Stanley Gibbons
SIMPLIFIED CATALOGUE

Stamps of the World

2009 Edition

IN COLOUR

An illustrated and priced five-volume guide to the postage stamps of the whole world, excluding changes of paper, perforation, shade and watermark

VOLUME 1

COUNTRIES A–C

STANLEY GIBBONS LTD
London and Ringwood

By Appointment to
Her Majesty the Queen
Stanley Gibbons Limited
London
Philatelists

74th Edition

Published in Great Britain by
Stanley Gibbons Ltd
Publications Editorial, Sales Offices and Distribution Centre
Parkside, Christchurch Road,
Ringwood, Hampshire BH24 3SH
Telephone 01425 472363

ISBN: 085259-686-3

Published as Stanley Gibbons Simplified Stamp Catalogue from 1934 to 1970, renamed Stamps of the World in 1971, and produced in two (1982-88), three (1989-2001), four (2002-2005) or five (from 2006) volumes as Stanley Gibbons Simplified Catalogue of Stamps of the World. This volume published October 2008

S.G. Item No. 2881 (09)

Pagination by Polestar Applied Solutions, England
Printed and bound in Italy by Lego SpA

Stanley Gibbons
SIMPLIFIED CATALOGUE
Stamps of the **World**

This popular catalogue is a straightforward listing of the stamps that have been issued everywhere in the world since the very first–Great Britain's famous Penny Black in 1840.

This edition, in which both the text and the illustrations have been captured electronically, is arranged completely alphabetically in a five-volume format. Volume 1 (Countries A–C), Volume 2 (Countries D–H), Volume 3 (Countries I–M), Volume 4 (Countries N–R) and Volume 5 (Countries S-Z).

Readers are reminded that the Catalogue Supplements, published in each issue of **Gibbons Stamp Monthly**, can be used to update the listings in **Stamps of the World** as well as our 22-part standard catalogue. To make the supplement even more useful the Type numbers given to the illustrations are the same in the Stamps of the World as in the standard catalogues. The first Catalogue Supplement to this Volume appeared in the September 2008 issue of **Gibbons Stamp Monthly**.

Gibbons Stamp Monthly can be obtained through newsagents or on postal subscription from Stanley Gibbons Publications, Parkside, Christchurch Road, Ringwood, Hants BH24 3SH.

The catalogue has many important features:

- The vast majority of illustrations are now in full colour to aid stamp identification.
- All miniature sheets are now included.
- As an indication of current values virtually every stamp is priced. Thousands of alterations have been made since the last edition.
- By being set out on a simplified basis that excludes changes of paper, perforation, shade, watermark, gum or printer's and date imprints it is particularly easy to use. (For its exact scope see "Information for users" pages following.)
- The thousands of colour illustrations and helpful descriptions of stamp designs make it of maximum appeal to collectors with thematic interests.
- Its catalogue numbers are the world-recognised Stanley Gibbons numbers throughout.
- Helpful introductory notes for the collector are included, backed by much historical, geographical and currency information.
- A very detailed index gives instant location of countries in this volume, and a cross-reference to those included in the other volumes.

Over 1,890 stamps and miniature sheets and 680 new illustrations have been added to the listings in this volume.

The listings in this edition are based on the standard catalogues: Part 1, Commonwealth & British Empire Stamps 1840–1970, Part 2 (Austria & Hungary) (6th edition), Part 3 (Balkans) (4th edition), Part 4 (Benelux) (5th edition), Part 5 (Czechoslovakia & Poland) (6th edition), Part 6 (France) (6th edition), Part 7 (Germany) (8th edition), Part 8 (Italy & Switzerland) (6th edition), Part 9 (Portugal & Spain) (5th edition), Part 10 (Russia) (6th edition), Part 11 (Scandinavia) (6th edition), Part 12 (Africa since Independence A-E) (2nd edition), Part 13 (Africa since Independence F-M) (1st edition), Part 14 (Africa since Independence N-Z) (1st edition), Part 15 (Central America) (3rd edition), Part 16 (Central Asia) (4th edition), Part 17 (China) (7th edition), Part 18 (Japan & Korea) (5th edition), Part 19 (Middle East) (6th edition), Part 20 (South America) (3rd edition), Part 21 (South-East Asia) (4th edition) and Part 22 (United States) (6th edition).

This edition includes major repricing for Benin, Cameroun, Central African Empire, Central African Republic, Comoro Islands, Congo (Brazzaville) (all since independence), Germany Part 7 and Japan and Korea Part 18.

Information for users

Aim

The aim of this catalogue is to provide a straightforward illustrated and priced guide to the postage stamps of the whole world to help you to enjoy the greatest hobby of the present day.

Arrangement

The catalogue lists countries in alphabetical order and there is a complete index at the end of each volume. For ease of reference country names are also printed at the head of each page.

Within each country, postage stamps are listed first. They are followed by separate sections for such other categories as postage due stamps, parcel post stamps, express stamps, official stamps, etc.

All catalogue lists are set out according to dates of issue of the stamps, starting from the earliest and working through to the most recent.

Scope of the Catalogue

The *Simplified Catalogue of Stamps of the World* contains listings of postage stamps only. Apart from the ordinary definitive, commemorative and air-mail stamps of each country – which appear first in each list – there are sections for the following where appropriate:

- postage due stamps
- parcel post stamps
- official stamps
- express and special delivery stamps
- charity and compulsory tax stamps
- newspaper and journal stamps
- printed matter stamps
- registration stamps
- acknowledgement of receipt stamps
- late fee and too late stamps
- military post stamps
- recorded message stamps
- personal delivery stamps

We receive numerous enquiries from collectors about other items which do not fall within the categories set out above and which consequently do not appear in the catalogue lists. It may be helpful, therefore, to summarise the other kinds of stamp that exist but which we deliberately exclude from this postage stamp catalogue.

We do *not* list the following:

Fiscal or revenue stamps: stamps used solely in collecting taxes or fees for non-postal purposes. Examples would be stamps which pay a tax on a receipt, represent the stamp duty on a contract or frank a customs document. Common inscriptions found include: Documentary, Proprietary, Inter. Revenue, Contract Note.

Local stamps: postage stamps whose validity and use are limited in area, say to a single town or city, though in some cases they provided, with official sanction, services in parts of countries not covered by the respective government.

Local carriage labels and Private local issues: many labels exist ostensibly to cover the cost of ferrying mail from one of Great Britain's offshore islands to the nearest mainland post office. They are not recognised as valid for national or international mail. Examples: Calf of Man, Davaar, Herm, Lundy, Pabay, Stroma. Items from some other places have only the status of tourist souvenir labels.

Telegraph stamps: stamps intended solely for the prepayment of telegraphic communication.

Bogus or "phantom" stamps: labels from mythical places or non-existent administrations. Examples in the classical period were Sedang, Counani, Clipperton Island and in modern times Thomond and Monte Bello Islands. Numerous labels have also appeared since the War from dissident groups as propaganda for their claims and without authority from the home governments. Common examples are labels for "Free Albania", "Free Rumania" and "Free Croatia" and numerous issues for Nagaland, Indonesia and the South Moluccas ("Republik Maluku Selatan").

Railway letter fee stamps: special stamps issued by railway companies for the conveyance of letters by rail. Example: Talyllyn Railway. Similar services are now offered by some bus companies and the labels they issue likewise do not qualify for inclusion in the catalogue.

Perfins ("perforated initials"): numerous postage stamps may be found with initial letters or designs punctured through them by tiny holes. These are applied by private and public concerns as a precaution against theft and do not qualify for separate mention.

Information for users

Labels: innumerable items exist resembling stamps but – as they do not prepay postage – they are classified as labels. The commonest categories are:

- propaganda and publicity labels: designed to further a cause or campaign;
- exhibition labels: particularly souvenirs from philatelic events;
- testing labels: stamp-size labels used in testing stamp-vending machines;
- Post Office training school stamps: British stamps overprinted with two thick vertical bars or SCHOOL SPECIMEN are produced by the Post Office for training purposes;
- seals and stickers: numerous charities produce stamp-like labels, particularly at Christmas and Easter, as a means of raising funds and these have no postal validity.

Cut-outs: items of postal stationary, such as envelopes, cards and wrappers, often have stamps impressed or imprinted on them. They may usually be cut out and affixed to envelopes, etc., for postal use if desired, but such items are not listed in this catalogue.

Collectors wanting further information about exact definitions are referred to *Philatelic Terms Illustrated*, published by Stanley Gibbons and containing many illustrations in colour.

There is also a priced listing of the postal fiscals of Great Britain in our *Commonwealth & British Empire Stamps 1840–1970* Catalogue and in Volume 1 of the *Great Britain Specialised* Catalogue (5th and later editions).

Prices are shown as follows:

10 means 10p (10 pence);
1.50 means £1.50 (1 pound and 50 pence);
For £100 and above, prices are in whole pounds.

Our prices are for stamps in fine condition, and in issues where condition varies we may ask more for the superb and less for the sub-standard.

The minimum catalogue price quoted is 10p. For individual stamps prices between 10p and 95p are provided as a guide for catalogue users. The lowest price charged for individual stamps purchased from Stanley Gibbons is £1.00.

The prices quoted are generally for the cheapest variety of stamps but it is worth noting that differences of watermark, perforation, or other details, outside the scope of this catalogue, may often increase the value of the stamp.

Prices quoted for mint issues are for single examples. Those in se-tenant pairs, strips, blocks or sheets may be worth more.

Where prices are not given in either column it is either because the stamps are not known to exist in that particular condition, or, more usually, because there is no reliable information as to value.

All prices are subject to change without prior notice and we give no guarantee to supply all stamps priced. Prices quoted for albums, publications, etc. advertised in this catalogue are also subject to change without prior notice.

Due to different production methods it is sometimes possible for new editions of Parts 2 to 22 to appear showing revised prices which are not included in that year's *Stamps of the World*.

Catalogue Numbers

Stanley Gibbons catalogue numbers are recognised universally and any individual stamp can be identified by quoting the catalogue number (the one at the left of the column) prefixed by the name of the country and the letters "S.G.". Do not confuse the catalogue number with the type numbers which refer to illustrations.

Prices

Prices in the left-hand column are for unused stamps and those in the right-hand column for used. Prices are given in pence and pounds:

100 pence (p) 1 pound (£1).

Unused Stamps

In the case of stamps from *Great Britain* and the *Commonwealth*, prices for unused stamps of Queen Victoria to King George V are for lightly hinged examples; unused prices of King Edward VIII to Queen Elizabeth II issues are for unmounted mint. The prices of unused Foreign stamps are for lightly hinged examples for those issued before 1946, thereafter for examples unmounted mint.

Used Stamps

Prices for used stamps generally refer to fine postally used examples, though for certain issues they are for cancelled-to-order.

Information for users

Guarantee

All stamps supplied by us are guaranteed originals in the following terms:

If not as described, and returned by the purchaser, we undertake to refund the price paid to us in the original transaction. If any stamp is certified as genuine by the Expert Committee of the Royal Philatelic Society, London, or by B.P.A. Expertising Ltd., the purchaser shall not be entitled to make any claim against us for any error, omission or mistake in such certificate.

Consumers' statutory rights are not affected by the above guarantee.

Currency

At the beginning of each country brief details give the currencies in which the values of the stamps are expressed. The dates, where given, are those of the earliest stamp issues in the particular currency. Where the currency is obvious, e.g. where the colony has the same currency as the mother country, no details are given.

Illustrations

Illustrations of any surcharges and overprints which are shown and not described are actual size; stamp illustrations are reduced to $\frac{3}{4}$ linear, *unless otherwise stated.*

"Key-Types"

A number of standard designs occur so frequently in the stamps of the French, German, Portuguese and Spanish colonies that it would be a waste of space to repeat them. Instead these are all illustrated on page xiv together with the descriptive names and letters by which they are referred to in the lists.

Type Numbers

These are the bold figures found below each illustration. References to "Type **6**", for example, in the lists of a country should therefore be understood to refer to the illustration below which the number **"6"** appears. These type numbers are also given in the second column of figures alongside each list of stamps, thus indicating clearly the design of each stamp. In the case of Key-Types – see above – letters take the place of the type numbers.

Where an issue comprises stamps of similar design, represented in this catalogue by one illustration, the corresponding type numbers should be taken as indicating this general design.

Where there are blanks in the type number column it means that the type of the corresponding stamps is that shown by the last number above in the type column of the same issue.

A dash (–) in the type column means that no illustration of the stamp is shown.

Where type numbers refer to stamps of another country, e.g. where stamps of one country are overprinted for use in another, this is always made clear in the text.

Stamp Designs

Brief descriptions of the subjects of the stamp designs are given either below or beside the illustrations, at the foot of the list of the issue concerned, or in the actual lists. Where a particular subject, e.g. the portrait of a well-known monarch, recurs frequently the description is not repeated, nor are obvious designs described.

Generally, the unillustrated designs are in the same shape and size as the one illustrated, except where otherwise indicated.

Surcharges and Overprints

Surcharges and overprints are usually described in the headings to the issues concerned. Where the actual wording of a surcharge or overprint is given it is shown in bold type.

Some stamps are described as being "Surcharged in words", e.g. **TWO CENTS**, and others "Surcharged in figures and words", e.g. **20 CENTS**, although of course many surcharges are in foreign languages and combinations of words and figures are numerous. There are often bars, etc., obliterating old values or inscriptions but in general these are only mentioned where it is necessary to avoid confusion.

No attention is paid in this catalogue to colours of overprints and surcharges so that stamps with the same overprints in different colours are not listed separately.

Numbers in brackets after the descriptions of overprinted or surcharged stamps are the catalogue numbers of the unoverprinted stamps.

Note – the words "inscribed" or "inscription" always refer to wording incorporated in the design of a stamp and not surcharges or overprints.

Coloured Papers

Where stamps are printed on coloured paper the description is given as e.g. "4 c. black on blue" – a stamp printed in black on blue paper. No attention is paid in this catalogue to difference in the texture of paper, e.g. laid, wove.

Information for users

Watermarks

Stamps having different watermarks, but otherwise the same, are not listed separately. No reference is therefore made to watermarks in this volume.

Stamp Colours

Colour names are only required for the identification of stamps, therefore they have been made as simple as possible. Thus "scarlet", "vermilion", "carmine" are all usually called red. Qualifying colour names have been introduced only where necessary for the sake of clearness.

Where stamps are printed in two or more colours the central portion of the design is in the first colour given, unless otherwise stated.

Perforations

All stamps are perforated unless otherwise stated. No distinction is made between the various gauges of perforation but early stamp issues which exist both imperforate and perforated are usually listed separately.

Where a heading states "Imperf. or perf". or "Perf. or rouletted" this does not necessarily mean that all values of the issue are found in both conditions.

Dates of Issue

The date given at the head of each issue is that of the appearance of the earliest stamp in the series. As stamps of the same design or issue are usually grouped together a list of King George VI stamps, for example, headed "1938" may include stamps issued from 1938 to the end of the reign.

Se-tenant Pairs

Many modern issues are printed in sheets containing different designs or face values. Such pairs, blocks, strips or sheets are described as being "se-tenant" and they are outside the scope of this catalogue, although reference to them may occur in instances where they form a composite design.

Miniature Sheets

As an increasing number of stamps are now only found in miniature sheets, Stamps of the World now lists these items.

"Appendix" Countries

We regret that, since 1968, it has been necessary to establish an Appendix (at the end of each country as appropriate) to which numerous stamps have had to be consigned. Several countries imagine that by issuing huge quantities of unnecessary stamps they will have a ready source of income from stamp collectors – and particularly from the less-experienced ones. Stanley Gibbons refuse to encourage this exploitation of the hobby and we do not stock the stamps concerned.

Two kinds of stamp are therefore given the briefest of mentions in the Appendix, purely for the sake of record. Administrations issuing stamps greatly in excess of true postal needs have the offending issues placed there. Likewise it contains stamps which have not fulfilled all the normal conditions for full catalogue listing.

These conditions are that the stamps must be issued by a legitimate postal authority, recognised by the government concerned, and are adhesives, valid for proper postal use in the class of service for which they are inscribed. Stamps, with the exception of such categories as postage dues and officials, must be available to the general public at face value with no artificial restrictions being imposed on their distribution.

The publishers of this catalogue have observed, with concern, the proliferation of 'artificial' stamp-issuing territories. On several occasions this has resulted in separately inscribed issues for various component parts of otherwise united states or territories.

Stanley Gibbons Publications have decided that where such circumstances occur, they will not, in the future, list these items in the SG catalogue without first satisfying themselves that the stamps represent a genuine political, historical or postal division within the country concerned. Any such issues which do not fulfil this stipulation will be recorded in the Catalogue Appendix only.

Stamps in the Appendix are kept under review in the light of any newly acquired information about them. If we are satisfied that a stamp qualifies for proper listing in the body of the catalogue it is moved there.

Information for users

"Undesirable Issues"

The rules governing many competitive exhibitions are set by the Federation Internationale de Philatelie and stipulate a downgrading of marks for stamps classed as "undesirable issues".

This catalogue can be taken as a guide to status. All stamps in the main listings and Addenda are acceptable. Stamps in the Appendix should not be entered for competition as these are the "undesirable issues".

Particular care is advised with Aden Protectorate States, Ajman, Bhutan, Chad, Fujeira, Khor Fakkan, Manama, Ras al Khaima, Sharjah, Umm al Qiwain and Yemen. Totally bogus stamps exist (as explained in Appendix notes) and these are to be avoided also for competition. As distinct from "undesirable stamps" certain categories are not covered in this catalogue purely by reason of its scope (see page viii). Consult the particular competition rules to see if such are admissable even though not listed by us.

Where to Look for More Detailed Listings

The present work deliberately omits details of paper, perforation, shade and watermark. But as you become more absorbed in stamp collecting and wish to get greater enjoyment from the hobby you may well want to study these matters.

All the information you require about any particular postage stamp will be found in the main Stanley Gibbons Catalogues.

Commonwealth countries before 1952 are covered by the Commonwealth & British Empire Stamps 1840–1952 published annually. Post-1952 Commonwealth Stamps are listed in the growing range of Commonwealth Country Catalogues.

For foreign countries you can easily find which catalogue to consult by looking at the country headings in the present book.

To the right of each country name are code letters specifying which volume of our main catalogues contains that country's listing.

The code letters are as follows:

Pt. 2 Part 2
Pt. 3 Part 3 etc.

(See page xiii for complete list of Parts.)

So, for example, if you want to know more about Chinese stamps than is contained in the *Simplified Catalogue of Stamps of the World* the reference to

CHINA Pt. 17

guides you to the Gibbons Part 17 *(China)* Catalogue listing for the details you require.

New editions of Parts 2 to 22 appear at irregular intervals.

Correspondence

Whilst we welcome information and suggestions we must ask correspondents to include the cost of postage for the return of any stamps submitted plus registration where appropriate. Letters should be addressed to The Catalogue Editor at Ringwood.

Where information is solicited purely for the benefit of the enquirer we regret we cannot undertake to reply.

Identification of Stamps

We regret we do not give opinions as to the genuineness of stamps, nor do we identify stamps or number them by our Catalogue.

Users of this catalogue are referred to our companion booklet entitled *Stamp Collecting – How to Identify Stamps.* It explains how to look up stamps in this catalogue, contains a full checklist of stamp inscriptions and gives help in dealing with unfamiliar scripts.

Stanley Gibbons would like to complement your collection

At Stanley Gibbons we offer a range of services which are designed to complement your collection.

Our modern stamp shop, the largest in Europe, together with our rare stamp department has one of the most comprehensive stocks of Great Britain in the world, so whether you are a beginner or an experienced philatelist you are certain to find something to suit your special requirements.

Alternatively, through our Mail Order services you can control the growth of your collection from the comfort of your own home. Our Postal Sales Department regularly sends out mailings of Special Offers. We can also help with your wants list—so why not ask us for those elusive items?

Why not take advantage of the many services we have to offer? Visit our premises in the Strand or, for more information, write to the appropriate address on page x.

Stanley Gibbons Holdings Plc

Stanley Gibbons Limited, Stanley Gibbons Auctions

399 Strand, London WC2R 0LX
Telephone 020 7836 8444, Fax 020 7836 7342,
E-mail: enquiries@stanleygibbons.co.uk
Website: www.stanleygibbons.com for all departments.

Auction and Specialist Stamp Departments.
Open Monday–Friday 9.30 a.m. to 5 p.m.

Shop. Open Monday–Friday 9 a.m. to 5.30 p.m. and Saturday 9.30 a.m. to 5.30 p.m.

Fraser's (a division of Stanley Gibbons Ltd)

399 Strand, London WC2R 0LX
Autographs, photographs, letters and documents

Telephone 020 7836 8444, Fax 020 7836 7342,
E-mail: info@frasersautographs.co.uk
Website: www.frasersautographs.com

Monday–Friday 9 a.m. to 5.30 p.m. and Saturday 10 a.m. to 4 p.m.

Stanley Gibbons Publications

Parkside, Christchurch Road, Ringwood, Hampshire BH24 3SH.
Telephone 01425 472363 (24 hour answer phone service), Fax 01425 470247,
E-mail: info@stanleygibbons.co.uk

Publications Mail Order. FREEPHONE 0800 611622
Monday–Friday 8.30 a.m. to 5 p.m.

Gibbons Stamp Monthly

Parkside, Christchurch Road, Ringwood, Hampshire BH24 3SH.
Subscriptions 01425 481049 Fax 01425 470247
E-mail: gsm@stanleygibbons.co.uk

Stanley Gibbons Publications Overseas Representation

Stanley Gibbons Publications are represented overseas by the following sole distributors (*) distributors (**) or licensees (***).

Australia*
Lighthouse Philatelic (Aust.) Pty. Ltd.
Locked Bag 5900 Botany DC, New South Wales, 2019 Australia.

Stanley Gibbons (Australia) Pty. Ltd.**
Level 6, 36 Clarence Street, Sydney, New South Wales 2000, Australia.

Belgium and Luxembourg**
Davo c/o Philac, Rue du Midi 48, Bruxelles, 1000 Belgium.

Canada**
Unitrade, 99 Floral Parkway, Toronto, Ontario, Canada M6L 2C4.

Denmark**
Samlerforum/Davo, Ostergade 3, DK 7470 Karup, Denmark.

Finland**
Davo c/o Kapylan Merkkiky Pohjolankatu 1 00610 Helsinki, Finland.

France*
Davo France (Casteilla), 10, Rue Leon Foucault, 78184 St. Quentin Yvelines Cesex, France.

Hong Kong**
Po-on Stamp Service, GPO Box 2498, Hong Kong.

Italy*
Ernesto Marini Srl, Via Struppa 300, I-16165, Genova GE, Italy.

Japan**
Japan Philatelic Co. Ltd., P.O. Box 2, Suginami-Minami, Tokyo, Japan.

Netherlands*
Davo Publications, P.O. Box 411, 7400 AK Deventer, Netherlands.

New Zealand***
Mowbray Collectables.
P.O. Box 80, Wellington, New Zealand.

Norway**
Davo Norge A/S, P.O. Box 738 Sentrum, N-0105, Oslo, Norway.

Saudi Arabia**
Arabian Stamps Centre, P.O. Box 54645, Riyadh 11524, Saudi Arabia.

Singapore**
Stamp Inc Collectibles Pte Ltd., 10 Ubi Cresent, #01-43 Ubi Tech Park, Singapore 408564.

Sweden*
Chr Winther Soerensen AB, Box 43, S-310 Knaered, Sweden.

U.S.A.**
Filatco Inc
P.O. Box 520 McLean
VA22101-0520
U.S.A.

Abbreviations

Anniv.	denotes	Anniversary
Assn.	,,	Association
Bis.	,,	Bistre
Bl.	,,	Blue
Bldg.	,,	Building
Blk.	,,	Black
Br.	,,	British or Bridge
Brn.	,,	Brown
B.W.I.	,,	British West Indies
C.A.R.I.F.T.A.	,,	Caribbean Free Trade Area
Cent.	,,	Centenary
Chest.	,,	Chestnut
Choc.	,,	Chocolate
Clar.	,,	Claret
Coll.	,,	College
Commem.	,,	Commemoration
Conf.	,,	Conference
Diag.	,,	Diagonally
E.C.A.F.E.	,,	Economic Commission for Asia and Far East
Emer.	,,	Emerald
E.P.T. Conference	,,	European Postal and Telecommunications Conference
Exn.		Exhibition
F.A.O.	,,	Food and Agriculture Organization
Fig.	,,	Figure
G.A.T.T.	,,	General Agreement on Tariffs and Trade
G.B.	,,	Great Britain
Gen.	,,	General
Govt.	,,	Government
Grn.	,,	Green
Horiz.	,,	Horizontal
H.Q.	,,	Headquarters
Imperf.	,,	Imperforate
Inaug.	,,	Inauguration
Ind.	,,	Indigo
Inscr.	,,	Inscribed or inscription
Int.	,,	International
I.A.T.A.	,,	International Air Transport Association
I.C.A.O.	,,	International Civil Aviation Organization
I.C.Y.	,,	International Co-operation Year
I.G.Y.	,,	International Geophysical Year
I.L.O.	,,	International Labour Office (or later, Organization)
I.M.C.O.	,,	Inter-Governmental Maritime Consultative Organization
I.T.U.	,,	International Telecommunication Union
Is.	,,	Islands
Lav.	,,	Lavender
Mar.	,,	Maroon
mm.	,,	Millimetres
Mult.	,,	Multicoloured

Mve.	denotes	Mauve
Nat.	,,	National
N.A.T.O.	,,	North Atlantic Treaty Organization
O.D.E.C.A.	,,	Organization of Central American States
Ol.	,,	Olive
Optd.	,,	Overprinted
Orge. or oran.	,,	Orange
P.A.T.A.	,,	Pacific Area Travel Association
Perf.	,,	Perforated
Post.	,,	Postage
Pres.	,,	President
P.U.	,,	Postal Union
Pur.	,,	Purple
R.	,,	River
R.S.A.	,,	Republic of South Africa
Roul.	,,	Rouletted
Sep.	,,	Sepia
S.E.A.T.O.	,,	South East Asia Treaty Organization
Surch.	,,	Surcharged
T.	,,	Type
T.U.C.	,,	Trades Union Congress
Turq.	,,	Turquoise
Ultram.	,,	Ultramarine
U.N.E.S.C.O.	,,	United Nations Educational, Scientific Cultural Organization
U.N.I.C.E.F.	,,	United Nations Children's Fund
U.N.O.	,,	United Nations Organization
U.N.R.W.A.	,,	United Nations Relief and Works Agency for Palestine Refugees in the Near East
U.N.T.E.A.	,,	United Nations Temporary Executive Authority
U.N.R.R.A.	,,	United Nations Relief and Rehabilitation Administration
U.P.U.	,,	Universal Postal Union
Verm.	,,	Vermilion
Vert.	,,	Vertical
Vio.	,,	Violet
W.F.T.U.	,,	World Federation of Trade Unions
W.H.O.	,,	World Health Organization
Yell.	,,	Yellow

Arabic Numerals

As in the case of European figures, the details of the Arabic numerals vary in different stamp designs, but they should be readily recognised with the aid of this illustration:

٠	١	٢	٣	٤
0	1	2	3	4
٥	٦	٧	٨	٩
5	6	7	8	9

Stanley Gibbons Stamp Catalogue
Complete List of Parts

1 Commonwealth & British Empire Stamps 1840–1970 (Annual)

Foreign Countries

2 Austria & Hungary (6th edition, 2002)
Austria · U.N. (Vienna) · Hungary

3 Balkans (4th edition, 1998)
Albania · Bosnia & Herzegovina · Bulgaria · Croatia · Greece & Islands · Macedonia · Rumania · Slovenia · Yugoslavia

4 Benelux (5th edition, 2003)
Belgium & Colonies · Luxembourg · Netherlands & Colonies

5 Czechoslovakia & Poland (6th edition, 2002)
Czechoslovakia · Czech Republic · Slovakia · Poland

6 France (6th edition, 2006)
France · Colonies · Post Offices · Andorra · Monaco

7 Germany (8th edition, 2008)
Germany · States · Colonies · Post Offices

8 Italy & Switzerland (6th edition, 2003)
Italy & Colonies · Liechtenstein · San Marino · Switzerland · U.N. (Geneva) · Vatican City

9 Portugal & Spain (5th edition, 2004)
Andorra · Portugal & Colonies · Spain & Colonies

10 Russia (6th edition, 2007)
Russia · Armenia · Azerbaijan · Belarus · Estonia · Georgia · Kazakhstan · Kyrgyzstan · Latvia · Lithuania · Moldova · Tajikistan · Turkmenistan · Ukraine · Uzbekistan · Mongolia

11 Scandinavia (6th edition, 2008)
Aland Islands · Denmark · Faroe Islands · Finland · Greenland · Iceland · Norway · Sweden

12 Africa since Independence A-E (2nd edition, 1983)
Algeria · Angola · Benin · Burundi · Cameroun · Cape Verdi · Central African Republic · Chad · Comoro Islands · Congo · Djibouti · Equatorial Guinea · Ethiopia

13 Africa since Independence F-M (1st edition, 1981)
Gabon · Guinea · Guinea-Bissau · Ivory Coast · Liberia · Libya · Malagasy Republic · Mali · Mauritania · Morocco · Mozambique

14 Africa since Independence N-Z (1st edition, 1981)
Niger Republic · Rwanda · St. Thomas & Prince · Senegal · Somalia · Sudan · Togo · Tunisia · Upper Volta · Zaire

15 Central America (3rd edition, 2007)
Costa Rica · Cuba · Dominican Republic · El Salvador · Guatemala · Haiti · Honduras · Mexico · Nicaragua · Panama

16 Central Asia (4th edition, 2006)
Afghanistan · Iran · Turkey

17 China (7th edition, 2006)
China · Taiwan · Tibet · Foreign P.O.s · Hong Kong · Macao

18 Japan & Korea (5th edition, 2008)
Japan · Korean Empire · South Korea · North Korea

19 Middle East (6th edition, 2005)
Bahrain · Egypt · Iraq · Israel · Jordan · Kuwait · Lebanon · Oman · Qatar · Saudi Arabia · Syria · U.A.E. · Yemen

20 South America (3rd edition, 1989)
Argentina · Bolivia · Brazil · Chile · Colombia · Ecuador · Paraguay · Peru · Surinam · Uruguay · Venezuela

21 South-East Asia (4th edition, 2004)
Bhutan · Burma · Indonesia · Kampuchea · Laos · Nepal · Philippines · Thailand · Vietnam

22 United States (6th edition, 2005)
U.S. & Possessions · Marshall Islands · Micronesia · Palau · U.N. (New York, Geneva, Vienna)

Thematic Catalogues

Stanley Gibbons Catalogues for use with **Stamps of the World.**
Collect Aircraft on Stamps (2nd edition to be published December 2008)
Collect Birds on Stamps (5th edition, 2003)
Collect Chess on Stamps (2nd edition, 1999)
Collect Fish on Stamps (1st edition, 1999)
Collect Fungi on Stamps (2nd edition, 1997)
Collect Motor Vehicles on Stamps (1st edition, 2004)
Collect Railways on Stamps (3rd edition, 1999)
Collect Shells on Stamps (out of print)
Collect Ships on Stamps (3rd edition, 2001)

Key-Types

(see note on page vii)

French Group

A. "Blanc."

B. "Mouchon."

C "Merson."

D. "Tablet."

E.

F.

G.

H.

"International Colonial Exhibition."

I. "Faidherbe."

J. "Palms."

K. "Balay."

L. "Natives."

M. "Figure."

German Group

N. "Yacht."

O. "Yacht."

Spanish Group

X. "Alfonso XII."

Y. "Baby."

Z. "Curly Head"

Portuguese Group

P. "Crown."

Q. "Embossed."

R. "Figures."

S. "Carlos."

T. "Manoel."

U. "Ceres."

V. "Newspaper."

W. "Due."

Stanley Gibbons One Country Albums

These albums have something the others do not... Stanley Gibbons catalogue numbers.

Ideal for the straightforward single country collection and the only Commonwealth one-country albums that feature **Stanley Gibbons catalogue numbers throughout.**

Available as separate volumes or in a great value set, all albums accommodate high-quality printed leaves featuring illustrations, Stanley Gibbons catalogue numbers and dates of issue. Supplements are produced annually to keep your collection up to date. Each volume is housed in a padded 4 or 22-ring maroon PVC binder, gold blocked on the spine and supplied with a self-adhesive title sheet. All album pages are 115gsm.

Great Britain Albums (with GB 4-ring binders)

R5250MAR	Volume 1 (1840-1970)	£32.97
R5252MAR	Volume 2 (1970-1990)	£33.97
R5254MAR	Volume 3 (1991-2004)	£33.97
R5255MAR	Volume 4 (2005-2007)	£36.97
R5250-SO	4 Volume Set Offer **Save £27.91**	£109.97

British Islands Albums (with 22-Ring binders)

R5524MAR	Guernsey Volume 1 (1941-1994)	£35.97
R5526MAR	Guernsey Volume 2 (1995-2004)	£35.97
R5529MAR	Guernsey Volume 3 (2005-2007)	£26.97
R5525MAR	Jersey Volume 1 (1941-1994)	£35.97
R5527MAR	Jersey Volume 2 (1995-2004)	£35.97
R5528MAR	Jersey Volume 3 (2005-2007)	£26.97
R5256MAR	Isle of Man Volume 1 (1958-1994)	£35.97
R5257MAR	Isle of Man Volume 2 (1995-2004)	£35.97
R5265MAR	Isle of Man Volume 3 (2005-2007)	£26.97

Guernsey, Jersey OR Isle of Man
3 Volume Set Offer **Save £16.94** £81.97

Commonwealth Albums (with 4-ring binders)

R5258MAR	Australia Vol. 1 (1913-1990)	£40.97
R5259MAR	Australia Vol. 2 (1991-2004)	£40.97
R5253MAR	Australia Vol. 3 (2005-2007)	£24.97
R5260MAR	Canada Vol. 1 (1851-1990)	£40.97
R5261MAR	Canada Vol. 2 (1991-2004)	£40.97
R5266MAR	Canada Vol. 3 (2005-2007)	£24.97
R5262MAR	New Zealand Vol. 1 (1855-1990)	£40.97
R5263MAR	New Zealand Vol. 2 (1991-2004)	£40.97
R5270MAR	New Zealand Vol. 3 (2005-2007)	£24.97

Australia, Canada OR New Zealand
3 Volume Set Offer **Save £21.94** £84.97

Stanley Gibbons Luxury Hingeless Albums

Featuring made-to-measure mounts designed to save you time and money

Our luxury hingeless album range offers the ultimate in quality, convenience and style. Handsomely bound in deeply padded navy blue leatherette, each album is richly embossed with the country's national crest on the cover and spine and presented in its own matching slipcase. Inside, the finest quality printed leaves have been expertly arranged with spaces for each stamp and selected illustrations and descriptions for your guidance. In addition, clear protective mounts are already in place to enable easy insertion of your stamps. Annual supplements help keep your album completely up to date.

GB

R5284	GB Volume 1 (1840-1970)	£110.75
R5285	GB Volume 2 (1971-1989)	£124.95
R5290	GB Volume 3 (1990-1999)	£102.95
R5295	GB Volume 4 (2000-2007)	£92.95
R5284-SO	GB 4-Volume Set Offer **Save £64.85**	£366.75

GB QEII

R5546	GB Q.E.II Volume 1 (1952-1989)	£122.25
R5581	GB Q.E.II Volume 2 (1990-1999)	£99.95
R5583	GB Q.E.II Volume 3 (2000-2007)	£99.95
R5546SO	GB Q.E.II Set Offer **Save £48.40**	£273.75

AUSTRALIA

R5280	Australia Volume 1 (1913-1965)	£81.50
R5281	Australia Volume 2 (1966-1985)	£104.25
R5291	Australia Volume 3 (1986-1999)	£114.25
R5297	Australia Volume 4 (2000-2007)	£104.95
R5280-SO	Australia Set Offer **Save £60.70**	£344.25

CANADA

R5282	Canada Volume 1 (1851-1969)	£103.95
R5283	Canada Volume 2 (1970-1985)	£117.95
R5293	Canada Volume 3 (1986-1999)	£122.95
R5298	Canada Volume 4 (2000-2006)	£97.25
R5260	Canada Volume 5 (2007)	£38.95
R5282-SO	Canada Set Offer **Save £72.80**	£408.25

NEW ZEALAND

R5288	New Zealand Volume 1 (1855-1967)	£98.95
R5289	New Zealand Volume 2 (1967-1985)	£116.95
R5296	New Zealand Volume 3 (1986-1995)	£104.25
R5561	New Zealand Volume 4 (1996-2002)	£115.25
R5530	New Zealand Volume 5 (2003-2007)	£89.75
R5288-SO	New Zealand Set Offer **Save £78.90**	£446.25

Prices correct as of September 2008. Prices subject to change.

STANLEY GIBBONS

Unit 7 Parkside, Christchurch Road, Ringwood, BH24 3SH

Tel: +44 (0)1425 472363 Fax: 01425 470247 Email: sales@stanleygibbons.com

STANLEY GIBBONS SIMPLIFIED CATALOGUE OF STAMPS OF THE WORLD—VOLUME 1 COUNTRIES A–C

ABU DHABI Pt. 1, Pt. 19

The largest of the Trucial States in the Persian Gulf. Treaty relations with Great Britain expired on 31 December 1966, when Abu Dhabi took over the postal services. On 18 July 1971, seven of the Gulf sheikhdoms, including Abu Dhabi, agreed to form the State of the United Arab Emirates. The federation came into being on 1 August 1972.

1964. 100 naye paise = 1 rupee.
1966. 1,000 fils = 1 dinar.

1 Shaikh Shakhbut bin Sultan

3 Ruler's Palace

1964.

1	1	5n.p. green	3·25	3·50
2		15n.p. brown	2·75	1·75
3		20n.p. blue	3·25	1·75
4		30n.p. orange	3·50	1·50
5	–	40n.p. violet	4·50	1·25
6	–	50n.p. bistre	6·00	2·75
7	–	75n.p. black	6·00	4·25
8	3	1r. green	4·00	2·00
9		2r. black	8·00	3·25
10	–	5r. red	19·00	10·00
11	–	10r. blue	24·00	14·00

DESIGNS: As Type **1**: 40 to 75n.p. Mountain gazelle; As Type **3**: 5, 10r. Oil rig and camels.

5 Saker Falcon

1965. Falconry.

12	5	20n.p. brown and blue	14·00	2·00
13	–	40n.p. brown and blue	17·00	3·00
14	–	2r. sepia and turquoise	28·00	14·00

DESIGNS: 40n.p., 2r. Other types of Saker falcon on gloved hand.

1966. Nos. 1/11 surch in new currency ("Fils" only on Nos. 5/7) and ruler's portrait obliterated with bars.

15	1	5f. on 5n.p. green	9·50	5·50
16		15f. on 15n.p. brown	12·00	9·50
17		20f. on 20n.p. blue	13·00	8·00
18		30f. on 30n.p. orange	12·00	19·00
19	–	40f. on 40n.p. violet	14·00	1·00
20	–	50f. on 50n.p. bistre	35·00	35·00
21	–	75f. on 75n.p. black	35·00	35·00
22	3	100f. on 1r. green	17·00	3·75
23		200f. on 2r. black	18·00	13·00
24	–	500f. on 5r. red	30·00	38·00
25	–	1d. on 10r. blue	48·00	65·00

9 Shaikh Zaid bin Sultan al Nahayyan

10

1967.

26	–	5f. red and green	40	15
27	–	15f. red and brown	50	15
28	–	20f. red and blue	75	15
29	–	35f. red and violet	80	25
30	9	40f. green	1·10	25
38	10	40f. green	1·40	40
31	9	50f. brown	1·60	40
39	10	50f. brown	2·40	55
32	9	60f. blue	5·00	1·80
40	10	60f. blue	26·00	8·25
33	9	100f. red	12·00	5·75
41	10	100f. red	29·00	16·00
34	–	125f. brown and green	1·50	1·10
35	–	200f. brown and blue	1·80	80
36	–	500f. violet and orange	3·25	1·20
37	–	1d. blue and green	9·00	2·10

DESIGNS—As Types **9/10**—VERT: 5f. to 35f. National flag. HORIZ: (47 × 27 mm); 125f. Mountain gazelle; 200f. Lanner falcon; 500f., 1d. Palace. Each with portrait of Ruler.

11 Human Rights Emblem and Shaikh Zaid

1968. Human Rights Year.

42	11	35f. multicoloured	1·60	65
43		60f. multicoloured	2·50	1·00
44		150f. multicoloured	6·50	2·30

12 Arms and Shaikh Zaid

1968. Anniv of Shaikh Zaid's Accession.

45	12	5f. multicoloured	2·00	50
46		10f. multicoloured	2·10	65
47		100f. multicoloured	5·75	1·20
48		125f. multicoloured	8·25	3·00

13 New Construction

1968. 2nd Anniv of Shaikh's Accession. "Progress in Abu Dhabi". Multicoloured.

49		5f. Type **13**	2·00	40
50		10f. Airport buildings (46½ × 34 mm)	4·00	80
51		35f. Shaikh Zaid, bridge and Northern goshawk (59 × 34 mm)	16·00	7·00

14 Petroleum Installations

1969. 3rd Anniv of Shaikh's Accession. Petroleum Industry. Multicoloured.

52		35f. Type **14**	1·50	50
53		60f. Marine drilling platform	2·50	1·00
54		125f. Separator platform, Zakum field	5·75	2·40
55		200f. Tank farm	10·50	5·75

15 Shaikh Zaid

1970.

56	–	5f. multicoloured	50	15
57	15	10f. multicoloured	75	15
58	–	25f. multicoloured	1·40	15
59	15	35f. multicoloured	1·80	25
60		50f. multicoloured	2·50	40
61	–	60f. multicoloured	2·75	50
62	15	70f. multicoloured	5·00	55
63	–	90f. multicoloured	6·00	1·10
64	–	125f. multicoloured	9·00	1·50
65	–	150f. multicoloured	9·00	1·80
66	–	500f. multicoloured	28·00	9·75
67	–	1d. multicoloured	49·00	16·00

DESIGNS: Nos. 56, 58, 61 and 63 as Type **15**, but frames changed, and smaller country name; 125f. Arab stallion; 150f. Mountain gazelle; 500f. Fort Jahili; 1d. Great Mosque.

No. 67 has face value in Arabic only.

17 Shaikh Zaid and "Mt. Fuji" (T. Hayashi)

1970. "Expo 70" World Fair, Osaka, Japan.

68	17	25f. multicoloured	1·80	90
69		35f. multicoloured	3·00	1·40
70		60f. multicoloured	5·75	1·80

18 Abu Dhabi Airport

19 Pres. G. A. Nasser

1970. 40th Anniv of Shaikh's Accession. Completion of Abu Dhabi Airport. Mult.

71		25f. Type **18**	1·80	65
72		60f. Airport entrance	5·00	1·60
73		150f. Aerial view of Abu Dhabi (vert)	11·50	3·75

1971. Gamal Nasser (President of Egypt) Commemoration.

74	19	25f. black on pink	5·00	2·75
75		35f. black on lilac	7·25	4·00

20 Military Land Rover Series II 88

1971. 5th Anniv of Shaikh's Accession. Defence Force. Multicoloured.

76		35f. Type **20**	4·00	1·10
77		60f. Patrol-boat "Baniyas"	5·75	1·60
78		125f. Armoured car	12·00	2·50
79		150f. Hawker Hunter FGA.76 jet fighters	16·00	5·00

1971. No. 60 surch.

80	15	5f. on 50f. multicoloured	70·00	55·00

22 Dome of the Rock

1972. Dome of the Rock, Jerusalem. Multicoloured.

81		35f. Type **22**	18·00	3·25
82		60f. Mosque entrance	29·00	6·50
83		125f. Mosque dome	55·00	16·00

1972. Provisional Issue. Nos. 56/67 optd **UAE** and arabic inscr.

84	–	5f. multicoloured	2·30	2·30
85	15	10f. multicoloured	2·30	1·40
86	–	25f. multicoloured	3·25	3·25
87	15	35f. multicoloured	4·50	4·00
88		50f. multicoloured	7·25	7·25
89	–	60f. multicoloured	8·25	8·25
90	15	70f. multicoloured	10·50	10·50
91	–	90f. multicoloured	14·00	14·00
92	–	125f. multicoloured	45·00	45·00
93	–	150f. multicoloured	60·00	60·00
94	–	500f. multicoloured	£140	£140
95	–	1d. multicoloured	£275	£275

For later issues see **UNITED ARAB EMIRATES**.

ADEN Pt. 1

Peninsula on southern coast of Arabia. Formerly part of the Indian Empire. A Crown Colony from 1 April 1937 to 18 January 1963, when Aden joined the South Arabian Federation, whose stamps it then used.

1937. 16 annas = 1 rupee.
1951. 100 cents = 1 shilling.

1 Dhow

1937.

1	1	½a. green	3·75	2·75
2		9p. green	3·75	3·00
3		1a. brown	3·75	1·50
4		2a. red	4·00	3·00
5		2½a. blue	4·50	2·00
6		3a. red	10·00	8·50
7		3½a. blue	7·50	4·50
8		8a. purple	24·00	8·00
9		1r. brown	48·00	9·50
10		2r. yellow	80·00	27·00
11		5r. purple	£160	95·00
12		10r. olive	£425	£425

2 King George VI and Queen Elizabeth

1937. Coronation.

13	2	1a. brown	65	1·25
14		2½a. blue	75	1·40
15		3½a. blue	1·00	2·75

3 Aidrus Mosque, Crater

1939.

16	3	½a. green	1·00	60
17	–	¾a. brown	2·00	1·25
18	–	1a. blue	40	40
19	–	1½a. red	1·50	60
20	3	2a. brown	40	25
21	–	2½a. blue	80	30
22	–	3a. brown and red	1·00	25
23	–	8a. orange	1·50	40
23a	–	14a. brown and blue	2·75	1·00
24	–	1r. green	3·00	2·25
25	–	2r. blue and mauve	8·00	2·25
26	–	5r. brown and olive	20·00	13·00
27	–	10r. brown and violet	35·00	14·00

DESIGNS: ¾a., 5r. Adenese Camel Corps; 1a., 2r. The Harbour; 1½a., 1r. Adenese dhow; 2½, 8a. Mukalla; 3, 14a., 10r. "Capture of Aden, 1839" (Capt. Rundle).

9 Houses of Parliament, London

1946. Victory.

28	9	1½a. red	20	1·60
29		2½a. blue	30	75

10

11 King George VI and Queen Elizabeth

1949. Royal Silver Wedding.

30	**10**	1½a. red	40	2·00
31	**11**	10r. purple	29·00	40·00

1949. 75th Anniv of U.P.U. As T **20/23** of Antigua surch with new values.

32	2½a. on 20c. blue	50	1·50
33	3a. on 30c. red	2·00	1·50
34	8a. on 50c. orange	1·40	2·00
35	1r. on 1s. blue	1·60	3·25

1951. Stamps of 1939 surch in cents or shillings.

36	5c. on 1a. blue	25	40
37	10c. on 2a. brown	15	45
38	15c. on 2½a. blue	30	1·25
39	20c. on 3a. brown and red	30	40
40	30c. on 8a. orange	40	65
41	50c. on 8a. orange	70	35
42	70c. on 14a. brown and blue	2·25	1·50
43	1s. on 1r. green	1·00	30
44	2s. on 2r. blue and mauve	12·00	3·50
45	5s. on 5r. brown and olive	22·00	12·00
46	10s. on 10r. brown and violet	29·00	13·00

13 Queen Elizabeth II

14 Minaret

15 Camel Transport

1953. Coronation.

47	**13**	15c. black and green	1·00	1·25

1953.

48	**14**	5c. green	20	10
49a		5c. turquoise	10	1·25
50	**15**	10c. orange	40	10
51		10c. red	10	30
52	–	15c. turquoise	1·25	60
79	–	15c. grey	70	3·75
80	–	25c. red	1·25	40
56	–	35c. blue	2·50	2·00
58	–	50c. blue	20	10
60	–	70c. grey	20	10
61a	–	70c. black	1·00	20
62	–	1s. brown and violet	30	10
63	–	1s. black and violet	1·50	10
64	–	1s.25 blue and black	4·00	60
65	–	2s. brown and red	1·25	50
66	–	2s. black and red	9·50	50
67	–	5s. brown and blue	1·50	1·00
68	–	5s. black and blue	8·00	1·25
69	–	10s. brown and green	1·75	8·00
70	–	10s. black and bronze	16·00	1·75
71	–	20s. brown and lilac	6·50	10·00
72	–	20s. black and lilac	55·00	14·00

DESIGNS—HORIZ: 15c. Crater; 25c. Mosque; 1s. Dhow building; 20s. (38 × 27 mm); Aden in 1572. VERT: 35c. Dhow; 50c. Map; 70c. Salt works; 1s.25, Colony's badge; 2s. Aden Protectorate Levy; 5s. Crater Pass; 10s. Tribesmen.

1954. Royal Visit. As No. 62 but inscr "ROYAL VISIT 1954".

73	1s. sepia and violet	60	60

1959. Revised Constitution. Optd **REVISED CONSTITUTION 1959** (in Arabic on No. 74).

74	15c. green (No. 53)	30	2·00
75	1s.25 blue and black (No. 64)	1·00	1·00

28 Protein Foods

1963. Freedom from Hunger.

76	**28**	1s.25 green	1·25	1·75

For later issues see **SOUTH ARABIAN FEDERATION**.

AFGHANISTAN Pt. 16

An independent country in Asia, to N.W. of Pakistan. Now a republic, the country was formerly ruled by monarchs from 1747 to 1973.

1871. 60 paisa = 12 shahi = 6 sanar = 3 abasi = 2 kran = 1 rupee.
1920. 60 paisa = 2 kran = 1 rupee.
1926. 100 poul (pul) = 1 afghani (rupee).

The issues from 1860 to 1892 (Types **1** to **16**) are difficult to classify because the values of each set are expressed in native script and are generally all printed in the same colour. As it is not possible to list these in an intelligible simplified form we would refer users to the detailed list in the Stanley Gibbons Part 16 (Central Asia) Catalogue.

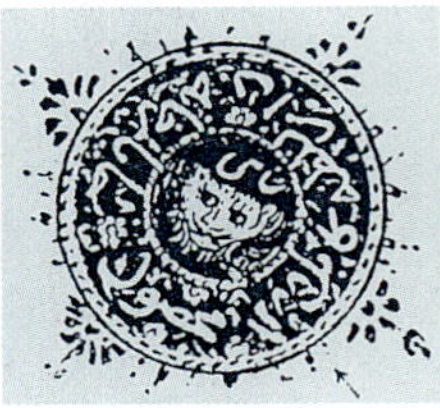
1

4

5

6

8

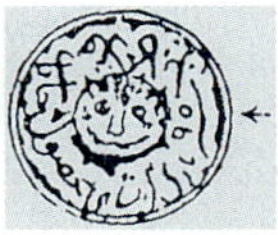
10

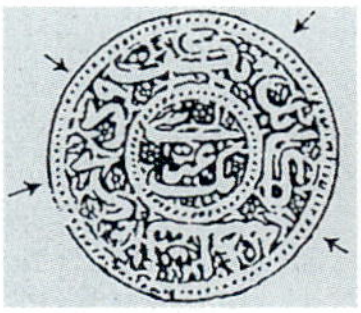
12

16

17 National Coat of Arms

1893. Dated "1310".

147	**17**	1a. black on green	3·25	3·25
148		1a. black on red	3·75	3·25
149a		1a. black on purple	3·75	3·50
150		1a. black on yellow	3·50	3·25
151		1a. black on orange	4·00	4·00
152		1a. black on blue	6·25	5·25

18 2 Abasi

1894. Undated.

153	**18**	2a. black on green	12·50	8·25
154		1r. black on green	15·00	13·00

20 1 Abasi

23

24 1 Abasi

1907. Imperf, roul or perf.

156a	**20**	1a. green	17·00	21·00
157	–	2a. blue	6·50	8·25
158	–	1r. green	45·00	23·00

The 2a. and 1r. are in similar designs.

1909. Perf.

165	**23**	2 paisa brown	13·00	4·50
166	**24**	1a. blue	5·25	2·10
168		1a. red	1·20	1·00
169	–	2a. green	3·00	2·50
170a	–	2a. bistre	2·75	3·00
171	–	1r. brown	5·00	5·25
172	–	1r. olive	7·75	7·75

The frames of the 2a. and 1r. differ from Type **24**.

27 Royal Star of Order of Independence

29 Crest of King Amanullah

(28)

1920. 1st Anniv of End of War of Independence. Size 39 × 47 mm.

173	**27**	10p. red	49·00	33·00
174		20p. purple	80·00	55·00
175		30p. green	£160	£160

1921. Size 23 × 29 mm.

177	**27**	10p. red	2·10	95
178		20p. purple	4·50	2·75
180b		30p. green	6·50	3·00

1923. 5th Independence Day. Optd with T **28**.

181	**27**	10p. red	41·00	41·00
181a		20p. brown	49·00	49·00
182		30p. green	60·00	60·00

1924. 6th Independence Day.

183	**29**	10p. brown (24 × 32 mm)	37·00	37·00

29a

30 Crest of King Amanullah

1924.

183b	**29a**	5k. blue	41·00	41·00
183c		5r. mauve	16·00	25·00

1925. 7th Independence Day.

184	**29**	10p. brown (29 × 37 mm)	60·00	45·00

1926. 7th Anniv of Independence.

185	**29**	10p. blue (26 × 33 mm)	6·50	8·25

1927. 8th Anniv of Independence.

186	**30**	10p. mauve	18·00	13·00

31

32

33

Types **31/3**, **36/37** and **41**, National Seal.

1927. Perf or imperf.

188A	**31**	15p. red	1·30	1·30
189A	**32**	30p. green	2·75	1·20
190B	**33**	60p. blue	3·00	2·10

See also Nos. 207A/13A.

34 Crest of King Amanullah

1928. 9th Anniv of Independence.

191	**34**	15p. red	5·00	5·00

36

37

1928.

193	**36**	10p. green	1·10	40
194	**37**	25p. red	1·20	80
195	–	40p. blue	1·20	80
196	–	50p. red	1·50	1·00

The frames of the 40 and 50p. differ from Type **37**. See also Nos. 207A/13A.

41

42 Independence Memorial

1929.

207A	**36**	10p. brown	1·50	1·30
208A	**31**	15p. blue	1·30	1·30
209A	**37**	25p. blue	1·30	1·20
210A	**41**	30p. green	1·30	1·20
211A	–	40p. red	1·60	1·50
212A	–	50p. blue	2·10	1·50
213A	**33**	60p. black	3·25	2·30

1931. 13th Independence Day.

214	**42**	20p. red	2·50	1·20

46 National Assembly Building

50 Mosque at Balkh

1932. Inauguration of National Council.

215	–	40p. brown (31 × 24 mm)	65	40
216	–	60p. violet (29 × 26 mm)	1·10	80
217	**46**	80p. red	1·50	1·20
218	–	1a. black (24 × 27 mm)	10·50	7·75
219	–	2a. blue (36 × 25 mm)	5·25	4·00
220	–	3a. green (36 × 24 mm)	5·50	3·75

DESIGNS: Nos. 215/16, 218/19, Council Chamber; 3a. National Assembly Building (different).

1932.

221	**50**	10p. brown	60	25
222	–	15p. brown	40	35
223	–	20p. red	65	25
224	–	25p. green	80	25
225	–	30p. red	80	25
226	–	40p. orange	1·00	50
227	–	50p. blue	1·50	1·30
228	–	60p. blue	1·30	90
229	–	80p. violet	2·50	2·10
230	–	1a. blue	4·50	80
231	–	2a. purple	5·00	2·30
232	–	3a. red	5·75	3·00

DESIGNS—32 × 23 mm: 15p. Kabul Fortress; 20, 25p. Parliament House, Darul Funun, Kabul; 40p. Memorial Pillar of Knowledge and Ignorance, Kabul; 1a. Ruins at Balkh; 2a. Minarets at Herat. 32 × 16 mm: 30p. Arch of Paghman. 23 × 32 mm: 60p. Minaret at Herat. 23 × 25 mm: 30p. Arch at Qalai Bust, near Kandahar; 50p. Independence Memorial, Kabul. 16 × 32 mm: 3a. Great Buddha at Bamian.

See also Nos. 237/51.

62 Independence Memorial

63 National Liberation Monument, Kabul

1932. 14th Independence Day.

233	**62**	1a. red	5·00	3·25

1932. Commemorative Issue.

234	**63**	80p. red	2·10	1·50

64 Arch of Paghman

1933. 15th Independence Day.

235	**64**	50p. blue	2·10	1·50

65 Independence Memorial

1934. 16th Independence Day.

236	**65**	50p. green	3·25	2·75

1934. As Nos. 219/20 and 221/30, but colours changed and new values.

237	**50**	10p. violet	25	15
238	–	15p. green	40	15
239	–	20p. mauve	40	15
240	–	25p. red	50	25
241	–	30p. orange	60	35
242	–	40p. black	65	35
243	–	45p. blue	2·10	1·60
244	–	45p. red	40	15
245	–	50p. red	75	25
246	–	60p. violet	80	40
247	–	75p. red	3·00	2·10
248	–	75p. blue	80	65
248b	–	80p. brown	1·30	80
249	–	1a. mauve	2·10	1·60
250	–	2a. grey	4·00	2·50
251	–	3a. blue	4·50	3·00

DESIGNS (new values)—34 × 23 mm: 45p. Royal Palace, Kabul. 20 × 34 mm: 75p. Hunters Canyon Pass, Hindu Kush.

68 Independence Memorial

69 Firework Display

1935. 17th Independence Day.

252	**68**	50p. blue	3·00	2·50

1936. 18th Independence Day.

253	**69**	50p. mauve	3·25	2·75

70 Independence Memorial and Mohamed Nadir Shah

71 Mohamed Nadir Shah

1937. 19th Independence Day. Perf or imperf.

254	**70**	50p. brown and violet	7·25	2·20

1938. 20th Independence Day. Perf or imperf.

255	**71**	50p. brown and blue	2·50	2·50

72 Aliabad Hospital

74 Mohamed Nadir Shah

1938. Obligatory Tax. Int Anti-cancer Fund.

256	**72**	10p. green	3·25	5·00
257	–	15p. blue	3·25	5·00

DESIGN—44 × 28 mm: 15p. Pierre and Marie Curie.

1939. 21st Independence Day.

258	**74**	50p. red	2·30	1·50

76 Darul Funun Parliament House, Kabul

79 Independence Memorial

82 Mohamed Zahir Shah

83 Sugar Mill, Baghlan

1939.

259	**76**	10p. purple (36½ × 24 mm)	25	20
260		15p. green (34 × 21 mm)	35	20
261		20p. purple (34 × 22½ mm)	40	25
262	–	25p. red	50	35
263	–	25p. green	35	25
264	–	30p. orange	40	25
265	–	35p. orange	1·50	1·00
266	–	40p. grey	80	50
267	**79**	45p. red	80	40
268		50p. orange	65	25
269		60p. violet	80	25
270	–	70p. violet	2·10	1·00
271	–	70p. purple	2·10	1·00
272	–	75p. blue	2·30	80
273	–	75p. purple	1·80	1·60
274	–	75p. red	3·00	3·00
275	–	80p. brown	1·50	1·00
276	**82**	1a. purple	1·60	80
277	–	1a. purple	1·60	1·00
278d	**83**	1a.25 blue	2·10	70
279a	–	2a. red	2·50	1·20
280	–	3a. blue	3·75	2·50

DESIGNS—31 × 19 mm: 25, 30p. Royal Palace, Kabul. 30 × 18 mm: 40p. Royal Palace, Kabul. 30 × 21 mm: 70p. Ruins at Qalai Bust, near Kandahar. 35½ × 21½ mm: 75p. Independence Memorial and Mohamed Nadir Shah. 34½ × 21 mm: 80p. As 75p. 35 × 20 mm: 1a. (No. 277), 2a. Mohamed Zahir Shah; 3a. As Type **82** but head turned more to left. 19 × 31 mm: 35p. Minarets at Herat.

85 Potez 25A2 over Kabul

1939. Air.

280a	**85**	5a. orange	5·75	4·50
280b		10a. blue	5·75	4·50
280c		20a. green	11·50	7·75

See also Nos. 300/2.

86 Mohamed Nadir Shah

87 Arch of Paghman

1940. 22nd Independence Day.

281	**86**	50p. green	2·10	1·50

1941. 23rd Independence Day.

282	–	15p. green	9·00	5·75
283	**87**	50p. brown	2·50	2·10

DESIGN: (19 × 29½ mm): 15p. Independence Memorial.

87b Mohamed Nadir Shah and Arch of Paghman

88 Independence Memorial and Mohamed Nadir Shah

1942. 24th Independence Day.

284	–	35p. green	3·75	3·75
285	**87b**	125p. blue	3·00	2·10

DESIGN—VERT: 35p. Independence Memorial in medallion.

1943. 25th Independence Day.

286	–	35p. red	14·00	12·50
287	**88**	1a.25 blue	3·25	2·50

DESIGN—HORIZ: 35p. Independence Memorial seen through archway and Mohamed Nadir Shah in oval frame.

89 Arch of Paghman

90 Independence Memorial and Mohamed Nadir Shah

1944. 26th Independence Day.

288	**89**	35p. red	1·30	75
289	**90**	1a.25 blue	2·30	2·00

91 Mohamed Nadir Shah and Independence Memorial

92 Arch of Paghman and Mohamed Nadir Shah

1945. 27th Independence Day.

290	**91**	35p. red	2·30	80
291	**92**	1a.25 blue	3·75	2·10

93 Independence Memorial

94 Mohamed Nadir Shah and Independence Memorial

1946. 28th Independence Day. Dated "1946".

292	–	15p. green	1·20	75
293	**93**	20p. mauve	2·10	90
294	–	125p. blue	3·25	2·10

DESIGNS—HORIZ: 15p. Mohamed Zahir Shah. VERT: 125p. Mohamed Nadir Shah.

1947. 29th Independence Day. Dated "1947".

295	–	15p. green	1·20	60
296	–	35p. mauve	1·30	80
297	**94**	125p. blue	3·25	2·00

DESIGNS—HORIZ: 15p. Mohamed Zahir Shah and ruins of Kandahar Fort; 35p. Mohamed Zahir Shah and Arch of Paghman.

95 Hungry Boy

96 Independence Memorial

1948. Child Welfare Fund.

298	**95**	35p. green	5·00	4·00
299	–	125p. blue	5·00	4·00

DESIGN—26 × 33½ mm: 125p. Hungry boy in vert frame.

See also No. 307.

1948. Air. As T **85** but colours changed.

300	**85**	5a. green	23·00	23·00
301		10a. orange	23·00	23·00
302		20a. blue	23·00	23·00

1948. 30th Independence Day. Dated "1948".

303	–	15p. green	80	35
304	**96**	20p. mauve	1·00	40
305	–	125p. blue	2·20	1·10

DESIGNS—VERT: 15p. Arch of Paghman. HORIZ: 125p. Mohamed Nadir Shah.

97 U.N. Symbol

1948. 3rd Anniv of U.N.O.

306	**97**	1a.25 blue	11·00	9·00

98 Hungry Boy

99 Victory Monument

1949. Obligatory Tax. Child Welfare Fund.

307	–	35p. orange	3·25	2·10
308	**98**	125p. blue	4·00	2·10

DESIGN—HORIZ: 35p. As Type **98** but 29 × 22½ mm.

1949. 31st Independence Day. Dated "1949" (Nos. 310/11).

309	**99**	25p. green	1·00	50
310	–	35p. mauve	1·20	65
311	–	1a.25 blue	2·30	1·30

DESIGNS—HORIZ: 35p. Mohamed Zahir Shah and ruins of Kandahar Fort; 1a.25, Independence Memorial and Mohamed Nadir Shah.

100 Arch of Paghman

1949. Obligatory Tax. 4th Anniv of U.N.O.

312	**100**	125p. green	15·00	9·00

101 King Mohamed Zahir Shah and Map of Afghanistan

1950. Obligatory Tax. Return of King Mohamed Zahir Shah from Visit to Europe.

313	**101**	125p. green	3·25	1·50

102 Hungry Boy

103 Mohamed Nadir Shah

1950. Obligatory Tax. Child Welfare Fund.

314	**102**	125p. green	4·50	2·50

1950. 32nd Independence Day.

315	**103**	35p. brown	65	40
316		125p. blue	1·80	60

104

1950. Obligatory Tax. 5th Anniv of U.N.O.
317 **104** 1a.25 blue . . . . 9·00 3·00

106

1950. 19th Anniv of Faculty of Medicine, Kabul.
318 **106** 35p. green (postage) . . . 1·20 75
319 – 1a.25 blue . . . . 4·25 2·30
320 **106** 35p. red (obligatory tax) 1·00 50
321 – 1a.25 black . . . . 7·00 2·30
DESIGN: Nos. 319 and 321, Sanatorium. Nos. 318 and 320 measure 38½ × 25½ mm and Nos. 319 and 321, 45 × 30 mm.

107 Minaret at Herat

109 Mohamed Zahir Shah

110 Mosque at Balkh

118

1951.
322 **107** 10p. brown and yellow . . 50 15
323 15p. brown and blue . . . 50 15
324 – 20p. black . . . . 9·75 5·25
325 **109** 25p. green 50 15
326 **110** 30p. red 60 15
327 **109** 35p. violet 65 15
328 – 40p. brown 65 15
329 – 45p. blue 65 15
330 – 50p. black . . . . 1·90 25
331 – 60p. black . . . . 1·50 25
332 – 70p. black, red and green 80 25
333 – 75p. red . . . . 1·20 50
334 – 80p. black and red . . . 2·10 90
335 – 1a. violet and green . . . 1·50 65
336 **118** 125p. black and purple . . 1·80 1·00
337 2a. blue . . . . 2·75 80
338 3a. blue and black . . . . 5·75 1·20
DESIGNS—19 × 29 mm: 20p. Buddha of Bamian; 45p. Maiwand Victory Monument; 60p. Victory Towers, Ghazni. 22 × 28 mm: 75, 80p., 1a. Mohamed Zahir Shah. 28 × 19 mm: 40p. Ruins at Qalai Bust; 70p. Flag. 30 × 19 mm: 50p. View of Kandahar.
See also Nos. 425/425k.

119 Douglas DC-3 over Kabul

1951. Air.
339 **119** 5a. red . . . . 3·25 65
339a 5a. green . . . . 1·80 40
340 10a. grey . . . . 7·50 1·80
341 20a. blue . . . . 10·50 3·00
See also Nos. 415a/b.

120 Shepherdess

121 Arch of Paghman

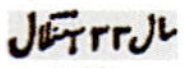
(122)

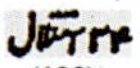
(123)

1951. Obligatory Tax. Child Welfare Fund.
342 **120** 35p. green . . . . 1·50 90
343 – 125p. blue . . . . 1·50 90
DESIGN—34½ × 44 mm: 125p. Young shepherd.

1951. 33rd Independence Day. Optd with T **122**.
344 **121** 35p. black and green . . 1·20 65
345 – 125p. blue . . . . 3·00 1·40
DESIGN (34 × 18½ mm): 125p. Mohamed Nadir Shah and Independence Memorial.
See also Nos. 360/1b and 418/19.

IMPERF STAMPS. From 1951 many issues were made available imperf from limited printings.

124 Flag of Pashtunistan

1951. Obligatory Tax. Pashtunistan Day.
346 **124** 35p. brown . . . . 1·50 80
347 – 125p. blue . . . . 3·00 2·10
DESIGN—42½ × 21½ mm: 125p. Afridi tribesman.

125 Dove and Globe

126 Avicenna (physician)

1951. Obligatory Tax. United Nations Day.
348 **125** 35p. mauve 80 40
349 – 125p. blue . . . . 2·10 1·60
DESIGN—VERT: 125p. Dove and globe.

1951. Obligatory Tax. 20th Anniv of Faculty of Medicine.
350 **126** 35p. mauve . . . . 7·75 1·50
351 125p. blue . . . . 3·00 4·00

127 Amir Sher Ali and First Stamp

128 Children and Postman

1951. Obligatory Tax. 76th Anniv of U.P.U.
352 **127** 35p. brown 65 40
353 – 35p. mauve 65 40
354 **127** 125p. blue . . . . 1·20 80
355 – 125p. blue . . . . 1·20 80
DESIGN: Nos. 353 and 355, Mohamed Zahir Shah and first stamp.

1952. Obligatory Tax. Child Welfare Fund.
356 **128** 35p. brown 80 65
357 – 125p. violet . . . . . . 1·60 1·00
DESIGN—HORIZ: 125p. Girl dancing (33 × 23 mm).

(129)

1952. Obligatory Tax. Birth Millenary of Avicenna (physician and philosopher). (a) Surch with T **129**.
358 **110** 40p. on 30p. red . . . . 5·25 3·00
(b) Surch **MILLIEME ANNIVERSAIRE DE BOALI SINAI BALKI 125 POULS** in frame.
359 **110** 125p. on 30p. red . . . . 7·50 3·50

1952. 34th Independence Day. As Nos. 344/5.
(a) Optd with T **123**.
360 35p. black and green . . . . 3·25 2·30
361 125p. blue . . . . 3·25 2·30
(b) Without opt.
361a 35p. black and green . . . 1·40 60
361b 125p. blue . . . . 3·00 1·20

131 Soldier and Flag of Pashtunistan

1952. Obligatory Tax. Pashtunistan Day.
362 **131** 35p. red 80 80
363 125p. blue . . . . 1·20 1·20

132 Orderly and Wounded Soldier

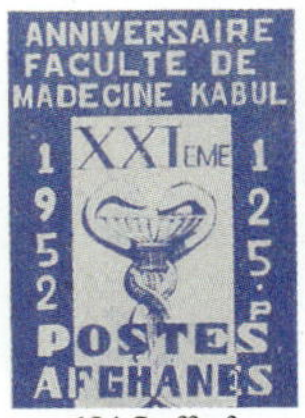
134 Staff of Aesculapius

133

1952. Obligatory Tax. Red Crescent Day.
364 **132** 10p. green 80 65

1952. Obligatory Tax. United Nations Day.
365 **133** 35p. red 80 65
366 125p. turquoise . . . . . 1·60 1·20

1952. Obligatory Tax. 21st Anniv of Faculty of Medicine.
367 **134** 35p. brown 75 50
368 125p. blue . . . . 2·00 1·30

135 Stretcher Bearers and Wounded

1953. Obligatory Tax. Red Crescent Day.
369 **135** 10p. green and brown . . 80 80
370 – 10p. brown and orange 80 80
DESIGN: No. 370, Wounded soldier, orderly and eagle.

136 Prince Mohamed Nadir

138 Flags of Afghanistan and Pashtunistan

137 Mohamed Nadir Shah and Flag-bearer

1953. Obligatory Tax. Children's Day.
371 **136** 35p. orange 40 25
372 125p. blue 80 60

1953. 35th Year of Independence. Inscr "1953".
373 **137** 35p. green 40 25
374 – 125p. violet 80 60
DESIGN—VERT: 125p. Independence Memorial and Mohamed Nadir Shah.

1953. Obligatory Tax. Pashtunistan Day. Inscr "1953".
375 **138** 35p. red 40 15
376 – 125p. blue 80 65
DESIGN—HORIZ: 125p. Badge of Pashtunistan (26 × 20 mm).

139 U.N. Emblem

140 Mohamed Nadir Shah

1953. Obligatory Tax. United Nations Day.
377 **139** 35p. mauve . . . . 1·00 80
378 125p. blue . . . . 2·10 1·50

1953. Obligatory Tax. 22nd Anniv of Faculty of Medicine.
379 **140** 35p. orange . . . . . . 1·50 1·50
380 – 125p. blue . . . . 3·00 3·00
DESIGN: 125p. As Type **140** but inscribed "1953" and with French inscription.
No. 379 was wrongly inscribed "23rd" in Arabic (the extreme right-hand figure in the second row of the inscription) and No. 380 was wrongly inscr "XXIII" and had the words "ANNIVERSAIRE" and "MEDECINE" wrongly spelt "ANNIVERAIRE" and "MADECINE". These mistakes were subsequently corrected but the corrected stamps are much rarer than the original issue.

141 Children's Band and Map of Afghanistan

1954. Obligatory Tax. Child Welfare Fund.
381 **141** 35p. violet 65 40
382 125p. blue . . . . 1·80 80

142 Mohamed Nadir Shah and Cannon

1954. 36th Independence Day.
383 **142** 35p. red 65 40
384 125p. blue . . . . 1·80 80

143 Hoisting the Flag

144

1954. Obligatory Tax. Pashtunistan Day.
385 **143** 35p. orange 65 40
386 125p. blue . . . . 1·80 80

1954. Red Crescent Day.
387 **144** 20p. red and blue 60 35

145 U.N. Flag and Map

146 Globe and Clasped Hands

1954. United Nations Day and 9th Anniv of U.N.O.
388 **145** 35p. red . . . . 1·20 1·20
389 125p. blue . . . . 3·25 2·20

1955. 10th Anniv of Signing of U.N. Charter.
390 **146** 35p. green . . . . 1·00 60
391 – 125p. blue . . . . 1·80 1·10
DESIGN—28½ × 36 mm. 125p. U.N. emblem and flags.
See also Nos. 403/4.

147 Amir Sher Ali and Mohamed Zahir Shah

1955. 85th Anniv of Postal Service.

392	147	35p.+15p. red	1·00	60
393		125p.+25p. grey	1·90	1·10

148 Children on Swing

149 Mohamed Nadir Shah (centre) and brothers

1955. Child Welfare Fund.

394	148	35p.+15p. green	1·20	75
395		125p.+25p. violet	2·50	1·20

1955. 37th Year of Independence.

396	149	35p. blue	65	40
397		35p. mauve	65	40
398	–	125p. violet	1·40	90
399	–	125p. purple	1·40	90

DESIGN: 125p. Mohamed Zahir Shah and battle scene.

150

151 Red Crescent

1955. Obligatory Tax. Pashtunistan Day.

400	150	35p. brown	60	25
401		125p. green	1·90	60

1955. Obligatory Tax. Red Crescent Day.

402	151	20p. red and grey	60	35

152 U.N. Flag

153 Child on Slide

1955. Obligatory Tax. 10th Anniv of United Nations.

403	152	35p. brown	90	60
404		125p. blue	1·80	1·10

1956. Children's Day.

405	153	35p.+15p. blue	90	40
406		140p.+15p. brown	2·30	80

154 Independence Memorial and Mohamed Nadir Shah

155 Exhibition Building

1956. 38th Year of Independence.

407	154	35p. green	60	35
408		140p. blue	2·30	90

1956. International Exhibition, Kabul.

409	155	50p. brown	80	40
410		50p. blue	80	40

156 Pashtun Square, Kabul

157 Mohamed Zahir Shah and Crescent

1956. Pashtunistan Day.

411	156	35p.+15p. violet	40	25
412		140p.+15p. brown	1·10	75

1956. Obligatory Tax. Red Crescent Day.

413	157	20p. green and red	40	25

158 Globe and Sun

159 Children on See-saw

1956. U.N. Day and 10th Anniv of Admission of Afghanistan into U.N.O.

414	158	35p.+15p. blue	1·20	1·10
415		140p.+15p. brown	2·10	1·80

1957. Air. As Nos. 339/40, but colours changed.

415a	119	5a. blue	2·10	60
415b		10a. violet	3·00	1·10

1957. Child Welfare Fund.

416	159	35p.+15p. red	80	60
417		140p.+15p. blue	1·60	1·50

1957. 39th Independence Day. As Nos. 344/5 but 35p. has longer Arabic opt (19 mm) and 125p. optd **39 em Anv.**

418	121	35p. black and green	65	35
419		125p. blue	1·00	75

162 Pashtu Flag

163 Red Crescent Headquarters, Kabul

1957. Pashtunistan Day.

420	162	50p. red	1·00	60
421		155p. violet	1·50	1·10

No. 421 is inscr "JOURNEE DU PASHTUNISTAN" beneath flag instead of Pushtu characters.

1957. Obligatory Tax. Red Crescent Day.

422	163	20p. blue and red	90	60

164 U.N. Headquarters, New York

166 Children Bathing

165 Buzkashi Game

1957. U.N. Day.

423	164	35p.+15p. brown	60	40
424		140p.+15p. blue	1·10	1·10

1957. As stamps of 1951, but colours changed and new value.

425	110	30p. brown	40	15
425a	–	40p. red	60	15
425b	–	50p. yellow	65	15
425c	–	60p. blue	80	15
425d	–	75p. violet	1·00	15
425e	–	80p. brown and violet	1·10	15
425f	–	1a. blue and red	1·80	15
425g	165	140p. purple and green	2·75	65
425k	118	2a. blue	5·75	80
425h		3a. black and orange	2·75	90

1958. Child Welfare Fund.

426	166	35p.+15p. red	65	40
427		140p.+15p. brown	80	65

167 Mohamed Nadir Shah and Old Soldier

1958. 40th Independence Day.

428	167	35p. green	40	25
429		140p. brown	1·20	1·00

168 Exhibition Buildings

1958. International Exhibition, Kabul.

430	168	35p. green	50	25
431		140p. red	1·20	1·00

169

170 President Bayar

1958. Pashtunistan Day.

432	169	35p.+15p. turquoise	40	25
433		140p.+15p. brown	1·00	65

1958. Visit of Turkish President.

434	170	50p. blue	35	15
435		100p. brown	65	35

171 Red Crescent and Map of Afghanistan

1958. Obligatory Tax. Red Crescent Day.

436	171	25p. red and green	40	15

172

1958. "Atoms for Peace".

437	172	50p. blue	60	50
438		100p. purple	90	65

173 Flags of U.N. and Afghanistan

174 UNESCO Headquarters, Paris

1958. U.N. Day.

439	173	50p. multicoloured	65	65
440		100p. multicoloured	1·40	1·20

1958. Inauguration of UNESCO Headquarters Building, Paris.

441	174	50p. green	80	65
442		100p. brown	80	80

175 Globe and Torch

1958. 10th Anniv of Declaration of Human Rights.

443	175	50p. mauve	50	50
444		100p. purple	1·00	1·20

176 Tug-of-War

1959. Child Welfare Fund.

445	176	35p.+15p. purple	60	35
446		165p.+15p. mauve	1·20	50

177 Mohamed Nadir Shah and Flags

1959. 41st Independence Day.

447	177	35p. red	60	50
448		165p. violet	1·50	65

178 Tribal Dance

1959. Pashtunistan Day.

449	178	35p.+15p. green	60	35
450		165p.+15p. orange	1·20	75

179 Badge-sellers

180 Horseman

1959. Obligatory Tax. Red Crescent Day.

451	179	25p. red and violet	40	15

1959. United Nations Day.

452	180	35p.+15p. orange	35	25
453		165p.+15p. green	65	40

181 "Uprooted Tree"

182 Buzkashi Game

183 Buzkashi Game

1960. World Refugee Year.

454	181	50p. orange	25	25
455		165p. blue	35	25
MS455a		108 × 80 mm. Nos. 454/5. Imperf	5·75	7·75
MS455b		As last, colours transposed	7·50	9·00

1960.

456	182	25p. pink	60	25
457		25p. violet	1·00	25
458		25p. olive	2·75	25
459		50p. turquoise	1·40	60
460		50p. blue	50	35
460a		50p. orange	50	35
461	183	100p. olive	80	25
462		150p. orange	65	35
463		175p. brown	2·50	50
464		2a. green	1·50	1·10

184 Children receiving Ball

1960. Child Welfare Fund.

465	184	75p.+25p. blue	90	35
466		175p.+25p. green	1·80	50

185 Douglas DC-6 over Mountains

1960. Air.

467	185	75p. violet	65	25
468		125p. blue	80	40
469		5a. olive	1·50	90

186 Independence Monument, Kabul

188 Insecticide Sprayer

187

1960. 42nd Independence Day.
470 **186** 50p. blue 40 25
471 175p. mauve . . . . . . 1·10 40

1960. Pashtunistan Day.
472 **187** 50p.+50p. red 60 30
473 175p.+50p. blue . . . . . 1·40 1·10

1960. Anti-Malaria Campaign Day.
474 **188** 50p.+50p. orange . . . . 1·30 1·20
475 175p.+50p. brown . . . . 3·50 2·75

189 Mohamed Zahir Shah

1960. King's 46th Birthday.
476 **189** 50p. brown 65 25
477 150p. red . . . . 1·60 60

190 Ambulance

1960. Red Crescent Day.
478 **190** 50p.+50p. violet & red . . 65 50
479 175p.+50p. blue & red . . 1·60 1·00

191 Teacher with Globe and Children

1960. Literacy Campaign.
480 **191** 50p. mauve 40 35
481 100p. green . . . . 1·10 50

192 Globe and Flags

195 Mir Wais Nika (patriot)

1960. U.N. Day.
482 **192** 50p. purple 25 15
483 175p. blue . . . . 1·00 65
MS483a 128 × 86 mm. Nos. 482/3. Imperf . . . . 6·25 4·50

1960. Olympic Games, Rome. Optd **1960** in figures and in Arabic and Olympic Rings.
484 **183** 175p. brown . . . . . . 1·80 2·10
MS484a 86 × 62 mm. No. 484. Imperf . . . . 6·25 8·25

1960. World Refugee Year. Nos. 454/5 surch **+25 Ps.**
485 **181** 50p.+25p. orange . . . . 1·80 1·80
486 165p.+25p. blue . . . . 1·80 1·80
MS486a 108 × 80 mm. Nos. 485/6. Imperf . . . . 6·25 6·50

1960. Mir Wais Nika Commemoration.
487 **195** 50p. mauve 65 40
488 175p. blue . . . . 1·20 50
MS488a 108 × 78 mm. Nos. 487/8. Imperf . . . . 3·75 3·75

The very numerous issues of Afghanistan which we do not list appeared between 21 April 1961 and 15 March 1964 (both dates inclusive), and were made available to the philatelic trade by an agency acting under the authority of a contract granted by the Afghanistan Government.

It later became evident that token supplies were only placed on sale in Kabul for a few hours and some of these sets contained stamps of very low denominations for which there was no possible postal use.

When the contract for the production of these stamps expired in 1963 it was not renewed and the Afghanistan Government set up a Philatelic Advisory Board to formulate stamp policy. The issues from No. 489 onwards were made in usable denominations and placed on sale without restriction in Afghanistan and distributed to the trade by the Philatelic Department of the G.P.O. in Kabul.

Issues not listed here will be found recorded in the Appendix at the end of this country. It is believed that some of the higher values from the agency sets were utilised for postage in late 1979.

196 Band Amir Lake

1961.
489 **196** 3a. blue 50 25
490 10a. purple . . . . 1·30 1·20

197 Independence Memorial

1963. 45th Independence Day.
491 **197** 25p. green 15 15
492 50p. orange 35 25
493 150p. mauve 50 35

198 Tribesmen

1963. Pashtunistan Day.
494 **198** 25p. violet 15 15
495 50p. blue 25 25
496 150p. brown 65 40

199 Assembly Building

1963. National Assembly.
497 **199** 25p. brown 15 15
498 50p. red 15 15
499 75p. brown 25 15
500 100p. olive 25 15
501 125p. lilac 40 15

200 Balkh Gate

201 Kemal Ataturk

1963.
502 **200** 3a. brown . . . . 1·00 25

1963. 25th Death Anniv of Kemal Ataturk.
503 **201** 1a. blue 15 15
504 3a. violet 65 50

202 Mohamed Zahir Shah

203 Afghan Stamp of 1878

1963. King's 49th Birthday.
505 **202** 25p. green 15 15
506 50p. grey 25 15
507 75p. red 35 25
508 100p. brown 50 25

1964. "Philately". Stamp Day.
509 **203** 1a.25 black, green & gold 25 15
510 5a. black, red and gold 60 40

204 Kabul International Airport

1964. Air. Inauguration of Kabul Int Airport.
511 **204** 10a. green and purple . . 80 25
512 20a. purple and green . . 1·00 40
513 50a. turquoise and blue 2·75 1·20

205 Kandahar International Airport

1964. Air. Inauguration of Kandahar Int Airport.
514 **205** 7a.75 brown 65 40
515 9a.25 blue 90 80
516 10a.50 green . . . . . . 1·20 1·00
517 13a.75 red . . . . 1·40 1·10

206 Unisphere and Flags

207 "Flame of Freedom"

1964. New York World's Fair.
518 **206** 6a. black, red and green 25 15

1964. 1st U.N. Human Rights Seminar, Kabul.
519 **207** 3a.75 multicoloured . . . 25 15

208 Snow Leopard

1964. Afghan Wildlife.
520 **208** 25p. blue and yellow . . . 1·80 25
521 – 50p. green and red . . . 2·10 25
522 – 75p. purple and blue . . . 2·50 25
523 – 5a. brown and green . . . 2·75 90
ANIMALS—VERT: 50p. Ibex. HORIZ: 75p. Argali; 5a. Yak.

209 Herat

210 Hurdling

1964. Tourist Publicity. Inscr "1964".
524 **209** 25p. brown and blue . . . 15 15
525 – 75p. blue and ochre . . . 15 15
526 – 3a. black, red and green 50 25
DESIGNS—VERT: 75p. Tomb of Gowhar Shad, Herat. HORIZ: 3a. Map and flag.

1964. Olympic Games, Tokyo.
527 **210** 25p. sepia, red and bistre 15 10
528 – 1a. sepia, red and blue . . 15 15
529 – 3a.75 sepia, red and green 40 25
530 – 5a. sepia, red and brown 50 35
MS530a 95 × 95 mm. Nos. 527/30. Imperf. (sold at 15a.) . . . . . 1·20 1·20
DESIGNS—VERT: 1a. Diving. HORIZ: 3a.75, Wrestling; 5a. Football.

211 Afghan Flag

212 Pashtu Flag

1964. 46th Independence Day.
531 **211** 25p. multicoloured . . . 15 15
532 75p. multicoloured . . . 35 15
On the above the Pushtu inscription "33rd Anniversary" is blocked out in gold.

1964. Pashtunistan Day.
533 **212** 100p. multicoloured . . . 25 15

213 Mohamed Zahir Shah

214 "Blood Transfusion"

1964. King's 50th Birthday.
534 **213** 1a.25 green and gold . . 25 15
535 3a.75 red and gold . . . 40 40
536 50a. black and gold . . . 3·50 2·30

1964. Red Crescent Day.
537 **214** 1a.+50p. red and black 35 25

215 Badges of Afghanistan and U.N.

1964. U.N. Day.
538 **215** 5a. blue, black and gold 25 15

216 Doves with Necklace

217 M. Jami

1964. Women's Day.
539 **216** 25p. blue, green and pink 60 35
540 75p. blue, green & lt blue 90 40
541 1a. blue, green and silver 1·20 60

1964. 550th Birth Anniv of Mowlana Jami (poet).
542 **217** 1a.50 cream, green & blk 1·00 80

218 Scaly-bellied Green Woodpecker

220 "The Red City"

219 I.T.U. Emblem and Symbols

1965. Birds. Multicoloured.
543 1a.25 Type **218** . . . . . . 3·00 40
544 3a.75 Lanceolated jay (vert) 5·25 90
545 5a. Himalayan monal pheasant (vert) . . . . . . 6·25 2·00

1965. Centenary of I.T.U.
546 **219** 5a. black, red and blue . . 50 35

1965. Tourist Publicity. Inscr "1965". Mult.
547 1a. Type **220** 25 10
548 3a.75 Bami Yan (valley and mountains) 40 15
549 5a. Band-E-Amir (lake and mountains) 60 25

221 I.C.Y. Emblem

1965. International Co-operation Year.
550 **221** 5a. multicoloured 50 35

222 Douglas DC-3 and Emblem

1965. 10th Anniv of Afghan Airlines (ARIANA).
551 **222** 1a.25 multicoloured . . . 35 10
552 – 5a. black, blue & purple 90 15
553 – 10a. multicoloured . . . 1·60 60
MS553a 90 × 90 mm. Nos. 551/3. Imperf . . . . 3·00 3·00
DESIGNS: 5a. Convair CV 240; 10a. Douglas DC-6A.

223 Mohamed Nadir Shah

224 Pashtu Flag

1965. 47th Independence Day.
554 **223** 1a. brown, black & green 40 15

1965. Pashtunistan Day.
555 **224** 1a. multicoloured 40 15

225 Promulgation of New Constitution

1965. New Constitution.
556 **225** 1a.50 black and green . . 40 15

226 Mohamed Zahir Shah

227 First Aid Post

1965. King's 51st Birthday.
557 **226** 1a.25 brown, blue & pink 25 15
558 6a. indigo, purple & blue 40 35
See also Nos. 579/80, 606/7 and 637/8.

1965. Red Crescent Day.
559 **227** 1a.50+50 brn, grn & red 35 25

228 U.N. and Afghan Flags

1965. U.N. Day.
560 **228** 5a. multicoloured 25 15

229 Fat-tailed Gecko

1966. Reptiles. Multicoloured.
561 3a. Type **229** . . . . 1·00 25
562 4a. "Agama caucasica" (lizard) . . . . 1·20 35
563 8a. "Testudo horsfieldi" (tortoise) . . . . 2·00 65

230 Cotton

231 Footballer

1966. Agriculture Day. Multicoloured.
564 1a. Type **230** 90 25
565 5a. Silkworm moth (caterpillar) . . . . 1·80 35
566 7a. Oxen . . . . 2·75 50

1966. World Cup Football Championship, England.
567 **231** 2a. black and red 75 25
568 6a. black and blue . . . . 1·30 35
569 12a. black and brown . . 2·75 75

232 Independence Memorial

1966. Independence Day.
570 **232** 1a. multicoloured 35 25
571 3a. multicoloured 90 35

233 Pashtu Flag

1966. Pashtunistan Day.
572 **233** 1a. blue 60 25

234 Founding Members

1966. Red Crescent Day.
573 **234** 2a.+1a. green and red . . 35 25
574 5a.+1a. brown & mve . . 75 35

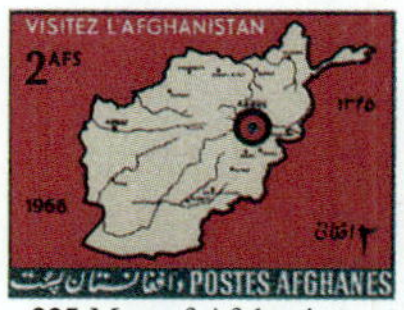

235 Map of Afghanistan

1966. Tourist Publicity. Multicoloured.
575 2a. Type **235** 25 25
576 4a. Bagh-i-Bala, former Palace of Abdur Rahman 50 35
577 8a. Tomb of Abdur Rahman, Kabul 75 75
MS578 111 × 80 mm. Nos. 575/7. Imperf . . . . 2·10 2·10

1966. King's 52nd Birthday. Portrait similar to T **226** but with position of inscr changed. Dated "1966".
579 1a. green 25 25
580 5a. brown 60 35

236 Mohamed Zahir Shah and U.N. Emblem

1966. U.N. Day. Inscr "20TH ANNIVERSAIRE DES REFUGIES".
581 **236** 5a. green, brown & emer 40 15
582 10a. red, green & yellow 80 15

237 Children Dancing

1966. Child Welfare Day.
583 **237** 1a.+1a. red and green . . 15 10
584 3a.+2a. brown & yell . . 35 15
585 7a.+3a. green & purple 55 35

238 Construction of Power Station

239 UNESCO Emblem

1967. Afghan Industrial Development. Mult.
586 2a. Type **238** 25 25
587 5a. Handwoven carpet (vert) 25 25
588 8a. Cement works 50 35

1967. 20th Anniv (1966) of UNESCO.
589 **239** 2a. multicoloured 25 15
590 6a. multicoloured 40 15
591 12a. multicoloured . . . 1·00 25

240 I.T.Y. Emblem

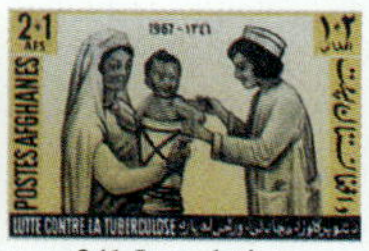

241 Inoculation

1967. International Tourist Year.
592 **240** 2a. black, blue and yellow 25 25
593 – 6a. black, blue and brown 50 25
MS594 110 × 70 mm. Nos. 592/3. Imperf. (sold at 10a.) . . . . . . 1·20 1·20
DESIGN: 6a. I.T.Y. emblem on map of Afghanistan.

1967. Anti-tuberculosis Campaign.
595 **241** 2a.+1a. black & yellow 25 25
596 5a.+2a. brown & pink . . 65 35

242 Hydroelectric Power Station, Dorunta

243 Rhesus Macaque

1967. Development of Electricity for Agriculture.
597 **242** 1a. lilac and green 15 15
598 – 6a. turquoise and brown 40 25
599 – 8a. blue and purple . . . 60 40
DESIGNS—VERT: 6a. Dam. HORIZ: 8a. Reservoir, Jalalabad.

1967. Wildlife.
600 **243** 2a. blue and buff 75 25
601 – 6a. sepia and green . . . 1·30 35
602 – 12a. brown and blue . . . 2·10 80
ANIMALS—HORIZ: 6a. Striped hyena; 12a. Goitred gazelles.

244 "Saving the Guns at Maiwand" (after R. Caton Woodville)

1967. Independence Day.
603 **244** 1a. brown and red . . . 35 25
604 2a. brown and mauve . . 60 25

245 Pashtu Dancers

1967. Pashtunistan Day.
605 **245** 2a. violet and purple . . . 60 25

1967. King's 53rd Birthday. Portrait similar to T **226** but with position of inscr changed. Dated "1967".
606 2a. brown 15 15
607 8a. blue 65 35

246 Red Crescent

247 U.N. Emblem and Fireworks

1967. Red Crescent Day.
608 **246** 3a.+1a. red, blk & ol . . 25 25
609 5a.+1a. red, blk & blue 40 25

1967. U.N. Day.
610 **247** 10a. multicoloured . . . 75 35

248 Wrestling

249 Said Jamal-ud-Din Afghan

1967. Olympic Games, Mexico City.
611 **248** 4a. purple and green . . . 50 25
612 – 6a. brown and red . . . 1·00 25
MS613 100 × 65 mm. Nos. 611/12 2·10 2·10
DESIGN: 6a. Wrestling throw.

1967. 70th Death Anniv of Said Afghan.
614 **249** 1a. purple 25 25
615 5a. brown 40 25

250 Bronze Vase

251 W.H.O. Emblem

1967. Archaeological Treasures (11th–12th century Ghasnavide era).
616 **250** 3a. brown and green . . . 35 15
617 – 7a. green and yellow . . . 65 25
MS618 65 × 100 mm. Nos. 616/17. Imperf . . . . 3·00 3·00
DESIGN: 7a. Bronze jar.

1968. 20th Anniv of W.H.O.
619 **251** 2a. blue and bistre . . . 25 25
620 7a. blue and red 50 35

252 Karakul Sheep

1968. Agricultural Day.
621 **252** 1a. black and yellow . . . 25 25
622 6a. brown, black and blue 1·00 35
623 12a. brown, sepia & blue 1·60 50

253 Road Map of Afghanistan

1968. Tourist Publicity. Multicoloured.
624 2a. Type **253** 25 25
625 3a. Victory Tower, Ghazni (21 × 31 mm) 35 25
626 16a. Mausoleum, Ghazni (21 × 31 mm) . . . . . . 1·20 60

254 Queen Humaira

255 Cinereous Vulture

1968. Mothers' Day.
627 **254** 2a.+2a. brown 35 25
628 7a.+2a. green 90 60

1968. Wild Birds. Multicoloured.
629 1a. Type **255** . . . . 1·80 65
630 6a. Eagle owl . . . . 4·25 2·00
631 7a. Greater flamingos . . . . 6·25 2·30

256 "Pig-sticking"

1968. Olympic Games, Mexico. Multicoloured.
632 2a. Olympic flame and rings (21 × 31 mm) 35 15
633 8a. Type **256** 65 40
634 12a. Buzkashi game . . . . 1·10 65

257 Flowers on Army Truck

1968. Independence Day.
635 **257** 6a. multicoloured 50 25

258 Pashtu Flag

259 Red Crescent

1968. Pashtunistan Day.
636 **258** 3a. multicoloured 45 25

1968. King's 54th Birthday. Portrait similar to T **226** but differently arranged and in smaller size (21 × 31 mm).
637 2a. blue 25 25
638 8a. brown 60 35

1968. Red Crescent Day.
639 **259** 4a.+1a. multicoloured . . 60 25

260 Human Rights Emblem

261 Maolala Djalalodine Balkhi

1968. U.N. Day and Human Rights Year.
640 **260** 1a. brown, bistre & green 25 25
641 2a. black, bistre & violet 25 25
642 6a. violet, bistre & purple 50 25
MS643 101 × 65 mm. **260** 10a. orange, bistre and purple. Imperf 1·80 1·80

1968. 695th Death Anniv of Maolala Djalalodine Balkhi (historian).
644 **261** 4a. mauve and green . . . 35 25

262 Temple Painting

263 I.L.O. Emblem

1969. Archaeological Treasures (Bagram era).
645 **262** 1a. red, yellow and green 35 25
646 – 3a. purple and violet . . . 90 25
MS647 101 × 66 mm. Nos. 6545/6. Imperf. (sold at 10a.) . . . . . 1·60 1·60
DESIGN: 3a. Carved vessel.

1969. 50th Anniv of I.L.O.
648 **263** 5a. black and yellow . . . 35 25
649 8a. black and blue 60 35

264 Red Cross Emblems

266 Mother and Child

1969. 50th Anniv of League of Red Cross Societies.
650 **264** 3a.+1a. multicoloured . . 65 35
651 5a.+1a. multicoloured . . 80 35

On Nos. 650/1 the commemorative inscr in English and Pushtu for the 50th anniv of the League of Red Cross Societies has been obliterated by gold bars.

1969. Mothers' Day.
654 **266** 1a.+1a. brown & yell . . 25 25
655 4a.+1a. violet & mve . . 40 35
MS656 121 × 81 mm. Nos. 654/5. Imperf. (sold at 10a.) . . . . . 2·10 2·10

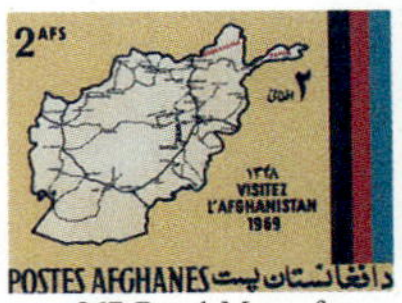

267 Road Map of Afghanistan

268 Bust (Hadda era)

1969. Tourist Publicity. Badakshan and Pamir Region. Multicoloured.
657 2a. Type **267** 60 25
658 4a. Pamir landscape 65 35
659 7a. Mountain mule transport 1·10 65
MS660 136 × 90 mm. Nos. 657/9. Imperf (sold at 15a.) . . . . . 2·50 2·50

1969. Archaeological Discoveries. Multicoloured.
661 1a. Type **268** 15 10
662 5a. Vase and jug (Bagram period) 40 15
663 10a. Statuette (Bagram period) 65 35

269 Mohamed Zahir Shah and Queen Humaira

270 Map and Rising Sun

1969. Independence Day.
664 **269** 5a. red, blue and gold . . 40 25
665 10a. green, purple & gold 75 40

1969. Pashtunistan Day.
666 **270** 2a. red and blue 25 15

271 Mohamed Zahir Shah

272 Red Crescent

1969. King's 55th Birthday.
667 **271** 2a. multicoloured 25 10
668 6a. multicoloured 60 25

1969. Red Crescent Day.
669 **272** 6a.+1a. multicoloured . . 80 25

273 U.N. Emblem, Afghan Arms and Flag

1969. United Nations Day.
670 **273** 5a. multicoloured 80 25

274 I.T.U. Emblem

275 Indian Crested Porcupine

1969. World Telecommunications Day.
671 **274** 6a. multicoloured 35 25
672 12a. multicoloured . . . 75 40

1969. Wild Animals. Multicoloured.
673 1a. Type **275** 50 35
674 3a. Wild boar . . . . 1·20 40
675 8a. Bactrian red deer . . . . 1·60 50

276 Footprint on the Moon

277 "Cancer the Crab"

1969. 1st Man on the Moon.
676 **276** 1a. multicoloured 25 25
677 3a. multicoloured 35 25
678 6a. multicoloured 50 25
679 10a. multicoloured . . . 75 40

1970. W.H.O. "Fight Cancer" Day.
680 **277** 2a. red, dp green & green 25 25
681 6a. red, deep blue & blue 50 25

278 Mirza Bedel

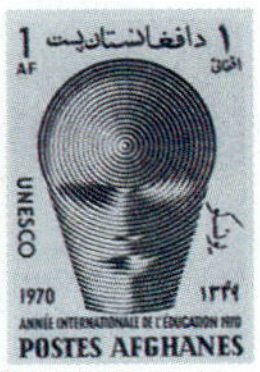

279 I.E.Y. Emblem

1970. 250th Death Anniv of Mirza Abdul Quader Bedel (poet).
682 **278** 5a. multicoloured 40 15

1970. International Education Year.
683 **279** 1a. black 25 25
684 6a. red 40 25
685 12a. green 90 40

280 Mother and Child

281 U.N. Emblem, Scales and Satellite

1970. Mothers' Day.
686 **280** 6a. multicoloured 35 25

1970. 25th Anniv of United Nations.
687 **281** 4a. blue, dp blue & yellow 25 25
688 6a. blue, deep blue & red 40 25

282 Road Map of Afghanistan with Location of Sites

283 Common Quail

1970. Tourist Publicity. Inscr "1970". Mult.
689 **282** 2a. black, green and blue 15 15
690 – 3a. multicoloured 25 15
691 – 7a. multicoloured 60 25
DESIGNS (36 × 26 mm): 3a. Lakeside mosque, Kabul; 7a. Arch of Paghman.

1970. Wild Birds. Multicoloured.
692 2a. Type **283** . . . . 2·10 65
693 4a. Golden eagle . . . . . . 4·00 1·00
694 6a. Common pheasant . . . 5·25 1·60

284 Shah Reviewing Troops

1970. Independence Day.
695 **284** 8a. multicoloured 40 25

285 Group of Pashtus

1970. Pashtunistan Day.
696 **285** 2a. blue and red 40 25

286 Mohamed Zahir Shah

287 Red Crescent Emblems

1970. King's 56th Birthday.
697 **286** 3a. violet and green . . . 25 25
698 7a. purple and blue . . . 75 35

1970. Red Crescent Day.
699 **287** 2a. black, red and gold 25 15

288 U.N. Emblem and Plaque

1970. United Nations Day.
700 **288** 1a. multicoloured 25 25
701 5a. multicoloured 25 25

289 Afghan Stamps of 1871

1970. Centenary of First Afghan Stamps.
702 **289** 1a. black, blue & orange 35 25
703 4a. black, yellow & blue 60 25
704 12a. black, blue and lilac 1·00 40

290 Global Emblem

1971. World Telecommunications Day.
705 **290** 12a. multicoloured . . . 65 40

291 "Callimorpha principalis"

1971. Butterflies and Moths. Multicoloured.
706 1a. Type **291** . . . . 1·30 60
707 3a. "Epizygaenella afghana" 2·75 1·20
708 5a. "Parnassius autocrator" 4·00 1·80

292 Lower half of old Kushan Statue

294 Pashtunistan Square, Kabul

293 Independence Memorial

1971. UNESCO Kushan Seminar.
709 **292** 6a. violet and yellow . . . 50 25
710 10a. purple and blue . . . 80 35

1971. Independence Day.
711 **293** 7a. multicoloured 60 25
712 9a. multicoloured 90 35

1971. Pashtunistan Day.
713 **294** 5a. purple 50 25

295 Mohamed Zahir Shah and Kabul Airport

1971. Air. Multicoloured.
714 50a. Type **295** . . . . 4·50 4·50
715 100a. King, airline emblem and Boeing 727 airplane 5·75 3·50

296 Mohamed Zahir Shah

297 Map, Nurse and Patients

1971. King's 57th Birthday.
716 **296** 9a. multicoloured 60 35
717 17a. multicoloured . . . 1·20 65

1971. Red Crescent Day.
718 **297** 8a. multicoloured 50 35

298 Emblem of Racial Equality Year

1971. United Nations Day.
719 **298** 24a. blue . . . . 1·50 80

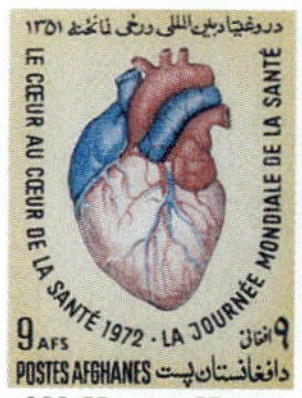

299 Human Heart

300 "Tulipa lanata"

1972. World Health Day and World Heart Month.
720 **299** 9a. multicoloured 90 35
721 12a. multicoloured . . . 1·80 40

1972. Afghan Flora and Fauna. Multicoloured.
722 7a. Type **300** . . . . 1·30 75
723 10a. Chukar partridge (horiz) 7·75 1·60
724 12a. Lynx (horiz) . . . . . 2·50 1·20
725 18a. "Allium stipitatum" . . 2·50 1·30

301 Buddha of Hadda

1972. Tourist Publicity.
726 **301** 3a. blue and brown . . . 60 25
727 – 7a. green and red 90 35
728 – 9a. purple and green . . . 1·30 40
DESIGNS: 7a. Greco-Bactrian seal, 250 B.C.; 9a. Greek temple, Ai-Khanum, 3rd–2nd century B.C.

302 King with Queen Humaira at Independence Parade

1972. Independence Day.
729 **302** 25a. multicoloured . . . 4·50 1·20

303 Wrestling

1972. Olympic Games, Munich. Various Wrestling Holds as T **303**.
730 4a. multicoloured 35 15
731 8a. multicoloured 60 25
732 10a. multicoloured 65 35
733 19a. multicoloured . . . . . 1·50 50
734 21a. multicoloured . . . . . 1·60 60
MS735 160 × 110 mm. Nos. 730/4. Imperf (sold at 60a.) . . . . . 3·25 3·25

304 Pathan and Mountain View

305 Mohamed Zahir Shah

1972. Pashtunistan Day.
736 **304** 5a. multicoloured 60 25

1972. King's 58th Birthday.
737 **305** 7a. blue, black and gold 75 25
738 14a. brown, black & gold 1·20 40

306 Ruined Town and Refugees

1972. Red Crescent Day.
739 **306** 7a. black, red and blue . . 65 25

307 E.C.A.F.E. Emblem

1972. U.N. Day. 25th Anniv of U.N. Economic Commission for Asia and the Far East.
740 **307** 12a. black and blue . . . 60 35

308 Ceramics

1973. Afghan Handicrafts. Multicoloured.
741 7a. Type **308** 40 25
742 9a. Embroidered coat (vert) 50 35
743 12a. Coffee set (vert) . . . 75 40
744 16a. Decorated boxes . . . . 1·10 50
MS745 110 × 110 mm. Nos. 741/4. Imperf (sold at 45a.) . . . . . 3·75 3·75

309 W.M.O. and Afghan Emblems

1973. Cent of World Meteorological Organization.
746 **309** 7a. green and mauve . . . 60 25
747 14a. red and blue . . . . 1·40 40

310 Emblems and Harvester

1973. 10th Anniv of World Food Programme.
748 **310** 14a.+7a. purple & blue 1·40 90

311 Al-Biruni

312 Association Emblem

1973. Birth Millenary of Abu-al Rayhan al-Biruni (mathematician and philosopher).
749 **311** 10a. multicoloured . . . 65 40

1973. Family Planning Week.
750 **312** 9a. purple and orange . . 65 25

313 Himalayan Monal Pheasant

1973. Birds. Multicoloured.
751 8a. Type **313** . . . . 3·00 2·10
752 9a. Great crested grebe . . 3·75 2·50
753 12a. Himalayan snowcock . . 4·50 3·25

314 Buzkashi Game

1973. Tourism.
754 **314** 8a. black 60 35

315 Firework Display

1973. Independence Day.
755 **315** 12a. multicoloured . . . 65 35

316 Landscape and Flag

1973. Pashtunistan Day.
756 **316** 9a. multicoloured 65 15

317 Red Crescent

1973. Red Crescent.
757 **317** 10a. multicoloured . . . 1·00 25

318 Kemal Ataturk

1973. 50th Anniv of Turkish Republic.
758 **318** 1a. blue 25 25
759 7a. brown . . . . 1·20 25

319 Human Rights Flame

1973. 25th Anniv of Declaration of Human Rights.
760 **319** 12a. blue, black and silver 60 40

320 Asiatic Black Bears

1974. Wild Animals. Multicoloured.
761 5a. Type **320** 65 15
762 7a. Afghan hound . . . . . 1·10 40
763 10a. Goitred gazelle . . . . 1·40 50
764 12a. Leopard . . . . 1·80 60
MS765 120 × 100 mm. Nos. 761/4. Imperf . . . . 10·50 10·50

321 "Workers"

1974. Labour Day.
766 **321** 9a. multicoloured 50 35

322 Arch of Paghman and Independence Memorial

1974. Independence Day.
767 **322** 4a. multicoloured 40 10
768 11a. multicoloured . . . 60 25

323 Arms of Afghanistan and Hands clasping Seedling

1974. 1st Anniv of Republic. Multicoloured.
769 4a. Type **323** 40 10
770 5a. Republican flag (36 × 26 mm) 60 15
771 7a. Gen. Mohammed Daoud (26 × 36 mm) 65 25
772 15a. Soldiers and arms . . . 1·20 35
MS773 Two sheets. Imperf (a) 120 × 80 mm. Nos. 769 and 772. (b) 100 × 100 mm. Nos. 770/1 3·75 3·75

324 Lesser Spotted Eagle

1974. Afghan Birds. Multicoloured.
774 1a. Type **324** . . . . 2·10 50
775 6a. White-fronted goose, ruddy shelduck and greylag goose . . . . 4·50 80
776 11a. Black crane and common coots . . . . . . 7·50 1·30

325 Flags of Pashtunistan and Afghanistan

1974. Pashtunistan Day.
777 **325** 5a. multicoloured 35 25

326 Republic's Coat of Arms

1974.
778 **326** 100p. green 80 25

327 Pres. Daoud

1974.
779 **327** 10a. multicoloured . . . 65 25
780 16a. multicoloured . . . 2·50 90
781 19a. multicoloured . . . 90 50
782 21a. multicoloured . . . 1·40 60
783 22a. multicoloured . . . 3·75 2·00
784 30a. multicoloured . . . 5·00 2·75

328 Arms and Centenary Years

1974. Centenary of U.P.U.
785 **328** 7a. green, black and gold 35 25

329 "UN" and U.N. Emblem

1974. United Nations Day.
786 **329** 5a. blue and ultramarine 40 15

330 Pres. Daoud

331 Minaret, Jam

1975.
787 **330** 50a. multicoloured . . . 2·75 1·40
788 100a. multicoloured . . . 5·75 2·50

1975. South Asia Tourist Year. Multicoloured.
789 7a. Type **331** 35 15
790 14a. "Griffon and Lady" (2nd century) 65 40
791 15a. Head of Buddha (4th–5th century) 80 40
MS792 130 × 90 mm. Nos. 789/91. Imperf . . . . 3·75 3·75

332 Afghan Flag

1975. Independence Day.
793 **332** 16a. multicoloured . . . 80 25

333 Rejoicing Crowd

1975. 2nd Anniv of Revolution.
794 **333** 9a. multicoloured 50 15
795 12a. multicoloured . . . 65 25

334 I.W.Y. Emblem

335 Rising Sun and Flag

1975. International Women's Year.
796 **334** 9a. black, blue and purple 50 15

1975. Pashtunistan Day.
797 **335** 10a. multicoloured . . . 40 15

336 Wazir M. Akbar Khan

1976. 130th Death Anniv of Akbar Khan (resistance leader).
798 **336** 15a. multicoloured . . . 60 40

337 Independence Monument and Arms

1976. Independence Day.
799 **337** 22a. multicoloured . . . 75 50

338 Pres. Daoud raising Flag

339 Mountain

1976. 3rd Anniv of Republic.
800 **338** 30a. multicoloured . . . 80 60

1976. Pashtunistan Day.
801 **339** 16a. multicoloured . . . 65 50

340 Arms

340a

1976.
802 – 25p. salmon 50 35
803 **340** 50p. green 60 25
803a **340a** 50p. rosine 60 25
804 **340** 1a. blue 65 10
DESIGN: 25p. As Type **340** but with Arms on left and inscription differently arranged.

341 Flag and Monuments on Open Book

1977. Independence Day.
805 **341** 20a. multicoloured . . . 75 65

342 Presidential Address

1977. Election of First President and New Constitution. Multicoloured.
806 7a. President Daoud and Election (45 × 27 mm) . . . 80 60
807 8a. Type **342** 90 75
808 10a. Inaugural ceremony . . 1·20 90
809 18a. Promulgation of new constitution (45 × 27 mm) 2·00 1·60
MS810 136 × 106 mm. Nos. 806/9. Imperf . . . . 3·75 3·75

343 Medal

1977. 80th Death Anniv of Sayed Jamaluddin (Afghan reformer).
811 **343** 12a. black, blue & gold 40 15

344 Crowd with Afghan Flag

346 Dome of the Rock

345 Dancers around Fountain

1977. Republic Day.
812 **344** 22a. multicoloured . . . 75 40

1977. Pashtunistan Day.
813 **345** 30a. multicoloured . . . 1·20 90

1977. Palestinian Welfare.
814 **346** 12a.+3a. black, gold and pink . . . . 2·10 60

347 Arms and Carrier Pigeon

1977.
815 **347** 1a. blue and black 40 15

348 President Daoud acknowledging Crowd

1978. 1st Anniv of Presidential Election.
816 **348** 20a. multicoloured . . . 2·10 1·20

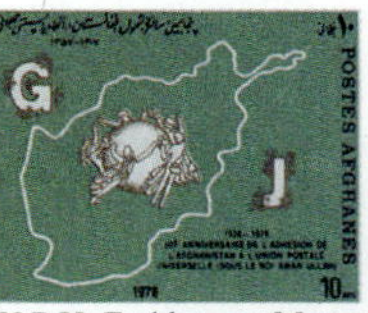

349 U.P.U. Emblem on Map of Afghanistan

1978. 50th Anniv of Admission to U.P.U.
817 **349** 10a. gold, green & black 40 15

350 Transmitting Aerial and Early Telephone

1978. 50th Anniv of Admission to I.T.U.
818 **350** 8a. multicoloured 40 15

351 Red Crescent, Red Cross and Red Lion Emblems

1978. Red Crescent.
819 **351** 3a. black . . . . 1·20 65

352 Arms

1978.
820 **352** 1a. red and gold . . . . 1·60 65
821 4a. red and gold . . . . 2·10 90

353 Ruin, Qalai Bust

1978. Independence Day. Multicoloured.
822 16a. Buddha, Bamian . . . . 1·20 50
823 22a. Type **353** . . . . 1·60 75
824 30a. Women in national costume . . . . 2·10 1·20

354 Afghans with Flag

355 Crest and Symbols of the Five Senses

1978. Pashtunistan Day.
825 **354** 7a. red and blue 50 15

1978. International Literacy Day.
826 **355** 20a. red 90 40

356 Flag

1978. "The Mail is in the Service of the People".
827 **356** 8a. red, gold and brown 65 15
828 9a. red, gold and brown 1·00 15

357 Martyr

358 President Mohammed Taraki

1978. "The People's Democratic Party Honours its Martyrs".
829 **357** 18a. green . . . . 1·00 40

1978. 14th Anniv of People's Democratic Party.
830 **358** 12a. multicoloured . . . 75 25

359 Emancipated Woman

1979. Women's Day.
831 **359** 14a. blue and red . . . . 1·20 50

360 Farmers planting Tree

1979. Farmers' Day.
832 **360** 1a. multicoloured 65 35

361 Map and Census Taking

1979. 1st Complete Population Census.
833 **361** 3a. black, blue and red . . 90 65

362 Pres. Taraki reading "Khalq"

1979. 1st Publication of "Khalq" (party newspaper).
834 **362** 2a. multicoloured 65 15

363 Pres. Taraki and Tank

364 Pres. Taraki

1979. 1st Anniv of Sawr Revolution (1st issue).
835 **363** 50p. multicoloured . . . 65 15

1979. 1st Anniv of Sawr Revolution (2nd issue). Multicoloured.
836 4a. Type **364** 40 10
837 5a. Revolutionary H.Q. and Tank Monument, Kabul (47 × 32 mm) 60 15
838 6a. Command room, Revolutionary H.Q. (vert) 65 15
839 12a. House where first Khalq Party Congress was held (vert) 80 25

365 Carpenter and Blacksmith

1979. Workers' Solidarity.
840 **365** 10a. multicoloured . . . 90 15

366 Children on Map of Afghanistan

1979. International Year of the Child.
841 **366** 16a. multicoloured . . . 1·80 90

367 Revolutionaries and Kabul Monuments

368 Afghans and Flag

1979. Independence Day.
842 **367** 30a. multicoloured . . . 1·60 90

1979. Pashtunistan Day.
843 **368** 9a. multicoloured 75 15

369 U.P.U. Emblem and Arms on Map

1979. Stamp Day.
844 **369** 15a. multicoloured . . . 65 25

370 Headstone and Tomb

1979. Martyrs' Day.
845 **370** 22a. multicoloured . . . 2·50 1·20

371 Doves around Globe

1979.
845a **371** 2a. blue and red . . . . 1·20 25

372 Woman with Baby, Dove and Rifle

374 Healthy Non-smoker and Prematurely Aged Smoker

373 Farmers receiving Land Grants

1980. International Women's Day.
846 **372** 8a. multicoloured . . . . 1·60 50

1980. Farmers' Day.
847 **373** 2a. multicoloured . . . . 2·10 65

1980. World Health Day. Anti-smoking Campaign.
848 **374** 5a. multicoloured . . . . 1·60 65

375 "Lenin speaking from Tribune"

1980. 110th Birth Anniv of Lenin.
849 **375** 12a. multicoloured . . . 2·50 80

376 Crowd and Clenched Fist

1980. 2nd Anniv of Sawr Revolution.
850 **376** 1a. multicoloured 65 15

377 Quarry Worker and Blacksmith

1980. Workers' Solidarity.
851 **377** 9a. multicoloured 50 15

378 Football

1980. Olympic Games, Moscow. Mult.
852 3a. Type **378** 60 15
853 6a. Wrestling 65 15
854 9a. Pigsticking 75 25
855 10a. Buzkashi 90 25

379 Soldiers attacking Fortress

1980. Independence Day.
856 **379** 3a. multicoloured 65 15

380 Pashtus with Flag

1980. Pashtunistan Day.
857 **380** 25a. multicoloured . . . 1·00 40

381 Post Office

1980. World U.P.U. Day.
858 **381** 20a. multicoloured . . . 1·00 40

382 Buzkashi

1980.

859 **382** 50a. multicoloured . . . 2·10 1·50
860 100a. multicoloured . . . 4·00 1·60

383 Arabic "H", Medina Mosque and Kaaba

1981. 1400th Anniv of Hegira.
861 **383** 13a.+2a. multicoloured . . 1·80 35

384 Mother and Child with Dove and Globe

1981. International Women's Day.
862 **384** 15a. multicoloured . . . 1·20 35

385 Ox Plough, Tractor and Planting Trees

1981. Farmers' Day.
863 **385** 1a. multicoloured . . . . 1·00 25

386 Urial

387 Crowd and Afghan Arms

1981. Protected Wildlife.
864 **386** 12a. multicoloured . . . 2·30 65

1981. 3rd Anniv of Sawr Revolution.
865 **387** 50p. brown 65 15

388 Road Workers in Ravine

389 Red Crescent enclosing Scenes of Disaster and Medical Aid

1981. Workers' Day.
866 **388** 10a. multicoloured . . . 90 35

1981. Red Crescent Day.
867 **389** 1a.+4a. multicoloured . . 65 80

390 Satellite Receiving Station

391 Map enclosing playing Children

1981. World Telecommunications Day.
868 **390** 9a. multicoloured 65 15

1981. International Children's Day.
869 **391** 15a. multicoloured . . . 90 40

392 Afghans and Monument

1981. Independence Day.
870 **392** 4a. multicoloured 90 15

393 Pashtus around Flag

394 Terracotta Horseman

1981. Pashtunistan Day.
871 **393** 2a. multicoloured 65 15

1981. World Tourism Day.
872 **394** 5a. multicoloured 65 15

395 Siamese Twins and I.Y.D.P. Emblem

1981. International Year of Disabled Persons.
873 **395** 6a.+1a. multicoloured . . 90 50

396 Harvesting

1981. World Food Day.
874 **396** 7a. multicoloured 80 15

397 Peace, Solidarity and Friendship Organization Emblem

398 Heads and Clenched Fist on Globe and Emblem

1981. Afro-Asian Peoples' Solidarity Meeting.
875 **397** 8a. blue 75 15

1981. International Anti-apartheid Year.
876 **398** 4a. multicoloured . . . . 1·00 25

399 Lion (bas-relief at Stara Zagora)

1981. 1300th Anniv of Bulgarian State.
877 **399** 20a. stone, purple and red 1·50 50

400 Mother rocking Cradle

1982. Women's Day.
878 **400** 6a. multicoloured 60 15

401 Farmers

402 Judas Tree

1982. Farmers' Day.
879 **401** 4a. multicoloured 65 15

1982. Plants. Multicoloured.
880 3a. Type **402** 35 15
881 4a. Hollyhock 60 15
882 16a. Rhubarb . . . . 1·20 35

403 Hands holding Flags and Tulip

404 Dimitrov

1982. 4th Anniv of Sawr Revolution.
883 **403** 1a. multicoloured . . . . 1·20 15

1982. Birth Centenary of Georgi Dimitrov (Bulgarian statesman).
884 **404** 30a. multicoloured . . . 2·30 80

405 Blacksmith, Factory Workers, Weaver and Labourer

1982. Workers' Day.
885 **405** 10a. multicoloured . . . 75 25

406 White Storks

407 Brandt's Hedgehog

1982. Birds. Multicoloured.
886 6a. Type **406** . . . . 1·60 50
887 11a. Eurasian goldfinches . . 2·10 60

1982. Animals. Multicoloured.
888 3a. Type **407** 60 15
889 14a. Cobra . . . . 1·50 25

408 National Monuments

409 Pashtus and Flag

1982. Independence Day.
890 **408** 20a. multicoloured . . . 1·20 50

1982. Pashtunistan Day.
891 **409** 32a. multicoloured . . . 2·50 75

410 Tourists

1982. World Tourism Day.
892 **410** 9a. multicoloured 80 35

411 Postman delivering Letter, Post Office and U.P.U. Emblem

1982. World U.P.U. Day.
893 **411** 4a. multicoloured 90 25

412 Family eating Meal

413 U.N. Emblem illuminating Globe

1982. World Food Day.
894 **412** 9a. multicoloured . . . . 1·40 35

1982. 37th Anniv of United Nations.
895 **413** 15a. multicoloured . . . 1·00 40

414 Earth Satellite Station

1982. I.T.U. Delegates' Conference, Nairobi.
896 **414** 8a. multicoloured 75 15

415 Dr. Robert Koch

416 Hand holding Torch, Globe and Scales

1982. Centenary of Discovery of Tubercle Bacillus.
897 **415** 7a. black, brown & pink 50 25

1982. 34th Anniv of Declaration of Human Rights.
898 **416** 5a. multicoloured 40 15

417 Lions

1982. Wild Animals. Multicoloured.
899 2a. Type **417** 40 15
900 7a. Asiatic wild asses 90 35
901 12a. Sable (vert) . . . . . . 2·00 50

418 Woman releasing Dove

419 Mir Alicher-e-Nawai (poet)

1983. International Women's Day.
902 **418** 3a. multicoloured 25 15

1983. "Mir Alicher-e-Nawai and his Times" Study Decade.
903 **419** 22a. multicoloured . . . 90 35

420 Distributing Land Ownership Documents

1983. Farmers' Day.
904 **420** 10a. multicoloured . . . 65 25

421 Revolution Monument

1983. 5th Anniv of Sawr Revolution.
905 **421** 15a. multicoloured . . . 65 25

422 World Map and Hands holding Cogwheel

1983. Labour Day.
906 **422** 20a. multicoloured . . . 65 25

423 Broadcasting Studio, Dish Aerial, Satellites and Television

1983. World Communications Year. Multicoloured.
907 4a. Type **423** 35 10
908 11a. Telecommunications headquarters 60 15

424 Hands holding Child

425 Arms and Map of Afghanistan

1983. International Children's Day.
909 **424** 25a. multicoloured . . . 50 20

1983. 2nd Anniv of National Fatherland Front.
910 **425** 1a. multicoloured 35 15

426 Apollo

427 Racial Segregation

1983. Butterflies. Multicoloured.
911 9a. Type **426** . . . . 1·00 75
912 13a. Swallowtail . . . . . . 2·30 1·30
913 21a. Small tortoiseshell (horiz) . . . . 3·00 1·60

1983. Anti-apartheid Campaign.
914 **427** 10a. multicoloured . . . 50 15

428 National Monuments

429 Pashtus with Flag

1983. Independence Day.
915 **428** 6a. multicoloured 40 15

1983. Pashtunistan Day.
916 **429** 3a. multicoloured 40 15

430 Afghan riding Camel

1983. World Tourism Day.
917 **430** 5a. multicoloured 40 25
918 – 7a. brown and black . . . 60 25
919 – 12a. multicoloured . . . 90 25
920 – 16a. multicoloured . . . 1·20 25
DESIGNS—VERT: 7a. Stone carving. 16a. Carved stele. HORIZ: 12a. Three statuettes.

431 Winter Landscape

1983. Multicoloured.
921 50a. Type **431** . . . . 1·60 35
922 100a. Woman with camel . . 3·75 40

432 "Communications"

1983. World Communications Year. Mult.
923 14a. Type **432** 65 15
924 15a. Ministry of Communications, Kabul 65 15

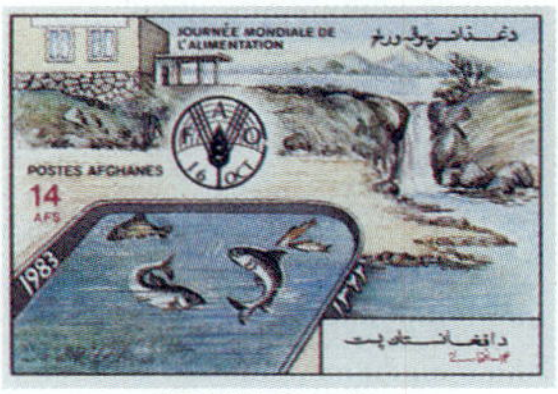
433 Fish Breeding

1983. World Food Day.
925 **433** 14a. multicoloured . . . 80 15

434 Football

1983. Sports. Multicoloured.
926 1a. Type **434** 25 25
927 18a. Boxing . . . . 1·00 35
928 21a. Wrestling . . . . 1·20 35

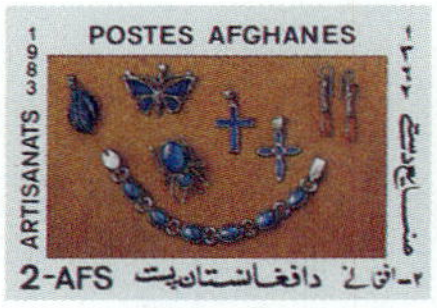
435 Jewellery

1983. Handicrafts. Multicoloured.
929 2a. Type **435** 15 10
930 8a. Polished stoneware . . . 35 15
931 19a. Furniture 60 15
932 30a. Leather goods . . . . . 1·40 15

436 Map, Sun, Scales and Torch

1983. 35th Anniv of Declaration of Human Rights.
933 **436** 20a. multicoloured . . . 90 15

437 Polytechnic Buildings and Emblem

1983. 20th Anniv of Kabul Polytechnic.
934 **437** 30a. multicoloured . . . 1·20 25

438 Ice Skating

439 Dove, Woman and Globe

1984. Winter Olympic Games, Sarajevo. Mult.
935 5a. Type **438** 25 10
936 9a. Skiing 35 10
937 11a. Speed skating 50 10
938 15a. Ice hockey 60 10
939 18a. Biathlon 65 15
940 20a. Ski jumping 80 15
941 22a. Bobsleigh . . . . 1·00 15

1984. International Women's Day.
942 **439** 4a. multicoloured 50 30

440 Ploughing with Tractor

1984. Farmers' Day. Multicoloured.
943 2a. Type **440** 15 10
944 4a. Digging irrigation channel 15 10
945 7a. Saddling donkey by water-mill 15 10
946 9a. Harvesting wheat 25 10
947 15a. Building haystack . . . 40 15
948 18a. Showing cattle 60 15
949 20a. Ploughing with oxen and sowing seed 75 15

441 "Luna I"

1984. World Aviation and Space Navigation Day. Multicoloured.
950 5a. Type **441** 35 25
951 8a. "Luna II" 40 25
952 11a. "Luna III" 50 25
953 17a. "Apollo XI" 65 25
954 22a. "Soyuz VI" 80 35
955 28a. "Soyuz VII" 80 35
956 34a. "Soyuz VI", "VII" and "VIII" . . . . 1·00 40
MS957 66 × 87 mm. 25a. Sergei Korolev (rocket designer) and rocket (29 × 41 mm) . . . . . 1·40 80

442 Flags, Soldier and Workers

443 Hunting Dog

1984. 6th Anniv of Sawr Revolution.
958 **442** 3a. multicoloured 40 15

1984. Animals. Multicoloured.
959 1a. Type **443** 10 10
960 2a. Argali 25 15
961 6a. Przewalski's horse (horiz) 60 15
962 8a. Wild boar 80 25
963 17a. Snow leopard (horiz) . . 1·60 25
964 19a. Tiger (horiz) . . . . . 2·75 25
965 22a. Indian elephant . . . . 3·00 35

444 Postal Messenger

1984. 19th U.P.U. Congress, Hamburg. Mult.
966 25a. Type **444** 90 15
967 35a. Post rider . . . . . . 1·40 35
968 40a. Bird with letter . . . . 1·80 35
MS969 97 × 66 mm. 50a. black 3·00 1·80
DESIGNS: At T **444**—35a. Post rider; 40a. Bird with letter; 25 × 37 mm—50a. Hamburg 1859 2s. stamp.

445 Antonov AN-2

1984. 40th Anniv of Ariana Airline. Mult.
970 1a. Type **445** 10 10
971 4a. Ilyushin Il-12 . . . . . 15 10
972 9a. Tupolev Tu-104A 60 15
973 10a. Ilyushin Il-18 . . . . . 80 15
974 13a. Yakovlev Yak-42 . . . 1·10 15
975 17a. Tupolev Tu-154 . . . . 1·40 15
976 21a. Ilyushin Il-86 . . . . . 1·60 15

446 Ettore Bugatti (motor manufacturer) and Bugatti Type 43 Sports car, 1927

1984. Motor Cars. Multicoloured.
977 2a. Type **446** 15 10
978 5a. Henry Ford and Ford Model A two-seater, 1903 35 10
979 8a. Rene Panhard (engineer) and Panhard Limosine, 1899 . . . . 60 10
980 11a. Gottlieb Daimler (engineer) and Daimler DB 18 saloon, 1935 . . . . . 75 10
981 12a. Karl Benz and Benz Viktoria two-seater (inscr "Victoria"), 1893 . . . . . 1·00 15
982 15a. Armand Peugeot (motor manufacturer) and Peugeot vis-a-vis, 1892 . . . . . . 1·10 15
983 22a. Louis Chevrolet (car designer) and Chevrolet Superior sedan, 1925 . . . 1·50 15

447 Open Book showing Monuments and Fortress

1984. Independence Day.
984 **447** 6a. multicoloured 40 15

448 Truck on Mountain Road and Pashtunistan Badge

1984. Pashtunistan Day.
985 **448** 3a. multicoloured 40 15

449 Arch at Qalai Bust

450 Pine Cone

1984. World Tourism Day. Multicoloured.
986 1a. Type **449** 10 10
987 2a. Ornamented belt 15 10
988 5a. Kabul monuments . . . 15 15
989 9a. Statuette (vert) 25 15
990 15a. Buffalo riders in snow 40 25
991 19a. Camel in ornate caparison 80 25
992 21a. Buzkashi players . . . . 1·00 25

1984. World Food Day. Multicoloured.
993 2a. Type **450** 15 10
994 4a. Walnuts 25 10
995 6a. Pomegranate 35 10
996 9a. Apples 50 10
997 13a. Cherries 60 15
998 15a. Grapes 75 15
999 26a. Pears . . . . 1·20 15

451 Globe and Emblem

1985. 20th Anniv (1984) of Peoples' Democratic Party.
1000 **451** 25a. multicoloured . . . 1·20 40

452 Cattle

453 Map and Geologist

1985. Farmers' Day. Multicoloured.
1001 1a. Type **452** 35 15
1002 3a. Mare and foal 35 15
1003 7a. Galloping horse 35 15
1004 8a. Grey horse (vert) . . . 60 25
1005 15a. Karakul sheep and sheepskins 90 25
1006 16a. Herder watching over cattle and sheep . . . . 1·10 35
1007 25a. Family with pack camels . . . . 1·50 40

1985. Geologists' Day.
1008 **453** 4a. multicoloured . . . 35 15

454 Satellite

1985. 20th Anniv of "Intelsat" Communications Satellite. Multicoloured.
1009 6a. Type **454** 50 15
1010 9a. "Intelsat III" 65 15
1011 10a. Rocket launch (vert) . . 90 15

455 "Visitors for Lenin" (V. Serov)

456 Revolutionaries with Flags

1985. 115th Birth Anniv of Lenin. Multicoloured.
1012 10a. Type **455** 65 25
1013 15a. "With Lenin" (detail, V. Serov) 80 25
1014 25a. Lenin and Red Army fighters . . . . 1·40 40
MS1015 90 × 21 mm. 50a. Lenin 2·30 1·40

1985. 7th Anniv of Sawr Revolution.
1016 **456** 21a. multicoloured . . . 1·00 15

457 Olympic Stadium and Moscow Skyline

1985. 12th World Youth and Students' Festival, Moscow. Multicoloured.
1017 7a. Type **457** 25 10
1018 12a. Festival emblem . . . 40 25
1019 13a. Moscow Kremlin . . . 50 35
1020 18a. Doll 65 60

458 Soviet Memorial, Berlin-Treptow, and Tank before Reichstag

1985. 40th Anniv of End of World War II. Multicoloured.
1021 6a. Type **458** 60 15
1022 9a. "Mother Homeland" war memorial, Volgograd, and fireworks over Moscow Kremlin 80 15
1023 10a. Cecilienhof Castle, Potsdam, and flags of United Kingdom, U.S.S.R. and U.S.A. . . . 1·10 15

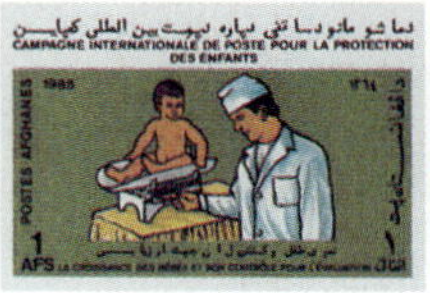
459 Weighing Baby

460 Purple Blewit

1985. UNICEF Child Survival Campaign. Mult.
1024 1a. Type **459** 10 15
1025 2a. Vaccinating child . . . 15 15
1026 4a. Breast-feeding baby . . 35 15
1027 5a. Mother and child . . . 40 15

1985. Fungi. Multicoloured.
1028 3a. Type **460** 15 10
1029 4a. Flaky-stemmed witches' mushroom 40 25
1030 7a. The blusher 60 35
1031 11a. Brown birch bolete . . 80 60
1032 12a. Common ink cap . . . 1·10 60
1033 18a. "Hypholoma sp." . . . 1·50 75
1034 20a. "Boletus aurantiacus" 1·60 75

461 Emblems

1985. United Nations Decade for Women.
1035 **461** 10a. multicoloured . . . 65 25

462 Evening Primrose

1985. "Argentina "85" International Stamp Exhibition, Buenos Aires. Flowers. Multicoloured.
1036 2a. Type **462** 15 10
1037 4a. Cockspur coral tree . . 35 15
1038 8a. "Tillandsia aeranthos" 60 15
1039 13a. Periwinkle 90 25
1040 18a. Marvel-of-Peru . . . . 1·30 35
1041 25a. "Cypella herbertii" . . 1·80 35
1042 30a. "Clytostoma callistegioides" . . . . . 2·30 35
MS1043 80 × 100 mm. 75a. "Sesbania punicea" (51 × 36 mm) 5·75 80

463 Building

1985. Independence Day.
1044 **463** 33a. multicoloured . . . 1·50 15

464 Dancers in Pashtunistan Square, Kabul

1985. Pashtunistan Day.
1045 **464** 25a. multicoloured . . . 1·50 15

465 Guldara Stupa

1985. 10th Anniv of World Tourism Organization. Multicoloured.
1046 1a. Type **465** 15 10
1047 2a. Mirwais tomb (vert) . . 15 10
1048 10a. Buddha of Bamian (vert) 60 10
1049 13a. No Gumbad mosque (vert) 80 10
1050 14a. Pule Kheshti mosque 90 15
1051 15a. Arch at Qalai Bust . . 1·00 15
1052 20a. Ghazni minaret (vert) 1·30 15

466 Boxing

1985. Sport. Multicoloured.
1053 1a. Type **466** 10 15
1054 2a. Volleyball 15 10
1055 3a. Football (vert) 50 10
1056 12a. Buzkashi 60 10
1057 14a. Weightlifting 65 15
1058 18a. Wrestling 75 15
1059 25a. Pigsticking . . . . . . 1·00 15

467 Fruit Stall

1985. World Food Day.
1060 **467** 25a. multicoloured . . . 90 15

468 Flags and U.N. Building, New York

469 Black-billed Magpie

1985. 40th Anniv of United Nations Organization.
1061 **468** 22a. multicoloured . . . 90 15

1985. Birds. Multicoloured.
1062 2a. Type **469** 25 10
1063 4a. Green woodpecker . . . 1·00 50
1064 8a. Common pheasants . . 1·10 50
1065 13a. Bluethroat, Eurasian goldfinch and hoopoe . . 1·60 90
1066 18a. Peregrine falcons . . . 2·00 1·00
1067 25a. Red-legged partridge 2·75 1·50
1068 30a. Eastern white pelicans (horiz) . . . . 3·50 1·70
MS1069 90 × 20 mm. 75a. Rose-ringed parakeets (29 × 41 mm) 7·50 80

470 Leopard and Cubs

1985. World Wildlife Fund. The Leopard. Mult.
1070 2a. Type **470** 40 25
1071 9a. Head of leopard . . . . 1·50 50
1072 11a. Leopard . . . . 2·50 80
1073 15a. Leopard cub . . . . . 3·75 1·20

471 Triumph 650 and Big Ben Tower

1985. Motorcycles. Multicoloured.
1074 2a. Type **471** 15 10
1075 4a. Motobecane and Eiffel Tower, Paris 35 10
1076 8a. Bultaco motorcycles and Don Quixote monument, Madrid 60 15
1077 13a. Honda and Mt. Fuji, Japan 90 15
1078 18a. Jawa and Old Town Hall clock, Prague . . . 1·10 25
1079 25a. MZ motorcycle and T.V. Tower, Berlin . . . 1·60 25
1080 30a. Motorcycle and Colosseum, Rome . . . . 2·00 25
MS1081 100 × 80 mm. 75a. Moskva Dneipr motorcycle and Red Square, Moscow . . . . . . 6·50 80

472 Crowd with Flags

1986. 21st Anniv of Peoples' Democratic Party.
1082 **472** 2a. multicoloured . . . 35 25

473 Lenin writing

1986. 27th Soviet Communist Party Congress, Moscow.
1083 **473** 25a. multicoloured . . . 80 40

474 "Vostok 1"

1986. 25th Anniv of First Manned Space Flight. Multicoloured.
1084 3a. Type **474** 25 15
1085 7a. Russian Cosmonaut Medal (vert) 25 15
1086 9a. Launch of "Vostok 1" (vert) 40 15
1087 11a. Yuri Gagarin (first man in space) (vert) . . . 50 15
1088 13a. Cosmonauts reading newspaper 60 25

1089 15a. Yuri Gagarin and Sergei Pavlovich Korolev (rocket designer) 60 25
1090 17a. Valentina Tereshkova (first woman in space) (vert) 75 25

475 Footballers

476 Lenin

1986. World Cup Football Championship, Mexico.
1091 **475** 3a. multicoloured 25 15
1092 – 4a. multicoloured (horiz) 35 15
1093 – 7a. multicoloured (horiz) 40 15
1094 – 11a. multicoloured . . . 65 15
1095 – 12a. mult (horiz) 80 25
1096 – 18a. multicoloured . . . 1·20 25
1097 – 20a. multicoloured . . . 1·40 25
MS1098 120 × 90 mm. 75a. multicoloured (39 × 26 mm) . . 4·50 80
DESIGNS: 4a. to 75a. Various footballing scenes.

1986. 116th Birth Anniv of Lenin.
1099 **476** 16a. multicoloured . . . 75 40

477 Delegates voting

1986. 1st Anniv of Supreme Council Meeting of Tribal Leaders.
1100 **477** 3a. brown, red and blue 25 15

478 Flags and Crowd

479 Worker with Cogwheel and Globe

1986. 8th Anniv of Sawr Revolution.
1101 **478** 8a. multicoloured . . . 40 15

1986. Labour Day.
1102 **479** 5a. multicoloured . . . 25 15

480 Patient receiving Blood Transfusion

481 St. Bernard

1986. International Red Cross/Crescent Day.
1103 **480** 7a. multicoloured . . . 50 25

1986. Pedigree Dogs. Multicoloured.
1104 5a. Type **481** 25 10
1105 7a. Rough collie 40 10
1106 8a. Spaniel 50 15
1107 9a. Long-haired dachshund 60 15
1108 11a. German shepherd . . . 65 25
1109 15a. Bulldog 90 25
1110 20a. Afghan hound . . . . 1·20 25

482 Tiger Barb

483 Mother and Children

1986. Fishes. Multicoloured.
1111 5a. Type **482** 25 15
1112 7a. Mbuna 40 15
1113 8a. Clown loach 50 15
1114 9a. Lisa 60 25
1115 11a. Figure-eight pufferfish 80 25
1116 15a. Six-barred distichodus 1·10 35
1117 20a. Sail-finned molly . . . 1·40 35

1986. World Children's Day. Multicoloured.
1118 1a. Type **483** 15 15
1119 3a. Woman holding boy and emblem 15 15
1120 9a. Circle of children on map (horiz) 40 15

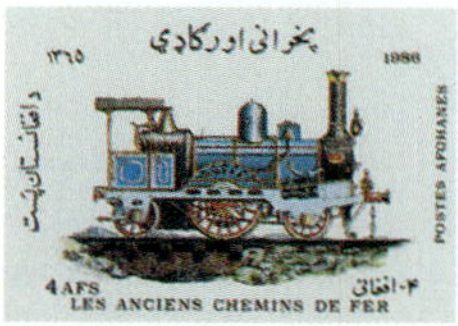
484 Italian Birkenhead Locomotive

1986. 19th-century Railway Locomotives. Mult.
1121 4a. Type **484** 25 10
1122 5a. Norris locomotive . . . 35 10
1123 6a. Stephenson "Patentee" type locomotive 40 15
1124 7a. Bridges Adams locomotive 50 15
1125 8a. Ansoldo locomotive . . 65 25
1126 9a. Locomotive "St. David" 80 25
1127 11a. Jones & Potts locomotive 90 25

485 Cobra

1986. Animals. Multicoloured.
1128 3a. Type **485** 15 10
1129 4a. Lizards (vert) 25 15
1130 5a. Praying mantis 35 15
1131 8a. Beetle (vert) 50 25
1132 9a. Spider 60 35
1133 10a. Snake 65 35
1134 11a. Scorpions 80 35
Nos. 1130/2 and 1134 are wrongly inscr "Les Reptiles".

486 Profiles on Globe

1986. World Youth Day.
1135 **486** 15a. multicoloured . . . 65 25

487 National Monuments

1986. Independence Day.
1136 **487** 10a. multicoloured . . . 50 25

488 11th-century Ship

1986. "Stockholmia 86" International Stamp Exhibition. Sailing Ships. Multicoloured.
1137 4a. Type **488** 40 15
1138 5a. Roman galley 50 25
1139 6a. English royal kogge . . 65 25
1140 7a. Early dhow 80 25
1141 8a. Nao . . . . 1·00 25
1142 9a. Ancient Egyptian ship 1·10 25
1143 11a. Medieval galeasse . . . 1·30 25
MS1144 86 × 64 mm. 50a. Early dhow (as 7a.) (41 × 29 mm) 4·00 80

489 Tribesmen

490 State Arms

1986. Pashtunistan Day.
1145 **489** 4a. multicoloured . . . 25 15

1986. Supreme Council Meeting of Tribal Leaders.
1146 **490** 3a. gold, blue and black 40 25

491 Labourer reading

492 Dove and U.N. Emblem

1986. World Literacy Day.
1147 **491** 2a. multicoloured . . . 25 15

1986. International Peace Year.
1148 **492** 12a. black and blue . . . 60 25

493 Tulips, Flame and Man with Rifle

494 Crowd and Flags

1986. Afghanistan Youth Day.
1149 **493** 3a. red and black . . . 40 25

1987. 9th Anniv of Sawr Revolution.
1150 **494** 3a. multicoloured . . . 25 15

495 Map and Dove

1987. National Reconciliation.
1151 **495** 3a. multicoloured . . . 25 15

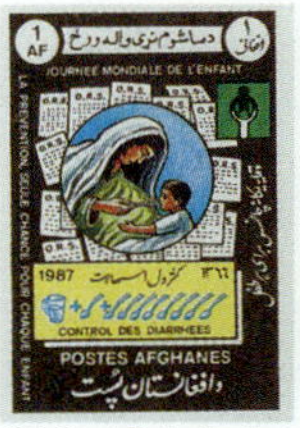
496 Oral Rehydration

498 "Pieris sp."

497 Conference Delegates

1987. International Children's Day. Multicoloured.
1152 1a. Type **496** 15 10
1153 5a. Weighing babies 15 10
1154 9a. Vaccinating babies . . . 35 15

1987. 1st Anniv of Tribal Conference.
1155 **497** 5a. multicoloured . . . 35 25

1987. Butterflies and Moths. Multicoloured.
1156 7a. Type **498** 60 35
1157 9a. Brimstone and unidentified butterfly . . . 75 35
1158 10a. Garden tiger moth (horiz) . . . . 1·00 50
1159 12a. "Parnassius sp." . . . 1·40 50
1160 15a. Butterfly (unidentified) (horiz) . . . . 1·50 65
1161 22a. Butterfly (unidentified) (horiz) . . . . 2·10 90
1162 25a. Butterfly (unidentified) 2·50 90

499 People on Hand

500 Khan Abdul Ghaffar Khan

1987. 1st Local Government Elections.
1163 **499** 1a. multicoloured . . . 25 15

1987. Pashtun and Baluch Day.
1164 **500** 4a. multicoloured . . . 25 15

501 "Sputnik 1"

1987. 30th Anniv of Launch of "Sputnik 1" (first artificial satellite). Multicoloured.
1165 10a. Type **501** 40 15
1166 15a. Rocket launch 60 15
1167 25a. "Soyuz"–"Salyut" space complex 80 15

502 Old and Modern Post Offices

1987. World U.P.U. Day.
1168 **502** 22a. multicoloured . . . 1·10 60

503 Monument and Arch of Paghman

1987. Independence Day.
1169 **503** 3a. multicoloured . . . 25 15

504 "Communications"

1987. United Nations Day.
1170 **504** 42a. multicoloured . . . 4·50 1·00

505 Lenin

506 Castor Oil Plant

1987. 70th Anniv of Russian Revolution.
1171 **505** 25a. multicoloured . . . 1·20 65

1987. Plants. Multicoloured.
1172 3a. Type **506** 15 15
1173 6a. Liquorice 35 15
1174 9a. Camomile 60 15
1175 14a. Thorn apple 80 15
1176 18a. Chicory . . . . 1·00 15

507 Field Mice

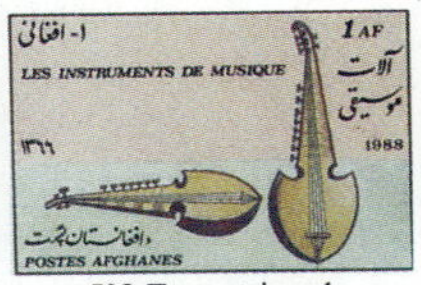
508 Four-stringed Instrument

1987. Mice. Multicoloured.
1177 2a. Type **507** 40 15
1178 4a. Brown and white mice (horiz) 50 15
1179 8a. Ginger mice (horiz) . . 60 15
1180 16a. Black mice (horiz) . . 1·00 15
1181 20a. Spotted and ginger mice (horiz) . . . . . . 1·20 15

1988. Musical Instruments. Multicoloured.
1182 1a. Type **508** 15 15
1183 3a. Drums 15 15
1184 5a. Two-stringed instruments with two pegs 25 15
1185 15a. Two-stringed instrument with ten pegs 60 15
1186 18a. Two-stringed instruments with fourteen or ten pegs 80 25
1187 25a. Four-stringed bowed instruments . . . . 1·20 25
1188 33a. Two-stringed bowed instruments . . . . 1·60 25

509 Mixed Arrangement

510 Emblems and Means of Communication

1988. Flowers. Multicoloured.
1189 3a. Type **509** 25 15
1190 5a. Tulips (horiz) 35 15
1191 7a. Mallows 50 25
1192 9a. Small mauve flowers . . 65 25
1193 12a. Marguerites . . . . . 1·20 35
1194 15a. White flowers . . . . 1·50 35
1195 24a. Red and blue flowers (horiz) . . . . 2·10 35

1988. 60th Anniv of Membership of U.P.U. and I.T.U.
1196 **510** 20a. multicoloured . . . 80 50

511 Tank Monument, Kabul, and Flags

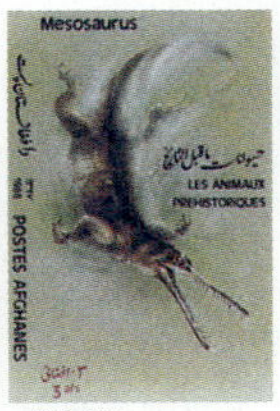
512 Mesosaurus

1988. 10th Anniv of Sawr Revolution.
1197 **511** 10a. multicoloured . . . 80 50

1988. Prehistoric Animals. Multicoloured.
1198 3a. Type **512** 15 10
1199 5a. Styracosaurus (horiz) . . 25 10
1200 10a. Uintatherium (horiz) 50 15
1201 15a. Protoceratops (horiz) 75 15
1202 20a. Stegosaurus (horiz) . . 1·00 25
1203 25a. Ceratosaurus . . . . . 1·30 25
1204 30a. Moa ("Dinornis maximus") . . . . 1·80 25

513 Baskets and Bowl of Fruit

1988. Fruit. Multicoloured.
1205 2a. Type **513** 25 15
1206 4a. Baskets of fruit . . . 35 15
1207 7a. Large basket of fruit . . 35 25
1208 8a. Bunch of grapes on branch (vert) 50 25
1209 16a. Buying fruit from market stall 80 35
1210 22a. Arranging fruit on market stall . . . . . . 1·20 35
1211 25a. Stallholder weighing fruit (vert) . . . . 1·80 35

514 Memorial Pillar of Knowledge and Ignorance, Kabul

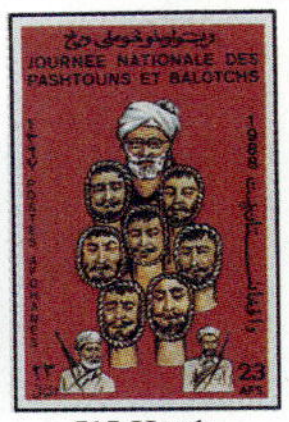
515 Heads encircled with Rope

1988. Independence Day.
1212 **514** 24a. multicoloured . . . 1·20 65

1988. Pashtunistan Day.
1213 **515** 23a. multicoloured . . . 90 60

516 Flags and Globe

517 Anniversary Emblem

1988. Afghan–Soviet Space Flight.
1214 **516** 32a. multicoloured . . . 1·20 50

1988. 125th Anniv of International Red Cross.
1215 **517** 10a. multicoloured . . . 80 50

518 Rocket and V. Tereshkova

1988. 25th Anniv of First Woman Cosmonaut Valentina Tereshkova's Space Flight. Mult.
1216 10a. Type **518** 80 35
1217 15a. Bird, globe and rocket (vert) 65 15
1218 25a. "Vostok 6" and globe 1·00 15

519 Decorated Metal Vessels

520 Indian Flag and Nehru

1988. Traditional Crafts. Multicoloured.
1219 2a. Type **519** 10 10
1220 4a. Pottery 15 10
1221 5a. Clothing (vert) 25 15
1222 9a. Carpets 35 15
1223 15a. Bags 35 25
1224 23a. Jewellery 90 25
1225 50a. Furniture . . . . . . 1·80 25

1988. Birth Centenary of Jawaharlal Nehru (Indian statesman).
1226 **520** 40a. multicoloured . . . 2·10 80

521 Emeralds

522 Ice Skating

1988. Gemstones. Multicoloured.
1227 13a. Type **521** 80 15
1228 37a. Lapis lazuli . . . . 1·80 35
1229 40a. Rubies . . . . 2·30 35

1988. Winter Olympic Games, Calgary. Mult.
1230 2a. Type **522** 15 15
1231 5a. Slalom 25 15
1232 9a. Two-man bobsleigh . . 50 15
1233 22a. Biathlon 90 15
1234 37a. Speed skating . . . . 1·90 15
MS1235 80 × 60 mm. 75a. Ice hockey 4·00 80

523 Old City

1988. International Campaign for Preservation of Old Sana'a, Yemen.
1236 **523** 32a. multicoloured . . . 1·50 1·10

524 Emblem

1989. 2nd Anniv of Move for Nat Reconciliation.
1237 **524** 4a. multicoloured . . . 25 15

525 Bishop and Game from "The Three Ages of Man" (attr. Estienne Porchier)

1989. Chess. Multicoloured.
1238 2a. Type **525** 25 15
1239 3a. Faience queen and 14th century drawing of Margrave Otto IV of Brandenburg and his wife playing chess 35 15
1240 4a. French king and game 40 15
1241 7a. King and game 65 25
1242 16a. Knight and game . . . 1·10 25
1243 24a. Arabian knight and "Great Chess" . . . . . 1·50 35
1244 45a. Bishop and teaching of game . . . . 2·75 40

Nos. 1240/4 show illustrations from King Alfonso X's "Book of Chess, Dice and Tablings".

526 "The Old Jew"

527 Euphrates Jerboa

1989. Picasso Paintings. Multicoloured.
1245 4a. Type **526** 35 25
1246 6a. "The Two Harlequins" 40 25
1247 8a. "Portrait of Ambrouse Vollar" 50 25
1248 22a. "Majorcan Woman" 1·20 25
1249 35a. "Acrobat on Ball" . . 2·30 25
MS1250 70 × 90 mm. 75a. "Horta de Ebro Factory". Imperf . . . . 4·00 80

1989. Animals. Multicoloured.
1251 3a. Type **527** 35 25
1252 4a. Asiatic wild ass 35 25
1253 14a. Lynx . . . . 1·00 35
1254 35a. Lammergeier . . . . . 3·50 1·50
1255 44a. Markhor . . . . 2·30 1·20
MS1256 70 × 90 mm. 100a. Oxus cobra . . . . 4·50 1·20

528 Bomb breaking, Dove and Woman holding Wheat

529 Cattle

1989. International Women's Day (1988).
1257 **528** 8a. multicoloured . . . 40 15

1989. Farmers' Day. Multicoloured.
1258 1a. Type **529** 25 15
1259 2a. Ploughing with oxen and tractors 25 15
1260 3a. Picking cotton 25 15

530 Dish Aerial

1989. World Meteorology Day. Multicoloured.
1261 27a. Type **530** . . . . . . 1·20 25
1262 32a. World Meteorological Organization emblem and state arms . . . . 1·60 25
1263 40a. Data-collecting equipment (vert) . . . . 2·10 25

531 Rejoicing Crowd

1989. 11th Anniv of Sawr Revolution.
1264 **531** 20a. multicoloured . . . 1·10 25

532 Outdoor Class

533 Eiffel Tower and Arc de Triomphe

1989. Teachers' Day.
1265 **532** 42a. multicoloured . . . 2·10 35

1989. Bicentenary of French Revolution.
1266 **533** 25a. multicoloured . . . 1·50 90

534 Transmission Mast

1989. 10th Anniv of Asia-Pacific Telecommunity.
1267 3a. Type **534** 15 15
1268 27a. Dish aerial . . . . . . 1·10 25

535 National Monuments

536 Pashtu

1989. Independence Day.
1269 **535** 25a. multicoloured . . . 1·20 35

1989. Pashtunistan Day.
1270 **536** 3a. multicoloured . . . 35 25

537 White Spoonbill

539 Mosque

538 Duchs Tourer, 1910

1989. Birds. Multicoloured.
1271 3a. Type **537** 25 15
1272 5a. Purple swamphen . . . 50 25

1273 10a. Eurasian bittern (horiz) 90 40
1274 15a. Eastern white pelican 1·20 50
1275 20a. Red-crested pochard 1·50 60
1276 25a. Mute swan 2·10 65
1277 30a. Great cormorant (horiz) 2·30 90

1989. Vintage Cars. Multicoloured.
1278 5a. Type **538** 40 25
1279 10a. Ford Model T touring car, 1911 75 25
1280 20a. Renault Type AX two-seater, 1911 1·20 25
1281 25a. Russo-Balte tourer, 1911 1·50 35
1282 30a. Fiat 509 tourer, 1926 1·80 35

1989. Multicoloured.
1283 1a. Type **539** 1·50 50
1284 2a. Minaret, Jam 3·00 75
1285 3a. Buzkashi (horiz) 4·50 90
1286 4a. Airplane over Hindu Kush (horiz) 6·00 1·00

1996. Nos. 1283/6 surch.
1287 300a. on 1a multicoloured (1283) (postage) 1·50 50
1288 600a. on 2a. multicoloured (1284) 3·00 75
1289 900a. on 3a. multicoloured (1285) 4·50 90
1290 1200a. on 4a. multicoloured (1286) (air) 6·00 1·00

NEWSPAPER STAMPS

N 35

1928.
N192 **N 35** 2p. blue 4·00 4·50

1929.
N205A **N 35** 2p. red 30 50

N 43

1932.
N215 **N 43** 2p. red 40 50
N216 2p. black 35 80
N217 2p. green 40 75
N219 2p. red 50 75

N 75 Coat-of-Arms

1939.
N259 **N 75** 2p. green 25 65
N260 2p. mauve (no gum) 15 1·00

1969. As Type N **75**, but larger and with different Pushtu inscr.
N652 100p. green 25 25
N653 150p. brown 35 25

OFFICIAL STAMPS

O 27

O 86

1909.
O173 **O 27** (–) red 1·20 1·20

1939. Design 22½ × 28 mm.
O281 **O 86** 15p. green 1·10 80
O282 30p. brown 1·50 1·50
O283 45p. red 1·20 1·20
O284 1a. mauve 2·00 1·80

1954. Design 24½ × 31 mm.
O285b **O 86** 50p. red 1·00 50

1965. Design 24 × 30½ mm.
O287 **O 86** 50p. pink 1·20 50

PARCEL POST STAMPS

P 27

1909.
P173 **P 27** 3s. brown 1·20 2·10
P174 3s. green 1·80 3·50
P175 1k. green 2·10 3·50
P176 1k. red 3·00 1·50
P177 1r. orange 6·50 2·00
P178 1r. grey 30·00
P179 1r. brown 3·50 3·50
P180 2r. red 4·00 4·00
P181 2r. blue 6·25 6·50

P 28 Old Habibia College, Kabul

1921.
P182 **P 28** 10p. brown 4·00 5·75
P183 15p. brown 5·75 6·50
P184 30p. purple 10·50 6·50
P185 1r. blue 12·50 12·50

1923. 5th Independence Day. Optd with T **28**.
P186 **P 28** 10p. brown 90·00
P187 15p. brown £100
P188 30p. purple £200

P 35

P 36

1928.
P192 **P 35** 2a. orange 6·50 5·00
P193 **P 36** 3a. green 10·50 10·50

1930.
P214 **P 35** 2a. green 7·50 7·50
P215 **P 36** 3a. brown 9·00 10·50

REGISTRATION STAMP

R 19

1894. Undated.
R155 **R 19** 2a. black on green 9·75 11·50

APPENDIX

The following stamps have either been issued in excess of postal needs or have not been available to the public in reasonable quantities at face value. Such stamps may later be given full listing if there is evidence of regular postal use.

1961.

Agriculture Day. Fauna and Flora. 2, 2, 5, 10, 15, 25, 50, 100, 150, 175p.

Child Welfare. Sports and Games. 2, 2, 5, 10, 15, 25, 50, 100, 150, 175p.

UNICEF Surch on 1961 Child Welfare issue. 2+25, 2+25, 5+25, 10+25, 15p.+25p.

Women's Day. 50, 175p.

Independence Day. Mohamed Nadir Shah. 50, 175p.

International Exhibition, Kabul. 50, 175p.

Pashtunistan Day. 50, 175p.

National Assembly. 50, 175p.

Anti-malaria Campaign. 50, 175p.

King's 47th Birthday. 50, 175p.

Red Crescent Day. Fruits. 2, 2, 5, 10, 15, 25, 50, 100, 150, 175p.

Afghan Red Crescent Fund. 1961 Red Crescent Day issue surch 2+25, 2+25, 5+25, 10+25, 15p.+25p.

United Nations Day. 1, 2, 3, 4, 50, 75, 175p.

Teachers' Day. Flowers and Educational Scenes. 2, 2, 5, 10, 15, 25, 50, 100, 150, 175p.

UNESCO 1961 Teachers' Day issue surch 2+25, 2+25, 5+25, 10+25, 15p.+25p.

1962.

15th Anniv (1961) of UNESCO 2, 2, 5, 10, 15, 25, 50, 75, 100p.

Ahmed Shah Baba. 50, 75, 100p.

Agriculture Day. Animals and Products. 2, 2, 5, 10, 15, 25, 50, 75, 100, 125p.

Independence Day. Marching Athletes. 25, 50, 150p.

Women's Day. Postage 25, 50p.; Air 100, 175p.

Pashtunistan Day. 25, 50, 150p.

Malaria Eradication. 2, 2, 5, 10, 15, 25, 50, 75, 100, 150, 175p.

National Assembly. 25, 50, 75, 100, 125p.

4th Asian Games, Djakarta, Indonesia. Postage 1, 2, 3, 4, 5p.; Air 25, 50, 75, 100, 150, 175p.

Children's Day. Sports and Produce. Postage 1, 2, 3, 4, 5p.; Air 75, 150, 200p.

King's 48th Birthday. 25, 50, 75, 100p.

Red Crescent Day. Fruits and Flowers. Postage 1, 2, 3, 4, 5p.; Air 25, 50, 100p.

Boy Scouts' Day. Postage 1, 2, 3, 4p.; Air 25, 50, 75, 100p.

1st Anniv of Hammarskjold's Death. Surch on 1961 UNESCO issue. 2+20, 2+20, 5+20, 10+20, 15+20, 25+20, 50+20, 75+20, 100p.+20p.

United Nations Day. Postage 1, 2, 3, 4, 5p.; Air 75, 100, 125p.

Teachers' Day. Sport and Flowers. Postage 1, 2, 3, 4, 5p.; Air 100, 150p.

World Meteorological Day. 50, 100p.

1963.

Famous Afghans Pantheon, Kabul. 50, 75, 100p.

Agriculture Day. Sheep and Silkworms. Postage 1, 2, 3, 4, 5p.; Air 100, 150, 200p.

Freedom from Hunger. Postage 2, 3, 300p.; Air 500p.

Malaria Eradication Fund. 1962 Malaria Eradication issue surch 2+15, 2+15, 5+15, 10+15, 15+15, 25+15, 50+15, 75+15, 100+15, 150+15, 175p.+15p.

World Meteorological Day. Postage 1, 2, 3, 4, 5p.; Air 200, 300, 400, 500p.

"GANEFO" Athletic Games, Djakarta, Indonesia. Postage 2, 3, 4, 5, 10p., 9a.; Air 300, 500p.

Red Cross Centenary Postage 2, 3, 4, 5, 10p.; Air 100, 200p., 4, 6a.

Nubian Monuments Preservation. Postage 100, 200, 500p.; Air 5a., 7a.50.

1964.

Women's Day (1963). 2, 3, 4, 5, 10p.

Afghan Boy Scouts and Girl Guides. Postage 2, 3, 4, 5, 10p.; Air 2, 2, 2a.50, 3, 4, 5, 12a.

Child Welfare Day (1963). Sports and Games. Postage 2, 3, 4, 5, 10p.; Air 200, 300p.

Afghan Red Crescent Society. Postage 100, 200p.; Air 5a., 7a.50.

Teachers' Day (1963). Flowers. Postage 2, 3, 4, 5, 10p.; Air 3a., 3a.50.

United Nations Day (1963). Postage 2, 3, 4, 5, 10p.; Air 100p., 2, 3a.

15th Anniv of Human Rights Declaration. Surch on 1964 United Nations Day issue. Postage 2+50, 3+50, 4+50, 5+50, 10p.+50p.; Air 100p.+50p., 2a.+50p., 3a.+50p.

UNICEF (dated 1963). Postage 100, 200p.; Air 5a. 7a.50.

Malaria Eradication (dated 1963). Postage 2, 3, 4, 5p., 10p. on 4p.; Air 2, 10a.

AITUTAKI Pt. 1

Island in the South Pacific.

1903. 12 pence = 1 shilling;
20 shillings = 1 pound.
1967. 100 cents = 1 dollar.

A. NEW ZEALAND DEPENDENCY

The British Government, who had exercised a protectorate over the Cook Islands group since the 1880s, handed the islands, including Aitutaki, to New Zealand administration in 1901. Cook Islands stamps were used from 1932 to 1972.

1903. Pictorial stamps of New Zealand surch **AITUTAKI.** and value in native language.
1 **23** ½d. green 4·50 6·50
2 **42** 1d. red 4·75 5·50
4 **26** 2½d. blue 12·00 12·00
5 **28** 3d. brown 18·00 15·00
6 **31** 6d. red 30·00 25·00
7 **34** 1s. orange 50·00 85·00

1911. King Edward VII stamps of New Zealand surch **AITUTAKI.** and value in native language.
9 **51** ½d. green 1·00 5·50
10 **53** 1d. red 3·00 13·00
11 **51** 6d. red 45·00 £130
12 1s. orange 50·00 £150

1916. King George V stamps of New Zealand surch **AITUTAKI.** and value in native language.
13a **62** 6d. red 7·50 27·00
14 1s. orange 12·00 90·00

1917. King George V stamps of New Zealand optd **AITUTAKI.**
19 **62** ½d. green 1·00 6·00
20 **53** 1d. red 4·25 30·00
21 **62** 1½d. grey 3·75 30·00
22 1½d. brown 80 7·00
15a 2½d. blue 1·75 15·00
16a 3d. brown 1·50 26·00
17a 6d. red 4·75 21·00
18a 1s. orange 12·00 32·00

1920. As 1920 pictorial stamps of Cook Islands but inscr "AITUTAKI".
30 ½d. black and green 2·00 17·00
31 1d. black and red 6·00 7·50
26 1½d. black and brown 6·00 12·00
32 2½d. black and blue 7·50 70·00
27 3d. black and blue 2·50 14·00
28 6d. brown and grey 5·50 14·00
29 1s. black and purple 9·50 16·00

B. PART OF COOK ISLANDS

On 9 August 1972 Aitutaki became a Port of Entry into the Cook Islands. Whilst remaining part of the Cook Islands, Aitutaki has a separate postal service.

1972. Nos. 227/8, 230, 233/4, 238, 240/1, 243 and 244 of Cook Islands optd **Aitutaki.**
33 **79** ½c. multicoloured 30 80
34 – 1c. multicoloured 70 1·40
35 – 2½c. multicoloured 2·25 7·00
36 – 4c. multicoloured 70 85
37 – 5c. multicoloured 2·50 7·50
38 – 10c. multicoloured 2·50 5·50
39 – 20c. multicoloured 3·75 1·00
40 – 25c. multicoloured 70 1·00
41 – 50c. multicoloured 2·75 2·75
42 – $1 multicoloured 4·00 5·50

1972. Christmas. Nos. 406/8 of Cook Islands optd **Aitutaki.**
43 **130** 1c. multicoloured 10 10
44 – 5c. multicoloured 15 15
45 – 10c. multicoloured 15 25

1972. Royal Silver Wedding. As Nos. 413 and 415 of Cook Islands, but inscr "COOK ISLANDS Aitutaki".
46 **131** 5c. black and silver 3·50 2·75
47 – 15c. black and silver 1·50 1·50

1972. No. 245 of Cook Islands optd **AITUTAKI.**
48 $2 multicoloured 50 75

1972. Nos. 227/8, 230, 233, 234, 238, 240, 241, 243 and 244 of Cook Islands optd **AITUTAKI** within ornamental oval.
49 **79** ½c. multicoloured 15 10
50 – 1c. multicoloured 15 10
51 – 2½c. multicoloured 20 10
52 – 4c. multicoloured 25 15
53 – 5c. multicoloured 25 15
54 – 10c. multicoloured 35 25
55 – 20c. multicoloured 1·25 50
56 – 25c. multicoloured 50 55
57 – 50c. multicoloured 75 90
58 – $1 multicoloured 1·25 1·75

13 "Christ Mocked" (Grunewald)

16 Red Hibiscus and Princess Anne

1973. Easter. Multicoloured.
59 1c. Type **13** 15 10
60 1c. "St. Veronica" (Van der Weyden) 15 10

61 1c. “The Crucified Christ with Virgin Mary, Saints and Angels” (Raphael) 15 10
62 1c. “Resurrection” (Piero della Francesca) 15 10
63 5c. “The Last Supper” (Master of Amiens) 20 15
64 5c. “Condemnation” (Holbein) 20 15
65 5c. “Christ on the Cross” (Rubens) 20 15
66 5c. “Resurrection” (El Greco) 20 15
67 10c. “Disrobing of Christ” (El Greco) 25 15
68 10c. “St. Veronica” (Van Oostsanen) 25 15
69 10c. “Christ on the Cross” (Rubens) 25 15
70 10c. “Resurrection” (Bouts) 25 15

1973. Silver Wedding Coinage. Nos. 417/23 of Cook Islands optd **AITUTAKI**.
71 **132** 1c. black, red and gold . . 10 10
72 – 2c. black, blue and gold . . 10 10
73 – 5c. black, green and silver 15 10
74 – 10c. black, blue and silver 20 10
75 – 20c. black, green and silver 30 15
76 – 50c. black, red and silver 50 30
77 – $1 black, blue and silver 70 45

1973. 10th Anniv of Treaty Banning Nuclear Testing. Nos. 236, 238, 240 and 243 of Cook Islands optd **AITUTAKI** within ornamental oval and **TENTH ANNIVERSARY CESSATION OF NUCLEAR TESTING TREATY**.
78 8c. multicoloured 15 15
79 10c. multicoloured 15 15
80 20c. multicoloured 30 20
81 50c. multicoloured 70 50

1973. Royal Wedding. Multicoloured.
82 25c. Type **16** 25 10
83 30c. Capt. Mark Phillips and blue hibiscus 25 10
MS84 114 × 65 mm. Nos. 82/3 . . . 50 40

17 “Virgin and Child” (Montagna)

1973. Christmas. “Virgin and Child” paintings by artists listed below. Multicoloured.
85 1c. Type **17** 10 10
86 1c. Crivelli 10 10
87 1c. Van Dyck 10 10
88 1c. Perugino 10 10
89 5c. Veronese (child at shoulder) 25 10
90 5c. Veronese (child on lap) . . 25 10
91 5c. Cima 25 10
92 5c. Memling 25 10
93 10c. Memling 25 10
94 10c. Del Colle 25 10
95 10c. Raphael 25 10
96 10c. Lotto 25 10

18 Rose-branch Murex

1974. Sea Shells. Multicoloured.
97 ½c. Type **18** . . . . 90 1·00
98 1c. New Caledonia nautilus 90 1·00
99 2c. Common or major harp 90 1·00
100 3c. Striped bonnet . . . . . 90 1·00
101 4c. Mole cowrie . . . . . . 90 1·00
102 5c. Pontifical mitre . . . . . 90 1·00
103 8c. Trumpet triton . . . . . 90 1·00
104 10c. Venus comb murex . . . 90 80
105 20c. Red-mouth olive . . . . 1·25 80
106 25c. Ruddy frog shell . . . . 1·25 80
107 60c. Widest pacific conch . . 4·00 1·25
108 $1 Maple-leaf triton or winged frog shell . . . . . 2·50 1·40
109 $2 Queen Elizabeth II and Marlin-spike auger . . . . 6·00 9·00
110 $5 Queen Elizabeth II and Tiger cowrie . . . . 29·00 10·00
The $2 and $5 are larger, 53 × 25 mm.

19 Bligh and H.M.S. “Bounty”

1974. William Bligh’s Discovery of Aitutaki. Multicoloured.
114 1c. Type **19** 60 60
115 1c. H.M.S. “Bounty” 60 60
116 5c. Bligh, and H.M.S. “Bounty” at Aitutaki . . . 1·00 1·00
117 5c. Aitutaki chart of 1856 . . 1·00 1·00
118 8c. Captain Cook and H.M.S. “Resolution” . . . 1·40 1·40
119 8c. Map of Aitutaki and inset location map . . . . . . 1·40 1·40
See also Nos. 123/8.

20 Aitutaki Stamps of 1903, Sand Map

1974. Centenary of U.P.U. Multicoloured.
120 25c. Type **20** 75 50
121 50c. Stamps of 1903 and 1920, and map . . . . . 1·00 75
MS122 66 × 75 mm. Nos. 120/1 1·25 2·75

1974. Air. As Nos. 114/119 in larger size (46 × 26 mm), additionally inscr “AIR MAIL”.
123 10c. Type **19** 60 65
124 10c. H.M.S. “Bounty” . . . 60 65
125 25c. Bligh, and H.M.S. “Bounty” at Aitutaki . . 70 75
126 25c. Aitutaki chart of 1856 70 75
127 30c. Captain Cook and H.M.S. “Resolution” . . . 80 85
128 30c. Map of Aitutaki and inset location map 80 85

21 “Virgin and Child” (Hugo van der Goes)
22 Churchill as Schoolboy

1974. Christmas. “Virgin and Child” paintings by artists named. Multicoloured.
129 1c. Type **21** 10 15
130 5c. Bellini 10 20
131 8c. Gerard David 10 20
132 10c. Antonello da Messina 10 15
133 25c. Joos van Cleve 20 30
134 30c. Master of the Life of St. Catherine 20 30
MS135 127 × 134 mm. Nos. 129/34 1·40 1·75

1974. Birth Centenary of Sir Winston Churchill. Multicoloured.
136 10c. Type **22** 20 25
137 25c. Churchill as young man 25 40
138 30c. Churchill with troops . . 25 45
139 50c. Churchill painting . . . 30 60
140 $1 Giving “V” sign 40 75
MS141 115 × 108 mm. Nos. 136/40 1·25 1·50

1974. Children’s Christmas Fund. Nos. 129/34 surch.
142 **21** 1c.+1c. multicoloured . . . 10 10
143 – 5c.+1c. multicoloured . . . 10 10
144 – 8c.+1c. multicoloured . . . 10 10
145 – 10c.+1c. multicoloured . . 10 10
146 – 25c.+1c. multicoloured . . 20 20
147 – 30c.+1c. multicoloured . . 20 20

24 Soviet and U.S. Flags

1975. “Apollo–Soyuz” Space Project. Mult.
148 25c. Type **24** 30 20
149 50c. Daedalus with space capsule 40 30
MS150 123 × 61 mm. Nos. 148/9 1·25 1·10

25 St. Francis
26 “The Descent” (detail, 15th-century Flemish School)

1975. Christmas. Multicoloured.
151 6c. Type **25** 10 10
152 6c. Madonna and Child . . . 10 10
153 6c. St. John 10 10
154 7c. King and donkey 10 10
155 7c. Madonna, Child and King 10 10
156 7c. Kings with gifts 10 10
157 15c. Madonna and Child . . 15 15
158 15c. St. Onufrius 15 15
159 15c. John the Baptist 15 15
160 20c. Shepherd and cattle . . 20 15
161 20c. Madonna and Child . . 20 15
162 20c. Shepherds 20 15
MS163 104 × 201 mm. Nos. 151/62 2·25 2·50
Stamps of the same value were printed together, se-tenant, each strip forming a composite design of a complete painting as follows: Nos. 151/3, “Madonna and Child with Saints Francis and John” (Lorenzetti); 154/6, “Adoration of the Kings” (Van der Weyden); 157/9, “Madonna and Child Enthroneth with Saints Onufrius and John the Baptist” (Montagna); 160/2, “Adoration of the Shepherds” (Reni).

1975. Children’s Christmas Fund. Nos. 151/62 surch.
164 **25** 6c.+1c. multicoloured . . . 10 10
165 – 6c.+1c. multicoloured . . . 10 10
166 – 6c.+1c. multicoloured . . . 10 10
167 – 7c.+1c. multicoloured . . . 10 10
168 – 7c.+1c. multicoloured . . . 10 10
169 – 7c.+1c. multicoloured . . . 10 10
170 – 15c.+1c. multicoloured . . 15 15
171 – 15c.+1c. multicoloured . . 15 15
172 – 15c.+1c. multicoloured . . 15 15
173 – 20c.+1c. multicoloured . . 20 20
174 – 20c.+1c. multicoloured . . 20 20
175 – 20c.+1c. multicoloured . . 20 20

1976. Easter. Multicoloured.
176 15c. Type **26** 15 10
177 30c. “The Descent” (detail) 20 15
178 35c. “The Descent” (detail) 25 20
MS179 87 × 67 mm. Nos. 176/8 forming a complete picture of “The Descent” . . . . 1·00 1·25

27 Left Detail
30 “The Visitation”

28 Cycling

1976. Bicentenary of American Revolution. Paintings by John Turnbull.
180 **27** 30c. multicoloured 20 10
181 – 30c. multicoloured 20 10
182 – 30c. multicoloured 20 10
183 – 35c. multicoloured 20 15
184 – 35c. multicoloured 20 15
185 – 35c. multicoloured 20 15
186 – 50c. multicoloured 20 15
187 – 50c. multicoloured 20 15
188 – 50c. multicoloured 20 15
MS189 132 × 120 mm. Nos. 180/8 1·75 1·10
PAINTINGS: Nos. 180/2, “The Declaration of Independence”; 183/5, “The Surrender of Lord Cornwallis at Yorktown”; 186/8, “The Resignation of General Washington”.
Stamps of the same value were printed together, se-tenant, each strip forming a composite design of the whole painting.

1976. Olympic Games, Montreal. Multicoloured.
190 15c. Type **28** 80 15
191 35c. Sailing 45 20
192 60c. Hockey . . . . 1·00 25
193 70c. Sprinting 70 30
MS194 107 × 97 mm. Nos. 190/3 2·50 1·25

1976. Royal Visit to the U.S.A. Nos. 190/3 optd **ROYAL VISIT JULY 1976.**
195 **28** 15c. multicoloured 50 15
196 – 35c. multicoloured 45 25
197 – 60c. multicoloured 80 40
198 – 70c. multicoloured 70 45
MS199 107 × 97 mm. Nos. 195/8 2·00 1·25

1976. Christmas.
200 **30** 6c. gold and green 10 10
201 – 6c. gold and green 10 10
202 – 7c. gold and purple 10 10
203 – 7c. gold and purple 10 10
204 – 15c. gold and blue 10 10
205 – 15c. gold and blue 10 10
206 – 20c. gold and violet . . . 15 15
207 – 20c. gold and violet . . . 15 15
MS208 128 × 96 mm. As Nos. 200/7 but with borders on three sides 1·00 1·40
DESIGNS: No. 201, Angel; 202, Angel; 203, Shepherds; 204, Joseph; 205, Mary and the Child; 206, Wise Man; 207, Two Wise Men.

Stamps of the same value were printed together, se-tenant, each pair forming a composite design.

1976. Children’s Christmas Fund. Nos. 200/7 surch.
209 **30** 6c.+1c. gold and green . . 10 10
210 – 6c.+1c. gold and green . . 10 10
211 – 7c.+1c. gold and purple . . 10 10
212 – 7c.+1c. gold and purple . . 10 10
213 – 15c.+1c. gold and blue . . 15 15
214 – 15c.+1c. gold and blue . . 15 15
215 – 20c.+1c. gold and violet . . 15 15
216 – 20c.+1c. gold and violet . . 15 15
MS217 128 × 96 mm. As Nos. 209/16 but with a premium of “+2c.” and borders on three sides . . . . 80 1·40

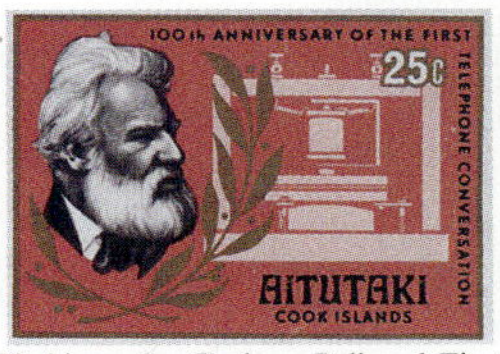
32 Alexander Graham Bell and First Telephone

1977. Centenary (1976) of Telephone.
218 **32** 25c. black, gold and red . . 20 15
219 – 70c. black, gold and lilac 40 40
MS220 116 × 59 mm. As Nos. 218/19 but with different colours . . . 70 1·00
DESIGN: 70c. Satellite and Earth station.

33 “Christ on the Cross” (detail)

1977. Easter. 400th Birth Anniv of Rubens. Mult.
221 15c. Type **33** 45 15
222 20c. “Lamentation for Christ” 60 20
223 35c. “Christ with Straw” . . 75 25
MS224 115 × 57 mm. Nos. 221/3. P 13 × 12½ . . . . 1·60 1·60

34 Captain Bligh, George III and H.M.S. “Bounty”

1977. Silver Jubilee. Multicoloured.
225 25c. Type **34** 35 35
226 35c. Rev. Williams, George IV and Aitutaki Church . . 40 40
227 50c. Union Jack, Queen Victoria and island map . . 45 45
228 $1 Balcony scene, 1953 . . . 50 50
MS229 130 × 87 mm. As Nos. 225/8 but with gold borders . . . . 1·25 1·25

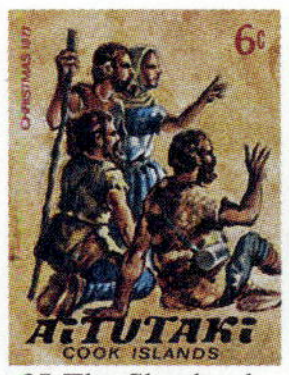

35 The Shepherds
37 Hawaiian Goddess

1977. Christmas. Multicoloured.
230 6c. Type **35** 10 10
231 6c. Angel 10 10
232 7c. Mary, Jesus and ox . . . 10 10
233 7c. Joseph and donkey . . . 10 10
234 15c. Three Kings 10 10
235 15c. Virgin and Child 10 10
236 20c. Joseph 10 10
237 20c. Mary and Jesus on donkey 10 10
MS238 130 × 95 mm. Nos. 230/7 70 1·25
Stamps of the same value were printed together, se-tenant, forming composite designs.

1977. Children’s Christmas Fund. Nos. 230/7 surch **+1c.**
239 6c.+1c. Type **35** 10 10
240 6c.+1c. Angel 10 10
241 7c.+1c. Mary, Jesus and ox 10 10
242 7c.+1c. Joseph and donkey 10 10
243 15c.+1c. Three Kings 15 10
244 15c.+1c. Virgin and Child 15 10

245 20c.+1c. Joseph 15 10
246 20c.+1c. Mary and Jesus on donkey 15 10
MS247 130 × 95 mm. As Nos. 239/46 but each with premium of "+2c." 70 85

1978. Bicentenary of Discovery of Hawaii. Mult.
248 35c. Type **37** 35 25
249 50c. Figurehead of H.M.S. "Resolution" (horiz) 60 40
250 $1 Hawaiian temple figure 70 70
MS251 168 × 75 mm. Nos. 248/50 1·50 1·75

38 "Christ on the Way to Calvary" (Martini)
39 The Yale of Beaufort

1978. Easter. Paintings from the Louvre, Paris. Mult.
252 15c. Type **38** 15 10
253 20c. "Pieta of Avignon" (E. Quarton) 20 10
254 35c. "The Pilgrims at Emmaus" (Rembrandt) 25 10
MS255 108 × 83 mm. Nos. 252/4 75 75

1978. Easter. Children's Charity. Designs as Nos. 252/4, but smaller (34 × 26 mm) and without margins, in separate miniature sheets 75 × 58 mm, each with a face value of 50c. + 5c.
MS256 As Nos. 252/4 Set of 3 sheets 1·00 1·00

1978. 25th Anniv of Coronation. Multicoloured.
257 $1 Type **39** 30 50
258 $1 Queen Elizabeth II 30 50
259 $1 Aitutaki ancestral statue 30 50
MS260 98 × 127 mm. Nos 257/9 × 2 75 75

Stamps from No. **MS**260 have coloured borders, the upper row in lavender and the lower in green.

40 "Adoration of the Infant Jesus"
41 "Captain Cook" (Nathaniel Dance)

1978. Christmas. 450th Death Anniv of Durer. Multicoloured.
261 15c. Type **40** 25 15
262 17c. "The Madonna with Child" 30 15
263 30c. "The Madonna with the Iris" 45 20
264 35c. "The Madonna of the Siskin" 45 25
MS265 101 × 109 mm. As Nos. 261/4 but each with premium of "+2c." 1·10 1·00

1979. Death Bicent of Captain Cook. Mult.
266 50c. Type **41** 1·00 80
267 75c. "H.M.S. 'Resolution' and 'Adventure' at Matavai Bay," Tahiti (W. Hodges) 1·75 95
MS268 94 × 58 mm. Nos. 266/7 2·00 2·25

42 Girl with Flowers
43 "Man writing a Letter" (painting by Gabriel Metsu)

1979. International Year of the Child. Multicoloured.
269 30c. Type **42** 20 15
270 35c. Boy playing guitar 30 20
271 65c. Children in canoe 40 30
MS272 104 × 80 mm. As Nos. 269/71, but each with a premium of "+3c." 70 1·00

1979. Death Centenary of Sir Rowland Hill. Multicoloured.
273 50c. Type **43** 45 45
274 50c. Sir Rowland Hill with Penny Black, 1903 ½d. and 1911 1d. stamps 45 45
275 50c. "Girl in Blue reading a Letter" (Jan Vermeer) 45 45
276 65c. "Woman writing a Letter" (Gerard Terborch) 50 50
277 65c. Sir Rowland Hill, with Penny Black, 1903 3d. and 1920 ½d. stamps 50 50
278 65c. "Lady reading a Letter" (Jan Vermeer) 50 50
MS279 151 × 85 mm. 30c. × 6. As Nos. 273/8 1·75 1·75

44 "The Burial of Christ" (left detail) (Quentin Metsys)
45 Einstein as a Young Man

1980. Easter. Multicoloured.
280 20c. Type **44** 40 25
281 30c. "The Burial of Christ" (centre detail) 50 35
282 35c. "The Burial of Christ" (right detail) 65 45
MS283 93 × 71 mm. As Nos. 280/2, but each with premium of "+2c." 75 75

1980. 25th Death Anniv of Albert Einstein (physicist). Multicoloured.
284 12c. Type **45** 60 60
285 12c. Atom and "E = mc²" equation 60 60
286 15c. Einstein in middle-age 65 65
287 15c. Cross over nuclear explosion (Test Ban Treaty, 1963) 65 65
288 20c. Einstein as an old man 75 75
289 20c. Hand preventing atomic explosion 75 75
MS290 113 × 118 mm. Nos 284/9 3·00 3·00

46 Ancestor Figure, Aitutaki
47 "Virgin and Child" (13th century)

1980. 3rd South Pacific Festival of Arts. Mult.
291 6c. Type **46** 10 10
292 6c. Staff god image, Rarotonga 10 10
293 6c. Trade adze, Mangaia 10 10
294 6c. Carved image of Tangaroa, Rarotonga 10 10
295 12c. Wooden image Aitutaki 10 10
296 12c. Hand club, Rarotonga 10 10
297 12c. Carved mace "god", Mangaia 10 10
298 12c. Fisherman's god, Rarotonga 10 10
299 15c. Ti'i image, Aitutaki 15 15
300 15c. Fisherman's god, Rarotonga (different) 15 15
301 15c. Carved mace "god", Cook Islands 15 15
302 15c. Carved image of Tangaroa, Rarotonga (different) 15 15
303 20c. Chief's headdress, Aitutaki 15 15
304 20c. Carved mace "god", Cook Islands (different) 15 15
305 20c. Staff god image, Rarotonga (different) 15 15
306 20c. Carved image of Tangaroa, Rarotonga (different) 15 15
MS307 134 × 194 mm. Nos. 291/306 1·60 1·75

1980. Christmas. Sculptures of "The Virgin and Child". Multicoloured.
308 15c. Type **47** 20 15
309 20c. 14th century 20 15
310 25c. 15th century 20 15
311 35c. 15th century (different) 30 20
MS312 82 × 120 mm. As Nos. 306/11 but each with premium of 2c. 70 80

48 "Mourning Virgin"
49 Gouldian Finch

1981. Easter. Details of Sculpture "Burial of Christ" by Pedro Roldan.
313 **48** 30c. gold and green 25 25
314 – 40c. gold and lilac 30 30
315 – 50c. gold and blue 30 30
MS316 107 × 60 mm. As Nos. 313/15 but each with premium of 2c. 75 85
DESIGNS: 40c. "Christ"; 50c. "Saint John".

1981. Birds (1st series). Multicoloured.
317 1c. Type **49** 45 30
318 1c. Common starling 45 30
319 2c. Golden whistler 50 30
320 2c. Scarlet robin 50 30
321 3c. Rufous fantail 60 30
322 3c. Peregrine falcon 60 30
323 4c. Java sparrow 70 30
324 4c. Barn owl 70 30
325 5c. Tahitian lory 70 30
326 5c. White-breasted wood swallow 70 30
327 6c. Purple swamphen 70 30
328 6c. Feral rock pigeon 70 30
329 10c. Chestnut-breasted mannikin 90 30
330 10c. Zebra dove 90 30
331 12c. Reef heron 1·00 40
332 12c. Common mynah 1·00 40
333 15c. Whimbrel (horiz) 1·25 40
334 15c. Black-browed albatross (horiz) 1·25 40
335 20c. Pacific golden plover (horiz) 1·50 55
336 20c. White tern (horiz) 1·50 55
337 25c. Pacific black duck (horiz) 1·75 70
338 25c. Brown booby (horiz) 1·75 70
339 30c. Great frigate bird (horiz) 2·00 85
340 30c. Pintail (horiz) 2·00 85
341 35c. Long-billed reed warbler 2·00 1·00
342 35c. Pomarine skua 2·00 1·00
343 40c. Buff-banded rail 2·25 1·25
344 40c. Spotted triller 2·25 1·25
345 50c. Royal albatross 2·25 1·50
346 50c. Stephen's lory 2·25 1·50
347 70c. Red-headed parrot-finch 5·50 3·00
348 70c. Orange dove 5·50 3·00
349 $1 Blue-headed flycatcher 4·50 3·75
350 $2 Red-bellied flycatcher 5·00 8·00
351 $4 Red munia 9·00 14·00
352 $5 Flat-billed kingfisher 9·00 16·00
See also Nos. 475/94.

50 Prince Charles
52 Footballers

1981. Royal Wedding. Multicoloured.
391 60c. Type **50** 30 40
392 80c. Lady Diana Spencer 40 55
393 $1.40 Prince Charles and Lady Diana (87 × 70 mm) 60 80

1981. International Year for Disabled Persons. Nos. 391/3 surch **+5c.**
394 60c.+5c. Type **50** 60 90
395 80c.+5c. Lady Diana Spencer 70 1·10
396 $1.40+5c. Prince Charles and Lady Diana 90 1·40

1981. World Cup Football Championship, Spain (1982). Football Scenes. Multicoloured.
397 12c. Ball to left of stamp 50 35
398 12c. Ball to right 50 35
399 15c. Ball to right 55 40
400 15c. Ball to left 55 40
401 20c. Ball to left 55 50
402 20c. Ball to right 55 50
403 25c. Type **52** 60 55
404 25c. "ESPANA 82" inscription 60 55
MS405 100 × 137 mm. 12c.+2c., 15c.+2c., 20c.+2c., 25c.+2c., each × 2. As Nos. 397/404 3·50 3·00

53 "The Holy Family"
54 Princess of Wales

1981. Christmas. Etchings by Rembrandt. Each brown and gold.
406 15c. Type **53** 45 45
407 30c. "Virgin with Child" 70 70
408 40c. "Adoration of the Shepherds" (horiz) 95 95
409 50c. "The Holy Family" (horiz) 1·25 1·25
MS410 Designs as Nos. 406/9 in separate miniature sheets, 65 × 82 mm or 82 × 65 mm, each with a face value of 80c.+5c. Set of 4 sheets 4·00 3·00

1982. 21st Birthday of Princess of Wales. Mult.
411 70c. Type **54** 2·00 60
412 $1 Prince and Princess of Wales 2·00 75
413 $2 Princess Diana (different) 3·25 1·50
MS414 82 × 91 mm. Nos. 411/13 6·00 2·75

1982. Birth of Prince William of Wales (1st issue). Nos. 391/3 optd.
415 60c. Type **50** 90 70
416 60c. Type **50** 90 70
417 80c. Lady Diana Spencer 1·10 80
418 80c. Lady Diana Spencer 1·10 80
419 $1.40 Prince Charles and Lady Diana 1·25 1·00
420 $1.40 Prince Charles and Lady Diana 1·25 1·00
OPTS: Nos. 415, 417 and 419, **21 JUNE 1982. PRINCE WILLIAM OF WALES.** Nos. 416, 418 and 420, **COMMEMORATING THE ROYAL BIRTH.**

1982. Birth of Prince William of Wales (2nd issue). As Nos. 411/13 but inscr "ROYAL BIRTH 21 JUNE 1982 PRINCE WILLIAM OF WALES".
421 70c. Type **54** 70 60
422 $1 Prince and Princess of Wales 80 75
423 $2 Princess Diana (different) 1·60 1·50
MS424 81 × 91 mm. Nos. 421/3 5·50 3·00

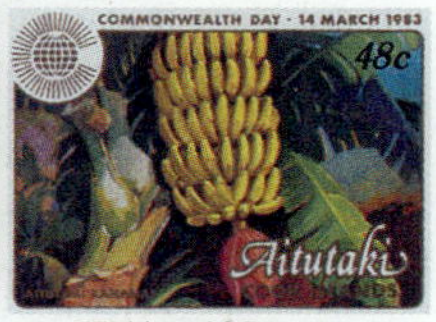

56 "Virgin and Child" (12th-century sculpture)
57 Aitutaki Bananas

1982. Christmas. Religious Sculptures. Multicoloured.
425 18c. Type **56** 70 70
426 36c. "Virgin and Child" (12th-century) 85 85
427 48c. "Virgin and Child" (13th-century) 1·00 1·00
428 60c. "Virgin and Child" (15th-century) 1·40 1·40
MS429 99 × 115 mm. As Nos. 425/8 but each with 2c. charity premium 2·50 2·75

1983. Commonwealth Day. Multicoloured.
430 48c. Type **57** 75 50
431 48c. Ancient Ti'i image 75 50
432 48c. Tourist canoeing 75 50
433 48c. Captain William Bligh and chart 75 50

58 Scouts around Campfire

1983. 75th Anniv of Boy Scout Movement. Mult.
434 36c. Type **58** 65 65
435 48c. Scout saluting 75 75
436 60c. Scouts hiking 80 80
MS437 78 × 107 mm. As Nos. 434/6 but each with premium of 3c. 1·50 1·75

1983. 15th World Scout Jamboree, Alberta, Canada. Nos. 434/6 optd **15TH WORLD SCOUT JAMBOREE.**
438 36c. Type **58** 80 45
439 48c. Scout saluting 1·00 55
440 60c. Scouts hiking 1·25 75
MS441 78 × 107 mm. As Nos. 438/40 but each with a premium of 3c. 1·50 2·00

60 Modern Sport Balloon
63 International Mail

1983. Bicentenary of Manned Flight.
442 **60** 18c. multicoloured 55 30
443 – 36c. multicoloured 75 50
444 – 48c. multicoloured 90 60
445 – 60c. multicoloured . . . . 1·00 80
MS446 – 64 × 80 mm. $2.50, mult (48½ × 28½ mm) . . . . 1·50 2·00
DESIGNS: 36c. to $2.50, showing different modern sports balloons.

1983. Various stamps surch (a) Nos. 335/48 and 352.
447 18c. on 20c. Pacific golden plover . . . . 2·75 1·25
448 18c. on 20c. White tern . . . 2·75 1·25
449 36c. on 25c. Pacific black duck . . . . 3·75 1·50
450 36c. on 25c. Brown booby . . 3·75 1·50
451 36c. on 30c. Great frigate bird . . . . 3·75 1·50
452 36c. on 30c. Pintail . . . . . 3·75 1·50
453 36c. on 35c. Long-billed reed warbler . . . . 3·75 1·50
454 36c. on 35c. Pomarine skua 3·75 1·50
455 48c. on 40c. Buff-banded rail 4·25 1·50
456 48c. on 40c. Spotted triller . . 4·25 1·50
457 48c. on 50c. Royal albatross 4·25 1·50
458 48c. on 50c. Stephen's lory 4·25 1·50
459 72c. on 70c. Red-headed parrot finch . . . . 7·50 3·00
460 72c. on 70c. Orange dove . . 7·50 3·00
461 $5.60 on $5 Flat-billed kingfisher (vert) . . . . . 21·00 10·00

(b) Nos. 392/3 and 412/3.
462 96c. on 80c. Lady Diana Spencer . . . . 3·00 2·50
463 96c. on $1 Prince and Princess of Wales . . . . 2·75 2·00
464 $1.20 on $1.40 Prince Charles and Lady Diana . . . . . 3·00 2·50
465 $1.20 on $2 Princess Diana 2·75 2·00

1983. World Communications Year. Multicoloured.
466 48c. Type **63** 65 50
467 60c. Telecommunications . . 95 70
468 96c. Space satellite . . . . . 1·40 1·00
MS469 126 × 53 mm. Nos. 466/8 2·50 2·50

64 "Madonna of the Chair"

1983. Christmas. 500th Birth Anniv of Raphael. Multicoloured.
470 36c. Type **64** 75 40
471 48c. "The Alba Madonna" 90 50
472 60c. "Conestabile Madonna" 1·25 70
MS473 95 × 116 mm. Nos. 470/2, but each with a premium of 3c. . . 2·75 1·40

1983. Christmas. 500th Birth Anniv of Raphael. Children's Charity. Designs as Nos. 470/2 in separate miniature sheets 46 × 47 mm, but with different frames and a face value of 85c.+5c. Imperf.
MS474 As Nos. 470/2 Set of 3 sheets 3·75 2·75

65 Gouldian Finch

66 Javelin throwing

1984. Birds (2nd series). Multicoloured.
475 2c. Type **65** . . . . 1·75 1·25
476 3c. Common starling . . . . 1·75 1·25
477 5c. Scarlet robin . . . . . . 1·75 1·40
478 10c. Golden whistler . . . . 2·25 1·40
479 12c. Rufous fantail . . . . . 2·25 1·40
480 18c. Peregrine falcon . . . . 2·25 1·75
481 24c. Barn owl . . . . 2·25 1·75
482 30c. Java sparrow . . . . . 2·25 1·50
483 36c. White-breasted wood swallow . . . . 2·25 1·50
484 48c. Tahitian lory . . . . . 2·25 1·50
485 50c. Feral rock pigeon . . . 2·50 2·50
486 60c. Purple swamphen . . . 2·50 2·00
487 72c. Zebra dove . . . . . . 3·00 2·50
488 96c. Chestnut-breasted mannikin . . . . 3·00 2·50
489 $1.20 Common mynah . . . 3·00 3·50
490 $2.10 Reef heron . . . . . 5·00 3·75
491 $3 Blue-headed flycatcher . . 7·00 6·00
492 $4.20 Red-bellied flycatcher 3·50 6·00
493 $5.60 Red munia . . . . . . 3·50 9·50
494 $9.60 Flat-billed kingfisher 7·50 12·00

1984. Olympic Games. Los Angeles. Multicoloured.
495 36c. Type **66** 35 35
496 48c. Shot-putting 40 45
497 60c. Hurdling 45 55
498 $2 Basketball . . . . 1·75 1·50
MS499 88 × 117 mm. As Nos. 495/8, but each with a charity premium of 5c. . . . . 3·00 3·50
DESIGNS: 48c. to $2, show Memorial Coliseum and various events.

1984. Olympic Gold Medal Winners. Nos. 495/8 optd.
500 36c. Type **66** (optd **Javelin Throw Tessa Sanderson Great Britain**) 35 35
501 48c. Shot-putting (optd **Shot Put Claudia Losch Germany**) 40 45
502 60c. Hurdling (optd **Heptathlon Glynis Nunn Australia**) 45 55
503 $2 Basketball (optd **Team Basketball United States**) 1·10 1·50

67 Captain William Bligh and Chart

1984. "Ausipex" International Stamp Exhibition, Melbourne. Multicoloured.
504 60c. Type **67** . . . . 4·00 3·75
505 96c. H.M.S. "Bounty" and map . . . . 4·00 4·00
506 $1.40 Aitutaki stamps of 1974, 1979 and 1981 with map . . . . 4·00 4·25
MS507 85 × 113 mm. As Nos. 504/6, but each with a premium of 5c. 7·50 4·00

1984. Birth of Prince Henry (1st issue). No. 391 optd **15-9-84 Birth Prince Henry** and surch also.
508 $3 on 60c. Type **50** . . . . . 2·00 3·25

69 The Annunciation

70 Princess Diana with Prince Henry

1984. Christmas. Details from Altarpiece, St Paul's Church, Palencia, Spain. Multicoloured.
509 36c. Type **69** 30 35
510 48c. The Nativity 40 45
511 60c. The Epiphany 45 50
512 96c. The Flight into Egypt 75 80
MS513 Designs as Nos. 509/12 in separate miniature sheets, each 45 × 53 mm and with a face value of 90c.+7c. Imperf. Set of 4 sheets 2·50 3·25

1984. Birth of Prince Henry (2nd issue). Mult.
514 48c. Type **70** . . . . 2·75 2·25
515 60c. Prince William with Prince Henry . . . . . . 2·75 2·25
516 $2.10 Prince and Princess of Wales with children . . . 3·50 4·50
MS517 113 × 65 mm. As Nos. 514/16, but each with a face value of 96c.+7c. . . . . . . 7·00 4·50

71 Grey Kingbird ("Gray Kingbird")

1985. Birth Bicentenary of John J. Audubon (ornithologist). Designs showing original paintings. Multicoloured.
518 55c. Type **71** . . . . 1·10 1·10
519 65c. Bohemian waxwing . . . 1·25 1·25
520 75c. Summer tanager . . . . 1·40 1·40
521 95c. Common cardinal ("Cardinal") . . . . 1·50 1·50
522 $1.15 White-winged crossbill 1·90 1·90

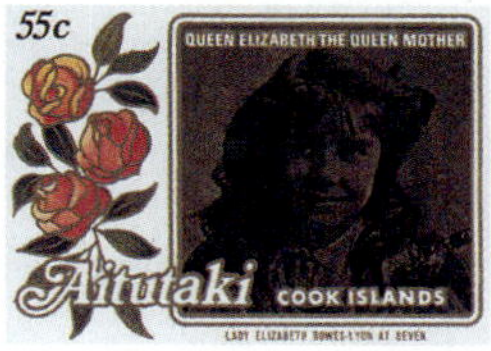

72 The Queen Mother, aged Seven

1985. Life and Times of Queen Elizabeth the Queen Mother. Multicoloured.
523 55c. Type **72** 45 50
524 65c. Engagement photograph, 1922 . . . . 50 55
525 75c. With young Princess Elizabeth 60 65
526 $1.30 With baby Prince Charles . . . . 1·00 1·10
MS527 75 × 49 mm. $3 Queen Mother on her 63rd birthday 2·25 2·40

73 "The Calmady Children" (T. Lawrence)

1985. International Youth Year. Multicoloured.
528 75c. Type **73** . . . . 3·00 2·75
529 90c. "Madame Charpentier's Children" (Renoir) . . . . 3·00 3·00
530 $1.40 "Young Girls at Piano" (Renoir) . . . . 3·75 4·00
MS531 103 × 104 mm. As Nos. 528/30, but each with a premium of 10c. . . . . 4·75 3·75

74 "Adoration of the Magi" (Giotto) and "Giotto" Spacecraft

1985. Christmas. Appearance of Halley's Comet (1st issue). Multicoloured.
532 95c. Type **74** . . . . 2·00 1·75
533 95c. As Type **74** but showing "Planet A" spacecraft . . . 2·00 1·75
534 $1.15 Type **74** . . . . 2·00 1·75
535 $1.15 As No. 533 . . . . . . 2·00 1·75
MS536 52 × 55 mm. $6.40. As Type **74** but without spacecraft (30 × 31 mm). Imperf . . . . . 14·00 8·50

75 Halley's Comet A.D. 684 (from "Nuremberg Chronicle")

1986. Appearance of Halley's Comet (2nd issue). Multicoloured.
537 90c. Type **75** . . . . 1·25 90
538 $1.25 Halley's Comet, 1066 (from Bayeux Tapestry) . . 1·60 1·10
539 $1.75 Halley's Comet, 1456 (from "Lucerne Chronicles") . . . . 1·90 1·50
MS540 107 × 82 mm. As Nos. 537/9, but each with a face value of 95c. 5·50 2·50
MS541 65 × 80 mm. $4.20, "Melencolia I" (Albrecht Dürer woodcut) (61 × 76 mm). Imperf 6·00 3·50

76 Queen Elizabeth II on Coronation Day (from photo by Cecil Beaton)

78 Prince Andrew and Miss Sarah Ferguson

77 Head of Statue of Liberty

1986. 60th Birthday of Queen Elizabeth II.
542 **76** 95c. multicoloured . . . . 2·00 2·25
MS543 58 × 68 mm. $4.20, As T **76**, but showing more of the portrait without oval frame . . . . . 5·50 5·50

1986. Centenary of Statue of Liberty. Mult.
544 $1 Type **77** . . . . 1·25 1·25
545 $2.75 Statue of Liberty at sunset . . . . 2·75 2·75
MS546 91 × 79 mm. As Nos. 544/5, but each with a face value of $1.25 3·25 2·50

1986. Royal Wedding.
547 **78** $2 multicoloured . . . . . 2·00 2·00
MS548 85 × 70 mm. Type **78** multicoloured . . . . 6·50 8·00

1986. "Stampex '86" Stamp Exhibition, Adelaide. No. **MS**507 with "Ausipex" emblems obliterated in gold.
MS549 As Nos. 504/6, but each with a premium of 5c. . . . . . . 11·00 12·00
The "Stampex '86" exhibition emblem is overprinted on the sheet margin.

1986. 86th Birthday of Queen Elizabeth the Queen Mother. Nos. 523/6 in miniature sheet, 132 × 82 mm.
MS550 Nos. 523/6 . . . . 11·00 10·00

79 "St. Anne with Virgin and Child"

83 Angels

1986. Christmas. Paintings by Durer. Multicoloured.
551 75c. Type **79** . . . . 1·25 1·25
552 $1.35 "Virgin and Child" . . 1·75 1·75
553 $1.95 "The Adoration of the Magi" . . . . 2·25 2·25
554 $2.75 "Madonna of the Rosary" . . . . 3·00 3·00
MS555 88 × 125 mm. As Nos. 551/4, but each with a face value of $1.65 13·00 14·00

1986. Visit of Pope John Paul II to South Pacific. Nos. 551/4 optd **NOVEMBER 21-24 1986 FIRST VISIT TO SOUTH PACIFIC** and surch also.
556 75c.+10c. Type **79** . . . . 2·75 2·50
557 $1.35+10c. "Virgin and Child" . . . . 3·25 3·00
558 $1.95+10c. "The Adoration of the Magi" . . . . . . 4·00 3·50
559 $2.75+10c. "Madonna of the Rosary" . . . . 5·00 5·00
MS560 88 × 125 mm. As Nos. 556/9, but each with a face value of $1.65+10c. . . . . 16·00 15·00

1987. Hurricane Relief Fund. Nos. 544/5, 547, 551/4 and 556/9 surch **HURRICANE RELIEF +50c**.
561 75c.+50c. Type **79** . . . . 3·25 2·75
562 75c.+10c.+50c. Type **79** . . . 4·00 3·50
563 $1+50c. Type **77** . . . . . 3·50 3·00
564 $1.35+50c. "Virgin and Child" (Durer) . . . . . 3·75 3·25
565 $1.35+10c.+50c. "Virgin and Child" (Durer) . . . . . 4·50 4·00
566 $1.95+50c. "The Adoration of the Magi" (Durer) . . . 4·50 4·00
567 $1.95+10c.+50c. "The Adoration of the Magi" (Durer) . . . . 5·00 4·50
568 $2+50c. Type **78** . . . . . 4·50 4·00
569 $2.75+50c. Statue of Liberty at sunset . . . . 5·00 4·50
570 $2.75+50c. "Madonna of the Rosary" (Durer) . . . . . 5·00 4·50
571 $2.75+10c.+50c. "Madonna of the Rosary" (Durer) . . 6·50 5·50

1987. Royal Ruby Wedding. Nos. 391/3 surch **2.50 Royal Wedding 40th Anniv**.
572 $2.50 on 60c. Type **50** . . . 2·00 2·50
573 $2.50 on 80c. Lady Diana Spencer . . . . 2·00 2·50
574 $2.50 on $1.40 Prince Charles and Lady Diana (87 × 70 mm) . . . . . . 2·00 2·50

1987. Christmas. Details of angels from "Virgin with Garland" by Rubens.
575 **83** 70c. multicoloured . . . . 2·00 2·00
576 – 85c. multicoloured . . . . 2·00 2·00
577 – $1.50 multicoloured . . . 2·25 2·25
578 – $1.85 multicoloured . . . 3·25 3·25
MS579 92 × 120 mm. As Nos. 575/8, but each with a face value of 95c. 12·00 13·00
MS580 96 × 85 mm. $6 "Virgin with Garland" (diamond, 56 × 56 mm) 11·00 13·00

84 Chariot Racing and Athletics

1988. Olympic Games, Seoul. Ancient and modern Olympic sports. Multicoloured.
581 70c. Type **84** . . . . 2·25 2·00
582 85c. Greek runners and football . . . . 2·50 2·25
583 95c. Greek wrestling and handball . . . . 2·50 2·25
584 $1.40 Greek hoplites and tennis . . . . 3·25 3·00
MS585 103 × 101 mm. As Nos. 581 and 584, but each with face value of $2 . . . . 8·00 8·50

1988. Olympic Medal Winners, Los Angeles. Nos. 581/4 optd.
586 70c. Type **84** (optd **FLORENCE GRIFFITH JOYNER UNITED STATES 100 M AND 200 M**) . . . . 2·00 2·00
587 85c. Greek runners and football (optd **GELINDO BORDIN ITALY MARATHON**) . . . . . 2·00 2·00
588 95c. Greek wrestling and handball (optd **HITOSHI SAITO JAPAN JUDO**) . . 2·00 2·00
589 $1.40 Greek hoplites and tennis (optd **STEFFI GRAF WEST GERMANY WOMEN'S TENNIS**) . . 4·50 4·00

85 "Adoration of the Shepherds" (detail)

1988. Christmas. Paintings by Rembrandt. Mult.
590 55c. Type **85** . . . . 2·00 1·75
591 70c. "The Holy Family" . . 2·25 2·00
592 85c. "Presentation in the Temple" . . . . 2·50 2·25
593 95c. "The Holy Family" (different) . . . . 2·50 2·25
594 $1.15 "Presentation in the Temple" (different) . . . 2·75 2·50
MS595 85 × 101 mm. $4.50, As Type **85** but 52 × 34 mm. . . . 5·50 6·50

86 H.M.S. "Bounty" leaving Spithead and King George III

1989. Bicentenary of Discovery of Aitutaki by Captain Bligh. Multicoloured.
596 55c. Type **86** . . . . 2·00 2·00
597 65c. Breadfruit plants . . . . 2·25 2·25
598 75c. Old chart showing Aitutaki and Captain Bligh 2·50 2·50
599 95c. Native outrigger and H.M.S. "Bounty" off Aitutaki . . . . 2·75 2·75
600 $1.65 Fletcher Christian confronting Bligh . . . . 3·50 3·50
MS601 94 × 72 mm. $4.20 "Mutineers casting Bligh adrift" (Robert Dodd) (60 × 45 mm) 8·00 9·50

87 "Apollo 11" Astronaut on Moon

1989. 20th Anniv of First Manned Landing on Moon. Multicoloured.
602 75c. Type **87** . . . . 2·75 2·00
603 $1.15 Conducting experiment on Moon . . . . 3·25 2·50
604 $1.80 Astronaut on Moon carrying equipment . . . . 4·00 3·50
MS605 105 × 86 mm. $6.40 Astronaut on Moon with U.S. flag (40 × 27 mm) . . . . 8·00 9·50

88 Virgin Mary

91 "Madonna of the Basket" (Correggio)

89 Human Comet striking Earth

1989. Christmas. Details from "Virgin in the Glory" by Titian. Multicoloured.
606 70c. Type **88** . . . . 2·50 2·00
607 85c. Christ Child . . . . . . 3·00 2·50
608 95c. Angel . . . . 3·25 2·75
609 $1.25 Cherubs . . . . 3·75 3·25
MS610 80 × 100 mm. $6 "Virgin in the Glory" (45 × 60 mm) . . . 8·00 9·50

1990. Protection of the Environment. Mult.
611 $1.75 Type **89** . . . . 2·25 2·25
612 $1.75 Comet's tail . . . . . 2·25 2·25
MS613 108 × 43 mm. Nos. 611/12 3·50 4·50
Nos. 611/12 were printed together, se-tenant, forming a composite design.

1990. 90th Birthday of Queen Elizabeth the Queen Mother. No. **MS**550 optd **Ninetieth Birthday**.
MS614 132 × 82 mm. Nos. 523/6 13·00 12·00

1990. Christmas. Religious Paintings. Mult.
615 70c. Type **91** . . . . 1·50 1·50
616 85c. "Virgin and Child" (Morando) . . . . 1·60 1·60
617 95c. "Adoration of the Child" (Tiepolo) . . . . . 1·75 1·75
618 $1.75 "Mystic Marriage of St. Catherine" (Memling) 2·50 2·75
MS619 165 × 93 mm. $6 "Donne Triptych" (Memling) (horiz) . . 12·00 13·00

1990. "Birdpex '90" Stamp Exhibition, Christchurch, New Zealand. Nos. 349/50 optd **Birdpex '90** and bird's head.
620 $1 Blue-headed flycatcher . . 4·50 4·50
621 $2 Red-bellied flycatcher . . 6·00 6·00

1991. 65th Birthday of Queen Elizabeth II. No. 352 optd **COMMEMORATING 65th BIRTHDAY OF H.M. QUEEN ELIZABETH II**.
622 $5 Flat-billed kingfisher . . . 12·00 12·00

93 "The Holy Family" (A. Mengs)

1991. Christmas. Religious Paintings. Mult.
623 80c. Type **93** . . . . 1·75 1·75
624 90c. "Virgin and the Child" (Lippi) . . . . 1·75 1·75
625 $1.05 "Virgin and Child" (A. Durer) . . . . 2·00 2·00
626 $1.75 "Adoration of the Shepherds" (G. de la Tour) 2·75 3·25
MS627 79 × 103 mm. "The Holy Family" (Michelangelo) . . . 12·00 13·00

94 Hurdling

1992. Olympic Games, Barcelona. Mult.
628 95c. Type **94** . . . . 1·75 1·50
629 $1.25 Weightlifting . . . . . 2·00 1·75
630 $1.50 Judo . . . . 2·50 2·25
631 $1.95 Football . . . . 2·75 2·75

95 Vaka Motu Canoe

1992. 6th Festival of Pacific Arts, Rarotonga. Sailing Canoes. Multicoloured.
632 30c. Type **95** 65 65
633 50c. Hamatafua 80 80
634 95c. Alia Kalia Ndrua . . . . 1·50 1·50
635 $1.75 Hokule'a Hawaiian . . 2·25 2·75
636 $1.95 Tuamotu Pahi . . . . 2·50 3·00

1992. Royal Visit by Prince Edward. Nos. 632/6 optd **ROYAL VISIT**.
637 30c. Type **95** . . . . 1·25 1·25
638 50c. Hamatafua . . . . . . 1·60 1·60
639 95c. Alia Kalia Ndrua . . . . 2·50 2·50
640 $1.75 Hokule'a Hawaiian . . 3·50 3·75
641 $1.95 Tuamotu Pahi . . . . 3·50 3·75

96 "Virgin's Nativity" (detail) (Reni)

1992. Christmas. Different details from "Virgin's Nativity" by Guido Reni.
642 **96** 80c. multicoloured . . . . 1·40 1·40
643 – 90c. multicoloured . . . . 1·60 1·60
644 – $1.05 multicoloured . . . 1·75 1·75
645 – $1.75 multicoloured . . . 2·50 3·00
MS646 – 101 × 86 mm. $6 multicoloured (as $1.05, but larger (36 × 46 mm)) . . . . 6·50 8·00

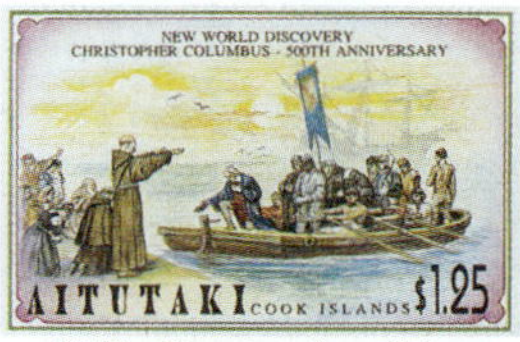

97 The Departure from Palos

1992. 500th Anniv of Discovery of America by Columbus. Multicoloured.
647 $1.25 Type **97** . . . . 2·25 2·50
648 $1.75 Map of voyages . . . 2·75 3·00
649 $1.95 Columbus and crew in New World . . . . 3·25 3·50

98 Queen Victoria and King Edward VII

1993. 40th Anniv of Coronation. Mult.
650 $1.75 Type **98** . . . . 3·50 3·00
651 $1.75 King George V and King George VI . . . . 3·50 3·00
652 $1.75 Queen Elizabeth II in 1953 and 1986 . . . . . 3·50 3·00

99 "Madonna and Child" (Nino Pisano)

1993. Christmas. Religious Sculptures. Mult.
653 80c. Type **99** 90 90
654 90c. "Virgin on Rosebush" (Luca della Robbia) . . . 1·00 1·00
655 $1.15 "Virgin with Child and St. John" (Juan Francisco Rustici) . . . . 1·40 1·40
656 $1.95 "Virgin with Child" (Miguel Angel) . . . . . 2·25 2·25
657 $3 "Madonna and Child" (Jacopo della Quercia) (32 × 47 mm) . . . . . . 3·25 4·00

100 Ice Hockey

1994. Winter Olympic Games, Lillehammer. Multicoloured.
658 $1.15 Type **100** . . . . . . 3·50 3·00
659 $1.15 Ski-jumping . . . . . 3·50 3·00
660 $1.15 Cross-country skiing 3·50 3·00

101 "Ipomoea pes–caprae"

103 "The Madonna of the Basket" (Correggio)

102 Cook Islands and U.S.A. Flags with Astronauts Collins, Armstrong and Aldrin

1994. Flowers. Multicoloured.
661 5c. Type **101** 10 10
662 10c. "Plumeria alba" 10 10
663 15c. "Hibiscus rosa-sinensis" 10 15
664 20c. "Allamanda cathartica" 15 20
665 25c. "Delonix regia" 20 25
666 30c. "Gardenia taitensis" . . 20 25
667 50c. "Plumeria rubra" . . . 35 40
668 80c. "Ipomoea littoralis" . . 60 65
669 85c. "Hibiscus tiliaceus" . . 60 65
670 90c. "Erythrina variegata" . . 65 70
671 $1 "Solandra nitida" 75 80
672 $2 "Cordia subcordata" . . . 1·50 1·60
673 $3 "Hibiscus rosa-sinensis" (different) (34 × 47 mm) . . 2·20 2·30
674 $5 As $3 (34 × 47 mm) . . . 3·75 4·00
675 $8 As $3 (34 × 47 mm) . . . 5·00 5·25
Nos. 671/5 include a portrait of Queen Elizabeth II at top right.

1994. 25th Anniv of First Manned Moon Landing. Multicoloured.
676 $2 Type **102** . . . . 7·50 7·50
677 $2 "Apollo 11" re-entering atmosphere and landing in sea . . . . 7·50 7·50

1994. Christmas. Religious Paintings. Mult.
678 85c. Type **103** . . . . 1·00 1·10
679 85c. "The Virgin and Child with Saints" (Memling) . . 1·00 1·10
680 85c. "The Virgin and Child with Flowers" (Dolci) . . . 1·00 1·10
681 85c. "The Virgin and Child with Angels" (Bergognone) 1·00 1·10
682 90c. "Adoration of the Kings" (Dosso) . . . . . 1·00 1·10
683 90c. "The Virgin and Child" (Bellini) . . . . 1·00 1·10
684 90c. "The Virgin and Child" (Schiavone) . . . . . . 1·00 1·10
685 90c. "Adoration of the Kings" (Dolci) . . . . . 1·00 1·10
No. 678 is inscribed "Corregio" in error.

104 Battle of Britain

1995. 50th Anniv of End of Second World War. Multicoloured.
686 $4 Type **104** . . . . 9·00 8·50
687 $4 Battle of Midway . . . . 9·00 8·50

105 Queen Elizabeth the Queen Mother

1995. 95th Birthday of Queen Elizabeth the Queen Mother.
688 **105** $4 multicoloured . . . . 7·50 8·00

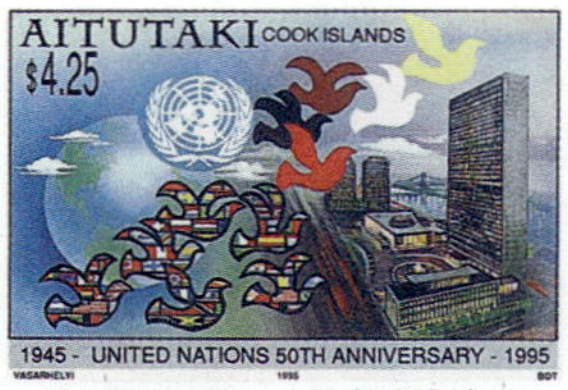

106 Globe, Doves, United Nations Emblem and Headquarters

1995. 50th Anniv of United Nations.
689 **106** $4.25 multicoloured . . . 5·50 7·00

107 Green Turtle

1995. Year of the Sea Turtle. Multicoloured.
690 95c. Type **107** . . . . 1·75 1·75
691 $1.15 Leatherback turtle . . 2·00 2·00
692 $1.50 Olive Ridley turtle . . 2·25 2·25
693 $1.75 Loggerhead turtle . . . 2·50 2·50

108 Queen Elizabeth II

1996. 70th Birthday of Queen Elizabeth II.
694 **108** $4.50 multicoloured . . . 8·50 8·00

109 Baron Pierre de Coubertin, Torch and Opening of 1896 Olympic Games

1996. Centenary of Modern Olympic Games. Multicoloured.
695 $2 Type **109** . . . . 5·00 5·00
696 $2 Athletes and American flag, 1996 . . . . 5·00 5·00

110 Princess Elizabeth and Lieut. Philip Mountbatten with King George VI and Queen Elizabeth, 1947

1997. Golden Wedding of Queen Elizabeth and Prince Philip.
697 **110** $2.50 multicoloured . . . 4·50 3·50
MS698 78 × 102 mm. **110** $6 multicoloured . . . . 8·00 8·50

111 Diana, Princess of Wales

1998. Diana, Princess of Wales Commemoration.
699 **111** $1 multicoloured . . . . 1·00 1·00
MS700 70 × 100 mm. $4 Diana, Princess of Wales . . . . . . 3·25 3·75

1998. Children's Charities. No. **MS**1427 surch **+$1 CHILDREN'S CHARITIES.**
MS701 70 × 100 mm. $4 + $1 Diana, Princess of Wales . . . . . . 3·75 4·50

1999. New Millennium. Nos. 632/6 optd **KIA ORANA THIRD MILLENNIUM**.
702 30c. Type **95** 50 50
703 50c. Hamatafua 60 60
704 95c. Alia Kalia Ndrua . . . 85 85
705 $1.75 Hokule'a Hawaiian . . 1·40 1·60
706 $1.95 Tuamotu Pahi . . . . 1·60 1·75

2000. Queen Elizabeth the Queen Mother's 100th Birthday. As T **277** of Cook Islands.
707 $3 blue and brown . . . . . 3·25 3·25
708 $3 multicoloured . . . . . . 3·25 3·25
709 $3 multicoloured . . . . . . 3·25 3·25
710 $3 green and brown . . . . 3·25 3·25
MS711 73 × 100 mm. $7.50 multicoloured . . . . 7·00 8·00
DESIGNS: No. 707, Queen Mother in evening dress and tiara; 708, Queen Mother in evening dress standing by table; 709, Queen Mother in Garter robes; 710, King George VI and Queen Elizabeth; **MS**711 Queen Mother holding lilies.

2000. Olympic Games, Sydney. As T **278** of Cook Islands. Multicoloured.
712 $2 Ancient Greek wrestlers 2·00 2·25
713 $2 Modern wrestlers . . . . 2·00 2·25
714 $2 Ancient Greek boxer . . . 2·00 2·25
715 $2 Modern boxers . . . . . 2·00 2·25
MS716 99 × 90 mm. $2.75 Olympic torch and Cook Island canoes 2·25 2·75

113 Blue Lorikeets and Flowers

2002. Endangered Species. Blue Lorikeet. Multicoloured.
717 80c. Type **113** . . . . 1·10 1·25
718 90c. Lorikeets and bananas 1·10 1·25
719 $1.15 Lorikeets on palm leaf 1·40 1·60
720 $1.95 Lorikeets in tree trunk 1·90 2·10

2003. "United We Stand". Support for Victims of 11 September 2001 Terrorist Attacks. Design as T **282** of Cook Islands. Multicoloured.
MS721 75 × 109 mm. $1.15 × 4 Twin Towers and flags of U.S.A. and Cook Islands . . . . 4·75 5·50

2005. Pope John Paul II Commemoration. As T **285** of Cook Islands. Multicoloured.
722 $1.95 Pope praying . . . . . 2·25 2·50

OFFICIAL STAMPS

1978. Nos. 98/105, 107/10 and 227/8 optd **O.H.M.S.** or surch also.
O 1 1c. multicoloured 90 10
O 2 2c. multicoloured . . . . . 1·00 10
O 3 3c. multicoloured . . . . . 1·00 10
O 4 4c. multicoloured . . . . . 1·00 10
O 5 5c. multicoloured . . . . . 1·00 10
O 6 8c. multicoloured . . . . . 1·25 10
O 7 10c. multicoloured . . . . . 1·50 15
O 8 15c. on 60c. multicoloured 2·75 20
O 9 18c. on 60c. multicoloured 2·75 20
O10 20c. multicoloured . . . . . 2·75 20
O11 50c. multicoloured . . . . . 1·00 55
O12 60c. multicoloured . . . . . 10·00 70
O13 $1 multicoloured (No. 108) 10·00 80
O14 $2 multicoloured . . . . . 9·00 75
O15 $4 on $1 mult (No. 228) . . 1·75 75
O16 $5 multicoloured . . . . . 11·00 1·25

1985. Nos. 351/2, 430/3, 475 and 477/94 optd **O.H.M.S.** or surch also.
O17 2c. Type **65** . . . . 1·25 1·50
O18 5c. Scarlet robin . . . . . . 1·50 1·50
O19 10c. Golden whistler . . . . 1·75 1·75
O20 12c. Rufous fantail . . . . . 1·90 2·00
O21 18c. Peregrine falcon . . . . 3·00 2·25
O22 20c. on 24 c Barn owl . . . 3·00 2·25
O23 30c. Java sparrow . . . . . 2·25 1·50
O24 40c. on 36c. White-breasted wood swallow . . . . 2·25 1·50
O25 50c. Feral rock pigeon . . . 2·25 1·50
O26 55c. on 48c. Tahitian lory . . 2·25 1·50
O27 60c. Purple swamphen . . . 2·50 1·75
O28 65c. on 72c. Zebra dove . . . 2·50 1·75
O38 75c. on 48c. Type **57** . . . 1·25 1·40
O39 75c. on 48c. Ancient Ti'i image . . . . 1·25 1·40
O40 75c. on 48c. Tourist canoeing . . . . 1·25 1·40
O41 75c. on 48c. Captain William Bligh and chart . . . . . 1·25 1·40
O29 80c. on 96c. Chestnut-breasted mannikin . . . . 2·50 1·75
O30 $1.20 Common mynah . . . 3·25 2·50
O31 $2.10 Reef heron . . . . . 4·25 3·75
O32 $3 Blue-headed flycatcher . . 6·00 6·00
O33 $4.20 Red-bellied flycatcher 7·00 7·00
O34 $5.60 Red munia . . . . . 8·00 8·00
O35 $9.60 Flat-billed kingfisher 13·00 13·00
O36 $14 on $4 Red munia (35 × 48 mm) . . . . . 15·00 15·00
O37 $18 on $5 Flat-billed kingfisher (35 × 48 mm) . . 17·00 17·00

AJMAN Pt. 19

One of the Trucial States in the Persian Gulf. On 18 July 1971, seven Gulf sheikhdoms, including Ajman, formed the State of the United Arab Emirates. The federation became effective on 1 August 1972.

1964. 100 naye paise = 1 rupee.
1967. 100 dirhams = 1 riyal.

1 Shaikh Rashid bin Humaid al Naimi and Arab Stallion

1964. Multicoloured. (a) Size 34½ × 23 mm.
1 1n.p. Type **1** 10 10
2 2n.p. Regal angelfish 10 10
3 3n.p. Dromedary 10 10
4 4n.p. Yellow-banded angelfish 10 10
5 5n.p. Tortoise 10 10
6 10n.p. Jewel cichlid 20 10
7 15n.p. White stork 30 10
8 20n.p. Black-headed gulls . . . 30 10
9 30n.p. Lanner falcon 45 20

(b) Size 42½ × 27 mm.
10 40n.p. Type **1** 20 20
11 50n.p. Regal angelfish 20 20
12 70n.p. Dromedary 30 20
13 1r. Yellow-banded angelfish 30 30
14 1r.50 Tortoise 55 45
15 2r. Jewel cichlid 75 65

(c) Size 53 × 34 mm.
16 3r. White stork . . . . 1·20 95
17 5r. Black-headed gulls . . . . 3·25 2·30
18 10r. Lanner falcon . . . . . 5·75 4·25

2 Kennedy in Football Kit

1964. Pres. Kennedy Commem. Perf or imperf.
19 **2** 10n.p. purple and green . . . 10 10
20 – 15n.p. violet and turquoise 10 10
21 – 50n.p. blue and brown . . . 20 10
22 – 1r. turquoise and sepia . . . 75 45
23 – 2r. olive and purple 75 45
24 – 3r. brown and green . . . . 1·10 75
25 – 5r. brown and violet . . . . 1·90 1·60
26 – 10r. brown and blue . . . . 3·75 2·75
MS26a 105 × 140 mm. Nos. 23/6 in new colours . . . . 19·00 9·50
DESIGNS—Various pictures of Kennedy: 15n.p. Diving; 50n.p. As naval officer; 1r. Sailing with Mrs. Kennedy; 2r. With Mrs. Eleanor Roosevelt; 3r. With wife and child; 5r. With colleagues; 10r. Full-face portrait.

3 Start of Race

1965. Olympic Games, Tokyo. Perf or imperf.
27 **3** 5n.p. slate, brown & mauve 10 10
28 – 10n.p. red, bronze and blue 10 10
29 **3** 15n.p. brown, violet & green 10 10
30 – 25n.p. black, blue and red . . 20 10
31 – 50n.p. slate, purple and blue 30 20
32 – 1r. blue, green and purple . . 45 30
33 – 1r.50 purple, violet and green 75 45
34 – 2r. blue, purple and ochre . . 95 55
35 – 3r. violet, brown and blue . . 1·40 85
36 – 5r. purple, green and yellow 2·40 1·40
MS36a 120 × 100 mm. Nos. 33/6 in new colours . . . . 9·50 6·50
DESIGNS: 10n.p., 1r.50, Boxing; 25n.p., 2r. Judo; 50n.p., 5r. Gymnastics; 1, 3r. Sailing.

4 First Gibbons Catalogue and Alexandria (U.S.) 5c. Postmaster's Stamp

1965. Stanley Gibbons Catalogue Centenary Exhibition, London. Multicoloured.
37 5n.p. Type **4** 10 10
38 10n.p. Austria (6k.) scarlet "Mercury" newspaper stamp 10 10
39 15n.p. British Guiana "One Cent", 1856 . . . . 10 10
40 25n.p. Canada "Twelvepence Black", 1851 . . . . . . 10 20
41 50n.p. Hawaii "Missionary" 2c., 1851 . . . . 20 20
42 1r. Mauritius "Post Office" 2d. blue, 1847 . . . . 40 20
43 3r. Switzerland "Double Geneva" 5c.+5c., 1843 . . . 1·20 55
44 5r. Tuscany 3 lire, 1860 . . . 2·10 95
MS44a Two sheets, each 124 × 99 mm. Nos. 37, 40/1, 44 and 38/9, 42/3 . . . . 7·50 7·50
The 5, 15 and 50n.p. and 3r. also include the First Gibbons Catalogue and the others, the Gibbons "Elizabethan" Catalogue.

1965. Pan Arab Games, Cairo. Perf or imperf. Nos. 29, 31 and 33/5 optd. (a) Optd **PAN ARAB GAMES CAIRO 1965**.
45 **3** 15n.p. brown, violet & green 10 10
46 – 50n.p. slate, purple and blue 40 40
47 – 1r.50 purple, violet & green 1·10 1·10
48 – 2r. blue, red and ochre . . . 1·60 1·60
49 – 3r. violet, brown and blue . . 2·40 2·40

(b) Optd as Nos. 45/9 but equivalent in Arabic.
50 **3** 15n.p. brown, violet & green 10 10
51 – 50n.p. slate, purple and blue 40 40
52 – 1r.50 purple, violet and green 1·10 1·10
53 – 2r. blue, red and ochre . . . 1·60 1·60
54 – 3r. violet, brown and blue . . 2·40 2·40

1965. Air. Designs similar to Nos. 1/9, but inscr "AIR MAIL". Mult. (a) Size 42½ × 25½ mm.
55 15n.p. Type **1** 10 10
56 25n.p. Regal angelfish 20 20
57 35n.p. Dromedary 20 20
58 50n.p. Yellow-banded angelfish 30 30
59 75n.p. Tortoise 45 45
60 1r. Jewel cichlid 65 65

(b) Size 53 × 34 mm.
61 2r. White stork . . . . 1·40 1·40
62 3r. Black-headed gull . . . . 1·90 1·90
63 5r. Lanner falcon . . . . . . 3·25 3·25

1966. Stamp Cent Exn, Cairo. Nos. 38/9 and 41/3 optd **STAMP CENTENARY EXHIBITION CAIRO, JANUARY 1966** and pyramid motif.
73 10n.p. multicoloured 10 10
74 15n.p. multicoloured 20 20
75 50n.p. multicoloured 40 40
76 1r. multicoloured 75 75
77 3r. multicoloured . . . . . . 2·30 2·30
MS78 Two sheets, each 124 × 99 mm. as **MS**44a . . . 6·00 3·25

8 Sir Winston Churchill and Tower Bridge

1966. Churchill Commemoration. Each design includes portrait of Churchill. Multicoloured.
79 25n.p. Type **8** 10 10
80 50n.p. Buckingham Palace . . . 20 10
81 75n.p. Blenheim Palace . . . 30 20
82 1r. British Museum 45 20
83 2r. St. Paul's Cathedral in wartime 85 45
84 3r. National Gallery and St. Martin in the Fields Church . . . . 1·30 65
85 5r. Westminster Abbey . . . . 2·10 1·10
86 7r.50 Houses of Parliament at night . . . . 3·25 1·60
MS87 101 × 120 mm. Nos. 85/6 23·00 12·00

9 Rocket

1966. Space Achievements. Multicoloured. (a) Postage. Size as T **9**.
88 1n.p. Type **9** 10 10
89 3n.p. Capsule 10 10
90 5n.p. Astronaut entering capsule in space 10 10
91 10n.p. Astronaut outside capsule in space 10 10

92	15n.p. Astronauts and globe	10	10
93	25n.p. Astronaut in space . .	10	10
MS94	98 × 88 mm. 1r. and 3r. in designs of 15n.p. and 10n.p. . .	4·25	3·75
	(b) Air. Size 38 × 38 mm.		
95	50n.p. As Type **9**	30	10
96	1r. Astronauts and globe . . .	45	20
97	3r. Astronaut outside capsule in space	1·40	45
98	5r. Capsule	2·40	85

1967. Various issues with currency names changed by overprinting in **Dh.** or **Riyals.** (a) Postage. Nos. 1/18 (1964 Definitives).

99	1d. on 1n.p.	10	10
100	2d. on 2n.p.	10	10
101	3d. on 3n.p.	10	10
102	4d. on 4n.p.	10	10
103	5d. on 5n.p.	10	10
104	10d. on 10n.p.	20	20
105	15d. on 15n.p.	20	20
106	20d. on 20n.p.	30	30
107	30d. on 30n.p.	45	45
108	40d. on 40n.p.	65	65
109	50d. on 50n.p.	85	85
110	70d. on 70n.p.	1·10	1·10
111	1r. on 1r.	1·50	1·50
112	1r.50 on 1r.50	2·40	2·40
113	2r. on 2r.	3·25	3·25
114	3r. on 3r.	1·90	1·90
115	5r. on 5r.	3·25	3·25
116	10r. on 10r.	6·50	6·50
	(b) Air. Nos. 55/63 (Airmails).		
117	15d. on 15n.p.	10	10
118	25d. on 25n.p.	20	20
119	35d. on 35n.p.	30	30
120	50d. on 50n.p.	40	40
121	75d. on 75n.p.	55	55
122	1r. on 1r.	75	75
123	2r. on 2r.	1·40	1·40
124	3r. on 3r.	2·30	2·30
125	5r. on 5r.	3·50	3·50

NEW CURRENCY SURCHARGES. Nos. 19/44 and 79/98 are known surch in new currency (dirhams and riyals), in limited quantities, but there is some doubt as to whether they were in use locally.

11 Fiat 1500 Saloon, 1962

1967. Transport.

135	**11**	1d. brown & blk (postage)	10	10
136	–	2d. blue and brown	10	10
137	–	3d. mauve and black . . .	10	10
138	–	4d. blue and brown	10	10
139	–	5d. green and black . . .	10	10
140	–	15d. blue and brown . . .	10	10
141	–	30d. brown and black . . .	20	10
142	–	50d. black and brown . . .	30	10
143	–	70d. violet and black . . .	40	10
144	**11**	1r. green and brown (air)	45	20
145	–	2r. mauve and black . . .	95	40
146	–	3r. black and brown . . .	1·40	55
147	–	5r. brown and black . . .	2·30	95
148	–	10r. blue and brown . . .	4·75	1·90

DESIGNS: 2d., 2r. Motor coach; 3d., 3r. Motor cyclist; 4d., 5r. Boeing 707 airliner; 5d., 10r. "Brasil" (liner); 15d. "Yankee" (sail training and cruise ship); 30d. Cameleer; 50d. Arab horse; 70d. Sikorsky S-58 helicopter.

OFFICIAL STAMPS

1965. Designs similar to Nos. 1/9, additionally inscr "ON STATE'S SERVICE". Multicoloured. (i) Postage. Size 43 × 26 mm.

O64	25n.p. Type **1**	20	10
O65	40n.p. Regal angelfish . . .	30	20
O66	50n.p. Dromedary	40	30
O67	75n.p. Yellow-banded angelfish	45	40
O68	1r. Tortoise	75	45
	(ii) Air. (a) Size 43 × 26 mm.		
O69	75n.p. Jewel cichlid	45	20
	(b) Size 53 × 34 mm.		
O70	2r. White stork	1·50	55
O71	3r. Black-headed gulls . . .	2·30	85
O72	5r. Lanner falcon	3·75	1·40

1967. Nos. O64/72 with currency names changed by overprinting in **Dh.** or **Riyals**.

O126	25d. on 25n.p.	20	20
O127	40d. on 40n.p.	30	20
O128	50d. on 50n.p.	40	20
O129	75d. on 75n.p. (No. O67)	45	40
O130	75d. on 75n.p. (No. O69)	75	50
O131	1r. on 1r.	55	70
O132	2r. on 2r.	3·75	2·20
O133	3r. on 3r.	7·50	3·25
O134	5r. on 5r.	13·50	6·50

For later issues see **UNITED ARAB EMIRATES**.

APPENDIX

From June 1967 very many stamp issues were made by a succession of agencies which had been awarded contracts by the Ruler, sometimes two agencies operating at the same time. Several contradictory statements were made as to the validity of some of these issues which appeared 1967–72 and for this reason they are only listed in abbreviated form.

1967.

50th Birth Anniv of President J. F. Kennedy. Air 10, 20, 40, 70d., 1r.50, 2, 3, 5r.

Paintings. Postage. Arab Paintings 1, 2, 3, 4, 5, 30, 70d.; Air. Asian Paintings 1, 2, 3, 5r.; Indian Painting 10r.

Tales from "The Arabian Nights". Postage 1, 2, 3, 10, 30, 50, 70d.; Air 90d., 1, 2, 3r.

World Scout Jamboree, Idaho. Postage 30, 70d., 1r.; Air 2, 3, 4r.

Olympic Games, Mexico (1968). Postage 35, 65, 75d., 1r.; Air 1r.25, 2, 3, 4r.

Winter Olympic Games, Grenoble (1968). Postage 5, 35, 60, 75d.; Air 1, 1r.25, 2, 3r.

Pres. J. F. Kennedy Memorial. Die-stamped on gold foil. Air 10r.

Paintings by Renoir and Terbrugghen. Air 35, 65d., 1, 2r. × 3.

1968.

Paintings by Velasquez. Air 1r. × 2, 2r. × 2.

Winter Olympic Games, Grenoble. Die-stamped on gold foil. Air 7r.

Paintings from Famous Galleries. Air 1r. × 4, 2r. × 6.

Costumes. Air 30d. × 2, 70d. × 2, 1r. × 2, 2r. × 2.

Olympic Games, Mexico. Postage 1r. × 4; Air 2r. × 4.

Satellites and Spacecraft. Air 30d. × 2, 70d. × 2, 1r. × 2, 2r. × 2, 3r. × 2.

Paintings. Hunting Dogs. Air 2r. × 6.

Paintings. Adam and Eve. Air 2r. × 4.

Human Rights Year. Kennedy Brothers and Martin Luther King. Air 1r. × 3, 2r. × 3.

Kennedy Brothers Memorial. Postage 2r.; Air 5r.

Sports Champions. Inter-Milano Football Club. Postage 5, 10, 15, 20, 25d.; Air 10r.

Sports Champions. Famous Footballers. Postage 15, 20, 50, 75d., 1r.; Air 10r.

Cats. Postage 1, 2, 3d.; Air 2, 3r.

Olympic Games, Mexico. Die-stamped on gold foil. 5r.

5th Death Anniv of Pres. J. F. Kennedy. On gold foil. Air 10r.

Paintings of the Madonna. Air 30, 70d., 1, 2, 3r.

Space Exploration. Postage 5, 10, 15, 20, 25d.; Air 15r.

Olympic Games, Mexico. Gold Medals. Postage 2r. × 4; Air 5r. × 4.

Christmas. Air 5r.

1969.

Sports Champions. Cyclists. Postage 1, 2, 5, 10, 15, 20d.; Air 12r.

Sports Champions. German Footballers. Postage 5, 10, 15, 20, 25d.; Air 10r.

Sports Champions. Motor-racing Drivers. Postage 1, 5, 10, 15, 25d.; Air 10r.

Motor-racing Cars. Postage 1, 5, 10, 15, 25d.; Air 10r.

Sports Champions. Boxers. Postage 5, 10, 15, 20d.; Air 10r.

Sports Champions. Baseball Players. Postage 1, 2, 5, 10, 15d.; Air 10r.

Birds. Air 1r. × 11.

Roses. 1r. × 6.

Wild Animals. Air 1r. × 6.

Paintings. Italian Old Masters. 5, 10, 15, 20d., 10r.

Paintings. Famous Composers. Air 5, 10, 25d., 10r.

Paintings. French Artists. 1r. × 4.

Paintings. Nudes. Air 2r. × 4.

Three Kings Mosaic. Air 1r. × 2, 3r. × 2.

Kennedy Brothers. Air 2, 3, 10r.

Olympic Games, Mexico. Gold Medal Winners. Postage 1, 2d., 10r.; Air 10d., 5, 10r.

Paintings of the Madonna. Postage 10d.; Air 10r.

Space Flight of "Apollo 9". Optd on 1968 Space Exploration issue. Air 15r.

Space Flight of "Apollo 10". Optd on 1968 Space Exploration issue. Air 15r.

1st Death Anniv of Gagarin. Optd on 1968 Space Exploration issue. 5d.

2nd Death Anniv of Edward White. Optd on 1968 Space Exploration issue. 10d.

1st Death Anniv of Robert Kennedy. Optd on 1969 Kennedy Brothers issue. Air 2r.

European Football Championship. Optd on 1968 Famous Footballers issue. Air 10r.

Olympic Games, Munich (1972). Optd on 1969 Mexico Gold Medal Winners issue. Air 10d., 5, 10r.

Moon Landing of "Apollo 11". Air 1, 2, 5r.

Moon Landing of "Apollo 11". Circular designs on gold or silver foil. Air 3r. × 3, 5r. × 3, 10r. × 14.

Paintings. Christmas. Postage 1, 2, 3, 4, 5, 15d.; Air 2, 3r.

1970.

"Apollo" Space Flights. Postage 1, 2, 4, 5, 10d.; Air 3, 5r.

Birth Bicentenary of Napoleon Bonaparte. Die-stamped on gold foil. Air 20r.

Paintings. Easter. Postage 5, 10, 12, 30, 50, 70d.; Air 1, 2r.

Moon Landing. Die-stamped on gold foil. Air 20r.

Paintings by Michelangelo. Postage 1, 2, 4, 5, 8, 10d.; Air 3, 5r.

World Cup Football Championship, Mexico. Air 25, 50, 75d., 1, 2, 3r.

"Expo 70" World Fair, Osaka, Japan. Japanese Paintings. Postage 1, 2, 3, 4, 5, 10, 15d.; Air 1, 5r.

Birth Bicent Napoleon Bonaparte. Postage 1, 2, 4, 5, 10d.; Air 3, 5r.

Paintings. Old Masters. Postage 1, 2, 5, 6, 10d.; Air 1, 2, 3r.

Space Flight of "Apollo 13". Air 50, 75, 80d., 1, 2, 3r.

World Cup Football Championship, Mexico. Die-stamped on gold foil. Air 20r.

Olympic Games, 1960–1972. Postage 15, 30, 50, 70d.; Air 2, 5r.

"Expo 70" World Fair, Osaka, Japan. Pavilions. Postage 1, 2, 3, 4, 10, 15d.; Air 1, 3r.

Brazil's Victory in World Cup Football Championship. Optd on 1970 World Football Cup issue. Air 25, 50, 75d., 1, 2, 3r.

"Gemini" and "Apollo" Space Flights. Postage 1, 2, 3, 4, 5, 6, 8, 10, 12, 15, 20, 25, 30, 35, 40, 50d.; Air 1, 1r.50, 2, 3r.

Vintage and Veteran Cars. Postage 1, 2, 4, 5, 8, 10d.; Air 2, 3r.

Pres. D. Eisenhower Commem. Postage 30, 50, 70d.; Air 1, 2, 3r.

Paintings by Ingres. Air 25, 30, 35, 50, 70, 85d., 1, 2r.

500th Birth Anniv (1971) of Albrecht Durer. Air 25, 30, 35, 50, 70, 85d., 1, 2r.

Christmas Paintings. Air 25, 30, 35, 50, 70, 85d., 1, 2r.

Winter Olympic Games, Sapporo, Japan (1972). Die-stamped on gold foil. Air 20r.

Meeting of Eisenhower and De Gaulle, 1942. Die-stamped on gold foil. Air 20r.

General De Gaulle Commem. Air 25, 50, 75d., 1, 2, 3r.

Winter Olympic Games, Sapporo, Japan (1972). Sports. Postage 1, 2, 5, 10d.; Air 3, 5r.

J. Rindt, World Formula 1 Motor-racing Champion. Die-stamped on gold foil. Air 20r.

1971.

"Philatokyo" Stamp Exhibition, Tokyo. Japanese Paintings. Air 25, 30, 35, 50, 70, 85d., 1, 2r.

Mars Space Project. Air 50, 75, 80d., 1, 2, 3r.

Napoleonic Military Uniforms. Postage 5, 10, 15, 20, 25, 30d.; Air 2, 3r.

Olympic Games, Munich (1972). Sports. Postage 10, 15, 25, 30, 40d.; Air 1, 2, 3r.

Paintings by Modern Artists. Air 25, 30, 35, 50, 70, 85d., 1, 2r.

Paintings by Famous Artists. Air 25, 30, 35, 50, 70, 85d., 1, 2r.

25th Anniv of United Nations. Optd on 1971 Modern Artists issue. Air 25, 30, 35, 50, 70, 85d., 1, 2r.

Olympic Games, Munich (1972). Sports. Postage 1, 2, 3, 4, 5, 6, 8, 10, 12, 15, 20, 25, 30, 35, 40, 50d.; Air 1, 1r.50, 2, 3r.

Butterflies. Air 25, 30, 35, 50, 70, 85d., 1, 2r.

Space Flight of "Apollo 14". Postage 15, 25, 50, 60, 70d.; Air 5r.

Winter Olympic Games, 1924–1968. Postage 30, 40, 50, 75d., 1r.; Air 2, 3r.

Signs of the Zodiac. 1, 2, 5, 10, 12, 15, 25, 30, 35, 45, 50, 60d.

Famous Men. Air 65, 70, 75, 80, 85, 90d., 1, 1r.25, 1r.50, 2, 2r.50, 3r.

Death Bicent of Beethoven. 20, 30, 40, 60d., 1r.50, 2r.

Dr. Albert Schweitzer Commem. 20, 30, 40, 60d., 1r.50, 2r.

Tropical Birds. Postage 1, 2, 3, 4, 5, 10d.; Air 2, 3r.

Paintings by French Artists. Postage 1, 2, 3, 4, 5, 10d.; Air 2, 3r.

Paintings by Modern Artists. Postage 1, 2, 3, 4, 5, 10d.; Air 2, 3r.

Paintings by Degas. Postage 1, 2, 3, 4, 5, 10d.; Air 2, 3r.

Paintings by Titian. Postage 1, 2, 3, 4, 5, 10d.; Air 2, 3r.

Paintings by Renoir. Postage 1, 2, 3, 4, 5, 10d.; Air 2, 3r.

Space Flight of "Apollo 15". Postage 25, 40, 50, 60d., 1r.; Air 6r.

"Philatokyo" Stamp Exhibition, Tokyo. Stamps. Postage 10, 15, 20, 30, 35, 50, 60, 80d.; Air 1, 2r.

Tropical Birds. Postage 1, 2, 3, 5, 7, 10, 12, 15, 20, 25, 30, 40d.; Air 50, 80d., 1, 3r.

Paintings depicting Venus. Postage 1, 2, 3, 4, 5, 10d.; Air 2, 3r.

13th World Scout Jamboree, Asagiri, Japan. Scouts. Postage 1, 2, 3, 5, 7, 10, 12, 15, 20, 25, 30, 35, 40, 50, 65, 80d.; Air 1, 1r.25, 1r.50, 2r.

Lions International Clubs. Optd on 1971 Famous Paintings issue. Air 25, 30, 35, 50, 70, 85d., 1, 2r.

13th World Scout Jamboree, Asagiri, Japan. Japanese Paintings. Postage 20, 30, 40, 60, 75d.; Air 3r.

25th Anniv of UNICEF Optd on 1971 Scout Jamboree (paintings) issue. Postage 20, 30, 40, 60, 75d.; Air 3r.

Christmas 1971. (1st series. Plain frames). Portraits of Popes. Postage 1, 2, 3, 4, 5, 10d.; Air 2, 3r.

Modern Cars. Postage 10, 15, 25, 40, 50d.; Air 3r.

Olympic Games, Munich (1972). Show-jumping. Embossed on gold foil. Air 20r.

Exploration of Outer Space. Postage 15, 25, 50, 60, 70d.; Air 5r.

Royal Visit of Queen Elizabeth II to Japan. Postage 1, 2, 3, 4, 5, 10d.; Air 2, 3r.

Meeting of Pres. Nixon and Emperor Hirohito of Japan in Alaska. Design as 3r. value of 1970 Eisenhower issue but value changed and optd with commemorative inscr. Air 5r. (silver opt), 5r. (gold opt).

"Apollo" Astronants. Postage 5, 20, 35, 40, 50d.; Air 1, 2, 3r.

Discoverers of the Universe. Astronomers and Space Scientists. Postage 5, 10, 15, 20, 25, 30d.; Air 2, 5r.

"ANPHILEX 71" Stamp Exn, New York. Air 2r.50.

Christmas 1971. Portraits of Popes (2nd series. Ornamental frames). Postage 1, 2, 3, 4, 5, 10d.; Air 2, 3r.

Royal Silver Wedding of Queen Elizabeth II and Prince Philip (1972). Air 1, 2, 3r.

Space Flight of "Apollo 16". Postage 20, 30, 40, 50, 60d.; Air 3, 4r.

Fairy Tales. "Baron Munchhausen" Stories. Postage 1, 2, 4, 5, 10d.; Air 3r.

World Fair, Philadelphia (1976). Paintings. Postage 25, 50, 75d.; Air 5r.

Fairy Tales. Stories of the Brothers Grimm. Postage 1, 2, 4, 5, 10d.; Air 3r.

European Tour of Emperor Hirohito of Japan. Postage 1, 2, 4, 5, 10d.; Air 6r.

13th World Scout Jamboree, Asagiri, Japan. Postage 5, 10, 15, 20, 25d.; Air 5r.

Winter Olympic Games, Sapporo, Japan (1972). Postage 5, 10, 15, 20, 25d.; Air 5r.

Olympic Games, Munich (1972). Postage 5, 10, 15, 20, 25d.; Air 5r.

"Japanese Life". Postage 10d. × 4, 20d. × 4, 30d. × 4, 40d. × 4, 50d. × 4; Air 3r. × 4.

Space Flight of "Apollo 15". Postage 5, 10, 15, 20, 25, 50d.; Air 1, 2, 3, 5r.

"Soyuz 11" Disaster. Air 50d., 1r., 1r.50.

"The Future in Space". Postage 5, 10, 15, 20, 25, 50d.

2500th Anniv of Persian Empire. Postage 10, 20, 30, 40, 50d., Air 3r.

Cats. Postage 10, 15, 20, 25d.; Air 50d., 1r.

50th Anniv of Tutankhamun Tomb Discovery. Postage 1, 2, 3, 4, 5, 6, 7, 8, 9, 10, 11, 12, 13, 14, 15, 16d.; Air 1r. × 4.

400th Birth Anniv of Johannes Kepler (astronomer). Postage 50d.; Air 5r.

Famous Men. Air. 1r. × 5.

1972.

150th Death Anniv of Napoleon Bonaparte (1971). Postage 10, 20, 30, 40d.; Air 1, 2, 3, 4r.

1st Death Anniv of General de Gaulle. Postage 10, 20, 30, 40d.; Air 1, 2, 3, 4r.

Wild Animals (1st series). Postage 5, 10, 15, 20, 25, 30, 35, 40d.

Tropical Fishes. Postage 5, 10, 15, 20, 25d.; Air 50, 75d., 1r.

Famous Musicians. Postage 5d. × 3, 10d. × 3, 15d. × 3, 20d. × 3, 25d. × 3, 30d. × 3, 35d. × 3, 40d. × 3.

Easter. Postage 5, 10, 15, 20, 25d.; Air 5r.

Wild Animals (2nd series). Postage 5, 10, 15, 20, 25d.; Air 5r.

"Tour de France" Cycle Race. Postage 5, 10, 15, 20, 25, 30, 35, 40, 45, 50, 55d.; Air 60, 65, 70, 75, 80, 85, 90, 95d., 1r.

Many other issues were released between 1 September 1971 and 1 August 1972, but their authenticity has been denied by the Ajman Postmaster-General. Certain issues of 1967–69 exist overprinted to commemorate other events but the Postmaster General states that these are unofficial.

Ajman joined the United Arab Emirates on 1 August 1972 and the Ministry of Communications assumed responsibility for the postal services. Further stamps inscribed "Ajman" issued after that date were released without authority and had no validity.

ALAND ISLANDS Pt. 11

Aland is an autonomous province of Finland. From 1984 separate stamps were issued for the area although stamps of Finland could also still be used there. On 1 January 1993 Aland assumed control of its own postal service and Finnish stamps ceased to be valid there.

1984. 100 pennia = 1 markka.
2002. 100 cents = 1 euro.

1 Fishing Boat

2 "Pommern" (barque) and Car Ferries, Mariehamn West Harbour

1984.

1 1 10p. mauve 15 20
2 20p. green 25 20
3 50p. green 25 20
4 – 1m. green 55 45
5 1 1m.10 blue 55 45
6 1m.20 black 55 55
7 1m.30 green 65 65
8 – 1m.40 multicoloured . . . . 1·20 80
9a – 1m.50 multicoloured . . . . 1·00 55
10 – 1m.90 multicoloured . . . . 1·00 95
12 – 3m. blue, green and black . 1·50 1·10
14 – 10m. black, chestnut & brn . 4·25 2·75
15 – 13m. multicoloured . . . . 6·00 5·00

DESIGNS—20 × 29 mm: 1m.50, Midsummer pole, Storby village. 21 × 31 mm: 13m. Rug, 1793. 26 × 32 mm: 3m. Map of Aland Islands. 30 × 20 mm: 1m. Farjsund Bridge. 31 × 21 mm: 1m.40, Aland flag; 1m.90, Mariehamn Town Hall. 32 × 26 mm: 10m. Seal of Aland showing St. Olaf (patron saint).

1984. 50th Anniv of Society of Shipowners.
16 2 2m. multicoloured . . . . . 4·75 2·30

3 Grove of Ashes and Hazels

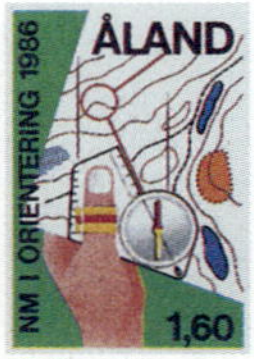

4 Map, Compass and Measuring Instrument

1985. Aland Scenes. Multicoloured.
17 2m. Type 3 . . . . 1·90 1·00
18 5m. Kokar Church and shore (horiz) . . . . 1·90 1·70
19 8m. Windmill and farm (horiz) 3·25 2·75

1986. Nordic Orienteering Championships, Aland.
20 4 1m.60 multicoloured . . . . 3·00 1·70

5 Clay Hands and Burial Mounds, Skamkulla

6 "Onnigeby" (drawing, Victor Westerholm)

1986. Archaeology. Multicoloured.
21 1m.60 Type 5 . . . . 1·90 80
22 2m.20 Bronze staff from Finby and Apostles . . . . 1·00 90
23 20m. Monument at ancient court site, Saltvik, and court in session (horiz) . . . . . 7·75 7·50

1986. Centenary of Onnigeby Artists' Colony.
24 6 3m.70 multicoloured . . . . 4·00 2·10

7 Eiders

8 Firemen in Horse-drawn Cart

1987. Birds. Multicoloured.
25 1m.70 Type 7 . . . . 7·75 7·25
26 2m.30 Tufted ducks . . . . . 3·75 2·75
27 12m. Velvet scoters . . . . . 5·00 4·75

1987. Centenary of Mariehamn Fire Brigade.
28 8 7m. multicoloured . . . . . 7·00 7·75

9 Meeting and Item 3 of Report

1987. 70th Anniv of Aland Municipalities Meeting, Finstrom.
29 9 1m.70 multicoloured . . . . 1·70 1·20

10 Loading Mail Barrels at Eckero

1988. 350th Anniv of Postal Service in Aland.
30 10 1m.80 multicoloured . . . . 2·40 1·70

11 Ploughing with Horses

12 Baltic Galleass "Albanus"

1988. Centenary of Agricultural Education in Aland.
31 11 2m.20 multicoloured . . . . 2·10 2·10

1988. Sailing Ships. Multicoloured.
32 1m.80 Type 12 . . . . 2·50 1·50
33 2m.40 Schooner "Ingrid" (horiz) . . . . 3·75 3·25
34 11m. Barque "Pamir" (horiz) 10·00 8·50

13 St. Olaf's Church, Jomala

14 Elder-flowered Orchid

1988.
35 13 1m.40 multicoloured . . . . 1·90 1·50

1989. Orchids. Multicoloured.
36 1m.50 Type 14 . . . . 2·50 1·60
37 2m.50 Narrow-leaved helleborine . . . . 3·25 2·20
38 14m. Lady's slipper . . . . . 11·50 10·00

15 Teacher and Pupils

16 St. Michael's Church, Finstrom

1989. 350th Anniv of First Aland School, Saltvik.
39 15 1m.90 multicoloured . . . . 1·50 1·30

1989.
40 16 1m.50 multicoloured . . . . 1·50 1·40

17 Baltic Herring

18 St. Andrew's Church, Lumparland

1990. Fishes. Multicoloured.
41 1m.50 Type 17 . . . . 1·30 1·00
42 2m. Northern pike . . . . . 1·30 1·00
43 2m.70 European flounder . . 1·30 1·40

1990.
44 18 1m.70 multicoloured . . . . 1·50 1·30

19 "St. Catherine" (fresco, St. Anna's Church, Kumlinge)

20 West European Hedgehog

1990.
45 19 2m. multicoloured 90 85

1991. Mammals. Multicoloured.
46 1m.60 Type 20 . . . . 1·30 85
47 2m.10 Eurasian red squirrel . . 1·30 1·00
48 2m.90 Roe deer . . . . 1·50 1·60

21 Volleyball

1991. Small Island Games, Mariehamn. Sheet 117 × 81 mm containing T 21 and similar vert designs. Multicoloured.
MS49 2m.10; Type 21; 2m.10; Shooting; 2m.10; Football; 2m.10, Running . . . . 5·00 4·75

22 Canoeing

23 "League of Nations Meeting, Geneva, 1921" (print by F. Rackwitz)

1991. Nordic Countries' Postal Co-operation. Tourism. Multicoloured.
50 2m.10 Type 22 . . . . 90 90
51 2m.90 Cycling . . . . 1·50 1·50

1991. 70th Anniv of Aland Autonomy.
52 23 16m. multicoloured . . . . 9·00 7·00

24 St. Mathias's Church, Vardo

25 Von Knorring (after Karl Jansson)

1991.
53 24 1m.80 multicoloured . . . . 1·50 1·00

1992. Birth Bicentenary of Rev. Frans Peter von Knorring (social reformer).
54 25 2 klass (1m.60) mult . . . . 1·30 90

26 Barque "Herzogen Cecilie" and Wheat Transport Route Map

27 Ranno Lighthouse

1992. 48th International Association of Cape Horners Congress, Mariehamn.
55 26 1 klass (2m.10) mult . . . . 2·00 1·50

1992. Lighthouses. Multicoloured.
56 2m.10 Type 27 . . . . 5·75 2·50
57 2m.10 Salskar . . . . 5·75 2·50
58 2m.10 Lagskar . . . . 5·75 2·50
59 2m.10 Market . . . . 5·75 2·50

28 "Lemland Landscape"

1992. Birth Cent of Joel Pettersson (painter). Mult.
60 2m.90 Type 28 . . . . 1·30 1·10
61 16m. "Self-portrait" . . . . . 6·50 6·25

29 Delegates processing to Church Service

30 St. Catherine's Church, Hammarland

1992. 70th Anniv of First Aland Provincial Parliament.
62 29 3m.40 multicoloured . . . . 1·90 1·50

1992.
63 30 1m.80 multicoloured . . . . 1·50 90

31 Arms

32 Fiddler

1993. Postal Autonomy. Multicoloured.
64 1m.60 Type 31 . . . . 1·20 85
MS65 129 × 80 mm. 1m.90 Cover with Kastelholm single-line postmark (26 × 35 mm); 1m.90 Mareinhamm Post Office; 1m.90 Post van leaving *Alfågeln* (ferry); 1m.90 Postal emblem (26 × 31 mm) . . . . 4·25 3·00

1993. Nordic Countries' Postal Co-operation. Tourism. Exhibits from Jan Karlsgarden Open-air Museum.
66 32 2m. red, pink and black . . 1·00 85
67 – 2m.30 blue, black and azure 1·00 1·00
DESIGN—HORIZ: 2m.30, Boat-house.

33 Saltvik Woman

34 Diabase Dyke, Sottunga

1993. Costumes. Multicoloured.
68 1m.90 Type 33 . . . . 1·30 85
69 3m.50 Eckero and Brando women and Mariehamn couple . . . . 1·50 1·50
70 17m. Finstrom couple . . . . 8·25 7·25

1993. Aland Geology. Multicoloured.
71 10p. Boulder field, Dano Gamlan 25 20
72 1m.60 Drumlin (hillock), Markusbole 75 75
73 2m. Type 34 . . . . 90 70
74 2m.30 Pitcher of Kallskar . . 90 75
75 2m.70 Pillow lava, Kumlinge 1·20 90
76 2m.90 Red Cow (islet), Lumpurn . . . . 1·30 1·30
77 3m.40 Erratic boulder, Torsskar, Kokar Osterbygge (horiz) . . . . 1·40 1·40
78 6m. Folded gneiss . . . . . . 2·50 2·30
79 7m. Pothole, Bano Foglo (horiz) . . . . 2·75 2·50

35 Mary Magdalene Church, Sottunga

37 Glanville's Fritillary ("Melitaea cinxia")

1993.
80 35 1m.80 multicoloured . . . . 1·30 1·20

1994. Butterflies. Multicoloured.
81 2m.30 Type 37 . . . . 1·30 1·20
82 2m.30 "Quercusia querqus" . . 1·30 1·10
83 2m.30 Clouded apollo ("Parnassius mnemosyne") 1·30 1·20
84 2m.30 "Hesperia comma" . . 1·30 1·10

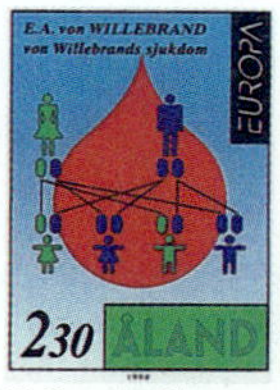

38 Genetic Diagram

39 Comb Ceramic and Pitted Ware Pottery

1994. Europa. Medical Discoveries. Multicoloured.
85 2m.30 Type **38** (discovery of Von Willebrand's disease (hereditary blood disorder)) 2·50 2·00
86 2m.90 Molecular diagram (purification of heparin by Erik Jorpes) 2·50 2·00

1994. The Stone Age.
87 **39** 2m.40 brown 1·00 1·20
88 – 2m.80 blue 1·20 1·30
89 – 18m. green 7·75 7·75
DESIGNS—VERT: 2m.80, Stone tools. HORIZ: 18m. Canoe and tent by river (reconstruction of Stone-age village, Langbergsoda).

40 St. John the Baptist's Church, Sund

42 "Skuta" (Cargo Sailing Boat)

1994.
90 **40** 2m. multicoloured 1·50 1·10

1995. Cargo Sailing Ships. Multicoloured.
91 2m.30 Type **42** 1·00 1·20
92 2m.30 "Sump" (well-boat) 1·00 1·20
93 2m.30 "Storbat" (farm boat) 1·00 1·20
94 2m.30 "Jakt" 1·00 1·20

43 National Colours and E.U. Emblem

44 Doves and Cliffs

1995. Admission of Aland Islands to European Union.
95 **43** 2m.90 multicoloured 1·70 1·30

1995. Europa. Peace and Freedom. Multicoloured.
96 2m.80 Type **44** 1·30 1·30
97 2m.90 Dove, night sky and island 1·30 1·40

45 Golf

46 Racing Dinghies

1995. Nordic Countries' Postal Co-operation. Tourism. With service indicator. Multicoloured.
98 2 klass (2m.) Type **45** 1·30 1·20
99 1 klass (2m.30) Sport fishing 1·50 1·20

1995. Optimist World Dinghy Championships, Mariehamn.
100 **46** 3m.40 multicoloured 2·00 1·40

47 St. George's Church, Geta

48 "St. Olaf" (Wooden Carving from Sund Church)

1995.
101 **47** 2m. multicoloured 1·30 90

1995. Birth Millenary of St. Olaf.
102 **48** 4m.30 multicoloured 1·90 2·00

49 Fish holding Flag in Mouth ("Greetings from Aland")

50 Landing on Branch

1996. Greetings Stamps. With service indicator. Multicoloured.
103 1 klass Type **49** 1·50 1·20
104 1 klass Bird holding flower in beak ("Congratulations") 1·50 1·20

1996. Endangered Species. The Eagle Owl. Multicoloured.
105 2m.40 Type **50** 1·00 1·20
106 2m.40 Perched on branch 1·00 1·10
107 2m.40 Adult owl 1·00 1·20
108 2m.40 Juvenile owl 1·00 1·10
Nos. 105/6 form a composite design.

51 Sally Salminen (novelist)

1996. Europa. Famous Women. Multicoloured.
109 2m.80 Type **51** 1·20 1·10
110 2m.90 Fanny Sundstrom (politician) 1·20 1·40

52 Choir

53 "Haircut"

1996. "Aland 96" Song and Music Festival, Mariehamn.
111 **52** 2m.40 multicoloured 1·30 1·10

1996. 150th Birth Anniv of Karl Jansson (painter).
112 **53** 18m. multicoloured 8·50 8·25

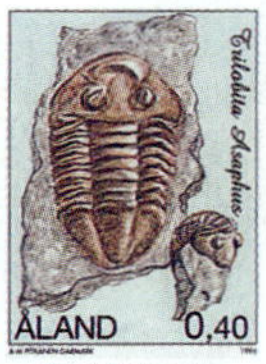

54 "Trilobita asaphus"

55 Brando Church

1996. Fossils. Multicoloured.
113 40p. Type **54** 25 35
114 9m. "Gastropoda euomophalus" 3·50 3·25

1996.
115 **55** 2m. multicoloured 1·30 1·00

56 Giant Isopod ("Saduria entomon") and Opossum Shrimp ("Mysis relicta")

57 Coltsfoot ("Tussilago farfara")

1997. Marine Survivors from the Ice Age. Multicoloured.
116 30p. Type **56** 25 25
117 2m.40 Four-horned sculpin ("Myotocephalus quadricornis") 1·30 1·00
118 4m.30 Ringed seal ("Phoca hispida botrica") 1·70 1·70

1997. Spring Flowers. Multicoloured.
119 2m.40 Type **57** 1·00 1·20
120 2m.40 Blue anemone ("Hepatica nobilis") 1·00 1·20
121 2m.40 Wood anemone ("Anemone nemorosa") 1·00 1·20
122 2m.40 Yellow anemone ("Anemone ranunculoides") 1·00 1·20

58 Floorball

59 The Devil's Dance

1997. 1st Women's Floorball World Championship, Mariehamn and Godby.
123 **58** 3m.40 multicoloured 2·00 1·30

1997. Europa. Tales and Legends.
124 **59** 2m.90 multicoloured 2·50 2·30

60 Kastelholm Castle and Arms

1997. 600th Anniv of Kalmar Union between Sweden, Denmark and Norway.
125 **60** 2m.40 multicoloured 1·20 1·30

61 Hologram of Schooner "Linden" and "75 Years"

1997. 75th Anniv of Aland Autonomy. Sheet 128 × 80 mm.
MS126 **61** 20m. multicoloured 10·00 9·00

62 "Thornbury" (freighter)

63 St George's Church, Mariehamn

1997. Steam Freighters. Multicoloured.
127 2m.80 Type **62** 1·20 1·20
128 3m.50 "Osmo" (freighter) 1·40 1·30

1997. 70th Anniv of Mariehamn Church.
129 **63** 1m.90 multicoloured 1·30 1·00

64 Man harvesting Apples

1998. Horticulture. Multicoloured.
130 2m. Type **64** 75 85
131 2m.40 Woman harvesting cucumbers 1·30 85

65 Boy on Moped

66 Midsummer Celebrations

1998. Youth Activities. Multicoloured.
132 2m.40 Type **65** 1·00 1·20
133 2m.40 Laptop computer 1·00 1·20
134 2m.40 CD disk and headphones 1·00 1·20
135 2m.40 Step aerobics 1·00 1·20

1998. Europa. National Festivals.
136 **66** 4m.20 multicoloured 2·75 1·80

67 "Isabella" (car ferry)

1998. Nordic Countries' Postal Co-operation. Shipping.
137 **67** 2m.40 multicoloured 1·30 1·00

68 Waves breaking

1998. International Year of the Ocean.
138 **68** 6m.30 multicoloured 3·00 2·40

69 Players

1998. Association of Tennis Professionals Senior Tour, Mariehamn. Self-adhesive.
139 **69** 2m.40 multicoloured 1·30 1·00

70 Schooner, Compass Rose and Knots

1998. Ninth International Sea Scout Camp, Bomarsund Fortress, Aland.
140 **70** 2m.80 multicoloured 1·40 1·10

71 Seffers Homestead, Onningeby

72 Eckero Church

1998. Traditional Porches. Multicoloured.
141 1m.60 Type **71** 65 65
142 2m. Labbas homestead, Storby 75 85
143 2m.90 Abras homestead, Bjorko 1·20 1·20

1998.
144 **72** 1m.90 multicoloured 1·30 85

73 Sword and Dagger

1999. Bronze Age Relics. Multicoloured.
145 2m. Type **73** 75 85
146 2m.20 "Ship" tumulus (vert) 90 1·00

74 Wardrobe

1999. Folk Art. Decorated Furniture. Mult.
147 2m.40 Type **74** 1·00 1·00
148 2m.40 Distaff 1·00 1·00
149 2m.40 Chest 1·00 1·00
150 2m.40 Spinning wheel 1·00 1·00

75 "'Pamir' and 'Passat' (barques) off Port Victoria" (R. Castor)

76 Cowslip

1999. 50th Anniv of Rounding of Cape Horn by "Pamir" on Last Wheat-carrying Voyage.
151 **75** 3m.40 multicoloured . . . 1·70 1·40

1999. Provincial Plant of Aland. Self-adhesive.
152 **76** 2m.40 multicoloured . . . 1·20 1·00

77 Ido Island, Kokar

1999. Europa. Parks and Gardens.
153 **77** 2m.90 multicoloured . . . 2·20 1·20
No. 153 is denominated both in markkas and in euros.

78 Racing Yachts

79 Puffed Shield Lichen ("Hypogymnia physodes")

1999. Sailing.
154 **78** 2m.70 multicoloured . . . 1·40 1·10

1999. Lichens. With service indicator. Mult.
155 2 klass (2m.) Type **79** . . . . 1·30 90
156 1 klass (2m.40) Common orange lichen ("Xanthoria parietina") . . . . 1·50 1·00

80 Loading Mail Plane

81 St. Bridget's Church, Lemland

1999. 125th Anniv of Universal Postal Union.
157 **80** 2m.90 multicoloured . . . 1·20 1·30

1999.
158 **81** 1m.90 multicoloured . . . 1·20 1·00

82 Runners

83 Arctic Tern (*Sterna paradisaea*)

1999. Finnish Cross-country Championships, Mariehamn.
159 **82** 3m.50 multicoloured . . . 1·50 1·30

DENOMINATION. From No. 162 to 207 Aland Islands stamps are denominated both in markkas and in euros. As no cash for the latter is in circulation, the catalogue continues to use the markka value.

2000. Sea Birds. Multicoloured.
162 1m.80 Type **83** 75 70
164 2m.20 Mew gull (*Larus canus*) (vert) 90 85
166 2m.60 Great black-backed gull (*Larus marinus*) . . . 1·00 95

84 International Peace Symbol and State Flag

2000. New Millennium Sheet. 100 × 80 mm. Multicoloured.
MS171 **84** 3m.40, yellow; 3m.40, red; 3m.40, blue; 3m.40, white . . . 8·00 5·25

85 Elk

86 "Building Europe"

2000. The Elk (*Alces alces*). Multicoloured.
172 2m.60 Type **85** . . . . 1·00 1·00
173 2m.60 With young . . . . . 1·00 1·00
174 2m.60 Beside lake . . . . . 1·00 1·00
175 2m.60 In snow . . . . 1·00 1·00

2000. Europa.
176 **86** 3m. multicoloured . . . . 2·20 1·60

87 Gymnast

88 Crew and *Linden* (schooner)

2000. Finno-Swedish Gymnastics Association Exhibition, Mariehamn. Self-adhesive.
177 **87** 2m.60 multicoloured . . . 1·30 1·00

2000. Visit by *Cutty Sark* Tall Ships' Race Competitors to Mariehamn.
178 **88** 3m.40 multicoloured . . . 1·60 1·20

89 Lange on prow of Longship

2000. Death Millenary of Hlodver Lange the Viking.
179 **89** 4m.50 multicoloured . . . 2·40 1·90

90 Wooden Ornamented Swiss-style House, Mariehamn

2000. 48th Death Anniv of Hilda Hongell (architect). Multicoloured.
180 3m.80 Type **90** . . . . 1·50 1·30
181 10m. House with central front entrance, Mariehamn 3·75 3·50

91 The Nativity

2000. 2000 Years of Christianity.
182 **91** 3m. multicoloured . . . . 1·50 1·20

92 Kokar Church

93 Steller's Eider in Flight

2000.
183 **92** 2m. multicoloured . . . . 1·20 95

2001. Endangered Species. The Steller's Eider (*Polysticta stelleri*). Multicoloured.
184 2m.70 Type **93** . . . . . . 1·00 1·20
185 2m.70 Duck and drake . . . 1·00 1·20
186 2m.70 Duck and drake swimming . . . . 1·00 1·20
187 2m.70 Drake swimming . . . 1·00 1·20

94 Swamp Horsetail (*Equisetum fluviatile*)

2001. Plants. Multicoloured.
188 1m.90 Type **94** 90 85
189 2m.80 Stiff clubmoss (*Lycopodium annotinum*) . . 1·20 1·20
190 3m.50 Polypody (*Polybodium vulgare*) . . . . 1·40 1·30

95 Heart and Graffiti on Brick Wall

2001. St. Valentine's Day.
200 **95** 3m.20 multicoloured . . . 1·40 1·30

96 Fisherman and Fish

2001. Europa. Water Resources.
201 **96** 3m.20 multicoloured . . . 2·10 1·90

97 Archipelago Windmill

98 Golden Retriever

2001. Windmills. Multicoloured.
202 3m. Type **97** . . . . 1·20 1·20
203 7m. Timbered windmill (horiz) . . . . 2·75 2·50
204 20m. Nest windmill (horiz) 8·00 7·50

2001. Puppies. Multicoloured.
205 2 klass (2m.30) Type **98** . . . 1·20 90
206 1 klass (2m.70) Wire-haired dachshund . . . . 1·40 1·00

99 Foglo Church

100 Smooth Snake (*Coronella Austriaca*)

2001.
207 **99** 2m. multicoloured 90 75

New Currency: 100 cents = 1 euro

2002. Endangered Animals. Multicoloured.
208 5c. Type **100** 25 20
209 70c. Great crested newt (*Triturus cristatus*) . . . . 1·40 1·50

101 Woman pushing Shopping Trolley

2002. Euro Currency.
210 **101** 60c. multicoloured . . . . 1·50 1·30

102 Tidying up Christmas

2002. St. Canute's Day.
211 **102** €2 multicoloured . . . . 4·75 4·50

103 Spiced Salmon and New Potatoes

2002. Traditional Dishes. Multicoloured.
212 1 klass (55c.) Type **103** . . . 1·40 1·20
213 1 klass (55c.) Fried herring, mashed potatoes and beetroot . . . . 1·40 1·20
214 1 klass (55c.) Black bread and butter . . . . 1·40 1·20
215 1 klass (55c.) Aland pancake with stewed prune sauce and whipped cream . . . . 1·40 1·20

104 Building

2002. Inauguration of New Post Terminal, Sviby.
216 **104** €1 multicoloured . . . . 2·50 2·20

105 Circus Elephant and Rider

2002. Europa. Circus.
217 **105** 40c. multicoloured . . . . 1·50 1·20

106 "Radar II" (sculpture, Stefan Lindfors)

2002. Nordic Countries' Postal Co-operation. Modern Art.
218 **106** €3 multicoloured . . . . 7·00 6·25

107 Kayaking

108 8th-century Buckle, Persby, Sud

2002.
219 **107** 90c. multicoloured . . . . 2·30 2·50

2002. Iron Age Jewellery found on Aland. Multicoloured.
220 2 klass. (45c.) Type **108** . . . 1·20 1·00
221 1 klass. (55c.) 8th-century pin, Sylloda, Saltvik . . . 1·40 1·20

109 Saltvik Church

110 Holmen

2002.
222 **109** 35c. multicoloured . . . . 1·00 85

2002. Janne Holmen (Olympic gold medallist, men's marathon).
223 **110** 1 klass. (55c.) mult . . . 1·40 1·20

111 *Cantharellus cibarius*

112 Tovis (kitten)

2003. Fungi. Multicoloured.
224 10c. Type **111** 25 30
225 50c. *Boletus edulis* . . . . . 1·30 95
226 €2.50 *Macrolepiota procera* 6·50 5·75

2003. Cat Photograph Competition Winners. Multicoloured.
227 2 klass (45c.) Type **112** . . . 1·20 1·10
228 1 klass (55c.) Randi (cat) (horiz) . . . . 1·40 1·30

113 "Landscape in Summer" (detail) (Elin Danielson-Gambogi)

114 "Freedom of Speech and Press" (Kurt Simons)

2003. Designs showing details of the painting. Multicoloured.
229 1 klass (55c.) Type **113** . . . 1·40 1·30
230 1 klass (55c.) Trees and flowers . . . . 1·40 1·30
231 1 klass (55c.) Sunset over sea 1·40 1·30
232 1 klass (55c.) Shoreline and boats . . . . 1·40 1·30

2003. Europa. Poster Art.
233 **114** 45c. multicoloured . . . . 1·70 1·30

115 "Pommern" (Arthur Victor Gregory)

2003. Centenary of *Pommern* (four mast steel barque, now museum). Self-adhesive.
234 **115** 55c. multicoloured . . . . 2·10 1·40

116 Two Boys

2003. "My Aland". Mark Levengood.
235 **116** 55c. multicoloured . . . . 1·40 1·30

117 Fiddle Player

118 Kumlinge Church

2003. 50th Anniv of Aland Folk Music Association.
236 **117** €1.10 multicoloured . . 2·50 2·10

2003.
237 **118** 40c. multicoloured . . . . 1·00 90

119 Children dressed as St. Lucia and her Attendants

2003. St. Lucia Celebrations.
238 **119** 60c. multicoloured . . . . 1·50 1·20

120 Ermine (*Mustela erminea*)

121 Fenja and Menja (giantesses)

2004. Predators. Multicoloured.
239 20c. Type **120** 65 50
240 60c. Fox (*Vulpes vulpes*) . . . 1·50 1·50
241 €3 Pine martin (*Martes martes*) . . . . 7·75 6·75

2004. Nordic Mythology. Sheet 105 × 70 mm.
MS250 **121** 55c. multicoloured 1·40 1·30
Stamps of a similar theme were issued by Denmark, Faroe Islands, Finland, Greenland, Iceland, Norway and Sweden.

122 Flag

2004. 50th Anniv of Aland Flag. Self-adhesive.
251 **122** 1klass (60c.) multicoloured . . . . . 1·40 1·30

123 *Cajsa* (longboat) and Passengers, 1986

124 Yacht moored in Inlet

2004. "My Aland". Mauno Koivisto (Finnish president 1982–94).
252 **123** 90c. multicoloured . . . . 2·20 2·00

2004. Europa. Holidays.
253 **124** 75c. multicoloured . . . . 1·80 1·60

125 Bomarsund Fortress

2004. 150th Anniv of Fall of Bomarsund Fortress. Sheet 170 × 95 mm containing Type **125** and similar vert designs.
MS254 75c. × 4, Type **125**; Bomarsund (different); Three soldiers; Six soldiers . . . . . 7·25 6·75

The stamps and margin of No. **MS**254 form a composite design of painting by A. Lourde-Laplace.

126 Storklyndan, Brando

2004. Landscapes. Multicoloured.
255 2 klass (50c.) Type **126** . . . 1·00 1·10
256 1 klass (60c.) Prästgardsnaset, Findstrom . . . . 1·70 1·30

127 Panathenaic Stadium, Athens

2004. Olympic Games, Athens.
257 **127** 80c. multicoloured . . . . 1·80 1·70

128 Father Christmas delivering Mail

2004. Christmas.
258 **128** 45c. multicoloured . . . . 1·20 1·10

129 Great Cormorant (*Phalacrocorax carbo sinensis*)

2005. Birds. Multicoloured.
259 15c. Type **129** 50 45
260 65c. Whooper swan (*Cygnus Cygnus*) . . . . 1·90 1·70
261 €4 Grey heron (*Ardea cinerea*) . . . . 9·50 8·25

130 Oakland Sport Chevrolet (1928) (⅔-size illustration)

2005. Vintage Cars. Multicoloured.
262 (60c.) Type **130** . . . . . . 1·70 1·30
263 (60c.) Ford V8 (1939) . . . . 1·70 1·30
264 (60c.) Buick Super 4D HT (1957) . . . . 1·70 1·30
265 (60c.) Volkswagen 1200 (1964) . . . . 1·70 1·30

131 Family and Bonfire

2005. Walpurgis Night. Self-adhesive.
266 **131** (50c.) multicoloured . . . 1·50 1·20

132 Fish

2005. Europa. Gastronomy.
267 **132** 90c. multicoloured . . . . 1·90 1·70

133 Bjorn Borg

135 *Linden* (schooner)

134 "A Visit to Bomarsund Fortress" (Fritz von Dardel)

2005. "My Aland". Bjorn Borg (tennis player).
268 **133** 55c. multicoloured . . . . 1·30 1·20

2005. 150th Anniv of Fall of Bomarsund Fortress (2004) (2nd series).
269 **134** €1.30 multicoloured . . 3·25 2·75

2005.
270 **135** 60c. multicoloured . . . . 1·70 1·40

136 Sando, Vardo

137 Boy and Girl Brownies

2005. Landscapes. Multicoloured.
271 70c. Type **136** . . . . 1·90 1·40
272 80c. Grondal, Geta . . . . . 2·20 2·00

2005. Christmas.
273 **137** 45c. multicoloured 90 75

138 *Potosia cuprea*

2006. Beetles.
274 40c. Type **138** 75 35
275 65c. *Coccinella septempunctata* . . . . . . 1·30 85
276 €2 *Oryctes nasicornis* . . . 4·50 3·00

139 Face

2006. Centenary of Women's Suffrage.
277 **139** 85c. multicoloured . . . . 2·40 2·00

140 Letesgubbe

2006. Nordic Mythology. Sheet 105 × 70 mm.
MS278 **140** 85c. multicoloured 2·40 2·40
Stamps of a similar theme were issued by Denmark, Greenland, Faroe Islands, Finland, Iceland, Norway and Sweden.

141 Bomarsund Fortress

2006. 150th Anniv of Demilitarization.

279	**141**	€1.50 multicoloured	4·25	4·00

142 Boy as King 143 Girl posting Letter

2006. Europa. Integration.

280	**142**	€1.30 multicoloured	3·75	3·50

2006. My Stamp. Self-adhesive.

281	**143**	1 klass multicoloured	1·75	1·50

144 Sail Boat

2006. "My Aland". Ake Lindman (actor and filmmaker).

282	**144**	75c. multicoloured	2·10	2·00

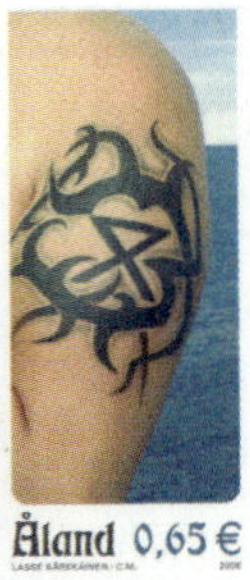

145 Soderby, Lemland 146 Tribal-style Tattoo (Thomas Dahlgren)

2006. Landscapes. Multicoloured.

283		55c. Type **145**	1·50	1·50
284		€1.20 Norra Essvik, Sottunga	3·50	3·25

2006. Tattoos. Multicoloured.

285		65c. Type **146**	2·10	2·00
286		65c. Seaman style (Mikael Sandholm)	2·10	2·00
287		65c. Floral (in memory of Tsunami disaster) (Linda Aberg)	2·10	2·00

147 Horse-drawn Sleigh 148 *Tripolium vulgare*

2006. Christmas. Inscribed "JULPOST 06".

288	**147**	(50c.) multicoloured	1·40	1·40

2007. Waterside Plants. Multicoloured.

289		80c. Type **148**	2·20	2·00
290		90c. *Lythrum salicaria*	2·60	2·50
291		€5 *Angelica archangelica*	12·50	12·00

149 Junkers F13

2007. Postal Transport. Multicoloured.

292		2klass Type **149**	1·60	1·50
293		1klass Saab 340	2·00	1·80

150 Skafto, Kumlinge

2007. Landscape.

294	**150**	2klass multicoloured	1·60	1·50

151 *Fillyjonks, Sea Monster and Cliffs* (painting by Tove Janson)

2007. Art.

295	**151**	85c. multicoloured	2·50	2·40

152 Scout Emblem and Window

2007. Europa. Centenary of Scouting.

296	**152**	70c. multicoloured	2·20	2·10

153 Bridal Crown (Titti Sundblom)

2007. Arts and Crafts. Multicoloured.

297		1klass Type **153**	2·20	2·00
298		1klass Flower print (Maria Korpi-Gordon and Adam Gordon)	2·20	2·00
299		1klass Ceramics (Judy Kuitunen)	2·20	2·00

154 Two Players

2007. Girls' Football in Aland. Self-adhesive.

300	**154**	1klass multicoloured	2·00	1·90

155 *Windmills* (Ture Bengtz)

2007. Birth Centenary of Ture Bengtz (artist and emigrant to USA). Emigration.

301	**155**	75c. multicoloured	2·10	2·00

156 Landscape, Kjusan, Hammarland

2007. SEPAC (small European mail services).

302	**156**	1klass multicoloured	2·00	1·90

157 Santa Claus (poster by Haddon Sundblom)

2007. Christmas. Inscr 'Julpost 07'.

303	**157**	(50c.) multicoloured	1·40	1·30

ALAOUITES Pt. 19

A coastal district of Syria, placed under French mandate in 1920. Became the Republic of Latakia in 1930. Incorporated with Syria in 1937.

100 centimes = 1 piastre.

1925. Stamps of France surch **ALAOUITES** and value in French and Arabic.

1	**11**	0p.10 on 2c. purple	2·00	7·00
2	**18**	0p.25 on 5c. orange	2·50	6·00
3	**15**	0p.75 on 15c. green	3·25	7·75
4	**18**	1p. on 20c. brown	2·30	6·00
5		1p.25 on 25c. blue	2·75	7·50
6		1p.50 on 30c. red	9·50	21·00
7		2p. on 35c. violet	65	6·50
8	**13**	2p. on 40c. red and blue	4·25	8·75
9		2p. on 45c. green and blue	9·25	21·00
10		3p. on 60c. violet and blue	2·00	11·50
11	**15**	3p. on 60c. violet	15·00	20·00
12		4p. on 85c. red	1·90	5·50
13	**13**	5p. on 1f. red and yellow	2·50	14·50
14		10p. on 2f. orange & grn	5·25	17·00
15		25p. on 5f. blue and buff	10·00	24·00

1925. "Pasteur" issue of France surch **ALAOUITES** and value in French and Arabic.

16	**30**	0p.50 on 10c. green	2·00	6·00
17		0p.75 on 15c. green	1·50	6·00
18		1p.50 on 30c. red	1·20	6·75
19		2p. on 45c. red	2·30	7·00
20		2p.50 on 50c. blue	3·50	7·75
21		4p. on 75c. blue	2·30	9·00

1925. Air. Stamps of France optd **ALAOUITES Avion** and value in French and Arabic.

22	**13**	2p. on 40c. red and blue	6·00	18·00
23		3p. on 60c. violet and blue	6·75	29·00
24		5p. on 1f. red and yellow	6·00	16·00
25		10p. on 2f. orange & green	6·00	18·00

1925. Pictorial stamps of Syria (1925) optd **ALAOUITES** in French and Arabic.

26		0p.10 violet	20	3·50
27		0p.25 black	1·30	5·25
28		0p.50 green	1·10	1·80
29		0p.75 red	1·20	5·00
30		1p. purple	80	2·30
31		1p.25 green	2·30	5·25
32		1p.50 pink	1·80	3·50
33		2p. brown	95	3·00
34		2p.50 blue	2·30	5·50
35		3p. brown	1·10	3·75
36		5p. violet	1·90	3·25
37		10p. purple	2·00	4·25
38		25p. blue	2·50	11·00

1925. Air. Nos. 33 and 35/37 optd **AVION** in French and Arabic.

40		2p. brown	2·00	6·75
41		3p. brown	1·00	6·25
42		5p. violet	1·10	6·50
43		10p. purple	95	5·75

1926. Air. Air stamps of Syria with airplane overprint optd **ALAOUITES** in French and Arabic.

44		2p. brown	1·80	8·25
45		3p. brown	1·60	8·25
46		5p. violet	1·60	8·25
47		10p. purple	1·50	8·75

See also Nos. 59/60 and 63.

1926. Pictorial stamps of 1925 surcharged.

53		05 on 0p.10 violet	15	5·00
54		2p. on 1p.25 green	11·00	7·50
48		3p.50 on 0p.75 red	85	3·75
49		4p. on 0p.25 black	1·30	3·50
56		4p.50 on 0p.75 red	2·30	6·00
50		6p. on 2p.50 blue	1·30	4·00
57		7p.50 on 2p.50 blue	2·00	2·50
51		12p. on 1p.25 green	3·00	8·25
58		15p. on 25p. blue	7·25	9·00
52		20p. on 1p.25 green	3·00	7·25

1929. Air. (a) Pictorial stamps of Syria optd with airplane and **ALAOUITES** in French and Arabic.

59		0p.50 green	2·00	7·00
60		1p. purple	3·25	15·00
61		25p. blue	20·00	48·00

(b) Nos. 54 and 58 of Alaouites optd with airplane.

62		2p. on 1p.25 green	2·50	8·25
63		15p. on 25p. blue	17·00	32·00

POSTAGE DUE STAMPS

1925. Postage Due stamps of France surch **ALAOUITES** and value in French and Arabic.

D26	D **11**	0p.50 on 10c. brown	1·20	8·25
D27		1p. on 20c. green	1·10	8·25
D28		2p. on 30c. red	1·00	8·50
D29		3p. on 50c. purple	1·20	8·75
D30		5p. on 1f. pur on yell	1·60	8·50

1925. Postage Due stamps of Syria (Nos. D192/6) optd **ALAOUITES** in French and Arabic.

D44		0p.50 brown on yellow	40	5·75
D45		1p. red on red	55	6·00
D46		2p. black on blue	80	7·00
D47		3p. brown on red	85	8·25
D48		5p. black on green	1·10	10·50

For later issues see **LATAKIA**.

ALBANIA Pt. 3

Albania, formerly part of the Turkish Empire, was declared independent on 28 November 1912, and this was recognized by Turkey in the treaty of 30 May 1913. After chaotic conditions during and after the First World War a republic was established in 1925. Three years later the country became a kingdom. From 7 April 1939 until December 1944, Albania was occupied, firstly by the Italians and then by the Germans. Following liberation a republic was set up in 1946.

1913. 40 paras = 1 piastre or grosch.
1913. 100 qint = 1 franc.
1947. 100 qint = 1 lek.

1913. Various types of Turkey optd with double-headed eagle and **SHQIPENIA**.

3	**28**	2pa. green (No. 271)	£225	£200
4		5pa. brown (No. 261)	£225	£200
2	**25**	10pa. green (No. 252)	£350	£300
5	**28**	10pa. green (No. 262)	£190	£130
12		10pa. green (No. 289)	£375	£375
11		10pa. on 20pa. red	£600	£600
6		20pa. red (No. 263)	£180	£110
13		20pa. red (No. 290)	£400	£350
7		1pi. blue (No. 264)	£130	£120
14a		1pi. blue (No. 291)	£900	£900
15		1pi. blk on red (No. D288)	£1500	£1500
8		2pi. black (No. 265)	£250	£200
14b		2pi. black (No. 292)		
1	**25**	2½pi. brown (No. 239)	£450	£350
9	**28**	5pi. purple (No. 267)	£700	£600
10		10pi. red (No. 268)	£2500	£2500

2

1913.

16	**2**	10pa. violet	8·00	6·00
17		20pa. red and grey	10·00	8·00
18		1g. grey	10·00	10·00
19		2g. blue and violet	12·00	9·50
20		5g. violet and blue	15·00	12·00
21		10g. blue and violet	15·00	12·00

3 4 Skanderbeg (after Heinz Kautsch)

1913. Independence Anniv.

22	**3**	10pa. black and green	2·75	1·75
23		20pa. black and red	3·00	2·75
24		30pa. black and violet	3·50	2·75
25		1g. black and blue	5·00	3·50
26		2g. black	8·00	6·00

1913.

27	**4**	2q. brown and yellow	1·00	1·00
28		5q. green and yellow	1·00	1·00
29		10q. red	1·10	1·10
30		25q. blue	1·25	1·25

31 50q. mauve and red . . . . 5·00 4·00
32 1f. brown . . . . 8·00 8·00

1914. Arrival of Prince William of Wied. Optd **7 Mars 1461 RROFTE MBRETI 1914.**
33 **4** 2q. brown and yellow . . . . 22·00 18·00
34 5q. green and yellow . . . . 22·00 18·00
35 10q. red and rose . . . . . 22·00 18·00
36 25q. blue . . . . 22·00 18·00
37 50q. mauve and rose . . . . 22·00 18·00
38 1f. brown . . . . 22·00 18·00

1914. Surch.
40 **4** 5pa. on 2q. brown & yellow 1·75 1·75
41 10pa. on 5q. green & yellow 1·75 1·75
42 20pa. on 10q. red . . . . . 2·25 1·75
43 1g. on 25q. blue . . . . . 2·75 2·50
44 2g. on 50q. mauve and red 3·50 3·50
45 5g. on 1f. brown . . . . . . 15·00 10·00

1914. Valona Provisional Issue. Optd **POSTE D'ALBANIE** and Turkish inscr in circle with star in centre.
45a **4** 2q. brown and yellow . . . £150 £150
45b 5q. green and yellow . . .
45c 10q. red and rose . . . . . 8·50 8·50
45d 25q. blue . . . . 8·50 8·50
45e 50q. mauve and red . . . . 8·50 8·50
45f 1f. brown £475
45g 5pa. on 2q. brown & yellow 25·00 25·00
45h 10pa. on 5q. green & yellow 50·00 50·00
45i 20pa. on 10q. red and rose 13·00 13·00
45j 1gr. on 25q. blue . . . . . 7·50 7·50
45k 2gr. on 50q. mauve and red 13·00 13·00
45l 5gr. on 1f. brown . . . . . 18·00 18·00

11

12

1917. Inscribed "SHQIPERIE KORCE VETQEVERITARE" or "REPUBLIKA KORCE SHQIPETARE" or "QARKU-POSTES-I-KORCES".
75 **11** 1c. brown and green . . . . 2·00 4·00
76 2c. brown and green . . . . 2·00 4·00
77 3c. grey and green . . . . . 2·00 4·00
78 5c. green and black . . . . 2·75 2·50
79 10c. red and black . . . . 2·75 2·50
72 25c. blue and black . . . . 9·00 6·25
80 50c. purple and black . . . 5·00 4·50
81 1f. brown and black . . . . 16·00 15·00

1918. No. 78 surch **QARKUI KORCES 25 CTS.**
81a 25c. on 5c. green and black 60·00 48·00

1919. Fiscal stamps used by the Austrians in Albania. Handstamped with control.
83 **12** (2)q. on 2h. brown . . . . 5·50 5·50
84 05q. on 16h. green . . . . 5·50 5·50
85 10q. on 8h. red . . . . . 5·50 5·50
86 25q. on 64h. blue . . . . 5·50 5·50
87a 50q. on 32h. violet . . . 5·50 5·50
88 1f. on 1.28k. brown on blue . . . . 8·00 8·00

Three sets may be made of this issue according to whether the handstamped control is a date, a curved comet or a comet with straight tail.

1919. No. 43 optd **SHKODER 1919.**
103 **4** 1g. on 25q. blue . . . . . 8·00 8·00

1919. Fiscal stamps surch **POSTAT SHQIPTARE** and new value.
104 **12** 10q. on 2h. brown . . . 4·50 4·50
111 10q. on 8h. red . . . . . 4·50 4·50
112 15q. on 8h. red . . . . . 4·50 4·50
113 20q. on 16h. green . . . 4·50 4·50
113b 25q. on 32h. violet . . . 4·50 4·50
107 25q. on 64h. blue . . . . 4·50 4·50
108 50q. on 32h. violet . . . 4·50 4·50
113c 50q. on 64h. blue . . . . 10·00 10·00
113d 1f. on 96h. orange . . . 6·00 6·00
113e 2f. on 160h. violet . . . 8·50 8·50

17 Prince William I

19 Skanderbeg

1920. Optd with double-headed eagle and **SHKORDA** or surch also.
114 **17** 1q. grey . . . . 21·00 40·00
115 2q. on 10q. red . . . . . 3·50 6·25
116 5q. on 10q. red . . . . . 3·25 6·25
117 10q. red . . . . 3·25 6·25
118 20q. brown . . . . 12·00 22·00
119 25q. blue £140 £275
120 25q. on 10q. red . . . . . 3·50 7·00
121 50q. violet . . . . 17·00 32·00
122 50q. on 10q. red . . . . . 3·50 7·00

1920. Optd with posthorn.
123 **19** 2q. orange . . . . 5·00 6·25
124 5q. green . . . . 6·75 11·00
125 10q. red . . . . 13·50 22·00
126 25q. blue . . . . 26·00 22·00
127 50q. green . . . . 5·00 7·50
128 1f. mauve . . . . 5·00 7·50

Stamps as Type **19** also exist optd **BESA** meaning "Loyalty".

1922. No. 123 surch with value in frame.
143 **19** 1q. on 2q. orange . . . . 3·50 2·00

24

1922. Views.
144 **24** 2q. orange (Gjinokaster) 80 1·75
145 5q. green (Kanina) 50 75
146 10q. red (Berat) 50 75
147 25q. blue (Veziri Bridge) 50 75
148 50q. green (Rozafat Fortress, Shkoder) . . . 60 75
149 1f. lilac (Korce) . . . . . 1·10 1·25
150 2f. green (Durres) . . . . 2·75 4·00

1924. Opening of National Assembly. Optd **TIRANE KALLNUER 1924** in frame with **Mbledhje Kushtetuese** above.
151 **24** 2q. orange . . . . 4·75 8·00
152 5q. green . . . . 4·75 8·00
153 10q. red . . . . 4·75 8·00
154 25q. blue . . . . 4·75 8·00
155 50q. green . . . . 4·75 8·00

1924. No. 144 surch with value and bars.
156 **24** 1 on 2q. orange . . . . . 2·50 3·75

1924. Red Cross. (a) Surch with small red cross and premium.
157 **24** 5q.+5q. green . . . . . . 7·50 7·50
158 10q.+5q. red . . . . 7·50 7·50
159 25q.+5q. blue . . . . 7·50 7·50
160 50q.+5q. green . . . . . . 7·50 7·50

(b) Nos. 157/60 with further surch of large red cross and premium.
161 **24** 5q.+5q.+5q. green . . . . 7·50 7·50
162 10q.+5q.+5q. red . . . . . 7·50 7·50
163 25q.+5q.+5q. blue . . . . 7·50 7·50
164 50q.+5q.+5q. green . . . . 7·50 7·50

1925. Return of Government to Capital in 1924. Optd **Triumf' i legalitetit 24 Dhetuer 1924.**
164a **24** 1 on 2q. orange (No. 156) 2·50 3·25
165 2q. orange . . . . 2·50 3·25
166 5q. green . . . . 2·50 3·25
167 10q. red . . . . 2·50 3·25
168 25q. blue . . . . 2·50 3·25
169 50q. green . . . . 2·50 3·25
170 1f. lilac . . . . 2·50 3·25

1925. Proclamation of Republic. Optd **Republika Shqiptare 21 Kallnduer 1925.**
171 **24** 1 on 2q. orange (No. 156) 2·50 3·25
172 2q. orange . . . . 2·50 3·25
173 5q. green . . . . 2·50 3·25
174 10q. red . . . . 2·50 3·25
175 25q. blue . . . . 2·50 3·25
176 50q. green . . . . 2·50 3·25
177 1f. lilac . . . . 2·50 3·25

1925. Optd **Republika Shqiptare.**
178 **24** 1 on 2q. orange (No. 156) 65 85
179 2q. orange 65 85
180 5q. green 65 85
181 10q. red 65 85
182 25q. blue 65 85
183 50q. green 65 85
184 1f. lilac . . . . 2·75 3·75
185 2f. green . . . . 2·75 3·75

32

1925. Air.
186 **32** 5q. green . . . . 3·25 3·25
187 10q. red . . . . 3·50 3·50
188 25q. blue . . . . 3·50 3·50
189 50q. green . . . . 5·00 5·00
190 1f. black and violet . . . . 8·25 8·25
191 2f. violet and olive . . . 11·00 11·00
192 3f. green and brown . . . 19·00 19·00

33 Pres. Ahmed Zogu, later King Zog I

34

1925.
193 **33** 1q. yellow 15 10
194 2q. brown 15 10
195 5q. green 15 10
196 10q. red 15 10
197 15q. brown 75 75
198 25q. blue 15 10
199 50q. green 75 30
200 **34** 1f. blue and red . . . . . 1·25 1·25
201 2f. orange and green . . . 1·75 1·25
202 3f. violet . . . . 3·50 3·00
203 5f. black and violet . . . . 4·25 4·75

1927. Air. Optd **Rep. Shqiptare.**
204 **32** 5q. green . . . . 10·00 10·00
205 10q. red . . . . 10·00 10·00
206 25q. blue . . . . 8·50 8·50
207 50q. green . . . . 8·00 8·00
208 1f. black and violet . . . . 8·00 8·00
209 2f. violet and olive . . . 9·75 9·75
210 3f. green and brown . . . 17·00 17·00

1927. Optd **A.Z.** and wreath.
211 **33** 1q. yellow 50 65
212 2q. brown 20 25
213 5q. green . . . . 1·10 35
214 10q. red 20 20
215 15q. brown . . . . 6·00 7·00
216 25q. blue 50 25
217 50q. green 50 25
218 **34** 1f. blue and red 50 25
219 2f. orange and green . . . 75 50
220 3f. violet and brown . . . 1·10 1·00
221 5f. black and violet . . . 1·75 2·00

1928. Inauguration of Vlore (Valona)-Brindisi Air Service. Optd **REP. SHQYPTARE Fluturim' i I-ar Vlone-Brindisi 21.IV.1928.**
222 **32** 5q. green . . . . 9·25 11·50
223 10q. red . . . . 9·25 11·50
224 25q. blue . . . . 9·25 9·50
225 50q. green . . . . 10·50 14·50
226 1f. black and violet . . . . 95·00 £110
227 2f. violet and olive . . . £100 £110
228 3f. green and brown . . . £100 £120

1928. Surch in figures and bars.
229 **33** 1 on 10q. red (No. 214) . . 50 40
230 5 on 25q. blue (No. 216) 50 40

39 Pres. Ahmed Zogu, later King Zog I

40

1928. National Assembly. Optd **Kujtim i Mbledhjes Kushtetuese 25.8.28.**
231 **39** 1q. brown . . . . 3·50 4·25
232 2q. grey . . . . 3·50 4·25
233 5q. green . . . . 3·50 4·25
234 10q. red . . . . 3·50 4·25
235 15q. brown . . . . 9·00 14·00
236 25q. blue . . . . 4·25 3·75
237 50q. lilac . . . . 6·75 5·00
238 **40** 1f. black and blue . . . . 4·25 3·75

1928. Accession of King Zog I. Optd **Mbretnia-Shqiptare Zog I 1.IX.1928.**
239 **39** 1q. brown . . . . 8·50 13·00
240 2q. grey . . . . 8·50 13·00
241 5q. green . . . . 6·50 11·00
242 10q. red . . . . 6·00 6·25
243 15q. brown . . . . 6·00 7·50
244 25q. blue . . . . 6·00 7·50
245 50q. lilac . . . . 6·75 8·75
246 **40** 1f. black and blue . . . . 8·25 11·00
247 2f. black and green . . . . 8·25 11·00

1928. Optd **Mbretnia-Shqiptare** only.
248 **39** 1q. brown 50 50
249 2q. grey 45 35
250 5q. green . . . . 2·50 50
251 10q. red 50 35
252 15q. brown . . . . 10·00 12·00
253 25q. blue 50 35
254 50q. lilac 75 35
255 **40** 1f. black and blue . . . . 1·50 1·90
256 2f. black and green . . . . 1·50 2·10
257 3f. olive and red . . . . . 4·00 2·75
258 5f. black and violet . . . 5·25 7·50

1929. Surch **Mbr. Shqiptare** and new value.
259 **33** 1 on 50q. green 25 40
260 5 on 25q. blue 30 40
261 15 on 10q. red 50 70

1929. King Zog's 35th Birthday. Optd **RROFT-MBRETI 8.X.1929.**
262 **33** 1q. yellow . . . . 4·50 6·75
263 2q. brown . . . . 4·50 6·75
264 5q. green . . . . 4·50 6·75
265 10q. red . . . . 4·50 6·75
266 25q. blue . . . . 4·50 6·75
267 50q. green . . . . 5·00 8·00
268 **34** 1f. blue and red . . . . . 8·00 12·00
269 2f. orange and green . . . 8·50 12·50

1929. Air. Optd **Mbr. Shqiptare.**
270 **32** 5q. green . . . . 8·00 12·00
271 10q. red . . . . 8·00 12·00
272 25q. blue . . . . 15·00 12·50
273 50q. green . . . . 45·00 60·00
274 1f. black and violet £250 £325
275 2f. violet and olive . . . £275 £350
276 3f. green and brown . . . £500 £550

49 Lake Butrinto

50 King Zog I

1930. 2nd Anniv of Accession of King Zog I.
277 **49** 1q. grey 15 20
278 2q. red 15 20
279 **50** 5q. green 15 15
280 10q. red 25 30
281 15q. brown 25 30
282 25q. blue 20 30
283 **49** 50q. green 40 45
284 – 1f. violet 85 60
285 – 2f. blue . . . . 1·00 60
286 – 3f. green . . . . 2·50 95
287 – 5f. brown . . . . 3·25 2·50

DESIGNS—VERT: 1, 2f. Ahmed Zog Bridge, River Mati. HORIZ: 3, 5f. Ruins of Zogu Castle.

53 Junkers F-13 (over Tirana)

1930. Air. T **53** and similar view.
288 **53** 5q. green . . . . 2·10 2·10
289 15q. red . . . . 2·10 2·10
290 20q. blue . . . . 2·10 2·10
291 50q. olive . . . . 3·75 3·75
292 – 1f. blue . . . . 6·25 6·25
293 – 2f. brown . . . . 21·00 21·00
294 – 3f. violet . . . . 24·00 24·00

1931. Air. Optd **TIRANE-ROME 6 KORRIK 1931.**
295 **53** 5q. green . . . . 9·00 9·00
296 15q. red . . . . 9·00 9·00
297 20q. blue . . . . 9·00 9·00
298 50q. olive . . . . 9·00 9·00
299 – 1f. blue . . . . 50·00 50·00
300 – 2f. brown . . . . 50·00 50·00
301 – 3f. violet . . . . 50·00 50·00

1934. 10th Anniv of Revolution. Optd **1924-24 Dhetuer-1934.**
302 **49** 1q. grey . . . . 2·00 3·50
303 2q. orange . . . . 2·00 3·50
304 **50** 5q. green . . . . 2·00 3·50
305 10q. red . . . . 2·00 3·50
306 15q. brown . . . . 2·00 3·50
307 25q. blue . . . . 3·00 3·75
308 **49** 50q. turquoise . . . . . . 3·00 3·75
309 – 1f. violet (No. 284) . . . . 4·00 7·50
310 – 2f. blue (No. 285) . . . . 8·00 13·00
311 – 3f. green (No. 286) . . . . 14·00 18·00

56 Horse and Flag of Skanderbeg

57 Albania in Chains

1937. 25th Anniv of Independence.
312 **56** 1q. violet 15 15
313 **57** 2q. brown 25 20
314 – 5q. green 40 20
315 **56** 10q. olive 45 50
316 **57** 15q. red 60 45
317 – 25q. blue . . . . 1·25 1·50
318 **56** 50q. green . . . . 1·75 2·00
319 **57** 1f. violet . . . . 5·00 5·25
320 – 2f. brown . . . . 8·00 8·50
MS320a 140 × 140 mm. 20q. purple (T **56**) . . . . 12·00 18·00

DESIGN: 5, 25q., 2f. As Type **57**, but eagle with opened wings (Liberated Albania).

58 Countess Geraldine Apponyi and King Zog

1938. Royal Wedding.
321 **58** 1q. purple 20 20
322 2q. brown 20 20
323 5q. green 20 25
324 10q. olive 50 50
325 15q. red 50 50
326 25q. blue 65 85
327 50q. green . . . . 3·50 2·75
328 1f. violet . . . . 4·75 3·75
MS328a 110 × 140 mm. 2 each 20q. purple, 30q. brown . . . . . . 20·00 27·00

59 National Emblems

60 King Zog

1938. 10th Anniv of Accession.

329 – 1q. purple 15 35
330 **59** 2q. red 25 35
331 – 5q. green 35 40
332 **60** 10q. brown 65 1·00
333 – 15q. red 65 1·00
334 **60** 25q. blue 85 1·10
335 **59** 50q. black 5·00 3·75
336 **60** 1f. green 7·50 5·50
MS336a 110×65 mm. 15q. red (333), 20q. green (**59**), 30q. violet (**60**) 16·00 25·00

DESIGN: 1, 5, 15q. As Type **60**, but Queen Geraldine's portrait.

ITALIAN OCCUPATION

1939. Optd **Mbledhja Kushtetuese 12-IV-1939 XVII**.

(a) Postage.

337 **49** 1q. grey 35 35
338 2q. red 35 35
339 **50** 5q. green 30 30
340 10q. red 30 30
341 15q. brown 70 75
342 25q. blue 80 95
343 **49** 50q. turquoise 1·00 1·25
344 – 1f. violet (No. 284) 2·00 2·75
345 – 2f. blue (No. 285) 2·25 3·00
346 – 3f. green 5·00 7·50
347 – 5f. brown 6·75 8·50

(b) Air. Optd as Nos. 337/47 or surch also.

348 **53** 5q. green 4·25 3·75
349 15q. red 3·00 3·75
350 20q. on 50q. olive 7·25 7·25

62 Gheg

64 Broken Columns, Botrint

63 King Victor Emmanuel

65 King and Fiat G18V on Tirana–Rome Service

1939.

351 **62** 1q. blue (postage) 40 25
352 – 2q. brown 30 10
353 – 3q. brown 30 10
354 – 5q. green 40 10
355 **63** 10q. brown 40 15
356 15q. red 50 15
357 25q. blue 50 25
358 30q. violet 80 60
359 – 50q. violet 1·10 60
360 – 65q. red 2·25 2·50
361 – 1f. green 2·50 1·50
362 – 2f. red 6·50 8·00
363 **64** 3f. black 10·00 14·50
364 – 5f. purple 12·00 18·00
365 **65** 20q. brown (air) 45·00 10·50

DESIGNS—SMALL: 2q. Tosk man; 3q. Gheg woman; 5, 65q. Profile of King Victor Emmanuel; 50q. Tosk woman. LARGE: 1f. Kruje Fortress; 2f. Bridge over River Kiri at Mes; 5f. Amphitheatre ruins, Berat.

66 Sheep Farming

67 King Victor Emmanuel

1940. Air.

366 **66** 5q. green 1·25 1·25
367 – 15q. red 1·75 1·60
368 – 20q. blue 4·00 2·40
369 – 50q. brown 4·50 4·75
370 – 1f. green 6·00 6·00
371 – 2f. black 13·50 14·00
372 – 3f. purple 55·00 24·00

DESIGNS: Savoia Marchetti S.M.75 airplane and—HORIZ: 20q. King of Italy and Durres harbour; 1f. Bridge over River Kiri at Mes. VERT: 15q. Aerial map; 50q. Girl and valley; 2f. Archway and wall, Durres; 3f. Women in North Eprius.

1942. 3rd Anniv of Italian Occupation.

373 **67** 5q. green 60 75
374 10q. brown 60 75
375 15q. red 75 1·25
376 25q. blue 75 1·25
377 65q. brown 1·75 2·00
378 1f. green 1·75 2·00
379 2f. purple 1·75 2·50

1942. No. 352 surch **1 QIND**.

380 1q. on 2q. brown 85 1·50

69

1943. Anti-tuberculosis Fund.

381 **69** 5q.+5q. green 50 85
382 10q.+10q. brown 50 85
383 15q.+10q. red 50 85
384 25q.+15q. blue 1·00 1·60
385 30q.+20q. violet 1·00 1·60
386 50q.+25q. orange 1·00 1·60
387 65q.+30q. grey 1·25 2·10
388 1f.+40q. brown 1·75 3·00

GERMAN OCCUPATION

1943. Postage stamps of 1939 optd **14 Shtator 1943** or surch also.

389 – 1q. on 3q. brn (No. 353) 90 4·25
390 – 2q. brown (No. 352) 90 4·25
391 – 3q. brown (No. 353) 90 4·25
392 – 5q. green (No. 354) 90 4·25
393 **63** 10q. brown 90 4·25
394 – 15q. red (No. 356) 90 4·25
395 – 25q. blue (No. 357) 90 4·25
396 – 30q. violet (No. 358) 90 4·25
397 – 50q. on 65q. brn (No. 360) 1·30 8·50
398 – 65q. red (No. 360) 1·30 8·50
399 – 1f. green (No. 361) 7·00 21·00
400 – 2f. red (No. 362) 8·75 75·00
401 **64** 3f. black 60·00 £200

71 War Refugees

1944. War Refugees' Relief Fund.

402 **71** 5q.+5q. green 2·75 16·00
403 10q.+5q. brown 2·75 16·00
404 15q.+5q. red 2·75 16·00
405 25q.+10q. blue 2·75 16·00
406 1f.+50q. green 2·75 16·00
407 2f.+1f. violet 2·75 16·00
408 3f.+1f.50 orange 2·75 16·00

INDEPENDENT STATE

1945. Nos. 353/8 and 360/2 surch **QEVERIJA DEMOKRAT. E SHQIPERISE 22-X-1944** and value.

409 30q. on 3q. brown 4·25 5·00
410 40q. on 5q. green 4·25 5·00
411 50q. on 10q. brown 4·25 5·00
412 60q. on 15q. red 4·25 5·00
413 80q. on 25q. blue 4·25 5·00
414 1f. on 30q. violet 4·25 5·00
415 2f. on 65q. brown 4·25 5·00
416 3f. on 1f. green 4·25 5·00
417 5f. on 2f. red 4·25 5·00

73

1945. 2nd Anniv of Formation of People's Army. Surch as T **73**.

418 **49** 30q. on 1q. grey 2·50 3·75
419 60q. on 1q. grey 2·50 3·75
420 80q. on 1q. grey 2·75 3·75
421 1f. on 1q. grey 6·00 7·50
422 2f. on 2q. red 7·50 8·75
423 3f. on 50q. grey 13·50 16·00
424 – 5f. on 2f. blue (No. 285) 20·00 25·00

1945. Red Cross Fund. Surch with Red Cross, **JAVA E K.K. SHQIPTAR 4-11 MAJ 1945** and value.

425 **69** 30q.+15q. on 5q.+5q. green 5·00 6·50
426 50q.+25q. on 10q.+10q. brown 5·00 6·50
427 1f.+50q. on 15q.+10q. red 14·00 16·00
428 2f.+1f. on 25q.+15q. blue 20·00 22·00

75 Permet Landscape

77 Globe, Dove and Olive Branch

1945.

429 – 20q. green 50 85
430 30q. orange 75 1·25
431 – 40q. brown 75 1·25
432 – 60q. red 1·00 1·75
433 – 1f. red 2·00 3·75
434 **75** 3f. blue 12·00 15·00

DESIGNS: 20q. Latinot; 40, 60q. Bridge at Berat; 1f. Permet landscape.

1946. Constitutional Assembly. Optd **ASAMBLEJA KUSHTETUESE 10 KALLNUER 1946**.

435 **75** 20q. green 1·25 1·25
436 30q. orange 1·75 1·75
437 – 40q. brown (No. 431) 2·00 2·00
438 – 60q. red (No. 432) 3·50 3·50
439 – 1f. red (No. 433) 12·00 12·00
440 – 3f. blue (No. 434) 20·00 20·00

PEOPLE'S REPUBLIC

1946. Int Women's Congress. Perf or imperf.

441 **77** 20q. mauve and red 85 85
442 40q. lilac and red 1·25 1·25
443 50q. violet and red 1·75 1·75
444 1f. blue and red 4·25 4·25
445 2f. blue and red 6·25 6·25

1946. Proclamation of Albanian People's Republic. Optd **REPUBLIKA POPULLORE E SHQIPERISE**.

446 **75** 20q. green 1·40 1·40
447 30q. orange 1·60 1·60
448 – 40q. brown (No. 431) 2·75 2·75
449 – 60q. red (No. 432) 5·50 5·50
450 – 1f. red (No. 433) 12·00 12·00
451 – 3f. blue (No. 434) 22·00 22·00

1946. Albanian Red Cross Congress. Surch **KONGRESI K.K.SH. 24-25-11-46** and premium.

452 **75** 20q.+10q. green 20·00 20·00
453 30q.+15q. orange 20·00 20·00
454 – 40q.+20q. brown 20·00 20·00
455 – 60q.+30q. red 20·00 20·00
456 – 1f.+50q. red 20·00 20·00
457 – 3f.+1f.50 blue 20·00 20·00

79 Athletes

80 Qemal Stafa

1946. Balkan Games.

458 **79** 1q. black 14·00 11·50
459 2q. green 14·00 11·50
460 5q. brown 14·00 11·50
461 10q. red 14·00 11·50
462 20q. blue 14·00 11·50
463 40q. lilac 16·00 11·50
464 1f. orange 32·00 30·00

1947. 5th Death Anniv of Qemal Stafa (Communist activist).

465 **80** 20q. dp brown & brown 9·00 9·00
466 28q. deep blue and blue 9·00 9·00
467 40q. dp brown & brown 9·00 9·00

81 Railway Construction

1947. Construction of Durres–Elbasan Railway.

468 **81** 1q. black and drab 5·00 1·25
469 4q. deep green and green 5·00 1·25
470 10q. dp brown & brown 5·25 1·60
471 15q. red and rose 5·25 1·60
472 20q. black and blue 12·00 1·75
473 28q. deep blue and blue 17·00 2·25
474 40q. red and purple 32·00 2·50
475 68q. dp brown & brown 40·00 22·00

82 Partisans

83 Enver Hoxha and Vasil Shanto

1947. 4th Anniv of Formation of People's Army. Inscr "1943–1947".

476 **82** 16q. brown 4·50 4·50
477 **83** 20q. brown 4·50 4·50
478 – 28q. blue 4·50 4·50
479 – 40q. brown and mauve 4·50 4·50

DESIGNS—HORIZ: 28q. Infantry column. VERT: 40q. Portrait of Vojo Kushi.

84 Ruined Conference Building

1947. 5th Anniv of Peza Conference.

480 **84** 2l. purple and mauve 6·00 4·00
481 2l.50 deep blue and blue 6·00 4·00

85 War Invalids

86 Peasants

1947. 1st Congress of War Invalids.

482 **85** 1l. red 10·00 10·00

1947. Agrarian Reform. Inscr "REFORMA AGRARE".

483 **86** 1l.50 purple 7·50 6·50
484 – 2l. brown 7·50 6·50
485 – 2l.50 blue 7·50 6·50
486 – 3l. red 7·50 6·50

DESIGNS—HORIZ: 2l. Banquet; 2l.50, Peasants rejoicing. VERT: 3l. Soldier being chaired.

87 Burning Village

1947. 3rd Anniv of Liberation. Inscr "29-XI-1944–1947".

487 **87** 1l.50 red 3·75 3·75
488 – 2l.50 purple 3·75 3·75
489 – 5l. blue 8·00 6·00
490 – 8l. mauve 12·00 8·00
491 – 12l. brown 20·00 14·00

DESIGNS: 2l.50, Riflemen; 5l. Machine-gunners; 8l. Mounted soldier; 12l. Infantry column.

1948. Nos. 429/34 surch **Lek** and value.

492 **75** 0l.50 on 30q. orange 35 35
493 1l. on 20q. green 90 90
494 – 2l.50 on 60q. red 2·50 2·25
495 – 3l. on 1f. red 3·00 3·00
496 – 5l. on 3f. blue 6·00 5·50
497 – 12l. on 40q. brown 15·00 12·50

88 Railway Construction

1948. Construction of Durres–Tirana Railway.

498 **88** 0l.50 red 2·50 1·00
499 1l. green 2·75 1·10
500 1l.50 red 4·25 1·10
501 2l.50 brown 5·25 2·00
502 5l. blue 10·00 2·75
503 8l. orange 16·00 4·75
504 12l. purple 20·00 8·00
505 20l. black 40·00 18·00

89 Parade of Infantrymen

90 Labourer, Globe and Flag

1948. 5th Anniv of People's Army.

506	**89**	2l.50 brown	3·00	2·50
507		5l. blue	5·00	4·50
508	–	8l. slate (Troops in action)	8·00	6·00

1949. Labour Day.

509	**90**	2l.50 brown	1·00	1·00
510		5l. blue	2·25	2·25
511		8l. purple	4·00	4·00

91 Soldier and Map

92 Albanian and Kremlin Tower

1949. 6th Anniv of People's Army.

512	**91**	2l.50 brown	1·10	1·10
513		5l. blue	2·25	2·25
514		8l. orange	4·00	4·00

1949. Albanian–Soviet Amity.

515	**92**	2l.50 brown	1·25	1·50
516		5l. blue	3·00	3·25

93 Gen. Enver Hoxha

94 Soldier and Flag

1949.

517	**93**	0l.50 purple	25	10
518		1l. green	30	10
519		1l.50 red	40	10
520		2l.50 brown	65	10
521		5l. blue	1·60	25
522		8l. purple	3·00	1·75
523		12l. purple	10·50	3·00
524		20l. slate	12·50	4·00

1949. 5th Anniv of Liberation.

525	**94**	2l.50 brown	70	70
526	–	3l. red	1·75	1·90
527	**94**	5l. violet	2·50	2·75
528	–	8l. black	5·25	5·50

DESIGN—HORIZ: 3, 8l. Street fighting.

96 Joseph Stalin

1949. Stalin's 70th Birthday.

529	**96**	2l.50 brown	1·00	1·25
530		5l. blue	1·90	2·50
531		8l. lake	4·25	5·50

97

98 Sami Frasheri

1950. 75th Anniv of U.P.U.

532	**97**	5l. blue	2·75	4·00
533		8l. purple	5·00	5·75
534		12l. black	9·00	10·00

1950. Literary Jubilee. Inscr "1950-JUBILEU I SHKRIMTAREVE TE RILINDJES".

535	**98**	2l. green	1·10	85
536	–	2l.50 brown	1·50	1·40
537	–	3l. red	1·75	2·00
538	–	5l. blue	3·00	3·00

PORTRAITS: 2l.50, A. Zako (Cajupi); 3l. Naim Frasheri; 5l. K. Kristoforidhi.

99 Vuno-Himare

100 Stafa and Shanto

1950. Air.

539	**99**	0l.50 black	90	90
540	–	1l. purple	90	90
541	–	2l. blue	1·60	1·60
542	**99**	5l. green	5·50	5·50
543	–	10l. blue	12·00	12·00
544	–	20l. violet	20·00	20·00

DESIGNS: Douglas DC-3 airplane over—1, 10l. Rozafat Shkodor; 2, 20l. Keshtjelle-Butrinto.

1950. Albanian Patriots.

545	–	2l. green	1·25	1·25
546	–	2l.50 violet	1·50	1·50
547	–	3l. red	2·50	2·25
548	–	5l. blue	3·00	2·50
549	**100**	8l. brown	8·00	7·25

PORTRAITS: 2l. Ahmet Haxhia, Hydajet Lezha, Naim Gjylbegu, Ndoc Mazi and Ndoc Deda; 2l.50, Asim Zeneli, Ali Demi, Kajo Karafili, Dervish Hakali and Asim Vokshi; 3l. Ataz Shehu, Baba Faja, Zoja Cure, Mustafa Matohiti and Gjok Doci; 5l. Perlat Rexhepi, Bako, Vojo Kushi, Reshit Collaku and Misto Mame.

101 Arms and Flags

102 Skanderbeg

1951. 5th Anniv of Republic.

550	**101**	2l.50 red	1·50	1·60
551		5l. blue	3·75	3·75
552		8l. black	5·50	5·75

1951. 483rd Death Anniv of Skanderbeg (patriot).

553	**102**	2l.50 brown	1·50	1·40
554		5l. violet	3·00	3·25
555		8l. bistre	4·75	4·75

103 Gen. Enver Hoxha and Assembly

104 Child and Globe

1951. 7th Anniv of Permet Congress.

556	**103**	2l.50 brown	90	90
557		3l. red	1·10	1·10
558		5l. blue	2·00	2·00
559		8l. mauve	3·75	3·75

1951. International Children's Day.

560	**104**	2l. green	1·50	1·10
561	–	2l.50 brown	1·75	1·50
562	–	3l. red	2·50	1·75
563	**104**	5l. blue	3·50	2·40

DESIGN—HORIZ: 2l.50, 3l. Nurse weighing baby.

105 Enver Hoxha and Meeting-house

1951. 10th Anniv of Albanian Communists.

564	**105**	2l.50 brown	55	55
565		3l. red	65	65
566		5l. blue	1·00	1·00
567		8l. black	2·25	2·25

106 Young Partisans

1951. 10th Anniv of Albanian Young Communists' Union. Inscr "1941–1951".

568	**106**	2l.50 brown	75	90
569	–	5l. blue	4·75	2·75
570	–	8l. red	3·50	3·50

DESIGNS: Schoolgirl, railway, tractor and factories; 8l. Miniature portraits of Stafa, Spiru, Mame and Kondi.

1952. Air. Surch in figures.

571	–	0.50l. on 2l. blue (No. 541)	£160	£130
572	**99**	0.50l. on 5l. green	35·00	25·00
573		2l.50 on 5l. green	£250	£140
574	–	2l.50 on 10l. blue (No. 543)	35·00	25·00

108 Factory

1953.

575	**108**	0l.50 brown	75	10
576	–	1l. green	75	10
577	–	2l.50 sepia	1·60	20
578	–	3l. red	2·00	35
579	–	5l. blue	3·75	90
580	–	8l. olive	4·00	1·10
581	–	12l. purple	5·50	1·40
582	–	20l. blue	12·50	3·25

DESIGNS—HORIZ: 1l. Canal; 2l.50, Girl and cotton mill; 3l. Girl and sugar factory; 5l. Film studio; 8l. Girl and textile machinery; 20l. Dam. VERT: 12l. Pylon and hydroelectric station.

109 Soldiers and Flags

1954. 10th Anniv of Liberation.

583	**109**	0l.50 lilac	15	15
584		1l. green	65	15
585		2l.50 brown	1·10	70
586		3l. red	2·00	85
587		5l. blue	2·75	1·25
588		8l. purple	5·25	3·50

110 First Albanian School

111

1956. 70th Anniv of Albanian Schools.

589	**110**	2l. purple	30	20
590	–	2l.50 green	85	30
591	–	5l. blue	1·60	1·25
592	**110**	10l. turquoise	4·25	3·50

DESIGN: 2l.50, 5l. Portraits of P. Sotiri, P. N. Luarasi and N. Naci.

1957. 15th Anniv of Albanian Workers' Party.

593	**111**	2l.50 brown	75	20
594	–	5l. blue	1·50	65
595	–	8l. purple	3·25	2·25

DESIGNS: 5l. Party headquarters, Tirana; 8l. Marx and Lenin.

112 Congress Emblem

1957. 4th World Trade Unions Congress, Leipzig.

596	**112**	2l.50 purple	50	20
597		3l. red	75	50
598		5l. blue	1·25	85
599		8l. green	3·50	2·25

113 Lenin and Cruiser "Aurora"

114 Raising the Flag

1957. 40th Anniv of Russian Revolution.

600	**113**	2l.50 brown	1·25	55
601		5l. blue	2·10	1·60
602		8l. black	3·60	2·25

1957. 45th Anniv of Proclamation of Independence.

603	**114**	1l.50 purple	75	30
604		2l.50 brown	1·10	75
605		5l. blue	3·00	1·40
606		8l. green	4·25	2·75

115 N. Veqilharxhi

116 L. Gurakuqi

1958. 160th Birth Anniv of Veqilharxhi (patriot).

607	**115**	2l.50 brown	80	30
608		5l. blue	1·50	60
609		8l. purple	3·25	1·50

1958. Removal of Ashes of Gurakuqi (patriot).

610	**116**	1l.50 green	20	20
611		2l.50 brown	75	60
612		5l. blue	1·10	75
613		8l. sepia	3·00	1·10

117 Freedom Fighters

118 Soldiers in Action

1958. 50th Anniv of Battle of Mashkullore.

614	**117**	2l.50 ochre	60	20
615	–	3l. green	80	20
616	**117**	5l. blue	1·25	75
617	–	8l. brown	2·50	1·50

DESIGN: 3, 8l. Tree and buildings.

1958. 15th Anniv of Albanian People's Army.

618	**118**	1l.50 green	20	15
619	–	2l.50 brown	60	25
620	**118**	8l. red	1·60	1·40
621	–	11l. blue	2·40	2·25

DESIGN: 2l.50, 11l. Tank-driver, sailor, infantryman and tanks.

119 Bust of Apollo and Butrinto Amphitheatre

120 F. Joliot-Curie and Council Emblem

1959. Cultural Monuments Week.

622	**119**	2l.50 brown	75	25
623		6l.50 green	3·00	1·40
624		11l. blue	4·25	2·50

1959. 10th Anniv of World Peace Council.

625	**120**	1l.50 red	2·25	80
626		2l.50 violet	5·00	2·00
627		11l. blue	10·50	6·00

121 Basketball

122 Soldier

1959. 1st National Spartacist Games.

628	**121**	1l.50 violet	75	35
629	–	2l.50 green	1·10	35
630	–	5l. red	1·75	1·40
631	–	11l. blue	6·25	3·75

DESIGNS: 2l.50, Football; 5l. Running; 11l. Runners with torches.

1959. 15th Anniv of Liberation.

632	**122**	1l.50 red	50	25
633	–	2l.50 brown	1·40	40
634	–	3l. green	1·60	50
635	–	6l.50 red	3·25	4·50
MS635a		141×96 mm. Nos. 632/5 but in red. Imperf	10·00	10·00

DESIGNS: 2l.50, Security guard. 3l. Harvester; 6l.50, Laboratory workers.

123 Mother and Child

124

1959. 10th Anniv of Declaration of Human Rights.
636 **123** 5l. blue . . . . 7·25 2·00
MS636a 72 × 65 mm. No. 636. Imperf . . . . 9·00 9·00

1960. 50th Anniv of International Women's Day.
637 **124** 2l.50 brown . . . . . . 1·00 55
638 11l. red . . . . 4·00 1·40

125 Congress Building

126 A. Moisiu

1960. 40th Anniv of Lushnje Congress.
639 **125** 2l.50 brown 55 25
640 7l.50 blue . . . . 1·50 80

1960. 80th Birth Anniv of Alexandre Moisiu (actor).
641 **126** 3l. brown 65 45
642 11l. green . . . . 2·25 80

127 Lenin

128 Vaso Pasha

1960. 90th Birth Anniv of Lenin.
643 **127** 4l. turquoise . . . . . . 1·75 35
644 11l. red . . . . 5·50 1·25

1960. 80th Anniv of Albanian Alphabet Study Association.
645 **128** 1l. olive 30 20
646 – 1l.50 brown 85 25
647 – 6l.50 blue . . . . . . 1·75 85
648 – 11l. red . . . . 4·25 1·60
DESIGNS: 1l.50, Jani Vreto; 6l.50, Sami Frasheri; 11l. Association statutes.

129 Frontier Guard

130 Family with Policeman

1960. 15th Anniv of Frontier Force.
649 **129** 1l.50 red 50 30
650 11l. blue . . . . 3·00 1·40

1960. 15th Anniv of People's Police.
651 **130** 1l.50 green 55 25
652 8l.50 brown . . . . 3·00 1·25

131 Normal School, Elbasan

132 Soldier and Cannon

1960. 50th Anniv of Normal School, Elbasan.
653 **131** 5l. green . . . . 2·50 1·40
654 6l.50 purple . . . . . . 2·50 1·40

1960. 40th Anniv of Battle of Vlore.
655 **132** 1l.50 brown 75 25
656 2l.50 purple . . . . . . 1·10 40
657 5l. blue . . . . 2·50 90

133 Tirana Clock Tower, Kremlin and Tupolev Tu-104A Jetliner

134 Federation Emblem

1960. 2nd Anniv of Tirana–Moscow Jet Air Service.
658 **133** 1l. brown . . . . 1·00 75
659 7l.50 blue . . . . 3·75 1·50
660 11l.50 grey . . . . . . 6·00 3·00

1960. 15th Anniv of World Democratic Youth Federation.
661 **134** 1l.50 blue 25 15
662 8l.50 red . . . . 1·40 55

135 Ali Kelmendi

136 Flags of Albania and Russia, and Clasped Hands

1960. 60th Birth Anniv of Kelmendi (Communist).
663 **135** 1l.50 olive 55 20
664 11l. purple . . . . 1·40 85

1961. 15th Anniv of Albanian-Soviet Friendship Society.
665 **136** 2l. violet 55 20
666 8l. purple . . . . 1·75 75

137 Marx and Lenin

1961. 4th Albanian Workers' Party Congress.
667 **137** 2l. red 55 20
668 8l. blue . . . . 1·60 80

138 Malsi e Madhe (Shkoder) Costume

139 European Otter

1961. Provincial Costumes.
669 **138** 1l. black 75 20
670 – 1l.50 purple . . . . . . 1·10 25
671 – 6l.50 blue . . . . . . 3·75 1·10
672 – 11l. red . . . . 7·25 2·40
COSTUMES: 1l.50, Malsi e Madhe (Shkoder) (female); 6l.50, Lume; 11l. Mirdite.

1961. Albanian Fauna.
673 **139** 2l.50 blue . . . . 4·00 1·00
674 – 6l.50 green . . . . 8·00 2·50
675 – 11l. brown . . . . . . 13·50 5·00
DESIGNS: 6l.50, Eurasian badger; 11l. Brown bear.

140 Dalmatian Pelicans

141 Cyclamen

1961. Albanian Birds.
676 **140** 1l.50 red on pink . . . . 3·50 60
677 – 7l.50 violet on blue . . . 5·75 1·60
678 – 11l. brown on pink . . . 8·75 2·00
BIRDS: 7l.50, Grey heron; 11l. Little egret.

1961. Albanian Flowers.
679 **141** 1l.50 purple and blue . . 2·50 50
680 – 8l. orange and purple . . 5·00 2·00
681 – 11l. red and green . . . . 8·00 2·50
FLOWERS: 8l. Forsythia; 11l. Lily.

142 M. G. Nikolla

143 Lenin and Marx on Flag

1961. 50th Birth Anniv of Nikolla (poet).
682 **142** 0l.50 brown 40 30
683 8l.50 green . . . . 2·00 1·40

1961. 20th Anniv of Albanian Workers' Party.
684 **143** 2l.50 red 90 25
685 7l.50 purple . . . . . . 2·00 90

144

145 Yuri Gagarin and "Vostok 1"

1961. 20th Anniv of Albanian Young Communists' Union.
686 **144** 2l.50 blue 90 25
687 7l.50 mauve . . . . . . 1·60 1·00

1962. World's First Manned Space Flight.
(a) Postage.
688 **145** 0l.50 blue 90 15
689 4l. purple . . . . 3·75 90
690 11l. green . . . . 9·00 3·00
(b) Air. Optd **POSTA AJRORE.**
691 **145** 0l.50 blue on cream . . . 35·00 35·00
692 4l. purple on cream . . . 35·00 35·00
693 11l. green on cream . . . 35·00 35·00

147 P. N. Luarasi

148 Campaign Emblem

1962. 50th Death Anniv of Petro N. Luarasi (patriot).
694 **147** 0l.50 blue 75 15
695 8l.50 brown . . . . . . 3·00 75

IMPERF STAMPS. Many Albanian stamps from No. 696 onwards exist imperf and/or in different colours from limited printings.

1962. Malaria Eradication.
696 **148** 1l.50 green 15 10
697 2l.50 red 20 10
698 10l. purple . . . . 1·10 65
699 11l. blue . . . . 1·60 90
MS699a 90 × 106 mm. Nos. 696/9 40·00 40·00

149 Camomile

150 Throwing the Javelin

1962. Medicinal Plants.
700 **149** 0l.50 yellow, green & blue 35 20
701 – 8l. green, yellow and grey 1·60 1·00
702 – 11l.50 violet, grn & ochre 2·75 1·25
PLANTS: 8l. Silver linden; 11l.50, Sage.

1962. Olympic Games, Tokyo, 1964 (1st issue). Inscr as in T **102**.
703 – 0l.50 black and blue . . . 20 15
704 – 2l.50 sepia and brown . . 70 15
705 – 3l. black and blue 90 20
706 **150** 9l. purple and red . . . . 2·50 75
707 – 10l. black and olive . . . 2·75 1·00
MS707a 81 × 63 mm. 15l. (as 3l.) 50·00 50·00
DESIGNS—VERT: 0l.50, Diving; 2l.50, Pole-vaulting; 10l. Putting the shot. HORIZ: 3l. Olympic flame.
See also Nos. 754/**MS**758a, 818/**MS**821a and 842/**MS**851a.

151 "Sputnik 1" in Orbit

152 Footballer and Ball in Net

1962. Cosmic Flights.
708 **151** 0l.50 yellow and violet . . 60 20
709 – 1l. sepia and green . . . 85 25
710 – 1l.50 yellow and red . . . 1·40 35
711 – 20l. blue and purple . . . 9·00 3·00
MS711a 101 × 76 mm. 14l. (+ 6l.) brown and blue (rocket) . . . 50·00 50·00
DESIGNS: 1l. Dog "Laika" and "Sputnik 2"; 1l.50, Artificial satellite and Sun; 20l. "Lunik 3" photographing Moon.

1962. World Cup Football Championship, Chile.
712 **152** 1l. violet and orange . . . 20 15
713 – 2l.50 blue and green . . . 1·00 20
714 **152** 6l.50 purple and brown 2·00 25
715 – 15l. purple and green . . 2·75 70
MS715a 82 × 66 mm. 20l. brown and green (as 713 but larger) . . . 50·00 50·00
DESIGN: 2l.50, 15l. As Type **152** but globe in place of ball in net.

153 "Europa" and Albanian Maps

154 Dardhe Woman

1962. Tourist Publicity.
716 **153** 0l.50 red, yellow & green 30 30
717 – 1l. red, purple and blue 1·40 1·40
718 – 2l.50 red, purple and blue 8·00 8·00
719 **153** 11l. red, yellow and grey 16·00 16·00
MS719a 82 × 63 mm. 7l. red, yellow and grey (**153**), 8l. red and grey (as 717) . . . . 50·00 50·00
DESIGN: 1, 2l.50, Statue and map.

1962. Costumes of Albania's Southern Region.
720 **154** 0l.50 red, purple and blue 25 10
721 – 1l. brown and buff . . . 30 15
722 – 2l.50 black, violet & grn 1·40 40
723 – 14l. red, brown and green 4·25 1·60
COSTUMES: 1l. Devoll man; 2l.50, Lunxheri woman; 14l. Gjirokaster man.

155 Chamois

156 Golden Eagle

1962. Albanian Animals.
724 **155** 0l.50 purple and green . . 50 15
725 – 1l. black and yellow . . . 1·40 30
726 – 1l.50 black and brown . . 2·00 35
727 – 15l. brown and green . . 20·00 3·75
MS727a 72 × 89 mm. 20l. brown and green (as 727 but larger) . . . £120 £120
ANIMALS—HORIZ. 1l. Lynx; 1l.50, Wild boar. VERT: 15l. Roe deer.

1962. 50th Anniv of Independence.
728 **156** 1l. brown and red 40 35
729 – 3l. black and brown . . . 1·75 75
730 – 16l. black and mauve . . 4·75 1·90
DESIGNS: 3l. I. Qemali; 16l. "RPSH" and golden eagle.

157 Revolutionaries

158 Henri Dunant and Globe

1963. 45th Anniv of October Revolution.
731 **157** 5l. violet and yellow . . . 1·10 55
732 – 10l. black and red . . . . 2·25 1·25
DESIGN: 10l. Statue of Lenin.

1963. Red Cross Centenary. Cross in red.
733 **158** 1l.50 black and red . . . 65 20
734 2l.50 black, red and blue 85 40
735 6l. black, red and green 1·60 90
736 10l. black, red and yellow 3·50 1·75

159 Stalin and Battle

160 Nikolaev and "Vostok 3"

1963. 20th Anniv of Battle of Stalingrad.
737 **159** 8l. black & grn (postage) 9·00 2·50
738 – 7l. red and green (air) . . 9·00 2·00
DESIGN: 7l. "Lenin" flag, map, tanks, etc.

1963. 1st "Team" Manned Space Flights.
739 **160** 2l.50 brown and blue . . 75 30
740 – 7l.50 black and blue . . . 1·75 1·00
741 – 20l. brown and violet . . 6·00 2·75
MS741a 88 × 73 mm. 25l. blue and brown (Popovich and Nikolaev) 35·00 35·00
DESIGNS—HORIZ: 7l.50, Globe, "Vostok 3" and "Vostok 4". VERT: 20l. P. Popovic and "Vostok 4".

161 Crawling Cockchafer

162 Policeman and Allegorical Figure

1963. Insects.
742 **161** 0l.50 brown and green . . 75 30
743 – 1l. brown and blue . . . 1·50 75
744 – 8l. purple and red . . . . 6·50 1·75
745 – 10l. black and yellow . . 8·00 3·25
INSECTS: 1l.50, Stagbeetle; 8l. "Procerus gigas" (ground beetle); 10l. "Cicindela albanica" (tiger beetle).

1963. 20th Anniv of Albanian Security Police.
746 **162** 2l.50 black, purple & red 90 50
747 7l.50 black, lake and red 3·25 80

163 Great Crested Grebe

164 Official Insignia and Postmark of 1913

1963. Birds. Multicoloured.
748 0l.50 Type **163** 80 25
749 3l. Golden eagle . . . . . . 2·00 30
750 6l.50 Grey partridge . . . . 3·25 1·10
751 11l. Western capercaillie . . . 6·75 1·75

1963. 50th Anniv of First Albanian Stamps.
752 **164** 5l. multicoloured . . . . 1·90 90
753 – 10l. green, black and red 3·50 1·60
DESIGN: 10l. Albanian stamps of 1913, 1937 and 1962.

165 Boxing

166 Gen. Enver Hoxha and Labinoti Council Building

1963. Olympic Games, Tokyo (1964) (2nd issue).
754 **165** 2l. green, red and yellow 65 65
755 – 3l. brown, blue & orange 85 25
756 – 5l. purple, brown and blue . . . . 1·25 35
757 – 6l. black, grey and green 1·75 90
758 – 9l. blue and brown . . . 3·50 1·40
MS758a 61 × 82 mm. 15l. mult (Torch, rings and map) . . . . . 25·00 25·00
SPORTS: 3l. Basketball; 5l. Volleyball; 6l. Cycling; 9l. Gymnastics.

1963. 20th Anniv of Albanian People's Army.
759 **166** 1l.50 yellow, black & red 40 20
760 – 2l.50 bistre, brown & blue 1·00 30
761 – 5l. black, drab & turq . . 1·90 90
762 – 6l. blue, buff and brown 2·75 1·40
DESIGNS: 2l.50, Soldier with weapons; 5l. Soldier attacking; 6l. Peacetime soldier.

167 Gagarin

1963. Soviet Cosmonauts. Portraits in yellow and brown.
763 **167** 3l. violet . . . . 1·00 20
764 – 5l. blue . . . . 1·40 40
765 – 7l. violet and grey . . . . 2·25 65
766 – 11l. blue and purple . . . 3·75 1·00
767 – 14l. blue and turquoise . . 4·75 1·40
768 – 20l. blue . . . . 7·25 3·50
COSMONAUTS: 5l. Titov; 7l. Nikolaev; 11l. Popovich; 14l. Bykovsky; 20l. Valentina Tereshkova.

168 Volleyball (Rumania)

1963. European Sports Events, 1963.
769 **168** 2l. red, black and olive . . 85 20
770 – 3l. bistre, black and red 85 30
771 – 5l. orange, black & green 1·25 65
772 – 7l. green, black and pink 1·90 85
773 – 8l. red, black and blue . . 3·50 1·10
SPORTS: 3l. Weightlifting (Sweden); 5l. Football (European Cup); 7l. Boxing (Russia); 8l. Ladies' Rowing (Russia).

169 Celadon Swallowtail

1963. Butterflies and Moths.
774 **169** 1l. black, yellow and red 75 25
775 – 2l. black, red and blue . . 90 30
776 – 4l. black, yellow & purple 2·00 85
777 – 5l. multicoloured . . . . 2·75 75
778 – 8l. black, red and brown 4·75 1·60
779 – 10l. orange, brown & blue 6·25 2·25
DESIGNS: 2l. Jersey tiger moth; 4l. Brimstone; 5l. Death's-head hawk moth; 8l. Orange tip; 10l. Peacock.

170 Lunik 1

1963. Air. Cosmic Flights.
780 **170** 2l. olive, yellow & orange 40 25
781 – 3l. multicoloured . . . . 1·00 25
782 – 5l. olive, yellow & purple 1·60 65
783 – 8l. red, yellow and violet 2·50 1·10
784 – 12l. red, orange and blue 4·50 3·50
DESIGNS: 3l. Lunik 2; 5l. Lunik 3; 8l. Venus 1; 12l. Mars 1.

171 Food Processing Works

172 Shield and Banner

1963. Industrial Buildings.
785 **171** 2l.50 red on pink 90 20
786 – 20l. green on green . . . 4·75 1·25
787 – 30l. purple on blue . . . 7·50 1·90
788 – 50l. bistre on cream . . . 9·50 3·50
DESIGNS—VERT: 20l. Naphtha refinery; 30l. Fruit-bottling plant. HORIZ: 50l. Copper-processing works.

1963. 1st Army and Defence Aid Assn Congress.
789 **172** 2l. multicoloured 70 25
790 8l. multicoloured . . . . 2·00 1·40

173 Young Men of Three Races

1963. 15th Anniv of Declaration of Human Rights.
791 **173** 3l. black and ochre . . . 65 55
792 5l. blue and ochre . . . 1·40 85
793 7l. violet and ochre . . . 2·25 1·40

174 Bobsleighing

175 Lenin

1963. Winter Olympic Games, Innsbruck. Inscr "1964".
794 **174** 0l.50 black and blue . . . 20 20
795 – 2l.50 black, red and grey 90 25
796 – 6l.50 black, yellow & grey 1·75 35
797 – 12l.50 red, black & green 3·50 1·60
MS797a 56 × 75 mm. 12l.50 black, green and blue (Ski jumper) (49 × 31 mm) . . . . 30·00 30·00
DESIGNS—VERT: 2l.50, Skiing; 12l.50, Figure-skating. HORIZ: 6l.50, Ice-hockey.

1964. 40th Death Anniv of Lenin.
798 **175** 5l. olive and bistre . . . 1·10 35
799 10l. olive and bistre . . . 1·50 85

176 Hurdling

177 Common Sturgeon

1964. "GANEFO" Games, Djakarta (1963).
800 **176** 2l.50 blue and lilac . . . 85 25
801 – 3l. brown and green . . . 1·25 30
802 – 6l.50 red and blue . . . . 1·60 40
803 – 8l. ochre and blue . . . . 2·50 90
SPORTS—HORIZ. 3l. Running; 6l.50, Rifle-shooting. VERT: 8l. Basketball.

1964. Fishes. Multicoloured.
804 0l.50 Type **177** 30 10
805 1l. Gilthead seabream 75 20
806 1l.50 Flat-headed grey mullet 1·00 30
807 2l.50 Common carp . . . . 1·50 50
808 6l.50 Atlantic mackerel . . . 3·00 1·25
809 10l. Lake Ochrid salmon . . 5·00 2·00

178 Eurasian Red Squirrel

1964. Forest Animals. Multicoloured.
810 1l. Type **178** 30 20
811 1l.50 Beech marten 50 25
812 2l. Red fox 70 30
813 2l.50 East European hedgehog 80 30
814 3l. Brown hare . . . . 1·00 70
815 5l. Golden jackal . . . . . . 1·75 70
816 7l. Wild cat . . . . 3·00 90
817 8l. Wolf . . . . 4·50 1·10

179 Lighting Olympic Torch

1964. Olympic Games, Tokyo (3rd issue). Inscr "DREJT TOKIOS".
818 **179** 3l. yellow, buff and green 30 15
819 – 5l. blue, violet and red . . 65 25
820 – 7l. lt blue, blue & yellow 90 30
821 – 10l. multicoloured . . . . 1·25 85
MS821a 81 × 91 mm. 15l. buff, blue and violet (as 820) (49 × 62 mm) 25·00 25·00
DESIGNS: 5l. Torch and globes; 7l. Olympic flag and Mt. Fuji; 10l. Olympic Stadium, Tokyo.

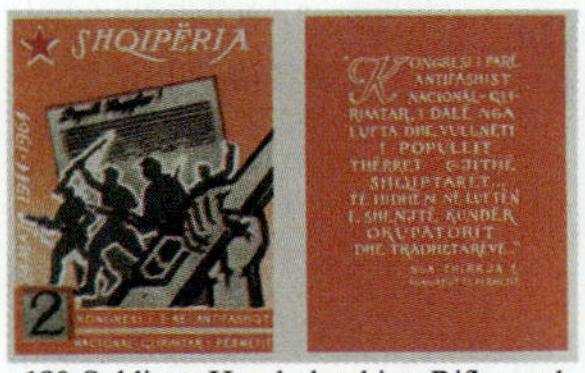

180 Soldiers, Hand clutching Rifle, and Inscription

1964. 20th Anniv of Permet Congress.
822 **180** 2l. sepia, red and orange 75 50
823 – 5l. multicoloured . . . . 2·00 1·50
824 – 8l. sepia, red and brown 3·50 3·00
DESIGNS (each with different inscription at right): 5l. Albanian Arms; 8l. Gen. Enver Hoxha.

181 Revolutionaries with Flag

183 Full Moon

1964. 40th Anniv of Revolution.
825 **181** 2l.50 black and red . . . 25 20
826 7l.50 black and mauve . . 1·00 45

1964. "Verso Tokyo" Stamp Exhibition, Rimini (Italy). Optd **Rimini 25-VI-64.**
827 10l. blue, violet, orange and black (No. 821) . . . . . 7·25 7·25

1964. Moon's Phases.
828 **183** 1l. yellow and violet . . . 30 15
829 – 5l. yellow and blue . . . 1·10 65
830 – 8l. yellow and blue . . . 1·75 85
831 – 11l. yellow and green . . 4·25 1·25
MS831a 67 × 78 mm. 15l. yellow and blue (New Moon) (34 × 39 mm). Imperf . . . . 25·00 25·00
PHASES: 5l. Waxing Moon; 8l. Half-Moon; 11l. Waning Moon.

184 Winter Wren

1964. Albanian Birds. Multicoloured.
832 0l.50 Type **184** 35 25
833 1l. Penduline tit 60 30
834 2l.50 Green woodpecker . . . 85 40
835 3l. Common treecreeper . . . 1·25 40
836 4l. Eurasian nuthatch . . . . 1·40 60
837 5l. Great tit . . . . 1·75 60
838 6l. Eurasian goldfinch . . . . 2·00 60
839 18l. Golden oriole . . . . . 4·75 2·10

1964. Air. Riccione "Space" Exhibition. Optd **Riccione 23-8-1964.**
840 **170** 2l. olive, yellow & orange 10·50 10·50
841 – 8l. red, yellow and violet (No. 783) . . . . . . 25·00 25·00

186 Running and Gymnastics

1964. Olympic Games, Tokyo.
842 **186** 1l. red, blue and green . . 20 15
843 – 2l. brown, blue and violet 25 20
844 – 3l. brown, violet and olive 35 20
845 – 4l. olive, turquoise & blue 50 25
846 – 5l. turquoise, purple & red 85 65
847 – 6l. ultram, lt blue & orge 1·00 75
848 – 7l. green, orange and blue 1·40 90
849 – 8l. grey, green and yellow 1·40 1·10
850 – 9l. lt blue, yellow & purple . . . . 1·40 1·25
851 – 10l. brown, green & turq 1·90 1·60
MS851a 70 × 96 mm. 20l. violet and bistre (Winners on Dais) (40 × 67 mm) . . . . 35·00 35·00
SPORTS: 2l. Weightlifting and judo; 3l. Horse-jumping and cycling; 4l. Football and water-polo; 5l. Wrestling and boxing; 6l. Various sports and hockey; 7l. Swimming and yachting; 8l. Basketball and volleyball; 9l. Rowing and canoeing; 10l. Fencing and pistol-shooting.

187 Chinese Republican Emblem

188 Karl Marx

1964. 15th Anniv of Chinese People's Republic. Inscr "I TETOR 1949 1964.".
852 **187** 7l. red, black and yellow 1·60 85
853 – 8l. black, red and yellow 2·75 1·25
DESIGN—HORIZ: 8l. Mao Tse-tung.

1964. Centenary of "First International".
854 **188** 2l. black, red and lavender 90 20
855 – 5l. slate . . . . 2·40 75
856 – 8l. black, red and buff . . 4·00 1·25
DESIGNS: 5l. St. Martin's Hall, London; 8l. F. Engels.

189 J. de Rada

190 Arms and Flag

1964. 150th Birth Anniv of Jeronim de Rada (poet).
857 **189** 7l. green . . . . 1·60 65
858 8l. violet . . . . 2·50 1·10

1964. 20th Anniv of Liberation.
859 **190** 1l. multicoloured 20 20
860 – 2l. blue, red and yellow 65 20
861 – 3l. brown, red and yellow 1·00 65
862 – 4l. green, red and yellow 1·40 85
863 – 10l. black, red and blue 3·50 1·60
DESIGNS—HORIZ: 2l. Industrial scene; 3l. Agricultural scene. 4l. Laboratory worker. VERT: 10l. Hands holding Constitution, hammer and sickle.

191 Mercury

192 Chestnut

1964. Solar System Planets. Multicoloured.
864 1l. Type **191** 25 20
865 2l. Venus 45 25
866 3l. Earth 70 30
867 4l. Mars 85 35
868 5l. Jupiter . . . . 1·10 40
869 6l. Saturn . . . . 1·60 50
870 7l. Uranus . . . . 1·90 65
871 8l. Neptune . . . . 2·00 1·25
872 9l. Pluto . . . . 2·10 1·60
MS872a 88 × 72 mm. 15l. Solar system and rocket (61 × 51 mm). Imperf . . . . 35·00 35·00

1965. Winter Fruits. Multicoloured.
873 1l. Type **192** 25 15
874 2l. Medlars 35 20
875 3l. Persimmon 75 25
876 4l. Pomegranate 95 35
877 5l. Quince . . . . 1·60 40
878 10l. Orange . . . . 2·75 1·10

193 "Industry"

194 Buffalo Grazing

1965. 20th Anniv of Albanian Trade Unions. Inscr "B.P.S.H. 1945–1965".
879 **193** 2l. red, pink and black . . 3·50 3·00
880 – 5l. black, grey and ochre 7·00 6·00
881 – 8l. blue, lt blue & black 8·50 6·50
DESIGNS: 5l. Set square, book and dividers ("Technocracy"); 8l. Hotel, trees and sunshade ("Tourism").

1965. Water Buffaloes.
882 **194** 1l. multicoloured 50 15
883 – 2l. multicoloured . . . . 1·10 20
884 – 3l. multicoloured . . . . 1·90 30
885 – 7l. multicoloured . . . . 4·50 1·10
886 – 12l. multicoloured . . . . 8·00 2·50
DESIGNS: 2l. to 12l. As Type **194**, showing different views of buffalo.

195 Coastal View

1965. Albanian Scenery. Multicoloured.
887 1l.50 Type **195** . . . . 1·60 80
888 2l.50 Mountain forest . . . . 2·75 1·10
889 3l. Lugina Peak (vert) . . . 3·50 1·40
890 4l. White River, Thethi (vert) 4·25 1·90
891 5l. Dry Mountain . . . . . 5·25 2·50
892 9l. Lake of Flowers, Lure . . 12·00 4·50

196 Frontier Guard

197 Rifleman

1965. 20th Anniv of Frontier Force.
893 **196** 2l.50 multicoloured . . . 1·40 85
894 12l.50 multicoloured . . . 8·00 3·50

1965. European Shooting Championships, Bucharest.
895 **197** 1l. purple, red and violet 20 15
896 – 2l. purple, ultram & blue 65 20
897 – 3l. red and pink 85 30
898 – 4l. multicoloured . . . . 1·25 30
899 – 15l. multicoloured . . . . 5·00 95
DESIGNS: 2, 15l. Rifle-shooting (different); 3l. "Target" map; 4l. Pistol-shooting.

198 I.T.U. Emblem and Symbols

199 Belyaev

1965. Centenary of I.T.U.
900 **198** 2l.50 mauve, black & grn 1·60 20
901 12l.50 blue, black & violet 6·00 1·40

1965. Space Flight of "Voskhod 2".
902 **199** 1l.50 brown and blue . . 20 10
903 – 2l. blue, ultram & lilac . . 30 15
904 – 6l.50 brown and mauve 1·25 35
905 – 20l. yellow, black & blue 4·50 1·25
MS906 71 × 86 mm. 20l. yellow, black and blue (as 905 but larger, 59 × 51 mm). Imperf . . . . 20·00 20·00
DESIGNS: 2l. "Voskhod 2"; 6l.50, Leonov; 20l. Leonov in space.

200 Marx and Lenin

201 Mother and Child

1965. Postal Ministers' Congress, Peking.
907 **200** 2l.50 sepia, red & yellow 75 30
908 7l.50 green, red & yellow 3·25 1·25

1965. International Children's Day. Multicoloured.
909 1l. Type **201** 25 15
910 2l. Children planting tree . . 45 20
911 3l. Children and construction toy (horiz) 75 20
912 4l. Child on beach 90 30
913 15l. Child reading book . . . 4·25 1·75

202 Wine Vessel

203 Fuchsia

1965. Albanian Antiquities. Multicoloured.
914 1l. Type **202** 20 10
915 2l. Helmet and shield 40 15
916 3l. Mosaic of animal (horiz) 85 25
917 4l. Statuette of man . . . . 1·60 30
918 15l. Statuette of headless and limbless man . . . . . . 4·25 1·60

1965. Albanian Flowers. Multicoloured.
919 1l. Type **203** 25 15
920 2l. Cyclamen 75 20
921 3l. Lilies . . . . 1·10 25
922 3l.50 Iris . . . . 1·40 25
923 4l. Dahlia . . . . 1·60 35
924 4l.50 Hydrangea . . . . . . 1·75 35
925 5l. Rose . . . . 2·00 70
926 7l. Tulips . . . . 2·75 90

(currency revaluation 10 (old) leks = 1 (new) lek.)

1965. Surch.
927 5q. on 30l. (No. 787) 20 20
928 15q. on 30l. (No. 787) . . . 45 20
929 25q. on 50l. (No. 788) . . . 65 25
930 80q. on 50l. (No. 788) . . . 2·10 90
931 1l.10 on 20l. (No. 786) . . . 3·25 1·10
932 2l. on 20l. (No. 786) . . . . 6·25 2·10

205 White Stork

206 "War Veterans" (after painting by B. Sejdini)

1965. Migratory Birds. Multicoloured.
933 10q. Type **205** 35 35
934 20q. European cuckoo . . . 65 35
935 30q. Hoopoe . . . . 1·10 50
936 40q. European bee-eater . . . 1·75 60
937 50q. European nightjar . . . 2·00 70
938 1l.50 Common quail . . . . 6·00 2·00

1965. War Veterans Conference.
939 **206** 25q. brown and black . . 3·25 85
940 65q. blue and black . . 7·25 1·75
941 1l.10 black . . . . 10·00 2·50

207 Hunter stalking Western Capercaillie

208 "Nerium oleander"

1965. Hunting.
942 **207** 10q. multicoloured . . . 85 25
943 – 20q. brown, sepia & grn 85 25
944 – 30q. multicoloured . . . 1·90 80
945 – 40q. purple and green . . 2·25 90
946 – 50q. brown, blue & black 2·00 55
947 – 1l. brown, bistre & green 4·25 1·00
DESIGNS: 20q. Shooting roe deer; 30q. Common pheasant; 40q. Shooting mallard; 50q. Dogs chasing wild boar; 1l. Hunter and brown hare.

1965. Mountain Flowers. Multicoloured.
948 10q. Type **208** 30 20
949 20q. "Myosotis alpestris" . . 40 20
950 30q. "Dianthus glacialis" . . 65 30
951 40q. "Nymphaea alba" . . . 1·25 40
952 50q. "Lotus corniculatus" . . 1·60 50
953 1l. "Papaver rhoeas" . . . . 3·75 1·60

209 Tourist Hotel, Fier

210 Freighter "Teuta"

1965. Public Buildings.
954 **209** 5q. black and blue . . . 10 10
955 – 10q. black and buff . . . 15 10
956 – 15q. black and green . . 20 10
957 – 25q. black and violet . . 75 15
958 – 65q. black and brown . . 1·25 35
959 – 80q. black and green . . 1·50 45
960 – 1l.10 black and purple . . 2·25 50
961 – 1l.60 black and blue . . . 3·00 1·25
962 – 2l. black and pink . . . 4·25 1·40
963 – 3l. black and grey . . . 8·00 2·40
BUILDINGS: 10q. Peshkopi Hotel; 15q. Sanatorium, Tirana; 25q. "House of Rest", Pogradec; 65q. Partisans Sports Palace, Tirana; 80q. "House of Rest", Dajti Mountain; 1l.10. Palace of Culture, Tirana; 1l.60, Adriatic Hotel, Durres; 2l. Migjeni Theatre, Shkoder; 3l. "A. Moisiu" Cultural Palace, Durres.

1965. Evolution of Albanian Ships.
964 **210** 10q. green and light green 40 20
965 – 20q. bistre and green . . 55 20
966 – 30q. ultramarine and blue 75 35
967 – 40q. violet and light violet 1·00 45
968 – 50q. red and rose . . . . 2·10 55
969 – 1l. brown and ochre . . . 4·25 1·00
DESIGNS: 20q. Punt; 30q. 19th-century sailing ship; 40q. 18th-century brig; 50q. Freighter "Vlora"; 1l. Illyrian galliots.

211 Head of Brown Bear

1965. Brown Bears. Different Bear designs as T **211**.
970 – 10q. brown and buff . . . 30 15
971 – 20q. brown and buff . . . 75 20
972 – 30q. brown, red and buff 1·00 35
973 – 35q. brown and buff . . . 1·25 40
974 – 40q. brown and buff . . . 1·60 45
975 **211** 50q. brown and buff . . . 2·50 50
976 – 55q. brown and buff . . . 3·50 85
977 – 60q. brown, red and buff 5·00 2·75
The 10q. to 40q. are vert.

212 Championships Emblem

213 Arms on Book

1965. 7th Balkan Basketball Championships, Tirana. Multicoloured.
978 10q. Type **212** 20 10
979 20q. Competing players . . . 40 15
980 30q. Clearing ball 85 20
981 50q. Attempted goal . . . . 2·10 25
982 1l.40 Medal and ribbon . . . 4·25 1·00

1966. 20th Anniv of Albanian People's Republic.
983 **213** 10q. gold, red and brown 15 10
984 – 20q. gold, blue & ultram 20 15
985 – 30q. gold, yellow and brown 75 20
986 – 60q. gold, lt grn & green 1·40 65
987 – 80q. gold, red and brown 2·25 75
DESIGNS (Arms and): 20q. Chimney stacks; 30q. Ear of corn; 60q. Hammer, sickle and open book; 80q. Industrial plant.

214 Cow

1966. Domestic Animals. Animals in natural colours; inscr in black: frame colours given.
988 **214** 10q. turquoise 30 20
989 – 20q. green 85 25
990 – 30q. blue . . . . 1·25 30
991 – 35q. lavender . . . . . 1·40 35
992 – 40q. pink . . . . 1·75 35
993 – 50q. yellow . . . . . . 2·00 40
994 – 55q. blue . . . . 2·25 70
995 – 60q. yellow . . . . . . 4·50 95
ANIMALS—HORIZ. 20q. Pig; 30q. Sheep; 35q. Goat; 40q. Dog. VERT: 50q. Cat; 55q. Horse; 60q. Ass.

215 Football

216 A. Z. Cajupi

1966. World Cup Football Championships (1st series).
996 **215** 5q. orange grey & buff 15 10
997 – 10q. multicoloured . . . 20 10
998 – 15q. blue, yellow & buff 25 15
999 – 20q. multicoloured . . . 35 20
1000 – 25q. sepia, red and buff 45 20
1001 – 30q. brown, green & buff 50 30
1002 – 35q. green, blue and buff 85 30
1003 – 40q. brown red and buff 90 35
1004 – 50q. multicoloured . . . 1·00 65
1005 – 70q. multicoloured . . . 1·40 90
DESIGNS—Footballer and map showing: 10q. Montevideo (1930); 15q. Rome (1934); 20q. Paris (1938); 25q. Rio de Janeiro (1950); 30q. Berne (1954); 35q. Stockholm (1958); 40q. Santiago (1962); 50q. London (1966); 70q. World Cup and football.
See also Nos. 1035/42.

1966. Birth Centenary of Andon Cajupi (poet).
1006 **216** 40q. indigo and blue . . 1·10 55
1007 1l.10 bronze and green 2·50 1·10

217 Painted Lady

218 W.H.O. Building

1966. Butterflies and Dragonflies. Multicoloured.
1008 10q. Type **217** 35 20
1009 20q. "Calopteryx virgo" . . 50 20
1010 30q. Pale clouded yellow . . 70 20
1011 35q. Banded agrion 85 25
1012 40q. Banded agrion (different) . . . . 1·10 30

1013 50q. Swallowtail . . . . . 1·50 40
1014 55q. Danube clouded yellow 2·00 50
1015 60q. Hungarian glider . . . 5·00 1·25
The 20, 35 and 40q. are dragonflies, remainder are butterflies.

1966. Inaug of W.H.O. Headquarters, Geneva.
1016 **218** 25q. black and blue . . 45 15
1017 – 35q. blue and orange . . 1·25 20
1018 – 60q. red, blue and green 1·60 35
1019 – 80q. blue, yellow & brn 2·75 65
DESIGNS—VERT: 35q. Ambulance and patient; 60q. Nurse and mother weighing baby. HORIZ: 80q. Medical equipment.

219 Leaf Star

1966. "Starfish". Multicoloured.
1020 15q. Type **219** 30 15
1021 25q. Spiny Star 50 20
1022 35q. Brittle Star . . . . . 1·10 25
1023 45q. Sea Star . . . . . . 1·60 30
1024 50q. Blood Star . . . . . 1·75 40
1025 60q. Sea Cucumber . . . . 2·25 40
1026 70q. Sea Urchin . . . . . 4·00 1·75

220 "Luna 10"

221 Water-level Map of Albania

1966. "Luna 10". Launching.
1027 **220** 20q. multicoloured . . . 70 20
1028 – 30q. multicoloured . . . 90 25
1029 **220** 70q. multicoloured . . . 1·75 35
1030 – 80q. multicoloured . . . 3·50 1·00
DESIGN: 30, 80q. Earth, Moon and trajectory of "Luna 10".

1966. International Hydrological Decade.
1031 **221** 20q. black, orge & red 50 20
1032 – 30q. multicoloured . . 1·00 25
1033 – 70q. black and violet . . 2·10 40
1034 – 80q. multicoloured . . . 2·75 1·25
DESIGNS: 30q. Water scale and fields; 70q. Turbine and electricity pylon; 80q. Hydrological decade emblem.

222 Footballers (Uruguay, 1930)

1966. World Cup Football Championship (2nd series). Inscriptions and values in black.
1035 **222** 10q. purple and ochre 20 10
1036 – 20q. olive and blue . . . 30 15
1037 – 30q. slate and red . . . 75 15
1038 – 35q. red and blue . . . 85 20
1039 – 40q. brown and green . . 1·00 20
1040 – 50q. green and brown . . 1·25 20
1041 – 55q. green and mauve . . 1·25 95
1042 – 60q. ochre and red . . . 2·50 1·40
DESIGNS—Various footballers representing World Cup winners: 20q. Italy, 1934; 30q. Italy, 1938; 35q. Uruguay, 1950; 40q. West Germany, 1954; 50q. Brazil, 1958; 55q. Brazil, 1962; 60q. Football and names of 16 finalists in 1966 Championship.

223 Tortoise

1966. Reptiles. Multicoloured.
1043 10q. Type **223** 20 15
1044 15q. Grass snake 30 20
1045 25q. Swamp tortoise 45 25
1046 30q. Lizard 55 30
1047 35q. Salamander 70 35
1048 45q. Green lizard . . . . . 1·25 40
1049 50q. Slow-worm . . . . . 1·25 75
1050 90q. Sand viper . . . . . 3·25 1·40

224 Siamese Cat

225 P. Budi (writer)

1966. Cats. Multicoloured.
1051 10q. Type **224** 25 15
1052 15q. Tabby 30 20
1053 25q. Kitten 90 30
1054 45q. Persian . . . . 1·75 40
1055 60q. Persian . . . . 2·25 90
1056 65q. Persian . . . . 2·50 1·00
1057 80q. Persian . . . . 3·25 1·25
Nos. 1053/7 are horiz.

1966. 400th Birth Anniv of P. Budi.
1058 **225** 25q. bronze and flesh . . 40 25
1059 1l.75 purple and green 3·25 1·90

226 UNESCO Emblem

1966. 20th Anniv of UNESCO Multicoloured.
1060 5q. Type **226** 20 15
1061 15q. Tulip and open book 35 20
1062 25q. Albanian dancers . . . 95 25
1063 1l.55 Jug and base of column . . . . 4·75 1·60

227 Borzoi

1966. Dogs. Multicoloured.
1064 10q. Type **227** 40 15
1065 15q. Kuvasz 50 20
1066 25q. Setter . . . . 1·25 25
1067 45q. Cocker spaniel . . . . 1·90 85
1068 60q. Bulldog . . . . 2·00 1·00
1069 65q. St. Bernard . . . . . 2·75 1·10
1070 80q. Dachshund . . . . . . 3·50 1·60

228 Hand holding Book

229 Ndre Mjeda (poet)

1966. 5th Workers Party Congress, Tirana. Multicoloured.
1071 15q. Type **228** 40 15
1072 25q. Emblems of agriculture and industry 85 15
1073 65q. Hammer and sickle, wheat and industrial skyline . . . . 1·90 35
1074 95q. Hands holding banner on bayonet and implements . . . . 3·25 65

1966. Birth Centenary of Ndre Mjeda.
1075 **229** 25q. brown and blue . . 65 20
1076 1l.75 brown and green 3·75 1·40

230 Hammer and Sickle

231 Young Communists and Banner

1966. 25th Anniv of Albanian Young Communists' Union. Multicoloured.
1077 15q. Type **230** 35 10
1078 25q. Soldier leading attack 75 10
1079 65q. Industrial worker . . . 1·60 30
1080 95q. Agricultural and industrial vista . . . . . 2·75 55

1966. 25th Anniv of Young Communists' Union. Multicoloured.
1081 5q. Manifesto (vert) 10 10
1082 10q. Type **231** 20 10
1083 1l.85 Partisans and banner (vert) . . . . 3·25 1·10

232 Golden Eagle

233 European Hake

1966. Birds of Prey. Multicoloured.
1084 10q. Type **232** 75 25
1085 15q. White-tailed sea eagle 1·10 40
1086 25q. Griffon vulture . . . . 1·90 90
1087 40q. Northern sparrow hawk . . . . 2·75 1·10
1088 50q. Osprey . . . . 3·50 1·40
1089 70q. Egyptian vulture . . . 4·75 2·00
1090 90q. Common kestrel . . . 5·25 2·75

1967. Fishes. Multicoloured.
1091 10q. Type **233** 30 15
1092 15q. Striped red mullet . . . 45 15
1093 25q. Opali . . . . 1·00 20
1094 40q. Atlantic wolffish . . . 1·25 30
1095 65q. Lumpsucker . . . . . 1·60 70
1096 80q. Swordfish . . . . . . 2·50 80
1097 1l.15 Short-spined sea-scorpion . . . . 2·75 1·40

234 Dalmatian Pelicans

1967. Dalmatian Pelicans. Multicoloured.
1098 10q. Type **234** 35 25
1099 15q. Three pelicans 75 35
1100 25q. Pelican and chicks at nest . . . . 2·00 55
1101 50q. Pelicans "taking off" and airborne . . . . . . 4·25 70
1102 2l. Pelican "yawning" . . . 11·00 3·50

235 "Camellia williamsi"

236 Congress Emblem

1967. Flowers. Multicoloured.
1103 5q. Type **235** 20 10
1104 10q. "Chrysanthemum indicum" 25 15
1105 15q. "Althaea rosea" . . . 30 15
1106 25q. "Abutilon striatum" . . 90 20
1107 35q. "Paeonia chinensis" . . 1·25 20
1108 65q. "Gladiolus gandavensis" . . . . . . 2·00 40
1109 80q. "Freesia hybrida" . . . 2·50 65
1110 1l.15 "Dianthus caryophyllus" . . . . . . 2·75 1·75

1967. 6th Trade Unions Congress, Tirana.
1111 **236** 25q. red, sepia and lilac 90 15
1112 1l.75 red, green and grey 4·00 1·60

237 Rose

1967. Roses.
1113 **237** 5q. multicoloured . . . 25 10
1114 – 10q. multicoloured . . . 55 10
1115 – 15q. multicoloured . . . 70 15
1116 – 25q. multicoloured . . . 85 15
1117 – 35q. multicoloured . . . 1·00 25
1118 – 65q. multicoloured . . . 1·50 40
1119 – 80q. multicoloured . . . 1·90 50
1120 – 1l.65 multicoloured . . . 4·50 1·25
DESIGNS: 10q. to 1l.65 Various roses as Type **237**.

238 Borsh Coast

1967. Albanian Riviera. Multicoloured.
1121 15q. Butrinti (vert) 40 20
1122 20q. Type **238** 50 20
1123 25q. Piqeras village 90 30
1124 45q. Coastal view . . . . . 1·40 30
1125 50q. Himara coast . . . . . 1·60 40
1126 65q. Fishing boat, Saranda 2·25 55
1127 80q. Dhermi . . . . 2·50 1·00
1128 1l. Sunset at sea (vert) . . 4·25 1·60

239 Fawn

1967. Roe Deer. Multicoloured.
1129 15q. Type **239** 50 15
1130 20q. Head of buck (vert) . . 50 20
1131 25q. Head of doe (vert) . . 95 20
1132 30q. Doe and fawn 95 25
1133 35q. Doe and new-born fawn . . . . 1·40 30
1134 40q. Young buck (vert) . . 1·40 35
1135 65q. Buck and doe (vert) . . 2·75 1·00
1136 70q. Running deer . . . . 3·50 1·40

240 Costumes of Malesia e Madhe Region

241 Battle Scene and Newspaper

1967. National Costumes. Multicoloured.
1137 15q. Type **240** 35 15
1138 20q. Zadrima 45 20
1139 25q. Kukesi 55 20
1140 45q. Dardhe 70 35
1141 50q. Myzeqe 75 70
1142 65q. Tirana . . . . 1·40 85
1143 80q. Dropulli . . . . 1·75 1·00
1144 1l. Laberise . . . . 2·25 1·25

1967. 25 Years of the Albanian Popular Press. Mult.
1145 25q. Type **241** 70 20
1146 75q. Newspapers and printery . . . . 1·90 50
1147 2l. Workers with newspaper 4·25 1·60

242 University, Torch and Open Book

243 Soldiers and Flag

1967. 10th Anniv of Tirana University.
1148 **242** 25q. multicoloured . . . 45 30
1149 1l.75 multicoloured . . . 2·75 1·10

1967. 25th Anniv of Albanian Democratic Front. Multicoloured.
1150 15q. Type **243** 25 15
1151 65q. Pick, rifle and flag . . 1·00 25
1152 1l.20 Torch and open book 1·90 75

244 Grey Rabbits

1967. Rabbit-breeding. Multicoloured.

1153	15q. Type **244**	20	10
1154	20q. Black and white rabbit (vert)	30	15
1155	25q. Brown hare	75	15
1156	35q. Brown rabbits	1·10	20
1157	40q. Common rabbits	1·40	20
1158	50q. Grey rabbit (vert)	1·75	65
1159	65q. Head of white rabbit (vert)	2·50	85
1160	1l. White rabbit	3·50	1·25

245 "Shkoder Wedding" (detail, Kole Idromeno)

1967. Albanian Paintings.

1161	**245** 15q. multicoloured	55	10
1162	– 20q. multicoloured	80	10
1163	– 25q. multicoloured	1·10	10
1164	– 45q. multicoloured	2·25	10
1165	– 50q. multicoloured	2·40	15
1166	– 65q. multicoloured	3·25	55
1167	– 80q. multicoloured	4·25	80
1168	– 1l. multicoloured	7·25	1·10

DESIGNS—VERT: 20q. "Head of the Prophet David" (detail, 16th-century fresco); 45q. Ancient mosaic head (from Durres); 50q. Detail, 16th-century icon (30 × 51 mm); 1l. "Our Sister" (K. Idromeno). HORIZ (51 × 30 mm): 25q. "Commandos of the Hakmarrja Battalion" (S. Shijaku); 65q. "Co-operative" (farm women, Z. Shoshi); 80q. "Street in Korce" (V. Mio).

246 Lenin and Stalin

1967. 50th Anniv of October Revolution. Mult.

1169	15q. Type **246**	20	15
1170	25q. Lenin with soldiers (vert)	65	15
1171	50q. Lenin addressing meeting (vert)	1·10	25
1172	1l.10 Revolutionaries	2·75	70

247 Common Turkey

248 First Aid

1967. Domestic Fowl. Multicoloured.

1173	15q. Type **247**	20	10
1174	20q. Goose	50	10
1175	25q. Hen	75	15
1176	45q. Cockerel	1·25	20
1177	50q. Helmeted guineafowl	1·40	50
1178	65q. Greylag goose (horiz)	1·90	65
1179	80q. Mallard (horiz)	2·50	85
1180	1l. Chicks (horiz)	3·50	1·25

1967. 6th Red Cross Congress, Tirana. Mult.

1181	15q.+5q. Type **248**	1·00	65
1182	25q.+5q. Stretcher case	1·90	1·00
1183	65q.+25q. Heart patient	5·00	3·50
1184	80q.+40q. Nurse holding child	8·75	5·25

249 Arms of Skanderbeg

1967. 500th Death Anniv of Castriota Skanderbeg (patriot) (1st issue). Multicoloured.

1185	10q. Type **249**	20	10
1186	15q. Skanderbeg	20	15
1187	25q. Helmet and sword	50	15
1188	30q. Kruja Castle	65	20
1189	35q. Petrela Castle	75	25
1190	65q. Berati Castle	1·40	30
1191	80q. Meeting of chiefs	1·75	65
1192	90q. Battle of Albulena	1·90	2·25

See also Nos. 1200/7.

250 Winter Olympic Emblem

1967. Winter Olympic Games, Grenoble. Mult.

1193	15q. Type **250**	15	10
1194	25q. Ice hockey	20	15
1195	30q. Figure skating	25	15
1196	50q. Skiing (slalom)	40	20
1197	80q. Skiing (downhill)	70	30
1198	1l. Ski jumping	1·60	40
MS1199	58 × 67 mm. 2l. As Type **250** but larger. Imperf	9·00	9·00

251 Skanderbeg Memorial, Tirana

1968. 500th Death Anniv of Castriota Skanderbeg (2nd issue). Multicoloured.

1200	10q. Type **251**	25	10
1201	15q. Skanderbeg portrait	30	15
1202	25q. Skanderbeg portrait (different)	90	15
1203	30q. Equestrian statue, Kruja (vert)	1·10	20
1204	35q. Skanderbeg and mountains	1·40	20
1205	65q. Bust of Skanderbeg	2·50	20
1206	80q. Title page of biography	2·75	85
1207	90q. "Skanderbeg battling with the Turks" (painting) (vert)	3·50	1·25

252 Alpine Dianthus

1968. Flowers. Multicoloured.

1208	15q. Type **252**	20	10
1209	20q. Chinese dianthus	25	15
1210	25q. Pink carnation	30	15
1211	50q. Red carnation and bud	85	20
1212	80q. Two red carnations	1·40	50
1213	1l.10 Yellow carnations	1·90	85

253 Ear of Wheat and Electricity Pylon

1968. 5th Agricultural Co-operative Congress. Mult.

1214	25q. Type **253**	40	15
1215	65q. Tractor (horiz)	1·25	45
1216	1l.10 Cow	1·90	40

254 Long-horned Goat

1968. Goats. Multicoloured.

1217	15q. Zane female	20	10
1218	20q. Kid	20	10
1219	25q. Long-haired capore	30	15
1220	30q. Black goat at rest	35	15
1221	40q. Kids dancing	75	20
1222	50q. Red and piebald goats	90	20
1223	80q. Long-haired ankara	1·60	30
1224	1l.40 Type **254**	2·75	85

The 15q., 20q. and 25q. are vert.

255 Zef Jubani

256 Doctor using Stethoscope

1968. 150th Birth Anniv of Zef Jubani (patriot).

1225	**255** 25q. brown and yellow	20	15
1226	1l.75 blue, black & vio	2·75	65

1968. 20th Anniv of W.H.O.

1227	**256** 25q. red and green	35	10
1228	– 65q. black, blue & yellow	75	20
1229	– 1l.10 brown and black	1·25	35

DESIGNS—HORIZ: 65q. Hospital and microscope. VERT: 1l.10, Mother feeding child.

257 Servicewoman

1968. 25th Anniv of Albanian Women's Union.

1230	**257** 15q. red and orange	25	15
1231	– 25q. turquoise and green	35	20
1232	– 60q. brown and ochre	1·00	30
1233	– 1l. violet and light violet	1·75	55

DESIGNS: 25q. Teacher; 60q. Farm-girl; 1l. Factory-worker.

258 Karl Marx

1968. 150th Birth Anniv of Karl Marx. Mult.

1234	15q. Type **258**	40	20
1235	25q. Marx addressing students	85	20
1236	65q. "Das Kapital", "Communist Manifesto" and marchers	1·60	65
1237	95q. Karl Marx	3·50	85

259 Heliopsis

1968. Flowers. Multicoloured.

1238	15q. Type **259**	10	10
1239	20q. Red flax	15	10
1240	25q. Orchid	20	10
1241	30q. Gloxinia	30	15
1242	40q. Orange lily	50	15
1243	80q. Hippeastrum	1·40	25
1244	1l.40 Purple magnolia	2·75	90

260 A. Frasheri and Torch

1968. 90th Anniv of Prizren Defence League.

1245	**260** 25q. black and green	40	15
1246	– 40q. multicoloured	95	20
1247	– 85q. multicoloured	1·60	40

DESIGNS: 40q. League headquarters; 85q. Frasheri's manifesto and partisans.

261 "Shepherd" (A. Kushi)

1968. Paintings in Tirana Gallery. Multicoloured.

1248	15q. Type **261**	15	10
1249	20q. "Tirana" (V. Mio) (horiz)	20	10
1250	25q. "Highlander" (G. Madhi)	25	15
1251	40q. "Refugees" (A. Buza)	75	15
1252	80q. "Partisans at Shahin Matrakut" (S. Xega)	1·40	50
1253	1l.50 "Old Man" (S. Papadhimitri)	2·75	1·00
1254	1l.70 "Shkoder Gate" (S. Rrota)	3·50	1·25
MS1255	90 × 114 mm. 2l.50 "Shkoder Costume" (Z. Colombi) (51 × 71 mm)	4·00	2·50

262 Soldiers and Armoured Vehicles

1968. 25th Anniv of People's Army. Multicoloured.

1256	15q. Type **262**	35	15
1257	25q. Sailor and naval craft	1·25	30
1258	65q. Pilot and Ilyushin Il-28 and Mikoyan Gurevich MiG-17 aircraft (vert)	2·50	85
1259	95q. Soldier and patriots	3·75	1·25

263 Common Squid

1968. Marine Fauna. Multicoloured.

1260	15q. Type **263**	25	10
1261	20q. Common lobster	20	10
1262	25q. Common northern whelk	65	15
1263	50q. Edible crab	1·00	40
1264	70q. Spiny lobster	1·40	65
1265	80q. Common green crab	1·75	85
1266	90q. Norwegian lobster	1·90	1·40

264 Relay-racing

1968. Olympic Games, Mexico. Multicoloured.

1267	15q. Type **264**	15	10
1268	20q. Running	20	10
1269	25q. Throwing the discus	25	10
1270	30q. Horse-jumping	30	15
1271	40q. High-jumping	35	15
1272	50q. Hurdling	40	20
1273	80q. Football	80	30
1274	1l.40 High diving	1·75	85
MS1275	90 × 81 mm. 2l. Olympic Stadium (64 × 54 mm.)	4·00	2·50

265 Enver Hoxha (Party Secretary)

266 Alphabet Book

1968. Enver Hoxha's 60th Birthday.
1276 **265** 25q. blue 35 25
1277 35q. purple 85 30
1278 80q. violet . . . . . . 1·75 90
1279 1l.10 brown . . . . . . 1·90 1·40
MS1280 80½ × 91 mm. **265** 1l.50 violet, red and gold. Imperf . . £120 £120

1968. 60th Anniv of Monastir Language Congress.
1281 **266** 15q. lake and green . . . 65 15
1282 85q. brown and green . . 3·25 55

267 Bohemian Waxwing

1968. Birds. Multicoloured.
1283 15q. Type **267** 55 20
1284 20q. Rose-coloured starling 75 20
1285 25q. River kingfishers . . . 1·10 30
1286 50q. Long-tailed tit . . . . 1·60 75
1287 80q. Wallcreeper . . . . . 3·25 90
1288 1l.10 Bearded reedling . . . 4·00 1·40

268 Mao Tse-tung

1968. Mao Tse-tung's 75th Birthday.
1289 **268** 25q. black, red and gold 85 30
1290 1l.75 black, red and gold 4·25 1·75

269 Adem Reka (dock foreman)

1969. Contemporary Heroes. Multicoloured.
1291 5q. Type **269** 10 10
1292 10q. Pjeter Lleshi (telegraph linesman) 15 10
1293 15q. M. Shehu and M. Kepi (fire victims) 20 15
1294 25q. Shkurte Vata (railway worker) . . . . 2·25 35
1295 65q. Agron Elezi (earthquake victim) . . . 95 25
1296 80q. Ismet Bruca (schoolteacher) . . . . . 1·25 40
1297 1l.30 Fuat Cela (blind Co-op leader) . . . . 1·90 50

270 Meteorological Equipment

1969. 20th Anniv of Albanian Hydro-meteorology. Multicoloured.
1298 15q. Type **270** 65 20
1299 25q. "Arrow" indicator . . 1·00 25
1300 1l.60 Meteorological balloon and isobar map . . . . . . 4·75 1·50

271 "Student Revolutionaries" (P. Mele)

272 "Self-portrait"

1969. Albanian Paintings since 1944. Mult.
1301 5q. Type **271** 15 10
1302 25q. "Partisans 1914" (F. Haxhiu) (horiz) . . . 20 10
1303 65q. "Steel Mill" (C. Ceka) (horiz) 75 15
1304 80q. "Reconstruction" (V. Kilica) (horiz) 85 30
1305 1l.10 "Harvest" (N. Jonuzi) (horiz) . . . . 1·40 35
1306 1l.15 "Seaside Terraces" (S. Kaceli) (horiz) . . . . 1·75 1·00
MS1307 111 × 91 mm. 2l. "Partisans' Meeting" (N. Zajmi). Imperf 2·50 2·00
SIZES: The 25q., 80q., 1l.10 and 1l.15 are 50 × 30 mm.

1969. 450th Death Anniv of Leonardo da Vinci.
1308 **272** 25q. agate, brown & gold 30 15
1309 – 35q. agate, brown & gold 65 20
1310 – 40q. agate, brown & gold 85 20
1311 – 1l. multicoloured . . . . 1·90 85
1312 – 2l. agate, brown & gold 3·75 1·75
MS1313 65 × 95 mm. 2l. multicoloured. Imperf . . . . 7·00 4·50
DESIGNS—VERT: 35q. "Lilies"; 1l. "Portrait of Beatrice"; 2l. "Portrait of a Lady". HORIZ: 40q. Design for "Helicopter".

273 Congress Building

1969. 25th Anniv of Permet Congress. Mult.
1314 25q. Type **273** 35 25
1315 2l.25 Two partisans . . . . 4·25 2·75
MS1316 95 × 101 mm. 1l. Albanian arms. Imperf . . . . 45·00 40·00

274 "Viola albanica"

1969. Flowers. Viola Family. Multicoloured.
1317 5q. Type **274** 10 10
1318 10q. "Viola hortensis" . . . 15 10
1319 15q. "Viola heterophylla" 20 15
1320 20q. "Viola hortensis" (different) 25 20
1321 25q. "Viola odorata" . . . 35 20
1322 80q. "Viola hortensis" (different) . . . . 1·25 85
1323 1l.95 "Viola hortensis" (different) . . . . 2·25 1·75

275 Plum

276 Throwing the Ball

1969. Fruit Trees. Blossom and Fruit. Mult.
1324 10q. Type **275** 15 20
1325 15q. Lemon 15 15
1326 25q. Pomegranate 50 15
1327 50q. Cherry . . . . 1·00 20
1328 80q. Apricot . . . . 1·75 85
1329 1l.20 Apple . . . . 2·75 1·40

1969. 16th European Basketball Championships, Naples. Multicoloured.
1330 10q. Type **276** 20 10
1331 15q. Trying for goal 20 10
1332 25q. Ball and net (horiz) . . 35 15
1333 80q. Scoring a goal . . . . 1·10 25
1334 2l.20 Intercepting a pass . . 2·75 1·00

277 Gymnastics

1969. National Spartakiad. Multicoloured.
1335 5q. Pickaxe, rifle, flag and stadium 15 10
1336 10q. Type **277** 15 10
1337 15q. Running 20 10
1338 20q. Pistol-shooting 25 15
1339 25q. Swimmer on starting block 30 15
1340 80q. Cycling . . . . 1·00 25
1341 95q. Football . . . . 1·25 45

278 Mao Tse-tung

1969. 20th Anniv of Chinese People's Republic. Multicoloured.
1342 25q. Type **278** . . . . . . 1·25 50
1343 85q. Steel ladle and control room (horiz) . . . . . . 4·00 1·25
1344 1l.40 Rejoicing crowd . . . 6·00 2·25

279 Enver Hoxha

1969. 25th Anniv of 2nd National Liberation Council Meeting, Berat. Multicoloured.
1345 25q. Type **279** 25 15
1346 80q. Star and Constitution 85 20
1347 1l.45 Freedom-fighters . . . 1·60 40

280 Entry of Provisional Government, Tirana

1969. 25th Anniv of Liberation. Multicoloured.
1348 25q. Type **280** 20 10
1349 30q. Oil refinery 35 10
1350 35q. Combine harvester . . 75 15
1351 45q. Hydroelectric power station . . . . 1·10 15
1352 55q. Soldier and partisans 1·60 65
1353 1l.10 People rejoicing . . . 2·75 1·25

281 Stalin

282 Head of Woman

1969. 90th Birth Anniv of Joseph Stalin.
1354 **281** 15q. lilac 15 10
1355 25q. blue 20 15
1356 1l. brown . . . . 1·10 30
1357 1l.10 blue . . . . 1·25 35

1969. Mosaics. (1st series). Multicoloured.
1358 15q. Type **282** 15 10
1359 25q. Floor pattern 20 10
1360 80q. Bird and tree 85 20
1361 1l.10 Diamond floor pattern 1·10 30
1362 1l.20 Corn in oval pattern 1·60 35
Nos. 1359/61 are horiz.
See also Nos. 1391/6, 1564/70 and 1657/62.

283 Manifesto and Congress Building

285 "Lilium cernum"

284 "25" and Workers

1970. 50th Anniv of Lushnje Congress.
1363 **283** 25q. black, red and grey 30 20
1364 – 1l.25 black, yell & grn 1·90 85
DESIGN: 1l.25, Lushnje postmark of 1920.

1970. 25th Anniv of Albanian Trade Unions.
1365 **284** 25q. multicoloured . . . 30 15
1366 1l.75 multicoloured . . . 1·90 90

1970. Lilies. Multicoloured.
1367 5q. Type **285** 25 10
1368 15q. "Lilium candidum" . . 40 10
1369 25q. "Lilium regale" . . . 70 20
1370 80q. "Lilium martagon" . . 1·75 30
1371 1l.10 "Lilium tigrinum" . . 2·25 75
1372 1l.15 "Lilium albanicum" 2·50 90
Nos. 1370/2 are horiz.

286 Lenin

1970. Birth Cent of Lenin. Each blk, silver & red.
1373 5q. Type **286** 10 10
1374 15q. Lenin making speech 15 15
1375 25q. As worker 20 15
1376 95q. As revolutionary . . . 95 35
1377 1l.10 Saluting . . . . . . 1·40 40
Nos. 1374/6 are horiz.

287 Frontier Guard

1970. 25th Anniv of Frontier Force.
1378 **287** 25q. multicoloured . . . 50 10
1379 1l.25 multicoloured . . . 2·00 75

288 Jules Rimet Cup

1970. World Cup Football Championship, Mexico. Multicoloured.
1380 5q. Type **288** 10 10
1381 10q. Aztec Stadium 15 10
1382 15q. Three footballers . . . 20 10
1383 25q. Heading goal 25 15
1384 65q. Two footballers 40 20
1385 80q. Two footballers . . . . 1·00 25
1386 2l. Two footballers . . . . 2·50 45
MS1387 81 × 74 mm. 2l. Mexican horseman and Mt. Popocatepetl 4·00 3·00
The design of **MS**1387 is larger, 56 × 45 mm.

289 New U.P.U. Headquarters Building

1970. New U.P.U. Headquarters Building, Berne.
1388 **289** 25q. blue, black and light blue 20 15
1389 1l.10 pink, black & orge 1·25 35
1390 1l.15 turq, blk & grn . . 1·40 45

290 Birds and Grapes

1970. Mosaics (2nd series). Multicoloured.
1391 5q. Type **290** 15 10
1392 10q. Waterfowl 20 10
1393 20q. Pheasant and tree stump 20 10
1394 25q. Bird and leaves 30 15
1395 65q. Fish 90 25
1396 2l.25 Peacock (vert) . . . . 2·25 85

291 Harvesters and Dancers

1970. 25th Anniv of Agrarian Reform.
1397 **291** 15q. lilac and black . . . 20 10
1398 – 25q. blue and black . . . 25 10
1399 – 80q. brown and black . . 85 20
1400 – 1l.30 brown and black . 1·25 35
DESIGNS: 25q. Ploughed fields and open-air conference; 80q. Cattle and newspapers; 1l.30, Combine-harvester and official visit.

292 Partisans going into Battle

1970. 50th Anniv of Battle of Vlore.
1401 **292** 15q. brown, orge & black 20 10
1402 – 25q. brown, yell & black 30 15
1403 – 1l.60 myrtle, grn & blk 1·40 85
DESIGNS: 25q. Victory parade; 1l.60, Partisans.

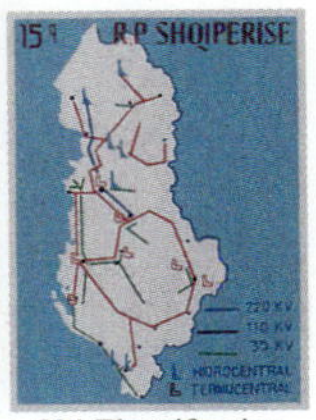

293 "The Harvesters" (I. Sulovari) 294 Electrification Map

1970. 25th Anniv of Liberation. Prize-winning Paintings. Multicoloured.
1404 5q. Type **293** 10 10
1405 15q. "Return of the Partisan" (D. Trebicka) (horiz) 15 10
1406 25q. "The Miners" (N. Zajmi) (horiz) 20 10
1407 65q. "Instructing the Partisans" (H. Nallbani) (horiz) 35 20
1408 95q. "Making Plans" (V. Kilica) (horiz) 85 50
1409 2l. "The Machinist" (Z. Shoshi) . . . . 2·50 90
MS1410 67 × 96 mm. 2l. "The Guerrilla" (S. Shijaku). (54 × 75 mm). Imperf . . . . . 3·50 2·50

1970. Rural Electrification Completion. Mult.
1411 15q. Type **294** 20 10
1412 25q. Lamp and graph . . . 25 15
1413 80q. Erecting power lines . . 85 20
1414 1l.10 Uses of electricity . . 1·40 50

295 Engels 296 Beethoven's Birthplace

295a Tractor Factory, Tirana

1970. 150th Birth Anniv of Friedrich Engels.
1415 **295** 25q. blue and bistre . . 25 15
1416 – 1l.10 purple and bistre 1·25 55
1417 – 1l.15 olive and bistre . . 1·25 70
DESIGNS: 1l.10, Engels as a young man; 1l.15, Engels making speech.

1971. Industry. Multicoloured.
1417a 10q. Type **295a** . . . . . £130 75·00
1417b 15q. Fertiliser factory, Fier £130 75·00
1417c 20q. Superphosphate factory, Lac (vert) . . . £130 75·00
1417d 25q. Cement factory, Elbasan . . . . £130 75·00

1970. Birth Bicentenary of Beethoven.
1418 **296** 5q. violet and gold . . . 20 10
1419 – 15q. purple and silver . . 20 20
1420 – 25q. green and gold . . 50 20
1421 – 65q. purple and silver . . 1·00 50
1422 – 1l.10 blue and gold . . . 1·50 50
1423 – 1l.80 black and silver . . 3·00 1·00
DESIGNS—VERT: Beethoven: 15q. In silhouette; 25q. As young man; 65q. Full-face; 1l.10, Profile. HORIZ: 1l.80, Stage performance of "Fidelio".

297 Republican Emblem

1971. 25th Anniv of Republic.
1424 **297** 15q. multicoloured . . . 10 10
1425 – 25q. multicoloured . . . 15 10
1426 – 80q. black, gold & green 90 15
1427 – 1l.30 black, gold & brn 1·25 65
DESIGNS: 25q. Proclamation; 80q. Enver Hoxha; 1l.30, Patriots.

298 "Storming the Barricades"

1971. Centenary of Paris Commune.
1428 – 25q. blue and deep blue 40 10
1429 – 50q. green and grey . . 50 20
1430 **298** 65q. chestnut and brown 80 20
1431 – 1l.10 lilac and violet . . 1·50 80
DESIGNS—VERT: 25q. "La Marseillaise"; 50q. Women Communards. HORIZ: 1l.10, Firing squad.

299 "Conflict of Race" 300 Tulip

1971. Racial Equality Year.
1432 **299** 25q. black and brown . . 20 15
1433 – 1l.10 black and red . . . 85 25
1434 – 1l.15 black and red . . . 95 30
DESIGNS—VERT: 1l.10, Heads of three races; 1l.15, Freedom fighters.

1971. Hybrid Tulips.
1435 **300** 5q. multicoloured . . . 15 10
1436 – 10q. multicoloured . . . 15 10
1437 – 15q. multicoloured . . . 20 10
1438 – 20q. multicoloured . . . 20 10
1439 – 25q. multicoloured . . . 55 15
1440 – 80q. multicoloured . . . 1·40 20
1441 – 1l. multicoloured . . . . 1·90 65
1442 – 1l.45 multicoloured . . . 3·50 1·40
DESIGNS: 10q. to 1l.45, Different varieties of tulips.

301 "Postrider" 302 Globe and Satellite (1970)

1971. 500th Birth Anniv of Albrecht Durer (painter and engraver).
1443 **301** 10q. black and green . . 15 10
1444 – 15q. black and blue . . 30 10
1445 – 25q. black and blue . . 50 15
1446 – 45q. black and purple . . 85 15
1447 – 65q. multicoloured . . . 1·25 25
1448 – 2l.40 multicoloured . . . 3·25 1·00
MS1449 93 × 90 mm. 2l.50 multicoloured. Imperf . . . . 5·00 3·50
DESIGNS—VERT: 15q. "Three Peasants"; 25q. "Peasant Dancers"; 45q. "The Bagpiper". HORIZ: 65q. "View of Kalchreut"; 2l.40, "View of Trient". LARGER: 2l.50, Self-portrait.

1971. Chinese Space Achievements. Multicoloured.
1450 60q. Type **302** 75 20
1451 1l.20 Public Building, Tirana 1·25 30
1452 2l.20 Globe and satellite (1971) . . . . 2·50 60
MS1453 65 × 112 mm. 2l.50 Globe and arrow. Imperf . . . . . . 5·00 3·50
The date on No. 1451 refers to the passage of Chinese satellite over Tirana.

303 Mao Tse-tung

1971. 50th Anniv of Chinese Communist Party. Multicoloured.
1454 25q. Type **303** 70 20
1455 1l.05 Party Birthplace (horiz) . . . . 1·75 70
1456 1l.20 Chinese celebrations (horiz) . . . . 2·50 1·00

304 Crested Tit

1971. Birds. Multicoloured.
1457 5q. Type **304** 25 20
1458 10q. European serin 30 20
1459 15q. Linnet 40 20
1460 25q. Firecrest 60 20
1461 45q. Rock thrush 90 25
1462 60q. Blue tit . . . . 1·40 60
1463 2l.40 Chaffinch . . . . . . 5·25 4·00

305 Running

1971. Olympic Games (1972). (1st issue). Mult.
1464 5q. Type **305** 10 10
1465 10q. Hurdling 15 10
1466 15q. Canoeing 15 10
1467 25q. Gymnastics 25 15
1468 80q. Fencing 55 25
1469 1l.05 Football . . . . . . 1·10 25
1470 3l.60 Diving . . . . 4·00 1·10
MS1471 70 × 83 mm. 2l. Runner breasting tape (47 × 54 mm). Imperf . . . . 4·00 3·00
See also Nos. 1522/**MS**1530.

306 Workers with Banner

1971. 6th Workers' Party Congress. Multicoloured.
1472 25q. Type **306** 25 15
1473 1l.05 Congress hall . . . . 1·40 95
1474 1l.20 "VI", flag, star and rifle (vert) . . . . 1·75 1·25

307 "XXX" and Red Flag 308 "Young Man" (R. Kuci)

1971. 30th Anniv of Albanian Workers' Party. Multicoloured.
1475 15q. Workers and industry (horiz) . . . . 2·50 15
1476 80q. Type **307** . . . . . . 1·00 75
1477 1l.55 Enver Hoxha and flags (horiz) . . . . 2·00 1·75

1971. Albanian Paintings. Multicoloured.
1478 5q. Type **308** 10 10
1479 15q. "Building Construction" (M. Fushekati) 15 10
1480 25q. "Partisan" (D. Jukniu) 20 10
1481 80q. "Fighter Pilots" (S. Kristo) (horiz) . . . . 1·00 20
1482 1l.20 "Girl Messenger" (A. Sadikaj) (horiz) . . . 1·40 65
1483 1l.55 "Medieval Warriors" (S. Kamberi) (horiz) . . . 2·00 1·25
MS1484 89 × 70 mm. 2l. "Partisans in the Mountains" (I. Lulani). Imperf . . . . 4·00 3·00

309 Emblems and Flags

1971. 30th Anniv of Albanian Young Communists' Union.
1485 **309** 15q. multicoloured . . . 15 10
1486 1l.35 multicoloured . . . 1·60 80

310 Village Girls

1971. Albanian Ballet "Halili and Hajria". Mult.
1487 5q. Type **310** 15 10
1488 10q. Parting of Halili and Hajria 20 10
1489 15q. Hajria before Sultan Suleiman 20 10
1490 50q. Hajria's marriage . . . 85 20
1491 80q. Execution of Halili . . 1·25 65
1492 1l.40 Hajria killing her husband . . . . 2·25 1·25

311 Rifle-shooting (Biathlon)

1972. Winter Olympic Games, Sapporo, Japan. Multicoloured.
1493 5q. Type **311** 10 10
1494 10q. Tobogganing 15 10
1495 15q. Ice-hockey 15 10
1496 20q. Bobsleighing 20 10
1497 50q. Speed skating 30 20
1498 1l. Slalom skiing . . . . . 1·10 30
1499 2l. Ski jumping . . . . . . 2·00 95
MS1500 71 × 91 mm. 2l.50 Figure skating. Imperf . . . . 4·00 3·00

312 Wild Strawberries

1972. Wild Fruits. Multicoloured.
1501 5q. Type **312** 15 10
1502 10q. Blackberries 15 10
1503 15q. Hazelnuts 20 10
1504 20q. Walnuts 25 15
1505 25q. Strawberry-tree fruit . . 30 15
1506 30q. Dogwood berries . . . 45 20
1507 2l.40 Rowanberries . . . . 2·50 1·10

313 Human Heart

314 Congress Delegates

1972. World Health Day. Multicoloured.
1508 1l.10 Type **313** . . . . . 1·10 30
1509 1l.20 Treatment of cardiac patient . . . . 1·25 75

1972. 7th Albanian Trade Unions Congress. Mult.
1510 25q. Type **314** 30 20
1511 2l.05 Congress Hall . . . . 1·90 1·00

315 Memorial Flame

1972. 30th Anniv of Martyrs' Day, and Death of Qemal Stafa.
1512 **315** 15q. multicoloured . . . 20 10
1513 – 25q. black, orge & grey 25 15
1514 – 1l.90 black and ochre . . 1·90 35
DESIGNS—VERT: 25q. "Spirit of Defiance" (statue). HORIZ: 1l.90, Qemal Stafa.

316 "Camellia japonica Kamelie"

1972. Camellias.
1515 **316** 5q. multicoloured . . . 15 10
1516 – 10q. multicoloured . . . 20 10
1517 – 15q. multicoloured . . . 20 10
1518 – 25q. multicoloured . . . 25 10
1519 – 45q. multicoloured . . . 40 15
1520 – 50q. multicoloured . . . 50 20
1521 – 2l.50 multicoloured . . . 3·50 2·25
DESIGNS: Nos. 1516/21, Various camellias as Type **316**.

317 High Jumping

1972. Olympic Games, Munich (2nd issue). Mult.
1522 5q. Type **317** 10 10
1523 10q. Running 10 10
1524 15q. Putting the shot . . . 15 10
1525 20q. Cycling 15 10
1526 25q. Pole-vaulting 20 10
1527 50q. Hurdling 35 15
1528 75q. Hockey 65 25
1529 2l. Swimming 90 75
MS1530 59 × 76 mm. 2l.50 High-diving (vert). Imperf . . . . . 4·00 3·00

318 Articulated bus

1972. Modern Transport. Multicoloured.
1531 15q. Type **318** 15 10
1532 25q. Czechoslovakian Class T699 diesel locomotive . . 2·00 15
1533 80q. Freighter "Tirana" . . 1·40 30
1534 1l.05 Motor-car 80 25
1535 1l.20 Container truck . . . 1·25 50

319 "Trial of Strength"

1972. 1st Nat Festival of Traditional Games. Mult.
1536 5q. Type **319** 10 10
1537 10q. Pick-a-back ball game 15 10
1538 15q. Leaping game 15 10
1539 25q. Rope game 20 10
1540 90q. Leap-frog 65 20
1541 2l. Women's throwing game 1·60 75

320 Newspaper "Mastheads"

1972. 30th Anniv of Press Day.
1542 **320** 15q. black and blue . . 20 10
1543 – 25q. green, red & black 25 15
1544 – 1l.90 black and mauve 1·90 95
DESIGNS: 25q. Printing-press and partisan; 1l.90, Workers with newspaper.

321 Location Map and Commemorative Plaque

1972. 30th Anniv of Peza Conference. Mult.
1545 15q. Type **321** 30 20
1546 25q. Partisans with flag . . 45 30
1547 1l.90 Conference Memorial 2·00 1·25

322 "Partisans Conference" (S. Capo)

1972. Albanian Paintings. Multicoloured.
1548 5q. Type **322** 10 10
1549 10q. "Head of Woman" (I. Lulani) (vert) 15 10
1550 15q. "Communists" (L. Shkreli) (vert) 15 10
1551 20q. "Nendorit, 1941" (S. Shijaku) (vert) 20 10
1552 50q. "Farm Woman" (Z. Shoshi) (vert) 65 20
1553 1l. "Landscape" (D. Trebicka) . . . . . . 1·25 50
1554 2l. "Girls with Bicycles" (V. Kilica) . . . . 2·50 1·25
MS1555 55 × 83 mm. 2l.30 "Folk Dance" (A. Buza) (vert, 40 × 67 mm). Imperf . . . . . 4·00 3·00

323 Congress Emblem

324 Lenin

1972. 6th Congress of Young Communists' Union.
1556 **323** 25q. gold, red and silver 30 15
1557 – 2l.05 multicoloured . . . 2·00 1·00
DESIGN: 2l.05, Young worker and banner.

1972. 55th Anniv of Russian October Revolution. Multicoloured.
1558 – 1l.10 multicoloured . . . 1·25 65
1559 **324** 1l.20 red, blk & pink . . 1·25 75
DESIGN: 1l.10, Hammer and Sickle.

325 Albanian Soldiers

1972. 60th Anniv of Independence.
1560 **325** 15q. blue, red and black 15 15
1561 – 25q. black, red & yellow 25 20
1562 – 65q. multicoloured . . . 45 20
1563 – 1l.25 black and red . . . 1·00 75
DESIGNS—VERT: 25q. Ismail Qemali; 1l.25, Albanian double-eagle emblem. HORIZ: 65q. Proclamation of Independence, 1912.

326 Cockerel (mosaic)

1972. Ancient Mosaics from Apolloni and Butrint (3rd series). Multicoloured.
1564 5q. Type **326** 10 10
1565 10q. Bird (vert) 15 10
1566 15q. Partridges (vert) . . . 20 10
1567 25q. Warrior's leg 25 15
1568 45q. Nude on dolphin (vert) 35 20
1569 50q. Fish (vert) 40 20
1570 2l.50 Warrior's head . . . . 3·25 1·75

327 Nicolas Copernicus

1973. 500th Birth Anniv of Copernicus. Mult.
1571 5q. Type **327** 10 10
1572 10q. Copernicus and signatures 15 10
1573 25q. Engraved portrait . . . 20 15
1574 80q. Copernicus at desk . . 1·00 25
1575 1l.20 Copernicus and planets 1·60 65
1576 1l.60 Planetary diagram . . 1·90 85

328 Policeman and Industrial Scene

1973. 30th Anniv of State Security Police.
1577 **328** 25q. black, blue & lt blue 30 20
1578 – 1l.80 multicoloured . . . 1·90 1·40
DESIGN: 1l.80, Prisoner under escort.

329/30 Cactus Flowers

1973. Cacti. As T **329/30**.
1579 **329** 10q. multicoloured . . . 10 10
1580 **330** 15q. multicoloured . . . 15 10
1581 – 20q. multicoloured . . . 20 10
1582 – 25q. multicoloured . . . 20 10
1583 – 30q. multicoloured . . . 4·50 1·75
1584 – 65q. multicoloured . . . 85 20
1585 – 80q. multicoloured . . . 1·00 25
1586 – 2l. multicoloured . . . . 1·90 85
Nos. 1579/86 were issued together se-tenant within the sheet and in alternate formats as Types **329/30**.

331 Common Tern

1973. Sea Birds. Multicoloured.
1587 5q. Type **331** 25 20
1588 15q. White-winged black tern 35 25
1589 25q. Black-headed gull . . . 40 25
1590 45q. Great black-headed gull 75 45
1591 80q. Slender-billed gull . . . 1·40 80
1592 2l.40 Sandwich tern . . . . 3·50 2·10

332 Postmark of 1913, and Letters

1973. 60th Anniv of First Albanian Stamps. Mult.
1593 25q. Type **332** . . . . . . 1·00 35
1594 11.80 Postman and postmarks . . . . 4·00 1·50

333 Albanian Woman

1973. 7th Albanian Women's Congress.
1595 **333** 25q. red and pink . . . 25 15
1596 – 11.80 black, orge & yell 1·75 1·40
DESIGN: 11.80, Albanian female workers.

334 "Creation of the General Staff" (G. Madhi)

1973. 30th Anniv of Albanian People's Army. Mult.
1597 25q. Type **334** . . . . . . 12·00 5·00
1598 40q. "August 1949" (sculpture by Sh. Haderi) (vert) . . . . 12·00 5·00
1599 60q. "Generation after Generation" (Statue by H. Dule) (vert) . . . . . 12·00 5·00
1600 80q. "Defend Revolutionary Victories" (M. Fushekati) 12·00 5·00

335 "Electrification" (S. Hysa)

1973. Albanian Paintings. Multicoloured.
1601 5q. Type **335** 10 10
1602 10q. "Textile Worker" (E. Nallbani) (vert) . . . 15 10
1603 15q. "Gymnastics Class" (M. Fushekati) 15 10
1604 50q. "Aviator" (F. Stamo) (vert) 65 15
1605 80q. "Downfall of Fascism" (A. Lakuriqi) 90 20
1606 11.20 "Koci Bako" (demonstrators (P. Mele)) (vert) . . . . 1·40 25
1607 11.30 "Peasant Girl" (Z. Shoshi) (vert) . . . . 1·75 30
MS1608 100 × 69 mm. 21.05 "Battle of Tendes se Qypit" (F. Haxhiu) (88 × 47 mm). Imperf . . . . . 4·00 3·00

336 "Mary Magdalene" **338** Weightlifting

337 Goalkeeper with Ball

1973. 400th Birth Anniv of Caravaggio. Paintings. Multicoloured.
1609 5q. Type **336** 10 10
1610 10q. "The Guitar Player" (horiz) 15 10
1611 15q. Self-portrait 20 10
1612 50q. "Boy carrying Fruit" 65 20
1613 80q. "Basket of Fruit" (horiz) 90 25
1614 11.20 "Narcissus" . . . . . 1·40 65
1615 11.30 "Boy peeling Apple" 2·25 90
MS1616 80 × 102 mm. 21.05 "Man in Feathered Hat". Imperf . . . 5·00 3·50

1973. World Cup Football Championship, Munich (1974) (1st issue). Multicoloured.
1617 **337** 5q. multicoloured . . . 10 10
1618 – 10q. multicoloured . . . 15 10
1619 – 15q. multicoloured . . . 15 10
1620 – 20q. multicoloured . . . 20 10
1621 – 25q. multicoloured . . . 25 15
1622 – 90q. multicoloured . . . 1·40 20
1623 – 11.20 multicoloured . . . 1·90 30
1624 – 11.25 multicoloured . . . 1·90 85
MS1625 80 × 50 mm. 21.05 multicoloured (Ball in net, and list of Championships). Imperf . . 5·00 3·50
DESIGNS: Nos. 1618/24 are similar to Type **337**, showing goalkeepers saving goals.
See also Nos. 1663/70.

1973. World Weightlifting Championships, Havana, Cuba.
1626 **338** 5q. multicoloured . . . 10 10
1627 – 10q. multicoloured . . . 15 10
1628 – 25q. multicoloured . . . 20 10
1629 – 90q. multicoloured . . . 90 25
1630 – 11.20 mult (horiz) . . . 1·10 35
1631 – 11.60 mult (horiz) . . . 1·60 40
DESIGNS: Nos. 1627/31 are similar to Type **338**, showing various lifts.

339 Ballet Scene **340** Mao Tse-tung

1973. "Albanian Life and Work". Multicoloured.
1632 5q. Cement Works, Kavaje 10 10
1633 10q. Ali Kelmendi truck factory and trucks (horiz) 15 10
1634 15q. Type **339** 20 10
1635 20q. Combine-harvester (horiz) 25 15
1636 25q. "Telecommunications" 25 15
1637 35q. Skier and hotel, Dajt (horiz) 35 15
1638 60q. Llogora holiday village (horiz) 50 20
1639 80q. Lake scene 65 25
1640 1l. Textile mill (horiz) . . . 50 20
1641 11.20 Furnacemen (horiz) . . 80 25
1642 21.40 Welder and pipeline (horiz) . . . . 2·00 50
1643 31. Skanderbeg Statue, Tirana . . . . 2·75 65
1644 51. Roman arches, Durres 4·25 1·75

1973. 80th Birth Anniv of Mao Tse-tung. Mult.
1645 85q. Type **340** . . . . . . 1·00 20
1646 11.20 Mao Tse-tung at parade . . . . 1·75 85

341 "Horse's Head" (Gericault)

1974. 150th Death Anniv of Jean-Louis Gericault (French painter).
1647 **341** 10q. multicoloured . . . 15 10
1648 – 15q. multicoloured . . . 15 10
1649 – 20q. black and gold . . 20 10
1650 – 25q. black, lilac and gold 25 15
1651 – 11.20 multicoloured . . . 1·60 30
1652 – 21.20 multicoloured . . . 3·50 1·25
MS1653 90 × 68 mm. 21.05 multicoloured. Imperf . . . . 4·00 3·00
DESIGNS—VERT: 15q. "Male Model" (Gericault); 20q. "Man and Dog"; 25q. "Head of a Negro"; 11.20, Self-portrait. HORIZ: 21.20, "Battle of the Giants".

342 "Lenin with Crew of the 'Aurora'" (D. Trebicka)

1974. 50th Death Anniv of Lenin. Multicoloured.
1654 25q. Type **342** 25 15
1655 60q. "Lenin" (P. Mele) (vert) . . . . 1·00 20
1656 11.20 "Lenin" (seated) (V. Kilica) (vert) . . . . 2·00 1·25

343 Duck

1974. Ancient Mosaics from Butrint, Pogradec and Apolloni (4th series). Multicoloured.
1657 5q. Duck (different) 10 10
1658 10q. Bird and flower 15 10
1659 15q. Ornamental basket and grapes 15 10
1660 25q. Type **343** 20 10
1661 40q. Donkey and cockerel 35 20
1662 21.50 Dragon . . . . 2·75 1·10

344 Shooting at Goal

1974. World Cup Football Championships, Munich (2nd issue).
1663 **344** 10q. multicoloured . . . 15 10
1664 – 15q. multicoloured . . . 15 10
1665 – 20q. multicoloured . . . 20 10
1666 – 25q. multicoloured . . . 25 10
1667 – 40q. multicoloured . . . 35 15
1668 – 80q. multicoloured . . . 1·00 25
1669 – 1l. multicoloured . . . . 1·25 25
1670 – 11.20 multicoloured . . . 1·60 45
MS1671 72 × 75 mm. 21.05 multicoloured (Trophy and names of competing countries). Imperf 4·00 3·00
DESIGNS: Nos. 1664/70, Players in action similar to Type **344**.

345 Memorial and Arms **346** "Solanum dulcamara"

1974. 30th Anniv of Permet Congress. Mult.
1672 25q. Type **345** 20 15
1673 11.80 Enver Hoxha and text 1·40 40

1974. Useful Plants. Multicoloured.
1674 10q. Type **346** 15 10
1675 15q. "Arbutus uva-ursi" (vert) 15 10
1676 20q. "Convallaria majalis" (vert) 15 10
1677 25q. "Colchicum autumnale" (vert) 20 10
1678 40q. "Borago officinalis" . . 75 20
1679 80q. "Saponaria officinalis" 1·40 25
1680 21.20 "Gentiana lutea" . . . 3·50 1·40

347 Revolutionaries

1974. 50th Anniv of 1924 Revolution.
1681 **347** 25q. mauve, black & red 20 15
1682 – 11.80 multicoloured . . . 1·25 40
DESIGN—VERT: 11.80, Prominent revolutionaries.

348 Redwing

1974. Song Birds. Multicoloured.
1683 10q. Type **348** 20 20
1684 15q. European robin 20 20
1685 20q. Western greenfinch . . 20 20
1686 25q. Northern bullfinch (vert) 45 20
1687 40q. Hawfinch (vert) 55 20
1688 80q. Blackcap (vert) . . . . 1·25 60
1689 21.20 Nightingale (vert) . . . 3·00 1·90

349 Globe and Post Office Emblem

1974. Centenary of Universal Postal Union. Multicoloured.
1690 **349** 85q. multicoloured . . . 1·00 50
1691 – 11.20 green, lilac & violet 1·50 75
MS1692 78 × 78 mm. 21.05 multicoloured. Imperf . . . . 22·00 22·00
DESIGNS—Vert: 11.20, U.P.U. emblem. Square: (70 × 70 mm.) 21.50, Text on globe.

350 "Widows" (Sali Shijaku)

1974. Albanian Paintings. Multicoloured.
1693 10q. Type **350** 10 10
1694 15q. "Road Construction" (Danish Jukniu) (vert) . . 20 10
1695 20q. "Fulfilling the Plans" (Clirim Ceka) 25 10
1696 25q. "The Call to Action" (Spiro Kristo) (vert) . . . 30 20
1697 40q. "The Winter Battle" (Sabaudin Xhaferi) . . . 40 20
1698 80q. "Three Comrades" (Clirim Ceka) (vert) . . . 80 50
1699 1l. "Step by Step, Aid the Partisans" (Guri Madhi) 1·00 60
1700 11.20 "At the War Memorial" (Kleo Nini) 1·25 70
MS1701 87 × 78 mm. 21.05 "Comrades" (Guri Madhi). Imperf . . . . 4·00 3·00

351 Chinese Festivities

1974. 25th Anniv of Chinese People's Republic. Multicoloured.
1702 **351** 85q. multicoloured . . . 85 25
1703 – 11.20 black, red and gold 1·25 30
DESIGN—VERT: 11.20, Mao Tse-tung.

352 Volleyball

1974. National Spartakiad. Multicoloured.
1704 10q. Type **352** 10 10
1705 15q. Hurdling 10 10
1706 20q. Hoop exercises 15 10
1707 25q. Stadium parade 15 10
1708 40q. Weightlifting 20 10
1709 80q. Wrestling 40 20
1710 1l. Rifle shooting 75 25
1711 11.20 Football 85 25

353 Berat

1974. 30th Anniv of 2nd Berat Liberal Council Meeting.
1712 **353** 25q. red and black . . . 20 15
1713 – 80q. yellow, brown and black 75 20
1714 – 1l. purple and black . . 1·10 50
DESIGNS—HORIZ: 80q. "Liberation" frieze. VERT: 1l. Council members walking to meeting.

354 Security Guards patrolling Industrial Plant

1974. 30th Anniv of Liberation. Multicoloured.
1715 25q. Type **354** 15 10
1716 35q. Chemical industry . . . 20 10
1717 50q. Agricultural produce 30 15
1718 80q. Cultural activities . . . 40 20
1719 1l. Scientific technology . . 80 25
1720 1l.20 Railway construction 2·50 50
MS1721 81 × 70 mm. 2l.05 Albanians with book (60 × 40 mm). Imperf . . . . . 4·00 3·00

355 Head of Artemis **356** Clasped hands

1974. Archaeological Discoveries. Multicoloured.
1722 **355** 10q. black, mauve & sil 10 10
1723 – 15q. black, green and silver 15 10
1724 – 20q. black, buff & silver 15 10
1725 – 25q. black, mauve & sil 20 10
1726 – 40q. multicoloured . . . 20 10
1727 – 80q. black, blue & silver 70 20
1728 – 1l. black, green & silver 90 20
1729 – 1l.20 black, sepia & sil 1·75 75
MS1730 96 × 96 mm. 2l.05 multicoloured. Imperf . . . 4·00 3·00
DESIGNS: 15q. Statue of Zeus; 20q. Statue of Poseidon; 25q. Illyrian helmet; 40q. Greek amphora; 80q. Bust of Agrippa; 1l. Bust of Demosthenes; 1l.20, Bust of Bilia. Square: (84 × 84 mm.) 2l.50, Head of Artemis and Greek vase.

1975. 30th Anniv of Albanian Trade Unions. Mult.
1731 25q. Type **356** 20 15
1732 1l.80 Workers with arms raised (horiz) . . . . . . 1·25 50

357 "Cichorium intybus"

1975. Albanian Flowers. Multicoloured.
1733 5q. Type **357** 10 10
1734 10q. "Sempervivum montanum" 10 10
1735 15q. "Aquilegia alpina" . . 10 10
1736 20q. "Anemone hortensis" 15 10
1737 25q. "Hibiscus trionum" . . 15 10
1738 30q. "Gentiana kochiana" 20 10
1739 35q. "Lavatera arborea" . . 20 10
1740 2l.70 "Iris graminea" . . . 1·90 70

358 Head of Jesus (detail, Doni Tondo)

1975. 500th Birth Anniv of Michelangelo. Mult.
1741 **358** 5q. multicoloured . . . 10 10
1742 – 10q. brown, grey & gold 10 10
1743 – 15q. brown, grey & gold 15 10
1744 – 20q. sepia, grey and gold 20 10
1745 – 25q. multicoloured . . . 20 10
1746 – 30q. brown, grey & gold 20 10
1747 – 1l.20 brn, grey & gold 85 30
1748 – 3l.90 multicoloured . . . 2·50 1·00
MS1749 77 × 86 mm. 2l.05 multicoloured. Imperf . . . . 4·50 3·00
DESIGNS: 10q. "The Heroic Captive"; 15q. "Head of Dawn"; 20q. "Awakening Giant" (detail); 25q. "Cumaenian Sybil" (detail, Sistine chapel); 30q. "Lorenzo di Medici"; 1l.20, Head and shoulders of "David"; 3l.90, "Delphic Sybil" (detail, Sistine chapel). 70 × 77 mm. 2l.05, Head of Michelangelo.

359 Horseman

1975. "Albanian Transport of the Past". Mult.
1750 5q. Type **359** 10 10
1751 10q. Horse and cart 15 10
1752 15q. Ferry 40 15
1753 20q. Barque 40 15
1754 25q. Horse-drawn cab . . . 30 15
1755 3l.35 Early car . . . . . . 2·75 85

360 Frontier Guard

1975. 30th Anniv of Frontier Force. Mult.
1756 25q. Type **360** 20 15
1757 1l.80 Guards patrolling industrial plant . . . . . 1·75 90

361 Patriot affixing Anti-fascist Placard

1975. 30th Anniv of "Victory over Fascism". Mult.
1758 25q. Type **361** 15 10
1759 60q. Partisans in battle . . . 30 10
1760 1l.20 Patriot defeating Nazi soldier . . . . 1·25 55

362 European Wigeon

1975. Albanian Wildfowl. Multicoloured.
1761 5q. Type **362** 20 20
1762 10q. Red-crested pochard 20 20
1763 15q. White-fronted goose . . 20 20
1764 20q. Pintail 20 20
1765 25q. Red-breasted merganser 20 20
1766 30q. Eider 35 20
1767 35q. Whooper swans . . . 45 20
1768 2l.70 Common shoveler . . 2·75 1·40

363 "Shyqyri Kanapari" (Musa Qarri)

1975. Albanian Paintings. People's Art Exhibition, Tirana. Multicoloured.
1769 5q. Type **363** 10 10
1770 10q. "Sea Rescue" (Agim Faja) 10 10
1771 15q. "28 November 1912" (Petri Ceno) (horiz) . . . 10 10
1772 20q. "Workers' Meeting" (Sali Shijaka) 15 10
1773 25q. "Shota Galica" (Ismail Lulani) 15 10
1774 30q. "Victorious Fighters" (Nestor Jonuzi) 20 15
1775 80q. "Partisan Comrades" (Vilson Halimi) 65 20
1776 2l.25 "Republic Day Celebration" (Fatmir Haxhiu) (horiz) . . . . 1·60 1·25
MS1777 68 × 98 mm. 2l.05 "Folk dance" (Abdurahim Buza). Imperf 3·00 2·00

364 Farmer with Declaration of Reform

1975. 30th Anniv of Agrarian Reform. Mult.
1778 15q. Type **364** 15 15
1779 2l. Agricultural scene . . . 1·40 75

365 Dead Man's Fingers **367** Power Lines leading to Village

366 Cycling

1975. Marine Corals. Multicoloured.
1780 5q. Type **365** 10 10
1781 10q. "Paramuricea chamaeleon" 15 10
1782 20q. Red Coral 15 10
1783 25q. Tube Coral or Sea Fan 30 15
1784 3l.70 "Cladocora cespitosa" 4·25 1·75

1975. Olympic Games, Montreal (1976). Mult.
1785 5q. Type **366** 10 10
1786 10q. Canoeing 10 10
1787 15q. Handball 15 10
1788 20q. Basketball 15 10
1789 25q. Water-polo 20 10
1790 30q. Hockey 20 10
1791 1l.20 Pole vaulting 85 25
1792 2l.05 Fencing . . . . 1·40 35
MS1793 73 × 77 mm. 2l.15 Games emblem and sportsmen. Imperf 6·00 6·00

1975. 5th Anniv of Electrification of Albanian Countryside. Multicoloured.
1794 **367** 15q. multicoloured . . . 15 15
1795 – 25q. violet, red and lilac 20 15
1796 – 80q. black, turq & green 85 20
1797 – 85q. buff, brn & ochre 1·25 85
DESIGNS: 25q. High power insulators; 80q. Dam and power station; 85q. T.V. pylons and emblems of agriculture and industry.

368 Berat

1975. Air. Tourist Resorts. Multicoloured.
1798 20q. Type **368** 25 15
1799 40q. Gjirokaster 40 20
1800 60q. Sarande 70 30
1801 90q. Durres 90 40
1802 1l.20 Krujae . . . . 1·25 50
1803 2l.40 Boga . . . . 2·40 1·00
1804 4l.05 Tirana . . . . 3·50 1·75

369 Child, Rabbit and Bear planting Saplings

1975. Children's Tales. Multicoloured.
1805 5q. Type **369** 10 10
1806 10q. Mrs. Fox and cub . . 10 10
1807 15q. Ducks in school . . . 15 10
1808 20q. Bears building 15 10
1809 25q. Animals watching television 20 10
1810 30q. Animals with log and electric light bulbs 20 10
1811 35q. Ants with spade and guitar 35 15
1812 2l.70 Boy and girl with sheep and dog . . . . . 1·90 85

370 Arms and Rejoicing Crowd

1976. 30th Anniv of Albanian People's Republic. Multicoloured.
1813 25q. Type **370** 20 15
1814 1l.90 Folk-dancers . . . . . 1·40 40

371 Ice Hockey

1976. Winter Olympic Games, Innsbruck. Mult.
1815 5q. Type **371** 10 10
1816 10q. Speed skating 15 10
1817 15q. Rifle shooting (biathlon) 20 10
1818 50q. Ski jumping 30 15
1819 1l.20 Skiing (slalom) 90 25
1820 2l.30 Bobsleighing . . . . . 1·90 45
MS1821 66 × 80 mm. 2l.15 Figure skating (pairs) . . . . 3·00 2·00

372 "Colchicum autumnale"

1976. Medicinal Plants. Multicoloured.
1822 5q. Type **372** 10 10
1823 10q. "Atropa belladonna" 15 10
1824 15q. "Gentiana lutea" . . . 15 10
1825 20q. "Aesculus hippocastanum" 15 10
1826 70q. "Polystichum filix" . . 35 20
1827 80q. "Althaea officinalis" 55 20
1828 2l.30 "Datura stamonium" 2·25 1·00

373 Wooden Bowl and Spoon

1976. Ethnographical Studies Conference, Tirana. Albanian Artifacts. Multicoloured.
1829 10q. Type **373** 10 10
1830 15q. Flask (vert) 15 10
1831 20q. Ornamental handles (vert) 20 10
1832 25q. Pistol and dagger . . . 25 10
1833 80q. Hand-woven rug (vert) 70 20
1834 1l.20 Filigree buckle and earrings . . . . 1·00 25
1835 1l.40 Jugs with handles (vert) . . . . 1·25 85

374 "Founding the Co-operatives" (Zef Shoshi)

1976. Albanian Paintings. Multicoloured.
1836 5q. Type **374** 10 10
1837 10q. "Going to Work" (Agim Zajmi) (vert) . . . 10 10
1838 25q. "Listening to Broadcast" (Vilson Kilica) 15 10
1839 40q. "Female Welder" (Sabaudin Xhaferi) (vert) 25 10
1840 50q. "Steel Workers" (Isuf Sulovari) (vert) 35 15
1841 1l.20 "1942 Revolt" (Lec Shkreli) (vert) 90 25
1842 1l.60 "Returning from Work" (Agron Dine) . . 1·25 35
MS1843 93 × 79 mm. 2l.05 "The Young Pioneer" (Andon Lakuriqi) 3·00 1·75

375 Demonstrators attacking Police

376 Party Flag, Industry and Agriculture

1976. 35th Anniv of Hoxha's Anti-fascist Demonstration. Multicoloured.
1844 25q. Type **375** 20 15
1845 1l.90 Crowd with flag . . . 1·40 55

1976. 7th Workers' Party Congress. Multicoloured.
1846 25q. Type **376** . . . . . 1·75 45
1847 1l.20 Hand holding Party symbols, and flag 85 30

377 Communist Advance

1976. 35th Anniv of Workers' Party. Mult.
1848 15q. Type **377** 20 10
1849 25q. Hands holding emblems and revolutionary army . . . 20 10
1850 80q. "Reconstruction" . . . 40 20
1851 1l.20 "Heavy Industry and Agriculture" 95 30
1852 1l.70 "The Arts" (ballet) . . 1·40 40

378 Young Communist

1976. 35th Anniv of Young Communists' Union. Multicoloured.
1853 80q. Type **378** . . . . . . 1·90 45
1854 1l.25 Young Communists in action 90 40

379 Ballet Dancers

1976. Albanian Ballet "Cuca e Malexe".
1855 **379** 10q. multicoloured . . . 10 10
1856 – 15q. multicoloured . . . 15 10
1857 – 20q. multicoloured . . . 20 10
1858 – 25q. multicoloured . . . 25 10
1859 – 80q. multicoloured . . . 45 20
1860 – 1l.20 multicoloured . . . 70 25
1861 – 1l.40 multicoloured . . . 85 30
MS1862 77 × 67 mm. 2l.05 multicoloured. Imperf . . . . 4·00 3·00
DESIGNS: 15q. to 2l.50, Various ballet scenes.

380 Bashtoves Castle

381 Skanderbeg's Shield and Spear

1976. Albanian Castles.
1863 **380** 10q. black and blue . . 10 10
1864 – 15q. black and green . . 10 10
1865 – 20q. black and grey . . 20 15
1866 – 25q. black and ochre . . 30 20
1867 – 80q. black, pink and red 90 50
1868 – 1l.20 black and blue . . 1·25 80
1869 – 1l.40 black, red & pink 1·75 90
DESIGNS: 15q. Gjirokaster; 20q. All Pash Tepelenes; 25q. Petreles; 80q. Berat; 1l.20, Durres; 1l.40, Krujes.

1977. Crest and Arms of Skanderbeg's Army. Mult.
1870 15q. Type **381** . . . . . . 1·25 70
1871 80q. Helmet, sword and scabbard . . . . 4·00 2·50
1872 1l. Halberd, spear, bow and arrows . . . . 6·00 3·00

382 Ilya Oiqi

383 Polyvinyl-chloride Plant, Vlore

1977. Albanian Heroes. Multicoloured.
1873 5q. Type **382** 10 10
1874 10q. Ilia Dashi 20 10
1875 25q. Fran Ndue Ivanaj . . . 75 30
1876 80q. Zeliha Allmetaj . . . . 1·25 35
1877 1l. Ylli Zaimi . . . . 1·50 50
1878 1l.90 Isuf Plloci . . . . . . 2·50 80

1977. 6th Five-year Plan. Multicoloured.
1879 15q. Type **383** 25 20
1880 25q. Naphtha plant, Ballsh 40 25
1881 65q. Hydroelectric station, Fjerzes 80 50
1882 1l. Metallurgical combinate, Elbasan . . . . 1·60 80

384 Shote Galica

385 Crowd and Martyrs' Monument, Tirana

1977. 50th Death Anniv of Shote Galica (Communist partisan).
1883 **384** 80q. red and pink . . . 80 40
1884 – 1l.25 grey and blue . . . 1·50 75
DESIGN: 1l.25, Shote Galica and father.

1977. 35th Anniv of Martyrs' Day. Multicoloured.
1885 25q. Type **385** 40 25
1886 80q. Clenched fist and Albanian flag . . . . . . 1·00 40
1887 1l.20 Bust of Qemal Stafa 1·75 70

386 Doctor calling at Village House

387 Workers outside Factory

1977. "Socialist Transformation of the Villages". Multicoloured.
1888 5q. Type **386** 10 10
1889 10q. Cowherd with cattle . . 15 10
1890 20q. Harvesting 20 20
1891 80q. Modern village . . . . 1·00 40
1892 2l.95 Tractor and greenhouse . . . . 3·50 70

1977. 8th Trade Unions Congress. Multicoloured.
1893 25q. Type **387** 25 20
1894 1l.80 Three workers with flags . . . . 1·50 80

388 Advancing Soldiers

1977. "All the People are Soldiers". Multicoloured.
1895 15q. Type **388** 20 10
1896 25q. Enver Hoxha and marching soldiers 25 10
1897 80q. Soldiers and workers 75 25
1898 1l. The Armed Forces . . . 1·00 35
1899 1l.90 Marching soldiers and workers . . . . 2·00 40

389 Two Girls with Handkerchiefs

391 "Beni Ecen Vet"

390 Armed Worker with Book

1977. National Costume Dances (1st series). Mult.
1900 5q. Type **389** 15 10
1901 10q. Two male dancers . . 15 10
1902 15q. Man and woman in kerchief dance 15 15
1903 25q. Two male dancers (different) 20 15
1904 80q. Two women dancers with kerchiefs 55 25
1905 1l.20 "Elbow dance" 85 30
1906 1l.55 Two women with kerchiefs (different) . . . 1·10 50
MS1907 56 × 74 mm. 2l.05 Sabre dance . . . . 4·00 3·00
See also Nos. 1932/6 and 1991/5.

1977. New Constitution.
1908 **390** 25q. gold, red and black 25 15
1909 – 1l.20 gold, red and black 1·10 35
DESIGN: 1l.20, Industrial and agricultural symbols and hand with book.

1977. Albanian Films.
1910 **391** 10q. green and grey . . 20 10
1911 – 15q. multicoloured . . . 30 10
1912 – 25q. green, black & grey 40 20
1913 – 80q. multicoloured . . . 1·00 50
1914 – 1l.20 brown and grey . . 1·50 60
1915 – 1l.60 multicoloured . . . 2·50 90
DESIGNS: 15q. "Rruge te Bardha"; 25q. "Rrugicat qe Kerkonin Diell"; 80q. "Ne Fillim te Veres"; 1l.20, "Lulekuqet Mbi Mure"; 1l.60, "Zonja nga Qyteti".

392 Rejoicing Crowd and Independence Memorial, Tirana

394 Pan Flute

393 "Farm Workers"

1977. 65th Anniv of Independence. Multicoloured.
1916 15q. Type **392** 15 15
1917 25q. Independence leaders marching in Tirana . . . 25 15
1918 1l.65 Albanians dancing under national flag . . . 1·25 45

1977. Paintings by V. Mio. Multicoloured.
1919 5q. Type **393** 10 10
1920 10q. "Landscape in the Snow" 10 10
1921 15q. "Sheep under a Walnut Tree, Springtime" 15 10
1922 25q. "Street in Korce" . . . 25 10
1923 80q. "Riders in the Mountains" 65 20
1924 1l. "Boats by the Seashore" 85 25
1925 1l.75 "Tractors Ploughing" 1·10 30
MS1926 67 × 102 mm. 2l.05 "Self-portrait" . . . . 4·00 2·50

1978. Folk Music Instruments.
1927 **394** 15q. red, black and green 30 15
1928 – 25q. yellow, black & vio 60 25
1929 – 80q. red, black and blue 1·50 40
1930 – 1l.20 yellow, blk & blue 3·00 60
1931 – 1l.70 lilac, black & grn 5·00 1·25
DESIGNS: 25q. Single-string goat's head fiddle; 80q. Trumpet; 1l.20, Drum; 1l.70, Bagpipes.

1978. National Costume Dances (2nd series). As T **389**. Multicoloured.
1932 5q. Girl dancers with scarves 10 10
1933 25q. Male dancers 20 15
1934 80q. Kneeling dancers . . . 40 20
1935 1l. Female dancers 70 25
1936 2l.30 Male dancers with linked arms . . . . . . 1·75 50

395 "Tractor Drivers" (D. Trebicka)

1978. Paintings of the Working Class. Mult.
1937 25q. Type **395** 15 10
1938 80q. "Steeplejack" (S. Kristo) 30 20
1939 85q. "A Point in the Discussion" (S. Milori) . . 35 20
1940 90q. "Oil Rig Crew" (A. Cini) (vert) 45 20
1941 1l.60 "Metal Workers" (R. Karanxha) 75 30
MS1942 73 × 99 mm. 2l.20 "The Political Discussion" (S. Sholla) 4·00 3·00

396 Boy and Girl

1978. International Children's Day. Multicoloured.
1943 5q. Type **396** 10 10
1944 10q. Boy and girl with pickaxe and rifle 15 10
1945 25q. Children dancing . . . 25 20
1946 1l.80 Classroom scene . . . 2·00 45

397 Woman with Pickaxe and Rifle

1978. 8th Women's Union Congress.
1947 **397** 25q. red and gold . . . 30 10
1948 – 1l.95 red and gold . . . 2·50 75
DESIGN: 1l.95, Peasant, Militia Guard and industrial installation.

398 Battle of Mostar Bridge **399** Guerillas and Flag

1978. Centenary of the League of Prizren.
1949 **398** 10q. multicoloured . . . 15 10
1950 – 25q. multicoloured . . . 20 15
1951 – 80q. multicoloured . . . 45 20
1952 – 1l.20 blue, black & vio 75 30
1953 – 1l.65 multicoloured . . . 1·00 40
1954 – 2l.60 lt grn, blk & grn 1·60 60
MS1955 75 × 69 mm. 2l.20 multicoloured . . . . 4·00 2·50
DESIGNS: 25q. Spirit of Skanderbeg; 80q. Albanians marching under national flag; 1l.20, Riflemen; 1l.65, Abdyl Frasheri (founder); 2l.20, League building, crossed rifles, pens and paper; 2l.60, League Headquarters, Prizren.

1978. 35th Anniv of People's Army.
1956 5q. Type **399** 35 15
1957 25q. Men of armed forces (horiz) 75 30
1958 1l.90 Men of armed forces, civil guards and Young Pioneers . . . . 4·00 1·50

1978. International Fair, Riccione. No. 1832 surch **3.30L. RICCIONE 78 26.8.78.**
1959 3l.30 on 25q. multicoloured 10·00 3·25

401 Man with Target Rifle **402** Kerchief Dance

1978. 32nd National Shooting Championships.
1960 **401** 25q. black and yellow . . 20 15
1961 – 80q. black and orange 40 20
1962 – 95q. black and red . . . 50 25
1963 – 2l.40 black and red . . . 1·75 50
DESIGNS—VERT: 80q. Woman with machine carbine; 2l.40, Pistol shooting. HORIZ: 95q. Shooting from prone position.

1978. National Folklore Festival, Gjirokaster. Mult.
1964 10q. Type **402** 10 10
1965 15q. Musicians 15 10
1966 25q. Fiddle player 20 15
1967 80q. Singers 45 20
1968 1l.20 Sabre dance 80 25
1969 1l.90 Girl dancers . . . . . 1·40 35

403 Enver Hoxha (after V. Kilica) **404** Woman with Wheatsheaf

1978. Enver Hoxha's 70th Birthday.
1970 **403** 80q. multicoloured . . . 65 20
1971 1l.20 multicoloured . . . 90 25
1972 2l.40 multicoloured . . . 1·40 65
MS1973 68 × 88 mm. **403** 2l.20 multicoloured . . . . 4·00 3·00

1978. Agriculture and Stock Raising. Multicoloured.
1974 15q. Type **404** 30 20
1975 25q. Woman with boxes of fruit 40 30
1976 80q. Shepherd and flock . . 1·25 60
1977 2l.60 Dairymaid and cattle 4·00 2·00

405 Pupils entering School **406** Dora D'Istria

1978.
1978 **405** 5q. brown, lt brn & gold 15 10
1979 – 10q. blue, lt bl & gold 20 10
1980 – 15q. violet, lilac and gold 30 15
1981 – 20q. brown, drab & gold 45 20
1982 – 25q. red, pink and gold 55 25
1983 – 60q. green, lt grn & gold 1·75 45
1984 – 80q. blue, lt blue & gold 2·50 55
1985 – 1l.20 magenta, mauve and gold . . . . . . 3·50 90
1986 – 1l.60 blue, lt blue & gold 12·00 1·40
1987 – 2l.40 grn, lt grn & gold 6·00 2·10
1988 – 3l. blue, lt blue & gold 7·50 3·75
DESIGNS: 10q. Telephone, letters, telegraph wires and switchboard operators; 15q. Pouring molten iron; 20q. Dancers, musical instruments, book and artist's materials; 25q. Newspapers, radio, television and broadcasting tower; 60q. Assistant in clothes shop; 80q. Militiamen and women, tanks, ships, aircraft and radar equipment; 1l.20, Industrial complex and symbols of industry; 1l.60, Train and truck; 2l.40, Workers hoeing fields, cattle and girl holding wheat sheaf; 3l. Microscope and nurse holding up baby.

1979. 150th Birth Anniv of Dora D'Istria (pioneer of women's rights).
1989 **406** 80q. green and black . . 85 20
1990 – 1l.10 grey and black . . 1·25 1·00
DESIGN: 1l.10, Full-face portrait.

1979. National Costume Dances (3rd series). As T **389**. Multicoloured.
1991 15q. Girl dancers with scarves 15 10
1992 25q. Male dancers 20 10
1993 80q. Girl dancers with scarves (different) 50 25
1994 1l.20 Male dancers with pistols 80 40
1995 1l.40 Female dancers with linked arms . . . . . . 1·25 45

407 Stone-built Galleried House **408** Aleksander Moissi

1979. Traditional Albanian Houses (1st series). Multicoloured.
1996 15q. Type **407** 15 10
1997 25q. Tower house (vert) . . 20 10
1998 80q. House with wooden galleries 85 25
1999 1l.20 Galleried tower house (vert) . . . . 1·25 40
2000 1l.40 Three-storied fortified house (vert) . . . . . . 1·75 65
MS2001 62 × 75 mm. 1l.90 Fortified tower house . . . . 4·00 3·00
See also Nos. 2116/19.

1979. Birth Centenary of Aleksander Moissi (actor).
2002 **408** 80q. green, black & gold 65 20
2003 – 1l.10 brown, blk & gold 1·00 25
DESIGN: 1l.10, Aleksander Moissi (different).

409 Vasil Shanto

1979. Anti-fascist Heroes (1st series). Multicoloured.
2004 15q. Type **409** 25 10
2005 25q. Qemal Stafa 30 15
2006 60q. Type **409** 80 20
2007 90q. As 25q. . . . . 1·25 60
See also Nos. 2052/5, 2090/3, 2126/9, 2167/70, 2221/4, 2274/7 and 2313/5.

410 Soldier, Crowd and Coat of Arms

1979. 35th Anniv of Permet Congress. Mult.
2008 25q. Soldier, factories and wheat 40 20
2009 1l.65 Type **410** . . . . . . 2·00 1·00

411 Albanian Flag

1979. 5th Albanian Democratic Front Congress.
2010 **411** 25q. multicoloured . . . 40 20
2011 1l.65 multicoloured . . . 2·00 1·00

412 "Ne Stervitje" (Arben Basha)

1979. Paintings. Multicoloured.
2012 15q. Type **412** 10 10
2013 25q. "Shtigje Lufte" (Ismail Lulani) 20 10
2014 80q. "Agim me Fitore" (Myrteza Fushekati) . . . 75 25
2015 1l.20 "Gjithe Populli ushtare" (Muhamet Deliu) 1·10 35
2016 1l.40 "Zjarret Ndezur Mbajme" (Jorgji Gjikopulli) . . . . 1·40 85
MS2017 78 × 103 mm. 1l.90 "Cajime Rrethime" (Fatmir Haxhiu) . . 4·00 3·00

413 Athletes round Party Flag **414** Founder-president

1979. 35th Anniv of Liberation Spartakiad. Mult.
2018 15q. Type **413** 10 10
2019 25q. Shooting 20 10
2020 80q. Girl gymnast 65 25
2021 1l.10 Football 90 35
2022 1l.40 High jump . . . . . 1·10 35

1979. Centenary of Albanian Literary Society.
2023 – 25q. black, brown and gold 20 15
2024 **414** 80q. black, brown and gold 45 20
2025 – 1l.20 black, blue & gold 70 30
2026 – 1l.55 black, vio & gold 95 40
MS2027 78 × 66 mm. 1l.90 black, buff and gold . . . . 3·00 2·50
DESIGNS: 25q. Foundation document and seal of 1880; 1l.20, Headquarters building, 1979; 1l.55, Headquarters building, 1879; 1l.90, Four founder members, book and quill.

415 Congress Building **417** Joseph Stalin

416 Workers and Industrial Complex

1979. 35th Anniv of Berat Congress. Multicoloured.
2028 25q. Arms and congress document 80 50
2029 1l.65 Type **415** . . . . . . 3·00 2·00

1979. 35th Anniv of Liberation. Multicoloured.
2030 25q. Type **416** 20 10
2031 80q. Wheat and hand grasping hammer and pickaxe 45 25
2032 1l.20 Open book, star and musical instrument . . . 60 30
2033 1l.55 Open book, compasses and gear wheel . . . . 1·00 45

1979. Birth Centenary of Joseph Stalin.
2034 **417** 80q. blue and red . . . 40 25
2035 – 1l.10 blue and red . . . 85 40
DESIGN: 1l.10, Stalin and Enver Hoxha.

418 Fireplace and Pottery, Korce

1980. Interiors (1st series). Multicoloured.
2036 25q. Type **418** 20 20
2037 80q. Carved bed alcove and weapons, Shkoder 50 40
2038 1l.20 Cooking hearth and carved chair, Mirdite . . 1·10 85
2039 1l.35 Turkish-style chimney, dagger and embroidered jacket, Gjirokaster . . . . 1·40 90
See also Nos. 2075/8.

419 Lacework

1980. Handicrafts. Multicoloured.
2040 25q. Pipe and flask 20 20
2041 80q. Leather handbags . . . 55 35
2042 1l.20 Carved eagle and embroidered rug 75 60
2043 1l.35 Type **419** 95 65

420 Aleksander Xhuvani

1980. Birth Centenary of Dr. Aleksander Xhuvani.
2044 **420** 80q. blue, grey and black 1·00 50
2045 1l. brown, grey and black . . . . 1·50 1·00

421 Insurrectionists

1980. 70th Anniv of Kosovo Insurrection.
2046 **421** 80q. black and red . . . 1·00 50
2047 – 1l. black and red . . . . 1·50 1·00
DESIGN: 1l. Battle scene.

422 "Soldiers and Workers helping Stricken Population" (D. Jukniu and L. Lulani)

1980. 1979 Earthquake Relief.
2048 **422** 80q. multicoloured . . . 1·00 50
2049 1l. multicoloured . . . . 1·50 1·00

423 Lenin

1980. 110th Birth Anniv of Lenin.
2050 **423** 80q. grey, red and pink 1·00 50
2051 1l. multicoloured . . . . 1·50 1·00

424 Misto Mame and Ali Demi

1980. Anti-fascist Heroes (2nd series). Mult.
2052 25q. Type **424** 25 10
2053 80q. Sadik Staveleci, Vojo Kushi and Xhoxhi Martini 60 30
2054 1l.20 Bule Naipi and Persefoni Kokedhima . . 90 60
2055 1l.35 Ndoc Deda, Hydajet Lezha, Naim Gjylbegu, Ndoc Mazi and Ahmet Haxhia . . . . 1·00 70

425 "Mirela"

1980. Children's Tales. Multicoloured.
2056 15q. Type **425** 10 10
2057 25q. "Shkarravina" 20 15
2058 80q. "Ariu Artist" 45 40
2059 2l.40 "Pika e Ujit" . . . . 2·25 1·40

426 "The Enver Hoxha Tractor Combine" (S. Shijaku and M. Fushekati)

1980. Paintings from Gallery of Figurative Arts, Tirana. Multicoloured.
2060 25q. Type **426** 20 15
2061 80q. "The Welder" (Harilla Dhima) 50 35
2062 1l.20 "Steel Erector (Petro Kokushta) 70 65
2063 1l.35 "Harvest Festival" (Pandeli Lena) 80 75
MS2064 65 × 82 mm. 1l.80 "Communists" (Vilson Kilica) (48 × 71 mm) . . . . 4·00 4·00

427 Decorated Door (Pergamen miniature)

1980. Art of the Middle Ages. Each black and gold.
2065 25q. Type **427** 15 10
2066 80q. Bird (relief) 45 25
2067 1l.20 Crowned lion (relief) 75 65
2068 1l.35 Pheasant (relief) . . . 80 75

428 Divjaka

1980. National Parks. Multicoloured.
2069 80q. Type **428** 45 30
2070 1l.20 Lura . . . . 1·00 75
2071 1l.60 Thethi . . . . 1·75 1·00
MS2072 89 × 90 mm. 1l.80 Llogara (77 × 80 mm) . . . . 4·00 4·00

429 Flag, Arms and rejoicing Albanians

1981. 35th Anniv of Albanian People's Republic. Multicoloured.
2073 80q. Type **429** 75 30
2074 1l. Crowd and flags outside People's Party headquarters 75 45

1981. Interiors (2nd series). Multicoloured.
2075 25q. As T **418** 20 15
2076 80q. Sleeping mats and spirit keg, Labara 45 30
2077 1l.20 Fireplace and covered dish mat . . . . 1·00 50
2078 1l.35 Interior and embroidered jacket, Dibres . . . . 1·25 65

430 Wooden Cot

1981. Folk Art. Multicoloured.
2079 25q. Type **430** 20 15
2080 80q. Bucket and flask . . . 60 30
2081 1l.20 Embroidered slippers 70 40
2082 1l.35 Jugs 80 85

431 Footballers

1981. World Cup Football Championship Eliminating Rounds. Multicoloured.
2083 25q. Type **431** . . . . . . 1·25 60
2084 80q. Tackle . . . . 3·75 1·75
2085 1l.20 Player kicking ball . . 5·25 2·25
2086 1l.35 Goalkeeper saving goal 6·25 2·75

432 Rifleman

433 Acrobats

1981. Cent of Battle of Shtimje. Each purple & red.
2087 80q. Type **432** 65 35
2088 1l. Albanian with sabre . . 80 50
MS2089 84 × 68 mm. 1l.80 Albanian with pistol . . . . 2·50 2·50

1981. Anti-fascist Heroes (3rd series). As T **424**. Multicoloured.
2090 25q. Perlat Rexhepi and Branko Kadia 20 15
2091 80q. Xheladin Beqiri and Hajdah Dushi 50 35
2092 1l.20 Koci Bako, Vasil Laci and Mujo Ulqinaku . . . 85 55
2093 1l.35 Mine Peza and Zoja Cure 95 70

1981. Children's Circus.
2094 – 15q. black, green & stone 15 10
2095 – 25q. black, blue and grey 20 15
2096 **433** 80q. black, mve & pink 45 35
2097 – 2l.40 black, orge & yell 1·60 1·40
DESIGNS: 15q. Monocyclists. 25q. Human pyramid; 2l.40, Acrobats spinning from marquee pole.

434 "Rallying to the Flag, December 1911" (A. Zajmi)

1981. Paintings. Multicoloured.
2098 25q. "Allies" (Sh. Hysa) (horiz) 20 15
2099 80q. "Azem Galica breaking the Ring of Turks" (A. Buza) (horiz) 50 30
2100 1l.20 Type **434** 70 45
2101 1l.35 "My Flag is my Heart" (L. Cefa) . . . . 1·10 90
MS2102 81 × 109 mm. 1l.80 "Unite under the Flag" (N. Vasia) (55 × 79 mm) . . . . 3·00 3·00

435 Weightlifting

1981. Albanian Participation in Inter Sports. Mult.
2103 25q. Rifle shooting 15 10
2104 80q. Type **435** 45 30
2105 1l.20 Volleyball 65 45
2106 1l.35 Football . . . . . . 1·00 70

436 Flag and Hands holding Pickaxe and Rifle

437 Industrial and Agricultural Symbols

1981. 8th Workers' Party Congress.
2107 **436** 80q. red, brown & black 55 35
2108 – 1l. red and black 70 50
DESIGN: 1l. Party flag, hammer and sickle.

1981. 40th Anniv of Workers' Party. Mult.
2109 80q. Type **437** . . . . . . 2·00 45
2110 2l.80 Albanian flag and hand holding pickaxe and rifle . . . . 2·00 1·25
MS2111 79 × 98 mm. 1l.80 Enver Hoxha and book (50 × 68 mm) 3·50 2·50

438 Pickaxe, Rifle and Young Communists Flag

439 F. S. Noli

1981. 40th Anniv of Young Communists' Union. Multicoloured.
2112 80q. Type **438** . . . . . . 1·25 40
2113 1l. Workers' Party flag and Young Communists emblem . . . . 2·00 85

1981. Birth Centenary of F. S. Noli (author).
2114 **439** 80q. green and gold . . 75 35
2115 1l.10 brown and gold . . 90 45

1982. Traditional Albanian Houses (2nd series). As T **407**, but vert. Multicoloured.
2116 25q. House in Bulqize . . . 25 15
2117 80q. House in Kosovo . . . 80 50
2118 1l.20 House in Bicaj . . . . 1·10 75
2119 1l.55 House in Mat . . . . 1·50 1·00

440 Map, Globe and Bacillus

1982. Centenary of Discovery of Tubercle Bacillus.
2120 **440** 80q. multicoloured . . . 1·75 80
2121 – 1l.10 brown & dp brown 3·00 1·50
DESIGN: 1l.10, Robert Koch (discoverer), microscope and bacillus.

441 "Prizren Castle" (G. Madhi)

1982. Paintings of Kosovo. Multicoloured.
2122 25q. Type **441** 25 20
2123 80q. "House of the Albanian League, Prizren" (K. Buza) (horiz) 75 60
2124 1l.20 "Mountain Gorge, Rogove" (K. Buza) . . . 1·25 75
2125 1l.55 "Street of the Hadhji, Zekes" (G. Madhi) . . . 1·75 1·00

1982. Anti-fascist Heroes (4th series). As T **424**. Multicoloured.
2126 25q. Hibe Palikuqi and Liri Gero 20 15
2127 80q. Mihal Duri and Kojo Karafili 60 40
2128 1l.20 Fato Dudumi, Margarita Tutulani and Shejnaze Juka 80 50
2129 1l.55 Memo Meto and Gjok Doci . . . . 1·10 75

442 Factories and Workers

1982. 9th Trade Unions Congress. Multicoloured.
2130 80q. Type **442** . . . . . . 1·50 75
2131 1l.10 Congress emblem . . . 2·00 1·00

443 Ship in Harbour

1982. Children's Paintings. Multicoloured.
2132 15q. Type **443** 25 15
2133 80q. Forest camp 75 45
2134 1l.20 House 90 70
2135 1l.65 House and garden . . 1·50 80

444 "Village Festival" (Danish Jukniu)

1982. Paintings from Gallery of Figurative Arts, Tirana. Multicoloured.
2136 25q. Type **444** 25 15
2137 80q. "The Hydroelectric Station Builders" (Ali Miruku) 60 40
2138 1l.20 "Steel Workers" (Clirim Ceka) . . . . . 1·00 60
2139 1l.55 "Oil Drillers" (Pandeli Lena) . . . . 1·25 85
MS2140 75 × 90 mm. 1l.90 "First Tapping of the Furnace" (Jorgji Gjikopulli) . . . . 3·50 2·50

445 "Voice of the People" (party newspaper)

447 Congress Emblem

446 Heroes of Peza Monument

1982. 40th Anniv of Popular Press. Multicoloured.
2141 80q. Type **445** . . . . . . 65·00 65·00
2142 1l.10 Hand duplicator producing first edition of "Voice of the People" . . 65·00 65·00

1982. 40th Anniv of Democratic Front. Mult.
2143 80q. Type **446** . . . . . . 2·50 1·50
2144 1l.10 Peza Conference building and marchers with flag . . . . 3·75 2·00

1982. 8th Young Communists' Union Congress.
2145 **447** 80q. multicoloured . . . 3·00 1·50
2146 1l.10 multicoloured . . . 4·50 2·25

448 Tapestry

1982. Handicrafts. Multicoloured.
2147 25q. Type **448** 25 15
2148 80q. Bags (vert) 60 40
2149 1l.20 Butter churns 85 55
2150 1l.55 Jug (vert) . . . . . . 1·25 1·10

449 Freedom Fighters

1982. 70th Anniv of Independence.
2151 **449** 20q. deep red, red & blk 20 15
2152 – 1l.20 black, grn & red 85 60
2153 – 2l.40 brown, buff and red . . . . 1·90 1·50
MS2154 90 × 89 mm. 1l.90 multicoloured . . . . 4·00 3·00
DESIGNS: 20q. Ismail Qemali (patriot) and crowd around building; 2l.40, Six freedom fighters. (58 × 55 mm) 1l.90, Independence Monument, Tirana.

450 Dhermi

1982. Coastal Views. Multicoloured.
2155 25q. Type **450** 20 15
2156 80q. Sarande 55 35
2157 1l.20 Ksamil 85 55
2158 1l.55 Lukove . . . . 1·10 1·00

451 Male Dancers

1983. Folk Dance Assemblies Abroad. Mult.
2159 25q. Type **451** 15 10
2160 80q. Male dancers and drummer 50 30
2161 1l.20 Musicians 70 40
2162 1l.55 Group of female dancers . . . . 1·00 90

452 Karl Marx

453 Electricity Generation

1983. Death Centenary of Karl Marx.
2163 **452** 80q. multicoloured . . . 1·00 50
2164 1l.10 multicoloured . . . 1·25 60

1983. Energy Development.
2165 **453** 80q. blue and orange . . 55 35
2166 – 1l.10 mauve and green 90 55
DESIGN: 1l.10, Gas and oil production.

1983. Anti-fascist Heroes (5th series). As T **424**. Multicoloured.
2167 25q. Asim Zeneli and Nazmi Rushiti 20 15
2168 80q. Shyqyri Ishmi, Shyqyri Alimerko and Myzafer Asqeriu 55 35
2169 1l.20 Qybra Sokoli, Qeriba Derri and Ylbere Bilibashi 90 55
2170 1l.55 Themo Vasi and Abaz Shehu . . . . 1·25 75

454 Congress Emblem

456 Soldier and Militia

455 Cycling

1983. 9th Women's Union Congress.
2171 **454** 80q. multicoloured . . . 60 50
2172 1l.10 multicoloured . . . 70 60

1983. Sport and Leisure. Multicoloured.
2173 25q. Type **455** 25 15
2174 80q. Chess . . . . 1·00 50
2175 1l.20 Gymnastics . . . . . 1·25 70
2176 1l.55 Wrestling . . . . . . 1·40 80

1983. 40th Anniv of People's Army.
2177 **456** 20q. gold and red . . . 20 15
2178 – 1l.20 gold and red . . . 85 50
2179 – 2l.40 gold and brown . . 1·75 1·40
DESIGNS: 1l.20, Soldier; 2l.40 Factory guard.

457 "Sunny Day" (Myrteza Fushekati)

1983. Paintings from Gallery of Figurative Arts, Tirana. Multicoloured.
2180 25q. Type **457** 20 15
2181 80q. "Morning Gossip" (Niko Progri) 55 40
2182 1l.20 "29th November, 1944" (Harilla Dhimo) . . 85 50
2183 1l.55 "Demolition" (Pandi Mele) . . . . 1·10 70
MS2184 111 × 74 mm. 1l.90 "Partisan Assault" (Sali Shijaku and Myrteza Fushekati) (99 × 59 mm) . . . . 7·00 6·00

1983. National Folklore Festival, Gjirokaster. As T **402**. Multicoloured.
2185 25q. Sword dance 25 15
2186 80q. Kerchief dance 75 45
2187 1l.20 Musicians . . . . . . 1·10 70
2188 1l.55 Women dancers with garlands . . . . 1·25 85

458 Enver Hoxha

1983. 75th Birthday of Enver Hoxha.
2189 **458** 80q. multicoloured . . . 45 35
2190 1l.20 multicoloured . . . 75 50
2191 1l.80 multicoloured . . . 1·40 85
MS2192 77 × 98 mm. 1l.90 multicoloured (as T **458** but with inscriptions differently arranged) 3·00 2·50

459 W.C.Y. Emblem and Globe

1983. World Communications Year.
2193 **459** 60q. multicoloured . . . 40 25
2194 1l.20 blue, orange & blk 65 45

460 "Combine to Triumph" (J. Keraj)

1983. Skanderbeg Epoch in Art. Multicoloured.
2195 25q. Type **460** 20 15
2196 80q. "The Heroic Resistance at Krujes" (N. Bakalli) . . 60 35
2197 1l.20 "United we are Unconquerable by our Enemies" (N. Progri) . . 90 55
2198 1l.55 "Assembly at Lezhe" (B. Ahmeti) . . . . . 1·25 70
MS2199 77 × 90 mm. 1l.90 "Victory over the Turks" (G. Madhi) . . 4·00 3·00

461 Amphitheatre, Butrint (Buthrotum)

1983. Graeco-Roman Remains in Illyria. Mult.
2200 80q. Type **461** . . . . . . 1·00 75
2201 1l.20 Colonnade, Apoloni Cesma (Apollonium) . . . 1·50 90
2202 1l.80 Vaulted gallery of amphitheatre, Dyrrah (Epidamnus) . . . . . . 1·90 1·25

462 Man's Head from Apoloni

463 Clock Tower, Gjirokaster

1984. Archaeological Discoveries (1st series). Mult.
2203 15q. Type **462** 20 15
2204 25q. Tombstone from Korce 25 15
2205 80q. Woman's head from Apoloni 55 35
2206 1l.10 Child's head from Tren 85 65
2207 1l.20 Man's head from Dyrrah 90 70
2208 2l.20 Bronze statuette of Eros from Dyrrah . . . . 1·75 1·25
See also Nos. 2258/61.

1984. Clock Towers.
2209 **463** 15q. purple 20 15
2210 – 25q. brown 25 15
2211 – 80q. violet 55 35
2212 – 1l.10 red 85 65
2213 – 1l.20 green 90 70
2214 – 2l.20 brown . . . . . . 1·75 1·25
DESIGNS: 25q. Kavaje; 80q. Elbasan; 1l.10, Tirana; 1l.20, Peqin; 2l.20, Kruje.

464 Student with Microscope

1984. 40th Anniv of Liberation (1st issue). Mult.
2215 15q. Type **464** 20 15
2216 25q. Soldier with flag . . . 25 15
2217 80q. Schoolchildren 65 35
2218 1l.10 Soldier, ships, airplanes and weapons . . 95 65
2219 1l.20 Workers with flag . . 1·10 75
2220 2l.20 Armed guards on patrol . . . . 4·00 1·75
See also Nos. 2255/6.

1984. Anti-fascist Heroes (6th series). As T **424**. Multicoloured.
2221 15q. Manush Alimani, Mustafa Matohiti and Kastriot Muco 15 10
2222 25q. Zaho Koka, Reshit Collaku and Maliq Muco 20 15
2223 1l.20 Lefter Talo, Tom Kola and Fuat Babani . . . 85 55
2224 2l.20 Myslysm Shyri, Dervish Hekali and Skender Caci . . . . . . 1·75 1·25

465 Enver Hoxha

1984. 40th Anniv of Permet Congress.
2225 **465** 80q. brown, orge & red 1·50 80
2226 – 1l.10 black, yell & lilac 1·75 1·25
DESIGN: 1l.10, Resistance fighter (detail of monument).

466 Children reading Comic

467 Football in Goal

1984. Children. Multicoloured.
2227 15q. Type **466** 20 15
2228 25q. Children with toys . . 25 20
2229 60q. Children gardening and rainbow 55 35
2230 2l.80 Children flying kite bearing Albanian arms . . 2·25 1·75

1984. European Football Championship Finals. Multicoloured.
2231 15q. Type **467** 40 20
2232 25q. Referee and football . . 60 30
2233 1l.20 Football and map of Europe . . . . 1·25 60
2234 2l.20 Football and pitch . . 3·50 1·75

468 "Freedom is Here" (Myrteza Fushekati)

1984. Paintings from Gallery of Figurative Arts, Tirana. Multicoloured.
2235 15q. Type **468** 20 15
2236 25q. "Morning" (Zamir Mati) (vert) 25 15
2237 80q. "My Darling" (Agim Zajmi) (vert) 70 40
2238 2l.60 "For the Partisans" (Arben Basha) . . . . . 2·00 1·75
MS2239 80 × 93 mm. 1l.90 "Albania" (Zamir Mati) . . . 7·00 5·00

469 Mulberry

471 Truck driving through Forest

470 Sabre Dance

1984. Flowers. Multicoloured.
2240 15q. Type **469** 25 15
2241 25q. Plantain 65 15
2242 1l.20 Hypericum . . . . . 3·25 1·10
2243 2l.20 Edelweiss . . . . . 6·25 2·50

1984. "Ausipex 84" International Stamp Exhibition, Melbourne. Sheet 72 × 88 mm.
MS2244 **470** 1l.90 multicoloured 3·00 3·00

1984. Forestry. Multicoloured.
2245 15q. Type **471** 40 25
2246 25q. Transporting logs on overhead cable 75 40
2247 1l.20 Sawmill in forest . . . 2·25 75
2248 2l.20 Lumberjack sawing down trees . . . . 3·00 1·60

472 Gjirokaster

473 Football

1984. "Eurphila '84" Int Stamp Exn, Rome.
2249 **472** 1l.20 multicoloured . . . 1·10 90

1984. 5th National Spartakiad. Multicoloured.
2250 15q. Type **473** 20 15
2251 25q. Running 25 15
2252 80q. Weightlifting 65 35
2253 2l.20 Pistol shooting . . . . 1·75 1·40
MS2254 70 × 90 mm. 1l.90 Opening ceremony . . . . 3·00 2·50

474 Agriculture and Industry

1984. 40th Anniv of Liberation (2nd issue). Mult.
2255 80q. Type **474** 80 40
2256 1l.10 Soldiers and flag . . . 1·25 60
MS2257 68 × 89 mm. 1l.90 Enver Hoxha making liberation speech 4·00 3·00

1985. Archaeological Discoveries (2nd series). As T **462**, showing Illyrian finds. Multicoloured.
2258 15q. Pot 25 15
2259 80q. Terracotta head of woman 65 35
2260 1l.20 Terracotta bust of Aphrodite . . . . 1·00 65
2261 1l.70 Bronze statuette of Nike . . . . 1·75 1·25

476 Kapo (bust)

477 Running

1985. 70th Birthday of Hysni Kapo (politician).
2262 **476** 90q. black and red . . . 90 60
2263 1l.10 black and blue . . 1·25 75

1985. "Olymphilex '85" Olympic Stamps Exhibition, Lausanne. Multicoloured.
2264 25q. Type **477** 25 15
2265 60q. Weightlifting 50 25
2266 1l.20 Football . . . . . . 1·10 65
2267 1l.50 Pistol shooting . . . . 1·60 1·10

478 Bach

479 Hoxha

1985. 300th Birth Anniv of Johann Sebastian Bach (composer).
2268 **478** 80q. orange, brn & blk 6·50 4·50
2269 – 1l.20 blue, dp blue & blk 7·50 5·50
DESIGN—1l.20, Bach's birthplace, Eisenach.

1985. Enver Hoxha Commemoration.
2270 **479** 80q. multicoloured . . . 1·00 80
MS2271 67 × 90 mm. **479** 1l.90 multicoloured . . . . 1·50 1·50

480 Frontier Guards

481 Scarf on Rifle Barrel

1985. 40th Anniv of Frontier Force. Multicoloured.
2272 25q. Type **480** 75 50
2273 80q. Frontier guard . . . . 1·75 1·00

1985. Anti-fascist Heroes (7th series). As T **424**. Multicoloured.
2274 25q. Mitro Xhani, Nimete Progonati and Kozma Nushi 40 25
2275 40q. Ajet Xhindoli, Mustafa Kacaci and Estref Caka 60 40
2276 60q. Celo Sinani, Llambro Andoni and Meleo Gosnishti 80 50
2277 1l.20 Thodhori Mastora, Fejzi Micoli and Hysen Cino . . . . 1·50 1·00

1985. 40th Anniv of V.E. (Victory in Europe) Day. Multicoloured.
2278 25q. Type **481** 75 50
2279 80q. Crumpled swastika and hand holding rifle butt . . 1·75 1·00

482 "Primary School" (Thoma Malo)

1985. Paintings from Gallery of Figurative Arts, Tirana. Multicoloured.
2280 25q. Type **482** 25 15
2281 80q. "Heroes and Mother" (Hysen Devolli) (vert) . . 90 35
2282 90q. "Mother writing" (Angjelin Dodmasej) (vert) 1·00 70
2283 1l.20 "Women off to Work" (Ksenofen Dilo) . . . . . 1·40 70
MS2284 74 × 88 mm. 1l.90 "Foundry Workers" (Mikel Gurashi) . . 4·00 3·00

483 Scoring a Goal

484 Oranges

1985. 10th World Basketball Championship, Spain.
2285 **483** 25q. blue and black . . 25 15
2286 – 80q. green and black . . 65 35
2287 – 1l.20 violet and black . . 1·00 70
2288 – 1l.60 red and black . . . 1·60 1·10
DESIGNS: 80q. Player running with ball; 1l.20, Defending goal; 1l.60, Defender capturing ball.

1985. Fruit Trees. Multicoloured.
2289 25q. Type **484** . . . . . . 1·50 55
2290 80q. Plums . . . . 2·25 80
2291 1l.20 Apples . . . . . . 3·25 1·50
2292 1l.60 Cherries . . . . . . 6·50 2·75

485 Kruja

1985. Architecture.
2293 **485** 25q. black and red . . . 25 15
2294 – 80q. black, grey and brown . . . . 1·25 35
2295 – 1l.20 black, brown & bl 1·75 65
2296 – 1l.60 black, brown & red 2·50 1·10
DESIGNS: 80q. Gjirokastra; 1l.20, Berat; 1l.60, Shkoder.

486 War Horse Dance

488 Dam across River Drin

487 State Arms

1985. National Folklore Festival. Dances.
2297 **486** 25q. brown, red & black 25 15
2298 – 80q. brown, red & black 65 35
2299 – 1l.20 brown, red & blk 1·00 65
2300 – 1l.60 brown, red & blk 1·60 1·10
MS2301 56 × 82 mm. 1l.90 multicoloured. Imperf . . . . 3·00 2·00
DESIGNS: 80q. Pillow dance; 1l.20, Ladies' kerchief dance; 1l.60, Men's one-legged pair dance; 1l.90, Fortress dance.

1986. 40th Anniv of Albanian People's Republic.
2302 **487** 25q. gold, red and black 60 40
2303 – 80q. multicoloured . . . 1·50 80
DESIGN: 80q. "Comrade Hoxha announcing the News to the People" (Vilson Kilica) and arms.

1986. Enver Hoxha Hydroelectric Power Station. Multicoloured.
2304 25q. Type **488** . . . . . . 2·50 1·00
2305 80q. Control building . . . 5·50 3·00

489 "Gymnospermium shqipetarum"

490 Maksim Gorki (writer)

1986. Flowers. Multicoloured.
2306 25q. Type **489** 60 40
2307 1l.20 "Leucojum valentinum" . . . . . . 3·00 1·50

1986. Anniversaries.
2308 **490** 25q. brown 25 15
2309 – 80q. violet . . . . . . 1·25 65
2310 – 1l.20 green . . . . . . 2·50 2·00
2311 – 2l.40 purple . . . . . . 4·25 2·75
MS2312 88 × 72 mm. 1l.90 violet, blue and yellow . . . . 4·75 3·00
DESIGNS: 25q. Type **490** (50th death anniv); 80q. Andre Ampere (physicist and mathematician, 150th death anniv); 1l.20, James Watt (inventor, 250th birth); 2l.40, Franz Liszt (composer, death cent). 88 × 72 mm. 1l.90, Heads of Gorki, Ampere, Watt and Liszt.

1986. Anti-fascist Heroes (8th series). As T **424**. Multicoloured.
2313 25q. Ramiz Aranitasi, Inajete Dumi and Laze Nuro Ferraj 80 60
2314 80q. Dine Kalenja, Kozma Naska, Met Hasa and Fahri Raalbani . . . . . 2·00 1·00
2315 1l.20 Hiqmet Buzi, Bajram Tusha, Mumin Selami and Hajredin Bylyshi . . . . 3·00 2·00

491 Trophy on Globe

1986. World Cup Football Championship, Mexico. Multicoloured.
2316 25q. Type **491** 30 20
2317 1l.20 Goalkeeper's hands and ball . . . . 1·25 1·00
MS2318 97 × 63 mm. 1l.90 Globe-football (40 × 32 mm) . . . . 3·00 2·50

492 Car Tyre within Ship's Wheel, Diesel Train and Traffic Lights

1986. 40th Anniv of Transport Workers' Day.
2319 **492** 1l.20 multicoloured . . . 4·25 1·25

493 Naim Frasheri (poet)

1986. Anniversaries. Multicoloured.
2320 30q. Type **493** (140th birth anniv) 50 15
2321 60q. Ndre Mjeda (poet, 120th birth anniv) . . . . 1·00 65
2322 90q. Petro Nini Luarasi (jounalist, 75th death anniv) . . . . 1·50 1·00
2323 1l. Andon Zaka Cajupi (poet, 120th birth anniv) 1·60 1·10
2324 1l.20 Millosh Gjergj Nikolla (Migjeni) (revolutionary writer, 75th birth anniv) 2·00 1·40
2325 2l.60 Urani Rumbo (women's education pioneer, 50th death anniv) 4·25 2·75

494 Congress Emblem

495 Party Stamp and Enver Hoxha's Signature

1986. 9th Workers' Party Congress, Tirana.
2326 **494** 30q. multicoloured . . . 5·75 4·25

1986. 45th Anniv of Workers' Party.
2327 **495** 30q. red, grey and gold 1·10 55
2328 – 1l.20 red, orange & gold 4·75 2·40
DESIGNS: 1l.20, Profiles of Marx, Engels, Lenin and Stalin and Tirana house where Party was founded.

496 "Mother Albania"

497 Marble Head of Aesculapius

1986.

2329	496	10q. blue	10	10
2330		20q. red	10	10
2331		30q. red	10	10
2332		50q. brown	20	15
2333		60q. green	25	15
2334		80q. red	30	20
2335		90q. blue	35	25
2336		1l.20 green	45	30
2337		1l.60 purple	60	40
2338		2l.20 green	85	55
2339		3l. brown	1·10	75
2340		6l. yellow	2·25	1·50

1987. Archaeological Discoveries. Multicoloured.

2341	30q. Type **497**	45	30
2342	80q. Terracotta figure of Aphrodite	1·10	75
2343	1l. Bronze figure of Pan	1·40	95
2344	1l.20 Limestone head of Jupiter	1·75	1·10

498 Monument and Centenary Emblem

499 Victor Hugo (writer, 185th birth anniv)

1987. Centenary of First Albanian School.

2345	**498**	30q. brown, lt brn & yell	30	20
2346	–	80q. multicoloured	80	55
2347	–	1l.20 multicoloured	1·25	85

DESIGNS: 80q. First school building; 1l.20, Woman soldier running, girl reading book and boy doing woodwork.

1987. Anniversaries.

2348	**499**	30q. vio, lavender & blk	30	20
2349	–	80q. brown, lt brn & blk	80	60
2350	–	90q. dp blue, blue & blk	90	65
2351	–	1l.30 dp grn, grn & brn	1·25	90

DESIGNS: 80q. Galileo Galilei (astronomer, 345th death); 90q. Charles Darwin (naturalist, 105th death); 1l.30. Miguel de Cervantes Saavedra (writer, 440th birth).

500 "Forsythia europaea"

501 Congress Emblem

1987. Flowers. Multicoloured.

2352	30q. Type **500**	30	20
2353	90q. "Moltkia doerfleri"	90	60
2354	2l.10 "Wulfenia baldacii"	2·10	1·40

1987. 10th Trade Unions Congress, Tirana.

2355	**501**	1l.20 dp red, red & gold	3·00	2·00

502 "The Bread of Industry" (Myrteza Fushekati)

1987. Paintings from Gallery of Figurative Arts, Tirana. Multicoloured.

2356	30q. Type **502**	25	20
2357	80q. "Partisan Gift" (Skender Kokobobo)	65	50
2358	1l. "Sowers" (Bujar Asllani) (horiz)	80	60
2359	1l.20 "At the Foundry" (Clirim Ceka) (horiz)	90	75

503 Throwing the Hammer

1987. World Light Athletics Championships, Rome. Multicoloured.

2360	30q. Type **503**	25	20
2361	90q. Running	75	55
2362	1l.10 Putting the shot	95	70
MS2363	85 × 59 mm. 1l.90 Runner, winners' podium and banner (64 × 24 mm)	1·50	1·50

504 Themistokli Germenji (revolutionary, 70th death)

1987. Anniversaries.

2364	**504**	30q. brown, red & black	35	25
2365	–	80q. red, scarlet & black	1·00	65
2366	–	90q. violet, red and black	1·10	75
2367	–	1l.30 green, red & black	1·60	1·10

DESIGNS: 80q. Bajram Curri (organizer of Albanian League, 125th birth); 90q. Aleks Stavre Drenova (poet, 40th death); 1l.30, Gjerasim Qiriazi (educational pioneer, 126th birth).

505 Emblem

506 National Flag

1987. 9th Young Communists' Union Congress, Tirana.

2368	**505**	1l.20 multicoloured	4·00	2·75

1987. 75th Anniv of Independence.

2369	**506**	1l.20 multicoloured	4·00	2·75

507 Post Office Emblem

508 Lord Byron (writer, bicentenary)

1987. 75th Anniv of Albanian Postal Administration. Multicoloured.

2370	90q. Type **507**	6·00	4·00
2371	1l.20 National emblem on bronze medallion	8·50	5·75

1988. Birth Anniversaries.

2372	**508**	30q. black and orange	2·75	2·25
2373	–	1l.20 black and mauve	10·50	8·50

DESIGN: 1l.20, Eugene Delacroix (painter, 190th anniv).

509 Oil Derrick, Tap, Houses and Wheat Ears

510 "Sideritis raeseri"

1988. 40th Anniv of W.H.O.

2374	**509**	90q. multicoloured	17·00	14·00
2375		1l.20 multicoloured	23·00	19·00

1988. Flowers. Multicoloured.

2376	30q. Type **510**	2·25	1·75
2377	90q. "Lunaria telekiana"	6·75	5·50
2378	2l.10 "Sanguisorba albanica"	16·00	13·00

511 Flag and Woman with Book

1988. 10th Women's Union Congress, Tirana.

2379	**511**	90q. black, red & orange	7·00	6·00

512 Footballers

513 Clasped Hands

1988. 8th European Football Championship, West Germany. Multicoloured.

2380	30q. Type **512**	65	50
2381	80q. Players jumping for ball	1·75	1·25
2382	1l.20 Tackling	2·50	1·90
MS2383	78 × 67 mm. 1l.90 Goalkeeper saving ball. Imperf	6·75	6·75

1988. 110th Anniv of League of Prizren. Mult.

2384	30q. Type **513**	6·50	6·50
2385	1l.20 League Headquarters, Prizren	27·00	27·00

514 Flag, Woman with Rifle and Soldier

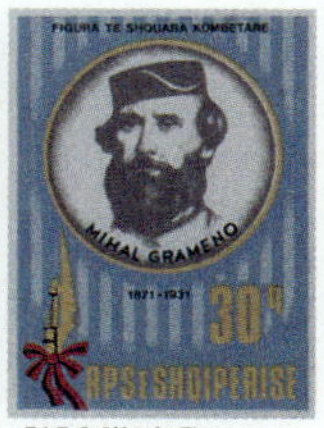

515 Mihal Grameno (writer)

1988. 45th Anniv of People's Army. Multicoloured.

2386	60q. Type **514**	15·00	15·00
2387	90q. Army monument, partisans and Labinot house	23·00	23·00

1988. Multicoloured.

2388	30q. Type **515**	5·50	5·50
2389	90q. Bajo Topulli (revolutionary)	16·00	16·00
2390	1l. Murat Toptani (sculptor and poet)	18·00	18·00
2391	1l.20 Jul Variboba (poet)	22·00	22·00

516 Migjeni

1988. 50th Death Anniv of Millosh Gjergj Nikolla (Migjeni) (writer).

2392	**516**	90q. silver and brown	6·75	6·00

517 "Dede Skurra"

518 Bride wearing Fezzes, Mirdita

1988. Ballads. Each black and grey.

2393	30q. Type **517**	5·00	5·00
2394	90q. "Young Omer"	15·00	15·00
2395	1l.20 "Gjergj Elez Alia"	19·00	19·00

1988. National Folklore Festival, Gjirokaster. Wedding Customs. Multicoloured.

2396	30q. Type **518**	9·00	9·00
2397	1l.20 Pan Dance, Gjirokaster	35·00	35·00

519 Hoxha

1988. 80th Birth Anniv of Enver Hoxha. Mult.

2398	90q. Type **519**	3·00	3·00
2399	1l.20 Enver Hoxha Museum (horiz)	4·00	4·00

520 Detail of Congress Document

1988. 80th Anniv of Monastir Language Congress. Multicoloured.

2400	60q. Type **520**	12·50	12·50
2401	90q. Alphabet book and Congress building	16·00	16·00

521 Steam Locomotive and Map showing 1947 Railway line

1989. Railway Locomotives. Multicoloured.

2402	30q. Type **521**	40	10
2403	90q. Polish steam locomotive and map of 1949 network	1·25	35
2404	1l.20 Diesel locomotive and 1978 network	1·60	45
2405	1l.80 Diesel locomotive and 1985 network	2·40	70
2406	2l.40 Czechoslovakian diesel-electric locomotive and 1988 network	3·25	90

522 Entrance to Two-storey Tomb

1989. Archaeological Discoveries in Illyria.

2407	**522**	30q. black, brown & grey	15	10
2408	–	90q. black and green	50	35
2409	–	2l.10 multicoloured	1·10	75

DESIGNS: 90q. Buckle showing battle scene; 2l.10, Earring depicting head.

523 Mother mourning Son

1989. "Kostandini and Doruntina" (folk tale). Mult.

2410	30q. Type **523**	15	10
2411	80q. Mother weeping over tomb and son rising from dead	45	30

2412 1l. Son and his sister on horseback 55 35
2413 1l.20 Mother and daughter reunited 65 45

524 "Aster albanicus"

525 Johann Strauss (composer, 90th death anniv)

1989. Flowers. Multicoloured.
2414 30q. Type **524** 15 10
2415 90q. "Orchis paparisti" . . 50 35
2416 2l.10 "Orchis albanica" . . 1·10 75

1989. Anniversaries. Each brown and gold.
2417 30q. Type **525** 15 10
2418 80q. Marie Curie (physicist, 55th death anniv) 45 30
2419 1l. Federico Garcia Lorca (writer, 53rd death anniv) 55 35
2420 1l.20 Albert Einstein (physicist, 110th birth anniv) 65 45

526 State Arms, Workers' Party Flag and Crowd

1989. 6th Albanian Democratic Front Congress, Tirana.
2421 **526** 1l.20 multicoloured . . . 5·00 4·00

527 Storming of the Bastille

1989. Bicentenary of French Revolution. Mult.
2422 90q. Type **527** 40 30
2423 1l.20 Monument 55 40

528 Galley

1989. Ships.
2424 **528** 30q. green and black . . 30 15
2425 – 80q. blue and black . . 75 35
2426 – 90q. blue and black . . 95 45
2427 – 1l.30 lilac and black . . 1·25 60
DESIGNS: 80q. Kogge; 90q. Schooner; 1l.30, "Tirana" (freighter).

529 Pjeter Bogdani (writer, 300th anniv)

530 Engels, Marx and Marchers

1989. Death Anniversaries. Multicoloured.
2428 30q. Type **529** 20 15
2429 80q. Gavril Dara (writer, centenary) 50 35
2430 90q. Thimi Mitko (writer, centenary (1990)) 60 40
2431 1l.30 Kole Idromeno (painter, 50th anniv) . . . 85 55

1989. 125th Anniv of "First International". Mult.
2432 90q. Type **530** 40 30
2433 1l.20 Factories, marchers and worker with pickaxe and rifle 55 40

531 Gymnastics

1989. 6th National Spartakiad.
2434 **531** 30q. black, orange & red 15 10
2435 – 80q. black, lt grn & grn 40 25
2436 – 1l. black, blue & dp blue 50 35
2437 – 1l.20 black, pur & red 55 35
DESIGNS: 80q. Football; 1l. Cycling; 1l.20, Running.

532 Soldier

533 Chamois

1989. 45th Anniv of Liberation. Multicoloured.
2438 30q. Type **532** 15 10
2439 80q. Date 35 25
2440 1l. State arms 45 30
2441 1l.20 Young couple 50 35

1990. Endangered Animals. The Chamois. Mult.
2442 10q. Type **533** 10 10
2443 30q. Mother and young . . 25 20
2444 80q. Chamois keeping lookout 65 50
2445 90q. Head of chamois . . . 70 55

534 Eagle Mask

1990. Masks. Multicoloured.
2446 30q. Type **534** 10 10
2447 90q. Sheep 35 25
2448 1l.20 Goat 50 35
2449 1l.80 Stork 70 45

535 Caesar's Mushroom

1990. Fungi. Multicoloured.
2450 30q. Type **535** 30 15
2451 90q. Parasol mushroom . . 85 40
2452 1l.20 Cep . . . . 1·10 50
2453 1l.80 "Clathrus cancelatus" 1·60 80

536 Engraving Die

1990. 150th Anniv of the Penny Black. Mult.
2454 90q. Type **536** 50 40
2455 1l.20 Mounted postal messenger 65 55
2456 1l.80 Mail coach passengers reading letters 95 80

537 Mascot and Flags

1990. World Cup Football Championship, Italy. Multicoloured.
2457 30q. Type **537** 15 10
2458 90q. Mascot running . . . 40 25
2459 1l.20 Mascot preparing to kick ball 55 35
MS2460 80 × 62 mm. 3l.30 Mascot as goalkeeper. Imperf . . . . 1·50 1·50

538 Young Van Gogh and Paintings

1990. Death Centenary of Vincent van Gogh (painter). Multicoloured.
2461 30q. Type **538** 15 10
2462 90q. Van Gogh and woman in field 40 25
2463 2l.10 Van Gogh in asylum 90 60
MS2464 88 × 73 mm. 2l.40 Van Gogh and "Wheatfield with Crows". Imperf . . . . 1·00 1·00

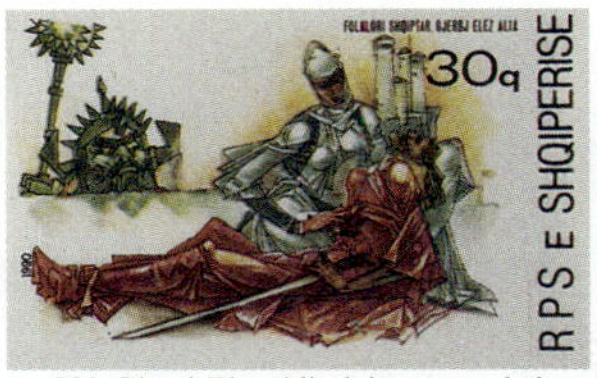

539 Gjergj Elez Alia lying wounded

1990. Gjergj Elez Alia (folk hero). Multicoloured.
2465 30q. Type **539** 15 10
2466 90q. Alia being helped onto horse 40 25
2467 1l.20 Alia fighting Bajloz . . 50 35
2468 1l.80 Alia on horseback and severed head of Bajloz . . 75 50

540 Mosque

541 Pirroja

1990. 2400th Anniv of Berat. Multicoloured.
2469 30q. Type **540** 10 10
2470 90q. Triadha's Church . . . 30 20
2471 1l.20 River 40 25
2472 1l.80 Onufri (artist) 60 40
2473 2l.40 Nikolla 80 55

1990. Illyrian Heroes. Each black.
2474 30q. Type **541** 10 10
2475 90q. Teuta 30 20
2476 1l.20 Bato 40 25
2477 1l.80 Bardhyli 65 45

542 School and "Globe" of Books

1990. International Literacy Year.
2478 **542** 90q. multicoloured . . . 30 20
2479 1l.20 multicoloured . . . 40 25

543 "Albanian Horsemen" (Eugene Delacroix)

1990. Albanians in Art. Multicoloured.
2480 30q. Type **543** 15 10
2481 1l.20 "Albanian Woman" (Camille Corot) 50 40
2482 1l.80 "Skanderbeg" (anon) 75 55

544 Boletini

545 Armorial Eagle

1991. 75th Death Anniv of Isa Boletini (revolutionary). Multicoloured.
2483 90q. Type **544** 20 15
2484 1l.20 Boletini and flag . . . 30 25

1991. 800th Anniv (1990) of Founding of Arberi State.
2485 **545** 90q. multicoloured . . . 20 15
2486 1l.20 multicoloured . . . 30 25

546 "Woman reading"

547 "Cistus albanicus"

1991. 150th Birth Anniv of Pierre Auguste Renoir (artist). Multicoloured.
2487 30q. Type **546** 15 10
2488 90q. "The Swing" 50 40
2489 1l.20 "The Boat Club" (horiz) 85 50
2490 1l.80 Still life (detail) (horiz) 95 70
MS2491 94 × 75 mm. 3l. "Portrait of Artist with Beard". Imperf . . 2·00 2·00

1991. Flowers. Multicoloured.
2492 30q. Type **547** 15 10
2493 90q. "Trifolium pilczii" . . 35 25
2494 1l.80 "Lilium albanicum" 75 55

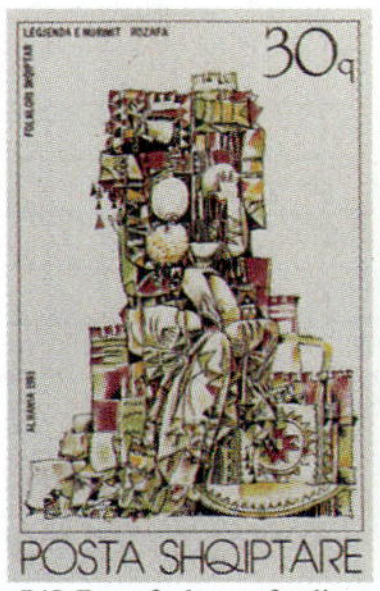

548 Rozafa breastfeeding Child

549 Mozart conducting

1991. Imprisonment of Rozafa (folk tale). Mult.
2495 30q. Type **548** 10 10
2496 90q. The three brothers talking to old man . . . 30 25
2497 1l.20 Building of walls around Rozafa 40 30
2498 1l.80 Figures symbolizing water flowing between stones 60 45

1991. Death Bicentenary of Wolfgang Amadeus Mozart (composer). Multicoloured.
2499 90q. Type **549** 30 25
2500 1l.20 Mozart and score . . 45 35
2501 1l.80 Mozart composing . . 65 50
MS2502 88 × 69 mm. 3l. Mozart medallion and score. Imperf . . 1·10 1·10

550 Vitus Bering

1992. Explorers. Multicoloured.

2503	30q. Type **550**	10	10
2504	90q. Christopher Columbus and his flagship "Santa Maria"	50	25
2505	1l.80 Ferdinand Magellan and his flagship "Vitoria"	90	50

551 Otto Lilienthal's Biplane Glider, 1896

1992. Aircraft.

2506	**551** 30q. black, red and blue	10	10
2507	– 80q. multicoloured . . .	25	20
2508	– 90q. multicoloured . . .	30	25
2509	– 1l.20 multicoloured . . .	40	30
2510	– 1l.80 multicoloured . . .	55	40
2511	– 2l.40 black, grey & mve	75	55

DESIGNS: 80q. Clement Ader's "Avion III", 1897; 90q. Wright Brothers' Type A, 1903; 1l.20, Concorde supersonic jetliner; 1l.80, Tupolev Tu-144 jetliner (wrongly inscr "114"); 2l.40, Dornier Do-31E (wrongly inscr "Dernier").

552 Ski Jumping

1992. Winter Olympic Games, Albertville. Mult.

2512	30q. Type **552**	10	10
2513	90q. Skiing	30	25
2514	1l.20 Ice skating (pairs) . .	40	30
2515	1l.80 Luge	60	45

553 "Europe" and Doves

1992. Admission of Albania to European Security and Co-operation Conference at Foreign Ministers' Meeting, Berlin. Multicoloured.

2516	90q. Type **553**	30	25
2517	1l.20 Members' flags and map of Europe	45	35

554 Envelopes and Emblem

1992. Admission of Albania to E.P.T. Conference. Multicoloured.

2518	90q. Type **554**	30	25
2519	1l.20 Emblem and tape reels	45	35

555 Everlasting Flame

1992. National Martyrs' Day. Multicoloured.

2520	90q. Type **555**	25	20
2521	4l.10 Poppies (horiz)	1·10	85

556 Pictograms

1992. European Football Championship, Sweden.

2522	**556** 30q. light green & green	10	10
2523	– 90q. red and blue . . .	35	25
2524	– 10l.80 ochre and brown	4·00	3·00
MS2525	90 × 69 mm. 5l. pink, ochre and green. Imperf	2·10	2·10

DESIGNS: 90q. to 5l., Different pictograms.

557 Lawn Tennis

1992. Olympic Games, Barcelona. Multicoloured.

2526	30q. Type **557**	10	10
2527	90q. Baseball	35	25
2528	1l.80 Table tennis	75	55
MS2529	89 × 69 mm. 5l. Torch bearer and running tracks. Imperf	2·10	2·10

558 Map and Doves

1992. European Unity.

2530	**558** 1l.20 multicoloured . . .	35	25

559 Native Pony

1992. Horses. Multicoloured.

2531	30q. Type **559**	10	10
2532	90q. Hungarian nonius . . .	25	20
2533	1l.20 Arab (vert)	35	25
2534	10l.60 Haflinger (vert) . . .	3·25	2·40

560 Map of Americas, Columbus and Ships

1992. Europa. 500th Anniv of Discovery of America by Columbus. Multicoloured.

2535	60q. Type **560**	60	20
2536	3l.20 Map of Americas and Columbus meeting Amerindians	1·10	1·85
MS2537	90 × 70 mm. 5l. Map of America and Columbus. Imperf	23·00	23·00

561 Mother Teresa and Child

562 Pope John Paul II

1992. Mother Teresa (Agnes Gonxhe Bojaxhi) (founder of Missionaries of Charity).

2538	**561** 40q. red	10	10
2539	60q. brown	10	10
2540	1l. violet	10	10
2541	1l.80 grey	10	10
2542	2l. red	15	10
2543	2l.40 green	15	10
2544	3l.20 blue	20	15
2545	5l. violet	25	20
2546	5l.60 purple	35	25
2547	7l.20 green	45	35
2548	10l. orange	55	40
2549	18l. orange	85	65
2550	20l. purple	30	25
2551	25l. green	1·00	75
2552	60l. green	85	65

1993. Papal Visit.

2555	**562** 16l. multicoloured . . .	95	70

1993. Nos. 2329/32 and 2335 surch **POSTA SHQIPTARE** and new value.

2556	**496** 3l. on 10q. blue	25	20
2557	6l.50 on 20q. red	50	35
2558	13l. on 30q. red	1·00	1·75
2559	20l. on 90q. blue	1·50	1·10
2560	30l. on 50q. brown . . .	2·25	1·75

564 Lef Nosi (first Postal Minister)

565 "Life Weighs Heavily on Man" (A. Zajmi)

1993. 80th Anniv of First Albanian Stamps.

2561	**564** 6l.50 brown and green	35	25

1993. Europa. Contemporary Art. Multicoloured.

2562	3l. Type **565**	30	25
2563	7l. "The Green Star" (E. Hila) (horiz)	70	55
MS2564	116 × 121 mm. 20l. "Gjirokaster" (B. Ahmeti). Imperf	1·60	1·60

566 Running

1993. Mediterranean Games, Agde and Roussillon (Languedoc), France. Multicoloured.

2565	3l. Type **566**	20	15
2566	16l. Canoeing	1·10	85
2567	21l. Cycling	1·40	1·10
MS2568	117 × 84 mm. 20l. Map of Mediterranean. Imperf	1·10	1·10

567 Bardhi

568 Mascot and Flags around Stadium

1993. 350th Death Anniv of Frang Bardhi (scholar).

2569	**567** 6l.50 brown and stone	45	35
MS2570	94 × 107 mm. 20l. brown and gold. Imperf	1·40	1·40

DESIGN: 20l. Bardhi writing at desk.

1994. World Cup Football Championship, U.S.A. Multicoloured.

2571	42l. Type **568**	50	40
2572	68l. Mascot kicking ball . .	80	60

569 Gjovalin Gjadri (construction engineer)

571 Richard Wagner

570 Emblem and Benz

1994. Europa. Discoveries and Inventions.

2573	**569** 50l. dp brn, ches & brn	70	55
2574	– 100l. dp brn, ches & brn	1·75	1·25
MS2575	60 × 80 mm. 150l. drab and brown. Imperf	2·00	2·00

DESIGN: 100l. Karl Ritter von Ghega (railway engineer); 150l. Sketch of traffic project.

1995. 150th Birth Anniv (1994) of Karl Benz (motor manufacturer). Multicoloured.

2576	5l. Type **570**	10	10
2577	10l. Mercedes-Benz C-class saloon, 1995 Daimler motor carriage, 1886 . . .	20	15
2578	60l. First four-wheel Benz motor-car, 1886	1·00	75
2579	125l. Mercedes-Benz 540 K cabriolet, 1936	2·10	1·60

1995. Composers. Each brown and gold.

2580	3l. Type **571**	10	10
2581	6l.50 Edvard Grieg	10	10
2582	11l. Charles Gounod . . .	20	15
2583	20l. Pyotr Tchaikovsky . .	35	25

572 Intersections

1995. 50th Anniv (1994) of Liberation.

2584	**572** 50l. black and red . . .	75	55

573 Ali Pasha

1995. 250th Birth Anniv (1994) of Ali Pasha of Tepelene (Pasha of Janina, 1788–1820).

2585	**573** 60l. black, yellow & brn	95	70
MS2586	80 × 60 mm. 100l. brown and orange (Administration building, Tepelene). Imperf . .	1·40	1·40

574 Veskopoja, 1744 (left half)

1995. 250th Anniv (1994) of Veskopoja Academy. Multicoloured.

2587	42l. Type **574**	60	45
2588	68l. Veskopoja, 1744 (right half)	1·00	75

Nos. 2587/8 were issued together, se-tenant, forming a composite design.

575 Olympic Rings and Map

1995. Centenary of International Olympic Committee. Sheet 60 × 80 mm. Imperf.

MS2589	**575** 80l. multicoloured	1·25	1·25

576 Palace of Europe, Strasbourg

1995. Admission of Albania to Council of Europe. Multicoloured.

2590	25l. Type **576**	30	25
2591	85l. State arms and map of Europe	1·40	1·10

577 Hands holding Olive Branch
579 Bee on Flower

578 Mice sitting around Table and Stork with Fox

1995. Europa. Peace and Freedom. Multicoloured.

2592	50l. Type **577**	80	60
2593	100l. Dove flying over hands	1·60	1·25
MS2594	80 × 60 mm. 150l. Figure stretching out hands. Imperf	2·50	2·50

1995. 300th Death Anniv of Jean de La Fontaine (writer). Multicoloured.

2595	2l. Type **578**	10	10
2596	3l. Stork with foxes around table	10	10
2597	25l. Frogs under tree	45	35
MS2598	80 × 60 mm. 60l. La Fontaine and animals. Imperf	1·00	75

1995. The Honey Bee. Multicoloured.

2599	5l. Type **579**	10	10
2600	10l. Bee and honeycomb	20	15
2601	25l. Bee on comb	45	35

580 Fridtjof Nansen
582 Male Chorus

581 Flags outside U.N. Building, New York

1995. Polar Explorers. Multicoloured.

2602	25l. Type **580**	55	45
2603	25l. James Cook	55	45
2604	25l. Roald Amundsen	55	45
2605	25l. Robert Scott	55	45

Nos. 2602/5 were issued together, se-tenant, forming a composite design.

1995. 50th Anniv of U.N.O. Multicoloured.

2606	2l. Type **581**	10	10
2607	100l. Flags flying to right outside U.N. building, New York	1·60	1·25

1995. National Folklore Festival, Berat. Mult.

2608	5l. Type **582**	10	10
2609	50l. Female participant	85	65

583 "Poet"
584 Church and Preacher, Berat Kruje

1995. Jan Kukuzeli (11th-century poet, musician and teacher). Abstract representations of Kukuzeli. Multicoloured.

2610	18l. Type **583**	30	25
2611	20l. "Musician"	35	25
MS2612	80 × 80 mm. 100l. "Teacher". Imperf	1·60	1·60

1995. 20th Anniv of World Tourism Organization. Multicoloured.

2613	18l. Type **584**	30	25
2614	20l. Street, Shkoder	35	25
2615	42l. Buildings, Gjirokaster	70	35

585 Paul Eluard
586 Louis, Film Reel and Projector

1995. Poets' Birth Centenaries. Multicoloured.

2616	25l. Type **585**	35	25
2617	50l. Sergei Yessenin	75	55

1995. Centenary of Motion Pictures. Lumiere Brothers (developers of cine camera). Mult.

2618	10l. Type **586**	25	20
2619	85l. Auguste, film reel and cinema audience	1·50	40

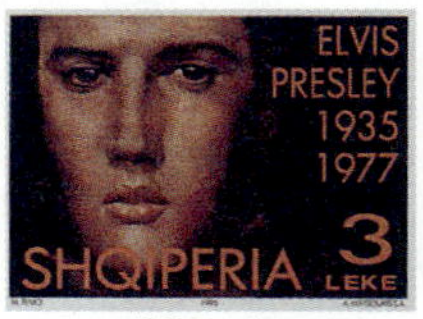

587 Presley

1995. 60th Birth Anniv of Elvis Presley (entertainer). Multicoloured.

2620	3l. Type **587**	10	10
2621	60l. Presley (different)	1·00	75

588 Banknotes of 1925
589 "5", Crumbling Star, Open Book and Peace Dove

1995. 70th Anniv of Albanian National Bank. Mult.

2622	10l. Type **588**	20	15
2623	25l. Modern banknotes	45	35

1995. 5th Anniv of Democratic Movement. Mult.

2624	5l. Type **589**	10	10
2625	50l. Woman planting tree	85	65

590 Mother Teresa
591 Football, Union Flag, Map of Europe and Stadium

1996. Europa. Famous Women. Mother Teresa (founder of Missionaries of Charity).

2626	**590** 25l. multicoloured	45	35
2627	100l. multicoloured	1·75	1·25
MS2628	60 × 80 mm. 150l. Mother Teresa (different). Imperf	2·50	2·50

1996. European Football Championship, England. Multicoloured.

2629	25l. Type **591**	65	35
2630	100l. Map of Europe, ball and player	1·75	1·25

592 Satellite and Radio Mast
593 Running

1996. Inaug of Cellular Telephone Network. Mult.

2631	10l. Type **592**	20	10
2632	60l. User, truck, container ship and mobile telephone (vert)	1·75	75

1996. Olympic Games, Atlanta, U.S.A. Mult.

2633	5l. Type **593**	10	10
2634	25l. Throwing the hammer	45	35
2635	60l. Long jumping	1·00	75
MS2636	60 × 80 mm. 100l. Games emblem. Imperf	1·75	1·75

594 Linked Hands
596 "The Naked Maja"

595 Gottfried Wilhelm Leibniz (350th)

1996. 75th Anniv of Albanian Red Cross.

2637	**594** 50l.+10l. mult	1·00	1·00

1996. Philosopher-mathematicians' Birth Annivs. Multicoloured.

2638	10l. Type **595**	20	[illegible]
2639	85l. Rene Descartes (400th)	1·50	[illegible]

1996. 250th Birth Anniv of Francisco de Goya (artist). Multicoloured.

2640	10l. Type **596**	20	10
2641	60l. "Dona Isabel Cobos de Porcel"	1·00	75
MS2642	80 × 60 mm. 100l. "Self-portrait" (24 × 29 mm)	1·75	1·75

597 Book Binding
598 Princess

1996. Christian Art Exhibition. Multicoloured.

2643	5l. Type **597**	10	10
2644	25l. Book clasp showing crucifixion	45	35
2645	85l. Book binding (different)	1·50	1·10

1996. 50th Anniv of UNICEF Children's Paintings. Multicoloured.

2646	5l. Type **598**	10	10
2647	10l. Woman	20	15
2648	25l. Sea life	45	35
2649	50l. Harbour	85	65

599 State Arms, Book and Fishta
600 Omar Khayyam and Writing Materials

1996. 125th Birth Anniv of Gjergj Fishta (writer and politician). Multicoloured.

2650	10l. Type **599**	20	15
2651	60l. Battle scene and Fishta	1·00	75

1997. 950th Birth Anniv of Omar Khayyam (astronomer and poet). Multicoloured.

2652	20l. Type **600**	35	25
2653	50l. Omar Khayyam and symbols of astronomy	85	65

Nos. 2652/3 are inscribed "850" in error.

601 Gutenberg
602 Pelicans

1997. 600th Birth Anniv of Johannes Gutenberg (printer). Multicoloured.

2654	20l. Type **601**	40	25
2655	60l. Printing press	1·00	75

Nos. 2654/5 were issued together, se-tenant, forming a composite design.

1997. The Dalmatian Pelican. Multicoloured.

2656	10l. Type **602**	20	15
2657	80l. Pelicans on shore and in flight	1·40	45

Nos. 2656/7 were issued together, se-tenant, forming a composite design.

603 Dragon
604 Konica

1997. Europa. Tales and Legends. "The Blue Pool". Multicoloured.

2658	30l. Type **603**	50	40
2659	100l. Dragon drinking from pool	1·75	1·25

1997. 55th Death Anniv of Faik Konica (writer and politician).

2660	**604** 10l. brown and black	20	15
2661	25l. blue and black	45	35
MS2662	60 × 80 mm. **604** 80l. brown	1·40	1·40

605 Male Athlete
606 Skanderberg

1997. Mediterranean Games, Bari. Multicoloured.
2663 20l. Type **605** 35 25
2664 30l. Female athlete and rowers 50 40
MS2665 60 × 80 mm. 100l. Discus-thrower, javelin-thrower and runner. Imperf . . . . 1·75 1·75

1997.
2666 **606** 5l. red and brown . . . 10 10
2667 10l. green and olive . . . 10 10
2668 20l. green and deep green 20 15
2669 25l. mauve and purple 25 20
2670 30l. violet and lilac . . . 30 25
2671 50l. grey and black . . . 50 40
2672 60l. lt brown & brown 60 45
2673 80l. lt brown & brown 80 60
2674 100l. red and lake . . . 1·00 75
2675 110l. blue and deep blue 1·10 85

1997. Mother Teresa (founder of Missionaries of Charity) Commemoration. No. 2627 optd **HOMAZH 1910–1997**.
2676 **590** 100l. multicoloured . . . 1·00 75

608 Codex Aureus (11th century)

609 Twin-headed Eagle (postal emblem)

1997. Codices (1st series). Multicoloured.
2677 10l. Type **608** 10 10
2678 25l. Codex Purpureus Beratinus (7th century) showing mountain and scribe 25 20
2679 60l. Codex Purpureus Beratinus showing church and scribe 60 45
See also Nos. 2712/14.

1997. 85th Anniv of Albanian Postal Service.
2680 **609** 10l. multicoloured . . . 10 10
2681 30l. multicoloured . . . 30 25
The 30l. differs from Type **609** in minor parts of the design.

610 Nikete of Ramesiana

611 Man sitting at Table

1998. Nikete Dardani, Bishop of Ramesiana (philosopher and composer).
2682 **610** 30l. multicoloured . . . 25 20
2683 100l. multicoloured . . . 85 65
There are minor differences of design between the two values.

1998. Legend of Pogradeci Lake. Multicoloured.
2684 30l. Type **611** 25 20
2685 50l. The Three Graces . . . 40 30
2686 60l. Women drawing water 50 40
2687 80l. Man of ice 70 55

612 Stylized Dancers

1998. Europa. National Festivals. Multicoloured.
2688 60l. Type **612** 50 40
2689 100l. Female dancer 85 65
MS2690 60 × 80 mm. 150l. Two dancers. Imperf . . . . 1·30 1·30

613 Abdyl Frasheri (founder)

614 Player with Ball

1998. 120th Anniv of League of Prizren. Mult.
2691 30l. Type **613** 25 15
2692 50l. Sulejman Vokshi and partisan 40 30
2693 60l. Iljaz Pashe Dibra and crossed rifles 50 35
2694 80l. Ymer Prizreni and partisans 70 50

1998. World Cup Football Championship, France. Multicoloured.
2695 60l. Type **614** 50 35
2696 100l. Player with ball (different) 85 65
MS2697 60 × 80 mm. 120l. Championship mascot. Imperf 1·10 1·10

615 Wrestlers in National Costume

616 Cacej

1998. European Junior Wrestling Championship. Multicoloured.
2698 30l. Type **615** 25 15
2699 60l. Ancient Greek wrestlers 25 15

1998. 90th Birth Anniv of Eqerem Cabej (linguist).
2700 **616** 60l. black and yellow . . 25 15
2701 80l. yellow, black & red 70 50

617 Diana, Princess of Wales

1998. Diana, Princess of Wales Commemoration. Multicoloured.
2702 60l. Type **617** 55 30
2703 100l. With Mother Teresa 90 45

618 Mother Teresa holding Child

1998. Mother Teresa (founder of Missionaries of Charity) Commemoration. Multicoloured.
2704 60l. Type **618** 55 30
2705 100l. Mother Teresa (vert) 90 45

619 Detail of Painting

1998. 150th Birth Anniv of Paul Gauguin (artist). Multicoloured.
2706 60l. Type **619** 55 30
2707 80l. "Women of Tahiti" . . 70 35
MS2708 60 × 80 mm. 120l. Face. Imperf . . . . 1·10 1·10

620 Epitaph

1998. 625th Anniv of Epitaph of Gllavenica (embroidery of dead Christ). Multicoloured.
2709 30l. Type **620** 25 10
2710 80l. Close-up of upper body 70 35
MS2711 80 × 60 mm. 100l. Detail of epitaph (24 × 29 mm) 90 90

621 Page of Codex

623 Koliqi

1998. Codices (2nd series). 11th-century Manuscripts. Multicoloured.
2712 30l. Type **621** 25 10
2713 50l. Front cover of manuscript 45 20
2714 80l. Page showing mosque 70 35

1998. "Italia '98" International Stamp Exhibition. No. **MS**2628 optd **Italia 98**.
MS2715 60 × 80 mm. 150l. mult 2·75 2·75

1998. 1st Death Anniv of Cardinal Mikel Koliqi (first Albanian Cardinal). Multicoloured.
2716 30l. Type **623** 25 15
2717 100l. Koliqi (different) . . . 90 45

624 George Washington (first President, 1789–97)

1999. American Anniversaries. Multicoloured.
2718 150l. Type **624** (death bicentenary) . . . . . . 1·40 70
2719 150l. Abraham Lincoln (President 1861–65, 190th birth anniv) . . . . . . 1·40 70
2720 150l. Martin Luther King Jr. (civil rights campaigner, 70th birth anniv) . . . . 1·40 70

625 Monk Seals

1999. The Monk Seal. Multicoloured.
2721 110l. Type **625** . . . . . . 1·00 50
2722 110l. Two seals (both facing left) . . . . 1·00 50
2723 150l. As No. 2722 but both facing right . . . . . . 1·40 70
2724 150l. As Type **625** but seal at back facing left and seal at front facing right 1·40 70
Nos. 2721/4 were issued together, se-tenant, forming a composite design.

1999. 50th Anniv of Council of Europe. No. 2590 surch **150 LEKE** and emblem.
2725 **576** 150l. on 25l. mult . . . 1·40 70

1999. "iBRA '99" International Stamp Exhibition, Nuremberg, Germany. No. 2496 surch **150 LEKE** in black (new value) and multicoloured (emblem).
2726 150l. on 90q. multicoloured 1·40 70

628 Dove, Airplane and NATO Emblem

629 Mickey Mouse

1999. 50th Anniv of North Atlantic Treaty Organization.
2727 **628** 10l. multicoloured . . . 10 10
2728 100l. multicoloured . . . 90 45
MS2729 69 × 85 mm. 250l. multicoloured . . . . 2·00 2·00

1999. Mickey Mouse (cartoon film character). Multicoloured.
2730 60l. Type **629** 55 30
2731 80l. Mickey writing letter . . 70 35
2732 110l. Mickey thinking . . . 1·00 50
2733 150l. Wearing black and red jumper . . . . 1·40 70

630 Thethi National Park, Shkoder

1999. Europa. Parks and Gardens. Multicoloured.
2734 90l. Type **630** 80 40
2735 310l. Lura National Park, Dibra . . . . 2·75 1·40
MS2736 80 × 60 mm. 350l. Divjaka National Park, Lushnje. Imperf 3·25 3·25

631 Coin

1999. Illyrian Coins. Multicoloured.
2737 10l. Type **631** 10 10
2738 20l. Coins from Labeateve, Bylisi and Scutari 20 10
2739 200l. Coins of King Monuni 1·75 90
MS2740 80 × 60 mm. 310l. Coin of King Gent (29 × 49 mm) . . . 2·75 2·75

1999. "Philexfrance 99" International Stamp Exhibition, Paris. No. 2512 surch with new value and Exhibition logo.
2741 **552** 150l. on 30q. mult . . . 1·40 70

633 Chaplin

634 Neil Armstrong on Moon

1999. 110th Birth Anniv of Charlie Chaplin (film actor and director). Multicoloured.
2742 30l. Type **633** 25 10
2743 50l. Raising hat 45 25
2744 250l. Dancing . . . . 2·25 1·10

1999. 30th Anniv of First Manned Moon Landing. Multicoloured.
2745 30l. Type **634** 25 10
2746 150l. Lunar module . . . . 1·40 70
2747 300l. Astronaut and American flag . . . . . 2·75 1·40
MS2748 60 × 80 mm. 280l. Launch of "Apollo 1" (25 × 29 mm) . . 2·50 2·50
Nos. 2745/7 were issued together, se-tenant, forming a composite design.

635 Prisoner behind Bars

636 Emblem

1999. The Nazi Holocaust.
2749 **635** 30l. multicoloured . . . 25 10
2750 150l. black and yellow 1·40 70

1999. 125th Anniv of Universal Postal Union.
2751 **636** 20l. multicoloured . . . 20 10
2752 60l. multicoloured . . . 55 30

1999. "China 1999" International Stamp Exhibition, Peking. No. 2497 surch **150 LEKE**.
2753 150l. on 11.20 multicoloured 1·40 70

638 Javelin

639 Madonna and Child

1999. 70th Anniv of National Athletic Championships. Multicoloured.

2754	10l. Type **638**	10	10
2755	20l. Discus	20	10
2756	200l. Running	1·90	85

1999. Icons by Onufri Shek (artist). Multicoloured.

2757	30l. Type **639**	25	10
2758	300l. The Resurrection	2·75	1·40

640 Bilal Golemi (veterinary surgeon)

1999. Birth Anniversaries. Multicoloured.

2759	10l. Type **640** (centenary)	10	10
2760	20l. Azem Galica (revolutionary) (centenary)	20	10
2761	50l. Viktor Eftimiu (writer) (centenary)	45	20
2762	300l. Lasgush Poradeci (poet) (centenary (2000))	2·75	1·40

641 Carnival Mask

1999. Carnivals. Multicoloured.

2763	30l. Type **641**	25	10
2764	300l. Turkey mask	2·75	1·40

642 Bell and Flowers

643 Woman's Costume, Librazhdi

2000. New Millennium. The Peace Bell. Mult.

2765	40l. Type **642**	35	15
2766	90l. Bell and flowers (different)	80	40

2000. Regional Costumes (1st series). Mult.

2767	5l. Type **643**	10	10
2768	10l. Woman's costume, Malesia E Madhe	10	10
2769	15l. Man's costume, Malesia E Madhe	15	10
2770	20l. Man's costume, Tropoje	20	10
2771	30l. Man's costume, Dumrea	30	15
2772	35l. Man's costume, Tirana	30	15
2773	40l. Woman's costume, Tirana	35	15
2774	45l. Woman's costume, Arbereshe	40	20
2775	50l. Man's costume, Gjirokastra	45	25
2776	55l. Woman's costume, Lunxheri	50	25
2777	70l. Woman's costume, Cameria	65	30
2778	90l. Man's costume, Laberia	80	40

See also Nos. 2832/43, 2892/2903, 2943/54, 3053/64, 3080/91 and 3171/82.

644 Majer

645 Donald Duck

2000. 150th Birth Anniv of Gustav Majer (etymologist).

2779	**644**	50l. green	45	25
2780		130l. red	1·25	65

2000. Donald and Daisy Duck (cartoon film characters). Multicoloured.

2781	10l. Type **645**	10	10
2782	30l. Donald Duck	30	15
2783	90l. Daisy Duck	80	40
2784	250l. Donald Duck	2·25	1·10

646 Early Racing Car

2000. Motor Racing. Multicoloured.

2785	30l. Type **646**	30	15
2786	30l. Two-man racing car	30	15
2787	30l. Racing car with wire nose	30	15
2788	30l. Racing car with solid wheels	30	15
2789	30l. Car No. 1	30	15
2790	30l. Car No. 2	30	15
2791	30l. White Formula 1 racing car (facing left)	30	15
2792	30l. Blue Formula 1 racing car	30	15
2793	30l. Red Formula 1 racing car	30	15
2794	30l. White Formula 1 racing car (front view)	30	15

647 Ristoz of Mborja Church, Korca

2000. Birth Bimillenary of Jesus Christ. Mult.

2795	15l. Type **647**	15	10
2796	40l. St. Kolli Church, Voskopoja	35	15
2797	90l. Church of Flori and Lauri, Kosovo	80	40
MS2798	80 × 60 mm. 250l. Fountain of Shengjin (mosaic), Tirana (37 × 37 mm)	2·75	2·75

648 "Building Europe"

650 Gustav Mahler (composer) (40th death anniv)

649 Wolf

2000. Europa. Multicoloured.

2799	130l. Type **648**	1·25	60
MS2800	60 × 80 mm. 300l. Detail of design showing boy holding star (24 × 29 mm)	3·40	3·40

2000. Animals. Multicoloured.

2801	10l. Type **649**	10	10
2802	40l. Brown bear	35	15
2803	90l. Wild boar	80	40
2804	220l. Red fox	2·00	1·00

2000. "WIPA 2000" International Stamp Exhibition, Vienna.

2805	**650**	130l. multicoloured	1·25	1·00

651 Footballer saving Ball

2000. European Football Championship, Belgium and The Netherlands. Multicoloured.

2806	10l. Type **651**	10	10
2807	120l. Footballer heading ball	1·10	55
MS2808	80 × 60 mm. 260l. Footballer kicking ball. Imperf	3·00	3·00

652 Musicans

2000. Paintings by Picasso. Multicoloured.

2809	30l. Type **652**	30	15
2810	40l. Abstract face	35	15
2811	250l. Two women running along beach	2·25	1·10
MS2812	60 × 80 mm. 400l. Painting of man (24 × 29 mm)	5·00	5·00

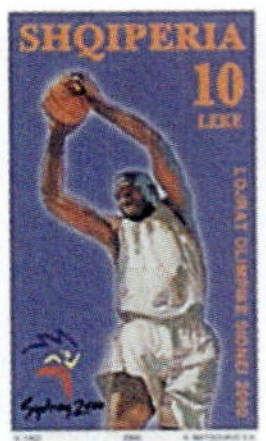

653 Basketball

655 "Self-portrait" (Picasso)

654 *LZ-1* (first Zeppelin airship) over Lake Constance, Friedrichshafen (first flight)

2000. Olympic Games, Sydney. Multicoloured.

2813	10l. Type **653**	10	10
2814	40l. Football	40	20
2815	90l. Athletics	85	45
2816	250l. Cycling	2·40	1·25

2000. Centenary of First Zeppelin Flight. Airship Development. Multicoloured.

2817	15l. Type **654**	15	10
2818	30l. Santos-Dumont airship *Ballon No. 5* and Eiffel Tower C attempted round trip from St. Cloud via Eiffel Tower, 1901	30	15
2819	300l. Beardmore airship *R-34* over New York (first double crossing of Atlantic)	2·75	1·25
MS2820	80 × 60 mm. 300l. Ferdinand von Zeppelin and airship (24 × 28 mm)	3·40	3·40

2000. "Espana 2000" World Stamp Exhibition, Madrid.

2821	**655**	130l. multicoloured	1·25	65

656 Yellow Gentian (*Gentiana lutea*)

658 Mother holding Child

657 Naim Frasheri (poet) and Landscape

2000. Medicinal Plants. Multicoloured.

2822	50l. Type **656**	50	25
2823	70l. Cross-leaved gentian (*Gentiana cruciata*)	65	35

2000. Personalities. Multicoloured.

2824	30l. Type **657**	20	15
2825	50l. Bajram Curri (revolutionary) and landscape	50	25

Nos. 2824/5 were issued together, se-tenant, forming a composite design.

2000. 50th Anniv of United Nations High Commission for Refugees. Multicoloured.

2826	50l. Type **658**	50	25
2827	90l. Mother breastfeeding child	85	40

659 Dede Ahmed Myftar Ahmataj

661 Southern Magnolia (*Magnolia gandiflora*)

2001. Religious Leaders. Multicoloured.

2828	90l. Type **65**	85	45
2829	90l. Dede Sali Njazi	85	45

2001. "For Kosovo". Nos. 2592/3 surch **PER KOSOVEN** and new value.

2830	80l.+10l. on 50l. multicoloured	85	45
2831	130l.+20l. on 100l. multicoloured	1·40	70

2001. Regional Costumes (2nd series). As T **643**. Multicoloured.

2832	20l. Man's costume, Tropoje	20	10
2833	20l. Woman's costume, Lume	20	10
2834	20l. Woman's costume, Mirdite	20	10
2835	20l. Man's costume, Lume	20	10
2836	20l. Woman's costume, Zadrime	20	10
2837	20l. Woman's costume, Shpati	20	10
2838	20l. Man's costume, Kruje	20	10
2839	20l. Woman's costume, Macukulli	20	10
2840	20l. Woman's costume, Dardhe	20	10
2841	20l. Man's costume, Lushnje	20	10
2842	20l. Woman's costume, Dropulli	20	10
2843	20l. Woman's costume, Shmili	20	10

2001. Scented Flowers. Multicoloured.

2844	10l. Type **661**	10	10
2845	20l. Virginia rose (*Rosa virginiana*)	20	10
2846	90l. *Dianthus barbatus*	85	45
2847	140l. Lilac (*Syringa vulgaris*)	1·25	65

662 Goofy in Shorts

2001. Goofy (cartoon film character). Multicoloured.

2848	20l. Type **662**	20	10
2849	50l. Goofy in blue hat	50	25
2850	90l. Goofy in red trousers	85	45
2851	140l. Goofy in purple waistcoat	1·25	65

663 Vincenzo Bellini

2001. Composers' Anniversaries. Multicoloured.

2852	90l. Type **663** (birth centenary)	85	45
2853	90l. Guiseppe Verdi (death centenary)	85	45
MS2854	90 × 90 mm. 300l. Bellini and Verdi (75 × 38 mm)	3·75	3·75

664 Cliffs and Stream

2001. Europa. Water Resources. Multicoloured.

2855	40l. Type **664**	40	20
2856	110l. Waterfall	1·10	55
2857	200l. Lake	1·90	95
MS2858	60 × 80 mm. 350l. Ripples (24 × 78 mm)	4·50	4·50

665 Horse

2001. Domestic Animals. Multicoloured.

2859	10l. Type **665**	10	10
2860	15l. Donkey	15	10
2861	80l. Siamese cat	75	40
2862	90l. Dog	85	45
MS2863	80 × 60 mm. 300l. Head of Siamese cat (49 × 29 mm)	3·75	3·75

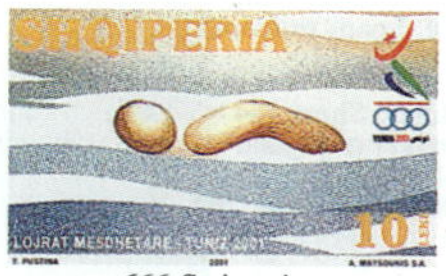

666 Swimming

2001. Mediterranean Games, Tunis. Multicoloured.

2864	10l. Type **666**	10	10
2865	90l. Athletics	85	45
2866	140l. Cycling	1·40	70
MS2867	60 × 80 mm. 260l. Discus (29 × 24 mm)	3·40	3·40

667 *Eole* (first powered take-off by Clement Ader, 1890)

2001. Aviation History. Multicoloured.

2868	40l. Type **667**	40	20
2869	40l. *Bleriot XI* (first powered crossing of English channel by Louis Bleriot, 1909)	40	20
2870	40l. *Spirit of St. Louis* (first solo non-stop crossing of North Atlantic from Paris to New York by Charles Lindbergh, 1927)	40	20
2871	40l. First flight to Tirana, 1925	40	20
2872	40l. Antonov AH-10 (first flight, 1956)	40	20
2873	40l. Concorde (first flight, 1969)	40	20
2874	40l. Concorde (first commercial flight, 1970)	40	20
2875	40l. Space shuttle *Colombia* (first flight, 1981)	40	20

668 Tabakeve **669** Dimitri of Arber

2001. Old Bridges.

2876	**668** 10l. multicoloured	10	10
2877	– 20l. multicoloured	20	10
2878	– 40l. multicoloured	40	20
2879	– 90l. black	85	45
MS2880	80 × 60 mm. 21.50 multicoloured	3·40	3·40

DESIGNS: 20l. Kamares; 40l. Golikut; 90l. Mesit. 49 × 22 mm—21.50, Tabakeve.

2001. Arms (1st series).

2881	20l. Type **669**	20	10
2882	45l. Balsha pricipality	45	25
2883	50l. Muzaka family	50	25
2884	90l. George Castriot (Skanderbeg)	85	45

See also Nos. 2921/4 and 2965/8.

670 Children encircling Globe

2001. United Nations Year of Dialogue among Civilizations. Multicoloured, background colours given.

2885	**670** 45l. red, yellow and black	40	20
2886	50l. orange and green	45	20
2887	120l. black and red	1·10	55

There are minor differences in Nos. 2886/7, with each colour forming a solid block above and below the central motif.

671 Award Ceremony (Medicins sans Frontieres, 1999 Peace Prize) and Medal

2001. Centenary of Nobel Prizes. Showing winners and Nobel medal. Multicoloured.

2888	10l. Type **671**	10	10
2889	20l. Wilhelm Konrad Rontgen (1901 Physics prize)	20	10
2890	90l. Ferid Murad (1998 Medicine Prize)	45	25
2891	200l. Mother Teresa (1979 Peace Prize)	2·00	1·00

2002. Regional Costumes (3rd series). As T **643**. Multicoloured.

2892	30l. Woman's costume, Gjakova	30	15
2893	30l. Woman's costume, Prizreni	30	15
2894	30l. Man's costume, Shkodra	30	15
2895	30l. Woman's costume, Shkodra	30	15
2896	30l. Man's costume, Berati	30	15
2897	30l. Woman's costume, Berati	30	15
2898	30l. Woman's costume, Elbasani	30	15
2899	30l. Man's costume, Elbasani	30	15
2900	30l. Woman's costume, Vlora	30	15
2901	30l. Man's costume, Vlora	30	15
2902	30l. Woman's costume, Gjirokastra	30	15
2903	30l. Woman's costume, Delvina	30	15

672 Bambi and Thumper **673** Fireplace

2002. Bambi (cartoon film character). Multicoloured.

2904	20l. Type **672**	20	40
2905	50l. Bambi alone amongst flowers	50	25
2906	90l. Bambi and Thumper looking right	90	45
2907	140l. Bambi with open mouth	1·40	70

2002. Traditional Fireplaces. T **673** and similar vert designs showing fireplaces. Multicoloured.

MS2908	30l. Type **673**; 40l. With columns at each side; 50l. With foliage arch; 90l. With three medallions in arch	4·25	4·25

674 Acrobatic Jugglers

2002. Europa. Circus. Multicoloured.

2909	40l. Type **674**	40	20
2910	90l. Female acrobat	90	45
2911	220l. Tightrope performers	2·25	1·10
MS2912	60 × 80 mm. 350l. Equestrienne performer (38 × 38 mm)	3·50	3·50

675 Heading the Ball

2002. Football World Championship, Japan and South Korea. Multicoloured.

2913	20l. Type **675**	20	10
2914	30l. Catching the ball	30	15
2915	90l. Kicking the ball from horizontal position	90	45
2916	120l. Player and ball	1·25	65
MS2917	80 × 60 mm. 360l. Emblem (50 × 30)	3·50	3·50

2002. Arms (2nd series). As T **669**. Multicoloured.

2918	20l. Gropa family	20	10
2919	45l. Skurra family	45	25
2920	50l. Bua family	50	25
2921	90l. Topia family	90	45

676 *Opuntia catingiola*

2002. Cacti. T **676** and similar triangular designs. Multicoloured.

MS2922	50l. Type **676**; 50l. *Neoporteria pseudoreicheana*; 50l. *Lobivia shaferi* 50l. *Hylocereus undatus*; 50l. *Borzicactus madisoniorum*	2·50	2·50

677 Blood Group Symbols with Wings

2002. 50th Anniv of Blood Bank Service. Multicoloured.

2923	90l. Type **677**	95	45
2924	90l. Blood group symbols containing figures	95	45

678 Naim Kryeziu (footballer)

2002. Sports Personalities. Multicoloured.

2925	50l. Type **678**	50	25
2926	50l. Riza Lushta (footballer)	50	25
2927	50l. Ymer Pampuri (weight lifter)	50	25
MS2928	61 × 81 mm. 300l. Loro BoriÇi (footballer) (vert). Imperf	3·00	3·00

679 Stamp, Torso and Emblem

2002. 50th Anniv International Federation of Stamp Dealers'Associations (IFSDA). Multicoloured.

2929	50l. Type **679**	50	25
2930	100l. Part of stamp enlarged and emblem	1·00	50

680 Statue of Liberty

2002. 1st Anniv of Attacks on World Trade Centre, New York. Multicoloured.

2931	100l. Type **680**	1·00	50
2932	150l. Burning towers and skyline	1·50	75
MS2933	61 × 81 mm. 350l. Statue of Liberty and World Trade Centre tower (vert)	3·50	3·50

681 Loggerhead Turtle (*Caretta caretta*)

2002. Fauna of Mediterranean Sea. Sheet 100 × 107 mm containing T **681** and similar horiz designs. Multicoloured.

MS2934	50l. Type **681**; 50l. Common dolphin (*Delphinus delphis*); 50l. Blue shark (*Prionace glaucai*); 50l. Fin whale (*Balenoptera physalus*); 50l. Ray (*Torpedo torpedo*); 50l. Octopus (*Octopus vulgaris*)	3·00	3·00

682 Tefta Tashko KoÇo

2002. Personalities. The Stage. Multicoloured.

2935	50l. Type **682** (singer)	50	25
2936	50l. Naim Frasheri (actor)	50	25
2937	50l. Kristaq Antoniu (singer)	50	25
2938	50l. Panajot KanaÇi (choreographer)	50	25

683 Flags **684** Satellite Dish and Outline of Stamp

2002. 90th Anniv of Independence. Multicoloured.

2939	20l. Type **683**	20	10
2940	90l. People and Albanian flag	95	45

2002. 90th Anniv of Albanian Post and Telecommunications. Multicoloured.

2941	20l. Type **684**	20	10
2942	90l. Airmail envelope and telegraph machine	95	45

2003. Regional Costumes (4th series). As T **643**. Multicoloured.

2943	30l. Woman's costume, Kelmendi	30	15
2944	30l. Man's costume, Zadrime	30	15
2945	30l. Woman's costume, Zerqani	30	15
2946	30l. Man's costume, Peshkopi	30	15
2947	30l. Man's costume, Malesia Tiranes	30	15
2948	30l. Woman's costume, Malesia Tiranes	30	15
2949	30l. Woman's costume, Fushe Kruje	30	15
2950	30l. Man's costume, Shpati	30	15
2951	30l. Woman's costume, Myzeqe	30	15
2952	30l. Woman's costume, Labinoti	30	15
2953	30l. Man's costume, Korce	30	15
2954	30l. Woman's costume, Laberi	30	15

685 Popeye and Bluto **687** Bearded Man

686 Port Palemo Castle

2003. Popeye (cartoon film character). Multicoloured.

2955	40l. Type **685**	40	20
2956	50l. Popeye running	50	25
2957	80l. Popeye and Olive Oyl	80	40
2958	150l. Popeye	1·50	70

2003. Castles. Sheet 118 × 98 mm. T **686** and similar horiz designs.

MS2959	10l. grey and black; 20l. green and black; 50l. grey and black; 20l. mauve and black	1·00	1·00

3181	40l. Man's costume, Zalle Dajt	80	80
3182	40l. Woman's costume, Zaranike Godolesh	80	80

Nos. 3183/94 have been left for 'Regional Costumes (8th series)' (Vert designs as T **643**), issued on 2 November 2007, not yet received.

733 Thethi National Park (Inscr 'Parku Kombetar I Thethit')

2007. Tourism. Multicoloured.

3195	40l. Type **733**	80	80
3196	50l. Luras Lake (Inscr 'Liqenet e Lures')	95	95
3197	60l. Canine's Castle (Inscr 'Kalaja Kanines')	1·20	1·20
3198	70l. Laguna Karavastase	1·40	1·40

734 Plane Tree

2007. Natural Heritage. Elbasan Plane Trees. Multicoloured.

3199	70l. Type **734**	1·40	1·40
3200	90l. Hollow tree	1·40	1·80

735 Pope Clement II

2007.

3201 **735**	30l. multicoloured	60	60
3202	90l. multicoloured	1·80	1·80

736 Leopold Senghor

2007. Birth Centenary (2006) of Leopold Sedar Senghor (poet and first President of Senegal 1960–80).

3203 **736**	40l. multicoloured	80	80
3204	80l. multicoloured	1·50	1·50

737 Team

2007. 60th Anniv of Albania as Balkan Football Champions.

3205 **737**	10l. multicoloured	20	20
3206	80l. multicoloured	1·50	1·50

738 Cannon

2007. World Heritage Site. Gjirokastra. Sheet 120 × 100 mm containing T **738** and similar vert designs. Multicoloured.

MS3207 10l. Type **738**; 20l. Flowers in a roundel; 30l. 'Kule' (building with tall basement, a first floor for use in the cold season, and a second floor for the warm season); 60l. Bridge ; 80l. Aerial view; 90l. Clock tower . . . 5·50 5·50

739 Soldier wearing Gas Mask

2007. 10th Anniv of Albania's Participation in International Military Missions. Multicoloured.

3208	10l. Type **739**	20	20
3209	100l. Soldiers in inflatable boat	1·90	1·90

740 Mother Teresa

2007. 10th Death Anniv of Agnes Ganzhou Bojaxhiu (Mother Teresa). Multicoloured.

3210 **740**	60l. multicoloured	1·20	1·20
3211	130l. multicoloured No.	2·50	2·50

MS3212 has been left for miniature sheet, not yet received.

741 Gaia (statue)

2007. Archaeology. Durres City. Multicoloured.

3213	30l. Type **741**	60	60
3214	120l. Gaia (close up)	2·30	2·30

No. **MS**3215 has been left for miniature sheet, not yet received.

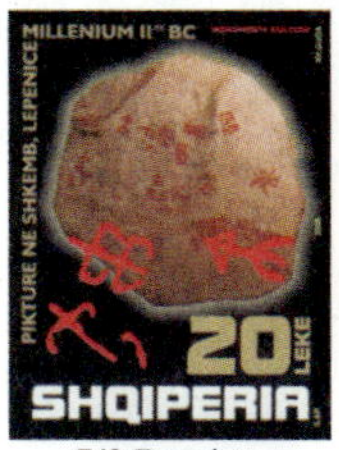

742 Drawings

2007. Cultural History. Tren Cave System (first occupied during Eneolithic period c. 2500–2000 BC). Multicoloured.

3216	20l. Type **742**	40	40
3217	100l. Drawings (different)	1·90	1·90
MS3218	81 × 61 mm. 300l. Cave (horiz)	6·00	6·00

743 Osman Kazazi

2007. Personalities (1st issue). Multicoloured.

3219	10l. Type **743** (politician)	20	20
3220	20l. Pjeter Arbnori (politician)	40	40
3221	60l. Llazar Sotir Gusho (Lagush Poradeci) (poet)	1·20	1·20
3222	100l. Cesk Zadeja (composer)	1·90	1·90

744 Abdurrahim Buza

2007. Personalities (2nd issue). Multicoloured.

3223	50l. Type **744** (artist)	95	95
3224	50l. Aleks Buda (historian)	95	95
3225	50l. Thimi Mitko (folklorist and nationalist)	95	95
3226	50l. Martin Camaj (writer)	95	95

745 Spheres as Player

2007. World Cup Football Championship, Germany. Multicoloured.

3227	30l. Type **745**	60	60
3228	60l. Triangles as player	1·20	1·20
3229	120l. Rectangles as player	2·30	2·30
MS3230	61 × 82 mm. 350l. Emblems	6·75	6·75

The stamp and margin of **MS**3230 form a composite design.

746 Ismail Kemal Bej Vlora (Ismail Qemali) (first head of state and government) and Arms

2007. 95th Anniv of Independence. Multicoloured.

3231	50l. Type **746**	95	95
3232	110l. Ismail Qemali	2·10	2·10

747 Garlic

2007. Domestic Plants. Multicoloured.

3233	80l. Type **747**	1·50	1·50
3234	80l. Onions	1·50	1·50
3235	80l. Peppers	1·50	1·50
3236	80l. Tomatoes	1·50	1·50

748 Blooms and Leaves

2007. *Wulfenia baldacci.* Multicoloured.

3237	70l. Type **748**	1·40	1·40
3238	100l. Flowers on single stem	1·90	1·90

749 Emblem

2007. 95th Anniv of National Post Office.

3239 **749**	80l. agate and vermilion	1·50	1·50
3240	90l. vermilion and black	1·80	1·80

750 New Road Surfacing

2007. Infrastructure Improvements. Sheet 133 × 107 mm containing T **750** and similar horiz designs. Multicoloured.

MS3241 10l. Type **750**; 20l. Durres port; 30l. New building, Tirana; 40l. Mother Teresa airport; 50l. Shkodra street, Hani i Hotit; 60l. Tepelene road, Gijirokastra; 70l. Fier road, Lushnje; 80l. Kalimash road, Morine . . . 6·75 6·75

EXPRESS LETTER STAMPS
ITALIAN OCCUPATION

E 67 King Victor Emmanuel

1940.

E373	E **67**	25q. violet	2·00	2·50
E374		50q. red	4·00	6·25

No. E374 is inscr "POSTAT EXPRES".

1943. Optd **14 Shtator 1943**.

E402	E **67**	25q. violet	20·00	30·00

POSTAGE DUE STAMPS

1914. Optd **TAKSE** through large letter **T**.

D33	**4**	2q. brown and yellow	6·00	2·00
D34		5q. green and yellow	6·00	3·75
D35		10q. red and pink	8·00	2·25
D36		25q. blue	10·00	2·50
D37		50q. mauve and red	11·00	4·50

1914. Nos. 40/4 optd **TAKSE**.

D46 **4**	10pa. on 5q. green & yell	2·75	2·50
D47	20pa. on 10q. red and pink	2·75	2·50
D48	1g. on 25q. blue	2·75	2·50
D49	2g. on 50q. mauve and red	2·75	2·50

1919. Fiscal stamps optd **TAXE**.

D89 **12**	4q. on 4h. pink	6·75	6·75
D90	10q. on 10k. red on grn	6·75	6·75
D91	20q. on 2k. orge on lilac	6·75	6·75
D92	50q. on 5k. brown on yell	6·75	6·75

D 20 Fortress of Shkoder

D 22

D 35

1920. Optd with posthorn.

D129	D **20**	4q. olive	75	75
D130		10q. red	1·50	4·75
D131		20q. brown	1·50	2·00
D132		50q. black	1·50	4·75

1922.

D141	D **22**	4q. black on red	85	1·75
D142		10q. black on red	85	1·75
D143		20q. black on red	85	1·75
D144		50q. black on red	85	1·75

1922. Optd **Republika Shiqiptare**.

D186	D **22**	4q. black on red	1·25	1·90
D187		10q. black on red	1·25	1·90
D188		20q. black on red	1·25	1·90
D189		50q. black on red	1·25	1·90

1925.

D204	D **35**	10q. blue	45	75
D205		20q. green	50	75
D206		30q. brown	75	2·00
D207		50q. dark brown	1·25	2·75

D 53 Arms of Albania

D 67

1930.

D288	D **53**	10q. blue	5·00	6·50
D289		20q. red	1·50	2·00
D290		30q. violet	1·50	2·00
D291		50q. green	1·50	2·00

1936. Optd **Takse**.

D312	**50**	10q. red	8·50	11·50

1940.

D373	D **67**	4q. red	20·00	25·00
D374		10q. violet	20·00	25·00
D375		20q. brown	20·00	25·00

D376		30q. blue	20·00	25·00
D377		50q. red	20·00	25·00

ALEXANDRETTA Pt. 6

The territory of Alexandretta. Autonomous under French control from 1923 to September 1938.

1938. 100 centiemes = 1 piastre.

1938. Stamps of Syria of 1930/1 optd **Sandjak d'Alexandrette** (Nos. 1, 4, 7 and 11) or **SANDJAK D'ALEXANDRETTE** (others), Nos. 7 and 11 surch also.

1		0p.10 purple	1·20	80
2		0p.20 red	1·20	80
3		0p.50 violet	1·20	80
4		0p.75 red	2·00	1·20
5		1p. brown	2·00	1·20
6		2p. violet	2·40	1·60
7		2p.50 on 4p. orange	6·25	2·00
8		3p. green	16·00	4·75
9		4p. orange	16·00	4·75
10		6p. black	20·00	4·75
11		12p.50 on 15p. red (No. 267)	14·00	6·00
12		25p. purple	35·00	12·00

1938. Air. Stamps of Syria of 1937 (Nos. 322 etc.) optd **SANDJAK D'ALEXANDRETTE**.

13		½p. violet	4·00	2·00
14		1p. black	4·00	2·00
15		2p. green	8·00	4·00
16		3p. blue	8·00	4·00
17		5p. mauve	24·00	10·00
18		10p. brown	24·00	10·00
19		15p. brown	32·00	12·00
20		25p. blue	47·00	16·00

1938. Death of Kemal Ataturk. Nos. 4, 5, 7, 9 and 11 optd **10-11-1938** in frame.

27		0p.75 red	80·00	39·00
28		1p. brown	39·00	20·00
29		2p.50 on 4p. orange	28·50	13·50
30		4p. orange	35·00	17·00
31		12p.50 on 15p. red	80·00	39·00

POSTAGE DUE STAMPS

1938. Postage Due stamps of Syria of 1925 optd **SANDJAK D'ALEXANDRETTE**.

D21	D 20	0p.50 brown on yellow	8·00	4·00
D22		1p. purple on pink	8·00	4·00
D23		2p. black on blue	24·00	6·25
D24		3p. black on red	32·00	9·50
D25		5p. black on green	39·00	14·00
D26		8p. black on blue	47·00	14·00

ALEXANDRIA Pt. 6

Issues of the French P.O. in this Egyptian port. The French Post Offices in Egypt closed on 31 March 1931.

1899. 100 centimes = 1 franc.
1921. 10 milliemes = 1 piastre.

1899. Stamps of France optd **ALEXANDRIE**.

1	10	1c. black on blue	1·60	1·00
2		2c. brown on yellow	2·50	2·50
3		3c. grey	2·00	2·50
4		4c. brown on grey	1·10	2·30
5		5c. green	3·25	2·30
7		10c. black on lilac	7·00	11·00
9		15c. blue	7·00	5·25
10		20c. red on green	9·00	8·25
11		25c. black on red	7·25	50
12		30c. brown	9·00	8·75
13		40c. red on yellow	13·50	10·50
15		50c. red	28·00	16·00
16		1f. olive	19·00	13·50
17		2f. brown on blue	75·00	85·00
18		5f. mauve on lilac	£120	90·00

1902. "Blanc", "Mouchon" and "Merson" key-types, inscr "ALEXANDRIE".

19	A	1c. grey	1·70	1·10
20		2c. purple	55	1·80
21		3c. red	65	1·50
22		4c. brown	15	1·30
24		5c. green	65	55
25	B	10c. red	2·50	1·10
26		15c. red	5·00	2·00
27		15c. orange	1·40	2·30
28		20c. brown	3·25	1·70
29		25c. blue	1·90	10
30		30c. mauve	4·75	3·50
31	C	40c. red and blue	4·50	2·00
32		50c. brown and lilac	8·75	70
33		1f. red and green	15·00	1·90
34		2f. lilac and buff	15·00	6·25
35		5f. blue and buff	19·00	11·00

1915. Red Cross. Surch **5c** and Red Cross.

36	B	10c. + 5c. red	15	4·75

1921. Surch thus, **15 Mill.**, in one line (without bars).

37	A	2m. on 5c. green	3·75	9·75
38		3m. on 3c. red	8·75	12·50
39	B	4m. on 10c. red	4·25	7·50
40	A	5m. on 1c. grey	12·50	12·50
41		5m. on 4c. brown	10·00	13·00
42	B	6m. on 15c. orange	2·75	7·50
43		8m. on 20c. brown	4·50	9·50
44		10m. on 25c. blue	2·75	6·00
45		12m. on 30c. mauve	13·00	21·00
46	A	15m. on 2c. purple	7·00	12·00
47	C	15m. on 40c. red and blue	15·00	21·00
48		15m. on 50c. brown & lilac	8·75	17·00
49		30m. on 1f. red and green	£120	£120
50		60m. on 2f. lilac and buff	£140	£140
51		150m. on 5f. blue and buff	£200	£225

1921. Surch thus, **15 MILLIEMES**, in two lines (without bars).

53	A	1m. on 1c. grey	3·75	5·50
54		2m. on 5c. green	3·25	4·75
55	B	4m. on 10c. red	4·50	7·00
65		4m. on 10c. green	2·50	4·75
56	A	5m. on 3c. orange	6·25	9·00
57	B	6m. on 15c. orange	2·75	5·50
58		8m. on 20c. brown	2·50	4·75
59		10m. on 25c. blue	2·30	3·25
60		10m. on 30c. mauve	6·50	6·00
61	C	15m. on 50c. brown & lilac	6·25	6·00
66	B	15m. on 50c. blue	2·75	2·30
62	C	30m. on 1f. red and green	5·00	3·75
63		60m. on 2f. lilac and buff	£1700	£1800
67		60m. on 2f. red and green	16·00	16·00
64		150m. on 5f. blue and buff	16·00	17·00

1925. Surch in milliemes with bars over old value.

68	A	1m. on 1c. grey	10	3·75
69		2m. on 5c. orange	20	2·75
70		2m. on 5c. green	3·00	4·50
71	B	4m. on 10c. green	90	4·75
72	A	5m. on 3c. red	1·50	3·75
73	B	6m. on 15c. orange	1·30	4·00
74		8m. on 20c. brown	95	4·25
75		10m. on 25c. blue	45	1·40
76		15m. on 50c. blue	2·30	1·50
77	C	30m. on 1f. red and green	1·50	85
78		60m. on 2f. red and green	3·50	7·75
79		150m. on 5f. blue and buff	5·00	8·75

1927. Altered key-types, inscr "Mm" below value.

80	A	3m. orange	2·75	5·25
81	B	15m. blue	2·50	1·50
82		20m. mauve	5·50	8·25
83	C	50m. red and green	11·50	16·00
84		100m. blue and yellow	14·50	18·00
85		250m. green and red	19·00	28·00

1927. Sinking Fund. As No. 81, colour changed, surch **+ 5 Mm Caisse d'Amortissement**.

86	B	15m.+5m. orange	3·25	8·50
87		15m.+5m. red	5·25	8·50
88		15m.+5m. brown	10·00	17·00
89		15m.+5m. lilac	14·00	26·00

POSTAGE DUE STAMPS

1922. Postage Due Stamps of France surch in milliemes.

D65	D 11	2m. on 5c. blue	1·30	6·75
D66		4m. on 10c. brown	3·00	6·75
D67		10m. on 30c. red	2·75	7·50
D68		15m. on 50c. purple	1·40	7·50
D69		30m. on 1f. pur on yell	1·20	11·00

D 10

1928.

D90	D 10	1m. grey	85	6·00
D91		2m. blue	3·25	5·75
D92		4m. pink	3·75	6·25
D93		5m. olive	3·50	5·50
D94		10m. red	4·00	6·25
D95		20m. purple	4·00	5·75
D96		30m. green	8·75	10·50
D97		40m. lilac	6·75	10·50

This set was issued for use in both Alexandria and Port Said.

ALGERIA Pt. 6, Pt. 12

French territory in N. Africa. Stamps of France were used in Algeria from July 1958 until 3 July 1962, when the country achieved independence following a referendum.

1924. 100 centimes = 1 franc.
1964. 100 centimes = 1 dinar.

1924. Stamps of France optd **ALGERIE**.

1	11	½c. on 1c. grey	50	1·60
2		1c. grey	50	2·30
3		2c. red	35	2·50
4		3c. red	55	2·30
5		4c. brown	50	1·90
6	18	5c. orange	1·00	60
7	11	5c. green	45	10
8	30	10c. green	1·30	1·20
9	18	10c. green	30	50
10	15	15c. green	1·40	1·30
11	30	15c. green	75	2·50
12	18	15c. brown	1·40	1·10
13		20c. brown	1·40	50
14		25c. blue	55	10
15	30	30c. red	85	65
16	18	30c. blue	35	10
17		30c. red*	45	1·50
18		35c. violet	1·50	1·60
19	13	40c. red and blue	1·90	2·00
20	18	40c. olive	1·40	1·70
21	13	45c. green and blue	1·10	2·30
22	30	45c. red	45	70
23		50c. blue	1·20	80
24	15	60c. violet	90	55
25		65c. red	25	55
26	30	75c. blue	40	35
27	15	80c. red	65	80
28		85c. red	40	35
29	13	1f. red and green	1·80	40
30	18	1f.05 red	50	1·50
31	13	2f. red and green	2·00	3·50
32		3f. violet and blue	1·90	3·00
33		5f. blue and yellow	8·50	12·00

*No. 17 was only issued pre-cancelled and the price in the unused column is for stamps with full gum.

3 Street in the Casbah

4 Mosque of Sidi Abderahman

5 Grand Mosque

6 Bay of Algiers

1926.

34	3	1c. green	25	1·30
35		2c. purple	25	1·20
36		3c. orange	10	1·20
37		5c. green	35	10
38		10c. mauve	40	10
39	4	15c. brown	35	20
40		20c. green	35	10
41		20c. red	1·50	10
45		25c. blue	1·00	35
46		30c. blue	1·00	1·40
47		30c. green	1·60	10
48		35c. violet	1·50	4·00
49		40c. green	10	10
50	5	45c. purple	50	10
51		50c. blue	40	10
53		50c. red	95	10
54		60c. green	40	75
55		65c. brown	2·00	1·50
56	3	65c. blue	1·80	20
57	5	75c. red	40	10
58		75c. blue	2·75	10
59		80c. orange	75	2·30
60		90c. red	2·00	2·00
61	6	1f. purple and green	90	10
62	5	1f.05 brown	60	2·30
63		1f.10 mauve	3·50	7·25
64	6	1f.25 ultramarine and blue	1·70	4·75
65		1f.50 ultramarine and blue	1·10	10
66		2f. brown and green	2·00	25
67		3f. red and mauve	3·50	1·40
68		5f. mauve and red	4·00	2·75
69		10f. red and brown	50·00	44·00
70		20f. green and violet	10·00	12·50

1926. Surch **½ centime**.

71	3	½c. on 1c. olive	10	1·70

1927. Wounded Soldiers of Moroccan War Charity Issue. Surch with star and crescent and premium.

72	3	5c.+5c. green	80	4·75
73		10c.+10c. mauve	90	4·50
74	4	15c.+15c. brown	1·20	4·50
75		20c.+20c. red	1·20	4·50
76		25c.+25c. green	80	4·75
77		30c.+30c. blue	1·60	4·50
78		35c.+35c. violet	50	4·50
79		40c.+40c. olive	80	4·50
80	5	50c.+50c. blue	1·00	4·75
81		80c.+80c. orange	95	4·75
82	6	1f.+1f. purple and green	1·20	4·75
83		2f.+2f. brown and green	24·00	50·00
84		5f.+5f. mauve and red	55·00	75·00

1927. Surch in figures.

85	4	10 on 35c. violet	30	90
86		25 on 30c. blue	50	10
87		30 on 25c. green	20	10
88	5	65 on 60c. green	85	85
89		90 on 80c. orange	15	10
90		1f.10 on 1f.05 brown	10	10
91	6	1f.50 on 1f.25 ultramarine and blue	90	90

1927. Surch **5c**.

92	11	5c. on 4c. brown (No. 5)	90	1·60

11 Railway Terminus, Oran

1930. Centenary of French Occupation.

93	11	5c.+5c. orange	7·50	25·00
94	–	10c.+10c. olive	6·25	19·00
95	–	15c.+15c. brown	4·25	18·00
96	–	25c.+25c. grey	4·25	19·00
97	–	30c.+30c. red	4·00	20·00
98	–	40c.+40c. green	3·50	18·00
99	–	50c.+50c. blue	4·00	17·00
100	–	75c.+75c. purple	3·00	18·00
101	–	1f.+1f. orange	4·00	19·00
102	–	1f.50+1f.50 blue	4·25	18·00
103	–	2f.+2f. red	3·00	18·00
104	–	3f.+3f. green	3·75	20·00
105	–	5f.+5f. red and green	7·25	50·00

DESIGNS—HORIZ: 10c. Constantine; 15c. Admiralty, Algiers; 25c. Algiers; 30c. Ruins of Timgad; 40c. Ruins of Djemila. VERT: 50c. Ruins of Djemila; 75c. Tlemcen; 1f. Ghardaia; 1f.50, Tolga; 2f. Tuaregs; 3f. Native quarter, Algiers; 5f. Mosque, Algiers.

12 Bay of Algiers, after painting by Verecque

1930. N. African International Philatelic Exn.

106	12	10f.+10f. brown	32·00	50·00

15 Admiralty and Penon Lighthouse, Algiers

1936.

107	A	1c. blue	25	1·30
108	F	2c. purple	20	65
109	B	3c. green	50	1·90
110	C	5c. mauve	40	10
111	15	10c. green	70	60
112	D	15c. red	35	10
113	G	20c. green	45	10
114	E	25c. purple	1·90	40
115	C	30c. green	45	15
116	D	40c. purple	70	15
117	G	45c. blue	1·10	3·25
118	15	50c. red	2·50	10
119	A	65c. brown	7·00	9·75
120		65c. red	1·90	30
121		70c. brown	75	85
122	F	75c. slate	75	15
124	B	90c. red	95	1·10
125	E	1f. brown	70	10
126	15	1f.25 violet	1·90	70
127		1f.25 red	70	1·90
128	F	1f.50 blue	2·30	75
129		1f.50 red	3·50	4·25
130	C	1f.75 orange	1·10	65
131	B	2f. purple	1·00	10
132	A	2f.25 green	19·00	26·00
133	E	2f.25 blue	1·90	2·00
134	C	2f.50 blue	2·00	3·25
135	G	3f. mauve	70	30
136	E	3f.50 blue	2·00	3·00
137	15	5f. slate	1·40	1·50
138	F	10f. orange	1·40	3·25
139	D	20f. blue	1·70	3·25

DESIGNS—HORIZ: A, In the Sahara; B, Arc de Triomphe, Lambese; C, Ghardaia, Mzab; D, Marabouts, Touggourt; E, El Kebir Mosque, Algiers. VERT: F, Colomb Bechar-Oued; G, Cemetery, Tlemcen.

17 Exhibition Pavilion

18 Constantine in 1837

1937. Paris International Exhibition.

140	17	40c. green	40	45
141		50c. red	30	30
142		1f.50 blue	50	85
143		1f.75 black	70	1·10

1937. Centenary of Capture of Constantine.

144	18	65c. red	75	10
145		1f. brown	1·90	35
146		1f.75 blue	15	70
147		2f.15 purple	25	30

19 Ruins of Roman Villa

1938. Centenary of Philippeville.

148	19	30c. green	1·50	2·50
149		65c. blue	50	45
150		75c. purple	1·40	2·75
151		3f. red	2·00	2·00
152		5f. brown	3·50	4·75

1938. 20th Anniv of Armistice Day. No. 132 surch **1918 - 11 Nov. - 1938 0.65 + 0.35**.

153		65c.+35c. on 2f.25 green	1·10	3·75

1938. Surch **0,25**.

154	15	25c. on 50c. red	20	10

22 Caillie, Lavigerie and Duveyrier

1939. Sahara Pioneers' Monument Fund.
155 **22** 30c.+20c. green 2·30 6·25
156 90c.+60c. red 1·30 4·50
157 2f.25+75c. blue 9·50 32·00
158 5f.+5f. black 11·00 60·00

23 "Extavia" (freighter) in Algiers Harbour

1939. New York World's Fair.
159 **23** 20c. green 1·10 3·75
160 40c. purple 1·50 4·25
161 90c. brown 1·80 50
162 1f.25 red 5·75 8·00
163 2f.25 blue 2·00 2·75

1939. Surch with new values and bars or cross.
173 **3** 50c. on 65c. blue 1·10 20
173c B 90c.+60c. red (No. 124) 65 15
164 **3** 1f. on 90c. red 70 10

25 Algerian Soldiers

26 Algiers

1940. Soldiers' Dependants' Relief Fund. Surch **+** and premium.
166 **25** 1f.+1f. blue 1·70 3·75
167 1f.+2f. red 1·70 5·25
168 1f.+4f. green 1·80 5·50
169 1f.+9f. brown 1·70 6·25

1941.
170 **26** 30c. blue 1·40 1·70
171 70c. brown 1·10 20
172 1f. red 1·10 20

28 Marshal Petain

1941.
174 **28** 1f. blue 60 1·50

1941. National Relief Fund. As No. 174, but surch **+4 f** and colour changed.
175 1f.+4f. black 90 4·00

1942. National Relief Fund. Surch **SECOURS NATIONAL +4f.**
176 1f.+4f. blue (No. 174) 50 5·00

1942. Various altered types. (a) As T **26**, but without "RF".
177 **26** 30c. blue 55 3·75
(b) As T **5**, but without "REPUBLIQUE FRANCAISE".
178 **5** 40c. grey 1·30 4·00
179 50c. red 75 1·30
(c) As No. 129 but without "RF".
180 F 1f.50 red 1·60 65

32 Arms of Oran

34 Marshal Petain

1942. Coats-of-Arms.
190 A 10c. lilac 1·10 3·25
191 **32** 30c. green 90 3·50
181 B 40c. violet 65 3·50
192 40c. lilac 1·60 3·25
182 **32** 60c. red 1·00 1·70
194 B 70c. blue 80 2·00
195 A 80c. green 95 3·25
183 B 1f.20 green 1·00 2·50
184 A 1f.50 red 20 25
198 **32** 2f. blue 25 80
186 B 2f.40 red 1·70 2·30
187 A 3f. blue 35 45
188 B 4f. blue 90 1·20
201 **32** 4f.50 purple 80 10
189 5f. green 1·10 1·30
ARMS: A, Algiers; B, Constantine.

1943.
202 **34** 1f.50 red 35 3·00

35 "La Marseillaise"

36 Allegory of Victory

1943.
203 **35** 1f.50 red 90 2·30
204 **36** 1f.50 blue 10 60

1943. Surch **2f.**
205 **32** 2f. on 5f. orange 25 1·00

38 Summer Palace, Algiers

39 Mother and Children

1943.
206 **38** 15f. grey 1·10 2·00
207 20f. green 1·50 2·00
208 50f. red 90 1·20
209 100f. blue 2·50 2·50
210 200f. brown 3·00 2·30

1943. Prisoners-of-war Relief Fund.
211 **39** 50c.+4f.50 pink 45 5·50
212 1f.50+8f.50 green 20 5·50
213 3f.+12f. blue 20 5·50
214 5f.+15f. brown 40 5·50

40 "Marianne"

41 Gallic Cock

1944.
215 **40** 10c. grey 10 75
216 30c. lilac 10 55
217 50c. red 10 10
218 80c. green 35 90
219 1f.20 lilac 60 1·80
220 1f.50 blue 10 10
221 2f.40 red 20 35
222 3f. violet 20 10
223 4f.50 black 40 10

1944.
224 **41** 40c. red 15 3·00
225 1f. green 20 15
226 2f. red 20 10
227 2f. brown 40 70
228 4f. blue 1·40 10
229 10f. black 85 2·50

1944. Surch **0f.30.**
230 **4** 0f.30 on 15c. brown 35 60
No. 230 was only issued pre-cancelled and the price in the unused column is for stamps with full gum.

1945. Types of France optd **ALGERIE.**
247 **239** 10c. black and blue 10 3·75
231 **217** 40c. mauve 10 50
232 50c. blue 15 10
248 – 50c. brown, yellow and red (No. 973) 60 40
233 **218** 60c. blue 40 70
236 **136** 80c. green 90 1·40
237 1f. blue 70 25
234 **218** 1f. red 60 20
238 **136** 1f.20 violet 70 3·50
235 **218** 1f.50 lilac 75 1·10
239 **136** 2f. brown 10 10
242 **219** 2f. green 75 10
240 **136** 2f.40 red 85 1·80
241 3f. orange 65 80
243 **219** 3f. red 40 10
244 4f.50 blue 1·70 35
245 5f. green 25 20
246 10f. blue 1·70 1·60

1945. Airmen and Dependants Fund. As No. 742 of France (bombers) optd **RF ALGERIE.**
249 **169** 1f.50+3f.50 blue 1·00 4·25

1945. Postal Employees War Victims' Fund. As No. 949 of France overprinted **ALGERIE.**
250 **223** 4f.+6f. brown 45 4·25

1945. Stamp Day. As No. 955 of France (Louis XI) optd **ALGERIE.**
251 **228** 2f.+3f. purple 95 4·00

1946. No. 184 surch **0f50 RF.**
252 50c. on 1f.50 red 10 20

1946. Type of France optd **ALGERIE** and surch **2F.**
253 **136** 2f. on 1f.50 brown 10 10

46 Potez 56 over Algiers

1946. Air.
254 **46** 5f. red 1·10 75
255 10f. blue 35 10
256 15f. green 60 70
257a 20f. brown 65 10
258 25f. violet 65 20
259 40f. black 1·20 1·40

1946. Stamp Day. As No. 975 of France (De la Varane), optd **ALGERIE.**
260 **241** 3f.+2f. red 65 6·00

47 Children at Spring

49 Arms of Constantine

1946. Charity. Inscr as in T **47.**
261 **47** 3f.+17f. green 1·30 6·50
262 4f.+21f. red 95 6·00
263 8f.+27f. purple 2·30 17·00
264 10f.+35f. blue 1·60 6·50
DESIGNS—VERT: 4f. Boy gazing skywards; 8f. Laurel-crowned head. HORIZ: 10f. Soldier looking at Algerian coast.

1947. Air. Surch **-10%.**
265 **46** "-10%" on 5f. red 15 55

1947. Stamp Day. As No. 1008 of France (Louvois), optd **ALGERIE.**
266 **253** 4f.50+5f.50 blue 20 5·25

1947. Various Arms.
267 **49** 10c. green and red 10 2·30
268 A 50c. black and orange 10 10
269 B 1f. blue and yellow 10 10
270 **49** 1f.30 black and blue 90 4·00
271 A 1f.50 violet and yellow 10 10
272 B 2f. black and green 10 10
273 **49** 2f.50 black and red 85 85
274 A 3f. red and green 10 50
275 B 3f.50 green and purple 35 10
276 **49** 4f. brown and green 10 10
277 A 4f.50 blue and red 10 10
278 5f. black and blue 20 10
279 B 6f. brown and red 10 10
280 8f. brown and blue 10 10
281 **49** 10f. pink and brown 20 10
282 A 15f. black and red 1·70 10
ARMS: A, Algiers; B, Oran. See also Nos. 364/8 and 381/3.

1947. Air. 7th Anniv of Gen. de Gaulle's Call to Arms. Surch with Lorraine Cross and **18 Juin 1940 + 10 Fr.**
283 **46** 10f.+10f. blue 2·75 5·75

1947. Resistance Movement. Type of France surch **ALGERIE+10f.**
284 **261** 5f.+10f. grey 1·00 5·50

1948. Stamp Day. Type of France (Arago) optd **ALGERIE.**
285 **267** 6f.+4f. green 85 6·25

1948. Air. 8th Anniv of Gen. de Gaulle's Call to Arms. Surch with Lorraine Cross and **18 JUIN 1940 + 10 Fr.**
286 **46** 5f.+10f. red 2·50 5·50

1948. General Leclerc Memorial. Type of France surch **ALGERIE + 4f.**
287 **270** 6f.+4f. red 1·10 5·00

57 Battleship "Richelieu"

58 White Storks over Minaret

1949. Naval Welfare Fund.
288 **57** 10f.+15f. blue 4·00 18·00
289 – 18f.+22f. red 7·00 18·00
DESIGN: 18f. Aircraft-carrier "Arromanches".

1949. Air.
290 **58** 50f. green 4·00 1·00
291 – 100f. brown 1·70 60
292 **58** 200f. red 8·00 3·75
293 – 500f. blue 26·00 40·00
DESIGN—HORIZ: 100, 500f. Dewoitine D-338 trimotor airplane over valley dwellings.

1949. Stamp Day. As No. 1054 of France (Choiseul) optd **ALGERIE.**
294 **278** 15f.+5f. mauve 30 6·00

60 French Colonials

61 Statue of Duke of Orleans

1949. 75th Anniv of U.P.U.
295 **60** 5f. green 1·20 4·50
296 15f. red 75 4·50
297 25f. blue 2·00 13·50

1949. Air. 25th Anniv of First Algerian Postage Stamp.
298 **61** 15f.+20f. brown 5·25 17·00

62 Grapes

63 Foreign Legionary

1950.
299 **62** 20f. purple, green & dp pur 75 40
300 – 25f. brown, green & black 1·30 30
301 – 40f. orange, green & brown 2·30 1·80
DESIGNS: 25f. Dates; 40f. Oranges and lemons.

1950. Stamp Day. As No. 1091 of France (Postman), optd **ALGERIE.**
302 **292** 12f.+3f. brown 1·70 7·50

1950. Foreign Legion Welfare Fund.
303 **63** 15f.+5f. green 1·50 7·00

64 R. P. de Foucauld and Gen. Laperrine

1950. 50th Anniv of French in the Sahara (25f.) and Unveiling of Monument to Abd-el-Kader (40f.).
304 **64** 25f.+5f. black and green 5·75 15·00
305 – 40f.+10f. dp brown & brn 4·25 15·00
DESIGN: 40f. Emir Abd-el-Kader and Marshal Bugeaud.

65 Col. C. d'Ornano

1951. Col. d'Ornano Monument Fund.
306 **65** 15f.+5f. purple, brn blk 1·00 5·00

1951. Stamp Day. As No. 1107 of France (Travelling Post Office sorting van), optd **ALGERIE.**
307 **300** 12f.+3f. brown 4·25 6·50

66 Apollo of Cherchel

67 Algerian War Memorial

1952.

308 **66** 10f. sepia 10 10
309 – 12f. brown 35 15
310 – 15f. blue 15 10
311 – 18f. red 30 20
312 – 20f. green 30 10
313 **66** 30f. blue 35 35
STATUES: 12, 18f. Isis of Cherchel; 15, 20f. Boy and eagle.

1952. Stamp Day. As No. 1140 of France (Mail Coach), optd **ALGERIE**.
314 **319** 12f.+3f. blue . . . . 1·90 7·75

1952. African Army Commemoration.
315 **67** 12f. green . . . . 95 2·50

68 Medaille Militaire

69 Fossil ("Berbericeras sekikensis")

1952. Military Medal Centenary.
316 **68** 15f.+5f. brown, yell & grn 1·80 6·50

1952. 19th Int Geological Convention, Algiers.
317 **69** 15f. red . . . . 2·30 6·00
318 – 30f. blue . . . . 1·30 3·50
DESIGN: 30f. Phonolite Dyke, Hoggar.

1952. 10th Anniv of Battle of Bir-Hakeim. As No. 1146 of France surch **ALGERIE+5 F**.
319 **325** 30f.+5f. blue . . . . . . 2·30 6·50

72 Bou-Nara

73 Members of Corps and Camel

1952. Red Cross Fund.
320 – 8f.+2f. red and blue . . . 80 4·50
321 **72** 12f.+3f. red . . . . 95 8·25
DESIGN: 8f. El-Oued and map of Algeria.

1952. 50th Anniv of Sahara Corps.
322 **73** 12f. brown . . . . 1·80 3·50

1953. Stamp Day. As No. 1161 of France (Count D'Argenson), optd **ALGERIE**.
323 **334** 12f.+3f. violet . . . . . 95 7·00

74 "Victory" of Cirta

75 E. Millon

1954. Army Welfare Fund.
324 **74** 15f.+5f. brown and sepia 40 3·50

1954. Military Health Service.
325 **75** 25f. sepia and green . . . 75 40
326 – 40f. red and brown . . . 65 15
327 – 50f. indigo and blue . . . 90 20
DOCTORS—VERT: 40f. F. Maillot. HORIZ: 50f. A. Laveran.

1954. Stamp Day. As No. 1202 of France (Lavalette), optd **ALGERIE**.
328 **346** 12f.+3f. red . . . . . . 65 5·00

76 French and Algerian Soldiers

77 Foreign Legionary

1954. Old Soldiers' Welfare Fund.
329 **76** 15f.+5f. sepia . . . . . . 1·30 4·75

1954. Foreign Legion Welfare Fund.
330 **77** 15f.+5f. green . . . . . . 2·30 6·50

78

79 Darguinah Hydroelectric Station

1954. 3rd International Congress of Mediterranean Citrus Fruit Culture.
331 **78** 15f. blue and indigo . . . 1·30 3·00

1954. 10th Anniv of Liberation. As No. 1204 of France ("D-Day") optd **ALGERIE**.
332 **348** 15f. red . . . . 55 1·80

1954. Inauguration of River Agrioun Hydroelectric Installations.
333 **79** 15f. purple . . . . 1·10 3·75

80 Courtyard of Bardo Museum

1954.

334 **80** 10f. brown & light brown 25 10
335 12f. orange and brown (I) 65 10
336 12f. orange and brown (II) 10 50
337 15f. blue and light blue . . 35 15
338 18f. carmine and red . . . 20 35
339 20f. green and light green 25 1·10
340 25f. lilac and mauve . . . 20 10
12f. "POSTES" and "ALGERIE" in orange (I) or in white (II).

1954. 150th Anniv of Presentation of First Legion of Honour. As No. 1223 of France, optd **ALGERIE**.
341 **356** 12f. green . . . . 30 3·50

81 Red Cross Nurses

82 St. Augustine

1954. Red Cross Fund. Cross in red.
342 **81** 12f.+3f. blue . . . . . . 2·75 8·00
343 – 15f.+5f. violet . . . . . 4·25 9·75
DESIGN: 15f. J.H. Dunant and Djemila ruins.

1954. 1600th Birth Anniv of St. Augustine.
344 **82** 15f. brown . . . . 1·20 2·50

83 Earthquake Victims and Ruins

84 Statue of Aesculapius and El Kettar Hospital

1954. Orleansville Earthquake Relief Fund. Inscr as in T **83**.
345 **83** 12f.+4f. brown . . . . . 1·40 6·00
346 15f.+5f. blue . . . . . 1·50 6·25
347 – 18f.+6f. mauve . . . . 1·70 6·25
348 – 20f.+7f. violet . . . . 1·80 6·50
349 – 25f.+8f. lake . . . . . 2·30 6·75
350 – 30f.+10f. turquoise . . . 1·70 8·00
DESIGNS—HORIZ: 18, 20f. Red Cross workers. 25, 30f. Stretcher-bearers.

1955. Stamp Day. As No. 1245 of France (Balloon Post), optd **ALGERIE**.
351 **364** 12f.+3f. blue . . . . . . 65 5·00

1955. 30th French Medical Congress.
352 **84** 15f. red 30 80

85 Ruins of Tipasa

86 Widows and Children

1955. Bimillenary of Tipasa.
353 **85** 50f. brown 35 10

1955. 50th Anniv of Rotary International. As No. 1235 of France optd **ALGERIE**.
354 **361** 30f. blue . . . . 45 2·30

1955. As Nos. 1238 and 1238b of France ("France") inscr "ALGERIE".
355 **362** 15f. red 15 10
356 20f. blue . . . . 1·50 1·80

1955. War Victims' Welfare Fund.
357 **86** 15f.+5f. indigo and blue . . 1·40 3·25

87 Grand Kabylie

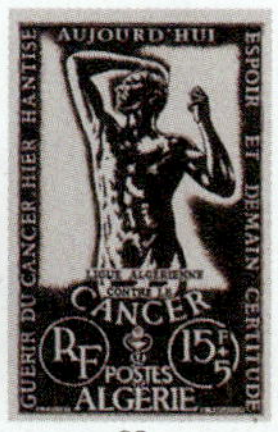
88

1955.

358 **87** 100f. indigo and blue . . . 1·10 15

1956. Anti-cancer Fund.
359 **88** 15f.+5f. brown . . . . . . 1·20 4·75

1956. Stamp Day. As No. 1279 of France ("Francis of Taxis"), optd **ALGERIE**.
360 **383** 12f.+3f. red . . . . . . 75 4·25

89 Foreign Legion Retirement Home, Sidi Bel Abbes

1956. Foreign Legion Welfare Fund.
361 **89** 15f.+5f. green . . . . . . 1·40 6·00

90 Marshal Franchet d'Esperey (after J. Ebstein)

1956. Birth Cent of Marshal Franchet d'Esperey.
362 **90** 15f. indigo and blue . . . 2·00 4·25

91 Marshal Leclerc and Memorial

1956. Marshal Leclerc Commemoration.
363 **91** 15f. brown and sepia . . . 25 3·75

1956. Various arms as T **49**.
364 1f. green and red 50 70
365 3f. blue and green . . . . 45 2·75
366 5f. blue and yellow 40 45
367 6f. green and red . . . . . 1·00 3·00
368 12f. blue and red . . . . . 1·00 4·25
DESIGNS: 1f. Bone; 3f. Mostaganem; 5f. Tlemcen; 6f. Algiers; 12f. Orleansville.

92 Oran

1956.

369 **92** 30f. purple . . . . 1·30 25
370 35f. red . . . . 1·70 5·00

1957. Stamp Day. As No. 1322 of France ("Felucca") optd **ALGERIE**.
371 **403** 12f.+3f. purple . . . . . 1·70 4·75

93 Electric Train Crossing Viaduct

1957. Electrification of Bone-Tebessa Railway Line.
372 **93** 40f. turquoise and green 1·20 10

94 Fennec Fox

1957. Red Cross Fund. Cross in red.
373 **94** 12f.+3f. brown . . . . . . 2·50 10·50
374 – 15f.+5f. sepia (White storks) . . . . 2·50 12·00

1957. 17th Anniv of Gen. de Gaulle's Call to Arms. Surch **18 JUIN 1940 + 5F**.
375 **91** 15f.+5f. red and carmine 60 5·00

96 Beni Bahdel Barrage, Tlemcen

97 "Horseman Crossing Ford" (after Delacroix)

1957. Air.
376 **96** 200f. red . . . . 7·25 10·00

1957. Army Welfare Fund. Inscr "OEUVRES SOCIALES DE L'ARMEE".
377 **97** 15f.+5f. red . . . . 3·50 11·00
378 – 20f.+5f. green . . . . . 3·25 11·50
379 – 35f.+10f. blue . . . . . 3·25 12·00
DESIGNS—HORIZ: 20f. "Lakeside View" (after Fromentin). VERT: 35f. "Arab Dancer" (after Chasseriau).

1958. Stamp Day. As No. 1375 of France (Rural Postal Service), optd **ALGERIE**.
380 **421** 15f.+5f. brown . . . . . 1·30 4·25

1958. Arms. As T **49** but inscr "REPUBLIQUE FRANCAISE" instead of "RF" at foot.
381 2f. red and blue . . . . . 50 4·00
382 6f. green and red . . . . . 36·00 60·00
383 10f. purple and green . . . 1·10 4·50
ARMS: 2f. Tizi-Ouzou; 6f. Algiers; 10f. Setif.

99 "Strelitzia Reginae"

100

1958. Algerian Child Welfare Fund.
384 **99** 20f.+5f. orge, vio & grn . . 2·75 6·25

1958. Marshal de Lattre Foundation.
385 **100** 20f.+5f. red, grn & bl . . 3·00 6·25

INDEPENDENT STATE

1962. Stamps of France optd **EA** and with bars obliterating "REPUBLIQUE FRANCAISE".
386 **344** 10c. green 95 40
387 **463** 25c. grey and red 70 30
393 – 45c. violet, purple and sepia (No. 1463) . . . . 6·75 4·50

394 – 50c. pur & grn (No. 1464) 6·75 4·50
395 – 1f. brown, blue and myrtle (No. 1549) . . . 4·50 1·80

103a Maps of Africa and Algeria

1962. War Orphans' Fund.
395a **103a** 1f.+9f. green, black and red £350

1962. As pictorial types of France but inscr "REPUBLIQUE ALGERIENNE".
396 – 5c. turquoise, grn & brn 25 10
397 **438** 10c. blue and sepia . . . 25 10
398 – 25c. red, slate & brown 55 15
399 – 95c. blue, buff and sepia 3·50 1·10
400 – 1f. sepia and green . . . 2·50 1·60
DESIGNS—VERT: 5c. Kerrata Gorges; 25c. Tlemcen Mosque; 95c. Oil derrick and pipeline at Hassi-Massaoud, Sahara. HORIZ: 1f. Medea.

104 Flag, Rifle and Olive Branch

1963. "Return of Peace". Flag in green and red. Inscription and background colours given.
401 **104** 5c. bistre 25 10
402 10c. blue 25 10
403 25c. red . . . . 1·90 30
404 95c. violet . . . . 1·80 75
405 – 1f. green . . . . 2·20 15
406 – 2f. brown . . . . 3·75 80
407 – 5f. purple . . . . 7·00 3·00
408 – 10f. black . . . . 25·00 14·50
DESIGN: 1f. to 10f. As Type **104** but with dove and broken chain added.

105 Campaign Emblem and Globe

1963. Freedom from Hunger.
409 **105** 25c. yellow, green and red 70 25

106 Clasped Hands

107 Map and Emblems

1963. National Solidarity Fund.
410 **106** 50c.+20c. red, grn & blk 1·40 65

1963. 1st Anniv of Independence.
411 **107** 25c. multicoloured 70 25

108 "Arab Physicians" (13th-century MS.)

109 Branch of Orange Tree

1963. 2nd Arab Physicians Union Congress.
412 **108** 25c. brown, green & bistre 2·10 55

1963.
413 **109** 8c. orange and bronze* 10 10
414 20c. orange and green* 25 15
415 40c. orange & turq* . . . 75 35
416 55c. orange and green* 95 55
*These stamps were only issued pre-cancelled, the unused prices being for stamps with full gum.

110 "Constitution"

111 "Freedom Fighters"

1963. Promulgation of Constitution.
417 **110** 25c. red, green and sepia 70 40

1963. 9th Anniv of Revolution.
418 **111** 25c. red, green and brown 70 25

112 Centenary Emblem

113 Globe and Scales of Justice

1963. Red Cross Centenary.
419 **112** 25c. blue, red and yellow 95 55

1963. 15th Anniv of Declaration of Human Rights.
420 **113** 25c. black and blue . . . 70 25

114 Labourers

116 Tractors

115 Map of Africa and Flags

1964. Labour Day.
421 **114** 50c. multicoloured . . . . 1·40 45

1964. 1st Anniv of Africa Day, and African Unity Charter.
422 **115** 45c. red, orange and blue 90 40

1964.
423 **116** 5c. purple 10 10
424 – 10c. brown 10 10
425 – 12c. green 50 25
426 – 15c. blue 45 25
427 – 20c. yellow 45 10
428 **116** 25c. red 55 10
429 – 30c. violet 55 15
430 – 45c. lake 70 25
431 – 50c. blue 70 10
432 – 65c. orange 90 25
433 **116** 85c. green . . . . 1·40 25
434 – 95c. red . . . . 1·80 25
DESIGNS: 10, 30, 65c. Apprentices; 12, 15, 45c. Research scientist; 20, 50, 95c. Draughtsman and bricklayer.

117 Rameses II in War Chariot, Abu Simbel

1964. Nubian Monuments Preservation.
435 **117** 20c. purple, red and blue 95 40
436 – 30c. ochre, turq & red . . 1·20 55
DESIGN: 30c. Heads of Rameses II.

118 Hertzian-wave Radio Transmitting Pylon

119 Fair Emblems

1964. Inauguration of Algiers–Annaba Radio-Telephone Service.
437 **118** 85c. black, blue & brown 2·10 65

1964. Algiers Fair.
438 **119** 30c. blue, yellow and red 55 25

120 Gas Plant

121 Planting Trees

1964. Inaug of Natural Gas Plant at Arzew.
439 **120** 25c. blue, yellow & violet 90 50

1964. Reafforestation Campaign.
440 **121** 25c. green, red and yellow 55 25

122 Children

123 Meharist Saddle

1964. Children's Charter.
441 **122** 15c. blue, green and red 50 25

1965. Saharan Handicrafts.
442 **123** 20c. multicoloured 55 25

124 Books Aflame

125 I.C.Y. Emblem

1965. Reconstitution of Algiers University Library.
443 **124** 20c.+5c. red, blk & grn 55 40

1965. International Co-operation Year.
444 **125** 30c. black, green and red 95 45
445 60c. black, green and blue 1·40 60

126 I.T.U. Emblem and Symbols

1965. Centenary of I.T.U.
446 **126** 60c. violet, ochre & green 95 50
447 95c. brown, ochre & lake 1·40 55

127 Musicians playing Rebbah and Lute

1965. Mohamed Racim's Miniatures (1st series). Multicoloured.
448 30c. Type **127** . . . . 1·80 65
449 60c. Musicians playing derbouka and tarr . . . . 2·75 1·50
450 5d. Algerian princess and sand gazelle . . . . 14·50 7·75
See also Nos. 471/3.

128 Cattle

1966. Rock-paintings of Tassili-N-Ajjer (1st series).
451 **128** 1d. brown, ochre & purple . . . . 5·25 2·75
452 – 1d. multicoloured . . . . 5·25 2·75
453 – 2d. dp brown, buff & brn 11·00 4·75
454 – 3d. multicoloured . . . . 12·00 6·25
DESIGNS—VERT: No. 452, Peuhl shepherd; 454, Peuhl girls. HORIZ: No. 453, Ostriches.
See also Nos. 474/7.

129 Pottery

130 Meteorological Instruments

1966. Grand Kahylie Handicrafts.
455 **129** 40c. brown, sepia and blue 55 40
456 – 50c. orange, green & bl 90 40
457 – 70c. black, red and blue 1·40 50
DESIGNS—HORIZ: 50c. Weaving. VERT: 70c. Jewellery.

1966. World Meteorological Day.
458 **130** 1d. purple, green and blue 1·40 50

131 Open Book, Cogwheel and Ear of Corn

132 W.H.O. Building

1966. Literacy Campaign.
459 **131** 30c. black and ochre . . . 50 25
460 – 60c. red, black and grey 75 40
DESIGN: 60c. Open primer, cogwheel and ear of corn.

1966. Inaug of W.H.O. Headquarters, Geneva.
461 **132** 30c. turq, grn & brn . . . 45 40
462 60c. slate, blue and brown 90 40

133 Mohammedan Scout Emblem and Banner

134 Soldiers and Battle Casualty

1966. 30th Anniv of Algerian Mohammedan Scouts, and 7th Arab Scout Jamboree, Jedaid (Tripoli). Multicoloured.
463 30c. Type **133** 70 40
464 1d. Jamboree emblem . . . . 1·80 65

1966. Freedom Fighters' Day.
465 **134** 30c.+10c. mult 95 65
466 95c.+10c. mult . . . . . 1·80 1·30

135 Massacre Victims

136 Emir Abd-el-Kader

1966. Deir Yassin Massacre (1948).
467 **135** 30c. black and red 55 25

1966. Return of Emir Abd-el-Kader's Remains.
468 **136** 30c. multicoloured 25 10
469 95c. multicoloured . . . . 1·10 40
See also Nos. 498/502.

137 UNESCO Emblems

138 Bardo Museum

1966. 20th Anniv of UNESCO.
470 **137** 1d. multicoloured . . . . 1·10 40

1966. Mohamed Racim's Miniatures (2nd series). As T **127**. Multicoloured.
471 1d. Horseman . . . . 4·50 1·50
472 1d.50 Algerian bride . . . . 6·75 2·00
473 2d. Barbarossa . . . . 10·00 3·50

1967. Rock-paintings of Tassili-N-Ajjer (2nd series). As T **128**.
474 1d. violet, buff and purple . . 4·50 1·90
475 2d. brown, buff and purple . 6·75 3·75
476 2d. brown, purple and buff 7·50 4·00
477 3d. brown, buff and black . . 10·50 5·50
DESIGNS: No. 474, Cow; No. 475, Antelope; No. 476, Archers; No. 477, Warrior.

1967. "Musulman Art". Multicoloured.
478 35c. Type **138** 45 25
479 95c. La Kalaa minaret (vert) 95 45
480 1d.30 Sedrata ruins . . . . . 1·70 65

139 Ghardaia

1967. Air.
481 **139** 1d. brown, green & purple 1·40 55
482 – 2d. brown, green and blue 3·25 1·40
483 – 5d. brown, green and blue 8·50 2·50
DESIGNS: 2d. Sud Aviation SE210 Caravelle over El Oued (Souf); 5d. Tipasa.

140 View of Moretti

1967. International Tourist Year. Multicoloured.
484 40c. Type **140** 70 40
485 70c. Tuareg, Tassili (vert) . . 1·40 55

141 Boy and Girl, and Red Crescent

142 Ostrich

1967. Algerian Red Crescent Organization.
486 **141** 30c.+10c. brn, red & grn 90 50

1967. Saharan Fauna. Multicoloured.
487 5c. Shiny-tailed Lizard (horiz) 50 40
488 20c. Type **142** 90 50
489 40c. Sand gazelle . . . . . . 1·40 65
490 70c. Fennec foxes (horiz) . . 1·90 1·00

143 Dancers with Tambourines

144 "Athletics"

1967. National Youth Festival.
491 **143** 50c. black, yellow & blue 95 40

1967. 5th Mediterranean Games, Tunis.
492 **144** 30c. black, blue and red 70 40

145 Skiing

146 Scouts supporting Jamboree Emblem

1967. Winter Olympic Games, Grenoble (1968).
493 **145** 30c. blue, green & ultram 95 40
494 – 95c. green, violet & brown 1·80 85
DESIGN—HORIZ (36 × 26 mm): 95c. Olympic rings and competitors.

1967.
498 **136** 5c. purple 25 10
499 10c. green 10 10
500 25c. orange 35 10
501 30c. black 45 10
502 30c. violet 45 10
496 50c. red 70 25
497 70c. blue 90 25
The 10c. value exists in two versions, differing in the figures of value and inscription at bottom right.

1967. World Scout Jamboree, Idaho.
503 **146** 1d. multicoloured . . . . 2·10 75

1967. No. 428 surch.
504 **116** 30c. on 25c. red 70 25

148 Kouitra

149 Nememcha Carpet

1968. Musical Instruments. Multicoloured.
505 30c. Type **148** 55 25
506 40c. Lute 90 40
507 1d.30 Rebbah . . . . 3·00 1·10

1968. Algerian Carpets. Multicoloured.
509 30c. Type **149** 95 55
510 70c. Guergour . . . . 1·80 85
511 95c. Djebel-Amour . . . . . 3·00 1·20
512 1d.30 Kalaa . . . . 3·75 1·40

150 Human Rights Emblem and Globe

1968. Human Rights Year.
513 **150** 40c. red, yellow and blue 75 40

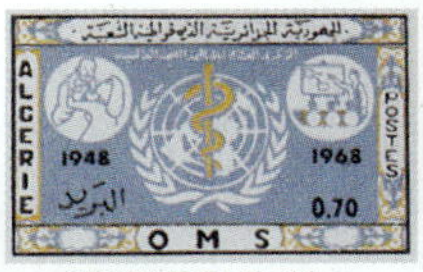

151 W.H.O. Emblem

152 Emigrant

1968. 20th Anniv of W.H.O.
514 **151** 70c. yellow, black & blue 90 40

1968. Emigration of Algerians to Europe.
515 **152** 30c. brown, slate & blue 55 25

153 Scouts holding Jamboree Emblem

154 Torch and Athletes

1968. 8th Arab Scouts Jamboree, Algiers.
516 **153** 30c. multicoloured 70 25

1968. Olympic Games, Mexico. Multicoloured.
517 30c. Type **154** 60 45
518 50c. Football . . . . 1·10 65
519 1d. Allegory of Games (horiz) 1·80 95

155 Barbary Sheep

156 "Neptune's Chariot", Timgad

1968. Protected Animals. Multicoloured.
520 40c. Type **155** 90 40
521 1d. Red deer . . . . 2·10 65

1968. Roman Mosaics. Multicoloured.
522 40c. "Hunting Scene" (Djemila) (vert) 70 25
523 95c. Type **156** . . . . 1·50 55

157 Miner

158 Opuntia

1968. "Industry, Energy and Mines".
524 **157** 30c. multicoloured 50 25
525 – 30c. silver and red 50 25
526 – 95c. red, black and silver 1·40 40
DESIGNS: No. 525, Coiled spring ("Industry"); No. 526, Symbol of radiation ("Energy").

1969. Algerian Flowers. Multicoloured.
527 25c. Type **158** 70 50
528 40c. Dianthus . . . . 1·10 65
529 70c. Rose . . . . 1·80 75
530 95c. Strelitzia . . . . 3·25 1·30
See also Nos. 621/4.

159 Djorf Torba Dam, Oued Guir

1969. Saharan Public Works. Multicoloured.
531 30c. Type **159** 70 25
532 1d.50 Route Nationale No. 51 . . . . 2·10 80

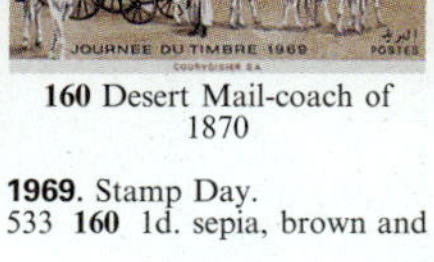

160 Desert Mail-coach of 1870

161 The Capitol, Timgad

1969. Stamp Day.
533 **160** 1d. sepia, brown and blue 2·75 85

1969. Roman Ruins in Algeria. Multicoloured.
534 30c. Type **161** 55 25
535 1d. Septimius Temple, Djemila (horiz) . . . . 1·50 60

162 I.L.O. Emblem

164 Carved Bookcase

1969. 50th Anniv of I.L.O.
536 **162** 95c. red, yellow and black 1·30 45

1969. No. 425 surch.
537 20c. on 12c. green 45 10

1969. Handicrafts. Multicoloured.
538 30c. Type **164** 50 25
539 60c. Copper tray 90 40
540 1d. Arab saddle . . . . . . 1·60 60

165 "Africa" Head

166 Astronauts on Moon

1969. 1st Pan-African Cultural Festival, Algiers.
541 **165** 30c. multicoloured 55 25

1969. 1st Man on the Moon.
542 **166** 50c. multicoloured . . . . 1·10 45

167 Bank Emblem

168 Flood Victims

1969. 5th Anniv of African Development Bank.
543 **167** 30c. black, yellow blue . . 55 25

1969. Aid for 1969 Flood Victims.
544 **168** 30c.+10c. black, flesh and blue 75 45
545 – 95c.+25c. brown, blue and purple . . . . 1·60 95
DESIGN: 95c. Helping hand for flood victims.

169 "Algerian Women" (Dinet)

1969. Dinet's Paintings. Multicoloured.
546 1d. Type **169** . . . . 2·10 85
547 1d.50 "The Look-outs" (Dinet) . . . . 2·75 1·20

170 "Mother and Child"

1969. "Protection of Mother and Child".
548 **170** 30c. multicoloured 70 40

171 "Agriculture"

172 Postal Deliveries by Donkey and Renault R4 Mail Van

1970. Four Year Plan.
549 **171** 25c. multicoloured 30 25
550 – 30c. multicoloured 55 25
551 – 50c. black and purple . . 55 25
DESIGNS: (LARGER, 49 × 23 mm): 30c. "Industry and Transport"; 50c. "Industry" (abstract).

1970. Stamp Day.
552 **172** 30c. multicoloured 70 25

173 Royal Prawn

174 Oranges

1970. Marine Life. Multicoloured.
553 30c. Type **173** 70 25
554 40c. Noble pen (mollusc) . . 90 40
555 75c. Neptune's basket . . . . 1·40 50
556 1d. Red coral . . . . 2·10 75

1970. "Expo 70" World Fair, Osaka, Japan. Multicoloured.
557 30c. Type **174** 70 25
558 60c. Algerian Pavilion . . . 70 40
559 70c. Bunches of grapes . . . 1·40 60

175 Olives and Bottle of Olive-oil

1970. World Olive-oil Year.
560 **175** 1d. multicoloured . . . . 1·90 80

176 New U.P.U. H.Q. Building

1970. Inaug of New U.P.U. Headquarters Building.
561 **176** 75c. multicoloured . . . . 1·10 40

177 Crossed Muskets

1970. Algerian 18th-century Weapons. Mult.
562 40c. Type **177** 90 65
563 75c. Sabre (vert) . . . . . . 1·60 85
564 1d. Pistol . . . . 2·30 1·10

178 Arab League Flag, Arms and Map

179 Lenin

1970. 25th Anniv of Arab League.
565 **178** 30c. multicoloured 55 25

1970. Birth Centenary of Lenin.
566 **179** 30c. bistre and ochre . . 2·75 40

180 Exhibition Palace

1970. 7th International Algiers Fair.
567 **180** 60c. green 70 40

181 I.E.Y. and Education Emblems

1970. International Education Year. Mult.
568 30c. Type **181** 55 25
569 3d. Illuminated Koran (30 × 41 mm) . . . . . . 3·50 1·80

182 Great Mosque, Tlemcen

1970. Mosques.
570 **182** 30c. multicoloured 45 25
571 – 40c. brown and bistre . . 55 25
572 – 1d. multicoloured . . . . 1·00 40
DESIGNS—VERT: 40c. Ketchaoua Mosque, Algiers; 1d. Sidi-Okba Mosque.

183 "Fine Arts"

1970. Algerian Fine Arts.
573 **183** 1d. orange, grn & lt grn 1·10 45

184 G.P.O., Algiers

186 "Racial Equality"

185 Hurdling

1971. Stamp Day.
574 **184** 30c. multicoloured . . . . 1·10 40

1971. 6th Mediterranean Games, Izmir (Turkey).
575 **185** 20c. grey and blue 50 25
576 – 40c. grey and green . . . 55 40
577 – 75c. grey and brown . . . 1·10 65
DESIGNS—VERT: 40c. Gymnastics; 75c. Basket-ball.

1971. Racial Equality Year.
578 **186** 60c. multicoloured 70 40

187 Symbols of Learning, and Students

1971. Inaug of Technological Institutes.
579 **187** 70c. multicoloured 90 30

188 Red Crescent Banner

1971. Red Crescent Day.
580 **188** 30c.+10c. red and green 70 40

189 Casbah, Algiers

1971. Air.
581 **189** 2d. multicoloured . . . . 2·50 1·10
582 – 3d. violet and black . . . 3·75 1·60
583 – 4d. multicoloured . . . . 4·25 2·00
DESIGNS: 3d. Port of Oran; 4d. Rhumel Gorges.

190 Aures Costume

191 UNICEF Emblem, Tree and Animals

1971. Regional Costumes (1st series). Multicoloured.
584 50c. Type **190** . . . . 1·30 60
585 70c. Oran . . . . 1·60 75
586 80c. Algiers . . . . 1·90 95
587 90c. Djebel-Amour . . . . . 2·30 1·10
See also Nos. 610/13 and 659/62.

1971. 25th Anniv of UNICEF.
588 **191** 60c. multicoloured 90 45

192 Lion of St. Mark's

1971. UNESCO "Save Venice" Campaign. Mult.
589 80c. Type **192** . . . . . . 1·40 55
590 1 d. 15 Bridge of Sighs . . . 2·30 95

193 Cycling

194 Book and Bookmark

1972. Olympic Games, Munich. Multicoloured.
591 25c. Type **193** 45 25
592 40c. Throwing the javelin (vert) 60 25
593 60c. Wrestling (vert) . . . . 1·10 50
594 1d. Gymnastics (vert) . . . . 1·60 55

1972. International Book Year.
595 **194** 1d.15 red, black and brown 90 45

195 Algerian Postmen

196 Jasmine

1972. Stamp Day.
596 **195** 40c. multicoloured 70 25

1972. Flowers. Multicoloured.
597 50c. Type **196** 70 40
598 60c. Violets 70 40
599 1d.15 Tuberose . . . . . . 2·10 65

197 Olympic Stadium

198 Festival Emblem

1972. Inaug of Cheraga Olympic Stadium.
600 **197** 50c. green, brown & violet 70 40

1972. 1st Festival of Arab Youth.
601 **198** 40c. brown, yellow & grn 55 25

199 Rejoicing Algerians

201 Child posting Letter

1972. 10th Anniv of Independence.
602 **199** 1d. multicoloured . . . . 1·30 60

1972. Regional Costumes (2nd series). As T **190**. Multicoloured.
610 50c. Hoggar . . . . 1·40 65
611 60c. Kabylie . . . . 1·80 65
612 70c. Mzab . . . . 1·90 85
613 90c. Tlemcen . . . . 2·40 1·10

1973. Stamp Day.
614 **201** 40c. multicoloured 55 25

202 Ho-Chi-Minh and Map

1973. "Homage to the Vietnamese People".
615 **202** 40c. multicoloured 90 40

203 Annaba Embroidery

1973. Algerian Embroidery. Multicoloured.
616 40c. Type **203** 55 25
617 60c. Algiers embroidery . . . 90 50
618 80c. Constantine embroidery 1·30 70

204 "Food Cultivation"

206 O.A.U. Emblem

205 Serviceman and Flag

1973. 10th Anniv of World Food Programme.
619 **204** 1d.15 multicoloured . . . 90 40

1973. National Service.
620 **205** 40c. multicoloured 55 25

1973. Algerian Flowers. As T **158**. Multicoloured.
621 30c. Type **158** 70 25
622 40c. As No. 529 . . . . . . 90 40
623 1d. As No. 528 . . . . . . 1·80 65
624 1d.15 As No. 530 . . . . . 2·75 1·10

1973. 10th Anniv of Organization of African Unity.
625 **206** 40c. multicoloured 55 25

207 Peasant Family

1973. Agrarian Revolution.
626 **207** 40c. multicoloured 70 25

208 Scout Badge on Map

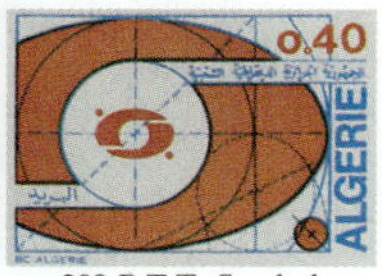
209 P.T.T. Symbol

1973. 24th World Scouting Congress, Nairobi, Kenya.
627 **208** 80c. mauve 75 40

1973. Inauguration of New P.T.T. Symbol.
628 **209** 40c. orange and blue . . 55 25

210 Conference Emblem

212 Young Workers

211 "Skikda Harbour"

1973. 4th Summit Conference of Non-Aligned Countries, Algiers.
629 **210** 40c. multicoloured 45 25
630 80c. multicoloured 90 40

1973. Opening of Skikda Port.
631 **211** 80c. multicoloured 70 25

1973. Volontariat Students' Volunteer Service.
632 **212** 40c. multicoloured 55 25

213 Arms of Algiers

1973. Millenary of Algiers.
633 **213** 2d. multicoloured . . . . 3·00 1·40

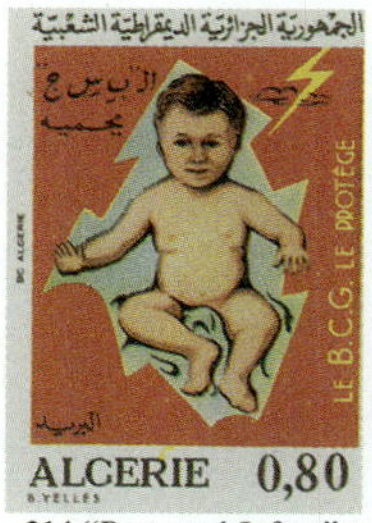
214 "Protected Infant"

1974. Anti-TB Campaign.
634 **214** 80c. multicoloured 90 45

215 Industrial Scene

1974. Four Year Plan.
635 **215** 80c. multicoloured 90 40

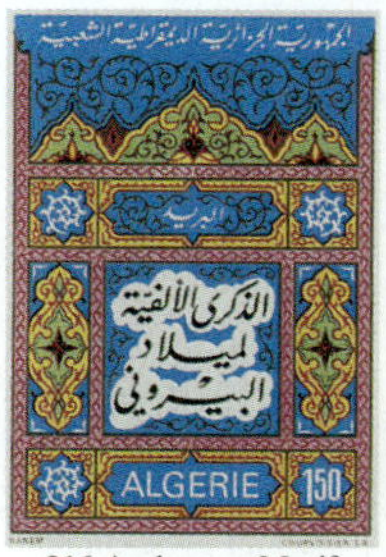
216 Arabesque Motif

1974. Birth Millenary of Abu-al Rayhan al-Biruni (mathematician and philosopher).
636 **216** 1d.50 multicoloured . . . 2·50 1·40

217 Map and Arrows

218 Upraised Weapon and Fist

1974. Meeting of Maghreb Committee for Co-ordination of Posts and Telecommunications, Tunis.
637 **217** 40c. multicoloured 55 25

1974. Solidarity with South African People's Campaign.
638 **218** 80c. black and red 70 25

219 Algerian Family

222 Automatic Stamp-vending Machine

220 Urban Scene

1974. Homage to Algerian Mothers.
639 **219** 85c. multicoloured 70 25

1974. Children's Drawings. Multicoloured.
640 70c. Type **220** 75 35
641 80c. Agricultural scene . . . 90 40
642 90c. Tractor and sunrise . . 1·10 65
Nos. 641/2 are size 49 × 33 mm.

1974. "Floralies 1974" Flower Show, Algiers. Nos. 623/4 optd **FLORALIES 1974**.
643 1d. multicoloured . . . . . 1·80 85
644 1d.15 multicoloured . . . . 2·30 1·30

1974. Stamp Day.
645 **222** 80c. multicoloured 80 35

223 U.P.U. Emblem on Globe

1974. Centenary of U.P.U.
646 **223** 80c. multicoloured 80 35

224 Revolutionaries

1974. 20th Anniv of Revolution. Multicoloured.
647 40c. Type **224** 55 25
648 70c. Armed soldiers (vert) . . 75 25
649 95c. Raising the flag (vert) . . 90 40
650 1d. Algerians looking to Independence . . . . . . 1·20 40

225 "Towards the Horizon"

226 Ewer

1974. "Horizon 1980".
651 **225** 95c. red, brown & black 75 40

1974. Algerian 17th-century Brassware. Mult.
652 50c. Type **226** 60 30
653 60c. Coffee pot 75 40
654 95c. Sugar basin . . . . . . 1·00 55
655 1d. Bath vessel . . . . 1·40 75

1975. No. 622 surch.
656 50c. on 40c. multicoloured . . 2·75 55

228 Games Emblem

1975. 7th Mediterranean Games (1st issue).
657 **228** 50c. violet, green & yellow 50 25
658 1d. orange, violet & blue 90 40
See also Nos. 671/5.

1975. Regional Costumes (3rd series). As T **190**. Multicoloured.
659 1d. Algiers . . . . 1·60 85
660 1d. The Hogger . . . . . . 1·60 85
661 1d. Oran . . . . 1·60 85
662 1d. Tlemcen . . . . 1·60 85

229 Labour Emblems

1975. 10th Anniv of Arab Labour Organization.
663 **229** 50c. brown 55 10

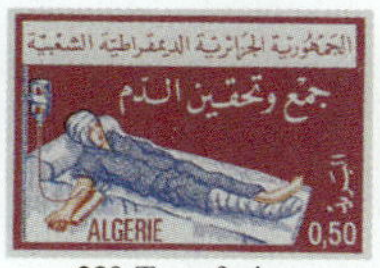
230 Transfusion

1975. Blood Collection and Transfusion Service.
664 **230** 50c. multicoloured 90 40

231 El Kantara Post Office

232 Policeman and Oil Rig on Map of Algeria

1975. Stamp Day.
665 **231** 50c. multicoloured 70 25

1975. Police Day.
666 **232** 50c. multicoloured . . . . 1·10 40

233 Ground Receiving Aerial

1975. Satellite Telecommunications. Mult.
667 50c. Type **233** 55 15
668 1d. Map of receiving sites . . 90 25
669 1d.20 Main and subsidiary ground stations . . . . . 1·20 50

234 Revolutionary with Flag

235 Swimming

1975. 20th Anniv of "Skikda" Revolution.
670 **234** 1d. multicoloured 75 40

1975. 7th Mediterranean Games, Algiers (2nd issue). Multicoloured.
671 25c. Type **235** 20 10
672 50c. Wrestling 45 25
673 70c. Football (vert) 70 30
674 1d. Athletics (vert) 90 40
675 1d.20 Handball (vert) . . . . 1·20 65
MS676 136 × 136 mm. Nos. 671/5 7·75 6·75

236 "Setif-Guelma-Kherrata"

237 Map of the Maghreb and A.P.U. Emblem

1975. 30th Anniv of Setif, Guelma and Kherrata Massacres (1st issue).
677 **236** 5c. black and orange . . 10 10
678 10c. black and green . . . 10 10
679 25c. black and blue . . . 25 10
680 30c. black and brown . . 45 10
681 50c. black and green . . . 45 10
682 70c. black and red 55 25
683 1d. black and red 90 40
See also No. 698.

1975. 10th Arab Postal Union Congress, Algiers.
684 **237** 1d. multicoloured 75 40

238 Mosaic, Palace of the Bey, Constantine

1975. Historic Buildings.
685 **238** 1d. multicoloured . . . . 1·10 40
686 – 2d. multicoloured . . . . 2·20 95
687 – 2d.50 black and brown . . 3·00 1·40
DESIGNS—VERT: 2d. Medersa Sidi-Boumedienne Oratory, Tlemcen. HORIZ: 2d.50, Palace of the Dey, Algiers.

239 University Building 240 Red-billed Fire Finch

1975. Millenary of Al-Azhar University, Cairo.
688 **239** 2d. multicoloured . . . . 2·10 80

1976. Algerian Birds (1st series). Multicoloured.
689 50c. Type **240** . . . . 1·30 65
690 1d.40 Black-headed bush shrike (horiz) . . . . . . 2·50 1·30
691 2d. Blue-tit . . . . 3·25 1·40
692 2d.50 Black-bellied sand-grouse (horiz) . . . . . . 3·75 2·00
See also Nos. 722/5.

241 Early and Modern Telephones 242 Map and Angolan Flag

1976. Telephone Centenary.
693 **241** 1d.40 multicoloured . . . 1·10 55

1976. "Solidarity with Republic of Angola".
694 **242** 50c. multicoloured 65 25

243 Child on Map 244 Postman

1976. Solidarity with People of Western Sahara.
695 **243** 50c. multicoloured 55 25

1976. Stamp Day.
696 **244** 1d.40 multicoloured . . . 1·10 40

245 People, Microscope and Slide 246 "Setif-Guelma-Kherrata"

1976. Campaign Against Tuberculosis.
697 **245** 50c. multicoloured . . . . 1·10 35

1976. 30th Anniv of Setif, Guelma and Kherrata Massacres (2nd issue).
698 **246** 50c. yellow and blue . . . 55 10

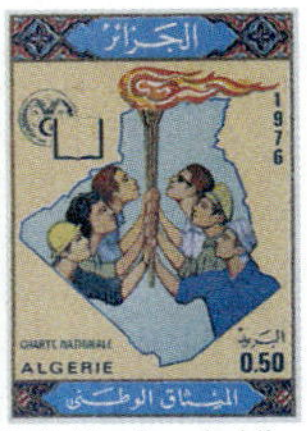

247 Ram's Head and Landscape 248 Algerians holding Torch

1976. Sheep Raising.
699 **247** 50c. multicoloured 65 25

1976. National Charter.
700 **248** 50c. multicoloured 55 25

249 Flag and Map 250 Map of Africa

1976. Solidarity with the Palestinian People.
701 **249** 50c. multicoloured 70 25

1976. 2nd Pan-African Commercial Fair, Algiers.
702 **250** 2d. multicoloured . . . . 1·70 65

251 Blind Man making Brushes

1976. Rehabilitation of the Blind. Multicoloured.
703 1d.20 Type **251** . . . . . . 1·40 45
704 1d.40 "The Blind Man" (E. Dinet) (horiz) . . . . . 2·10 65

252 Open Book

1976. The Constitution.
705 **252** 2d. multicoloured . . . . 1·70 65

253 Soldiers planting Seedlings

1976. Protection against Saharan Encroachment.
706 **253** 1d.40 multicoloured . . . 1·40 55

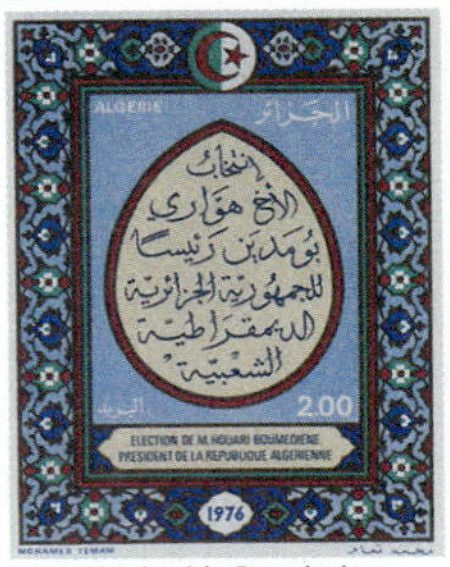

254 Arabic Inscription

1976. Election of President Boumedienne.
707 **254** 2d. multicoloured . . . . 1·70 65

255 Map of Telephone Centres 256 "Pyramid" of Heads

1977. Inauguration of Automatic Telephone Dialling System.
708 **255** 40c. multicoloured 50 25

1977. 2nd General Population and Housing Census.
709 **256** 60c. on 50c. mult 60 25

257 Museum Building 258 El Kantara Gorges

1977. Sahara Museum, Ouargla.
710 **257** 60c. multicoloured 75 40

1977.
711 **258** 20c. green and cream . . 10 10
712 60c. mauve and cream . . 25 10
713 1d. brown and cream . . 60 25

259 Assembly in Session

1977. National Assembly.
714 **259** 2d. multicoloured . . . . 1·40 55

260 Soldiers with Flag 261 Soldier with Flag

1977. Solidarity with People of Zimbabwe.
715 **260** 2d. multicoloured . . . . 1·40 50

1977. Solidarity with People of Namibia.
716 **261** 3d. multicoloured . . . . 2·30 75

262 "Winter"

1977. Roman Mosaics. "The Seasons". Mult.
717 1d.20 Type **262** . . . . . . 1·60 85
718 1d.40 "Autumn" . . . . . . 1·60 85
719 2d. "Summer" . . . . 2·50 1·30
720 3d. "Spring" . . . . 3·50 1·70
MS721 101 × 145 mm. Nos. 717/20 13·50 12·00

1977. Algerian Birds (2nd series). As T **240**. Multicoloured.
722 60c. Tristram's warbler . . . 1·20 70
723 1d.40 Moussier's redstart (horiz) . . . . 2·10 1·10
724 2d. Temminck's horned lark (horiz) . . . . 3·25 1·50
725 3d. Hoopoe . . . . 4·00 2·00

263 Horseman 264 Ribbon and Games Emblem

1977. "The Cavaliers" (performing horsemen). Multicoloured.
726 2d. Type **263** . . . . 2·10 85
727 5d. Three horsemen (horiz) 4·75 1·90

1977. 3rd African Games, Algiers (1978) (1st issue). Multicoloured.
728 60c. Type **264** 55 25
729 1d.40 Symbolic design and emblem . . . . 1·50 50
See also Nos. 740/4.

265 Tessala el Merdja

1977. Socialist Agricultural Villages.
730 **265** 1d.40 multicoloured . . . 1·00 40

266 12th-century Almohad Dirham

1977. Ancient Coins. Multicoloured.
731 60c. Type **266** 70 40
732 1d.40 12th-century Alomhad dinar . . . . 1·30 65
733 2d. 11th-century Almorarid dinar . . . . 1·90 95

267 Cherry ("Cerasus avium") 269 Children with Traffic Signs opposing Car

1978. Fruit Tree Blossom. Multicoloured.
734 60c. Type **267** 70 25
735 1d.20 "Persica vulgaris" (peach) . . . . 1·10 75
736 1d.30 "Amygdalus communis" (almond) . . . 1·10 75
737 1d.40 "Malus communis" (crab apple) . . . . 1·60 80

1978. Surch.
738 **236** 60c. on 50c. black & grn 70 25

1978. Road Safety for Children.
739 **269** 60c. multicoloured 60 25

270 Boxing and Map of Africa

272 Ka'aba, Mecca

271 Patient returning to Family

1978. 3rd African Games, Algiers (2nd issue). Multicoloured.

740	40c. Sports emblems and volleyball (horiz)	25	10
741	60c. Olympic rings and table tennis symbol	40	25
742	1d.20 Basketball symbol (horiz)	1·00	40
743	1d.30 Hammerthrowing symbol	1·00	5·00
744	1d.40 Type **270**	1·30	60

1978. Anti-tuberculosis Campaign.

745 **271**	60c. multicoloured	60	25

1978. Pilgrimage to Mecca.

746 **272**	60c. multicoloured	70	25

273 Road-building

1978. African Unity Road.

747 **273**	60c. multicoloured	70	25

274 Triangular Brooch

275 President Houari Boumedienne

1978. Jewellery (1st series). Multicoloured.

748	1d.20 Type **274**	1·20	55
749	1d.35 Circular brooch	1·50	70
750	1d.40 Anklet	1·80	80

See also Nos. 780/2 and 833/5.

1979. President Boumedienne Commem (1st issue).

751 **275**	60c. brown, red & turq	55	25

See also No. 753.

276 Books and Hands holding Torch

1979. National Liberation Front Party Congress.

752 **276**	60c. multicoloured	55	25

277 President Houari Boumedienne

1979. President Boumedienne Commem (2nd issue).

753 **277**	1d.40 multicoloured	1·40	50

278 Arabic Inscription

279 White Storks

1979. Election of President Chadli Bendjedid.

754 **278**	2d. multicoloured	1·60	40

1979. Air.

755 **279**	10d. blue, black and red	6·75	2·50

280 Ben Badis

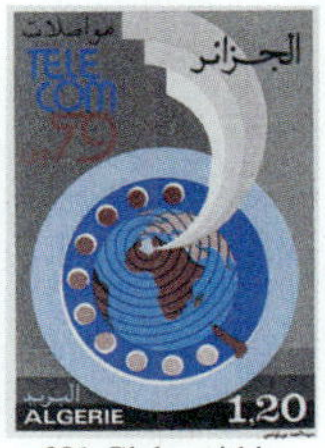

281 Globe within Telephone Dial

1979. 90th Birth Anniv of Sheikh Abdelhamid Ben Badis (journalist and education pioneer).

756 **280**	60c. multicoloured	55	25

1979. "Telecom 79" Exhibition. Multicoloured.

757	1d.20 Type **281**	90	35
758	1d.40 Sound waves	1·20	45

282 Children dancing on Globe

1979. International Year of the Child. Mult.

759	60c. Picking Dates	55	10
760	1d.40 Type **282** (vert)	1·10	45

283 Kabylie Nuthatch

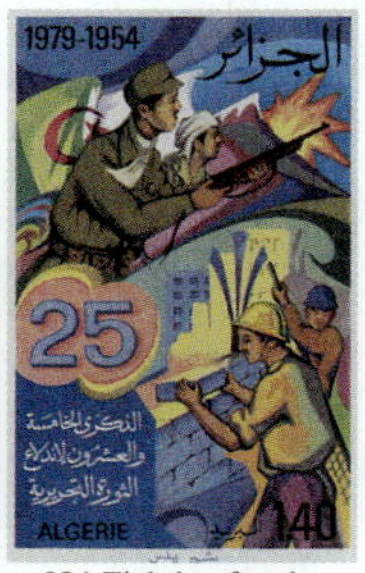

284 Fighting for the Revolution and Construction work

1979.

761 **283**	1d.40 multicoloured	2·00	95

1979. 25th Anniv of Revolution. Multicoloured.

762	1d.40 Type **284**	1·00	30
763	3d. Algerians with flag	1·70	85

285 Arabic Inscription

1979. 1400th Anniv of Hegira.

764 **285**	3d. gold, turquoise & blue	2·10	80

286 Return of Dionysus (right detail)

287 Books

1980. Dionysus Mosaic, Setif. Multicoloured.

765	1d.20 Type **286**	1·30	40
766	1d.35 Centre detail	1·30	55
767	1d.40 Left detail	1·60	80

Nos. 765/7 were issued together, se-tenant, forming a composite design.

1980. Day of Knowledge.

768 **287**	60c. brown, yellow & grn	55	10

288 Five Year Plan

1980. Extraordinary Congress of National Liberation Front Party.

769 **288**	60c. multicoloured	55	25

289 Olympic Flame

1980. Olympic Games, Moscow. Multicoloured.

770	50c. Type **289**	50	10
771	1d.40 Olympic sports (horiz)	95	45

290 Figures supporting O.P.E.C. Emblem

1980. 20th Anniv of Organization of Petroleum Exporting Countries.

772 **290**	60c. green, blue and red	65	10
773 –	1d.40 green and blue	1·20	45

DESIGN: 1d.40, O.P.E.C. emblem on world map.

291 Aures

1980. World Tourism Conference, Manila. Mult.

774	50c. Type **291**	50	25
775	1d. El Oued	90	25
776	1d.40 Tassili	1·10	40
777	2d. Algiers	1·90	65

292 Ibn Sina

1980. Birth Millenary of Ibn Sina (Avicenna) (philosopher).

778 **292**	3d. multicoloured	2·10	80

293 Earthquake Devastation

1980. El Asnam Earthquake Relief.

779 **293**	3d. multicoloured	2·10	55

1980. Jewellery (2nd series). As T **274**. Mult.

780	60c. Necklace	60	25
781	1d.40 Earrings and bracelet	1·10	55
782	2d. Diadem (horiz)	1·60	70

294 Emblem

1981. Five Year Plan.

783 **294**	60c. multicoloured	40	10

295 Basket-worker

1981. Traditional Arts. Multicoloured.

784	40c. Type **295**	35	10
785	60c. Spinning	45	20
786	1d. Copper-smith	75	25
787	1d.40 Jeweller	1·20	40

296 Cedar "Cedrus atlantica"

1981. World Tree Day. Multicoloured.

788	60c. Type **296**	45	10
789	1d.40 Cypress "Cupressus dupreziana"	1·10	40

297 Mohamed Bachir el Ibrahimi

298 Children and Blackboard (Basic Schooling)

1981. Day of Knowledge.
790 **297** 60c. multicoloured 45 10
791 **298** 60c. multicoloured 45 10

299 Archer, Dog and Internal Organs

1981. 12th Int Hydatidological Congress, Algiers.
792 **299** 2d. multicoloured . . . . 1·80 55

300 Dish Aerial and Caduceus

301 "Disabled"

1981. World Telecommunications Day.
793 **300** 1d.40 multicoloured . . . 1·10 25

1981. International Year of Disabled People.
794 **301** 1d.20 blue, red & orange 90 25
795 – 1d.40 multicoloured . . . 1·00 30
DESIGN: 1d.40, Disabled people and hand holding flower.

302 "Papilio machaon"

1981. Butterflies. Multicoloured.
796 60c. Type **302** 70 35
797 1d.20 "Rhodocera rhamni gonepteryx rhamni" . . . 1·20 50
798 1d.40 "Charaxes jasius" . . . 1·60 85
799 2d. "Papilio podalirius" . . . 2·10 90

303 Mediterranean Monk Seal

304 Man holding Ear of Wheat

1981. Nature Protection. Multicoloured.
800 60c. Type **303** 80 40
801 1d.40 Barbary ape . . . . . 1·60 85

1981. World Food Day.
802 **304** 2d. multicoloured . . . . 1·30 50

305 Cattle, Jabbaren

1981. Cave Paintings. Multicoloured.
803 60c. Mouflon, Tan Zoumaitek 55 25
804 1d. Type **305** 95 40
805 1d.60 Cattle, Iherir (horiz) . . 1·30 55
806 2d. One-horned bull, Jabbaren (horiz) . . . . . 1·80 85

306 Galley

1981. Algerian Ships of 17th and 18th Centuries. Multicoloured.
807 60c. Type **306** 80 50
808 1d.60 Xebec . . . . 1·80 1·00

307 Footballers with Cup

308 Microscope

1982. World Cup Football Championship, Spain. Multicoloured.
809 80c. Type **307** 60 25
810 2d.80 Footballers and ball (horiz) . . . . 1·90 75

1982. Centenary of Discovery of Tubercle Bacillus.
811 **308** 80c. blue, lt blue & orge 55 25

309 Mirror

1982. Popular Traditional Arts. Multicoloured.
812 80c. Type **309** 60 25
813 2d. Whatnot . . . . 1·30 40
814 2d.40 Chest (48 × 32 mm) . . 1·70 75

310 New Mosque, Algiers

311 "Callitris articulata"

1982. Views of Algeria before 1830 (1st series). Size 32 × 22 mm.
815 **310** 80c. brown 45 15
816 – 2d.40 violet . . . . . . 1·20 50
817 – 3d. green . . . . 1·60 65
DESIGNS: 2d.40, Sidi Boumedienne Mosque, Tlemcen; 3d. Garden of Dey, Algiers.
See also Nos. 859/62, 873/5, 880/2, 999/1001, 1054/6 and 1075/86.

1982. Medicinal Plants. Multicoloured.
818 50c. Type **311** 45 10
819 80c. "Artemisia herba-alba" 55 25
820 1d. "Ricinus communis" . . 90 35
821 2d.40 "Thymus fontanesii" 1·90 75

312 Independence Fighter

313 Congress House

1982. 20th Anniv of Independence. Mult.
822 50c. Type **312** 40 15
823 80c. Modern soldiers 55 25
824 2d. Algerians and symbols of prosperity . . . . 1·40 55
MS825 74 × 82 mm. 5d. Sun rising over flames (31 × 39 mm) . . . 4·25 4·00

1982. Soumman Congress.
826 **313** 80c. multicoloured 55 15

314 Scout and Guide releasing Dove

315 Child

1982. 75th Anniv of Boy Scout Movement.
827 **314** 2d.80 multicoloured . . . 1·90 55

1982. Palestinian Children.
828 **315** 1d.60 multicoloured . . . 95 30

316 Waldrapp

1982. Nature Protection. Multicoloured.
829 50c. Type **316** 70 40
830 80c. Houbara bustard (vert) 95 65
831 2d. Tawny eagle . . . . . . 2·20 1·10
832 2d.40 Lammergeier (vert) . . 2·75 1·40

317 Mirror

318 "Abies numidica"

1983. Silver Work.
833 **317** 50c. silver, black and red 35 10
834 – 1d. multicoloured 55 40
835 – 2d. silver, black, & purple 1·20 60
DESIGNS—VERT. 1d. Perfume flasks. HORIZ: 2d. Belt buckle.

1983. World Tree Day. Multicoloured.
836 80c. Type **318** 70 25
837 2d.80 "Acacia raddiana" . . 2·10 75

319 Mineral

320 Customs Officer

1983. Mineral Resources.
838 **319** 70c. multicoloured 90 35
839 80c. multicoloured . . . . 1·00 50
840 1d.20 mult (horiz) . . . . 1·20 65
841 2d.40 mult (horiz) . . . . 2·50 1·20

1983. 30th Anniv of Customs Co-operation Council.
842 **320** 80c. multicoloured 70 25

321 Emir Abdelkader

1983. Death Centenary of Emir Abdelkader.
843 **321** 4d. multicoloured . . . . 2·30 95

322 Fly Agaric

323 Ibn Khaldoun

1983. Mushrooms. Multicoloured.
844 50c. Type **322** 80 25
845 80c. Death cap . . . . . . 1·10 65
846 1d.40 "Pleurotus eryngii" . . 2·40 1·00
847 2d.80 "Terfezia leonis" . . . 3·75 1·70

1983. Ibn Khaldoun Commemoration.
848 **323** 80c. multicoloured 70 25

324 W.C.Y. Emblem and Post Office

1983. World Communications Year. Mult.
849 80c. Type **324** 55 25
850 2d.40 W.C.Y. emblem and telephone switch box . . . 1·50 65

325 Goat and Tassili Mountains

1983. Tassili World Patrimony. Multicoloured.
851 50c. Type **325** 40 10
852 80c. Touaregs 55 25
853 2d.40 Rock paintings . . . . 1·40 55
854 2d.80 Rock formation . . . 1·80 75

326 Sloughi

1983. Sloughi. Multicoloured.
855 80c. Type **326** 80 35
856 2d.40 Sloughi . . . . 2·10 1·00

327 Symbols of Economic Progress

1983. 5th National Liberation Front Party Congress. Multicoloured.
857 80c. Type **327** 80 35
MS858 75 × 82 mm. 5d. Party emblem (31 × 38 mm) . . . . 4·25 4·00

1984. Views of Algeria before 1830 (2nd series). As T **310**.
859 10c. blue 10 10
860 1d. purple 45 10
861 2d. blue 95 45
862 4d. red . . . . 2·10 65

DESIGNS: 10c. Oran; 1d. Sidi Abderahmane Mosque, Et Taalibi; 2d. Bejaia; 4d. Constantine.

328 Jug

329 Fountain

1984. Pottery. Multicoloured.
863 80c. Type **328** 55 25
864 1d. Dish (horiz) 75 40
865 2d. Lamp . . . . 1·40 60
866 2d.40 Jug (horiz) . . . . . 1·60 75

1984. Fountains of Old Algiers.
867 **329** 50c. multicoloured 20 10
868 – 80c. multicoloured 55 40
869 – 2d.40 multicoloured . . . 1·30 65
DESIGNS: 80c., 2d.40, Different fountains.

330 Dove, Flames and Olympic Rings

331 Stallion

1984. Olympic Games, Los Angeles.
870 **330** 1d. multicoloured 90 40

1984. Horses. Multicoloured.
871 80c. Type **331** 70 40
872 2d.40 Mare . . . . 1·90 1·00

1984. Views of Algeria before 1830 (3rd series). As T **310**.
873 5c. purple 10 10
874 20c. blue 10 10
875 70c. violet 40 25
DESIGNS: 5c. Mustapha Pacha; 20c. Bab Azzoun; 70c. Mostaganem.

332 Lute

1984. Musical Instruments. Multicoloured.
876 80c. Type **332** 55 25
877 1d. Drum 90 40
878 2d.40 One-stringed instrument 1·80 75
879 2d.80 Bagpipes . . . . . . 2·00 1·00

1984. Views of Algeria before 1830 (4th series). As T **310**.
880 30c. red and black 25 10
881 40c. black 25 10
882 50c. brown 25 10
DESIGNS: 30c. Algiers from Admiralty; 40c. Kolea; 50c. Algiers from aqueduct.

333 Partisans in Mountains and Flag

1984. 30th Anniv of Revolution. Multicoloured.
883 80c. Type **333** 70 25
MS884 75 × 82 mm. 5d. Algerian flags (31 × 39 mm) . . . . . . 4·25 4·00

334 Map of M'Zab Valley

1984. M'Zab Valley. Multicoloured.
885 80c. Type **334** 65 10
886 2d.40 M'Zab town . . . . . 1·70 60

335 Coffee Pot

336 Blue-finned Tuna

1985. Ornamental Tableware.
887 **335** 80c. black, silver & yellow 55 25
888 – 2d. black, silver and green 1·20 60
889 – 2d.40 black, silver & pink 1·60 70
DESIGNS—HORIZ: 2d. Bowl. VERT: 2d.40, Lidded jar.

1985. Fishes. Multicoloured.
890 50c. Type **336** 55 25
891 80c. Gilthead seabream . . . 95 40
892 2d.40 Dusky grouper . . . . 2·20 1·10
893 2d.80 Smooth hound . . . . 2·75 1·20

337 Birds in Flight and Emblem

1985. National Games.
894 **337** 80c. multicoloured 65 25

338 Stylized Trees

339 Algiers Casbah

1985. Environmental Protection. Multicoloured.
895 80c. Type **338** 80 25
896 1d.40 Stylized waves 90 40

1985.
897 **339** 20c. blue and cream . . . 10 10
898 80c. green and cream . . 55 10
899 2d.40 brown and cream 1·70 10

340 Dove within "40"

341 Figures linking arms and Emblem

1985. 40th Anniv of U.N.O.
900 **340** 1d. multicoloured 90 25

1985. 1st National Youth Festival.
901 **341** 80c. multicoloured 70 25

342 Figures linking arms on Globe and Dove

343 O.P.E.C. Emblem

1985. International Youth Year. Multicoloured.
902 80c. Type **342** 60 25
903 1d.40 Doves making globe with laurels 90 35

1985. 25th Anniv of Organization of Petroleum Exporting Countries.
904 **343** 80c. multicoloured 70 25

344 Mother and Children

1985. Family Planning. Multicoloured.
905 80c. Type **344** 55 25
906 1d.40 Doctor weighing baby 90 40
907 1d.70 Mother breast-feeding baby . . . . 1·10 50

345 Chetaibi Bay

1985. Tourist Sites.
908 **345** 80c. blue, green & brown 45 25
909 – 2d. brown, green & blue 1·30 40
910 – 2d.40 brown, green & bl 1·60 65
DESIGNS—VERT: 2d. El Meniaa. HORIZ: 2d.40, Bou Noura.

346 "Palm Grove"

1985. Paintings by N. Dinet. Multicoloured.
911 2d. Type **346** . . . . 1·50 75
912 3d. "Palm Grove" (different) 2·10 1·20

347 Line Pattern

1985. Weavings. Multicoloured.
913 80c. Type **347** 70 45
914 1d.40 Diamond pattern . . . 1·40 65
915 2d.40 Patterned horizontal stripes . . . . 2·00 1·10
916 2d.80 Vertical and horizontal stripes . . . . 2·50 1·60

348 "Felis margarita"

349 Oral Vaccination

1986. Wild Cats. Multicoloured.
917 80c. Type **348** 80 45
918 1d. Caracal . . . . 1·00 60
919 2d. Wild cat . . . . 1·90 1·10
920 2d.40 Serval (vert) . . . . . 2·50 1·40

1986. UNESCO Child Survival Campaign. Mult.
921 80c. Type **349** 55 25
922 1d.40 Sun behind mother and baby . . . . 1·20 55
923 1d.70 Children playing . . . 1·50 75

350 Industrial Skyline, Clasped Hands and Emblem

351 Books and Crowd

1986. 30th Anniv of Algerian General Workers' Union.
924 **350** 2d. multicoloured . . . . 1·50 55

1986. National Charter.
925 **351** 4d. multicoloured . . . . 2·75 1·20

352 Emblem on Book and Drawing Instruments

353 Children playing

1986. Disabled Persons' Day.
926 **352** 80c. multicoloured 70 30

1986. Anti-tuberculosis Campaign.
927 **353** 80c. multicoloured 70 35

354 Sombrero on Football

355 Courtyard with Fountain

1986. World Cup Football Championship, Mexico. Multicoloured.
928 2d. Type **354** . . . . 1·40 55
929 2d.40 Players and ball . . . 1·60 70

1986. Traditional Dwellings. Multicoloured.
930 80c. Type **355** 70 30
931 2d.40 Courtyard with two beds of shrubs . . . . . . 1·80 1·00
932 3d. Courtyard with plants in tall pot . . . . 2·30 1·30

356 Heart forming Drop over Patient

357 Transmission Mast as Palm Tree

1986. Blood Donors.
933 **356** 80c. multicoloured . . . . 1·40 40

1986. Opening of Hertzian Wave Communications (Southern District).
934 **357** 60c. multicoloured 45 25

358 Studded Gate

1986. Mosque Gateways. Multicoloured.
935 2d. Type **358** . . . . 1·30 55
936 2d.40 Ornate gateway . . . . 1·60 75

359 Dove

1986. International Peace Year.
937 **359** 2d.40 multicoloured . . . 1·60 55

360 Girl dancing

361 "Narcissus tazetta"

1986. Folk Dances. Multicoloured.
938 80c. Type **360** 70 25
939 2d.40 Woman with purple dress dancing . . . . . . 1·70 65
940 2d.80 Veiled sword dancer . . 1·90 85

1986. Flowers. Multicoloured.
941 80c. Type **361** 70 30
942 1d.40 "Iris unguicularis" . . 1·20 55
943 2d.40 "Capparis spinosa" . . 1·70 90
944 2d.80 "Gladiolus segetum" 2·10 1·10

362 "Algerian Family"

363 Earrings

1987. Paintings by Mohammed Issiakhem in National Museum. Multicoloured.
945 2d. Type **362** . . . . . . 1·50 75
946 5d. "Man and Books" . . . 3·50 2·00

1987. Jewellery from Aures. Multicoloured.
947 1d. Type **363** 75 40
948 1d.80 Bangles . . . . . . 1·20 60
949 2d.90 Brooches . . . . . . 1·70 1·10
950 3d.30 Necklace (horiz) . . . 2·00 1·20

364 Boy and Girl

1987. Rock Carvings. Multicoloured.
951 1d. Type **364** 90 55
952 2d.90 Goat . . . . . . 2·00 1·30
953 3d.30 Animals . . . . . . 2·30 1·40

365 Baby holding Syringe "Umbrella"

366 Workers and Circles

1987. African Vaccination Year.
954 **365** 1d. multicoloured 55 25

1987. Voluntary Service.
955 **366** 1d. multicoloured 55 30

367 People and Buildings

1987. 3rd General Population Census.
956 **367** 1d. multicoloured 55 25

368 1962 War Orphans Fund Stamps and Magnifying Glass

1987. 25th Anniv of Independent Algeria Stamps.
957 **368** 1d.80 multicoloured . . . 1·80 60

369 Hand holding Torch

370 Actors in Spotlight

1987. 25th Anniv of Independence. Multicoloured.
958 1d. Type **369** 55 25
MS959 75 × 82 mm. 5d. Sun, dove and "25" (32 × 39 mm) . . . . 3·50 3·25

1987. Amateur Theatre Festival, Mostaganem. Multicoloured.
960 1d. Type **370** 55 85
961 1d.80 Theatre 90 55

371 Discus Thrower

372 Greater Flamingo

1987. Mediterranean Games, Lattaquie. Mult.
962 1d. Type **371** 55 30
963 2d.90 Tennis player (vert) . . 1·50 70
964 3d.30 Footballer . . . . . . 1·80 95

1987. Birds. Multicoloured.
965 1d. Type **372** 75 40
966 1d.80 Purple swamphen . . . 1·30 80
967 2d.50 Black-shouldered kite 2·00 95
968 2d.90 Red kite . . . . . . 1·90 85

373 Reservoir

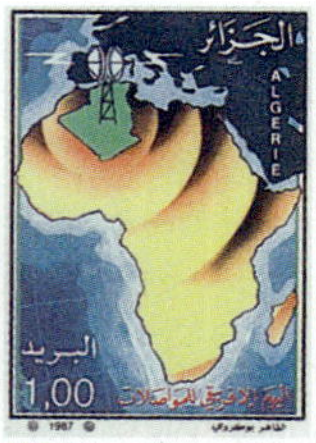

374 Map, Transmitter and Radio Waves

1987. Agriculture. Multicoloured.
969 1d. Type **373** 60 25
970 1d. Forestry (36 × 28 mm) . . 60 25
971 1d. Foodstuffs (25 × 37 mm) 60 25
972 1d. Erecting hedge against desert (25 × 37 mm) 55 25

1987. African Telecommunications Day.
973 **374** 1d. multicoloured 70 25

375 Motorway

1987. Transport. Multicoloured.
974 2d.90 Type **375** . . . . . . 1·50 60
975 3d.30 Diesel locomotive and passenger train . . . . . . 2·75 1·20

376 Houari Boumedienne University, Algiers

1987. Universities. Multicoloured.
976 1d. Type **376** 55 25
977 2d.50 Oran University . . . 1·30 45
978 2d.90 Constantine University 1·50 60
979 3d.30 Emir Abdelkader University, Constantine (vert) . . . . 1·90 75

377 Wheat, Sun and Farmer ploughing with Oxen

378 Emblem as Sun above Factories

1988. 10th Anniv of International Agricultural Development Fund.
980 **377** 1d. multicoloured 70 25

1988. Autonomy of State-owned Utilities.
981 **378** 1d. multicoloured 55 25

379 Woman's Face and Emblem

380 Globe, Flag, Wood Pigeon and Scout Salute

1988. International Women's Day.
982 **379** 1d. multicoloured 55 25

1988. 75th Anniv of Arab Scouting.
983 **380** 2d. multicoloured . . . . 1·10 45

381 Bau-Hanifia

382 Running

1988. Spas. Multicoloured.
984 1d. Type **381** 55 25
985 2d.90 Chellala . . . . . . 1·50 55
986 3d.30 Righa-Ain Tolba . . . 1·70 70

1988. Olympic Games, Seoul.
987 **382** 2d.90 multicoloured . . . 1·90 90

383 Pencil and Globe

384 Barbary Ape

1988. International Literacy Day.
988 **383** 2d.90 multicoloured . . . 1·40 70

1988. Endangered Animals. Barbary Ape. Mult.
989 50c. Type **384** 80 40
990 90c. Ape family . . . . . . 1·20 65
991 1d. Ape's head and shoulders (vert) . . . . 1·60 85
992 1d.80 Ape in tree (vert) . . . 2·75 1·50

385 Family Group

386 Different Races raising Fists

1988. 40th Anniv of W.H.O.
993 **385** 2d.90 multicoloured . . . 1·30 60

1988. Anti-apartheid Campaign.
994 **386** 2d.50 multicoloured . . . 1·20 50

387 Emblem

388 Man irrigating Fields

1988. 6th National Liberation Front Party Congress.
995 **387** 1d. multicoloured 55 25

1988. Agriculture. Multicoloured.
996 1d. Type **388** 55 25
997 1d. Fields, cattle and man picking fruit 55 25

389 Constantine

390 Courtyard

1989.
998 **389** 1d. deep green and green 40 85

1989. Views of Algeria before 1830 (5th series). As T **310**.
999 2d.50 green 90 25
1000 2d.90 green . . . . 1·00 25
1001 5d. brown and black . . . . 2·10 40
DESIGNS: 2d.50, Bay; 2d.90, Harbour; 5d. View of harbour through archway.

1989. National Achievements. Multicoloured.
1002 1d. Type **390** 55 25
1003 1d. Flats (housing) 55 25
1004 1d. Gateway, Timimoun (tourism) 55 25
1005 1d. Dish aerial and telephones (communications) 55 25

391 Oran Es Senia Airport

1989. Airports. Multicoloured.
1006 2d.90 Type **391** . . . . . . 1·20 45
1007 3d.30 Tebessa airport . . . 1·40 60
1008 5d. Tamanrasset airport (vert) . . . . 2·10 1·20

392 Irrigation

1989. Development of South. Multicoloured.
1009 1d. Type **392** 50 25
1010 1d.80 Ouargla secondary school 70 40
1011 2d.50 Gas complex, Hassi R'mel (vert) . . . . . . 1·10 50

393 Soldiers at Various Tasks

395 Mother and Baby

394 Locusts and Crop Spraying

1989. 20th Anniv of National Service.
1012 **393** 2d. multicoloured . . . 1·30 65

1989. Anti-locusts Campaign.
1013 **394** 1d. multicoloured . . . 55 25

1989. International Children's Day.
1014 **395** 1d.+30c. mult 65 40

396 Moon

1989. 20th Anniv of First Manned Landing on Moon. Multicoloured.
1015 2d.90 Type **396** . . . . . . 1·20 50
1016 4d. Astronaut on moon . . 1·50 80

397 Globe and Emblem

1989. Centenary of Interparliamentary Union.
1017 **397** 2d.90 mauve, brn & gold 1·20 40

398 Fruits and Vegetables

1989. National Production.
1018 **398** 2d. multicoloured . . . 75 40
1019 – 3d. multicoloured . . . 1·10 60
1020 – 5d. multicoloured . . . 1·90 1·10
DESIGNS: 3, 5d. Various fruits and vegetables.

399 Atlantic Bonito

400 "35" and Soldier with Rifle

1989. Fishes. Multicoloured.
1021 1d. Type **399** 60 30
1022 1d.80 John dory . . . . . 1·10 45
1023 2d.90 Red seabream . . . . 1·60 60
1024 3d.30 Swordfish . . . . . . 1·80 75

1989. 35th Anniv of Revolution.
1025 **400** 1d. multicoloured . . . 50 15

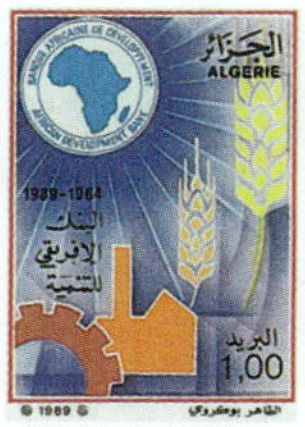
401 Bank Emblem, Cogwheel, Factory and Wheat

402 Satan's Mushroom

1989. 25th Anniv of African Development Bank.
1026 **401** 1d. multicoloured . . . 45 25

1989. Fungi. Multicoloured.
1027 1d. Type **402** 70 30
1028 1d.80 Yellow stainer . . . . 1·20 45
1029 2d.90 Parasol mushroom . . 1·90 75
1030 3d.30 Saffron milk cap . . 2·20 95

403 Emblem

404 Sun, Arm and Face

1990. 10th Anniv of Pan-African Postal Union.
1031 **403** 1d. multicoloured . . . 50 25

1990. Rational Use of Energy.
1032 **404** 1d. multicoloured . . . 60 25

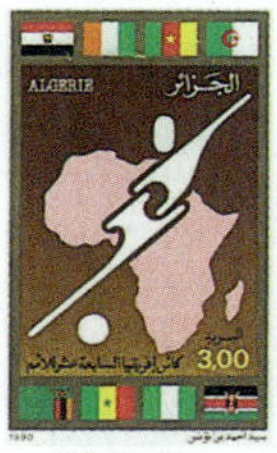
405 Emblem

406 Ceramics

1990. African Nations Cup Football Championship.
1033 **405** 3d. multicoloured . . . 1·30 50

1990. Industries. Multicoloured.
1034 2d. Type **406** 70 35
1035 2d.90 Car maintenance . . . 1·10 45
1036 3d.30 Fishing . . . . 1·70 65

407 Pictogram and Olympic Rings

408 Pylons on Map

1990. World Cup Football Championship, Italy. Multicoloured.
1037 2d.90 Type **407** . . . . . . 1·10 50
1038 5d. Trophy, ball and flag . . 1·90 95

1990. Rural Electrification.
1039 **408** 2d. multicoloured . . . 80 30

409 Young Workers

410 Members' Flags

1990. Youth. Multicoloured.
1040 2d. Type **409** 80 30
1041 3d. Youth in crowd (vert) 1·20 45

1990. Arab Maghreb Union Summit Conference.
1042 **410** 1d. multicoloured . . . 50 25

411 Anniversary Emblem

1990. 30th Anniv of O.P.E.C.
1043 **411** 2d. multicoloured . . . 80 30

412 House and Hand holding Coin

413 Flag, Rifle and Hands with Broken Manacles

1990. Savings Day.
1044 **412** 1d. multicoloured . . . 40 15

1990. Namibian Independence.
1045 **413** 3d. multicoloured . . . 1·00 30

414 Duck

415 Dome of the Rock and Palestinians

1990. Domestic Animals. Multicoloured.
1046 1d. Type **414** 50 15
1047 2d. Hare (horiz) 95 35
1048 2d.90 Common turkey . . . 1·30 55
1049 3d.30 Red junglefowl (horiz) 1·60 75

1990. Palestinian "Intifada" Movement.
1050 **415** 1d.+30c. mult 60 40

416 Crowd with Banners

417 Families in Countryside

1990. 30th Anniv of 11 December 1960 Demonstration.
1051 **416** 1d. multicoloured . . . 30 10

1990. Campaign against Respiratory Diseases.
1052 **417** 1d. multicoloured . . . 30 10

418 Sunburst, Torch and Open Book

420 "Jasminum fruticans"

419 Bejaia

1991. 2nd Anniv of Constitution.
1053 **418** 1d. multicoloured . . . 30 10

1991. Views of Algeria before 1830 (6th series). As T **310**.
1054 1d.50 red 50 10
1055 4d.20 green . . . . 1·40 55
DESIGNS: 1d.50, Kolea; 4d.20, Constantine.

1991. Air. Multicoloured.
1056 10d. Type **419** . . . . . . 2·75 1·20
1057 20d. Annaba . . . . 5·50 2·75

1991. Flowers. Multicoloured.
1058 2d. Type **420** 70 30
1059 4d. "Dianthus crinitus" . . 1·40 55
1060 5d. "Cyclamen africanum" 1·80 80

421 "Trip to the Country" (Mehdi Medrar)

1991. Children's Drawings. Multicoloured.
1061 3d. Type **421** 90 25
1062 4d. "Children playing" (Ouidad Bounab) . . . . 1·20 40

422 Emblem

1991. 3rd Anniv of Arab Maghreb Union Summit Conference, Zeralda.
1063 **422** 1d. multicoloured . . . 30 10

423 Figures and Emblem

1991. 40th Anniv of Geneva Convention on Status of Refugees.
1064 **423** 3d. multicoloured . . . 1·00 35

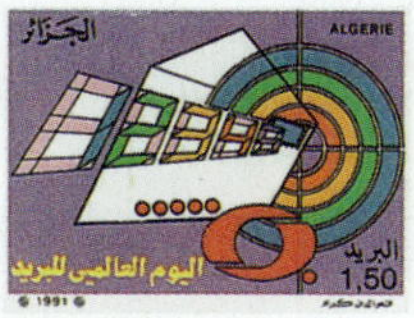
424 Coded Letter and Target

1991. World Post Day (1065) and "Telecom 91" International Telecommunications Exhibition, Geneva (1066). Multicoloured.
1065 1d.50 Type **424** 55 25
1066 4d.20 Exhibition and I.T.U. emblems (vert) . . . . . 1·20 45

425 Spanish Festoon

1991. Butterflies. Multicoloured.
1067 2d. Type **425** 60 30
1068 4d. "Melitaea didyma" . . . 1·00 45
1069 6d. Red admiral . . . . . . 1·40 65
1070 7d. Large tortoiseshell . . . 1·70 95

426 Chest Ornament

427 Woman

1991. Silver Jewellery from South Algeria. Mult.

1071	3d. Necklaces	60	30
1072	4d. Type **426**	80	45
1073	5d. Enamelled ornament	90	65
1074	7d. Bangles (horiz)	1·50	1·00

1992. Views of Algeria before 1830. As previous issues and new values. Size 30½ × 21 mm.

1075	5c. purple	60	30
1076	10c. blue	70	1·80
1077	20c. blue	90	50
1078	30c. red and black	1·30	35
1079	50c. brown	1·30	35
1080	70c. lilac	1·80	85
1081	80c. brown	2·00	75
1082	1d. brown	1·50	65
1083	2d. blue	2·75	1·30
1084	3d. green	3·75	95
1085	4d. red	5·25	1·30
1086	6d.20 blue	90	25
1087	7d.50 red	1·20	25

DESIGNS: 5c., 6d.20, As No. 873; 10c., 7d.50, As No. 859; 20c. As No. 1000; 30c. As No. 1001; 50c. As No. 882; 70c. As No. 875; 80c. Type **310**; 1d. As No. 860; 2d. As No. 861; 3d. As No. 817; 4d. As No. 1055.

1992. International Women's Day.

1095 **427**	1d.50 multicoloured	40	10

428 Dorcas Gazelle

429 Algiers

1992. Gazelles. Multicoloured.

1096	1d.50 Type **428**	40	10
1097	6d.20 Edmi gazelle	1·10	60
1098	8d.60 Addra gazelle	1·50	75

1992.

1099 **429**	1d.50 brown & lt brown	25	10
1132	2d. blue	30	10
1147	3d. blue	50	10

430 Runners

431 Doves and Flags

1992. Olympic Games, Barcelona.

1100 **430**	6d.20 multicoloured	1·20	45

1992. 30th Anniv of Independence.

1101 **431**	5d. green, red and black	90	30

432 "Ajuga iva"

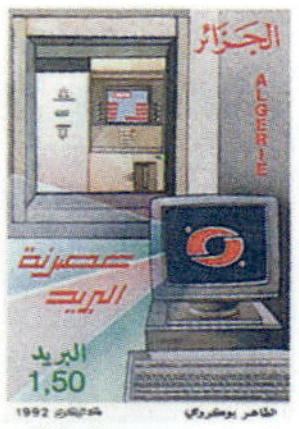
433 Computerized Post Office Equipment

1992. Medicinal Plants. Multicoloured.

1102	1d.50 Type **432**	25	10
1103	5d.10 Buckthorn	90	40
1104	6d.20 Milk thistle	1·20	50
1105	8d.60 French lavender	1·60	70

1992. World Post Day. Modernization of Postal Service.

1106 **433**	1d.50 multicoloured	40	10

434 Boudiaf

1992. Mohammed Boudiaf (chairman of Committee of State) Commemoration.

1107 **434**	2d. multicoloured	45	25
1108	8d.60 multicoloured	1·50	75

435 2nd-century B.C. Numidian Coin

1992. Coinage. Multicoloured.

1109	1d.50 Type **435**	20	10
1110	2d. 14th-century Zianide dinar	30	15
1111	5d.10 11th-century Almoravid dinar	85	40
1112	6d.20 19th-century Emir Abd-el-Kader coin	1·20	55

436 Short-snouted Seahorse

437 Algiers Door Knocker

1992. Marine Animals. Multicoloured.

1113	1d.50 Type **436**	35	10
1114	2d.70 Loggerhead turtle	55	25
1115	6d.20 Mediterranean moray	1·20	55
1116	7d.50 Lobster	1·40	70

1993. Door Knockers. Multicoloured.

1117	2d. Type **437**	30	10
1118	5d.60 Constantine	90	35
1119	8d.60 Tlemcen	1·40	70

438 Medlar Blossom

1993. Fruit-tree Blossom. Multicoloured.

1120	4d.50 Type **438**	80	40
1121	8d.60 Quince (vert)	1·40	70
1122	11d. Apricot (vert)	1·80	95

439 Patrol Boat, Emblem and Flag

440 Grain Storage Jar

1993. 20th Anniv of Coastguard Service.

1123 **439**	2d. multicoloured	95	35

1993. Traditional Utensils. Multicoloured.

1124	2d. Type **440**	50	10
1125	5d.60 Grindstone	90	50
1126	8d.60 Oil-press	1·40	65

441 Mauretanian Royal Mausoleum, Tipaza

442 Jijelienne Coast

1993. Mausoleums. Multicoloured.

1127	8d.60 Type **441**	1·10	50
1128	12d. Royal Mausoleum, El Khroub	1·80	80

1993. Air.

1129 **442**	50d. green, brown & blue	5·75	2·00

443 Annaba

444 Chameleon

1993. Ports. Multicoloured.

1130	2d. Type **443**	40	10
1131	8d.60 Arzew	1·40	50

1993. Reptiles. Multicoloured.

1133	2d. Type **444**	50	10
1134	8d.60 Desert monitor (horiz)	1·60	85

445 Tipaza

446 Map, Processing Plant and Uses of Hydrocarbons

1993. Tourism. Multicoloured.

1135	2d. Type **445**	40	10
1136	8d.60 Kerzaz	1·10	50

1993. 30th Anniv of Sonatrach (National Society for Transformation and Commercialization of Hydrocarbons).

1137 **446**	2d. multicoloured	50	10

447 Dove, Flag and "18"

448 Crown of Statue of Liberty, Football, U.S. Flag and Trophy

1994. National Chahid Day.

1138 **447**	2d. multicoloured	55	10

1994. World Cup Football Championship, U.S.A.

1139 **448**	8d.60 multicoloured	2·75	85

449 Monkey Orchid

450 Hoggar Script on Stone

1994. Orchids. Multicoloured.

1140	5d.60 Type **449**	1·20	65
1141	8d.60 "Orphrys lutea"	1·50	85
1142	11d. Bee orchid	2·20	1·30

1994. Ancient Communication. Multicoloured.

1143	3d. Type **450**	80	25
1144	10d. Abizar stele	1·80	75

451 Flags and Olympic Rings

452 Figures and City on Globe

1994. Cent of International Olympic Committee.

1145 **451**	12d. multicoloured	1·90	65

1994. World Population Day.

1146 **452**	3d. multicoloured	50	10

453 Sandstone

454 Brooches

1994. Minerals. Multicoloured.

1148	3d. Type **453**	55	25
1149	5d. Cipolin	90	45
1150	10d. Turitella shells in chalk	2·00	1·00

1994. Saharan Silver Jewellery. Multicoloured.

1151	3d. Type **454**	65	15
1152	5d. Belt (horiz)	1·10	40
1153	12d. Bracelets (horiz)	2·75	1·00

455 Soldiers

456 Ladybirds on Leaves

1994. 40th Anniv of Revolution.

1154 **455**	3d. multicoloured	45	10

1994. Insects. Multicoloured.

1155	3d. Type **456**	50	15
1156	12d. Beetle ("Buprestidae") on plant	1·90	75

457 Virus and Family

1994. World Anti-AIDS Campaign Day.

1157 **457**	3d. black, blue & mauve	50	10

458 Algiers

459 Southern Algeria

1994. Regional Dances. Multicoloured.

1158	3d. Type **458**	50	10
1159	10d. Constantine	1·30	65
1160	12d. Alaoui	1·40	75

1995. 20th Anniv of World Tourism Organization.

1161 **459**	3d. multicoloured	40	10

460 Honey Bee on Comb — **461** Dahlia

1995. Bee-keeping. Multicoloured.
1162 3d. Type **460** 40 10
1163 13d. Bee on flower (horiz) 1·50 85

1995. Flowers. Multicoloured.
1164 3d. Type **461** 55 10
1165 10d. Zinnias . . . . 1·60 70
1166 13d. Lilac . . . . 1·80 85

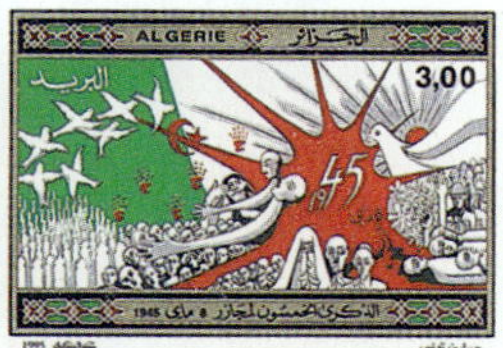
462 Circular Design — **463** Doves, Graves, Victims and Soldiers

1995. Stucco Work from Sedrata (4th century after Hegira).
1167 **462** 3d. brown 30 10
1168 – 4d. green 50 10
1169 – 5d. brown 55 25
DESIGNS—4d. Circular design within square; 5d. Stylized flowers.

1995. 50th Anniv of End of Second World War. Multicoloured.
1170 3d. Type **463** 40 10
MS1171 70 × 80 mm. 13d. National flag on dove (25 × 27 mm) . . 4·50 3·50

464 Water Pollution — **465** Players and Anniversary Emblem

1995. Environmental Protection. Multicoloured.
1172 3d. Type **464** 35 10
1173 13d. Air pollution . . . . . 1·50 65

1995. Centenary of Volleyball.
1174 **465** 3d. multicoloured . . . 30 10

466 Map and Pylon — **467** Children and Schoolbag Contents

1995. Electrification.
1175 **466** 3d. multicoloured . . . 35 10

1995. National Solidarity.
1176 **467** 3d.+50c. mult 50 35

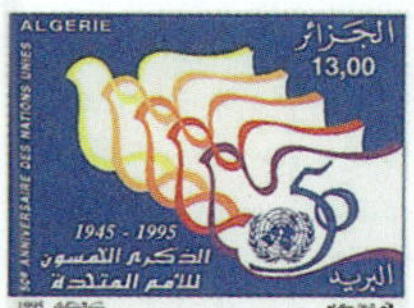

468 Doves and Anniversary Emblem — **469** Pitcher from Lakhdaria

1995. 50th Anniv of U.N.O.
1177 **468** 13d. multicoloured . . . 1·40 75

1995. Traditional Pottery.
1178 **469** 10d. brown . . . . . . 1·10 40
1179 – 20d. brown . . . . . . 2·10 65
1180 – 21d. brown . . . . . . 2·10 65
1181 – 30d. brown . . . . . . 3·00 90
DESIGNS: 20d. Water jug (Aokas); 21d. Jar (Larbaa nath Iraten); 30d. Jar (Ouadhia).

470 Common Shelduck

1995. Water Birds. Multicoloured.
1182 3d. Type **470** 55 25
1183 5d. Common snipe 90 35

471 Doves flying over Javelin Thrower and Olympic Rings

1996. Centenary of Modern Olympic Games and Olympic Games, Atlanta.
1184 **471** 20d. multicoloured . . . 2·20 1·10

472 Fringed Bag — **473** Pasteur Institute

1996. Handicrafts. Leather Bags. Multicoloured.
1185 5d. Type **472** . . . . 1·20 50
1186 16d. Shoulder bag with handle (vert) . . . . . . 2·20 95

1996. Centenary (1994) of Algerian Pasteur Institute.
1187 **473** 5d. multicoloured . . . 55 20

474 Arabic Script and Computer

1996. Scientific and Technical Education Day. Multicoloured.
1188 5d. Type **474** 55 25
1189 16d. Dove, fountain pen and symbols (vert) . . . . . 1·40 60
1190 23d. Pencil, pen, dividers and satellite over Earth on pages of open book (vert) . . . . 2·40 1·10

475 Iron Ore, Djebel Quenza

1996. Minerals. Multicoloured.
1191 10d. Type **475** . . . . . . 1·20 50
1192 20d. Gold, Tirek-Amesmessa 2·20 95

476 "Pandoriana pandora"

1996. Butterflies. Multicoloured.
1193 5d. Type **476** 65 25
1194 10d. "Coenonympha pamphilus" . . . . 1·10 50
1195 20d. Painted lady . . . . 2·30 1·10
1196 23d. Marbled white . . . . 2·50 1·30

477 Globe, Drug Addict and Drugs

1996. World Anti-drugs Day.
1197 **477** 5d. multicoloured . . . 50 15

478 "Woman with Pigeons"

1996. Paintings by Ismail Samsom. Multicoloured.
1198 20d. Type **478** . . . . . . 1·50 80
1199 30d. "Interrogation" . . . . 2·30 1·30

479 Ambulance and Paramedic holding Child (Medical Aid) — **480** Children, Syringe and Pens

1996. Civil Defence. Multicoloured.
1200 5d. Type **479** 50 25
1201 23d. Globe resting in cupped hands (natural disaster prevention) (vert) . . . . 1·80 85

1996. 50th Anniv of UNICEF Multicoloured.
1202 5d. Type **480** 40 10
1203 10d. Family holding pencil, key, syringe and flower 90 35

481 Dar Hassan Pacha — **482** Minbar Inscription, Nedroma Mosque

1996. Algiers Courtyards. Multicoloured.
1204 5d. Type **481** 40 15
1205 10d. Dar Kedaoudj el Amia 75 40
1206 20d. Palais des Rais . . . . 1·50 90
1207 30d. Villa Abdellatif . . . . 2·40 1·40

1997. Mosque Carvings. Multicoloured.
1208 5d. Type **482** 40 15
1209 23d. Doors, Ketchaoua Mosque, Algiers . . . . 1·80 95

483 Outline Map, Graph and Roofs over People — **484** Soldiers controlling Crowd with Flags

1997. 4th General Population and Housing Census.
1210 **483** 5d. multicoloured . . . 40 10

1997. 35th Anniv of Oargla Protest.
1211 **484** 5d. multicoloured . . . 40 10

485 Doves above Crowd with Flags

1997. 35th Anniv of Victory Day.
1212 **485** 5d. multicoloured . . . 40 10

486 "Ficaria verna"

1997. Flowers. Multicoloured.
1213 5d. Type **486** 50 20
1214 16d. Honeysuckle . . . . . 1·20 70
1215 23d. Common poppy . . . 1·80 1·00

487 "No Smoking" Sign on Map — **488** Crowd and Map

1997. World No Smoking Day.
1216 **487** 5d. multicoloured . . . 40 10

1997. Legislative Elections.
1217 **488** 5d. multicoloured . . . 40 10

489 "Buthus occitanus"

1997. Scorpions. Multicoloured.
1218 5d. Type **489** 45 15
1219 10d. "Androctonus australis" 80 45

490 Crowd with Flags

1997. 35th Anniv of Independence. Multicoloured.
1220 5d. Type **490** 40 10
MS1221 70 × 80 mm. 10d. National flag behind doves and "35" between broken chain-link (25 × 36 mm) . . . . 1·10 85

491 Zakaria

1997. 20th Death Anniv of Moufdi Zakaria (poet).
1222 **491** 5d. multicoloured . . . 40 10

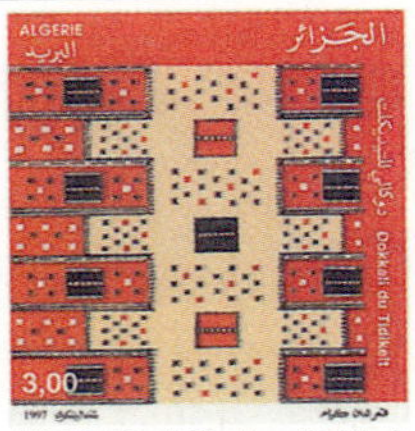
492 Dokkali Design, Tidikelt

1997. Textiles. Multicoloured.
1223 3d. Type **492** 30 10
1224 5d. Tellis design, Aures . . 45 25
1225 10d. Bou Taleb design, M'Sila 80 40
1226 20d. Ddil design, Ait-Hichem . . . . 1·50 85

493 Map, Emblem and Rainbow

1997. 25th Anniv of Pan-Arab Security Forces Organization.
1227 **493** 5d. multicoloured . . . 40 15

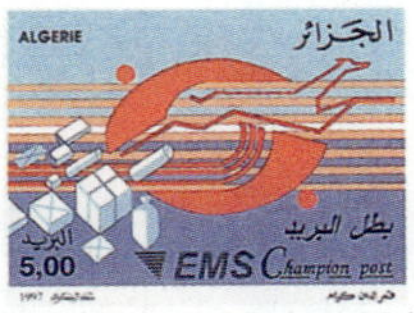
494 Packages and Express Mail Service Emblem

1997. World Post Day.
1228 **494** 5d. multicoloured . . . 40 15

495 Rising Sun on Map

1997. Local Elections.
1229 **495** 5d. multicoloured . . . 40 15

496 Tenes Lighthouse

1997. Lighthouses. Multicoloured.
1230 5d. Type **496** 50 25
1231 10d. Cap Caxine, Algiers (vert) . . . . 1·00 50

497 Mail Plane and Mail Van

1997. 1st Anniv of Aeropostale.
1232 **497** 5d. multicoloured . . . 50 15

498 Variable Scallop

1997. Sea Shells. Multicoloured.
1233 5d. Type **498** 55 15
1234 10d. "Bolinus brandaris" . . 1·00 40
1235 20d. "Hinia reticulata" (vert) . . . . 1·90 80

499 National Flag and Columned Facade

500 Flag, Ballot Box, Constitution and People

1997. Inauguration of Council of the Nation (upper parliamentary chamber).
1236 **499** 5d. multicoloured . . . 40 15

1997. Completion of Government Reform. Mult.
1237 5d. Type **500** (presidential election) 40 15
1238 5d. Constitution and torch (constitution referendum) 40 15
1239 5d. Ballot box and voting papers (elections to National Assembly (lower chamber of Parliament)) 40 15
1240 5d. Flag, sun and rose (local elections) 40 15
1241 5d. Flag and Parliament (elections to National Council (upper chamber)) 40 15
Nos. 1237/41 were issued together, se-tenant, forming a composite design.

501 Exhibition Emblem

1998. "Expo 98" World's Fair, Lisbon. Multicoloured.
1242 5d. Type **501** 40 15
MS1243 80 × 70 mm. 24d. Mosaic of fishes (40 × 31 mm) Imperf . . 2·00 1·80

502 Aerial Bombardment

1998. 40th Anniv of Bombing of Sakiet Sidi Youcef.
1244 **502** 5d. multicoloured . . . 40 15

503 Archives Building

1998. National Archives.
1245 **503** 5d. multicoloured . . . 40 15

504 Lalla Fadhma N'Soumeur

1998. International Women's Day.
1246 **504** 5d. multicoloured . . . 35 15

505 Players and Eiffel Tower

506 View from Land

1998. World Cup Football Championship, France.
1247 **505** 24d. multicoloured . . . 1·90 55

1998. Algiers Kasbah. Multicoloured.
1248 5d. Type **506** 40 30
1249 10d. Street 80 40
1250 24d. View from sea (horiz) 1·50 95

507 Crescent and Flag

1998. Red Crescent.
1251 **507** 5d.+1d. red, green and black 45 25

508 Battle Scene

1998. 150th Anniv of Insurrection of the Zaatcha.
1252 **508** 5d. multicoloured . . . 40 15

509 Parent and Child and Hand holding Rose

510 "Tourism and the Environment"

1998. International Children's Day. National Solidarity. Multicoloured.
1253 5d.+1d. Type **509** 45 25
1254 5d.+1d. Children encircling emblem (horiz) 45 25

1998. Tourism. Multicoloured.
1255 5d. Type **510** 40 15
1256 10d. Young tourists and methods of transportation (horiz) 90 35
1257 24d. Taghit (horiz) . . . . 1·80 95

511 Map of North Africa and Arabia

1998. Arab Post Day.
1258 **511** 5d. multicoloured . . . 90 10

512 Interpol and Algerian Police Force Emblems

1998. 75th Anniv of Interpol.
1259 **512** 5d. multicoloured . . . 40 10

513 Provisional Government and State Flag

1998. 40th Anniv of Creation of Provisional Government of Algerian Republic.
1260 **513** 5d. multicoloured . . . 40 15

514 Arrows leading from Algeria around the World

1998. National Diplomacy Day.
1261 **514** 5d. multicoloured . . . 40 10

515 Dove and Olympic Rings

1998. 35th Anniv of Algerian Olympic Committee.
1262 **515** 5d. multicoloured . . . 40 10

516 Osprey

1998. Birds. Multicoloured.
1263 5d. Type **516** 55 25
1264 10d. Audouin's gull . . . . 1·10 45
1265 24d. Shag (vert) . . . . . . 2·20 1·10
1266 30d. Common cormorant (vert) . . . . 2·75 1·40

517 Anniversary Emblem and Profiles

518 Comb

1998. 50th Anniv of Universal Declaration of Human Rights. Multicoloured.
1267 5d. Type **517** 55 10
1268 24d. Anniversary emblem, dove and people . . . 2·00 90

1999. Spinning and Weaving Implements. Mult.
1269 5d. Type **518** 50 25
1270 10d. Carding (horiz) 90 40
1271 20d. Spindle . . . . 1·90 90
1272 24d. Loom . . . . 2·20 1·00

519 Dove, Torch, Flag and Soldiers

1999. National Chahid Day.
1273 **519** 5d. multicoloured . . . 40 15

520 Pear

1999. Fruit Trees. Multicoloured.
1274 5d. Type **520** 45 25
1275 10d. Plum 80 45
1276 24d. Orange (vert) . . . . . 2·00 1·10

521 Calligraphy

522 14th-century Ceramic Mosaic, Tlemcen

1999. Presidential Election.
1277 **521** 5d. multicoloured . . . 40 15

1999. Crafts. Multicoloured.
1278 5d. Type **522** 45 25
1279 10d. 11th-century ceramic mosaic, Kalaa des Beni Hammad 80 40
1280 20d. Cradle (horiz) . . . . 1·80 90
1281 24d. Table with raised rim (horiz) . . . . 2·00 1·00

523 Pictograms on Map of Africa and South African Flag

524 Gneiss

1999. 7th African Games, Johannesburg. Mult.
1282 5d. Type **523** 45 25
1283 10d. Pictograms of athletes and South African flag (horiz) 90 40

1999. Minerals. Multicoloured.
1284 5d. Type **524** 40 25
1285 20d. Granite . . . . 1·60 90
1286 24d. Sericite schist . . . . . 2·00 1·10

525 Emblem

526 Family and Map of Africa

1999. Organization of African Unity Summit, Algiers.
1287 **525** 5d. multicoloured . . . 40 15

1999. 40th Anniv of Organization of African Unity Convention on Refugees.
1288 **526** 5d. multicoloured . . . 40 15

527 Emblem and Police Officers

1999. Police Day.
1289 **527** 5d. multicoloured . . . 90 15

528 Linked Hands and "2000"

1999. International Year of Culture and Peace.
1290 **528** 5d. multicoloured . . . 40 15

529 Dentex Seabream

1999. Fishes. Multicoloured.
1291 5d. Type **529** 55 25
1292 10d. Striped red mullet . . . 95 45
1293 20d. Pink dentex . . . . . 2·00 1·00
1294 24d. White seabream . . . 2·75 1·20

530 Rainbow

1999. Referendum.
1295 **530** 5d. multicoloured . . . 40 15

531 Emblem and Rainbow

1999. 125th Anniv of Universal Postal Union. Mult.
1296 5d. Type **531** 55 15
1297 5d. Globe, satellite and stamps 55 15

532 Woman's Face

1999. Rural Women's Day.
1298 **532** 5d. multicoloured . . . 55 15

533 Partisans and Helicopters

534 Chaoui

1999. 45th Anniv of Revolution. Multicoloured.
1299 5d. Type **533** 55 20
1300 5d. Partisans and fires . . . 55 20
Nos. 1299/300 were issued together, se-tenant, forming a composite design.

1999. Folk Dances. Multicoloured.
1301 5d. Type **534** 55 25
1302 10d. Targuie . . . . 1·00 45
1303 24d. M'zab . . . . 2·00 1·10

535 Doves

536 Chaffinches

2000. New Millennium. Mult. Self-adhesive.
1304 5d. Type **535** (peace) . . . 55 40
1305 5d. Plants and tree (environment) 55 40
1306 5d. Umbrella over ears of grain (food security) . . . 55 40
1307 5d. Wind farm (new energy sources) 55 40
1308 5d. Globe and ballot box (democracy) 55 40
1309 5d. Microscope (health) . . 55 40
1310 5d. Cargo ship at quayside (commerce) 55 40
1311 5d. Space satellite, dish aerial, jet plane and train (communications) 55 40
1312 5d. Astronaut and lunar buggy on Moon (space) 55 40
1313 5d. Film cave paintings, mandolin and music notes (culture) 55 40
1314 5d. Outline of dove (peace) 55 40
1315 5d. Hand above flora and fauna (environment) . . . 55 40
1316 5d. Space satellites, computer and printed circuits forming maps of Europe and Africa (communications) . . . 55 40
1317 5d. Sun, clouds, flame and water (new energy sources) 55 40
1318 5d. Hand holding seedling (food security) 55 40
1319 5d. Staff of Aesculapius and heart (health) 55 40
1320 5d. Arrows around globe (communication) 55 40
1321 5d. Cave paintings, book, painting and violin (culture) 55 40
1322 5d. Parthenon and envelopes (democracy) 55 40
1323 5d. Space satellite, solar system, space shuttle and astronaut (space) 55 40

2000. Birds. Multicoloured.
1324 5d. Type **536** 50 35
1325 5d. Northern serin (horiz) 50 35
1326 10d. Northern bullfinch (horiz) 95 60
1327 24d. Eurasian goldfinch . . 2·50 1·40

537 Emblem

2000. "EXPO 2000" World's Fair, Hanover.
1328 **537** 5d. multicoloured . . . 50 30

538 Sydney Opera House and Sports Pictograms

2000. Olympic Games, Sydney.
1329 **538** 24d. multicoloured . . . 2·20 85

539 Emblem

540 Crowd, Linked Hands and White Doves

2000. Telethon 2000 (fundraising event).
1330 **539** 5d. multicoloured . . . 50 25

2000. "Concorde Civile". Multicoloured.
1331 5d. Type **540** 50 15
1332 10d. Hands releasing doves (horiz) 95 40
1333 20d. Flag, doves and hands forming heart (horiz) . . 1·90 80
1334 24d. Doves and clasped hands above flowers . . . 2·20 1·00

541 Building

2000. National Library.
1335 **541** 5d. multicoloured . . . 50 20

542 Hand holding Blood Droplet

2000. Blood Donation Campaign.
1336 **542** 5d. multicoloured . . . 50 25

543 Lock

2000. Touareg Cultural Heritage. Multicoloured.
1337 5d. Type **543** 50 40
1338 10d. Lock (vert) 95 40

544 Mohamed Racim (artist)

2000. Personalities. Multicoloured.
1339 10d. Type **544** 95 40
1340 10d. Mohammed Dib (writer) 95 40
1341 10d. Mustapha Kateb (theatre director) 95 40
1342 10d. Ali Maachi (musician) 95 40

545 Cock-chafer

546 Jug

2000. Insects. Multicoloured.
1343 5d. Type **545** 50 30
1344 5d. Carpet beetle 50 30
1345 10d. Drugstore beetle . . . 95 55
1346 24d. Carabus . . . . 2·50 1·20

2000. Roman Artefacts, Tipasa. Multicoloured.
1347 5d. Type **546** 50 25
1348 10d. Vase 95 50
1349 24d. Jug . . . . 2·40 1·10

547 *Limodorum abortivum*

2000. Orchids. Multicoloured.
1350 5d. Type **547** 50 25
1351 10d. *Orchis papilionacea* . . 95 50
1352 24d. *Orchis provincialis* . . 2·40 1·10

548 Greylag Goose (*Anser anser*)

2001. Waterfowl. Multicoloured.
1353 5d. Type **548** 50 25
1354 5d. Avocet (*Recurvirostra avosetta*) (vert) 50 25
1355 10d. Eurasian bittern (*Botaurus stellaris*) (vert) 95 55
1356 24d. Western curlew (*Numenius arquata*) . . . 2·50 1·10

549 Painted Table

550 Forest, Belezma National Park, Batna

2001. Traditional Crafts. Multicoloured.
1357 5d. Type **549** 50 25
1358 10d. Decorated shelf (horiz) 95 60
1359 24d. Ornate mirror . . . . 2·40 95

2001. National Parks. Multicoloured.
1360 5d. Type **550** 50 25
1361 10d. Headland, Gouraya National Park, Bejaia (horiz) 95 45
1362 20d. Forest and mountains, Theneit el Had National Park, Tissemsilt (horiz) 1·90 80
1363 24d. El Tarf National Park 2·40 1·00

551 St. Augustine as Child (statue)

2001. St. Augustine of Hippo Conference, Algiers and Annaba. Multicoloured.
1364 5d. Type **551** 50 25
1365 24d. 4th-century Christian mosaic (43 × 31 mm) . . . 2·40 1·10

552 Obverse and Reverse of Ryal Boudjou, 1830

2001. Coins. Multicoloured.
1366 5d. Type **552** 50 25
1367 10d. Obverse and reverse of Double Boudjou, 1826 . . 95 45
1368 24d. Obverse and reverse of Ryal Drahem, 1771 . . . 2·40 1·00

553 Emblem and Scouts

2001. National Scouts' Day.
1369 **553** 5d. multicoloured . . . 50 30

554 Child throwing Stones

555 Asthma Sufferer

2001. Intifida.
1370 **554** 5d. multicoloured . . . 50 15

2001. National Asthma Day.
1371 **556** 5d. multicoloured . . . 45 15

556 Hopscotch

2001. Children's Games. Multicoloured.
1372 5d. Type **556** 50 15
1373 5d. Jacks 50 15
1374 5d. Spinning top 50 15
1375 5d. Marbles 50 15

557 Runners

2001. 50th Anniv of Mediterranean Games. Multicoloured.
1376 5d. Type **557** 45 15
1377 5d. Race winners and tile decoration 45 15

558 Emblem

559 Burning Lorry

2001. 15th World Festival of Youth and Students, Algiers.
1378 **558** 5d. multicoloured . . . 45 15

2001. Freedom Fighters' Day.
1379 **559** 5d. multicoloured . . . 45 15

560 Tree of Pencils

561 Children encircling Globe

2001. Teacher's Day.
1380 **560** 5d. multicoloured . . . 45 15

2001. United Nations Year of Dialogue among Civilisations.
1381 **561** 5d. multicoloured . . . 45 15

562 Dove and Explosion

2001. National Immigration Day. 40th Anniv of Demonstrations in Paris.
1382 **562** 5d. multicoloured . . . 45 20

563 El Mokrani

564 Bab el Oued (flood damaged town)

2001. Resistance Fighters. Multicoloured.
1383 5d. Type **563** 45 20
1384 5d. Cheikh Bouamama . . . 45 20

2001. Flood Victims Relief Fund.
1385 **564** 5d.+5d. multicoloured 90 40

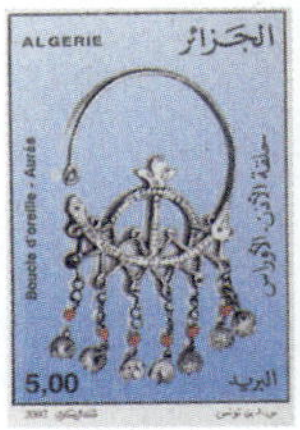
565 Earring

567 Flag, Doves and Soldiers

566 Ball, Net and Goalkeeper

2002. Silver Jewellery from Aures Region. Multicoloured.
1386 5d. Type **565** 45 25
1387 5d. Fibula 45 25
1388 24d. Pendant . . . . 1·60 1·10

2002. World Cup Football Championship, Japan and South Korea. Multicoloured.
1389 5d. Type **566** 45 25
1390 24d. Monk holding football (vert) . . . . 1·80 1·60

2002. 40th Anniv of Victory Day.
1391 **567** 5d. multicoloured . . . 45 30

568 Ksar Sidi Ouali Tamentit, Touat

2002. Fortified Castles. Multicoloured.
1392 5d. Type **568** 45 30
1393 5d. Ksar Ighzar, Gourara 45 30

569 Basket, Ball and Players

571 Book Illustration

570 Child and Table

2002. World Basketball Championship, Indianapolis, U.S.A.
1394 **569** 5d. multicoloured . . . 45 10

2002. Children's Day. Multicoloured.
1395 5d. Type **570** 45 10
1396 5d. Two girls 45 10

2002. 14th Death Anniv of Mohamed Temmam (artist and musician). Multicoloured.
1397 10d. Type **571** 90 40
1398 10d. Self-portrait 90 40

572 Anniversary Emblem

573 Calcite

2002. 40th Anniv of Independence. Multicoloured.
1399 5d. Type **572** 45 10
1400 24d. Flags and crowd . . . 1·30 1·00

2002. Minerals. Multicoloured.
1401 5d. Type **573** 30 10
1402 5d. Feldspar 30 10
1403 5d. Galena (horiz) 30 10
1404 5d. Conglomerate (pudding stone) (horiz) 30 10

574 Cherchell

2002. Lighthouses. Multicoloured.
1405 5d. Type **574** 30 10
1406 10d. Cap de Fer 60 40
1407 24d. Rachgoun island . . . 1·50 1·00

575 Postal Emblem

2002. Re-organization of Algerian Posts.
1408 **575** 5d. multicoloured . . . 30 10

576 Small Jug

2002. Pots. Multicoloured.
1409 5d. Type **576** 30 10
1410 5d. Pot for cooking cous-cous 30 10
1411 5d. Two-handled jar 30 10
1412 5d. Oil lamp 30 10

577 Dove and Rainbow

2002. International Day of Tolerance.
1413 **577** 24d. multicoloured . . . 1·50 1·00

578 *Venus verrucosa*

2002. Shells. Multicoloured.
1414 5d. Type **578** 30 10
1415 5d. *Acanthocardia aculeate* 30 10
1416 5d. *Xenophora crispa* 30 10
1417 5d. *Epitonium commune* . . 30 10

579 *Eucalyptus globules*

580 Eiffel Tower, Paris and Martyr's Monument, Algiers

2002. Medicinal Plants. Multicoloured.
1418 5d. Type **579** 30 10
1419 10d. Mallow (*Malva sylvestris*) 60 40
1420 24d. Laurel (*Laurus nobilis*) 1·50 1·00

2003. Djazair 2003, Year of Algeria in France. Multicoloured.
1421 5d. Type **580** 30 15
1422 24d. French and Algerian flags (horiz) . . . . . . 1·50 1·00

581 Emblem

2003. 10th Arab Games.
1423 **581** 5d. multicoloured . . . 30 10

582 El Maadjen, Relizane (oasis)

2003. International Year of Freshwater. Multicoloured.
1424 5d. Type **582** 30 10
1425 10d. Traditional well, M'zab valley 60 40
1426 24d. Kesria (irrigation), Timimoun . . . . 1·50 1·00

583 Slave Sale Contract (5 June 494)

2003. Vandal Carved Tablets. Multicoloured.
1427 10d. Type **583** 60 40
1428 24d. Mathematical chart (5 April 493) (vert) . . . 1·50 1·00

584 Building Facade, Face and Books **585** *Rumina decollate*

2003. Student's Day.
1429 **584** 5d. multicoloured . . . 30 10

2003. Snails. Multicoloured.
1430 5d. Type **585** 30 10
1431 24d. *Helix aspera* . . . . . 1·50 1·00

586 Candle, Map of Africa and Members' Flags **587** *Ulva lactuca*

2003. 1st Anniv of African Union.
1432 **586** 5d. multicoloured . . . 30 10

2003. Seaweeds. Multicoloured.
1433 5d. Type **587** 30 10
1434 24d. *Gymnogongrus crenulatus* . . . . 1·50 1·00

588 Ploughing with Oxen **590** Heart, Hand, Foot and Eye

589 Maouche Mohand Amokrane (founder) and Emblem

2003. Roman Mosaics. Multicoloured.
1435 5d. Type **588** 30 10
1436 10d. Ulysses and the Sirens 60 40
1437 24d. Hunting scene . . . . 1·50 1·00

2003. 40th Anniv of Algerian Olympic Committee.
1438 **589** 5d. multicoloured . . . 30 10

2003. World Diabetes Awareness Day.
1439 **590** 5d. multicoloured . . . 30 10

591 Ruins **592** Doors

2003. Support for Earthquake Victims (21 May 2003).
1440 **591** 5d.+5d. multicoloured 60 40

2003. Decorative Art. Multicoloured.
1441 5d. Type **592** 30 15
1442 10d. Window 60 40
1443 24d. Ceiling . . . . 1·50 1·00

593 Flags

2003. 45th Anniv of Algeria—China Diplomatic Relations.
1444 **593** 5d. multicoloured . . . 30 10

594 Hurdler **595** Woman with Raised Arms

2004. Olympic Games, Athens. Multicoloured.
1445 5d. Type **594** 30 10
1446 10d. Parthenon and hand holding Olympic torch . . 60 40

2004. Women's Day.
1447 **595** 5d. multicoloured . . . 30 10

596 Juba I **598** Entrance to Presidential Palace

597 Olive Tree

2004. Numidian Kings. Each brown, bronze and black.
1448 5d. Type **596** 30 10
1449 5d. Juba II 30 10
1450 5d. Micipsa 30 10
1451 5d. Massinassa 30 10
1452 5d. Jugurtha 30 10

2004. Tree Day. Multicoloured.
1453 5d. Type **597** 30 10
1454 10d. Date palm (vert) . . . 60 40

2004. Presidential Elections.
1455 **598** 24d. multicoloured . . . 1·50 1·00

599 Player catching Ball

2004. Centenary of FIFA (Federation Internationale de Football Association). Multicoloured.
1456 5d. Type **599** 30 10
1457 24d. Anniversary emblem 1·50 1·00

600 Dromedary

2004.
1458 **600** 24d. multicoloured . . . 1·50 1·00

601 Giving and Receiving Blood **602** Tradesmen

2004. International Blood Donation Day.
1459 **601** 5d. vermilion and black 30 10

2004. Acquiring a Trade.
1460 **602** 5d. multicoloured . . . 30 10

603 Chess Pieces and Board

2004. 80th Anniv of World Chess Federation (FIDE).
1461 **603** 5d. multicoloured . . . 30 10

604 Emblems and Currency **605** Yellow Rose

2004. 40th Anniv of CNEP Bank. Multicoloured.
1462 5d. Type **604** 30 10
1463 24d. Harbour . . . . 1·50 1·00

2004. Roses. Multicoloured.
1464 15d. Type **605** . . . . . . 1·30 65
1465 20d. Yellow rose (different) 1·40 85
1466 30d. Orange rose . . . . . 1·80 1·30
1467 50d. Pink rose . . . . . . 2·75 2·10

606 Map and Flags

2004. 6th Pan African Conference, Algiers.
1470 **606** 24d. multicoloured . . . 1·50 1·00

607 In Tehaq Rock Formation

2004. Tourism. Sahara. Multicoloured.
1471 5d. Type **607** 30 15
1472 24d. Ekanassay (vert) . . . 1·50 1·00

608 TeleFood Emblem, Houses and Flowers

2004. World Food Day. TeleFood (UN food agency). Multicoloured.
1473 5d.+1d. Type **608** 35 25
1474 5d.+1d. House and fruit trees 35 25

609 Group of Six

2004. 50th Anniv of Revolution. Multicoloured.
1475 15d. Type **609** . . . . . . 1·30 65
MS1476 70 × 80 mm. 30d. Emblem (30 × 40 mm) . . . . 1·80 1·80

610 Satellite and Earth

2004. 2nd Anniv of Launch of D'ALSAT 1 Satellite.
1477 **610** 30d. multicoloured . . . 1·80 1·30

611 Rainbow and Plants

2004. Protection of the Environment.
1478 **611** 15d. multicoloured . . . 1·10 60

612 Rabah Bitat

2004. 4th Death Anniv of Rabah Bitat (politician).
1479 **612** 15d. multicoloured . . . 1·10 60

613 Wood Pigeon (*Columba palumbus*)

2005. Pigeons. Multicoloured.
1480 10d. Type **613** 60 35
1481 15d. Rock dove (*Columba livia*) . . . . 1·10 60

614 *Echium australis*

615 Eye and Hands

2005. Flowers. Multicoloured.
1482 15d. Type **614** . . . . . . 1·30 65
1483 30d. *Borago officinalis* . . . 1·80 1·30

2005. National Day for the Disabled.
1484 **615** 15d. multicoloured . . . 1·10 60

616 Emblem

2005. Arab League Summit, Algeria (1485). 60th Anniv of Arab League (1486). Multicoloured.
1485 15d. Type **616** . . . . . . 1·10 60
1486 30d. Emblem and "2005–1945" (vert) . . . . . . 1·80 1·30

617 Medersa D'Alger

2005. Medersa (seats of learning). Multicoloured.
1487 10d. Type **617** 60 35
1488 15d. Medersa de Constantine . . . . . . 1·10 60
1489 30d. Medersa de Tlemcen 1·80 1·30

618 Emblem

619 Workers and Hand holding Apple

2005. World Intellectual Property Day.
1490 **618** 15d. multicoloured . . . 1·10 60

2005. World Day for Safety and Health at Work.
1491 **619** 15d. multicoloured . . . 1·10 60

620 "60" and Dove

2005. 60th Anniv of Massacre.
1492 **620** 15d. multicoloured . . . 1·10 60

621 Medal and Stylized Sports

622 Lakhdar Ben Khlouf

2005. 15th Mediterranean Games, Almeria. Multicoloured.
1493 15d. Type **621** . . . . . . 1·10 60
1494 30d. Emblem (horiz) . . . . 1·80 1·30

2005. Poets. Multicoloured.
1495 10d. Type **622** 60 35
1496 15d. Ben M'sayeb . . . . . 1·10 60
1497 20d. Si Mohand Ou M'Hand . . . . 1·40 85
1498 30d. Aissa El Djermouni . . 1·80 1·30

623 Children

2005. International Day against Drug Abuse.
1499 **623** 15d. multicoloured . . . 1·10 60

624 Student and Soldiers

626 Emblem

625 Cheetah

2005. 50th Anniv of UGEMA (General Union of the Algerian Moslem Students).
1500 **624** 15d. multicoloured . . . 1·10 60

2005. Cheetah (inscr "Guepard"). Multicoloured.
1501 15d. Type **625** . . . . . . 1·10 60
1502 30d. Standing . . . . 1·80 1·30

2005. World Information Society Summit, Tunis.
1503 **626** 15d. multicoloured . . . 1·10 60

627 "50" and Soldiers

628 Phare Fort

2005. 50th Anniv of Uprising.
1504 **627** 15d. multicoloured . . . 1·10 60

2005. Forts. Multicoloured.
1505 10d. Type **628** 60 35
1506 15d. Cap Matifou . . . . . 1·10 60
1507 30d. Santa Cruz . . . . . 1·80 1·30

629 Emblem and Runners

630 Clasped Hands

2005. International Year of Sports Education.
1508 **629** 30d. multicoloured . . . 1·80 1·30

2005. National Reconciliation.
1509 **630** 15d. multicoloured . . . 1·10 60

631 Flag

2005. Referendum.
1510 **631** 15d. multicoloured . . . 1·10 60

632 Flag, Emblem and Buildings

2005. Recovery of National Sovereignty.
1511 **632** 30d. multicoloured . . . 1·80 1·30

633 Saddle

2005. Emir Abdelkader's Possessions. Multicoloured.
1512 15d. Type **633** . . . . . . 1·10 60
1513 30d. Boots . . . . 1·80 1·30
1514 40d. Jacket (vert) . . . . . 2·40 1·70
1515 50d. Seal (vert) . . . . . . 2·75 2·10

634 Miguel de Cervantes

635 Amputee

2005. Miguel de Cervantes Saavedra (writer) Commemoration.
1516 **634** 30d. multicoloured . . . 1·80 1·30

2005. Anti-Personnel Mine Destruction Campaign.
1517 **635** 30d. multicoloured . . . 1·80 1·30

636 Emblem

637 Ptolemy

2005. International AIDS Awareness Day.
1518 **636** 30d. multicoloured . . . 1·80 1·30

2005. Kings. Multicoloured.
1519 15d. Type **637** . . . . . . 1·10 60
1520 30d. Syphax . . . . 1·80 1·30

638 Building Facade

2006. Posts.
1521 **638** 30d. multicoloured . . . 1·80 1·30

639 *Ciconia ciconia*

2006. Waterside Birds. Multicoloured.
1522 10d. Type **639** 60 35
1523 15d. *Ciconia nigra* . . . . . 1·10 60
1524 20d. *Platalea leucorodia* . . 1·40 85
1525 30d. *Grus grus* . . . . . . 1·80 1·30

640 Skier

2006. Winter Olympic Games, Turin.
1526 **640** 15d. multicoloured . . . 1·10 60

641 Aissat Idir (founder)

642 Ball and Globe

2006. 50th Anniv of UGTA Trade Union.
1527 **641** 15d. multicoloured . . . 1·10 60

2006. World Cup Football Championship, Germany.
1528 **642** 30d. multicoloured . . . 1·80 1·30

643 Airport

2006. New Air Terminal, Algiers.
1529 **643** 30d. multicoloured . . . 1·80 1·30

645 Students

2006. 50th Anniv of Student's Day.
1532 **645** 20d. multicoloured . . . 1·40 85

646 Trees

2006. International Environment Day.
1533 **646** 30d. multicoloured . . . 1·80 1·30

647 Powder Holder

2006. Poire a Poudre (powder holders). Multicoloured.
1534 15d. Type **647** . . . . . . 1·10 60
1535 20d. Powder holder (different) . . . . 1·40 85

648 Map

649 Emblem

2006. 50th Anniv of La Soummam Congress.
1536 **648** 20d. multicoloured . . . 1·40 85

2006. 16th Arab School Games.
1537 **649** 30d. multicoloured . . . 1·80 1·30

650 Dunes and Oasis

2006. International Year of Deserts and Desertification.
1538 **650** 15d. multicoloured . . . 1·10 60

651 Traditional Designs

2007. Algiers-Arab Cultural Capital-2007. Mult.
1539 15d. Type **651** . . . . 1·10 60
1540 30d. "2007" . . . . 1·80 1·30

652 L'ilot d'Arzew

2007. Lighthouses. Multicoloured.
1541 15d. Type **652** . . . . . . 1·10 60
1542 20d. Cap Sigli . . . . . . 1·40 85
1543 38d. Ras-Afia . . . . 2·20 1·50

653 Women

653a Mohamed Ameziane Belhaddad

2007. Development of Women's Employment.
1544 **653** 15d. multicoloured . . . 1·10 60

2007. Mohamed Ameziane Belhaddad Commemoration.
1545 **653a** 15d. multicoloured . . 1·10 60

654 Ksar de Kenadsa

2007. Cultural Heritage. Multicoloured.
1546 15d. Type **654** . . . . . . 1·10 60
1547 15d. Ksar de Temacine (vert) . . . . 1·10 60

655 Emblem, Map and 'JEUX AFRO-ASIATIQUES D'ALGER'

2007. Sport Events in Algiers. Multicoloured.
1548 15d. Type **655** . . . . . . 1·10 60
1549 15d. Emblem, map and 'ALL AFRICAN GAMES' (vert) . . . . . 1·10 60

656 Count Landon's Garden, Biskra

2007. Gardens. Multicoloured.
1550 15d. Type **656** . . . . . . 1·10 60
1551 20d. Ibn Badis garden, Oran 1·40 85
1552 38d. Jardin d' Essai du Hamma, Algiers . . . . 2·20 1·50

657 Theatre de Setif

2007. Theatres. Multicoloured.
1553 15d. Type **657** . . . . . . 1·10 60
1554 15d. Theatre d'Oranen, Oran . . . . 1·10 60
1555 20d. Theatre de Annaba (*horiz*) . . . . 1·40 85
1556 38d. Theatre d'Algers . . . 2·20 1·50

658 Demonstrators

2007. 45th Anniv of Festival of Independence and Youth. Multicoloured.
1556 15d. Type **658** . . . . . . 1·10 60
MS1557 60 × 77 mm. 20d. Satellite, computer and inkwell. Imperf 1·40 1·40

659 Bottle

660 Emblem

2007. Ceramics. Multicoloured.
1558 15d. Type **659** . . . . . . 1·10 60
1559 15d. Two handled jug . . . 1·10 60
1560 20d. Censer . . . . 1·40 85
1561 38d. Oil lamp (horiz) . . . 2·20 1·50

2007. 45th Anniv of National Police. Multicoloured.
1562 15d. Type **660** . . . . . . 1·10 60
1563 38d. Policeman and patrol vehicle . . . . 2·20 1·50

661 Hyena

2007. Endangered Species. Multicoloured.
1564 15d. Type **661** . . . . . . 1·10 60
1565 38d. White-tailed red fox . . 2·20 1·50

662 Encyclopaedia of Algerian Postage Stamps

2007.
1566 **662** 15d. multicoloured . . . 1·10 60

663 Ahmed Bey

664 Emblem

2007. Ahmed Bey (resistance fighter) Commemoration.
1567 **663** 15d. multicoloured . . . 1·10 60

2007. National Artisans' Day.
1568 **664** 15d. multicoloured . . . 1·10 60

665 Nile Tilapia

2007. Nile Tilapia (*Oreochromis niloticus*).
1569 **665** 15d. multicoloured . . . 1·10 60

666 Abd el-kader

668 Doves and Emblem

667 Emblem

2007. Birth Bicentenary of Abd al-Qadir al-Jaza'iri (Abd el-kader) (Islamic scholar, Sufi, political and military leader). Sheet 158 × 108 mm containing T **666** and similar vert designs.
MS1570 15d. Type **666**; 15d. Facing left; 38d. Wearing medals and belt 3·25 3·25

2008. Census.
1571 **667** 15d. multicoloured . . . 1·10 60

2008. 50th Anniv of Bombing of Sakiet Sid Youcef, Tunisia.
1572 **668** 15d. multicoloured . . . 1·10 60
A stamp of a similar design was issued by Tunisia.

POSTAGE DUE STAMPS

1926. As Postage Due stamps of France, but inscr "ALGERIE".
D 34 **D 11** 5c. blue . . . . . . 45 4·25
D 35 10c. brown 45 95
D 36 20c. olive . . . . . . 1·00 4·25
D 37 25c. red . . . . 85 4·75
D 38 30c. red 30 10
D 39 45c. green . . . . . . 2·00 5·25
D 40 50c. purple 10 10
D 41 60c. green . . . . . . 1·80 6·50
D 42 1f. red on yellow . . . 50 85
D249 1f.50 lilac . . . . . . 1·60 5·00
D 43 2f. mauve . . . . . . 70 1·90
D250 2f. blue . . . . 2·30 4·75
D 44 3f. blue . . . . 70 1·60
D251 5f. red . . . . 1·90 5·00
D252 5f. green . . . . . . 3·75 5·00

1926. As Postage Due stamps of France, but inscr "ALGERIE".
D45 **D 19** 1c. olive . . . . 10 3·75
D46 10c. violet . . . . . . 75 1·80
D47 30c. bistre 65 10
D48 60c. red . . . . 1·10 10
D49 1f. violet . . . . 8·00 1·80
D50 2f. blue . . . . 9·75 2·25

1927. Nos. D36, D39 and D37 surch.
D92 **D 11** 60 on 20c. olive . . . . 1·20 45
D93 2f. on 45c. green . . . 2·50 4·25
D94 3f. on 25c. red . . . . 1·00 5·50

1927. Nos. D45/8 surch.
D95 **D 19** 10c. on 30c. bistre . . . 2·30 12·00
D96 1f. on 1c. olive . . . . 1·20 3·50
D97 1f. on 60c. red . . . 10·00 10
D98 2f. on 10c. violet . . . 6·00 38·00

1942. As 1926 issue, but without "RF".
D181 **D 11** 30c. red . . . . 1·90 4·75
D182 2f. mauve . . . . . . 2·75 4·00

1944. No. 208 surch **TAXE P. C. V. DOUANE 20Fr.**
D230 **38** 20f. on 50f. red . . . . 2·30 4·75

1944. Surch **T 0.50.**
D231 **4** 50c. on 20c. green . . . . 1·40 4·00

1947. Postage Due Stamps of France optd **ALGERIE.**
D283 10c. brown (No. D985) . . 10 4·00
D284 30c. purple (No. D986) . . 35 4·00

D 53

1947.
D285 **D 53** 20c. red . . . . 15 4·50
D286 60c. blue . . . . . . 35 4·75
D287 1f. brown . . . . . . 10 4·00
D288 1f.50 olive . . . . . . 80 6·00
D289 2f. red . . . . 15 3·25
D290 3f. violet . . . . . . 35 3·50
D291 5f. blue . . . . 30 1·30
D292 6f. black . . . . . . 30 3·00
D293 10f. purple 80 95
D294 15f. myrtle . . . . . 2·00 4·75
D295 20f. green . . . . . . 1·10 1·30
D296 30f. red . . . . 4·25 4·75
D297 50f. black . . . . . . 4·75 6·75
D298 100f. blue . . . . . . 20·00 18·00

INDEPENDENT STATE

1962. Postage Due stamps of France optd **EA** and with bar obliterating "REPUBLIQUE FRANCAISE".
D391 **D 457** 5c. mauve . . . . . 20·00 17·00
D392 10c. red . . . . . . 20·00 17·00
D393 20c. brown . . . . . 20·00 17·00
D394 50c. green . . . . . 40·00 34·00
D395 1f. green . . . . . . 60·00 55·00
The above also exist with larger overprint applied with handstamps.

D 107 Scales of Justice

D 200 Ears of Corn

1963.
D411 **D 107** 5c. red and olive . . 10 10
D412 10c. olive and red . . 10 10
D413 20c. blue and black 50 30
D414 50c. brown and green 1·10 75
D415 1f. violet and orange 2·20 1·80

1968. No. D415 surch.
D508 **D 107** 60c. on 1f. violet and orange 80 60

1972.
D603 **D 200** 10c. brown 10 10
D604 20c. brown 10 10
D605 40c. orange 25 10
D606 50c. blue 30 10
D607 80c. brown 65 30
D608 1d. green 85 50
D609 2d. blue . . . . . . 1·60 95
D610 3d. violet 50 25
D611 4d. purple 55 40

D 644 Post Office

2006. Postage Due.
D1530 D **644** 5d. blue 15 10
D1531 10d. green 20 10

ALLENSTEIN Pt. 7

A district of E. Prussia retained by Germany as the result of a plebiscite in 1920. Stamps issued during the plebiscite period.

100 pfennig = 1 mark.

1920. Stamps of Germany inscr "DEUTSCHES REICH" optd **PLEBISCITE OLSZTYN ALLENSTEIN**.
1 **17** 5pf. green 45 90
2 10pf. red 45 90
3 **24** 15pf. violet 45 90
4 15pf. purple . . . . 6·25 10·50
5 **17** 20pf. blue . . . . 45 1·10
6 30pf. black & orge on buff 45 1·10
7 40pf. black and red . . . 45 90
8 50pf. black & pur on buff 45 90
9 75pf. black and green . . . 45 90
10 **18** 1m. red . . . . 1·60 2·75
11 1m.25 green . . . . 1·80 3·00
12 1m.50 brown . . . . . . 1·10 2·75
13b **20** 2m.50 red . . . . 2·75 8·75
14 **21** 3m. black . . . . 2·75 3·50

1920. Stamps of Germany inscr "DEUTSCHES REICH" optd **TRAITE DE VERSAILLES** etc. in oval.
15 **17** 5pf. green 45 90
16 10pf. red 45 90
17 **24** 15pf. violet 45 90
18 15pf. purple . . . . 23·00 40·00
19 **17** 20pf. blue . . . . 70 1·40
20 30pf. black & orge on buff 45 90
21 40pf. black and red 45 90
22 50pf. black & pur on buff 45 90
23 75pf. black and green . . . 70 1·40
24 **18** 1m. red . . . . 1·60 2·20
25 1m.25 green . . . . 1·60 2·50
26 1m.50 brown . . . . . . 1·30 2·20
27 **20** 2m.50 red . . . . 2·75 4·50
28 **21** 3m. black . . . . 1·80 2·20

ALSACE AND LORRAINE Pt. 7

Stamps used in parts of France occupied by the German army in the war of 1870–71, and afterwards temporarily in the annexed provinces of Alsace and Lorraine.

100 pfennig = 1 mark

1

1870.
1 **1** 1c. green . . . . 60·00 £110
3 2c. brown . . . . 80·00 £140
5 4c. grey . . . . 80·00 80·00
8 5c. green . . . . 55·00 8·75
10 10c. brown . . . . 70·00 13·00
14 20c. blue . . . . 70·00 10·50
16 25c. brown . . . . £110 80·00

For 1940 issues see separate lists for Alsace and Lorraine under German Occupations.

ALWAR Pt. 1

A state of Rajputana, N. India. Now uses Indian stamps.

12 pies = 1 anna; 16 annas = 1 rupee

1 Native Dagger

1877. Roul or perf.
1b **1** ¼a. blue . . . . 4·75 1·10
5 ¼a. green . . . . 5·00 2·50
2c 1a. brown . . . . 3·25 1·50

ANDORRA Pt. 6, Pt. 9

An independent state in the Pyrenees under the joint suzerainty of France and Spain.

FRENCH POST OFFICES

1931. 100 centimes = 1 franc.
2002. 100 cents = 1 euro.

1931. Stamps of France optd **ANDORRE**.
F 1 **11** ½c. on 1c. grey . . . . . 30 5·75
F 2 1c. grey 35 65
F 3 2c. red . . . . 35 7·00
F 4 3c. orange . . . . 40 3·75
F 5 5c. green . . . . 80 7·25
F 6 10c. lilac . . . . 3·00 8·75
F 7 **18** 15c. brown . . . . 7·50 7·75
F 8 20c. mauve . . . . 12·50 12·50
F 9 25c. brown . . . . 9·25 11·50
F10 30c. green . . . . 9·00 13·50
F11 40c. blue . . . . 11·00 17·00
F12 **15** 45c. violet . . . . 16·00 20·00
F13 50c. red . . . . 13·00 14·00
F14 65c. green . . . . 25·00 38·00
F15 75c. mauve . . . . 25·00 35·00
F16 **18** 90c. red . . . . 30·00 41·00
F17 **15** 1f. blue . . . . 36·00 41·00
F18 **18** 1f.50 blue . . . . 40·00 49·00
F19 **13** 2f. red and green . . . . 35·00 60·00
F20 3f. mauve and red . . . . 80·00 95·00
F21 5f. blue and buff £100 £180
F22 10f. green and red £200 £250
F23 20f. mauve and green . . . £250 £275

F **3** Our Lady's Chapel, Meritxell

F **5** St. Michael's Church, Engolasters

1932.
F24 F **3** 1c. slate . . . . 20 2·30
F25 2c. violet . . . . 60 2·00
F26 3c. brown . . . . 65 2·20
F27 5c. green . . . . 35 2·30
F28 A 10c. lilac . . . . 1·40 2·75
F29 F **3** 15c. red . . . . 2·00 2·75
F30 A 20c. mauve . . . . 11·50 13·50
F31 F **5** 25c. brown . . . . 4·75 6·25
F32 A 25c. brown . . . . 11·50 30·00
F33 30c. green . . . . 3·00 3·75
F34 40c. blue . . . . 8·25 3·25
F35 40c. brown . . . . 1·20 3·50
F36 45c. red . . . . 12·00 23·00
F37 45c. green . . . . 6·25 19·00
F38 F **5** 50c. mauve . . . . 9·50 9·25
F39 A 50c. violet . . . . 6·00 17·00
F40 50c. green . . . . 1·70 9·00
F41 55c. violet . . . . 25·00 60·00
F42 60c. brown . . . . 1·60 6·50
F43 F **5** 65c. green . . . . 42·00 44·00
F44 A 65c. blue . . . . 16·00 29·00
F45 70c. red . . . . 1·70 5·00
F46 F **5** 75c. violet . . . . 8·75 10·00
F47 A 75c. blue . . . . 3·25 14·50
F48 80c. green . . . . 17·00 60·00
F49 B 80c. green . . . . 1·60 5·50
F50 90c. red . . . . 7·75 7·25
F51 90c. green . . . . 5·50 13·00
F52 1f. green . . . . 28·00 19·00
F53 1f. red . . . . 26·00 29·00
F54 1f. blue . . . . 1·30 3·00
F55 1f. 20 violet . . . . . . 1·20 5·75
F56 F **3** 1f. 25 mauve . . . . . . 50·00 55·00
F57 1f.25 red . . . . 6·00 17·00
F58 B 1f.30 brown . . . . . . 1·60 5·75
F59 C 1f.50 blue . . . . 25·00 32·00
F60 B 1f.50 red . . . . 95 5·75
F61 1f.75 violet . . . . . . 80·00 95·00
F62 1f.75 blue . . . . 46·00 55·00
F63 2f. mauve . . . . 9·00 20·00
F64 F **3** 2f. red . . . . 1·80 7·50
F65 2f. green . . . . 1·10 7·50
F66 2f.15 violet . . . . . . 46·00 65·00
F67 2f.25 blue . . . . 8·75 26·00
F68 2f.40 red . . . . 1·30 5·75
F69 2f.50 black . . . . . . 11·50 31·00
F70 2f.50 blue . . . . 2·40 9·00
F71 B 3f. brown . . . . 24·00 36·00
F72 F **3** 3f. brown . . . . 2·10 6·00
F73 4f. blue . . . . 1·50 5·50
F74 4f.50 violet . . . . . . 1·20 7·25
F75 C 5f. brown . . . . 1·70 6·00
F76 10f. violet . . . . . . 2·30 6·00
F78 15f. blue . . . . 1·10 3·50
F79 20f. red . . . . 1·80 3·25
F81 A 50f. blue . . . . 2·50 8·00
DESIGNS—HORIZ: A, St. Anthony's Bridge; C, Andorra la Vella. VERT: B, Valley of Sant Julia.

1935. No. F38 surch **20c**.
F82 F **5** 20c. on 50c. purple . . . 10·00 24·00

F **9**

F **13** Andorra la Vella

F **10**

F **14** Councillor Jaume Bonell

1936.
F83 F **9** 1c. black . . . . 35 2·75
F84 2c. blue . . . . 30 2·75
F85 3c. brown . . . . 40 2·75
F86 5c. red . . . . 20 2·75
F87 10c. blue . . . . 20 2·75
F88 15c. mauve . . . . 2·30 4·25
F89 20c. green . . . . 25 2·75
F90 30c. red . . . . 30 6·00
F91 30c. black . . . . 1·40 5·75
F92 35c. green . . . . 45·00 70·00
F93 40c. brown . . . . 85 5·50
F94 50c. green . . . . 95 5·75
F95 60c. blue . . . . 1·50 5·75
F96 70c. violet . . . . 1·30 5·75

1944.
F 97 F **10** 10c. violet . . . . 10 3·50
F 98 30c. red . . . . 20 3·25
F 99 40c. blue . . . . 40 3·50
F100 50c. red . . . . 15 4·00
F101 60c. black . . . . 35 3·50
F102 70c. mauve . . . . 25 5·00
F103 80c. green . . . . 10 5·00
F104 1f. blue . . . . 65 2·10
F105 D 1f. purple . . . . 25 5·50
F106 1f.20 blue . . . . 15 5·50
F107 1f.50 red . . . . 10 5·00
F108 2f. green . . . . 10 3·25
F109 E 2f.40 red . . . . 15 3·50
F110 2f.50 red . . . . 2·30 5·25
F111 3f. brown . . . . 55 2·50
F112 D 3f. red . . . . 2·20 4·25
F113 E 4f. blue . . . . 35 5·50
F114 4f. green . . . . 50 6·50
F115 D 4f. brown . . . . 1·20 9·00
F116 E 4f.50 brown . . . . . . 50 5·00
F117 F **13** 4f.50 blue . . . . 3·00 17·00
F118 5f. blue . . . . 45 5·50
F119 5f. green . . . . 1·10 5·75
F120 E 5f. green . . . . 1·60 10·00
F121 5f. violet . . . . 2·75 6·50
F122 F **13** 6f. red . . . . 35 3·25
F123 6f. purple . . . . 30 5·00
F124 E 6f. green . . . . 1·90 6·50
F125 F **13** 8f. blue . . . . 1·30 7·00
F126 E 8f. brown . . . . 55 3·00
F127 F **13** 10f. green . . . . 40 5·00
F128 10f. blue . . . . 75 1·30
F129 12f. red . . . . 55 6·50
F130 12f. green . . . . 70 5·00
F131 F **14** 15f. purple . . . . 30 5·75
F132 F **13** 15f. red . . . . 50 3·00
F133 15f. brown . . . . 3·50 2·00
F134 F **14** 18f. blue . . . . 1·50 10·50
F135 F **13** 18f. red . . . . 7·25 23·00
F136 F **14** 20f. blue . . . . 95 5·75
F137 20f. violet . . . . 2·50 8·75
F138 25f. red . . . . 1·90 9·00
F139 25f. blue . . . . 1·00 7·50
F140 30f. blue . . . . 13·50 22·00
F141 40f. green . . . . 1·50 8·00
F142 50f. brown . . . . 85 3·75
DESIGNS—HORIZ: D, Church of St. John of Caselles; E, House of the Valleys.

F **15** Chamois and Pyrenees

F **16** Les Escaldes

1950. Air.
F143 F **15** 100f. blue . . . . . . 45·00 42·00

1955.
F144 F **16** 1f. blue (postage) . . . 10 2·30
F145 2f. green . . . . 40 1·80
F146 3f. red . . . . 55 1·50
F147 5f. brown . . . . 60 1·70
F148 – 6f. green . . . . 2·10 2·50
F149 – 8f. red . . . . 2·30 2·75
F150 – 10f. violet . . . . 4·00 2·50
F151 – 12f. blue . . . . 2·20 1·80
F152 – 15f. red . . . . 2·75 1·90
F153 – 18f. blue . . . . 2·20 3·25
F154 – 20f. violet . . . . 2·40 1·50
F155 – 25f. brown . . . . 3·00 3·50
F156 – 30f. blue . . . . 19·00 25·00
F157 – 35f. blue . . . . 10·00 12·50
F158 – 40f. green . . . . 27·00 46·00
F159 – 50f. red . . . . 3·75 3·50
F160 – 65f. violet . . . . 5·00 25·00
F161 – 70f. brown . . . . 5·25 19·00
F162 – 75f. blue . . . . 35·00 80·00

F163 – 100f. green (air) . . . 7·75 9·50
F164 – 200f. red . . . . 13·00 15·00
F165 – 500f. blue . . . . 75·00 55·00
DESIGNS—VERT: 15f. to 25f. Gothic cross, Andorra la Vella; 100f. to 500f. East Valira River. HORIZ: 6f. to 12f. Santa Coloma Church; 30f. to 75f. Les Bons village.

New currency. 100 (old) francs = 1 (new) franc.

F **21**

F **22** Gothic Cross, Meritxell

1961.
F166 F **21** 1c. grey, blue and slate (postage) . . . 60 1·40
F167 2c. lt orge, blk & orge 60 1·40
F168 5c. lt grn, blk & grn 40 1·40
F169 10c. pink, blk & red 45 40
F170a 12c. yell, pur & grn 1·90 4·00
F171 15c. lt bl, blk & bl . . 70 1·40
F172 18c. pink, blk & mve 1·30 2·75
F173 20c. lt yell, brn & yell 75 30
F174 F **22** 25c. blue, vio & grn 95 85
F175 30c. pur, red & grn 95 50
F175a 40c. green and brown 1·20 1·70
F176 45c. blue, ind & grn 14·50 29·00
F176a 45c. brown, bl & vio 1·20 2·50
F177 50c. multicoloured . . 1·90 1·30
F177a 60c. brown & chestnut 1·40 1·80
F178 65c. olive, bl & brn 16·00 48·00
F179 85c. multicoloured . . 15·00 31·00
F179a 90c. green, bl & brn 1·10 3·00
F180 1f. blue, brn & turq 1·60 1·10

F181 – 2f. green, red and purple (air) . . . . 2·00 1·80
F182 – 3f. purple, bl & grn 2·20 2·10
F183 – 5f. orange, pur & red 3·00 1·60
F184 – 10f. green and blue . . 5·50 4·50
DESIGNS—As Type F **22**: 60c. to 1f. Engolasters Lake; 2f. to 10f. Incles Valley.

F **23** "Telstar" Satellite and part of Globe

1962. 1st Trans-Atlantic TV Satellite Link.
F185 F **23** 50c. violet and blue . . 80 2·50

F **24** "La Sardane" (dance)

1963. Andorran History (1st issue).
F186 F **24** 20c. purple, mve & grn 2·75 5·75
F187 – 50c. red and green . . 5·75 11·00
F188 – 1f. green, blue & brn 7·75 18·00
DESIGNS—LARGER (48½ × 27 mm): 50c. Charlemagne crossing Andorra. (48 × 27 mm): 1f. Foundation of Andorra by Louis le Debonnaire.
See also Nos. F190/1.

F **25** Santa Coloma Church and Grand Palais, Paris

1964. "PHILATEC 1964" International Stamp Exhibition, Paris.
F189 F **25** 25c. green, pur & brn 95 2·75

1964. Andorran History (2nd issue). As Nos. F187/8, inscribed "1964".
F190 60c. green, chestnut and brown . . . . 6·75 28·00
F191 1f. blue, sepia and brown 11·50 28·00
DESIGNS (48½ × 27 mm): 60c. "Napoleon re-establishes the Andorran Statute, 1806"; 1f. "Confirmation of the Co-government, 1288".

F **26** Virgin of Santa Coloma

F **27** "Syncom", Morse Key and Pleumeur-Bodou centre

1964. Red Cross Fund.
F192 F **26** 25c.+10c. red, green and blue . . . . 10·50 33·00

1965. Centenary of I.T.U.
F193 F **27** 60c. violet, blue and red . . . . 3·25 7·00

F **28** Andorra House, Paris

F **29** Chair-lift

1965. Opening of Andorra House, Paris.
F194 F **28** 25c. brown, olive & bl 85 2·00

1966. Winter Sports.
F195 F **29** 25c. green, purple & bl 80 2·75
F196 – 40c. brown, blue & red 1·80 3·50
DESIGN—HORIZ: 40c. Ski-lift.

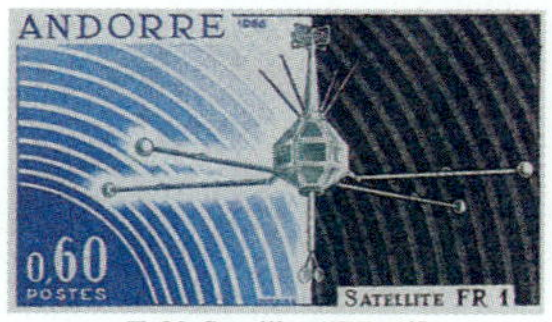

F **30** Satellite "FR 1"

1966. Launching of Satellite "FR 1".
F197 F **30** 60c. blue, emer & grn 1·10 3·75

F **31** Europa "Ship"

F **32** Cogwheels

1966. Europa.
F198 F **31** 60c. brown . . . . . . 2·75 5·50

1967. Europa.
F199 F **32** 30c. indigo and blue 2·10 4·25
F200 60c. red and purple . . 3·25 9·00

F **33** "Folk Dancers" (statue)

F **34** Telephone and Dial

1967. Centenary (1966) of New Reform.
F201 F **33** 30c. green, olive & slate 95 3·00

1967. Inaug of Automatic Telephone Service.
F202 F **34** 60c. black, violet & red 1·10 3·25

F **35** Andorran Family

1967. Institution of Social Security.
F203 F **35** 2f.30 brown & purple 4·75 16·00

F **36** "The Temptation"

F **37** Downhill Skiing

1967. 16th-century Frescoes in House of the Valleys (1st series).
F204 F **36** 25c. red and black . . 65 2·50
F205 – 30c. purple and violet 70 3·00
F206 – 60c. blue and indigo 1·10 4·00
FRESCOES: 30c. "The Kiss of Judas"; 60c. "The Descent from the Cross".
See also Nos. F210/12.

1968. Winter Olympic Games, Grenoble.
F207 F **37** 40c. purple, orge & red 70 3·25

F **38** Europa "Key"

1968. Europa.
F208 F **38** 30c. blue and slate . . 3·25 6·25
F209 60c. violet & brown . . 6·50 11·50

1968. 16th-century Frescoes in House of the Valleys (2nd series). Designs as Type F **36**.
F210 25c. deep green and green 60 2·75
F211 30c. purple and brown . . . 95 4·25
F212 60c. brown and red . . . . 1·90 5·75
FRESCOES: 25c. "The Beating of Christ"; 30c. "Christ Helped by the Cyrenians"; 60c. "The Death of Christ".

F **39** High Jumping

1968. Olympic Games, Mexico.
F213 F **39** 40c. brown and blue 1·60 3·25

F **40** Colonnade

F **41** Canoeing

1969. Europa.
F214 F **40** 40c. grey, blue and red 7·25 9·25
F215 70c. red, green and blue . . . . 11·00 19·00

1969. World Kayak-Canoeing Championships, Bourg-St. Maurice.
F216 F **41** 70c. dp blue, bl & grn 1·40 4·50

F **41a** "Diamond Crystal" in Rain Drop

F **42** "The Apocalypse"

1969. European Water Charter.
F217 F **41a** 70c. black, blue and ultramarine . . . . 3·50 8·50

1969. Altar-screen, Church of St. John of Caselles (1st series). "The Revelation of St. John".
F218 F **42** 30c. red, violet & brn 75 1·80
F219 – 40c. bistre, brn & grey 1·10 2·30
F220 – 70c. purple, lake & red 1·60 3·00
DESIGNS: 40c. Angel "clothed with cloud with face as the sun, and feet as pillars of fire" (Rev. 10); 70c. Christ with sword and stars, and seven candlesticks.
See also Nos. F225/7, F233/5 and F240/2.

F **43** Handball Player

F **44** "Flaming Sun"

1970. 7th World Handball Championships, France.
F221 F **43** 80c. blue, brn & dp bl 1·90 4·50

1970. Europa.
F222 F **44** 40c. orange . . . . . 5·00 3·50
F223 80c. violet . . . . . . 11·50 11·50

F **45** Putting the Shot

F **46** Ice Skaters

1970. 1st European Junior Athletic Championships, Paris.
F224 F **45** 80c. purple and blue 2·20 4·75

1970. Altar-screen, Church of St. John of Caselles (2nd series). Designs as Type F **42**.
F225 30c. violet, brown and red 1·40 2·10
F226 40c. green and violet . . . 1·30 2·50
F227 80c. red, blue and green . . 2·75 3·50
DESIGNS: 30c. Angel with keys and padlock; 40c. Angel with pillar; 80c. St. John being boiled in cauldron of oil.

1971. World Ice Skating Championships, Lyon.
F228 F **46** 80c. violet, pur & red 2·50 4·25

F **47** Western Capercaillie

F **48** Europa Chain

1971. Nature Protection.
F229 F **47** 80c. multicoloured . . 4·00 5·00
F230 – 80c. brown, green & bl 4·25 5·50
DESIGN: No. F230, Brown bear.

1971. Europa.
F231 F **48** 50c. red . . . . 7·25 10·50
F232 80c. green . . . . . . 12·00 17·00

1971. Altar-screen, Church of St. John of Caselles (3rd series). As Type F **42**.
F233 30c. green, brown and myrtle . . . . 1·50 4·00
F234 50c. brown, orange and lake 1·90 4·50
F235 90c. blue, purple and brown 3·50 6·00
DESIGNS: 30c. St. John in temple at Ephesus; 50c. St. John with cup of poison; 90c. St. John disputing with pagan philosophers.

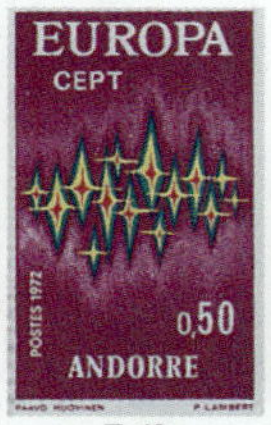

F **49** "Communications"

F **50** Golden Eagle

1972. Europa.
F236 F **49** 50c. multicoloured . . 7·50 7·25
F237 90c. multicoloured . . 12·00 16·00

1972. Nature Protection.
F238 F **50** 60c. olive, green & pur 3·75 5·50

F **51** Rifle-shooting

F **52** General De Gaulle

1972. Olympic Games, Munich.
F239 F **51** 1f. purple . . . . . . 2·75 4·00

1972. Altar-screen, Church of St. John of Caselles (4th series). As Type F **42**.
F240 30c. purple, grey and green 1·10 2·00
F241 50c. grey and blue . . . . 1·40 2·50
F242 90c. green and blue . . . . 2·20 3·50
DESIGNS: 30c. St. John in discussion with bishop; 50c. St. John healing a cripple; 90c. Angel with spear.

1972. 5th Anniv of Gen. De Gaulle's Visit to Andorra.
F243 F **52** 50c. blue . . . . . . 3·25 5·00
F244 – 90c. red . . . . 4·50 6·75
DESIGN: 90c. Gen. De Gaulle in Andorra la Vella, 1967.
See also Nos. F434/5.

F **53** Europa "Posthorn"

1973. Europa.
F245 F **53** 50c. multicoloured . . 7·00 9·00
F246 90c. multicoloured . . 7·50 18·00

F **54** "Virgin of Canolich" (wood carving)

F **55** Lily

1973. Andorran Art.
F247 F **54** 1f. lilac, blue and drab 2·50 3·75

1973. Pyrenean Flowers (1st series). Multicoloured.
F248 30c. Type F **55** . . . . . . 90 2·75
F249 50c. Columbine . . . . . . 2·00 4·00
F250 90c. Wild pinks . . . . . . 1·40 2·75
See also Nos. F253/5 and F264/6.

F **56** Blue Tit ("Mesange Bleue")

F **57** "The Virgin of Pal"

1973. Nature Protection. Birds. Multicoloured.
F251 90c. Type F **56** . . . . . . 2·50 4·50
F252 1f. Lesser spotted woodpecker ("Pic Epeichette") . . . . . . 2·75 5·00
See also Nos. F259/60.

1974. Pyrenean Wild Flowers (2nd series). As Type F **55**. Multicoloured.
F253 45c. Iris . . . . 45 3·50
F254 65c. Tobacco Plant . . . . 55 4·00
F255 90c. Narcissus . . . . . . 1·30 4·25

1974. Europa. Church Sculptures. Mult.
F256 50c. Type F **57** . . . . . . 12·00 9·25
F257 90c. "The Virgin of Santa Coloma" . . . . 17·00 15·00

F **58** Arms of Andorra

F **59** Letters crossing Globe

1974. Meeting of Co-Princes, Cahors.
F258 F **58** 1f. blue, violet & orge 90 5·00

1974. Nature Protection. Birds. As Type F **56**. Multicoloured.
F259 60c. Citril finch ("Venturon Montagnard") . . . . . 4·00 6·25
F260 80c. Northern bullfinch ("Boureuil") . . . . . . 3·25 6·00

1974. Centenary of U.P.U.
F261 F **59** 1f.20 red, grey & brn 2·20 3·75

F 60 "Calvary"

1975. Europa. Paintings from La Cortinada Church. Multicoloured.
F262 80c. Type F **60** . . . . . . 7·00 13·00
F263 1f.20 "Coronation of St. Martin" (horiz) . . . 10·00 20·00

1975. Pyrenean Flowers (3rd series). As Type F **55**.
F264 60c. multicoloured . . . . 55 2·75
F265 80c. multicoloured . . . . 1·70 3·50
F266 1f.20 yellow, red and green 1·00 2·75
DESIGNS: 60c. Gentian; 80c. Anemone; 1f.20, Colchicum.

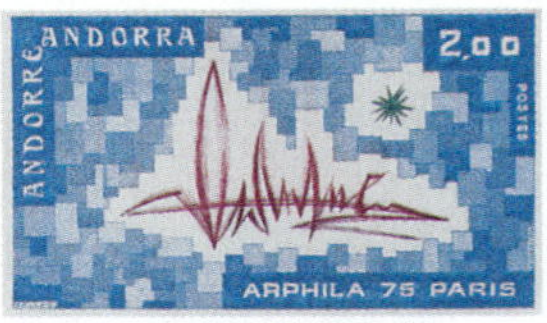

F **61** "Arphila" Motif

1975. "Arphila 75" International Stamp Exhibition, Paris.
F267 F **61** 2f. red, green and blue 1·60 4·00

F **62** Pres. Pompidou (Co-prince of Andorra)

F **63** "La Pubilla" and Emblem

1976. President Pompidou of France Commem.
F268 F **62** 80c. black and violet 80 2·75

1976. International Women's Year.
F269 F **63** 1f.20 black, pur & bl 2·00 3·25

F **64** Skier

F **65** Telephone and Satellite

1976. Winter Olympic Games, Innsbruck.
F270 F **64** 1f.20 black, green & bl 1·10 3·00

1976. Telephone Centenary.
F271 F **65** 1f. green, black and red 1·60 3·25

F **66** Catalan Forge

1976. Europa.
F272 F **66** 80c. brown, blue & grn 2·00 3·50
F273 – 1f.20 red, green & blk 3·75 4·50
DESIGN: 1f.20, Andorran folk-weaving.

F **67** Thomas Jefferson

F **68** Ball-trap (clay pigeon) Shooting

1976. Bicentenary of American Revolution.
F274 F **67** 1f.20 dp grn, brn & grn 1·10 3·00

1976. Olympic Games, Montreal.
F275 F **68** 2f. brown, violet & grn 1·50 3·50

F **69** New Chapel

1976. New Chapel of Our Lady, Meritxell.
F276 F **69** 1f. green, purple & brn 90 2·75

F **70** Apollo

F **71** Stoat

1976. Nature Protection. Butterflies. Mult.
F277 80c. Type F **70** . . . . . . 2·75 5·75
F278 1f.40 Camberwell beauty . . 2·50 5·00

1977. Nature Protection.
F279 F **71** 1f. grey, black & blue 2·10 3·25

F **72** Church of St. John of Caselles

F **73** Book and Flowers

1977. Europa.
F280 F **72** 1f. purple, green & bl 5·50 4·75
F281 – 1f.40 indigo, grn & bl 9·00 5·50
DESIGN: 1f.40, St. Vicens Chateau.

1977. 1st Anniv of Institute of Andorran Studies.
F282 F **73** 80c. brown, green & bl 1·00 2·50

F **74** St. Roma

1977. Reredos, St. Roma's Chapel, Les Bons.
F283 F **74** 2f. multicoloured . . . 2·50 3·00

F **75** General Council Assembly Hall

F **76** Eurasian Red Squirrel

1977. Andorran Institutions.
F284 F **75** 1f.10 red, blue & brn 2·50 3·50
F285 – 2f. brown and red . . 2·50 3·50
DESIGN—VERT. 2f. Don Guillem d'Areny Plandolit.

1978. Nature Protection.
F286 F **76** 1f. brown, grn & olive 1·00 2·50

F **77** Escalls Bridge

1978. 700th Anniv of Parity Treaties (1st issue).
F287 F **77** 80c. green, brown & bl 65 2·40
See also No. F292.

F **78** Church at Pal

1978. Europa.
F288 F **78** 1f. brown, green & red 5·75 4·25
F289 – 1f.40 brown, bl & red 8·25 5·50
DESIGN: 1f.40, Charlemagne's House.

F **79** "Virgin of Sispony"

1978. Andorran Art.
F290 F **79** 2f. multicoloured . . . 2·00 3·00

F **80** Tribunal Meeting

1978. Tribunal of Visura.
F291 F **80** 1f.20 multicoloured . . 1·70 2·50

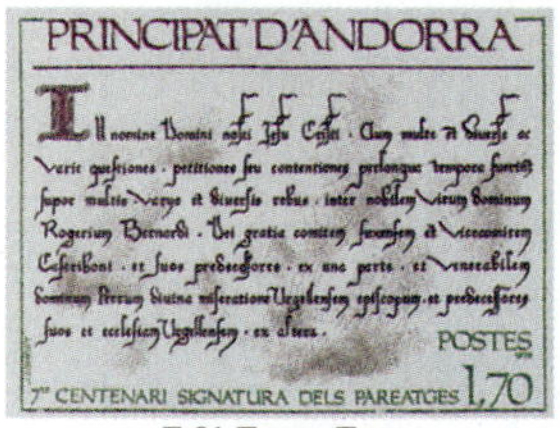

F **81** Treaty Text

1978. 700th Anniv of Parity Treaties (2nd issue).
F292 F **81** 1f.50 brown, grn & red 95 2·50

F **82** Chamois

F **83** Rock Ptarmigans ("Perdiu Blanca")

1978. Nature Protection.
F293 F **82** 1f. brown, lt brn & bl 65 2·10

1979. Nature Protection.
F294 F **83** 1f.20 multicoloured . . 1·10 2·75

F **84** Early 20th Century Postman and Church of St. John of Caselles

F **85** Wall painting, Church of St. Cerni, Nagol

1979. Europa.
F295 F **84** 1f.20 black, brn & grn 2·00 4·25
F296 – 1f.70 brown, grn & mve . . . . 2·50 5·00
DESIGN: 1f.70, Old French Post Office, Andorra.

1979. Pre-Romanesque Art.
F297 F **85** 2f. green, pink and brown . . . . 1·30 2·50
See also No. F309.

F **86** Boy with Sheep

F **87** Co-princes Monument (Luigiteruggi)

1979. International Year of the Child.
F298 F **86** 1f.70 multicoloured . . 70 2·50

1979. Co-princes Monument.
F299 F **87** 2f. dp green, grn & red 1·30 2·75

F **88** Judo

F **89** Cal Pal, La Cortinada

1979. World Judo Championships, Paris.
F300 F **88** 1f.30 black, dp bl & bl 85 2·30

1980.
F301 F **89** 1f.10 brown, bl & grn 50 2·10

F **90** Cross-country Skiing

F **91** Charlemagne

1980. Winter Olympics, Lake Placid.
F302 F **90** 1f.80 ultram, bl & red 1·10 2·75

1980. Europa.
F303 F **91** 1f.30 brn, chest & red 65 3·00
F304 – 1f.80 green and brown 95 3·00
DESIGN: 1f.80, Napoleon I.

F **93** Dog's-tooth Violet

F **94** Cyclists

1980. Nature Protection. Multicoloured.
F306 1f.10 Type F **93** . . . . . 40 2·10
F305 1f.30 Pyrenean lily . . . . 40 2·10

1980. World Cycling Championships.
F307 F **94** 1f.20 violet, mve & brn 65 2·20

F **95** House of the Valleys

1980. 400th Anniv of Restoration of House of the Valleys (meeting place of Andorran General Council).
F308 F **95** 1f.40 brown, vio & grn 70 2·10

1980. Pre-Romanesque Art. As Type F **85**. Mult.
F309 2f. Angel (wall painting, Church of St. Cerni, Nagol) (horiz) . . . . . 70 2·75

F **97** Shepherds' Huts, Mereig

1981. Architecture.
F310 F **97** 1f.40 brown and blue 80 1·50

F **98** Bear Dance (Emcamp Carnival)
F **99** Bonelli's Warbler

1981. Europa.
F311 F **98** 1f.40 black, green & bl 1·10 2·00
F312 – 2f. black, blue and red 95 3·00
DESIGN: 2f. El Contrapas (dance).

1981. Nature Protection. Birds. Multicoloured.
F313 1f.20 Type F **99** . . . . . 80 2·40
F314 1f.40 Wallcreeper . . . . . 80 2·40

F **100** Fencing

1981. World Fencing Championships, Clermont-Ferrand.
F315 F **100** 2f. blue and black . . 55 2·50

F **101** Chasuble of St. Martin (miniature)

1981. Art.
F316 F **101** 3f. multicoloured . . 95 2·20

F **102** Fountain, Sant Julia de Loria
F **103** Symbolic Disabled

1981. International Decade of Drinking Water.
F317 F **102** 1f.60 blue and brown 45 2·20

1981. International Year of Disabled Persons.
F318 F **103** 2f.30 blue, red & grn 50 2·50

F **104** Scroll and Badge (creation of Andorran Executive Council, 1981)
F **105** Footballer running to right

1982. Europa.
F319 F **104** 1f.60 blue, brn & orge 1·30 2·50
F320 – 2f.30 blue, blk & orge 1·10 1·90
DESIGN: 2f.30, Hat and cloak (creation of Land Council, 1419).

1982. World Cup Football Championship, Spain.
F321 F **105** 1f.60 brown and red 1·20 2·10
F322 – 2f.60 brown and red 1·80 2·20
DESIGN: 2f.60, Footballer running to left.

F **106** 1f.25 Stamp, 1933

1982. 1st Official Exhibition of Andorran Postage Stamps.
MSF323 F **106** 5f. black and red 1·80 3·50

F **107** Wall Painting, La Cortinada Church

1982. Romanesque Art.
F324 F **107** 3f. multicoloured . . 80 4·25

F **108** Wild Cat
F **109** Dr. Robert Koch

1982. Nature Protection.
F325 F **108** 1f.80 blk, grn & grey 1·30 3·25
F326 – 2f.60 brown & green 1·20 3·50
DESIGN: 2f.60, Scots Pine.

1982. Centenary of Discovery of Tubercle Bacillus.
F327 F **109** 2f.10 lilac . . . . . . 1·10 2·50

F **110** St. Thomas Aquinas
F **111** Montgolfier and Charles Balloons over Tuileries, Paris

1982. St. Thomas Aquinas Commemoration.
F328 F **110** 2f. deep brown, brown and grey . . . . . 95 2·30

1983. Bicentenary of Manned Flight.
F329 F **111** 2f. green, red and brown . . . . . . 65 2·30

F **112** Silver Birch

1983. Nature Protection.
F330 F **112** 1f. red, brown and green . . . . 1·40 3·25
F331 – 1f.50 green, bl & brn 1·20 3·25
DESIGN: 1f.50, Brown trout.

F **113** Mountain Cheesery

1983. Europa.
F332 F **113** 1f. purple and violet 2·30 3·25
F333 – 2f.60 red, mve & pur 2·50 3·50
DESIGN: 2f.60, Catalan forge.

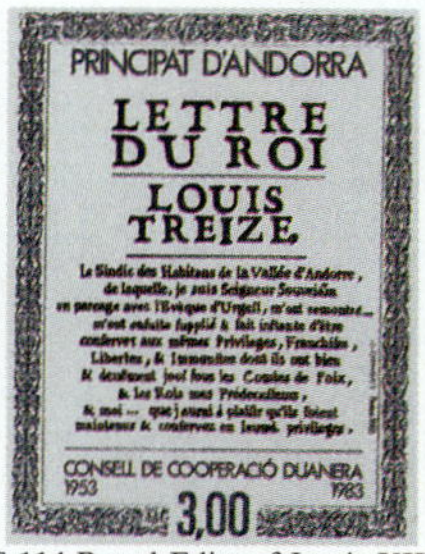

F **114** Royal Edict of Louis XIII

1983. 30th Anniv of Customs Co-operation Council.
F334 F **114** 3f. black and slate . . 1·30 4·75

F **115** Early Coat of Arms

1983. Inscr "POSTES".
F335 F **115** 5c. green and red . . 1·10 3·50
F336 10c. dp green & green 95 1·60
F337 20c. violet and mauve 1·00 1·10
F338 30c. purple and violet 85 2·30
F339 40c. blue & ultram . . 1·00 2·30
F340 50c. black and red . . 1·10 2·20
F341 1f. lake and red . . . 1·20 2·20
F342 1f.90 green . . . . . 2·40 4·25
F343 2f. red and brown . . 1·40 1·30
F344 2f.10 green . . . . . 1·40 2·40
F345 2f.20 red . . . . . . 50 3·25
F346 2f.30 red . . . . . . 1·30 3·25
F347 3f. green and mauve 1·50 3·50
F348 4f. orange and brown 2·75 5·50
F349 5f. brown and red . . 1·90 5·00
F350 10f. red and brown 4·00 5·50
F351 15f. green & dp green 5·00 7·75
F352 20f. blue and brown 3·50 8·00
For design as Type F **115** but inscribed "LA POSTE" see Nos. F446/9.

F **116** Wall Painting, La Cortinada Church
F **117** Plandolit House

1983. Romanesque Art.
F354 F **116** 4f. multicoloured . . 1·30 3·50

1983.
F355 F **117** 1f.60 brown & green 40 1·50

F **118** Snowflakes and Olympic Torch

1984. Winter Olympic Games, Sarajevo.
F356 F **118** 2f.80 red, blue & grn 85 2·40

F **119** Pyrenees and Council of Europe Emblem

1984. Work Community of Pyrenees Region.
F357 F **119** 3f. blue and brown . . 80 2·75

F **120** Bridge

1984. Europa.
F358 F **120** 2f. green . . . . . . 3·00 3·25
F359 2f.80 red . . . . . . 3·50 4·00

F **121** Sweet Chestnut

1984. Nature Protection.
F360 F **121** 1f.70 grn, brn & pur 85 3·25
F361 – 2f.10 green & brown 1·00 3·25
DESIGN: 2f.10, Walnut.

F **122** Centre Members

1984. Pyrenean Cultures Centre, Andorra.
F362 F **122** 3f. blue, orange & red 70 2·75

F **123** "St. George" (detail of fresco, Church of St. Cerni, Nagol)

1984. Pre-Romanesque Art.
F363 F **123** 5f. multicoloured . . 1·40 3·50

F **124** Sant Julia Valley
F **125** Title Page of "Le Val d'Andorre" (comic opera)

1985.
F364 F **124** 2f. green, olive & brn 65 2·50

1985. Europa.
F365 F **125** 2f.10 green . . . . . 2·40 3·00
F366 – 3f. brown & dp brown 3·25 4·25
DESIGN: 3f. Musical instruments within frame.

F **126** Teenagers holding up ball
F **127** Mallard

1985. International Youth Year.
F367 F **126** 3f. red and brown . . 70 2·75

1985. Nature Protection. Multicoloured.
F368 1f.80 Type F **127** . . . . . 1·10 2·75
F369 2f.20 Eurasian goldfinch . . 1·00 3·25

F **128** St. Cerni and Angel (fresco, Church of St. Cerni, Nagol)

1985. Pre-Romanesque Art.
F370 F **128** 5f. multicoloured . . 1·30 3·50

F **130** 1979 Europa Stamp

1986. Inauguration of Postal Museum.
F381 F **130** 2f.20 brown & green 80 2·75

F **131** Ansalonga

F **132** Players

1986. Europa.
F382 F **131** 2f.20 black and blue 1·90 3·25
F383 – 3f.20 black and green 3·00 4·00
DESIGN: 3f.20, Pyrenean chamois.

1986. World Cup Football Championship, Mexico.
F384 F **132** 3f. grn, blk & dp grn 1·10 3·00

F **133** Angonella Lakes

1986.
F385 F **133** 2f.20 multicoloured 65 2·50

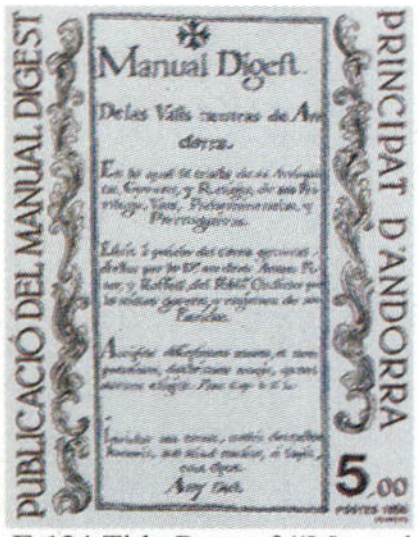

F **134** Title Page of "Manual Digest", 1748

1986. "Manual Digest".
F386 F **134** 5f. black, grn & brn 95 3·50

F **135** Dove with Twig

F **136** St. Vincent's Chapel, Enclar

1986. International Peace Year.
F387 F **135** 1f.90 blue and indigo 75 2·50

1986.
F388 F **136** 1f.90 brn, blk & grn 55 2·50

F **137** Arms

F **138** Meritxell Chapel

1987. Visit of French Co-prince (French president).
F389 F **137** 2f.20 multicoloured 1·10 3·50

1987. Europa.
F390 F **138** 2f.20 purple and red 4·25 3·50
F391 – 3f.40 violet and blue 6·25 4·75
DESIGN: 3f.40, Ordino.

F **139** Ransol

F **140** Horse

1987.
F392 F **139** 1f.90 multicoloured 95 3·00

1987. Nature Protection. Multicoloured.
F393 1f.90 Type F **140** . . . . . 1·30 3·75
F394 2f.20 Isabel (moth) . . . . 1·50 3·75

F **141** Arualsu (fresco, La Cortinada Church)

1987. Romanesque Art.
F395 F **141** 5f. multicoloured . . 1·40 3·75

F **142** Walker with Map by Signpost

1987. Walking.
F396 F **142** 2f. pur, grn & dp grn 60 2·30

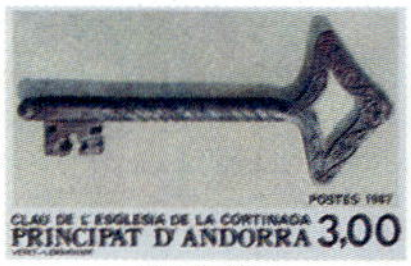

F **143** Key

F **144** Arms

1987. La Cortinada Church Key.
F397 F **143** 3f. multicoloured . . 1·10 3·00

1988.
F398 F **144** 2f.20 red . . . . . . 65 2·50
F399 2f.30 red . . . . . . 2·75 4·00
F400 2f.50 red . . . . . . 3·50 4·00
F401 2f.80 red . . . . . . 80 3·75
Nos. F400/1 are inscribed "LA POSTE".

F **145** Bronze Boot and Mountains

F **146** Players

1988. Archaeology.
F407 F **145** 3f. multicoloured . . 85 3·25

1988. Rugby.
F408 F **146** 2f.20 blk, yell & grn 70 4·00

F **147** Enclar Aerial

F **148** Les Escaldes Hot Spring

1988. Europa. Transport and Communications. Each green, brown and blue.
F409 2f.20 Type F **147** . . . . . 2·75 3·00
F410 3f.60 Hand pointing to map on screen (tourist information) . . . . . . 3·75 4·50

1988.
F411 F **148** 2f.20 blue, brn & grn 60 2·50

F **149** Ansalonga Pass

F **150** Pyrenean Shepherd Dog

1988.
F412 F **149** 2f. blue, green & olive 55 2·50

1988. Nature Protection. Multicoloured.
F413 2f. Type F **150** . . . . . . 1·80 4·00
F414 2f.20 Hare . . . . 1·90 4·00

F **151** Fresco, Andorra La Vella Church

1988. Romanesque Art.
F415 F **151** 5f. multicoloured . . 1·40 3·50

F **152** Birds

F **153** Pal

1989. Bicentenary of French Revolution.
F416 F **152** 2f.20 violet, blk & red 1·00 2·50

1989.
F417 F **153** 2f.20 violet and blue 70 2·50

F **154** The Strong Horse

1989. Europa. Children's Games. Each brown and cream.
F418 2f.20 Type F **154** . . . . . 2·40 3·00
F419 3f.60 The Handkerchief . . 3·00 4·25

F **155** Wounded Soldiers

F **156** Archaeological Find and St. Vincent's Chapel, Enclar

1989. 125th Anniv of International Red Cross.
F420 F **155** 3f.60 brn, blk & red 95 3·00

1989. Archaeology.
F421 F **156** 3f. multicoloured . . 95 3·00

F **157** Wild Boar

1989. Nature Protection.
F422 F **157** 2f.20 blk, grn & brn 1·40 3·00
F423 – 3f.60 black, green and deep green . . . . 1·80 4·00
DESIGN: 3f.60, Palmate newt.

F **158** Retable of St. Michael de la Mosquera, Encamp

1989.
F424 F **158** 5f. multicoloured . . 1·70 4·75

F **159** La Margineda Bridge

1990.
F425 F **159** 2f.30 blue, brn & turq 70 2·40

F **160** Llorts Iron Ore Mines

1990.
F426 F **160** 3f.20 multicoloured 95 2·75

F **161** Exterior of Old Post Office, Andorra La Vella

1990. Europa. Post Office Buildings.
F427 F **161** 2f.30 red and black 2·50 3·00
F428 – 3f.20 violet and red 3·50 4·25
DESIGN: 3f.20, Interior of modern post office.

F **162** Censer, St. Roma's Chapel, Les Bons

F **163** Wild Roses

1990.
F429 F **162** 3f. multicoloured . . 85 2·75

1990. Nature Protection. Multicoloured.
F430 2f.30 Type F **163** . . . . . 1·30 2·75
F431 3f.20 Otter (horiz) . . . . 1·40 3·00

F **164** Tobacco-drying Sheds, Les Bons

1990.
F432 F **164** 2f.30 yell, blk & red 65 2·40

F **165** Part of Mural from Santa Coloma Church

1990.
F433 F **165** 5f. multicoloured . . 1·20 3·25

1990. Birth Centenary of Charles de Gaulle (French statesman). As Nos. F243/4 but values and inscriptions changed.
F434 F **52** 2f.30 blue . . . . . . 2·10 3·00
F435 3f.20 red . . . . 2·50 3·25

F **166** Coin from St. Eulalia's Church, Encamp

1990.
F436 F **166** 3f.20 multicoloured 75 2·75

F **167** Chapel of Sant Roma Dels Vilars
F **168** Emblem and Track

1991.
F437 F **167** 2f.50 blue, blk & grn 70 2·40

1991. 4th European Small States Games.
F438 F **168** 2f.50 multicoloured 50 2·40

F **169** Television Satellite
F **170** Bottles

1991. Europa. Europe in Space. Multicoloured.
F439 2f.50 Type F **169** . . . . . 2·75 3·50
F440 3f.50 Globe, telescope and eye (horiz) . . . . 4·00 4·50

1991. Artefacts from Tomb of St. Vincent of Enclar.
F441 F **170** 3f.20 multicoloured 95 2·50

F **171** Sheep

1991. Nature Protection.
F442 F **171** 2f.50 brown, bl & blk 1·80 4·00
F443 – 3f.50 brn, mve & blk 1·90 4·00
DESIGN: 3f.50, Pyrenean cow.

F **172** Players

1991. World Petanque Championship, Engordany.
F444 F **172** 2f.50 blk, bistre & red 85 2·40

F **173** Mozart, Quartet and Organ Pipes

1991. Death Bicentenary of Wolfgang Amadeus Mozart (composer).
F445 F **173** 3f.40 blue, blk & turq 1·50 2·75

1991. As Type F **115** but inscr "LA POSTE".
F446 F **115** 2f.20 green . . . . . 1·20 3·50
F447 2f.40 green . . . . . 3·00 4·00
F448 2f.50 red . . . . . . 1·30 3·50
F449 2f.70 green . . . . . 2·75 3·25
F450 2f.80 red . . . . . . 2·75 3·25
F451 3f. red . . . . 2·75 3·00

F **174** "Virgin of the Remedy of Sant Julia and Sant Germa"
F **175** Slalom

1991.
F455 F **174** 5f. multicoloured . . 1·40 3·25

1992. Winter Olympic Games, Albertville. Mult.
F456 2f.50 Type F **175** . . . . 2·50 2·30
F457 3f.40 Figure skating . . . . 2·50 2·75

F **176** St. Andrew's Church, Arinsal

1992.
F458 F **176** 2f.50 black and buff 1·40 1·90

F **177** Navigation Instrument and Columbus's Fleet
F **178** Canoeing

1992. Europa. 500th Anniv of Discovery of America by Columbus. Multicoloured.
F459 2f.50 Type F **177** . . . . . 3·50 3·25
F460 3f.40 Fleet, Columbus and Amerindians . . . . . . 5·50 4·75

1992. Olympic Games, Barcelona. Multicoloured.
F461 2f.50 Type F **178** . . . . . 2·10 2·20
F462 3f.40 Shooting . . . . . . 2·10 2·20

F **179** Globe Flowers
F **180** "Martyrdom of St. Eulalia" (altarpiece, St. Eulalia's Church, Encamp)

1992. Nature Protection. Multicoloured.
F463 2f.50 Type F **179** . . . . . 1·60 2·10
F464 3f.40 Griffon vulture ("El Voltor") (horiz) . . . . . 2·10 2·50

1992.
F465 F **180** 4f. multicoloured . . 1·10 2·30

F **181** "Ordino Arcalis 91" (Mauro Staccioli)

1992. Modern Sculpture. Multicoloured.
F466 5f. Type F **181** . . . . . . 1·40 2·50
F467 5f. "Storm in a Teacup" (Dennis Oppenheim) (horiz) . . . . 2·10 2·50

F **182** Grau Roig
F **183** "Estructures Autogeneradores" (Jorge du Bon)

1993. Ski Resorts. Multicoloured.
F468 2f.50 Type F **182** . . . . . 2·10 2·40
F469 2f.50 Ordino . . . . 2·75 2·75
F470 2f.50 Soldeu el Tarter . . . 2·20 2·40
F471 3f.40 Pal . . . . 2·20 2·40
F472 3f.40 Arinsal . . . . 2·20 2·40

1993. Europa. Contemporary Art.
F473 F **183** 2f.50 dp bl, bl & vio 2·10 2·75
F474 – 3f.40 multicoloured 2·30 3·00
DESIGN—HORIZ: 3f.40, "Fisicromia per Andorra" (Carlos Cruz-Diez).

F **184** Common Blue
F **185** Cyclist

1993. Nature Protection. Butterflies. Multicoloured.
F475 2f.50 Type F **184** . . . . . 2·75 2·75
F476 4f.20 "Nymphalidae" . . . 2·75 3·50

1993. Tour de France Cycling Road Race.
F477 F **185** 2f.50 multicoloured 2·10 2·75

F **186** Smiling Hands

1993. 10th Anniv of Andorran School.
F478 F **186** 2f.80 multicoloured 2·30 2·75

F **187** "A Pagan Place" (Michael Warren)

1993. Modern Sculpture.
F479 F **187** 5f. black and blue . . 3·00 2·50
F480 – 5f. multicoloured 3·00 2·50
DESIGN: No. F480, "Pep, Lu, Canolic, Ton, Meritxell, Roma, Anna, Pau, Carles, Eugenia... and Others" (Erik Dietman).

F **188** Cross-country Skiing
F **189** Constitution Monument

1994. Winter Olympic Games, Lillehammer, Norway.
F481 F **188** 3f.70 multicoloured 1·60 1·90

1994. 1st Anniv of New Constitution.
F482 F **189** 2f.80 multicoloured 1·60 1·60
F483 – 3f.70 blk, yell & mve 2·30 2·75
DESIGN: 3f.70, Stone tablet.

F **190** AIDS Virus

1994. Europa. Discoveries and Inventions. Mult.
F484 2f.80 Type F **190** . . . . . 1·70 2·00
F485 3f.70 Radio mast . . . . . 2·20 2·50

F **191** Competitors' Flags and Football
F **192** Horse Riding

1994. World Cup Football Championship, U.S.A.
F486 F **191** 3f.70 multicoloured 1·60 1·90

1994. Tourist Activities. Multicoloured.
F487 2f.80 Type F **192** . . . . . 1·80 1·80
F488 2f.80 Mountain biking . . . 1·80 1·80
F489 2f.80 Climbing . . . . . . 1·80 1·80
F490 2f.80 Fishing . . . . 1·80 1·80

F **193** Scarce Swallowtail
F **194** "26 10 93"

1994. Nature Protection. Butterflies. Multicoloured.
F491 2f.80 Type F **193** . . . . . 2·10 2·10
F492 4f.40 Small tortoiseshell . . 2·75 2·75

1994. Meeting of Co-princes.
F493 F **194** 2f.80 multicoloured 1·40 1·50

F 269 Legend of Lake Engolasters

F 270 Globe and Books

2001. Legends. Multicoloured.
F581 3f. Type F **269** . . . . . . 1·50 1·50
F582 3f. Lords before King (foundation of Andorra) 1·50 1·50

2001. World Book Day.
F583 F **270** 3f.80 multicoloured 1·60 1·60

F 271 Water Splash

F 272 Raspberry

2001. Europa. Water Resources.
F584 F **271** 3f. multicoloured . . 1·70 1·70

2001. Multicoloured.
F585 3f. Type F **272** . . . . . . 1·40 1·40
F586 4f.40 Jay (horiz) . . . . . 1·90 1·90

F 273 Profiles talking

2001. European Year of Languages.
F587 F **273** 3f.80 multicoloured 1·60 1·60

F 274 Trumpeter

2001. Jazz Festival, Escaldes-Engordany.
F588 F **274** 3f. multicoloured . . 1·20 40

F 275 Kitchen

2001.
F589 F **275** 5f. multicoloured . . 1·60 1·20

F 276 Chapel

2001. 25th Anniv of Chapel of Our Lady, Meritxell.
F590 F **276** 3f. multicoloured . . 1·20 40

F 277 Hotel Pla

2001.
F591 F **277** 15f.50 black, violet and green . . . . . 5·00 2·00

F 278 Cross

F 279 State Arms

2001. Grossa Cross (boundary cross at the crossroads between Avinguda Meritxell and Carrer Bisbe Iglesias).
F592 F **278** 2f.70 multicoloured 80 40

New Currency
100 cents = 1 euro

2002. (a) With Face Value. Ordinary gum.
F593 F **279** 1c. multicoloured . . 20 20
F594 2c. multicoloured . . 20 20
F595 5c. multicoloured . . 20 20
F596 60c. multicoloured . . 1·30 1·30

(b) No value expressed.
F598 F **279** (46c.) multicoloured 80 80
F599 (46c.) multicoloured 80 80

(ii) Size 17 × 23 mm. Self-adhesive gum.
F599a (52c.) multicoloured . . . 1·00 1·00
Nos. F598/9 were sold at the rate for inland letters up to 20 grammes.

F 280 The Legend of Meritxell

F 281 Pedestrians on Crossing

2002. Legends. Designs as Nos. F525, F531/3 and F581/2 but with values in new currency as Type F **280**. Multicoloured.
F600 10c. Type F **280** 40 15
F601 20c. Wrestlers (The Fountain of Esmelicat) 40 15
F602 41c. The Piper (La joueurde cornemuse) . . 80 40
F603 45c. Legend of Saint Vincent Castle 75 75
F604 48c. Port Rat (horiz) . . 80 80
F604a 48c. The Cave of Ourses 80 80
F604b 49c. The Testament of Ilop 80 80
F604c 50c. El tresor de la font del Manego . . . . . 2·10 2·10
F605 50c. The Seven-armed Cross 80 50
F610 €1 Lords before King (foundation of Andorra) 1·60 80
F611 €2 Legend of Lake Engolasters . . . . . 3·25 1·60
F612 €5 The White Lady . . . 15·00 9·50

2002. Schools' Road Safety Campaign.
F615 F **281** 69c. multicoloured . . 1·60 80

F 282 Skier

2002. Winter Olympic Games, Salt Lake City, U.S.A.
F616 F **282** 58c. multicoloured . . 1·20 80

F 283 Hotel Rosaleda

F 284 Water Droplet and Clouds

2002.
F617 F **283** 46c. multicoloured . . 80 80

2002. World Water Day.
F618 F **284** 67c. multicoloured . . 1·20 80

F 285 Clown

2002. Europa. Circus.
F619 F **285** 46c. multicoloured . . 1·60 1·20

F 286 Myrtle

F 287 Seated Nude (Josep Viladomat)

2002.
F620 F **286** 46c. multicoloured . . 1·20 80

2002.
F621 F **287** €2.26 multicoloured 5·00 3·25

F 288 Mountains from Tunnel Entrance

2002. Completion of the Envalira Road Tunnel between Andorra and France.
F622 F **288** 46c. multicoloured . . 1·20 80

F 289 Mural (detail) (Santa Coloma Church, Andorra la Vella)

2002.
F623 F **289** €1.02 multicoloured 2·00 1·60

F 290 Arms of Escaldes – Engordany

F 291 State Arms

2003. Arms. No value expressed. Self-adhesive.
F624 F **290** (46c.) multicoloured 1·20 40
No. F624 was sold at the rate for inland letters up to 20 grammes.

2003. Legends. "Legende du pin de la Margineda". Vert design as Type F **280**.
F625 69c. multicoloured . . . . 1·20 80

2003. 10th Anniv of Constitution.
F626 F **291** €2.36 multicoloured 5·00 3·25

F 292 Les Bons

F 293 Hotel Mirador

2003. Architecture.
F627 F **292** 67c. multicoloured . . 1·60 1·20

2003.
F628 F **293** €1.02 multicoloured 2·00 1·60

F 294 Man, Dog and Sheep

F 296 Cyclist and Map

F 295 Dancers and Fire

2003. Europa. Poster Art.
F629 F **294** 46c. multicoloured . . 1·20 80

2003. Fires of St. John the Baptist Festival.
F630 F **295** 50c. multicoloured . . 1·20 80

2003. Centenary of Tour de France (cycle race).
F631 F **296** 50c. multicoloured . . 1·20 80

F 297 Pole Vault

F 298 *Greixa sparassis crispa*

2003. World Athletics Championship, Paris.
F632 F **297** 90c. multicoloured . . 1·60 1·20

2003.
F633 F **298** 45c. multicoloured . . 80 80

F 299 Red Currant

2003.
F634 F **299** 75c. multicoloured . . 1·60 1·20

F 300 Telephone, Satellite and Globe

2003. Centenary of First Telephone in Andorra.
F635 F **300** 50c. multicoloured . . 1·20 80

F 301 "Maternity" (Paul Gauguin)

2003.
F636 F **301** 75c. multicoloured . . 1·60 1·20

F 302 St. Anthony's Market

F 303 Children

2004.
F637 F **302** 50c. multicoloured . . 80 80

2004.
F638 F **303** 50c. multicoloured . . 80 80

F **304** Hotel Valira

2004.
F639 F **304** €1.11 multicoloured 1·80 1·80

F **305** Woman and Andorra Sign F **306** Madriu-Perafita-Claror Valley

2004. Europa. Holidays.
F640 F **305** 50c. orange, red and black 80 80

2004. UNESCO World Heritage Site.
F641 F **306** 75c. multicoloured . . 1·20 1·20

F **307** Poblet de Fontaneda

2004.
F642 F **307** 50c. multicoloured . . 80 80

F **308** Runner and Swimmer

2004. Olympic Games, Athens 2004.
F643 F **308** 90c. multicoloured . . 1·50 1·50

F **309** "Pont de la Margineda"(sketch)

2004. Arts. Margineda Bridge by Joaquim Mir (Spanish artist). Multicoloured.
F644 €1 Type F **309** . . . . . 1·60 1·60
F645 €2 "Pont de la Margineda" (painting) . . 3·25 3·25

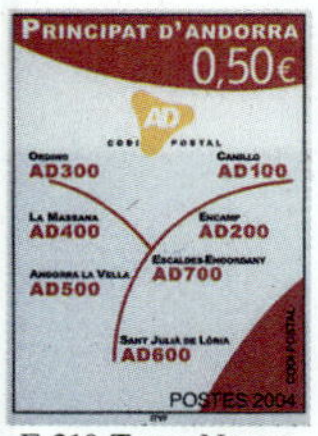

F **310** Town Names and Post Codes F **311** Emblem

2004. Introduction of Postal Codes.
F646 F **310** 50c. vermilion, black and lemon 80 80

2004. 10th Anniv of Entry into Council of Europe.
F647 F **311** €2.50 multicoloured 4·00 4·00

F **312** Children's Nativity F **313** Three Kings visiting Child

2004. Christmas.
F648 F **312** 50c. black, brown and bistre 80 80

2005.
F649 F **313** 50c. multicoloured . . 80 80

F **314** Mountains and Lake

2005. World Heritage Site. Madriu-Claror-Perafita Valley.
F650 F **314** 50c. multicoloured . . 80 80

F **315** Tengmalm's Owl (*Aegolius funereus*) F **316** Bottle, Glass, Jug and Fruit

2005.
F651 F **315** 90c. multicoloured . . 1·50 1·50

2005. Europa. Gastronomy.
F652 F **316** 55c. multicoloured . . 90 90

F **317** Marksman F **318** Mountain Hut, Bordes d'Ensegur

2005. Small States of Europe Games. Sheet 151 × 70 mm containing Type F **317** and similar vert designs. Each black and magenta.
MSF653 53c. Type F **317**; 55c. Runner; 82c. Swimmer; €1 Diver 4·25 4·25

2005.
F654 F **318** €2.50 multicoloured 3·50 3·50

F **319** Motorcycle

2005.
F655 F **319** €2.50 sepia, brown and black . . . . . 3·50 3·50

F **320** "Prats de Santa Coloma" (Joaquim Mir)

2005. Art.
F656 F **320** 82c. multicoloured . . 1·70 1·70

F **321** Hostel Calones

2005.
F657 F **321** €1.98 multicoloured 4·00 4·00

F **322** Lorry in Snow (Josep Alsina)

2005. Photography.
F658 F **322** 53c. multicoloured . . 1·00 1·00

F **323** Emblem

2005. Centenary of Rotary International.
F659 F **323** 55c. multicoloured . . 1·10 1·10

F **324** "Adoration of the Shepherds" (A. Viladomat)

2005. Christmas.
F660 F **324** €1.22 multicoloured 2·40 2·40

F **325** *Ursus arctos* F **326** Alpine Skier

2006. Fauna. Multicoloured.
F661 53c. Type F **325** . . . . . 1·00 1·00
F662 53c. *Rupicapra pyrenaica* (vert) . . . . 1·00 1·00

2006. Winter Olympic Games, Turin. Multicoloured.
F663 55c. Type F **326** . . . . . 1·10 1·10
F664 75c. Cross country skier . . 1·50 1·50

F **326a** Tobacco Leaves F **328** Coloured blocks

F **327** Napoleon (½-size illustration)

2006. Tobacco Museum, Sant Julia de Loria.
F665 F **326a** 82c. multicoloured 1·70 1·70

2006. Bicentenary of Napoleon's Decree restoring Statute of Co-Principality.
F666 F **327** 53c. blue, azure and black . . . . 1·00 1·00

2006. Europa. Integration.
F667 F **328** 53c. multicoloured . . 1·00 1·00

F **329** Sorteny Valley Nature Reserve F **330** Pablo Casals

2006.
F668 F **329** 55c. multicoloured . . 1·10 1·10

2006. 130th Birth Anniv of Pablo Casals (cellist).
F669 F **330** 90c. multicoloured . . 1·80 1·80

F **331** Model T Ford

2006.
F670 F **331** 85c. multicoloured . . 1·70 1·70

F **332** "Montserrat Procession" (Josep Borrell)

2006.
F671 F **332** €1.30 multicoloured 2·60 2·60

F **333** Reredos (retable), Sant Marti de la Cortinada, Ordino

2006.
F672 F **333** 54c. multicoloured . . 1·10 1·10

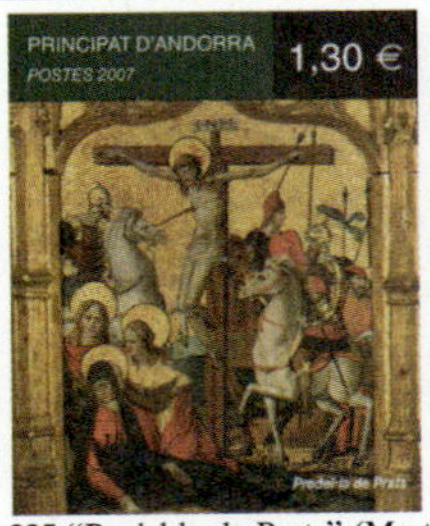

F **335** "Predel-la de Prats" (Master of Canillo)

2007.

F675	F **335**	€1.30 multicoloured	2·60	2·60

F **336** Heart enclosing Rose

2007. Saint George.

F676	F **336**	86c. multicoloured . .	2·75	2·75

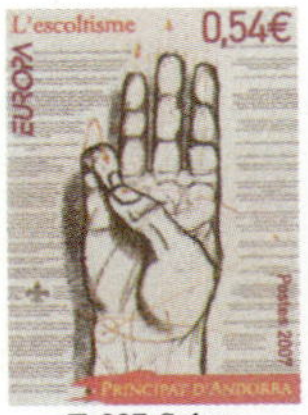

F **337** Salute

F **338** Virgin, Meritxell

2007. Europa. Centenary of Scouting.

F677	F **337**	54c. multicoloured . .	2·25	2·25

2007. Twinning of Meritxell and Sabart. Multicoloured.

F678	54c. Type F **338**	1·75	1·75
F679	54c. Virgin, Sabart	1·75	1·75

F **339** 'Pinette'

2007.

F680	F **339**	60c. multicoloured . .	2·00	2·00

F **340** Players

2007. Rugby World Cup, France.

F681	F **340**	85c. multicoloured . .	2·75	2·75

F **341** Vall del Comapedrosa

2007.

F682	F **341**	€3.04 multicoloured	9·50	9·50

No. F683 and Type F **341** have been left for 'El Cedre', issued on 5 November 2007, not yet received.

No. F684 and Type F **342** have been left for 'La Barma de la Marginada', issued on 12 November 2007, not yet received.

F **343** Altarpiece, Sant Marti de la Cortinada

2007. Christmas.

F685	F **343**	54c. multicoloured . .	1·75	1·75

F **344** *Vulpes vulpes* (red fox)

2008. Fauna. Multicoloured.

F686	54c. Type F **344**	1·75	1·75
F687	60c. *Sus scrofa* (wild boar) (*vert*)	2·00	2·00

POSTAGE DUE STAMPS

1931. Postage Due stamps of France optd **ANDORRE**.

FD24	D **11**	5c. blue	85	4·75
FD25		10c. brown	75	3·25
FD26		30c. red	55	4·25
FD27		50c. purple	80	4·75
FD28		60c. green	12·50	43·00
FD29		1f. brown on yellow	80	6·00
FD30		2f. mauve	7·00	36·00
FD31		3f. mauve	1·30	7·75

1931. Postage Due stamps of France optd **ANDORRE**.

FD32	D **43**	1c. green	50	4·50
FD33		10c. red	5·00	11·50
FD34		60c. red	22·00	40·00
FD35		1f. green	55·00	95·00
FD36		1f.20 on 2f. blue . . .	17·00	£140
FD37		2f. brown	£130	£190
FD38		5f. on 1f. purple . . .	55·00	95·00

FD **7**

FD **10**

FD **11** Wheat Sheaves

1935.

FD82	FD **7**	1c. green	1·10	7·75

1937.

FD 97	FD **10**	5c. blue	3·75	14·00
FD 98		10c. brown	3·25	26·00
FD 99		2f. mauve	7·00	13·50
FD100		5f. orange	19·00	35·00

1943.

FD101a	FD **11**	10c. brown . . .	60	1·80
FD102		30c. mauve . . .	1·80	2·50
FD103		50c. green	1·00	2·75
FD104		1f. blue	2·00	4·25
FD105		1f.50 red	5·00	12·50
FD106		2f. blue	2·00	4·50
FD107		3f. red	2·40	8·50
FD108		4f. violet	4·75	13·00
FD109		5f. mauve	3·75	12·50
FD110		10f. orange . . .	5·50	13·00
FD111		20f. brown	7·25	19·00

1946. As Type FD **11**, but inscr "TIMBRE-TAXE".

FD143	10c. brown	25	6·25
FD144	1f. blue	95	3·50
FD145	2f. blue	80	3·50
FD146	3f. brown	1·90	5·25
FD147	4f. violet	2·50	6·25
FD148	5f. red	1·30	5·00
FD149	10f. orange	2·50	6·50
FD150	20f. brown	6·25	11·50
FD151	50f. green	48·00	43·00
FD152	100f. green	60·00	£140

1961. As Nos. FD143/52 but new values and colours.

FD185	5c. red	2·75	7·25
FD186	10c. orange	4·75	15·00
FD187	20c. brown	11·00	25·00
FD188	50c. green	19·00	41·00

1964. Designs as Nos. D1650/6 of France, but inscr "ANDORRE".

FD192	5c. red, green and purple	30	3·50
FD193	10c. blue, grn & pur . . .	70	3·50
FD194	15c. red, green and brown	80	3·50
FD195	20c. purple, green & turq	90	3·75
FD196	30c. blue, grn & brn . . .	70	2·00
FD197	40c. yellow, red and green	1·90	2·50
FD198	50c. red, green and blue	1·50	1·50

FD **129** Holly Berries

1985. Fruits.

FD371	FD **129**	10c. red and green	1·60	2·40
FD372	–	20c. brown & blue	1·60	2·40
FD373	–	30c. green and red	1·60	2·40
FD374	–	40c. brown & blk	1·60	2·50
FD375	–	50c. olive & violet	1·60	2·50
FD376	–	1f. green and blue	1·60	2·50
FD377	–	2f. red and brown	1·70	2·75
FD378	–	3f. purple & green	1·90	3·00
FD379	–	4f. olive and blue	2·00	3·25
FD380	–	5f. olive and red	2·30	3·75

DESIGNS: 20c. Wild plum; 30c. Raspberry; 40c. Dogberry; 50c. Blackberry; 1f. Juniper; 2f. Rose Hip; 3f. Elder; 4f. Bilberry; 5f. Strawberry.

SPANISH POST OFFICES

1928. 100 centimos = 1 peseta.
2002. 100 cents = 1 euro.

1928. Stamps of Spain optd **CORREOS ANDORRA**.

1	**68**	2c. green	60	75
2		5c. red	95	1·90
3		10c. green	1·80	2·40
5		15c. blue	1·90	2·10
6		20c. violet	1·90	2·10
7		25c. red	4·00	7·50
8		30c. brown	18·00	13·00
9		40c. blue	13·00	12·50
10		50c. orange	14·50	14·00
11	**69**	1p. grey	18·00	19·00
12		4p. red	£120	£120
13		10p. brown	£140	£150

2 House of the Valleys

3 General Council of Andorra

1929.

14	**2**	2c. green	1·20	1·10
26		2c. brown	55	80
15	–	5c. purple	2·30	2·50
27	–	5c. brown	85	1·90
16	–	10c. green	2·30	2·50
17	–	15c. blue	2·75	3·00
30	–	15c. green	3·50	4·00
18	–	20c. violet	2·75	3·50
33	–	25c. red	1·70	1·80
20	**2**	30c. brown	80·00	75·00
34		30c. red	1·70	2·10
21	–	40c. blue	5·50	3·25
36	**2**	45c. red	1·00	1·20
22	–	50c. orange	5·50	3·25
38	**2**	60c. blue	3·25	3·50
23	**3**	1p. slate	14·50	18·00
39		4p. purple	34·00	34·00
40		10p. brown	42·00	42·00

DESIGNS: 5, 40c. Church of St. John of Caselles; 10, 20, 50c. Sant Julia de Loria; 15, 25c. Santa Coloma Church.

7 Councillor Manuel Areny Bons

11 Map

1948.

41	F	2c. olive	55	1·20
42		5c. orange	55	1·20
43		10c. blue	55	1·20
44	**7**	20c. purple	4·75	3·00
45		25c. orange	2·75	1·50
46	G	30c. green	10·50	3·75
47	H	50c. green	15·00	6·50
48	I	75c. blue	13·00	7·75
49	H	90c. purple	1·90	3·50
50	I	1p. red	13·00	5·75
51	G	1p.35 violet	6·50	6·25
52	**11**	4p. blue	10·50	11·00
53		10p. brown	18·00	12·00

DESIGNS—VERT: F. Edelweiss; G. Arms; H. Market Place, Ordino; I. Shrine near Meritxell Chapel.

12 Andorra La Vella

13 St. Anthony's Bridge

1951. Air.

54	**12**	1p. brown	15·00	10·00

1963.

55	**13**	25c. brown and black . . .	25	25
56	–	70c. black and green	25	35
57	–	1p. lilac and grey	35	60
58	–	2p. violet and lilac	50	90
59	–	2p.50 deep red and purple	35	55
60	–	3p. slate and black	85	1·20
61	–	5p. purple and brown . . .	2·40	2·20
62	–	6p. red and brown	3·00	2·50

DESIGNS—VERT: 70c. Anyos meadows (wrongly inscr "AYNOS"); 1p. Canillo; 2p. Santa Coloma Church; 2p.50, Arms; 6p. Virgin of Meritxell. HORIZ: 3p. Andorra la Vella; 5p. Ordino.

14 Daffodills

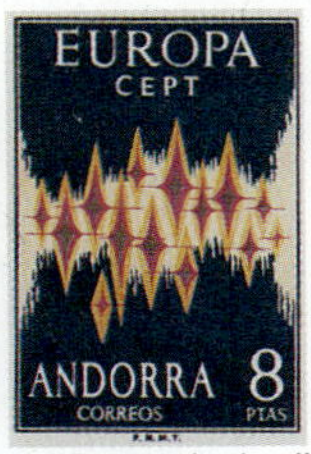

15 "Communications"

1966. Pyrenean Flowers.

63	**14**	50c. blue and slate	10	50
64	–	1p. purple and brown . . .	1·20	60
65	–	5p. blue and green	2·30	2·40
66	–	10p. slate and violet . . .	95	1·90

DESIGNS: 1p. Carnation; 5p. Narcissus; 10p. Anemone (wrongly inscr "HELEBORUS CONI").

1972. Europa.

67	**15**	8p. multicoloured	80·00	65·00

16 Encamp Valley

17 Volleyball

1972. Tourist Views. Multicoloured.

68	1p. Type **16**	50	60
69	1p.50 La Massana	60	60
70	2p. Skis and snowscape, Pas de la Casa	1·30	1·20
71	5p. Lake Pessons (horiz) . . .	1·70	1·20

1972. Olympic Games, Munich. Multicoloured.

72	2p. Type **17**	35	35
73	5p. Swimming (horiz)	50	60

18 St. Anthony's Auction

1972. Andorran Customs. Multicoloured.

74	1p. Type **18**	25	25
75	1p.50 "Les Caramelles" (choir)	25	25
76	2p. Nativity play (Christmas)	15	25
77	5p. Giant cigar (vert)	70	60
78	8p. Carved shrine, Meritxell (vert)	95	80
79	15p. "La Marratxa" (dance)	1·80	1·60

19 "Peoples of Europe"

20 "The Nativity"

1973. Europa.

80	**19**	2p. black, red and blue . .	25	35
81	–	8p. red, brown and black . .	85	85

DESIGN: 8p. Europa "Posthorn".

1973. Christmas. Frescoes from Meritxell Chapel. Multicoloured.

82	2p. Type **20**	25	35
83	5p. "Adoration of the Kings"	80	1·20

21 "Virgin of Ordino"

22 Oak Cupboard and Shelves

1974. Europa. Sculptures. Multicoloured.
84 2p. Type **21** . . . . 1·60 1·50
85 8p. Cross . . . . 2·75 3·00

1974. Arts and Crafts. Multicoloured.
86 10p. Type **22** . . . . 2·20 2·40
87 25p. Crown of the Virgin of the Roses . . . . 3·25 4·00

23 U.P.U. Monument, Berne

1974. Centenary of Universal Postal Union.
88 **23** 15p. multicoloured . . . . 90 1·40

24 "The Nativity"

1974. Christmas. Carvings from Meritxell Chapel. Multicoloured.
89 2p. Type **24** 70 65
90 5p. "Adoration of the Kings" 1·70 1·20

25 19th-century Postman and Church of St. John of Caselles
26 "Peasant with Knife"

1975. "Espana 75" Int Stamp Exhibition, Madrid.
91 **25** 3p. multicoloured 20 35

1975. Europa. 12th-century Romanesque Paintings from La Cortinada Church. Multicoloured.
92 3p. Type **26** . . . . 1·40 1·70
93 12p. "Christ" . . . . 2·75 3·50

27 Cathedral and Consecration Text

1975. 1100th Anniv of Consecration of Urgel Cathedral.
94 **27** 7p. multicoloured . . . . . 85 1·60

28 "The Nativity"

1975. Christmas. Paintings from La Cortinada Church. Multicoloured.
95 3p. Type **28** 30 30
96 7p. "Adoration of The Kings" 55 80

29 Copper Cauldron
30 Slalom Skiing

1976. Europa. Multicoloured.
97 3p. Type **29** 25 55
98 12p. Wooden marriage chest (horiz) 70 80

1976. Olympic Games, Montreal. Multicoloured.
99 7p. Type **30** 25 50
100 15p. Canoeing (horiz) 60 95

31 "The Nativity"

1976. Christmas. Carvings from La Massana Church. Multicoloured.
101 3p. Type **31** 10 25
102 25p. "Adoration of the Kings" . . . . 60 1·30

32 Ansalonga

1977. Europa. Multicoloured.
103 3p. Type **32** 25 35
104 12p. Xuclar 60 85

33 Boundary Cross
34 Map of Andorran Post Offices

1977. Christmas. Multicoloured.
105 5p. Type **33** 25 35
106 12p. St. Michael's Church, Engolasters . . . . 60 1·10

1978. 50th Anniv of Spanish Post Offices. Sheet 105 × 149 mm containing T **34** and similar vert designs. Multicoloured.
MS107 5p. Type **34**; 10p. Postman delivering letter, 1923; 20p. Spanish Post Office, Andorra la Vella, 1928; 25p. Andorran arms 55 1·50

35 House of the Valleys

1978. Europa. Multicoloured.
108 5p. Type **35** 10 30
109 12p. Church of St. John of Caselles 50 80

36 Crown, Mitre and Crook
37 "Holy Family"

1978. 700th Anniv of Parity Treaties.
110 **36** 5p. multicoloured 25 40

1978. Christmas. Frescoes in St. Mary's Church, Encamp. Multicoloured.
111 5p. Type **37** 20 25
112 25p. "Adoration of the Kings" 50 60

38 Young Woman's Costume
39 Old Mail Bus

1979. Local Costumes. Multicoloured.
113 3p. Type **38** 10 10
114 5p. Young man's costume . . 10 20
115 12p. Newly-weds 25 35

1979. Europa.
116 **39** 5p. green & blue on yellow 25 25
117 – 12p. lilac and red on yellow 55 70
DESIGN: 12p. Pre-stamp letters.

40 Drawing of Boy and Girl
41 Agnus Dei, Santa Coloma Church

1979. International Year of the Child.
118 **40** 19p. blue, red and black 35 55

1979. Christmas. Multicoloured.
119 **41** 8p. Santa Coloma Church 10 25
120 25p. Type **41** 35 55

42 Pere d'Urg
43 Antoni Fiter i Rosell

1979. Bishops of Urgel, Co-princes of Andorra (1st series).
121 **42** 1p. blue and brown 10 10
122 – 5p. red and violet 10 20
123 – 13p. brown and green . . . 20 35
DESIGNS: 5p. Joseph Caixal; 13p. Joan Benlloch.
See also Nos. 137/8, 171, 182 and 189.

1980. Europa.
124 **43** 8p. brown, ochre and green 10 20
125 – 19p. black, green & dp grn 35 55
DESIGN: 19p. Francesc Cairat i Freixes.

44 Skiing

1980. Olympic Games, Moscow.
126 **44** 5p. turquoise, red and blk 10 20
127 – 8p. multicoloured 10 20
128 – 50p. multicoloured 25 80
DESIGNS: 8p. Boxing; 50p. Shooting.

45 Nativity
46 Santa Anna Dance

1980. Christmas. Multicoloured.
129 10p. Type **45** 10 20
130 22p. Epiphany 10 50

1981. Europa. Multicoloured.
131 12p. Type **46** 25 35
132 30p. Festival of the Virgin of Canolich 35 55

47 Militia Members

1981. 50th Anniv of People's Militia.
133 **47** 30p. green, grey and black 25 55

48 Handicapped Child learning to Write

1981. International Year of Disabled Persons.
134 **48** 50p. multicoloured 40 75

49 "The Nativity"
50 Arms of Andorra

1981. Christmas. Carvings from Encamp Church. Multicoloured.
135 12p. Type **49** 10 25
136 30p. "The Adoration" . . . 35 55

1981. Bishops of Urgel, Co-princes of Andorra (2nd series). As T **42**.
137 7p. purple and blue 10 20
138 20p. brown and green 25 50
DESIGNS: 7p. Salvador Casanas; 20p. Josep de Boltas.

1982. With "PTA" under figure of value.
139 **50** 1p. mauve 10 10
140 3p. brown 10 10
141 7p. red 10 10
142 12p. red 10 20
143 15p. blue 20 20
144 20p. green 20 20
145 30p. red 25 40
146 50p. green (25 × 31 mm) . . 60 50
147 100p. blue (25 × 31 mm) . . 1·90 1·00
See also Nos. 203/6.

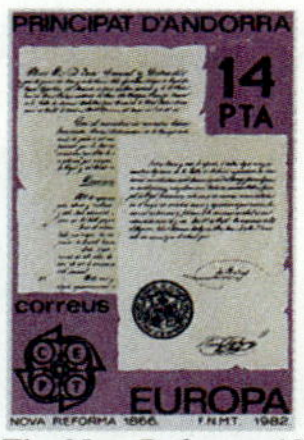

51 The New Reforms, 1866

1982. Europa. Multicoloured.
154 14p. Type **51** 30 35
155 33p. Reform of the Institutions, 1981 . . . . . 40 65

52 Footballers

1982. World Cup Football Championship, Spain. Multicoloured.
156 14p. Type **52** 50 55
157 33p. Tackle . . . . 1·10 1·10

53 Arms and 1929 1p. stamp

1982. National Stamp Exhibition.
158 **53** 14p. black and green . . . 25 40

119 Drais Velocipede, 1818

1997. Bicycle Museum (1st series). Multicoloured.
252 32p. Type **119** 40 45
253 65p. Michaux velocipede, 1861 . . . . 85 80
See also Nos. 258/9 and 264/5.

120 The Bear and The Smugglers

121 Dove and Cultural Symbols

1997. Europa. Tales and Legends.
254 **120** 65p. multicoloured . . . 1·20 1·10

1997. National UNESCO Commission.
255 **121** 32p. multicoloured . . . 25 35

122 Catalan Crib Figure

1997. Christmas.
256 **122** 32p. multicoloured . . . 25 35

123 Giant Slalom

1998. Winter Olympic Games, Nagano, Japan.
257 **123** 35p. multicoloured . . . 25 35

1998. Bicycle Museum (2nd series). As T **119**. Multicoloured.
258 35p. Kangaroo bicycle, Great Britain, 1878 . . . . . . 40 45
259 70p. The Swallow, France, 1889 . . . . 85 95

124 Harlequins of Canillo

1998. Europa. National Festivals.
260 **124** 70p. multicoloured . . . 1·00 1·00

125 Front Page of First Edition and Landscape

1998. 250th Anniv of "Manual Digest".
261 **125** 35p. multicoloured . . . 25 35

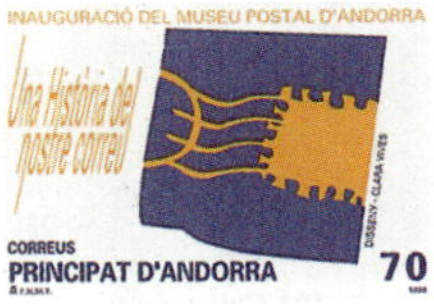
126 Emblem

1998. Inauguration of Postal Museum.
262 **126** 70p. violet and yellow . . 50 70

127 St. Lucia Fair

1998. Christmas.
263 **127** 35p. multicoloured . . . 25 35

1999. Bicycle Museum (3rd series). As T **119**. Multicoloured.
264 35p. Salvo tricycle, 1878 (vert) 35 45
265 70p. Rudge tricycle, Coventry, England 90 95

128 Mules

1999. Postal History.
266 **128** 35p. black and brown . . 25 35

129 Palace of Human Rights, Strasbourg

1999. 50th Anniv of Council of Europe.
267 **129** 35p. multicoloured . . . 25 35

130 Vall d'Incles National Park, Canillo

1999. Europa. Parks and Gardens.
268 **130** 70p. multicoloured . . . 1·00 1·00

131 Rull House, Sispony

1999.
269 **131** 35p. multicoloured . . . 25 55

132 Angel (detail of altarpiece, St. Serni's Church, Canillo)

133 Santa Coloma Church

1999. Christmas.
270 **132** 35p. brown and light brown 25 55

1999. European Heritage.
271 **133** 35p. multicoloured . . . 25 60

134 "Building Europe"

2000. Europa.
272 **134** 70p. multicoloured . . . 1·00 1·00

135 Angonella Lakes, Ordino

2000.
273 **135** 35p. multicoloured . . . 25 35

136 Casa Lacruz

2000. 131st Birth Anniv of Josep Cadafalch (architect).
274 **136** 35p. multicoloured . . . 25 35

137 Dinner Service

138 Hurdling

2000. D'Areny-Plandolit Museum.
275 **137** 70p. multicoloured . . . 50 65

2000. Olympic Games, Sydney.
276 **138** 70p. multicoloured . . . 50 65

139 United Nations Headquarters, Strasbourg

2000. 50th Anniv of United Nations Declaration of Human Rights.
277 **139** 70p. multicoloured . . . 50 65

140 Gradual, St. Roma, Les Bons

141 "Quadre de les Animes" (Joan Casanovas)

2000. 25th Anniv of the National Archives.
278 **140** 35p. multicoloured . . . 25 35

2000. Christmas.
279 **141** 35p. multicoloured . . . 25 35

142 Rec del Sola

2001. Natural Heritage.
280 **142** 40p. multicoloured . . . 25 40

143 Roc del Metge (thermal spring), Escaldes-Engordany

2001. Europa. Water Resources.
281 **143** 75p. multicoloured . . . 1·00 80

144 Casa Palau, Sant

145 Part of Sanctuary, Julia de Loria Meritxell

2001.
282 **144** 75p. multicoloured . . . 50 80

2001. 25th Anniv of Chapel of Our Lady, Meritxell.
283 **145** 40p. multicoloured . . . 25 40

146 Building

2001. 10th Anniv of National Auditorium, Ordino.
284 **146** 75p. multicoloured . . . 50 80

147 Angel (detail of altarpiece, Church of St. John of Caselles)

2001. Christmas.
285 **147** 40p. multicoloured . . . 25 40

New Currency
100 cents = 1 euro

148 State Arms

2002.
286 **148** 25c. orange 30 40
286a 27c. blue 40 40
286b 28c. blue 45 45
286c 29c. sepia 45 45
286d 30c. carmine 45 45
287 50c. red 40 90
288 52c. yellow 70 60
289 53c. green . . . . 1·20 1·10
289a 57c. blue . . . . 1·30 1·30
289b 58c. black . . . . . . 1·30 1·30
290 77c. orange . . . . . . 1·30 1·30
291 78c. magenta . . . . . 1·30 1·30

149 Alpine Accentor (*Prunella collaris*)

2002. Native Birds. Multicoloured.
300 25c. Type **149** 30 40
301 50c. Snow finch (*Montifringilla nivalis*) . . . 60 80

150 Emblem

2002. International Year of the Mountain.
302 **150** 50c. multicoloured 50 80

151 Tightrope Walker

2002. Europa. Circus.
303 **151** 50c. multicoloured . . . . 9·00 90

152 Casa Fusile, Escaldes-Engordany
153 Pinette Minim

2002. Architectural Heritage. Multicoloured.
304 €1.80 Type **152** . . . . . . 2·40 3·25
305 €2.10 Farga Rossell Iron Museum, La Massana . . 3·00 3·00

2002. History of the Motor Car (1st series). Multicoloured.
306 25c. Type **153** 35 60
307 50c. Rolls Royce Silver Wraith 50 80
See also Nos. 317/18 and 324/5.

154 Placa Benlloch, Areny-Plandolit

2002. Christmas.
308 **154** 25c. multicoloured 25 50

155 Painted Medallion

2002. Cultural Heritage. Romanesque Murals from Santa Coloma Church, Andorra la Vella.
309 25c. Type **155** 35 35
310 50c. Part of damaged fresco showing seated figure . . . 70 70
311 75c. Frieze . . . . 1·10 1·10

156 Sassanat Bridge

2003.
312 **156** 26c. multicoloured 30 50

157 State Arms

2003. 10th Anniv of Constitution.
313 **157** 76c. multicoloured . . . . 80 1·30

158 Man drinking, Donkey and Market Stalls
159 Northern Wheatear (*Oenanthe oenanthe*)

2003. Europa. Poster Art.
314 **158** 76c. multicoloured . . . . 1·00 1·20

2003. Native Birds.
315 **159** 50c. multicoloured 30 50

160 Multicoloured Stripes

2003. 10th Anniv of Andorras' Membership of United Nations.
316 **160** 76c. multicoloured 80 85

161 Carter (1908)

2003. History of the Motor Car (2nd series). Multicoloured.
317 51c. Type **161** 70 70
318 76c. Peugeot (1928) (horiz) 1·10 1·10

162 Roadside Cross, Andorra la Vella

2003. Christmas.
319 **162** 26c. multicoloured 30 30

163 "Fira del Bestiar" (Joaquim Mir)

2004.
320 **163** 27c. multicoloured 30 30

164 "L'Escorxador" (Joaquim Mir)
165 Coaches and Skiers in Snow

2004.
321 **164** 52c. multicoloured 55 65

2004. Europa. Holidays.
322 **165** 77c. black 80 95

166 Chaffinch (*Fringilla coelebs*)

2004. Native Birds.
323 **166** 27c. multicoloured 30 30

167 Simca 508 C (1939)

2004. History of the Motor Car (3rd series).
324 €1.90 Type **167** . . . . . . 2·50 2·50
325 €2.19 Messerschmitt KR 1 (1955) . . . . 3·25 3·25

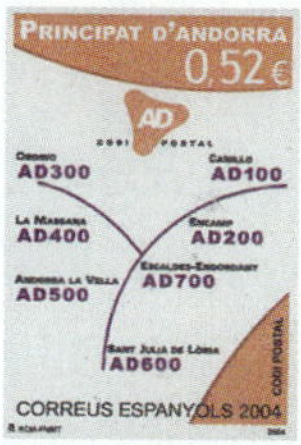

168 Map showing Postal Districts

2004. Introduction of Postal Codes.
326 **168** 52c. orange, magenta and black 55 55

169 Stars and Flag as Jigsaw Pieces

2004. 10th Anniv of Entry into Council of Europe.
327 **169** 52c. multicoloured 55 55

170 Nativity

2004. Christmas.
328 **170** 27c. multicoloured 30 30

171 Madriu-Perafita-Claror Valley
172 "Endless" (Mark Brusse)

2005. UNESCO World Heritage Site.
329 **171** 28c. multicoloured 30 30

2005.
330 **172** 53c. multicoloured 60 60

173 Glass, Flowers, Jug and Tureen

2005. Europa. Gastronomy.
331 **173** 78c. multicoloured 80 80

174 Cyclist
175 Shrine

2005. Small States of Europe Games.
332 **174** €1.95 brown and black 3·00 3·00

2005. 25th Anniv of Caritas Andorra (humanitarian organization).
333 **175** 28c. multicoloured 30 30

176 Dipper (*Cinclus cinclus*)

2005. Native Birds.
334 **176** €2.21 multicoloured . . 3·25 3·25

177 The Nativity (Sergei Mas)

2005. Christmas.
335 **177** 28c. multicoloured 55 55

178 Skiers

2006. Winter Olympic Games, Turin.
336 **178** 29c. multicoloured 55 55

179 "Ruta del Hierro" (sculpture) (Satora Sato)

2006. Cultural Heritage.
337 **179** 78c. multicoloured . . . . 1·40 1·40

180 Stylized People of Many Colours and Abilities

2006. Europa. Integration.
338 **180** 57c. multicoloured . . . . 1·10 1·10

181 Grey Partridge (*Perdix perdix*)

2006. Natural Heritage.
339 **181** €2.39 multicoloured . . 4·75 4·75

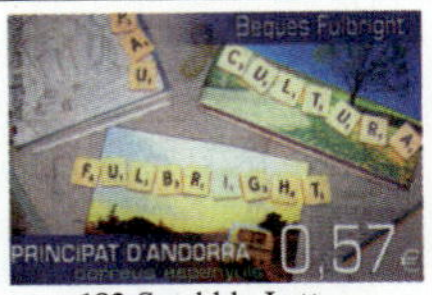

182 Scrabble Letters

2006. Fulbright Scholarships.

340	**182**	57c. multicoloured	1·10	1·10

183 Head Containing World Map

2006. 60th Anniv of UNESCO and 10th Anniv of CNAU.

341	**183**	€2.33 multicoloured	4·75	4·75

184 Nativity

2006. Christmas.

342	**184**	29c. multicoloured	55	55

185 "Encamp 1994" (F. Galobardes)

2007. Cultural Heritage.

343	**185**	30c. multicoloured	55	55

186 Doves and Emblem

187 'La Familia Jordino' (sculpture by Rachid Khimoune)

2007. Europa. Centenary of Scouting.

344	**186**	58c. multicoloured	2·25	2·25

2007. Cultural Heritage. The Iron Route (historical trail).

345	**187**	€2.43 multicoloured	8·25	8·25

188 Capercaillie (*Tetrao urogallus*)

2007. Natural Heritage.

346	**188**	€2.49 multicoloured	8·50	8·50

189 *Casa de la Vall* (Francesc Galobardes)

2007. Cultural Heritage.

347	**189**	78c. multicoloured	3·00	3·00

190 Stylized Figures

2007. 25th Anniv of Andorra Red Cross.

348	**190**	30c. carmine and black	1·40	1·40

191 "Lamb kneeling before Infant Jesus" (painting by Sergi Mas)

2007. Christmas.

349	**191**	30c. multicoloured	1·40	1·40

192 *Gypaetus barbatus* (Lammergeier or bearded vulture)

2008. Natural Heritage.

350	**192**	31c. multicoloured	1·40	1·40

193 *Carro Vortiu* (sculpture by Jordi Casamajor)

2008. Cultural Heritage.

351	**193**	60c. multicoloured	2·40	2·40

EXPRESS LETTER STAMPS

1928. Express Letter stamp of Spain optd **CORREOS ANDORRA**.

E15	E **53**	20c. red	42·00	48·00

E 4 Lammergeier over Pyrenees

E 12 Eurasian Red Squirrel (after Durer) and Arms

1929.

E41	E **4**	20c. red	4·50	6·25

1949.

E54	E **12**	25c. red	2·40	3·50

ANGOLA Pt. 9, Pt. 12

Republic of Southern Africa. Independent of Portugal since 11 November 1975.

1870. 1000 reis = 1 milreis.
1913. 100 centavos = 1 escudo.
1932. 100 centavos = 1 angolar.
1954. 100 centavos = 1 escudo.
1977. 100 lweis = 1 kwanza.

1870. "Crown" key-type inscr "ANGOLA".

7	P	5r. black	1·60	1·10
17		10r. yellow	16·00	9·25
31		10r. green	6·00	3·25
9		20r. bistre	1·70	1·50
26		20r. red	14·00	10·50
10		25r. red	8·25	6·00
27		25r. purple	9·00	3·75
19b		40r. blue	£180	£130
33		40r. yellow	8·25	3·75
12		50r. green	40·00	11·00
30		50r. blue	36·00	8·00
21a		100r. lilac	3·75	2·40
22		200r. orange	3·00	1·50
23a		300r. brown	3·75	2·40

1886. "Embossed" key-type inscr "PROVINCIA DE ANGOLA".

35	Q	5r. black	9·75	4·50
36		10r. green	9·75	4·50
37		20r. red	13·00	9·25
39		25r. mauve	9·75	3·00
40		40r. brown	12·00	5·50
41		50r. blue	15·00	3·00
42		100r. brown	21·00	7·75
43		200r. violet	28·00	9·50
44		300r. orange	29·00	10·50

1894. "Figures" key-type inscr "ANGOLA".

49	R	5r. orange	2·30	1·00
62		10r. mauve	3·25	2·00
63		15r. brown	4·00	1·80
54		20r. lavender	4·00	1·80
74		25r. green	4·00	1·80
66		50r. blue	5·00	2·40
67		75r. red	8·50	7·25
68		80r. green	9·75	5·25
69		100r. brown on buff	9·75	5·25
70		150r. red on rose	16·00	10·50
77		200r. blue on blue	16·00	10·50
78		300r. blue on brown	16·00	10·50

1894. No. N51 with circular surch **CORREIOS DE ANGOLA 25 REIS**.

79b	V	25r. on 2½r. brown	46·00	46·00

1898. "King Carlos" key-type inscr "ANGOLA".

80	S	2½r. grey	40	35
81		5r. orange	40	35
82		10r. green	40	35
83		15r. brown	2·30	1·20
142		15r. green	1·20	1·10
84		20r. lilac	50	40
85		25r. green	1·20	50
143		25r. red	60	35
86		50r. blue	2·10	70
144		50r. brown	5·75	1·90
145		65r. blue	6·00	4·25
87		75r. red	7·25	4·50
146		75r. purple	2·30	1·50
88		80r. mauve	7·25	2·30
89		100r. blue on blue	1·40	1·00
147		115r. brown on pink	8·00	5·50
148		130r. brown on yellow	8·00	5·50
90		150r. brown on buff	7·50	4·50
91		200r. purple on pink	4·25	1·30
92		300r. blue on pink	4·75	3·75
149		400r. blue on yellow	4·25	2·75
93		500r. black on blue	4·75	3·75
94		700r. mauve on yellow	23·00	11·50

1902. "Embossed", "Figures" and "Newspaper" key-types of Angola surch.

98	R	65r. on 5r. orange	6·50	4·50
100		65r. on 10r. mauve	8·00	4·50
102		65r. on 20r. violet	6·50	4·50
104		65r. on 25r. green	9·75	6·00
95	Q	65r. on 40r. brown	8·00	4·50
96		65r. on 300r. orange	8·00	4·50
106		115r. on 10r. green	6·50	3·75
109	R	115r. on 80r. green	24·00	6·00
111		115r. on 100r. brn on buff	9·75	5·25
113		115r. on 150r. red on rose	8·00	7·25
108	Q	115r. on 200r. violet	6·50	3·75
120	R	130r. on 15r. brown	4·50	3·75
116	Q	130r. on 50r. blue	9·25	3·75
124	R	130r. on 75r. red	4·75	3·25
118	Q	130r. on 100r. brown	6·00	3·75
126	R	130r. on 300r. blue on brn	13·00	11·00
136	V	400r. on 2½r. brown	1·20	1·10
127	Q	400r. on 5r. black	9·50	7·25
128		400r. on 20r. red	47·00	30·00
130		400r. on 25r. mauve	16·00	8·50
131	R	400r. on 50r. pale blue	6·50	4·00
133		400r. on 200r. blue on blue	6·50	5·50

1902. "King Carlos" key-type of Angola optd **PROVISORIO**.

138	S	15r. brown	1·60	1·10
139		25r. green	1·30	60
140		50r. blue	2·00	1·00
141		75r. red	3·25	3·00

1905. No. 145 surch **50 REIS** and bar.

150	S	50r. on 65r. blue	3·00	1·60

1911. "King Carlos" key-type optd **REPUBLICA**.

151	S	2½r. grey	40	30
152		5r. orange	40	30
153		10r. green	40	30
154		15r. green	35	35
155		20r. lilac	40	30
156		25r. red	40	30
157		50r. brown	1·10	85
232		50r. blue (No. 140)	1·10	95
224		75r. purple	1·10	75
234		75r. red (No. 141)	1·40	1·10
225		100r. blue on blue	1·60	1·60
160		115r. brown on pink	1·60	95
161		130r. brown on yellow	1·60	95
226		200r. purple on pink	1·50	1·00
163		400r. blue on yellow	2·20	95
164		500r. black on blue	2·20	1·10
165		700r. mauve on yellow	2·20	1·40

1912. "King Manoel" key-type inscr "ANGOLA" optd **REPUBLICA**.

166	T	2½r. lilac	40	30
167		5r. black	40	30
168		10r. green	40	30
169		20r. red	40	30
170		25r. brown	40	30
171		50r. blue	1·10	85
172		75r. brown	1·20	1·10
173		100r. brown on green	1·60	1·20
174		200r. green on pink	1·60	1·20
175		300r. black on blue	1·60	1·20

1912. "King Carlos" key-type of Angola optd **REPUBLICA** and surch.

176	S	2½ on 15r. green	2·50	1·60
177		5 on 15r. green	3·00	1·60
178		10 on 15r. green	1·90	1·60
179		25 on 75r. red (No. 141)	36·00	28·00
180		25 on 75r. purple	3·00	3·00

1913. Surch **REPUBLICA ANGOLA** and value in figures on "Vasco da Gama" issues of

(a) Portuguese Colonies.

181	¼c. on 2½r. green	75	45
182	½c. on 5r. red	75	45
183	1c. on 10r. purple	75	45
184	2½c. on 25r. green	75	45
185	5c. on 50r. blue	75	45
186	7½c. on 75r. brown	3·00	2·50
187	10c. on 100r. brown	1·60	1·10
188	15c. on 150r. bistre	95	80

(b) Macao.

189	¼c. on ½a. green	1·10	95
190	½c. on 1a. red	1·10	95
191	1c. on 2a. purple	95	70
192	2½c. on 4a. green	80	60
193	5c. on 8a. blue	80	65
194	7½c. on 12a. brown	3·50	1·60
195	10c. on 16a. brown	1·40	95
196	15c. on 24a. bistre	1·25	95

(c) Timor.

197	¼c. on ½a. green	1·10	95
198	½c. on 1a. red	1·10	95
199	1c. on 2a. purple	90	70
200	2½c. on 4a. green	1·90	60
201	5c. on 8a. blue	1·10	75
202	7½c. on 12a. brown	3·50	1·60
203	10c. on 16a. brown	1·40	95
204	15c. on 24a. bistre	1·30	95

1914. "Ceres" key-type inscr "ANGOLA".

296	U	¼c. olive	20	15
297		½c. black	20	15
298		1c. green	20	15
299		1½c. brown	25	20
300		2c. red	25	20
301		2c. grey	35	30
281		2½c. violet	20	15
303		3c. orange	15	15
304		4c. red	15	15
305		4½c. grey	15	15
284a		5c. blue	20	15
307		6c. mauve	15	15
308		7c. blue	15	15
309		7½c. brown	25	20
288		8c. grey	20	20
311		10c. brown	20	15
312		12c. brown	35	30
313		12c. green	35	30
291		15c. purple	20	15
314		15c. pink	20	15
315		20c. green	85	70
316		24c. blue	70	60
317		25c. brown	90	70
217		30c. brown on green	1·20	1·10
318		30c. green	35	30
218		40c. brown on pink	1·20	1·10
319		40c. blue	70	35
219		50c. orange on pink	4·75	3·50
320		50c. purple	70	35
321		60c. blue	90	55
322		60c. red	43·00	26·00
322a		80c. pink	85	45
220		1e. green on blue	3·25	2·20
323		1e. red	85	45
325		1e. blue	1·40	85
326		2e. purple	1·20	60
327		5e. brown	7·25	5·75
328		10e. pink	16·00	13·00
329		20e. green	55·00	36·00

1914. Provisional stamps of 1902 optd **REPUBLICA**.

233	S	50r. on 65r. blue	3·00	2·10
256	Q	115r. on 10r. green	1·50	1·20
258	R	115r. on 80r. green	1·00	90
261		115r. on 100r. brn on buff	1·20	1·10
263		115r. on 150r. red on rose	90	90
266	Q	115r. on 200r. violet	1·30	1·10
267	R	130r. on 15r. brown	1·00	90
246	Q	130r. on 50r. blue	9·50	9·50
269	R	130r. on 75r. red	1·80	1·10
273	Q	130r. on 100r. brown	80	70
274	R	130r. on 300r. blue on brn	80	70
254	V	400r. on 2½r. brown	55	45

1919. Stamps of 1911, 1912 or 1914 surch.

332	S	¼c. on 75r. purple	1·10	95
331	T	½c. on 75r. brown	90	75
336		1c. on 50r. blue	95	85
335	S	2½c. on 100r. blue on blue	1·10	80
334		2½c. on 100r. brown on grn	1·40	1·10
337		4c. on 130r. brown on yell	1·10	80
339	U	$04 on 15c. purple	1·10	80
340		$04 on 15c. pink	9·00	
341	T	$00.5 on 75r. brown	1·10	90
342	U	$00.5 on 7½c. brown	80	70

1925. Nos. 136 and 133 surch **Republica 40 C.**

345	V	40c. on 400r. on 2½r. brn	55	55
343	R	40c. on 400r. on 200r. blue on blue	60	45

1931. "Ceres" key-type of Angola surch.

347	U	50c. on 60c. red	1·10	95
348		70c. on 80c. pink	2·20	1·40
349		70c. on 1e. blue	1·80	1·40
350		1e.40 on 2e. purple	1·30	80

17 Ceres

1932.

351	17	1c. brown	15	15
352		5c. sepia	20	20
353		10c. mauve	20	20
354		15c. black	20	20
355		20c. grey	20	20
356		30c. green	20	20
357		35c. green	4·75	2·50
358		40c. red	30	15
359		45c. blue	85	70
360		50c. brown	20	15
361		60c. olive	65	20
362		70c. brown	65	20
363		80c. green	40	15
364		85c. red	2·50	1·20
365		1a. red	60	20
366		1a.40 blue	5·75	2·20
367		1a.75 blue	8·00	3·00
368		2a. mauve	2·50	30
369		5a. green	5·75	95
370		10a. brown	11·00	3·00
371		20a. orange	26·00	3·00

1934. Surch.

380	17	5c. on 80c. green (A)	65	30
419		5c. on 80c. green (B)	60	40
413		10c. on 45c. blue	1·10	70
381		10c. on 80c. green	85	45
414		15c. on 45c. blue	1·10	70
382		15c. on 80c. green	1·20	45
415		20c. on 85c. red	1·10	70
374		30c. on 1a.40 blue	1·90	1·40
416		35c. on 85c. red	1·10	70
417		50c. on 1a.40 blue	1·10	70
418		60c. on 1a. red	4·75	4·75
375		70c. on 2a. mauve	2·30	1·40
376		80c. on 5a. green	3·50	1·40

(A) surch **0,05 Cent.** in one line; (B) surch **5 CENTAVOS** in two lines.

1935. "Due" key-type surch **CORREIOS** and new value.

377	W	5c. on 6c. brown	1·20	85
378		30c. on 50c. grey	1·20	85
379		40c. on 50c. grey	1·20	85

22 Vasco da Gama

27 Airplane over Globe

1938. Name and value in black.

383	22	1c. olive (postage)	15	15
384		5c. brown	20	20
385		10c. red	20	20
386		15c. purple	20	20
387		20c. grey	20	20
388	–	30c. purple	30	30
389	–	35c. green	60	45
390	–	40c. brown	20	15
391	–	50c. mauve	30	15
392	–	60c. black	60	20
393	–	70c. violet	60	20
394	–	80c. orange	60	20
395	–	1a. red	50	20
396	–	1a.75 blue	1·20	60
397	–	2a. red	1·70	65
398	–	5a. olive	7·25	65
399	–	10a. blue	14·50	70
400	–	20a. brown	22·00	1·70
401	27	10c. red (air)	30	30
402		20c. violet	30	20
403		50c. orange	30	20
404		1a. blue	30	20
405		2a. red	60	20
406		3a. green	55	35
407		5a. brown	5·25	80
408		9a. red	4·25	8·50
409		10a. mauve	5·75	1·10

DESIGNS: 30c. to 50c. Mousinho de Albuquerque; 60c. to 1a. "Fomento" (symbolizing Progress); 1a.75, 2, 5a. Prince Henry the Navigator; 10, 20a. Afonso de Albuquerque.

28 Portuguese Colonial Column

31 Arms of Angola

1938. President's Colonial Tour.

410	28	80c. green	1·70	1·20
411		1a.75 blue	11·50	3·50
412		20a. brown	32·00	17·00

1945. Nos. 394/6 surch.

420	5c. on 80c. orange	50	35
421	50c. on 1a. red	50	35
422	50c. on 1a.75 blue	50	35

1947. Air.

423a	31	1a. brown	5·75	3·00
423b		2a. green	6·25	3·00
423c		3a. orange	6·25	3·00
423d		3a.50 orange	12·50	3·00
423e		5a. green	40·00	14·50
423f		6a. pink	40·00	9·50
423g		9a. red	£140	£140
423h		10a. green	95·00	60·00
423i		20a. blue	£130	60·00
423j		50a. black	£200	£140
423k		100a. yellow	£250	£225

32 Sao Miguel Fortress, Luanda

33 Our Lady of Fatima

1948. Tercentenary of Restoration of Angola. Inscr "Tricentenario da Restauracao de Angola 1648–1948".

424	32	5c. violet	15	10
425	–	10c. brown	45	15
426	–	30c. green	15	10
427	–	50c. purple	15	10
428	–	1a. red	45	10
429	–	1a.75 blue	70	10
430	–	2a. green	70	10
431	–	5a. black	2·30	35
432	–	10a. mauve	5·50	45
433	–	20a. blue	11·50	2·50

MS433a 162 × 225 mm. Nos. 424/33 (sold at 42a.50) . . . 60·00 60·00

DESIGNS—HORIZ: 10c. Our Lady of Nazareth Hermitage, Luanda; 1a. Surrender of Luanda; 5a. Inscribed Rocks of Yelala; 20a. Massangano Fortress. VERT (portraits): 30c. Don John IV; 50c. Salvador Correia de Sa Benevides; 1a.75, Diogo Cao; 7a. Manuel Cerveira Pereira; 10a. Paulo Dias de Novais.

1948. Honouring Our Lady of Fatima.

434	33	50c. red	1·80	1·10
435		3a. blue	7·00	2·20
436		6a. orange	22·00	5·50
437		9a. red	60·00	7·00

35 River Chiumbe

36 Pedras Negras

1949.

438	35	20c. blue	30	15
439	36	40c. brown	30	10
440	–	50c. red	30	10
441	–	2a.50 blue	1·80	30
442	–	3a.50 grey	1·80	1·40
443	–	15a. green	14·50	1·40
444	–	50a. green	80·00	5·00

DESIGNS—As T **35**: 50c. Luanda; 2a.50, Bandeira; 3a.50, Mocamedes; 50a. Braganza Falls. 31 × 26 mm: 15a. River Cubal.

37 Aircraft and Globe

38 "Tentativa Feliz"

1949. Air.

445	37	1a. orange	50	10
446		2a. brown	1·10	10
447		3a. mauve	1·40	15
448		6a. green	2·50	50
449		9a. purple	3·50	1·20

1949. Centenary of Founding of Mocamedes.

450	38	1a. purple	5·75	65
451		4a. green	14·50	1·80

39 Letter and Globe

40 Reproduction of "Crown" key-type

1949. 75th Anniv of U.P.U.

452	39	4a. green	7·25	1·60

1950. Philatelic Exhibition and 80th Anniv of First Angolan Stamp.

453	40	50a. green	1·00	30
454		1a. red	1·00	50
455		4a. black	3·25	1·30

MS455a 120 × 79 mm. Nos. 453/5 (sold at 6a.50) . . . 15·00 11·50

41 Bells and Dove

42 Angels holding Candelabra

1950. Holy Year.

456	41	1a. violet	70	15
457	42	4a. black	3·25	60

43 Dark Chanting Goshawk

44 Our Lady of Fatima

1951. Birds. Multicoloured.

458	5c. Type **43**	30	15
459	10c. Racquet-tailed roller	30	15
460	15c. Bateleur	45	15
461	20c. European bee eater	45	30
462	50c. Giant kingfisher	45	15
463	1a. Anchieta's barbet	45	15
464	1a.50 African open-bill stork	65	15
465	2a. Southern ground hornbill	65	15
466	2a.50 African skimmer	95	15
467	3a. Shikra	65	15
468	3a.50 Senham's bustard	95	15
469	4a. African golden oriole	1·00	15
470	4a.50 Magpie shrike	1·00	15
471	5a. Red-shouldered glossy starling	3·50	35
472	6a. Sharp-tailed glossy starling	5·00	95
473	7a. Fan-tailed whydah	5·75	1·20
474	10a. Half-collared kingfisher	23·00	1·60
475	12a.50 White-crowned shrike	6·25	2·00
476	15a. White-winged starling	5·75	2·00
477	20a. Southern yellow-billed hornbill	55·00	5·00
478	25a. Violet starling	20·00	4·25
479	30a. Sulphur-breasted bush shrike	20·00	5·00
480	40a. Secretary bird	29·00	7·00
481	50a. Peach-faced lovebird	70·00	14·50

The 10, 15 and 20c., 2a.50, 3a., 4a.50, 12a.50 and 30a. are horiz, the remainder vert.

1951. Termination of Holy Year.

482	44	4a. orange	2·30	1·10

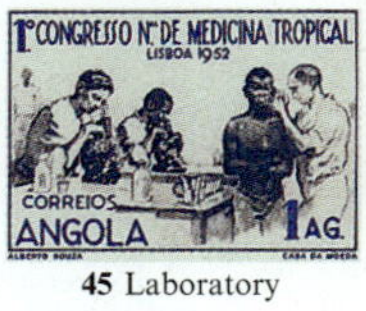

45 Laboratory

46 The Sacred Face

1952. 1st Tropical Medicine Congress, Lisbon.

483	45	1a. grey and blue	80	30

1952. Missionary Art Exhibition.

484	46	10c. blue and flesh	15	15
485		50c. green and stone	65	15
486		2a. purple and flesh	2·30	45

47 Leopard

48 Stamp of 1853 and Colonial Arms

1953. Angolan Fauna. Multicoloured.

487	5c. Type **47**	15	15
488	10c. Sable antelope (vert)	15	15
489	20c. African elephant (vert)	15	15
490	30c. Eland (vert)	15	15
491	40c. Crocodile	15	15
492	50c. Impala (vert)	15	15
493	1a. Mountain zebra (vert)	20	15
494	1a.50 Sitatunga (vert)	20	15
495	2a. Black rhinoceros	20	15
496	2a.30 Gemsbok (vert)	20	15
497	2a.50 Lion (vert)	30	15
498	3a. African buffalo	35	15
499	3a.50 Springbok (vert)	35	15
500	4a. Blue wildebeest (vert)	12·50	15
501	5a. Hartebeest (vert)	60	15
502	7a. Warthog (vert)	85	15
503	10a. Waterbuck (vert)	1·80	15
504	12a.50 Hippopotamus (vert)	4·75	95
505	15a. Greater kudu (vert)	5·75	95
506	20a. Giraffe (vert)	7·25	60

1953. Portuguese Stamp Centenary.

507	48	50c. multicoloured	45	35

49 Father M. da Nobrega and Sao Paulo

50 Route of President's Tour

1954. 4th Centenary of Sao Paulo.

508	49	1e. black and buff	30	15

1954. Presidential Visit.

509	50	35c. multicoloured	10	10
510		4e.50 multicoloured	70	35

51 Map of Angola

52 Col. A. de Paiva

1955. Map mult. Angola territory in colour given.

511	51	5c. white	15	15
512		20c. salmon	15	15
513		50c. blue	15	15
514		1e. orange	15	15
515		2e.30 yellow	80	30
516		4e. blue	1·60	15
517		10e. green	1·40	15
518		20e. white	2·75	1·20

1956. Birth Centenary of De Paiva.

519	52	1e. black, blue and orange	30	20

53 Quela Chief

54 Father J. M. Antunes

1957. Natives. Multicoloured.

520	5c. Type **53**	15	15
521	10c. Andulo flute player	15	15
522	15c. Dembos man and woman	15	15
523	20c. Quissama dancer (male)	15	15
524	30c. Quibala family	15	15
525	40c. Bocolo dancer (female)	15	15
526	50c. Quissama woman	15	15
527	80c. Cuanhama woman	20	15
528	1e.50 Luanda widow	1·70	15
529	2e.50 Bocolo dancer (male)	1·70	15
530	4e. Muquixe man	85	15
531	10e. Cabinda chief	1·60	30

1957. Birth Centenary of Father Antunes.

532	54	1e. multicoloured	60	30

55 Exhibition Emblem, Globe and Arms

1958. Brussels International Exhibition.
533 **55** 1e.50 multicoloured 50 45

56 "Securidaca longipedunculata"

57 Native Doctor and Patient

1958. 6th Int Tropical Medicine Congress.
534 **56** 2e.50 multicoloured . . . . 1·90 65

1958. 75th Anniv of Maria Pia Hospital, Luanda.
535 **57** 1e. brown, black and blue 35 20
536 – 1e.50 multicoloured 85 45
537 – 2e.50 multicoloured . . . . 1·60 80
DESIGNS: 1e.50, 17th-century doctor and patient; 2e.50, Present-day doctor, orderly and patients.

58 Welwitschia (plant)

1959. Centenary of Discovery of Welwitschia.
538 **58** 1e.50 multicoloured 70 35
539 – 2e.50 multicoloured . . . . 1·10 45
540 – 5e. multicoloured . . . . . 1·80 45
541 – 10e. multicoloured . . . . 5·50 1·40
DESIGNS: 2e.50, 5, 10e. Various types of Welwitschia ("Welwitschia mirabilis").

59 Old Map of West Africa

1960. 500th Death Anniv of Prince Henry the Navigator.
542 **59** 2e.50 multicoloured 45 20

60 "Agriculture" (distribution of seeds)

61

1960. 10th Anniv of African Technical Co-operation Commission.
543 **60** 2e.50 multicoloured 50 20

1961. Angolan Women. As T **61**. Portraits multicoloured; background colours given.
544 10c. green 10 10
545 15c. blue 10 10
546 30c. yellow 10 10
547 40c. grey 10 10
548 60c. brown 10 10
549 1e.50 turquoise 15 10
550 2e. lilac 80 10
551 2e.50 lemon 80 10
552 3e. pink . . . . 3·00 20
553 4e. olive . . . . 1·40 20
554 5e. blue 95 20
555 7e.50 yellow . . . . 1·30 65
556 10e. buff 95 50
557 15e. brown . . . . 1·40 65
558 25e. red . . . . 2·00 95
559 50e. grey . . . . 4·25 2·00

62 Weightlifting

1962. Sports. Multicoloured.
560 50e. Flying 15 15
561 1e. Rowing 85 15
562 1e.50 Water polo 60 20
563 2e.50 Throwing the hammer 70 20
564 4e.50 High jumping 60 45
565 15e. Type **62** . . . . 1·40 1·10

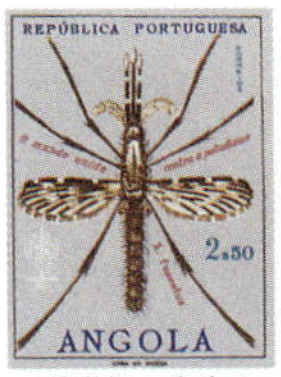

63 "Anopheles funestus" (mosquito)

64 Gen. Norton de Matos (statue)

1962. Malaria Eradication.
566 **63** 2e.50 multicoloured . . . . 1·30 60

1962. 50th Anniv of Nova Lisboa.
567 **64** 2e.50 multicoloured 45 20

65 Red Locusts

1963. 15th Anniv of Int Locust Eradication Service.
568 **65** 2e.50 multicoloured . . . . 1·30 35

66 Arms of St. Paul of the Assumption, Luanda

67 Rear-Admiral A. Tomas

1963. Angolan Civic Arms (1st series). Mult.
569 5c. Type **66** 15 15
570 10c. Massangano 15 15
571 30c. Muxima 15 15
572 50c. Carmona 15 15
573 1e. Salazar 50 15
574 1e.50 Malanje 95 15
575 2e. Henry of Carvalho . . . 50 15
576 2e.50 Mocamedes . . . . . 3·00 45
577 3e. Novo Redondo 70 15
578 3e.50 St. Salvador (Congo) 80 15
579 5e. Luso 70 20
580 7e.50 St. Philip (Benguela) . . 95 80
581 10e. Lobito . . . . 1·20 70
582 12e.50 Gabela . . . . 1·30 1·20
583 15e. Sa da Bandeira . . . . 1·30 1·20
584 17e.50 Silva Porto . . . . . 2·20 1·90
585 20e. Nova Lisboa . . . . . 2·20 1·60
586 22e.50 Cabinda . . . . . . 2·20 1·90
587 30e. Serpa Pinto . . . . . . 2·50 2·50
See also Nos. 589/610.

1963. Presidential Visit.
588 **67** 2e.50 multicoloured 45 15

68 Arms of Sanza-Pombo

69 Map of Africa, Boeing 707 and Lockheed Super Constellation Airliners

1963. Angolan Civic Arms (2nd series). Mult.
589 15c. Type **68** 15 15
590 20c. St. Antonio do Zaire . . 15 15
591 25c. Ambriz 15 15
592 40c. Ambrizete 15 15
593 50c. Catete 15 15
594 70c. Quibaxe 15 15
595 1e. Maquela do Zombo . . . 15 15
596 1e.20 Bembe 15 15
597 1e.50 Caxito 50 15
598 1e.80 Dondo 50 45
599 2e.50 Damba . . . . 1·90 15
600 4e. Cuimba 45 15
601 6e.50 Negage 45 30
602 7e. Quitexe 65 45
603 8e. Mucaba 65 50
604 9e. 31 de Janeiro 95 80
605 11e. Novo Caipemba . . . . 1·10 95
606 14e. Songo . . . . 1·20 1·10
607 17e. Quimbele . . . . 1·30 1·20
608 25e. Noqui . . . . 1·60 1·20
609 35e. Santa Cruz . . . . . . 2·30 1·90
610 50e. General Freire . . . . . 3·00 1·60

1963. 10th Anniv of T.A.P. Airline.
611 **69** 1e. multicoloured 85 30

70 Bandeira Cathedral

71 Dr. A. T. de Sousa

1963. Angolan Churches. Multicoloured.
612 10c. Type **70** 10 10
613 20c. Landana 10 10
614 30c. Luanda (Cathedral) . . 10 10
615 40c. Gabela 10 10
616 50c. St. Martin, Bay of Tigers (Chapel) 10 10
617 1e. Melange (Cathedral) (horiz) 15 15
618 1e.50 St. Peter, Chibia . . . 15 15
619 2e. Benguela (horiz) 20 15
620 2e.50 Jesus, Luanda 20 15
621 3e. Camabatela (horiz) . . . 30 15
622 3e.50 Cabinda Mission . . . 45 15
623 4e. Vila Folgares (horiz) . . 45 20
624 4e.50 Arrabida, Lobito (horiz) 60 20
625 5e. Cabinda 60 30
626 7e.50 Cacuso, Malange (horiz) 95 50
627 10e. Lubanga Mission . . . 1·20 50
628 12e.50 Huila Mission (horiz) 1·40 80
629 15e. Island Cape, Luanda (horiz) . . . . 1·60 85

1964. Centenary of National Overseas Bank.
630 **71** 2e.50 multicoloured 60 30

72 Arms and Palace of Commerce, Luanda

1964. Cent of Luanda Commercial Association.
631 **72** 1e. multicoloured 20 15

73 I.T.U. Emblem and St. Gabriel

74 Boeing 707 over Petroleum Refinery

1965. Centenary of I.T.U.
632 **73** 2e.50 multicoloured 85 45

1965. Air. Multicoloured.
633 1e.50 Type **74** 80 10
634 2e.50 Cambabe Dam 85 10
635 3e. Salazar Dam . . . . . . 1·20 10
636 4e. Captain Trofilo Duarte Dam . . . . 1·20 15
637 4e.50 Creveiro Lopes Dam . . 85 15
638 5e. Cuango Dam 85 20
639 6e. Quanza Bridge . . . . . 1·40 30
640 7e. Captain Trofilo Duarte Railway Bridge . . . . . 2·00 30
641 8e.50 Dr. Oliveira Salazar Bridge . . . . 2·50 80
642 12e.50 Captain Silva Carvalho Railway Bridge 2·50 1·10
Nos. 634/42 are horiz and each design includes a Boeing 707 airliner overhead.

75 Fokker F.27 Friendship over Luanda Airport

1965. 25th Anniv of Direccao dos Transportes Aereos (Angolan airline).
643 **75** 2e.50 multicoloured 85 20

76 Arquebusier, 1539

77 St. Paul's Hospital, Luanda, and Sarmento Rodrigues Commercial and Industrial School

1966. Portuguese Military Uniforms. Multicoloured.
644 50c. Type **76** 10 10
645 1e. Arquebusier, 1640 . . . . 10 10
646 1e.50 Infantry officer, 1777 15 10
647 2e. Infantry standard-bearer, 1777 . . . . 25 10
648 2e.50 Infantryman, 1777 . . 25 10
649 3e. Cavalry officer, 1783 . . 35 10
650 4e. Trooper, 1783 . . . . . 40 15
651 4e.50 Infantry officer, 1807 50 25
652 5e. Infantryman, 1807 . . . 60 25
653 6e. Cavalry officer, 1807 . . 85 25
654 8e. Trooper, 1807 . . . . . 1·20 40
655 9e. Infantryman, 1873 . . . 1·20 60

1966. 40th Anniv of National Revolution.
656 **77** 1e. multicoloured 35 15

78 Emblem of Brotherhood

79 Mendes Barata and Cruiser "Don Carlos I"

1966. Centenary of Brotherhood of the Holy Spirit.
657 **78** 1e. multicoloured 25 15

1967. Centenary of Military Naval Assn. Mult.
658 1e. Type **79** 65 35
659 2e.50 Augusto de Castilho and sail/steam corvette "Mindelo" 85 35

80 Basilica of Fatima

81 17th-century Map and M. C. Pereira (founder)

1967. 50th Anniv of Fatima Apparitions.
660 **80** 50c. multicoloured 25 15

1967. 350th Anniv of Benguela.
661 **81** 50c. multicoloured 25 15

82 Town Hall, Uige-Carmona

83 "The Three Orders"

1967. 50th Anniv of Uige-Carmona.
662 **82** 1e. multicoloured 15 15

1967. Portuguese Civil and Military Orders. Mult.
663 50c. Type **83** 15 15
664 1e. "Tower and Sword" . . . 15 15
665 1e.50 "Avis" 15 15
666 2e. "Christ" 15 15
667 2e.50 "St. James of the Sword" 15 15
668 3e. "Empire" 25 15
669 4e. "Prince Henry" 35 35
670 5e. "Benemerencia" 40 35
671 10e. "Public Instruction" . . 75 85
672 20e. "Agricultural and Industrial Merit" . . . . . 1·60 95

84 Belmonte Castle

85 Francisco Inocencio de Souza Countinho

1968. 500th Birth Anniv of Pedro Cabral (explorer). Multicoloured.
673 50c. Our Lady of Hope (vert) 15 15
674 1e. Type **84** 25 15
675 1e.50 St. Jeronimo's hermitage (vert) 35 15
676 2e.50 Cabral's fleet (vert) 90 15

1969. Bicent of Novo Redondo (Angolan city).
677 **85** 2e. multicoloured 20 10

86 Gunboat "Loge" and Admiral Coutinho

87 Compass

1969. Birth Centenary of Admiral Gago Coutinho.
678 **86** 2e.50 multicoloured 75 25

1969. 500th Birth Anniv of Vasco da Gama (explorer).
679 **87** 1e. multicoloured 25 15

88 L. A. Rebello de Silva

89 Gate of Jeronimos

1969. Cent of Overseas Administrative Reforms.
680 **88** 1e.50 multicoloured 15 15

1969. 500th Birth Anniv of King Manoel I.
681 **89** 3e. multicoloured 25 15

90 "Angolasaurus bocagei"

91 Marshal Carmona

1970. Fossils and Minerals. Multicoloured.
682 50c. Type **90** 40 15
683 1e. Ferro-meteorite 40 15
684 1e.50 Dioptase 65 40
685 2e. "Gondwanidium validium" 65 40
686 2e.50 Diamonds 65 40
687 3e. Estromatolitos 65 40
688 3e.50 Giant-toothed shark ("Procarcharodon megalodon") 1·10 65
689 4e. Dwarf lungfish ("Microceratodus angolensis") 1·10 65
690 4e.50 Muscovite (mica) 1·10 65
691 5e. Barytes 1·10 65
692 6e. "Nostoceras helicinum" 2·10 90
693 10e. "Rotula orbiculus angolensis" 2·20 1·30

1970. Birth Centenary of Marshal Carmona.
694 **91** 2e.50 multicoloured 35 15

92 Cotton-picking

1970. Centenary of Malanje Municipality.
695 **92** 2e.50 multicoloured 40 25

93 Mail Steamers "Infante Dom Henrique" and "Principe Perfeito" and 1870 5r. Stamp

94 Map and Emblems

1970. Stamp Centenary. Multicoloured.
696 1e.50 Type **93** (postage) 40 25
697 4e.50 Beyer-Garratt steam locomotive and 25r. stamp of 1870 2·20 2·20
698 2e.50 Fokker F.27 Friendship and Boeing 707 mail planes and 10r. stamp of 1870 (air) 1·50 65
MS699 150 × 105 mm. Nos. 696/8 (sold at 15e.) 9·50 9·50

1971. 5th Regional Soil and Foundation Engineering Conference, Luanda.
700 **94** 2e.50 multicoloured 25 15

96 16th-century Galleon at Mouth of Congo

1972. 400th Anniv of Camoens' "The Lusiads" (epic poem).
704 **96** 1e. multicoloured 50 15

97 Sailing Yachts

1972. Olympic Games, Munich.
705 **97** 50c. multicoloured 50 15

98 Fairey IIID Seaplane "Santa Cruz" near Fernando de Noronha

1972. 50th Anniv of 1st Flight Lisbon–Rio de Janeiro.
706 **98** 1e. multicoloured 25 15

99 W.M.O. Emblem

1974. Centenary of W.M.O.
707 **99** 1e. multicoloured 35 15

100 Dish Aerials

1974. Inauguration of Satellite Communications Station Network.
708 **100** 2e. multicoloured 35 25

101 Doris Harp

1974. Sea Shells. Multicoloured.
709 25c. Type **101** 10 10
710 30c. West African murex 10 10
711 50c. Scaly-ridged venus 10 10
712 70c. Filose latirus 15 10
713 1e. "Cymbium cisium" 15 10
714 1e.50 West African helmet 15 10
715 2e. Rat cowrie 15 10
716 2e.50 Butterfly cone 25 10
717 3e. Bubonian conch 35 15
718 3e.50 "Tympanotonus fuscatus" 40 15
719 4e. Great ribbed cockle 40 15
720 5e. Lightning moon 50 15
721 6e. Lion's-paw scallop 60 25
722 7e. Giant tun 75 25
723 10e. Rugose donax 1·00 40
724 25e. Smith's distorsio 3·00 1·10
725 30e. "Olivancilaria acuminata" 3·00 1·30
726 35e. Giant hairy melongena 3·25 1·70
727 40e. Wavy-leaved turrid 4·50 1·80
728 50e. American sundial 5·75 2·20

1974. Youth Philately. No. 511 optd **1974 FILATELIA JUVENIL**.
729 **51** 5c. multicoloured 15 60

103 Arm with Rifle and Star

104 Diquiche-ua-Puheue Mask

1975. Independence.
730 **103** 1e.50 multicoloured 10 10

1975. Angolan Masks. Multicoloured.
731 50c. Type **104** 10 10
732 3e. Bui ou Congolo mask 15 10

105 Workers

107 Pres. Agostinho Neto

1976. Workers' Day.
733 **105** 1e. multicoloured 10 10

1976. Stamp Day. Optd **DIA DO SELO 15 Junho 1976 REP. POPULAR DE**.
734 **51** 10e. multicoloured 1·50 1·25

1976. 1st Anniv of Independence.
735 **107** 50c. black and grey 10 10
736 2e. purple and grey 10 10
737 3e. blue and grey 10 10
738 5e. brown and buff 15 10
739 10e. brown and drab 25 10
MS740 59 × 75 mm. No. 739, but without President's name. Imperf 2·00

1976. St. Silvestre Games. Optd **S Silvestre Rep. Popular de**.
741 **62** 15e. multicoloured 55 35

1977. Nos. 518, 724/5 and 728 optd **REPUBLICA POPULAR DE**.
742 20e. Type **51** 3·50 3·50
743 25e. "Cymatium trigonum" 60 15
744 30e. "Olivancilaria acuminata" 75 25
745 50e. "Solarium granulatum" 1·25 40

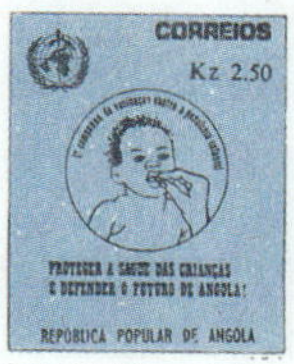

111 Child receiving Vaccine

112 Map of Africa and Flag

1977. Polio Vaccination Campaign.
746 **111** 2k.50 blue and black 10 10

1977. MPLA Congress.
747 **112** 6k. multicoloured 20 15

113 Human Rights Flame

114 Emblem

1979. 30th Anniv of Declaration of Human Rights.
748 **113** 2k.50 yellow, red & black 15 10

1979. International Anti-apartheid Year.
749 **114** 1k. multicoloured 10 10

115 Child raising Arms to Light

117 Pres. Agostinho Neto

1980. International Year of the Child (1979).
750 **115** 3k.50 multicoloured 15 10

1980. Nos. 697/8 optd **REPUBLICA POPULAR DE**.
751 4e.50 multicoloured (postage) 2·75 1·75
752 2e.50 multicoloured (air) 15 10

1980. National Heroes Day. Multicoloured.
753 4k.50 Type **117** 15 10
754 50k. Pres. Neto with machine-gun 1·25 70

118 Arms and Workers

119 "The Liberated Angolan" (A. Vaz de Carvalho)

1980. "Popular Power".
755 **118** 40k. blue and black 1·00 55

1980. 5th Anniv of Independence.
756 **119** 5k.50 multicoloured 15 10

120 Running

121 Millet

1980. Olympic Games, Moscow.
757 **120** 9k. pink and red 20 10
758 – 12k. light blue and blue 30 10
DESIGN: 12k. Swimming.

1980. Angolan Produce. Multicoloured.
759 50l. Type **121** 10 10
760 5k. Coffee 15 10
761 7k.50 Sunflower 20 10
762 13k.50 Cotton 30 15
763 14k. Petroleum 30 15
764 16k. Diamonds 35 20

1981. Nos. 708, 713/16 and 718/27 with "REPUBLICA PORTUGUESA" inscr obliterated.
(a) Dish aerials.
765 **100** 2e. multicoloured 10 10

(b) Sea Shells. Multicoloured.
766 1e. "Cymbium cisium" 10 10
767 1e.50 West African helmet 15 10
768 2e. Rat cowrie 20 10
769 2e.50 Butterfly cone 25 10
770 3e.50 "Tympanotonus fuscatus" 30 10
771 4e. Great ribbed cockle 35 15
772 5e. Lightning moon 40 15
773 6e. Lion's-paw scallop 45 20
774 7e. Giant tun 50 20
775 10e. Rugose donax 70 25
776 25e. Smith's distorsio 1·75 30
777 30e. "Olivancilaria acuminata" 1·90 65
778 35e. Giant hairy melongena 2·40 90
779 40e. Wavy-leaved turrid 3·00 1·00

122 Prisoner and Protesting Crowd

1981. 5th Anniv of Soweto Riots in South Africa.
780 **122** 4k.50 black, red & silver . . . 20 15

123 Basketball and Volleyball

1981. 2nd Central African Games. Multicoloured.
781 50l. Cycling and Tennis . . . 10 10
782 5k. Judo and Boxing 20 15
783 6k. Type **123** 25 15
784 10k. Handball and football 40 20
MS784a 116 × 129 mm. 15k. Swimming and javelin. Imperf 80 85

124 Statuette   125 "Charaxes kahldeni f. homeyri"

1981. "Turipex 81".
785 **124** 9k. multicoloured 40 20

1982. Butterflies. Multicoloured.
787 50l. Type **125** 10 10
788 1k. "Abantis gambesiaca" . . 10 10
789 5k. "Catacroptera cloanthe" . . 25 30
790 9k. "Myrina ficedula" (vert) 60 25
791 10k. "Colotis danae" 60 25
792 15k. "Acraea acrita bella" . . 80 30
793 100k. "Precis hierta cebrese" 5·25 2·40
MS793a 154 × 104 mm. Nos. 787/93. Imperf (sold at 30k.) . . . . . 1·40 1·40

126 "Silence of Night"

1982. 5th Anniv of Admission to United Nations. Multicoloured.
794 5k.50 Type **126** 25 15
795 7k.50 "Cotton Fields" . . . 35 15

127 Worker and Building   129 Angolan Woman and Emblem

128 "Albizzia versicolor"

1982. 20th Anniv of Angola Laboratory of Engineering. Multicoloured.
797 9k. Laboratory building (horiz) 40 20
798 13k. Type **127** (Research in construction materials) . . 45 25
799 100k. Geotechnical equipment 4·00 2·25

1983. Flowers (1st series). Multicoloured.
800 5k. "Dichrostachys glomerata" 25 10
801 12k. "Amblygonocarpus obtusangulus" 45 20
802 50k. Type **128** . . . . 2·00 1·10

1983. 1st Angolan Women's Organization Congress.
803 **129** 20k. multicoloured . . . 80 25

130 M'pungi (horn)

1983. World Communications Year. Multicoloured.
804 6k.50 Type **130** 25 20
805 12k. Mondu (drum) 50 45

131 Spear breaking Chain around South Africa

1983. 30th Anniv of Organization of African Unity.
806 **131** 6k.50 multicoloured . . . 30 25

132 "Antestiopsis lineaticollis intricata"

1983. "Brasiliana 83" International Stamp Exn, Rio de Janeiro. Harmful Insects. Multicoloured.
807 4k.50 Type **132** 25 15
808 6k.50 "Stephanoderes hampei" 35 25
809 10k. "Zonocerus variegatus" 60 45

133 Map of Africa and E.C.A. Emblem

1983. 25th Anniv of Economic Commission for Africa.
810 **133** 10k. multicoloured . . . 45 40

134 Collecting Mail   136 Dove

135 "Parasa karschi"

1983. 185th Anniv of Postal Service. Multicoloured.
811 50l. Type **134** 10 10
812 3k.50 Unloading mail from aircraft (horiz) 20 15
813 5k. Sorting mail (horiz) . . . 35 25
814 15k. Posting letter 85 80
815 30k. Collecting mail from private box (horiz) . . . . 1·75 1·50
MS816 142 × 78 mm. Nos. 812, 813 and 815 . . . . 2·20 1·90

1984. Moths. Multicoloured.
817 50l. Type **135** 10 10
818 1k. "Diaphone angolensis" 10 10
819 3k.50 "Choeropais jucunda" 30 15
820 6k.50 "Hespagarista rendalli" 50 35
821 15k. "Euchromia guineensis" 95 80
822 17k.50 "Mazuca roseistriga" 1·10 95
823 20k. "Utetheisa callima" . . 1·40 1·25

1984. 1st National Union of Angolan Workers Congress.
824 **136** 30k. multicoloured . . . 1·75 1·50

137 Flag and Agostinho Neto

1984. 5th National Heroes Day. Multicoloured.
825 10k.50 Type **137** 50 45
826 36k.50 Flag and Agostinho Neto (different) . . . . . 1·60 1·50

138 Southern Ground Hornbill

1984. Birds. Multicoloured.
827 10k.50 Type **138** 90 90
828 14k. Palm-nut vulture . . . . 1·25 1·25
829 16k. Goliath heron . . . . . 1·50 1·50
830 19k.50 Eastern white pelican 1·75 1·75
831 22k. African spoonbill . . . 2·00 2·00
832 26k. South African crowned crane . . . . 2·40 2·40

139 Greater Kudu

1984. Mammals. Multicoloured.
833 1k. Type **139** 10 10
834 4k. Springbok 25 15
835 5k. Chimpanzee 30 25
836 10k. African buffalo 55 50
837 15k. Sable antelope 80 65
838 20k. Aardvark . . . . 1·25 1·10
839 25k. Spotted hyena . . . . . 1·50 1·25

140 Sao Pedro da Barra Fortress

1985. Monuments. Multicoloured.
840 5k. Type **140** 25 20
841 12k.50 Nova Oerias ruins . . 60 55
842 18k. Antiga cathedral ruins, M'Banza Kongo 80 75
843 26k. Massangano fortress . . 1·25 1·10
844 39k. Escravatura museum . . 1·75 1·60

141 Flags on World Map   142 Flags and "XXV"

1985. 5th Anniv of Southern Africa Development Co-ordination Conference. Multicoloured.
845 1k. Type **141** 10 10
846 11k. Offshore drilling . . . . 1·25 50
847 57k. Conference session . . . 2·50 2·40

1985. 25th Anniv of National Union of Angolan Workers.
848 **142** 77k. multicoloured . . . 3·50 3·25

143 "Lonchocarpas sericeus"

1985. Medicinal Plants. Multicoloured.
849 1k. Type **143** 10 10
850 4k. "Gossypium sp." 20 15
851 11k. Senna 50 45
852 25k.50 "Gloriosa superba" 1·10 1·00
853 55k. "Cochlospermum angolensis" . . . . 2·50 2·40

144 Map of Angola as Dove and Conference Emblem

1984. Ministerial Conference of Non-aligned Countries, Luanda.
854 **144** 35k. multicoloured . . . 1·60 1·50

145 Dove and U.N. Emblem

1985. 40th Anniv of U.N.O.
855 **145** 12k.50 multicoloured . . 60 55

146 Cement Works

1985. 10th Anniv of Independence. Multicoloured.
856 50l. Type **146** 10 10
857 5k. Timber yard 20 15
858 7k. Quartz 30 25
859 10k. Iron works 50 45
MS860 210 × 123 mm. Nos. 856/9 1·10 95

147 Emblem, Open Book, Soldier, Farmer and Factory

1985. 2nd MPLA Congress.
861 **147** 20k. multicoloured . . . 90 85

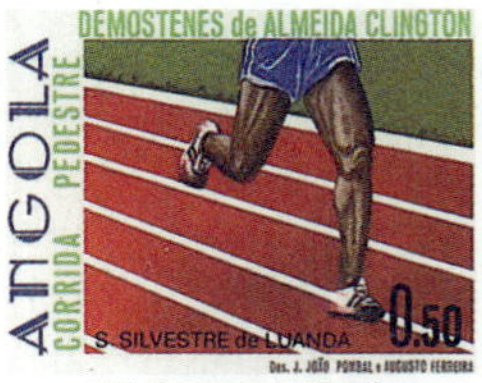

148 Runner on Track

1985. 30th Anniv of Demostenes de Almeida Clington Races. Multicoloured.
862 50l. Type **148** 10 10
863 5k. Two runners on road . . 20 15
864 6k.50 Three runners on road 30 25
865 10k. Two runners on track 50 45

149 Map, Stadium and Players

150 Crowd

1986. World Cup Football Championship, Mexico.

866 **149**	50l. multicoloured	10	10
867	– 3k.50 multicoloured	15	15
868	– 5k. multicoloured	30	25
869	– 7k. multicoloured	35	30
870	– 10k. multicoloured	50	45
871	– 18k. multicoloured	85	70

DESIGNS: 3k.50 to 18k. Different footballers.

1986. 25th Anniv of Armed Independence Movement.

872 **150**	15k. multicoloured	75	70

151 Soviet Space Project

1985. 25th Anniv of First Man in Space. Mult.

873	50l. Type **151**	10	10
874	1k. "Voskhod 1"	10	10
875	5k. Cosmonaut on space walk	20	15
876	10k. Moon vehicle	50	45
877	13k. "Soyuz"–"Apollo" link-up	60	55

152 National Flag and U.N. Emblem

1986. 10th Anniv of Angolan Membership of U.N.O.

878 **152**	22k. multicoloured	1·00	90

153 People at Work

155 Ouioca

154 Lecturer and Students (Faculty of Engineering)

1986. 30th Anniv of Popular Movement for the Liberation of Angola. Multicoloured.

879	5k. Type **153**	20	15
880	5k. Emblem and people (29 × 36 mm)	20	15
881	5k. Soldiers fighting	20	15

Nos. 879/81 were printed together, se-tenant, forming a composite design.

1986. 10th Anniv of Agostinho Neto University. Multicoloured.

882	50l. Type **154**	10	10
883	7k. Students and Judges (Faculty of Law)	30	25
884	10k. Students using microscopes and surgeons operating (Faculty of Medicine)	50	45

1987. Traditional Hairstyles. Multicoloured.

885	1k. Type **155**	10	10
886	1k.50 Luanda	10	10
887	5k. Humbe	20	15
888	7k. Muila	35	25
889	20k. Muila (different)	80	70
890	30k. Lunda, Dilolo	1·25	1·00

156 "Lenin in the Smolny Institute" (detail, Serov)

157 Pambala Beach

1987. 70th Anniv of Russian Revolution.

891 **156**	15k. multicoloured	60	25

1987. Scenic Spots. Multicoloured.

892	50l. Type **157**	10	10
893	1k.50 Quedas do Dala (waterfalls)	10	10
894	3k.50 Black Feet Rocks, Pungo Adongo (vert)	15	10
895	5k. Cuango River valley	20	15
896	10k. Luanda shore (vert)	40	35
897	20k. Serra da Leba road	80	75

158 Emblem

159 Dancers

1988. 2nd Angolan Women's Organization Congress. Multicoloured.

898	2k. Type **158**	10	10
899	10k. Women engaged in various pursuits	40	35

1988. 10th Anniv of Vitoria Carnival. Mult.

900	5k. Type **159**	15	10
901	10k. Revellers	40	35

160 Augusto N'Gangula (child revolutionary)

1989. Pioneers. Multicoloured.

902	12k. Type **160** (20th death anniv)	50	45
903	15k. Pioneers (25th anniv (1988) of Agostinho Neto Pioneers Organization)	60	55

161 Luanda 1st August Sports Club (1979–81)

1989. 10th National Football League Championship. Championship Winners. Multicoloured.

904	5k. Type **161**	15	15
905	5k. Luanda Petro Atletico (1982, 1984, 1986–88)	15	15
906	5k. Benguela 1st May Sports Club (1983, 1985)	15	15

162 Watering Cabbages

1990. 10th Anniv (1987) of International Fund for Agricultural Development.

907 **162**	10k. multicoloured	35	30

163 19th-century Middle-class Houses, Luanda

1990. Historical Buildings. Multicoloured.

908	1k. Type **163**	10	10
909	2k. Cidade Alta railway station, Luanda	1·75	30
910	5k. National Anthropology Museum	20	15
911	15k. Palace of Ana Joaquina dos Santos	55	50
912	23k. Iron Palace	80	75
913	36k. Meteorological observatory (vert)	1·25	1·10
914	50k. Governor's palace	1·75	1·60

164 "General Machado" and Route Map

1990. Benguela (915) and Luanda Railways. Mult.

915	5k. Type **164**	45	30
916	12k. Beyer-Garratt steam locomotive (facing left)	80	75
917	12k. Beyer-Garratt steam locomotive (facing right)	80	75
918	14k. Mikado steam locomotive	1·25	95
MS919	88 × 69 mm. 25k. Diesel-electric locomotive (39 × 29 mm)	1·70	1·50

165 Hydroelectric Production

1990. 10th Anniv of Southern Africa Development Co-ordinating Conference. Multicoloured.

920	5k. Type **165**	20	15
921	9k. Oil industry	90	30

166 Map in Envelope

1990. 10th Anniv of Pan-African Postal Union. Multicoloured.

922	4k. Type **166**	15	10
923	10k. Map consisting of stamps and envelopes	35	30

167 "Muxima"

1990. "Stamp World London 90" International Stamp Exn. Paintings by Raul Indipwo. Multicoloured.

924	6k. "Three Graces" (horiz)	20	15
925	9k. Type **167**	30	25

168 Antelope

1990. Protected Animals. Sable Antelope. Mult.

926	5k. Type **168**	2·40	1·90
927	5k. Male and female	2·40	1·90
928	5k. Female	2·40	1·90
929	5k. Female and young	2·40	1·90

169 Porcelain Rose

170 Zebra Drinking

1990. "Belgica 90" International Stamp Exhibition, Brussels. Flowers. Multicoloured.

930	5k. Type **169**	20	15
931	8k. Indian carnation	30	25
932	10k. Allamanda	35	30
MS933	113 × 139 mm. 40k. Hibiscus and "Manneqin Pis", Brussels (49 × 39 mm)	1·40	1·20

1990. International Literacy Year. Multicoloured.

934	5k. Type **170**	20	15
935	5k. Butterfly	20	15
936	5k. Horse's head	20	15
MS937	210 × 260 mm. 30 × 1k. Composite jungle-scene showing various animals and plants	2·50	2·20

171 Flag and People

1990. 10th Anniv of People's Assembly.

938 **171**	10k. multicoloured	35	30

172 Dove, Flag and Workers

174 Marimba

173 Uniform, 1961

1990. 3rd Popular Movement for the Liberation of Angola-Labour Party Congress.

939 **172**	14k. multicoloured	50	45

1991. 30th Anniv of Armed Independence Movement. Freedom Fighters' Uniforms. Mult.

940	6k. Type **173**	20	15
941	6k. Pau N'Dulo, 1962–63	20	15
942	6k. Military uniform, 1968	20	15
943	6k. Military uniform from 1972	20	15

1991. Musical Instruments. Multicoloured.

944	6k. Type **174**	10	10
945	6k. Ngoma ya Mucupela (double-ended drum)	10	10
946	6k. Ngoma la Txina (floor-standing drum)	10	10
947	6k. Kissange	10	10

175 Iona National Park

1991. African Tourism Year. Multicoloured.

948	3k. Type **175**	10	10
949	7k. Kalandula Falls	10	10
950	35k. Lobito Bay	70	30
951	60k. "Welwitschia mirabilis"	65	55

176 Kabir of the Dembos

1991. "Espamer '91" Spain–Latin America Stamp Exhibition, Buenos Aires. Dogs. Multicoloured.
953 5k. Type **176** 10 10
954 7k. Ombua 20 10
955 11k. Kabir massongo 15 10
956 12k. Kawa tchowe 15 10

177 Judo

178 Mother and Child

1991. Olympic Games, Barcelona (1992) (1st issue). Multicoloured.
957 4k. Type **177** 10 10
958 6k. Yachting 10 10
959 10k. Marathon 15 10
960 100k. Swimming . . . . . . 1·10 95

1991. 13th Anniv of Angolan Red Cross. Mult.
961 20k.+5k. Type **178** 30 20
962 40k.+5k. Zebra and foal . . 50 40

179 Quadrant and Galleon

1991. "Iberex '91" Stamp Exhibition. Navigational Instruments. Multicoloured.
963 5k. Type **179** 15 10
964 15k. Astrolabe and caravel . . 30 10
965 20k. Cross-staff and caravel . 50 20
966 50k. Navigation chart by Fran-cisco Rodrigues and galleon . . . . 1·50 60

180 Common Eagle Ray

181 Mukixi wa Mbwesu Mask

1992. Rays. Multicoloured.
967 40k. Type **180** 35 25
968 50k. Spotted eagle ray . . . 40 35
969 66k. Manta ray 55 40
970 80k. Brown ray 65 50
MS971 112 × 140 mm. 25k. "Atlantic manta" 15 15

1992. Quioca Painted Masks (1st series).
972 – 60k. orange and brown . . 15 10
973 – 100k. black, verm & red . 25 20
974 **181** 150k. pink and orange . . 35 30
975 – 250k. red and brown . . . 60 50
DESIGNS: 60k. Kalelwa mask; 100k. Mikixe wa Kino mask; 250k. Cikunza mask.
See also Nos. 1006/7 and 1021/4.

182 "Ptaeroxylon obliquum"

184 Dimba House

183 King and Missionaries

1992. "Lubrapex 92" Brazilian–Portuguese Stamp Exhibition, Lisbon. Medicinal Plants. Each brown, stone and deep brown.
976 200k. Type **182** 45 35
977 300k. "Spondias mombin" 70 55
978 500k. "Parinari curatellifolia" 1·25 1·00
979 600k. "Cochlospermum angolense" . . . . 1·40 1·10

1992. 500th Anniv (1991) of Baptism of First Angolans. Multicoloured.
980 150k. Type **183** 35 30
981 420k. Ruins of M'Banza Congo Church . . . . . . 1·00 80
982 470k. Muxima Church . . . 1·10 90
983 500k. Cross superimposed on children's faces . . . . . 1·25 1·00

1992. "Expo '92" World's Fair, Seville. Traditional Houses. Multicoloured.
984 150k. Type **184** 35 30
985 330k. Cokwe house 80 65
986 360k. Mbali house 85 70
987 420k. Ambwela house . . . 1·00 80
988 500k. House of the Upper Zambezi . . . . 1·25 1·00

185 Lovebirds

1992. Nature Protection. Peach-faced Lovebirds. Multicoloured.
989 150k. Type **185** 35 30
990 200k. Birds feeding 45 35
991 250k. Bird in hand 60 50
992 300k. Bird on perch 70 55

186 "Crucifixion"

1992. Visit of Pope John Paul II. Sheet 151 × 90 mm containing T **186** and similar vert design plus two labels.
MS993 340k. Type **186** 370k. "The Lost Soul" . . . . 1·40 1·10

187 Hurdling

1992. Olympic Games, Barcelona (2nd issue). Mult.
994 120k. Type **187** 30 25
995 180k. Cycling 45 35
996 240k. Roller hockey 55 45
997 360k. Basketball 85 70

188 Women with Nets

190 Crowd with Ballot Papers around Ballot Box

189 "Santa Maria"

1992. Fishing. Multicoloured.
998 65k. Type **188** 20 10
999 90k. Fishermen pulling in nets 30 15
1000 100k. Fishermen checking traps 35 20
1001 120k. Fishing canoes . . . 30 25

1992. 500th Anniv of Discovery of America by Columbus and Genova 92 International Thematic Stamp Exhibition. Sheet 95 × 70 mm.
MS1002 **189** 500k. multicoloured 50 40

1992. 1st Free Elections. Multicoloured.
1003 120k. Type **190** 30 25
1004 150k. Doves, map, people and ballot box 35 30
1005 200k. Dove, crowd and ballot box 45 35

1992. Quioca Painted Masks (2nd series). As T **181**.
1006 72k. brown, black and yellow 15 10
1007 80k. red, black and brown 20 15
1008 120k. pink, black and red 30 25
1009 210k. black and yellow . . . 50 40
DESIGNS: 72k. Cihongo mask; 80k. Mbwasu mask; 120k. Cinhanga mask; 210k. Kalewa mask.

191 Mail Van

1992. Introduction of Express Mail Service in Angola. Multicoloured.
1010 450k. Type **191** 55 45
1011 550k. Boeing 707 airplane 65 50

192 Weather Balloon

193 Rayed Hat

1993. World Meteorology Day. Meteorological Instruments. Multicoloured.
1012 250k. Type **192** 10 10
1013 470k. Actinometer 10 10
1014 500k. Rain-gauge 10 10

1993. Molluscs. Multicoloured.
1015 210k. Type **193** 10 10
1016 330k. Bubonian conch . . . 15 10
1017 400k. African pelican's foot 15 10
1018 500k. White spindle 20 15
MS1019 70 × 90 mm. 1000k. "Pusionella nifat" 40 30

194 Leopard

1993. Africa Day. Sheet 95 × 70 mm.
MS1020 **194** 1500k. multicoloured 60 45

1993. Quioca Art (1st series). As T **181**.
1021 72k. grey, red and brown 10 10
1022 210k. pink and brown . . . 10 10
1023 420k. black, brown & orge 10 10
1024 600k. black, red and brown 10 10
DESIGNS: 72k. Men with vehicles; 210k. Rider on antelope; 420k. Bird-plane; 600k. Carrying "soba".
See also Nos. 1038/41 and 1050/3.

195 "Sansevieria cylindrica"

196 Atlantic Hawksbill Turtle laying Eggs and Green Turtle

1993. Cacti and Succulents. Multicoloured.
1025 360k. Type **195** 10 10
1026 400k. Milk-bush 10 10
1027 500k. Indian fig 10 10
1028 600k. "Dracaena aubryana" 10 10

1993. Sea Turtles. Multicoloured.
1029 180k. Type **196** 10 10
1030 450k. Head of Atlantic hawksbill turtle and newly hatched turtles 10 10
1031 550k. Leather-back turtle . . 10 10
1032 630k. Loggerhead turtles . . 15 10
Nos. 1029/32 were issued together, se-tenant, forming a composite design.

197 People Dancing

1993. Union of Portuguese speaking Capital Cities. Sheet 95 × 71 mm.
MS1033 **197** 1500k. multicoloured 20 10

198 Vimbundi Pipe

199 St. George's Mushroom

1993. Tobacco Pipes. Multicoloured.
1034 72k. Type **198** 10 10
1035 200k. Vimbundi pipe (different) 10 10
1036 420k. Mutopa calabash water pipe 10 10
1037 600k. Pexi carved-head pipe 10 10

1993. Quioca Art (2nd series). As T **181**.
1038 300k. brown and orange . . 10 10
1039 600k. red and brown . . . 10 10
1040 800k. black, orange and deep orange 15 10
1041 1000k. orange and brown 20 15
DESIGNS: 300k. Leopard and dog; 600k. Rabbits; 800k. Birds; 1000k. Birds and cockerel.

1993. Fungi. Multicoloured.
1042 300k. Type **199** 55 15
1043 500k. Death cap 90 30
1044 600k. "Amanita vaginata" 1·10 35
1045 1000k. Parasol mushroom 1·90 60

200 "Cinganji" (figurine of dancer, Bie province)

201 Orgy

1994. National Culture Day. "Hong Kong '94" International Stamp Exhibition. Multicoloured.
1046 500k. Type **200** 10 10
1047 1000k. Chief's staff with carved woman's head (Bie province) 20 15
1048 1200k. Statuette of traveller riding ox (Huambo province) 25 20
1049 2200k. Corn pestle (Ovimbundu) 45 35

1994. Quioca Art (3rd series). As T **181**.
1050 500k. multicoloured 10 10
1051 2000k. red and brown . . . 40 30
1052 2500k. red and brown . . . 50 40
1053 3000k. carmine and red . . 60 50

DESIGNS: 500k. Bird on plant; 2000k. Plant with roots; 2500k. Plant; 3000k. Fern.

1994. AIDS Awareness Campaign. Multicoloured.
1054 500k. Type **201** 10 10
1055 1000k. Masked figure using infected syringe passing box of condoms to young couple 10 10
1056 3000k. Victims 20 15

202 Flag, Arrows and Small Ball

1994. World Cup Football Championship, U.S.A. Multicoloured.
1057 500k. Type **202** 10 10
1058 700k. Flag, four arrows and large ball 10 10
1059 2200k. Flag, goal net and ball 10 10
1060 2500k. Flag, ball and boot 10 10

203 Brachiosaurus

1994. "Philakorea 1994" International and "Singpex '94" Stamp Exhibitions. Dinosaurs. Multicoloured.
1061 1000k. Type **203** 10 10
1062 3000k. Spinosaurus 10 10
1063 5000k. Ouranosaurus . . . 10 10
1064 10000k. Lesothosaurus . . . 15 10
MS1065 102 × 145 mm. 19000k. Lesothosaurus and map (43 × 34 mm) 20 10

204 Brown Snake Eagle, Ostrich, Yellow-billed Stork and Pink-backed Pelican

1994. Tourism. Multicoloured.
1066 2000k. Type **204** 10 10
1067 4000k. Animals 10 10
1068 8000k. Women 10 10
1069 10000k. Men 10 10

205 Dual-service Wall-mounted Post Box

1994. Post Boxes. Multicoloured.
1070 5000k. Type **205** 10 10
1071 7500k. Wall-mounted philatelic post box 10 10
1072 10000k. Free-standing post box 10 10
1073 21000k. Multiple service wall-mounted post box . . 25 15

206 "Heliothis armigera" (moth)

1994. Insects. Multicoloured.
1074 5000k. Type **206** 10 10
1075 6000k. "Bemisia tabasi" . . 10 10
1076 10000k. "Dysdercus sp." (bug) 10 10
1077 27000k. "Spodoptera exigua" (moth) 25 15

207 "100"

1994. Cent of International Olympic Committee.
1078 **207** 27000k. red, yell & blk 25 20

208 Pot

1995. Traditional Ceramics. With service indicator. Multicoloured. (a) INLAND POSTAGE. Inscr "PORTE NACIONAL".
1079 (1°) Type **208** 10 10
1080 (2°) Pot with figure of woman on lid 10 10

(b) INTERNATIONAL POSTAGE. Inscr "PORTE INTERNACIONAL".
1081 (1°) Pot with man's head on lid 20 15
1082 (2°) Duck-shaped pot . . . 25 20

209 Making Fire

1995. The !Kung (Khoisan tribe). Multicoloured.
1083 10000k. Type **209** 10 10
1084 15000k. Tipping darts with poison 15 10
1085 20000k. Smoking 20 15
1086 25000k. Hunting 20 15
1087 28000k. Women and children 25 20
1088 30000k. Painting animals on walls 25 20

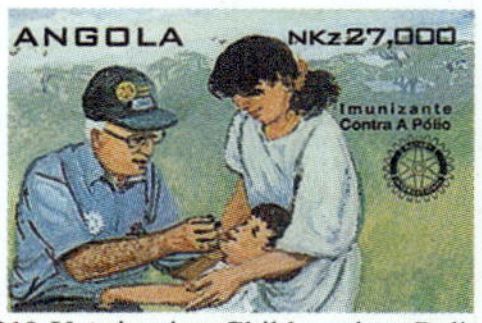

210 Vaccinating Child against Polio

1995. 90th Anniv of Rotary International. Multicoloured. (a) Inscr in Portuguese.
1089 27000k. Type **210** 15 10
1090 27000k. Examining baby . . 15 10
1091 27000k. Giving child vaccination 15 10

(b) Inscr in English.
1092 27000k. Type **210** 15 10
1093 27000k. As No. 1090 . . . 15 10
1094 27000k. As No. 1091 . . . 15 10
MS1095 Two sheets, each 110 × 80 mm. 81000k. Dove flying over map. (a) Inscr in Portuguese; (b) Inscr in English Set of 2 sheets 90 75

Nos. 1089/91 and 1092/4 respectively were issued together, se-tenant, forming composite designs.

211 "Sputnik 1" (satellite)

1995. World Telecommunications Day. Mult.
1096 27000k. Type **211** 15 10
1097 27000k. "Intelsat" satellite and space shuttle 15 10
MS1098 100 × 80 mm. Nos. 1096/7 30 20

212 Doves above Baby on Daisy-covered Map

1995. 20th Anniv of Independence.
1099 **212** 2900k. multicoloured . . 65 50

213 Child, Containers and Fork-lift Truck

1996. Goods Transportation. Multicoloured.
1100 200k. Type **213** 10 10
1101 1265k. Sailing boats and "Mount Cameroon" (ferry) 25 25
1102 2583k. Fork-lift trucks loading and unloading "Mount Cameroon" (ferry) 90 50
1103 2583k. Truck 60 50
MS1104 106 × 76 mm. 1265k. Ferry 25 25

214 Women in Agriculture

1996. 4th World Conference on Women, Peking (1995). Multicoloured.
1105 375k. Type **214** 10 10
1106 1106k. Women in education 25 20
1107 1265k. Women in business 30 25
1108 2900k. Dimba servant girl (vert) 65 50
MS1109 106 × 76 mm. 1500k. Traditional education (vert) . . 35 30

215 Verdant Hawk Moth

1996. Flora and Fauna. Multicoloured.
1110 1500k. Type **215** 10 10
1111 1500k. Western honey buzzard 10 10
1112 1500k. Bateleur 10 10
1113 1500k. Common kestrel . . 10 10
1114 4400k. Water lily 20 15
1115 4400k. Red-crested turaco 20 15
1116 4400k. Giraffe 20 15
1117 4400k. African elephant . . 20 15
1118 5100k. Panther toad 20 15
1119 5100k. Hippopotamus . . . 20 15
1120 5100k. Cattle egret 20 15
1121 5100k. Lion 20 15
1122 6000k. African hunting ("wild") dog 25 20
1123 6000k. Helmeted turtle . . . 25 20
1124 6000k. African pygmy goose 25 20
1125 6000k. Egyptian plover . . 25 20
MS1126 100 × 70 mm. 12000k. Spotted hyena 50 40

Nos. 1111/13, 1115/17, 1119/21 and 1123/5 respectively were issued together, se-tenant, forming composite designs.

216 California Quail

1997. Birds. Multicoloured.
1127 5500k. Type **216** 20 15
1128 5500k. Prairie chicken ("Greater Prairie Chicken") 20 15
1129 5500k. Indian blue quail ("Painted Quail") 20 15
1130 5500k. Golden pheasant . . 20 15
1131 5500k. Crested wood partridge ("Roulroul Partridge") 20 15
1132 5500k. Ceylon spurfowl ("Ceylon Sourfowl") . . . 20 15
1133 5500k. Himalayan snowcock 20 15
1134 5500k. Temminck's tragopan ("Temminicks Tragopan") 20 15
1135 5500k. Lady Amherst's pheasant 20 15
1136 5500k. Great curassow . . . 20 15
1137 5500k. Red-legged partridge 20 15
1138 5500k. Himalayan monal pheasant ("Impeyan Pheasant") 20 15
1139 5500k. Anna's hummingbird 20 15
1140 5500k. Blue-throated hummingbird 20 15
1141 5500k. Broad-tailed hummingbird 20 15
1142 5500k. Costa's hummingbird 20 15
1143 5500k. White-eared hummingbird 20 15
1144 5500k. Calliope hummingbird 20 15
1145 5500k. Violet-crowned hummingbird 20 15
1146 5500k. Rufous hummingbird 20 15
1147 5500k. Crimson topaz ("Crimson Topaz Hummingbird") 20 15
1148 5500k. Broad-billed hummingbird 20 15
1149 5500k. Frilled coquette ("Frilled Coquette Hummingbird") 20 15
1150 5500k. Ruby-throated hummingbird 20 15
MS1151 Two sheets, each 100 × 70 mm. (a) 12000k. Ring-necked pheasant; (b) 12000k. Racquet-tailed hummingbird Set of 2 sheets . . . . 1·40 1·20

217 Lions attacking Zebra

1996. African Wildlife. Multicoloured.
1152 180k. Type **217** 10 10
1153 180k. Lions watching zebras 10 10
1154 180k. African hunting dogs attacking gnu 10 10
1155 180k. Pack of hunting dogs chasing herd of gnu . . 10 10
1156 450k. Lions stalking isolated zebra 10 10
1157 450k. Male lion 10 10
1158 450k. Hunting dogs surrounding gnu 10 10
1159 450k. Close-up of African hunting dog 10 10
1160 550k. Cheetah 10 10
1161 550k. Cheetah chasing springbok 10 10
1162 550k. Leopard 10 10
1163 550k. Leopard stalking oryx 10 10
1164 630k. Cheetah running beside herd of springbok 10 10
1165 630k. Cheetah overpowering springbok 10 10
1166 630k. Leopard approaching oryx 10 10
1167 630k. Leopard leaping at oryx 10 10

Nos. 1152/67 were issued together, se-tenant, in sheetlets with each horizontal strip forming a composite design of lions, cheetah, hunting dogs or leopard attacking prey.

218 Couple with Elderly Woman

1996. 50th Anniv of U.N.O. Multicoloured.
1168 3500k. Type **218** 15 10
1169 3500k. Children at water pump 15 10
MS1170 104 × 74 mm. 8000k. Unloading sacks from ship . . 35 25

219 "Styrbjorn" (Swedish sail warship), 1789

1996. Ships. Multicoloured.
1171 6000k. Type **219** 35 20
1172 6000k. U.S.S. "Constellation" (United States frigate), 1797 . . . 35 20
1173 6000k. "Taureau" (French torpedo-boat), 1865 . . . 35 20
1174 6000k. French bomb ketch 35 20
1175 6000k. "Sardegna" (Italian battleship), 1881 . . . 35 20
1176 6000k. H.M.S. "Glasgow" (frigate), 1867 . . . . 35 20
1177 6000k. U.S.S. "Essex" (frigate), 1812 . . . . . 35 20
1178 6000k. H.M.S. "Inflexible" (battleship), 1881 . . . 35 20
1179 6000k. H.M.S. "Minotaur" (ironclad), 1863 . . . . 35 20
1180 6000k. "Napoleon" (French steam ship of the line), 1854 . . . . 35 20

1181 6000k. "Sophia Amalia" (Danish galleon), 1650 . . 35 20
1182 6000k. "Massena" (French battleship), 1887 . . . . 35 20
MS1183 Two sheets, each 105 × 74 mm. (a) 12000k. "Royal Prince" (English galleon), 1666 (vert); (b) 12000k. H.M.S. "Tremendous" (British ship of the line), 1806 (vert) Set of 2 sheets 1·40 1·20

220 Mask and Drilling Platform

1996. 20th Anniv of Sonangol. Multicoloured.
1184 1000k. Type **220** 30 10
1185 1000k. Storage tanks and mask of woman's face . . 10 10
1186 2500k. Mask with beard and gas bottles 10 10
1187 5000k. Refuelling airplane and mask of monkey's face 20 15

221 Slaves in Ship's Hold

1996. "Brapex 96" National Stamp Exhibition, Recife, Brazil. Multicoloured.
1188 20000k. Type **221** 10 10
1189 20000k. Ship capsizing . . . 20 10
1190 30000k. Boats punting out to ship 30 15
1191 30000k. Inspection of slaves 20 15
MS1192 100 × 70 mm. 50000k. Boats (close-up of detail of No. 1190) 30 20

222 Mission Church, Huila

223 Handball

1996. Churches. Multicoloured.
1193 5000k. Type **222** 10 10
1194 10000k. Church of Our Lady, PoPulo 10 10
1195 10000k. Church of Our Lady, Nazare 10 10
1196 25000k. St. Adriao's Church 10 10

1996. Olympic Games, Atlanta, U.S.A. Mult.
1197 5000k. Type **223** 10 10
1198 10000k. Swimming (horiz) 10 10
1199 25000k. Athletics 10 10
1200 35000k. Shooting (horiz) . . 15 10
MS1201 76 × 106 mm. 65000k. Basketball (horiz) 25 15

224 Dolphins, and Angola on Map of Africa

1996. 40th Anniv of Popular Movement for the Liberation of Angola (MPLA).
1202 **224** 30000k. multicoloured 15 10
The face value of No. 1202 is wrongly inscr as "300.00.00".

225 AVE, Spain

1997. Trains. Multicoloured.
1203 100000k. Type **225** 60 50
1204 100000k. "Hikari", Japan 60 50
1205 100000k. "Warbonnet" diesel locomotives, U.S.A. 60 50
1206 100000k. "Deltic" diesel locomotive, Great Britain 60 50
1207 100000k. "Eurostar", France and Great Britain 60 50
1208 100000k. ETR 450, Italy . . 60 50
1209 140000k. Class E1300 diesel locomotive, Morocco . . 85 70
1210 140000k. ICE, Germany . . 85 70
1211 140000k. Class X2000, Sweden 85 70
1212 140000k. TGV, France . . . 85 70
1213 250000k. Steam locomotive 1·10 90
1214 250000k. Garratt steam locomotive . . . . 1·10 90
1215 250000k. General Electric electric locomotive . . . . 1·10 90
MS1216 Two sheets. (a) 106 × 76 mm. 11000k. Via Rail diesel locomotive, Canada (49 × 37 mm); (b) 76 × 106 mm. 11000k. Canadian Pacific steam locomotive, Canada (37 × 49 mm) Set of 2 sheets . . . . 1·20 1·20
Nos. 1203/8 were issued together, se-tenant, forming a composite design.

226 Thoroughbred

1997. Horses. Multicoloured.
1217 100000k. Type **226** 45 35
1218 100000k. Palomino and Appaloosa 45 35
1219 100000k. Grey and white Arabs 45 35
1220 100000k. Arab colt 45 35
1221 100000k. Thoroughbred colt 45 35
1222 100000k. Mustang (with hind quarters of another mustang) 45 35
1223 100000k. Head of mustang and hind quarters of Furioso 45 35
1224 100000k. Head and shoulders of Furioso . . . 45 35
1225 120000k. Thoroughbred . . 55 45
1226 120000k. Arab and palomino 55 45
1227 120000k. Arab and Chincoteague 55 45
1228 120000k. Pintos 55 45
1229 120000k. Przewalski's Horse 55 45
1230 120000k. Thoroughbred colt 55 45
1231 120000k. Arabs 55 45
1232 120000k. New Forest pony 55 45
1233 140000k. Selle Francais . . 65 50
1234 140000k. Fjord 65 50
1235 140000k. Percheron 65 50
1236 140000k. Italian heavy draught horse 65 50
1237 140000k. Shagya Arab . . . 65 50
1238 140000k. Avelignese 65 50
1239 140000k. Czechoslovakian warmblood 65 50
1240 140000k. New Forest pony 65 50
MS1241 Two sheets, each 100 × 70 mm. (a) 215000k. Thoroughbred mother and foal; (b) 220000k. Head and shoulders of thoroughbred Set of 2 sheets 2·00 2·00
Stamps of the same value were issued together, se-tenant, Nos. 1217/24 and 1225/32 respectively forming composite designs.

227 Jules Rimet Trophy (Uruguay, 1930)

1997. World Cup Football Championship, France.
1242 **227** 100000k. black 45 35
1243 – 100000k. black 45 35
1244 – 100000k. multicoloured 45 35
1245 – 100000k. multicoloured 45 35
1246 – 100000k. black 45 35
1247 – 100000k. multicoloured 45 35
1248 – 100000k. black 45 35
1249 – 100000k. black 45 35
1250 – 100000k. multicoloured 45 35
1251 – 100000k. multicoloured 45 35
1252 – 100000k. black 45 35
MS1253 Two sheets. (a) 127 × 102 mm. 220000k. multicoloured (Angola team); (b) 76 × 102 mm. 250000k. multicoloured (Angola team, 1997) Set of 2 sheets . . . 2·00 2·00
DESIGNS—Victory celebrations: No. 1243, Germany (1954); 1244, Brazil (1970); 1245, Maradona holding trophy (Argentina, 1986); 1246, Brazil (1994). Official team photographs: 1247, Germany (1954); 1248, Uruguay (1958); 1249, Italy (1938); 1250, Brazil (1962); 1251, Brazil (1970); 1252, Uruguay (1930).

228 House Insurance

230 Royal Assyrian ("Terinos terpander")

229 Coral

1998. 20th Anniv of ENSA Insurance. Mult.
1254 240000k. Type **228** . . . . 1·10 90
1255 240000k. Forklift truck carrying egg (industrial risks) . . . . 1·10 90
1256 240000k. Egg on cross (personal accidents) . . . 1·10 90
1257 240000k. Egg on waves (pleasure boating) . . . . 1·10 90
MS1258 99 × 155 mm. 350000k. Emblem (59 × 39 mm) . . . . 1·50 1·50

1998. "Expo '98" World's Fair, Lisbon, Portugal. Multicoloured.
1259 100000k. Type **229** 45 35
1260 100000k. Sea urchin 45 35
1261 100000k. Seahorses 45 35
1262 100000k. Sea anemone . . . 45 35
1263 240000k. Sea slug . . . . . 1·10 90
1264 240000k. Finger coral . . . 1·10 90

1998. Butterflies. Multicoloured.
1265 120000k. Type **230** 55 45
1266 120000k. Wanderer ("Bematistes aganice") . . 55 45
1267 120000k. Great orange-tip ("Hebomoia glaucippe") 55 45
1268 120000k. Alfalfa butterfly ("Colias eurytheme") . . 55 45
1269 120000k. Red-banded perelite ("Pereute leucodrosime") 55 45
1270 120000k. Large copper ("Lycaena dispar") . . . 55 45
1271 120000k. Malachite ("Metamorpha stelenes") 55 45
1272 120000k. Tiger swallowtail ("Papilio glaucus") . . . 55 45
1273 120000k. Monarch ("Danaus plexippus") . . 55 45
1274 120000k. Grecian shoemaker ("Catonephele numili") 55 45
1275 120000k. Silver-studded blue ("Plebejus argus") 55 45
1276 120000k. Common eggfly ("Hypolimnas bolina") . . 55 45
1277 120000k. Brazilian dynastor ("Dynastor napolean") (horiz) 55 45
1278 120000k. Saturn butterfly ("Zeuxidia amethystus") (horiz) 55 45
1279 120000k. Pipevine swallowtail ("Battus philenor") (horiz) 55 45
1280 120000k. Orange-barred sulphur ("Phoebis philea") (horiz) 55 45
1281 120000k. African monarch ("Danaus chrysippus") (horiz) 55 45
1282 120000k. Green-underside blue ("Glaucopsyche alexis") (horiz) 55 45
MS1283 Three sheets. (a) 68 × 98 mm. 250000k. Gold-banded forester ("Euphaedra neophron"); (b) 98 × 68 mm. 250000k. Hewitson's uraneis ("Uraneis ucubis") on "Armillaria straminea" (fungus); (c) 98 × 68 mm. 250000k. Brown hairstreak ("Thecla betulae") (horiz) Set of 3 sheets . . . 1·90 1·90
Nos. 1265/70, 1271/6 and 1277/82 respectively were issued together, se-tenant, forming composite designs.

231 British Tortoiseshell

1998. Cats and Dogs. Multicoloured.
1284 140000k. Type **231** 65 55
1285 140000k. Chinchilla 65 55
1286 140000k. Russian blue . . . 65 55
1287 140000k. Black persian (longhair) (wrongly inscribed "Longhiar") . . 65 55
1288 140000k. British red tabby 65 55
1289 140000k. Birman 65 55
1290 140000k. West Highland white terrier 65 55
1291 140000k. Red setter 65 55
1292 140000k. Dachshund . . . 65 55
1293 140000k. St. John water-dog 65 55
1294 140000k. Shetland sheep-dog 65 55
1295 140000k. Dalmatian 65 55
MS1296 Two sheets, each 91 × 73 mm. (a) 500000k. Turkish van (swimming cat); (b) 500000k. Labrador retriever Set of 2 sheets 2·00 2·00

232 Dolphin, Yacht and Container Ship

1998. 1st Anniv of Government of Unity and National Reconciliation. Multicoloured.
1297 100000k. Type **232** 45 35
1298 100000k. Yacht, dolphin and container ship (different) 45 35
1299 100000k. Yacht, container ship and railway line . . 45 35
1300 100000k. Coastline and electricity pylons 45 35
1301 200000k. Grapes, goat and railway 95 75
1302 200000k. Village 95 75
1303 200000k. Tractor, grapes and railway 95 75
1304 200000k. Coal train 95 75
1305 200000k. Railway line with branch and pylons . . . 95 75
1306 200000k. Elephant and tip of tree 95 75
1307 200000k. Edge of coastline with pylon 95 75
1308 200000k. Tree trunk and coastline 95 75
Nos. 1297/1308 were issued together, se-tenant, forming a composite design.

233 Ostrich, Children and Blackboard

1998. Decade of Education in Africa. Sheet 100 × 70 mm.
MS1309 **233** 400000k. mult . . . 2·00 2·00

234 Lion

1998. Animals of the Grande Porte. Multicoloured.
1310 100000k. Type **234** 45 35
1311 100000k. Hippopotamus ("Hippopotamus amphibius") 45 35
1312 100000k. African elephant ("Loxodonta africana") 45 35
1313 100000k. Giraffe ("Giraffa camelopardalis") 45 35
1314 220000k. African buffalo ("Synceros caffer") . . . 1·00 80
1315 220000k. Gorilla ("Gorilla gorilla") . . . . 1·00 80
1316 220000k. White rhinoceros ("Ceratotherium simum") 1·00 80
1317 220000k. Gemsbok ("Oryx gazella") . . . . 1·00 80
There are errors in the Latin inscriptions.

235 Man kicking Football

1998. Eradication of Polio in Angola. Sheet 100 × 70 mm.
MS1318 **235** 500000k. mult . . . 2·00 2·00

236 Diana, Princess of Wales

237 "Pagurites sp."

1998. Diana, Princess of Wales Commemoration. Multicoloured.

1319 100000k. Type **236** 45 35
1320 100000k. Wearing white balldress 45 35
1321 100000k. Holding handbag 45 35
1322 100000k. Wearing black evening dress 45 35
1323 100000k. Holding bouquet (white jacket) 45 35
1324 100000k. Wearing pearl necklace (looking down) 45 35
1325 100000k. Wearing pearl necklace (head raised) 45 35
1326 100000k. Speaking, wearing green velvet jacket 45 35
1327 100000k. Wearing sunglasses 45 35
1328 100000k. Wearing black jacket and white blouse 45 35
1329 100000k. Wearing green blouse 45 35
1330 100000k. Holding flowers (black jacket) 45 35
1331 150000k. With young girl amputee 70 55
1332 150000k. With two amputees 70 55
1333 150000k. Walking through minefield 70 55
MS1334 76 × 106 mm. 400000k. In mine protective clothing 2·70 2·70

1998. International Year of the Ocean. Mult.

1335 100000k. Type **237** 45 35
1336 100000k. "Callinectes marginatus" (crab) 45 35
1337 100000k. "Thais forbesi" 45 35
1338 100000k. "Ostrea tulipa" 45 35
1339 100000k. "Balanus amphitrite" 45 35
1340 100000k. "Uca tangeri" 45 35
1341 170000k. "Littorina angulifera" 80 65
1342 170000k. Great hairy melongena ("Semifusus morio") 80 65
1343 170000k. "Thais coronata" 80 65
1344 170000k. "Cerithium atratum" on red branch 80 65
1345 170000k. "Ostrea tulipa" (different) 80 65
1346 170000k. "Cerithium atratum" on green branch 80 65
MS1347 Two sheets, each 85 × 110 mm. (a) 300000k. "Goniopsis" (crab) (horiz); (b) 300000k. Shell Set of 2 sheets 3·50 3·50

238 Mangos

1998. "Portugal 98" International Stamp Exhibition, Lisbon. Fruit and Vegetables. Multicoloured.

1348 100000k. Type **238** 45 35
1349 100000k. Guava 45 35
1350 120000k. Chillies 55 45
1351 120000k. Sweet corn 55 45
1352 140000k. Sliced bananas 65 55
1353 140000k. Avocadoes 65 55

239 Bimba Canoe

1998. Canoes. Multicoloured.

1354 250000k. Type **239** 1·10 90
1355 250000k. Sailing canoe, Ndongo 1·10 90
1356 250000k. Building canoes in Ndongo 1·10 90

240 "Titanic"

1998. The "Titanic" (liner that sank on maiden voyage, 1912). Sheet 200 × 160 mm containing T **240** and similar designs. Multicoloured.

MS1357 350000k. Type **240**; 350000k. Stern of "Titanic"; 350000k. "Titanic" under full steam (75 × 30 mm); 350000k. Bow of "Titanic" (37 × 60 mm) 3·50 3·50

241 Ultralight Plane

1998. Aircraft. Multicoloured.

1358 150000k. Type **241** 70 55
1359 150000k. Gyroplane 70 55
1360 150000k. Business jet 70 55
1361 150000k. Convertible plane 70 55
1362 150000k. Chuterplane 70 55
1363 150000k. Twin-rotor craft 70 55
1364 150000k. Skycrane 70 55
1365 150000k. British Aerospace/ Aerospatiale Concorde Supersonic airliner 70 55
1366 150000k. Flying boat 70 55
1367 200000k. Boeing 737-100 70 55
1368 200000k. Ilyushin Il-62M 70 55
1369 250000k. Pedal-powered plane 70 55
1370 250000k. Sail plane 70 55
1371 250000k. Aerobatic plane 70 55
1372 250000k. Hang-gliding 70 55
1373 250000k. Balloon 70 55
1374 250000k. Glidercraft 70 55
1375 250000k. Model airplane 70 55
1376 250000k. Air racing 70 55
1377 250000k. Solar-celled plane 70 55
MS1378 Four sheets. (a) 110 × 85 mm. 1000000k. Boeing 777 (84 × 28 mm); (b) 85 × 110 mm. 1000000k. Space shuttle Columbia (28 × 84 mm); (c) 100 × 70 mm. 1000000k. Boeing 737-200 (84 × 28 mm); (d) 100 × 70 mm. 1000000k. Boeing 747-300 (84 × 28 mm) Set of 4 sheets 3·00 3·00

Nos. 1358/66 and 1369/77 respectively were issued together, se-tenant, forming composite designs.

242 Parasaurolophus

243 Head

1998. Prehistoric Animals. Multicoloured.

1379 120000k. Type **242** 55 45
1380 120000k. Elaphosaurus 55 45
1381 120000k. Iguanodon 55 45
1382 120000k. Maiasaura 55 45
1383 120000k. Brontosaurus 55 45
1384 120000k. Plateosaurus 55 45
1385 120000k. Brachiosaurus 55 45
1386 120000k. Anatosaurus 55 45
1387 120000k. Tyrannosaurus rex 55 45
1388 120000k. Carnotaurus 55 45
1389 120000k. Corythosaurus 55 45
1390 120000k. Stegosaurus 55 45
1391 120000k. Iguanodon (different) 55 45
1392 120000k. Hadrosaurus (horiz) 55 45
1393 120000k. Ouranosaurus (horiz) 55 45
1394 120000k. Hypsilophodon (horiz) 55 45
1395 120000k. Brachiosaurus (horiz) 55 45
1396 120000k. Shunosaurus (horiz) 55 45
1397 120000k. Amargasaurus (horiz) 55 45
1398 120000k. Tuojiangosaurus (horiz) 55 45
1399 120000k. Monoclonius 55 45
1400 120000k. Struthiosaurus (horiz) 55 45
MS1401 Two sheets, each 85 × 110 mm. (a) 550000k. Tyrannosaurus (different); (b) 550000k. Triceratops Set of 2 sheets 2·40 2·40

1999. Endangered Species. The Lesser Flamingo (*Phoenicopterus minor*). Multicoloured.

1402 300000k. Type **243** 1·40 1·10
1403 300000k. Flamingo with wings outstretched 1·40 1·10
1404 300000k. Flamingo facing left 1·40 1·10
1405 300000k. Front view of flamingo 1·40 1·10

244 Hyacinth Macaw (*Anodorhynchus hyacinthinus*)

1999. Animals and Birds. Multicoloured.

1406 300000k. Type **244** 1·40 1·10
1407 300000k. Penguin (*Spheniscifformes*) (vert) 1·40 1·10
1408 300000k. Przewalski's horse (*Equus caballus przewalski*) (wrongly inscr "Equis") 1·40 1·10
1409 300000k. American bald eagle (*Haliaetus leucocephalus*) (vert) 1·40 1·10
1410 300000k. Spectacled bear (*Tremarctos ornatus*) 1·40 1·10
1411 300000k. Jay (*Aphelocoma*) 1·40 1·10
1412 300000k. Bare-legged scops owl (*Otus insularis*) 1·40 1·10
1413 300000k. Whale-headed stork (*Balaeniceps rex*) 1·40 1·10
1414 300000k. Atlantic ridley turtle (*Lepidochelys kempii*) 1·40 1·10
1415 300000k. Canadian river otter (*Lutra canadensis*) 1·40 1·10
1416 300000k. Swift fox (*Vulpes velox hebes*) 1·40 1·10
1417 300000k. Deer (*Odocoileus*) 1·40 1·10
1418 300000k. Orang-utan (*Pongo pygmaeus*) 1·40 1·10
1419 300000k. Golden lion tamarin (*Leontopithecus rosalia rosalia*) (inscr "Leontopitecus") 1·40 1·10
1420 300000k. Tiger (*Panthera tigris altaica*) 1·40 1·10
1421 300000k. Polecat (wrongly inscr "Tragelaphus eurycerus") 1·40 1·10
MS1422 Two sheets, each 110 × 85 mm. (a) 1000000k. Brown bear (*Ursus arctos horribilis*): (b) 1000000k. Giant panda (*Ailuropoda melanoleuca*) 9·50 9·50

245 Satellite circling Earth

1999. International Telecommunications Day.

1423 **245** 500000k. multicoloured 90 70

246 Waterfall, Andulo, Bie

1999. Waterfalls. Multicoloured.

1424 500000k. Type **246** 90 70
1425 500000k. Chiumbo, Lunda 90 70
1426 500000k. Ruacana, Cunene 90 70
1427 500000k. Coemba, Moxico 90 70

247 Emblem

1999. "Afrobasket '99" (Men's African Basketball Championship). Multicoloured.

1428 15000000k. Type **247** 70 55
1429 15000000k. Ball teetering on the edge of net, and players' hands 70 55
1430 15000000k. Hand scooping ball from edge of net 70 55
1431 15000000k. Flower holding ball 70 55
MS1432 95 × 83 mm. 25000000k. Enlarged detail from No. 1441 (39 × 29 mm) 1·25 1·25

248 African Continent

1999. South African Development Community (S.A.D.C.).

1433 **248** 1000000k. multicoloured 50 40

249 Duke and Duchess of York, 1923

250 Ekuikui II

1999. 100th Birthday of Queen Elizabeth, the Queen Mother. Multicoloured.

1434 **249** 200000k. black and gold 10 10
1435 – 200000k. mult 10 10
1436 – 200000k. mult 10 10
1437 – 200000k. mult 10 10
MS1438 154 × 157 mm. 500000k. Queen Mother in academic robes (37 × 50 mm) 25 25

DESIGNS: No. 1447, Portrait of Queen Mother wearing Star of the Garter; 1448, Queen Mother wearing fur stole; 1449, Queen Mother wearing blue hat.

1999. Rulers. Multicoloured.

1439 500000k. Type **250** 25 20
1440 500000k. Mvemba Nzinga 25 20
1441 500000k. Mwata Yamvu Nawej II 25 20
1442 500000k. Njinga Mbande 25 20
MS1443 104 × 76 mm. 1000000k. Mandume Ndemufayo 50 50

251 13th-century B.C. Pharaonic Barque

1999. Ships. Multicoloured.

1444 950000k. Type **251** 50 40
1445 950000k. Flemish carrack, 1480 50 40
1446 950000k. H.M.S. *Beagle* (Darwin), 1830 50 40
1447 950000k. *North Star* (paddle-steamer), 1852 50 40
1448 950000k. *Fram* (schooner, Amundsen and Nansen), 1892 50 40
1449 950000k. *Unyo Maru* (sail/ steam freighter), 1909 (inscr "Unyon") 50 40
1450 950000k. *Juan Sebastian de Elcano* (cadet schooner), 1927 50 40
1451 950000k. *Tovarishch*, (three-masted cadet barque), 1933 50 40
1452 950000k. *Bucentaur* (Venetian state galley), 1728 50 40
1453 950000k. *Clermont* (first commercial paddle-steamer), 1807 50 40
1454 950000k. *Savannah* (paddle-steamer), 1819 50 40
1455 950000k. *Dromedary* (steam tug), 1844 50 40
1456 950000k. *Iberia* (steam freighter), 1881 50 40
1457 950000k. *Gluckauf* (tanker), 1886 50 40
1458 950000k. *Cidade de Paris* (ocean steamer), 1888 50 40
1459 950000k. *Mauretania* (liner), 1906 50 40
1460 950000k. *La Gloire* (first armoured-hull ship), 1859 50 40
1461 950000k. *L'Ocean*, (French battery ship), 1868 50 40
1462 950000k. *Dandolo* (Italian cruiser), 1876 (inscr "Dandalo") and stern of H.M.S. *Dreadnought* 50 40
1463 950000k. H.M.S. *Dreadnought* (battleship), 1906 50 40
1464 950000k. *Bismarck* (battleship), 1939 and stern of U.S.S. *Cleveland* 50 40
1465 950000k. U.S.S. *Cleveland* (cruiser), 1946 50 40
1466 950000k. U.S.S. *Boston* (first guided-missile cruiser), 1942 and stern of U.S.S. *Long Beach* 50 40

1467 950000k. U.S.S. *Long Beach* (first nuclear-powered cruiser), 1959 . . . . . . 50 40
MS1468 Four sheets, each 75×70 mm. (a) 5000000k. 18th-century junk; (b) 5000000k. *Madre de Dios* (carrack) (wrongly inscr "Deus"), 1609; (c) 5000000k. Catamaran, 1861; (d) 5000000k. *Natchez* (Mississippi paddle-steamer), 1870 . . . . 9·50 9·50

Nos. 1474/5, 1476/7 and 1478/9 respectively were issued together, se-tenant, forming a composite design.

252 Fly Agaric (*Amanita muscaria*)

1999. Fungi. Multicoloured.
1469 1000000k. Type **252** (wrongly inscr "Aminita") 50 40
1470 1000000k. Bronze boletus (*Boletus*) 50 40
1471 1000000k. Lawyer's wig (*Coprinus comatus*) . . . 50 40
1472 1000000k. The blusher (*Amanita rubescens*) (inscr "Aminita") 50 40
1473 1000000k. Slimy-branded cort (*Cortinarius collinitus*) 50 40
1474 1000000k. Devil's boletus (*Boletus satanas*) 50 40
1475 1000000k. Parasol mushroom (*Lepiota procera*) 50 40
1476 1000000k. Trumpet agaric (*Clitocybe geotropa*) . . . 50 40
1477 1000000k. *Morchella crassipes* 50 40
1478 1000000k. *Boletus rufescens* 50 40
1479 1000000k. Death cap (*Amanita phalloides*) . . . 50 40
1480 1000000k. *Collybia iocephala* 50 40
1481 1000000k. *Tricholoma aurantium* 50 40
1482 1000000k. *Cortinarius violaceus* 50 40
1483 1000000k. *Mycena polygramma* 50 40
1484 1000000k. *Psalliota augusta* 50 40
1485 1000000k. *Russula nigricans* 50 40
1486 1000000k. Granulated boletus (*Boletus granulatus*) 50 40
1487 1000000k. *Mycena strobilinoides* 50 40
1488 1000000k. Caesar's mushroom (*Amanita caesarea*) 50 40
1489 1000000k. Fly agaric (*Amanita muscaria*) (different) 50 40
1490 1000000k. *Boletus crocipodius* 50 40
1491 1000000k. Cracked green russula (*Russula virescens*) 50 40
1492 1000000k. Saffron milk cap (*Lactarius deliciosus*) . . . 50 40
1493 1250000k. Caesar's mushroom (*Amanita caesarea*) (different) . . . 60 50
1495 1250000k. Red cracked boletus (*Boletus chrysenteron*) (wrongly inscr "chrysenteron") . . 60 50
1496 1250000k. Butter mushroom (*Boletus luteus*) 60 50
1497 1250000k. Lawyer's wig (*Coprinus comatus*) (different) 60 50
1498 1250000k. Witch's hat (*Hygrocybe conica*) . . . 60 50
1499 1250000k. *Psalliota xanthoderma* 60 50
MS1500 Two sheets, each 75×105 mm. (a) 5000000k. *Mycena lilacifolia*; (b) 5000000k. *Psalliota haemorrhoidaria* . . 5·00 5·00

253 Mercury and Venus

1999. 30th Anniv of First Manned Moon Landing. Multicoloured.
1501 3500000k. Type **253** 70 55
1502 3500000k. Jupiter 70 55
1503 3500000k. Neptune and Pluto 70 55
1504 3500000k. Earth and Mars 70 55
1505 3500000k. Saturn 70 55
1506 3500000k. Uranus 70 55
1507 3500000k. Explorer 17 satellite, 1963 . . . . . 70 55
1508 3500000k. Intelsat 4A satellite, 1975 . . . . . 70 55
1509 3500000k. GOES-D (Geostationary Operational Environmental Satellite), 1980 . . . . 70 55
1510 3500000k. Intelsat 2 satellite, 1966 . . . . 70 55
1511 3500000k. Navstar 2 (Navigation System with Timing And Ranging), 1978 . . . . 70 55
1512 3500000k. S.M.S. (Solar Maximum Mission) satellite, 1980 . . . . . 70 55
1513 3500000k. Earth and astronaut walking in space 70 55
1514 3500000k. Mariner 8 spacecraft 70 55
1515 3500000k. Viking 10 spacecraft 70 55
1516 3500000k. Ginga satellite . . 70 55
1517 3500000k. Soyuz 19 spacecraft (inscr "satelite") 70 55
1518 3500000k. Voyager spacecraft 70 55
1519 3500000k. Hubble space telescope (vert) 70 55
1520 3500000k. Launch of space shuttle *Atlantis* (vert) . . 70 55
1521 3500000k. Uhuru satellite (vert) 70 55
1522 3500000k. Mir space station (vert) 70 55
1523 3500000k. Gemini 7 spacecraft (vert) 70 55
1524 3500000k. Venera 7 spacecraft (vert) 70 55
MS1525 Five sheets (a) 95×85 mm. 6000000k. Astronaut from Apollo 17 walking on moon (vert); (b) 95×85 mm. 6000000k. Astronaut driving moon buggy (vert); (c) 85×110 mm. 12000000k. Launch of commercial satellite SBS 4 (vert); (d) 85×110 mm. Neil Armstrong (astronaut) (vert); (e) 110×85 mm. 12000000k. Earth and *Columbia* spacecraft . . . . 10·00 10·00

No. 1523 is inscribed "GEMNI" in error.

254 "Night Attack by 47 Ronins"

1999. 150th Death Anniv of Katushika Hokusai (artist). Multicoloured.
1526 3500000k. Type **254** 70 55
1527 3500000k. "Usigafuchi no Kudan" 70 55
1528 3500000k. Sketch of seated man 70 55
1529 3500000k. Sketch of animals and birds 70 55
1530 3500000k. "Autumn Pheasant" 70 55
1531 3500000k. Rural landscape 70 55
1532 3500000k. "Survey of the region" 70 55
1533 3500000k. Kabuki theatre 70 55
1534 3500000k. Sketch of hen . . 70 55
1535 3500000k. Sketch of wheelwright 70 55
1536 3500000k. "Excursion to Enoshima" 70 55
1537 3500000k. Sumida River landscape 70 55
MS1538 Two sheets, each 100×70 mm. (a) 12000000k. Japanese calligraphy between woman and child (vert); (b) 12000000k. Woman dressing hair (vert) . . . . 5·00 5·00

255 SNCF Class 242 Steam Locomotive

2000. "PHILEX FRANCE 99" International Stamp Exhibition, Paris. Locomotives. Two sheets, each 111×80 mm containing T **255** and similar horiz design. Multicoloured.
MS1539 (a) 12k. Type **255** (b) 12k. Prototype Linear Propulsion Hover Train . . . . 3·50 3·50

256 Zebra

2000. Fauna. Multicoloured.
1540 1k.50 Type **256** 45 35
1541 2k. Short-tailed fruit bat . . 65 50
1542 3k. California condor . . . 95 75
1543 5k.50 Lion . . . . 1·70 1·40
MS1544 Eight sheets:— 140×179 mm. (a) 3k.50×6, Florida white-tailed deer; Turkey; Beaver; Bullfrog; Manatee; Greenback cutthroat trout; (b) 3k.50×6, White-faced sapajou; Toucan; Eyelash viper; Tree frog; Golden lion tamarin; Harpy eagle: —140×179 mm. (vert) (c) 3k.50×6, Mountain gorilla; Black rhino; Cape buffalo; Jackson chameleon; Cape cobra; Meerkats; (d) 3k.50×6, Kangaroo; Koala; Rainbow bee-eater; Red-eyed tree frog; Townsville blue-eye; Snake-necked tortoise:—107×77 mm. (vert) (e) 12k. Cheetah; (g) 12k. Orang-utan: —70×100 mm. (vert) 12k. Ring-tailed lemur . . . . 23·00 23·00

257 Harpy Eagle

2000. Birds. Multicoloured.
1545 1k.50 Type **257** 70 55
1546 2k. Andean condor 65 50
1547 3k. Lappet-faced vulture (vert) 95 75
1547a 5k.50 Vulture . . . . . . 1·60 1·20
MS1548 Eight sheets 128×127 mm. (a) 3k.50×6, American kestrel (*Falco sparverius*) (inscr "sperterius"); Spectacled owl (*Pulsatrix perspicillata*); White-tailed kite (*Eleanus leucurus*) (inscr "Elemus"); Boobook owl (*Ninox novaeseelandiae*) (inscr "novaseseelandiar"); *Polemaetus bellicosus* (inscr "Polmactus"); Caracara (*Polyborus plancus*); (b) 3k.50×6, Northern goshawk (*Accipiter gentiles*) (inscr "Acolpiler genttlis"); Hawk owl (*Surnia ulula*) (wrongly inscr "Surnis"); Peregrine falcon (*Falco prregrinus*); Eastern screech owl (*Otus asio*); African fish eagle (*Haliaeetus vocifer*) (inscr "Haliaectus"); Laughing falcon (*Herpetotheres cachinnans*) (inscr "Herpetothers"):—85×127 mm. (c) 6k.50×3, Verreaux's eagle; Bonelli's eagle; African fish eagle: —127×85 mm. (d) 6k.50×3, Bald eagle (vert); Tawny eagle (vert); Eagle (vert); (e) 85×110 mm. 12k. Lanner falcon (vert); (f) 110×85 mm. 12k. King vultures; (g) 85×111 mm. 15k. Secretary bird (*Sagittarius serpentarius*); (h) 15k. Golden eagle (*Aquila chrysaetos*) (inscr "chrysectos") 14·50 14·50

258 Zebra (*Equs zebra*)

2000. Animals and Birds. Multicoloured.
1549 1k.50 Type **258** 55 45
1550 1k.50 Golden palm weaver (*Ploceus xanthops*) 55 45
1551 1k.50 Hunting dog (*Lycaon pictus*) 55 45
1552 1k.50 Cheetah (*Acinonyx jubatus*) 55 45
1553 1k.50 Gemsbok (*Oryx gazelle*) 55 45
1554 1k.50 Cape fox (*Vulpes chama*) (inscr "Otocyon megalotis") 55 45
1555 1k.50 Giraffe (*Giraffa camelopardalis*) 55 45
1556 1k.50 Golden jackal (*Canis aureus*) (inscr "adustus") 55 45
1557 1k.50 Potto (*Perodicticus potto*) 55 45
1558 1k.50 Lion (*Panthera leo*) 55 45
1559 1k.50 Lilac-breasted roller (*Coracias caudate*) (inscr "Coracus") 55 45
1560 1k.50 Bat-eared fox (*Otocyon megalotis*) . . . 55 45
1561 2k. Ostrich (*Struthio camelus*) . . . . 1·30 1·00
1562 2k. African wild cat (*Felis lybica*) . . . . 1·30 1·00
1563 2k. Impala (*Aepyceros melampus*) . . . . 1·30 1·00
1564 2k. Savanna monkey (*Cercopithecus aethiops*) 1·30 1·00
1565 2k. Black rhino (*Diceros bicornis*) . . . . 1·30 1·00
1566 2k. Baboon (*Papio*) . . . . 1·30 1·00
1567 2k. Caracal (*Felis caracal*) 1·30 1·00
1568 2k. Secretary bird (*Sagittarius serpentarius*) 1·30 1·00
1569 2k. Warthog (*Phacochoerus aethiopicus*) . . . . . . 1·30 1·00
1570 2k. Afro-Australian fur seal (*Arctocephalus pusillus*) . . 1·30 1·00
1571 2k. Malachite kingfisher (*Alcedo cristata*) . . . . . 1·30 1·00
1572 2k. Hippopotamus (*Hippopotamus amphibious*) . . . . . . 1·30 1·00
MS1573 Two sheets. (a) 85×110 mm.12k. Savanna monkey (vert); (b) 110×85 mm. 12k. Elephant (*Loxodonta Africana*) (vert) . . . . 13·00 13·00

259 Flowers and Birds (Lai-Ji)

2000. Millennium (1st issue). Cultural Events of the 16th-century. Multicoloured.
1574 2k.50 Type **259** 85 70
1575 2k.50 "Last Judgement", Orvieto Cathedral (Luca Signorelli) 85 70
1576 2k.50 "Enchanted Garden" (Hieronymus Bosch) . . . 85 70
1577 2k.50 Machiavelli (author of O Principe (beginning of modern politics)) 85 70
1578 2k.50 Illustration from Utopia (Sir Thomas More) 85 70
1579 2k.50 Martin Luther (church reform) 85 70
1580 2k.50 Charles I of Spain (holy Roman Emperor (unification of Europe)) 85 70
1581 2k.50 "School of Athens" (Rafael) 85 70
1582 2k.50 Juan Sebastion Elcano (first circumnavigation of the world) 85 70
1583 2k.50 Henry VIII (separation from Catholic church) 85 70
1584 2k.50 Spanish conquering Aztecs and Incas (exploration of Americas) 85 70
1585 2k.50 Plasencia Cathedral (beginning of Romanesque architecture) 85 70
1586 2k.50 Potatoes (first introduction into Europe) 85 70
1587 2k.50 Astrolabe (Copernicus' theory of the universe) 85 70
1588 2k.50 Priest and courtiers (Portuguese-Japanese trade) 85 70
1589 2k.50 "Self Portrait" (Albrecht Durer (death, 1528)) (60×40 mm) . . . 85 70
1590 2k.50 Woman, hourglass, inkwell and cross (declaration of rights of indigenous Americans by Queen Isabel of Castille) 85 70

260 Henry II of Germany

2000. Millennium (2nd issue). Monarchs and Popes. Multicoloured.
MS1591 Twelve sheets:— 165 × 198 mm. (a) 3k. × 4, Type **260**; Marina Mniszech, Queen Consort of Tsar Lzhedmitry (false Dmitri); Tsar Ivan IV; Tsar Ivan III; (b) 3k. × 4, Charles II of England; Lady Jane Grey; Leopold III of Belgium; Louis XV of France; (c) 3k. × 6, James I of England; James II of England; James VI of Scotland; Brian Boru, King of Ireland; William I of Prussia (inscr "William I of Germany"); Edward VI of England; (d) 3k. × 6, Pope Nicholas II; Pope Pascal II; Pope Sergius IV; Pope Victor II; Pope Victor III; Pope Urban III; Pope Innocent II; (e) 3k. × 6, Pope John XIII; Pope Agapetus II; Pope John XVIII; Pope Lucius II; (f) 3k. × 6, Pope Celestine II; Pope Clement II; Pope Clement III; Pope Gelasius II; Pope Benedict VII; Pope Gregory V:— 109 × 129 mm. (g) 12k. William IV of England; (h) 12k. Tsar Fyodor I; (i) 12k. Tsar Lzhedmitry; (j) 12k. Pope Gregory VII; (k) 12k. Pope Leo XIII; (l) 12k. Pope Leo IX . . . 16·00 16·00

261 Damaged Building, Kuito

2000. Buildings and People. Multicoloured.
1592 3k. Type **261** 75 60
1593 3k. People and Kunje–Kuito road 75 60
1594 4k. Post Office building . . 1·00 80
1595 4k. Police headquarters . . 1·00 80
1596 5k. Damaged apartments . . 1·10 85
1597 5k. Independence Plaza . . 1·10 85
1598 6k. Children . . . . 1·20 95
1599 6k. Man carrying sack . . . 1·20 95

262 Trees

2000. Children's Paintings. Multicoloured.
1600 3k. Type **262** 75 60
1601 4k. Wall . . . . 1·00 80
1602 5k. Rural scene . . . . . . 1·30 1·10

263 Directorate of Communications, Telephones and Telegraphs, Luanda

2000. Postal Buildings. Multicoloured.
1603 5k. Type **263** 85 65
1604 5k. ETP building, Mbanza Congo 85 65
1605 5k. CTT building, Namibe 85 65
1606 8k. ECP building, Luanda 1·30 1·00
1607 8k. ETP building, Lobito . . 1·30 1·00
1608 8k. ECP building, Luanda (different) . . . . 1·30 1·00

264 Tank, Rifle and Dove

2001. 25th Anniv of Independence. Sheet 140 × 47 mm containing T **264** and similar horiz design. Multicoloured.
MS1609 12k. Type **264**; 12k. Dove, mattock and tractor . . . . 3·25 3·25

265 Radio Studio

2001. 25th Anniv of Public Radio (MS1613a, MS1613c) and Television (others). Four sheets containing T **265** and similar multicoloured designs.
MS1610 (a) 154 × 80 mm. 9k.50, Type **265**; 9k.50, Reporter in war zone; 9k.50 Carrying stretcher from burning aeroplane. (b) 154 × 80 mm. 9k.50, Television studio; 9k.50, Cameraman filming tank; 9k.50, Women and children crossing water. (c) 99 × 60 mm. 12k. Reporter in war zone (detail) (42 × 28 mm). (d) 99 × 60 mm. 12k. Cameraman filming tank (detail) (28 × 42 mm) (vert) . . . . . 10·50 10·50

266 Hands holding Book

2001. Africa Day. Multicoloured.
1611 10k. Type **266** . . . . . . 1·30 1·00
1612 10k. Hands and xylophone 1·30 1·00
MS1613 130 × 90 mm. 30k. Map of Africa . . . . 4·00 4·00

267 *Nicolaia speciosa*

2001. Flowers. Belgica 2001 International Stamp Exhibition. Multicoloured.
1614 8k. Type **267** . . . . 1·00 85
1615 9k. *Allamanda cathartica* (inscr "cathartca") . . . 1·10 85
1616 10k. *Welwitschia mirabilis* 1·30 1·00
1617 10k. *Tagetes patula* . . . . 1·30 1·00
MS1618 130 × 90 mm. 30k. No. 1616 4·00 4·00

268 Man wearing Dark Glasses

2001. Total Eclipse of the Sun, 21 June 2001. Sheet 130 × 90 mm.
MS1619 **268** 30k. multicoloured 4·00 4·00

269 West African Lungfish (*Protopterus annectens*)

2001. Freshwater Fish. Multicoloured.
1620 11k. Type **269** . . . . . . 1·10 90
1621 17k. *Protopterus amphibious* 1·90 1·50
1622 18k. *Tilapia ruweti* . . . . 1·90 1·50
MS1623 130 × 90 mm. 36k. Red-breasted tilapia (*Tilapia rendalli*) 4·00 4·00

270 Ovambo Efundula, Cunene

2001. Traditional Dances. Multicoloured.
1624 11k. Type **270** . . . . . . 1·10 90
1625 11k. Massembo, Luanda . . 1·10 90
1626 17k. Macolo Batuque, Uige 1·90 1·50
1627 18k. Mukixi, Lunda Tchokwe . . . . 1·90 1·50
1628 18k. Humbi Puberdade, Namibe . . . . 1·90 1·50
MS1629 130 × 90 mm. 36k. Carnival Juvenil, Luanda . . . . 4·00 4·00

271 Hand-woven Hat, Banda

2001. Woven Crafts. Sheet 130 × 90 mm containing T **271** and similar horiz design. Multicoloured.
MS1630 17k. Type **271**; 18k. Hat with extensions, Kijinga . . . 3·75 3·75

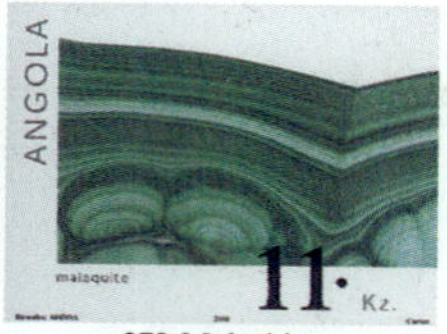

272 Malachite

2001. Minerals. Multicoloured.
1631 11k. Type **272** . . . . . . 1·10 90
1632 11k. Hematite . . . . . . 1·10 90
1633 18k. Diamond . . . . . . 1·90 1·50
1634 18k. Psilomelane . . . . . 1·90 1·50

273 Mwana Mpwevo

2002. Masks. Multicoloured.
1635 10k. Type **273** (Ngangela animistic ritual) . . . . . 1·00 1·50
1636 11k. Mukixi (Cokwe circumcision ritual) . . . 1·10 1·50
1637 11k. Mbunda (comic) . . . 1·10 1·50
1638 17k. Mwana Pwo (Cokwe circumcision ritual) . . . 1·90 1·50
1639 18k. Likisi-Cinganji (supernatural incarnation) 1·90 1·50
MS1640 90 × 80 mm. 36k. Ndemba (Bakongo circumcision ritual) 4·00 4·00

274 Players and Football

2002. Football World Cup Championship, Japan and South Korea. Multicoloured.
1641 35c. Type **274** . . . . . . 3·75 3·00
1642 37c. Players and ball (different) . . . . . . 4·00 3·25
MS1643 55 × 120 mm. Nos. 1641/2 7·25 7·25

275 Figure with Target on Chest

2002. Socialist International Congress. Multicoloured.
1644 10k. Type **275** (abolition of the death penalty) . . . . 1·00 80
1645 10k. Woman (end to violence against women) 1·00 80
1646 10k. Faces (combating poverty) . . . . 1·00 80
1647 10k. Map and dollar sign (eliminate foreign debt) 1·00 80
1648 10k. Map ("Africa in Peril" combating poverty) . . . 1·00 80
MS1649 40 × 30 mm. Nos. 1644/7 5·00 5·00

276 National Map, Rainbow and Dove

2002. Peace and Reconciliation Commission.
1650 **276** 35k. multicoloured . . . 2·00 1·60

277 Python (*Python anchietae*) (inscr "pithon")

2002. Reptiles. Multicoloured.
1651 21k. Type **277** . . . . . . 1·20 95
1652 35k. *Lacerta* (lizard) . . . . 1·90 1·50
1653 37k. *Naja Nigicollis* . . . 2·10 1·60
1654 40k. *Crocodylus niloticus* . . 2·20 1·70

278 Lighthouse, Barra do Dande

2002. Lighthouses and Buoys. Multicoloured.
1655 45k. Type **278** . . . . . . 2·20 1·70
1656 45k. Snake Head lighthouse, Soyo . . . . 2·20 1·70
1657 45k. Tafe lighthouse, Cabinda Bay . . . . . . 2·20 1·70
1658 45k. Moita Seca lighthouse, South Margin Bay . . . 2·20 1·70
1659 45k. Red buoy no. 9, Luanda Bay . . . . . . 2·20 1·70
1660 45k. Green buoy no. 1, Luanda Bay . . . . . . 2·20 1·70

279 Partial Eclipse (one third)

2002. Total Eclipse of the Sun (21 June 2001). Sheet 155 × 80 mm containing T **279** and similar horiz designs showing stages of eclipse. Multicoloured.
MS1661 21k. Type **279**; 35k. Two thirds; 37k. Total eclipse . . . 5·25 5·25

280 Antonio Manuel (17th-century Congolese ambassador to Pope Paul V) and Lion

2002. Angola—Italy Friendship. Multicoloured.
1662 35k. Type **280** . . . . . . 1·90 1·50
1663 45k. Antonio Manuel and papal plaque . . . . . . 2·20 1·70
MS1664 120 × 72 mm. Nos. 1662/3 4·00 4·00

281 Omolingui (Ovimbundo water pot)

2002. Pottery. Multicoloured.
1665 27k. Type **281** . . . . . . 1·50 1·20
1666 45k. Mulondo (Luvale drinking jar) . . . . . . 2·20 1·70
1667 47k. Ombya Yo Tuma (Ovimbundo food pot) . . 2·50 2·00
MS1668 120 × 72 mm. 51k. Sanga (Bakongo drinking vessel) . . . 2·75 2·75

282 Trees, Satellite Dish and UN Emblem

2003. 3rd United Nations Science, Technology and Development Meeting.
1669 **282** 50k. multicoloured . . . 2·75 2·20

283 Stylized Bi-plane

2003. Centenary of Powered Flight.
1670 **283** 25k. multicoloured 1·40 1·10

284 Antonio Jacinto

2003. Writers. Multicoloured.
1671 27k. Type **284** 1·50 1·20
1672 45k. Antonio Agostinho Neto 2·20 1·70
MS1673 121 × 90 mm. 27k. Antonio Jacinto wearing cap; 45k. Agostinho Neto as younger man 3·75 3·75

285 Two Antelope

2003. Sable Antelope (*Hippotragus niger*). Multicoloured.
1674 27k. Type **285** 1·50 1·20
1675 45k. Two antelope with straight horns 2·20 1·70
1676 47k. One antelope with curved horns 2·50 2·00

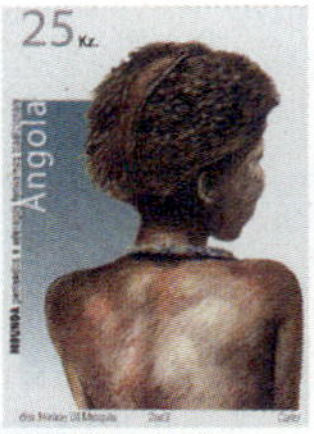

286 Mbunda Woman

2003. Traditional Women's Hairstyles. Sheet 130 × 120 mm containing T **286** and similar vert designs.
MS1677 25k. × 6, Type **286**; Soyo; Huila; Humbi; Cabinda; Quipungu 8·00 8·00

287 Musicians (detail, "Ascensao") (Jorge Afonso)

2003. Christmas. Multicoloured.
1678 27k. Type **287** 1·50 1·20
1679 27k. "AdoraÇao dos Pastores" (Andre Reinoso) 1·50 1·20
1680 45k. Holy Family (detail, "AdoraÇao dos Pastores") (Josefa de Obidos) 2·20 1·70
1681 45k. Cherubs (detail, "AdoraÇao dos Pastores") (Josefa de Obidos) 2·20 1·70
MS1682 110 × 92 mm. Nos. 1678/81 7·50 7·50

288 Bryde's Whale (*Balaenoptera edeni*)

2003. Marine Mammals. Multicoloured.
1683 27k. Type **288** 1·50 1·20
1684 45k. Heaviside's dolphin (*Cephalorhynchus heavisidii*) 2·20 1·70
MS1685 120 × 84 mm. 27k. Type **288**; 47k. Pilot whale (Globicephala melaena) (inscr "Giobiocephaia") 4·00 4·00

289 Tawny Eagle (*Aquila rapax*)

2003. Eagles. Multicoloured.
1686 20k. Type **289** 1·00 80
1687 20k. Martial eagle (*Hieraaetus bellicosus*) (inscr "Polemaetus") 1·00 80
1688 25k. African fish eagle (*Haliaeetus vocifer*) 1·40 1·10
1689 25k. Bateleur (*Terathopius ecaudatus*) 1·40 1·10
MS1690 120 × 80 mm. 45k. Verreaux's eagle (*Aquila verreauxi*) 2·20 2·20

290 Chess Pieces

2003. Chess. Multicoloured.
1691 45k. Type **290** 2·20 1·70
1692 45k. Board and pieces 2·20 1·70

291 Pope John Paul II

2003. 25th Anniv of the Pontificate of Pope John Paul II. Multicoloured.
1693 27k. Type **291** 1·50 1·20
1694 27k. Pope John Paul II with raised hand 1·50 1·20

292 *Adansonia digitata*

2004. Southern African Development Community. Plants. Multicoloured.
1695 27k. Type **292** 1·20 95
1695a 27k. *Psidium guayava* 1·20 95
1696 45k. *Carica papaya* 2·00 1·60
1697 45k. *Cymbopogon citrates* 2·00 1·60
MS1698 129 × 105 mm. Nos. 1695/7 5·25 5·25

293 Basketball

2004. Olympic Games, Athens. Multicoloured.
1699 27k. Type **293** 1·20 95
1700 27k. Handball 1·20 95
1701 45k. Running 2·00 1·60
1702 45k. Volleyball 2·00 1·60

294 Humpback Whales (*Megaptera novaeangliae*)

2004. Sea Mammals. Multicoloured.
1703 27k. Type **294** 1·20 95
1704 27k. Heaviside's dolphin (*Cephalorhynchus heavisidii*) 1·20 95
1705 45k. Bottlenose dolphin (*Tursiops truncates*) 2·00 1·60
MS1706 135 × 80 mm. 99k. *Megaptera novaeangliae* (different) 4·25 4·25
Nos. 1703/5 were issued together, se-tenant, forming a composite design.

295 Saddle Tanker (Benguela)

2004. Trains. Multicoloured.
1707 27k. Type **295** 1·20 95
1708 27k. Diesel locomotive (Mocamedes) 1·20 95
1709 27k. Locomotive CFB 225 (Benguela) 1·20 95

296 Fireman and Campaign Emblem

2004. Fire Emergency Phone Number Publicity Campaign. Multicoloured.
1710 27k. Type **296** 1·20 95
1711 27k. Fire appliance 1·20 95
1712 45k. Fire appliance facing right 2·00 1·60
MS1713 130 × 80 mm. Nos. 1710/12 4·25 4·25

297 Globe and Footballers

2004. Centenary of FIFA (Federation Internationale de Football Association).
1714 **297** 45k. multicoloured 2·00 1·60

298 Three Kings

2004. Christmas. Multicoloured.
1715 27k. Type **298** 1·20 95
1716 45k. Nativity 2·00 1·60
Nos. 1715/16 were issued together, se-tenant, forming a composite design.

299 Family of Monkeys

2004. Colobus Monkey (*Colobus angolensis*). Multicoloured.
1717 27k. Type **299** 1·20 95
1718 27k. Mother and baby 1·20 95
1719 27k. Male 1·20 95
1720 27k. Facing left 1·20 95

300 Woman and City Skyline

2005. 50th Anniv of Rotary of Luanda. Multicoloured.
1721 45k. Type **300** 2·00 1·60
1722 51k. Woman and countryside 2·20 1·70
MS1723 120 × 80 mm. Nos. 1721/2 4·25 3·25

APPENDIX

1995.

90th Anniv of Rotary International (on gold foil). 81000k.

CHARITY TAX STAMPS

Used on certain days of the year as an additional tax on internal letters. If one was not used in addition to normal postage, postage due stamps were used to collect the deficiency and the fine.

1925. Marquis de Pombal Commemorative stamps of Portugal but inscr "ANGOLA".
C343 C **73** 15c. violet 90 85
C344 – 15c. violet 90 85
C345 C **75** 15c. violet 90 85

C **15**

C **29**

C **52** Old Man

1929.
C347 C **15** 50c. blue 4·50 1·50

1939. No gum.
C413 C **29** 50c. green 2·40 20
C414 1a. red 3·50 1·60

1955. Heads in brown.
C646 C **52** 50c. orange 15 10
C647 – 1e. red (Boy) 15 10
C648 – 1e.50 green (Girl) 15 10
C522 – 2e.50 blue (Old woman) 60 35

1957. Surch.
C535 C **52** 10c. on 50c. orange 20 15
C534 30c. on 50c. orange 25 25

C **58** Mother and Child

C **75** "Full Employment"

C **65** Yellow, White and Black Men

1959.
C538 C **58** 10c. black and orange 20 15
C539 – 30c. black and slate 20 15
DESIGN: 30c. Boy and girl.

1962. Provincial Settlement Committee.
C568 C **65** 50c. multicoloured 25 15
C569 1e. multicoloured 40 15

1965. Provincial Settlement Committee.
C643 C **75** 50e. multicoloured 20 15
C644 1e. multicoloured 20 15
C645 2e. multicoloured 25 15

C **95** Planting Tree

1972. Provincial Settlement Committee.
C701 C **95** 50c. red and brown 15 15
C702 – 1e. black and green 15 15
C703 – 2e. black and brown 15 15
DESIGNS: 1e. Agricultural workers; 2e. Corncobs and flowers.

NEWSPAPER STAMP

1893. "Newspaper" key-type inscr "ANGOLA".
N51 V 2½r. brown 2·30 1·10

POSTAGE DUE STAMPS

1904. "Due" key-type inscr "ANGOLA".
D150 W 5r. green 30 30
D151 10r. grey 30 30
D152 20r. brown 65 35
D153 30r. orange 65 35
D154 50r. brown 85 55
D155 60r. brown 7·50 4·00
D156 100r. mauve 3·25 2·10
D157 130r. blue 3·25 2·10

D158	200r. red	9·25	5·00
D159	500r. lilac	7·75	4·25

See also Nos. D343/52.

1911. Nos. D150/9 optd **REPUBLICA**.

D166	W 5r. green	25	20
D167	10r. grey	25	20
D168	20r. brown	25	20
D169	30r. orange	40	20
D170	50r. brown	40	20
D171	60r. brown	1·10	70
D172	100r. mauve	1·10	70
D173	130r. blue	1·30	85
D174	200r. red	1·50	85
D175	500r. lilac	1·70	1·50

1921. Values in new currency.

D343	W ½c. green	25	20
D344	1c. grey	25	20
D345	2c. brown	25	20
D346	3c. orange	25	20
D347	5c. brown	25	20
D348	6c. brown	25	20
D349	10c. mauve	35	30
D350	13c. blue	70	65
D351	20c. red	70	65
D352	50c. grey	70	65

1925. Marquis de Pombal stamps of Angola, as Nos. C343/5, optd **MULTA**.

D353	C **73** 30c. violet	90	85
D354	– 30c. violet	90	85
D355	C **75** 30c. violet	90	85

1949. Surch **PORTEADO** and value.

D438	**17** 10c. on 20c. grey	25	20
D439	20c. on 30c. green	45	40
D440	30c. on 50c. brown	70	60
D441	40c. on 1a. red	1·00	95
D442	50c. on 2a. mauve	1·50	1·40
D443	1a. on 5a. green	1·70	1·60

D 45

1952. Numerals in red, name in black.

D483	D **45** 10c. brown and olive	20	15
D484	30c. green and blue	20	15
D485	50c. brown & lt brn	20	15
D486	1a. blue, green & orge	40	40
D487	2a. brown and red	55	50
D488	5a. brown and blue	55	50

ANGRA — Pt. 9

A district of the Azores, which used the stamps of the Azores except from 1892 to 1905.

1000 reis = 1 milreis.

1892. As T **4** of Funchal, inscr "ANGRA".

16	5r. yellow	2·75	1·80
5	10r. mauve	3·25	1·80
6	15r. brown	3·75	2·75
7	20r. violet	3·75	2·75
8	25r. green	4·50	75
9	50r. blue	7·75	4·00
10	75r. red	8·75	5·25
11	80r. green	10·00	9·75
24	100r. brown on yellow	38·00	14·00
13	150r. red on rose	50·00	41·00
14	200r. blue on blue	50·00	41·00
15	300r. blue on brown	50·00	41·00

1897. "King Carlos" key-type inscr "ANGRA".

28	S 2½r. grey	70	45
29	5r. red	70	45
30	10r. green	70	45
31	15r. brown	8·75	6·00
43	15r. green	85	60
32	20r. lilac	1·80	1·30
33	25r. green	2·75	1·20
44	25r. red	65	60
34	50r. blue	5·25	1·70
46	65r. blue	1·20	60
35	75r. red	3·25	1·60
47	75r. brown on yellow	13·00	10·50
36	80r. mauve	1·40	1·20
37	100r. blue on blue	2·50	1·70
48	115r. red on pink	2·50	2·00
49	130r. brown on cream	2·40	2·00
38	150r. brown on yellow	2·40	1·70
50	180r. grey on pink	3·00	2·75
39	200r. purple on pink	4·75	4·75
40	300r. blue on pink	7·25	6·25
41	500r. black on blue	15·00	13·00

ANGUILLA — Pt. 1

St. Christopher, Nevis and Anguilla were granted Associated Statehood on 27 February 1967, but following a referendum Anguilla declared her independence and the St. Christopher authorities withdrew. On 7 July 1969, the Anguilla post office was officially recognised by the Government of St. Christopher, Nevis and Anguilla and normal postal communications via St. Christopher were resumed.

By the Anguilla Act of 27 July 1971, the island was restored to direct British control.

100 cents = 1 West Indian dollar.

1967. Nos. 129/44 of St. Kitts-Nevis optd **Independent Anguilla** and bar.

1	– ½c. sepia and blue	42·00	26·00
2	**33** 1c. multicoloured	45·00	9·50
3	– 2c. multicoloured	45·00	2·00
4	– 3c. multicoloured	45·00	4·50
5	– 4c. multicoloured	45·00	5·50
6	– 5c. multicoloured	£160	27·00
7	– 6c. multicoloured	75·00	13·00
8	– 10c. multicoloured	45·00	7·50
9	– 15c. multicoloured	85·00	15·00
10	– 20c. multicoloured	£160	17·00
11	– 25c. multicoloured	12·00	28·00
12	– 50c. multicoloured	£2750	£550
13	– 60c. multicoloured	£3500	£1100
14	– $1 yellow and blue	£2250	£475
15	– $2.50 multicoloured	£1900	£350
16	– $5 multicoloured	£2000	£350

Owing to the limited stocks available for overprinting, the sale of the stamps was personally controlled by the Postmaster and no orders from the trade were accepted.

2 Mahogany Tree, The Quarter

1967.

17	**2** 1c. green, brown and orange	10	1·00
18	– 2c. turquoise and black	10	2·00
19	– 3c. black and green	10	10
20	– 4c. blue and black	10	10
21	– 5c. multicoloured	10	10
22	– 6c. red and black	10	10
23	– 10c. multicoloured	15	10
24	– 15c. multicoloured	2·50	20
25	– 20c. multicoloured	1·25	2·25
26	– 25c. multicoloured	60	20
27	– 40c. green, blue and black	1·00	25
28	– 60c. multicoloured	4·50	4·50
29	– $1 multicoloured	1·75	3·25
30	– $2.50 multicoloured	2·00	5·50
31	– $5 multicoloured	3·00	4·25

DESIGNS: 2c. Sombrero Lighthouse; 3c. St. Mary's Church; 4c. Valley Police Station; 5c. Old Plantation House, Mt. Fortune; 6c. Valley Post Office; 10c. Methodist Church, West End; 15c. Wall Blake Airport; 20c. Beech A90 King Air aircraft over Sandy Ground; 25c. Island harbour; 40c. Map of Anguilla; 60c. Hermit crab and starfish; $1, Hibiscus; $2.50, Local scene; $5, Spiny lobster.

17 Yachts in Lagoon

1968. Anguillan Ships. Multicoloured.

32	10c. Type **17**	20	10
33	15c. Boat on beach	25	10
34	25c. Schooner "Warspite"	35	15
35	40c. Schooner "Atlantic Star"	40	20

18 Purple-throated Carib

1968. Anguillan Birds. Multicoloured.

36	10c. Type **18**	65	15
37	15c. Bananaquit	80	20
38	25c. Black-necked stilt (horiz)	85	20
39	40c. Royal tern (horiz)	90	30

19 Guides' Badge and Anniversary Years

1968. 35th Anniv of Anguillan Girl Guides. Mult.

40	10c. Type **19**	10	10
41	15c. Badge and silhouettes of guides (vert)	15	10
42	25c. Guides' badge and Headquarters	20	15
43	40c. Association and proficiency badges (vert)	25	15

20 The Three Kings

1968. Christmas.

44	**20** 1c. black and red	10	10
45	– 10c. black and blue	10	10
46	– 15c. black and brown	15	10
47	– 40c. black and blue	15	10
48	– 50c. black and green	20	15

DESIGNS—VERT: 10c. The Wise Men; 15c. Holy Family and manger. HORIZ: 40c. The Shepherds; 50c. Holy Family and donkey.

21 Bagging Salt

1969. Anguillan Salt Industry. Multicoloured.

49	10c. Type **21**	25	10
50	15c. Packing salt	30	10
51	40c. Salt pond	35	10
52	50c. Loading salt	35	10

1969. Expiration of Interim Agreement on Status of Anguilla. Nos. 17/22, 23, 24 and 26/7 optd **INDEPENDENCE JANUARY 1969**.

52a	1c. green, brown and orange	10	40
52b	2c. green and black	10	40
52c	3c. black and green	10	40
52d	4c. blue and black	10	40
52e	5c. multicoloured	10	20
52f	6c. red and black	10	20
52g	10c. multicoloured	10	30
52h	15c. multicoloured	90	30
52i	25c. multicoloured	80	30
52j	40c. green, blue and black	1·00	40

The remaining values of the 1967 series, nos. 17/31, also come with this overprint but these are outside the scope of this catalogue.

22 "The Crucifixion" (Studio of Massys)

1969. Easter Commemoration. Multicoloured.

53	25c. Type **22**	25	15
54	40c. "The Last Supper" (ascribed to Roberti)	35	15

23 Amaryllis

1969. Flowers of the Caribbean. Multicoloured.

55	10c. Type **23**	15	20
56	15c. Bougainvillea	20	25
57	40c. Hibiscus	30	50
58	50c. "Cattleya" orchid	1·25	1·60

24 Superb Gaza, Channelled Turban, Chestnut Turban and Carved Star Shell

1969. Sea Shells. Multicoloured.

59	10c. Type **24**	20	20
60	15c. American thorny oysters	20	20
61	40c. Scotch, royal and smooth scotch bonnets	30	30
62	50c. Atlantic trumpet triton	40	30

1969. Christmas. Nos. 17 and 25/8 optd with different seasonal emblems.

63	1c. green, brown and orange	10	10
64	20c. multicoloured	20	10
65	25c. multicoloured	20	10
66	40c. green, blue and black	25	15
67	60c. multicoloured	40	20

30 Spotted Goatfish

1969. Fishes. Multicoloured.

68	10c. Type **30**	30	15
69	15c. Blue-striped grunt	45	15
70	40c. Nassau grouper	55	20
71	50c. Banded butterflyfish	65	20

31 "Morning Glory"

32 "The Crucifixion" (Masaccio)

1970. Flowers. Multicoloured.

72	10c. Type **31**	25	10
73	15c. Blue petrea	35	10
74	40c. Hibiscus	50	20
75	50c. "Flame Tree"	60	25

1970. Easter. Multicoloured.

76	10c. "The Ascent to Calvary" (Tiepolo) (horiz)	15	10
77	20c. Type **32**	20	10
78	40c. "Deposition" (Rosso Fiorentino)	25	15
79	60c. "The Ascent to Calvary" (Murillo) (horiz)	25	15

33 Scout Badge and Map

1970. 40th Anniv of Scouting in Anguilla. Multicoloured.

80	10c. Type **33**	15	15
81	15c. Scout camp, and cubs practising first aid	20	20
82	40c. Monkey bridge	25	30
83	50c. Scout H.Q. building and Lord Baden-Powell	35	30

34 Boatbuilding

1970. Multicoloured.

84	1c. Type **34**	30	40
85	2c. Road construction	30	40
86	3c. Quay, Blowing Point	30	20
87	4c. Broadcaster, Radio Anguilla	30	50
88	5c. Cottage Hospital extension	40	50
89	6c. Valley Secondary School	30	50
90	10c. Hotel extension	30	30
91	15c. Sandy Ground	30	30
92	20c. Supermarket and cinema	70	30
93	25c. Bananas and mangoes	35	1·00
94	40c. Wall Blake Airport	4·00	3·25
95	60c. Sandy Ground jetty	65	3·50
96	$1 Administration buildings	1·25	1·40
97	$2.50 Livestock	1·50	4·00
98	$5 Sandy Hill Bay	3·25	3·75

35 "The Adoration of the Shepherds" (Reni)

1970. Christmas. Multicoloured.

99	1c. Type **35**	10	10
100	20c. "The Virgin and Child" (Gozzoli)	30	20
101	25c. "Mystic Nativity" (detail, Botticelli)	30	20
102	40c. "The Santa Margherita Madonna" (detail, Mazzola)	40	25
103	50c. "The Adoration of the Magi" (detail, Tiepolo)	40	25

36 "Ecce Homo" (detail, Correggio)

1971. Easter. Paintings. Multicoloured.

104	10c. Type **36**	25	10
105	15c. "Christ appearing to St Peter" (detail, Carracci)	25	10
106	40c. "Angels weeping over the Dead Christ" (detail, Guercino) (horiz)	30	10
107	50c. "The Supper at Emmaus" (detail, Caravaggio) (horiz)	30	15

37 "Hypolimnas misippus"

1971. Butterflies. Multicoloured.

108	10c. Type **37**	1·60	70
109	15c. "Junonia evarete"	1·60	80
110	40c. "Agraulis vanillae"	2·00	1·25
111	50c. "Danaus plexippus"	2·00	1·50

38 "Magnanime" and "Aimable" in Battle

39 "The Ansidei Madonna" (detail, Raphael)

1971. Sea-battles of the West Indies. Multicoloured.

112	10c. Type **38**	1·10	1·40
113	15c. H.M.S. "Duke", "Glorieux" and H.M.S. "Agamemnon"	1·25	1·60
114	25c. H.M.S. "Formidable" and H.M.S. "Namur" against "Ville de Paris"	1·50	1·75
115	40c. H.M.S. "Canada"	1·60	1·90
116	50c. H.M.S. "St. Albans" and wreck of "Hector"	1·75	2·00

Nos. 112/116 were issued together, se-tenant, forming a composite design.

1971. Christmas. Multicoloured.

117	20c. Type **39**	25	30
118	25c. "Mystic Nativity" (detail, Botticelli)	25	30
119	40c. "Adoration of the Shepherds" (detail, ascr to Murillo)	30	40
120	50c. "The Madonna of the Iris" (detail, ascr to Durer)	35	70

40 Map of Anguilla and St. Martin by Thomas Jefferys, 1775

41 "Jesus Buffeted"

1972. Caribbean Maps depicting Anguilla. Multicoloured.

121	10c. Type **40**	25	10
122	15c. Samuel Fahlberg's Map, 1814	35	15
123	40c. Thomas Jefferys' Map, 1775 (horiz)	50	25
124	50c. Captain E. Barnett's Map, 1847 (horiz)	60	25

1972. Easter. Multicoloured.

125	10c. Type **41**	25	25
126	15c. "The Way of Sorrows"	30	30
127	25c. "The Crucifixion"	30	30
128	40c. "Descent from the Cross"	35	35
129	50c. "The Burial"	40	40

42 Loblolly Tree

44 Flight into Egypt

1972. Multicoloured.

130	1c. Spear fishing	10	40
131	2c. Type **42**	10	40
132	3c. Sandy Ground	10	40
133	4c. Ferry at Blowing Point	1·75	20
134	5c. Agriculture	15	1·00
135	6c. St. Mary's Church	25	20
136	10c. St. Gerard's Church	25	40
137	15c. Cottage hospital extension	25	30
138	20c. Public library	30	35
139	25c. Sunset at Blowing Point	40	2·00
140	40c. Boat building	5·00	1·50
141	60c. Hibiscus	4·00	4·00
142	$1 Magnificent frigate bird ("Man-o'-War")	10·00	8·00
143	$2.50 Frangipani	5·00	10·00
144	$5 Brown pelican	16·00	17·00
144a	$10 Green-back turtle	15·00	18·00

1972. Royal Silver Wedding. As T **52** of Ascension, but with Schooner and Common dolphin in background.

145	25c. green	50	75
146	40c. brown	50	75

1972. Christmas. Multicoloured.

147	1c. Type **44**	10	10
148	20c. Star of Bethlehem	20	20
149	25c. Holy Family	20	20
150	40c. Arrival of the Magi	20	25
151	50c. Adoration of the Magi	25	25

45 "The Betrayal of Christ"

1973. Easter. Multicoloured.

152	1c. Type **45**	10	10
153	10c. "The Man of Sorrows"	10	10
154	20c. "Christ bearing the Cross"	10	15
155	25c. "The Crucifixion"	15	15
156	40c. "The Descent from the Cross"	15	15
157	50c. "The Resurrection"	15	20
MS158	140 × 141 mm. Nos. 152/7. Bottom panel in gold and mauve	70	80

46 "Santa Maria"

1973. Columbus Discovers the West Indies. Multicoloured.

159	1c. Type **46**	10	10
160	20c. Early map	1·50	1·25
161	40c. Map of voyages	1·60	1·40
162	70c. Sighting land	1·90	1·75
163	$1.20 Landing of Columbus	2·50	2·25
MS164	193 × 93 mm. Nos. 159/63	6·00	7·00

47 Princess Anne and Captain Mark Phillips

49 "The Crucifixion" (Raphael)

48 "The Adoration of the Shepherds" (Reni)

1973. Royal Wedding. Multicoloured. Background colours given.

165	**47**	60c. green	20	15
166		$1.20 mauve	30	15

1973. Christmas. Multicoloured.

167	1c. Type **48**	10	10
168	10c. "The Madonna and Child with Saints Jerome and Dominic" (Filippino Lippi)	10	10
169	20c. "The Nativity" (Master of Brunswick)	15	15
170	25c. "Madonna of the Meadow" (Bellini)	15	15
171	40c. "Virgin and Child" (Cima)	20	20
172	50c. "Adoration of the Kings" (Geertgen)	20	20
MS173	148 × 149 mm. Nos. 167/72	80	1·60

1974. Easter.

174	**49**	1c. multicoloured	10	10
175	–	15c. multicoloured	10	10
176	–	20c. multicoloured	15	15
177	–	25c. multicoloured	15	15
178	–	40c. multicoloured	15	15
179	–	$1 multicoloured	20	25
MS180		123 × 141 mm. Nos. 174/9	1·00	1·25

DESIGNS: 15c. to $1, Details of Raphael's "Crucifixion".

50 Churchill Making "Victory" Sign

1974. Birth Centenary of Sir Winston Churchill. Multicoloured.

181	1c. Type **50**	10	10
182	20c. Churchill with Roosevelt	20	20
183	25c. Wartime broadcast	20	20
184	40c. Birthplace, Blenheim Palace	30	30
185	60c. Churchill's statue	30	35
186	$1.20 Country residence, Chartwell	45	55
MS187	195 × 96 mm. Nos. 181/6	1·40	2·50

51 U.P.U. Emblem

1974. Centenary of U.P.U.

188	**51**	1c. black and blue	10	10
189		20c. black and orange	15	15
190		25c. black and yellow	15	15
191		40c. black and mauve	20	25
192		60c. black and green	30	40
193		$1.20 black and blue	50	60
MS194		195 × 96 mm. Nos. 188/93	1·25	2·25

52 Anguillan pointing to Star

1974. Christmas. Multicoloured.

195	1c. Type **52**	10	10
196	20c. Child in Manger	10	20
197	25c. King's offering	10	20
198	40c. Star over map of Anguilla	15	20
199	60c. Family looking at star	15	20
200	$1.20 Angels of Peace	20	30
MS201	177 × 85 mm. Nos. 195/200	1·00	2·00

53 "Mary, John and Mary Magdalene" (Matthias Grunewald)

55 "Madonna, Child and the Infant John the Baptist" (Raphael)

54 Statue of Liberty

1975. Easter. Details from Isenheim Altarpiece, Colmar Museum. Multicoloured.

202	1c. Type **53**	10	10
203	10c. "The Crucifixion"	15	15
204	15c. "St. John the Baptist"	15	15
205	20c. "St. Sebastian and Angels"	15	20
206	$1 "The Entombment" (horiz)	20	35
207	$1.50 "St. Anthony the Hermit"	25	45
MS208	134 × 127 mm. Nos. 202/7 (imperf)	1·00	2·00

1975. Bicentenary of American Revolution. Mult.

209	1c. Type **54**	10	10
210	10c. The Capitol	20	10
211	15c. "Congress voting for Independence" (Pine and Savage)	30	15
212	20c. Washington and map	30	15
213	$1 Boston Tea Party	45	40
214	$1.50 Bicentenary logo	50	60
MS215	198 × 97 mm. Nos. 209/14	1·25	2·50

1975. Christmas. "Madonna and Child" paintings by artists named. Multicoloured.

216	1c. Type **55**	10	10
217	10c. Cima	15	10
218	15c. Dolci	20	15
219	20c. Durer	20	20
220	$1 Bellini	35	25
221	$1.50 Botticelli	45	35
MS222	130 × 145 mm. Nos. 216/21	2·00	2·25

1976. New Constitution. Nos. 130 etc optd **NEW CONSTITUTION 1976** or surch also.

223	1c. Spear fishing	30	40
224	2c. on 1c. Spear fishing	30	40
225	2c. Type **42**	7·50	1·75
226	3c. on 40c. Boat building	75	70
227	4c. Ferry at Blowing Point	1·00	1·00
228	5c. on 40c. Boat building	30	50
229	6c. St. Mary's Church	30	50
230	10c. on 20c. Public library	30	50
231	10c. St. Gerard's Church	7·50	4·75
232	15c. Cottage Hospital extension	30	1·25
233	20c. Public library	30	50
234	25c. Sunset at Blowing Point	30	50
235	40c. Boat building	1·00	70
236	60c. Hibiscus	70	70
237	$1 Magnificent frigate bird	6·50	2·25
238	$2.50 Frangipani	2·25	2·25
239	$5 Brown pelican	8·00	8·50
240	$10 Green-back turtle	3·00	6·00

57 Almond

1976. Flowering Trees. Multicoloured.

241	1c. Type **57**	10	10
242	10c. Autograph	20	20
243	15c. Calabash	20	20
244	20c. Cordia	20	20
245	$1 Papaya	30	45
246	$1.50 Flamboyant	35	55
MS247	194 × 99 mm. Nos. 241/6	1·50	2·00

58 The Three Marys

1976. Easter. Showing portions of the Altar Frontal Tapestry, Rheinau. Multicoloured.

248	1c. Type **58**	10	10
249	10c. The Crucifixion	10	10
250	15c. Two Soldiers	15	15
251	20c. The Annunciation	15	15
252	$1 The complete tapestry (horiz)	65	65
253	$1.50 The Risen Christ	80	80
MS254	138 × 130 mm. Nos. 248/53 (imperf)	1·75	2·10

59 French Ships approaching Anguilla

1976. Bicentenary of Battle of Anguilla. Mult.

255	1c. Type **59**	10	10
256	3c. "Margaret" (sloop) leaving Anguilla	1·25	35
257	15c. Capture of "Le Desius"	1·50	55
258	25c. "La Vaillante" forced aground	1·50	80
259	$1 H.M.S. "Lapwing"	2·00	1·25
260	$1.50 "Le Desius" burning	2·25	1·75
MS261	205 × 103 mm. Nos. 255/60	7·50	6·00

60 "Christmas Carnival" (A. Richardson)

1976. Christmas. Children's Paintings. Mult.

262	1c. Type **60**	10	10
263	3c. "Dreams of Christmas Gifts" (J. Connor)	10	10
264	15c. "Carolling" (P. Richardson)	15	15
265	25c. "Candle-light Procession" (A. Mussington)	20	20
266	$1 "Going to Church" (B. Franklin)	30	30
267	$1.50 "Coming Home for Christmas" (E. Gumbs)	40	40
MS268	232 × 147 mm. Nos. 262/7	1·50	1·75

61 Prince Charles and H.M.S. "Minerva" (frigate)

1977. Silver Jubilee. Multicoloured.

269	25c. Type **61**	15	10
270	40c. Prince Philip landing by launch at Road Bay, 1964	15	10
271	$1.20 Coronation scene	20	20
272	$2.50 Coronation regalia and map of Anguilla	25	30
MS273	145 × 96 mm. Nos. 269/72	65	90

62 Yellow-crowned Night Heron

1977. Multicoloured.

274	1c. Type **62**	30	1·25
275	2c. Great barracuda	30	2·50
276	3c. Queen or pink conch	2·00	3·25
277	4c. Spanish bayonet (flower)	40	70
278	5c. Honeycomb trunkfish	1·50	30
279	6c. Cable and Wireless building	30	30
280	10c. American kestrel ("American Sparrow Hawk")	5·00	3·00
281	15c. Ground orchid	2·75	1·75
282	20c. Stop-light parrotfish	3·25	75
283	22c. Lobster fishing boat	50	60
284	35c. Boat race	1·40	70
285	50c. Sea bean	90	50
286	$1 Sandy Island	60	50
287	$2.50 Manchineel	1·00	1·00
288	$5 Ground lizard	2·00	1·75
289	$10 Red-billed tropic bird	9·00	4·25

63 "The Crucifixion" (Massys)

1977. Easter. Paintings by Castagno ($1.50) or Ugolino (others). Multicoloured.

291	1c. Type **63**	10	10
292	3c. "The Betrayal"	10	10
293	22c. "The Way to Calvary"	20	20
294	30c. "The Deposition"	25	25
295	$1 "The Resurrection"	50	50
296	$1.50 "The Crucifixion"	65	65
MS297	192 × 126 mm. Nos. 291/6	1·60	1·75

1977. Royal Visit. Nos. 269/72 optd **ROYAL VISIT TO WEST INDIES.**

298	25c. Type **61**	10	10
299	40c. Prince Philip landing at Road Bay, 1964	10	15
300	$1.20 Coronation scene	20	25
301	$1.50 Coronation regalia and map of Anguilla	25	35
MS302	145 × 96 mm. Nos. 298/301	80	60

65 "Le Chapeau de Paille"

1977. 400th Birth Anniv of Rubens. Multicoloured.

303	25c. Type **65**	15	15
304	40c. "Helene Fourment and her Two Children"	20	25
305	$1.20 "Rubens and his Wife"	60	65
306	$2.50 "Marchesa Brigida Spinola-Doria"	75	95
MS307	90 × 145 mm. Nos. 303/6	2·00	2·10

1977. Christmas. Nos. 262/7 with old date blocked out and additionally inscr "1977", some also surch.

308	1c. Type **60**	10	10
309	5c. on 3c. "Dreams of Christmas Gifts"	10	10
310	12c. on 15c. "Carolling"	15	15
311	18c. on 25c. "Candle-light Procession"	20	20
312	$1 "Going to Church"	45	45
313	$2.50 on $1.50 "Coming Home for Christmas"	90	90
MS314	232 × 147 mm. Nos. 308/13	2·50	2·50

1978. Easter. Nos. 303/6 optd **EASTER 1978.**

315	25c. Type **65**	15	20
316	40c. "Helene Fourment with her Two Children"	15	20
317	$1.20 "Rubens and his Wife"	35	40
318	$2.50 "Marchesa Brigida Spinola-Doria"	45	60
MS319	93 × 145 mm. Nos. 315/18	1·25	1·50

68 Coronation Coach at Admiralty Arch

1978. 25th Anniv of Coronation. Multicoloured.

320	22c. Buckingham Palace	10	10
321	50c. Type **68**	10	10
322	$1.50 Balcony scene	15	15
323	$2.50 Royal coat of arms	25	25
MS324	138 × 92 mm. Nos. 320/3	60	60

1978. Anniversaries. Nos. 283/4 and 287 optd **VALLEY SECONDARY SCHOOL 1953–1978** and Nos. 285/6 and 288 optd **ROAD METHODIST CHURCH 1878–1978**, or surch also.

325	22c. Lobster fishing boat	20	15
326	35c. Boat race	30	20
327	50c. Sea bean	30	30
328	$1 Sandy Island	35	40
329	$1.20 on $5 Ground lizard	40	45
330	$1.50 on $2.50 Manchineel	45	55

71 Mother and Child

1978. Christmas. Children's Paintings. Mult.

331	5c. Type **71**	10	10
332	12c. Christmas masquerade	15	10
333	18c. Christmas dinner	15	10
334	22c. Serenading	15	10
335	$1 Child in manger	45	20
336	$2.50 Family going to church	90	40
MS337	191 × 101 mm. Nos. 331/6	1·60	1·75

1979. International Year of the Child. As Nos. 331/6, but additionally inscr "1979 INTERNATIONAL YEAR OF THE CHILD" and emblem. Borders in different colours.

338	5c. Type **71**	10	10
339	12c. Christmas masquerade	10	10
340	18c. Christmas dinner	10	10
341	22c. Serenading	10	10
342	$1 Child in manger	30	30
343	$2.50 Family going to church	50	50
MS344	205 × 112 mm. Nos. 338/43	2·25	2·50

1979. Nos. 274/7 and 279/80 surch.

345	12c. on 2c. Great barracuda	50	50
346	14c. on 4c. Spanish bayonet	50	50
347	18c. on 3c. Queen conch	80	55
348	25c. on 6c. Cable and Wireless building	55	50
349	38c. on 10c. American kestrel	2·50	70
350	40c. on 1c. Type **62**	2·50	70

73 Valley Methodist Church

1979. Easter. Church Interiors. Multicoloured.

351	5c. Type **73**	10	10
352	12c. St. Mary's Anglican Church, The Valley	10	10
353	18c. St. Gerard's Roman Catholic Church, The Valley	15	15
354	22c. Road Methodist Church	15	15
355	$1.50 St. Augustine's Anglican Church, East End	60	60
356	$2.50 West End Methodist Church	75	75
MS357	190 × 105 mm. Nos. 351/6	1·75	2·25

74 Cape of Good Hope 1d. "Woodblock" of 1881

1979. Death Centenary of Sir Rowland Hill. Multicoloured.

358	1c. Type **74**	10	10
359	1c. U.S.A. "inverted Jenny" of 1918	10	10
360	22c. Penny Black ("V.R." Official)	15	15
361	35c. Germany 2m, "Graf Zeppelin" of 1928	20	20
362	$1.50 U.S.A. $5 "Columbus" of 1893	40	60
363	$2.50 Great Britain £5 orange of 1882	60	95
MS364	187 × 123 mm. Nos. 358/63	1·25	2·40

75 Wright "Flyer I" (1st powered Flight, 1903)

1979. History of Powered Flight. Multicoloured.

365	5c. Type **75**	20	10
366	12c. Louis Bleriot at Dover after Channel crossing, 1909	25	10
367	18c. Vickers FB-27 Vimy (1st non-stop crossing of Atlantic, 1919)	30	15
368	22c. Ryan NYP Special "Spirit of St Louis" (1st solo Atlantic flight by Charles Lindbergh, 1927)	30	20
369	$1.50 Airship LZ 127 "Graf Zeppelin", 1928	65	60
370	$2.50 Concorde, 1979	3·25	90
MS371	200 × 113 mm. Nos. 365/70	3·50	3·25

76 Sombrero Island

1979. Outer Islands. Multicoloured.

372	5c. Type **76**	15	10
373	12c. Anguillita Island	15	10
374	18c. Sandy Island	15	15
375	25c. Prickly Pear Cays	15	15
376	$1 Dog Island	40	40
377	$2.50 Scrub Island	60	70
MS378	180 × 91 mm. Nos. 372/7	2·75	2·25

77 Red Poinsettia

1979. Christmas. Multicoloured.

379	22c. Type **77**	15	20
380	35c. Kalanchoe	20	30
381	$1.50 Cream poinsettia	40	50
382	$2.50 White poinsettia	60	70
MS383	146 × 164 mm. Nos. 379/82	1·75	2·25

78 Exhibition Scene

1979. "London 1980" International Stamp Exhibition (1st issue). Multicoloured.

384	35c. Type **78**	15	20
385	50c. Earls Court Exhibition Centre	15	25
386	$1.50 Penny Black and Two-penny Blue stamps	25	60
387	$2.50 Exhibition Logo	45	95
MS388	150 × 94 mm. Nos. 384/7	1·40	2·00

See also Nos. 407/9.

79 Games Site

1980. Winter Olympic Games, Lake Placid, U.S.A. Multicoloured.

389	5c. Type **79**	10	10
390	18c. Ice hockey	20	10
391	35c. Ice skating	20	20
392	50c. Bobsleighing	20	20
393	$1 Skiing	20	35
394	$2.50 Luge-tobogganing	40	80
MS395	136 × 128 mm. Nos. 389/94	1·00	2·00

80 Salt ready for "Reaping"

1980. Salt Industry. Multicoloured.
396 5c. Type **80** 10 10
397 12c. Tallying salt 10 10
398 18c. Unloading salt flats 15 15
399 22c. Salt storage heap 15 15
400 $1 Salt for bagging and grinding 30 40
401 $2.50 Loading salt for export 50 70
MS402 180 × 92 mm. Nos. 396/401 1·10 1·75

1980. Anniversaries. Nos. 280, 282 and 287/8 optd **50th Anniversary Scouting 1980** (10c., $2.50) or **75th Anniversary Rotary 1980** (others).
403 10c. American kestrel 1·75 15
404 20c. Stop-light parrotfish 1·00 20
405 $2.50 Manchineel 1·75 1·25
406 $5 Ground lizard 2·50 1·90

83 Palace of Westminster and Great Britain 1970 9d. "Philympia" Commemoration

1980. "London 1980" International Stamp Exhibition (2nd issue). Multicoloured.
407 50c. Type **83** 55 75
408 $1.50 City Hall, Toronto and "Capex 1978" stamp of Canada 85 1·25
409 $2.50 Statue of Liberty and 1976 "Interphil" stamp of U.S.A. 1·10 1·40
MS410 157 × 130 mm. Nos. 407/9 2·25 3·00

84 Queen Elizabeth the Queen Mother

85 Brown Pelicans ("Pelican")

1980. 80th Birthday of The Queen Mother.
411 **84** 35c. multicoloured 70 40
412 50c. multicoloured 85 50
413 $1.50 multicoloured 1·50 1·50
414 $3 multicoloured 2·25 2·50
MS415 160 × 110 mm. Nos. 411/14 5·50 4·75

1980. Christmas. Birds. Multicoloured.
416 5c. Type **85** 30 10
417 22c. Great blue heron ("Great Grey Heron") 75 20
418 $1.50 Barn swallow ("Swallow") 1·75 60
419 $3 Ruby-throated hummingbird ("Hummingbird") 2·25 1·40
MS420 126 × 160 mm. Nos. 416/19 10·00 7·50

1980. Separation from St. Kitts. Nos. 274, 277, 280/9, 334 and 418/19 optd **SEPARATION 1980** or surch also.
421 1c. Type **62** 20 80
422b 2c. on 4c. Spanish bayonet 20 80
423 5c. on 15c. Ground orchid 1·50 80
424 5c. on $1.50 Barn swallow 1·50 80
425 5c. on $3 Ruby-throated hummingbird 1·50 80
426 10c. American kestrel 1·75 80
427 12c. on $1 Sandy Island 20 80
428 14c. on $2.50 Manchineel 20 80
429 15c. Ground orchid 1·50 80
430 18c. on $5 Ground lizard 25 80
431 20c. Stop-light parrotfish 25 80
432 22c. Lobster fishing boat 25 80
433 25c. on 15c. Ground orchid 1·50 85
434 35c. Boat race 30 85
435 38c. on 22c. Serenading 30 85
436 40c. on 1c. Type **62** 30 85
437 50c. Sea bean 35 95
438 $1 Sandy Island 50 1·25
439 $2.50 Manchineel 1·25 3·00
440 $5 Ground lizard 2·25 4·00
441 $10 Red-billed tropic bird 5·00 6·00
442 $10 on 6c. Cable and Wireless Building 5·00 6·00

87 First Petition for Separation, 1825

1980. Separation from St. Kitts. Multicoloured.
443 18c. Type **87** 10 10
444 22c. Referendum ballot paper, 1967 15 10
445 35c. Airport blockade, 1967 30 15
446 50c. Anguillan flag 60 20
447 $1 Separation celebration, 1980 40 35
MS448 178 × 92 mm. Nos. 443/7 1·40 1·25

88 "Nelson's Dockyard" (R. Granger Barrett)

1981. 175th Death Anniv of Lord Nelson. Mult.
449 22c. Type **88** 2·50 50
450 35c. "Ships in which Nelson Served" (Nicholas Pocock) 2·50 70
451 50c. "H.M.S. Victory" (Monamy Swaine) 3·00 1·50
452 $3 "Battle of Trafalgar" (Clarkson Stanfield) 3·75 6·50
MS453 82 × 63 mm. $5 "Horatio Nelson" (L. F. Abbott) and coat of arms 3·00 3·25

89 Minnie Mouse being chased by Bees

1981. Easter. Walt Disney Cartoon Characters. Multicoloured.
454 1c. Type **89** 10 10
455 2c. Pluto laughing at Mickey Mouse 10 10
456 3c. Minnie Mouse tying ribbon round Pluto's neck 10 10
457 5c. Minnie Mouse confronted by love-struck bird who fancies her bonnet 10 10
458 7c. Dewey and Huey admiring themselves in mirror 10 10
459 9c. Horace Horsecollar and Clarabelle Cow out for a stroll 10 10
460 10c. Daisy Duck with hat full of Easter eggs 10 10
461 $2 Goofy unwrapping Easter hat 1·40 1·40
462 $3 Donald Duck in his Easter finery 1·60 1·60
MS463 134 × 108 mm. $5 Chip and Dale making off with hat 3·50 3·50

90 Prince Charles, Lady Diana Spencer and St. Paul's Cathedral

1981. Royal Wedding. Multicoloured.
464 50c. Type **90** 15 20
465 $2.50 Althorp 30 50
466 $3 Windsor Castle 35 60
MS467 90 × 72 mm. Buckingham Palace 1·25 1·50

91 Children playing in Tree

1981. 35th Anniv of UNICEF Multicoloured.
470 5c. Type **91** 20 30
471 10c. Children playing by pool 20 30
472 15c. Children playing musical instruments 20 30
473 $3 Children playing with pets 2·50 3·00
MS474 78 × 106 mm. Children playing football (vert) 3·50 5·00

1981. Christmas. Designs as T **89** showing scenes from Walt Disney's cartoon film "The Night before Christmas".
475 1c. multicoloured 10 10
476 2c. multicoloured 10 10
477 3c. multicoloured 10 10
478 5c. multicoloured 15 10
479 7c. multicoloured 15 10
480 10c. multicoloured 15 10
481 12c. multicoloured 15 10
482 $2 multicoloured 3·75 1·25
483 $3 multicoloured 3·75 1·60
MS484 130 × 105 mm. $5 multicoloured 5·50 3·50

92 Red Grouper

1982. Multicoloured.
485 1c. Type **92** 15 1·00
486 5c. Ferry service, Blowing Point 30 1·00
487 10c. Island dinghies 20 60
488 15c. Majorettes 20 60
489 20c. Launching boat, Sandy Hill 40 60
490 25c. Corals 1·50 50
491 30c. Little Bay cliffs 30 75
492 35c. Fountain Cave interior 1·50 30
493 40c. Sunset over Sandy Island 30 75
494 45c. Landing at Sombrero 50 30
495 60c. Seine fishing 3·25 3·25
496 75c. Boat race at sunset, Sandy Ground 1·00 2·00
497 $1 Bagging lobster at Island Harbour 2·25 2·00
498 $5 Brown pelicans 16·00 13·00
499 $7.50 Hibiscus 11·00 15·00
500 $10 Queen triggerfish 16·00 15·00

1982. No. 494 surch **50c.**
501 50c. on 45c. Landing at Sombrero 50 35

94 Anthurium and "Heliconius charithonia"

95 Lady Diana Spencer in 1961

1982. Easter. Flowers and Butterflies. Multicoloured.
502 10c. Type **94** 1·10 15
503 35c. Bird of paradise and "Junonia evarete" 2·00 40
504 75c. Allamanda and "Danaus plexippus" 2·25 70
505 $3 Orchid tree and "Biblis hyperia" 3·50 2·25
MS506 65 × 79 mm. $5 Amaryllis and "Dryas julia" 2·75 3·50

1982. 21st Birthday of Princess of Wales. Mult.
507 10c. Type **95** 50 20
508 30c. Lady Diana Spencer in 1968 1·75 25
509 40c. Lady Diana in 1970 50 30
510 60c. Lady Diana in 1974 55 35
511 $2 Lady Diana in 1981 80 1·10
512 $3 Lady Diana in 1981 (different) 5·50 1·40
MS513 72 × 90 mm. $5 Princess of Wales 7·50 3·00
MS514 125 × 125 mm. As Nos. 507/12, but with buff borders 8·50 6·50

96 Pitching Tent

1982. 75th Anniv of Boy Scout Movement. Multicoloured.
515 10c. Type **96** 45 20
516 35c. Scout band 85 50
517 75c. Yachting 1·25 90
518 $3 On parade 3·00 2·75
MS519 90 × 72 mm. $5 Cooking 4·50 4·00

1982. World Cup Football Championship, Spain. Horiz designs as T **89** showing scenes from Walt Disney's cartoon film "Bedknobs and Broomsticks".
520 1c. multicoloured 10 10
521 3c. multicoloured 10 10
522 4c. multicoloured 10 10
523 5c. multicoloured 10 10
524 7c. multicoloured 10 10
525 9c. multicoloured 10 10
526 10c. multicoloured 10 10
527 $2.50 multicoloured 2·25 1·75
528 $3 multicoloured 2·25 2·00
MS529 126 × 101 mm. $5 multicoloured 9·00 8·50

1982. Commonwealth Games, Brisbane. Nos. 487, 495/6 and 498 optd **COMMONWEALTH GAMES 1982.**
530 10c. Island dinghies 15 25
531 60c. Seine fishing 45 60
532 75c. Boat race at sunset, Sandy Ground 60 80
533 $5 Brown pelicans 3·25 3·75

1982. Birth Cent of A. A. Milne (author). As T **89**.
534 1c. multicoloured 25 20
535 2c. multicoloured 25 20
536 3c. multicoloured 25 20
537 5c. multicoloured 35 20
538 7c. multicoloured 35 25
539 10c. multicoloured 50 15
540 12c. multicoloured 60 20
541 20c. multicoloured 90 25
542 $5 multicoloured 9·00 9·50
MS543 120 × 93 mm. $5 multicoloured 7·50 9·00
DESIGNS—HORIZ: 1c. to $5 Scenes from various "Winnie the Pooh" stories.

98 Culture

1983. Commonwealth Day. Multicoloured.
544 10c. Type **98** 10 15
545 35c. Anguilla and British flags 30 30
546 75c. Economic co-operation 60 1·00
547 $2.50 Salt industry (salt pond) 3·75 4·50
MS548 76 × 61 mm. World map showing positions of Commonwealth countries 2·50 2·50

99 "I am the Lord Thy God"

101 Montgolfier Hot Air Balloon, 1783

100 Leatherback Turtle

1983. Easter. The Ten Commandments. Mult.
549 1c. Type **99** 10 10
550 2c. "Thou shalt not make any graven image" 10 10
551 3c. "Thou shalt not take My Name in vain" 10 10
552 10c. "Remember the Sabbath Day" 25 10
553 35c. "Honour thy father and mother" 65 20
554 60c. "Thou shalt not kill" 1·00 40
555 75c. "Thou shalt not commit adultery" 1·25 50
556 $2 "Thou shalt not steal" 2·75 1·50
557 $2.50 "Thou shalt not bear false witness" 3·00 1·50
558 $5 "Thou shalt not covet" 4·25 2·75
MS559 126 × 102 mm. $5 "Moses receiving the Tablets" (16th-century woodcut) 2·75 3·00

1983. Endangered Species. Turtles. Multicoloured.
560 10c. Type **100** 3·50 80
561 35c. Hawksbill turtle 6·50 1·25

562	75c. Green turtle	7·50	3·50
563	$1 Loggerhead turtle	8·50	7·50
MS564	93×72 mm. $5 Leatherback turtle (different)	22·00	4·00

1983. Bicentenary of Manned Flight. Multicoloured.

565	10c. Type **101**	50	50
566	60c. Blanchard and Jefferies crossing English Channel by balloon, 1785	1·25	85
567	$1 Henri Giffard's steam-powered dirigible airship, 1852	1·75	1·50
568	$2.50 Otto Lillienthal and biplane glider, 1890–96	2·50	3·00
MS569	72×90 mm. $5 Wilbur Wright flying round Statue of Liberty, 1909	2·75	3·50

102 Boys' Brigade Band and Flag

1983. Centenary of Boys' Brigade. Multicoloured.

570	10c. Type **102**	50	15
571	$5 Brigade members marching	3·50	2·75
MS572	96×115 mm. Nos. 570/1	3·25	4·50

1983. 150th Anniv of Abolition of Slavery (1st issue). Nos. 487, 493 and 497/8 optd **150TH ANNIVERSARY ABOLITION OF SLAVERY ACT.**

573	10c. Island dinghies	20	10
574	40c. Sunset over Sandy Island	30	25
575	$1 Bagging lobster at Island Harbour	70	50
576	$5 Brown pelicans	8·50	2·75

See also Nos. 616/23.

104 Jiminy on Clock ("Cricket on the Hearth")

1983. Christmas. Walt Disney Cartoon Characters. Multicoloured.

577	1c. Type **104**	10	10
578	2c. Jiminy with fiddle ("Cricket on the Hearth")	10	10
579	3c. Jiminy among toys ("Cricket on the Hearth")	10	10
580	4c. Mickey as Bob Cratchit ("A Christmas Carol")	10	10
581	5c. Donald Duck as Scrooge ("A Christmas Carol")	10	10
582	6c. Mini and Goofy in "The Chimes"	10	10
583	10c. Goofy sees an imp appearing from bells ("The Chimes")	10	10
584	$2 Donald Duck as Mr. Pickwick ("The Pickwick Papers")	3·25	2·75
585	$3 Disney characters as Pickwickians ("The Pickwick Papers")	3·75	2·25
MS586	130×104 mm. Donald Duck as Mr. Pickwick with gifts ("The Pickwick Papers")	10·00	11·00

105 100 Metres Race

1984. Olympic Games, Los Angeles. Multicoloured.
(A) Inscr "1984 Los Angeles".

587A	1c. Type **105**	10	10
588A	2c. Long jumping	10	10
589A	3c. Shot-putting	10	10
590A	4c. High jumping	10	10
591A	5c. 400 metres race	10	10
592A	6c. Hurdling	10	10
593A	10c. Discus-throwing	10	10
594A	$1 Pole-vaulting	3·25	1·25
595A	$4 Javelin-throwing	6·00	3·50
MS596A	117×93 mm. $5 1500 metres race	7·50	4·50

(B) Inscr "1984 Olympics Los Angeles" and Olympic emblem.

587B	1c. Type **105**	10	10
588B	2c. Long jumping	10	10
589B	3c. Shot-putting	10	10
590B	4c. High jumping	10	10
591B	5c. 400 metres race	10	10
592B	6c. Hurdling	10	10
593B	10c. Discus-throwing	10	10
594B	$1 Pole-vaulting	3·75	3·00
595B	$4 Javelin-throwing	7·50	8·50
MS596B	117×93 mm. $5 1500 metres race	7·50	4·50

106 "Justice"

1984. Easter. Multicoloured.

597	10c. Type **106**	15	10
598	25c. "Poetry"	20	20
599	35c. "Philosophy"	30	30
600	40c. "Theology"	30	30
601	$1 "Abraham and Paul"	85	95
602	$2 "Moses and Matthew"	1·60	2·25
603	$3 "John and David"	2·25	3·00
604	$4 "Peter and Adam"	2·50	3·00
MS605	83×110 mm. $5 "Astronomy"	3·50	3·00

Nos. 597/605 show details from "La Stanza della Segnatura" by Raphael.

1984. Nos. 485, 491, 498/500 surch.

606	25c. on $7.50 Hibiscus	65	35
607	35c. on 30c. Little Bay cliffs	50	40
608	60c. on 1c. Type **92**	55	45
609	$2.50 on $5 Brown pelicans	3·00	1·50
610	$2.50 on $10 Queen triggerfish	1·75	1·50

108 1913 1d. Kangaroo Stamp

1984. "Ausipex 84" International Stamp Exhibition. Multicoloured.

611	10c. Type **108**	40	30
612	75c. 1914 6d. Laughing Kookaburra	1·25	1·25
613	$1 1932 2d. Sydney Harbour Bridge	1·75	1·75
614	$2.50 1938 10s. King George VI	2·25	3·75
MS615	95×86 mm. $5 £1 Bass and £2 Admiral King	5·00	7·00

109 Thomas Fowell Buxton

1984. 150th Anniv of Abolition of Slavery (2nd issue). Multicoloured.

616	10c. Type **109**	10	10
617	25c. Abraham Lincoln	25	25
618	35c. Henri Christophe	35	35
619	60c. Thomas Clarkson	50	50
620	75c. William Wilberforce	60	60
621	$1 Olaudah Equiano	70	70
622	$2.50 General Charles Gordon	1·60	1·60
623	$5 Granville Sharp	3·00	3·00
MS624	150×121 mm. Nos. 616/23	7·50	10·00

1984. Universal Postal Union Congress, Hamburg. Nos. 486/7 and 498 optd **U.P.U. CONGRESS HAMBURG 1984** or surch also (No 626).

625	5c. Ferry service, Blowing Point	30	10
626	20c. on 10c. Island dinghies	30	15
627	$5 Brown pelicans	5·50	3·50

1984. Birth of Prince Henry. Nos. 507/12 optd **PRINCE HENRY BIRTH 15.9.84.**

628	10c. Type **95**	20	10
629	30c. Lady Diana Spencer in 1968	40	25
630	40c. Lady Diana in 1970	20	30
631	60c. Lady Diana in 1974	30	45
632	$2 Lady Diana in 1981	75	1·25
633	$3 Lady Diana in 1981 (different)	1·25	1·75
MS634	72×90 mm. $5 Princess of Wales	2·00	3·00
MS635	125×125 mm. As Nos. 628/33, but with buff borders	2·50	4·00

112 Christmas in Sweden

1984. Christmas. Walt Disney Cartoon Characters. National Scenes. Multicoloured.

636	1c. Type **112**	10	10
637	2c. Italy	10	10
638	3c. Holland	10	10
639	4c. Mexico	10	10
640	5c. Spain	10	10
641	10c. Disneyland, U.S.A.	10	10
642	$1 Japan	3·00	2·00
643	$2 Anguilla	4·00	4·75
644	$4 Germany	6·50	8·00
MS645	126×102 mm. $5 England	7·00	5·00

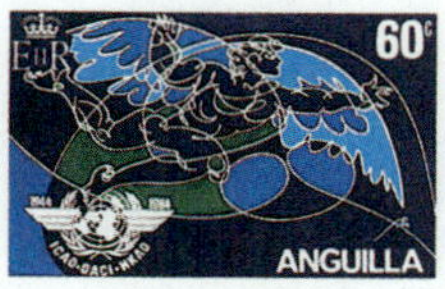

113 Icarus in Flight

1984. 40th Anniv of International Civil Aviation Authority. Multicoloured.

646	60c. Type **113**	60	75
647	75c. "Solar Princess" (abstract)	80	90
648	$2.50 I.C.A.O. emblem (vert)	2·25	3·00
MS649	65×49 mm. $5 Map of air routes serving Anguilla	3·00	4·50

114 Barn Swallow

115 The Queen Mother visiting King's College Hospital, London

1985. Birth Bicentenary of John J. Audubon (ornithologist). Multicoloured.

650	10c. Type **114**	80	65
651	60c. American wood stork ("Woodstork")	1·50	1·25
652	75c. Roseate tern	1·50	1·25
653	$5 Osprey	4·50	6·00
MS654	Two sheets, each 73×103 mm. $4 Western tanager (horiz); (b) $4 Solitary vireo (horiz) Set of 2 sheets	8·50	5·00

1985. Life and Times of Queen Elizabeth the Queen Mother. Multicoloured.

655	10c. Type **115**	10	10
656	$2 The Queen Mother inspecting Royal Marine Volunteer Cadets, Deal	80	1·25
657	$3 The Queen Mother outside Clarence House	1·10	1·50
MS658	56×85 mm. $5 At Ascot, 1979	1·75	2·50

116 White-tailed Tropic Bird

1985. Birds. Multicoloured.

659	5c. Brown pelican	1·75	1·75
660	10c. Mourning dove ("Turtle Dove")	1·75	1·75
661	15c. Magnificent frigate bird (inscr "Man-o-War")	1·75	1·75
662	20c. Antillean crested hummingbird	1·75	1·75
663	25c. Type **116**	1·75	1·75
664	30c. Caribbean elaenia	1·75	1·75
665	35c. Black-whiskered vireo	7·50	5·00
665a	35c. Lesser Antillean bullfinch	3·00	1·75
666	40c. Yellow-crowned night heron	1·75	1·75
667	45c. Pearly-eyed thrasher	1·75	1·75
668	50c. Laughing gull	1·75	1·75
669	65c. Brown booby	1·75	1·75
670	80c. Grey kingbird	2·25	3·00
671	$1 Audubon's shearwater	2·25	3·00
672	$1.35 Roseate tern	1·75	3·00
673	$2.50 Bananaquit	5·50	8·00
674	$5 Belted kingfisher	4·25	8·00
675	$10 Green-backed heron ("Green Heron")	7·00	10·00

1985. 75th Anniv of Girl Guide Movement. Nos. 486, 491, 496 and 498 optd **GIRL GUIDES 75TH ANNIVERSARY 1910–1985** and anniversary emblem.

676	5c. Ferry service, Blowing Point	30	30
677	30c. Little Bay cliffs	40	35
678	75c. Boat race at sunset, Sandy Ground	60	85
679	$5 Brown pelicans	9·00	8·50

118 Goofy as Huckleberry Finn Fishing

1985. 150th Birth Anniv of Mark Twain (author). Walt Disney cartoon characters in scenes from "Huckleberry Finn". Multicoloured.

680	10c. Type **118**	70	20
681	60c. Pete as Pap surprising Huck	2·25	85
682	$1 "Multiplication tables"	2·75	1·25
683	$3 The Duke reciting Shakespeare	4·00	4·00
MS684	127×102 mm. $5 "In school but out"	8·50	8·00

119 Hansel and Gretel (Mickey and Minnie Mouse) awakening in Forest

1985. Birth Bicentenaries of Grimm Brothers (folklorists). Designs showing Walt Disney cartoon characters in scenes from "Hansel and Gretel". Multicoloured.

685	5c. Type **119**	55	55
686	50c. Hansel and Gretel find the gingerbread house	1·50	60
687	90c. Hansel and Gretel meeting the Witch	2·00	1·00
688	$4 Hansel and Gretel captured by the Witch	3·50	5·00
MS689	128×101 mm. $5 Hansel and Gretel riding on swan	8·00	9·00

120 Statue of Liberty and "Danmark" (Denmark)

1985. Centenary of the Statue of Liberty (1986). The Statue of Liberty and Cadet ships.

690	10c. Type **120**	1·00	85
691	20c. "Eagle" (U.S.A.)	1·25	90
692	60c. "Amerigo Vespucci" (Italy)	1·60	1·50
693	75c. "Sir Winston Churchill" (Great Britain)	1·60	1·50
694	$2 "Nippon Maru" (Japan)	1·75	4·00
695	$2.50 "Gorch Fock" (West Germany)	1·75	4·00
MS696	96×69 mm. $5 Statue of Liberty (vert)	7·00	4·50

1985. 80th Anniv of Rotary (10, 35c.) and International Youth Year (others). Nos. 487, 491 and 497 optd or surch **80TH ANNIVERSARY ROTARY 1985** and emblem (10, 35c.) or **INTERNATIONAL YOUTH YEAR** and emblem ($1, $5).

697	10c. Island dinghies	25	15
698	35c. on 30c. Little Bay cliffs	55	30
699	$1 Bagging lobster at Island Harbour	1·25	80
700	$5 on 30c. Little Bay cliffs	4·00	4·50

123 Johannes Hevelius (astronomer) and Mayan Temple Observatory

1986. Appearance of Halley's Comet. Multicoloured.
701 5c. Type **123** 55 55
702 10c. "Viking Lander" space vehicle on Mars, 1976 . . 55 55
703 60c. Comet in 1664 (from "Theatri Cosmicum", 1668) 1·50 85
704 $4 Comet over Mississippi riverboat, 1835 (150th birth anniv of Mark Twain) . . 4·50 5·00
MS705 101 × 70 mm. $5 Halley's Comet over Anguilla . . . . . 4·50 6·00

124 "The Crucifixion"

125 Princess Elizabeth inspecting Guards, 1946

1986. Easter.
706 **124** 10c. multicoloured 20 20
707 – 25c. multicoloured 35 35
708 – 45c. multicoloured 65 65
709 – $4 multicoloured . . . . 3·25 3·75
MS710 – 93 × 75 mm. $5 multicoloured (horiz) . . . . . 5·50 7·50
DESIGNS: 25c. to $5 Different stained glass windows from Chartres Cathedral.

1986. 60th Birthday of Queen Elizabeth II.
711 **125** 20c. black and yellow . . 40 20
712 – $2 multicoloured . . . . 1·75 1·50
713 – $3 multicoloured . . . . 1·75 1·75
MS714 – 120 × 85 mm. $5 black and brown . . . . 2·75 3·75
DESIGNS: $2 Queen at Garter Ceremony; $3 At Trooping the Colour; $5 Duke and Duchess of York with baby Princess Elizabeth, 1926.

1986. "Ameripex" International Stamp Exhibition, Chicago. Nos. 659, 667, 671, 673 and 675 optd **AMERIPEX 1986**.
715 5c. Brown pelican 60 75
716 45c. Pearly-eyed thrasher . . 1·25 45
717 $1 Audubon's shearwater . . 2·00 1·10
718 $2.50 Bananaquit . . . . . 2·75 3·00
719 $10 Green-backed heron . . 6·50 8·50

127 Prince Andrew and Miss Sarah Ferguson

130 Christopher Columbus with Astrolabe

129 Trading Sloop

1986. Royal Wedding. Multicoloured.
720 10c. Type **127** 50 15
721 35c. Prince Andrew 85 35
722 $2 Miss Sarah Ferguson . . 2·25 1·50
723 $3 Prince Andrew and Miss Sarah Ferguson (diffferent) 2·50 2·00
MS724 119 × 90 mm. $6 Westminster Abbey . . . . 5·50 6·50

1986. International Peace Year. Nos. 616/23 optd **INTERNATIONAL YEAR OF PEACE**.
725 10c. Type **109** 90 60
726 25c. Abraham Lincoln . . . 1·25 50
727 35c. Henri Christophe . . . 1·40 55
728 60c. Thomas Clarkson . . . 2·00 80
729 75c. William Wilberforce . . 2·00 1·00
730 $1 Olaudah Equiano . . . 2·00 1·25
731 $2.50 General Gordon . . . 3·50 4·75
732 $5 Granville Sharp . . . . 4·25 7·00
MS733 150 × 121 mm. Nos. 725/32 15·00 17·00

1986. Christmas. Ships. Multicoloured.
734 10c. Type **129** . . . . 1·75 60
735 45c. "Lady Rodney" (cargo liner) . . . . 3·25 1·10
736 80c. "West Derby" (19th-century sailing ship) 4·25 2·50
737 $3 "Warspite" (local sloop) 8·50 10·00
MS738 130 × 100 mm. $4 Boat-race day (vert) . . . . 17·00 19·00

1986. 500th Anniv (1992) of Discovery of America by Columbus (1st issue). Multicoloured.
739 5c. Type **130** 60 60
740 10c. Columbus on board ship 1·00 60
741 35c. "Santa Maria" . . . . 2·10 1·10
742 80c. King Ferdinand and Queen Isabella of Spain (horiz) . . . . 1·50 1·75
743 $4 Caribbean Indians smoking tobacco (horiz) . . 3·25 5·00
MS744 Two sheets, each 96 × 66 mm. (a) $5 Caribbean manatee (horiz). (b) $5 Dragon tree Set of 2 sheets . . . . . 15·00 17·00
See also Nos. 902/6.

131 "Danaus plexippus"

1987. Easter. Butterflies. Multicoloured.
745 10c. Type **131** . . . . 1·50 70
746 80c. "Anartia jatrophae" . . 4·00 2·75
747 $1 "Heliconius charithonia" 4·25 2·75
748 $2 "Junonia evarete" . . . . 7·00 8·50
MS749 90 × 69 mm. $6 "Dryas julia" 11·00 13·00

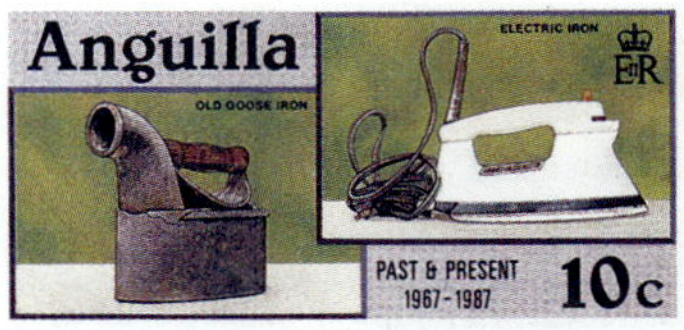

132 Old Goose Iron and Modern Electric Iron

1987. 20th Anniv of Separation from St. Kitts-Nevis. Multicoloured.
750 10c. Type **132** 70 40
751 35c. Old East End School and Albena Lake-Hodge Comprehensive College . . 75 45
752 45c. Past and present markets 85 50
753 80c. Previous sailing ferry and new motor ferry, Blowing Point . . . . . . 2·50 1·25
754 $1 Original mobile post office and new telephone exchange . . . . 2·50 1·40
755 $2 Open-air meeting, Burrowes Park and House of Assembly in session . . 2·75 3·25
MS756 159 × 127 mm. Nos. 750/5 12·00 15·00

1987. "Capex '87" International Stamp Exhibition, Toronto. Nos. 665a, 667, 670 and 675 optd **CAPEX'87**.
757 35c. Lesser Antillean bullfinch . . . . 2·25 80
758 45c. Pearly-eyed thrasher . . 2·25 80
759 80c. Grey kingbird . . . . . 3·25 1·25
760 $10 Green-backed heron . . 11·00 13·00

1987. 20th Anniv of Independence. Nos. 659, 661/4 and 665a/75 optd **20 YEARS OF PROGRESS 1967–1987**, No. 762 surch also.
761 5c. Brown pelican . . . . . 2·75 2·75
762 10c. on 15c. Magnificent frigate bird . . . . . . 2·75 2·75
763 15c. Magnificent frigate bird 3·00 3·00
764 20c. Antillean crested hummingbird . . . . . . 3·00 3·00
765 25c. Type **116** . . . . . . 3·00 3·00
766 30c. Caribbean elaenia . . . 3·00 3·00
767 35c. Lesser Antillean bullfinch . . . . 3·00 3·00
768 40c. Yellow-crowned night heron . . . . 3·00 3·00
769 45c. Pearly-eyed thrasher . . 3·00 3·00
770 50c. Laughing gull . . . . . 3·00 3·00
771 65c. Brown booby . . . . . 3·25 3·25
772 80c. Grey kingbird . . . . . 3·25 3·25
773 $1 Audubon's shearwater . . 3·25 3·25
774 $1.35 Roseate tern . . . . 3·75 4·00
775 $2.50 Bananaquit . . . . . 4·50 6·00
776 $5 Belted kingfisher . . . . 6·00 8·50
777 $10 Green-backed heron . . 8·00 11·00

135 Wicket Keeper and Game in Progress

1987. Cricket World Cup. Multicoloured.
778 10c. Type **135** . . . . . . 2·25 80
779 35c. Batsman and local Anguilla team . . . . . . 2·25 70
780 45c. Batsman and game in progress . . . . 2·75 75
781 $2.50 Bowler and game in progress . . . . 5·00 8·50
MS782 100 × 75 mm. $6 Batsman and game in progress (different) 15·00 16·00

136 West Indian Top Shell

1987. Christmas. Sea Shells and Crabs. Mult.
783 10c. Type **136** . . . . 1·50 55
784 35c. Ghost crab . . . . . . 2·25 60
785 50c. Spiny Caribbean vase . . 3·00 1·40
786 $2 Great land crab . . . . . 6·00 8·00
MS787 101 × 75 mm. $6 Queen or pink conch . . . . 12·00 13·00

1987. Royal Ruby Wedding. Nos. 665a, 671/2 and 675 optd **40TH WEDDING ANNIVERSARY H.M. QUEEN ELIZABETH II H.R.H. THE DUKE OF EDINBURGH**.
788 35c. Lesser Antillean bullfinch . . . . 1·50 55
789 $1 Audubon's shearwater . . 2·25 80
790 $1.35 Roseate tern . . . . . 2·50 90
791 $10 Green-backed heron . . 6·50 8·50

138 "Crinum erubescens"

139 Relay Racing

1988. Easter. Lilies. Multicoloured.
792 30c. Type **138** 60 25
793 45c. Spider lily 70 25
794 $1 "Crinum macowanii" . . 1·75 85
795 $2.50 Day lily . . . . 2·00 3·00
MS796 100 × 75 mm. $6 Easter lily 2·75 4·50

1988. Olympic Games, Seoul. Multicoloured.
797 35c. Type **139** 45 30
798 45c. Windsurfing 55 45
799 50c. Tennis . . . . 1·50 1·10
800 80c. Basketball . . . . . . 6·50 2·75
MS801 104 × 78 mm. $6 Athletics 3·00 4·50

140 Common Sea Fan

1988. Christmas. Marine Life. Multicoloured.
802 35c. Type **140** . . . . 1·00 30
803 80c. Coral crab . . . . . . 1·75 70
804 $1 Grooved brain coral . . . 2·00 1·00
805 $1.60 Queen triggerfish . . . 2·75 3·25
MS806 103 × 78 mm. $6 West Indian spiny lobster . . . . 3·00 4·50

1988. Visit of Princess Alexandra. Nos. 665a, 670/1 and 673 optd **H.R.H. PRINCESS ALEXANDRA'S VISIT NOVEMBER 1988**.
807 35c. Lesser Antillean bullfinch . . . . 2·50 70
808 80c. Grey kingbird . . . . . 3·25 1·40
809 $1 Audubon's shearwater . . 3·25 1·60
810 $2.50 Bananaquit . . . . . 5·00 5·50

142 Wood Slave

1989. Lizards. Multicoloured.
811 45c. Type **142** . . . . 1·75 50
812 80c. Slippery back . . . . . 2·50 85
813 $2.50 "Iguana delicatissima" 4·50 4·75
MS814 101 × 75 mm. $6 Tree lizard 14·00 4·75

143 "Christ Crowned with Thorns" (detail) (Bosch)

144 University Arms

1989. Easter. Religious Paintings. Multicoloured.
815 35c. Type **143** 80 25
816 80c. "Christ bearing the Cross" (detail) (Gerard David) . . . . 1·25 75
817 $1 "The Deposition" (detail) (Gerard David) . . . . 1·40 80
818 $1.60 "Pieta" (detail) (Rogier van der Weyden) . . . . 2·00 2·75
MS819 103 × 77 mm. $6 "Crucified Christ with the Virgin Mary and Saints" (detail) (Raphael) . . . 2·75 4·25

1989. 40th Anniv of University of the West Indies.
820 **144** $5 multicoloured . . . . 3·75 4·25

1989. 20th Anniv of First Manned Landing on Moon. Nos. 670/2 and 674 optd **20TH ANNIVERSARY MOON LANDING**.
821 80c. Grey kingbird . . . . . 2·75 90
822 $1 Audubon's shearwater . . 2·75 1·00
823 $1.35 Roseate tern . . . . 3·00 1·75
824 $5 Belted kingfisher . . . . 7·50 10·00

146 Lone Star (house), 1930

1989. Christmas. Historic Houses. Multicoloured.
825 5c. Type **146** . . . . 50 1·00
826 35c. Whitehouse, 1906 . . . 1·00 45
827 45c. Hodges House . . . . . 1·10 50
828 80c. Warden's Place . . . . 1·75 1·75
MS829 102 × 77 mm. $6 Wallblake House, 1787 . . . . 3·75 6·00

147 Bigeye ("Blear Eye")

1990. Fishes. Multicoloured.
830B 5c. Type **147** 60 75
831B 10c. Long-spined squirrelfish ("Redman") 60 75
832A 15c. Stop-light parrotfish ("Speckletail") 60 60
833A 25c. Blue-striped grunt . . 70 80
834A 30c. Yellow jack 70 80
835B 35c. Red hind 75 75
836A 40c. Spotted goatfish . . . 90 80
837A 45c. Queen triggerfish ("Old wife") 90 60
838A 50c. Coney ("Butter fish") 90 80
839A 65c. Smooth trunkfish ("Shell fish") . . . . . . 1·00 80
840A 80c. Yellow-tailed snapper 1·25 90
841A $1 Banded butterflyfish ("Katy") . . . . 1·25 1·00
842A $1.35 Nassau grouper . . . 1·50 1·50
843A $2.50 Blue tang ("Doctor fish") . . . . 2·25 3·50
844A $5 Queen angelfish . . . . 3·00 5·00
845A $10 Great barracuda . . . 4·75 8·00

148 The Last Supper

149 G.B. 1840 Penny Black

1990. Easter. Multicoloured.
846 35c. Type **148** . . . . 1·25 40
847 45c. The Trial . . . . 1·25 40

848 $1.35 The Crucifixion . . . . 3·00 2·25
849 $2.50 The Empty Tomb . . . 3·50 5·00
MS850 114 × 84 mm. $6 The Resurrection . . . . 11·00 13·00

1990. "Stamp World London 90" International Stamp Exhibition. Multicoloured.
851 25c. Type **149** . . . . 1·25 35
852 50c. G.B. 1840 Twopenny Blue . . . . 1·75 50
853 $1.50 Cape of Good Hope 1861 1d. "woodblock" (horiz) . . . . 3·00 3·25
854 $2.50 G.B. 1882 £5 (horiz) . . 3·50 4·25
MS855 86 × 71 mm. $6 Penny Black and Twopence Blue (horiz) . . 12·00 15·00

1990. Anniversaries and Events. Nos. 841/4 optd.
856 $1 Banded butterflyfish (optd **EXPO '90**) . . . . 1·50 1·00
857 $1.35 Nassau grouper (optd **1990 INTERNATIONAL LITERACY YEAR**) . . . 1·60 1·25
858 $2.50 Blue tang (optd **WORLD CUP FOOTBALL CHAMPIONSHIPS 1990**) 6·00 6·00
859 $5 Queen angelfish (optd **90TH BIRTHDAY H.M. THE QUEEN MOTHER**) 11·00 11·00

151 Mermaid Flag

1990. Island Flags. Multicoloured.
860 50c. Type **151** . . . . 1·75 60
861 80c. New Anguilla official flag . . . . 2·25 1·00
862 $1 Three Dolphins flag . . . 2·50 1·10
863 $5 Governor's official flag . . 7·00 9·00

152 Laughing Gulls

1990. Christmas. Sea Birds. Multicoloured.
864 10c. Type **152** 60 50
865 35c. Brown booby . . . . . 1·00 50
866 $1.50 Bridled tern . . . . . 2·00 2·00
867 $3.50 Brown pelican . . . . 3·25 4·75
MS868 101 × 76 mm. $6 Least tern 8·50 11·00

1991. Easter. Nos. 846/9 optd **1991**.
869 35c. Type **148** . . . . 1·50 60
870 45c. The Trial . . . . 1·60 60
871 $1.35 The Crucifixion . . . . 3·00 2·00
872 $2.50 The Empty Tomb . . . 4·25 7·50
MS873 114 × 84 mm. $6 The Resurrection . . . . 12·00 14·00

154 Angel

155 Angels with Palm Branches outside St. Gerard's Church

1991. Christmas.
874 **154** 5c. violet, brown & black 1·00 1·00
875 – 35c. multicoloured . . . . 2·50 55
876 – 80c. multicoloured . . . . 2·50 2·25
877 – $1 multicoloured . . . . 3·50 2·25
MS878 – 131 × 97 mm. $5 multicoloured . . . . 11·00 13·00
DESIGNS—VERT: 35c. Father Christmas. HORIZ: 80c. Church and house; $1 Palm trees at night; $5 Anguilla village.

1992. Easter. Multicoloured.
879 30c. Type **155** . . . . 1·25 45
880 45c. Angels singing outside Methodist Church . . . . 1·50 45
881 80c. Village (horiz) . . . . 2·50 90
882 $1 Congregation going to St. Mary's Church . . . 2·50 1·00
883 $5 Dinghy regatta (horiz) . . 6·50 9·50

1992. No. 834 surch **$1.60**.
884 $1.60 on 30c. Yellow jack . . 2·75 2·25

157 Anguillan Flags

1992. 25th Anniv of Separation from St. Kitts-Nevis. Multicoloured.
885 80c. Type **157** . . . . 2·75 1·50
886 $1 Present official seal . . . 2·75 1·50
887 $1.60 Anguillan flags at airport . . . . 4·00 3·75
888 $2 Royal Commissioner's official seal . . . . . . 4·00 4·50
MS889 116 × 117 mm. $10 "Independent Anguilla" overprinted stamps of 1967 (85 × 85 mm) . . . . 14·00 15·00

158 Dinghy Race

1992. Sailing Dinghy Racing.
890 **158** 20c. multicoloured . . . . 1·75 75
891 – 35c. multicoloured . . . . 2·25 65
892 – 45c. multicoloured . . . . 2·50 65
893 – 80c. multicoloured . . . . 3·25 4·50
894 – 80c. black and blue . . . 3·25 4·50
895 – $1 multicoloured . . . . 3·25 2·75
MS896 – 129 × 30 mm. $6 multicoloured . . . . 9·00 11·00
DESIGNS—VERT: 35c. Stylized poster; 80c. (No. 893) "Blue Bird" in race; 80c. (No. 894) Construction drawings of "Blue Bird" by Douglas Pyle; $1 Stylized poster (different). HORIZ: 45c. Dinghies on beach. (97 × 32 mm)—$6 Composite designs as 20 and 45c. values.

159 Mucka Jumbie on Stilts

1992. Christmas. Local Traditions. Mult.
897 20c. Type **159** . . . . 1·00 40
898 70c. Masqueraders . . . . . 2·00 60
899 $1.05 Baking in old style oven . . . . 2·25 1·25
900 $2.40 Collecting presents from Christmas tree . . . 4·00 6·00
MS901 128 × 101 mm. $5 As No. 900 3·75 6·00

160 Columbus landing in New World

1992. 500th Anniv of Discovery of America by Columbus (2nd issue).
902 **160** 80c. multicoloured . . . . 3·00 1·25
903 – $1 black and brown . . . 3·00 1·25
904 – $2 multicoloured . . . . 4·00 4·50
905 – $3 multicoloured . . . . 4·50 6·50
MS906 – 78 × 54 mm. $6 multicoloured . . . . 11·00 12·00
DESIGNS—VERT: $1 Christopher Columbus; $6 Columbus and map of West Indies. HORIZ: $2 Fleet of Columbus; $3 "Pinta".

161 "Kite Flying" (Kyle Brooks)

163 Lord Great Chamberlain presenting Spurs of Charity to Queen

162 Salt Picking

1993. Easter. Children's Paintings. Mult.
907 20c. Type **161** . . . . 2·00 75
908 45c. "Clifftop Village Service" (Kara Connor) . . 2·50 70
909 80c. "Morning Devotion on Sombrero" (Junior Carty) 3·25 1·40
910 $1.50 "Hill Top Church Service" (Leana Harris) . . 4·50 7·00
MS911 90 × 110 mm. $5 "Good Friday Kites" (Marvin Hazel and Kyle Brooks) (39 × 53 mm) . . 5·50 7·50

1993. Traditional Industries. Mult.
912 20c. Type **162** . . . . 3·50 1·25
913 80c. Tobacco growing . . . 2·75 1·25
914 $1 Cotton picking . . . . . 2·75 1·25
915 $2 Harvesting sugar cane . . 4·75 7·00
MS916 111 × 85 mm. $6 Fishing 12·00 14·00

1993. 40th Anniv of Coronation. Mult.
917 80c. Type **163** . . . . 2·25 80
918 $1 The Benediction . . . . . 2·50 90
919 $2 Queen Elizabeth II in Coronation robes . . . . 3·25 3·50
920 $3 St. Edward's Crown . . . 3·75 4·50
MS921 114 × 95 mm. $6 The Queen and Prince Philip in Coronation coach . . . . 13·00 14·00

164 Carnival Pan Player

1993. Anguilla Carnival. Multicoloured.
922 20c. Type **164** 80 40
923 45c. Revellers dressed as pirates 90 50
924 80c. Revellers dressed as stars 1·25 40
925 $1 Mas dancing . . . . . . 2·25 80
926 $2 Masked couple . . . . . 3·50 4·50
927 $3 Revellers dressed as commandos . . . . 4·25 6·00
MS928 123 × 94 mm. $5 Revellers in fantasy costumes . . . . . . 12·00 14·00

165 Mucka Jumbies Carnival Characters

167 Princess Alexandra, 1988

166 Travelling Branch Post Van at Sandy Ground

1993. Christmas. Multicoloured.
929 20c. Type **165** . . . . 1·25 80
930 35c. Local carol singers . . . 1·60 70
931 45c. Christmas home baking 1·75 70
932 $3 Decorating Christmas tree 5·50 7·50
MS933 123 × 118 mm. $4 Mucka Jumbies and carol singers (58½ × 47 mm) . . . . 3·50 5·00

1994. Delivering the Mail. Multicoloured.
934 20c. Type **166** . . . . 2·00 80
935 45c. "Betsy R" (mail schooner) at The Forest (vert) . . . . 2·50 80
936 80c. Mail van at old Post Office . . . . 3·00 1·60
937 $1 Jeep on beach, Island Harbour (vert) . . . . . 3·00 1·60
938 $4 New Post Office . . . . . 4·75 8·00

1994. Royal Visitors. Multicoloured.
939 45c. Type **167** . . . . 1·75 75
940 50c. Princess Alice, 1960 . . 1·75 75
941 80c. Prince Philip, 1993 . . . 2·50 1·50
942 $1 Prince Charles, 1973 . . . 2·75 1·50
943 $2 Queen Elizabeth II, 1994 3·50 5·00
MS944 162 × 90 mm. Nos. 939/43 12·00 13·00

168 "The Crucifixion"

170 "The Nativity" (Gustave Dore)

169 Cameroun Player and Pontiac Silverdome, Detroit

1994. Easter. Stained-glass Windows. Multicoloured.
945 20c. Type **168** . . . . 1·00 50
946 45c. "The Empty Tomb" . . 1·40 45
947 80c. "The Resurrection" . . 2·00 90
948 $3 "Risen Christ with Disciples" . . . . 4·50 7·50

1994. World Cup Football Championship, U.S.A. Multicoloured.
949 20c. Type **169** 85 50
950 70c. Argentine player and Foxboro Stadium, Boston 1·50 70
951 $1.80 Italian player and RFK Memorial Stadium, Washington . . . . 2·50 3·00
952 $2.40 German player and Soldier Field, Chicago . . 3·50 4·00
MS953 112 × 85 mm. $6 American and Colombian players . . . . 11·00 12·00

1994. Christmas. Religious Paintings. Mult.
954 20c. Type **170** . . . . 1·00 80
955 30c. "The Wise Men guided by the Star" (Dore) . . . 1·25 80
956 35c. "The Annunciation" (Dore) . . . . 1·25 80
957 45c. "Adoration of the Shepherds" (detail) (Poussin) . . . . 1·40 80
958 $2.40 "The Flight into Egypt" (Dore) . . . . . 4·50 6·00

171 Pair of Zenaida Doves

1995. Easter. Zenaida Doves. Multicoloured.
959 20c. Type **171** 50 40
960 45c. Dove on branch 75 50
961 50c. Guarding nest 80 55
962 $5 With chicks . . . . 5·50 7·00

172 Trygve Lie (first Secretary-General) and General Assembly

1995. 50th Anniv of United Nations. Multicoloured.
963 20c. Type **172** 30 30
964 80c. Flag and building showing "50" 60 65
965 $1 Dag Hammarskjold and U Thant (former Secretary-Generals) and U.N. Charter 70 75
966 $5 U.N. Building (vert) . . . 4·00 7·00

173 Anniversary Emblem and Map of Anguilla

1995. 25th Anniv of Caribbean Development Bank. Multicoloured.

967	45c. Type **173**	1·50	1·75
968	$5 Bank building and launches	3·00	4·25

174 Blue Whale

1995. Endangered Species. Whales. Multicoloured.

969	20c. Type **174**	2·50	85
970	45c. Right whale (vert)	2·75	75
971	$1 Sperm whale	3·25	1·75
972	$5 Humpback whale	8·50	9·00

175 Palm Tree

1995. Christmas. Multicoloured.

973	10c. Type **175**	90	90
974	25c. Balloons and fishes	1·25	60
975	45c. Shells	1·50	60
976	$5 Fishes in shape of Christmas tree	9·00	10·00

176 Deep Water Gorgonia

177 Running

1996. Corals. Multicoloured.

977	20c. Type **176**	1·75	80
978	80c. Common sea fan	2·75	1·00
979	$5 Venus sea fern	8·00	10·00

1996. Olympic Games, Atlanta. Multicoloured.

980	20c. Type **177**	1·00	60
981	80c. Javelin throwing and wheelchair basketball	3·00	1·25
982	$1 High jumping and hurdles	1·50	1·25
983	$3.50 Olympic rings and torch with Greek and American flags	5·50	5·50

178 Siege of Sandy Hill Fort

1996. Bicentenary of the Battle for Anguilla. Multicoloured.

984	60c. Type **178**	1·25	1·00
985	75c. French troops destroying church (horiz)	1·25	1·00
986	$1.50 Naval battle (horiz)	2·75	2·50
987	$4 French troops landing at Rendezvous Bay	4·00	5·50

179 Gooseberry

1997. Fruit. Multicoloured.

988	10c. Type **179**	50	60
989	20c. West Indian cherry	60	30
990	40c. Tamarind	75	30
991	50c. Pomme-surette	80	40
992	60c. Sea almond	90	55
993	75c. Sea grape	1·00	85
994	80c. Banana	1·10	85
995	$1 Genip	1·25	1·00
996	$1.10 Coco plum	1·40	1·60
997	$1.25 Pope	1·75	2·00
998	$1.50 Pawpaw	1·75	2·00
999	$2 Sugar apple	2·25	3·00
1000	$3 Soursop	3·00	3·75
1001	$4 Pomegranate	3·50	4·25
1002	$5 Cashew	4·00	5·00
1003	$10 Mango	7·00	8·00

180 West Indian Iguanas hatching

1997. Endangered Species. West Indian Iguanas. Multicoloured.

1004	20c. Type **180**	1·75	1·50
1005	50c. On rock	2·00	1·60
1006	75c. On branch	2·25	2·00
1007	$3 Head of West Indian iguana	3·25	4·00

181 "Juluca, Rainbow Deity"

1997. Ancient Stone Carvings from Fountain Cavern. Multicoloured.

1008	30c. Type **181**	55	35
1009	$1.25 "Lizard with front legs extended"	1·10	1·00
1010	$2.25 "Chief"	1·75	2·50
1011	$2.75 "Jocahu, the Creator"	2·25	3·00

182 Diana, Princess of Wales

1998. Diana, Princess of Wales Commemoration. Multicoloured.

1012	15c. Type **182**	2·00	1·25
1013	$1 Wearing yellow blouse	2·75	1·60
1014	$1.90 Wearing tiara	3·00	3·00
1015	$2.25 Wearing blue short-sleeved Red Cross blouse	3·25	3·25

183 "Treasure Island" (Valarie Alix)

1998. International Arts Festival. Multicoloured.

1016	15c. Type **183**	60	60
1017	30c. "Posing in the Light" (Melsadis Fleming) (vert)	60	40
1018	$1 "Pescadores de Anguilla" (Juan Garcia) (vert)	90	80
1019	$1.50 "Fresh Catch" (Verna Hart)	1·25	1·75
1020	$1.90 "The Bell Tower of St. Mary's" (Ricky Racardo Edwards) (vert)	1·50	2·25

184 Roasting Corn-cobs on Fire

1998. Christmas. "Hidden Beauty of Anguilla". Children's Paintings. Multicoloured.

1021	15c. Type **184**	35	30
1022	$1 Fresh fruit and market stallholder	80	50
1023	$1.50 Underwater scene	1·00	1·25
1024	$3 Cacti and view of sea	1·60	2·50

185 University of West Indies Centre, Anguilla

1998. 50th Anniv of University of West Indies. Multicoloured.

1025	$1.50 Type **185**	80	90
1026	$1.90 Man with torch and University arms	1·10	1·50

186 Sopwith Camel and Bristol F2B Fighters

1998. 80th Anniv of Royal Air Force. Multicoloured.

1027	30c. Type **186**	1·00	50
1028	$1 Supermarine Spitfire Mk II and Hawker Hurricane Mk I	2·00	90
1029	$1.50 Avro Lancaster	2·25	2·25
1030	$1.90 Panavia Tornado F3 and Harrier GR7	2·75	3·00

187 Saturn 5 Rocket and "Apollo 11" Command Module

1999. 30th Anniv of First Manned Landing on Moon. Multicoloured.

1031	30c. Type **187**	55	35
1032	$1 Astronaut Edwin Aldrin, Lunar Module "Eagle" and first footprint on Moon	1·00	70
1033	$1.50 Lunar Module leaving Moon's surface	1·00	1·00
1034	$1.90 Recovery of Command Module	1·40	2·00

188 Albena Lake Hodge

189 Library and Resource Centre

1999. Anguillan Heroes and Heroines (1st series). Each black, green and cream.

1035	30c. Type **188**	40	30
1036	$1 Collins O. Hodge	80	65
1037	$1.50 Edwin Wallace Rey	1·00	1·25
1038	$1.90 Walter G. Hodge	1·25	2·00

1999. Modern Architecture. Multicoloured.

1039	30c. Type **189**	45	35
1040	65c. Parliamentary building and Court House	65	60
1041	$1 Caribbean Commercial Bank	1·00	80
1042	$1.50 Police Headquarters	2·25	2·00
1043	$1.90 Post Office	1·75	2·50

190 Beach Barbeque and Fireworks

1999. Christmas and New Millennium. Mult.

1044	30c. Type **190**	55	30
1045	$1 Musicians around globe	1·25	55
1046	$1.50 Family at Christmas dinner	1·75	1·75
1047	$1.90 Celebrations around decorated shrub	2·00	2·50

191 Shoal Bay (East)

2000. Beaches. Multicoloured.

1048	15c. Type **191**	30	40
1049	30c. Maundys Bay	35	30
1050	$1 Rendezvous Bay	75	50
1051	$1.50 Meads Bay	1·00	1·25
1052	$1.90 Little Bay	1·25	1·75
1053	$2 Sandy Ground	1·25	1·75
MS1054	144 × 144 mm. Nos. 1048/53	4·25	4·75

192 Toy Banjo (Casey Reid)

2000. Easter. Indigenous Toys. Multicoloured.

1055	25c. Type **192**	40	30
1056	30c. Spinning top (Johniela Harrigan)	40	30
1057	$1.50 Catapult (Akeem Rogers)	1·10	1·10
1058	$1.90 Roller (Melisa Mussington)	1·40	1·75
1059	$2.50 Killy Ban (trap) (Casey Reid)	1·75	2·25
MS1060	145 × 185 mm. 75c. Rag Doll (Jahia Esposito) (vert); $1 Kite (Javed Maynard) (vert); $1.25, Cricket ball (Jevon Lake) (vert); $4 Pond boat (Corvel Flemming) (vert)	4·75	5·50

193 Lanville Harrigan

2000. West Indies Cricket Tour and 100th Test Match at Lord's. Multicoloured.

1061	$2 Type **193**	2·00	2·00
1062	$4 Cardigan Connor	3·00	4·00
MS1063	119 × 102 mm. $6 Lord's Cricket Ground (horiz)	9·00	9·00

2000. "The Stamp Show 2000" International Stamp Exhibition, London. Beaches. As No. **MS**1054, but with exhibition logo on bottom margin. Mult.

MS1064	144 × 144 mm. Nos. 1048/53	4·75	6·00

194 Prince William and Royal Family after Trooping the Colour

2000. 18th Birthday of Prince William. Mult.

1065	30c. Type **194**	1·50	50
1066	$1 Prince and Princess of Wales with sons	2·25	85
1067	$1.90 With Prince Charles and Prince Harry	2·75	2·75
1068	$2.25 Skiing with father and brother	3·25	3·25
MS1069	125 × 95 mm. $8 Prince William as pupil at Eton	7·00	8·00

195 Queen Elizabeth the Queen Mother and Prince William

2000. 100th Birthday of Queen Elizabeth the Queen Mother. Showing different portraits. Multicoloured.

1070	30c. Type **195**	65	40
1071	$1.50 Island scene	1·50	1·00
1072	$1.90 Clarence House	1·75	1·60
1073	$5 Castle of Mey	3·25	4·00

196 "Anguilla Montage" (Weme Caster)

2000. International Arts Festival. Multicoloured.

1074	15c. Type **196**	30	40
1075	30c. "Serenity" (Damien Carty)	35	35
1076	65c. "Inter Island Cargo" (Paula Walden)	55	45
1077	$1.50 "Rainbow City where Spirits find Form" (Fiona Percy)	1·25	1·50
1078	$1.90 "Sailing Silver Seas" (Valerie Carpenter)	1·40	2·00
MS1079	75 × 100 mm. $7 "Historic Anguilla" (Melsadis Fleming) (42 × 28 mm)	4·75	6·00

197 Dried Flower Arrangement

2000. Christmas. Flower and Garden Show.

1080 **197**	15c. multicoloured	25	25
1081	– 25c. multicoloured	30	25
1082	– 30c. multicoloured	30	25
1083	– $1 multicoloured	75	60
1084	– $1.50 multicoloured	1·25	1·50
1085	– $1.90 multicoloured	1·50	2·25

DESIGNS: 25c. to $1.90, Different floral arrangements.

198 Winning Primary School Football Team (Bank Sponsorship)

2000. 15th Anniv of National Bank of Anguilla. Multicoloured.

1086	30c. Type **198**	30	25
1087	$1 *De-Chan* (yacht) (Bank sponsorship) (vert)	70	60
1088	$1.50 Bank crest (vert)	1·25	1·50
1089	$1.90 New Bank Headquarters	1·50	2·00

199 Ebenezer Methodist Church in 19th Century

2000. 170th Anniv of Ebenezer Methodist Church.

1090 **199**	30c. brown and black	30	20
1091	– $1.90 multicoloured	1·50	2·00

DESIGN: $1.90, Church in 2000.

200 Soroptomist Day Care Centre

2001. United Nations Women's Human Rights Campaign. Multicoloured.

1092	25c. Type **200**	30	30
1093	30c. Britannia Idalia Gumbs (Anguillan politician) (vert)	30	30
1094	$2.25 "Caribbean Woman II" (Leisel Renee Jobity) (vert)	1·60	2·25

201 John Paul Jones and U.S.S. *Ranger* (frigate)

2001. 225th Anniv of American War of Independence. Multicoloured.

1095	30c. Type **201**	1·25	60
1096	$1 George Washington and Battle of Yorktown	1·50	1·00
1097	$1.50 Thomas Jefferson and submission of Declaration of Independence to Congress	2·00	2·50
1098	$1.90 John Adams and the signing of the Treaty of Paris	2·00	2·50

202 Bahama Pintail

2001. Anguillian Birds. Multicoloured.

1099	30c. Type **202**	75	50
1100	$1 Black-faced grassquit (vert)	1·00	80
1101	$1.50 Common noddy	1·60	1·60
1102	$2 Black-necked stilt (vert)	2·00	2·25
1103	$3 Kentish plover ("Snowy Plover")	2·50	2·75
MS1104	124 × 88 mm. 25c. Snowy egret; 65c. Red-billed tropic bird; $1.35, Greater yellowlegs; $2.25, Sooty tern	6·00	6·00

203 "Children encircling Globe" (Urska Golob)

2001. U.N. Year of Dialogue among Civilisations.

1105 **203**	$1.90 multicoloured	1·60	2·25

204 Triangle

2001. Christmas. Indigenous Musical Instruments. Multicoloured.

1106	15c. Type **204**	25	30
1107	25c. Maracas	35	35
1108	30c. Guiro (vert)	35	35
1109	$1.50 Marimba	1·25	1·25
1110	$1.90 Tambu (hand drum) (vert)	1·50	1·75
1111	$2.50 Bass pan	2·00	2·50
MS1112	110 × 176 mm. 75c. Banjo (vert); $1 Quatro (vert); $1.25, Ukelele (vert); $3 Cello (vert)	5·00	6·00

205 Sombrero Lighthouse, 1962

206 Artist, Entertainer and Sportsmen

2002. Commissioning of New Sombrero Lighthouse. Multicoloured.

1113	30c. Type **205**	75	55
1114	$1.50 Old and new lighthouses (horiz)	1·75	1·75
1115	$1.90 New, fully-automated lighthouse, 2001	2·00	2·25

2002. 20th Anniv of Social Security Board. Multicoloured (except 30c.).

1116	30c. Type **206** (ultramarine and blue)	40	30
1117	75c. Anguillans of all ages	70	65
1118	$2.50 Anguillan workers (horiz)	2·25	2·75

207 H.M.S. *Antrim* (destroyer), 1967

2002. Ships of the Royal Navy. Multicoloured.

1119	30c. Type **207**	60	45
1120	50c. H.M.S. *Formidable* (aircraft carrier), 1939	80	60
1121	$1.50 H.M.S. *Dreadnought* (battleship), 1906	1·25	1·50
1122	$2 H.M.S. *Warrior* (ironclad), 1860	1·75	2·00
MS1123	102 × 77 mm. H.M.S. *Ark Royal* (aircraft carrier), 1981 (vert)	6·50	7·00

208 Princess Elizabeth with Prince Charles

2002. Golden Jubilee. Multicoloured.

1124	30c. Type **208**	40	30
1125	$1.50 Queen Elizabeth wearing white coat	1·10	1·10
1126	$1.90 Queen Elizabeth in evening dress	1·75	1·75
1127	$5 Wearing yellow hat and coat	4·25	4·50
MS1128	106 × 75 mm. $8 Queen Elizabeth sitting at desk	8·50	9·50

209 Valley Health Centre

2002. Centenary of Pan American Health Organization. Multicoloured.

1129	30c. Type **209**	45	25
1130	$1.50 Centenary of PAHO logo	1·25	1·60

210 *Finance* (sloop)

2003. Past Sailing Vessels of Anguilla. Multicoloured.

1131	15c. Type **210**	40	40
1132	30c. *Tiny Gull*	50	30
1133	65c. *Lady Laurel* (schooner)	70	40
1134	75c. *Spitfire* (gaff rigged sloop)	70	40
1135	$1 *Liberator* (schooner)	90	50
1136	$1.35 *Excelsior* (schooner)	1·00	70
1137	$1.50 *Rose Millicent*	1·25	1·00
1138	$1.90 *Betsy R.* (sloop)	1·40	1·10
1139	$2 *Sunbeam R.* (sloop)	1·50	1·40
1140	$2.25 *New London*	1·75	1·90
1141	$3 *Ismay* (schooner)	2·25	2·50
1142	$10 *Warspite* (schooner)	7·00	7·50

211 Stone Pestle

2003. Artifacts of Anguilla. Multicoloured.

1143	30c. Type **211**	50	25
1144	$1 Frog worked shell ornament	1·00	60
1145	$1.50 Pottery	1·25	1·10
1146	$1.90 Mask worked shell ornament	1·50	1·75

212 Frangipani Beach Club

2003. Hotels of Anguilla. Multicoloured.

1147	75c. Type **212**	70	45
1148	$1 Pimms, Cap Juluca	85	55
1149	$1.35 Cocoloba Beach Resort	1·00	80
1150	$1.50 Malliouhana Hotel	1·25	1·10
1151	$1.90 Carmiar Beach Club	1·40	1·40
1152	$3 Covecastles	2·00	2·50

213 "Eudice's Garden" (Eunice Summer)

2004. International Arts Festival. Multicoloured.

1153	15c. Type **213**	40	30
1154	30c. "Hammocks" (Lisa Davenport)	50	30
1155	$1 "Conched Out" (Richard Shaffett)	90	70
1156	$1.50 "Islands Rhythms"(Carol Garvin)	1·10	1·10
1157	$1.90 "Party at the Beach"(Jean–Pierre Ballagny)	1·40	1·40
1158	$3 "Shoal Bay before Luis"(Jacqueline Mariethoz)	2·00	2·50

214 Athlete (400 Metres)

2004. Olympic Games, Athens. Multicoloured.

1159	30c. Type **214**	50	30
1160	$1 Laser dinghies (sailing)	90	60
1161	$1.50 Gymnastics (rings)	1·10	1·10
1162	$1.90 The Acropolis, Athens, Pierre de Coubertin (founder of modern Olympics) and Dimetrios Vikelas (first IOC President) (horiz)	1·40	1·75

215 Goat

2004. Goats of Anguilla. Multicoloured.

1163	30c. Type **215**	50	30
1164	50c. Black and white goat	60	35
1165	$1 Black and tan goat (vert)	90	60
1166	$1.50 Chestnut goat	1·10	1·10
1167	$1.90 Chestnut and white goat (vert)	1·40	1·50
1168	$2.25 Two kids	1·75	2·00

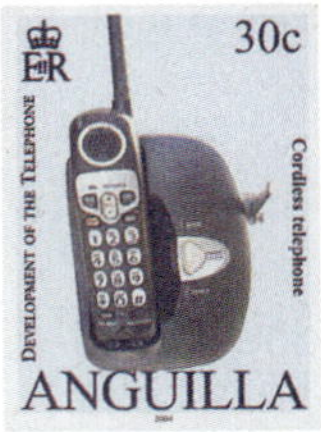

216 Cordless Telephone

2004. Development of the Telephone. Multicoloured.

1169	30c. Type **216**	30	20
1170	$1 Touch tone telephone	90	70
1171	$1.50 Cellular phone	1·25	1·40
1172	$1.90 Circular dial telephone (horiz)	1·60	1·75
1173	$3.80 Magneto telephone	3·25	3·50

217 Santa baking in Traditional Rock Oven

2004. Christmas. Multicoloured.

1174	30c. Type **217**	30	20
1175	$1.50 Santa climbing coconut tree	1·25	1·40
1176	$1.90 Santa's string band	1·40	1·60
1177	$3.80 Santa delivering gifts by donkey	2·75	3·00
MS1178	107 × 76 mm. $8 Santa delivering gifts by boat	6·00	7·00

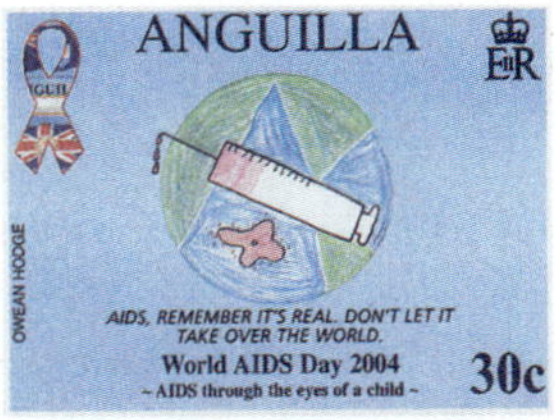

218 "AIDS, Remember it's Real. Don't let it take over the World" (Owean Hodge)

2005. World AIDS Day 2004—"AIDS through the Eyes of a Child". Children's paintings. Multicoloured.

1179	30c. Type **218**	30	20
1180	$1.50 "Arm Yourself against AIDS" (Lydia Fleming)	1·25	1·40
1181	$1.90 "AIDS is Your Concern" (Nina Rodriguez)	1·40	1·60
MS1182	144 × 144 mm. 15c. Classroom (Kenswick Richardson); 75c. Dancer, Schoolgirl, Teacher, Smoker (Toniquewah Ruan); $1 Girls and Tree (Elizabeth Anne Orchard); $2 "Even I can get AIDS" (Tricia Watty-Beard)	3·00	3·25

219 Arms of Anguilla and Rotary Emblem

2005. Centenary of Rotary International and 25th Anniv of Anguilla Rotary Club. Multicoloured.

1183	30c. Type **219**	30	20
1184	$1 Brown pelican and palm tree (District 7020)	80	70
1185	$1.50 Paul Harris (founder)	1·25	1·40
1186	$1.90 Children on slide (School Playground Project)	1·40	1·60

220 Grey Dog

2005. Dogs of Anguilla. Multicoloured.

1187	30c. Type **220**	30	20
1188	$1.50 Black and tan dog with puppy (vert)	1·25	1·40
1189	$1.90 Black and tan dog (vert)	1·40	1·60
1190	$2.25 Tan dog	1·70	1·80

221 Air Anguilla Cessna 402

2006. Early Airlines. Multicoloured.

1191	30c. Type **221**	40	30
1192	40c. LIAT DHC Dash 8	45	30
1193	60c. Winair Foxtrot DHC Twin Otter	70	40
1194	$1 Anguilla Airways Piper Aztec	1·00	70
1195	$1.50 St. Thomas Air Transport Piper Aztec	1·40	1·60
1196	$1.90 Carib Air Service Piper Aztec	1·90	2·10

222 *Appias drusillia*

2006. Butterflies. Multicoloured.

1197	30c. Type **222**	40	30
1198	$1.50 *Danaus plexippus megalippe*	1·25	1·40
1199	$1.90 *Phoebis sennae*	1·70	1·80
1200	$2.75 *Papilio demoleus*	2·40	2·50
MS1201	126 × 88 mm. 40c. *Aphrissa statira*; 60c. *Eurema elathea*; $1 *Danaus plexippus megalippe*; $3 *Agraulis vanillae*	4·75	5·00

223 Soroptimist International Logo

2007. 25th Anniv (2006) of Anguilla Soroptimist Club. Multicoloured.

1202	$1.90 Type **223**	1·70	1·80
1203	$2.75 Alecia Ballin	2·75	2·50

ANJOUAN — Pt. 6

One of the Comoro Is. between Madagascar and the East coast of Africa. Used stamps of Madagascar from 1914 and became part of the Comoro Islands in 1950.

100 centimes = 1 franc.

1892. "Tablet" key-type inscr "SULTANAT D'ANJOUAN".

1	D	1c. black on blue	1·10	1·75
2		2c. brown on buff	1·90	2·00
3		4c. brown on grey	3·00	2·50
4		5c. green on green	5·50	5·75
5		10c. black on lilac	7·00	5·50
14		10c. red	22·00	23·00
6		15c. blue	8·75	7·75
15		15c. grey	13·00	14·50
7		20c. red on green	8·75	10·50
8		25c. black on pink	8·75	10·50
16		25c. blue	15·00	19·00
9		30c. brown on grey	20·00	21·00
17		35c. black on yellow	8·00	8·00
10		40c. red on yellow	30·00	25·00
18		45c. black on green	85·00	90·00
11		50c. red on pink	29·00	36·00
19		50c. brown on blue	18·00	29·00
12		75c. brown on orange	25·00	40·00
13		1f. green	60·00	75·00

1912. Surch in figures.

20	D	05 on 2c. brown on buff	2·75	3·75
21		05 on 4c. brown on grey	1·40	2·75
22		05 on 15c. blue	1·40	2·75
23		05 on 20c. red on green	1·70	4·75
24		05 on 25c. black on pink	1·50	3·25
25		05 on 30c. brown on grey	2·50	2·75
26		10 on 40c. red on yellow	1·40	1·70
27		10 on 45c. black on green	1·10	1·60
28		10 on 50c. red on pink	2·30	7·50
29		10 on 75c. brown on orange	2·00	6·00
30		10 on 1f. green	3·75	5·75

ANNAM AND TONGKING — Pt. 6

Later part of Indo-China and now included in Vietnam.

100 centimes = 1 franc.

1888. Stamps of French Colonies, "Commerce" type, surch **A & T** and value in figures.

1	J	1 on 2c. brown on yellow	60·00	48·00
2		1 on 4c. lilac on grey	50·00	30·00
3		5 on 10c. black on lilac	45·00	44·00

ANTIGUA — Pt. 1

One of the Leeward Islands, Br. W. Indies. Used general issues for Leeward Islands, concurrently with Antiguan stamps until 1 July 1956. Ministerial Government introduced on 1 January 1960. Achieved Associated Statehood on 3 March 1967 and Independence within the Commonwealth on 1 November 1981.

Nos. 718/21 and 733 onwards are inscribed "Antigua and Barbuda".

1862. 12 pence = 1 shilling;
20 shillings = 1 pound.
1951. 100 cents = 1 West Indian dollar.

1

3

1862.

5	1	1d. mauve	£130	60·00
25		1d. red	£225	3·75
29		6d. green	60·00	£120

1879.

21	3	½d. green	3·00	16·00
22		2½d. brown	£190	55·00
27		2½d. blue	7·00	14·00
23		4d. blue	£275	15·00
28		4d. brown	2·25	3·00
30		1s. mauve	£160	£140

4

5

8

1903.

31	4	½d. black and green	3·75	6·50
41		½d. green	3·50	4·50
32		1d. black and red	8·00	1·25
43		1d. red	8·50	2·25
45		2d. purple and brown	4·75	32·00
34		2½d. black and blue	9·50	16·00
46		2½d. blue	17·00	16·00
47		3d. green and brown	6·50	19·00
48		6d. purple and black	7·50	40·00
49		1s. blue and purple	19·00	70·00
50		2s. green and violet	95·00	£110
39		2s.6d. black and purple	23·00	55·00
40	5	5s. green and violet	80·00	£120

1913. Head of King George V.

51	5	5s. green and violet	80·00	£130

1916. Optd **WAR STAMP**.

52	4	½d. green	3·25	2·50
54		1½d. orange	1·00	1·25

1921.

62	8	½d. green	2·75	50
63		1d. red	4·00	50
64		1d. violet	5·50	1·50
67		1½d. orange	5·00	7·00
68		1½d. red	8·00	1·75
69		1½d. brown	3·00	60
70		2d. grey	3·75	75
72		2½d. yellow	6·50	17·00
73		2½d. blue	9·00	5·50
74		3d. purple on yellow	7·00	8·50
56		4d. black and red on yellow	2·25	5·50
75		6d. purple	5·50	6·50
57		1s. black on green	4·25	9·00
58		2s. purple and blue on blue	13·00	24·00
78		2s.6d. black and red on blue	38·00	28·00
79		3s. green and violet	45·00	95·00
80		4s. black and red	48·00	70·00
60		5s. green and red on yellow	8·50	50·00
61		£1 purple and black on red	£225	£325

9 Old Dockyard, English Harbour

10 Government House, St. John's

1932. Tercentenary. Designs with medallion portrait of King George V.

81	9	½d. green	3·75	7·50
82	–	1d. red	4·25	7·50
83	–	1½d. brown	3·25	4·75
84	10	2d. grey	5·50	22·00
85	–	2½d. blue	5·50	8·50
86		3d. orange	5·50	12·00
87	–	6d. violet	15·00	12·00
88	–	1s. olive	19·00	28·00
89	–	2s.6d. purple	50·00	70·00
90	–	5s. black and brown	£100	£130

DESIGNS—HORIZ: 6d. to 2s.6d. Nelson's "Victory"; 5s. Sir Thomas Warner's "Conception".

13 Windsor Castle

1935. Silver Jubilee.

91	13	1d. blue and red	2·75	3·50
92		1½d. blue and grey	2·75	65
93		2½d. brown and blue	6·50	1·25
94		1s. grey and purple	8·50	14·00

1937. Coronation. As T **2** of Aden.

95	1d. red	70	2·50
96	1½d. brown	60	2·50
97	2½d. blue	2·00	2·75

15 English Harbour

16 Nelson's Dockyard

1938.

98	15	½d. green	40	1·25
99	16	1d. red	3·00	3·00
100a		1½d. brown	2·75	2·75
101	15	2d. grey	1·00	80
102	16	2½d. blue	1·00	80
103	–	3d. orange	1·00	1·00
104	–	6d. violet	3·50	1·25
105	–	1s. black and brown	6·00	2·00
106a	–	2s.6d. purple	29·00	16·00
107	–	5s. olive	14·00	9·00
108	16	10s. mauve	16·00	28·00
109	–	£1 green	30·00	45·00

DESIGNS—HORIZ: 3d., 2s.6d., £1, Fort James. VERT: 6d., 1s., 5s. St. John's Harbour.

1946. Victory. As T **9** of Aden.

110	1½d. brown	20	10
111	3d. orange	20	50

1949. Silver Wedding. As T **10/11** of Aden.

112	2½d. blue	50	2·75
113	5s. green	12·00	11·00

20 Hermes, Globe and Forms of Transport

21 Hemispheres, Jet-powered Vickers Viking Airliner and Steamer

22 Hermes and Globe

23 U.P.U. Monument

1949. 75th Anniv of U.P.U.

114 **20** 2½d. blue 40 60
115 **21** 3d. orange . . . . 2·00 2·50
116 **22** 6d. purple . . . . 45 2·25
117 **23** 1s. brown . . . . 45 1·25

24 Arms of University

25 Princess Alice

1951. Inauguration of B.W.I. University College.

118 **24** 3c. black and brown . . . 45 1·50
119 **25** 12c. black and violet . . . 80 1·75

1953. Coronation. As T **13** of Aden.

120 2c. black and green 30 75

27 Martello Tower

1953. Designs as 1938 issues but with portrait of Queen Elizabeth II as in T **27**.

120a – ½c. brown 30 30
121 **15** 1c. grey 30 80
122 **16** 2c. green 30 10
123 3c. black and yellow . . . 40 20
153 **15** 4c. red . . . . 30 1·25
154 **16** 5c. black and lilac 20 10
155 – 6c. yellow 60 30
156 **27** 8c. blue 30 20
157 – 12c. violet 55 20
129 – 24c. black and brown . . 2·50 15
130 **27** 48c. purple and blue . . . 7·50 2·75
131 – 60c. purple . . . . 7·50 80
132 – $1.20 olive . . . . 3·00 70
133 **16** $2.40 purple . . . . . . 11·00 12·00
134 – $4.80 slate . . . . 16·00 24·00

DESIGNS—HORIZ: ½, 6, 60c., $4.80, Fort James. VERT: 12, 24c., $1.20, St John's Harbour.

28 Federation Map

1958. Inaug of British Caribbean Federation.

135 **28** 3c. green . . . . 1·25 30
136 6c. blue . . . . 1·40 2·75
137 12c. red . . . . 1·60 75

1960. New Constitution. Nos. 123 and 157 optd COMMEMORATION ANTIGUA CONSTITUTION.

138 **16** 3c. black and yellow . . . 15 15
139 – 12c. violet 15 15

30 Nelson's Dockyard and Admiral Nelson

1961. Restoration of Nelson's Dockyard.

140 **30** 20c. purple and brown . . 70 1·50
141 30c. green and blue . . . . 1·10 1·75

31 Stamp of 1862 and R.M.S.P. "Solent I" at English Harbour

1962. Stamp Centenary.

142 **31** 3c. purple and green . . . 85 10
143 10c. blue and green 95 10
144 12c. sepia and green . . . 1·00 10
145 50c. brown and green . . . 1·50 2·00

1963. Freedom from Hunger. As T **28** of Aden.

146 12c. green 15 15

33 Red Cross Emblem

1963. Centenary of Red Cross.

147 **33** 3c. red and black 30 75
148 12c. red and blue . . . . 45 1·25

34 Shakespeare and Memorial Theatre, Stratford-upon-Avon

1964. 400th Birth Anniv of Shakespeare.

164 **34** 12c. brown 30 10

1965. No. 157 surch **15c.**

165 15c. on 12c. violet 10 10

36 I.T.U. Emblem

1965. Centenary of I.T.U.

166 **36** 2c. blue and red 25 15
167 50c. yellow and blue . . . 75 95

37 I.C.Y. Emblem

1965. International Co-operation Year.

168 **37** 4c. purple and turquoise . . 20 10
169 15c. green and lavender . . 30 20

38 Sir Winston Churchill, and St. Paul's Cathedral in Wartime

1966. Churchill Commemoration. Designs in black, red and gold with background in colours given.

170 **38** ½c. blue . . . . 10 1·75
171 4c. green 55 10
172 25c. brown . . . . 1·40 45
173 35c. violet . . . . 1·40 55

39 Queen Elizabeth II and Duke of Edinburgh

1966. Royal Visit.

174 **39** 6c. black and blue . . . . 1·50 1·10
175 15c. black and mauve . . . 1·50 1·40

40 Footballer's Legs, Ball and Jules Rimet Cup

1966. World Cup Football Championship.

176 **40** 6c. multicoloured 20 75
177 35c. multicoloured 60 25

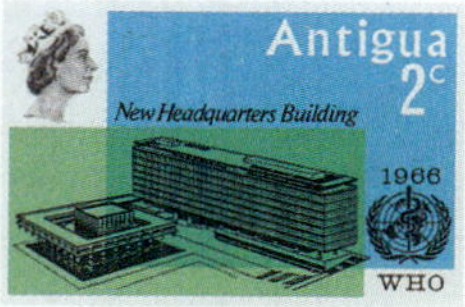

41 W.H.O. Building

1966. Inaug of W.H.O. Headquarters, Geneva.

178 **41** 2c. black, green and blue 20 25
179 15c. black, purple & brn 1·10 25

42 Nelson's Dockyard

1966.

180 **42** ½c. green and blue 10 75
181 – 1c. purple and mauve . . . 10 30
182 – 2c. blue and orange . . . 10 20
183a – 3c. red and black 15 15
184a – 4c. violet and brown . . . 15 30
185 – 5c. blue and green 10 10
186 – 6c. orange and purple . . 1·00 30
187 – 10c. green and red . . . 15 10
188a – 15c. brown and blue . . . 55 10
189 – 25c. blue and brown . . . 35 20
190a – 35c. mauve and brown . . 60 1·00
191a – 50c. green and black . . . 70 2·25
192 – 75c. blue and ultramarine 3·00 2·50
193b – $1 mauve and green . . . 1·25 5·00
194 – $2.50 black and mauve 5·00 7·50
195 – $5 green and violet . . . 7·00 6·50

DESIGNS: 1c. Old Post Office, St John's; 2c. Health Centre; 3c. Teachers' Training College; 4c. Martello Tower, Barbuda; 5c. Ruins of Officers' Quarters, Shirley Heights; 6c. Government House, Barbuda; 10c. Princess Margaret School; 15c. Air terminal building; 25c. General Post Office; 35c. Clarence House; 50c. Government House, St. John's; 75c. Administration building; $1 Court-house, St. John's; $2.50, Magistrates' Court; $5 St. John's Cathedral.

54 "Education"

55 "Science"

56 "Culture"

1966. 20th Anniv of UNESCO.

196 **54** 4c. violet, yellow & orange 15 10
197 **55** 25c. yellow, violet and olive 35 10
198 **56** $1 black, purple and orange . . . . 80 2·25

57 State Flag and Maps

1967. Statehood. Multicoloured.

199 4c. Type **57** 10 10
200 15c. State Flag 10 20
201 25c. Premier's Office and State Flag 10 25
202 35c. As 15c. 15 25

60 Gilbert Memorial Church

1967. Attainment of Autonomy by the Methodist Church.

203 **60** 4c. black and red 10 10
204 – 25c. black and green . . . 15 15
205 – 35c. black and blue 15 15

DESIGNS: 25c. Nathaniel Gilbert's House; 35c. Caribbean and Central American map.

63 Coat of Arms

66 Tracking Station

64 "Susan Constant" (settlers' ship)

1967. 300th Anniv of Treaty of Breda and Grant of New Arms.

206 **63** 15c. multicoloured 15 10
207 35c. multicoloured 15 10

1967. 300th Anniv of Barbuda Settlement.

208 **64** 4c. blue 40 10
209 – 6c. purple . . . . 40 1·25
210 **64** 25c. green 45 20
211 – 35c. black 45 25

DESIGN: 6, 35c. Blaeu's Map of 1665.

1968. N.A.S.A. Apollo Project. Inauguration of Dow Hill Tracking Station.

212 **66** 4c. blue, yellow and black 10 10
213 – 15c. blue, yellow and black 20 10
214 – 25c. blue, yellow and black 20 10
215 – 50c. blue, yellow and black 30 40

DESIGNS: 15c. Antenna and spacecraft taking off; 25c. Spacecraft approaching Moon; 50c. Re-entry of space capsule.

70 Limbo-dancing

1968. Tourism. Multicoloured.

216 ½c. Type **70** 10 20
217 15c. Water-skier and bathers 30 10
218 25c. Yachts and beach . . . 30 10
219 35c. Underwater swimming 30 10
220 50c. Type **70** . . . . 35 1·10

74 Old Harbour in 1768

1968. Opening of St. John's Deep Water Harbour.

221 **74** 2c. blue and red 10 40
222 – 15c. green and sepia . . . 35 10
223 – 25c. yellow and blue . . . 40 10
224 – 35c. salmon and emerald 50 10
225 **74** $1 black . . . . 90 2·00

DESIGNS: 15c. Old harbour in 1829; 25c. Freighter and chart of new harbour; 35c. New harbour.

78 Parliament Buildings

1969. Tercentenary of Parliament. Multicoloured.

226 4c. Type **78** 10 10
227 15c. Antigua Mace and bearer 20 10
228 25c. House of Representative's Room . . 20 10
229 50c. Coat of arms and Seal of Antigua . . . . 30 1·60

82 Freight Transport

1969. 1st Anniv of Caribbean Free Trade Area.

230	**82** 4c. black and purple	10	10
231	15c. black and blue	20	30
232	– 25c. brown, black & ochre	25	30
233	– 35c. chocolate, blk & brn	25	30

DESIGN—VERT: 25, 35c. Crate of cargo.

84 Island of Redonda (Chart)

1969. Centenary of Redonda Phosphate Industry. Multicoloured.

249	15c. Type **84**	20	10
250	25c. View of Redonda from the sea	20	10
251	50c. Type **84**	45	75

86 "The Adoration of the Magi" (Marcillat)

1969. Christmas. Stained Glass Windows. Mult.

252	6c. Type **86**	10	10
253	10c. "The Nativity" (unknown German artist, 15th century)	10	10
254	35c. Type **86**	25	10
255	50c. As 10c.	50	40

1970. Surch **20c** and bars.

256	20c. on 25c. (No. 189)	10	10

89 Coat of Arms — 90 Sikorsky S-38 Flying Boat

1970. Coil Stamps.

257A	**89** 5c. blue	10	25
258A	10c. green	10	25
259A	25c. red	20	25

1970. 40th Anniv of Antiguan Air Services. Multicoloured.

260	5c. Type **90**	50	10
261	20c. Dornier Do-X flying boat	80	10
262	35c. Hawker Siddeley H.S.748	1·00	10
263	50c. Douglas C-124C Globemaster II	1·00	1·50
264	75c. Vickers Super VC-10	1·25	2·00

91 Dickens and Scene from "Nicholas Nickleby"

1970. Death Centenary of Charles Dickens.

265	**91** 5c. bistre, sepia and black	10	10
266	– 20c. turq, sepia & blk	20	10
267	– 35c. blue, sepia and black	30	10
268	– $1 red, sepia and black	75	70

DESIGNS: All stamps show Dickens and scene from: 20c. "Pickwick Papers"; 35c. "Oliver Twist"; $1 "David Copperfield".

92 Carib Indian and War Canoe

1970. Multicoloured.

323	½c. Type **92**	20	50
270	1c. Columbus and "Nina"	30	1·50
271	2c. Sir Thomas Warner's emblem and "Concepcion"	40	3·25
325	3c. Viscount Hood and H.M.S. "Barfleur"	35	1·25
273	4c. Sir George Rodney and H.M.S. "Formidable"	40	3·00
274	5c. Nelson and H.M.S. "Boreas"	50	40
275	6c. William IV and H.M.S. "Pegasus"	1·75	4·00
276	10c. "Blackbeard" and pirate ketch	80	20
277	15c. Collingwood and H.M.S. "Pelican"	7·50	1·00
278	20c. Nelson and H.M.S. "Victory"	1·25	40
279	25c. "Solent I" (paddle-steamer)	1·25	40
280	35c. George V (when Prince George) and H.M.S. "Canada" (screw corvette)	1·75	80
281	50c. H.M.S. "Renown" (battle cruiser)	4·00	6·00
331	75c. "Federal Maple" (freighter)	7·50	3·00
332	$1 "Sol Quest" (yacht) and class emblem	3·00	1·75
333	$2.50 H.M.S. "London" (destroyer)	2·75	6·50
285	$5 "Pathfinder" (tug)	2·50	6·00

93 "The Small Passion" (detail) (Durer) — 94 4th King's Own Regiment, 1759

1970. Christmas.

286	**93** 3c. black and blue	10	10
287	– 10c. purple and pink	10	10
288	**93** 35c. black and red	30	10
289	– 50c. black and lilac	45	50

DESIGN: 10, 50c. "Adoration of the Magi" (detail)(Durer).

1970. Military Uniforms (1st series). Mult.

290	½c. Type **94**	10	10
291	10c. 4th West India Regiment, 1804	50	10
292	20c. 60th Regiment, The Royal American, 1809	75	10
293	35c. 93rd Regiment, Sutherland Highlanders, 1826–34	1·00	10
294	75c. 3rd West India Regiment, 1851	1·75	2·00
MS295	128 × 164 mm. Nos. 290/4	4·50	2·10

See also Nos. 303/8, 313/18, 353/8 and 380/5.

95 Market Woman casting Vote — 96 "The Last Supper"

1971. 20th Anniv of Adult Suffrage.

296	**95** 5c. brown	10	10
297	– 20c. olive	10	10
298	– 35c. purple	10	10
299	– 50c. blue	15	30

DESIGNS: People voting: 20c. Executive; 35c. Housewife; 50c. Artisan.

1971. Easter. Works by Durer.

300	**96** 5c. black grey and red	10	10
301	– 35c. black, grey and violet	10	10
302	– 75c. black, grey and gold	20	30

DESIGNS: 35c. "The Crucifixion"; 75c. "The Resurrection".

1971. Military Uniforms (2nd series). As T **94**. Multicoloured.

303	½c. Private, 12th Regiment, The Suffolk (1704)	10	10
304	10c. Grenadier, 38th Regiment, South Staffordshire (1751)	35	10
305	20c. Light Company, 5th Regiment, Royal Northumberland Fusiliers (1778)	50	10
306	35c. Private, 48th Regiment, The Northamptonshire (1793)	60	10
307	75c. Private, 15th Regiment, East Yorks (1805)	1·00	3·00
MS308	127 × 144 mm. Nos. 303/7	4·50	6·50

97 "Madonna and Child" (detail, Veronese)

1971. Christmas. Multicoloured.

309	3c. Type **97**	10	10
310	5c. "Adoration of the Shepherds" (detail, Veronese)	10	10
311	35c. Type **97**	25	10
312	50c. As 5c.	40	30

1972. Military Uniforms (3rd series). As T **94**. Multicoloured.

313	½c. Battalion Company Officer, 25th Foot, 1815	10	10
314	10c. Sergeant, 14th Foot, 1837	85	10
315	20c. Private, 67th Foot, 1853	1·60	15
316	35c. Officer, Royal Artillery, 1854	1·90	20
317	75c. Private, 29th Foot, 1870	2·25	4·00
MS318	125 × 141 mm. Nos. 313/17	7·00	8·50

98 Reticulated Cowrie Helmet

1972. Shells. Multicoloured.

319	3c. Type **98**	50	10
320	5c. Measled cowrie	50	10
321	35c. West Indian fighting conch	1·40	15
322	50c. Hawk-wing conch	1·60	3·00

99 St. John's Cathedral, Side View

1972. Christmas and 125th Anniv of St. John's Cathedral. Multicoloured.

335	35c. Type **99**	20	10
336	50c. Cathedral interior	25	25
337	75c. St. John's Cathedral	30	60
MS338	165 × 102 mm. Nos. 335/7	65	1·00

1972. Royal Silver Wedding. As T **52** of Ascension, but with floral background.

339	20c. blue	15	15
340	35c. blue	15	15

101 Batsman and Map

1972. 50th Anniv of Rising Sun Cricket Club. Multicoloured.

341	5c. Type **101**	55	15
342	35c. Batsman and wicket-keeper	65	10
343	$1 Club badge	1·00	2·25
MS344	88 × 130 mm. Nos. 341/3	3·25	7·50

102 Yacht and Map — 103 "Episcopal Coat of Arms"

1972. Inauguration of Antigua and Barbuda Tourist Office in New York. Multicoloured.

345	35c. Type **102**	15	10
346	50c. Yachts	20	15
347	75c. St. John's G.P.O.	25	25
348	$1 Statue of Liberty	25	25
MS349	100 × 94 mm. Nos. 346, 348	75	1·25

1973. Easter. Multicoloured.

350	**103** 5c. Type **103**	10	10
351	– 35c. "The Crucifixion"	15	10
352	– 75c. "Arms of 1st Bishop of Antigua"	25	30

Nos. 350/2 show different stained-glass windows from St. John's Cathedral.

1973. Military Uniforms (4th series). As T **94**. Multicoloured.

353	½c. Private, Zachariah Tiffin's Regiment of Foot, 1701	10	10
354	10c. Private, 63rd Regiment of Foot, 1759	40	10
355	20c. Light Company Officer, 35th Regiment of Foot, 1828	50	15
356	35c. Private, 2nd West India Regiment, 1853	65	15
357	75c. Sergeant, 49th Regiment, 1858	1·00	1·25
MS358	127 × 145 mm. Nos. 353/7	3·75	3·25

104 Butterfly Costumes

1973. Carnival. Multicoloured.

359	5c. Type **104**	10	10
360	20c. Carnival street scene	15	10
361	35c. Carnival troupe	20	10
362	75c. Carnival Queen	30	30
MS363	134 × 95 mm. Nos. 359/62	65	1·00

105 "Virgin of the Milk Porridge" (Gerard David)

1973. Christmas. Multicoloured.

364	3c. Type **105**	10	10
365	5c. "Adoration of the Magi" (Stomer)	10	10
366	20c. "The Granducal Madonna" (Raphael)	15	10
367	35c. "Nativity with God the Father and Holy Ghost" (Battista)	20	10
368	$1 "Madonna and Child" (Murillo)	40	60
MS369	130 × 128 mm. Nos. 364/8	1·10	1·75

106 Princess Anne and Captain Mark Phillips

1973. Royal Wedding.

370	**106** 35c. multicoloured	10	10
371	– $2 multicoloured	25	25
MS372	78 × 100 mm. Nos. 370/1	50	40

The $2 is as Type **106** but has a different border.

1973. Nos. 370/1 optd **HONEYMOON VISIT DECEMBER 16TH 1973.**

373	**106** 35c. multicoloured	15	10
374	– $2 multicoloured	30	30
MS375	78 × 100 mm. Nos. 373/4	55	55

108 Coat of Arms of Antigua and University

1974. 25th Anniv of University of West Indies. Multicoloured.
376 5c. Type **108** 15 10
377 20c. Extra-mural art 20 10
378 35c. Antigua campus 20 10
379 75c. Antigua chancellor 25 35

1974. Military Uniforms (5th series). As T **94**. Multicoloured.
380 ½c. Officer, 59th Foot, 1797 10 10
381 10c. Gunner, Royal Artillery, 1800 35 10
382 20c. Private, 1st West India Regiment, 1830 50 10
383 35c. Officer, 92nd Foot, 1843 60 10
384 75c. Private, 23rd Foot, 1846 75 2·25
MS385 125 × 145 mm. Nos. 380/4 2·25 2·50

109 English Postman, Mailcoach and Westland Dragonfly Helicopter

1974. Centenary of U.P.U. Multicoloured.
386 ½c. Type **109** 10 10
387 1c. Bellman, mail steamer "Orinoco" and satellite 10 10
388 2c. Train guard, post-bus and hydrofoil 10 10
389 5c. Swiss messenger, Wells Fargo coach and Concorde 60 30
390 20c. Postilion, Japanese postmen and carrier pigeon 35 10
391 35c. Antiguan postman, Sikorsky S-88 flying boat and tracking station 45 15
392 $1 Medieval courier, American express train and Boeing 747-100 1·75 2·00
MS393 141 × 161 mm. Nos. 386/92 3·50 2·50
On the ½c. English is spelt "Enlish" and on the 2c. Postal is spelt "Fostal".

110 Traditional Player

111 Footballers

1974. Antiguan Steel Bands.
394 **110** 5c. dp red, red and black 10 10
395 – 20c. brown, lt brn & blk 10 10
396 – 35c. lt green, green & blk 10 10
397 – 75c. blue, dp blue & blk 20 1·10
MS398 115 × 108 mm. Nos. 394/7 35 1·25
DESIGNS—HORIZ: 20c. Traditional band; 35c. Modern band. VERT: 75c. Modern player.

1974. World Cup Football Championships.
399 **111** 5c. multicoloured 10 10
400 – 35c. multicoloured 15 10
401 – 75c. multicoloured 30 30
402 – $1 multicoloured 35 40
MS403 135 × 130 mm. Nos. 399/402 85 90
Nos. 400/2 show various footballing designs similar to Type **111**.

1974. Earthquake Relief Fund. Nos. 400/2 and 397 optd or surch **EARTHQUAKE RELIEF**.
404 35c. multicoloured 20 10
405 75c. multicoloured 30 25
406 $1 multicoloured 40 30
407 $5 on 75c. deep blue, blue and black 1·25 2·00

113 Churchill as Schoolboy and School College Building, Harrow

114 "Madonna of the Trees" (Bellini)

1974. Birth Centenary of Sir Winston Churchill. Multicoloured.
408 5c. Type **113** 15 10
409 35c. Churchill and St. Paul's Cathedral 20 10
410 75c. Coat of arms and catafalque 30 65
411 $1 Churchill, "reward" notice and South African escape route 45 1·00
MS412 107 × 82 mm. Nos. 408/11 1·00 1·50

1974. Christmas. "Madonna and Child" paintings by named artists. Multicoloured.
413 ½c. Type **114** 10 10
414 1c. Raphael 10 10
415 2c. Van der Weyden 10 10
416 3c. Giorgione 10 10
417 5c. Mantegna 10 10
418 20c. Vivarini 20 10
419 35c. Montagna 30 10
420 75c. Lorenzo Costa 55 1·10
MS421 139 × 126 mm. Nos. 413/20 95 1·40

1975. Nos. 390/2 and 331 surch.
422 50c. on 20c. multicoloured 1·25 2·00
423 $2.50 on 35c. multicoloured 2·00 5·50
424 $5 on $1 multicoloured 6·50 7·00
425 $10 on 75c. multicoloured 2·00 7·50

116 Carib War Canoe, English Harbour, 1300

1975. Nelson's Dockyard. Multicoloured.
427 5c. Type **116** 20 10
428 15c. Ship of the line, English Harbour, 1770 80 15
429 35c. H.M.S "Boreas" at anchor, and Lord Nelson, 1787 1·25 15
430 50c. Yachts during "Sailing Week", 1974 1·25 1·50
431 $1 Yacht Anchorage, Old Dockyard, 1970 1·50 2·25
MS432 130 × 134 mm. As Nos. 427/31, but in larger format, 43 × 28 mm 3·25 2·00

117 Lady of the Valley Church

1975. Antiguan Churches. Multicoloured.
433 5c. Type **117** 10 10
434 20c. Gilbert Memorial 10 10
435 35c. Grace Hill Moravian 15 10
436 50c. St. Phillips 20 20
437 $1 Ebenezer Methodist 35 50
MS438 91 × 101 mm. Nos. 435/7 65 1·25

118 Map of 1721 and Sextant of 1640

1975. Maps of Antigua. Multicoloured.
439 5c. Type **118** 30 15
440 20c. Map of 1775 and galleon 55 15
441 35c. Maps of 1775 and 1955 70 15
442 $1 1973 maps of Antigua and English Harbour 1·40 2·25
MS443 130 × 89 mm. Nos. 439/42 3·00 3·25

119 Scout Bugler

1975. World Scout Jamboree, Norway. Mult.
444 15c. Type **119** 25 15
445 20c. Scouts in camp 30 15
446 35c. "Lord Baden-Powell" (D. Jagger) 50 20
447 $2 Scout dancers from Dahomey 1·50 2·25
MS448 145 × 107 mm. Nos. 444/7 3·25 3·50

120 "Eurema elathea"

1975. Butterflies. Multicoloured.
449 ½c. Type **120** 10 30
450 1c. "Danaus plexippus" 10 30
451 2c. "Phoebis philea" 10 30
452 5c. "Hypolimnas misippus" 20 10
453 20c. "Eurema proterpia" 75 40
454 35c. "Battus polydamas" 1·40 50
455 $2 "Cynthia cardui" 4·00 9·00
MS456 147 × 94 mm. Nos. 452/5 6·00 11·00
No. 452 is incorrectly captioned "Marpesia petreus thetys".

121 "Madonna and Child" (Correggio)

122 Vivian Richards

1975. Christmas. "Madonna and Child" paintings by artists named. Multicoloured.
457 ½c. Type **121** 10 10
458 1c. El Greco 10 10
459 2c. Durer 10 10
460 3c. Antonello 10 10
461 5c. Bellini 10 10
462 10c. Durer (different) 10 10
463 35c. Bellini (different) 40 10
464 $2 Durer (different again) 1·00 1·00
MS465 138 × 119 mm. Nos. 461/4 1·50 1·60

1975. World Cricket Cup Winners. Multicoloured.
466 5c. Type **122** 1·25 20
467 35c. Andy Roberts 2·25 60
468 $2 West Indies team (horiz) 4·25 8·00

123 Antillean Crested Hummingbird

1976. Multicoloured.
469A ½c. Type **123** 40 50
470A 1c. Imperial amazon ("Imperial Parrot") 1·40 50
471A 2c. Zenaida dove 1·40 50
472A 3c. Loggerhead kingbird 1·40 60
473A 4c. Red-necked pigeon 1·40 2·00
474A 5c. Rufous-throated solitaire 2·00 10
475A 6c. Orchid tree 30 2·00
476A 10c. Bougainvillea 30 10
477A 15c. Geiger tree 35 10
478A 20c. Flamboyant 35 35
479A 25c. Hibiscus 40 15
480A 35c. Flame of the wood 40 40
481A 50c. Cannon at Fort James 55 60
482A 75c. Premier's Office 60 2·00
483A $1 Potworks Dam 75 1·00
484A $2.50 Diamond irrigation scheme (44 × 28 mm) 1·00 5·00
485B $5 Government House (44 × 28 mm) 1·50 7·50
486A $10 Coolidge International Airport (44 × 28 mm) 3·50 8·00

124 Privates, Clark's Illinois Regiment

1976. Bicentenary of American Revolution. Mult.
487 ½c. Type **124** 10 10
488 1c. Rifleman, Pennsylvania Militia 10 10
489 2c. Powder horn 10 10
490 5c. Water bottle 10 10
491 35c. American flags 50 10
492 $1 "Montgomery" (American brig) 1·00 40
493 $5 "Ranger" (privateer sloop) 1·75 2·25
MS494 71 × 84 mm. $2.50, Congress flag 1·00 1·40

125 High Jump

1976. Olympic Games, Montreal.
495 **125** ½c. brown, yellow & black 10 10
496 – 1c. violet, blue and black 10 10
497 – 2c. green and black 10 10
498 – 15c. blue and black 15 10
499 – 30c. brown, yell & blk 20 15
500 – $1 orange, red and black 40 40
501 – $2 red and black 60 80
MS502 88 × 138 mm. Nos. 498/501 1·75 1·25
DESIGNS: 1c. Boxing; 2c. Pole vault; 15c. Swimming; 30c. Running; $1 Cycling; $2 Shot put.

126 Water Skiing

1976. Water Sports. Multicoloured.
503 ½c. Type **126** 10 10
504 1c. Sailing 10 10
505 2c. Snorkeling 10 10
506 20c. Deep sea fishing 50 10
507 50c. Scuba diving 75 35
508 $2 Swimming 1·25 1·25
MS509 89 × 114 mm. Nos. 506/8 1·75 1·75

127 French Angelfish

1976. Fishes. Multicoloured.
510 15c. Type **127** 40 15
511 30c. Yellow-finned grouper 55 30
512 50c. Yellow-tailed snapper 70 50
513 90c. Shy hamlet 90 1·50

128 The Annunciation

130 Royal Family

129 Mercury and U.P.U. Emblem

1976. Christmas. Multicoloured.
514 8c. Type **128** 10 10
515 10c. The Holy Family 10 10
516 15c. The Magi 10 10
517 50c. The Shepherds 20 25
518 $1 Epiphany scene 30 50

1976. Special Events, 1976. Multicoloured.
519 ½c. Type **129** 10 10
520 1c. Alfred Nobel 10 10
521 10c. Space satellite 30 10
522 50c. Viv Richards and Andy Roberts 3·50 1·75
523 $1 Bell and telephones 1·00 2·00
524 $2 Yacht "Freelance" 2·25 4·50
MS525 127 × 101 mm. Nos. 521/4 7·50 13·00

1977. Silver Jubilee. Multicoloured. (a) Perf.
526 10c. Type **130** 10 10
527 30c. Royal Visit, 1966 10 10
528 50c. The Queen enthroned 15 15
529 90c. The Queen after Coronation 15 25
530 $2.50 Queen and Prince Charles 30 55
MS531 116 × 78 mm. $5 Queen and Prince Philip 65 85

(b) Roul × imperf. Self-adhesive.
532 50c. As 90c. 35 75
533 $5 The Queen and Prince Philip 2·00 3·75
Nos. 532/3 come from booklets.

131 Making Camp

1977. Caribbean Scout Jamboree, Jamaica. Mult.

534	½c. Type **131**	10	10
535	1c. Hiking	10	10
536	2c. Rock-climbing	10	10
537	10c. Cutting logs	15	10
538	30c. Map and sign reading	40	10
539	50c. First aid	65	25
540	$2 Rafting	1·25	2·50
MS541	127 × 114 mm. Nos. 538/40	3·00	4·00

132 Carnival Costume

134 "Virgin and Child Enthroned" (Tura)

1977. 21st Anniv of Carnival. Multicoloured.

542	10c. Type **132**	10	10
543	30c. Carnival Queen	25	10
544	50c. Butterfly costume	30	15
545	90c. Queen of the band	40	25
546	$1 Calypso King and Queen	40	30
MS547	140 × 120 mm. Nos. 542/6	1·10	1·60

1977. Royal Visit. Nos. 526/30 optd **ROYAL VISIT 28TH OCTOBER 1977.**

548	10c. Type **130**	10	10
549	30c. Royal Visit, 1966	15	10
550	50c. The Queen enthroned	20	10
551	90c. The Queen after Coronation	30	20
552	$2.50 Queen and Prince Charles	50	35
MS553	116 × 178 mm. $5 Queen and Prince Philip	1·00	1·00

1977. Christmas. Paintings by artists listed. Mult.

554	½c. Type **134**	10	20
555	1c. Crivelli	10	20
556	2c. Lotto	10	20
557	8c. Pontormo	15	10
558	10c. Tura (different)	15	10
559	25c. Lotto (different)	30	10
560	$2 Crivelli (different)	85	1·00
MS561	144 × 118 mm. Nos. 557/60	1·75	2·75

135 Pineapple

1977. 10th Anniv of Statehood. Multicoloured.

562	10c. Type **135**	10	10
563	15c. State flag	60	20
564	50c. Police band	2·50	80
565	90c. Premier V. C. Bird	55	80
566	$2 State Coat of Arms	90	2·00
MS567	129 × 99 mm. Nos. 563/6	3·50	3·00

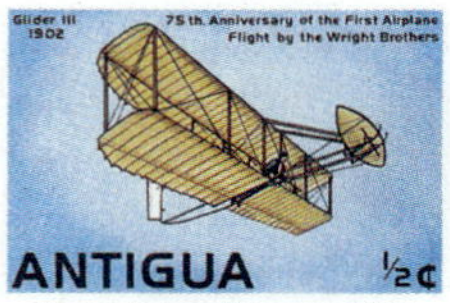

136 Wright Glider III, 1902

1978. 75th Anniv of Powered Flight. Mult.

568	½c. Type **136**	10	10
569	1c. Wright Flyer I, 1903	10	10
570	2c. Launch system and engine	10	10
571	10c. Orville Wright (vert)	30	10
572	50c. Wright Flyer III, 1905	60	15
573	90c. Wilbur Wright (vert)	80	30
574	$2 Wright Type B, 1910	1·00	80
MS575	90 × 75 mm. $2.50, Wright Flyer I on launch system	1·25	2·75

137 Sunfish Regatta

138 Queen Elizabeth and Prince Philip

1978. Sailing Week. Multicoloured.

576	10c. Type **137**	20	10
577	50c. Fishing and work boat race	35	20
578	90c. Curtain Bluff race	60	35
579	$2 Power boat rally	1·10	1·25
MS580	110 × 77 mm. $2.50, Guadeloupe–Antigua race	1·50	1·75

1978. 25th Anniv of Coronation. Mult. (a) Perf.

581	10c. Type **138**	10	10
582	30c. Crowning	10	10
583	50c. Coronation procession	15	10
584	90c. Queen seated in St. Edward's Chair	20	15
585	$2.50 Queen wearing Imperial State Crown	40	40
MS586	114 × 104 mm. $5 Queen and Prince Philip	80	80

(b) Roul × imperf. Self-adhesive. Horiz designs as Type **138**.

587	25c. Glass Coach	15	30
588	50c. Irish State Coach	25	50
589	$5 Coronation Coach	1·75	3·00

Nos. 587/9 come from booklets.

140 Player running with Ball

141 Petrea

1978. World Cup Football Championship, Argentina. Multicoloured.

590	10c. Type **140**	15	10
591	15c. Players in front of goal	15	10
592	$3 Referee and player	2·00	1·75
MS593	126 × 88 mm. 25c. Player crouching with ball; 30c. Players heading ball; 50c. Players running with ball; $2 Goalkeeper diving. All horiz	3·25	2·50

1978. Flowers. Multicoloured.

594	25c. Type **141**	25	10
595	50c. Sunflower	35	20
596	90c. Frangipani	60	30
597	$2 Passion flower	1·25	2·00
MS598	118 × 85 mm. $2.50, Hibiscus	1·40	1·60

142 "St. Ildefonso receiving the Chasuble from the Virgin" (Rubens)

1978. Christmas. Multicoloured.

599	8c. Type **142**	10	10
600	25c. "The Flight of St. Barbara" (Rubens)	20	10
601	$2 "Madonna and Child, with St. Joseph, John the Baptist and Donor"	65	55
MS602	170 × 113 mm. $4 "The Annunciation" (Rubens)	1·25	1·50

The painting shown on No. 601 is incorrectly attributed to Rubens on the stamp. The artist was Sebastiano del Piombo.

143 1d. Stamp of 1863

144 "The Deposition from the Cross" (painting)

1979. Death Centenary of Sir Rowland Hill. Mult.

603	25c. Type **143**	10	10
604	50c. 1840 Penny Black	20	15
605	$1 Mail coach and woman posting letter, c. 1840	30	20
606	$2 Modern transport	1·10	60
MS607	108 × 82 mm. $2.50, Sir Rowland Hill	80	90

1979. Easter. Works by Durer.

608	**144**	10c. multicoloured	10	10
609	–	50c. multicoloured	35	20
610	–	$4 black, mauve and yellow	1·00	90
MS611	–	114 × 99 mm. $2.50, multicoloured	80	80

DESIGNS: 50c., $2.50, "Christ on the Cross–The Passion" (wood engravings) (both different); $4 "Man of Sorrows with Hands Raised" (wood engraving).

145 Toy Yacht and Child's Hand

147 Cook's Birthplace, Marton

146 Yellow Jack

1979. International Year of the Child. Mult.

612	25c. Type **145**	10	10
613	50c. Rocket	25	15
614	90c. Car	40	25
615	$2 Toy train	1·00	90
MS616	80 × 112 mm. $5 Aeroplane	1·10	1·10

Nos. 612/16 also show the hands of children of different races.

1979. Fishes. Multicoloured.

617	30c. Type **146**	35	15
618	50c. Blue-finned tuna	40	25
619	90c. Sailfish	60	40
620	$3 Wahoo	1·75	1·75
MS621	122 × 75 mm. $2.50, Great barracuda	1·50	1·40

1979. Death Bicentenary of Captain Cook. Mult.

622	25c. Type **147**	65	25
623	50c. H.M.S. "Endeavour"	1·25	60
624	90c. Marine chronometer	75	80
625	$3 Landing at Botany Bay	1·75	3·00
MS626	110 × 85 mm. $2.50, H.M.S. "Resolution"	2·25	1·50

148 The Holy Family

149 Javelin Throwing

1979. Christmas. Multicoloured.

627	8c. Type **148**	10	10
628	25c. Virgin and Child on ass	15	10
629	50c. Shepherd and star	25	35
630	$4 Wise Men with gifts	85	2·50
MS631	113 × 94 mm. $3 Angel with trumpet	1·00	1·50

1980. Olympic Games, Moscow. Multicoloured.

632	10c. Type **149**	20	10
633	25c. Running	20	10
634	$1 Pole vault	50	50
635	$2 Hurdles	70	1·75
MS636	127 × 96 mm. $3 Boxing (horiz)	80	90

150 Mickey Mouse and Airplane

1980. International Year of the Child. Walt Disney Cartoon Characters. Multicoloured.

637	½c. Type **150**	10	10
638	1c. Donald Duck driving car (vert)	10	10
639	2c. Goofy driving taxi	10	10
640	3c. Mickey and Minnie Mouse on motorcycle	10	10
641	4c. Huey, Dewey and Louie on a bicycle for three	10	10
642	5c. Grandma Duck and truck of roosters	10	10
643	10c. Mickey Mouse in jeep (vert)	10	10
644	$1 Chip and Dale in yacht	2·00	2·00
645	$4 Donald Duck riding toy train (vert)	4·00	6·50
MS646	101 × 127 mm. $2.50, Goofy flying biplane	4·50	3·25

1980. "London 1980" International Stamp Exhibition. Nos. 603/6 optd **LONDON 1980**.

647	25c. Type **143**	25	15
648	50c. Penny Black	35	35
649	$1 Stage-coach and woman posting letter, c. 1840	60	70
650	$2 Modern mail transport	3·25	3·00

152 "David" (statue, Donatello)

1980. Famous Works of Art. Multicoloured.

651	10c. Type **152**	10	10
652	30c. "The Birth of Venus" (painting, Botticelli) (horiz)	30	15
653	50c. "Reclining Couple" (sarcophagus), Cerveteri (horiz)	40	40
654	90c. "The Garden of Earthly Delights" (painting by Bosch) (horiz)	55	65
655	$1 "Portinari Altarpiece" (painting, van der Goes) (horiz)	65	75
656	$4 "Eleanora of Toledo and her Son, Giovanni de'Medici" (painting, Bronzino)	1·75	3·00
MS657	99 × 124 mm. $5 "The Holy Family" (painting, Rembrandt)	2·50	1·75

153 Anniversary Emblem and Headquarters, U.S.A.

1980. 75th Anniv of Rotary International. Mult.

658	30c. Type **153**	30	30
659	50c. Rotary anniversary emblem and Antigua Rotary Club banner	40	50
660	90c. Map of Antigua and Rotary emblem	60	70
661	$3 Paul P. Harris (founder) and Rotary emblem	2·00	3·50
MS662	102 × 78 mm. $5 Antiguan flags and Rotary emblems	1·25	2·00

154 Queen Elizabeth the Queen Mother

155 Ringed Kingfisher

1980. 80th Birthday of The Queen Mother.

663	**154**	10c. multicoloured	40	10
664		$2.50 multicoloured	1·50	1·75
MS665		68 × 90 mm. As T **154**. $3 multicoloured	1·75	2·25

1980. Birds. Multicoloured.

666	10c. Type **155**	70	30
667	30c. Plain pigeon	1·00	50
668	$1 Green-throated carib	1·50	2·00
669	$2 Black-necked stilt	2·00	4·00
MS670	73 × 73 mm. $2.50, Roseate tern	7·00	4·50

1980. Christmas. Walt Disney's "Sleeping Beauty". As T **150**. Multicoloured.

671	½c. The Bad Fairy with her raven	10	10
672	1c. The good fairies	10	10
673	2c. Aurora	10	10
674	4c. Aurora pricks her finger	10	10
675	8c. The prince	10	10
676	10c. The prince fights the dragon	15	10

677 25c. The prince awakens Aurora with a kiss 20 20
678 $2 The prince and Aurora's betrothal 2·25 2·25
679 $2.50 The prince and princess 2·50 2·50
MS680 126 × 101 mm. $4 multicoloured (vert) 5·00 3·25

156 Diesel Locomotive No. 15

1981. Sugar Cane Railway Locomotives. Mult.
681 25c. Type **156** 15 15
682 50c. Narrow-gauge steam locomotive 30 30
683 90c. Diesel locomotives Nos. 1 and 10 55 60
684 $3 Steam locomotive hauling sugar cane 2·00 2·25
MS685 82 × 111 mm. $2.50, Antiguan sugar factory, railway yard and sheds 1·75 1·75

1981. Independence. Nos. 475/6 and 478/86 optd **"INDEPENDENCE 1981"**.
686B 6c. Orchid tree 10 30
687B 10c. Bougainvillea 10 10
688B 20c. Flamboyant 10 10
689B 25c. Hibiscus 15 15
690B 35c. Flame of the wood 20 20
691B 50c. Cannon at Fort James 35 35
692B 75c. Premier's Office 40 60
693B $1 Potworks Dam 55 70
694B $2.50 Irrigation scheme, Diamond Estate 75 1·75
695B $5 Government House 1·40 3·00
696B $10 Coolidge International Airport 3·25 5·50

158 "Pipes of Pan"

1981. Birth Centenary of Picasso. Multicoloured.
697 10c. Type **158** 10 10
698 50c. "Seated Harlequin" 30 30
699 90c. "Paulo as Harlequin" 55 55
700 $4 "Mother and Child" 2·00 2·00
MS701 115 × 140 mm. $5 "Three Musicians" (detail) 1·75 2·75

159 Prince Charles and Lady Diana Spencer

160 Prince of Wales at Investiture, 1969

1981. Royal Wedding (1st issue). Multicoloured.
702 25c. Type **159** 10 10
703 50c. Glamis Castle 10 10
704 $4 Prince Charles skiing 80 80
MS705 96 × 82 mm. $5 Glass coach 80 80

1981. Royal Wedding (2nd issue). Multicoloured. Roul × imperf. Self-adhesive.
706 25c. Type **160** 15 25
707 25c. Prince Charles as baby, 1948 15 25
708 $1 Prince Charles at R.A.F. College, Cranwell, 1971 25 50
709 $1 Prince Charles attending Hill House School, 1956 25 50
710 $2 Prince Charles and Lady Diana Spencer 50 75
711 $2 Prince Charles at Trinity College, 1967 50 75
712 $5 Prince Charles and Lady Diana (different) 1·00 1·50

161 Irene Joshua (founder)

1981. 50th Anniv of Antigua Girl Guide Movement. Multicoloured.
713 10c. Type **161** 15 10
714 50c. Campfire sing-song 45 35
715 90c. Sailing 75 65
716 $2.50 Animal tending 1·75 2·00
MS717 110 × 85 mm. $5 Raising the flag 4·50 3·00

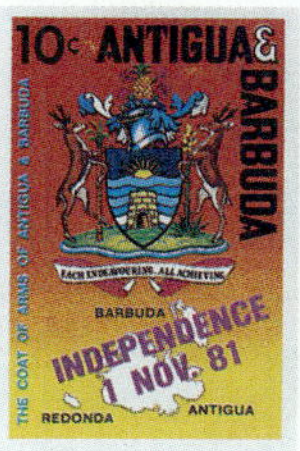

162 Antigua and Barbuda Coat of Arms

163 "Holy Night" (Jacques Stella)

1981. Independence. Multicoloured.
718 10c. Type **162** 25 10
719 50c. Pineapple, with Antigua and Barbuda flag and map 2·00 60
720 90c. Prime Minister Vere Bird 55 55
721 $2.50 St. John's Cathedral (38 × 25 mm) 1·50 3·50
MS722 105 × 79 mm. $5 Map of Antigua and Barbuda (42 × 42 mm) 4·50 2·75

1981. Christmas. Paintings. Multicoloured.
723 8c. Type **163** 15 10
724 30c. "Mary with Child" (Julius Schnorr von Carolfeld) 40 15
725 $1 "Virgin and Child" (Alonso Cano) 75 90
726 $3 "Virgin and Child" (Lorenzo di Credi) 1·10 3·75
MS727 77 × 111 mm. $5 "Holy Family" (Pieter von Avon) 2·50 4·50

164 Swimming

1981. International Year of Disabled People. Sports for the Disabled. Multicoloured.
728 10c. Type **164** 10 10
729 50c. Discus-throwing 20 30
730 90c. Archery 40 55
731 $2 Baseball 1·00 1·40
MS732 108 × 84 mm. $4 Basketball 5·00 2·75

165 Scene from Football Match

1982. World Cup Football Championship, Spain.
733 **165** 10c. multicoloured 30 10
734 – 50c. multicoloured 60 35
735 – 90c. multicoloured 1·10 70
736 – $4 multicoloured 3·50 3·50
MS737 – 75 × 92 mm. $5 multicoloured 8·50 10·00
DESIGNS: 50c. to $5, Scenes from various matches.

166 Airbus Industrie A300

167 Cordia

1982. Coolidge International Airport. Mult.
738 10c. Type **166** 10 10
739 50c. Hawker-Siddeley H.S.748 30 30
740 90c. De Havilland D.H.C.6 Twin Otter 60 60
741 $2.50 Britten Norman Islander 1·75 1·75
MS742 99 × 73 mm. $5 Boeing 747-100 (horiz) 2·75 4·00

1982. Death Centenary of Charles Darwin. Fauna and Flora. Multicoloured.
743 10c. Type **167** 30 10
744 50c. Small Indian mongoose (horiz) 60 40
745 90c. Corallita 1·00 75
746 $2 Mexican bulldog bat (horiz) 2·50 3·25
MS747 107 × 85 mm. $5 Carribbean monk seal 7·50 8·00

168 Queen's House, Greenwich

1982. 21st Birthday of Princess of Wales. Mult.
748 90c. Type **168** 45 45
749 $1 Prince and Princess of Wales 65 50
750 $4 Princess Diana 3·00 2·00
MS751 102 × 75 mm. $5 Type **169** 3·75 2·50

170 Boy Scouts decorating Streets for Independence Parade

1982. 75th Anniv of Boy Scout Movement. Multicoloured.
752 10c. Type **170** 25 10
753 50c. Boy Scout giving helping hand during street parade 60 40
754 90c. Boy Scouts attending H.R.H. Princess Margaret at Independence Ceremony 1·00 75
755 $2.20 Cub Scout giving directions to tourists 1·90 2·75
MS756 102 × 72 mm. $5 Lord Baden-Powell 5·50 5·50

1982. Birth of Prince William of Wales. Nos. 748/50 optd **ROYAL BABY 21.6.82.**
757 90c. Type **168** 45 45
758 $1 Prince and Princess of Wales 50 50
759 $4 Princess Diana 2·00 1·50
MS760 102 × 75 mm. $5 Type **169** 2·40 2·50

172 Roosevelt in 1940

1982. Birth Centenary of Franklin D. Roosevelt. (Nos. 761, 763 and 765/6) and 250th Birth Anniv of George Washington (others). Multicoloured.
761 10c. Type **172** 20 10
762 25c. Washington as blacksmith 45 15
763 45c. Churchill, Roosevelt and Stalin at Yalta Conference 1·75 40
764 60c. Washington crossing the Delaware (vert) 1·00 40
765 $1 "Roosevelt Special" train (vert) 1·75 90
766 $3 Portrait of Roosevelt (vert) 1·40 2·40
MS767 92 × 87 mm. $4 Roosevelt and Wife 2·00 1·75
MS768 92 × 87 mm. $4 Portrait of Washington (vert) 2·00 1·75
No. **MS**768 also exists imperf.

173 "Annunciation"

1982. Christmas. Religious Paintings by Raphael. Multicoloured.
769 10c. Type **173** 10 10
770 30c. "Adoration of the Magi" 15 15
771 $1 "Presentation at the Temple" 50 50
772 $4 "Coronation of the Virgin" 2·10 2·25
MS773 95 × 124 mm. $5 "Marriage of the Virgin" 2·75 2·50

174 Tritons and Dolphins

1983. 500th Birth Anniv of Raphael. Details from "Galatea" Fresco. Multicoloured.
774 45c. Type **174** 20 25
775 50c. Sea nymph carried off by Triton 25 30
776 60c. Winged angel steering dolphins (horiz) 30 35
777 $4 Cupids shooting arrows (horiz) 1·60 2·00
MS778 101 × 125 mm. $5 Galatea pulled along by dolphins 1·50 2·25

175 Pineapple Produce

1983. Commonwealth Day. Multicoloured.
779 25c. Type **175** 15 15
780 45c. Carnival 20 25
781 60c. Tourism 30 35
782 $3 Airport 1·00 1·50

176 T.V. Satellite Coverage of Royal Wedding

1983. World Communications Year. Multicoloured.
783 15c. Type **176** 40 20
784 50c. Police communications 2·25 1·50
785 60c. House-to-train telephone call 2·25 1·50
786 $3 Satellite earth station with planets Jupiter and Saturn 4·75 5·00
MS787 100 × 90 mm. $5 "Comsat" satellite over West Indies 2·00 3·75

177 Bottle-nosed Dolphin

1983. Whales. Multicoloured.
788 15c. Type **177** 85 20
789 50c. Fin whale 1·75 1·25
790 60c. Bowhead whale 2·00 1·25
791 $3 Spectacled porpoise 3·75 4·25
MS792 122 × 101 mm. $5 Narwhal 8·50 6·00

178 Cashew Nut

1983. Fruits and Flowers. Multicoloured.
793 1c. Type **178** 15 1·00
794 2c. Passion fruit 15 1·00
795 3c. Mango 15 1·00
796 5c. Grapefruit 20 75
797a 10c. Pawpaw 30 20
798 15c. Breadfruit 75 20
799 20c. Coconut 50 20
800a 25c. Oleander 75 20
801 30c. Banana 60 40
802a 40c. Pineapple 75 30
803a 45c. Cordia 85 40
804 50c. Cassia 90 60
805 60c. Poui 1·50 1·00
806a $1 Frangipani 2·00 1·50
807a $2 Flamboyant 3·50 4·50
808 $2.50 Lemon 3·75 6·50
809 $5 Linum vitae 5·00 13·00
810 $10 National flag and coat of arms 8·00 17·00

179 Dornier Do-X Flying Boat

1983. Bicentenary of Manned Flight. Mult.
811 30c. Type **179** . . . . 1·00 30
812 50c. Supermarine S.6B seaplane . . . . 1·25 60
813 60c. Curtiss F-9C Sparrowhawk biplane and airship U.S.S. "Akron" . . 1·40 85
814 $4 Hot-air balloon "Pro Juventute" . . . . 3·25 5·00
MS815 80 × 105 mm. $5 Airship LZ-127 "Graf Zeppelin" . . . 1·75 2·25

180 "Sibyls and Angels" (detail) (Raphael)

1983. Christmas. 500th Birth Anniv of Raphael.
816 **180** 10c. multicoloured 30 20
817 – 30c. multicoloured 65 35
818 – $1 multicoloured . . . . 1·50 1·25
819 – $4 multicoloured . . . . 3·00 5·00
MS820 – 101 × 103 mm. $5 multicoloured . . . . 1·50 2·25
DESIGNS—HORIZ: 10c. to $4, Different details from "Sibyls and Angels". VERT: $5 "The Vision of Ezekiel".

181 John Wesley (founder) **182** Discus

1983. Bicentenary of Methodist Church (1984). Multicoloured.
821 15c. Type **181** 25 15
822 50c. Nathaniel Gilbert (founder in Antigua) . . . 70 50
823 60c. St. John Methodist Church steeple 75 65
824 $3 Ebenezer Methodist Church, St. John's . . . . 2·00 4·00

1984. Olympic Games, Los Angeles. Multicoloured.
825 25c. Type **182** 20 15
826 50c. Gymnastics 35 30
827 90c. Hurdling 65 70
828 $3 Cycling . . . . 2·50 3·75
MS829 82 × 67 mm. $5 Volleyball 2·75 3·00

183 "Booker Vanguard" (freighter)

1984. Ships. Multicoloured.
830 45c. Type **183** . . . . 1·00 55
831 50c. S.S. "Canberra" (liner) 1·25 80
832 60c. Yachts . . . . 1·50 1·00
833 $4 "Fairwind" (cargo liner) 3·00 7·00
MS834 107 × 80 mm. $5 18th-century British man-of-war (vert) . . . . 1·75 3·50

184 Chenille **187** Abraham Lincoln

1984. Universal Postal Union Congress, Hamburg. Multicoloured.
835 15c. Type **184** 40 15
836 50c. Shell flower 80 70
837 60c. Anthurium . . . . . . 85 1·10
838 $3 Angels trumpet . . . . . 2·75 6·50
MS839 100 × 75 mm. $5 Crown of Thorns . . . . 1·50 3·25

1984. Various stamps surch. (a) Nos. 702/4.
840 $2 on 25c. Type **159** . . . . 2·50 2·50
841 $2 on 50c. Glamis Castle . . 2·50 2·50
842 $2 on $4 Prince Charles skiing . . . . 2·50 2·50
MS843 96 × 82 mm. $2 on $5 Glass coach . . . . 4·00 4·00

(b) Nos. 748/50.
844 $2 on 90c. Type **168** . . . . 2·00 2·00
845 $2 on $1 Prince and Princess of Wales . . . . 2·00 2·00
846 $2 on $4 Princess Diana . . 2·00 2·00
MS847 102 × 75 mm. Type **169** 4·00 4·00

(c) Nos. 757/9.
848 $2 on 90c. Type **168** . . . . 2·00 2·00
849 $2 on $1 Prince and Princess of Wales . . . . 2·00 2·00
850 $2 on $4 Princess Diana . . 2·00 2·00
MS851 102 × 75 mm. $2 on $5 Type **169** . . . . 4·00 4·00

(d) Nos. 779/82.
852 $2 on 25c. Type **175** . . . . 2·75 1·25
853 $2 on 45c. Carnival . . . . 2·75 1·25
854 $2 on 60c. Tourism . . . . . 2·75 1·25
855 $2 on $3 Airport . . . . . . 2·75 1·25

1984. Presidents of the United States of America. Multicoloured.
856 10c. Type **187** 15 10
857 20c. Harry S. Truman . . . 20 15
858 30c. Dwight D. Eisenhower 30 25
859 40c. Ronald W. Reagan . . . 50 30
860 90c. Gettysburg Address, 1863 . . . . 90 75
861 $1.10 Formation of N.A.T.O.,1949 . . . . . . 1·25 1·25
862 $1.50 Eisenhower during the war . . . . 1·60 1·75
863 $2 Reagan and Caribbean Basin Initiative . . . . . 1·75 2·00

188 View of Moravian Mission

1984. 150th Anniv of Abolition of Slavery. Multicoloured.
864 40c. Type **188** 90 50
865 50c. Antigua Courthouse, 1823 . . . . 1·00 65
866 60c. Planting sugar-cane, Monks Hill . . . . 1·10 75
867 $3 Boiling house, Delaps' estate . . . . 4·25 6·00
MS868 95 × 70 mm. $5 Loading sugar, Willoughby Bay . . . . 6·50 4·75

189 Rufous-sided Towhee **190** Grass-skiing

1984. Songbirds. Multicoloured.
869 40c. Type **189** . . . . 1·25 85
870 50c. Parula warbler . . . . . 1·40 1·10
871 60c. House wren . . . . . . 1·50 1·50
872 $2 Ruby-crowned kinglet . . 2·00 3·75
873 $3 Common flicker ("Yellow-shafted Flicker") . . . . 2·75 5·00
MS874 76 × 76 mm. $5 Yellow-breasted chat . . . . 2·50 6·00

1984. "Ausipex" International Stamp Exhibition, Melbourne, Australian Sports. Multicoloured.
875 $1 Type **190** . . . . 1·25 1·50
876 $5 Australian football . . . 3·75 5·50
MS877 108 × 78 mm. $5 Boomerang-throwing . . . . 2·50 4·00

191 "The Virgin and Infant with Angels and Cherubs" **192** "The Blue Dancers"

1984. 450th Death Anniv of Correggio (painter). Multicoloured.
878 25c. Type **191** 40 20
879 60c. "The Four Saints" . . . 80 50
880 90c. "St. Catherine" . . . . 1·10 90
881 $3 "The Campori Madonna" 2·25 4·25
MS882 90 × 60 mm. $5 "St. John the Baptist" . . . . 2·00 2·75

1984. 150th Birth Anniv of Edgar Degas (painter). Multicoloured.
883 15c. Type **192** 35 15
884 50c. "The Pink Dancers" . . 80 60
885 70c. "Two Dancers" . . . . 1·10 85
886 $4 "Dancers at the Bar" . . 2·50 4·75
MS887 90 × 60 mm. "The Folk dancers" (40 × 27 mm) . . . . 2·00 2·75

193 Sir Winston Churchill **194** Donald Duck fishing

1984. Famous People. Multicoloured.
888 60c. Type **193** . . . . 1·10 1·50
889 60c. Mahatma Gandhi . . . 1·10 1·50
890 60c. John F. Kennedy . . . 1·10 1·50
891 60c. Mao Tse-tung . . . . . 1·10 1·50
892 $1 Churchill with General De Gaulle, Paris, 1944 (horiz) 1·25 1·75
893 $1 Gandhi leaving London by train, 1931 (horiz) . . . 1·25 1·75
894 $1 Kennedy with Chancellor Adenauer and Mayor Brandt, Berlin, 1963 (horiz) 1·25 1·75
895 $1 Mao Tse-tung with Lin Piao, Peking, 1969 (horiz) 1·25 1·75
MS896 114 × 80 mm. $5 Flags of Great Britain, India, the United States and China . . . . . . 9·00 4·50

1984. Christmas. 50th Birthday of Donald Duck. Walt Disney Cartoon Characters. Multicoloured.
897 1c. Type **194** 10 10
898 2c. Donald Duck lying on beach 10 10
899 3c. Donald Duck and nephews with fishing rods and fishes 10 10
900 4c. Donald Duck and nephews in boat 10 10
901 5c. Wearing diving masks . . 10 10
902 10c. In deckchairs reading books 10 10
903 $1 With toy shark's fin . . . 2·25 1·25
904 $2 In sailing boat . . . . . 2·50 3·00
905 $5 Attempting to propel boat 5·50 6·00
MS906 Two sheets, each 125 × 100 mm. (a) $5 Nephews with crayon and paintbrushes (horiz). (b) $5 Donald Duck in deckchair Set of 2 sheets . . . 9·00 13·00

195 Torch from Statue in Madison Square Park, 1885

1985. Centenary (1986) of Statue of Liberty (1st issue). Multicoloured.
907 25c. Type **195** 30 20
908 30c. Statue of Liberty and scaffolding ("Restoration and Renewal") (vert) . . . 30 20
909 50c. Frederic Bartholdi (sculptor) supervising construction, 1876 . . . . 40 40
910 90c. Close-up of statue . . . 60 75
911 $1 Statue and cadet ship ("Operation Sail", 1976) (vert) . . . . 1·60 1·40
912 $3 Dedication ceremony, 1886 . . . . 1·75 3·00
MS913 110 × 80 mm. $5 Port of New York . . . . 3·75 3·75
See also Nos. 1110/19.

196 Arawak Pot Sherd and Indians making Clay Utensils

1985. Native American Artefacts. Multicoloured.
914 15c. Type **196** 15 10
915 50c. Arawak body design and Arawak Indians tattooing 30 40
916 60c. Head of the god "Yocahu" and Indians harvesting manioc 40 50
917 $3 Carib war club and Carib Indians going into battle 1·25 2·50
MS918 97 × 68 mm. $5 Taino Indians worshipping stone idol 1·50 2·50

197 Triumph 2hp "Jap", 1903

1985. Centenary of the Motorcycle. Multicoloured.
919 10c. Type **197** 65 15
920 30c. "Indian Arrow", 1949 1·10 40
921 60c. BMW "R100RS", 1976 1·60 1·25
922 $4 Harley-Davidson "Model II", 1916 . . . . 5·50 9·00
MS923 90 × 93 mm. $5 Laverda "Jota", 1975 . . . . 5·50 7·00

198 Slavonian Grebe ("Horned Grebe")

1985. Birth Bicentenary of John J. Audubon (ornithologist) (1st issue). Multicoloured. Designs showing original paintings.
924 90c. Type **198** . . . . 1·75 1·25
925 $1 British storm petrel ("Least Petrel") . . . . . 2·00 1·25
926 $1.50 Great blue heron . . . 2·50 3·25
927 $3 Double-crested cormorant 3·75 6·00
MS928 103 × 72 mm. $5 White-tailed tropic bird (vert) . . . . 7·00 6·00
See also Nos. 990/4.

199 "Anaea cyanea"

1985. Butterflies. Multicoloured.
929 25c. Type **199** . . . . 1·00 30
930 60c. "Leodonta dysoni" . . . 2·25 1·25
931 90c. "Junea doraete" . . . . 2·75 1·50
932 $4 "Prepona pylene" . . . . 7·50 10·50
MS933 132 × 105 mm. $5 "Caerois gerdtrudlus" . . . . 4·50 6·50

200 Cessna 172D Skyhawk

1985. 40th Anniv of International Civil Aviation Organization. Multicoloured.
934 30c. Type **200** . . . . 1·25 30
935 90c. Fokker D.VII . . . . . 2·75 1·25
936 $1.50 SPAD VII . . . . . . 3·75 3·25
937 $3 Boeing 747-100 . . . . . 5·50 7·50
MS938 97 × 83 mm. $5 De Havilland D.H.C.6 twin otter . . . . . . 4·50 6·50

201 Maimonides **203** The Queen Mother attending Church

202 Young Farmers with Produce

1985. 850th Birth Anniv of Maimonides (physician, philosopher and scholar).
939 **201** $2 green . . . . 4·00 3·25
MS940 70 × 84 mm. Type **201** $5 brown . . . . 7·00 4·50

1985. International Youth Year. Multicoloured.
941 25c. Type **202** 25 20
942 50c. Hotel management trainees 40 50
943 60c. Girls with goat and boys with football ("Environment") . . . . . 1·00 70
944 $3 Windsurfing ("Leisure") 2·75 5·50
MS945 102 × 72 mm. $5 Young people with Antiguan flags . . 2·75 3·25

1985. Life and Times of Queen Elizabeth the Queen Mother. Multicoloured.
946 $1 Type **203** 45 60
947 $1.50 Watching children playing in London garden 60 85
948 $2.50 The Queen Mother in 1979 . . . . 90 1·40
MS949 56 × 85 mm. $5 With Prince Edward at Royal Wedding, 1981 5·50 3·00
Stamps as Nos. 946/8, but with face values of 90c., $1 and $3 exist from additional sheetlets with changed background colours.

204 Magnificent Frigate Bird

206 Bass Trombone

205 Girl Guides Nursing

1985. Marine Life. Multicoloured.
950 15c. Type **204** . . . . 1·00 30
951 45c. Brain coral . . . . . . 2·00 95
952 60c. Cushion star . . . . . 2·25 1·75
953 $3 Spotted moray . . . . . 7·00 9·00
MS954 110 × 80 mm. $5 Elkhorn coral . . . . 9·00 7·00

1985. 75th Anniv of Girl Guide Movement. Multicoloured.
955 15c. Type **205** 75 20
956 45c. Open-air Girl Guide meeting . . . . 1·40 60
957 60c. Lord and Lady Baden-Powell . . . . 1·75 90
958 $3 Girl Guides gathering flowers . . . . 4·25 4·50
MS959 67 × 96 mm. $5 Barn swallow (Nature study) . . . . 6·50 8·50

1985. 300th Birth Anniv of Johann Sebastian Bach (composer).
960 **206** 25c. multicoloured . . . . 1·40 55
961 – 50c. multicoloured . . . . 1·75 1·10
962 – $1 multicoloured . . . . 3·25 1·75
963 – $3 multicoloured . . . . 6·00 7·00
MS964 – 104 × 73 mm. $5 black and grey . . . . 4·50 4·75
DESIGNS:50c. English horn; $1 Violino piccolo; $3 Bass rackett; $5 Johann Sebastian Bach.

207 Flags of Great Britain and Antigua

1985. Royal Visit. Multicoloured.
965 60c. Type **207** . . . . 1·00 65
966 $1 Queen Elizabeth II (vert) 1·50 1·25
967 $4 Royal Yacht "Britannia" 3·25 7·00
MS968 110 × 83 mm. $5 Map of Antigua . . . . 3·00 3·25

1985. 150th Birth Anniv of Mark Twain (author). As T **118** of Anguilla showing Walt Disney cartoon characters in scenes from "Roughing It". Multicoloured.
969 25c. Donald Duck and Mickey Mouse meeting Indians . . . . 1·00 20
970 50c. Mickey Mouse, Donald Duck and Goofy canoeing 1·50 55
971 $1.10 Goofy as Pony Express rider . . . . 2·50 2·25
972 $1.50 Donald Duck and Goofy hunting buffalo . . 3·00 3·75
973 $2 Mickey Mouse and silver mine . . . . 3·50 4·50
MS974 127 × 101 mm. $5 Mickey Mouse driving stagecoach . . . 8·00 7·50

1985. Birth Bicentenaries of Grimm Brothers (folklorists). As T **119** of Anguilla showing Walt Disney cartoon characters in scenes from "Spindle, Shuttle and Needle". Multicoloured.
975 30c. The Prince (Mickey Mouse) searches for a bride 1·25 40
976 60c. The Prince finds the Orphan Girl (Minnie Mouse) . . . . 1·75 80
977 70c. The Spindle finds the Prince . . . . 2·00 1·40
978 $1 The Needle tidies the Girl's house . . . . . . 2·50 1·75
979 $3 The Prince proposes . . . 4·75 7·50
MS980 125 × 101 mm. $5 The Orphan Girl and spinning wheel on Prince's horse . . . . . . 8·00 7·50

208 Benjamin Franklin and U.N. (New York) 1953 U.P.U. 5c. Stamp

1985. 40th Anniv of United Nations Organization. Multicoloured.
981 40c. Type **208** . . . . 1·00 70
982 $1 George Washington Carver (agricultural chemist) and 1982 Nature Conservation 28c. stamp 2·00 2·00
983 $3 Charles Lindbergh (aviator) and 1978 I.C.A.O. 25c. stamp . . . . 4·75 7·50
MS984 101 × 77 mm. $5 Marc Chagall (artist) (vert) . . . . 6·50 4·75
Nos. 981/4 each include a United Nations (New York) stamp design.

209 "Madonna and Child" (De Landi)

211 Tug

210 Football, Boots and Trophy

1985. Christmas. Religious Paintings. Mult.
985 10c. Type **209** 30 15
986 25c. "Madonna and Child" (Berlinghiero) 55 25
987 60c. "The Nativity" (Fra Angelico) 70 60
988 $4 "Presentation in the Temple" (Giovanni di Paolo) . . . . 1·75 4·25
MS989 113 × 81 mm. $5 "The Nativity" (Antoniazzo Romano) 3·00 3·75

1986. Birth Bicentenary of John J. Audubon (ornithologist) (2nd issue). As T **198** showing original paintings. Multicoloured.
990 60c. Mallard . . . . 2·25 1·50
991 90c. North American black duck ("Dusky Duck") . . 2·75 2·00
992 $1.50 Pintail ("Common Pintail") . . . . 3·50 4·50
993 $3 American wigeon ("Wigeon") . . . . 4·75 6·50
MS994 102 × 73 mm. Eider ("Common Eider") . . . . . 7·00 5·50

1986. World Cup Football Championship, Mexico. Multicoloured.
995 30c. Type **210** . . . . 1·50 40
996 60c. Goalkeeper (vert) . . . 2·00 85
997 $1 Referee blowing whistle (vert) . . . . 2·50 1·75
998 $4 Ball in net . . . . 6·50 9·00
MS999 87 × 76 mm. $5 Two players competing for ball . . . . . 8·50 7·50

1986. Appearance of Halley's Comet (1st issue). As T **123** of Anguilla. Multicoloured.
1000 5c. Edmond Halley and Old Greenwich Observatory 30 20
1001 10c. Messerschmitt Me 163B Komet (fighter aircraft), 1944 . . . . 30 15
1002 60c. Montezuma (Aztec emperor) and Comet in 1517 (from "Historias de las Indias de Neuva Espana") . . . . 1·50 70
1003 $4 Pocahontas saving Capt. John Smith and Comet in 1607 . . . . 4·50 5·50
MS1004 101 × 70 mm. $5 Halley's Comet over English Harbour, Antigua . . . . 3·50 3·75
See also Nos. 1047/51.

1986. 60th Birthday of Queen Elizabeth II. As T **125** of Anguilla.
1005 60c. black and yellow . . . 30 35
1006 $1 multicoloured 50 55
1007 $4 multicoloured . . . . . 1·40 1·90
MS1008 120 × 85 mm. $5 black and brown . . . . 2·00 3·00
DESIGNS: 60c. Wedding photograph, 1947; $1 Queen at Trooping the Colour; $4 In Scotland; $5 Queen Mary and Princess Elizabeth, 1927.

1986. Local Boats. Multicoloured.
1009 30c. Type **211** 25 20
1010 60c. Game fishing boat . . 45 35
1011 $1 Yacht 75 60
1012 $4 Lugger with auxiliary sail 2·50 3·25
MS1013 108 × 78 mm. $5 Boats under construction . . . . . . 3·00 4·00

212 "Hiawatha" express

1986. "Ameripex '86" International Stamp Exhibition, Chicago. Famous American Trains. Multicoloured.
1014 25c. Type **212** . . . . . . 1·25 50
1015 50c. "Grand Canyon" express . . . . 1·50 80
1016 $1 "Powhattan Arrow" express . . . . 1·75 1·75
1017 $3 "Empire State" express 3·00 6·00
MS1018 116 × 87 mm. $5 Southern Pacific "Daylight" express . . 6·00 11·00

213 Prince Andrew and Miss Sarah Ferguson

214 Fly-specked Cerith

1986. Royal Wedding. Multicoloured.
1019 45c. Type **213** 70 35
1020 60c. Prince Andrew 80 45
1021 $4 Prince Andrew with Prince Philip . . . . . . 2·75 3·50
MS1022 88 × 88 mm. $5 Prince Andrew and Miss Sarah Ferguson (different) . . . . 5·00 4·50

1986. Sea Shells. Multicoloured.
1023 15c. Type **214** 75 50
1024 45c. Smooth Scotch bonnet 1·75 1·25
1025 60c. West Indian crown conch . . . . 2·00 2·00
1026 $3 Ciboney murex . . . . . 6·50 10·00
MS1027 109 × 75 mm. $5 Colourful Atlantic moon (horiz) . . . . 7·50 8·50

215 Water Lily

1986. Flowers. Multicoloured.
1028 10c. Type **215** 20 15
1029 15c. Queen of the night . . 20 15
1030 50c. Cup of gold 55 55
1031 60c. Beach morning glory 70 70
1032 70c. Golden trumpet 80 80
1033 $1 Air plant . . . . 90 1·10
1034 $4 Purple wreath . . . . . 1·75 3·00
1035 $4 Zephyr lily . . . . . . 2·00 3·75
MS1036 Two sheets, each 102 × 72 mm. (a) $4 Dozakie. (b) $5 Four o'clock flower Set of 2 sheets . . . . 5·00 7·50

1986. World Cup Football Championship Winners, Mexico. Nos. 995/8 optd **WINNERS Argentina 3 W.Germany 2**.
1037 30c. Type **210** . . . . . . 1·25 40
1038 60c. Goalkeeper (vert) . . . 1·75 75
1039 $1 Referee blowing whistle (vert) . . . . 2·25 1·10
1040 $4 Ball in net . . . . 5·50 4·50
MS1041 87 × 76 mm. $5 Two players competing for ball . . . . . . 5·50 4·00

217 "Hygrocybe occidentalis var. scarletina"

(218)

1986. Mushrooms. Multicoloured.
1042 10c. Type **217** 30 25
1043 50c. "Trogia buccinalis" . . 70 55
1044 $1 "Collybia subpruinosa" 1·25 1·25
1045 $4 "Leucocoprinus brebissonii" . . . . 3·00 4·50
MS1046 102 × 82 mm. $5 "Pyrrhoglossum pyrrhum" . . 13·00 11·00

1986. Appearance of Halley's Comet (2nd issue). Nos. 1000/3 optd with T **218**.
1047 5c. Edmond Halley and Old Greenwich Observatory 20 10
1048 10c. Messerschmitt Me 163B Komet (fighter aircraft), 1944 . . . . 50 10
1049 60c. Montezuma (Aztec emperor) and Comet in 1517 (from "Historias de las Indias de Neuva Espana") . . . . 1·25 65
1050 $4 Pocahontas saving Capt. John Smith and Comet in 1607 . . . . 4·50 4·00
MS1051 101 × 70 mm. $5 Halley's Comet over English Harbour, Antigua . . . . 6·00 6·50

219 Auburn "Speedster" (1933)

1986. Centenary of First Benz Motor Car. Mult.
1052 10c. Type **219** 15 10
1053 15c. Mercury "Sable" (1986) 20 10
1054 50c. Cadillac (1959) 55 30
1055 60c. Studebaker (1950) . . . 70 45
1056 70c. Lagonda "V-12" (1939) 80 55
1057 $1 Adler "Standard" (1930) 1·10 75
1058 $3 DKW (1956) . . . . . . 2·50 2·50
1059 $4 Mercedes "500K" (1936) 3·00 3·00
MS1060 Two sheets, each 99 × 70 mm. (a) $5 Daimler (1896). (b) $5 Mercedes "Knight" (1921) Set of 2 sheets . . . . 9·00 6·50

220 Young Mickey Mouse playing Santa Claus

1986. Christmas. Designs showing Walt Disney cartoon characters as babies. Multicoloured.
1061 25c. Type **220** 60 35
1062 30c. Mickey and Minnie Mouse building snowman 70 40
1063 40c. Aunt Matilda and Goofy baking 75 45
1064 60c. Goofy and Pluto . . . 1·00 85
1065 70c. Pluto, Donald and Daisy Duck carol singing 1·10 1·00
1066 $1.50 Donald Duck, Mickey Mouse and Pluto stringing popcorn . . . . 1·75 2·50
1067 $3 Grandma Duck and Minnie Mouse . . . . . 3·00 4·50
1068 $4 Donald Duck and Pete 3·25 4·50
MS1069 Two sheets, each 127 × 102 mm. (a) $5 Goofy, Donald Duck and Minnie Mouse playing with reindeer. (b) $5 Mickey Mouse, Donald and Daisy Duck playing with toys Set of 2 sheets . . . . 13·00 14·00

221 Arms of Antigua

222 "Canada I" (1981)

1986.

1070 **221** 10c. blue 50 50
1071 – 25c. red 75 75
DESIGN: 25c. Flag of Antigua.

1987. America's Cup Yachting Championship. Multicoloured.
1072 30c. Type **222** 45 20
1073 60c. "Gretel II" (1970) . . . 60 50
1074 $1 "Sceptre" (1958) . . . . 85 1·00
1075 $3 "Vigilant" (1893) . . . . 2·25 3·00
MS1076 113 × 84 mm. $5 "Australia II" defeating "Liberty" (1983) (horiz) . . . . 4·00 5·00

223 Bridled Burrfish

1987. Marine Life. Multicoloured.
1077 15c. Type **223** . . . . . . 2·50 50
1078 30c. Common noddy ("Brown Noddy") . . . . 4·50 60
1079 40c. Nassau grouper . . . . 3·00 70
1080 50c. Laughing gull . . . . 5·50 1·50
1081 60c. French angelfish . . . 3·50 1·50
1082 $1 Porkfish . . . . 3·50 1·75
1083 $2 Royal tern . . . . 7·50 6·00
1084 $3 Sooty tern . . . . 7·50 8·00
MS1085 Two sheets, each 120 × 94 mm. (a) $5 Banded butterflyfish. (b) $5 Brown booby Set of 2 sheets . . . . 17·00 14·00
Nos. 1078, 1080 and 1083/5 are without the World Wildlife Fund logo shown on Type **223**.

224 Handball

1987. Olympic Games, Seoul (1988) (1st issue). Multicoloured.
1086 10c. Type **224** 60 10
1087 60c. Fencing 85 35
1088 $1 Gymnastics . . . . . . 1·25 80
1089 $3 Football . . . . 2·50 4·00
MS1090 100 × 72 mm. $5 Boxing gloves . . . . 3·50 4·25
See also Nos. 1222/6.

225 "The Profile"

1987. Birth Centenary of Marc Chagall (artist). Multicoloured.
1091 10c. Type **225** 30 15
1092 30c. "Portrait of the Artist's Sister" 45 30
1093 40c. "Bride with Fan" . . . 50 40
1094 60c. "David in Profile" . . 55 45
1095 90c. "Fiancee with Bouquet" 75 60
1096 $1 "Self Portrait with Brushes" 75 65
1097 $3 "The Walk" . . . . . 1·75 2·25
1098 $4 "Three Candles" . . . . 2·00 2·50
MS1099 Two sheets, each 110 × 95 mm. (a) $5 "Fall of Icarus" (104 × 89 mm). (b) $5 "Myth of Orpheus" (104 × 89 mm). Imperf Set of 2 sheets . . . . 6·50 6·00

226 "Spirit of Australia" (fastest powerboat), 1978

1987. Milestones of Transportation. Multicoloured.
1100 10c. Type **226** 80 40
1101 15c. Werner von Siemens's electric locomotive, 1879 1·50 50
1102 30c. U.S.S. "Triton" (first submerged circum-navigation), 1960 . . . . 1·25 50
1103 50c. Trevithick's steam carriage (first passenger-carrying vehicle), 1801 . . 1·75 60
1104 60c. U.S.S. "New Jersey" (battleship), 1942 . . . . 1·75 85
1105 70c. Draisaine bicycle, 1818 2·00 1·00
1106 90c. "United States" (liner) (holder of Blue Riband), 1952 . . . . 1·75 1·00
1107 $1.50 Cierva C.4 (first autogyro), 1923 . . . . 1·75 2·75
1108 $2 Curtiss NC-4 flying boat (first transatlantic flight), 1919 . . . . 2·00 3·00
1109 $3 "Queen Elizabeth 2" (liner), 1969 . . . . . 3·50 4·50

227 Lee Iacocca at Unveiling of Restored Statue

228 Grace Kelly

1987. Centenary of Statue of Liberty (1986) (2nd issue). Multicoloured.
1110 15c. Type **227** 15 15
1111 30c. Statue at sunset (side view) 20 20
1112 45c. Aerial view of head . . 30 30
1113 50c. Lee Iacocca and torch 35 35
1114 60c. Workmen inside head of Statue (horiz) 35 35
1115 90c. Restoration work (horiz) 50 50
1116 $1 Head of Statue 55 55
1117 $2 Statue at sunset (front view) . . . . 1·00 1·50
1118 $3 Inspecting restoration work (horiz) . . . . . 1·25 2·00
1119 $5 Statue at night . . . . . 2·00 3·50

1987. Entertainers. Multicoloured.
1120 15c. Type **228** 90 40
1121 30c. Marilyn Monroe . . . 2·75 80
1122 45c. Orson Welles 90 60
1123 50c. Judy Garland 90 65
1124 60c. John Lennon . . . . . 4·25 1·25
1125 $1 Rock Hudson . . . . . 1·40 1·10
1126 $2 John Wayne . . . . . . 2·50 2·00
1127 $3 Elvis Presley . . . . . . 10·00 4·50

229 Scouts around Camp Fire and Red Kangaroo

1987. 16th World Scout Jamboree, Australia. Mult.
1128 10c. Type **229** 65 20
1129 60c. Scouts canoeing and blue-winged kookaburra 1·25 80
1130 $1 Scouts on assault course and ring-tailed rock wallaby . . . . 1·00 85
1131 $3 Field kitchen and koala 1·50 4·25
MS1132 103 × 78 mm. $5 Flags of Antigua, Australia and Scout Movement . . . . 3·25 3·50

230 Whistling Frog

1987. "Capex '87" International Stamp Exhibition, Toronto. Reptiles and Amphibians. Mult.
1133 30c. Type **230** 55 20
1134 60c. Croaking lizard 75 40
1135 $1 Antiguan anole . . . . . 1·00 70
1136 $3 Red-footed tortoise . . . 2·00 3·00
MS1137 106 × 76 mm. $5 Ground lizard . . . . 2·25 2·75

1987. 10th Death Anniv of Elvis Presley (entertainer). No. 1127 optd **10th ANNIVERSARY 16th AUGUST 1987**.
1138 $3 Elvis Presley . . . . . . 8·00 4·75

232 House of Burgesses, Virginia ("Freedom of Speech")

1987. Bicentenary of U.S. Constitution. Mult.
1139 15c. Type **232** 10 10
1140 45c. State Seal, Connecticut 20 25
1141 60c. State Seal, Delaware . . 25 35
1142 $4 Governor Morris (Pennsylvania delegate) (vert) . . . . 1·75 2·25
MS1143 105 × 75 mm. $5 Roger Sherman (Connecticut delegate) (vert) . . . . 2·00 2·75

233 "Madonna and Child" (Bernardo Daddi)

234 Wedding Photograph, 1947

1987. Christmas. Religious Paintings. Mult.
1144 45c. Type **233** 50 15
1145 60c. St. Joseph (detail, "The Nativity" (Sano di Pietro)) 65 30
1146 $1 Virgin Mary (detail, "The Nativity" (Sano di Pietro)) 85 55
1147 $4 "Music-making Angel" (Melozzo da Forli) . . 2·25 3·50
MS1148 99 × 70 mm. $5 "The Flight into Egypt" (Sano di Pietro) 2·25 2·75

1988. Royal Ruby Wedding.
1149 **234** 25c. brown, black and blue 30 15
1150 – 60c. multicoloured . . . 60 40
1151 – $2 brown, black and green . . . . 1·10 1·10
1152 – $3 multicoloured . . . . 1·50 1·60
MS1153 - 107 × 77 mm. $5 multicoloured . . . . 2·50 2·75
DESIGNS: 60c. Queen Elizabeth II; $2 Princess Elizabeth and Prince Philip with Prince Charles at his christening, 1948; $3 Queen Elizabeth (from photo by Tim Graham), 1980; $5 Royal family, 1952.

235 Great Blue Heron

1988. Birds of Antigua. Multicoloured.
1154 10c. Type **235** 45 40
1155 15c. Ringed kingfisher (horiz) 50 40
1156 50c. Bananaquit (horiz) . . 90 50
1157 60c. American purple gallinule ("Purple Gallinule") (horiz) 90 50
1158 70c. Blue-hooded euphonia (horiz) . . . . 1·00 55
1159 $1 Brown-throated conure ("Caribbean Parakeet") 1·25 75
1160 $3 Troupial (horiz) . . . . 2·50 3·50
1161 $4 Purple-throated carib ("Hummingbird") (horiz) 2·50 3·50
MS1162 Two sheets, each 115 × 86 mm. (a) $5 Greater flamingo. (b) $5 Brown pelican Set of 2 sheets . . . . 4·50 5·50

236 First Aid at Daycare Centre, Antigua

1988. Salvation Army's Community Service. Multicoloured.
1163 25c. Type **236** 80 65
1164 30c. Giving penicillin injection, Indonesia . . . 80 65
1165 40c. Children at daycare centre, Bolivia 90 75
1166 45c. Rehabilitation of the handicapped, India . . . 90 75
1167 50c. Training blind man, Kenya . . . . 1·00 1·25
1168 60c. Weighing baby, Ghana 1·00 1·25
1169 $1 Training typist, Zambia 1·40 1·75
1170 $2 Emergency food kitchen, Sri Lanka . . . . 2·00 3·50
MS1171 152 × 83 mm. $5 General Eva Burrows . . . . 3·75 4·50

237 Columbus's Second Fleet, 1493

1988. 500th Anniv (1992) of Discovery of America by Columbus (1st issue). Multicoloured.
1172 10c. Type **237** 80 40
1173 30c. Painos. Indian village and fleet 80 45
1174 45c. "Santa Mariagalante" (flagship) and Painos. village . . . . 1·00 45
1175 60c. Painos Indians offering Columbus fruit and vegetables 80 50
1176 90c. Painos Indian and Columbus with scarlet macaw . . . . 2·00 1·00
1177 $1 Columbus landing on island . . . . 1·50 1·00
1178 $3 Spanish soldier and fleet 2·25 3·00
1179 $4 Fleet under sail . . . . 2·50 3·00
MS1180 Two sheets, each 110 × 80 mm. (a) $5 Queen Isabella's cross. (b) $5 Gold coin of Ferdinand and Isabella Set of 2 sheets . . . . 6·50 7·00
See also Nos. 1267/71, 1360/8, 1503/11, 1654/60 and 1670/1.

Antigua & Barbuda 30c
238 "Bust of Christ"

1988. Easter. 500th Birth Anniv of Titian (artist). Multicoloured.
1181 30c. Type **238** 40 20
1182 40c. "Scourging of Christ" 45 25
1183 45c. "Madonna in Glory with Saints" 45 25
1184 50c. "The Averoldi Polyptych" (detail) . . . 45 35
1185 $1 "Christ Crowned with Thorns" 70 55
1186 $2 "Christ Mocked" . . . . 1·10 1·25
1187 $3 "Christ and Simon of Cyrene" . . . . 1·50 1·75
1188 $4 "Crucifixion with Virgin and Saints" . . . . . . 1·75 2·25
MS1189 Two sheets, each 110 × 95 mm. (a) $5 "Ecce Homo" (detail). (b) $5 "Noli me Tangere" (detail) Set of 2 sheets . . . . 7·00 8·50

239 Two Yachts rounding Buoy

1988. Sailing Week. Multicoloured.
1190 30c. Type **239** 35 20
1191 60c. Three yachts 50 40
1192 $1 British yacht under way 60 55
1193 $3 Three yachts (different) 1·10 2·50
MS1194 103 × 92 mm. $5 Two yachts . . . . 1·75 3·25

240 Mickey Mouse and Diver with Porpoise

1988. Disney EPCOT Centre, Orlando, Florida. Designs showing cartoon characters and exhibits. Multicoloured.

1195 1c. Type **240** 10 10
1196 2c. Goofy and Mickey Mouse with futuristic car (vert) 10 10
1197 3c. Mickey Mouse and Goofy as Atlas (vert) 10 10
1198 4c. Mickey Mouse and "Eda-phosaurus" (prehistoric reptile) 10 10
1199 5c. Mickey Mouse at Journey into Imagination exhibit 15 10
1200 10c. Mickey Mouse collecting vegetables (vert) 20 10
1201 25c. Type **240** 55 25
1202 30c. As 2c. 55 25
1203 40c. As 3c. 60 30
1204 60c. As 4c. 85 50
1205 70c. As 5c. 95 60
1206 $1.50 As 10c. 2·00 2·00
1207 $3 Goofy and Mickey Mouse with robot (vert) 2·50 2·75
1208 $4 Mickey Mouse and Clarabelle at Horizons exhibit 2·50 2·75
MS1209 Two sheets, each 125 × 99 mm. (a) $5 Mickey Mouse and monorail (vert). (b) $5 Mickey Mouse flying over EPCOT Centre Set of 2 sheets 7·00 6·50

1988. Stamp Exhibitions. Nos. 1083/4 optd.

1210 $2 Royal tern (optd **Praga '88**, Prague) 5·50 2·75
1211 $3 Sooty tern (optd **INDEPENDENCE 40**, Israel) 5·50 3·50
MS1212 Two sheets, each 120 × 94 mm. (a) $5 Banded butterflyfish (optd **"OLYMPHILEX '88"**, Seoul). (b) $5 brown booby (optd **"FINLANDIA 88"**, Helsinki). Set of 2 sheets 17·00 10·00

242 Jacaranda

243 Gymnastics

1988. Flowering Trees. Multicoloured.

1213 10c. Type **242** 30 20
1214 30c. Cordia 40 20
1215 50c. Orchid tree 60 40
1216 90c. Flamboyant 70 50
1217 $1 African tulip tree 75 55
1218 $2 Potato tree 1·40 1·60
1219 $3 Crepe myrtle 1·60 2·00
1220 $4 Pitch apple 1·75 2·75
MS1221 Two sheets, each 106 × 76 mm. (a) $5 Cassia. (b) $5 Chinaberry Set of 2 sheets 5·00 6·00

1988. Olympic Games, Seoul (2nd issue). Mult.

1222 40c. Type **243** 30 25
1223 60c. Weightlifting 40 30
1224 $1 Water polo (horiz) 80 50
1225 $3 Boxing (horiz) 1·50 2·25
MS1226 114 × 80 mm. $5 Runner with Olympic torch 2·00 3·00

244 "Danaus plexippus"

1988. Caribbean Butterflies. Multicoloured.

1227 1c. Type **244** 60 1·00
1228 2c. "Greta diaphanus" 70 1·00
1229 3c. "Calisto archebates" 70 1·00
1230 5c. "Hamadryas feronia" 85 1·00
1231 10c. "Mestra dorcas" 1·00 30
1232 15c. "Hypolimnas misippus" 1·50 30
1233 20c. "Dione juno" 1·60 30
1234 25c. "Heliconius charithonia" 1·60 30
1235 30c. "Eurema pyro" 1·60 30
1236 40c. "Papilio androgeus" 1·60 30
1237 45c. "Anteos maerula" 1·60 30
1238 50c. "Aphrissa orbis" 1·75 45
1239 60c. "Astraptes xagua" 2·00 60
1240 $1 "Heliopetes arsalte" 2·25 1·00
1241 $2 "Polites baracoa" 3·25 3·75
1242 $2.50 "Phocides pigmalion" 4·00 5·00
1243 $5 "Prepona amphitoe" 5·50 7·50
1244 $10 "Oarisma nanus" 7·50 11·00
1244a $20 "Parides lycimenes" 15·00 20·00

245 President Kennedy and Family

1988. 25th Death Anniv of John F. Kennedy (American statesman). Multicoloured.

1245 1c. Type **245** 10 10
1246 2c. Kennedy commanding "PT109" 10 10
1247 3c. Funeral cortege 10 10
1248 4c. In motorcade, Mexico City 10 10
1249 30c. As 1c. 35 15
1250 60c. As 4c. 1·00 40
1251 $1 As 3c. 1·10 75
1252 $4 As 2c. 3·00 3·50
MS1253 105 × 75 mm. $5 Kennedy taking presidential oath of office 2·50 3·25

246 Minnie Mouse carol singing

1988. Christmas. "Mickey's Christmas Chorale". Design showing Walt Disney cartoon characters. Multicoloured.

1254 10c. Type **246** 40 30
1255 25c. Pluto 55 45
1256 30c. Mickey Mouse playing ukelele 55 45
1257 70c. Donald Duck and nephew 90 80
1258 $1 Mordie and Ferdie carol singing 90 1·00
1259 $1 Goofy carol singing 90 1·00
1260 $1 Chip n'Dale sliding off roof 90 1·00
1261 $1 Two of Donald Duck's nephews at window 90 1·00
1262 $1 As 10c. 90 1·00
1263 $1 As 25c. 90 1·00
1264 $1 As 30c. 90 1·00
1265 $1 As 70c. 90 1·00
MS1266 Two sheets, each 127 × 102 mm. (a) $7 Donald Duck playing trumpet and Mickey and Minnie Mouse in carriage. (b) $7 Mickey Mouse and friends singing carols on roller skates (horiz) Set of 2 sheets 8·50 8·50

Nos. 1258/65 were printed together, se-tenant, forming a composite design.

247 Arawak Warriors

1989. 500th Anniv of Discovery of America by Columbus (1992) (2nd issue). Pre-Columbian Arawak Society. Multicoloured.

1267 $1.50 Type **247** 1·10 1·40
1268 $1.50 Whip dancers 1·10 1·40
1269 $1.50 Whip dancers and chief with pineapple 1·10 1·40
1270 $1.50 Family and camp fire 1·10 1·40
MS1271 71 × 84 mm. $6 Arawak chief 2·75 3·00

Nos. 1267/70 were printed together, se-tenant, forming a composite design.

248 De Havilland Comet 4 Airliner

1989. 50th Anniv of First Jet Flight. Mult.

1272 10c. Type **248** 90 45
1273 30c. Messerschmitt Me 262 fighter 1·50 45
1274 40c. Boeing 707 airliner 1·50 45
1275 60c. Canadair CL-13 Sabre (inscr "F-86") fighter 1·90 55
1276 $1 Lockheed F-104 Starfighters 2·25 1·10
1277 $2 McDonnell Douglas DC-10 airliner 3·00 3·00
1278 $3 Boeing 747-300/400 airliner 3·25 4·50
1279 $4 McDonnell Douglas F-4 Phantom II fighter 3·25 4·50
MS1280 Two sheets, each 114 × 83 mm. (a) $7 Grumman F-14A Tomcat fighter. (b) $7 Concorde airliner Set of 2 sheets 9·50 12·00

249 "Festivale"

1989. Caribbean Cruise Ships. Multicoloured.

1281 25c. Type **249** 1·75 50
1282 45c. "Southward" 2·00 50
1283 50c. "Sagafjord" 2·00 50
1284 60c. "Daphne" 2·00 60
1285 75c. "Cunard Countess" 2·25 1·00
1286 90c. "Song of America" 2·50 1·10
1287 $3 "Island Princess" 4·00 5·50
1288 $4 "Galileo" 4·00 5·50
MS1289 (a) 113 × 87 mm. $6 "Norway". (b) 111 × 82 mm. $6 "Oceanic" Set of 2 sheets 7·00 11·00

250 "Fish swimming by Duck half-submerged in Stream"

1989. Japanese Art. Paintings by Hiroshige. Mult.

1290 25c. Type **250** 1·00 50
1291 45c. "Crane and Wave" 1·25 50
1292 50c. "Sparrows and Morning Glories" 1·40 50
1293 60c. "Crested Blackbird and Flowering Cherry" 1·50 60
1294 $1 "Great Knot sitting among Water Grass" 1·75 80
1295 $2 "Goose on a Bank of Water" 2·50 2·50
1296 $3 "Black Paradise Flycatcher and Blossoms" 3·00 3·00
1297 $4 "Sleepy Owl perched on a Pine Branch" 3·00 3·00
MS1298 Two sheets, each 102 × 75 mm. (a) $5 "Bullfinch flying near a Clematis Branch". (b) $5 "Titmouse on a Cherry Branch" Set of 2 sheets 9·00 9·50

251 Mickey and Minnie Mouse in Helicopter over River Seine

1989. "Philexfrance 89" International Stamp Exhibition, Paris. Walt Disney cartoon characters in Paris. Multicoloured.

1299 1c. Type **251** 10 10
1300 2c. Goofy and Mickey Mouse passing Arc de Triomphe 10 10
1301 3c. Mickey Mouse painting picture of Notre Dame 10 10
1302 4c. Mickey and Minnie Mouse with Pluto leaving Metro station 10 10
1303 5c. Minnie Mouse as model in fashion show 10 10
1304 10c. Daisy Duck, Minnie Mouse and Clarabelle as Folies Bergere dancers 10 10
1305 $5 Mickey and Minnie Mouse shopping in street market 7·00 7·00
1306 $6 Mickey and Minnie Mouse, Jose Carioca and Donald Duck at pavement cafe 7·00 7·00
MS1307 Two sheets, each 127 × 101 mm. (a) $5 Mickey and Minnie Mouse in hot air balloon. (b) $5 Mickey Mouse at Pompidou Centre cafe (vert) Set of 2 sheets 11·00 13·00

252 Goalkeeper

1989. World Cup Football Championship, Italy (1990). Multicoloured.

1308 15c. Type **252** 85 30
1309 25c. Goalkeeper moving towards ball 90 30
1310 $1 Goalkeeper reaching for ball 2·00 1·25
1311 $4 Goalkeeper saving goal 3·50 5·00
MS1312 Two sheets, each 75 × 105 mm. (a) $5 Three players competing for ball (horiz). (b) $5 Ball and player' legs (horiz) Set of 2 sheets 8·00 10·00

253 "Mycena pura"

1989. Fungi. Multicoloured.

1313 10c. Type **253** 75 50
1314 25c. "Psathyrella tuberculata" (vert) 1·10 40
1315 50c. "Psilocybe cubensis" 1·50 60
1316 60c. "Leptonia caeruleocapitata" (vert) 1·50 70
1317 75c. "Xeromphalina tenuipes" (vert) 1·75 1·10
1318 $1 "Chlorophyllum molybdites" (vert) 1·75 1·25
1319 $3 "Marasmius haematocephalus" 2·75 3·75
1320 $4 "Cantharellus cinnabarinus" 2·75 3·75
MS1321 Two sheets, each 88 × 62 mm. (a) $6 "Leucopaxillus gracillimus" (vert). (b) $6 "Volvariella volvacea" Set of 2 sheets 13·00 15·00

254 Desmarest's Hutia

1989. Local Fauna. Multicoloured.

1322 25c. Type **254** 80 50
1323 45c. Caribbean monk seal 2·50 1·00
1324 80c. Mustache bat (vert) 1·50 1·00
1325 $4 American manatee (vert) 3·50 5·50
MS1326 113 × 87 mm. $5 West Indian giant rice rat 7·00 9·00

255 Goofy and Old Printing Press

258 Launch of "Apollo II"

256 Mickey Mouse and Donald Duck with Camden and Amboy Locomotive "John Bull", 1831

1989. "American Philately". Walt Disney cartoon characters with stamps and the logo of the American Philatelic Society. Multicoloured.

1327 1c. Type **255** 10 10
1328 2c. Donald Duck cancelling first day cover for Mickey Mouse 10 10

1329 3c. Donald Duck's nephews reading recruiting poster for Pony Express riders 10 10
1330 4c. Morty and Ferdie as early radio broadcasters 10 10
1331 5c. Donald Duck and water buffalo watching television 10 10
1332 10c. Donald Duck with stamp album 10 10
1333 $4 Daisy Duck with computer system . . . . 4·75 6·00
1334 $6 Donald's nephews with stereo radio, trumpet and guitar . . . . 6·00 7·00
MS1335 Two sheets, each 127 × 102 mm. (a) $5 Donald's nephews donating stamps to charity. (b) $5 Minnie Mouse flying mailplane upside down (horiz) Set of 2 sheets . . . . 11·00 13·00

1989. "World Stamp Expo '89" International Stamp Exhibition, Washington. Walt Disney cartoon characters and locomotives. Mult.
1336 25c. Type **256** 90 50
1337 45c. Mickey Mouse and friends with "Atlantic", 1832 . . . . 1·10 50
1338 50c. Mickey Mouse and Goofy with "William Crooks", 1861 . . . . . 1·10 50
1339 60c. Mickey Mouse and Goofy with "Minnetonka", 1869 . . . 1·10 65
1340 $1 Chip n'Dale with "Thatcher Perkins", 1863 1·40 75
1341 $2 Mickey and Minnie Mouse with "Pioneer", 1848 . . . . 2·25 2·25
1342 $3 Mickey Mouse and Donald Duck with cog railway locomotive "Peppersass", 1869 . . . 3·00 4·00
1343 $4 Mickey Mouse with Huey, Dewey and Louie aboard N.Y. World's Fair "Gimbels Flyer", 1939 . . 3·25 4·00
MS1344 Two sheets, each 127 × 101 mm. (a) $6 Mickey Mouse and locomotive "Thomas Jefferson", 1835 (vert). (b) $6 Mickey Mouse and friends at Central Pacific "Golden Spike" ceremony, 1869 Set of 2 sheets 7·50 9·00

1989. 20th Anniv of First Manned Landing on Moon. Multicoloured.
1346 10c. Type **258** 50 30
1347 45c. Aldrin on Moon . . . 1·25 30
1348 $1 Module "Eagle" over Moon (horiz) . . . . . . 1·75 1·10
1349 $4 Recovery of "Apollo II" crew after splashdown (horiz) . . . . 2·75 5·00
MS1350 107 × 77 mm. $5 Astronaut Neil Armstrong . . . . 4·50 5·50

259 "The Small Cowper Madonna" (Raphael)

260 Star-eyed Hermit Crab

1989. Christmas. Paintings by Raphael and Giotto. Multicoloured.
1351 10c. Type **259** 30 15
1352 25c. "Madonna of the Goldfinch" (Raphael) . . 45 20
1353 30c. "The Alba Madonna" (Raphael) 45 20
1354 50c. Saint (detail, "Bologna Altarpiece") (Giotto) . . 65 30
1355 60c. Angel (detail, "Bologna Altarpiece") (Giotto) . . 70 35
1356 70c. Angel slaying serpent (detail, "Bologna Altarpiece") (Giotto) . . 80 40
1357 $4 Evangelist (detail, "Bologna Altarpiece") (Giotto) . . . . 3·00 4·50
1358 $5 "Madonna of Foligno" (detail) (Raphael) . . . . 3·00 4·50
MS1359 Two sheets, each 71 × 96 mm. (a) $5 "The Marriage of the Virgin" (detail) (Raphael). (b) $5 Madonna and Child (detail, "Bologna Altarpiece") (Giotto) Set of 2 sheets . . . . 9·00 12·00

1990. 500th Anniv (1992) of Discovery of America by Columbus (3rd issue). New World Natural History–Marine Life. Multicoloured.
1360 10c. Type **260** 45 20
1361 20c. Spiny lobster 65 25
1362 25c. Magnificent banded fanworm 65 25
1363 45c. Cannonball jellyfish . . 80 40
1364 60c. Red-spiny sea star . . . 1·00 60
1365 $2 Peppermint shrimp . . . 2·00 2·50
1366 $3 Coral crab . . . . 2·25 3·75
1367 $4 Branching fire coral . . . 2·25 3·75
MS1368 Two sheets, each 100 × 69 mm. (a) $5 Common sea fan. (b) $5 Portuguese man-of-war Set of 2 sheets . . . . 8·00 9·00

261 "Vanilla mexicana"

262 Queen Victoria and Queen Elizabeth II

1990. "Expo '90" International Garden and Greenery Exhibition, Osaka. Orchids. Multicoloured.
1369 15c. Type **261** 75 50
1370 45c. "Epidendrum ibaguense" . . . . 1·10 50
1371 50c. "Epidendrum secundum" . . . . 1·25 55
1372 60c. "Maxillaria conferta" . 1·40 55
1373 $1 "Oncidium altissimum" . 1·50 1·00
1374 $2 "Spiranthes lanceolata" . 2·00 2·50
1375 $3 "Tonopsis utricularioides" . . . . . 2·25 3·50
1376 $5 "Epidendrum nocturnum" . . . . . . 3·25 4·50
MS1377 Two sheets, each 102 × 70 mm. (a) $6 "Octomeria graminifolia". (b) $6 "Rodriguezia lanceolata" Set of 2 sheets . . 6·50 8·00

1990. 150th Anniv of the Penny Black.
1378 **262** 45c. green . . . . 1·00 40
1379 – 60c. mauve . . . . . . 1·25 65
1380 – $5 blue . . . . 3·75 5·50
MS1381 102 × 80 mm. Type **262** $6 purple . . . . 5·00 6·50
DESIGNS: 60c., $5 As Type **262**, but with different backgrounds.

263 "Britannia" (mail paddle-steamer), 1840

1990. "Stamp World London '90" International Stamp Exhibition.
1382 **263** 50c. green and red . . . 1·00 35
1383 – 75c. brown and red . . . 1·50 90
1384 – $4 blue and red . . . . 4·00 5·50
MS1385 – 104 × 81 mm. $6 brown and red . . . . 3·75 6·00
DESIGNS: 75c. Travelling Post Office sorting van, 1892; $4 Short S.23 Empire "C" Class flying boat "Centaurus", 1938; $6 Post Office underground railway, London, 1927.

264 Flamefish

1990. Reef Fishes. Multicoloured.
1386 10c. Type **264** 65 55
1387 15c. Coney 80 55
1388 50c. Long-spined squirrelfish 1·25 60
1389 60c. Sergeant major . . . . 1·25 60
1390 $1 Yellow-tailed snapper . . 1·50 85
1391 $2 Rock beauty . . . . . . 2·25 2·75
1392 $3 Spanish hogfish . . . . 2·75 3·75
1393 $4 Striped parrotfish . . . . 2·75 3·75
MS1394 Two sheets, each 90 × 70 mm. (a) $5 Black-barred soldierfish. (b) $4 Four-eyed butterflyfish Set of 2 sheets . . 10·00 11·00

265 "Voyager 2" passing Saturn

266 Queen Mother in Evening Dress

1990. Achievement in Space. Multicoloured.
1395 45c. Type **265** . . . . . . 1·00 85
1396 45c. "Pioneer 11" photographing Saturn . . 1·10 85
1397 45c. Astronaut in transporter . . . . 1·10 85
1398 45c. Space shuttle "Columbia" . . . . 1·10 85
1399 45c. "Apollo 10" command module on parachutes . . 1·10 85
1400 45c. "Skylab" space station 1·10 85
1401 45c. Astronaut Edward White in space . . . . . 1·10 85
1402 45c. "Apollo" spacecraft on joint mission . . . . . 1·10 85
1403 45c. "Soyuz" spacecraft on joint mission . . . . . . 1·10 85
1404 45c. "Mariner 1" passing Venus . . . . 1·10 85
1405 45c. "Gemini 4" capsule . . 1·10 85
1406 45c. "Sputnik 1" . . . . . 1·10 85
1407 45c. Hubble space telescope 1·10 85
1408 45c. North American X-15 rocket plane . . . . . . 1·10 85
1409 45c. Bell XS-1 airplane . . . 1·10 85
1410 45c. "Apollo 17" astronaut and lunar rock formation 1·10 85
1411 45c. Lunar Rover . . . . . 1·10 85
1412 45c. "Apollo 14" lunar module . . . . 1·10 85
1413 45c. Astronaut Buzz Aldrin on Moon . . . . 1·10 85
1414 45c. Soviet "Lunokhod" lunar vehicle . . . . . . 1·10 85

1990. 90th Birthday of Queen Elizabeth the Queen Mother.
1415 **266** 15c. multicoloured . . . 55 20
1416 – 35c. multicoloured . . . 75 25
1417 – 75c. multicoloured . . . 1·00 85
1418 – $3 multicoloured . . . . 2·50 3·50
MS1419 – 67 × 98 mm. mult . . . 4·00 4·50
DESIGNS: Nos. 1416/19, Recent photographs of the Queen Mother.

267 Mickey Mouse as Animator

1990. Mickey Mouse in Hollywood. Walt Disney cartoon characters. Multicoloured.
1420 25c. Type **267** 60 25
1421 45c. Minnie Mouse learning lines while being dressed 80 25
1422 50c. Mickey Mouse with clapper board 90 30
1423 60c. Daisy Duck making-up Mickey Mouse . . . . . 1·00 35
1424 $1 Clarabelle Cow as Cleopatra . . . . 1·25 70
1425 $2 Mickey Mouse directing Goofy and Donald Duck 1·75 2·25
1426 $3 Mickey Mouse directing Goofy as birdman . . . 2·25 3·50
1427 $4 Donald Duck and Mickey Mouse editing film . . . . 2·25 3·50
MS1428 Two sheets, each 132 × 95 mm. (a) $5 Minnie Mouse, Daisy Duck and Clarabelle as musical stars. (b) $5 Mickey Mouse on set as director Set of 2 sheets. . . . . . . 7·00 9·00

268 Men's 20 Kilometres Walk

269 Huey and Dewey asleep ("Christmas Stories")

1990. Olympic Games, Barcelona (1992) (1st issue). Multicoloured.
1429 50c. Type **268** 75 40
1430 75c. Triple jump . . . . . 1·00 75
1431 $1 Men's 10,000 metres . . 1·25 85
1432 $5 Javelin . . . . 3·50 6·00
MS1433 100 × 70 mm. $6 Athlete lighting Olympic flame at Los Angeles Olympics . . . . . . 5·50 7·00
See also Nos. 1553/61 and 1609/17.

1990. International Literacy Year. Walt Disney cartoon characters illustrating works by Charles Dickens. Multicoloured.
1434 15c. Type **269** 65 35
1435 45c. Donald Duck as Poor Jo looking at grave ("Bleak House") . . . . 1·00 45
1436 50c. Dewey as Oliver asking for more ("Oliver Twist") 1·10 50
1437 60c. Daisy Duck as The Marchioness ("Old Curiosity Shop") . . . . 1·25 55
1438 $1 Little Nell giving nosegay to her grandfather ("Little Nell") . . . . 1·40 85
1439 $2 Scrooge McDuck as Mr. Pickwick ("Pickwick Papers") . . . . 2·00 2·50
1440 $3 Minnie Mouse as Florence and Mickey Mouse as Paul ("Dombey and Son") . . . . 2·25 3·50
1441 $5 Minnie Mouse as Jenny Wren ("Our Mutual Friend") . . . . 2·75 4·50
MS1442 Two sheets, each 126 × 102 mm. (a) $6 Artful Dodger picking pocket ("Oliver Twist"). (b) $6 Unexpected arrivals at Mr. Peggoty's ("David Copperfield") Set of 2 sheets 10·00 12·00

1990. World Cup Football Championship Winners, Italy. Nos. 1308/11 optd **Winners West Germany 1 Argentina 0**.
1443 15c. Type **252** 75 40
1444 25c. Goalkeeper moving towards ball 75 40
1445 $1 Goalkeeper reaching for ball . . . . 1·75 1·60
1446 $4 Goalkeeper saving goal . 3·75 5·50
MS1447 Two sheets, each 75 × 105 mm. (a) $5 Three players competing for ball (horiz). (b) $5 Ball and players' legs (horiz) Set of 2 sheets . . . . 9·50 11·00

271 Pearly-eyed Thrasher

1990. Birds. Multicoloured.
1448 10c. Type **271** 45 30
1449 25c. Purple-throated carib 45 35
1450 50c. Common yellowthroat 50 40
1451 60c. American kestrel . . . 1·00 70
1452 $1 Yellow-bellied sapsucker 1·00 80
1453 $2 American purple gallinule ("Purple Gallinule") . . . 2·00 2·25
1454 $3 Yellow-crowned night heron . . . . 2·10 3·00
1455 $4 Blue-hooded euphonia 2·10 3·00
MS1456 Two sheets, each 76 × 60 mm. (a) $6 Brown pelican. (b) $6 Magnificent frigate bird Set of 2 sheets . . . . 14·00 16·00

272 "Madonna and Child with Saints" (detail, Sebastiano del Piombo)

1990. Christmas. Paintings by Renaissance Masters. Multicoloured.
1457 25c. Type **272** 80 30
1458 30c. "Virgin and Child with Angels" (detail, Grunewald) (vert) 90 30
1459 40c. "The Holy Family and a Shepherd" (detail, Titian) . . . . 1·00 30
1460 60c. "Virgin and Child" (detail, Lippi) (vert) . . . . 1·40 40
1461 $1 "Jesus, St. John and Two Angels" (Rubens) . . . . 1·75 70
1462 $2 "Adoration of the Shepherds" (detail, Vincenzo Catena) . . . . 2·50 2·75
1463 $4 "Adoration of the Magi" (detail, Giorgione) . . . . 4·00 5·50
1464 $5 "Virgin and Child adored by Warrior" (detail, Vincenzo Catena) . . . . 4·00 5·50
MS1465 Two sheets, each 71 × 101 mm. (a) $6 "Allegory of the Blessings of Jacob" (detail, Rubens) (vert). (b) $6 "Adoration of the Magi" (detail, Fra Angelico) (vert) Set of 2 sheets . . . . . 6·50 7·50

273 "Rape of the Daughters of Leucippus" (detail)

1991. 350th Death Anniv of Rubens. Mult.
1466 25c. Type **273** . . . . . . 1·00 40
1467 45c. "Bacchanal" (detail) . . 1·50 45

1468 50c. "Rape of the Sabine Women" (detail) . . . . 1·50 50
1469 60c. "Battle of the Amazons" (detail) . . . . 1·60 65
1470 $1 "Rape of the Sabine Women" (different detail) 2·00 1·00
1471 $2 "Bacchanal" (different detail) . . . . 2·50 2·50
1472 $3 "Rape of the Sabine Women" (different detail) 3·50 4·25
1473 $4 "Bacchanal" (different detail) . . . . 3·50 5·00
MS1474 Two sheets, each 101 × 71 mm. (a) $6 "Rape of Hippoda-meia" (detail). (b) $6 "Battle of the Amazons" (different detail) Set of 2 sheets . . . . 8·50 10·00

274 U.S. Troops cross into Germany, 1944

1991. 50th Anniv of Second World War. Mult.
1475 10c. Type **274** . . . . . . 1·10 65
1476 15c. Axis surrender in North Africa, 1943 . . . . . . 1·25 50
1477 25c. U.S. tanks invade Kwalajalein, 1944 . . . . 1·25 50
1478 45c. Roosevelt and Churchill meet at Casablanca, 1943 2·50 70
1479 50c. Marshal Badoglio, Prime Minister of Italian anti-fascist government, 1943 . . . . 1·50 70
1480 $1 Lord Mountbatten, Supreme Allied Commander South-east Asia, 1943 . . . . 3·00 1·50
1481 $2 Greek victory at Koritza, 1940 . . . . 2·25 2·75
1482 $4 Anglo-Soviet mutual assistance pact, 1941 . . . 3·25 4·25
1483 $5 Operation Torch landings, 1942 . . . . . 3·25 4·25
MS1484 Two sheets, each 108 × 80 mm. (a) $6 Japanese attack on Pearl Harbor, 1941. (b) $6 U.S.A.A.F. daylight raid on Schweinfurt, 1943 Set of 2 sheets 9·00 11·00

275 Locomotive "Prince Regent", Middleton Colliery, 1812

1991. Cog Railways. Multicoloured.
1485 25c. Type **275** . . . . . . 1·25 55
1486 30c. Snowdon Mountain Railway . . . . 1·25 55
1487 40c. First railcar at Hell Gate, Manitou Pike's Peak Railway, U.S.A . . 1·40 65
1488 60c. P.N.K.A. rack railway, Java . . . . 1·60 70
1489 $1 Green Mountain Railway, Maine, 1883 . . 2·00 1·00
1490 $2 Rack locomotive "Pike's Peak", 1891 . . . . . . 3·00 3·00
1491 $4 Vitznau–Rigi Railway, Switzerland, and Mt. Rigi hotel local post stamp . . 3·75 4·75
1492 $5 Leopoldina Railway, Brazil . . . . 3·75 4·75
MS1493 Two sheets, each 100 × 70 mm. (a) $6 Electric towing locomotives, Panama Canal. (b) $6 Gornergracht Railway, Switzerland (vert) Set of 2 sheets . . . . 12·00 13·00

276 "Heliconius charithonia"

1991. Butterflies. Multicoloured.
1494 10c. Type **276** 65 50
1495 35c. "Marpesia petreus" . . 1·10 50
1496 50c. "Anartia amathea" . . 1·25 60
1497 75c. "Siproeta stelenes" . . 1·50 1·00
1498 $1 "Battus polydamas" . . 1·75 1·10
1499 $2 "Historis odius" . . . 2·25 2·75
1500 $4 "Hypolimnas misippus" 3·25 4·25
1501 $5 "Hamadryas feronia" . . 3·25 4·25
MS1502 Two sheets. (a) 73 × 100 mm. $6 "Vanessa cardui" caterpillar (vert) (b) 100 × 73 mm. $6 "Danaus plexippus" caterpillar (vert) Set of 2 sheets . . . . 14·00 16·00

277 Hanno the Phoenician, 450 B.C.

1991. 500th Anniv of Discovery of America by Columbus (1992) (4th issue). History of Exploration.
1503 **277** 10c. multicoloured . . . 70 40
1504 – 15c. multicoloured . . . 80 40
1505 – 45c. multicoloured . . . 1·25 50
1506 – 60c. multicoloured . . . 1·40 60
1507 – $1 multicoloured . . . . 1·75 85
1508 – $2 multicoloured . . . . 2·25 2·75
1509 – $4 multicoloured . . . . 3·00 4·00
1510 – $5 multicoloured . . . . 3·00 4·00
MS1511 – Two sheets, each 106 × 76 mm. (a) $6 black and red. (b) $6 black and red Set of 2 sheets 7·00 9·00
DESIGNS—HORIZ: 15c. Pytheas the Greek, 325 B.C.; 45c. Erik the Red discovering Greenland, 985 A.D.; 60c. Leif Eriksson reaching Vinland, 1000 A.D.; $1 Scylax the Greek in the Indian Ocean, 518 A.D.; $2 Marco Polo sailing to the Orient, 1259 A.D.; $4 Ship of Queen Hatshepsut of Egypt, 1493 B.C.; $5 St. Brendan's coracle, 500 A.D. VERT: $6 (No. **MS**1511a) Engraving of Columbus as Admiral; $6 (No. **MS**1511b) Engraving of Columbus bare-headed.

278 "Camille Roulin" (Van Gogh)

1991. Death Centenary (1990) of Vincent van Gogh (artist). Multicoloured.
1512 5c. Type **278** 70 85
1513 10c. "Armand Roulin" . . . 70 60
1514 15c. "Young Peasant Woman with Straw Hat sitting in the Wheat" . . 85 50
1515 25c. "Adeline Ravoux" . . 1·00 50
1516 30c. "The Schoolboy" . . . 1·00 50
1517 40c. "Doctor Gachet" . . . 1·10 50
1518 50c. "Portrait of a Man" . . 1·25 50
1519 75c. "Two Children" . . . 1·75 80
1520 $2 "The Postman Joseph Roulin" . . . . 2·75 2·75
1521 $3 "The Seated Zouave" . . 3·75 4·00
1522 $4 "L'Arlesienne" . . . . 4·00 4·50
1523 $5 "Self-Portrait, November/December 1888" . . . . 4·00 4·50
MS1524 Three sheets, each 102 × 76 mm. (a) $5 "Farmhouse in Provence" (horiz). (b) $5 "Flowering Garden" (horiz). (c) $6 "The Bridge at Trinquetaille" (horiz) Imperf Set of 3 sheets 16·00 18·00

279 Mickey Mouse as Champion Sumo Wrestler

1991. "Philanippon '91" International Stamp Exhibition, Tokyo. Walt Disney cartoon characters participating in martial arts. Multicoloured.
1525 10c. Type **279** 80 20
1526 15c. Goofy using the tonfa (horiz) 90 25
1527 45c. Donald Duck as a Ninja (horiz) . . . . . 1·60 50
1528 60c. Mickey armed for Kung fu . . . . 2·00 65
1529 $1 Goofy with Kendo sword 2·50 1·25
1530 $2 Mickey and Donald demonstrating Aikido (horiz) . . . . 3·00 3·00
1531 $4 Mickey and Donald in Judo bout (horiz) . . . . 4·00 5·00
1532 $5 Mickey performing Yabusame (mounted archery) . . . . 4·00 5·00
MS1533 Two sheets, each 127 × 102 mm. (a) $6 Mickey delivering Karate kick (horiz). (b) $6 Mickey demonstrating Tamashiwara Set of 2 sheets 10·00 12·00

280 Queen Elizabeth and Prince Philip in 1976

1991. 65th Birthday of Queen Elizabeth II. Multicoloured.
1534 15c. Type **280** 30 10
1535 20c. The Queen and Prince Philip in Portugal, 1985 30 10
1536 $2 Queen Elizabeth II . . . 1·50 1·50
1537 $4 The Queen and Prince Philip at Ascot, 1986 . . 2·75 3·25
MS1538 68 × 90 mm. $4 The Queen at National Theatre, 1986, and Prince Philip . . . . 3·25 4·00

1991. 10th Wedding Anniv of Prince and Princess of Wales. As T **280**. Multicoloured.
1539 10c. Prince and Princess of Wales at party, 1986 . . . 40 10
1540 40c. Separate portraits of Prince, Princess and sons 80 25
1541 $1 Prince Henry and Prince William . . . . 1·10 70
1542 $5 Princess Diana in Australia and Prince Charles in Hungary . . . 4·25 4·50
MS1543 68 × 90 mm. $4 Prince Charles in Hackney and Princess and sons in Majorca, 1987 . . 5·00 5·50

281 Daisy Duck teeing-off

1991. Golf. Walt Disney cartoon characters. Mult.
1544 10c. Type **281** 70 50
1545 15c. Goofy playing ball from under trees 75 50
1546 45c. Mickey Mouse playing deflected shot . . . . . . 1·25 50
1547 60c. Mickey hacking divot out of fairway . . . . . 1·50 65
1548 $1 Donald Duck playing ball out of pond . . . . 1·75 1·10
1549 $2 Minnie Mouse hitting ball over pond . . . . . 2·50 2·75
1550 $4 Donald in a bunker . . . 3·25 4·00
1551 $5 Goofy trying snooker shot into hole . . . . . . 3·25 4·00
MS1552 Two sheets, each 127 × 102 mm. (a) $6 Grandma Duck in senior tournament. (b) $6 Mickey and Minnie Mouse on course (horiz) Set of 2 sheets 10·00 12·00

282 Moose receiving Gold Medal

1991. 50th Anniv of Archie Comics, and Olympic Games, Barcelona (1992) (2nd issue). Multicoloured.
1553 10c. Type **282** 55 40
1554 25c. Archie playing polo on a motorcycle (horiz) . . . 85 40
1555 40c. Archie and Betty at fencing class . . . . . . 1·10 45
1556 60c. Archie joining girls' volleyball team . . . . . 1·40 65
1557 $1 Archie with tennis ball in his mouth . . . . 1·75 1·10
1558 $2 Archie running marathon 2·50 3·00
1559 $4 Archie judging women's gymnastics (horiz) . . . . 3·75 4·50
1560 $5 Archie watching the cheer-leaders . . . . . . 3·75 4·50
MS1561 Two sheets, each 128 × 102 mm. (a) $6 Archie heading football. (b) $6 Archie catching baseball (horiz) Set of 2 sheets . . . . 11·00 13·00

283 Presidents De Gaulle and Kennedy, 1961

1991. Birth Centenary of Charles de Gaulle (French statesman). Multicoloured.
1562 10c. Type **283** 80 50
1563 15c. General De Gaulle with President Roosevelt, 1945 (vert) 80 50
1564 45c. President De Gaulle with Chancellor Adenauer, 1962 (vert) . . 1·25 50
1565 60c. De Gaulle at Arc de Triomphe, Liberation of Paris, 1944 (vert) . . . . 1·50 65
1566 $1 General De Gaulle crossing the Rhine, 1945 1·75 1·25
1567 $2 General De Gaulle in Algiers, 1944 . . . . . . 2·50 3·00
1568 $4 Presidents De Gaulle and Eisenhower, 1960 . . . . 3·25 4·50
1569 $5 De Gaulle returning from Germany, 1968 (vert) . . 3·25 4·50
MS1570 Two sheets. (a) 76 × 106 mm. $6 De Gaulle with crowd. (b) 106 × 76 mm. $6 De Gaulle and Churchill at Casablanca, 1943 Set of 2 sheets 14·00 13·00

284 Parliament Building and Map

1991. 10th Anniv of Independence.
1571 **284** 10c. multicoloured . . . 75 50
MS1572 87 × 97 mm. $6 Old Post Office, St. Johns, and stamps of 1862 and 1981 (50 × 37 mm) 6·00 7·50

285 Germans celebrating Reunification

1991. Anniversaries and Events. Multicoloured.
1573 25c. Type **285** 30 30
1574 75c. Cubs erecting tent . . . 70 50
1575 $1.50 "Don Giovanni" and Mozart . . . . 5·00 3·00
1576 $2 Chariot driver and Gate at night . . . . 1·10 2·00
1577 $2 Lord Baden-Powell and members of 3rd Antigua Methodist cub pack (vert) 3·00 2·75
1578 $2 Lilienthal's signature and glider "Flugzeug Nr. 5" 3·25 2·75
1579 $2.50 Driver in Class P36 steam locomotive (vert) 6·00 4·00
1580 $3 Statues from podium . . 1·75 3·25
1581 $3.50 Cubs and camp fire 2·50 3·25
1582 $4 St. Peter's Cathedral, Salzburg . . . . 9·00 7·50
MS1583 Two sheets. (a) 100 × 72 mm. $4 Detail of chariot and helmet; (b) 89 × 117 mm. $5 Antiguan flag and Jamboree emblem (vert) Set of 2 sheets 8·00 11·00
ANNIVERSARIES AND EVENTS: Nos. 1573, 1576, 1580, **MS**1583a, Bicentenary of Brandenburg Gate, Germany; 1574, 1577, 1581, **MS**1583b, 17th World Scout Jamboree, Korea; 1575, 1582, Death bicentenary of Mozart (composer); 1578, Centenary of Otto Lilienthal's gliding experiments; 1579, Centenary of Trans-Siberian Railway.

286 "Nimitz" Class Carrier and "Ticonderoga" Class Cruiser

1991. 50th Anniv of Japanese Attack on Pearl Harbor. Multicoloured.
1585 $1 Type **286** . . . . . . 2·25 1·75
1586 $1 Tourist launch . . . . . 2·25 1·75
1587 $1 U.S.S. "Arizona" memorial . . . . 2·25 1·75
1588 $1 Wreaths on water and aircraft . . . . 2·25 1·75

1589	$1 White tern	2·25	1·75
1590	$1 Mitsubishi A6M Zero-Sen fighters over Pearl City	2·25	1·75
1591	$1 Mitsubishi A6M Zero-Sen fighters attacking	2·25	1·75
1592	$1 Battleship Row in flames	2·25	1·75
1593	$1 U.S.S. "Nevada" (battleship) underway	2·25	1·75
1594	$1 Mitsubishi A6M Zero-Sen fighters returning to carriers	2·25	1·75

287 "The Annunciation"

1991. Christmas. Religious Paintings by Fra Angelico. Multicoloured.

1595	10c. Type **287**	40	30
1596	30c. "Nativity"	65	30
1597	40c. "Adoration of the Magi"	75	30
1598	60c. "Presentation in the Temple"	1·00	45
1599	$1 "Circumcision"	1·25	65
1600	$3 "Flight into Egypt"	2·50	3·50
1601	$4 "Massacre of the Innocents"	2·50	4·00
1602	$5 "Christ teaching in the Temple"	2·50	4·00

MS1603 Two sheets, each 102 × 127 mm. (a) $6 "Adoration of the Magi" (Cook Tondo). (b) $6 "Adoration of the Magi" (different) Set of 2 sheets . . . 13·00 14·00

288 Queen Elizabeth II and Bird Sanctuary

1992. 40th Anniv of Queen Elizabeth II's Accession. Multicoloured.

1604	10c. Type **288**	1·25	40
1605	30c. Nelson's Dockyard	1·50	40
1606	$1 Ruins on Shirley Heights	1·50	70
1607	$5 Beach and palm trees	3·00	4·25

MS1608 Two sheets, each 75 × 98 mm. (a) $6 Beach. (b) $6 Hillside foliage Set of 2 sheets . . . 8·50 9·00

289 Mickey Mouse awarding Swimming Gold Medal to Mermaid

1992. Olympic Games, Barcelona (3rd issue). Walt Disney cartoon characters. Multicoloured.

1609	10c. Type **289**	70	30
1610	15c. Huey, Dewey and Louie with kayak	80	30
1611	30c. Donald Duck and Uncle Scrooge in yacht	1·00	35
1612	50c. Donald and horse playing water polo	1·40	50
1613	$1 Big Pete weightlifting	2·00	85
1614	$2 Donald and Goofy fencing	3·00	3·00
1615	$4 Mickey and Donald playing volleyball	4·00	4·50
1616	$5 Goofy vaulting	4·00	4·50

MS1617 Four sheets, each 123 × 98 mm. (a) $6 Mickey playing football. (b) $6 Mickey playing basketball (horiz). (c) $6 Minnie Mouse on uneven parallel bars (horiz). (d) $6 Mickey, Goofy and Donald judging gymnastics (horiz) Set of 4 sheets . . . 14·00 15·00

290 Pteranodon

1992. Prehistoric Animals. Mult.

1618	10c. Type **290**	65	40
1619	15c. Brachiosaurus	65	40
1620	30c. Tyrannosaurus Rex	85	40
1621	50c. Parasaurolophus	1·00	50
1622	$1 Deinonychus (horiz)	1·50	1·00
1623	$2 Triceratops (horiz)	2·00	2·00
1624	$4 Protoceratops hatching (horiz)	2·25	2·75
1625	$5 Stegosaurus (horiz)	2·25	2·75

MS1626 Two sheets, each 100 × 70 mm. (a) $6 Apatosaurus (horiz). (b) $6 Allosaurus (horiz) Set of 2 sheets . . . 8·50 9·50

291 "Supper at Emmaus" (Caravaggio)

1992. Easter. Religious Paintings. Multicoloured.

1627	10c. Type **291**	60	25
1628	15c. "The Vision of St. Peter" (Zurbaran)	75	25
1629	30c. "Christ driving the Money-changers from the Temple" (Tiepolo)	1·00	40
1630	40c. "Martyrdom of St. Bartholomew" (detail) (Ribera)	1·25	50
1631	$1 "Christ driving the Money-changers from the Temple" (detail) (Tiepolo)	2·00	1·00
1632	$2 "Crucifixion" (detail) (Altdorfer)	3·00	3·00
1633	$4 "The Deposition" (detail) (Fra Angelico)	4·00	5·00
1634	$5 "The Deposition" (different detail) (Fra Angelico)	4·00	5·00

MS1635 Two sheets. (a) 102 × 71 mm. $6 "The Last Supper" (detail, Masip). (b) 71 × 102 mm. $6 "Crucifixion" (detail, Altdorfer) (vert) Set of 2 sheets . . . 9·50 12·00

292 "The Miracle at the Well" (Alonso Cano)

1992. "Granada '92" International Stamp Exhibition, Spain. Spanish Paintings. Multicoloured.

1636	10c. Type **292**	50	30
1637	15c. "The Poet Luis de Goingora y Argote" (Velazquez)	65	30
1638	30c. "The Painter Francisco Goya" (Vincente Lopez Portana)	85	40
1639	40c. "Maria de las Nieves Michaela Fourdinier" (Luis Paret y Alcazar)	95	50
1640	$1 "Carlos III eating before his Court" (Alcazar) (horiz)	1·75	1·25
1641	$2 "Rain Shower in Granada" (Antonio Munoz Degrain) (horiz)	2·50	2·75
1642	$4 "Sarah Bernhardt" (Santiago Rusinol i Prats)	3·50	4·00
1643	$5 "The Hermitage Garden" (Joaquim Mir Trinxet)	3·50	4·00

MS1644 Two sheets, each 120 × 95 mm. (a) $6 "The Ascent of Monsieur Boucle's Montgolfier Balloon in the Gardens of Aranjuez" (Antonio Carnicero) (112 × 87 mm). (b) $6 "Olympus: Battle with the Giants" (Francisco Bayeu y Subías) (112 × 87 mm). Imperf Set of 2 sheets . . . 14·00 15·00

293 "Amanita caesarea"

1992. Fungi. Multicoloured.

1645	10c. Type **293**	70	40
1646	15c. "Collybia fusipes"	85	40
1647	30c. "Boletus aereus"	1·25	40
1648	40c. "Laccaria amethystina"	1·25	50
1649	$1 "Russula virescens"	2·00	1·25
1650	$2 "Tricholoma equestre" ("Tricholoma auratum")	2·75	2·75
1651	$4 "Calocybe gambosa"	3·50	4·00
1652	$5 "Lentinus tigrinus" ("Panus tigrinus")	3·50	4·00

MS1653 Two sheets, each 100 × 70 mm. (a) $6 "Clavariadelphus truncatus". (b) $6 "Auricularia auricula-judae" Set of 2 sheets . . . 12·00 13·00

294 Memorial Cross and Huts, San Salvador

1992. 500th Anniv of Discovery of America by Columbus (5th issue). World Columbian Stamp "Expo '92", Chicago. Multicoloured.

1654	15c. Type **294**	30	20
1655	30c. Martin Pinzon with telescope	45	25
1656	40c. Christopher Columbus	65	35
1657	$1 "Pinta"	2·50	1·25
1658	$2 "Nina"	2·75	2·75
1659	$4 "Santa Maria"	3·50	5·50

MS1660 Two sheets, each 108 × 76 mm. (a) $6 Ship and map of West Indies. (b) $6 Sea monster Set of 2 sheets . . . 8·50 11·00

295 Antillean Crested Hummingbird and Wild Plantain

1992. "Genova '92" International Thematic Stamp Exhibition. Hummingbirds and Plants. Multicoloured.

1661	10c. Type **295**	35	50
1662	25c. Green mango and parrot's plantain	50	40
1663	45c. Purple-throated carib and lobster claws	70	45
1664	60c. Antillean mango and coral plant	80	55
1665	$1 Vervain hummingbird and cardinal's guard	1·10	85
1666	$2 Rufous-breasted hermit and heliconia	1·75	2·00
1667	$4 Blue-headed hummingbird and red ginger	3·00	3·50
1668	$5 Green-throated carib and ornamental banana	3·00	3·50

MS1669 Two sheets, each 100 × 70 mm. (a) $6 Bee hummingbird and jungle flame. (b) $6 Western streamertail and bignonia Set of 2 sheets . . . 10·00 12·00

296 Columbus meeting Amerindians

1992. 500th Anniv of Discovery of America by Columbus (6th issue). Organization of East Caribbean States. Multicoloured.

1670	$1 Type **296**	85	65
1671	$2 Ships approaching island	1·40	1·60

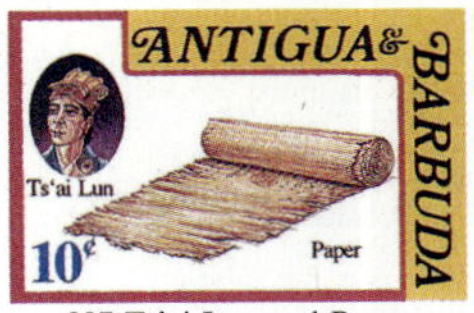

297 Ts'ai Lun and Paper

1992. Inventors and Inventions. Mult.

1672	10c. Type **297**	25	25
1673	25c. Igor Sikorsky and "Bolshoi Baltiskii" (first four-engined airplane)	1·50	40
1674	30c. Alexander Graham Bell and early telephone	55	45
1675	40c. Johannes Gutenberg and early printing press	55	45
1676	60c. James Watt and stationary steam engine	3·50	1·25
1677	$1 Anton van Leeuwenhoek and early microscope	1·75	1·40
1678	$4 Louis Braille and hands reading braille	4·50	5·00
1679	$5 Galileo and telescope	4·50	5·00

MS1680 Two sheets, each 100 × 73 mm. (a) $6 Edison and Latimer's phonograph. (b) $6 "Clermont" (first commercial paddle-steamer) Set of 2 sheets . . . 9·50 12·00

298 Elvis looking Pensive

1992. 15th Death Anniv of Elvis Presley. Mult.

1681	$1 Type **298**	1·75	1·10
1682	$1 Wearing black and yellow striped shirt	1·75	1·10
1683	$1 Singing into microphone	1·75	1·10
1684	$1 Wearing wide-brimmed hat	1·75	1·10
1685	$1 With microphone in right hand	1·75	1·10
1686	$1 In Army uniform	1·75	1·10
1687	$1 Wearing pink shirt	1·75	1·10
1688	$1 In yellow shirt	1·75	1·10
1689	$1 In jacket and bow tie	1·75	1·10

299 Madison Square Gardens

1992. Postage Stamp Mega Event, New York. Sheet 100 × 70 mm.

MS1690 **299** $6 multicoloured . . . 4·25 5·50

300 "Virgin and Child with Angels" (detail) (School of Piero della Francesca)

301 Russian Cosmonauts

1992. Christmas. Details of the Holy Child from various paintings. Multicoloured.

1691	10c. Type **300**	60	30
1692	25c. "Madonna degli Alberelli" (Giovanni Bellini)	90	30
1693	30c. "Madonna and Child with St. Anthony Abbot and St. Sigismund" (Neroccio)	95	30
1694	40c. "Madonna and the Grand Duke" (Raphael)	1·00	30
1695	60c. "The Nativity" (Georges de la Tour)	1·50	60
1696	$1 "Holy Family" (Jacob Jordaens)	1·75	1·00

1697 $4 "Madonna and Child Enthroned" (Magaritone) 3·75 4·75
1698 $5 "Madonna and Child on a Curved Throne" (Byzantine school) 3·75 4·75
MS1699 Two sheets, each 76 × 102 mm. (a) $6 "Madonna and Child" (Domenco Ghirlando). (b) $6 "The Holy Family" (Pontormo) Set of 2 sheets 9·50 12·00

1992. Anniversaries and Events. Mult.
1700 10c. Type **301** 70 60
1701 40c. "Graf Zeppelin" (airship), 1929 1·50 65
1702 45c. Bishop Daniel Davis 50 40
1703 75c. Konrad Adenauer making speech 65 65
1704 $1 Bus Mosbacher and "Weatherly" (yacht) 1·25 1·25
1705 $1.50 Rain forest 1·40 1·50
1706 $2 Tiger 6·00 4·00
1707 $2 National flag, plant and emblem (horiz) 4·50 3·00
1708 $2 Members of Community Players company (horiz) 2·00 3·00
1709 $2.25 Women carrying pots 2·00 3·00
1710 $3 Lions Club emblem 2·25 3·25
1711 $4 Chinese rocket on launch tower 4·00 4·50
1712 $4 West German and N.A.T.O. flags 4·50 4·75
1713 $6 Hugo Eckener (airship pioneer) 4·50 5·50
MS1714 Four sheets, each 100 × 71 mm. (a) $6 Projected European space station. (b) $6 Airship LZ-129 "Hindenburg", 1936. (c) $6 Brandenburg Gate on German flag. (d) $6 "Danaus plexippus" (butterfly) Set of 4 sheets 21·00 22·00

ANNIVERSARIES AND EVENTS: Nos. 1700, 1711, **MS**1714a, International Space Year; 1701, 1713, **MS**1714b, 75th death anniv of Count Ferdinand von Zeppelin; 1702, 150th anniv of Anglican Diocese of North-eastern Caribbean and Aruba; 1703, 1712, **MS**1714c, 25th death anniv of Konrad Adenauer (German statesman); 1704, Americas Cup yachting championship; 1705/6, **MS**1714d, Earth Summit '92, Rio; 1707, 50th anniv of Inter-American Institute for Agricultural Co-operation; 1708, 40th anniv of Cultural Development; 1709, United Nations World Health Organization Projects; 1710, 75th anniv of International Association of Lions Clubs.

302 Boy Hiker resting

304 Cardinal's Guard

303 Goofy playing Golf

1993. Hummel Figurines. Multicoloured.
1715 15c. Type **302** 35 15
1716 30c. Girl sitting on fence 55 25
1717 40c. Boy hunter 65 35
1718 50c. Boy with umbrella 75 45
1719 $1 Hikers at signpost 1·25 75
1720 $2 Boy hiker with pack and stick 1·75 2·25
1721 $4 Girl with young child and goat 2·75 3·50
1722 $5 Boy whistling 2·75 3·50
MS1723 Two sheets, each 97 × 122 mm. (a) $1.50 × 4, As Nos. 1715/18. (b) $1.50 × 4, As Nos. 1719/22 Set of 2 sheets 13·00 14·00

1993. Opening of Euro-Disney Resort, Paris. Multicoloured.
1724 10c. Type **303** 80 30
1725 25c. Chip and Dale at Davy Crockett's campground 1·00 30
1726 30c. Donald Duck at the Cheyenne Hotel 1·00 35
1727 40c. Goofy at the Santa Fe Hotel 1·10 35
1728 $1 Mickey and Minnie Mouse at the New York Hotel 2·25 1·25
1729 $2 Mickey, Minnie and Goofy in car 2·75 2·75
1730 $4 Goofy at Pirates of the Caribbean 4·00 5·00
1731 $5 Donald at Adventureland 4·00 5·00
MS1732 Four sheets, each 127 × 102 mm. (a) $6 Mickey in bellboy outfit. (b) $6 Mickey on star (vert). (c) $6 Mickey on opening poster (vert). (d) $6 Mickey and balloons on opening poster (vert) Set of 2 sheets 16·00 18·00

1993. Flowers. Multicoloured.
1733 15c. Type **304** 1·00 40
1734 25c. Giant granadilla 1·10 40
1735 30c. Spider flower 1·10 40
1736 40c. Gold vine 1·25 40
1737 $1 Frangipani 2·00 1·25
1738 $2 Bougainvillea 2·75 2·75
1739 $4 Yellow oleander 3·75 4·50
1740 $5 Spicy jatropha 3·75 4·50
MS1741 Two sheets, each 100 × 70 mm. (a) $6 Birdlime tree. (b) Fairy lily Set of 2 sheets 9·00 12·00

305 "The Destiny of Marie de' Medici" (upper detail)

1993. Bicentenary of the Louvre, Paris. Paintings by Peter Paul Rubens. Multicoloured.
1742 $1 Type **305** 95 85
1743 $1 "The Birth of Marie de' Medici" 95 85
1744 $1 "The Education of Marie de' Medici" 95 85
1745 $1 "The Destiny of Marie de' Medici" (lower detail) 95 85
1746 $1 "Henry VI receiving the Portrait of Marie" 95 85
1747 $1 "The Meeting of the King and Marie at Lyons" 95 85
1748 $1 "The Marriage by Proxy" 95 85
1749 $1 "The Birth of Louis XIII" 95 85
1750 $1 "The Capture of Juliers" 95 85
1751 $1 "The Exchange of the Princesses" 95 85
1752 $1 "The Regency" 95 85
1753 $1 "The Majority of Louis XIII" 95 85
1754 $1 "The Flight from Blois" 95 85
1755 $1 "The Treaty of Angouleme" 95 85
1756 $1 "The Peace of Angers" 95 85
1757 $1 "The Reconciliation of Louis and Marie de' Medici" 95 85
MS1758 70 × 100 mm. $6 "Helene Faurment with a Coach" (52 × 85 mm) 5·50 7·00
Nos. 1742/57 depict details from "The Story of Marie de' Medici".

306 St. Lucia Amazon ("St. Lucia Parrot")

1993. Endangered Species. Multicoloured.
1759 $1 Type **306** 90 90
1760 $1 Cahow 90 90
1761 $1 Swallow-tailed kite 90 90
1762 $1 Everglade kite ("Everglades Kite") 90 90
1763 $1 Imperial amazon ("Imperial Parrot") 90 90
1764 $1 Humpback whale 90 90
1765 $1 Plain pigeon ("Puerto Rican Plain Pigeon") 90 90
1766 $1 St. Vincent amazon ("St. Vincent Parrot") 90 90
1767 $1 Puerto Rican amazon ("Puerto Rican Parrot") 90 90
1768 $1 Leatherback turtle 90 90
1769 $1 American crocodile 90 90
1770 $1 Hawksbill turtle 90 90
MS1771 Two sheets, each 100 × 70 mm. (a) $6 As No. 1764. (b) West Indian manatee Set of 2 sheets 8·00 10·00
Nos. 1759/70 were printed together, se-tenant, with the background forming a composite design.

307 Queen Elizabeth II at Coronation (photograph by Cecil Beaton)

1993. 40th Anniv of Coronation (1st issue).
1772 **307** 30c. multicoloured 60 60
1773 – 40c. multicoloured 70 70
1774 – $2 blue and black 1·75 2·00
1775 – $4 multicoloured 2·25 2·50
MS1776 70 × 100 mm. $6 multicoloured 5·00 6·00
DESIGNS: 40c. Queen Elizabeth the Queen Mother's Crown, 1937; $2 Procession of heralds; $4 Queen Elizabeth II and Prince Edward. (28½ × 42½ mm)—$6 "Queen Elizabeth II" (detail) (Dennis Fildes).

308 Princess Margaret and Antony Armstrong-Jones

1993. 40th Anniv of Coronation (2nd issue).
1777/1808 $1 × 32 either grey and black or multicoloured 26·00 28·00
DESIGNS: Various views as Type **308** from each decade of the reign.

309 Edward Stanley Gibbons and Catalogue of 1865

1993. Famous Professional Philatelists (1st series).
1809 **309** $1.50 brown, black & grn 1·25 1·25
1810 – $1.50 multicoloured 1·25 1·25
1811 – $1.50 multicoloured 1·25 1·25
1812 – $1.50 multicoloured 1·25 1·25
1813 – $1.50 multicoloured 1·25 1·25
1814 – $1.50 multicoloured 1·25 1·25
MS1815 98 × 69 mm. $3 black; $3 black 5·50 6·50
DESIGNS: No. 1810, Theodore Champion and France 1849 1f. stamp; 1811, J. Walter Scott and U.S.A. 1918 24c. "Inverted Jenny" error; 1812, Hugo Michel and Bavaria 1849 1k. stamp; 1813, Alberto and Giulio Bolaffi with Sardinia 1851 5c. stamp; 1814, Richard Borek and Brunswick 1865 1gr. stamp; **MS**1815, Front pages of "Mekeel's Weekly Stamp News" in 1891 (misdated 1890) and 1993.
See also No. 1957.

310 Paul Gascoigne

311 Grand Inspector W. Heath

1993. World Cup Football Championship, U.S.A. (1st issue). English Players. Multicoloured.
1816 $2 Type **310** 1·50 1·40
1817 $2 David Platt 1·50 1·40
1818 $2 Martin Peters 1·50 1·40
1819 $2 John Barnes 1·50 1·40
1820 $2 Gary Lineker 1·50 1·40
1821 $2 Geoff Hurst 1·50 1·40
1822 $2 Bobby Charlton 1·50 1·40
1823 $2 Bryan Robson 1·50 1·40
1824 $2 Bobby Moore 1·50 1·40
1825 $2 Nobby Stiles 1·50 1·40
1826 $2 Gordon Banks 1·50 1·40
1827 $2 Peter Shilton 1·50 1·40
MS1828 Two sheets, each 135 × 109 mm. (a) $6 Bobby Moore holding World Cup. (b) $6 Gary Lineker and Bobby Robson Set of 2 sheets 9·00 11·00
See also Nos. 2039/45.

1993. Anniversaries and Events. Multicoloured.
1829 10c. Type **311** 2·00 1·00
1830 15c. Rodnina and Oulanov (U.S.S.R.) (pairs figure skating) (horiz) 1·25 50
1831 30c. Present Masonic Hall, St. John's (horiz) 2·25 1·00
1832 30c. Willy Brandt with Helmut Schmidt and George Leber (horiz) 70 40
1833 30c. "Cat and Bird" (Picasso) (horiz) 70 40
1834 40c. Previous Masonic Hall, St. John's (horiz) 2·25 1·00
1835 40c. "Fish on a Newspaper" (Picasso) (horiz) 70 50
1836 40c. Early astronomical equipment 70 50
1837 40c. Prince Naruhito and engagement photographs (horiz) 70 50
1838 60c. Grand Inspector J. Jeffery 3·00 1·25
1839 $1 "Woman combing her Hair" (W. Slewinski) (horiz) 1·25 1·25
1840 $3 Masako Owada and engagement photographs (horiz) 2·50 3·00
1841 $3 "Artist's Wife with Cat" (Konrad Kryzanowski) (horiz) 2·50 3·00
1842 $4 Willy Brandt and protest march (horiz) 3·00 3·50
1843 $4 Galaxy 3·00 3·50
1844 $5 Alberto Tomba (Italy) (giant slalom) (horiz) 3·00 3·50
1845 $5 "Dying Bull" (Picasso) (horiz) 3·00 3·50
1846 $5 Pres. Clinton and family (horiz) 3·00 3·50
MS1847 Seven sheets. (a) 106 × 75 mm. $5 Copernicus. (b) 106 × 75 mm. $6 Womens' 1500 metre speed skating medallists (horiz). (c) 106 × 75 mm. $6 Willy Brandt at Warsaw Ghetto Memorial (horiz). (d) 106 × 75 mm. $6 "Woman with a Dog" (detail) (Picasso) (horiz). (e) 106 × 75 mm. $6 Masako Owada. (f) 70 × 100 mm. $6 "General Confusion" (S. I. Witkiewicz). (g) 106 × 75 mm. $6 Pres. Clinton taking the Oath (42½ × 57 mm) Set of 7 sheets 25·00 28·00

ANNIVERSARIES AND EVENTS: Nos. 1829, 1831, 1834, 1838, 150th anniv of St. John's Masonic Lodge No. 492; 1830, 1844, **MS**1847b, Winter Olympic Games '94, Lillehammer; 1832, 1842, **MS**1847c, 80th birth anniv of Willy Brandt (German politician); 1833, 1835, 1845, **MS**1847d, 20th death anniv of Picasso (artist); 1836, 1843, **MS**1847a, 450th death anniv of Copernicus (astronomer); 1837, 1840, **MS**1847e, Marriage of Crown Prince Naruhito of Japan; 1839, 1841, **MS**1847f, "Polska '93" International Stamp Exhibition, Poznan; 1846, **MS**1847g, Inauguration of U.S. President William Clinton.

312 Hugo Eckener and Dr. W. Beckers with Airship "Graf Zeppelin" over Lake George, New York

1993. Aviation Anniversaries. Multicoloured.
1848 30c. Type **312** 1·00 70
1849 40c. Chicago World's Fair from "Graf Zeppelin" 1·00 1·00
1850 40c. Gloster Whittle E.28/39, 1941 1·00 1·00
1851 40c. George Washington writing balloon mail letter (vert) 1·00 1·00
1852 $4 Pres. Wilson and Curtiss JN-4 Jenny 3·75 4·50
1853 $5 Airship "Hindenburg" over Ebbets Field baseball stadium, 1937 3·75 4·50

1854 $5 Gloster Meteor in dogfight . . . . 3·75 4·50

MS1855 Three sheets. (a) 86 × 105 mm. $6 Hugo Eckener (vert). (b) 105 × 86 mm. $6 Consolidated PBY-5 Catalina flying boat (57 × 42½ mm). (c) 105 × 86 mm. $6 Alexander Hamilton, Washington and John Jay watching Blanchard's balloon, 1793 (horiz) Set of 3 sheets . . 16·00 18·00

ANNIVERSARIES: Nos. 1848/9, 1853, **MS**1855a, 125th birth anniv of Hugo Eckener (airship commander); 1850, 1854, **MS**1855b, 75th anniv of Royal Air Force; 1851/2, **MS**1855c, Bicentenary of first airmail flight.

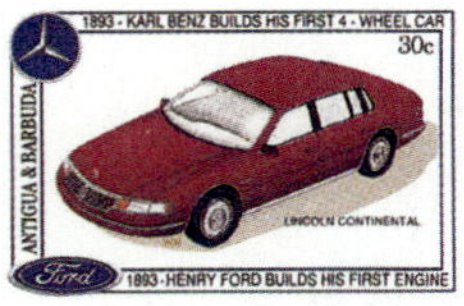

313 Lincoln Continental

1993. Centenaries of Henry Ford's First Petrol Engine (Nos. 1856, 1858), and Karl Benz's First Four-wheeled Car (others). Multicoloured.

1856 30c. Type **313** . . . . 1·00 75
1857 40c. Mercedes racing car, 1914 . . . . 1·00 75
1858 $4 Ford "GT40", 1966 . . . 4·00 4·50
1859 $5 Mercedes Benz "gull-wing" coupe, 1954 . . . 4·00 4·50

MS1860 Two sheets. (a) 114 × 87 mm. $6 Ford's Mustang emblem. (b) 87 × 114 mm. $6 Germany 1936 12pf. Benz and U.S.A. 1968 12c. Ford stamps Set of 2 sheets . . . . 9·00 12·00

314 "The Musical Farmer", 1932

1993. Mickey Mouse Film Posters. Mult.

1861 10c. Type **314** 75 30
1862 15c. "Little Whirlwind", 1941 . . . . 85 35
1863 30c. "Pluto's Dream House", 1940 . . . . . . 1·00 40
1864 40c. "Gulliver Mickey", 1934 . . . . 1·00 40
1865 50c. "Alpine Climbers", 1936 . . . . 1·00 50
1866 $1 "Mr. Mouse Takes a Trip", 1940 . . . . . . 1·50 1·00
1867 $2 "The Nifty Nineties", 1941 . . . . 2·25 2·50
1868 $4 "Mickey Down Under", 1948 . . . . 3·25 4·50
1869 $5 "The Pointer", 1939 . . 3·25 4·50

MS1870 Two sheets, each 125 × 105 mm. (a) $6 "The Simple Things", 1953. (b) $6 "The Prince and the Pauper", 1990 Set of 2 sheets . . . . 11·00 14·00

315 Marie and Fritz with Christmas Tree

1993. Christmas. Mickey's Nutcracker. Walt Disney cartoon characters in scenes from "The Nutcracker". Multicoloured.

1871 10c. Type **315** 75 40
1872 15c. Marie receives Nutcracker from Godfather Drosselmeir . . 80 40
1873 20c. Fritz breaks Nutcracker 80 40
1874 30c. Nutcracker with sword 90 40
1875 40c. Nutcracker and Marie in the snow 95 40
1876 50c. Marie and the Prince meet Sugar Plum Fairy 1·00 60
1877 60c. Marie and Prince in Crystal Hall . . . . . . 1·00 60
1878 $3 Huey, Dewey and Louie as Cossack dancers . . . 3·25 4·00
1879 $6 Mother Ginger and her puppets . . . . 4·50 6·50

MS1880 Two sheets, each 127 × 102 mm. (a) $6 Marie and Prince in sleigh. (b) $6 The Prince in sword fight (vert) Set of 2 sheets 9·00 12·00

316 "Hannah and Samuel" (Rembrandt)

1993. Famous Paintings by Rembrandt and Matisse. Multicoloured.

1881 15c. Type **316** 40 30
1882 15c. "Guitarist" (Matisse) 40 30
1883 30c. "The Jewish Bride" (Rembrandt) 55 30
1884 40c. "Jacob wrestling with the Angel" (Rembrandt) 60 30
1885 60c. "Interior with a Goldfish Bowl" (Matisse) 80 50
1886 $1 "Mlle Yvonne Landsberg" (Matisse) . . 1·25 80
1887 $4 "The Toboggan" (Matisse) . . . . 3·00 4·25
1888 $5 "Moses with the Tablets of the Law" (Rembrandt) 3·00 4·25

MS1889 Two sheets. (a) 124 × 99 mm. $6 "The Blinding of Samson by the Philistines" (detail) (Rembrandt). (b) 99 × 124 mm. $6 "The Three Sisters" (detail) (Matisse) Set of 2 sheets . . . . 9·50 12·00

317 Hong Kong 1981 $1 Golden Threadfin Bream Stamp and Sampans, Shau Kei Wan

1994. "Hong Kong '94" International Stamp Exhibition (1st issue). Multicoloured.

1890 40c. Type **317** 80 80
1891 40c. Antigua 1990 $2 Rock beauty stamp and sampans, Shau Kei Wan 80 80

Nos. 1890/1 were printed together, se-tenant, forming a composite design.

See also Nos. 1892/7 and 1898/1905.

318 Terracotta Warriors

1994. "Hong Kong '94" International Stamp Exhibition (2nd issue). Qin Dynasty Terracotta Figures. Multicoloured.

1892 40c. Type **318** 75 60
1893 40c. Cavalryman and horse 75 60
1894 40c. Warriors in armour . . 75 60
1895 40c. Painted bronze chariot and team 75 60
1896 40c. Pekingese dog 75 60
1897 40c. Warriors with horses 75 60

319 Mickey Mouse in Junk

320 Sumatran Rhinoceros lying down

1994. "Hong Kong '94" International Stamp Exhibition (3rd issue). Walt Disney cartoon characters. Multicoloured.

1898 10c. Type **319** 70 30
1899 15c. Minnie Mouse as mandarin 75 35
1900 30c. Donald and Daisy Duck on houseboat . . . 90 45
1901 50c. Mickey holding bird in cage . . . . 1·10 60
1902 $1 Pluto and ornamental dog . . . . 1·75 1·00
1903 $2 Minnie and Daisy celebrating Bun Festival 2·50 2·50
1904 $4 Goofy making noodles 3·50 4·50
1905 $5 Goofy pulling Mickey in rickshaw . . . . . . 3·50 4·50

MS1906 Two sheets, each 133 × 109 mm. (a) $5 Mickey and Donald on harbour ferry (horiz). (b) $5 Mickey in traditional dragon dance (horiz) Set of 2 sheets . . . . 7·00 9·00

1994. Centenary (1992) of Sierra Club (environmental protection society). Endangered Species. Multicoloured.

1907 $1.50 Type **320** . . . . . . 1·25 1·25
1908 $1.50 Sumatran rhinoceros feeding . . . . 1·25 1·25
1909 $1.50 Ring-tailed lemur on ground . . . . 1·25 1·25
1910 $1.50 Ring-tailed lemur on branch . . . . 1·25 1·25
1911 $1.50 Red-fronted brown lemur on branch . . . 1·25 1·25
1912 $1.50 Head of red-fronted brown lemur . . . . . 1·25 1·25
1913 $1.50 Head of red-fronted brown lemur in front of trunk . . . . 1·25 1·25
1914 $1.50 Sierra Club Centennial emblem 80 80
1915 $1.50 Head of Bactrian camel . . . . 1·25 1·25
1916 $1.50 Bactrian camel . . . 1·25 1·25
1917 $1.50 African elephant drinking . . . . 1·25 1·25
1918 $1.50 Head of African elephant . . . . 1·25 1·25
1919 $1.50 Leopard sitting upright . . . . 1·25 1·25
1920 $1.50 Leopard in grass (emblem at right) . . . . 1·25 1·25
1921 $1.50 Leopard in grass (emblem at left) . . . . . 1·25 1·25

MS1922 Four sheets. (a) 100 × 70 mm. $1.50, Sumatran rhinoceros (horiz). (b) 70 × 100 mm. $1.50, Ring-tailed lemur (horiz). (c) 70 × 100 mm. $1.50, Bactrian camel (horiz). (d) 100 × 70 mm. $1.50, African elephant (horiz) Set of 4 sheets 6·00 8·00

321 West Highland White Terrier

1994. Dogs of the World. Chinese New Year ("Year of the Dog"). Multicoloured.

1923 50c. Type **321** 75 65
1924 50c. Beagle 75 65
1925 50c. Scottish terrier 75 65
1926 50c. Pekingese 75 65
1927 50c. Dachshund 75 65
1928 50c. Yorkshire terrier . . . 75 65
1929 50c. Pomeranian 75 65
1930 50c. Poodle 75 65
1931 50c. Shetland sheepdog . . 75 65
1932 50c. Pug 75 65
1933 50c. Shih Tzu 75 65
1934 50c. Chihuahua 75 65
1935 75c. Mastiff 75 65
1936 75c. Border collie 75 65
1937 75c. Samoyed 75 65
1938 75c. Airedale terrier . . . 75 65
1939 75c. English setter 75 65
1940 75c. Rough collie 75 65
1941 75c. Newfoundland 75 65
1942 75c. Weimarana 75 65
1943 75c. English springer spaniel 75 65
1944 75c. Dalmatian 75 65
1945 75c. Boxer 75 65
1946 75c. Old English sheepdog 75 65

MS1947 Two sheets, each 93 × 58 mm. (a) $6 Welsh corgi. (b) $6 Labrador retriever Set of 2 sheets . . . . 9·00 12·00

322 "Spiranthes lanceolata"

323 Hermann E. Sieger, Germany 1931 1m. Zeppelin Stamp and Airship LZ-127 "Graf Zeppelin"

1994. Orchids. Multicoloured.

1948 10c. Type **322** 70 60
1949 20c. "Ionopsis utricularioides" . . . . . 1·00 50
1950 30c. "Tetramicra canaliculata" . . . . . . 1·25 50
1951 50c. "Oncidium picturatum" 1·50 65
1952 $1 "Epidendrum difforme" 2·00 1·25
1953 $2 "Epidendrum ciliare" . . 3·00 2·75
1954 $4 "Epidendrum ibaguense" 4·00 4·25
1955 $5 "Epidendrum nocturnum" . . . . . . 4·00 4·25

MS1956 Two sheets, each 100 × 73 mm. (a) $6 "Rodriguezia lanceolato". (b) $6 "Encyclia cochleata" Set of 2 sheets . . . 9·00 12·00

1994. Famous Professional Philatelists (2nd series).

1957 **323** $1.50 multicoloured . . 2·75 2·50

324 "Danaus plexippus"

325 Bottlenose Dolphin

1994. Butterflies. Multicoloured.

1958 10c. Type **324** 85 75
1959 15c. "Appias drusilla" . . . 1·00 45
1960 30c. "Eurema lisa" . . . . 1·25 55
1961 40c. "Anaea troglodyta" . . 1·25 60
1962 $1 "Urbanus proteus" . . . 2·00 1·25
1963 $2 "Junonia evarete" . . . 2·75 2·75
1964 $4 "Battus polydamas" . . 3·50 4·50
1965 $5 "Heliconius charitonia" 3·50 4·50

MS1966 Two sheets, each 102 × 72 mm. (a) $6 "Phoebis sennae". (b) $6 "Hemiargus hanno" Set of 2 sheets . . . . 9·00 12·00

No. 1959 is inscribed "Appisa drusilla" and No. 1965 "Heliconius charitonius", both in error.

1994. Marine Life. Multicoloured.

1967 50c. Type **325** 75 75
1968 50c. Killer whale 75 75
1969 50c. Spinner dolphin 75 75
1970 50c. Oceanic sunfish 75 75
1971 50c. Caribbean reef shark and short fin pilot whale 75 75
1972 50c. Copper-banded butterflyfish 75 75
1973 50c. Mosaic moray 75 75
1974 50c. Clown triggerfish . . . 75 75
1975 50c. Red lobster 75 75

MS1976 Two sheets, each 106 × 76 mm. (a) $6 Seahorse. (b) $6 Swordfish ("Blue Marlin") (horiz) Set of 2 sheets . . . . 11·00 12·00

326 Edwin Aldrin (astronaut)

1994. 25th Anniv of First Manned Moon Landing. Multicoloured.

1977 $1.50 Type **326** . . . . . . 1·75 1·50
1978 $1.50 First lunar footprint . 1·75 1·50
1979 $1.50 Neil Armstrong (astronaut) . . . . 1·75 1·50
1980 $1.50 Aldrin stepping onto Moon . . . . 1·75 1·50
1981 $1.50 Aldrin and equipment 1·75 1·50
1982 $1.50 Aldrin and U.S.A. flag 1·75 1·50
1983 $1.50 Aldrin at Tranquility Base . . . . 1·75 1·50
1984 $1.50 Moon plaque . . . . 1·75 1·50
1985 $1.50 "Eagle" leaving Moon 1·75 1·50
1986 $1.50 Command module in lunar orbit . . . . . . 1·75 1·50
1987 $1.50 First day cover of U.S.A. 1969 10c. First Man on Moon stamp . . 1·75 1·50
1988 $1.50 Pres. Nixon and astronauts . . . . 1·75 1·50

MS1989 72 × 102 mm. $6 Armstrong and Aldrin with postal official 4·00 5·00

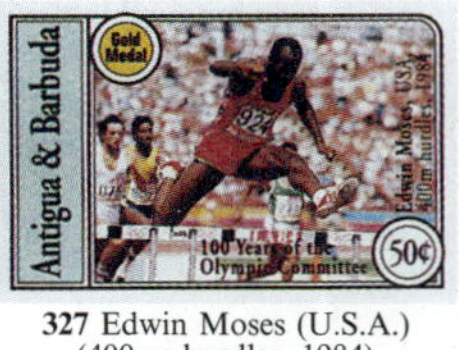

327 Edwin Moses (U.S.A.) (400 m hurdles, 1984)

1994. Centenary of International Olympic Committee. Gold Medal Winners. Multicoloured.

1990 50c. Type **327** 40 30
1991 $1.50 Steffi Graf (Germany) (tennis, 1988) . . . . . 1·75 1·75

MS1992 79 × 110 mm. $6 Johann Olav Koss (Norway) (500, 1500 and 10,000 metre speed skating), 1994 . . . . 5·00 5·50

328 Antiguan Family

1994. International Year of the Family.
1993 **328** 90c. multicoloured . . . 1·00 1·00

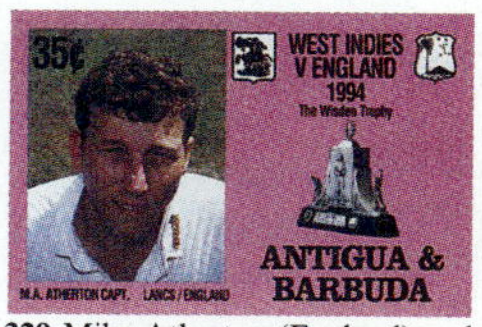

329 Mike Atherton (England) and Wisden Trophy

1994. Centenary (1995) of First English Cricket Tour to the West Indies. Multicoloured.
1994 35c. Type **329** . . . . . . 1·00 65
1995 75c. Viv Richards (West Indies) (vert) . . . . . . 1·75 1·25
1996 $1.20 Richie Richardson (West Indies) and Wisden Trophy . . . . 2·25 2·50
MS1997 80 × 100 mm. $3 English team, 1895 (black and brown) 2·50 3·00

330 Entrance Bridge, Songgwangsa Temple

1994. "Philakorea '94" International Stamp Exhibition, Seoul. Multicoloured.
1998 40c. Type **330** 50 40
1999 75c. Long-necked bottle . . 70 75
2000 75c. Punch'ong ware jar with floral decoration . . 70 75
2001 75c. Punch'ong ware jar with blue dragon pattern 70 75
2002 75c. Ewer in shape of bamboo shoot 70 75
2003 75c. Punch'ong ware green jar 70 75
2004 75c. Pear-shaped bottle . . 70 75
2005 75c. Porcelain jar with brown dragon pattern . . 70 75
2006 75c. Porcelain jar with floral pattern 70 75
2007 90c. Song-op Folk Village, Cheju 70 75
2008 $3 Port Sogwipo . . . . . 1·75 2·25
MS2009 104 × 71 mm. $4 Ox herder playing flute (vert) . . . . . . 3·25 4·00

331 Short S.25 Sunderland (flying boat)

1994. 50th Anniv of D-Day. Multicoloured.
2010 40c. Type **331** . . . . . . 1·00 40
2011 $2 Lockheed P-38 Lightning fighters attacking train . . 2·75 2·75
2012 $3 Martin B-26 Marauder bombers . . . . 3·25 3·75
MS2013 108 × 78 mm. $6 Hawker Typhoon fighter bomber . . . 6·00 6·50

332 Travis Tritt

1994. Stars of Country and Western Music. Multicoloured.
2014 75c. Type **332** 70 70
2015 75c. Dwight Yoakam . . . 70 70
2016 75c. Billy Ray Cyrus 70 70
2017 75c. Alan Jackson 70 70
2018 75c. Garth Brooks 70 70
2019 75c. Vince Gill 70 70
2020 75c. Clint Black 70 70
2021 75c. Eddie Rabbit 70 70
2022 75c. Patsy Cline 70 70
2023 75c. Tanya Tucker 70 70
2024 75c. Dolly Parton 70 70
2025 75c. Anne Murray 70 70
2026 75c. Tammy Wynette . . . 70 70
2027 75c. Loretta Lynn 70 70
2028 75c. Reba McEntire 70 70
2029 75c. Skeeter Davis 70 70
2030 75c. Hank Snow 70 70
2031 75c. Gene Autry 70 70
2032 75c. Jimmie Rodgers 70 70
2033 75c. Ernest Tubb 70 70
2034 75c. Eddy Arnold 70 70
2035 75c. Willie Nelson 70 70
2036 75c. Johnny Cash 70 70
2037 75c. George Jones 70 70
MS2038 Three sheets. (a) 100 × 70 mm. $6 Hank Williams Jr. (b) 100 × 70 mm. $6 Hank Williams Sr. (c) 70 × 100 mm. $6 Kitty Wells (horiz) Set of 3 sheets 14·00 14·00

333 Hugo Sanchez (Mexico)

1994. World Cup Football Championship, U.S.A. (2nd issue). Multicoloured.
2039 15c. Type **333** 75 30
2040 35c. Jurgen Klinsmann (Germany) . . . . 1·25 45
2041 65c. Antiguan player . . . 1·50 55
2042 $1.20 Cobi Jones (U.S.A.) . 2·00 1·75
2043 $4 Roberto Baggio (Italy) . 3·25 4·00
2044 $5 Bwalya Kalusha (Zambia) . . . . 3·25 4·00
MS2045 Two sheets. (a) 72 × 105 mm. $6 Maldive Islands player (vert). (b) 107 × 78 mm. $6 World Cup trophy (vert) Set of 2 sheets . . . . 8·00 9·00
No. 2040 is inscribed "Klinsman" in error.

334 Sir Shridath Ramphal

1994. 1st Recipients of Order of the Caribbean Community. Multicoloured.
2046 65c. Type **334** 50 40
2047 90c. William Demas 65 60
2048 $1.20 Derek Walcott . . . . 2·00 1·50

335 Pair of Magnificent Frigate Birds

1994. Birds. Multicoloured.
2049 10c. Type **335** 55 45
2050 15c. Bridled quail dove . . 65 40
2051 30c. Magnificent frigate bird chick hatching 85 70
2052 40c. Purple-throated carib (vert) 85 70
2053 $1 Male magnificent frigate bird in courtship display (vert) . . . . 1·10 1·25
2054 $1 Broad-winged hawk (vert) . . . . 1·10 1·25
2055 $3 Young magnificent frigate bird . . . . 2·25 3·25
2056 $4 Yellow warbler . . . . . 2·25 3·25
MS2057 Two sheets. (a) 70 × 100 mm. $6 Female magnificent frigate bird (vert). (b) 100 × 70 mm. $6 Black-billed whistling duck ducklings Set of 2 sheets . . . . 8·00 9·00
Nos. 2049, 2051, 2053 and 2055 also show the W.W.F. Panda emblem.

336 "The Virgin and Child by the Fireside" (Robert Campin)

337 Magnificent Frigate Bird

1994. Christmas. Religious Paintings. Multicoloured.
2058 15c. Type **336** 80 30
2059 35c. "The Reading Madonna" (Giorgione) . . 1·10 30
2060 40c. "Madonna and Child" (Giovanni Bellini) . . . . 1·25 30
2061 45c. "The Litta Madonna" (Da Vinci) . . . . 1·25 30
2062 65c. "The Virgin and Child under the Apple Tree" (Lucas Cranach the Elder) 1·60 55
2063 75c. "Madonna and Child" (Master of the Female Half-lengths) . . . . . . 1·75 70
2064 $1.20 "An Allegory of the Church" (Alessandro Allori) . . . . 2·25 2·00
2065 $5 "Madonna and Child wreathed with Flowers" (Jacob Jordaens) . . . . 3·75 5·50
MS2066 Two sheets. (a) 123 × 88 mm. $6 "Madonna and Child with Commissioners" (detail) (Palma Vecchio) (b) 88 × 123 mm. $6 "The Virgin Enthroned with Child" (detail) (Bohemian master) Set of 2 sheets 7·50 9·00

1995. Birds. Multicoloured.
2067 15c. Type **337** 30 10
2068 25c. Blue-hooded euphonia 40 15
2069 35c. Eastern meadowlark ("Meadowlark") 45 20
2070 40c. Red-billed tropic bird 45 20
2071 45c. Greater flamingo . . . 45 25
2072 60c. Yellow-faced grassquit 50 30
2073 65c. Yellow-billed cuckoo 50 30
2074 70c. Purple-throated carib 55 35
2075 75c. Bananaquit 55 35
2076 90c. Painted bunting 65 40
2077 $1.20 Red-legged honeycreeper 90 55
2078 $2 Northern jacana ("Jacana") . . . . 1·50 1·00
2079 $5 Greater Antillean bullfinch . . . . 3·25 3·00
2080 $10 Caribbean elaenia . . . 6·00 6·50
2081 $20 Brown trembler ("Trembler") . . . . . . 10·00 11·00

338 Head of Pachycephalosaurus

1995. Prehistoric Animals. Multicoloured.
2082 15c. Type **338** 60 60
2083 20c. Head of afrovenator . . 60 60
2084 65c. Centrosaurus 80 80
2085 75c. Kronosaurus (horiz) . . 80 80
2086 75c. Ichthyosaurus (horiz) 80 80
2087 75c. Plesiosaurus (horiz) . . 80 80
2088 75c. Archelon (horiz) . . . 80 80
2089 75c. Pair of tyrannosaurus (horiz) 80 80
2090 75c. Tyrannosaurus (horiz) 80 80
2091 75c. Parasaurolophus (horiz) 80 80
2092 75c. Pair of parasaurolophus (horiz) 80 80
2093 75c. Oviraptor (horiz) . . . 80 80
2094 75c. Protoceratops with eggs (horiz) 80 80
2095 75c. Pteranodon and protoceratops (horiz) . . 80 80
2096 75c. Pair of protoceratops (horiz) 80 80
2097 90c. Pentaceratops drinking 1·00 1·00
2098 $1.20 Head of tarbosaurus 1·25 1·25
2099 $5 Head of styracosaurus 3·25 4·00
MS2100 Two sheets, each 101 × 70 mm. (a) $6 Head of Corythosaurus (horiz). (b) $6 Head of Carnotaurus (horiz) Set of 2 sheets . . . . 9·50 12·00

339 Al Oerter (U.S.A.) (discus – 1956, 1960, 1964, 1968)

1995. Olympic Games, Atlanta (1996). Previous Gold Medal Winners (1st issue). Multicoloured.
2101 15c. Type **339** 60 30
2102 20c. Greg Louganis (U.S.A.) (diving – 1984, 1988) . . 60 30
2103 65c. Naim Suleymanoglu (Turkey) (weightlifting – 1988) 75 50
2104 90c. Louise Ritter (U.S.A.) (high jump – 1988) . . . 1·00 70
2105 $1.20 Nadia Comaneci (Rumania) (gymnastics – 1976) . . . . 2·00 1·40
2106 $5 Olga Bondarenko (Russia) (10,000 metres – 1988) . . . . 3·25 5·00
MS2107 Two sheets, each 106 × 76 mm. (a) $6 United States crew (eight-oared shell — 1964). (b) $6 Lutz Hessilch (Germany) (cycling — 1988) (vert) Set of 2 sheets . . . . 11·00 12·00
No. 2106 is inscribed "BOLDARENKO" in error.
See also Nos. 2302/23.

340 Map of Berlin showing Russian Advance

1995. 50th Anniv of End of Second World War in Europe. Multicoloured.
2108 $1.20 Type **340** . . . . . . 1·40 1·25
2109 $1.20 Russian tank and infantry . . . . 1·40 1·25
2110 $1.20 Street fighting in Berlin . . . . 1·40 1·25
2111 $1.20 German tank exploding . . . . 1·40 1·25
2112 $1.20 Russian air raid . . . 1·40 1·25
2113 $1.20 German troops surrendering . . . . . . 1·40 1·25
2114 $1.20 Hoisting the Soviet flag on the Reichstag . . 1·40 1·25
2115 $1.20 Captured German standards . . . . 1·40 1·25
MS2116 104 × 74 mm. $6 Gen. Konev (vert) . . . . 4·50 5·50
See also Nos. 2132/8.

341 Signatures and Earl of Halifax

342 Woman buying Produce from Market

1995. 50th Anniv of United Nations. Multicoloured.
2117 75c. Type **341** . . . . . . 70 1·00
2118 90c. Virginia Gildersleeve 70 1·00
2119 $1.20 Harold Stassen . . . 70 1·00
MS2120 100 × 70 mm. $6 Pres. Franklin D. Roosevelt . . . . 3·50 4·25
Nos. 2117/19 were printed together, se-tenant, forming a composite design.

1995. 50th Anniv of F.A.O. Multicoloured.
2121 75c. Type **342** . . . . . . 70 1·00
2122 90c. Women shopping . . . 70 1·00
2123 $1.20 Women talking . . . 70 1·00
MS2124 100 × 70 mm. $6 Tractor 3·00 3·75
Nos. 2121/3 were printed together, se-tenant, forming a composite design.

343 Beach and Rotary Emblem

344 Queen Elizabeth the Queen Mother

1995. 90th Anniv of Rotary International.
2125 **343** $5 multicoloured . . . . 3·50 4·00
MS2126 74 × 104 mm. $6 National flag and emblem . . . . 3·50 4·00

1995. 95th Birthday of Queen Elizabeth the Queen Mother.
2127 – $1.50 brown, light brown and black . . . . . . 1·50 1·50
2128 **344** $1.50 multicoloured . . 1·50 1·50
2129 – $1.50 multicoloured . . 1·50 1·50
2130 – $1.50 multicoloured . . 1·50 1·50
MS2131 100 × 127 mm. $6 multicoloured . . . . 5·50 5·50
DESIGNS: No. 2127, Queen Elizabeth the Queen Mother (pastel drawing); 2129, At desk (oil painting); 2130, Wearing green dress; **MS**2131, Wearing blue dress.

1995. 50th Anniv of End of Second World War in the Pacific. As T **340**. Multicoloured.
2132 $1.20 Gen. Chang Kai-Shek and Chinese guerrillas . . 1·10 1·25
2133 $1.20 Gen. Douglas MacArthur and beach landing . . . . 1·10 1·25
2134 $1.20 Gen. Claire Chennault and U.S. fighter aircraft 1·10 1·25
2135 $1.20 Brig. Orde Wingate and supply drop . . . . . 1·10 1·25
2136 $1.20 Gen. Joseph Stilwell and U.S. supply plane . . 1·10 1·25
2137 $1.20 Field-Marshal Bill Slim and loading cow into plane . . . . 1·10 1·25
MS2138 108 × 76 mm. $3 Admiral Nimitz and aircraft carrier . . 2·75 3·50

345 Family ("Caring")

1995. Tourism. Sheet 95 × 72 mm, containing T **345** and similar horiz designs. Multicoloured.
MS2139 $2 Type **345**; $2 Market trader ("Marketing"); $2 Workers and housewife ("Working"); $2 Leisure pursuits ("Enjoying Life") 5·50 7·00

346 Purple-throated Carib

347 Original Church, 1845

1995. Birds. Multicoloured.
2140 75c. Type **346** 1·00 85
2141 75c. Antillean crested hummingbird 1·00 85
2142 75c. Bananaquit 1·00 85
2143 75c. Mangrove cuckoo 1·00 85
2144 75c. Troupial 1·00 85
2145 75c. Green-throated carib 1·00 85
2146 75c. Yellow warbler 1·00 85
2147 75c. Antillean euphonia ("Blue-hooded Euphonia") 1·00 85
2148 75c. Scaly-breasted thrasher 1·00 85
2149 75c. Burrowing owl 1·00 85
2150 75c. Carib grackle 1·00 85
2151 75c. Adelaide's warbler 1·00 85
2152 75c. Ring-necked duck 1·00 85
2153 75c. Ruddy duck 1·00 85
2154 75c. Green-winged teal 1·00 85
2155 75c. Wood duck 1·00 85
2156 75c. Hooded merganser 1·00 85
2157 75c. Lesser scaup 1·00 85
2158 75c. Black-billed whistling duck ("West Indian Tree Duck") 1·00 85
2159 75c. Fulvous whistling duck 1·00 85
2160 75c. Bahama pintail 1·00 85
2161 75c. Northern shoveler 1·00 85
2162 75c. Masked duck 1·00 85
2163 75c. American wigeon 1·00 85
MS2164 Two sheets, each 104 × 74 mm. (a) $6 American purple gallinule. (b) $6 Heads of Blue-winged teal Set of 2 sheets 13·00 13·00
Nos. 2140/51 and 2152/63 respectively were printed together, se-tenant, forming composite designs.

1995. 150th Anniv of Greenbay Moravian Church. Multicoloured.
2165 20c. Type **347** 70 30
2166 60c. Church in 1967 1·00 40
2167 75c. Present church 1·25 50
2168 90c. Revd. John Buckley (first minister of African descent) 1·40 60
2169 $1.20 Bishop John Ephraim Knight (longest-serving minister) 1·75 1·75
2170 $2 As 75c. 2·75 3·50
MS2171 110 × 81 mm. $6 Front of present church 4·50 6·00

348 Mining Bees

1995. Bees. Multicoloured.
2172 90c. Type **348** 1·00 70
2173 $1.20 Solitary bee 1·40 90
2174 $1.65 Leaf-cutter bee 2·00 2·00
2175 $1.75 Honey bees 2·00 2·00
MS2176 110 × 80 mm. $6 Solitary mining bee 4·00 5·00

349 Narcissus

1995. Flowers. Multicoloured.
2177 75c. Type **349** 80 80
2178 75c. Camellia 80 80
2179 75c. Iris 80 80
2180 75c. Tulip 80 80
2181 75c. Poppy 80 80
2182 75c. Peony 80 80
2183 75c. Magnolia 80 80
2184 75c. Oriental lily 80 80
2185 75c. Rose 80 80
2186 75c. Pansy 80 80
2187 75c. Hydrangea 80 80
2188 75c. Azaleas 80 80
MS2189 80 × 100 mm. $6 Calla lily 4·00 5·00
No. 2186 is inscribed "Pansie" in error.

350 Somali

1995. Cats. Multicoloured.
2190 45c. Type **350** 75 60
2191 45c. Persian and butterflies 75 60
2192 45c. Devon rex 75 60
2193 45c. Turkish angora 75 60
2194 45c. Himalayan 75 60
2195 45c. Maine coon 75 60
2196 45c. Ginger non-pedigree 75 60
2197 45c. American wirehair 75 60
2198 45c. British shorthair 75 60
2199 45c. American curl 75 60
2200 45c. Black non-pedigree and butterfly 75 60
2201 45c. Birman 75 60
MS2202 104 × 74 mm. $6 Siberian kitten (vert) 7·50 7·50
Nos. 2190/2201 were printed together, se-tenant, forming a composite design.

351 The Explorer Tent

1995. 18th World Scout Jamboree, Netherlands. Tents. Multicoloured.
2203 $1.20 Type **351** 1·60 1·60
2204 $1.20 Camper tent 1·60 1·60
2205 $1.20 Wall tent 1·60 1·60
2206 $1.20 Trail tarp 1·60 1·60
2207 $1.20 Miner's tent 1·60 1·60
2208 $1.20 Voyager tent 1·60 1·60
MS2209 Two sheets, each 76 × 106 mm. (a) $6 Scout and camp fire. (b) $6 Scout with back pack (vert) Set of 2 sheets 8·50 10·00

352 Trans-Gabon Diesel-electric Train

1995. Trains of the World. Multicoloured.
2210 35c. Type **352** 1·00 65
2211 65c. Canadian Pacific diesel-electric locomotive 1·50 90
2212 75c. Santa Fe Railway diesel-electric locomotive, U.S.A. 1·60 1·00
2213 90c. High Speed Train, Great Britain 1·60 1·00
2214 $1.20 TGV express train, France 1·60 1·60
2215 $1.20 Diesel-electric locomotive, Australia 1·60 1·60
2216 $1.20 Pendolino "ETR 450" electric train, Italy 1·60 1·60
2217 $1.20 Diesel-electric locomotive, Thailand 1·60 1·60
2218 $1.20 Pennsylvania Railroad Type K4 steam locomotive, U.S.A. 1·60 1·60
2219 $1.20 Beyer-Garratt steam locomotive, East African Railways 1·60 1·60
2220 $1.20 Natal Government steam locomotive 1·60 1·60
2221 $1.20 Rail gun, American Civil War 1·60 1·60
2222 $1.20 Locomotive "Lion" (red livery), Great Britain 1·60 1·60
2223 $1.20 William Hedley's "Puffing Billy" (green livery), Great Britain 1·60 1·60
2224 $6 Amtrak high speed diesel locomotive, U.S.A. 3·75 4·50
MS2225 Two sheets, each 110 × 80 mm. (a) $6 Locomotive "Iron Rooster", China (vert). (b) $6 "Indian-Pacific" diesel-electric locomotive, Australia (vert) Set of 2 sheets 13·00 13·00

353 Dag Hammarskjold (1961 Peace)

1995. Cent of Nobel Prize Trust Fund. Mult.
2226 $1 Type **353** 1·10 1·10
2227 $1 Georg Wittig (1979 Chemistry) 1·10 1·10
2228 $1 Wilhelm Ostwald (1909 Chemistry) 1·10 1·10
2229 $1 Robert Koch (1905 Medicine) 1·10 1·10
2230 $1 Karl Ziegler (1963 Chemistry) 1·10 1·10
2231 $1 Alexander Fleming (1945 Medicine) 1·10 1·10
2232 $1 Hermann Staudinger (1953 Chemistry) 1·10 1·10
2233 $1 Manfred Eigen (1967 Chemistry) 1·10 1·10
2234 $1 Arno Penzias (1978 Physics) 1·10 1·10
2235 $1 Shmuel Agnon (1966 Literature) 1·10 1·10
2236 $1 Rudyard Kipling (1907 Literature) 1·10 1·10
2237 $1 Aleksandr Solzhenitsyn (1970 Literature) 1·10 1·10
2238 $1 Jack Steinberger (1988 Physics) 1·10 1·10
2239 $1 Andrei Sakharov (1975 Peace) 1·10 1·10
2240 $1 Otto Stern (1943 Physics) 1·10 1·10
2241 $1 John Steinbeck (1962 Literature) 1·10 1·10
2242 $1 Nadine Gordimer (1991 Literature) 1·10 1·10
2243 $1 William Faulkner (1949 Literature) 1·10 1·10
MS2244 Two sheets, each 100 × 70 mm. (a) $6 Elie Wiesel (1986 Peace) (vert). (b) $6 The Dalai Lama (1989 Peace) (vert) Set of 2 sheets 8·00 9·50

354 Elvis Presley

1995. 60th Birth Anniv of Elvis Presley. Mult.
2245 $1 Type **354** 1·25 95
2246 $1 Holding microphone in right hand 1·25 95
2247 $1 In blue shirt and with neck of guitar 1·25 95
2248 $1 Wearing blue shirt and smiling 1·25 95
2249 $1 On wedding day 1·25 95
2250 $1 In army uniform 1·25 95
2251 $1 Wearing red shirt 1·25 95
2252 $1 Wearing white shirt 1·25 95
2253 $1 In white shirt with microphone 1·25 95
MS2254 101 × 71 mm. $6 "Ghost" image of Elvis amongst the stars 7·00 5·50

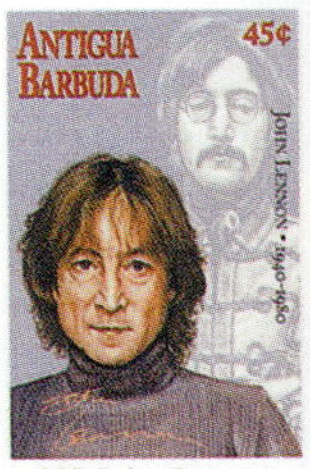

355 John Lennon and Signature

357 "Rest on the Flight into Egypt" (Paolo Veronese)

1995. 15th Death Anniv of John Lennon (entertainer). Multicoloured.
2255 45c. Type **355** 50 40
2256 50c. In beard and spectacles 50 50
2257 65c. Wearing sunglasses 55 55
2258 75c. In cap with heart badge 65 65
MS2259 103 × 73 mm. $6 As 75c. 5·50 6·50

1995. Hurricane Relief. Nos. 2203/8 optd **"Hurricane Relief"**.
2260 $1.20 Type **351** 1·25 1·25
2261 $1.20 Camper tent 1·25 1·25
2262 $1.20 Wall tent 1·25 1·25
2263 $1.20 Trail tarp 1·25 1·25
2264 $1.20 Miner's tent 1·25 1·25
2265 $1.20 Voyager tent 1·25 1·25
MS2266 Two sheets, each 76 × 106 mm. (a) $6 Scout and camp fire. (b) $6 Scout with back pack (vert) Set of 2 sheets 12·00 15·00

1995. Christmas. Religious Paintings. Multicoloured.
2267 15c. Type **357** 30 30
2268 35c. "Madonna and Child" (Van Dyck) 40 40
2269 65c. "Sacred Conversation Piece" (Veronese) 60 50
2270 75c. "Vision of St. Anthony" (Van Dyck) 70 60
2271 90c. "Virgin and Child" (Van Eyck) 80 65
2272 $6 "The Immaculate Conception" (Giovanni Tiepolo) 3·00 4·25
MS2273 Two sheets. (a) 101 × 127 mm. $5 "Christ appearing to his Mother" (detail) (Van der Weyden). (b) 127 × 101 mm. $6 "The Infant Jesus and Young St. John" (Murillo) Set of 2 sheets 7·50 9·00

358 "Hygrophoropsis aurantiaca"

360 Florence Griffith Joyner (U.S.A.) (Gold – track, 1988)

359 H.M.S. "Resolution" (Cook)

1996. Fungi. Multicoloured.
2274 75c. Type **358** 60 70
2275 75c. "Hygrophorus bakerensis" 60 70
2276 75c. "Hygrophorus conicus" 60 70
2277 75c. "Hygrophorus miniatus" ("Hygrocybe miniata") 60 70
2278 75c. "Suillus brevipes" 60 70
2279 75c. "Suillus luteus" 60 70
2280 75c. "Suillus granulatus" 60 70
2281 75c. "Suillus caerulescens" 60 70
MS2282 Two sheets, each 105 × 75 mm. (a) $6 "Conocybe filaris". (b) $6 "Hygrocybe flavescens" Set of 2 sheets 7·00 8·00

1996. Sailing Ships. Multicoloured.
2283 15c. Type **359** 70 40
2284 25c. "Mayflower" (Pilgrim Fathers) 70 40
2285 45c. "Santa Maria" (Columbus) 1·00 40
2286 75c. "Aemilia" (Dutch galleon) 1·00 90
2287 75c. "Sovereign of the Seas" (English galleon) 1·00 90
2288 90c. H.M.S. "Victory" (Nelson) 1·25 90
2289 $1.20 As No. 2286 1·50 1·60
2290 $1.20 As No. 2287 1·50 1·60
2291 $1.20 "Royal Louis" (French galleon) 1·50 1·60
2292 $1.20 H.M.S. "Royal George" (ship of the line) 1·50 1·60
2293 $1.20 "Le Protecteur" (French frigate) 1·50 1·60
2294 $1.20 As No. 2288 1·50 1·60
2295 $1.50 As No. 2285 1·50 1·60
2296 $1.50 "Vitoria" (Magellan) 1·60 1·75
2297 $1.50 "Golden Hind" (Drake) 1·60 1·75
2298 $1.50 As No. 2284 1·60 1·75
2299 $1.50 "Griffin" (La Salle) 1·60 1·75
2300 $1.50 Type **359** 1·60 1·75
MS2301 Two sheets. (a) 102 × 72 mm. $6 U.S.S. "Constitution" (frigate). (b) 98 × 67 mm. $6 "Grande" "Hermine" (Cartier) Set of 2 sheets 7·50 9·00

1996. Olympic Games, Atlanta. Previous Medal Winners (2nd issue). Multicoloured.
2302 65c. Type **360** 60 60
2303 75c. Olympic Stadium, Seoul (1988) (horiz) 65 65
2304 90c. Allison Jolly and Lynne Jewell (U.S.A.) (Gold – yachting, 1988) (horiz) 70 70
2305 90c. Wolfgang Nordwig (Germany) (Gold – pole vaulting, 1972) 70 75
2306 90c. Shirley Strong (Great Britain) (Silver – 100 metres hurdles, 1984) 70 75
2307 90c. Sergei Bubka (Russia) (Gold – pole vault, 1988) 70 75

2308 90c. Filbert Bayi (Tanzania) (Silver – 3000 metres steeplechase, 1980) . . . 70 75
2309 90c. Victor Saneyev (Russia) (Gold – triple jump, 1968, 1972, 1976) 70 75
2310 90c. Silke Renk (Germany) (Gold – javelin, 1992) . . 70 75
2311 90c. Daley Thompson (Great Britain) (Gold – decathlon, 1980, 1984) . . 70 75
2312 90c. Robert Richards (U.S.A.) (Gold – pole vault, 1952, 1956) 70 75
2313 90c. Parry O'Brien (U.S.A.) (Gold – shot put, 1952, 1956) 70 75
2314 90c. Ingrid Kramer (Germany) (Gold – women's platform diving, 1960) 70 75
2315 90c. Kelly McCormick (U.S.A.) (Silver – women's springboard diving, 1984) 70 75
2316 90c. Gary Tobian (U.S.A.) (Gold – men's springboard diving, 1960) 70 75
2317 90c. Greg Louganis (U.S.A.) (Gold – men's diving, 1984 and 1988) 70 75
2318 90c. Michelle Mitchell (U.S.A.) (Silver – women's platform diving, 1984 and 1988) 70 75
2319 90c. Zhou Jihong (China) (Gold – women's platform diving, 1984) 70 75
2320 90c. Wendy Wyland (U.S.A.) (Bronze – women's platform diving, 1984) 70 75
2321 90c. Xu Yanmei (China) (Gold – women's platform diving, 1988) 70 75
2322 90c. Fu Mingxia (China) (Gold – women's platform diving, 1992) 70 75
2323 $1.20 2000 metre tandem cycle race (horiz) . . . . 1·00 1·00
MS2324 Two sheets, each 106×76 mm. (a) $5 Bill Toomey (U.S.A.) (Gold—Decathlon, 1968) (horiz). (b) $6 Mark Lenzi (U.S.A.) (Gold—Men's springboard diving, 1992) Set of 2 sheets . . . . 7·00 8·00

Nos. 2305/13 and 2314/22 respectively were printed together, se-tenant, with the background forming a composite design.

361 Black Skimmer

1996. Sea Birds. Multicoloured.
2325 75c. Type **361** 70 75
2326 75c. Black-capped petrel . . 70 75
2327 75c. Sooty tern 70 75
2328 75c. Royal tern 70 75
2329 75c. Pomarine skua ("Pomarine Jaeger") . . 70 75
2330 75c. White-tailed tropic bird 70 75
2331 75c. Northern gannet . . . 70 75
2332 75c. Laughing gull 70 75
MS2333 Two sheets, each 105×75 mm. (a) $5 Magnificent frigate bird ("Great Frigate Bird"). (b) $6 Brown pelican Set of 2 sheets . . . . 7·50 9·00

362 Mickey and Goofy on Elephant ("Around the World in Eighty Days")

1996. Novels of Jules Verne. Walt Disney cartoon characters in scenes from the books. Multicoloured.
2334 1c. Type **362** 15 25
2335 2c. Mickey, Donald and Goofy entering cave ("A Journey to the Centre of the Earth") 20 25
2336 5c. Mickey and Minnie driving postcart ("Michel Strogoff") 30 25
2337 10c. Mickey, Donald and Goofy in space rocket ("From the Earth to the Moon") 40 20
2338 15c. Mickey and Goofy in balloon ("Five Weeks in a Balloon") 40 20
2339 20c. Mickey and Goofy in China ("Around the World in Eighty Days") 40 20
2340 $1 Mickey, Goofy and Pluto on island ("The Mysterious Island") . . . 2·00 85
2341 $2 Mickey, Pluto, Goofy and Donald on Moon ("From the Earth to the Moon") . . . . 2·50 2·50
2342 $3 Mickey being lifted by bird ("Captain Grant's Children") . . . . 3·00 3·25
2343 $5 Mickey with seal and squid ("Twenty Thousand Leagues Under the Sea") 4·25 5·00
MS2344 Two sheets, each 124×99 mm. (a) $6 Mickey on "Nautilus" ("Twenty Thousand Leagues Under the Sea"). (b) $6 Mickey and Donald on raft ("A Journey to the Centre of the Earth") Set of 2 sheets . . . . 11·50 11·50

363 Bruce Lee

1996. "CHINA '96" 9th Asian International Stamp Exhibition, Peking. Bruce Lee (actor). Multicoloured.
2345 75c. Type **363** 70 70
2346 75c. Bruce Lee in white shirt and red tie 70 70
2347 75c. In plaid jacket and tie 70 70
2348 75c. In mask and uniform 70 70
2349 75c. Bare-chested 70 70
2350 75c. In mandarin jacket . . 70 70
2351 75c. In brown jumper . . . 70 70
2352 75c. In fawn shirt 70 70
2353 75c. Shouting 70 70
MS2354 76×106 mm. $5 Bruce Lee 3·75 4·00

364 Queen Elizabeth II

1996. 70th Birthday of Queen Elizabeth II. Multicoloured.
2355 $2 Type **364** . . . . 1·25 1·50
2356 $2 With bouquet . . . . . 1·25 1·50
2357 $2 In Garter robes . . . . 1·25 1·50
MS2358 96×111 mm. $6 Wearing white dress . . . . 5·50 6·00

365 Ancient Egyptian Cavalryman

1996. Cavalry through the Ages. Multicoloured.
2359 60c. Type **365** 50 55
2360 60c. 13th-century English knight 50 55
2361 60c. 16th-century Spanish lancer 50 55
2362 60c. 18th-century Chinese cavalryman 50 55
MS2363 100×70 mm. $6 19th-century French cuirassier 3·25 3·75

366 Girl in Red Sari

367 Tomb of Zachariah and "Verbascum sinuatum"

1996. 50th Anniv of UNICEF Multicoloured.
2364 75c. Type **366** 60 60
2365 90c. South American mother and child 70 70
2366 $1.20 Nurse with child . . . 90 1·00
MS2367 114×74 mm. $6 Chinese child . . . . 3·25 3·75

1996. 3000th Anniv of Jerusalem. Multicoloured.
2368 75c. Type **367** 65 65
2369 90c. Pool of Siloam and "Hyacinthus orientalis" 75 75
2370 $1.20 Hurva Synagogue and "Ranunculus asiaticus" 1·10 1·10
MS2371 66×80 mm. $6 Model of Herrod's Temple and "Cerics siliquastrum" . . . . 5·50 5·50

368 Kate Smith

1996. Cent of Radio. Entertainers. Mult.
2372 65c. Type **368** 50 50
2373 75c. Dinah Shore 60 60
2374 90c. Rudy Vallee 70 70
2375 $1.20 Bing Crosby . . . . 90 1·00
MS2376 72×104 mm. $6 Jo Stafford (28×42 mm) . . . . 3·25 3·75

369 "Madonna Enthroned"

1996. Christmas. Religious Paintings by Filippo Lippi. Multicoloured.
2377 60c. Type **369** 70 40
2378 90c. "Adoration of the Child and Saints" . . . 80 55
2379 $1 "The Annunciation" . . 95 70
2380 $1.20 "Birth of the Virgin" 1·10 1·10
2381 $1.60 "Adoration of the Child" . . . . 1·50 1·75
2382 $1.75 "Madonna and Child" 1·75 2·00
MS2383 Two sheets, each 76×106 mm. (a) $6 "Madonna and Child" (different). (b) $6 "The Circumcision" Set of 2 sheets 10·00 11·00

370 Robert Preston ("The Music Man")

1997. Broadway Musical Stars. Multicoloured.
2384 $1 Type **370** 90 90
2385 $1 Michael Crawford ("Phantom of the Opera") 90 90
2386 $1 Zero Mostel ("Fiddler on the Roof") 90 90
2387 $1 Patti Lupone ("Evita") 90 90
2388 $1 Raul Julia ("Threepenny Opera") 90 90
2389 $1 Mary Martin ("South Pacific") 90 90
2390 $1 Carol Channing ("Hello Dolly") 90 90
2391 $1 Yul Brynner ("The King and I") 90 90
2392 $1 Julie Andrews ("My Fair Lady") 90 90
MS2393 106×76 mm. $6 Mickey Rooney ("Sugar Babies") . . . 4·00 5·00

371 Goofy and Wilbur

1997. Walt Disney Cartoon Characters. Mult.
2394 1c. Type **371** 10 10
2395 2c. Donald and Goofy in boxing ring 10 10
2396 5c. Donald, Panchito and Jose Carioca 10 10
2397 10c. Mickey and Goofy playing chess 20 15
2398 15c. Chip and Dale with acorns 20 15
2399 20c. Pluto and Mickey . . . 20 15
2400 $1 Daisy and Minnie eating ice-cream 90 75
2401 $2 Daisy and Minnie at dressing table . . . . . . 1·50 1·75
2402 $3 Gus Goose and Donald 2·00 2·50
MS2403 Two sheets. (a) 102×127 mm. $6 Goofy. (b) 127×102 mm. Donald Duck playing guitar (vert) Set of 2 sheets 8·00 8·50

372 Charlie Chaplin as Young Man

1997. 20th Death Anniv of Charlie Chaplin (film star). Multicoloured.
2404 $1 Type **372** 70 70
2405 $1 Pulling face 70 70
2406 $1 Looking over shoulder 70 70
2407 $1 In cap 70 70
2408 $1 In front of star 70 70
2409 $1 In "The Great Dictator" 70 70
2410 $1 With movie camera and megaphone 70 70
2411 $1 Standing in front of camera lens 70 70
2412 $1 Putting on make-up . . . 70 70
MS2413 76×106 mm. $6 Charlie Chaplin . . . . 4·00 4·25

Nos. 2404/12 were printed together, se-tenant, with the backgrounds forming a composite design.

373 "Charaxes porthos"

1997. Butterflies. Multicoloured.
2414 90c. Type **373** 65 50
2415 $1.10 "Charaxes protoclea protoclea" 70 80
2416 $1.10 "Byblia ilithyia" . . . 70 80
2417 $1.10 Black-headed tchagra (bird) 70 80
2418 $1.10 "Charaxes nobilis" . . 70 80
2419 $1.10 "Pseudacraea boisduvali trimeni" . . . 70 80
2420 $1.10 "Charaxes smaragdalis" 70 80
2421 $1.10 "Charaxes lasti" . . . 70 80
2422 $1.10 "Pseudacrea poggei" 70 80
2423 $1.10 "Graphium colonna" 70 80
2424 $1.10 Carmine bee eater (bird) 70 80
2425 $1.10 "Pseudacraea eurytus" 70 80
2426 $1.10 "Hypolimnas monteironis" 70 80
2427 $1.10 "Charaxes anticlea" 70 80
2428 $1.10 "Graphium leonidas" 70 80
2429 $1.10 "Graphium illyris" . . 70 80
2430 $1.10 "Nephronia argia" . . 70 80
2431 $1.10 "Graphium policenes" 70 80
2432 $1.10 "Papilio dardanus" . . 70 80
2433 $1.20 "Aethiopana honorius" 70 80
2434 $1.60 "Charaxes hadrianus" 1·00 1·10
2435 $1.75 "Precis westermanni" 1·25 1·40
MS2436 Three sheets, each 106×76 mm. (a) $6 "Charaxes lactitinctus" (horiz). (b) $6 "Eupheadra neophron". (c) $6 "Euxanthe tiberius" (horiz) Set of 3 sheets . . . . 11·00 13·00

Nos. 2415/23 and 2424/32 respectively were printed together, se-tenant, with the backgrounds forming a composite design.
No. 2430 is inscribed "Nepheronia argia" in error.

374 Convent of The Companions of Jesus, Morelia, Mexico

1997. 50th Anniv of UNESCO Multicoloured.
2437 60c. Type **374** 60 35
2438 90c. Fortress at San Lorenzo, Panama (vert) 70 50
2439 $1 Canaima National Park, Venezuela (vert) 80 55
2440 $1.10 Aerial view of church with tower, Guanajuato, Mexico (vert) 80 90
2441 $1.10 Church facade, Guanajuato, Mexico (vert) 80 90
2442 $1.10 Aerial view of churches with domes, Guanajuato, Mexico (vert) 80 90
2443 $1.10 Jesuit Missions of the Chiquitos, Bolivia (vert) 80 90
2444 $1.10 Huascaran National Park, Peru (vert) 80 90
2445 $1.10 Jesuit Missions of La Santisima, Paraguay (vert) 80 90
2446 $1.10 Cartagena, Colombia (vert) 80 90
2447 $1.10 Fortification, Havana, Cuba (vert) 80 90
2448 $1.20 As No. 2444 (vert) . . 85 90
2449 $1.60 Church of San Fransisco, Guatemala (vert) . . . . 1·25 1·40
2450 $1.65 Tikal National Park, Guatemala . . . . . . 1·50 1·60
2451 $1.65 Rio Platano Reserve, Honduras . . . . . . 1·50 1·60
2452 $1.65 Ruins of Copan, Honduras . . . . 1·50 1·60
2453 $1.65 Antigua ruins, Guatemala . . . . 1·50 1·60
2454 $1.65 Teotihuacan, Mexico 1·50 1·60
2455 $1.75 Santo Domingo, Dominican Republic (vert) 1·60 1·75
MS2456 Two sheets, each 127 × 102 mm. (a) $6 Tikal National Park, Guatemala. (b) $6 Teotihuacan pyramid, Mexico Set of 2 sheets . . . . 9·00 9·50
No. 2446 is inscribed "Columbia" in error.

375 Red Bishop

1997. Endangered Species. Multicoloured.
2457 $1.20 Type **375** . . . . . 1·25 1·25
2458 $1.20 Yellow baboon . . . 1·25 1·25
2459 $1.20 Superb starling . . . 1·25 1·25
2460 $1.20 Ratel . . . . 1·25 1·25
2461 $1.20 Hunting dog . . . . 1·25 1·25
2462 $1.20 Serval . . . . 1·25 1·25
2463 $1.65 Okapi . . . . 1·40 1·40
2464 $1.65 Giant forest squirrel 1·40 1·40
2465 $1.65 Lesser masked weaver 1·40 1·40
2466 $1.65 Small-spotted genet 1·40 1·40
2467 $1.65 Yellow-billed stork . . 1·40 1·40
2468 $1.65 Red-headed agama . . 1·40 1·40
MS2469 Three sheets, each 106 × 76 mm. (a) $6 South African crowned crane. (b) $6 Bat-eared fox. (c) $6 Malachite kingfisher Set of 3 sheets . . . . . . 14·00 15·00
Nos. 2457/62 and 2463/8 respectively were printed together, se-tenant, with the backgrounds forming composite designs.

376 Child's Face and UNESCO Emblem

1997. 10th Anniv of Chernobyl Nuclear Disaster. Multicoloured.
2470 $1.65 Type **376** . . . . . . 1·25 1·40
2471 $2 As Type **376**, but inscr "CHABAD'S CHILDREN OF CHERNOBYL" at foot 1·50 1·60

377 Paul Harris and James Grant

1997. 50th Death Anniv of Paul Harris (founder of Rotary International).
2472 $1.75 Type **377** . . . . . . 1·25 1·50
MS2473 78 × 107 mm. $6 Group study exchange, New Zealand 3·50 4·00

378 Queen Elizabeth II

1997. Golden Wedding of Queen Elizabeth and Prince Philip. Multicoloured.
2474 $1 Type **378** . . . . 1·00 1·00
2475 $1 Royal coat of arms . . . 1·00 1·00
2476 $1 Queen Elizabeth and Prince Philip at reception 1·00 1·00
2477 $1 Queen Elizabeth and Prince Philip in landau . . 1·00 1·00
2478 $1 Balmoral . . . . 1·00 1·00
2479 $1 Prince Philip . . . . . . 1·00 1·00
MS2480 100 × 71 mm. $6 Queen Elizabeth with Prince Philip in naval uniform . . . . 4·00 4·50

379 Kaiser Wilhelm I and Heinrich von Stephan

1997. "Pacific '97" International Stamp Exhibition, San Francisco. Death Centenary of Heinrich von Stephan (founder of the U.P.U.).
2481 **379** $1.75 blue . . . . 1·10 1·40
2482 – $1.75 brown . . . . . . 1·10 1·40
2483 – $1.75 mauve . . . . . . 1·10 1·40
MS2484 82 × 119 mm. $6 violet 3·75 4·50
DESIGNS: No. 2482, Von Stephan and Mercury; 2483, Carrier pigeon and loft; **MS**2484, Von Stephan and 15th-century Basle messenger.
No. 2483 is inscribed "PIDGEON" in error.

380 The Two Ugly Sisters and their Mother

1997. 175th Anniv of Brothers Grimm's Third Collection of Fairy Tales. Cinderella. Multicoloured.
2485 $1.75 Type **380** . . . . . . 1·40 1·50
2486 $1.75 Cinderella and her Fairy Godmother . . . . 1·40 1·50
2487 $1.75 Cinderella and the Prince . . . . 1·40 1·50
MS2488 124 × 96 mm. $6 Cinderella trying on slipper . . . . 4·00 4·50

381 "Marasmius rotula"

1997. Fungi. Multicoloured.
2489 45c. Type **381** 50 30
2490 65c. "Cantharellus cibarius" 60 40
2491 70c. "Lepiota cristata" . . . 60 40
2492 90c. "Auricularia mesenteric" 70 50
2493 $1 "Pholiota alnicola" . . . 75 55
2494 $1.65 "Leccinum aurantiacum" . . . . . . 1·10 1·25
2495 $1.75 "Entoloma serrulatum" . . . . . . 1·25 1·40
2496 $1.75 "Panaeolus sphinctrinus" . . . . . . 1·25 1·40
2497 $1.75 "Volvariella bombycina" . . . . . . 1·25 1·40
2498 $1.75 "Conocybe percincta" . . 1·25 1·40
2499 $1.75 "Pluteus cervinus" . . 1·25 1·40
2500 $1.75 "Russula foetens" . . 1·25 1·40
MS2501 Two sheets, each 106 × 76 mm. (a) $6 "Amanita cothurnata". (b) $6 "Panellus serotinus" Set of 2 sheets . . . 7·50 8·50

382 "Odontoglossum cervantesii"

1997. Orchids of the World. Multicoloured.
2502 45c. Type **382** 50 30
2503 65c. "Phalaenopsis" Medford Star 60 40
2504 75c. "Vanda Motes" Resplendent 65 45
2505 90c. "Odontonia" Debutante 70 50
2506 $1 "Iwanagaara" Apple Blossom 75 55
2507 $1.65 "Cattleya" Sophia Martin . . . . 1·10 1·25
2508 $1.65 Dogface Butterfly . . 1·10 1·25
2509 $1.65 "Laeliocattleya" Mini Purple . . . . 1·10 1·25
2510 $1.65 "Cymbidium" Showgirl . . . . 1·10 1·25
2511 $1.65 "Brassolaeliocattleya" Dorothy Bertsch . . . . 1·10 1·25
2512 $1.65 "Disa Blackii" . . . . 1·10 1·25
2513 $1.65 "Paphiopedilum leeanum" . . . . 1·10 1·25
2514 $1.65 "Paphiopedilum macranthum" . . . . . . 1·10 1·25
2515 $1.65 "Brassocattleya" Angel Lace . . . . 1·10 1·25
2516 $1.65 "Saphrolae liocattleya" Precious Stones . . . . 1·10 1·25
2517 $1.65 Orange Theope Butterfly . . . . 1·10 1·25
2518 $1.65 "Promenaea xanthina" 1·10 1·25
2519 $1.65 "Lycaste macrobulbon" . . . . . 1·10 1·25
2520 $1.65 "Amestella philippinensis" . . . . . 1·10 1·25
2521 $1.65 "Masdevallia" Machu Picchu . . . . 1·10 1·25
2522 $1.65 "Phalaenopsis" Zuma Urchin . . . . 1·10 1·25
2523 $2 "Dendrobium victoria-reginae" . . . . 1·40 1·60
MS2524 Two sheets, each 76 × 106 mm. (a) "Mitonia" Seine. (b) "Pouphiopedilum gratrixanum" Set of 2 sheets 7·50 8·50
Nos. 2507/14 and 2515/22 respectively were printed together, se-tenant, with the backgrounds forming composite designs.

383 Maradona holding World Cup Trophy, 1986

1997. World Cup Football Championship, France (1998).
2525 **383** 60c. multicoloured . . . 50 35
2526 – 75c. brown 60 45
2527 – 90c. multicoloured . . . 70 50
2528 – $1 brown 75 75
2529 – $1 brown 75 75
2530 – $1 brown 75 75
2531 – $1 black 75 75
2532 – $1 brown 75 75
2533 – $1 brown 75 75
2534 – $1 brown 75 75
2535 – $1 brown 75 75
2536 – $1.20 multicoloured . . 75 75
2537 – $1.65 multicoloured . . 1·10 1·25
2538 – $1.75 multicoloured . . 1·10 1·40
MS2539 Two sheets, each 102 × 127 mm. (a) $6 multicoloured. (b) $6 mult Set of 2 sheets . . . . 7·50 8·50
DESIGNS—HORIZ: No. 2526, Fritzwalter, West Germany, 1954; 2527, Zoff, Italy, 1982; 2536, Moore, England, 1966; 2537, Alberto, Brazil, 1970; 2538, Matthaus, West Germany, 1990; **MS**2539 (b) West German players celebrating, 1990. VERT: No. 2528, Ademir, Brazil, 1950; 2529, Eusebio, Portugal, 1966; 2530, Fontaine, France, 1958; 2531, Schillaci, Italy, 1990; 2532, Leonidas, Brazil, 1938; 2533, Stabile, Argentina, 1930; 2534, Nejedly, Czechoslovakia, 1934; 2535, Muller, West Germany, 1970; **MS**2539 (a) Bebeto, Brazil.

384 Scottish Fold Kitten

1997. Cats and Dogs. Multicoloured.
2540 $1.65 Type **384** . . . . . . 1·40 1·25
2541 $1.65 Japanese bobtail . . . 1·40 1·25
2542 $1.65 Tabby manx . . . . 1·40 1·25
2543 $1.65 Bicolor American shorthair . . . . 1·40 1·25
2544 $1.65 Sorrel Abyssinian . . 1·40 1·25
2545 $1.65 Himalayan blue point 1·40 1·25
2546 $1.65 Dachshund . . . . . 1·40 1·25
2547 $1.65 Staffordshire terrier 1·40 1·25
2548 $1.65 Shar-pei . . . . . . 1·40 1·25
2549 $1.65 Beagle . . . . 1·40 1·25
2550 $1.65 Norfolk terrier . . . 1·40 1·25
2551 $1.65 Golden retriever . . . 1·40 1·25
MS2552 Two sheets, each 107 × 77 mm. (a) $6 Red tabby (vert). (b) $6 Siberian husky (vert) Set of 2 sheets . . . . 7·50 8·50

385 Original Drawing by Trevithick, 1803

1997. Railway Locomotives of the World. Multicoloured.
2553 $1.65 Type **385** . . . . . . 1·40 1·25
2554 $1.65 William Hedley's "Puffing Billy", (1813–14) 1·40 1·25
2555 $1.65 Crampton locomotive of French Nord Railway, 1858 . . . . 1·40 1·25
2556 $1.65 Lawrence Machine Shop locomotive, U.S.A., 1860 . . . . 1·40 1·25
2557 $1.65 Natchez and Hamburg Railway steam locomotive "Mississippi", U.S.A., 1834 . . . . 1·40 1·25
2558 $1.65 Bury "Coppernob" locomotive, Furness Railway, 1846 . . . . . 1·40 1·25
2559 $1.65 David Joy's "Jenny Lind", 1847 . . . . . 1·40 1·25
2560 $1.65 Schenectady Atlantic locomotive, U.S.A., 1899 1·40 1·25
2561 $1.65 Kitsons Class 1800 tank locomotive, Japan, 1881 . . . . 1·40 1·25
2562 $1.65 Pennsylvania Railroad express frieght . . . . . 1·40 1·25
2563 $1.65 Karl Golsdorf's 4 cylinder locomotive, Austria . . . . 1·40 1·25
2564 $1.65 Series "E" locomotive, Russia, 1930 . . . . . 1·40 1·25
MS2565 Two sheets, each 72 × 100 mm. (a) $6 George Stephenson "Patentee" type locomotive, 1843. (b) $6 Brunel's trestle bridge over River Lynher, Cornwall Set of 2 sheets . . . 7·50 8·50
No. 2554 is dated "1860" in error.

386 "The Angel leaving Tobias and his Family" (Rembrandt)

1997. Christmas. Religious Paintings. Multicoloured.
2566 15c. Type **386** 20 15
2567 25c. "The Resurrection" (Martin Knoller) 30 20
2568 60c. "Astronomy" (Raphael) 50 40
2569 75c. "Music-making Angel" (Melozzo da Forli) . . . 60 55
2570 90c. "Amor" (Parmigianino) 70 60

2571 $1.20 "Madonna and Child with Saints" (Rosso Fiorentino) 80 85
MS2572 Two sheets, each 105 × 96 mm. (a) $6 "The Wedding of Tobias" (Gianantonio and Francesco Guardi) (horiz). (b) $6 "The Portinari Altarpiece" (Hugo van der Goes) (horiz) Set of 2 sheets . . . . 7·50 8·50

387 Diana, Princess of Wales

1998. Diana, Princess of Wales Commemoration. Multicoloured (except Nos. 2574 and 2581/2).
2573 $1.65 Type **387** . . . . . . 1·10 1·10
2574 $1.65 Wearing hoop earrings (red and black) . . . 1·10 1·10
2575 $1.65 Carrying bouquet . . 1·10 1·10
2576 $1.65 Wearing floral hat . . 1·10 1·10
2577 $1.65 With Prince Harry . . 1·10 1·10
2578 $1.65 Wearing white jacket 1·10 1·10
2579 $1.65 In kitchen . . . . . . 1·10 1·10
2580 $1.65 Wearing black and white dress . . . . 1·10 1·10
2581 $1.65 Wearing hat (brown and black) . . . . . . 1·10 1·10
2582 $1.65 Wearing floral print dress (brown and black) 1·10 1·10
2583 $1.65 Dancing with John Travolta . . . . 1·10 1·10
2584 $1.65 Wearing white hat and jacket . . . . 1·10 1·10
MS2585 Two sheets, each 70 × 100 mm. (a) $6 Wearing red jumper. (b) $6 Wearing black dress for papal audience (brown and black) Set of 2 sheets . . . . . 7·50 8·00

388 Yellow Damselfish

1998. Fishes. Multicoloured.
2586 75c. Type **388** 55 40
2587 90c. Barred hamlet 65 50
2588 $1 Yellow-tailed damselfish ("Jewelfish") 70 55
2589 $1.20 Blue-headed wrasse . . 75 60
2590 $1.50 Queen angelfish . . . 85 85
2591 $1.65 Jackknife-fish 90 95
2592 $1.65 Spot-finned hogfish . . 90 95
2593 $1.65 Sergeant major . . . 90 95
2594 $1.65 Neon goby 90 95
2595 $1.65 Jawfish 90 95
2596 $1.65 Flamefish 90 95
2597 $1.65 Rock beauty 90 95
2598 $1.65 Yellow-tailed snapper 90 95
2599 $1.65 Creole wrasse 90 95
2600 $1.65 Slender filefish . . . 90 95
2601 $1.65 Long-spined squirrelfish 90 95
2602 $1.65 Royal gramma ("Fairy Basslet") . . . 90 95
2603 $1.75 Queen triggerfish . . . 1·00 1·10
MS2604 Two sheets, each 80 × 110 mm. (a) $6 Porkfish. (b) $6 Black-capped basslet Set of 2 sheets . . . . 7·50 8·50
Nos. 2591/6 and 2597/2602 respectively were printed together, se-tenant, with the backgrounds forming composite designs.

389 First Church and Manse, 1822–40

1998. 175th Anniv of Cedar Hall Moravian Church. Multicoloured.
2605 20c. Type **389** 20 20
2606 45c. Cedar Hall School, 1840 . . . . 35 30
2607 75c. Hugh A. King, minister 1945–53 . . . . 55 45
2608 90c. Present Church building 65 50
2609 $1.20 Water tank, 1822 . . 75 65
2610 $2 Former Manse, demolished 1978 . . . . 1·25 1·50
MS2611 100 × 70 mm. $6 Present church building (different) (50 × 37 mm.) . . . . 3·25 4·00

390 Europa Point Lighthouse, Gibraltar
391 Pooh and Tigger (January)

1998. Lighthouses of the World. Multicoloured.
2612 45c. Type **390** 50 40
2613 65c. Tierra del Fuego, Argentina (horiz) 60 40
2614 75c. Point Loma, California, U.S.A. (horiz) 70 45
2615 90c. Groenpoint, Cape Town, South Africa . . . 80 45
2616 $1 Youghal, Cork, Ireland 85 55
2617 $1.20 Launceston, Tasmania, Australia . . . 90 75
2618 $1.65 Point Abino, Ontario, Canada (horiz) . . . . . 1·25 1·50
2619 $1.75 Great Inagua, Bahamas . . . . 1·40 1·75
MS2620 99 × 70 mm. $6 Cap Hatteras, North Carolina, U.S.A. 5·00 5·50
No. 2613 is inscribed "Terra Del Fuego" in error.

1998. Through the Year with Winnie the Pooh. Multicoloured.
2621 $1 Type **391** 85 85
2622 $1 Pooh and Piglet indoors (February) 85 85
2623 $1 Piglet hang-gliding with scarf (March) 85 85
2624 $1 Tigger, Pooh and Piglet on pond (April) 85 85
2625 $1 Kanga and Roo with posy of flowers (May) . . 85 85
2626 $1 Pooh on balloon and Owl (June) 85 85
2627 $1 Pooh, Eeyore, Tigger and Piglet gazing at stars (July) 85 85
2628 $1 Pooh and Piglet by stream (August) 85 85
2629 $1 Christopher Robin going to school (September) . . 85 85
2630 $1 Eeyore in fallen leaves (October) 85 85
2631 $1 Pooh and Rabbit gathering pumpkins (November) 85 85
2632 $1 Pooh and Piglet skiing (December) 85 85
MS2633 Four sheets, each 126 × 101 mm. (a) $6 Pooh, Rabbit and Piglet with blanket (Spring). (b) $6 Pooh by pond (Summer). (c) $6 Pooh sweeping fallen leaves (Autumn). (d) $6 Pooh and Eeyore on ice (Winter) Set of 4 sheets 16·00 16·00

392 Miss Nellie Robinson (founder)

1998. Centenary of Thomas Oliver Robinson Memorial School.
2634 **392** 20c. green and black . . 20 15
2635 – 45c. multicoloured . . . 40 25
2636 – 65c. green and black . . 55 45
2637 – 75c. multicoloured . . . 60 55
2638 – 90c. multicoloured . . . 70 60
2639 – $1.20 brown, green and black . . . . 90 1·10
MS2640 106 × 76 mm. $6 brown 3·25 3·75
DESIGNS—HORIZ: 45c. School photo, 1985; 65c. Former school building, 1930–49; 75c. Children with Mrs. Natalie Hurst (present headmistress); $1.20, Present school building, 1950. VERT: 90c. Miss Ina Loving (former teacher); $6 Miss Nellie Robinson (different).

393 Spotted Eagle Ray

1998. International Year of the Ocean. Multicoloured.
2641/65 40c. × 25 Type **393**; Manta ray; Hawksbill turtle; Jellyfish; Queen angelfish; Octopus; Emperor angelfish; Regal angelfish; Porkfish; Racoon butterflyfish; Atlantic barracuda; Sea horse; Nautilus; Trumpetfish; White tip shark; Sunken Spanish galleon; Black-tip shark; Long-nosed butterflyfish; Green moray eel; Captain Nemo; Treasure chest; Hammerhead shark; Divers; Lionfish; Clownfish . . . . . .
2666/77 75c. × 12 Maroon-tailed conure; Cocoi heron; Common tern; Rainbow lory ("Rainbow Lorikeet"); Saddleback butterflyfish; Goatfish and cat shark; Blue shark and stingray; Majestic snapper; Nassau grouper; Black-cap gramma and blue tang; Stingrays; Stingrays and giant starfish . . . . . .
2641/77 Set of 37 . . . . 12·00 14·00
MS2678 Two sheets. (a) 68 × 98 mm. $6 Humpback whale. (b) 98 × 68 mm. $6 Fiddler ray Set of 2 sheets . . . . 7·00 7·50
Nos. 2641/65 and 2666/77 respectively were printed together, se-tenant, with the backgrounds forming composite designs.

394 "Savannah" (paddle-steamer)

1998. Ships of the World. Multicoloured.
2679 $1.75 Type **394** . . . . . . 1·25 1·40
2680 $1.75 Viking longship . . . 1·25 1·40
2681 $1.75 Greek galley . . . . 1·25 1·40
2682 $1.75 Sailing clipper . . . . 1·25 1·40
2683 $1.75 Dhow . . . . 1·25 1·40
2684 $1.75 Fishing catboat . . . 1·25 1·40
MS2685 Three sheets, each 100 × 70 mm. (a) $6 13th-century English warship (41 × 22 mm). (b) $6 Sailing dory (22 × 41 mm). (c) $6 Baltimore clipper (41 × 22 mm) Set of 3 sheets . . . . 11·00 12·00

395 Flags of Antigua and CARICOM

1998. 25th Anniv of Caribbean Community.
2686 **395** $1 multicoloured . . . . 1·25 1·25

396 Ford, 1896

1998. Classic Cars. Multicoloured.
2687 $1.65 Type **396** . . . . . . 1·00 1·10
2688 $1.65 Ford A, 1903 . . . . 1·00 1·10
2689 $1.65 Ford T, 1928 . . . . 1·00 1·10
2690 $1.65 Ford T, 1922 . . . . 1·00 1·10
2691 $1.65 Ford Blackhawk, 1929 1·00 1·10
2692 $1.65 Ford Sedan, 1934 . . 1·00 1·10
2693 $1.65 Torpedo, 1911 . . . . 1·00 1·10
2694 $1.65 Mercedes 22, 1913 . . 1·00 1·10
2695 $1.65 Rover, 1920 . . . . . 1·00 1·10
2696 $1.65 Mercedes-Benz, 1956 1·00 1·10
2697 $1.65 Packard V-12, 1934 1·00 1·10
2698 $1.65 Opel, 1924 . . . . . 1·00 1·10
MS2699 Two sheets, each 70 × 100 mm. (a) $6 Ford, 1908 (60 × 40 mm). (b) $6 Ford, 1929 (60 × 40 mm) Set of 2 sheets . . 7·50 8·00

397 Lockheed-Boeing General Dynamics Yf-22

1998. Modern Aircraft. Multicoloured.
2700 $1.65 Type **397** . . . . . . 1·10 1·25
2701 $1.65 Dassault-Breguet Rafale BO 1 . . . . . . 1·10 1·25
2702 $1.65 MiG 29 . . . . 1·10 1·25
2703 $1.65 Dassault-Breguet Mirage 2000D . . . . . 1·10 1·25
2704 $1.65 Rockwell B-1B "Lancer" . . . . 1·10 1·25
2705 $1.65 McDonnell-Douglas C-17A . . . . 1·10 1·25
2706 $1.65 Space Shuttle . . . . 1·10 1·25
2707 $1.65 SAAB "Grippen" . . 1·10 1·25
2708 $1.65 Eurofighter EF-2000 1·10 1·25
2709 $1.65 Sukhoi SU 27 . . . . 1·10 1·25
2710 $1.65 Northrop B-2 . . . . 1·10 1·25
2711 $1.65 Lockheed F-117 "Nighthawk" . . . . . . 1·10 1·25
MS2712 Two sheets, each 110 × 85 mm. (a) $6 F18 Hornet. (b) $6 Sukhoi SU 35 Set of 2 sheets 7·50 8·00
No. **MS**2712b is inscribed "Sukhi" in error.

398 Karl Benz (internal-combustion engine)
399 Stylized Americas

1998. Millennium Series. Famous People of the Twentieth Century. Inventors. Multicoloured.
2713 $1 Type **398** 80 80
2714 $1 Early Benz car and Mercedes-Benz racing car (53 × 38 mm) 80 80
2715 $1 Atom bomb mushroom cloud (53 × 38 mm) . . . 80 80
2716 $1 Albert Einstein (theory of relativity) 80 80
2717 $1 Leopold Godowsky Jr. and Leopold Damrosch Mannes (Kodachrome film) 80 80
2718 $1 Camera and transparencies (53 × 38 mm) 80 80
2719 $1 Heinkel He 178 (first turbo jet plane) (53 × 38 mm) 80 80
2720 $1 Dr. Hans Pabst von Ohain (jet turbine engine) 80 80
2721 $1 Rudolf Diesel (diesel engine) 80 80
2722 $1 Early Diesel engine and forms of transport (53 × 38 mm) 80 80
2723 $1 Zeppelin airship (53 × 38 mm) 80 80
2724 $1 Count Ferdinand von Zeppelin (airship pioneer) 80 80
2725 $1 Wilhelm Conrad Rontgen (X-rays) 80 80
2726 $1 X-ray of hand (53 × 38 mm) 80 80
2727 $1 Launch of Saturn rocket (53 × 38 mm) 80 80
2728 $1 Wernher von Braun (rocket research) 80 80
MS2729 Two sheets, each 106 × 76 mm. (a) $6 Hans Geiger (Geiger counter). (b) $6 William Shockley (research into semi-conductors) Set of 2 sheets . . 7·50 8·00
No. 2713 is inscribed "CARL BENZ" in error.

1998. 50th Anniv of Organization of American States.
2730 **399** $1 multicoloured 70 70

400 "Figures on the Seashore"

1998. 25th Death Anniv of Pablo Picasso (painter). Multicoloured.
2731 $1.20 Type **400** 75 70
2732 $1.65 "Three Figures under a Tree" (vert) 85 90
2733 $1.75 "Two Women running on the Beach" . . . . . 95 1·10
MS2734 126 × 102 mm. $6 "Bullfight" . . . . 3·25 3·50

401 Dino 246 GT-GTS

1998. Birth Centenary of Enzo Ferrari (car manufacturer). Multicoloured.
2735 $1.75 Type **401** . . . . . . 2·25 2·25
2736 $1.75 Front view of Dino 246 GT-GTS . . . . . . 2·25 2·25
2737 $1.75 365 GT4 BB . . . . 2·25 2·25
MS2738 104 × 72 mm. $6 Dino 246 GT-GTS (91 × 34 mm) . . . . 6·00 6·00

402 Scout Handshake

1998. 19th World Scout Jamboree, Chile. Multicoloured.
2739 90c. Type **402** 60 55
2740 $1 Scouts hiking 75 70
2741 $1.20 Scout salute . . . . . 90 1·10
MS2742 68 × 98 mm. $6 Lord Baden-Powell . . . . 3·25 3·50

403 Mahatma Gandhi 405 Diana, Princess of Wales

404 McDonnell Douglas Phantom F-GR1

1998. 50th Death Anniv of Mahatma Gandhi. Multicoloured.
2743 90c. Type **403** 75 60
2744 $1 Gandhi seated 90 75
2745 $1.20 As young man . . . . . 1·25 1·10
2746 $1.65 At primary school in Rajkot, aged 7 . . . . . 1·75 1·90
MS2747 100 × 70 mm. $6 Gandhi with staff . . . . 3·75 4·00

1998. 80th Anniv of Royal Air Force. Multicoloured.
2748 $1.75 Type **404** . . . . . . 1·25 1·40
2749 $1.75 Two Sepecat Jaguar GR1As . . . . 1·25 1·40
2750 $1.75 Panavia Tornado F3 . . 1·25 1·40
2751 $1.75 McDonnell Douglas Phantom F-GR2 . . . . 1·25 1·40
MS2752 Two sheets, each 90 × 68 mm. (a) $6 Golden eagle (bird) and Bristol F2B Fighter. (b) $6 Hawker Hurricane and EF-2000 Eurofighter Set of 2 sheets . . . . 8·00 8·50

1998. 1st Death Anniv of Diana, Princess of Wales.
2753 **405** $1.20 multicoloured . . 1·00 1·00

406 Brown Pelican

1998. Sea Birds of the World. Multicoloured.
2754 15c. Type **406** 30 20
2755 25c. Dunlin 40 20
2756 45c. Atlantic puffin 50 25
2757 75c. King eider 65 70
2758 75c. Inca tern 65 70
2759 75c. Little auk ("Dovekie") 65 70
2760 75c. Ross's gull 65 70
2761 75c. Common noddy ("Brown Noddy") 65 70
2762 75c. Marbled murrelet . . . 65 70
2763 75c. Northern gannet . . . 65 70
2764 75c. Razorbill 65 70
2765 75c. Long-tailed skua ("Long-tailed Jaegar") . . 65 70
2766 75c. Black guillemot 65 70
2767 75c. Whimbrel 65 70
2768 75c. American oystercatcher ("Oystercatcher") 30 35
2769 90c. Pied cormorant 65 70
MS2770 Two sheets, each 100 × 70 mm. (a) $6 Black skimmer. (b) $6 Wandering albatross Set of 2 sheets . . . 7·50 8·00

Nos. 2757/68 were printed together, se-tenant, with the backgrounds forming a composite design.

No. 2760 is inscribed "ROSS' BULL" in error.

407 Border Collie

1998. Christmas. Dogs. Multicoloured.
2771 15c. Type **407** 30 20
2772 25c. Dalmatian 40 20
2773 65c. Weimaraner 55 40
2774 75c. Scottish terrier 60 40
2775 90c. Long-haired dachshund 70 50
2776 $1.20 Golden retriever . . . 90 90
2777 $2 Pekingese . . . . 1·60 1·90
MS2778 Two sheets, each 75 × 66 mm. (a) $6 Dalmatian. (b) $6 Jack Russell terrier Set of 2 sheets . . . . 7·50 8·00

408 Mickey Mouse Sailing

1999. 70th Birthday of Mickey Mouse. Walt Disney characters participating in water sports. Multicoloured.
2779 $1 Type **408** 80 80
2780 $1 Mickey and Goofy sailing 80 80
2781 $1 Goofy windsurfing . . . 80 80
2782 $1 Mickey sailing and seagull 80 80
2783 $1 Goofy sailing 80 80
2784 $1 Mickey windsurfing . . . 80 80
2785 $1 Goofy running with surfboard 80 80
2786 $1 Mickey surfing 80 80
2787 $1 Donald Duck holding surfboard 80 80
2788 $1 Donald on surfboard (face value at right) . . . 80 80
2789 $1 Minnie Mouse surfing in green shorts 80 80
2790 $1 Goofy surfing 80 80
2791 $1 Goofy in purple shorts waterskiing 80 80
2792 $1 Mickey waterskiing . . . 80 80
2793 $1 Goofy waterskiing with Mickey 80 80
2794 $1 Donald on surfboard (face value at left) 80 80
2795 $1 Goofy in yellow shorts waterskiing 80 80
2796 $1 Minnie in pink shorts surfing 80 80
MS2797 Four sheets, each 127 × 102 mm. (a) $6 Goofy (horiz). (b) $6 Donald Duck. (c) $6 Minnie Mouse. (d) $6 Mickey Mouse Set of 4 sheets . . . . 14·00 15·00

409 Hell's Gate Steel Orchestra, 1996

1999. 50th Anniv of Hell's Gate Steel Orchestra. Multicoloured.
2798 20c. Type **409** 20 15
2799 60c. Orchestra members, New York, 1992 . . . . 40 35
2800 75c. Orchestra members with steel drums, 1950 . . 50 45
2801 90c. Eustace Henry, 1964 . . 60 50
2802 $1.20 Alston Henry playing double tenor . . . . . . 85 1·10
MS2803 Two sheets. (a) 100 × 70 mm. $4 Orchestra members, 1950 (vert). (b) 70 × 100 mm. $4 Eustace Henry, 1964 (vert) Set of 2 sheets . . . 5·50 6·00

410 Tulips 411 Elle Macpherson

1999. Flowers. Multicoloured.
2804 60c. Type **410** 40 30
2805 75c. Fuschia 50 35
2806 90c. Morning glory (horiz) . . 60 60
2807 90c. Geranium (horiz) . . . 60 60
2808 90c. Blue hibiscus (horiz) . . 60 60
2809 90c. Marigolds (horiz) . . . 60 60
2810 90c. Sunflower (horiz) . . . 60 60
2811 90c. Impatiens (horiz) . . . 60 60
2812 90c. Petunia (horiz) 60 60
2813 90c. Pansy (horiz) 60 60
2814 90c. Saucer magnolia (horiz) 60 60
2815 $1 Primrose (horiz) 70 70
2816 $1 Bleeding heart (horiz) . . 70 70
2817 $1 Pink dogwood (horiz) . . 70 70
2818 $1 Peony (horiz) 70 70
2819 $1 Rose (horiz) 70 70
2820 $1 Hellebores (horiz) . . . 70 70
2821 $1 Lily (horiz) 70 70
2822 $1 Violet (horiz) 70 70
2823 $1 Cherry blossom (horiz) . . 70 70
2824 $1.20 Calla lily 75 75
2825 $1.65 Sweet pea . . . . . . 90 1·10
MS2826 Two sheets. (a) 76 × 100 mm. $6 Sangria lily. (b) 106 × 76 mm. $6 Zinnias Set of 2 sheets . . . . 7·50 8·00

Nos. 2806/14 and 2815/23 respectively were each printed together, se-tenant, forming composite designs.

1999. "Australia '99" International Stamp Exhibition, Melbourne (1st issue). Elle Macpherson (model). Multicoloured.
2827 $1.20 Type **411** 75 80
2828 $1.20 Lying on couch . . . 75 80
2829 $1.20 In swimsuit 75 80
2830 $1.20 Looking over shoulder 75 80
2831 $1.20 Wearing cream shirt 75 80
2832 $1.20 Wearing stetson . . . 75 80
2833 $1.20 Wearing black T-shirt 75 80
2834 $1.20 Holding tree branch 75 80

See also Nos. 2875/92.

412 "Luna 2" Moon Probe 413 John Glenn entering "Mercury" Capsule, 1962

1999. Satellites and Spacecraft. Multicoloured.
2835 $1.65 Type **412** . . . . . . 1·10 1·10
2836 $1.65 "Mariner 2" space probe . . . . 1·10 1·10
2837 $1.65 "Giotto" space probe 1·10 1·10
2838 $1.65 Rosat satellite . . . . 1·10 1·10
2839 $1.65 International Ultraviolet Explorer . . . 1·10 1·10
2840 $1.65 "Ulysses" space probe 1·10 1·10
2841 $1.65 "Mariner 10" space probe . . . . 1·10 1·10
2842 $1.65 "Luna 9" Moon probe . . . . 1·10 1·10
2843 $1.65 Advanced X-ray Astrophysics Facility . . 1·10 1·10
2844 $1.65 "Magellan" space probe . . . . 1·10 1·10
2845 $1.65 "Pioneer – Venus 2" space probe . . . . . . 1·10 1·10
2846 $1.65 Infra-red Astronomy Satellite . . . . 1·10 1·10
MS2847 Two sheets, each 106 × 76 mm. (a) $6 "Salyut 1" space station (horiz). (b) $6 "MIR" space station (horiz) Set of 2 sheets . . . . . 7·50 8·00

Nos. 2835/40 and 2841/46 repectively were each printed together, se-tenant, with the backgrounds forming composite designs.

1999. John Glenn's Return to Space. Multicoloured.
2848 $1.75 Type **413** . . . . . . 1·25 1·25
2849 $1.75 Glenn in "Mercury" mission spacesuit . . . . 1·25 1·25
2850 $1.75 Fitting helmet for "Mercury" mission . . . 1·25 1·25
2851 $1.75 Outside pressure chamber . . . . 1·25 1·25

414 Brachiosaurus

1999. Prehistoric Animals. Multicoloured.
2852 65c. Type **414** 65 40
2853 75c. Oviraptor (vert) 70 40
2854 $1 Homotherium 80 45
2855 $1.20 Macrauchenia (vert) 90 60
2856 $1.65 Struthiomimus . . . . 1·00 1·00
2857 $1.65 Corythosaurus . . . . 1·00 1·00
2858 $1.65 Dsungaripterus . . . 1·00 1·00
2859 $1.65 Compsognathus . . . 1·00 1·00
2860 $1.65 Prosaurolophus . . . 1·00 1·00
2861 $1.65 Montanoceratops . . 1·00 1·00
2862 $1.65 Stegosaurus . . . . . 1·00 1·00
2863 $1.65 Deinonychus . . . . . 1·00 1·00
2864 $1.65 Ouranosaurus . . . . 1·00 1·00
2865 $1.65 Leptictidium . . . . 1·00 1·00
2866 $1.65 Ictitherium . . . . . 1·00 1·00
2867 $1.65 Plesictis . . . . . . 1·00 1·00
2868 $1.65 Hemicyon . . . . . . 1·00 1·00
2869 $1.65 Diacodexis . . . . . 1·00 1·00
2870 $1.65 Stylinodon . . . . . 1·00 1·00
2871 $1.65 Kanuites . . . . . . 1·00 1·00
2872 $1.65 Chriacus . . . . . . 1·00 1·00
2873 $1.65 Argyrolagus . . . . . 1·00 1·00
MS2874 Two sheets, each 110 × 85 mm. (a) $6 Eurhinodelphis. (b) $6 Pteranodon Set of 2 sheets . . . . . . 7·50 8·00

Nos. 2856/64 and 2865/73 respectively were each printed together, se-tenant, with the backgrounds forming composite designs.

415 Two White Kittens

1999. "Australia '99" International Stamp Exhibition, Melbourne (2nd issue). Cats. Mult.
2875 35c. Type **415** 30 20
2876 45c. Kitten with string . . . 40 25
2877 60c. Two kittens under blanket 50 35
2878 75c. Two kittens in basket 60 45
2879 90c. Kitten with ball 70 50
2880 $1 White kitten 80 60
2881 $1.65 Two kittens playing 1·00 1·00
2882 $1.65 Black and white kitten 1·00 1·00
2883 $1.65 Black kitten and sleeping cream kitten . . 1·00 1·00
2884 $1.65 White kitten with green string . . . . 1·00 1·00
2885 $1.65 Two sleeping kittens 1·00 1·00
2886 $1.65 White kitten with black tip to tail . . . . . 1·00 1·00
2887 $1.65 Kitten with red string 1·00 1·00
2888 $1.65 Two long-haired kittens . . . . 1·00 1·00
2889 $1.65 Ginger kitten . . . . 1·00 1·00
2890 $1.65 Kitten playing with mouse . . . . 1·00 1·00
2891 $1.65 Kitten asleep on blue cushion . . . . 1·00 1·00
2892 $1.65 Tabby kitten . . . . 1·00 1·00
MS2893 Two sheets, each 70 × 100 mm. (a) $6 Cat carrying kitten in mouth. (b) $6 Kitten in tree Set of 2 sheets . . . . . . 7·50 8·00

416 Early Leipzig–Dresden Railway Carriage and Caroline Islands 1901 Yacht Type 5m. Stamp

1999. "iBRA '99" International Stamp Exhibition, Nuremberg. Multicoloured.
2894 $1 Type **416** 70 60
2895 $1.20 Golsdorf steam locomotive and Caroline Islands 1901 Yacht type 1m. 80 70
2896 $1.65 Early Leipzig–Dresden Railway carriage and Caroline Islands 1899 20pf. optd on Germany 1·00 1·10
2897 $1.90 Golsdorf steam locomotive and Caroline Islands 1901 Yacht type 5pf. and 20pf. . . . . . 1·40 1·75
MS2898 165 × 110 mm. $6 Registration label for Ponape, Caroline Islands . . . . 3·25 3·50

417 "People on Balcony of Sazaido" (Hokusai)

1999. 150th Death Anniv of Katsushika Hokusai (Japanese artist). Multicoloured.

2899	$1.65 Type **417**	1·00	1·00
2900	$1.65 "Nakahara in Sagami Province"	1·00	1·00
2901	$1.65 "Defensive Positions" (two wrestlers)	1·00	1·00
2902	$1.65 "Defensive Positions" (three wrestlers)	1·00	1·00
2903	$1.65 "Mount Fuji in Clear Weather"	1·00	1·00
2904	$1.65 "Nihonbashi in Edo"	1·00	1·00
2905	$1.65 "Asakusa Honganji"	1·00	1·00
2906	$1.65 "Dawn at Isawa in Kai Province"	1·00	1·00
2907	$1.65 "Samurai with Bow and Arrow" (with arrows on ground)	1·00	1·00
2908	$1.65 "Samurai with Bow and Arrow" (trees in background)	1·00	1·00
2909	$1.65 "Kajikazawa in Kai Province"	1·00	1·00
2910	$1.65 "A Great Wave"	1·00	1·00
MS2911	Two sheets, each 100×71 mm. (a) $6 "A Netsuke Workshop" (vert). (b) $6 "Gotenyama at Shinagawa on Tokaido Highway" (vert) Set of 2 sheets	7·50	8·00

No. 2903 is inscribed "MOUNT FUGI" in error.

418 Sophie Rhys-Jones

419 Three Children

1999. Royal Wedding. Multicoloured.

2912	$3 Type **418**	1·75	2·00
2913	$3 Sophie and Prince Edward	1·75	2·00
2914	$3 Prince Edward	1·75	2·00
MS2915	108×78 mm. $6 Prince Edward with Sophie Rhys-Jones and Windsor Castle (horiz)	3·25	3·50

1999. 10th Anniv of United Nations Rights of the Child Convention. Multicoloured.

2916	$3 Type **419**	1·75	2·00
2917	$3 Adult hand holding child's hand	1·75	2·00
2918	$3 Dove and U.N. Headquarters	1·75	2·00
MS2919	112×70 mm. $6 Dove	3·25	3·50

Nos. 2916/18 were printed together, se-tenant, forming a composite design.

420 Crampton Type Railway Locomotive, 1855–69

1999. "PhilexFrance '99" International Stamp Exhibition, Paris. Railway Locomotives. Two sheets, each 106×81 mm, containing T **420** and similar design. Multicoloured.

MS2920	(a) $6 Type **420**. (b) $6 Compound type No. 232-U1 steam locomotive, 1949 Set of 2 sheets	7·50	8·00

421 Three Archangels from "Faust"

1999. 250th Birth Anniv of Johann von Goethe (German writer).

2921	**421** $1.75 purple, mauve and black	1·10	1·25
2922	– $1.75 blue, violet and black	1·10	1·25
2923	– $1.75 green and black	1·10	1·25
MS2924	– 79×101 mm. $6 black and brown	3·25	3·50

DESIGNS: No. 2922, Von Goethe and Von Schiller; 2923, Faust reclining with spirits; **MS**2924 Wolfgang von Goethe.

422 "Missa Ferdie" (fishing launch)

423 Fiery Jewel

1999. Local Ships and Boats. Multicoloured.

2925	25c. Type **422**	25	20
2926	45c. Yachts in 32nd Annual Antigua International Sailing Week	40	25
2927	60c. "Jolly Roger" (tourist ship)	50	40
2928	90c. "Freewinds" (cruise liner) (10th anniv of first visit)	70	60
2929	$1.20 "Monarch of the Seas" (cruise liner)	95	1·10
MS2930	98×62 mm. $4 "Freewinds" (11th anniv of maiden voyage) (50×37 mm)	2·75	3·00

1999. Butterflies. Multicoloured.

2931	65c. Type **423**	60	40
2932	75c. Hewitson's blue hairstreak	70	45
2933	$1 California dog face (horiz)	80	80
2934	$1 Small copper (horiz)	80	80
2935	$1 Zebra swallowtail (horiz)	80	80
2936	$1 White "M" hairstreak (horiz)	80	80
2937	$1 Old world swallowtail (horiz)	80	80
2938	$1 Buckeye (horiz)	80	80
2939	$1 Apollo (horiz)	80	80
2940	$1 Sonoran blue (horiz)	80	80
2941	$1 Purple emperor (horiz)	80	80
2942	$1.20 Scarce bamboo page (horiz)	90	90
2943	$1.65 Paris peacock (horiz)	1·25	1·40
MS2944	Two sheets. (a) 85×110 mm. $6 Monarch. (b) 110×85 mm. $6 Cairns birdwing (horiz) Set of 2 sheets	7·50	5·00

Nos. 2933/41 were printed together, se-tenant, forming a composite design.

424 "Madonna and Child in Wreath of Flowers" (Rubens)

1999. Christmas. Religious Paintings.

2945	**424** 15c. multicoloured	20	10
2946	– 25c. black, stone & yellow	25	15
2947	– 45c. multicoloured	40	25
2948	– 60c. multicoloured	50	30
2949	– $2 multicoloured	1·50	1·60
2950	– $4 black, stone & yell	2·75	3·25
MS2951	– 76×106 mm. $6 multicoloured	3·50	3·75

DESIGNS: 25c. "Shroud of Christ held by Two Angels" (Durer); 45c. "Madonna and Child enthroned between Two Saints" (Raphael); 60c. "Holy Family with Lamb" (Raphael); $2 "The Transfiguration" (Raphael); $4 "Three Putti holding Coat of Arms" (Durer); $6 "Coronation of St. Catharine" (Rubens).

425 Katharine Hepburn (actress)

2000. Senior Celebrities of the 20th Century. Mult.

2952	90c. Type **425**	55	55
2953	90c. Martha Graham (dancer)	55	55
2954	90c. Eubie Blake (jazz pianist)	55	55
2955	90c. Agatha Christie (novelist)	55	55
2956	90c. Eudora Welty (American novelist)	55	55
2957	90c. Helen Hayes (actress)	55	55
2958	90c. Vladimir Horowitz (concert pianist)	55	55
2959	90c. Katharine Graham (newspaper publisher)	55	55
2960	90c. Pablo Casals (cellist)	55	55
2961	90c. Pete Seeger (folk singer)	55	55
2962	90c. Andres Segovia (guitarist)	55	55
2963	90c. Frank Lloyd Wright (architect)	55	55

426 Sir Cliff Richard

2000. 60th Birthday of Sir Cliff Richard (entertainer).

2964	**426** $1.65 multicoloured	1·00	1·00

427 Charlie Chaplin

2000. Charlie Chaplin (actor and director) Commemoration. Showing film scenes. Mult.

2965	$1.65 Standing in street (*Modern Times*)	90	90
2966	$1.65 Hugging man (*The Gold Rush*)	90	90
2967	$1.65 Type **427**	90	90
2968	$1.65 Wielding tools (*Modern Times*)	90	90
2969	$1.65 With hands on hips (*The Gold Rush*)	90	90
2970	$1.65 Wearing cape (*The Gold Rush*)	90	90

428 Streamertail

2000. "The Stamp Show 2000" International Stamp Exhibition, London. Birds of the Caribbean. Mult.

2971	75c. Type **428**	50	35
2972	90c. Yellow-bellied sapsucker	60	40
2973	$1.20 Rufous-tailed jacamar	75	75
2974	$1.20 Scarlet macaw	75	75
2975	$1.20 Yellow-crowned amazon ("Yellow-fronted Amazon")	75	75
2976	$1.20 Golden conure ("Queen-of-Bavaria")	75	75
2977	$1.20 Nanday conure	75	75
2978	$1.20 Jamaican tody	75	75
2979	$1.20 Smooth-billed ani	75	75
2980	$1.20 Puerto Rican woodpecker	75	75
2981	$1.20 Ruby-throated hummingbird	75	75
2982	$1.20 Common ground dove	75	75
2983	$1.20 American wood ibis ("Wood Stork")	75	75
2984	$1.20 Saffron finch	75	75
2985	$1.20 Green-backed heron	75	75
2986	$1.20 Lovely cotinga	75	75
2987	$1.20 St. Vincent amazon ("St. Vincent Parrot")	75	75
2988	$1.20 Cuban grassquit	75	75
2989	$1.20 Red-winged blackbird	75	75
2990	$2 Spectacled owl	1·40	1·50
MS2991	Two sheets, each 80×106 mm. (a) $6 Vermillion flycatcher (50×37 mm). (b) $6 Red-capped manakin (37×50 mm) Set of 2 sheets	7·00	7·50

Nos. 2974/81 and 2982/9 were each printed together, se-tenant, with the backgrounds forming composite designs.

No. 2981 is inscribed "Arhilochus colubria" in error.

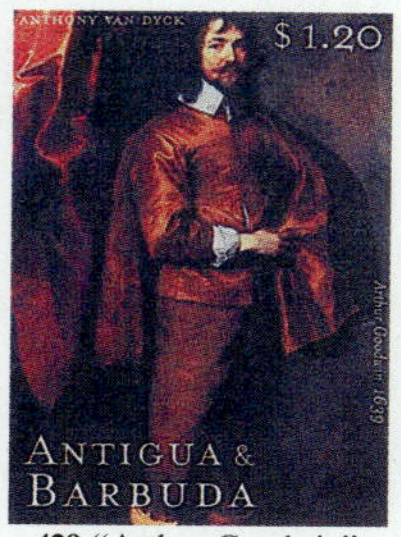

429 "Arthur Goodwin"

2000. 400th Birth Anniv of Sir Anthony Van Dyck (Flemish painter). Multicoloured.

2992	$1.20 Type **429**	75	75
2993	$1.20 "Sir Thomas Wharton"	75	75
2994	$1.20 "Mary Villiers, Daughter of Duke of Buckingham"	75	75
2995	$1.20 "Christina Bruce, Countess of Devonshire"	75	75
2996	$1.20 "James Hamilton, Duke of Hamilton"	75	75
2997	$1.20 "Henry Danvers, Earl of Danby"	75	75
2998	$1.20 "Marie de Raet, Wife of Philippe le Roy"	75	75
2999	$1.20 "Jacomo de Cachiopin"	75	75
3000	$1.20 "Princess Henrietta of Lorraine attended by a Page"	75	75
3001	$1.20 "Portrait of a Man"	75	75
3002	$1.20 "Portrait of a Woman"	75	75
3003	$1.20 "Philippe le Roy, Seigneur de Ravels"	75	75
3004	$1.20 "Charles I in State Robes"	75	75
3005	$1.20 "Queen Henrietta Maria" (in white dress)	75	75
3006	$1.20 "Queen Henrietta Maria with Sir Jeffrey Hudson"	75	75
3007	$1.20 "Charles I in Armour"	75	75
3008	$1.20 "Queen Henrietta Maria in Profile facing right"	75	75
3009	$1.20 "Queen Henrietta Maria" (in black dress)	75	75
MS3010	Six sheets. (a) 102×128 mm. $5 "Charles I on Horseback". (b) 102×128 mm. $5 "Charles I Hunting". (c) 128×102 mm. $5 "Charles I with Queen Henrietta Maria". (d) 128×102 mm. $5 "Charles I" (from Three Aspects portrait). (e) 102×128 mm. $6 "William, Lord Russell". (f) 102×128 mm. $6 "Two Sons of Duke of Lennox" Set of 6 sheets	17·00	19·00

No. 2994 is inscribed "Mary Villers", 3002 "Portrait of a Women", 3005 "Henrieta Maria" and **MS**3010f "Duke of Lenox", all in error.

430 *Eupolea miniszeki*

2000. Butterflies. Multicoloured.

3011	$1.65 Type **430**	90	90
3012	$1.65 *Heliconius doris*	90	90
3013	$1.65 *Evenus coronata*	90	90
3014	$1.65 *Papilio anchisiades*	90	90
3015	$1.65 *Syrmatia dorilas*	90	90
3016	$1.65 *Morpho patroclus*	90	90
3017	$1.65 *Mesosemia loruhama*	90	90
3018	$1.65 *Bia actorion*	90	90
3019	$1.65 *Anteos clorinde*	90	90
3020	$1.65 *Menander menande*	90	90
3021	$1.65 *Catasticta manco*	90	90
3022	$1.65 *Urania leilus*	90	90
3023	$1.65 *Theope eudocia* (vert)	90	90
3024	$1.65 *Uranus sloanus* (vert)	90	90
3025	$1.65 *Helicopis cupido* (vert)	90	90
3026	$1.65 *Papilio velovis* (vert)	90	90
3027	$1.65 *Graphium androcles* (vert)	90	90
3028	$1.65 *Mesene phareus* (vert)	90	90
MS3029	Three sheets. (a) 110×85 mm. $6 *Graphium encelades*. (b) 110×85 mm. $6 *Graphium milon*. (c) 85×110 mm. $6 *Hemlargus isola* (vert) Set of 3 sheets	9·50	10·00

Nos. 3011/16, 3017/22 and 3023/8 were each printed together, se-tenant, with the backgrounds forming composite designs.

431 Boxer

432 *Epidendrum pseudepidendrum*

2000. Cats and Dogs. Multicoloured.
3030 90c. Type **431** 60 40
3031 $1 Alaskan malamute . . . 70 45
3032 $1.65 Bearded collie 90 90
3033 $1.65 Cardigan Welsh corgi 90 90
3034 $1.65 Saluki (red) 90 90
3035 $1.65 Basset hound 90 90
3036 $1.65 White standard poodle 90 90
3037 $1.65 Boston terrier 90 90
3038 $1.65 Long-haired blue and white cat (horiz) 90 90
3039 $1.65 Snow shoe (horiz) . . 90 90
3040 $1.65 Persian (horiz) 90 90
3041 $1.65 Chocolate lynx point (horiz) 90 90
3042 $1.65 Brown and white sphynx (horiz) 90 90
3043 $1.65 White tortoiseshell (horiz) 90 90
3044 $2 Wirehaired pointer . . . 1·10 1·10
3045 $4 Saluki (black) . . . . . 2·00 2·25
MS3046 Two sheets. (a) 106 × 71 mm. $6 Cavalier King Charles spaniel. (b) 111 × 81 mm. $6 Lavender tortie Set of 2 sheets 7·50 8·00

2000. Flowers of the Caribbean. Multicoloured.
3047 45c. Type **432** 35 25
3048 65c. *Odontoglossum cervantesii* 50 30
3049 75c. *Cattleya dowiana* . . . 60 35
3050 90c. *Beloperone guttata* . . 70 40
3051 $1 *Colliandra haematocephala* 75 50
3052 $1.20 *Brassavola nodosa* . . 85 65
3053 $1.65 *Pseudocalymna alliaceum* . . . . 1·00 1·00
3054 $1.65 *Datura candida* . . . 1·00 1·00
3055 $1.65 *Ipomoea tuberosa* . . 1·00 1·00
3056 $1.65 *Allamanda cathartica* . 1·00 1·00
3057 $1.65 *Aspasia epidendroides* 1·00 1·00
3058 $1.65 *Maxillaria cucullata* . 1·00 1·00
3059 $1.65 *Anthurium andreanum* 1·00 1·00
3060 $1.65 *Doxantha unguiscati* . 1·00 1·00
3061 $1.65 *Hibiscus rosa-sinensis* 1·00 1·00
3062 $1.65 *Canna indica* . . . . 1·00 1·00
3063 $1.65 *Heliconius umilis* . . 1·00 1·00
3064 $1.65 *Strelitzia reginae* . . 1·00 1·00
3065 $1.65 *Masdevallia coccinea* . 1·00 1·00
3066 $1.65 *Paphinia cristata* . . 1·00 1·00
3067 $1.65 *Vanilla planifolia* . . 1·00 1·00
3068 $1.65 *Cattleya forbesii* . . 1·00 1·00
3069 $1.65 *Lycaste skinneri* . . . 1·00 1·00
3070 $1.65 *Cattleya percivaliana* 1·00 1·00
MS3071 Three sheets, each 74 × 103 mm. (a) $6 *Cattleya leopoldiie*. (b) $6 *Strelitzia reginae*. (c) $6 *Rossioglossum grande* Set of 3 sheets . . . . 9·50 10·00
No. 3061 is inscribed "rosa-senensis" and **MS**3071b "regenae", both in error.

433 Prince William

2000. 18th Birthday of Prince William. Multicoloured.
3072 $1.65 Prince William waving 1·00 1·00
3073 $1.65 Wearing Eton school uniform . . . . 1·00 1·00
3074 $1.65 Wearing grey suit . . 1·00 1·00
3075 $1.65 Type **433** . . . . . 1·00 1·00
MS3076 100 × 80 mm. $6 Princess Diana with Princes William and Harry (37 × 50 mm) . . . . . 3·50 3·75

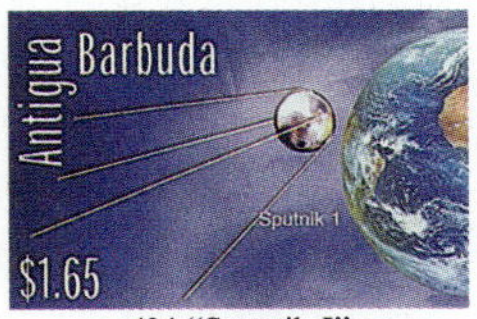

434 "Sputnik I"

2000. "EXPO 2000" World Stamp Exhibition, Anaheim, U.S.A. Space Satellites. Multicoloured.
3077 $1.65 Type **434** . . . . . 1·00 1·00
3078 $1.65 "Explorer I" . . . . 1·00 1·00
3079 $1.65 "Mars Express" . . . 1·00 1·00
3080 $1.65 "Lunik I Solnik" . . 1·00 1·00
3081 $1.65 "Ranger 7" . . . . 1·00 1·00
3082 $1.65 "Mariner 4" . . . . 1·00 1·00
3083 $1.65 "Mariner 10" . . . . 1·00 1·00
3084 $1.65 "Soho" . . . . 1·00 1·00
3085 $1.65 "Mariner 2" . . . . 1·00 1·00
3086 $1.65 "Giotto" . . . . . . 1·00 1·00
3087 $1.65 "Exosat" . . . . . . 1·00 1·00
3088 $1.65 "Pioneer Venus" . . . 1·00 1·00
MS3089 Two sheets, each 106 × 76 mm. (a) $6 "Vostok I". (b) $6 Hubble Space Telescope Set of 2 sheets . . . . . . 7·50 8·00
Nos. 3077/82 and 3083/8 were each printed together, se-tenant, with the backgrounds forming composite designs.

435 Alexei Leonov (Commander of "Soyuz 19")

436 Anna Karina in *Une Femme est Une Femme*, 1961

2000. 25th Anniv of "Apollo–Soyuz" Joint Project. Multicoloured.
3090 $3 Type **435** . . . . 1·75 2·00
3091 $3 "Soyuz 19" . . . . . . 1·75 2·00
3092 $3 Valeri Kubasov ("Soyuz 19" engineer) . . . . . . 1·75 2·00
MS3093 71 × 88 mm. $6 Alexei Leonov and Thomas Stafford (Commander of "Apollo 18") 3·25 3·50

2000. 50th Anniv of Berlin Film Festival. Designs showing actors, directors and film scenes. Mult.
3094 $1.65 Type **436** . . . . . 1·00 1·00
3095 $1.65 *Carmen Jones*, 1955 . . 1·00 1·00
3096 $1.65 *Die Ratten*, 1955 . . . 1·00 1·00
3097 $1.65 *Die Vier im Jeep*, 1951 1·00 1·00
3098 $1.65 Sidney Poitier in *Lilies of the Field*, 1963 . . . . 1·00 1·00
3099 $1.65 *Invitation to the Dance*, 1956 . . . . . . 1·00 1·00
MS3100 97 × 103 mm. $6 Kate Winslet in *Sense and Sensibility*, 1996 . . . . 3·25 3·50
No. 3096 is inscribed "GOLDER BERLIN BEAR" and **MS**3100 shows the award date "1966" in error.

437 George Stephenson and *Locomotion No. 1*, 1825

2000. 175th Anniv of Stockton and Darlington Line (first public railway). Multicoloured.
3101 $3 Type **437** . . . . 2·00 2·25
3102 $3 Camden and Amboy Railroad locomotive *John Bull*, 1831 . . . . 2·00 2·25

438 Statue of Johann Sebastian Bach

439 Albert Einstein

2000. 250th Death Anniv of Johann Sebastian Bach (German composer). Sheet 77 × 88 mm.
MS3103 **438** $6 multicoloured . . 3·50 3·75

2000. Election of Albert Einstein (mathematical physicist) as *Time Magazine* "Man of the Century". Sheet 117 × 91 mm.
MS3104 **439** $6 multicoloured . . 3·25 3·50

440 LZ-1 Airship, 1900

2000. Centenary of First Zeppelin Flight.
3105 **440** $3 brown, black and blue . . . . 1·75 2·00
3106 – $3 brown, black and blue . . . . 1·75 2·00
3107 – $3 multicoloured . . . . 1·75 2·00
MS3108 93 × 66 mm. $6 multicoloured . . . . 3·25 3·50
DESIGNS: No. 3106, LZ-2, 1906; 3107, LZ-3, 1906. (50 × 37 mm)—No. **MS**3108, LZ-7 *Deutschland*, 1910.
Nos. 3105/7 were printed together, se-tenant, with the backgrounds forming a composite design.

441 Marcus Latimer Hurley (cycling), St. Louis (1904)

2000. Olympic Games, Sydney. Multicoloured.
3109 $2 Type **441** . . . . 1·40 1·40
3110 $2 Diving . . . . 1·40 1·40
3111 $2 Flaminio Stadium, Rome (1960) and Italian flag . . 1·40 1·40
3112 $2 Ancient Greek javelin thrower . . . . 1·40 1·40

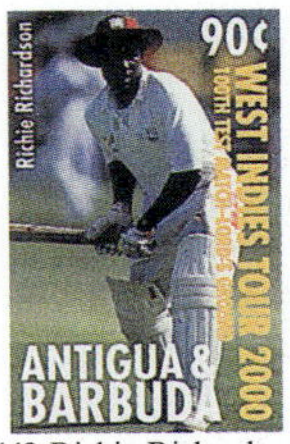

442 Richie Richardson

2000. West Indies Cricket Tour and 100th Test Match at Lord's. Multicoloured.
3113 90c. Type **442** 75 40
3114 $5 Viv Richards . . . . . 3·25 3·50
MS3115 121 × 104 mm. $6 Lord's Cricket Ground (horiz) . . . . 3·50 3·75
No. 3114 is inscribed "Viv Richard" in error.

443 Outreach Programme at Sunshine Home for Girls

2000. Girls Brigade. Multicoloured.
3116 20c. Type **443** 20 15
3117 60c. Ullida Rawlins Gill (International Vice President) (vert) 40 30
3118 75c. Officers and girls . . . 50 35
3119 90c. Girl with flag (vert) . . 70 50
3120 $1.20 Members of 8th Antigua Company with flag (vert) . . . . 95 1·10
MS3121 102 × 124 mm. $5 Girl Brigade badge (vert) . . . . . 3·00 3·25

444 Lady Elizabeth Bowes-Lyon as Young Girl

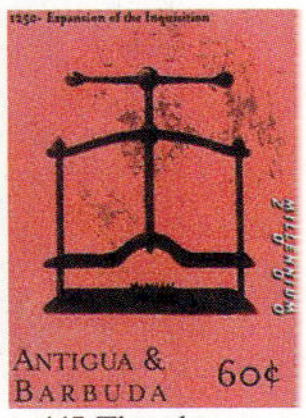

445 Thumbscrew (Expansion of Inquisition, 1250)

2000. "Queen Elizabeth the Queen Mother's Century".
3122 **444** $2 multicoloured . . . . 1·40 1·40
3123 – $2 black and gold . . . 1·40 1·40
3124 – $2 black and gold . . . 1·40 1·40
3125 – $2 multicoloured . . . . 1·40 1·40
MS3126 153 × 157 mm. $6 multicoloured . . . . 3·50 3·75
DESIGNS: No. 3123, Queen Elizabeth in 1940; 3124, Queen Mother with Princess Anne, 1951; 3125, Queen Mother in Canada, 1989; **MS**3126, Queen Mother inspecting guard of honour.
No. **MS**3126 also shows the Royal Arms embossed in gold.

2000. New Millennium. People and Events of Thirteenth Century (1250–1300). Multicoloured (except No. 3127).
3127 60c. Type **445** (black and red) 40 40
3128 60c. Chartres Cathedral (completed, 1260) 40 40
3129 60c. Donor's sculpture, Naumberg (completed, 1260) 40 40
3130 60c. Delegates (Simon de Montfort's Parliament, 1261) 40 40
3131 60c. "Maesta" (Cimabue) (painted 1270) 40 40
3132 60c. Marco Polo (departure from Venice, 1271) . . . 40 40
3133 60c. "Divine Wind" (Kamikaze wind saves Japan from invasion, 1274) 40 40
3134 60c. St. Thomas Aquinas (died 1274) 40 40
3135 60c. Arezzo Cathedral (completed 1277) 40 40
3136 60c. Margrethe ("The Maid of Norway") (crowned Queen of Scotland, 1286) 40 40
3137 60c. Jewish refugees (Expulsion of Jews from England, 1290) 40 40
3138 60c. Muslim horseman (capture of Acre, 1291) . . 40 40
3139 60c. Moshe de Leon (compiles *The Zohar*, 1291) 40 40
3140 60c. Knights in combat (German Civil War, 1292–98) 40 40
3141 60c. Kublai Khan (died 1294) 40 40
3142 60c. Dante (writes *La Vita Nuova*, 1295) (59 × 39 mm) 40 40
3143 60c. "Autumn Colours on Quiao and Hua Mountains" (Zhan Mengfu) (painted 1296) 40 40

446 "Admonishing the Court Ladies" (after Ku K'ai-Chih)

2000. New Millennium. Two Thousand Years of Chinese Paintings. Multicoloured.
3144 25c. Type **446** 20 20
3145 25c. Ink on silk drawing from Zhan Jadashan . . . 20 20
3146 25c. Ink and colour on silk drawing from Mawangdui Tomb 20 20
3147 25c. "Scholars collating Texts" (attr Yang Zihua) 20 20
3148 25c. "Spring Outing" (attr Zhan Ziqian) 20 20
3149 25c. "Portrait of the Emperors" (attr Yen Liben) 20 20
3150 25c. "Sailing Boats and Riverside Mansion" (attr Li Sixun) 20 20
3151 25c. "Two Horses and Groom" (Han Kan) . . . 20 20
3152 25c. "King's Portrait" (attr Wu Daozi) 20 20
3153 25c. "Court Ladies wearing Flowered Headdresses" (attr Zhou Fang) 20 20
3154 25c. "Distant Mountain Forest" (mountain) (Juran) 20 20
3155 25c. "Mount Kuanglu" (Jiang Hao) 20 20
3156 25c. "Pheasant and Small Birds" (Huang Jucai) . . 20 20
3157 25c. "Deer among Red Maples" (anon) 20 20
3158 25c. "Distant Mountain Forest" (river and fields) (Juran) 20 20
3159 25c. "Literary Gathering" (Han Huang) (57 × 39 mm) 20 20
3160 25c. "Birds and Insects" (Huang Quan) 20 20
No. 3148 is inscribed "SPRINTING", No. 3150 "MASION" and No. 3153 "HEADRESSES", all in error.

447 King Donald III of Scotland

2000. Monarchs of the Millennium.
3161 **447** $1.65 black, stone and brown . . . . 1·00 1·00
3162 – $1.65 black, stone and brown . . . . 1·00 1·00
3163 – $1.65 black, stone and brown . . . . 1·00 1·00
3164 – $1.65 black, stone and brown . . . . 1·00 1·00
3165 – $1.65 black, stone and brown . . . . 1·00 1·00
3166 – $1.65 black, stone and brown . . . . 1·00 1·00

3167 – $1.65 multicoloured . . 1·00 1·00
3168 – $1.65 multicoloured . . 1·00 1·00
3169 – $1.65 multicoloured . . 1·00 1·00
3170 – $1.65 multicoloured . . 1·00 1·00
3171 – $1.65 multicoloured . . 1·00 1·00
3172 – $1.65 multicoloured . . 1·00 1·00
MS3173 – Two sheets, each 115×135 mm. (a) $6 mult. (b) $6 mult Set of 2 sheets . . . . . 7·50 8·00

DESIGNS: No. 3162, King Duncan I of Scotland; 3163, King Duncan II of Scotland; 3164, King Macbeth of Scotland; 3165, King Malcolm III of Scotland; 3166, King Edgar of Scotland; 3167, King Charles I of England and Scotland; 3168, King Charles II of England and Scotland; 3169, Prince Charles Edward Stuart ("The Young Pretender"); 3170, King James II of England and VII of Scotland; 3171, King James II of Scotland; 3172, King James III of Scotland; MS3173a, King Robert I of Scotland; MS3173b, Queen Anne of Great Britain.

No. 3169 is inscribed "George III 1760–1820 Great Britain" in error.

2000. Popes of the Millennium. As T **447**. Each black, yellow and green.
3174 $1.65 Alexander VI (bare-headed) . . . . . . 1·00 1·00
3175 $1.65 Benedict XIII . . . . 1·00 1·00
3176 $1.65 Boniface IX . . . . . 1·00 1·00
3177 $1.65 Alexander VI (wearing cap) . . . . 1·00 1·00
3178 $1.65 Clement VIII . . . . 1·00 1·00
3179 $1.65 Clement VI . . . . . 1·00 1·00
3180 $1.65 John Paul II . . . . 1·00 1·00
3181 $1.65 Benedict XV . . . . 1·00 1·00
3182 $1.65 John XXIII . . . . . 1·00 1·00
3183 $1.65 Pius XI . . . . . . 1·00 1·00
3184 $1.65 Pius XII . . . . . 1·00 1·00
3185 $1.65 Paul VI . . . . . . 1·00 1·00
MS3186 Two sheets, each 115×135 mm. (a) $6 Pius II (black, yellow and black). (b) $6 Pius VII (black, yellow and black) Set of 2 sheets . . . . 7·50 8·00

No. 3181 is inscribed "BENIDICT XV" in error.

448 Agouti

2000. Fauna of the Rain Forest. Multicoloured.
3187 75c. Type **448** 60 35
3188 90c. Capybara 70 40
3189 $1.20 Basilisk lizard 80 55
3190 $1.65 Green violetear ("Green Violet-Ear Hummingbird") . . . . . 1·00 1·00
3191 $1.65 Harpy eagle . . . . . 1·00 1·00
3192 $1.65 Three-toed sloth . . . 1·00 1·00
3193 $1.65 White uakari monkey . 1·00 1·00
3194 $1.65 Anteater . . . . . . 1·00 1·00
3195 $1.65 Coati . . . . 1·00 1·00
3196 $1.75 Red-eyed tree frog . . 1·00 1·00
3197 $1.75 Black spider monkey . 1·00 1·00
3198 $1.75 Emerald toucanet . . 1·00 1·00
3199 $1.75 Kinkajou . . . . . . 1·00 1·00
3200 $1.75 Spectacled bear . . . 1·00 1·00
3201 $1.75 Tapir . . . . 1·00 1·00
3202 $2 Heliconid butterfly . . . 1·25 1·25
MS3203 Two sheets. (a) 90×65 mm. $6 Keel-billed toucan (horiz). (b) 65×90 mm. $6 Scarlet macaw Set of 2 sheets . . . . . 7·50 8·00

Nos. 3190/5 and 3196/201 were printed together, se-tenant, forming composite designs.

449 "Sea Cliff" Submarine

2000. Submarines. Multicoloured.
3204 65c. Type **449** 40 30
3205 75c. "Beaver Mark IV" . . 50 35
3206 90c. "Reef Ranger" 60 40
3207 $1 "Cubmarine" 70 45
3208 $1.20 "Alvin" 80 55
3209 $2 H.M.S. *Revenge* . . . . 1·25 1·40
3210 $2 *Walrus*, Netherlands . . 1·25 1·40
3211 $2 U.S.S. *Los Angeles* . . . 1·25 1·40
3212 $2 *Daphne*, France . . . . 1·25 1·40
3213 $2 U.S.S. *Ohio* . . . . . . 1·25 1·40
3214 $2 U.S.S. *Skipjack* . . . . 1·25 1·40
3215 $3 "Argus", Russia . . . . 1·60 1·75
MS3216 Two sheets, each 107×84 mm. (a) $6 "Trieste". (b) $6 Type 209 U-boat, Germany Set of 2 sheets . . . . 7·50 8·00

Nos. 3209/14 were printed together, se-tenant, with the backgrounds forming a composite design.

450 German Lookout

2000. 60th Anniv of Battle of Britain. Multicoloured (except No. 3222).
3217 $1.20 Type **450** . . . . . . 1·00 1·00
3218 $1.20 Children's evacuation train . . . . 1·00 1·00
3219 $1.20 Evacuating hospital patients . . . . 1·00 1·00
3220 $1.20 Hawker Hurricane (fighter) . . . . 1·00 1·00
3221 $1.20 Rescue team . . . . 1·00 1·00
3222 $1.20 Churchill cartoon (black) . . . . 1·00 1·00
3223 $1.20 King George VI and Queen Elizabeth inspecting bomb damage 1·00 1·00
3224 $1.20 Barrage balloon above Tower Bridge . . . . . . 1·00 1·00
3225 $1.20 Bristol Blenheim (bomber) . . . . 1·00 1·00
3226 $1.20 Prime Minister Winston Churchill . . . . 1·00 1·00
3227 $1.20 Bristol Blenheim and barrage balloons . . . . 1·00 1·00
3228 $1.20 Heinkel (fighter) . . . 1·00 1·00
3229 $1.20 Supermarine Spitfire (fighter) . . . . 1·00 1·00
3230 $1.20 German rescue launch 1·00 1·00
3231 $1.20 Messerschmitt 109 (fighter) . . . . 1·00 1·00
3232 $1.20 R.A.F. rescue launch 1·00 1·00
MS3233 Two sheets, each 90×60 mm. (a) $6 Junkers 87B (dive bomber). (b) $6 Supermarine Spitfires at dusk Set of 2 sheets 10·00 11·00

No. **MS**3233a is inscribed "JUNKERS 878" in error.

451 "The Defence of Cadiz" (Zurbaran)

2000. "Espana 2000" International Stamp Exhibition, Madrid. Paintings from the Prado Museum. Mult.
3234 $1.65 Type **451** 90 90
3235 $1.65 "The Defence of Cadiz" (General and galleys) 90 90
3236 $1.65 "The Defence of Cadiz" (officers) 90 90
3237 $1.65 "Vulcan's Forge" (Vulcan) (Velazquez) . . . 90 90
3238 $1.65 "Vulcan's Forge" (working metal) 90 90
3239 $1.65 "Vulcan's Forge" (workers with hammers) 90 90
3240 $1.65 "Family Portrait" (three men) (Adriaen Key) 90 90
3241 $1.65 "Family Portrait" (one man) 90 90
3242 $1.65 "Family Portrait" (three women) 90 90
3243 $1.65 "The Devotion of Rudolf I" (horseman with lantern) (Rubens and Jan Wildens) 90 90
3244 $1.65 "The Devotion of Rudolf I" (priest on horseback) 90 90
3245 $1.65 "The Devotion of Rudolf I" (huntsman) . . 90 90
3246 $1.65 "The Concert" (lute player) (Vincente Gonzalez) 90 90
3247 $1.65 "The Concert" (lady with fan) 90 90
3248 $1.65 "The Concert" (two gentlemen) 90 90
3249 $1.65 "The Adoration of the Magi" (Wise Man) (Juan Maino) 90 90
3250 $1.65 "The Adoration of the Magi" (two Wise Men) 90 90
3251 $1.65 "The Adoration of the Magi" (Holy Family) . . 90 90
MS3252 Three sheets. (a) 115×90 mm. $6 "The Deliverance of St. Peter" (Jose de Ribera) (horiz). (b) 110×90 mm. $6 "The Fan Seller" (Jose del Castillo). (c) 110×90 mm. $6 "Family in a Garden" (Jan van Kessel the Younger) Set of 3 sheets . . . 9·50 10·00

Nos. 3246/8 are inscribed "Gonzlez" with No. 3248 additionally inscribed "Francisco Rizi", all in error.

452 Two Angels

2000. Christmas and Holy Year. Multicoloured.
3253 25c. Type **452** 20 15
3254 45c. Heads of two angels looking down 35 25
3255 90c. Heads of two angels, one looking up 60 40
3256 $1.75 Type **452** . . . . . . 1·10 1·25
3257 $1.75 As 45c. . . . . 1·10 1·25
3258 $1.75 As 90c. . . . . 1·10 1·25
3259 $1.75 As $5 . . . . 1·10 1·25
3260 $5 Two angels with drapery 3·00 3·50
MS3261 110×120 mm. $6 Holy Child . . . . 3·25 3·50

453 "Dr. Ephraim Bueno" (Rembrandt)

2000. Bicentenary of Rijksmuseum, Amsterdam. Dutch Paintings. Multicoloured.
3262 $1 Type **453** 60 60
3263 $1 "Woman writing a Letter" (Frans van Meris de Oude) 60 60
3264 $1 "Mary Magdalen" (Jan van Scorel) 60 60
3265 $1 "Anna Coddle" (Maerten van Heemskerck) 60 60
3266 $1 "Cleopatra's Banquet" (Gerard Lairesse) 60 60
3267 $1 "Titus in Friar's Habit" (Rembrandt) 60 60
3268 $1.20 "Saskia" (Rembrandt) 70 70
3269 $1.20 "In the Month of July" (Paul Joseph Constantin Gabriel) . . . 70 70
3270 $1.20 "Maria Trip" (Rembrandt) 70 70
3271 $1.20 "Still Life with Flowers" (Jan van Huysum) 70 70
3272 $1.20 "Haesje van Cleyburgh" (Rembrandt) 70 70
3273 $1.20 "Girl in a White Kimono" (George Hendrick Breitner) . . . 70 70
3274 $1.65 "Man and Woman at a Spinning Wheel" (Pieter Pietersz) 90 90
3275 $1.65 "Self-portrait" (Rembrandt) 90 90
3276 $1.65 "Jeremiah lamenting the Destruction of Jerusalem" (Rembrandt) 90 90
3277 $1.65 "The Jewish Bride" (Rembrandt) 90 90
3278 $1.65 "Anna accused by Tobit of stealing a Kid" (Rembrandt) 90 90
3279 $1.65 "The Prophetess Anna" (Rembrandt) . . . 90 90
MS3280 Three sheets, each 118×88 mm. (a) $6 "Doubting Thomas" (Hendrick ter Brugghen). (b) $6 "Still Life with Cheeses" (Floris van Dijck); (c) $6 "Isaac Blessing Jacob" (Govert Flinck) Set of 3 sheets . . . . 9·50 10·00

454 "Starmie No. 121"

2001. Characters from "Pokemon" (children's cartoon series). Multicoloured.
3281 $1.75 Type **454** . . . . . . 1·10 1·10
3282 $1.75 "Misty" . . . . 1·10 1·10
3283 $1.75 "Brock" . . . . 1·10 1·10
3284 $1.75 "Geodude No. 74" . . 1·10 1·10
3285 $1.75 "Krabby No. 98" . . 1·10 1·10
3286 $1.75 "Ash" . . . . 1·10 1·10
MS3287 74×114 mm. $6 "Charizard No. 6" . . . . 3·25 3·50

455 Blue-toothed Entoloma

456 Map and Graphs

2001. "Hong Kong 2001" Stamp Exhibition. Tropical Fungi. Multicoloured.
3288 25c. Type **455** 30 20
3289 90c. Common morel 60 40
3290 $1 Red cage fungus 75 45
3291 $1.65 Copper trumpet . . . 90 90
3292 $1.65 Field mushroom ("Meadow Mushroom") 90 90
3293 $1.65 Green gill ("Green-gilled Parasol") 90 90
3294 $1.65 The panther 90 90
3295 $1.65 Death cap 90 90
3296 $1.65 Royal boletus ("King Bolete") 90 90
3297 $1.65 Lilac fairy helmet ("Lilac Bonnet") 90 90
3298 $1.65 Silky volvar 90 90
3299 $1.65 Agrocybe mushroom ("Poplar Field Cap") . . 90 90
3300 $1.65 Saint George's mushroom 90 90
3301 $1.65 Red-stemmed tough shank 90 90
3302 $1.65 Fly agaric 90 90
3303 $1.75 Common fawn agaric ("Fawn Shield-Cap") . . 1·00 1·00
MS3304 Two sheets, each 70×90 mm. (a) $6 Yellow parasol. (b) $6 Mutagen milk cap Set of 2 sheets . . . . 7·50 8·00

Nos. 3291/6 and 3297/302 were each printed together, se-tenant, with the backgrounds forming composite designs.

2001. Population and Housing Census.
3305 **456** 15c. multicoloured . . . 15 10
3306 – 25c. multicoloured . . . 20 15
3307 – 65c. multicoloured . . . 55 50
3308 – 90c. multicoloured . . . 70 70
MS3309 – 55×50 mm. $6 multicoloured (Map and census logo) . . . . 3·50 3·75

DESIGNS: 25c. to 90c. Map and different form of graph.

457 "Yuna (Bath-house Women)" (detail)

2001. "PHILANIPPON 2001" International Stamp Exhibition, Tokyo. Traditional Japanese Paintings. Multicoloured.
3310 45c. Type **457** 30 25
3311 60c. "Yuna (Bath-house Women)" (different detail) 40 30
3312 65c. "Yuna (Bath-house Women)" (different detail) 40 30
3313 75c. "The Hikone Screen" (detail) 50 35
3314 $1 "The Hikone Screen" (different detail) 60 45
3315 $1.20 "The Hikone Screen" (different detail) 70 55
3316 $1.65 Galleon and Dutch merchants with horse . . 90 90
3317 $1.65 Galleon and merchants with tiger . . 90 90
3318 $1.65 Merchants unpacking goods 90 90
3319 $1.65 Merchants with parasol and horse 90 90
3320 $1.65 Women packing food 90 90
3321 $1.65 Picnic under the cherry tree 90 90
3322 $1.65 Palanquins and resting bearers 90 90
3323 $1.65 Women dancing . . . 90 90

3324	$1.65 Three samurai	90	90
3325	$1.65 One samurai	90	90
MS3326	Three sheets, each 80 × 110 mm. (a) $6 "Harunobu Suzuki" (Shiba Kokani) (38 × 50 mm). (b) $6 "Daruma" (Tsujo Kako) (38 × 50 mm). (c) $6 "Visiting a Shrine on a Rainy Night" (Harunobu Suziki) (38 × 50 mm) Set of 3 sheets	9·50	10·00

Nos. 3316/19 ("The Namban Screen" by Kano Nizen) and Nos. 3320/5 ("Merry-making under the Cherry Blossoms" by Kano Naganobu) were each printed together, se-tenant, with both sheetlets forming the entire painting.

458 Lucille Ball leaning on Mantelpiece

2001. Scenes from *I Love Lucy* (American T.V. comedy series). Eight sheets each containing multicoloured design as T **458**.

MS3327	(a) 118 × 92 mm. $6 Type **458**. (b) 98 × 120 mm. $6 Desi Arnaz laughing. (c) 93 × 130 mm. $6 William Frawley at table. (d) 114 × 145 mm. $6 Lucille Ball with William Frawley. (e) 114 × 145 mm. $6 Lucille Ball in blue dress. (f) 119 × 111 mm. $6 Lucille Ball sitting at table. (g) 128 × 100 mm. $6 Lucille Ball as scarecrow. (h) 93 × 125 mm. $6 William Frawley shouting at Desi Arnaz (horiz) Set of 8 sheets	22·00	24·00

459 *Hintleya burtii*

2001. Caribbean Orchids. Multicoloured.

3328	45c. Type **459**	40	25
3329	75c. *Neomoovea irrovata*	50	35
3330	90c. *Comparettia speciosa*	60	40
3331	$1 *Cypripedium crapeanum*	70	45
3332	$1.20 *Trichoceuos muralis* (vert)	75	75
3333	$1.20 *Dracula rampira* (vert)	75	75
3334	$1.20 *Psychopsis papilio* (vert)	75	75
3335	$1.20 *Lycaste clenningiana* (vert)	75	75
3336	$1.20 *Telipogon nevuosus* (vert)	75	75
3337	$1.20 *Masclecallia ayahbacana* (vert)	75	75
3338	$1.65 *Cattleya dowiana* (vert)	90	90
3339	$1.65 *Dendiobium cruentum* (vert)	90	90
3340	$1.65 *Bulbophyllum lobb* (vert)	90	90
3341	$1.65 *Chysis laevis* (vert)	90	90
3342	$1.65 *Ancistrochilus rothschildicanus* (vert)	90	90
3343	$1.65 *Angraecum sororium* (vert)	90	90
3344	$1.65 *Rhyncholaelia glanca* (vert)	90	90
3345	$1.65 *Oncidium barbatum* (vert)	90	90
3346	$1.65 *Phaius tankervillege* (vert)	90	90
3347	$1.65 *Ghies brechtiana* (vert)	90	90
3348	$1.65 *Angraecum leonis* (vert)	90	90
3349	$1.65 *Cycnoches loddigesti* (vert)	90	90
MS3350	Two sheets. (a) 68 × 104 mm. $6 *Symphalossum sanquinem* (vert). (b) 104 × 68 mm. $6 *Trichopilia fragrans* (vert) Set of 2 sheets	7·50	8·00

460 Yellowtail Damselfish

2001. Tropical Marine Life. Multicoloured.

3351	25c. Type **460**	20	15
3352	45c. Indigo hamlet	30	25
3353	65c. Great white shark	45	30
3354	90c. Bottle-nose dolphin	60	50
3355	90c. Palette surgeonfish	60	50
3356	$1 Octopus	65	50
3357	$1.20 Common dolphin	70	70
3358	$1.20 Franklin's gull	70	70
3359	$1.20 Rock beauty	70	70
3360	$1.20 Bicoloured angelfish	70	70
3361	$1.20 Beaugregory	70	70
3362	$1.20 Banded butterflyfish	70	70
3363	$1.20 Common tern	70	70
3364	$1.20 Flying fish	70	70
3365	$1.20 Queen angelfish	70	70
3366	$1.20 Blue-striped grunt	70	70
3367	$1.20 Porkfish	70	70
3368	$1.20 Blue tang	70	70
3369	$1.65 Red-footed booby	90	90
3370	$1.65 Bottle-nose dolphin	90	90
3371	$1.65 Hawksbill turtle	90	90
3372	$1.65 Monk seal	90	90
3373	$1.65 Great white shark (inscr "Bull Shark")	90	90
3374	$1.65 Lemon shark	90	90
3375	$1.65 Dugong	90	90
3376	$1.65 White-tailed tropicbird	90	90
3377	$1.65 Bull shark	90	90
3378	$1.65 Manta ray	90	90
3379	$1.65 Green turtle	90	90
3380	$1.65 Spanish grunt	90	90
MS3381	Four sheets. (a) 68 × 98 mm. $5 Sailfish. (b) 68 × 98 mm. $5 Brown pelican and beaugregory (vert). (c) 98 × 68 mm. $6 Queen triggerfish. (d) 96 × 68 mm. $6 Hawksbill turtle Set of 4 sheets	12·00	13·00

Nos. 3357/62, 3363/8, 3369/74 and 3375/80 were each printed together, se-tenant, the backgrounds forming composite designs.

461 *Freewinds* (liner) and Police Band, Antigua

2001. Work of *Freewinds* (Church of Scientology flagship) in Caribbean. Multicoloured.

3382	30c. Type **461**	40	30
3383	45c. At anchor off St. Barthelemy	45	30
3384	75c. At sunset	70	60
3385	90c. Off Bonaire	90	90
3386	$1.50 *Freewinds* anchored off Bequia	1·25	1·40
MS3387	Two sheets, each 85 × 60 mm. (a) $4 *Freewinds* alongside quay, Curacao. (b) $4 Decorated with lights Set of 2 sheets	5·50	6·00

462 Young Queen Victoria in Blue Dress

2001. Death Centenary of Queen Victoria. Multicoloured.

3388	$2 Type **462**	1·40	1·40
3389	$2 Queen Victoria wearing red head-dress	1·40	1·40
3390	$2 Queen Victoria with jewelled hair ornament	1·40	1·40
3391	$2 Queen Victoria, after Chalon, in brooch	1·40	1·40
MS3392	70 × 82 mm. $5 Queen Victoria in old age	3·00	3·50

463 "Water Lilies"

2001. 75th Death Anniv of Claude-Oscar Monet (French painter). Multicoloured.

3393	$2 Type **463**	1·25	1·40
3394	$2 "Rose Portals, Giverny"	1·25	1·40
3395	$2 "Water Lily Pond, Harmony in Green"	1·25	1·40
3396	$2 "Artist's Garden, Irises"	1·25	1·40
MS3397	136 × 111 mm. $5 "Jerusalem Artichoke Flowers" (vert)	3·00	3·25

No. 3396 is inscribed "Artists's" in error.

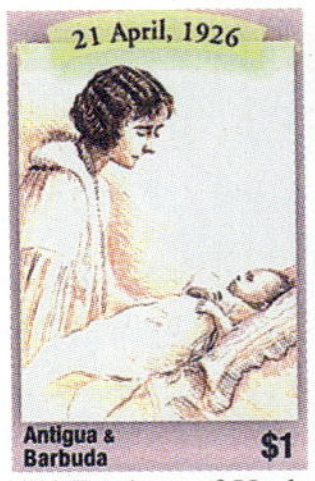

464 Duchess of York with Baby Princess Elizabeth (1926)

465 Verdi in Top Hat

2001. 75th Birthday of Queen Elizabeth II. Multicoloured.

3398	$1 Type **464**	75	75
3399	$1 Queen in Coronation robes (1953)	75	75
3400	$1 Young Princess Elizabeth (1938)	75	75
3401	$1 Queen Elizabeth in Garter robes (1956)	75	75
3402	$1 Princess Elizabeth with pony (1939)	75	75
3403	$1 Queen Elizabeth in red dress and pearls (1985)	75	75
MS3404	90 × 72 mm. $6 Princess Elizabeth and Queen Elizabeth (1940)	3·50	3·75

2001. Death Centenary of Giuseppe Verdi (Italian composer). Multicoloured.

3405	$2 Type **465**	1·75	1·75
3406	$2 Don Carlos and part of opera score	1·75	1·75
3407	$2 Conductor and score for *Aida*	1·75	1·75
3408	$2 Musicians and score for *Rigoletto*	1·75	1·75
MS3409	77 × 117 mm. $5 Verdi in evening dress	4·50	4·75

Nos. 3405/8 were printed together, se-tenant, the backgrounds forming a composite design.

466 "Georges-Henri Manuel"

2001. Death Centenary of Henri de Toulouse-Lautrec (French painter). Multicoloured.

3410	$2 Type **466**	1·25	1·40
3411	$2 "Louis Pascal"	1·25	1·40
3412	$2 "Romain Coolus"	1·25	1·40
3413	$2 "Monsieur Fourcade"	1·25	1·40
MS3414	67 × 84 mm. $5 "Dancing at the Moulin de la Galette"	3·00	3·25

No 3412 is inscribed "ROMAN" in error.

467 Marlene Dietrich smoking

2001. Birth Centenary of Marlene Dietrich (actress and singer).

3415	**467**	$2 black, purple and red	1·25	1·40
3416	–	$2 black, purple and red	1·25	1·40
3417	–	$2 multicoloured	1·25	1·40
3418	–	$2 black, purple and red	1·25	1·40

DESIGNS: No. 3416, Marlene Dietrich, in evening gown, sitting on settee; 3417, In black dress; 3418, Sitting on piano.

468 Collared Peccary

2001. Vanishing Fauna of the Caribbean. Multicoloured.

3419	25c. Type **468**	30	20
3420	30c. Baird's tapir	30	20
3421	45c. Agouti	40	25
3422	75c. Bananaquit	50	35
3423	90c. Six-banded armadillo	60	40
3424	$1 Roseate spoonbill	75	45
3425	$1.80 Mouse opossum	1·25	1·40
3426	$1.80 Magnificent black frigate bird	1·25	1·40
3427	$1.80 Northern jacana	1·25	1·40
3428	$1.80 Painted bunting	1·25	1·40
3429	$1.80 Haitian solenodon	1·25	1·40
3430	$1.80 St. Lucia iguana	1·25	1·40
3431	$2.50 West Indian iguana	1·60	1·75
3432	$2.50 Scarlet macaw	1·60	1·75
3433	$2.50 Cotton-topped tamarin	1·60	1·75
3434	$2.50 Kinkajou	1·60	1·75
MS3435	Two sheets. (a) 117 × 85 mm. $6 Ocelot (vert). (b) 162 × 116 mm. $6 King vulture (vert) Set of 2 sheets	7·50	8·00

469 Sara Crewe (*The Little Princess*) reading a Letter

2001. Shirley Temple Films. Multicoloured. Showing film scenes. (a) *The Little Princess*. Multicoloured.

3436	$1.50 Type **469**	90	90
3437	$1.50 Sara in pink dressing gown	90	90
3438	$1.50 Sara cuddling doll	90	90
3439	$1.50 Sara as Princess on throne	90	90
3440	$1.50 Sara talking to man in frock coat	90	90
3441	$1.50 Sara blowing out candles	90	90
3442	$1.80 Sara with Father (horiz)	1·00	1·00
3443	$1.80 Sara scrubbing floor (horiz)	1·00	1·00
3444	$1.80 Sara and friend with Headmistress (horiz)	1·00	1·00
3445	$1.80 Sara with Queen Victoria (horiz)	1·00	1·00
MS3446	106 × 76 mm. $6 Sara with wounded Father	3·25	3·50

(b) *Baby, Take a Bow*.

3447	$1.65 Shirley in dancing class (horiz)	90	90
3448	$1.65 Shirley cuddling Father (horiz)	90	90
3449	$1.65 Shirley at bedtime with parents (horiz)	90	90
3450	$1.65 Shirley in yellow dress with Father (horiz)	90	90
3451	$1.65 Shirley and Father at Christmas party (horiz)	90	90
3452	$1.65 Shirley and gangster looking in cradle (horiz)	90	90
3453	$1.65 Shirley in spotted dress	90	90
3454	$1.65 Shirley on steps with gangster	90	90
3455	$1.65 Shirley with gangster holding gun	90	90
3456	$1.65 Shirley with Mother	90	90
MS3457	106 × 76 mm. $6 Shirley in spotted dress	3·25	3·50

470 Rudolph Valentino in *Blood and Sand*, 1922

2001. 75th Death Anniv of Rudolph Valentino (Italian film actor).

3458	**470**	$1 brown and black	70	70
3459	–	$1 lilac and black	70	70
3460	–	$1 brown and black	70	70
3461	–	$1 brown and black	70	70
3462	–	$1 red and black	70	70
3463	–	$1 lilac and black	70	70
3464	–	$1 multicoloured	70	70
3465	–	$1 multicoloured	70	70
3466	–	$1 multicoloured	70	70
3467	–	$1 multicoloured	70	70

3468 – $1 multicoloured 70 70
3469 – $1 multicoloured 70 70
MS3470 Two sheets. (a) 90 × 125 mm. $6 multicoloured. (b) 68 × 95 mm. $6 multicoloured Set of 2 sheets . . . . 7·50 8·00

DESIGNS: No. 3459, In *Eyes of Youth* with Clara Kimbal Young, 1919; 3460, In *All Night Long* with Carmel Meyers, 1918; 3461, Valentino in 1926; 3462, In *Camille* with Alla Nazimova, 1921; 3463, In *Cobra* with Nita Naldi, 1925; 3464, In *The Son of the Sheik* with Vilma Banky, 1926; 3465, In *The Young Rajah*, 1922; 3466, In *The Eagle* with Vilma Banky, 1925; 3467, In *The Sheik* with Agnes Ayres, 1921; 3468, In *A Sainted Devil*, 1924; 3469, In *Monsieur Beaucaire*, 1924; MS3470, (a) Valentino with Natacha Rambova. (b) In *The Four Horseman of the Apocalypse*, 1921.

Nos. 3464 and 3466 are inscribed "BLANKY" and No. 3467 "AYERS", all in error.

471 Queen Elizabeth

472 Melvin Calvin, 1961

2001. Golden Jubilee (1st issue).
3471 **471** $1 multicoloured . . . . 1·00 1·00

No. 3471 was printed in sheetlets of 8, containing two vertical rows of four, separated by a large illustrated central gutter. Both the stamp and the illustration on the central gutter are made up of a collage of miniature flower photographs.

See also Nos. 3535/8.

2001. Centenary of Nobel Prizes. Chemistry Winners. Multicoloured.
3472 $1.50 Type **472** 90 90
3473 $1.50 Linus Pauling, 1954 90 90
3474 $1.50 Vincent du Vigneaud, 1955 . . . . 90 90
3475 $1.50 Richard Synge, 1952 90 90
3476 $1.50 Archer Martin, 1952 90 90
3477 $1.50 Alfred Werner, 1913 90 90
3478 $1.50 Robert Curl Jr., 1996 90 90
3479 $1.50 Alan Heeger, 2000 . . 90 90
3480 $1.50 Michael Smith, 1993 90 90
3481 $1.50 Sidney Altman, 1989 90 90
3482 $1.50 Elias Corey, 1990 . . 90 90
3483 $1.50 William Giauque, 1949 . . . . 90 90
MS3484 Three sheets, each 107 × 75 mm. (a) $6 Ernest Rutherford, 1908. (b) $6 Ernst Fischer, 1973. (c) $6 American volunteers, International Red Cross (Peace Prize, 1944) Set of 3 sheets . . . . 9·50 10·00

473 "Madonna and Child with Angels" (Filippo Lippi)

474 Final between Uruguay and Brazil, Brazil 1950

2001. Christmas. Italian Religious Paintings. Multicoloured.
3485 25c. Type **473** 20 15
3486 45c. "Madonna of Corneto Tarquinia" (Lippi) . . . 35 25
3487 50c. "Madonna and Child" (Domenico Ghirlandaio) 35 25
3488 75c. "Madonna and Child" (Lippi) 60 35
3489 $4 "Madonna Delceppo" (Lippi) . . . . 2·50 3·00
MS3490 106 × 136 mm. $6 "Madonna enthroned with Angels and Saints" (Lippi) . . . . . 3·25 3·50

2001. World Cup Football Championship, Japan and Korea (2002). Multicoloured.
3491 $1.50 Type **474** 90 90
3492 $1.50 Ferenc Puskas (Hungary), Switzerland 1954 . . . . 90 90
3493 $1.50 Raymond Kopa (France), Sweden 1958 . . 90 90
3494 $1.50 Mauro (Brazil), Chile 1962 . . . . 90 90
3495 $1.50 Gordon Banks (England), England 1966 90 90
3496 $1.50 Pele (Brazil), Mexico 1970 . . . . 90 90
3497 $1.50 Daniel Passarella (Argentina), Argentina 1978 . . . . 90 90
3498 $1.50 Karl-Heinz Rummenigge (Germany), Spain 1982 . . . . 90 90
3499 $1.50 World Cup Trophy, Mexico 1986 . . . . . . 90 90
3500 $1.50 Diego Maradona (Argentina), Italy 1990 . . 90 90
3501 $1.50 Roger Milla (Cameroun), U.S.A. 1994 90 90
3502 $1.50 Zinedine Zidane (France), France 1998 . . 90 90
MS3503 Two sheets, each 88 × 75 mm. (a) $6 Detail of Jules Rimet Trophy, Uruguay, 1930. (b) $6 Detail of World Cup Trophy, Japan/Korea, 2002 Set of 2 sheets 7·50 8·00

No. 3500 is inscribed "Deigo" in error.

475 Battle of Nashville, 1864

2002. American Civil War. Multicoloured.
3504 45c. Type **475** 55 55
3505 45c. Capture of Atlanta, 1864 . . . . 55 55
3506 45c. Battle of Spotsylvania, 1864 . . . . 55 55
3507 45c. Battle of The Wilderness, 1864 . . . . 55 55
3508 45c. Battle of Chickamauga Creek, 1863 . . . . . 55 55
3509 45c. Battle of Gettysburg, 1863 . . . . 55 55
3510 45c. Lee and Jackson at Chancellorsville, 1863 . . 55 55
3511 45c. Battle of Fredericksburg, 1862 . . 55 55
3512 45c. Battle of Antietam, 1862 . . . . 55 55
3513 45c. Second Battle of Bull Run, 1862 . . . . . . 55 55
3514 45c. Battle of Five Forks, 1865 . . . . 55 55
3515 45c. Seven Days' Battles, 1862 . . . . 55 55
3516 45c. First Battle of Bull Run, 1861 . . . . 55 55
3517 45c. Battle of Shiloh, 1862 55 55
3518 45c. Battle of Seven Pines, 1862 . . . . 55 55
3519 45c. Bombardment of Fort Sumter, 1861 . . . . . 55 55
3520 45c. Battle of Chattanooga, 1863 . . . . 55 55
3521 45c. Grant and Lee at Appomattox, 1865 . . . 55 55
3522 50c. General Ulysses S. Grant (vert) 55 55
3523 50c. President Abraham Lincoln (vert) 55 55
3524 50c. President Jefferson Davis (vert) 55 55
3525 50c. General Robert E. Lee (vert) 55 55
3526 50c. General George Custer (vert) 55 55
3527 50c. Admiral Andrew Hull Foote (vert) 55 55
3528 50c. General "Stonewall" Jackson (vert) 55 55
3529 50c. General Jeb Stuart (vert) 55 55
3530 50c. General George Meade (vert) 55 55
3531 50c. General Philip Sheridan (vert) 55 55
3532 50c. General James Longstreet (vert) 55 55
3533 50c. General John Mosby (vert) 55 55
MS3534 Two sheets, each 105 × 76 mm. (a) $6 Confederate ironclad *Merrimack* attacking *Cumberland* (Federal sloop) (51 × 38 mm). (b) $6 *Monitor* (Federal ironclad) Set of 2 sheets 9·50 10·00

476 Queen Elizabeth presenting Rosettes

2002. Golden Jubilee (2nd issue). Multicoloured.
3535 $2 Type **476** . . . . 1·75 1·75
3536 $2 Queen Elizabeth at garden party . . . . . . 1·75 1·75
3537 $2 Queen Elizabeth in evening dress . . . . . . 1·75 1·75
3538 $2 Queen Elizabeth in cream coat . . . . 1·75 1·75
MS3539 76 × 108 mm. $6 Princesses Elizabeth and Margaret as bridesmaids . . . . 3·50 3·75

477 U.S. Flag as Statue of Liberty and Antigua & Barbuda Flag

478 Sir Vivian Richards waving Bat

2002. "United We Stand". Support for Victims of 11 September 2001 Terrorist Attacks.
3540 **477** $2 multicoloured . . . . 1·25 1·40

2002. 50th Birthday of Sir Vivian Richards (West Indian cricketer). Multicoloured.
3541 25c. Type **478** 70 30
3542 30c. Sir Vivian Richards receiving presentation from Antigua Cricket Association 80 35
3543 50c. Sir Vivian Richards wearing sash 90 45
3544 75c. Sir Vivian Richards batting . . . . 1·10 70
3545 $1.50 Sir Vivian Richards and Lady Richards . . . 1·75 1·75
3546 $1.80 Sir Vivian Richards with enlarged action photograph of himself . . 2·00 2·25
MS3547 Two sheets, each 68 × 95 mm. (a) $6 Sir Vivian Richards with guard of honour. (b) $6 Sir Vivian Richards in Indian traditional dress Set of 2 sheets . . . . 10·00 10·50

479 Thick-billed Parrot

2002. Flora and Fauna. Multicoloured.
3548 50c. Type **479** 40 30
3549 75c. Lesser long-nosed bat 50 35
3550 90c. Quetzal 60 60
3551 90c. Two-toed sloth 60 60
3552 90c. Lovely cotinga 60 60
3553 90c. *Pseudolycaena marsyas* (butterfly) 60 60
3554 90c. Magenta-throated woodstar 60 60
3555 90c. *Automeris rubrescens* (moth) 60 60
3556 90c. *Bufo periglenes* (toad) 60 60
3557 90c. Collared peccary . . . 60 60
3558 90c. Tamandua anteater . . 60 60
3559 $1 St. Lucia parrot 70 70
3560 $1 Cuban kite 70 70
3561 $1 West Indian whistling-duck 70 70
3562 $1 *Euremа amelia* (butterfly) 70 70
3563 $1 Scarlet ibis 70 70
3564 $1 Black-capped petrel . . 70 70
3565 $1 *Cnemidophorus vanzoi* (lizard) 70 70
3566 $1 Cuban solenodon 70 70
3567 $1 *Papilio thersites* (butterfly) 70 70
3568 $1.50 Montserrat oriole . . 95 95
3569 $1.80 *Leptotes perkinsae* (butterfly) . . . . 1·25 1·40
MS3570 Two sheets, each 110 × 85 mm. (a) $6 Olive Ridley turtle. (b) $6 Margay Set of 2 sheets . . . . 7·50 8·00

Nos. 3550/8 and 3559/67 were each printed together, se-tenant, with the backgrounds forming composite designs.

480 Community Players wearing Straw Hats

2002. 50th Anniv of Community Players. Multicoloured. Showing scenes from various productions.
3571 20c. Type **480** 25 20
3572 25c. Men in suits with women in long dresses . . 25 20
3573 30c. In *Pirates of Penzance* 25 20
3574 75c. Female choir 50 35
3575 90c. In Mexican dress . . . 60 40
3576 $1.50 Members at a reception . . . . 95 1·10
3577 $1.80 Production in the open air . . . . 1·25 1·40
MS3578 Two sheets, each 76 × 84 mm. (a) $4 Mrs. Edie Hill-Thibou (former President) (vert). (b) $4 Miss Yvonne Maginley (Acting President and Director of Music) (vert) Set of 2 sheets . . 5·50 6·00

481 Mount Fuji, Japan

482 Cross-country Skiing

2002. International Year of Mountains. Mult.
3579 $2 Type **481** . . . . 1·25 1·40
3580 $2 Machu Picchu, Peru . . 1·25 1·40
3581 $2 The Matterhorn, Switzerland . . . . 1·25 1·40

2002. Winter Olympic Games, Salt Lake City. Multicoloured.
3582 $2 Type **482** . . . . 1·25 1·40
3583 $2 Pairs figure skating . . . 1·25 1·40
MS3584 84 × 114 mm. Nos. 3582/3 2·25 2·50

483 Amerigo Vespucci wearing Skullcap

2002. 500th Anniv of Amerigo Vespucci's Third Voyage. Multicoloured.
3585 $2.50 Type **483** . . . . . . 1·60 1·75
3586 $2.50 Vespucci as an old man . . . . 1·60 1·75
3587 $2.50 16th-century map . . 1·60 1·75
MS3588 49 × 68 mm. $5 Vespucci holding dividers (vert) . . . . 3·00 3·25

484 *Spirit of St. Louis* and Charles Lindbergh (pilot)

2002. 75th Anniv of First Solo Transatlantic Flight. Multicoloured.
3589 $2.50 Type **484** . . . . . . 1·60 1·75
3590 $2.50 *Spirit of St. Louis* at Le Bourget, Paris, 1927 1·60 1·75
3591 $2.50 Charles Lindbergh in New York ticker-tape parade, 1927 . . . . 1·60 1·75
MS3592 80 × 110 mm. $6 Charles Lindbergh wearing flying helmet 3·25 3·50

485 Princess Diana

2002. 5th Death Anniv of Diana, Princess of Wales. Multicoloured.
3593 $1.80 Type **485** . . . . . . 1·10 1·25
3594 $1.80 Princess Diana in tiara (looking left) . . . . . 1·10 1·25
3595 $1.80 Wearing hat . . . . . 1·10 1·25
3596 $1.80 Princess Diana wearing pearl drop earrings and black dress 1·10 1·25
3597 $1.80 Wearing tiara (facing front) . . . . 1·10 1·25
3598 $1.80 Princess Diana wearing pearl drop earrings . . . . 1·10 1·25
MS3599 91 × 106 mm. $6 Princess Diana . . . . 3·25 3·50

486 Kennedy Brothers

2002. Presidents John F. Kennedy and Ronald Reagan Commemoration. Multicoloured.
3600 $1.50 Type **486** 90 90
3601 $1.50 John Kennedy with Danny Kaye (American entertainer) 90 90

3602 $1.50 Delivering Cuban Blockade speech, 1962 . . 90 90
3603 $1.50 With Jacqueline Kennedy 90 90
3604 $1.50 Meeting Bill Clinton (future president) 90 90
3605 $1.50 Family at John Kennedy's funeral 90 90
3606 $1.50 President and Mrs. Reagan with Pope John Paul II, 1982 . . . . 90 90
3607 $1.50 As George Gipp in *Knute Rockne - All American*, 1940 . . . . 90 90
3608 $1.50 With General Matthew Ridgeway, Bitburg Military Cemetery, Germany, 1985 90 90
3609 $1.50 With George H. Bush and Secretary Mikhail Gorbachev of U.S.S.R., 1988 . . . . 90 90
3610 $1.50 Presidents Reagan, Ford, Carter and Nixon at the White House, 1981 90 90
3611 $1.50 Horse riding with Queen Elizabeth, Windsor, 1982 . . . . 90 90
MS3612 Two sheets, each 88 × 22 mm. (a) $6 President Kennedy at press conference (vert). (b) $6 President Reagan (vert) Set of 2 sheets . . . . 7·50 8·00

487 Red-billed Tropicbird

2002. Endangered Species of Antigua. Multicoloured.
3613 $1.50 Type **487** 90 90
3614 $1.50 Brown pelican 90 90
3615 $1.50 Magnificent frigate bird 90 90
3616 $1.50 Ground lizard 90 90
3617 $1.50 West Indian whistling duck 90 90
3618 $1.50 Antiguan racer snake 90 90
3619 $1.50 Spiny lobster 90 90
3620 $1.50 Hawksbill turtle . . . 90 90
3621 $1.50 Queen conch 90 90

488 Elvis Presley

2002. 25th Death Anniv of Elvis Presley (American entertainer).
3622 **488** $1 multicoloured . . . . 1·40 1·25

489 Cheerleader Teddy

2002. Centenary of the Teddy Bear. Girl Teddies. Multicoloured.
3623 $2 Type **489** . . . . 1·25 1·40
3624 $2 Figure skater . . . . 1·25 1·40
3625 $2 Ballet dancer . . . . 1·25 1·40
3626 $2 Aerobics instructor . . . 1·25 1·40

490 "Croconaw No. 159"

2002. Pokemon (children's cartoon series). Mult.
3627 $1.50 Type **490** 90 90
3628 $1.50 "Mantine No. 226" 90 90
3629 $1.50 "Feraligatr No. 160" 90 90
3630 $1.50 "Qwilfish No. 211" 90 90
3631 $1.50 "Remoraid No. 223" 90 90
3632 $1.50 "Quagsire No. 195" 90 90
MS3633 80 × 106 mm. $6 "Chinchou No. 170" . . . . 3·25 3·50

491 Charlie Chaplin

492 Bob Hope

2002. 25th Death Anniv of Charlie Chaplin (British actor). Each black, grey and light grey.
3634 $1.80 Type **491** . . . . 1·25 1·40
3635 $1.80 Wearing waistcoat and spotted bow-tie . . . . 1·25 1·40
3636 $1.80 In top hat . . . . 1·25 1·40
3637 $1.80 Wearing coat and bowler hat . . . . 1·25 1·40
3638 $1.80 Charlie Chaplin in old age . . . . 1·25 1·40
3639 $1.80 With finger on chin 1·25 1·40
MS3640 90 × 105 mm. $6 Charlie Chaplin as The Tramp . . . . 3·50 3·75

2002. Bob Hope (American entertainer) Commemoration. Designs showing him entertaining American troops. Multicoloured.
3641 $1.50 Type **492** . . . . 1·10 1·25
3642 $1.50 Wearing base hat,Vietnam, 1972 . . . . 1·10 1·25
3643 $1.50 On board U.S.S. *John F. Kennedy* (aircraft carrier) . . . . 1·10 1·25
3644 $1.50 With hawk badge on sleeve, Berlin, 1948 . . . 1·10 1·25
3645 $1.50 Wearing desert fatigues . . . . 1·10 1·25
3646 $1.50 In white cap and stars on collar . . . . 1·10 1·25

493 Lee Strasberg

494 Marlene Dietrich

2002. 20th Death Anniv of Lee Strasberg (pioneer of "Method Acting").
3647 **493** $1 black and stone . . . 75 75

2002. 10th Death Anniv of Marlene Dietrich (actress and singer). Each black and grey.
3648 $1.50 Type **494** 90 90
3649 $1.50 Wearing top hat 90 90
3650 $1.50 In chiffon dress . . . 90 90
3651 $1.50 Resting chin on left hand 90 90
3652 $1.50 In cloche hat 90 90
3653 $1.50 Wearing black evening gloves 90 90
MS3654 83 × 108 mm. $6 Marlene Dietrich wearing chiffon scarf 3·25 3·50

495 Ferrari 801, 1957

2002. Ferrari Racing Cars. Multicoloured.
3655 20c. Type **495** 20 20
3656 25c. Ferrari 256, 1959 . . . 25 20
3657 30c. Ferrari 246 P, 1960 . . 25 20
3658 90c. Ferrari 246, 1966 . . . 60 50
3659 $1 Ferrari 312 B2, 1971 . . 70 55
3660 $1.50 Ferrari 312, 1969 . . 90 90
3661 $2 Ferrari F310 B, 1997 . . 1·25 1·40
3662 $4 Ferrari F2002, 2002 . . 2·25 2·50

496 Antigua & Barbuda Flag

2002. 21st Anniv of Independence. Multicoloured.
3663 25c. Type **496** 35 25
3664 30c. Antigua & Barbuda coat of arms (vert) . . . 35 25
3665 $1.50 Mount St. John's Hospital under construction . . . . 1·25 1·25
3666 $1.80 Parliament Building, St. John's . . . . 1·40 1·60
MS3667 Two sheets, each 77 × 81 mm. (a) $6 Sir Vere Bird (Prime Minister, 1967–94) (38 × 51 mm). (b) $6 Lester Bird (Prime Minister since 1994) (38 × 51 mm) Set of 2 sheets . . . 7·50 8·00

497 Juan Valeron (Spain)

2002. World Cup Football Championship, Japan and Korea. Multicoloured.
3668 $1.65 Type **497** 90 90
3669 $1.65 Iker Casillas (Spain) 90 90
3670 $1.65 Fernando Hierro (Spain) 90 90
3671 $1.65 Gary Kelly (Ireland) 90 90
3672 $1.65 Damien Duff (Ireland) 90 90
3673 $1.65 Matt Holland (Ireland) 90 90
3674 $1.65 Pyo Lee (South Korea) 90 90
3675 $1.65 Ji Sung Park (South Korea) 90 90
3676 $1.65 Jung Hwan Ahn (South Korea) 90 90
3677 $1.65 Filippo Inzaghi (Italy) 90 90
3678 $1.65 Paolo Maldini (Italy) 90 90
3679 $1.65 Dammiano Tommasi (Italy) 90 90
MS3680 Four sheets, each 82 × 82 mm. (a) $3 Jose Camacho (Spanish coach); $3 Raul Gonzales Blanco (Spain). (b) $3 Robbie Keane (Ireland); $3 Mick McCarthy (Irish coach). (c) $3 Guus Hiddink (South Korean coach); $3 Chul Sang Yoo (South Korea). (d) $3 Francesco Totti (Italy); $3 Giovanni Trapattoni (Italian coach) Set of 4 sheets 12·00 13·00
No. MS3680a is inscribed "Carlos Gamarra" in error.

498 "Coronation of the Virgin" (Domenico Ghirlandaio)

2002. Christmas. Religious Paintings. Multicoloured.
3681 25c. Type **498** 20 15
3682 45c. "Adoration of the Magi" (detail) (D. Ghirlandaio) 30 25
3683 75c. "Annunciation" (Simone Martini) (vert) 50 35
3684 90c. "Adoration of the Magi" (different detail) (D. Ghirlandaio) 60 40
3685 $5 "Madonna and Child" (Giovanni Bellini) . . . . 3·00 3·50
MS3686 76 × 110 mm. $6 "Madonnna and Child" (S. Martini) . . . . 3·25 3·50

499 Antiguan Racer Snake Head

2002. Endangered Species. Antiguan Racer Snake. Multicoloured.
3687 $1 Type **499** 70 70
3688 $1 Coiled Antiguan racer snake with tail at right . . 70 70
3689 $1 Antiguan racer snake with pebbles and leaves 70 70
3690 $1 Coiled Antiguan racer snake with tail at left . . 70 70

500 Magnificent Frigate Bird

2002. Fauna and Flora. Multicoloured.
3691 $1.50 Type **500** 90 90
3692 $1.50 Sooty tern 90 90
3693 $1.50 Bananaquit 90 90
3694 $1.50 Yellow-crowned night heron 90 90
3695 $1.50 Greater flamingo . . . 90 90
3696 $1.50 Belted kingfisher . . . 90 90
3697 $1.50 Killer whale 90 90
3698 $1.50 Sperm whale 90 90
3699 $1.50 Minke whale 90 90
3700 $1.50 Blainville's beaked whale 90 90
3701 $1.50 Blue whale 90 90
3702 $1.50 Cuvier's beaked whale 90 90
3703 $1.80 *Epidendrum fragans* 1·10 1·10
3704 $1.80 *Dombeya wallichii* . . 1·10 1·10
3705 $1.80 *Abebuia serratifolia* . . 1·10 1·10
3706 $1.80 *Cryptostegia grandiflora* . . . . 1·10 1·10
3707 $1.80 *Hylocereus undatus* . . 1·10 1·10
3708 $1.80 *Rodriguezia lanceolata* 1·10 1·10
3709 $1.80 *Diphthera festiva* . . . 1·10 1·10
3710 $1.80 *Hypocrita dejanira* . . 1·10 1·10
3711 $1.80 *Eupseudosoma involutum* . . . . 1·10 1·10
3712 $1.80 *Composia credula* . . 1·10 1·10
3713 $1.80 *Citherania magnifica* 1·10 1·10
3714 $1.80 *Divana diva* . . . . 1·10 1·10
MS3715 Four sheets, each 75 × 45 mm. (a) $5 Snowy egret. (b) $5 *Rothschildia orizaba* (moth). (c) $6 Humpback whale. (d) $6 *Ionopsis utricularioides* (flower) Set of 4 sheets 12·00 13·00
Nos. 3691/6 (birds), 3697/702 (whales), 3703/8 (moths) and 3709/14 (flowers) were each printed together, se-tenant, with the backgrounds forming composite designs.

501 Dr. Margaret O'garro

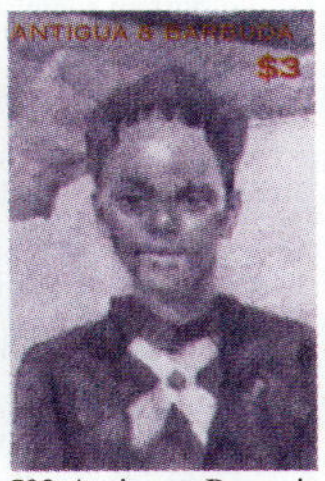

502 Antiguan Brownie

2002. Centenary of Pan American Health Organization. Health Professionals. Multicoloured.
3716 $1.50 Type **501** 90 90
3717 $1.50 Ineta Wallace (nurse) 90 90
3718 $1.50 Vincent Edwards (public health official) . . 90 90

2002. 20th World Scout Jamboree, Thailand. Each lilac and brown (Nos. 3719/21) or multicoloured (others).
3719 $3 Type **502** . . . . 1·75 1·90
3720 $3 Brownie with badge on cap . . . . 1·75 1·90
3721 $3 Brownie without badge on cap . . . . 1·75 1·90
3722 $3 Robert Baden-Powell on horseback, 1896 (horiz) 1·75 1·90
3723 $3 Ernest Thompson Seton (founder, Boy Scouts of America), 1910, and American scout badge (horiz) . . . . 1·75 1·90
3724 $3 First black scout troop, Virginia, 1928 (horiz) . . 1·75 1·90
MS3725 Two sheets. (a) 80 × 113 mm. $6 Ernest Thompson Seton. (b) 110 × 83 mm. $6 Scout salute Set of 2 sheets . . . . 7·50 8·00
Nos. 3719/21 were printed together, se-tenant, forming a composite design.

503 Scene from *2001: A Space Odyssey* (Arthur C. Clarke)

2002. Famous Science Fiction Authors. Three sheets, each 150 × 108 mm, containg vert designs as T **503**. Multicoloured.
MS3726 Three sheets. (a) $6 Type **503**. (b) $6 Scene from *The Monuments of Mars* (Richard C. Hoagland). (c) $6 Nostradamus with globe Set of 3 sheets . . . 9·50 10·00

504 "Goat and Kids" (Liu Jiyou)

2003. Chinese New Year ("Year of the Goat").
3727 **504** $1.80 multicoloured . . 1·10 1·10

505 "Lucretia"

2003. 450th Death Anniv of Lucas Cranach the Elder (artist). Multicoloured.
3728 75c. Type **505** 50 35
3729 90c. "Venus and Cupid" (detail) 60 40
3730 $1 "Judith with Head of Holofernes" (c. 1530) . . . 70 60
3731 $1.50 "Portrait of a Young Lady" (detail) . . . . . 90 1·00
MS3732 152 × 188 mm. $2 "Portrait of the Wife of a Jurist"; $2 "Portrait of a Jurist"; $2 "Johannes Cuspinian"; $2 "Portrait of Anna Cuspinian" 3·50 3·75
MS3733 120 × 100 mm. $6 "Judith with Head of Holofernes" (c. 1532) . . . . 3·50 3·75

506 "A High Class Maid training in a Samurai Household"

2003. Japanese Art of Taiso Yoshitoshi. Multicoloured.
3734 25c. Type **506** 25 15
3735 50c. "A Castle-Toppler known as a Keisei" . . . 40 25
3736 $1 "Stylish Young Geisha battling a Snowstorm on her Way to Work" . . . 70 55
3737 $5 "A Lady in Distress being treated with Moxa" 3·00 3·50
MS3738 178 × 140 mm. $2 "A Lady of the Imperial Court wearing Four Layers of Robes"; $2 "Young Mother adoring her Infant Son"; $2 "Lady-in-Waiting looking amused over a Veranda in the Household of a Great Lord"; $2 "A High Ranking Courtesan known as an "Oiran", waiting for a Private Assignation" . . . . 5·00 5·50
MS3739 135 × 67 mm. $6 "A Girl teasing her Cat" . . . . . . 3·25 3·50

507 "Boats at Martigues"

2003. 50th Death Anniv of Raoul Dufy (artist). Multicoloured.
3740 90c. Type **507** 60 40
3741 $1 "Harvesting" 70 45
3742 $1.80 "Sailboats in the Port of Le Havre" . . . . . . 1·10 1·10
3743 $5 "The Big Bather" (vert) 3·00 3·50
MS3744 173 × 124 mm. $2 "The Beach and the Pier at Trouville"; $2 "Port with Sailing Ships"; $2 "Black Cargo"; $2 "Nice, The Bay of Anges" . . . . 5·00 5·50
MS3745 Two sheets, each 95 × 76 mm. (a) $6 "Vence". (b) $6 "The Interior with an Open Window". Both Imperf . . . . 7·50 8·00

508 Queen Elizabeth II at Trooping the Colour

509 Prince William

2003. 50th Anniv of Coronation. Multicoloured.
MS3746 155 × 93 mm. $3 Type **508**; $3 Queen wearing fawn beret with single feather; $3 Queen wearing feathered hat . . . . 5·50 6·00
MS3747 105 × 75 mm. $6 Princess Elizabeth . . . . 3·50 3·75

2003. 21st Birthday of Prince William of Wales. Multicoloured.
MS3748 147 × 77 mm. $3 Type **509**; $3 Prince william wearing polo helmet; $3 Wearing blue T-shirt 5·50 3·75
MS3749 67 × 97 mm. $6 As teenager holding bouquet . . . . 3·50 3·75

510 Tamarind Tree, Parham

2003. Centenary of Salvation Army in Antigua. Multicoloured.
3750 30c. Type **510** 40 25
3751 90c. Salvation Army pre-school 80 45
3752 $1 Meals on wheels (horiz) 95 65
3753 $1.50 St. John Citadel band (horiz) . . . . 1·40 1·40
3754 $1.80 Salvation Army Citadel (horiz) . . . . . 1·75 2·00
MS3755 146 × 78 mm. $6 As Type **510** but without badge and centenary inscription . . . . . 4·25 4·50

511 First Anglican Scout Troop, 1931

512 Cesar Garin (1903)

2003. 90th Anniv of Antigua and Barbuda Scouts Association. Multicoloured (except No. 3756).
3756 30c. Type **511** (black and brown) 25 20
3757 $1 National Scout Camp, 2002 . . . . 70 55
3758 $1.50 Woodbadge Training course, 2000 (horiz) . . . 90 90
3759 $1.80 Visitors to National Camp, 1986 (horiz) . . . 1·10 1·10
MS3760 136 × 96 mm. 90c. Edris George; 90c. Theodore George; 90c. Edris James (all Deputy Commissioners) . . . . 1·60 1·75
MS3761 74 × 101 mm. $6 Scout leader demonstrating semaphore 3·25 3·50

2003. Centenary of Tour de France Cycle Race. Past winners. Multicoloured.
MS3762 160 × 100 mm. $2 Type **512**; $2 Caricature of Henri Cornet (1904); $2 Louis Trousselier (1905); $2 Rene Pottier (1906) 7·00 7·00
MS3763 160 × 100 mm. $2 Lucien Petit-Breton (1907); $2 Lucien Petit-Breton (1908); $2 Francois Faber (1909); $2 Octave Lapize (1910) . . . . 7·00 7·00
MS3764 160 × 100 mm. $2 Gustave Garrigou (1911); $2 Odile Defraye (1912); $2 Phillipe Thys (1913); $2 Phillipe Thys (1914) . . . . . 7·00 7·00
MS3765 Three sheets, each 100 × 70 mm. (a) $6 Henri Desgranges (editor of *L'Auto*). (b) $6 Pierre Giffard (editor of *Le Velo*). (c) $6 Le Compte de Dion (sponsor) Set of 3 sheets . . . 12·00 13·00

513 Frigate Bird and Emblem

2003. 30th Anniv of CARICOM.
3766 **513** $1 multicoloured . . . . 1·00 80

514 Cadillac Eldorado Convertible (1955)

2003. Centenary of General Motors Cadillac. Multicoloured.
MS3767 110 × 150 mm. $2 Type **514**; $2 Cadillac Series 60 (1937); $2 Cadillac Eldorado (1959); $2 Cadillac Eldorado (2002) . . . 5·00 5·50
MS3768 102 × 76 mm. $6 Cadillac Eldorado (1953) . . . . 3·25 3·50

515 Chutes de Carbet Waterfall, Guadeloupe

2003. International Year of Freshwater. Multicoloured.
MS3769 94 × 180 mm. $2 Type **515**; $2 Foot of Chutes de Carbet waterfall; $2 Rapids at foot of Chutes de Carbet waterfall . . 3·25 3·50
MS3770 96 × 67 mm. $6 Waterfall, Ocho Rios, Jamaica (vert) . . 3·25 3·50

516 Corvette Convertible (1954)

2003. 50th Anniv of General Motors Chevrolet Corvette. Multicoloured.
MS3771 110 × 151 mm. $2 Type **516**; $2 Corvette Sting Ray (1964); $2 Corvette Sting Ray Convertible (1964); $2 Corvette Convertible (1998) . . . . 5·00 5·50
MS3772 102 × 74 mm. $6 Corvette Convertible (1956) . . . . . . 3·25 3·50

517 *Flyer I* (first manned powered flight), 1903

2003. Centenary of Powered Flight. Multicoloured.
MS3773 176 × 106 mm. $2 Type **517**; $2 Paul Cornu's helicopter on first helicopter flight, 1907; $2 E.B. Ely's biplane making first landing on ship, 1911; $2 Curtiss A-1 (first seaplane), 1911 . . . . 5·00 5·50
MS3774 176 × 106 mm. $2 Bell X-5 research aircraft with variable wings, 1951; $2 Convair XFY-1 vertical take-off and landing; $2 North American X-15 rocket aircraft, 1959; $2 Alexei Leonov on first spacewalk, 1965 . . . 5·00 5·50
MS3775 176 × 106 mm. $2 Concorde, 1969; $2 Martin X-24 Lifting Body Vehicle Pre-Space Shuttle, 1969; $2 Apollo-Soyuz, 1975; $2 Viking Robot Mars Expedition, 1976 . . . . . . 3·25 3·50
MS3776 Three sheets, each 106 × 76 mm. (a) $6 Boeing Model 200 Monomail with retractable landing gear, 1930. (b) $6 Bell XS-1 rocket plane breaking sound barrier, 1947. (c) $6 Grumman X-29 with forward swept wings, 1984 . . . . 3·25 3·50

2003. As Nos. 2067/81, with overprint smaller and bird inscriptions in English only.
3777 $5 Greater Antillean bullfinch . . . . 2·00 2·10
3778 $10 Caribbean elaenia . . . 4·25 4·50

518 *Psychopsis papilio*

2003. Orchids. Multicoloured.
MS3779 96 × 138 mm. $2.50 Type **518**; $2.50 *Amesiella philippinensis*; $2.50 *Maclellanara* "Pagan Dove Song"; $2.50 *Phalaenopsis* "Little Hal" . . . 5·50 6·00
MS3780 205 × 124 mm. $2.50 *Daeliocattleya* "Amber Glow"; $2.50 *Hygrochilus parishii*; $2.50 *Dendrobium crystallinum*; $2.50 *Disa* hybrid (all horiz) . . . . . 5·50 6·00
MS3781 98 × 68 mm. $5 *Cattleya deckeri* (horiz) . . . . 3·25 3·50

519 Bull Shark

2003. Sharks. Multicoloured.
MS3782 128 × 128 mm. $2 Type **519**; $2 Grey reef shark; $2 Black tip shark; $2 Leopard shark . . . 5·00 5·50
MS3783 88 × 88 mm. $5 Great white shark . . . . 3·25 3·50

520 Esmeralda

2003. Butterflies. Multicoloured.
MS3784 105 × 86 mm. $2 Type **520**; $2 Tiger pierid; $2 Blue night butterfly; $2 *Charaxes nobilis* 5·00 5·50
MS3785 205 × 132 mm. $2.50 Orange-barred sulphur; $2.50 Scarce bamboo page; $2.50 *Charaxes latona*; $2.50 Hewitson's blue hairstreak . . . . 6·00 6·50
MS3786 98 × 68 mm. $5 *Diaethia merdionalis* . . . . 3·25 3·50

521 Apes

2003. Centenary of Circus Clowns. Multicoloured.
MS3787 119 × 195 mm. $1.80 Type **521**; $1.80 Mo Lite; $1.80 Gigi; $1.80 "Buttons" M. C. Bride 4·25 4·50
MS3788 145 × 218 mm. $1.80 Chun Group; $1.80 Casselly Sisters (acrobats); $1.80 Oliver Groszer; $1.80 Keith Nelson (sword swallower) 4·25 4·50
No. **MS**3787 is cut in the shape of a clown on a bicycle and No. **MS**3788 in the shape of a circus elephant.

522 "Madonna and Child" (detail) (Bartolommeo Vivarini)

2003. Christmas. Multicoloured.
3789 25c. Type **522** 20 10
3790 30c. "Holy Family" (detail) (Pompeo Girolano Batoni) 25 15
3791 45c. "Madonna and Child" (detail) (Benozzo Gozzoli) 35 25
3792 50c. "Madonna and Child" (detail) (Benozzo Gozzoli), Calci Parish Church 35 25
3793 75c. "Madonna and Child giving Blessings" (Benozzo Gozzoli) 50 35
3794 90c. "Madonna and Child" (detail) (Master of the Female Half-Figures) 60 40
3795 $2.50 "The Benois Madonna" (detail) (da Vinci) 1·50 1·75
MS3796 70 × 110 mm. $6 "The Virgin and Child with Angels" (Rosso Fiorentino) 3·25 3·50

523 Blue and Yellow Macaw ("Blue and Gold Macaw")

2003. Birds. Multicoloured.
MS3797 96 × 137 mm. $2.50 Type **523**; $2.50 Green-winged macaw; $2.50 Rainbow lory ("Green-naped Lorikeet"); $2.50 Lesser sulphur-crested cockatoo 5·50 6·00
MS3798 205 × 133 mm. $2.50 Chestnut-fronted macaw ("Severe Macaw"); $2.50 Blue-headed parrot; $2.50 Budgerigar; $2.50 Sun conure (all horiz) 5·50 6·00
MS3799 98 × 68 mm. $5 Waldrapp ("Bald Ibis") (horiz) 3·25 3·50

524 Diana Monkey

2004. Chinese New Year ("Year of the Monkey"). Multicoloured.
MS3800 152 × 95 mm. $1.50 Type **524**; $1.50 Mandrill; $1.50 Lar gibbon; $1.50 Red howler monkey 3·25 3·50

525 Mountain Landscape

2004. Hong Kong 2004 International Stamp Exhibition. Paintings by Ren Xiong. Multicoloured.
MS3801 131 × 138 mm. $1.50 Type **525**; $1.50 "Myriad Bamboo in Misty Rain"; $1.50 Winter landscape; $1.50 House and tree 3·25 3·50
MS3802 170 × 137 mm. $1.50 "Myriad Sceptres worshipping Heaven"; $1.50 Misty mountain landscape; $1.50 Maple and cherry trees; $1.50 Mountain landscape with two streams; $1.50 "Myriad Valleys with competing Streams"; $1.50 Myriad lights 5·00 5·50
MS3803 74 × 153 mm. $2.50 Bird singing from flowering cherry branch; $2.50 Bird in maple tree 3·00 3·25
Nos. **MS**3801/2 show paintings from *The Ten Myriads* album and No. **MS**3803 paintings from *Album after the Poems of Yao Xie.*

526 Binky skating

2004. *Arthur the Aardvark* by Marc Brown (children's books and TV programme). T **526** and similar vert designs. Multicoloured.
MS3804 150 × 183 mm. $1.50 Type **526**; $150 Buster skating; $1.50 Francine skating; $1.50 D.W.; $1.50 Sue Ellen; $1.50 Muffy skating 5·00 5·50
MS3805 150 × 183 mm. $1.80 Binky in baseball game; $1.80 Muffy with bat; $1.80 Francine running; $1.80 Buster catching ball 4·00 4·50
MS3806 150 × 183 mm. $2.50 Arthur hitting ball; $2.50 Sue Ellen with bat; $2.50 Binky holding bat; $2.50 Arthur with bat raised 4·00 4·50
No. **MS**3804 shows Arthur characters skating and **MS**3805/6 show them playing baseball.

527 "Freedom of Speech"

2004. 25th Death Anniv of Norman Rockwell (artist) (2003). T **527** and similar vert designs. Multicoloured.
MS3807 135 × 145 mm. $2 Type **527**; $2 "Freedom to Worship"; $2 "Freedom from Want"; $2 "Freedom from Fear" 5·00 5·50
MS3808 62 × 82 mm. $6 "Do Unto Others as you would have them Do Unto You". Imperf 5·00 5·50
No. **MS**3807 shows a series of posters and **MS**3808 a painting for Saturday Evening Post cover, 1961.

528 "Woman with a Flower"

2004. 30th Death Anniv of Pablo Picasso (artist). T **528** and similar vert designs. Multicoloured.
MS3809 177 × 127 mm. $2 Type **528**; $2 "Marie-Therese Seated"; $2 The Red Armchair (Marie-Therese) Seated"; $2 "The Dream (Marie-Therese) Seated" 5·00 5·50
MS3810 58 × 69 mm. $5 "Bust of a Girl (Marie-Therese)". Imperf 3·25 3·50

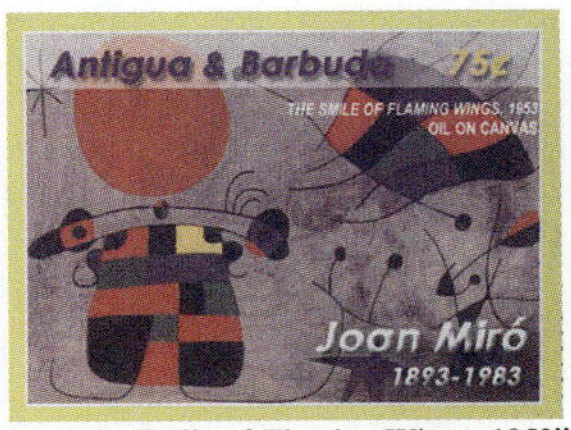

529 "The Smile of Flaming Wings, 1953"

2004. 20th Death Anniv of Joan Miro (artist). Multicoloured.
3811 75c. Type **529** 50 35
3812 90c. "The Bird's Song in the Dew of the Moon, 1955" 60 40
3813 $1 "Dancer II, 1957" (vert) 70 45
3814 $4 "Painting, 1954" (vert) 2·50 3·00
MS3815 Sheet 181 × 152 mm containing four different $2 designs, each entitled "Painting Based on a Collage, 1933" 4·75 5·50
MS3816 Two sheets. (a) 102 × 83 mm. $5 "Bather, 1932". (b) 83 × 102 mm. $6 "Flame in Space and Nude Woman, 1932." Both imperf. Set of 2 sheets 6·25 6·75

530 "Vaite Goupil"

2004. Death Centenary of Paul Gauguin (2003) (artist). Multicoloured.
3817 25c. Type **530** 25 20
3818 30c. "Autoportrait. Pres du Golgotha" 25 20
3819 75c. "Le Moulin David A Pont-Aven" (horiz) 60 40
3820 $2.50 "Moisson en Bretagne" 1·75 1·90
MS3821 77 × 62 mm. $4 "Cavaliers sur la Plage". Imperf 2·50 2·75

531 Felipe de Borbon and Letizia Ortiz

2004. Marriage of Crown Prince Felipe de Borbon and Letizia Ortiz. Multicoloured.
3822 30c. Type **531** 25 15
3823 50c. Felipe de Borbon and Letizia Ortiz in gardens 35 25
3824 75c. Letizia Ortiz 50 30
3825 90c. Felipe de Borbon 60 40
3826 $1 Felipe de Borbon and Letizia Ortiz wearing dark coats 70 55
3827 $5 Felipe de Borbon and Letizia Ortiz at social function 3·00 3·25
MS3828 190 × 174 mm. $1.80 Family photo; $1.80 Felipe de Borbon swearing allegiance to the Flag; $1.80 Felipe de Borbon with father and grandfather; $1.80 With King Juan Carlos I and Queen Sofia (horiz); $1.80 As No. 3824; $1.80 As No. 3825 6·00 6·50
MS3829 Six sheets, each 138 × 123 mm. (a) $5 Family photo. (b) $5 Felipe de Borbon with father and grandfather. (c) $5 Felipe de Borbon and Letizia Ortiz laughing. (d) $6 With King Juan Carlos I and Queen Sofia (horiz). (e) $6 Felipe de Borbon swearing allegiance to the Flag. (f) $6 Letizia Ortiz reading news Set of 6 sheets 17·00 18·00

532 Dove carrying Olive Branch

2004. United Nations International Year of Peace. Sheet 146 × 86 mm containing T **532** and similar horiz designs. Multicoloured.
MS3830 $3 Type **532**; $3 Dove with olive branch and globe; $3 Dove with olive branch and United Nations emblem 5·50 6·00

533 King Class 4-6-0

2004. Bicentenary of Steam Locomotives. Six sheets containing T **533** and similar multicoloured designs.
MS3831 Three sheets. (a) 147 × 175 mm. $1 Type **533**; $1 Argentinian 11B Class 2-8-0; $1 Baldwin Mikado; $1 Track signal; $1 Signal block instrument; $1 Forders Sidings signal box; $1 Signal on line; $1 Signal in snow; $1 Interior of signal box; $1 Two light signals. (b) 147 × 176 mm. $1 Class 2-4-0T, Douglas–Port Erin line; $1 Class 4-8-2S, South African; $1 Class 2-8-2, China; $1 St. Pancras Station; $1 Ulverston Station; $1 Bolton Station; $1 Liverpool Street Station; $1 Cannon Street Station; $1 Malvern Station. (c) 146 × 177 mm. $1 Evening Star (horiz); $1 Indian Railways XC Pacific (horiz); $1 German Kreigslokomotive (horiz); $1 Bullied Light Pacific and Corfe Castle (horiz); $1 Copper cap chimney (horiz); $1 Tallylyn Railway (horiz); $1 Preservation volunteers (horiz); $1 Class Y7 0-4-0T (horiz); $1 Asmara Locoshed and Breda 0-4-0, Eritrea (horiz) Set of 3 sheets 14·00 15·00
MS3832 Three sheets, each 97 × 67 mm. (a) $5 Settle–Carlisle line (horiz). (b) $6 Lake Egridir (horiz). (c) $6 Douro Valley railway (horiz) Set of 3 sheets 9·00 9·50

534 Pope John Paul II and Mother Teresa

2004. 25th Anniv of the Pontificate of Pope John Paul II. Sheet 162 × 152 mm containing T **534** and similar horiz designs. Multicoloured.
MS3833 $1.80 Type **534**; $1.80 At the Wailing Wall; $1.80 With Pres. George W. Bush; $1.80 Waving with left hand; $1.80 Waving with right hand . . . . 7·50 7·50

535 Poster of 1964 Olympic Games, Tokyo

2004. Olympic Games, Athens. Multicoloured.

3834	$1 Type **535**	70	50
3835	$1.65 Commemorative medal of 1964 Olympic Games, Tokyo	1·00	1·00
3836	$1.80 Fencing (horiz) . . .	1·10	1·25
3837	$2 Pankration (wrestling, Greek art) (horiz)	1·25	1·40

536 Milan Galic (Yugoslav player)

2004. European Football Championship 2004, Portugal. Commemoration of First European Football Championship (1960). T **536** and similar multicoloured designs.
MS3838 147 × 86 mm. $2 Type **536**; $2 Slava Metreveli (USSR player); $2 Igor Netto (USSR player); $2 Parc des Princes stadium . . . 4·75 5·50
MS3839 98 × 85 mm. $6 USSR football team, 1960 (50 × 37 *mm*) 3·25 3·50

537 Derrick Tysoe (Durham Light Infantry)

2004. 60th Anniv of D-Day Landings.

3840	**537**	30c. multicoloured . . .	25	20
3841	–	45c. multicoloured . . .	30	20
3842	–	$1.50 multicoloured . .	95	95
3843	–	$3 multicoloured	1·75	1·90

MS3844 Two sheets, each 177 × 107 mm. (a) $2 purple, mauve and black; $2 multicoloured; $2 purple; $2 lilac and black. (b) $2 deep blue and black; $2 blue and black; $2 slate violet and black Set of 2 sheets . . . . . 9·00 9·50
MS3845 Two sheets, each 100 × 69 mm. (a) $6 purple and black. (b) $6 brown and black Set of 2 sheets . . . . . . 7·50 8·00

DESIGNS: No. 3840 Type **537**; No. 3841 Lt. Gen. Walter Bedell Smith; 3842 Les Perry, 1st Battalion, Suffolk Regiment; 3843 Major Gen. Percy Hobart; **MS**3844 (a) $2 Tiger II tank; $2 Kurt Meyer and tactics; $2 Canadian infantry; $2 British infantry; (b) $2 Hamilcar and Tetrarch tank; $2 Horsa Glider and soldiers; $2 Beachheads; $2 Soldiers and civilians; **MS**3845 (a) $6 Mulberry Harbour; (b) $6 Sherman tank.

538 Queen Juliana

2004. Queen Juliana of the Netherlands. Sheet, 170 × 180 mm, containing T **538** and similar horiz designs. Multicoloured.
MS3846 $2 Type **538**; $2 With Prince Bernhard; $2 With Princess Beatrix; $2 With Princess Irene; $2 With Princess Margriet; $2 With Princess Christina . . . . . . 7·50 8·00

539 Mike Bibby

2004. National Basketball Association, China. Sheet, 204 × 140 mm, containing T **539** and similar vert designs. Multicoloured.
MS3847 Type **539**; $1.50 Jim Jackson; $1.50 Tracy McGrady; $1.50 Chris Webber; $1.50 Peja Stojakovic; $1.50 Yao Ming . . 7·00 7·00

540 Zinedine Zidane (France)

2004. Centenary of FIFA (Federation Internationale de Football Association). T **540** and similar horiz designs. Multicoloured.
MS3848 193 × 97 mm. $2 Type **540**; $2 Roberto Baggio (Italy); $2 Franz Beckenbaur (Germany); $2 Ossie Ardiles (Argentina) . . . 3·50 3·75
MS3849 108 × 87 mm. $6 Jimmy Greaves (England) . . . . . . 3·50 3·75

541 George Herman "Babe" Ruth

542 John Denver

2004. Centenary of Baseball World Series. Sheet 127 × 118 mm containing T **541** and similar vert designs showing portraits of George Herman Ruth Jr ("Babe Ruth"). Multicoloured.
MS3850 $1.80 Type **541**; $1.80 Wearing crown; $1.80 Wearing striped cap; $1.80 Holding baseball bat over shoulder . . 3·50 3·75

2004. John Denver Commemoration. Sheet 117 × 107 mm containing T **542** and similar vert designs. Multicoloured.
MS3851 $1.50 Type **542**; $1.50 John Denver (wearing pale waistcoat); $1.50 Wearing dark waistcoat; $1.50 Facing left . . . . . . 3·25 3·50

543 "If you had wider shoulders…"

2004. "The Family Circus" (cartoon). T **543** and similar vert designs. Multicoloured.
MS3852 115 × 176 mm. $2 Type **543**; $2 "Billy attacked me too hard!" (red border); $2 "Who tee-peed the mummies?"; $2 "Looking out there makes me realize its indeed the little things that count" . . 4·25 4·50
MS3853 115 × 176 mm. $2 "Billy attacked me too hard!" (purple border); $2 "His ears came from where his eyes are"; $2 "Tennessee!"; $2 "One candy, or one bowl?" . . . . 4·25 4·50
MS3854 176 × 115 mm. $2 "Someday I might travel to another planet, but I'm not sure why"; $2 "Adam and Eve were lucky. They didn't have any history to learn"; $2 "My backpack is too full. Will somebody help me to stand up?"; $2 "I tripped because one foot tried to hug the other foot" . . 4·25 4·50
MS3855 176 × 115 mm. $2 "If you don't put enough stamps on it the mailman will only take it part way"; $2 "Gee, Grandma, you have a lot of thoughts on your wall"; $2 "Shall I play for you, pa-rum-pa-rum-pummm…"; $2 "You have to do that when you're married" . . . . 4·25 4·50
MS3856 192 × 105 mm. $2 Billy; $2 Jeffy; $2 PJ; $2 Dolly . . . . 4·25 4·50

544 People holding Balloons forming AIDS Ribbon

2004. World AIDS Day.

3857	**544**	$2 multicoloured	1·25	1·40

545 "Madonna in Floral Wreath" (Bruegel the Elder with Rubens)

546 Santa on Skis

2004. Christmas. Multicoloured. (a) As T **545**.

3858	20c. Type **545**	20	15
3859	25c. "Madonna and Child" (detail) (Mabuse (Jan Gossaert))	20	25
3860	$1 "Floral Wreath with Virgin and Child" (detail) (Daniel Seghers)	70	45
3861	$1.80 "Madonna and Child" (detail) (Andrea Mantegna)	1·10	1·25

MS3862 70 × 100 mm. $6 "Madonna in a Floral Wreath" (Daniel Seghers) . . . . 3·25 3·50

(b) As T **546**.

3863	30c. Type **546**	25	15
3864	45c. Santa ornament with arms raised	30	25
3865	50c. Santa on chimney . . .	35	25

547 American Pit (inscr "Pitt") Bull Terrier

2005. Cats and Dogs. Multicoloured.

3866	30c. Type **547**	30	20
3867	75c. Golden Persian	50	40
3868	90c. Maltese (dog)	60	45
3869	$1 Calico shorthair (cat) . .	70	60
3870	$1.50 Siamese	90	90
3871	$1.50 Rottweiler	90	90
3872	$3 Tabby Persian	1·75	2·00
3873	$3 Australian terrier	1·75	2·00

MS3874 Two sheets, each 100 × 70 mm. (a) $5 Turkish cat. (b) $5 German shepherd dog (horiz) . . . . 6·00 6·50

548 Yellowtail Damselfish

2005. Tropical Sea Life. Multicoloured.
MS3875 143 × 84 mm. $2 Type **548**; $2 French angelfish; $2 Horseshoe crab; $2 Emerald mithrax crab 4·75 5·00
MS3876 100 × 70 mm. $6 Spanish hogfish . . . . 3·25 3·50
The stamps within **MS**3875 form a composite design of a coral reef.

549 Figure-of-eight Butterfly

2005. Insects. Multicoloured.
MS3877 143 × 83 mm. $2 Type **549**; $2 Honey bee; $2 Migratory grasshopper; $2 Hercules beetle 4·75 5·00
MS3878 100 × 70 mm. $5 Cramer's mesene butterfly (vert) . . . . 3·00 3·25

550 Mammuthus imperator

2005. Prehistoric Animals. Multicoloured.
MS3879 Three sheets, each 140 × 110 mm. (a) $2 Type **550**; $2 Brontops; $2 Hyracotherium; $2 Propaleotherium. (b) $2.50 Ceratosaurs; $2.50 Coelurosaurs; $2.50 Ornitholestes; $2.50 Baryonyx. (c) $3 Plateosaurus; $3 Yangchuanosaurus; $3 Ceolophysis; $3 Lystrosaurus 15·00 16·00
MS3880 Three sheets, each 98 × 70 mm. (a) $4 Triceratops. (b) $5 Stegosaurus. (c) $6 Coelodonta 6·00 6·25
The stamps within Nos. **MS**3879a/c each form composite background designs.

551 Uruguay Team, 1930

2005. 75th Anniv of First World Cup Football Championship, Uruguay. Multicoloured.

3881	$2.50 Type **551**	1·50	1·60
3882	$2.50 Hector Castro scoring goal against Argentina, World Cup final, 1930 . .	1·50	1·60
3883	$2.50 Estadio Centenario . .	1·50	1·60
3884	$2.50 Hector Castro	1·50	1·60

MS3885 111 × 86 mm. $6 Players after victory of Uruguay, 1930 3·25 3·50

552 Bust of Von Schiller (C. L. Richter), Central Park, New York

2005. Death Bicentenary of Friedrich von Schiller (poet and dramatist). Multicoloured.

3886 $3 Type **552** . . . . 1·75 2·00
3887 $3 Modern performance of *Kabale und Liebe* . . . . 1·75 2·00
3888 $3 Von Schiller's birthplace, Marbach, Germany . . . 1·75 2·00
MS3889 66 × 95 mm. $6 Von Schiller and statue, Lincoln Park, Chicago 3·25 3·50

553 *Misterio en la Isla de los Monstruos*, 1961

2005. Death Centenary of Jules Verne (writer). Posters from films of Jules Verne's novels. Multicoloured.

3890 $2 Type **553** . . . . 1·25 1·40
3891 $2 *Journey to the Centre of the Earth*, 1961 . . . . . 1·25 1·40
3892 $2 *From the Earth to the Moon*, 1956 . . . . . . 1·25 1·40
3893 $2 *Los Diablos del Mar*, 1961 . . . . 1·25 1·40
MS3894 103 × 97 mm. $5 Michael Strogoff (56 × 41 mm) . . . . 3·00 3·25

554 British attempting to Board Spanish Ship *Santisima Trinidad*

2005. Bicentenary of the Battle of Trafalgar. Multicoloured.

3895 90c. Type **554** . . . . . . 1·00 70
3896 $1 Sailors clinging to wreckage and HMS *Royal Sovereign*, *Santa Ana*, HMS *Mars*, Fouguex and HMS *Temeraire* . . . . . 1·25 90
3897 $1.50 HMS *Britannia* firing on crippled French *Bucentaure* . . . . . . 1·50 1·50
3898 $1.80 French *Redoubtable* and HMS *Victory* . . . . 1·75 2·00
MS3899 90 × 122 mm. $6 Crew of HMS *Victory* firing during battle 4·75 5·00

555 Ronald Reagan **556** Defeated German Soldiers, Red Square, 9 May 1945

2005. Ronald Reagan (US President 1981–9) Commemoration.

3900 **555** $1.50 multicoloured . . 90 90

2005. 60th Anniv of Victory in Europe Day. Multicoloured.

3901 $1.50 Type **556** 90 90
3902 $1.50 General Montgomery . . 90 90
3903 $1.50 Marshal Zhukov . . . 90 90
3904 $1.50 General Bradley . . . 90 90

557 Churchill, Roosevelt and Stalin at Yalta Summit, 1945

2005. 60th Anniv of Victory in Japan Day. Multicoloured.

3905 $2 Type **557** . . . . 1·25 1·25
3906 $2 US troops raising flag on Mt. Suribachi . . . . . . 1·25 1·25
3907 $2 Gen. McArthur signing Japanese surrender documents . . . . 1·25 1·25
3908 $2 Surrendering Japanese officials, 2 September 1945 1·25 1·25

558 "Mother Hen and her Brood" (Wang Ning)

2005. Chinese New Year ("Year of the Rooster"). Multicoloured.

3909 $1 Type **558** 70 75
MS3910 75 × 105 mm. $4 "Mother Hen and her Brood" (Wang Ning) 2·50 2·75

559 Dwight Howard, Orlando Magic

2005. US National Basketball Association Players. Multicoloured.

3911 75c. Type **559** 70 55
3912 75c. Lucious Harris, Cleveland Cavaliers . . . 70 55
3913 75c. Emeka Okafor, Charlotte Bobcats 70 55
3914 75c. Antonio McDyess, Detroit Pistons 70 55
3915 75c. Ray Allen, Seattle Supersonics 70 55

560 Pope John Paul II with Rabbi Meir Lau (Chief Rabbi of Israel, 1993–2003) **561** Italy 1979 World Rotary Congress Stamp

2005. Pope John Paul II Commemoration.

3916 **560** $3 multicoloured . . . . 2·75 2·75

2005. Centenary of Rotary International. Multicoloured.

3917 $3 Type **561** . . . . 1·75 1·90
3918 $3 Paul Harris medallion and "Sow the Seeds of Love" . . . . 1·75 1·90
3919 $3 Paul Harris (founder), Tokyo, 1935 . . . . . . 1·75 1·90
MS3920 100 × 70 mm. $6 Young African children (horiz) . . . . 3·25 3·50

562 Albert Einstein

2005. 50th Death Anniv of Albert Einstein (physicist). Multi.

3921 $3 Type **562** . . . . 1·75 1·90
3922 $3 On bicycle . . . . 1·75 1·90
3923 $3 Albert Einstein (grey background) . . . . . . 1·75 1·90

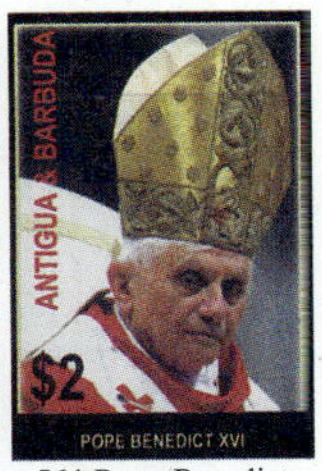

563 Hans Christian Andersen **564** Pope Benedict XVI

2005. Birth Bicentenary of Hans Christian Andersen (writer). Multicoloured.

3924 $3 Type **563** . . . . 1·75 1·90
3925 $3 Statue in Central Park, New York . . . . 1·75 1·90
3926 $3 Tombstone . . . . . . 1·75 1·90
MS3927 100 × 70 mm. $6 Hans Christian Andersen seated in chair 3·25 3·50

2005. Election of Pope Benedict XVI.

3928 **564** $2 multicoloured . . . . 1·75 1·75

565 Gilbert's Memorial Methodist Church

2005. Christmas. Churches. Multicoloured.

3929 25c. Type **565** 25 15
3930 30c. The People's Church, Barbuda 30 20
3931 30c. Tyrell's Roman Catholic Church 30 20
3932 45c. St. Barnabas Anglican Church 35 20
3933 50c. St. Peter's Anglican Church 40 30
3934 75c. Spring Gardens Moravian Church 50 40
3935 75c. St. Steven's Anglican Church 50 40
3936 90c. Pilgrim Holiness Church (vert) 60 45
3937 90c. Holy Family Catholic Cathedral 60 45
3938 $1 Ebenezer Methodist Church 70 75
MS3939 Two sheets, each 100 × 70 mm. (a) $5 St. John's Cathedral. (b) $5 Service at Spring Gardens Moravian Church (vert) 6·00 5·50

566 The Joiners Loft, Nelson's Dockyard

2005. National Parks of Antigua. Multicoloured

3940 20c. Type **566** 15 20
3941 20c. Pay Office, Nelson's Dockyard (vert) 15 20
3942 30c. Bakery, Nelson's Dockyard 30 20
3943 30c. Admirals House Museum, Nelson's Dockyard 30 20
3944 75c. Devil's Bridge National Park 50 40
3945 75c. View from Shirley Heights Lookout, Nelson's Dockyard National Park 50 40
3946 90c. Green Castle Hill National Park 60 45
3947 90c. Fort Berkeley, Nelson's Dockyard National Park 60 45
3948 $1.50 Pigeon Point Beach, Nelson's Dockyard National Park 90 90
3949 $1.50 Half Moon Bay National Park 90 90
3950 $1.80 Cannon at Fort Berkeley . . . . 1·10 1·25
MS3951 Two sheets, (a) 96 × 67 mm. $5 Frigate birds nesting at Codrington Lagoon National Park, Barbuda. (b) 65 × 96 mm. $5 Cannon and Admirals House Museum, Nelson's Dockyard (vert) . . . . 6·00 6·50

567 Yellowstone National Park

2006. National Parks of the USA. Multicoloured.

3952 $1.50 Type **567** 90 90
3953 $1.50 Olympic National Park 90 90
3954 $1.50 Glacier National Park 90 90
3955 $1.50 Grand Canyon National Park 90 90
3956 $1.50 Yosemite National Park 90 90
3957 $1.50 Great Smoky Mountains National Park 90 90
MS3958 95 × 70 mm. $6 Mount Rainier National Park (42 × 28 mm) . . . . 3·25 3·50

568 Bishop John Ephraim Knight **570** Marilyn Monroe

569 Princess Elizabeth

2006. 250th Anniv of Moravian Church in Antigua. Moravian Church Antigua Conference. Multicoloured.

3959 30c. Type **568** 25 15
3960 $1 John Andrew Buckley (minister 1856–79) 70 55
3961 $1.50 Old Spring Gardens Moravian Church, 1854–1963 (horiz) 90 90
MS3962 Three sheets, each 95 × 60 mm. (a) $5 Westerby Memorial, St. John's. (b) $5 Sandbox Tree (site of beginnings of Antigua Moravian Church). (c) $5 Spring Gardens Teachers College, 1854–1958 (horiz) . . 5·50 6·00

2006. 80th Birthday of Queen Elizabeth II. Multicoloured.

3963 $2 Type **569** . . . . . . 1·10 1·10
3964 $2 Princess Elizabeth wearing cream dress and pearl necklace . . . . . 1·10 1·10
3965 $2 Princess Elizabeth wearing white blouse . . 1·10 1·10
3966 $2 Queen Elizabeth II wearing diadem and red dress . . . . 1·10 1·10
MS3967 120 × 120 mm. $6 Queen Elizabeth II wearing diadem and drop earrings . . . . 3·00 3·25

2006. 80th Birth Anniv of Marilyn Monroe (actress).

3968 **570** $3 multicoloured . . . . 1·75 1·75

571 Austria 2s.20 Ice Hockey Stamp

2006. Winter Olympic Games, Turin. Showing Austrian stamps issued for 1964 Olympic Games, Innsbruck (Nos. 3964/6) or poster (No. 3967). Multicoloured.

3969 75c. Type **571** 50 40
3970 75c. Poster for Winter Olympic Games, Sapporo, 1972 (vert) 50 40
3971 90c. Japan 1972 Winter Olympics 20y. skiing stamp (vert) 60 40
3972 90c. (1s.80) Figure skating stamp 60 40

3973 $2 4s. Bobsleighing stamp 1·25 1·25
3974 $3 Poster for Winter Olympic Games, Innsbruck, 1964 (vert) . . 1·75 1·75

572 Benjamin Franklin

2006. Washington 2006 International Stamp Exhibition. Showing Benjamin Franklin. Multicoloured.
MS3975 Two sheets, each 140 × 152 mm. (a) $3 × 4 Type **572**, Wearing red in oval portrait in gold frame (84 × 93 mm) (imperf); USA 1847 5c. stamp; Close-up portrait. (b) $3 × 3 Round portraits in gold frames: Wearing red; Sitting at desk; In close-up . . . . . . 11·00 12·00

573 Mozart's Viola

2006. 250th Birth Anniv of Wolfgang Amadeus Mozart (composer). Multicoloured.
3976 $3 Type **573** . . . . 1·75 1·75
3977 $3 Mozart aged eleven . . . 1·75 1·75
3978 $3 Young Mozart . . . . . . 1·75 1·75
3979 $3 Mozart in Verona, 1770 1·75 1·75

574 Elvis Presley in "Charro!"

2006. 50th Anniv of Elvis Presley's Film Debut. Sheet 190 × 127 mm containing T **574** and similar vert designs showing film posters. Multicoloured.
3980 $3 Type **574** . . . . 1·75 1·75
3981 $3 "Follow That Dream" 1·75 1·75
3982 $3 "G I Blues" . . . . 1·75 1·75
3983 $3 "Blue Hawaii" . . . . . 1·75 1·75

575 Leaders after Garbage Collection Race, 2002

2006. 75th Anniv of Antigua and Barbuda Girl Guides. Multicoloured.
3984 25c. Type **575** 20 10
3985 30c. Girl guides colour party (horiz) 25 15
3986 45c. Uniformed and non-uniformed members . . . 30 20
3987 50c. Girl guides marching band (horiz) 30 25
3988 $1 Leeward Islands leaders training camp, 1946 (horiz) 70 55
MS3989 Three sheets, each 100 × 70 mm. (a) $5 Enrolment ceremony, 2006 (horiz). (b) $5 Girl guides gathering at Fort James, 1935 (horiz). (c) $5 Lisa Simon, Assistant Commissioner . . . 8·25 8·50

576 HS-748 Hawker Siddely Avro

2006. 50th Anniv of LIAT (Leeward Islands Air Transport) Airline. Multicoloured.
3990 30c. Type **576** 25 15
3991 50c. BN2 Islanders on ground 30 20
3992 50c. BN2 Norman Islander 30 20
3993 50c. Beechcraft Twin Bonanza (vert) 30 20
3994 $1.50 BAC111-orange and HS748-pink/lilac on ground 90 90
3995 $2.50 Present brand DH8-300 50 seater De Havilland on ground . . 1·60 1·40
MS3996 70 × 100 mm. $5 Sir Frank Delisle (founder) and first Beechcraft Twin Bonanza N9614R (vert) . . . . 2·75 3·00

577 Magnificent Frigate Bird

2006. 25th Anniv of Independence. Multicoloured.
3997 25c. Type **577** 20 10
3998 25c. Fallow deer hinds . . . 20 10
3999 25c. Fallow deer stag on beach 20 10
4000 25c. Magnificent frigate birds in flight and on nest 20 10
4001 30c. Pineapple 25 15
4002 $1 National flag 70 55
4003 $1.50 Coat of Arms 90 90
MS4004 100 × 70 mm. $5 New Parliament building (38 × 49 mm) 2·75 3·00

578 JSC Shuttle Mission Simulator (SMS)

2006. Space Anniversaries. Multicoloured. (a) 25th Anniv of First Flight of Space Shuttle "Columbia".
4005 $2 Type **578** . . . . 1·25 1·25
4006 $2 STS-1 prime crew during classroom session . . . . 1·25 1·25
4007 $2 STS-1 "Columbia" on launch pad . . . . 1·25 1·25
4008 $2 STS-1 "Columbia" blast-off . . . . 1·25 1·25
4009 $2 Pre-touchdown landing of "Columbia" at Edwards AFB, California 1·25 1·25
4010 $2 Space shuttle "Columbia" landing at Edwards Air Force Base 1·25 1·25

(b) 40th Anniv of "Luna 9" Moon Landing.
4011 $3 Molniya 8K78M rocket on launch vehicle . . . . 1·75 1·75
4012 $3 "Luna 9" flight apparatus . . . . 1·75 1·75
4013 $3 Image of Moon's surface transmitted by "Luna 9" 1·75 1·75
4014 $3 "Luna 9" capsule . . . . 1·75 1·75

(c) 30th Anniv (2005) of "Apollo-Soyuz" Test Project.
4015 $3 "Apollo" crew boarding transfer van . . . . . . 1·75 1·75
4016 $3 Handshake after "Apollo-Soyuz" linkup . . 1·75 1·75
4017 $3 Display of ASTP commemorative plaque 1·75 1·75
4018 $3 Recovery of ASTP Apollo command module 1·75 1·75
MS4019 Three sheets, each 100 × 70 mm. (a) $6 Calipso satellite. (b) $6 SS *Atlantis* docking on Space Station "MIR". (c) $6 Artist's concept of a NASA spaceship to orbit the Moon 9·00 9·75

579 Dalai Lama (Tibetan leader)

581 Bauble

580 "Landscape with the Baptism of the Eunuch" (detail)

2006. Civil Rights. Multicoloured.
4020 $2 Type **579** . . . . 1·25 1·25
4021 $2 Abraham Lincoln (slavery abolitionist) . . . 1·25 1·25
4022 $2 Susan Anthony (women's suffragist) . . . . 1·25 1·25
4023 $2 Harriet Tubman (slave liberator) . . . . 1·25 1·25
4024 $2 Mahatma Gandhi (Indian leader) . . . . . 1·25 1·25
4025 $2 Nelson Mandela (anti-apartheid leader) . . . . 1·25 1·25
4026 $2 Rosa Parks (civil rights activist) . . . . 1·25 1·25
MS4027 70 × 100 mm. $5 Martin Luther King (civil rights leader) 2·75 3·00

2006. 400th Birth Anniv of Rembrandt Harmenszoon van Rijn (artist). Multicoloured.
4028 50c. Type **580** 30 20
4029 75c. "Landscape with a Coach" (detail) 50 40
4030 $1 "River Landscape with Ruins" (detail) 70 55
4031 $2 "Landscape with a Castle" (detail) . . . . . 1·25 1·25
4032 $2 "Samson Posing the Riddle to the Wedding Guests" (detail, Samson's bride) . . . . 1·25 1·25
4033 $2 "Samson Posing the Riddle to the Wedding Guests" (detail, two men) 1·25 1·25
4034 $2 "Samson Posing the Riddle to the Wedding Guests" (detail, two guests listening) . . . . . 1·25 1·25
4035 $2 "Samson Posing the Riddle to the Wedding Guests" (detail, woman) 1·25 1·25
4036 $2 "The Holy Family (detail, man sitting at table) . . . . 1·25 1·25
4037 $2 "The Good Samaritan arriving at the Inn" (detail) . . . . 1·25 1·25
4038 $2 "Rebecca Taking Leave of her Family" (detail) . . 1·25 1·25
4039 $2 "The Holy Family" (detail, man sitting) . . . 1·25 1·25
MS4040 Two sheets, each 70 × 100 mm. (a) $5 "Self-Portrait". (b) $5 "Rembrandt's Mother". Both imperf . . . . 5·50 6·00

2006. Christmas. Multicoloured.
4041 30c. Type **581** 25 15
4042 90c. Gold star 65 50
4043 $1 Red bell 70 55
4044 $1.50 Miniature tree 90 75
MS4045 100 × 150 mm. $2 × 4 As Nos. 4041/4 . . . . 5·00 4·50
MS4046 100 × 70 mm. $6 Santa on beach with wrapped presents 3·00 2·75

Nos. 4041/5 show Christmas tree decorations.

Stamps from **MS**4045 are in similar designs to Nos. 4041/4 but have the country inscription at top and no coloured panel at the foot of the stamp.

The background of **MS**4045 forms a composite design showing a decorated Christmas tree.

582 Betty Boop

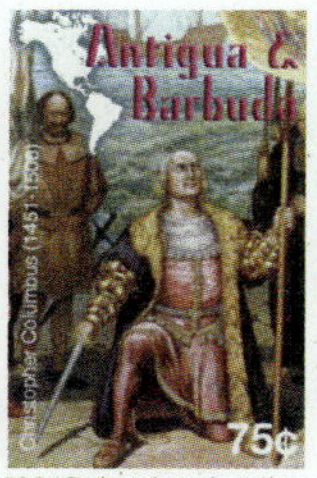

583 Columbus landing in New World

2006. Betty Boop. Multicoloured.
4047 $1.50 Type **582** 90 75
4048 $1.50 Leaning forward . . . 90 75
4049 $1.50 Holding mirror . . . 90 75
4050 $1.50 Holding microphone 90 75
4051 $1.50 Seated, looking over shoulder 90 75
4052 $1.50 Wearing red heart garter 90 75
MS4053 70 × 100 mm. $3 "BETTY BOOP"; $3 With yellow fur stole 3·00 2·75

2007. 500th Death Anniv of Christopher Columbus. Multicoloured.
4054 75c. Type **583** 50 40
4055 90c. Christopher Columbus 60 45
4056 $2 Columbus (portrait in oval frame) . . . . 1·25 1·25
4057 $3 Columbus (in profile) . . 1·75 1·75
MS4058 100 × 70 mm. $6 *Nina*, *Pinta* and *Santa Maria* . . . . . . 3·00 3·25

584 National Flags forming Knot

2007. Centenary of World Scout Movement. Multicoloured.
4059 $4 Type **584** . . . . 2·25 2·25
MS4060 110 × 80 mm. $6 National flags forming knot . . . . . . 3·00 3·25

585 Ensign Kennedy

2007. 90th Birth Anniv of John F. Kennedy (American President 1960–3). Multicoloured.
4061 $3 Type **585** . . . . 1·75 1·75
4062 $3 Kennedy and crew members . . . . 1·75 1·75
4063 $3 Kennedy at the USS *PT-109* . . . . 1·75 1·75
4064 $3 Kennedy in the South Pacific . . . . 1·75 1·75
4065 $3 Campaigning on crutches 1·75 1·75
4066 $3 "The New Congressman" 1·75 1·75
4067 $3 John F. Fitzgerald, Joseph Kennedy and John F. Kennedy . . . . . . 1·75 1·75
4068 $3 "Celebrating Victory" . . 1·75 1·75

Nos. 4061/4 (showing John Kennedy in the Navy, 1941–5) and 4065/8 (showing his election to the House of Representatives, 1947–53).

586 *Alamanda*

587 *Callicore maimuna* (figure-of-eight butterfly)

2007. Flowers. Multicoloured.
4069 75c. Type **586** 50 40
4070 90c. *Bidens sulphurea* . . . 60 45
4071 $1 *Alstroemeria caryophyllacea* 70 55
4072 $2 *Canna limbata* (*horiz*) . . 1·25 1·25
4073 $2 *Gazania rigens* (*horiz*) . . 1·25 1·25
4074 $2 *Gloriosa rothschildiana* (*horiz*) . . . . 1·25 1·25
4075 $2 *Hibiscus sinensis* (*horiz*) 1·25 1·25
4076 $4 *Bougainvillea* . . . . . . 2·25 2·25
MS4077 100 × 70 mm. $6 *Caesalpinia pulcherrima* . . . . 3·00 3·25

2007. Butterflies of the Caribbean. Multicoloured.
4078 75c. Type **587** 50 40
4079 90c. *Dismorphia amphione* (tiger pierid) 60 45

4080	$1 *Eryphanis polyxena* (purple mort bleu)	70	55
4081	$4 *Colobura dirce* (mosaic butterfly)	2·25	2·25
MS4082	130×108 mm. $2×4 *Actinote pellenea* (small lacewing); *Anteos clorinde* (clorinde); *Morpho peleides* (common morpho); *Anartia jatrophae* (white peacock)	4·50	4·50
MS4083	70×99 mm. $5 *Catonephele numilia* (Grecian shoemaker)	2·75	2·75

The stamps and margins of No. **MS**4082 form a composite design of palm tree foliage.

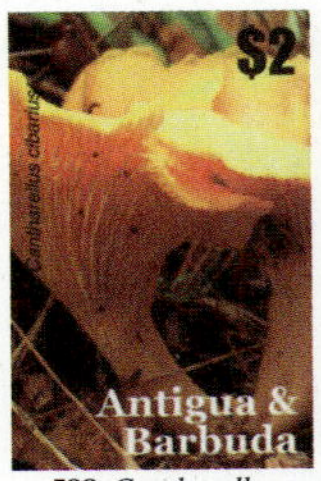

588 *Cantharellus cibarius*

590 Kenneth Benjamin

589 *Oncidium flexuosum*

2007. Mushrooms of the Caribbean. Multicoloured.

MS4084	131×108 mm. $2×4 Type **588**; *Auricularia auricula-judae*; *Mycena acicula*; *Peziza vesiculosa*	4·50	4·50
MS4085	100×70 mm. $6 *Pleurotus djamor*	3·00	3·25

The stamps and margins of No. **MS**4084 form a composite design.

2007. Orchids. Multicoloured.

4086	$3 Type **589**	1·75	1·75
4087	$3 *Paphiopedilum Pinocchio*	1·75	
4088	$3 *Cattleyopsis lindenii*	1·75	1·75
4089	$3 *Cattleyopsis cubensis*	1·75	1·75
MS4090	100×70 mm. $6 *Osmoglossum pulchellum* (*vert*)	3·00	3·25

2007. World Cup Cricket, West Indies. Famous West Indian Cricketers. Multicoloured.

4091	25c. Type **590**	15	10
4092	30c. Anderson Roberts	20	15
4093	90c. Ridley Jacobs	60	45
4094	$1 Curtly Ambrose	70	55
4095	$1.50 Richard (Richie) Richardson	90	75
MS4096	117×90 mm. $5 Sir Vivian Richards	2·75	3·00

591 Princess Elizabeth and Duke of Edinburgh

2007. Diamond Wedding of Queen Elizabeth II and Duke of Edinburgh. Multicoloured.

4097	$1.50 Type **591**	90	75
4098	$1.50 Wedding shoes	90	75
MS4099	101×70 mm. $6 On wedding day with family (*vert*)	3·00	3·25

592 Camellias and Butterfly

2007. 50th Death Anniv of Qi Baishi (artist). Paintings on Fans. Multicoloured.

4100	$1.50 Type **592**	90	75
4101	$1.50 Two shrimps and arrowhead leaves	90	75
4102	$1.50 Gourd and ladybug	90	75
4103	$1.50 Bird	90	75
4104	$1.50 Landscape	90	75
4105	$1.50 Five shrimps	90	75
MS4106	(a) 102×72 mm. $3 Chrysanthemums; $3 Maple leaves (both vert). (b) 72×102 mm. $6 Wisteria (*vert*)	7·00	7·50

593 Ferrari 365 GTS4, 1969

2007. Ferrari Classic Cars. Multicoloured.

4107	$1.40 Type **593**	85	70
4108	$1.40 Superamerica, 2005	85	70
4109	$1.40 F1 90, 1990	85	70
4110	$1.40 400 Automatic, 1976	85	70
4111	$1.40 250 GT Coupe, 1954	85	70
4112	$1.40 156 F2, 1960	85	70
4113	$1.40 312 P, 1972	85	70
4114	$1.40 D 50, 1956	85	70

594 Concorde 01 rolled out, Filton, 20 Sept 1971

2007. Concorde. Multicoloured.

4115	$1.50 Type **594**	90	75
4116	$1.50 Concorde 01 (G-AXDN) in flight (green border)	90	75
4117	$1.50 As Type **594** (violet border)	90	75
4118	$1.50 As No. 4116 (magenta)	90	75
4119	$1.50 As Type **594** (green border)	90	75
4120	$1.50 As No. 4116 (violet border)	90	75
4121	$1.50 Concorde and London Eye (green inscr)	90	75
4122	$1.50 Concorde and Sydney Opera House (black inscr)	90	75
4123	$1.50 As No. 4121 (magenta inscr)	90	75
4124	$1.50 As No. 4122 (orange inscr)	90	75
4125	$1.50 As No. 4121 (black inscr)	90	75
4126	$1.50 As No. 4122 (blue inscr)	90	75

Nos. 4115/20 show Concorde 01, the first pre-production aircraft.

Nos. 4121/6 commemorate the London to Sydney flight record set on 13 February 1985. The colours given for Nos. 4121/6 are those of the country inscription 'ANTIGUA & BARBUDA'.

595 NH-90 Helicopter

2007. Centenary of the Helicopter. Multicoloured.

4127	$1.50 Type **595**	90	75
4128	$1.50 BO 105 helicopter carrying pipes	90	75
4129	$1.50 NH-90 helicopter on ground	90	75
4130	$1.50 AS-61 helicopter 6-15 over sea	90	75
4131	$1.50 BO 105 helicopter and lighthouse	90	75
4132	$1.50 AS-61 helicopter 6-26	90	75
MS4133	100×71 mm. $6 Bell UH-1 Iroquois 'Huey' troop carrier (*vert*)	3·00	3·25

596 Pope Benedict XVI

597 Elvis Presley

598 Diana, Princess of Wales

2007. 80th Birthday of Pope Benedict XVI.

4134 **596**	$1.40 multicoloured	85	70

2007. 30th Death Anniv of Elvis Presley. Multicoloured.

4135	$1.50 Type **597**	90	75
4136	$1.50 Wearing striped shirt, seen in profile	90	75
4137	$1.50 Holding guitar, wearing jacket and bow tie	90	75
4138	$1.50 Wearing striped shirt, smiling	90	75
4139	$1.50 Wearing red shirt	90	75
4140	$1.50 Holding guitar, seen in half-profile	90	75

2007. 10th Death Anniv of Diana, Princess of Wales. Multicoloured.

4141	$2 Type **598**	1·25	1·25
4142	$2 Wearing pale mauve and drop earrings	1·25	1·25
4143	$2 Wearing purple jacket with black edging on collar	1·25	1·25
4144	$2 Wearing brownish grey and white dress and hat	1·25	1·25
MS4145	70×100 mm. $6 Wearing headscarf	3·00	2·75

599 *Strelitzia parvifolia* (bird of paradise)

600 John W. Ashe, Antigua & Barbuda

2007. Plants and Trees. Multicoloured.

4146	15c. Type **599**	15	10
4147	20c. *Thespesia populnea* (seaside mahoe)	20	15
4148	30c. *Hibiscus rosa sinensis*	25	15
4149	50c. *Agave karatto*	30	20
4150	70c. *Barringtonia asiatica*	45	35
4151	75c. *Cocos nucifera* (coconut)	50	40
4152	90c. *Prosopis chilensis* (mesquite) (*horiz*)	60	45
4153	$1 *Tamarindus indica*	70	55
4154	$1.50 *Capparis cynophallophora* (black willow) (*horiz*)	90	75
4155	$1.80 Baobab (*horiz*)	1·10	1·10
4156	$2 *Petrea volubilis*	1·25	1·25
4157	$2.50 *Opuntia cochenillifera* (cactus) (*horiz*)	1·50	1·50
4158	$5 *Hymenaea courbaril* (locust fruit) (*horiz*)	2·75	3·00
4159	$10 *Caesalpinia ciliata* (Barbuda black warri)	5·25	5·50
4160	$20 *Ricinus communis* (castor oil plant)	10·00	10·50

2007. Holocaust Remembrance. Multicoloured.

4161	$1.40 Type **600**	85	70
4162	$1.40 Alfred Capelle, Marshall Islands	85	70
4163	$1.40 Masao Nakayama, Micronesia	85	70
4164	$1.40 Gilles Noghes, Monaco	85	70
4165	$1.40 Baatar Choisuren, Mongolia	85	70
4166	$1.40 Filipe Chiduma, Mozambique	85	70
4167	$1.40 Marlene Moses, Nauru	85	70
4168	$1.40 Franciscus Majoor, Netherlands	85	70

601 Antigua and Barbuda on Bauble

2007. Christmas. Multicoloured.

4169	30c. Type **601**	25	15
4170	90c. Decorated palm tree and parade dancers on beach	65	50
4171	$1 Cake decorations	70	55
4172	$1.50 Parade costume	90	75

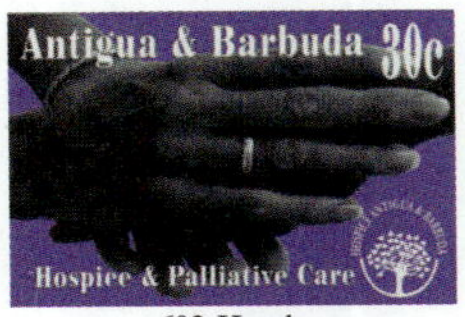

602 Hands

2007. World Hospice and Palliative Care Day. Multicoloured.

4173	30c. Type **602**	25	15
4174	30c. Clock	25	15

ANTIOQUIA Pt. 20

One of the states of the Granadine Confederation. A department of Colombia from 1886, now uses Colombian stamps.

100 centavos = 1 peso.

1

5

6

1868. Various arms designs. Imperf.

1 **1**	2½c. blue	£450	£225
2 –	5c. green	£350	£200
3 –	10c. lilac	£850	£385
4 –	1p. red	£300	£185

1869. Various frames. Imperf.

5 **5**	2½c. blue	2·50	2·00
6	5c. green	3·25	3·00
8	10c. mauve	4·00	2·00
9	20c. brown	4·50	3·00
10 **6**	1p. red	7·50	7·50

7

15

1873. Arms designs inscr "E.S." (or "Eo. So." or "Estado Soberano") "de Antioquia". Imperf.

11 **7**	1c. green	2·00	1·50
12 –	5c. green	2·50	1·60
13 –	10c. mauve	16·00	12·00
14 –	20c. brown	4·00	2·50
15 –	50c. blue	1·00	80
16 –	1p. red	2·50	2·50
17 –	2p. black on yellow	5·00	5·00
18 –	5p. black on red	25·00	20·00

The 5p. is larger (25½×31½ mm).

1875. Imperf.

20 **15**	1c. black on green	60	60
43	1c. mauve	1·00	1·00
21	1c. black	60	60
52	1c. green	1·00	1·00
22 –	2½c. blue (Arms)	80	80
23 –	5c. green ("Liberty")	6·00	5·00
25 –	10c. mauve (J. Berrio)	8·00	7·00

20 Condor

21 Liberty

23 Liberty

25 Liberty

1879. Imperf.

30 **20**	2½c. blue	3·00	3·00
38	2½c. green	80	1·00
45	2½c. black on buff	3·00	3·00
39 **21**	5c. green	85	1·00
40	5c. violet	1·75	1·00
32 –	10c. violet (Arms)	£250	£200
36 **23**	10c. violet	50·00	16·00

41		10c. red	1·00	1·00
42	21	20c. brown	1·25	1·25

1883. Various frames. Head of Liberty to left. Imperf.

53	25	5c. brown	4·00	2·00
47		5c. yellow	3·00	2·50
48		5c. green	55·00	40·00
49		10c. green	2·00	2·00
50		10c. mauve	3·50	3·50
55		10c. blue	4·00	3·50
51		20c. blue	2·50	2·50

28

31

1886. Imperf.

57	28	1c. green on pink	50	50
65		1c. red on lilac	30	30
58		2½c. black on orange	35	40
66		2½c. mauve on pink	50	40
59		5c. blue on buff	2·00	75
67		5c. red on green	2·25	2·25
68		5c. lake on buff	1·00	80
60		10c. red on buff	1·00	60
69		10c. brown on green	1·00	80
61		20c. purple on buff	1·00	60
62		50c. yellow on buff	2·00	2·00
63		1p. yellow on green	4·00	4·00
64		2p. green on lilac	4·00	4·00

1888. Various sizes and frames. Inscr "MEDELLIN". Imperf.

70	31	2½c. black on yellow	15·00	12·00
71		2½c. red on white	2·50	2·50
72		5c. black on yellow	2·00	2·00
73		5c. red on orange	1·75	1·75

34

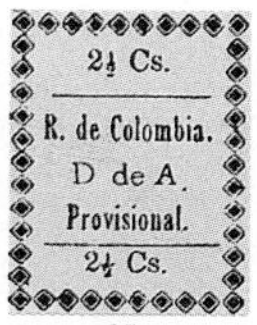
35

1889. Arms in various frames.

74	34	1c. black on red	10	10
75		2½c. black on blue	20	15
76		5c. black on yellow	45	25
77		10c. black on green	50	40
95		10c. brown	25	25
78		20c. blue	1·00	1·00
79		50c. brown	2·00	2·00
80		50c. green	1·75	1·75
81		1p. red	1·00	1·00
82		2p. black on mauve	7·50	6·00
83		5p. black on red	10·00	7·50

1890. Perf.

84	35	2½c. black on buff	1·00	1·00
85		5c. black on yellow	1·00	1·00
86		10c. black on buff	4·75	4·75
87		10c. black on red	5·00	5·00
88		20c. black on yellow	5·00	5·00

36

37

1892.

89	36	1c. brown on buff	50	40
90		1c. blue	20	20
91		2½c. violet on lilac	30	30
92		2½c. green	30	30
93		5c. black	80	60
94		5c. red	20	20

1896.

96	37	2c. grey	40	40
107		2c. red	25	40
97		2½c. brown	40	40
108		2½c. blue	25	40
98		3c. red	50	50
109		3c. olive	25	40
99		5c. green	25	20
110		5c. yellow	20	30
100		10c. lilac	45	45
111		10c. brown	50	60
101		20c. brown	70	70
112		20c. blue	75	1·00
102		50c. sepia	90	90
113		50c. red	1·00	1·40
103		1p. black and blue	10·00	10·00
114		1p. black and red	10·00	10·00
104		2p. black and orange	40·00	40·00
115		2p. black and green	35·00	35·00
105		5p. black and mauve	50·00	50·00

39 Gen. Cordoba

43

1899.

118	39	½c. blue	10	10
119		1c. blue	10	10
120		2c. black	10	10
121		3c. red	10	10
122		4c. brown	10	10
123		5c. green	10	10
124		10c. red	10	10
125		20c. violet	10	10
126		50c. yellow	10	10
127		1p. green	10	15
128		2p. green	10	20

1901. Various frames.

132	43	1c. red	10	15
133		1c. brown	25	25
134		1c. blue	25	25

Nos. 132 and 134 also exist with "CENTAVO" inside the rectangle below figure "1".

46

47

48 Girardot

1902.

138	46	1c. red	10	10
139		1c. blue	10	10
140		2c. blue	10	10
141		2c. violet	10	10
142		3c. green	10	10
143		4c. purple	10	10
144	47	5c. red	10	10
145		10c. mauve	10	10
147		20c. green	15	15
148		30c. red	15	10
149	48	40c. blue	15	10
150		50c. brown on yellow	20	20
152	–	1p. black and violet	40	45
153	–	2p. black and red	40	45
154	–	5p. black and blue	50	55

DESIGN: 1p. to 5p. Dr. J. Felix de Restrepo.
No. 145 also exists with smaller head.

54

55

56 Zea

1903.

159	54	4c. brown	10	10
160		5c. blue	10	10
161	55	10c. yellow	10	10
162		20c. lilac	10	10
163		30c. brown	30	30
164		40c. green	30	30
165		50c. red	10	15
166	56	1p. green	25	20
167		2p. mauve (Rovira)	25	20
168		3p. blue (La Pola)	30	30
169		4p. red (Restrepo)	50	30
170		5p. brown (Madrid)	50	40
171		10p. red (Corral)	2·25	2·25

ACKNOWLEDGEMENT OF RECEIPT STAMPS

AR 53

1902.

AR157	AR 53	5c. black on red	30	20
AR158		5c. green	10	10

REGISTRATION STAMPS

R 38

1896.

R106	R 38	2½c. pink	50	50
R117		2½c. blue	60	60

R 41 Gen. Cordoba

R 42

1899.

R130	R 41	2½c. blue	10	10
R131	R 42	10c. red	10	10

R 52

1902.

R156	R 52	10c. violet on green	10	10

TOO LATE STAMPS

L 40 Gen. Cordoba

L 51

1899.

L129	L 40	2½c. green	10	10

1901. As T 43, but inscr "RETARDO" at sides.

L137a		2½c. purple	60	60

1902.

L155	L 51	2½c. lilac	10	10

ARBE Pt. 8

During the period of D'Annunzio's Italian Regency of Carnaro (Fiume), separate issues were made for Arbe (now Rab).

100 centesimi = 1 lira.

1920. No. 148, etc of Fiume optd **ARBE**.

1B	5c. green	4·50	5·25
2B	10c. red	10·50	11·50
3B	20c. brown	24·00	18·00
4B	25c. blue	14·50	18·00
5	50c. on 20c. brown	26·00	18·00
6	55c. on 5c. green	26·00	18·00

EXPRESS LETTER STAMPS

1920. Nos. E163/4 of Fiume optd **ARBE**.

E7	30c. on 20c. brown	95·00	55·00
E8	50c. on 5c. green	95·00	55·00

ARGENTINA Pt. 20

A republic in the S.E. of S. America formerly part of the Spanish Empire.

1858. 100 centavos = 1 peso.
1985. 100 centavos = 1 austral.
1992. 100 centavos = 1 peso.

1 Argentine Confederation

3 Argentine Confederation

1858. Imperf.

1	1	5c. red	1·60	9·50
2		10c. green	2·25	55·00
3		15c. blue	16·00	£140

1862. Imperf.

10	3	5c. red	20·00	24·00
8		10c. green	£160	75·00
9		15c. blue	£325	£250

5 Rivadavia

6 Rivadavia

1864. Imperf.

24	5	5c. red	£250	65·00
14	6	10c. green	£1700	£1000
15	5	15c. blue	£8000	£3500

1864. Perf.

16	5	5c. red	35·00	14·00
17	6	10c. green	80·00	35·00
18	5	15c. blue	£160	75·00

9 Rivadavia

10 Gen. Belgrano

11 Gen. San Martin

1867. Perf.

28	9	5c. red	12·00	75
29	10	10c. green	35·00	5·00
30a	11	15c. blue	50·00	15·00

12 Balcarce

22 Sarsfield

24 Lopez

1873. Portraits. Perf.

31	12	1c. violet	4·00	2·25
32	–	4c. brown (Moreno)	5·50	45
33	–	30c. orange (Alvear)	£120	17·00
34	–	60c. black (Posadas)	£120	5·50
35	–	90c. blue (Saavedra)	28·00	2·50

1877. Surch with large figure of value.

37	9	1 on 5c. red	55·00	17·00
38		2 on 5c. red	£110	70·00
39	10	8 on 10c. green	£140	35·00

1876. Roul.

36	9	5c. red	£170	70·00
40		8c. lake	28·00	30
41	10	16c. green	9·00	1·25
42	22	20c. blue	9·50	3·50
43	11	24c. blue	19·00	3·50

1877. Perf.

46	24	2c. green	4·75	1·00
44	9	8c. lake	4·75	15
45	11	24c. blue	8·50	50
47	–	25c. lake (Alvear)	25·00	7·00

1882. Surch **1/2 (PROVISORIO)**.

51	9	½ on 5c. red	1·00	90

29

33

1882.

52	29	½c. brown	1·60	90
55		1c. red	4·00	1·25
54		12c. blue	65·00	10·00

1884. Surch **1884** and value in figures or words.

90	9	½c. on 5c. red	3·00	2·25
92	11	½c. on 15c. blue	2·25	1·75
94		1c. on 15c. blue	7·00	5·50
100	9	4c. on 5c. red	10·00	6·00

1884.

101	33	½c. brown	1·00	50
102		1c. red	6·00	50
103		12c. blue	28·00	1·40

34 Urquiza

45 Mitre

1888. Portrait types, inscr "CORREOS ARGENTINOS".

108	34	½c. blue	55	50
110	–	2c. green (Lopez)	10·00	7·00
111	–	3c. green (Celman)	1·90	70
113	–	5c. red (Rivadavia)	9·00	65
114	–	6c. red (Sarmiento)	24·00	16·00
115	–	10c. brown (Avellaneda)	16·00	1·25
116	–	15c. orange (San Martin)	16·00	1·75
117a	–	20c. green (Roca)	13·00	1·40
118	–	25c. violet (Belgrano)	16·00	1·75
119	–	30c. brown (Dorrego)	24·00	2·75
120a	–	40c. grey (Moreno)	24·00	3·25
121	45	50c. blue	85·00	9·00

60 Paz

51 Rivadavia

1888. Portrait types, inscr "CORREOS Y TELEGRAFOS" except No. 126.

137	60	½c. green	10	15
122	–	½c. blue (Urquiza)	30	15
123	–	1c. brown (Sarsfield)	95	20
125	–	2c. violet (Derqui)	95	15
126	–	3c. green (Celman)	2·25	45
127	51	5c. red	3·00	20
129	–	6c. blue (Sarmiento)	1·60	60
130	–	10c. brown (Avellaneda)	1·90	30
131	–	12c. blue (Alberti)	4·75	1·25
132	–	40c. grey (Moreno)	4·50	90
133	–	50c. orange (Mitre)	4·50	90
134	–	60c. black (Posadas)	17·00	3·00

1890. No. 131 surch **1/4** and bars.

135	¼ on 12c. blue	40	35

52 Rivadavia

63 La Madrid

61 Rivadavia

1890.

128a	52	5c. red	2·25	15

1891. Portraits.

139	–	1p. blue (San Martin)	45·00	6·50
140	63	5p. blue	£225	24·00
141	–	20p. green (G. Brown)	£325	70·00

1891.

138	61	8c. red	1·40	25

65 Rivadavia

66 Belgrano

67 San Martin

1892.

142	65	½c. blue	20	15
143		1c. brown	40	15
144		2c. green	25	15
145		3c. orange	70	15
146		5c. red	70	15
147	66	10c. red	5·50	15
148		12c. blue	2·75	15
149		16c. slate	6·50	60
150		24c. sepia	11·00	60
257		30c. orange	8·00	50
151		50c. green	10·00	50
188		80c. lilac	12·00	50
152a	67	1p. red	10·00	80
190		1p.20 black	9·50	4·00
153		2p. green	17·00	8·00
154		5p. blue	42·00	3·00

70 Fleet of Columbus

71 "Liberty" and Shield

1892. 4th Centenary of Discovery of America by Columbus.

219	70	2c. blue	12·50	4·50
220		5c. blue	26·00	5·00

1899.

221	71	½c. brown	15	15
222		1c. green	10	10
223		2c. grey	10	10
224		3c. orange	95	15
225		4c. yellow	1·75	15
226		5c. red	10	10
227		6c. black	1·10	20
228		10c. green	1·75	15
229a		12c. blue	1·10	30
230		12c. green	1·10	30
231		15c. blue	3·00	15
232		16c. orange	8·50	4·25
233		20c. red	2·25	15
234		24c. purple	4·00	80
235		30c. red	4·25	20
237		50c. blue	5·50	15
238		1p. black and blue	16·00	80
239		5p. black and orange	65·00	11·00
240		10p. black and green	60·00	11·00
241		20p. black and red	£225	32·00

The peso values are larger (19 × 32 mm).

73 Port Rosario

74 Gen. San Martin

1902. Completion of Port Rosario Docks.

290	73	5c. blue	80	2·00

1908.

291	74	½c. violet	15	10
292		1c. brown	20	10
293		2c. brown	60	10
294		3c. green	75	35
295		4c. mauve	1·50	35
296		5c. red	35	10
297		6c. green	85	25
298		10c. green	1·75	10
299		12c. brown	45	40
300		12c. blue	1·40	10
301		15c. green	1·90	90
302		20c. blue	1·40	10
303		24c. red	3·75	70
304		30c. red	6·00	70
305		50c. black	5·50	45
306		1p. red and blue	13·00	1·90

The 1p. is larger (21½ × 27 mm) with portrait at upper left.

76 Pyramid of May

80 Saavedra

78 Azcuenaga and Alberti

1910. Cent of Deposition of the Spanish Viceroy.

366	76	½c. blue and grey	40	10
367	–	1c. black and green	40	10
368	–	2c. black and green	30	10
369	78	3c. green	85	10
370	–	4c. green and blue	85	15
371	80	5c. red	70	10
372	–	10c. black and brown	2·00	15
373	–	12c. blue	1·60	25
374	–	20c. black and brown	3·75	40
375	–	24c. blue and brown	2·00	1·00
376	–	30c. black and lilac	2·00	75
377	–	50c. black and red	5·00	1·00
378	–	1p. blue	12·00	3·50
379	–	5p. purple and orange	80·00	35·00
380	–	10p. black and orange	£100	75·00
381	–	20p. black and blue	£170	£100

DESIGNS—VERT: 50c. Crowds on 25 May 1810; 10p. Centenary Monument; 20p. San Martin. HORIZ: 1c. Pena and Vieytes; 2c. Meeting at Pena's house; 4c. Fort of the Viceroys, Buenos Aires; 10c. Distribution of cockades; 12c. Congress Building; 20c. Castelli and Matheu; 24c. First National Council; 30c. Belgrano and Larrea; 1p. Moreno and Paso; 5p. "Oath of the Junta".

90 Sarmiento

91 Ploughman

1911. Birth Centenary of Pres. Sarmiento.

382	90	5c. black and brown	70	40

1911.

383	91	5c. red	40	15
384		12c. blue	4·50	20

92 Ploughman

94

1911.

395	92	½c. violet	20	20
396		1c. brown	20	15
397		2c. brown	40	15
398		3c. green	50	20
399		4c. purple	40	20
400		5c. red	20	15
401		10c. green	60	15
402		12c. blue	1·60	10
403		20c. blue	5·00	1·25
404		24c. brown	3·75	20
405		30c. red	2·00	70
406		50c. black	6·00	70
408	94	1p. red and blue	7·00	1·10
409		5p. green and grey	22·00	7·00
410		10p. blue and violet	85·00	10·00
411		20p. red and blue	£200	70·00

95 Dr. F. N. Laprida

97 San Martin

96 Declaration of Independence

1916. Centenary of Independence.

417	95	½c. violet	20	15
418		1c. brown	25	15
419		2c. brown	20	15
420		3c. green	50	15
421		4c. purple	75	15
422	96	5c. red	35	15
423		10c. green	1·60	15
424	97	12c. blue	75	15
425		20c. blue	1·25	15
426		24c. red	2·00	85
427		30c. red	2·00	40
428		50c. black	3·75	50
429		1p. red and blue	11·00	4·50
430		5p. green and grey	£130	45·00
431		10p. blue and violet	£130	85·00
432		20p. red and grey	£190	75·00

98 San Martin

100 Dr. Juan Pujol

1917.

433	98	½c. violet	20	15
434		1c. buff	20	15
435		2c. brown	20	15
436		3c. green	70	15
454		4c. purple	30	15
455		5c. red	15	15
456		10c. green	1·75	15
457	–	12c. blue	1·40	15
458	–	20c. blue	1·75	15
459	–	24c. red	5·00	2·25
460	–	30c. red	5·00	70
461	–	50c. black	4·50	70
445	–	1p. red and blue	4·50	20
446	–	5p. green and grey	19·00	3·50
447	–	10p. blue and violet	45·00	11·00
448	–	20p. red and grey	81·00	17·00

The 12c. to 20p. values are larger (21 × 27 mm).

1918. Birth Centenary of Juan Pujol, 1st P.M.G. of Argentina.

449	100	5c. grey and bistre	80	30

102 Mausoleum of Belgrano

103 Creation of Argentine Flag

1920. Death Centenary of Gen. Manuel Belgrano.

478	102	2c. red	50	15
479	103	5c. blue and red	50	15
480	–	12c. blue and green	1·00	75

DESIGN—VERT: 12c. Gen. Belgrano.

106 General Urquiza

107 General Mitre

108

1920. Gen. Urquiza's Victory at Cepada.

488	106	5c. blue	30	10

1921. Birth Centenary of Gen. Mitre.

490	107	2c. brown	35	10
491		5c. blue	35	10

1921. 1st Pan-American Postal Congress.

492	108	3c. lilac	1·50	65
493		5c. blue	2·00	20
494		10c. brown	2·50	90
495		12c. red	4·50	1·90

1921. As T **108**, but smaller. Inscr "BUENOS AIRES AGOSTO DE 1921".

496	5c. red	2·25	25

1921. As No. 496, but inscr "REPUBLICA ARGENTINA" at foot.

511	5c. red	1·75	25

112

114 B. Rivadavia

1923. With or without stop below "c".

513	112	½c. purple	15	15
530		1c. brown	15	15
515		2c. brown	35	15
532		3c. green	15	15
533		4c. red	50	15
518		5c. red	15	15
535		10c. green	35	15
520		12c. blue	45	15
537		20c. blue	85	15
538		24c. brown	2·00	1·00
539		25c. violet	1·00	15
540		30c. red	2·00	15
541		50c. black	2·00	15
542	–	1p. red and blue	2·25	15
543	–	5p. green and lilac	17·00	70
544	–	10p. blue and red	38·00	3·75
545	–	20p. lake and slate	55·00	8·50

The peso values are larger (21 × 27 mm).

1926. Rivadavia Centenary.

546	114	5c. red	50	15

115 Rivadavia

116 San Martin

117 G.P.O., 1926

118 G.P.O., 1826

1926. Postal Centenary.

547	115	3c. green	15	15
548	116	5c. red	10	15
549	117	12c. blue	1·00	20
550	118	25c. brown	1·75	15

120 Biplane and Globe

122

1928. Air.

558	120	5c. red	1·75	50
559		10c. blue	2·75	85
560	–	15c. brown	2·50	90
561	120	18c. violet	4·25	3·25
562	–	20c. blue	2·75	90
563	–	24c. blue	4·25	3·00
564	122	25c. violet	4·25	1·40
565		30c. red	5·50	1·00
566	–	35c. red	4·25	1·25
567a	120	36c. brown	3·25	1·40
568	–	50c. black	4·50	65
569	–	54c. brown	4·25	2·10
570	–	72c. green	5·50	2·10
571	122	90c. purple	10·00	1·90
572		1p. red and blue	12·00	70
573		1p.08 blue and red	17·00	4·75
574	–	1p.26 green and violet	23·00	9·00
575	–	1p.80 red and blue	23·00	9·00
576	–	3p.60 blue and grey	48·00	21·00

DESIGNS—VERT: 15, 20, 24, 54, 72c. Yellow-headed Caracara over sea. HORIZ: 35, 50c., 1p.26, 1p.80, 3p.60, Andean Condor on mountain top.

124 Arms of Argentina and Brazil

125 Torch illuminating New World

1928. Centenary of Peace with Brazil.

577	**124**	5c. red	1·00	35
578		12c. blue	1·60	70

1929. "Day of the Race" issue.

579	**125**	2c. brown	85	20
580	–	5c. red	95	15
581	–	12c. blue	2·25	75

DESIGNS: 5c. Symbolical figures, Spain and Argentina; 12c. American offering laurels to Columbus.

"ZEPPELIN" 1er VUELO 1930
(128)

1930. Air. "Zeppelin" Europe–Pan-America Flight. Optd with T **128**.

587	–	20c. blue (No. 562)	10·00	5·50
588	–	50c. black (No. 568)	18·00	8·50
589	**122**	90c. purple	9·00	6·50
584		1p. red and blue	20·00	13·00
585	–	1p.80 (No. 575)	60·00	32·00
586	–	3p.60 (No. 576)	£170	95·00

129 Soldier and Civilian Insurgents

130 The Victorious March, 6 September 30

1930. Revolution of 6 September 1930.

592	**129**	½c. violet	20	15
611	**130**	½c. mauve	15	10
593	**129**	1c. green	25	15
612	**130**	1c. black	1·00	40
594		2c. lilac	35	15
595	**129**	3c. green	50	25
613	**130**	3c. green	50	25
596	**129**	4c. violet	40	25
614	**130**	4c. lake	40	20
597	**129**	5c. red	20	15
615	**130**	5c. red	15	10
598	**129**	10c. black	85	35
616	**130**	10c. green	1·00	25
599		12c. blue	85	25
600		20c. buff	85	20
601	**130**	24c. brown	3·25	1·50
602		25c. green	4·25	1·50
603		30c. violet	6·00	2·00
604		50c. black	9·00	2·75
605		1p. red and blue	17·00	10·00
606		2p. orange and black	30·00	10·00
607		5p. black and green	90·00	40·00
608		10p. blue and lake	£120	50·00
609		20p. blue and green	£325	£120
610		50p. violet and green	£900	£650

1931. 1st Anniv of 1930 Revolution. Optd **6 Septembre 1930 - 1931**.

617	**112**	3c. green (postage)	25	25
618		10c. green	70	70
619		30c. red	3·75	3·75
620		50c. black	3·75	3·75
621		1p. red and blue	4·25	3·75
622	**130**	2p. orange and black	15·00	8·50
622	**112**	5p. green and lilac	75·00	23·00
624	**129**	18c. violet (air)	2·25	1·75
625	–	72c. green (No. 570)	21·00	13·00
626	**122**	90c. purple	16·00	12·00
627	–	1p.80 red & bl (No. 575)	40·00	30·00
628	–	3p.60 bl & grey (No. 576)	60·00	45·00

1932. Zeppelin Air stamps. Optd **GRAF ZEPPELIN 1932**.

629	**120**	5c. red	2·50	1·60
630		18c. violet	12·00	7·50
631	**122**	90c. purple	35·00	20·00

134 Refrigerating Plant

135 Port La Plata

1932. 6th International Refrigerating Congress.

632	**134**	3c. green	50	25
633		10c. red	1·25	15
634		12c. blue	3·50	1·40

1933. 50th Anniv of La Plata City.

635	**135**	3c. brown and green	1·00	25
636	–	10c. purple and orange	60	20
637	–	15c. blue	4·00	2·00
638	–	20c. brown and lilac	2·00	1·00
639	–	30c. red and green	16·00	6·00

DESIGNS: 10c. President J. A. Roca; 15c. Municipal buildings; 20c. La Plata Cathedral; 30c. Dr. D. Rocha.

139 Christ of the Andes

141 "Liberty" with Arms of Brazil and Argentina

1934. 32nd Int Eucharistic Congress, Buenos Aires.

640	**139**	10c. red	85	25
641	–	15c. blue	1·60	55

DESIGN—HORIZ: 15c. Buenos Aires Cathedral.

1935. Visit of President Vargas of Brazil. Inscr "MAYO DE 1935".

642	**141**	10c. red	85	25
643	–	15c. blue	1·60	55

DESIGN: 15c. Clasped hands and flags.

143 D. F. Sarmiento

146 Prize Bull

151 With Boundary Lines

1935. Portraits.

644		½c. purple (Belgrano)	15	10
645		1c. brown (Type **143**)	15	10
646		2c. brown (Urquiza)	15	10
647		3c. green (San Martin)	15	10
648		4c. grey (G. Brown)	10	10
653b		5c. brown (Moreno)	60	10
650		6c. green (Alberdi)	15	10
653d		10c. red (Rivadavia)	25	10
651		12c. purple (Mitre)	10	10
708		15c. grey (Martin Guemes)	80	10
652		20c. blue (Juan Martin Guemes)	80	10
653		20c. blue (Martin Guemes)	80	10

See also Nos. 671 etc.

1935. Philatelic Exhibition, Buenos Aires (Ex. Fl. B.A.). Sheet 83 × 100 mm.
MS654 **112** 10c. green × 4 (sold at 1p.) 55·00 27·00

1936. Production and Industry.

676	**146**	15c. blue	60	15
677a		20c. blue (19½ × 26 mm)	15	15
755		20c. blue (22 × 33 mm)	1·50	15
656	–	25c. red and pink	40	15
757	–	30c. brown and yellow	40	15
658	–	40c. purple and mauve	35	15
659	–	50c. red and salmon	25	15
660	**151**	1p. blue and brown	19·00	75
760	–	1p. blue and brown	3·00	15
661	–	2p. blue and purple	85	15
662	–	5p. green and blue	11·50	75
763	–	10p. black and purple	11·50	1·60
764	–	20p. brown and blue	11·00	1·60

DESIGNS—VERT: 25c. Ploughman; 50c. Oil well; 1p. (No. 760) as Type **151** but without country boundaries; 5p. Iguazu Falls; 10p. Grapes; 20p. Cotton plant. HORIZ: 30c. Patagonian ram; 40c. Sugar cane and factory; 2p. Fruit products.

157

158 Pres. Sarmiento

1936. Pan-American Peace Conference.

665	**157**	10c. red	50	15

1938. President's 50th Death Anniv.

666	**158**	3c. green	40	40
667		5c. red	40	40
668		15c. blue	75	40
669		50c. orange	2·25	80

159 "Presidente Sarmiento"

160 Allegory of the Post

1939. Last Voyage of Cadet Ship "Presidente Sarmiento".

670	**159**	5c. green	85	10

1939. Portraits as T **143**.

671	–	2½c. black	15	10
672	–	3c. grey (San Martin)	40	10
672a	–	3c. grey (Moreno)	15	10
673	–	4c. green	10	10
894	–	5c. brown (16½ × 22½ mm)	10	10
674	–	8c. orange	10	10
678	–	10c. purple	15	10
675	–	12c. red	10	10
895	–	20c. lilac (21 × 27 mm)	20	10
895b	–	20c. lilac (19½ × 25½ mm)	15	10

PORTRAITS: 2½c. L. Braille; 4c. G. Brown; 5c. Jose Hernandez; 8c. N. Avellaneda; 10c. B. Rivadavia; 12c. B. Mitre; 20c. G. Brown.

1939. 11th U.P.U. Congress, Buenos Aires.

679	**160**	5c. red	15	10
680	–	15c. grey	40	25
681	–	20c. blue	40	10
682	–	25c. green	85	35
683	–	50c. brown	2·25	80
684	–	1p. purple	4·50	1·75
685	–	2p. mauve	20·00	11·50
686	–	5p. violet	46·00	23·00

DESIGNS—VERT: 20c. Seal of Argentina; 1p. Symbols of postal communications; 2p. Argentina, "Land of Promise" from a pioneer painting. HORIZ: 15c. G.P.O.; 25c. Iguazu Falls; 50c. Mt. Bonete; 5p. Lake Frias.

1939. International Philatelic Exhibition, Buenos Aires. Two sheets se-tenant horiz or vert, each comprising Nos. 679, 681/3 arranged differently.
MS686a Two sheets, 190 × 95 mm or 95 × 190 mm 6·00 6·00

165 Working-class Family and New Home

167 North and South America

1939. 1st Pan-American Housing Congress.

687	**165**	5c. green	20	10

1940. 50th Anniv of Pan-American Union.

688	**167**	15c. blue	35	10

168 Corrientes Type 5

1940. Centenary of First Adhesive Postage Stamps and Philatelic Exhibition, Cordoba. Sheet 111 × 111 mm containing early Argentine issues as T **168**.
MS688a 5c. blue (Type **168**); 5c. blue (Cordoba T **3**); 5c. red (Type **1**); 5c. red (Type **3**); 10c. blue (Buenos Aires T **1**) 10·00 6·00

169 Airplane and Envelope

1940. Air.

689	**169**	30c. orange	7·00	10
690	–	50c. brown	9·50	15
691	**169**	1p. red	3·50	10
692	–	1p.25 green	80	10
693	**169**	2p.50 blue	2·75	40

DESIGNS—VERT: 50c. "Mercury"; 1p.25, Douglas DC-2 in clouds.

172 Gen. French, Col. Beruti and Rosette of the "Legion de Patricios"

1941. 131st Anniv of Rising against Spain.

694	**172**	5c. blue	40	10

173 Marco M. de Avellaneda

174 Statue of Gen. J. A. Roca

1941. Death Centenary of Avellaneda (patriot).

695	**173**	5c. blue	40	10

1941. Dedication of Statue of Gen. Roca.

696	**174**	5c. green	40	10

175 Pellegrini (founder) and National Bank

176 Gen. Juan Lavalle

1941. 50th Anniv of National Bank.

697	**175**	5c. lake	40	10

1941. Death Centenary of Gen. Lavalle.

698	**176**	5c. blue	40	10

177 New P.O. Savings Bank

178 Jose Manuel Estrada

1942. Inauguration of P.O. Savings Bank.

699	**177**	1c. green	40	10

1942. Birth Centenary of Estrada (patriot).

700	**178**	5c. purple	50	10

180 G.P.O., Buenos Aires

181 Proposed Columbus Lighthouse

1942. Postage and Express Stamps.

717	**180**	35c. blue	5·50	15
746		35c. blue	1·10	15

No. 717 is inscr "PALACIO CENTRAL DE CORREOS Y TELEGRAFOS" and No. 746 "PALACIO CENTRAL DE CORREOS Y TELECOMUNICACIONES".

1942. 450th Anniv of Discovery of America by Columbus.

721	**181**	15c. blue	4·00	15

182 Dr. Paz (founder of "La Prensa")

183 Flag of Argentina and Books

184 Arms of Argentina

1942. Birth Centenary of Dr. Jose C. Paz.

722	**182**	5c. blue	40	15

1943. 1st National Book Fair.

723	**183**	5c. blue	20	15

1943. Revolution of 4 June 1943.

724	**184**	5c. red	20	15
725		15c. green	60	15
726		20c. blue (larger)	80	15

185 National Independence House

186 Head of Liberty, Money-box and Laurels

1943. Restoration of Tucuman Museum.
727 **185** 5c. green 35 15

1943. 1st Savings Bank Conference.
728 **186** 5c. brown 40 10

187 Buenos Aires in 1800

1944. Export Day.
729 **187** 5c. black 40 10

188 Postal Union of the Americas and Spain

189 Alexander Graham Bell

191 Liner, Warship and Yacht

1944. Postmen's Benefit Fund. Inscr "PRO-CARTERO".
730 – 3c.+2c. black and violet 1·10 1·10
731 **188** 5c.+5c. black and red . . 85 20
732 **189** 10c.+5c. black and orge 1·10 35
733 – 25c.+15c. black and brn 2·40 75
734 – 1p.+50c. black and green 10·00 7·75
DESIGNS: 3c. Samuel Morse; 25c. Rowland Hill; 1p. Columbus landing in America.

1944. Naval Week.
735 **191** 5c. blue 75 10

192 Argentina

193 Arms of Argentina

1944. San Juan Earthquake Relief Fund.
736 **192** 5c.+10c. black & olive . . 60 50
737 5c.+50c. black and red . . 3·50 1·10
738 5c.+1p. black & orange 7·00 5·50
739 5c.+20p. black & blue . . 28·00 23·00

1944. 1st Anniv of Revolution of 4 June 1943.
740 **193** 5c. blue 40 15

193a National Flag

1944. National Anthem and Aid for La Rioja and Catamarca Provinces. Two sheets 75×110 mm each containing T **193a**.
MS740a 5c.+1p. blue and plum 1·60 1·60
MS740b 5c.+50p. blue and indigo £300 £325

194 Archangel Gabriel

195 Cross of Palermo

196 Allegory of Savings

1944. 4th National Eucharistic Congress.
741 **194** 3c. green 50 15
742 **195** 5c. red 50 15

1944. 20th Anniv of Universal Savings Day.
743 **196** 5c. black 40 15

197 Reservists

1944. Reservists' Day.
744 **197** 5c. blue 40 15

198 Bernardino Rivadavia

199 Rivadavia's Mausoleum

1945. Rivadavia's Death Centenary.
770 **198** 3c. green 15 15
771 – 5c. red 15 15
772 **199** 20c. blue 15 15
DESIGN—As Type **198**: 5c. Rivadavia and Scales of Justice.

200 San Martin

201 Monument to Andes Army, Mendoza

1945.
773 **200** 5c. red 10 10

1946. "Homage to the Unknown Soldier of Independence".
776 **201** 5c. purple 15 15

202 Pres. Roosevelt

203 "Affirmation"

1946. 1st Death Anniv of Pres. Franklin Roosevelt.
777 **202** 5c. grey 10 10

1946. Installation of Pres. Juan Peron.
778 **203** 5c. blue 15 15

204 Airplane over Iguazu Falls

1946. Air.
779 **204** 15c. red 15 10
780 – 25c. green 20 10
DESIGN: 25c. Airplane over Andes.

205 "Flight"

1946. Aviation Week.
781 **205** 15c. green on green . . . 55 10
782 – 60c. purple on buff . . . 55 15
DESIGN: 60c. Hand upholding globe.

207 "Argentina and Populace"

1946. 1st Anniv of Peron's Defeat of Counter-revolution.
783 **207** 5c. mauve 20 10
784 10c. green 30 10
785 15c. blue 60 25
786 50c. brown 60 40
787 1p. red . . . . 1·25 1·10

208 Money-box and Map

209 Industry

1946. Annual Savings Day.
788 **208** 30c. red 35 10

1946. Industrial Exhibition.
789 **209** 5c. purple 10 10

210 Argentine–Brazil International Bridge

211 South Pole

1947. Opening of Bridge between Argentina and Brazil.
790 **210** 5c. green 25 25

1947. 43rd Anniv of 1st Argentine Antarctic Mail.
791 **211** 5c. violet 60 15
792 20c. red . . . . 1·25 15

212 "Justice"

213 Icarus Falling

1947. 1st Anniv of Col. Juan Peron's Presidency.
793 **212** 5c. purple and buff . . . 10 10

1947. "Week of the Wing".
794 **213** 15c. purple 15 10

214 "Presidente Sarmiento"

215 Cervantes and "Don Quixote"

1947. 50th Anniv of Launching of Cadet Ship "Presidente Sarmiento".
795 **214** 5c. blue 50 10

1947. 400th Birth Anniv of Cervantes.
796 **215** 5c. green 10 10

216 Gen. San Martin and Urn

1947. Arrival from Spain of Ashes of Gen. San Martin's Parents.
797 **216** 5c. green 10 10

217 Young Crusaders

218 Statue of Araucarian Indian

1947. Educational Crusade for Universal Peace.
798 **217** 5c. green 10 10
799 20c. brown 30 10

1948. American Indian Day.
801 **218** 25c. brown 25 10

219 Phrygian Cap and Sprig of Wheat

220 "Stop"

1948. 5th Anniv of Anti-isolationist Revolution of 4 June 1943.
802 **219** 5c. blue 10 10

1948. Safety First Campaign.
803 **220** 5c. yellow and brown . . 15 10

221 Posthorn and Oak Leaves

222 Argentine Farmers

1948. Bicent of Postal Service in Rio de la Plata.
804 **221** 5c. mauve 15 15

1948. Agriculture Day.
805 **222** 10c. brown 15 15

223 "Liberty and Plenty"

225 Statue of Atlas

226 Map, Globe and Compasses

1948. Re-election of President Peron.
806 **223** 25c. red 15 15

1948. Air. 4th Meeting of Pan-American Cartographers.
807 **225** 45c. brown 35 10
808 **226** 70c. green 65 15

226a Buenos Aires

1948. Bicentenary of Postal Service in Rio de la Plata (2nd issue). Two sheets containing designs as T **226a**.
MS808a 144×101 mm. (horiz designs). 15c. green (Mail coach, 1865); 45c. brown (Type **226a**); 55c. brown (First train, 1857); 85c. ultramarine (Sailing ship, 1767)
MS808b 102×144 mm (vert designs). 85c. brown (Domingo de Basavilibaso); 1p.50 green (Postrider, 1748); 1p.20 indigo (Sailing ship, 1798); 1p.90 purple (Courier in the Andes, 1772) Price for 2 sheets . . . . 13·00 13·00

227 Winged Railway Wheel

1949. 1st Anniv of Nationalization of Argentine Railways.
809 **227** 10c. blue 25 10

228 Head of Liberty

1949. Constitution Day.
810 **228** 1p. purple and red . . . 80 15

229 Trophy and Target **230** "Intercommunication"

1949. Air. International Shooting Championship.
811 **229** 75c. brown 65 15

1949. 75th Anniv of U.P.U.
812 **230** 25c. green and olive . . . 20 15

231 San Martin **233** Stamp Designer

232 San Martin at Boulogne

1950. San Martin's Death Cent. Dated "1850 1950".
813 – 10c. purple and blue . . . 15 10
814 **231** 20c. brown and red . . . 15 10
815 **232** 25c. brown 15 10
816 – 50c. blue and green . . . 40 10
817 – 75c. green and brown . . 40 10
818 – 1p. green . . . . 1·00 20
819 – 2p. purple 85 35
MS819a 120 × 150 mm. Nos. 813/14 and 816/17. Imperf . . . . . 1·60 1·10
DESIGNS—As Type **231**: 10, 50, 75c. Portraits of San Martin; 2p. San Martin Mausoleum. As Type **232**: 1p. House where San Martin died.

1950. Int Philatelic Exhibition, Buenos Aires.
820 **233** 10c.+10c. violet (postage) 15 15
821 – 45c.+45c. blue (air) . . . 40 25
822 – 70c.+70c. brown 60 40
823 – 1p.+1p. red . . . . . . 1·75 1·60
824 – 2p.50+2p.50 olive . . . . 9·50 7·00
825 – 5p.+5p. green . . . . . . 11·00 8·50
MS825a 120 × 150 mm. Nos. 820/2. Imperf . . . . 3·50 3·50
DESIGNS: 45c. Engraver; 70c. Proofing; 1p. Printer; 2p.50, Woman reading letter; 5p. San Martin.

234 S. America and Antarctic **235** Douglas DC-3 and Andean Condor

1951.
826 **234** 1p. blue and brown . . . 50 15

1951. Air. 10th Anniv of State Airlines.
827 **235** 20c. olive 30 20

236 Pegasus and Steam Locomotive

1951. Five-year Plan.
828 **236** 5c. brown (postage) . . . 15 15
829 – 25c. green 45 10
830 – 40c. purple 40 15
831 – 20c. blue (air) 25 15
DESIGNS—HORIZ: 25c. "President Peron" (liner) and common dolphin. VERT: 20c. Douglas DC-4 and Andean condor; 40c. Head of Mercury and telephone.

237 Woman Voter and "Argentina" **238** "Piety"

1951. Women's Suffrage in Argentina.
832 **237** 10c. purple 10 10

1951. Air. Eva Peron Foundation Fund.
833 **238** 2p.45+7p.55 olive . . . . 20·00 13·50

239 Eva Peron **240** Eva Peron

1952. (a) Size 20 × 26 mm.
834 **239** 1c. brown 10 10
835 5c. grey 10 10
836 10c. red 10 10
837 20c. red 10 10
838 25c. green 10 10
839 40c. purple 15 10
841 45c. blue 25 10
840 50c. bistre 25 10

(b) Size 22 × 33 mm. Without inscr "EVA PERON".
842 **240** 1p. brown 35 10
843 1p.50 green . . . . 1·75 10
844 2p. red 50 10
845 3p. blue 85 15

(c) Size 22 × 33 mm. Inscr "EVA PERON".
846 **240** 1p. brown 35 10
847 1p.50 green . . . . 1·10 10
848 2p. red . . . . 1·25 10
849 3p. blue . . . . 1·75 45

(d) Size $30\frac{1}{2}$ × 40 mm. Inscr "EVA PERON".
850 **240** 5p. brown . . . . 1·75 40
851 **239** 10p. red . . . . 4·75 1·40
852 **240** 20p. green . . . . 8·00 3·25
853 **239** 50p. blue . . . . 14·00 7·75

241 Indian Funeral Urn **242** Rescue Ship "Uruguay"

1953. 4th Centenary of Santiago del Estero.
854 **241** 50c. green 15 10

1953. 50th Anniv of Rescue of the "Antarctic".
855 **242** 50c. blue . . . . 1·25 40

243 Planting Flag in S. Orkneys **244** "Telegraphs"

1954. 50th Anniv of Argentine P.O. in South Orkneys.
856 **243** 1p.45 blue 85 40

1954. International Telecommunications Conference. Symbolical designs inscr as in T **244**.
857 **244** 1p.50 purple 40 15
858 – 3p. blue . . . . 1·10 25
859 – 5p. red . . . . 1·60 35
DESIGNS—VERT: 3p. "Radio". HORIZ: 5p. "Television".

245 Pediment, Buenos Aires Stock Exchange **246** Eva Peron

1954. Centenary of Argentine Stock Exchange.
860 **245** 1p. green 30 10

1954. 2nd Death Anniv of Eva Peron.
861 **246** 3p. red . . . . 1·60 20

247 San Martin **249** Wheat

250 Mt. Fitz Roy **248** "Prosperity"

1954.
862 **247** 20c. red 10 10
863 40c. red 30 10
868 – 50c. blue (33 × 22 mm) 60 10
869 – 50c. blue (32 × 21 mm) 70 10
870 **249** 80c. brown 25 10
871 – 1p. brown 30 10
872 – 1p.50 blue 25 10
873 – 2p. red 35 10
874 – 3p. purple 35 10
875a – 5p. green . . . . 6·25 10
876 – 10p. green and grey . . 6·25 10
877 **250** 20p. violet . . . . 9·25 40
1018 – 22p. blue . . . . 1·40 10
878 – 50p. indigo and blue ($30\frac{1}{2}$ × $40\frac{1}{2}$ mm) . . . 8·00 80
1023 – 50p. blue ($29\frac{1}{2}$ × 40 mm) 6·25 40
1287 – 50p. blue ($22\frac{1}{2}$ × $32\frac{1}{2}$ mm) . . . 1·00 10
DESIGNS—As Type **249**: HORIZ: 50c. Port of Buenos Aires; 1p. Cattle; 2p. Eva Peron Foundation; 3p. El Nihuil Dam. As Type **250**: VERT: 1p.50, 22p. Industrial Plant; 5p. Iguazu Falls; 50p. San Martin. HORIZ: 10p. Humahuaca Ravine.
For 43p. in the design of the 1p.50 and 22p. see No. 1021.
For 65c. in same design see No. 1313.

1954. Centenary of Argentine Corn Exchange.
867 **248** 1p.50 grey 65 10

251 Clasped Hands and Congress Emblem **252** Father and Son with Model Airplane

1955. Productivity and Social Welfare Congress.
879 **251** 3p. brown 90 10

1955. 25th Anniv of Commercial Air Services.
880 **252** 1p.50 grey 80 10

253 "Liberation" **254** Forces Emblem

1955. Anti-Peronist Revolution of 16 Sept. 1955.
881 **253** 1p.50 olive 20 10

1955. Armed Forces Commemoration.
882 **254** 3p. blue 35 10

255 Gen. Urquiza (after J. M. Blanes) **256** Detail from "Antiope" (Correggio)

1956. 104th Anniv of Battle of Caseros.
883 **255** 1p.50 green 25 10

1956. Infantile Paralysis Relief Fund.
884 **256** 20c.+30c. grey 20 10

257 Coin and Die **258** Corrientes Stamp of 1856

259 Dr. J. G. Pujol **260** Cotton, Chaco

1956. 75th Anniv of National Mint.
885 **257** 2p. brown and sepia . . . 20 10

1956. Centenary of 1st Argentine Stamps.
886 **258** 40c. blue and green . . . 15 10
887 2p.40 mauve and brown 20 10
888 **259** 4p.40 blue 50 15
The 40c. shows a 1r. stamp of 1856.

1956. New Provinces.
889 – 50c. blue 10 10
890 **260** 1p. lake 20 10
891 – 1p.50 green 30 10
DESIGNS—HORIZ: 50c. Lumbering, La Pampa. VERT: 1p.50, Mate tea plant, Misiones.

261 "Liberty" **262** Detail from "Virgin of the Rocks" (Leonardo)

1956. 1st Anniv of Revolution.
892 **261** 2p.40 mauve 25 10

1956. Air. Infantile Paralysis Victims, Gratitude for Help.
893 **262** 1p. purple 30 10

1956. Argentine Stamp Centenary (2nd issue) and Corrientes Stamp Centenary Exhibition. Nos. 886/7 but in litho and colours changed and No. 888 in sheet.
MS893a 147 × 169 mm. 40c. indigo and green; 2p.40 claret and purple; 4p.40 blue . . . . 2·50 2·25

264 Esteban Echeverria (writer)

265 F. Ameghino (anthropologist)

266 Roque Saenz Pena (statesman)

267 Franklin

1956.
896 **264** 2p. purple 20 10
897 **265** 2p.40 brown 30 10
898 **266** 4p.40 green 45 10

1956. 250th Birth Anniv of Benjamin Franklin.
899 **267** 40c. blue 25 10

268 "Hercules" (sail frigate)

269 Admiral G. Brown

1957. Death Cent of Admiral Guillermo Brown.
900 **268** 40c. blue (postage) . . . 50 10
901 – 2p.40 green 40 10
902 – 60c. grey (air) 75 10
903 – 1p. mauve 20 10
904 **269** 2p. brown 25 10
DESIGNS—HORIZ: 60c. "Zefiro" and "Nancy" (sail warships) at Battle of Montevideo; 1p. L. Rosales and T. Espora. VERT: 2p.40, Admiral Brown in later years.

270 Church of Santo Domingo

271 Map of the Americas and Badge of Buenos Aires

1957. 150th Anniv of Defence of Buenos Aires.
905 **270** 40c. green 10 10

1957. Air. Inter-American Economic Conference.
906 **271** 2p. purple 35 10

272 "La Portena", 1857

273 Globe, Flag and Compass Rose

1957. Centenary of Argentine Railways.
907 **272** 40c. sepia (postage) . . . 45 10
908 – 60c. grey (air) 45 10
DESIGN: 60c. Diesel locomotive.

1957. Air. Int Tourist Congress, Buenos Aires.
909 **273** 1p. brown 15 10
910 – 2p. turquoise 20 10
DESIGN: 2p. Symbolic key of tourism.

274 Head of Liberty

275

1957. Reform Convention.
911 **274** 40c. red 10 10

1957. Air. International Correspondence Week.
912 **275** 1p. blue 15 10

276 "Wealth in Oil"

277 La Plata Museum

1957. 50th Anniv of Argentine Oil Industry.
913 **276** 40c. blue 15 10

1958. 75th Anniv of Founding of La Plata.
914 **277** 40c. black 15 10

278 Health Emblem and Flower

1958. Air. Child Welfare.
915 **278** 1p.+50c. red 20 20

279 Stamp of 1858 and River Ferry

280 Stamp of 1858

1958. Centenary of Argentine Confederation Stamps and Philatelic Exhibition, Buenos Aires.
916 **279** 40c.+20c. purple and green (postage) 45 20
917 – 2p.40+1p.20 blue and black 40 25
918 – 4p.40+2p.20 pur & bl . . 60 40
919 **280** 1p.+50c. blue and olive (air) 40 35
920 2p.+1p. violet and red . . 55 45
921 3p.+1p.50 brown & grn 60 55
922 5p.+2p.50 red and olive 1·00 85
923 10p.+5p. sepia & olive . . 1·50 1·40
DESIGNS—HORIZ: 2p.40, Magnifier, stamp album and stamp of 1858; 4p.40, P.O. building of 1858.

281 Steam Locomotive and Arms of Argentina and Bolivia

282 Douglas DC-6 over Map of Argentine-Bolivian Frontier

1958. Argentine–Bolivian Friendship.
(a) Inauguration of Yacuiba–Santa Cruz Railway.
924 **281** 40c. red and slate 35 10
(b) Exchange of Presidential Visits.
925 **282** 1p. brown 15 10

283 "Liberty and Flag"

284 Farman H.F.20 Biplane

1958. Transfer of Presidential Mandate. Head of "Liberty" in grey; inscr black; flag yellow and blue; background colours given.
926 **283** 40c. buff 10 10
927 1p. salmon 15 10
928 2p. green 25 10

1958. 50th Anniv of Argentine Aero Club.
929 **284** 2p. brown 20 10

285 National Flag Monument, Rosario

286 Map of Antarctica

1958. 1st Anniv of Inauguration of National Flag Monument.
930 **285** 40c. grey and blue 10 10

1958. International Geophysical Year.
931 **286** 40c. black and red 50 10

287 Confederation Stamp and "The Santa Fe Mail" (after J. L. Palliere)

1958. Cent of Argentine Confederation Stamps.
932 – 40c. grn & blue (postage) 15 10
933 – 80c. blue & yellow (air) 40 10
934 **287** 1p. blue and orange . . . 20 10
DESIGNS: 40c. First local Cordoba 5c. stamp of 1858 and mail coach; 80c. Buenos Aires Type **1** of 1858 and "View of Buenos Aires" (after Deroy).

288 Aerial view of Flooded Town

1958. Flood Disaster Relief Fund. Inscr as in T **288**.
935 **288** 40c.+20c. brn (postage) 15 10
936 – 1p.+50c. plum (air) . . . 20 10
937 – 5p.+2p.50 blue 50 20
DESIGNS—HORIZ: 1p. Different aerial view of flooded town; 5p. Truck in flood water and garage.

289 Child receiving Blood

290 U.N. Emblem and "Dying Captive" (after Michelangelo)

1958. Leukaemia Relief Campaign.
938 **289** 1p.+50c. red and black . . 15 10

1959. 10th Anniv of Declaration of Human Rights.
939 **290** 40c. grey and brown . . . 10 10

291 Hawker Siddeley Comet 4

1959. Air. Inauguration of Comet Jet Airliners by Argentine National Airlines.
940 **291** 5p. black and green . . . 25 10

292 Orchids and Globe

293 Pope Pius XII

1959. 1st Int Horticultural Exn, Buenos Aires.
941 **292** 1p. purple 15 10

1959. Pope Pius XII Commemoration.
942 **293** 1p. black and yellow . . . 15 10

294 William Harvey

1959. 21st International Physiological Science Congress. Medical Scientists.
943 **294** 50c. green 10 10
944 – 1p. red 15 10
945 – 1p.50 brown 20 10
PORTRAITS: 1p. Claude Bernard; 1p.50, Ivan P. Pavlov.

295 Creole Horse

296 Tierra del Fuego

1959.
946 – 10c. green 10 10
947 – 20c. purple 10 10
948 – 50c. ochre 10 10
950 **295** 1p. red 10 10
1016 – 1p. brown 10 10
1027 – 1p. brown 10 10
1035 – 2p. red 35 10
951 – 3p. blue 10 10
1036 – 4p. red 40 10
952 **296** 5p. brown 25 10
1037 – 8p. red 25 10
1286 – 10p. brown 50 10
1038 – 10p. red 70 10
1017 – 12p. purple 90 10
954 – 20p. green . . . . 2·40 10
1039 – 20p. red 30 10
1019 – 23p. green . . . . . . 4·00 10
1020 – 25p. lilac . . . . 1·25 10
1021 – 43p. lake . . . . 5·50 10
1022 – 45p. brown . . . . . . 3·25 10
1025 – 100p. blue . . . . 6·25 20
1026 – 300p. violet . . . . . . 3·25 10
1032 – 500p. green . . . . . . 1·60 30
1290 – 1000p. blue . . . . . . 4·50 90
DESIGNS—As Type **295**—HORIZ: 10c. Spectacled caiman; 20c. Llama; 50c. Puma. VERT: 2, 4, 8, 10p. (No 1038), 20p. (No. 1039) San Martin. As Type **296**—HORIZ: 3p. Zapata Hill, Catamarca; 300p. Mar del Plata (40 × 29½ mm). VERT: 1p. (No. 1016) Sunflowers; 1p. (No. 1027) Sunflower (22 × 32 mm); 10p. (No. 1286) Inca Bridge, Mendoza; 12, 23, 25p. Red quebracho tree; 20p. (No. 954) Lake Nahuel Huapi; 43, 45p. Industrial plant (30 × 39½ mm); 100p. Ski-jumper; 500p. Red deer (stag); 1,000p. Leaping salmon.
For these designs with face values in revalued currency, see Nos. 1300 etc.

298 Runner

299

1959. 3rd Pan-American Games, Chicago. Designs embody torch emblem. Centres and torch in black.
955 **298** 20c.+10c. green (postage) 10 10
956 – 50c.+20c. yellow 15 15
957 – 1p.+50c. purple 15 15
958 – 2p.+1p. blue (air) 30 15
959 – 3p.+1p.50 olive 45 30
DESIGNS—VERT: 50c. Basketball; 1p. Boxing. HORIZ: 2p. Rowing; 3p. High-diving.

1959. Red Cross Hygiene Campaign.
960 **299** 1p. red, blue and black 10 10

300 Child with Toys

1959. Mothers' Day.
961 **300** 1p. red and black 10 10

301 Buenos Aires 1p. stamp of 1859

1959. Stamp Day.
962 **301** 1p. blue and grey 10 10

302 B. Mitre and J. J. de Urquiza

303 Andean Condor

1959. Centenary of Pact of San Jose de Flores.
963 **302** 1p. plum 10 10

1960. Child Welfare. Birds.
964 **303** 20c.+10c. blue (postage) 70 15
965 – 50c.+20c. violet 70 15
966 – 1p.+50c. brown . . . . . 1·00 25
967 – 2p.+1p. mauve (air) . . . 70 30
968 – 3p.+1p.50 green 70 50
BIRDS: 50c. Fork-tailed flycatcher; 1p. Magellanic woodpecker; 2p. Red-winged tinamou; 3p. Greater rhea.

304 "Uprooted Tree"

305 Abraham Lincoln

1960. World Refugee Year.
969 **304** 1p. red and brown . . . 10 10
970 4p.20 purple and green . . 15 10
MS971 113 × 85 mm. No. 969/70 with premium added for aid to refugees 1p.50c. and 4p.20+2p.10. Imperf . . . . 80 1·00

1960. 150th Birth Anniv of Abraham Lincoln.
972 **305** 5p. blue 25 15

306 Saavedra and Chapter Hall, Buenos Aires

307 Dr. L. Drago

1960. 150th Anniv of May Revolution.
973 **306** 1p. purple (postage) . . . 10 10
974 – 2p. green 10 10
975 – 4p.20 green and grey . . 20 10
976 – 10p.70 blue and slate . . 40 15
977 – 1p.80 brown (air) 10 10
978 – 5p. purple and brown . . 30 10
MS979 Two sheets each 104 × 156 mm. Nos. 973/4, 977 in red-brown. Nos. 975/6, 978 in green . . . . 2·50 1·50
DESIGNS—Chapter Hall and: 1p.80, Moreno; 2p. Paso; 4p.20, Alberti and Azcuenaga; 5p. Belgrano and Castelli; 10p.70, Larrea and Matheu.

1960. Birth Centenary of Drago.
980 **307** 4p.20 brown 15 10

308 "Five Provinces"

309 "Market Place 1810" (Buenos Aires)

1960. Air. New Argentine Provinces.
981 **308** 1p.80 blue and red . . . 10 10

1960. Air. Inter-American Philatelic Exhibition, Buenos Aires ("EFIMAYO") and 150th Anniv of Revolution. Inscr "EFIMAYO 1960".
982 **309** 2p.+1p. lake 15 10
983 – 6p.+3p. grey 35 20
984 – 10p.70+5p.30 blue 60 35
985 – 20p.+10p. turquoise . . . 75 60
DESIGNS: 6p. "The Water Carrier"; 10p.70, "The Landing Place"; 20p. "The Fort".

310 J. B. Alberdi

311 Seibo (Argentine National Flower)

1960. 150th Birth Anniv of J. B. Alberdi (statesman).
986 **310** 1p. green 10 10

1960. Air. Chilean Earthquake Relief Fund. Inscr "AYUDA CHILE".
987 **311** 6p.+3p. red 30 25
988 – 10p.70+5p.30 red 40 35
DESIGN: 10p.70, Copihue (Chilean national flower).

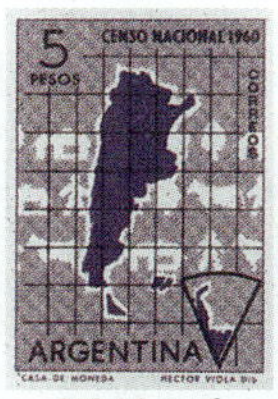

312 Map of Argentina

313 Galleon

1960. Census.
989 **312** 5p. lilac 40 10

1960. 8th Spanish-American P.U. Congress.
990 **313** 1p. green (postage) . . . 40 10
991 5p. brown 85 20
992 1p.80 purple (air) 40 10
993 10p.70 turquoise . . . . 1·10 30

1960. Air. U.N. Day. Nos. 982/5 optd **DIA DE LAS NACIONES UNIDAS 24 DE OCTUBRE**.
994 **309** 2p.+1p. red 20 15
995 – 6p.+3p. black 25 25
996 – 10p.70+5p.30 blue . . . 50 40
997 – 20p.+10p. turquoise . . . 70 65

315 Blessed Virgin of Lujan

316 Jacaranda

1960. 1st Inter-American Marian Congress.
998 **315** 1p. blue 10 10

1960. International Thematic Stamp Exhibition ("TEMEX"). Inscr "TEMEX-61".
999 **316** 50c.+50c. blue 10 10
1000 – 1p.+1p. turquoise . . . 10 10
1001 – 3p.+3p. brown 30 20
1002 – 5p.+5p. brown 50 30
FLOWERS: 1p. Passion flowers; 3p. Hibiscus; 5p. Black lapacho.

317 Argentine Scout Badge

318 "Shipment of Cereals" (after B. Q. Martin)

1961. International Scout (Patrol) Camp.
1003 **317** 1p. red and black . . . 15 10

1961. Export Campaign.
1004 **318** 1p. brown 15 10

319 Emperor Penguin and Chick

320 "America"

1961. Child Welfare. Inscr "PRO-INFANCIA".
1005 – 4p.20+2p.10 brown (postage) . . . . . . 1·00 75
1006 **319** 1p.80+90c. black (air) . . 60 50
DESIGN: 4p.20, Blue-eyed cormorant.

1961. 150th Anniv of Battle of San Nicolas.
1007 **320** 2p. black 55 10

321 Dr. M. Moreno

322 Emperor Trajan

1961. 150th Death Anniv of Dr. M. Moreno.
1008 **321** 2p. blue 15 10

1961. Visit of President of Italy.
1009 **322** 2p. green 15 10

1961. Americas Day. Nos. 999/1002 optd **14 DE ABRIL DE LAS AMERICAS**.
1010 **316** 50c.+50c. blue 10 10
1011 – 1p.+1p. turquoise . . . 15 10
1012 – 3p.+3p. brown 20 20
1013 – 5p.+5p. brown 40 35

324 Tagore

325 San Martin Monument, Madrid

1961. Birth Centenary of Rabindranath Tagore (Indian poet).
1014 **324** 2p. violet on green . . . 20 10

1961. Inaug of Spanish San Martin Monument.
1015 **325** 1p. black 15 10

331a Gen. Belgrano (after monument by Rocha, Buenos Aires)

1961. Gen. Manuel Belgrano Commemoration.
1034 **331a** 2p. blue 15 10

333 Antarctic Scene

1961. 10th Anniv of San Martin Antarctic Base.
1044 **333** 2p. black 50 10

334 Conquistador and Sword

335 Sarmiento Statue (Rodin)

1961. 4th Centenary of Jujuy City.
1045 **334** 2p. red and black . . . 15 10

1961. 150th Birth Anniv of Sarmiento.
1046 **335** 2p. violet 15 10

336 Cordoba Cathedral

343 15c. Stamp of 1862

1961. "Argentina 62" International Philatelic Exn.
1047 **336** 2p.+2p. purple (postage) 20 15
1048 – 3p.+3p. green 30 15
1049 – 10p.+10p. blue 85 50
MS1050 86 × 86 mm. Nos. 1047/9 each indigo. Imperf . . . . . 1·50 1·50
1059 **343** 6p.50+6p.50 blue and turquoise (air) 40 30
DESIGNS—HORIZ: 10p. Buenos Aires Cathedral. VERT: 3p. As Type **343** but showing 10c. value and different inscr.

337

338 "The Flight into Egypt" (after Ana Maria Moncalvo)

1961. World Town-planning Day.
1052 **337** 2p. blue and yellow . . . 15 10

1961. Child Welfare.
1053 **338** 2p.+1p. brown & lilac 15 10
1054 10p.+5p. purple & mve 50 15

339 Belgrano Statue (C. Belleuse)

340 Mounted Grenadier

1962. 150th Anniv of National Flag.
1055 **339** 2p. blue 15 10

1962. 150th Anniv of Gen. San Martin's Mounted Grenadiers.
1056 **340** 2p. red 15 10

341 Mosquito and Emblem

342 Lujan Basilica

1962. Malaria Eradication.
1057 **341** 2p. black and red . . . 10 10

1962. 75th Anniv of Coronation of the Holy Virgin of Lujan.
1058 **342** 2p. black and brown . . 10 10

344 Juan Jufre (founder)

345 UNESCO Emblem

1962. 400th Anniv of San Juan.
1060 **344** 2p. blue 10 10

1962. Air. 15th Anniv of UNESCO.
1061 **345** 13p. brown and ochre 30 15

346 "Flight"

347 Juan Vucetich (fingerprints pioneer)

1962. 50th Anniv of Argentine Air Force.
1062 **346** 2p. blue, black & purple 15 10

1962. Vucetich Commem.
1063 **347** 2p. green 15 10

348 19th-century Mail Coach

350 U.P.A.E. Emblem

1962. Air. Postman's Day.
1064 **348** 5p.60 black and drab . . 15 10

1962. Air. Surch **AEREO** and value.
1065 **296** 5p.60 on 5p. brown . . 30 15
1066 18p. on 5p. brn on grn 1·00 20

1962. Air. 50th Anniv of Postal Union of Latin America.
1067 **350** 5p.60 blue 10 10

351 Pres. Sarmiento

352 Chalk-browed Mockingbird

1962.
1073 **351** 2p. green 45 10
1069 – 4p. red 60 10
1075 – 6p. red . . . . 1·40 10
1071 – 6p. brown 10 10
1072 – 90p. bistre . . . . . . 2·00 15
PORTRAITS: 4, 6p. Jose Hernandez; 90p. G. Brown.

1962. Child Welfare.
1076 **352** 4p.+2p. sepia, turquoise and brown . . . . . 1·25 75
1077 – 12p.+6p. brown, yellow and slate . . . . . 2·00 1·25
DESIGN—VERT: 12p. Rufous-collared sparrow.
See also Nos. 1101/2, 1124/5, 1165/6, 1191/2, 1214/15, 1264/5, 1293/4, 1394/5, 1415/16 and 1441/2.

353 Skylark 3 Glider

354 "20 de Febrero" Monument, Salta

1963. Air. 9th World Gliding Championships, Junin.
1078 **353** 5p.60 black and blue . . 20 10
1079 – 11p. black, red and blue 40 10
DESIGN: 11p. Super Albatross glider.

1963. 150th Anniv of Battle of Salta.
1080 **354** 2p. green 15 10

355 Cogwheels

356 National College

1963. 75th Anniv of Argentine Industrial Union.
1081 **355** 4p. red and grey 10 10

1963. Centenary of National College, Buenos Aires.
1082 **356** 4p. black and buff . . . 10 10

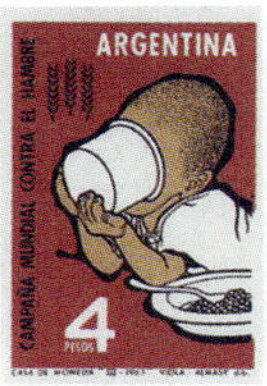

357 Child drinking Milk

358 "Flight"

1963. Freedom from Hunger.
1083 **357** 4p. ochre, black and red 15 10

1963. Air. (a) As T **358**.
1084 **358** 5p.60 green, mve & pur 35 10
1085 7p. black & yellow (I) 45 10
1086 7p. black & yellow (II) 4·25 75
1087 11p. purple, green & blk 45 15
1088 18p. blue, red and mauve 1·10 25
1089 21p. grey, red and brown 1·50 35
Two types of 7p. I, "ARGENTINA" reads down, and II, "ARGENTINA" reads up as in Type **358**.

(b) As T **358** but inscr "REPUBLICA ARGENTINA" reading down.
1147 12p. lake and brown . . . . 1·50 15
1148 15p. blue and red . . . . . 1·50 15
1291 26p. ochre 25 15
1150 27p.50 green and black . . 2·25 30
1151 30p.50 brown and blue . . 2·25 35
1292 40p. lilac . . . . 2·25 15
1153 68p. green . . . . 2·75 25
1154 78p. blue 55 35
See also Nos. 1374/80 in revalued currency.

359 Football

360 Frigate "La Argentina" (after Bouchard)

1963. 4th Pan-American Games, Sao Paulo.
1090 **359** 4p.+2p. green, black and pink (postage) . . 20 10
1091 – 12p.+6p. purple, black and salmon 30 25
1092 – 11p.+5p. red, black and green (air) 35 25
DESIGNS: 11p. Cycling; 12p. Show-jumping.

1963. Navy Day.
1093 **360** 4p. blue 80 10

361 Assembly House and Seal

1963. 150th Anniv of 1813 Assembly.
1094 **361** 4p. black and blue . . . 15 10

362 Battle Scene

1963. 150th Anniv of Battle of San Lorenzo.
1095 **362** 4p. black & green on grn 20 10

363 Queen Nefertari (bas-relief)

1963. UNESCO Campaign for Preservation of Nubian Monuments.
1096 **363** 4p. black, green & buff 25 10

364 Government House

365 "Science"

1963. Presidential Installation.
1097 **364** 5p. brown and pink . . 15 10

1963. 10th Latin-American Neurosurgery Congress.
1098 **365** 4p. blue, black & brown 20 10

366 Blackboards

367 F. de las Carreras (President of Supreme Court)

1963. "Alliance for Progress".
1099 **366** 5p. red, black and blue 15 10

1963. Centenary of Judicial Power.
1100 **367** 5p. green 15 10

1963. Child Welfare. As T **352**. Mult.
1101 4p.+2p. Vermilion flycatcher (postage) 35 25
1102 11p.+5p. Great kiskadee (air) 75 75

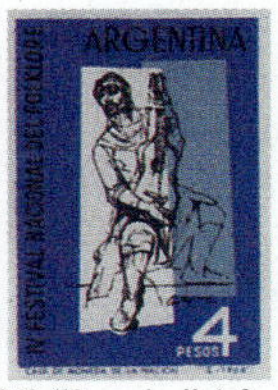

368 Kemal Ataturk

369 "Payador" (after Castagnino)

1963. 25th Death Anniv of Kemal Ataturk.
1103 **368** 12p. grey 30 10

1964. 4th National Folklore Festival.
1104 **369** 4p. black, blue & ultram 15 10

370 Map of Antarctic Islands

1964. Antarctic Claims Issue.
1105 **370** 2p. bl & ochre (postage) 80 30
1106 – 4p. bistre and blue . . 1·25 35
1107 – 18p. bl & bistre (air) . . 2·25 55
DESIGNS—VERT: (30 × 39½ mm): 4p. Map of Argentina and Antarctica. HORIZ: (as Type **291**): 18p. Map of "Islas Malvinas" (Falkland Islands).

371 Jorge Newbery in Airplane

1964. 50th Death Anniv of Jorge Newbery (aviator).
1108 **371** 4p. green 15 10

372 Pres. Kennedy

373 Father Brochero

1964. President Kennedy Memorial Issue.
1109 **372** 4p. blue and mauve . . 15 10

1964. 50th Death Anniv of Father J. G. Brochero.
1110 **373** 4p. brown 15 10

374 U.P.U. Monument, Berne

375 Soldier of the Patricios Regiment

1964. Air. 15th U.P.U. Congress, Vienna.
1111 **374** 18p. purple and red . . 50 20

1964. Army Day.
1112 **375** 4p. multicoloured . . . 50 15
See also Nos. 1135, 1170, 1201, 1223, 1246, 1343, 1363, 1399, 1450, 1515, 1564, 1641 and 1678.

376 Pope John XXIII

377 Olympic Stadium

1964. Pope John Commemoration.
1113 **376** 4p. black and orange . . 20 10

1964. Olympic Games, Tokyo.
1114 **377** 4p.+2p. brown, yellow and red (postage) . . 15 15
1115 – 12p.+6p. black & green 30 30
1116 – 11p.+5p. blk & bl (air) 40 40
DESIGNS—VERT: 11p. Sailing; 12p. Fencing.

378 University Arms

379 Olympic Flame and Crutch

1964. 350th Anniv of Cordoba University.
1117 **378** 4p. yellow, blue & black 15 10

1964. Air. Invalids Olympic Games, Tokyo.
1118 **379** 18p.+9p. multicoloured 35 45

380 "The Discovery of America" (Florentine woodcut)

381 Pigeons and U.N. Headquarters

1964. Air. "Columbus Day" (or "Day of the Race").
1119 **380** 13p. black and drab . . 35 15

1964. United Nations Day.
1120 **381** 4p. ultramarine and blue 15 10

382 J. V. Gonzalez (medallion)

383 Gen. J. Roca

1964. Birth Centenary of J. V. Gonzalez.
1121 **382** 4p. red 15 10

1964. 50th Death Anniv of General Julio Roca.
1122 **383** 4p. blue 15 10

384 "Market-place, Montserrat Square" (after C. Morel)

385 Icebreaker "General San Martin" and Bearded Penguin

1964. "Argentine Painters".
1123 **384** 4p. sepia 25 10

1964. Child Welfare. As T **352**. Multicoloured.
1124 4p.+2p. Red-crested cardinal (postage) 65 35
1125 18p.+9p. Chilean swallow (air) . . . . 1·25 80

1965. "National Territory of Tierra del Fuego, Antarctic and South Atlantic Isles".
1126 – 2p. purple (postage) . . 50 10
1127 **385** 4p. blue . . . . 2·00 40
1128 – 11p. red (air) 85 15
DESIGNS: 2p. General Belgrano Base (inscr "BASE DE EJERCITO" etc); 11p. Teniente Matienzo Joint Antarctic Base (inscr "BASE CONJUNTA" etc).

1965. Air. 1st Rio Plata Philatelists' Day. Optd **PRIMERAS JORNADAS FILATELICAS RIOPLATENSES**.
1129 **358** 7p. black & yellow (II) 15 15

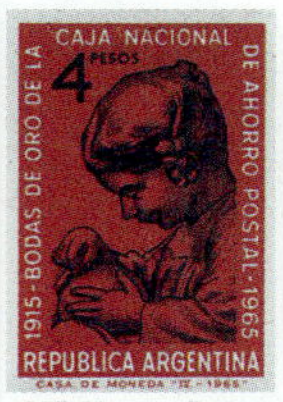

387 Young Saver

388 I.T.U. Emblem

1965. 50th Anniv of National Postal Savings Bank.
1130 **387** 4p. black and red . . . 10 10

1965. Air. Centenary of I.T.U.
1131 **388** 18p. multicoloured . . . 40 15

389 I.Q.S.Y. Emblem

390 Soldier of the "Pueyrredon Hussars"

1965. Int Quiet Sun Year and Space Research.
1132 **389** 4p. black, orange and blue (postage) 15 10
1133 – 18p. red (air) 55 20
1134 – 50p. blue 80 35
DESIGNS—VERT: 18p. Rocket launching. HORIZ: 50p. Earth, trajectories and space phenomena (both inscr "INVESTIGACIONES ESPACIALES").

1965. Army Day (29 May).
1135 **390** 8p. multicoloured . . . 70 15
See also Nos. 1170, 1201, 1223, 1246, 1343, 1363, 1399, 1450, 1515, 1564 and 1641.

391 Ricardo Guiraldes

392 H. Yrigoyen (statesman)

1965. Argentine Writers (1st series). Each brown.
1136 8p. Type **391** 35 10
1137 8p. E. Larreta 35 10
1138 8p. L. Lugones 35 10
1139 8p. R. J. Payro 35 10
1140 8p. R. Rojas 35 10
See also Nos 1174/8.

1965. Hipolito Yrigoyen Commemoration.
1141 **392** 8p. black and red . . . 15 10

393 "Children looking through a Window"

1965. International Mental Health Seminar.
1142 **393** 8p. black and brown . . 15 10

394 Ancient Map and Funeral Urn

395 Mgr. Dr. J. Cagliero

1965. 400th Anniv of San Miguel de Tucuman.
1143 **394** 8p. multicoloured . . . 15 10

1965. Cagliero Commemoration.
1144 **395** 8p. violet 15 10

396 Dante (statue in Church of the Holy Cross, Florence)

397 Sail Merchantman "Mimosa"

1965. 700th Birth Anniv of Dante.
1145 **396** 8p. blue 15 10

1965. Centenary of Welsh Colonisation of Chubut and Foundation of Rawson.
1146 **397** 8p. black and red . . . 65 20

398 Police Emblem on Map of Buenos Aires

1965. Federal Police Day.
1155 **398** 8p. red 15 10

399 Schoolchildren

1965. 81st Anniv of Law 1420 (Public Education).
1156 **399** 8p. black and green . . 15 10

400 St. Francis's Church, Catamarca

401 R. Dario (Nicaraguan poet)

1965. Brother Mamerto Esquiu Commemoration.
1157 **400** 8p. brown and yellow . . 15 10

1965. 50th Death Anniv of Ruben Dario.
1158 **401** 15p. violet on grey . . . 15 10

402 "The Orange-seller" (detail)

1966. Prilidiano Pueyrredon's Paintings. Designs show details from the original works, each green.
1159 8p. Type **402** 55 45
1160 8p. "A Halt at the Village Grocer's Shop" 55 45
1161 8p. "San Fernando Landscape" 75 45
1162 8p. "Bathing Horses on the Banks of the River Plate" 55 45

403 Rocket "Centaur" and Antarctic Map

404 Dr. Sun Yat-sen

1966. Air. Rocket Launches in Antarctica.
1163 **403** 27p.50 red, black & blue 65 25

1966. Birth Centenary of Dr. Sun Yat-sen.
1164 **404** 8p. brown 45 25

1966. Child Welfare. As T **352**, inscr "R. ARGENTINA". Multicoloured.
1165 8p.+4p. Southern lapwing (postage) . . . . 1·00 55
1166 27p.50+12p.50 Rufous hornero (air) . . . . . 1·25 85

405 "Rivadavia" 5c. stamp of 1864

1966. 2nd Rio Plata Philatelists Days and Exhibition. Miniature sheet containing designs as T **405**.
MS1167 141 × 100 mm. 4p. red and grey (T **405**); 5p. green and grey (10c. stamp); 8p. blue and grey (15c. stamp) 75 90

406 "Human Races"

1966. Inaug of W.H.O. Headquarters, Geneva.
1168 **406** 8p. black and brown . . 15 10

407 Magellan Gull

1966. Air. 50th Anniv of Naval Aviation School, Puerto Militar.
1169 **407** 12p. multicoloured . . . 40 25

1966. Army Day (29 May). As T **390**.
1170 8p. multicoloured 65 15
DESIGN: 8p. Militiaman of Guemes's "Infernals".

408 Arms of Argentina

1966. Air. "Argentina '66" Philatelic Exhibition, Buenos Aires.
1171 **408** 10p.+10p. multicoloured 1·50 1·10

409

1966. 150th Anniv of Independence. Sheet of 25 (5 × 5) comprising different 10p. designs–national, federal and provincial arms and maps, as T **409**. Inscr "1816–1966". Multicoloured.
MS1172 Sheet of 25 stamps . . . 25·00

410 "Charity" Emblem

1966. Argentine Charities.
1173 **410** 10p. blue, black & green 25 15

1966. Argentine Writers (2nd series). Portraits as T **391**. Each green.
1174 10p. H. Ascasubi 40 10
1175 10p. Estanislao del Campo 40 10
1176 10p. M. Cane 40 10
1177 10p. Lucio V. Lopez 40 10
1178 10p. R. Obligado 40 10

411 Anchor

1966. 25th Anniv of Argentine Mercantile Marine.
1179 **411** 4p. multicoloured . . . 25 15

412 L. Agote

413 Map and Flags of the American States

1966. Argentine Scientists. Each violet.
1180 10p. Type **412** 40 10
1181 10p. J. B. Ambrosetti . . . 40 10
1182 10p. M. I. Lillo 40 10
1183 10p. F. P. Moreno 40 10
1184 10p. F. J. Muniz 40 10

1966. 7th American Armies Conf, Buenos Aires.
1185 **413** 10p. multicoloured . . . 15 10

414 Bank Facade

415 La Salle Statue and College

1966. 75th Anniv of Argentine National Bank.
1186 **414** 10p. green 10 10

1966. 75th Anniv of La Salle College, Buenos Aires.
1187 **415** 10p. black and brown . . 10 10

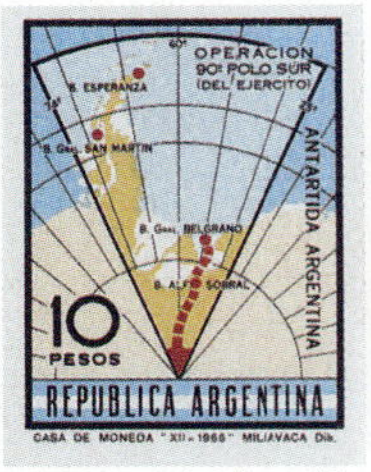
416 Antarctic Map with Expedition Route

417 Gen. J. M. de Pueyrredon

1966. Argentine South Pole Expedition, 1965–66.
1188 **416** 10p. multicoloured . . . 80 50

1966. Gen. J. M. de Pueyrredon Commemoration.
1189 **417** 10p. red 10 10

418 Gen. J. G. de Las Heras

419 Ancient Pot

1966. Gen. Juan G. de Las Heras Commemoration.
1190 **418** 10p. black 10 10

1967. Child Welfare. As T **352**, inscr "R. ARGENTINA". Multicoloured.
1191 10p.+5p. Scarlet-headed blackbird (horiz) (postage) 80 60
1192 15p.+7p. Blue and yellow tanager (air) . . . . . . 1·25 90

1967. 20th Anniv of UNESCO.
1193 **419** 10p. multicoloured . . . 15 10

420 "The Meal" (after F. Fader)

1967. Fernando Fader (painter).
1194 **420** 10p. brown 15 10

421 Juana Azurduy de Padilla

422 Schooner "Invencible"

1967. Famous Argentine Women. Each sepia.
1195 6p. Type **421** 30 10
1196 6p. J. M. Gorriti 30 10
1197 6p. C. Grierson 30 10
1198 6p. J. P. Manson 30 10
1199 6p. A. Storni 30 10

1967. Navy Day.
1200 **422** 20p. multicoloured . . . 1·25 20

1967. Army Day (29 May). As T **390**.
1201 20p. multicoloured 75 15
DESIGN: 20p. Soldier of the Arribenos Regiment.

423 M. Belgrano (6p.) and J. G. de Artigas (22p.)

1967. 3rd Rio Plata Philatelists Days and Exhibition. Sheet 63 × 55 mm comprising designs as T **423**.
MS1202 6p. and 22p. each brown and grey 35 40

424 Suitcase and Dove

425 PADELAI Emblem and Sun

1967. International Tourist Year.
1203 **424** 20p. multicoloured . . . 15 10

1967. 75th Anniv of PADELAI (Argentine Children's Welfare Association).
1204 **425** 20p. multicoloured . . . 15 10

426 Teodoro Fels's Bleriot XI

427 Ferreyra's Oxwagon and Skyscrapers

1967. Air. 50th Anniv of 1st Argentine–Uruguay Airmail Flight.
1205 **426** 26p. brown, olive & blue 30 10

1967. Centenary of Villa Maria.
1206 **427** 20p. multicoloured . . . 15 10

428 "General San Martin" (from statue by M. P. Nunez de Ibarra)

429 Interior of Museum

1967. 150th Anniv of Battle of Chacabuco.
1207 **428** 20p. brown and yellow 45 15
1208 – 40p. blue 70 15
DESIGN—(48 × 31 mm)—HORIZ: 40p. "Battle of Chacabuco" (from painting by P. Subercaseaux).

1967. 10th Anniv of Government House Museum.
1209 **429** 20p. blue 15 10

430 Pedro Zanni and "Provincia de Buenos Aires"

1967. Aeronautics Week.
1210 **430** 20p. multicoloured . . . 15 10

431 Cadet Ship "General Brown" (from painting by E. Biggeri)

432 Ovidio Lagos and Front Page of "La Capital" (newspaper)

1967. "Temex 67" Stamp Exhibition and 95th Anniv of Naval Military School.
1211 **431** 20p. multicoloured . . . 1·00 20

1967. Centenary of "La Capital".
1212 **432** 20p. brown 15 10

433 St. Barbara (from altar-painting, Segovia, Spain)

434 "Sivori's Wife"

1967. Artillery Day (4 Dec).
1213 **433** 20p. red 15 10

1967. Child Welfare. Bird designs as T **352**. Multicoloured.
1214 20p.+10p. Amazon kingfisher (postage) . . . 75 40
1215 26p.+13p. Toco toucan (air) 1·00 60

1968. 50th Death Anniv of Eduardo Sivori (painter).
1216 **434** 20p. green 15 10

435 "Almirante Brown" Scientific Station

436 Man in Wheelchair

1968. "Antarctic Territories".
1217 – 6p. multicoloured . . . 60 15
1218 **435** 20p. multicoloured . . . 85 20
1219 – 40p. multicoloured . . . 1·10 55
DESIGNS—VERT (22½ × 32 mm): 6p. Map of Antarctic radio-postal stations. HORIZ (as Type **435**): 40p. Aircraft over South Pole ("Trans-Polar Round Flight").

1968. Rehabilitation Day for the Handicapped.
1220 **436** 20p. black and green . . 20 10

437 "St. Gabriel" (detail from "The Annunciation" by Leonardo da Vinci)

438 Children and W.H.O. Emblem

1968. St. Gabriel (patron saint of army communications).
1221 **437** 20p. mauve 15 10

1968. 20th Anniv of W.H.O.
1222 **438** 20p. blue and red . . . 15 10

1968. Army Day (29 May). As T **390**.
1223 20p. multicoloured 85 15
DESIGN: 20p. Iriarte's artilleryman.

439 Full-rigged Cadet Ship "Libertad" (E. Biggeri)

1968. Navy Day.
1224 **439** 20p. multicoloured . . . 65 15

440 G. Rawson and Hospital

1968. Centenary of Guillermo Rawson Hospital.
1225 **440** 6p. bistre 15 10

441 Vito Dumas and "Legh II"

1968. Air. Vito Dumas' World Voyage in Yacht "Legh II".
1226 **441** 68p. multicoloured . . . 60 20

442 Children using Zebra crossing

1968. Road Safety.
1227 **442** 20p. multicoloured . . . 20 10

443 "O'Higgins greeting San Martin" (P. Subercaseaux)

1968. 150th Anniv of Battle of the Maipu.
1228 **443** 40p. blue 55 20

444 Dr. O. Magnasco (lawyer)

445 "The Sea" (E. Gomez)

446 "Grandmother's Birthday" (P. Lynch)

1968. Magnasco Commemoration.
1229 **444** 20p. brown 20 10

1968. Children's Stamp Design Competition.
1230 **445** 20p. multicoloured . . . 20 15
1231 **446** 20p. multicoloured . . . 20 15

447 Mar del Plata at Night

448 Mounted Gendarme

1968. 4th Plenary Assembly of Int Telegraph and Telephone Consultative Committee, Mar del Plata.
1232 **447** 20p. black, yellow and blue (postage) 25 15
1233 – 40p. black, mauve and blue (air) 35 15
1234 – 68p. multicoloured . . . 50 25

DESIGNS (as Type **447**): 40p. South America in Assembly hemisphere. (Larger, 40 × 30 mm): 68p. Assembly emblem.

1968. National Gendarmerie.
1235 **448** 20p. multicoloured . . . 30 10

449 Coastguard Cutter "Lynch"

450 A. de Anchorena and "Pampero"

1968. National Maritime Prefecture (Coastguard).
1236 **449** 20p. black, grey and blue 65 10

1968. Aeronautics Week.
1237 **450** 20p. multicoloured . . . 30 10

451 St. Martin of Tours (A. Guido)

452 Bank Emblem

1968. St. Martin of Tours (patron saint of Buenos Aires).
1238 **451** 20p. brown and lilac . . 15 10

1968. Municipal Bank of Buenos Aires.
1239 **452** 20p. black, green & yell 15 10

453 Anniversary and A.L.P.I. Emblems

1968. 25th Anniv of "Fight Against Polio Association" (A.L.P.I.).
1240 **453** 20p. green and red . . . 20 10

454 "My Grandmother's Birthday" (Patricia Lynch)

1968. 1st "Solidarity" Philatelic Exn, Buenos Aires.
1241 **454** 40p.+20p. multicoloured 75 30

455 "The Potter Woman" (Ramon Gomez Cornet)

456 Emblem of State Coalfields

1968. Cent of Whitcomb Gallery, Buenos Aires.
1242 **455** 20p. red 15 10

1968. Coal and Steel Industries. Multicoloured.
1243 20p. Type **456** 15 10
1244 20p. Ladle and emblem of Military Steel-manufacturing Agency ("FM") 15 10

457 Illustration from Schmidl's book "Journey to the River Plate and Paraguay"

1969. Ulrich Schmidl Commemoration.
1245 **457** 20p. yellow, red & black 15 10

1969. Army Day (29 May). As T **390**.
1246 20p. Sapper, Buenos Aires Army, 1856 . . . . . . 70 15

459 Sail Frigate "Hercules"

1969. Navy Day.
1247 **459** 20p. multicoloured . . . 1·00 20

460 "Freedom and Equality" (from poster by S. Zagorski)

461 I.L.O. Emblem within Honeycomb

1969. Human Rights Year.
1254 **460** 20p. black and yellow . . 15 10

1969. 50th Anniv of I.L.O.
1255 **461** 20p. multicoloured . . . 15 10

462 P. N. Arata (biologist)

463 Dish Aerial and Satellite

1969. Argentine Scientists.
1256 **462** 6p. brown on yellow . . 35 15
1257 – 6p. brown on yellow . . 35 15
1258 – 6p. brown on yellow . . 35 15
1259 – 6p. brown on yellow . . 35 15
1260 – 6p. brown on yellow . . 35 15
PORTRAITS: No. 1257, M. Fernandez (zoologist); 1258, A. P. Gallardo (biologist); 1259, C. M. Hicken (botanist); 1260, E. L. Holmberg (botanist).

1969. Satellite Communications.
1261 **463** 20p. blk & yell (postage) 25 15
1262 – 40p. blue (air) 55 20
DESIGN—HORIZ: 40p. Earth station and dish aerial.

464 Nieuport 28 and Route Map

1969. 50th Anniv of 1st Argentine Airmail Service.
1263 **464** 20p. multicoloured . . . 20 10

1969. Child Welfare. As T **352**, inscr "R. ARGENTINA". Multicoloured.
1264 20p.+10p. White-faced whistling duck (postage) 1·00 45
1265 26p.+13p. Lineated woodpecker (air) . . . . 1·00 45

465 College Entrance

466 General Pacheco (from painting by R. Guidice)

1969. Centenary of Argentine Military College.
1266 **465** 20p. multicoloured . . . 15 10

1969. Death Centenary of General Angel Pacheco.
1267 **466** 20p. green 15 10

467 Bartolome Mitre and Logotypes of "La Nacion"

468 J. Aguirre

1969. Centenary of Newspapers "La Nacion" and "La Prensa".
1268 **467** 20p. black, emer & grn 50 15
1269 – 20p. black orange & yell 50 15
DESIGN: No. 1269 "The Lantern" (masthead) and logotypes of "La Prensa".

1969. Argentine Musicians.
1270 **468** 6p. green and blue . . . 65 15
1271 – 6p. green and blue . . . 65 15
1272 – 6p. green and blue . . . 65 15
1273 – 6p. green and blue . . . 65 15
1274 – 6p. green and blue . . . 65 15
MUSICIANS: No. 1271, F. Boero; 1272, C. Gaito; 1273, C. L. Buchardo; 1274, A. Williams.

469 Hydro-electric Project on Rivers Limay and Neuquen

1969. National Development Projects. Mult.
1275 6p. Type **469** (postage) . . . 50 10
1276 20p. Parana–Santa Fe river tunnel 60 15
1277 26p. Atomic power plant, Atucha (air) . . . . . . 1·00 40

470 Lieut. B. Matienzo and Nieuport 28 Biplane

1969. Aeronautics Week.
1278 **470** 20p. multicoloured . . . 50 10

471 Capital "L" and Lions Emblem

1969. 50th Anniv of Lions International.
1279 **471** 20p. olive, orge & green 50 10

472 "Madonna and Child" (after R. Soldi)

1969. Christmas.
1280 **472** 20p. multicoloured . . . 55 15

1970. Child Welfare. As T **352**, but differently arranged and inscr "REPUBLICA ARGENTINA". Multicoloured.
1293 20c.+10c. Slender-tailed woodstar (postage) . . . 85 55
1294 40c.+20c. Chilean flamingo (air) 90 70
See also Nos. 1394/5, 1415/16 and 1441/2.

474 "General Belgrano" (lithograph by Gericault)

1970. Birth Bicent of General Manuel Belgrano.
1295 **474** 20c. brown 45 15
1296 – 50c. black, flesh & blue 80 25
DESIGN—HORIZ (56 × 15 mm): 50c. "Monument to the Flag" (bas-relief by Jose Fioravanti).

475 Early Fire Engine

1970. Air. Centenary of Buenos Aires Fire Brigade.
1297 **475** 40c. multicoloured . . . 60 10

476 Naval Schooner "Juliet", 1814

1970. Navy Day.
1298 **476** 20c. multicoloured . . . 1·25 20

477 San Jose Palace

478 General Belgrano

1970. President Justo de Urquiza Commemoration.
1299 **477** 20c. multicoloured . . . 15 10

1970. Revalued currency. Previous designs with values in centavos and pesos as T **478**. Inscr "REPUBLICA ARGENTINA" or "ARGENTINA".
1300 1c. green (No. 1016) . . 15 10
1301 – 3c. red (No. 951) . . . 15 10
1302 **296** 5c. blue 15 10
1303 **478** 6c. blue 15 10
1304 – 8c. green 15 10
1305 – 10c. brown (No. 1286)* 45 10
1306 – 10c. red (No. 1286) . . 1·25 10
1307 – 10c. brown (No. 1286)* 55 10
1308 **478** 10c. brown 20 10
1309 – 25c. brown 40 10
1310 **478** 30c. purple 10 10
1311 – 50c. red 80 10
1312 **478** 60c. yellow 10 10
1313 – 65c. brown (No. 878) 85 10
1314 – 70c. blue 10 10
1315 – 90c. green (No. 878) . . 2·00 10
1316a – 1p. brown (as No. 1027, but 23 × 29 mm) 40 10
1317 – 1p.15 blue (No. 1072) 80 10
1318 – 1p.20 orange (No. 878) 80 10
1319 – 1p.20 red 35 10
1320 – 1p.80 brn (as No. 1072) 30 10
1321 **478** 1p.80 blue 20 10
1322 – 2p. brown 20 10
1323 – 2p.70 bl (as No. 878) 25 10
1323a **478** 3p. grey 15 10
1392 – 4p.50 green (as No. 1288) (G. Brown) 40 10
1325 – 5p. green (as No. 1032) 95 10
1326 – 6p. red 25 10
1327 – 6p. green 25 10
1328 – 7p.50 grn (as No. 878) 85 10
1329 – 10p. blue (as No. 1033) 1·25 10
1329a – 12p. green 25 10
1329b – 12p. red 25 10
1330 – 13p.50 red (as No. 1072) . . . . 1·00 10
1331 – 13p.50 red (as No. 1072 but larger, 16 × 24 mm) 40 10
1332 – 15p. red 25 10
1333 – 15p. blue 25 10
1334 – 20p. red 40 10
1335 – 22p.50 blue (as No. 878) (22 × 32½ mm) . . . 1·00 10
1393 – 22p.50 blue (as No. 878) (26 × 39 mm) 40 10

1336	–	30p. red	40	10
1337	478	40p. green	70	15
1338	–	40p. red	40	10
1339	478	60p. blue	80	20
1340	–	70p. blue	1·00	20
1340a	478	90p. green	55	30
1340b	–	100p. red	55	25
1340c	–	110p. red	35	15
1340d	–	120p. red	30	20
1340e	–	130p. red	40	25

DESIGNS—VERT (as Type **478**): 25, 50, 70c., 1p.20, 2, 6, 12, 15p. (No. 1332), 20, 30, 40p. (No. 1338), 100, 110, 120, 130p. General Jose de San Martin; 15p. (No. 1333), 70p. Guillermo Brown.

*No. 1307 differs from Nos. 1305/6 in being without imprint. It also has "CORREOS" at top right.

482 Wireless Set of 1920 and Radio "Waves"

1970. 50th Anniv of Argentine Radio Broadcasting.
1341 **482** 20c. multicoloured . . . 15 10

483 Emblem of Education Year

485 "United Nations"

484 "Liberation Fleet leaving Valparaiso" (A. Abel)

1970. Air. International Education Year.
1342 **483** 68c. black and blue . . . 30 15

1970. Military Uniforms. As T **390**. Multicoloured.
1343 20c. Military courier, 1879 75 25

1970. 150th Anniv of Peruvian Liberation.
1344 **484** 26c. multicoloured . . . 1·40 20

1970. 25th Anniv of U.N.
1345 **485** 20c. multicoloured . . . 15 10

486 Cordoba Cathedral

1970. 400th Anniv of Tucuman Diocese.
1346 **486** 50c. blk & grey (postage) 85 10
1347 – 40c. multicoloured (air) 85 20
DESIGN—HORIZ: 40c. Chapel, Sumampa.

487 Planetarium

1970. Air. Buenos Aires Planetarium.
1348 **487** 40c. multicoloured . . . 40 15

488 "Liberty" and Mint Building

1970. 25th Anniv of State Mint Building, Buenos Aires.
1349 **488** 20c. black, green & gold 15 10

489 "The Manger" (H. G. Gutierrez) (½-size illustration)

1970. Christmas.
1350 **489** 20c. multicoloured . . . 25 10

490 Jorge Newbery and Morane Saulnier Type L Airplane

1970. Air. Aeronautics Week.
1351 **490** 26c. multicoloured . . . 40 15

491 St. John Bosco and College Building

1970. Salesian Mission in Patagonia.
1352 **491** 20c. black and green . . 15 10

492 "Planting the Flag"

1971. 5th Anniv of Argentine Expedition to the South Pole.
1353 **492** 20c. multicoloured . . . 1·25 35

493 Dorado (½-size illustration)

1971. Child Welfare. Fishes. Multicoloured.
1354 20c.+10c. Type **493** (postage) 65 45
1355 40c.+20c. River Plate pejerry (air) 55 35

494 Einstein and Scanners

495 E. I. Alippi

1971. Electronics in Postal Development.
1356 **494** 25c. multicoloured . . . 30 10

1971. Argentine Actors and Actresses. Each black and brown.
1357 15c. Type **495** 40 10
1358 15c. J. A. Casaberta 40 10
1359 15c. R. Casaux 40 10
1360 15c. Angelina Pagano . . . 40 10
1361 15c. F. Parravicini 40 10

496 Federation Emblem

1971. Inter-American Regional Meeting of International Roads Federation.
1362 **496** 25c. black and blue . . . 15 10

1971. Army Day. As T **390**.
1363 25c. multicoloured . . . . . 1·00 15
DESIGN: 25c. Artilleryman of 1826.

1971. Navy Day. As T **476**.
1364 25c. multicoloured . . . . . 1·75 20
DESIGN: Sloop "Carmen".

498 "General Guemes" (L. Gigli)

1971. 150th Death Anniv of General M. de Guemes. Multicoloured.
1365 25c. Type **498** 55 20
1366 25c. "Death of Guemes" (A. Alice) (84 × 29 mm) 55 20

499 Order of the Peruvian Sun

1971. 150th Anniv of Peruvian Independence.
1367 **499** 31c. yellow, black & red 40 10

500 Stylized Tulip

501 Dr. A. Saenz (founder) (after Jose Gut)

1971. 3rd Int and 8th Nat Horticultural Exhibition.
1368 **500** 25c. multicoloured . . . 25 15

1971. 150th Anniv of Buenos Aires University.
1369 **501** 25c. multicoloured . . . 20 15

502 Arsenal Emblem

1971. 30th Anniv of Fabricaciones Militares (Arsenals).
1370 **502** 25c. multicoloured . . . 20 15

503 Road Transport

1971. Nationalized Industries.
1371 **503** 25c. mult (postage) . . . 35 10
1372 – 65c. multicoloured . . . 90 35
1373 – 31c. yell, blk & red (air) 45 25

DESIGNS: 31c. Refinery and formula ("Petrochemicals"); 65c. Tree and paper roll ("Paper and Cellulose").

1971. Air. Revalued currency. Face values in centavos.

1374	358	45c. brown	2·50	15
1375		68c. red	30	15
1376a		70c. blue	1·60	15
1377		90c. green	1·75	15
1378		1p.70 blue	55	10
1379		1p.95 green	55	15
1380		2p.65 purple	55	15

504 Constellation and Telescope

1971. Centenary of Cordoba Observatory.
1381 **504** 25c. multicoloured . . . 25 15

505 Capt. D. L. Candelaria and Morane Saulnier Type P Airplane

1971. 25th Aeronautics and Space Week.
1382 **505** 25c. multicoloured . . . 40 10

506 "Stamps" (Mariette Lydis)

507 "Christ in Majesty" (tapestry by Butler)

1971. 2nd Charity Stamp Exhibition.
1383 **506** 1p.+50c. multicoloured 35 35

1971. Christmas.
1384 **507** 25c. multicoloured . . . 20 10

1972. Child Welfare. As T **352**, but differently arranged and inscr "REPUBLICA ARGENTINA".
1394 25c.+10c. Saffron finch (vert) 90 40
1395 65c.+30c. Rufous-bellied thrush (horiz) . . . . . . 1·10 50

508 "Maternity" (J. Castagnino)

1972. 25th Anniv of UNICEF.
1396 **508** 25c. black and brown . . 20 15

509 Treaty Emblem, "Libertad" (liner) and Almirante Brown Base

1972. 10th Anniv of Antarctic Treaty.
1397 **509** 25c. multicoloured . . . 1·25 20

510 Postman's Mail Pouch

1972. Bicentenary of 1st Buenos Aires Postman.
1398 **510** 25c. multicoloured . . . 15 10

1972. Army Day. As T **390**. Multicoloured.
1399 25c. Sergeant of Negro and Mulatto Battalion (1806–7) 65 15

1972. Navy Day. As T **476**. Multicoloured.
1400 25c. Brigantine "Santisima Trinidad" . . . . 1·40 20

512 Sonic Balloon **513** Oil Pump

1972. National Meteorological Service.
1401 **512** 25c. multicoloured . . . 25 15

1972. 50th Anniv of State Oilfields (Y.P.F.).
1402 **513** 45c. black, blue & gold 80 10

514 Forest Centre

1972. 7th World Forestry Congress, Buenos Aires.
1403 **514** 25c. black, blue & lt bl 45 10

515 Arms and Cadet Ship "Presidente Sarmiento"

1972. Centenary of Naval School.
1404 **515** 25c. multicoloured . . . 1·25 20

516 Baron A. de Marchi, Balloon and Voisin "Boxkite" **517** Bartolome Mitre

1972. Aeronautics Week.
1405 **516** 25c. multicoloured . . . 40 10

1972. 150th Birth Anniv of General Bartolome Mitre.
1406 **517** 25c. blue 20 10

518 Heart and Flower **519** "Martin Fierro" (J. C. Castignino)

1972. World Health Day.
1407 **518** 90c. blk, violet & blue 45 15

1972. Int Book Year and Cent of "Martin Fierro" (poem by Jose Hernandez). Multicoloured.
1408 50c. Type **519** 25 15
1409 90c. "Spirit of the Gaucho" (V. Forte) 50 20

520 Iguazu Falls

1972. American Tourist Year.
1410 **520** 45c. multicoloured . . . 30 10

521 "Wise Man on Horseback" (18th-century wood-carving) **522** Cockerel Emblem

1972. Christmas.
1411 **521** 50c. multicoloured . . . 40 10

1973. 150th Anniv of Federal Police Force.
1412 **522** 50c. multicoloured . . . 20 10

523 Bank Emblem and First Coin **525** Presidential Chair

524 Douglas DC-3 Aircraft and Polar Map

1973. 150th Anniv of Provincial Bank of Buenos Aires.
1413 **523** 50c. multicoloured . . . 15 10

1973. 10th Anniv of 1st Argentine Flight to South Pole.
1414 **524** 50c. multicoloured . . . 90 20

1973. Child Welfare. As T **473**, but differently arranged and inscr "R. ARGENTINA". Mult.
1415 50c.+25c. Crested screamer (vert) 85 50
1416 90c.+45c. Saffron-cowled blackbird (horiz) . . . . 1·25 75

1973. Presidential Inauguration.
1417 **525** 50c. multicoloured . . . 20 10

526 San Martin and Bolivar

1973. San Martin's Farewell to People of Peru. Multicoloured.
1418 50c. Type **526** 25 15
1419 50c. "San Martin" (after Gil de Castro) (vert) 25 15

527 "Eva Peron – Eternally with her People"

1973. Eva Peron Commemoration.
1420 **527** 70c. multicoloured . . . 20 15

528 "House of Viceroy Sobremonte" (H. de Virgilio)

1973. 4th Centenary of Cordoba.
1421 **528** 50c. multicoloured . . . 20 10

529 "Woman" (L. Spilimbergo)

1973. Philatelists' Day. Argentine Paintings. Mult.
1422 15c.+15c. "Nature Study" (A. Guttero) (horiz) . . . 50 10
1423 70c. Type **529** 80 15
1424 90c.+90c. "Nude" (M. C. Victorica) (horiz) 85 70
See also Nos. 1434/6 and 1440.

530 "La Argentina" (sail frigate) **531** Early and Modern Telephones

1973. Navy Day.
1425 **530** 70c. multicoloured . . . 1·25 20

1973. 25th Anniv of National Telecommunications Enterprise (E.N.T.E.L.).
1426 **531** 70c. multicoloured . . . 35 10

532 Quill Pen of Flags **533** Lujan Basilica

1973. 12th International Latin Notaries Congress.
1427 **532** 70c. multicoloured . . . 25 15

1973.
1428 **533** 18c. brown and yellow 15 10
1429 50c. purple and black 15 10
1429a 50c. blue and brown . . 15 10
1430 50c. purple 15 10

1973. Transfer of Presidency of General Juan Peron. No. 1318 optd **TRANSMISION DEL MANDO PRESIDENCIAL 12 OCTUBRE 1973**.
1431 1p.20 orange 80 15

535 "Virgin and Child" (stained-glass window)

1973. Christmas. Multicoloured.
1432 70c. Type **535** 30 10
1433 1p.20 "The Manger" (B. Venier) 60 15

1974. Argentine Paintings. As T **529**. Mult.
1434 50c. "Houses" (E. Daneri) (horiz) 30 10
1435 70c. "The Lama" (J. B. Planas) 35 15
1436 90c. "Homage to the Blue Grotto" (E. Pettoruti) (horiz) 50 20

536 View of Mar del Plata

1974. Centenary of Mar del Plata.
1437 **536** 70c. multicoloured . . . 30 10

537 "Fray Justo Santa Maria de Oro" (anon.) **538** Weather Contrasts

1974. Birth Bicentenary of Fray Justo Santa Maria de Oro.
1438 **537** 70c. multicoloured . . . 20 10

1974. Cent of World Meteorological Organization.
1439 **538** 1p.20 multicoloured . . 40 10

1974. "Prenfil 74" Philatelic Press Exhibition, Buenos Aires. As No. 1435.
1440 70c.+30c. multicoloured . . 20 20

1974. Child Welfare. As T **352** but differently arranged and inscr "REPUBLICA ARGENTINA". Multicoloured.
1441 70c.+30c. Double-collared seedeater 65 45
1442 1p.20+60c. Hooded siskin 1·10 65

539 B. Roldan **540** O.E.A. Member Countries

1974. Birth Centenary of Belisario Roldan (writer).
1443 **539** 70c. brown and blue . . 10 10

1974. 25th Anniv of Organization of American States' Charter.
1444 **540** 1p.38 multicoloured . . 15 10

541 Posthorn Emblem

1974. Creation of State Posts and Telecommunications Enterprise (E.N.C.O.T.E.L.).
1445 **541** 1p.20 blue, black & gold 40 10

542 Flags of Member Countries

543 El Chocon Hydro-electric Complex

1974. 6th Meeting of River Plate Countries' Foreign Ministers.
1446 **542** 1p.38 multicoloured . . 15 15

1974. Nationalized Industries. Multicoloured.
1447 70c. Type **543** 35 10
1448 1p.20 Blast furnace, Somisa steel mills 55 25
1449 4p.50 General Belgrano Bridge (61 × 25 mm) . . . 2·75 60

1974. Army Day. As T **390**. Multicoloured.
1450 1p.20 Mounted Grenadier 70 15
See also Nos. 1515 and 1564.

544 A. Mascias and Bleriot XI

1974. Air Force Day.
1451 **544** 1p.20 multicoloured . . 75 15

545 Brigantine "Belgrano"

1974. 150th Anniv of San Martin's Departure into Exile.
1452 **545** 1p.20 multicoloured . . 1·25 20

546 San Francisco Convent, Santa Fe

1974. 400th Anniv of Santa Fe.
1453 **546** 1p.20 multicoloured . . 45 10

547 Symbolic Posthorn

1974. Centenary of U.P.U.
1454 **547** 2p.65 multicoloured . . 70 10

548 Mariano Necochea

1974. 150th Anniv of Battles of Junin and Ayacucho. Sheet 143 × 134 mm comprising T **548** and similar vert designs. Multicoloured.
MS1455 (a) 1p. Type **548**; (b) 1p.20 San Martin; (c) 1p.70 Manuel Isidoro Suarez; (d) 1p.90 Juan Pascual Pringles; (e) 2p.70 Latin American flags; (f) 4p.50 Jose Felix Bogado . . . . 3·25 3·00

549 Congress Building, Buenos Aires

1974.
1456 **549** 30p. purple and yellow 1·50 10

550 Boy examining Stamp

1974. International Year of Youth Philately.
1457 **550** 1p.70 black and yellow 40 10

551 "Christmas in Peace" (V. Campanella)

1974. Christmas. Multicoloured.
1458 1p.20 Type **551** 35 10
1459 2p.65 "St. Anne and the Virgin Mary" 40 15

552 "Space Monsters" (R. Forner)

1975. Contemporary Argentine Paintings. Mult.
1460 2p.70 Type **552** 80 15
1461 4p.50 "Sleep" (E. Centurion) . . . . . 1·50 25

553 Cathedral and Weaver, Catamarca (½-size illustration)

1975. Tourist Views (1st series). Multicoloured.
1462 1p.20 Type **553** 25 15
1463 1p.20 Street scene and carved pulpit, Jujuy . . . 25 15
1464 1p.20 Monastery and tree-felling, Salta 25 15
1465 1p.20 Dam and vase, Santiago del Estero . . . 25 15
1466 1p.20 Colombres Museum and farm cart, Tucuman 25 15
See also Nos. 1491/3.

554 "We're Vaccinated Now" (M. L. Alonso)

555 "Don Quixote" (Zuloaga)

1975. Children's Vaccination Campaign.
1467 **554** 2p. multicoloured . . . 50 15

1975. Air. "Espana 75" International Stamp Exhibition, Madrid.
1468 **555** 2p.75 black, yell & red 60 15

556 Hugo S. Acuna and South Orkneys Base (¾-size illustration)

1975. Antarctic Pioneers. Multicoloured.
1469 2p. Type **556** 45 10
1470 2p. Francisco P. Moreno and Quetrihue Peninsula 45 10
1471 2p. Capt. Carlos M. Moyano and Cerra Torre, Santa Cruz 45 10
1472 2p. Lt. Col. Luis Piedra Buena and naval cutter "Luisito" in the Antarctic 1·40 25
1473 2p. Ensign Jose M. Sobral and "Snow Hill" House 45 10

557 Valley of the Moon, San Juan Province

559 Eduardo Bradley and Balloon

1975.
1474 **557** 50p. multicoloured . . 1·75 10
1474a 300p. multicoloured . . 2·10 40
1474b – 500p. multicoloured . . 4·25 85
1474c – 1000p. multicoloured 3·75 1·00
DESIGNS—HORIZ: 500p. Admiral Brown Antarctic Station; 1000p. San Francisco Church, Salta.

1975. Air. Surch.
1475 **358** 9p.20 on 5p.60 green, mauve and purple . . 90 10
1476 19p.70 on 5p.60 green, mauve and purple . . 1·10 20
1477 100p. on 5p.60 green, mauve and purple . . 2·75 40

1975. Air Force Day.
1478 **559** 6p. multicoloured . . . 60 15

560 Sail Frigate "25 de Mayo"

1975. Navy Day.
1479 **560** 6p. multicoloured . . . 90 20

561 "Oath of the 33 Orientales on the Beach of La Agraciada" (J. Blanes)

1975. 150th Anniv of Uruguayan Independence.
1480 **561** 6p. multicoloured . . . 30 15

1975. Air. Surch. **REVALORIZADO** and value.
1481 **358** 9p.20 on 5p.60 green, mauve and purple . . 85 15
1482 19p.70 on 5p.60 green, mauve and purple . . 1·00 30

563 Flame Emblem

1975. 30th Anniv of Pres. Peron's Seizure of Power.
1483 **563** 6p. multicoloured . . . 35 15

1975. Surch **REVALORIZADO** and value.
1484 **533** 5p. on 18c. brown & yell 45 10

565 Bridge and Flags of Argentina and Uruguay

1975. "International Bridge" between Colon (Argentina) and Paysandu (Uruguay).
1485 **565** 6p. multicoloured . . . 50 15

566 Posthorn Emblem

568 "The Nativity" (stained-glass window)

1975. Introduction of Postal Codes.
1486 **566** 10p. on 20c. yellow, black and green . . . 35 10

1975. Nos. 951 and 1288 surch **REVALORIZADO** and value.
1487 6c. on 3p. blue 15 10
1488 30c. on 90p. bistre 15 10

1975. Christmas.
1489 **568** 6p. multicoloured . . . 30 15

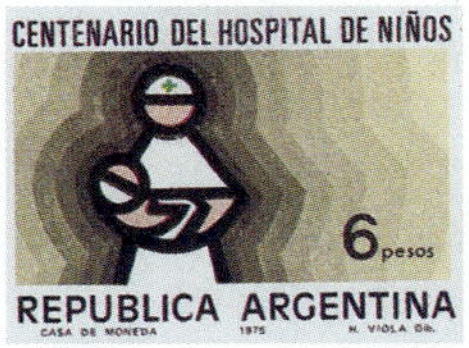

569 Stylized Nurse and Child

570 "Numeral"

1975. Centenary of Children's Hospital.
1490 **569** 6p. multicoloured . . . 35 10

1975. Tourist Views (2nd series). As T **553**. Mult.
1491 6p. Mounted patrol and oil rig, Chubut 55 15
1492 6p. Glacier and sheep-shearing, Santa Cruz . . 55 15
1493 6p. Lake Lapataia, Tierra del Fuego, and Antarctic scene 55 15

1976.
1494 **570** 12c. grey and black . . . 10 10
1495 50c. slate and green . . 10 10
1496 1p. red and black . . . 10 10
1497 4p. blue and black . . 15 10
1498 5p. yellow and black . . 15 10
1499 6p. brown and black . . 15 10
1500 10p. grey and violet . . 20 10
1501 27p. green and black . . 55 10
1502 30p. blue and black . . 75 10
1503 45p. yellow and black . . 75 10
1504 50p. green and black . . 75 10
1505 100p. green and red . . 1·10 10

571 Airliner in Flight

1976. 25th Anniv of "Aerolineas Argentinas".
1513 **571** 30p. multicoloured . . . 90 15

572 Sail Frigate "Heroina" and Map of Malvinas

1976. Argentine Claims to Falkland Islands (Malvinas).
1514 **572** 6p. multicoloured . . . 85 20

1976. Army Day. As T **390**. Multicoloured.
1515 12p. Infantryman of Conde's 7th Regiment . . 50 15

573 Louis Braille

574 Plush-crested Jay

1976. Louis Braille (inventor of characters for the Blind) Commemoration.
1516 **573** 19p.70 blue 30 15

1976. Argentine Philately. Multicoloured.
1517 7p.+3p.50 Type **574** 60 35
1518 13p.+6p.50 Yellow-collared macaw 80 35
1519 20p.+10p. "Begonia micranthera" 65 40
1520 40p.+20p. "Echinopsis shaferi" (teasel) 90 55

575 Schooner "Rio de la Plata"

1976. Navy Day.
1521 **575** 12p. multicoloured . . . 1·00 20

576 Dr. Bernardo Houssay (Medicine)

1976. Argentine Nobel Prize Winners.
1522 **576** 10p. black, orge & grey 30 10
1523 – 15p. black, yell & grey 35 15
1524 – 20p. black, brn & grey 50 25
DESIGNS: 15p. Dr. Luis Leloir (chemistry); 20p. Dr. Carlos Lamas (peace).

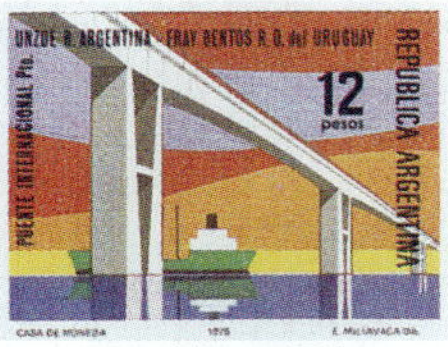

577 Bridge and Ship

1976. "International Bridge" between Unzue (Argentina) and Fray Bentos (Uruguay).
1525 **577** 12p. multicoloured . . . 30 10

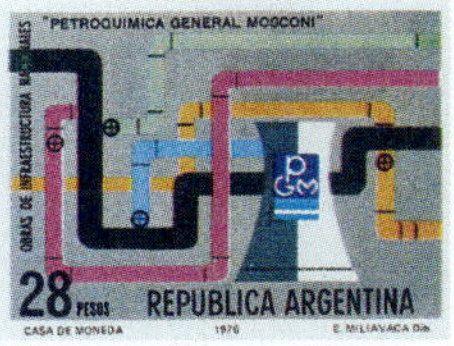

578 Cooling Tower and Pipelines

1976. General Mosconi Petrochemical Project.
1526 **578** 28p. multicoloured . . . 45 15

579 Teodoro Fels and Bleriot XI

1976. Air Force Day.
1527 **579** 15p. multicoloured . . . 40 10

580 "Nativity" (E. Chiapetto)

1976. Christmas.
1528 **580** 20p. multicoloured . . . 50 10

581 Dr. D. Velez Sarsfield (statesman)

582 Conference Emblem

1977. Death Cent (1975) of Dr. D. V. Sarsfield.
1529 **581** 50p. brown and red . . 60 15

1977. United Nations Water Conference.
1530 **582** 70p. multicoloured . . . 45 25

583 "The Visit" (Horacio Butler)

1977. Plastic Arts. Multicoloured.
1531 50p. Type **583** 50 15
1532 70p. "Consecration" (M. P. Caride) (vert) 70 25

584 World Cup Emblem

585 City of La Plata Museum

1977. World Cup Football Championship, Argentina. Multicoloured.
1533 30p. Type **584** 50 15
1534 70p. Stadium and flags (vert) 65 30

1977.

1535	**585**	5p. black and brown	10	10
1536	–	10p. black and blue	10	10
1538	–	20p. black and yellow	10	10
1539	–	40p. black and blue	20	10
1540	–	50p. black and yellow	40	10
1541	–	50p. black and brown	25	10
1542	–	100p. black and pink	35	10
1543	–	100p. black and orange	10	10
1544	–	100p. black and green	10	10
1545	–	200p. black and blue	25	20
1546	–	280p. black and lilac	4·50	15
1547b	–	300p. black and yellow	85	10
1548	–	480p. black and yellow	80	20
1549b	–	500p. black and green	60	15
1550	–	520p. black and orange	90	20
1551	–	800p. black and purple	1·10	25
1552a	–	1000p. black and gold	1·60	35
1553	–	1000p. black and yellow	1·25	35
1554	–	2000p. multicoloured	1·00	35

DESIGNS—HORIZ: 10p. House of Independence, Tucuman; 20p. Type **585**; 50p. (No. 1541), Cabildo, Buenos Aires; 100p. (Nos. 1542/3), Columbus Theatre, Buenos Aires; 280p., 300p. Rio Grande Museum Chapel, Tierra del Fuego; 480p., 520p., 800p. San Ignacio Mission Church ruins; 500p. Candonga Chapel; 1000p. General Post Office, Buenos Aires (No. 1552 39 × 29 mm, No. 1553 32 × 21 mm); 2000p. Civic Centre, Bariloche. VERT: 40p. Cabildo, Salta; 50p. (No. 1540), Cabildo, Buenos Aires; 200p. Monument to the Flag, Rosario.

586 Morse Key and Satellite

1977. "Argentine Philately". Multicoloured.
1560 10p.+5p. Type **586** 25 15
1561 20p.+10p. Old and modern mail vans 45 25
1562 60p.+30p. Old and modern ships . . . . 1·25 75
1563 70p.+35p. SPAD XIII and Boeing 707 aircraft . . . 85 60

1977. Army Day. As T **390**. Multicoloured.
1564 30p. Trooper of 16th Lancers 50 15

587 Schooner "Sarandi"

1977. Navy Day.
1565 **587** 30p. multicoloured . . . 1·25 20

1977. 150th Anniv of Uruguay Post Office. As No. 1325 but colour changed. Surch **100 PESOS 150 ANIV. DEL CORREO NACIONAL DEL URUGUAY.**
1566 100p. on 5p. brown 90 40

1977. "Argentina '77" Exhibition. As No. 1474c, but inscr "EXPOSICION ARGENTINA '77".
1567 160p.+80p. multicoloured 1·60 1·25

589 Admiral Guillermo Brown

1977. Birth Bicent of Admiral Guillermo Brown.
1568 **589** 30p. multicoloured . . . 40 15

590 Civic Centre, Santa Rosa (La Pampa)

1977. Provinces of the Argentine. Multicoloured.
1569 30p. Type **590** 40 20
1570 30p. Sierra de la Ventana (Buenos Aires) 40 20
1571 30p. Skiers at Chapelco, San Martin de los Andes (Neuquen) 40 20
1572 30p. Lake Fonck (Rio Negro) 40 20

591 Savoia S.16 ter Flying Boat over Rio de la Plata

1977. Air Force and 1926 Buenos Aires–New York Flight Commemoration.
1573 **591** 40p. multicoloured . . . 35 15

592 Jet Fighter Outline

1977. 50th Anniv of Military Aviation Factory.
1574 **592** 30p. blue, pale blue and black 30 10

593 "The Adoration of the Kings" (stained-glass window, Holy Sacrament Basilica, Buenos Aires)

1977. Christmas.
1575 **593** 100p. multicoloured . . 75 20

1978. World Cup Football Championship, Argentina. Sheet 102 × 133 mm containing No. 1567 × 4 optd **Argentina 78** and logo.
MS1576 160p.+80p. multicoloured 15·00 15·00

595 World Cup Emblem

1978. World Cup Football Championship, Argentina.
1577 **595** 200p. green and blue . . 55 20

596 Rosario

1978. World Cup Football Championship (3rd issue). Match Sites. Multicoloured.
1578 50p. Type **596** 20 15
1579 100p. Cordoba 40 15
1580 150p. Mendoza 50 15
1581 200p. Mar del Plata 50 25
1582 300p. Buenos Aires . . . . 2·00 75

597 Children and Institute Emblem

1978. 50th Anniv of Inter-American Children's Institute.
1583 **597** 100p. multicoloured . . 40 15

598 "The Working Day" (B. Quinquela Martin)

600 Hooded Siskin

1978. Argentine Art. Multicoloured.
1584 100p. Type **598** 65 15
1585 100p. "Bust of an Unknown Woman" (Orlando Pierri) 2·00 75

599 Players from Argentina, Hungary, France and Italy (Group One)

1978. World Cup Football Championship, Argentina. Multicoloured.
1586 100p. Type **599** 35 10
1587 200p. Group Two players 45 15

1588 300p. Group Three players 65 20
1589 400p. Group Four players 1·00 30
MS1590 89 × 60 mm. 700p. black and flesh . . . . 2·40 1·60
DESIGN: (39 × 26 mm) 700p. River Plate Stadium.

1978. Inter-American Philatelic Exhibition. Mult.
1591 50p.+50p. Type **600** . . . . 1·75 1·50
1592 100p.+100p. Double-collared seedeater . . . . 2·00 2·00
1593 150p.+150p. Saffron-cowled blackbird . . . . 2·50 2·10
1594 200p.+200p. Vermilion flycatcher . . . . 2·75 2·40
1595 500p.+500p. Great kiskadee 7·00 5·75

601 Young Tree with Support

1978. Technical Co-operation among Developing Countries Conference, Buenos Aires.
1596 **601** 100p. multicoloured . . 30 15

602 River Plate Stadium

1978. Argentina's Victory in World Cup Football Championship. Sheet 88 × 60 mm.
MS1597 **602** 1000p. black, stone and red . . . . 3·25 1·75

603 Bank Emblems of 1878 and 1978

1978. Centenary of Bank of Buenos Aires.
1598 **603** 100p. multicoloured . . 30 15

604 General Manuel Savio and Steel Production

1978. 30th Death Anniv of General Manuel Savio (director of military manufacturing).
1599 **604** 100p. multicoloured . . 30 15

605 San Martin **606** Numeral

1978. Birth Bicentenary of Gen. San Martin.
1600 **605** 2000p. green . . . . . 3·25 30
1600a 10000p. blue . . . . . 3·00 35

1978.
1601 **606** 150p. blue and light blue 40 20
1602 180p. blue and light blue 40 10
1603 200p. blue and light blue 30 15

607 Chessboard, Pawn and Queen **608** Argentine Flag supporting Globe

1978. 23rd Chess Olympiad, Buenos Aires.
1604 **607** 200p. multicoloured . . 2·00 65

1978. 12th Int Cancer Congress, Buenos Aires.
1605 **608** 200p. multicoloured . . 80 20

609 "Correct Franking"

1978. Postal Publicity.
1606 **609** 20p. blue 15 10
1607 – 30p. green 15 10
1608 – 50p. red 25 10
DESIGN—VERT: 30p. "Collect postage stamps". HORIZ: 50p. "Indicate the correct post code".

610 Push-pull Tug

1978. 20th Anniv of Argentine River Fleet. Mult.
1609 100p. Type **610** 40 15
1610 200p. Tug "Legador" . . . 90 25
1611 300p. Tug "Rio Parana Mini" 95 30
1612 400p. River passenger ship "Ciudad de Parana" . . . 1·25 25

611 Bahia Blanca and Arms

1978. 150th Anniv of Bahia Blanca.
1613 **611** 200p. multicoloured . . 45 15

612 "To Spain" (Arturo Dresco)

1978. Visit of King and Queen of Spain.
1614 **612** 300p. multicoloured . . 1·75 25

613 Stained-glass Window, San Isidro Cathedral, Buenos Aires

1978. Christmas.
1615 **613** 200p. multicoloured . . 60 15

614 "Chacabuco Slope" (Pedro Subercaseaux)

1978. Birth Bicent of General Jose de San Martin.
1616 500p. Type **614** . . . . . . 1·25 35
1617 1000p. "The Embrace of Maipo" (Pedro Subercaseaux) (vert) . . . 2·25 50

615 San Martin Stamp of 1877 and U.P.U. Emblem

1979. Cent of Argentine Membership of U.P.U.
1618 **615** 200p. blue, black & brn 35 15

616 Mariano Moreno (revolutionary)

1979. Celebrities.
1619 **616** 200p. yellow, blk & red 45 15
1620 – 200p. blue, blk & dp bl 45 15
DESIGNS: No. 1620, Adolfo Alsina (statesman).

617 "Still Life" (Ernesto de la Carcova)

1979. Argentine Paintings. Multicoloured.
1621 200p. Type **617** 60 15
1622 300p. "The Washer-woman" (F. Brughetti) 80 20

618 Balcarce Antenna and Radio Waves

1979. 3rd Inter-American Telecommunications Conference.
1623 **618** 200p. multicoloured . . 35 15

619 Rosette **620** Olives

1979.
1624 **619** 240p. blue and brown 35 10
1625 260p. blue and black 35 10
1626 290p. blue and brown 40 10
1627 310p. blue and purple 45 10
1628 350p. blue and red . . 60 15
1629 450p. blue and ultram 55 15
1630 600p. blue and green 50 20
1631 700p. blue and black 50 20
1632 800p. blue and orange 45 10
1632a 1100p. blue and grey 65 10
1632b 1500p. blue and black 40 10
1632c 1700p. blue and green 50 10

1979. Agricultural Products. Multicoloured.
1633 100p. Type **620** 25 10
1634 200p. Tea 50 25
1635 300p. Sorghum 65 40
1636 400p. Flax . . . . 1·00 55

621 "75" and Symbol

1979. 75th Anniv of Argentine Automobile Club.
1637 **621** 200p. multicoloured . . 35 15

622 Laurel Leaves and Army Emblem

1979. Naming of Village Subteniente Berdina, Tucuman.
1638 **622** 200p. multicoloured . . 30 15

623 Wheat Exchange and Emblem

1979. 125th Anniv of Wheat Exchange, Buenos Aires.
1639 **623** 200p. blue, gold & black 30 15

624 "Uruguay" (sail/steam gunboat)

1979. Navy Day.
1640 **624** 250p. multicoloured . . 1·00 20

1979. Army Day. As T **390**. Multicoloured.
1641 200p. Trooper of Mounted Chasseurs, 1817 . . . . . 1·00 20

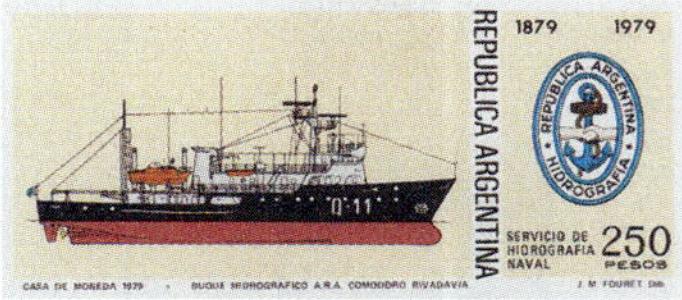

625 "Comodoro Rivadavia" (hydrographic survey ship)

1979. Naval Hydrographic Service.
1642 **625** 250p. multicoloured . . 1·00 20

626 Tree and Man Symbol

1979. Ecology Day.
1643 **626** 250p. multicoloured . . 55 15

627 SPAD XIII and Vicente Almandos

1979. Air Force Day.
1644 **627** 250p. multicoloured . . 80 20

628 "Military Occupation of Rio Negro by Gen. Julio A. Roca's Expedition" (detail, J. M. Blanes)

1979. Centenary of Conquest of the Desert.
1645 **628** 250p. multicoloured . . 70 20

629 Caravel "Magdalena"

1979. "Buenos Aires '80" International Stamp Exhibition. Multicoloured.
1646 400p.+400p. Type **629** . . . 2·50 2·10
1647 500p.+500p. Three-masted sailing ship . . . . . . 8·50 4·50
1648 600p.+600p. Corvette "Descubierta" . . . . . 8·00 6·75
1649 1500p.+1500p. Yacht "Fortuna" . . . . 17·00 8·75

630 Rowland Hill

631 Francisco de Viedma y Narvaez Monument (A. Funes and J. Agosta)

1979. Death Centenary of Sir Rowland Hill.
1650 **630** 300p. black, grey & red 45 20

1979. Bicentenary of Founding of Viedma and Carmen de Patagones Towns.
1651 **631** 300p. multicoloured . . 45 20

632 Pope Paul VI

633 Molinas Church

1979. Election of Pope John Paul I.
1652 **632** 500p. black 80 35
1653 – 500p. black 80 35
DESIGN: No. 1653, Pope John Paul I.

1979. Churches. Multicoloured.
1654 100p.+50p. Purmamarca Church 30 15
1655 200p.+100p. Type **633** . . . 45 20
1656 300p.+150p. Animana Church 50 35
1657 400p.+200p. San Jose de Lules Church 75 50

1979. 75th Anniv of Rosario Philatelic Society. No. 1545 optd **75 ANIV. SOCIEDAD FILATELICA DE ROSARIO**.
1658 200p. blue and black . . . 70 20

635 Children's Faces, and Sun on Map of Argentina

1979. Resettlement Policy.
1659 **635** 300p. yellow, black & bl 50 20

636 Stained-glass Window, Salta Cathedral

1979. Christmas.
1660 **636** 300p. multicoloured . . 55 20

637 Institute Emblem

1979. Centenary of Military Geographical Institute.
1661 **637** 300p. multicoloured . . 70 20

638 General Mosconi and Oil Rig

1979. Birth Centenary of General Enrique Mosconi.
1662 **638** 1000p. blue and black 1·75 50

639 Buenos Aires 3p. Stamp of 1858

1979. Prenfil 80 International Exhibition of Philatelic Literature and Journalism, Buenos Aires. Four sheets 89 × 60 mm containing designs as T **639**.
MS1663 (a) 250p.+250p. black, stone and vermilion; (b) 750p.+750p. flesh and black; (c) 1000p.+1000p. multicoloured; (d) 2000p.+2000p. black, green and vermilion . . . . 12·00 12·00
DESIGNS—VERT: 750p. Rowland Hill; 2000p. International Year of the Child emblem. HORIZ: 1000p. Argentine 5c. Columbus stamp of 1892.

640 Rotary Emblem and Globe

1979. 75th Anniv of Rotary International.
1664 **640** 300p. multicoloured . . 1·00 25

641 Girl with Ruddy Ground Doves

642 Guillermo Brown

1979. International Year of the Child.
1665 **641** 500p. brown, blue & blk 90 40
1666 – 1000p. multicoloured . . 1·25 30
DESIGN: 1000p. "Family".

1980.
1667 **642** 5000p. black . . . . . . 2·75 20
1668 30000p. black and blue 2·00 50

643 I.T.U. Emblem and Microphone

1980. Regional Administrative Conference on Broadcasting, Buenos Aires.
1669 **643** 500p. blue, gold & ultram 80 30

644 Organization of American States Emblem

1980. Day of the Americas.
1670 **644** 500p. multicoloured . . 50 20

645 Angel

1980. Centenary of Argentinian Red Cross.
1671 **645** 500p. multicoloured . . 60 20

646 Salto Grande Hydro-electric Complex

1980. National Development Projects. Mult.
1672 300p. Type **646** 90 35
1673 300p. Zarate-Brazo Largo bridge 90 35
1674 300p. Dish aerials, Balcarce 50 20

647 Hipolito Bouchard and Sail Frigate "La Argentina"

1980. Navy Day.
1675 **647** 500p. multicoloured . . 1·25 30

648 "Villarino" and Woodcut of San Martin Theodore by Gericault

1980. Centenary of Return of General Jose de San Martin's Remains.
1676 **648** 500p. multicoloured . . 1·25 30

649 "Gazeta de Buenos-Ayres" and Signature of Dr. Mariano Moreno (first editor)

1980. Journalists' Day.
1677 **649** 500p. multicoloured . . 60 20

650 Part of Mural

1980. 400th Anniv of Buenos Aires. Sheet 249 × 103 mm containing T **650** and similar vert designs forming a composite design depicting the ceramic mural by Rodolfo Franco in Cathedral Underground Station.
MS1678 500p. × 14 multicoloured 7·00 5·50

651 Soldier feeding Dove

1980. Army Day.
1679 **651** 500p. green, blk & gold 60 30

652 Lt. Gen. Aramburu

1980. 10th Death Anniv of Lt. Gen. Pedro Eugenio Aramburu.
1680 **652** 500p. yellow and black 50 20

653 Gen. Juan Gregorio de Las Heras

1980. National Heroes.
1681 **653** 500p. stone and black . . 60 20
1682 – 500p. yellow, blk & pur 60 20
1683 – 500p. mauve and black 60 20
DESIGNS: No. 1682, Bernardino Rivadavia; 1683, Brigadier-General Jose Matias Zapiola.

654 University of La Plata

1980. 75th Anniv of La Plata University.
1684 **654** 500p. multicoloured . . 60 20

655 Major Francisco de Arteaga and Avro 504K

1980. Air Force Day.
1685 **655** 500p. multicoloured . . 75 20

656 Flag and "Pencil" Figure
658 Congress Emblem

1980. National Census.
1686 **656** 500p. black and blue . . 1·25 20

657 King Penguin

1980. 75th Anniv of Argentine Presence in South Orkneys and 150th Anniv of Political and Military Command for the Malvinas. Two sheets each 151 × 174 mm containing T **657** and similar vert designs. Multicoloured.
MS1687 Two sheets (a) 150p. × 12 Centre two stamps depict South Orkneys Naval Station; (b) 500p. × 12 Centre two stamps depict "Puerto Soledad 1829" by Luisa Vernet . . . . 22·00 15·00

1980. National Marian Congress, Mendoza.
1688 **658** 700p. multicoloured . . 50 15

659 Heart pierced by Cigarette
661 Radio Antenna and Call Sign

660 Part of Mural

1980. Anti-smoking Campaign.
1689 **659** 700p. multicoloured . . 60 20

1980. Buenos Aires 80 International Stamp Exhibition. Sheet 251 × 105 mm containing T **660** and similar vert designs forming a composite design depicting the ceramic mural by Alfredo Guido in the 9th July Underground Station.
MS1690 500p. × 14 multicoloured 7·00 5·00

1980. Radio Amateurs.
1691 **661** 700p. blue, black & green 50 15

662 Academy Emblem
663 Commemorative Medallion

1980. 50th Anniv of Technical Military Academy.
1692 **662** 700p. multicoloured . . 50 15

1980. Christmas. 150th Anniv of Appearance of Holy Virgin to St. Catherine Laboure.
1693 **663** 700p. multicoloured . . 50 15

664 Plan of Lujan Cathedral and Outline of Virgin
665 Simon Bolivar

1980. Christmas. 350th Anniv of Appearance of Holy Virgin at Lujan.
1694 **664** 700p. green and brown 50 15

1980. 150th Death Anniv of Simon Bolivar.
1695 **665** 700p. multicoloured . . 50 15

666 Football and Flags of Competing Nations

1981. Gold Cup Football Competition, Montevideo.
1696 **666** 1000p. multicoloured . . 85 20

667 "Lujan Landscape" (Marcos Tiglio)

1981. Paintings. Multicoloured.
1697 1000p. Type **667** 70 20
1698 1000p. "Effect of Light on Lines" (Miguel Angel Vidal) 70 20

668 Congress Emblem

1981. International Congress on Medicine and Sciences applied to Sport.
1699 **668** 1000p. blue, brown & blk 45 15

669 Esperanza Army Base, Antarctica

1981. 20th Anniv of Antarctic Treaty. Mult.
1700 1000p. Type **669** . . . . . 1·50 50
1701 2000p. Map of Vicecomodoro Marambio Island and De Havilland Twin Otter airplane (59½ × 25 mm) . . . . . 2·00 80
1702 2000p. Icebreaker "Almirante Irizar" . . . 3·00 95

670 Military Club

1981. Centenary of Military Club. Multicoloured.
1703 1000p. Type **670** 60 20
1704 2000p. Blunderbusses . . . 80 25

671 "Minuet" (Carlos E. Pellegrini)

1981. "Espamer '81" International Stamp Exhibition, Buenos Aires (1st issue).
1705 **671** 500p.+250p. purple, gold and brown 60 45
1706 – 700p.+350p. green, gold and brown 80 70
1707 – 800p.+400p. brown, gold and deep brown . . . 1·00 80
1708 – 1000p.+500p. mult . . . 1·25 1·10
DESIGNS: 700p. "La Media Cana" (Carlos Morel); 800p. "Cielito" (Carlos E. Pellegrini); 1000p. "El Gato" (Juan Leon Palliere).
See also Nos. 1719 and 1720/1.

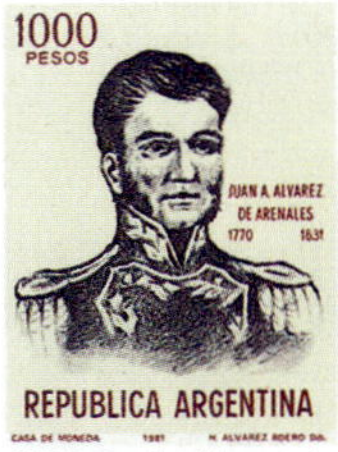

672 Juan A. Alvarez de Arenales

1981. Celebrities' Anniversaries.
1709 **672** 1000p. black, yell & brn 70 20
1710 – 1000p. blk, pink & lilac 70 20
1711 – 1000p. black, pale green and green 70 20
DESIGNS: No. 1709, Type **672** (patriot, 150th death anniv); 1710, Felix G. Frias (writer and politician, death centenary); 1711, Jose E. Uriburu (statesman, 150th birth centenary).

1981. 50th Anniv of Bahia Blanca Philatelic and Numismatic Society. No. 1553 optd **50 ANIV DE LA ASOCIACION FILATELICA Y NUMISMATICA DE BAHIA BLANCA.**
1712 1000p. black and yellow . . 1·60 65

674 World Map divided into Time Zones and Sun

1981. Centenary of Naval Observatory.
1713 **674** 1000p. multicoloured . . 55 30

675 "St. Cayetano" (detail, stained-glass window, San Cayetano Basilica)

1981. 500th Death Anniv of St. Cayetano (founder of Teatino Order).
1714 **675** 1000p. multicoloured . . 45 20

676 Pablo Castaibert and Bleriot XI

1981. Air Force Day.
1715 **676** 1000p. multicoloured . . 75 20

677 First Argentine Blast Furnace, Sierra de Palpala

1981. 22nd Latin American Steel-makers Congress, Buenos Aires.
1716 **677** 1000p. multicoloured . . 45 20

678 Emblem of National Directorate for Special Education
679 Sperm Whale and Map of Argentina and Antarctica

1981. International Year of Disabled People.
1717 **678** 1000p. multicoloured . . 50 20

1981. Campaign against Indiscriminate Whaling.
1718 **679** 1000p. multicoloured . . 2·25 25

680 "Espamer 81" Emblem and 15th-century Caravel

1981. "Espamer 81" International Stamp Exhibition, Buenos Aires (2nd issue).
1719 **680** 1300p. pink, brn & blk 95 20

681 "San Martin at the Battle of Bailen" (equestrian statuette)
682 Argentine Army Emblem

1981. "Espamer 81" International Stamp Exhibition, Buenos Aires (3rd issue).
1720 **681** 1000p. multicoloured . . 20 15
1721 1500p. multicoloured . . 60 15

1981. Argentine Army. 175th Anniv of Infantry Regiment No. 1 "Patricios". Multicoloured.
1722 1500p. Type **682** 55 20
1723 1500p. "Patricios" badge . . 55 20

1981. Philatelic Services Course, Postal Union of the Americas and Spain Technical Training School, Buenos Aires. Optd **CURSO SUPERIOR DE ORGANIZACION DE SERVICIOS FILATELICOS-UPAE-BUENOS AIRES-1981.**
1724 **680** 1300p. pink, brn & blk 1·10 20

684 Football

1981. Espamer 81 International Stamp Exhibition, Buenos Aires (4th issue). Sheet 137×130 mm containing T **684** and similar vert designs. Multicoloured.
MS1725 2000p. Type **684**; 3000p. Tackle; 5000p. Dribbling; 15000p. Goalkeeper . . . . 6·00 5·00

685 "Patacon" (one peso piece)

1981. Centenary of First Argentine Coins.
1726 **685** 2000p. silver, blk & pur 55 15
1727 – 3000p. gold, black & bl 70 20
DESIGN: 3000p. Argentine oro (five pesos piece).

686 Stained-glass Window, Church of Our Lady of Mercy, Tucuman

1981. Christmas.
1728 **686** 1500p. multicoloured . . 75 20

687 "Drive Carefully"

688 Francisco Luis Bernardez

1981. Road Safety. Multicoloured.
1729 1000p. "Observe traffic lights" . . . . 1·40 20
1730 2000p. Type **687** 90 25
1731 3000p. Zebra Crossing ("Cross at the white lines") (horiz) . . . . . . 1·00 35
1732 4000p. Headlights ("Don't dazzle") (horiz) . . . . . 1·25 45

1982. Authors. Multicoloured.
1733 1000p. Type **688** . . . . . 1·25 20
1734 2000p. Lucio V. Mansilla 85 25
1735 3000p. Conrado Nale Roxlo 1·10 35
1736 4000p. Victoria Ocampo . . 1·25 45

689 Emblem

690 Dr. Robert Koch

1982. 22nd American Air Force Commanders Conference, Buenos Aires.
1737 **689** 2000p. multicoloured . . 85 25

1982. 25th World Tuberculosis Conf, Buenos Aires.
1738 **690** 2000p. brown, red & blk 60 25

691 Pre-Columbian Artwork and Signature of Hernando de Lerma (founder)

1982. 400th Anniv of Salta City.
1739 **691** 2000p. green, blk & gold 80 25
MS1740 89×60 mm. **691** 5000p. green, black and gold (39×26 mm) . . . . 2·50 2·50

1982. Argentine Invasion of the Falkland Islands. Optd **LAS MALVINAS SON ARGENTINAS**.
1741 **619** 1700p. blue and green 60 20

693 "Poseidon with Trophies of War" (sculpture) and Naval Centre Arms

1982. Centenary of Naval Centre.
1742 **693** 2000p. multicoloured . . 90 25

694 "Chorisia speciosa"

695 Juan C. Sanchez

1982. Flowers. Multicoloured.
1743 200p. "Zinnia peruviana" 10 10
1744 300p. "Ipomoea purpurea" 10 10
1745 400p. "Tillandsia aeranthos" 10 10
1746 500p. Type **694** 10 10
1747 800p. "Oncidium bifolium" 10 10
1748 1000p. "Erythrina crista-galli" 10 10
1749 2000p. "Jacaranda mimosifolia" 15 10
1750 3000p. "Bauhinia candicans" 50 10
1751 5000p. "Tecoma stans" . . 60 10
1752 10000p. "Tabebuia ipe" . . 90 15
1753 20000p. "Passiflora coerulea" . . . . 1·00 20
1754 30000p. "Aristolochia littoralis" . . . . 1·25 30
1755 50000p. "Oxalis enneaphylla" . . . . . . 2·40 40

1982. 10th Death Anniv of Lt. Gen. Juan C. Sanchez.
1761 **695** 5000p. multicoloured . . 80 25

696 Don Luis Verne (first Commander)

1982. 153rd Anniv of Political and Military Command for the Malvinas.
1762 **696** 5000p. black and brown 1·25 50
1763 – 5000p. light bl, blk & bl 90 35
DESIGN (82×28 mm): No. 1763, Map of the South Atlantic Islands.

697 Pope John Paul II

698 San Martin

1982. Papal Visit.
1764 **697** 5000p. multicoloured . . 1·00 55

1982.
1765 **698** 50000p. brown and red 4·00 50

699 "The Organ Player" (detail, Aldo Severi)

700 "Gen. de Sombras" (Sylvia Sieburger)

1982. Paintings. Multicoloured.
1766 2000p. Type **699** 65 20
1767 3000p. "Flowers" (Santiago Cogorno) 70 25

1982. "Argentine Philately". Tapestries. Mult.
1768 1000p.+500p. Type **700** . . 20 15
1769 2000p.+1000p. "Interpretation of a Rectangle" (Silke Haupt) 30 20
1770 3000p.+1500p. "Canal" (detail, Beatriz Bongliani) (horiz) . . . . 1·10 40
1771 4000p.+2000p. "Pueblito de Tilcara" (Tana Sachs) (horiz) 75 55

701 Petrol Pump and Sugar Cane

704 Map of Africa showing Namibia

703 Belt Buckle with Argentine Scout Emblem

1982. Alconafta (petrol-alcohol mixture) Campaign.
1772 **701** 2000p. multicoloured . . 40 10

1982. 50th Anniv of Tucuman Philatelic Society. No. 1751 optd **50 ANIVERSARIO SOCIEDAD FILATELICA DE TUCUMAN**.
1773 5000p. multicoloured . . . 1·60 90

1982. 75th Anniv of Boy Scout Movement.
1774 **703** 5000p. multicoloured . . 1·00 25

1982. Namibia Day.
1775 **704** 5000p. multicoloured . . 55 15

705 Rio Tercero Nuclear Power Station

1982. Atomic Energy. Multicoloured.
1776 2000p. Type **705** 40 10
1777 2000p. Control room of Rio Tercero power station . . 40 10

706 Our Lady of Itati, Corrientes

707 "Sidereal Tension" (M. A. Agatiello)

1982. Churches and Cathedrals of the North-east Provinces.
1778 **706** 2000p. green and black 50 15
1779 – 3000p. grey and purple 60 15
1780 – 5000p. blue and purple 80 20
1781 – 10000p. brown and black 1·25 40
DESIGNS—VERT: 3000p. Resistencia Cathedral, Chaco. HORIZ: 5000p. Formosa Cathedral; 10000p. Ruins of San Ignacio, Misiones.

1982. Art. Multicoloured.
1782 2000p. Type **707** 60 20
1783 3000p. "Sugerencia II" (E. MacEntyre) 70 20
1784 5000p. "Storm" (Carlos Silva) . . . . 1·00 25

708 Games Emblem and Santa Fe Bridge

1982. 2nd "Southern Cross" Games, Rosario and Santa Fe.
1785 **708** 2000p. blue and black 45 10

709 Volleyball

1982. 10th Men's Volleyball World Championship.
1786 **709** 2000p. multicoloured . . 30 10
1787 5000p. multicoloured . . 60 20

710 Road Signs

1982. 50th Anniv of National Roads Administration.
1788 **710** 5000p. multicoloured . . 60 20

711 Monument to the Army of the Andes

1982. Centenary of "Los Andes" Newspaper.
1789 **711** 5000p. multicoloured . . 50 20

712 La Plata Cathedral

714 Dr. Carlos Pellegrini (founder) (after J. Sorolla y Bastida)

713 First Oil Rig

1982. Centenary of La Plata. Multicoloured.
1790 5000p. Type **712** 50 20
1791 5000p. Municipal Palace . . 50 20
MS1792 120×115 mm. 2500p.×6 (a) Cathedral; (b) Allegorical head (top); (c) Observatory; (d) Municipal Palace; (e) Allegorical head (bottom); (f) Natural Sciences Museum . . . . . . 1·60 1·25

1982. 75th Anniv of Discovery of Oil in Comodoro Rivadavia.
1793 **713** 5000p. multicoloured . . 50 25

1982. Cent of Buenos Aires Jockey Club. Mult.
1794 5000p. Jockey Club emblem 55 20
1795 5000p. Type **714** 55 20

715 Cross of St. Damian, Assisi

716 "St. Vincent de Paul" (stained-glass window, Our Lady of the Miraculous Medal, Buenos Aires)

1982. 800th Birth Anniv of St. Francis of Assisi.

1796	**715**	5000p. multicoloured . .	1·00	20

1982. Christmas.

1797	**716**	3000p. multicoloured . .	1·40	40

717 Pedro B. Palacios

1982. Authors. Each red and green.

1798	1000p. Type **717**	15	10
1799	2000p. Leopoldo Marechal	20	10
1800	3000p. Delfina Bunge de Galvez	25	10
1801	4000p. Manuel Galvez . . .	50	15
1802	5000p. Evaristo Carriego . .	65	15

718 Argentine Flag and Map of South Atlantic Islands (½-size illustration)

1983. 1st Anniv of Argentine Invasion of Falkland Islands.

1803	**718**	20000p. multicoloured	95	35

719 Sitram (automatic message transmission service) Emblem

1983. Information Technology. Multicoloured.

1804	5000p. Type **719**	1·00	20
1805	5000p. Red Arpac (data communications system) emblem	1·00	20

720 Naval League Emblem

1983. Navy Day. 50th Anniv of Naval League.

1806	**720**	5000p. multicoloured . .	50	15

721 Allegorical Figure (Victor Rebuffo)

1983. 25th Anniv of National Arts Fund.

1807	**721**	5000p. multicoloured . .	45	15

722 Golden Saloon

1983. 75th Anniv of Columbus Theatre, Buenos Aires. Multicoloured.

1808	5000p. Type **722**	70	15
1809	10000p. Stage curtain . . .	90	20

(Currency reform. 10000 (old) pesos = 1 (new) peso.)

723 Marbles

1983. Argentine Philately. Children's Games (1st series). Multicoloured.

1810	20c.+10c. Type **723**	15	10
1811	30c.+15c. Skipping	30	15
1812	50c.+25c. Hopscotch	40	25
1813	1p.+50c. Boy with kite . . .	60	40
1814	2p.+1p. Boy with spinning top	70	55

See also Nos. 1870/4.

724 Maned Wolf

1983. Protected Animals (1st series). Mult.

1815	1p. Type **724**	35	10
1816	1p.50 Pampas deer	55	15
1817	2p. Giant anteater	60	15
1818	2p.50 Jaguar	75	25

See also Nos 1883/87.

1983. Flowers. As T **694** but inscr in new currency. Multicoloured.

1819	5c. Type **694**	40	10
1820	10c. "Erythrina crista-galli"	10	10
1821	20c. "Jacaranda mimosifolia"	10	10
1822	30c. "Bauhinia candicans"	35	10
1823	40c. "Eichhornia crassipes"	10	10
1824	50c. "Tecoma stans" . . .	10	10
1825	1p. "Tabebuia ipe" . . .	10	10
1826	1p.80 "Mutisia retusa" . . .	15	10
1827	2p. "Passiflora coerulea" . .	20	10
1828	3p. "Aristolochia littoralis"	30	10
1829	5p. "Oxalis enneaphylla" . .	50	10
1830	10p. "Alstroemeria aurantiaca"	40	10
1831	20p. "Ipomoea purpurea"	40	10
1832	30p. "Embothrium coccineum"	40	15
1833	50p. "Tillandsia aeranthos"	45	15
1834	100p. "Oncidium bifolium"	65	15
1835	300p. "Cassia carnaval" . .	1·60	45

725 "Founding of City of Catamarca" (detail, Luis Varela Lezana)

1983. 300th Anniv of San Fernando del Valle de Catamarca.

1836	**725**	1p. multicoloured . . .	30	10

726 Brother Mamerto Esquiu

727 Bolivar (painting by Herrera Toro after engraving by C. Turner)

1983. Death Centenary of Brother Mamerto Esquiu, Bishop of Cordoba.

1837	**726**	1p. black, red and grey	30	10

1983. Birth Bicentenary of Simon Bolivar.

1838	**727**	1p. multicoloured . . .	30	10
1839	–	2p. red and black . . .	60	15

DESIGN: 2p. Bolivar (engraving by Kepper).

728 San Martin

729 Gen. Toribio de Luzuriaga

1983.

1840	**728**	10p. green and black . .	2·50	45
1841	–	20p. blue and black . .	90	40
1842	**728**	50p. brown and blue . .	2·00	45
1843	–	200p. black and blue . .	1·25	45
1844	–	500p. blue and brown . .	1·75	25

DESIGNS: 20, 500p. Guillermo Brown; 200p. Manuel Belgrano.

1983. Birth Bicentenary (1982) of Gen. Toribio de Luzuriaga.

1845	**729**	1p. multicoloured . . .	30	10

730 Grand Bourg House, Buenos Aires

1983. 50th Anniv of Sanmartinian National Institute.

1846	**730**	2p. brown and black . .	55	15

731 Dove and Rotary Emblem

1983. Rotary International South American Regional Conference, Buenos Aires.

1847	**731**	1p. multicoloured . . .	55	20

732 Running Track and Games Emblem

1983. 9th Pan-American Games, Venezuela.

1848	**732**	1p. red, green & black	35	15
1849	–	2p. multicoloured . . .	60	25

DESIGN: 2p. Games emblem.

733 W.C.Y. Emblem

734 "The Squash Peddler" (Antonio Berni)

1983. World Communications Year (1st issue).

1850	**733**	2p. multicoloured . . .	55	20

See also Nos. 1853/6 and 1857.

1983. Argentine Paintings. Multicoloured.

1851	1p. Type **734**	35	10
1852	2p. "Figure in Yellow" (Luis Seoane)	55	20

735 Ox-drawn Wagon

736 "Central Post Office, Buenos Aires" (Lola Frexas)

1983. World Communications Year (2nd issue). Mail Transport. Multicoloured.

1853	1p. Type **735**	45	10
1854	2p. Horse-drawn mail cart	50	15
1855	4p. Locomotive "La Portena"	1·25	50
1856	5p. Tram	1·25	50

1983. World Communications Year (3rd issue).

1857	**736**	2p. multicoloured . . .	35	15

737 Rockhopper Penguin

738 Coin of 1813

1983. Fauna and Pioneers of Southern Argentina. Multicoloured.

1858a	2p. Type **737**	40	25
1858b	2p. Wandering albatross	40	25
1858c	2p. Black-browed albatross	40	25
1858d	2p. Macaroni penguin . .	40	25
1858e	2p. Luis Piedra Buena (after Juan R. Mezzadra)	40	15
1858f	2p. Carlos Maria Moyano (after Mezzadra)	40	15
1858g	2p. Luis Py (after Mezzadra)	40	15
1858h	2p. Augusto Lasserre (after Horacio Alvarez Boero)	40	15
1858i	2p. Light-mantled sooty albatross	40	25
1858j	2p. Leopard seal	40	15
1858k	2p. Crabeater seal	40	15
1858l	2p. Weddell seal	40	15

1983. Transfer of Presidency.

1859	**738**	2p. silver, black and blue	35	15

739 "Christmas Manger" (tapestry by Silke)

1983. Christmas. Multicoloured.
1860 2p. Type **739** 35 15
1861 3p. Stained-glass window, San Carlos de Bariloche Church 55 20

740 Printing Cylinder and Newspaper

1984. Centenary of "El Dia" Newspaper.
1862 **740** 4p. multicoloured . . . 40 15

741 Compass Rose

1984. "Espana 84" (Madrid) and "Argentina 85" (Buenos Aires) International Stamp Exhibitions (1st issue). Multicoloured.
1863 5p.+2p.50 Type **741** 50 15
1864 5p.+2p.50 Arms of Spain and Argentine Republic 50 15
1865 5p.+2p.50 Arms of Christopher Columbus . . 50 15
1866 5p.+2p.50 "Nina" . . . . . 1·25 45
1867 5p.+2p.50 "Pinta" . . . . . 1·25 45
1868 5p.+2p.50 "Santa Maria" . . 1·25 45
See also Nos. 1906/10, 1917/18 and 1920/4.

742 College

1984. Centenary of Alejandro Carbo Teacher Training College, Cordoba.
1869 **742** 10p. multicoloured . . . 40 15

1984. Argentine Philately. Children's Games (2nd series). As T **723**. Multicoloured.
1870 2p.+1p. Blind man's buff . . 20 15
1871 3p.+1p.50 Girls throwing hoop 30 25
1872 4p.+2p. Leap frog 40 35
1873 5p.+2p.50 Boy rolling hoop 55 45
1874 6p.+3p. Ball and stick . . . 60 55

743 Rowing and Basketball

1984. Olympic Games, Los Angeles. Mult.
1875 5p. Type **743** 25 15
1876 5p. Weightlifting and discus 25 15
1877 10p. Cycling and swimming 45 20
1878 10p. Pole vault and fencing 45 20

744 Wheat

1984. Food Supplies. Multicoloured.
1879 10p. Type **744** (18th F.A.O. Latin American Regional Conference, Buenos Aires) 40 20
1880 10p. Sunflowers (World Food Day) 40 20
1881 10p. Maize (3rd National Maize Congress, Pergamino) 40 20

745 Stock Exchange

1984. Centenary of Rosario Stock Exchange.
1882 **745** 10p. multicoloured . . . 40 20

1984. Protected Animals (2nd series). As T **724**. Multicoloured.
1883 20p. Brazilian merganser . . 65 20
1884 20p. Black-fronted piping guan 65 20
1885 20p. Hooded grebes 65 20
1886 20p. Vicunas 65 20
1887 20p. Chilean guemal 65 20

746 Festival Emblem

1984. 1st Latin American Theatre Festival, Cordoba.
1888 **746** 20p. multicoloured . . . 25 15

747 "Apostles' Communion" (detail, Fra Angelico)

1984. 50th Anniv of Buenos Aires International Eucharist Congress.
1889 **747** 20p. multicoloured . . . 25 15

748 Antonio Oneto and Railway Station (Puerto Deseado)

1984. City Centenaries. Multicoloured.
1890 20p. Type **748** 75 25
1891 20p. 19th-century view and sail/steam corvette "Parana" (Ushuaia) . . . 1·25 35

749 Glacier

1984. World Heritage Site. Los Glaciares National Park. Multicoloured.
1892 20p. Glacier (different) . . . 30 10
1893 30p. Type **749** 40 15

1984. 50th Anniv of Buenos Aires Philatelic Centre. No. 1830 optd **1934–50°ANIVERSARIO-1984 CENTRO FILATELICO BUENOS-AIRES**.
1894 10p. multicoloured 20 15

751 "Jesus and the Star" (Diego Aguero)

1984. Christmas. Multicoloured.
1895 20p. Type **751** 30 15
1896 30p. "The Three Kings" (Leandro Ruiz) 40 15
1897 50p. "The Holy Family" (Maria Castillo) (vert) . . 60 20

752 "Sheds (La Boca)" (Marcos Borio)

753 Angel J. Carranza (historian, 150th)

1984. Argentine Paintings. Multicoloured.
1898 20p. Type **752** 30 20
1899 20p. "View of the Zoo" (Fermin Eguia) (horiz) . . 35 20
1900 20p. "Floodlit Congress Building" (Francisco Travieso) 30 20

1985. Birth Anniversaries.
1901 **753** 10p. deep blue & blue 40 10
1902 – 20p. deep brown & brn 40 10
1903 – 30p. deep blue & blue 45 15
1904 – 40p. black and green . . 70 15
DESIGNS: 20p. Estanislao del Campo (poet, 150th); 30p. Jose Hernandez (journalist, 150th); 40p. Vicente Lopez y Planes (President of Argentine Confederation 1827–28, birth bicent).

754 Guemes and "Infernal" (soldier)

1985. Birth Bicentenary of General Martin Miguel de Guemes (Independence hero).
1905 **754** 30p. multicoloured . . . 30 15

755 Teodoro Fels's Bleriot XI Gnome

1985. "Argentina '85" International Stamp Exhibition, Buenos Aires (2nd issue). First Airmail Flights. Multicoloured.
1906 20p. Type **755** (Buenos Aires–Montevideo, 1917) 30 10
1907 40p. Junkers F-13L (Cordoba–Villa Dolores, 1925) 50 15
1908 60p. Saint-Exupery's Latecoere 25 (first Bahia Blanca-Comodoro Rivadavia, 1929) 75 25
1909 80p. "Graf Zeppelin" airship (Argentina-Germany, 1934) . . . . . 1·10 45
1910 100p. Consolidated PBY-5A Catalina amphibian (to Argentine Antarctic, 1952) 1·25 60

756 Central Bank

1985. 50th Anniv of Central Bank, Buenos Aires.
1911 **756** 80p. multicoloured . . . 40 20

757 Jose A. Ferreyra and "Munequitas Portenas"

1985. Argentine Film Directors. Multicoloured.
1912 100p. Type **757** 45 25
1913 100p. Leopoldo Torre Nilsson and "Martin Fierro" 45 25

758 "Carlos Gardel" (Hermenegildo Sabat)

1985. 50th Death Anniv of Carlos Gardel (entertainer). Multicoloured.
1914 200p. Type **758** 65 25
1915 200p. "Carlos Gardel" (Carlos Alonso) 65 25
1916 200p. "Carlos Gardel" (Aldo Severi and Martiniano Arce) 65 25

759 "The Arrival" (Pedro Figari)

1985. "Argentina '85" International Stamp Exhibition (3rd issue). Multicoloured.
1917 20c. Type **759** 65 25
1918 30c. "Mail Coach Square" (detail, Cesareo B. de Quiros) 75 25
MS1919 146×74 mm. 20c. (29×39 mm), 30c. (39×29 mm) Details of "Halt in the Country" (Prilidiano Pueyrredon) . . . . 1·75 1·75

760 Cover of 1917 Teodoro Fels Flight

1985. "Argentina '85" International Stamp Exhibition (4th issue). Multicoloured.
1920 10c. Type **760** 40 15
1921 10c. Cover of 1925 Cordoba–Villa Dolores flight 40 15
1922 10c. Cover of 1929 Saint-Exupery flight 40 15
1923 10c. Cover of 1934 "Graf Zeppelin" flight 40 15
1924 10c. Cover of 1952 Antarctic flight 40 15

1985. Flowers. As T **694** but with currency expressed as "A". Multicoloured.
1930 ½c. "Oxalis enneaphylla" 40 10
1931 1c. "Alstroemeria aurantiaca" 10 10
1932 2c. "Ipomoea purpurea" 10 10
1933 3c. "Embothrium coccineum" 10 10
1934a 5c. "Tillandsia aeranthos" 10 10
1927 8½c. "Erythrina crista-galli" 25 10
1935a 10c. "Oncidium bifolium" 40 10
1936a 20c. "Chorisia speciosa" 35 10
1937 30c. "Cassia carnaval" . . 40 10
1938 50c. "Zinnnia peruviana" 65 10
1941 1a. "Begonia micranthera var. Hieronymi" 80 10
1941a 2a. "Bauhinia candicans" 10 10
1942 5a. "Gymnocalycium bruchii" 10 10
1942a 10a. "Eichhornia crassipes" 10 10
1942b 20a. "Mutisia retusa" . . . 10 10
1942c 50a. Passion flower 10 10
1943 100a. "Alstroemeria aurantiaca" 10 10
1943a 300a. "Ipomoea purpurea" 10 10
1943b 500a. "Embothrium coccineum" 10 10
1943c 1000a. "Aristolochia littoralis" 20 10

1943d 5000a. "Erythrina crista-galli" . . . . 1·25 10
1943e 10000a. "Jacaranda mimosifolia" . . . . . 4·00 55

No. 1927 is 15 × 23 mm, the remainder 22 × 32 mm.

761 "Woman with Bird" (Juan del Prete)

762 Musical Bow

1985. Argentine Paintings. Multicoloured.

1944 20c. Type **761** 75 30
1945 30c. "Illuminated Fruits" (Fortunato Lacamera) . . 75 30

1985. Traditional Musical Instruments. Mult.

1946 20c. Type **762** 60 20
1947 20c. Long flute with drum accompaniment 60 20
1948 20c. Frame drum 60 20
1949 20c. Pan's flute 60 20
1950 20c. Jew's harp 60 20

763 Juan Bautista Alberdi (writer)

1985. Anniversaries.

1951 10c. Type **763** (death centenary (1984)) 25 15
1952 20c. Nicolas Avellaneda (President 1874–80, death centenary) 50 25
1953 30c. Brother Luis Beltran (Independence hero, birth bicentenary (1984)) . . . 75 25
1954 40c. Ricardo Levene (historian) (birth centenary) 90 25

764 Roller Skaters

1985. International Youth Year.

1955 **764** 20c. black and blue . . . 60 20
1956 – 30c. multicoloured . . . 65 30

MS1957 146 × 74 mm. 1a. multicoloured. Imperf . . . . 1·25 1·40

DESIGNS: 30c. "Disappointment". 137 × 66 mm "Halt in the Country" (Prilidiano Pueyrredon).

765 "Rothschildia jacobaeae"

1985. Argentine Philately. Butterflies.

1958 5c.+2c. Type **765** 35 10
1959 10c.+5c. "Heliconius erato phyllis" 55 20
1960 20c.+10c. "Precis evarete hilaris" . . . . 1·10 40
1961 25c.+13c. "Cyanopepla pretiosa" . . . . 1·40 55
1962 40c.+20c. "Papilio androgeus" . . . . 1·75 90

766 Forclaz Windmill (Entre Rios)

768 "Birth of Our Lord" (Carlos Cortes)

767 Hand holding White Stick

1985. Tourism. Argentine Provinces. Mult.

1963 10c. Type **766** 40 10
1964 10c. Sierra de la Ventana (Buenos Aires) 40 10
1965 10c. Potrero de los Funes artificial lake (San Luis) 40 10
1966 10c. Church belfry (North-west Argentina) 40 10
1967 10c. Magellanic penguins, Punta Tombo (Chubut) 1·00 30
1968 10c. Sea of Mirrors (Cordoba) 40 10

1985. National Campaign for the Prevention of Blindness.

1969 **767** 10c. multicoloured . . . 40 10

1985. Christmas. Multicoloured.

1970 10c. Type **768** 30 15
1971 20c. "Christmas" (Hector Viola) 80 25

769 Rio Gallegos Cathedral

1985. Centenary of Rio Gallegos.

1972 **769** 10c. multicoloured . . . 50 10

770 Grape Harvesting

1986. 50th Anniv of Grape Harvest Nat Festival.

1973 **770** 10c. multicoloured . . . 40 10

771 House of Valentin Alsina (Italian Period)

1986. Buenos Aires Architecture, 1880–1930. Mult.

1974 20c. Type **771** 55 20
1975 20c. 1441 Calle Cerrito (French period) 55 20
1976 20c. Customs House (Academic period) (horiz) 55 20
1977 20c. House, Avenido de Mayo (Art Nouveau) . . 55 20
1978 20c. Isaac Fernandez Blanco Museum (National Restoration period) (horiz) 55 20

772 Jubany Base

773 "Foundation of Nereid" (detail, Lola Mora)

1986. Argentine Antarctic Research. Mult.

1979 10c. Type **772** 60 20
1980 10c. Kerguelen fur seal . . . 60 20
1981 10c. Southern sealion . . . 60 20
1982 10c. General Belgrano Base 60 20
1983 10c. Pintado petrel . . . . 1·00 40
1984 10c. Black-browed albatross 1·00 40
1985 10c. King penguin . . . . . 1·00 40
1986 10c. Giant petrel . . . . . 1·00 40
1987 10c. Hugo Alberto Acuna (explorer) 60 20
1988 10c. Magellanic penguin . . 1·00 40
1989 10c. Magellan snipe . . . . 1·00 40
1990 10c. Capt. Augustin Servando del Castillo (explorer) 60 20

1986. Sculpture. Multicoloured.

1991 20c. Type **773** 85 25
1992 30c. "Work Song" (detail, Rogelio Yrurtia) . . . . 1·25 40

774 Dr. Alicia Moreau de Justo (suffragist, d. 1986)

775 Dr. Francisco Narciso Laprida

1986. Anniversaries.

1993 **774** 10c. black, yellow & brn 30 10
1994 – 10c. black, turq & blue 30 10
1995 – 30c. black, red & mauve 65 30

DESIGNS: No. 1994, Dr. Emilio Ravignani (historian, birth centenary); 1995, Indira Gandhi (Prime Minister of India, 1st death anniv).

1986. Birth Bicentenaries of Independence Heroes. Each brown, yellow and black.

1996 20c. Type **775** 50 45
1997 20c. Brig. Gen. Estanislao Lopez 50 45
1998 20c. Gen. Francisco Ramirez 50 45

776 Namuncura

777 Drawing by Nazarena Pastor

1986. Birth Centenary of Ceferino Namuncura (first Indian seminary student).

1999 **776** 20c. multicoloured . . . 25 15

1986. Argentine Philately. Children's Drawings. Multicoloured.

2000 5c.+2c. Type **777** 15 15
2001 10c.+5c. Girl and boy holding flowers and balloon (Tatiana Valleistein) (horiz) 20 20
2002 20c.+10c. Boy and girl (Juan Manel Flores) 70 70
2003 25c.+13c. Town and waterfront (Marcelo E. Pezzuto) (horiz) . . . 85 85
2004 40c.+20c. Village (Esteban Diehl) (horiz) . . . . . 1·00 1·00

1986. No. 1825 surch **A0,10**.

2005 10c. on 1p. "Tabebuia ipe" 65 30

779 Argentine Team (value top left)

1986. Argentina, World Cup Football Championship (Mexico) Winners. Multicoloured.

2006 75c. Type **779** . . . . . . 1·10 1·10
2007 75c. Argentine team (value top right) . . . . . . 1·10 1·10
2008 75c. Argentine team (value bottom left) . . . . . . 1·10 1·10
2009 75c. Argentine team (value bottom right) . . . . . 1·10 1·10
2010 75c. Player shooting for goal 1·10 1·10
2011 75c. Player tackling and goalkeeper on ground . . 1·10 1·10
2012 75c. Player number 11 . . . 1·10 1·10
2013 75c. Player number 7 . . . 1·10 1·10
2014 75c. Crowd and Argentina player . . . . 1·10 1·10
2015 75c. West German player . . 1·10 1·10
2016 75c. Goalkeeper on ground 1·10 1·10
2017 75c. Footballers' legs . . . 1·10 1·10
2018 75c. Hand holding World Cup trophy . . . . . . 1·10 1·10
2019 75c. Raised arm and crowded stadium . . . . 1·10 1·10
2020 75c. People with flags and cameras . . . . 1·10 1·10
2021 75c. Player's body and crowd . . . . 1·10 1·10

Nos. 2006/13 were printed together se-tenant in a sheetlet of eight stamps arranged in two blocks, each block forming a composite design. Nos. 2014/21 were similarly arranged in a second sheetlet.

780 Municipal Building

1986. Centenary of San Francisco City.

2022 **780** 20c. multicoloured . . . 50 20

781 Old Railway Station

1986. Centenary of Trelew City.

2023 **781** 20c. multicoloured . . . 1·00 45

782 Emblem and Colours

1986. Mutualism Day.

2024 **782** 20c. multicoloured . . . 25 15

783 "Primitive Retable" (Aniko Szabo)

1986. Christmas. Multicoloured.

2025 20c. Type **783** 50 10
2026 30c. "Everybody's Tree" (Franca Delacqua) . . . 60 15

784 St. Rosa of Lima

785 Municipal Building

1986. 400th Birth Anniv of St. Rosa de Lima.
2027 **784** 50c. multicoloured . . . 80 20

1986. Anniversaries. Multicoloured.
2028 20c. Type **785** (bicentenary of Rio Cuarto city) . . . 40 10
2029 20c. Palace of Justice, Cordoba (50th anniv) . . 40 10

786 Marine Biology

1987. 25th Anniv of Antarctic Treaty. Mult.
2030 20c. Type **786** 80 20
2031 30c. Study of native birds 1·75 30
MS2032 159 × 89 mm. As Nos. 2030/1 but each 39 × 49 mm 75 75

787 Emblem

1987. Centenary of National Mortgage Bank.
2033 **787** 20c. yellow, brown & blk 20 15

788 Stylized Pine Trees

1987. Argentine Co-operative Movement.
2034 **788** 20c. multicoloured . . . 20 15

789 Pope

1987. 2nd Visit of Pope John Paul II.
2035 **789** 20c. blue and red . . . 40 10
2036 – 80c. brown and green . . 1·00 55
MS2037 160 × 90 mm. 1a. multicoloured (34 × 45 mm) . . 15 15
DESIGNS: 80c. Pope in robes with Crucifix; 1a. Pope and children.

790 Flag forming "PAZ" (peace)

1987. International Peace Year.
2038 **790** 20c. blue, dp blue & blk 45 15
2039 – 30c. multicoloured . . . 55 20
DESIGN: 30c. "Pigeon" (sculpture, Victor Kaniuka).

791 "Polo Players" (Alejandro Moy)

792 "Supplicant" (Museum of Natural Sciences, La Plata)

1987. World Polo Championships, Palermo.
2040 **791** 20c. multicoloured . . . 80 15

1987. 14th International Museums Council General Conference, Buenos Aires. Multicoloured.
2041 25c. Conference emblem . . 45 15
2042 25c. Shield of Potosi (National History Museum, Buenos Aires) 45 15
2043 25c. Statue of St. Bartholomew (Enrique Larreta Spanish Art Museum, Buenos Aires) 45 15
2044 25c. Cudgel with animal design (Patagonia Museum, San Carlos de Bariloche) 45 15
2045 25c. Type **792** 45 15
2046 25c. Grate from Argentine Confederation House (Entre Rios Historical Museum, Parana) 45 15
2047 25c. Statue of St. Joseph (Northern Historical Museum, Salta) 45 15
2048 25c. Funeral urn (Provincial Archaeological Museum, Santiago del Estero) . . . 45 15

793 Pillar Box

794 Spotted Metynis ("Metynnis maculatus")

1987. No value expressed. (a) Inscr "C" and "TARIFA INTERNA/HASTA 10 GRAMOS".
2049 **793** (18c.) red, black & yell 1·25 15
(b) Inscr "C" and "TARIFA INTERNA/DE 11 A 20 GRAMOS".
2050 **793** (33c.) black, yell & grn 1·60 15

1987. Argentine Philately. River Fishes. Mult.
2051 10c.+5c. Type **794** 35 10
2052 10c.+5c. Black-finned pearlfish ("Cynolebias nigripinnis") 35 10
2053 10c.+5c. Solar's leporinus ("Leporinus solarii") . . 35 10
2054 10c.+5c. Red-flanked bloodfin ("Aphyocharax rathbuni") 35 10
2055 10c.+5c. Bronze catfish ("Corydoras aeneus") . . 35 10
2056 10c.+5c. Giant hatchetfish ("Thoracocharax securis") 35 10
2057 10c.+5c. Black-striped pearlfish ("Cynolebias melanotaenia") 35 10
2058 10c.+5c. Chanchito cichlid ("Cichlasoma facetum") 35 10
2059 20c.+10c. Silver tetra ("Tetragonopterus argente") 65 25
2060 20c.+10c. Buenos Aires tetra ("Hemigrammus caudovittatus") 65 25
2061 20c.+10c. Two-spotted astyanax ("Astyanax bimaculatus") 65 25
2062 20c.+10c. Black widow tetra ("Gymnocorymbus ternetzi") 65 25
2063 20c.+10c. Trahira ("Hoplias malabaricus") 65 25
2064 20c.+10c. Blue-finned tetra ("Aphyocharax rubripinnis") 65 25
2065 20c.+10c. Agassiz's dwarf cichlid ("Apistogramma agassizi") 65 25
2066 20c.+10c. Fanning pyrrhulina ("Pyrrhulina rachoviana") 65 25

795 College Facade and Arms (½-size illustration)

1987. 300th Anniv of Montserrat College, Cordoba and Montserrat/87 National Stamp Exhibition. Sheet 75 × 110 mm. Imperf.
MS2067 **795** 1a. multicoloured 10 10

796 Jorge Luis Borges (writer)

1987. Anniversaries. Multicoloured.
2068 20c. Type **796** (1st death anniv) 25 10
2069 30c. Armando Discepolo, (dramatist and theatre director, birth cent) . . . 40 15
2070 50c. Dr Carlos Alberto Pueyrredon (historian, birth centenary) 65 20

797 Drawing by Leonardo da Vinci

1987. "The Post, a Medium for Communication and Prevention of Addictions".
2071 **797** 30c. multicoloured . . . 40 15

798 "The Sower" (Julio Vanzo)

1987. 75th Anniv of Argentine Farmers' Union.
2072 **798** 30c. multicoloured . . . 40 15

799 Basketball

800 Col. Maj. Ignacio Alvarez Thomas

1987. 10th Pan-American Games, Indianapolis. Multicoloured.
2073 20c. Type **799** 40 10
2074 30c. Rowing 45 15
2075 50c. Dinghies 65 15

1987. Anniversaries. Multicoloured.
2076 25c. Type **800** (birth bicent) 35 10
2077 25c. Col. Manuel Dorrego (birth bicentenary) 35 10
2078 50c. 18th-century Spanish map of Falkland Islands (death bicentenary of Jacinto de Altolaguirre, governor of Islands) (horiz) 60 20
2079 50c. "Signing the Accord" (Rafael del Villar) (50th anniv of House of Accord Museum, San Nicolas) (horiz) 60 20

801 Children as Nurse and Mother

1987. UNICEF Child Vaccination Campaign.
2080 **801** 30c. multicoloured . . . 40 15

802 Balloon

803 "Nativity" (tapestry, Alisia Frega)

1987. Anniversaries. Multicoloured.
2081 50c. Type **802** (50th anniv of LRA National Radio) . . 40 20
2082 50c. Celendonio Galvan Moreno (first editor) (50th anniv of "Postas Argentinas" magazine) . . 40 20
2083 1a. Dr. Jose Marco del Pont (founder) (centenary of Argentine Philatelic Society) 60 25

1987. Christmas. Multicoloured.
2084 50c. Type **803** 35 25
2085 1a. Doves and flowers (tapestry, Silvina Trigos) 45 25

804 Crested Oropendola, Baritu National Park

1987. National Parks (1st series). Multicoloured.
2086 50c. Type **804** . . . . . . 1·00 40
2087 50c. Otter, Nahuel Huapi National Park 65 30
2088 50c. Night monkey, Rio Pilcomayo National Park 65 30
2089 50c. Kelp goose, Tierra del Fuego National Park . . 1·00 40
2090 50c. Alligator, Iguazu National Park 65 30
See also Nos. 2150/4, 2222/6 and 2295/9.

805 "Caminito" (Jose Canella)

1988. Historical and Tourist Sites. Multicoloured.
2090a 3a. "Purmamarca" (Nestor Martin) (33 × 22 mm) . . 60 20
2091 5a. Type **805** . . . . . . 1·75 30
2092 10a. "Old Almacen" (Jose Canella) (A) . . . . . . 3·25 1·50
2092a 10a. "Old Almacen" (Jose Canella) (B) . . . . . . 1·00 45
2095 20a. "Ushuaia" (Nestor Martin) (vert) . . . . . 2·75 1·10
2099 50a. Type **805** 75 10
10a. A. Inscr "Viejo Almacen". B. Inscr "El Viejo Almacen".

806 "Minstrel singing in a Grocer's Shop" (Carlos Morel)

1988. Argentine Paintings. Multicoloured.
2105 1a. Type **806** 50 15
2106 1a. "Curuzu" (detail, Candido Lopez) 50 15

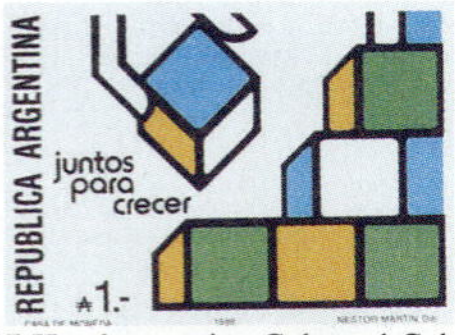

807 Hand arranging Coloured Cubes

1988. Argentine–Brazil Economic Co-operation.
2107 **807** 1a. multicoloured . . . 45 15

808 St. Anne's Chapel, Corrientes

1988. 400th Annivs of Corrientes and Alta Gracia. Multicoloured.
2108 1a. Type **808** 45 15
2109 1a. Alta Gracia church . . . 45 15

809 Men Stacking Sacks

1988. Labour Day. Details of mural "Cereals" (Nueve de Julio station, Buenos Aires underground railway). Multicoloured.
2110 50c. Type **809** 70 70
2111 50c. Sacks 70 70
2112 50c. Men unloading truck 70 70
2113 50c. Horse and cart 70 70
Nos. 2110/13 were printed together, se-tenant, forming a composite design.

810 Steam Locomotive "Yatay" and Tender, 1888 (½-size illustration)

1988. "Prenfil '88" Philatelic Literature Exhibition, Buenos Aires (1st issue). Railways. Multicoloured.
2114 1a.+50c. Type **810** 35 35
2115 1a.+50c. Electric passenger coach, 1914 . . . . . . 35 35
2116 1a.+50c. Type B-15 locomotive and tender, 1942 35 35
2117 1a.+50c. Type GT-22 diesel locomotive, 1988 . . . . 35 35
See also Nos. 2134/7.

811 Running

1988. Olympic Games, Seoul. Multicoloured.
2118 1a. Type **811** 35 10
2119 2a. Football 45 15
2120 3a. Hockey 55 20
2121 4a. Tennis 65 35

812 Bank Facade

1988. Centenary of Bank of Mendoza.
2122 **812** 2a. multicoloured . . . 20 15

813 Arms of Guemes and National Guard Emblem

814 "St. Cayetano (patron saint of workers)" (C. Quaglia)

1988. 50th Anniv of National Guard.
2123 **813** 2a. multicoloured . . . 20 15

1988. Philatelic Anniversaries and Events. Mult.
2124 2a. Type **814** (50th anniv of Liniers (Buenos Aires) Philatelic Circle) 45 15
2125 3a. "Our Lady of Carmen (patron saint of Cuyo)" (window, Carlos Quaglia) (50th anniv of West Argentina Philatelic Society) 60 20
MS2126 145 × 73 mm. 5a. "Love" (mural, Antonio Berni) (Li-men 88 national stamp exhibition, Buenos Aires) (39 × 29 mm) 50 50

815 Sarmiento (after Mario Chierico) and Cathedral of the North School

1988. Death Centenary of Domingo Faustino Sarmiento (President, 1868–74).
2127 **815** 3a. multicoloured . . . 35 20

816 "San Isidro" (Enrique Castro)

1988. Horse Paintings. Multicoloured.
2128 2a.+1a. Type **816** 60 60
2129 2a.+1a. "Waiting" (Gustavo Solari) 60 60
2130 2a.+1a. "Beside the Pond" (F. Romero Carranza) . . 60 60
2131 2a.+1a. "Mare and Colt" (Enrique Castro) 60 60
2132 2a.+1a. "Under the Tail" (Enrique Castro) 60 60

1988. 21st International Urological Society Congress. No. 2091 optd **XXI CONGRESO DE LA SOCIEDAD INTERNACIONAL DE UROLOGIA SIU 88**.
2133 **805** 5a. multicoloured . . . 2·00 1·50

818 Cover of "References de la Poste"

819 "Immaculate Conception"

1988. "Prenfil '88" Philatelic Literature Exhibition, Buenos Aires (2nd issue). Designs showing magazine covers. Multicoloured.
2134 1a.+1a. Type **818** 60 30
2135 1a.+1a. "Cronaca Filatelica" 55 20
2136 1a.+1a. "Co Fi" 75 35
2137 2a.+2a. "Postas Argentinas" 55 20

1988. Arbrafax 88 Argentinian–Brazilian Stamp Exhibition, Buenos Aires. Sheet 156 × 80 mm containing T **819** and similar horiz design. Multicoloured.
MS2138 2a.+2a. "Candle Delivery at San Ignacio" (Leonie Matthis); 3a.+3a. Type **819** . . . . . . 1·00 1·00

820 Underground Train

1988. 75th Anniv of Buenos Aires Underground Railway.
2139 **820** 5a. multicoloured . . . 1·25 75

821 "Virgin of Tenderness"

1988. Christmas. Virgins in Ucrania Cathedral, Buenos Aires. Multicoloured.
2140 5a. Type **821** 60 40
2141 5a. "Virgin of Protection" 60 40

822 Ushuaia and St. John

1989. Death Centenary (1988) of St. John Bosco (founder of Salesian Brothers).
2142 **822** 5a. multicoloured . . . 35 10

823 "Rincon de los Areneros" (Justo Lynch)

1989. Paintings. Multicoloured.
2143 5a. Type **823** 35 10
2144 5a. "Blancos" (Fernando Fader) 35 10

824 "Crowning with Thorns" and Church of Our Lady of Carmen, Tandil

1989. Holy Week. Multicoloured.
2145 2a. Type **824** 15 10
2146 2a. "Jesus of Nazareth" and Buenos Aires Cathedral 15 10
2147 3a. "Our Lady of Sorrows" and Humahuaca Church, Jujuy 15 10
2148 3a. "Jesus Meets His Mother" (statue) and La Quebrada Church, San Luis 15 10

825 Shattering Drinking Glass

1989. Anti-alcoholism Campaign.
2149 **825** 5a. multicoloured . . . 25 10

1989. National Parks (2nd series). As T **804**. Mult.
2150 5a. Crested gallito ("Gallito Capeton"), Lihue Calel National Park 75 20
2151 5a. Lizard, El Palmar National Park 50 20
2152 5a. Tapirs, Calilegua National Park 60 20
2153 5a. Howler monkey, Chaco National Park 65 20
2154 5a. Magellanic woodpecker ("Carpintero Negro Patagonico"), Los Glaciares National Park 75 20

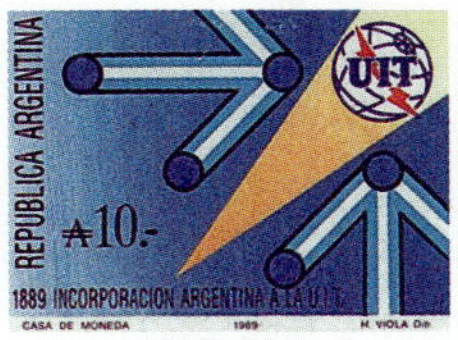

826 Emblem

1989. Cent of Argentine Membership of I.T.U.
2155 **826** 10a. multicoloured . . . 40 10

827 Class 1A Glider Entries

1989. World Model Airplane Championships, La Cruz-Embals-Cordoba. Multicoloured.
2156 5a. Type **827** 35 10
2157 5a. Class 1B rubber-powered entries 35 10
2158 10a. Class 1C petrol-engined entries 35 10

828 Otuno ("Diplomystes viedmensis")

1989. Argentine Philately. Fishes. Multicoloured.
2159 10a.+5a. Type **828** 30 25
2160 10a.+5a. Striped galaxiid ("Haplochiton taeniatus") 30 25
2161 10a.+5a. Creole perch ("Jenyns percichthys tucha") 30 25
2162 10a.+5a. River Plate galaxiid ("Galaxias platei") 30 25
2163 10a.+5a. Brown trout ("Salmo fario") 30 25

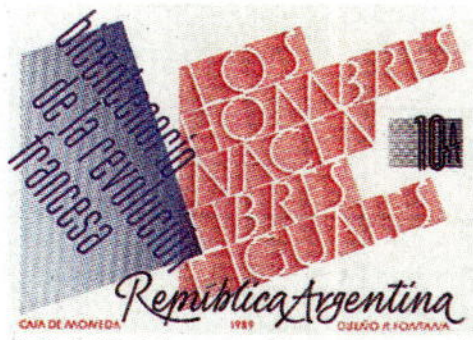

829 "All Men are Born Free and Equal"

1989. Bicentenary of French Revolution.
2164 **829** 10a. red, blue and black 35 10
2165 – 15a. black, red and blue 35 10
MS2166 146 × 74 mm. 25a. multicoloured . . . . 2·00 2·00
DESIGNS: 15a. "Marianne" (Gandon) and French flag; 25a. "Liberty guiding the People" (detail, E. Delacroix).

830 "Weser" (steamer)

1989. Immigration. Multicoloured.
2167 150a. Type **830** 90 35
2168 200a. Immigrants' hostel . . 40 35
MS2169 155 × 80 mm. As Nos. 2167/8 but each 35 × 25 mm 5·00 5·00

831 "Republic" (bronze bust)

1989. Transference of Presidency. Unissued stamp surch as in T **831**.

2170 **831** 300a. on 50a. mult . . . 60 55

832 Arms of Columbus and Title Page of "Book of Privileges"

1989. "Espamer '90" Spain–Latin America Stamp Exhibition. Chronicles of Discovery. Each yellow, black and red.

2171 100a.+50a. Type **832** . . . 30 30
2172 150a.+50a. Illustration from "New Chronicle and Good Government" (Guaman Poma de Ayala) 40 40
2173 200a.+100a. Illustration from "Discovery and Conquest of Peru" (Pedro de Cieza de Leon) 60 60
2174 250a.+100a. Illustration from "A Journey to the River Plate" (Ulrico Schmidl) 70 70

833 Fr. Guillermo Furlong and Title Page of "Los Jesuitas"

1989. Birth Anniversaries.

2175 **833** 150a. black, light green and green (centenary) 30 25
2176 – 150a. black, buff and brown (centenary) . . 30 25
2177 – 200a. black, light blue and blue (bicentenary) 40 35

DESIGNS: No. 2176, Dr. Gregorio Alvarez (physician) and title page of "Canto A Chos Mala"; 2177, Brigadier Gen. Enrique Martinez and "Battle of Maipu" (detail of lithograph, Theodore Gericault).

834 Wooden Mask from Atajo

835 "Policewoman with Children" (Diego Molinari)

1989. America. Pre-Columbian Artefacts. Mult.

2178 200a. Type **834** 65 35
2179 300a. Urn from Punta de Balastro 85 55

1989. Federal Police Week. Winning entries in a schools' painting competition.

2180 100a. Type **835** 20 15
2181 100a. "Traffic policeman" (Carlos Alberto Sarago) 20 15
2182 150a. "Adults and child by traffic lights" (Roxana Andrea Osuna) 30 25
2183 150a. "Policeman and child stopping traffic at crossing" (Pablo Javier Quaglia) 30 25

836 "Dream of Christmas" (Maria Carballido)

1989. Christmas. Multicoloured.

2184 200a. Type **836** 40 35
2185 200a. "Cradle Song for Baby Jesus" (Gato Frias) 40 35
2186 300a. "Christ of the Hills" (statue, Chipo Cespedes) (vert) 85 55

837 "Battle of Vuelta de Obligado" (Ulde Todo)

1989.

2187 **837** 300a. multicoloured . . 1·25 45

838 Port Building

1990. Cent of Buenos Aires Port. Multicoloured.

2188 200a. Type **838** . . . . . . 1·50 75
2189 200a. Crane and bows of container and sailing ships 1·50 75
2190 200a. Truck on quay and ships in dock . . . . . . 1·50 75
2191 200a. Van and building . . 1·50 75

Nos. 2188/91 were printed together, se-tenant, forming a composite design.

839 Aconcagua Peak and Los Horcones Lagoon

1990. Aconcagua International Fair. Mult.

2192 500a. Type **839** 60 35
2193 500a. Aconcagua Peak and Los Horcones Lagoon (right-hand detail) 60 35

Nos. 2192/3 were printed together, se-tenant, forming a composite design.

840 "75" and Girl with Savings Box

1990. 75th Anniv of National Savings and Insurance Fund.

2194 **840** 1000a. multicoloured . . 20 15

841 Footballer in Striped Shirt

1990. World Cup Football Championship, Italy. Multicoloured.

2195 2500a. Type **841** . . . . . 1·25 1·00
2196 2500a. Upper body of footballer in blue shirt . . . . 1·25 1·00
2197 2500a. Ball and footballers' legs . . . . 1·25 1·00
2198 2500a. Lower body of footballer . . . . 1·25 1·00

Nos. 2195/8 were printed together, se-tenant, forming a composite design.

842 Flowers

1990. Anti-drugs Campaign.

2199 **842** 2000a. multicoloured . . 85 30

843 School Emblem and Pellegrini

1990. Centenary of Carlos Pellegrini Commercial High School.

2200 **843** 2000a. multicoloured . . 65 30

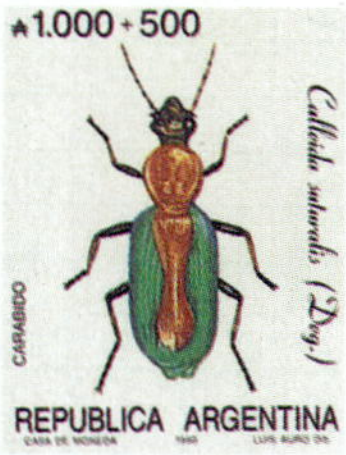

844 "Calleida suturalis"

1990. Argentine Philately. Insects. Multicoloured.

2201 1000a.+500a. Type **844** . . 60 35
2202 1000a.+500a. "Adalia bipunctata" 60 35
2203 1000a.+500a. "Hippodamia convergens" 60 35
2204 1000a.+500a. "Nabis punctipennis" 60 35
2205 1000a.+500a. "Podisus nigrispinus" 60 35

845 Letters and Globe

1990. International Literacy Year.

2206 **845** 2000a. multicoloured . . 85 30

846 Marcos Zar and Savoia S-16 Flying Boat

1990. Air. Aerofildae 90 National Air Mail Exhibition, Buenos Aires. Sheet 158 × 78 mm containing T **846** and similar horiz design. Multicoloured.

MS2207 2000a.+ 2000a. Type **846**; 3000a.+3000a. Capt. Antonio Parodi and biplane . . . . . 12·00 12·00

847 Players

1990. World Basketball Championship. Mult.

2208 2000a. Type **847** 85 30
MS2209 5000a. Detail of No. 2208 (29 × 39 mm) . . . . 8·00 7·00

848 Junkers Ju 52/3m

1990. Air. 50th Anniv of LADE (airline). Mult.

2210 2500a. Type **848** . . . . . 1·25 45
2211 2500a. Grumman SA-16 Albatross flying boat . . 1·25 45
2212 2500a. Fokker Friendship 1·25 45
2213 2500a. Fokker Fellowship 1·25 45

849 Arms of West Indies Maritime Post

1990. 14th Postal Union of the Americas and Spain Congress, Buenos Aires.

2214 **849** 3000a. brown & black 85 50
2215 – 3000a. multicoloured . . 1·50 75
2216 – 3000a. multicoloured . . 1·50 75
2217 – 3000a. multicoloured . . 1·25 50

DESIGNS: No. 2215, Sailing packet and despatch boat; 2216, "Rio Carcarana" (cargo liner); 2217, Boeing 707 airplane and mail van.

850 "Descubierta"

1990. Espamer 91 Spain–Latin America Stamp Exhibition, Buenos Aires. Sheet 109 × 114 mm containing T **850** and similar vert designs. Multicoloured.

MS2218 2000a.+1000a. × 4: Type **850**; Alejandro Malaspina (explorer) and "Atrevide"; Amerindians; Artist drawing Amerindians . . . . 13·00 13·00

851 "Hamelia erecta" and Iguazu Falls

1990. America. Natural World. Multicoloured.

2219 3000a. Type **851** . . . . . 1·50 45
2220 3000a. Sea cow, Puerto Deseado . . . . 1·50 45

852 U.P.U. Emblem on "Stamp"

1990. World Post Day.

2221 **852** 3000a. multicoloured . . 95 45

1990. National Parks (3rd series). As T **804**. Mult.

2222 3000a. Anteater, El Rey National Park . . . . . 1·25 45
2223 3000a. Black-necked swans ("Cisne de Cuello Negro"), Laguna Blanca National Park . . . . . 2·00 70
2224 3000a. Black-chested buzzard eagle ("Aguila Mora"), Lanin National Park . . . . 2·00 70

2225 3000a. Armadillo, Perito Moreno National Park . . 1·25 45
2226 3000a. Pudu, Puelo National Park . . . . 1·25 45

853 Hands (after Michelangelo) and Army Emblem

1990. Cent of Salvation Army in Argentina (2227) and Nat University of the Littoral (2228). Mult.
2227 3000a. Type **853** . . . . . 1·10 50
2228 3000a. University building and emblem . . . . . . 1·10 50

854 Archangel Gabriel

856 "Landscape" (Pio Collivadino)

855 Putting the Shot

1990. Christmas. Stained-glass windows by Carlos Quaglia from Church of Immaculate Conception, Villaguay. Multicoloured.
2229 3000a. Dove's wing and hand 85 50
2230 3000a. Dove and Mary . . 85 50
2231 3000a. Type **854** 85 50
2232 3000a. Lower half of Mary and open book 85 50
2233 3000a. Joseph 85 50
2234 3000a. Star, shepherds and head of Mary 85 50
2235 3000a. Manger 85 50
2236 3000a. Baby Jesus in Mary's arms 85 50
2237 3000a. Joseph with two doves and Mary 85 50
2238 3000a. Simeon 85 50
2239 3000a. Lower halves of Joseph and Mary 85 50
2240 3000a. Lower half of Simeon and altar 85 50
Nos. 2229/32, 2233/6 and 2237/40 were printed together in se-tenant sheetlets of four stamps, each sheetlet forming a composite design of stained glass windows entitled "Incarnation of Son of God", "The Birth of Christ" and "Presentation of Jesus in the Temple".

1990. Espamer 91 Spain–Latin America Stamp Exhibition, Buenos Aires (2nd issue) and Olympic Games, Barcelona (1992). Sheet 103 × 125 mm containing T **855** and similar vert designs. Multicoloured.
MS2241 2000a.+2000a. × 4: Type **855**; High jumping; Hurdling; Pole vaulting . . . . 18·00 18·00

1991. Paintings. Multicoloured.
2242 4000a. Type **856** 90 45
2243 4000a. "Weeping Willows" (Atilio Malinverno) (horiz) 90 45

857 Juan Manuel Fangio

1991. Espamer 91 Spain–Latin America Stamp Exhibition, Buenos Aires (3rd issue). Racing Drivers. Sheet 104 × 125 mm containing T **857** and similar vert designs. Multicoloured.
MS2244 2500a.+2500a. × 4: Type **857**; Juan Manuel Bordeau; Carlos Alberto Reutemann; Oscar and Juan Galvez . . . . . . 9·00 9·00

858 Rosas

860 "Hernan, the Pirate" (Jose Salinas)

859 Freestyle Gymnastics

1991. Return of Remains of Brig. Gen. Juan Manuel de Rosas.
2245 **858** 4000a. multicoloured . . 80 35

1991. Espamer 91 Spain–Latin America Stamp Exhibition, Buenos Aires (4th issue) and Olympic Games, Barcelona (1992) (2nd issue). Gymnastics. Sheet 103 × 125 mm containing T **859** and similar vert designs. Multicoloured.
MS2246 2500a.+2500a. × 4: Type **859**; Asymmetric bars; Beam; Hoop exercise . . . . . 9·00 9·00

1991. Comic Strips. Each black and blue.
2247 4000a. Type **860** . . . . . 1·40 70
2248 4000a. "Don Fulgencio" (Lino Palacio) . . . . . 1·40 70
2249 4000a. "Tablas Medicas de Salerno" (Oscar Conti) . . 1·40 70
2250 4000a. "Buenos Aires en Camiseta" (Alejandro del Prado) . . . . 1·40 70
2251 4000a. "Girls!" (Jose Divito) 1·40 70
2252 4000a. "Langostino" (Eduardo Ferro) . . . . 1·40 70
2253 4000a. "Mafalda" (Joaquin Lavado) . . . . 1·40 70
2254 4000a. "Mort Cinder" (Alberto Breccia) . . . . 1·40 70

861 "Flags" (Maria Augustina Ferreyra)

1991. 700th Anniv of Swiss Confederation.
2255 **861** 4000a. multicoloured . . 80 30

862 Divine Child Mayor

1991. 400th Anniv of La Rioja City.
2256 **862** 4000a. multicoloured . . 80 30

863 Eduardo Bradley, Angel Zuloaga and Balloon "Eduardo Newbery"

1991. 75th Anniv of Crossing of Andes by Balloon.
2257 **863** 4000a. multicoloured . . 90 35

864 "Vitoria" (Magellan's galleon)

1991. America. Voyages of Discovery. Mult.
2258 4000a. Type **864** . . . . . 1·25 40
2259 4000a. Juan Diaz de Solis's fleet . . . . 1·25 40

865 "Virgin of the Valley, Catamarca" (top half)

1991. Christmas. Stained-glass Windows from Church of Our Lady of Lourdes, Santos Lugares, Buenos Aires. Multicoloured.
2260 4000a. Type **865** . . . . . 1·10 40
2261 4000a. "Virgin of the Valley" (bottom half) . . 1·10 40
2262 4000a. Church and "Virgin of the Rosary of the Miracle, Cordoba" (top half) . . . . 1·10 40
2263 4000a. "Virgin of the Rosary of the Miracle" (bottom half) . . . . . . 1·10 40
Nos. 2260/3 were issued together, se-tenant, Nos. 2260/1 and 2262/3 forming composite designs.

866 Enrique Pestalozzi (editor) and Masthead

1991. Centenaries. Multicoloured.
2264 4000a. Type **866** ("Argentinisches Tageblatt" (1989)) 85 40
2265 4000a. Leandro Alem (founder) and flags (Radical Civic Union) . . 85 40
2266 4000a. Marksman (Argentine Shooting Federation) 85 40
2267 4000a. Dr. Nicasio Etchepareborda (first professor) and emblem (Buenos Aires Faculty of Odontology) 85 40
2268 4000a. Dalmiro Huergo and emblem (Graduate School of Economics) 85 40

867 Gen. Juan Lavalle and Medal

1991. Anniversaries. Multicoloured.
2269 4000a. Type **867** (150th death anniv) 85 40
2270 4000a. Gen. Jose Maria Paz and Battle of Ituzaingo medal (birth bicentenary) 85 40
2271 4000a. Dr. Marco Avellaneda and opening words of "Ode to the 25th May" (politician and writer, 150th death anniv) 85 40
2272 4000a. William Henry Hudson and title page of "Far Away and Long Ago" (writer, 150th birth anniv) 85 40

868 "Castor" (rocket)

1991. "Iberoprenfil '92" Iberia–Latin America Philatelic Literature Exhibition, Buenos Aires (1st issue). Multicoloured.
2273 4000a.+4000a. Type **868** . . 2·00 1·00
2274 4000a.+4000a. "Lusat-1" satellite . . . . 2·00 1·00
See also Nos. 2313/14 and 2325/8.

869 Guiana Crested Eagle ("Morphnu guianensis")

870 Gaucho with Woman

1991. Birds. Multicoloured.
2275 4000a. Type **869** . . . . . 1·50 1·00
2276 4000a. Green-winged macaw ("Ara chloroptera") . . . 1·50 1·00
2277 4000a. Lesser rhea ("Pterocnemia pennata") 1·50 1·00

1992. Abrafex 92 Argentinian–Brazilian Stamp Exhibition, Porto Algere, Brazil. Sheet 103 × 126 mm containing T **870** and similar vert designs. Multicoloured.
MS2278 38c. Type **870**; 38c. Gaucho with horse; 38c. Gaucho in grocer's shop; 38c. Ranch owner 7·00 7·00

871 Golden Tops

1992. Fungi.
2279 10c. Type **871** 50 10
2280 25c. Common ink cap . . . 70 20
2281 38c. Type **871** . . . . . . 1·75 25
2282 48c. As 25c. . . . . 1·75 30
2283 50c. Granulated boletus . . 1·75 30
2284 51c. Common morel . . . . 1·75 40
2285 61c. Fly agaric . . . . . . 2·25 45
2286 68c. Lawyer's wig . . . . . 2·25 40
2289 1p. As 61c. . . . . 3·00 40
2290 1p.25 As 50c. . . . . . . 3·25 40
2293 2p. As 51c. . . . . 6·50 60
For redrawn, smaller, designs see Nos. 2365/77.

1992. National Parks (4th series). As T **804**. Multicoloured.
2295 38c. Chucao tapaculo ("Chucao"), Los Alerces National Park . . . . . 1·25 85
2296 38c. Opossum, Los Arrayanes National Park 1·00 40
2297 38c. Giant armadillo, Formosa Nature Reserve 1·00 40
2298 38c. Cavy, Petrified Forests Natural Monument . . . 1·00 40
2299 38c. James's flamingo ("Parina chica"), Laguna de los Pozuelos Natural Monument . . . . 1·25 85

872 Soldier and Truck

1992. National Heroes Commem. Multicoloured.
2300 38c. Type **872** 75 40
2301 38c. "General Belgrano" (cruiser) 90 40
2302 38c. FMA Pucara fighter . . 90 40

873 "Carnotaurus sastrei" **874** "Tileforo Areco"

1992. Dinosaurs. Multicoloured.
2303 38c.+38c. Type **873** . . . . 2·25 1·25
2304 38c.+38c. "Amargasaurus cazaui" . . . . 2·25 1·25

1992. Birth Centenary (1991) of Florencio Molina Campios (painter). Multicoloured.
2305 38c. Type **874** . . . . . . 1·10 45
2306 38c. "In the Shade" (horiz) 1·10 45

875 Deer

1992. Conference on Environment and Development, Rio de Janeiro. Sheet 85 × 82 mm containing T **875** and similar square designs. Multicoloured.
MS2307 38c. Type **875**; 38c. Birds; 38c. Butterflies; 38c. Whale . . 12·00 12·00

876 General Lucio N. Mansilla and "San Martin" (frigate)

1992. Birth Anniversaries. Multicoloured.
2308 38c. Type **876** (bicentenary) 1·10 50
2309 38c. Jose Manuel Estrada (historian, 150th) 85 40
2310 38c. General Jose I. Garmendia (150th) . . 85 40

877 Hearts as Flowers

1992. Anti-drugs Campaign.
2311 **877** 38c. multicoloured . . . 85 40

878 Steam Pump Fire Engine and Calaza

1992. 140th Birth Anniv of Col. Jose Calaza (founder of fire service).
2312 **878** 38c. multicoloured . . . 1·10 50

879 "The Party"

1992. "Iberoprenfil '92" Iberia–Latin America Philatelic Literature Exhibition, Buenos Aires (2nd issue). Paintings by Raul Soldi. Multicoloured.
2313 76c.+76c. Type **879** . . . . 3·50 1·75
2314 76c.+76c. "Church of St. Anne of Glew" . . . 3·50 1·75

880 Columbus, European Symbols and "Santa Maria"

1992. America. 500th Anniv of Discovery of America by Columbus. Multicoloured.
2315 38c. Type **880** . . . . . . 1·25 40
2316 38c. American symbols and Columbus . . . . 1·25 40

1992. 50th Anniv of Neuquen and Rio Negro Philatelic Centre. Unissued stamp as T **871** optd **50°ANIVERSARIO CENTRO FILATELICO DE NEUQUEN Y RIO NEGRO**. Multicoloured.
2317 1p.77 Verdigris agaric . . . 4·50 2·50

882 "God Pays You" **883** Flags of Paraguay and Argentina as Stamps

1992. Argentine Films. Advertising posters. Mult.
2318 38c. Type **882** . . . . . . 1·00 40
2319 38c. "The Turbid Waters" 1·00 40
2320 38c. "Un Guapo del 900" 1·00 40
2321 38c. "The Truce" . . . . . 1·00 40
2322 38c. "The Official Version" 1·00 40

1992. "Parafil '92" Paraguay–Argentina Stamp Exhibition, Buenos Aires.
2323 **883** 76c.+76c. mult . . . . . 3·00 1·50

884 Angel and Baby Jesus **885** Punta Mogotes Lighthouse

1992. Christmas.
2324 **884** 38c. multicoloured . . . 1·00 40

1992. "Iberoprenfil '92" Iberia–Latin America Philatelic Literature Exhibition, Buenos Aires (3rd issue). Lighthouses. Multicoloured.
2325 38c. Type **885** . . . . . . 1·00 50
2326 38c. Rio Negro . . . . . . 1·00 50
2327 38c. San Antonio . . . . . 1·00 50
2328 38c. Cabo Blanco . . . . . 1·00 50

886 Campaign Emblem **887** "Sac-B" Research Satellite

1992. Anti-AIDS Campaign.
2329 **886** 10c. black, red and blue 80 15
2330 – 26c. multicoloured . . . 1·60 25
DESIGN: 26c. AIDS cloud over house of life.

1992. International Space Year.
2331 **887** 38c. multicoloured . . . 80 40

888 "The Lord of the Miracle" (Matriz Church, Salta)

1992. 400th Anniv of Arrival of the "Lord of the Miracle" in America. Sheet 72 × 112 mm.
MS2332 **888** 76c. multicoloured 7·00 4·50

889 Footballers and Emblem

1993. Centenary of Argentine Football Assn.
2333 **889** 38c. multicoloured . . . 1·25 60

890 Arquebusier and Arms of Francisco de Arganaras (founder) **892** Order of San Martin

891 Government Tower, Poznan

1993. 400th Anniv of Jujuy.
2334 **890** 38c. multicoloured . . . 1·00 40

1993. International Stamp Exhibitions. Sheet 84 × 119 mm containing T **891** and similar square designs. Multicoloured.
MS2335 38c. Type **891** (Polska 93); 48c."Christ the Redeemer" (Statue), Rio de Janeiro (Brasiliana 93); 76c. Palace dome, Bangkok (Bangkok 1993) . . . 6·60 6·60

1993. Anniversaries. Multicoloured.
2336 38c. Type **892** (50th anniv) 85 45
2337 38c. Entrance to and emblem of National History Academy (centenary) 85 45

893 Flag-bearer and Arms of Gendarmerie **895** Snowy Egret ("Egretta thula")

894 Luis Candelaria and Morane Saulnier Type P Monoplane

1993. National Heroes Commemoration. Mult.
2338 38c. Type **893** . . . . . . 1·00 40
2339 38c. "Rio Iguazu" (coastguard corvette) . . 1·00 40

1993. 75th Anniv of First Flight over the Andes.
2340 **894** 38c. multicoloured . . . 1·25 40

1993. Paintings of Birds by Axel Amuchastegui. Multicoloured.
2341 38c.+38c. Type **895** . . . . 1·60 1·60
2342 38c.+38c. Scarlet-headed blackbird ("Amblyramphus holosericeus") . . . . . 1·60 1·60
2343 38c.+38c. Red-crested cardinal ("Paroaria coronata") . . . . 1·60 1·60
2344 38c.+38c. Amazon kingfisher ("Chloroceryle amazona") 1·60 1·60

896 "Coming Home" (Adriana Zaefferer)

1993. Paintings. Multicoloured.
2345 38c. Type **896** 90 40
2346 38c. "The Old House" (Norberto Russo) 90 40

897 Pato

1993. 40th Anniv of Declaration of Pato as National Sport.
2347 **897** 1p. multicoloured . . . 2·40 65

898 Segurola's Pacara ("Enterolobium contortisiliquum")

1993. Old Trees in Buenos Aires. Multicoloured.
2348 75c. Type **898** (Puan and Baldomero Fernandez Moreno Streets) . . . . . 1·25 40
2349 75c. Pueyrredon's carob tree ("Prosopis alba") (Pueyrredon Square) . . . 1·25 40
2350 1p.50 Alvear's coral tree ("Erythrina falcata") (Lavalle Square) . . . . 2·50 80
2351 1p.50 Avellaneda's magnolia ("Magnolia grandiflora") (Adolfo Berro Avenue) . . 2·50 80

899 Southern Right Whale

1993. America. Endangered Animals. Mult.
2352 50c. Type **899** . . . . . . 1·25 55
2353 75c. Commerson's dolphin 1·75 80

900 Star, Leaf and Bell (Christmas)

1993. Christmas and New Year. Festive Symbols. Multicoloured.
2354 75c. Type **900** . . . . . . 1·25 40
2355 75c. Leaf, sun and moon (New Year) . . . . . . 1·25 40
2356 75c. Leaf and fir tree (Christmas) . . . . 1·25 40
2357 75c. Fish and moon (New Year) . . . . 1·25 40
Nos. 2354/7 were issued together, se-tenant, forming a composite design.

901 Cave Painting

1993. Cave of Hands, Santa Cruz.
2358 **901** 1p. multicoloured . . . 2·00 40

902 Emblem

1994. New Argentine Post Emblem.
2359 **902** 75c. multicoloured . . . 1·25 40

903 Brazil Player **904** Golden Tops

1994. World Cup Football Championship, U.S.A. (1st issue). Multicoloured.
2360 25c. German player 30 20
2361 50c. Type **903** 90 45
2362 75c. Argentine player . . . 1·40 50
2363 1p. Italian player . . . . . 1·90 75
MS2364 151 × 99 mm. 1p.50 As No. 2362 but 39 × 49 mm . . . 4·75 4·75
See also Nos. 2380/3.

1994. Fungi. Multicoloured.
2365 10c. Type **904** 20 10
2366 25c. Common ink cap . . . 55 20
2369 50c. Granulated boletus . . 1·25 50
2374 1p. Fly agaric . . . . . . 2·75 1·10
2377 2p. Common morel . . . . . 5·25 2·25

905 Argentine Player with Ball (Matias Taylor)

1994. World Cup Football Championship, U.S.A. (2nd issue). Winning entries in children's competition. Multicoloured.
2380 75c. Type **905** . . . . . . 1·40 50
2381 75c. Tackle (Torcuato Santiago Gonzalez Agote) 1·40 50
2382 75c. Players (Julian Lisenberg) (horiz) . . . . 1·40 50
2383 75c. Match scene (Maria Paula Palma) (horiz) . . . 1·40 50

906 Black-throated Finch

1994. Animals of the Falkland Islands (Islas Malvinas). Multicoloured.
2384 25c. Type **906** 55 40
2385 50c. Gentoo penguins . . . 1·10 75
2386 75c. Falkland Islands flightless steamer ducks 1·60 1·10
2387 1p. Southern elephant-seal 1·75 60

907 Town Arms

1994. Anniversaries. Multicoloured.
2388 75c. Type **907** (400th anniv of San Luis) . . . . . . 1·25 50
2389 75c. Arms (3rd anniv of provincial status of Tierra del Fuego, Antarctica and South Atlantic Islands) . . 1·25 50

908 Ladislao Jose Biro

1994. Inventors. Multicoloured.
2390 75c. Type **908** (ball-point pen) . . . . 1·25 50
2391 75c. Raul Pateras de Pescara (helicopter) . . . . . . 1·25 50
2392 75c. Quirino Cristiani (animated films) . . . . . 1·25 50
2393 75c. Enrique Finochietto (surgical instruments) . . 1·25 50

909 Star, Purple Bauble and Bell

1994. UNICEF Children's Fund in Argentina. Multicoloured.
2394 50c. Type **909** 85 45
2395 75c. Bell, red bauble and star . . . . 1·25 50

910 Children holding Globe (Ivana Mirna de Caro)

1994. "Care of the Planet". Children's Painting Competition. Multicoloured.
2396 25c. Type **910** 30 20
2397 25c. Girl polishing sunbeam and boy tending tree (Elena Tsouprik) 30 20
2398 50c. Children of all races around globe (Estefania Navarro) (horiz) 60 45
2399 50c. Globe as house (Maria Belen Gidoni) (horiz) . . 60 45

911 Star and Angel (The Annunciation)

1994. Christmas. Multicoloured.
2400 50c. Type **911** 60 45
2401 75c. Madonna and Child (Nativity) . . . . 1·25 50

912 Running

1995. 12th Pan-American Games, Mar del Plata. Multicoloured.
2402 75c. Type **912** . . . . . . 1·25 45
2403 75c. Cycling . . . . 1·25 45
2404 75c. Diving . . . . 1·25 45
2405 1p.25 Football (vert) . . . . 2·00 60
2406 1p.25 Gymnastics (vert) . . 2·00 60

913 Postal Emblem

1995. Self-adhesive.
2407 **913** 25c. yellow, blue & black 3·75 50
2408 75c. yellow, blue & black 1·25 50

914 National Congress Building and "The Republic Triumphant" (statue, detail)

1995. New Constitution, August 1994.
2409 **914** 75c. multicoloured . . . 1·25 40

915 Letters and Disk

1995. 21st International Book Fair.
2410 **915** 75c. multicoloured . . . 1·25 50

916 Bay-winged Cowbird

1995. Birds. Multicoloured.
2412 5p. Hooded siskin . . . . . 10·50 7·50
2413 9p.40 Type **916** . . . . . . 21·00 15·00
2414 10p. Rufous-collared sparrow . . . . 20·00 13·50

917 Clouds seen through Atrium

1995. Centenary of Argentine Engineers' Centre, Buenos Aires.
2420 **917** 75c. multicoloured . . . 1·25 45

918 Antoine de Saint-Exupery (pilot and writer)

1995. Aerofila 96 Latin American Airmail Exhibition. Sheet 130 × 90 mm containing T **918** and similar multicoloured design.
MS2421 25c.+25c. Type **918**; 75c.+75c. Illustration from "The Little Prince" . . . . 12·00 12·00

919 "Bahia Aguirre" (supply ship)

1995. Argentine Antarctic. Sheet 171 × 91 mm containing T **919** and similar horiz design. Multicoloured.
MS2422 75c.+25c. Type **919**; 1p.25+75c. Lockheed C-130 Hercules transport plane . . . 11·50 11·50

920 Jose Marti

1995. Revolutionaries' Anniversaries. Mult.
2423 1p. Type **920** (death cent) 1·60 45
2424 1p. Antonio de Sucre (birth bicentenary) . . . . . . 1·60 45

921 Greater Rhea **922** Cave Painting (Patagonia)

1995. Birds. Multicoloured.
2425 5c. Type **921** 15 10
2425a 10c. Giant wood rail ("ipecae") 15 10
2426 25c. King penguin 45 20
2427 50c. Toco toucan 85 45
2428 75c. Andean condor . . . 1·40 75
2429 1p. Barn owl . . . . . . 1·75 1·00
2430 2p. Olivaceous cormorant 3·50 2·00
2431 2p.75 Southern lapwing . . 5·00 2·75
2432 3p.25 Southern lapwing . . 4·00 3·00

1995. Animals. As T **921**. Multicoloured.
2436 25c. Alligator 30 20
2437 50c. Red fox 60 45
2438 75c. Anteater . . . . 1·25 75
2439 75c. Vicuna . . . . 1·25 75
2440 75c. Sperm whale . . . . . 1·25 75

1995. Archaeology. Multicoloured.
2441 75c. Type **922** . . . . . . 1·25 40
2442 75c. Stone mask (Tafi culture, Tucuman) . . . . 1·25 40
2443 75c. Anthropomorphic vase (Catamarca) . . . . . . 1·25 40
2444 75c. Woven cloth (North Patagonia) . . . . 1·25 40

923 Peron

1995. Birth Centenary of Juan Peron (President, 1946–55 and 1973–74).
2445 **923** 75c. blue and bistre . . . 1·25 40

924 Postal Emblem on Sunflower

1995.
2446 **924** 75c. multicoloured . . . 1·25 40

925 "50" Emblem

1995. Anniversaries. Sheet 110 × 80 mm containing T **925** and similar horiz designs. Multicoloured.
MS2447 75c. Type **925** (50th anniv of United Nations Organization); 75c. "50" and emblem (50th anniv of International Civil Aviation Organization); 75c. "50" and emblem (50th anniv of Food and Agriculture Organization); 75c. "75" and emblem (75th anniv of International Labour Organization) . . . . 11·50 11·50

926 Christmas Tree

1995. Christmas. Multicoloured.
2448 75c. Type **926** . . . . . . 1·25 40
2449 75c. "1996" . . . . . . 1·25 40
2450 75c. Glasses of champagne . . 1·25 40
2451 75c. Present . . . . . . 1·25 40
2452 75c. Type **926** . . . . . . 1·25 40

927 "Les 400 Coups" (dir. Francois Truffaut)

1995. Centenary of Motion Pictures. Each black, grey and orange.
2453 75c. "Battleship Potemkin" (dir. Sergei Eisenstein) . . 1·25 40
2454 75c. "Casablanca" (dir. Michael Curtiz) . . . . 1·25 40
2455 75c. "Bicycle Thieves" (dir. Vittorio de Sica) . . . . 1·25 40
2456 75c. Charlie Chaplin in "Limelight" . . . . . . 1·25 40
2457 75c. Type **927** . . . . . . 1·25 40
2458 75c. "Chronicle of an Only Child" (dir. Leonardo Favio) . . . . 1·25 40

928 Horse-drawn Mail Coach

1995. America (1994). Postal Transport. Mult.
2459 75c. Type **928** . . . . . . 1·25 40
2460 75c. Early postal van . . . 1·25 40

929 Dirigible Airship

1995. The Sky. Multicoloured.
2461 25c. Type **929** 55 20
2462 25c. Kite 55 20
2463 25c. Hot-air balloon 55 20
2464 50c. Balloons 85 45
2465 50c. Paper airplane 85 45
2466 75c. Airplane . . . . 1·25 45
2467 75c. Helicopter . . . . . . 1·25 45
2468 75c. Parachute . . . . . . 1·25 45

930 Ancient Greek and Modern Runners

1996. Multicoloured. (a) Centenary of Modern Olympic Games. Horiz designs.
2471 75c. Type **930** . . . . . . 1·25 35
2472 1p. "The Discus Thrower" (ancient Greek statue, Miron) and modern thrower . . . . 1·60 50
(b) Olympic Games. Vert designs.
2473 75c. Torch bearer (Buenos Aires, 2004) . . . . . . 1·25 35
2474 1p. Rowing (Atlanta, 1996) 1·60 50

931 Francisco Muniz (founder of Academy of Medicine and Public Hygiene Council)

1996. Physicians' Anniversaries. Multicoloured.
2475 50c. Type **931** (birth bicentenary (1995)) . . . 85 45
2476 50c. Ricardo Gutierrez (founder of Children's Hospital and co-founder of periodical "La Patria Argentina", death centenary) 85 45
2477 50c. Ignacio Pirovano (death centenary (1995)) 85 45
2478 50c. Esteban Maradona (birth centenary (1995) and first death anniv) . . 85 45

932 Mosaic Map of Jerusalem (left-hand detail)

1996. 3000th Anniv of Jerusalem. Multicoloured.
2479 75c. Type **932** . . . . . 1·25 40
2480 75c. Map (right-hand detail) 1·25 40
Nos. 2479/80 were issued together, se-tenant, forming a composite design.

933 Capybaras

1996. America. Endangered Species. Mult.
2481 75c. Type **933** . . . . . . 1·50 45
2482 75c. Guanacos . . . . . . 1·50 45

934 Ramon Franco's Seaplane "Plus Ultra"

1996. "Aerofila '96" Latin American Airmail Exhibition. Aircraft. Multicoloured.
2483 25c.+25c. Type **934** . . . . 1·25 60
2484 25c.+25c. Alberto Santos-Dumont's biplane "14 bis" . . . . 1·25 60
2485 50c.+50c. Charles Lindbergh's "Spirit of St. Louis" . . . . 2·50 1·25
2486 50c.+50c. Eduardo Olivero's biplane "Buenos Aires" 2·50 1·25

1996. As Nos. 2407/8. Self-adhesive. Imperf.
2486a **913** 25c. yellow and blue . . 3·75 50
2486b 75c. yellow and blue . . 1·25 70

935 Dusky-legged Guan, Diamante National Park

1996. National Parks. Multicoloured.
2487 75c. Type **935** . . . . . . 1·25 45
2488 75c. Mountain viscacha, El Leoncito Nature Reserve 1·60 70
2489 75c. Marsh deer, Otamendi Nature Reserve . . . . . 1·25 45
2490 75c. Red-spectacled amazon, San Antonio Nature Reserve . . . . 1·60 70

936 Dragon

1996. Murals from Buenos Aires Underground Railway. Multicoloured.
2491 1p.+50c. Type **936** . . . . 3·00 1·75
2492 1p.50+1p. Bird . . . . . . 5·00 2·50

937 "San Antonio" (tank landing ship)

1996. Cent of Port Belgrano Naval Base. Mult.
2493 25c. Type **937** 65 20
2494 50c. "Rosales" (corvette) . . 1·25 45
2495 75c. "Hercules" (destroyer) 1·75 70
2496 1p. "25 de Mayo" (aircraft carrier) . . . . 2·50 1·00

938 Decorative Panel

1996. Carousel. Multicoloured.
2497 25c. Type **938** 55 20
2498 25c. Child on horse 55 20
2499 25c. Carousel 55 20
2500 50c. Fairground horses . . . 85 20
2501 50c. Child in airplane . . . 85 20
2502 50c. Pig 85 20
2503 75c. Child in car . . . . . 1·25 45

939 Head Post Office, Buenos Aires

940 "Adoration of the Wise Men" (Gladys Rinaldi)

1996. Size $24\frac{1}{2} \times 34\frac{1}{2}$ mm. Self-adhesive. Imperf.
2504 **939** 75c. multicoloured . . . 90 70
See also Nos. 2537/8.

1996. Christmas. Tapestries. Multicoloured.
2505 75c. Type **940** . . . . . . 1·25 45
2506 1p. Abstract (Norma Bonet de Maekawa) (horiz) . . 1·60 70

941 Melchior Base

1996. Argentinian Presence in Antarctic. Mult.
2507 75c. Type **941** . . . . . . 1·40 45
2508 1p.25 "Irizar" (ice-breaker) 2·75 70

942 "Vahine no te Miti" (Gauguin)

1996. Cent of National Gallery of Fine Arts. Mult.
2509 75c. Type **942** . . . . . . 1·25 45
2510 1p. "The Nymph surprised" (Edouard Manet) . . . . 1·60 65
2511 1p. "Figure of Woman" (Amedeo Modigliani) . . 1·60 65
2512 1p.25 "Woman lying down" (Pablo Picasso) (horiz) . . 2·00 75

943 Granite Mining, Cordoba

1997. Mining Industry. Multicoloured.
2513 75c. Type **943** . . . . . . 1·25 45
2514 1p.25 Borax mining, Salta 2·00 65

944 "They amuse Themselves in Dancing" (Raul Soldi)

1997. America (1996). National Costume.
2515 **944** 75c. multicoloured . . . 1·25 45

945 Arms, Sabre and Shako

1997. Centenary of Repatriation of General San Martin's Sabre.
2516 **945** 75c. multicoloured . . . 1·25 45

946 Match Scene

1997. 29th World Rugby Youth Championship, Argentina.
2517 **946** 75c. multicoloured . . . 1·25 45

947 "Fortuna" (yacht)

1997. 50th Anniv of Buenos Aires to Rio de Janeiro Regatta.
2518 **947** 75c. multicoloured . . . 90 30

948 Ceres Design, France (1849–52)

1997. "Mevifil '97" First Int Exn of Philatelic Audio-visual and Computer Systems. Mult.
2519 50c.+50c. Type **948** . . . . 1·60 1·25
2520 50c.+50c. Queen Isabella II design, Spain (1851) . . . 1·60 1·25
2521 50c.+50c. Rivadavia design, Argentine Republic (1864) 1·60 1·25
2522 50c.+50c. Paddle-steamer design, Buenos Aires (1858) . . . . 1·60 1·25

Nos. 2519/22 were issued together, se-tenant, with the centre of the block forming the composite design of an eye.

949 Museum

1997. Centenary of National History Museum, Buenos Aires.
2523 **949** 75c. multicoloured . . . 1·25 45

950 Seal and Oak Leaf

951 Carcano (after Dolores Capdevila)

1997. Centenary of La Plata National University.
2524 **950** 75c. multicoloured . . . 1·25 45

1997. 50th Death Anniv (1996) of Ramon Carcano (postal reformer).
2525 **951** 75c. multicoloured . . . 1·25 45

952 Cabo Virgenes Lighthouse

1997. Lighthouses. Multicoloured.
2526 75c. Type **952** . . . . . . 1·25 45
2527 75c. Isla Pinguino . . . . . 1·25 45
2528 75c. San Juan de Salvamento . . . . 1·25 45
2529 75c. Punta Delgada . . . . 1·25 45

953 Condor and Olympic Rings

1997. Inclusion of Buenos Aires in Final Selection Round for 2004 Olympic Games.
2530 **953** 75c. multicoloured . . . 1·25 45

954 Lacroze Company Suburban Service, 1912

1997. Centenary of First Electric Tramway in Buenos Aires. Illustrations from "History of the Tram" by Marcelo Mayorga. Multicoloured.
2531 75c. Type **954** . . . . . . 1·40 70
2532 75c. Lacroze Company urban service, 1907 . . . 1·40 70
2533 75c. Anglo Argentina Company tramcar, 1930 1·40 70
2534 75c. City of Buenos Aires Transport Corporation tramcar, 1942 . . . . . . 1·40 70
2535 75c. Fabricaciones Militares tramcar, 1956 . . . . . . 1·40 70
2536 75c. Electricos de Sur Company tramcar, 1908 1·40 70

Nos. 2531/6 were issued together, se-tenant, showing a composite design of a tram in a city street.

1997. As No. 2504 but size 23 × 35 mm. Self-adhesive. Imperf.
2537 **939** 25c. multicoloured . . . 70 20
2538 75c. multicoloured . . . 1·40 20

955 Monument (by Mauricio Molina)

1997. Inauguration of Monument to Joaquin Gonzalez (politician) at La Rioja.
2539 **955** 75c. multicoloured . . . 1·25 45

956 Alberto Ginastera (after Carlos Nine)

1997. Composers. Multicoloured.
2540 75c. Type **956** . . . . . 1·25 45
2541 75c. Astor Piazzolla (after Carlos Alonso) . . . . . 1·25 45
2542 75c. Anibal Troilo (after Hermenegildo Sabat) . . 1·25 45
2543 75c. Atahualpa Yupanqui (after Luis Scafati) . . . 1·25 45

957 "Tren a las Nubes", Salta

1997. Trains. Multicoloured.
2544 50c.+50c. Type **957** . . . . 1·60 80
2545 50c.+50c. Preserved steam locomotive, Buenos Aires 1·60 80
2546 50c.+50c. Patagonian express "La Trochita" Rio Negro–Chubut . . . 1·60 80
2547 50c.+50c. Austral Fueguino Railway locomotive No. 2, Tierra del Fuego 1·60 80

958 Eva Peron (after Raul Manteola)

1997. 50th Anniv of Women's Suffrage.
2548 **958** 75c. pink and grey . . . 1·25 45

959 Jorge Luis Borges and Maze

1997. Writers. Multicoloured.
2549 1p. Type **959** . . . . 1·60 50
2550 1p. Julio Cortazar and hopscotch grid . . . . . 1·60 50

1997. 70th Anniv of Air Mail in Argentina. No. **MS**2421 optd **1927 1997 ANIVERSARIO AEROPOSTA ARGENTINA** in margin.
MS2551 25c.+25c. multicoloured; 75c.+75c. multicoloured . . . 11·50 7·00

961 Members' Flags and Southern Cross

1997. Mercosur (South American Common Market).
2552 **961** 75c. multicoloured . . . 1·25 45

962 "Presidente Sarmiento" (Hugo Leban)

1997. Centenary of Launch of "Presidente Sarmiento" (cadet ship). Multicoloured.
2553 75c. Type **962** . . . . . . 2·00 35
MS2554 150 × 100 mm. 75c. "Presidente Sarmiento" at sea; 75c. Figurehead (vert) . . . . 4·00 70

963 Guevara

1997. 30th Death Anniv of Ernesto "Che" Guevara (revolutionary).
2555 **963** 75c. brown, red & black 1·25 45

964 Vicuna (Julian Chiapparo)

1997. "Draw an Ecostamp" Children's Competition Winners. Multicoloured.
2556 50c. Type **964** 80 20
2557 50c. Vicuna (Leandro Lopez Portal) 80 20
2558 75c. Seal (Andres Lloren) (horiz) . . . . 1·25 45
2559 75c. Ashy-headed goose (Jose Saccone) (horiz) . . 1·25 45

965 "Nativity" (Mary Jose)

1997. Christmas. Tapestries of the Nativity. Designs by artists named. Mult. (a) Size 45 × 34 mm.
2560 75c. Type **965** . . . . . . 1·25 45

(b) Size 44 × 27 mm. Self-adhesive. Imperf.
2561 25c. Elena Aguilar 40 20
2562 25c. Silvia Pettachi 40 20
2563 50c. Ana Escobar 80 20
2564 50c. Alejandra Martinez . . 80 20
2565 75c. As No. 2560 but with inscriptions differently arranged . . . . 1·25 45
2566 75c. Nidia Martinez . . . . 1·25 45

966 Mother Teresa

1997. Mother Teresa (founder of the Missionaries of Charity) Commemoration.
2567 **966** 75c. multicoloured . . . 1·25 45

967 Houssay

1998. 50th Anniv (1997) of Award to Bernardo Houssay of Nobel Prize for Medicine and Physiology.
2568 **967** 75c. multicoloured . . . 90 70

968 Mountaineers

1998. Cent of First Ascent of Mt. Aconcagua.
2569 **968** 1p.25 multicoloured . . 1·25 1·00

969 San Martin de los Andes and Lake Lacar

1998. Centenary of San Martin de los Andes.

2570	**969**	75c. multicoloured . . .	90	70

970 Grenadier Monument (Juan Carlos Ferraro)

1998. Declaration as National Historical Monument of Palermo Barracks of General San Martin Horse Grenadiers. Multicoloured.

2571	75c. Type **970**	90	70
2572	75c. Sevres urn with portrait of San Martin	90	70
2573	75c. Regiment coat of arms	90	70
2574	75c. Main facade of barracks	90	70

971 Globe and Baby

1998. Protection of Ozone Layer.

2575	**971**	75c. multicoloured . . .	90	70

972 Postman, 1920

1998. America. The Postman. Multicoloured.

2576	75c. Type **972**	90	70
2577	75c. Postman, 1998	90	70

973 "El Reino del Reves"

1998. Stories by Maria Elena Walsh. Illustrations by Eduardo and Ricardo Fuhrmann. Multicoloured. Self-adhesive.

2578	75c. Type **973**	90	70
2579	75c. "Zoo Loco"	90	70
2580	75c. "Dailan Kifki"	90	70
2581	75c. "Manuelita"	90	70

974 St Peter's, Fiambala, Catamarca

1998. Historic Chapels. Multicoloured.

2582	75c. Type **974**	90	70
2583	75c. Huacalera, Jujuy . . .	90	70
2584	75c. St. Dominic's, La Rioja	90	70
2585	75c. Tumbaya, Jujuy . . .	90	70

975 Raised Hands

1998. White Helmets (volunteer humanitarian workers).

2586	**975**	1p. multicoloured . . .	1·25	1·00

976 Argentine Player

1998. World Cup Football Championship, France. Multicoloured.

2587	75c. Type **976**	90	70
2588	75c. Croatian player	90	70
2589	75c. Jamaican player . . .	90	70
2590	75c. Japanese player	90	70

977 Typewriter, Camera, Pen, Computer and Satellite

1998. Journalism Day.

2591	**977**	75c. multicoloured . . .	90	70

978 Corrientes 1860 3c. Stamps and Postal Emblem

1998. 250th Anniv of Establishment of Regular Postal Service in Rio de la Plata (Spanish dominion in South America). Multicoloured.

2592	75c. Type **978**	90	70
2593	75c. Buenos Aires Post Office and pillar box . . .	90	70

979 Jesuit Ruins, San Ignacio Mini

1998. Mercosur Missions.

2594	**979**	75c. multicoloured . . .	90	70

980 Aberdeen Angus

1998. Cattle. Multicoloured.

2595	25c. Type **980**	30	20
2596	25c. Brahman	30	20
2597	50c. Hereford	60	45
2598	50c. Criolla	60	45
2599	75c. Holando-Argentina . .	90	70
2600	75c. Shorthorn	90	70

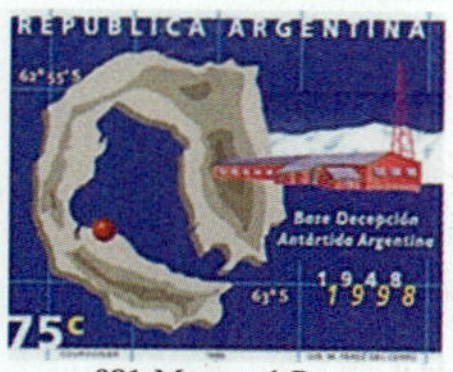

981 Map and Base

1998. 50th Anniv of Decepcion Antarctic Base.

2601	**981**	75c. multicoloured . . .	90	70

982 Anniversary Emblem

1998. 50th Anniv of State of Israel.

2602	**982**	75c. multicoloured . . .	90	70

983 Bridge in Japanese Garden, Buenos Aires

1998. Cent of Argentina–Japan Friendship Treaty.

2603	**983**	75c. multicoloured . . .	90	70

984 Facade and clock

1998. 70th Anniv of Head Post Office, Buenos Aires. Multicoloured.

2604	75c. Type **984**	90	70
2605	75c. Capital and bench . . .	90	70

985 Patoruzu (Quinterno)

986 Heart with Arms holding Baby

1998. Comic Strip Characters. Multicoloured.

2606	75c. Type **985**	90	70
2607	75c. Matias (Sendra)	90	70
2608	75c. Clemente (Caloi) . . .	90	70
2609	75c. El Eternauta (Oesterheld Solano Lopez)	90	70
2610	75c. Loco Chavez (Trillo Altuna)	90	70
2611	75c. Inodoro Pereyra (Fontanarrosa)	90	70
2612	75c. Tia Vicenta (Landru)	90	70
2613	75c. Gaturro (Nik)	90	70

1998. 220th Anniv of Dr. Pedro de Elizalde Children's Hospital.

2614	**986**	75c. multicoloured . . .	90	70

987 Post Banner and Pennant, 1785, and Arms of Maritime Post

1998. "Espamer '98" Iberian–Latin American Stamp Exhibition, Buenos Aires. Mult. Self-adhesive.

2615	25c. Type **987**	30	20
2616	75c. Mail brigantine	1·25	70
2617	75c.+75c. Mail brigantine (different)	2·50	1·75
2618	1p.25+1p.25 Mail brig . . .	4·25	3·00

988 Passport and Wallenberg

1998. Raoul Wallenberg (Swedish diplomat in Hungary who helped Jews escape, 1944–45) Commemoration.

2619	**988**	75c. multicoloured . . .	90	70

989 Aguada Culture Bird

1998. 50th Anniv of Organization of American States.

2620	**989**	75c. multicoloured . . .	90	70

990 Eoraptor

1998. Prehistoric Animals. Multicoloured.

2621	75c. Type **990**	90	70
2622	75c. Gasparinisaura	90	70
2623	75c. Giganotosaurus	90	70
2624	75c. Patagosaurus	90	70

Nos. 2621/4 were issued together, se-tenant, forming a composite design.

991 Child as Angel, Stars and Score

993 Postman

992 Juan Figueroa (founder) and First Issue

1998. Christmas.

2625	**991**	75c. multicoloured . . .	90	70

1998. Centenary of "El Liberal" (newspaper).

2626	**992**	75c. multicoloured . . .	90	70

1998. Postmen. Size 25 × 35 mm. Multicoloured. Self-adhesive.

2627	25c. Type **993**	30	20
2628	75c. Modern postman . . .	90	70

For 75c. in reduced size see No. 2640.

1998. Birds. As T **921**. Multicoloured. Self-adhesive.

2629	60c. Red-tailed comet . . .	75	60

994 Child (painting, Francisco Ramirez)

1998. 50th Anniv of Universal Declaration of Human Rights.

2635	**994**	75c. multicoloured . . .	90	70

995 Enrique Julio (founder) and Newspaper Offices

1998. Cent of "La Nueva Provincia" (newspaper).

2636	**995**	75c. multicoloured . . .	90	70

996 "Haggadah" of Pessah (exhibit) and Carving on Cathedral

1998. Permanent Exhibition commemorating Holocaust Victims, Buenos Aires Cathedral.

2637	**996**	75c. multicoloured . . .	90	70

1999. Postmen. Size 21 × 27 mm. Mult. Self-adhesive.

2638	25c. Type **993**	30	20
2639	50c. Postman, 1950	60	45
2640	75c. As No. 2628	90	70

997 Oil-smeared Magellanic Penguin

1999. International Year of the Ocean. Mult.

2641	50c. Type **997**	60	45
2642	75c. Dolphins (horiz) . . .	90	70

998 Buildings and Draughtsman's Instruments

1999. National Arts Fund.

2643	**998**	75c. multicoloured . . .	90	70

999 Computer and Book

1999. 25th Book Fair, Buenos Aires. Multicoloured.

2644	75c. Type **999**	90	70
2645	75c. Obelisk, compact disk case and readers	90	70

Nos. 2644/5 were issued together, se-tenant, forming a composite design.

1000 Rugby Balls and Player

1999. Centenary of Argentine Rugby Union. Multicoloured.

2646	75c. Type **1000**	90	70
MS2647	120 × 90 mm. 1p.50 19th-century and modern players	1·80	1·40

1001 Glass, La Giralda

1002 Pierre de Coubertin, 1924 Olympic Gold Medal and Olympic Rings

1999. Cafes. Multicoloured. Self-adhesive.

2648	25c. Type **1001**	30	20
2649	75c. Two glasses, Cafe Homero Manzi	90	70
2650	75c. Hatstand, Confiteria Ideal	90	70
2651	1p.25 Cup and saucer, Cafe Tortoni	1·50	1·00

1999. 75th Anniv of Argentine Olympic Committee.

2652	**1002**	75c. multicoloured . . .	90	70

1003 Enrico Caruso (Italian tenor)

1999. Opera. Multicoloured.

2653	75c. Type **1003** (125th birth anniv and centenary of American debut)	90	70
2654	75c. Singer and musical instruments	90	70
2655	75c. Buenos Aires Opera House	90	70
2656	75c. Scene from "El Matrero" (Felipe Boero)	90	70

1004 Rosario Vera Penaloza (educationist)

1999. America (1998). Famous Women. Mult.

2659	75c. Type **1004**	90	70
2660	75c. Julieta Lanteri (women's rights campaigner)	90	70

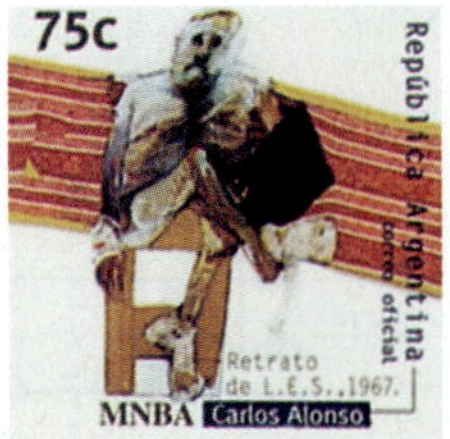

1005 "Portrait of L. E. S." (Carlos Alonso)

1999. Paintings. Two sheets each 150 × 100 mm containing multicoloured designs as T **1005**.

MS2661	Two sheets. (a) 75c. "Anarchy of Year 20" (Luis Felipe Noe) (78 × 39 mm); 75c. Type **1005**. (b) 75c. "Typical Orchestra" (Antonio Berni) (69 × 49 mm); 75c. Unititled (Aida Carballo) (39 × 49 mm)	9·50	9·50

1006 Local Road Network

1999. Bulk Mailing Stamps. Mult. Self-adhesive.

2662	35c. Type **1006**	40	30
2663	40c. Town plan	50	40
2664	50c. Regional map	60	45

1007 Carrier Pigeon

1999.

2665	**1007**	75c. multicoloured . . .	90	70

1008 Boxer

1999. Dogs. Multicoloured.

2666	25c. Type **1008**	20	20
2667	25c. Old English sheepdog	30	20
2668	50c. Welsh collie	60	45
2669	50c. St. Bernard	60	45
2670	75c. German shepherd . . .	90	70
2671	75c. Siberian husky	90	70

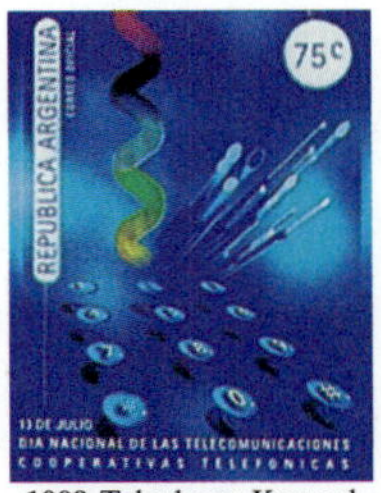

1009 Telephone Keypad

1999. National Telecommunications Day.

2672	**1009**	75c. multicoloured . . .	90	70

1010 College Gates

1999. 150th Anniv of Justo Jose de Urquiza College, Concepcion del Uruguay.

2673	**1010**	75c. multicoloured . . .	90	70

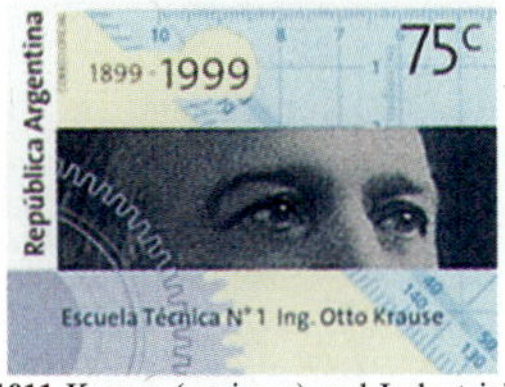

1011 Krause (engineer) and Industrial Instruments

1999. Centenary of Technical School No. 1 Otto Krause.

2674	**1011**	75c. multicoloured . . .	90	70

1012 Nativity

1999. Bethlehem 2000.

2675	**1012**	75c. blue, gold and red	90	70

1013 Brotherhood among Men

1999. America. A New Millennium without Arms. Multicoloured.

2676	75c. Type **1013**	90	70
2677	75c. Liberty Tree (vert) . .	90	70

1014 Coypu ("Myocastor coypus"), Mburucuya National Park

1999. National Parks. Multicoloured.

2678	50c. Type **1014**	60	50
2679	50c. Andean condor, Quebrada de los Condoritos National Park	60	50
2680	50c. Vicuna, San Guillermo National Park	60	50
2681	75c. Puma, Sierra de las Quijadas National Park	90	70
2682	75c. Argentine grey fox ("Dusicyon griseus"), Talampaya National Park	90	70

1015 Map of the Americas, Road Network and Wickerwork

1999. 40th Anniv of Inter-American Development Bank.

2683	**1015**	75c. multicoloured . . .	90	70

1016 "Evidencias VI" (Carlos Gallardo)

1999. 125th Anniv of Universal Postal Union.

2684	**1016**	1p.50 multicoloured . .	1·75	1·40

1017 "Fournier" and Map

1999. 50th Anniv of Sinking of the "Fournier" (minesweeper) in Antarctica.

2685	**1017**	75c. multicoloured . . .	90	70

1018 "Nothofagus pumillio"

1999. Trees (1st series). Multicoloured.

2686	75c. Type **1018**	90	70
2687	75c. "Prosopis caldenia" . .	90	70
2688	75c. "Schinopsis balansae"	90	70
2689	75c. "Cordia trichotoma"	90	70

Nos. 2686/9 were issued together, se-tenant, forming a composite design.

1019 Latecoere 25 Mailplane

1999. 50th Anniv of World Record for Consecutive Parachute Jumps. Multicoloured.
2690 75c. Type **1019** 90 70
2691 75c. Parachutists 90 70

1020 Accordionist "The Tango"

1999. The New Millennium. Three sheets each 150 × 100 mm containing multicoloured designs as T **1020**.
MS2692 Three sheets. (a) 50, 75c. "The Tango"; (b) 50, 75c. Jorge Luis Borges (writer); (c) 50, (horiz), 75c. Football . . . . . 11·50 11·50

1021 Boca Juniors Club Supporters

1999. Football. Multicoloured. (a) Size 42 × 33 mm.
2693 75c. Type **1021** 90 70
2694 75c. River Plate Club supporters 90 70

(b) Size 37 × 34 mm (1p.50) or 37 × 27 mm (others)
(i) Boca Juniors.
2695 25c. Two players and ball 30 25
2696 50c. Club badge 60 50
2697 50c. Players hugging 60 50
2698 75c. Supporters and balloons 90 70
2699 75c. Club banner 90 70
2700 75c. Players 90 70
2701 1p.50 Player making high kick . . . . 1·75 1·40

(ii) River Plate.
2702 25c. Stadium 30 25
2703 50c. Players arriving on pitch 60 50
2704 50c. Supporters waving flags 60 50
2705 75c. Club badge 90 70
2706 75c. Trophy 90 70
2707 75c. Supporters with banner 90 70
2708 1p.50 Player preparing to kick ball . . . . 1·75 1·40

Nos. 2695/708 are self-adhesive.

1022 Planisphere of Central South America (Pierre Descelliers, 1546)

1999. Maps. Multicoloured.
2709 25c.+25c. Type **1022** 60 60
2710 50c.+50c. 17th-century map of estuary of the River Plate (Claes Voogt) . . . 1·25 1·25
2711 50c.+50c. Buenos Aires (Military Geographical Institute, 1910) . . . . . 1·25 1·25
2712 75c.+75c. Mouth of Riachuelo river and Buenos Aires harbour (satellite picture, 1999) . . 1·75 1·75

1023 Valdivielso and St. Peter's Cathedral, Rome

1999. Canonization of Hector Valdivielso Saez (Brother of the Christian Schools).
2713 **1023** 75c. multicoloured . . . 90 70

1024 "San Francisco Xavier" (brig)

1999. Bicentenary of Manuel Belgrano Naval Academy.
2714 **1024** 75c. multicoloured . . . 90 70

1025 "Uruguay"

1999. 125th Anniv of Launch of "Uruguay" (sail/steam corvette). Sheet 150 × 100 mm.
MS2715 **1025** 1p.50 multicoloured 4·75 4·75

1026 Holy Family

1999. Christmas. Multicoloured.
2716 25c. Wise Man (29 × 29 mm) 30 25
2717 25c. Bell (29 × 29 mm) . . . 30 25
2718 50c. Two kings and camels (39 × 29 mm) 60 50
2719 50c. Holly leaf (39 × 29 mm) 60 50
2720 75c. Angel with star (39 × 30 mm) 90 70
2721 75c. Star (29 × 30 mm) . . . 90 70
2722 75c. Nativity (39 × 29 mm) 90 70
2723 75c. Tree decorations (29 × 29 mm) 90 70
2724 75c. Type **1026** 90 70

1027 Grape on Vine

2000. Wine Making. Multicoloured.
2725 25c. Type **1027** 35 30
2726 25c. Glass and bottle of wine 35 30
2727 50c. Wine bottles 70 55
2728 50c. Cork screw and cork 70 55

1028 Mathematical Symbol and "2000"

2000. International Mathematics Year.
2729 **1028** 75c. multicoloured . . . 1·00 80

1029 White-fronted Dove

2000. Doves and Pigeon. Mult. Self-adhesive.
2730 75c. Type **1029** . . . . . . 1·00 80
2731 75c. Picazuro pigeon (*Columba picazuro*) . . . 1·00 80
2732 75c. Picui dove (*Columbina picni*) . . . . 1·00 80
2733 75c. Eared dove (*Fenaida auriculata*) . . . . 1·00 80

1030 *Venda coerulea*

2000. Bangkok 2000 International Stamp Exhibition. Plants. Sheet 100 × 76 mm containing T **1030** and similar horiz design. Multicoloured.
MS2734 25c. Type **1030**; 75c. Coral tree . . . . 1·20 1·20

1031 Open Book (CONABIP Library)

2000. Libraries. Multicoloured.
2735 25c. Type **1031** 35 35
2736 50c. Building facade (Jujuy library) 70 55
2737 75c. Hands and braille book (Argentine Library for the Blind) . . . . 1·00 80
2738 $1 Open book and building (National Library) . . . 2·10 1·60

No. 2737 has an inscription in braille across the stamp.

1032 Caravel, Compass Rose and Letter

2000. 500th Anniv of the Discovery of Brazil. Multicoloured.
2739 25c. Type **1032** 35 30
2740 75c. Pedro Alvares Cabral (discoverer) and map of South America . . . . . 1·00 80

1033 Lieutenant General Luis Maria Campos (founder)

2000. Centenary of the Higher Military Academy.
2741 **1033** 75c. multicoloured . . . 1·00 80

1034 Penny Black and *La Portena* (steam locomotive), 1857

2000. The Stamp Show 2000 International Stamp Exhibition, London. Sheet 99 × 76 mm containing T **1034** and similar horiz design. Multicoloured.
MS2742 25c. Type **1034**; 75c. Two 1862 15c. stamps and modern pillar box . . . . 1·20 1·20

1035 Convention Emblem

2000. 91st Rotary International Convention, Buenos Aires.
2743 **1035** 75c. multicoloured . . . 1·00 80

1036 Futuristic Houses and Emblems (Rocio Casado)

2000. "Stampin' the Future". Winning Entries in Children's International Painting Competition. Mult.
2744 25c. Type **1036** 35 30
2745 50c. Sea and clouds (Carolina Cacerez) (vert) 70 55
2746 75c. Flower (Valeria A. Pizarro) . . . . 1·00 80
2747 $1 Flying cars (Cristina Ayala Castro) (vert) . . . 1·40 1·10

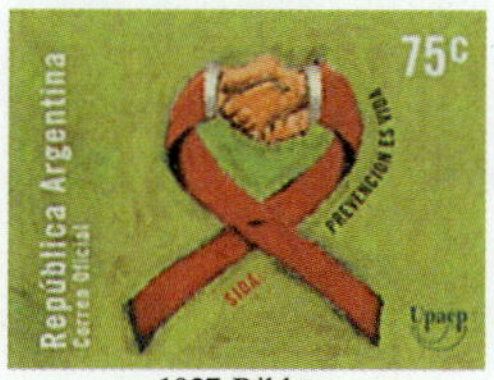

1037 Ribbon

2000. America. AIDS Awareness. Multicoloured.
2748 75c. Type **1037** . . . . . . 1·00 80
2749 75c. Arms circling faces . . 1·00 80

1038 Potez 25 Biplane

2000. Birth Centenary of Antoine de Saint-Exupery (novelist and pilot). Multicoloured.
2750 25c. Type **1038** 35 30
2751 50c. Late 28 . . . . 70 55

1039 Potez 25 Biplane

2000. "Aerofila 2000" Mercosur Air Philately Exhibition, Buenos Aires. Multicoloured.
2752 25c. As Type **1039** 35 30
2753 25c. Antoine de Saint-Exupery (novelist and pilot) (29 × 29 mm) . . . 35 30
2754 50c. Late 28 . . . . 70 55
2755 50c. Henri Guillaumet, Almonacid and Jean Mermoz (aviation pioneers) (29 × 29 mm) . . 70 55
2756 50c. Map of South America and tail of Late 25 (39 × 39 mm) 70 55
2757 $1 Late 25 and cover (39 × 29 mm) . . . . . . 1·40 1·10

1040 Illia

2000. Birth Centenary of Arturo U. Illia (President, 1963–66).
2758 **1040** 75c. multicoloured . . . 1·00 80

1041 San Martin **1042** Siku Pipes

2000. 150th Death Anniv of General Jose de San Martin.
2759 **1041** 75c. multicoloured . . . 1·00 80

2000. Argentine Culture. Multicoloured.

2760	10c. Ceremonial axe	15	10
2761	25c. Type **1042**	35	30
2762	50c. Andean loom	70	55
2763	60c. Pampeana poncho . .	80	60
2764	75c. Funeral mask	1·00	80
2765	$1 Basket	1·40	1·10
2766	$2 Kultun ritual drum . . .	2·75	2·25
2767	$3.25 Ceremonial tiger mask	4·50	3·50
2768	$5 Funeral urn	7·00	5·50
2770	$9.40 Suri ceremonial costume	13·00	10·00

1043 Sarsfield, Signature and Cordoba Province Arms

2000. Birth Bicentenary of Dalmacio Velez Sarsfield (lawyer).
2775 **1043** 75c. multicoloured . . . 1·00 80

1044 Windsurfing

2000. Olympic Games, Sydney. Multicoloured.

2776	75c. Type **1044**	1·00	80
2777	75c. Hockey	1·00	80
2778	75c. Volleyball	1·00	80
2779	75c. High jump and pole vault	1·00	80

1045 Argentine Petiso

2000. "Espana 2000" International Stamp Exhibition, Madrid. Horses. Multicoloured.

2780	25c. Type **1045**	35	30
2781	25c. Carriage horse	35	30
2782	50c. Peruvian horse	70	55
2783	50c. Criolla	70	55
2784	75c. Saddle horse	1·00	80
2785	75c. Polo horse	1·00	80

MS2786 100 × 75 mm. 25c. Stagecoach (39 × 29 mm); 75c. Horse's head (39 × 29 mm) . . 1·20 1·20

1046 Man on Bicycle and Las Nereidas Fountain

2000. Transportation. Multicoloured.

2787	25c.+25c. Type **1046**	70	55
2788	50c.+50c. *Graf Zeppelin* over Buenos Aires	1·25	1·00
2789	50c.+50c. *Ganz* (diesel locomotive)	1·40	1·10
2790	75c.+75c. Tram	2·10	1·75

1047 Nuclear Reactor

2000. 50th Anniv of National Commission for Atomic Energy.
2791 **1047** 75c. multicoloured . . . 1·00 80

1048 "Filete" (left-hand detail)

2000. Fileteado (painting genre) (Nos. 2792/3) and Tango (dance) (Nos. 2794/5). Multicoloured.

2792	75c. Type **1048**	1·00	80
2793	75c. "Filete" (right-hand detail) (Brunetti brothers)	1·00	80
2794	75c. Tango orchestra . . .	1·00	80
2795	75c. Couple dancing	1·00	80

1049 Human Bodies on Jigsaw

2000. 40th Anniv of Organ Donation Publicity Campaign.
2796 **1049** 75c. multicoloured . . . 1·00 60

1050 "Birth of Jesus" (stained glass window, Sanctuary of Our Lady of the Rosary, New Pompeii)

2000. Christmas.
2797 **1050** 75c. multicoloured . . . 1·00 60

1051 *Commelina erecta*

2000. Medicinal Plants. Multicoloured.

2798	75c. Type **1051**	1·00	60
2799	75c. *Senna corymbosa* . . .	1·00	60
2800	75c. *Mirabilis jalapa* . . .	1·00	60
2801	75c. *Eugenia uniflora* . . .	1·00	60

1052 Human-shaped Vessel, Cienaga

2000. Traditional Crafts. Multicoloured.

2802	75c. Type **1052**	1·00	60
2803	75c. Painted human-shaped vase, Vaquerias	1·00	60
2804	75c. Animal-shaped vessel, Condorhuasi	1·00	60
2805	75c. Human-shaped vase, Candelaria	1·00	60

1053 "U. P." Unidad Postal

2001. Postal Agents' Stamps. Multicoloured, background colours given. Self-adhesive gum.

2806	**1053**	10c. turquoise	15	10
2807		25c. green	35	20
2808		60c. yellow	80	45
2809		75c. red	1·00	60
2810		$1 blue	1·40	80
2811		$3 red	4·00	2·40
2812		$3.25 yellow	4·50	2·75
2813		$5.50 mauve	7·50	4·50

Nos. 2806/13 were issued for use by Postal Agents as opposed to branches of the Argentine Post Office.

1054 *Megatherium americanum* ("Megaterio")

2001. Cainozoic Mammals. Multicoloured.

2820	75c. Type **1054**	80	45
2821	75c. *Doedicurus clavcaudatus* ("Gliptodonte")	80	45
2822	75c. *Macrauchenia patachonica* ("Macrauqueria")	80	45
2823	75c. *Toxodon platensis* ("Toxodonte")	80	45

1055 Map, South Polar Skua and San Martin Base

2001. 50th Anniv of San Martín and Brown Antarctic Bases. Multicoloured.

2824	75c. Type **1055**	80	45
2825	75c. Blue-eyed cormorant, map and Brown Base . .	80	45

1056 Bees on Clover Flower

2001. Apiculture. Multicoloured.

2826	75c. Type **1056**	80	45
2827	75c. Bees on honeycomb . .	80	45
2828	75c. Bees and bee-keeper attending hives	80	45
2829	75c. Jar of honey and swizzle	80	45

Nos. 2826/9 were issued together, se-tenant, forming a composite design.

1057 Scientist with Fossilized Bones

2001. 50th Anniv of Argentine Antarctic Institute. Sheet 150 × 99 mm containing T **1057** and similar horiz design. Multicoloured.
MS2830 75c. Type **1057**; 75c. Scientist and surveying equipment 1·80 1·80

1058 Dornier Do-j Wal Flying Boat *Plus Ultra* and Route Map

2001. 75th Anniv of Major Ramon Franco's Flight from Spain to Argentina.
2831 **1058** 75c. multicoloured . . . 80 45

1059 Horse's Bridle Fittings

2001. Silver Work. Each blue, silver and black.

2832	75c. Type **1059**	80	45
2833	75c. Stirrups	80	45
2834	75c. Spurs	80	45
2835	75c. Rastra (gaucho belt decoration)	80	45

1060 "Washerwoman by the Banks of Belgrano" (detail, Prilidiano Pueyrredon)

2001. Belgica 2001 International Stamp Exhibition, Brussels. 500th Anniv of European Postal Service. Sheet 99 × 75 mm containing T **1060** and similar horiz design. Multicoloured.
MS2836 25c. Type **1060**; 75c. "Hay Harvest" (detail, Pieter Bruegel, the Elder) . . . . 1·20 1·20

1061 Goalkeeper catching Ball

2001. Under 20's World Youth Football Championship, Argentine Republic. Multicoloured.

2837	75c. Type **1061**	80	45
2838	75c. Player kicking ball . .	80	45

1062 People and Buildings

2001. National Census.
2839 **1062** 75c. multicoloured . . . 80 45

1063 SAC-C Satellite, Seagulls and Sunflowers

2001. Environmental Protection. Satellite Tracking Project.
2840 **1063** 75c. multicoloured . . . 80 45

1064 Puma

2001. Wild Cats. Multicoloured.
2841 25c. Type **1064** 35 20
2842 25c. Jaguar 35 20
2843 50c. Jaguarundi 70 50
2844 50c. Ocelot 70 50
2845 75c. Geoffroy's Cat 80 45
2846 75c. Kodkod 80 45

1065 "Bandoneon Recital" (painting, Aldo Severi)

2001.
2847 **1065** 75c. multicoloured . . . 80 45

1066 Couple dancing the Tango

2001. PHILA NIPPON 01 International Stamp Exhibition, Tokyo. Sheet 100 × 75 mm containing T **1066** and similar horiz design. Multicoloured.
MS2848 75c. Type **1066**; 75c. Kabuki performer . . . . . . 1·90 1·90

1067 Discepolo

2001. Birth Centenary of Enriques Santos Discepolo (actor and lyric writer).
2849 **1067** 75c. multicoloured . . . 80 45

1068 Courtyard, Caroya Estancia, Angel and Chapel, Estancia Santa Catalina

2001. UNESCO World Heritage Sites. Mult.
2850 75c. Type **1068** 80 45
2851 75c. Emblem and chapel, Estancia La Candelaria, dome of Estancia Alta Gracia and belfry, Estancia Jesus Maria . . 80 45

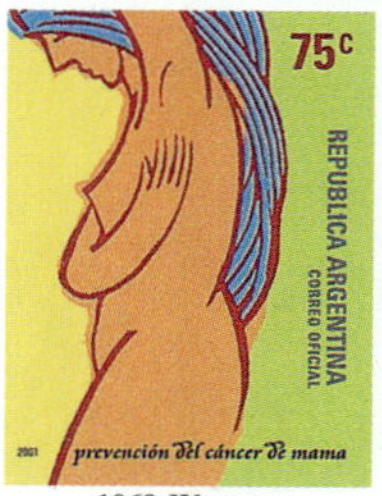

1069 Woman

2001. Breast Cancer Awareness.
2852 **1069** 75c. multicoloured . . . 80 45

1070 Burmeister's Porpoise

2001. Marine Mammals. Multicoloured.
2853 25c.+25c. Type **1070** 70 70
2854 50c.+50c. La Plata River dolphin . . . . 1·40 1·40
2855 50c.+50c. Minke whale . . . 1·40 1·40
2856 75c.+75c. Humpback whale 2·10 2·10

1071 Alfa Romeo 159 Alfetta, Spain, 1951

2001. Formula 1 Racing Cars driven by Juan Manuel Fangio. Multicoloured.
2857 75c. Type **1071** . . . . . . 1·00 60
2858 75c. Mercedes Benz W 196, France, 1954 . . . . . 1·00 60
2859 75c. Lancia-Ferrari D50, Monaco, 1956 . . . . . 1·00 60
2860 75c. Maserati 250 F, Germany, 1957 . . . . . 1·00 60

1072 Palo Santo Tree (*Bulnesia sarmientoi*)

2001. Mercosur (South American Common Market).
2861 **1072** 75c. multicoloured . . . 1·00 60

1073 Justo Jose de Urquiza

2001. Birth Anniversaries. Multicoloured.
2862 75c. Type **1073** (politician) (bicentenary) . . . . . . 1·00 60
2863 75c. Roque Saenz Pena (President 1910—14) (150th anniv) . . . . . . 1·00 60

1074 18th-century Mail Courier

2001. HAFNIA 01 International Stamp Exhibition, Copenhagen. Sheet 100 × 75 mm containing T **1074** and similar horiz design. Multicoloured.
MS2864 25c. Type **1074**; 75c. 17th-century mail courier . . . 1·20 1·20

1075 "La Pobladora" Carriage (Enrique Udaondo Graphic Museum Complex)

2001. Museums. Multicoloured.
2865 75c. Type **1075** . . . . . . 1·00 60
2866 75c. Ebony and silver crucifix (Brigadier General Juan Martin de Pueyrredon Museum) (vert) . . . . 1·00 60
2867 75c. Funerary urn (Emilio and Duncan Wagner Museum of Anthropological and Natural Sciences) (vert) 1·00 60
2868 75c. Skeleton of Carnotaurus sastrei (Argentine Natural Science Museum) . . . . 1·00 60

1076 "The Power of the Most High will Overshadow You" (Martin La Spina)

2001. Christmas.
2869 **1076** 75c. multicoloured . . . 1·00 60

1077 Carola Lorenzini and Focke Wulf 44-J

2001. Aviation. Multicoloured.
2870 75c. Type **1077** . . . . . . 1·00 60
2871 75c. Jean Mermoz and Arc-en-Ciel . . . . 1·00 60

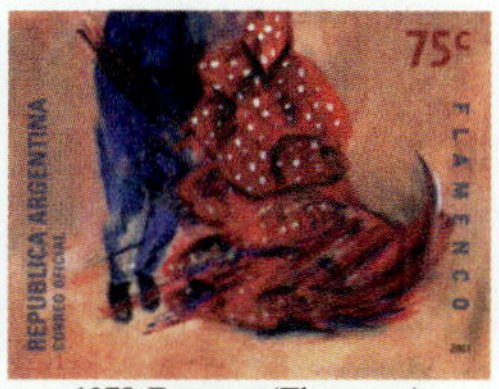

1078 Dancers (Flamenco)

2001. Dances. Multicoloured.
2872 75c. Type **1078** . . . . . . 1·00 60
2873 75c. Dancers (purple skirt) (Vals) . . . . 1·00 60
2874 75c. Dancers (orange skirt) (Zamba) . . . . 1·00 60
2875 75c. Dancers (Tango) . . . 1·00 60

1079 Scene from "Apollon Musagete" (Igor Stravinsky)

2001. National Day of the Dancer.
2876 **1079** 75c. multicoloured . . . 1·00 60

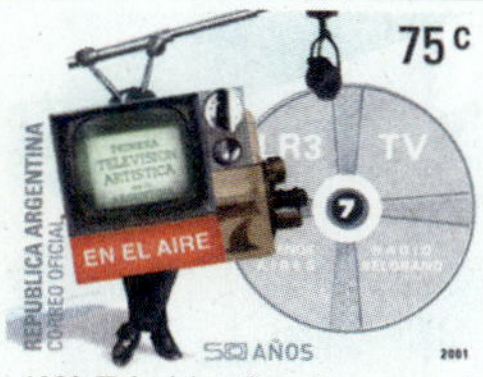

1080 Television Set, Camera and Microphone

2001. 50th Anniv of Television in Argentina. Multicoloured.
2877 75c. Type **1080** . . . . . . 1·00 60
2878 75c. Television set and video tapes . . . . 1·00 60
2879 75c. Satellite dish and astronaut . . . . 1·00 60
2880 75c. Colour television cables and remote control . . . 1·00 60

1081 Consolidated PBY-5A Catalina (amphibian) and Cancellation

2002. 50th Anniv of Argentine Antarctic Programme. Multicoloured.
2881 75c. Type **1081** (first air and sea courier service) . . . 1·00 60
2882 75c. *Chiriguano* (minesweeper) and buildings (foundation of Esparanza Base) . . . . 1·00 60

1082 House and Flag

2002. America. Education and Literacy Campaign. Multicoloured.
2883 75c. Type **1082** . . . . . . 1·00 60
2884 75c. Children playing hopscotch . . . . 1·00 60

1083 Two-banded Plover (*Charadrius falklandicus*)

2002. Birds. Multicoloured.
2885 50c. Type **1083** 70 40
2886 50c. Dolphin gull (*Larus scoresbii*) 70 40
2887 75c. Ruddy-headed goose (*Chloephaga rubidiceps*) (vert) . . . . 1·00 60
2888 75c. King penguin (*Aptenodytes patagonicus*) (vert) . . . . 1·00 60

1084 Flags of Championship Winners and Football

2002. 20th-century World Cup Football Champions. Multicoloured.
2889 75c. Type **1084** . . . . . . 1·00 60
2890 75c. Argentine footballer . . 1·00 60

1085 Parana River and Emblem

2002. Anniversaries. Multicoloured.

2891 25c. Type **1085** (150th anniv of Rosario City) 35 20
2892 25c. National flag and monument 35 20
2893 50c. Mount Fitzroy (150th birth anniv of Francisco Pascasio Moreno (Perito) (explorer and founder of Argentine Scouts movement)) 70 40
2894 50c. Dr. Moreno 70 40
2895 75c. Flower and view of city (centenary of foundation San Carlos de Bariloche) 1·00 60
2896 75c. Capilla San Eduardo (St. Edward's chapel) and city plan . . . . 1·00 60

1086 Fruit, Mother, Boy, Bread and Health Centre

2002. Centenary of Pan-American Health Organization.

2897 **1086** 75c. multicoloured . . . 90 55

1087 Cosme Mariano Argerich, 1758–1820

2002. Doctors. Multicoloured.

2898 50c. Type **1087** 55 30
2899 50c. Jose Maria Ramos Mejia, 1849–1914 . . . . 55 30
2900 50c. Salvador Mazza, 1886–1946 . . . . 55 30
2901 50c. Carlos Arturo Giananonio, 1926–1995 55 30

1088 Hill of Seven Colours, Jujuy

2002. Landscapes. Multicoloured.

2902 75c. Type **1088** 90 55
2903 75c. Iguazu waterfall, Misiones 90 55
2904 75c. Talampaya National Park 90 55
2905 75c. Agoncagua mountain, Mendoza 90 55
2906 75c. Rosedal Park, Buenos Aires 90 55
2907 75c. San Jorge lighthouse, Chubut 90 55
2908 75c. Perito Moreno glacier, Santa Cruz 90 55
2909 75c. Lapataia Bay, Tierra del Fuego 90 55

See also Nos. 2980/7 and 3022/9.

1089 Pampas Deer (*Ozotoceros bezoarticus*)

2002. Endangered Species. Multicoloured.

2910 $1 Type **1089** . . . . 1·10 65
2911 $1 Vicuna (*Vicugna vicugna*) 1·10 65
2912 $1 Southern pudu (*Pudu pudu*) . . . . 1·10 65
2913 $1 Chaco peccary (*Catgonus wagneri*) . . . . 1·10 65

1090 Eva Peron

2002. 50th Death Anniv of Eva Peron. Multicoloured.

2914 75c. Type **1090** 90 55
2915 75c. In cameo 90 55
2916 75c. At microphone 90 55
2917 75c. In profile wearing earrings 90 55

1091 Argentine Footballer

2002. Philakorea 2002 International Stamp Exhibition. Sheet 100 × 75 mm containing T **1091** and similar horiz design. Multicoloured.

MS2918 $1.50 Type **1091**; $1.50 Korean footballer . . . . . . 3·25 3·25

1092 Boa Constrictor (*Boa lampalagua*)

2002. Reptiles. Multicoloured.

2919 25c.+25c. Type **1092** 55 55
2920 50c.+50c. Caiman (*Caiman yacare*) . . . . 1·10 1·10
2921 50c.+50c. Argentine black and white tegu (*Tupinambis merianae*) . . 1·10 1·10
2922 75c.+75c. Red-footed tortoise (*Chelonoidis carbonaria*) . . . . 1·60 1·60

1093 Whale's Head

2002. Mercosur (South American Common Market). Multicoloured.

2923 75c. Type **1093** 90 55
2924 75c. Whale's tail 90 55

1094 *Edessa meditabunda*

2002. Insects. Multicoloured.

2925 25c. Type **1094** 25 10
2926 50c. *Elaeochlora viridis* . . . 55 30
2927 75c. *Chrysodina aurata* . . . 90 55
2928 75c. *Steirastoma breve* . . . 1·10 65

1095 Players, Ball and Net

2002. World Men's Volleyball Championships. Multicoloured.

2929 75c. Type **1095** 90 55
2930 75c. Two players ball and net 90 55
2931 75c. Hands, net, ball and head 90 55
2932 75c. Players congratulating one another 90 55

1096 Roadway

2002. 50th Anniv of Argentine Highways Department.

2933 **1096** 75c. multicoloured . . . 90 55

1097 Roberto Arlt

2002. Death Anniversaries. Multicoloured.

2934 75c. Type **1097** (writer, 60th) 90 55
2935 75c. Luis Sandrini (actor and director, 22nd) . . . 90 55
2936 75c. Nini Marshall (actor, 6th) 90 55
2937 75c. Beatriz Guido (writer, 14th) 90 55

1098 Immigrant Hotel, Mother and Child

2002. Immigration. Multicoloured.

2938 75c. Type **1098** 90 55
2939 75c. Two men and ship . . 90 55
2940 75c. Two men and immigrant hotel 90 55
2941 75c. Horse-drawn farm implement and family . . 90 55

Nos. 2938/41 were issued in horizontal se-tenant strips of four stamps within the sheet, each pair (2938/9 and 2940/1) forming a composite design.

1099 Envelope, Horse-drawn Coach and Head

2002. 50th Anniv of Argentine Federation of Philatelic Entities (FAEF). Multicoloured.

2942 75c. Type **1099** . . . . . .
2943 75c. Flag, figure, ship and arms 90 55

1100 Joseph leading Donkey carrying Mary and Jesus

2002. Christmas.

2944 **1100** 75c. multicoloured . . . 90 55

1101 Andres Chazarreta (composer)

2002. Folklorists. Multicoloured.

2945 75c. Type **1101** 90 55
2946 75c. Gustavo "Cuchi" Leguizamon (songwriter) 90 55
2947 75c. Carlos Vega (guitarist) 90 55
2948 75c. Armando Tejada Gomez (poet and songwriter) 90 55

1102 Girl (rod puppet)

2002. Puppets. Multicoloured.

2949 75c. Type **1102** 90 55
2950 75c. Fish and king (marionettes) 90 55
2951 75c. Man (marote puppet) 90 55
2952 75c. Figures (shadow puppets) 90 55

1103 Cabbage containing Hands

2003. "Pro Huerta" (communal gardens initiative). Multicoloured.

2953 75c. Type **1103** 95 55
2954 75c. Street map as corn cob (vert) 95 55

1104 Woven Bag and Band

2003. Mercosur (South American Common Market). Multicoloured.

2955 75c. Type **1104** (Pilaga and Toba people, Formosa province) 95 55
2956 75c. Basketwork sieve (Mbya people, Misiones province) and wooden servers (Wichi people, Salta province) 95 55

1105 Squirrel Cuckoo (*Piaya cayana*) (Colonia Benitez reserve) (⅔-size illustration)

2003. National Parks. Multicoloured.

2957 50c. Type **1105** 50 30
2958 50c. Grey brocket (*Mazama gouzoupira*) (Copo park) 50 30

2959 50c. Guanaco (*Lama guanicoe*) (Los Cardones) . . 50 30
2960 75c. Magellanic penguin (*Speniscus magellanicus*) (Monte Leon) 95 55
2961 75c. *Tinamotis pentlandii* (Campo de los Alisos) . . 95 55

1106 "Composition with Rag Grid" (Kenneth Kemble)

2003. Art. Multicoloured.
2962 25c. Type **1106** 30 15
2963 25c. "Painting" (Roberto Aizenberg) (vert) 35 15
2964 50c. "Screen" (Romulo Maccio) (vert) 60 35
2965 75c. "La Gioconda" (Guillemo Roux) 95 55
2966 75c. "To Flee" (Antonio Segui) 95 55
2967 $1 "San P." (Xul Solar) (vert) . . . . 1·20 70

1107 Hockey Player

2003. Sport. Multicoloured.
2968 75c. Type **1107** (Women's Hockey World Champions, 2002) 95 55
2969 75c. Footballer (World Blind Football Champions, 2002) 95 55
No. 2969 was embossed with the face value in Braille.

1108 Mago Fafa (Broccoli)

2003. Cartoons. Sheet 156 × 120 mm containing T **1108** and similar vert designs. Multicoloured.
MS2970 25c. Type **1108**; 25c. Astronauta (Crist); 50c. Hijitus (Garcia Ferre); 50c. Savarese (Mandrafina and Robin Wood); 75c. Sonoman (Oswal); 75c. El Tipito (Daniel Paz and Rudy); 75c. La Vaca Aurora (Mirco); 75c. Diogenes y el Linyera (Tabare) 4·25 4·25

1109 19th-century Soup Tureen

2003. Silver Work. Multicoloured.
2971 75c. Type **1109** 95 55
2972 75c. Kettle, *mate de campana* and drinking tube 95 55
2973 75c. Chocolate pot and jug 95 55
2974 75c. 19th-century sugar bowl 95 55
Nos. 2971/4 were issued together, se-tenant, forming a composite design.

1110 Empanadas

2003. Traditional Foods. Multicoloured.
2975 75c. Type **1110** (turnovers) 95 55
2976 75c. Locro (corn and bean stew) 95 55
2977 75c. Parillada (mixed grill) 95 55
2978 75c. Pastilitos (miniature pastries) 95 55

1111 El Elastico (elastic)

2003. Children's Games. Sheet 108 × 88 mm containing T **1111** and similar horiz designs. Multicoloured.
MS2979 50c. × 4 Type **1111**; La escondida (hide and seek); La mancha (tag); Martin pescador (Martin the fisherman) . . . . 2·50 2·50

2003. Landscapes. As T **1088**. Multicoloured.
2980 75c. Mbigua marsh, Formosa 95 55
2981 75c. Dead Man's salt flat, Catamarca 95 55
2982 75c. Quilmes ruins, Tucuman 95 55
2983 75c. Ibera marshland, Corrientes 95 55
2984 75c. Moon Valley, Ischigualasto park, San Juan 95 55
2985 75c. Mar del Plata city, Buenos Aires 95 55
2986 75c. Caleu Caleu, La Pampa 95 55
2987 75c. Lanin National Park, Neuqueen 95 55

1112 Velocipede (1855) (⅔-size illustration)

2003. Evolution of the Bicycle. Multicoloured.
2988 25c.+25c. Type **1112** 60 60
2989 50c.+50c. Penny farthing (1867) . . . . 1·20 1·20
2990 50c.+50c. Touring bicycle 1·20 1·20
2991 75c.+75c. Racing bicycle . . 1·90 1·90

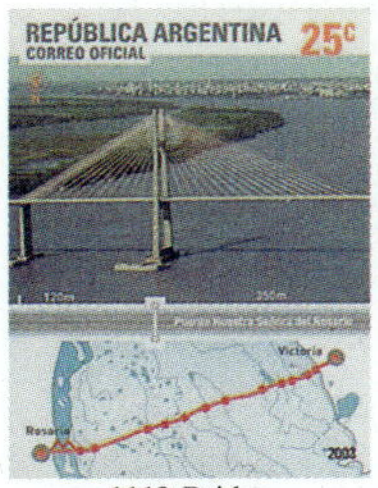

1113 Bridge

2003. Inauguration of Nuestra Senora de Rosario Bridge over Parana River. Multicoloured.
2992 25c. Type **1113** 30 15
2993 75c. Ship and bridge 95 55
Nos. 2992/3 were issued together, se-tenant, forming a composite design of the bridge.

1114 Provincial Emblem

2003. Rio Negro Province.
2994 **1114** 75c. multicoloured . . . 95 55

1115 Dr. Vicente Fidel Lopez

2003. Anniversaries. Multicoloured.
2995 75c. Type **1115** (politician) (death centenary) 95 55
2996 75c. General San Martin Regiment (centenary of modern regiment) 95 55
2997 75c. Script and Bautista Alberdi (constitutional pioneer) (150th anniv of constitution) 95 55
2998 75c. Presidential palace and symbols of office 95 55

1116 Demon Mask

2003. Bangkok 2003 International Stamp Exhibition. Sheet 150 × 100 mm containing T **1116** and similar vert design. Multicoloured.
MS2999 75c. × 2 Type **1116** (Quebrada de Humahuaca carnival, Argentine); Spirit mask (Phi Ta Khon festival, Thailand) 1·90 1·90

1117 Andean Condor (*Vultur gryphus*)

2003. America. Flora and Fauna. Multicoloured.
3000 75c. Type **1117** 95 55
3001 75c. *Nothofagus pumilio* (tree), forest and mountains 95 55

1118 Map, Laboratory and Tres Hermanos Mountain

2003. 50th Anniv of Jubany Antarctic Base.
3002 **1118** 75c. multicoloured . . . 95 55

1119 Cattle

2003. National Products. Multicoloured.
3003 75c. Type **1119** (livestock) 95 55
3004 75c. Soya beans (agriculture) 95 55
3005 75c. Telecobalt therapy machines (nuclear medicine) 95 55
3006 75c. Drums and bars (aluminium production) 95 55

1120 Corvette *Uruguay*

2003. Centenary of Rescue of Swedish Scientists by Argentine Corvette *Uruguay*. Multicoloured.
3007 75c. Type **1120** 95 55
MS3008 150 × 99 mm. 75c. × 2 Swedish ship (40 × 30 mm); Captain Julian Irizar and *Uruguay* (40 × 30 mm) . . . . 1·90 1·90

1121 The Nativity (clay figures)

2003. Christmas. Multicoloured.
3009 75c. Type **1121** 95 55
3010 75c. "Guacho Birth" (wooden carving) (Eloy Lopez) 95 55

1122 Savings Bank Building, Cordoba

2003. 20th-Century Architecture. Multicoloured.
3011 75c. Type **1122** 95 55
3012 75c. Bank, San Miguel de Tucuman 95 55
3013 75c. Minetti Palace, Rosario 95 55
3014 75c. Barolo Palace, Buenos Aires 95 55

1123 Helicopter over Orcados Base

2004. Centenary of Orcados Base and Orcados del Sud Post Office, Antarctica. Multicoloured.
3015 75c. Type **1123** 95 55
MS3016 150 × 100 mm. 75c. × 2, 5 cent 1904 stamp and "Orcados del Sud" 1904 postmark; Orcados meteorological observatory, 1904 1·90 1·90

1124 Llama, Cave Painting, Painted Door and Rio Grande Valley

2004. UNESCO World Heritage Site. Quebrada de Humahuaca. Multicoloured.
3017 75c. Type **1124** 95 55
3018 75c. Church, festival procession and valley . . 95 55
Nos. 3017/18 were issued together, se-tenant, forming a composite design.

1125 Green Forest

2004. America. Endangered Species. Destruction of the Rainforest. Multicoloured.
3019 75c. Type **1125** 95 55
3020 75c. Dying forest 95 55
Nos. 3019/20 were issued together, se-tenant, forming a composite design.
The centre of No. 3020 has been removed to simulate burning.

1126 Masthead of First Edition and Modern Copy

2004. Centenary of "La Voz del Interior" Newspaper.
3021 **1126** 75c. multicoloured . . . 95 55

2004. Landscapes. As T **1088**. Multicoloured.
3022 75c. Drying peppers, Molinas, Salta 95 55
3023 75c. Man leading donkey, Pampa del Indio Park, Chaco 95 55
3024 75c. Dam on Rio Dulce river, Rio Hondo, Santiago del Estero . . . 95 55
3025 75c. Bridge over Setubal lagoon, Santa Fe de la Vera Cruz 95 55
3026 75c. San Roque lake, Cordoba 95 55
3027 75c. Palm Grove National Park, Entre Rios 95 55
3028 75c. Potero de los Funes, San Luis 95 55
3029 75c. Tronador mountain, Rio Negro 95 55

1127 Street Football

2004. Centenary of FIFA (Federation Internationale de Football Association). Paintings by Ruben Ramonda. Multicoloured.
3030 75c. Type **1127** 95 55
3031 75c. The Tunnel 95 55

1128 "Back from Fishing" (Joaquin Sorolla y Bastida)

2004. Espana 2004 International Stamp Exhibition, Valencia. Sheet 150 × 100 mm containing T **1128** and similar multicoloured design.
MS3032 75c. Type **1128**; 75c. "At Rest in the Pampa" (Angel Della Valle) (vert) . . . . 1·90 1·90

1129 Compass in Case

2004. 125th Anniv of Naval Hydro-Graphic Service. Multicoloured.
3033 75c. Type **1129** 95 55
3034 75c. Sextant 95 55
3035 75c. Cabo Virgenes lighthouse 95 55
3036 75c. *Puerto Deseado* (hydro-graphic ship) 95 55

1130 Performing Dogs

2004. Circus. Sheet 109 × 88 mm containing T **1130** and similar horiz designs. Multicoloured.
MS3037 50c. Type **1130**; 50c. Trapeze artiste; 50c. Clown riding unicycle; 50c. Equestrienne . . 2·50 2·50
The stamps of No. **MS**3037 form a composite design of a circus ring.

1131 Isidorito

2004. *Patorutzito* (character from graphic magazine by Dante Quinterno). Designs showing characters. Multicoloured.
3038 75c. Patoruzito (20 × 60 mm) 95 55
3039 75c. Pamperito (20 × 60 mm) 95 55
3040 75c. Isidorito (30 × 29 mm) 95 55
3041 75c. Malen 95 55
3042 75c. Upita 95 55
3043 75c. Chacha 95 55
MS3044 167 × 118 mm. 25c. Type **1131**; 25c. Upita (different); 50c. Patoruzito; 50c. Malen (different); 75c. Pamperito; 75c. Chacha plus 2 stamp size labels 3·75 3·75
The stamps and labels contained in **MS**3044 form a composite design.

1132 Woman and Guide Dog

2004. Working Dogs. Multicoloured.
3045 75c. Type **1132** 95 55
3046 75c. Rescue dog (horiz) . . 95 55

1133 *Patagonotothen ramsay*

2004. Endangered Species. Fish. Multicoloured.
3047 75c. Type **1133** 95 55
3048 75c. *Bathyraja griseocauda* 95 55
3049 75c. *Salilota australis* . . . 95 55
3050 75c. *Dissostichus eleginoides* 95 55

1134 Cycling

2004. Olympic Games, Athens 2004. Multicoloured.
3051 75c. Type **1134** 95 55
3052 75c. Judo 95 55
3053 75c. Swimming 95 55
3054 75c. Tennis 95 55

1135 *Villarino*

2004. Naval Carriers. Multicoloured.
3055 25c.+25c. Type **1135** 30 30
3056 50c.+50c. *Pampa* 60 60
3057 50c.+50c. *Bahia Thetis* . . . 60 60
3058 75c.+75c. *Cabo de Hornis* 1·90 1·90
Nos. 3055/8 were issued together, se-tenant, forming a composite design.

1136 Queen Palm Fruit (*Syagrus romanzoffiana*)

2004. Singapore 2004 International Stamp Exhibition. Fruit. Sheet 150 × 100 mm containing T **1136** and similar vert designs.
MS3059 75c. × 2, Type **1136**; Mango 1·90 1·90

1137 El Pehuen

2004. Legends and Traditions. Multicoloured.
3060 75c. Type **1137** (legend of araucaria tree) 95 55
3061 75c. La Yacumama (Diaguita water goddess) 95 55
3062 75c. La Pachamama (earth goddess) 95 55
3063 75c. La Difunta Correa (legend of mother who died of thirst) 95 55

1138 Early Students and Microscope

2004. Centenaries. Multicoloured.
3064 75c. Type **1138** (Agronomy and Veterinary Science Institute) 95 55
3065 75c. Jose san Martin (statue) and road and rail bridges over Nequen river (Neuqin city) 95 55
3066 75c. Monument and cover of "La Coleccionista" (Rosario Philatelic Association) 95 55

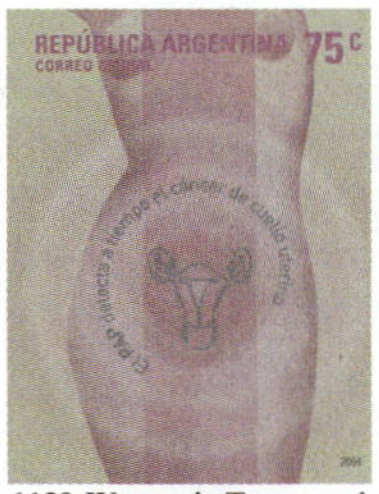

1139 Woman's Torso and Campaign Emblem

2004. Cervical Cancer Awareness Campaign.
3067 **1139** 75c. multicoloured . . . 95 55

1140 Hourglass containing Clear Water

2004. Mercosur. Water Conservation Campaign. Multicoloured.
3068 75c. Type **1140** 95 55
3069 75c. Hourglass containing contaminated water . . . 95 55

1141 Mary

2004. Christmas. Multicoloured.
3070 75c. Type **1141** 95 55
3071 75c. The Nativity 95 55

1142 Reverse

2004. 1813 One Ounce Gold Coin. Multicoloured.
3072 75c. Type **1142** 95 55
3073 75c. Obverse 95 55
Nos. 3072/3 were issued together, se-tenant, forming a composite design.

1143 "Spanish Grammar for Americans" and Andres Bello (author)

2004. 3rd International Spanish Language Congress.
3074 **1143** 75c. multicoloured . . . 95 55

1144 Exchange Building

2004. 150th Anniv of Buenos Aires Commodities Exchange.
3075 **1144** 75c. multicoloured . . . 95 55

1145 "Aloysia citriodora"

2004. Aromatic Plants. Multicoloured.
3076 75c. Type **1145** 95 55
3077 75c. "Minthostachys mollis" 95 55
3078 75c. "Tagetes minuta" . . . 95 55
3079 75c. "Lippia turbinate" . . 95 55

1146 Emblem and Scout

2005. 12th Pan American Scout Jamboree, Mendoza.
3080 **1146** 75c. multicoloured . . . 95 55

1147 Ram Klong Yao Dance (Thailand)

2005. 50th Anniv of Thailand—Argentina Diplomatic Relations. Multicoloured.

3081	75c. Type **1147**	95	55
3082	75c. Tango (Argentina)	95	55

1148 "Woman in Red Sweater"

2005. Birth Centenary of Alberto Berni (artist). Details from painting. Multicoloured.

3083	75c. Type **1148**	95	55
MS3084	150 × 99 mm. 75c. × 2 Face (detail); Baby and men wearing hats (detail) (horiz)	1·90	1·90

The stamps and margin of No. **MS**3084 form a composite design of "Manifestation".

1149 Rotary International Emblem, Children and Vaccine

2005. Centenary of Rotary International (charitable organization). Eradication of Polio Campaign.

3085	**1149**	75c. multicoloured	95	55

1150 Silvina Ocampo

2005. Mercosaur. Writers. Multicoloured.

3086	75c. Type **1150** (1903–1993)	95	55
3087	75c. Ezequiel Martinez Estrada (1895–1964)	95	55

1151 Sedan Graciela

2005. National Motor Industry. Multicoloured.

3088	75c. Type **1151**	95	55
3089	75c. Justicalista sport	95	55
3090	75c. Rastrojero diesel	95	55
3091	75c. Siam di Tella 1500	95	55
3092	75c. Torino 380W	95	55

1152 Jose Antonio Balseiro (founder) and Nuclear Reactor

2005. 50th Anniv of Balseiro Institute. International Year of Physics. Multicoloured.

3093	75c. Type **1152**	95	55
3094	75c. Albert Einstein and frontispiece of *Theory of Special Relativity*	95	55

1153 Pope John Paul II

2005. Pope John Paul II Commemoration. Multicoloured.

3095	75c. Type **1153**	95	55
MS3096	150 × 99 mm. 75c. × 2, (each 40 × 50 mm) Wearing mitre and carrying pastoral staff; Saying farewell	1·90	1·90

1154 Workers at Machines and Demonstrators

2005. Anniversaries. Multicoloured.

3097	75c. Type **1154** (75th anniv of Workers Confederation)	95	55
3098	75c. Mar del Plata and *La Capital* (centenary of *La Capital* newspaper)	95	55
3099	75c. Alfredo Palacios (centenary of Sunday blue law)	95	55

1155 Cesar Milstein

2005. Cesar Milstein (Nobel Prize for Medicine, 1984) Commemoration.

3100	**1155**	75c. multicoloured	95	55

1156 Orestes Liberti (1st Commander) and Horse-drawn Fire Engine

2005. Volunteer Fire Fighters. Multicoloured.

3101	75c. Type **1156**	95	55
3102	75c. Fighting fire and modern engine	95	55

1157 Early and Modern Red Cross Workers

2005. 125th Anniv of Argentine Red Cross Society.

3103	**1157**	75c. multicoloured	95	55

1158 Abyssinian

2005. Cats. Sheet 117 × 166 mm containing T **1158** and similar horiz designs. Multicoloured.

MS3104	25c. Birman; 25c. Siamese; 50c. Oriental shorthair; 50c. Persian; 75c. Type **1158**; 75c. European shorthair	3·75	3·75

1159 Juan Filloy

2005. 5th Death Anniv of Juan Filloy (writer).

3105	**1159**	75c. multicoloured	95	55

1160 Malbec (⅔-size illustration)

2005. Tourism. Wine. Multicoloured.

3106	75c. Type **1160** (Mendoza, Tupungato Valley)	95	55
3107	75c. Merlot (Rio Negro, Alto Valle de Rio Negro)	95	55
3108	75c. Syrah (San Juan - Zonda Valley)	95	55
3109	75c. Torrontes (Salta - Cafayate, Calchaquies Valleys)	95	55

See also Nos. 3202/4.

1161 Our Lady of the Rosary Candonga Chapel, Sierras Chicas, Cordoba

2005. Places of Worship. Multicoloured.

3110	75c. Type **1161**	95	55
3111	75c. Al Ahmad Mosque, Buenos Aires	95	55
3112	75c. Israelite Congregation of Argentine Temple, Buenos Aires	95	55
3113	75c. Vision of the Middle Buddhist Temple, Buenos Aires	95	55

1162 Pulperia Perucho, Gral, Lavalle, Mendoza

2005. Stores (Pulperias). Multicoloured.

3114	75c. Type **1162**	95	55
3115	75c. El Torito, Baradero, Buenos Aires	95	55
3116	75c. Impini, Larroque, Entre Rios	95	55
3117	75c. Pulperia de Cacho di Catarina	95	55

1163 *Rio De la Plata* (merchant vessel) (⅔-size illustration)

2005. Ships. Multicoloured.

3118	25c.+25c. Type **1163**	60	40
3119	50c.+50c. *Libertad* (passenger ship)	1·20	80
3120	50c.+50c. *Camopo Duran* (tanker)	1·20	80
3121	75c.+75c. *Isla Soledad* (container ship)	1·90	1·10

Nos. 3118/21 were issued together, se-tenant, forming a composite design.

1164 Julio Bocca (dancer)

2005. Colon Theatre. Multicoloured.

3122	75c. Type **1164**	95	55
3123	75c. Theatre orchestra, opera singers and choir	95	55

1165 Ice Flow

2005. 1st Anniv of Antarctic Treaty Secretariat, Buenos Aires (3124). General Hernan Pujato's Expeditions to Antarctica (**MS**3125). Mult.

3124	75c. Type **1165**	95	55
MS3125	150 × 100 mm. 75c. × 2, Divers and boat; General Pujato and team members	1·90	1·90

1166 Virgin and Child (detail)

2005. Christmas. Showing parts of the painting "Retablo" by Elena Strorni. Multicoloured.

3126	75c. Type **1166**	95	55
MS3127	150 × 100 mm. 75c. × 4, The Annunciation (40 × 40 mm); The Nativity (40 × 40 mm); Three Wise Men (40 × 40 mm); Presenting Jesus in the temple (40 × 40 mm)	4·00	4·00

1167 Solar Panel and Light Bulb

2005. Alternative Energy. Multicoloured.

3128	75c. Type **1167**	95	55
3129	$4 Wind generators	5·00	3·00

1168 Mar de Plata Port and Summit Emblem

2005. 4th Americas' Summit.

3130	**1168**	75c. multicoloured	95	55

1169 German Immigrants, Canada de Gomez, Santa Fe

2005. Immigration. Multicoloured.
3131 75c. Type **1169** 95 55
3132 75c. Slovakian women and children, Immigrant Hotel, Buenos Aires 95 55
3133 75c. Welsh immigrants, Chubut Central Railway, Trelew 95 55
3134 75c. Jewish colony, Moises Ville, Santa Fe 95 55

1170 Luis Angel Firpo

2005. Sport. Boxers. Multicoloured.
3135 75c. Type **1170** 95 55
3136 75c. Nicolino Locche 95 55

1171 Man (film, "Ivan & Eva")

2005. Design. Multicoloured.
3137 75c. Type **1171** 95 55
3138 75c. Dress (Nadine Zlotogora) (clothes and textile) (vert) 95 55
3139 75c. Aluminium chair (Ricardo Blanco) (industrial design) (vert) 95 55
3140 75c. CD case (Claudia Smith) (graphic design) 95 55

1172 Bartolme Mitre

2006. Death Centenary of Bartolme Mitre (journalist and president 1862–8).
3141 **1172** 75c. multicoloured 60 30

1173 Snow-covered City

2006. Centenary of Esquel.
3142 **1173** 75c. multicoloured 60 30

1175 Ramon Carrillo

1176 Guitar

2006. Birth Centenary of Ramon Carrillo (health care specialist).
3151 **1175** 75c. multicoloured 60 30

2006. Mercosur. Musical Instruments. Mult.
3152 75c. Type **1176** 60 30
3153 $3.50 Drum 2·10 1·10

1177 1 de Mayo Lighthouse

2006. Lighthouses. Multicoloured.
3154 75c. Type **1177** 60 30
3155 75c. Ano Nuevo 60 30
3156 75c. El Rincon 60 30
3157 75c. Recalada a Bahia Blanca 60 30

1178 Escuela de Mecanica de la Armada (concentration camp) (1976)

2006. "From Horror to Hope". 30th Anniv of Military Dictatorship. Sheet 151 × 99 mm containing T **1178** and similar vert design. Multicoloured.
MS3158 75c. × 2, Type **1178**; Escuela de Mecanica de la Armada (memorial museum) (2006) 1·20 1·20

1179 Crown

2006. 18th-century Religious Silverware. Multicoloured.
3159 75c. Type **1179** 60 30
3160 75c. Candelabra 60 30
3161 75c. Chalice 60 30
3162 75c. Viaticum 60 30

1180 Toyota Corolla WRC (Luis Perez Companc—Rally Nacional A8 category)

2006. National Motor Racing Champions. Multicoloured.
3163 75c. Type **1180** 60 30
3164 75c. Ford Falcon (Juan Manuel Silva—Turismo Carretera category) 60 30
3165 75c. Ford Focus (Gabriel Ponce de Leon—Turismo Competición 2000 category) 60 30
3166 75c. Ford Escort (Patricio di Palma—Class 3 Nacional category) 60 30

1181 Springer Spaniel

2006. Dogs. Sheet 117 × 166 mm containing T **1181** and similar horiz designs. Multicoloured.
MS3167 25c. Type **1181**; 25c. Yorkshire terrier; 50c. Argentine dogo (Argentinian mastiff); 50c. Miniature schnauzer; 75c. Poodle; 75c. Chow 2·75 2·75
No. **MS**3167 also contains two illustrated stamp size labels forming a composite design.

2006. World Cup Football Championship, Germany. Multicoloured.
3172 $4 Football in net 2·40 1·20
Type **1182**, Nos. 3168/71 and **MS**3173 have been left, not yet received.

1183 Knotted Cigarette (½-size illustration)

2006. World Health Organization No Tobacco Day.
3174 **1183** 75c. multicoloured 60 30

1184 Lizard Outline and Dead Tree

1185 Mauricio Borensztein (Tato Bores) (actor)

2006. International Year of Deserts and Desertification. Multicoloured.
3175 75c. Type **1184** 60 30
3176 75c. *Lilotaemus* (lizard) and *Calycera crassifolia* 60 30

2006. Personalities. Multicoloured.
3177 75c. Type **1185** 60 30
3178 75c. Rodolfo Walsh (journalist) 60 30

1186 Alpine Skiing

2006. Winter Sports. Multicoloured.
3179 75c. Type **1186** 60 30
3180 75c. Snowboarding 60 30
3181 75c. Cross-country skiing 60 30
3182 75c. Biathlon 60 30

1187 Musician

2006. Tango. Multicoloured.
3183 75c. Type **1187** 60 30
3184 $4 Dancers 2·40 1·20
Stamps of a similar design were issued by France.

1188 Patoruzito riding Pamperito

2006. Patoruzito (character from graphic magazine by Dante Quinterno). Opening of "Patoruzito—La Gran Adventura" (film).
3185 **1188** 75c. multicoloured 60 30

1189 Taruca (*Hippocamelus antisensis*) (½-size illustration)

2006. Natural Monuments. Multicoloured.
3186 75c. Type **1189** 60 30
3187 75c. Southern right whale (*Eubaluena australis*) 60 30
3188 75c. Huemul (*Hippocamelus bisculus*) 60 30
3189 75c. Jaguar (*Panthera onca*) 60 30

1190 House as Money Box and Plug connected to Sun (Florencia Tovi)

2006. America. Energy Conservation. Winning Designs in Children's Drawing Competition. Multicoloured.
3190 75c. Type **1190** 60 30
3191 75c. Window, table and standard lamp (Camila Suarez) 60 30

1191 "The Re-conquest of Buenos Aires" (Charles Fouqueray)

2006. Bicentenary of British Invasion and Defeat. Sheet 99 × 75 mm.
MS3192 **1191** 1p.50 multicoloured 1·00 1·00

1192 Flags as Ribbons

2006. 30th Council of the Common Market. Mercosur and Associate States' Presidents' Summit.
3193 **1192** 3p.50 multicoloured 2·25 1·10

1193 Ciudad de Buenos Aires (½-size illustration)

2006. River Transport. Multicoloured.
3194 25c.+25c. Type **1193** 35 20
3195 50c.+50c. Lambare 65 35
3196 50c.+50c. Madrid 65 35
3197 75c.+75c. Rawson 1·00 50

1194 "150 Anos"

2006. 150th Anniv of First Argentine Stamp. Multicoloured.
3198 75c. Type **1194** 60 30
MS3199 151 × 99 mm. $1.50 As Type **3** (1856 1 real stamp) (40 × 40 mm) 1·00 1·00

1195 Colorado River Basin

1196 Legion de Patricios Rifleman (1806–9)

2006. 30th Anniv of Comite Interjurisdiccional de Rio Colorado (COIRCO) (inter-jurisdictional committee on the Colorado river).
3200 **1195** 75c. multicoloured 60 30

2006. Bicentenary of Infantry Corps "Patricios".
3201 **1196** 75c. multicoloured 60 30

2006. Tourism. Wine. As T **1160**. Multicoloured.
3202 75c. Syrah (Catamarcaungato Valley) 60 30
3203 75c. Torrontes Riojano (La Rioja) 60 30
3204 75c. Pinot noir (Neuquen) 60 30

1197 Cadets

2006. Centenary of Ramon L. Falcon Cadet School.
3205 **1197** 75c. multicoloured . . . 60 30

1198 Puente San Roque Gonzalez de Santa Cruz, between Argentina and Paraguay (⅔-size illustration)

2006. International Bridges in Argentina. Multicoloured.
3206 75c. Type **1198** 60 30
3207 75c. Puente Presidente Tancredo Neves, between Argentina and Brazil . . 60 30

1199 "Madona y Paloma"

2006. Christmas. Paintings by Alfredo Guttero. Multicoloured.
3208 75c. Type **1199** 60 30
3209 75c. "Anunciacion" (horiz) 60 30

1200 Research Activities

2006. National Institute of Farming Technology.
3210 **1200** 75c. multicoloured . . . 60 30

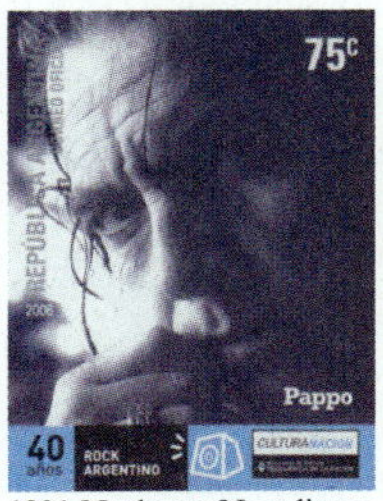

1201 Norberto Napolitano (Pappo)

2006. 40th Anniv of Argentinean Rock Music. Multicoloured.
3211 75c. Type **1201** 60 30
3212 75c. Luca George (Luca) Prodan 60 30
3213 75c. Miguel Angel Peralta (Miguel Abuelo) 60 30
3214 75c. Jose Alberto Iglesias (Tanguito) 60 30

1202 Valentin Sayhueque

2006. Caciques (tribal chiefs). Multicoloured.
3215 75c. Type **1202** (Huilliche people) 60 30
3216 75c. Casimiro Bigua (Tehuelche people) . . . 60 30

1203 *Hercules* (detail from painting *Combate de Marin Garcia* by Emilio Biggeri)

2007. 150th Death Anniv of Admiral William Brown.
3217 **1203** 75c. multicoloured . . . 60 30

1204 Grapes (Neuquen)

2007. Tourism. Wine. Multicoloured.
3218 75c. Type **1204** 60 30
3219 75c. Grapes (Catamarca) . . 60 30
3220 75c. Grapes (La Rioja) . . . 60 30
3221 3p.25 Bottle (Neuquen) . . 2·25 1·40
3222 3p.25 Bottle (Catamarca) . . 2·25 1·40
3223 3p.25 Bottle (La Rioja) . . 2·25 1·40

1205 1982 18 pesos Stamp and Ofincina Radiopostal Islas Malvinas Postmark

2007. 25th Anniv of South Atlantic Conflict. Multicoloured.
3224 75c. Type **1205** 60 30
3225 75c. IAI Dagger Fighter aircraft 60 30
3226 75c. Battle Cruiser *General Belgrano* 60 30
3227 75c. Decorated veteran . . . 60 30
3228 75c. Decoration awarded to all veterans (*vert*) 60 30

1206 Postal Workers (detail from painting by Jose Murcia)

2007. 50th Anniv of Postal and Telecommunications Workers Federation (FOECYT).
3229 **1206** 75c. multicoloured . . . 60 30

1207 *Phalacrocorax atriceps* (Imperial or blue-eyed cormorant)

2007. Argentina in Antarctica. Multicoloured.
3230 75c. Type **1207** 60 30
3231 75c. *Leptonychotes weddellii* (Weddell seal) 60 30
3232 75c. *Sterna vittata* (Antarctic tern) 60 30
3233 75c. *Sterna vittata* (Antarctic tern) 60 30
3234 75c. *Pysoscelis adeliae* (Adelie penguin) 60 30
3235 75c. *Chionis alba* (snowy or yellow-billed sheathbill) 60 30
3236 75c. *Pygoscelis papua* (gentoo penguins) 60 30
3237 75c. *Pygoscelis papua* (gentoo penguins) 60 30
3238 4p. *Almirante Irizar* (ice breaker) . . . . 2·60 1·60

Nos. 3232/3 and 3236/7 were issued together, se-tenant, forming a composite design.

1208 Latin American Art Museum, Buenos Aires

2007. Architecture. Multicoloured.
3239 75c. Type **1208** 60 30
3240 3p.25. High Mountain Archaeological Museum, Salta . . . . 2·25 1·40

1209 Rocking Horse

2007. Toys. Multicoloured.
3241 75c. Type **1209** 60 30
3242 75c. Tea set 60 30
3243 75c. Train set 60 30
3244 75c. Soldiers 60 30

1210 Emblem

2007. National Road Safety Campaign.
3245 **1210** 75c. red and silver . . . 60 30

1211 Argentine Bases

2007. International Polar Year. Sheet 150 × 98 mm.
MS3246 **1211** 4p. multicoloured 2·60 1·60

1212 *Combate de Santo Domingo* (Eleodora Marenco)

2007. Bicentenary of Defence of Buenos Aires.
3247 **1212** 75c. multicoloured . . . 60 30

1213 Radiation and Fluorescence Detectors

2007. Pierre Auger Observatory.
3248 **1213** 75c. multicoloured . . . 60 30

1214 St. Jose de Calasanz and Pupils (stained glass window, San Jose de Calasanz Church, Buenos Aires)

2007. 450th Birth Anniv of Jose de Calasanz (founder of first free school in modern Europe).
3249 **1214** 1p. multicoloured . . . 60 30

1215 Campfire

2007. Centenary of Scouting. Multicoloured.
3250 25c.+25c. Type **1215** 35 20
3251 50c.+50c. Tent and scout saluting 65 35
3252 75c.+75c. Scout wearing pack . . . . 1·00 50
3253 1p.+1p. Scouts pulling guy rope . . . . 1·30 70

Nos. 3250/3 were issued together, se-tenant, forming a composite design.

1216 *El Chaco* (meteorite) (Illustration reduced. Actual size 60 × 40 mm)

2007. Meteorites of Campo Del Cielo. Sheet 148 × 99 mm.
MS3254 **1216** 6p. multicoloured 4·00 4·00

1217 *Homero Manzi* (Hermenegildo Sabat)

2007. Birth Centenary of Homero Nicolas Manzione Prestera (Homero Manzi) (lyricist).
3255 **1217** 1p. multicoloured . . . 65 35

1218 Road leading to S. C. de Bariloche (Rio Negro)

2007. Tourism. National Route 40. Sheet 496 × 99 mm containing T **1218** and similar horiz designs. Multicoloured.
MS3256 50c. Type **1218**; 50c. Abra El Acay (40 × 30 mm); 1p. Road to Perito Moreno (Santa Cruz) (70 × 30 mm); 1p. *La Trochita* locomotive (Chubut) (40 × 30 mm); 1p. Lanin volcano (Neuquen) (40 × 30 mm), 1p. Rio Grande (Mendoza) (50 × 30 mm); 1p. Goats, San Jose Jachal (San Juan) (40 × 30 mm); 1p. Cuesta de Miranda (La Rioja) (50 × 30 mm); 1p. Capel Nuestra Senora del Transito (Catamarca); 1p. Ruins of Quilmes (Tucuman); 1p. Road leading to Oratorio (Jujuy) (40 × 30 mm) . . . . 6·00 6·00

1219 Houses with Blocked and Free-flowing Chimneys (Julieta Saavedra Barrgan)

2007. Carbon Monoxide Inhalation Prevention Campaign. Winning Designs in Children's Drawing Competition. Multicoloured.
3257 1p. Type **1219** 65 35
3258 1p. Dirty and clean flames (Efrain Osvaldo Rost) (vert) 65 35
3259 1p. Engineer and gas cooker (Camila Micaela Alvarez Petrone) (vert) 65 35
3260 1p. Smoking fire (Leandro Ventancour) 65 35

1220 Accordion

2007. 150th Anniv of Argentine–Germany Bilateral Relations. Sheet 150 × 100 mm.
MS3261 **1220** 4p. multicoloured 2·60 1·60

1221 Emblem

2007. Centenary of Club Atletico San Lorenzo de Almagro.
3262 **1221** 1p. multicoloured . . . 65 35

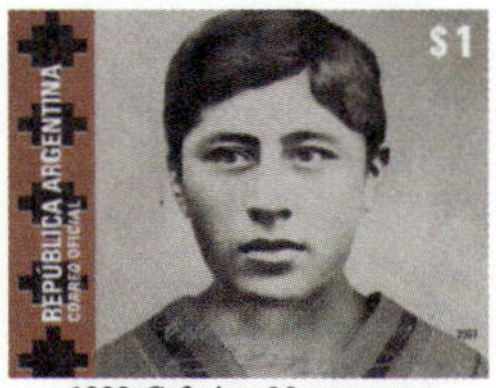

1222 Ceferino Namuncura

2007. Beatification of Ceferino Namuncura.
3263 **1222** 1p. multicoloured . . . 65 35

1223 *Corrientes esquina Uruguay* (Horacio Cuppola)

2007. Contemporary Art. Multicoloured.
3264 1p. Type **1223** 65 35
3265 1p. *Dialogo* (Liliana Porter) (vert) 65 35
3266 1p. *0611* (detail) (Pablo Siqier) 65 35
3267 1p. *Imaginando el estupor* (detail) (Marta Minujin) (vert) 65 35

1224 Three Wise Men

2007. Christmas. Showing detail from *The Birth* (stained glass window)). Multicoloured.
3268 25c. Type **1224** 15 10
3269 1p. Holy Family 65 35

1225 Early Drilling Site

2007. Centenary of Oil and Gas Discovery in Argentina.
3270 **1225** 1p. multicoloured . . . 65 35

1226 *Pampero* (balloon) and River Plate

2007. Centenary of Aaron de Anchorena and Jorge Newbery's Balloon Flight across the River Plate.
3271 **1226** 1p. multicoloured . . . 65 35

1227 Ceremonial Staff

2007. Presidential Inauguration. 24th Anniv of Democracy.
3272 **1227** 1p. multicoloured . . . 65 35

1228 Accordionist and Dancers

2007. Festivals. Multicoloured.
3273 1p. Type **1228** (National Chamame (dance) festival) 65 35
3274 1p. Ponchos and dancers (National and International Poncho festival) 65 35
3275 1p. Horseman, fireworks, guitar and dancers (National and International Dressage and Folklore festival) . . 65 35
3276 1p. Snow Queen and skier (National Snow festival) 65 35

BULK MAIL STAMPS

BP 999 Post Office Building, Buenos Aires

1999. Bulk Mail. Self-adhesive. Imperf.
BP2644 **BP 999** $7 black and blue 8·50 8·50
BP2645 $11 black and red 14·00 14·00
BP2646 $16 black and yellow . . . . 20·00 20·00
BP2647 $23 black and green . . . . . 28·00 28·00

BP 1069

2001. Bulk Mail. Additionally overprinted **UP.** Imperf.
BP2853 **BP 1069** $7 black and blue . . . . . 8·50 8·50
BP2854 $11 black and red . . . . . 14·00 14·00

EXPRESS SERVICE MAIL

E 999 Express Service Emblem

1999. Self-adhesive.
E2644 **E 999** 8p.75 blue and silver 12·00 9·50
E2645 – 17p.50 blue and gold 24·00 19·00
DESIGN: 24-hour service emblem.
No. E2644 was for express service mail and No. E2645 for use on 24-hour express service mail.

OFFICIAL STAMPS

1884. Optd **OFICIAL.**
O66 **33** ½c. brown . . . . 8·00 6·00
O69 1c. red 45 15
O70 **24** 2c. green 45 15
O71 – 4c. brown (No. 32) . . . 45 15
O72 **9** 8c. red 45 15
O73 **10** 10c. green . . . . 42·00 22·00
O76 **33** 12c. blue 70 60
O77 **10** 16c. green . . . . 1·90 75
O78 **22** 20c. blue . . . . 8·00 6·00
O79 **11** 24c. blue (roul) . . . . 1·40 85
O80 24c. blue (perf) . . . . . 1·25 70
O81 – 25c. red (No. 47) . . . . 9·50 6·50
O82 – 30c. orange (No. 33) . . . 17·00 12·00
O83 – 60c. black (No. 34) . . . 12·00 7·50
O84 – 90c. blue (No. 35) . . . . 8·50 6·50

O 73

1901.
O275 **O 73** 1c. grey 25 10
O276 2c. brown 35 15
O277 5c. red 45 15
O278 10c. green 50 15
O279 30c. blue . . . . . 3·50 85
O280 50c. orange . . . . . 1·90 65

1938. (a) Optd **SERVICIO OFICIAL** in two lines.
O668 **143** 1c. brown (No. 645) . . 10 10
O669 – 2c. brown (No. 646) . . 10 10
O670 – 3c. green (No. 647) . . 10 10
O679 – 3c. grey (No. 672) . . . 10 10
O771 – 3c. grey (No. 672a) . . 3·00 1·25
O671 – 5c. brown (No. 653b) 10 10
O782 **200** 5c. red (No. 773) . . . 10 10
O667 – 10c. red (No. 653d) . . 10 10
O773 – 10c. purple (No. 678) 10 10
O681 **146** 15c. blue (No. 676) . . 10 10
O774 – 15c. grey (No. 708) . . 10 10
O683 **146** 20c. blue (19½ × 26 mm) 50 10
O872 **247** 20c. red 10 10
O813 – 25c. (No. 673) 10 10
O674 – 40c. (No. 658) 10 10
O675 – 50c. (No. 659) 10 10
O676 **152** 1p. (No. 760) 10 10
O827 **234** 1p. (No. 826) 35 10
O778 – 2p. (No. 661) 10 10
O779 – 5p. (No. 662) 15 10
O780 – 10p. (No. 763) 25 10
O781 – 20p. (No. 764) 80 20

(b) Optd **SERVICIO OFICIAL** in one line.
O897 – 20c. lilac (No. 895) . . . 15 10

1953. Eva Peron stamps optd **SERVICIO OFICIAL.**
O854 **239** 5c. grey 10 10
O855 10c. red 10 10
O856 20c. red 10 10
O857 25c. green 10 10
O858 40c. purple 10 10
O859 45c. blue 15 10
O860 50c. bistre 10 10
O862 **240** 1p. brown (No. 846) . . 10 10
O863 1p.50 green (No. 847) 25 10
O864 2p. red (No. 848) . . . 20 10
O865 3p. blue (No. 849) . . . 45 15
O866 5p. brown 70 40
O867 **239** 10p. red . . . . 4·00 3·00
O868 **240** 20p. green . . . . . . 32·00 20·00

1955. Stamps of 1954 optd **SERVICIO OFICIAL** in one line.
O869 **247** 20c. red 10 10
O870 40c. red 10 10
O880 – 1p. brown (No. 871) . . 10 10
O882 – 3p. purple (No. 874) . . 10 10
O883 – 5p. green (No. 875) . . 30 10
O884 – 10p. green and grey (No. 876) 40 10
O886 **250** 20p. violet 75 15

1955. Various stamps optd. (a) Optd **S. OFICIAL.**
O 896 – 5c. brown (No. 894) 10 10
O 955 – 10c. green (No. 946) 10 10
O 956 – 20c. purple (No. 947) 10 10
O 879 – 50c. blue (No. 868) . . 20 10
O 957 – 50c. ochre (No. 948) 10 10
O1034 – 1p. brn (No. 1016) . . 10 10
O 899 **264** 2p. purple 10 10
O1050 – 2p. red (No. 1035) . . 10 10
O 959 – 3p. blue (No. 951) . . 15 10
O1051 – 4p. red (No. 1036) . . 15 10
O 961 **296** 5p. brown 20 10
O1052 – 8p. red (No. 1037) . . 15 10
O 962 – 10p. brown (No. 1286) 15 10
O1053 – 10p. red (No. 1038) . . 15 10
O1036 – 12p. dull purple (No. 1028) 40 10
O 964 – 20p. green (No. 954) 50 10
O1055 – 20p. red (No. 1039) . . 20 10
O1037 – 22p. blue (No. 1018) 50 10
O1038 – 23p. green (No. 1019) 95 10
O1039 – 25p. lilac (No. 1020) 50 10
O1040 – 43p. lake (No. 1021) 1·40 65
O1041 – 45p. brn (No. 1022) . . 1·40 65
O1042 – 50p. blue (No. 1023) 2·40 95
O1043 – 50p. blue (No. 1287) 3·25 95
O1045 – 100p. blue (No. 1289) 1·60 65
O1046 – 300p. violet (No. 1026) 4·75 2·25

(b) Optd **SERVICIO OFICIAL.**
O 900 **265** 2p.40 brown 20 10
O 958 – 3p. blue (No. 951) . . 15 10
O 901 **266** 4p.40 green 25 10
O 960 **296** 5p. brown 20 10
O 887 – 50p. ind & bl (No. 878) 1·60 65
O1049 – 500p. grn (No. 1032) 7·75 3·75

For lists of stamps optd **M.A., M.G., M.H., M.I., M.J.I., M.M., M.O.P.** or **M.R.C.** for use in ministerial offices see the Stanley Gibbons Catalogue Part 20 (South America).

1963. Nos. 1068, etc., optd **S. OFICIAL.**
O1076 **351** 2p. green 20 10
O1080 – 4p. red (No. 1069) . . 15 10
O1081 – 6p. red (No. 1070) . . 25 10
O1078 – 90p. bistre (No. 1288) 4·00 2·00

RECORDED MESSAGE STAMPS

RM 166 Winged Messenger

1939. Various symbolic designs inscr "CORREOS FONOPOSTAL".
RM688 **RM 166** 1p.18 blue . . . 16·00 8·00
RM689 – 1p.32 blue . . . 16·00 8·00
RM690 – 1p.50 brown . . . 48·00 24·00
DESIGNS—VERT: 1p.32, Head of Liberty and National Arms. HORIZ: 1p.50, Record and winged letter.

TELEGRAPH STAMPS USED FOR POSTAGE

PT 34

PT 35 (Sun closer to "NACIONAL")

1887.
PT104 **PT 34** 10c. red 50 10
PT105 **PT 35** 10c. red 50 10
PT106 **PT 34** 40c. blue 60 10
PT107 **PT 35** 40c. blue 60 15

ARMENIA Pt. 10

Formerly part of Transcaucasian Russia. Temporarily independent after the Russian revolution of 1917. From 12 March 1922, Armenia, Azerbaijan and Georgia formed the Transcaucasian Federation. Issues for the federation were superseded by those of the Soviet Union in 1924.

With the dissolution of the Soviet Union in 1991 Armenia once again became independent.

NOTE. Only one price is given for Nos. 3/245, which applies to unused or cancelled to order. Postally used copies are worth more.

All the overprints and surcharges were handstamped and consequently were applied upright or inverted indiscriminately, some occurring only inverted.

1919. 100 kopeks = 1 rouble.
1994. 100 luma = 1 dram.

NATIONAL REPUBLIC

28 May 1918 to 2 December 1920 and 18 February to 2 April 1921.

1919. Arms type of Russia and unissued Postal Savings Bank stamp (No. 6) surch. Imperf or perf. (a) Surch thus **k. 60 k** with or without stops.
3 **22** 60k. on 1k. orange 65
6 – 60k. on 1k. red on buff . . . 12·00

(b) Surch in figures only.
7 **22** 60k. on 1k. orange . . . . . 30·00
8 120k. on 1k. orange . . . . 30·00

(6)

(8)

1919. Stamps of Russia optd as T 6 in various sizes, with or without frame. Imperf or perf. (a) Arms types.
53B **22** 1k. orange . . . . 12·50
54B 2k. green . . . . 3·00
55B 3k. red . . . . 2·40
11B **23** 4k. red 80
12B **22** 5k. red . . . . 1·30
13B **23** 10k. blue 90
14B **22** 10k. on 7k. blue . . . . 1·20
15B **10** 15k. blue and purple . . 1·50
16B **14** 20k. red and blue . . . 1·60
17B **10** 25k. mauve and green . . 2·00
45B 35k. green and purple . . 2·20
19B **14** 50k. green and purple . . 1·00
30aB **22** 60k. on 1k. orange (No. 3) . . . . . . 2·50
31B **10** 70k. orange and brown . 1·00
32B **15** 1r. orange and brown . . 2·20
33B **11** 3r.50 green and brown . 3·50
23B **20** 5r. green and blue . . . 5·00
62B **11** 7r. yellow and black . . 40·00
24B 7r. pink and green . . . 9·00
52B **20** 10r. grey, red and yellow 11·00

(b) Romanov type.
63B 4k. red (No. 129) . . . 2·00

(c) Unissued Postal Savings Bank stamp.
64A 1k. red on buff . . . . . 6·50

1920. Stamps of Russia surch as T 8 in various types and sizes. Imperf or perf. (a) Arms types.
94B **22** 1r. on 60k. on 1k. orange (No. 3) . . . 4·50
65B 1r. on 1k. orange . . . 3·25
66B 3r. on 3k. red . . . . 2·10
67B 3r. on 4k. red . . . . 7·25
97B 5r. on 2k. green . . . . 2·50
69B **23** 5r. on 4k. red . . . . 1·30
70B **22** 5r. on 5k. red . . . . 1·80
71B 5r. on 7k. blue . . . . 1·20
72B **23** 5r. on 10k. blue . . . . 1·60
73B **22** 5r. on 10 on 7k. blue . . 2·10
74B **10** 5r. on 14k. red and blue 2·30
75B 5r. on 15k. blue and purple . . . . 2·10
76B **14** 5r. on 20k. red and blue 2·10
76aB **10** 5r. on 20 on 14k. red and blue . . . . . 8·50
77B 5r. on 25k. mauve and green . . . . 8·50
111B **22** 5r. on 3 r .on 5k. red . . 11·00
78B **10** 10r. on 25k. mauve and green . . . . 2·00
79B 10r. on 35k. green and purple . . . . 1·50
80B **14** 10r. on 50k. green and purple . . . . 4·00

80aB **9** 25r. on 1k. orange . . . 40·00
80bB 25r. on 3k. red . . . . 40·00
80cB 25r. on 5k. purple . . . 40·00
80dB **22** 25r. on 10 on 7k. blue 40·00
80eB **10** 25r. on 15k. blue and purple . . . . 40·00
81B **14** 25r. on 20k. red and blue . . . . 4·50
82B **10** 25r. on 25k. mauve and green . . . . 3·75
83B 25r. on 35k. green and purple . . . . 2·75
84B **14** 25r. on 50k. green and purple . . . . 3·50
85B **10** 25r. on 70k. orange and brown . . . . 5·00
104aB **9** 50r. on 1k. orange . . . 45·00
104bB 50r. on 3k. red . . . . 48·00
85bB **10** 50r. on 4k. red . . . . 45·00
104cB **14** 50r. on 5k. purple . . . 48·00
85cB **10** 50r. on 15k. blue and purple . . . . 45·00
85dB **14** 50r. on 20k. red and blue . . . . 45·00
85eB **10** 50r. on 35k. green & purple . . . . 45·00
85fB **14** 50r. on 50k. green & purple . . . . 25·00
105B **10** 50r. on 70k. orange and brown . . . . 6·25
106B **15** 50r. on 1r. orange and brown . . . . 6·50
107B 100r. on 1r. orange and brown . . . . 6·00
108B **11** 100r. on 3r.50 green and brown . . . . 18·00
88B **20** 100r. on 5r. green and blue . . . . 15·00
89B **11** 100r. on 7r. yellow and black . . . . 19·00
90B 100r. on 7r. pink and green . . . . 10·00
93B **20** 100r. on 10r. grey, red and yellow . . . . . 15·00

(b) Romanov issue of 1913.
112 1r. on 1k. orange . . . . . 10·50
113 3r. on 3k. red . . . . . . 13·00
114 5r. on 4k. red . . . . . . 5·50
115 5r. on 10 on 7k. brown . . 3·25
116 5r. on 14k. green . . . . 39·00
117 5r. on 20 on 14k. green . . 5·25
118 25r. on 4k. red . . . . . 6·50
118a 100r. on 1k. orange . . . . 65·00
119 100r. on 2k. green . . . . 65·00
120 100r. on 3r. violet . . . . 65·00

(c) War Charity issues of 1914 and 1915.
121 **15** 25r. on 1k. green and red on yellow . . . . 39·00
122 25r. on 3k. green and red on rose . . . . 39·00
123 50r. on 7k. green and brown on buff . . . . 48·00
124 50r. on 10k. brown and blue . . . . 48·00
125 100r. on 1k. green and red on yellow . . . . 48·00
126 100r. on 1k. grey and brown . . . . 48·00
127 100r. on 3k. green and red on rose . . . . 48·00
128 100r. on 7k. green and brown on buff . . . . 48·00
129 100r. on 10k. brown and blue . . . . 48·00

1920. Arms types of Russia optd as T 6 in various sizes with or without frame, and surch as T 8 or with value only in various types and sizes. Imperf or perf.
155B **22** 1r. on 60k. on 1k. orange (No. 3) . . . 1·30
156A 3r. on 3k. red . . . . . 2·50
157A 5r. on 2k. green . . . . 1·10
141A **23** 5r. on 4k. red . . . . . 4·50
158A **22** 5r. on 5k. red . . . . . 4·25
142A **23** 5r. on 10k. blue . . . . 4·50
143A **22** 5r. on 10 on 7k. blue . . 4·50
144A **10** 5r. on 15k. blue & pur 2·40
145A **14** 5r. on 20k. red and blue 2·40
132B **10** 10r. on 15k. blue & pur 12·00
145aB **14** 10r. on 20k. red & blue 1·20
146A **10** 10r. on 25k. mauve and green . . . . 2·40
147B 10r. on 35k. green and purple . . . . 1·20
148A **14** 10r. on 50k. green and purple . . . . 3·00
159A **10** 10r. on 70k. orange and brown . . . . 14·00
163A **22** 10r. on 5r. on 5k. red 30·00
164A **10** 10r. on 5r. on 25k. mauve and green . . 32·00
165A 10r. on 5r. on 35k. green and purple . . 11·00
138A 25r. on 70k. orange and brown . . . . 8·00
161B **15** 50r. on 1r. orange and brown . . . . 2·75
135B **11** 100r. on 3r.50 green and brown . . . . 3·00
151A **20** 100r. on 5r. green & bl 8·00
136A **11** 100r. on 7r. pink and green . . . . 9·00
154aA **20** 100r. on 10r. grey, red and yellow . . . . 12·00
166A 100r. on 25r. on 5r, green and blue . . . 30·00

1920. Stamps of Russia optd as T 6 in various sizes, with or without frame and surch **10**. Perf. (a) Arms types.
168 **14** 10 on 20k. red and blue . . 30·00
169 **10** 10 on 25k. mauve and green . . . . 30·00
170 10 on 35k. green and purple . . . . 20·00
171 **14** 10 on 50k. green and purple . . . . 24·00

(b) Romanov type.
172 10 on 4k. red (No. 129) . . . 48·00

1920. Stamps of Russia optd with monogram as in T 8 in various types and sizes and surch **10**. Imperf or perf. (a) Arms types.
173 **23** 10 on 4k. red . . . . . . 48·00
174 **22** 10 on 5k. red . . . . . . 48·00
175 **10** 10 on 15k. blue & purple 48·00
176 **14** 10 on 20k. red and blue 45·00
176a **10** 10 on 20 on 14k. red and blue . . . . 24·00
177 10 on 25k. mauve & green 24·00
178 10 on 35k. green & purple 24·00
179 **14** 10 on 50k. green & purple 24·00

(b) Romanov type.
181 10 on 4k. red (No. 129) . . . 60·00

11

12 Mt. Ararat

Stamps in Types **11**, **12** and a similar horizontal type showing a woman spinning were printed in Paris to the order of the Armenian National Government, but were not issued in Armenia as the Bolshevists had assumed control. (Price 10p. each).

SOVIET REPUBLIC

2 December 1920 to 18 February 1921 and 2 April 1921 to 12 March 1922.

(13)

1921. Arms types of Russia surch with T **13**. Perf.
182 **15** 5000r. on 1r. orange and brown . . . . 6·50
183 **11** 5000r. on 3r.50 grn & brn 6·50
184 **20** 5000r. on 5r. green & blue 6·50
185 **11** 5000r. on 7r. pink and green . . . . 6·50
186 **20** 5000r. on 10r. grey, red & yellow . . . . 6·50

14 Common Crane

16 Village Scene

1922. Unissued stamps surch in gold kopeks. Imperf.
187 **14** 1 on 250r. red . . . . . . 9·75
188 1 on 250r. slate . . . . . 13·00
189 **16** 2 on 500r. red . . . . . . 5·25
190 3 on 500r. slate . . . . . 5·25
191 – 4 on 1000r. red . . . . . 5·25
192 – 4 on 1000r. slate . . . . . 9·75
193 – 5 on 2000r. slate . . . . 30·00
194 – 10 on 2000r. red . . . . . 30·00
195 – 15 on 5000r. red . . . . . 23·00
196 – 20 on 5000r. slate . . . . 5·25

DESIGNS (sizes in mm): 1000r. Woman at well (17 × 26); 2000r. Erivan railway station (35 × 24½); 5000r. Horseman and Mt. Ararat (39½ × 24½).

17 Soviet Emblems

18 Wall Sculpture at Ani

19 Mt. Aragatz

1922. Unissued stamps as T **17/19** surch in gold kopeks in figures. Imperf or perf.
210 **17** 1 on 1r. green . . . . . 9·75
198 **18** 2 on 2r. slate . . . . . . 15·00
212 – 3 on 3r. red . . . . . . 18·00
213 – 4 on 25r. green . . . . . 3·75
201 – 5 on 50r. red . . . . . . 5·00
215 – 10 on 100r. orange . . . 13·00
203 – 15 on 250r. blue . . . . 2·20
204a **19** 20 on 500r. purple . . . 3·00
205 – 35 on 20,000r. red . . . . 24·00
206a – 50 on 25,000r. green . . . 48·00
209 – 50r. on 25,000r. blue . . . 6·50

DESIGNS (sizes in mm): 3r. (29 × 22) and 250r. (21 × 35) Soviet emblems; 25r. (30 × 22½); 100r. (34½ × 23) and 20,000r. (43 × 27) Mythological sculptures, Ani. 50r. (25½ × 37). Armenian soldier; 25,000r. (45½ × 27½) Mt. Ararat.

The above and other values were not officially issued without the surcharges.

TRANSCAUCASIAN FEDERATION ISSUES FOR ARMENIA

1923. As T **19**, etc., surch in gold kopeks in figures. Imperf or perf.
219 – 1 on 250r. blue . . . . . 6·50
217 **19** 2 on 500r. purple . . . . 6·50
218 – 3 on 20000r. lake . . . . 13·00

26 Mt. Ararat and Soviet Emblems

28 Ploughing

1923. Unissued stamps in various designs as T **26/28** surch in Transcaucasian roubles in figures. Perf.
227 **26** 10,000r. on 50r. green and red . . . . 1·80
228 – 15,000r. on 300r. blue and buff . . . . 1·80
229 – 25,000r. on 400r. blue and pink . . . . 1·80
240B – 30,000r. on 500r. violet and lilac . . . . 2·00
231 – 50,000r. on 1000r. blue 1·80
232 – 75,000r. on 3000r. black and green . . . . 2·00
233 – 100,000r. on 2000r. black and grey . . . . 2·40
243 – 200,000r. on 4000r. black and brn . . . . 1·20
235 – 300,000r. on 5000r. black and red . . . . 3·25
245 **28** 500,000r. on 10,000r. black and red . . . . 1·50

DESIGNS (sizes in mm): 300r. (26 × 35) Star over Mt. Ararat; 400r. (26 × 34½) Soviet emblems; 500r. (26 × 34½) Crane (bird); 1000r. (19 × 25) Peasant in print; 2000r. (26 × 31) Human-headed bird from old bas-relief; 3000r. (26½ × 36) Sower; 4000r. (26 × 31½) Star and dragon; 5000r. (26 × 32) Blacksmith.

INDEPENDENT REPUBLIC

31 Mount Ararat and National Colours

1992. Independence Day.
246 **31** 20k. multicoloured 15 15
247 2r. multicoloured 70 70
248 5r. multicoloured . . . . 1·70 1·70
MS249 80 × 80 mm. 7r. multicoloured (Mt. Ararat and eagle) . . . . 43·00 43·00

32 Dish Aerial and World Map

1992. Inauguration of International Direct-dial Telephone System.
250 **32** 50k. multicoloured . . . . 3·00 3·00

33 Ancient Greek Wrestling **34** National Flag

1992. Olympic Games, Barcelona. Multicoloured.
251 40k. Type **33** 10 35
252 3r.60 Boxing 40 40
253 5r. Weightlifting 60 60
254 12r. Gymnastics (ring exercises) . . . . 1·40 1·40

1992.
255 **34** 20k. multicoloured (postage) 10 10
256 – 1r. black 15 15
257 – 3r. brown 45 45
258 – 3r. brown 30 30
259 – 5r. black 60 60
260 – 20r. grey 65 65
261 – 2r. blue (air) 30 30
DESIGNS: 1r. Goddess Waroubini statuette from Orgov radio-optical telescope; 2r. Zvartnots Airport, Yerevan; 3r. (No. 257) Goddess Anahit; 3r. (No. 258) Runic inscription Karmir-Blour; 5r. U.P.U. Monument, Berne, Switzerland; 20r. Silver cup from Karashamb.
See also Nos. 275/82.

35 "Noah's Descent from Mt. Ararat"

1993. 175th Birth Anniv of Hovhannes Aivazovsky (painter). Sheet 95 × 63 mm.
MS262 **35** 7r. multicoloured . . . 2·10 2·10

36 Engraved 10th-century Tombstone, Makenis **37** Garni Canyon

1993. Armenian Cultural History. Multicoloured.
263 40k. Type **36** 10 10
264 80k. Illuminated page from Gospel of 1295 . . . . . . 20 20
265 3r.60 13th-century bas-relief, Gandzasar 75 75
266 5r. "Glorious Mother of God" (18th-century painting, H. Hovnatanian) 1·30 1·30

1993. Landscapes. Multicoloured.
268 40k. Type **37** 10 10
269 80k. Shaki Falls, Zangezur 10 10
270 3r.60 River Arpa gorge, Vike 35 35
271 5r. Lake Sevan (horiz) . . . 50 50
272 12r. Mount Ararat (horiz) . . 1·20 1·20

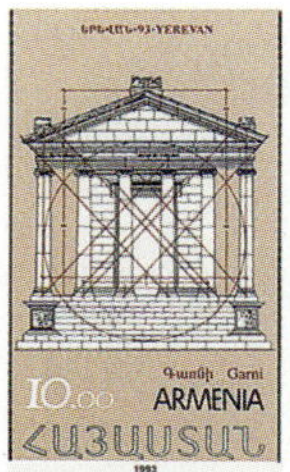

38 Temple of Garni **39** Reliquary for Arm of St. Thaddeus (17th century)

1993. "YEREVAN '93" International Stamp Exn.
273 **38** 10r. red, black and brown 60 60
MS274 133 × 111 mm. No. 273 × 6 plus two labels . . . . 4·50 4·25

1994. As T **34** but new currency.
275 10l. agate and brown 10 10
277 50l. deep brown and brown 60 60
280 10d. brown and grey 60 60
282 25d. gold and red . . . . . 1·50 1·50
DESIGNS: 10l. Shivini, Sun God (Karmir-Blour); 50l. Tayshaba, God of the Elements (Karmir-Blour); 10d. Khaldi, Supreme God (Karmir-Blour); 25d. National arms.

1994. Treasures of Etchmiadzin (seat of Armenian church). Multicoloured.
286 3d. Descent from the Cross (9th-century wooden panel) 10 10
287 5d. Gilded silver reliquary of Holy Cross of Khotakerats (1300) 10 10
288 12d. Cross with St. Karapet's right hand (14th century) 50 50
289 30d. Type **39** . . . . 1·00 1·00
290 50d. Gilded silver chrism vessel (1815) . . . . 1·40 1·40

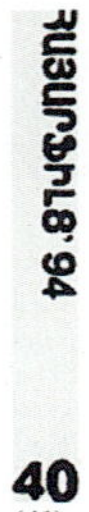

(40) (41)

1994. Stamp Exhibitions, Yerevan. (a) "Armenia '94" National Exn. No. 273 surch with T **40**.
291 **38** 40d. on 10r. red, blk & brn 3·75 3·75
(b) "Armenia–Argentina" Exhibition. No. 273 surch with T **41**.
292 **38** 40d. on 10r. red, blk & brn 3·75 3·75

42 Cancelled Stamps of 1919 **43** Stadium and Arms of National Committee

1994. 75th Anniv of First Stamp Issue.
293 **42** 16d. multicoloured 30 30

1994. Olympic Committees. Multicoloured.
294 30d. Type **43** 45 45
295 40d. Olympic rings (centenary of Int Olympic Committee) 65 65

44 Haroutune Shmavonian **45** Ervand Otian

1994. Bicentenary of "Azdarar" (first Armenian periodical).
296 **44** 30d. brown and green . . . 40 40

1994. 125th Birth Anniversaries.
297 **45** 50d. drab and brown . . . 30 30
298 – 50d. brown 30 30
DESIGN—HORIZ: 50d. Levon Shant.

46 "Cross" (from Gospel) **47** Vazgen I

1995. 1700th Anniv (2001) of Christianity in Armenia (1st issue). Works of art. Multicoloured.
299 60d. Type **46** 55 55
300 70d. "St. Bartholomew and St. Thaddeus the Apostles" (Hovnatan Hovnatanian) (45 × 39 mm) 55 55
301 70d. "Kings Abhar and Trdat" (Mkrtoum Hovnatanian) (45 × 39 mm) 55 55
302 80d. "St. Gregory the Illuminator" 70 70
303 90d. "The Baptism of Armenian People" (H. Aivazovsky) 85 85
MS304 97 × 71 mm. 400d. black and ochre ("Echmiadzin Monastery" (detail of engraving by Jacob Peeters)) . . . . 2·75 2·75
See also Nos. **MS**331, 362/**MS**367, 382/**MS**387 and **MS**401.

1995. 1st Death Anniv of Vazgen I (Patriarch of Armenian Orthodox Church).
305 **47** 150d. black and grey . . . 70 70

48 Black-polished Pottery **49** Red Kite and Oak

1995. Museum Artefacts (1st series). Multicoloured.
306 30d. Type **48** 25 25
307 60d. Silver horn 50 50
308 130d. Gohar carpet . . . . . 1·20 1·20
See also Nos. 332/4.

1995. Birds and Trees. Multicoloured.
309 40d. Type **49** 40 55
310 60d. Golden eagle and juniper 50 60

50 Workers building "Honeycomb" Map

1995. Hyastan All-Armenian Fund.
311 **50** 90d. multicoloured 65 65

51 Rainbows around U.N. Emblem

1995. 50th Anniv of U.N.O.
312 **51** 90d. multicoloured 65 65

52 Commander P. Kitsook (408th Rifle Division)

1995. 50th Anniv of End of Second World War. (a) Size 40 × 23 mm. Each black, orange and blue.
313 60d. Type **52** 40 40
314 60d. Commanders S. Chernikov, N. Tavartkeladze and V. Penkovsky (76th Mountain Rifle Red-banner (51st Guard) Division) . . 40 40
315 60d. Commanders S. Zakian, H. Babayan and I. Lyudnikov (390th Rifle Division) 40 40
316 60d. Commanders A. Vasilian, M. Dobrovolsky, Y. Grechany and G. Sorokin (409th Rifle Division) 40 40
317 60d. Commanders A. Sargissian and N. Safarian (89th Taman Triple Order Bearer Rifle Division) 40 40
(b) Size 23 × 35 mm. Each blue, orange and brown.
318 60d. Marshal Hovhannes Baghramian 60 60
319 60d. Admiral Hovhannes Issakov 60 60
320 60d. General Marshal Hamazasp Babajanian . . 60 60
321 60d. Marshal Sergey Khoudyakov 60 60
MS322 120 × 90 mm. 300d. "Return of the Hero" (Mariam Aslamazian) . . . . 2·50 2·50

53 Ghevond Alishan (historian and geographer)

1995. Writers' Anniversaries.
323 **53** 90d. green and black . . . 55 55
324 – 90d. sepia, brown & yellow 55 55
325 – 90d. blue and red 60 60
DESIGNS: No. 323, Type **53** (175th birth); 324, Grigor Artsruni (journalist, 150th birth); 325, Franz Werfel (50th death).

54 Sports and Concert Complex **55** Katsian and Spectators watching Flight

1995. Yerevan.
326 – 60d. black and orange . . 30 30
327 – 80d. black and pink . . . 40 40
328 **54** 90d. black and buff . . . 45 45
329 – 100d. black and buff . . . 60 60
330 – 120d. black and pink . . . 80 80
MS331 90 × 65 mm. 400d. multicoloured . . . . 2·40 2·40
DESIGNS—As T **54**: 60d. Brandy distillery and wine cellars; 80d. Abovian Street; 400d. Panoramic view of Yerevan. 60 × 23 mm: 100d. Baghramian Avenue; 120d. Republic Square.
No. **MS**331 also commemorates the 1700th anniv (2001) of Christianity in Armenia.

1995. Museum Artefacts (2nd series). As T **48**. Mult.
332 40d. Four-wheeled carriages (horiz) 25 25
333 60d. Bronze model of solar system 45 45
334 90d. Tombstone from Loriberd 65 65

1995. Air. 86th Anniv of Artiom Katsian's 1909 World Record for Range and Altitude.
335 **55** 90d. ochre, brown and blue 60 60

(56) **57** Griboedov

1996. No. 275 surch as T **56**.
336 40d. on 10l. agate and brown 95 95
337 100d. on 10l. agate and brown . . . . 2·30 2·30
338 150d. on 10l. agate and brown . . . . 3·50 3·50
339 200d. on 10l. agate and brown . . . . 5·00 5·00

1996. Birth Bicentenary of Aleksandr Griboedov (historian).
340 **57** 90d. stone, brown and red 65 65

58 Hayrik Khrimian (patriarch of Armenian Orthodox Church, 175th birth anniv (1995))

1996. Anniversaries.
341 **58** 90d. blue & brn (postage) 55 55
342 – 90d. multicoloured 55 55
343 – 90d. grey, blue & red (air) 55 55
DESIGNS—HORIZ: No. 342, Lazar Serebryakov (Admiral of the Fleet, and 19th-century Russian warships, birth bicentenary (1995)). VERT: No. 343, Nelson Stepanian (Second World War pilot, 50th death anniv (1994)).

59 Opening Frame from First Armenian Film

1996. Centenary of Motion Pictures.
344 **59** 60d. black, grey and blue . . . 40 40

60 Angel and Red Cross

61 Wild Goats

1996. 75th Anniv of Armenian Red Cross Society.
345 **60** 60d. multicoloured 40 40

1996. Mammals. Multicoloured.
346 40d. Type **61** 60 20
347 60d. Leopards 55 65

62 Nansen and "Fram"

1996. Centenary of Return of Fridtjof Nansen's Arctic Expedition.
348 **62** 90d. multicoloured 70 70

63 Cycling

64 Torch Bearer

1996. Olympic Games, Atlanta. Multicoloured.
349 40d. Type **63** 25 25
350 60d. Triple jumping 40 40
351 90d. Wrestling 70 70
Nos. 349/51 were issued together, se-tenant, the backgrounds forming a composite design showing ancient Greek athletes.

1996. Centenary of Modern Olympic Games.
352 **64** 60d. multicoloured 35 35

65 Genrikh Kasparian (first prize winner, "Chess in USSR" competition, 1939)

66 Tigran Petrosian (World chess champion, 1963–69) and Tigran Petrosian Chess House, Yerevan

1996. 32nd Chess Olympiad, Yerevan. Designs showing positions from previous games. Mult.
353 40d. Type **65** 35 35
354 40d. Tigran Petrosian v. Mikhail Botvinnik (World Championship, Moscow, 1963) 35 35
355 40d. Gary Kasparov v. Anatoly Karpov (World Championship, Leningrad, 1986) 35 35
356 40d. Olympiad emblem . . . 35 35

1996.
357 **66** 90d. multicoloured 65 65

67 Goats

1996. The Wild Goat. Multicoloured.
358 70d. Type **67** 35 35
359 100d. Lone female 45 45
360 130d. Lone male 60 60
361 350d. Heads of male and female . . . . 1·70 1·70

68 Church of the Holy Mother, Samarkand, Uzbekistan

1997. 1700th Anniv (2001) of Christianity in Armenia (2nd issue). Armenian Apostolic Overseas Churches. Multicoloured.
362 100d. Type **68** 50 50
363 100d. Church of the Holy Mother, Kishinev, Moldova 50 50
364 100d. St. Hripsime's Church, Yalta, Ukraine 50 50
365 100d. St. Catherine's Church, St. Petersburg, Russia . . . 50 50
366 100d. Church, Lvov, Ukraine 50 50
MS367 92 × 66 mm. 500d. St. George of Echmiadzin's Church, Tbilisi, Georgia . . . 2·50 2·50

69 Man operating Printing Press

1997. 225th Anniv of First Printing Press in Armenia.
368 **69** 70d. multicoloured 85 85

70 Jivani and Mount Ararat

1997. 150th Birth Anniv of Jivani (folk singer).
369 **70** 90d. multicoloured 45 45

71 Babajanian and Score of "Heroic Ballad"

1997. 75th Birth Anniv (1996) of Arno Babajanian (composer and pianist).
370 **71** 90d. black, lilac & purple 45 45

72 Countryside (Gevorg Bashinjaghian)

1997. Exhibits in National Gallery of Armenia (1st series). Multicoloured.
371 150d. Type **72** 75 75
372 150d. "One of My Dreams" (Eghishe Tadevossian) . . 75 75
373 150d. "Portrait of Natalia Tehumian" (Hakob Hovnatanian) (vert) . . . 75 75
374 150d. "Salome" (Vardges Sureniants) (vert) 75 75
See also Nos. 390/2 and 512/13.

73 Mamulian

74 St. Basil's Cathedral, Moscow

1997. Birth Centenary of Rouben Mamulian (film director).
375 **73** 150d. multicoloured . . . 80 80

1997. "Moscow 97" Int Stamp Exhibition.
376 **74** 170d. multicoloured . . . 85 85

75 Hayk and Bel

76 Charents

1997. Europa. Tales and Legends. Multicoloured.
377 170d. Type **75** . . . . 2·00 2·00
378 250d. The Song of Vahagn 2·50 2·50

1997. Birth Centenary of Eghishe Charents (poet).
379 **76** 150d. brown and red . . . 75 75

77 "Iris lycotis"

78 St. Gregory the Illuminator Cathedral, Anthelias, Libya

1997. Irises. Multicoloured.
380 40d. Type **77** 15 15
381 170d. "Iris elegantissima" . . 75 75

1997. 1700th Anniv (2001) of Christianity in Armenia (3rd issue). Armenian Overseas Educational Centres. Multicoloured.
382 100d. Type **78** 50 50
383 100d. St. Khach Armenian Church, Nakhijevan, Rostov-on-Don 50 50
384 100d. St. James's Monastery, Jerusalem (horiz) 50 50
385 100d. Nercissian School, Tblisi, Georgia (60 × 21 mm) 50 50
386 100d. San Lazzaro Mekhitarian Congregation, Venice (horiz) 50 50
MS387 90 × 45 mm. 500d. Lazarian Seminary, Moscow (horiz) . . 2·40 2·40

79 Baby Jesus, Angel and Mary

80 Eagle and Demonstrator with Flag

1997. Christmas.
388 **79** 40d. multicoloured 30 30

1998. 10th Anniv of Karabakh Movement.
389 **80** 250d. multicoloured . . . 1·60 1·60

1998. Exhibits in National Gallery of Armenia (2nd series). As T **72**. Multicoloured.
390 150d. "Family. Generations" (Yervand Kochar) (vert) 75 75
391 150d. "Tartar Women's Dance" (Alexander Bazhbeouk-Melikian) . . . 75 75
392 150d. "Spring in Our Yard" (Haroutiun Kalents) (vert) 75 75

81 Diana, Princess of Wales

82 Eiffel Tower, Ball and Pitch

1998. Diana, Princess of Wales Commemoration.
393 **81** 250d. multicoloured . . . 90 90

1998. World Cup Football Championship, France.
394 **82** 250d. multicoloured . . . 1·20 1·20

83 Couple leaping through Flames (Trndez)

1998. Europa. National Festivals. Multicoloured.
395 170d. Type **83** . . . . 1·30 1·30
396 250d. Girls in traditional costume (Ascension) . . . 2·20 2·20

84 Southern Swallowtail

85 Ayrarat Couple

1998. Insects. Multicoloured.
397 170d. Type **84** 85 85
398 250d. "Rethera komarovi" (moth) . . . . 1·20 1·20

1998. Traditional Costumes (1st series). Mult.
399 170d. Type **85** 85 85
400 250d. Vaspurakan family . . 1·20 1·20
See also Nos. 408/9, 492/3, 591/2 and 620/1.

86 St. Forty Children's Church, Milan

1998. 1700th Anniv (2001) of Christianity in Armenia (4th issue). Sheet 143 × 71 mm. Multicoloured.
MS401 100d. Type **86**; 100d. St. Sargis's Church, London; 100d. St. Vardan's Cathedral, New York; 100d. St. Hovhannes's Cathedral, Paris; 100d. St. Gregory the Illuminator's Cathedral, Buenos Aires . . . 2·50 2·50

87 Fissure in Earth's Surface

1998. 10th Anniv of Armenian Earthquake.
402 **87** 250d. black, red and lilac 1·20 1·20

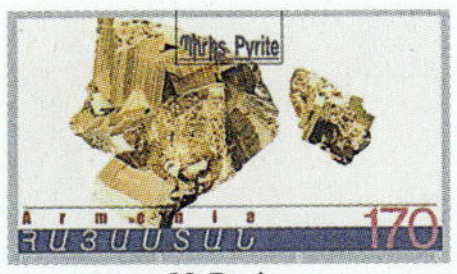

88 Pyrite

1998. Minerals. Multicoloured.
403 170d. Type **88** 90 90
404 250d. Agate . . . . 1·30 1·30

89 Briusov

90 Parajanov

1998. 125th Birth Anniv of Valery Briusov (Russian translator of Armenian works).
405 **89** 90d. multicoloured 45 45

1999. 75th Birth Anniv of Sergei Parajanov (film director and artist). Sheet 74 × 65 mm.
MS406 **90** 500d. multicoloured 2·75 2·75
MS407 As No. **MS**406 but with emblem in margin of "iBRA" International Stamp Exhibition, Nuremberg, Germany . . . . 3·00 3·00

1999. Traditional Costumes (2nd series). As T **85**.
408 170d. Mother and child from Karin 90 90
409 250d. Zangezour couple . . . 1·30 1·30

91 Khosrov Reserve

1999. Europa. Parks and Gardens. Multicoloured.
410 170d. Type **91** 85 85
411 250d. Dilijan Reserve . . . . 1·00 1·00

92 Anniversary Emblem on Flag

1999. 50th Anniv of Council of Europe.
412 **92** 170d. multicoloured . . . 1·80 1·80

93 Medieval Kogge and Map

1999. Ships of the Armenian Kingdom of Cilicia (11–14th centuries). Multicoloured.
413 170d. Type **93** 85 85
414 250d. Medieval single-masted sailing ships . . . . 1·30 1·30
415 250d. As No. 414 but with emblem of "Philexfrance 99" International Stamp Exhibition, Paris, France, in lower right corner . . . 1·30 1·30

94 Armenian Gampr

1999. Domestic Pets. Multicoloured.
416 170d. Type **94** 85 85
417 250d. Turkish van cat . . . 1·30 1·30
418 250d. As No. 417 but with emblem of "China 1999" International Stamp Exhibition, Peking, China, in lower right corner . . . 1·40 1·40

95 Obverse and Reverse of Medal

1999. 1st Pan-Armenian Games, Yerevan. Sheet 58 × 40 mm.
MS419 **95** 250d. multicoloured 2·20 2·20

96 St. Gregory the Illuminator's Church, Cairo

1999. 1700th Anniv (2001) of Christianity in Armenia (5th issue). Sheet 121 × 65 mm containing T **96** and similar horiz designs. Multicoloured.
MS420 70d. Type **96**; 70d. St. Gregory the Illuminator's Church, Singapore; 70d. St. Khach's Church, Suchava; 70d. St. Saviour's Church, Worcester; 70d. Church of the Holy Mother, Madras . . . . 1·90 1·90

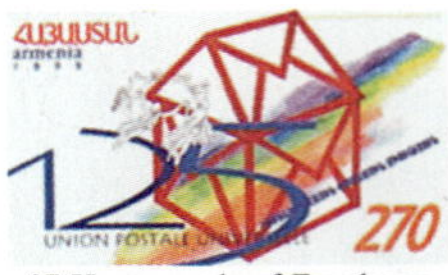

97 House made of Envelopes

1999. 125th Anniv of Universal Postal Union.
421 **97** 270d. multicoloured . . . 1·60 1·60

98 Karen Demirchyan (Speaker of the National Assembly)

2000. Commemoration of Victims of Attack on National Assembly. Multicoloured.
422 250d. Type **98** . . . . 1·40 1·40
423 250d. Vazgen Sargsyan (Prime Minister) . . . . . 1·40 1·40
MS424 60 × 40 mm. 540d. Demirchyan Sargsyan, Yuri Bakshyan, Ruben Mirochyan, Henrik Abrahamyan, Armenak Armenakyan, Leonard Petrossyan and Mikael Kotanyan . . . . 3·00 3·00

99 Sevan Trout

101 "Building Europe"

100 The Liar Hunter

2000. Fishes. Multicoloured.
425 50d. Type **99** 35 35
426 270d. Sevan barbel . . . . . 1·50 1·50

2000. National Fairy Tales. Multicoloured.
427 70d. Type **100** 40 40
428 130d. The King and the Peddler 70 70

2000. Europa.
429 **101** 40d. multicoloured . . . 35 35
430 500d. multicoloured . . . 4·25 4·25

102 St. Gayane Church, Vagharshapat

2000. 1700th Anniv (2001) of Christianity in Armenia (6th issue). Sheet 121 × 65 mm containing T **102** and similar horiz designs. Multicoloured.
MS431 70d. Type **102**; 70d. Etchmiadzin Cathedral, Vagharshapat; 70d. Church of the Holy Mother, Khor Virap; 70d. St. Shoghakat Church, Vagharshapat; 70d. St. Hrip'sime Church, Vagharshapat . . . . 2·75 2·75

103 Basketball

2000. Olympic Games, Sydney. Multicoloured.
432 10d. Type **103** 10 10
433 30d. Tennis 25 25
434 500d. Weightlifting . . . . . 4·25 4·25

104 Quartz

2000. Minerals. Multicoloured.
435 170d. Type **104** . . . . . . 1·30 1·30
436 250d. Molybdenite . . . . . 1·90 1·90

105 Shnorhali

106 Adoration of the Magi

2000. 900th Birth Anniv of Nerses Shnorhali (writer and musician).
437 **105** 270d. multicoloured . . . 1·60 1·60

2000. Christmas.
438 **106** 170d. multicoloured . . . 1·00 1·00

107 Issahakian

2000. 125th Birth Anniv of Avetik Issahakian (poet).
439 **107** 130d. multicoloured . . . 60 60

108 Dhol

109 Viktor Hambartsoumian (astrophysicist)

2000. Musical Instruments. Multicoloured.
440 170d. Type **108** 95 95
441 250d. Duduk (wind instrument) . . . . 1·30 1·30

2000. New Millennium. Famous Armenians. Mult.
442 110d. Type **109** 65 65
443 110d. Abraham Alikhanov (physicist) 65 65
444 110d. Andranik Iossifan (electrical engineer) 65 65
445 110d. Sargis Saltikov (metallurgist) 65 65
446 110d. Samval Kochariants (electrical engineer) 65 65
447 110d. Artem Mikoyan (aircraft designer) 65 65
448 110d. Norayr Sisisakian (biochemist) 65 65
449 110d. Ivan Knunyants (chemist) 65 65
450 110d. Nikoghayos Yenikolopian (physical chemist) 65 65
451 110d. Nikoghayos Adonts (historian) 65 65
452 110d. Manouk Abeghian (folklore scholar) 65 65
453 110d. Hovhannes Toumanian (poet) 65 65
454 110d. Hrachya Ajarian (linguist) 65 65
455 110d. Gevorg Emin (poet) . . 65 65
456 110d. Yervand Lalayan (anthropologist) 65 65
457 110d. Daniel Varoujan (poet) 65 65
458 110d. Paruyr Sevak (poet) . . 65 65
459 110d. William Saroyan (dramatist and novelist) . . 65 65
460 110d. Hamo Beknazarian (film director) 65 65
461 110d. Alexandre Tamanian (architect) 65 65
462 110d. Vahram Papazian (actor) 65 65
463 110d. Vasil Tahirov (viticulturist) 65 65
464 110d. Leonid Yengibarian (mime artist) 65 65
465 110d. Haykanoush Danielian (singer) 65 65
466 110d. Sergo Hambartsoumian (weight lifter) 65 65
467 110d. Hrant Shahinian (gymnast) 65 65
468 110d. Toros Toramanian (architect) 65 65
469 110d. Komitas (composer) . . 65 65
470 110d. Aram Khachatourian (composer) 65 65
471 110d. Martiros Sarian (artist) 65 65
472 110d. Avet Terterian (composer) 65 65
473 110d. Alexandre Spendiarian (composer) 65 65
474 110d. Arshile Gorky (artist) 65 65
475 110d. Minas Avetissian (artist) 65 65
476 110d. (Levon Orbeli physiologist) 65 65
477 110d. Hripsimeh Simonian (ceramics artist) 65 65

110 Soldiers

2001. 1550th Anniv of Battle of Avarayr. Sheet 90 × 65 mm containing T **110** and similar vert design. Multicoloured.
MS478 170d. Type **110**; 270d. Vardan Mamikonian . . . . . 3·00 3·00

111 Narekatsi and Text

2001. Millenary of A Record of Lamentations by Grigor Narekatsi.
479 **111** 25d. multicoloured . . . 55 55

112 Lake Sevan

2001. Europa. Water Resources. Multicoloured.
480 50d. Type **112** 25 25
481 500d. Spandarian Reservoir 2·75 2·75

113 Emblem

2001. Armenian Membership of Council of Europe.
482 **113** 240d. multicoloured . . . 1·10 1·10

114 Trophy

2001. 2nd Pan-Armenian Games. Sheet 58 × 40 mm.
MS483 **114** 300d. multicoloured 2·20 2·20

115 Persian Squirrel

2001. Endangered Species. Persian Squirrel (*Sciurus persicus*). Multicoloured.
484 40d. Type **115** 40 40
485 50d. Adult sitting on branch with young in tree hole . . 50 50
486 80d. Head of squirrel 85 85
487 120d. On ground . . . . . . 1·30 1·30

116 Cathedral Facade

2001. 1700th Anniv of Christianity in Armenia (7th issue). St. Gregory the Illuminator Cathedral, Yerevan. Multicoloured.
488 50d. Type **116** 35 35
489 205d. Interior elevation of Cathedral (44 × 30 mm) . . 1·40 1·40
490 240d. Exterior elevation of Cathedral (44 × 30 mm) . . 1·70 1·70

117 Lazarian and Institute

2001. Death Bicentenary of Hovhannes Lazarian (founder of Institute of Oriental Languages, Moscow).
491 **117** 300d. multicoloured . . . 1·70 1·70
A stamp in a similar design was issued by Russia.

2001. Traditional Costumes (3rd series). As T **85**. Multicoloured.
492 50d. Javakhch couple 40 40
493 250d. Artzakh couple . . . . 1·70 1·70

118 Emblem

119 Children encircling Globe

2001. 6th World Wushu Championships, Yerevan.
494 **118** 180d. black . . . . 1·00 1·00

2001. United Nations Year of Dialogue among Civilizations.
495 **119** 275d. multicoloured . . . 1·60 1·60

120 Emblem

2001. 10th Anniv of Commonwealth of Independent States.
496 **120** 205d. multicoloured . . . 1·20 1·20

121 Profiles

2001. European Year of Languages.
497 **121** 350d. multicoloured . . . 2·30 2·30

122 Flag

2001. 10th Anniv of Independence.
498 **122** 300d. multicoloured . . . 1·70 1·70

123 Cart

2001. Transport. Multicoloured.
499 180d. Type **123** . . . . . . 1·30 1·30
500 205d. Phaeton . . . . 1·40 1·40

124 *Hypericum perforatum*

125 Eagle

2001. Medicinal Plants. Multicoloured.
501 85d. Type **124** 60 60
502 205d. *Thymus serpyllum* . . . 1·50 1·50

2002.
503 **125** 10d. brown 10 10
504 25d. green 20 20
506 50d. blue 35 35
507 70d. rose 20 20
508 300d. blue . . . . 1·50 1·50
509 500d. brown . . . . 1·90 1·90

126 Calendar Belt (2000 B.C.) and Copper Works

2002. Traditional Production. Multicoloured.
510 120d. Type **126** 75 75
511 350d. Beer vessels (7th century B.C.) and modern brewing equipment . . . . 2·10 2·10

2002. Exhibits in National Gallery of Armenia (3rd series). Vert designs as T **72**.
512 200d. black, grey and green 1·00 1·00
513 200d. black, grey and red . . 1·00 1·00
DESIGNS: No. 512, "Lily" (Edgar Chahine); 513, "Salome" (sculpture, Hakob Gurjian).

127 Football and Maps of Japan and South Korea

2002. World Cup Football Championships, Japan and South Korea.
514 **127** 350d. multicoloured . . . 1·90 1·90

128 Pushman and "The Silent Order" (detail, painting)

2002. 125th Birth Anniv of Hovsep Pushman (artist). Sheet 75 × 65 mm.
MS515 **128** 650d. multicoloured 3·50 3·50

129 Technical Drawings, Tevossian and Factory

2002. Birth Centenary of Hovhannes Tevossian (metallurgical engineer).
516 **129** 350d. multicoloured . . . 1·90 1·90

130 Birds, Playing Cards, Ribbons and Magician's Hat

132 Ani Cathedral

131 Aivazian

2002. Europa. Circus. Multicoloured.
517 70d. Type **130** 40 40
518 500d. Clown juggling . . . . 2·10 2·10

2002. Birth Centenary of Artemy Aivazian (composer).
519 **131** 600d. multicoloured . . . 3·25 3·25

2002. Sheet 90 × 60 mm.
MS520 **132** 550d. multicoloured 2·75 2·75

133 Kaputjugh Mountain

2002. International Year of Mountains.
521 **133** 350d. multicoloured . . . 2·10 2·10

134 Armenian Lizard (*Lacerta armeniaca*)

2002. Reptiles. Multicoloured.
522 170d. Type **134** . . . . . . 1·10 1·10
523 220d. Radde's viper (*Vipera raddei*) . . . . 1·40 1·40

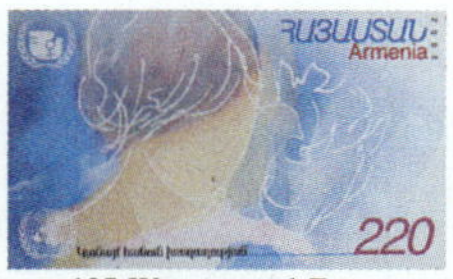
135 Woman and Dove

2002. United Nations Development Fund for Women.
524 **135** 220d. multicoloured . . . 1·60 1·60

136 Steam Locomotive

2002. Centenary of Alexandrapol–Yerevan Railway.
525 **136** 350d. multicoloured . . . 2·50 2·50

137 *Galanthus artjuschenkoae*

2002. Flowers. Multicoloured.
526 150d. Type **137** . . . . . . 1·00 1·00
527 200d. *Merendera mirzoevae* 1·50 1·50

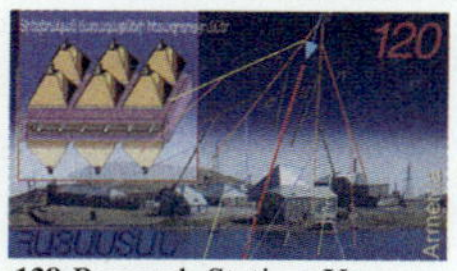
138 Research Station, Yerevan Physics Institute

2002. Space Research. Multicoloured.
528 120d. Type **138** 85 85
529 220d. Orion 1 and Orion 2 space observatories . . . . 1·50 1·50

139 "Handle with Care" (Artak Baghdassaryan)

140 Aram Khachatourian

2003. Europa. Poster Art. Multicoloured.
530 170d. Type **139** . . . . . . 1·30 1·30
531 250d. "Armenia our Home" (Kearen Kojoyan) . . . . 1·70 1·70

2003. Birth Centenary of Aram Khachatourian (composer).
532 **140** 350d. multicoloured . . . 1·90 1·90

141 Armenian Gull (*Larus Armenicus*)

2003. World Environment Day. Rehabilitation of Lake Gilli.
533 **141** 220d. multicoloured . . . 1·30 1·30

142 Viaduct and Emblem

2003. 10th Anniv of TRACEA (transport corridor Europe–Caucasus–Asia) Programme. Sheet 74 × 55 mm.
MS534 **142** 480d. multicoloured 2·75 2·75

143 Horse-drawn Cart, Map of Route and First Postal Seal

2003. 175th Anniv of First Armenian Postal Dispatch.
535 **143** 70d. multicoloured . . . 40 40

144 Siamanto and Script

146 Vahan Tekeyan

145 Coins and Currency Notes

2003. 125th Birth Anniv of Siamanto (Atom Yarchanyan) (writer).
536 **144** 350d. multicoloured . . . 1·90 1·90

2003. 10th Anniv of Armenian Currency.
537 **145** 170d. multicoloured . . . 95 95

2003. 125th Birth Anniv of Vahan Tekeyan (writer).
538 **146** 200d. multicoloured . . . 1·10 1·10

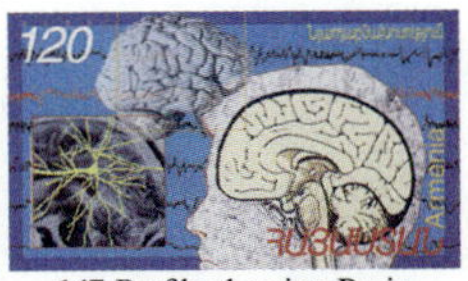

147 Profile showing Brain

2003. Neurophysiology.
539 **147** 120d. multicoloured . . . 65 65

148 Sports and Culture Complex, Yerevan

2003. 3rd Armenian Games. Sheet 58 × 40 mm.
MS540 **148** 350d. multicoloured 2·00 2·00

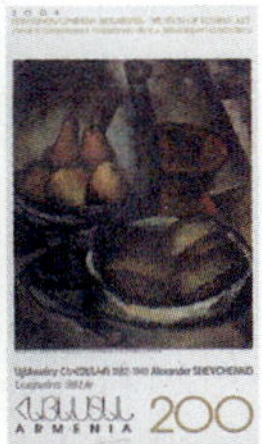

149 "The Baptism" (6–7th century), Gospel of Ejmiatsin

150 "Still Life" (Alexander Shevchenko)

2003. Armenian Miniatures. Sheet 65 × 74 mm.
MS541 **149** 550d. multicoloured 3·25 3·25

2004. Art. Multicoloured.
542 200d. Type **150** . . . . . . 1·20 1·20
543 220d. "In a Restaurant" (Konstantin Roudakon) . . 1·30 1·30

151 "100" and Football

2004. Centenary of FIFA (Federation Internationale de Football Association).
544 **151** 350d. multicoloured . . . 1·70 1·70

152 White Voskehat Grapes

2004. Grapes. Multicoloured.
545 170d. Type **152** . . . . . 1·00 1·00
546 220d. Black Areni grapes . . 1·20 1·20

153 17th-century Frescos, Vifliem Church

155 Aramayis Yerznkian

154 *The Cat and the Dog*, 1937

2004. 400th Anniv of New Julfa (Armenian settlement in Iran). Sheet 55 × 56 mm.
MS547 **153** 590d. multicoloured 3·00 3·00

2004. Animated Films. Multicoloured.
548 70d. Type **154** 40 40
549 120d. *Foxbook*, 1975 . . . . 70 70

2004. 125th Birth Anniv of Aramayis Yerznkian (politician).
550 **155** 220d. multicoloured . . . 1·10 1·10

156 Karabakh Horse

2005.
551 **156** 350d. multicoloured . . . 1·80 1·80

157 Hand and Olympic Rings

158 Hands enclosing Seedling

2005. Olympic Games, Athens (2004). Multicoloured.
552 70d. Type **157** 40 40
553 170d. Hand as runner . . . 1·00 1·00
554 350d. Hand as pistol . . . . 2·10 2·10

2005. International Day against Desertification.
555 **158** 360d. multicoloured . . . 1·90 1·90

159 Laboratory Vessel and Chemical Formula

2005. Chemistry.
556 **159** 220d. multicoloured . . . 1·10 1·10

160 Michael Nalbandian and Script

2005. 175th Birth Anniv of Michael Nalbandian (writer).
557 **160** 220d. multicoloured . . . 1·10 1·10

161 Mouratsan and Forest

2005. 150th Birth Anniv of Grigor Ter–Hovhanissian (Mouratsan) (writer).
558 **161** 350d. multicoloured . . . 1·80 1·80

162 Tigran petrossian

2005. 75th Birth Anniv of Tigran Petrossian (chess player).
559 **162** 220d. multicoloured . . . 1·10 1·10

163 Man sitting on Flower

164 Goshavank Church

2005. Europa. Holidays (2004). Multicoloured.
560 70d. Type **163** 25 25
561 350d. Footprint in sand . . . 1·70 1·70

2005. Goshavank Monastery (12th–13th century). Sheet 84 × 84 mm.
MS562 **164** 480d. multicoloured 2·40 2·40

165 Armen Tigranian, Musical Scores and Landscape

2005. 125th Birth Anniv of Armen Tigranian (composer and musician).
563 **165** 220d. multicoloured . . . 1·10 1·10

166 Xachkar (cross)

2005. 90th Anniv of Armenian Genocide.
564 **166** 350d. multicoloured . . . 1·90 1·90

167 Mother Armenia (statue)

169 "Self Portrait"

168 Anushavan Arzumanian

2005. 60th Anniv of End of World War II.
565 **167** 350d. multicoloured . . . 1·90 1·90

2005. Birth Centenary of Anushavan Arzumanian (economist).
566 **168** 220d. multicoloured . . . 1·10 1·10

2005. 125th Birth Anniv of Martiros Sarian (artist). Multicoloured.
567 170d. Type **169** 80 80
568 200d. "Mount Aragats" . . . 90 90

170 Lavash Bread

172 Alphabet and Mesrob Mashots (inventor) (statue)

171 Fragment of 16th-century Khachkar

2005. Europa. Gastronomy. Multicoloured.
569 70d. Type **170** 25 25
570 350d. Harisa porridge . . . . 1·90 1·90

2005. Mother's Day.
571 **171** 350d. multicoloured . . . 1·90 1·90

2005. 1600th Anniv of Armenian Alphabet.
572 **172** 70d. multicoloured . . . 25 25

173 Vardan Ajemian (actor and theatre director)

174 Carpet (Artzakh) (19th-century)

2005. Anniversaries. Multicoloured.
573 70d. Type **173** (birth centenary) 25 25
574 170d. Anania Shirakatsi (scientist) (1400th birth anniv) 80 80

2005. Carpets. Multicoloured.
575 60d. Type **174** 15 15
576 350d. Carpet (Zangezour) (1904) . . . . 1·90 1·90
MS577 92 × 65 mm. 480d. Carpet (Artzakh) (18th-century) (28 × 42 mm) . . . . 2·50 2·50

175 Mher Mkrtchian (actor)

2005. Anniversaries. Multicoloured.
578 120d. Type **175** (75th birth anniv) 45 45
579 350d. Artem Mikoyan (aircraft designer) (birth centenary) . . . . 1·90 1·90

176 Armenian and Russian Flags and Arms

2006. Year of Armenia in Russia.
580 **176** 350d. multicoloured . . . 90 90
A stamp of the same design was issued by Russia.

177 Alexandre Melik-Pashaev (conductor)

2006. Birth Centenaries. Multicoloured.
581 70d. Type **177** 25 25
582 170d. Vakhtang Ananian (writer) 80 80

178 Emblem

2006. Winter Olympic Games, Turin. Multicoloured.
583 120d. Type **178** 45 45
584 170d. Map of Italy on skis 80 80

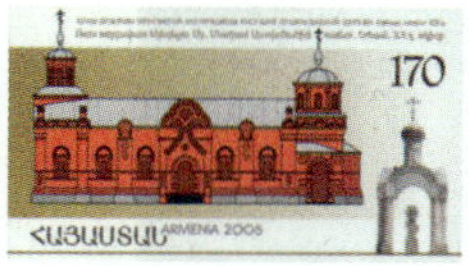

179 Cathedral Facade

2006. St. Mary's Cathedral of Russian Orthodox.
585 **179** 170d. multicoloured . . . 80 80

180 Raphael Patakanian

181 "P" and Emblem

2006. 175th Birth Anniv of Raphael Patkanian (writer).
586 **180** 220d. multicoloured . . . 1·10 1·10

2006. 50th Anniv of Europa Stamps. Multicoloured.
587 70d. Type **181** 20 20
588 70d. "T" and emblem . . . 20 20
589 70d. "C" and emblem . . . 20 20
590 70d. "E" and emblem . . . 20 20

2006. Traditional Costumes (4th series). As T **85**.
591 170d. Sassoun family 60 60
592 200d. Shatakhk couple . . . 65 65

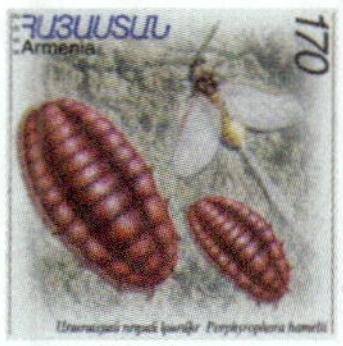

182 *Porphyrophora hamelii*

183 Spiridon Melikian

2006. Insects. Multicoloured.
593 170d. Type **182** 60 60
594 220d. *Procerus fallettianus* . . 70 70

2006. 125th (2005) Birth Anniv of Spiridon Melikian (composer).
595 **183** 350d. multicoloured . . . 90 90

184 "Adoration of the Magi" (1391), Gospel of Vostan

2006. Armenian Miniatures (2nd series). Sheet 75 × 65 mm.
MS596 **184** 480d. multicoloured 1·40 1·40

185 "15"

186 Dove

2006. 15th Anniv of Republic of Armenia. Sheet 70 × 70 mm.
MS597 **185** 480d. multicoloured 5·75 5·75

2006. Peace.
598 **186** 50d. multicoloured . . . 1·00 1·00

187 "To Jerusalem" (1211), Gospel of Haghpat

2006. Armenian Miniatures (3rd series). Sheet 65 × 76 mm.
MS599 **187** 220d. multicoloured 2·75 2·75

188 Watch Mechanism

2006. Europa. Integration. Multicoloured.
600 200d. Type **188** . . . . . . 2·75 2·75
601 350d. Golden key and rusty keys . . . . 4·50 4·50

189 Ball, Trophy, Flags and Emblem

2006. World Cup Football Championship, Germany.
602 **189** 350d. multicoloured . . . 4·50 4·50

190 Boghos Nubar

2006. Centenary of General Benevolent Union. Sheet 110 × 77 mm containing T **190** and similar vert designs. Multicoloured.
MS603 120d. × 3, Type **190** (benefactor); Minutes of first meeting; Alex Manoogian (benefactor) . . . . 4·50 4·50

191 Sergey Merkurov and "Naked" (sculpture)

2006. 125th Birth Anniv of Sergey Merkurov (artist and sculptor).
604 **191** 230d. multicoloured . . . 2·75 2·75

192 *Testudo horsfieldii*

193 Trophy

2007. Endangered Species. *Testudo horsfieldii*. Multicoloured.
605 70d. Type **192** 95 95
606 70d. Facing left 95 95
607 70d. Facing right 95 95
608 70d. Amongst leaves 95 95

2007. Armenia—37th World Chess Olympiad Champions. Multicoloured.
609 170d. Type **193** . . . . . . 2·20 2·20
610 220d. Medal . . . . 2·75 2·75
611 280d. Chess pieces . . . . . 2·75 2·75
612 350d. Queen . . . . 4·50 4·50

194 Decorated Tree

195 Clown and Circus Building

2007. Christmas and New Year.
613 **194** 70d. multicoloured . . . 95 95

2007. 50th Anniv of National Circus Collective.
614 **195** 70d. multicoloured . . . 95 95

196 Stepan Shahumian Monument

2007. Armenian Settlements. Stepanavan. Multicoloured.
615 110d. Type **196** . . . . . . 1·40 1·40
616 120d. Memorial fountain . . 1·50 1·50
617 170d. Rock of Lori Bridge 2·25 2·25
618 200d. Bear Rock . . . . . . 2·50 2·50

197 Sculpture

2007. 50th Anniv of Yerevan Mathematical Machines Scientific Research Institute.
619 **197** 120d. multicoloured . . . 1·50 1·50

2007. Traditional Costumes (5th series). As T **85**.
620 170d. Taron couple . . . . . 2·25 2·25
621 230d. Shirak couple . . . . 2·75 2·75

198 Voski

2007. Apricot (*Armeniaca vulgaris*). Multicoloured.
622 230d. Type **198** . . . . . . 2·25 2·25
623 230d. Yerevani . . . . 2·25 2·25
624 230d. Ghevondi . . . . . . 2·25 2·25
625 230d. Karmir Nakhijevanik 2·25 2·25
626 230d. Deghin Nakhijevanik 2·25 2·25
627 230d. Khosroveni karmir . . 2·25 2·25
628 230d. Deghnanush vaghahas 2·25 2·25
629 230d. Vaghahas vardaguyn 2·25 2·25
630 230d. Karmreni . . . . . . 2·25 2·25
631 230d. Sateni deghin . . . . . 2·25 2·25

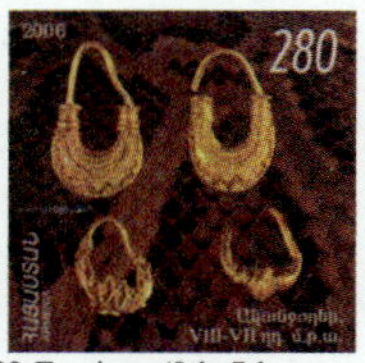

199 Earrings (8th–7th century BC)

2007. Jewellery. Multicoloured.
632 280d. Type **199** . . . . . . 2·75 2·75
633 280d. Pendant (3rd century BC) . . . . 2·75 2·75
634 280d. Earrings with pendants (10th–11th century) . . . . 2·75 2·75
635 280d. Gospel with encrusted cover (1484) . . . . 2·75 2·75
636 280d. Chalice (1623) . . . . 2·75 2·75
637 280d. Mitre (1765) . . . . . 2·75 2·75
638 280d. Dove-shaped vessel (1797) . . . . 2·75 2·75
639 280d. Knar-diadem (19th century) . . . . 2·75 2·75
640 280d. Bracelet (early 20th century) . . . . 2·75 2·75
641 280d. Incensory (19th century) . . . . 2·75 2·75

200 "Pallas Athena or Armoured Figure"

2007. 400th Birth Anniv (2006) of Rembrandt Harmenszoon van Rijn (artist). Multicoloured.
642 70d. Type **200** 95 95
643 350d. "Portrait of an Old Man" . . . . 4·50 4·50
MS644 128 × 89 mm. 70d. "Self Portrait with Saskia"; 170d. "Juno"; 280d. "Woman with Fan"; 350d. "Portrait of Jan Six" 10·00 10·00

201 Mozart as a Young Man (detail)

2007. 250th Birth Anniv (2006) of Wolfgang Amadeus Mozart (composer and musician). Multicoloured.
645 70d. Type **201** 20 20
646 350d. Mozart facing left (vert) . . . . 4·50 4·50
MS647 128 × 89 mm. 70d. Mozart and score (42 × 28 mm); 170d. Mozart and script (42 × 28 mm); 280d. Mozart and stringed instrument (42 × 28 mm); 350d. Mozart as young man (28 × 42 mm) . . . . 10·00 10·00

202 Artashes Shahinian

2007. Birth Centenary of Artashes Shahinian (scientist).
648 **202** 230d. multicoloured . . . 1·90 1·90

203 Blue Mosque

2007.
649 **203** 350d. multicoloured . . . 4·50 4·50

204 'L'Ange au Sourire' (the angel with a smile), Rheims Cathedral

205 Apricot

2007. Year of Armenia in France. Multicoloured.
650 70d. Type **204** . . . . 1·00 1·00
651 350d. The Nativity (15th-century miniature) . . 4·50 4·50

2007.
652 **205** 350d. multicoloured . . . 4·25 4·25

206 Tirgran the Great

207 Hands

2007.
653 **206** 50d. multicoloured . . . 80 80
654 60d. multicoloured . . . 90 90
655 70d. multicoloured . . . 1·00 1·00
656 120d. multicoloured . . . 1·80 1·80

2007. Centenary of Scouting.
657 **207** 350d. multicoloured . . . 4·50 4·50

208 Gusan Sheram

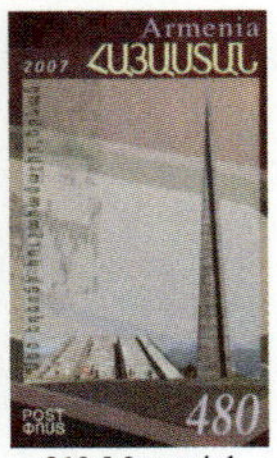

210 Memorial

209 Margar Sedrakyan

2007. 150th Birth Anniv of Talyan Grigor Karapet (Gusan Sheram) (composer and singer).
658 **208** 280d. multicoloured . . . 3·75 3·75

2007. Birth Centenary of Margar Sedrakyan (Cognac maker).
659 **209** 170d. multicoloured . . . 2·30 2·30

2007. 40th Anniv of Genocide Museum. Sheet 74 × 65 mm.
MS660 **210** 480d. multicoloured 6·00 6·00

211 *Sparrows* (Yeva Karapetyan)

2007. Children's Drawings.
661 **211** 35d. multicoloured . . . 1·00 1·00

212 Gevorg Bashinjaghyan and *Gyughakan Tesaran*

2007. 150th Birth Anniv of Gevorg Bashinjaghyan (artist). Multicoloured.
662 160d. Type **212** . . . . . . 2·30 2·30
663 220d. *Aragats* . . . . 3·00 3·00

213 Jean Garzou in his Studio

2007. Birth Centenary of Garnik Zulumyan (Jean Garzou) (artist). Multicoloured.
664 180d. Type **213** . . . . . . 2·50 2·50
665 220d. *Portrait of Seda* (*vert*) 2·75 2·75

214 Hands holding Trophy

2007. Pan Armenian Games, Yerevan. Sheet 40 × 58 mm.
MS666 **214** 360d. multicoloured 4·75 4·75

215 Norayr Sisakyan

2007. Birth Centenary of Norayr Sisakyan (biochemist).
667 **215** 120d. multicoloured . . . 1·60 1·60

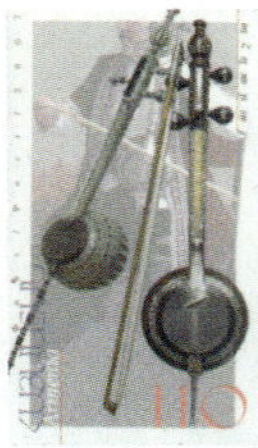
216 Kamancha

217 *Pelecanus crispus* (Dalmatian pelican)

2007. Traditional Instruments.
668 **216** 110d. multicoloured . . . 1·60 1·60

2007. Endangered Species. Multicoloured.
669 120d. Type **217** . . . . . . 1·50 1·50
670 200d. *Aegypius monachus* (Eurasian black vulture) . . 2·75 2·75

218 Matenadaran

2007. Matenadaran Manuscript and Book Depository.
671 **218** 200d. multicoloured . . . 2·50 2·50

219 Bagrat Nalbandyan

2007. Bagrat Nalbandyan (communications commissar) Commemoration.
672 **219** 230d. multicoloured . . . 3·00 3·00

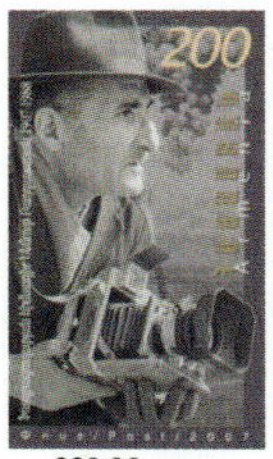

220 Nemrut Baghdasaryan

222 *Aphrodite* (Greek)

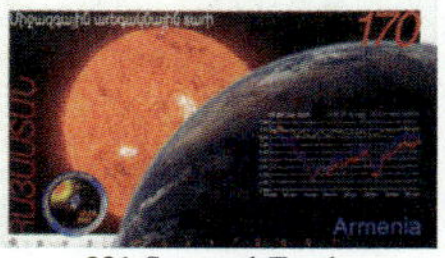

221 Sun and Earth

2007. Birth Centenary of Nemrut Baghdasaryan (photojournalist).
673 **220** 200d. multicoloured . . . 2·50 2·50

2007. International Year of Solar Physics. 50th Anniv of Geophysics.
674 **221** 170d. multicoloured . . . 2·30 2·30

2007. Statues. Multicoloured.
675 70d. Type **222** . . . . . . 1·00 1·00
676 350d. *Anahit* (Armenian) . . 4·50 4·50
Stamps of the same design were issued by Greece.

ARUBA Pt. 4

An island in the Caribbean, formerly part of Netherlands Antilles. In 1986 became an autonomous country within the Kingdom of the Netherlands.

100 cents = 1 gulden.

1 Map

1986. New Constitution.
1 **1** 25c. yellow, blue and black . . 70 35
2 – 45c. multicoloured 90 70
3 – 55c. black, grey and red . . . 1·10 75
4 – 100c. multicoloured . . . . . 1·75 1·60
DESIGNS—VERT: 45c. Aruban arms; 55c. National anthem. HORIZ: 100c. Aruban flag.

2 House

1986.
5 **2** 5c. black and yellow 10 10
6 – 15c. black and blue 35 20
7 – 20c. black and grey 20 15
8 – 25c. black and violet 30 30
9 – 30c. black and red 65 45
10 – 35c. black and bistre 65 45
12 – 45c. black and blue 65 35
14 – 55c. black and grey 75 45
15 – 60c. black and blue 90 65
16 – 65c. black and blue . . . . . 1·00 85
18 – 75c. black and brown 90 70
20 – 85c. black and orange . . . 1·00 75
21 – 90c. black and green . . . . 1·10 80
22 – 100c. black and brown . . . 1·10 85
23 – 150c. black and green . . . . 2·00 1·50
24 – 250c. black and green . . . . 3·25 2·75
DESIGNS: 15c. Clock tower; 20c. Container crane; 25c. Lighthouse; 30c. Snake; 35c. Burrowing owl; 45c. Caribbean vase (shell); 55c. Frog; 60c. Water-skier; 65c. Fisherman casting net; 75c. Hurdy-gurdy; 85c. Pot; 90, 250c. Different cacti; 100c. Maize; 150c. Watapana Tree.

3 People and Two Ropes

1986. "Solidarity". Multicoloured.
25 30c.+10c. Type **3** 85 55
26 35c.+15c. People and three ropes . . . . 1·00 65
27 60c.+25c. People and one rope 1·40 1·00

4 Dove between Scenes of Peace and War

1986. International Peace Year. Multicoloured.
28 60c. Type **4** . . . . 1·00 75
29 100c. Doves flying over broken barbed wire . . . . 1·50 1·10

5 Boy and Caterpillar

6 Engagement Picture

1986. Child Welfare. Multicoloured.
30 45c.+20c. Type **5** . . . . . . 1·10 75
31 70c.+25c. Boy and shell . . . 1·60 1·10
32 100c.+40c. Girl and butterfly 2·10 1·50

1987. Golden Wedding of Princess Juliana and Prince Bernhard.
33 **6** 135c. orange, black and gold 2·10 1·40

7 Queen Beatrix and Prince Claus

1987. Royal Visit. Multicoloured.
34 55c. Type **7** 90 55
35 60c. Prince Willem-Alexander 1·00 65

8 Woman looking at Beach

1987. Tourism. Multicoloured.
36 60c. Type **8** . . . . 1·10 80
37 100c. Woman looking at desert landscape . . . . 1·75 1·10

9 Child with Book on Beach

10 Plantation

1987. Child Welfare. Multicoloured.
38 25c.+10c. Type **9** 80 45
39 45c.+20c. Children drawing Christmas tree . . . . . . 1·10 70
40 70c.+30c. Child gazing at Nativity crib . . . . 1·60 1·10

1988. "Aloe vera". Multicoloured.
41 45c. Type **10** 80 55
42 60c. Stem and leaves of plant 1·00 70
43 100c. Harvesting aloes . . . . 1·60 1·00

11 25c. Coin

12 Bananaquits, Country Scene and "Love"

1988. Coins. Multicoloured.
44 25c. Type **11** 55 35
45 55c. Square 50c. coin . . . . 1·00 70
46 65c. 5c. and 10c. coins . . . . 1·25 80
47 150c. 1 gulden coin . . . . . 2·10 1·50

1988. Greetings Stamps. Multicoloured.
48 70c. Type **12** 90 65
49 135c. West Indian crown conch, West Indian chank (shells), seaside scene and "Love" . . . . 1·75 1·25

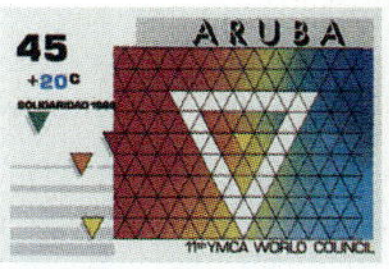

13 White Triangle on Shaded Background

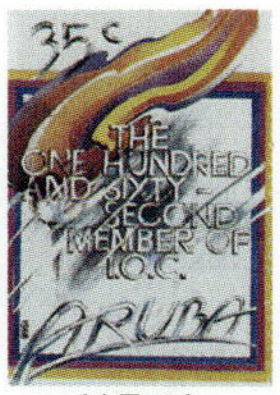

14 Torch

1988. "Solidarity". 11th Y.M.C.A. World Council. Multicoloured.
50 45c.+20c. Type **13** . . . . . . 1·00 70
51 60c.+25c. Interlocking triangles 1·40 1·00
52 100c.+50c. Shaded triangle on white background . . . . . 1·90 1·40

1988. Olympic Games, Seoul. Multicoloured.
53 35c. Type **14** 70 35
54 100c. Games and Olympic emblems . . . . 1·40 1·10

15 Jacks

16 Children

1988. Child Welfare. Toys. Multicoloured.
55 45c.+20c. Type **15** . . . . . 1·00 70
56 70c.+30c. Spinning top . . . . 70 1·00
57 100c.+50c. Kite . . . . 2·00 1·40

1989. Carnival. Multicoloured.
58 45c. Type **16** 85 55
59 60c. Girl in costume . . . . . 1·00 70
60 100c. Lights . . . . 1·90 1·10

17 Maripampun

18 Emblem

1989. Maripampun. Multicoloured.
61 35c. Type **17** 70 45
62 55c. Seed pods . . . . 1·00 70
63 200c. Pod distributing seeds 2·75 2·10

1989. Universal Postal Union.
64 **18** 250c. multicoloured . . . . 3·50 2·25

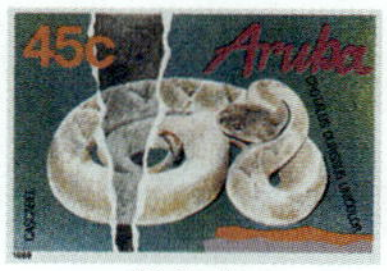
19 Snake

1989. South American Rattlesnake.
65 **19** 45c. multicoloured 70 45
66 – 55c. multicoloured 80 55
67 – 60c. multicoloured . . . . . 1·00 65
DESIGNS: 55, 60c. Snake (different).

20 Spoon in Child's Hand

21 Violin, Tambour and Cuatro Players

1989. Child Welfare. Multicoloured.
68 45c +20c. Type **20** 90 65
69 60c.+30c. Child playing football . . . . 1·10 80
70 100c.+50c. Child's hand in adult's hand (vert) . . . . 2·00 1·40

1989. New Year. Dande Musicians. Multicoloured.
71 25c. Type **21** 55 30
72 70c. Guitar and cuatro players and singer with hat 90 65
73 150c. Cuatro, accordion and wiri players . . . . 1·75 1·40

22 Tractor and Natural Vegetation

1990. Environmental Protection. Multicoloured.
74 45c. Type **22** 75 55
75 55c. Face and wildlife (vert) 90 65
76 100c. Marine life . . . . . . 1·60 1·10

23 Giant Caribbean Anemone and Pederson's Cleaning Shrimp

24 Ball

1990. Marine Life. Multicoloured.
77 60c. Type **23** . . . . 1·00 70
78 70c. Queen angelfish and red coral . . . . 1·10 1·00
79 100c. Banded coral shrimp, fire sponge and yellow boring sponge . . . . 1·90 1·50

1990. World Cup Football Championship, Italy. Multicoloured.
80 35c. Type **24** 65 35
81 200c. Mascot . . . . 2·75 2·10

25 Emblem of Committee of Tanki Leendert Association Youth Centre

26 Clay Painting Stamps

1990. "Solidarity". Multicoloured.
82 55c.+25c. Type **25** . . . . . 1·40 1·10
83 100c.+50c. Emblem of Foundation for Promotion of Responsible Parenthood 2·40 1·90

1990. Archaeology. Multicoloured.
84 45c. Type **26** 70 55
85 60c. Stone figure 90 70
86 100c. Dabajuroid-style jar . . 1·60 1·25

27 Sailboards and Fishes

28 Mountain and Shoreline

1990. Child Welfare. Multicoloured.
87 45c.+20c. Type **27** . . . . . 1·00 75
88 60c.+30c. Parakeets and coconut trees . . . . 1·25 1·10
89 100c.+50c. Kites and lizard . . 2·10 1·75

1991. Landscapes. Multicoloured.
90 55c. Type **28** 90 65
91 65c. Cacti and Haystack mountain . . . . 1·00 1·25
92 100c. House, mountain and ocean, Jaburibari . . . . . 1·60 1·25

29 Woman holding Herbs ("Carer")

30 "Ocimum sanctum"

1991. Women and Work. Multicoloured.
93 35c. Type **29** 65 35
94 70c. Women and kitchen ("Housewife") . . . . . . 1·00 85
95 100c. Women and telephone ("Woman in the World") 1·40 2·25

1991. Medicinal Plants. Multicoloured.
96 65c. Type **30** 85 75
97 75c. "Jatropha gossypifolia" 1·00 90
98 95c. "Croton flavens" . . . . 1·40 1·10

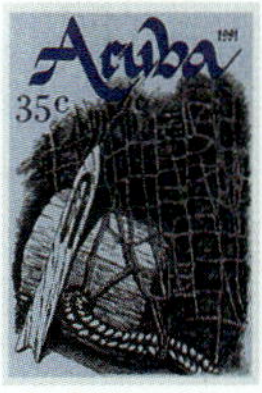
31 Fishing Net, Float and Needle

32 Child's Hand taking Book from Shelf

1991. Traditional Crafts.
99 **31** 35c. black, ultram & blue 65 35
100 – 250c. black, lilac & purple 3·50 2·75
DESIGNS: 250c. Hat, straw and hat-block.

1991. Child Welfare. Multicoloured.
101 45c.+25c. Type **32** . . . . . 1·00 80
102 60c.+35c. Child's finger pointing to letter "B" . . . 1·50 1·10
103 100c.+50c. Child reading . . 2·10 1·75

33 Toucan saying "Welcome"

34 Government Decree of 1892 establishing first Aruban Post Office

1991. Tourism. Multicoloured.
104 35c. Type **33** 65 45
105 70c. Aruban youth welcoming tourist . . . . 1·00 80
106 100c. Windmill and Bubali swamp . . . . 1·50 1·25

1992. Centenary of Postal Service (1st issue). Mult.
107 60c. Type **34** 90 75
108 75c. Lt.-Governor's building (mail service office, 1892–1908) (horiz) . . . . . 1·10 80
109 80c. Present Oranjestad P.O. (horiz) . . . . 1·40 1·00
See also Nos. 117/19.

35 Equality of Sexes

1992. Equality. Multicoloured.
110 100c. Type **35** . . . . 1·50 1·10
111 100c. People of different races (equality of nations) . . . 1·50 1·10

36 Aruban Flag, Guide Emblem and Girl Guides

37 Columbus, Map and Clouds

1992. "Solidarity". Multicoloured.
112 55c.+30c. Type **36** . . . . . 1·50 1·10
113 100c.+50c. Open hand with Cancer Fund emblem . . . 2·10 1·00

1992. 500th Anniv of Discovery of America by Columbus. Multicoloured.
114 30c. Type **37** 55 35
115 40c. Caravel (from navigation chart, 1525) 65 50
116 50c. Indians, queen conch shell and 1540 map . . . . 1·00 65

38 "I Love Post" (Jelissa Boekhoudt)

1992. Child Welfare. Centenary of Postal Service (2nd issue). Children's Drawings. Multicoloured.
117 50c.+30c. Type **38** . . . . . 1·25 95
118 70c.+35c. Airplane dropping letters (Marianne Fingal) 1·40 1·10
119 100c.+50c. Pigeon carrying letter in beak (Minorenti Jacobs) (vert) . . . . . . 2·10 1·75

39 Seroe Colorado Bridge

41 Rocks at Ayo

1992. Natural Bridges. Multicoloured.
120 70c. Type **39** . . . . 1·00 75
121 80c. Natural Bridge . . . . 1·25 90

1993. Rock Formations. Multicoloured.
123 50c. Type **41** 75 65
124 60c. Casibari 80 75
125 100c. Ayo (different) . . . . 1·25 1·10

42 Traditional Instruments

43 Sailfish dinghy

1993. Cock's Burial (part of St. John's Feast celebrations). Multicoloured.
126 40c. Type **42** 65 55
127 70c. "Cock's Burial" (painting, Leo Kuiperi) . . 95 80
128 80c. Verses of song, yellow flag, and calabashes . . . 1·10 1·00

1993. Sports. Multicoloured.
129 50c. Type **43** 70 65
130 65c. Land sailing 90 80
131 75c. Sailboard . . . . 1·00 90

44 Young Iguana

1993. The Iguana. Multicoloured.
132 35c. Type **44** 55 50
133 60c. Young adult 80 70
134 100c. Adult (vert) . . . . . 1·25 1·10

45 Aruban House, Landscape and Cacti

1993. Child Welfare. Multicoloured.
135 50c.+30c. Type **45** . . . . . 1·00 90
136 75c.+40c. Face, bridge and sea (vert) . . . . 1·50 1·40
137 100c.+50c. Bridge, buildings and landscape . . . . . . 1·90 1·75

46 Owls

47 Athlete

1994. The Burrowing Owl. Multicoloured.
138 5c. Type **46** 30 20
139 10c. Pair with young 50 35
140 35c. Owl with locust in claw (vert) 85 70
141 40c. Owl (vert) . . . . 1·00 90

1994. Centenary of Int Olympic Committee. Mult.
142 50c. Type **47** 70 65
143 90c. Baron Pierre de Coubertin (founder) . . . 90 1·10

48 Family in House

49 Flags of U.S.A. and Aruba, Ball and Players

1994. "Solidarity". Int Year of The Family. Mult.
144 50c.+35c. Type **48** . . . . . 1·10 1·00
145 100c.+50c. Family outside house . . . . 2·00 1·90

1994. World Cup Football Championship, U.S.A. Multicoloured.
146 65c. Type **49** 90 80
147 150c. Mascot . . . . 2·00 1·75

50 West Indian Cherry

51 Children with Umbrella sitting on Anchor (shelter and security)

1994. Wild Fruits. Multicoloured.
148 40c. Type **50** 70 55
149 70c. Geiger tree 95 80

150 85c. "Pithecellobium unguis-cati" . . . . 1·25 1·10
151 150c. Sea grape . . . . . . 2·25 1·75

1994. Child Welfare. Influence of the Family. Mult.
152 50c.+30c. Type **51** . . . . . 1·10 1·00
153 80c.+35c. Children in smiling sun (warmth of nurturing home) . . . . 1·50 1·40
154 100c.+50c. Child flying on owl (wisdom guiding the child) . . . . 1·90 1·75

52 Government Building, 1888

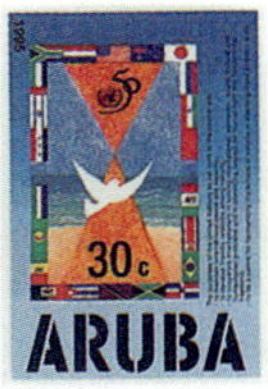

53 Dove, Emblem and Flags

1995. Historic Buildings. Multicoloured.
155 35c. Type **52** 50 45
156 60c. Ecury Residence, 1929 (vert) 85 70
157 100c. Protestant Church, 1846 (vert) . . . . 1·25 1·10

1995. 50th Anniv of U.N.O. Multicoloured.
158 30c. Type **53** 55 45
159 200c. Emblem, flags, globe and doves . . . . 2·50 2·40

54 Casanova II and Rosettes

55 Cowpea

1995. Interpaso Horses. Multicoloured.
160 25c. Type **54** 50 35
161 75c. Horse performing Paso Fino . . . . 1·10 90
162 80c. Horse performing Figure 8 (vert) . . . . 1·10 1·00
163 90c. Girl on horseback (vert) 1·25 1·10

1995. Vegetables. Multicoloured.
164 25c. Type **55** 40 35
165 50c. Apple cucumber 80 65
166 70c. Okra 95 80
167 85c. Pumpkin . . . . 1·25 1·00

56 Hawksbill Turtle

57 Children holding Balloons outside House (Christina Trejo)

1995. Turtles. Multicoloured.
168 15c. Type **56** 50 20
169 50c. Green turtle 80 50
170 95c. Loggerhead turtle . . . . 1·50 1·10
171 100c. Leatherback turtle . . . 1·60 1·10

1995. Child Welfare. Children's Drawings. Mult.
172 50c.+25c. Type **57** . . . . . 1·10 80
173 70c.+35c. Children at seaside (Julysses Tromp) . . . . . 1·40 1·10
174 100c.+50c. Children and adults gardening (Ronald Tromp) . . . . 2·10 1·60

58 Henry Eman

59 Woman

1996. 10th Anniv of Internal Autonomy. Politicians. Multicoloured.
175 100c. Type **58** . . . . 1·25 1·10
176 100c. Juancho Irausquin . . 1·25 1·10
177 100c. Shon Eman . . . . . 1·25 1·10
178 100c. Betico Croes . . . . . 1·25 1·10

1996. America. Traditional Costumes. Mult.
179 65c. Type **59** 90 70
180 70c. Man 95 70
181 100c. Couple dancing (horiz) 1·40 1·10

60 Running

61 Mathematical Instruments, "G" and Rising Sun

1996. Olympic Games, Atlanta. Multicoloured.
182 85c. Type **60** . . . . 1·10 90
183 130c. Cycling . . . . 1·75 1·60

1996. "Solidarity". 75th Anniv of Freemasons' Lodge El Sol Naciente. Multicoloured.
184 60c.+30c. Type **61** . . . . . 1·25 1·00
185 100c.+50c. Globes on top of columns and doorway . . 1·90 1·75

62 Livia Ecury (teacher and nurse)

63 Rabbits at Bus-stop

1996. Anniversaries. Multicoloured.
186 60c. Type **62** (5th death) . . 90 80
187 60c. Laura Wernet-Paskel (teacher and politician, 85th birth) 90 80
188 60c. Lolita Euson (poet, 2nd death) 90 80

1996. Child Welfare. Comic Strips. Multicoloured.
189 50c.+25c. Type **63** . . . . . 1·00 80
190 70c.+35c. Mother accompanying young owl to school . . . . 1·40 1·25
191 100c.+50c. Boy flying kite with friend . . . . 1·75 1·60

64 Children at the Seaside and Words on Signpost

65 Postman on Bicycle, 1936–57

1997. "Year of Papiamento" (Creole language). Multicoloured.
192 50c. Type **64** 75 60
193 140c. Sunrise over ocean . . 1·90 2·10

1997. America. The Postman. Multicoloured.
194 60c. Type **65** 90 80
195 70c. Postman delivering package by jeep, 1957–88 1·00 80
196 80c. Postman delivering letter from motor scooter, 1995 1·25 1·00

66 Decorated Cunucu House

1997. Aruban Architecture. Multicoloured.
197 30c. Type **66** 45 40
198 65c. Bannistered steps . . . . 1·00 80
199 100c. Arends Building (vert) 1·40 1·25

67 Merlin and Lighthouse

68 Passengers approaching Cruise Liner

1997. "Pacific 97" International Stamp Exhibition, San Francisco. Multicoloured.
200 90c. Type **67** . . . . 1·10 1·10
201 90c. Windswept trees and dolphin . . . . 1·10 1·10
202 90c. Iguana on rock and cacti 1·10 1·10
203 90c. Three types of fishes and one dolphin . . . . 1·10 1·10
204 90c. Two dolphins and fishes 1·10 1·10
205 90c. Burrowing owl on shore, turtle and lionfish . . . . 1·10 1·10
206 90c. Stingray, rock beauty, angelfishes, squirrelfish and coral reef . . . . . . 1·10 1·10
207 90c. Diver and stern of shipwreck . . . . 1·10 1·10
208 90c. Shipwreck, reef and fishes . . . . 1·10 1·10

Nos. 200/8 were issued together, se-tenant, forming a composite design.

1997. Cruise Tourism. Multicoloured.
209 35c. Type **68** 50 40
210 50c. Passengers disembarking 70 60
211 150c. Cruise liner at sea and launch at shore . . . . . 2·00 1·75

69 Coral Tree

1997. Trees. Multicoloured.
212 50c. Type **69** 70 60
213 60c. "Cordia dentata" . . . 90 80
214 70c. "Tabebuia billbergii" . . 1·00 80
215 130c. Lignum vitae . . . . . 1·75 1·60

70 Girl among Aloes

1997. Child Welfare. Child and Nature. Mult.
216 50c.+25c. Type **70** . . . . . 1·00 85
217 70c.+35c. Boy and butterfly (vert) . . . . 1·40 1·25
218 100c.+50c. Girl swimming underwater by coral reef 1·90 1·75

71 Fort Zoutman

72 Stages of Eclipse

1998. Bicentenary of Fort Zoutman.
219 **71** 30c. multicoloured 50 40
220 250c. multicoloured . . . . 3·00 2·75

Each design consists of alternating strips in brown tones or black and white. When the 250c. is laid on top of the 30c., the brown strips form a composite design of the fort in its early years and the black and white strips a composite design of the fort after 1929, when various alterations were made.

1998. Total Solar Eclipse. Multicoloured.
221 85c. Type **72** . . . . 1·10 1·00
222 100c. Globe showing path of eclipse and map of Aruba plotting duration of total darkness . . . . 1·40 1·25

73 Globe, Emblem and Wheelchair balanced on Map of Aruba

1998. "Solidarity" Anniversaries. Multicoloured.
223 60c.+30c. Type **73** (50th anniv of Lions Club of Aruba) . . . . 1·25 1·00
224 100c.+50c. Boy reading, emblem and grandmother in rocking chair (60th anniv of Rotary Club of Aruba) . . . . 1·90 1·75

74 Tropical Mockingbird

1998. Birds. Multicoloured.
225 50c. Type **74** 70 65
226 60c. American kestrel (vert) 95 80
227 70c. Troupial (vert) . . . . . 1·10 90
228 150c. Bananaquit . . . . . 2·10 1·90

75 Villagers processing Corn

76 Ribbon Dance

1998. World Stamp Day.
229 **75** 225c. multicoloured . . . . 3·25 2·75

1998. Child Welfare. Multicoloured.
230 50c.+25c. Type **76** . . . . . 1·00 90
231 80c.+40c. Boy playing cuarta (four-string guitar) . . . . 1·75 1·60
232 100c. + 50c. Basketball . . . 2·00 1·75

77 Two Donkeys

1999. The Donkey. Multicoloured.
233 40c. Type **77** 60 50
234 65c. Two adults and foal . . 1·00 90
235 100c. Adult and foal . . . . 1·40 1·40

78 "Opuntia wentiana"

79 Creole Dog

1999. Cacti. Multicoloured.
236 50c. Type **78** 70 65
237 60c. "Lemaireocereus griseus" 95 80
238 70c. "Cephalocereus lanuginosus" ("Cadushi di carona") . . . . 1·00 90
239 75c. "Cephalocereus lanuginosus" ("Cadushi") 1·10 1·00

1999. Creole Dogs ("Canis familiaris"). Mult.
240 40c. Type **79** 60 50
241 60c. White dog standing on rock 90 80
242 80c. Dog sitting by sea . . . 1·10 1·00
243 165c. Black and tan dog sitting on rock . . . . . . 2·10 2·00

80 Indian Cave Drawings and Antique Map

1999. 500 Years of Cultural Diversity. Mult.
244 150c. Type **80** . . . . 1·75 1·60
245 175c. Indian cave drawings and carnival headdress . . 2·10 2·00
MS246 90 × 60 mm. Nos. 244/5 4·00 4·00

81 Public Library and Children

1999. 50th Anniv of Public Library Service. Mult.
247 70c. Type **81** 90 80
248 100c. Library, Santa Cruz . . 1·25 1·25

82 Boy with Fisherman

83 Three Wise Men

1999. Child Welfare. Multicoloured.

249	60c.+30c. Type **82**	1·00	1·00
250	80c.+40c. Man reading to children	1·50	1·40
251	100c.+50c. Woman with child (vert)	1·90	1·75

1999. Christmas. Multicoloured. Self-adhesive.

252	40c. Type **83**	50	45
253	70c. Shepherds	95	90
254	100c. Holy Family	1·40	1·25

84 *Norops lineatus*

2000. Reptiles. Multicoloured.

255	40c. Type **84**	55	50
256	60c. Greeen iguana (vert)	90	80
257	75c. Annulated snake (vert)	1·00	90
258	150c. Racerunner	1·75	1·75

85 Flags

2000. America. A.I.D.S. Awareness. Multicoloured.

259	75c. Type **85**	95	90
260	175c. Ribbon on globe (vert)	2·10	2·00

86 Bank Facade

2000. Anniversaries. Multicoloured.

261	150c. Type **86** (75th anniv of Aruba Bank)	1·90	1·75
262	165c. Chapel (250th anniv of Alto Vista Chapel)	2·25	2·00

87 West Indian Top Shell

2000. Aspects of Aruba. Multicoloured.

263	15c. Type **87**	20	20
264	25c. Guadirikiri cave	40	35
265	35c. Mud-house (vert)	50	50
267	55c. Cacti	75	70
269	85c. Hooiberg	1·00	1·00
271	100c. Gold smelter, Balashi (vert)	1·25	1·25
272	250c. Rock crystal	3·25	3·25
275	500c. Conchi	5·75	5·50

88 Children at Beach Playground

2000. "Solidarity". Multicoloured.

280	75c.+35c. Type **88**	1·40	1·25
281	100c.+50c. Children building sandcastles	2·10	1·90

89 "Solar Energy" (Nikki Johanna Teresia Willems)

2000. Child Welfare. "Stampin' the Future". Winning Entries in Children's International Painting Competition. Multicoloured.

282	60c.+30c. Type **89**	1·25	1·25
283	80c.+40c. "Environmental Protection" (Samantha Jeanne Tromp)	1·50	1·40
284	100c.+50c. "Future Vehicles" (Jennifer Huntington)	2·10	1·90

90 Cat

2001. Domestic Animals. Multicoloured.

285	5c. Type **90**	15	15
286	30c. Tortoise	35	35
287	50c. Rabbit	60	60
288	200c. Brown-throated conure	2·40	2·40

91 Shaman preparing for Sun Ceremony

2001. 40 Years of Mascaruba (amateur theatre group). Depicting scenes from *Macuarima*, History or Legend? (musical play). Mult.

289	60c. Type **91**	70	70
290	150c. Love scene between Guadarikiri and Blanco	1·75	1·75

92 Ford Model A Roadster, 1930

2001. Motor Cars. Multicoloured.

291	25c. Type **92**	30	30
292	40c. Citroen Comerciale saloon, 1933	45	45
293	70c. Plymouth Pick-up, 1948	90	90
294	75c. Edsel corsair convertable, 1959	1·00	1·00

93 Rock Drawings

94 Pedestrians using Crossing

2001. Universal Postal Union. United Nations Year of Dialogue among Civilizations.

295	**93** 175c. multicoloured	2·40	2·40

2001. Child Welfare. International Year of Volunteers. Multicoloured.

296	40c. + 20c. Type **94**	80	80
297	60c. + 30c. Boys walking dogs	1·10	1·10
298	100c. + 50c. Children putting litter in bin	2·00	2·00

95 Dakota Airport, 1950

2002. Queen Beatrix Airport. Multicoloured.

299	30c. Type **95**	45	45
300	75c. Queen Beatrix Airport, 1972	1·10	1·10
301	175c. Queen Beatrix Airport, 2000	2·50	2·50

Dakota Airport was re-named Princess Beatrix Airport in 1955 and Queen Beatrix Airport in 1972.

96 Prince Willem-Alexander and Princess Maxima

2002. Wedding of Crown Prince Willem-Alexander to Maxima Zorreguieta. Multicoloured.

302	60c. Type **96**	85	85
303	300c. Prince Willem-Alexander and Princess Máxima facing right	4·25	4·25

97 Tap and Water Droplet

98 Hand holding Quill Pen

2002. 70th Anniv of Water Company (W. E. B.). Multicoloured.

304	60c. Type **97**	85	85
305	85c. Water pipes (horiz)	1·25	1·25
306	165c. Water meter and meter reader	2·25	2·25

2002. America. Literacy Campaign. Multicoloured.

307	25c. Type **98**	35	35
308	100c. Alphabet on wall and boy on step-ladder	1·40	1·40

99 *U-156* Submarine firing on Lago Oil Refinery

100 Boy, Iguana and Goat

2002. Second World War. Multicoloured.

309	60c. Type **99**	85	85
310	75c. *Pedernales* (oil-tanker) in flames	1·00	1·00
311	150c. "Boy" Ecury (resistance fighter) (statue) (vert)	2·10	2·10

2002. Child Welfare. Animals. Multicoloured.

312	40c.+20c. Type **100**	85	85
313	60c.+30c. Girl, turtle and crab (horiz)	1·00	1·00
314	100c.+50c. Pelicans, boy and parakeet	2·10	2·10

101 House at Fontein

2003. Mud Houses. Multicoloured.

315	40c. Type **101**	30	30
316	60c. House at Ari Kok	45	45
317	75c. House at Fontein	55	55

102 The Trupialen Boys Choir

2003. 50th Anniv of "De Trupialen" (boys' organization). Multicoloured.

318	30c. Type **102**	10	10
319	50c. Puppet theatre posters	20	20
320	100c. Organization emblems	35	35

103 *Schomburgkia humboldtii*

2003. Orchids. Multicoloured.

321	75c. Type **103**	25	25
322	500c. *Brassavola nodosa*	1·80	1·80

104 Orange-barred Sulphur Butterfly

105 Hawksbill Turtle (*Eretmochelys imbricate*)

2003. Butterflies. Multicoloured.

323	40c. Type **104**	15	15
324	75c. Monarch	30	30
325	85c. Hairstreak	30	30
326	175c. Gulf fritillary	60	60

2003. Endangered Species. Turtles. Multicoloured.

327	25c. Type **105**	10	10
328	60c. Leatherback turtle (*Dermochelys coricea*) (horiz)	20	20
329	75c. Green turtle (*Chelonia mydas*)	30	30
330	150c. Loggerhead turtle (*Caretta caretta*) (horiz)	55	55

106 Baseball

2003. Child Welfare. Children and Sport.

331	40c.+20c. Type **106**	40	40
332	60c.+30c. Volleyball	60	60
333	100c.+50c. Football	1·00	1·00

107 Masks and Headdresses

108 Sandwich Tern (*Sterna sandvicensis*)

2004. 50th Anniv of Carnival. Multicoloured.

334	60c. Type **107**	40	40
335	75c. Woman's face (vert)	55	55
336	150c. Heads wearing carnival headdresses	1·00	1·00

2004. Birds. Multicoloured.

337	70c. Type **108**	50	55
338	75c. Brown pelican (*Pelecanus occidentalis*)	55	55
339	80c. Frigate bird (*Fregata magnificens*)	55	55
340	90c. Laughing gull (*Larus atricilla*)	60	60

109 Parrotfish

110 Children holding Maracas

2004. Fish. Multicoloured.

341	40c. Type **109**	30	30
342	60c. Queen angelfish	40	40
343	75c. Squirrelfish	55	55
344	100c. Small-mouthed grunt	70	70

2004. Child Welfare. Musical Instruments. Multicoloured.

345	60c.+30c. Type **110**	50	50
346	85c.+40c. Three children and steel drum	70	70
347	100c.+50c. Boy playing wiri and girl holding tambourine	85	85

111 Presents and Decorated Tree

112 Interconnecting Islands (Aruba, Curacao, Bonaire, Saba, St. Maarten and St. Eustatius)

2004. Christmas and New Year. Multicoloured.

348	50c. Type **111**	30	30
349	85c. Parcels, carol singers and candle	50	50
350	125c. Fireworks	70	70

2004. 50th Anniv of Charter of the Kingdom (statute establishing partial autonomy). Multicoloured.

351	160c. Type **112**	90	90
352	165c. Kingdom Statute monument	95	95

113 Sun and Flower

2004. Greetings Stamps. Multicoloured.

353	60c. Type **113** ("Thank you")	40	40
354	75c. Two rabbits ("Love")	55	55
355	135c. Fish ("Get well soon")	75	75
356	215c. Balloons ("Congratulations")	1·30	1·30

114 Race Car and Spectators

2005. Drag Racing. Multicoloured.

357	60c. Type **114**	40	40
358	85c. Parachute opening at race end	60	60
359	185c. Race start	1·10	1·10

115 Queen Beatrix and Prince Claus — **116** Sunset

2005. 25th Anniv of Coronation of Queen Beatrix. Sheet 144 × 75 mm containing T **115** and similar vert designs. Multicoloured.

MS360 30c. Type **115**; 60c. Seated; 75c. With Nelson Mandela; 105c.Wearing glasses; 215c. Wearing hat . . . 3·00 3·00

2005. Tourism. Sunsets. Multicoloured.

361	60c. Type **116**	35	35
362	100c. Palm tree	60	60
363	205c. Pelicans	1·30	1·30

117 American Kestrel (*Falco sparverius*) — **118** *Acropora cervicornis*

2005. Birds. Multicoloured.

364	60c. Type **117**	35	35
365	75c. Burrowing owl (*Athene cunicularia*)	50	50
366	135c. Osprey (*Pandion haliaetus*)	75	75
367	200c. Common caracara (*Polyborus plancus*)	1·20	1·20
MS368	110 × 70 mm. Nos. 364/7	2·75	2·75

2005. Corals. Multicoloured.

369	60c. Type **118**	35	35
370	75c. *Millepora complanata*	45	45
371	100c. *Iciligorgia schrammi*	60	60
372	215c. *Diploria strigosa*	1·40	1·40

119 Girl and Stamps

2005. Child Welfare. Philately. Multicoloured.

373	75c. Type **119**	45	45
374	85c. Boy holding magnifier and album	50	50
375	125c. Boy putting stamps in album	80	80

120 "House of Savaneta" (Jean George Pandellis)

2006. Art. Multicoloured.

376	60c. Type **120**	30	30
377	75c. "Haf di Rei" (Mateo Hayde)	45	45
378	185c. "Landscape" (Julie Oduber)	1·20	1·20

121 Emblem — **122** Tree and Log Bridge

2006. 50th Anniv of YMCA. Multicoloured.

379	75c. Type **121**	45	45
380	205c. Children at play (horiz)	1·40	1·40

2006. Washington 2006 International Stamp Exhibition. Sheet 98 × 88 mm containing T **122** and similar multicoloured design.

MS381 500c. × 2, Type **122**; Cacti and boats (vert) . . . 5·50 5·50

The stamps and margins of **MS**381 form a composite design.

123 Goalkeeper

2006. World Cup Football Championship, Germany. Multicoloured.

382	75c. Type **123**	45	45
383	215c. Hands holding globe as football	1·25	1·20

124 Surf Boards, Boats, Windsurfers and Kitesurfer

2006. 20th Anniv of Hi-Winds Windsurfing Competition. Multicoloured.

384	60c. Type **124**	40	40
385	100c. Leaping kitesurfer	65	65
386	125c. Windsurfers	75	75

125 Fire Hazards

2006. Fire Prevention. Multicoloured.

387	60c. Type **125**	40	40
388	100c. Firefighters	65	65
389	205c. Fire appliances	1·40	1·40

126 House and Goat

2006. Arikok National Park. Multicoloured.

390	75c. Type **126**	45	45
391	100c. Cacti, valley and eagle (vert)	65	65
392	200c. Cacti and owl	1·20	1·20

127 Dancers and Boar

2007. New Year. Year of the Pig. Sheet 78 × 62 mm containing T **127** and similar multicoloured design.

MS393 205c. Type **127**; 215c. Dragon (*vert*) . . . 6·00 6·00

The stamp and margin of **MS393** form a composite design.

128 Luciana Maria Koolman and Original Building

2007. 50th Anniv of Casa Cuna Children's Home Foundation. Multicoloured.

394	50c. Type **128**	75	75
395	125c. Children enclosed in hands	1·90	1·90
396	150c. New building	2·10	2·10

129 Museum of Antiquities

2007. Museums. Multicoloured.

397	70c. Type **129**	90	90
398	85c. Numismatic museum	1·20	1·20
399	100c. Archaeological museum	1·50	1·50
400	135c. Historical museum	1·90	1·90

EXPRESS MAIL SERVICE

E **40** Globe, Planets and Aruban Arms

1993.

E122	E **40** 200c. multicoloured	2·75	2·10

ASCENSION Pt. 1

An island in South Atlantic. A dependency of St. Helena.

1922. 12 pence = 1 shilling;
20 shillings = 1 pound.
1971. 100 pence = 1 pound.

1922. Stamps of St. Helena of 1912 optd **ASCENSION**.

1	½d. black and green	4·75	21·00
2	1d. green	4·75	20·00
3	1½d. red	17·00	48·00
4	2d. black and slate	17·00	13·00
5	3d. blue	13·00	21·00
6	8d. black and purple	27·00	50·00
9	1s. black on green	28·00	48·00
7	2s. black and blue on blue	95·00	£120
8	3s. black and violet	£140	£160

2 Badge of St. Helena

1924.

10	**2** ½d. black	4·00	16·00
11	1d. black and green	5·50	11·00
12	1½d. red	9·00	30·00
13	2d. black and grey	18·00	10·00
14	3d. blue	8·00	16·00
15	4d. black on yellow	48·00	80·00
15d	5d. purple and green	14·00	24·00
16	6d. black and purple	50·00	£100
17	8d. black and violet	15·00	45·00
18	1s. black and brown	21·00	55·00
19	2s. black and blue on blue	60·00	90·00
20	3s. black on blue	85·00	90·00

3 Georgetown — **4** Ascension Island

1934. Medallion portrait of King George V (except 1s.).

21	**3** ½d. black and violet	90	80
22	**4** 1d. black and green	1·75	1·25
23	– 1½d. black and red	1·75	2·25
24	**4** 2d. black and orange	1·75	2·50
25	– 3d. black and blue	1·75	1·50
26	– 5d. black and blue	2·25	3·25
27	**4** 8d. black and brown	4·25	4·75
28	– 1s. black and red	18·00	9·00
29	**4** 2s.6d. black and purple	45·00	40·00
30	– 5s. black and brown	50·00	55·00

DESIGNS—HORIZ: 1½d. The Pier; 3d. Long Beach; 5d. Three Sisters; 1s. Sooty tern ("Wideawake Fair"); 5s. Green mountain.

1935. Silver Jubilee. As T **13** of Antigua.

31	1½d. blue and red	3·50	9·00
32	2d. blue and grey	11·00	25·00
33	5d. green and blue	19·00	28·00
34	1s. grey and purple	23·00	32·00

1937. Coronation. As T **2** of Aden.

35	1d. green	50	1·40
36	2d. orange	1·00	60
37	3d. blue	1·00	50

10 The Pier

1938.

38b	A ½d. black and violet	1·25	2·50
39	B 1d. black and green	42·00	9·50
39b	1d. black and orange	45	60
39d	C 1d. black and green	60	1·50
40b	**10** 1½d. black and red	85	80
40d	1½d. black and pink	70	1·00
41a	B 2d. black and orange	80	40
41c	2d. black and red	1·00	1·75
42	D 3d. black and blue	£100	27·00
42b	3d. black and grey	70	80
42d	B 4d. black and blue	4·50	3·00
43	C 6d. black and blue	9·00	2·25
44a	A 1s. black and brown	4·75	2·00
45	**10** 2s.6d. black and red	42·00	9·50
46a	D 5s. black and brown	38·00	30·00
47a	C 10s. black and purple	42·00	55·00

DESIGNS: A, Georgetown; B, Green Mountain; C, Three Sisters; D, Long Beach.

1946. Victory. As T **9** of Aden.

48	2d. orange	40	1·00
49	4d. blue	40	60

1948. Silver Wedding. As T **10/11** of Aden.

50	3d. black	50	30
51	10s. mauve	50·00	50·00

1949. U.P.U. As T **20/23** of Antigua.

52	3d. red	1·00	2·00
53	4d. blue	4·00	1·50
54	6d. olive	2·00	3·50
55	1s. black	2·00	1·50

1953. Coronation. As T **13** of Aden.

56	3d. black and grey	1·00	1·50

19 Water Catchment

1956.

57	**19** ½d. black and brown	10	50
58	– 1d. black and mauve	3·00	1·75
59	– 1½d. black and orange	1·00	1·00
60	– 2d. black and red	3·50	2·25
61	– 2½d. black and brown	1·75	2·50
62	– 3d. black and blue	4·00	1·25
63	– 4d. black and turquoise	1·25	2·00
64	– 6d. black and blue	1·25	2·50
65	– 7d. black and olive	2·25	1·50
66	– 1s. black and red	1·00	1·25
67	– 2s.6d. black and purple	27·00	6·50
68	– 5s. black and green	35·00	17·00
69	– 10s. black and purple	48·00	35·00

DESIGNS: 1d. Map of Ascension; 1½d. Georgetown; 2d. Map showing Atlantic cables; 2½d. Mountain road; 3d. White-tailed tropic bird ("Boatswain Bird"); 4d. Yellow-finned tuna; 6d. Rollers on seashore; 7d. Turtles; 1s. Land crab; 2s.6d. Sooty tern ("Wideawake"); 5s. Perfect Crater; 10s. View of Ascension from north-west.

28 Brown Booby

1963. Birds. Multicoloured.

70	1d. Type **28**	1·50	30
71	1½d. White-capped noddy ("Black Noddy")	2·00	1·00
72	2d. White tern ("Fairy Tern")	1·25	30
73	3d. Red-billed tropic bird	1·75	30
74	4½d. Common noddy ("Brown Noddy")	1·75	30
75	6d. Sooty tern ("Wideawake Tern")	1·25	30
76	7d. Ascension frigate bird ("Frigate bird")	1·25	30
77	10d. Blue-faced booby ("White Booby")	1·25	50
78	1s. White-tailed tropic bird ("Yellow-billed Tropicbird")	1·25	30
79	1s.6d. Red-billed tropic bird	4·50	1·75
80	2s.6d. Madeiran storm petrel	8·50	11·00
81	5s. Red-footed booby (brown phase)	9·00	11·00

82 10s. Ascension frigate birds ("Frigate birds") . . . . . 13·00 12·00
83 £1 Red-footed booby (white phase) . . . . 20·00 13·00

1963. Freedom from Hunger. As T **28** of Aden.
84 1s.6d. red 75 40

1963. Centenary of Red Cross. As T **33** of Antigua.
85 3d. red and black . . . . . . 1·75 1·25
86 1s.6d. red and blue . . . . . 3·25 2·25

1965. Centenary of I.T.U. As T **36** of Antigua.
87 3d. mauve and violet 50 65
88 6d. turquoise and brown . . . 75 65

1965. I.C.Y. As T **37** of Antigua.
89 1d. purple and turquoise . . . 40 60
90 6d. green and lavender 60 90

1966. Churchill Commemoration. As T **38** of Antigua.
91 1d. blue 50 75
92 3d. green . . . . 2·25 1·25
93 6d. brown . . . . 2·75 1·50
94 1s.6d. violet . . . . 3·50 2·00

1966. World Cup Football Championship. As T **40** of Antigua.
95 3d. multicoloured . . . . . . 1·50 60
96 6d. multicoloured . . . . . . 1·50 80

1966. Inauguration of W.H.O. Headquarters, Geneva. As T **41** of Antigua.
97 3d. black, green and blue . . . 1·75 1·00
98 1s.6d. black, purple and ochre 4·75 2·00

36 Satellite Station

44 Human Rights Emblem and Chain Links

37 B.B.C. Emblem

1966. Opening of Apollo Communication Satellite Earth Station.
99 **36** 4d. black and violet . . . 10 10
100 8d. black and green . . . 15 15
101 1s.3d. black and brown . . 15 20
102 2s.6d. black and blue . . . 15 20

1966. Opening of B.B.C. Relay Station.
103 **37** 1d. gold and blue 10 10
104 3d. gold and green 15 15
105 6d. gold and violet 15 15
106 1s.6d. gold and red 15 15

1967. 20th Anniv of UNESCO As T **54/56** of Antigua.
107 3d. multicoloured . . . . . 2·00 1·50
108 6d. yellow, violet and olive 2·75 2·00
109 1s.6d. black, purple and orange . . . . 4·50 2·50

1968. Human Rights Year.
110 **44** 6d. orange, red and black 15 15
111 1s.6d. blue, red and black 20 25
112 2s.6d. green, red and black 20 30

45 Black Durgon ("Ascension Black-Fish")

1968. Fishes (1st series).
113 **45** 4d. black, grey and blue . . 30 40
114 – 8d. multicoloured 35 70
115 – 1s.9d. multicoloured . . . 40 80
116 – 2s.3d. multicoloured . . . 40 85
DESIGNS: 8d. Scribbled filefish ("Leather-jacket"); 1s.9d. Yellow-finned tuna; 2s.3d. Short-finned mako.
See also Nos. 117/20 and 126/9.

1969. Fishes (2nd series). As T **45**. Multicoloured.
117 4d. Sailfish 75 90
118 6d. White seabream ("Old wife") . . . . 1·00 1·25
119 1s.6d. Yellowtail . . . . . . 1·25 2·50
120 2s.11d. Rock hind ("Jack") 1·50 3·00

46 H.M.S. "Rattlesnake"

1969. Royal Navy Crests (1st series).
121 **46** 4d. multicoloured 60 30
122 – 9d. multicoloured 75 35
123 – 1s.9d. blue and gold . . . 1·10 45
124 – 2s.3d. multicoloured . . . 1·25 55
MS125 165 × 105 mm. Nos. 121/4 6·50 13·00
DESIGNS: 9d. H.M.S. "Weston"; 1s.9d. H.M.S. "Undaunted"; 2s.3d. H.M.S. "Eagle".
See also Nos. 130/3, 149/52, 154/7 and 166/9.

1970. Fishes (3rd series). As T **45**. Multicoloured.
126 4d. Wahoo . . . . 4·50 2·75
127w 9d. Ascension jack ("Coalfish") . . . . 3·00 1·25
128 1s.9d. Pompouno dolphin 5·50 3·50
129w 2s.3d. Squirrelfish ("Soldier") . . . . 5·50 3·50

1970. Royal Navy Crests (2nd series). As T **46**. Multicoloured.
130 4d. H.M.S. "Penelope" . . . 1·00 1·00
131 9d. H.M.S. "Carlisle" . . . 1·25 1·50
132 1s.6d. H.M.S. "Amphion" . . 1·75 2·00
133 2s.6d. H.M.S. "Magpie" . . 1·75 2·00
MS134 159 × 96 mm. Nos. 130/3 11·00 15·00

50 Early Chinese Rocket

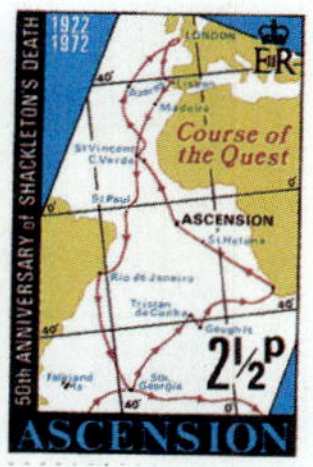

51 Course of the "Quest"

1971. Decimal Currency. Evolution of Space Travel. Multicoloured.
135 ½p. Type **50** 15 20
136 1p. Medieval Arab astronomers 20 20
137 1½p. Tycho Brahe's observatory, quadrant and supernova (horiz) 30 30
138 2p. Galileo, Moon and telescope (horiz) 40 30
139 2½p. Isaac Newton, instruments and apple (horiz) . . . . 1·25 1·00
140 3½p. Harrison's chronometer and H.M.S. "Deptford" (frigate), 1735 (horiz) . . . 2·25 1·50
141 4½p. Space rocket taking off 1·25 1·00
142 5p. World's largest telescope, Palomar (horiz) . . . . . 1·00 1·00
143 7½p. World's largest radio telescope, Jodrell Bank (horiz) . . . . 4·00 1·75
144 10p. "Mariner VII" and Mars (horiz) . . . . 3·50 1·75
145 12½p. "Sputnik II" and Space dog, Laika (horiz) . . . . 5·00 2·00
146 25p. Walking in Space . . . 6·00 2·25
147 50p. "Apollo XI" crew on Moon (horiz) . . . . . . 5·00 2·75
148 £1 Future Space Research station (horiz) . . . . . . 5·00 4·50

1971. Royal Navy Crests (3rd series). As T **46**. Mult.
149 2p. H.M.S. "Phoenix" . . . 1·00 30
150 4p. H.M.S. "Milford" . . . 1·25 55
151 9p. H.M.S. "Pelican" . . . 1·50 80
152 15p. H.M.S. "Oberon" . . . 1·50 1·00
MS153 151 × 104 mm. Nos. 149/52 4·75 15·00

1972. Royal Navy Crests (4th series). As T **46**. Mult.
154 1½p. H.M.S. "Lowestoft" . . 50 50
155 3p. H.M.S. "Auckland" . . . 55 75
156 6p. H.M.S. "Nigeria" . . . . 60 1·25
157 17½p. H.M.S. "Bermuda" . . 90 2·50
MS158 157 × 93 mm. Nos. 154/7 2·25 7·50

1972. 50th Anniv of Shackleton's Death. Mult.
159 2½p. Type **51** 30 60
160 4p. Shackleton and "Quest" (horiz) 35 60
161 7½p. Shackleton's cabin and "Quest" (horiz) 35 65
162 11p. Shackleton statue and memorial 40 80
MS163 139 × 114 mm. Nos. 159/62 1·25 6·00

52 Land Crab and Short-finned Mako

1972. Royal Silver Wedding. Multicoloured.
164 **52** 2p. violet 15 10
165 16p. red 35 30

1973. Royal Naval Crests (5th series). As T **46**. Multicoloured.
166 2p. H.M.S. "Birmingham" 2·00 1·50
167 4p. H.M.S. "Cardiff" . . . 2·25 1·50
168 9p. H.M.S. "Penzance" . . . 3·00 1·75
169 13p. H.M.S. "Rochester" . . 3·25 1·75
MS170 109 × 152 mm. Nos. 166/9 28·00 10·00

53 Green Turtle

1973. Turtles. Multicoloured.
171 4p. Type **53** . . . . 2·75 1·75
172 9p. Loggerhead turtle . . . . 3·00 2·00
173 12p. Hawksbill turtle . . . . 3·25 2·25

54 Sergeant, R.M. Light Infantry, 1900

1973. 50th Anniv of Departure of Royal Marines from Ascension. Multicoloured.
174 2p. Type **54** . . . . 1·50 1·50
175 6p. R.M. Private, 1816 . . . 2·25 2·00
176 12p. R.M. Light Infantry Officer, 1880 . . . . . . 2·50 2·50
177 20p. R.M. Artillery Colour Sergeant, 1910 . . . . . 3·00 2·75

1973. Royal Wedding. As T **47** of Anguilla. Multicoloured. Background colours given.
178 2p. brown 15 10
179 18p. green 20 20

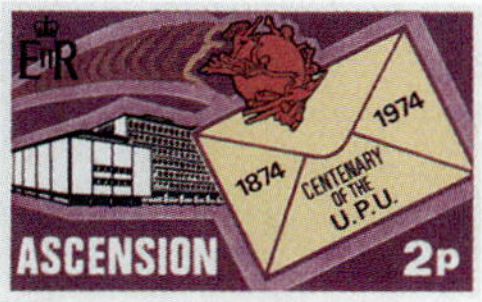

55 Letter and H.Q., Berne

1974. Centenary of Universal Postal Union. Mult.
180 2p. Type **55** 20 30
181 9p. Hermes and U.P.U. monument 30 45

56 Churchill as a Boy, and Birthplace, Blenheim Palace

1974. Birth Centenary of Sir Winston Churchill. Multicoloured.
182 5p. Type **56** 20 35
183 25p. Churchill as statesman, and U.N. Building 30 75
MS184 93 × 87 mm. Nos. 182/3 1·00 2·50

57 "Skylab 3" and Photograph of Ascension

1975. Space Satellites. Multicoloured.
185 2p. Type **57** 20 30
186 18p. "Skylab 4" Command module and photograph . . 30 40

58 U.S.A.F. Lockheed C-141A Starlifter

1975. Wideawake Airfield. Multicoloured.
187 2p. Type **58** 80 65
188 5p. R.A.F. Lockheed C-130 Hercules 80 85
189 9p. Vickers Super VC-10 . . 80 1·40
190 24p. U.S.A.F. Lockheed C-5A Galaxy . . . . . . 1·25 2·50
MS191 144 × 99 mm. Nos. 187/90 17·00 22·00

1975. "Apollo-Soyuz" Space Link. Nos. 141 and 145/6 optd **APOLLO-SOYUZ LINK 1975**.
192 4½p. multicoloured 15 20
193 12½p. multicoloured 15 25
194 25p. multicoloured 25 40

60 Arrival of Royal Navy, 1815

1975. 160th Anniv of Occupation. Multicoloured.
195 2p. Type **60** 25 25
196 5p. Water supply, Dampiers Drip 25 40
197 9p. First landing, 1815 . . . 25 60
198 15p. The garden on Green Mountain 35 85

61 Yellow Canaries ("Canary")

1976. Multicoloured.
199 1p. Type **61** . . . . 40 1·50
200 2p. White tern ("Fairy Tern") (vert) . . . . 50 1·50
201 3p. Common waxbill ("Waxbill") . . . . 50 1·50
202 4p. White-capped noddy ("Black Noddy") (vert) . . 50 1·50
203 5p. Common noddy ("Brown Noddy") . . . . 70 1·50
204 6p. Common mynah . . . . 70 1·50
205 7p. Madeiran storm petrel (vert) . . . . 70 1·50
206 8p. Sooty tern . . . . 70 1·50
207 9p. Blue-faced booby ("White Booby") (vert) . . . . . 70 1·50
208 10p. Red-footed booby . . . 70 1·50
209 15p. Red-necked spurfowl ("Red-throated Francolin") (vert) . . . . 85 1·50
210 18p. Brown booby (vert) . . 85 1·50
211 25p. Red-billed tropic bird ("Red-billed Bo'sun Bird") 90 1·50
212 50p. White-tailed tropic bird ("Yellow-billed Tropic Bird") . . . . 1·00 1·75
213 £1 Ascension frigate-bird (vert) . . . . 1·00 2·25
214 £2 Boatswain Bird Island Sanctuary (50 × 38 mm) . . 2·00 5·00

63 G.B. Penny Red with Ascension Postmark

1976. Festival of Stamps, London.
215 **63** 5p. red, black and brown 15 15
216 – 9p. green, black and brown 15 20
217 – 25p. multicoloured . . . 25 45
MS218 133 × 121 mm. No. 217 with St. Helena No. 318 and Tristan da Cunha No. 206 . . . . . . 1·50 2·00
DESIGNS—VERT: 9p. ½d. stamp of 1922. HORIZ: 25p. "Southampton Castle" (liner).

64 U.S. Base, Ascension

1976. Bicentenary of American Revolution. Multicoloured.

219	8p. Type **64**	30	40
220	9p. NASA Station at Devils Ashpit	30	45
221	25p. "Viking" landing on Mars	40	80

65 Visit of Prince Philip, 1957 **66** Tunnel carrying Water Pipe

1977. Silver Jubilee. Multicoloured.

222	8p. Type **65**	15	15
223	12p. Coronation Coach leaving Buckingham Palace (horiz)	20	20
224	25p. Coronation Coach (horiz)	35	40

1977. Water Supplies. Multicoloured.

225	3p. Type **66**	15	15
226	5p. Breakneck Valley wells	20	20
227	12p. Break tank (horiz)	30	35
228	25p. Water catchment (horiz)	45	65

67 Mars Bay Location, 1877

1977. Centenary of Visit of Professor Gill (astronomer). Multicoloured.

229	3p. Type **67**	15	20
230	8p. Instrument sites, Mars Bay	15	25
231	12p. Sir David and Lady Gill	20	40
232	25p. Maps of Ascension	60	70

68 Lion of England **70** Flank of Sisters, Sisters' Red Hill and East Crater

1978. 25th Anniv of Coronation.

233	**68**	25p. yellow, brown and silver	35	50
234	–	25p. multicoloured	35	50
235	–	25p. yellow, brown and silver	35	50

DESIGNS: No 234, Queen Elizabeth II; No 235, Green turtle.

1978. Ascension Island Volcanic Rock Formations. Multicoloured.

236	3p. Type **70**	15	20
237	5p. Holland's Crater (Hollow Tooth)	20	30
238	12p. Street Crater, Lower Valley Crater and Bear's Back	25	40
239	15p. Butt Crater, Weather Post and Green Mountain	30	45
240	25p. Flank of Sisters, Thistle Hill and Two Boats Village	35	50
MS241	185 × 100 mm. Nos. 236/40, each × 2	2·00	5·00

Nos. 236/40 were issued as a se-tenant strip within the sheet, forming a composite design.

71 "The Resolution" (H. Roberts) **72** St. Mary's Church, Georgetown

1979. Bicentenary of Captain Cook's Voyages, 1768–79. Multicoloured.

242	3p. Type **71**	25	25
243	8p. Cook's chronometer	25	40
244	12p. Green turtle	30	50
245	25p. Flaxman/Wedgwood medallion of Cook	30	70

1979. Ascension Day. Multicoloured.

246	8p. Type **72**	10	20
247	12p. Map of Ascension	15	30
248	50p. "The Ascension" (painting by Rembrandt)	30	90

73 Landing Cable, Comfortless Cove

1979. 80th Anniv of Eastern Telegraph Company's Arrival on Ascension.

249	**73**	3p. black and red	10	10
250	–	8p. black and green	15	15
251	–	12p. black and yellow	20	20
252	–	15p. black and violet	20	25
253	–	25p. black and brown	25	35

DESIGNS—HORIZ: 8p. C.S. "Anglia"; 15p. C.S. "Seine"; 25p. Cable and Wireless earth station. VERT: 12p. Map of Atlantic cable network.

74 1938 6d. Stamp

1979. Death Centenary of Sir Rowland Hill.

254	**74**	3p. black and blue	10	10
255	–	8p. black, green and pale green	15	20
256	–	12p. black, blue and pale blue	15	25
257	–	50p. black and red	40	90

DESIGNS—HORIZ: 8p. 1956 5s. definitive. VERT: 12p. 1924 3s. stamp; 50p. Sir Rowland Hill.

75 "Anogramma ascensionis"

1980. Ferns and Grasses. Multicoloured.

258	3p. Type **75**	10	15
259	6p. "Xiphopteris ascensionense"	10	20
260	8p. "Sporobolus caespitosus"	10	20
261	12p. "Sporobolus durus" (vert)	15	30
262	18p. "Dryopteris ascensionis" (vert)	15	40
263	24p. "Marattia purpurascens" (vert)	20	55

76 17th-Century Bottle Post

1980. "London 1980" International Stamp Exhibition. Multicoloured.

264	8p. Type **76**	15	20
265	12p. 19th-century chance calling ship	20	25
266	15p. "Garth Castle" (regular mail service from 1863)	20	30
267	50p. "St. Helena" (mail services, 1980)	60	90
MS268	102 × 154 mm. Nos. 264/7	1·00	2·40

77 H.M. Queen Elizabeth the Queen Mother

1980. 80th Birthday of The Queen Mother.

269	**77**	15p. multicoloured	40	40

78 Lubbock's Yellowtail

1980. Fishes. Multicoloured.

270	3p. Type **78**	15	25
271	10p. Resplendent angelfish	20	25
272	25p. Bicoloured butterflyfish	25	55
273	40p. Marmalade razorfish	40	75

79 H.M.S. "Tortoise"

1980. 150th Anniv of Royal Geographical Society. Multicoloured.

274	10p. Type **79**	20	40
275	15p. "Wideawake Fair"	25	45
276	60p. Mid-Atlantic Ridge (38 × 48 mm)	65	1·25

80 Green Mountain Farm, 1881

1981. Green Mountain Farm. Multicoloured.

277	12p. Type **80**	15	35
278	15p. Two Boats, 1881	15	40
279	20p. Green Mountain and Two Boats, 1981	20	50
280	30p. Green Mountain Farm, 1981	30	70

81 Cable and Wireless Earth Station

1981. "Space Shuttle" Mission and Opening of 2nd Earth Station.

281	**81**	15p. black, blue and pale blue	30	35

82 Poinsettia

83 Solanum

1981. Flowers. Multicoloured.

282A	1p. Type **82**	70	1·25
283B	2p. Clustered wax flower	50	1·25
284B	3p. Kolanchoe (vert)	50	1·25
285A	4p. Yellow pops	80	1·25
286A	5p. Camels foot creeper	80	1·25
287A	8p. White oleander	80	1·25
288B	10p. Ascension lily (vert)	45	75
289A	12p. Coral plant (vert)	1·50	1·10
290B	15p. Yellow allamanda	50	75
291B	20p. Ascension euphorbia	1·00	75
292A	30p. Flame of the forest (vert)	1·25	1·25
293A	40p. Bougainvillea "King Leopold"	1·25	3·00
294A	50p. Type **83**	1·25	3·25
295B	£1 Ladies petticoat	2·00	3·00
296A	£2 Red hibiscus	3·75	6·00

Nos. 294/6 are as Type **83**.

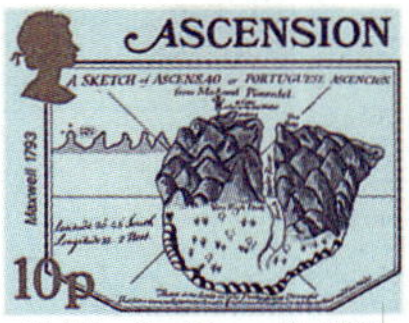

84 Map by Maxwell, 1793

1981. Early Maps of Ascension.

297	**84**	10p. black, gold and blue	20	35
298	–	12p. black, gold and green	20	35
299	–	15p. black, gold and stone	20	35
300	–	40p. black, gold and yellow	50	70
MS301	–	79 × 64 mm. 5p. × 4 multicoloured	60	75

DESIGNS: 12p. Maxwell, 1793 (different); 15p. Ekeberg and Chapman, 1811; 40p. Campbell, 1819; miniature sheet, Linschoten, 1599.

Stamps from **MS**301 form a composite design.

85 Wedding Bouquet from Ascension **87** "Interest"

1981. Royal Wedding. Multicoloured.

302	10p. Type **85**	15	15
303	15p. Prince Charles in Fleet Air Arm flying kit	30	30
304	50p. Prince Charles and Lady Diana Spencer	65	90

1981. 25th Anniv of Duke of Edinburgh Award Scheme. Multicoloured.

305	5p. Type **87**	15	15
306	10p. "Physical activities"	15	15
307	15p. "Service"	20	20
308	40p. Duke of Edinburgh	45	45

88 Scout crossing Rope Bridge

1982. 75th Anniv of Boy Scout Movement.

309	**88**	10p. black, blue and light blue	15	35
310	–	15p. black, brown and yellow	15	50
311	–	25p. black, mve & lt mve	20	60
312	–	40p. black, red and orange	30	85
MS313	–	121 × 121 mm. 10, 15, 25, 40p. As Nos. 309/12 (each diamond 40 × 40 mm)	1·00	2·50

DESIGNS: 15p. 1st Ascension Scout Group flag; 25p. Scouts learning to use radio; 40p. Lord Baden-Powell.

89 Charles Darwin

1982. 150th Anniv of Charles Darwin's Voyage. Multicoloured.

314	10p. Type **89**	20	40
315	12p. Darwin's pistols	20	50
316	15p. Rock crab	25	55
317	40p. H.M.S. "Beagle"	60	95

90 Fairey Swordfish Torpedo Bomber

1982. 40th Anniv of Wideawake Airfield. Multicoloured.

318	5p. Type **90**	75	35
319	10p. North American B-25C Mitchell	1·00	40
320	15p. Boeing EC-135N Aria	1·25	55
321	50p. Lockheed C-130 Hercules	1·75	1·10

91 Ascension Coat of Arms

1982. 21st Birthday of Princess of Wales. Mult.

322	12p. Type **91**	25	25
323	15p. Lady Diana Spencer in Music Room, Buckingham Palace	25	25
324	25p. Bride and Earl Spencer leaving Clarence House	40	40
325	50p. Formal portrait	75	75

1982. Commonwealth Games, Brisbane. Nos. 290/1 optd **1st PARTICIPATION COMMONWEALTH GAMES 1982.**

326	15p. Yellow allamanda	30	40
327	20p. Ascension euphorbia	40	45

94 Bush House, London

1982. Christmas. 50th Anniv of B.B.C. External Broadcasting. Multicoloured.

328	5p. Type **94**	15	20
329	10p. Atlantic relay station	20	30
330	25p. Lord Reith, first Director-General	30	60
331	40p. King George V making his first Christmas broadcast, 1932	45	75

95 "Marasmius echinosphaerus"

1983. Fungi. Multicoloured.

332	7p. Type **95**	40	30
333	12p. "Chlorophyllum molybdites"	50	45
334	15p. "Leucocoprinus cepaestripes"	60	50
335	20p. "Lycoperdon marginatum"	70	65
336	50p. "Marasmiellus distantifolius"	90	1·25

96 Aerial View of Georgetown

1983. Island Views (1st series). Multicoloured.

337	12p. Type **96**	15	25
338	15p. Green Mountain farm	15	25
339	20p. Boatswain Bird Island	20	40
340	60p. Telemetry Hill by night	40	80

See also Nos. 367/70.

97 Westland Wessex 5 Helicopter of No. 845 Naval Air Squadron

1983. Bicentenary of Manned Flight. British Military Aircraft. Multicoloured.

341	12p. Type **97**	40	65
342	15p. Avro Vulcan B.2 of No. 44 Squadron	40	75
343	20p. Hawker Siddeley Nimrod M.R.2P of No. 20 Squadron	40	85
344	60p. Handey Page Victor K2 of No. 55 Squadron	60	2·00

98 Iguanid

1983. Introduced Species. Multicoloured.

345	12p. Type **98**	25	30
346	15p. Common rabbit	30	35
347	20p. Cat	40	45
348	60p. Donkey	75	1·40

99 Speckled Tellin

1983. Sea Shells. Multicoloured.

349	7p. Type **99**	15	20
350	12p. Lion's paw scallop	15	30
351	15p. Lurid cowrie	15	35
352	20p. Ascension nerite	20	45
353	50p. Miniature melo	40	1·10

100 1922 1½d. Stamp **101** Prince Andrew

1984. 150th Anniv of St. Helena as a British Colony. Multicoloured.

354	12p. Type **100**	15	45
355	15p. 1922 2d. stamp	15	50
356	20p. 1922 8d. stamp	20	55
357	60p. 1922 1s. stamp	50	1·40

1984. Visit of Prince Andrew. Sheet 124 × 90 mm. MS358 12p. Type **101**; 70p. Prince Andrew in naval uniform 1·00 1·60

102 Naval Semaphore

1984. 250th Anniv of "Lloyd's List" (newspaper). Multicoloured.

359	12p. Type **102**	50	30
360	15p. "Southampton Castle" (liner)	55	35
361	20p. Pier head	55	45
362	70p. "Dane" (screw steamer)	1·25	1·50

103 Penny Coin and Yellow-finned Tuna

1984. New Coinage. Multicoloured.

363	12p. Type **103**	35	35
364	15p. Twopenny coin and donkey	40	40
365	20p. Fifty pence coin and green turtle	45	50
366	70p. Pound coin and sooty tern	80	1·75

1984. Island Views (2nd series). As T **96**. Mult.

367	12p. The Devil's Riding-school	20	30
368	15p. St. Mary's Church	25	35
369	20p. Two Boats Village	25	45
370	70p. Ascension from the sea	80	1·50

104 Bermuda Cypress **105** The Queen Mother with Prince Andrew at Silver Jubilee Service

1985. Trees. Multicoloured.

371	7p. Type **104**	20	20
372	12p. Norfolk Island pine	25	30
373	15p. Screwpine	25	35
374	20p. Eucalyptus	25	45
375	65p. Spore tree	70	1·40

1985. Life and Times of Queen Elizabeth the Queen Mother. Multicoloured.

376	12p. With the Duke of York at Balmoral, 1924	25	35
377	15p. Type **105**	25	40
378	20p. The Queen Mother at Ascot	30	55
379	70p. With Prince Henry at his christening (from photo by Lord Snowdon)	80	1·75
MS380	91 × 73 mm. 75p. Visiting the "Queen Elizabeth 2" at Southampton, 1968	1·10	1·60

106 32 Pdr. Smooth Bore Muzzle-loader, c. 1820, and Royal Marine Artillery Hat Plate, c. 1816

1985. Guns on Ascension Island. Multicoloured.

381	12p. Type **106**	40	90
382	15p. 7 inch rifled muzzle-loader, c. 1866, and Royal Cypher on barrel	40	1·00
383	20p. 7 pdr rifled muzzle-loader, c. 1877, and Royal Artillery Badge	40	1·25
384	70p. 5.5 inch gun, 1941, and crest from H.M.S. "Hood"	80	3·00

107 Guide Flag **108** "Clerodendrum fragrans"

1985. 75th Anniv of Girl Guide Movement and International Youth Year. Multicoloured.

385	12p. Type **107**	40	70
386	15p. Practising first aid	40	80
387	20p. Camping	40	90
388	70p. Lady Baden-Powell	1·00	2·50

1985. Wild Flowers. Multicoloured.

389	12p. Type **108**	30	75
390	15p. Shell ginger	30	90
391	20p. Cape daisy	35	90
392	70p. Ginger lily	70	2·50

109 Newton's Reflector Telescope **110** Princess Elizabeth in 1926

1986. Appearance of Halley's Comet. Mult.

393	12p. Type **109**	40	1·10
394	15p. Edmond Halley and Old Greenwich Observatory	40	1·25
395	20p. Short's Gregorian telescope and comet, 1759	40	1·25
396	70p. Ascension satellite tracking station and ICE spacecraft	1·25	3·50

1986. 60th Birthday of Queen Elizabeth II. Mult.

397	7p. Type **110**	15	25
398	15p. Queen making Christmas broadcast, 1952	20	40
399	20p. At Garter ceremony, Windsor Castle, 1983	25	50
400	35p. In Auckland, New Zealand, 1981	35	80
401	£1 At Crown Agents' Head Office, London, 1983	1·00	2·25

111 1975 Space Satellites 2p. Stamp

1986. "Ameripex '86" International Stamp Exhibition, Chicago. Designs showing previous Ascension stamps. Multicoloured.

402	12p. Type **111**	25	70
403	15p. 1980 "London 1980" International Stamp Exhibition 50p.	25	80
404	20p. 1976 Bicentenary of American Revolution 8p.	30	1·00
405	70p. 1982 40th anniv of Wideawake Airfield 10p.	70	2·25
MS406	60 × 75 mm. 75p. Statue of Liberty	2·00	2·75

112 Prince Andrew and Miss Sarah Ferguson

1986. Royal Wedding. Multicoloured.

407	15p. Type **112**	25	50
408	35p. Prince Andrew aboard H.M.S. "Brazen"	50	1·00

113 H.M.S. "Ganymede" (c. 1811)

1986. Ships of the Royal Navy. Multicoloured.

409	1p. Type **113**	55	1·50
410	2p. H.M.S. "Kangaroo" (c.1811)	60	1·50
411	4p. H.M.S. "Trinculo" (c.1811)	60	1·50
412	5p. H.M.S. "Daring" (c.1811)	60	1·50
413	9p. H.M.S. "Thais" (c.1811)	70	1·50
414	10p. H.M.S. "Pheasant" (1819)	70	1·50
415	15p. H.M.S. "Myrmidon" (1819)	80	1·75
416	18p. H.M.S. "Atholl" (1825)	90	1·75
417	20p. H.M.S. "Medina" (1830)	90	1·75
418	25p. H.M.S. "Saracen" (1840)	1·00	2·00
419	30p. H.M.S. "Hydra" (c.1845)	1·00	2·00
420	50p. H.M.S. "Sealark" (1849)	1·00	2·50
421	70p. H.M.S. "Rattlesnake" (1868)	1·00	3·00
422	£1 H.M.S. "Penelope" (1889)	1·25	3·75
423	£2 H.M.S. "Monarch" (1897)	2·50	6·50

114 Cape Gooseberry

1987. Edible Bush Fruits. Multicoloured.

424	12p. Type **114**	65	90
425	15p. Prickly pear	65	1·00
426	20p. Guava	70	1·10
427	70p. Loquat	1·10	2·75

115 Ignition of Rocket Motors **116** Captains in Full Dress raising Red Ensign

1987. 25th Anniv of First American Manned Earth Orbit. Multicoloured.
428 15p. Type **115** 55 75
429 18p. Lift-off 60 80
430 25p. Re-entry 75 95
431 £1 Splashdown . . . . . . 2·50 3·25
MS432 92 × 78 mm. 70p. "Friendship 7" capsule . . . . 1·75 2·00

1987. 19th-century Uniforms (1st series). Royal Navy, 1815–20. Multicoloured.
433 25p. Type **116** 50 60
434 25p. Surgeon and seamen . . 50 60
435 25p. Seaman with water-carrying donkey 50 60
436 25p. Midshipman and gun . . 50 60
437 25p. Commander in undress uniform surveying 50 60
See also Nos. 478/82.

117 "Cynthia cardui"

1987. Insects (1st series). Multicoloured.
438 15p. Type **117** 55 65
439 18p. "Danaus chrysippus" . . 60 75
440 25p. "Hypolimnas misippus" . 75 85
441 £1 "Lampides boeticus" . . . 2·00 2·50
See also Nos. 452/5 and 483/6.

118 Male Ascension Frigate Birds

1987. Sea Birds (1st series). Multicoloured.
442 25p. Type **118** . . . . . . 1·60 1·90
443 25p. Juvenile Ascension frigate bird, brown booby and blue-faced boobies . . 1·60 1·90
444 25p. Male Ascension frigate bird and blue-faced boobies 1·60 1·90
445 25p. Female Ascension frigate bird . . . . 1·60 1·90
446 25p. Adult male feeding juvenile Ascension frigate bird . . . . 1·60 1·90
Nos. 442/6 were printed together, se-tenant, forming a composite design.
See also Nos. 469/73.

1987. Royal Ruby Wedding. Nos. 397/401 optd **40TH WEDDING ANNIVERSARY.**
447 7p. Type **110** 15 15
448 15p. Queen making Christmas broadcast, 1952 20 20
449 20p. At Garter ceremony, Windsor Castle, 1983 . . . 25 25
450 35p. In Auckland, New Zealand, 1981 . . . . . 40 45
451 £1 At Crown Agents' Head Office, London, 1983 . . . 1·00 1·10

1988. Insects (2nd series). As T **117**. Multicoloured.
452 15p. "Gryllus bimaculatus" (field cricket) 50 50
453 18p. "Ruspolia differens" (bush cricket) 55 55
454 25p. "Chilomenus lunata" (ladybird) 70 70
455 £1 "Diachrysia orichalcea" (moth) . . . . 2·25 2·25

120 Bate's Memorial, St. Mary's Church

1988. 150th Death Anniv of Captain William Bate (garrison commander, 1828–38). Multicoloured.
456 9p. Type **120** 35 35
457 15p. Commodore's Cottage . 45 45
458 18p. North East Cottage . . 50 50
459 25p. Map of Ascension . . . 70 70
460 70p. Captain Bate and marines . . . . 1·75 1·75

121 H.M.S. "Resolution" (ship of the line), 1667

1988. Bicentenary of Australian Settlement. Ships of the Royal Navy. Multicoloured.
461 9p. Type **121** . . . . 1·00 45
462 18p. H.M.S. "Resolution" (Captain Cook), 1772 . . . 1·50 70
463 25p. H.M.S. "Resolution" (battleship), 1892 . . . . 1·50 85
464 65p. H.M.S. "Resolution" (battleship), 1916 . . . . 2·50 1·50

1988. "Sydpex '88" National Stamp Exhibition, Sydney. Nos. 461/4 optd **SYDPEX 88 30.7.88 - 7.8.88.**
465 9p. Type **121** 50 40
466 18p. H.M.S. "Resolution" (Captain Cook), 1772 . . . 75 60
467 25p. H.M.S. "Resolution" (battleship), 1892 . . . . 85 70
468 65p. H.M.S. "Resolution" (battleship), 1916 . . . . 1·60 1·40

1988. Sea Birds (2nd series). Sooty Tern. As T **118.** Multicoloured.
469 25p. Pair displaying . . . . 1·60 1·60
470 25p. Turning egg . . . . . . 1·60 1·60
471 25p. Incubating egg . . . . 1·60 1·60
472 25p. Feeding chick . . . . . 1·60 1·60
473 25p. Immature sooty tern . . 1·60 1·60
Nos. 469/73 were printed together, se-tenant, forming a composite design of a nesting colony.

123 Lloyd's Coffee House, London, 1688 **124** Two Land Crabs

1988. 300th Anniv of Lloyd's of London. Mult.
474 8p. Type **123** 25 35
475 18p. "Alert IV" (cable ship) (horiz) 65 70
476 25p. Satellite recovery in space (horiz) 80 90
477 65p. "Good Hope Castle" (cargo liner) on fire off Ascension, 1973 . . . . 1·75 2·00

1988. 19th-century Uniforms (2nd series). Royal Marines 1821–34. As T **116.** Multicoloured.
478 25p. Marines landing on Ascension, 1821 . . . . 1·10 1·60
479 25p. Officer and Marine at semaphore station, 1829 . 1·10 1·60
480 25p. Sergeant and Marine at Octagonal Tank, 1831 . 1·10 1·60
481 25p. Officers at water pipe tunnel, 1833 . . . . . 1·10 1·60
482 25p. Officer supervising construction of barracks, 1834 . . . . 1·10 1·60

1989. Insects (3rd series). As T **117.** Mult.
483 15p. "Trichoptilus wahlbergi" (moth) 75 50
484 18p. "Lucilia sericata" (fly) 80 55
485 25p. "Alceis ornatus" (weevil) 1·10 70
486 £1 "Polistes fuscatus" (wasp) 3·00 2·40

1989. Ascension Land Crabs. Multicoloured.
487 15p. Type **124** 40 45
488 18p. Crab with claws raised 45 50
489 25p. Crab on rock 60 70
490 £1 Crab in surf . . . . . . 2·25 2·50
MS491 98 × 101 mm. Nos. 487/90 3·50 3·75

125 1949 75th Anniversary of U.P.U. 1s. Stamp

1989. "Philexfrance '89" International Stamp Exhibition, Paris, and "World Stamp Expo '89", Washington (1st issue). Sheet 104 × 86 mm.
MS492 **125** 75p. multicoloured 1·50 1·75
See also Nos. 498/503.

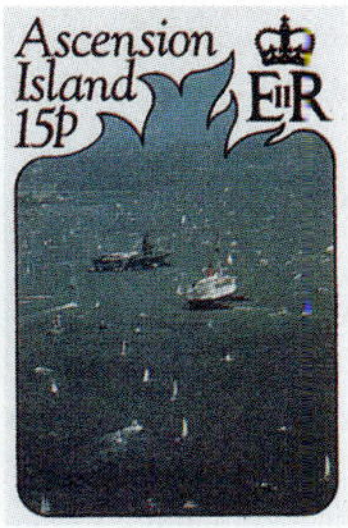

126 "Apollo 7" Tracking Station, Ascension **127** "Queen Elizabeth 2" (liner) and U.S.S. "John F. Kennedy" (aircraft carrier) in New York Harbour

1989. 20th Anniv of First Manned Landing on Moon. Multicoloured.
493 15p. Type **126** 65 45
494 18p. Launch of "Apollo 7" (30 × 30 mm) 70 50
495 25p. "Apollo 7" emblem (30 × 30 mm) 90 70
496 70p. "Apollo 7" jettisoning expended Saturn rocket . . 1·75 1·75
MS497 101 × 83 mm. £1 Diagram of "Apollo 11" mission . . . . . 2·00 2·10

1989. "Philexfrance 89" International Stamp Exhibition, Paris, and "World Stamp Expo '89", Washington (1st issue). Designs showing Statue of Liberty and Centenary celebrations. Multicoloured.
498 15p. Type **127** 50 50
499 15p. Cleaning statue 50 50
500 15p. Statue of Liberty . . . 50 50
501 15p. Crown of statue 50 50
502 15p. Warships and New York skyline 50 50
503 15p. "Jean de Vienne" (French destroyer) and skyscrapers 50 50

128 Devil's Ashpit Tracking Station

1989. Closure of Devil's Ashpit Tracking Station, Ascension. Multicoloured.
504 18p. Type **128** 80 50
505 25p. Launch of shuttle "Atlantis" 80 55

129 Bubonian Conch

1989. Sea Shells. Multicoloured.
506 8p. Type **129** 40 30
507 18p. Giant tun 70 50
508 25p. Doris loup 90 65
509 £1 Atlantic trumpet triton . . 2·75 2·50

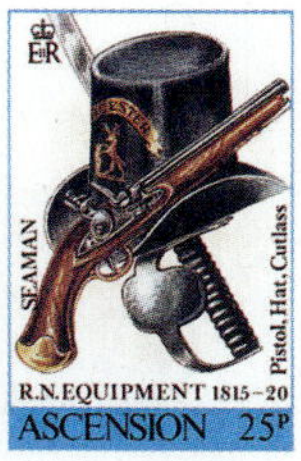

130 Donkeys **131** Seaman's Pistol, Hat and Cutlass

1989. Ascension Wildlife. Multicoloured.
510 18p. Type **130** 75 75
511 25p. Green turtle 75 85

1990. Royal Navy Equipment, 1815–20. Mult.
512 25p. Type **131** 70 70
513 25p. Midshipman's belt plate, button, sword and hat . . 70 70
514 25p. Surgeon's hat, sword and instrument chest . . . 70 70
515 25p. Captain's hat, telescope and sword 70 70
516 25p. Admiral's epaulette, megaphone, hat and pocket 70 70
See also Nos. 541/5.

132 Pair of Ascension Frigate Birds with Young **134** "Queen Elizabeth, 1940" (Sir Gerald Kelly)

133 Penny Black and Twopence Blue

1990. Endangered Species. Ascension Frigate Bird. Multicoloured.
517 9p. Type **132** . . . . . . 1·50 1·00
518 10p. Fledgeling . . . . . . 1·50 1·00
519 11p. Adult male in flight . . 1·50 1·00
520 15p. Female and immature birds in flight . . . . . . 1·75 1·25

1990. "Stamp World London 90" International Stamp Exhibition. Multicoloured.
521 9p. Type **133** 50 40
522 18p. Ascension postmarks used on G.B. stamps . . . 70 60
523 25p. Unloading mail at Wideawake Airfield 95 85
524 £1 Mail van and Main Post Office . . . . 2·25 2·75

1990. 90th Birthday of Queen Elizabeth the Queen Mother.
525 **134** 25p. multicoloured . . . 75 75
526 – £1 black and lilac . . . . 2·25 2·25
DESIGN—29 × 37 mm: £1 King George VI and Queen Elizabeth with Bren-gun carrier.

136 "Madonna and Child" (sculpture, Dino Felici) **137** "Garth Castle" (mail steamer), 1910

1990. Christmas. Works of Art. Multicoloured.
527 8p. Type **136** 70 70
528 18p. "Madonna and Child" (anon) . . . . 1·25 1·25
529 25p. "Madonna and Child with St. John" (Johann Gebhard) . . . . 1·75 1·75
530 65p. "Madonna and Child" (Giacomo Gritti) . . . . . 3·00 4·00

1990. Maiden Voyage of "St. Helena II". Mult.
531 9p. Type **137** 90 90
532 18p. "St. Helena I" during Falkland Islands campaign, 1982 . . . . 1·25 1·25
533 25p. Launch of "St. Helena II" . . . . 1·75 1·75
534 70p. Duke of York launching "St. Helena II" . . . . . 3·00 4·25
MS535 100 × 100 mm. £1 "St. Helena II" and outline map of Ascension . . . . 3·50 5·00

1991. 175th Anniv of Occupation. Nos. 418, 420 and 422 optd **BRITISH FOR 175 YEARS.**
536 25p. H.M.S. "Saracen" (1840) . . . . 2·00 2·50
537 50p. H.M.S. "Sealark" (1849) 2·50 3·25
538 £1 H.M.S. "Penelope" (1889) 3·75 4·75

139 Queen Elizabeth II at Trooping the Colour

1991. 65th Birthday of Queen Elizabeth II and 70th Birthday of Prince Philip. Multicoloured.
539 25p. Type **139** 1·25 1·60
540 25p. Prince Philip in naval uniform 1·25 1·60

1991. Royal Marines Equipment, 1821–1844. As T **131**. Multicoloured.
541 25p. Officer's shako, epaulettes, belt plate and button 1·10 1·60
542 25p. Officer's cap, sword, epaulettes and belt plate 1·10 1·60
543 25p. Drum major's shako and staff 1·10 1·60
544 25p. Sergeant's shako, chevrons, belt plate and canteen 1·10 1·60
545 25p. Drummer's shako and side-drum 1·10 1·60

140 B.B.C. World Service Relay Station

1991. 25th Anniv of B.B.C. Atlantic Relay Station. Multicoloured.
546 15p. Type **140** 90 1·10
547 18p. Transmitters at English Bay 1·00 1·25
548 25p. Satellite receiving station (vert) 1·25 1·40
549 70p. Antenna support tower (vert) 2·50 4·00

141 St. Mary's Church

1991. Christmas. Ascension Churches. Mult.
550 8p. Type **141** 55 55
551 18p. Interior of St. Mary's Church 1·00 1·00
552 25p. Our Lady of Ascension Grotto 1·25 1·25
553 65p. Interior of Our Lady of Ascension Grotto 2·75 5·00

142 Black Durgon ("Blackfish")

1991. Fishes. Multicoloured.
554 1p. Type **142** 85 60
555 2p. Sergeant major ("Five finger") 1·00 60
556 4p. Resplendent angelfish 1·25 70
557 5p. Derbio ("Silver fish") 1·25 70
558 9p. Spotted scorpionfish ("Gurnard") 1·50 80
559 10p. St. Helena parrotfish ("Blue dad") 1·50 80
560 15p. St. Helena butterflyfish ("Cunning fish") 2·00 1·00
561 18p. Rock hind ("Grouper") 2·00 1·00
562 20p. Spotted moray 2·00 1·25
563 25p. Squirrelfish ("Hardback soldierfish") 2·00 1·25
564 30p. Blue marlin 2·00 1·40
565 50p. Wahoo 2·50 2·00
566 70p. Yellow-finned tuna 2·50 2·75
567 £1 Blue shark 3·00 3·50
568 £2.50 Bottlenose dolphin 6·50 7·00

143 Holland's Crater

1992. 40th Anniv of Queen Elizabeth II's Accession. Multicoloured.
569 9p. Type **143** 30 30
570 15p. Green Mountain 50 50
571 18p. Boatswain Bird Island 60 60
572 25p. Three portraits of Queen Elizabeth 80 80
573 70p. Queen Elizabeth II 2·00 2·00
The portraits shown on the 25p. are repeated from the three lower values of the set.

144 Compass Rose and "Eye of the Wind" (cadet brig)

1992. 500th Anniv of Discovery of America by Columbus and Re-enactment Voyages. Mult.
574 9p. Type **144** 1·25 80
575 18p. Map of re-enactment voyages and "Soren Larsen" (cadet brigantine) 1·75 1·25
576 25p. "Santa Maria", "Pinta" and "Nina" 2·25 1·50
577 70p. Columbus and "Santa Maria" 3·75 3·50

145 Control Tower, Wideawake Airfield

146 Hawker Siddeley Nimrod

1992. 50th Anniv of Wideawake Airfield. Multicoloured.
578 15p. Type **145** 65 75
579 18p. Nose hangar 70 80
580 25p. Site preparation by U.S. Army engineers 90 1·00
581 70p. Laying fuel pipeline 2·25 2·50

1992. 10th Anniv of Liberation of Falkland Islands. Aircraft. Multicoloured.
582 15p. Type **146** 1·50 1·75
583 18p. Vickers VC-10 landing at Ascension 1·50 1·75
584 25p. Westland Wessex HU Mk 5 helicopter lifting supplies 2·00 1·75
585 65p. Avro Vulcan B.2 over Ascension 3·25 4·75
MS586 116 × 116 mm. 15p.+3p. Type **146**; 18p.+4p. As No. 583; 25p.+5p. As No. 584; 65p.+13p. As No. 585 4·75 6·00
The premiums on No. **MS**586 were for the S.S.A.F.A.

147 "Christmas in Great Britain and Ascension"

1992. Christmas. Children's Paintings. Mult.
587 8p. Type **147** 80 1·00
588 18p. "Santa Claus riding turtle" 1·25 1·50
589 25p. "Nativity" 1·50 1·75
590 65p. "Nativity with rabbit" 2·75 5·00

148 Male Canary Singing

1993. Yellow Canary. Multicoloured.
591 15p. Type **148** 75 70
592 18p. Adult male and female 85 80
593 25p. Young birds calling for food 95 95
594 70p. Adults and young birds on the wing 2·50 3·75

149 Sopwith Snipe

1993. 75th Anniv of Royal Air Force. Multicoloured.
595 20p. Type **149** 2·00 1·75
596 25p. Supermarine Southampton 2·00 1·75
597 30p. Avro Type 652 Anson 2·00 1·90
598 70p. Vickers-Armstrong Wellington 3·25 4·50
MS599 110 × 77 mm. 25p. Westland Lysander; 25p. Armstrong-Whitworth Meteor ("Gloster Meteor"); 25p. De Havilland D.H.106 Comet; 25p. Hawker Siddeley H.S.801 Nimrod 3·00 4·00

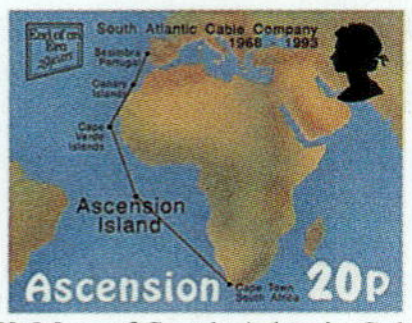

150 Map of South Atlantic Cable

1993. 25th Anniv of South Atlantic Cable Company. Multicoloured.
600 20p. Type **150** 80 90
601 25p. "Sir Eric Sharpe" laying cable 90 1·00
602 30p. Map of Ascension 1·00 1·25
603 70p. "Sir Eric Sharpe" (cable ship) off Ascension 2·25 2·75

151 Lanatana Camara

1993. Local Flowers. Multicoloured.
604 20p. Type **151** 1·50 1·00
605 25p. Moonflower 1·60 1·10
606 30p. Hibiscus 1·60 1·25
607 70p. Frangipani 3·00 3·25

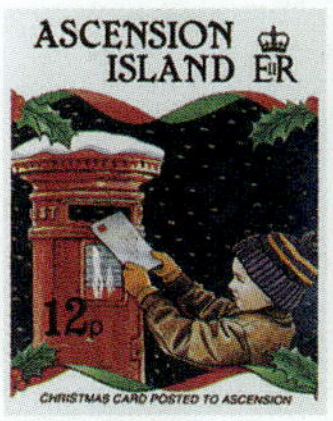

152 Posting Christmas Card to Ascension

153 Ichthyosaurus

1993. Christmas. Multicoloured.
608 12p. Type **152** 45 45
609 20p. Loading mail onto R.A.F. Lockheed TriStar at Brize Norton 75 60
610 25p. TriStar over South Atlantic 85 70
611 30p. Unloading mail at Wideawake Airfield 1·10 80
612 65p. Receiving card and Georgetown Post Office 1·60 2·75
MS613 161 × 76 mm. Nos. 608/12 9·00 9·00

1994. Prehistoric Aquatic Reptiles. Mult.
614 12p. Type **153** 70 1·10
615 20p. Metriorhynchus 85 1·25
616 25p. Mosasaurus 90 1·40
617 30p. Elasmosaurus 90 1·50
618 65p. Plesiosaurus 1·75 2·75

1994. "Hong Kong '94" International Stamp Exhibition. Nos. 614/18 optd **HONG KONG '94** and emblem.
619 12p. Type **153** 85 1·40
620 20p. Metriorhynchus 1·10 1·50
621 25p. Mosasaurus 1·10 1·75
622 30p. Elasmosaurus 1·25 1·90
623 65p. Plesiosaurus 2·25 3·50

155 Young Green Turtles heading towards Sea

1994. Green Turtles. Multicoloured.
624 20p. Type **155** 2·00 2·00
625 25p. Turtle digging nest 2·00 2·00
626 30p. Turtle leaving sea 2·00 2·00
627 65p. Turtle swimming 3·50 5·50
MS628 116 × 90 mm. 30p. Turtle leaving sea (different); 30p. Turtle digging nest (different); 30p. Young turtles heading towards sea (different); 30p. Young turtle leaving nest 9·50 10·00

156 "Yorkshireman" (tug)

1994. Civilian Ships used in Liberation of Falkland Islands, 1982. Multicoloured.
629 20p. Type **156** 2·50 2·00
630 25p. "St. Helena I" (minesweeper support ship) 2·50 2·00
631 30p. "British Esk" (tanker) 2·50 2·25
632 65p. "Uganda" (hospital ship) 4·50 5·50

157 Sooty Tern Chick

1994. Sooty Tern. Multicoloured.
633 20p. Type **157** 90 1·50
634 25p. Juvenile bird 95 1·50
635 30p. Brooding adult 1·10 1·60
636 65p. Adult male performing courting display 1·75 2·75
MS637 77 × 58 mm. £1 Flock of sooty terns 3·50 5·50

158 Donkey Mare with Foal

159 "Leonurus japonicus"

1994. Christmas. Donkeys. Multicoloured.
638 12p. Type **158** 1·40 1·25
639 20p. Juvenile 1·75 1·60
640 25p. Foal 1·75 1·60
641 30p. Adult and cattle egrets 1·75 1·75
642 65p. Adult 3·25 4·50

1995. Flowers. Multicoloured.
643 20p. Type **159** 2·50 2·00
644 25p. "Catharanthus roseus" (horiz) 2·50 2·00
645 30p. "Mirabilis jalapa" 2·75 2·25
646 65p. "Asclepias curassavica" (horiz) 3·50 5·00

160 Two Boats and Green Mountain

1995. Late 19th-century Scenes. Each in cinnamon and brown.
647 12p. Type **160** 50 80
648 20p. Island Stewards' Store 70 90
649 25p. Navy headquarters and barracks 90 1·10
650 30p. Police office 1·75 1·75
651 65p. Pierhead 2·00 3·50

161 5.5-inch Coastal Battery

1995. 50th Anniv of End of Second World War. Multicoloured.
652 20p. Type **161** 1·50 2·00
653 25p. Fairey Swordfish aircraft 1·75 2·00
654 30p. H.M.S. "Dorsetshire" (cruiser) 1·75 2·25
655 65p. H.M.S. "Devonshire" (cruiser) 3·50 4·25
MS656 75 × 85 mm. £1 Reverse of 1939–45 War Medal (vert) 2·50 3·25

162 Male and Female "Lampides boeticus"

1995. Butterflies. Multicoloured.
657 20p. Type **162** . . . . . 1·25 1·25
658 25p. "Vanessa cardui" . . . 1·40 1·40
659 30p. Male "Hypolimnas misippus" . . . . 1·40 1·40
660 65p. "Danaus chrysippus" . . 2·50 3·00
MS661 114 × 85 mm. £1 "Vanessa atalanta" . . . . 3·50 3·25
No. **MS**661 includes the "Singapore '95" International Stamp Exhibition logo on the sheet margin.

163 "Santa Claus on Boat" (Phillip Stephens)

1995. Christmas. Children's Drawings. Mult.
662 12p. Type **163** . . . . . 1·50 1·25
663 20p. "Santa sitting on Wall" (Kelly Lemon) . . . . . 1·75 1·60
664 25p. "Santa in Chimney" (Mario Anthony) . . . . . 1·75 1·60
665 30p. "Santa riding Dolphin" (Verena Benjamin) . . . . 1·75 1·60
666 65p. "Santa in Sleigh over Ascension" (Tom Butler) 3·25 4·50

164 "Cypraea lurida oceanica"

1996. Molluscs. Multicoloured.
667 12p. Type **164** . . . . . . 2·50 2·75
668 25p. "Cypraea spurca sanctaehelenae" . . . . . 2·75 3·00
669 30p. "Harpa doris" . . . . 2·75 3·00
670 65p. "Umbraculum umbraculum" . . . . . 3·50 3·75
Nos. 667/70 were printed together, se-tenant, forming a composite design.

165 Queen Elizabeth II and St. Mary's Church

1996. 70th Birthday of Queen Elizabeth II. Mult.
671 20p. Type **165** 55 60
672 25p. The Residency 60 60
673 30p. The Roman Catholic Grotto 70 70
674 65p. The Exiles' Club . . . . 1·75 1·75

166 American Army Jeep

1996. "CAPEX '96" International Stamp Exhibition, Toronto. Island Transport. Multicoloured.
675 20p. Type **166** . . . . . 1·25 1·25
676 25p. Citroen 7.5hp two-seater car, 1924 . . . . 1·40 1·40
677 30p. Austin ten tourer car, 1930 . . . . 1·40 1·40
678 65p. Series 1 Land Rover . . 2·50 3·00

167 Madeiran Storm Petrel

168 Pylons

1996. Birds and their Young. Multicoloured.
679 1p. Type **167** 50 60
680 2p. Red-billed tropic bird . . 50 60
681 4p. Common mynah 50 60
682 5p. House sparrow 50 60
683 7p. Common waxbill 65 65
684 10p. White tern 70 70
685 12p. Red-necked spurfowl . . 80 80
686 15p. Common noddy ("Brown Noddy") 90 90
687 20p. Yellow canary . . . . . 1·00 1·00
688 25p. White-capped noddy ("Black Noddy") . . . . 1·00 1·00
689 30p. Red-footed booby . . . 1·25 1·25
690 40p. White-tailed tropic bird ("Yellow-billed Tropicbird") . . . . . . 1·50 1·50
691 65p. Brown booby . . . . . 2·00 2·25
692 £1 Blue-faced booby ("Masked Booby") . . . . 2·50 2·75
693 £2 Sooty tern . . . . . . 4·50 5·00
694 £3 Ascension frigate bird . . 6·50 7·00
See also Nos. 726/7.

1996. 30th Anniv of B.B.C. Atlantic Relay Station. Multicoloured.
695 20p. Type **168** 75 75
696 25p. Pylons (different) . . . 80 80
697 30p. Pylons and station buildings 90 90
698 65p. Dish aerial, pylon and beach . . . . 1·90 1·90

169 Santa Claus on Dish Aerial

1996. Christmas. Santa Claus. Multicoloured.
699 12p. Type **169** 50 50
700 20p. Playing golf 75 75
701 25p. In deck chair 75 75
702 30p. On top of aircraft . . . 85 85
703 65p. On funnel of "St. Helena II" (mail ship) 1·90 2·25

170 Date Palm

171 Red Ensign and "Maersk Ascension" (tanker)

1997. "Hong Kong '97" International Stamp Exhibition. Trees. Multicoloured.
704 20p. Type **170** 75 75
705 25p. Mauritius hemp 85 85
706 30p. Norfolk Island pine . . 95 95
707 65p. Dwarf palm . . . . . 2·00 2·50

1997. "HONG KONG '97" International Stamp Exhibition. Sheet 130 × 90 mm containing design as No. 691. Multicoloured.
MS708 65p. Brown booby . . . 1·50 1·50

1997. Flags. Multicoloured.
709 12p. Type **171** 80 80
710 25p. R.A.F. flag and Tristar airliner . . . . 1·10 1·10
711 30p. N.A.S.A. emblem and Space Shuttle "Atlantis" landing . . . . 1·25 1·25
712 65p. White Ensign and H.M.S. "Northumberland" (frigate) . . . . 2·00 2·75

172 "Solanum sodomaeum"

1997. Wild Herbs. Multicoloured.
713 30p. Type **172** . . . . . . 1·00 1·25
714 30p. "Ageratum conyzoides" . 1·00 1·25
715 30p. "Leonurus sibiricus" . . 1·00 1·25
716 30p. "Cerastium vulgatum" 1·00 1·25
717 30p. "Commelina diffusa" . . 1·00 1·25
Nos. 713/17 were printed together, se-tenant, with the backgrounds forming a composite design.

1997. Return of Hong Kong to China. Sheet 130 × 90 mm containing design as No. 692, but with "1997" imprint date.
MS718 £1 Blue-faced booby . . 2·00 2·10

173 Queen Elizabeth II

1997. Golden Wedding of Queen Elizabeth and Prince Philip. Multicoloured.
719 20p. Type **173** . . . . . . 1·50 1·60
720 20p. Prince Philip on horseback . . . . 1·50 1·60
721 25p. Queen Elizabeth with polo pony . . . . 1·50 1·60
722 25p. Prince Philip in Montserrat . . . . 1·50 1·60
723 30p. Queen Elizabeth and Prince Philip . . . . . 1·50 1·60
724 30p. Prince William and Prince Harry on horseback 1·50 1·60
MS725 110 × 70 mm. $1.50, Queen Elizabeth and Prince Philip in landau (horiz) . . . . 3·50 3·50
Nos. 719/20, 721/2 and 723/4 respectively were printed together, se-tenant, with the backgrounds forming composite designs.

1997. Birds and their Young. As Nos. 683 and 687, but smaller, size 20 × 24 mm. Multicoloured.
726 15p. Common waxbill . . . 1·50 1·75
727 35p. Yellow canary . . . . . 1·75 2·00

174 Black Marlin

1997. Gamefish. Multicoloured.
728 12p. Type **174** 50 60
729 20p. Atlantic sailfish 75 80
730 25p. Swordfish 85 90
731 30p. Wahoo . . . . 95 1·00
732 £1 Yellowfin tuna . . . . . 2·50 3·00

175 Interior of St. Mary's Church

176 "Cactoblastis cactorum" (caterpillar and moth)

1997. Christmas. Multicoloured.
733 15p. Type **175** 75 75
734 35p. Falklands memorial window showing Virgin and child . . . . 1·40 1·40
735 40p. Falklands memorial window showing Archangel 1·50 1·60
736 50p. Pair of stained glass windows . . . . 1·75 2·00

1998. Biological Control using Insects. Mult.
737 15p. Type **176** . . . . . . 1·50 1·25
738 35p. "Teleonemia scrupulosa" (lace-bug) . . . . . . 2·00 1·90
739 40p. "Neltumius arizonensis" (beetle) . . . . 2·00 2·00
740 50p. "Algarobius prosopis" (beetle) . . . . 2·25 2·50

177 Diana, Princess of Wales, 1985

1998. Diana, Princess of Wales Commemoration. Sheet 145 × 70 mm, containing T **177** and similar vert designs. Multicoloured.
MS741 35p. Type **177**; 35p. Wearing yellow blouse, 1992; 35p. Wearing grey jacket, 1984; 35p. Carrying bouquets (sold at £1.40 + 20p. charity premium) . . . . . . 3·75 3·75

178 Fairey Fawn

1998. 80th Anniv of Royal Air Force. Mult.
742 15p. Type **178** . . . . . . 1·00 85
743 35p. Vickers Vernon . . . . 1·60 1·50
744 40p. Supermarine Spitfire F.22 . . . . 1·75 1·75
745 50p. Bristol Britannia C.2 . . 1·90 2·25
MS746 110 × 77 mm. 50p. Blackburn Kangaroo; 50p. S.E.5a; 50p. Curtiss Kittyhawk III; 50p. Boeing Fortress II . . . . 4·75 4·75

179 Barn Swallow

180 Cricket

1998. Migratory Birds. Multicoloured.
747 15p. Type **179** 90 90
748 25p. House martin . . . . . 1·25 1·25
749 35p. Cattle egret . . . . . . 1·40 1·50
750 40p. Eurasian swift ("Swift") 1·50 1·75
751 50p. Allen's gallinule . . . . 1·75 2·00

1998. Sporting Activities. Multicoloured.
752 15p. Type **180** . . . . 2·50 1·50
753 35p. Golf . . . . 3·25 1·75
754 40p. Football . . . . 1·75 2·00
755 50p. Shooting . . . . 1·75 2·00

181 Children in Nativity Play

1998. Christmas. Multicoloured.
756 15p. Type **181** . . . . 1·00 1·00
757 35p. Santa Claus arriving on Ascension . . . . 1·50 1·50
758 40p. Santa Claus on carnival float . . . . 1·50 1·50
759 50p. Carol singers . . . . . 1·50 1·50

182 Curtiss C-46 Commando

1999. Aircraft. Multicoloured.
760 15p. Type **182** . . . . 1·25 1·25
761 35p. Douglas C-47 Dakota . . 1·75 2·00
762 40p. Douglas C-54 Skymaster 1·75 2·00
763 50p. Consolidated Liberator Mk. V . . . . 1·75 2·00
MS764 120 × 85 mm. $1.50, Consolidated Liberator LB-30 8·00 8·00
No. **MS**764 also commemorates the 125th birth anniv of Sir Winston Churchill.

183 "Glengorm Castle" (mail ship), 1929

1999. "Australia '99" World Stamp Exhibition, Melbourne. Ships. Multicoloured.
765 15p. Type **183** . . . . 1·25 1·25
766 35p. "Gloucester Castle" (mail ship), 1930 . . . . . 1·75 2·00
767 40p. "Durham Castle" (mail ship), 1930 . . . . 1·75 2·00
768 50p. "Garth Castle" (mail ship), 1930 . . . . 1·75 2·00
MS769 121 × 82 mm. £1 H.M.S. "Endeavour" (Cook) . . . . . 2·75 3·00

184 Pair of White Terns ("Fairy Terns")

1999. Endangered Species. White Tern ("Fairy Tern"). Multicoloured.
770 10p. Type **184** 40 55
771 10p. On branch 40 55
772 10p. Adult and fledgeling . . 40 55
773 10p. In flight 40 55

185 Prince Edward and Miss Sophie Rhys-Jones

186 Command and Service Modules

1999. Royal Wedding. Multicoloured.
774 50p. Type **185** . . . . 1·25 1·50
775 £1 Engagement photograph 2·25 2·75

1999. 30th Anniv of First Manned Landing on Moon. Multicoloured.
776 15p. Type **186** . . . . 75 1·10
777 35p. Moon from "Apollo 11" 1·25 1·60
778 40p. Devil's Ashpit Tracking Station and command module . . . . 1·25 1·60
779 50p. Lunar module leaving Moon . . . . 1·25 1·60
MS780 90 × 80 mm. $1.50, Earth as seen from Moon (circular, 40 mm diam) . . . . 3·75 5·00

187 King George VI, Queen Elizabeth and Prime Minister Winston Churchill, 1940

1999. "Queen Elizabeth the Queen Mother's Century". Multicoloured.
781 15p. Type **187** . . . . 1·25 1·25
782 35p. With Prince Charles at Coronation, 1953 . . . . 1·75 1·75
783 40p. On her 88th Birthday, 1988 . . . . 1·75 1·75
784 50p. With Guards' drummers, 1988 . . . . 1·75 1·75
MS785 145 × 70 mm. £1.50, Lady Elizabeth Bowes-Lyon, and "Titanic" (liner) (black) . . . 3·50 5·00

188 Babies with Toys

1999. Christmas. Multicoloured.
786 15p. Type **188** . . . . 1·25 1·25
787 35p. Children dressed as clowns . . . . 1·75 1·75
788 40p. Getting ready for bed 1·75 1·75
789 50p. Children dressed as pirates . . . . 1·75 1·75

189 "Anglia" (cable ship), 1900

1999. Centenary of Cable & Wireless Communications plc on Ascension.
790 **189** 15p. black, brown and bistre . . . . 1·50 1·50
791 – 35p. black, brown and bistre . . . . 2·00 2·00
792 – 40p. multicoloured . . . 2·00 2·00
793 – 50p. black, brown and bistre . . . . 2·00 2·00
MS794 - - 105 × 90 mm. £1.50, multicoloured . . . . 3·50 4·00
DESIGNS: 35p. "Cambria" (cable ship), 1910; 40p. Cable network map; 50p. "Colonia" (cable ship), 1910; £1.50, "Seine" (cable ship), 1899.

190 Baby Turtles

2000. Turtle Project on Ascension. Multicoloured.
795 15p. Type **190** . . . . 1·25 1·25
796 35p. Turtle on beach . . . . 1·75 1·75
797 40p. Turtle with tracking device . . . . 1·75 1·75
798 50p. Turtle heading for sea 1·75 1·75
MS799 197 × 132 mm. 25p. Head of turtle; 25p. Type **190**; 25p. Turtle on beach; 25p. Turtle entering sea (each 40 × 26 mm) . . . . . . 5·00 5·50

2000. "The Stamp Show 2000" International Stamp Exhibition, London. As No. **MS**799, but with "The Stamp Show 2000" added to the bottom right corner of the margin.
MS800 197 × 132 mm. 25p. Head of turtle; 25p. Type **190**; 25p. Turtle on beach; 25p. Turtle entering sea (each 40 × 26 mm) . . . . . . 2·75 3·25

191 Prince William as Toddler, 1983

2000. 18th Birthday of Prince William. Mult.
801 15p. Type **191** . . . . 1·00 1·00
802 35p. Prince William in 1994 1·50 1·50
803 40p. Skiing at Klosters, Switzerland (horiz) . . . . 1·50 1·50
804 50p. Prince William in 1997 (horiz) . . . . 1·50 1·50
MS805 175 × 95 mm. 10p. As baby with toy mouse (horiz) and Nos. 801/4 . . . . 5·50 6·00

192 Royal Marine and Early Fort, 1815

2000. Forts. Multicoloured.
806 15p. Type **192** . . . . 1·50 1·50
807 35p. Army officer and Fort Thornton, 1817 . . . . . . 2·25 2·25
808 40p. Soldier and Fort Hayes, 1860 . . . . 2·25 2·25
809 50p. Naval lieutenant and Fort Bedford, 1940 . . . . 2·25 2·25

193 Ships and Dockside Crane ("I saw Three Ships")

2000. Christmas. Carols. Multicoloured.
810 15p. Type **193** . . . . 1·25 1·00
811 25p. Choir and musicians on beach ("Silent Night") . . 1·50 1·00
812 40p. Donkeys and church ("Away in a Manger") . . 2·25 1·75
813 90p. Carol singers outside church ("Hark the Herald Angels Sing") . . . . . . 3·75 6·00

194 Green Turtle

2001. "Hong Kong 2001" Stamp Exhibition. Sheet 150 × 90 mm, containing T **194**. Multicoloured.
MS814 25p. Type **194**; 40p. Loggerhead turtle . . . . . . 2·50 3·00

195 Captain William Dampier

196 Alfonso de Albuquerque

2001. Centenary of Wreck of the *Roebuck*. Mult.
815 15p. Type **195** . . . . 1·50 1·50
816 35p. Construction drawing (horiz) . . . . 2·00 2·00
817 40p. Cave dwelling at Dampier's Drip (horiz) . . 2·00 2·00
818 50p. Map of Ascension . . . 2·50 2·50

2001. 500th Anniv of the Discovery of Ascension Island. Multicoloured.
819 15p. Type **196** . . . . 1·75 1·75
820 35p. Portuguese caravel . . . 2·50 2·50
821 40p. Cantino map . . . . . 2·50 2·50
822 50p. Rear Admiral Sir George Cockburn . . . . 2·50 2·50

197 Great Britain 1d. Stamp used on Ascension, 1855

2001. Death Centenary of Queen Victoria. Mult.
823 15p. Type **197** . . . . 1·25 1·25
824 25p. Navy church parade, 1901 (horiz) . . . . . . 1·50 1·50
825 35p. H.M.S. *Phoebe* (cruiser) (horiz) . . . . 2·00 2·00
826 40p. The Red Lion, 1863 (horiz) . . . . 2·00 2·00
827 50p. "Queen Victoria" . . . 2·00 2·00
828 65p. Sir Joseph Hooker (botanist) . . . . 2·00 2·75
MS829 105 × 80 mm. £1.50, Queen Victoria's coffin on the steps of St. George's Chapel, Windsor (horiz) . . . . 3·75 4·75

198 Islander Hostel

2001. "BELGICA 2001" International Stamp Exhibition, Brussels. Tourism. Multicoloured.
830 35p. Type **198** . . . . 2·00 2·25
831 35p. The Residency . . . . . 2·00 2·25
832 40p. The Red Lion . . . . . 2·00 2·25
833 40p. Turtle Ponds . . . . . 2·00 2·25

199 Female Ascension Frigate Bird

2001. Birdlife World Bird Festival (1st series). Ascension Frigate Birds. Multicoloured.
834 15p. Type **199** . . . . 1·25 1·25
835 35p. Fledgeling . . . . . . 1·75 1·75
836 40p. Male bird in flight (horiz) . . . . 1·75 1·75
837 50p. Male bird with pouch inflated (horiz) . . . . . 1·75 1·75
MS838 175 × 80 mm. 10p. Male and female birds on rock (horiz) and Nos. 834/7 . . . . 5·00 6·00
See also Nos. 889/94 and 921/**MS**926.

200 Princess Elizabeth and Dog

2002. Golden Jubilee.
839 **200** 15p. agate, mauve and gold . . . . 1·25 1·25
840 – 35p. multicoloured . . . 1·75 1·75
841 – 40p. multicoloured . . . 1·75 1·75
842 – 50p. multicoloured . . . 1·75 2·00
MS843 – 162 × 95 mm. Nos. 839/42 and 60p. multicoloured . . . . 5·50 6·50
DESIGNS—HORIZ: 35p. Queen Elizabeth wearing tiara, 1978; 40p. Princess Elizabeth, 1946; 50p. Queen Elizabeth visiting Henley-on-Thames, 1998. VERT: (38 × 51 mm)—50p. Queen Elizabeth after Annigoni.

201 Royal Marines landing at English Bay

2002. 20th Anniv of Liberation of the Falkland Islands. Multicoloured.
844 15p. Type **201** 80 85
845 35p. Weapons testing . . . . 1·25 1·40
846 40p. H.M.S. *Hermes* (aircraft carrier) . . . . 1·25 1·40
847 50p. R.A.F. Vulcan at Wideawake Airfield . . . . 1·25 1·50

202 Duchess of York at Harrow Hospital, 1931

204 "Ecce Ancilla Dominii" (Dante Rossetti)

203 Travellers Palm and Vinca

2002. Queen Elizabeth the Queen Mother Commemoration.
848 **202** 35p. black, gold and purple . . . . 1·00 1·10
849 – 40p. multicoloured . . . 1·00 1·25
MS850 – 145 × 70 mm. 50p. brown and gold; £1 multicoloured . . 4·75 5·50
DESIGNS: 40p. Queen Mother on her birthday, 1997; 50p. Duchess of York, 1925; £1 Queen Mother, Scrabster, 1992.

2002. Island Views. Multicoloured.
851 10p. Type **203** 30 35
852 15p. Broken Tooth (volcanic crater) and Mexican poppy 40 45
853 20p. St. Mary's Church and Ascension lily 50 55
854 25p. Boatswain Bird Island and goatweed 60 65
855 30p. Cannon and Mauritius hemp 70 75
856 35p. The Guest House and frangipani 80 85
857 40p. Wideawake tern and Ascension spurge 90 95
858 50p. The Pier Head and lovechaste . . . . 1·25 1·40
859 65p. Sisters' Peak and yellowboy . . . . 1·50 1·75
860 90p. Two Boats School and Persian lilac . . . . . . 2·00 2·25
861 £2 Green turtle and wild currant . . . . 4·00 4·25
862 £5 Wideawake Airfield and coral tree . . . . 10·00 10·50

2002. Christmas. Religious Paintings. Mult.
863 15p. Type **204** 70 70
864 25p. "The Holy Family and Shepherd" (Titian) (horiz) 95 95
865 35p. "Christ carrying the Cross" (A. Bergognone) . . 1·25 1·25
866 75p. Sketch for "The Ascension" (Benjamin West) . . . . 2·50 3·00

205 Ariane 4 Rocket on Gantry

207 Queen Elizabeth II

206 Coronation Coach in Procession

2003. Ariane Downrange Station. Multicoloured.
867 35p. Type **205** . . . . 1·40 1·25
868 40p. Map of Ariane Downrange stations (horiz) 1·50 1·25
869 65p. Automated Transfer Vehicle (ATV) in Space (horiz) . . . . 2·50 2·50
870 90p. Launch of Ariane 5 . . 3·75 4·25
MS871 170 × 88 mm. Nos. 867/70 8·25 8·50

2003. 50th Anniv of Coronation. Multicoloured.
872 40p. Type **206** . . . . 1·50 1·00
873 £1 Newly crowned Queen with bishops and peers . . 3·25 3·75
MS874 95 × 115 mm. As Nos. 872/3 4·75 4·75
Nos. 872/3 have red frame; stamps from **MS**874 have no frame and country name in mauve panel.

2003.
875 **207** £3 black, green and myrtle . . . . 6·50 7·00

208 Prince William at Tidworth Polo Club and on Skiing Holiday, 2002

2003. 21st Birthday of Prince William of Wales. Multicoloured.
876 75p. Type **208** . . . . 2·75 2·75
877 75p. On Raleigh International Expedition, 2000 and at Queen Mother's 101st Birthday, 2001 . . . . . . 2·75 2·75

209 Bleriot XI

2003. Centenary of Powered Flight. Multicoloured.
878 15p. Type **209** 75 75
879 20p. Vickers VC-10 . . . . . 80 80
880 35p. BAe Harrier FRS Mk1 1·40 1·40
881 40p. Westland Sea King HAS Mk. 4 helicopter . . . . . 1·50 1·50
882 50p. Rockwell Space Shuttle 1·50 1·50
883 90p. General Dynamics F-16 Fighting Falcon . . . . . 3·00 3·50
MS884 115 × 65 mm. £1.50 Fairey Swordfish Mk II. . . . . . . 5·00 5·50

210 Casting Vote into Ballot Box

2003. Christmas. First Anniv of Democracy on Ascension. Multicoloured.
885 15p. Type **210** 75 55
886 25p. Island Council session 90 65
887 40p. Students ("HIGHER EDUCATION") . . . . . 1·40 1·10
888 £1 Government Headquarters 2·75 3·50

211 Adult with Fledgling

2004. Birdlife International (2nd series). Masked Booby. Multicoloured.
889 15p. Type **211** 80 75
890 35p. Pair (vert) . . . . . . 1·40 1·00
891 40p. In flight (vert) . . . . . 1·40 1·25
892 50p. Adult calling . . . . . 1·50 1·50
893 90p. Masked booby . . . . . 3·00 3·50
MS894 175 × 80 mm. Nos. 889/93 7·00 7·50

212 *Bougainvillea glabra* (orange)

2004. Bicentenary of the Royal Horticultural Society. Multicoloured.
895 15p. Type **212** 75 75
896 35p. *Bougainvillea glabra* (pink) . . . . 1·40 1·00
897 40p. *Bougainvillea glabra* (white) . . . . 1·50 1·10
898 90p. *Bougainvillea spectabilis* (red) . . . . 2·75 3·50
MS899 105 × 80 mm. £1.50 *Pteris adscensionis* . . . . 4·50 5·00

213 Blue Marlin

2004. Sport Fishing (1st series). Multicoloured.
900 15p. Type **213** 75 75
901 35p. Swordfish . . . . 1·40 1·00
902 40p. Sailfish . . . . 1·50 1·10
903 90p. White marlin . . . . . 2·75 3·50
MS904 61 × 51 mm. £1.50 Blue marlin . . . . 4·50 5·00
See also Nos. 927/**MS**931.

214 Moon over Hummock Point

2004. Lunar Eclipse. Multicoloured.
905 15p. Type **214** 75 75
906 25p. Yellow moon over Sisters Peak (North side) 1·25 90
907 35p. Orange moon over Daly's Craggs . . . . . . 1·50 1·00
908 £1.25 Red moon and birds over Mars Bay . . . . . 3·75 4·50
MS909 130 × 55 mm. £1.25 As No. 908 . . . . 4·00 4·50

215 MV *Ascension*

2004. Merchant Ships. Multicoloured.
910 15p. Type **215** 75 65
911 35p. *St. Helena* (mail ship) 1·40 1·00
912 40p. *Caronia* (mail ship) . . . 1·50 1·25
913 £1.25 MV *Maersk Gannet* . . 3·75 4·50

216 British Carronade on Sliding Carriage

2005. Bicentenary of Battle of Trafalgar (1st issue). Multicoloured.
914 15p. Type **216** 75 65
915 25p. Royal Marine drummer boy, 1805 (vert) . . . . . 1·25 90
916 35p. HMS *Britannia* (vert) . . 1·40 1·25
917 40p. Admiral Nelson . . . . 1·50 1·25
918 50p. HMS *Neptune* and *Santissima Trinidad* . . . . 1·60 1·50
919 90p. HMS *Victory* . . . . . 2·75 3·50
MS920 120 × 80 mm. £1 Lord Nelson (vert); £1 *Neptune* (vert) 6·50 7·00
No. 919 contains traces of powdered wood from HMS *Victory*.
See also Nos. 937/9.

217 White Tern ("Fairy Tern")

2005. Birdlife International (3rd series). "The Sea Birds Return". Multicoloured.
921 15p. Type **217** 55 55
922 35p. White-tailed tropic bird 1·10 1·10
923 40p. Brown booby . . . . . 1·25 1·40
924 50p. Common noddy ("Brown Noddy") . . . . 1·40 1·40
925 £1.25 Red-billed tropic bird 3·25 3·50
MS926 170 × 80 mm. Nos. 921/5 6·75 7·00

218 Yellowfin Tuna

2005. Sport Fishing (2nd series). Tuna. Mult.
927 35p. Type **218** . . . . 1·10 1·10
928 40p. Skipjack tuna . . . . . 1·25 1·25
929 50p. Albacore tuna . . . . . 1·40 1·40
930 £1.25 Bigeye tuna . . . . . 3·25 3·50
MS931 61 × 51 mm. £1.50 Yellowfin tuna hunting herrings . . . . 4·00 4·50

219 Pope John Paul II **220** *The Little Fir Tree*

2005. Pope John Paul II Commemoration.
932 **219** 40p. multicoloured . . . 1·75 1·75

2005. Christmas. Birth Bicentenary of Hans Christian Andersen (writer). Multicoloured.
933 15p. Type **220** 70 70
934 25p. *The Mail-Coach Passengers* 90 80
935 35p. *The Little Match Girl* . . 1·25 1·10
936 £1.25 *The Snow Man* . . . . 4·00 4·50

221 HMS *Victory*

2005. Bicentenary of the Battle of Trafalgar (2nd issue). Multicoloured.
937 40p. Type **221** . . . . 1·50 1·40
938 65p. Ships engaged in battle (horiz) . . . . 2·50 3·00
939 90p. "Admiral Lord Nelson" 3·50 4·00

222 Black Jack

2006. Sport Fishing (3rd series). Jacks. Multicoloured.
940 20p. Type **222** 80 80
941 35p. Almaco jack . . . . . 1·40 ·25
942 50p. Horse-eye jack . . . . 1·75 ·75
943 £1 Rainbow runner . . . . . 3·25 3·75
MS944 61 × 50 mm. £1.50 Longfin crevalle jack . . . . 4·00 4·50

223 Princess Elizabeth

2006. 80th Birthday of Queen Elizabeth II. Multicoloured.
945 20p. Type **223** 80 80
946 40p. Queen Elizabeth II, c. 1952 . . . 1·60 1·25
947 50p. Queen Elizabeth II . . . 1·75 1·60
948 £1.30 Wearing Garter robes 4·25 4·50
MS949 144 × 75 mm. £1 Queen, c. 1952; £1 Queen in 1960s 6·00 6·25

224 HMS *Beagle* (175th anniv of Darwin's voyage)

2006. Exploration and Innovation. Anniversaries. Multicoloured.
950 20p. Type **224** 80 80
951 20p. Charles Darwin (originator of theory of evolution) 80 80
952 35p. *Great Britain* (steam/sail) 1·40 1·40
953 35p. Isambard Kingdom Brunel (engineer, birth bicentenary) . . . . 1·40 1·40
954 40p. *Nina* (Columbus) . . . 1·60 1·60
955 40p. Christopher Columbus (discoverer of New World, 500th death anniv) . . . . 1·60 1·60
956 50p. World map with lines of magnetic variation . . . . 1·60 1·60
957 50p. Edmund Halley (astronomer, 350th birth anniv) and Halley's comet 1·60 1·60
Nos. 950/1, 952/3, 954/5 and 956/7 were each printed together, se-tenant, forming a composite background design.

225 Long Beach ("Greetings from Ascension")

2006. Christmas. Views of Ascension Island. Multicoloured.
958 15p. Type **225** 70 70
959 25p. Coastal rocks at sunset ("Merry Christmas") . . . 1·10 1·10
960 35p. Dewpond ("Seasons Greetings") . . . . 1·40 1·10
961 £1.25 Coast and Boatswain Bird Island ("Happy New Year") . . . . 4·00 4·50

226 Resplendent Angelfish

2007. Endangered Species. Resplendent Angelfish (*Centropyge resplendens*). Multicoloured.
962 35p. Type **226** . . . . 1·40 1·10
963 40p. Shoal of resplendent angelfish . . . . 1·60 1·60
964 50p. Three angelfish near red coral and rocks . . . . . 1·60 1·60
965 £1.25 Large male angelfish and three smaller females 4·00 4·50

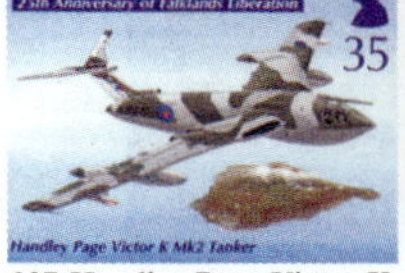

227 Handley Page Victor K Mk2 Tanker **229** Mother Teresa and Princess Diana, Rome, 1992

228 Ascension Scouts forming Fleur-de-Lis Emblem

2007. 25th Anniv of the Liberation of the Falkland Islands. Multicoloured.

966 35p. Type **227** . . . . . . 1·20 90
967 40p. HMS *Dumbarton Castle* (offshore patrol vessel) and Chinook helicopter . . . . 1·40 1·40
968 50p. HMS *Fearless* with helicopter and landing craft 1·40 1·40
969 £1.25 Vulcan XM607 taking off . . . . 4·00 4·50
MS970 Two sheets, each 183 × 89 mm. (a) As Type **227**; 40p. Vickers VC10 Transport; 50p. Nimrod MR2 Maritime Reconnaissance; As No. 969. (b) 35p. RFA *Tidespring* refuelling HMS *Antrim*; As No. 967; As No. 968; £1.25 *Atlantic Conveyor* and Harrier fighter . . . . . . 16·00 16·00

Stamps from the two miniature sheets **MS**970a/b do not have white borders.

The 50p. stamp from **MS**970(a) has an incorrect spelling "Reconaissance".

2007. Centenary of Scouting. Multicoloured.

971 35p. Type **228** . . . . . . 1·20 90
972 40p. Scouts rescuing stranded turtle . . . . 1·40 1·40
973 50p. Ascension Scout Troop sitting on gun from HMS *Hood* . . . . 1·40 1·40
974 £1.25 Scouts on top of their Land Rover near Butt Crater . . . . 4·00 4·50

2007. 10th Death Anniv of Diana, Princess of Wales.

975 **229** 50p. multicoloured . . . 1·40 1·40

230 Engagement Photograph, July 1947

2007. Diamond Wedding of Queen Elizabeth II and Duke of Edinburgh. Multicoloured.

976 35p. Type **230** . . . . 1·20 90
977 90p. Wedding programme . . 3·75 2·75
978 £1.25 Queen and Duke of Edinburgh at St. Paul's Cathedral for 80th birthday Thanksgiving Service . . . 4·00 4·50

231 BOU Base Camp near Mars Bay

2007. 50th Anniv of the British Ornithologists' Union Centenary Expedition (1957–9). Multicoloured.

979 15p. Type **231** 50 55
980 15p. Peter Mundy's drawing of extinct flightless rail, 1656 . . . . 50 55
981 25p. Team member recording sooty tern ('Wideawake') 85 90
982 25p. Sooty terns ('Wideawake') 85 90
983 40p. BOU outpost, Boatswainbird Island . . . 1·80 1·90
984 40p. Masked booby . . . . 1·80 1·90
985 50p. Team members with expedition dinghy *Overdraft* . . . . 2·10 2·20
986 50p. Red-footed booby . . . 2·10 2·20

232 *Lampides boeticus* (long-tailed blue butterfly)

2008. Fauna and their Eggs. Multicoloured.

987 15p. Type **232** 45 50
988 20p. *Cheilomenes lunata* (ladybird) 60 65
989 25p. *Panulirus echinatus* (spiny lobster) 75 80
990 30p. *Schistocerca gregaria* (desert locust) 90 85
991 35p. *Chelonia mydas* (green turtle) . . . . 1·10 1·20
992 40p. *Gecarcinus lagostoma* (landcrab) . . . . 1·20 1·30
993 50p. *Sula sula* (red-footed booby) . . . . 1·50 1·60
994 65p. *Hemdactylus mercatorius* (coconut-palm gecko) . . . 1·90 2·00
995 90p. *Estrilda astrild* (common waxbill) . . . . 2·75 3·00
996 £1 *Stegastes lubbocki* (yellowtail damselfish) . . 3·00 3·25
997 £2.50 *Oceanodroma castro* (Madeiran storm-petrel) . . 7·50 7·75
998 £5 *Francolinus afer* (red-necked francolin) . . . . . 15·00 15·50

233 Bluntnose Sixgill Shark

2008. Sharks. Multicoloured.

999 35p. Type **233** . . . . . . 1·10 1·20
1000 40p. Scalloped hammerhead 1·20 1·30
1001 50p. Shortfin mako . . . .
1002 £1.25 Whale shark . . . . 3·75 4·00
MS1003 70 × 45 mm. £1.50 Bigeye thresher . . . . 4·50 4·50

POSTAGE DUE STAMPS

D 1 Outline Map of Ascension

1986.

D1 D **1** 1p. deep brown and brown 15 20
D2 2p. brown and orange . . 15 20
D3 5p. brown and orange . . 15 20
D4 7p. black and violet . . . 20 30
D5 10p. black and blue . . . 25 35
D6 25p. black and green . . 65 75

AUSTRALIA Pt. 1

An island continent to the S.E. of Asia. A Commonwealth consisting of the states of New S. Wales, Queensland, S. Australia, Tasmania, Victoria and W. Australia.

1913. 12 pence = 1 shilling;
20 shillings = 1 pound.
1966. 100 cents = 1 dollar.

1 Eastern Grey Kangaroo

3

1913.

1 **1** ½d. green . . . . 6·50 3·75
2 1d. red . . . . 10·00 1·00
35 2d. grey . . . . 35·00 6·50
36 2½d. blue . . . . 23·00 10·00
37 3d. olive . . . . 28·00 4·75
6 4d. orange . . . . 60·00 22·00
8 5d. brown . . . . 55·00 32·00
38 6d. blue . . . . 55·00 7·50
73 6d. brown . . . . 24·00 1·75
133 9d. violet . . . . 29·00 1·50
40 1s. green . . . . 38·00 4·25
41 2s. brown . . . . £190 14·00
134 2s. purple . . . . 5·50 60
135 5s. grey and yellow . . . £130 13·00
136 10s. grey and pink . . . £325 £130
15 £1 brown and blue . . . £1800 £1900
137 £1 grey £550 £225
138 £2 black and pink . . . £2750 £450

1913.

20 **3** ½d. green . . . . 3·75 1·00
94 ½d. orange . . . . 2·25 1·40
17 1d. red . . . . 2·50 4·50
57 1d. violet . . . . 5·00 1·50
125 1d. green . . . . 1·75 20
59a 1½d. brown . . . . 6·50 60
61 1½d. green . . . . 4·00 80
77 1½d. red . . . . 2·25 40
62 2d. orange . . . . 12·00 1·00
127 2d. red . . . . 1·75 10
98 2d. brown . . . . 9·00 9·50
128 3d. blue . . . . 18·00 1·25
22 4d. orange . . . . 27·00 2·50
64 4d. violet . . . . 13·00 15·00
65 4d. blue . . . . 48·00 7·50
129 4d. olive . . . . 18·00 1·25
92 4½d. violet . . . . 18·00 3·75
130 5d. brown . . . . 15·00 20
131 1s.4d. blue . . . . 50·00 3·50

4 Laughing Kookaburra

8 Parliament House, Canberra

1913.

19 **4** 6d. purple . . . . 75·00 50·00

1927. Opening of Parliament House.

105 **8** 1½d. lake 50 50

1928. National Stamp Exhibition, Melbourne.

106 **4** 3d. blue . . . . 4·25 6·50
MS106a 65 × 70 mm. No. 106 × 4 £110 £200

9 De Havilland Hercules and Pastoral Scene

10 Black Swan

1929. Air.

115 **9** 3d. green . . . . 8·00 4·00

1929. Centenary of Western Australia.

116 **10** 1½d. red . . . . 1·25 1·60

11 "Capt. Chas Sturt" (J. H. Crossland)

13 The "Southern Cross" above Hemispheres

1930. Centenary of Sturt's Exploration of River Murray.

117 **11** 1½d. red . . . . 1·00 1·00
118 3d. blue . . . . 4·25 7·50

1930. Surch in words.

119 **3** 2d. on 1½d. red . . . . . 1·50 1·00
120 5d. on 4½d. violet . . . . 7·00 11·00

1931. Kingsford Smith's Flights.

121 **13** 2d. red (postage) . . . . . 1·00 1·00
122 3d. blue . . . . 4·75 5·00
123 6d. violet (air) . . . . . . 5·50 15·00

1931. Air. As T **13** but inscr "AIR MAIL SERVICE".

139 6d. brown . . . . 14·00 14·00

1931. Air. No. 139 optd **O S**.

139a 6d. brown . . . . 25·00 48·00

17 Superb Lyrebird

18 Sydney Harbour Bridge

1932.

140 **17** 1s. green . . . . 35·00 2·50

1932. Opening of Sydney Harbour Bridge.

144 **18** 2d. red . . . . 3·00 1·40
142 3d. blue . . . . 5·50 7·50
143 5s. green £400 £190

19 Laughing Kookaburra

20 Melbourne and River Yarra

1932.

146 **19** 6d. brown . . . . 16·00 55

1934. Centenary of Victoria.

147 **20** 2d. red . . . . 2·50 1·75
148 3d. blue . . . . 4·00 5·50
149 1s. black . . . . 45·00 20·00

21 Merino Ram

22 Hermes

1934. Death Centenary of Capt. John Macarthur (founder of Australian sheep-farming).

150 **21** 2d. red . . . . 6·50 1·50
151 3d. blue . . . . 10·00 14·00
152 9d. purple . . . . 27·00 45·00

1934.

153b **22** 1s.6d. purple . . . . . . 2·00 1·40

23 Cenotaph, Whitehall

24 King George V on "Anzac"

1935. 20th. Anniv of Gallipoli Landing.

154 **23** 2d. red . . . . 1·75 30
155 1s. black . . . . 48·00 42·00

1935. Silver Jubilee.

156 **24** 2d. red . . . . 2·00 30
157 3d. blue . . . . 6·00 9·00
158 2s. violet . . . . 30·00 45·00

25 Amphitrite and Telephone Cable

26 Site of Adelaide, 1836; Old Gum Tree, Glenelg; King William Street, Adelaide

1936. Opening of Submarine Telephone Cable to Tasmania.

159 **25** 2d. red . . . . 1·25 50
160 3d. blue . . . . 3·25 2·75

1936. Centenary of South Australia.

161 **26** 2d. red . . . . 2·00 40
162 3d. blue . . . . 6·00 3·50
163 1s. green . . . . 12·00 8·50

27 Wallaroo

28 Queen Elizabeth

29 King George VI

30 King George VI

31 King George VI

33 Merino Ram

38 Queen Elizabeth

40 King George VI and Queen Elizabeth

1937.

228 **27** ½d. orange 20 10
165 **28** 1d. green 80 50
180 – 1d. green . . . . 4·75 60
181 – 1d. purple . . . . 1·50 50
182 **29** 1½d. purple . . . . 4·75 10·00
183 1½d. green . . . . 1·00 1·75
167 **30** 2d. red 80 50
184 – 2d. red . . . . 3·75 20
185 **30** 2d. purple . . . . 50 1·75
186 **31** 3d. blue . . . . 45·00 3·75
187 3d. brown 40 10
188 – 4d. green . . . . 1·00 10

189 33 5d. purple . . . . 50 2·00
190a – 6d. brown . . . . 1·75 10
191 – 9d. brown . . . . 1·00 30
192 – 1s. green . . . . 1·25 10
175 31 1s.4d. mauve . . . . . . 2·00 2·50
176a 38 5s. purple . . . . 3·75 2·50
177 – 10s. purple . . . . 42·00 16·00
178 40 £1 slate . . . . 60·00 35·00

DESIGNS—As Type **28**: 4d. Koala; 6d. Kookaburra; 1s. Lyrebird. As Type **33**: 9d. Platypus. As Type **38**: 10s. King George VI.

Nos. 180 and 184 are as Types **28** and **30** but with completely shaded background.

41 Governor Phillip at Sydney Cove (J. Alcott)　**42** A.I.F. and Nurse

1937. 150th Anniv of New South Wales.
193 41 2d. red . . . . 2·25 30
194 3d. blue . . . . 6·00 2·25
195 9d. purple . . . . 18·00 10·00

1940. Australian Imperial Forces.
196 42 1d. green . . . . 1·75 2·50
197 2d. red . . . . 1·75 1·50
198 3d. blue . . . . 12·00 10·00
199 6d. purple . . . . 23·00 20·00

1941. Surch with figures and bars.
200 30 2½d. on 2d. red 75 70
201 31 3½d. on 3d. blue . . . . 1·00 2·25
202 33 5½d. on 5d. purple . . . . 4·00 5·50

46a Queen Elizabeth

47 King George VI　**48** King George VI

49 King George VI　**50** Emu

1942.
203 46a 1d. purple . . . . 1·25 10
204 1½d. green . . . . 1·50 10
205 47 2d. purple . . . . 1·00 1·75
206 48 2½d. red 40 10
207 49 3½d. blue . . . . 1·00 60
208 50 5½d. grey . . . . 1·00 20

52 Duke and Duchess of Gloucester　**53** Star and Wreath

1945. Royal Visit.
209 52 2½d. red 15 10
210 3½d. blue . . . . 20 1·10
211 5½d. grey . . . . 25 1·10

1946. Victory. Inscr "PEACE 1945".
213 53 2½d. red 15 10
214 – 3½d. blue . . . . 45 1·50
215 – 5½d. green 50 90

DESIGNS—HORIZ: 3½d. Flag and dove. VERT: 5½d. Angel.

56 Sir Thomas Mitchell and Queensland

1946. Centenary of Mitchell's Central Queensland Exploration.
216 56 2½d. red 15 10
217 3½d. blue . . . . 50 1·25
218 1s. green 50 50

57 Lt. John Shortland, R.N.　**58** Steel Foundry

1947. 150th Anniv of City of Newcastle.
219 57 2½d. lake 15 10
220 58 3½d. blue . . . . 50 1·25
221 – 5½d. green 50 65

DESIGNS—As Type **58**: HORIZ: 5½d. Coal carrier cranes.

60 Queen Elizabeth II when Princess

1947. Wedding of Princess Elizabeth.
222a 60 1d. purple 10 10

61 Hereford Bull　**61a** Hermes and Globe

62 Aboriginal Art　**62a** Commonwealth Coat of Arms

1948.
223 61 1s.3d. brown . . . . . 1·75 1·10
223a 61a 1s.6d. brown 70 10
224 62 2s. brown . . . . 1·50 10
224a 62a 5s. red . . . . 3·00 20
224b 10s. purple . . . . . . 15·00 85
224c £1 blue . . . . 32·00 3·75
224d £2 green . . . . 80·00 14·00

63 William J. Farrer　**64** Ferdinand von Mueller

1948. W. J. Farrer (wheat research) Commem.
225 63 2½d. red 30 10

1948. Sir Ferdinand von Mueller (botanist) Commemoration.
226 64 2½d. red 20 10

65 Boy Scout　**66** "Henry Lawson" (Sir Lionel Lindsay)

1948. Pan-Pacific Scout Jamboree, Wonga Park.
227 65 2½d. lake 20 10

For 3½d. value dates "1952–53", see No. 254.

1949. Henry Lawson (poet) Commemoration.
231 66 2½d. purple 30 10

67 Mounted Postman and Convair CV 240 Aircraft　**68** John, Lord Forrest of Bunbury

1949. 75th Anniv of U.P.U.
232 67 3½d. blue 40 60

1949. John, Lord Forrest (explorer and politician) Commemoration.
233 68 2½d. red 30 10

69 Queen Elizabeth　**70** King George VI

81 King George VI　**80** King George VI

71 Aborigine　**82** King George VI

1950.
236 69 1½d. green 40 40
237 2d. green 15 10
234 70 2½d. red 10 10
237c 2½d. brown 15 35
235 3d. red 15 25
237d 3d. green 15 10
247 81 3½d. purple 10 10
248 4½d. red . . . . 15 1·25
249 6½d. brown . . . . 15 1·00
250 6½d. green 10 35
251 80 7½d. blue 15 80
238 71 8½d. brown . . . . 20 1·00
252 82 1s.0½d. blue 60 60
253 71 2s.6d. brown (21 × 25½ mm) . . . . 1·50 70

72 Reproduction of First Stamp of N.S.W.　**73** Reproduction of First Stamp of Victoria

1950. Centenary of Australian States Stamps.
239 72 2½d. purple 25 10
240 73 2½d. purple 25 10

75 Sir Henry Parkes　**77** Federal Parliament House, Canberra

1951. 50th Anniv of Commonwealth. Inscr as in T **75** and **77**.
241 75 3d. lake 60 10
242 – 3d. lake 60 10
243 – 5½d. blue . . . . 30 2·25
244 77 1s.6d. brown 50 50

DESIGNS—As Type **70**: No. 242, Sir Edmund Barton. As Type **77**: No. 243, Opening first Federal Parliament.

78 E. H. Hargraves　**79** C. J. Latrobe

1951. Centenaries. Discovery of Gold in Australia and of Responsible Government in Victoria.
245 78 3d. purple 50 10
246 79 3d. purple 50 10

1952. Pan-Pacific Scout Jamboree, Greystanes. As T **65** but dated "1952–53".
254 65 3½d. lake 20 10

83 Butter　**86** Queen Elizabeth II

1953. Food Production. Inscr "PRODUCE FOOD!".
255 83 3d. green 30 10
256 – 3d. green (Wheat) 30 10
257 – 3d. green (Beef) 30 10
258 83 3½d. red 30 10
259 – 3½d. red (Wheat) 30 10
260 – 3½d. red (Beef) 30 10

1953.
261 86 1d. purple 15 15
261a 2½d. blue 20 15
262 3d. green 20 10
263 3½d. red 20 10
263a 6½d. orange . . . . . . 2·50 50

87 Queen Elizabeth II

1953. Coronation.
264 87 3½d. red 40 10
265 7½d. violet . . . . 75 1·40
266 2s. green . . . . 2·50 1·40

88 Young Farmers and Calf

1953. 25th Anniv of Australian Young Farmers' Clubs.
267 88 3½d. brown and green . . . 10 10

89 Lt.-Gov. D. Collins　**90** Lt.-Gov. W. Paterson

91 Sullivan Cove, Hobart, 1804　**92** Stamp of 1853

1953. 150th Anniv of Settlement in Tasmania.
268 89 3½d. purple 30 10
269 90 3½d. purple 30 10
270 91 2s. green . . . . 1·25 2·75

1953. 1st Centenary of Tasmania Postage Stamps.
271 92 3d. red 10 40

93 Queen Elizabeth II and Duke of Edinburgh

94 Queen Elizabeth II　**95** "Telegraphic Communications"

1954. Royal Visit.
272 93 3½d. red 20 10
273 94 7½d. purple . . . . 30 1·25
274 93 2s. green 60 65

1954. Centenary of Telegraph.
275 95 3½d. brown 10 10

96 Red Cross and Globe　**97** Mute Swan

1954. 40th Anniv of Australian Red Cross Society.
276 96 3½d. blue and red 10 10

1954. Centenary of Western Australian Stamps.
277 97 3½d. black 20 10

98 Locomotives of 1854 and 1954

1954. Centenary of Australian Railways.

278	**98**	3½d. purple	30	10

99 Territory Badge **100** Olympic Games Symbol

1954. Australian Antarctic Research.

279	**99**	3½d. black	15	10

1954. Olympic Games Propaganda.

280	**100**	2s. blue	1·00	1·00
280a		2s. green	1·75	2·25

101 Rotary Symbol, Globe and Flags **103** American Memorial, Canberra

1955. 50th Anniv of Rotary International.

281	**101**	3½d. red	10	10

1955. Australian–American Friendship.

283	**103**	3½d. blue	10	10

101a Queen Elizabeth II **102** Queen Elizabeth II

1955.

282a	**101a**	4d. lake	20	10
282b		7½d. violet	60	1·50
282c		10d. blue	60	1·25
282	**102**	1s.0½d. blue	1·25	1·25
282d		1s.7d. brown	1·25	45

104 Cobb & Co. Coach (from etching by Sir Lionel Lindsay)

1955. Mail-coach Pioneers Commemoration.

284	**104**	3½d. sepia	25	10
285		2s. brown	50	1·40

105 Y.M.C.A. Emblem and Map of the World

1955. World Centenary of Y.M.C.A.

286	**105**	3½d. green and red	10	10

106 Florence Nightingale and Young Nurse **107** Queen Victoria

1955. Nursing Profession Commemoration.

287	**106**	3½d. lilac	10	10

1955. Centenary of South Australian Postage Stamps.

288	**107**	3½d. green	10	10

108 Badges of N.S.W., Victoria and Tasmania

1956. Centenary of Responsible Government in N.S.W., Victoria and Tasmania.

289	**108**	3½d. lake	10	10

109 Arms of Melbourne **110** Olympic Torch and Symbol

111 Collins Street, Melbourne

1956. Olympic Games, Melbourne.

290	**109**	4d. red	25	10
291	**110**	7½d. blue	50	1·40
292	**111**	1s. multicoloured	60	30
293	–	2s. multicoloured	85	1·40

DESIGN—As Type **111**: 2s. Melbourne across River Yarra.

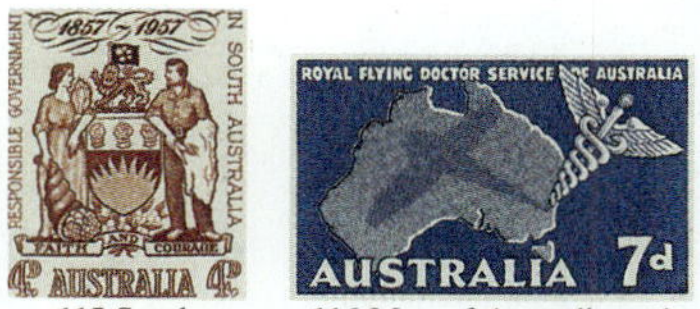

115 South Australia Coat of Arms **116** Map of Australia and Caduceus

1957. Centenary of Responsible Government in South Australia.

296	**115**	4d. brown	10	10

1957. Royal Flying Doctor Service of Australia.

297	**116**	7d. blue	15	10

117 "The Spirit of Christmas" (after Sir Joshua Reynolds)

1957. Christmas.

298	**117**	3½d. red	10	20
299		4d. purple	10	10

118 Lockheed Super Constellation Airliner

1958. Inaug of Australian "Round-the-World" Air Service.

301	**118**	2s. blue	75	1·00

119 Hall of Memory, Sailor and Airman

1958.

302	**119**	5½d. lake	40	30
303	–	5½d. lake	40	30

No. 303 shows a soldier and servicewoman instead of the sailor and airman.

120 Sir Charles Kingsford Smith and the "Southern Cross" **122** The Nativity

121 Silver Mine, Broken Hill

1958. 30th Anniv of 1st Air Crossing of the Tasman Sea.

304	**120**	8d. blue	60	1·00

1958. 75th Anniv of Founding of Broken Hill.

305	**121**	4d. brown	30	10

1958. Christmas Issue.

306	**122**	3½d. red	20	30
307		4d. violet	20	10

124 Queen Elizabeth II **126** Queen Elizabeth II

127 Queen Elizabeth II **128** Queen Elizabeth II **129** Queen Elizabeth II

1959.

308	–	1d. purple	10	10
309	**124**	2d. brown	50	20
311	**126**	3d. turquoise	15	10
312	**127**	3½d. green	15	15
313	**128**	4d. red	1·75	10
314	**129**	5d. blue	1·00	10

No. 308 shows a head and shoulders portrait as in Type **128** and is vert.

131 Numbat **137** Christmas Bells

142 Aboriginal Stockman

1959.

316	**131**	6d. brown	1·50	10
317	–	8d. brown	75	10
318	–	9d. sepia	1·50	55
319	–	11d. blue	1·00	15
320	–	1s. green	1·75	40
321	–	1s.2d. purple	1·00	15
322	**137**	1s.6d. red on yellow	1·50	1·00
323	–	2s. blue	70	10
324	–	2s.3d. green on yellow	1·00	10
324a	–	2s.3d. green	2·50	75
325	–	2s.5d. brown on yellow	3·50	75
326	–	3s. red	1·00	20
327	**142**	5s. brown	11·00	2·25

DESIGNS—As Type **131**: VERT: 8d. Tiger Cat; 9d. Eastern grey kangaroo; 11d. Common rabbit bandicoot; 1s. Platypus. HORIZ: 1s.2d. Thylacine. As Type **137**: 2s. Flannel flower; 2s.3d. Wattle; 2s.5d. Banksia (plant); 3s. Waratah.

143 Postmaster Isaac Nichols boarding the Brig "Experiment"

1959. 150th Anniv of Australian P.O.

331	**143**	4d. slate	15	10

144 Parliament House, Brisbane, and Arms of Queensland **145** "The Approach of the Magi"

1959. Centenary of Queensland Self-Government.

332	**144**	4d. lilac and green	10	10

1959. Christmas.

333	**145**	5d. violet	10	10

146 Girl Guide and Lord Baden-Powell **147** "The Overlanders" (after Sir Daryl Lindsay)

1960. 50th Anniv of Girl Guide Movement.

334	**146**	5d. blue	30	15

1960. Centenary of Northern Territory Exploration.

335	**147**	5d. mauve	40	15

148 "Archer" and Melbourne Cup **149** Queen Victoria

1960. 100th Melbourne Cup Race Commemoration.

336	**148**	5d. sepia	20	10

1960. Centenary of Queensland Stamps.

337	**149**	5d. green	25	10

150 Open Bible and Candle **151** Colombo Plan Bureau Emblem

1960. Christmas Issue.

338	**150**	5d. lake	10	10

1961. Colombo Plan.

339	**151**	1s. brown	10	10

152 Melba (after bust by Sir Bertram Mackennal) **153** Open Prayer Book and Text

1961. Birth Centenary of Dame Nellie Melba (singer).

340	**152**	5d. blue	30	15

1961. Christmas Issue.

341	**153**	5d. brown	10	10

154 J. M. Stuart **155** Flynn's Grave and Nursing Sister

1962. Centenary of Stuart's South to North Crossing of Australia.

342	**154**	5d. red	15	10

1962. 50th Anniv of Australian Inland Mission.

343	**155**	5d. multicoloured	30	15

156 "Woman" **157** "Madonna and Child"

1962. "Associated Country Women of the World" Conference, Melbourne.
344 **156** 5d. green 10 10

1962. Christmas.
345 **157** 5d. violet 15 10

158 Perth and Kangaroo Paw (plant) **160** Queen Elizabeth II

1962. British Empire and Commonwealth Games, Perth. Multicoloured.
346 5d. Type **158** 40 10
347 2s.3d. Arms of Perth and running track . . . . . . 1·50 2·75

1963. Royal Visit.
348 **160** 5d. green 35 10
349 – 2s.3d. lake . . . . 1·50 3·00
DESIGN: 2s.3d. Queen Elizabeth II and Duke of Edinburgh.

162 Arms of Canberra and W. B. Griffin (architect) **163** Centenary Emblem

1963. 50th Anniv of Canberra.
350 **162** 5d. green 15 10

1963. Centenary of Red Cross.
351 **163** 5d. red, grey and blue . . 40 10

164 Blaxland, Lawson and Wentworth on Mount York

1963. 150th Anniv of First Crossing of Blue Mountains.
352 **164** 5d. blue 15 10

165 "Export"

1963. Export Campaign.
353 **165** 5d. red 10 10

1963. As T **160** but smaller $17\frac{1}{2} \times 21\frac{1}{2}$ mm "5D" at top right replacing "ROYAL VISIT 1963" and oak leaves omitted.
354 5d. green 75 10
354c 5d. red 55 10

167 Tasman and "Heemskerk" **173** "Peace on Earth..."

1963. Navigators.
355 **167** 4s. blue . . . . 3·00 55
356 – 5s. brown . . . . 3·25 1·75
357 – 7s.6d. olive . . . . 19·00 16·00
358 – 10s. purple . . . . 25·00 5·00
359 – £1 violet . . . . 32·00 16·00
360 – £2 sepia . . . . 55·00 75·00

DESIGNS—As Type **167**: 7s.6d. Captain Cook; 10s. Flinders and "Investigator". $20\frac{1}{2} \times 5\frac{1}{2}$ mm: 5s. Dampier and "Roebuck"; £1 Bass and "Tom Thumb" (whale boat); £2 Admiral King and "Mermaid" (survey cutter).

1963. Christmas.
361 **173** 5d. blue 10 10

174 "Commonwealth Cable" **176** Black-backed Magpie

1963. Opening of COMPAC (Trans-Pacific Telephone Cable).
362 **174** 2s.3d. multicoloured . . . 1·00 2·75

1964. Birds.
363 – 6d. multicoloured . . . . 1·00 25
364 **176** 9d. black, grey and green 1·00 2·75
365 – 1s.6d. multicoloured . . . 75 1·40
366 – 2s. yellow, black and pink 1·40 50
367 – 2s.5d. multicoloured . . . 1·75 3·50
368 – 2s.6d. multicoloured . . . 2·50 3·75
369 – 3s. multicoloured . . . . 2·50 1·75
BIRDS—HORIZ: 6d. Yellow-tailed thornbill; 2s.6d. Scarlet robin. VERT: 1s.6d. Galah (cockatoo); 2s. Golden whistler (Thickhead); 2s.5d. Blue wren; 3s. Straw-necked ibis.

182 Bleriot XI Aircraft (type flown by M. Guillaux, 1914)

1964. 50th Anniv of 1st Australian Airmail Flight.
370 **182** 5d. green 30 10
371 2s.3d. red . . . . 1·50 2·75

183 Child looking at Nativity Scene **184** "Simpson and his Donkey"

1964. Christmas.
372 **183** 5d. red, blue, buff and black 10 10

1965. 50th Anniv of Gallipoli Landing.
373 **184** 5d. brown 50 10
374 8d. blue . . . . 75 2·50
375 2s.3d. purple . . . . . . 1·50 2·50

185 "T-elecommunications" **186** Sir Winston Churchill

1965. Centenary of I.T.U.
376 **185** 5d. black, brown and blue 40 10

1965. Churchill Commemoration.
377 **186** 5d. multicoloured 15 10

187 General Monash **188** Hargrave and "Multiplane" Seaplane (1902)

1965. Birth Centenary of General Sir John Monash (engineer and soldier).
378 **187** 5d. multicoloured 15 10

1965. 50th Death Anniv of Lawrence Hargrave (aviation pioneer).
379 **188** 5d. multicoloured 15 10

189 I.C.Y. Emblem **190** "Nativity Scene"

1965. International Co-operation Year.
380 **189** 2s.3d. green and blue . . 65 1·50

1965. Christmas.
381 **190** 5d. multicoloured 15 10

191 Queen Elizabeth II **192** Blue-faced Honeyeater

1966. Decimal currency. As earlier issues but with values in cents and dollars as in T **191/2**. Also some new designs.
382 **191** 1c. brown 25 10
383 2c. green 70 10
384 3c. green 70 10
404 3c. black, pink and green 45 1·25
385 4c. red 20 10
405 4c. black, brown and red 35 60
405a 5c. black, brown and blue 40 10
386 – 5c. multicoloured (as 363) 25 10
386c **191** 5c. blue 70 10
387 **192** 6c. multicoloured . . . . 1·25 1·00
387a **191** 6c. orange . . . . 1·00 10
388 – 7c. multicoloured 60 10
388a **191** 7c. purple . . . . 1·50 10
389 – 8c. multicoloured . . . . 60 1·00
390 – 9c. multicoloured 60 20
391 – 10c. multicoloured . . . 60 10
392 – 13c. multicoloured . . . 1·50 25
393 – 15c. multicoloured (as 365) . . . . 1·25 1·50
394 – 20c. yellow, black and pink (as 366) . . . . 2·00 15
395 – 24c. multicoloured . . . 65 1·25
396 – 25c. multicoloured (as 368) . . . . 2·00 30
397 – 30c. multicoloured (as 369) . . . . 4·50 1·25
398 **167** 40c. blue . . . . 3·00 10
399 – 50c. brown (as 356) . . 3·00 10
400 – 75c. olive (as 357) . . 1·00 1·00
401 – $1 purple (as 358) . . . 1·50 20
402 – $2 violet (as 359) . . . 6·00 1·00
403 – $4 brown (as 360) . . . 5·50 6·50
DESIGNS—VERT: 7c. White-tailed Dascyllus ("Humbug fish"); 8c. Copper-banded butterflyfish ("Coral fish"); 9c. Hermit crab; 10c. Orange clownfish ("Anemone fish"); 13c. Red-necked avocet. HORIZ: 24c. Azure kingfisher.

200 "Saving Life"

1966. 75th Anniv of Royal Life Saving Society.
406 **200** 4c. black, lt bl & bl . . . 15 10

201 "Adoration of the Shepherds" **202** "Eendracht"

1966. Christmas.
407 **201** 4c. black and olive . . . 10 10

1966. 350th Anniv of Dirk Hartog's Landing in Australia.
408 **202** 4c. multicoloured 10 10

203 Open Bible **204** Ancient Keys and Modern Lock

1967. 150th Anniv of British and Foreign Bible Society in Australia.
409 **203** 4c. multicoloured 10 10

1967. 150th Anniv of Australian Banking.
410 **204** 4c. black, blue and green 10 10

205 Lions Badge and 50 Stars **206** Y.W.C.A. Emblem

1967. 50th Anniv of Lions International.
411 **205** 4c. black, gold and blue 10 10

1967. World Y.W.C.A. Council Meeting, Monash University, Melbourne.
412 **206** 4c. multicoloured 10 10

207 Anatomical Figures

1967. 5th World Gynaecology and Obstetrics Congress, Sydney.
413 **207** 4c. black, blue and violet 10 10

1967. No. 385 surch.
414 **191** 5c. on 4c. red 35 10

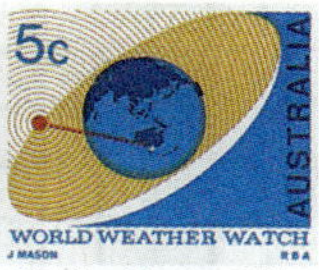

209 Christmas Bells and Gothic Arches **211** Satellite in Orbit

1967. Christmas. Multicoloured.
415 5c. Type **209** 20 10
416 25c. Religious symbols (vert) 1·00 1·90

1968. World Weather Watch. Multicoloured.
417 5c. Type **211** 30 10
418 20c. World weather map . . 1·10 2·75

213 Radar Antenna **214** Kangaroo Paw (Western Australia)

1968. World Telecommunications via Intelsat II.
419 **213** 25c. blue, black and green 1·25 2·50

1968. State Floral Emblems. Multicoloured.
420 6c. Type **214** . . . . 45 1·25
421 13c. Pink Heath (Victoria) . . 50 70
422 15c. Tasmanian Blue Gum (Tasmania) 70 40
423 20c. Sturt's Desert Pea (South Australia) . . . . . . 1·50 75
424 25c. Cooktown Orchid (Queensland) . . . . . . 1·10 75
425 30c. Waratah (New South Wales) 50 10

220 Soil Sample Analysis

1968. International Soil Science Congress and World Medical Association Assembly. Mult.
426 5c. Type **220** 10 10
427 5c. Rubber-gloved hands, syringe and head of Hippocrates 10 10

222 Athlete carrying Torch and Sunstone Symbol

224 Houses and Dollar Signs

1968. Olympic Games, Mexico City. Mult.
428 5c. Type **222** 30 10
429 25c. Sunstone symbol and Mexican flag . . . . . . 40 1·50

1968. Building and Savings Societies Congress.
430 **224** 5c. multicoloured 10 40

225 Church Window and View of Bethlehem

226 Edgeworth David (geologist)

1968. Christmas.
431 **225** 5c. multicoloured 10 10

1968. Famous Australians (1st series).
432 **226** 5c. green on myrtle . . . 25 20
433 – 5c. black on blue 25 20
434 – 5c. brown on buff 25 20
435 – 5c. violet on lilac 25 20
DESIGNS: No. 433, A. B. Paterson (poet); No. 434, Albert Namatjira (artist); No. 435, Caroline Chrisholm (social worker).

Nos. 432/5 were only issued in booklets and exist with one or two sides imperf.

See also Nos. 446/9, 479/82, 505/8, 537/40, 590/5, 602/7 and 637/40.

230 Macquarie Lighthouse

231 Pioneers and Modern Building, Darwin

1968. 150th Anniv of Macquarie Lighthouse.
436 **230** 5c. black and yellow . . . 30 70

1969. Centenary of Northern Territory Settlement.
437 **231** 5c. brown, olive and ochre 10 10

232 Melbourne Harbour

1969. 6th Biennial Conference of International Association of Ports and Harbours, Melbourne.
438 **232** 5c. multicoloured 20 10

233 Concentric Circles (symbolizing Management, Labour and Government)

1969. 50th Anniv of I.L.O.
439 **233** 5c. multicoloured 15 10

234 Sugar Cane

238 "The Nativity" (stained glass window)

1969. Primary Industries. Multicoloured.
440 7c. Type **234** . . . . 50 1·50
441 15c. Timber . . . . 75 2·50
442 20c. Wheat 30 60
443 25c. Wool . . . . 50 1·50

1969. Christmas. Multicoloured.
444 5c. Type **238** 20 10
445 25c. "Tree of Life", Christ in crib and Christmas Star (abstract) . . . . 1·00 2·00

240 Edmund Barton

244 Capt. Ross Smith's Vickers Vimy, 1919

1969. Famous Australians (2nd series). Prime Ministers.
446 **240** 5c. black on green 40 20
447 – 5c. black on green 40 20
448 – 5c. black on green 40 20
449 – 5c. black on green 40 20
DESIGNS: No. 447, Alfred Deakin; 448, J. C. Watson; 449, G. H. Reid.

Nos. 446/9 were only issued in booklets and only exist with one or two adjacent sides imperf.

1969. 50th Anniv of 1st England–Australia Flight.
450 **244** 5c. multicoloured 15 10
451 – 5c. red, black and green . . 15 10
452 – 5c. multicoloured 15 10
DESIGNS: No. 451, Lt. H. Fysh and Lt. P. McGinness on 1919 survey with Ford Model T runabout; 452, Capt. Wrigley and Sgt. Murphy in Royal Aircraft Factory B.E.2E taking off to meet the Smiths.

247 Symbolic Track and Diesel Locomotive

1970. Sydney–Perth Standard Gauge Railway Link.
453 **247** 5c. multicoloured 15 10

248 Australian Pavilion, Osaka

1970. World Fair, Osaka.
454 **248** 5c. multicoloured 15 10
455 – 20c. red and black 35 65
DESIGN: 20c., "Southern Cross" and "from the Country of the south with warm feelings" (message).

251 Australian Flag

1970. Royal Visit.
456 – 5c. black and ochre . . . 35 15
457 **251** 30c. multicoloured . . . . 1·10 2·50
DESIGN: 5c. Queen Elizabeth II and Duke of Edinburgh.

252 Lucerne Plant, Bull and Sun

1970. 11th International Grasslands Congress, Queensland.
458 **252** 5c. multicoloured 10 80

253 Captain Cook and H.M.S. "Endeavour"

259 Sturt's Desert Rose

1970. Bicentenary of Captain Cook's Discovery of Australia's East Coast. Multicoloured.
459 5c. Type **253** 35 10
460 5c. Sextant and H.M.S. "Endeavour" 35 10
461 5c. Landing at Botany Bay 35 10
462 5c. Charting and exploring 35 10
463 5c. Claiming possession . . 35 10
464 30c. Captain Cook, H.M.S. "Endeavour", sextant, aborigines and kangaroo (63 × 30 mm) . . . . . . 1·25 2·50
MS465 157 × 129 mm. Nos. 459/64. Imperf . . . . 7·50 9·00

Nos. 459/63 were issued together, se-tenant, forming a composite design.

1970. Coil Stamps. Multicoloured.
465a 2c. Type **259** 40 20
466 4c. Type **259** . . . . 85 1·75
467 5c. Golden wattle 20 10
468 6c. Type **259** . . . . 1·25 1·00
468b 7c. Sturt's desert pea . . . 40 70
468d 10c. As 7c. . . . . 60 1·25

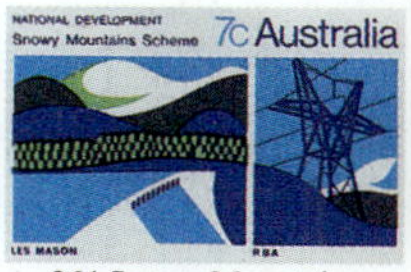

264 Snowy Mountains Scheme

265 Rising Flames

1970. National Development (1st series). Mult.
469 7c. Type **264** 20 80
470 8c. Ord River scheme 10 15
471 9c. Bauxite to aluminium . . 15 15
472 10c. Oil and natural gas . . . 30 10
See also Nos. 541/4.

1970. 16th Commonwealth Parliamentary Association Conference, Canberra.
473 **265** 6c. multicoloured 10 10

266 Milk Analysis and Dairy Herd

267 "The Nativity"

1970. 18th International Dairy Congress, Sydney.
474 **266** 6c. multicoloured 10 10

1970. Christmas.
475 **267** 6c. multicoloured 10 10

268 U.N. "Plant" and Dove of Peace

269 Boeing 707 and Avro 504

1970. 25th Anniv of United Nations.
476 **268** 6c. multicoloured 15 10

1970. 50th Anniv of QANTAS Airline.
477 **269** 6c. multicoloured 30 10
478 – 30c. multicoloured . . . . 70 1·50
DESIGN: 30c. Avro 504 and Boeing 707.

1970. Famous Australians (3rd series). As T **226**.
479 6c. blue 50 20
480 6c. black on brown 50 20
481 6c. purple on pink 50 20
482 6c. red on pink 50 20
DESIGNS: No. 479, The Duigan brothers (pioneer aviators); 480, Lachlan Macquarie (Governor of New South Wales); 481, Adam Lindsay Gordon (poet); 482, E. J. Eyre (explorer).

271 "Theatre"

1971. "Australia–Asia". 28th International Congress of Orientalists, Canberra. Multicoloured.
483 7c. Type **271** 45 60
484 15c. "Music" . . . . 70 1·00
485 20c. "Sea Craft" 65 90

272 The Southern Cross

273 Market "Graph"

1971. Centenary of Australian Natives' Association.
486 **272** 6c. black, red and blue . . 10 10

1971. Centenary of Sydney Stock Exchange.
487 **273** 6c. multicoloured 10 10

274 Rotary Emblem

275 Dassault Mirage Jets and De Havilland D.H.9A Biplane

1971. 50th Anniv of Rotary International in Australia.
488 **274** 6c. multicoloured 15 10

1971. 50th Anniv of R.A.A.F.
489 **275** 6c. multicoloured 60 10

276 Draught-horse, Cat and Dog

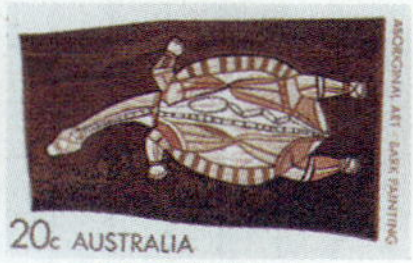

277 Bark Painting

1971. Animals. Multicoloured.
490 6c. Type **276** 20 10
491 12c. Vet and lamb ("Animal Science") 45 20
492 18c. Red Kangaroo ("Fauna Conservation") . . . . . 1·00 35
493 24c. Guide-dog ("Animals Aid to Man") . . . . . . 80 1·50

The 6c. commemorates the Centenary of the Australian R.S.P.C.A.

1971. Aboriginal Art. Multicoloured.
494 20c. Type **277** 20 20
495 25c. Body decoration 20 55
496 30c. Cave painting (vert) . . 40 20
497 35c. Grave posts (vert) . . . 30 15

278 The Three Kings and the Star

280 Cameo Brooch

1971. Christmas. Colours of star and colour of "AUSTRALIA" given.
498 **278** 7c. blue, mauve and brown 50 15
499 7c. mauve, brown and white 50 15
500 7c. mauve, white and black . . . . 2·75 80
501 7c. black, green and black 50 15
502 7c. lilac, green and mauve 50 15

503	7c. black, brown and white	50	15
504	7c. blue, mauve and green	14·00	2·25

1972. Famous Australians. (4th series). As T **240**. Prime Ministers.

505	7c. blue	30	20
506	7c. blue	30	20
507	7c. red	30	20
508	7c. red	30	20

DESIGNS: No. 505, Andrew Fisher; 506, W. M. Hughes; 507, Joseph Cook; 508, S. M. Bruce.

1972. 50th Anniv of Country Women's Association.

509	**280**	7c. multicoloured	20	10

281 Fruit **282** Worker in Wheelchair

1972. Primary Industries. Multicoloured.

510	20c. Type **281**	1·00	2·50
511	25c. Rice	1·00	4·00
512	30c. Fish	1·00	1·00
513	35c. Beef	2·25	75

1972. Rehabilitation of the Disabled.

514	**282**	12c. brown and green	10	10
515	–	18c. green and orange	85	35
516	–	24c. blue and brown	15	10

DESIGNS—HORIZ: 18c. Patient and teacher. VERT: 24c. Boy playing with ball.

283 Telegraph Line **284** Athletics

1972. Centenary of Overland Telegraph Line.

517	**283**	7c. multicoloured	15	15

1972. Olympic Games, Munich. Multicoloured.

518	7c. Type **284**	20	25
519	7c. Rowing	20	25
520	7c. Swimming	20	25
521	35c. Equestrian	1·25	3·50

285 Numerals and Computer Circuit

1972. 10th Int Congress of Accountants, Sydney.

522	**285**	7c. multicoloured	15	15

286 Australian-built Harvester

1972. Pioneer Life. Multicoloured.

523	5c. Pioneer family (vert)	10	10
524	10c. Water-pump (vert)	20	10
525	15c. Type **286**	15	10
526	40c. House	15	30
527	50c. Stage-coach	35	20
528	60c. Morse key (vert)	30	80
529	80c. "Gem" (paddle-steamer)	30	80

287 Jesus with Children **288** "Length"

1972. Christmas. Multicoloured.

530	7c. Type **287**	30	10
531	35c. Dove and spectrum motif (vert)	2·75	5·00

1973. Metric Conversion. Multicoloured.

532	7c. Type **288**	40	60
533	7c. "Volume"	40	60
534	7c. "Mass"	40	60
535	7c. "Temperature" (horiz)	40	60

289 Caduceus and Laurel Wreath **291** Shipping

1973. 25th Anniv of World Health Organization.

536	**289**	7c. multicoloured	30	15

1973. Famous Australians (5th series). As T **226**.

537	7c. brown and black	35	45
538	7c. lilac and black	35	45
539	7c. brown and black	35	45
540	7c. lilac and black	35	45

PORTRAITS: No. 537, William Wentworth (statesman and explorer); 538, Isaac Isaacs (1st Australian-born Governor-General); 539, Mary Gilmore (writer); 540, Marcus Clarke (author).

1973. National Development (2nd series). Mult.

541	20c. Type **291**	1·50	2·75
542	25c. Iron ore and steel	1·50	2·75
543	30c. Beef roads	1·50	2·75
544	35c. Mapping	2·25	2·75

292 Banded Coral Shrimp **293** Children at Play

1973. Marine Life and Gemstones. Multicoloured.

545	1c. Type **292**	10	10
546	2c. Fiddler crab	10	10
547	3c. Coral crab	10	10
548	4c. Mauve stinger	15	55
549	6c. Chrysoprase (vert)	15	50
550	7c. Agate (vert)	20	10
551	8c. Opal (vert)	20	10
552	9c. Rhodonite (vert)	50	15
552a	10c. Star sapphire (vert)	75	10

1973. 50th Anniv of Legacy (welfare organization).

553	**293**	7c. brown, red and green	30	10

294 John baptizing Jesus **295** Sydney Opera House

1973. Christmas. Multicoloured.

554	7c. Type **294**	35	10
555	30c. The Good Shepherd	1·75	2·25

1973. Architecture.

556	**295**	7c. blue and pale blue	30	15
557	–	10c. ochre and brown	60	70
558	–	40c. grey, brown and black	1·00	2·50
559	–	50c. multicoloured	1·25	2·75

DESIGNS—HORIZ: 10c. Buchanan's Hotel, Townsville; 40c. Como House, Melbourne. VERT: 50c. St. James's Church, Sydney.

296 Wireless Receiver and Speaker **297** Common Wombat

1973. 50th Anniv of Regular Radio Broadcasting.

560	**296**	7c. blue, red and black	15	10

1974. Animals. Multicoloured.

561	20c. Type **297**	25	10
562	25c. Short-nosed echidna (inscr "Spiny Anteater")	60	60
563	30c. Brush-tailed possum	60	15
564	75c. Pygmy (inscr "Feather-tailed") glider	80	1·00

298 "Sergeant of Light Horse" (G. Lambert) **299** Supreme Court Judge

1974. Australian Paintings. Multicoloured.

565	$1 Type **298**	1·00	10
566	$2 "Red Gums of the Far North" (H. Heysen) (horiz)	1·25	25
566a	$4 "Shearing the Rams" (Tom Roberts) (horiz)	2·00	2·25
567	$5 "McMahon's Point" (Sir Arthur Streeton)	5·00	2·25
567a	$10 "Coming South" (Tom Roberts)	5·50	3·50

1974. 150th Anniv of Australia's Third Charter of Justice.

568	**299**	7c. multicoloured	20	10

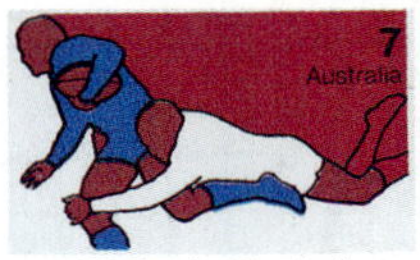

300 Rugby Football

1974. Non-Olympic Sports. Multicoloured.

569	7c. Type **300**	40	50
570	7c. Bowls	40	50
571	7c. Australian football (vert)	40	50
572	7c. Cricket (vert)	40	50
573	7c. Golf (vert)	40	50
574	7c. Surfing (vert)	40	50
575	7c. Tennis (vert)	40	50

301 "Transport of Mails" **302** Letter "A" and W. C. Wentworth (co-founder)

1974. Centenary of U.P.U. Multicoloured.

576	7c. Type **301**	40	20
577	30c. Three-part version of T **301** (vert)	85	1·90

1974. 150th Anniv of First Independent Newspaper, "The Australian".

578	**302**	7c. black and brown	50	40

1974. No. 551 surch.

579	9c. on 8c. multicoloured	15	15

304 "The Adoration of the Magi" **305** "Pre-school Education"

1974. Christmas. Woodcuts by Durer.

580	**304**	10c. black on cream	25	10
581	–	35c. black on cream	80	1·00

DESIGN: 35c. "The Flight into Egypt".

1974. Education in Australia. Multicoloured.

582	5c. Type **305**	25	40
583	11c. "Correspondence Schools"	25	60
584	15c. "Science Education"	40	40
585	60c. "Advanced Education" (vert)	50	2·00

306 "Road Safety" **307** Australian Women's Year Emblem

1975. Environment Dangers. Multicoloured.

586	10c. Type **306**	50	50
587	10c. "Pollution" (horiz)	50	50
588	10c. "Bush Fires" (horiz)	50	50

1975. International Women's Year.

589	**307**	10c. blue, green and violet	20	15

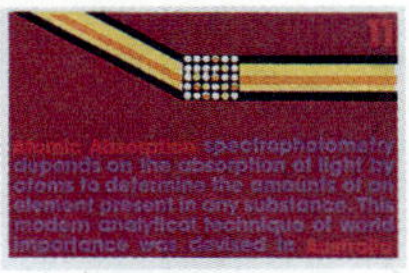

308 J. H. Scullin **309** Atomic Absorption Spectrophotometry

1975. Famous Australians (6th series). Prime Ministers. Multicoloured.

590	10c. Type **308**	25	35
591	10c. J. A. Lyons	25	35
592	10c. Earle Page	25	35
593	10c. Arthur Fadden	25	35
594	10c. John Curtin	25	35
595	10c. J. B. Chifley	25	35

1975. Scientific Development. Multicoloured.

596	11c. Type **309**	70	75
597	24c. Radio astronomy	1·25	2·00
598	33c. Immunology	1·25	2·00
599	48c. Oceanography	1·50	2·75

310 Logo of Australian Postal Commission

1975. Inauguration of Australian Postal and Telecommunications Commissions.

600	**310**	10c. black, red and grey	25	10
601	–	10c. black, orange and grey	25	10

DESIGN: No. 601, Logo of Australian Telecommunications Commission.

311 Edith Cowan **312** "Helichrysum thomsonii"

1975. Famous Australians (7th series). Australian Women. Multicoloured.

602	10c. Type **311**	40	55
603	10c. Louisa Lawson	40	55
604	10c. "Henry Richardson" (pen name of Ethel Richardson)	40	55
605	10c. Catherine Spence	40	55
606a	10c. Constance Stone	40	55
607	10c. Truganini	40	55

1975. Wild Flowers. Multicoloured.

608	18c. Type **312**	25	10
609	45c. "Callistemon teretifolius" (horiz)	50	10

313 "Tambaran" House and Sydney Opera House **314** Epiphany Scene

1975. Independence of Papua New Guinea. Mult.
610 18c. Type **313** 20 10
611 25c. "Freedom" (bird in flight) (horiz) . . . . . . 50 1·50

1975. Christmas.
612 **314** 15c. multicoloured 35 10
613 – 45c. violet, blue and silver 90 2·75
DESIGN—HORIZ: 45c. "Shining Star".

315 Australian Coat of Arms

1976. 75th Anniv of Nationhood.
614 **315** 18c. multicoloured 40 20

316 Telephone-user, c. 1878

1976. Centenary of Telephone.
615 **316** 18c. multicoloured 20 15

317 John Oxley

1976. 19th Century Explorers. Multicoloured.
616 18c. Type **317** 35 50
617 18c. Hume and Hovell . . . 35 50
618 18c. John Forrest 35 50
619 18c. Ernest Giles 35 50
620 18c. William Gosse 35 50
621 18c. Peter Warburton 35 50

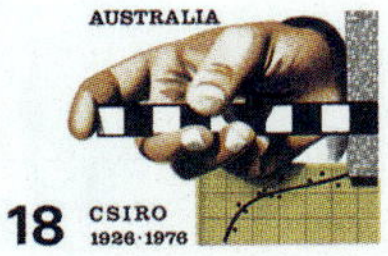

318 Measuring Stick, Graph and Computer Tape

1976. 50th Anniv of Commonwealth Scientific and Industrial Research Organization.
622 **318** 18c. multicoloured 20 15

319 Football

1976. Olympic Games, Montreal. Multicoloured.
623 18c. Type **319** 20 20
624 18c. Gymnastics (vert) . . . 20 20
625 25c. Diving (vert) 35 80
626 40c. Cycling . . . . 90 1·25

320 Richmond Bridge, Tasmania

321 Blamire Young (designer of first Australian stamp)

1976. Australian Scenes. Multicoloured.
627 5c. Type **320** 20 10
628 25c. Broken Bay, N.S.W . . 65 10
629 35c. Wittenoom Gorge, W.A 45 20
630 50c. Mt. Buffalo, Victoria (vert) 90 20
631 70c. Barrier Reef . . . . . 1·25 1·25
632 85c. Ayers Rock, N.T . . . 1·50 2·25

1976. National Stamp Week.
633 **321** 18c. multicoloured 15 15
MS634 101 × 112 mm. Nos. 633 × 4 75 2·00

322 "Virgin and Child" (detail, Simone Contarini)

1976. Christmas.
635 **322** 15c. mauve and blue . . . 20 10
636 – 45c. multicoloured 50 90
DESIGN: 45c. Toy koala bear and decorations.

323 John Gould

1976. Famous Australians. (8th series). Scientists. Multicoloured.
637 18c. Type **323** 35 50
638 18c. Thomas Laby 35 50
639 18c. Sir Baldwin Spencer . . 35 50
640 18c. Griffith Taylor 35 50

324 "Music"

325 Queen Elizabeth II

1977. Performing Arts. Multicoloured.
641 20c. Type **324** 15 25
642 30c. Drama 20 35
643 40c. Dance 25 40
644 60c. Opera . . . . 1·50 1·75

1977. Silver Jubilee. Multicoloured.
645 18c. Type **325** 30 10
646 45c. The Queen and Duke of Edinburgh 70 90

326 Fielder and Wicket Keeper

327 Parliament House

1977. Centenary of Australia–England Test Cricket.
647 18c. Type **326** 50 65
648 18c. Umpire and batsman . . 50 65
649 18c. Fielders 50 65
650 18c. Batsman and umpire . . 50 65
651 18c. Bowler and fielder . . . 50 65
652 45c. Batsman facing bowler 65 1·25

1977. 50th Anniv of Opening of Parliament House, Canberra.
653 **327** 18c. multicoloured 15 10

328 Trade Union Workers

329 Surfing Santa

1977. 50th Anniv of Australian Council of Trade Unions.
654 **328** 18c. multicoloured 15 10

1977. Christmas. Multicoloured.
655 15c. Type **329** 25 10
656 45c. Madonna and Child . . 75 1·25

330 National Flag

1978. Australia Day.
657 **330** 18c. multicoloured 20 15

331 Harry Hawker and Sopwith Atlantic

1978. Early Australian Aviators. Multicoloured.
658 18c. Type **331** 30 50
659 18c. Bert Hinkler and Avro Type 581 Avian 30 50
660 18c. Sir Charles Kingsford Smith and "Southern Cross" 30 50
661 18c. Charles Ulm and "Southern Cross" 30 50
MS662 100 × 112 mm. Nos. 658/61 × 2. Imperf . . . . 75 1·75

332 Piper PA-31 Navajo landing at Station Airstrip

1978. 50th Anniv of Royal Flying Doctor Service.
663 **332** 18c. multicoloured 20 15

333 Illawarra Flame Tree

334 Sturt's Desert Rose and Map

1978. Trees. Multicoloured.
664 18c. Type **333** 20 15
665 25c. Ghost gum . . . . . . 35 1·40
666 40c. Grass tree . . . . 45 2·00
667 45c. Cootamundra wattle . . 45 70

1978. Establishment of State Government for the Northern Territory.
668 **334** 18c. multicoloured 20 15

335 Hooded Plover

336 1928 3d. National Stamp Exhibition Commemorative

1978. Birds (1st series). Multicoloured.
669 1c. Spotted-sided ("Zebra") finch 10 20
670 2c. Crimson finch 10 20
671 5c. Type **335** 50 10
672 15c. Forest kingfisher (vert) 20 20
673 20c. Australian dabchick ("Little Grebe") 70 10
674 20c. Yellow robin ("Eastern Yellow Robin") 75 10
675 22c. White-tailed kingfisher (22 × 29 mm) 30 10
676 25c. Masked ("Spur-wing") plover . . . . 1·00 1·25
677 30c. Pied oystercatcher . . . 1·00 25
678 40c. Variegated ("Lovely") wren (vert) 30 45
679 50c. Flame robin (vert) . . . 1·00 70
680 55c. Comb-crested jacana ("Lotus-Bird") . . . . . . 1·40 60
See also Nos. 734/40.

1978. 50th Anniv of National Stamp Week, and National Stamp Exhibition.
694 **336** 20c. multicoloured 15 15
MS695 78 × 113 mm. No. 694 × 4 75 1·75

337 "The Madonna and the Child" (after van Eyck)

338 "Tulloch"

1978. Christmas. Multicoloured.
696 15c. Type **337** 30 10
697 25c. "The Virgin and Child" (Marmion) 45 55
698 55c. "The Holy Family" (del Vaga) 70 90

1978. Horse-racing. Multicoloured.
699 20c. Type **338** 30 10
700 35c. "Bernborough" (vert) . . 45 85
701 50c. "Phar Lap" (vert) . . . 60 1·25
702 55c. "Peter Pan" . . . . . . 60 1·10

339 Raising the Flag, Sydney Cove, 26 January 1788

340 "Canberra" (paddle-steamer)

1979. Australia Day.
703 **339** 20c. multicoloured 15 15

1979. Ferries and Murray River Steamers. Mult.
704 20c. Type **340** 25 10
705 35c. "Lady Denman" . . . . 45 1·00
706 50c. "Murray River Queen" (paddle-steamer) . . . . . 65 1·40
707 55c. "Curl Curl" (hydrofoil) 70 1·25

341 Port Campbell, Victoria

1979. National Parks. Multicoloured.
708 20c. Type **341** 40 40
709 20c. Uluru, Northern Territory 40 40
710 20c. Royal, New South Wales 40 40
711 20c. Flinders Ranges, South Australia 40 40
712 20c. Nambung, Western Australia 40 40
713 20c. Girraween, Queensland (vert) 40 40
714 20c. Mount Field, Tasmania (vert) 40 40

342 "Double Fairlie" Type Locomotive, Western Australia

1979. Steam Railways. Multicoloured.
715 20c. Type **342** 30 10
716 35c. Locomotive, Puffing Billy Line, Victoria 60 70
717 50c. Locomotive, Pichi Richi Line, South Australia . . . 70 1·50
718 55c. Locomotive, Zig Zag Railway, New South Wales 80 1·40

343 Symbolic Swan

1979. 150th Anniv of Western Australia.
719 **343** 20c. multicoloured 15 15

344 Children playing on Slide

345 Letters and Parcels

1979. International Year of the Child.
720 **344** 20c. multicoloured 15 10

1979. Christmas. Multicoloured.
721 15c. "Christ's Nativity" (Eastern European icon) 15 10
722 25c. Type **345** 15 65
723 55c. "Madonna and Child" (Buglioni) 25 80

346 Fly-fishing

347 Matthew Flinders

1979. Fishing.
724 **346** 20c. multicoloured 15 10
725 – 35c. blue and violet . . . 25 70
726 – 50c. multicoloured 35 90
727 – 55c. multicoloured 35 85
DESIGNS: 35c. Spinning; 50c. Deep sea game-fishing; 55c. Surf-fishing.

1980. Australia Day.
728 **347** 20c. multicoloured 20 10

348 Dingo

1980. Dogs. Multicoloured.
729 20c. Type **348** 35 10
730 25c. Border collie 35 50
731 35c. Australian terrier 40 70
732 50c. Australian cattle dog . . 70 1·75
733 55c. Australian kelpie . . . . 70 1·40

1980. Birds (2nd series). As T **335**. Multicoloured.
734 10c. Golden-shouldered parrot (vert) 50 10
734b 18c. Spotted catbird (vert) 50 1·50
735 28c. Australian bee eater ("Rainbow Bird") (vert) 50 20
736 35c. Regent bower bird (vert) 50 10
737 45c. Masked wood swallow 50 10
738 60c. Australian king parrot ("King Parrot") (vert) . . 50 15
739 80c. Rainbow pitta . . . . 1·00 75
740 $1 Black-backed magpie ("Western Magpie") (vert) 1·00 10

349 Queen Elizabeth II

350 "Once a jolly Swagman camp'd by a Billabong"

1980. Birthday of Queen Elizabeth II.
741 **349** 22c. multicoloured 30 20

1980. Folklore. "Waltzing Matilda". Multicoloured.
742 22c. Type **350** 30 20
743 22c. "And he sang as he shoved that jumbuck in his tuckerbag" 30 20
744 22c. "Up rode the squatter mounted on his thoroughbred" 30 20
745 22c. "Down came the troopers one, two, three" 30 20
746 22c. "And his ghost may be heard as you pass by that billabong" 30 20

351 High Court Building, Canberra

352 Salvation Army

1980. Opening of High Court Building.
747 **351** 22c. multicoloured 20 20

1980. Community Welfare. Multicoloured.
748 22c. Type **352** 30 30
749 22c. St. Vincent de Paul Society (vert) 30 30
750 22c. Meals on Wheels (vert) 30 30
751 22c. "Life. Be in it" 30 30

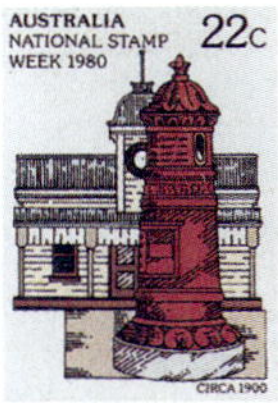

353 Postbox, c. 1900

354 "Holy Family" (painting, Prospero Fontana)

1980. National Stamp Week. Multicoloured.
752 22c. Type **353** 30 20
753 22c. Postman, facing left . . 30 20
754 22c. Ford Model T mail van 30 20
755 22c. Postman, facing right . . 30 20
756 22c. Postman and postbox . . 30 20
MS757 95 × 100 mm. Nos. 752, 754 and 756 . . . . 1·10 1·60

1980. Christmas. Multicoloured.
758 15c. "The Virgin Enthroned" (Justin O'Brien) (detail) . . 15 10
759 28c. Type **354** 25 40
760 60c. "Madonna and Child" (sculpture by School of M. Zuern) . . . . 50 1·10

355 Commonwealth Aircraft Factory Wackett, 1941

1980. Australian Aircraft. Multicoloured.
761 22c. Type **355** 30 10
762 40c. Commonwealth Aircraft Factory Winjeel, 1955 . . 50 75
763 45c. Commonwealth Aircraft Factory Boomerang, 1944 50 85
764 60c. Government Aircraft Factory Nomad, 1975 . . 65 1·40

356 Flag in shape of Australia

1981. Australia Day.
765 **356** 22c. multicoloured 20 20

357 Caricature of Darby Munro (jockey)

358 1931 Kingsford Smith's Flights 6d. Commemorative

1981. Sporting Personalities. Caricatures. Mult.
766 22c. Type **357** 20 10
767 35c. Victor Trumper (cricket) 40 60
768 55c. Sir Norman Brookes (tennis) . . . . 40 1·00
769 60c. Walter Lindrum (billiards) . . . . 40 1·25

1981. 50th Anniversary of Official Australia–U.K. Airmail Service.
770 **358** 22c. lilac, red and blue . . 15 10
771 – 60c. lilac, red and blue . . 40 90
DESIGN—HORIZ: 60c. As T **358**, but format changed.

359 Apex Emblem and Map of Australia

1981. 50th Anniv of Apex (young men's service club).
772 **359** 22c. multicoloured 20 20

360 Queen's Personal Standard for Australia

361 "Licence Inspected"

1981. Birthday of Queen Elizabeth II.
773 **360** 22c. multicoloured 20 20

1981. Gold Rush Era. Sketches by S. T. Gill. Mult.
774 22c. Type **361** 20 25
775 22c. "Puddling" 20 25
776 22c. "Quality of washing stuff" 20 25
777 22c. "On route to deposit gold" 20 25

362 "On the Wallaby Track" (Fred McCubbin)

1981. Paintings. Multicoloured.
778 $2 Type **362** . . . . 1·00 30
779 $5 "A Holiday at Mentone, 1888" (Charles Conder) . . 4·00 1·25

363 Thylacine

363a Blue Mountain Tree Frog

363b "Papilio ulysses" (butterfly)

1981. Wildlife. Multicoloured.
781 1c. Lace monitor 10 20
782 3c. Corroboree frog 10 10
783 4c. Regent skipper (butterfly) (vert) 55 80
784 5c. Queensland hairy-nosed wombat (vert) 10 10
785 10c. Cairns birdwing (butterfly) (vert) 60 10
786 15c. Eastern snake-necked tortoise . . . . 1·00 75
787 20c. MacLeay's swallowtail (butterfly) (vert) 80 35
788 24c. Type **363** 45 10
789 25c. Common rabbit-bandicoot (inscr "Greater Bilby") (vert) 40 80
790a 27c. Type **363a** . . . . . . 1·00 30
791 27c. Type **363b** . . . . . . 1·00 30
792 30c. Bridle nail-tailed wallaby (vert) 90 20
792a 30c. Chlorinda hairstreak (butterfly) (vert) . . . . . 1·00 20
793 35c. Blue tiger (butterfly) (vert) . . . . 1·00 30
794 40c. Smooth knob-tailed gecko 45 30
795 45c. Big greasy (butterfly) (vert) . . . . 1·00 30
796 50c. Leadbeater's possum 50 10
797 55c. Stick-nest rat (vert) . . 50 30
798 60c. Wood white (butterfly) (vert) . . . . 1·10 30
799 65c. Yellow-faced whip snake . . . . 1·75 1·50
800 70c. Crucifix toad . . . . . 65 1·75
801 75c. Eastern water dragon 1·25 90
802 80c. Amaryllis azure (butterfly) (vert) . . . . . 1·40 2·00
803 85c. Centralian blue-tongued lizard . . . . 1·10 1·25
804 90c. Freshwater crocodile 1·60 1·25
805 95c. Thorny devil . . . . . 1·60 2·00
806 $1 Sword-grass brown (butterfly) (vert) . . . . . 1·40 30

364 Prince Charles and Lady Diana Spencer

365 "Cortinarius cinnabarinus"

1981. Royal Wedding.
821 **364** 24c. multicoloured 20 10
822 60c. multicoloured . . . . 55 1·00

1981. Australian Fungi. Multicoloured.
823 24c. Type **365** 25 10
824 35c. "Coprinus comatus" . . 45 1·10
825 55c. "Armillaria luteobubalina" . . . . . . 60 1·25
826 60c. "Cortinarius austro-venetus" . . . . 70 1·40

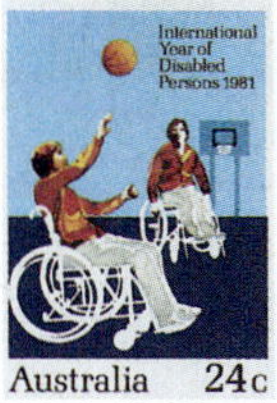

366 Disabled People playing Basketball

367 "Christmas Bush for His Adorning"

1981. International Year for Disabled Persons.
827 **366** 24c. multicoloured 20 20

1981. Christmas. Scenes and Verses from Carols by W. James and J. Wheeler. Multicoloured.
828 18c. Type **367** 20 10
829 30c. "The Silver Stars are in the Sky" 25 25
830 60c. "Noeltime" 40 90

368 Globe depicting Australia

369 "Ragamuffin" ocean racing yacht

1981. Commonwealth Heads of Government Meeting, Melbourne.
831 **368** 24c. black, blue and gold 15 10
832 60c. black, blue and silver 45 75

1981. Yachts. Multicoloured.
833 24c. Type **369** 25 10
834 35c. "Sharpie" 40 55
835 55c. "12 Metre" . . . . . . 55 1·00
836 60c. "Sabot" . . . . 80 1·25

370 Aborigine, Governor Phillip (founder of N.S.W., 1788) and Post World War II Migrant

1982. Australia Day. "Three Great Waves of Migration".
837 **370** 24c. multicoloured 35 25

371 Humpback Whale

372 Queen Elizabeth II

1982. Whales. Multicoloured.
838 24c. Sperm whale 30 10
839 35c. Black (inscr "Southern") right whale (vert) 40 60

840 55c. Blue whale (vert) . . . . 60 1·50
841 60c. Type **371** . . . . 70 1·50

1982. Birthday of Queen Elizabeth II.
842 **372** 27c. multicoloured 35 15

373 "Marjorie Atherton" **374** Radio Announcer and 1930-style Microphone

1982. Roses. Multicoloured.
843 27c. Type **373** 30 15
844 40c. "Imp" 40 60
845 65c. "Minnie Watson" . . . 70 2·00
846 75c. "Satellite" . . . . 70 1·25

1982. 50th Anniv of ABC (Australian Broadcasting Commission). Multicoloured.
847 27c. Type **374** 30 65
848 27c. ABC logo 30 65

375 Forbes Post Office **376** Early Australian Christmas Card

1982. Historic Australian Post Offices. Mult.
849 27c. Type **375** 30 40
850 27c. Flemington Post Office 30 40
851 27c. Rockhampton Post Office 30 40
852 27c. Kingston S. E. Post Office (horiz) 30 40
853 27c. York Post Office (horiz) 30 40
854 27c. Launceston Post Office 30 40
855 27c. Old Post and Telegraph Station, Alice Springs (horiz) 30 40

1982. Christmas. Multicoloured.
856 21c. Bushman's Hotel with Cobb's coach arriving (horiz) 25 10
857 35c. Type **376** 40 60
858 75c. Little girl offering Christmas pudding to swagman . . . . 60 1·60

377 Boxing

1982. Commonwealth Games, Brisbane.
859 **377** 27c. stone, yellow and red 20 25
860 – 27c. yellow, stone and green 20 25
861 – 27c. stone, yellow and brown 20 25
862 – 75c. multicoloured . . . . 50 1·25
MS863 130 × 95 mm. Nos. 859/61 1·25 1·75
DESIGNS: No. 860, Archery; No. 861, Weight-lifting; No. 862, Pole-vaulting.

378 Sydney Harbour Bridge 5s. Stamp of 1932 **379** "Yirawala" Bark Painting

1982. National Stamp Week.
864 **378** 27c. multicoloured 35 30

1982. Opening of Australian National Gallery.
865 **379** 27c. multicoloured 30 25

380 Mimi Spirits Dancing **381** "Eucalyptus calophylla" "Rosea"

1982. Aboriginal Culture. Music and Dance.
866 **380** 27c. multicoloured 20 10
867 – 40c. multicoloured 30 60
868 – 65c. multicoloured . . . . 45 1·00
869 – 75c. multicoloured . . . . 50 1·00
DESIGN: 40c. to 75c. Aboriginal bark paintings of Mimi Spirits.

1982. Eucalyptus Flowers. Multicoloured.
870 1c. Type **381** 10 30
871 2c. "Eucalyptus casia" . . . 10 30
872 3c. "Eucalyptus ficifolia" . . 1·25 2·00
873 10c. "Eucalyptus globulus" 1·25 2·00
874 27c. "Eucalyptus forrestiana" 30 40

382 Shand Mason Steam Fire Engine, 1891

1983. Historic Fire Engines. Multicoloured.
875 27c. Type **382** 35 10
876 40c. Hotchkiss fire engine, 1914 . . . . 45 75
877 65c. Ahrens-Fox fire engine, 1929 . . . . 70 1·60
878 75c. Merryweather manual fire appliance, 1851 . . . . 70 1·40

383 H.M.S. "Sirius" **384** Stylized Kangaroo and Kiwi

1983. Australia Day. Multicoloured.
879 27c. Type **383** 40 75
880 27c. H.M.S. "Supply" . . . 40 75

1983. Closer Economic Relationship Agreement with New Zealand.
881 **384** 27c. multicoloured 30 30

385 Equality and Dignity **386** R.Y. "Britannia" passing Sydney Opera House

1983. Commonwealth Day. Multicoloured.
882 27c. Type **385** 20 25
883 27c. Liberty and Freedom . . 20 25
884 27c. Social Justice and Co-operation 20 25
885 75c. Peace and Harmony . . 50 1·50

1983. Birthday of Queen Elizabeth II.
886 **386** 27c. multicoloured 50 30

387 "Postal and Telecommunications Services" **388** Badge of the Order of St. John

1983. World Communications Year.
887 **387** 27c. multicoloured 30 30

1983. Centenary of St. John Ambulance in Australia.
888 **388** 27c. black and blue . . . 35 30

389 Jaycee Members and Badge **390** "The Bloke"

1983. 50th Anniv of Australian Jaycees.
889 **389** 27c. multicoloured 30 30

1983. Folklore. "The Sentimental Bloke" (humorous poem by C. J. Dennis). Multicoloured.
890 27c. Type **390** 40 50
891 27c. "Doreen—The Intro" . . 40 50
892 27c. "The Stror' at Coot" . . 40 50
893 27c. "Hitched" 40 50
894 27c. "The Mooch o' Life" . . 40 50

391 Nativity Scene

1983. Christmas. Children's Paintings. Mult.
895 24c. Type **391** 20 10
896 35c. Kookaburra 35 45
897 85c. Father Christmas in sleigh over beach . . . . . 90 1·40

392 Sir Paul Edmund de Strzelecki

1983. Explorers of Australia. Multicoloured.
898 30c. Type **392** 25 40
899 30c. Ludwig Leichhardt . . . 25 40
900 30c. William John Wills and Robert O'Hara Burke . . 25 40
901 30c. Alexander Forrest . . . 25 40

393 Cook Family Cottage, Melbourne

1984. Australia Day.
902 **393** 30c. black and stone . . . 30 35

394 Charles Ulm, "Faith in Australia" and Trans-Tasman Cover

1984. 50th Anniv of First Official Airmail Flights. New Zealand–Australia and Australia–Papua New Guinea. Multicoloured.
903 45c. Type **394** . . . . 75 1·25
904 45c. As Type **394** but showing flown cover to Papua New Guinea . . . . 75 1·25

395 Thomson "Steamer", 1898

1984. Veteran and Vintage Cars. Multicoloured.
905 30c. Type **395** 50 70
906 30c. Tarrant two seater, 1906 50 70
907 30c. Gordon & Co "Australian Six" two seater, 1919 . . . . 50 70
908 30c. Summit tourer, 1923 . . 50 70
909 30c. Chic two seater, 1924 . . 50 70

396 Queen Elizabeth II **397** "Cutty Sark"

1984. Birthday of Queen Elizabeth II.
910 **396** 30c. multicoloured 30 35

1984. Clipper Ships. Multicoloured.
911 30c. Type **397** 35 25
912 45c. "Orient" (horiz) 50 80
913 75c. "Sobraon" (horiz) . . . 70 1·75
914 85c. "Thermopylae" . . . . 70 1·50

398 Freestyle **399** Coral Hopper

1984. Skiing. Multicoloured.
915 30c. Type **398** 30 45
916 30c. Downhill racer 30 45
917 30c. Slalom (horiz) 30 45
918 30c. Nordic (horiz) 30 45

1984. Marine Life. Multicoloured.
919 2c. Type **399** 10 30
920 3c. Jimble 40 30
921 5c. Tasselled frogfish ("Anglerfish") 15 10
922 10c. Rough stonefish . . . . 1·00 50
923 20c. Red handfish 65 40
924 25c. Orange-lipped cowrie . . 45 40
925 30c. Choat's wrasse 45 40
926 33c. Leafy seadragon 65 10
927 40c. Red velvetfish . . . . . 85 1·75
928 45c. Textile or cloth of gold cone . . . . 1·50 50
929 50c. Clown surgeonfish . . . 80 50
930 55c. Bennet's nudibranch . . 80 50
931 60c. Zebra lionfish . . . . . 1·50 70
932 65c. Banded stingray . . . . 1·50 2·25
933 70c. Southern blue-ringed octopus . . . . 1·50 1·75
934 80c. Pineconefish ("Pineapple fish") . . . . 1·25 1·75
935 85c. Royal angelfish 90 70
936 90c. Crab-eyed goby . . . . 1·60 75
937 $1 Crown of thorns starfish 1·50 80

400 Before the Event **401** Australian 1913 1d. Kangaroo Stamp

1984. Olympic Games, Los Angeles. Multicoloured.
941 30c. Type **400** 25 40
942 30c. During the event 25 40
943 30c. After the event (vert) . . 25 40

1984. "Ausipex '84" International Stamp Exhibition, Melbourne.
944 **401** 30c. multicoloured 35 30
MS945 126 × 175 mm. 30c. × 7, Victoria 1850 3d. "Half Length"; New South Wales 1850 1d. "Sydney View"; Tasmania 1853 1d.; South Australia 1855 1d.; Western Australia 1854 1d. "Black Swan"; Queensland 1860 6d.; Type **401** . . . . 3·50 4·50

402 "Angel" (stained-glass window, St. Francis's Church, Melbourne) **403** "Stick Figures" (Cobar Region)

1984. Christmas. Stained-glass Windows. Mult.
946 24c. "Angel and Child" (Holy Trinity Church, Sydney) 15 10
947 30c. "Veiled Virgin and Child" (St. Mary's Catholic Church, Geelong) 20 10
948 40c. Type **402** 30 70
949 50c. "Three Kings" (St. Mary's Cathedral, Sydney) 40 85
950 85c. "Madonna and Child" (St. Bartholomew's Church, Norwood) . . . . 50 1·40

1984. Bicentenary (1988) of Australian Settlement (1st issue). The First Australians. Multicoloured.
951 30c. Type **403** 20 45
952 30c. "Bunjil" (large figure), Grampians 20 45
953 30c. "Quikans" (tall figures), Cape York 20 45
954 30c. "Wandjina Spirit and Baby Snakes" (Gibb River) 20 45
955 30c. "Rock Python" (Gibb River) 20 45
956 30c. "Silver Barramundi" (fish) (Kakadu National Park) 20 45
957 30c. Bicentenary emblem . . 20 45
958 85c. "Rock Possum" (Kakadu National Park) 50 1·40

See also Nos. 972/5, 993/6, 1002/7, 1019/22, 1059/63, 1064/6, 1077/81, 1090/2, 1110, 1137/41, 1145/8 and 1149.

404 Yellow-tufted Honeyeater

405 "Musgrave Ranges" (Sidney Nolan)

1984. 150th Anniv of Victoria.
959 30c. Type **404** 40 65
960 30c. Leadbeater's possum . . 40 65

1985. Australia Day. Birth Bicentenary of Dorothea Mackellar (author of poem "My Country"). Multicoloured.
961 30c. Type **405** 50 80
962 30c. "The Walls of China" (Russell Drysdale) 50 80

406 Young People of Different Races and Sun

407 Royal Victorian Volunteer Artillery

1985. International Youth Year.
963 **406** 30c. multicoloured 40 30

1985. 19th-Century Australian Military Uniforms. Multicoloured.
964 33c. Type **407** 50 70
965 33c. Western Australian Pinjarrah Cavalry 50 70
966 33c. New South Wales Lancers 50 70
967 33c. New South Wales Contingent to the Sudan 50 70
968 33c. Victorian Mounted Rifles 50 70

408 District Nurse of early 1900s

410 Abel Tasman and Journal Entry

409 Sulphur-crested Cockatoos

1985. Centenary of District Nursing Services.
969 **408** 33c. multicoloured 45 35

1985. Multicoloured, background colour given.
970 **409** 1c. flesh . . . . 1·50 2·75
971 33c. turquoise 45 55

1985. Bicentenary (1988) of Australian Settlement (2nd issue). Navigators. Multicoloured.
972 33c. Type **410** 45 35
973 33c. Dirk Hartog's "Eendracht" (detail, Aert Anthonisz) 45 35
974 33c. "William Dampier" (detail, T. Murray) 45 35
975 90c. Globe and hand with extract from Dampier's journal . . . . 1·00 2·50
MS976 150 × 115 mm. As Nos. 972/5, but with cream-coloured margins . . . . . . 3·25 4·50

411 Sovereign's Badge of Order of Australia

412 Tree, and Soil running through Hourglass ("Soil")

1985. Queen Elizabeth II's Birthday.
977 **411** 33c. multicoloured 40 30

1985. Conservation. Multicoloured.
978 33c. Type **412** 25 20
979 50c. Washing on line and smog ("air") 50 85
980 80c. Tap and flower ("water") . . . . 65 1·50
981 90c. Chain encircling flames ("energy") . . . . 80 2·00

413 "Elves and Fairies" (Annie Rentoul and Ida Rentoul Outhwaite)

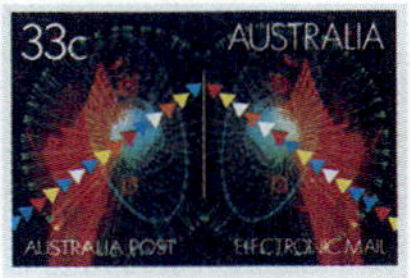

414 Dish Aerials

1985. Classic Australian Children's Books. Mult.
982 33c. Type **413** 50 75
983 33c. "The Magic Pudding" (Norman Lindsay) 50 75
984 33c. "Ginger Meggs" (James Charles Bancks) 50 75
985 33c. "Blinky Bill" (Dorothy Wall) 50 75
986 33c. "Snugglepot and Cuddlepie" (May Gibbs) 50 75

1985. Electronic Mail Service.
987 **414** 33c. multicoloured 35 30

415 Angel in Sailing Ship

1985. Christmas. Multicoloured.
988 27c. Angel with holly wings 25 10
989 33c. Angel with bells 30 10
990 45c. Type **415** 40 35
991 55c. Angel with star 50 70
992 90c. Angel with Christmas tree bauble . . . . 75 1·75

416 Astrolabe ("Batavia", 1629)

417 Aboriginal Wandjina Spirit, Map of Australia and Egg

1985. Bicentenary (1988) of Australian Settlement (3rd issue). Relics from Early Shipwrecks. Multicoloured.
993 33c. Type **416** 35 15
994 50c. German beardman jug ("Vergulde Draeck", 1656) 60 1·00
995 90c. Wooden bobbins ("Batavia", 1629) and encrusted scissors ("Zeewijk", 1727) . . . . 1·00 3·25
996 $1 Silver and brass buckle ("Zeewijk", 1727) . . . . 1·00 2·25

1986. Australia Day.
997 **417** 33c. multicoloured 40 30

418 AUSSAT Satellite, Moon and Earth's Surface

419 H.M.S. "Buffalo"

1986. AUSSAT National Communications Satellite System. Multicoloured.
998 33c. Type **418** 40 15
999 80c. AUSSAT satellite in orbit . . . . 1·00 2·25

1986. 150th Anniv of South Australia. Mult.
1000 33c. Type **419** . . . . . . 70 1·00
1001 33c. "City Sign" sculpture (Otto Hajek), Adelaide . . 70 1·00

Nos. 1000/1 were printed together se-tenant, the background of each horiz pair showing an extract from the colony's Letters Patent of 1836.

420 "Banksia serrata"

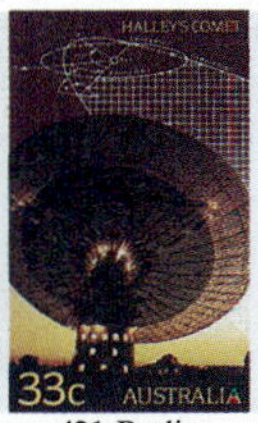

421 Radio Telescope, Parkes, and Diagram of Comet's Orbit

1986. Bicentenary (1988) of Australian Settlement (4th issue). Cook's Voyage to New Holland. Multicoloured.
1002 33c. Type **420** 60 35
1003 33c. "Hibiscus meraukensis" 60 35
1004 50c. "Dillenia alata" . . . . 90 1·10
1005 80c. "Correa reflexa" . . . 1·75 2·75
1006 90c. "Joseph Banks" (botanist) (Reynolds) and Banks with Dr. Solander 2·25 2·75
1007 90c. "Sydney Parkinson" (self-portrait) and Parkinson drawing . . . 2·25 2·75

1986. Appearance of Halley's Comet.
1008 **421** 33c. multicoloured . . . 50 35

422 Queen Elizabeth II

423 Brumbies (wild horses)

1986. 60th Birthday of Queen Elizabeth.
1009 **422** 33c. multicoloured . . . 55 35

1986. Australian Horses. Multicoloured.
1010 33c. Type **423** 60 15
1011 80c. Mustering . . . . . . 1·50 2·25
1012 90c. Show-jumping . . . . 1·50 2·50
1013 $1 Child on pony . . . . . 1·75 2·25

424 "The Old Shearer stands"

425 "King George III" (A. Ramsay) and Convicts

1986. Folklore. Scenes and Verses from the Folksong "Click go the Shears". Multicoloured.
1014 33c. Type **424** 55 80
1015 33c. "The ringer looks around" 55 80
1016 33c. "The boss of the board" 55 80
1017 33c. "The tar-boy is there" 55 80
1018 33c. "Shearing is all over" 55 80

Nos. 1014/18 were printed together, se-tenant, forming a composite design.

1986. Bicentenary (1988) of Australian Settlement (5th issue). Convict Settlement in New South Wales. Multicoloured.
1019 33c. Type **425** 60 65
1020 33c. "Lord Sydney" (Gilbert Stuart) and convicts . . . 60 65
1021 33c. "Captain Arthur Phillip" (F. Wheatley) and ship 60 65
1022 $1 "Captain John Hunter" (W. B. Bennett) and aborigines . . . . 1·75 5·50

426 Red Kangaroo

427 Royal Bluebell

1986. Australian Wildlife (1st series). Mult.
1023 36c. Type **426** 70 95
1024 36c. Emu 70 95
1025 36c. Koala 70 95
1026 36c. Laughing kookaburra ("Kookaburra") 70 95
1027 36c. Platypus 70 95

See also Nos. 1072/6.

1986. Alpine Wildflowers. Multicoloured.
1028 3c. Type **427** 50 75
1029 5c. Alpine marsh marigold 2·00 3·25
1030 25c. Mount Buffalo sunray 2·00 3·25
1031 36c. Silver snow daisy . . . 45 30

428 Pink Enamel Orchid

429 "Australia II" crossing Finishing Line

1986. Native Orchids. Multicoloured.
1032 36c. Type **428** 70 20
1033 55c. "Dendrobium nindii" 1·25 1·25
1034 90c. Duck orchid . . . . . 2·00 3·75
1035 $1 Queen of Sheba orchid 2·00 2·50

1986. Australian Victory in America's Cup, 1983. Multicoloured.
1036 36c. Type **429** 75 75
1037 36c. Boxing kangaroo flag of winning syndicate . . . 75 75
1038 36c. America's Cup trophy 75 75

430 Dove with Olive Branch and Sun

431 Mary and Joseph

1986. International Peace Year.
1039 **430** 36c. multicoloured . . . 65 40

1986. Christmas. Scenes from children's nativity play. Multicoloured.
1040 30c. Type **431** 40 30
1041 36c. Three Wise Men leaving gifts 50 45
1042 60c. Angels (horiz) . . . . 90 1·50
MS1043 147 × 70 mm. 30c. Three angels and shepherd (horiz); 30c. Kneeling shepherds (horiz); 30c. Mary, Joseph and three angels; 30c. Innkeeper and two angels; 30c. Three Wise Men (horiz) 3·50 3·75

432 Australian Flag on Printed Circuit Board

433 Aerial View of Yacht

1987. Australia Day. Multicoloured.

1044	36c. Type **432**	55	75
1045	36c. "Australian Made" Campaign logos	55	75

1987. America's Cup Yachting Championship. Multicoloured.

1046	36c. Type **433**	30	20
1047	55c. Two yachts tacking	60	1·00
1048	90c. Two yachts beating	80	2·50
1049	$1 Two yachts under full sail	90	1·50

434 Grapes and Melons

435 Livestock

1987. Australian Fruit. Multicoloured.

1050	36c. Type **434**	30	20
1051	65c. Tropical and sub-tropical fruits	80	1·50
1052	90c. Citrus fruit, apples and pears	1·25	2·50
1053	$1 Stone and berry fruits	1·25	1·60

1987. Agricultural Shows. Multicoloured.

1054	36c. Type **435**	60	20
1055	65c. Produce	1·00	1·75
1056	90c. Sideshows	1·25	3·00
1057	$1 Competitions	1·50	2·40

436 Queen Elizabeth in Australia, 1986

1987. Queen Elizabeth II's Birthday.

1058 **436**	36c. multicoloured	55	60

437 Convicts on Quay

438 "At the Station"

1987. Bicentenary (1988) of Australian Settlement (6th issue). Departure of the First Fleet. Multicoloured.

1059	36c. Type **437**	80	1·10
1060	36c. Royal Marines officer and wife	80	1·10
1061	36c. Sailors loading supplies	80	1·10
1062	36c. Officers being ferried to ships	80	1·10
1063	36c. Fleet in English Channel	80	1·10

See also Nos. 1064/6, 1077/81 and 1090/2.

1987. Bicentenary (1988) of Australian Settlement (7th issue). First Fleet at Tenerife. As T **437**. Multicoloured.

1064	36c. Ferrying supplies, Santa Cruz	70	1·00
1065	36c. Canary Islands fishermen and departing fleet	70	1·00
1066	$1 Fleet arriving at Tenerife	1·75	2·25

Nos. 1064/5 were printed together, se-tenant, forming a composite design.

1987. Folklore. Scenes and Verses from Poem "The Man from Snowy River". Multicoloured.

1067	36c. Type **438**	80	1·10
1068	36c. "Mountain bred"	80	1·10
1069	36c. "That terrible descent"	80	1·10
1070	36c. "At their heels"	80	1·10
1071	36c. "Brought them back"	80	1·10

Nos. 1067/71 were printed together, se-tenant, forming a composite background design of mountain scenery.

1987. Australian Wildlife (2nd series). As T **426**. Multicoloured.

1072	37c. Common brushtail possum	55	85
1073	37c. Sulphur-crested cockatoo ("Cockatoo")	55	85
1074	37c. Common wombat	55	85
1075	37c. Crimson rosella ("Rosella")	55	85
1076	37c. Echidna	55	85

1987. Bicentenary (1988) of Australian Settlement (8th issue). First Fleet at Rio de Janeiro. As T **437**. Multicoloured.

1077	37c. Sperm whale and fleet	80	1·10
1078	37c. Brazilian coast	80	1·10
1079	37c. British officers in market	80	1·10
1080	37c. Religious procession	80	1·10
1081	37c. Fleet leaving Rio	80	1·10

Nos. 1077/81 were printed together, se-tenant, forming a composite design.

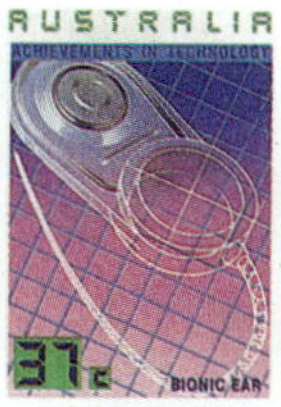

439 Bionic Ear

440 Catching Crayfish

1987. Australian Achievements in Technology. Mult.

1082	37c. Type **439**	30	15
1083	53c. Microchips	55	45
1084	63c. Robotics	60	70
1085	68c. Ceramics	65	75

1987. "Aussie Kids". Multicoloured.

1086	37c. Type **440**	40	35
1087	55c. Playing cat's cradle	60	75
1088	90c. Young football supporters	1·00	2·50
1089	$1 Children with kangaroo	1·00	1·50

1987. Bicentenary (1988) of Australian Settlement (9th issue). First Fleet at Cape of Good Hope. As T **437**. Multicoloured.

1090	37c. Marine checking list of livestock	65	1·00
1091	37c. Loading livestock	65	1·00
1092	$1 First Fleet at Cape Town	1·50	2·25

Nos. 1090/1 were printed together, se-tenant, forming a composite design.

441 Detail of Spearthrower, Western Australia

1987. Aboriginal Crafts. Multicoloured.

1093	3c. Type **441**	1·10	1·50
1094	15c. Shield pattern, New South Wales	5·00	7·00
1095	37c. Basket weave, Queensland	1·10	1·50
1096	37c. Bowl design, Central Australia	90	1·25
1097	37c. Belt pattern, Northern Territory	1·10	1·50

442 Grandmother and Granddaughters with Candles

443 Koala with Stockman's Hat and Eagle dressed as Uncle Sam

1987. Christmas. Designs showing carol singing by candlelight. Multicoloured.

1098	30c. Type **442**	50	65
1099	30c. Father and daughters	50	65
1100	30c. Four children	50	65
1101	30c. Family	50	65
1102	30c. Six teenagers	50	65
1103	37c. Choir (horiz)	50	65
1104	63c. Father and two children (horiz)	85	1·25

1988. Bicentenary of Australian Settlement (10th issue). Arrival of First Fleet. As T **437**. Mult.

1105	37c. Aborigines watching arrival of Fleet, Botany Bay	65	90
1106	37c. Aborigine family and anchored ships	65	90
1107	37c. Fleet arriving at Sydney Cove	65	90
1108	37c. Ship's boat	65	90
1109	37c. Raising the flag, Sydney Cove, 26 January 1788	65	90

Nos. 1105/9 were printed together, se-tenant, forming a composite design.

1988. Bicentenary of Australian Settlement (11th issue). Joint issue with U.S.A.

1110 **443**	37c. multicoloured	60	35

444 "Religion" (A. Horner)

445 "Government House, Sydney, 1790" (George Raper)

1988. "Living Together". Designs showing cartoons. Multicoloured (except 30c.).

1111	1c. Type **444**	50	70
1112	2c. "Industry" (P. Nicholson)	50	60
1113	3c. "Local Government" (A. Collette)	50	60
1114	4c. "Trade Unions" (Liz Honey)	10	20
1115	5c. "Parliament" (Bronwyn Halls)	50	50
1116	10c. "Transport" (Meg Williams)	30	50
1117	15c. "Sport" (G. Cook)	1·50	60
1118	20c. "Commerce" (M. Atcherson)	70	1·00
1119	25c. "Housing" (C. Smith)	45	40
1120	30c. "Welfare" (R. Tandberg) (black and lilac)	55	1·25
1121	37c. "Postal Services" (P. Viska)	60	50
1121b	39c. "Tourism" (J. Spooner)	60	50
1122	40c. "Recreation" (R. Harvey)	70	70
1123	45c. "Health" (Jenny Coopes)	70	1·25
1124	50c. "Mining" (G. Haddon)	70	50
1125	53c. "Primary Industry" (S. Leahy)	1·75	2·00
1126	55c. "Education" (Victoria Roberts)	1·50	2·00
1127	60c. "Armed Forces" (B. Green)	1·50	70
1128	63c. "Police" (J. Russell)	2·50	1·40
1129	65c. "Telecommunications" (B. Petty)	1·50	2·50
1130	68c. "The Media" (A. Langoulant)	2·25	3·25
1131	70c. "Science and Technology" (J. Hook)	1·75	1·75
1132	75c. "Visual Arts" (G. Dazeley)	1·00	1·00
1133	80c. "Performing Arts" (A. Stitt)	1·25	1·00
1134	90c. "Banking" (S. Billington)	1·50	1·50
1135	95c. "Law" (C. Aslanis)	1·00	2·00
1136	$1 "Rescue and Emergency" (M. Leunig)	1·10	1·00

1988. Bicentenary of Australian Settlement (12th issue). "The Early Years, 1788–1809". Mult.

1137	37c. Type **445**	65	1·00
1138	37c. "Government Farm, Parramatta, 1791" ("The Port Jackson Painter")	65	1·00
1139	37c. "Parramatta Road, 1796" (attr Thomas Watling)	65	1·00
1140	37c. "View of Sydney Cove, c. 1800" (detail) (Edward Dayes)	65	1·00
1141	37c. "Sydney Hospital, 1803", (detail) (George William Evans)	65	1·00

Nos. 1137/41 were printed together, se-tenant, forming a composite background design from the painting "View of Sydney from the East Side of the Cove, c. 1808" by John Eyre.

446 Queen Elizabeth II (from photo by Tim Graham)

1988. Queen Elizabeth II's Birthday.

1142 **446**	37c. multicoloured	50	40

447 Expo '88 Logo

1988. "Expo '88" World Fair, Brisbane.

1143 **447**	37c. multicoloured	50	40

448 New Parliament House

1988. Opening of New Parliament House, Canberra.

1144 **448**	37c. multicoloured	50	40

449 Early Settler and Sailing Clipper

1988. Bicentenary of Australian Settlement (13th issue). Multicoloured.

1145	37c. Type **449**	75	1·00
1146	37c. Queen Elizabeth II with British and Australian Parliament Buildings	75	1·00
1147	$1 W. G. Grace (cricketer) and tennis racquet	1·50	2·25
1148	$1 Shakespeare, John Lennon (entertainer) and Sydney Opera House	1·50	2·25

Stamps in similar designs were also issued by Great Britain.

450 Kiwi and Koala at Campfire

1988. Bicentenary of Australian Settlement (14th issue).

1149 **450**	37c. multicoloured	65	40

A stamp in a similar design was also issued by New Zealand.

451 "Bush Potato Country" (Turkey Tolsen Tjupurrula and David Corby Tjapaltjarri)

1988. Art of the Desert. Aboriginal Paintings from Central Australia. Multicoloured.

1150	37c. Type **451**	25	30
1151	55c. "Courtship Rejected" (Limpi Puntungka Tjapangati)	45	70
1152	90c. "Medicine Story" (artist unknown)	65	2·40
1153	$1 "Ancestor Dreaming" (Tim Leura Tjapaltjarri)	65	1·50

452 Basketball

1988. Olympic Games, Seoul. Multicoloured.

1154	37c. Type **452**	50	40
1155	65c. Athlete crossing finish line	60	1·75
1156	$1 Gymnast with hoop	85	1·75

453 Rod and Mace

1988. 34th Commonwealth Parliamentary Conference, Canberra.
1157 **453** 37c. multicoloured . . . 50 60

454 Necklace by Peter Tully

1988. Australian Crafts. Multicoloured.
1158 2c. Type **454** . . . . 4·00 5·50
1159 5c. Vase by Colin Levy . . 4·00 5·50
1160 39c. Teapot by Frank Bauer 50 35

455 Pinnacles Desert

1988. Panorama of Australia. Multicoloured.
1161 39c. Type **455** 70 40
1162 55c. Flooded landscape, Arnhem Land . . . . . 1·00 1·00
1163 65c. Twelve Apostles, Victoria . . . . 1·50 2·50
1164 70c. Mountain Ash wood 1·50 2·50

456 "The Nativity" (Danielle Hush)

1988. Christmas. Multicoloured.
1165 32c. Type **456** 35 10
1166 39c. "Koala as Father Christmas" (Kylie Courtney) 35 10
1167 63c. "Christmas Cockatoo" (Benjamin Stevenson) . . 70 1·40

457 Sir Henry Parkes **458** Bowls

1989. Australia Day. Centenary of Federation Speech by Sir Henry Parkes (N.S.W. Prime Minister).
1168 **457** 39c. multicoloured . . . 45 40

1989. Sports. Multicoloured.
1169 1c. Type **458** 10 50
1170 2c. Tenpin-bowling 10 20
1171 3c. Australian football . . . 1·00 1·00
1172 5c. Kayaking and canoeing 15 10
1174 10c. Sailboarding 15 15
1176 20c. Tennis 20 25
1179 39c. Fishing 45 40
1180 41c. Cycling 40 35
1181 43c. Skateboarding 50 40
1184 55c. Kite-flying 50 45
1186 65c. Rock-climbing 80 70
1187 70c. Cricket . . . . 1·90 80
1188 75c. Netball . . . . 70 1·50
1189 80c. Squash . . . . 1·00 65
1190 85c. Diving . . . . 1·75 80
1191 90c. Soccer . . . . 1·75 1·50
1192 $1 Fun-run . . . . 1·00 50
1193 $1.10 Golf . . . . 3·00 1·00
1194 $1.20 Hang-gliding . . . . 4·00 1·10

459 Merino

1989. Sheep in Australia. Multicoloured.
1195 39c. Type **459** 70 50
1196 39c. Poll Dorset 70 50
1197 85c. Polwarth . . . . 1·40 2·75
1198 $1 Corriedale . . . . 1·40 1·50

460 Adelaide Botanic Garden

1989. Botanic Gardens. Multicoloured.
1199 $2 Noroo, New South Wales . . . . 1·50 30
1200 $5 Mawarra, Victoria . . . 4·25 60
1201 $10 Type **460** . . . . . . 7·50 1·00
1201a $20 "A View of the Artist's House and Garden in Mills Plains, Van Diemen's Land" (John Glover) . . . . 15·00 8·00

461 "Queen Elizabeth II" (sculpture, John Dowie) **462** Arrival of Immigrant Ship, 1830s

1989. Queen Elizabeth II's Birthday.
1202 **461** 39c. multicoloured . . . 55 50

1989. Colonial Development (1st issue). Pastoral Era 1810–1850. Multicoloured.
1203 39c. Type **462** 55 60
1204 39c. Pioneer cottage and wool dray 55 60
1205 39c. Squatter's homestead 55 60
1206 39c. Shepherd with flock (from Joseph Lycett's "Views of Australia") . . 55 60
1207 39c. Explorer in desert (after watercolour by Edward Frome) 55 60
See also Nos. 1254/8 and 1264/8.

463 Gladys Moncrieff and Roy Rene **464** "Impression" (Tom Roberts)

1989. Australian Stage and Screen Personalities. Multicoloured.
1208 39c. Type **463** 45 40
1209 85c. Charles Chauvel and Chips Rafferty . . . . . 1·00 2·00
1210 $1 Nellie Stewart and J. C. Williamson . . . . 1·00 1·25
1211 $1.10 Lottie Lyell and Raymond Longford . . . 1·00 1·50

1989. Australian Impressionist Paintings. Mult.
1212 41c. Type **464** 45 50
1213 41c. "Impression for Golden Summer" (Sir Arthur Streeton) 45 50
1214 41c. "All on a Summer's Day" (Charles Conder) (vert) 45 50
1215 41c. "Petit Dejeuner" (Frederick McCubbin) . . 45 50

465 Freeways

1989. The Urban Environment.
1216 **465** 41c. black, purple and green . . . . 80 1·40
1217 – 41c. black, purple and mauve . . . . 80 1·25
1218 – 41c. black, purple and blue . . . . 80 1·40
DESIGNS: No. 1217, City buildings, Melbourne; No. 1218, Commuter train at platform.

466 Hikers outside Youth Hostel

1989. 50th Anniv of Australian Youth Hostels.
1219 **466** 41c. multicoloured . . . 55 50

467 Horse Tram, Adelaide, 1878

1989. Historic Trams. Multicoloured.
1220 41c. Type **467** 70 70
1221 41c. Steam tram, Sydney, 1884 . . . . 70 70
1222 41c. Cable tram, Melbourne, 1886 . . . . 70 70
1223 41c. Double-deck electric tram, Hobart, 1893 . . . 70 70
1224 41c. Combination electric tram, Brisbane, 1901 . . . 70 70

468 "Annunciation" (15th-century Book of Hours) **469** Radio Waves and Globe

1989. Christmas. Illuminated Manuscripts. Mult.
1225 36c. Type **468** 40 15
1226 41c. "Annunciation to the Shepherds" (Wharncliffe Book of Hours, c. 1475) 50 15
1227 80c. "Adoration of the Magi" (15th-century Parisian Book of Hours) 1·25 1·90

1989. 50th Anniv of Radio Australia.
1228 **469** 41c. multicoloured . . . 55 50

470 Golden Wattle **471** Australian Wildflowers

1990. Australia Day.
1229 **470** 41c. multicoloured . . . 55 50

1990. Greetings Stamps.
1230 **471** 41c. multicoloured . . . 65 65
1231 43c. multicoloured . . . 50 50

472 Dr. Constance Stone (first Australian woman doctor), Modern Doctor and Nurses

1990. Centenary of Women in Medical Practice.
1232 **472** 41c. multicoloured . . . 50 45

473 Greater Glider **474** "Stop Smoking"

1990. Animals of the High Country. Multicoloured.
1233 41c. Type **473** 60 45
1234 65c. Tiger cat ("Spotted-tailed Quoll") . . . . . . 90 1·50
1235 70c. Mountain pygmy-possum . . . . 95 1·50
1236 80c. Brush-tailed rock-wallaby . . . . 1·10 1·50

1990. Community Health. Multicoloured.
1237 41c. Type **474** 55 55
1238 41c. "Drinking and driving don't mix" 55 55
1239 41c. "No junk food, please" 55 55
1240 41c. "Guess who's just had a check up?" 55 55

475 Soldiers from Two World Wars **476** Queen at Australian Ballet Gala Performance, London, 1988

1990. "The Anzac Tradition". Multicoloured.
1241 41c. Type **475** 50 40
1242 41c. Fighter pilots and munitions worker 50 40
1243 65c. Veterans and Anzac Day parade 85 90
1244 $1 Casualty evacuation, Vietnam, and disabled veteran . . . . 1·25 1·40
1245 $1.10 Letters from home and returning troopships 1·40 1·50

1990. Queen Elizabeth II's Birthday.
1246 **476** 41c. multicoloured . . . 65 45

477 New South Wales 1861 5s. Stamp

1990. 150th Anniv of the Penny Black. Designs showing stamps. Multicoloured.
1247 41c. Type **477** 60 75
1248 41c. South Australia 1855 unissued 1s. 60 75
1249 41c. Tasmania 1853 4d. . . 60 75
1250 41c. Victoria 1867 5s. . . . 60 75
1251 41c. Queensland 1897 unissued 6d. 60 75
1252 41c. Western Australia 1855 4d. with inverted frame 60 75
MS1253 122 × 85 mm. Nos. 1247/52 3·50 4·50

478 Gold Miners on Way to Diggings

1990. Colonial Development (2nd issue). Gold Fever. Multicoloured.
1254 41c. Type **478** . . . . . . 85 1·00
1255 41c. Mining camp . . . . . 85 1·00
1256 41c. Panning and washing for gold . . . . 85 1·00
1257 41c. Gold Commissioner's tent . . . . 85 1·00
1258 41c. Moving gold under escort . . . . 85 1·00

479 Glaciology Research

1990. Australian–Soviet Scientific Co-operation in Antarctica. Multicoloured.
1261 41c. Type **479** 65 40
1262 $1.10 Krill (marine biology research) . . . . 1·60 1·50
MS1263 85 × 65 mm. Nos. 1261/2 2·25 2·25
Stamps in similar designs were also issued by Russia.

480 Auctioning Building Plots

1990. Colonial Development (3rd issue). Boomtime. Multicoloured.
1264 41c. Type **480** 55 55
1265 41c. Colonial mansion . . . 55 55
1266 41c. Stock exchange 55 55
1267 41c. Fashionable society . . 55 55
1268 41c. Factories 55 55

481 "Salmon Gums" (Robert Juniper)

482 "Adelaide Town Hall" (Edmund Gouldsmith)

1990. "Heidelberg and Heritage" Art Exhibition. Multicoloured.

1269 28c. Type **481** . . . . . . 2·50 3·25
1270 43c. "The Blue Dress" (Brian Dunlop) 40 45

1990. 150th Anniv of Local Government.

1271 **482** 43c. multicoloured . . . 75 50

483 Laughing Kookaburras and Gifts

1990. Christmas. Multicoloured.

1272 38c. Type **483** 50 25
1273 43c. Baby Jesus with koalas and wallaby (vert) 50 25
1274 80c. Possum on Christmas tree . . . . 1·50 2·50

484 National Flag

485 Black-necked Stork

1991. Australia Day. 90th Anniv of Australian Flag.

1275 **484** 43c. blue, red and grey 50 40
1276 – 90c. multicoloured . . . 1·10 1·25
1277 – $1 multicoloured . . . . . 1·25 1·40
1278 – $1.20 red, blue and grey 1·60 1·75

DESIGNS: 90c. Royal Australian Navy ensign; $1 Royal Australian Air Force standard; $1.20, Australian merchant marine ensign.

1991. Waterbirds. Multicoloured.

1279 43c. Type **485** 75 40
1280 43c. Black swan (horiz) . . 75 40
1281 85c. Cereopsis goose ("Cape Barren") . . . . 2·00 2·25
1282 $1 Chestnut-breasted teal ("Chestnut Teal") (horiz) 2·00 1·75

486 Recruitment Poster (Women's Services)

1991. Anzac Day. 50th Anniversaries.

1283 **486** 43c. multicoloured . . . 60 40
1284 – 43c. black, green & brn 60 40
1285 – $1.20 multicoloured . . 2·25 2·00

DESIGNS: 43c. (No. 1284) Patrol (Defence of Tobruk); $1.20, "V-P Day Canberra" (Harold Abbot) (Australian War Memorial).

487 Queen Elizabeth at Royal Albert Hall, London

489 "Bondi" (Max Dupain)

488 "Tectocoris diophthalmus" (bug)

1991. Queen Elizabeth II's Birthday.

1286 **487** multicoloured 80 50

1991. Insects. Multicoloured.

1287 43c. Type **488** 75 45
1288 43c. "Cizara ardeniae" (hawk moth) 75 45
1289 80c. "Petasida ephippigera" (grasshopper) . . . . . . 2·00 2·00
1290 $1 "Castiarina producta" (beetle) . . . . 2·00 1·50

1991. 150 Years of Photography in Australia.

1291 **489** 43c. black, brown and blue 75 65
1292 – 43c. black, green & brn 75 65
1293 – 70c. black, green & brn 1·25 1·10
1294 – $1.20 black, brn & grn 1·75 1·50

DESIGNS: No. 1292, "Gears for the Mining Industry, Vickers Ruwolt, Melbourne" (Wolfgang Sievers): 1293, "The Wheel of Youth" (Harold Cazneaux): 1294, "Teacup Ballet" (Olive Cotton).

490 Singing Group

491 Puppy

1991. Australian Radio Broadcasting. Designs showing listeners and scenes from radio programmes. Multicoloured.

1295 43c. Type **490** 60 45
1296 43c. "Blue Hills" serial . . . 60 45
1297 85c. "The Quiz Kids" . . . 1·25 1·25
1298 $1 "Argonauts' Club" children's programme . . 1·50 1·40

1991. Domestic Pets. Multicoloured.

1299 43c. Type **491** 70 45
1300 43c. Kitten 70 45
1301 70c. Pony . . . . 1·40 2·50
1302 $1 Sulphur-crested cockatoo 1·90 1·50

492 George Vancouver (1791) and Edward Eyre (1841)

493 "Seven Little Australians" (Ethel Turner)

1991. Exploration of Western Australia.

1303 **492** $1.05 multicoloured . . 1·00 1·10
MS1304 100 × 65 mm. No. 1303 1·25 1·40

1991. Australian Writers of the 1890s. Multicoloured.

1305 43c. Type **493** 50 45
1306 75c. "On Our Selection" (Steele Rudd) . . . . . . 80 1·00
1307 $1 "Clancy of the Overflow" (poem, A. B. Paterson) (vert) . . . . 1·10 1·00
1308 $1.20 "The Drover's Wife" (short story, Henry Lawson) (vert) . . . . . 1·25 1·60

494 Shepherd

1991. Christmas. Multicoloured.

1309 38c. Type **494** 40 15
1310 43c. Infant Jesus 45 15
1311 90c. Wise Man . . . . . . 1·50 1·75

495 Parma Wallaby

1992. Threatened Species. Multicoloured. Ordinary or self-adhesive gum.

1312 45c. Type **495** 80 70
1313 45c. Ghost bat 80 70
1314 45c. Long-tailed dunnart . . 80 70
1315 45c. Little pygmy-possum 80 70
1316 45c. Dusky hopping-mouse 80 70
1317 45c. Squirrel glider 80 70

496 Basket of Wild Flowers

1992. Greetings Stamp.

1318 **496** 45c. multicoloured . . . 50 50

497 Noosa River, Queensland

1992. Wetlands and Waterways. Multicoloured.

1319 20c. Type **497** . . . . . . 1·75 2·25
1320 45c. Lake Eildon, Victoria 40 45

498 "Young Endeavour" (brigantine)

1992. Australia Day and 500th Anniv of Discovery of America by Columbus (**MS**1337). Multicoloured. Sailing Ships.

1333 45c. Type **498** 80 50
1334 45c. "Britannia" (yacht) (vert) 80 50
1335 $1.05 "Akarana" (cutter) (vert) . . . . 1·75 2·75
1336 $1.20 "John Louis" (pearling lugger) . . . . 2·00 2·00
MS1337 147 × 64 mm. Nos. 1333/6 4·75 5·25

499 Bombing of Darwin

1992. 50th Anniv of Second World War Battles. Multicoloured.

1338 45c. Type **499** 70 45
1339 75c. Anti-aircraft gun and fighters, Milne Bay . . . 1·25 1·50
1340 75c. Infantry on Kokoda Trail . . . . 1·25 1·50
1341 $1.05 H.M.A.S. "Australia" (cruiser) and U.S.S. "Yorktown" (aircraft carrier), Coral Sea . . . . 1·50 1·75
1342 $1.20 Australians advancing, El Alamein . . . . . . 1·75 1·60

500 "Helix Nebula"

1992. International Space Year. Multicoloured.

1343 45c. Type **500** 85 45
1344 $1.05 "The Pleiades" . . . 2·00 1·25
1345 $1.20 "Spiral Galaxy, NGC 2997" . . . . 2·25 1·50
MS1346 133 × 70 mm. Nos. 1343/5 4·50 4·50

501 Hunter Valley, New South Wales

1992. Vineyard Regions. Multicoloured.

1347 45c. Type **501** 80 90
1348 45c. North-east Victoria . . 80 90
1349 45c. Barossa Valley, South Australia 80 90
1350 45c. Coonawarra, South Australia 80 90
1351 45c. Margaret River, Western Australia 80 90

502 3½d. Stamp of 1953

503 Salt Action

1992. Queen Elizabeth II's Birthday.

1352 **502** 45c. multicoloured . . . 1·00 60

1992. Land Conservation. Multicoloured.

1353 45c. Type **503** . . . . . . 85 1·10
1354 45c. Farm planning . . . . 85 1·10
1355 45c. Erosion control . . . . 85 1·10
1356 45c. Tree planting . . . . . 85 1·10
1357 45c. Dune care . . . . . . 85 1·10

504 Cycling

1992. Olympic Games and Paralympic Games (No. 1359), Barcelona. Multicoloured.

1358 45c. Type **504** 60 45
1359 $1.20 High jumping . . . . 1·50 1·60
1360 $1.20 Weightlifting . . . . 1·50 1·60

505 Echidna

506 Sydney Harbour Tunnel (value at left)

1992. Australian Wildlife (1st series). Multicoloured.

1361 30c. Saltwater crocodile . . 25 20
1362 35c. Type **505** 65 30
1363 40c. Platypus . . . . . . 1·75 25
1364 50c. Koala 60 35
1365 60c. Common bushtail possum . . . . 1·25 1·25
1366 70c. Laughing kookaburra ("Kookaburra") . . . . 2·25 1·00
1367 85c. Australian pelican ("Pelican") 75 70
1368a 90c. Eastern grey kangaroo 2·00 2·00
1369 95c. Common wombat . . . 1·00 2·50
1370a $1.20 Major Mitchell's cockatoo ("Pink Cockatoo") . . . . . . 2·00 1·10
1371 $1.35 Emu . . . . 1·75 2·25

See also Nos. 1453/8.

1992. Opening of Sydney Harbour Tunnel. Mult.

1375b 45c. Type **506** . . . . . 1·75 1·75
1376b 45c. Sydney Harbour Tunnel (value at right) 1·75 1·75

Nos. 1375/6 were printed together, se-tenant, forming a composite design.

507 Warden's Courthouse, Coolgardie

508 Bowler of 1892

1992. Centenary of Discovery of Gold at Coolgardie and Kalgoorlie. Multicoloured.

1377 45c. Type **507** 70 45
1378 45c. Post Office, Kalgoorlie 70 45
1379 $1.05 York Hotel, Kalgoorlie . . . . 1·60 2·00
1380 $1.20 Town Hall, Kalgoorlie 1·90 2·00

1992. Centenary of Sheffield Shield Cricket Tournament. Multicoloured.

1381 45c. Type **508** . . . . . . 1·00 50
1382 $1.20 Batsman and wicket-keeper . . . . 2·00 2·50

509 Children's Nativity Play

1992. Christmas. Multicoloured.

1383	40c. Type **509**	55	15
1384	45c. Child waking on Christmas Day	60	15
1385	$1 Children carol singing	1·90	1·75

510 "Ghost Gum, Central Australia" (Namatjira)

1993. Australia Day. Paintings by Albert Namatjira. Multicoloured.

1386	45c. Type **510**	90	1·40
1387	45c. "Across the Plain to Mount Giles"	90	1·40

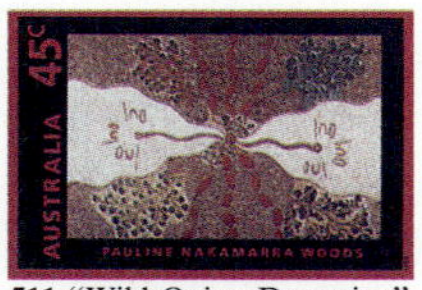

511 "Wild Onion Dreaming" (Pauline Nakamarra Woods)

1993. "Dreamings". Paintings by Aboriginal Artists. Multicoloured.

1388	45c. Type **511**	60	30
1389	75c. "Yam Plants" (Jack Wunuwun) (vert)	1·10	95
1390	85c. "Goose Egg Hunt" (George Milpurrurru) (vert)	1·25	1·40
1391	$1 "Kalumpiwarra-Ngulalintji" (Rover Thomas)	1·40	1·40

512 Uluru (Ayers Rock) National Park

1993. World Heritage Sites (1st series). Multicoloured.

1392	45c. Type **512**	80	30
1393	85c. Rain forest, Fraser Island	2·00	1·60
1394	95c. Beach, Shark Bay	2·00	1·60
1395	$2 Waterfall, Kakadu	3·00	2·25

See also Nos. 1582/5.

513 Queen Elizabeth II on Royal Visit, 1992

514 H.M.A.S. "Sydney" (cruiser, launched 1934) in Action

1993. Queen Elizabeth II's Birthday.

1396	**513** 45c. multicoloured	70	60

1993. Second World War Naval Vessels. Mult.

1397	45c. Type **514**	80	45
1398	85c. H.M.A.S. "Bathurst" (mine-sweeper)	1·60	1·75
1399	$1.05 H.M.A.S. "Arunta" (destroyer)	1·75	2·75
1400	$1.20 "Centaur" (hospital ship) and tug	2·00	2·75

515 "Work in the Home"

516 "Centenary Special", Tasmania, 1971

1993. Working Life in the 1890s. Mult.

1401	45c. Type **515**	55	50
1402	45c. "Work in the Cities"	55	50
1403	$1 "Work in the Country"	1·10	1·25
1404	$1.20 Trade Union banner	1·50	2·00

1993. Australian Trains. Multicoloured.

1405	45c. Type **516**	65	85
1406	45c. "Spirit of Progress", Victoria	65	85
1407	45c. "Western Endeavour", Western Australia, 1970	65	85
1408	45c. "Silver City Comet", New South Wales	65	85
1409	45c. Cairns–Kuranda tourist train, Queensland	65	85
1410	45c. "The Ghan", Northern Territory	65	85

Nos. 1405/10 also come self-adhesive.

517 "Black Cockatoo Feather" (Fiona Foley)

518 Conference Emblem

1993. International Year of Indigenous Peoples. Aboriginal Art. Multicoloured.

1417	45c. Type **517**	35	30
1418	75c. "Ngarrgooroon Country" (Hector Jandany) (horiz)	60	1·50
1419	$1 "Ngak Ngak" (Ginger Riley Munduwalawala) (horiz)	75	1·60
1420	$1.05 "Untitled" (Robert Cole)	90	2·50

1993. Inter-Parliamentary Union Conference and 50th Anniv of Women in Federal Parliament. Multicoloured.

1421	45c. Type **518**	75	1·50
1422	45c. Dame Enid Lyons and Senator Dorothy Tangney	75	1·50

519 Ornithocheirus

520 "Goodwill"

1993. Prehistoric Animals. Multicoloured.

1423	45c. Type **519**	60	50
1424	45c. Leaellynasaura (25 × 30 mm)	60	50
1425	45c. Timimus (26 × 33 mm)	60	50
1426	45c. Allosaurus (26 × 33 mm)	60	50
1427	75c. Muttaburrasaurus (30 × 50 mm)	1·00	90
1428	$1.05 Minmi (50 × 30 mm)	1·50	1·50
MS1429	166 × 73 mm. Nos. 1423/8	5·50	6·50

Nos. 1423/4 also come self-adhesive.

1993. Christmas. Multicoloured.

1432	40c. Type **520**	50	15
1433	45c. "Joy"	55	15
1434	$1 "Peace"	1·90	1·75

521 "Shoalhaven River Bank—Dawn" (Arthur Boyd)

1994. Australia Day. Landscape Paintings. Mult.

1435	45c. Type **521**	50	20
1436	85c. "Wimmera" (Sir Sidney Nolan)	1·10	1·10
1437	$1.05 "Lagoon, Wimmera" (Nolan)	1·25	1·50
1438	$2 "White Cockatoos with Flame Trees" (Boyd) (vert)	2·00	2·50

522 Teaching Lifesaving Techniques

1994. Centenary of Organized Life Saving in Australia. Multicoloured.

1439	45c. Type **522**	60	45
1440	45c. Lifeguard on watch	60	45
1441	95c. Lifeguard team	1·25	1·40
1442	$1.20 Lifeguards on surf boards	1·60	1·75

Nos. 1439/40 also come self-adhesive.

523 Rose

524 Bridge and National Flags

1994. Greetings Stamps. Flower photographs by Lariane Fonseca. Multicoloured.

1445	45c. Type **523**	40	45
1446	45c. Tulips	40	45
1447	45c. Poppies	40	45

1994. Opening of Friendship Bridge between Thailand and Laos.

1448	**524** 95c. multicoloured	1·25	1·40

525 "Queen Elizabeth II" (Sir William Dargie)

526 "Family in Field" (Bobbie-Lea Blackmore)

1994. Queen Elizabeth II's Birthday.

1449	**525** 45c. multicoloured	70	70

1994. International Year of the Family. Children's Paintings. Multicoloured.

1450	45c. Type **526**	55	30
1451	75c. "Family on Beach" (Kathryn Teoh)	1·00	1·25
1452	$1 "Family around Fire" (Maree McCarthy)	1·25	1·50

1994. Australian Wildlife (2nd series). As T **505**. Multicoloured. Ordinary or self-adhesive gum.

1459	45c. Kangaroo	60	85
1460	45c. Female kangaroo with young	60	85
1461	45c. Two kangaroos	60	85
1462	45c. Family of koalas on branch	60	85
1463	45c. Koala on ground	60	85
1464	45c. Koala asleep in tree	60	85

527 Suffragettes

1994. Centenary of Women's Emancipation in South Australia.

1465	**527** 45c. multicoloured	60	60

528 Bunyip from Aboriginal Legend

1994. The Bunyip (mythological monster). Mult.

1466	45c. Type **528**	55	70
1467	45c. Nature spirit bunyip	55	70
1468	90c. "The Bunyip of Berkeley's Creek" (book illustration)	1·00	1·75
1469	$1.35 Bunyip as natural history	1·40	2·25

529 "Robert Menzies" (Sir Ivor Hele)

530 Lawrence Hargrave and Box Kites

1994. Wartime Prime Ministers. Multicoloured.

1470	45c. Type **529**	1·10	1·40
1471	45c. "Arthur Fadden" (William Dargie)	1·10	1·40
1472	45c. "John Curtin" (Anthony Dattilo-Rubbo)	1·10	1·40
1473	45c. "Francis Forde" (Joshua Smith)	1·10	1·40
1474	45c. "Joseph Chifley" (A. D. Colquhoun)	1·10	1·40

1994. Aviation Pioneers.

1475	**530** 45c. brown, green and cinnamon	80	50
1476	– 45c. brown, red and lilac	80	50
1477	– $1.35 brown, violet and blue	2·50	3·25
1478	– $1.80 brown, deep green and green	2·75	3·50

DESIGNS: No. 1476, Ross and Keith Smith with Vickers Vimy (first England–Australia flight); 1477, Ivor McIntyre, Stanley Goble and Fairey IIID seaplane (first aerial circumnavigation of Australia); 1478, Freda Thompson and De Havilland Moth Major "Christopher Robin" (first Australian woman to fly solo from England to Australia).

531 Scarlet Macaw

532 "Madonna and Child" (detail)

1994. Australian Zoos. Endangered Species. Mult.

1479	45c. Type **531**	75	55
1480	45c. Cheetah (25 × 30 mm)	75	55
1481	45c. Orang-utan (26 × 37 mm)	75	55
1482	45c. Fijian crested iguana (26 × 37 mm)	75	55
1483	$1 Asian elephants (49 × 28 mm)	2·00	1·60
MS1484	166 × 73 mm. Nos. 1479/83	4·50	4·50

Nos. 1479/80 also come self-adhesive.

1994. Christmas. "The Adoration of the Magi" by Giovanni Toscani. Multicoloured.

1487	40c. Type **532**	60	15
1488	45c. "Wise Man and Horse" (detail) (horiz)	60	15
1489	$1 "Wise Man and St. Joseph" (detail) (horiz)	1·50	1·00
1490	$1.80 Complete painting (49 × 29 mm)	2·00	2·75

533 Yachts outside Sydney Harbour

534 Symbolic Kangaroo

1994. 50th Sydney to Hobart Yacht Race. Mult.

1491	45c. Type **533**	1·00	80
1492	45c. Yachts passing Tasmania coastline	1·00	80

Nos. 1491/92 also come self-adhesive.

1994. Self-adhesive. Automatic Cash Machine Stamps.

1495	**534** 45c. gold, emerald and green	55	80
1496	45c. gold, green and blue	55	80
1497	45c. gold, green and lilac	55	80
1498	45c. gold, emerald and green	55	80
1499	45c. gold, emerald and green	55	80
1500	45c. gold, green and pink	55	80
1501	45c. gold, green and red	55	80
1502	45c. gold, green and brown	55	80

535 "Back Verandah" (Russell Drysdale)

1995. Australia Day. Paintings. Multicoloured.

1503	45c. Type **535**	60	45
1504	45c. "Skull Springs Country" (Guy Grey-Smith)	60	45
1505	$1.05 "Outcamp" (Robert Juniper)	1·60	1·50
1506	$1.20 "Kite Flying" (Ian Fairweather)	1·75	1·50

536 Red Heart and Rose

537 "Endeavour" Replica at Sea

1995. St. Valentine's Day. Multicoloured.

1507 45c. Type **536** 55 55
1508 45c. Gold and red heart with rose 55 55
1509 45c. Gold heart and roses 85 85

1995. Completion of "Endeavour" Replica. Mult.

1510 45c. Type **537** . . . . . . 1·50 1·50
1511 45c. "Captain Cook's Endeavour" (detail) (Oswald Brett) . . . . . 1·50 1·50

538 Coalport Plate and Bracket Clock, Old Government House, Parramatta

1995. 50th Anniv of Australian National Trusts.

1514 **538** 45c. blue and brown . . 45 45
1515 – 45c. green and brown . . 45 45
1516 – $1 red and blue . . . . 1·00 95
1517 – $2 green and blue . . . 1·90 1·90

DESIGNS: No. 1515, Steiner doll and Italian-style chair, Ayers House, Adelaide; 1516, "Advance Australia" teapot and parian-ware statuette, Victoria; 1517, Silver bowl and china urn, Old Observatory, Perth.

539 Light Opal (hologram)

1995. Opals. Multicoloured.

1518 $1.20 Type **539** . . . . . . 3·50 1·25
1519 $2.50 Black opal (hologram) 4·50 3·75

540 Queen Elizabeth II at Gala Concert, 1992

541 Sir Edward Dunlop and P.O.W. Association Badge

1995. Queen Elizabeth II's Birthday.

1520 **540** 45c. multicoloured . . . 75 75

1995. Australian Second World War Heroes (1st series). Mult. Ordinary or self-adhesive gum.

1521 45c. Type **541** 60 60
1522 45c. Mrs. Jessie Vasey and War Widows' Guild badge 60 60
1523 45c. Sgt. Tom Derrick and Victoria Cross 60 60
1524 45c. Flt. Sgt. Rawdon Middleton and Victoria Cross 60 60

See also Nos. 1545/8.

542 Children and Globe of Flags

543 "The Story of the Kelly Gang"

1995. 50th Anniv of United Nations.

1529 **542** 45c. multicoloured . . . 75 75

1995. Centenary of Cinema. Scenes from Films. Multicoloured. (a) Size 23 × 35 mm.

1530 45c. Type **543** . . . . . . 1·25 1·25
1531 45c. "On Our Selection" . . 1·25 1·25
1532 45c. "Jedda" . . . . 1·25 1·25
1533 45c. "Picnic at Hanging Rock" . . . . 1·25 1·25
1534 45c. "Strictly Ballroom" . . 1·25 1·25

(b) Self-adhesive. Size 19 × 30½ mm.

1535 45c. Type **543** . . . . . . 1·40 1·50
1536 45c. "On Our Selection" . . 1·40 1·50
1537 45c. "Jedda" . . . . 1·40 1·50
1538 45c. "Picnic at Hanging Rock" . . . . 1·40 1·50
1539 45c. "Strictly Ballroom" . . 1·40 1·50

544 Man in Wheelchair flying Kite

545 Koala with Cub

1995. People with Disabilities. Multicoloured.

1540 45c. Type **544** . . . . . . 1·25 1·25
1541 45c. Blind woman playing violin . . . . 1·25 1·25

1995. 50th Anniv of Peace in the Pacific. Designs as 1946 Victory Commemoration (Nos. 213/15) redrawn with new face values.

1542 **53** 45c. red 80 60
1543 – 45c. green 80 60
1544 – $1.50 blue . . . . 2·25 2·25

DESIGNS—VERT: No. 1543, Angel. HORIZ: No. 1544, Flag and dove.

1995. Australian Second World War Heroes (2nd series). As T **541**. Multicoloured.

1545 45c. Sister Ellen Savage and George Medal . . . . . 1·25 1·25
1546 45c. Chief Petty Officer Percy Collins and Distinguished Service Medal and Bar . . . . . 1·25 1·25
1547 45c. Lt-Comm. Leon Goldsworthy and George Cross . . . . 1·25 1·25
1548 45c. Warrant Officer Len Waters and R.A.A.F. wings . . . . 1·25 1·25

1995. Australia–China Joint Issue. Endangered Species. Multicoloured.

1549 45c. Type **545** . . . . . . 70 1·00
1550 45c. Giant panda with cubs 70 1·00
MS1551 Two sheets, each 106 × 70 mm. (a) No. 1549. (b) No. 1550 Set of 2 sheets . . . 2·00 2·25

546 Father Joseph Slattery, Thomas Lyle and Walter Filmer (Radiology)

1995. Medical Scientists. Multicoloured.

1552 45c. Type **546** . . . . . . 1·25 1·25
1553 45c. Dame Jean Macnamara and Sir Macfarlane Burnet (viruses) . . . . . 1·25 1·25
1554 45c. Fred Hollows (ophthalmology) (vert) . . 1·25 60
1555 $2.50 Sir Howard Florey (antibiotics) (vert) . . . . 5·50 6·00

547 Flatback Turtle

548 "Madonna and Child"

1995. Marine Life. Multicoloured. Ordinary or self-adhesive gum.

1556 45c. Type **547** 55 55
1557 45c. Flame angelfish and nudibranch 55 55
1558 45c. Potato grouper ("Potato cod") and hump-headed wrasse ("Maori wrasse") 55 55
1559 45c. Giant trevally 55 55
1560 45c. Black marlin 55 55
1561 45c. Mako and tiger sharks 55 55
MS1562 166 × 73 mm. Nos. 1556/61 3·50 3·00

1995. Christmas. Stained-glass Windows from Our Lady Help of Christians Church, Melbourne. Multicoloured.

1569 40c. Type **548** 80 15
1570 45c. "Angel carrying the Gloria banner" 80 15
1571 $1 "Rejoicing Angels" . . . 2·75 2·50

No. 1569 also comes self-adhesive.

549 "West Australian Banksia" (Margaret Preston)

1996. Australia Day. Paintings. Multicoloured.

1573 45c. Type **549** . . . . . . 1·00 30
1574 85c. "The Babe is Wise" (Lina Bryans) . . . . . . 2·00 2·25
1575 $1 "The Bridge in Curve" (Grace Cossington Smith) (horiz) . . . . 2·25 2·00
1576 $1.20 "Beach Umbrellas" (Vida Lahey) (horiz) . . . 2·50 3·25

550 Gold Heart and Rose

1996. St. Valentine's Day.

1577 **550** 45c. multicoloured . . . 1·00 1·00

551 Bristol Type 156 Beaufighter and Curtiss P-40E Kittyhawk I

1996. Military Aviation. Multicoloured.

1578 45c. Type **551** . . . . . . 1·75 1·75
1579 45c. Hawker Sea Fury and Fairey Firefly . . . . . . 1·75 1·75
1580 45c. Bell Kiowa helicopters 1·75 1·75
1581 45c. Government Aircraft Factory Hornets . . . . 1·75 1·75

552 Tasmanian Wilderness

1996. World Heritage Sites (2nd series). Mult.

1582 45c. Type **552** 80 45
1583 75c. Willandra Lakes . . . 1·75 1·75
1584 95c. Naracoorte Fossil Cave 2·00 2·75
1585 $1 Lord Howe Island . . . 2·00 1·75

553 Australian Spotted Cuscus

555 North Melbourne Players

554 Head of Queen Elizabeth II

1996. Australia–Indonesia Joint Issue. Mult.

1586 45c. Type **553** . . . . . . 1·25 1·60
1587 45c. Indonesian bear cuscus 1·25 1·60
MS1588 106 × 70 mm. Nos. 1586/7 2·50 3·00

1996. Queen Elizabeth II's Birthday.

1589 **554** 45c. multicoloured . . . 1·00 75

1996. Centenary of Australian Football League. Players from different teams. Multicoloured. Ordinary or self-adhesive gum.

1606 45c. Type **555** 50 90
1607 45c. Brisbane (red and yellow shirt) 50 90
1608 45c. Sydney (red and white shirt) 50 90
1609 45c. Carlton (black shirt with white emblem) . . . 50 90
1610 45c. Adelaide (black, red and yellow shirt) 50 90
1611 45c. Fitzroy (yellow, red and blue shirt) 50 90
1612 45c. Richmond (black shirt with yellow diagonal stripe) 50 90
1613 45c. St. Kilda (red, white and black shirt) 50 90
1614 45c. Melbourne (black shirt with red top) 50 90
1615 45c. Collingwood (black and white vertical striped shirt) 50 90
1616 45c. Fremantle (green, red, white and blue shirt) . . 50 90
1617 45c. Footscray (blue, white and red shirt) 50 90
1618 45c. West Coast (deep blue shirt with yellow stripes) 50 90
1619 45c. Essendon (black shirt with red stripe) 50 90
1620 45c. Geelong (black and white horizontal striped shirt) 50 90
1621 45c. Hawthorn (black and yellow vertical striped shirt) 50 90

556 Leadbeater's Possum

1996. Fauna and Flora (1st series). Central Highlands Forest, Victoria. Multicoloured.

1622 5c. Type **556** 10 10
1623 10c. Powerful owl 65 20
1624 $2 Blackwood wattle . . . 1·40 1·50
1625 $5 Soft tree fern and mountain ash (30 × 50 mm) . . . . 3·50 3·75

See also Nos. 1679/90, 1854/66, 2126/9, 2200/3, 2272/6 and 2377/80.

1996. "China '96" 9th Asian International Stamp Exhibition, Peking. Sheet 120 × 65 mm, containing Nos. 1453b, 1454b and 1455b. Multicoloured.

MS1626 45c. Kangaroo; 45c. Female kangaroo with young; 45c. Two kangaroos . . . . 2·00 2·25

557 Edwin Flack (800 and 1500 metres gold medal winner, 1896)

1996. Centennial Olympic Games and 10th Paralympic Games, Atlanta. Multicoloured.

1627 45c. Type **557** 70 70
1628 45c. Fanny Durack (100 metres freestyle swimming gold medal winner, 1912) 70 70
1629 $1.05 Wheelchair athletes . . 1·60 1·60

558 "Animalia" (Graeme Base)

1996. 50th Anniv of Children's Book Council Awards. Designs taken from book covers. Ordinary or self-adhesive gum. Multicoloured.

1630 45c. Type **558** 60 60
1631 45c. "Greetings from Sandy Beach" (Bob Graham) . . 60 60
1632 45c. "Who Sank the Boat?" (Pamela Allen) 60 60
1633 45c. "John Brown, Rose and the Midnight Cat" (Jenny Wagner, illustrated by Ron Brooks) 60 60

559 American Bald Eagle, Kangaroo and Olympic Flame

560 Margaret Windeyer

1996. Passing of Olympic Flag to Sydney.
1638 **559** 45c. multicoloured . . . 55 50

1996. Centenary of the National Council of Women.
1639 **560** 45c. purple and yellow 50 50
1640 – $1 blue and yellow . . . 1·25 2·00
DESIGN: $1 Rose Scott.

561 Pearl

1996. Pearls and Diamonds. Multicoloured.
1641 45c. Type **561** 60 50
1642 $1.20 Diamond . . . . . . 1·40 1·50
The pearl on the 45c. is shown as an exelgram (holographic printing on ultra thin plastic film) and the diamond on the $1.20 as a hologram, each embossed on to the stamp.

562 Silhouettes of Female Dancer and Musician on Rural Landscape

1996. 50th Anniv of Arts Councils. Multicoloured.
1643 20c. Type **562** . . . . . . 2·00 2·25
1644 45c. Silhouettes of female dancer and male dancer on landscape 35 40

563 Ginger Cats

1996. Australian Pets. Multicoloured.
1645 45c. Type **563** 75 75
1646 45c. Blue heeler dogs . . . 75 75
1647 45c. Sulphur-crested cockatoo (30 × 25 mm) . . 75 75
1648 45c. Duck with ducklings (25 × 30 mm) 75 75
1649 45c. Dog and cat (25 × 30 mm) 75 75
1650 45c. Ponies (30 × 50 mm) . . 75 75
MS1651 166 × 73 mm. Nos. 1645/50 4·00 4·00
Nos. 1645/6 also come self-adhesive.

564 Ferdinand von Mueller

1996. Australia–Germany Joint Issue. Death Centenary of Ferdinand von Mueller (botanist).
1654 **564** $1.20 multicoloured . . 1·25 1·60

565 Willem de Vlamingh

566 Madonna and Child

1996. 300th Anniv of the Visit of Willem de Vlamingh to Western Australia.
1655 **565** 45c. multicoloured . . . 1·00 1·50

1996. Christmas. Multicoloured.
1656 40c. Type **566** 55 15
1657 45c. Wise man with gift . . 55 15
1658 $1 Shepherd boy with lamb 1·25 1·50
No. 1656 also comes self-adhesive.

567 "Landscape '74" (Fred Williams)

1997. Australia Day. Contemporary Paintings. Multicoloured.
1660 85c. Type **567** . . . . . . 1·10 1·10
1661 90c. "The Balcony 2" (Brett Whiteley) . . . . 1·10 1·10
1662 $1.20 "Fire Haze at Gerringong" (Lloyd Rees) 1·40 1·40

568 Sir Donald Bradman

569 Red Roses

1997. Australian Legends (1st series). Sir Donald Bradman (cricketer). Multicoloured.
1663 45c. Type **568** 55 55
1664 45c. Bradman playing stroke 55 55
See also Nos. 1731/42, 1838/9, 1947/50, 2069/70, 2160/4, 2264/7, 2348/9, 2473/8, 2577/81 and 2741/58.

1997. St. Valentine's Day. Ordinary or self-adhesive gum.
1665 **569** 45c. multicoloured . . . 50 50

570 Ford Coupe Utility, 1934

571 May Wirth and Horse

1997. Classic Cars. Multicoloured. Ordinary or self-adhesive gum.
1667 45c. Type **570** 60 70
1668 45c. Holden 48-215 (FX) sedan, 1948 . . . . . . 60 70
1669 45c. Austin Lancer sedan, 1958 . . . . 60 70
1670 45c. Chrysler Valiant "R" Series sedan, 1962 . . . . 60 70

1997. 150th Anniv of the Circus in Australia. Multicoloured.
1675 45c. Type **571** 55 65
1676 45c. Con Colleano on tightrope 55 65
1677 45c. Clowns 55 65
1678 45c. Acrobats 55 65

1997. Fauna and Flora (2nd series). Kakadu Wetlands, Northern Territory. As T **556**. Mult.
1679 20c. Saltwater crocodile . . 15 20
1680 25c. Northern dwarf tree frog 20 25
1681 45c. Comb-crested jacana ("Jacana") 75 75
1682 45c. Mangrove kingfisher ("Little Kingfisher") . . . 75 75
1683 45c. Brolga 75 75
1684 45c. Black-necked stork ("Jabiru") 75 75
1685 $1 "Cressida cressida" (butterfly) 70 75
1686 $10 Kakadu Wetlands (50 × 30 mm) . . . . . . 7·00 5·00
MS1686a 106 × 70 mm. No. 1686 11·00 11·00
Nos. 1681/84 also come self-adhesive.

572 Royal Wedding 1d. Stamp of 1947

573 Hand holding Globe and Lion's Emblem

1997. Queen Elizabeth II's Birthday.
1691 **572** 45c. purple 60 60

1997. 50th Anniv of First Australian Lions Club.
1692 **573** 45c. blue, brown and purple 50 50

574 Doll holding Teddy Bear (Kaye Wiggs)

575 Police Rescue Helicopter

1997. Dolls and Teddy Bears. Multicoloured.
1693 45c. Type **574** 45 50
1694 45c. Teddy bear standing (Jennifer Laing) 45 50
1695 45c. Doll wearing white dress with teddy bear (Susie McMahon) 45 50
1696 45c. Doll in brown dress and bonnet (Lynda Jacobson) 45 50
1697 45c. Teddy bear sitting (Helen Williams) 45 50

1997. Emergency Services. Multicoloured.
1698 45c. Type **575** . . . . . . 1·25 1·00
1699 45c. Emergency Service volunteers carrying victim 1·25 1·00
1700 $1.05 Fire service at fire . . 2·50 2·25
1701 $1.20 Loading casualty into ambulance . . . . 2·50 2·00

576 George Peppin Jnr (breeder) and Merino Sheep

1997. Bicentenary of Arrival of Merino Sheep in Australia. Multicoloured.
1702 45c. Type **576** . . . . . . 70 1·00
1703 45c. Pepe chair, cloth and wool logo . . . . 70 1·00

577 Dumbi the Owl

1997. "The Dreaming". Cartoons from Aboriginal Stories. Multicoloured.
1704 45c. Type **577** 65 30
1705 $1 The Two Willy-Willies 1·50 1·10
1706 $1.20 How Brolga became a Bird . . . . 1·50 2·00
1707 $1.80 Tuggan-Tuggan . . . 2·10 3·25

578 "Rhoetosaurus brownei"

579 Spotted-tailed Quoll

1997. Prehistoric Animals. Multicoloured.
1708 45c. Type **578** 45 60
1709 45c. "Mcnamaraspis kaprios" 45 60
1710 45c. "Ninjemys oweni" . . 45 60
1711 45c. "Paracyclotosaurus davidi" 45 60
1712 45c. "Woolungasaurus glendowerensis" 45 60

1997. Nocturnal Animals. Multicoloured.
1713 45c. Type **579** 70 90
1714 45c. Barking owl 70 90
1715 45c. Platypus (30 × 25 mm) 70 90
1716 45c. Brown antechinus (30 × 25 mm) 70 90
1717 45c. Dingo (30 × 25 mm) . . 70 90
1718 45c. Yellow-bellied glider (50 × 30 mm) 70 90
MS1719 166 × 78 mm. Nos. 1713/18 4·75 4·75
Nos. 1713/14 also come self-adhesive.

580 Woman

1997. Breast Cancer Awareness Campaign.
1722 **580** 45c. multicoloured . . . 1·25 60

581 Two Angels

1997. Christmas. Children's Nativity Play. Mult.
1723 40c. Type **581** 50 15
1724 45c. Mary 55 15
1725 $1 Three Kings . . . . . . 1·25 1·50
No. 1723 also comes self-adhesive.

582 "Flying Cloud" (clipper) (J. Scott)

1998. Ship Paintings. Multicoloured.
1727 45c. Type **582** 60 30
1728 85c. "Marco Polo" (full-rigged ship) (T. Robertson) . . . . . 1·00 1·00
1729 $1 "Chusan I" (steamship) (C. Gregory) . . . . . . 1·25 1·10
1730 $1.20 "Heather Belle" (clipper) . . . . 1·50 1·75

583 Betty Cuthbert (1956)

584 "Champagne" Rose

1998. Australian Legends (2nd series). Olympic Gold Medal Winners. Multicoloured. Ordinary or self-adhesive gum.
1731 45c. Type **583** 55 65
1732 45c. Betty Cuthbert running 55 65
1733 45c. Herb Elliott (1960) . . 55 65
1734 45c. Herb Elliott running . . 55 65
1735 45c. Dawn Fraser (1956, 1960 and 1964) 55 65
1736 45c. Dawn Fraser swimming 55 65
1737 45c. Marjorie Jackson (1952) 55 65
1738 45c. Marjorie Jackson running 55 65
1739 45c. Murray Rose (1956) . . 55 65
1740 45c. Murray Rose swimming 55 65
1741 45c. Shirley Strickland (1952 and 1956) 55 65
1742 45c. Shirley Strickland hurdling 55 65

1998. Greeting Stamp. Ordinary or self-adhesive gum.
1755 **584** 45c. multicoloured . . . 55 50

585 Queen Elizabeth II

1998. Queen Elizabeth II's Birthday.
1757 **585** 45c. multicoloured . . . 50 50

586 Sea Hawk (helicopter) landing on Frigate

1998. 50th Anniv of Royal Australian Navy Fleet Air Arm.
1758 **586** 45c. multicoloured . . . 50 50

587 Sheep Shearer and Sheep

1998. Farming. Multicoloured. Ordinary or self-adhesive gum.
1759 45c. Type **587** 45 50
1760 45c. Barley and silo 45 50
1761 45c. Farmers herding beef cattle 45 50
1762 45c. Sugar cane harvesting 45 50
1763 45c. Two dairy cows 45 50

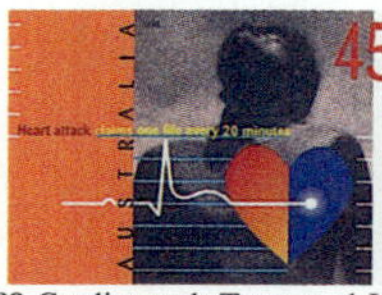

588 Cardiograph Trace and Heart

1998. Heart Disease Awareness.
1769 **588** 45c. multicoloured . . . 50 50

589 Johnny OKeefe ("The Wild One", 1958)

1998. Australian Rock and Roll. Multicoloured. Ordinary or self-adhesive gum.
1770 45c. Type **589** 55 50
1771 45c. Col Joye ("Oh Yeah Uh Huh", 1959) 55 50
1772 45c. Little Pattie ("He's My Blonde Headed Stompie Wompie Real Gone Surfer Boy", 1963) . . . 55 50
1773 45c. Normie Rowe ("Shakin all Over", 1965) 55 50
1774 45c. Easybeats ("She's so Fine", 1965) 55 50
1775 45c. Russell Morris ("The Real Thing", 1969) . . . 55 50
1776 45c. Masters Apprentices ("Turn Up Your Radio", 1970) 55 50
1777 45c. Daddy Cool ("Eagle Rock", 1971) 55 50
1778 45c. Billy Thorpe and the Aztecs ("Most People I know think I'm Crazy", 1972) 55 50
1779 45c. Skyhooks ("Horror Movie", 1974) 55 50
1780 45c. AC/DC ("It's a Long Way to the Top", 1975) 55 50
1781 45c. Sherbet ("Howzat", 1976) 55 50

590 Yellow-tufted Honeyeater ("Helmeted Honeyeater")

1998. Endangered Species. Multicoloured.
1794 5c. Type **590** 45 45
1795 5c. Orange-bellied parrot . . 45 45
1796 45c. Red-tailed cockatoo ("Red-tailed Black-Cockatoo") 80 80
1797 45c. Gouldian finch 80 80

591 French Horn and Cello Players

1998. Youth Arts, Australia. Multicoloured.
1798 45c. Type **591** 50 50
1799 45c. Dancers 50 50

592 "Phalaenopsis rosenstromii"

1998. Australia–Singapore Joint Issue. Orchids. Multicoloured.
1800 45c. Type **592** 55 40
1801 85c. "Arundina graminifolia" . . . . . . 1·00 1·00
1802 $1 "Grammatophyllum speciosum" . . . . 1·40 1·25
1803 $1.20 "Dendrobium phalaenopsis" . . . . . 1·50 1·60
MS1804 138 × 72 mm. Nos. 1800/3 4·00 3·75

593 Flying Angel with Teapot (cartoon by Michael Leunig)

1998. "The Teapot of Truth" (cartoons by Michael Leunig). Multicoloured.
1805 45c. Type **593** 70 75
1806 45c. Two birds in heart-shaped tree 70 75
1807 45c. Pouring tea 70 75
1808 $1 Mother and child (29 × 24 mm) . . . . . . 1·25 1·25
1809 $1.20 Cat with smiling face (29 × 24 mm) . . . . . . 1·50 1·60

594 Red Lacewing

595 Flinders' Telescope and Map of Tasmania

1998. Butterflies. Multicoloured. Ordinary or self-adhesive gum.
1815 45c. Type **594** 75 85
1816 45c. Dull oakblue 75 85
1817 45c. Meadow argus 75 85
1818 45c. Ulysses butterfly . . . 75 85
1819 45c. Common red-eye . . . 75 85

1998. Bicentenary of the Circumnavigation of Tasmania by George Bass and Matthew Flinders. Multicoloured.
1820 45c. Type **595** 65 50
1821 45c. Sextant and letter from Bass 65 50

596 Weedy Seadragon

597 Rose of Freedom

1998. International Year of the Ocean. Multicoloured.
1822 45c. Type **596** 65 65
1823 45c. Bottlenose dolphin . . 65 65
1824 45c. Fiery squid (24 × 29 mm) 65 65
1825 45c. Manta ray (29 × 24 mm) 65 65
1826 45c. White pointer shark (29 × 49 mm) 65 65
1827 45c. Southern right whale (49 × 29 mm) 65 65
MS1828 166 × 73 mm. Nos. 1822/7 2·75 2·75
Nos. 1822/3 also come self-adhesive.

1998. 50th Anniv of Universal Declaration of Human Rights.
1831 **597** 45c. multicoloured . . . 50 50

598 Three Kings

1998. Christmas. Multicoloured.
1832 40c. Type **598** 40 15
1833 45c. Nativity scene 40 15
1834 $1 Mary and Joseph . . . . 1·10 1·10
No. 1832 also comes self-adhesive.

599 Australian Coat of Arms

1999. 50th Anniv of Australian Citizenship. Ordinary or self-adhesive gum.
1837 **599** 45c. multicoloured . . . 40 40

600 Arthur Boyd

1999. Australian Legends (3rd series). Arthur Boyd (painter). Multicoloured. Ordinary or self-adhesive gum.
1838 45c. Type **600** 50 50
1839 45c. "Nebuchadnezzer on fire falling over Waterfall" (Arthur Boyd) 50 50

601 Red Roses

1999. Greetings Stamp. Romance. Ordinary or self-adhesive gum.
1843 **601** 45c. multicoloured . . . 40 40

602 Elderly Man and Grandmother with Boy

1999. International Year of Older Persons. Mult.
1844 45c. Type **602** 50 50
1845 45c. Elderly woman and grandfather with boy 50 50

603 "Polly Woodside" (barque)

604 Olympic Torch and 1956 7½d. Stamp

1999. Sailing Ships. Multicoloured.
1846 45c. Type **603** 60 35
1847 85c. "Alma Doepel" (topsail schooner) . . . . 1·00 1·10
1848 $1 "Enterprize" replica (topsail schooner) . . . . 1·25 1·10
1849 $1.05 "Lady Nelson" replica (topsail schooner) . . . . 1·40 1·90

1999. Australia—Ireland Joint Issue. "Polly Woodside" (barque). Sheet 137 × 72 mm. Mult.
MS1850 45c. Type **603**; 30p. Type **374** of Ireland (No. **MS**1850 was sold at $1.25 in Australia) 1·25 1·40

1999. Australia—Canada. Joint Issue. "Marco Polo" (emigrant ship). Sheet 160 × 95 mm. Mult.
MS1851 85c. As No. 1728; 46c. Type **701** of Canada (No. **MS**1851 was sold at $1.30 in Australia) 1·25 1·40

1999. "Australia '99" International Stamp Exhibition, Melbourne. Two sheets, each 142 × 76 mm, containing designs as Nos. 398/403 and all with face value of 45c.
MS1852 (a) 45c. ultramarine (Type **167**); 45c. grey (Captain Cook); 45c. brown (Flinders). (b) 45c. red (Type **168**); 45c. brown (Bass); 45c. purple (King) Set of 2 sheets . . . . 2·50 2·75

1999. Olympic Torch Commemoration.
1853 **604** $1.20 multicoloured . . 1·10 1·10

605 "Correa reflexa" (native fuchsia)

607 "Here's Humphrey"

606 Queen Elizabeth II with The Queen Mother

1999. Fauna and Flora (3rd series). Coastal Environment. Multicoloured.
1854 45c. Type **605** 50 50
1855 45c. "Hibbertia scandens" (guinea flower) 50 50
1856 45c. "Ipomoea pre-caprae" (beach morning glory) . . 50 50
1857 45c. "Wahlenbergia stricta" (Australian bluebells) . . 50 50
1858 70c. Humpback whales and zebra volute shell (29 × 24 mm) 60 70
1859 90c. Brahminy kite and checkerboard helmet shell (29 × 24 mm) 65 70
1860 90c. Fraser Island and chambered nautilus (29 × 24 mm) 65 70
1861 $1.05 Loggerhead turtle and melon shell (29 × 24 mm) 75 80
1862 $1.20 White-bellied sea eagle and Campbell's stromb shell (29 × 24 mm) 85 90
Nos. 1859/60 were printed together, se-tenant, forming a composite design.
Nos. 1854/7 also come self-adhesive.

1999. Queen Elizabeth II's Birthday.
1870 **606** 45c. multicoloured . . . 50 50

1999. Children's Television Programmes. Multicoloured. Ordinary or self-adhesive gum.
1871 45c. Type **607** 45 45
1872 45c. "Bananas in Pyjamas" 45 45
1873 45c. "Mr. Squiggle" 45 45
1874 45c. "Play School" (teddy bears) 45 45
1875 45c. "Play School" (clock, toy dog and doll) 45 45

608 Obverse and Reverse of 1899 Sovereign

1999. Centenary of the Perth Mint.
1881 **608** $2 gold, blue and green 2·00 1·75

609 Lineout against New Zealand

610 Drilling at Burn's Creek and Rock Bolting in Tumut 2 Power Station Hall

1999. Centenary of Australian Test Rugby. Mult.
1882 45c. Type **609** 50 40
1883 45c. Kicking the ball against England 50 40
1884 $1 Try against South Africa (horiz) . . . . 1·00 85
1885 $1.20 Passing the ball against Wales (horiz) . . 1·10 1·25
Nos. 1882/3 also come self-adhesive.

1999. 50th Anniv of Snowy Mountain Scheme (hydro-electric project). Multicoloured. Ordinary or self-adhesive gum.
1888 45c. Type **610** 65 65
1889 45c. English class for migrant workers, Cooma 65 65
1890 45c. Tumut 2 Tailwater Tunnel and Eucumbene Dam 65 65
1891 45c. German carpenters and Island Bend Dam 65 65

611 Calligraphy Pen and Letter

612 Sydney Olympic Emblem

1999. Greetings Stamps. Multicoloured.
1896 45c. Type **611** 65 65
1897 45c. Wedding rings 65 65
1898 45c. Birthday cake 65 65
1899 45c. Christmas decoration 65 65
1900 45c. Teddy bear 65 65
1901 $1 Koala . . . . 1·25 1·25
See also No. 1921.

1999. Olympic Games, Sydney (2000) (1st issue).
1902 **612** 45c. multicoloured . . . 1·25 50
See also Nos. 2015/24.

613 Australia Post Symbol, 1975

1999. "Sydney Design '99" International Congress and Exhibition. Multicoloured.
1903 45c. Type **613** 45 30
1904 90c. Embryo chair, 1988 . . 80 80
1905 $1.35 Possum skin textile, c.1985 . . . . 1·25 1·25
1906 $1.50 Storey Hall, R.M.I.T. University, 1995 . . . . 1·25 1·50

614 Magnificent Tree Frog

615 Madonna and Child

1999. National Stamp Collecting Month, Small Pond Life. Multicoloured. Ordinary or self-adhesive gum.
1907 45c. Type **614** 55 55
1908 45c. Sacred kingfisher . . . 55 55
1909 45c. Roth's tree frog (29 × 24 mm) 55 55
1910 45c. Dragonfly (29 × 24 mm) 55 55
1911 50c. Javelin frog (24 × 29 mm) 65 65
1912 50c. Northern dwarf tree frog (24 × 29 mm) 65 65
MS1913 166 × 73 mm. Nos. 1907/12 3·00 3·25

1999. Christmas. Multicoloured.
1918 40c. Type **615** 50 30
1919 $1 Tree of Life (horiz) . . . 1·00 1·00
No. 1918 also comes self-adhesive.

616 Fireworks and Hologram

617 Rachel Thomson (college administrator)

1999. Millennium Greetings stamp.
1921 **616** 45c. multicoloured . . . 50 50

2000. New Millennium. "Face of Australia". Mult.
1922 45c. Nicholle and Meghan Triandis (twin babies) . . 50 60
1923 45c. David Willis (cattleman) 50 60
1924 45c. Natasha Bramley (scuba diver) 50 60
1925 45c. Cyril Watson (Aborigine boy) 50 60
1926 45c. Mollie Dowdall (wearing red hat) (vineyard worker) 50 60
1927 45c. Robin Dicks (flying instructor) 50 60
1928 45c. Mary Simons (retired nurse) 50 60
1929 45c. Peta and Samantha Nieuwerth (mother and baby) 50 60
1930 45c. John Matthews (doctor) 50 60
1931 45c. Edith Dizon-Fitzimmons (wearing drop earrings) (music teacher) 50 60
1932 45c. Philippa Weir (wearing brown hat) (teacher) . . 50 60
1933 45c. John Thurgar (in bush hat and jacket) (farmer) 50 60
1934 45c. Miguel Alzona (with face painted) (schoolboy) 50 60
1935 45c. Type **617** 50 60
1936 45c. Necip Akarsu (wearing blue shirt) (postmaster) 50 60
1937 45c. Justin Allan (R.A.N. sailor) 50 60
1938 45c. Wadad Dennaoui (wearing checked shirt) (student) 50 60
1939 45c. Jack Laity (market gardener) 50 60
1940 45c. Kelsey Stubbin (wearing cricket cap) (schoolboy) 50 60
1941 45c. Gianna Rossi (resting chin on hand) (church worker) 50 60
1942 45c. Paris Hansch (toddler) 50 60
1943 45c. Donald George Whatham (in blue shirt and tie) (retired teacher) 50 60
1944 45c. Stacey Coull (wearing pendant) 50 60
1945 45c. Alex Payne (wearing cycle helmet) (schoolgirl) 50 60
1946 45c. John Lodge (Salvation Army member) 50 60

618 Walter Parker

2000. Australian Legends (4th series). "The Last Anzacs". Multicoloured. Ordinary of sels-adhesive gum.
1951 45c. Type **618** 35 40
1952 45c. Roy Longmore 35 40
1953 45c. Alec Campbell 35 40
1954 45c. 1914–15 Star (medal) 35 40

619 Scenes from "Cloudstreet" (play) (Perth Festival)

620 Coast Banksia, False Sarsaparilla and Swamp Bloodwood (plants)

2000. Arts Festivals. Multicoloured.
1955 45c. Type **619** 55 55
1956 45c. Belgian dancers from Rosas Company (Adelaide Festival) 55 55
1957 45c. "Guardian Angel" (sculpture) and dancer (Sydney Festival) 55 55
1958 45c. Musician and Balinese dancer (Melbourne Festival) 55 55
1959 45c. Members of Vusa Dance Company of South Africa (Brisbane Festival) 55 55

2000. Gardens. Multicoloured. Ordinary or self-adhesive gum.
1965 45c. Type **620** 35 40
1966 45c. Eastern spinebill on swamp bottlebrush in foreground 35 40
1967 45c. Border of cannas . . . 35 40
1968 45c. Roses, lake and ornamental bridge 35 40
1969 45c. Hibiscus with bandstand in background 35 40

621 Queen Elizabeth II in 1996

2000. Queen Elizabeth II's Birthday.
1970 **621** 45c. multicoloured . . . 65 50

622 Medals and Korean Landscape

2000. 50th Anniv of Korean War.
1971 **622** 45c. multicoloured . . . 50 50

623 Daisy

624 Taking the Vote, New South Wales

2000. Nature and Nation. Greeting stamps. Mult.
1972 45c. Type **623** 45 50
1973 45c. Australia on globe . . 45 50
1974 45c. Red kangaroo and flag 45 50
1975 45c. Sand, sea and sky . . . 45 50
1976 45c. Rainforest 45 50

2000. Centenary of Commonwealth of Australia Constitution Act. Multicoloured.
1977 45c. Type **624** 45 40
1978 45c. Voters waiting for results, Geraldton, Western Australia 45 40
1979 $1.50 Queen Victoria (29 × 49 mm) . . . . . . 1·40 1·40
1980 $1.50 Women dancing ("The Fair New Nation") (29 × 49 mm) . . . . . . 1·40 1·40
MS1981 155 × 189 mm. Nos. 1977/80 3·25 3·25

625 Sydney Opera House, New South Wales

2000. International Stamps. Views of Australia (1st series). Multicoloured.
1982 50c. Type **625** 90 30
1983 $1 Nandroya Falls, Queensland . . . . 1·60 50
1984 $1.50 Sydney Harbour Bridge, New South Wales 2·00 1·00
1985 $2 Cradle Mountain, Tasmania . . . . 2·25 1·00
1986 $3 The Pinnacles, Western Australia . . . . 2·50 1·25
1987 $4.50 Flinders Ranges, South Australia (51 × 24 mm) . . . . . . 3·75 2·75
1988 $5 Twelve Apostles, Victoria (51 × 24 mm) . . . . . . 4·00 3·00
1989 $10 Devils Marbles, Northern Territory (51 × 24 mm) . . . . . . 8·25 5·50
Nos. 1982/9 were intended for international postage which, under changes in Australian tax laws from 1 July 2000, remained exempt from General Sales Tax.
From 1 february 2001 only international stamps were valid on overseas mail and from that date could not be used on items posted to Australian addresses.
See also Nos. 2121/4, 2195/7 and 2219/22.

626 Tennis Player in Wheelchair

627 Sir Neville Howse (first Australian recipient of Victoria Cross, 1900)

2000. Paralympic Games, Sydney (1st issue). Multicoloured. Ordinary or self-adhesive gum.
1990 45c. Type **626** 50 50
1991 45c. Amputee sprinting . . 50 50
1992 49c. Basketball player in wheelchair 50 50
1993 49c. Blind cyclist 50 50
1994 49c. Amputee putting the shot 50 50
See also Nos. 2053/4.

2000. Cent of Australia's First Victoria Cross Award.
2000 **627** 45c. multicoloured . . . 60 50
2001 – 45c. brown, gold and black 60 50
2002 – 45c. multicoloured . . . 60 50
2003 – 45c. multicoloured . . . 60 50
2004 – 45c. brown, gold and black 60 50
DESIGNS: No. 2001, Sir Roden Cutler, 1941; 2002, Victoria Cross; 2003, Private Edward Kenna, 1945; 2004, Warrant Officer Keith Payne, 1969.

628 Water Polo

629 Olympic Flag, Flame and Parthenon

2000. Olympic Games, Sydney (2nd issue). Multicoloured. Ordinary or self-adhesive gum. Competitors highlighted in varnish.
2005 45c. Type **628** 40 50
2006 45c. Hockey 40 50
2007 45c. Swimming 40 50
2008 45c. Basketball 40 50
2009 45c. Cycling (triathlon) . . . 40 50
2010 45c. Horse riding 40 50
2011 45c. Tennis 40 50
2012 45c. Gymnastics 40 50
2013 45c. Running 40 50
2014 45c. Rowing 40 50
Nos. 2005/14 were printed together, se-tenant, with the backgrounds forming a composite design.

2000. Transfer of Olympic Flag from Sydney to Athens. Joint issue with Greece. Multicoloured.
2025 45c. Type **629** 50 40
2026 $1.50 Olympic Flag, Flame and Sydney Opera House 1·50 1·50
Stamps in similar designs were issued by Greece.

630 Ian Thorpe (Men's 400m Freestyle Swimming)

631 Martian Terrain

2000. Australian Gold Medal Winners at Sydney Olympic Games. Multicoloured.
2027A 45c. Type **630** 45 45
2028A 45c. Australian team (Men's 4 × 100 m Freestyle Swimming Relay) . . . 45 45
2029A 45c. Michael Diamond (Men's Trap Shooting) 45 45
2030A 45c. Australian team (Three Day Equestrian Event) 45 45
2031A 45c. Susie O'Neill (Women's 200 m Freestyle Swimming) 45 45
2032A 45c. Australian team (Men's 4 × 200 m Freestyle Swimming Relay) . . . 45 45
2033A 45c. Simon Fairweather (Men's Individual Archery) 45 45
2034A 45c. Australian team (Men's Madison Cycling) 45 45
2035A 45c. Grant Hackett (Men's 1500 m Freestyle Swimming) 45 45
2036A 45c. Australian team (Women's Water Polo) 45 45
2037A 45c. Australian team (Women's Beach Volleyball) 45 45
2038A 45c. Cathy Freeman (Women's 400 m Athletics) 45 45
2039A 45c. Lauren Burns (Women's under 49 kg Taekwondo) 45 45
2040A 45c. Australian team (Women's Hockey) 45 45
2041A 45c. Australian crew (Women's 470 Dinghy Sailing) 45 45
2042A 45c. Australian crew (Men's 470 Dinghy Sailing) 45 45

2000. Stamp Collecting Month. Exploration of Mars. Multicoloured. (a) Ordinary gum.
2043 45c. Type **631** 45 45
2044 45c. Astronaut using thruster 45 45
2045 45c. Spacecraft (50 × 30 mm) 45 45
2046 45c. Flight crew (30 × 25 mm) 45 45
2047 45c. Launch site (30 × 50 mm) 45 45
2048 45c. Robots on kelp rod (25 × 30 mm) 45 45
MS2049 166 × 73 mm. Nos. 2043/8 2·50 2·50
(b) Self-adhesive. Designs 21 × 32 mm.
2050 45c. Type **631** 45 45
2051 45c. Astronaut using thruster 45 45

632 Cathy Freeman with Olympic Torch and Ring of Flames

2000. Opening Ceremony, Olympic Games, Sydney.
2052 **632** 45c. multicoloured . . . 1·00 50

633 Blind Athlete carrying Olympic Torch

2000. Paralympic Games, Sydney (2nd issue). Multicoloured.
2053 45c. Type **633** 55 50
2054 45c. Paralympic Games logo 55 50

634 Siobhan Paton (swimmer)

635 "Sleep in Heavenly Peace"

2000. Siobhan Paton, Paralympian of the Year.
2055 **634** 45c. multicoloured . . . 1·00 60

2000. Christmas. "Silent Night" (carol). Multicoloured. (a) Ordinary gum.
2056 40c. Type **635** 50 25
2057 45c. "All is Calm, All is Bright" 50 25
MS2058 165 × 75 mm. Nos. 2056/7 1·00 1·00

(b) Self-adhesive.
2059 40c. Type **635** 45 35

(c) International Mail. As T **625** inscr "Season's Greetings".
2060 80c. Byron Bay, New South Wales 70 85

2001. International Mail. No. 1901 optd **International POST**.
2061 $1 Koala . . . . 1·60 80

637 Parade passing Federation Arch, Sydney

2001. Centenary of Federation. Multicoloured. (a) Ordinary gum.
2062 49c. Type **637** 45 40
2063 49c. Edmund Barton (first Federal Prime Minister) 45 40
2064 $2 "Australia For Ever" (song sheet) and celebration picnic (50 × 30 mm) . . . . . . 1·75 2·00
2065 $2 State Banquet, Sydney (30 × 50 mm) . . . . . 1·75 2·00
MS2066 166 × 73 mm. Nos. 2062/5 4·25 4·75

(b) Self-adhesive.
2067 49c. Type **637** 60 60
2068 49c. Edmund Barton (first Federal Prime Minister) 60 60

638 Slim Dusty with Guitar in 1940s

2001. Australian Legends (5th series). Slim Dusty (country music singer). Multicoloured. Ordinary or self-adhesive gum.
2069 45c. Type **638** 50 50
2070 45c. Slim Dusty wearing "Sundowner" hat 50 50

639 Light Horse Parade, 1940, and Command Post, New Guinea, 1943

2001. Centenary of Australian Army. Multicoloured.
2073 45c. Type **639** 75 50
2074 45c. Soldier carrying Rwandan child and officers on the Commando Selection Course 75 50

640 Entry Canopy, Skylights and Site Plan

2001. Opening of the National Museum, Canberra. Multicoloured.
2075 49c. Type **640** 50 50
2076 49c. Skylights and "Pangk" (wallaby sculpture) . . . 50 50

2001. Sir Donald Bradman (cricketer) Commemoration. Nos. 1663/4 additionally inscribed "1908–2001" in red. Multicoloured.
2077 45c. Type **568** 50 50
2078 45c. Bradman playing stroke 50 50

641 "Khe Sanh" (Cold Chisel), 1978

2001. Australian Rock and Pop Music. Multicoloured. Ordinary or self-adhesive gum.
2089 45c. Type **641** 60 45
2090 45c. "Down Under" (Men at Work), 1981 . . . . . 60 45
2091 45c. "Power and the Passion" (Midnight Oil), 1983 . . . . 60 45
2092 45c. "Original Sin" (INXS), 1984 . . . . 60 45
2093 45c. "You're the Voice" (John Farnham), 1986 . . 60 45
2094 45c. "Don't Dream it's Over" (Crowded House), 1986 . . . . 60 45
2095 45c. "Treaty" (Yothu Yindi), 1991 . . . . . . 60 45
2096 45c. "Tomorrow" (Silverchair), 1994 . . . . 60 45
2097 45c. "Confide in Me" (Kylie Minogue), 1994 . . . . 60 45
2098 45c. "Truly, Madly, Deeply" (Savage Garden), 1997 . . 60 45

642 Queen Elizabeth II holding Bouquet

643 Party Balloons

2001. Queen Elizabeth II's Birthday.
2099 **642** 45c. multicoloured . . . 1·25 55

2001. "Colour My Day". Greetings Stamps. (a) Domestic Mail.
2100 45c. Type **643** 30 35
2101 45c. Smiling Flower 30 35
2102 45c. Hologram and party streamers 30 35

(b) International Mail.
2103 $1 Kangaroo and joey . . . 1·00 80
2104 $1.50 The Bayulu Banner 1·40 1·75

644 "Opening of the First Federal Parliament" (Charles Nuttall)

2001. Centenary of Federal Parliament. Paintings. Multicoloured.
2105 45c. Type **644** 50 40
2106 $2.45 "Prince George opening the First Parliament of the Commonwealth of Australia" (Tom Roberts) 2·25 2·50
MS2107 Two sheets, each 166 × 75 mm. (a) No. 2105. (b) No. 2106 Set of 2 sheets . . . 2·50 2·75

645 Telecommunications Tower

2001. Outback Services. Multicoloured. Ordinary or self-adhesive gum.
2108 45c. Type **645** 80 75
2109 45c. Road train 80 75
2110 45c. School of the Air pupil 80 75
2111 45c. Outback family and mail box 80 75
2112 45c. Royal Flying Doctor Service aircraft and ambulance 80 75

646 Dragon Boat and Hong Kong Convention and Exhibition Centre

2001. Joint Issue with Hong Kong. Dragon Boat Racing. Multicoloured. (a) Domestic Mail.
2118 45c. Type **646** 50 45

(b) International Mail.
2119 $1 Dragon boat and Sydney Opera House . . . . . . 1·00 1·00
MS2120 115 × 70 mm. Nos. 2118/19 1·40 1·40

2001. International Stamps. Views of Australia (2nd series). As T **625**. Multicoloured.
2125 50c. The Three Sisters, Blue Mountains, New South Wales 55 30
2122 $1 The Murrumbidgee River, Australian Capital Territory . . . . 1·25 40
2123 $1.50 Four Mile Beach, Port Douglas, Queensland . . 1·75 1·00
2124 $20 Uluru Rock at dusk, Northern Territory (52 × 24 mm) . . . . . . 16·00 15·00

647 Variegated Wren ("Variegated Fairy-Wren")

649 Christmas Tree

648 Daniel Solander (Swedish botanist) and Mango Tree

2001. Fauna and Flora (4th series). Desert Birds. Multicoloured. Ordinary or self-adhesive gum.
2130 45c. Type **647** 50 50
2131 45c. Painted finch ("Painted Firetail") 50 50
2132 45c. Crimson chat 50 50
2133 45c. Budgerigar 50 50

2001. Australia–Sweden Joint Issue. Daniel Solander's Voyage with Captain Cook. Multicoloured. (a) Domestic Mail.
2134 45c. Type **648** 50 50

(b) International Mail.
2135 $1.50 H.M.S. *Endeavour* on reef and Kapok tree . . . 1·75 1·75

2001. Christmas (1st issue). Multicoloured. (a) Domestic Mail.
2136 40c. Type **649** 40 35

(b) International Mail.
2137 80c. Star . . . . 1·00 1·00
See also Nos. 2157/8.

650 Australia on Globe

2001. Commonwealth Heads of Government Meeting (No. 2138) and Commonwealth Parliamentary Conference (No. 2139). Mult.
2138 45c. Type **650** 50 50
2139 45c. Southern Cross 50 50

651 Wedge-tailed Eagle

2001. Centenary of Birds of Australia. Birds of Prey. Multicoloured.
2140 49c. Type **651** 60 50
2141 49c. Australian kestrel ("Nankeen Kestrel") . . . 65 50
2142 98c. Red goshawk (vert) . . 1·25 1·25
2143 98c. Spotted harrier (vert) 1·25 1·25

652 Cockatoos dancing to Animal Band

653 "Adoration of the Magi"

2001. National Stamp Collecting Month. "Wild Babies" (cartoons). Multicoloured. Ordinary or self-adhesive gum.
2144 45c. Type **652** 45 45
2145 45c. Kevin Koala with birthday cake 45 45
2146 45c. Ring-tailed possums eating 45 45
2147 45c. Bilbies at foot of tree 45 45
2148 45c. James Wombat on rope ladder 45 45
2149 45c. Wallaby, echidna and platypus on rope ladder 45 45
MS2150 Two sheets, each 175 × 75 mm. (a) Nos. 2144/6. (b) 2147/9. Ordinary gum . . . . 2·50 2·50

2001. Christmas (2nd issue). Miniatures from "Wharncliffe Hours Manuscript". Multicoloured.
2157 40c. Type **653** 75 30
2158 45c. "Flight into Egypt" . . 75 35
No. 2157 also comes self-adhesive.

654 Sir Gustav Nossal (immunologist)

2002. Australian Legends. (6th series). Medical Scientists. Ordinary or self-adhesive gum. Multicoloured.
2165 45c. Type **654** 40 40
2166 45c. Nancy Millis (microbiologist) 40 40
2167 45c. Peter Doherty (immunologist) 40 40
2168 45c. Fiona Stanley (epidemiologist) 40 40
2169 45c. Donald Metcalf (haematologist) 40 40

655 Queen Elizabeth in 1953

2002. Golden Jubilee. Multicoloured.
2170 45c. Type **655** 50 35
2171 $2.45 Queen Elizabeth in Italy, 2000 . . . . 2·25 3·00
MS2172 160 × 77 mm. Nos. 2170/1 2·75 3·25

656 Steven Bradbury (Men's 1000m Short Track Speed Skating)

2002. Australian Gold Medal Winners at Salt Lake City Winter Olympic Games. Multicoloured.
2173 45c. Type **656** 60 60
2174 45c. Alisa Camplin (Women's Aerials Freestyle Skiing) 60 60

657 Austin 7 and Bugatti Type 40, Australian Grand Prix, Phillip Island, 1928

658 Macquarie Lighthouse

2002. Centenary of Motor Racing in Australia and New Zealand. Ordinary or self-adhesive gum. Multicoloured.

2175	45c. Type **657**	60	50
2176	45c. Jaguar Mark II, Australian Touring Car Championship, Mallala, 1963	60	50
2177	45c. Repco-Brabham, Tasman Series, Sandown, 1966	60	50
2178	45c. Holden Torana and Ford Falcon, Hardie-Ferodo 500, Bathurst, 1972	60	50
2179	45c. William's Ford, Australian Grand Prix, Calder, 1980	60	50
2180	45c. Benetton-Renault, Australian Grand Prix, Albert Park, 2001	60	50

2002. Lighthouses. Multicoloured.

2187	45c. Type **658**	65	35
2188	49c. Cape Naturaliste	80	65
2189	49c. Troubridge Island	80	65
2190	$1.50 Cape Bruny	2·00	1·60

Nos. 2188/9 also come self-adhesive.

659 Nicolas Baudin, Kangaroo, *Geographe* (ship) and Map

2002. Australia—France Joint Issue. Bicentenary of Flinders—Baudin Meeting at Encounter Bay. Multicoloured. (a) Domestic Mail.

2193	45c. Type **659**	50	40

(b) International Mail.

2194	$1.50 Matthew Flinders, Port Lincoln Parrot, *Investigator* (ship) and Map	1·75	1·75

2002. International Stamps. Views of Australia (3rd series). As T **625**. Multicoloured.

2195	50c. Walker Flat, River Murray, South Australia	55	40
2196	$1 Mt. Roland, Tasmania	1·00	75
2197	$1.50 Cape Leveque, Western Australia	1·40	1·25

Nos. 2195/6 also come self-adhesive.

660 Desert Star Flower

2002. Fauna and Flora (5th series). Great Sandy Desert. Multicoloured.

2200	50c. Type **660**	40	45
2201	$1 Bilby	80	85
2202	$1.50 Thorny Devil	1·20	1·30
2203	$2 Great Sandy Desert landscape (50 × 30 mm)	1·60	1·70

No. 2200 also comes self-adhesive.

661 "Ghost Gum, Mt Sonder" (Albert Namatjira)

2002. Birth Centenary of Albert Namatjira (artist). Multicoloured. Nos. 2204/7, ordinary or self-adhesive gum.

2209	45c. Type **661**	40	45
2210	45c. "Mt Hermannsburg"	40	45
2211	45c. "Glen Helen Country"	40	45
2212	45c. "Simpsons Gap"	40	45
MS2208	133 × 70 mm. Nos. 2204/7	1·75	1·40

662 *Nelumbo nucifera*

2002. Australia–Thailand Joint Issue. 50th Anniv of Diplomatic Relations. Water Lilies. Multicoloured. (a) Domestic Mail.

2213	45c. Type **662**	40	35

(b) International Mail.

2214	$1 *Nymphaea immutabilis*	85	75
MS2215	107 × 70 mm. Nos. 2214/15	1·25	1·40

663 Star, Presents and Baubles

664 Lilly-pilly

2002. International Greetings. Multicoloured.

2216	90c. Type **663**	75	80
2217	$1.10 Koala	90	95
2218	$1.65 "Puja" (painting by Ngarralja Tommy May)	1·30	1·40

2002. International Stamps. Views of Australia (4th series). As T **625**. Multicoloured.

2219	$1.10 Coonawarra, South Australia	90	95
2220	$1.65 Gariwerd (Grampians), Victoria	1·30	1·40
2221	$2.20 National Library, Canberra	1·80	1·90
2222	$3.30 Cape York, Queensland	2·75	3·00

2002. "Bush Tucker". Edible Plants from the Outback. Multicoloured. Ordinary or self-adhesive gum.

2228	49c. Type **664**	55	55
2229	49c. Honey Grevillea	55	55
2230	49c. Quandong	55	55
2231	49c. Acacia seeds	55	55
2232	49c. Murnong	55	55

665 Bunyip

666 "Wakeful"

2002. Stamp Collecting Month. *The Magic Rainforest*, (book by John Marsden). Multicoloured. Nos. 2233/8, ordinary or self-adhesive gum.

2233	45c. Type **665**	50	50
2234	45c. Fairy on branch	50	50
2235	45c. Gnome with sword	50	50
2236	45c. Goblin with stock whip	50	50
2237	45c. Wizard	50	50
2238	45c. Sprite	50	50
MS2239	170 × 90 mm. Nos. 2234/9	2·75	2·75

2002. Champion Racehorses. Multicoloured.

2246	45c. Type **666**	75	75
2247	45c. "Rising Fast"	75	75
2248	45c. "Manikato"	75	75
2249	45c. "Might and Power"	75	75
2250	45c. "Sunline"	75	75

667 Nativity

2002. Christmas. Multicoloured.

2251	40c. Type **667**	75	35
2252	45c. The Three Wise Men	75	35

No. 2251 also comes self-adhesive.

668 Two Daisies

2003. Greetings Stamps. Some adapted from previous issues. Multicoloured.

2254	50c. Type **668**	40	45
2255	50c. Wedding rings and yellow roses	40	45
2256	50c. Hearts and pink roses	40	45
2257	50c. Birthday cake and present	40	45
2258	50c. Seated teddy bear	40	45
2259	50c. Balloons	40	45
2260	50c. Red kangaroo and flag	40	45
2261	50c. Australia on globe	40	45
2262	50c. Sports car	40	45
2263	$1 Wedding rings and pink rose	80	85

669 Margaret Court with Wimbledon Trophy

2003. Australian Legends (7th series). Tennis Players. Ordinary or self-adhesive gum. Multicoloured.

2264	50c. Type **669**	65	50
2265	50c. Margaret Court in action	65	50
2266	50c. Rod Laver with Wimbledon Trophy	65	50
2267	50c. Rod Laver in action	65	50

670 Blue Orchid

672 "Hari Withers" Camellia

671 Snapper and Fishing from Beach

2003. Fauna and Flora (6th series). Rainforest, Daintree National Park. Multicoloured. Ordinary or self-adhesive gum.

2272	50c. Orange-thighed tree frog	60	45
2273	50c. Green-spotted triangle (butterfly)	60	45
2274	50c. Striped possum	60	45
2275	50c. Yellow-bellied sunbird	60	45
2276	$1.45 Type **670**	1·25	1 10

2003. Angling in Australia. Multicoloured.

2282	50c. Type **671**	60	60
2283	50c. Murray cod and flooded wood	60	60
2284	50c. Brown trout and fly-fishing	60	60
2285	50c. Yellow-finned tuna and sea-fishing from launch	60	60
2286	50c. Barramundi and anglers in mangrove swamp	60	60

2003. Australian Horticulture. Multicoloured. (a) Size 25 × 36 mm. Ordinary gum.

2287	50c. Type **672**	55	50
2288	50c. "Victoria Gold" rose	55	50
2289	50c. "Superb" grevillea	55	50
2290	50c. "Bush Tango" kangaroo paw	55	50
2291	50c. "Midnight" rhododendron	55	50

(b) Size 21 × 33 mm. Self-adhesive.

2292	50c. Type **672**	50	50
2293	50c. "Victoria Gold" rose	50	50
2294	50c. "Superb" grevillea	50	50
2295	50c. "Bush Tango" kangaroo paw	50	50
2296	50c. "Midnight" rhododendron	50	50

673 "Ned Kelly" (Sir Sidney Nolan)

2003. Australian Paintings (1st series). Multicoloured.

2297	$1 Type **673**	1·10	1·10
2298	$1 "Family Home, Suburban Exterior" (Howard Arkley)	1·10	1·10
2299	$1.45 "Cord Long Drawn, Expectant" (Robert Jacks)	1·40	1·40
2300	$2.45 "Girl" (Joy Hester)	2·25	2·50

674 Queen Elizabeth II, 1953 (photograph by Cecil Beaton)

2003. 50th Anniv of Coronation. Multicoloured.

2301	50c. Type **674**	75	45
2302	$2.45 St. Edward's Crown	2·50	3·00
MS2303	105 × 70 mm. Nos. 2301/2	3·25	3·25

No. 2301 also comes self-adhesive.

675 Untitled Painting by Ningura Napurrula

2003. International Stamps. Art of Papunya Tula Movement. Showing untitled paintings by Aboriginal artists. Multicoloured.

2305	$1.10 Type **675**	90	95
2306	$1.65 Naata Nungurrayi	1·30	1·40
2307	$2.20 Graham Tjupurrula (55 × 24 mm)	1·90	1·90
2308	$3.30 Dini Campbell Tjampitjinpa (55 × 24 mm)	3·00	3·00

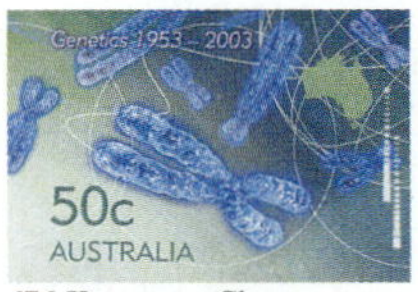

676 Kangaroo Chromosomes

2003. 50th Anniv of Discovery of DNA. Multicoloured.

2309	50c. Type **676**	70	55
2310	50c. DNA double helix	70	55

677 *Oscar W* (paddle-steamer)

2003. 150th Anniv of Murray River Shipping. Multicoloured. Ordinary or self-adhesive gum.

2311	50c. Type **677**	60	50
2312	50c. *Marion* (paddle-steamer)	60	50
2313	50c. *Ruby* (paddle-steamer)	60	50
2314	50c. *Pyap* (cruise vessel)	60	50
2315	50c. *Adelaide* (paddle-steamer)	60	50

678 Christmas Tree

2003. Greetings Stamps. Peace and Goodwill. Design, adapted from Christmas 2001 (1st issue) (Nos. 2136/7). Multicoloured. (a) Domestic Mail.

2321	50c. Type **678**	40	45

(b) International Mail.

2322	90c. Star	75	80

679 Sir Samuel Griffith (first Chief Justice)

2003. Centenary of High Court of Australia.

2323	**679**	50c. purple, black and red	55	45
2324	–	$1.45 vermilion, red and black	1·50	1·50
MS2325		105 × 70 mm. Nos. 2323/4	2·00	2·00

DESIGN: $1.45, "JUSTICE".

680 Ulysses Butterfly

2003. Stamp Collecting Month. Bugs and Butterflies. Multicoloured. Ordinary or self-adhesive gum.

2326 50c. Type **680** 50 45
2327 50c. Leichhardt's grasshopper 50 45
2328 50c. Vedalia ladybird . . . 50 45
2329 50c. Green mantid and captured damselfly . . . 50 45
2330 50c. Emperor gum moth caterpillar 50 45
2331 50c. Fiddler beetle 50 45
MS2332 170 × 85 mm. Nos. 2326/31 2·75 2·50

681 Hands passing Ball and Players

2003. Rugby World Cup Championship, Australia. Multicoloured. (a) Domestic Mail.

2339 50c. Type **681** 55 45

(b) International Mail.

2340 $1.10 Trophy (Webb Ellis Cup) and Telstra Stadium 1·10 1·00
2341 $1.65 Hand grasping ball and player taking shot at goal . . . . 1·50 2·00
MS2342 115 × 70 mm. Nos. 2339/41 2·75 3·00

682 "Active with ASTHMA" and Silhouettes of Sportspeople

2003. National Asthma Week Campaign.

2343 **682** 50c. multicoloured . . . 1·00 45

683 Mary, Baby Jesus and Angels

2003. Christmas. Multicoloured.

2344 45c. Type **683** 45 15
2345 50c. Three Wise Men . . . 45 15
2346 90c. Angel appearing to shepherds 80 90
No. 2344 also comes self-adhesive.

684 Joan Sutherland as *Lucia di Lammermoor*, 1980

2004. Australian Legends (8th series). Dame Joan Sutherland (opera singer). Multicoloured. Ordinary or self-adhesive gum.

2350 50c. Type **684** 80 80
2351 50c. Joan Sutherland . . . 80 80

685 Aboriginal shell necklace and bracelet

2004. Bicentenary of Settlement of Hobart, Tasmania. Multicoloured.

2352 50c. Type **685** 70 55
2353 50c. Cheshunt House, Deloraine 70 55
2354 $1 "Mount Wellington and Hobart Town from Kangaroo Point" (John Glover) . . . . 1·40 1·50
2355 $1 Mountains, south west Tasmania . . . . . . 1·40 1·50
MS2356 135 × 72 mm. Nos. 2352/5 3·75 3·75

686 Ross Bridge, Tasmania, 1836

2004. Landmark Bridges. Multicoloured. Ordinary or self-adhesive gum.

2357 50c. Type **686** 85 70
2358 50c. Lockyer Creek Bridge, Queensland, 1911 . . . . 85 70
2359 50c. Sydney Harbour Bridge, 1932 . . . . . . 85 70
2360 50c. Birkenhead Bridge, Adelaide, 1940 . . . . . 85 70
2361 50c. Bolte Bridge, Melbourne, 1999 . . . . 85 70

687 Stylized "Southern Cross"

689 Queen Elizabeth II (from photo by Dorothy Wilding)

688 Solar Systems CS500 Dish ("solar")

2004. Greetings Stamp.

2367 **687** 50c. multicoloured . . . 55 45

2004. Renewable Energy. Multicoloured. Ordinary or self-adhesive gum.

2368 50c. Type **688** 75 75
2369 50c. Wind turbines ("wind") 75 75
2370 50c. Snowy Mountains Hydro-electric Scheme ("hydro") 75 75
2371 50c. Sugar cane field, bagasse (waste plant fibre) and sugar mill ("biomass") 75 75

2004. 50th Anniv of Royal Tour to Australia.

2376 **689** 50c. purple, black and grey . . . . 1·25 55

690 Red Lacewing

692 Shaw Savill Lines *Dominion Monarch*

691 Cockatoos and Aircraft

2004. Fauna and Flora (7th series). Rainforest Butterflies. Multicoloured.

2377 5c. Type **690** 15 10
2378 10c. Blue-banded eggfly . . 15 10
2379 75c. Cruiser . . . . 1·00 35
2380 $2 Ulysses and red lacewing butterflies and Daintree Rainforest (50 × 30 mm) 3·00 2·25

2004. Australian Innovations. Multicoloured. Ordinary or self-adhesive gum.

2381 50c. Type **691** (black box flight recorder, 1961) . . 85 70
2382 50c. Pregnant woman (ultrasound imaging equipment, 1976) 85 70
2383 50c. Driver's hands on wheel (Racecam TV sport coverage, 1979) 85 70
2384 50c. Kangaroo with joey and car (baby safety capsule, 1984) 85 70
2385 50c. Portion of banknote and tree (polymer banknotes, 1988) 85 70

2004. "Bon Voyage". Ocean Liners. Advertising posters. Multicoloured.

2391 50c. Type **692** 90 45
2392 $1 Union Steam Ship Co. *Awatea* . . . . 1·50 85
2393 $1.45 Orient Line *Ormonde* & *Orsova* . . . . 2·00 2·00
2394 $2 Aberdeen & Commonwealth Line liner passing under bridge . . . 2·75 2·75
No. 2395 also comes self-adhesive.

693 Eureka Flag (Southern Cross)

2004. 150th Anniv of Eureka Stockade. Multicoloured.

2396 50c. Type **693** 60 45
2397 $2.45 Peter Lalor (gold diggers leader) and detail from "Swearing allegiance to the Southern Cross 1854" (Alphonse Doudiet) 2·75 2·50
MS2398 106 × 69 mm. Nos. 2396/7 3·25 3·25

694 Koala

2004. "Impressions". Australian Wildlife and Heritage. Multicoloured.

2399 $1 Type **694** . . . . . . 1·50 1·00
2400 $1 Little penguin . . . . . 1·50 1·00
2401 $1.45 Clown anemonefish (horiz) . . . . 1·75 1·50
2402 $2.45 Gold Coast (horiz) . . 2·75 2·75

695 Swimming

2004. Olympic Games, Athens, Greece. Multicoloured.

2403 50c. Type **695** 60 45
2404 $1.65 Sprinting . . . . . . 1·75 1·90
2405 $1.65 Cycling . . . . 2·50 1·90

696 Ian Thorpe (Men's 400m Freestyle Swimming)

2004. Australian Gold Medal Winners at Olympic Games, Athens. Multicoloured.

2406 50c. Type **696** 80 70
2407 50c. Women's 4 × 100m relay team 80 70
2408 50c. Sara Carrigan (Road Race Cycling) 80 70
2409 50c. Petria Thomas (Women's 100m Butterfly Swimming) 80 70
2410 50c. Suzanne Balogh (Women's Trap Shooting) 80 70
2411 50c. Ian Thorpe (Men's 200m Freestyle Swimming) 80 70
2412 50c. Jodie Henry (Women's 100m Freestyle Swimming) 80 70
2413 50c. Anna Meares (Women's 500m Time Trial Cycling) 80 70
2414 50c. James Tomkins and Drew Ginn (Men's Pair Rowing) 80 70
2415 50c. Grant Hacket (Men's 1500m Freestyle Swimming) 80 70
2416 50c. Women's 4 × 100m Medley Relay Swimming Team 80 70
2417 50c. Chantelle Newberry (Women's 10m Platform Diving) 80 70
2418 50c. Men's 4000m pursuit cycling team 80 70
2419 50c. Ryan Bayley (Men's Individual Sprint Cycling) 80 70
2420 50c. Graeme Brown and Stuart O'Grady (Men's Madison Cycling) 80 70
2421 50c. Ryan Bayley (Men's Keirin Cycling) 80 70
2422 50c. Men's hockey team . . 80 70

697 Entrance Beach, Broome, Western Australia

2004. International Stamps. Coastlines. Multicoloured.

2423 $1.20 Type **697** . . . . . . 1·25 50
2424 $1.80 Mt. William National Park, Tasmania . . . . . 1·75 90
2425 $2.40 Potato Point, Bodalla, New South Wales . . . . 2·25 1·50
2426 $3.60 Point Gibbon, Eyre Peninsula, South Australia 3·00 2·75

698 Sheet of Early Australian Stamp (No. 16) (½-size illustration)

2004. Treasures from the Archives (1st series). Ordinary or self-adhesive gum.

2427 **698** $5 multicoloured . . . . 6·00 5·50
See also No. 2555.

699 Stephenson 2-4-0 (Melbourne–Sandridge, 1854)

2004. 150th Anniv of Australian Railways. Multicoloured. Ordinary or self-adhesive gum.

2429 50c. Type **699** 90 90
2430 50c. Locomotive No. 1 (Sydney–Parramatta, 1855) 90 90
2431 50c. B12 Class locomotive (Helidon–Toowoomba, 1867) 90 90
2432 50c. G Class train (Kalgoorlie–Port Augusta, 1917) 90 90
2433 50c. *The Ghan* (Alice Springs–Darwin, 2004) . . 90 90

700 "Ezzie" (black and white cat)

702 Mary and Jesus

701 Mick Doohan (Repsol)

2004. Stamp Collecting Months. Cats and Dogs. Multicoloured. (a) Ordinary gum.

2439 50c. Type **700** 75 60
2440 50c. "Tinkerbell" (ginger and white kitten) 75 60
2441 50c. "Max" (Labrador puppy) 75 60
2442 50c. "Bridie" and "Lily" (West Highland terriers) 75 60
2443 $1 "Edward" (Jack Russell terrier) . . . . 1·75 1·50
MS2444 170 × 85 mm. Nos. 2439/43 4·25 3·25

(b) Self-adhesive.

2445 50c. "Max" (Labrador puppy) 70 70
2446 50c. Type **700** 70 70
2447 50c. "Bridie" and "Lily" (West Highland Terriers) 70 70

2448 50c. "Tinkerbell" (ginger and white kitten) 70 70
2449 $1 "Edward" (Jack Russell terrier) . . . . 1·50 1·50

2004. Formula 1 Motorcycle Racing. Multicoloured. Ordinary or self-adhesive gum.
2455 50c. Type **701** 60 65
2456 50c. Wayne Gardner (Racing Honda) 60 65
2457 50c. Troy Bayliss (Ducati) 60 65
2458 50c. Daryl Beattie (Team Suzuki) 60 65
2459 50c. Garry McCoy (Red Bull) 60 65

2004. Christmas. Multicoloured. (a) Domestic mail.
2460 45c. Type **702** 40 15
2461 50c. The Angel and the shepherds 45 15

(b) International mail.
2462 $1 The Three Wise Men (horiz) 80 80

(c) Self-adhesive.
2464 $1 The Three Wise Men (horiz) 80 85

703 Tennis Player and Match, Warehousemen's Cricket Ground, Melbourne, c. 1905

2005. Centenary of Australian Open Tennis Championships. Multicoloured.
2465 50c. Type **703** 70 45
2466 $1.80 Woman player and match, Melbourne Park, c. 2005 . . . . . . 2·50 2·75

704 Prue Acton

705 Princess Parrot

2005. Australian Legends (9th series). Fashion Designers. Multicoloured. Ordinary or self-adhesive gum.
2473 50c. Type **704** 60 70
2474 50c. Jenny Bannister 60 70
2475 50c. Collette Dinnigan . . . 60 70
2476 50c. Akira Isogawa 60 70
2477 50c. Joe Saba 60 70
2478 50c. Carla Zampatti 60 70

2005. Australian Parrots. Multicoloured. Ordinary or self-adhesive gum.
2484 50c. Type **705** 80 70
2485 50c. Rainbow lorikeet . . . 80 70
2486 50c. Green rosella 80 70
2487 50c. Red-capped parrot . . 80 70
2488 50c. Purple-crowned lorikeet 80 70

706 Sir Donald Bradman's Cap

707 Bumble Bee Toy

2005. Sporting Treasures. Multicoloured.
2489 50c. Type **706** . . . . . . 1·00 85
2490 50c. Lionel Rose's boxing gloves . . . . 1·00 85
2491 $1 Marjorie Jackson's running spikes . . . . . 1·50 1·50
2492 $1 Phar Lap's racing silks 1·50 1·50

2005. Greetings Stamps (1st series). "Marking the Occasion". Multicoloured.
2493 50c. Type **707** 85 85
2494 50c. Red roses 85 85
2495 50c. Wrapped presents . . . 85 85
2496 50c. Kangaroos at sunset . . 85 85
2497 50c. Bouquet of white flowers 85 85
2498 $1 Hand holding bouquet of cream roses . . . . . . 1·50 1·25
2499 $1.10 Koala . . . . 1·50 1·25
2500 $1.20 Shell on sandy beach 1·60 1·60
2501 $1.80 Sydney Opera House 2·50 2·75

Nos. 2493/8 are for domestic use and 2499/51 are for international use.

See also Nos. 2556/7.

708 Greater Blue Mountains Area, New South Wales

710 Rotary Emblem and Man supporting Globe

709 Tribrachidium

2005. World Heritage Sites. Multicoloured.
2502 50c. Type **708** . . . . . . 1·00 85
2503 50c. Blenheim Palace, England . . . . 1·00 85
2504 50c. Wet Tropics, Queensland . . . . 1·00 85
2505 50c. Stonehenge, England 1·00 85
2506 $1 Purnululu National Park, West Australia . . . . . 1·75 1·50
2507 $1 Heart of Neolithic Orkney, Scotland . . . . 1·75 1·50
2508 $1.80 Uluru-Kata Tjuta National Park, Northern Territories . . . . 2·50 2·75
2509 $1.80 Hadrian's Wall, England . . . . 2·50 2·75

Nos. 2502/7 are for domestic use and 2508/9 are for international use.

Stamps in similar designs were also issued by Great Britain.

2005. Creatures of the Slime (Ediacaran fossils). Multicoloured.
2510 50c. Type **709** 85 85
2511 50c. Dickinsonia 85 85
2512 50c. Spriggina 85 85
2513 50c. Kimberella 85 85
2514 50c. Inaria 85 85
2515 $1 Charniodiscus 1.501 . . 1·50 1·50
MS2516 170 × 210 mm. Nos. 2510/15 5·00 5·50

2005. Centenary of Rotary International. Ordinary or self-adhesive gum.
2517 **710** 50c. multicoloured . . . 1·00 85

711 Obverse of Coin showing Head of Queen Victoria

2005. 150th Anniv of First Australian Coin. Design showing one sovereign coin and Sydney Mint building. Multicoloured.
2519 50c. Type **711** 85 85
2520 $2.45 Reverse of coin showing olive wreath . . 3·25 3·25
MS2521 105 × 69 mm. As Nos. 2519/20 but coins in gold foil 4·00 4·25

712 Queen at Opening Ceremony for Commonwealth Heads of Government Meeting, Queensland, 2002

2005. Queen's Birthday.
2522 **712** 50c. multicoloured . . . 1·00 60

713 Superb Lyrebird

2005. International Stamps. Bush Wildlife. Multicoloured.
2523 $1 Type **713** . . . . 1·50 60
2524 $1.10 Laughing kookaburra 1·50 65
2525 $1.20 Koala . . . . 1·60 80
2526 $1.80 Red kangaroo . . . . 2·50 1·50

Nos. 2524/6 also come self-adhesive.

714 Sturt's Desert Pea

2005. Australian Wildflowers (1st series). Multicoloured. Ordinary or self-adhesive gum.
2530 50c. Type **714** 85 85
2531 50c. Coarse-leaved mallee 85 85
2532 50c. Common fringe lily . . 85 85
2533 50c. Swamp daisy 85 85

See also Nos. 2590/MS2594 and 2759/62.

715 Vineyard

2005. Australian Wine. Multicoloured.
2538 50c. Type **715** 85 85
2539 50c. Ripening grapes . . . 85 85
2540 $1 Harvesting grapes . . . 1·50 1·50
2541 $1 Casks of wine . . . . . 1·50 1·50
2542 $1.45 Glasses of red and white wine and cheese . . 2·25 2·50

Nos. 2538/9 also come self-adhesive.

716 Snowgum

2005. Native Trees. Multicoloured. Ordinary or self-adhesive gum.
2550 50c. Type **716** 60 65
2551 50c. Wollemi pine 60 65
2552 50c. Boab 60 65
2553 50c. Karri 60 65
2554 50c. Moreton Bay fig . . . 60 65

717 1888 20s. New South Wales Stamps (½-size illustration)

2005. Treasures from the Archives (2nd issue).
2555 **717** $5 multicoloured . . . . 7·00 7·00

718 Christmas Tree with Lights

2005. Greetings Stamps. "Marking the Occasion" (2nd series). Multicoloured.
2556 45c. Type **718** 85 85
2557 50c. Map of Australia with stars 85 85

719 Chloe the Chicken

720 Madonna and Child

2005. Stamp Collecting Month. "Down on the Farm". Multicoloured.
2565 50c. Type **719** 60 70
2566 50c. Lucy the Lamb . . . 60 70
2567 50c. Gilbert the Goat . . . 60 70
2568 50c. Ralph the Piglet . . . 60 70
2569 50c. Abigail the Cow . . . 60 70
2570 $1 Harry the Horse . . . . 1·25 1·40
MS2564 170 × 85 mm. Nos. 2558/63 5·00 5·50

Nos. 2558/2563 also come self-adhesive.

2005. Christmas. Multicoloured. Ordinary or self-adhesive gum. (i) Domestic mail.
2571 45c. Type **720** 75 15

(ii) International Mail.
2572 $1 Adoring angel (horiz) . . 1·25 85

721 Emblem

722 Mrs. Norm Everage, 1969

2006. Commonwealth Games, Melbourne (1st issue). Ordinary or self-adhesive gum.
2575 **721** 50c. multicoloured . . . 60 45

See also Nos. 2596/2600 and MS2607/MS2623.

2006. Australian Legends (10th series). Barry Humphries (satirist and actor). Multicoloured. Ordinary or self-adhesive gum.
2582 50c. Type **722** 75 60
2583 50c. As Mrs. Edna Everage, 1973 . . . . 75 60
2584 50c. As Dame Edna Everage, 1982 . . . . . 75 60
2585 50c. As Dame Edna Everage, 2004 . . . . . 75 60
2586 50c. Barry Humphries . . . 75 60

723 Red Rose

2006. Greetings Stamp. Roses. Ordinary or self-adhesive gum.
2587 **723** 50c. multicoloured . . . 50 45

724 *Pincushion Hakea*

2006. Australian Wildflowers (2nd series). Multicoloured.
2590 $1 Type **724** 85 50
2591 $2 Donkey orchid . . . . . 1·70 1·25
2592 $5 Mangles kangaroo paw (49 × 29 mm) . . . . . . 4·25 4·50
2593 $10 Waratah (49 × 29 mm) 8·75 9·00
MS2594 105 × 70 mm. $10 As No. 2593 (49 × 29 mm) . . . . 8·75 9·00

725 Dale Begg-Smith

2006. Dale-Begg Smith's Gold Medal for Men's Moguls Skiing at Winter Olympic Games, Turin.
2595 **725** 50c. multicoloured . . . 65 55

726 Athlete at Start

2006. Commonwealth Games, Melbourne (2nd issue). Multicoloured. (a) Ordinary gum. (i) Domestic Mail.
2596 50c. Type **726** 50 45

(ii) International Post.
2597 $1.25 Cyclist . . . . 2·25 2·00
2598 $1.85 Netball . . . . 2·75 3·25
MS2599 142 × 75 mm. Nos. 2596/8 5·50 5·50

(b) Self-adhesive.
2600 50c. Type **726** 50 45

727 Platypus

2006. International Post. Native Wildlife. Multicoloured.
2601 5c. Type **727** 10 10
2602 25c. Short-beaked echidna 20 25
2603 $1.25 Common wombat . . 1·50 1·10
2604 $1.85 Tasmanian devil . . . 2·00 1·60
2605 $2.50 Greater bilby . . . . 2·75 2·00
2606 $3.70 Dingo . . . . 3·75 3·25

728 Tram with Feathered "Wings" (Opening Ceremony)

2006. Commonwealth Games (3rd issue). Seventeen sheets each 180 × 200 mm containing horiz designs as T **728** showing opening/closing ceremonies (Nos. **MS**2607, **MS**2622) or Australian gold medal winners (others). Multicoloured.
MS2607 50c. × 5 No. 1 Opening Ceremony . . . . 2·75 3·25
MS2608 50c. × 5 No. 2 . . . . 2·75 3·25
MS2609 50c. × 10 No. 3 . . . . 5·00 6·00
MS2610 50c. × 5 No. 4 . . . . 2·75 3·25
MS2611 50c. × 10 No. 5 . . . . 5·00 6·00
MS2612 50c. × 5 No. 6 . . . . 2·75 3·25
MS2613 50c. × 5 No. 7 . . . . 2·75 3·25
MS2614 50c. × 10 No. 8 . . . . 5·00 6·00
MS2615 50c. × 5 No. 9 . . . . 2·75 3·25
MS2616 50c. × 10 No. 10 . . . . 5·00 6·00
MS2617 50c. × 5 No. 11 . . . . 2·75 3·25
MS2618 50c. × 10 No. 12 . . . . 5·00 6·00
MS2619 50c. × 10 No. 13 . . . . 5·00 6·00
MS2620 50c. × 10 No. 14 . . . . 5·00 6·00
MS2621 50c. × 5 No. 15 . . . . 2·75 3·25
MS2622 50c. × 5 No. 16 Closing Ceremony . . . . 2·75 3·25
MS2623 50c. × 10 No. 17 Most memorable moment Kerryn McCann's Marathon victory 5·00 6·00
Nos. **MS**2607/23 are numbered from 1 to 17 at the foot of the sheet.

729 "Queen Elizabeth II in Garter Robes" (Pietro Annigoni)

2006. 80th Birthday of Queen Elizabeth II. Multicoloured. (a) Ordinary gum.
2624 50c. Type **729** 65 45
2625 $2.45 Queen Elizabeth II (photo by Cecil Beaton) 3·50 3·75
MS2626 105 × 70 mm. Nos. 2624/5 4·00 4·00
No. **MS**2626 also commemorates the 50th anniversary of the portrait by Annigoni.

(b) Self-adhesive.
2627 50c. Type **729** 75 65

730 Point Lonsdale, Victoria, 1902

731 Koala with Cub

2006. Lighthouses of the 20th Century. Ordinary or self-adhesive gum. Multicoloured.
2628 50c. Type **730** 90 90
2629 50c. Cape Don, Northern Territory, 1916 . . . . . . 90 90
2630 50c. Wollongong Head, New South Wales, 1937 . . . 90 90
2631 50c. Casuarina Point, West Australia, 1971 . . . . . 90 90
2632 50c. Point Cartwright, Queensland, 1979 . . . . 90 90

2006. International Stamps. "Greetings from Australia". Ordinary or self-adhesive gum. Multicoloured.
2638 $1.25 Type **731** . . . . . 1·60 1·25
2639 $1.85 Royal Exhibition Building, Melbourne . . . 2·40 2·75

732 Boy heading Ball ("PLAY")

2006. World Cup Football Championship, Germany. Soccer in Australia. Ordinary gum. Multicoloured.
(i) Domestic Mail.
2642 50c. Type **732** 60 70
2643 50c. Player kicking ball ("GOAL") 60 70

(ii) International Post.
2644 $1.25 Goalkeeper ("SAVE") 1·60 1·25
2645 $1.85 Player with ball ("SHOT") . . . . 2·40 2·75
MS2646 Circular 170 × 170 mm. Nos. 2642/5 . . . . 4·75 4·75

(b) Self-adhesive.
2647 50c. Type **732** 65 60
2648 50c. As No. 2643 . . . . . 65 60

733 Kate sorting Mail

2006. "Postie Kate". Ordinary or self-adhesive gum. Multicoloured.
2649 50c. Type **733** 70 70
2650 50c. On motorcycle, giving letter to woman 70 70
2651 50c. With van, delivering parcel 70 70
2652 50c. Riding motorcycle, passing mailbox 70 70
2653 50c. With mail satchel on shoulder 70 70

734 Blue Whale

2006. Endangered Species. Whales. Multicoloured. (a) Ordinary gum. (i) Domestic Mail.
2659 50c. Type **734** 75 60
2660 50c. Humpback whale . . . 75 60

(ii) International Post.
2661 $1.25 Fin whale . . . . . . 1·75 1·25
2662 $1.85 Southern bottlenose whale . . . . 2·75 2·75
MS2663 69 × 66 mm. Nos. 2659/62 5·50 5·00

(b) Self-adhesive. (i) Domestic Mail.
2664 50c. Type **734** 75 65
2665 50c. As No. 2660 . . . . . 75 65

(ii) International Post.
2666 $1.25 As No. 2661 . . . . 1·60 1·60
2667 $1.85 As No. 2662 . . . . 2·40 2·40

2006. Le Salon du Timbre Stamp Exhibition, Paris. No. **MS**2646 inscr "LE SALON DU TIMBRE & DE L'ECRIT 17 AU 25 JUIN 2006 PARC FLORAL DE PARIS www.salondutimbre.fr" on sheet margin.
MS2668 Circular 170 × 170 mm. Nos. 2642/5 . . . . 4·25 4·50

735 Surfing

2006. Extreme Sports. Multicoloured.
2669 50c. Type **735** 70 50
2670 $1 Snowboarding . . . . . 1·40 1·10
2671 $1.45 Skateboarding . . . . 1·75 1·90
2672 $2 Freestyle motoX . . . . 2·75 3·00

736 Ford TT Truck, 1917

2006. Driving through the Years. Multicoloured. (a) Ordinary or self-adhesive gum.
2678 50c. Type **736** 70 70
2679 50c. Holden FE, 1956 . . . 70 70
2680 50c. Morris 850 (Mini Minor), 1961 . . . . . . 70 70
2681 50c. Holden Sandman HX panel van, 1976 . . . . . 70 70
2682 50c. Toyota LandCruiser FJ60, 1985 . . . . 70 70

737 "Sunbury Rock Festival" (1972)

2006. Rock Posters (1st series). Multicoloured. (a) Ordinary or self-adhesive gum.
2683 50c. Type **737** 70 70
2684 50c. "Magic Dirt" (2002) . . 70 70
2685 50c. "Masters Apprentices" (1969) 70 70
2686 50c. "Goanna's Spirit of Place" (1983) 70 70
2687 50c. "Angels/Sports/Paul Kelly" (c. 1979) 70 70
2688 50c. "Midnight Oil" (c. 1979) 70 70
2689 50c. "Big Day Out" (2003) 70 70
2690 50c. "Apollo Bay Music Festival" (1999) 70 70
2691 50c. "Rolling Stones Australian Tour" (1973) 70 70
2692 50c. "Mental as Anything" (1990) 70 70
See also Nos. 2808/11.

738 White Shark

2006. Stamp Collecting Month. Dangerous Australians. Multicoloured. (a) Ordinary gum.
2703 50c. Type **738** 70 70
2704 50c. Eastern brown snake 70 70
2705 50c. Box jellyfish 70 70
2706 50c. Saltwater crocodile . . 70 70
2707 50c. Blue-ringed octopus . . 70 70
2708 $1 Yellow-bellied sea snake 1·25 1·25
MS2709 130 × 90 mm. Nos. 2703/8 3·75 3·75

(b) Self-adhesive.
2710 50c. Type **738** 70 70
2711 50c. As No. 2704 . . . . . 70 70
2712 50c. As No. 2705 . . . . . 70 70
2713 50c. As No. 2706 . . . . . 70 70
2714 50c. As No. 2707 . . . . . 70 70
2715 $1 As No. 2708 . . . . . . 1·25 1·25

739 "In Melbourne Tonight"

2006. 50th Anniv of Television in Australia. Multicoloured. (a) Ordinary or self-adhesive gum.
2716 50c. Type **739** 70 70
2717 50c. "Homicide" 70 70
2718 50c. "Dateline" 70 70
2719 50c. "Neighbours" 70 70
2720 50c. "Kath and Kim" . . . 70 70

2006. China 2006 Stamp and Coin Expo. Two sheets, each 110 × 80 mm containing No. 2638, design on sheet margin given.
MS2726 **731** (a) $1.25 multicoloured (Great Wall of China). (b) $1.25 multicoloured (Sydney Opera House) . . . . 3·00 3·00

740 2s. Melbourne across River Yarra Stamp

2006. 50th Anniv of Olympic Games, Melbourne. Showing Australia 1956 Olympic Games stamps and contemporary photographs of Melbourne. Multicoloured.
2727 50c. Type **740** 80 80
2728 50c. River Yarra, Melbourne 80 80
2729 $1 1s. Collins Street stamp 1·40 1·40
2730 $1 Collins Street, Melbourne 1·40 1·40

741 Virgin Mary and Baby Jesus

742 Victorious Australian Cricketers

2006. Christmas. Multicoloured. (a) Ordinary gum. (i) Domestic mail.
2731 45c. Type **741** 80 30
2732 50c. Magi with gift 80 35

(ii) International Mail.
2733 $1.05 Young shepherd with lamb . . . . 1·40 1·10

(b) Self-adhesive. Smaller design 22 × 33 mm. (i) Domestic mail.
2734 45c. Type **741** 70 45

(ii) International Mail.
2735 $1.05 As No. 2733 . . . . 1·25 1·10

2007. "Australia wins the Ashes". Multicoloured. (a) Ordinary gum. (i) Domestic Mail.
2736 50c. Type **742** 70 70

(ii) International Post.
2737 $1.85 Australian team with Ashes Urn . . . . 2·10 2·25
MS2738 160 × 80 mm. Nos. 2736/7 3·00 3·25

(b) Self-adhesive. (i) Domestic Mail.
2739 50c. As No. 2736 . . . . . 70 70

(ii) International Post.
2740 $1.85 As No. 2737 . . . . 2·10 2·25

743 Scobie Breasley (jockey), 1936

744 Tasmanian Christmas Bell

2007. Australian Legends (11th series). Legends of Australian Horse Racing. Multicoloured. (a) Ordinary gum.
2741 50c. Type **743** 70 70
2742 50c. Scobie Breasley on "Santa Claus" after winning English Derby . . 70 70
2743 50c. Bart Cummings (trainer) holding binoculars, 1966 . . . . 70 70
2744 50c. Bart Cummings holding Melbourne Cup 70 70
2745 50c. Roy Higgins (jockey), 1965 . . . . 70 70
2746 50c. Roy Higgins riding "Light Fingers" to win Melbourne Cup, 1965 . . 70 70
2747 50c. Bob Ingham (breeder), c. 1972 . . . . 70 70
2748 50c. Bob Ingham leading "Lonhro", 2004 . . . . . 70 70
2749 50c. George Moore (jockey), 1957 . . . . 70 70
2750 50c. George Moore riding "Tulloch", 1960 . . . . . 70 70
2751 50c. John Tapp (race commentator), 1972 . . . 70 70
2752 50c. John Tapp at microphone, 1998 . . . . 70 70

(b) Self-adhesive.
2753 50c. Type **743** 70 70
2754 50c. As No. 2743 . . . . . 70 70
2755 50c. As No. 2746 . . . . . 70 70
2756 50c. As No. 2748 . . . . . 70 70
2757 50c. As No. 2749 . . . . . 70 70
2758 50c. As No. 2751 . . . . . 70 70

2007. Australian Wildflowers (3rd series). Multicoloured. Ordinary or self-adhesive gum.
2759 50c. Type **744** 70 70
2760 50c. Green spider flower . . 70 70
2761 50c. Sturt's desert rose . . 70 70
2762 50c. *Phebalium whitei* . . . 70 70

745 Swimmer

2007. 12th FINA (Federation Internationale de Natation) World Championships, Melbourne. Ordinary or self-adhesive gum.
2767 **745** 50c. multicoloured . . . 70 70

746 Maria Island, Tasmania

2007. International Post. Island Jewels. Multicoloured. (a) Ordinary gum.

2769	10c. Type **746**	15	10
2770	30c. Rottnest Island, West Australia	45	40
2771	$1.30 Green Island, Queensland	2·00	2·10
2772	$1.95 Fraser Island, Queensland	2·50	2·25
2773	$2.60 Kangaroo Island, South Australia	3·25	3·00
2774	$3.85 Lord Howe Island, New South Wales	3·75	3·50
	(b) Self-adhesive gum.		
2775	$1.30 As No. 2771	2·00	2·10
2776	$1.95 As No. 2772	2·50	2·25

747 Female Lifeguard with Reel

2007. Year of the Surf Lifesaver. Multicoloured. (a) Ordinary gum.

2777	50c. Type **747**	50	45
2778	50c. Male lifeguards	50	45
2779	$1 Surf boat	2·00	2·10
2780	$2 "Nippers" (life saving club's children's programme)	2·50	2·25
	(b) Self-adhesive gum.		
2781	50c. As No. 2778	50	45
2782	50c. Type **747**	50	45
MS2783	160 × 90 mm. $2.45 Inflatable rescue boat × 2	6·50	6·75

748 Aries

749 "At the Beach" (Percy Trompf)

2007. Signs of the Zodiac. Multicoloured. Ordinary or self-adhesive gum.

2784	50c. Type **748**	70	70
2785	50c. Taurus	70	70
2786	50c. Gemini	70	70
2787	50c. Cancer	70	70
2788	50c. Leo	70	70
2789	50c. Virgo	70	70
2790	50c. Libra	70	70
2791	50c. Scorpio	70	70
2792	50c. Sagittarius	70	70
2793	50c. Capricorn	70	70
2794	50c. Aquarius	70	70
2795	50c. Pisces	70	70

2007. Poster Art (2nd series). Nostalgic Tourism. Showing 1930s tourism posters. Multicoloured.

2808	50c. Type **749**	70	70
2809	$1 "Fishing" (John Vickery)	1·30	1·30
2810	$2 "Riding in the Country" (James Northfield)	2·75	2·75
2811	$2.45 "Winter Sport" (James Northfield)	3·25	3·25

750 Queen Elizabeth II in Australia, March 2006

2007. Queen's Birthday.

2812	**750** 50c. multicoloured	1·00	1·00

751 *Admella* (steamship), 1859

2007. Historic Shipwrecks. Multicoloured.

2813	50c. Type **751**	70	70
2814	$1 *Loch Ard* (clipper), 1878	1·30	1·30
2815	$2 *Dunbar* (clipper), 1857	2·75	2·75

752 Yellow-footed Rock-wallaby

753 "The Burning Bicycle"

2007. International Post. "Country to Coast". Multicoloured.

2816	$1.30 Type **752**	1·80	1·80
2817	$1.95 Sydney Harbour Bridge	2·75	2·75

2007. Circus: Under the Big Top. Multicoloured. Ordinary or self-adhesive gum.

2818	50c. Type **753**	70	70
2819	50c. "The Inside-out Man"	70	70
2820	50c. "The Dental Trapeze"	70	70
2821	50c. "The Banana Lady"	70	70
2822	50c. "The Human Cannonball"	70	70

754 Big Golden Guitar, Tamworth, New South Wales

755 Sydney Harbour Bridge

2007. 'Big Things' (roadside advertising models). Multicoloured. Ordinary or self-adhesive gum.

2828	50c. Type **754**	70	70
2829	50c. Big lobster, Kingston SE, South Australia	70	70
2830	50c. Big banana, Coffs Harbour, New South Wales	70	70
2831	50c. Big Merino ram, Goulburn, New South Wales	70	70
2832	50c. Big pineapple, Nambour, Queensland	70	70

2007. International Post. 75th Anniv of Sydney Harbour Bridge. Sheet 130 × 90 mm.

MS2838	**755** (a) $1.95 × 2 multicoloured. (b) $1.95 × 2 multicoloured (emblem and '15 JUNE 2007 SYDNEY NSW 2000' inscr in gold on sheet margin) Set of 2 sheets	11·00	11·00

756 Grey-headed flying-fox

2007. Threatened Wildlife. Multicoloured. (i) Domestic mail.

2839	50c. Type **756**	70	70
2840	50c. Mountain Pygmy-possum	70	70
	(ii) International Post.		
2841	$1.25 Flatback turtle	1·80	1·80
2842	$1.30 Wandering albatross	1·80	1·80

757 Former ICI House, Melbourne, 1973

2007. Landmarks: Modernist Australian Architecture. Multicoloured.

2843	50c. Type **757**	70	70
2844	50c. Academy of Science, Canberra, 1958	70	70
2845	$1 Council House, Perth, 1962	1·30	1·30
2846	$2.45 Sydney Opera House, 1973	3·25	3·25
MS2847	90 × 90 mm. Nos. 2843/6	5·75	5·75

758 Delicatessen, Dairy Produce Hall, Queen Victoria Market, Melbourne

759 APEC Logo and Half Globe

2007. Market Feast. Multicoloured. Ordinary or self-adhesive gum.

2848	50c. Type **758**	70	70
2849	50c. Banana seller, Rusty's Market, Cairns	70	70
2850	50c. Sydney Fish Market	70	70
2851	50c. Vegetable stall, Adelaide Central Market	70	70
2852	50c. Potato seller, Hume Murray Farmers Market, Albury Wodonga	70	70

2007. 'BANGKOK 2007' International Stamp Exhibition. Sheet as No. **MS**2838 with 'BANGKOK 2007' emblem inscr in gold on sheet margin.

MS2857a	130 × 90 mm. **755** $1.95 × 2 multicoloured	11·00	11·00

2007. Asia-Pacific Economic Cooperation Forum, Australia. Ordinary or self-adhesive gum.

2858	**759** 50c. multicoloured	70	70

760 SAS Soldiers, Helicopter and Parachutist

2007. 50th Anniv of the Special Air Service.

2860	**760** 50c. multicoloured	70	70

761 Brisbane Botanic Gardens, Mt. Coot-tha

2007. Australian Botanic Gardens. Multicoloured. Ordinary or self-adhesive gum.

2861	50c. Type **761**	70	70
2862	50c. Kings Park and Botanic Garden, Perth	70	70
2863	50c. Royal Botanic Gardens and Domain, Sydney	70	70
2864	50c. Royal Botanic Gardens, Melbourne	70	70
2865	50c. Botanic Gardens of Adelaide	70	70

2007. Collectors International Fair, Prague. No. **MS**2838 inscr 'SBERATEL SAMMLER COLLECTOR' and emblem on sheet margin.

MS2871	130 × 90 mm. **755** $1.95 × 2 multicoloured	5·00	5·25

762 Sputnik (first satellite), 1957

763 Family Picnic outside Caravan, 1950s

2007. Stamp Collecting Month. Blast Off! 50 Years in Space. Multicoloured.

2872	50c. Type **762**	70	70
2873	50c. Cosmonaut Alexei Leonov on first space walk, 1965	70	70
2874	50c. Neil Armstrong walking on Moon, 1969	70	70
2875	50c. *Voyager* space probe, 1977	70	70
2876	50c. International Space Station, 1998	70	70
2877	$1 Hubble Space Telescope and galaxy, 1990	1·30	1·30
MS2878	160 × 90 mm. Nos. 2872/7 and as No. 2877 but 51 × 37 mm	6·25	6·50

Nos. 2872/6 also come self-adhesive.

2007. Caravanning through the Years. Multicoloured. Ordinary or self-adhesive gum.

2884	50c. Type **763**	70	70
2885	50c. Family with kangaroos outside caravan, 1960s	70	70
2886	50c. Family outside caravan, 1970s	70	70
2887	50c. Woman and girl outside caravan, 1980s	70	70
2888	50c. Elderly couple sitting outside caravan, c. 2007	70	70

764 Surfing Santa Stamp Design by Roger Roberts, 1977

765 Red Rose

2007. Christmas. 50 Years of Christmas Stamps. Multicoloured designs showing Christmas stamp designs from previous years redrawn without the face values. (a) Ordinary gum. (i) Domestic Mail.

2894	45c. Type **764**	60	60
2895	45c. Bush Nativity (Baby Jesus with koalas and wallaby) by Marg Towt, 1990	60	60
2896	45c. 'Madonna and Child' by Vivienne Goodman, 1996	60	60
2897	50c. 'The Spirit of Christmas' (Infant Samuel from painting by Joshua Reynolds), 1957 (horiz)	70	70
	(ii) International Post.		
2898	$1.10 Madonna and Child from stained-glass window, 1984	1·50	1·50
	(b) Self-adhesive. (i) Domestic Mail.		
2899	45c. As Type **764**	60	60
2900	45c. As No. 2895	60	60
2901	45c. As No. 2896	60	60
2902	50c. As No. 2897	70	70
	(ii) International Post.		
2903	$1.10 As No. 2898	1·50	1·50
MS2904	156 × 100 mm. As No. 2899 and Nos. 2900/3	4·00	4·25

2008. Greetings stamp. 'Love Blooms'. Ordinary or self-adhesive gum.

2905	**765** 50c. multicoloured	70	70

766 Dame Elisabeth Murdoch

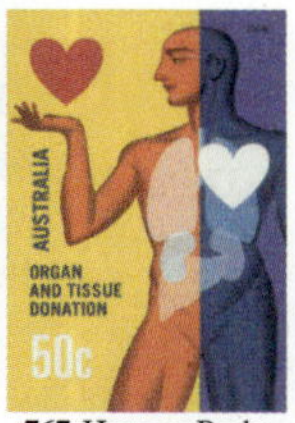

767 Human Body showing Organs

2008. Australian Legends (12th series). Philanthropists. Multicoloured. Ordinary or self-dhesive gum.

2907	50c. Type **766**	75	75
2908	50c. Victor Smorgon and Loti Smorgon	75	75
2909	50c. Lady (Mary) Fairfax	75	75
2910	50c. Frank Lowy	75	75

2008. Organ and Tissue Donation. Ordinary or self-adhesive gum.

2915	**767** 50c. multicoloured	75	75

768 Scout Camp

2008. Centenary of Scouting in Australia. T **768** and similar horiz designs. Multicoloured. (a) Ordinary gum. (i) Domestic Mail.

2917	50c. Type **768**	75	75
	(ii) International Post.		
2918	$1.35 Scouts in circle	1·90	1·90
2919	$2 Lord Baden-Powell (founder)	2·75	2·75
	(b) Self-adhesive. (i) Domestic Mail.		
2920	50c. As Type **768**	75	75

(ii) International Post.
2921 $1.35 As No. 2918 . . . . 1·90 1·90
2922 $2 As No. 2919 . . . . . . 2·75 2·75

769 Hanging Rock, Grose River Gorge, New South Wales

770 Pope Benedict XVI

2008. International Post. 'Gorgeous Australia'. Multicoloured. (a) Ordinary gum.
2923 $1.35 Type **769** . . . . . . 1·90 1·90
2924 $2 Walpa Gorge, Northern Territory . . . . . . 2·75 2·75
2925 $2.70 Katherine Gorge, Northern Territory (horiz) 3·50 3·50
2926 $4 Geikie Gorge, West Australia (horiz) . . . . 5·50 5·50
(b) Self-adhesive
2927 $1.35 As Type 769 . . . . . 1·90 1·90
2928 $2 As No. 2924 . . . . . . 2·75 2·75

2008. World Youth Day, Sydney. Multicoloured. (a) Ordinary gum (i) Domestic Mail.
2929 50c. Type **770** 75 75
(ii) International Post
2930 $1.35 Pope holding crosier 1·90 1·90
2931 $2 Pope giving blessing . . 2·75 2·75
(b) Self-adhesive. (ii) International Post
2932 $1.35 As No. 2930 . . . . 1·90 1·90
2933 $2 As No. 2931 . . . . . . 2·75 2·75

2008. Canberra Stamp Show. Sheet 130 × 90 mm containing No. 2919 × 2. Multicoloured.
MS2934 $2 × 2 Lord Baden-Powell 5·50 5·50

771 Bulldogs

772 Face Shovel in Mine

2008. Centenary of Rugby League. Multicoloured. (a) Ordinary gum.
2935 50c. Type **771** 75 75
2936 50c. Titans 75 75
2937 50c. Sharks 75 75
2938 50c. Knights 75 75
2939 50c. Cowboys 75 75
2940 50c. Broncos 75 75
2941 50c. Sea Eagles 75 75
2942 50c. Storm 75 75
2943 50c. Roosters 75 75
2944 50c. Raiders 75 75
2945 50c. Rabbitohs 75 75
2946 50c. Panthers 75 75
2947 50c. Dragons 75 75
2948 50c. Eels 75 75
2949 50c. Wests Tigers 75 75
2950 50c. Warriors 75 75
(b) Self-adhesive.
2951 50c. As No. 2942 . . . . . 75 75
2952 50c. As No. 2937 . . . . . 75 75
2953 50c. As No. 2943 . . . . . 75 75
2954 50c. As Type **771** 75 75
2955 50c. As No. 2938 . . . . . 75 75
2956 50c. As No. 2939 . . . . . 75 75
2957 50c. As No. 2945 . . . . . 75 75
2958 50c. As No. 2944 . . . . . 75 75
2959 50c. As No. 2948 . . . . . 75 75
2960 50c. As No. 2949 . . . . . 75 75
2961 50c. As No. 2947 . . . . . 75 75
2962 50c. As No. 2941 . . . . . 75 75
2963 50c. As No. 2940 . . . . . 75 75
2964 50c. As No. 2936 . . . . . 75 75
2965 50c. As No. 2946 . . . . . 75 75
2966 50c. As No. 2950 . . . . . 75 75

2008. Heavy Haulers. Multicoloured. (a) Ordinary or self-adhesive gum.
2967 50c. Type **772** 75 75
2968 50c. 200 tonne mine haul truck 75 75
2969 50c. Road train 75 75
2970 50c. Ore train, West Australia 75 75
2971 50c. MS *Berge Stahl* (world?s largest bulk carrier) 75 75

773 Veterans marching

774 Queen Elizabeth II at Official Dinner, Parliament House, Canberra, 2006

2008. 'Lest We Forget': ANZAC Day. Multicoloured. (a) Ordinary gum.
2977 50c. Type **773** 75 75
2978 50c. Laying wreaths at war memorial 75 75
2979 50c. Playing the *Last Post* 75 75
2980 50c. War veteran and young boy 75 75
2981 50c. Young Australians at Gallipoli 75 75
MS2982 160 × 90 mm. Nos. 2977/81 3·75 3·75
(b) Self-adhesive.
2983 50c. As Type **773** 75 75
2984 50c. As No. 2978 . . . . . 75 75
2985 50c. As No. 2979 . . . . . 75 75
2986 50c. As No. 2980 . . . . . 75 75
2987 50c. As No. 2981 . . . . . 75 75

2008. Queen's Birthday. Multicoloured. (i) Domestic Mail.
2988 50c. Type**774** 75 75
(ii) International Post.
2989 $2 Sovereign's badge, Order of Australia . . . . . 2·75 2·75
MS2990 106 × 70 mm. Nos. 2988/9 3·50 3·50

775 Balloons over Sydney, New South Wales

2008. 'Up Up and Away'. 150th Anniv of First Hot Air Balloon Flight in Australia. Multicoloured. Ordinary or self adhesive gum.
2991 50c. Type **775** 75 75
2992 50c. Orange and white balloons over Mt. Feathertop, Victoria . . . 75 75
2993 50c. Multicoloured balloons over the Western MacDonnell Ranges, Northern Territories . . . 75 75
2994 50c. Balloons over Canberra, Australian Central Territory 75 75

2008. WSC Israel 2008 World Stamp Championship, Tel-Aviv. Sheet 130 × 90 mm containing No. 2979 × 4. Multicoloured.
MS2999 50c. × 4 Playing *The Last Post* . . . . 3·00 3·00

OFFICIAL STAMPS

1931. Optd **O.S.** (a) Kangaroo issue.
O133 **1** 6d. brown . . . . 24·00 20·00
(b) King George V issue.
O128 **3** ½d. orange . . . . 4·75 1·50
O129 1d. green . . . . 3·25 45
O130 2d. red . . . . 12·00 55
O131 3d. blue . . . . 7·50 4·00
O126 4d. olive . . . . 16·00 3·00
O132 5d. brown . . . . 35·00 27·00
(c) Various issues.
O123 **13** 2d. red . . . . 55·00 19·00
O134 **18** 2d. red . . . . 5·00 2·00
O124 **13** 3d. blue . . . . £200 27·00
O135 **18** 3d. blue . . . . 14·00 5·00
O136 **17** 1s. green . . . . 42·00 27·00

POSTAGE DUE STAMPS

D 1

D 3

1902. White space below value at foot.
D1 D **1** ½d. green . . . . 3·25 4·50
D2 1d. green . . . . 13·00 8·00
D3 2d. green . . . . 45·00 9·00
D4 3d. green . . . . 35·00 23·00
D5 4d. green . . . . 42·00 12·00
D6 6d. green . . . . 55·00 9·50
D7 8d. green . . . . 95·00 75·00
D8 5s. green . . . . £180 70·00

1902. White space filled in.
D22 D **3** ½d. green . . . . 10·00 8·00
D23 1d. green . . . . 10·00 3·00
D24 2d. green . . . . 27·00 3·00
D25 3d. green . . . . 65·00 16·00
D26 4d. green . . . . 55·00 13·00
D17 5d. green . . . . 50·00 10·00
D28 6d. green . . . . 55·00 10·00
D29 8d. green . . . . £120 50·00
D18 10d. green . . . . 75·00 17·00
D19 1s. green . . . . 55·00 14·00
D20 2s. green . . . . £100 18·00
D33 5s. green . . . . £250 22·00
D43 10s. green £1800 £1800
D44 20s. green £4000 £2250

1908. As Type D **3**, but stroke after figure of value, thus "5/-".
D58 D **3** 1s. green . . . . 75·00 9·00
D60 2s. green £1000 £6000
D59 5s. green . . . . £225 48·00
D61 10s. green £2500 £15000
D62 20s. green £6500 £30000

D 7

D **10**

1909.
D132 D **7** ½d. red and green . . . 3·00 2·50
D133 1d. red and green . . . 2·50 3·00
D 93 1½d. red and green . . 1·50 9·00
D121 2d. red and green . . . 5·50 1·25
D134 3d. red and green . . . 1·75 3·00
D109 4d. red and green . . . 6·50 3·25
D124 5d. red and green . . . 12·00 4·00
D137 6d. red and green . . . 2·50 2·00
D126 7d. red and green . . . 2·25 3·00
D127 8d. red and green . . . 4·00 16·00
D139 10d. red and green . . 3·25 1·75
D128 1s. red and green . . . 17·00 1·75
D 70 2s. red and green . . . 70·00 9·50
D 71 5s. red and green . . . 90·00 13·00
D 72 10s. red and green . . . £250 £150
D 73 £1 red and green . . . £475 £275

1953.
D140 D **10** 1s. red and green . . 5·50 2·25
D130 2s. red and green . . 14·00 8·00
D131a 5s. red and green . . 12·00 70

AUSTRALIAN ANTARCTIC TERRITORY Pt. 1

By an Order in Council of 7 February 1933, the territory S. of latitude 60°S. between 160th and 145th meridians of East longitude (excepting Adelie Land) was placed under Australian administration. Until 1957 stamps of Australia were used from the base.

1957. 12 pence = 1 shilling;
20 shillings = 1 pound.
1966. 100 cents = 1 dollar.

1 1954 Expedition at Vestfold Hills and Map

1957.
1 **1** 2s. blue 80 50

2 Members of Shackleton Expedition at S. Magnetic Pole, 1909

3 Weazel and Team

1959.
2 **2** 5d. on 4d. black and sepia . . 60 15
3 **3** 8d. on 7d. black and blue . . 1·75 2·25
4 – 1s. myrtle . . . . 2·25 2·00
5 – 2s.3d. green . . . . 7·00 4·00
DESIGNS—VERT (as Type **3**): 1s. Dog-team and iceberg; 2s.3d. Map of Antarctica and emperor penguins.

6

7 Sir Douglas Mawson (Expedition leader)

1961.
6 **6** 5d. blue . . . . 1·00 20

1961. 50th Anniv of 1911–14 Australian Antarctic Expedition.
7 **7** 5d. myrtle 35 20

8 Aurora and Camera Dome

11 Sastrugi (Snow Ridges)

1966. Multicoloured.
8 1c. Type **8** 70 30
9 2c. Emperor penguins . . . . 3·00 80
10 4c. Ship and iceberg . . . . 1·00 90
11 5c. Banding southern elephant-seals . . . . 2·25 1·75
12 7c. Measuring snow strata . . 80 80
13 10c. Wind gauges . . . . . . 1·00 1·10
14 15c. Weather balloon . . . . 5·00 2·00
15 20c. Bell Trooper helicopter (horiz) . . . . 7·50 2·50
16 25c. Radio operator (horiz) . . 1·75 2·25
17 50c. Ice-compression tests (horiz) . . . . 2·50 4·00
18 $1 Parahelion ("mock sun") (horiz) . . . . 19·00 12·00

1971. 10th Anniv of Antarctic Treaty.
19 **11** 6c. blue and black . . . . . 75 1·00
20 – 30c. multicoloured . . . . . 2·75 6·00
DESIGN: 30c. Pancake ice.

12 Capt. Cook, Sextant and Compass

13 Plankton

1972. Bicentenary of Cook's Circumnavigation of Antarctica. Multicoloured.
21 7c. Type **12** . . . . 1·00 75
22 35c. Chart and H.M.S. "Resolution" . . . . 3·50 2·00

1973. Multicoloured.
23 1c. Type **13** 30 20
24 5c. Mawson's De Havilland Gipsy Moth, 1931 . . . . 55 80
25 7c. Adelie penguin . . . . . 1·50 80
26 8c. De Havilland Fox Moth, 1934–37 . . . . 60 1·00
27 9c. Leopard seal (horiz) . . . 40 1·00
28 10c. Killer whale (horiz) . . . 2·25 2·00
29 20c. Wandering albatross ("Albatross") (horiz) . . 1·25 1·00
30 25c. Wilkins's Lockheed Vega "San Francisco", 1928 (horiz) . . . . 55 1·00
31 30c. Ellsworth's Northrop Gamma "Polar Star", 1935 55 1·00
32 35c. Christensen's Avro Type 581 Avian, 1934 (horiz) . . . . 55 1·00
33 50c. Byrd's Ford Trimotor "Floyd Bennett", 1929 . . 55 1·25
34 $1 Sperm whale . . . . 75 1·40

14 Admiral Byrd (expedition leader), Ford Trimotor "Floyd Bennett" and Map of South Pole

15 "Thala Dan" (supply ship)

1979. 50th Anniv of First Flight over South Pole. Multicoloured.
35 20c. Type **14** 25 60
36 55c. Admiral Byrd, aircraft and Antarctic terrain . . . 50 1·25

1979. Ships. Multicoloured.
37 1c. "Aurora" (horiz) 15 10
38 2c. "Penola" (Rymill's ship) . . 40 10
39 5c. Type **15** 30 40
40 10c. H.M.S. "Challenger" (survey ship) (horiz) . . . . 50 1·25
41 15c. "Morning" (bow view) (whaling ship) (horiz) . . . 2·00 3·00
42 15c. "Nimrod" (stern view) (Shackleton's ship) (horiz) 1·40 1·75
43 20c. "Discovery II" (supply ship) (horiz) . . . . . . 1·50 1·50

44 22c. "Terra Nova" (Scott's ship) 1·00 1·25
45 25c. "Endurance" (Shackleton's ship) 60 1·00
46 30c. "Fram" (Amundsen's ship) (horiz) 60 1·75
47 35c. "Nella Dan" (supply ship) 80 1·75
48 40c. "Kista Dan" (supply ship) 1·25 2·00
49 45c. "L'Astrolabe" (D'Urville's ship) (horiz) 70 1·50
50 50c. "Norvegia" (supply ship) (horiz) 70 70
51 55c. "Discovery" (Scott's ship) 1·00 2·00
52 $1 H.M.S. "Resolution" (Cook's ship) 1·75 2·50

No. 41 is incorrectly inscr "S.Y. Nimrod".

16 Sir Douglas Mawson in Antarctic Terrain

17 Light-mantled Sooty Albatross

1982. Birth Centenary of Sir Douglas Mawson (Antarctic explorer). Multicoloured.
53 27c. Type **16** 25 25
54 75c. Sir Douglas Mawson and map of Australian Antarctic Territory 75 1·50

1983. Regional Wildlife. Multicoloured.
55 27c. Type **17** 60 90
56 27c. King cormorant ("Macquarie Island shag") 60 90
57 27c. Southern elephant seal 60 90
58 27c. Royal penguin 60 90
59 27c. Dove prion ("Antarctic prion") 60 90

18 Antarctic Scientist

19 Prismatic Compass and Lloyd-Creak Dip Circle

1983. 12th Antarctic Treaty Consultative Meeting. Canberra.
60 **18** 27c. multicoloured 55 75

1984. 75th Anniv of Magnetic Pole Expedition. Multicoloured.
61 30c. Type **19** 30 30
62 85c. Aneroid barometer and theodolite 70 1·25

20 Dog Team pulling Sledge

21 Prince Charles Mountains near Mawson Station

1984. Antarctic Scenes. Multicoloured.
63 2c. Summer afternoon, Mawson Station 20 70
64 5c. Type **20** 20 30
65 10c. Late summer evening, MacRobertson Land 20 40
66 15c. Prince Charles Mountains 20 60
67 20c. Summer morning, Wilkesland 20 1·25
68 25c. Sea-ice and iceberg 60 1·50
69 30c. Mount Coates 25 50
70 33c. "Iceberg Alley", Mawson 25 1·00
71 36c. Early winter evening, Casey Station 50 50
72 45c. Brash ice (vert) 70 2·00
73 60c. Midwinter shadows, Casey Station 50 65
74 75c. Coastline 3·00 2·75
75 85c. Landing strip 2·50 3·00
76 90c. Pancake ice (vert) 75 80
77 $1 Emperor penguins 3·00 1·50

1986. 25th Anniv of Antarctic Treaty.
78 **21** 36c. multicoloured 1·25 1·10

22 Hourglass Dolphins and "Nella Dan"

23 "Antarctica"

1988. Environment, Conservation and Technology. Multicoloured.
79 37c. Type **22** 1·10 1·25
80 37c. Emperor penguins and Davis Station 1·10 1·25
81 37c. Crabeater seal and Hughes 500D helicopters 1·10 1·25
82 37c. Adelie penguins and tracked vehicle 1·10 1·25
83 37c. Grey-headed albatross and photographer 1·10 1·25

1989. Antarctic Landscape Paintings by Sir Sidney Nolan. Multicoloured.
84 39c. Type **23** 1·25 1·50
85 39c. "Iceberg Alley" 1·25 1·50
86 60c. "Glacial Flow" 2·00 2·25
87 80c. "Frozen Sea" 2·50 2·75

24 "Aurora Australis"

1991. 30th Anniv of Antarctic Treaty (43c.) and Maiden Voyage of "Aurora Australis" (research ship) ($1.20). Multicoloured.
88 43c. Type **24** 75 60
89 $1.20 "Aurora Australis" off Heard Island 2·75 4·25

25 Adelie Penguin and Chick

26 Head of Husky

1992. Antarctic Wildlife. Multicoloured.
90 45c. Type **25** 45 40
91 75c. Elephant seal with pup 70 65
92 85c. Hall's giant petrel ("Northern giant petrel") on nest with fledgeling 80 75
93 95c. Weddell seal and pup 90 85
94 $1 Royal penguin 90 85
95 $1.20 Emperor penguins with chicks (vert) 1·25 1·10
96 $1.40 Fur seal 1·25 1·40
97 $1.50 King penguin (vert) 1·40 1·75

1994. Departure of Huskies from Antarctica. Multicoloured.
104 45c. Type **26** 1·50 75
105 75c. Dogs pulling sledge (horiz) 1·75 2·00
106 85c. Husky in harness 2·00 2·25
107 $1.05 Dogs on leads (horiz) 2·25 2·50

27 Humpback Whale with Calf

1995. Whales and Dolphins. Multicoloured.
108 45c. Type **27** 1·75 80
109 45c. Pair of hourglass dolphins (vert) 1·75 1·75
110 45c. Pair of minke whales (vert) 1·75 1·75
111 $1 Killer whale 3·00 3·00
MS112 146×64 mm. Nos. 108/11 6·50 6·50

Nos. 109/10 were printed together, se-tenant, forming a composite design.

28 "Rafting Sea Ice" (Christian Clare Robertson)

29 Apple Huts

1996. Paintings by Christian Clare Robertson. Multicoloured.
113 45c. Type **28** 90 1·00
114 45c. "Shadow on the Plateau" 90 1·00
115 $1 "Ice Cave" 1·90 1·90
116 $1.20 "Twelve Lake" 2·25 2·25

1997. 50th Anniv of Australian National Antarctic Research Expeditions (A.N.A.R.E.). Multicoloured.
117 45c. Type **29** 85 85
118 45c. Tuning a radio receiver 85 85
119 95c. Summer surveying 1·40 1·75
120 $1.05 Scientists in cage above sea ice 1·50 1·75
121 $1.20 Scientists and tents 1·60 1·90

30 "Aurora Australis" (research ship)

1998. Antarctic Transport. Multicoloured.
122 45c. Type **30** 1·75 1·60
123 45c. "Skidoo" 1·75 1·60
124 $1 Helicopter lifting quad motorcycle (vert) 3·50 2·75
125 $2 Hagglunds tractor and trailer (vert) 3·50 3·50

31 Sir Douglas Mawson (expedition leader, 1911–14) and "Aurora" (research ship)

1999. Restoration of Mawson's Huts, Cape Denison. Each including a background drawing of a hut. Multicoloured.
126 45c. Type **31** 1·25 1·25
127 45c. Huts in blizzard 1·25 1·25
128 90c. Husky team 2·00 2·25
129 $1.35 Conservation in progress 2·00 2·25

32 Emperor Penguins

2000. Penguins. Multicoloured.
130 45c. Type **32** 1·75 1·75
131 45c. Adelie penguins 1·75 1·75

33 Adelie Penguins with Egg

2001. Centenary of Australian Antarctic Exploration. Multicoloured.
132 5c. Type **33** 55 65
133 5c. Louis Bernacchi (physicist) 55 65
134 5c. *Nimrod* (Shackleton) 55 65
135 5c. Mackay, Edgeworth David and Mawson at South Magnetic Pole, 1909 55 65
136 5c. Taylor and Debenham (geologists) 55 65
137 10c. Early radio set 55 65
138 10c. Lockheed-Vega aircraft and husky team 55 65
139 10c. Sir Douglas Mawson 55 65
140 10c. Members of BANZARE Expedition, 1929–31 55 65
141 10c. Hoisting Union Jack 55 65
142 25c. Hoisting Australian flag, 1948 60 70
143 25c. Hagglund vehicle and helicopter 60 70
144 25c. *Aurora australis* over Casey 60 70
145 25c. Scientist with weather balloon 60 70
146 25c. Modern Antarctic clothing and "apple" hut 60 70
147 45c. *Nella Dan* (supply ship) and emperor penguins 65 75
148 45c. Male and female scientists taking ice sample 65 75
149 45c. Scientist using satellite phone 65 75
150 45c. Weddell seal and tourists 65 75
151 45c. Satellite photograph of Antarctica 65 75

Nos. 132/51 were printed together, se-tenant, with the backgrounds forming a composite design.

Each stamp carries an inscription on the reverse, printed over the gum.

34 Female Leopard Seal and Pup

2001. Endangered Species. Leopard Seal. Mult.
152 45c. Type **34** 1·25 1·25
153 45c. Male seal on ice floe chasing adelie penguins 1·00 1·10
154 45c. Female seal and pup swimming underwater 1·00 1·10
155 45c. Adult seal chasing adelie penguins underwater 1·00 1·10

35 Light Detection and Ranging Equipment, Davis Base

2002. Antarctic Research. Multicoloured.
156 45c. Type **35** 1·25 1·25
157 45c. Magnified diatom and coastline, Casey Base 1·25 1·25
158 45c. Wandering albatross, Macquarie Base 1·25 1·25
159 45c. Adelie penguin, Mawson Base 1·25 1·25

36 *Kista Dan* in Heavy Seas

2003. Antarctic Supply Ships. Multicoloured.
160 50c. Type **36** 1·40 1·60
161 50c. *Magga Dan* entering pack ice 1·60 1·60
162 $1 *Thala Dan* and iceberg (vert) 2·25 1·75
163 $1.45 *Nella Dan* unloading in Antarctic (vert) 2·75 3·00

37 Naming Ceremony, 1954

2004. 50th Anniv of Mawson Station. Multicoloured.
164 50c. Type **37** 1·25 1·40
165 50c. Mawson Station, 2004 1·25 1·40
166 $1 Accomodation "caravan", 1950s 1·75 1·75
167 $1.45 Emperor penguin rookery 2·40 2·75

38 Hughes 500 Helicopter

2005. Aviation in the Australian Antarctic Territory. Multicoloured.
168 50c. Type **38** 1·25 1·40
169 50c. De Haviland DHC-2 Beaver 1·25 1·40
170 $1 Pilatus PC06 Porter 1·75 1·75
171 $1.45 Douglas DC-3/Dakota C-47 2·40 2·75

39 Mackerel Icefish

2006. Fish of the Australian Antarctic Territory. Multicoloured.
172 50c. Type **39** 90 1·00
173 50c. Lanternfish 90 1·00
174 $1 Eaton's skate 1·60 1·60
175 $1 Patagonian toothfish 1·60 1·60

40 Royal Penguins

2007. Endangered Species. Royal Penguins (*Eudyptes schlegeli*). Multicoloured.

176		50c. Type **40**	70	70
177		50c. Penguin with egg	70	70
178		$1 Two penguins sparring	1·30	1·30
179		$1 Pair snuggling together	1·30	1·30

AUSTRIA Pt. 2

A state of Central Europe, part of the Austro-Hungarian Monarchy and Empire until 1918. At the end of the First World War the Empire was dismembered and German-speaking Austria became a Republic.

Austria was absorbed into the German Reich in 1938 and remained part of Germany until 1945. Following occupation by the four Allied Powers the Austrian Republic was re-established on 14 May 1945.

1850. 60 kreuzer = 1 gulden.
1858. 100 kreuzer = 1 gulden.
1899. 100 heller = 1 krone.
1925. 100 groschen = 1 schilling.
1938. 100 pfennig = 1 German reichsmark.
1945. 100 groschen = 1 schilling.
2002. 100 cents = 1 euro.

1 Arms of Austria

4

5

1850. Imperf.

6a	**1**	1k. yellow	£1400	£110
7		2k. black	£1700	75·00
8a		3k. red	£475	2·75
9		6k. brown	£1000	5·50
10		9k. blue	£1200	2·75

For stamps in Type **1** with values in "CENTES", see Lombardy and Venetia.

1858.

22a	**5**	2k. yellow	£1200	55·00
23	**4**	3k. black	£2000	£275
24		3k. green	£1500	£170
25a	**5**	5k. red	£450	1·50
26a		10k. brown	£900	3·25
27a		15k. blue	£900	1·90

For stamps in Types **4** and **5** with values in "SOLDI", see Lombardy and Venetia.

The portraits on Austrian stamps to 1906 are of the Emperor Francis Joseph I.

10

12 Arms of Austria

1860.

33	**10**	2k. yellow	£450	29·00
34		3k. green	£375	27·00
35		5k. red	£275	70
36		10k. brown	£350	1·90
37		15k. blue	£450	1·30

1863.

45	**12**	2k. yellow	£200	13·00
46		3k. green	£200	13·00
47		5k. red	60·00	40
48		10k. blue	£250	3·25
49		15k. brown	£250	1·80

A H 14

A H 16

20

1867.

59	A H **14**	2k. yellow	13·00	85
60		3k. green	90·00	85
62		5k. red	8·75	40
63		10k. blue	£160	85
64		15k. brown	8·75	6·75
AH56a		25k. grey	55·00	17·00
66	A H **16**	50k. brown	35·00	£130

1883.

70c	**20**	2k. brown	7·00	35
71c		3k. green	7·00	35
72c		5k. red	44·00	15
73c		10k. blue	4·50	35
74b		20k. grey	70·00	3·25
75a		50k. mauve	£325	85·00

23

24

25

1890.

79	**23**	1k. grey	2·20	25
80		2k. brown	35	25
81		3k. green	55	25
82		5k. red	55	25
83		10k. blue	1·30	25
84		12k. purple	2·75	35
85		15k. purple	2·50	35
86		20k. green	35·00	2·50
87		24k. blue	2·75	1·30
88		30k. brown	2·75	65
89		50k. mauve	7·00	8·50
90	**24**	1g. blue	2·50	3·00
105		1g. lilac	46·00	4·75
91		2g. red	3·50	17·00
106		2g. green	16·00	42·00

1891. Figures in black.

92	**25**	20k. green	1·80	25
93		24k. blue	3·00	85
94		30k. brown	1·80	25
95		50k. mauve	1·80	35

27

28

29

30

1899. Corner numerals in black on heller values.

107	**27**	1h. mauve	1·30	15
108		2h. grey	2·75	60
140		3h. brown	90	15
141		5h. green	90	15
142		6h. orange	90	15
143	**28**	10h. red	90	15
144		20h. brown	1·30	15
145		25h. blue	1·30	15
146		30h. mauve	3·00	80
147	**29**	35h. green	1·50	25
148		40h. green	3·50	4·25
149		50h. blue	7·00	10·00
150		60h. brown	3·50	85
119ac	**30**	1k. red	5·75	20
120c		2k. lilac	55·00	45
121c		4k. green	10·00	14·50

33

35

1904. Types as before, but with corners containing figures altered as T **33** and **35**. Figures in black on white on 10h. to 30h. only.

169	**33**	1h. purple	20	35
170		2h. black	20	25
171		3h. brown	35	15
183		5h. green	30	15
173		6h. orange	40	15
160	**28**	10h. red	2·20	15
161		20h. brown	35·00	95
162		25h. blue	34·00	95
163		30h. mauve	55·00	1·90
178	**35**	35h. green	3·50	35
179		40h. purple	3·50	95
180		50h. blue	3·50	3·75
181		60h. brown	3·50	85
168		72h. red	2·75	1·90

1906. Figures on plain white ground and stamps printed in one colour.

184	**28**	10h. red	45	15
185		12h. violet	1·30	85
186		20h. brown	3·75	15
187		25h. blue	3·75	50
188		30h. red	9·00	40

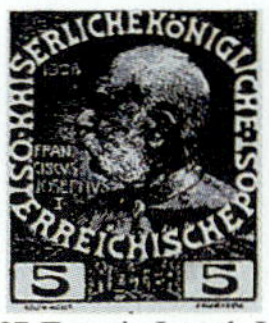
37 Francis Joseph I

38 Francis Joseph I

41 Schonbrunn

42 Francis Joseph I

1908. 60th Anniv of Emperor's Accession.

189A	–	1h. black	30	15
190A	–	2h. violet	30	15
191B	–	3h. purple	20	15
192B	**37**	5h. green	20	15
193A	–	6h. brown	70	85
194B	**37**	10h. red	20	15
195A	–	12h. red	1·30	1·30
196B	–	20h. brown	2·20	40
197B	**37**	25h. blue	2·00	40
198B	–	30h. green	4·75	60
199A	–	35h. grey	3·50	25
200	**38**	50h. green	1·10	25
201	–	60h. red	30	20
202	**38**	72h. brown	2·75	40
203	–	1k. violet	13·00	25
204	**41**	2k. green and red	21·00	40
205	–	5k. purple and brown	44·00	6·00
206	**42**	10k. brown, blue & ochre	£180	70·00

DESIGNS—As Type **37**: 1h. Charles VI; 2h. Maria Theresa; 3h. Joseph II; 6h. Leopold II; 12h. Francis I; 20h. Ferdinand; 30h. Francis Joseph I in 1848; 35h. Same in 1878. As Type **38**: 60h. Francis Joseph I on horseback; 1k. Same in ceremonial robes. As Type **41**: 5k. Hofburg.

45

47

1910. 80th Birthday of Francis Joseph I. As issue of 1908 but with dates added as T **45**.

223		1h. black	4·50	8·50
224		2h. violet	6·25	17·00
225		3h. purple	5·75	12·50
226		5h. green	70	55
227		6h. brown	4·50	12·50
228		10h. red	30	55
229		12h. red	4·50	12·50
230		20h. brown	9·25	13·50
231		25h. blue	2·20	2·75
232		30h. green	4·75	8·50
233		35h. grey	4·75	8·50
234		50h. green	7·00	13·00
235		60h. red	7·00	13·00
236		1k. violet	7·50	15·00
237		2k. green and red	£150	£225
238		5k. purple and brown	£120	£200
239		10k. brown, blue and ochre	£200	£350

1914. War Charity Funds.

240	**47**	5h.+(2h.) green	25	55
241		10h.+(2h.) red	25	65

48 Cavalry

1915. War Charity Funds.

242	–	3h.+1h. brown	15	45
243	**48**	5h.+2h. green	15	15
244	–	10h.+2h. red	15	15
245	–	20h.+3h. green	75	2·10
246	–	35h.+3h. blue	2·20	5·00

DESIGNS: 3h. Infantry; 10h. Artillery; 20h. Battleship "Viribus Unitas" (Navy); 35h. Lohner Pfeilflieger B-1 biplane (Air Force).

49 Imperial Austrian Crown

50 Francis Joseph I

51 Arms of Austria

52

1916.

247	**49**	3h. violet	10	10
248		5h. green	10	10
249		6h. orange	30	65
250		10h. red	15	10
251		12h. blue	35	1·40
252	**50**	15h. red	50	15
253		20h. brown	3·00	25
254		25h. blue	5·25	40
255		30h. slate	4·50	65
256	**51**	40h. olive	20	25
257		50h. green	20	15
258		60h. blue	20	15
259		80h. brown	35	15
260		90h. purple	35	15
261		1k. red on yellow	35	20
262aa	**52**	2k. blue	20	40
263aa		3k. red	35	85
264a		4k. green	2·20	1·50
265aa		10k. violet	13·00	29·00

On Nos. 254/5 the portrait is full face. The 1k. has floral sprays each side of the coat-of-arms.

60 Charles I

1917.

290	**60**	15h. red	15	10
291a		20h. green	15	10
292		25h. blue	60	15
293		30h. violet	45	15

1918. Air. Optd **FLUGPOST** or surch also.

296A	**52**	1k.50 on 2k. mauve	1·80	6·75
297B		2k.50 on 3k. brown	8·75	25·00
298A		4k. grey	5·75	17·00

1918. Optd **Deutschosterreich.**

299	**49**	3h. violet	20	20
300		5h. green	20	20
301		6h. orange	30	1·70
302		10h. red	20	10
303		12h. blue	35	2·50
304	**60**	15h. red	35	1·20
305		20h. green	15	15
306		25h. blue	30	20
307		30h. violet	20	20
308	**51**	40h. olive	20	20
309		50h. green	70	1·50
310		60h. blue	70	1·50
311		80h. brown	35	35
312		90h. red	35	50
313		1k. red on yellow	35	35
314	**52**	2k. blue	30	25
315		3k. red	40	85
316		4k. green	1·50	3·00
317		10k. violet	9·25	24·00

64 Posthorn

65 Republican Arms

66 "New Republic"

1919. Imperf or perf.

336	**64**	3h. grey	15	15
337	**65**	5h. green	15	15
338		5h. grey	15	15
339	**64**	6h. orange	35	50
340	**65**	10h. red	15	15
342	**64**	12h. blue	20	85
343a		15h. brown	20	15
344	**66**	20h. green	20	15
346	**65**	25h. blue	20	15
347	**64**	25h. violet	20	15
348	**66**	30h. brown	20	15
349		40h. violet	20	15
350		40h. red	20	15
351	**65**	45h. green	25	85
352	**66**	50h. blue	15	15
353	**64**	60h. green	15	15
354	**65**	1k. red on yellow	15	15
355		1k. blue	15	15

67 Parliament Building

71 Republican Arms

1919.

356	**67**	2k. black and red	35	85
357		2½k. bistre	35	40
358		3k. brown and blue	30	30
359		4k. black and red	30	30
360		5k. black	30	30
361		7½k. purple	45	55
362		10k. brown and green	45	55

363		20k. brown and violet	35	40
364		50k. violet on yellow	90	1·50

1920.

402	71	80h. red	20	15
403		1k. brown	20	15
404		1½k. green	35	15
405		2k. blue	20	15
406		3k. black and green	25	25
407		4k. claret and red	25	15
408		5k. red and lilac	25	15
409		7½k. brown and orange	35	30
410		10k. blue and violet	35	30

The frames of the 3 to 10k. differ.

1920. Issues for Carinthian Plebiscite. Optd **Karnten Abstimmung** (T **65/7** in new colours). (a) Perf.

411	65	5h. (+10h.) grey on yell	90	1·70
412		10h. (+20h.) red on pink	90	1·30
413	64	15h. (+30h.) brn on yell	65	1·10
414	66	20h. (+40h.) green on bl	65	1·10
415	64	25h. (+50h.) pur on pink	65	95
416	66	30h. (+60h.) brn on buff	2·75	3·50
417		40h. (+80h.) red on yell	70	1·10
418		50h. (+100h.) indigo on blue	70	85
419	64	60h. (+120h.) green on bl	2·20	4·00
420	71	80h. (+160h.) red	70	1·00
421		1k. (+2k.) brown	70	1·10
422		2k. (+4k.) blue	70	1·10

(b) Imperf.

423	67	2½k. (+5k.) brown	90	1·30
424		3k. (+6k.) green & blue	1·10	1·50
425		4k. (+8k.) violet & red	1·80	1·90
426		5k. (+10k.) blue	1·30	1·70
427		7½k. (+15k.) green	1·30	1·70
428		10k. (+20k.) red & green	1·80	1·60
429		20k. (+40k.) pur & lilac	1·90	2·30

The plebiscite was to decide whether Carinthia should be part of Austria or Yugoslavia, and the premium was for a fund to promote a vote in favour of remaining in Austria. The result was a vote for Austria.

1921. Flood Relief Fund. Optd **Hochwasser 1920** (colours changed).

430	65	5h. (+10h.) grey on yell	45	65
431		10h. (+20h.) brown	45	65
432	64	15h. (+30h.) grey	45	65
433	66	20h. (+40h.) green on yell	45	65
434	64	25h. (+50h.) blue on yell	45	65
435	66	30h. (+60h.) purple on bl	90	1·30
436		40h. (+80h.) brn on red	1·10	1·50
437		50h. (+100h.) green on bl	1·80	2·50
438	64	60h. (+120h.) pur on yell	45	1·40
439	71	80h. (+160h.) blue	80	1·20
440		1k. (+2k.) orange on blue	65	1·00
441		1½k. (+3k.) green on yell	40	75
442		2k. (+4k.) brown	40	75
443	67	2½k. (+5k.) blue	45	75
444		3k. (+6k.) red & green	45	75
445		4k. (+8k.) brown & lilac	1·80	2·30
446		5k. (+10k.) green	45	85
447		7½k. (+15k.) red	55	95
448		10k. (+20k.) green & blue	50	1·00
449		20k. (+40k.) pur & red	1·10	1·50

80 Pincers and Hammer

81 Ear of Corn

1922.

461	81	½k. brown	15	75
462	80	1k. brown	20	15
463		2k. blue	15	15
464	81	2½k. brown	15	15
465	80	4k. purple	35	1·10
466		5k. green	15	15
467	81	7½k. violet	15	15
468	80	10k. red	15	10
469	81	12½k. green	15	15
470		15k. turquoise	15	15
471		20k. blue	15	10
472		25k. red	15	10
473	80	30k. grey	15	15
474		45k. red	15	15
475		50k. brown	10	15
476		60k. green	10	15
477		75k. blue	10	10
478		80k. yellow	10	10
479	81	100k. grey	10	10
480		120k. brown	25	15
481		150k. orange	10	10
482		160k. green	10	10
483		180k. red	30	15
484		200k. pink	10	10
485		240k. violet	30	15
486		300k. blue	15	10
487		400k. green	1·80	35
488		500k. yellow	20	15
489		600k. slate	25	15
490		700k. brown	4·50	15
491		800k. violet	2·75	2·20
492	80	1000k. mauve	7·00	25
493		1200k. red	5·25	50
494		1500k. orange	7·00	20
495		1600k. slate	8·75	2·50
496		2000k. blue	12·50	1·70
497		3000k. blue	26·00	2·10
498		4000k. blue on blue	18·00	3·75

82

85 Mozart

1922.

499	82	20k. sepia	20	15
500		25k. blue	20	15
501		50k. red	20	15
502		100k. green	20	15
503		200k. purple	20	15
504		500k. orange	90	1·30
505		1000k. violet on yellow	35	15
506		2000k. green on yellow	45	15
507		3000k. red	35·00	85
508		5000k. black	8·75	1·70
509		10,000k. brown	10·50	5·50

1922. Musicians' Fund.

519b	–	2½k. brown	12·50	10·00
520	85	5k. blue	1·80	2·50
521	–	7½k. black	2·75	3·75
522	–	10k. purple	4·00	5·00
523b	–	25k. green	7·00	9·25
524	–	50k. red	4·00	5·00
525	–	100k. green	10·50	12·50

COMPOSERS: 2½k. Haydn; 7½k. Beethoven; 10k. Schubert; 25k. Bruckner; 50k. J. Strauss; 100k. Wolf.

87 Hawk

88 W. Kress

1922. Air.

546	87	300k. red	55	1·60
547		400k. green	7·00	19·00
548		600k. olive	40	1·20
549		900k. red	40	1·30
550	88	1200k. purple	40	1·30
551		2400k. slate	40	1·40
552		3000k. brown	6·25	10·00
553		4800k. blue	5·75	10·00

89 Bregenz

90 "Art the Comforter"

1923. Artists' Charity Fund.

554	89	100k. green	6·25	12·00
555	–	120k. blue	7·00	8·50
556	–	160k. purple	7·00	8·50
557	–	180k. purple	7·00	8·50
558	–	200k. red	7·00	8·50
559	–	240k. brown	7·00	8·50
560	–	400k. brown	6·50	8·75
561	–	600k. green	6·50	9·25
562	–	1000k. black	8·75	12·00

DESIGNS: 120k. Salzburg; 160k. Eisenstadt; 180k. Klagenfurt; 200k. Innsbruck; 240k. Linz; 400k. Graz; 600k. Melk; 1000k. Vienna.

1924. Artists' Charity Fund.

563	90	100k.+300k. green	6·50	8·50
564	–	300k.+900k. brown	6·50	8·50
565	–	500k.+1500k. purple	6·50	8·50
566	–	600k.+1800k. turquoise	13·00	17·00
567	–	1000k.+3000k. brown	18·00	23·00

DESIGNS: 300k. "Agriculture and Handicraft"; 500k. "Mother Love"; 600k. "Charity"; 1000k. "Fruitfulness".

91

92 Plains

93 Minorite Church, Vienna

1925.

568	91	1g. grey	45	15
569		2g. red	65	15
570		3g. red	90	15
571		4g. blue	1·50	15
572		5g. brown	2·50	15
573		6g. blue	2·75	15
574		7g. brown	2·40	15
575		8g. green	7·00	15
576	92	10g. brown	65	15
577		15g. red	65	15
578		16g. blue	65	15
579		18g. green	1·80	65
580	–	20g. violet	1·60	15
581	–	24g. red	1·80	50
582	–	30g. brown	1·60	15
583	–	40g. blue	2·75	15
584	–	45g. brown	3·50	15
585	–	50g. grey	5·25	40
586	–	80g. blue	11·50	4·75
587	93	1s. green	39·00	1·70
588	–	2s. red	14·00	11·00

DESIGN—As T **92**—20g. to 80g. Golden eagle on mountains.

96 Airman and Hansa Brandenburg C-1

97 De Havilland D.H.34 and Common Crane

1925. Air.

616	96	2g. brown	65	1·30
617		5g. red	35	35
618		6g. blue	1·50	1·70
619		8g. green	1·80	2·10
620	97	10g. red	2·20	3·00
621	96	10g. orange	2·75	2·10
622	97	15g. red	1·10	1·50
623	96	15g. mauve	90	95
624		20g. brown	16·00	8·50
625		25g. violet	6·25	9·25
626	97	30g. purple	1·30	3·00
627	96	30g. bistre	15·00	10·00
628	97	50g. grey	1·90	3·25
629	96	50g. blue	25·00	15·00
630		80g. green	4·50	4·25
631	97	1s. blue	16·00	8·50
632		2s. green	2·75	4·25
633		3s. brown	60·00	65·00
634		5s. blue	18·00	27·00
635		10s. brown on grey (25 × 32 mm)	10·50	21·00

98 Siegfried and Dragon

99 Dr. Michael Hainisch

1926. Child Welfare. Scenes from the Nibelung Legend.

636	98	3g.+2g. brown	70	85
637	–	8g.+2g. blue	25	50
638	–	15g.+5g. red	25	50
639	–	20g.+5g. green	45	65
640	–	24g.+6g. violet	45	65
641	–	40g.+10g. brown	4·50	4·75

DESIGNS: 8g. Gunther's voyage; 15g. Kriemhild and Brunhild; 20g. Hagen and the Rhine maidens; 24g. Rudiger and the Nibelungs; 40g. Dietrich's fight with Hagen.

1928. 10th Anniv of Republic and War Orphans and Invalid Children's Fund.

642	99	10g. (+10g.) brown	5·25	12·50
643		15g. (+15g.) red	5·25	12·50
644		30g. (+30g.) black	5·25	12·50
645		40g. (+40g.) blue	5·25	12·50

100 Gussing

101 National Library, Vienna

1929. Views. Size 25½ × 21½ mm.

646	100	10g. orange	1·30	15
647		10g. brown	1·30	15
648	–	15g. purple	90	1·40
649	–	16g. black	55	15
650	–	18g. green	90	65
651	–	20g. black	1·80	10
653	–	24g. purple	7·00	60
654	–	30g. violet	8·75	30
655	–	40g. blue	14·00	15
656	–	50g. violet	38·00	25
657	–	60g. green	35·00	40
658	101	1s. brown	8·75	40
659	–	2s. green	15·00	12·50

VIEWS—As T **100**: 15g. Hochosterwitz; 16, 20g. Durnstein; 18g. Traunsee; 24g. Salzburg; 30g. Seewiesen; 40g. Innsbruck; 50g. Worthersee; 60g. Hohenems. As T **101**: 2s. St. Stephen's Cathedral, Vienna.

See also Nos. 678/91.

102 Pres. Wilhelm Miklas

104 Johann Nestroy

1930. Anti-tuberculosis Fund.

660	102	10g. (+10g.) brown	12·50	23·00
661		20g. (+20g.) red	12·50	23·00
662		30g. (+30g.) purple	12·50	23·00
663		40g. (+40g.) blue	12·50	23·00
664		50g. (+50g.) green	12·50	23·00
665		1s. (+1s.) brown	12·50	23·00

1930. Rotarian Congress. Optd with Rotary Int emblem and **CONVENTION WIEN 1931**.

666	100	10g. (+10g.) brown	44·00	60·00
667	–	20g. (+20g.) grey (No. 651)	44·00	60·00
668	–	30g. (+30g.) vio (No. 654)	44·00	60·00
669	–	40g. (+40g.) bl (No. 655)	44·00	60·00
670	–	50g. (+50g.) vio (No. 656)	44·00	60·00
671	101	1s. (+1s.) brown	44·00	60·00

1931. Austrian Writers and Youth Unemployment Fund.

672	–	10g. (+10g.) purple	18·00	34·00
673	–	20g. (+20g.) grey	18·00	34·00
674	104	30g. (+30g.) red	18·00	34·00
675	–	40g. (+40g.) blue	18·00	34·00
676	–	50g. (+50g.) green	18·00	34·00
677	–	1s. (+1s.) brown	18·00	34·00

DESIGNS: 10g. F. Raimund; 20g. E. Grillparzer; 40g. A Stifter; 50g. L. Anzengruber; 1s. P. Rosegger.

105

106 Dr. Ignaz Seipel

1932. Designs as No. 646 etc, but size reduced to 20½ × 16 mm as T **105**.

678	105	10g. brown	90	15
679	–	12g. green	2·00	15
680	–	18g. green	2·00	2·50
681	–	20g. black	1·40	10
682	–	24g. red	5·75	15
683	–	24g. violet	3·50	15
684	–	30g. violet	18·00	15
685	–	30g. red	6·25	15
686	–	40g. blue	22·00	1·30
687	–	40g. violet	8·75	35
688	–	50g. violet	26·00	40
689	–	50g. blue	8·75	40
690	–	60g. green	70·00	3·25
691	–	64g. green	29·00	40

DESIGNS (new values): 12g. Traunsee; 64g. Hohenems.

1932. Death of Dr. Seipel (Chancellor), and Ex-servicemen's Fund.

692	106	50g. (+50g.) blue	16·00	25·00

107 Hans Makart

108 The Climb

1932. Austrian Painters.

693	–	12g. (+12g.) green	22·00	46·00
694	–	24g. (+24g.) purple	22·00	46·00
695	–	30g. (+30g.) red	22·00	46·00
696	107	40g. (+40g.) grey	22·00	46·00
697	–	64g. (+64g.) brown	22·00	46·00
698	–	1s. (+1s.) red	22·00	46·00

DESIGNS: 12g. F. G. Waldmuller; 24g. Von Schwind; 30g. Alt; 64g. Klimt; 1s. A. Egger-Lienz.

1933. International Ski Championship Fund.

699	108	12g. (+12g.) green	8·75	15·00
700	–	24g. (+24g.) violet	£110	£160
701	–	30g. (+30g.) red	16·00	26·00
702	–	50g. (+50g.) blue	£110	£150

DESIGNS: 24g. Start; 30g. Race; 50g. Ski jump.

109 "The Honeymoon" (M. von Schwind)

111 John Sobieski

1933. International Philatelic Exn, Vienna (WIPA).

703	109	50g. (+50g.) blue	£180	£225
MS705		127 × 105 mm. As No. 703 (+1s.60 admission) in block of four	£3500	£3750

1933. 250th Anniv of Relief of Vienna and Pan-German Catholic Congress.

706	–	12g. (+12g.) green	28·00	38·00
707	–	24g. (+24g.) violet	26·00	34·00
708	–	30g. (+30g.) red	26·00	34·00
709	111	40g. (+40g.) grey	38·00	60·00
710	–	50g. (+50g.) blue	26·00	34·00
711	–	64g. (+64g.) brown	31·00	60·00

DESIGNS—VERT: 12g. Vienna in 1683; 24g. Marco d'Aviano; 30g. Count von Starhemberg; 50g. Charles of Lorraine; 64g. Burgomaster Liebenberg.

1933. Winter Relief Fund. Surch with premium and **Winterhilfe** (5g.) or **WINTERHILFE** (others).

712	**91**	5g.+2g. green	35	75
713	–	12g.+3g. blue (as 679)	55	85
714	–	24g.+6g. brn (as 682)	35	75
715	**101**	1s.+50g. red	39·00	55·00

114

115

1934.

716	**114**	1g. violet	15	15
717		3g. red	15	15
718	–	4g. green	15	15
719	–	5g. purple	15	15
721	–	6g. blue	30	15
722	–	8g. green	30	15
723	–	12g. brown	30	10
724	–	20g. brown	30	15
725	–	24g. turquoise	30	15
726	–	25g. violet	40	30
727	–	30g. red	40	15
728	–	35g. red	65	50
729	**115**	40g. grey	95	35
730		45g. brown	90	25
731	–	60g. blue	1·10	35
732	–	64g. brown	1·60	15
733	–	1s. purple	2·00	65
735	–	2s. green	3·50	6·75
736	–	3s. orange	18·00	21·00
737	–	5s. black	28·00	50·00

DESIGNS (Austrian costumes of the districts named)—As Type **114**: 1, 3g. Burgenland; 4, 5g. Carinthia; 6, 8g. Lower Austria; 12, 20g. Upper Austria; 24, 25g. Salzburg; 30, 35g. Styria (Steiermark). As Type **115**: 40, 45g. Tyrol; 60, 64g. Vorarlberg; 1s. Vienna; 2s. Army officer and soldiers. 30 × 31 mm: 3s. Harvesters; 5s. Builders.

117 Chancellor Dollfuss

118 Anton Pilgram

1934. Dollfuss Mourning Stamp.

738	**117**	24g. black	70	40

See also No. 762.

1934. Welfare Funds. Austrian Architects.

739	**118**	12g. (+12g.) black	12·50	21·00
740	–	24g. (+24g.) violet	12·50	21·00
741	–	30g. (+30g.) red	12·50	21·00
742	–	40g. (+40g.) brown	12·50	21·00
743	–	60g. (+60g.) blue	12·50	21·00
744	–	64g. (+64g.) green	12·50	21·00

DESIGNS: 24g. Fischer von Erlach; 30g. J. Prandtauer; 40g. A. von Siccardsburg and E. van der Null; 60g. H. von Ferstel; 64g. Otto Wagner.

119 "Mother and Child" (J. Danhauser)

1935. Mothers Day.

745	**119**	24g. blue	55	35

1935. 1st Anniv of Assassination of Dr. Dollfuss.

762	**117**	24g. blue	1·30	1·00

121 Maria Worth Castle, Carinthia

122 Zugspitze Aerial Railway

1935. Air. Designs showing Junkers airplane (except 10s.) and landscape.

763	–	5g. purple	45	65
764	**121**	10g. orange	45	50
765	–	15g. green	90	1·70
766	–	20g. blue	20	50
767	–	25g. purple	45	40
768	–	30g. red	45	40
769	–	40g. green	45	40
770	–	50g. blue	45	75
771	–	60g. sepia	45	1·40
772	–	80g. brown	55	1·40
773	–	1s. red	45	1·30
774	–	2s. green	3·25	6·75
775	–	3s. brown	9·75	21·00
776	**122**	5s. green	5·25	17·00
777	–	10s. blue	65·00	£110

DESIGNS—As T **121**: 5g. Gussing Castle; 15g. Durnstein; 20g. Hallstatt; 25g. Salzburg; 30g. Dachstein Mts.; 40g. Wettersee; 50g. Stuben am Arlberg; 60g. St. Stephen's Cathedral, Vienna; 80g. Minorite Church, Vienna. As T **122**: 1s. River Danube; 2s. Tauern railway viaduct; 3s. Grossglockner mountain roadway; 10s. Glider and yachts on the Attersee.

1935. Winter Relief Fund. As Nos. 719, 723, 725 and 733, but colours changed, surch **Winterhilfe** (778/80) or **WINTERHILFE** (781) and premium.

778		5g.+2g. green	45	85
779		12g.+3g. blue	70	1·30
780		24g.+6g. brown	45	85
781		1s.+50g. red	44·00	65·00

123 Prince Eugene of Savoy (born 1663, not 1667 as given)

124 Slalom Course Skier

1935. Welfare Funds. Austrian Heroes.

782	**123**	12g. (+12g.) brown	13·00	21·00
783	–	24g. (+24g.) green	13·00	21·00
784	–	30g. (+30g.) purple	13·00	21·00
785	–	40g. (+40g.) blue	13·00	21·00
786	–	60g. (+60g.) blue	13·00	21·00
787	–	64g. (+64g.) violet	13·00	21·00

PORTRAITS: 24g. Baron von Laudon; 30g. Archduke Charles; 40g. Field-Marshal Radetzky; 60g. Vice-Admiral von Tegetthoff; 64g. Field-Marshal Conrad von Hotzendorff.

1936. International Ski Championship Fund. Inscr "WETTKAMPFE 1936".

788	**124**	12g. (+12g.) green	3·00	4·25
789	–	24g. (+24g.) violet	4·50	6·00
790	–	35g. (+35g.) red	29·00	50·00
791	–	60g. (+60g.) blue	29·00	50·00

DESIGNS: 24g. Skier on mountain slope; 35g. Woman slalom course skier; 60g. View of Maria Theresienstrasse, Innsbruck.

125 Madonna and Child

1936. Mothers' Day.

792	**125**	24g. blue	45	50

126 Chancellor Dollfuss

127 "St. Martin sharing Cloak"

1936. 2nd Anniv of Assassination of Dr. Dollfuss.

793	**126**	10s. blue	£950	£1100

1936. Winter Relief Fund. Inscr "WINTERHILFE 1936/37".

794	**127**	5g.+2g. green	25	65
795	–	12g.+3g. violet	25	65
796	–	24g.+6g. blue	25	65
797	–	1s.+1s. red	7·00	12·50

DESIGNS: 12g. "Healing the sick"; 24g. "St. Elizabeth feeding the hungry"; 1s. "Warming the poor".

128 J. Ressel

129 Mother and Child

1936. Welfare Funds. Austrian Inventors.

798	**128**	12g. (+12g.) brown	4·50	7·50
799	–	24g. (+24g.) violet	4·50	7·50
800	–	30g. (+30g.) red	4·50	7·50
801	–	40g. (+40g.) black	4·50	7·50
802	–	60g. (+60g.) blue	4·50	7·50
803	–	64g. (+64g.) green	4·50	7·50

PORTRAITS: 24g. Karl Ritter von Ghega; 30g. J. Werndl; 40g. Carl Freih. Auer von Welsbach; 60g. R. von Lieben; 64g. V. Kaplan.

1937. Mothers' Day.

804	**129**	24g. red	45	40

130 "Maria Anna"

131 "Child Welfare"

1937. Centenary of Regular Danube Services of Danube Steam Navigation Co. Paddle-steamers.

805	**130**	12g. red	1·10	40
806	–	24g. blue	1·10	40
807	–	64g. green	1·10	85

DESIGNS: 24g. "Helios"; 64g. "Oesterreich".

1937. Winter Relief Fund. Inscr "WINTERHILFE 1937 1938".

808	**131**	5g.+2g. green	25	50
809	–	12g.+3g. brown	25	50
810	–	24g.+6g. blue	25	50
811	–	1s.+1s. red	3·50	8·50

DESIGNS: 12g. "Feeding the Children"; 24g. "Protecting the Aged"; 1s. "Nursing the Sick".

132 Steam Locomotive "Austria", 1837

133 Dr. G. Van Swieten

1937. Railway Centenary.

812	**132**	12g. brown	25	15
813	–	25g. violet	95	1·30
814	–	35g. red	2·40	2·75

DESIGNS: 25g. Steam locomotive, 1936; 35g. Electric locomotive.

1937. Welfare Funds. Austrian Doctors.

815	**133**	5g. (+5g.) brown	2·20	4·75
816	–	8g. (+8g.) red	2·20	4·75
817	–	12g. (+12g.) brown	2·20	4·75
818	–	20g. (+20g.) green	2·20	4·75
819	–	24g. (+24g.) violet	2·20	4·75
820	–	30g. (+30g.) red	2·20	4·75
821	–	40g. (+40g.) olive	2·20	4·75
822	–	60g. (+60g.) blue	2·20	4·75
823	–	64g. (+64g.) purple	2·20	4·75

DESIGNS: 8g. L. A. von Auenbrugg; 12g. K. von Rokitansky; 20g. J. Skoda; 25g. F. von Hebra; 30g. F. von Arlt; 40g. J. Hyrtl; 60g. T. Billroth; 64g. T. Meynert.

134 Nosegay and Signs of the Zodiac

1937. Christmas Greetings.

824		12g. green	20	25
825	**134**	24g. red	20	25

ALLIED OCCUPATION. Nos. 826/905 were issued in the Russian Zone of occupation and Nos. 906/22 were a joint issue for use in the British, French and American zones.

1945. Hitler portrait stamps of Germany optd.

(a) Optd **Osterreich** only.

826	**173**	5pf. green	35	40
827		8pf. red	50	1·30

(b) Optd **Osterreich** and bar.

828	**173**	6pf. violet	35	40
829		12pf. red	50	60

(137)

(140)

1945. 1941 and 1944 Hitler stamps of Germany optd as T **137**.

830	**137**	1pf. grey	4·25	7·50
831		3pf. brown	2·50	5·00
832		4pf. grey	13·00	29·00
833		5pf. green	3·00	5·00
834		6pf. violet	35	85
835		8pf. red	1·10	1·70
836		10pf. brown	3·50	5·50
837		12pf. red	45	1·00
838		15pf. red	1·40	3·00
839		16pf. green	29·00	60·00
840		20pf. blue	3·25	5·75
841		24pf. brown	30·00	65·00
842	**173**	25pf. blue	2·75	5·00
843		30pf. green	2·75	5·00
844		40pf. mauve	3·25	5·75
845	**225**	42pf. green	6·00	12·50
846	**173**	50pf. green	4·75	9·25
847		60pf. brown	5·25	12·00
848		80pf. blue	4·25	10·50
853	**182**	1rm. green	26·00	46·00
850		2rm. violet	24·00	46·00
855		3rm. red	44·00	90·00
856		5rm. blue	£350	£650

1945. Stamps of Germany surch **OSTERREICH** and new value.

857	**186**	5pf. on 12+88pf. green	70	2·10
858	–	6pf. on 6+14pf. brown and blue (No. 811)	7·75	18·00
859	**220**	8pf. on 42+108pf. brn	1·20	3·25
860	–	12pf. on 3+7pf. blue (No. 810)	85	2·10

1945. 1941 and 1944 Hitler stamps of Germany optd as T **140**.

862	**173**	5pf. green	85	4·25
863		6pf. violet	85	3·25
864		8pf. red	70	2·50
865		12pf. red	85	3·00
866		30pf. green	8·75	21·00
867a	**225**	42pf. green	24·00	42·00

141 New National Arms

142 New National Arms

1945.

868	**141**	3pf. brown	15	15
869		4pf. blue	15	35
870		5pf. green	15	40
871		6pf. purple	15	20
872		8pf. orange	15	20
873		10pf. brown	15	20
874		12pf. red	15	20
875		15pf. orange	15	20
876		16pf. green	15	40
877		20pf. blue	15	20
878		24pf. orange	15	35
879		25pf. blue	15	35
880		30pf. green	15	20
881		38pf. blue	15	25
882		40pf. purple	15	25
883		42pf. grey	25	35
884		50pf. green	15	40
885		60pf. red	15	35
886		80pf. violet	15	35
887	**142**	1rm. green	25	85
888		2rm. violet	25	85
889		3rm. purple	35	1·30
890		5rm. brown	45	1·70

Nos. 877/86 are 24 × 28 mm.

144 Allegorical of the Home Land

145 Posthorn

1945. Austrian Welfare Charities.

905	**144**	1s.+10s. green	1·10	3·25

1945.

906	**145**	1g. blue	15	60
907		3g. orange	15	20
908		4g. brown	15	20
909		5g. green	15	20
910		6g. purple	15	20
911		8g. red	15	20
912		10g. grey	15	20
913		12g. brown	15	20
914		15g. red	15	20
915		20g. brown	15	20
916		25g. blue	15	20
917		30g. mauve	15	20
918		40g. blue	15	20
919		60g. olive	15	25
920		1s. violet	25	65
921		2s. yellow	50	1·70
922		5s. blue	70	2·10

146 Salzburg

148 Durnstein

1945. Views as T **146/8**.

No.	Type	Description	Unused	Used
923	–	3g. blue	15	15
924	–	4g. red	15	15
925	–	5g. red	15	15
926	**146**	6g. green	15	15
927	–	8g. brown	15	15
928	–	8g. purple	15	15
929	–	8g. green	15	15
930	–	10g. green	15	15
931	–	10g. purple	15	15
932	–	12g. brown	15	15
933	–	15g. blue	15	15
934	–	16g. brown	15	15
935	–	20g. blue	15	15
936	–	24g. green	15	15
937	–	25g. grey	15	15
938	–	30g. red	15	15
939	–	30g. blue	45	40
940	–	35g. red	15	15
941	–	38g. green	15	35
942	–	40g. grey	15	15
943	–	42g. red	15	15
944	–	45g. blue	35	65
945	–	50g. blue	20	15
946	–	50g. purple	60	60
947	–	60g. blue	15	20
948	–	60g. violet	2·50	3·00
949	–	70g. blue	35	40
950	–	80g. brown	35	60
951	–	90g. green	1·70	2·50
952A	**148**	1s. brown	85	90
953A	–	2s. grey	3·50	5·00
954A	–	3s. green	1·10	1·70
955A	–	5s. red	1·70	3·25

DESIGNS—As Type **146**: 3g. Lermoos; 4g. Iron-ore mine, Erzberg; 5g. Leopoldsberg, Vienna; 8g. (927), Prater Woods, Vienna; 8g. (928/9), Town Hall Park, Vienna; 10g. (930/1), Hochosterwitz; 12g. Schafberg; 15g. Forchtenstein; 16g. Gesauseeingang. 23½ × 29 mm: 20g. Gebhartsberg; 24g. Holdrichsmuhle, near Modling; 25g. Vent im Otztal; 30g. (938/9), Neusiedler Lake; 35g. Belvedere Palace, Vienna; 38g. Langbath Lake; 40g. Mariazell; 42g. Traunstein; 45g. Burg Hartenstein; 50g. (945/6), Silvretta Peaks, Vorarlberg; 60g. (947/8), Semmering; 70g. Badgastein; 80g. Kaisergebirge; 90g. Wayside shrine near Tragoss. As T **148**: 2s. St. Christof; 3s. Heiligenblut; 5s. Schonbrunn Palace, Vienna.

See also Nos. 1072/86a.

1946. 1st Anniv of U.N.O. No. 938 surch **26. JUNI 1945+20 g 26. JUNI 1946** and globe.

No.	Type	Description	Unused	Used
971		30g.+20g. red	3·00	5·50

151 Dr. Karl Renner

1946. 1st Anniv of Establishment of Renner Government.

No.	Type	Description	Unused	Used
972	**151**	1s.+1s. green	3·00	7·50
973		2s.+2s. violet	3·00	7·50
974		3s.+3s. purple	3·00	7·50
975		5s.+5s. brown	3·00	7·50
MS976		Four sheets, each 180 × 155 mm, each with block of 8 of one value (972/5) and Arms in centre. Imperf Set 4 sheets	£2250	£11000

152 Dagger and Map

(153)

1946. "Anti-Fascist" Exhibition.

No.	Type	Description	Unused	Used
977	**152**	5g.+3g. sepia	45	1·10
978	–	6g.+4g. green	35	85
979	–	8g.+6g. orange	35	85
980	–	12g.+12g. blue	35	85
981	–	30g.+30g. violet	35	75
982	–	42g.+42g. brown	35	90
983	–	1s.+1s. red	45	1·30
984	–	2s.+2s. red	85	2·20

DESIGNS: 6g. Broom sweeping Nazi and Fascist emblems; 8g. St. Stephen's Cathedral in flames; 12g. Hand and barbed wire; 30g. Hand strangling snake; 42g. Hammer and broken column; 1s. Hand and Austrian flag; 2s. Eagle and smoking Nazi emblem.

1946. Congress of Society for Promotion of Cultural and Economic Relations with the Soviet Union. No. 932 optd with T **153**.

No.	Type	Description	Unused	Used
985		12g. brown	25	55

154 Mare and Foal

155 Ruprecht's Church, Vienna

1946. Austria Prize Race Fund.

No.	Type	Description	Unused	Used
986	**154**	16g.+16g. red	2·50	5·75
987	–	24g.+24g. violet	2·20	5·00
988	–	60g.+60g. green	2·20	5·00
989	–	1s.+1s. blue	2·20	5·00
990	–	2s.+2s. brown	4·75	9·25

DESIGNS: 24g. Two horses' heads; 60g. Racehorse clearing hurdle; 1s. Three racehorses; 2s. Three horses' heads.

1946. 950th Anniv of First recorded use of name "Osterreich".

No.	Type	Description	Unused	Used
991	**155**	30g.+70g. red	45	90

156 Statue of Duke Rudolf

157 Franz Grillparzer (dramatic poet)

1946. St. Stephen's Cathedral Reconstruction Fund. Architectural and Sculptural designs.

No.	Type	Description	Unused	Used
992	**156**	3g.+12g. brown	20	75
993	–	5g.+20g. purple	20	75
994	–	6g.+24g. blue	20	75
995	–	8g.+32g. green	20	75
996	–	10g.+40g. blue	15	85
997	–	12g.+48g. violet	45	1·50
998	–	30g.+1s.20 red	1·30	2·10
999	–	50g.+1s.80 blue	1·90	4·00
1000	–	1s.+5s. purple	2·20	5·00
1001	–	2s.+10s. brown	4·00	10·00

DESIGNS: 5g. Tomb of Frederick III; 6g. Pulpit; 8g. Statue of St. Stephen; 10g. Statue of Madonna and Child; 12g. Altar; 30g. Organ; 50g. Anton Pilgram; 1s. N.E. Tower; 2s. S.W. Spire.

1947. Famous Austrians.

No.	Type	Description	Unused	Used
1002	–	12g. green	25	15
1003	**157**	18g. purple	20	15
1004	–	20g. green	45	25
1005	–	40g. brown	9·25	5·25
1006	–	40g. green	8·75	8·50
1007	–	60g. lake	45	40

PORTRAITS: 12g. Franz Schubert (composer); 20g. Carl Michael Ziehrer (composer); 40g. (No. 1005), Adalbert Stifter (poet); 40g. (No. 1006), Anton Bruckner (composer); 60g. Friedrich Amerling (painter).

158 Harvesting

159 Airplane over Hinterstoder

1947. Vienna Fair Fund.

No.	Type	Description	Unused	Used
1009	**158**	3g.+2g. brown	45	85
1010	–	8g.+2g. green	45	85
1011	–	10g.+5g. slate	45	85
1012	–	12g.+8g. violet	45	85
1013	–	18g.+12g. olive	45	85
1014	–	30g.+10g. purple	45	85
1015	–	35g.+15g. red	50	1·20
1016	–	60g.+20g. blue	70	1·30

DESIGNS: 8g. Logging; 10g. Factory; 12g. Pithead; 18g. Oil wells; 30g. Textile machinery; 35g. Foundry; 60g. Electric cables.

1947. Air.

No.	Type	Description	Unused	Used
1017	–	50g. brown	30	85
1018	–	1s. purple	35	85
1019	–	2s. green	40	1·30
1020	**159**	3s. brown	3·00	5·75
1021	–	4s. green	2·40	5·75
1022	–	5s. blue	2·40	5·75
1023	–	10s. blue	1·10	9·25

DESIGNS—Airplane over: 50g. Windmill at St. Andra; 1s. Heidentor; 2s. Gmund; 4s. Pragraten; 5s. Torsaule; 10s. St. Charles's Church, Vienna.

160 Beaker (15th century)

161 Racehorse

1947. National Art Exhibition Fund.

No.	Type	Description	Unused	Used
1024	**160**	3g.+2g. brown	40	65
1025	–	8g.+2g. green	40	65
1026	–	10g.+5g. red	40	65
1027	–	12g.+8g. violet	40	65
1028	–	18g.+12g. brown	40	75
1029	–	20g.+10g. violet	40	70
1030	–	30g.+10g. green	40	70
1031	–	35g.+15g. red	40	85
1032	–	48g.+12g. purple	40	85
1033	–	60g.+20g. blue	45	95

DESIGNS: 8g. Statue of "Providence" (Donner); 10g. Benedictine Monastery, Melk; 12g. "Wife of Dr. Brante of Vienna"; 18g. "Children in a Window" (Waldmuller); 20g. Belvedere Palace Gateway; 30g. Figure of "Egeria" on fountain at Schonbrunn; 35g. National Library, Vienna; 48g. "Copper Printer's (Ernst Rohm) Workshop" (Ferdinand Schmutzer); 60g. "Girl in Straw Hat" (Amerling).

1947. Vienna Prize Race Fund.

No.	Type	Description	Unused	Used
1034	**161**	60+20g. blue on pink	20	85

163 Prisoner-of-war

165 Globe and Tape Machine

1947. Prisoners-of-war Relief Fund.

No.	Type	Description	Unused	Used
1063	**163**	8g.+2g. green	20	50
1064	–	12g.+8g. brown	20	55
1065	–	18g.+12g. black	20	55
1066	–	35g.+15g. purple	20	55
1067	–	60g.+20g. blue	20	55
1068	–	1s.+40g. brown	30	1·10

DESIGNS: 12g. Letter from home; 18g. Gruesome camp visitor; 35g. Soldier and family reunited; 60g. Industry beckons returned soldier; 1s. Soldier sowing.

1947. Nos. 934 and 941 surch.

No.	Type	Description	Unused	Used
1069		75g. on 38g. green	35	95
1070		1s.40 on 16g. brown	15	25

1947. Telegraph Centenary.

No.	Type	Description	Unused	Used
1071	**165**	40g. violet	25	40

1947. Currency Revaluation. (a) As T **146**.

No.	Type	Description	Unused	Used
1072		3g. red (Lermoos)	25	20
1073		5g. red (Leopoldsberg)	25	15
1074		10g. red (Hochosterwitz)	25	15
1075		15g. red (Forchtenstein)	2·20	1·90
		(b) As T **146** but larger (23½ × 29 mm).		
1076		20g. red (Gebhartsberg)	45	15
1077		30g. red (Neusiedler Lake)	65	25
1078		40g. red (Mariazell)	60	15
1079		50g. red (Silvretta Peaks)	85	15
1080		60g. red (Semmering)	10·00	2·00
1081		70g. red (Badgastein)	3·50	20
1082		80g. red (Kaisergebirge)	3·50	20
1083		90g. red (Wayside shrine, Tragoss)	4·25	1·00
		(c) As T **148**.		
1084		1s. violet (Durnstein)	70	15
1085		2s. violet (St. Christof)	85	25
1086		3s. violet (Heiligenblut)	17·00	1·50
1086a		5s. violet (Schonbrunn)	17·00	2·10

Nos. 1072/86a in new currency replaced previous issue at rate of 3s. (old) = 1s. (new).

166 Sacred Olympic Flame

167 Laabenbach Viaduct, Neulenbach

1948. Fund for Entries to 5th Winter Olympic Games, St. Moritz.

No.	Type	Description	Unused	Used
1087	**166**	1s.+50g. blue	40	65

1948. Reconstruction Fund.

No.	Type	Description	Unused	Used
1088	**167**	10g.+5g. grey	20	25
1089	–	20g.+10g. violet	20	25
1090	–	30g.+10g. green	45	45
1091	–	40g.+20g. green	30	25
1092	–	45g.+20g. blue	30	25
1093	–	60g.+30g. red	30	25
1094	–	75g.+35g. purple	20	25
1095	–	80g.+40g. purple	40	25
1096	–	1s.+50g. blue	40	25
1097	–	1s.40+70g. lake	55	80

DESIGNS (showing reconstruction): 20g. Vermunt Lake Dam; 30g. Danube Port, Vienna; 40g. Erzberg open-cast mine; 45g. Southern Railway Station, Vienna; 60g. Flats; 75g. Vienna Gas Works; 80g. Oil refinery; 1s. Mountain roadway; 1s.40, Parliament Building.

169 Violets

170 Vorarlberg Montafon

1948. Anti-tuberculosis Fund.

No.	Type	Description	Unused	Used
1098	**169**	10g.+5g. violet, mauve and green	35	30
1099	–	20g.+10g. green, light green and yellow	25	25
1100	–	30g.+10g. brown, yellow and green	3·25	3·25
1101	–	40g.+20g. green, yellow and orange	65	70
1102	–	45g.+20g. purple, mauve and yellow	25	25
1103	–	60g.+30g. red, mauve and green	25	25
1104	–	75g.+35g. green, pink and yellow	25	25
1105	–	80g.+40g. blue, pink and green	35	30
1106	–	1s.+50g. blue, ultramarine and green	40	35
1107	–	1s.40+70g. green, blue and yellow	1·70	1·70

FLOWERS: 20g. Anemone; 30g. Crocus; 40g. Primrose; 45g. Pasque flower; 60g. Rhododendron; 75g. Wild rose; 80g. Cyclamen; 1s. Gentian; 1s.40, Edelweiss.

1948. Provincial Costumes.

No.	Type	Description	Unused	Used
1108	–	3g. grey	75	1·00
1109	–	5g. green	25	15
1110	–	10g. blue	25	15
1111	–	15g. brown	45	15
1112	**170**	20g. green	25	15
1113	–	25g. brown	25	15
1114	–	30g. red	2·75	15
1115	–	30g. violet	65	15
1116	–	40g. violet	2·75	15
1117	–	40g. green	45	15
1118	–	45g. blue	2·75	60
1119	–	50g. brown	90	15
1120	–	60g. red	45	15
1121	–	70g. green	50	15
1122	–	75g. blue	5·25	55
1123	–	80g. rose	55	20
1124	–	90g. purple	42·00	40
1125	–	1s. blue	11·50	20
1126	–	1s. red	95·00	20
1127	–	1s. green	40	20
1128	–	1s.20 violet	65	20
1129	–	1s.40 brown	3·75	25
1130	–	1s.45 red	1·90	20
1131	–	1s.50 blue	1·40	20
1132	–	1s.60 red	55	20
1133	–	1s.70 blue	3·25	65
1134	–	2s. green	1·30	20
1135	–	2s.20 slate	6·50	20
1136	–	2s.40 blue	1·40	20
1137	–	2s.50 brown	4·75	1·80
1138	–	2s.70 brown	95	70
1139	–	3s. lake	2·75	20
1140	–	3s.50 green	26·00	20
1141	–	4s.50 purple	95	70
1142	–	5s. purple	1·40	20
1143	–	7s. olive	7·00	1·50
1144	–	10s. grey	40·00	6·25

DESIGNS—As T **170**: 3g. "Tirol Inntal"; 5g. "Salzburg Pinzgau"; 10, 75g. "Steiermark Salzkammergut" (different designs); 15g. "Burgenland Lutzmannsburg"; 25g., 1s.60, "Wien 1850" (two different designs); 30g. (2) "Salzburg Pongau"; 40g. (2) "Wien 1840"; 45g. "Karnten Lesachtal"; 50g. "Vorarlberg Bregenzerwald"; 60g. "Karnten Lavanttal"; 70g. "Niederosterreich Wachau"; 80g. "Steiermark Ennstal"; 90g. "Steiermark Mittelsteier"; 1s. (3) "Tirol Pustertal"; 1s.20, "Niederosterreich Wienerwald"; 1s.40, "Oberosterreich Innviertel"; 1s.45, "Wilter bei Innsbruck"; 1s.50, "Wien 1853"; 1s.70, "Ost Tirol Kals"; 2s. "Oberosterreich"; 2s.20, "Ischl 1820"; 2s.40, "Kitzbuhel"; 2s.50, "Obersteiermark 1850"; 2s.70, "Kleines Walsertal"; 3s. "Burgenland"; 3s.50, "Niederosterreich 1850"; 4s.50, "Gailtal"; 5s. "Zillertal"; 7s. "Steiermark Sulmtal". 25 × 35 mm: 10s. "Wien 1850".

172 Kunstlerhaus

173 Hans Makart

1948. 80th Anniv of Creative Artists' Association.

No.	Type	Description	Unused	Used
1145	**172**	20g.+10g. green	9·00	7·00
1146	**173**	30g.+15g. brown	2·75	2·50
1147	–	40g.+20g. blue	2·75	2·50
1148	–	50g.+25g. violet	5·00	4·75
1149	–	60g.+30g. red	6·25	4·25

1150 – 1s.+50g. blue . . . . . 6·25 6·00
1151 – 1s.40+70g. brown . . . 16·00 17·00
PORTRAITS: 40g. K. Kundmann; 50g. A. von Siccardsburg; 60g. H. Canon; 1s. W. Unger; 1s.40, Friedr. Schmidt.

174 St. Rupert

175 Pres. Renner

1948. Salzburg Cathedral Reconstruction Fund.
1152 **174** 20g.+10g. green . . . . 9·00 9·25
1153 – 30g.+15g. brown . . . . 2·75 3·50
1154 – 40g.+20g. green . . . . 3·25 3·50
1155 – 50g.+25g. brown 65 80
1156 – 60g.+30g. red 65 80
1157 – 80g.+40g. purple 65 80
1158 – 1s.+50g. blue . . . . 80 1·10
1159 – 1s.40+70g. green . . . . 2·75 3·00
DESIGNS: 30, 40, 50, 80g. Views of Salzburg Cathedral; 60g. St. Peter's; 1s. Cathedral and Fortress; 1s.40, Madonna.

1948. 30th Anniv of Republic.
1160 **175** 1s. blue . . . . 3·00 2·50
See also Nos. 1224 and 1333.

176 F. Gruber and J. Mohr

177 Boy and Hare

1948. 130th Anniv of Composition of Carol "Silent Night, Holy Night".
1161 **176** 60g. brown . . . . . . 6·25 5·75

1949. Child Welfare Fund.
1162 **177** 40g.+10g. purple . . . . 18·00 21·00
1163 – 60g.+20g. red . . . . . 18·00 21·00
1164 – 1s.+25g. blue . . . . . 18·00 21·00
1165 – 1s.40+35g. green . . . . 23·00 24·00
DESIGNS: 60g. Two girls and apples in boot; 1s. Boy and birthday cake; 1s.40, Girl praying before candle.

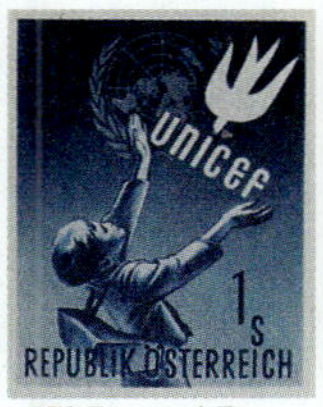

178 Boy and Dove

179 Johann Strauss

1949. U.N. Int. Children's Emergency Fund.
1166 **178** 1s. blue . . . . 13·50 3·00

1949. 50th Death Anniv of Johann Strauss the Younger (composer).
1167 **179** 1s. blue . . . . 3·50 3·00
See also Nos. 1174, 1207 and 1229.

180 Esperanto Star

181 St. Gebhard

1949. Esperanto Congress, Vienna.
1168 **180** 20g. green 90 85

1949. Birth Millenary of St. Gebhard (Bishop of Vorarlberg).
1169 **181** 30g. violet . . . . 2·00 1·90

182 Seal of Duke Friedrich II, 1230

183 Allegory of U.P.U.

1949. Prisoners-of-war Relief Fund. Arms.
1170 **182** 40g.+10g. yell & brn . . 13·00 11·50
1171 – 60g.+15g. pink & pur . . 11·50 8·75
1172 – 1s.+25g. red & blue . . 11·50 8·75
1173 – 1s.60+40g. pink and green . . . . 14·00 13·50
ARMS: 60g. Princes of Austria, 1450; 1s. Austria, 1600; 1s.60, Austria, 1945.

1949. Death Centenary of Johann Strauss the Elder (composer). Portrait as T **179**.
1174 30g. purple . . . . 2·00 2·20

1949. 75th Anniv of U.P.U.
1175 **183** 40g. green . . . . 4·50 4·00
1176 – 60g. red . . . . 5·00 3·50
1177 – 1s. blue . . . . 10·00 7·75
DESIGNS: 60g. Children holding "75"; 1s. Woman's head.

185 Magnifying Glass and Covers

186 M. M. Daffinger

1949. Stamp Day.
1206 **185** 60g.+15g. brown . . . . 3·75 2·75

1949. 50th Death Anniv of Karl Millocker (composer). Portrait as T **179**.
1207 1s. blue . . . . 26·00 13·00

1950. 160th Birth Anniv of Moritz Michael Daffinger (painter).
1208 **186** 60g. brown . . . . . . 9·75 7·00

187 A. Hofer

1950. 140th Death Anniv of Andreas Hofer (patriot).
1209 **187** 60g. violet . . . . 16·00 11·50
See also Nos. 1211, 1223, 1232, 1234, 1243, 1253, 1288 and 1386.

188 Stamp of 1850

189 Arms of Austria and Carinthia

1950. Austrian Stamp Centenary.
1210 **188** 1s. black on yellow . . . 2·00 1·70

1950. Death Centenary of Josef Madersperger (sewing machine inventor). Portrait as T **187**.
1211 60g. violet . . . . 8·50 4·25

1950. 30th Anniv of Carinthian Plebiscite.
1212 **189** 60g.+15g. grn & brn . . 45·00 33·00
1213 – 1s.+25g. red & orange 45·00 39·00
1214 – 1s.70+40g. blue and turquoise . . . . . . 50·00 44·00
DESIGNS: 1s. Carinthian waving Austrian flag; 1s.70, Hand and ballot box.

190 Rooks

191 Philatelist

1950. Air.
1215 **190** 60g. violet . . . . . . 4·00 3·50
1216 – 1s. violet (Barn swallows) . . . . . . 25·00 20·00
1217 – 2s. blue (Black-headed gulls) . . . . . . 18·00 7·50
1218 – 3s. turquoise (Great cormorants) £160 £100
1219 – 5s. brown (Common buzzard) £150 £110
1220 – 10s. purple (Grey heron) 70·00 55·00
1221 – 20s. sepia (Golden eagle) 12·00 5·75

1950. Stamp Day.
1222 **191** 60g.+15g. green . . . . 12·00 8·75

1950. Birth Centenary of Alexander Girardi (actor). Portrait as T **187**.
1223 30g. blue . . . . 2·00 1·50

192 Dr. Renner

193 Miner

1951. Death of Pres. Karl Renner.
1224 **192** 1s. black on lemon . . . 1·60 45

1951. Reconstruction Fund.
1225 **193** 40g.+10g. purple . . . . 19·00 17·00
1226 – 60g.+15g. green . . . . 19·00 17·00
1227 – 1s.+25g. brown . . . . 19·00 17·00
1228 – 1s.70+40g. blue . . . . 19·00 17·00
DESIGNS: 60g. Bricklayer; 1s. Bridge-builder; 1s.70, Telegraph engineer.

1951. 150th Birth Anniv of Joseph Lanner (composer). Portrait as T **179**.
1229 60g. green . . . . 5·75 2·50

194 Martin Johann Schmidt

195 Scout Badge

1951. 150th Death Anniv of Schmidt (painter).
1230 **194** 1s. red . . . . 8·00 3·50

1951. Boy Scout Jamboree.
1231 **195** 1s. red, yellow & green 5·75 4·50

1951. 10th Death Anniv of Wilhelm Kienzl (composer). Portrait as T **187**.
1232 1s.50 blue . . . . 3·75 2·00

196 Laurel Branch and Olympic Emblem

197 Schrammel

1952. 6th Winter Olympic Games, Oslo.
1233 **196** 2s.40+60g. green . . . . 25·00 22·00

1952. 150th Birth Anniv of Karl Ritter von Ghega (railway engineer). Portrait as T **187**.
1234 1s. green . . . . 8·50 2·10

1952. Birth Cent of Josef Schrammel (composer).
1235 **197** 1s.50 blue . . . . 8·50 2·10
See also No. 1239.

198 Cupid and Letter

199 Breakfast Pavilion

1952. Stamp Day.
1236 **198** 1s.50+35g. purple . . . 25·00 21·00

1952. Bicentenary of Schonbrunn Menagerie.
1237 **199** 1s.50 green . . . . . . 7·75 2·40

200

202

1952. Int Union of Socialist Youth Camp, Vienna.
1238 **200** 1s.50 blue . . . . 8·25 1·50

1952. 150th Birth Anniv of Nikolaus Lenau (writer). Portrait as T **197**.
1239 1s. green . . . . 8·50 2·10

1952. International Children's Correspondence.
1240 **202** 2s.40 blue . . . . 14·50 3·00

203 "Christus Pantocrator" (sculpture)

204 Hugo Wolf

1952. Austrian Catholics' Day.
1241 **203** 1s.+25g. olive . . . . . 13·50 12·50

1953. 50th Death Anniv of Wolf (composer).
1242 **204** 1s.50 blue . . . . 8·75 1·80

1953. President Korner's 80th Birthday. As T **187** but portrait of Korner.
1243 1s.50 blue . . . . 8·50 1·30
For 1s.50 black, see No. 1288.

1953. 60th Anniv of Austrian Trade Union Movement. As No. 955 (colour changed) surch **GEWERKSCHAFTS BEWEGUNG 60 JAHRE 1s+25g.**
1244 1s.+25g. on 5s. blue . . . . 3·25 3·00

206 Linz National Theatre

207 Meeting-house, Steyr

1953. 150th Anniv of Linz National Theatre.
1245 **206** 1s.50 turquoise . . . . . 20·00 2·50

1953. Vienna Evangelical School Rebuilding Fund.
1246 **207** 70g.+15g. purple 25 25
1247 – 1s.+25g. blue 25 25
1248 – 1s.50+40g. brown . . . 75 75
1249 – 2s.40+60g. green . . . . 3·50 3·50
1250 – 3s.+75g. lilac . . . . . 8·75 8·50
DESIGNS: 1s. J. Kepler (astronomer); 1s.50, Lutheran Bible, 1534; 2s.40, T. von Hansen (architect); 3s. School after reconstruction.

208 Child and Christmas Tree

209

1953. Christmas.
1251 **208** 1s. green . . . . 1·50 40
See also No. 1266.

1953. Stamp Day.
1252 **209** 1s.+25g. brown . . . . 8·50 7·75

1954. 150th Birth Anniv of M. Von Schwind (painter). As T **187** but portrait of Von Schwind.
1253 1s.50 lilac . . . . 18·00 2·75

210 Baron K. von Rokitansky
212 Surgeon with Microscope

1954. 150th Birth Anniv of Von Rokitansky (anatomist).
1254 **210** 1s.50 violet . . . . . . 20·00 3·00
See also No. 1264.

1954. Avalanche Fund. As No. 953 (colour changed) surch **LAWINENOPFER 1954 1s+20g.**
1255 1s.+20g. blue 30 30

1954. Health Service Fund.
1256 – 30g.+10g. violet . . . . 1·50 1·40
1257 **212** 70g.+15g. brown 30 30
1258 – 1s.+25g. blue 30 30
1259 – 1s.45+35g. green 65 60
1260 – 1s.50+35g. red . . . . . 6·25 6·50
1261 – 2s.40+60g. purple . . . 7·50 8·00
DESIGNS: 30g. Boy patient and sun-ray lamp; 1s. Mother and children; 1s.45, Operating theatre; 1s.50, Baby on scales; 2s.40, Red Cross nurse and ambulance.

213 Esperanto Star
214 J. M. Rottmayr von Rosenbrunn

1954. 50th Anniv of Esperanto in Austria.
1262 **213** 1s. green and brown . . 5·50 50

1954. Birth Tercentenary of Rottmayr von Rosenbrunn (painter).
1263 **214** 1s. green . . . . 15·00 3·50

1954. 25th Death Anniv of Dr. Auer von Welsbach (inventor). Portrait as T **210**.
1264 1s.50 blue . . . . 36·00 3·00

216 Great Organ, Church of St. Florian
217 18th-century River Boat

1954. 2nd International Congress of Catholic Church Music, Vienna.
1265 **216** 1s. brown . . . . 2·75 50

1954. Christmas. As No. 1251, but colour changed.
1266 **208** 1s. blue . . . . 4·75 75

1954. Stamp Day.
1267 **217** 1s.+25g. green . . . . . 8·25 7·25

218 Arms of Austria and Newspapers

1954. 150th Anniv of State Printing Works and 250th Anniv of "Wiener-Zeitung" (newspaper).
1268 **218** 1s. black and red . . . . 3·25 45

219 "Freedom"

1955. 10th Anniv of Re-establishment of Austrian Republic.
1269 – 70g. purple . . . . . . 1·80 30
1270 – 1s. blue . . . . 6·75 30
1271 **219** 1s.45 red . . . . . . 11·50 4·00
1272 – 1s.50 brown . . . . . . 29·00 40
1273 – 2s.40 green . . . . . . 11·50 7·00
DESIGNS: 70g. Parliament Buildings; 1s. Western Railway terminus, Vienna; 1s.50, Modern houses; 2s.40, Limberg Dam.

1955. Austrian State Treaty. As No. 888, but colour changed, optd **STAATSVERTRAG 1955**.
1274 **142** 2s. grey . . . . 3·25 70

221 "Strength through Unity"

1955. 4th World Trade Unions Congress, Vienna.
1275 **221** 1s. blue . . . . 3·25 2·75

222 "Return to Work"

1955. Returned Prisoners-of-war Relief Fund.
1276 **222** 1s.+25g. brown . . . . 3·00 2·50

223 Burgtheater, Vienna

1955. Re-opening of Burgtheater and State Opera House, Vienna.
1277 **223** 1s.50 brown . . . . . . 4·75 40
1278 – 2s.40 blue (Opera House) 6·00 3·00

224 Globe and Flags
225 Stamp Collector

1955. 10th Anniv of U.N.O.
1279 **224** 2s.40 green . . . . . . 17·00 3·50

1955. Stamp Day.
1280 **225** 1s.+25g. brown . . . . 4·50 4·00

226 Mozart
227

1956. Birth Bicentenary of Mozart (composer).
1281 **226** 2s.40 blue . . . . 6·25 1·50

1956. Admission of Austria into U.N.
1282 **227** 2s.40 brown . . . . . . 15·00 2·50

228
229 Vienna and Five New Towns

1956. 5th World Power Conference, Vienna.
1283 **228** 2s.40 blue . . . . 13·50 3·00

1956. 23rd International Town Planning Congress.
1284 **229** 1s.45 red, black & green 4·00 1·00

230 J. B. Fischer von Erlach
231 "Stamp Day"

1956. Birth Tercentenary of Fischer von Erlach (architect).
1285 **230** 1s.50 brown . . . . . . 1·10 1·20

1956. Stamp Day.
1286 **231** 1s.+25g. red . . . . . . 3·75 3·50

1956. Hungarian Relief Fund. As No. 1173, but colours changed, surch **1956 1.50 +50 UNGARNHILFE.**
1287 1s.50+50g. on 1s.60+40g. red and grey 80 70

1957. Death of Pres. Korner. As No. 1243, but colour changed.
1288 1s.50 black . . . . 2·30 1·80

233 J. Wagner von Jauregg
234 Anton Wildgans

1957. Birth Centenary of Wagner von Jauregg (psychiatrist).
1289 **233** 2s.40 brown . . . . . . 5·25 2·75

1957. 25th Death Anniv of Anton Wildgans (poet).
1290 **234** 1s. blue 40 30

235 Daimber (1907), Graf and Stift (1957) Post Buses

1957. 50th Anniv of Postal Coach Service.
1291 **235** 1s. black on yellow . . . 50 35

237 Mt. Gasherbrum II
236 Mariazell Basilica

1957. Austrian Himalaya–Karakorum Expedition, 1956.
1293 **237** 1s.50 blue 55 40

1957. Buildings. (a) Size 20½ × 24½ mm.
1295 – 20g. purple 25 25
1296 – 30g. green 35 25
1297 – 40g. red 25 15
1298 – 50g. grey 65 15
1299 – 60g. brown 40 15
1300 – 70g. blue 40 15
1301 – 80g. brown 35 15
1302 **236** 1s. brown 90 15
1303 – 1s. brown 70 15
1304 – 1s.20 purple 85 25
1305 – 1s.30 green 60 15
1306 – 1s.40 blue 70 25
1307 – 1s.50 red 10 20
1308 – 1s.80 blue 80 20
1309 – 2s. blue . . . . 4·50 15
1310 – 2s. blue 80 15
1311 – 2s.20 green . . . . . . 1·00 25
1312 – 2s.50 violet . . . . . . 1·60 60
1313 – 3s. blue . . . . 1·20 15
1314 – 3s.40 green . . . . . . 1·50 85
1315 – 3s.50 mauve . . . . . . 1·20 15
1316 – 4s. violet . . . . 2·00 15
1317 – 4s.50 green . . . . . . 2·30 65
1318 – 5s.50 green . . . . . . 2·30 45
1319 – 6s. violet . . . . 1·90 15
1320 – 6s.40 blue . . . . 2·10 1·00
1321 – 8s. purple . . . . 2·10 40

(b) Larger.
1322 – 10s. green . . . . 4·00 40
1323 – 20s. purple . . . . . . 4·75 85

(c) Smaller, size 17½ × 21 mm.
1324 – 50g. grey 25 15
1325 **236** 1s. brown 35 20
1326 – 1s.50 purple 35 20

DESIGNS: 20g. Old Courtyard, Morbisch; 30g. Vienna Town Hall; 40g. Porcia Castle, Spittal; 50g. Heiligenstadt flats; 60g. Lederer Tower, Wells; 70g. Archbishop's Palace, Salzburg; 80g. Old farmhouse, Pinzgau; 1s. (1303) Millstatt; 1s.20, Corn Measurer's House, Bruck-on-the-Mur; 1s.30, Schattenburg Castle; 1s.40, Klagenfurt Town Hall; 1s.50, "Rabenhof" Flats, Erdberg, Vienna; 1s.80, Mint Tower, Hall-in-Tyrol; 2s. (1309) Christkindl Church; 2s. (1310) Dragon Fountain, Klagenfurt; 2s.20, Beethoven's House, Heiligenstadt, Vienna; 2s.50, Danube Bridge, Linz; 3s. "Swiss Portal", Imperial Palace, Vienna; 3s.40, Stein Gate, Krems-on-the-Danube; 3s.50, Esterhazy Palace, Eisenstadt; 4s. Vienna Gate, Hainburg; 4s.50, Schwechat Airport; 5s.50, Chur Gate, Feldkirch; 6s. Graz Town Hall; 6s.40, "Golden Roof", Innsbruck; 8s. Steyr Town Hall. 22 × 28½ mm: 10s. Heidenreichstein Castle. 28½ × 37½ mm: 20s. Melk Abbey.

238 Post Office, Linz

1957. Stamp Day.
1327 **238** 1s.+25g. green . . . . . 3·75 3·25

239 Badgastein

1958. International Alpine Ski Championships, Badgastein.
1328 **239** 1s.50 blue 35 25

240 Vickers Viscount 800
241 Mother and Child

1958. Austrian Airlines Inaugural Flight, Vienna–London.
1329 **240** 4s. red 90 35

1958. Mothers' Day.
1330 **241** 1s.50 blue 35 25

242 Walther von der Vogelweide (after 12th-century manuscript)
243 Dr. O. Redlich

1958. 3rd Austrian Choir Festival, Vienna.
1331 **242** 1s.50 multicoloured . . . 35 25

1958. Birth Cent of Dr. Oswald Redlich (historian).
1332 **243** 2s.40 blue 75 50

1958. 40th Anniv of Republic. As T **175** but inscr "40 JAHRE".
1333 **175** 1s.50 green 80 65

244 Post Office, Kitzbuhel

1958. Stamp Day.
1334 **244** 2s.40+60g. blue . . . . 1·20 95

245 "E" building on Map of Europe

246 Monopoly Emblem and Cigars

1959. Europa.
1335 **245** 2s.40 green . . . . . . 1·10 45

1959. 175th Anniv of Austrian Tobacco Monopoly.
1336 **246** 2s.40 brown 60 35

247 Archduke Johann

248 Western Capercailie

1959. Death Cent of Archduke Johann of Austria.
1337 **247** 1s.50 green 40 30

1959. International Hunting Congress, Vienna.
1338 **248** 1s. purple 45 25
1339 – 1s.50 blue (Roebuck) . . 60 20
1340 – 2s.40 grn (Wild boar) . . 80 95
1341 – 3s.50 brown (Red deer family) 70 50

249 Haydn

250 Tyrolean Eagle

1959. 150th Death Anniv of Haydn.
1342 **249** 1s.50 purple 55 30

1959. 150th Anniv of Tyrolese Rising.
1343 **250** 1s.50 red 35 25

251 Microwave Transmitting Aerial, Zugspitze

252 Handball Player

1959. Inaug of Austrian Microwave Network.
1344 **251** 2s.40 blue 50 30

1959. Sports.
1345 – 1s. violet 35 25
1346 **252** 1s.50 green 70 35
1347 – 1s.80 red 45 35
1348 – 2s. purple 30 20
1349 – 2s.20 blue 45 35
DESIGNS: 1s. Runner; 1s.80, Gymnast; 2s. Hurdling; 2s.20, Hammer thrower.

253 Orchestral Instruments

254 Roman Coach

1959. Vienna Philharmonic Orchestra's World Tour.
1350 **253** 2s.40 black and blue . . 55 40

1959. Stamp Day.
1351 **254** 2s.40+60g. blk & mve . . 90 80

255 Refugees

256 Pres. Adolf Scharf

1960. World Refugee Year.
1352 **255** 3s. turquoise 70 50

1960. President's 70th Birthday.
1353 **256** 1s.50 green 65 30

257 Youth Hostellers

258 Dr. Eiselsberg

1960. Youth Hostels Movement.
1354 **257** 1s. red 30 25

1960. Birth Cent of Dr. Anton Eiselsberg (surgeon).
1355 **258** 1s.50 sepia and cream . . 80 30

259 Gustav Mahler

260 Jakob Prandtauer

1960. Birth Centenary of Gustav Mahler (composer).
1356 **259** 1s.50 brown 80 30

1960. 300th Birth Anniv of Jakob Prandtauer (architect).
1357 **260** 1s.50 brown 80 30

261 Grossglockner Highway

262 Ionic Capital

1960. 25th Anniv of Grossglockner Alpine Highway.
1358 **261** 1s.80 blue 80 55

1960. Europa.
1359 **262** 3s. black . . . . 2·20 1·40

263 Griffen, Carinthia

1960. 40th Anniv of Carinthian Plebiscite.
1360 **263** 1s.50 green 50 30

264 Examining Proof of Engraved Stamp

1960. Stamp Day.
1361 **264** 3s.+70g. brown . . . . 1·50 1·30

265 "Freedom"

267 Transport and Multi-unit Electric Train

266 Hansa Brandenburg C-1

1961. Austrian Freedom Martyrs' Commem.
1362 **265** 1s.50 red 35 25

1961. "LUPOSTA" Exhibition, Vienna, and 1st Austrian Airmail Service Commemoration.
1363 **266** 5s. blue . . . . 1·20 85

1961. European Transport Ministers' Meeting.
1364 **267** 3s. olive and red 75 65

268 "Mower in the Alps" (Detail, A. Egger-Lienz)

269 Observatory on Sonnblick Mountain

1961. Centenary of Kunstlerhaus, Vienna. Inscr as in T **268**.
1365 **268** 1s. purple and brown . . 25 25
1366 – 1s.50 lilac and brown . . 30 25
1367 – 3s. green and brown . . 1·00 95
1368 – 5s. violet and brown . . 1·20 85
PAINTINGS: 1s.50, "The Kiss" (after A. von Pettenkofen). 3s. "Portrait of a Girl" (after A. Romako). 5s. "The Triumph of Ariadne" (detail of Ariadne, after Hans Makart).

1961. 75th Anniv of Sonnblick Meteorological Observatory.
1369 **269** 1s.80 blue 45 35

270 Lavanttaler Colliery

271 Mercury

1961. 15th Anniv of Nationalized Industries. Inscr "JAHRE VERSTAATLICHTE UNTERNEHMUNGEN".
1370 **270** 1s. black 25 20
1371 – 1s.50 green 25 20
1372 – 1s.80 red 70 65
1373 – 3s. mauve 85 80
1374 – 5s. blue . . . . 1·10 1·00
DESIGNS: 1s.50, Turbine; 1s.80, Industrial plant; 3s. Steelworks, Linz; 5s. Oil refinery, Schwechat.

1961. World Bank Congress, Vienna.
1375 **271** 3s. black 70 50

272 Arms of Burgenland

273 Liszt

1961. 40th Anniv of Burgenland.
1376 **272** 1s.50 red, yellow & sepia 35 25

1961. 150th Birth Anniv of Franz Liszt (composer).
1377 **273** 3s. brown 70 45

274 Rust Post Office

1961. Stamp Day.
1378 **274** 3s.+70g. green . . . . . 1·30 1·30

275 Court of Accounts

1961. Bicentenary of Court of Accounts.
1379 **275** 1s. sepia 30 25

276 Glockner-Kaprun Power Station

1962. 15th Anniv of Electric Power Nationalization. Inscr as in T **276**.
1380 **276** 1s. blue 25 20
1381 – 1s.50 purple 35 30
1382 – 1s.80 green 80 80
1383 – 3s. brown 70 55
1384 – 4s. red 75 60
1385 – 6s.40 black . . . . . . 1·80 1·70
DESIGNS: 1s.50, Ybbs-Persenbeug (Danube); 1s.80, Luner See; 3s. Grossraming (Enns River); 4s. Bisamberg Transformer Station; 6s.40, St. Andra Power Stations.

1962. Death Cent of Johann Nestroy (playwright). Portrait as T **187**.
1386 1s. violet 25 15

277 F. Gauermann

278 Scout Badge and Handclasp

1962. Death Cent of Friedrich Gauermann (painter).
1387 **277** 1s.50 blue 30 25

1962. 50th Anniv of Austrian Scout Movement.
1388 **278** 1s.50 green 55 35

279 Forest and Lake

1962. "The Austrian Forest".
1389 **279** 1s. grey 30 20
1390 – 1s.50 brown 50 35
1391 – 3s. myrtle . . . . 1·50 1·20
DESIGNS: 1s.50, Deciduous forest; 3s. Fir and larch forest.

280 Electric Locomotive and Steam Locomotive "Austria" (1837)

1962. 125th Anniv of Austrian Railways.
1392 **280** 3s. black and buff . . . 1·50 1·00

281 Engraving Die

282 Postal Officials of 1863

1962. Stamp Day.
1393 **281** 3s.+70g. violet . . . . . 1·70 1·70

1963. Centenary of Paris Postal Conference.
1394 **282** 3s. sepia and yellow . . 85 70

283 Hermann Bahr

284 St. Florian (statue)

1963. Birth Centenary of Hermann Bahr (writer).
1395 **283** 1s.50 sepia and blue . . 35 25

1963. Cent of Austrian Voluntary Fire Brigade.
1396 **284** 1s.50 black and pink . . 70 50

285 Flag and Emblem

1963. 5th Austrian Trade Unions Federation Congress.
1397 **285** 1s.50 red, sepia & grey 35 15

286 Crests of Tyrol and Austria

1963. 600th Anniv of Tyrol as an Austrian Province.
1398 **286** 1s.50 multicoloured . . . 35 15

287 Prince Eugene of Savoy

288 Centenary Emblem

1963. Birth Tercent of Prince Eugene of Savoy.
1399 **287** 1s.50 violet 35 25

1963. Centenary of Red Cross.
1400 **288** 3s. silver, red and black 70 45

289 Skiing (slalom)

1963. Winter Olympic Games, Innsbruck, 1964. Centres black; inscr gold; background colours given.
1401 **289** 1s. grey 20 15
1402 – 1s.20 blue 30 25
1403 – 1s.50 grey 25 20
1404 – 1s.80 purple 45 40
1405 – 2s.20 green 80 80
1406 – 3s. slate 65 45
1407 – 4s. blue . . . . 1·00 90
DESIGNS: 1s.20, Skiing (biathlon); 1s.50, Ski jumping; 1s.80, Figure skating; 2s.20, Ice hockey; 3s. Tobogganing; 4s. Bobsleighing.

290 Vienna "101" P.O. and Railway Shed

291 "The Holy Family" (Josef Stammel)

1963. Stamp Day.
1408 **290** 3s.+70g. black & drab 80 80

1963. Christmas.
1409 **291** 2s. green 45 25

292 Nasturtium

1964. Int Horticultural Exn, Vienna. Mult.
1410 1s. Type **292** 25 15
1411 1s.50 Peony 25 15
1412 1s.80 Clematis 35 30
1413 2s.20 Dahlia 75 65
1414 3s. Convolvulus 65 50
1415 4s. Mallow . . . . 1·20 85

293 Gothic Statue and Stained-glass Window

1964. Romanesque Art Exhibition, Vienna.
1416 **293** 1s.50 blue and black . . 35 25

294 Pallas Athene and Interior of Assembly Hall, Parliament Building

1964. 2nd Parliamentary and Scientific Conference, Vienna.
1417 **294** 1s.80 black and green . . 40 30

295 "The Kiss" (Gustav Klimt)

1964. Re-opening of "Viennese Secession" Exn Hall.
1418 **295** 3s. multicoloured 70 55

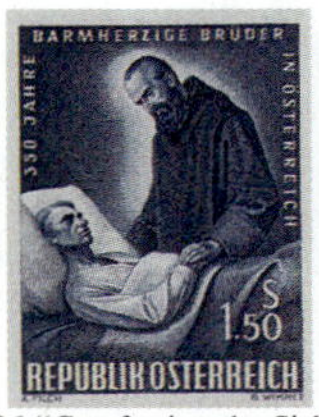

296 "Comforting the Sick"

1964. 350th Anniv of Order of Brothers of Mercy in Austria.
1419 **296** 1s.50 blue 35 25

297 "Bringing News of the Victory at Kunersdorf" (Bellotto)

1964. 15th U.P.U. Congress, Vienna. Paintings.
1420 **297** 1s. purple 20 15
1421 – 1s.20 brown 30 25
1422 – 1s.50 blue 30 20
1423 – 1s.80 violet 45 35
1424 – 2s.20 black 60 45
1425 – 3s. purple 55 45
1426 – 4s. green 80 60
1427 – 6s.40 purple . . . . . 2·20 1·70
PAINTINGS: 1s.20, "Changing Horses" (Hormann); 1s.50, "The Wedding Trip" (Schwind); 1s.80, "Postboys returning Home" (Raffalt); 2s.20, "The Vienna Mail Coach" (Klein); 3s. "Changing Horses" (Gauermann); 4s. "Postal Tracked-vehicle in Mountain Village" (Pilch); 6s.40, "Saalbach Post Office and Post-bus" (Pilch).

298 Vienna, from the Hochhaus (N.)

299 "Workers"

1964. "WIPA" Stamp Exhibition, Vienna (1965) (1st issue). Multicoloured.
1428 1s.50+30g. Type **298** 40 40
1429 1s.50+30g. N.E. 40 40
1430 1s.50+30g. E. 40 40
1431 1s.50+30g. S.E. 40 40
1432 1s.50+30g. S. 40 40
1433 1s.50+30g. S.W. 40 40
1434 1s.50+30g. W. 40 40
1435 1s.50+30g. N.W. 40 40
The designs show a panoramic view of Vienna, looking to different points of compass (indicated on stamps). The inscription reads "Vienna welcomes you to WIPA 1965".
See also Nos. 1447/52.

1964. Centenary of Austrian Workers' Movement.
1436 **299** 1s. black 30 25

300 Europa "Flower"

301 Radio Receiver Dial

1964. Europa.
1437 **300** 3s. blue . . . . 1·40 65

1964. 40th Anniv of Austrian Broadcasting Service.
1438 **301** 1s. sepia and red 25 25

302 Old Printing Press

1964. 6th International Graphical Federation Congress, Vienna.
1439 **302** 1s.50 black and drab . . 35 25

303 Post-bus Station, St. Gilgen

1964. Stamp Day.
1440 **303** 3s.+70g. multicoloured 1·00 85

304 Dr. Adolf Scharf

305 "Reconstruction"

1965. Pres. Scharf Commemoration.
1441 **304** 1s.50 blue and black . . 35 30

1965. "20 Years of Reconstruction".
1442 **305** 1s.80 lake 35 35

306 University Seal, 1365

307 "St. George" (after engraving by Altdorfer)

1965. 600th Anniv of Vienna University.
1443 **306** 3s. red and gold 65 40

1965. Danubian Art.
1444 **307** 1s.80 blue 40 30

308 I.T.U. Emblem, Morse Key and T.V. Aerial

309 F. Raimund

1965. Centenary of I.T.U.
1445 **308** 3s. violet 65 35

1965. 175th Birth Anniv of Ferdinand Raimund (actor and playwright).
1446 **309** 3s. purple 65 30

310 Egyptian Hieroglyphs on Papyrus

311 Gymnasts with Wands

1965. "WIPA" Stamp Exhibition, Vienna (2nd issue). "Development of the Letter".
1447 **310** 1s.50+40g. black and pink 40 30
1448 – 1s.80+50g. black and yellow 45 40
1449 – 2s.20+60g. black and lilac 85 85
1450 – 3s.+80g. black & yell . . 70 50
1451 – 4s.+1s. black & blue . . 1·00 1·00
1452 – 5s.+1s.20 black & grn . . 1·50 1·30
DESIGNS: 1s.80, Cuneiform writing; 2s.20, Latin; 3c. Ancient letter and seal; 4s.19th-century letter; 5s. Typewriter.

1965. 4th Gymnaestrada, Vienna.
1453 **311** 1s.50 black and blue . . 35 25
1454 – 3s. black and brown . . 60 35
DESIGNS: 3s. Girls exercising with tambourines.

312 Dr. I. Semmelweis

313 F. G. Waldmuller (self-portrait)

1965. Death Cent of Ignaz Semmelweis (physician).
1455 **312** 1s.50 lilac 30 15

1965. Death Cent of F. G. Waldmuller (painter).
1456 **313** 3s. black 60 35

314 Red Cross and Gauze **315** Flag and Crowned Eagle

1965. Red Cross Conference, Vienna.
1457 **314** 3s. red and black 65 30

1965. 50th Anniv of Austrian Towns Union.
1458 **315** 1s.50 multicoloured . . . 35 25

316 Austrian Flag, U. N. Emblem and Headquarters

1965. 10th Anniv of Austria's Membership of U.N.O.
1459 **316** 3s. sepia, red and blue 65 40

317 University Building **318** Bertha von Suttner

1965. 150th Anniv of University of Technology, Vienna.
1460 **317** 1s.50 violet 35 20

1965. 60th Anniv of Nobel Peace Prize Award to Bertha von Suttner (writer).
1461 **318** 1s.50 black 35 25

319 Postman delivering Mail

1965. Stamp Day.
1462 **319** 3s.+70g. green 90 85

320 Postal Code Map

1966. Introduction of Postal Code System.
1463 **320** 1s.50 black, red & yell 35 15

321 P.T.T. Headquarters **322** M. Ebner-Eschenbach

1966. Centenary of Austrian Posts and Telegraphs Administration.
1464 **321** 1s.50 black on cream . . 35 25

1966. 50th Death Anniv of Maria Ebner-Eschenbach (writer).
1465 **322** 3s. purple 60 30

323 Big Wheel **324** Josef Hoffmann

1966. Bicentenary of Vienna Prater.
1466 **323** 1s.50 green 40 30

1966. 10th Death Anniv of Josef Hoffmann (architect).
1467 **324** 3s. brown 60 30

325 Bank Emblem

1966. 150th Anniv of Austrian National Bank.
1468 **325** 3s. brown, grn & drab 60 25

326 Arms of Wiener Neustadt

1966. "Wiener Neustadt 1440–93" Art Exhibition.
1469 **326** 1s.50 multicoloured . . . 35 20

327 Puppy **328** Columbine

1966. 120th Anniv of Vienna Animal Protection Society.
1470 **327** 1s.80 black and yellow 35 25

1966. Alpine Flora. Multicoloured.
1471 1s.50 Type **328** 25 20
1472 1s.80 Turk's cap 30 25
1473 2s.20 Wulfenia 45 40
1474 3s. Globe flower 55 45
1475 4s. Orange lily 70 65
1476 5s. Alpine anemone . . . . 1·00 85

329 Fair Building

1966. Wels International Fair.
1477 **329** 3s. blue 60 25

330 Peter Anich **331** "Suffering"

1966. Death Bicent of Peter Anich (cartographer).
1478 **330** 1s.80 black 35 20

1966. 15th International Occupational Health Congress, Vienna.
1479 **331** 3s. black and red 60 25

332 "Eunuchus" by Terence (engraving, Johann Gruninger)

1966. Austrian National Library, Vienna. Mult.
1480 1s.50 Type **332** (Theatre collection) 25 25
1481 1s.80 Detail of title page of Willem Blaeu's atlas (Cartography collection) 30 20
1482 2s.20 "Herrengasse, Vienna" (Anton Stutzinger (Pictures and portraits collection)) 40 30
1483 3s. Illustration from Rene of Anjou's "Livre du Cuer d'Amours Espris" (Manuscripts collection) 55 35

333 Young Girl

1966. Austrian "Save the Children" Fund.
1484 **333** 3s. black and blue . . . 60 30

334 Strawberries **335** 16th-century Postman

1966. Fruits. Multicoloured.
1485 50g. Type **334** 35 30
1486 1s. Grapes 25 20
1487 1s.50 Apple 35 25
1488 1s.80 Blackberries 60 50
1489 2s.20 Apricots 70 55
1490 3s. Cherries 65 50

1966. Stamp Day.
1491 **335** 3s.+70g. multicoloured 75 65

336 Arms of Linz University **337** Skater of 1867

1966. Inauguration of Linz University.
1492 **336** 3s. multicoloured 60 40

1967. Centenary of Vienna Skating Assn.
1493 **337** 3s. indigo and blue . . . 60 25

338 Dancer with Violin **339** Dr. Schonherr

1967. Centenary of "Blue Danube" Waltz.
1494 **338** 3s. purple 60 30

1967. Birth Cent of Dr. Karl Schonherr (poet).
1495 **339** 3s. brown 60 30

340 Ice Hockey Goalkeeper

1967. World Ice Hockey Championships, Vienna.
1496 **340** 3s. blue and green . . . 60 50

341 Violin and Organ **343** "Madonna" (Gothic wood-carving)

342 "Mother and Children" (aquarelle, Peter Fendi)

1967. 125th Anniv of Vienna Philharmonic Orchestra.
1497 **341** 3s.50 blue 65 30

1967. Mother's Day.
1498 **342** 2s. multicoloured 30 25

1967. "Gothic Art in Austria" Exhibition, Krems.
1499 **343** 3s. green 60 25

344 Jewelled Cross **345** "The White Swan" (from Kokoschkas tapestry "Cupid and Psyche")

1967. "Salzburg Treasures" Exhibition, Salzburg Cathedral.
1500 **344** 3s.50 multicoloured . . . 65 30

1967. "Art of the Nibelungen District" Exhibition, Pochlarn.
1501 **345** 2s. multicoloured 30 25

346 Vienna

1967. 10th European Talks, Vienna.
1502 **346** 3s. black and red 60 35

347 Champion Bull

1967. Centenary of Ried Fair.
1503 **347** 2s. purple 35 25

348 Colorado Potato Beetle

1967. 6th Int Plant Protection Congress, Vienna.
1504 **348** 3s. multicoloured 65 40

349 Locomotive No. 671

1967. Centenary of Brenner Railway.
1505 **349** 3s.50 green and brown 65 40

350 "Christ" (fresco detail)

1967. Lambach Frescoes.
1506 **350** 2s. multicoloured 30 20

351 Prater Hall, Vienna

352 Rector's Medallion and Chain

1967. International Trade Fairs Congress, Vienna.
1507 **351** 2s. purple and cream . . 50 45

1967. 275th Anniv of Fine Arts Academy, Vienna.
1508 **352** 2s. brown, yellow & blue 50 45

353 Bible on Rock (from commemorative coin of 1717)

355 Memorial, Vienna

354 Forest Trees

1967. 450th Anniv of the Reformation.
1509 **353** 3s.50 blue 70 50

1967. 100 Years of Austrian University Forestry Studies.
1510 **354** 3s.50 green 55 40

1967. 150th Anniv of Land Registry.
1511 **355** 2s. green 35 30

356 "St. Leopold" (stained-glass window, Heiligenkreuz Monastery)

357 "Music and Art"

1967. Margrave Leopold the Holy.
1512 **356** 1s.80 multicoloured . . . 35 30

1967. 150th Anniv of Academy of Music and Dramatic Art, Vienna.
1513 **357** 3s.50 black and violet . . 65 50

358 St. Mary's Altar, Nonnberg Convent, Salzburg

359 "The Letter-carrier" (from playing-card)

1967. Christmas.
1514 **358** 2s. green 35 25

1967. Stamp Day.
1515 **359** 3s.50+80g. mult . . . . 1·00 95

360 Ski Jump, Stadium and Mountains

1968. Winter University Games, Innsbruck.
1516 **360** 2s. blue 35 25

361 C. Sitte

362 Mother and Child

1968. 125th Birth Anniv of Camillo Sitte (architect).
1517 **361** 2s. brown 30 25

1968. Mothers' Day.
1518 **362** 2s. olive 30 25

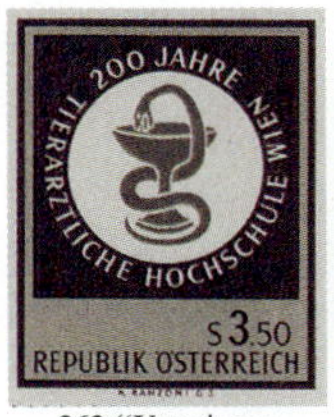

363 "Veterinary Medicine"

364 Bride with Lace Veil

1968. Bicentenary of Vienna Veterinary College.
1519 **363** 3s.50 gold, pur & drab 70 50

1968. Centenary of Vorarlberg Lace.
1520 **364** 3s.50 blue 65 45

365 Etrich Limousine

1968. "IFA Wien 1968" Airmail Stamp Exhibition, Vienna.
1521 **365** 2s. brown 40 35
1522 – 3s.50 green 70 65
1523 – 5s. blue . . . . 1·30 1·00
DESIGNS: 3s.50, Sud Aviation Caravelle; 5s. Douglas DC-8.

366 Horse-racing

1968. Centenary of Freudenau Gallop Races.
1524 **366** 3s.50 brown 65 45

367 Landsteiner

368 P. Rosegger

1968. Birth Centenary of Dr. Karl Landsteiner (physician and pathologist).
1525 **367** 3s.50 blue 65 40

1968. 50th Death Anniv of Peter Rosegger (writer).
1526 **368** 2s. green 30 25

369 A. Kauffmann (self-portrait)

370 Statue of Young Man (Helenenberg site)

1968. Exhibition of Angelica Kauffmann's Paintings, Bregenz.
1527 **369** 2s. violet 40 30

1968. Magdalensberg Excavations, Carinthia.
1528 **370** 2s. black and green . . . 30 25

371 "The Bishop" (Romanesque carving)

372 K. Moser

1968. 750th Anniv of Graz-Seckau Diocese.
1529 **371** 2s. grey 35 25

1968. 50th Death Anniv of Koloman Moser (graphic artist).
1530 **372** 2s. brown and red . . . 35 25

373 Human Rights Emblem

374 Arms and Provincial Shields

1968. Human Rights Year.
1531 **373** 1s.50 red, green & grey 65 30

1968. 50th Anniv of Republic. Multicoloured.
1532 2s. Type **374** 40 35
1533 2s. Karl Renner (first President of Second Republic) 40 35
1534 2s. First Article of Constitution 40 35

375 Crib, Oberndorf, Salzburg

376 Mercury

1968. 150th Anniv of "Silent Night, Holy Night" (carol).
1535 **375** 2s. green 35 25

1968. Stamp Day.
1536 **376** 3s.50+80g. green 75 75

377 Fresco (Troger), Melk Monastery

378 "Madonna and Child"

1968. Baroque Frescoes. Designs showing frescoes in locations given. Multicoloured.
1537 2s. Type **377** 50 45
1538 2s. Altenburg Monastery . . 50 45
1539 2s. Rohrenbach-Greillenstein 50 45
1540 2s. Ebenfurth Castle 50 45
1541 2s. Halbthurn Castle 50 45
1542 2s. Maria Treu Church, Vienna 50 45
Nos. 1537/9 are the work of Anton Troger and Nos. 1540/2 that of Franz Maulbertsch.

1969. 500th Anniv of Vienna Diocese. Statues in St. Stephen's Cathedral, Vienna.
1543 **378** 2s. blue 45 45
1544 – 2s. grey 45 45
1545 – 2s. green 45 45
1546 – 2s. purple 45 45
1547 – 2s. black 45 45
1548 – 2s. brown 45 45
DESIGNS: No. 1544, "St. Christopher"; No. 1545, "St. George"; No. 1546, "St. Paul"; No. 1547, "St. Sebastian"; No. 1548, "St. Stephen".

379 Parliament Building, Vienna

1969. Interparliamentary Union Meeting, Vienna.
1549 **379** 2s. green 30 25

380 Colonnade

1969. Europa.
1550 **380** 2s. multicoloured 75 25

381 "Council Members"

382 Soldiers

1969. 20th Anniv of Council of Europe.
1551 **381** 3s.50 multicoloured . . . 70 50

1969. Austrian Armed Forces.
1552 **382** 2s. brown and red . . . 35 25

383 "Don Giovanni"

1969. Centenary of State Opera, Vienna. Sheet 182 × 212 mm. T **383** and similar scenes.
MS1553 2s. × 8 each brown, red and gold . . . . 5·50 5·50
DESIGNS—Scenes from Opera and Ballet: "Don Giovanni" (Mozart), "The Magic Flute" (Mozart), "Fidelio" (Beethoven), "Lohengrin" (Wagner), "Don Carlos" (Verdi), "Carmen" (Bizet), "Der Rosenkavlier" (R. Strauss) and "Swan Lake" (Tchaikovsky).

384 Maximilian's Armour

385 Viennese "Privilege" Seal

1969. "Maximilian I" Exhibition, Innsbruck.
1554 **384** 2s. black 35 25

1969. 19th International Union of Local Authorities Congress, Vienna.
1555 **385** 2s. red, brown & ochre 30 25

386 Young Girl

387 Hands clasping Spanner

1969. 20th Anniv of "SOS" Children's Villages Movement.
1556 **386** 2s. brown and green . . 30 25

1969. 50th Anniv of Int Labour Organization.
1557 **387** 2s. green 30 25

388 Austrian "Flag" encircling Globe

389 "El Cid killing a Bull" (Goya)

1969. "Austrians Living Abroad" Year.
1558 **388** 3s.50 red and green . . . 65 40

1969. Bicentenary of Albertina Art Collection, Vienna. Multicoloured.
1559 2s. Type **389** 40 40
1560 2s. "Young Hare" (Durer) 40 40
1561 2s. "Madonna with Pomegranate" (Raphael) 40 40
1562 2s. "The Painter and the Amateur" (Bruegel) . . . 40 40
1563 2s. "Rubens's Son, Nicholas" (Rubens) . . . 40 40
1564 2s. "Self-portrait" (Rembrandt) 40 40
1565 2s. "Madame de Pompadour" (detail, Guerin) 40 40
1566 2s. "The Artist's Wife" (Schiele) 40 40

390 Pres. Jonas

391 Posthorn and Lightning over Globe

1969. Pres. Franz Jonas's 70th Birthday.
1567 **390** 2s. blue and grey 30 25

1969. 50th Anniv of Post and Telegraph Employees Union.
1568 **391** 2s. multicoloured 30 25

392 Savings Bank (c. 1450)

393 "The Madonna" (Egger-Lienz)

1969. 150th Anniv of Austrian Savings Bank.
1569 **392** 2s. green and silver . . . 30 25

1969. Christmas.
1570 **393** 2s. purple and yellow . . 25 25

394 Unken, Salzburg, Post-house Sign (after F. Zeller)

395 J. Schoffel

1969. Stamp Day.
1571 **394** 3s.50+80g. black, red and stone 70 70

1970. 60th Death Anniv of Josef Schoffel ("Saviour of the Vienna Woods").
1572 **395** 2s. purple 30 25

396 St. Clement Hofbauer

398 Krimml Waterfalls

397 Chancellor Leopold Figl

1970. 150th Death Anniv of St. Clement Hofbauer (theologian).
1573 **396** 2s. brown and green . . 30 25

1970. 25th Anniv of Austrian Republic.
1574 **397** 2s. olive 35 25
1575 – 2s. brown 35 25
DESIGN: No. 1575, Belvedere Castle.

1970. Nature Conservation Year.
1576 **398** 2s. green 70 50

399 Oldest University Seal

401 Tower Clock, 1450–1550

400 "Musikverein" Organ

1970. 300th Anniv of Leopold Franz University, Innsbruck.
1577 **399** 2s. black and red 30 25

1970. Centenary of "Musikverein" Building.
1578 **400** 2s. purple and gold . . . 30 25

1970. Antique Clocks.
1579 **401** 1s.50 brown and cream 30 25
1580 – 1s.50 green & lt green . . 30 25
1581 – 2s. blue and pale blue . . 35 30
1582 – 2s. red and purple . . . 35 30
1583 – 3s.50 brown and buff . . 75 65
1584 – 3s.50 purple and lilac . . 75 65
DESIGNS: No. 1580, Empire "lyre" clock, 1790–1815; No. 1581, Pendant ball clock, 1600–50; No. 1582, Pocket-watch and signet, 1800–30; No. 1583, Bracket clock, 1720–60; No. 1584, "Biedermeier" pendulum clock and musical-box, 1820–50.

402 "The Beggar Student" (Millocker)

403 Scene from "The Gipsy Baron" (J. Strauss)

1970. Famous Operettas.
1585 **402** 1s.50 turquoise & green 30 25
1586 – 1s.50 blue and yellow . . 30 25
1587 – 2s. purple and pink . . . 35 30
1588 – 2s. brown and green . . 35 30
1589 – 3s.50 blue and light blue 75 65
1590 – 3s.50 blue and buff . . 75 65
OPERETTAS: No. 1586, "Die Fledermaus" (Johann Strauss the younger); 1587, "A Waltz Dream" (O. Straus); 1588, "The Birdseller" (C. Zeller); 1589, "The Merry Widow" (F. Lehar); 1590, "Two Hearts in Waltz-time" (R. Stoiz).

1970. 25th Anniv of Bregenz Festival.
1591 **403** 3s.50 blue, buff & ult . . 65 45

404 Festival Emblem

405 T. Koschat

1970. 50th Anniv of Salzburg Festival.
1592 **404** 3s.50 multicoloured . . . 65 45

1970. 125th Birth Anniv of Thomas Koschat (composer and poet).
1593 **405** 2s. brown 30 30

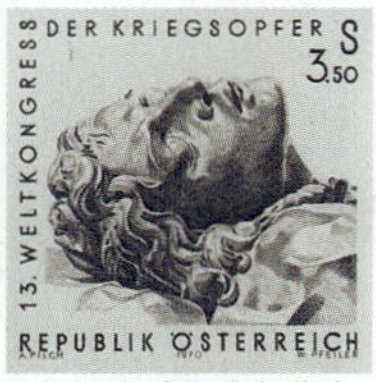

406 "Head of St. John", from sculpture "Mount of Olives", Ried Church (attributed to T. Schwanthaler)

1970. 13th World Veterans Federation General Assembly.
1594 **406** 3s.50 sepia 65 40

407 Climbers and Mountains

1970. "Walking and Mountaineering".
1595 **407** 2s. blue and mauve . . . 30 25

408 A. Cossmann

1970. Birth Cent of Alfred Cossmann (engraver).
1596 **408** 2s. brown 30 25

409 Arms of Carinthia

410 U.N. Emblem

1970. 50th Anniv of Carinthian Plebiscite.
1597 **409** 2s. multicoloured 30 25

1970. 25th Anniv of United Nations.
1598 **410** 3s.50 blue and black . . 65 40

411 "Adoration of the Shepherds" (carving, Garsten Monastery)

1970. Christmas.
1599 **411** 2s. blue 30 25

412 Saddle, Harness and Posthorn

413 Pres. K. Renner

1970. Stamp Day.
1600 **412** 3s.50+80g. black, yellow and grey 75 75

1970. Birth Centenary of Pres. Renner.
1601 **413** 2s. purple 30 25

414 Beethoven (after painting by Waldmuller)

415 E. Handel-Mazzetti

1970. Birth Bicentenary of Beethoven.
1602 **414** 3s.50 black and stone . . 65 45

1971. Birth Centenary of Enrica Handel-Mazzetti (novelist).
1603 **415** 2s. brown 30 25

416 "Safety for Children"

1971. Road Safety.
1604 **416** 2s. multicoloured 35 25

417 Florentine Bowl, c. 1580

1971. Austrian Art Treasures (1st series). Sculpture and Applied Art.
1605 **417** 1s.50 green and grey . . 40 25
1606 – 2s. purple and grey . . . 45 30
1607 – 3s.50 yellow, brn & grey 85 65
DESIGNS: 2s. Ivory equestrian statuette of Joseph I, 1693 (Matthias Steinle); 3s.50, Salt-cellar, c. 1570 (Cellini).
See also Nos. 1609/11, 1632/4 and 1651/3.

418 Shield of Trade Association

419 "Jacopo de Strada" (Titian)

1971. 23rd International Chamber of Commerce Congress, Vienna.
1608 **418** 3s.50 multicoloured . . . 65 35

1971. Austrian Art Treasures (2nd series).
1609 **419** 1s.50 purple 30 25
1610 – 2s. black 35 30
1611 – 3s.50 brown 75 65
PAINTINGS: 2s. "The Village Feast" (Brueghel); 3s.50, "Young Venetian Woman" (Durer).

420 Notary's Seal

421 "St. Matthew" (altar sculpture)

1971. Austrian Notarial Statute Cent Congress.
1612 **420** 3s.50 purple and brown 65 35

1971. "Krems Millennium of Art" Exhibition.
1613 **421** 2s. brown and purple . . 30 25

422 Dr. A. Neilreich

423 Singer with Lyre

1971. Death Cent of Dr. August Neilreich (botanist).
1614 **422** 2s. brown 30 25

1971. International Choir Festival, Vienna.
1615 **423** 4s. blue, gold & lt blue 70 50

424 Arms of Kitzbuhel

1971. 700th Anniv of Kitzbuhel.
1616 **424** 2s.50 multicoloured . . . 40 25

425 Stock Exchange Building

1971. Bicentenary of Vienna Stock Exchange.
1617 **425** 4s. brown 70 40

426 Old and New Fair Halls

427 O.G.B. Emblem

1971. "50 Years of Vienna International Fairs".
1618 **426** 2s.50 purple 40 25

1971. 25th Anniv of Austrian Trade Unions Federation.
1619 **427** 2s. multicoloured 30 25

428 Arms and Insignia

429 "Marcus" Veteran Car

1971. 50th Anniv of Burgenland Province.
1620 **428** 4s. multicoloured 30 25

1971. 75th Anniv of Austrian Automobile, Motor Cycle and Touring Club.
1621 **429** 4s. black and green . . . 70 50

430 Europa Bridge, Brenner Highway

431 Iron-ore Workings, Erzberg

1971. Inauguration of Brenner Highway.
1622 **430** 4s. blue 70 50

1971. 25 Years of Nationalized Industries.
1623 **431** 1s.50 brown 35 25
1624 – 2s. blue 35 25
1625 – 4s. green 80 75
DESIGNS: 2s. Nitrogen Works, Linz; 4s. Iron and Steel works, Linz.

432 Electric Train on the Semmering Line

433 E. Tschermak-Seysenegg

1971. Railway Anniversaries.
1626 **432** 2s. purple 40 25

1971. Birth Centenary of Dr. E. Tshermak-Seysenegg (biologist).
1627 **433** 2s. purple and grey . . . 30 25

434 Angling

435 "The Infant Jesus as Saviour" (from miniature by Durer)

1971. Sports.
1628 **434** 2s. brown 30 25

1971. Christmas.
1629 **435** 2s. multicoloured 35 25

436 "50 Years"

1971. 50th Anniv of Austrian Philatelic Clubs Association.
1630 **436** 4s.+1s.50 pur & gold . . 95 85

437 Franz Grillparzer (from miniature by Daffinger)

438 Roman Fountain, Friesach

1972. Death Centenary of Grillparzer (dramatist).
1631 **437** 2s. black, brown & stone 35 25

1972. Austrian Art Treasures (3rd series). Fountains.
1632 **438** 1s.50 purple 30 25
1633 – 2s. brown 35 25
1634 – 2s.50 green 60 50
DESIGNS: 2s. Lead Fountain, Heiligenkreuz Abbey; 2s.50. Leopold Fountain, Innsbruck.

439 Hofburg Palace

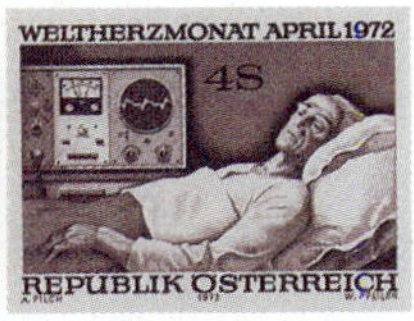
440 Heart Patient

1972. 4th European Postal Ministers' Conf, Vienna.
1635 **439** 4s. violet 75 50

1972. World Heart Month.
1636 **440** 4s. brown 70 50

441 "Woman's Head" (sculpture, Gurk Cathedral)

442 Vienna Town Hall and Congress Emblem

1972. 900th Anniv of Gurk Diocese.
1637 **441** 2s. purple and gold . . . 35 25

1972. 9th International Public and Co-operative Economy Congress, Vienna.
1638 **442** 4s. black, red and yellow 70 50

443 Lienz–Pelos Pylon Line

1972. 25th Anniv of Electric Power Nationalization.
1639 **443** 70g. violet and grey . . 20 15
1640 – 2s.50 brown and grey . . 45 30
1641 – 4s. blue and grey 80 55
DESIGNS: 2s.50, Vienna-Semmering Power Station; 4s. Zemm Dam and lake.

444 Runner with Torch

445 "Hermes" (C. Laib)

1972. Passage of the Olympic Torch through Austria.
1642 **444** 2s. brown and red . . . 35 25

1972. "Late Gothic Art" Exhibition, Salzburg.
1643 **445** 2s. purple 35 25

446 Pears

448 University Arms

447 "Spanish Walk"

1972. Amateur Gardeners' Congress, Vienna.
1644 **446** 2s.50 multicoloured . . . 45 25

1972. 400th Anniv of the Spanish Riding School, Vienna. Sheet 136 × 181 mm containing T **447** and similar square designs each in purple, red and gold.
MS1645 2s. Type **447**; 2s. "Piaffe"; 2s.50 "Levade"; 2s.50 "On the long rein"; 4s. "Capriole"; 4s. "Courbette" . . . . 3·25 3·25

1972. Cent of University of Agriculture, Vienna.
1646 **448** 2s. multicoloured 35 25

449 Old University Buildings (after F. Danreiter)

450 C. M. Ziehrer

1972. 350th Anniv of Paris Lodron University, Salzburg.
1647 **449** 4s. brown 70 25

1972. 50th Death Anniv of Carl M. Ziehrer (composer and conductor).
1648 **450** 2s. red 35 25

451 "Virgin and Child", Inzersdorf Church

1972. Christmas.
1649 **451** 2s. purple and green . . 35 25

452 18th-century Viennese Postman

1972. Stamp Day.
1650 **452** 4s.+1s. green 95 85

453 State Sledge of Maria Theresa

1972. Austrian Art Treasures (4th series). Carriages from the Imperial Coach House.
1651 **453** 1s.50 brown and bistre 55 25
1652 – 2s. green and bistre . . . 30 30
1653 – 2s.50 purple and bistre 60 50
DESIGNS: 2s. Coronation landau; 2s.50, Hapsburg State Coach.

454 Telephone Network **456** A. Petzold

455 "Drug Addict"

1972. Completion of Austrian Telephone System Automation.
1654 **454** 2s. black and yellow . . 35 25

1973. Campaign against Drug Abuse.
1655 **455** 2s. multicoloured 50 35

1973. 50th Death Anniv of Alfons Petzold (writer).
1656 **456** 2s. purple 40 25

457 Korner **458** McDonell DC-9

1973. Birth Centenary of Pres. Theodor Korner (President, 1951–57).
1657 **457** 2s. purple and grey . . . 35 25

1973. Austrian Aviation Anniversaries.
1658 **458** 2s. blue and red 40 25

459 Otto Loewi **460** "Succour"

1973. Birth Cent of Otto Loewi (pharmacologist).
1659 **459** 4s. violet 70 50

1973. 25th Anniv of National Federation of Austrian Social Insurance Institutes.
1660 **460** 2s. blue 35 25

461 Telephone Dial within Posthorn **463** Military Pentathlon

462 Fair Emblem

1973. Europa.
1661 **461** 2s.50 black, yell & orge 90 30

1973. 25th Dornbirn Fair.
1662 **462** 2s. multicoloured 35 25

1973. 25th Anniv of International Military Sports Council and 23rd Military Pentathlon Championships, Wiener Neustadt.
1663 **463** 4s. green 70 50

464 Leo Slezak **465** Main Entrance, Hofburg Palace

1973. Birth Centenary of Leo Slezak (operatic tenor).
1664 **464** 4s. brown 70 50

1973. 39th International Statistical Institute's Congress, Vienna.
1665 **465** 2s. brown, red and grey 35 25

466 "Admiral Tegetthof Icebound" (J. Payer) **467** I.U.L.C.S. Arms

1973. Centenary of Discovery of Franz Josef Land.
1666 **466** 2s.50 green 45 30

1973. 13th International Union of Leather Chemists' Societies Congress, Vienna.
1667 **467** 4s. multicoloured 70 50

468 "Academy of Sciences, Vienna" (B. Bellotto) **469** Max Reinhardt

1973. Cent of Int Meteorological Organization.
1668 **468** 2s.50 violet 45 30

1973. Birth Centenary of Max Reinhardt (theatrical director).
1669 **469** 2s. purple 35 25

470 F. Hanusch

1973. 50th Death Anniv of Ferdinand Hanusch (politician).
1670 **470** 2s. purple 35 25

471 Light Harness Racing

1973. Centenary of Vienna Trotting Assn.
1671 **471** 2s. green 35 25

472 Radio Operator

1973. 50th Anniv of International Criminal Police Organization (Interpol).
1672 **472** 4s. violet 70 50

473 Petzval Camera Lens

1973. "Europhot" (professional photographers) Congress, Vienna.
1673 **473** 2s.50 multicoloured . . . 45 40

474 Aqueduct, Hollen Valley

1973. Centenary of Vienna's 1st Mountain-spring Aqueduct.
1674 **474** 2s. brown, red & blue . . 35 25

475 Almsee **476** "The Nativity" (stained-glass window, St. Erhard Church, Bretenau)

1973. Views. (a) Size 23 × 29 mm.
1674a – 20g. blue and light blue 50 35
1675 – 50g. green & lt green 20 15
1676 – 1s. sepia and brown . . 25 15
1677 – 1s.50 purple and pink 40 15
1678 – 2s. indigo and blue . . 45 15
1679 – 2s.50 deep lilac & lilac 60 15
1680 – 3s. ultramarine & blue 65 15
1680a – 3s.50 brown & orange 75 20
1681 **475** 4s. violet and lilac . . . 75 20
1681a – 4s.20 black and grey . . 1·00 85
1682 – 4s.50 dp green & green 90 20
1683 – 5s. violet and lilac . . 90 15
1683a – 5s.50 blue and violet . . 1·50 1·10
1683b – 5s.60 olive and green 1·50 1·70
1684 – 6s. lilac and pink . . . 1·40 15
1684a – 6s.50 blue & turquoise 1·40 25
1685 – 7s. deep green & green 1·60 15
1685a – 7s.50 purple & mauve 1·90 35
1686 – 8s. brown and pink . . 1·80 40
1686a – 9s. red and pink . . . 2·00 50
1687 – 10s. myrtle and green 2·10 15
1688 – 11s. red and orange . . 2·00 30
1688a – 12s. sepia and brown 2·40 60
1688b – 14s. myrtle and green 2·75 50
1688c – 16s. brown and orange 2·75 60
1688d – 20s. green and bistre . . 3·50 65

(b) Size 28 × 37 mm.
1689 – 50s. violet and grey . . . . 9·50 1·80

(c) Size 17 × 20 mm.
1690 – 3s. ultramarine and blue 55 35

DESIGNS: 20g. Friedstadt Keep, Muhlviertel; 50g. Zillertal; 1s. Kahlenbergerdorf, Vienna; 1s.50, Bludenz; 2s. Old bridge, Finstermunz; 2s.50, Murau, Styria; 3s. Bischofsmutze and Alpine farm; 3s.50, Osterkirche, Oberwart; 4s.20, Hirschegg, Kleinwalsertal; 4s.50, Windmill, Retz; 5s. Ruins of Aggstein Castle; 5s.50, Peace Chapel, Stoderzinken; 5s.60, Riezlern, Kleinwalsertal; 6s. Lindauer Hut, Ratikon Massif; 6s.50, Villach, Carinthia; 7s. Falkenstein Castle; 7s.50, Hohensalzburg Fortress; 8s. Votive column, Reiteregg, Styria; 9s. Asten valley; 10s. Neusiedlersee; 11s. Enns; 12s. Kufstein Fortress; 14s. Weiszsee, Salzburg; 16s. Bad Tatzmannsdorf open-air museum; 20s. Myra Falls, Muggendorf; 50s. Hofburg, Vienna.

1973. Christmas.
1691 **476** 2s. multicoloured 40 25

477 "Archangel Gabriel" (carving by Lorenz Luchsperger) **478** Dr. Fritz Pregl

1973. Stamp Day.
1692 **477** 4s.+1s. purple 85 85

1973. 50th Anniv of Award of Nobel Prize for Chemistry to Fritz Pregl.
1693 **478** 4s. blue 70 50

479 Telex Machine and Globe **480** Hugo Hofmannsthal

1974. 50th Anniv of Radio Austria.
1694 **479** 2s.50 blue & ultramarine 45 30

1974. Birth Cent of Hugo Hofmannsthal (writer).
1695 **480** 4s. blue 70 50

481 Anton Bruckner (composer)

1974. Inaug of Bruckner Memorial Centre, Linz.
1696 **481** 4s. brown 70 50

482 Vegetables

1974. 2nd Int Horticultural Show, Vienna. Mult.
1697 2s. Type **482** 40 30
1698 2s.50 Fruit 60 50
1699 4s. Flowers 80 65

483 Head from Ancient Seal **484** Karl Kraus

1974. 750th Anniv of Judenburg.
1700 **483** 2s. multicoloured 35 25

1974. Birth Centenary of Karl Kraus (poet).
1701 **484** 4s. red 70 50

485 "St. Michael" (wood-carving, Thomas Schwanthaler)
486 "King Arthur" (statue, Innsbruck)

1974. "Sculptures by the Schwanthaler Family" Exhibition, Reichersberg.
1702 **485** 2s.50 green 50 30

1974. Europa.
1703 **486** 2s.50 blue and brown . . 1·00 30

487 Early De Dion-Bouton Motor-tricycle
489 I.R.U. Emblem

488 Mask of Satyr's Head

1974. 75th Anniv of Austrian Association of Motoring, Motor Cycling and Cycling.
1704 **487** 2s. brown and grey . . . 35 25

1974. "Renaissance in Austria" Exhibition, Schallaburg Castle.
1705 **488** 2s. black, brown & gold 35 25

1974. 14th International Road Haulage Union Congress, Innsbruck.
1706 **489** 4s. black and orange . . 70 50

490 F. A. Maulbertsch
491 Gendarmes of 1849 and 1974

1974. 205th Birth Anniv of Franz Maulbertsch (painter).
1707 **490** 2s. brown 35 25

1974. 125th Anniv of Austrian Gendarmerie.
1708 **491** 2s. multicoloured 35 25

492 Fencing

1974. Sports.
1709 **492** 2s.50 black and orange 45 30

493 Transport Emblems

1974. European Transport Ministers' Conference, Vienna.
1710 **493** 4s. multicoloured 75 50

494 "St. Virgilius" (wood-carving)
495 Pres. F. Jonas

1974. 1200 Years of Christianity in Salzburg.
1711 **494** 2s. blue 35 25

1974. Pres. Franz Jonas Commemoration.
1712 **495** 2s. black 35 25

496 F. Stelzhamer
497 Diving

1974. Death Cent of Franz Stelzhamer (poet).
1713 **496** 2s. blue 35 25

1974. 13th European Swimming, Diving and Water-polo Championships.
1714 **497** 4s. brown and blue . . . 70 50

498 F. R. von Hebra (founder of German scientific dermatology)
499 A. Schonberg

1974. 30th Meeting of German-speaking Dermatologists Association, Graz.
1715 **498** 4s. brown 70 50

1974. Birth Cent of Arnold Schonberg (composer).
1716 **499** 2s.50 purple 45 30

500 Broadcasting Studios, Salzburg
501 E. Eysler

1974. 50th Anniv of Austrian Broadcasting.
1717 **500** 2s. multicoloured 35 25

1974. 25th Death Anniv of Edmund Eysler (composer).
1718 **501** 2s. green 35 25

502 19th-century Postman and Mail Transport

1974. Centenary of U.P.U.
1719 **502** 2s. brown and mauve . . 40 25
1720 – 4s. blue and grey 75 50
DESIGN: 4s. Modern postman and mail transport.

503 Sports Emblem

1974. 25th Anniv of Football Pools in Austria.
1721 **503** 70g. red, black and green 25 15

504 Steel Gauntlet grasping Rose

1974. Nature Protection.
1722 **504** 2s. multicoloured 55 35

505 C. D. von Dittersdorf
506 Mail Coach and P.O., 1905

1974. 175th Death Anniv of Carl Ditters von Dittersdorf (composer).
1723 **505** 2s. green 35 25

1974. Stamp Day.
1724 **506** 4s.+2s. blue . . . . . . 1·00 85

507 "Virgin Mary and Child" (wood-carving)
508 F. Schmidt

1974. Christmas.
1725 **507** 2s. brown and gold . . . 35 25

1974. Birth Centenary of Franz Schmidt (composer).
1726 **508** 4s. black and stone . . . 70 50

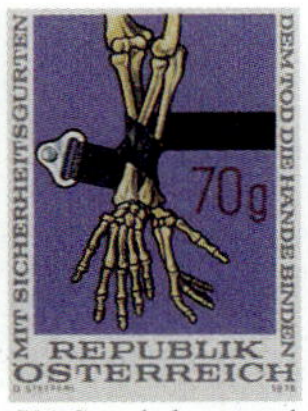

509 "St. Christopher and Child" (altarpiece)
511 Seat-belt around Skeletal Limbs

510 Slalom

1975. European Architectural Heritage Year and 125th Anniv of Austrian Commission for Preservation of Monuments.
1727 **509** 2s.50 brown and grey . . 50 30

1975. Winter Olympics, Innsbruck (1976) (1st issue). Multicoloured.
1728 1s.+50g. Type **510** 25 25
1729 1s.50+70g. Ice hockey . . . 30 30
1730 2s.+90g. Ski-jumping . . . 50 45
1731 4s.+1s.90 Bobsleighing . . . 1·00 85
See also Nos. 1747/50.

1975. Car Safety-belts Campaign.
1732 **511** 70g. multicoloured . . . 20 15

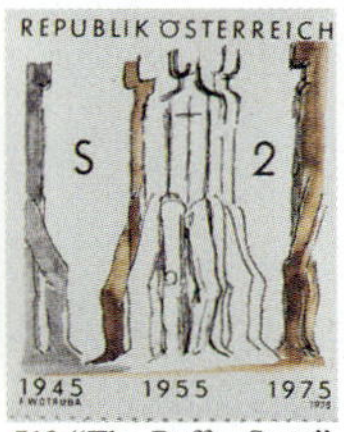

512 Stained-glass Window, Vienna Town Hall
513 "The Buffer State"

1975. 11th European Communities' Day.
1733 **512** 2s.50 multicoloured . . . 50 45

1975. 30th Anniv of Foundation of Austrian Second Republic.
1734 **513** 2s. black and brown . . 35 25

514 Forest Scene

1975. 50th Anniv of Foundation of Austrian Forests Administration.
1735 **514** 2s. green 50 35

515 "The High Priest" (M. Pacher)
516 Gosaukamm Cable-way

1975. Europa.
1736 **515** 2s.50 multicoloured . . . 55 30

1975. 4th International Ropeways Congress, Vienna.
1737 **516** 2s. blue and red 35 25

517 J. Misson

1975. Death Centenary of Josef Misson (poet).
1738 **517** 2s. brown and red . . . 35 25

518 "Setting Sun"
520 L. Fall

519 F. Porsche

1975. Nat Pensioners' Assn Meeting, Vienna.
1739 **518** 1s.50 multicoloured . . . 30 25

1975. Birth Centenary of Prof. Ferdinand Porsche (motor engineer).
1740 **519** 1s.50 purple & green . . 30 20

1975. 50th Death Anniv of Leo Fall (composer).
1741 **520** 2s. violet 35 25

521 Judo "Shoulder Throw"
522 Heinrich Angeli

1975. World Judo Championships, Vienna.
1742 **521** 2s.50 multicoloured . . . 45 30

1975. 50th Death Anniv of Heinrich Angeli (court painter).
1743 **522** 2s. purple 35 25

523 J. Strauss

1975. 150th Birth Anniv of Johann Strauss the Younger (composer).
1744 **523** 4s. brown and ochre . . 55 40

524 "The Cellist" 525 "One's Own House"

1975. 75th Anniv of Vienna Symphony Orchestra.
1745 **524** 2s.50 blue and silver . . 50 30

1975. 50th Anniv of Austrian Building Societies.
1746 **525** 2s. multicoloured 35 25

1975. Winter Olympic Games, Innsbruck (1976) (2nd issue). As T **510**. Multicoloured.
1747 70g.+30g. Figure-skating (pairs) 25 25
1748 2s.+1s. Cross-country skiing 45 45
1749 2s.50+1s. Tobogganing . . . 50 45
1750 4s.+2s. Rifle-shooting (biathlon) . . . . 1·00 85

526 Scene on Folding Fan

1975. Bicentenary of Salzburg State Theatre.
1751 **526** 1s.50 multicoloured . . . 30 25

527 Austrian Stamps of 1850, 1922 and 1945 528 "Virgin and Child" (Schottenaltar, Vienna)

1975. Stamp Day. 125th Anniv of Austrian Postage Stamps.
1752 **527** 4s.+2s. multicoloured . . 1·00 95

1975. Christmas.
1753 **528** 2s. lilac and gold 40 25

529 "Spiralbaum" (F. Hundertwasser) 531 Dr. R. Barany

530 Old Theatre Building

1975. Modern Austrian Art.
1754 **529** 4s. multicoloured . . . . 1·10 75

1976. Bicentenary of the Burgtheatre, Vienna. Sheet 130 × 60 mm containing T **530** and similar horiz design.
MS1755 3s. blue (Type **530**); 3s. brown (Interior of the modern theatre) . . . . 1·50 1·40

1976. Birth Centenary of Dr. Robert Barany (Nobel prizewinner for Medicine, 1915).
1756 **531** 3s. brown and blue . . . 65 35

532 Ammonite Fossil 533 9th-century Coronation Throne

1976. Cent Exn, Vienna Natural History Museum.
1757 **532** 3s. multicoloured 65 35

1976. Millenary of Carinthia.
1758 **533** 3s. black and yellow . . 65 35

534 Stained-glass Window, Klosterneuburg 535 "The Siege of Linz" (contemporary engraving)

1976. Babenberg Exhibition, Lilienfeld.
1759 **534** 3s. multicoloured 65 35

1976. 350th Anniv of the Peasants' War in Upper Austria.
1760 **535** 4s. black and green . . . 70 50

536 Bowler delivering Ball

1976. 11th World Skittles Championships, Vienna.
1761 **536** 4s. black and orange . . 70 50

537 "St. Wolfgang" (altar painting by Michael Pacher) 538 Tassilo Cup, Kremsmunster

1976. International Art Exhibition, St. Wolfgang.
1762 **537** 6s. purple . . . . 1·10 70

1976. Europa.
1763 **538** 4s. multicoloured 70 50

539 Fair Emblem 540 Constantin Economo

1976. 25th Austrian Timber Fair, Klagenfurt.
1764 **539** 3s. multicoloured 65 35

1976. Birth Centenary of Constantin Economo (brain specialist).
1765 **540** 3s. brown 55 30

541 Bohemian Court Chancellery, Vienna 542 Arms of Lower Austria

1976. Centenary of Administrative Court.
1766 **541** 6s. brown . . . . 1·00 70

1976. Millenary of Austria. Sheet 135 × 180 mm containing T **542** and similar vert designs showing provincial arms.
MS1767 2s. × 9 multicoloured . . 3·75 3·75
DESIGNS: Arms of Lower Austria, Upper Austria, Styria, Carinthia, Vorarlberg, Salzburg, Burgenland and Vienna.

543 Cancer the Crab

1976. Fight against Cancer.
1768 **543** 2s.50 multicoloured . . . 45 30

544 U.N. Emblem and Bridge 545 Punched Tapes and Map of Europe

1976. 10th Anniv of U.N. Industrial Development Organization.
1769 **544** 3s. blue and gold 65 35

1976. 30th Anniv of Austrian Press Agency.
1770 **545** 1s.50 multicoloured . . . 25 15

546 V. Kaplan

1976. Birth Centenary of Viktor Kaplan (inventor of turbine).
1771 **546** 2s.50 multicoloured . . . 40 25

547 "The Birth of Christ" (Konrad von Friesach)

1976. Christmas.
1772 **547** 3s. multicoloured 60 30

548 Postilion's Hat and Posthorn

1976. Stamp Day.
1773 **548** 6s.+2s. black & lilac . . 1·30 1·20

549 R. M. Rilke 550 "Augustin the Piper" (Arik Brauer)

1976. 50th Death Anniv of Rainer Maria Rilke (poet).
1774 **549** 3s. violet 60 35

1976. Austrian Modern Art.
1775 **550** 6s. multicoloured . . . . 1·10 70

551 City Synagogue 552 N. J. von Jacquin

1976. 150th Anniv of Vienna City Synagogue.
1776 **551** 1s.50 multicoloured . . . 30 20

1977. 250th Birth Anniv of Nikolaus Joseph Freiherrn von Jacquin (botanist).
1777 **552** 4s. brown 70 55

553 Oswald von Wolkenstein 555 A. Kubin

554 Handball

1977. 600th Birth Anniv of Oswald von Wolkenstein (poet).
1778 **553** 3s. multicoloured 60 30

1977. World Indoor Handball Championships, Group B, Austria.
1779 **554** 1s.50 multicoloured . . . 30 20

1977. Birth Centenary of Alfred Kubin (writer and illustrator).
1780 **555** 6s. blue . . . . 1·10 70

556 Cathedral Spire 558 I.A.E.A. Emblem

557 F. Herzmanovsky-Orlando

1977. 25th Anniv of Re-opening of St. Stephen's Cathedral, Vienna.
1781 **556** 2s.50 brown 55 35
1782 – 3s. blue 65 45
1783 – 4s. purple 90 70
DESIGNS: 3s. West front; 4s. Interior.

1977. Birth Centenary of Fritz Herzmanovsky-Orlando (writer).
1784 **557** 6s. green and gold . . . 1·00 70

1977. 20th Anniv of Int Atomic Energy Agency.
1785 **558** 3s. lt blue, gold & blue 60 30

559 Arms of Schwanenstadt

561 Globe (Vincenzo Coronelli)

560 Attersee

1977. 350th Anniv of Schwanenstadt.
1786 **559** 3s. multicoloured 60 30

1977. Europa.
1787 **560** 6s. green . . . . 1·90 70

1977. 5th International Symposium and 25th Anniv of Coronelli World Federation of Globe Friends.
1788 **561** 3s. black and stone . . . 60 30

562 Canoeist

1977. World "White Water" Canoe Championships.
1789 **562** 4s. multicoloured 70 50

563 "The Samaritan" (Francesco Bassano)

1977. 50th Anniv of Austrian Workers' Samaritan Federation.
1790 **563** 1s.50 multicoloured . . . 30 25

564 Papermakers' Arms

565 "Freedom"

1977. 17th Conference of European Committee of Pulp and Paper Technology.
1791 **564** 3s. multicoloured 60 30

1977. Martyrs for Austrian Freedom.
1792 **565** 2s.50 blue and red . . . 45 30

566 Steam Locomotive, "Austria", 1837

1977. 140th Anniv of Austrian Railways. Mult.
1793 1s.50 Type **566** 40 30
1794 2s.50 Type 214 steam locomotive, 1928 . . . . 65 40
1795 3s. Type 1044 electric locomotive, 1974 . . . . 90 65

567 "Madonna and Child" (wood carving, Mariastein Pilgrimage Church)

1977. Christmas.
1796 **567** 3s. multicoloured 65 35

568 "Danube Maiden" (Wolfgang Hutter)

569 Emanuel Herrmann (inventor of postcard)

1977. Austrian Modern Art.
1797 **568** 6s. multicoloured . . . . 1·10 70

1977. Stamp Day.
1798 **569** 6s.+2s. brown and cinnamon . . . . . . 1·30 1·30

570 Egon Friedell

1978. Birth Centenary of Egon Friedell (writer).
1799 **570** 3s. black and blue . . . 60 30

571 Underground Train

1978. Opening of Vienna Underground Railway.
1800 **571** 3s. multicoloured 75 40

572 Rifleman and Skier

1978. Biathlon World Championships, Hochfilzen.
1801 **572** 4s. multicoloured 70 50

573 Aztec Feather Shield

1978. 30th Anniv of Museum of Ethnology, Vienna.
1802 **573** 3s. multicoloured 55 30

574 Leopold Kunschak

575 "Mountain Peasants"

1978. 25th Death Anniv of Leopold Kunschak (politician).
1803 **574** 3s. blue 60 30

1978. Birth Centenary of Suitbert Lobisser (wood engraver).
1804 **575** 3s. brown and stone . . 55 30

576 Black Grouse, Hunting Satchel and Fowling Piece

577 Map of Europe and Austrian Parliament Building

1978. International Hunting Exn, Marchegg.
1805 **576** 6s. blue, brown & turq 1·10 50

1978. 3rd Interparliamentary European Security Conference, Vienna.
1806 **577** 4s. multicoloured 70 50

578 Riegersburg Castle, Styria

1978. Europa.
1807 **578** 6s. purple . . . . 2·00 70

579 "Admont Pieta" (Salzburg Circle Master)

580 Ort Castle

1978. "Gothic Art in Styria" Exhibition.
1808 **579** 2s.50 black and ochre . . 40 30

1978. 700th Anniv of Gmunden Town Charter.
1809 **580** 3s. multicoloured 65 30

581 Face surrounded by Fruit and Flowers

582 Franz Lehar and Villa at Bad Ischl

1978. 25th Anniv of Austrian Association for Social Tourism.
1810 **581** 6s. multicoloured . . . . 1·10 70

1978. International Lehar Congress.
1811 **582** 6s. blue . . . . 1·10 70

583 Tools and Globe

1978. 15th Congress of International Federation of Building and Wood Workers.
1812 **583** 1s.50 black, yellow & red 25 20

584 Knights Jousting

1978. 700th Anniv of Battle of Durnkrut and Jedenspeigen.
1813 **584** 3s. multicoloured 55 30

585 Bridge over River Drau

586 City Seal, 1440

1978. 1100th Anniv of Villach.
1814 **585** 3s. multicoloured 55 30

1978. 850th Anniv of Graz.
1815 **586** 4s. brown, green & grey 70 50

587 Angler

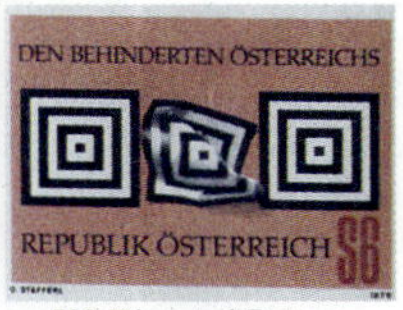

588 Distorted Pattern

1978. 25th Sport Fishing Championships, Vienna.
1816 **587** 4s. multicoloured 70 45

1978. Handicapped People.
1817 **588** 6s. black and brown . . 1·00 65

589 Concrete Chain

590 "Grace" (Albin Egger-Lienz)

1978. 9th International Concrete and Prefabrication Industry Congress, Vienna.
1818 **589** 2s.50 multicoloured . . . 40 25

1978. European Family Congress.
1819 **590** 6s. multicoloured . . . . 1·00 65

591 Lise Meitner

592 Victor Adler (bust, Anton Hamek)

1978. Birth Centenary of Lise Meitner (physicist).
1820 **591** 6s. violet . . . . 1·10 70

1978. 60th Death Anniv of Victor Adler (statesman).
1821 **592** 3s. black and red 55 30

593 Franz Schubert (after Josef Kriehuber)

594 "Madonna and Child" (Martino Altomonte, Wilhering Collegiate Church)

1978. 150th Death Anniv of Franz Schubert (composer).
1822 **593** 6s. brown . . . . 1·20 70

1978. Christmas.
1823 **594** 3s. multicoloured 55 30

595 Postbus, 1913

1978. Stamp Day.
1824 **595** 10s.+5s. multicoloured 2·40 1·90

596 "Archduke Johann Hut, Grossglockner" (E. T. Compton)

1978. Centenary of Austrian Alpine Club.
1825 **596** 1s.50 violet and gold . . 25 20

597 "Adam" (Rudolf Hausner)

598 Bound Hands

1978. Austrian Modern Art.
1826 **597** 6s. multicoloured . . . . 1·10 65

1978. 30th Anniv of Declaration of Human Rights.
1827 **598** 6s. purple . . . . 1·00 65

599 "CCIR"

1979. 50th Anniv of International Radio Consultative Committee.
1828 **599** 6s. multicoloured 90 60

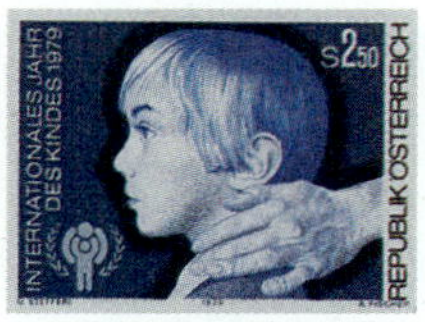

600 Adult protecting Child

1979. International Year of the Child.
1829 **600** 2s.50 multicoloured . . . 45 30

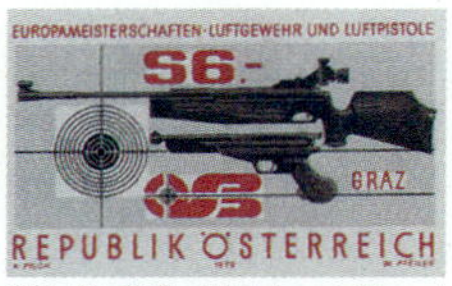

601 Air Rifle, Pistol and Target

1979. Centenary of Austrian Shooting Club, and European Air Rifle and Air Pistol Shooting Championships.
1830 **601** 6s. multicoloured . . . . 1·00 65

602 "Franz I" (paddle-steamer)

1979. 150th Anniv of Danube Steam Navigation Company.
1831 **602** 1s.50 blue 35 25
1832 – 2s.50 brown 50 35
1833 – 3s. red 70 35
DESIGNS: 2s.50, Pusher tug "Linz"; 3s. "Theodor Korner" (passenger vessel).

603 Skater

1979. World Ice Skating and Dancing Championships. Vienna.
1834 **603** 4s. multicoloured 70 45

604 Fashion Drawing by Theo Zache, 1900

605 Wiener Neustadt Cathedral

1979. 50th Viennese Int Ladies' Fashion Week.
1835 **604** 2s.50 multicoloured . . . 40 30

1979. 700th Anniv of Wiener Neustadt Cathedral.
1836 **605** 4s. blue and grey 70 45

606 Relief from Emperor Joseph II Monument, Vienna

607 Population Graph

1979. Bicentenary of Education for the Deaf.
1837 **606** 2s.50 green, black & gold 45 30

1979. 150th Anniv of Austrian Central Statistical Office.
1838 **607** 2s.50 multicoloured . . . 45 30

608 Laurenz Koschier (postal reformer)

609 Section through Diesel Engine

1979. Europa.
1839 **608** 6s. brown and ochre . . 1·80 65

1979. 13th Congress of International Combustion Engine Council.
1840 **609** 4s. multicoloured 70 45

610 Town Arms of Ried, Braunau and Scharding

1979. Bicentenary of Innviertel District.
1841 **610** 3s. multicoloured 55 30

611 Water Pollution

1979. Prevention of Water Pollution.
1842 **611** 2s.50 green and grey . . 45 30

612 Arms of Rottenmann

613 Jodok Fink

1979. 700th Anniv of Rottenmann.
1843 **612** 3s. multicoloured 55 30

1979. 50th Death Anniv of Jodok Fink (politician).
1844 **613** 3s. brown 55 30

614 Arms of Wels and Returned Soldiers League Badge

615 Flower

1979. 5th European Meeting of Returned Soldiers.
1845 **614** 4s. green and black . . . 70 45

1979. U.N. Conference on Science and Technology for Development, Vienna.
1846 **615** 4s. blue 70 45

616 Vienna International Centre

1979. Opening of U.N.O. Vienna Int Centre.
1847 **616** 6s. slate . . . . 1·10 65

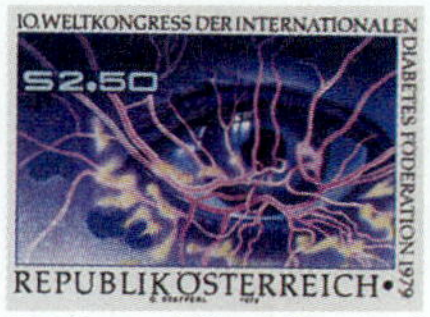

617 Eye and Blood Vessels of Diabetic

1979. 10th World Congress of International Diabetes Federation, Vienna.
1848 **617** 2s.50 multicoloured . . . 45 30

618 Stanzer Valley seen from Arlberg Road Tunnel

1979. 16th World Road Congress, Vienna.
1849 **618** 4s. multicoloured 70 45

619 Steam-driven Printing Press

1979. 175th Anniv of State Printing Works.
1850 **619** 3s. black and stone . . . 45 35

620 Richard Zsigmondy

1979. 50th Death Anniv of Dr. Richard Zsigmondy (Nobel Prize winner for Chemistry).
1851 **620** 6s. brown . . . . 1·00 65

621 Bregenz Festival and Congress Hall

1979. Bregenz Festival and Congress Hall.
1852 **621** 2s.50 lilac 45 35

622 Burning Match

1979. "Save Energy".
1853 **622** 2s.50 multicoloured . . . 45 30

623 Lions Emblem

1979. 25th European Lions Forum, Vienna.
1854 **623** 4s. yellow, gold and lilac 70 45

624 Wilhelm Exner (founder)

625 "The Suffering Christ" (Hans Fronius)

1979. Centenary of Industrial Museum and Technical School, Vienna.
1855 **624** 2s.50 dp purple & purple 45 30

1979. Austrian Modern Art.
1856 **625** 4s. black and stone . . . 70 45

626 Series 52 Goods Locomotive

627 August Musger

1979. Centenary of Raab (Gyor)–Odenburg (Sopron)-Ebenfurt Railway.
1857 **626** 2s.50 multicoloured . . . 70 45

1979. 50th Death Anniv of August Musger (pioneer of slow-motion photography).
1858 **627** 2s.50 black and grey . . 45 30

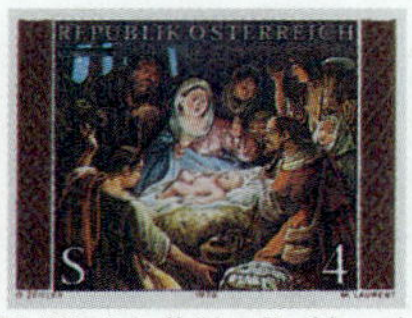

628 "Nativity" (detail of icon by Moses Subotic, St. Barbara Church, Vienna)

1979. Christmas.
1859 **628** 4s. multicoloured 70 45

629 Neue Hofburg, Vienna

1979. "WIPA 1981" International Stamp Exhibition, Vienna (1st issue). Inscr "1. Phase".
1860 **629** 16s.+8s. multicoloured 3·50 3·25
See also No. 1890.

630 Arms of Baden **631** Loading Exports

1980. 500th Anniv of Baden.
1861 **630** 4s. multicoloured 70 45

1980. Austrian Exports.
1862 **631** 4s. blue, red and black 70 45

632 Rheumatic Hand holding Stick

1980. Fight against Rheumatism.
1863 **632** 2s.50 red and blue . . . 45 30

633 Emblems of 1880 and 1980

1980. Centenary of Austrian Red Cross.
1864 **633** 2s.50 multicoloured . . . 45 30

634 Kirchschlager **635** Robert Hamerling

1980. Pres. Rudolf Kirchschlager's 65th Birthday.
1865 **634** 4s. brown and red . . . 70 50

1980. 150th Birth Anniv of Robert Hamerling (writer).
1866 **635** 2s.50 green 45 30

636 Town Seal **637** "Maria Theresa as a Young Woman" (Andreas Moller)

1980. 750th Anniv of Hallein.
1867 **636** 4s. black and red 70 45

1980. Death Bicentenary of Empress Maria Theresa.
1868 **637** 2s.50 purple 60 35
1869 – 4s. blue 90 50
1870 – 6s. brown . . . . 1·40 95

DESIGNS: 4s. "Maria Theresa with St. Stephen's Crown" (Martin van Meytens); 6s. "Maria Theresa as Widow" (Joseph Ducreux).

638 Flags of Treaty Signatories **639** St. Benedict (statue, Meinrad Guggenbichler)

1980. 25th Anniv of Austrian State Treaty.
1871 **638** 4s. multicoloured 70 45

1980. Congress of Austrian Benedictine Orders, Mariazell.
1872 **639** 2s.50 green 45 30

640 "Hygieia" (Gustav Klimt) **641** Dish Aerial, Aflenz

1980. 175th Anniv of Hygiene Education.
1873 **640** 4s. multicoloured 70 45

1980. Inauguration of Aflenz Satellite Communications Earth Station.
1874 **641** 6s. multicoloured . . . . 1·10 65

642 Steyr (copperplate engraving, 1693)

1980. Millenary of Steyr.
1875 **642** 4s. brown, black & gold 70 45

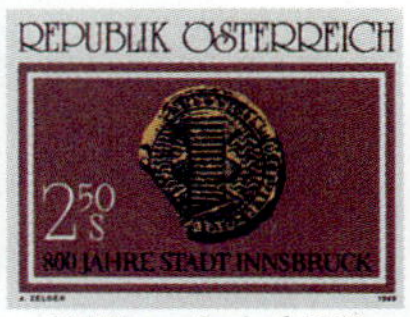

643 Oil Driller **644** Town Seal of 1267

1980. 50th Anniv of Oil Production in Austria.
1876 **643** 2s.50 multicoloured . . . 45 30

1980. 800th Anniv of Innsbruck.
1877 **644** 2s.50 yellow, blk & red 45 30

645 Ducal Crown

1980. 800th Anniv of Elevation of Styria to Dukedom.
1878 **645** 4s. multicoloured 70 45

646 Leo Ascher **647** "Abraham" (illustration from "Viennese Genesis")

1980. Birth Cent of Leo Ascher (composer).
1879 **646** 3s. violet 55 30

1980. 10th Congress of International Organization for Study of the Old Testament.
1880 **647** 4s. multicoloured 70 45

648 Robert Stolz **649** Falkenstein Railway Bridge

1980. Europa and Birth Centenary of Robert Stolz (composer).
1881 **648** 6s. red . . . . 1·80 55

1980. 11th International Association of Bridge and Structural Engineering Congress, Vienna.
1882 **649** 4s. multicoloured 70 45

650 "Moon Figure" (Karl Brandstatter) **651** Customs Officer

1980. Austrian Modern Art.
1883 **650** 4s. multicoloured 70 45

1980. 150th Anniv of Customs Service.
1884 **651** 2s.50 brown and red . . 40 30

652 Masthead of 1810

1980. 350th Anniv of "Linzer Zeitung" (Linz newspaper).
1885 **652** 2s.50 black, red & gold 40 30

653 Frontispiece of Waidhofen Municipal Book **654** Heads

1980. 750th Anniv of Waidhofen.
1886 **653** 2s.50 multicoloured . . . 40 30

1980. 25th Anniv of Federal Army.
1887 **654** 2s.50 green and red . . . 40 30

655 Alfred Wegener **656** Robert Musil

1980. Birth Centenary of Alfred Wegener (explorer and geophysicist).
1888 **655** 4s. blue 70 45

1980. Birth Centenary of Robert Musil (writer).
1889 **656** 4s. brown 70 45

1980. "WIPA 1981" International Stamp Exhibition, Vienna (2nd issue). Inscr "2. Phase".
1890 **629** 16s.+8s. mult . . . . . 3·50 3·25

657 "Adoration of the Kings" (stained-glass window, Viktring Collegiate Church) **658** Ribbon in National Colours

1980. Christmas.
1891 **657** 4s. multicoloured 70 45

1981. 25th Anniv of General Social Insurance Act.
1892 **658** 2s.50 red, green & black 35 25

659 Unissued Design for 1926 Child Welfare Stamps **660** Disabled Person operating Machine Tool

1981. Birth Centenary of Wilhelm Dachauer (artist).
1894 **659** 3s. brown 45 30

1981. 3rd European Regional Conference of Rehabilitation International.
1895 **660** 6s. brown, blue and red 90 65

661 Sigmund Freud **662** Long-distance Heating System

1981. 125th Birth Anniv of Sigmund Freud (psychoanalyst).
1896 **661** 3s. purple 50 35

1981. 20th International Union of Long-distance Heat Distributors Congress, Vienna.
1897 **662** 4s. multicoloured 65 45

663 "Azzo and his Vassals" (cover of Monastery's "bearskin" Manuscript) **664** Maypole

1981. Kuenring Exhibition, Zwettl Monastery.
1898 **663** 3s. multicoloured 50 30

1981. Europa.
1899 **664** 6s. multicoloured . . . . 2·20 70

665 Early Telephone

1981. Centenary of Austrian Telephone System.
1900 **665** 4s. multicoloured 65 45

666 "The Frog King"

1981. Art Education in Schools.
1901 **666** 3s. multicoloured 50 30

667 Research Centre

1981. 25th Anniv of Seibersdorf Research Centre.
1902 **667** 4s. blue, dp blue & orge 65 50

668 Town Hall and Seal

669 Johann Florian Heller (chemist)

1981. 850th Anniv of St. Veit-on-Glan.
1903 **668** 4s. yellow, brown & red 65 45

1981. 11th Int Clinical Chemistry Congress, Vienna.
1904 **669** 6s. brown 90 65

670 Boltzmann

671 Otto Bauer

1981. 75th Death Anniv of Ludwig Boltzmann (physicist).
1905 **670** 3s. green 50 30

1981. Birth Centenary of Otto Bauer (writer and politician).
1906 **671** 4s. multicoloured 65 45

672 Chemical Balance

673 Impossible Construction (M. C. Escher)

1981. International Pharmaceutical Federation Congress, Vienna.
1907 **672** 6s. black, brown and red 90 65

1981. 10th International Austrian Mathematicians' Congress, Innsbruck.
1908 **673** 4s. lt blue, blue & dp blue 65 45

674 "Coronation of Virgin Mary" (detail)

675 Compass Rose

1981. 500th Anniv of Michael Pacher's Altarpiece at St. Wolfgang, Abersee.
1909 **674** 3s. blue 50 30

1981. 75th Anniv of Graz S.E. Exhibition.
1910 **675** 4s. multicoloured 65 45

676 "Holy Trinity" (illuminated MS, 12th century)

1981. 16th International Congress of Byzantine Scholars, Vienna.
1911 **676** 6s. multicoloured 90 65

677 Josef II

678 Hans Kelsen

1981. Bicentenary of Toleration Act (giving freedom of worship to Protestants).
1912 **677** 4s. black, blue & bistre 65 45

1981. Bicentenary of Hans Kelsen (law lecturer and contributor to shaping of Austrian Constitution).
1913 **678** 3s. red 50 30

679 Full and Empty Bowls and F.A.O. Emblem

1981. World Food Day.
1914 **679** 6s. multicoloured 90 65

680 "Between the Times" (Oscar Asboth)

681 Workers and Emblem

1981. Austrian Modern Art.
1915 **680** 4s. multicoloured 65 45

1981. 7th International Catholic Employees' Meeting, Vienna-Lainz.
1916 **681** 3s. multicoloured 50 30

682 Hammer-Purgstall

1981. 125th Death Anniv of Josef Hammer-Purgstall (orientalist).
1917 **682** 3s. multicoloured 50 30

683 Julius Raab

684 Stefan Zweig

1981. 90th Birth Anniv of Julius Raab (politician).
1918 **683** 6s. purple 85 65

1981. Birth Centenary of Stefan Zweig (writer).
1919 **684** 4s. lilac 60 45

685 Christmas Crib, Burgenland

1981. Christmas.
1920 **685** 4s. multicoloured 60 45

686 Arms of St. Nikola

1981. 800th Anniv of St. Nikola-on-Danube.
1921 **686** 4s. multicoloured 60 45

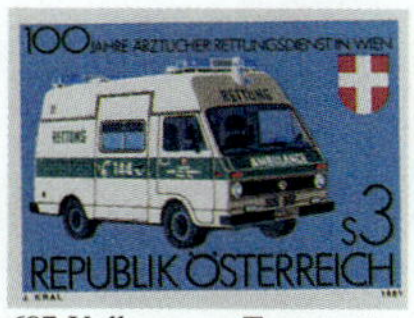

687 Volkswagen Transporter Ambulance

1981. Cent of Vienna's Emergency Medical Service.
1922 **687** 3s. multicoloured 50 35

688 Skier

689 Dorotheum Building

1982. Alpine Skiing World Championship, Schladming-Haus.
1923 **688** 4s. multicoloured 60 40

1982. 275th Anniv of Dorotheum Auction, Pawn and Banking Society.
1924 **689** 4s. multicoloured 60 40

690 Lifesaving

691 St. Severin

1982. 25th Anniv of Austrian Water Lifesaving Service.
1925 **690** 5s. blue, red & light blue 75 50

1982. "St. Severin and the End of the Roman Period" Exhibition, Enns.
1926 **691** 3s. multicoloured 50 30

692 Sebastian Kneipp (pioneer of holistic medicine)

693 Printers' Coat-of-arms

1982. International Kneipp Congress, Vienna.
1927 **692** 4s. multicoloured 60 45

1982. 500th Anniv of Printing in Austria.
1928 **693** 4s. multicoloured 60 45

694 Urine Analysis from "Canon Medicinae" by Avicenna

695 St. Francis preaching to Animals (miniature)

1982. 5th European Union for Urology Congress, Vienna.
1929 **694** 6s. multicoloured 85 65

1982. "Franciscan Art and Culture in the Middle Ages" Exhibition, Krems-Stein.
1930 **695** 3s. multicoloured 45 30

696 Haydn and Birthplace, Rohrau

697 Globe within Milk Churn

1982. "Joseph Haydn and His Time" Exhibition, Eisenstadt.
1931 **696** 3s. green 50 35

1982. World Dairying Day.
1932 **697** 7s. multicoloured . . . . 1·10 80

698 Town Arms (1804 flag)

699 Tennis Player

1982. 800th Anniv of Gfohl.
1933 **698** 4s. multicoloured 60 45

1982. 80th Anniv of Austrian Lawn Tennis Assn.
1934 **699** 3s. multicoloured 55 35

700 Main Square, Langenlois

701 Town Arms

1982. 900th Anniv of Langenlois.
1935 **700** 4s. multicoloured 60 45

1982. 800th Anniv of Weiz.
1936 **701** 4s. multicoloured 90 40

702 Linz–Freistadt–Budweis Horse-drawn Railway

1982. Europa.
1937 **702** 6s. brown . . . . 2·40 70

703 Ignaz Seipel **704** Postbus

1982. 50th Death Anniv of Ignaz Seipel (Federal Chancellor).
1938 **703** 3s. purple 50 30

1982. 75th Anniv of Post-bus Service.
1939 **704** 4s. multicoloured 60 45

705 Rocket Launch

1982. Second U.N. Conference on the Exploration and Peaceful Uses of Outer Space, Vienna.
1940 **705** 4s. multicoloured 60 45

706 Globe (Federal Office for Standardization and Surveying, Vienna)

1982. Geodesists' Day.
1941 **706** 3s. multicoloured 45 30

707 Great Bustard ("Grosstrappe")

1982. Endangered Animals. Multicoloured.
1942 3s. Type **707** 50 50
1943 4s. Eurasian beaver 65 60
1944 6s. Western capercaillie ("Auerhahn") 90 85

708 Institute Building, Laxenburg

1982. 10th Anniv of International Institute for Applied Systems Analysis.
1945 **708** 3s. black and brown . . 40 30

709 St. Apollonia (patron saint of dentists)

1982. 70th International Dentists Federation Congress, Vienna.
1946 **709** 4s. multicoloured 60 45

710 Emmerich Kalman **711** Max Mell

1982. Birth Cent of Emmerich Kalman (composer).
1947 **710** 3s. blue 45 35

1982. Birth Centenary of Max Mell (writer).
1948 **711** 3s. multicoloured 45 30

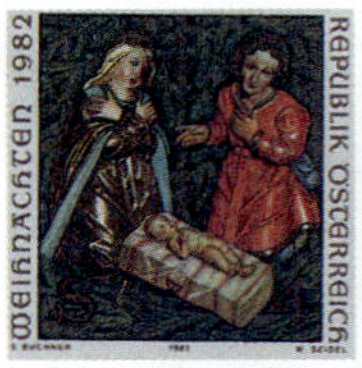

712 Christmas Crib, Damuls Church **713** Aerial View of Bosphorus

1982. Christmas.
1949 **712** 4s. multicoloured 60 45

1982. Centenary of St. George's Austrian College, Istanbul.
1950 **713** 4s. multicoloured 60 45

714 "Mainz-Weber" Mailbox, 1870

1982. Stamp Day.
1951 **714** 6s.+3s. multicoloured . . 1·50 1·40

715 "Muse of the Republic" (Ernst Fuchs) **716** Bank, Vienna

1982. Austrian Modern Art.
1952 **715** 4s. red and violet 60 45

1983. Centenary of Postal Savings Bank.
1953 **716** 4s. yellow, black and blue 60 45

717 Hildegard Burjan

1983. Birth Centenary of Hildegard Burjan (founder of Caritas Socialis (religious sisterhood)).
1954 **717** 4s. red 60 45

718 Linked Arms

1983. World Communications Year.
1955 **718** 7s. multicoloured . . . . 1·00 70

719 Young Girl **720** Josef Matthias Hauer

1983. 75th Anniv of Children's Friends Organization.
1956 **719** 4s. black, blue and red 60 45

1983. Birth Centenary of Josef Matthias Hauer (composer).
1957 **720** 3s. purple 40 35

721 Douglas DC-9-80 Super Eighty

1983. 25th Anniv of Austrian Airlines.
1958 **721** 6s. multicoloured 85 65

722 Hands protecting Workers

1983. Cent of Government Work Inspection Law.
1959 **722** 4s. grn, dp grn & brn . . 60 45

723 Wels (engraving, Matthaeus Merian)

1983. "Millenary of Upper Austria" Exn, Wels.
1960 **723** 3s. multicoloured 40 30

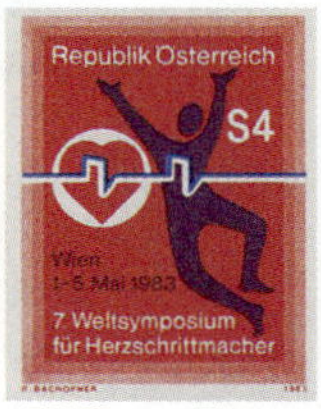

724 Human Figure, Heart and Electrocardiogram **725** Monastery Arms

1983. 7th World Symposium on Pacemakers.
1961 **724** 4s. red, mauve and blue 60 45

1983. 900th Anniv of Gottweig Monastery.
1962 **725** 3s. multicoloured 45 30

726 Weitra

1983. 800th Anniv of Weitra.
1963 **726** 4s. black, red and gold 60 45

727 Cap, Stick, Ribbon and Emblems

1983. 50th Anniv of MKV and CCV Catholic Students' Organizations.
1964 **727** 4s. multicoloured 60 45

728 Glopper Castle and Town Arms **729** Hess

1983. 650th Anniv of Hohenems Town Charter.
1965 **728** 4s. multicoloured 60 45

1983. Europa. Birth Centenary of Viktor Franz Hess (physicist and Nobel Prize winner).
1966 **729** 6s. green . . . . 2·40 70

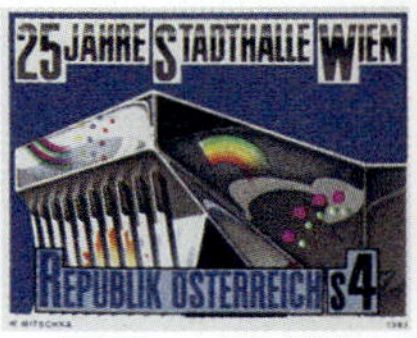

730 Vienna City Hall **731** Kiwanis Emblem and View of Vienna

1983. 25th Anniv of Vienna City Hall.
1967 **730** 4s. multicoloured 60 45

1983. Kiwanis International, World and European Conference, Vienna.
1968 **731** 5s. multicoloured 75 50

732 Congress Emblem **733** Hasenauer and Natural History Museum, Vienna

1983. 7th World Psychiatry Congress, Vienna.
1969 **732** 4s. multicoloured 60 40

1983. 150th Birth Anniv of Carl Freiherr von Hasenauer (architect).
1970 **733** 3s. brown 45 30

734 Institute for Promotion of Trade and Industry, Linz

1983. 27th International Professional Competition for Young Skilled Workers, Linz.
1971 **734** 4s. multicoloured 65 45

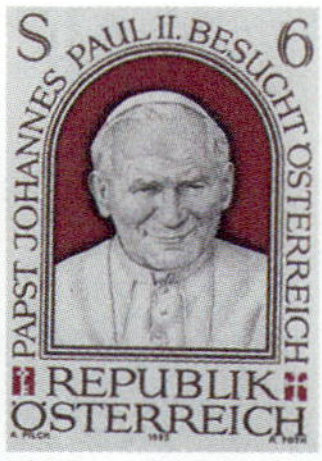

735 Symbols of Penicillin V Efficacy and Cancer **736** Pope John Paul II

1983. 13th Int Chemotherapy Congress, Vienna.
1972 **735** 5s. red and green 70 50

1983. Papal Visit.
1973 **736** 6s. black, red and gold 95 65

737 "Relief of Vienna, 1683" (Franz Geffels)

1983. 300th Anniv of Relief of Vienna. Sheet 90 × 70 mm.
MS1974 **737** 6s. multicoloured . . 1·20 1·00

738 Spectrum around Cross

739 Vienna Town Hall

1983. Austrian Catholics' Day.
1975 **738** 3s. multicoloured 50 30

1983. Centenary of Vienna Town Hall.
1976 **739** 4s. multicoloured 65 40

740 Karl von Terzaghi

1983. Birth Centenary of Karl von Terzaghi (soil mechanics and foundations engineer).
1977 **740** 3s. blue 50 30

741 Initials of Federation

1983. 10th Austrian Trade Unions Federation Congress.
1978 **741** 3s. red and black 50 30

742 "Evening Sun in Burgenland" (Gottfried Kumpf)

743 Tram No. 5, 1883

1983. Austrian Modern Art.
1979 **742** 4s. multicoloured 60 45

1983. Centenary of Modling–Hinterbruhl Electric Railway.
1980 **743** 3s. multicoloured 55 35

744 Boy looking at Stamped Envelope

1983. Stamp Day.
1981 **744** 6s.+3s. multicoloured . . 1·50 1·40

745 Francisco Carolinum Museum, Linz

1983. 150th Anniv of Upper Austrian Provincial Museum.
1982 **745** 4s. multicoloured 65 45

746 Crib by Johann Giner the Elder, Kitzbuhel Church

1983. Christmas.
1983 **746** 4s. multicoloured 65 45

747 Parliament Building

748 "St. Nicholas" (Maria Freund)

1983. Centenary of Parliament Building, Vienna.
1984 **747** 4s. blue 65 45

1983. Youth Stamp.
1985 **748** 3s. multicoloured 50 30

749 Wolfgang Pauli

1983. 25th Death Anniv of Wolfgang Pauli (Nobel Prize winner for Physics).
1986 **749** 6s. brown 90 65

750 Gregor Mendel

1984. Death Cent of Gregor Mendel (geneticist).
1987 **750** 4s. ochre and brown . . 60 45

751 Hanak at Work

1984. 50th Death Anniv of Anton Hanak (sculptor).
1988 **751** 3s. brown and black . . 45 30

752 Disabled Skier

1984. 3rd World Winter Games for the Disabled, Innsbruck.
1989 **752** 4s.+2s. multicoloured . . 1·00 95

753 Memorial, Wollersdorf

1984. 50th Anniv of 1934 Insurrections.
1990 **753** 4s.50 red and black . . . 70 50

754 Founders' Stone

755 Geras Monastery

1984. 900th Anniv of Reichersberg Monastery.
1991 **754** 3s.50 stone, brown & bl 55 40

1984. Monasteries and Abbeys.

1992	–	50g. yellow, black & grey	20	20
1993	–	1s. yellow, black & mve	20	15
1994	–	1s.50 yellow, red & blue	25	20
1995	–	2s. yellow, green & black	40	20
1996	**755**	3s.50 yellow, sep & brn	70	15
1997	–	4s. yellow, purple & red	70	15
1998	–	4s.50 yellow, lilac & blue	75	15
1999	–	5s. yellow, purple & orge	75	15
2000	–	5s.50 yell, dp vio & vio	1·10	25
2001	–	6s. yellow, green & emer	1·00	15
2002	–	7s. yellow, green & blue	1·40	20
2003	–	7s.50 yell, dp brn & brn	1·40	25
2004	–	8s. yellow, blue and red	1·50	25
2005	–	10s. yellow, red & grey	1·80	25
2006	–	11s. yellow, black & brn	1·90	45
2007	–	12s. yellow, brn & orge	2·75	85
2008	–	17s. yellow, ultram & bl	3·25	75
2009	–	20s. yellow, brown & red	4·00	1·30

DESIGNS: 50g. Vorau Monastery; 1s. Wettingen Abbey, Mehrerau; 1s.50, Monastery of Teutonic Order, Vienna; 2s. Michaelbeuern Benedictine Monastery, Salzburg; 4s. Stams Monastery; 4s.50, Schlagl Monastery; 5s. St. Paul's Monastery, Lavanttal; 5s.50, St. Gerold's Priory, Vorarlberg; 6s. Rein Monastery; 7s. Loretto Monastery; 7s.50, Dominican Monastery, Vienna; 8s. Cistercian Monastery, Zwettl; 10s. Premonstratensian Monastery, Wilten; 11s. Trappist Monastery, Engelszell; 12s. Monastery of the Hospitallers, Eisenstadt; 17s. St. Peter's Abbey, Salzburg; 20s. Wernberg Convent, Carinthia.

756 Cigar Band showing Tobacco Plant

757 Kostendorf

1984. Bicentenary of Tobacco Monopoly.
2012 **756** 4s.50 multicoloured . . . 70 50

1984. 1200th Anniv of Kostendorf.
2013 **757** 4s.50 multicoloured . . . 70 50

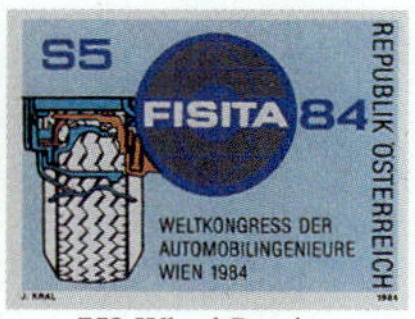

758 Wheel Bearing

1984. 20th International Federation of Automobile Engineers' Associations World Congress, Vienna.
2014 **758** 5s. multicoloured 75 50

759 Bridge

760 Archduke Johann (after Schnorr von Carolsfeld)

1984. Europa. 25th Anniv of E.P.T. Conference.
2015 **759** 6s. blue and ultramarine 2·20 70

1984. 125th Death Anniv of Archduke Johann.
2016 **760** 4s.50 multicoloured . . . 70 50

761 Aragonite

762 Binding of "Das Buch vom Kaiser", by Max Herzig

1984. "Ore and Iron in the Green Mark" Exhibition, Eisenerz.
2017 **761** 3s.50 multicoloured . . . 50 35

1984. Lower Austrian "Era of Emperor Franz Joseph: From Revolution to Grunderzeit" Exhibition, Grafenegg Castle.
2018 **762** 3s.50 red and gold . . . 55 35

763 Upper City Tower and Arms

764 Dionysus (Virunum mosaic)

1984. 850th Anniv of Vocklabruch.
2019 **763** 4s.50 multicoloured . . . 70 50

1984. Centenary of Carinthia Provincial Museum, Klagenfurt.
2020 **764** 3s.50 stone, brn & grey 50 35

765 "Meeting of Austrian Army with South Tyrolean Reserves" (detail, Schnorr von Carolsfeld)

766 Ralph Benatzky

1984. "Jubilee of Tyrol Province" Exhibition.
2021 **765** 3s.50 multicoloured . . . 50 35

1984. Birth Cent of Ralph Benatzky (composer).
2022 **766** 4s. brown 60 45

767 Flood Control Barriers

768 Christian von Ehrenfels

1984. Centenary of Flood Control Systems.
2023 **767** 4s.50 green 70 50

1984. 125th Death Anniv of Christian von Ehrenfels (philosopher).
2024 **768** 3s.50 multicoloured . . . 50 35

769 Models of European Monuments

1984. 25th Anniv of Minimundus (model world), Worthersee.
2025 **769** 4s. yellow and black . . 60 45

770 Blockheide Eibenstein National Park

1984. Natural Beauty Spots.
2026 **770** 4s. pink and olive . . . 60 45

771 Electric Train on Schanatobel Bridge (Arlberg Railway Centenary)

1984. Railway Anniversaries.
2027 **771** 3s.50 brown, gold & red 70 45
2028 – 4s.50 blue, silver and red 80 50
DESIGN: 4s.50, Electric train on Falkenstein Bridge (75th anniv of Tauern Railway).

772 Johann Georg Stuwer's Ascent in Montgolfier Balloon

1984. Bicentenary of First Manned Balloon Flight in Austria.
2029 **772** 6s. multicoloured . . . . 1·00 70

773 Lake Neusiedl

1984. Natural Beauty Spots.
2030 **773** 4s. purple and blue . . . 60 45

774 Palace of Justice, Vienna

775 "Joseph Hyrtl" (window, Innsbruck Anatomy Institute)

1984. 20th Int Bar Assn Congress, Vienna.
2031 **774** 7s. multicoloured . . . . 1·10 80

1984. 7th European Anatomists' Congress, Innsbruck.
2032 **775** 6s. multicoloured 90 60

776 "Window" (Karl Korab)

777 Clock of Imms (astrolabe)

1984. Austrian Modern Art.
2033 **776** 4s. multicoloured 60 40

1984. 600th Birth Anniv of Johannes von Gmunden (astronomer and mathematician).
2034 **777** 3s.50 multicoloured . . . 55 40

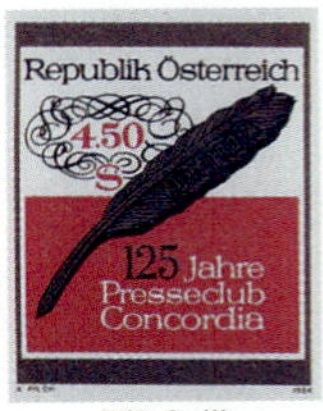

778 Quill

779 Fanny Elssler

1984. 125th Anniv of Concordia Press Club.
2035 **778** 4s.50 black, gold & red 70 50

1984. Death Centenary of Fanny Elssler (dancer).
2036 **779** 4s. multicoloured 65 40

780 "Holy Family" (detail, Aggsbach Old High Altar)

1984. Christmas.
2037 **780** 4s.50 multicoloured . . . 70 50

781 Detail from Burial Chamber Wall of Seschemnofer III

782 Coat of Arms

1984. Stamp Day.
2038 **781** 6s.+3s. multicoloured . . 1·50 1·40

1985. 400th Anniv of Graz University.
2039 **782** 3s.50 multicoloured . . . 50 35

783 Dr. Lorenz Bohler

1985. Birth Centenary of Prof. Dr. Lorenz Bohler (surgeon).
2040 **783** 4s.50 purple 70 50

784 Ski Jumping, Skiing and Emblem

1985. World Nordic Skiing Championship, Seefeld.
2041 **784** 4s. multicoloured 65 45

785 Linz Cathedral

786 Alban Berg

1985. Bicentenary of Linz Diocese.
2042 **785** 4s.50 multicoloured . . . 70 50

1985. Birth Centenary of Alban Berg (composer).
2043 **786** 6s. blue 90 70

787 Institute Emblem

788 Stylized "B" and Clouds

1985. 25th Anniv of Institute for Vocational Advancement.
2044 **787** 4s.50 multicoloured . . . 70 50

1985. 2000th Anniv of Bregenz.
2045 **788** 4s. black, ultram & blue 60 45

789 1885 Registration Label

790 Josef Stefan

1985. Centenary of Registration Labels in Austria.
2046 **789** 4s.50 black, yell & grey 70 50

1985. 150th Birth Anniv of Josef Stefan (physicist).
2047 **790** 6s. brown, stone and red 90 65

791 St. Leopold (Margrave and patron saint)

792 "The Story-teller"

1985. Lower Austrian Provincial Exhibition, Klosterneuburg Monastery.
2048 **791** 3s.50 multicoloured . . . 50 35

1985. 150th Birth Anniv of Franz Defregger (artist).
2049 **792** 3s.50 multicoloured . . . 50 35

793 Barbed Wire, Broken Tree and New Shoot

794 Johann Joseph Fux (composer)

1985. 40th Anniv of Liberation.
2050 **793** 4s.50 multicoloured . . . 70 50

1985. Europa. Music Year.
2051 **794** 6s. brown and grey . . . 1·90 70

795 Flags and Caduceus

797 Bishop's Gate, St. Polten

796 Town and Arms

1985. 25th Anniv of European Free Trade Association.
2052 **795** 4s. multicoloured 60 45

1985. Millenary of Boheimkirchen.
2053 **796** 4s.50 multicoloured . . . 70 50

1985. Bicentenary of St. Polten Diocese.
2054 **797** 4s.50 multicoloured . . . 70 55

798 Johannes von Nepomuk Church, Innsbruck

799 Garsten (copperplate, George Matthaus Fischer)

1985. Gumpp Family (architects) Exn, Innsbruck.
2055 **798** 3s.50 multicoloured . . . 55 40

1985. Millenary of Garsten.
2056 **799** 4s.50 multicoloured . . . 70 50

800 U.N. Emblem and Austrian Arms

1985. 40th Anniv of U.N.O. and 30th Anniv of Austrian Membership.
2057 **800** 4s. multicoloured 65 45

801 Association Headquarters, Vienna

1985. 13th International Suicide Prevention Association Congress, Vienna.
2058 **801** 5s. brown, lt yell & yell 75 55

802 Woodland

1985. Forestry Year. Sheet 90 × 70 mm.
MS2059 **802** 6s. multicoloured . . 1·50 1·20

803 Operetta Emblem and Spa Building

804 Fireman and Emblem

1985. 25th Bad Ischl Operetta Week.
2060 **803** 3s.50 multicoloured . . . 60 45

1985. 8th International Fire Brigades Competition, Vocklabruck.
2061 **804** 4s.50 black, green & red 95 50

805 Grossglockner Mountain Road

1985. 50th Anniv of Grossglockner Mountain Road.
2062 **805** 4s. multicoloured 60 50

806 Chessboard as Globe

807 "Founding of Konigstetten" (August Stephan)

1985. World Chess Association Congress, Graz.
2063 **806** 4s. multicoloured 60 45

1985. Millenary of Konigstetten.
2064 **807** 4s.50 multicoloured . . . 70 50

808 Webern Church and Arms of Hofkirchen and Taufkircher

1985. 1200th Anniversaries of Hofkirchen, Weibern and Taufkirchen.
2065 **808** 4s.50 multicoloured . . . 70 50

809 Dr. Adam Politzer

1985. 150th Birth Anniv of Dr. Adam Politzer (otologist).
2066 **809** 3s.50 violet 55 35

810 Emblem and View of Vienna

1985. International Association of Forwarding Agents World Congress, Vienna.
2067 **810** 6s. multicoloured 95 65

811 "Clowns Riding High Bicycles" (Paul Flora)

1985. Austrian Modern Art.
2068 **811** 4s. multicoloured 65 45

812 St. Martin, Patron Saint of Burgenland

1985. 25th Anniv of Eisenstadt Diocese.
2069 **812** 4s.50 black, bistre & red 70 50

813 Roman Mounted Courier

1985. 50th Anniv of Stamp Day.
2070 **813** 6s.+3s. multicoloured . . 1·50 1·40

814 Hanns Horbiger

815 "Adoration of the Christ Child" (marble relief)

1985. 125th Birth Anniv of Hanns Horbiger (design engineer).
2071 **814** 3s.50 purple and gold . . 55 40

1985. Christmas.
2072 **815** 4s.50 multicoloured . . . 65 40

816 Aqueduct

1985. 75th Anniv of Second Vienna Waterline.
2073 **816** 3s.50 black, red & blue 55 40

818 Chateau de la Muette (headquarters)

1985. 25th Anniv of Organization of Economic Co-operation and Development.
2080 **818** 4s. black, gold & mauve 60 45

819 Johann Bohm

1986. Birth Centenary of Johann Bohm (founder of Austrian Trade Unions Federation).
2081 **819** 4s.50 black and red . . . 70 50

820 Dove and Globe

1986. International Peace Year.
2082 **820** 6s. multicoloured 90 60

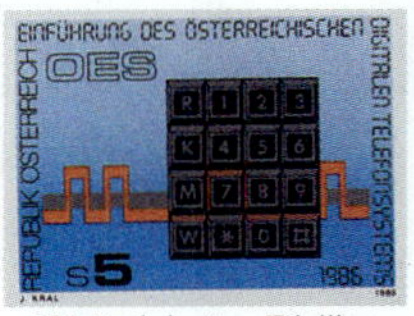

821 Push-button Dialling

1986. Introduction of Digital Preselection Telephone System.
2083 **821** 5s. multicoloured 70 50

822 Albrechtsberger and Organ

1986. 250th Birth Anniv of Johann Georg Albrechtsberger (composer).
2084 **822** 3s.50 multicoloured . . . 50 40

823 Main Square and Arms

1986. 850th Anniv of Korneuburg.
2085 **823** 5s. multicoloured 75 45

824 Kokoschka (self-portrait)

825 Council Flag

1986. Birth Centenary of Oskar Kokoschka (artist).
2086 **824** 4s. black and pink . . . 65 40

1986. 30th Anniv of Membership of Council of Europe.
2087 **825** 6s. black, red and blue 90 65

826 Holzmeister and Salzburg Festival Hall

1986. Birth Centenary of Professor Clemens Holzmeister (architect).
2088 **826** 4s. grey, brown & lt brn 60 45

827 Road, Roll of Material, and Congress Emblem

1986. 3rd International Geotextile Congress, Vienna.
2089 **827** 5s. multicoloured 75 50

828 Schlosshof Palace (after Bernardo Bellotto) and Prince Eugene

1986. "Prince Eugene and the Baroque Era" Exhibition, Schlosshof and Niederweiden.
2090 **828** 4s. multicoloured 60 45

829 St. Florian Monastery

1986. Upper Austrian "World of Baroque" Exhibition, St. Florian Monastery.
2091 **829** 4s. multicoloured 60 45

830 Herberstein Castle and Styrian Arms

1986. "Styria – Bridge and Bulwark" Exhibition, Herberstein Castle, near Stubenberg.
2092 **830** 4s. multicoloured 60 45

831 Large Pasque Flower

1986. Europa.
2093 **831** 6s. multicoloured . . . . 1·80 70

832 Wagner and Scene from Opera "Lohengrin"

1986. International Richard Wagner (composer) Congress, Vienna.
2094 **832** 4s. multicoloured 60 45

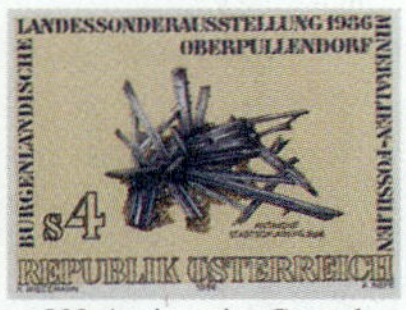

833 Antimonite Crystal

1986. Burgenland "Mineral and Fossils" Exhibition, Oberpullendorf.
2095 **833** 4s. multicoloured 60 45

834 Martinswall, Zirl

1986. Natural Beauty Spots.
2096 **834** 5s. brown and blue . . . 80 50

835 Waidhofen

1986. 800th Anniv of Waidhofen on Ybbs.
2097 **835** 4s. multicoloured 65 45

836 Tschauko Falls, Ferlach

1986. Natural Beauty Spots.
2098 **836** 5s. green and brown . . 75 50

837 19th-century Steam and Modern Articulated Trams

1986. Cent of Salzburg Local Transport System.
2099 **837** 4s. multicoloured 65 45

838 Enns and Seals of Signatories

1986. 800th Anniv of Georgenberg Treaty (between Duke Leopold V of Austria and Duke Otakar IV of Styria).
2100 **838** 5s. multicoloured 75 50

839 Tandler **840** "Observatory, 1886" (A. Heilmann)

1986. 50th Death Anniv of Julius Tandler (social reformer).
2101 **839** 4s. multicoloured 60 45

1986. Centenary of Sonnblick Observatory.
2102 **840** 4s. black, blue and gold 60 45

841 Man collecting Mandragora (from "Codex Tacuinum Sanitatis") **842** Fire Assistant

1986. 7th European Anaesthesia Congress, Vienna.
2103 **841** 5s. multicoloured 75 50

1986. 300th Anniv of Vienna Fire Brigade.
2104 **842** 4s. multicoloured 95 50

843 Stoessl **844** Viennese Hunting Tapestry (detail)

1986. 50th Death Anniv of Otto Stoessl (writer).
2105 **843** 4s. multicoloured 60 45

1986. 5th International Oriental Carpets and Tapestry Conference, Vienna and Budapest.
2106 **844** 5s. multicoloured 75 50

845 Minister in Pulpit **846** "Decomposition" (Walter Schmogner)

1986. 125th Anniv of Protestants Act and 25th Anniv of Protestants Law.
2107 **845** 5s. black and violet . . . 75 50

1986. Austrian Modern Art.
2108 **846** 4s. multicoloured 65 45

847 Liszt, Birthplace and Score

1986. 175th Birth Anniv of Franz Liszt (composer).
2109 **847** 5s. green and brown . . 75 50

848 Aerial View of Vienna (½-size illustration)

1986. European Security and Co-operation Conference Review Meeting, Vienna. Sheet 90 × 70 mm.
MS2110 **848** 6s. multicoloured . . 1·40 1·10

849 Strettweg Religious Carriage

1986. 175th Anniv of Styrian Joanneum Museum.
2111 **849** 4s. multicoloured 60 45

850 "Nuremberg Letter Messenger" (16th century woodcut) **852** Headquarters

851 "Adoration of the Shepherds" (woodcut, Johann Georg Schwanthaler)

1986. Stamp Day.
2112 **850** 6s.+3s. multicoloured . . 1·50 1·40

1986. Christmas.
2113 **851** 5s. brown and gold . . . 75 50

1986. 40th Anniv of Federal Chamber of Trade and Industry.
2114 **852** 5s. multicoloured 75 50

853 Foundry Worker

1986. Austrian World of Work (1st series).
2115 **853** 4s. multicoloured 60 45
See also Nos. 2144, 2178, 2211, 2277, 2386, 2414, 2428, 2486, 2520, 2572 and 2605.

854 "The Educated Eye"

1987. Centenary of Adult Education in Vienna.
2116 **854** 5s. multicoloured 75 50

855 "Large Blue Madonna" (Anton Faistauer)

1987. Painters' Birth Centenaries. Multicoloured.
2117 4s. Type **855** 60 45
2118 6s. "Self-portrait" (Albert Paris Gutersloh) 95 70

856 Hundertwasser House, Vienna

1987. Europa and "Europalia 1987 Austria" Festival, Belgium.
2119 **856** 6s. multicoloured . . . . 2·20 1·20

857 Ice Hockey Players

1987. World Ice Hockey Championships, Vienna, and 75th Anniv of Austrian Ice Hockey Association.
2120 **857** 5s. multicoloured 85 50

858 Austria Centre

1987. Inaug of Austria Conference Centre, Vienna.
2121 **858** 5s. multicoloured 90 50

859 Salzburg **860** Machine Shop, 1920

1987. 700th Anniv of Salzburg Town Charter.
2122 **859** 5s. multicoloured 95 55

1987. Upper Austrian "Work–Men–Machines, the Route to Industrialized Society" Exhibition, Steyr.
2123 **860** 4s. black and red 65 40

861 Man and Woman **862** "Adele Bloch-Bauer I" (detail, Gustav Klimt)

1987. Equal Rights for Men and Women.
2124 **861** 5s. multicoloured 80 50

1987. Lower Austrian "Era of Emperor Franz Joseph: Splendour and Misery" Exhibition, Grafenegg Castle.
2125 **862** 4s. multicoloured 65 45

863 Archbishop and Salzburg

1987. 400th Anniv of Election of Prince Wolf Dietrich von Raitenau as Archbishop of Salzburg.
2126 **863** 4s. multicoloured 60 45

864 Schnitzler **865** Lace and Arms

1987. 125th Birth Anniv of Arthur Schnitzler (dramatist).
2127 **864** 6s. multicoloured 85 65

1987. 1100th Anniv of Lustenau.
2128 **865** 5s. multicoloured 80 50

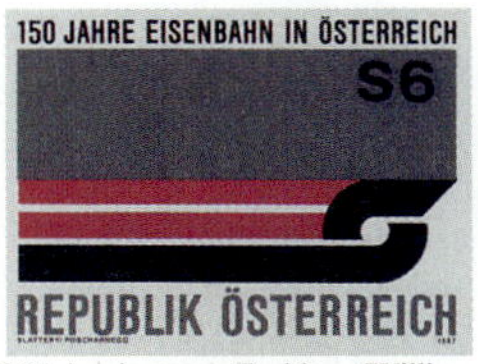

866 Anniversary Emblem (William Slattery)

1987. 150th Anniv of Austrian Railways. Sheet 90 × 70 mm.
MS2129 **866** 6s. silver, red and black 1·40 1·10

867 Dachstein Giant Ice Cave

1987. Natural Beauty Spots.
2130 **867** 5s. green and black . . . 80 50

868 Engraver at Work **869** Dr. Karl Josef Bayer (chemist)

1987. 8th European Association of Engravers and Flexographers International Congress, Vienna.
2131 **868** 5s. brown, pink and grey 80 50

1987. 8th International Light Metal Meeting, Leoben and Vienna.
2132 **869** 5s. multicoloured 80 50

870 Passenger Ferry

871 Office Building, Vienna

1987. Centenary of 1st Achensee Steam Service.
2133 **870** 4s. multicoloured 60 45

1987. 10th Anniv of Office of Ombudsmen.
2134 **871** 5s. black, yellow and red 75 50

872 Schrodinger

873 Freistadt Town Square

1987. Birth Cent of Erwin Schrodinger (physicist).
2135 **872** 5s. brown, cream and bistre 80 50

1987. 125th Anniv of Freistadt Exhibitions.
2136 **873** 5s. multicoloured 80 50

874 Arbing Church

1987. 850th Anniv of Arbing.
2137 **874** 5s. multicoloured 80 50

875 Gauertal and Montafon Valleys, Voralberg

1987. Natural Beauty Spots.
2138 **875** 5s. brown and yellow . . 80 50

876 Cyclist

877 Emblem

1987. World Cycling Championship, Vienna and Villach.
2139 **876** 5s. multicoloured 80 55

1987. World Congress of International Institute of Savings Banks, Vienna.
2140 **877** 5s. multicoloured 80 55

878 Hofhaymer at Organ

880 Lammergeier ("Bartgeier")

879 Haydn and Salzburg

1987. 450th Death Anniv of Paul Hofhaymer (composer and organist).
2141 **878** 4s. blue, black and gold 60 45

1987. 250th Birth Anniv of Michael Haydn (composer).
2142 **879** 4s. lilac 60 45

1987. 25th Anniv of Alpine Zoo, Innsbruck.
2143 **880** 4s. multicoloured 60 45

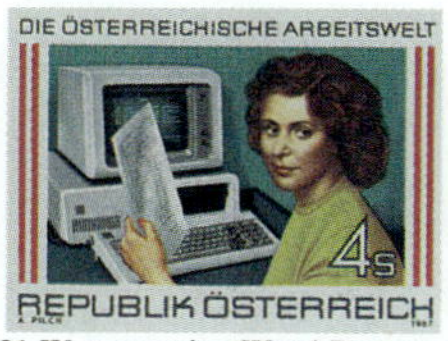

881 Woman using Word Processor

1987. Austrian World of Work (2nd series).
2144 **881** 4s. multicoloured 65 45

882 "Tree Goddesses" (Arnulf Neuwirth)

1987. Austrian Modern Art.
2145 **882** 5s. multicoloured 80 50

883 Lottery Wheel

884 Helmer

1987. Bicentenary of Gambling Monopoly.
2146 **883** 5s. multicoloured 80 50

1987. Birth Centenary of Oskar Helmer (politician).
2147 **884** 4s. multicoloured 60 45

885 Gluck

886 Stagecoach and Passengers (lithograph, Carl Schuster)

1987. Death Bicentenary of Christoph Willibald Gluck (composer).
2148 **885** 5s. brown and ochre . . 80 50

1987. Stamp Day.
2149 **886** 6s.+3s. multicoloured . . 1·50 1·40

887 Josef Mohr and Franz Xaver Gruber (composers of "Silent Night")

1987. Christmas.
2150 **887** 5s. multicoloured . . . . 1·00 50

888 Bosco and Boys

889 Cross-country Sledging

1988. International Educational Congress of St. John Bosco's Salesian Brothers, Vienna.
2151 **888** 5s. purple and orange . . 80 50

1988. 4th World Winter Games for the Disabled, Innsbruck.
2152 **889** 5s.+2s.50 multicoloured 1·20 1·10

890 Mach

891 "Village with Bridge"

1988. 150th Birth Anniv of Ernst Mach (physicist and philosopher).
2153 **890** 6s. multicoloured 85 60

1988. 25th Death Anniv of Franz von Zulow (artist).
2154 **891** 4s. multicoloured 65 45

892 "The Confiscation" (Ferdinand Georg Waldmuller)

1988. "Patriotism and Protest: Viennese Biedermeier and Revolution" Exhibition, Vienna.
2155 **892** 4s. multicoloured 65 45

893 Barbed Wire, Flag and Crosses

1988. 50th Anniv of Annexation of Austria by Germany.
2156 **893** 5s. green, brown and red 80 50

894 Steam Locomotive "Aigen", Muhlkreis Railway, 1887

895 European Bee Eater

1988. Railway Centenaries. Multicoloured.
2157 4s. Type **894** 70 45
2158 5s. Modern electric tram and Josefsplatz stop (Viennese Local Railways Stock Corporation) . . . 85 50

1988. 25th Anniv of World Wildlife Fund, Austria.
2159 **895** 5s. multicoloured 85 50

896 Decanter and Beaker

897 Late Gothic Silver Censer

1988. Styrian "Glass and Coal" Exn, Barnbach.
2160 **896** 4s. multicoloured 65 45

1988. Lower Austrian "Art and Monastic Life at the Birth of Austria" Exhibition, Seitenstetten Benedictine Monastery.
2161 **897** 4s. multicoloured 60 45

898 Taking Casualty to Volkswagen Transporter Ambulance and Red Cross

900 Mattsee Monastery

899 Dish Aerials, Aflenz

1988. 125th Anniv of Red Cross.
2162 **898** 12s. black, red and green 1·80 1·20

1988. Europa. Telecommunications.
2163 **899** 6s. multicoloured . . . . 2·20 60

1988. Salzburg "Bajuvars from Severin to Tassilo" Exhibition, Mattsee Monastery.
2164 **900** 4s. multicoloured 65 45

901 Weinberg Castle

902 Horvath

1988. Upper Austrian "Muhlviertel: Nature, Culture, Life" Exhibition, Weinberg Castle, near Kefermarkt.
2165 **901** 4s. multicoloured 65 45

1988. 50th Death Anniv of Odon von Horvath (writer).
2166 **902** 6s. black and bistre . . . 1·00 60

903 Stockerau Town Hall

1988. 25th Anniv of Stockerau Festival.
2167 **903** 5s. multicoloured 80 50

904 Motorway

905 Brixlegg

1988. Completion of Tauern Motorway.
2168 **904** 4s. multicoloured 65 45

1988. 1200th Anniv of Brixlegg.
2169 **905** 5s. multicoloured 85 50

906 Klagenfurt (after Matthaus Merian)

1988. 400th Anniv of Regular Postal Services in Carinthia.
2170 **906** 5s. multicoloured 80 50

907 Parish Church and Dean's House

1988. 1200th Anniv of Brixen im Thale, Tyrol.
2171 **907** 5s. multicoloured 80 50

908 Krimml Waterfalls, Upper Tauern National Park

1988. Natural Beauty Spots.
2172 **908** 5s. black and blue . . . 80 50

909 Town Arms

1988. 1100th Anniv of Feldkirchen, Carinthia.
2173 **909** 5s. multicoloured 80 50

910 Feldbach

1988. 800th Anniv of Feldbach.
2174 **910** 5s. multicoloured 80 50

911 Ansfelden

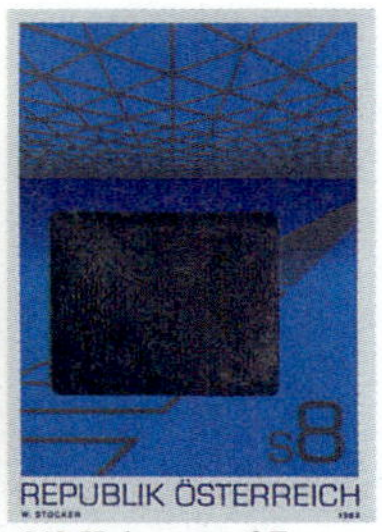

912 Hologram of Export Emblem

1988. 1200th Anniv of Ansfelden.
2175 **911** 5s. multicoloured 80 50

1988. Federal Economic Chamber Export Congress.
2176 **912** 8s. multicoloured . . . . 2·10 1·90

913 Concert Hall

1988. 75th Anniv of Vienna Concert Hall.
2177 **913** 5s. multicoloured 80 50

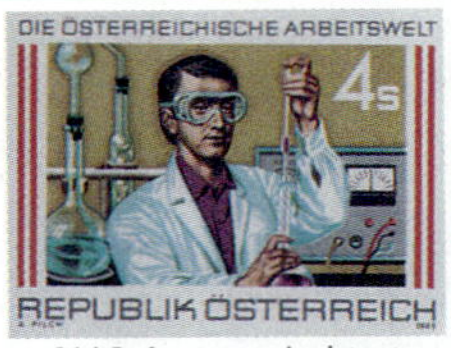

914 Laboratory Assistant

1988. Austrian World of Work (3rd series).
2178 **914** 4s. multicoloured 65 45

915 "Guards" (Giselbert Hoke)

916 Schonbauer

1988. Austrian Modern Art.
2179 **915** 5s. multicoloured 80 50

1988. Birth Centenary of Dr. Leopold Schonbauer (neurosurgeon and politician).
2180 **916** 4s. multicoloured 70 45

917 Carnation

918 Loading Railway Mail Van at Pardubitz Station, 1914

1988. Cent of Austrian Social Democratic Party.
2181 **917** 4s. multicoloured 65 50

1988. Stamp Day.
2182 **918** 6s.+3s. multicoloured . . 1·50 1·40

919 "Nativity" (St. Barbara's Church, Vienna)

920 "Madonna" (Lucas Cranach)

1988. Christmas.
2183 **919** 5s. multicoloured 80 50

1989. 25th Anniv of Diocese of Innsbruck.
2184 **920** 4s. multicoloured 60 45

921 Margrave Leopold II leading Abbot Sigibold and Monks to Melk (detail of fresco, Paul Troger)

1989. 900th Anniv of Melk Benedictine Monastery.
2185 **921** 5s. multicoloured 80 50

922 Marianne Hainisch

923 Glider and Paraskier

1989. 150th Birth Anniv of Marianne Hainisch (women's rights activist).
2186 **922** 6s. multicoloured 95 65

1989. World Gliding Championships, Wiener Neustadt, and World Paraskiing Championships, Damuls.
2187 **923** 6s. multicoloured 95 65

924 "The Painting"

926 Wittgenstein

925 "Bruck an der Leitha" (17th-century engraving, Georg Vischer)

1989. 50th Death Anniv of Rudolf Jettmar (painter).
2188 **924** 5s. multicoloured 80 50

1989. 750th Anniv of Bruck an der Leitha.
2189 **925** 5s. multicoloured 80 50

1989. Birth Centenary of Ludwig Wittgenstein (philosopher).
2190 **926** 5s. multicoloured 80 50

927 Holy Trinity Church, Stadl-Paura

928 Suess (after Josef Kriehuber) and Map

1989. 250th Death Anniv of Johann Michael Prunner (architect).
2191 **927** 5s. multicoloured 80 50

1989. 75th Death Anniv of Eduard Suess (geologist and politician).
2192 **928** 6s. multicoloured 90 70

929 "Judenburg" (17th-century engraving, Georg Vischer)

930 Steam Engine (Vinzenz Prick)

1989. Upper Styrian "People, Coins, Markets" Exhibition, Judenburg.
2193 **929** 4s. multicoloured 65 45

1989. Lower Austrian "Magic of Industry" Exhibition, Pottenstein.
2194 **930** 4s. blue and gold 65 45

931 Radstadt

1989. 700th Anniv of Radstadt.
2195 **931** 5s. multicoloured 80 50

932 Wooden Salt Barge from Viechtau

1989. Europa. Children's Toys.
2196 **932** 6s. multicoloured . . . . 1·90 70

933 "St. Adalbero and Family before Madonna and Child" (Monastery Itinerary Book)

935 Hansa Brandenburg C-1 Mail Biplane at Vienna, 1918

934 "Gisela" (paddle-steamer)

1989. Upper Austrian "Graphic Art" Exhibition and 900th Anniv of Lambach Monastery Church.
2197 **933** 4s. multicoloured 65 45

1989. 150th Anniv of Passenger Shipping on Traunsee.
2198 **934** 5s. multicoloured . . . . 1·00 50

1989. Stamp Day.
2199 **935** 6s.+3s. multicoloured . . 1·50 1·40

936 St. Andra (after Matthaus Merian)

1989. 650th Anniv of St. Andra.
2200 **936** 5s. multicoloured 80 50

937 Strauss

938 Locomotive

1989. 125th Birth Anniv of Richard Strauss (composer).
2201 **937** 6s. red, brown and gold 95 70

1989. Centenary of Achensee Steam Rack Railway.
2202 **938** 5s. multicoloured 90 50

939 Parliament Building, Vienna

1989. Centenary of Interparliamentary Union.
2203 **939** 6s. multicoloured 95 65

940 Anniversary Emblem

1989. Centenary of National Insurance in Austria.
2204 **940** 5s. multicoloured 80 50

941 U.N. Building, Vienna

1989. 10th Anniv of U.N. Vienna Centre.
2205 **941** 8s. multicoloured . . . . 1·20 80

942 Lusthaus Water, Prater Woods, Vienna

1989. Natural Beauty Spots.
2206 **942** 5s. black and buff . . . 80 65

943 Wildalpen and Hammerworks

1989. 850th Anniv of Wildalpen.
2207 **943** 5s. multicoloured 80 50

944 Emblem **946** "Tree of Life" (Ernst Steiner)

945 Palace of Justice, Vienna

1989. 33rd Congress of European Organization for Quality Control, Vienna.
2208 **944** 6s. multicoloured 90 70

1989. 14th Congress of Int Assn of Criminal Law.
2209 **945** 6s. multicoloured 90 65

1989. Austrian Modern Art.
2210 **946** 5s. multicoloured 80 50

947 Bricklayer **948** Ludwig Anzengruber (150th birth anniv)

1989. Austrian World of Work (4th series).
2211 **947** 5s. multicoloured 80 50

1989. Writers' Anniversaries. Multicoloured.
2212 4s. Type **948** 60 50
2213 4s. Georg Trakl (75th death anniv) 60 50

949 Fried **950** "Adoration of the Shepherds" (detail, Johann Carl von Reslfeld)

1989. 125th Birth Anniv of Alfred Fried (Peace Movement worker).
2214 **949** 6s. multicoloured 95 70

1989. Christmas.
2215 **950** 5s. multicoloured 80 50

951 "Courier" (Albrecht Durer) **952** Streif Downhill and Ganslern Slalom Runs

1990. 500th Anniv of Regular European Postal Services.
2216 **951** 5s. chocolate, cinnamon and brown 85 50

1990. 50th Hahnenkamm Ski Championships, Kitzbuhel.
2217 **952** 5s. multicoloured 80 50

953 Sulzer **954** Emich

1990. Death Centenary of Salomon Sulzer (creator of modern Synagogue songs).
2218 **953** 4s.50 multicoloured . . . 75 50

1990. 50th Death Anniv of Friedrich Emich (microchemist).
2219 **954** 6s. purple and green . . 85 65

955 Emperor Friedrich III (miniature by Ulrich Schreier)

1990. 500th Anniv of Linz as Capital of Upper Austria.
2220 **955** 5s. multicoloured 80 50

956 University Seals

1990. 625th Anniv of Vienna University and 175th Anniv of Vienna University of Technology.
2221 **956** 5s. red, gold and lilac . . 80 50

957 South Styrian Vineyards

1990. Natural Beauty Spots.
2222 **957** 5s. black and yellow . . 80 50

958 Parish Church **959** 1897 May Day Emblem

1990. 1200th Anniv of Anthering.
2223 **958** 7s. multicoloured . . . . 1·20 80

1990. Centenary of Labour Day.
2224 **959** 4s.50 multicoloured . . . 70 50

960 "Our Dear Housewife of Seckau" (relief) **961** Ebene Reichenau Post Office

1990. 850th Anniv of Seckau Abbey.
2225 **960** 4s.50 blue 70 50

1990. Europa. Post Office Buildings.
2226 **961** 7s. multicoloured . . . . 2·20 80

962 Thematic Stamp Motifs **963** Makart (self-portrait)

1990. Stamp Day.
2227 **962** 7s.+3s. multicoloured . . 1·50 1·40

1990. 150th Birth Anniv of Hans Makart (painter).
2228 **963** 4s.50 multicoloured . . . 70 55

964 Schiele (self-portrait) **965** Raimund

1990. Birth Centenary of Egon Schiele (painter).
2229 **964** 5s. multicoloured 85 70

1990. Birth Bicentenary of Ferdinand Raimund (actor and playwright).
2230 **965** 4s.50 multicoloured . . . 70 50

966 "The Hundred Guilden Note" (Rembrandt)

1990. 2nd Int Christus Medicus Congress, Bad Ischl.
2231 **966** 7s. multicoloured . . . . 1·20 80

967 Hardegg

1990. 700th Anniv of Hardegg's Elevation to Status of Town.
2232 **967** 4s.50 multicoloured . . . 70 50

968 Oberdrauburg (copperplate engraving, Freiherr von Valvasor) **970** Zdarsky skiing

969 Church and Town Hall

1990. 750th Anniv of Oberdrauburg.
2233 **968** 5s. multicoloured 85 50

1990. 850th Anniv of Gumpoldskirchen.
2234 **969** 5s. multicoloured 85 50

1990. 50th Death Anniv of Mathias Zdarsky (developer of alpine skiing).
2235 **970** 5s. multicoloured 80 55

971 "Telegraph", 1880, and "Anton Chekhov", 1978

1990. 150th Anniv of Modern (metal) Shipbuilding in Austria.
2236 **971** 9s. multicoloured . . . . 1·50 1·00

972 Perkonig **973** "Man of Rainbows" (Robert Zeppel-Sperl)

1990. Birth Centenary of Josef Friedrich Perkonig (writer).
2237 **972** 5s. sepia, brown & gold 80 50

1990. Austrian Modern Art.
2238 **973** 5s. multicoloured 80 50

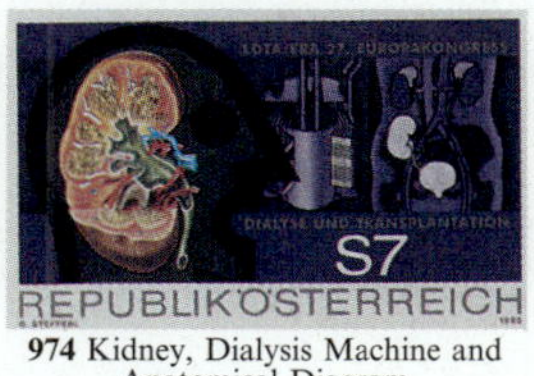

974 Kidney, Dialysis Machine and Anatomical Diagram

1990. 27th European Dialysis and Transplantation Federation Congress, Vienna.
2239 **974** 7s. multicoloured . . . . 1·20 80

975 Werfel

1990. Birth Centenary of Franz Werfel (writer).
2240 **975** 5s. multicoloured 80 50

976 U.N. and Austrian Flags

1990. 30th Anniv of Austrian Participation in U.N. Peace-keeping Forces.
2241 **976** 7s. multicoloured . . . . 1·20 80

977 Arms of Provinces

1990. 45th Anniv of First Provinces Conference (established Second Republic as Federal State).
2242 **977** 5s. multicoloured 80 50

978 University Seal **979** Vogelsang

1990. 150th Anniv of Mining University, Leoben.
2243 **978** 4s.50 black, red & green 70 45

1990. Death Centenary of Karl von Vogelsang (Christian social reformer).
2244 **979** 4s.50 multicoloured . . . 70 45

980 Metal Workers

1990. Centenary of Metal, Mining and Energy Trade Union.
2245 **980** 5s. multicoloured 80 50

981 Player **982** Greenhouse

1990. 3rd World Ice Curling Championships, Vienna.
2246 **981** 7s. multicoloured . . . . 1·20 80

1990. Re-opening of Schonbrunn Greenhouse.
2247 **982** 5s. multicoloured 80 50

983 "Birth of Christ" **984** Grillparzer

1990. Christmas. Detail of Altarpiece by Master Nikolaus of Verdun, Klosterneuburg Monastery.
2248 **983** 5s. multicoloured 80 50

1991. Birth Bicent of Franz Grillparzer (dramatist).
2249 **984** 4s.50 multicoloured . . . 80 50

985 Skier **986** Kreisky

1991. World Alpine Skiing Championships, Saalbach-Hinterglemm.
2250 **985** 5s. multicoloured 80 50

1991. 80th Birth Anniv of Bruno Kreisky (Chancellor, 1970–82).
2251 **986** 5s. multicoloured 80 55

987 Schmidt and Vienna Town Hall

1991. Death Centenary of Friedrich von Schmidt (architect).
2252 **987** 7s. multicoloured . . . . 1·20 85

988 Fountain, Vienna

1991. Anniversaries. Multicoloured.
2253 4s.50 Type **988** (250th death anniv of Georg Raphael Donner (sculptor)) . . . 65 55
2254 5s. "Kitzbuhel in Winter" (birth centenary of Alfons Walde (artist and architect)) 70 65
2255 7s. Vienna Stock Exchange (death centenary of Theophil von Hansen (architect)) 95 85
See also No. 2269.

989 M. von Ebner-Eschenbach

1991. 75th Death Anniv of Marie von Ebner-Eschenbach (writer).
2256 **989** 4s.50 purple 70 50

990 Mozart

1991. Death Bicentenary of Wolfgang Amadeus Mozart (composer). Sheet 115 × 69 mm containing T **990** and similar vert design, each purple, mauve and gold.
MS2257 5s. Type **990**; 5s. "The Magic Flute" (statue, Vienna) 2·30 1·90

991 Obir Stalactite Caverns, Eisenkappel

1991. Natural Beauty Spots.
2258 **991** 5s. multicoloured 80 50

992 Spittal an der Drau (after Matthaus Merian)

1991. 800th Anniv of Spittal an der Drau.
2259 **992** 4s.50 multicoloured . . . 70 50

993 "ERS-1" European Remote Sensing Satellite

1991. Europa. Europe in Space.
2260 **993** 7s. multicoloured . . . . 2·30 80

994 "Garden Party" (Anthoni Bays)

1991. Vorarlberg "Clothing and People" Exhibition, Hohenems.
2261 **994** 5s. multicoloured 80 50

995 Grein

1991. 500th Anniv of Grein Town Charter.
2262 **995** 4s.50 multicoloured . . . 70 50

996 Bedding Plants forming Arms

1991. 1200th Anniv of Tulln.
2263 **996** 5s. multicoloured 80 50

997 Military History Museum

1991. Vienna Museum Centenaries. Multicoloured.
2264 5s. Type **997** 80 60
2265 7s. Museum of Art History 1·10 90

998 "B" and "P" **999** Tunnel Entrance

1991. Stamp Day.
2266 **998** 7s.+3s. brown, sepia and black . . . . 1·50 1·70

This is the first of a series of ten annual stamps, each of which will illustrate two letters. The complete series will spell out the words "Briefmarke" and "Philatelie".

1991. Opening of Karawanken Road Tunnel between Carinthia and Slovenia.
2267 **999** 7s. multicoloured . . . . 1·00 80

1000 Town Hall

1991. 5th Anniv of St. Polten as Capital of Lower Austria.
2268 **1000** 5s. multicoloured . . . 85 50

1991. 150th Birth Anniv of Otto Wagner (architect). As T **988**. Multicoloured.
2269 4s.50 Karlsplatz Station, Vienna City Railway . . 70 50

1001 Rowing

1991. Junior World Canoeing Championships and World Rowing Championships, Vienna.
2270 **1001** 5s. multicoloured . . . 80 50

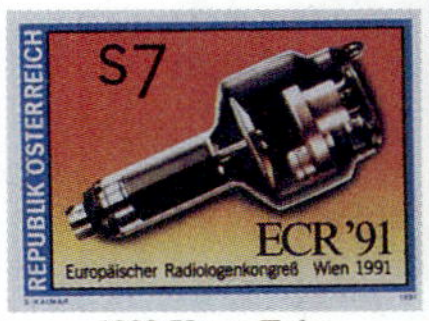

1002 X-ray Tube **1003** Paracelsus

1991. European Radiology Congress, Vienna.
2271 **1002** 7s. multicoloured . . . 1·00 80

1991. 450th Death Anniv of Theophrastus Bombastus von Hohenheim (Paracelsus) (physician and scientist).
2272 **1003** 4s. black, red & brown 70 50

1004 "Mir" Space Station **1005** Almabtrieb (driving cattle from mountain pastures) (Zell, Tyrol)

1991. "Austro Mir 91" Soviet–Austrian Space Flight.
2273 **1004** 9s. multicoloured . . . 1·40 1·30

1991. Folk Customs and Art (1st series). Mult.
2274 4s.50 Type **1005** 70 50
2275 5s. Vintage Crown (Neustift, Vienna) 75 60
2276 7s. Harvest monstrance (Nestelbach, Styria) . . . 1·10 85
See also Nos. 2305/7, 2349/51, 2363/5, 2393/5, 2418, 2432/3, 2450, 2482, 2491, 2500/1, 2508, 2524, 2546, 2547, 2550, 2552, 2569, 2581, 2587, 2595, 2718, 2776 and 2815.

1006 Weaver

1991. Austrian World of Work (5th series).
2277 **1006** 4s.50 multicoloured . . 70 50

1007 "The General" (Rudolf Pointner) **1008** Raab

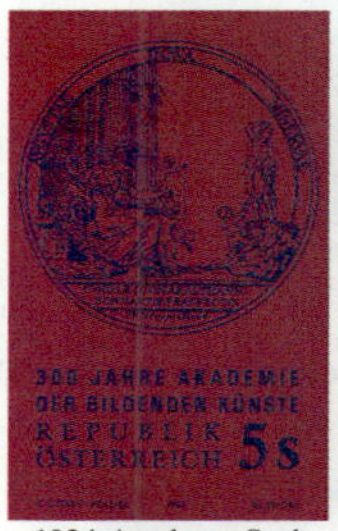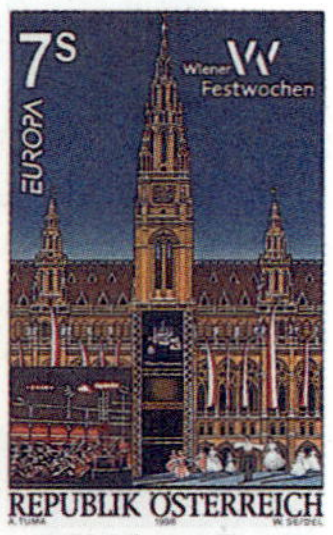**1991.** Austrian Modern Art.
2278 **1007** 5s. multicoloured . . . 80 55

1991. Birth Centenary of Julius Raab (Chancellor, 1953–61).
2279 **1008** 4s.50 brown & chestnut 70 50

1009 "Birth of Christ" (detail of fresco, Baumgartenberg Church)

1991. Christmas.
2280 **1009** 5s. multicoloured . . . 80 60

1010 Clerks

1992. Centenary of Trade Union of Clerks in Private Enterprise.
2281 **1010** 5s.50 multicoloured . . 85 60

1011 Emblems of Games and Olympic Rings

1992. Winter Olympic Games, Albertville, and Summer Games, Barcelona.
2282 **1011** 7s. multicoloured . . . 1·20 85

1012 Competitor

1992. 8th World Toboggan Championships on Natural Runs, Bad Goisern.
2283 **1012** 5s. multicoloured . . . 80 50

1013 Hollow Stone, Klostertal

1992. Natural Beauty Spots.
2284 **1013** 5s. multicoloured . . . 80 50

1014 Saiko

1015 "Athlete with Ball" (Christian Attersee)

1992. Birth Centenary of George Saiko (writer).
2285 **1014** 5s.50 brown 85 60

1992. Centenary of Workers' Sport Movement.
2286 **1015** 5s.50 multicoloured . . 85 65

1016 Franz Joseph Muller (chemist and mineralogist)

1992. Scientific Anniversaries. Multicoloured.
2287 5s. Type **1016** (250th birth anniv) 75 60
2288 5s.50 Paul Kitaibel (botanist, 175th death anniv) 85 65
2289 6s. Christian Doppler (physicist) (150th anniv of observation of Doppler Effect) 95 75
2290 7s. Richard Kuhn (chemist, 25th death anniv) . . . . 1·10 90

1017 Angels playing Instruments

1992. 150th Death Anniv of Vienna Philharmonic Orchestra. Sheet 90 × 70 mm.
MS2291 **1017** 5s.50 black, brown and gold . . . . 1·20 1·00

1018 First and Present Emblems

1992. Centenary of Railway Workers' Trade Union.
2292 **1018** 5s.50 red and black . . 85 60

1019 Hanrieder

1020 Scenes from "The Birdseller" (Zeller) and "The Beggar Student" (Millocker)

1992. 150th Birth Anniv of Norbert Hanrieder (writer).
2293 **1019** 5s.50 lilac & brown . . 85 55

1992. 150th Birth Anniversaries of Carl Zeller and Karl Millocker (composers).
2294 **1020** 6s. multicoloured . . . 95 85

1021 Foundry and Process

1992. Ironworks Day. 40th Anniv of First LD-Process Steel Works, Linz.
2295 **1021** 5s. multicoloured . . . 80 50

1022 Woodcut of the Americas by Sebastian Munster (from "Geographia Universalis" by Claudius Ptolomaus)

1992. Europa. 500th Anniv of Discovery of America by Columbus.
2296 **1022** 7s. multicoloured . . . 2·40 85

1023 Dredger

1024 Rieger

1992. Centenary of Treaty for International Regulation of the Rhine.
2297 **1023** 7s. multicoloured . . . 1·30 85

1992. Centenary of Adoption of Pseudonym Reimmichl by Sebastian Rieger (writer).
2298 **1024** 5s. brown 80 50

1025 Flags and Alps

1026 Dr. Anna Dengel

1992. Alpine Protection Convention.
2299 **1025** 5s.50 multicoloured . . 85 70

1992. Birth Centenary of Dr. Anna Dengel (founder of Medical Missionary Sisters).
2300 **1026** 5s.50 multicoloured . . 85 55

1027 "R" and "H"

1992. Stamp Day.
2301 **1027** 7s.+3s. multicoloured 1·40 1·50
See note below No. 2266.

1028 Town Hall

1992. 750th Anniv of First Documentation of Lienz as a Town.
2302 **1028** 5s. multicoloured . . . 80 50

1029 "Billroth in Lecture Room" (A. F. Seligmann)

1030 Waldheim

1992. Austrian Surgery Society International Congress, Eisenstadt.
2303 **1029** 6s. multicoloured . . . 90 70

1992. Presidency of Dr. Kurt Waldheim.
2304 **1030** 5s.50 black, red & grey 85 65

1992. Folk Customs and Art (2nd series). As T **1005**. Multicoloured.
2305 5s. Target with figure of Zieler, Lower Austria, 1732 . . . . 70 65
2306 5s.50 Chest, Carinthia . . . 80 75
2307 7s. Votive tablet from Venser Chapel, Vorarlberg 1·00 85

1031 Bridge over Canal

1992. Completion of Marchfeld Canal System.
2308 **1031** 5s. multicoloured . . . 80 50

1032 "The Purification of Sea Water" (Peter Pongratz)

1992. Austrian Modern Art.
2309 **1032** 5s.50 multicoloured . . 85 60

1033 Gateway, Hofburg Palace (venue)

1992. 5th Int Ombudsmen's Conference, Vienna.
2310 **1033** 5s.50 multicoloured . . 85 55

1034 Academy Seal

1035 "The Annunciation"

1992. 300th Anniv of Academy of Fine Arts, Vienna.
2311 **1034** 5s. blue and red 80 60

1992. Death Bicentenary of Veit Koniger (sculptor).
2312 **1035** 5s. multicoloured . . . 80 60

1036 "Birth of Christ" (Johann Georg Schmidt)

1992. Christmas.
2313 **1036** 5s.50 multicoloured . . 85 50

1037 Earth and Satellite

1992. Birth Centenary of Hermann Potocnik (alias Noordung) (space travel pioneer).
2314 **1037** 10s. multicoloured . . . 1·50 1·30

1038 Dome of Michael Wing, Hofburg Palace, Vienna

1039 Emergency Vehicle's Flashing Lantern

1993. Architects' Anniversaries. Multicoloured.
2315 5s. Type **1038** (Joseph Emanuel Fischer von Erlach, 300th birth) . . . 75 50
2316 5s.50 Kinsky Palace, Vienna (Johann Lukas von Hildebrandt, 325th birth) 85 65
2317 7s. State Opera House, Vienna (Eduard van der Null and August Siccard von Siccardsburg, 125th death annivs) . . . . . . 1·20 75

1993. 25th Anniv of Radio-controlled Emergency Medical Service.
2318 **1039** 5s. multicoloured . . . 80 55

1040 Wilder Kaiser Massif, Tyrol

1993. Natural Beauty Spots.
2319 **1040** 6s. multicoloured . . . 90 80

1041 Mitterhofer Typewriter

1993. Death Centenary of Peter Mitterhofer (typewriter pioneer).
2320 **1041** 17s. multicoloured . . . 2·40 2·20

1042 "Strada del Sole" (record sleeve)

1993. "Austro Pop" (1st series). Rainhard Fendrich (singer).
2321 **1042** 5s.50 multicoloured . . 80 60
See also Nos. 2356 and 2368.

1043 Games Emblem

1993. Winter Special Olympics, Salzburg and Schladming.
2322 **1043** 6s.+3s. multicoloured 1·20 1·30

1044 Sealsfield

1045 Girl realizing her Rights

1993. Birth Bicent of Charles Sealsfield (novelist).
2323 **1044** 10s. red, blue and gold 1·40 1·00

1993. Ratification of U.N. Convention on Children's Rights.
2324 **1045** 7s. multicoloured . . . 1·00 85

1046 "Death" (detail of sculpture, Josef Stammel), Admont Monastery, Styria

1047 "Flying Harlequin" (Paul Flora)

1993. Monasteries and Abbeys.
2325 – 1s. brown, black & grn 20 15
2326 **1046** 5s.50 black, yell & grn 1·10 25
2327 – 6s. black, mauve & yell 1·00 25
2328 – 7s. brown, black & grey 1·40 40
2329 – 7s.50 brown, bl & blk 1·40 50
2330 – 8s. orange, black & bl 1·60 60
2331 – 10s. black, blue & orge 2·00 55
2332 – 20s. black, blue & yell 3·50 65
2333 – 26s. orange, black & bis 4·50 1·70
2334 – 30s. red, yellow & black 6·00 1·10

DESIGNS: 1s. The Annunciation (detail of crosier of Abbess), St. Gabriel Benedictine Abbey, Bertholdstein; 6s. St. Benedict of Nursia (glass painting), Mariastern Abbey, Gwiggen; 7s. Marble lion, Franciscan Monastery, Salzburg; 7s.50, Virgin Mary (detail of cupola painting by Paul Troger), Altenburg Monastery; 8s. Early Gothic doorway, Wilhering Monastery; 10s. "The Healing of St. Peregrinus" (altarpiece), Maria Luggau Monastery; 20s. Hartmann Crosier, St. Georgenberg Abbey, Fiecht; 26s. "Master Dolorosa" (sculpture), Franciscan Monastery, Schwaz; 30s. Madonna and Child, Monastery of the Scottish Order, Vienna.

1993. Europa. Contemporary Art.
2345 **1047** 7s. multicoloured . . . 2·30 85

1048 Silhouette, Script and Signature

1049 "Hohentwiel" (lake steamer) and Flags

1993. 150th Birth Anniv of Peter Rosegger (writer and newspaper publisher).
2346 **1048** 5s.50 black and green 80 55

1993. Lake Constance European Region.
2347 **1049** 6s. multicoloured . . . 1·10 70

1050 Knights in Battle and "I"s

1051 Human Rights Emblem melting Bars

1993. Stamp Day.
2348 **1050** 7s.+3s. gold, black and blue . . . . 1·40 1·40
See note below No. 2266.

1993. Folk Customs and Art (3rd series). As T **1005**. Multicoloured.
2349 5s. Corpus Christi Day procession, Hallstatt, Upper Austria 70 50
2350 5s.50 Drawing the block (log), Burgenland 80 60
2351 7s. Aperschnalzen (whipping the snow away), Salzburg 1·00 80

1993. U.N. World Conf on Human Rights, Vienna.
2352 **1051** 10s. multicoloured . . . 1·40 1·10

1052 Jagerstatter

1053 Train approaching Wolfgangsee

1993. 50th Death Anniv of Franz Jagerstatter (conscientious objector).
2353 **1052** 5s.50 multicoloured . . 80 55

1993. Centenary of Schafberg Cog Railway.
2354 **1053** 6s. multicoloured . . . 95 70

1054 "Self-portrait with Doll"

1993. Birth Centenary of Rudolf Wacker (artist).
2355 **1054** 6s. multicoloured . . . 80 70

1993. "Austro Pop" (2nd series). Ludwig Hirsch (singer and actor). As T **1042**. Multicoloured.
2356 5s.50 "Die Omama" (record sleeve) 80 60

1055 "Concert in Dornbacher Park" (Balthasar Wigand)

1993. 150th Anniv of Vienna Male Choral Society.
2357 **1055** 5s. multicoloured . . . 70 55

1056 "Easter" (Max Weiler)

1057 "99 Heads" (detail, Friedensreich Hundertwasser)

1993. Austrian Modern Art.
2358 **1056** 5s.50 multicoloured . . 80 55

1993. Council of Europe Heads of State Conference, Vienna.
2359 **1057** 7s. multicoloured . . . 1·40 85

1058 Statue of Athene, Parliament Building

1060 "Birth of Christ" (Krainburg Altar, Styria)

1059 Workers

1993. 75th Anniv of Austrian Republic.
2360 **1058** 5s. multicoloured . . . 80 60

1993. Cent of 1st Austrian Trade Unions Congress.
2361 **1059** 5s.50 multicoloured . . 80 55

1993. Christmas.
2362 **1060** 5s.50 multicoloured . . 80 50

1994. Folk Customs and Art (4th series). As T **1005**. Multicoloured.
2363 5s.50 Rocking cradle, Vorarlberg 75 60
2364 6s. Carved sleigh, Styria . . 85 70
2365 7s. Godparent's bowl and lid, Upper Austria . . . . 1·00 85

1061 Winter Sports

1994. Winter Olympic Games, Lillehammer, Norway.
2366 **1061** 7s. multicoloured . . . 95 85

1062 Early Production of Coins

1994. 800th Anniv of Vienna Mint.
2367 **1062** 6s. multicoloured . . . 80 60

1994. "Austro Pop" (3rd series). Falco (Johann Holzel) (singer). As T **1042**. Multicoloured.
2368 6s. "Rock Me Amadeus" (record sleeve) 85 60

1063 "Reclining Lady" (detail, Herbert Boeckl)

1994. Birth Centenary of Herbert Boeckl (painter).
2369 **1063** 5s.50 multicoloured . . 85 60

1064 N.W. Tower of City Wall

1994. 800th Anniv of Wiener Neustadt.
2370 **1064** 6s. multicoloured . . . 80 60

1065 Lurgrotte (caves), Styria

1994. Natural Beauty Spots.
2371 **1065** 6s. multicoloured . . . 90 60

1066 Lake Rudolf (Teleki–Hohnel expedition to Africa, 1887)

1994. Europa. Discoveries.
2372 **1066** 7s. multicoloured . . . 2·00 85

1067 "E" and "L" as Ruins in Landscape

1994. Stamp Day.
2373 **1067** 7s.+3s. multicoloured 1·40 1·40
See note below No. 2266.

1068 "Allegory of Theology, Justice, Philosophy and Medicine" (detail of fresco, National Library)

1994. 300th Birth Anniv of Daniel Gran (artist).
2374 **1068** 20s. multicoloured . . . 3·00 2·20

1069 Scene from "The Prodigal Son" (opera, Benjamin Britten)

1994. 25th Anniv of Carinthian Summer Festival, Ossiach and Villach.
2375 **1069** 5s.50 gold and red . . 80 55

1070 Steam Locomotive and Diesel Railcar (Gailtal)

1994. Railway Centenaries. Multicoloured.
2376 5s.50 Type **1070** 95 75
2377 6s. Steam locomotive and diesel railcar (Murtal) . . 1·10 75

1071 Gmeiner and Children

1072 Seitz (bust, G. Ambrosi)

1994. 75th Birth Anniv of Hermann Gmeiner (founder of S.O.S. children's villages).
2378 **1071** 7s. multicoloured . . . 95 85

1994. 125th Birth Anniv of Karl Seitz (acting President, 1920).
2379 **1072** 5s.50 multicoloured . . 80 60

1073 Bohm

1075 Franz Theodor Csokor (dramatist and poet)

1074 Ethnic Minorities on Map

1994. Birth Centenary of Karl Bohm (conductor).
2380 **1073** 7s. blue and gold . . . 95 85

1994. Legal and Cultural Protection of Ethnic Minorities.
2381 **1074** 5s.50 multicoloured . . 90 85

1994. Writers' Anniversaries. Multicoloured.
2382 6s. Type **1075** (25th death anniv) 80 60
2383 7s. Joseph Roth (novelist, birth cent) 95 70

1076 "Head" (Franz Ringel)

1077 Money Box

1994. Austrian Modern Art.
2384 **1076** 6s. multicoloured . . . 85 60

1994. 175th Anniv of Savings Banks in Austria.
2385 **1077** 7s. multicoloured . . . 95 85

1078 Air Hostess and Child

1994. Austrian World of Work (6th series).
2386 **1078** 6s. multicoloured . . . 80 70

1079 Coudenhove-Kalergi and Map of Europe

1994. Birth Cent of Richard Coudenhove-Kalergi (founder of Paneuropa Union).
2387 **1079** 10s. multicoloured . . . 1·40 1·10

1080 "Birth of Christ" (Anton Wollenek)

1081 Map and Austrian and E.U. Flags

1994. Christmas.
2388 **1080** 6s. multicoloured . . . 80 55

1995. Austria's Entry into E.U.
2389 **1081** 7s. multicoloured . . . 95 85

1082 Loos House, Michaelerplatz, Vienna

1995. 125th Birth Anniv of Adolf Loos (architect).
2390 **1082** 10s. multicoloured . . . 1·40 1·10

1083 Sporting Activities

1995. 50th Anniv of Austrian Gymnastics and Sports Association.
2391 **1083** 6s. multicoloured . . . 80 55

1084 Workers

1995. 75th Anniv of Workers' and Employees' Chambers (advisory body).
2392 **1084** 6s. multicoloured . . . 80 55

1995. Folk Costumes and Art (5th series). As T **1005**. Multicoloured.
2393 5s.50 Belt, Carinthia 75 55
2394 6s. Costume of Hiata (vineyard guard), Vienna 90 60
2395 7s. Gold bonnet, Wachau 95 85

1085 State Seal

1086 Heft Ironworks

1995. 50th Anniv of Second Republic.
2396 **1085** 6s. multicoloured . . . 80 55

1995. Carinthian "History of Mining and Industry" Exhibition, Heft, Huttenberg.
2397 **1086** 5s.50 multicoloured . . 80 55

1087 Hiker in Mountains

1995. Centenary of Friends of Nature.
2398 **1087** 5s.50 multicoloured . . 80 55

1088 Heidenreichstein National Park

1995. Natural Beauty Spots.
2399 **1088** 6s. multicoloured . . . 80 65

1089 Woman and Barbed Wire around Skull

1090 Map, Woman and Child and Transport

1995. Europa. Peace and Freedom.
2400 **1089** 7s. multicoloured . . . 2·20 85

1995. Meeting of European Ministers of Transport Conference, Vienna.
2401 **1090** 7s. multicoloured . . . 95 85

1091 "F" and "A" on Vase of Flowers

1093 St. Gebhard (stained-glass window, Martin Hausle)

1092 Set for "The Flying Dutchman"

1995. Stamp Day.
2402 **1091** 10s.+5s. mult . . . . . 2·00 2·20
See note below No. 2266.

1995. 50th Bregenz Festival.
2403 **1092** 6s. multicoloured . . . 80 60

1995. Death Millenary of St. Gebhard, Bishop of Konstanz (patron saint of Vorarlberg chuches).
2404 **1093** 7s.50 multicoloured . . 1·00 85

1094 Members' Flags

1095 Loschmidt

1995. 50th Anniv of U.N.O.
2405 **1094** 10s. multicoloured . . . 1·40 95

1995. Death Centenary of Josef Loschmidt (physical chemist).
2406 **1095** 20s. black, stone & brn 3·50 2·30

1096 K. Leichter

1097 Scene from "Jedermann" (Hugo von Hofmannsthal)

1995. Birth Cent of Kathe Leichter (sociologist).
2407 **1096** 6s. cream, black & red 80 55

1995. 75th Anniv of Salzburg Festival.
2408 **1097** 6s. multicoloured . . . 80 60

1098 "European Scene" (Adolf Frohner)

1995. Austrian Modern Art.
2409 **1098** 6s. multicoloured . . . 80 70

1099 Franz von Suppe and "The Beautiful Galatea"

1995. Composers' Anniversaries. Scenes from operettas. Multicoloured.
2410 6s. Type **1099** (death cent) 80 65
2411 7s. Nico Dostal and "The Hungarian Wedding" (birth centenary) 95 75

1100 University Building

1995. 25th Anniv of Klagenfurt University.
2412 **1100** 5s.50 multicoloured . . 80 60

1101 Hollenburg Castle

1995. 75th Anniv of Carinthian Referendum.
2413 **1101** 6s. multicoloured . . . 80 60

1102 Postman

1995. Austrian World of Work (7th series).
2414 **1102** 6s. multicoloured . . . 80 60

1103 Anton von Webern (50th death) **1104** Christ Child

1995. Composers' Anniversaries.
2415 **1103** 6s. blue and orange . . 80 55
2416 – 7s. red and orange . . 95 80
DESIGN: 7s. Ludwig van Beethoven (225th birth).

1995. Christmas. 300th Anniv of Christkindl Church.
2417 **1104** 6s. multicoloured . . . 80 55

1996. Folk Customs and Art (6th series). As T **1005**.
2418 6s. multicoloured 85 60
DESIGN: 6s. Masked figures Roller and Scheller (Imst masquerades, Tyrol).

1105 Empress Maria Theresia and Academy Building

1996. 250th Anniv of Theresian Academy, Vienna.
2419 **1105** 6s. multicoloured . . . 85 60

1106 Ski Jumping

1996. World Ski Jumping Championships, Tauplitz and Bad Mitterndorf.
2420 **1106** 7s. multicoloured . . . 1·00 80

1107 Terminal

1996. Completion of West Terminal, Vienna International Airport.
2421 **1107** 7s. multicoloured . . . 1·00 80

1108 Hohe Tauern National Park

1996. Natural Beauty Spots.
2422 **1108** 6s. multicoloured . . . 85 70

1109 "Mother and Child" (Peter Fendi) **1110** Organ and Music

1996. Artists' Birth Bicentenaries. Multicoloured.
2423 6s. Type **1109** 85 65
2424 7s. "Self-portrait" (Leopold Kupelwieser) . . . . . . 1·00 90

1996. Death Cent of Anton Bruckner (composer).
2425 **1110** 5s.50 multicoloured . . 85 80

1111 Kollmitz Castle (from copper engraving)

1996. 300th Death Anniv of Georg Vischer (cartographer and engraver).
2426 **1111** 10s. black and stone . . 1·50 1·20

1112 Old Market Square

1996. 800th Anniv of Klagenfurt.
2427 **1112** 6s. multicoloured . . . 95 65

1113 Hotel Chef and Waitress

1996. Austrian World of Work (8th series).
2428 **1113** 6s. multicoloured . . . 85 75

1114 Paula von Preradovic (writer) **1115** "M" and "T" and Bluebirds (mosaic)

1996. Europa. Famous Women.
2429 **1114** 7s. stone, brown & grey 1·00 85

1996. Stamp Day.
2430 **1115** 10s.+5s. mult . . . . . 2·20 2·20
See note below No. 2266.

1116 Mascot with Olympic Flag

1996. Olympic Games, Atlanta.
2431 **1116** 10s. multicoloured . . . 1·50 1·20

1996. Folk Customs and Art (7th series). As T **1005**.
2432 5s.50 Flower-bedecked poles, Salzburg 85 70
2433 7s. Tyrol militia . . . . . . 1·00 1·00

1117 Landscape

1996. 75th Anniv of Burgenland.
2434 **1117** 6s. multicoloured . . . 85 75

1118 Mountaineers **1119** Deed of Otto III, 996

1996. Cent of Austrian Mountain Rescue Service.
2435 **1118** 6s. multicoloured . . . 85 65

1996. Millenary of Austria. Multicoloured.
2436 6s. Type **1119** 90 80
2437 6s. Archduke Joseph II (after Georg Weikert) and Archduchess Maria Theresia (after Martin van Meytens) 90 80
2438 7s. "Duke Heinrich II" (stained-glass window, Monastery of the Holy Cross) . . . . 1·00 1·00
2439 7s. Arms in flames (1848 Revolution) . . . . . . 1·00 1·00
2440 7s. Rudolf IV, the Founder 1·00 1·00
2441 7s. Karl Renner (first Federal Republic president) . . . . 1·00 1·00
2442 10s. Archduke Maximilian I (Holy Roman Emperor) (miniature from Statute Book of Order of the Golden Fleece) . . . . . 1·40 1·40
2443 10s. Seal and signature of Leopold Figl (State Treaty of 1955) . . . . . 1·40 1·40
2444 20s. Imperial crown of Rudolf II . . . . . . 2·75 2·75
2445 20s. State arms, stars of Europe and "The Horsebreaker" (bronze by Josef Lax) (Austria and Europe) . . . . 2·75 2·75

1120 "Power Station" (Reinhard Artberg)

1996. Austrian Modern Art.
2446 **1120** 7s. multicoloured . . . 1·00 90

1121 Children of Different Nations

1996. 50th Anniv of UNICEF.
2447 **1121** 10s. multicoloured . . . 1·50 1·20

1122 Nativity and Vienna Town Hall

1996. Christmas.
2448 **1122** 6s. multicoloured . . . 85 60

1123 Kramer

1997. Birth Centenary of Theodor Kramer (poet).
2449 **1123** 5s.50 blue 85 60

1997. Folk Customs and Art (8th series). As T **1005**. Multicoloured.
2450 7s. Epiphany carol singers, Eisenstadt Burgenland . . 1·00 75

1124 Vineyards on the Nussberg, Vienna

1997. Natural Beauty Spots.
2451 **1124** 6s. multicoloured . . . 85 65

1125 Academy and Light

1997. 150th Anniv of Austrian Academy of Sciences, Vienna.
2452 **1125** 10s. multicoloured . . . 1·50 1·00

1126 Emblem

1997. 50th Anniv of Verbund Electricity Company.
2453 **1126** 6s. multicoloured . . . 85 65

1127 The Cruel Rosalia of Forchtenstein

1128 Stage Set for "Die tote Stadt"

1997. Myths and Legends.
2454 – 6s.50 grn, pink & blk . . . 1·50 55
2455 **1127** 7s. black, stone & brn 1·40 65
2456 – 8s. orange, blk & lilac 1·40 1·00
2457 – 9s. black, stone & pur 1·70 1·40
2458 – 10s. black, grey & red 1·90 1·50
2459 – 13s. black, brn & pur 2·50 1·80
2460 – 14s. black, lt blue & bl 2·40 1·80
2461 – 20s. green, blk & stone 3·75 2·50
2462 – 22s. black, bl & stone 3·75 3·50
2463 – 23s. black, ochre and green . . . . . . 5·00 3·50
2464 – 25s. stone, black and yellow . . . . . . 4·50 3·00
2465 – 32s. black, brn & pink 6·25 4·50
DESIGNS: 6s.50, Lindworm of Klagenfurt; 8s. The Black Lady of Hardegg; 9s. Charming Augustin; 10s. Basilisk of Vienna; 13s. The Pied Piper of Korneuburg; 14s. The Strudengau Water-nymph; 20s. St. Notburga; 22s. Witches Whirl; 23s. Loaf Agony; 25s. St. Konrad and Altems Castle; 32s. The Discovery of Erzberg (Mountain of Ore).

1997. Birth Cent of Erich Korngold (composer).
2470 **1128** 20s. black, blue & gold 3·50 2·00

1129 Stadium, Badge and Players

1997. Rapid Vienna, National Football Champions, 1995–96.
2471 **1129** 7s. multicoloured . . . 1·00 80

1130 Red Deer

1997. Hunting and the Environment. Deer Feeding in Winter.
2472 **1130** 7s. multicoloured . . . 1·00 75

1131 Canisius and Children (altar by Josef Bachlechner in Innsbruck Seminary)

1997. 400th Death Anniv of St. Petrus Canisius (patron saint of Innsbruck).
2473 **1131** 7s.50 multicoloured . . 1·10 85

1132 Johannes Brahms (after L. Michalek)

1997. Composers' Anniversaries.
2474 **1132** 6s. violet and gold . . . 85 80
2475 – 10s. purple and gold . . 1·50 1·10
DESIGNS: 6s. Type **1132** (death centenary); 10s. Franz Schubert (birth bicentenary).

1133 "A" and "E"

1134 The Four Friends

1997. Stamp Day.
2476 **1133** 7s. multicoloured . . . 1·00 80
See note below No. 2266.

1997. Europa. Tales and Legends. "The Town Band of Bremen" by the Brothers Grimm.
2477 **1134** 7s. multicoloured . . . 2·00 1·00

1135 1850 9k. Stamp and Postman

1997. "WIPA 2000" International Stamp Exhibition, Vienna (1st issue).
2478 **1135** 27s.+13s. mult . . . . 6·00 6·50
See also Nos. 2521, 2543, **MS**2551 and **MS**2564.

1136 Train on Hochschneeberg Line

1997. Railway Anniversaries. Multicoloured.
2479 6s. Type **1136** (centenary of Hochschneeberg rack-railway) 85 70
2480 7s.50 Steam locomotive "Licaon" and viaduct near Mattersburg (150th anniv of Odenburg–Wiener Neustadt line) . . 1·20 90

1137 Cogwheels

1138 Waggerl (self-portrait)

1997. 125th Anniv of Austrian Technical Supervisory Association.
2481 **1137** 7s. multicoloured . . . 1·00 85

1997. Folk Customs and Art (9th series). As T **1005**. Multicoloured.
2482 6s.50 Tyrolean brass band 1·00 85

1997. Birth Centenary of Karl Waggerl (writer).
2483 **1138** 7s. green, yellow & blue 1·00 80

1139 Adolf Lorenz (founder of German Society of Orthopaedia)

1997. Orthopaedics Congress, Vienna.
2484 **1139** 8s. multicoloured . . . 1·20 1·00

1140 Emblem

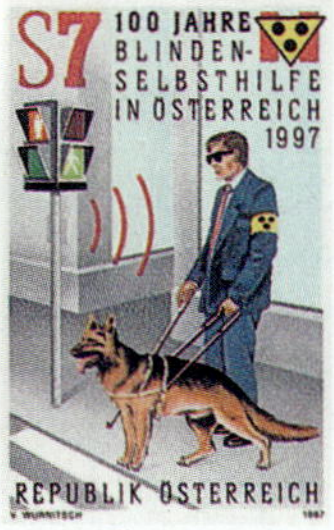

1142 Blind Man with Guide Dog

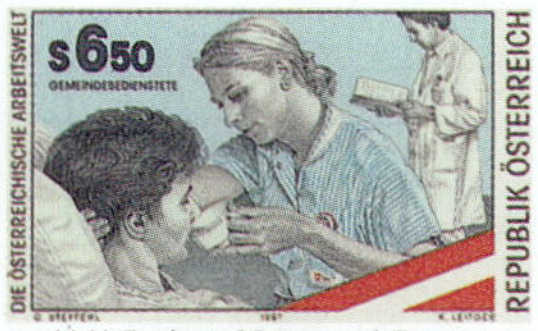

1141 Patient, Nurse and Doctor

1997. 125th Anniv of College of Agricultural Sciences, Vienna.
2485 **1140** 9s. multicoloured . . . 1·40 1·00

1997. Austrian World of Work (9th series).
2486 **1141** 6s.50 multicoloured . . 1·00 1·00

1997. Cent of Austrian Association for the Blind.
2487 **1142** 7s. multicoloured . . . 1·00 80

1143 "House in Wind" (Helmut Schickhofer)

1997. Austrian Modern Art.
2488 **1143** 7s. multicoloured . . . 1·00 75

1144 Klestil

1145 Werner

1997. 65th Birthday of Pres. Thomas Klestil.
2489 **1144** 7s. multicoloured . . . 1·00 85

1997. 75th Birth Anniv of Oskar Werner (actor).
2490 **1145** 7s. black, orge & grey 1·00 90

1997. Folk Customs and Art (10th series). As T **1005**. Multicoloured.
2491 6s.50 Tower wind-band, Upper Austria . . . . . 1·00 75

1146 Glowing Light

1997. 25th Anniv of Light in Darkness (umbrella organization of children's charities).
2492 **1146** 7s. blue . . . . 1·00 80

1147 "Mariazell Madonna"

1997. Christmas.
2493 **1147** 7s. multicoloured . . . 1·00 75

1148 Kalkalpen National Park

1998. Natural Beauty Spots.
2494 **1148** 7s. multicoloured . . . 95 75

1149 Courting Pair

1998. Hunting and the Environment. Preservation of Breeding Habitat of the Black Grouse.
2495 **1149** 9s. multicoloured . . . 1·30 1·40

1150 Ice Skaters

1998. Winter Olympic Games, Nagano, Japan.
2496 **1150** 14s. multicoloured . . . 1·90 1·80

1151 Austrian Poster Exposition Advertising Poster, 1928

1152 Alois Senefelder (inventor) on Lithographic Stone

1998. Birth Cent of Joseph Binder (designer).
2497 **1151** 7s. multicoloured . . . 1·10 90

1998. Bicentenary of Invention of Lithography (printing process).
2498 **1152** 7s. blue, yellow & black 1·10 80

1153 Facade

1155 "St. Florian" (glass painting)

1154 Player and Team Emblem

1998. Centenary of Vienna Secession (exn hall).
2499 **1153** 8s. brown, gold & blue 1·20 90

1998. Folk Customs and Art (11th series). As T **1005**. Multicoloured.
2500 6s.50 Fiacre, Vienna . . . . 1·00 75
2501 7s. Palm Sunday procession, Thaur, Tyrol . . . . . . 1·00 80

1998. Austria Memphis Football Club.
2502 **1154** 7s. multicoloured . . . 1·10 85

1998. St. Florian, Patron Saint of Firemen.
2503 **1155** 7s. multicoloured . . . 1·10 85

1156 Rupertus Cross

1998. 1200th Anniv of Salzburg Archdiocese.
2504 **1156** 7s. multicoloured . . . 1·10 80

1157 Series Yv Locomotive No. 2, 1895

1998. Centenary of Completion of Ybbs Valley Railway.
2505 **1157** 6s.50 multicoloured . . 1·00 90

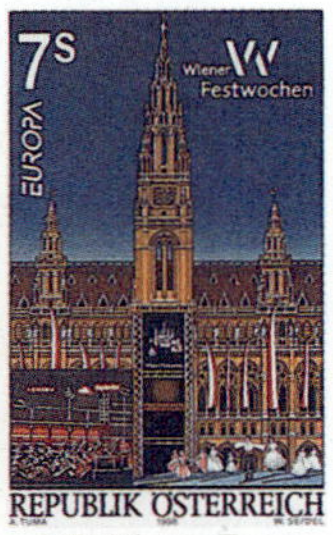

1158 "Tyrolia" (Ferdinand Cosander) **1159** Vienna Town Hall (Viennese festive weeks)

1998. 175th Anniv of Tyrol Ferdinandeum (state museum), Innsbruck.
2506 **1158** 7s. multicoloured . . . 1·10 80

1998. Europa. National Festivals.
2507 **1159** 7s. multicoloured . . . 2·20 90

1998. Folk Customs and Art (12th series). As T **1005**. Multicoloured.
2508 6s.50 Samson and the dwarves, Salzburg . . . . 1·00 95

1160 Christine Lavant

1998. 25th Death Anniv of Christine Lavant (poet).
2509 **1160** 7s. multicoloured . . . 1·00 80

1161 Electric Railcar No. 1 **1162** "R" and "L"

1998. Centenary of Postlingberg Railway.
2510 **1161** 6s.50 multicoloured . . 1·00 90

1998. Stamp Day.
2511 **1162** 7s. multicoloured . . . 1·00 1·10
See note below No. 2266.

1163 Presidency Emblem **1164** Railcar No. 5090

1998. Austrian Presidency of E.U.
2512 **1163** 7s. multicoloured . . . 1·00 1·00

1998. Centenary of Pinzgau Railway.
2513 **1164** 6s.50 multicoloured . . 1·00 90

1165 Volksoper, Vienna

1998. Centenary of Volksoper (theatre) and 50th Death Anniv of Franz Lehar (composer).
2514 **1165** 6s.50 multicoloured . . 1·00 1·00

1166 Empress Elisabeth (after Franz Winterhalter)

1998. Death Centenary of Empress Elisabeth.
2515 **1166** 7s. multicoloured . . . 1·20 1·00

1167 School Building

1998. Centenary of Vienna Business School.
2516 **1167** 7s. multicoloured . . . 1·00 1·00

1168 Kudlich and Farmers **1169** "My Garden" (Hans Staudacher)

1998. 175th Birth Anniv of Hans Kudlich (promoter of 1848 "Peasants' Liberation" Law).
2517 **1168** 6s.50 multicoloured . . 1·00 1·00

1998. Austrian Modern Art.
2518 **1169** 7s. multicoloured . . . 1·00 95

1170 Town Hall and Arms

1998. 350th Anniv of Declaration of Eisenstadt as a Free Town.
2519 **1170** 7s. multicoloured . . . 1·00 1·10

1171 Photographer and Reporter

1998. Austrian World of Work (10th series). Art, Media and Freelances.
2520 **1171** 6s.50 multicoloured . . 95 85

1172 1929 2s. Stamp and Post Van

1998. "WIPA 2000" International Stamp Exhibition, Vienna (2nd issue).
2521 **1172** 32s.+13s. mult . . . . 6·75 6·75

1173 "Nativity" (fresco, Tainach Church) **1174** Cross-country Skiing

1998. Christmas.
2522 **1173** 7s. multicoloured . . . 1·00 80

1999. World Nordic Skiing Championships, Ramsau.
2523 **1174** 7s. multicoloured . . . 1·00 1·00

1999. Folk Customs and Art (13th series). As T **1005**. Multicoloured.
2524 6s.50 Walking pilgrimage to Mariazell . . . . 1·00 1·00

1175 Stingl Rock, Bohemian Forest

1999. Natural Beauty Spots.
2525 **1175** 7s. multicoloured . . . 1·00 1·10

1176 Books and Compact Disc

1999. Centenary of Austrian Patent Office.
2526 **1176** 7s. multicoloured . . . 1·00 90

1177 Player and Club Emblem

1999. SK Puntigamer Sturm Graz Football Club.
2527 **1177** 7s. multicoloured . . . 1·00 1·10

1178 Palace Facade

1999. World Heritage Site. Schonbrunn Palace, Vienna.
2528 **1178** 13s. multicoloured . . . 1·90 2·20

1179 Partridges

1999. Hunting and the Environment. Living Space for Grey Partridges.
2529 **1179** 6s.50 multicoloured . . 1·00 1·10

1180 Snowboarder

1999. 50th Anniv of Austrian General Sport Federation.
2530 **1180** 7s. multicoloured . . . 1·00 1·00

1181 Council Building, Strasbourg

1999. 50th Anniv of Council of Europe.
2531 **1181** 14s. multicoloured . . . 2·10 1·80
No. 2531 is denominated both in Austrian schillings and in euros.

1182 Steyr Type 50 Baby Saloon

1999. Birth Centenary of Karl Jenschke (engineer and car manufacturer).
2532 **1182** 7s. multicoloured . . . 1·00 90

1183 "St. Martin" (marble relief, Peuerbach Church)

1999. Ancient Arts and Crafts (1st series).
2533 **1183** 8s. brown, blue & orange . . . . 1·30 1·10
See also Nos. 2542, 2575, 2600 and 2602.

1184 Symbols of Aid and Emblem

1999. 125th Anniv of Diakonie (professional charitable services).
2534 **1184** 7s. multicoloured . . . 1·00 1·00

1185 Johann Strauss, the Younger

1999. Composers' Death Anniversaries. Mult.
2535 7s. Type **1185** (centenary) 1·00 90
2536 8s. Johann Strauss, the Elder (150th anniv) . . . 1·20 1·20

1186 Rural Gendarmes

1188 "K" and "I"

1187 Donau-auen National Park

1999. 150th Anniv of National Gendarmerie.
2537 **1186** 7s. multicoloured . . . 1·00 1·00

1999. Europa. Parks and Gardens.
2538 **1187** 7s. multicoloured . . . 1·00 95

1999. Stamp Day.
2539 **1188** 7s. multicoloured . . . 1·00 1·00
See note below No. 2266.

1189 Iron Stage Curtain

1999. Centenary of Graz Opera.
2540 **1189** 6s.50 multicoloured . . 1·00 1·00

1190 Couple on Bench

1999. International Year of the Elderly.
2541 **1190** 7s. multicoloured . . . 1·00 1·00

1191 "St. Anne with Mary and Child Jesus" (wood-carving, St. George's Church, Purgg)

1999. Ancient Arts and Crafts (2nd series).
2542 **1191** 9s. multicoloured . . . 1·40 1·30

1192 1949 25g. Stamp and Vienna Airport

1999. "WIPA 2000" International Stamp Exhibition, Vienna (3rd issue).
2543 **1192** 32s.+16s. mult . . . . 7·50 7·25

1193 "Security throughout Life"

1194 "Cafe Girardi" (Wolfgang Herzig)

1999. 14th Congress of Federation of Austrian Trade Unions.
2544 **1193** 6s.50 multicoloured . . 1·00 1·00

1999. Austrian Modern Art.
2545 **1194** 7s. multicoloured . . . 1·00 90

1999. Folk Customs and Art (14th series). As T **1005**. Multicoloured.
2546 8s. Pumpkin Festival, Lower Austria . . . . 1·20 1·30

1999. Folk Customs and Art (15th series). As T **1005**. Multicoloured.
2547 7s. The Pummerin (great bell of St. Stephen's Cathedral) ringing in the New Year . . . . 1·90 1·40

1195 Institute and Fossils

1999. 150th Anniv of National Institute of Geology.
2548 **1195** 7s. multicoloured . . . 1·00 1·00

1196 "Nativity" (altar painting, Pinkafeld Church)

1999. Christmas.
2549 **1196** 7s. multicoloured . . . 1·00 90

2000. Folk Customs and Art (16th series). As T **1005**. Multicoloured.
2550 7s. Chapel procession, Carinthia . . . . 95 1·00

2000. "WIPA 2000" International Stamp Exhibition, Vienna (4th issue). Sheet 150 × 95 mm.
MS2551 27s.+13s. No. 2478; 32s.+13s. No. 2521; 32s.+16s. No. 2543 . . . . 27·00 19·00

2000. Folk Customs and Art (17th series). As T **1005**. Multicoloured.
2552 6s.50 Three men wearing masks (Cavalcade of Beautiful Masks, Telfs) 1·00 90

1197 *Zantadeschica aethiopica*

2000. International Garden Show, Graz.
2553 **1197** 7s. multicoloured . . . 1·00 1·00

1198 Ibex

2000. Hunting and the Environment. Return of Ibex to Austrian Mountains.
2554 **1198** 7s. multicoloured . . . 1·00 1·00

1199 Players

2000. F.C. Tirol Innsbruck, National Football Champion 2000.
2555 **1199** 7s. multicoloured . . . 1·00 1·00

1200 Mt. Grossglockner and Viewing Point

2000. Bicentenary of First Ascent of Mt. Grossglockner.
2556 **1200** 7s. multicoloured . . . 1·00 1·00

1201 Weisssee Lake

2000. Natural Beauty Spots.
2557 **1201** 7s. multicoloured . . . 1·00 1·30

1202 "Building Europe"

1203 Junkers Airplane and Air Traffic Control Tower

2000. Europa.
2558 **1202** 7s. multicoloured . . . 1·20 1·20

2000. 75th Anniv of Civil Aviation at Klagenfurt Airport.
2559 **1203** 7s. multicoloured . . . 1·10 1·00

1204 Madonna of Altenmarkt (statue) and Glass Roof, Palm House, Burggarten, Vienna

2000. 150th Anniv of Protection of Historic Monuments.
2560 **1204** 8s. multicoloured . . . 1·30 1·20

1205 Illuminated Letter and Text

2000. Life of St. Malachy (treatise) by St. Bernard of Clairvaux.
2561 **1205** 9s. multicoloured . . . 1·70 1·50

1206 "E" and "E"

2000. Stamp Day.
2562 **1206** 7s. multicoloured . . . 1·10 1·10
See note below No. 2266.

1207 1850 9 Kreuzer and 2000 Stamp Day Stamps

2000. 150th Anniv of Austrian Stamps.
2563 **1207** 7s. multicoloured . . . 1·10 1·30

2000. "WIPA 2000" International Stamp Exhibition, Vienna (5th series). Sheet 65 × 90 mm.
MS2564 10s. As No. 2462a . . . 30·00 21·00

1208 "Confetti"

2000. *Confetti* (children's television programme).
2565 **1208** 7s. multicoloured . . . 1·00 1·00

1209 "Blue Blues"

2000. Death Commemoration of Friedensreich Hundertwasser (artist). Sheet 129 × 126 mm, containing four versions of T **1209** identified by the colours of the vertical strips at the top of the design.
MS2566 7s. silver; 7s. red; 7s. mauve; 7s. black . . . . 6·25 4·25

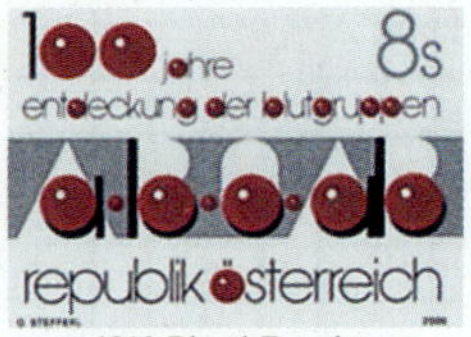

1210 Blood Droplets

2000. Centenary of Discovery of Blood Groups by Karl Landsteiner (pathologist).
2567 **1210** 8s. pink, silver & black 1·20 1·20

1211 Daimler Cannstatter Bus

2000. Centenary of First Regular Bus Route between Purkersdorf and Gablitz.
2568 **1211** 9s. black, blue and light blue . . . . 1·50 1·40

2000. Folk Customs and Art (18th series). As T **1005**. Multicoloured.
2569 7s. Men on raft (International Rafting Meeting, Carinthia) . . . 1·10 1·00

1212 Dachstein River and Hallstatt

2000. Natural Beauty Spots.
2570 **1212** 7s. multicoloured . . . 1·10 1·00

1213 String Instrument and Emblem

2000. Centenary of Vienna Symphony Orchestra.
2571 **1213** 7s. multicoloured . . . 1·10 1·00

1214 Dinghies

2000. Olympic Games, Sydney.
2572 **1214** 9s. multicoloured . . . 1·50 1·60

1215 Old and Modern Paper Production Methods

2000. Austrian World of Work (11th series). Printing and Paper.
2573 **1215** 6s.50 multicoloured . . 1·00 1·10

1216 "Turf Turkey" (Ida Szigethy)

2000. Austrian Modern Art.
2574 **1216** 7s. multicoloured . . . 1·10 1·00

1217 Codex 965 (National Library)

2000. Ancient Arts and Crafts (3rd series).
2575 **1217** 8s. multicoloured . . . 1·30 1·30
See also Nos. 2600 and 2602.

1218 Child receiving Vaccination

1219 Urania Building, Vienna

2000. Bicentenary of Vaccination in Austria.
2576 **1218** 7s. black and cinnamon 1·10 1·00

2000. 50th Anniv of Adult Education Association.
2577 **1219** 7s. brown, grey & gold 1·10 1·00

1220 The Nativity (altar piece, Ludesch Church)

2000. Christmas.
2578 **1220** 7s. multicoloured . . . 1·00 1·00

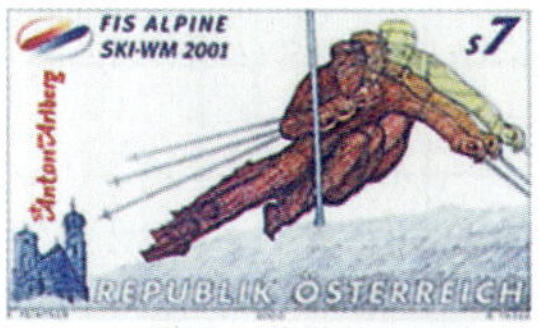

1221 Downhill Skier

2000. World Skiing Championship (2001), St. Anton am Arlberg.
2579 **1221** 7s. multicoloured . . . 1·10 1·30

1222 Pair of Mallards

2001. Hunting and the Environment. Protection of Wetlands.
2580 **1222** 7s. multicoloured . . . 1·10 1·00

2001. Folk Customs and Art (19th series). As T **1005**. Multicoloured.
2581 8s. Boat mill, Mureck, Styria . . . . 1·20 1·20

1223 Steam Locomotive No. 3

2001. Centenary of Zillertal Railway.
2582 **1223** 7s. multicoloured . . . 1·10 1·00

1224 Players and Club Emblem

2001. SV Casino Salzburg, National Football Champion.
2583 **1224** 7s. multicoloured . . . 1·10 1·00

1225 Rolf Rudiger

2001. *Confetti* (children's television programme).
2584 **1225** 7s. multicoloured . . . 1·10 1·00

1226 Monoplane and Airport

2001. 75th Anniv of Salzburg Airport.
2585 **1226** 14s. multicoloured . . . 2·30 2·10

1227 Baerenschuetz Gorge

2001. Natural Beauty Spots.
2586 **1227** 7s. multicoloured . . . 1·10 1·00

2001. Folk Customs and Art (20th series). As T **1005**. Multicoloured.
2587 7s. Lent season cloth from Eastern Tyrol . . . . . . 1·10 1·20

1228 Water Droplet

1230 Air Balloon

1229 Post Office Railway Car

2001. Europa. Water Resources.
2588 **1228** 15s. multicoloured . . . 3·50 3·00

2001. Stamp Day.
2589 **1229** 20s.+10s. mult . . . . 7·25 6·00

2001. Centenary of Austrian Flying Club.
2590 **1230** 7s. multicoloured . . . 1·10 1·00

1231 Refugee

2001. 50th Anniv of United Nations High Commissioner for Refugees.
2591 **1231** 21s. multicoloured . . . 4·00 3·50

1232 Kalte Rinne Viaduct

2001. UNESCO World Heritage Site. The Semmering Railway.
2592 **1232** 35s. multicoloured . . . 7·25 7·50

1233 "Seppl" (mascot) (Michelle Schneeweiss)

2001. 7th International Hiking Olympics, Seefeld.
2593 **1233** 7s. multicoloured . . . 1·10 1·00

1234 Field Post Office at Famagusta

2001. Army Postal Services Abroad.
2594 **1234** 7s. multicoloured . . . 1·10 1·20

2001. Folk Customs and Art (21st series). As T **1005**. Multicoloured.
2595 7s. Rifle and Clubhouse, Preberschiessen, Salzburg (Rifleman's gathering) . . 1·10 1·00

1235 "Taurus" (Railway Engine)

2001. Conversion of East–West Railway to Four-tracked Railway.
2596 **1235** 7s. multicoloured . . . 1·10 1·00

1236 19th-century Theatrical Scene

2001. Birth Bicentenary of Johann Nestroy (playwright and actor).
2597 **1236** 7s. multicoloured . . . 1·10 1·00

1237 "The Continents" (detail Helmut Leherb)

2001. Austrian Modern Art.
2598 **1237** 7s. multicoloured . . . 1·10 1·00

1238 "False Friends" (Von Fuehrich)

2001. 125th Death Anniv of Joseph Ritter von Fuehrich (artist and engraver).
2599 **1238** 8s. deep green & green 1·30 1·10

1239 Pluviale (embroidered religious robe)   **1240** Dobler

2001. Ancient Arts and Crafts (4th series).
2600 **1239** 10s. multicoloured . . . 1·90 1·70

2001. Birth Bicentenary of Leopold Ludwig Dobler (magician and inventor).
2601 **1240** 7s. multicoloured . . . 1·10 1·00

1241 Dalmatik (religious vestment) (Carmelite Monastery, Silbergrasse, Vienna)

2001. Ancient Arts and Crafts (5th series).
2602 **1241** 7s. multicoloured . . . 1·10 1·20

1242 Building and Scientific Equipment

2001. 150th Anniv of the Central Institute for Meteorology and Geodynamics, Vienna.
2603 **1242** 12s. multicoloured . . . 2·40 2·00

1243 Cat

2001.
2604 **1243** 19s. multicoloured . . . 4·25 3·25

1244 Civil Servants

2001. Austrian World of Work (12th series). Civil Service.
2605 **1244** 7s. multicoloured . . . 1·10 1·30

1245 Figure of Infant Jesus   **1246** House of the Basilisk, Vienna

2001. Christmas. Glass Shrine, Fitzmoos Church.
2606 **1245** 7s. multicoloured . . . 1·00 1·00

New Currency

2002. Tourism.
2607 – 4c. multicoloured . . . 10 10
2608 – 7c. blue and black . . . 20 15
2609 – 13c. multicoloured . . . 25 25
2610 – 17c. violet and black . . 35 35
2611 – 20c. multicoloured . . . 35 35
2612 – 25c. multicoloured . . . 45 45
2613 – 27c. blue and black . . 55 50
2614 – 45c. multicoloured . . . 80 80
2615 **1246** 51c. multicoloured . . . 95 65
2616 – 55c. multicoloured . . . 95 90
2617 – 58c. multicoloured . . . 1·10 80
2618 – 73c. multicoloured . . . 1·40 1·00
2619 – 75c. multicoloured . . . 1·40 1·10
2620 – 87c. multicoloured . . . 1·60 1·20
2621 – €1 multicoloured . . . 1·80 1·50
2622 – €1.25 multicoloured 2·30 2·00
2623 – €2.03 multicoloured 3·75 2·50
2626 – €3.75 multicoloured 6·75 6·00

DESIGNS: 4c. As No. 2615; 7c. As No. 2623; 13c. As No. 2620; 17c. As No. 2617; 20c. Yachts, Worthersee, Carintha; 25c. Crucifixes on rock, Mondsee, Upper Austria; 27c. As No. 2618; 45c. Snow covered chalet, Jungholz, Kleinwasler; 55c. Gothic houses, Steyr, Upper Austria; 58c. Wine cellars, Hadres, Lower Austria; 73c. Alpine chalet, Salzburg; 75c. Boat on Bodensee, Voralberg; 87c. Alpach Valley, Tyrol; €1 Farmhouse, Rossegg, Styria; €1.25 Wine press building, Eisenburg, Burgenland; €2.03 Heligenkreuz, Lower Austria; €3.75 Gothic shrine, Hochhosterwitz, Carinthia.

1247 Stars, Map of Europe and €1 Coin

2002. Euro Currency.
2630 **1247** €3.27 multicoloured 7·25 6·75

No. 2630 is printed on the back under the gum with examples of Austrian schilling coins.

1248 Skiers and Olympic Rings

2002. Winter Olympic Games, Salt Lake City, U.S.A.
2631 **1248** 73c. multicoloured . . . 1·70 1·60

1249 Bouquet of Flowers

2002.
2632 **1249** 87c. multicoloured . . . 1·90 1·80

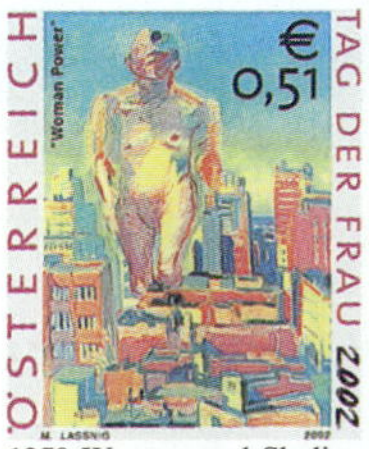

1250 Woman and Skyline

2002. Women's Day.
2633 **1250** 51c. multicoloured . . . 2·00 1·80

1251 Mel and Lucy

2002. "Philis" (children's stamp awareness programme) (1st issue).
2634 **1251** 58c. multicoloured . . . 1·60 1·50

See also Nos. 2639 and 2662.

1252 Red Roses

2002. Greetings Stamp.
2635 **1252** 58c. multicoloured . . . 1·40 1·30

1253 Kubin

2002. 125th Birth Anniv of Alfred Kubin (artist).
2636 **1253** 87c. black and buff . . 1·90 1·80

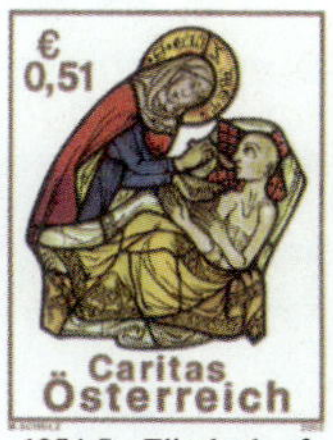

1254 St. Elizabeth of Thuringia and Sick Man

2002. Caritas (Catholic charity organization).
2637 **1254** 51c. multicoloured . . . 1·40 1·30

1255 Tiger, Clown and Circus Tent

2002. Europa. The Circus.
2638 **1255** 87c. multicoloured . . . 2·40 2·20

1256 Sisko and Mauritius

2002. "Philis" (children's stamp awareness programme) (2nd issue).
2639 **1256** 58c. multicoloured . . . 1·50 1·40

1257 The Nativity

2002. 800th Anniv of Lilienfeld Abbey.
2640 **1257** €2.03 multicoloured 4·50 4·25

1258 Mimi

2002. *Confetti* (children's television programme).
2641 **1258** 51c. multicoloured . . . 1·30 1·20

1259 Railway Carriage, 1919

2002. Stamp Day.
2642 **1259** €1.60+80c. multicoloured . . . . 6·25 5·75

1260 Cheetah, Zebra and Orang-utan

2002. 250th Anniv of Schonbrunn Zoo. Mult.
2643 51c. Type **1260** . . . . . . 1·10 1·00
2644 58c. Gulls, flamingos and pelicans . . . . 1·30 1·20
2645 87c. Lion, turtle and crocodile . . . . 1·90 1·80
2646 €1.38 Elephant, birds and fish . . . . 3·00 2·75

Nos. 2643/6 were issued together, se-tenant, forming a composite design.

1261 Teddy Bears

2002. Centenary of the Teddy Bear.
2647 **1261** 51c. multicoloured . . . 1·40 1·30

1262 Chair No. 14 (Michael Thonet)

2002. 75th Anniv of "Design Austria" (design group) (1st issue).
2648 **1262** €1.38 multicoloured 3·00 3·00

See also Nos. 2661 and 2670.

1263 Crystal Cup

2002. Ancient Arts and Crafts.
2649 **1263** €1.60 multicoloured 3·50 3·25

1264 Museum Buildings

2002. Museumsquartier (MQ), Messepalast, Vienna.
2650 **1264** 58c. multicoloured . . . 1·60 1·10

1265 Figures supporting Emblem

2002. 50th Anniv of Union of Austrians Abroad.
2651 **1265** €2.47 multicoloured 4·75 4·75

1266 Clown Doctor

2002. "Rote Nasen" (Red Noses (charity)).
2652 **1266** 51c. multicoloured . . . 1·30 95

1267 Head

2002. Linzer Klangwolke (sound and light performance), Linz.
2653 **1267** 58c. multicoloured . . . 1·40 1·10

1268 Graf & Stift Typ 40/45

2002.
2654 **1268** 51c. multicoloured . . . 1·10 95

1269 Dog

2002.
2655 **1269** 51c. multicoloured . . . 1·10 95

1270 Steam Locomotive 109

2002.
2656 **1270** 51c. multicoloured . . . 1·10 95

1271 "Schutzenhaus" (Karl Goldammer)

2002. Austrian Modern Art.
2657 **1271** 51c. multicoloured . . . 1·30 95

1272 Lottery Ball

2002. 250th Anniv of Austrian Lottery. Sheet 72 × 90 mm.
MS2658 **1272** 87c. multicoloured 1·60 1·70

1273 Thayatal National Park

2002.
2659 **1273** 58c. multicoloured . . . 1·30 1·10

1274 Puch 175 SV

2002.
2660 **1274** 58c. multicoloured . . . 1·40 1·10

1275 "Eye"

2002. 75th Anniv of "Design Austria" (design group) (2nd issue). Winning Entry in Design Competition.
2661 **1275** €1.38 multicoloured 3·00 2·75

1276 Edison and Gogo

2002. "Philis" (children's stamp awareness programme) (3rd issue).
2662 **1276** 58c. multicoloured . . . 1·60 1·10

1277 Crib Aureola, Thaur, Tyrol

2002. Christmas.
2663 **1277** 51c. multicoloured . . . 1·10 95

1278 Emblem

2003. Make-up Rate Stamp.
2664 **1278** 45c. yellow, silver and black . . . . 1·10 95

1279 Amphitheatre on River Mur

2003. Graz, Cultural Capital of Europe, 2003.
2665 **1279** 58c. multicoloured . . . 1·30 1·10

1280 Billy Wilder **1281** Heart, Linked Rings and Doves

2003. 1st Death Anniv of Billy Wilder (film director).
2666 **1280** 58c. multicoloured . . . 1·40 1·10

2003. Greetings Stamp. Wedding.
2667 **1281** 58c. multicoloured . . . 1·40 1·10

1282 Kasperl

2003. Confetti (children's television programme). 45th Anniv of Kasperl (puppet).
2668 **1282** 51c. multicoloured . . . 1·10 95

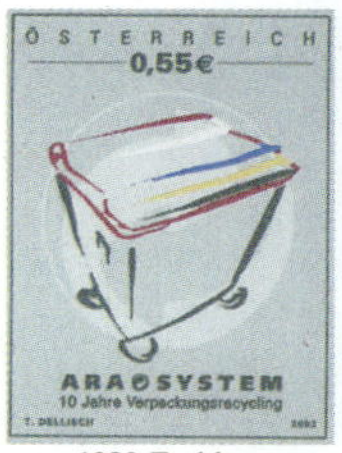

1283 Emblem **1284** Carafe and Glasses (Adolf Loos)

2003. 10th Anniv of Recycling Enterprise.
2669 **1283** 55c. multicoloured . . . 1·00 1·00

2003. 75th Anniv of "Design Austria" (design group) (3rd issue).
2670 **1284** €1.38 blue, black and orange . . . . 2·40 2·75

1285 Seated Pandas

2003. Schönbrunn Zoo's Acquisition of Pandas from People's Republic of China. Sheet 110 × 76 mm containing T **1285** and similar multicoloured design.
MS2671 75c. Pandas nuzzling (40 × 34 mm) (horiz); €1 Type **1285** . . . . 4·00 3·25

1286 St. George's Monastery

2003. Millenary of St. George's Monastery, Carintha.
2672 **1286** 87c. multicoloured . . . 1·60 1·70

1287 Marcel Prawy

2003. Marcel Prawy Commemoration (musician). Sheet 100 × 100 mm.
MS2673 **1287** €1.75 multicoloured 3·00 3·25

1288 Face

2003. Europa. Poster Art.
2674 **1288** €1.02 multicoloured 2·20 1·90

1289 Siemens M 320 Postal Wagon

2003. Stamp Day.
2675 **1289** €2.54+€1.26 multicoloured . . . . 7·75 7·00

1290 Series 5045 Locomotive "Blue Flash"

2003.
2676 **1290** 75c. multicoloured . . . 1·70 1·40

1291 Bridge over Salzach River

2003. Centenary of Oberndorf–Laufen Bridge.
2677 **1291** 55c. multicoloured . . . 1·70 1·00

A stamp of the same design was issued by Germany.

1292 Ford Model T

2003. Centenary of Ford Motor Company. Sheet 150 × 81 mm containing T **1292** and similar horiz designs. Multicoloured.
MS2678 Type **1292**; 55c. Henry Ford; 55c. Ford Streetka . . . 3·75 3·25

1293 Keith Richards

2003. Rolling Stones. Sheet 101 × 101 mm containing T **1291** and similar vert designs. Multicoloured.
MS2679 Type **1293**; 55c. Mick Jagger; 55c. Charlie Watts; 55c. Ronnie Woods . . . . 5·50 4·25

1294 Panther Airport Fire Appliance

2003.
2688 **1294** 55c. multicoloured . . . 1·30 1·00

1295 Apostle and Scribe

1296 "Prenez le temps d'aimer" (Take time to enjoy) (Kiki Kogelnik)

2003. Year of the Bible.
2689 **1295** 55c. multicoloured . . . 95 1·00

2003.
2690 **1296** 55c. multicoloured . . . 1·30 1·00

1297 Lake

2003. UNESCO World Heritage Site. Lake Neusiedlersee.
2691 **1297** €1 multicoloured . . . 2·20 1·90

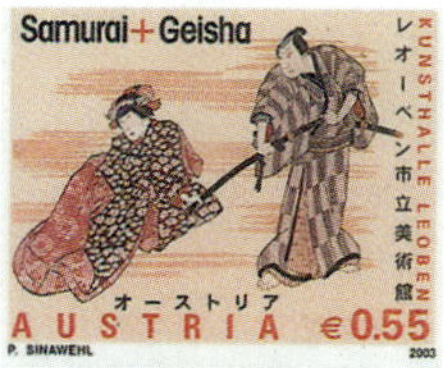

1298 Geisha and Samurai

2003. Japan Exhibition, Leoben.
2692 **1298** 55c. multicoloured . . . 1·30 1·00

1299 Princess Turandot

2003. Performance of Puccini's Opera *Turandot*, St. Margarethen Roman Quarry.
2693 **1299** 55c. multicoloured . . . 1·30 1·00

1300 Family (Eva Wallner)

1301 Water Tower

2003. Children's Stamp.
2694 **1300** 55c. multicoloured . . . 1·30 1·00

2003. 50th Anniv Local Government Conference, Wiener Neustadt.
2695 **1301** 55c. multicoloured . . . 95 1·00

1302 TomTom (cartoon character) and Bouquet

2003. Greetings stamp.
2696 **1302** 55c. multicoloured . . . 1·40 1·00

1303 TomTom throwing Parcel from Hot Air Balloon

2003.
2697 **1303** 55c. multicoloured . . . 1·00 1·00

1304 Werner Schlager

2003. Werner Schlager, World Table Tennis Champion, 2003.
2698 **1304** 55c. multicoloured . . . 1·60 1·00

1305 Stylized Head (Cornelia Zell)

2003. Jugend-Phila '03 International Youth Stamp Exhibition, Graz.
2699 **1305** 55c. multicoloured . . . 1·00 1·00

1306 Fan and "Elisabeth"

2003. Elisabeth, the Musical (musical based on life of Empress Elisabeth).
2700 **1306** 55c. multicoloured . . . 1·40 1·00

1307 "Judith"

1309 Grand Piano

1308 Hands enclosing Light

2003. 185th Death Anniv of Gustav Klimt (artist). Sheet 80 × 100 mm.
MS2701 **1308** €2.10 multicoloured 4·00 4·00

2003. 30th Anniv of "Licht ins Dunkel" (Bringing light into darkness) (fund raising campaign).
2702 **1308** 55c. multicoloured . . . 1·60 1·40

2003. 175th Anniv of Bosendorfer (piano manufacturer).
2703 **1309** 75c. multicoloured . . . 1·00 1·00

1310 Oscar Peterson

2003. 78th Birth Anniv of Oscar Peterson (pianist).
2704 **1310** €1.25 multicoloured 2·40 2·30

1311 Stained Glass Window

2003. Christmas.
2705 **1311** 55c. multicoloured . . . 1·40 1·00

1312 Postal Emblem

2003. Greeting Stamps. T **1312** and similar design. Each yellow, black and gold.
2706 55c. Type **1312** . . . . . . 1·00 1·00
2707 55c. Postal emblem (horiz) 1·00 1·00
Nos. 2706/7 could be personalised by the addition of photograph or logo, replacing the design shown on the stamp.

1313 Ricardo Muti

2004. Vienna Philharmonic Orchestra's New Year Concert conducted by Ricardo Muti (principal conductor, La Scala Milan).
2708 **1313** €1 multicoloured . . . 2·20 1·90

1314 Seiji Ozawa

2004. 2nd Anniv of Seija Ozawa's Appointment as Musical Director of Vienna State Opera House.
2709 **1314** €1 multicoloured . . . 2·20 1·90

1315 Jose Carreras

2004. 30th Anniv of Jose Carreras Association with Vienna State Opera House.
2710 **1315** €1 multicoloured . . . 1·90 1·90

1316 Gerard Hanappi

2004. Centenary of Austrian Football. Sheet 196 × 113 mm containing T **1316** and similar vert designs. Multicoloured.
MS2711 55c. × 10, Type **1316**; Mathias Sindelar; Football and anniversary emblem; Bruno Pezzey; Ernst Ocwirk; Walter Zeman; Herbert Prohaska; Hans Krankl; Andreas Herzog; Anton Polster . . . . 10·50 10·50

1317 Crucifixion (Werner Berg)

2004. Easter.
2712 **1317** 55c. multicoloured . . . 1·00 1·00

1318 Dancers

2004. Life Ball (AIDS charity).
2713 **1318** 55c. multicoloured . . . 1·10 1·00

1319 Cardinal Franz Konig

2004. Cardinal Franz Konig Commemoration.
2714 **1319** €1 multicoloured . . . 2·20 1·90

1320 Emperor Franz Joseph and Empress Elisabeth

1321 Catholics' Day Emblem

2004. 150th Anniv of the Marriage of Emperor Franz Joseph and Empress Elisabeth. Sheet 157 × 109 mm containing T **1320** and similar vert designs. Multicoloured.
MS2715 €1.25 Type **1320**; €1.50 Wedding procession; €1.75 Emperor Franz Joseph and Empress Elisabeth (35 × 42 mm) 8·75 8·50

2004. Catholics' Day. Sheet 110 × 160 mm containing T **1321** and similar vert designs. Multicoloured.
MS2716 55c. Type **1321**; €1.25 Pope John Paul II; €1.25 Magna Mater Austriae (Romanesque statue) (Chapel of Grace, Basilica, Mariazell); €1.25 Mother of God on Column of the Blessed Virgin (Basilica, Mariazell); €1.25 Virgin Mary (Treasury Altar, Basilica, Mariazell); €1.25 Crucifix (High Altar, Basilica, Mariazell) . . . 13·50 13·00

1322 Mail Plane

2004. Stamp Day.
2717 **1322** €2.65+€1.30 multicoloured . . . . 7·75 7·50

2004. Folk Customs and Art (22nd series). As T **1005**. Multicoloured.
2718 55c. Barrel sliding, Kosterneuburgs . . . . . 1·00 1·00

1323 Joe Zawinul (musician)

2004.
2719 **1323** 55c. multicoloured . . . 1·00 1·00

1324 Sun and Flowers

2004. Europa. Holidays.
2720 **1324** 75c. multicoloured . . . 1·50 1·40

1325 Holy Sepulchre, Jerusalem

2004. Papal Order of the Holy Sepulchre.
2721 **1325** 125c. multicoloured . . 2·30 2·30

1326 Imperial and Royal Southern State Railway Locomotive *Engerth*

2004.
2722 **1326** 55c. multicoloured . . . 1·20 1·00

1327 Fireworks and Bubbles

1328 Theodor Herzl

2004. Danube Island Festival, Vienna.
2723 **1327** 55c. multicoloured . . . 1·00 1·00

2004. Death Centenary of Theodor Herzl (writer and Zionist pioneer).
2724 **1328** 55c. multicoloured . . . 1·70 1·00
A stamp of the same design was issued by Israel and Hungary.

1329 Arnold Schwarzenegger (governor of California)

2004.
2725 **1329** 100c. multicoloured . . 2·75 2·50

1330 Ernst Happel

2004. 12th Death Anniv of Ernst Happel (football trainer).
2726 **1330** 100c. black and scarlet 3·00 2·50

1331 Tom Turbo (bicycle) (Andreas Wolkerstorfer)

2004. Tom Turbo (character from children's television series). Winning Entry in Children's Drawing Competition.
2727 **1331** 55c. multicoloured . . . 1·20 1·00

1332 TomTom (cartoon character) greeting Snail

2004. Greetings Stamp.
2728 **1332** 55c. multicoloured . . . 1·40 1·00

1333 Town Hall and Steam Tram

2004. Incorporation of Floridsdorf into Vienna.
2729 **1333** 55c. multicoloured . . . 1·40 1·00

1334 Crystal

2004. Crystal Worlds (tourist attraction), Wattens. Sheet 147 × 85 mm containing T **1334** and similar horiz design. Multicoloured.
MS2730 375c. × 2, Type **1334**; Swan 14·00 14·00
The stamps of **MS**2730 have crystals applied to the surface.

1335 Hermann Maier

2004. Hermann Maier—World Champion Giant Slalom Skier.
2731 **1335** 55c. multicoloured . . . 1·70 1·00

1336 "Kaspar Winterbild" (Josef Bramer)

2004.
2732 **1336** 55c. multicoloured . . . 1·10 1·00

2004. No. 2607 surch BASILISK.
2733 55c. on 51c. multicoloured 1·70 1·60

1338 "Die Wartende" (Sylvia Gredenberg)

2004.
2734 **1338** 55c. multicoloured . . . 1·00 1·00

1339 "Junge Sonnenblume" (Max Weiler)

2004. Sheet 80 × 100 mm.
MS2735 **1339** €2.10 multicoloured 4·00 4·00

1340 Campaign Poster (Friedensreich Hundertwasser)

2004. 20th Anniv of Campaign to save Danube Meadows (now National Park).
2736 **1340** 55c. multicoloured . . . 2·20 1·00

1341 Soldier and National Arms

2004. 50th Anniv of Federal Army.
2737 **1341** 55c. multicoloured . . . 1·10 1·00

1342 Nikolaus Harnoncourt

2004. 75th Birthday of Nikolaus Harnoncourt (musician).
2738 **1342** €1 multicoloured . . . 1·90 1·90

1343 Salzburg Christmas Market

2004. Christmas.
2739 **1343** 55c. multicoloured . . . 1·00 1·00

1344 Lorin Maazel

2005. Vienna Philharmonic Orchestra's New Year Concert conducted by Lorin Maazel.
2740 **1344** €1 multicoloured . . . 1·80 1·90

1345 Herbert von Karajan

2005. 10th Anniv of Herbert von Karajan Centre.
2741 **1345** 55c. blue, black and deep blue . . . . . 1·00 1·00

1346 Stephan Eberharter

2005. Stephan Eberharter—World Champion Skier.
2742 **1346** 55c. multicoloured . . . 1·60 1·00

2005. Nos. 2607, 2609/10, 2613, 2617/18, 2620 and 2623 variously surch.
2743 55c. on 4c. multicoloured . . 1·10 1·00
2744 55c. on 13c. multicoloured 1·10 1·00
2745 55c. on 17c. multicoloured 1·10 1·00
2746 55c. on 27c. multicoloured 1·10 1·00
2747 55c. on 58c. multicoloured 1·10 1·00
2748 55c. on 73c. multicoloured 1·10 1·00
2749 55c. on 87c. multicoloured 1·10 1·00
2750 55c. on €2.03 multicoloured 1·10 1·00

1355 Globe and Rotary Emblem

2005. Centenary of Rotary International (charitable organization).
2751 **1355** 55c. multicoloured . . . 1·10 1·00

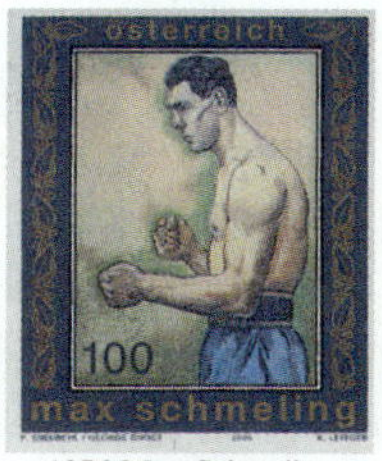

1356 Max Schmeling

2005. Death Centenary of Max Schmeling (boxer).
2752 **1356** 100c. multicoloured . . 2·10 1·90

1357 "Venus in Front of the Mirror" (Peter Paul Rubens)

2005. Liechtenstein Museum, Garden Palace, Vienna.
2753 **1357** 125c. multicoloured . . 2·75 2·30

1358 Carl Djerassi

2005. 82nd Birth Anniv of Carl Djerassi (chemist and writer). Sheet 60 × 80 mm.
MS2754 **1358** 100c. multicoloured 2·10 1·90

1359 Pope John Paul II **1360** Taurus

2005. Pope John Paul II Commemoration.
2755 **1359** €1 multicoloured . . . 2·10 1·90

2005. Astrology (1st issue). Multicoloured. Self-adhesive gum.
2756 55c. Type **1360** . . . . . . 1·10 1·00
2757 55c. Gemini . . . . 1·10 1·00
2758 55c. Cancer . . . . 1·10 1·00
2759 55c. Rooster (Year of the Rooster) (Chinese astrology) (yellow) . . . . 1·10 1·00
See also Nos. 2772/5, 2784/7 and 2799/2802.

1361 Post Office Building and Carriages

2005. Imperial Post Office in Jerusalem (1859–1914).
2760 **1361** 100c. multicoloured . . 1·90 1·90

1362 Saint Florian **1363** Tracks

2005. Saints (1st issue). Saint Florian (National Patron Saint).
2761 **1362** 55c. multicoloured . . . 1·10 1·00
See also Nos. 2767, 2829, 2857 and 2890.

2005. 60th Anniv of Liberation of Mauthausen Concentration Camp.
2762 **1363** 55c. multicoloured . . . 1·10 1·00

1364 State Arms

2005. 60th Anniv of Second Republic and 50th Anniv of State Treaty. Sheet 120 × 80 mm containing T **1364** and similar multicoloured design.
MS2763 55c. × 2, Type **1364**; Seals and signatures on treaty (42 × 35 mm) . . . . 2·30 2·10

1365 Heidi Klum

2005. Life Ball (AIDS charity).
2764 **1365** 75c. multicoloured . . . 1·80 1·40

1366 Junkers F 13 Flying Boat

2005. Stamp Day.
2765 **1366** 265c.+130c. mult . . . 8·75 7·50

1367 Waiter in Cup of Coffee

2005. Europa. Gastronomy.
2766 **1367** 75c. multicoloured . . . 1·80 1·40

1368 Saint Joseph **1370** Melman, Marty, Alex and Gloria (characters)

1369 Jochen Rindt

2005. Saints (2nd issue).
2767 **1368** 55c. multicoloured . . . 1·10 1·00

2005. 25th Death Anniv of Karl Jochen Rindt (1970—Formula 1 World Champion).
2768 **1369** 55c. multicoloured . . . 1·20 1·00

2005. *Madagascar* (animated film).
2769 **1370** 55c. multicoloured . . . 1·20 1·00

1371 Peacock Butterfly (*Inachis io*)

2005.
2770 **1371** 55c. multicoloured . . . 1·20 1·00

1372 Edelweiss

2005. Vorarlberg Embroidery.
2771 **1372** 375c. green . . . . . . 7·75 7·00

2005. Astrology (2nd issue). As T **1360**. Multicoloured. Self-adhesive.
2772 55c. Leo . . . . 1·10 1·00
2773 55c. Virgo . . . . 1·10 1·00
2774 55c. Libra . . . . 1·10 1·00
2775 55c. As No. 2759 (rosine) 1·10 1·00

2005. Customs and Art (23rd series). As T **1005**. Multicoloured.
2776 55c. Game of dice, Frankenburg . . . . . . 1·10 1·00

1373 Nikki Lauda

2005. Nikki Lauda (Formula 1 World Champion—1975, 1977 and 1984).
2777 **1373** 55c. multicoloured . . . 1·20 1·00

1374 Pumpkin

2005. Halloween.
2778 **1374** 55c. multicoloured . . . 1·10 1·00

1375 "Houses" (Egon Schiele)

2005. Art. Sheet 100 × 80 mm.
MS2779 **1375** 210c. multicoloured 4·25 4·00

1376 ET 10.103 Railcar

2005. Centenary of Montafon Railway.
2780 **1376** 55c. multicoloured . . . 1·20 1·00

1377 Presentation of Deed

2005. Landhaus (provincial government building), Klagenfurt.
2781 **1377** 75c. multicoloured . . . 1·50 1·40

1378 "Master of the Woods" (Karl Hodina)

2005.
2782 **1378** 55c. multicoloured . . . 1·10 1·00

1379 Adalbert Stifter

2005. Birth Bicentenary of Adalbert Stifter (writer).
2783 **1379** 55c. multicoloured . . . 1·90 1·00

2005. Astrology (3rd issue). As T **1360**. Multicoloured. Self-adhesive.
2784 55c. Scorpio . . . . 1·10 1·00
2785 55c. Sagittarius . . . . . . 1·10 1·00
2786 55c. Capricorn . . . . . . 1·10 1·00
2787 55c. As No. 2759 . . . . . 1·10 1·00

1380 National Theatre

2005. 50th Anniv of Re-opening of National Theatre and Opera House. Sheet 130 × 60 mm containing T **1380** and similar horiz design.
MS2788 55c. sepia and agate; 55c. indigo and black . . . . . . 2·10 2·10
DESIGNS: 55c. × 2, Type **1380**; State Opera House.

1381 Hills

2005. Restoration of Sattler's Cyclorama of Salzburg. Sheet 155 × 56 mm containing T **381** and similar horiz design. Multicoloured.
MS2789 125c. × 2, Type **1381**; Townscape . . . . 4·75 4·75

1382 "Nude" (Veronika Zillner)

1383 Aslan (character)

2005.
2790 **1382** 55c. multicoloured . . . 1·10 1·00

2005. *The Chronicles of Narnia* (film of book by C. S. Lewis).
2791 **1383** 55c. multicoloured . . . 1·20 1·00

1384 "Maria Heimsuchung" (Reinhold Stecher)

2005. Advent.
2792 **1384** 55c. multicoloured . . . 1·10 1·00

1385 Shields

2005. 800th Anniv of Order of Teutonic Knights.
2793 **1385** 55c. multicoloured . . . 1·10 1·00

1386 Snow-covered Houses

2005. Christmas.
2794 **1386** 55c. multicoloured . . . 1·10 1·00

1387 Mariss Jansons

2006. Vienna Philharmonic Orchestra's New Year Concert conducted by Mariss Jansons.
2795 **1387** 75c. multicoloured . . . 1·50 1·40

1388 Building Facade

2006. Austria's Presidency of European Union.
2796 **1388** 75c. multicoloured . . . 1·50 1·40

1389 "Post" Philatelic Shop

2006. Greeting Stamp.
2797 **1389** 55c. multicoloured . . . 1·10 1·00

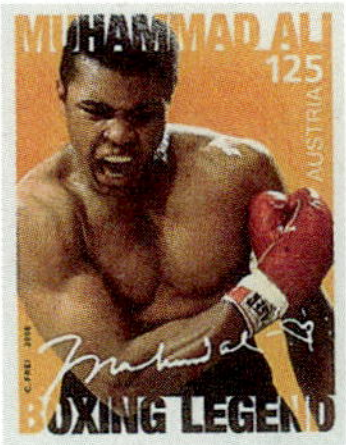

1390 Muhammad Ali

1391 Dog ("Year of the Dog")

2006. Muhammad Ali (boxer).
2798 **1390** €1.25 multicoloured 2·75 2·30

2006. Astrology (4th issue). Multicoloured. Self-adhesive.
2799 55c. Type **1391** . . . . . . 1·10 1·00
2800 55c. Aquarius . . . . 1·10 1·00
2801 55c. Pisces . . . . 1·10 1·00
2802 55c. Aries . . . . 1·10 1·00

1392 Wolfgang Mozart

2006. 250th Birth Anniv of Wolfgang Amadeus Mozart (composer and musician).
2803 **1392** 55c. red and silver . . . 1·20 1·00

1393 Europa (sculpture) (R. Chavanon)

1394 "Lost in her Dreams" (Friedrich von Amerling)

2006. 50th Anniv of Europa Stamps.
2804 **1393** 125c. multicoloured . . 2·40 2·30

2006. Liechtenstein Museum, Garden Palace, Vienna.
2805 **1394** 125c. multicoloured . . 2·40 2·30
A stamp of the same design was issued by Liechtenstein.

1395 Meteorite

2006. Post from another World. Meteorite H-chondrite on Stamps. Sheet 81 × 60 mm.
MS2806 **1395** 375c. multicoloured 7·75 7·00
No. **MS**2806 contains ground meteorite dust and is sold in a folder.

1396 Almaz and Karl Heinz Bohm (founders)

2006. 25th Anniv of Menschen fur Menschen (charity).
2807 **1396** 100c. multicoloured . . 1·90 1·90

1397 Initiation

1398 Couch

2006. Freemasonry in Austria. Sheet 81 × 61 mm.
MS2808 **1397** 100c. multicoloured 2·40 2·40

2006. 150th Birth Anniv of Sigmund Freud (psychoanalysis).
2809 **1398** 55c. multicoloured . . . 1·20 1·00

1399 Franz Beckenbauer (Andy Warhol)

1402 Falco

2006. Franz Beckenbauer (footballer).
2810 **1399** 75c. multicoloured . . . 1·70 1·50

2006. Flood Relief. No. 2612 surch **75+425 HOCH WASSER HILFE 2006**.
2811 75c.+425c. on 25c. multicoloured . . . . . . 8·75 8·50
The surcharge was for the victims of the Marchfeld floods.

2006. No. 2608 surch **HEILIGENKREUZ NIEDEROSTERRICH** and tree.
2812 55c. on 7c. multicoloured . . 1·10 1·00

2006. Hans Holzl (Falco) (rock musician) Commemoration.
2813 **1402** 55c. multicoloured . . . 1·20 1·10

1403 Naomi Campbell

2006. Life Ball (AIDS charity).
2814 **1403** 75c. multicoloured . . . 1·75 1·50

2006. Customs and Art (24th series). As T **1005**. Multicoloured.
2815 55c. Weitensfeld Kranzlreiten (race) . . . 1·20 1·10

1404 Emblem

2006. Privatization of Post Office.
2816 **1404** 55c. multicoloured . . . 1·20 1·10

1405 Jim Clark

2006. Formula I Motor Racing Legends. Sheet 140 × 185 mm containing T **1405** and similar horiz designs. Multicoloured.
MS2817 55c. × 4, Type **1405**; Jacky Ickx; Jackie Stewart; Alain Prost; 75c. × 2, Stirling Moss; Mario Andretti; 100c. Bruce McLaren; 125c. Jack Brabham . . . . . 12·50 12·50
See also No. **MS**2868.

1406 Saint Hemma

2006.
2818 **1406** 55c. multicoloured . . . 1·20 1·10

1407 Emblem

2006. 60th Anniv of Federal Chamber of Industry and Commerce.
2819 **1407** 55c. silver, vermilion and black . . . . . 1·50 1·40

1408 Mozart

2006. 250th Birth Anniv of Wolfgang Amadeus Mozart (composer and musician). Viva Mozart Exhibition, Salzburg.
2820 **1408** 55c. multicoloured . . . 1·20 1·10

1409 Ottfried Fischer

2006. Ottfried Fischer (actor).
2821 **1409** 55c. multicoloured . . . 1·20 1·10

1410 Figures

2006. Europa. Integration.
2822 **1410** 75c. multicoloured . . . 1·70 1·50

1411 Airbus A310-300

2006. Stamp Day.
2823 **1411** 265c.+130c. multicoloured . . . . 9·00 9·00

1412 St. Anne's Column, Innsbruck

2006.
2824 **1412** 55c. multicoloured . . . 1·20 1·10

1413 K. K. STB Reihe 106 Locomotive

2006. Centenary of Pyhrn Railway.
2825 **1413** 55c. multicoloured . . . 1·20 1·10

1414 Fireworks over Victoria Harbour, Hong Kong

2006. Fireworks. Sheet 146 × 85 mm containing T **1414** and similar horiz design. Multicoloured.
MS2826 €3.75 × 2, Type **1414**; Fireworks over Giant Ferris Wheel, Vienna, Austria . . . . 15·00 15·00
MS2826 has crystals applied to the surface of the stamps and was sold in a folder.
Stamps of a similar design were issued by Hong Kong.

1415 European Lynx (*Lynx lynx*)

2006. Fauna.
2827 **1415** 55c. multicoloured . . . 1·20 1·10

1416 Emblem

2006. WIPA 2008 International Stamp Exhibition.
2828 **1416** 55c.+20c. multicoloured 1·70 1·50

1417 Saint Gebhard

2006. Saints (3rd issue).
2829 **1417** 55c. multicoloured . . . 1·20 1·10

1418 Steyr 220 Motor Car

2006.
2830 **1418** 55c. multicoloured . . . 1·20 1·10

1419 KTM R 125 Tarzan Motorbike

2006.
2831 **1419** 55c. multicoloured . . . 1·20 1·10

1420 Benjamin Raich

2006. Benjamin Raich—World Champion Skier.
2832 **1420** 55c. multicoloured . . . 1·20 1·10

1421 Piano

2006. Musical Instruments. Multicoloured.
2833 55c. Type **1421** . . . . . . 1·20 1·10
2834 55c. Guqin . . . . 1·20 1·10
Stamps of a similar design were issued by China.

1422 "Young Boy" (Cornelia Schlesinger)

2006.
2835 **1422** 55c. multicoloured . . . 1·20 1·10

1423 Alte Saline (salt refinery) and Saint Rupert

1424 "Homo sapiens" (detail) (Valentin Oman)

2006. German and Austrian Philatelic Exhibition, Bad Reichenhall.
2836 **1423** 55c.+20c. multicoloured 1·70 1·50

2006. Modern Art.
2837 **1424** 55c. multicoloured . . . 1·20 1·10

1425 Pond Turtle

1426 Bald Ibis

2006. Self-adhesive.
2838 **1425** 55c. multicoloured . . . 1·20 1·10

2006. Fauna. Multicoloured. Self-adhesive.
2839 55c. Type **1426** . . . . . . 1·20 1·10
2840 55c. Brown bear . . . . . 1·20 1·10

1427 "The Holy Family at Rest" (Franz Weiss)

1428 "Christkindl Pilgrimage Church" (Reinhold Stecher)

2006. Christmas (1st issue).
2841 **1427** 55c. multicoloured . . . 1·20 1·10

2006. Christmas (2nd issue).
2842 **1428** 55c. multicoloured . . . 1·20 1·10

1429 "Ferdinand Square" (T. Chyshkovskii)

2006. 750th Anniv of Lvov.
2843 **1429** 55c. multicoloured . . . 1·20 1·10
A stamp of a similar design was issued by Ukraine.

1430 Michael Schumacher

1430a Michael Schumacher

2006. Michael Schumacher (Formula 1 World Champion–1994/5 and 2000/4).
2844 **1430** 75c. multicoloured . . 1·75 1·75
2844a **1430a** 75c. multicoloured . . 1·75 1·75
No. 2844a has different (incorrect) championship year dates and includes designer and year of issue at lower margin.

1431 "Zinnoberroten Merkur" (No. N13 "Mercury")

2006. Centenary of National Stamp and Coin Dealers' Association.
2845 **1431** 55c. cerise and gold . . 1·20 1·10

1432 Zubin Mehta

2007. Vienna Philharmonic Orchestra's New Year Concert conducted by Zubin Mehta.
2846 **1432** 75c. multicoloured . . . 2·50 2·50

1433 Alpine Flowers

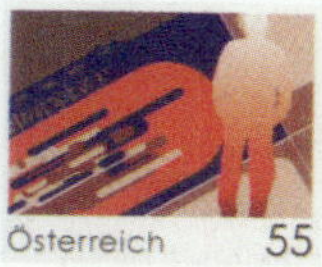

1434 Symbols of Technology and Figure

2007. Flowers. Multicoloured.
2847 55c. Type **1433** . . . . . . 1·25 1·25
2848 75c. Hellebores . . . . . . 2·40 2·40
2849 €1.25 Spring flowers . . . 5·00 5·00

2007. Mankind and Technology. Self-adhesive.
2850 **1434** 55c. multicoloured . . . 1·25 1·25

1435 Fire and Earth

1437 Roe Deer

1436 Outline of Robert Baden-Powell

2007. Lower Austrian Provincial Exhibition.
2851 **1435** 55c. multicoloured . . . 1·25 1·25

2007. Centenary of Scouting. Sheet 170 × 130 mm containing T **1436** and similar horiz designs. Multicoloured.
MS2852 55c. × 4, Type **1436**; Campfire; Tent; Guitar . . . . 5·00 5·00

2007.
2853 **1437** 75c. multicoloured . . . 2·40 2·40

1438 "Portrait of a Lady" (Bernardino Zaganelli da Cottignola)

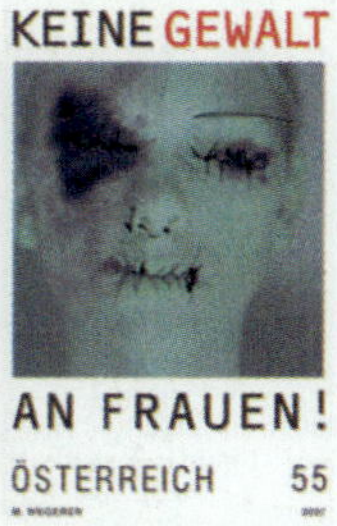

1439 Injured Woman

2007.
2854 **1438** €1.25 multicoloured 5·00 5·00

2007. Stop Violence against Women Campaign.
2855 **1439** 55c. multicoloured . . . 1·25 1·25

1440 Easter Rattles

2007. Traditional Customs.
2856 **1440** 55c. multicoloured . . . 1·25 1·25

1441 Saint Klemens Maria Holbauer

2007. Saints (4th issue).
2857 **1441** 55c. multicoloured . . . 1·25 1·25

1442 Emblem

2007. WIPA 2008 International Stamp Exhibition.
2858 **1442** 55c.+20c. multicoloured 1·75 1·75

1443 Roses

2007. Mourning Stamp. No value expressed.
2859 **1443** (55c.) multicoloured . . 1·25 1·25

1444 Flowers

2007. Greetings Stamp. No value expressed.
2860 **1444** (55c.) multicoloured . . 1·25 1·25

1445 Salamander (*Salamandra salamandra*)

2007. Fauna. Multicoloured. Self-adhesive.
2861 55c. Type **1445** . . . . . . 1·25 1·25
2862 55c. Crayfish (*Astacus astacus*) . . . . 1·25 1·25

1446 Pope Benedict XVI

2007. 80th Birth Anniv of Pope Benedict XVI.
2863 **1446** 100c. multicoloured . . 2·50 2·50

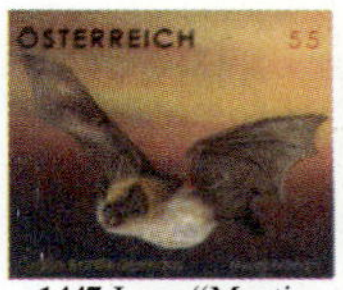

1447 Inscr "Myotis brandtii" 1448 Violet

2007. Whiskered Bat. Self-adhesive.
2864 **1447** 55c. multicoloured . . . 1·25 1·25
No. 2864 is described as "Whiskered Bat", that is Myotis mystacinus but is inscribed "Myotis brandtii", that is Brandt's Bat.

2007.
2865 **1448** 100c. multicoloured . . 2·50 2·20

1449 'The Good Samaritan' (fresco, Franciscan Monastery, Schwaz)

2007. 80th Anniv of Austrian Workers Samaritan Federation (medical assistance organization).
2866 **1449** 55c. multicoloured . . . 1·25 1·25

1450 'Untitled' (painting by Hermann Nitsch) (Illustration reduced. Actual size 60 × 80 mm)

2007. Modern Art. Sheet 61 × 80 mm. Imperf.
MS2867 **1450** 100c. scarlet and black 2·25 2·25

2007. Formula I Motor Racing Legends. Sheet 140 × 185 mm containing horiz designs (size 50 × 32 mm) as T **1405**. Multicoloured.
MS2868 55c. × 8, Phil Hill; Clay Regazzoni; Gerhard Berger; Juan Manuel Fangio; John Surtees; Mika Hakkinen; Graham Hill; Emerson Fittipaldi . . . . . . 10·00 10·00

1451 Krause & Comp Electric Locomotive

2007. Centenary of Mariazell Narrow Gauge Railway.
2869 **1451** 55c. multicoloured . . . 1·25 1·25

1452 Church Facade and Tower

2007. 850th Anniv of Mariazell Basilica.
2870 **1452** 55c. multicoloured . . . 1·25 1·25

1453 Trix and Flix

2007. European Football Championships (Euro 2008), Austria and Switzerland. Sheet 100 × 80 mm containing T **1453** and similar horiz designs. Multicoloured.
MS2871 20c. Type **1453**; 25c. Holding trophy; 30c.Tackling for the ball; 35c.With arms around each other . . . . 2·50 2·50

1454 'Self-portrait' (painting by Angelika Kauffmann)

2007. Modern Art. Sheet 81 × 101 mm.
MS2872 **1454** 210c. scarlet and black 4·75 4·75

1455 *Wien* (steamer) (painting by Harry Heusser)

2007. Stamp Day.
2873 **1455** 265c.+130c. multicoloured . . . . 9·00 9·00

1456 Globe as Scout 1457 Ignaz Pleyel

2007. Europa. Centenary of Scouting.
2874 **1456** 55c. multicoloured . . . 1·25 1·25

2007. 250th Birth Anniv of Ignaz Joseph Pleyel (composer).
2875 **1457** £1 multicoloured . . . 2·25 2·25

1458 Shrek and Fiona 1459 Museum Building

2007. 'Shrek the Third' (animated film).
2876 **1458** 55c. multicoloured . . . 1·25 1·25

2007. Essel Museum. Self-adhesive.
2877 **1459** 55c. multicoloured . . . 1·25 1·25

1460 Wilhelm Kienzl

2007. 150th Birth Anniv of Wilhelm Kienzl (composer).
2878 **1460** 75c. multicoloured . . . 1·90 1·90

1461 U Series Steam Locomotive

2007. Bregenz Forest Railway.
2879 **1461** 75c. multicoloured . . . 1·90 1·90

1462 'Man' (Astrid Bernhart)

2007.
2880 **1462** 55c. multicoloured . . . 1·25 1·25

1463 Dandelion

2007. Flora. Multicoloured.
2881 4c. Type **1463** 25 25
2882 10c. Scottish laburnum . . . 30 30
2883 65c. Gelder rose . . . . . 1·50 1·50
2884 115c. *Gentiana ciliate* . . . 2·40 2·40
2885 140c. Clematis . . . . . . 2·75 2·75

1464 *Haliaeetus albicilla* (white-tailed eagle)

2007.
2886 **1464** 55c. multicoloured . . . 1·25 1·25

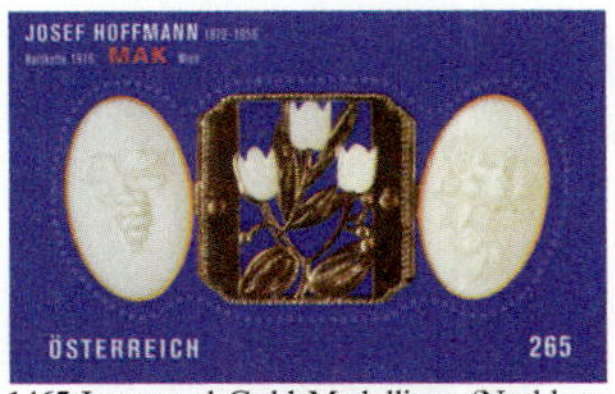

1465 Ivory and Gold Medallions (Necklace, 1916) (½-size illustration)

2007. Josef Hoffman (designer and architect) Commemoration. Sheet 81 × 51 mm. Imperf.
MS2887 **1465** 265c. multicoloured 6·25 6·25

1466 Oil Derrick

2007. 75th Anniv of Austrian Oil Production.
2888 **1466** 75c. multicoloured . . . 1·75 1·75
No. 2888 was impregnated with scent of oil which was released by rubbing part of the design.

1467 Stag and Hind

2007. Birth Bicentenary of Friedrich Gauermann (artist).
2889 **1467** 55c. multicoloured . . . 1·25 1·25

1468 Saint Rupert

2007. Saints (5th issue).
2890 **1468** 55c. multicoloured . . . 1·25 1·25

1469 Niki Hosp

2007. Niki Hosp–Women's World Cup Alpine Ski Champion, 2006–2007.
2891 **1469** 55c. multicoloured . . . 1·25 1·25

1470 *Lucanus cervus* (stag beetle)

1471 Key

2007. Self-adhesive.
2892 **1470** 75c. multicoloured . . . 1·90 1·90

2007. Michel Blumelhuber (iron and steel carver) Commemoration.
2893 **1471** 75c. multicoloured . . . 1·90 1·90

1472 Christiane Horbiger

2007. Christiane Horbiger (actress and recipient of Cross of Honour for Science and Art).
2894 **1472** 55c. multicoloured . . . 1·25 1·25

1473 Scene from 'Queen of Spades' (Peter Illyich Tchaikovsky)

2007. Vienna State Opera Opening Nights (1st issue).
2895 **1473** 55c. multicoloured . . . 1·25 1·25
See also No. 2914.

1474 Nativity (altar painting, Oberwollan)

1475 Clownfish

2007. Christmas. Multicoloured.
2896 55c. Type **1474** . . . . . . 1·25 1·25
2897 65c. Nativity (icon, Church of St. Barbara) . . . . . 1·50 1·50

2007. 50th Anniv of Haus des Meeres (Aqua Terra Zoo).
2898 **1475** 55c. multicoloured . . . 1·25 1·25

1476 Thomas Gottschalk

2007. Thomas Gottschalk and 'Wetten dass?' (TV presenter and game show).
2899 **1476** 65c. multicoloured . . . 1·50 1·50

1477 *Cypripedium calceolus* (lady's slipper orchid)

1478 Vienna

2008.
2900 **1477** 15c. multicoloured . . . 40 40

2008. EURO 2008 Football Championships (1st issue). Venues. Sheet 150 × 90 mm containing T **1478** and similar square designs. Multicoloured.
MS2901 55c. × 4, Type **1478**; Salzburg; Klagenfurt; Innsbruck, 65c. × 4, Zurich; Basel; Bern; Geneva . . . . 11·00 11·00
The stamps of No. **MS**2901 share a common background design.
See also Nos. 2903/4, 2906/7, 2909, 2910, 2917 and 2918.

1479 Emblem and St Stephen's Cathedral

2008. WIPA 2008 International Stamp Exhibition.
2902 **1479** 55c.+20c. multicoloured 1·75 1·75
See also Nos. 2828 and 2858.

1480 Trix and Flix (mascots)

1481 *Portrait of Martina* (Hans Robert Pippal)

2008. EURO 2008 Football Championships (2nd issue). Multicoloured. Self-adhesive.
2903 55c. Type **1480** . . . . . . 1·25 1·25
2904 65c. Emblem . . . . 1·50 1·50

2008. Modern Art.
2905 **1481** 65c. multicoloured . . . 1·50 1·50

1482 Trix and Flix (Alexandra Payer)

2008. EURO 2008 Football Championships (3rd issue). Children's Drawings. Multicoloured.
2906 55c. Type **1482** . . . . . . 1·25 1·25
2907 55c. Footballs as map of Europe (Corina Payr) . . 1·25 1·25

2008. WIPA 2008 International Stamp Exhibition. Gold. Sheet 126 × 73 mm containing triangular designs as T **1479**. Multicoloured.
MS2908 55c. As No. 2828; 55c. As No. 2858; 65c. As No. 2902 . . 4·25 4·25

1483 Map of Europe, Football and Euro Stars (Saskia Puchegger)

2008. EURO 2008 Football Championships (4th issue). Children's Drawings.
2909 **1483** 65c. multicoloured . . . 1·50 1·50

1484 *Defence* (Maria Lassnig)

2008. EURO 2008 Football Championships (5th issue).
2910 **1484** 55c. multicoloured . . . 1·25 1·25

1485 *Hyla arborea* (tree frog)

2008. Fauna. Multicoloured. Self-adhesive.
2911 65c. Type **1485** . . . . . . 1·50 1·50
2912 65c. *Alcedo atthis* (kingfisher) . . . . 1·50 1·50

1486 Aircraft Tail

2008. 50th Anniv of Austrian Airlines.
2913 **1486** 140c. multicoloured . . 1·60 1·60
No. 2913 includes an area, which when scratched, could win a prize.

1487 Scene from *La Forza del Destino* (Giuseppe Verdi)

2008. Vienna State Opera Opening Nights (2nd issue).
2914 **1487** 55c. multicoloured . . . 1·25 1·25

1488 *Princess Marie Franziska von Liechtenstein* (Friedrich von Amerling)

2008.
2915 **1488** 125c. multicoloured . . 1·40 1·40
A stamp of a similar design was issued by Liechtenstein.

1489 Imaginary Landscape

2008. Modern Art. Sysanne Sculler (Soshana).
2916 **1489** 55c. multicoloured . . . 1·25 1·25

1490 Football

2008. EURO 2008 Football Championships (6th issue). Self-adhesive.
2917 **1490** 375c. multicoloured . . 3·75 3·75
No. 2917 is made from a synthetic mixture containing polyurethane, as the original ball used for the EURO 2008 (known as the 'Europass').

1491 Football Field, Ball and Player's Legs

2008. EURO 2008 Football Championships (7th issue).
2918 **1491** 55c. multicoloured . . . 1·25 1·25

1492 Lindwurm (symbol of Klagenfurt) on Football and Karawanken Mountains (Bolona Jencic)

2008. EURO 2008 Football Championships (8th issue). Children's Drawings.
2919 **1492** 125c. multicoloured . . 2·40 2·40

1493 View from River

2008. World Heritage Site. Wachau.
2920 **1493** 100c. multicoloured . . 2·25 2·25

1494 Austrian and Swiss Flags, Alps and Turf (Stefan Gritsch)

2008. EURO 2008 Football Championships (9th issue). Children's Drawings.
2921 **1494** 55c. multicoloured . . . 1·25 1·25

1495 Football wearing Lederhosen (Vanessa Schennach)

2008. EURO 2008 Football Championships (10th issue). Children's Drawings.
2922 **1495** 100c. multicoloured . . 2·25 2·25

IMPERIAL JOURNAL STAMPS

J 18

J 21 Arms of Austria

J 22 Arms of Austria

1853. Imperf.
J67 1k. blue . . . . 34·00 1·80
J15 2k. green . . . . £2250 70·00
J68 2k. brown . . . . 26·00 2·00
J32 4k. brown £550 £1400
The 2k. green has different corner ornaments.

For similar values in black or red, see Lombardy and Venetia Imperial Journal stamps, Nos. J22/4.

1890. Imperf.

J76	J 21	1k. brown	14·00	1·70
J77		2k. green	13·00	2·50

1890. Perf.

J78	J 22	25k. red	£120	£250

NEWSPAPER STAMPS

N 2 Mercury

N 8 Francis Joseph I

N 11 Francis Joseph I

1851. Imperf.

N11b	N 2	(0.6k.) blue	£200	£130
N12		(6k.) yellow	£29000	£9500
N13		(6k.) red	£49000	£78000
N14		(30k.) red	£25000	£14000

1858. Imperf.

N28	N 8	(1k.05) blue	£700	£750
N29		(1k.05) lilac	£950	£375

1861. Imperf.

N38	N 11	(1k.05) grey	£200	£190

N 13 Arms of Austria

AHN 17 Mercury

N 19 Mercury

1863. Imperf.

N44	N 13	(1k.05) lilac	55·00	19·00

1867. Imperf.

AHN58b	AHN 17	(1k.) lilac	60	40

1880. Imperf.

N69	N 19	½k. green	11·50	1·50

N 31 Mercury

N 43 Mercury

1899. Imperf.

N122	N 31	2h. blue	20	15
N123		6h. orange	2·50	2·50
N124		10h. brown	1·60	1·20
N125		20h. pink	1·70	2·30

1908. Imperf.

N207c	N 43	2h. blue	1·30	20
N208c		6h. orange	5·50	70
N209c		10h. red	5·50	70
N210c		20h. brown	5·50	50

N 53 Mercury

N 54 Mercury

1916. Imperf.

N266	N 53	2h. brown	20	35
N267		4h. green	45	1·90
N268		6h. blue	40	2·30
N269		10h. orange	90	2·30
N270		30h. red	45	2·40

1916. For Express. Perf.

N271	N 54	2h. red on yellow	1·00	3·75
N272		5h. green on yellow	1·00	3·75

N 61 Mercury

N 68 Mercury

1917. For Express. Perf.

N294	N 61	2h. red on yellow	30	50
N295		5h. green on yellow	30	50

1919. Optd **Deutschosterreich**. Imperf.

N318	N 53	2h. brown	10	30
N319		4h. green	40	1·50
N320		6h. blue	20	1·50
N321		10h. orange	40	1·60
N322		30h. red	20	95

1919. For Express. Optd **Deutschosterreich**. Perf.

N334	N 61	2h. red on yellow	10	25
N335		5h. green on yellow	10	25

1920. Imperf.

N365	N 68	2h. violet	15	20
N366		4h. brown	15	30
N367		5h. slate	15	20
N368		6h. blue	15	20
N369		8h. green	15	40
N370		9h. bistre	15	20
N371		10h. red	15	20
N372		12h. blue	15	50
N373		15h. mauve	15	25
N374		18h. turquoise	15	35
N375		20h. orange	15	35
N376		30h. brown	15	20
N377		45h. green	15	70
N378		60h. red	25	25
N379		72h. brown	35	70
N380		90h. violet	35	95
N381		1k.20 red	35	1·00
N382		2k.40 green	35	1·00
N383		3k. grey	35	60

1921. For Express. No. N334 surch **50 50**.

N450	N 61	50 on 2h. red on yell	20	40

N 78 Mercury

N 79 Posthorn and Arrow

1921. Imperf.

N452	N 78	45h. grey	20	40
N453		75h. red	20	70
N454		1k.50 green	20	90
N455		1k.80 blue	20	1·10
N456		2k.25 brown	30	1·40
N457		3k. green	30	95
N458		6k. purple	30	1·20
N459		7k.50 brown	50	1·70

1921. For Express. Perf.

N460	N 79	50h. lilac on yellow	30	1·90

POSTAGE DUE STAMPS

D 26

D 44

1894. Perf.

D 96	D 26	1k. brown	2·75	1·50
D 97		2k. brown	3·75	3·00
D 98		3k. brown	4·25	1·50
D 99		5k. brown	4·25	75
D100		6k. brown	3·50	6·75
D101		7k. brown	1·60	6·50
D102		10k. brown	4·50	90
D103		20k. brown	1·50	7·25
D104		50k. brown	46·00	75·00

1899. As Type D 26, but value in heller. Perf or imperf.

D126	D 26	1h. brown	50	30
D127		2h. brown	50	35
D128		3h. brown	50	30
D129		4h. brown	1·00	50
D130		5h. brown	85	45
D131		6h. brown	70	30
D132		10h. brown	80	30
D133		12h. brown	85	90
D134		15h. brown	1·30	1·10
D135		20h. brown	1·90	60
D136		40h. brown	2·75	80
D137		100h. brown	21·00	2·40

1908. Perf.

D210b	D 44	1h. red	1·00	1·90
D211c		2h. red	35	40
D212c		4h. red	30	25
D213c		6h. red	30	30
D214c		10h. red	50	25
D215c		14h. red	5·25	2·75
D216c		20h. red	10·50	20
D217c		25h. red	9·50	6·25
D218c		30h. red	10·00	40
D219c		50h. red	23·00	50
D220c		100h. red	25·00	80
D221c		5k. violet	95·00	16·00
D222c		10k. violet	£300	4·75

D 55

D 56

1916.

D273	D 55	5h. red	10	20
D274		10h. red	10	20
D275		15h. red	10	20
D276		20h. red	10	20
D277		25h. red	20	1·30
D278		30h. red	20	50
D279		40h. red	20	60
D280		50h. red	1·20	2·40
D281	D 56	1k. blue	30	50
D282		5k. blue	3·00	4·00
D283		10k. blue	3·50	1·90

1916. Nos. 189/90 optd **PORTO** or surch **15 15** also.

D284		1h. black	10	20
D285		15 on 2h. violet	30	60

1917. Unissued stamps as T **50** surch **PORTO** and value.

D286	50	10 on 24h. blue	2·10	70
D287		15 on 36h. violet	60	20
D288		20 on 54h. orange	40	50
D289		50 on 42h. brown	40	40

The above differ from Type **50** by showing a full-face portrait.

1919. Optd **Deutschosterreich**.

D323	D 55	5h. red	15	20
D324		10h. red	15	20
D325		15h. red	30	60
D326		20h. red	30	50
D327		25h. red	10·50	24·00
D328		30h. red	15	40
D329		40h. red	30	95
D330		50h. red	30	1·90
D331	D 56	1k. blue	5·75	14·50
D332		5k. blue	11·50	14·50
D333		10k. blue	13·50	4·50

D 69

D 70

1920. Imperf or perf (D **69**), perf (D **70**).

D384	D 69	5h. pink	20	40
D385		10h. pink	20	30
D386		15h. pink	20	1·60
D387		20h. pink	20	40
D388		25h. pink	30	1·60
D389		30h. pink	20	40
D390		40h. pink	20	35
D391		50h. pink	20	40
D392		80h. pink	20	50
D393A	D 70	1k. blue	20	40
D394A		1½k. blue	20	40
D395A		2k. blue	20	40
D396A		3k. blue	25	95
D397A		4k. blue	20	1·10
D398A		5k. blue	20	50
D399A		8k. blue	50	1·20
D400A		10k. blue	50	50
D401A		20k. blue	1·00	1·90

1921. No. 343a surch **Nachmarke 7½ K.** Perf.

D451	64	7½k. on 15h. brown	20	30

D 83

D 86

1921.

D510	D 83	1k. brown	20	40
D511		2k. brown	20	50
D512		4k. brown	20	85
D513		5k. brown	20	40
D514		7½k. brown	25	1·10
D515	–	10k. blue	20	50
D516	–	15k. blue	25	70
D517	–	20k. blue	25	75
D518	–	50k. blue	20	70

The 10k. to 50k. are larger (22 × 30 mm).

1922.

D526	D 83	10k. turquoise	25	60
D527		15k. turquoise	20	90
D528		20k. turquoise	25	70
D529		25k. turquoise	20	1·50
D530		40k. turquoise	20	50
D531		50k. turquoise	25	1·60
D532	D 86	100k. purple	15	20
D533		150k. purple	15	20
D534		200k. purple	15	20
D535		400k. purple	15	20
D536		600k. purple	30	60
D537		800k. purple	20	20
D538		1000k. purple	20	20
D539		1200k. purple	2·50	4·75
D540		1500k. purple	40	50
D541		1800k. purple	5·25	12·50
D542		2000k. purple	85	1·20
D543		3000k. purple	12·50	27·00
D544		4000k. purple	10·50	21·00
D545		6000k. purple	16·00	36·00

D 94

D 120

1925.

D589	D 94	1g. red	15	15
D590		2g. red	15	15
D591		3g. red	20	15
D592		4g. red	20	15
D593		5g. red	15	10
D594		6g. red	35	50
D595		8g. red	35	25
D596		10g. blue	35	10
D597		12g. blue	20	15
D598		14g. blue	20	15
D599		15g. blue	15	10
D600		16g. blue	40	20
D601		18g. blue	1·60	4·00
D602		20g. blue	35	10
D603		23g. blue	1·00	20
D604		24g. blue	3·00	15
D605		28g. blue	2·50	30
D606		30g. blue	85	15
D607		31g. blue	3·00	30
D608		35g. blue	3·50	20
D609		39g. blue	3·75	15
D610		40g. blue	2·50	2·75
D611		60g. blue	1·80	2·20
D612	–	1s. green	5·25	1·50
D613	–	2s. green	36·00	4·50
D614	–	5s. green	£150	49·00
D615	–	10s. green	55·00	5·25

DESIGN: 1 to 10s. Horiz bands of colour.

1935.

D746	D 120	1g. red	20	20
D747		2g. red	30	25
D748		3g. red	20	20
D749		5g. red	20	20
D750	–	10g. blue	20	20
D751	–	12g. blue	20	15
D752	–	15g. blue	35	60
D753	–	20g. blue	40	20
D754	–	24g. blue	80	20
D755	–	30g. blue	80	20
D756	–	39g. blue	1·00	20
D757	–	60g. blue	1·10	1·30
D758	–	1s. green	2·10	40
D759	–	2s. green	5·25	1·20
D760	–	5s. green	8·25	5·25
D761	–	10s. green	12·50	80

DESIGNS: 10 to 60g. As Type D **120** but with background of horizontal lines; 1 to 10s. As last, but with positions of figures, arms and inscriptions reversed.

D 143

D 162

1945.

D891	D 143	1pf. red	15	20
D892		2pf. red	15	20
D893		3pf. red	15	20
D894		5pf. red	15	20
D895		10pf. red	15	20
D896		12pf. red	15	25
D897		20pf. red	15	25
D898		24pf. red	15	40
D899		30pf. red	15	50
D900		60pf. red	15	45
D901		1rm. violet	15	50
D902		2rm. violet	15	90
D903		5rm. violet	20	95
D904		10rm. violet	20	1·20

1946. Optd **PORTO**.

D956	145	3g. orange	10	15
D957		5g. green	10	15
D958		6g. purple	10	15
D959		8g. red	10	15
D960		10g. grey	10	25
D961		12g. brown	10	15
D962		15g. red	10	20
D963		20g. brown	10	15
D964		25g. blue	10	20
D965		30g. mauve	10	15
D966		40g. blue	10	25
D967		60g. green	10	25
D968		1s. violet	15	30
D969		2s. yellow	60	1·20
D970		5s. blue	60	90

1947.

D1035	D 162	1g. brown	15	45
D1036		2g. brown	15	45
D1037		3g. brown	15	45
D1038		5g. brown	15	15
D1039		8g. brown	15	35
D1040		10g. brown	15	15
D1041		12g. brown	15	15
D1042		15g. brown	15	35
D1043		16g. brown	45	1·00
D1044		17g. brown	35	1·00
D1045		18g. brown	35	1·20
D1046		20g. brown	95	20
D1047		24g. brown	40	1·20
D1048		30g. brown	15	30
D1049		36g. brown	85	1·60
D1050		40g. brown	15	15
D1051		42g. brown	1·00	1·50
D1052		48g. brown	1·00	1·50
D1053		50g. brown	85	20
D1054		60g. brown	25	60
D1055		70g. brown	15	30
D1056		80g. brown	4·75	2·50
D1057		1s. blue	15	15
D1058		1s.15 blue	4·25	40
D1059		1s.20 blue	4·25	1·60
D1060		2s. blue	40	30
D1061		5s. blue	45	30
D1062		10s. blue	50	40

D 184

D 817

1949.

D1178 D 184 1g. red 20 15
D1179 2g. red 25 20
D1180 4g. red 50 50
D1181 5g. red . . . . . . 2·10 55
D1182 8g. red . . . . . . 2·50 2·50
D1183 10g. red 40 15
D1184 20g. red 40 15
D1185 30g. red 40 15
D1186 40g. red 20 15
D1187 50g. red 40 15
D1188 60g. red . . . . . . 13·00 70
D1189 63g. red . . . . . . 5·50 5·00
D1190 70g. red 40 15
D1191 80g. red 40 45
D1192 90g. red 45 45
D1193 1s. violet 80 20
D1194 1s.20 violet 75 60
D1195 1s.35 violet 45 35
D1196 1s.40 violet 75 55
D1197 1s.50 violet 75 20
D1198 1s.65 violet 75 60
D1199 1s.70 violet 60 60
D1200 2s. violet 95 20
D1201 2s.50 violet 85 20
D1202 3s. violet 85 30
D1203 4s. violet . . . . . 1·20 1·50
D1204 5s. violet . . . . . 2·00 30
D1205 10s. violet . . . . . 2·10 30

1985.

D2074 D 817 10g. yellow & black 15 15
D2075 20g. red and black 15 15
D2076 50g. orange & black 15 30
D2077 1s. blue and black 20 45
D2078 2s. brown and black 35 60
D2079 3s. violet and black 45 75
D2080 5s. yellow & black 1·00 1·00
D2081 10s. green & black 1·70 1·50

AUSTRIAN TERRITORIES ACQUIRED BY ITALY Pt. 2

Italian territory acquired from Austria at the close of the war of 1914–18, including Trentino and Trieste.

1918. 100 heller = 1 krone.
1918. 100 centesimi = 1 lira.
1919. 100 centesimi = 1 corona.

TRENTINO

1918. Stamps of Austria optd **Regno d'Italia Trentino 3 nov 1918.**

1 49 3h. purple . . . . 1·90 2·10
2 5h. green . . . . 1·50 1·50
3 6h. orange . . . . 30·00 25·00
4 10h. red . . . . 2·00 1·50
5 12h. green . . . . 85·00 80·00
6 60 15h. brown . . . . 2·50 2·50
7 20h. green . . . . 1·50 1·75
8 25h. blue . . . . 23·00 21·00
9 30h. violet . . . . 6·75 6·75
10 51 40h. green . . . . 32·00 32·00
11 50h. green . . . . 18·00 17·00
12 60h. blue . . . . 23·00 25·00
13 80h. brown . . . . 35·00 40·00
14 90h. red £850 £850
15 1k. red on yellow . . . . 35·00 38·00
16 52 2k. blue £180 £190
17 4k. green £1400 £1300
18 10k. violet £65000

1918. Stamps of Italy optd **Venezia Tridentina.**

19 30 1c. brown . . . . 40 1·25
20 31 2c. brown . . . . 40 1·25
21 37 5c. green . . . . 70 1·25
22 10c. red . . . . 70 1·25
23 41 20c. orange . . . . 1·10 1·90
24 39 40c. brown . . . . 35·00 35·00
25 33 45c. olive . . . . 17·00 24·00
26 39 50c. mauve . . . . 21·00 26·00
27 34 1l. brown and green . . . . 21·00 26·00

1919. Stamps of Italy surch **Venezia Tridentina** and value.

28 37 5h. on 5c. green . . . . . 70 1·10
29 10h. on 10c. red . . . . . 70 1·10
30 41 20h. on 20c. orange . . . . 70 1·10

VENEZIA GIULIA

For use in Trieste and territory, Gorizia and province, and in Istria.

1918. Stamps of Austria optd **Regno d'Italia Venezia Giulia 3. XI. 18.**

31 49 3h. purple 90 90
32 5h. green 90 90
33 6h. orange . . . . 1·10 1·10
34 10h. red 55 55
35 12h. green . . . . 1·10 1·10
36 60 15h. brown 55 55
37 20h. green 55 55
38 25h. blue . . . . 3·50 3·50
39 30h. purple . . . . 1·50 1·50
40 51 40h. green . . . . 40·00 60·00
41 50h. green . . . . 2·10 3·00
42 60h. blue . . . . 11·00 11·00
43 80h. brown . . . . 3·50 5·50
44 1k. red on yellow . . . . 3·50 6·75
45 52 2k. blue . . . . 85·00 £110
46 3k. red £140 £160
47 4k. green £210 £250
48 10k. violet £23000 £24000

1918. Stamps of Italy optd **Venezia Giulia.**

49 30 1c. brown . . . . 55 1·00
50 31 2c. brown . . . . 55 1·00
51 37 5c. green 55 55
52 10c. red 55 55
53 41 20c. orange 55 55
54 39 25c. blue 55 55
55 40c. brown . . . . 4·25 5·50
56 33 45c. green . . . . 75 1·25
57 39 50c. mauve . . . . 1·75 2·50
58 60c. red . . . . 27·00 30·00
59 34 1l. brown and green . . . . 14·00 14·00

1919. Stamps of Italy surch **Venezia Giulia** and value.

60 37 5h. on 5c. green 90 90
61 41 20h. on 20c. orange 70 70

EXPRESS LETTER STAMPS

1919. Express Letter stamp of Italy optd **Venezia Giulia.**

E60 E 35 25c. red . . . . 21·00 23·00

POSTAGE DUE STAMPS

1918. Postage Due Stamps of Italy optd **Venezia Giulia.**

D60 D 12 5c. mauve and orange 15 55
D61 10c. mauve & orange 15 55
D62 20c. mauve & orange 70 1·10
D63 30c. mauve & orange 1·50 1·90
D64 40c. mauve & orange 14·00 16·00
D65 50c. mauve & orange 35·00 45·00
D66 1l. mauve and blue . . £110 £120

GENERAL ISSUE

For use throughout the liberated area of Trentino, Venezia Giulia and Dalmatia.

1919. Stamps of Italy surch in new currency.

62 30 1ce. di cor on 1c. brown . . 90 90
64 31 2ce. di cor on 2c. brown . . 90 90
65 37 5ce. di cor on 5c. green . . 90 90
67 10ce. di cor on 10c. red . . 90 90
68 41 20ce. di cor on 20c. orange 90 90
70 39 25ce. di cor on 25c. blue . . 90 90
71 40ce. di cor on 40c. brown 90 90
72 33 45ce. di cor on 45c. green 90 90
73 39 50ce. di cor on 50c. mauve 90 90
74 60ce. di cor on 60c. red . . 90 1·50
75 34 1cor. on 1l. brown & green 90 1·50
76 una corona on 1l. brn & grn 2·00 5·50
82 5cor. on 5l. blue and red . . 21·00 25·00
83 10cor. on 10l. green & red 21·00 25·00

EXPRESS LETTER STAMPS

1919. Express Letter stamps of Italy surch in new currency.

E76 E 35 25ce. di cor on 25c. red 70 1·10
E77 E 41 30ce. di cor on 30c. red and blue . . . . . . 70 1·10

POSTAGE DUE STAMPS

1919. Postage Due stamps of Italy surch in new currency.

D76 D 12 5ce. di cor on 5c. mauve and orange . . 40 90
D77 10ce. di cor. on 10c. mauve and orange . . 40 90
D78 20ce. di cor on 20c. mauve and orange . . 40 90
D79 30ce. di cor on 30c. mauve and orange . . 40 90
D80 40ce. di cor on 40c. mauve and orange . . 40 90
D81 50ce. di cor on 50c. mauve and orange . . 40 90
D82 una corona on 1l. mauve and blue . . . 40 1·50
D86 1cor. on 1l. mve & blue 3·00 3·50
D83 due corona on 2l. mauve and blue . . . 35·00 48·00
D87 2cor. on 2l. mve & blue 17·00 26·00
D84 cinque corona on 5l. mauve and blue . . . 35·00 45·00
D88 5cor. on 5l. mve & blue 18·00 26·00

AUSTRO-HUNGARIAN MILITARY POST Pt. 2

A. GENERAL ISSUES

100 heller = 1 krone.

1915. Stamps of Bosnia and Herzegovina optd **K.U.K. FELDPOST.**

1 25 1h. olive 40 80
2 2h. blue 40 80
3 3h. lake 40 80
4 5h. green 40 40
5 6h. black 40 80
6 10h. red 25 45
7 12h. olive . . . . 40 1·00
8 20h. brown 50 75
9 25h. blue . . . . 50 1·00
10 30h. red . . . . 2·75 9·50
11 26 35h. green . . . . 1·90 7·00
12 40h. violet . . . . 1·90 7·00
13 45h. brown . . . . 1·90 7·00
14 50h. blue . . . . 1·90 7·00
15 60h. purple . . . . 50 4·00
16 72h. blue . . . . 2·00 7·25
17 25 1k. brown on cream . . . . 2·00 6·75
18 2k. indigo on blue . . . . 2·00 7·50
19 26 3k. red on green . . . . . 21·00 60·00
20 5k. lilac on grey . . . . . 18·00 55·00
21 10k. blue on grey £170 £375

2 Francis Joseph

1915.

22 2 1h. green 15 25
23 2h. blue 10 30
24 3h. red 15 25
25 5h. green 15 25
26 6h. black 15 35
27 10h. red 15 25
28 10h. blue 10 30
29 12h. green 15 40
30 15h. red 15 20
31 20h. brown 25 50
32 20h. green 25 60
33 25h. blue 15 30
34 30h. red 20 60
35 35h. green 25 85
36 40h. violet 25 85
37 45h. brown 25 85
38 50h. deep green 25 85
39 60h. purple 30 85
40 72h. blue 35 85
41 80h. brown 25 35
42 90h. red . . . . 65 1·90
43 – 1k. purple on cream . . . . 1·25 3·75
44 – 2k. green on blue . . . . . 90 1·75
45 – 3k. red on green . . . . . 70 1·00
46 – 4k. violet on grey . . . . . 70 1·00
47 – 5k. violet on grey . . . . . 21·00 25·00
48 – 10k. blue on grey . . . . . 2·75 10·50

The kronen values are larger, with profile portrait.

1917. As 1917 issue of Bosnia, but inscr "K.u.K. FELDPOST".

49 1h. blue 90 20
50 2h. orange 90 20
51 3h. grey 90 20
52 5h. green 90 20
53 6h. violet 15 25
54 10h. brown 10 20
55 12h. blue 15 20
56 15h. red 15 20
57 20h. brown 15 20
58 25h. blue 20 45
59 30h. grey 15 20
60 40h. bistre 15 20
61 50h. green 10 20
62 60h. red 15 30
63 80h. blue 15 20
64 90h. purple 25 85
65 2k. red on buff 15 25
66 3k. green on blue . . . . . 70 2·10
67 4k. red on green . . . . . 14·50 26·00
68 10k. violet on grey . . . . . 1·10 7·50

The kronen values are larger and the border is different.

1918. Imperial and Royal Welfare Fund. As 1918 issue of Bosnia, but inscr "K. UND K. FELDPOST".

69 40 10h. (+10h.) green 25 90
70 – 20h. (+10h.) red 25 90
71 40 45h. (+10h.) blue 25 90

NEWSPAPER STAMPS

N 4 Mercury

1916.

N49 N 4 2h. blue 15 30
N50 6h. orange . . . . 35 1·40
N51 10h. red . . . . 60 1·40
N52 20h. brown . . . . 75 1·40

B. ISSUES FOR ITALY

100 centesimi = 1 lira.

1918. General Issue stamps of 1917 surch in figs and words.

1 2c. on 1h. blue 10 25
2 3c. on 2h. orange 10 25
3 4c. on 3h. grey 10 25
4 6c. on 5h. green 10 25
5 7c. on 6h. violet 10 25
6 11c. on 10h. brown 10 25
7 13c. on 12h. blue 10 25
8 16c. on 15h. red 10 25
9 22c. on 20h. brown 10 25
10 27c. on 25h. blue 30 65
11 32c. on 30h. grey 10 50
12 43c. on 40h. bistre 15 55
13 53c. on 50h. green 15 30
14 64c. on 60h. red 20 65
15 85c. on 80h. blue 15 35
16 95c. on 90h. purple 15 35
17 2l.11 on 2k. red on buff . . . 25 55
18 3l.16 on 3k. green on blue . . 60 1·40
19 4l.22 on 4k. red on green . . . 75 1·60

NEWSPAPER STAMPS

1918. Newspaper stamps of General Issue surch in figs and words.

N20 N 4 3c. on 2h. blue 15 40
N21 7c. on 6h. orange . . . 35 1·00
N22 11c. on 10h. red 35 95
N23 22c. on 20h. brown . . . 30 95

1918. For Express. Newspaper stamps of Bosnia surch in figs and words.

N24 N 35 3c. on 2h. red on yell 5·50 11·50
N25 6c. on 5h. green on yell 5·50 11·50

POSTAGE DUE STAMPS

1918. Postage Due stamps of Bosnia surch in figs and words.

D20 D 35 6c. on 5h. red . . . . 3·50 5·50
D21 11c. on 10h. red . . . . 2·10 4·50
D22 16c. on 15h. red . . . . 80 2·25
D23 27c. on 25h. red . . . . 80 2·25
D24 32c. on 30h. red . . . . 80 2·25
D25 43c. on 40h. red . . . . 80 2·25
D26 53c. on 50h. red . . . . 80 2·25

C. ISSUES FOR MONTENEGRO

100 heller = 1 krone.

1917. Nos. 28 and 30 of General Issues optd **K.U.K. MILIT. VERWALTUNG MONTENEGRO.**

1 2 10h. blue . . . . 9·50 9·00
2 15h. red . . . . 11·50 9·00

D. ISSUES FOR ROMANIA

100 bani = 1 leu.

1917. General Issue stamps of 1917 optd **BANI** or **LEI.**

1 3b. grey . . . . 1·90 2·40
2 5b. green . . . . 1·90 2·00
3 6b. violet . . . . 1·90 1·90
4 10b. brown 15 75
5 12b. blue . . . . 1·10 1·50
6 15b. red . . . . 1·10 1·90
7 20b. brown 15 75
8 25b. blue 15 30
9 30b. grey 40 65
10 40b. bistre 15 65
11 50b. green 40 70
12 60b. red 40 70
13 80b. blue 15 45
14 90b. purple 40 65
15 2l. red on buff 50 90
16 3l. green on blue . . . . . 65 1·10
17 4l. red on green . . . . . . 65 1·10

3 Charles I

1918.

18 3 3b. grey 15 70
19 5b. green 15 55
20 6b. violet 20 45
21 10b. brown 25 60
22 12b. blue 20 60
23 15b. red 20 50
24 20b. brown 20 45
25 25b. blue 20 45
26 30b. grey 20 45
27 40b. bistre 20 45
28 50b. green 25 60
29 60b. red 25 65
30 80b. blue 15 50
31 90b. purple 25 75
32 2l. red on buff 25 90
33 3l. green on blue 35 90
34 4l. red on green . . . . . . 40 1·00

E. ISSUES FOR SERBIA

100 heller = 1 krone.

1916. Stamps of Bosnia optd **SERBIEN.**

22 25 1h. olive . . . . 2·00 3·50
23 2h. blue . . . . 2·00 3·50
24 3h. lake . . . . 1·90 3·25
25 5h. green 25 75
26 6h. black . . . . 1·25 2·10
27 10h. red 25 70
28 12h. olive . . . . 1·25 2·10
29 20h. brown . . . . 65 1·40
30 25h. blue . . . . 65 1·25
31 30h. red . . . . 65 1·25
32 26 35h. green . . . . 65 1·25
33 40h. violet . . . . 65 1·25
34 45h. brown . . . . 65 1·25
35 50h. blue . . . . 65 1·25
36 60h. brown . . . . 65 1·25
37 72h. blue . . . . 65 1·25
38 25 1k. brown on cream . . . . 70 1·50
39 2k. indigo on blue . . . . 70 1·50
40 26 3k. red on green . . . . . 70 1·60
41 5k. lilac on grey . . . . . 1·00 1·25
42 10k. blue on grey . . . . . 10·25 25·00

AUSTRO-HUNGARIAN POST OFFICES IN THE TURKISH EMPIRE Pt. 2

Various Austro-Hungarian P.O.s in the Turkish Empire. Such offices had closed by 15 December 1914 except for several in Albania which remained open until 1915.

A. LOMBARDY AND VENETIA CURRENCY

100 soldi = 1 florin.

1

2

3

1867.

1	1	2s. yellow	1·50	29·00
9		3s. green	95	24·00
10		5s. red	35	17·00
11		10s. blue	95·00	1·20
5		15s. brown	24·00	7·00
6		25s. lilac	25·00	37·00
7a	2	50s. brown	1·10	60·00

1883.

14	3	2s. black and brown	15	30
15		3s. black and green	1·10	2·75
16		5s. black and red	15	50
17		10s. black and blue	65	50
18		20s. black and grey	5·50	8·00
19		50s. black and mauve	90	18·00

B. TURKISH CURRENCY

40 paras = 1 piastre.

1886. Surch **10 PARA 10**.

21a	3	10p. on 3s. green	60	9·00

1888. Nos. 71/75a of Austria surch.

22	20	10pa. on 3k. green	3·00	6·00
23		20pa. on 5k. red	60	4·50
24		1pi. on 10k. blue	36·00	1·20
25		2pi. on 20k. grey	1·80	3·00
26		5pi. on 50k. purple	3·00	12·00

1890. Stamps of Austria of 1890, the kreuzer values with lower figures of value removed, surch at foot.

27	23	8pa. on 2k. brown	15	50
28		10pa. on 3k. green	45	50
29		20pa. on 5k. red	20	50
30		1pi. on 10k. blue	30	15
31		2pi. on 20k. olive	5·25	26·00
32		5pi. on 50k. mauve	8·00	65·00
33	24	10pi. on 1g. blue	9·50	33·00
37		10pi. on 1g. lilac	11·00	22·00
34		20pi. on 2g. red	11·50	50·00
38		20pi. on 2g. green	35·00	65·00

1890. Stamps of Austria of 1891, with lower figures of value removed, surch at foot.

35	25	2pi. on 20k. green	4·50	1·30
36		5pi. on 50k. mauve	2·10	2·75

1900. Stamps of Austria of 1899, the heller values with lower figures of value removed, surch at foot.

46	27	10pa. on 5h. green	3·25	1·40
40	28	20pa. on 10h. red	4·50	65
48		1pi. on 25h. blue	2·40	40
49	29	2pi. on 50h. blue	4·25	1·40
43d	30	5pi. on 1k. red	1·40	20
44d		10pi. on 2k. lavender	2·40	1·60
45d		20pi. on 4k. green	2·50	3·50

1903. Stamps of Austria of 1899, with all figures of value removed, surch at top and at foot.

55	27	10pa. green	50	1·60
56	28	20pa. red	80	80
57		30pa. mauve	50	3·50
58		1pi. blue	60	30
59	29	2pi. blue	60	80

11 Francis Joseph I

12 Francis Joseph I

1908. 60th Anniv of Emperor's Accession.

60	11	10pa. green on yellow	15	30
61		20pa. red on pink	20	30
62		30pa. brown on buff	30	50
63		60pa. purple on blue	50	3·25
70		1pi. ultramarine on blue	30	50
65	12	2pi. red on yellow	15	15
66		5pi. brown on grey	50	80
67		10pi. green on yellow	90	1·60
68		20pi. blue on grey	1·70	3·25

POSTAGE DUE STAMPS

1902. Postage Due stamps as Type D 32 of Austria, but with value in heller, surch with new value.

D50	D 32	10pa. on 5h. green	1·10	2·50
D51		20pa. on 10h. green	1·50	3·25
D52		1pi. on 20h. green	2·75	4·00
D53		2pi. on 40h. green	2·75	4·00
D54		5pi. on 100h. green	3·75	2·75

D 13

1908.

D71A	D 13	¼pi. green	2·50	8·75
D72A		½pi. green	1·60	8·00
D73A		1pi. green	1·80	7·25
D74A		1½pi. green	95	19·00
D75A		2pi. green	1·50	16·00
D76A		5pi. green	1·80	11·50
D77A		10pi. green	15·00	£120
D78A		20pi. green	10·50	£140
D79A		30pi. green	15·00	13·00

C. FRENCH CURRENCY

100 centimes = 1 franc.

1903. Stamps of Austria surch **CENTIMES** or **FRANC**.

F1	27	5c. on 5h. green and black	1·50	5·75
F2	28	10c. on 10h. red and black (No. 143)	1·20	6·25
F3		25c. on 25h. blue and black (No. 145)	35·00	35·00
F4	29	50c. on 50h. blue and black	16·00	£225
F5	30	1f. on 1k. red	1·50	£160
F6		2f. on 2k. lilac	10·50	£375
F7		4f. on 4k. green	11·00	£650

1904. Stamps of Austria surch **CENTIMES**.

F14	33	5c. on 5h. green	2·20	3·00
F13	28	10c. on 10h. red and black (No. 160)	65	5·75
F10		25c. on 25h. blue and black (No. 176)	60	39·00
F11	35	50c. on 50h. blue	1·10	£180

1906. Type of Austria surch **CENTIMES**.

F15	28	10c. on 10h. red (No. 184)	1·20	46·00
F16		15c. on 15h. violet and black (as No. 185)	90	42·00

No. F16 was not issued without the surch.

1908. 60th Anniv of Emperor's Accession. As T **11/12** but in centimes or franc.

F17	11	5c. green on yellow	20	1·10
F18		10c. red on pink	45	1·40
F19		15c. brown on buff	60	7·75
F20		25c. blue on blue	17·00	7·00
F21	12	50c. red on yellow	2·75	38·00
F22		1f. brown on grey	3·50	55·00

AZERBAIJAN Pt. 10

Formerly part of the Russian Empire. Became independent on 27 May 1918, following the Russian Revolution. Soviet troops invaded the country on 27 April 1920, and a Soviet Republic followed. From 1 October 1923 stamps of the Transcaucasian Federation were used but these were superseded by those of the Soviet Union in 1924.

With the dissolution of the Soviet Union in 1991, Azerbaijan once again became an independent state.

1919. 100 kopeks = 1 rouble.
1992. 100 qopik = 1 manat.
2006. 1 manat = 100 qepik.

1 Standard-bearer

6 Famine Supplies

3 "Labour"

4 Petroleum Well

1919. Imperf. Various designs.

1B	1	10k. multicoloured	20	20
2B	–	20k. multicoloured	20	20
3B	–	40k. olive, black and yellow	20	20
4B	–	60k. orange, black & yellow	20	25
5B	–	1r. blue, black and yellow	30	30
6B	–	2r. red, black and yellow	30	30
7B	–	5r. blue, black and yellow	40	55
8B	–	10r. olive, black & yellow	60	60
9B	–	25r. blue, black and red	1·00	1·00
10B	–	50r. olive, black and red	1·30	1·10

DESIGNS—HORIZ: 40k. to 1r. Reaper; 2r. to 10r. Citadel, Baku; 25r., 50r. Temple of Eternal Fires.

1921. Imperf.

11	3	1r. green	35	75
12	4	2r. brown	50	80
13	–	5r. brown	35	75
14	–	10r. grey	50	85
15	–	25r. orange	35	75
16	–	50r. violet	35	75
17	–	100r. orange	40	80
18	–	150r. blue	40	80
19	–	250r. violet and buff	40	80
20	–	400r. blue	40	80
21	–	500r. black and lilac	40	80
22	–	1000r. red and blue	40	80
23	–	2000r. black and blue	40	80
24	–	3000r. brown and blue	40	80
25	–	5000r. green on olive	55	50

DESIGNS—HORIZ: 5r., 3000r. Bibi Eibatt Oilfield; 100r., 5000r. Goukasoff House (State Museum of Arts); 400r., 1000r. Hall of Judgment, Khan's Palace. VERT: 10r., 2000r. Minaret of Friday Mosque, Khan's Palace, Baku; 25r., 250r. Globe and Workers; 50r. Malden's Tower, Baku; 150r., 500r. Blacksmiths.

1921. Famine Relief. Imperf.

26	6	500r. blue	50	1·50
27	–	1000r. brown	85	2·50

DESIGN—VERT: 1000r. Starving family.

For stamps of the above issues surch with new values, see Stanley Gibbons Part 10 (Russia) Catalogue.

13 Azerbaijan Map and Flag

16 Maiden's Tower, Baku

1992. Independence.

83	13	35q. multicoloured	90	90

1992. Unissued stamp showing Caspian Sea surch **AZARBAYCAN** and new value.

84B	25q. on 15k. multicoloured	45	45
85B	35q. on 15k. multicoloured	65	65
86B	50q. on 15k. multicoloured	85	85
87B	1m.50 on 15k. multicoloured	2·75	2·75
88B	2m.50 on 15k. multicoloured	4·25	4·25

1992. Dated "1992".

89	16	10q. green and black	15	15
90		20q. red and black	15	15
91		50q. yellow and black	20	20
92		1m.50 blue and black	85	85

See also Nos. 101/4.

17 Akhalteka Horse

1993. Horses. Multicoloured.

93	20q. Type **17**	10	10
94	30q. Kabarda horse	10	10
95	50q. Qarabair horse	10	10
96	1m. Don horse	10	10
97	2m.50 Yakut horse	45	45
98	5m. Orlov horse	85	85
99	10m. Diliboz horse	1·70	1·70
MS100	80 × 60 mm. 8m. Qarabag horse	1·70	1·70

1993. Dated "1993".

101	16	50q. blue and black	25	25
102		1m. mauve and black	15	15
103		2m.50 yellow and black	30	30
104		5m. green and black	55	55

18 "Tulipa eichleri"

20 Map of Nakhichevan

19 Russian Sturgeon

1993. Flowers. Multicoloured.

105	25q. Type **18**	10	10
106	50q. "Puschkinia scilloides"	10	10
107	1m. "Iris elegantissima"	15	15
108	1m.50 "Iris acutiloba"	20	20
109	5m. "Tulipa florenskyii"	70	70
110	10m. "Iris reticulata"	1·30	1·30
MS111	78 × 58 mm. 10m. *Muscari elecostomum* (31 × 39 mm)	1·20	1·20

1993. Fishes. Multicoloured.

112	25q. Type **19**	10	10
113	50q. Stellate sturgeon	10	10
114	1m. Iranian roach	15	10
115	1m.50 Caspian roach	25	25
116	5m. Caspian trout	90	90
117	10m. Black-backed shad	1·80	1·80
MS118	76 × 58 mm. 10m. Beluga (*Huso huso*) (39 × 31 mm)	1·60	1·20

1993. 70th Birthday of President Heydar Aliev.

119	–	25m. black and red	1·50	1·50
120	20	25m. multicoloured	1·50	1·50
MS121a		110 × 90 mm. Nos. 119/20 (map inscr "Naxcivan")	9·50	9·50

DESIGN: No. 119, President Aliev.

21 Government Building, Baku

1993.

122	21	25q. black and yellow	15	15
123		30q. black and green	15	15
124		50q. black and blue	30	30
125		1m. black and red	60	60

22 Flags, and Dish Aerials on Maps

1993. Azerbaijan–Iran Telecommunications Co-operation.

126	22	15q. multicoloured	80	80

23 National Colours and Islamic Crescent

24 State Arms

1994. National Day.

127	23	5m. multicoloured	35	35

1994.

128	24	8m. multicoloured	65	65

25 Sirvan Palace

26 Fuzuli

1994. Baku Architecture.

129	25	2m. red, silver and black	15	15
130	–	4m. green, silver and black	25	25
131	–	8m. blue, silver and black	55	55

DESIGNS: 4m. 15th-century tomb; 8m. Divan-Khana.

1994. 500th Birth Anniv (1992) of Mohammed ibn Suleiman Fuzuli (poet).

132	**26**	10m. multicoloured	45	45

1994. No. 126 surch **IRAN–AZERBAYGAN** and value.

133	**22**	2m. on 15q. multicoloured	30	30
134		20m. on 15q. multicoloured	85	85
135		25m. on 15q. multicoloured	1·00	1·00
136		50m. on 15q. multicoloured	2·40	2·40

1994. Nos. 122/5 surch.

137	**21**	5m. on 1m. black and red	30	30
138		10m. on 30q. black & grn	30	30
139		15m. on 30q. black & grn	30	30
140		20m. on 50q. black & blue	30	30
141		25m. on 1m. black & red	35	35
142		40m. on 50q. black & blue	65	65
143		50m. on 25q. black & yell	85	85
144		100m. on 25q. black & yell	1·70	1·70

29 Rasulzade

1994. 110th Birth Anniv of Mammed Amin Rasulzade (politician).

145	**29**	15m. brown, ochre & black	85	85

30 Mamedquluzade

32 Laumontite

31 Temple of the Fire Worshippers of Atashgah

1994. 125th Birth Anniv of Jalil Mamedquluzade (writer).

146	**30**	20m. black, gold and blue	85	85

1994. 115th Anniv of Nobel Partnership to Exploit Black Sea Oil. Multicoloured.

147		15m. Type **31**	25	25
148		20m. Oil wells	35	35
149		25m. "Zoroastr" (first oil tanker in Caspian Sea)	40	40
150		50m. Nobel brothers and Petr Bilderling (partners)	1·00	1·00
MS151		110 × 73 mm. No. 150	1·10	1·10

1994. Minerals. Multicoloured.

152		5m. Type **32**	25	25
153		10m. Epidot calcite	40	40
154		15m. Andradite	65	65
155		20m. Amethyst	85	85
MS156		120 × 110 mm. Nos. 152/5	2·10	2·10

33 Players

1994. World Cup Football Championship, U.S.A.

157	**33**	5m. multicoloured	10	10
158	–	10m. multicoloured	10	10
159	–	20m. multicoloured	25	25
160	–	25m. multicoloured	35	35
161	–	30m. multicoloured	40	40
162	–	50m. multicoloured	70	70
163	–	80m. multicoloured	1·10	1·10
MS164		90 × 65 mm. 100m. multicoloured (31 × 39 mm)	1·30	1·30

DESIGNS: 10m. to 100m. Match scenes.

34 Posthorn

1994.

165	**34**	5m. red and black	10	10
166		10m. green and black	10	10
167		20m. blue and black	30	20
168		25m. yellow and black	30	30
169		40m. brown and black	55	55

35 Coelophysis and Segisaurus

1994. Prehistoric Animals. Multicoloured.

170		5m. Type **35**	10	15
171		10m. Pentaceratops and tyrannosaurids	10	15
172		20m. Segnosaurus and oviraptor	40	40
173		25m. Albertosaurus and corythosaurus	50	50
174		30m. Igaunodons	60	60
175		50m. Stegosaurus and allosaurus	1·10	1·10
176		80m. Tyrannosaurus and saurolophus	1·70	1·70
MS177		81 × 61 mm. 100m. Phobetor (39 × 31 mm)	1·80	1·80

36 Nesting Grouse

1994. The Caucasian Black Grouse. Multicoloured.

178		50m. Type **36**	60	60
179		80m. Grouse on mountain	95	95
180		100m. Pair of grouse	1·40	1·40
181		120m. Grouse in spring meadow	2·00	2·00

1994. No. 84 further surch **400 M.**

182		400m. on 25q. on 15k. mult	1·60	1·60

38 "Kapitan Razhabov" (tug)

1994. Ships. Multicoloured.

183		50m. Type **38**	30	30
184		50m. "Azerbaijan" (ferry)	30	30
185		50m. "Merkuri 1" (ferry)	30	30
186		50m. "Tovuz" (container ship)	30	30
187		50m. "Ganzha" (tanker)	30	30

Nos. 183/7 were issued together, se-tenant, the backgrounds of which form a composite design of a map.

39 Pres. Aliev

1994. President Haidar Aliev. Sheet 102 × 72 mm.

MS188	**39**	150m. multicoloured	2·40	2·40

40 White-tailed Sea Eagle

1994. Birds of Prey. Multicoloured.

189		10m. Type **40**	60	60
190		15m. Imperial eagle	70	70
191		20m. Tawny eagle	85	85
192		25m. Lammergeier (vert)	1·00	1·00
193		50m. Saker falcon (vert)	2·40	2·40
MS194		83 × 64 mm. 100m. Golden eagle (*Aquila chrysaetos*) (39 × 31 mm)	1·60	1·60

Nos. 190/1 and **MS**194 are wrongly inscr "Aguila".

41 "Felis libica caudata"

1994. Wild Cats. Multicoloured.

195		10m. Type **41**	60	60
196		15m. Manul cat	70	70
197		20m. Lynx	85	85
198		25m. Leopard (horiz)	1·00	1·00
199		50m. Tiger (horiz)	2·40	2·40
MS200		64 × 56 mm. 100m. Tiger with cub (31 × 39 mm)	1·60	1·60

No. 197 is wrongly inscribed "Felis lyns lyns".

42 Ancient Greek and Modern Javelin Throwers

1994. Centenary of Int Olympic Committee. Mult.

201		100m. Type **42**	60	60
202		100m. Ancient Greek and modern discus throwers	60	60
203		100m. Baron Pierre de Coubertin (founder of modern games) and flame	60	60

1995. Nos. 89/92 and 101/4 surch.

204	**15**	250m. on 10q. green & blk	50	50
205		250m. on 20q. red & black	50	50
206		250m. on 50q. yell & blk	50	50
207		250m. on 1m.50 bl & blk	50	50
208		500m. on 50q. blue & blk	1·10	1·10
209		500m. on 1m. mve & blk	1·10	1·10
210		500m. on 2m.50 yellow and black	1·10	1·10
211		500m. on 5m. green & blk	1·10	1·10

44 Apollo

1995. Butterflies. Multicoloured.

212		10m. Type **44**	30	30
213		25m. "Zegris menestho"	70	70
214		50m. "Manduca atropos"	1·40	1·40
215		60m. "Pararge adrastoides"	1·80	1·80
MS216		103 × 157 mm. Nos. 212/15	4·25	4·25

45 Aleksei Urmanov (Russia) (gold, men's figure skating)

46 Mary Cleave

1995. Winter Olympic Games, Lillehammer, Norway, Medal Winners. Multicoloured.

217		10m. Type **45**	10	10
218		25m. Nancy Kerrigan (U.S.A.) (silver, women's figure skating)	25	25
219		40m. Bonnie Blair (U.S.A.) (gold, women's 500m. speed skating) (horiz)	40	45
220		50m. Takanori Kano (Japan) (gold, men's ski jumping) (horiz)	40	40
221		80m. Philip Laros (Canada) (silver, men's freestyle skiing)	75	75
222		100m. German team (gold, three-man bobsleigh)	1·00	1·00
MS223		102 × 71 mm. 200m. Katya Seizinger (Germany) (gold, women's skiing)	2·20	2·20

1995. 25th Anniv (1994) of First Manned Moon Landing. Female Astronauts. Two sheets, each 137 × 78 mm, containing T **46** and similar vert designs. Multicoloured.

MS224		(a) 100m. Type **46**; 100m. Valentina Tereshkova; 100m. Tamara Jernigen; 100m. Wendy Lawrence. (b) 100m. Mae Jemison; 100m. Cathy Coleman; 100m. Ellen Shulman; 100m. Mary Weber	3·75	3·75

1995. Nos. 165/7 surch.

225	**34**	100m. on 5m. red & black	15	15
226		250m. on 10m. grn & blk	45	45
227		500m. on 20m. blue & blk	90	90

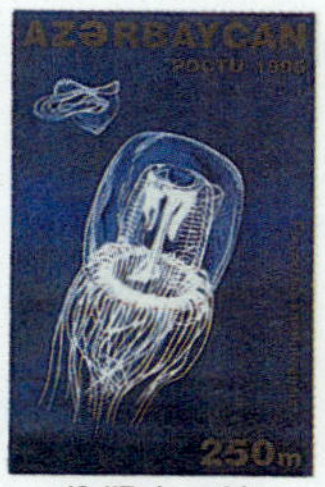

48 "Polyorchis karafutoensis"

1995. Marine Animals. Multicoloured.

228		50m. "Loligo vulgaris" (horiz)	15	15
229		100m. "Orchistoma pileus" (horiz)	40	40
230		150m. "Pegea confoederata" (horiz)	60	60
231		250m. Type **48**	1·00	1·00
232		300m. "Agalma okeni"	1·20	1·20
MS233		89 × 60 mm. 500m. *Corolla spectabilis* (39 × 31 mm)	1·60	1·60

49 Matamata Turtle

1995. Tortoises and Turtles. Multicoloured.

234		50m. Type **49**	15	15
235		100m. Loggerhead turtle	40	40
236		150m. Leopard tortoise	60	60
237		250m. Indian star tortoise	1·00	1·00
238		300m. Hermann's tortoise	1·20	1·20
MS239		79 × 65 mm. 500m. Alligator-snapping turtle (*Macroclemys temmincki*) (31 × 39 mm)	1·70	1·70

50 Uzeyir Hacibeyov (composer, 110th)

53 Charles's Hydrogen Balloon, 1783

1995. Birth Anniversaries.

240	**50**	250m. silver and black	40	40
241	–	400m. gold and black	60	60

DESIGN: 400m. Vakhid (poet, centenary).

1995. Nos. 84/88 surch.

242		200m. on 2m.50 on 15k. mult	60	60
243		400m. on 25q. on 15k. mult	1·00	1·00
244		600m. on 35q. on 15k. mult	1·80	1·80
245		800m. on 50q. on 15k. mult	2·30	2·30
246		1000m. on 1m.50 on 15k. multicoloured	3·00	3·00

1995. Nos. 168/9 surch.

247	**34**	400m. on 25m. yell & blk	1·10	1·10
248		900m. on 40m. brn & blk	2·50	2·50

1995. History of Airships. Multicoloured.

249		100m. Type **53**	15	15
250		150m. Tissandier Brothers' electrically-powered airship, 1883	30	30
251		250m. J.-B. Meusnier's elliptical balloon design, 1784 (horiz)	50	50
252		300m. Baldwin's dirigible airship, 1904 (horiz)	60	60

253 400m. U.S. Navy dirigible airship, 1917 (horiz) . . . 85 85
254 500m. Pedal-powered airship, 1909 (horiz) . . . . 1·00 1·00
MS255 79 × 62 mm. 800m. First rigid dirigible airship by Hugo Eckener, 1924 (horiz) . . . . 1·70 1·70
No. 249 is wrongly dated.

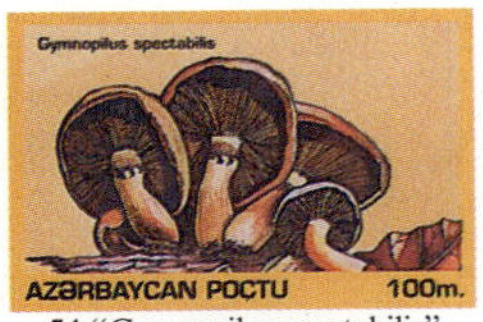

54 "Gymnopilus spectabilis"

1995. Fungi. Multicoloured.
256 100m. Type **54** 35 35
257 250m. Fly agaric 95 95
258 300m. Parasol mushroom . . 1·10 1·10
259 400m. "Hygrophorus spectosus" . . . . 1·40 1·40
MS260 110 × 80 mm. 500m. Fly agaric (different) . . . . 2·40 2·40
The 250m. and 500m. are wrongly inscr "agaris".

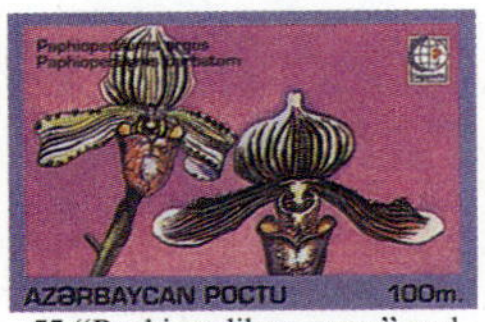

55 "Paphiopedilum argus" and "Paphiopedilum barbatum"

1995. "Singapore '95" International Stamp Exhibition. Orchids. Multicoloured.
261 100m. Type **55** 35 35
262 250m. "Maxillaria picta" . . 95 95
263 300m. "Laeliocattleya" . . . 1·10 1·10
264 400m. "Dendrobium nobile" 1·40 1·40
MS265 110 × 80 mm. 500m. *Cattleya gloriette* . . . . 1·30 1·30

56 Pres. Aliev and U.N. Secretary-General Boutros Boutros Ghali

1995. 50th Anniv of U.N.O.
266 **56** 250m. multicoloured . . . 2·10 2·10

57 Players

58 American Bald Eagle

1995. World Cup Football Championship, France (1998). Multicoloured.
267 100m. Type **57** 35 35
268 150m. Dribbling 50 50
269 250m. Tackling 85 85
270 300m. Preparing to kick ball 1·00 1·00
271 400m. Contesting for ball . . 1·30 1·30
MS272 79 × 60 mm. 600m. Goalkeeper diving for ball . . . 2·20 2·20

1995. Air.
273 **58** 2200m. multicoloured . . . 2·50 2·50

59 Persian

60 Horse

1995. Cats. Multicoloured.
274 100m. Type **59** 15 15
275 150m. Chartreux 30 30
276 250m. Somali 50 50
277 300m. Longhair Scottish fold 60 60
278 400m. Cymric 85 85
279 500m. Turkish angora . . . 1·00 1·00
MS280 85 × 75 mm. 800m. Birman (31 × 39 mm) . . . . 1·70 1·70

1995. Flora and Fauna. Multicoloured.
281 100m. Type **60** 15 15
282 200m. Grape hyacinths (vert) 40 40
283 250m. Beluga 50 50
284 300m. Golden eagle 60 60
285 400m. Tiger 75 75
286 500m. Georgian black grouse nesting . . . . 1·00 1·00
287 1000m. Georgian black grouse in meadow . . . . 2·00 2·00

61 Lennon and Signature

1995. 15th Death Anniv of John Lennon (entertainer).
288 **61** 500m. multicoloured . . . 1·10 1·10

62 Early Steam Locomotive, U.S.A.

1996. Railway Locomotives. Multicoloured.
289 100m. Type **62** 45 45
290 100m. New York Central Class J3 locomotive . . . 45 45
291 100m. Steam locomotive on bridge 45 45
292 100m. Steam locomotive No. 1959, Germany . . . 45 45
293 100m. Steam locomotive No. 4113, Germany . . . 45 45
294 100m. Steam locomotive, Italy 45 45
295 100m. Class 59 steam locomotive, Japan 45 45
296 100m. Class QJ steam locomotive, China 45 45
297 100m. Class Sn 23 steam locomotive, China 45 45
MS298 110 × 80 mm. 500m. Electric train (vert) . . . . 2·75 2·75

63 Operating Theatre and Topcubasov

1996. Birth Centenary of M. Topcubasov (surgeon).
299 **63** 300m. multicoloured . . . 1·00 1·00

64 Feast and Woman wearing Traditional Costume

1996. New Year.
300 **64** 250m. multicoloured . . . 90 90

65 Carl Lewis (athletics, Los Angeles, 1984)

1996. Olympic Games, Atlanta. Previous Gold Medallists. Multicoloured.
301 50m. Type **65** (wrongly inscr "1994") 15 15
302 100m. Mohammed Ali (Cassius Clay) (boxing, Rome, 1960) 35 35
303 150m. Li Ning (gymnastics, Los Angeles, 1984) . . . 55 55
304 200m. Said Aouita (5000m, Los Angeles, 1984) 70 70
305 250m. Olga Korbut (gymnastics, Munich, 1972) 90 90
306 300m. Nadia Comaneci (gymnastics, Montreal, 1976) . . . . 1·10 1·10
307 400m. Greg Louganis (diving, Los Angeles, 1984) . . . . 1·30 1·30
MS308 74 × 104 mm. 500m. Nazim Goussinev (bantamweight boxing, Barcelona, 1992) (vert) . . . . 1·80 1·80

66 "Maral-Gol"

1996. 5th Death Anniv of G. Aliev (painter). Mult.
309 100m. "Reka Cura" 55 55
310 200m. Type **66** . . . . 1·10 1·10

67 Behbudov and Globe

1996. 7th Death Anniv of Resid Behbudov (singer).
311 **67** 100m. multicoloured . . . 95 95

68 Mammadaliev and Flasks

69 National Flag and Government Building

1996. 1st Death Anniv of Yusif Mammadaliev (scientist).
312 **68** 100m. multicoloured . . . 95 95

1996. 5th Anniv of Republic.
313 **69** 250m. multicoloured . . . 90 90

70 Dome of the Rock

1996. 3000th Anniv of Jerusalem. Multicoloured.
314 100m. Praying at the Wailing Wall 70 70
315 250m. Interior of church . . 1·70 1·70
316 300m. Type **70** . . . . 2·00 2·00
MS317 73 × 104 mm. 500m. Montefiore Windmill . . . . . 3·50 3·50

71 German Shepherd

1996. Dogs. Multicoloured.
318 50m. Type **71** 10 10
319 100m. Basset hounds 40 40
320 150m. Collies 60 60
321 200m. Bull terriers 85 85
322 300m. Boxers . . . . 1·30 1·30
323 400m. Cocker spaniels . . . 1·70 1·70
MS324 70 × 80 mm. 500m. Shar-pei (38 × 30 mm) . . . . 2·10 2·10

72 Shaft-tailed Whydah

73 "Burgundy"

1996. Birds. Multicoloured.
325 50m. Type **72** 10 10
326 100m. Blue-naped mousebird 40 40
327 150m. Asian black-headed oriole 60 60
328 200m. Golden oriole 85 85
329 300m. Common starling . . . 1·30 1·30
330 400m. Yellow-fronted canary 1·70 1·70
MS331 60 × 80 mm. 500m. European bee eater (*Merops apaister*) (31 × 39 mm) . . . . 2·10 2·10

1996. Roses. Multicoloured.
332 50m. Type **73** 10 10
333 100m. "Virgo" 40 40
334 150m. "Rose Gaujard" . . . 60 60
335 200m. "Luna" 85 85
336 300m. "Lady Rose" . . . . 1·30 1·30
337 400m. "Landora" . . . . . 1·70 1·70
MS338 90 × 70 mm. 500m. "Luxor" (39 × 31 mm) . . . . 2·10 2·10

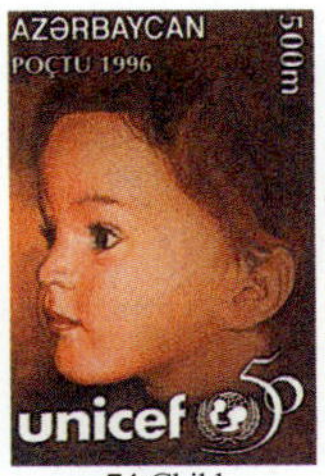

74 Child

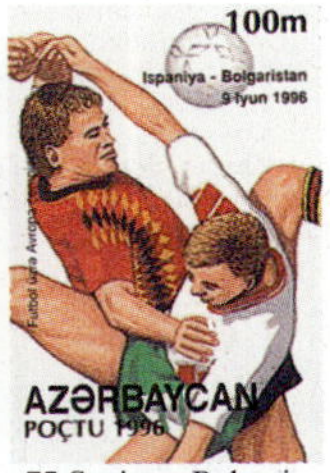

75 Spain v. Bulgaria

1996. 50th Anniv of UNICEF.
339 **74** 500m. multicoloured . . . 90 90

1996. European Football Championship, England. Multicoloured.
340 100m. Type **75** 25 25
341 150m. Rumania v. France . . 40 40
342 200m. Czech Republic v. Germany 50 50
343 250m. England v. Switzerland 70 70
344 300m. Croatia v. Turkey . . 75 75
345 400m. Italy v. Russia . . . . 1·10 1·10
MS346 110 × 80 mm. 500m. Detail of cup . . . . 1·40 1·40

76 Chinese Junk

1996. Ships. Multicoloured.
347 100m. Type **76** 25 25
348 150m. "Danmark" (Danish full-rigged cadet ship) . . . 40 40
349 200m. "Nippon-Maru II" (Japanese cadet ship) . . . 60 60
350 250m. "Mircea" (Rumanian barque) 75 75
351 300m. "Kruzenshtern" (Russian cadet barque) . . 95 95
352 400m. "Ariadne" (German cadet schooner) . . . . . 1·30 1·30
MS353 107 × 77 mm. 500m. *Tovarishch* (Russian four-masted cadet barque) (vert) . . . . . 2·75 2·75

77 Baxram Gur killing Dragon (fountain by A. Shulgin at Baku)

79 Bulls

78 Nariman Narimanov (politician and writer)

1997.

354 **77** 100m. purple and black . . 35 35
356 250m. black and yellow . . 40 40
357 400m. black and red . . . 55 55
358 500m. black and green . . 65 65
359 1000m. black and blue . . 1·30 1·30

1997. Anniversaries. Multicoloured.
365 250m. Type **78** (125th birth anniv (1995)) 80 80
366 250m. Fatali Xoyskin (politician, 120th birth anniv (1995)) 80 80
367 250m. Aziz Mammed-Kerim ogli Aliyev (politician, birth centenary) 80 80
368 250m. Ilyas Afendiyev (writer, 1st death anniv) . . 80 80

1997. Qobustasn Rock Carvings. Sheet 127 × 84 mm containing T **79** and similar vert designs. Multicoloured.
MS369 500m. Type **79**; 500m. Goats; 500m. Dancers . . . . 4·50 4·50

1997. Red Cross. Various stamps optd **Red Cross** and cross. (a) Nos. 93/99.
370 20q. multicoloured 10 10
371 30q. multicoloured 10 10
372 50q. multicoloured 10 10
373 1m. multicoloured 35 35
374 2m.50 multicoloured . . . . 1·00 1·00
375 5m. multicoloured . . . . . 2·00 2·00
376 10m. multicoloured . . . . . 4·25 4·25
MS377 80 × 60 mm. 8m. multicoloured . . . . 4·25 4·25

(b) Nos. 195/9.
378 10m. multicoloured 40 40
379 15m. multicoloured 70 70
380 20m. multicoloured 95 95
381 25m. multicoloured . . . . . 1·20 1·20
382 50m. multicoloured . . . . . 2·40 2·40
MS383 64 × 56 mm. 100m. multicoloured . . . . 4·25 4·25

1997. 50th Anniv of Rotary Club International in Azerbaijan. Various stamps optd **50th Anniversary of the Rotary Club** and emblem. (a) Nos. 314/16.
384 100m. multicoloured 95 95
385 250m. multicoloured . . . . 2·20 2·20
386 300m. multicoloured . . . . 2·75 2·75
MS387 74 × 103 mm. 500m. multicoloured . . . . 2·50 2·50

(b) Nos. 347/52.
388 100m. multicoloured 40 40
389 150m. multicoloured 70 70
390 200m. multicoloured 85 85
391 250m. multicoloured . . . . 1·10 1·10
392 300m. multicoloured . . . . 1·30 1·30
393 400m. multicoloured . . . . 1·70 1·70
MS394 106 × 76 mm. 500m. multicoloured . . . . 4·50 4·50

82 Dog

1997. "The Town Band of Bremen" by the Brothers Grimm. Multicoloured.
395 250m. Type **82** . . . . 1·50 1·50
396 250m. Donkey and cat . . . 1·50 1·50
397 250m. Rooster . . . . 1·50 1·50
MS398 125 × 96 mm. 500m. Animals frightening robbers from hideaway 3·50 3·50
Nos. 395/7 were issued together, se-tenant, forming a composite design.

83 Seal Pup

1997. The Caspian Seal. Multicoloured.
399 250m. Type **83** 65 65
400 250m. Bull and mountain peak 65 65
401 250m. Bull and gull 65 65
402 250m. Cow (profile) 65 65
403 250m. Cow (full face) 65 65
404 250m. Young seal (three-quarter face) 65 65
MS405 106 × 77 mm. 500m. Cow (vert) . . . . 3·50 3·50
Nos. 399/404 were issued together, se-tenant, forming a composite design.

84 Tanbur

1997. Traditional Musical Instruments. Mult.
406 250m. Type **84** 60 60
407 250m. Gaval (tambourine) . . 60 60
408 500m. Jang (harp) . . . . . 1·20 1·20

85 19th-century Oil Derricks, Aspheron Peninsula

86 Sirvani

1997. 125th Anniv of First Industrial Oil Well in Azerbaijan. Sheet 115 × 91 mm containing T **85** and similar vert design. Multicoloured.
MS409 500m. Type **85**; 500m. Modern drilling platform, Caspian Sea . . . . 2·50 2·50

1997. 870th Birth Anniv (1996) of Xanqani Sirvani (poet).
410 **86** 250m. multicoloured . . . 85 85

87 Taza-pir Mosque, Baku

1997. Mosques. Multicoloured.
411 250m. Type **87** 75 75
412 250m. Momuna-Xatun Mosque, Nakhichevan . . 75 75
413 250m. Govharaga Mosque, Shusha 75 75

88 Rasulbekov and Baku T.V. Tower

90 Katarina Wit, East Germany

89 Italy, 1938

1997. 80th Birth Anniv of G. D. Rasulbekov (former Minister of Telecommunications).
414 **88** 250m. multicoloured . . . 75 75

1997. World Cup Football Championship, France (1998).
415 **89** 250m. black 70 70
416 – 250m. multicoloured . . . 70 70
417 – 250m. black 70 70
418 – 250m. multicoloured . . . 70 70
419 – 250m. multicoloured . . . 70 70
420 – 250m. multicoloured . . . 70 70
MS421 85 × 90 mm. 1500m. black and blue (Tofiq Bahramov (referee)) . . . . 3·25 3·25

DESIGNS—World Champion Teams: No. 416, Argentina, 1986; 417, Uruguay, 1930 (wrongly inscr "1980"); 418, Brazil, 1994; 419, England, 1966; 420, West Germany, 1990.

1997. Winter Olympic Games, Nagano, Japan. Mult.
422 250m. Type **90** (figure skating gold medal, 1984 and 1988) 3·75 50
423 250m. Elvis Stoyko, Canada (figure skating silver medal, 1994) 50 50
424 250m. Midori Ito, Japan (figure skating silver medal, 1992) 50 50
425 250m. Azerbaijan flag and silhouettes of sports . . . 50 50
426 250m. Olympic torch and mountain 50 50
427 250m. Kristin Yamaguchi, U.S.A. (figure skating gold medal, 1992) 50 50
428 250m. John Curry, Great Britain (figure skating gold medal, 1976) 50 50
429 250m. Cen Lu, China (figure skating bronze medal, 1994) 50 50
MS430 76 × 106 mm. 500m. Yekaterina Gordeyeva and Sergi Grinkov, Russia (figure skating gold medal, 1984 and 1988) . . 3·00 3·00

91 Diana, Princess of Wales

1998. Diana, Princess of Wales Commem. Mult.
431 400m. Type **91** 50 50
432 400m. Wearing black polo-neck jumper 50 50

92 Aliyev and Mountain Landscape

1998. 90th Birth Anniv of Hasan Aliyev (ecologist).
433 **92** 500m. multicoloured . . . 85 85

93 Tourist Map, Flag and Pres. Aliev

1998. 75th Birthday of President Haidar Aliev. Sheet 114 × 89 mm.
MS434 **93** 500m. multicoloured 2·10 2·10

1998. "Israel 98" International Stamp Exhibition, Tel Aviv. No. **MS**369 optd **98** and emblem on each stamp and "Israel 98–WORLD STAMP EXHIBITION TEL–AVIV 13–21 MAY 1998" in margin.
MS435 500m. × 3 multicoloured 5·50 5·50

95 Ashug Alesker (singer)

1998. Birth Anniversaries. Multicoloured.
436 250m. Type **95** (175th anniv) 60 60
437 250m. Magomedhuseyn Shakhriyar (poet, 90th anniv) 60 60
438 250m. Qara Qarayev (composer, 80th anniv) . . 60 60

96 Bul-Bul

97 Mickey and Minnie Mouse playing Chess

1998. Birth Centenary of Bul-Bul (Murtuz Meshadirza ogli Mamedov) (singer).
439 **96** 500m. multicoloured . . . 85 85

1998. World Rapid Chess Championship, Georgia. Multicoloured.
440 250m. Type **97** . . . . 2·10 2·10
441 500m. Mickey, Minnie, pawn and rook . . . . 2·40 2·40
442 500m. Goofy, bishop and knight . . . . 2·40 2·40
443 500m. Donald Duck, king and bishop . . . . 2·40 2·40
444 500m. Pluto, rook, pawn and clockwork pawn . . . . . 2·40 2·40
445 500m. Minnie and queen . . 2·40 2·40
446 500m. Daisy Duck, bishop and king . . . . 2·40 2·40
447 500m. Goofy, Donald and pawn . . . . 2·40 2·40
448 500m. Mickey, queen and rook . . . . 2·40 2·40
MS449 Two sheets, each 127 × 101 mm. (a) 4000m. Mickey, Minnie, Pluto and queen; (b) 4000m. Donald, Mickey and pawn 19·00 19·00

98 Preparing Pastries

1998. Europa. National Festivals: New Year. Mult.
450 1000m. Type **98** . . . . . . 1·20 1·20
451 3000m. Acrobat and wrestlers 3·00 3·00

1999. "iBRA" International Stamp Exhibition, Nuremberg, Germany. Nos. 450/1 optd with exhibition emblem.
452 1000m. multicoloured 75 75
453 3000m. multicoloured . . . . 2·30 2·30

100 Greater Flamingo, Gizilagach National Park

101 14th-century Square Tower

1999. Europa. Parks and Gardens. Multicoloured.
454 1000m. Type **100** . . . . . . 1·20 1·20
455 3000m. Stag, Girkan National Park . . . . . . 3·00 3·00

1999. Towers at Mardakyan.
456 **101** 1000m. black and blue . . 60 60
457 – 3000m. black and red . . 2·30 1·90
DESIGN: 3000m. 13th-century round tower.
See also Nos. 547 and 557.

102 President Aliev and Flag

1999. 75th Anniv of Nakhichevan Autonomous Region. Multicoloured.
460 1000m. Type **102** . . . . . . 1·00 1·00
461 1000m. Map of Nakhichevan 1·00 1·00
MS462 110 × 90 mm. Nos. 460/1 1·90 1·90

103 Cabbarli

1999. Birth Centenary of Cafar Cabbarli (dramatist).
463 **103** 250m. multicoloured . . . 75 75

104 40k. Stamp

1999. 80th Anniv of First Azerbaijani Stamps. Sheet 131 × 106 mm containing T **104** and similar multicoloured designs showing stamps of 1919.
MS464 500m. 10k. stamp (Type **1**) (25 × 35 mm); 500m. Type **104**; 500m. 5r. stamp; 500m. 50r. stamp (Type **2**) . . . . 3·25 3·25

105 Flag, Pigeon and Emblem on Scroll

106 Caravanserai Inner Court and Maiden's Tower, Baku

1999. 125th Anniv of Universal Postal Union. Multicoloured.
465 250m. Type **105** 10 10
466 300m. Satellite, computer and emblem . . . . 3·00 3·00

1999. 19th-century Caravanserais. Multicoloured.
467 500m. Type **106** . . . . . . 1·30 1·30
468 500m. Camels outside caravanserai, Sheki . . . . 1·30 1·30

107 Anniversary Emblem

1999. 50th Anniv of Council of Europe.
469 **107** 1000m. multicoloured . . 95 95

108 Beybur Khan's Son fighting Camel

1999. 1300th Anniv of Kitabi Dada Qorqud (folk epic). Sheet 90 × 125 mm containing T **108** and similar horiz designs. Multicoloured.
MS470 1000m. Type **108**; 1000m. Wounded Tural slumped on horse; 1000m. Gaza Khan asleep beside horse . . . . 2·75 2·75

109 "Building Europe"

111 14th-century Square Tower, Ramana

110 Phaeton

2000. Europa.
471 **109** 1000m. multicoloured . . 90 90
472 3000m. multicoloured . . 3·25 3·25

2000. Baku City Transport. Sheet 111 × 88 mm containing T **110** and similar horiz designs. Multicoloured.
MS473 500m. Type **110**; 500m. Konka; 500m. Electric tram; 500m. Trolleybus . . . . . . 3·50 3·50

2000. Towers of Mardakyan.
474 **111** 100m. black and orange 40 40
475 – 250m. black and green . . 1·00 1·00
DESIGN: 250m. 14th-century round tower, Nardaran.
See also Nos. 499/500.

112 Wrestling

114 Satellite Picture of Azerbaijan and Emblem

113 Duck flying

2000. Olympic Games, Sydney. Multicoloured.
476 500m. Type **112** 95 95
477 500m. Weightlifting 95 95
478 500m. Boxing 95 95
479 500m. Relay 95 95

2000. The Ferruginous Duck. Multicoloured.
480 500m. Type **113** 70 70
481 500m. Ducks in water and standing on rocks 70 70
482 500m. Duck standing on rock and others swimming by grasses 70 70
483 500m. Ducks at sunset . . . 70 70

2000. 50th Anniv of World Meteorological Organization.
484 **114** 1000m. multicoloured . . 85 85

115 Quinces

2000. Fruits. Multicoloured.
485 500m. Type **115** 75 75
486 500m. Pomegranates (*Punica granatum*) 75 75
487 500m. Peaches (*Persica*) . . 75 75
488 500m. Figs (*Ficus carica*) . . 75 75

116 Ringed-necked Pheasant

2000. The Ringed-necked Pheasant (*Phasanus colchicus*). Sheet 102 × 72 mm.
MS489 **116** 2000m. multicoloured 2·50 2·50

117 Rasul-Rza

2000. 90th Birth Anniv of Rasul-Rza (poet).
490 **117** 250m. multicoloured . . . 80 80

118 Levantine Viper

2000. Reptiles. Multicoloured.
491 500m. Type **118** . . . . . . 1·10 1·10
492 500m. Rock lizard (*Lacerta saxicola*) (wrongly inscr "Laserta saxcola") . . . . 1·10 1·10
493 500m. Ottoman viper (*Vipera xanthina*) . . . . 1·10 1·10
494 500m. Toad-headed agama (*Phrynocephalus mystaceus*) 1·10 1·10
MS495 90 × 63 mm. 500m. Watersnake (*Natrix tessellate*) and sunwatcher (*Phrynocephalus helioscopus*) (vert) . . . . . . 1·30 1·30

119 Rahman

2000. 90th Birth Anniv of Sabit Rahman (writer).
496 **119** 1000m. multicoloured . . 1·40 1·40

120 Emblem

2000. UNESCO International Year of Culture and Peace.
497 **120** 3000m. multicoloured . . 2·75 2·75

121 Namig Abullayev (gold, freestyle flyweight wrestling)

2001. Olympic Games, Sydney. Medal Winners. Sheet 99 × 127 mm containing T **121** and similar horiz designs. Multicoloured.
MS498 1000m. Type **121**; 1000m. Zemifira Meftahaddinova (gold, skeet shooting); 1000m. Vugar Alakbarov (bronze, middle-weight boxing) . . . . 3·00 3·00

122 Seal, Lesser White-fronted Goose and Oil Rig

2001. Europa. Water Resources. The Caspian Sea. Multicoloured.
499 1000m. Type **122** . . . . . . 1·00 1·00
500 3000m. Sturgeon, crab and oil rig . . . . 3·25 3·25

123 Building and Flags

2001. Admission of Azerbaijan to Council of Europe.
501 **123** 1000m. multicoloured . . 1·00 1·00

2001. Towers of Sheki. As T **111**.
502 100m. black and lilac 30 30
503 250m. black and yellow . . . 80 80
DESIGNS: 100m. 18th-century round tower; 250m. Ruin of 12th-century tower.

124 Refugee Camp

2001. 50th Anniv of United Nations High Commissioner for Refugees. Sheet 100 × 73 mm.
MS504 **124** 3000m. black and blue 2·50 2·50

125 Tusi, Globe and Books

2001. 800th Birth Anniv of Nasraddin Tusi (mathematician and astronomer). Sheet 110 × 78 mm.
MS505 **125** 3000m. multicoloured 2·50 2·50

126 Handshake and Emblem

128 Short-eared Owl (*Asio flammeus*)

127 Yuri Gagarin, "Vostok 1" and Globe

2001. 10th Anniv of Union of Independent States.
506 **126** 1000m. multicoloured . . 1·00 1·00

2001. 40th Anniv of First Manned Space Flight. Sheet 83 × 56 mm.
MS507 **127** 3000m. multicoloured 2·20 2·20

2001. Owls. Multicoloured.
508 1000m. Type **128** 75 75
509 1000m. Tawny owl (*Strix aluco*) 75 75
510 1000m. Scops owl (*Otus scops*) 75 75
511 1000m. Long-eared owl (*Asio otus*) 75 75
512 1000m. Eagle owl on branch (*Bubo bubo*) 75 75
513 1000m. Little owl (*Athene noctua*) 75 75
MS514 91 × 68 mm. 1000m. Eagle owl (*Bubo bubo*) in flight . . . 1·90 1·90

129 Pres. Heydar Aliyev

2001. 10th Anniv of Independence.
515 **129** 5000m. multicoloured . . 7·75 7·75

130 Pres. Vladimir Putin and Pres. Heydar Aliyev

2001. Visit of President Putin to Azerbaijan.
516 **130** 1000m. multicoloured . . 85 80

131 Emblem and Athletes

2002. 10th Anniv of National Olympic Committee.
517 **131** 3000m. multicoloured . . 2·20 2·20

132 Circus Performers

133 Presidents Heydar Aliyev and Jiang Zemin

2002. Europa. Circus. Multicoloured.
518 1000m. Type **132** . . . . . . 1·00 1·00
519 3000m. Equestrian juggler and trapeze artist . . . . 3·25 3·25

2002. 10th Anniv of Azerbaijan--China Diplomatic Relations.
520 **133** 1000m. multicoloured . . 90 90

134 Molla Panah Vagif's Mausoleum, Susa

136 Emblem

2002. Towers of Karabakh.
521 **134** 100m. black and green . . 20 20
522 – 250m. black and cinnamon 50 50
DESIGNS: 250m. 19th-century mosque, Aghdam.

2002. 10th Anniv of Azermarka Stamp Company. No. 83 surch **Azermarka 1992--2002 1000m.**
523 **13** 1000m. on 35q. multicoloured 85 85

2002. 10th Anniv of New Azerbaijan Party.
524 **136** 3000m. multicoloured . . 2·20 2·20

137 African Monarch (*Danaus chrysippus*)

2002. Butterflies and Moths. Multicoloured.
525 1000m. Type **137** (inscr "Danais") 95 95
526 1000m. Southern swallowtail (*Papilio alexanor*) 95 95
527 1000m. *Thaleropis jonia* . . . 95 95
528 1000m. Red admiral (*Vanessa atalanta*) 95 95
529 1000m. *Argynnis alexandra* 95 95
530 1000m. *Brahmaea christoph* (moth) 95 95

138 Pres. Heydar Aliyev and Pope John Paul II

2002. Pope John Paul II's Visit to Azerbaijan. Sheet 80 × 65 mm.
MS531 **138** 1500m. multicoloured 2·00 2·00

139 Telegraph Machine, Building Facade and Emblem

2002. 70th Anniv of Baku Telegraph Office.
532 **139** 3000m. multicoloured . . 2·00 2·00

140 Gadjiyev and Piano

2002. 80th Birth Anniv of Ruaf Gadjiyev (composer).
533 **140** 5000m. multicoloured . . 2·50 2·50

141 Bearded Men with Swords, Black Pawns, White Pawn and White Rook

2002. European Junior Chess Championships, Baku. Showing chess board and views of Baku. Multicoloured.
534 1500m. Type **141** . . . . . . 1·20 1·20
535 1500m. Two knights on horseback . . . . 1·20 1·20
536 1500m. Two elephants . . . 1·20 1·20
537 1500m. Black rook, black pawn, bearded men with swords and fallen knight 1·20 1·20
Nos. 534/7 were issued together, se-tenant, forming a composite design showing a chess game and views of ancient Baku.

142 World Trade Centre, New York, U.S.A. and Azerbaijan Flags and Globe

2002. 1st Anniv of Attack on World Trade Centre, New York. Sheet 130 × 65 mm containing vert design as T **142**. Multicoloured.
MS538 1500m. × 3 Type **142** . . 2·30 2·30

143 Turkish Football Team

2002. Football World Cup Championship, Japan and South Korea. Sheet 102 × 110 mm.
MS539 **143** 5000m. multicoloured 3·50 3·50

144 Dove, Woman, Flag and Emblems

145 Siamese Fighting Fish (*Betta splendens*)

2002. United Nations Development Fund for Women.
540 **144** 3000m. multicoloured . . 2·10 2·10

2002. Aquarium Fish. Multicoloured.
541 100m. Type **145** 75 75
542 100m. Blue discus (*Symphysodon aequifasciatus*) 75 75
543 100m. Freshwater angelfish (*Pterophyllum scalare*) . . . 75 75
544 100m. Black moor (*Carassius auratus auratus*) 75 75
545 100m. Boeseman's rainbowfish (*Melanotaenia boesemani*) 75 75
546 1000m. Firemouth cichlid (*Cichlasoma meeki*) 75 75

2003. Towers of Karabakh. As T **101**.
547 250m. black and blue 45 45
DESIGN: No. 547, Askeran tower and fortress.

146 Bomb and Scissors ("Stop Terrorism")

2003. Europa. Poster Art. Multicoloured.
548 1000m. Type **146** 85 85
549 3000m. Wrestlers ("Sport is the Health of the Nation") 2·50 2·50

147 Flag and UPU Emblem

2003. 10th Anniv of Azerbaijan Membership of Universal Postal Union.
550 **147** 3000m. multicoloured . . 2·10 2·10

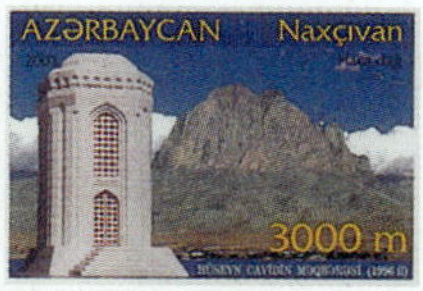

148 H. Djavid Mausoleum and Hacha Mountain

2003. Nakhichevan.
551 **148** 3000m. multicoloured . . 2·10 2·10

149 Map and Pipeline

2003. Baku–Tbilisi–Jeychan Oil Pipeline.
552 **149** 3000m. multicoloured . . 2·10 2·10

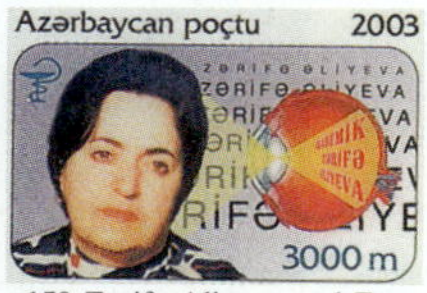

150 Zarifa Aliyeva and Eye

2003. 80th Birth Anniv of Zarifa Aliyeva (ophthalmologist).
553 **150** 3000m. multicoloured . . 2·10 2·10

151 Heydar Aliyev

2003. 80th Birth Anniv of Pres. Heydar Aliyev. Sheet 130 × 160 mm.
MS554 **151** 10000m. multicoloured 6·00 6·00

2003. Nos. 131 and 168 surch.
555 500m. on 25m. yellow and black 50 50
556 1000m. on 8m. blue, silver and black . . . . 1·00 1·00

2003. Towers of Karabakh. As T **101**.
557 1000m. black 75 75
DESIGN: No. 557, Archway, walls and tower, Shusha Town.

153 QAZ-11-73 Saloon Car

2003. Cars. Sheet 100 × 77 mm containing T **153** and similar horiz designs. Multicoloured.
MS558 500m. × 4 Type **153**; QAZ-M-20 Pobeda; QAZ 12 Zim; QAZ-21 Volga (inscr "Volqa") 2·40 2·00

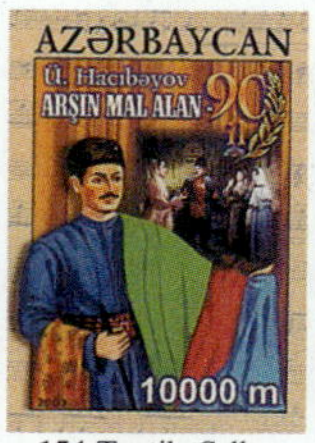

154 Textile Seller

2003. 90th Anniv of U. Hajibekov's Musical Comedy "Arshin Mal Alan".
559 **154** 10000m. multicoloured . . 5·00 5·00

2003. Nos. 91, 129, 130, 152/5, 165 and 169 surch.
560 500m. on 50q. yellow and black 40 40
561 500m. on 2m. red, silver and black 40 40
562 500m. on 4m. green, silver and black 40 40
563 500m. on 5m. multicoloured 40 40
564 500m. on 10m. multicoloured 40 40
565 500m. on 15m. multicoloured 40 40
566 500m. on 20m. multicoloured 40 40
567 500m. on 5m. red and black 40 40
568 500m. on 40m. brown and black 40 40

155 Bear (*Ursus arctos*) (inscr "arctors")

2003. Sheki National Park. Sheet 106 × 84 mm containing T **155** and similar horiz designs. Multicoloured.
MS569 3000m. Type **155**; Racoon (*Procyon lotor*); Wild boar (*Sus scrofa*); Fox (*Vulpes vulpes*) . . 6·75 6·75

156 Map and Monument

157 Dove of Peace (sculpture)

2004. 80th Anniversary of Nakhichevan Autonomous Republic.
570 **156** 3000m. multicoloured . . 1·70 1·70

2004. Samgayit Town.
571 **157** 500m. blue and black . . 60 60

158 Geygel Lake

2004. Europa. Holidays. Multicoloured.
572 1000m. Type **158** 85 85
573 3000m. Baku at night . . . . 2·50 2·50

159 Molla Cuma

2004. 150th Birth Anniversary of Molla Cuma (singer).
574 **159** 500m. multicoloured . . . 75 75

160 High Jump

2004. Olympic Games, 2004, Greece. Multicoloured.
575 500m. Type **160** 70 70
576 500m. Wrestlers 70 70
577 500m. Runner 70 70
578 500m. Greek vase 70 70
Nos. 575/8 were issued together, se-tenant, forming a composite design.

161 World Cup Trophy

2004. Centenary of FIFA (Federation Internationale de Football Association). Multicoloured.
579 500m. Type **161** 70 70
580 500m. Player facing left . . . 70 70
581 500m. Player facing right . . 70 70
582 500m. Goalkeeper 70 70
Nos. 579/82 were issued together, se-tenant, forming a composite design.

162 Heydar Aliyev

163 Mosques and Camels

2004. Heydar Aliyev Commemoration (president, 1993–2003) (1st issue).
583 **162** 500m. multicoloured 60 60
See also Nos. **MS**590, 607 and 632.

2004. The Great Silk Route.
584 **163** 3000m. multicoloured . . 2·10 2·10

164 Carpet and Couple wearing 19th-century Costume, Baku

166 Heydar Aliyev

165 Globe, Honeywell DDP 516 and Modern Computer

2004. Traditional Costumes. Carpets and 19th-century costumes.
585 500m. Type **164** 65 65
586 500m. Couple holding instruments, Karabakh . . 65 65
587 500m. Woman wearing long headdress, man with cane, Nakhichevan 65 65
588 500m. Man with dagger . . . 65 65

2004. 35th Anniv of the Internet.
589 **165** 3000m. multicoloured . . 1·80 1·80

2004. Heydar Aliyev Commemoration (president, 1993–2003) (2nd issue). Sheet 60 × 80 mm.
MS590 **166** 1000m. multicoloured 5·50 5·50

167 Leopard in Tree

2005. Endangered Species. Leopards. Multicoloured.
591 1000m. Type **167** 80 80
592 1000m. Two cubs 80 80
593 1000m. Adult 80 80
594 1000m. Mother and cubs . . 80 80

2005. Nos. 212/15 surch **1000 mm.**
595 1000m. on 10m. multicoloured 60 60
596 1000m. on 25m. multicoloured 60 60
597 1000m. on 50m. multicoloured 60 60
598 1000m. on 60m. multicoloured 60 60

169 Ministry Building and Emblem

170 Observatory

2005. 5th Anniv of Ministry of Taxes.
599 **169** 3000m. multicoloured . . 2·50 1·80

2005. Shemakha Town.
600 **170** 500m. mauve and black 1·40 45

171 *Cephalanthera rubra*

173 Heydar Aliyev

172 Aircraft, Tanks and Oil Tankers

2005. Orchids. Multicoloured.
601 500m. Type **171** 40 40
602 1000m. *Orchis papilionacea* 85 85
603 1500m. *Epipactis atrorubens* 1·30 1·30
604 3000m. *Orchis purpurea* . . . 3·00 3·00
MS605 135 × 190 mm. Nos. 601/4 3·75 3·75

2005. 60th Anniv of the End of World War II.
606 **172** 1000m. multicoloured . . 60 60

2005. Heydar Aliyev (president, 1993–2003) Commemoration (3rd issue).
607 **173** 1000m. multicoloured . . 60 60

174 Pilaf

2005. Europa. Gastronomy. Multicoloured.
608 1000m. Type **174** 70 70
609 3000m. Dolmasi . . . . . . 3·00 3·00

175 Rock Paintings and Academy Building

2005. 60th Anniv of Academy of Science.
610 **175** 1000m. multicoloured . . 45 45

176 Astronaut

2005. 40th Anniv of First Space Walk. Sheet 86 × 58 mm.
MS611 **176** 3000m. multicoloured 2·00 2·00

177 Computers and Emblem

2005. Tunis 2005 (World Summit on Information Society).
612 **177** 1000m. multicoloured . . 45 45

178 Pope John Paul II

2005. Pope John Paul II Commemoration.
613 **178** 3000m. multicoloured . . 2·00 2·00

179 *Paravespula germanica*

2005. Insects. Sheet 101 × 80 mm containing T **179** and similar horiz designs. Multicoloured.
MS614 500m. Type **179**; 1000m. *Bombus terrestris*; 1500m. *Vespa crabro*; 3000m. *Apis mellifera caucasica* . . . . 3·25 3·25

180 Emblem and Nos. 450/1

2005. 50th Anniv of Europa Stamps. Showing previous Europa stamps. Multicoloured.
615 3000m. Type **180** . . . . . . 1·40 1·40
616 3000m. Emblem and Nos. 471/2 . . . . 1·40 1·40
617 3000m. Emblem and Nos. 548/9 . . . . 1·40 1·40
618 3000m. Emblem and Nos. 1167/8 of West Germany . . . . 1·40 1·40
MS619 Four sheets, each 88 × 88 mm. (a) As No. 615; (b) As No. 616; (c) As No. 617; (d) As No. 618 . . . . 5·00 5·00

Note: On 1 January 2006 the manat was re-valued at the rate 1 new manat = 5000 old manat.

NEW CURRENCY

1 manat (m) = 100 qepik (q)

2006. Nos. 131, 110, 114, 168, 521, 113, 457, 146 and 127/8 surch.
620 5q. on 8m. blue, silver and black (No. 131) . . . . . 1·00 1·00
621 10q. on 1m. multicoloured (No. 110) . . . . 1·30 1·30
622 10q. on 1m. multicoloured (No. 114) . . . . 1·30 1·30
623 10q. on 25m. yellow and black (No. 168) . . . . . 1·30 1·30
624 10q. on 100m. black and green (No. 521) . . . . . 1·30 1·30
625 20q. on 50q. multicoloured (No. 113) . . . . 1·75 1·75
626 20q. on 3000m. black and scarlet (No. 457) . . . . . 1·75 1·75
627 20q. on 20m. black, gold and blue (No. 146) . . . . . 1·75 1·75
628 60q. on 5m. multicoloured (No. 127) . . . . 2·50 2·50
629 60q. on 8m. multicoloured (No. 128) . . . . 2·50 2·50

182 19th-century Mosque, Lankaran

183 Emblem

2006. Towns.
630 **182** 10q. blue and black . . . 1·00 1·00
631 – 20q. buff and brown . . . 1·50 1·50
DESIGNS: Type **182**; 20q. 9th-century fortress, Lachin.
See also Nos. 652/3.

2006. Heydar Aliyev (president, 1993–2003) Commemoration (4th issue).
632 **162** 60q. multicoloured . . . 4·25 4·25

2006. 30th Anniv of OPEC Fund for International Development.
633 **183** 5q. multicoloured . . . . 1·00 1·00

184 Hands from Many Nations

185 Emblem

2006. Europa. Integration. Multicoloured.
634 20q. Type **184** . . . . 2·50 2·50
635 60q. Globe enclosed in star 7·50 7·50

2006. World Cup Football Championship, Germany. Multicoloured.
636 20q. Type **185** . . . . 1·50 1·50
637 60q. Player and map of Germany . . . . 1·40 1·40

186 Samad Vurgun

2006. Writers Birth Centenaries. Multicoloured.
638 10q. Type **186** 80 80
639 60q. Suleyman Rustam . . . 2·40 2·40

187 Russian Flag and Arms and St. Basil's Cathedral, Moscow

2006. Year of Russia in Azerbaijan. Multicoloured.
640 10q. Type **187** . . . . 1·00 1·00
641 20q. Azerbaijan flag and arms and Taza Pir mosque, Baku . . . . 1·30 1·30

642 30q. Azerbaijan flag and arms and Maiden Tower, Baku . . . . 1·50 1·50
643 60q. Russian flag and arms and Kremlin, Moscow . . 2·50 2·50

188 Gulustan Mausoleum, Nakhichivan (13th-century)

189 Globe and Binary Code

2006.
644 **188** 20q. multicoloured . . . 1·40 1·40

2006. World Information Organization Day.
645 **189** 1m. multicoloured . . . . 6·00 6·00

190 Khan (1867)

2006. Karabakh Horses. Multicoloured.
646 20q. Type **190** . . . . 1·50 1·50
647 20q. Zaman (1952) . . . . . 1·50 1·50
648 20q. Sarvan (1987) . . . . . 1·50 1·50
649 20q. Gar-gar (2001) . . . . . 1·50 1·50
MS650 122 × 94 mm. Size 52 × 37 mm. Nos. 646/9 . . . 9·00 9·00
MS651 82 × 65 mm. 60q. Rearing horse (vert) . . . . 6·50 6·50

2006. Towns. As T **182**. Multicoloured.
652 10q. lilac and black . . . . 1·00 1·00
653 20q. pink and black . . . . 1·50 1·50
DESIGNS: 10q. Sumuggala tower, Gakh; 20q. Nizami's mausoleum, Ganja.

2006. 50th Anniv of Europa Stamps. Nos. 608/609 surch. Multicoloured.
654 20q. on 1000m. multicoloured (Type **174**) . . . . 2·50 2·50
655 60q. on 3000m. multicoloured (Dolmasi) . . . . 8·00 8·00

192 Emblem

2006. 15th Anniv of Regional Concord of Communication.
656 **192** 20q. multicoloured . . . 1·60 1·60

193 Arms and Flag

2006. 15th Anniv of Independence.
657 **193** 20q. multicoloured . . . 1·60 1·60

194 Fire Appliance AMO-F15 (1926)

2006. Fire Engines. Sheet 101 × 76 mm containing T **194** and similar horiz designs showing fire engines. Multicoloured.
MS658 10q. Type **194**; 20q. PMQ-1 (1932); 60q. PMQ-9 (1950); 1m. ATS 2,5 (1998) . . . . 10·50 10·50

195 Pigeons and Tower

2007. Pigeons. Multicoloured.
659 20q. Type **195** . . . . 1·60 1·60
660 20q. Iridescent pigeons and domes . . . . 1·60 1·60
661 20q. Brown and white pigeons and oil derricks . . 1·60 1·60
662 20q. White pigeon, brown and white pigeon and buildings . . . . 1·60 1·60
663 20q. Dark pigeons and gateways . . . . 1·60 1·60
664 20q. Spotted pigeons and windmills . . . . 1·60 1·60
MS665 54 × 78 mm. 1m. White pigeon with feathered feet (vert) 5·00 5·00
The stamp and margins of **MS**665 form a composite design.

196 Baku Customs' Building

197 Monument to Victims

2007. Bicentenary of Baku Customs Services (20q.) or 15th Anniv of Azerbaijan Customs Services (60q.). Multicoloured.
666 20q. Type **196** . . . . 1·60 1·60
667 60q. Azerbaijan Customs' building . . . . 4·50 4·50

2007. 15th Anniv of Khojali Tragedy. Sheet 99 × 72 mm.
MS668 **197** 1m. multicoloured . . 6·25 6·25

198 Emblem

2007. Europa. Centenary of Scouting. Multicoloured.
669 20q. Type **198** . . . . 2·50 2·50
670 60q. Emblem on kite . . . . 7·00 7·00

199 Symbols of Azerbaijan and Japan

200 Mosque, Goycay

2007. Azerbaijan—Japan Friendly Relations.
671 **199** 1m. multicoloured . . . . 5·50 5·50

2007. Towns.
672 **200** 10q. yellow and black . . 1·00 1·00

2007
60qəp
(201)

2007
60qəp
(202)

60qəp
(203)

2007. Nos. 551 and 613 surch as T **201**, 615/18 surch as T **202** and 570 surch as T **203**.
673 60q. on 3000m. multicoloured (No. 551) . . . . 4·50 4·50
674 60q. on 3000m. multicoloured (No. 570) . . . . 4·50 4·50
675 60q. on 3000m. multicoloured (No. 613) . . . . 4·50 4·50
676 60q. on 3000m. multicoloured (No. 615) . . . . 3·75 3·75
677 60q. on 3000m. multicoloured (No. 616) . . . . 3·75 3·75
678 60q. on 3000m. multicoloured (No. 617) . . . . 3·75 3·75
679 60q. on 3000m. multicoloured (No. 618) . . . . 3·75 3·75

204 Dog Fight

2007. Azim Azimzade (artist) Commemoration. Paintings. Multicoloured.
680 20q. Type **204** . . . . . . 1·50 1·50
681 20q. Wedding . . . . 1·50 1·50

205 Emblem

2007. 15th Anniv of Azermarka (postal company).
682 **205** 50q. multicoloured . . . 3·75 3·75

206 Polar Bear Cub

2007. Polar Bear (*Ursus maritimus*). Multicoloured.
683 60q. Type **206** . . . . 4·50 4·50
MS684 76 × 122 mm 1m. Cub with stick (*vert*) . . . . 8·50 8·50
No. **MS**684 was cut around in the shape of a bear cub.

207 *Gagea alexeenkoana*

2007. Local Flora. Two sheets containing T **207** and similar horiz designs. Multicoloured.
MS685 182 × 50 mm 10q. Type **207**; 20q. *Centaurea ficher*; 40q. *Galanthus caucasicus*; 60q. *Ophrys caucasica* . . . . 7·00 7·00
MS686 50 × 54 mm 1m. *Ophrys caucasica* (different) . . . . 6·50 6·50
The stamp and margin of No. **MS**686 form a composite design.

208 Huseyn Cavid

2007. 160th Birth Anniv of Huseyn Cavid.
687 **208** 20q. multicoloured . . . 1·60 1·60

209 Khudafarin Bridge, Jabrail

2007. Azim Azimzade (artist) Commemoration. Bridges. Multicoloured.
688 10q. Type **209** 80 80
689 20q. Gazanchi, Nakhchivan 1·60 1·60
690 30q. Gudyalchay, Guba . . . 2·40 2·40
691 50q. Ganjachay, Ganja . . . 3·00 3·00
MS692 74 × 58 mm 60q. 11th century bridge, Jabrail . . . 4·00 4·00
The stamps and margin of No. **MS**692 form a composite design.

15m
10
qəp
2007
(210)

2007. No. 145 surch as T **210**.
693 10q. on 15m. brown, ochre and black . . . . 1·20 1·20

211 11th-century Bridge, Jabrail

212 Sputnik

2007. Towns.
694 **211** 10q. pink and black . . . 90 90
695 – 20q. emerald and black 1·00 1·00
DESIGNS: 10q. Type **211**; 20q. Fortress, Kalbajar.

2007. 50th Anniv of Space Exploration. Sheet 100 × 72 mm.
MS696 **212** 1m. multicoloured . . 6·75 6·75

213 Karim Karimov

2007. 90th Birth Anniv of Karim Karimov (Chairman of the Aeronautics Commission). Sheet 61 × 76 mm.
MS697 **213** 1m. multicoloured . . 6·25 6·25

214 Judo

2008. Olympic Games, Beijing. Showing stylized athletes. Multicoloured.
698 20q. Type **214** . . . . . . 1·60 1·60
699 30q. Weight lifting . . . . . 2·20 2·20
700 40q. Wrestling . . . . 3·25 3·25
701 60q. Boxing . . . . 4·00 4·00

AZORES Pt. 9

A group of islands in the Atlantic Ocean.

1868. 1000 reis = 1 milreis.
1912. 100 centavos = 1 escudo.
2002. 100 cents = 1 euro.

NOTE. Except where otherwise stated, Nos. 1/393 are all stamps of Portugal optd **ACORES**.

1868. Curved value labels. Imperf.
1 **14** 5r. black £3000 £1900
2 10r. yellow £13000 £9000
3 20r. bistre £170 £150
4 50r. green £170 £150
5 80r. orange £190 £160
6 100r. purple £190 £160

1868. Curved value labels. Perf.
7 **14** 5r. black . . . . 60·00 60·00
9 10r. yellow . . . . 80·00 60·00
10 20r. bistre . . . . 60·00 55·00
11 25r. pink . . . . 60·00 9·50
12 50r. green £180 £170
13 80r. orange £180 £170
14 100r. lilac £180 £170
16 120r. blue £150 £100
17 240r. lilac £550 £350

1871. Straight value labels.
38 **15** 5r. black . . . . 11·50 7·75
39 10r. yellow . . . . 37·00 29·00
73 10r. green . . . . 70·00 60·00
29 15r. brown . . . . 15·00 14·00
31 20r. bistre . . . . 26·00 15·00

109		20r. red	90·00	75·00
32		25r. pink	14·50	3·75
33		50r. green	75·00	30·00
54		50r. blue	£130	75·00
101b		80r. orange	65·00	50·00
103		100r. mauve	50·00	45·00
25		120r. blue	£140	£120
49		150r. blue	£160	£120
104		150r. yellow	50·00	45·00
26		240r. lilac	£750	£600
50		300r. lilac	75·00	55·00
94		1000r. black	£120	£100

1880.

58	16	5r. black	23·00	11·00
61		25r. grey	46·00	7·25
61b		25r. brown	46·00	7·25
60	17	25r. grey	£120	37·00
67	16	50r. blue	£140	34·00

1882.

136	19	5r. grey	26·00	9·00
125		10r. green	24·00	11·50
139		20r. red	27·00	15·00
126		25r. brown	24·00	3·50
141		25r. mauve	28·00	2·40
142		50r. blue	21·00	3·50
128		500r. black	£150	£130
129		500r. mauve	£120	85·00

1894. Prince Henry the Navigator.

143	32	5r. orange	2·75	2·40
144		10r. red	2·75	2·40
145		15r. brown	3·50	3·25
146		20r. lilac	3·50	3·25
147		25r. green	4·00	3·50
148		50r. blue	9·75	5·50
149		75r. red	18·00	7·50
150		80r. green	21·00	8·00
151		100r. brown on buff	21·00	6·50
152		150r. red	28·00	15·00
153		300r. blue on buff	33·00	23·00
154		500r. purple	60·00	35·00
155		1000r. black on buff	£180	90·00

1895. St. Anthony of Padua.

156	35	2½r. black	2·40	95
157	–	5r. orange	7·50	2·30
158	–	10r. mauve	7·50	3·50
159	–	15r. brown	11·50	5·50
160	–	20r. grey	12·50	7·50
161	–	25r. purple and green	8·00	2·30
162	37	50r. brown and blue	26·00	11·50
163		75r. brown and red	38·00	32·00
164		80r. brown and green	43·00	38·00
165		100r. black and brown	43·00	34·00
166	–	150r. red and brown	90·00	80·00
167	–	200r. blue and brown	95·00	85·00
168	–	300r. black and brown	£120	85·00
169	–	500r. brown & green	£170	£120
170	–	1000r. lilac and green	£275	£350

1898. Vasco da Gama stamps as Nos. 378/385 of Portugal but inscr "ACORES".

171		2½r. green	2·75	1·00
172		5r. red	5·00	1·20
173		10r. purple	5·50	2·30
174		25r. green	5·50	2·30
175		50r. blue	7·75	7·50
176		75r. brown	16·00	11·00
177		100r. brown	21·00	11·50
178		150r. bistre	34·00	23·00

1906. "King Carlos" key-type inscr "ACORES" and optd with letters **A**, **H** and **PD** in three of the corners.

179	S	2½r. grey	35	30
180		5r. orange	35	30
181		10r. green	35	30
182		20r. lilac	55	40
183		25r. red	55	30
184		50r. blue	4·75	3·75
185		75r. brown on yellow	1·70	1·00
186		100r. blue on blue	1·60	1·10
187		200r. purple on pink	1·80	1·10
188		300r. blue on pink	5·25	4·50
189		500r. black on blue	12·50	11·00

7 King Manoel

1910.

190	7	2½r. lilac	35	30
191		5r. black	35	30
192		10r. green	35	30
193		15r. brown	70	50
194		20r. red	95	80
195		25r. brown	35	35
196		50r. blue	2·40	1·20
197		75r. brown	2·40	1·20
198		80r. grey	2·40	1·20
199		100r. brown on green	2·40	3·00
200		200r. green on pink	3·75	3·00
201		300r. black on blue	3·75	2·20
202		500r. brown and olive	7·50	8·00
203		1000r. black and blue	17·00	15·00

1910. Optd **REPUBLICA**.

204	7	2½r. lilac	30	25
205		5r. black	30	25
206		10r. green	35	25
207		15r. brown	1·50	1·10
208b		20r. red	1·50	1·10
209		25r. brown	30	20
210a		50r. blue	1·00	95
211		75r. brown	1·10	75
212		80r. grey	1·10	75
213		100r. brown on green	95	75
214		200r. green on orange	95	75
215		300r. black on blue	2·75	1·80
216		500r. brown and green	3·50	2·50
217		1000r. black and blue	8·75	5·50

1911. Vasco da Gama stamps of Azores optd **REPUBLICA**, some surch also.

218		2½r. green	50	35
219		15r. on 5r. red	50	35
220		25r. green	50	35
221		50r. blue	1·70	1·20
222		75r. brown	1·50	1·40
223		80r. on 150r. brown	1·50	1·50
224		100r. brown	1·70	1·50
225		1000r. on 10r. purple	21·00	12·00

1911. Postage Due stamps optd or surch **REPUBLICA ACORES**.

226	D 48	5r. black	1·00	90
227		10r. mauve	2·20	90
228		20r. orange	4·25	3·00
229		200r. brown on buff	18·00	16·00
230		300r. on 50r. grey	17·00	15·00
231		500r. on 100r. red on pink	17·00	14·50

1912. "Ceres" type.

250	56	¼c. brown	45	35
273		½c. black	45	40
252		1c. green	85	65
274		1c. brown	45	40
254		1½c. brown	85	65
255		1½c. green	45	40
256		2c. red	65	50
257		2c. orange	45	40
258		2½c. lilac	65	50
259		3c. red	45	40
278		3c. blue	35	25
260		3½c. green	45	40
261		4c. green	45	40
401		4c. orange	45	35
262		5c. blue	65	50
280		5c. brown	45	40
264		6c. purple	45	40
282		6c. brown	45	40
403		6c. red	30	20
265		7½c. brown	5·25	3·00
266		7½c. blue	1·50	1·40
267		8c. grey	65	50
283		8c. green	65	45
284		8c. orange	80	75
268		10c. brown	5·25	2·20
285		10c. red	95	70
286		12c. blue	2·10	1·50
287		12c. green	70	60
288		13½c. blue	2·10	1·50
249		14c. blue on yellow	1·80	1·50
269		15c. purple	65	50
289		15c. black	45	40
290		16c. blue	75	70
243		20c. brown on green	9·75	5·50
291		20c. brown	70	60
292		20c. green	95	75
293		20c. drab	65	50
294		24c. blue	70	45
295		25c. pink	55	40
244		30c. brown on pink	60·00	48·00
245		30c. brown on yellow	1·80	1·50
296		30c. brown	1·50	1·30
406		32c. green	2·20	1·50
298		36c. red	65	50
299		40c. blue	80	55
300		40c. brown	1·50	80
407		40c. green	1·20	60
408		48c. pink	2·75	2·30
246		50c. orange on orange	5·25	1·50
247		50c. orange on yellow	5·00	2·20
302		50c. yellow	1·50	90
410		50c. red	2·75	2·30
303		60c. blue	1·40	1·20
304		64c. blue	4·00	2·10
411		64c. red	3·75	2·10
305		75c. pink	4·00	3·00
412		75c. red	3·75	2·75
306		80c. purple	2·00	1·60
307		80c. lilac	2·10	1·50
413		80c. green	3·75	2·30
308		90c. blue	2·00	1·60
309		96c. red	6·00	2·75
248		1e. green on blue	13·50	6·00
310		1e. lilac	2·00	1·60
314		1e. purple	3·00	2·50
414		1e. red	32·00	22·00
311		1e.10 brown	2·20	1·60
312		1e.20 green	2·50	1·60
315		1e.20 buff	6·50	4·75
415		1e.25 blue	2·10	1·80
316		1e.50 purple	7·75	5·25
317		1e.50 lilac	6·75	5·50
400		1e.60 blue	3·25	1·40
313		2e. green	8·00	5·25
319		2e.40 green	55·00	24·00
320		3e. pink	65·00	39·00
321		3e.20 green	7·75	7·50
322		5e. green	14·50	8·00
323		10e. pink	39·00	22·00
324		20e. blue	95·00	65·00

1925. C. C. Branco Centenary.

325	65	2c. orange	20	20
326		3c. green	20	20
327		4c. blue	20	20
328		5c. red	20	20
329	–	10c. blue	20	20
330	–	16c. orange	30	20
331	67	25c. red	30	20
332	–	32c. green	40	40
333	67	40c. black and green	40	40
334		48c. purple	95	95
335	–	50c. green	95	80
336	–	64c. brown	95	80
337	–	75c. grey	95	80
338	67	80c. brown	95	80
339	–	96c. red	1·10	95
340	–	1e.50 blue on blue	1·10	95
341	67	1e.60 blue	1·20	1·10
342	–	2e. green on green	2·00	1·70
343	–	2e.40 red on orange	2·75	1·90
344	–	3e.20 black on green	4·75	4·25

1926. 1st Independence Issue.

345	76	2c. black and orange	30	25
346	–	3c. black and blue	30	25
347	76	4c. black and green	30	25
348	–	5c. black and brown	30	25
349	76	6c. black and orange	30	25
350	–	15c. black and green	60	60
351	77	20c. black and violet	60	60
352	–	25c. black and red	60	60
353	77	32c. black and green	60	60
354	–	40c. black and brown	60	60
355	–	50c. black and olive	1·30	1·30
356	–	75c. black and red	1·40	1·40
357	–	1e. black and violet	1·70	1·70
358	–	4e.50 black and green	7·00	7·00

1927. 2nd Independence Issue.

359	80	2c. black and brown	35	35
360	–	3c. black and blue	25	25
361	80	4c. black and orange	25	25
362	–	5c. black and brown	25	25
363	–	6c. black and brown	25	25
364	–	15c. black and brown	25	25
365	80	25c. black and grey	1·00	1·00
366	–	32c. black and green	1·00	1·00
367	–	40c. black and green	60	60
368	–	96c. black and red	2·50	2·50
369	–	1e.60 black and blue	2·75	2·75
370	–	4e.50 black and yellow	7·00	2·50

1928. 3rd Independence Issue.

371	–	2c. black and blue	25	20
372	84	3c. black and green	25	20
373	–	4c. black and red	25	20
374	–	5c. black and olive	25	20
375	–	6c. black and brown	25	20
376	84	15c. black and grey	50	50
377	–	16c. black and purple	60	60
378	–	25c. black and blue	60	60
379	–	32c. black and green	65	65
380	–	40c. black and brown	65	65
381	–	50c. black and red	1·40	1·30
382	84	80c. black and grey	1·40	1·30
383	–	96c. black and red	3·50	2·50
384	–	1e. black and mauve	3·50	2·50
385	–	1e.60 black and blue	3·50	2·50
386	–	4e.50 black and yellow	9·50	6·75

1929. "Ceres" type surch **ACORES** and new value.

387	56	4c. on 25c. pink	60	60
388		4c. on 60c. blue	1·20	1·10
389		10c. on 25c. pink	1·20	1·10
390		12c. on 25c. pink	1·10	1·10
391		15c. on 25c. pink	1·10	1·10
392		20c. on 25c. pink	1·90	1·90
393		40c. on 1e.10 brown	3·75	3·75

14 10r. Stamp of 1868

1980. 112th Anniv of First Azores Stamps.

416	14	6e.50 black, yellow & red	20	10
417	–	19e.50 blk, purple & blue	95	60
MS418		140 × 115 mm. Nos. 416/17 (sold at 30e.)	4·00	4·00

DESIGN: 19e.50, 100r. stamp of 1868.

15 Map of the Azores

1980. World Tourism Conference, Manila, Philippines. Multicoloured.

419		50c. Type **15**	10	10
420		1e. Church	10	10
421		5e. Windmill	50	10
422		6e.50 Traditional costume	55	15
423		8e. Coastal scene	80	35
424		30e. Coastal village	1·80	65

16 St. Peter's Cavalcade, Sao Miguel Island

1981. Europa. Folklore.

425	16	22e. multicoloured	1·40	70
MS426		140 × 116 mm. No. 425 × 2	7·00	7·00

17 Bulls attacking Spanish Soldiers

1981. 400th Anniv of Battle of Salga. Mult.

427		8e.50 Type **17**	50	10
428		33e.50 Friar Don Pedro leading attack	1·90	80

18 "Myosotis azorica"

1981. Regional Flowers. Multicoloured.

429		4e. Type **18**	15	10
430		7e. "Tolpis azorica"	25	15
431		8e.50 "Ranunculus azoricus"	40	15
432		10e. "Lactuca watsoniana"	55	15
433		12e.50 "Hypericum foliosum"	25	10
434		20e. "Platanthera micranta"	70	40
435		27e. "Vicia dennesiana"	2·50	1·10
436		30e. "Rubus hochstetterorum"	80	30
437		33e.50 "Azorina vidalii"	3·25	1·00
438		37e.50 "Vaccinium cylindraceum"	1·10	60
439		50e. "Laurus azorica"	1·60	80
440		100e. "Juniperus brevifolia"	2·20	85

19 Embarkation of the Heroes of Mindelo

20 Chapel of the Holy Ghost

1982. Europa. Multicoloured.

445	19	33e.50 multicoloured	1·90	75
MS446		140 × 113 mm. No. 445 × 3	16·00	16·00

1982. Regional Architecture. Multicoloured.

447		27e. Type **20**	1·30	65
448		33e.50 Chapel of the Holy Ghost (different)	1·80	90

21 Geothermal Power Station, Pico Vermeilho, Sao Miguel

1983. Europa.

449	21	37e.50 multicoloured	1·50	65
MS450		114 × 140 mm. No. 449 × 3	17·00	17·00

22 Flag of Azores

1983. Flag.

451	22	12e.50 multicoloured	75	10

23 Two "Holy Ghost" Jesters, Sao Miguel

1984. Traditional Costumes. Multicoloured.

452		16e. Type **23**	55	10
453		51e. Two women wearing Terceira cloak	1·90	1·20

23a Bridge

1984. Europa.
454 **23a** 51e. multicoloured . . . . 2·00 1·10
MS455 114 × 139 mm. No. 454 × 3 16·00 16·00

24 "Megabombus ruderatus"

1984. Insects (1st series). Multicoloured.
456 16e. Type **24** 35 10
457 35e. Large white (butterfly) 1·00 55
458 40e. "Chrysomela banksi" (leaf beetle) . . . . 1·40 50
459 51e. "Phlogophora interrupta" (moth) . . . . 1·60 90

1985. Insects (2nd series). As T **24**. Multicoloured.
460 20e. "Polyspilla polyspilla" (leaf beetle) 35 10
461 40e. "Sphaerophoria nigra" (hover fly) . . . . 1·00 45
462 46e. Clouded yellow (butterfly) . . . . 1·40 65
463 60e. Southern grayling (butterfly) . . . . 1·60 75

25 Drummer **26** Jeque

1985. Europa. Music Year.
464 **25** 60e. multicoloured . . . . 2·20 95
MS465 140 × 114 mm. No. 464 × 3 18·00 18·00

1985. Traditional Boats. Multicoloured.
466 40e. Type **26** . . . . 1·30 70
467 60e. Bote . . . . 1·80 80

27 Northern Bullfinch

1986. Europa.
468 **27** 68e.50 multicoloured . . . 2·40 1·00
MS469 140 × 114 mm. No. 468 × 3 14·50 14·50

28 Alto das Covas Fountain, Terceira

1986. Regional Architecture. Drinking Fountains. Multicoloured.
470 22e.50 Type **28** 55 10
471 52e.50 Faja de Baixo, Sao Miguel . . . . 1·80 80
472 68e.50 Portoes de S. Pedro, Terceira . . . . 2·50 1·00
473 100e. Agua d'Alto, Sao Miguel . . . . 3·50 90

29 Ox Cart, Santa Maria

1986. Traditional Carts. Multicoloured.
474 25e. Type **29** 55 10
475 75e. Ram cart, Sao Miguel 2·50 1·30

30 Regional Assembly Building (Correia Fernandes and Luis Miranda)

1987. Europa. Architecture.
476 **30** 74e.50 multicoloured . . . 2·30 1·00
MS477 140 × 114 mm. No. 476 × 4 18·00 18·00

31 Santa Cruz, Graciosa

1987. Windows and Balconies. Multicoloured.
478 51e. Type **31** . . . . 1·60 80
479 74e.50 Ribeira Grande, Sao Miguel . . . . 2·00 80

32 A. C. Read's Curtiss NC-4 Flying Boat, 1919

1987. Historic Airplane Landings in the Azores. Multicoloured.
480 25e. Type **32** 50 10
481 57e. E. F. Christiansen's Dornier Do-X flying boat, 1932 . . . . 1·80 1·00
482 74e.50 Italo Balbo's Savoia Marchetti S-55X flying boat, 1933 . . . . 2·50 95
483 125e. Charles Lindbergh's Lockheed 8 Sirius seaplane "Tingmissartoq", 1933 . . 3·00 1·30

33 19th-century Mule-drawn Omnibus

1988. Europa. Transport and Communications.
484 **33** 80e. multicoloured . . . . 2·40 85
MS485 140 × 112 mm. As No. 484 × 4 but with cream background 14·50 14·50

34 Wood Pigeon

1988. Nature Protection. Birds (1st series). Mult.
486 27e. Type **34** 55 15
487 60e. Eurasian woodcock . . 1·80 80
488 80e. Roseate tern . . . . . . 1·90 85
489 100e. Common buzzard . . . 2·50 90
See also Nos. 492/5 and 500/3.

35 Azores Arms

1988. Coats-of-arms. Multicoloured.
490 55e. Type **35** . . . . 1·50 70
491 80e. Bettencourt family arms 2·00 90

1989. Nature Protection (2nd series). Goldcrest. As T **34**. Multicoloured.
492 30e. Goldcrest perched on branch 80 20
493 30e. Pair 80 20
494 30e. Goldcrest on nest . . . 80 20
495 30e. Goldcrest with outspread wings 80 20

36 Boy in Boat

1989. Europa. Children's Games and Toys.
496 **36** 80e. multicoloured . . . . 2·00 90
MS497 139 × 112 mm. 80e. × 2, Type **36**; 80e. × 2, Boy with toy boat . . . . 16·00 16·00

37 Pioneers

1989. 550th Anniv of Portuguese Settlement in Azores. Multicoloured.
498 29e. Type **37** 50 15
499 87e. Settler breaking land . . 2·20 1·00

1990. Nature Protection (3rd series). Northern Bullfinch. As T **34**. Multicoloured.
500 32e. Two bullfinches . . . . 1·00 25
501 32e. Bullfinch on branch . . 1·00 25
502 32e. Bullfinch landing on twig 1·00 25
503 32e. Bullfinch on nest . . . . 1·00 25

38 Vasco da Gama P.O.

1990. Europa. P.O. Buildings.
504 **38** 80e. multicoloured . . . . 1·50 80
MS505 139 × 111 mm. 80e. × 2, Type **38**; 80e. × 2, Maia Post Office . . . . 14·50 14·50

39 Cart Maker

1990. Traditional Occupations. Multicoloured.
506 5e. Type **39** 15 10
507 10e. Viol maker 15 10
508 32e. Potter 50 20
509 35e. Making roof tiles . . . 50 15
510 38e. Carpenter 50 20
511 60e. Tinsmith . . . . 1·50 65
512 65e. Laying pavement mosaics . . . . 1·20 60
513 70e. Quarrying . . . . 1·30 65
514 85e. Basket maker . . . . . 1·30 55
515 100e. Cooper . . . . 2·10 95
516 110e. Shaping stones . . . . 1·30 65
517 120e. Boat builders . . . . . 1·60 80

40 "Hermes" Spaceplane

1991. Europa. Europe in Space.
520 **40** 80e. multicoloured . . . . 1·50 85
MS521 140 × 112 mm. 80e. × 2, Type **40**; 80e. × 2, "Sanger" spaceplane . . . . 13·50 13·50

41 "Helena" (schooner)

1991. Inter-island Transport. Multicoloured.
522 35e. Type **41** 50 10
523 60e. Beech Model 18 airplane, 1947 . . . . 95 45
524 80e. "Cruzeiro do Canal" (ferry), 1987 . . . . 1·50 75
525 110e. British Aerospace ATP airliner, 1991 . . . . . . 1·80 80

42 "Santa Maria" off Azores

1992. Europa. 500th Anniv of Discovery of America by Columbus.
526 **42** 85e. multicoloured . . . . 1·30 65

43 "Insulano" (steamer, 1868)

1992. The Empresa Insulana de Navegacao Shipping Fleet. Multicoloured.
527 38e. Type **43** 50 15
528 65e. "Carvalho Araujo" (ferry, 1930) 95 50
529 85e. "Funchal" (ferry, 1961) 1·20 65
530 120e. "Terceirense" (freighter, 1948) . . . . 1·60 70

44 Ox-mill

1993. Traditional Grinders. Multicoloured.
531 42e. Type **44** 50 20
532 130e. Hand-mill . . . . . . 1·90 90

45 "Two Sirens at the Entrance of a Grotto" (Antonio Dacosta) **46** Main Entrance, Praia da Vitoria Church, Terceira

1993. Europa. Contemporary Art.
533 **45** 90e. multicoloured . . . . 1·40 65
MS534 140 × 112 mm. 90e. × 2, Type **45**; 90e. × 2, "Acorinan III" 6·50 6·50

1993. Doorways. Multicoloured.
535 42e. Type **46** 50 20
536 70e. South door, Praia da Vitoria Church 90 45
537 90e. Main door, Ponta Delgada Church, Sao Miguel . . . . 1·20 50
538 130e. South door, Ponta Delgada Church . . . . . 1·60 65

47 Floral Decoration, Our Lady of Sorrows, Caloura, Sao Miguel

1994. Tiles. Multicoloured.
539 40e. Type **47** 40 20
540 70e. Decoration of crosses, Our Lady of Sorrows, Caloura, Sao Miguel . . . 90 40

541 100e. "Adoration of the Wise Men", Our Lady of Hope Monastery, Ponta Delgada, Sao Miguel . . . . 1·20 60
542 150e. "St. Bras" (altar frontal), Our Lady of Anjos, Santa Maria . . . 1·70 80

48 Monkey and Explorer with Model Caravel

1994. Europa. Discoveries. Multicoloured.
543 **48** 100e. multicoloured . . . . 1·20 60
MS544 140 × 112 mm. 100e. × 2, Type **48**; 100e. × 2, Armadilo and explorer with model caravel . . 5·50 5·50

49 Doorway, St. Barbaras Church, Cedros, Faial

1994. Manoeline Architecture. Multicoloured.
545 45e. Type **49** 45 20
546 140e. Window, Ribeira Grande, Sao Miguel . . . 1·50 80

50 Aristides Moreira da Motta

1995. Centenary of Decree decentralizing Government of the Azores and Madeira Islands. Pro-autonomy activists. Multicoloured.
547 42e. Type **50** 45 20
548 130e. Gil Mont' Alverne de Sequeira . . . . 1·40 65

51 Santana Palace, Ponta Delgada

1995. Architecture of Sao Miguel. Multicoloured.
549 45e. Type **51** 45 20
550 80e. Chapel of Our Lady of the Victories, Furnas . . . 80 35
551 95e. Hospital, Ponta Delgada 95 40
552 135e. Ernesto do Canto's villa, Furnas . . . . 1·20 60

52 Contendas Lighthouse, Terceira (½-size illustration)

1996. Lighthouses. Multicoloured.
553 47e. Type **52** 40 20
554 78e. Molhe Lighthouse, Sao Miguel 85 45
555 98e. Arnel Lighthouse, Sao Miguel 95 50
556 140e. Santa Clara Lighthouse, Sao Miguel . . 1·30 65
MS557 110 × 140 mm. 200e. Ponta da Barca Lighthouse, Graciosa 2·50 2·50

53 Natalia Correia (poet)

1996. Europa. Famous Women.
558 **53** 98e. multicoloured 95 50
MS559 140 × 112 mm. No. 558 × 3 2·30 2·30

54 Bird eating Grapes (St. Peter's Church, Ponta Delgada)

1997. Gilded Wooden Altarpieces. Multicoloured.
560 49e. Type **54** 45 20
561 80e. Cherub (St. Peter of Alcantara Convent, Sao Roque) 80 30
562 100e. Cherub with wings (All Saints Church, Jesuit College, Ponta Delgada) 90 50
563 140e. Caryatid (St. Joseph's Church, Ponta Delgada) 1·30 70

55 Island of the Seven Cities

1997. Europa. Tales and Legends.
564 **55** 100e. multicoloured . . . . 1·00 50
MS565 140 × 106 mm. No. 564 × 3 3·00 3·00

56 Emperor and Empress and young Bulls (Festival of the Holy Spirit)

1998. Europa. National Festivals.
566 **56** 100e. multicoloured 90 45
MS567 140 × 109 No. 566 × 3 . . 2·50 2·50

57 Spotted Dolphin

1998. "Expo '98" World's Fair, Lisbon. Marine Life. Multicoloured.
568 50e. Type **57** 45 20
569 140e. Sperm whale (79 × 30 mm) . . . . . . 1·20 65

58 Mt. Pico Nature Reserve

1999. Europa. Parks and Gardens.
570 **58** 100e. multicoloured 85 45
MS571 154 × 109 mm. No. 570 × 3 3·00 3·00

59 "Emigrants" (Domingos Rebelo)

1999. Paintings. Multicoloured.
572 51e. Type **59** 45 20
573 95e. "Portrait of Vitorino Nemesio" (Antonio Dacosta) (vert) 80 45
574 100e. "Cattle loose on the Alto das Covas" (Ze van der Hagen Bretao) . . . 85 45
575 140e. "Vila Franca Island" (Duarte Maia) . . . . 1·10 65

60 "Building Europe"

2000. Europa.
576 **60** 100e. multicoloured 85 45
MS577 154 × 108 mm. No. 576 × 3 2·50 2·50

61 Fishermen retrieving Mail Raft

2000. History of Mail Delivery in the Azores. Mult.
578 85e. Type **61** 70 35
579 140e. Zeppelin airship dropping mail sacks . . . 1·10 60

62 Coast Line

2001. Europa. Water Resources.
580 **62** 105e. multicoloured 85 45
MS581 140 × 110 mm. No. 580 × 3 2·20 2·20

63 Arch and Town

2001. UNESCO World Heritage Site, Angra do Heroismo. Multicoloured.
582 53e. Type **63** 40 20
583 85e. Monument and town . . 70 35
584 140e. Balcony and view over town . . . . 1·10 60
MS585 140 × 112 mm. 350e. Map of town . . . . 2·40 2·40

64 Clown

2002. Europa. Circus.
586 **64** 54c. multicoloured 85 40
MS587 140 × 110 mm. No. 586 × 3 3·00 3·00

65 Faial Island, Azores

2002. Windmills. Multicoloured.
588 43c. Type **65** 65 30
589 54c. Onze-Lieve-Vrouw-Lombeek, Roosdaal . . . 80 40
Stamps of a similar design were issued by Belgium.

66 Birds (Sebastiao Rodrigues)

2003. Europa. Poster Art.
590 **66** 55c. multicoloured 80 40
MS591 140 × 113 mm. No. 591 × 2 75 75

67 Pineapple Groves

2003. Sao Miguel Island. Multicoloured.
592 30c. Type **67** 35 20
593 43c. Vineyards and grapes . . 65 30
594 55c. Date growing 80 40
595 70c. Coffee growing . . . . 1·00 50
MS596 140 × 112 mm. €1 Dancers and ceramic figure; €2 Fruit and ceramic bird (Espirito Santos festival) . . . . 4·00 4·00

68 Figures, Flowers and Island

2004. Europa. Holidays.
597 **68** 56c. multicoloured 75 40
MS598 141 × 112 mm. No. 597 × 2 1·50 1·50

69 Blue Marlin (*Makaira nigricans*)

2004. Endangered Species. Atlantic Marlin. Multicoloured.
599 30c. Type **69** 25 15
600 30c. Fin, body and tail . . . 25 15
601 30c. White marlin (*Tetrapturus albidus*) . . . 25 15
602 30c. Back and tail 25 15
Nos. 599/602 were issued together, se-tenant, forming a composite design.

70 Torresmos (marinated pork)

2005. Europa. Gastronomy. Multicoloured.
603 57c. Type **70** 80 40
MS604 125 × 95 mm. 57c. × 2, *Polvo guisado* (octopus) × 2 . . . . . 1·60 1·60

71 Cow

2005. Tourism. Multicoloured.
605 30c. Type **71** 40 20
606 30c. Arched window and lake 40 20
607 45c. Decorated house 60 30
608 45c. Windmill 60 30

609		57c. Whale's tail	80	40
610		74c. Pineapple and hot spring	1·00	1·00
MS611		125 × 95 mm. 30c. Santo Cristo dos Milagres (statue); €1.55 Bird	2·50	2·50

Nos. 605/10 were issued together, se-tenant, forming a composite design.

72 Figures standing on Head (Joao Dinis)

2006. Europa. Integration. Winning Entries in ANACED (association for art and creativity by and for people with disabilities) Painting Competition. Multicoloured.

612		60c. Type **72**	1·40	70
MS613		125 × 95 mm. 60c. × 2, One legged figure; Figures with irregular outlines	2·75	2·75

73 Crabs, Lucky Strike

2006. Hydrothermal Springs. Multicoloured.

614		20c. Type **73**	35	15
615		30c. Fish, Lucky Strike	50	25
616		75c. Plumes, Rainbow	2·25	1·10
617		€2 Fish tower, Rainbow	4·50	2·25
MS618		125 × 95 mm. €2 No. 617	4·50	4·50

74 Mountain

2006. Wine from Pico Island. Multicoloured.

619		30c. Type **74**	50	25
620		60c. Terraces	1·30	65
621		75c. Wine barrel	1·70	90
622		€1 Harvesting	2·50	1·20
MS623		125 × 95 mm. 45c. Young vines; 60c. Harvesting; 75c. Winery; €1 Barrels	6·25	6·25

75 Scarf

2007. Europa. Centenary of Scouting. Multicoloured.

624		61c. Type **75**	1·40	1·40
MS625		125 × 95 mm. 61c. × 2, Reef knot; Scouts in camp	2·75	2·75

The stamps of **MS**625 form a composite design.

76 Sao Miguel

2007. Windmills. Multicoloured.

626		30c. Type **76**	65	65
627		45c. Sao Jorge	90	90
628		61c. Corvo	1·40	1·40
629		75c. Blue windmill, Sao Jorge	1·50	1·50
MS630		125 × 95 mm. 45c. Sao Miguel (different); €2 Red windmill, Sao Jorge	5·50	5·50

77 Capelinhos Volcano

2007. 50th Anniv of Eruption of Capelinhos Volcano, Faial Island. Multicoloured.

631		30c. Type **77**	65	65
632		75c. Erupting volcano and lighthouse	1·50	1·50
MS633		125 × 95 mm. €2.45 Island showing lighthouse (80 × 30 mm)	5·75	5·75

The stamp and margin of **MS**633 form a composite design.

CHARITY TAX STAMPS

Used on certain days of the year as an additional postal tax on internal letters. The proceeds were devoted to public charities. If one was not affixed in addition to the ordinary postage, postage due stamps were used to collect the deficiency and the fine.

1911. No. 206 optd **ASSISTENCIA**.

C218a	**7**	10r. green	1·40	90

1913. No. 252 optd **ASSISTENCIA**.

C250	**56**	1c. green	3·75	2·75

1915. For the Poor. Charity stamp of Portugal optd **ACORES**.

C251	C **58**	1c. red	50	35

1925. No. C251 surch **15 ctvs**.

C325	C **58**	15c. on 1c. red	65	65

1925. Portuguese Army in Flanders issue of Portugal optd **ACORES**.

C345	C **71**	10c. red	90	90
C346		10c. green	90	90
C347		10c. blue	90	90
C348		10c. brown	90	90

1925. As Marquis de Pombal issue of Portugal, inscr "ACORES".

C349	C **73**	20c. green	90	90
C350	–	20c. green	90	90
C351	C **75**	20c. green	90	90

NEWSPAPER STAMPS

1876. Stamps of Portugal optd **ACORES**.

N146	N **16**	2r. black	4·25	2·20
N150b	N **17**	2½r. green	4·25	2·20
N150a		2½r. brown	4·25	2·20

PARCEL POST STAMPS

1921. Stamps of Portugal optd **ACORES**.

P325	P **59**	1c. brown	40	35
P326		2c. orange	40	35
P327		5c. brown	40	35
P328		10c. brown	60	35
P329		20c. blue	60	35
P330		40c. red	60	35
P331		50c. black	80	1·50
P332		60c. blue	80	1·50
P333		70c. brown	2·10	1·80
P334		80c. blue	2·10	1·80
P335		90c. violet	2·10	1·80
P336		1e. green	2·10	1·80
P337		2e. lilac	3·50	2·75
P338		3e. olive	6·00	3·00
P339		4e. blue	7·25	3·00
P340		5e. lilac	7·50	5·75
P341		10e. brown	31·00	17·00

POSTAGE DUE STAMPS

Nos. D179/351 are stamps of Portugal overprinted **ACORES**.

1904.

D179	D **49**	5r. brown	1·00	90
D180		10r. orange	1·00	90
D181		20r. mauve	1·60	1·20
D182		30r. green	1·60	1·20
D183		40r. lilac	2·75	1·80
D184		50r. red	4·25	3·25
D185		100r. blue	5·50	4·75

1911. As last, optd **REPUBLICA**.

D218	D **49**	5r. brown	45	45
D219		10r. orange	45	45
D220		20r. mauve	70	60
D221		30r. green	70	60
D222		40r. lilac	1·10	70
D223		50r. red	5·25	5·25
D224		100r. blue	1·90	1·90

1918. Value in centavos.

D325	D **49**	½c. brown	55	50
D326		1c. orange	55	50
D327		2c. purple	55	50
D328		3c. green	55	50
D329		4c. lilac	55	50
D330		5c. red	55	50
D331		10c. blue	55	50

1922.

D332	D **49**	½c. green	30	30
D333		1c. green	45	30
D334		2c. green	45	35
D335		3c. green	70	35
D336		8c. green	70	35
D337		10c. green	70	35
D338		12c. green	70	35
D339		16c. green	75	35
D340		20c. green	50	35
D341		24c. green	75	35
D342		32c. green	75	35
D343		36c. green	75	50
D344		40c. green	75	50
D345		48c. green	75	50
D346		50c. green	75	50
D347		60c. green	80	55
D348		72c. green	80	55
D349		80c. green	4·00	3·25
D350		1e.20 green	4·50	3·75

1925. Portuguese Army in Flanders.

D351	D **72**	20c. brown	90	75

1925. As Nos. C349/51, optd **MULTA**.

D352	D **73**	40c. green	90	85
D353	–	40c. green	90	85
D354	D **75**	40c. green	90	85

BADEN Pt. 7

In S.W. Germany. Formerly a Grand Duchy, now part of the German Federal Republic.

60 kreuzer = 1 gulden.

1

2

1851. Imperf.

1	**1**	1k. black on buff	£550	£275
8		1k. black on white	£450	31·00
3		3k. black on yellow	£275	18·00
9		3k. black on green	£350	7·00
10		3k. black on blue	£1600	35·00
5		6k. black on green	£900	55·00
11		6k. black on orange	£600	28·00
6		9k. black on red	£225	31·00

1860. Shaded background behind Arms. Perf.

13	**2**	1k. black	90·00	31·00
16		3k. blue	95·00	19·00
17		6k. orange	£110	70·00
22		6k. blue	£180	£110
19		9k. red	£275	£200
25		9k. brown	£110	£130

1862. Uncoloured background behind Arms.

27		1k. black	55·00	14·00
28		3k. red	55·00	1·80
30		6k. blue	10·50	19·00
33		9k. brown	16·00	31·00
36		18k. green	£450	£550
38		30k. orange	33·00	£2250

1868. "K R." instead of "KREUZER".

39		1k. green	4·50	5·25
41		3k. red	2·75	1·80
44		7k. blue	22·00	40·00

For issues of 1947 to 1964 see Germany: Allied Occupation (French Zone).

RURAL POSTAGE DUE STAMPS

D 4

1862.

D39	D **4**	1k. black on yellow	4·50	£350
D40		3k. black on yellow	2·75	£160
D41		12k. black on yellow	40·00	£15000

BAGHDAD Pt. 1

A city in Iraq. Special stamps issued during British occupation in the War of 1914–18.

16 annas = 1 rupee.

1917. Various issues of Turkey surch **BAGHDAD IN BRITISH OCCUPATION** and new value in annas.

A. Pictorial issues of 1913.

1	**32**	½a. on 2pa. red	£180	£225
2	**34**	½a. on 5pa. purple	£130	£140
3	–	½a. on 10pa. green (No. 516)	£750	£950
4	**31**	½a. on 10pa. green	£1300	£1500
5	–	1a. on 20pa. red (No. 504)	£500	£600
6	–	2a. on 1pi. blue (No. 518)	£225	£250

B. As last, but optd with small star.

7	–	1a. on 20pa. red	£350	£400
8	–	2a. on 1pi. blue	£4000	£4500

C. Postal Jubilee issue.

9	**60**	½a. on 10pa. red	£550	£650
10b		1a. on 20pa. blue	£1200	£1500
11b		2a. on 1pi. black & violet	£140	£150

D. Optd with Turkish letter "B".

12	**30**	2a. on 1pi. blue	£550	£700

E. Optd with star and Arabic date within crescent.

13	**30**	½a. on 10pa. green	£130	£140
14		1a. on 20pa. red	£500	£550
15	**23**	1a. on 20pa. red	£550	£650
16	**21**	1a. on 20pa. red (No. N185)	£4750	£6000
17	**30**	2a. on 1pi. blue	£140	£160
18	**21**	2a. on 1pi. blue	£225	£275

F. Optd as last, but with date between star and crescent.

19	**23**	½a. on 10pa. green	£150	£180
20	**60**	½a. on 10pa. red	£225	£250
21	**30**	1a. on 20pa. red	£150	£180
22	**28**	1a. on 20pa. red	£550	£600
23	**15**	1a. on 10pa. on 20pa. red	£250	£275
24	**30**	2a. on 1pi. blue	£225	£275
25	**28**	2a. on 1pi. blue	£1800	£2000

BAHAMAS Pt. 1

A group of islands in the Br. W. Indies, S.E. of Florida. Self-Government introduced on 7 January 1964. The islands became an independent member of the British Commonwealth on 10 July 1973.

1859. 12 pence = 1 shilling;
20 shillings = 1 pound.
1966. 100 cents = 1 dollar.

1

2

3

1859. Imperf.

2	**1**	1d. red	60·00	£1500

1860. Perf.

33	**1**	1d. red	55·00	15·00
26	**2**	4d. red	£300	60·00
31		6d. violet	£160	60·00
39ba	**3**	1s. green	8·00	8·00

1883. Surch **FOURPENCE**.

45	**2**	4d. on 6d. violet	£550	£400

5

6 Queen's Staircase, Nassau

1884.

48	**5**	1d. red	7·00	2·50
52		2½d. blue	9·50	2·25
53		4d. yellow	9·50	4·00
54		6d. mauve	6·00	30·00
56		5s. green	65·00	75·00
57		£1 red	£275	£225

1901.

111	**6**	1d. black and red	1·75	2·00
76a		3d. purple on buff	5·50	5·50
77		3d. black and brown	2·00	2·25
59		5d. black and orange	8·50	48·00
78		5d. black and mauve	2·75	5·50
113		2s. black and blue	19·00	22·00
61		3s. black and green	38·00	60·00

7

8

1902.

71	**7**	½d. green	5·00	3·00
62		1d. red	1·50	2·00
63		2½d. blue	6·50	1·25
64		4d. yellow	15·00	60·00
66		6d. brown	3·50	24·00
67		1s. black and red	20·00	50·00
69		5s. purple and blue	65·00	85·00
70		£1 green and black	£250	£325

1912.

115	**8**	½d. green	50	40
116		1d. red	1·00	15
117		1½d. brown	9·00	1·00
118		2d. grey	1·50	2·25
119		2½d. blue	1·00	2·25
120		3d. purple on yellow	6·50	16·00
121		4d. yellow	1·50	4·00
122		6d. brown	70	1·25
123		1s. black and red	2·75	5·50
124		5s. purple and blue	35·00	65·00
125		£1 green and black	£170	£325

1917. Optd **1.1.17.** and Red Cross.

90	**6**	1d. black and red	40	2·00

1918. Optd **WAR TAX** in one line.

96	**8**	½d. green	1·75	1·75
97		1d. red	2·00	35
93	**6**	1d. black and red	3·50	5·50
98		3d. purple on yellow	1·00	1·50

100		3d. black and brown	60	4·00
99	8	1s. black and red	9·00	2·75

1919. Optd **WAR CHARITY 3.6.18.**

101	6	1d. black and red	30	2·50

1919. Optd **WAR TAX** in two lines.

102	8	½d. green	30	1·25
103		1d. red	1·50	1·50
105	6	3d. black and brown	75	8·00
104	8	1s. black and red	22·00	48·00

16

17 Seal of the Colony

1920. Peace Celebration.

106	16	½d. green	1·00	5·50
107		1d. red	2·75	1·00
108		2d. grey	2·75	7·50
109		3d. brown	2·75	9·00
110		1s. green	12·00	35·00

1930. Tercentenary of the Colony.

126	17	1d. black and red	2·25	2·75
127		3d. black and brown	4·25	15·00
128		5d. black and violet	4·25	15·00
129		2s. black and blue	18·00	50·00
130		3s. black and green	45·00	85·00

1931. As T **17**, but without dates at top.

131b		2s. black and blue	11·00	5·00
132a		3s. black and green	9·00	3·50

1935. Silver Jubilee. As T **13** of Antigua.

141		1½d. blue and red	1·00	3·50
142		2½d. brown and blue	5·00	9·50
143		6d. blue and olive	7·00	14·00
144		1s. grey and purple	7·00	13·00

19 Greater Flamingo (in flight)

1935.

145	19	8d. blue and red	6·00	3·25

1937. Coronation. As T **2** of Aden.

146		½d. green	15	15
147		1½d. brown	30	1·10
148		2½d. blue	50	1·10

20 King George VI

21 Sea Garden, Nassau

1938.

149	20	½d. green	1·50	1·25
149e		½d. purple	1·00	2·50
150		1d. red	8·50	2·50
150ab		1d. grey	60	70
151		1½d. brown	1·50	1·25
152		2d. grey	18·00	4·00
152b		2d. red	1·00	65
152c		2d. green	1·75	80
153		2½d. blue	3·25	1·50
153a		2½d. violet	1·25	1·25
154		3d. violet	16·00	3·00
154a		3d. blue	70	1·25
154b		3d. red	70	3·25
158	21	4d. blue and orange	1·00	1·00
159	–	6d. green and blue	75	1·00
160	–	8d. blue and red	9·50	2·50
154c	20	10d. orange	2·50	20
155c		1s. black and red	15·00	75
156b		5s. purple and blue	28·00	22·00
157a		£1 green and black	60·00	55·00

DESIGNS—As Type **21**: 6d. Fort Charlotte; 8d. Greater flamingos.

1940. Surch **3d.**

161	20	3d. on 2½d. blue	1·50	1·75

1942. 450th Anniv of Landing of Columbus. Optd **1492 LANDFALL OF COLUMBUS 1942.**

162	20	½d. green	30	60
163		1d. grey	30	60
164		1½d. brown	40	60
165		2d. red	50	65
166		2½d. blue	50	65
167		3d. blue	30	65
168	21	4d. blue and orange	40	90
169	–	6d. green & blue (No. 159)	40	1·75
170	–	8d. blue and red (No. 160)	1·50	70
171	20	1s. black and red	8·50	4·25
172a	17	2s. black and blue	8·00	10·00
173		3s. black and green	8·00	6·50
174a	20	5s. purple and blue	23·00	14·00
175a		£1 green and black	30·00	25·00

1946. Victory. As T **9** of Aden.

176		1½d. brown	10	60
177		3d. blue	10	60

26 Infant Welfare Clinic

1948. Tercentenary of Settlement of Island of Eleuthera. Inscr as in T **26**.

178	26	½d. orange	40	1·50
179	–	1d. olive	40	35
180	–	1½d. yellow	40	80
181	–	2d. red	40	40
182	–	2½d. brown	70	75
183	–	3d. blue	2·50	85
184	–	4d. black	60	70
185	–	6d. green	2·50	80
186	–	8d. violet	1·25	70
187	–	10d. red	1·25	35
188	–	1s. brown	2·75	50
189	–	2s. purple	4·25	8·50
190	–	3s. blue	11·00	8·50
191	–	5s. mauve	18·00	4·50
192	–	10s. grey	15·00	11·00
193	–	£1 red	15·00	16·00

DESIGNS: 1d. Agriculture; 1½d. Sisal; 2d. Straw work; 2½d. Dairy; 3d. Fishing fleet; 4d. Island settlement; 6d. Tuna fishing; 8d. Paradise Beach; 10d. Modern hotels; 1s. Yacht racing; 2s. Water sports—skiing; 3s. Shipbuilding; 5s. Transportation; 10s. Salt production; £1 Parliament Buildings.

1948. Silver Wedding. As T **10/11** of Aden.

194		1½d. brown	20	25
195		£1 grey	38·00	32·00

1949. 75th Anniv of U.P.U. As T **20/23** of Antigua.

196		2½d. violet	35	75
197		3d. blue	2·25	3·25
198		6d. blue	55	3·00
199		1s. red	55	75

1953. Coronation. As T **13** of Aden.

200		6d. black and blue	1·50	60

42 Infant Welfare Clinic

43 Queen Elizabeth II

1954. Designs as Nos. 178/93 but with portrait of Queen Elizabeth II and without commemorative inscr as in T **42**.

201	42	½d. black and red	10	1·50
202	–	1d. olive and brown	10	30
203	–	1½d. blue and black	15	80
204	–	2d. brown and green	15	30
205	–	3d. black and red	65	1·25
206	–	4d. turquoise and purple	30	30
207	–	5d. brown and blue	1·40	2·25
208	–	6d. blue and black	2·25	20
209	–	8d. black and lilac	70	40
210	–	10d. black and blue	30	10
211	–	1s. blue and brown	1·50	10
212	–	2s. orange and black	2·00	70
213	–	2s.6d. black and blue	3·50	2·00
214	–	5s. green and orange	19·00	75
215	–	10s. black and slate	26·00	2·50
216	–	£1 black and violet	24·00	6·50

DESIGNS: 1½d. Hatchet Bay, Eleuthera; 4d. Water sports—skiing; 5d. Dairy; 6d. Transportation; 2s. Sisal; 2s.6d. Shipbuilding; 5s. Tuna fishing. Other values the same as for the corresponding values in Nos. 178/93.

1959. Centenary of 1st Bahamas Postage Stamp.

217	43	1d. black and red	45	20
218		2d. black and green	45	1·00
219		6d. black and blue	55	40
220		10d. black and brown	55	1·00

44 Christ Church Cathedral

1962. Centenary of Nassau.

221	44	8d. green	50	55
222	–	10d. violet	50	25

DESIGN: 10d. Nassau Public Library.

1963. Freedom from Hunger. As T **28** of Aden.

223		8d. sepia	40	40

1963. Bahamas Talks. Nos. 209/10 optd **BAHAMAS TALKS 1962.**

224		8d. black and lilac	50	75
225		10d. black and blue	50	75

1963. Centenary of Red Cross. As T **33** of Antigua.

226		1d. red and black	50	50
227		10d. red and blue	1·75	2·50

1964. New Constitution. Nos. 201/16 optd **NEW CONSTITUTION 1964.**

228	42	½d. black and red	15	1·50
229	–	1d. olive and brown	15	15
230	–	1½d. blue and black	70	1·50
231	–	2d. brown and green	15	20
232	–	3d. black and red	2·00	1·75
233	–	4d. turquoise and purple	70	55
234	–	5d. brown and blue	70	1·50
235	–	6d. blue and black	3·25	30
236	–	8d. black and lilac	70	30
237	–	10d. black and blue	30	15
238	–	1s. blue and brown	1·50	15
239	–	2s. brown and black	2·00	1·75
240	–	2s.6d. black and blue	3·00	2·75
241	–	5s. green and orange	7·00	3·25
242	–	10s. black and slate	7·00	5·50
243	–	£1 black and violet	7·50	19·00

1964. 400th Birth Anniv of Shakespeare. As T **34** of Antigua.

244		6d. turquoise	30	10

1964. Olympic Games, Tokyo. No. 211 surch **8d.** and Olympic rings.

245		8d. on 1s. blue and brown	45	15

49 Colony's Badge

1965.

247	49	½d. multicoloured	15	2·25
248	–	1d. slate, blue and orange	30	1·00
249	–	1½d. red, green and brown	15	2·75
250	–	2d. slate, green and blue	15	10
251	–	3d. red, blue and purple	4·00	20
252	–	4d. green, blue and brown	4·75	3·00
253	–	6d. green, blue and red	1·25	10
254	–	8d. purple, blue & bronze	50	30
255	–	10d. brown, green and violet	25	10
256a	–	1s. multicoloured	40	10
257	–	2s. brown, blue and green	1·00	1·25
258	–	2s.6d. olive, blue and red	2·50	3·00
259	–	5s. brown, blue and green	2·75	1·00
260	–	10s. red, blue and brown	16·00	3·50
261	–	£1 brown, blue and red	19·00	9·00

DESIGNS: 1d. Out Island regatta; 1½d. Hospital; 2d. High School; 3d. Greater flamingo; 4d. R.M.S. "Queen Elizabeth"; 6d. "Development"; 8d. Yachting; 10d. Public square; 1s. Sea garden; 2s. Old cannons at Fort Charlotte; 2s.6d. Sikorsky S-38 flying boat, 1929, and Boeing 707 airliner; 5s. Williamson film project, 1914, and undersea post office, 1939; 10s. Queen or pink conch; £1 Columbus's flagship.

1965. Centenary of I.T.U. As T **36** of Antigua.

262		1d. green and orange	15	10
263		2s. purple and olive	65	45

1965. No. 254 surch **9d.**

264		9d. on 8d. purple, blue & bronze	30	15

1965. I.C.Y. As T **37** of Antigua.

265		½d. purple and turquoise	10	1·10
266		1s. green and lavender	30	40

1966. Churchill Commemoration. As T **38** of Antigua.

267		½d. blue	10	75
268		2d. green	50	30
269		10d. brown	85	85
270		1s. violet	85	1·40

1966. Royal Visit. As T **39** of Antigua but inscr "to the Caribbean" omitted.

271		6d. black and blue	1·00	50
272		1s. black and mauve	1·25	1·25

1966. Decimal currency. Nos. 247/61 surch.

273	49	1c. on ½d. multicoloured	10	30
274	–	2c. on 1d. slate, blue and orange	75	30
275	–	3c. on 2d. slate, green and blue	10	10
276	–	4c. on 3d. red, blue and purple	2·00	20
277	–	5c. on 4d. green, blue and brown	2·00	3·00
278	–	8c. on 6d. green, blue and red	20	20
279	–	10c. on 8d. purple, blue and bronze	30	75
280	–	11c. on 1½d. red, green and brown	15	30
281	–	12c. on 10d. brown, green and violet	15	10
282	–	15c. on 1s. multicoloured	25	10
283	–	22c. on 2s. brown, blue and green	60	1·25
284	–	50c. on 2s.6d. olive, blue and red	1·00	1·40
285	–	$1 on 5s. brown, blue and green	1·75	1·50
286	–	$2 on 10s. red, blue and brown	7·50	4·50
287	–	$3 on £1 brown, blue and red	7·50	4·50

1966. World Cup Football Championships. As T **40** of Antigua.

288		8c. multicoloured	35	15
289		15c. multicoloured	40	25

1966. Inauguration of W.H.O. Headquarters, Geneva. As T **41** of Antigua.

290		11c. black, green and blue	50	90
291		15c. black, purple and ochre	50	50

1966. 20th Anniv of UNESCO As T **54/6** of Antigua.

292		3c. multicoloured	10	10
293		15c. yellow, violet and olive	35	20
294		$1 black, purple and orange	1·10	2·00

1967. As Nos. 247/51, 253/9 and 261 but values in decimal currency, and new designs for 5c. and $2.

295	49	1c. multicoloured	10	3·25
296	–	2c. slate, blue and green	50	60
297	–	3c. slate, green and violet	10	10
298	–	4c. red, light blue and blue	4·75	50
299	–	5c. black, blue and purple	1·00	3·50
300	–	8c. green, blue and brown	25	10
301	–	10c. purple, blue and red	30	70
302	–	11c. red, green and blue	25	80
303	–	12c. brown, green and olive	25	10
304	–	15c. multicoloured	55	10
305	–	22c. brown, blue and red	70	65
306	–	50c. olive, blue and green	2·25	1·00
307	–	$1 maroon, blue and purple	2·00	60
308	–	$2 multicoloured	13·00	3·00
309	–	$3 brown, blue and purple	3·75	2·00

NEW DESIGNS: 5c. "Oceanic"; $2 Conch shell (different).

69 Bahamas Crest

1967. Diamond Jubilee of World Scouting. Mult.

310		3c. Type **69**	35	15
311		15c. Scout badge	40	15

71 Globe and Emblem

1968. Human Rights Year. Multicoloured.

312		3c. Type **71**	10	10
313		12c. Scales of Justice and emblem	20	10
314		$1 Bahamas Crest and emblem	70	80

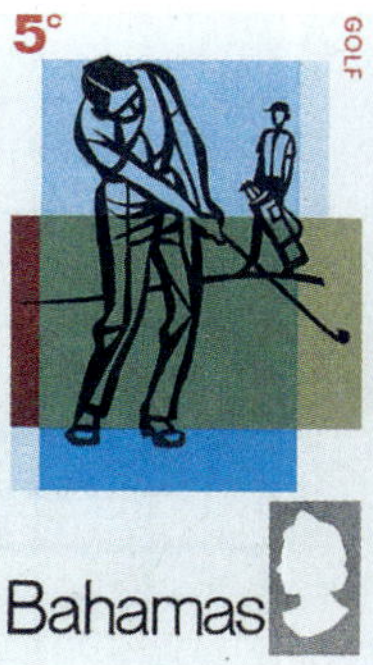

74 Golf

1968. Tourism. Multicoloured.

315		5c. Type **74**	1·75	1·75
316		11c. Yachting	1·25	40
317		15c. Horse-racing	1·75	45
318		50c. Water-skiing	2·50	6·50

78 Racing Yacht and Olympic Monument

1968. Olympic Games, Mexico City.
319 **78** 5c. brown, yellow and green 40 75
320 – 11c. multicoloured 40 25
321 – 50c. multicoloured . . . . 60 1·75
322 **78** $1 grey, blue and violet . . 2·00 3·75
DESIGNS: 11c. Long jumping and Olympic Monument; 50c. Running and Olympic Monument.

81 Legislative Building

1968. 14th Commonwealth Parliamentary Conference. Multicoloured.
323 3c. Type **81** 10 30
324 10c. Bahamas Mace and Westminster Clock Tower (vert) 15 30
325 12c. Local straw market (vert) 15 25
326 15c. Horse-drawn surrey . . 20 35

85 Obverse and reverse of $100 Gold Coin

1968. Gold Coins commemorating the first General Election under the New Constitution.
327 **85** 3c. red on gold 40 40
328 – 12c. green on gold 45 50
329 – 15c. purple on gold . . . 50 60
330 – $1 black on gold . . . . . 1·25 3·25
OBVERSE AND REVERSE OF: 12c. $50 gold coin; 15c. $20 gold coins; $1, $10 gold coin.

89 First Flight Postcard of 1919

1969. 50th Anniv of Bahamas Airmail Services.
331 **89** 12c. multicoloured 50 50
332 – 15c. multicoloured . . . . 60 1·75
DESIGN: 15c. Sikorsky S-38 flying boat of 1929.

91 Game-fishing Boats

1969. Tourism. One Millionth Visitor to Bahamas. Multicoloured.
333 3c. Type **91** 25 10
334 11c. Paradise Beach 35 15
335 12c. "Sunfish" sailing boats 35 15
336 15c. Rawson Square and parade 45 25
MS337 130 × 96 mm. Nos. 333/6 2·75 3·50

92 "The Adoration of the Shepherds" (Louis le Nain)

1969. Christmas. Multicoloured.
338 3c. Type **92** 10 20
339 11c. "The Adoration of the Shepherds" (Poussin) . . . 15 30
340 12c. "The Adoration of the Kings" (Gerard David) . . 15 20
341 15c. "The Adoration of the Kings" (Vincenzo Foppa) 20 65

93 Badge of Girl Guides

1970. Diamond Jubilee of Girl Guides' Association. Multicoloured.
342 3c. Type **93** 30 10
343 12c. Badge of Brownies . . . 45 20
344 15c. Badge of Rangers . . . 50 35

94 New U.P.U. Headquarters and Emblem

1970. New U.P.U. Headquarters Building.
345 **94** 3c. multicoloured 10 40
346 15c. multicoloured 20 60

95 Coach and Globe

1970. "Goodwill Caravan". Multicoloured.
347 3c. Type **95** 75 20
348 11c. Diesel train and globe 1·50 60
349 12c. "Canberra" (liner), yacht and globe . . . . 1·50 60
350 15c. B.A.C. One Eleven airliner and globe . . . . 1·50 1·75
MS351 165 × 125 mm. Nos. 347/50 9·50 17·00

96 Nurse, Patients and Greater Flamingo

1970. Centenary of British Red Cross. Multicoloured.
352 3c. Type **96** 75 50
353 15c. Hospital and blue marlin 75 1·75

97 "The Nativity" (detail, Pittoni)

1970. Christmas. Multicoloured.
354 3c. Type **97** 15 15
355 11c. "The Holy Family" (detail, Anton Raphael Mengs) 20 25
356 12c. "The Adoration of the Shepherds" (detail, Giorgione) 20 20
357 15c. "The Adoration of the Shepherds" (detail, School of Seville) 30 75
MS358 114 × 140 mm. Nos. 354/7 1·40 4·25

98 International Airport

1971. Multicoloured.
359 1c. Type **98** 10 30
360 2c. Breadfruit 15 35
361 3c. Straw market 15 30
362 4c. Hawksbill turtle . . . . 1·75 10·00
363 5c. Nassau grouper 60 60
364 6c. As 4c. . . . . 45 1·25
365 7c. Hibiscus . . . . 2·00 5·00
366 8c. Yellow elder . . . . . . 60 1·50
367 10c. Bahamian sponge boat 55 30
368 11c. Greater flamingos . . . 2·50 3·25
369 12c. As 7c. . . . . 2·00 3·00
370 15c. Bonefish 55 55
466 16c. As 7c. 70 35
371 18c. Royal poinciana . . . 65 65
467a 21c. As 2c. . . . . 80 1·25
372 22c. As 18c. . . . . 2·75 15·00
468 25c. As 4c. 90 40
469 40c. As 10c. . . . . 8·00 75
470 50c. Post Office, Nassau . . 1·50 1·75
471 $1 Pineapple (vert) . . . . 1·50 2·50
399 $2 Crawfish (vert) . . . . . 1·50 6·00
473 $3 Junkanoo (vert) . . . . 1·50 9·00

99 Snowflake

101 Shepherd

100 High Jumping

1971. Christmas.
377 **99** 3c. purple, orange and gold 10 10
378 – 11c. blue and gold 20 15
379 – 15c. multicoloured 20 20
380 – 18c. blue, ultram & gold 25 25
MS381 126 × 95 mm. Nos. 377/80 1·25 1·50
DESIGNS: 11c. "Peace on Earth" (doves); 15c. Arms of Bahamas and holly; 18c. Starlit lagoon.

1972. Olympic Games, Munich. Multicoloured.
382 10c. Type **100** 35 60
383 11c. Cycling . . . . 1·50 75
384 15c. Running 60 75
385 18c. Sailing . . . . 95 1·25
MS386 127 × 95 mm. Nos. 382/5 3·25 3·00

1972. Christmas. Multicoloured.
387 3c. Type **101** 10 10
388 6c. Bells 10 10
389 15c. Holly and Cross 15 20
390 20c. Poinsettia 25 45
MS391 108 × 140 mm. Nos. 387/90 80 2·75

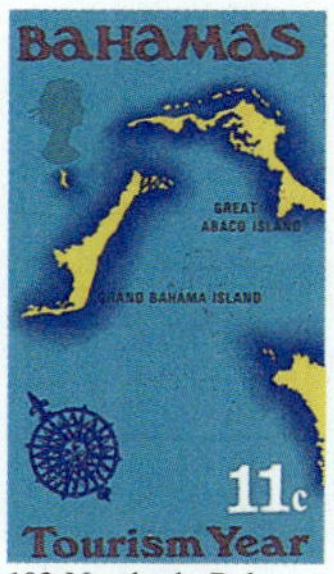

102 Northerly Bahama Islands

1972. Tourism Year of the Americas. Sheet 133 × 105 mm, containing T **102**.
MS392 11, 15, 18 and 50c. multicoloured . . . . 3·00 3·25
The four designs are printed, se-tenant in **MS**392, forming a composite map design of the Bahamas.

1972. Royal Silver Wedding. As T **52** of Ascension, but with mace and galleon in background.
393 11c. pink 15 15
394 18c. violet 15 20

104 Weather Satellite

1973. Centenary of I.M.O./W.M.O. Multicoloured.
410 15c. Type **104** 50 25
411 18c. Weather radar 60 35

105 C. A. Bain (national hero)

106 "The Virgin in Prayer" (Sassoferrato)

1973. Independence. Multicoloured.
412 3c. Type **105** 10 10
413 11c. Coat of arms 15 10
414 15c. Bahamas flag 20 15
415 $1 Governor-General, M. B. Butler . . . . 65 1·00
MS416 86 × 121 mm. Nos. 412/15 1·75 1·75

1973. Christmas. Multicoloured.
417 3c. Type **106** 10 10
418 11c. "Virgin and Child with St. John" (Filippino Lippi) 15 15
419 15c. "A Choir of Angels" (Simon Marmion) 15 15
420 18c. "The Two Trinities" (Murillo) 25 25
MS421 120 × 99 mm. Nos. 417/20 1·75 1·40

107 "Agriculture and Sciences"

1974. 25th Anniv of University of West Indies. Multicoloured.
422 15c. Type **107** 20 25
423 18c. "Arts, Engineering and General Studies" 25 30

108 U.P.U. Monument, Berne

1974. Centenary of U.P.U.
424 **108** 3c. multicoloured 10 15
425 – 13c. multicoloured (vert) 20 25
426 – 14c. multicoloured 20 30
427 – 18c. multicoloured (vert) 25 40
MS428 128 × 95 mm. Nos. 424/7 80 1·60
DESIGNS—As Type **108** but showing different arrangements of the U.P.U. Monument.

109 Roseate Spoonbills

1974. 15th Anniv of Bahamas National Trust. Mult.
429 13c. Type **109** . . . . 1·60 1·10
430 14c. White-crowned pigeon 1·60 75
431 21c. White-tailed tropic birds 2·00 1·25
432 36c. Cuban amazon ("Bahamian parrot") . . . 2·50 6·50
MS433 123 × 120 mm. Nos. 429/32 9·50 13·00

110 "The Holy Family" (Jacques de Stella)

1974. Christmas. Multicoloured.
434 8c. Type **110** 10 10
435 10c. "Madonna and Child" (16th-century Brescian School) 15 15
436 12c. "Virgin and Child with St. John the Baptist and St. Catherine" (Previtali) 15 15
437 21c. "Virgin and Child with Angels" (Previtali) . . . 25 30
MS438 126 × 105 mm. Nos. 434/7 1·00 1·40

111 "Anteos maerula"

1975. Butterflies. Multicoloured.
439 3c. Type **111** 25 15
440 14c. "Eurema nicippe" . . . 80 50
441 18c. "Papilio andraemon" . . 95 65
442 21c. "Euptoieta hegesia" . . 1·10 85
MS443 194 × 94 mm. Nos. 439/42 7·50 6·50

112 Sheep Husbandry

1975. Economic Diversification. Multicoloured.
444 3c. Type **112** 10 10
445 14c. Electric-reel fishing (vert) 20 15
446 18c. Farming 25 20
447 21c. Oil refinery (vert) . . . 80 35
MS448 127 × 94 mm. Nos. 444/7 1·25 1·50

113 Rowena Rand (evangelist)

1975. International Women's Year.
449 **113** 14c. brown, lt blue & bl 20 50
450 – 18c. yellow, grn & brn . . 25 75
DESIGN: 18c. I.W.Y. symbol and harvest symbol.

114 "Adoration of the Shepherds" (Perugino)

1975. Christmas. Multicoloured.
451 3c. Type **114** 15 60
452 8c. "Adoration of the Magi" (Ghirlandaio) 20 10
453 18c. As 8c. 55 90
454 21c. Type **114** 60 95
MS455 142 × 107 mm. Nos. 451/4 2·25 4·50

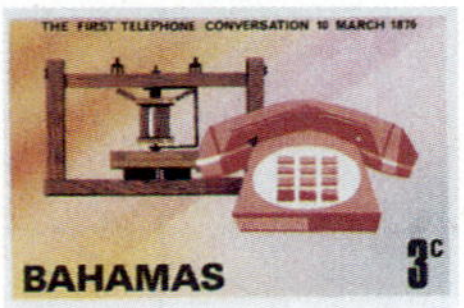

115 Telephones, 1876 and 1976

1976. Centenary of Telephone. Multicoloured.
456 3c. Type **115** 20 50
457 16c. Radio-telephone link, Deleporte 40 50
458 21c. Alexander Graham Bell 50 65
459 25c. Satellite . . . . 60 1·00

116 Map of North America

1976. Bicentenary of American Revolution. Mult.
475 16c. Type **116** 30 30
476 $1 John Murray, Earl of Dunmore . . . . 1·50 1·75
MS477 127 × 100 mm. Nos. 476 × 4 6·00 7·50

117 Cycling

118 "Virgin and Child" (detail, Lippi)

1976. Olympic Games, Montreal.
478 **117** 8c. mauve, blue and light blue . . . . 1·25 20
479 – 16c. orange, brown and light blue 35 30
480 – 25c. blue, mauve and light blue 45 50
481 – 40c. brown, orange and blue . . . . 55 1·60
MS482 100 × 126 mm. Nos. 478/81 3·00 3·00
DESIGNS: 16c. Jumping; 25c. Sailing; 40c. Boxing.

1976. Christmas. Multicoloured.
483 3c. Type **118** 10 10
484 21c. "Adoration of the Shepherds" (School of Seville) 20 15
485 25c. "Adoration of the Kings" (detail, Foppa) . . 20 20
486 40c. "Virgin and Child" (detail, Vivarini) 35 40
MS487 107 × 127 mm. Nos. 483/6 1·00 2·00

119 Queen beneath Cloth of Gold Canopy

1977. Silver Jubilee. Multicoloured.
488 8c. Type **119** 10 10
489 16c. The Crowning 15 15
490 21c. Taking the Oath 15 15
491 40c. Queen with sceptre and orb 25 30
MS492 122 × 90 mm. Nos. 488/91 80 1·25

120 Featherduster

1977. Marine Life. Multicoloured.
493 3c. Type **120** 40 15
494 8c. Porkfish and cave 60 20
495 16c. Elkhorn coral 70 40
496 21c. Soft coral and sponge 80 55
MS497 119 × 93 mm. Nos. 493/6 2·75 4·50

121 Scouts around Campfire and Home-made Shower

1977. 6th Caribbean Scout Jamboree. Multicoloured.
498 16c. Type **121** 75 30
499 21c. Boating scenes 85 35

1977. Royal Visit. Nos. 488/91 optd **Royal Visit October 1977**.
500 8c. Type **119** 15 10
501 16c. The Crowning 20 15
502 21c. Taking the Oath 25 25
503 40c. Queen with sceptre and orb 30 40
MS504 122 × 90 mm. Nos. 500/3 1·25 1·50

123 Virgin and Child

124 Public Library, Nassau (Colonial)

1977. Christmas. Multicoloured.
505 3c. Type **123** 10 10
506 16c. The Magi 20 25
507 21c. Nativity scene 25 40
508 25c. The Magi and star . . . 30 45
MS509 136 × 74 mm. Nos. 505/8 75 1·75

1978. Architectural Heritage.
510 **124** 3c. black and green . . . 10 10
511 – 8c. black and blue 15 10
512 – 16c. black and mauve . . 20 20
513 – 18c. black and pink . . . 25 30
MS514 91 × 91 mm. Nos. 510/13 70 1·60
DESIGNS: 8c. St. Matthew's Church (Gothic); 16c. Government House (Colonial); 18c. Hermitage, Cat Island (Spanish).

125 Sceptre, St. Edward's Crown and Orb

127 Child reaching for Adult

126 Coat of Arms within Wreath and Three Ships

1978. 25th Anniv of Coronation. Multicoloured.
515 16c. Type **125** 15 10
516 $1 Queen in Coronation regalia 50 65
MS517 147 × 96 mm. Nos. 515/16 1·25 1·00

1978. Christmas.
532 **126** 5c. gold, lake and red . . 15 10
533 – 21c. gold, deep blue and blue 30 25
MS534 95 × 95 mm. Nos. 532/3 1·50 5·00
DESIGN: 21c. Three angels with trumpets.

1979. International Year of the Child. Multicoloured.
535 5c. Type **127** 20 15
536 16c. Boys playing leapfrog . . 40 45
537 21c. Girls skipping 50 60
538 25c. Bricks with I.Y.C. emblem 50 75
MS539 101 × 125 mm. Nos. 535/8 1·40 3·25

128 Sir Rowland Hill and Penny Black

1979. Death Centenary of Sir Rowland Hill. Multicoloured.
540 10c. Type **128** 30 10
541 21c. Printing press, 1840, and 6d. stamp of 1862 . . . . 40 30
542 25c. Great Britain 1856 6d. with "A 05" (Nassau) cancellation, and 1840 2d. Blue 40 50
543 40c. Early mailboat and 1d. stamp of 1859 . . . . . . 45 70
MS544 115 × 80 mm. Nos. 540/3 2·00 3·25

129 Commemorative Plaque and Map of Bahamas

1979. 250th Anniv of Parliament. Multicoloured.
545 16c. Type **129** 35 10
546 21c. Parliament buildings . . 40 15
547 25c. Legislative Chamber . . 40 15
548 $1 Senate Chamber . . . . . 80 1·00
MS549 116 × 89 mm. Nos. 545/8 2·50 3·75

130 Goombay Carnival Headdress

132 Virgin and Child

131 Landfall of Columbus, 1492

1979. Christmas.
550 **130** 5c. multicoloured 10 10
551 – 10c. multicoloured 15 10
552 – 16c. multicoloured 20 10
553 – 21c. multicoloured 20 20
554 – 25c. multicoloured 25 20
555 – 40c. multicoloured 30 45
MS556 50 × 88 mm. Nos. 550/5 2·00 3·00
DESIGNS: 10c. to 40c. Various Carnival costumes.

1980. Multicoloured.
557 1c. Type **131** . . . . 1·25 2·50
558 3c. Blackbeard the pirate . . 30 2·50
559 5c. Eleutheran Adventurers (Articles and Orders, 1647) 30 1·25
560 10c. Ceremonial mace 20 40
561 12c. The Loyalists, 1783–88 30 2·00
562 15c. Slave trading, Vendue House . . . . 5·50 1·25
563 16c. Wrecking in the 1800s 1·75 1·25
564 18c. Blockade running (American Civil War) . . . 2·50 2·50
565 21c. Bootlegging, 1919–29 . . 60 2·50
566 25c. Pineapple cultivation . . 40 2·50
567 40c. Sponge clipping . . . . 70 1·50
568 50c. Tourist development . . 75 1·50
569 $1 Modern agriculture . . . 75 4·25
570 $2 Modern air and sea transport . . . . 4·25 5·50
571 $3 Banking (Central Bank) 1·25 4·00
572 $5 Independence, 10 July 1973 . . . . 1·50 6·00

1980. Christmas. Straw-work. Multicoloured.
573 5c. Type **132** 10 10
574 21c. Three Kings 25 10
575 25c. Angel 25 15
576 $1 Christmas tree 75 85
MS577 168 × 105 mm. Nos. 573/6 1·25 2·25

133 Disabled Persons with Walking Stick

1981. International Year of Disabled People. Mult.
578 5c. Type **133** 10 10
579 $1 Disabled person in wheelchair . . . . 1·25 1·25
MS580 120 × 60 mm. Nos. 578/9 1·40 2·50

134 Grand Bahama Tracking Site

1981. Space Exploration. Multicoloured.
581 10c. Type **134** 30 15
582 20c. Satellite view of Bahamas (vert) 60 50
583 25c. Satelite view of Eleuthera 65 60
584 50c. Satellite view of Andros and New Province (vert) 1·00 1·25
MS585 115 × 99 mm. Nos. 581/4 2·25 2·25

135 Prince Charles and Lady Diana Spencer

1981. Royal Wedding. Multicoloured.
586 30c. Type **135** . . . . 1·25 30
587 $2 Prince Charles and Prime Minister Pindling . . . . . 1·25 1·25
MS588 142 × 120 mm. Nos. 586/7 5·00 1·25

136 Bahamas Pintail ("Bahama Duck")

1981. Wildlife (1st series). Birds. Multicoloured.

589	5c. Type **136**	1·50	60
590	20c. Reddish egret	2·00	60
591	25c. Brown booby	2·00	65
592	$1 Black-billed whistling duck ("West Indian Tree Duck")	4·00	7·50
MS593	100 × 74 mm. Nos. 589/92	8·50	8·50

See also Nos. 626/30, 653/7 and 690/4.

1981. Commonwealth Finance Ministers' Meeting. Nos. 559/60, 566 and 568 optd **COMMONWEALTH FINANCE MINISTERS' MEETING 21–23 SEPTEMBER 1981.**

594	5c. Eleutheran Adventures (Articles and Orders, 1647)	15	15
595	10c. Ceremonial mace	20	20
596	25c. Pineapple cultivation	50	60
597	50c. Tourist development	85	1·50

138 Poultry

1981. World Food Day. Multicoloured.

598	5c. Type **138**	20	10
599	20c. Sheep	35	35
600	30c. Lobsters	45	50
601	50c. Pigs	75	1·50
MS602	115 × 63 mm. Nos. 598/601	1·50	3·25

139 Father Christmas

141 Greater Flamingo (male)

140 Robert Koch

1981. Christmas. Multicoloured.

603	5c. Type **139**	55	85
604	5c. Mother and child	55	85
605	5c. St. Nicholas, Holland	55	85
606	25c. Lussibruden, Sweden	70	95
607	25c. Mother and child (different)	70	95
608	25c. King Wenceslas, Czechoslovakia	70	95
609	30c. Mother with child on knee	70	95
610	30c. Mother carrying child	70	95
611	$1 Christkindl Angel, Germany	1·00	1·50

1982. Centenary of Discovery of Tubercle Bacillus by Robert Koch.

612	**140** 5c. black, brown and lilac	70	50
613	– 16c. black, brown & orge	1·50	50
614	– 21c. multicoloured	1·50	55
615	– $1 multicoloured	3·00	7·50
MS616	94 × 97 mm. Nos. 612/15	6·00	7·50

DESIGNS: 16c. Stylised infected person; 21c. Early and modern microscopes; $1 Mantoux test.

1982. Greater Flamingos. Multicoloured.

617	25c. Type **141**	1·60	1·00
618	25c. Female	1·60	1·00
619	25c. Female with nestling	1·60	1·00
620	25c. Juvenile	1·60	1·00
621	25c. Immature bird	1·60	1·00

142 Lady Diana Spencer at Ascot, June, 1981

143 House of Assembly Plaque

1982. 21st Birthday of Princess of Wales. Mult.

622	16c. Bahamas coat of arms	20	10
623	25c. Type **142**	45	15
624	40c. Bride and Earl Spencer arriving at St. Paul's	60	20
625	$1 Formal portrait	1·00	1·25

1982. Wildlife (2nd series). Mammals. As T **136**. Multicoloured.

626	10c. Buffy flower bat	1·00	15
627	16c. Bahamian hutia	1·25	25
628	21c. Common racoon	1·50	55
629	$1 Common dolphin	3·00	1·90
MS630	115 × 76 mm. Nos. 626/9	6·00	3·50

1982. 28th Commonwealth Parliamentary Association Conference. Multicoloured.

631	5c. Type **143**	15	10
632	25c. Association coat of arms	50	35
633	40c. Coat of arms	80	60
634	50c. House of Assembly	1·10	75

144 Wesley Methodist Church, Baillou Hill Road

1982. Christmas. Churches. Multicoloured.

635	5c. Type **144**	10	20
636	12c. Centreville Seventh Day Adventist Church	15	20
637	15c. The Church of God of Prophecy, East Street	15	30
638	21c. Bethel Baptist Church, Meeting Street	15	30
639	25c. St. Francis Xavier Catholic Church, Highbury Park	15	50
640	$1 Holy Cross Anglican Church, Highbury Park	60	3·00

145 Prime Minister Lyndon O. Pindling

1983. Commonwealth Day. Multicoloured.

641	5c. Type **145**	10	10
642	25c. Bahamian and Commonwealth flags	50	40
643	35c. Map showing position of Bahamas	50	50
644	$1 Ocean liner	1·10	1·40

1983. Nos. 562/5 surch.

645	20c. on 15c. Slave trading, Vendue House	50	35
646	31c. on 21c. Bootlegging, 1919–29	60	55
647	35c. on 16c. Wrecking in the 1800s	70	60
648	80c. on 18c. Blockade running (American Civil War)	80	1·40

147 Customs Officers and "Queen Elizabeth 2" (liner)

148 Raising the National Flag

1983. 30th Anniv of Customs Co-operation Council. Multicoloured.

649	31c. Type **147**	1·50	45
650	$1 Customs officers and Lockheed JetStar airliner	3·50	2·75

1983. 10th Anniv of Independence.

651	**148** $1 multicoloured	1·00	1·40
MS652	105 × 65 mm. No. 651	1·00	1·40

1983. Wildlife (3rd series). Butterflies. As T **136**.

653	5c. multicoloured	1·50	20
654	25c. multicoloured	2·25	40
655	31c. black, yellow and red	2·25	55
656	50c. multicoloured	2·50	85
MS657	120 × 80 mm. Nos. 653/6	6·50	6·00

DESIGNS: 5c. "Atalopedes carteri"; 25c. "Ascia monuste"; 31c. "Phoebis agarithe"; 50c. "Dryas julia".

149 "Loyalist Dreams"

151 "Christmas Bells" (Monica Pinder)

150 Consolidated Catalina

1983. Bicentenary of Arrival of American Loyalists in the Bahamas. Multicoloured.

658	5c. Type **149**	10	10
659	31c. New Plymouth, Abaco (horiz)	30	50
660	35c. New Plymouth Hotel (horiz)	40	70
661	50c. "Island Hope"	45	90
MS662	111 × 76 mm. Nos. 658/61	1·25	2·50

1983. Air. Bicentenary of Manned Flight. Mult.

663	10c. Type **150**	55	15
664	25c. Avro Tudor IV	75	30
665	31c. Avro Lancastrian	85	45
666	35c. Consolidated Commodore	1·00	50

For these stamps without the Manned Flight logo, see Nos. 699/702.

1983. Christmas. Children's Paintings. Multicoloured.

667	5c. Type **151**	15	10
668	20c. "Flamingo" (Cory Bullard)	35	30
669	25c. "Yellow Hibiscus with Christmas Candle" (Monique Bailey)	45	40
670	31c. "Santa goes-a-sailing" (Sabrina Seiler) (horiz)	55	45
671	35c. "Silhouette scene with Palm Trees" (James Blake)	60	50
672	50c. "Silhouette scene with Pelicans" (Erik Russell) (horiz)	70	70

152 1861 4d. Stamp

153 "Trent I" (paddle-steamer)

1984. 125th Anniv of First Bahamas Postage Stamp. Multicoloured.

673	5c. Type **152**	25	10
674	$1 1859 1d. stamp	1·75	1·50

1984. 250th Anniv of "Lloyd's List" (newspaper). Multicoloured.

675	5c. Type **153**	50	10
676	31c. "Orinoco II" (mail ship), 1886	1·00	60
677	35c. Cruise liners in Nassau harbour	1·10	75
678	50c. "Oropesa" (container ship)	1·40	1·60

154 Running

155 Bahamas and Caribbean Community Flags

1984. Olympic Games, Los Angeles.

679	**154** 5c. green, black and gold	15	20
680	– 25c. blue, black and gold	50	50
681	– 31c. red, black and gold	55	60
682	– $1 brown, black and gold	6·00	7·00
MS683	115 × 80 mm. Nos. 679/82	6·00	8·00

DESIGNS: 25c. Shot-putting; 31c. Boxing; $1 Basketball.

1984. 5th Conference of Caribbean Community Heads of Government.

684	**155** 50c. multicoloured	1·00	1·00

156 Bahama Woodstar

157 "The Holy Virgin with Jesus and Johannes" (19th-century porcelain plaque after Titian)

1984. 25th Anniv of National Trust. Multicoloured.

685	31c. Type **156**	3·75	3·75
686	31c. Belted kingfishers, greater flamingos and "Eleutherodactylus planirostris" (frog)	3·75	3·75
687	31c. Black-necked stilts, greater flamingos and "Phoebis sennae" (butterfly)	3·75	3·75
688	31c. "Urbanus proteus" (butterfly) and "Chelonia mydas" (turtle)	3·75	3·75
689	31c. Osprey and greater flamingos	3·75	3·75

Nos. 685/9 were printed together in horiz strips of 5 forming a composite design.

1984. Wildlife (4th series). Reptiles and Amphibians. As T **136**.

690	5c. Allens' Cay iguana	85	20
691	25c. Curly-tailed lizard	1·75	60
692	35c. Greenhouse frog	2·00	85
693	50c. Atlantic green turtle	2·25	3·50
MS694	112 × 82 mm. Nos. 690/3	6·25	7·50

1984. Christmas. Religious Paintings. Multicoloured.

695	5c. Type **157**	30	10
696	31c. "Madonna with Child in Tropical Landscape" (aquarelle, Anais Colin)	80	60
697	35c. "The Holy Virgin with the Child" (miniature on ivory, Elena Caula)	1·00	65
MS698	116 × 76 mm. Nos. 695/7	2·25	4·00

1985. Air. As Nos. 663/6, but without Manned Flight logo.

699	10c. Type **150**	80	50
700	25c. Avro Tudor IV	95	50
701	31c. Avro Lancastrian	95	60
702	35c. Consolidated Commodore	1·40	1·10

158 Brownie Emblem and Queen or Pink Conch

1985. International Youth Year. 75th Anniv of Girl Guide Movement. Multicoloured.

703	5c. Type **158**	60	50
704	25c. Tents and coconut palm	1·25	1·00
705	31c. Guide salute and greater flamingos	1·90	1·50
706	35c. Ranger emblem and marlin	1·90	1·50
MS707	95 × 74 mm. Nos. 703/6	5·50	7·50

159 Killdeer Plover

1985. Birth Bicent of John J. Audubon (ornithologist). Multicoloured.

708 5c. Type **159** . . . . 1·00 60
709 31c. Mourning dove (vert) . . 2·25 60
710 35c. "Mourning dove" (John J. Audubon) (vert) . . . . 2·25 65
711 $1 "Killdeer Plover" (John J. Audubon) . . . . 4·00 4·50

160 The Queen Mother at Christening of Peter Phillips, 1977 **162** Queen Elizabeth II

161 Ears of Wheat and Emblems

1985. Life and Times of Queen Elizabeth the Queen Mother. Multicoloured.

712 5c. Visiting Auckland, New Zealand, 1927 . . . . . . 45 20
713 25c. Type **160** 70 40
714 35c. The Queen Mother attending church 75 55
715 50c. With Prince Henry at his christening (from photo by Lord Snowdon) . . . . . 1·50 2·00
MS716 91 × 73 mm. $1.25, In horse-drawn carriage, Sark . . . . . 2·75 1·90

1985. 40th Anniv of U.N.O. and F.A.O.

717 **161** 25c. multicoloured . . . . 1·00 70

1985. Commonwealth Heads of Government Meeting, Nassau. Multicoloured.

718 31c. Type **162** . . . . 3·00 3·75
719 35c. Bahamas Prime Minister's flag and Commonwealth emblem . . 3·00 3·75

163 "Grandma's Christmas Bouquet" (Alton Roland Lowe)

1985. Christmas. Paintings by Alton Roland Lowe. Multicoloured.

736 5c. Type **163** 60 40
737 25c. "Junkanoo Romeo and Juliet" (vert) . . . . 1·50 1·00
738 31c. "Bunce Gal" (vert) . . . 1·75 1·50
739 35c. "Home for Christmas" . . 1·75 2·75
MS740 110 × 68 mm. Nos. 736/9 . . 2·75 3·25

1986. 60th Birthday of Queen Elizabeth II. As T **110** of Ascension. Multicoloured.

741 10c. Princess Elizabeth aged one, 1927 . . . . 15 15
742 25c. The Coronation, 1953 . . 30 30
743 35c. Queen making speech at Commonwealth Banquet, Bahamas, 1985 . . . . . 35 40
744 40c. In Djakova, Yugoslavia, 1972 . . . . 35 45
745 $1 At Crown Agents Head Office, London, 1983 . . . 80 1·40

164 1980 1c. and 18c. Definitive Stamps

1986. "Ameripex '86" International Stamp Exn, Chicago.

746 **164** 5c. multicoloured . . . . 1·00 70
747 – 25c. multicoloured . . . . 2·25 50
748 – 31c. multicoloured . . . . 2·50 60
749 – 50c. multicoloured . . . . 3·25 5·50
750 – $1 black, green and blue . . 3·50 6·50
MS751 80 × 80 mm. No. 750 . . 4·00 4·00

DESIGNS—HORIZ: (showing Bahamas stamps)—25c. 1969 50th Anniv of Bahamas Airmail Service pair; 31c. 1976 Bicentenary of American Revolution 16c., 50c. 1981 Space Exploration miniature sheet. VERT: $1 Statue of Liberty.

No. 750 also commemorates the Centenary of the Statue of Liberty.

1986. Royal Wedding. As T **112** of Ascension. Mult.

756 10c. Prince Andrew and Miss Sarah Ferguson 20 20
757 $1 Prince Andrew . . . . . 1·25 2·10

165 Rock Beauty (juvenile)

1986. Fishes. Multicoloured.

758A 5c. Type **165** 75 75
759A 10c. Stoplight parrotfish . . 80 1·00
760A 15c. Jackknife-fish . . . . 1·50 1·50
761A 20c. Flamefish . . . . . . 1·25 1·25
762A 25c. Peppermint basslet ("Swissguard basslet") . . 1·50 1·50
763A 30c. Spot-finned butterflyfish . . . . . . 1·10 1·50
764A 35c. Queen triggerfish . . . 1·10 2·75
765B 40c. Four-eyed butterflyfish 1·40 1·60
766A 45c. Royal gramma ("Fairy basslet") . . . . 1·50 1·25
767A 50c. Queen angelfish . . . 2·00 3·75
797 60c. Blue chromis . . . . . 2·75 6·00
769B $1 Spanish hogfish . . . . 2·75 3·00
799 $2 Harlequin bass . . . . 3·00 8·50
771A $3 Black-barred soldierfish 6·00 7·00
772A $5 Cherub angelfish ("Pygmy angelfish") . . . 6·50 8·00
773A $10 Red hind . . . . . . 19·00 25·00

166 Christ Church Cathedral, Nassau, 1861

1986. 125th Anniv of City of Nassau. Diocese and Cathedral. Multicoloured.

774 10c. Type **166** 30 20
775 40c. Christ Church Cathedral, 1986 . . . . 70 80
MS776 75 × 100 mm. Nos. 774/5 4·00 6·00

167 Man and Boy looking at Crib

1986. Christmas. International Peace Year. Mult.

777 10c. Type **167** 35 20
778 40c. Mary and Joseph journeying to Bethlehem 85 75
779 45c. Children praying and Star of Bethlehem . . . 95 1·00
780 50c. Children exchanging gifts 1·00 2·50
MS781 95 × 90 mm. Nos. 777/80 8·50 11·00

168 Great Isaac Lighthouse **169** Anne Bonney

1987. Lighthouses. Multicoloured.

782 10c. Type **168** . . . . . . 2·75 85
783 40c. Bird Rock lighthouse . . 5·50 1·75
784 45c. Castle Island lighthouse 5·50 2·00
785 $1 "Hole in the Wall" lighthouse . . . . 8·00 12·00

1987. Pirates and Privateers of the Caribbean. Multicoloured.

786 10c. Type **169** . . . . 3·50 1·50
787 40c. Edward Teach ("Blackbeard") . . . . . 6·00 3·75
788 45c. Captain Edward England . . . . 6·00 3·75
789 50c. Captain Woodes Rogers 7·00 8·50
MS790 75 × 95 mm. $1.25, Map of Bahamas and colonial coat of arms . . . . 12·00 4·75

170 Boeing 737

1987. Air. Aircraft. Multicoloured.

800 15c. Type **170** . . . . 3·00 1·50
801 40c. Boeing 757-200 . . . . 4·00 2·25
802 45c. Airbus Industrie A300 B4-200 . . . . 4·00 2·25
803 50c. Boeing 747-200 . . . . 4·50 4·50

171 "Norway" (liner) and Catamaran **173** King Ferdinand and Queen Isabella of Spain

172 "Cattleyopsis lindenii"

1987. Tourist Transport. Multicoloured.

804 40c. Type **171** . . . . 2·25 2·25
805 40c. Liners and speedboat . . 2·25 2·25
806 40c. Game fishing boat and cruising yacht . . . . . . 2·25 2·25
807 40c. Game fishing boat and racing yachts . . . . . . 2·25 2·25
808 40c. Fishing boat and schooner . . . . 2·25 2·25
809 40c. Hawker Siddeley H.S.748 airliner . . . . . 2·25 2·25
810 40c. Boeing 737 and Boeing 727-200 airliners . . . . 2·25 2·25
811 40c. Beech 200 Super King Air aircraft and radio beacon . . . . 2·25 2·25
812 40c. Aircraft and Nassau control tower . . . . . . 2·25 2·25
813 40c. Helicopter and parked aircraft . . . . 2·25 2·25

Nos. 804/8 and 809/13 were each printed together, se-tenant, forming composite design.

1987. Christmas. Orchids. Multicoloured.

814 10c. Type **172** . . . . 1·75 60
815 40c. "Encyclia lucayana" . . 3·00 1·50
816 45c. "Encyclia hodgeana" . . 3·00 1·50
817 50c. "Encyclia lleidae" . . . 3·00 3·00
MS818 120 × 92 mm. Nos. 814/17 9·50 11·00

1988. 500th Anniv (1992) of Discovery of America by Columbus (1st issue). Multicoloured.

819 10c. Type **173** 85 60
820 40c. Columbus before Talavera Committee . . . 1·75 1·75
821 45c. Lucayan village . . . . 1·90 1·90
822 50c. Lucayan potters . . . . 2·00 3·50
MS823 65 × 50 mm. $1.50, Map of Antilles, c. 1500 . . . . 6·00 3·75

See also Nos. 844/8, 870/4, 908/12 and 933/7.

174 Whistling Ducks in Flight

1988. Black-billed Whistling Duck. Multicoloured.

824 5c. Type **174** . . . . 2·25 1·75
825 10c. Whistling duck in reeds 2·25 1·75
826 20c. Pair with brood . . . . 4·00 2·75
827 45c. Pair wading . . . . . . 6·00 3·25

175 Grantstown Cabin, c.1820

1988. 150th Anniv of Abolition of Slavery. Multicoloured.

828 10c. Type **175** 50 30
829 40c. Basket-making, Grantstown . . . . 1·25 95

176 Olympic Flame, High Jumping, Hammer throwing, Basketball and Gymnastics

1988. Olympic Games, Seoul. Designs taken from painting by James Martin. Multicoloured.

830 10c. Type **176** 90 50
831 40c. Athletics, archery, swimming, long jumping, weightlifting and boxing . . 90 60
832 45c. Javelin throwing, gymnastics, hurdling and shot put 90 60
833 $1 Athletics, hurdling, gymnastics and cycling . . 3·50 5·00
MS834 113 × 85 mm. Nos. 830/3 5·50 3·25

1988. 300th Anniv of Lloyd's of London. As T **123** of Ascension. Multicoloured.

835 10c. "Lloyd's List" of 1740 30 15
836 40c. Freeport Harbour (horiz) 2·00 60
837 45c. Space shuttle over Bahamas (horiz) . . . . . 2·00 60
838 $1 "Yarmouth Castle" (freighter) on fire . . . . . 3·00 1·90

177 "Oh Little Town of Bethlehem" **178** Cuban Emerald

1988. Christmas. Carols. Multicoloured.

839 10c. Type **177** 55 30
840 40c. "Little Donkey" . . . . 1·50 75
841 45c. "Silent Night" . . . . . 1·50 90
842 50c. "Hark the Herald Angels Sing" . . . . 1·60 2·25
MS843 88 × 108 mm. Nos. 839/42 2·75 2·75

1989. 500th Anniv (1992) of Discovery of America by Columbus (2nd issue). As T **173**. Multicoloured.

844 10c. Columbus drawing chart 2·25 85
845 40c. Types of caravel . . . . 3·25 1·75
846 45c. Early navigational instruments . . . . 3·25 1·75
847 50c. Arawak artefacts . . . . 3·25 5·00
MS848 64 × 64 mm. $1.50, Caravel under construction (from 15th-cent "Nuremburg Chronicles") . . . . 2·50 2·50

1989. Hummingbirds. Multicoloured.

849 10c. Type **178** . . . . 1·75 1·25
850 40c. Ruby-throated hummingbird . . . . 3·00 2·00
851 45c. Bahama woodstar . . . 3·00 2·00
852 50c. Rufous hummingbird . . 3·25 4·50

179 Teaching Water Safety

1989. 125th Anniv of Int Red Cross. Mult.

853 10c. Type **179** . . . . 1·75 50
854 $1 Henri Dunant (founder) and Battle of Solferino . . 3·75 4·50

1989. 20th Anniv of First Manned Landing on Moon. As T **126** of Ascension. Multicoloured.

855 10c. "Apollo 8" Communications Station, Grand Bahama . . . . . 1·25 50
856 40c. Crew of "Apollo 8" (30 × 30 mm) . . . . . . 2·00 90
857 45c. "Apollo 8" emblem (30 × 30 mm) . . . . . . 2·00 90
858 $1 The Earth seen from "Apollo 8" . . . . 2·75 5·00
MS859 100 × 83 mm. $2 "Apollo 11" astronauts in training, Manned Spacecraft Centre, Houston . . 5·00 6·00

180 Church of the Nativity, Bethlehem

1989. Christmas. Churches of the Holy Land. Multicoloured.
860 10c. Type **180** . . . . 1·25 30
861 40c. Basilica of the Annunciation, Nazareth . . 2·25 70
862 45c. Tabgha Church, Galilee 2·25 70
863 $1 Church of the Holy Sepulchre, Jerusalem . . . 4·00 6·50
MS864 92 × 109 mm. Nos. 860/3 9·00 9·50

181 1974 U.P.U. Centenary 13c. Stamp and Globe

1989. "World Stamp Expo '89" International Stamp Exhibition, Washington. Multicoloured.
865 10c. Type **181** 70 40
866 40c. New U.P.U. Headquarters Building 3c. and building . . . . 1·40 85
867 45c. 1986 "Ameripex '86" $1 and Capitol, Washington 1·40 90
868 $1 1949 75th anniv of U.P.U. 2½d. and Boeing 737 airliner . . . . 5·50 7·00
MS869 107 × 80 mm. $2 Map showing route of Columbus, 1492 (30 × 38 mm) . . . . 10·00 14·00

1990. 500th Anniv (1992) of Discovery of America by Columbus (3rd issue). As T **173**. Multicoloured.
870 10c. Launching caravel . . . 1·75 80
871 40c. Provisional ship . . . . 2·75 2·00
872 45c. Shortening sail . . . . . 2·75 2·00
873 50c. Lucayan fisherman . . . 2·75 4·00
MS874 70 × 61 mm. $1.50, Departure of Columbus, 1492 5·50 7·00

182 Bahamas Flag, O.A.S. Headquarters and Centenary Logo

1990. Centenary of Organization of American States.
875 **182** 40c. multicoloured . . . . 2·00 2·25

183 Supermarine Spitfire Mk I "Bahamas I"

1990. "Stamp World London 90" International Stamp Exhibition, London. Presentation Fighter Aircraft. Sheet 107 × 78 mm. containing T **183**. Multicoloured.
MS876 $1 Type **183**; $1 Hawker Hurricane Mk IIc "Bahamas V" 9·50 7·50

184 Teacher with Boy

1990. International Literacy Year. Multicoloured.
877 10c. Type **184** . . . . 1·00 50
878 40c. Three boys in class . . . 1·75 1·25
879 50c. Teacher and children with books . . . . 1·75 5·00

1990. 90th Birthday of Queen Elizabeth the Queen Mother. As T **134** of Ascension.
880 40c. multicoloured . . . . . 1·50 50
881 $1.50 black and ochre . . . 2·75 6·00
DESIGNS—21 × 36 mm: 40c. "Queen Elizabeth 1938" (Sir Gerald Kelly); 29 × 37 mm: $1.50, Queen Elizabeth at garden party, France, 1938.

185 Cuban Amazon preening

186 The Annunciation

1990. Cuban Amazon ("Bahamian Parrot"). Mult.
882 10c. Type **185** . . . . 1·25 85
883 40c. Pair in flight . . . . . . 2·25 1·50
884 45c. Cuban amazon's head 2·25 1·50
885 50c. Perched on branch . . . 2·50 3·75
MS886 73 × 63 mm. $1.50, Feeding on berries . . . . 8·00 10·00

1990. Christmas. Multicoloured.
887 10c. Type **186** 65 50
888 40c. The Nativity . . . . . 1·25 70
889 45c. Angel appearing to Shepherds . . . . 1·25 70
890 $1 The Three Kings . . . . 3·00 6·00
MS891 94 × 110 mm. Nos. 887/90 12·00 12·00

187 Green-backed Heron ("Green Heron")

189 The Annunciation

188 Radar Plot of Hurricane Hugo

1991. Birds. Multicoloured.
892 5c. Type **187** . . . . 1·00 1·25
893 10c. Turkey vulture . . . . . 1·75 1·50
976 15c. Osprey . . . . 1·00 70
895 20c. Clapper rail . . . . . . 1·25 80
978 25c. Royal tern 80 70
979 30c. Key West quail dove . . 6·00 1·25
898 40c. Smooth-billed ani . . . 2·00 55
899 45c. Burrowing owl . . . . . 3·25 80
900 50c. Hairy woodpecker . . . 2·75 80
983 55c. Mangrove cuckoo . . . 2·00 80
902 60c. Bahama mockingbird . . 2·75 1·75
903 70c. Red-winged blackbird 2·75 1·75
904 $1 Thick-billed vireo . . . . 3·25 1·50
905 $2 Bahama yellowthroat . . 6·00 6·50
988 $5 Stripe-headed tanager . . 6·50 9·00
907 $10 Greater Antillean bullfinch . . . . 14·00 16·00

1991. 500th Anniv (1992) of Discovery of America by Columbus (4th issue). As T **173**. Multicoloured.
908 15c. Columbus navigating by stars . . . . 1·75 85
909 40c. Fleet in mid-Atlantic . . 2·50 2·25
910 55c. Lucayan family worshipping at night . . . 2·50 2·50
911 60c. Map of First Voyage . . 3·25 5·00
MS912 56 × 61 mm. $1.50, "Pinta"'s look-out sighting land . . . . 6·00 7·00

1991. 65th Birthday of Queen Elizabeth II and 70th Birthday of Prince Philip. As T **139** of Ascension. Multicoloured.
913 15c. Prince Philip . . . . . 1·00 1·50
914 $1 Queen Elizabeth II . . . 1·75 2·00

1991. International Decade for Natural Disaster Reduction. Multicoloured.
915 15c. Type **188** . . . . 1·25 65
916 40c. Diagram of hurricane . . 1·75 1·50
917 55c. Flooding caused by Hurricane David, 1979 . . 2·00 2·25
918 60c. U.S. Dept of Commerce weather reconnaissance Lockhead WP-3D Orion 2·75 4·00

1991. Christmas. Multicoloured.
919 15c. Type **189** . . . . . . 1·00 30
920 55c. Mary and Joseph travelling to Bethlehem . . 2·00 1·00
921 60c. Angel appearing to the shepherds . . . . 2·00 1·50
922 $1 Adoration of the kings . . 3·25 4·50
MS923 92 × 108 mm. Nos. 919/22 9·00 9·50

190 First Progressive Liberal Party Cabinet

1992. 25th Anniv of Majority Rule. Multicoloured.
924 15c. Type **190** 75 40
925 40c. Signing of Independence Constitution . . . . 1·60 1·10
926 55c. Prince of Wales handing over Constitutional Instrument (vert) . . . . 1·75 1·50
927 60c. First Bahamian Governor-General, Sir Milo Butler (vert) . . . . 2·00 3·50

1992. 40th Anniv of Queen Elizabeth II's Accession. As T **143** of Ascension. Multicoloured.
928 15c. Queen Elizabeth with bouquet 60 30
929 40c. Queen Elizabeth with flags . . . . 1·10 70
930 55c. Queen Elizabeth at display . . . . 1·10 90
931 60c. Three portraits of Queen Elizabeth . . . . 1·25 1·50
932 $1 Queen Elizabeth II . . . 1·50 2·50

1992. 500th Anniv of Discovery of America by Columbus (5th issue). As T **173**. Multicoloured.
933 15c. Lucayans sighting fleet 1·75 1·00
934 40c. "Santa Maria" and dolphins . . . . 2·50 1·75
935 55c. Lucayan canoes approaching ships . . . . 2·50 2·25
936 60c. Columbus giving thanks for landfall . . . . 3·00 4·25
MS937 61 × 57 mm. $1.50, Children at Columbus Monument . . . 3·50 6·00

191 Templeton, Galbraith and Hansberger Ltd Building

1992. 20th Anniv of Templeton Prize for Religion.
938 **191** 55c. multicoloured . . . . 1·50 1·75

192 Pole Vaulting

194 Mary visiting Elizabeth

193 Arid Landscape and Starving Child

1992. Olympic Games, Barcelona. Multicoloured.
939 15c. Type **192** 60 50
940 40c. Javelin . . . . 1·00 90
941 55c. Hurdling . . . . 1·10 1·25
942 60c. Basketball . . . . . . 8·00 5·00
MS943 70 × 50 mm. $2 Sailing 7·50 9·00

1992. International Conference on Nutrition, Rome. Multicoloured.
944 15c. Type **193** . . . . 1·25 75
945 55c. Seedling, cornfield and child . . . . 2·00 2·00

1992. 500th Anniv of Discovery of America by Columbus (6th issue). Sheet 65 × 65 mm, containing vert design as T **173**. Multicoloured.
MS946 $2 Columbus landing in Bahamas . . . . 7·50 8·00

1992. Christmas. Multicoloured.
947 15c. Type **194** 40 20
948 55c. The Nativity . . . . . 1·10 1·00
949 60c. Angel and shepherds . . 1·25 1·50
950 70c. Wise Men and star . . 1·40 2·50
MS951 95 × 110 mm. Nos. 947/50 6·50 7·50

1992. Hurricane Relief. No. MS876 showing each stamp surch **HURRICANE RELIEF+$1**.
MS952 $1+$1 Type **183**; $1+$1 Hawker Hurricane Mk IIc "Bahamas V" . . . . 12·00 15·00

196 Flags of Bahamas and U.S.A. with Agricultural Worker

1993. 50th Anniv of The Contract (U.S.A.–Bahamas farm labour programme). Each including national flags. Multicoloured.
953 15c. Type **196** . . . . 1·75 70
954 55c. Onions . . . . 2·25 1·50
955 60c. Citrus fruit . . . . . . 2·50 2·50
956 70c. Apples . . . . 2·75 3·25

1993. 75th Anniv of Royal Air Force. As T **149** of Ascension. Multicoloured.
957 15c. Westland Wapiti IIA . . 1·75 85
958 40c. Gloster Gladiator I . . . 2·25 1·00
959 55c. De Havilland Vampire F.3 . . . . 2·50 1·75
960 70c. English Electric Lightning F.3 . . . . . 3·00 5·00
MS961 110 × 77 mm. 60c. Avro Shackleton M.R.2; 60c. Fairey Battle; 60c. Douglas Boston III; 60c. De Havilland D.H.9a . . 8·50 9·50

197 1978 Coronation Anniversary Stamps

198 "Lignum vitae" (national tree)

1993. 40th Anniv of Coronation. Multicoloured.
962 15c. Type **197** 70 50
963 55c. Two examples of 1953 Coronation stamp . . . . 1·75 1·75
964 60c. 1977 Silver Jubilee 8c. and 16c. stamps . . . . . 1·75 2·00
965 70c. 1977 Silver Jubilee 21c. and 40c. stamps . . . . . 2·00 2·75

1993. 20th Anniv of Independence. Mult.
966 15c. Type **198** 30 20
967 55c. Yellow elder (national flower) 90 90
968 60c. Blue marlin (national fish) . . . . 1·25 1·25
969 70c. Greater flamingo (national bird) . . . . . . 2·00 3·00

199 Cordia

200 The Annunciation

1993. Environment Protection (1st series). Wildflowers. Multicoloured.
970 15c. Type **199** . . . . 1·50 50
971 55c. Seaside morning glory 3·00 1·25
972 60c. Poinciana . . . . 3·25 2·25
973 70c. Spider lily . . . . . . 3·75 4·50
See also Nos. 1017/21, 1035/8, 1084/7, 1121/4, 1149/53 and 1193/6.

1993. Christmas. Multicoloured.
990 15c. Type **200** 75 50
991 55c. Angel and shepherds . . 2·25 1·75
992 60c. Holy Family . . . . . 2·25 2·50
993 70c. Three Kings . . . . . . 2·75 3·75
MS994 86 × 106 mm. $1 Virgin Mary and Child . . . . 5·50 7·50

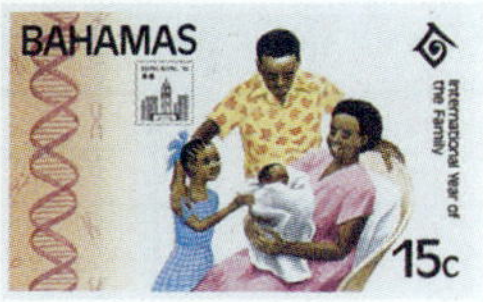

201 Family

1994. "Hong Kong '94" International Stamp Exhibition. International Year of the Family. Multicoloured.
995 15c. Type **201** . . . . 1·50 40
996 55c. Children doing homework . . . . 2·50 1·25
997 60c. Grandfather and grandson fishing . . . . . 2·75 1·75
998 70c. Grandmother teaching grandchildren the Lord's Prayer . . . . 3·25 5·00

202 Flags of Bahamas and Great Britain

1994. Royal Visit. Multicoloured.
999 15c. Type **202** . . . . . . 1·25 50
1000 55c. Royal Yacht "Britannia" . . . . . . 2·50 1·75
1001 60c. Queen Elizabeth II . . 2·50 1·90
1002 70c. Queen Elizabeth and Prince Philip . . . . . . 2·50 4·50

203 Yachts

1994. 40th Anniv of National Family Island Regatta. Multicoloured.
1003 15c. Type **203** 80 40
1004 55c. Dinghies racing . . . . 1·75 1·25
1005 60c. Working boats . . . . 1·75 1·75
1006 70c. Sailing sloop . . . . . 2·25 4·00
MS1007 76 × 54 mm. $2 Launching sloop (vert) . . . . 8·00 9·00

204 Logo and Bahamas 1968 Olympic Games Stamp

1994. Centenary of International Olympic Committee. Multicoloured.
1008 15c. Type **204** . . . . . . 1·75 50
1009 55c. 1976 Olympic Games stamps (vert) . . . . . . 2·75 1·25
1010 60c. 1984 Olympic Games stamps . . . . 2·75 2·25
1011 70c. 1992 Olympic Games stamps (vert) . . . . . . 3·00 4·50

205 Star of Order

1994. First Recipients of Order of the Caribbean Community. Sheet 90 × 69 mm.
MS1012 **205** $2 multicoloured . . 5·50 6·50

206 "Calpodes ethlius" and Canna

207 Spot-finned Hogfish and Spanish Hogfish

1994. Butterflies and Flowers. Multicoloured.
1013 15c. Type **206** . . . . . . 1·10 55
1014 55c. "Phoebis sennae" and cassia . . . . 2·00 1·50
1015 60c. "Anartia jatrophae" and passion flower . . . 2·25 2·25
1016 70c. "Battus devilliersi" and calico flower . . . . . . 2·25 3·00

1994. Environment Protection (2nd series). Marine Life. Multicoloured.
1017 40c. Type **207** . . . . . . 1·00 1·25
1018 40c. Tomate and long-spined squirrelfish . . . . 1·00 1·25
1019 40c. French angelfish . . . 1·00 1·25
1020 40c. Queen angelfish . . . . 1·00 1·25
1021 40c. Rock beauty . . . . . 1·00 1·25
MS1022 57 × 55 mm. $2 Rock beauty, Queen angelfish and windsurfer . . . . 6·00 7·00
Nos. 1017/21 were printed together, se-tenant, with the backgrounds forming a composite design.

208 Angel

1994. Christmas. Multicoloured.
1023 15c. Type **208** 30 30
1024 55c. Holy Family . . . . . 90 1·10
1025 60c. Shepherds . . . . . . 1·10 1·40
1026 70c. Wise Men . . . . . . 1·25 2·50
MS1027 73 × 85 mm. Jesus in manger . . . . 3·50 5·00

209 Lion and Emblem

210 Kirtlands Warbler on Nest

1995. 20th Anniv of the College of the Bahamas. Multicoloured.
1028 15c. Type **209** 30 30
1029 70c. Queen Elizabeth II and College building . . . . 1·25 1·75

1995. 50th Anniv of End of Second World War. As T **161** of Ascension. Multicoloured.
1030 15c. Bahamian infantry drilling 75 50
1031 55c. Consolidated PBY-5A Catalina flying boat . . . 2·00 1·25
1032 60c. Bahamian women in naval operations room . . 2·00 2·25
1033 70c. Consolidated B-24 Liberator bomber . . . . 2·50 3·75
MS1034 75 × 85 mm. $2 Reverse of 1939–45 War Medal (vert) . . 3·00 4·00

1995. Environment Protection (3rd series). Endangered Species. Kirtland's Warbler. Mult.
1035 15c. Type **210** 55 75
1036 15c. Singing on branch 55 75
1037 25c. Feeding chicks 55 75
1038 25c. Catching insects 55 75
MS1039 73 × 67 mm. $2 On branch 7·50 8·50
No. **MS**1039 does not show the W.W.F. Panda emblem.

211 Eleuthera Cliffs

1995. Tourism. Multicoloured.
1040 15c. Type **211** . . . . . . 1·75 50
1041 55c. Clarence Town, Long Island . . . . 2·75 1·25
1042 60c. Albert Lowe Museum 3·00 2·50
1043 70c. Yachts . . . . 3·25 6·00

212 Pigs and Chick

1995. 50th Anniv of F.A.O. Multicoloured.
1044 15c. Type **212** . . . . . . 1·50 50
1045 55c. Seedling and hand holding seed . . . . 2·00 1·10
1046 60c. Family with fruit and vegetables . . . . 2·50 2·25
1047 70c. Fishes and crustaceans 3·50 4·50

213 Sikorsky S-55 Helicopter, Sinai, 1957

1995. 50th Anniv of United Nations. Multicoloured.
1048 15c. Type **213** 70 50
1049 55c. Ferret armoured car, Sinai, 1957 . . . . 1·25 1·25
1050 60c. Fokker F.27 Friendship (airliner), Cambodia, 1991–93 . . . . 1·50 2·00
1051 70c. Lockheed C-130 Hercules (transport) . . . 1·60 2·75

214 St. Agnes Anglican Church

1995. Christmas. Churches. Multicoloured.
1052 15c. Type **214** 30 25
1053 55c. Church of God, East Street 90 90
1054 60c. Sacred Heart Roman Catholic Church . . . . 95 1·25
1055 70c. Salem Union Baptist Church . . . . 1·10 1·75

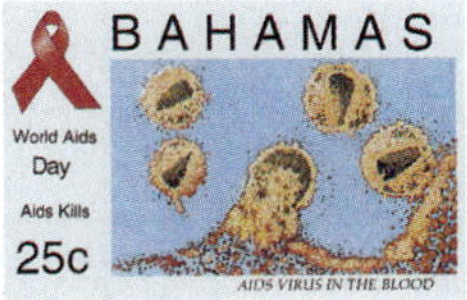

215 Microscopic View of AIDS Virus

1995. World AIDS Day. Multicoloured.
1056 25c. Type **215** 60 50
1057 70c. Research into AIDS . . 1·00 1·50

216 Sunrise Tellin

1996. Sea Shells. Multicoloured.
1058 5c. Type **216** 30 75
1059 10c. Queen conch 35 75
1060 15c. Angular triton 55 40
1061 20c. True tulip 70 45
1062 25c. Reticulated cowrie-helmet 70 60
1063 30c. Sand dollar 80 60
1063a 35c. As 30c. . . . . 1·50 55
1064 40c. Lace short-frond murex . . . . 1·00 60
1065 45c. Inflated sea biscuit . . 1·25 60
1066 50c. West Indian top shell . 1·10 70
1067 55c. Spiny oyster . . . . . 1·50 75
1068 60c. King helmet . . . . . 2·00 90
1068a 65c. As 45c. . . . . 2·50 1·25
1069 70c. Lion's paw . . . . . 1·60 1·00
1069a 80c. As 55c. . . . . 2·50 1·50
1070 $1 Crown cone . . . . . 2·25 1·75
1071 $2 Atlantic partridge tun . 3·50 4·00
1072 $5 Wide-mouthed purpura 8·00 9·00
1073 $10 Atlantic trumpet triton 21·00 21·00

217 East Goodwin Lightship with Marconi Apparatus on Mast

1996. Centenary of Radio. Multicoloured.
1074 15c. Type **217** . . . . . . 2·00 80
1075 55c. Newspaper headline concerning Dr. Crippen 2·50 1·25
1076 60c. "Philadelphia" (liner) and first readable transatlantic message . . 2·50 2·00
1077 70c. Guglielmo Marconi and "Elettra" (yacht) . . . . 3·00 4·00
MS1078 80 × 47 mm. $2 "Titanic" and "Carpathia" (liners) . . . 7·50 8·50

218 Swimming

219 Green Anole

1996. Centenary of Modern Olympic Games. Multicoloured.
1079 15c. Type **218** 40 35
1080 55c. Running 90 90
1081 60c. Basketball . . . . . . 1·75 1·75
1082 70c. Long jumping . . . . 1·40 2·50
MS1083 73 × 86 mm. $2 Javelin throwing . . . . 3·00 4·00

1996. Environment Protection (4th series). Reptiles. Multicoloured.
1084 15c. Type **219** 55 50
1085 55c. Little Bahama bank boa . . . . 1·10 1·00
1086 60c. Inagua freshwater turtle 1·50 1·75
1087 70c. Acklins rock iguana . . 1·75 2·75
MS1088 85 × 105 mm. Nos. 1084/7 4·50 5·50

220 The Annunciation

221 Department of Archives Building

1996. Christmas. Multicoloured.
1089 15c. Type **220** . . . . . . 1·25 40
1090 55c. Joseph and Mary travelling to Bethlehem 2·50 1·00
1091 60c. Shepherds and angel . . 2·50 1·50
1092 70c. Adoration of the Magi 2·75 4·00
MS1093 70 × 87 mm. $2 Presentation in the Temple . . . . 3·00 3·75

1996. 25th Anniv of Archives Department.
1094 **221** 55c. multicoloured . . . 1·50 1·00
MS1095 83 × 54 mm. $2 multicoloured . . . . 4·75 6·50

1997. "HONG KONG '97" International Stamp Exhibition. Sheet 130 × 90 mm, containing design as No. 1070, but with "1997" imprint date. Multicoloured.
MS1096 $1 Crown cone . . . . 3·00 3·50

1997. Return of Hong Kong to China. Sheet 130 × 90 mm, containing design as No. 1069, but with "1997" imprint date.
MS1097 70c. Lion's paw . . . . 2·00 2·50

1997. Golden Wedding of Queen Elizabeth and Prince Philip. As T **173** of Ascension. Multicoloured.
1114 50c. Queen Elizabeth II in Bonn, 1992 . . . . 2·00 2·25
1115 50c. Prince Philip and Prince Charles at Trooping the Colour . . . . 2·00 2·25
1116 60c. Prince Philip . . . . . 2·00 2·25
1117 60c. Queen at Trooping the Colour . . . . 2·00 2·25
1118 70c. Queen Elizabeth and Prince Philip at polo, 1970 . . . . 2·00 2·25
1119 70c. Prince Charles playing polo . . . . 2·00 2·25
MS1120 110 × 70 mm. $2 Queen Elizabeth and Prince Philip in landau (horiz) . . . . 6·50 7·00

222 Underwater Scene

1997. Environment Protection (5th series). International Year of the Reefs.
1121 **222** 15c. multicoloured . . . 1·25 60
1122 – 55c. multicoloured . . . 2·25 1·00
1123 – 60c. multicoloured . . . 2·25 1·75
1124 – 70c. multicoloured . . . 2·50 3·00
DESIGNS: 55c. to 70c. Different children's paintings of underwater scenes.

223 Angel

223a Wearing Grey Jacket, 1988

1997. Christmas. Multicoloured.
1125 15c. Type **223** . . . . . . 1·25 40
1126 55c. Mary and Baby Jesus 2·00 80

1127 60c. Shepherd . . . . . . 2·00 1·25
1128 70c. King . . . . 2·50 3·75
MS1129 74 × 94 mm. $2 Baby Jesus wrapped in swaddling-bands. 7·00 7·00

1998. Diana, Princess of Wales Commemoration.
1130 **223a** 15c. multicoloured . . . 50 50
MS1131 145 × 70 mm. 15c. As No. 1130; 55c. Wearing striped jacket, 1983; 60c. In evening dress, 1983; 70c. Meeting crowds, 1993 2·50 2·75

1998. 80th Anniv of the Royal Air Force. As T **178** of Ascension. Multicoloured.
1132 15c. Handley Page Hyderabad 55 40
1133 55c. Hawker Demon . . . . 1·00 85
1134 60c. Gloster Meteor F.8 . . 1·10 1·25
1135 70c. Lockheed Neptune MR.1 . . . . 1·40 2·25
MS1136 110 × 76 mm. 50c. Sopwith Camel; 50c. Short 184 (seaplane); 50c. Supermarine Spitfire PR.19; 50c. North American Mitchell III 4·00 4·25

224 Newsletters

1998. 50th Anniv of Organization of American States. Multicoloured.
1137 15c. Type **224** 30 30
1138 55c. Headquarters building and flags, Washington . . 70 80

225 Start of Declaration and Birds

1998. 50th Anniv of Universal Declaration of Human Rights.
1139 **225** 55c. blue and black . . . 1·50 1·00

226 University Arms and Graduates

1998. 50th Anniv of University of the West Indies.
1140 **226** 55c. multicoloured . . . 1·50 1·00

227 Supreme Court Building

1998. 25th Anniv of Independence. Multicoloured.
1141 15c. Type **227** . . . . . . 1·00 50
1142 55c. Nassau Library . . . . 1·75 1·00
1143 60c. Government House . . 1·90 1·50
1144 70c. Gregory Arch . . . . 2·00 3·00
MS1145 70 × 55 mm. $2 Island Regatta, George Town . . . . 3·50 5·00

228 "Disney Magic" (cruise liner) at Night

1998. Disney Cruise Line's Castaway Cay Holiday Development. Multicoloured.
1146 55c. Type **228** . . . . . . 2·00 2·00
1147 55c. "Disney Magic" by day 2·00 2·00

229 "Ryndam" (cruise liner)

1998. Holland America Line's Half Moon Cay Holiday Development.
1148 **229** 55c. multicoloured . . . 2·25 1·50

230 Barrel Pink Rose

1998. Environment Protection (6th series). Roses. Multicoloured.
1149 55c. Type **230** 1·50 1·60
1150 55c. Yellow cream . . . . . 1·50 1·60
1151 55c. Seven sisters . . . . . 1·50 1·60
1152 55c. Big red . . . . 1·50 1·60
1153 55c. Island beauty . . . . . 1·50 1·60
MS1154 100 × 70 mm. No. 1153 1·50 1·75

231 The Annunciation

1998. Christmas. Multicoloured.
1155 15c. Type **231** 50 30
1156 55c. Shepherds . . . . . . 1·00 70
1157 60c. Three Kings . . . . . 1·25 1·10
1158 70c. The Flight into Egypt 1·50 2·75
MS1159 87 × 67 mm. The Nativity 3·00 4·00

232 Killer Whale and other Marine Life

1998. International Year of the Ocean. Multicoloured.
1160 15c. Type **232** 65 50
1161 55c. Tropical fish 85 90

233 Timothy Gibson (composer)

1998. 25th Anniv of "March on Bahamaland" (national anthem).
1162 **233** 60c. multicoloured . . . 1·00 1·25

234 Head of Greater Flamingo and Chick

1999. 40th Anniv of National Trust (1st issue). Inagua National Park. Multicoloured.
1163 55c. Type **234** . . . . . . 1·50 1·60
1164 55c. Pair with two chicks . . 1·50 1·60
1165 55c. Greater flamingos asleep or stretching wings 1·50 1·60
1166 55c. Greater flamingos feeding . . . . 1·50 1·60
1167 55c. Greater flamingos in flight . . . . 1·50 1·60
Nos. 1163/7 were printed together, se-tenant, with the backgrounds forming a composite design.
See also Nos. 1173/7, 1198/1202 and 1207/11.

235 Arawak Indian Canoe

1999. "Australia '99" World Stamp Exhibition, Melbourne. Maritime History. Multicoloured.
1168 15c. Type **235** 40 30
1169 55c. "Santa Maria" (Columbus), 1492 . . . . 2·00 1·25
1170 60c. "Queen Anne's Revenge" (Blackbeard), 1716 . . . . 2·25 1·75
1171 70c. "The Banshee" (Confederate paddle-steamer) running blockade 2·50 3·50
MS1172 110 × 66 mm. $2 Firing on American ships, 1776 . . . . 3·25 4·25

1999. 40th Anniv of National Trust (2nd issue). Exuma Cays Land and Sea Park. As T **234**. Mult.
1173 55c. Dolphin . . . . 1·50 1·75
1174 55c. Angelfish and parrotfish 1·50 1·75
1175 55c. Queen triggerfish . . . 1·50 1·75
1176 55c. Turtle . . . . 1·50 1·75
1177 55c. Lobster . . . . 1·50 1·75
Nos. 1173/7 were printed together, se-tenant, with the backgrounds forming a composite design.

236 Society Headquarters Building

1999. 40th Anniv of Bahamas Historical Society.
1178 **236** $1 multicoloured . . . . 1·50 2·25

1999. 30th Anniv of First Manned Landing on Moon. As T **186** of Ascension. Multicoloured.
1179 15c. Constructing ascent module 45 40
1180 65c. Diagram of command and service module . . . 1·25 1·25
1181 70c. Lunar module descending . . . . 1·25 1·75
1182 80c. Lunar module preparing to dock with service module . . . . . 1·25 2·50
MS1183 90 × 80 mm. $2 Earth as seen from Moon (circular, 40 mm diam) . . . . 3·25 4·25

1999. "Queen Elizabeth the Queen Mother's Century". As T **187** of Ascension. Multicoloured.
1184 15c. Visiting Herts Hospital, 1940 . . . . 60 35
1185 65c. With Princess Elizabeth, Hyde Park, 1944 . . . . 1·50 1·00
1186 70c. With Prince Andrew, 1997 . . . . 1·50 1·50
1187 80c. With Irish Guards' mascot, 1997 . . . . . 1·50 1·75
MS1188 145 × 70 mm. $2 Lady Elizabeth Bowes-Lyon with her brother David, 1904, and England World Cup team celebrating, 1966. . . . . 4·50 5·00

237 "Delaware" (American mail ship), 1880

1999. 125th Anniv of U.P.U. Ships. Multicoloured.
1189 15c. Type **237** . . . . . . 1·50 50
1190 65c. "Atlantis" (liner), 1923 2·50 1·50
1191 70c. "Queen of Bermuda 2" (liner), 1937 . . . . . . 2·50 2·25
1192 80c. U.S.S. "Saufley" (destroyer), 1943 . . . . 2·75 3·25

238 "Turtle Pond" (Green Turtle)

1999. Environment Protection (7th series). Marine Life Paintings by Ricardo Knowles. Multicoloured.
1193 15c. Type **238** 50 35
1194 65c. "Turtle Cliff" (Loggerhead turtle) . . . 1·25 1·00
1195 70c. "Barracuda" . . . . . 1·40 1·40
1196 80c. "Coral Reef" . . . . . 1·50 2·25
MS1197 90 × 75 mm. $2 "Atlantic Bottle-nosed Dolphins" . . . . 3·25 4·50
The 65c. is inscribed "GREEN TURTLES" in error.

1999. 40th Anniv of National Trust (3rd issue). Birds. As T **234**. Multicoloured.
1198 65c. Bridled tern and white-tailed tropic bird . . . . 1·75 1·75
1199 65c. Louisiana heron . . . 1·75 1·75
1200 65c. Bahama woodstar . . . 1·75 1·75
1201 65c. Black-billed whistling duck . . . . 1·75 1·75
1202 65c. Cuban amazon . . . . 1·75 1·75
Nos. 1198/1202 were printed together, se-tenant, with the backgrounds forming a composite design.

239 Man on Elephant Float

1999. Christmas. Junkanoo Festival. Multicoloured.
1203 15c. Type **239** 50 30
1204 65c. Man in winged costume 1·00 1·00
1205 70c. Man in feathered mask 1·25 1·25
1206 80c. Man blowing conch shell . . . . 1·50 2·00

1999. 40th Anniv of National Trust (4th issue). Flora and Fauna. As T **234**. Multicoloured.
1207 65c. Foxglove . . . . . . 2·00 2·00
1208 65c. Vole . . . . 2·00 2·00
1209 65c. Cuban amazon . . . . 2·00 2·00
1210 65c. Lizard . . . . 2·00 2·00
1211 65c. Red hibiscus . . . . . 2·00 2·00
Nos. 1207/11 were printed together, se-tenant, with the backgrounds forming a composite design.

240 New Plymouth

2000. Historic Fishing Villages. Multicoloured.
1212 15c. Type **240** . . . . . . 1·00 40
1213 65c. Cherokee Sound . . . 1·90 1·00
1214 70c. Hope Town . . . . . 2·25 1·75
1215 80c. Spanish Wells . . . . 2·50 3·00

241 Gold Medal Winning Bahamas Women's Relay Team

2000. "The Golden Girls" winners of 4 × 100 metre Relay at I.A.A.F. World Track and Field Championship '99, Spain. Sheet 100 × 55 mm.
MS1216 **241** $2 multicoloured . . 3·00 3·50

242 Prickly Pear

2000. Medicinal Plants (1st series). Multicoloured.
1217 15c. Type **242** 35 30
1218 65c. Buttercup . . . . . . 1·25 1·25
1219 70c. Shepherd's needle . . . 1·25 1·50
1220 80c. Five fingers . . . . . 1·40 2·25
See also Nos. 1282/5 and 1324/7.

243 Re-arming and Re-fuelling Spitfire

2000. "The Stamp Show 2000" International Stamp Exhibition, London. 60th Anniv of Battle of Britain. Multicoloured.
1221 15c. Type **243** 70 45
1222 65c. Sqdn. Ldr. Stanford-Tuck's Hurricane Mk I 1·40 1·40
1223 70c. Dogfight between Spitfires and Heinkel IIIs 1·60 1·75
1224 80c. Flight of Spitfires attacking . . . . 1·60 2·25
MS1225 90 × 70 mm. $2 Presentation Spitfire Bahamas . . . . . . 3·50 4·00

244 Teachers' and Salaried Workers' Co-operative Credit Union Building

2000. Co-operatives Movement in Bahamas. Sheet 90 × 50 mm.
MS1226 **244** $2 multicoloured . . 3·50 4·00

245 Swimming

2000. Olympic Games, Sydney. Each inscribed with details of previous Bahamian participation. Mult.
1227 15c. Type **245** 50 30
1228 65c. Triple jump 1·40 1·25
1229 70c. Women's 4 × 100 m relay 1·40 1·40
1230 80c. Sailing 1·50 2·25

246 *Encyclia cochleata*

2000. Christmas. Orchids. Multicoloured.
1231 15c. Type **246** 55 30
1232 65c. *Encyclia plicata* 1·40 1·25
1233 70c. *Bletia purpurea* 1·60 1·60
1234 80c. *Encyclia gracilis* 1·75 2·25

247 Cuban Amazon and Primary School Class

2000. Bahamas Humane Society. Multicoloured.
1235 15c. Type **247** 1·25 50
1236 65c. Cat and Society stall 2·25 1·25
1237 70c. Dogs and veterinary surgery 2·75 2·25
1238 80c. Goat and animal rescue van 2·75 3·00

248 "Meadow Street, Inagua"

2001. Early Settlements. Paintings by Ricardo Knowles. Multicoloured.
1239 15c. Type **248** 40 30
1240 65c. "Bain Town" 1·25 1·00
1241 70c. "Hope Town, Abaco" 1·40 1·40
1242 80c. "Blue Hills" 1·50 2·25

249 Lynden Pindling presenting Independence Constitution, 1972

2001. Sir Lynden Pindling (former Prime Minister) Commemoration. Multicoloured.
1243 15c. Type **249** 50 40
1244 65c. Sir Lynden Pindling with Bahamas flag 1·40 1·50

250 "Cocoaplum"

2001. Edible Wild Fruits. Paintings by Alton Roland Lowe. Multicoloured.
1245 15c. Type **250** 35 25
1246 65c. "Guana Berry" 1·25 1·10
1247 70c. "Mastic" 1·25 1·25
1248 80c. "Seagrape" 1·50 2·25

251 Reddish Egret

2001. Birds and their Eggs. Multicoloured.
1249 5c. Type **251** 40 40
1250 10c. American purple gallinule 50 40
1251 15c. Antillean nighthawk 60 20
1252 20c. Wilson's plover 70 30
1253 25c. Killdeer plover 75 35
1254 30c. Bahama woodstar 80 40
1255 40c. Bahama swallow 90 50
1256 50c. Bahama mockingbird 1·00 65
1257 60c. Black-cowled oriole 1·25 75
1258 65c. Great lizard cuckoo 1·25 80
1259 70c. Audubon's shearwater 1·40 1·00
1260 80c. Grey kingbird 1·50 1·10
1261 $1 Bananaquit 1·75 1·40
1262 $2 Yellow warbler 3·50 3·50
1263 $5 Greater Antillean bullfinch 7·00 7·50
1264 $10 Roseate spoonbill 13·00 15·00

252 H.M.S. *Norfolk* (cruiser), 1933

2001. Royal Navy Ships connected to Bahamas. Multicoloured.
1265 15c. Type **252** 90 40
1266 25c. H.M.S. *Scarborough* (sloop), 1930s 1·25 50
1267 50c. H.M.S. *Bahamas* (frigate), 1944 1·75 1·25
1268 65c. H.M.S. *Battleaxe* (frigate), 1979 2·00 1·75
1269 70c. H.M.S. *Invincible* (aircraft carrier), 1997 2·00 2·00
1270 80c. H.M.S. *Norfolk* (frigate), 2000 2·00 2·75

253 "Adoration of the Shepherds"

2001. Christmas. Paintings by Rubens. Mult.
1271 15c. Type **253** 55 25
1272 65c. "Adoration of the Magi" (with Van Dyck) 1·40 1·10
1273 70c. "Holy Virgin in Wreath of Flowers" (with Breughel) 1·50 1·40
1274 80c. "Holy Virgin adored by Angels" 1·60 2·00

2002. Golden Jubilee. As T **200** of Ascension.
1275 15c. black, green and gold 35 25
1276 65c. multicoloured 1·10 95
1277 70c. multicoloured 1·25 1·25
1278 80c. multicoloured 1·25 1·75
MS1279 162 × 95 mm. Nos. 1275/8 and $2 multicoloured 6·50 6·50
DESIGNS—HORIZ: 15c. Princess Elizabeth; 65c. Queen Elizabeth in Bonn, 1992; 70c. Queen Elizabeth with Prince Edward, 1965; 80c. Queen Elizabeth at Sandringham, 1996. VERT (38 × 51 mm)—$2 Queen Elizabeth after Annigoni.

254 Avard Moncur (athlete)

2002. Award of BAAA Most Outstanding Male Athlete Title to Avard Moncur. Sheet 65 × 98 mm.
MS1280 **254** $2 multicoloured 3·25 3·50

255 Statue of Liberty with U.S. and Bahamas Flags

2002. In Remembrance. Victims of Terrorist Attacks on U.S.A. (11 September 2001).
1281 **255** $1 multicoloured 3·00 3·00

2002. Medicinal Plants (2nd series). As T **242**. Multicoloured.
1282 15c. Wild sage 50 35
1283 65c. Seaside maho 1·40 1·10
1284 70c. Sea ox-eye 1·50 1·40
1285 80c. Mexican poppy 1·50 1·75

2002. Queen Elizabeth the Queen Mother Commemoration. As T **202** of Ascension.
1286 15c. brown, gold and purple 60 40
1287 65c. multicoloured 1·40 1·50
MS1288 145 × 70 mm. 70c. black and gold; 80c. multicoloured 3·50 3·50
DESIGNS: 15c. Queen Elizabeth at American Red Cross Club, London, 1944; 65c. Queen Mother at Remembrance Service, 1989; 70c. Queen Elizabeth, 1944; 80c. Queen Mother at Cheltenham Races, 2000.

256 Rice Bird and Rice

2002. Illustrations from *The Natural History of Carolina, Florida and the Bahama Islands* by Mark Catesby (1747). Multicoloured.
1289 15c. Type **256** 75 45
1290 25c. Alligator and red mangrove 80 50
1291 50c. Parrot fish 1·25 90
1292 65c. Ilathera duck and sea ox-eye 1·50 1·50
1293 70c. Flamingo and gorgonian coral 1·60 1·75
1294 80c. Crested bittern and inkberry 1·75 2·00

257 "While Shepherds watched their Flocks"

2002. Christmas. Scenes from Carols. Multicoloured.
1295 15c. Type **257** 60 25
1296 65c. "We Three Kings" 1·40 1·10
1297 70c. "Once in Royal David's City" 1·50 1·50
1298 80c. "I saw Three Ships" 1·60 2·00

258 Flamingo on Nest

2003. Inagua National Park Wetlands. Flamingos. Multicoloured.
1299 15c. Type **258** 70 45
1300 25c. Flock of flamingos feeding 90 50
1301 50c. Group of flamingos 1·50 1·00
1302 65c. Group of flamingos walking 1·75 1·75
1303 70c. Flamingos taking-off 1·90 1·90
1304 80c. Flamingos in flight 2·00 2·50

259 Captain Edward Teach ("Blackbeard")

260 Dinghies

2003. Pirates. Multicoloured.
1305 15c. Type **259** 80 45
1306 25c. Captain "Calico Jack" Rackham 1·25 50
1307 50c. Anne Bonney 1·75 1·10
1308 65c. Captain Woodes Rogers 2·00 1·75
1309 70c. Sir John Hawkins 2·25 2·25
1310 80c. Captain Bartholomew Roberts ("Black Bart") 2·50 3·00

2003. 50th Anniv of Family Island Regatta. Multicoloured.
1311 15c. Type **260** 75 40
1312 65c. *New Courageous* (racing sloop) 1·75 1·40
1313 70c. *New Susan Chase* (racing sloop) 1·90 1·75
1314 80c. *Tida Wave* (racing sloop) 2·00 2·25

2003. 50th Anniv of Coronation. As T **206** of Ascension. Multicoloured.
1315 65c. Queen with crown, orb and sceptre 1·50 1·40
1316 80c. Royal family on Buckingham Palace balcony 2·00 2·25
MS1317 95 × 115 mm. 15c. As 65c.; 70c. As 80c. 2·25 2·50
Nos. 1315/16 have red frame; stamps from MS1317 have no frame and country name in mauve panel.

2003. Medicinal Plants (3rd series). As T **242**.
1318 15c. *Asystasia* 40 25
1319 65c. *Cassia* 1·40 1·25
1320 70c. *Lignum vitae* 1·50 1·50
1321 80c. Snowberry 1·60 1·75

2003. Centenary of Powered Flight. As T **209** of Ascension. Multicoloured.
1322 15c. Piper Cub 60 30
1323 25c. De Havilland Tiger Moth 85 55
1324 50c. Lockheed SR-71A Blackbird 1·50 1·10
1325 65c. Supermarine S6B 1·60 1·40
1326 70c. North American P-51D Mustang "Miss America" 1·75 1·60
1327 80c. Douglas DC-3 Dakota 1·90 2·00

261 Interior with Stained Glass Window

2003. Christmas. St. Matthew's Church, Nassau. Multicoloured.
1328 15c. Type **261** 50 25
1329 65c. Church interior (horiz) 1·50 1·10
1330 70c. St. Matthew's Church (horiz) 1·60 1·50
1331 80c. Church tower 1·75 2·00

262 "Crawfishin"

2003. "Waters of Life". Paintings by Alton Lowe. Multicoloured.
1332 15c. Type **262** 50 25
1333 65c. "Summer" 1·50 1·25
1334 70c. "The Whelkers" 1·60 1·60
1335 80c. "Annual Visit" 1·75 2·00

263 Egrets on Dead Tree

2004. Wetlands (2nd series). Harrold and Wilson Ponds, New Providence Island. Multicoloured.
1336 15c. Type **263** 55 30
1337 25c. Green-backed heron and duck 75 50
1338 50c. Birdwatchers in canoes 1·40 1·10
1339 65c. Egret and Bahama pintail ducks 1·75 1·60
1340 70c. Egret and Louisiana heron 1·90 2·00
1341 80c. Birdwatchers with binoculars and telescope 2·00 2·50

264 Methodist Church, Cupid's Cay, Governor's Harbour

2004. 300th Birth Anniv of John Wesley (founder of Methodist Church) (2003). Multicoloured.

1342	15c. Type **264**	45	25
1343	25c. Church, Grants Town, Nassau	60	35
1344	50c. Wooden Chapel, Marsh Harbour (vert)	1·25	1·10
1345	65c. Ebeneezer Methodist Church	1·50	1·50
1346	70c. Trinity Methodist Church	1·75	2·00
1346a	80c. Portrait by Antonius Roberts (vert)	1·90	2·25

265 Cattleya

2004. Bicentenary of the Royal Horticultural Society. Multicoloured.

1347	15c. Type **265**	45	25
1348	65c. Hibiscus	1·25	1·00
1349	70c. Canna	1·40	1·40
1350	80c. Thunbergia	1·50	1·75

266 Elbow Reef Lighthouse

267 Boxing

2004. Lighthouses (1st series). Multicoloured.

1351	15c. Type **266**	50	30
1352	50c. Great Stirrup	1·40	1·00
1353	65c. Great Isaac	1·50	1·10
1354	70c. Hole in the Wall	1·60	1·60
1355	80c. Hog Island	1·75	1·90

See also Nos. 1396/1400.

2004. Olympic Games, Athens. Multicoloured.

1356	15c. Type **267**	40	25
1357	50c. Swimming	1·00	80
1358	65c. Tennis	1·10	1·10
1359	70c. Relay racing	1·25	1·40

268 "Anticipation"

2004. Christmas. Junkanoo Festival. Multicoloured.

1360	15c. Type **268**	30	20
1361	25c. "First Time"	40	25
1362	50c. "On The Move" (vert)	80	60
1363	65c. "I'm Ready" (vert)	90	80
1364	70c. "Trumpet Player" (vert)	1·00	1·00
1365	80c. "Drummer Boy" (vert)	1·10	1·40

269 RMS *Mauretania*

2004. Merchant Ships. Multicoloured.

1366	15c. Type **269**	65	30
1367	25c. MV *Adonia*	85	40
1368	50c. MS *Royal Princess*	1·50	85
1369	65c. SS *Queen of Nassau*	1·60	1·40
1370	70c. RMS *Transvaal Castle*	1·75	1·75
1371	80c. SS *Norway*	1·90	2·00

2005. Medicinal Plants (4th series). As T **242**. Multicoloured.

1372	15c. Aloe vera	25	20
1373	25c. Red stopper	35	25
1374	50c. Blue flower	65	65
1375	65c. Bay lavender	90	1·00

270 Commando Squadron

2005. 25th Anniv of the Royal Bahamas Defence Force. Multicoloured.

1376	15c. Type **270**	45	25
1377	25c. HMBS *Abaco*	65	30
1378	50c. HMBS *Bahamas*	1·10	1·00
1379	65c. Officers and marines in uniform	1·40	1·60

2005. Bicentenary of Battle of Trafalgar. Multicoloured (except **MS**1386) designs as T **216** of Ascension.

1380	15c. Tower Sea Service pistols, 1801 RN Pattern (vert)	50	25
1381	25c. Royal Marine, 1805 (vert)	70	40
1382	50c. HMS *Boreas* off Bahamas, 1787	1·25	1·00
1383	65c. "Death of Nelson" (A. W. Devis)	1·50	1·25
1384	70c. HMS *Victory*	1·75	1·75
1385	80c. *Achille* surrendering to HMS *Polyphemus*	1·90	2·25
MS1386	120 × 78 mm. $1 Admiral Collingwood (brown, black and grey) (vert); $1 HMS *Polyphemus* (vert)	5·50	6·00

No. 1384 contains traces of powdered wood from HMS *Victory*.

271 William Curry

273 College Entrance, Nassau

272 Flags of EU and Bahamas and Map

2005. Abaco—Key West Connections. Mult.

1387	15c. Type **271**	30	20
1388	25c. Captain John Bartlum's House (horiz)	45	35
1389	50c. Captain John Bartlum	90	85
1390	65c. Captain Tuggy Roberts' House (horiz)	1·25	1·40

2005. 50th Anniv of First Europa Stamp. Designs, all showing flags of EU and Bahamas, outline Map of Western Europe and different seascapes. Multicoloured.

1391	15c. Type **272**	45	35
1392	25c. Seascape with bands of thin high cloud	65	60
1393	50c. Seascape with small island	1·25	1·40
1394	$5 Seascape with clouds	9·00	9·50
MS1395	120 × 77 mm. Nos. 1391/4	10·00	11·00

2005. Lighthouses (2nd series). As T **266**. Multicoloured.

1396	15c. Bird Rock	75	35
1397	50c. Castle Island	1·50	80
1398	65c. San Salvador	1·75	1·40
1399	70c. Great Inagua	1·90	1·90
1400	80c. Cay Lobos	2·00	2·25

2005. Pope John Paul II Commemoration. As T **219** of Ascension.

1401	$1 multicoloured	2·00	2·00

2005. 30th Anniv of the College of the Bahamas. Sheet 81 × 88 mm.

MS1402	**273** $2 multicoloured	3·25	3·50

2005. Christmas. Birth Bicentenary of Hans Christian Andersen (writer). As T **220** of Ascension. Multicoloured.

1403	15c. *The Little Fir Tree*	55	30
1404	25c. *The Princess and the Pea*	75	55
1405	50c. *The Tin Soldier*	1·50	1·50
1406	65c. *Thumbelina*	1·60	1·60

274 Bahama Nuthatch

2006. BirdLife International. Bahama Nuthatch (*Sitta insularis*). Multicoloured.

1407	15c. Type **274**	50	25
1408	25c. On thick branch (facing left)	70	30
1409	50c. On tree trunk (facing right)	1·25	85
1410	65c. On thin branch among pine needles	1·50	1·10
1411	70c. Nuthatch seen from underside	1·60	1·60
1412	80c. On tree trunk near hole (facing left)	1·75	2·00
MS1413	170 × 85 mm. Nos. 1407/12	6·50	7·00

The stamps within No. **MS**1413 form a composite design showing nuthatches in Caribbean pine trees.

2006. 80th Birthday of Queen Elizabeth II. As T **223** of Ascension. Multicoloured.

1414	15c. Princess Elizabeth	45	25
1415	25c. Queen Elizabeth II, c. 1952	65	30
1416	50c. Wearing blue feathered hat	1·10	85
1417	65c. Wearing hat with brim raised at one side	1·40	1·40
MS1418	144 × 75 mm. $1.50 As No. 1415; $1.50 As No. 1416	6·00	6·50

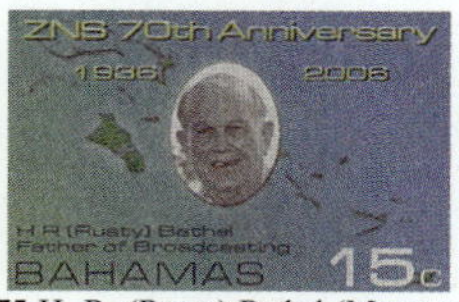

275 H. R. (Rusty) Bethel (Manager, ZNS Radio 1945–70)

2006. 70th Anniv of Broadcasting in the Bahamas. Multicoloured.

1419	15c. Type **275**	45	25
1420	25c. New Broadcasting Corporation of the Bahamas logo	65	30
1421	50c. National Headquarters of Broadcasting Corporation of the Bahamas	1·10	80
1422	65c. ZNS Nassau Radio stations building	1·40	1·25
1423	70c. Radio mast and map of Bahamas	1·50	1·50
1424	80c. "ZNS Radio" (70th anniv) and microphone	1·60	1·75

276 Amaryllis (*Hippeastrum puniceum*)

2006. Flowers of the Bahamas. Paintings by Alton Roland Lowe. Multicoloured.

1425	5c. Type **276**	15	15
1426	10c. *Barleria cristata*	20	15
1427	25c. Desert rose (*Adenium obesum*)	40	20
1428	35c. Poor man's orchid (*Bauhinia* sp.)	55	25
1429	40c. Frangipani (*Plumeria* sp.)	60	30
1430	55c. Herald's trumpet (*Beaumontia grandiflora*)	75	35
1431	65c. Oleander (*Nerium oleander*)	90	50
1432	75c. Bird of Paradise (*Strelitzia reginae*)	1·25	90
1433	80c. *Plumbago capensis*	1·25	90
1434	90c. Rose (*Rosa* sp.)	1·40	1·00
1435	$1 Rubber vine (*Cryptostegia madagascariensis*)	1·60	1·10
1436	$2 Star of Bethlehem (*Jatropha integerrima*)	3·25	3·00
1437	$5 Angel's trumpet (*Brugmansia suaveolens*)	7·50	8·00
1438	$10 Wine lily (*Crinum* sp.)	15·00	16·00

277 *Centrosema virginianum* (blue pea)

2006. Wild Flowering Vines. Paintings by Alton Roland Lowe. Multicoloured.

1439	15c. Type **277**	40	25
1440	50c. *Urechites lutea* (allamanda)	90	60
1441	65c. *Ipomoea indica* (morning glory)	1·10	1·10
1442	70c. *Ipomoea microdactyla* (sky vine)	1·25	1·50

278 Christmas Sunday

2006. Christmas. Multicoloured.

1443	15c. Type **278**	40	25
1444	25c. Christmas dinner	60	30
1445	50c. Bay Street shopping	1·00	1·60
1446	65c. Boxing Day Junkanoo	1·25	85
1447	70c. Watch Night service	1·40	1·40
1448	80c. New Year's Day Junkanoo	1·50	1·75

279 Blainville's Beaked Whale

2007. Endangered Species. Blainville's Beaked Whale (*Mesoplodon densirostris*). Multicoloured.

1449	15c. Type **279**	40	25
1450	25c. Three whales	60	30
1451	50c. Whales just beneath surface	1·00	60
1452	60c. Two whales	1·10	65

280 Princess Elizabeth and Lt. Philip Mountbatten, 1949

2007. Diamond Wedding of Queen Elizabeth II and Prince Philip. Multicoloured.

1453	15c. Type **280**	10	10
1454	25c. Princess Elizabeth riding in carriage on her wedding day, 1949	35	25
1455	50c. Princess Elizabeth and Prince Philip waving from balcony on wedding day, 1949	85	60
1456	65c. Princess Elizabeth, Prince Philip and Queen Mary	1·20	90
MS1457	125 × 85 mm. $5 Wedding portrait (42 × 56 mm)	8·25	8·25

281 Bahamas Scouts at Church Service

2007. Centenary of Scouting. Multicoloured.

1458	15c. Type **281**	1·20	70
1459	25c. Scout in adventure playground	1·75	1·00
1460	50c. Scout barbecue	3·00	1·75
1461	65c. Bahamas girl scouts on parade	3·25	1·90
MS1462	90 × 65 mm. 70c. Scouts playing ball (*vert*); 80c. Lord Baden-Powell (*vert*)		

282 Scouts repairing Causeway ('Service')

283 Flower Decoration

2007. 20th Anniv of Governor-General's Youth Award. Multicoloured.

1463	15c. Type **282**	10	10
1464	25c. Painting ('Skills')	35	25

1465 50c. Kayaking ('Physical Recreation') 70 50
1466 65c. Hiking ('Adventurous Journey') 95 60
1467 70c. Conch shell emblem 1·40 1·50

2007. Christmas. Tree Decorations. Multicoloured.
1468 15c. Type **283** 10 10
1469 25c. Sea shells decoration 35 25
1470 50c. Sea shells decoration (different) 70 50
1471 65c. Bow and sea shells decoration 90 60
1472 70c. Gold woven decoration 1·20 1·40
1473 80c. 'Angel' made from sea shells 1·50 1·60

284 Choir

2007. 300th Birth Anniv of Charles Wesley. Multicoloured.
1474 15c. Type **284** 25 15
1475 50c. Charles and John Wesley (evangelists) (vert) 75 50
1476 65c. Revd. Charles Wesley and *Hymns and Sacred Poems* (vert) 95 60
1477 70c. Harbour Island Methodist Church (horiz) 1·40 1·50

285 *Heliconius charitonius* (zebra longwing)

2008. Bahamas Butterflies. Multicoloured.
1478 15c. Type **285** 10 10
1479 25c. *Dryas julia carteri* (Julia) 35 25
1480 50c. *Phoebis sennae* (cloudless sulphur) 85 60
1481 65c. *Danaus gilippus berenice* (The Queen) 1·20 90
1482 70c. *Urbanus proteus* (long-tailed skipper) 1·40 1·50
1483 80c. *Dione vanillae insularis* (Gulf fritillary) 1·50 1·60
MS1484 170 × 75 mm. Nos. 1478/83 4·00 4·25

SPECIAL DELIVERY STAMPS

1916. Optd **SPECIAL DELIVERY**.
S2 **6** 5d. black and orange 50 9·00
S3 5d. black and mauve 30 3·25

BAHAWALPUR Pt. 1

A former Indian Feudatory state which joined Pakistan in 1947 and continued to use its own stamps until 1953.

12 pies = 1 anna, 16 annas = 1 rupee.

(1)

2 Amir Muhammad Bahawal Khan I Abbasi

1947. Nos. 265/8, 269a/77 and 259/62 of India optd with Type **1**.
1 **100a** 3p. slate 24·00
2 ½a. purple 24·00
3 9p. green 24·00
4 1a. red 24·00
5 **101** 1½a. violet 24·00
6 2a. red 24·00
7 3a. violet 24·00
8 3½a. blue 24·00
9 **102** 4a. brown 24·00
10 6a. green 24·00
11 8a. violet 24·00
12 12a. lake 24·00
13 14a. purple 65·00
14 **93** 1r. grey and brown 29·00
15 2r. purple and brown £1800
16 5r. green and blue £1800
17 10r. purple and red £1800

1948. Bicentenary Commemoration.
18 **2** ½a. black and red 3·00 4·25

4 H. H. the Amir of Bahawalpur

5 The Tombs of the Amirs

1948.
19 **4** 3p. black and blue 2·00 20·00
20 ½a. black and red 2·00 20·00
21 9p. black and green 2·00 20·00
22 1a. black and red 2·00 20·00
23 1½a. black and violet 3·00 16·00
24 **5** 2a. green and red 3·00 20·00
25 – 4a. orange and brown 3·00 20·00
26 – 6a. violet and blue 3·50 20·00
27 – 8a. red and violet 3·50 20·00
28 – 12a. green and red 3·75 30·00
29 – 1r. violet and brown 19·00 42·00
35 – 1r. green and orange 1·75 18·00
30 – 2r. green and red 50·00 70·00
36 – 2r. black and red 1·75 22·00
31 – 5r. black and violet 50·00 85·00
37 – 5r. brown and blue 1·90 40·00
32 – 10r. red and black 32·00 £100
38 – 10r. brown and green 2·00 45·00
DESIGNS—HORIZ: 6a. Fort Derawar from the lake; 8a. Nur-Mahal Palace; 12a. Sadiq-Garh Palace. 46 × 32 mm: 10r. Three generations of Rulers. VERT (As Type **5**): 4a. Mosque in Sadiq-Garh; 1, 2, 5r. H.H. the Amir of Bahawalpur.

12 H.H. the Amir of Bahawalpur and Mohammed Ali Jinnah

1948. 1st Anniv of Union with Pakistan.
33 **12** 1½a. red and green 1·50 4·00

13 Soldiers of 1848 and 1948

14 Irrigation

1948. Centenary of Multan Campaign.
34 **13** 1½a. black and red 1·25 10·00

1949. Silver Jubilee of Accession of H.H. the Amir of Bahawalpur.
39 **14** 3p. black and blue 10 8·00
40 – ½a. black and orange 10 8·00
41 – 9p. black and green 10 8·00
42 – 1a. black and red 10 8·00
DESIGNS: ½a. Wheat; 9p. Cotton; 1a. Sahiwal bull.

17 U.P.U. Monument, Berne

1949. 75th Anniv of U.P.U.
43 **17** 9p. black and green 20 1·25
44 1a. black and mauve 20 1·25
45 1½a. black and orange 20 1·25
46 2½a. black and blue 20 1·25

OFFICIAL STAMPS

O **4** Eastern White Pelicans

1945. As Type O **4** with Arabic opt.
O1 – ½a. black and green 5·50 14·00
O2 – 1a. black and red 3·75 11·00
O7 – 1a. black and brown 55·00 65·00
O3 – 2a. black and violet 3·25 12·00
O4 O **4** 4a. black and olive 12·00 26·00
O5 – 8a. black and brown 26·00 18·00
O6 – 1r. black and orange 26·00 18·00

DESIGNS: ½a. Panjnad Weir; 1a. (No. O2), Camel and calf; 1a. (No. O7), Baggage camels; 2a. Blackbuck antelopes; 8a. Friday Mosque, Fort Derawar; 1r. Temple at Pattan Munara.

(O 8)

1945. Types as Nos. O1, etc., in new colours and without Arabic opt. (a) Surch as Type O **8**.
O11 ½a. on 8a. black and purple (as No. O5) 5·50 7·00
O12 1½a. on 5r. black and orange (as No. O6) 40·00 11·00
O13 1½a. on 2r. black and blue (as No. O1) £130 8·50

(b) Optd **SERVICE** and Arabic inscription.
O14 ½a. black and red (as No. O1) 1·25 11·00
O15 1a. black and red (as No. O2) 2·00 13·00
O16 2a. black and orange (as No. O3) 3·25 45·00

1945. As Type **4** but inscr "SERVICE" at left.
O17 3p. black and blue 4·00 11·00
O18 1½a. black and violet 20·00 8·00

O **11** Allied Banners

1946. Victory.
O19 O **11** 1½a. green and grey 3·50 4·25

1948. Stamps of 1948 with Arabic opt as in Type O **4**.
O20 **4** 3p. black and blue 80 12·00
O21 1a. black and red 80 11·00
O22 **5** 2a. green and red 80 12·00
O23 – 4a. orange and brown 80 16·00
O24 – 1r. green and orange 80 18·00
O25 – 2r. black and red 80 24·00
O26 – 5r. chocolate and blue 80 40·00
O27 – 10r. brown and green 80 40·00

1949. 75th Anniv of U.P.U. optd as in Type O **4**.
O28 **17** 9p. black and green 15 4·50
O29 1a. black and mauve 15 4·50
O30 1½a. black and orange 15 4·50
O31 2½a. black and blue 15 4·50

BAHRAIN Pt. 1, Pt. 19

An archipelago in the Persian Gulf on the Arabian coast. An independent shaikhdom with Indian and later British postal administration. The latter was closed on 1 January 1966, when the Bahrain Post Office took over.

1933. 12 pies = 1 anna; 16 annas = 1 rupee.
1957. 100 naya paise = 1 rupee.
Stamps of India optd **BAHRAIN**.

1933. King George V.
1 **55** 3p. grey 3·50 45
2 **56** ½a. green 7·50 3·25
15 **79** ½a. green 4·50 1·75
3 **80** 9p. green 3·75 3·50
4 **57** 1a. brown 7·00 2·50
16 **81** 1a. brown 10·00 40
5 **82** 1a.3p. mauve 10·00 2·75
6 **70** 2a. orange 10·00 19·00
17 **59** 2a. orange 45·00 7·50
7 **62** 3a. blue 19·00 55·00
18 3a. red 4·75 60
8 **83** 3a.6p. blue 3·75 30
9 **71** 4a. green 18·00 55·00
19 **63** 4a. olive 5·00 40
10 **65** 8a. mauve 6·00 30
11 **66** 12a. red 7·50 1·25
12 **67** 1r. brown and green 16·00 10·00
13 2r. red and orange 28·00 35·00
14w 5r. blue and violet £120 £140
36w 15r. brown and green 70·00 75·00
37 25r. slate and purple £120 90·00

1938. King George VI.
20 **91** 3p. slate 16·00 4·50
21 ½a. brown 7·00 20
22 9p. green 11·00 9·00
23 1a. red 10·00 20
24 **92** 2a. red 5·00 3·50
26 – 3a. green (No. 253) 12·00 8·00
27 – 3a.6p. blue (No. 254) 6·00 5·00
28 – 4a. brown (No. 255) £150 70·00
30 – 8a. violet (No. 257) £200 35·00
31 – 12a. red (No. 258) £130 45·00
32 **93** 1r. slate and brown 5·50 1·75
33 2r. purple and brown 15·00 8·00
34 5r. green and blue 15·00 13·00
35 10r. purple and red 75·00 42·00

1942. King George VI.
38 **100a** 3p. slate 3·00 2·50
39 ½a. mauve 4·25 3·00
40 9p. green 15·00 19·00
41 1a. red 6·50 1·00
42 **101** 1a.3p. bistre 8·50 21·00
43 1½a. violet 6·00 8·00
44 2a. red 6·00 1·50
45 3a. violet 18·50 7·50
46 3½a. blue 4·75 21·00
47 **102** 4a. brown 4·00 2·00
48 6a. green 17·00 12·00
49 8a. violet 7·00 4·00
50 12a. purple 9·50 6·00

Stamps of Great Britain surch **BAHRAIN** and new value in Indian currency.

1948. King George VI.
51 **128** ½a. on ½d. green 50 1·25
71 ½a. on ½d. orange 2·50 2·75
52 1a. on 1d. red 50 3·00
72 1a. on 1d. blue 3·00 20
53 1½a. on 1½d. brown 50 3·75
73 1½a. on 1½d. green 3·00 13·00
54 2a. on 2d. orange 50 20
74 2a. on 2d. brown 1·50 30
55 2½a. on 2½d. blue 50 4·50
75 2½a. on 2½d. red 3·00 14·00
56 3a. on 3d. violet 50 10
76 **129** 4a. on 4d. blue 4·00 1·50
57 6a. on 6d. purple 50 10
58 **130** 1r. on 1s. brown 1·25 10
59 **131** 2r. on 2s.6d. green 5·50 4·75
60 5r. on 5s. red 5·50 4·75
60a – 10r. on 10s. blue (No. 478a) 80·00 60·00

1948. Silver Wedding.
61 **137** 2½a. on 2½d. blue 1·00 2·50
62 **138** 15r. on £1 blue 30·00 48·00

1948. Olympic Games.
63 **139** 2½a. on 2½d. blue 1·00 4·00
64 **140** 3a. on 3d. violet 1·00 3·75
65 – 6a. on 6d. purple 1·50 3·75
66 – 1r. on 1s. brown 2·50 4·00

1949. U.P.U.
67 **143** 2½a. on 2½d. blue 60 2·25
68 **144** 3a. on 3d. violet 70 4·00
69 – 6a. on 6d. purple 60 3·00
70 – 1r. on 1s. brown 1·25 2·75

1951. Pictorial stamps (Nos. 509/11).
77 **147** 2r. on 2s.6d. green 26·00 12·00
78 – 5r. on 5s. red 14·00 4·25
79 – 10r. on 10s. blue 30·00 8·50

1952. Queen Elizabeth II.
97 **154** ½a. on ½d. orange 10 15
81 1a. on 1d. blue 10 10
82 1½a. on 1½d. green 10 30
83 2a. on 2d. brown 30 10
84 **155** 2½a. on 2½d. red 20 1·75
85 3a. on 3d. lilac 3·00 10
86 4a. on 4d. blue 13·00 30
99 **157** 6a. on 6d. purple 50 75
88 **160** 12a. on 1s.3d. green 3·25 20
89 1r. on 1s.6d. blue 3·25 10

1953. Coronation.
90 **161** 2½a. on 2½d. red 1·25 75
91 – 4a. on 4d. blue 2·25 6·50
92 **163** 12a. on 1s.3d. green 3·25 4·50
93 – 1r. on 1s.6d. blue 7·50 50

1955. Pictorial stamps (Nos. 595a/598a).
94 **166** 2r. on 2s.6d. brown 5·50 2·00
95 – 5r. on 5s. red 13·00 2·75
96 – 10r. on 10s. blue 20·00 2·75

1957. Queen Elizabeth II.
102 **157** 1n.p. on 5d. brown 10 10
103 **154** 3n.p. on ½d. orange 50 3·00
104 6n.p. on 1d. blue 50 3·00
105 9n.p. on 1½d. green 50 3·25
106 12n.p. on 2d. pale brown 30 70
107 **155** 15n.p. on 2½d. red 30 15
108 20n.p. on 3d. lilac 30 10
109 25n.p. on 4d. blue 1·25 2·50
110 **157** 40n.p. on 6d. purple 40 10
111 50n.p. on 9d. olive 3·75 4·50
112 75n.p. on 1s.3d. green 2·50 50

1957. World Scout Jubilee Jamboree.
113 **170** 15n.p. on 2½d. red 25 35
114 **171** 25n.p. on 4d. blue 30 35
115 – 75n.p. on 1s.3d. green 40 45

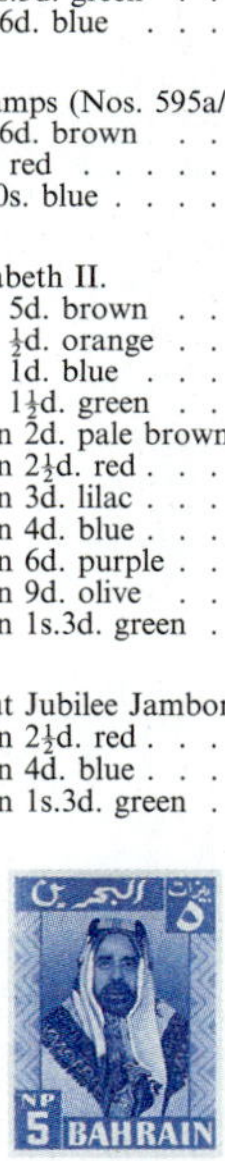

16 Shaikh Sulman bin Hamed al-Khalifa

1960.
117 **16** 5n.p. blue 20 10
118 15n.p. orange 20 10
119 20n.p. violet 20 10
120 30n.p. bistre 20 10
121 40n.p. grey 20 10
122 50n.p. green 20 10
123 75n.p. brown 30 15

124	–	1r. black	3·00	30
125	–	2r. red	3·00	2·25
126	–	5r. blue	5·00	3·00
127	–	10r. green	12·00	5·50

The rupee values are larger, 27×32½ mm.

18 Shaikh Isa bin Sulman al-Khalifa

19 Air Terminal, Muharraq

1964.

128	18	5n.p. blue	10	10
129		15n.p. orange	10	70
130		20n.p. violet	10	10
131		30n.p. bistre	10	10
132		40n.p. slate	15	10
133		50n.p. green	15	1·50
134		75n.p. brown	25	10
135	19	1r. black	11·00	2·25
136		2r. red	11·00	2·75
137	–	5r. blue	14·00	15·00
138	–	10r. myrtle	14·00	15·00

DESIGN—As Type **19**: 5r., 10r. Deep water harbour.

21 Sheikh Isa bin Sulman al-Khalifa

22 Ruler and Bahrain Airport

1966.

139	21	5f. green	15	15
140		10f. red	15	15
141		15f. blue	15	15
142		20f. purple	25	15
143	22	30f. black and green	35	15
144		40f. black and blue	40	15
145	–	50f. black and red	60	25
146	–	75f. black and violet	75	35
147	–	100f. blue and yellow	2·50	1·00
148	–	200f. green and orange	11·00	2·10
149	–	500f. brown and yellow	9·25	3·75
150	–	1d. multicoloured	17·00	8·50

DESIGNS—As Type **22**: 50f., 75f. Ruler and Mina Sulman deep-water harbour. VERT (26½×42½ mm): 100f. Pearl-diving; 200f. Lanner falcon and horse-racing; 500f. Serving coffee, and ruler's palace. LARGER (37×52½ mm): 1d. Ruler, crest, date palm, horse, dhow, pearl necklace, mosque, coffee-pot and Bab-al-Bahrain (gateway).

23 Produce

24 W.H.O. Emblem and Map of Bahrain

1966. Trade Fair and Agricultural Show.

151	23	10f. turquoise and red	40	10
152		20f. lilac and green	60	10
153		40f. blue and brown	1·70	40
154		200f. red and blue	8·00	3·75

1968. 20th Anniv of W.H.O.

155	24	20f. black and grey	75	50
156		40f. black and turquoise	2·50	1·50
157		150f. black and red	11·00	5·00

25 View of Isa Town

1968. Inauguration of Isa New Town. Mult.

158		50f. Type **25**	3·75	1·10
159		80f. Shopping centre	5·50	2·10
160		120f. Stadium	8·50	3·75
161		150f. Mosque	10·00	5·00

26 Symbol of Learning

1969. 50th Anniv of School Education in Bahrain.

162	26	40f. multicoloured	1·50	90
163		60f. multicoloured	3·00	1·50
164		150f. multicoloured	8·00	3·75

27 Dish Aerial and Map of Persian Gulf

1969. Opening of Satellite Earth Station, Ras Abu Jarjour. Multicoloured.

165		20f. Type **27**	2·20	50
166		40f. Dish aerial and palms (vert)	4·50	85
167		100f. Type **27**	10·00	3·75
168		150f. As 40f.	17·00	5·50

28 Arms, Map and Manama Municipality Building

1970. 2nd Arab Cities Organization Conf, Manama.

169	28	30f. multicoloured	2·10	2·10
170		150f. multicoloured	11·50	11·50

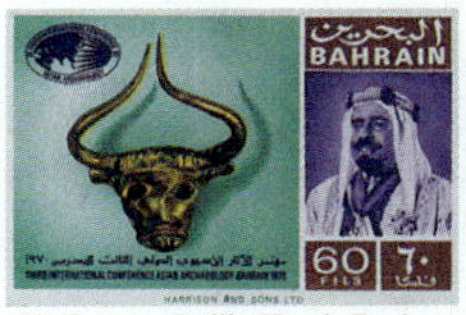

29 Copper Bull's Head, Barbar

1970. 3rd International Asian Archaeology Conference, Bahrain. Multicoloured.

171		60f. Type **29**	3·75	2·00
172		80f. Palace of Dilmun excavations	5·75	2·50
173		120f. Desert gravemounds	7·25	3·25
174		150f. Dilmun seal	8·50	4·25

30 Vickers Super VC-10 Airliner, Big Ben, London, and Bahrain Minaret

1970. 1st Gulf Aviation Vickers Super VC-10 Flight, Doha–London.

175	30	30f. multicoloured	2·50	75
176		60f. multicoloured	5·00	1·70
177		120f. multicoloured	9·25	5·00

31 I.E.Y. Emblem and Open Book

1970. International Education Year. Multicoloured.

178		60f. Type **31**	4·25	4·25
179		120f. Emblem and Bahraini children	8·50	8·50

32 Allegory of Independence

34 Human Heart

33 Arab Dhow with Arab League and U.N. Emblems

1971. Independence Day and 10th Anniv of Ruler's Accession. Multicoloured.

180		30f. Type **32**	1·80	1·00
181		60f. Government House	3·75	1·80
182		120f. Arms of Bahrain	9·25	4·50
183		150f. Arms of Bahrain (gold background)	12·50	6·25

1972. Bahrain's Membership of Arab League and U.N. Multicoloured.

184		30f. Type **33**	4·50	4·50
185		60f. Type **33**	7·50	7·50
186		120f. Dhow sails (vert)	10·00	10·00
187		150f. As 120f.	18·00	18·00

1972. World Health Day.

188	34	30f. multicoloured	4·50	4·50
189		60f. multicoloured	9·25	9·25

35 F.A.O. and U.N. Emblems

1973. 10th Anniv of World Food Programme.

190	35	30f. brown, red and green	4·25	4·25
191		60f. brown, lt brown & grn	8·00	8·00

36 "Races of the World"

1973. 25th Anniv of Declaration of Human Rights.

192	36	30f. blue, brown and black	5·00	5·00
193		60f. red, brown and black	7·50	7·50

38 Flour Mill

1973. National Day. "Progress in Bahrain". Mult.

195		30f. Type **38**	1·80	50
196		60f. Muharraq Airport	2·50	90
197		120f. Sulmaniya Medical Centre	5·00	2·75
198		150f. Aluminium Smelter	5·00	3·00

39 U.P.U. Emblem within Letters

1974. Admission of Bahrain to U.P.U. Mult.

199		30f. Type **39**	1·80	1·80
200		60f. U.P.U. emblem on letters	3·25	3·25
201		120f. Ruler and emblem on dove with letter in beak (37×28 mm)	3·25	3·25
202		150f. As 120f. (37×28 mm)	4·50	4·50

40 Traffic Lights and Directing Hands

1974. International Traffic Day.

203	40	30f. multicoloured	3·75	3·75
204		60f. multicoloured	6·75	6·75

41 U.P.U. "Stamp" and Mail Transport

1974. Centenary of U.P.U.

205	41	30f. multicoloured	1·00	1·00
206		60f. multicoloured	1·20	1·20
207		120f. multicoloured	3·25	3·25
208		150f. multicoloured	4·00	4·00

42 Emblem and Sitra Power Station

43 Costume and Headdress

1974. National Day. Multicoloured.

209		30f. Type **42**	65	25
210		60f. Type **42**	2·10	1·10
211		120f. Emblem and Bahrain Dry Dock	3·50	2·20
212		150f. As 120f.	4·50	3·00

1975. Bahrain Women's Costumes.

213	43	30f. multicoloured	65	65
214	–	60f. multicoloured	1·50	1·60
215	–	120f. multicoloured	3·25	3·25
216	–	150f. multicoloured	3·75	3·75

DESIGNS: Nos. 214/16, Costumes as Type **43**.

44 Jewelled Pendant

45 Women planting "Flower"

1975. Costume Jewellery. Multicoloured.

217		30f. Type **44**	85	85
218		60f. Gold crown	2·00	2·00
219		120f. Jewelled necklace	3·75	3·75
220		150f. Gold necklace	5·00	5·00

1975. International Women's Year. Multicoloured.

221		30f. Type **45**	1·80	85
222		60f. Woman holding I.W.Y. emblem	5·00	1·80

46 Head of Horse

1975. Horses. Multicoloured.

223a	60f. Type **46**	5·75	5·75
223b	60f. Grey	5·75	5·75
223c	60f. Grey with foal (horiz)	5·75	5·75
223d	60f. Close-up of Arab with grey	5·75	5·75
223e	60f. Grey and herd of browns (horiz)	5·75	5·75
223f	60f. Grey and brown (horiz)	5·75	5·75
223g	60f. Arabs riding horses (horiz)	5·75	5·75
223h	60f. Arab leading grey beside sea (horiz)	5·75	5·75

47 National Flag

48 Map of Bahrain within Cog and Laurel

1976.

224	47	5f. red, pink and blue	25	25
225		10f. red, pink & green	25	25
226		15f. red, pink & black	25	25
227		20f. red, pink & brown	40	25
227a	48	25f. black and grey	50	25
228		40f. black and blue	50	35
228a		50f. green, black & olive	50	40
228b		60f. black and green	85	50
229		80f. black and mauve	1·30	60
229b		100f. black and red	1·30	75
230		150f. black and yellow	2·50	1·20
231		200f. black and yellow	3·00	1·40

49 Concorde Taking off

1976. 1st Commercial Flight of Concorde. Mult.

232	80f. Type **49**	3·50	2·50
233	80f. Concorde landing	3·50	2·50
234	80f. Concorde en route	3·50	2·50
235	80f. Concorde on runway	3·50	2·50
MS236	154 × 115 mm. Nos. 232/5. Imperf	14·50	14·50

50 Soldier, Crest and Flag

52 Shaikh Isa bin Sulman al-Khalifa

51 King Khalid of Saudi Arabia and Shaikh of Bahrain with National Flags

1976. Defence Force Cadets' Day.

237	50	40f. multicoloured	2·30	2·30
238		80f. multicoloured	4·25	4·25

1976. Visit to Bahrain of King Khalid of Saudi Arabia.

239	51	40f. multicoloured	1·80	1·30
240		80f. multicoloured	3·75	3·00

1976.

241	52	300f. green and pale green	4·25	2·10
242		400f. purple and pink	5·75	3·00
243		500f. blue and pale blue	7·25	3·75
244		1d. black and grey	12·50	6·75
244a		2d. violet and lilac	23·00	12·50
244b		3d. brown and pink	37·00	18·00

53 Ministry of Housing Emblem, Designs for Houses and Mosque

1976. National Day.

245	53	40f. multicoloured	1·70	75
246		80f. multicoloured	3·75	1·50

54 A.P.U. Emblem

1977. 25th Anniv of Arab Postal Union.

247	54	40f. multicoloured	1·70	1·30
248		80f. multicoloured	3·75	2·50

55 Dogs on Beach

1977. Saluki Dogs. Multicoloured.

249a	80f. Type **55**	3·00	3·00
249b	80f. Dog and dromedaries	3·00	3·00
249c	80f. Dog and antelope	3·00	3·00
249d	80f. Dog on lawn of building	3·00	3·00
249e	80f. Head of dog	3·00	3·00
249f	80f. Heads of two dogs	3·00	3·00
249g	80f. Dog in scrubland	3·00	3·00
249h	80f. Dogs fighting	3·00	3·00

56 Arab Students and Candle

1977. International Literacy Day.

250	56	40f. multicoloured	1·70	1·30
251		80f. multicoloured	3·75	2·50

57 Shipyard Installations and Arab Flags

1977. Inauguration of Arab Shipbuilding and Repair Yard Co.

252	57	40f. multicoloured	1·70	1·30
253		80f. multicoloured	3·75	2·50

58 Microwave Antenna

1978. 10th World Telecommunications Day.

254	58	40f. multicoloured	1·70	1·30
255		80f. silver, dp blue & blue	3·75	1·70

59 Child being helped to Walk

60 Boom Dhow

1979. International Year of the Child. Mult.

256	50f. Type **59**	1·70	1·20
257	100f. Hands protecting child	3·75	2·20

1979. Dhows. Multicoloured.

258	100f. Type **60**	5·00	5·00
259	100f. Baghla	5·00	5·00
260	100f. Shu'ai (horiz)	5·00	5·00
261	100f. Ghanja (horiz)	5·00	5·00
262	100f. Kotia	5·00	5·00
263	100f. Sambuk	5·00	5·00
264	100f. Jaliboot (horiz)	5·00	5·00
265	100f. Zarook (horiz)	5·00	5·00

61 Dome of Mosque, Mecca

1980. 1400th Anniv of Hejira.

266	61	50f. multicoloured	85	40
267		100f. multicoloured	1·80	1·40
268		150f. multicoloured	2·10	1·70
269		200f. multicoloured	3·00	2·30
MS270		84 × 91 mm. No. 267 (sold at 200f.)	8·00	8·00

62 Arab with Gyr Falcon

1980. Falconry. Multicoloured.

271	100f. Type **62**	3·25	1·80
272	100f. Arab looking at Lanner falcon on wrist	3·25	1·80
273	100f. Peregrine falcon resting with outstretched wings	3·25	1·80
274	100f. Peregrine falcon in flight	3·25	1·80
275	100f. Gyr falcon on pillar (with camels in background) (vert)	3·25	1·80
276	100f. Gyr falcon on pillar (closer view) (vert)	3·25	1·80
277	100f. Close-up of gyr falcon facing right (vert)	3·25	1·80
278	100f. Close-up of Lanner falcon full-face (vert)	3·25	1·80

63 Map and I.Y.D.P. Emblem

1981. International Year for Disabled Persons.

279	63	50f. multicoloured	2·10	60
280		100f. multicoloured	4·25	2·10

64 Jubilee Emblem

1981. 50th Anniv of Electrical Power in Bahrain.

281	64	50f. multicoloured	1·50	65
282		100f. multicoloured	3·50	1·50

65 Carving

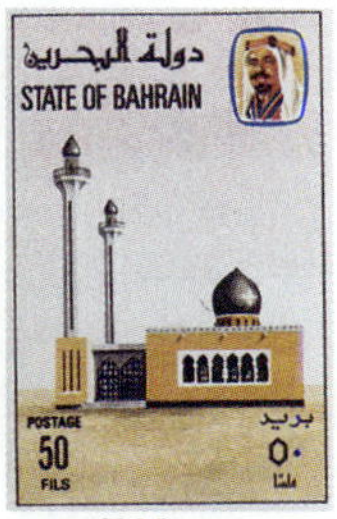

66 Mosque

1981. Handicrafts. Multicoloured.

283	50f. Type **65**	1·30	50
284	100f. Pottery	1·70	90
285	150f. Weaving	2·20	1·70
286	200f. Basket-making	3·25	2·10

1981. Mosques.

287	66	50f. multicoloured	1·30	50
288	–	100f. multicoloured	1·70	90
289	–	150f. multicoloured	2·20	1·70
290	–	200f. multicoloured	3·25	2·10

DESIGNS: 100f. to 200f. As Type **66** but showing different mosques.

67 Shaikh Isa bin Sulman al-Khalifa

69 Flags and Clasped Hands encircling Emblem

68 Dorcas Gazelle

1981. 20th Anniv of Coronation of Shaikh Isa bin Sulman al-Khalifa.

291	67	15f. gold, grey and mauve	60	60
292		50f. gold, grey and red	1·20	1·20
293		100f. gold, grey and brown	2·00	2·00
294		150f. gold, grey and blue	3·25	3·25
295		200f. gold, grey and blue	3·75	3·75

1982. Al-Areen Wildlife Park. Multicoloured.

296	100f. Goitred gazelle	2·10	2·10
297	100f. Type **68**	2·10	2·10
298	100f. Dhub lizard	2·10	2·10
299	100f. Brown hares	2·10	2·10
300	100f. Arabian oryx	2·10	2·10
301	100f. Addax	2·10	2·10

1982. 3rd Supreme Council Session of Gulf Co-operation Council.

302	69	50f. multicoloured	90	90
303	–	100f. multicoloured	2·50	2·50

70 Madinat Hamad

1983. Opening of Madinat Hamad New Town. Multicoloured.

304	50f. Type **70**	1·70	50
305	100f. View of Madinat Hamad (different)	3·00	1·70

71 Shaikh Isa bin Sulman al-Khalifa

1983. Bicentenary of Al-Khalifa Dynasty. Mult.

306	100f. Type **71**	1·00	1·00
307	100f. Cartouche of Ali bin Khalifa al-Khalifa	1·00	1·00
308	100f. Isa bin Ali al-Khalifa	1·00	1·00
309	100f. Hamad bin Isa al-Khalifa	1·00	1·00
310	100f. Salman bin Hamad al-Khalifa	1·00	1·00
311	100f. Cartouche of Ahmed bin Mohammed al-Khalifa	1·00	1·00
312	100f. Cartouche of Salman bin Ahmed al-Khalifa	1·00	1·00
313	100f. Cartouche of Abdullah bin Ahmed al-Khalifa	1·00	1·00
314	100f. Cartouche of Mohammed bin Khalifa al-Khalifa	1·00	1·00
MS315	109 × 83 mm. 500f. Type **71** (60 × 38 mm)	9·25	9·25

72 G.C.C. and Traffic and Licensing Directorate Emblems

1984. Gulf Co-operation Council Traffic Week.

316	72	15f. multicoloured	40	15
317		50f. multicoloured	1·30	40
318		100f. multicoloured	1·80	85

73 Hurdling

1984. Olympic Games, Los Angeles. Multicoloured.

319	15f. Type **73**	25	25
320	50f. Show-jumping	85	85
321	100f. Swimming	1·70	1·70
322	150f. Fencing	2·10	2·10
323	200f. Shooting	3·50	3·50

74 Manama and Emblem

1984. Centenary of Postal Services.

324	**74**	15f. multicoloured	40	15
325		50f. multicoloured	1·30	40
326		100f. multicoloured	2·10	1·10

75 Narrow-barred Spanish Mackerel

1985. Fishes. Multicoloured.

327	100f. Type **75**	1·70	1·70
328	100f. Crocodile needlefish (three fishes)	1·70	1·70
329	100f. Sombre sweetlips (fish swimming to left, blue and lilac background)	1·70	1·70
330	100f. White-spotted rabbitfish (two fishes, blue and lilac background)	1·70	1·70
331	100f. Grey mullet (two fishes, green and pink background)	1·70	1·70
332	100f. Two-banded seabream (green and grey background)	1·70	1·70
333	100f. River seabream (blue background)	1·70	1·70
334	100f. Malabar grouper (green background)	1·70	1·70
335	100f. Small-toothed emperor (pink anemone background)	1·70	1·70
336	100f. Golden trevally (fish swimming to right, blue and lilac background)	1·70	1·70

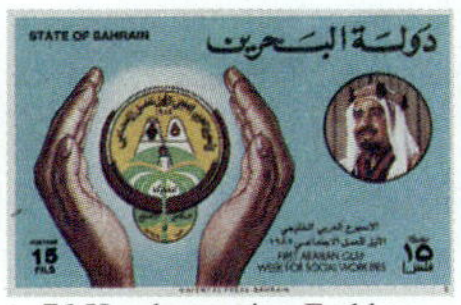
76 Hands cupping Emblem

1985. Arabian Gulf States Social Work Week.

337	**76**	15f. multicoloured	35	35
338		50f. multicoloured	1·00	1·00
339		100f. multicoloured	2·30	2·30

77 I.Y.Y. Emblem

1986. International Youth Year.

340	**77**	15f. multicoloured	35	35
341		50f. multicoloured	1·00	1·00
342		100f. multicoloured	2·30	2·30

78 Aerial View of Causeway

1986. Opening of Saudi–Bahrain Causeway. Mult.

343	15f. Type **78**	35	35
344	50f. Aerial view of island	1·00	1·00
345	100f. Aerial view of road bridge	1·70	1·70

79 Shaikh Isa bin Sulman al-Khalifa

1986. 25th Anniv of Accession of Shaikh Isa bin Sulman al-Khalifa.

346	**79**	15f. multicoloured	35	35
347		50f. multicoloured	1·00	1·00
348		100f. multicoloured	1·70	1·70
MS349		148 × 110 mm. Nos. 346/8	6·75	6·75

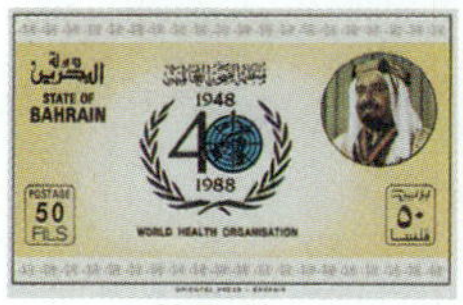
80 Emblem

1988. 40th Anniv of W.H.O.

350	**80**	50f. multicoloured	60	60
351		150f. multicoloured	1·70	1·70

81 Centre

1988. Opening of Ahmed al-Fateh Islamic Centre.

352	**81**	50f. multicoloured	60	60
353		150f. multicoloured	1·70	1·70

82 Running

1988. Olympic Games, Seoul. Multicoloured.

354	50f. Type **82**	35	25
355	80f. Dressage	65	40
356	150f. Fencing	1·40	1·00
357	200f. Football	2·20	1·70

83 Emblem in "1988"

1988. 9th Supreme Council Meeting of Gulf Co-operation Council.

358	**83**	50f. multicoloured	60	60
359		150f. multicoloured	1·70	1·70

84 Arab leading Camel

85 Shaikh Isa bin Sulman al-Khalifa

1989. Camels. Multicoloured.

360	150f. Type **84**	1·30	1·30
361	150f. Arab leading camel (different)	1·30	1·30
362	150f. Head of camel and pump-head	1·30	1·30
363	150f. Close-up of Arab on camel	1·30	1·30
364	150f. Arab riding camel	1·30	1·30
365	150f. Two Arab camel-riders	1·30	1·30
366	150f. Head of camel and camel-rider (horiz)	1·30	1·30
367	150f. Camels at rest in camp (horiz)	1·30	1·30
368	150f. Camels with calf (horiz)	1·30	1·30
369	150f. Heads of three camels (horiz)	1·30	1·30
370	150f. Camel in scrubland (horiz)	1·30	1·30
371	150f. Arab on camel (horiz)	1·30	1·30

1989. Multicoloured, colour of frame given.

372	**85**	25f. green	25	15
373		40f. grey	35	15
374		50f. pink	35	15
375		60f. brown	40	15
376		75f. mauve	60	15
377		80f. green	60	15
378		100f. orange	85	25
379		120f. violet	90	25
380		150f. grey	1·20	40
381		200f. blue	1·40	60
MS382		167 × 132 mm. Nos. 372/81	7·25	7·25

86 Houbara Bustards

1990. The Houbara Bustard. Multicoloured.

383	150f. Type **86**	1·20	1·20
384	150f. Two bustards (facing each other)	1·20	1·20
385	150f. Chicks and eggs	1·20	1·20
386	150f. Adult and chick	1·20	1·20
387	150f. Adult (vert)	1·20	1·20
388	150f. In flight	1·20	1·20
389	150f. Adult (facing right)	1·20	1·20
390	150f. Young bird (vert)	1·20	1·20
391	150f. Adult (facing left)	1·20	1·20
392	150f. Bird in display plumage	1·20	1·20
393	150f. Two bustards in display plumage	1·20	1·20
394	150f. Two bustards with bridge in background	1·20	1·20

87 Anniversary Emblem

1990. 40th Anniv of Gulf Air.

395	**87**	50f. multicoloured	40	25
396		80f. multicoloured	65	40
397		150f. multicoloured	1·30	85
398		200f. multicoloured	1·80	1·20

88 Anniversary Emblem

1990. 50th Anniv of Bahrain Chamber of Commerce and Industry.

399	**88**	50f. multicoloured	40	25
400		80f. multicoloured	60	40
401		150f. multicoloured	1·30	75
402		200f. multicoloured	1·40	1·00

89 I.L.Y. Emblem

1990. International Literacy Year.

403	**89**	50f. multicoloured	40	25
404		80f. multicoloured	60	40
405		150f. multicoloured	1·10	75
406		200f. multicoloured	1·50	1·00

90 Crested Lark

1991. Birds. Multicoloured.

407	150f. Type **90**	1·00	1·00
408	150f. Hoopoe ("Upupa epops")	1·00	1·00
409	150f. White-cheeked bulbul ("Pycnonotus leucogenys")	1·00	1·00
410	150f. Turtle dove ("Streptopelia turtur")	1·00	1·00
411	150f. Collared dove ("Streptopelia decaocto")	1·00	1·00
412	150f. Common kestrel ("Falco tinnunculus")	1·00	1·00
413	150f. House sparrow ("Passer domesticus") (horiz)	1·00	1·00
414	150f. Great grey shrike ("Lanius excubitor") (horiz)	1·00	1·00
415	150f. Rose-ringed parakeet ("Psittacula krameri")	1·00	1·00

91 Shaikh Isa bin Sulman al-Khalifa

1991. 30th Anniv of Amir's Coronation.

416	**91**	50f. multicoloured	35	25
417	A	50f. multicoloured	35	25
418	**91**	80f. multicoloured	50	35
419	A	80f. multicoloured	50	35
420	**91**	150f. multicoloured	1·10	65
421	A	150f. multicoloured	1·10	65
422	**91**	200f. multicoloured	1·40	85
423	A	200f. multicoloured	1·40	85
MS424		134 × 114 mm. **91** 500f. multicoloured; A 500f. multicoloured	8·50	8·50

DESIGN: A, The Amir and sunburst.

92 White Stork ("Ciconia ciconia")

1992. Migratory Birds. Multicoloured.

425	150f. Type **92**	90	90
426	150f. European bee eater ("Merops apiaster")	90	90
427	150f. Common starling ("Sturnus vulgaris")	90	90
428	150f. Grey hypocolius ("Hypocolius ampelinus")	90	90
429	150f. European cuckoo ("Cuculus canorus")	90	90
430	150f. Mistle thrush ("Turdus viscivorus")	90	90
431	150f. European roller ("Coracias garrulus")	90	90
432	150f. Eurasian goldfinch ("Carduelis carduelis")	90	90
433	150f. Red-backed shrike ("Lanius collurio")	90	90
434	150f. Redwing ("Turdus iliacus") (horiz)	90	90
435	150f. Pied wagtail ("Motacilla alba") (horiz)	90	90
436	150f. Golden oriole ("Oriolus oriolus") (horiz)	90	90
437	150f. European robin ("Erithacus rubecula")	90	90
438	150f. Nightingale ("Luscinia luscinia")	90	90
439	150f. Spotted flycatcher ("Muscicapa striata")	90	90
440	150f. Barn swallow ("Hirundo rustica")	90	90

93 Start of Race

1992. Horse-racing. Multicoloured.

441	150f. Type **93**	1·00	1·00
442	150f. Parading in paddock	1·00	1·00
443	150f. Galloping around bend	1·00	1·00
444	150f. Galloping past national flags	1·00	1·00
445	150f. Galloping past spectator stand	1·00	1·00
446	150f. Head-on view of horses	1·00	1·00
447	150f. Reaching winning post	1·00	1·00
448	150f. A black and a grey galloping	1·00	1·00

94 Show-jumping

1992. Olympic Games, Barcelona. Multicoloured.

449	50f. Type **94**	35	35
450	80f. Running	65	65
451	150f. Karate	1·30	1·30
452	200f. Cycling	1·70	1·70

95 Airport

1992. 60th Anniv of Bahrain International Airport.

453	**95**	50f. multicoloured	35	35
454		80f. multicoloured	65	65
455		150f. multicoloured	1·30	1·30
456		200f. multicoloured	1·70	1·70

96 Girl skipping

98 Artillery Gun Crew

97 Cable-cars and Pylons

1992. Children's Paintings. Multicoloured.

457	50f. Type **96**	35	25
458	80f. Women	50	35
459	150f. Women preparing food (horiz)	1·00	65
460	200f. Pearl divers (horiz)	1·30	90

1992. Expansion of Aluminium Industry. Mult.

461	50f. Type **97**	35	35
462	80f. Worker in aluminium plant	65	65
463	150f. Aerial view of aluminium plant	1·30	1·30
464	200f. Processed aluminium	1·70	1·70

1993. 25th Anniv of Bahrain Defence Force. Mult.

465	50f. Type **98**	35	35
466	80f. General Dynamics Fighting Falcon jet fighters, tanks and patrol boat	60	60
467	150f. "Ahmed al Fatah" (missile corvette) (horiz)	1·20	1·20
468	200f. Fighting Falcon over Bahrain (horiz)	1·50	1·50

99 Satellite View of Bahrain

100 Purple Heron

1993. World Meteorological Day. Multicoloured.

469	50f. Type **99**	50	50
470	150f. Satellite picture of world (horiz)	1·30	1·30
471	200f. Earth seen from space	2·00	2·00

1993. Water Birds. Multicoloured.

472	150f. Type **100**	1·30	1·30
473	150f. Moorhen ("Gallinula chloropus")	1·30	1·30
474	150f. Socotra cormorant ("Phalacrocorax nigrogularis")	1·30	1·30
475	150f. Crab plover ("Dromas ardeola")	1·30	1·30
476	150f. River kingfisher ("Alcedo atthis")	1·30	1·30
477	150f. Northern lapwing ("Vanellus vanellus")	1·30	1·30
478	150f. Oystercatcher ("Haematopus ostralegus") (horiz)	1·30	1·30
479	150f. Black-crowned night heron ("Nycticorax nycticorax")	1·30	1·30
480	150f. Caspian tern ("Sterna caspia") (horiz)	1·30	1·30
481	150f. Ruddy turnstone ("Arenaria interpres") (horiz)	1·30	1·30
482	150f. Water rail ("Rallus aquaticus") (horiz)	1·30	1·30
483	150f. Mallard ("Anas platyrhyncos) (horiz)	1·30	1·30
484	150f. Lesser black-backed gull ("Larus fuscus") (horiz)	1·30	1·30

101 Fawn

1993. The Goitered Gazelle. Multicoloured.

485	25f. Type **101**	90	90
486	50f. Doe walking	1·80	1·80
487	50f. Doe with ears pricked	1·80	1·80
488	150f. Male gazelle	5·50	5·50

102 "Lycium shawii"

103 Children and Silhouettes of Parents' Heads

1993. Wild Flowers. Multicoloured.

489	150f. Type **102**	85	85
490	150f. "Alhagi maurorum"	85	85
491	150f. Caper-bush ("Caparis spinosa")	85	85
492	150f. "Cistanche phelypae"	85	85
493	150f. "Asphodelus tenuifolius"	85	85
494	150f. "Limonium axillare"	85	85
495	150f. "Cynomorium coccineum"	85	85
496	150f. "Calligonum polygonoides"	85	85

1994. International Year of the Family.

497	**103**	50f. multicoloured	35	35
498		80f. multicoloured	60	60
499		150f. multicoloured	1·20	1·20
500		200f. multicoloured	1·50	1·50

104 "Lepidochrysops arabicus"

105 Anniversary Emblem

1994. Butterflies. Multicoloured.

501	50f. Type **104**	25	25
502	50f. "Ypthima bolanica"	25	25
503	50f. Desert grass yellow ("Eurema brigitta")	25	25
504	50f. "Precis limnoria"	25	25
505	50f. Small tortoiseshell ("Aglais urticae")	25	25
506	50f. Protomedia ("Colotis protomedia")	25	25
507	50f. Clouded mother-of-pearl (Salamis anacardii")	25	25
508	50f. "Byblia ilithyia"	25	25
509	150f. Swallowtail ("Papilio machaon") (horiz)	75	75
510	150f. Blue ("Agrodiaetus loewii") (horiz)	75	75
511	150f. Painted lady ("Vanessa cardui") (horiz)	75	75
512	150f. Chequered swallowtail ("Papilio demoleus") (horiz)	75	75
513	150f. Guineafowl ("Hamanumida daedalus") (horiz)	75	75
514	150f. "Funonia orithya" (horiz)	75	75
515	150f. "Funonia chorimine" (horiz)	75	75
516	150f. "Colias croceus" (horiz)	75	75

1994. 75th Anniv of International Red Cross and Red Crescent.

517	**105**	50f. multicoloured	35	35
518		80f. multicoloured	60	60
519		150f. multicoloured	1·20	1·20
520		200f. multicoloured	1·50	1·50

106 Goalkeeper

1994. World Cup Football Championship, U.S.A. Multicoloured.

521	50f. Type **106**	40	40
522	80f. Players	65	65
523	150f. Players' legs	1·30	1·30
524	200f. Player on ground	1·70	1·70

107 Earth Station

1994. 25th Anniv of Ras Abu Jarjour Satellite Earth Station.

525	**107**	50f. multicoloured	60	60
526		80f. multicoloured	65	65
527		150f. multicoloured	1·40	1·40
528		200f. multicoloured	1·70	1·70

108 Children on Open Book, Pen as Torch and School

109 Dove with "Olive Branch" of Members' Flags

1994. 75th Anniv of Education in Bahrain.

529	**108**	50f. multicoloured	35	35
530		80f. multicoloured	60	60
531		150f. multicoloured	1·20	1·20
532		200f. multicoloured	1·50	1·50

1994. 15th Gulf Co-operation Council Supreme Council Session, Bahrain.

533	**109**	50f. multicoloured	35	35
534		80f. multicoloured	60	60
535		150f. multicoloured	1·10	1·10
536		200f. multicoloured	1·40	1·40

110 Date Palm in Bloom

1995. The Date Palm.

537	80f. Type **110**	60	60
538	100f. Date palm with unripened dates	65	65
539	200f. Dates ripening	1·20	1·20
540	250f. Date palm trees with ripened dates	1·70	1·70
MS541	134 × 126 mm. 500f. Dates, coffee pot, cups and date palms (65 × 47 mm)	3·25	3·25

111 Campaign Emblem

1995. World Health Day. Anti-poliomyelitis Campaign.

542	**111**	80f. multicoloured	40	40
543		200f. multicoloured	1·20	1·20
544		250f. multicoloured	1·60	1·60

112 Exhibition Emblem

114 Headquarters, Cairo

113 Crops

1995. 1st National Industries Exhibition.

545	**112**	80f. multicoloured	40	40
546		200f. multicoloured	1·20	1·20
547		250f. multicoloured	1·60	1·60

1995. 50th Anniv of F.A.O. Multicoloured.

548	80f. Type **113**	40	40
549	200f. Field of crops	1·20	1·20
550	250f. Field of cabbages	1·60	1·60

1995. 50th Anniv of Arab League.

551	**114**	80f. multicoloured	40	40
552		200f. multicoloured	1·20	1·20
553		250f. multicoloured	1·60	1·60

115 U.N. Headquarters and Map of Bahrain

1995. 50th Anniv of U.N.O.

554	**115**	80f. multicoloured	40	40
555		100f. multicoloured	60	60
556		200f. multicoloured	1·30	1·30
557		250f. multicoloured	1·50	1·50

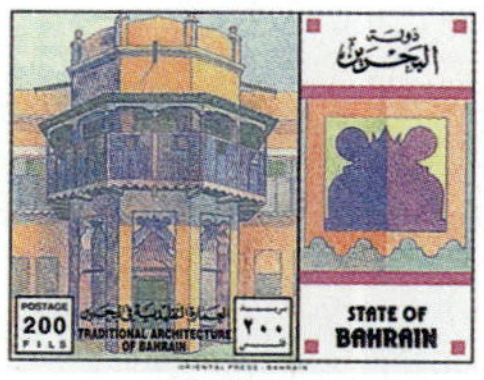

116 Tower

1995. Traditional Architecture. Multicoloured.

558	200f. Type **116**	1·00	1·00
559	200f. Balcony	1·00	1·00
560	200f. Doorway	1·00	1·00
561	200f. Multi-storied facade	1·00	1·00
562	200f. Entrance flanked by two windows	1·00	1·00
563	200f. Three arched windows	1·00	1·00

117 National Flag and Shaikh Isa Bin Sulman al-Khalifa

118 Bookcase and Open Book

1995. National Day.

564	**117**	80f. multicoloured	40	40
565		100f. multicoloured	60	60
566		200f. multicoloured	1·30	1·30
567		250f. multicoloured	1·60	1·60

1996. 50th Anniv of Public Library.

568	**118**	80f. multicoloured	40	40
569		200f. multicoloured	1·40	1·40
570		250f. multicoloured	1·60	1·60

119 Divers on Dhow

1996. Pearl Diving. Multicoloured.
571 80f. Type **119** 40 40
572 100f. Divers 50 50
573 200f. Diver on sea-bed and dhow . . . . 1·00 1·00
574 250f. Diver with net . . . . 1·40 1·40
MS575 119 × 119 mm. 500f. Diving equipment (70 × 70 mm) . . . 3·25 3·25

120 Globe, Ship and Olympic Rings

1996. Olympic Games, Atlanta.
576 **120** 80f. multicoloured 40 40
577 100f. multicoloured . . . 60 60
578 200f. multicoloured . . . 1·30 1·30
579 250f. multicoloured . . . 1·60 1·60

121 Interpol Emblem and Map, Arms and Flag of Bahrain

1996. 24th Anniv of Membership of International Criminal Police (Interpol).
580 **121** 80f. multicoloured 40 40
581 100f. multicoloured . . . 60 60
582 200f. multicoloured . . . 1·30 1·30
583 250f. multicoloured . . . 1·60 1·60

122 Anniversary Emblems in English and Arabic

1996. 25th Anniv of Aluminium Bahrain.
584 **122** 80f. multicoloured 35 35
585 100f. multicoloured . . . 40 40
586 200f. multicoloured . . . 1·00 1·00
587 250f. multicoloured . . . 1·30 1·30

123 National Flag, Map and Shaikh Isa bin Sulman al-Khalifa

1996. 35th Anniv of Amir's Accession.
588 **123** 80f. multicoloured 40 40
589 100f. multicoloured . . . 60 60
590 200f. multicoloured . . . 1·30 1·30
591 250f. multicoloured . . . 1·60 1·60

124 Tanker, Refinery and Storage Tanks

1997. 60th Anniv of Bahrain Refinery.
592 **124** 80f. multicoloured 40 40
593 200f. multicoloured . . . 1·10 1·10
594 250f. multicoloured . . . 1·50 1·50

125 Kuheilaan Weld umm Zorayr

1997. Arab Horses at Amiri Stud. Multicoloured.
595 200f. Musannaan (white horse), Al-Jellabieh and Rabdaan . . . . 1·10 1·10
596 200f. Type **125** . . . . . . 1·10 1·10
597 200f. Al-Jellaby . . . . . . 1·10 1·10
598 200f. Musannaan (brown horse) . . . . 1·10 1·10
599 200f. Kuheilaan Aladiyat . . 1·10 1·10
600 200f. Kuheilaan Aafas . . . 1·10 1·10
601 200f. Al-Dhahma . . . . . 1·10 1·10
602 200f. Mlolshaan . . . . . . 1·10 1·10
603 200f. Al-Kray . . . . 1·10 1·10
604 200f. Krush . . . . 1·10 1·10
605 200f. Al Hamdaany . . . . 1·10 1·10
606 200f. Hadhfaan . . . . . . 1·10 1·10
607 200f. Rabda . . . . 1·10 1·10
608 200f. Al-Suwaitieh . . . . . 1·10 1·10
609 200f. Al-Obeyah . . . . . . 1·10 1·10
610 200f. Al-Shuwaimeh . . . . 1·10 1·10
611 200f. Al-Ma'anaghieh . . . . 1·10 1·10
612 200f. Al-Tuwaisah . . . . . 1·10 1·10
613 200f. Wadhna . . . . 1·10 1·10
614 200f. Al-Saqlawieh . . . . . 1·10 1·10
615 200f. Al-Shawafah . . . . . 1·10 1·10

126 Championship Emblem

1997. 9th World Men's Junior Volleyball Championship.
616 **126** 80f. multicoloured 40 40
617 100f. multicoloured . . . 60 60
618 200f. multicoloured . . . 1·10 1·10
619 250f. multicoloured . . . 1·40 1·40

127 Emblem

1997. 10th Anniv of Montreal Protocol (on reduction of use of chlorofluorocarbons).
620 **127** 80f. multicoloured 40 40
621 100f. multicoloured . . . 60 60
622 200f. multicoloured . . . 1·10 1·10
623 250f. multicoloured . . . 1·40 1·40

128 Close-up of Support

1997. Inauguration of Shaikh Isa bin Salman Bridge between Manama and Muharraq. Multicoloured.
624 80f. Type **128** 40 40
625 200f. Distant view of middle section . . . . 1·20 1·20
626 250f. View of complete bridge (75 × 26 mm) . . . . . 1·40 1·40
MS627 137 × 116 mm. 500f. As No. 626 . . . . 3·00 3·00

129 Complex at Night

1998. Inauguration of Urea Plant at Gulf Petrochemical Industries Co Complex. Mult.
628 80f. Type **129** 40 40
629 200f. Refining towers . . . . 1·20 1·20
630 250f. Aerial view of complex 1·40 1·40

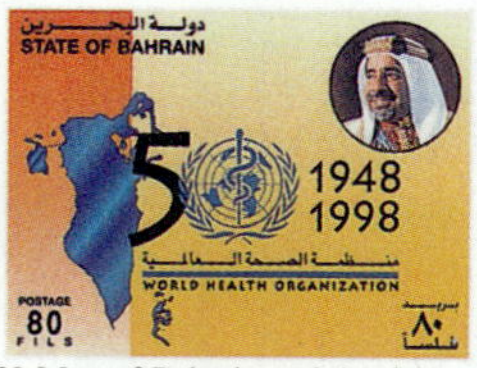

130 Map of Bahrain and Anniversary Emblem

1998. 50th Anniv of W.H.O.
631 **130** 80f. multicoloured 40 40
632 200f. multicoloured . . . 1·20 1·20
633 250f. multicoloured . . . 1·40 1·40

131 Emblem

1998. World Cup Football Championship, France. Multicoloured.
634 80f. Type **131** 40 40
635 200f. Globes and football forming "98" (vert) . . . . 1·20 1·20
636 250f. Footballers and globe (vert) . . . . 1·40 1·40

132 Football

1998. 14th Arabian Gulf Cup Football Championship, Bahrain. Multicoloured.
637 80f. Type **132** 40 40
638 200f. Close-up of football . . 1·20 1·20
639 250f. As No. 638 . . . . . . 1·40 1·40

133 Emblem and Koran

1999. Holy Koran Reading Competition.
640 **133** 100f. multicoloured . . . 60 60
641 200f. multicoloured . . . 1·30 1·30
642 250f. multicoloured . . . 1·40 1·40

134 Shaikh Isa bin Sulman al-Khalifa and State Flag

1999. Shaikh Isa bin Sulman al-Khalifa Commemoration. Multicoloured.
643 100f. Type **134** 60 60
644 200f. Shaikh and map of Bahrain (41 × 31 mm) . . . 1·30 1·30
645 250f. Shaikh, map of Bahrain and state flag . . . . . . 1·40 1·40
MS646 125 × 170 mm. 500f. Type **134** (67 × 102 mm) . . . 3·25 3·25

135 Emblem

1999. International Year of the Elderly. Mult.
647 100f. Type **135** 60 60
648 200f. Emblem and flame . . 1·30 1·30
649 250f. Emblem (different) . . 1·40 1·40

136 Emblem

1999. 10th Anniv of Bahrain Stock Exchange. Multicoloured.
650 100f. Type **136** 60 60
651 200f. Shaikh Isa bin Salman Bridge and emblem . . . . 1·30 1·30
652 250f. Globe and emblem . . 1·40 1·40

137 Shaikh Isa bin Salman and Shaikh Hamad bin Isa holding Flag

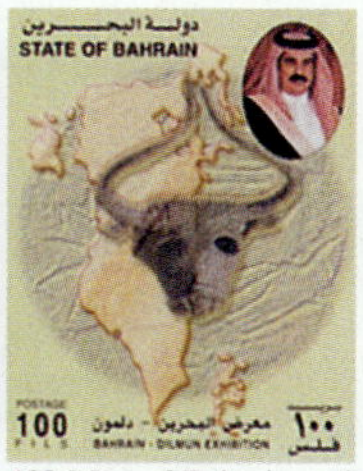

138 Map of Bahrain and Animal Skull

1999. National Day. Multicoloured.
653 100f. Type **137** 60 60
654 200f. Shaikh Hamad bin Isa and flag . . . . 1·30 1·30
655 250f. Shaikh Hamad bin Isa and globe . . . . 1·40 1·40
MS656 115 × 155 mm. 500f. As Type **137** (56 × 96 mm) . . . . 3·00 3·00

2000. Dilmun Exhibition. Multicoloured.
657 100f. Type **138** 60 60
658 200f. Map of Bahrain superimposed over animal skull 1·30 1·30
659 250f. Map of Bahrain and artefact . . . . 1·40 1·40

139 Map of Bahrain and Emblem

2000. 50th Anniv of Gulf Air. Multicoloured.
660 100f. Type **139** 90 90
661 200f. Map of Bahrain and emblem in circle . . . . . 1·80 1·80
662 250f. Map of Bahrain, emblem and eagles . . . . 2·20 2·20

140 Emblem

2000. "Made in Bahrain 2000" Exhibition. Multicoloured.
663 100f. Type **140** 90 90
664 200f. Type **140** . . . . 1·80 1·80
665 250f. Oil refinery . . . . . . 2·20 2·20

141 Minarets and Fort

2000. Millennium. Multicoloured.
666 100f. Type **141** . . . . 1·00 1·00
667 100f. Dhows and factories . . 1·00 1·00
668 100f. Man harvesting dates 1·00 1·00
669 100f. Fort, globe and dish aerial . . . . 1·00 1·00
670 200f. Lake and bridge . . . 1·80 1·80
671 200f. Modern building and woman . . . . 1·80 1·80
672 200f. Dhows, jug and wicker basket . . . . 1·80 1·80
673 200f. Horseman and falconer 1·80 1·80
674 250f. Pearl divers . . . . . . 2·20 2·20
675 250f. Opening clams . . . . 2·20 2·20

676 250f. Fishermen . . . . . . 2·20 2·20
677 250f. Man mending fishing nets . . . . 2·20 2·20

142 Emblem

2000. 21st Gulf Co-operation Council Supreme Council Session, Bahrain. Multicoloured.
678 100f. Type **142** 90 90
679 200f. Members' flags . . . . 1·80 1·80

143 Stained-glass Window

2001. 10th Anniv of Beit Al Qur'an (Islamic institution). Multicoloured.
680 100f. Type **143** 60 60
681 200f. Beit Al Qur'an by night 1·20 1·20
682 250f. Facade . . . . 1·60 1·60
MS683 170 × 80 mm. 500f. Subjects as Nos. 680/2 but forming composite design. Imperf . . . 3·00 3·00

144 Building

2001. 25th Anniv of Ministry of Housing and Agriculture. Multicoloured.
684 100f. Type **144** 60 60
685 150f. Sculpture and building 90 90
686 200f. Building viewed through arch . . . . 1·20 1·20
687 250f. Tall, arched building . . 1·60 1·60

145 Emblem and Stylized Figures

2001. International Year of Volunteers. Multicoloured.
688 100f. Type **145** 60 60
689 150f. Hands encircling emblem 90 90
690 200f. Star pattern and emblem . . . . 1·20 1·20
691 250f. Paper cut figures . . . 1·60 1·60

146 Emblem

2002. Arab Women's Day. Multicoloured.
692 100f. Type **146** 60 60
693 200f. Elliptical shapes and emblem . . . . 1·30 1·30
694 250f. Women (horiz) . . . . 1·60 1·60

147 Football and Emblem

148 Shaikh Hamad Bin Isa Al Khalifa

2002. World Cup Football Championship, Japan and South Korea. Sheet 124 × 64 mm containing T **147** and similar vert designs. Multicoloured.
MS695 100f. Type **147**; 200f. Earth, football and emblem; 250f. Football and white peaks . . . 3·25 3·25

2002. Multicoloured, background colour given.
(a) Size 22 × 28 mm.
696 **148** 25f. brown 10 10
697 40f. purple 25 25
698 50f. grey 30 30
699 60f. blue 40 40
700 80f. blue 50 50
701 100f. orange 60 60
702 125f. mauve 75 75
703 150f. orange 85 85
704 200f. green . . . . 1·30 1·30
705 250f. pink . . . . 1·60 1·60
706 300f. brown . . . . . . 1·80 1·80
707 400f. green . . . . 2·50 2·50
(b) 26 × 36 mm.
708 500f. mauve . . . . 3·00 3·00
709 1d. orange . . . . 6·25 6·25
710 2d. blue . . . . 12·50 12·50
711 3d. brown . . . . 18·00 18·00
MS712 246 × 162 mm. Nos. 696/711 50·00 50·00

149 Stylized Teacher, Child and Symbols of Communication

2002. World Teacher's Day.
713 **149** 100f. multicoloured . . . 50 50
714 200f. multicoloured . . . 1·00 1·00

150 Emblem

2002. Parliamentary Election, 2002. Multicoloured.
715 100f. Type **150** 50 50
716 200f. Hand posting voting slip (vert) . . . . 1·00 1·00

151 Shaikh Hamad Bin Isa Al Khalifa and Flag

2002. National Day. Multicoloured.
717 100f. Type **151** 50 50
718 200f. Shaikh Hamad Bin Isa and flag (different) (vert) 1·00 1·00
719 250f. As No. 718 but with maroon background (vert) 1·30 1·30

152 Bahrain

2003. Arab Summit Conference, Sharm el-Sheikh, Egypt. Designs representing landmarks from each state.
720 100f. Type **152** 50 50
721 100f. Sudan 50 50
722 100f. Saudi Arabia 50 50
723 100f. Djibouti 50 50
724 100f. Algeria 50 50
725 100f. Tunisia 50 50
726 100f. UAE 50 50
727 100f. Jordan 50 50
728 200f. Comoros . . . . . . 1·00 1·00
729 200f. Qatar . . . . 1·00 1·00
730 200f. Palestine . . . . . . 1·00 1·00
731 200f. Oman . . . . 1·00 1·00
732 200f. Iraq . . . . 1·00 1·00
733 200f. Somalia . . . . 1·00 1·00
734 200f. Syria . . . . 1·00 1·00
735 250f. Yemen . . . . 1·30 1·30
736 250f. Mauritania . . . . . . 1·30 1·30
737 250f. Egypt . . . . 1·30 1·30
738 250f. Libya . . . . 1·30 1·30
739 250f. Lebanon . . . . 1·30 1·30
740 250f. Kuwait . . . . 1·30 1·30
MS741 120 × 103 mm. 500f. Buildings surrounding Holy Kabba. Imperf . . . . . . 2·50 2·50

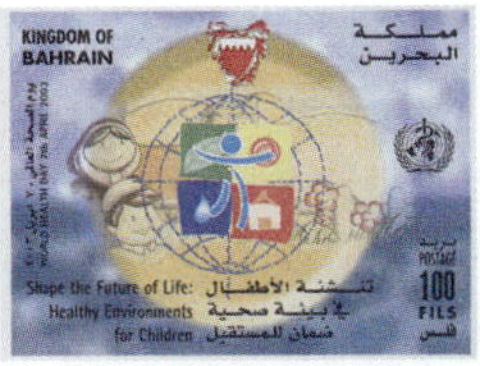

153 Children, Emblem and Flowers

2003. World Health Day. Multicoloured.
742 100f. Type **153** 60 60
743 200f. Stylized figures and emblem . . . . 1·30 1·30

154 Swan

2003. World Environment Day. Flora and Fauna. Multicoloured.
744 100f. Type **154** 60 60
745 100f. Peacock 60 60
746 100f. Flamingos 60 60
747 100f. Ostrich 60 60
748 200f. *Rumex vesicarius* . . 1·00 1·00
749 200f. *Arnebia hispidissima* . . 1·00 1·00
750 200f. *Capparis spinosa* . . . 1·00 1·00
751 200f. *Cassia italica* . . . . 1·00 1·00
752 250f. Crab . . . . 1·30 1·30
753 250f. Turtle . . . . 1·30 1·30
754 250f. Sting ray . . . . . . 1·30 1·30
755 250f. Shark . . . . 1·30 1·30

155 Girl Writing

2003. Children's Day. Multicoloured.
756 100f. Type **155** 60 60
757 150f. Girl painting 80 80
758 200f. Children playing (horiz) 1·00 1·00
759 250f. School class (horiz) . . 1·30 1·30

156 Shaikh Hamad Bin Isa Al Khalifa on Horseback

2003. National Day.
760 **156** 100f. multicoloured . . . 60 60
761 200f. multicoloured . . . 1·00 1·00
762 250f. multicoloured . . . 1·30 1·30
MS763 125 × 167 mm. **156** 500f. multicoloured (57 × 87 mm) . . 2·75 2·75

157 Mother and Baby

2004. Mothers' Day. Multicoloured.
764 100f. Type **157** 50 50
765 200f. Mother and child reading . . . . 1·00 1·00

158 Computer Model of Formula One Car (½-size illustration)

2004. Bahrain Formula One Grand Prix. Sheet 180 × 180 mm containing T **158** and similar multicoloured designs.
MS766 100f. Type **158**; 150f. Model facing right; 200f. Side view; 250f. Rear view; 500f. Shakir tower, Bahrain International Circuit (40 × 40 mm) . . . . 6·50 6·50

159 Healthy Figures reaching for Drug Abuser

2004. International Day against Drug Abuse. Multicoloured.
767 100f. Type **159** 30 30
768 150f. Shrunken arm 45 45
769 200f. Needles and seated figure 60 60
770 250f. Healthy hands reaching to diseased hand 70 70

160 Running

2004. Olympic Games, Athens 2004. Sheet 211 × 65 mm containing T **160** and similar horiz designs. Multicoloured.
MS771 100f. Type **160**; 150f. Swimming; 200f. Windsurfing; 250f. Pistol Shooting . . . . . 2·00 2·00

161 Hands holding Emblem

2004. 25th Session of Arabian Gulf States Co-operation Supreme Council. Multicoloured.
772 100f. Type **161** 30 30
773 200f. Emblem with flags as ribbons 60 60
774 250f. Emblem on background of flags 70 70
MS775 201 × 100 mm. 500f. Symbols of Gulf States (175 × 34 mm) 2·75 2·75

162 Amaryllis Flower and Fair Emblem

2005. Bahrain Garden Fair. Multicoloured.

776		100f. Type **162**	30	
777		200f. Rose	60	60
778		250f. Jasmine	70	70

163 Scales and Court Building

2005. Inauguration of Constitutional Court.

779	**163**	100f. multicoloured	30	30
780		200f. multicoloured	60	60
791		250f. multicoloured	70	70

164 Statuette

2005. 50th Anniv of Discovery of Dilmon Civilization. Multicoloured.

782		100f. Type **164**	30	30
783		100f. Engraved seals	30	30
784		100f. Horseman (statue)	30	30
785		200f. pot spilling jewellery	60	60
786		200f. Two decorated pots	60	60
787		200f. Cylindrical vase and pot with lid	60	60
788		250f. Walls and gateway (horiz)	75	75
789		250f. Aerial view (horiz)	75	75
790		250f. Walls and steps (horiz)	75	75
MS791		Two sheets. (a) 195 × 155 mm. Nos. 782/90. (b) 140 × 105 mm. 500f. Sheikh Salman Bin Hamad Al Khalifa and archaeologists (88 × 58 mm)	6·50	6·50

165 King Hamad bin Isa Al Khalifa

2005. National Day. Multicoloured.

792		100f. Type **165**	30	30
793		200f. Flag and King Al Khalifa (vert)	60	60
794		250f. Towers and King Al Khalifa	75	75

166 Flag

2006. 25th Anniv of Gulf Co-operation Council. Multicoloured.

795		100f. Type **166**	30	30
MS796		165 × 105 mm. 500f. Flags of member states. Imperf	6·75	6·75

Stamps of similar designs were issued by Kuwait, Oman, Qatar, Saudi Arabia and United Arab Emirates.

167 Emblem

2006. World Cup Football Championship, Germany. Multicoloured.

797		100f. Type **167**	30	30
798		200f. Globe and balls	60	60
799		250f. Emblem (different)	75	75

168 King Hamad Bin Isa Al Khalifa

2006. National Day. Accession of King Hamad Bin Isa Al Khalifa. Multicoloured.

800		100f. Type **168**	30	30
801		200f. Facing front	60	60
802		250f. Facing left	75	75
803		500f. As Type **168** (40 × 54 mm)	1·50	1·50

169 Figures under Umbrella

2007. Consumer Protection Day. Multicoloured.

804		100f. Type **169**	30	30
805		200f. Flags as umbrella	60	60

170 King Hamad Bin Isa Al Khalifa

2007. National Day. Multicoloured.

806		100f. Type **170**	30	30
807		200f. Seated (horiz)	60	60
808		250f. King Hamad Bin Isa Al Khalifa and previous rulers (horiz)	90	90
MS809		125 × 201 mm. 100f. × 2, No. 806 × 2; Horiz. 200f. × 2, No. 807 × 2	1·80	1·80

WAR TAX STAMPS

T 36 "War Effort"

T 37 "War Effort"

1973.

T192	**T 36**	5f. blue and cobalt	£100	65·00

1973.

T194a	**T 37**	5f. blue	4·25	35

BAMRA — Pt. 1

A state in India. Now uses Indian stamps.

12 pies = 1 anna; 16 annas = 1 rupee.

1

8

1888.

1	**1**	¼a. black on yellow	£475	
2		½a. black on red	85·00	
3		1a. black on blue	65·00	
4		2a. black on green	90·00	£375
5		4a. black on yellow	80·00	£375
6		8a. black on red	48·00	

1890. Imperf.

10	**8**	¼a. black on red	2·00	2·75
11		½a. black on green	3·50	3·50
30		1a. black on yellow	4·50	3·25
16		2a. black on red	4·50	4·75
19		4a. black on red	11·00	8·00
22		8a. black on red	14·00	19·00
25		1r. black on red	20·00	21·00

BANGLADESH — Pt. 1

Formerly the Eastern wing of Pakistan. Following a landslide victory at the Pakistan General Election in December 1970 by the Awami League party the National Assembly was suspended. Unrest spread throughout the eastern province culminating in the intervention of India on the side of the East Bengalis. The new state became effective after the surrender of the Pakistan army in December 1971.

1971. 100 paisa = 1 rupee.
1972. 100 paisa = 1 taka.

1 Map of Bangladesh

3 "Martyrdom"

1971.

1	**1**	10p. indigo, orange and blue	10	10
2	–	20p. multicoloured	10	10
3	–	50p. multicoloured	10	10
4	–	1r. multicoloured	10	10
5	–	2r. turquoise, blue and red	25	35
6	–	3r. light green, green and blue	30	55
7	–	5r. multicoloured	50	1·00
8	–	10r. gold, red and blue	1·00	2·00

DESIGNS: 20p. "Dacca University Massacre"; 50p. "75 Million People"; 1r. Flag of Independence; 2r. Ballot box; 3r. Broken chain; 5r. Shaikh Majibur Rahman; 10r. "Support Bangla Desh" and map.

1971. Liberation. Nos. 1 and 7/8 optd **BANGLADESH LIBERATED.**

9		10p. indigo, orange and blue	20	10
10		5r. multicoloured	1·75	2·25
11		10r. gold, red and blue	2·75	3·75

The remaining values of the original issue were also overprinted and placed on sale in Great Britian but were not issued in Bangladesh.

On 1 February 1972 the Agency placed on sale a further issue in the flag, map and Sheikh Mujib designs in new colours and new currency (100 paisa = 1 taka). This issue proved to be unacceptable to the Bangladesh authorities who declared them to be invalid for postal purposes, no supplies being sold within Bangladesh. The values comprise 1, 2, 3, 5, 7, 10, 15, 20, 25, 40, 50, 75p., 1, 2 and 5t.

1972. In Memory of the Martyrs.

12	**3**	20p. green and red	30	50

4 Flames of Independence

5 Doves of Peace

1972. 1st Anniv of Independence.

13	**4**	20p. lake and red	25	10
14		60p. blue and red	40	45
15		75p. violet and red	45	55

1972. Victory Day.

16	**5**	20p. multicoloured	20	10
17		60p. multicoloured	30	55
18		75p. multicoloured	30	55

6 "Homage to Martyrs"

7 Embroidered Quilt

8 Court of Justice

9 Flame Emblem

1973. In Memory of the Martyrs.

19	**6**	20p. multicoloured	15	10
20		60p. multicoloured	30	40
21		1t.35 multicoloured	65	1·75

1973.

22	**7**	2p. black	10	1·00
23	–	3p. green	20	1·00
24	–	5p. brown	20	10
25	–	10p. black	20	10
26	–	20p. green	50	10
27	–	25p. mauve	3·25	10
28	–	50p. purple	2·25	30
29	–	60p. grey	1·75	1·25
30	–	75p. orange	1·25	1·25
31	–	90p. brown	1·50	2·00
32	**8**	1t. violet	6·00	30
33	–	2t. green	6·00	65
34	–	5t. blue	7·50	2·50
35	–	10t. pink	8·00	4·75

DESIGNS—As Type **7**: 3p. Jute field; 5p. Jack fruit; 10p. Bullocks ploughing; 20p. Rakta jaba (flower); 25p. Tiger; 60p. Bamboo grove; 75p. Plucking tea; 90p. Handicrafts. (28 × 22 mm): 50p. Hilsa (fish). As Type **8**. VERT: 2t. Date tree. HORIZ: 5t. Fishing boat; 10t. Sixty-dome mosque, Bagerhat.

See also Nos. 49/51a, 64/75 and 711.

1973. 25th Anniv of Declaration of Human Rights.

36	**9**	10p. multicoloured	10	10
37		1t.25 multicoloured	20	20

10 Family, Map and Graph

11 Copernicus and Heliocentric System

1974. First Population Census.

38	**10**	20p. multicoloured	10	10
39		25p. multicoloured	10	10
40		75p. multicoloured	20	20

1974. 500th Birth Anniv of Copernicus.

41	**11**	25p. orange, violet and black	10	10
42		75p. orange, green and black	25	50

12 U.N. H.Q. and Bangladesh Flag

13 U.P.U. Emblem

1974. Bangladesh's Admission to the U.N.

43	**12**	25p. multicoloured	10	10
44		1t. multicoloured	35	40

1974. Centenary of Universal Postal Union. Mult.

45		25p. Type **13**	10	10
46		1t.25 Mail runner	20	15
47		1t.75 Type **13**	20	25
48		5t. As 1t.25	80	1·60

14 Courts of Justice

1974. As Nos. 32/5 with revised inscriptions.

49	**14**	1t. violet	1·50	10
50	–	2t. olive	2·00	2·00
51	–	5t. blue	7·00	70
51a	–	10t. pink	20·00	14·00

For these designs redrawn to 32 × 20 mm or 20 × 32 mm, see Nos. 72/5 and, to 35 × 22 mm, see No. 711.

15 Tiger

16 Symbolic Family

1974. Wildlife Preservation. Multicoloured.
52 25p. Type **15** 70 10
53 50p. Tiger cub 1·00 70
54 2t. Tiger in stream 1·75 3·50

1974. World Population Year. "Family Planning for All". Multicoloured.
55 25p. Type **16** 15 10
56 70p. Village family 25 50
57 1t.25 Heads of family (horiz) 40 1·10

17 Radar Antenna

19 Telephones of 1876 and 1976

18 Woman's Head

1975. Inauguration of Betbunia Satellite Earth Station.
58 **17** 25p. black, silver and red 10 10
59 1t. black, silver and blue 20 70

1975. International Women's Year.
60 **18** 50p. multicoloured 10 10
61 2t. multicoloured 25 1·00

1976. As Nos. 24/31 and 49/51a but redrawn in smaller size.
64 – 5p. green 20 10
65 – 10p. black 20 10
66 – 20p. green 1·50 10
67 – 25p. mauve 4·00 10
68 – 50p. purple 3·75 10
69 – 60p. grey 40 40
70 – 75p. green 1·75 3·25
71 – 90p. brown 40 60
72 **14** 1t. violet 2·00 10
73 – 2t. green 9·00 10
74 – 5t. blue 3·25 3·00
75 – 10t. red 8·50 4·00

Nos. 64/71 are 23 × 18 mm (50p.) or 18 × 23 mm (others) and Nos. 72/75 are 20 × 32 mm (2t.) or 32 × 20 mm (others).

For the 10t. redrawn to 35 × 22 mm, see No. 711.

1976. Centenary of Telephone.
76 **19** 2t.25 multicoloured 25 20
77 – 5t. red, green and black 55 65
DESIGN: 5t. Alexander Graham Bell.

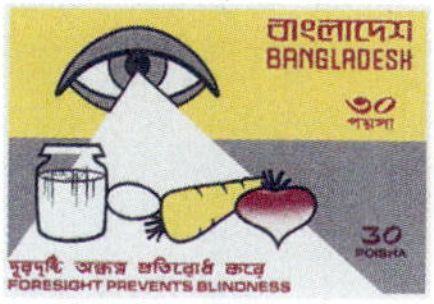

20 Eye and Nutriments

1976. Prevention of Blindness.
78 **20** 30p. multicoloured 50 10
79 2t.25 multicoloured 1·40 2·75

21 Liberty Bell

1976. Bicentenary of American Revolution. Mult.
80 30p. Type **21** 10 10
81 2t.25 Statue of Liberty 20 25
82 5t. "Mayflower" 40 50
83 10t. Mount Rushmore 40 80
MS84 167 × 95 mm. No. 83 1·50 3·00

22 Industry, Science, Agriculture and Education

23 Hurdling

1976. 25th Anniv of Colombo Plan.
85 **22** 30p. multicoloured 15 10
86 2t.25 multicoloured 35 1·00

1976. Olympic Games, Montreal. Multicoloured.
87 25p. Type **23** 10 10
88 30p. Running (horiz) 10 10
89 1t. Pole vaulting 15 10
90 2t.25 Swimming (horiz) 30 45
91 3t.50 Gymnastics 55 1·25
92 5t. Football 1·00 2·00

24 The Blessing

25 Qazi Nazrul Islam (poet)

1977. Silver Jubilee. Multicoloured.
93 30p. Type **24** 10 10
94 2t.25 Queen Elizabeth II 20 25
95 10t. Queen Elizabeth and Prince Philip 70 85
MS96 114 × 127 mm. Nos. 93/5 80 1·50

1977. Qazi Nazrul Islam Commemoration.
97 **25** 40p. green and black 10 10
98 – 2t.25 brown, red & lt brn 50 30
DESIGN—HORIZ: 2t.25, Head and shoulders portrait.

26 Bird with Letter

1977. 15th Anniv of Asian–Oceanic Postal Union.
99 **26** 30p. red, blue and grey 10 10
100 2t.25 red, blue and grey 20 25

27 Sloth Bear

28 Campfire and Tent

1977. Animals. Multicoloured.
101 40p. Type **27** 15 10
102 1t. Spotted deer 15 10
103 2t.25 Leopard (horiz) 30 20
104 3t.50 Gaur (horiz) 30 35
105 4t. Indian elephant (horiz) 80 50
106 5t. Tiger (horiz) 90 75

The Bengali numerals on the 40p. resemble "80", and that on the 4t. resembles "8".

1978. First National Scout Jamboree.
107 **28** 40p. red, blue and pale blue 25 10
108 – 3t.50 lilac, green and blue 80 30
109 – 5t. green, blue and red 95 45
DESIGNS—HORIZ: 3t.50, Scout stretcher-team. VERT: 5t. Scout salute.

29 "Michelia champaca"

1978. Flowers. Multicoloured.
110 40p. Type **29** 20 10
111 1t. "Cassia fistula" 25 15
112 2t.25 "Delonix regia" 30 30
113 3t.50 "Nymphaea nouchali" 35 60
114 4t. "Butea monosperma" 35 80
115 5t. "Anthocephalus indicus" 35 85

30 St. Edward's Crown and Sceptres

32 Fenchuganj Fertiliser Factory

31 Sir Alan Cobham's De Havilland D.H.50

1978. 25th Anniv of Coronation. Multicoloured.
116 40p. Type **30** 10 10
117 3t.50 Balcony scene 15 30
118 5t. Queen Elizabeth and Prince Philip 25 50
119 10t. Coronation portrait by Cecil Beaton 45 80
MS120 89 × 121 mm. Nos. 116/19 1·10 1·50

1978. 75th Anniv of Powered Flight.
121 **31** 40p. multicoloured 15 10
122 – 2t.25 brown and blue 25 45
123 – 3t.50 brown and yellow 25 65
124 – 5t. multicoloured 2·50 3·50
DESIGNS: 2t.25, Captain Hans Bertram's seaplane "Atlantis"; 3t.50, Wright brothers' Flyer III; 5t. Concorde.

1978.
125 – 5p. brown 10 10
126 **32** 10p. blue 10 10
127 – 15p. orange 10 10
128 – 20p. red 10 10
129 – 25p. blue 15 10
130 – 30p. green 2·75 10
131 – 40p. purple 30 10
132 – 50p. black 4·75 1·50
134 – 80p. brown 20 10
136 – 1t. violet 7·00 10
137 – 2t. blue 2·50 3·25
DESIGNS—HORIZ: 5p. Lalbag Fort; 25p. Jute on a boat; 40, 50p. Baitul Mukarram Mosque; 1t. Dotara (musical instrument); 2t. Karnaphuli Dam. VERT: 15p. Pineapple; 20p. Bangladesh gas; 30p. Banana tree; 80p. Mohastan Garh.

33 Tawaf-E-Ka'aba, Mecca

35 Moulana Abdul Hamid Khan Bhashani

34 Jasim Uddin

1978. Pilgrimage to Mecca. Multicoloured.
140 40p. Type **33** 20 10
141 3t. Pilgrims in Wuquf, Arafat (horiz) 60 45

1979. 3rd Death Anniv of Jasim Uddin (poet).
142 **34** 40p. multicoloured 20 50

1979. 3rd Death Anniv of Moulana Abdul Hamid Khan Bhashani (national leader).
143 **35** 40p. multicoloured 40 30

36 Sir Rowland Hill

37 Children with Hoops

1979. Death Centenary of Sir Rowland Hill.
144 **36** 40p. blue, red and light blue 10 10
145 – 3t.50 multicoloured 35 30
146 – 10t. multicoloured 80 1·00
MS147 176 × 96 mm. Nos. 144/6 2·25 2·75
DESIGNS: 3t.50, Sir Rowland Hill and first Bangladesh stamp; 10t. Sir Rowland Hill and Bangladesh U.P.U. stamp.

1979. International Year of the Child. Multicoloured.
148 40p. Type **37** 10 10
149 3t.50 Boy with kite 35 35
150 5t. Children jumping 50 50
MS151 170 × 120 mm. Nos. 148/50 1·50 2·75

38 Rotary International Emblem

40 A. K. Fazlul Huq

39 Canal Digging

1980. 75th Anniv of Rotary International.
152 **38** 40p. black, red and yellow 20 10
153 – 5t. gold and blue 65 45
DESIGN: 5t. Rotary emblem (different).

1980. Mass Participation in Canal Digging.
154 **39** 40p. multicoloured 40 30

1980. 18th Death Anniv of A. K. Fazlul Huq (national leader).
155 **40** 40p. multicoloured 30 30

41 Early Forms of Mail Transport

1980. "London 1980" International Stamp Exhibition. Multicoloured.
156 1t. Type **41** 15 10
157 10t. Modern forms of mail transport 1·25 90
MS158 140 × 95 mm. Nos. 156/7 1·40 2·00

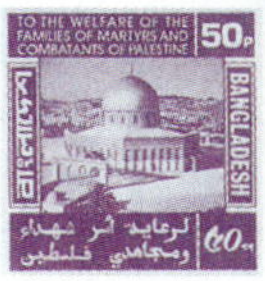

42 Dome of the Rock

43 Outdoor Class

1980. Palestinian Welfare.
159 **42** 50p. lilac 70 30

1980. Education.
160 **43** 50p. multicoloured 40 30

44 Beach Scene

1980. World Tourism Conference, Manila. Mult.
161 50p. Type **44** 35 50
162 5t. Beach scene (different) . . 65 1·10
MS163 140 × 88 mm. Nos. 161/2 1·00 1·50

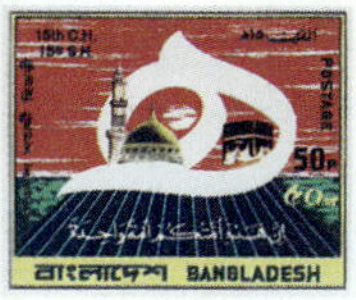 
45 Mecca 46 Begum Roquiah

1980. Moslem Year 1400 A. H. Commemoration.
164 **45** 50p. multicoloured 20 20

1980. Birth Centenary of Begum Roquiah (campaigner for women's rights).
165 **46** 50p. multicoloured 10 10
166 2t. multicoloured 35 20

47 Spotted Deer and Scout Emblem 49 Queen Elizabeth the Queen Mother

1981. 5th Asia–Pacific and 2nd Bangladesh Scout Jamboree.
167 **47** 50p. multicoloured 25 15
168 5t. multicoloured . . . . . 1·00 2·00

1981. 2nd Population Census. Nos. 38/40 optd **2nd. CENSUS 1981.**
169 **10** 20p. multicoloured 10 10
170 25p. multicoloured 10 10
171 75p. multicoloured 20 30

1981. 80th Birthday of the Queen Mother.
172 **49** 1t. multicoloured 15 15
173 15t. multicoloured . . . . 1·75 2·50
MS174 95 × 73 mm. Nos. 172/3 2·00 2·50

50 Revolutionary with Flag and Sub-machine-gun 52 Kemal Ataturk in Civilian Dress

51 Bangladesh Village and Farm Scenes

1981. 10th Anniv of Independence. Mult.
175 50p. Type **50** 15 10
176 2t. Figures on map symbolizing Bangladesh life style 25 45

1981. U.N. Conference on Least Developed Countries, Paris.
177 **51** 50p. multicoloured 35 15

1981. Birth Centenary of Kemal Ataturk (Turkish statesman).
178 50p. Type **52** 45 30
179 1t. Kemal Ataturk in uniform 80 1·25

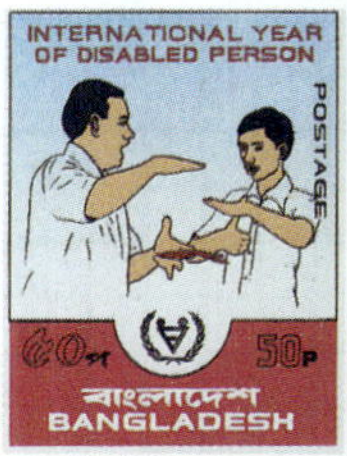 
53 Deaf People using Sign Language 54 Farm Scene and Wheat Ear

1981. Int Year for Disabled Persons. Mult.
180 50p. Type **53** 40 20
181 2t. Disabled person writing (horiz) . . . . 85 2·50

1981. World Food Day.
182 **54** 50p. multicoloured . . . . 50 1·00

55 River Scene 56 Dr. M. Hussain

1982. 10th Anniv of Human Environment Conference.
183 **55** 50p. multicoloured . . . . 50 1·00

1982. 1st Death Anniv of Dr. Motahar Hussain (educationist).
184 **56** 50p. multicoloured . . . . 50 1·00

57 Knotted Rope surrounding Bengali "75"

1982. 75th Anniv of Boy Scout Movement and 125th Birth Anniv of Lord Baden-Powell. Multicoloured.
185 50p. Type **57** 50 30
186 2t. Lord Baden-Powell (vert) 2·00 4·50

সম্মিলিত
সশস্ত্র বাহিনী দিবস
২১ নভেম্বর,৮২
(58)

60 Metric Scales

59 Captain Mohiuddin Jahangir

1982. Armed Forces' Day. No. 175 optd with T **58**.
187 50p. Type **50** . . . . 3·50 3·00

1983. Heroes and Martyrs of the Liberation. Multicoloured, background colour of commemorative plaque given.
188 50p. Type **59** (orange) . . . 30 45
189 50p. Sepoy Hamidur Rahman (green) 30 45
190 50p. Sepoy Mohammed Mustafa Kamal (red) . . . 30 45
191 50p. Muhammed Ruhul Amin (yellow) 30 45
192 50p. Flt. Lt. M. Matiur Rahman (brown) 30 45
193 50p. Lance-Naik Munshi Abdur Rob (brown) . . . 30 45
194 50p. Lance-Naik Nur Mouhammad (green) . . . 30 45

1983. Introduction of Metric Weights and Measures. Multicoloured.
195 50p. Type **60** 40 30
196 2t. Weights, jug and tape measure (horiz) . . . . . 1·75 2·75

61 Dr. Robert Koch 63 Dr. Muhammed Shahidulla

62 Open Stage Theatre

1983. Centenary (1982) of Robert Koch's Discovery of Tubercle Bacillus. Multicoloured.
197 50p. Type **61** . . . . 1·00 40
198 1t. Microscope, slide and X-ray . . . . 2·25 3·50

1983. Commonwealth Day. Multicoloured.
199 1t. Type **62** 10 15
200 3t. Boat race 20 30
201 10t. Snake dance 50 90
202 15t. Picking tea . . . . . . 60 1·50

1983. Dr. Muhammed Shahidulla (Bengali scholar) Commemoration.
203 **63** 50p. multicoloured . . . . 75 1·00

64 Magpie Robin

1983. Birds of Bangladesh. Multicoloured.
204 50p. Type **64** 75 40
205 2t. White-throated kingfisher (vert) . . . . 1·00 2·00
206 3t.75 Lesser flame-backed woodpecker (vert) . . . . 1·25 2·50
207 5t. White-winged wood duck 1·40 2·75
MS208 165 × 110 mm. Nos. 240/7 (sold at 13t.) . . . . 5·00 13·00

65 "Macrobrachium rosenbergii"

1983. Marine Life. Multicoloured.
209 50p. Type **65** 40 30
210 2t. White pomfret . . . . . 60 1·25
211 3t.75 Rohu . . . . 75 1·50
212 5t. Climbing perch . . . . . 90 2·50
MS213 119 × 98 mm. Nos. 209/12 (sold at 13t.) . . . . 2·50 6·00

1983. Visit of Queen Elizabeth II. No. 95 optd **Nov. '83 Visit of Queen.**
214 10t. Queen Elizabeth and Prince Philip . . . . . . 4·50 6·00

67 Conference Hall, Dhaka

1983. 14th Islamic Foreign Ministers' Conference, Dhaka. Multicoloured.
215 50p. Type **67** 35 30
216 5t. Old Fort, Dhaka . . . . 1·25 3·00

68 Early Mail Runner 69 Carrying Mail by Boat

1983. World Communications Year. Multicoloured.
217 50p. Type **68** 30 15
218 5t. Sailing ship, steam train and Boeing 707 airliner . . 2·00 1·50
219 10t. Mail runner and dish aerial (horiz) . . . . . . 2·75 4·50

1983. Postal Communications.
220 **69** 5p. blue 10 40
221 – 10p. purple 10 40
222 – 15p. blue 20 40
223 – 20p. black . . . . 1·20 40
224 – 25p. grey 20 40
225 – 30p. brown 20 40
226 – 50p. brown 75 10
227 – 1t. blue 75 10
228 – 2t. green 75 10
228a – 3t. brown . . . . 3·00 70
229 – 5t. purple . . . . 2·00 1·00
DESIGNS—HORIZ (22 × 17 mm): 10p. Counter, Dhaka G.P.O.; 15p. I.W.T.A. Terminal, Dhaka; 20p. Inside railway travelling post office; 30p. Emptying pillar box; 50p. Mobile post office van. (30 × 19 mm): 1t. Kamalapur Railway Station, Dhaka; 2t. Zia International Airport; 3t. Sorting mail by machine; 5t. Khulna G.P.O. VERT (17 × 22 mm): 25p. Delivering a letter.

প্রথম বাংলাদেশ জাতীয় ডাকটিকিট প্রদর্শনী-১৯৮৪
(70)

1984. 1st National Stamp Exhibition (1st issue). Nos. 161/2 optd with T **70** (5t.) or **First Bangladesh National Philatelic Exhibition—1984** (50p.).
230 **44** 50p. multicoloured . . . . 1·50 2·00
231 – 5t. multicoloured . . . . . 2·00 2·75

71 Girl with Stamp Album (⅔-size illustration)

1984. 1st National Stamp Exhibition (2nd issue). Multicoloured.
232 50p. Type **71** . . . . 65 1·25
233 7t.50 Boy with stamp album 1·10 2·00
MS234 98 × 117 mm. Nos. 232/3 (sold at 10t.) . . . . 3·00 4·00

72 Sarus Crane and Gavial 73 Eagle attacking Hen with Chicks

1984. Dhaka Zoo. Multicoloured.
235 1t. Type **72** . . . . 1·75 85
236 2t. Common peafowl and tiger . . . . 2·50 4·25

1984. Centenary of Postal Life Insurance. Mult.
237 1t. Type **73** 50 25
238 5t. Bangladesh family and postman's hand with insurance cheque . . . . 1·50 2·25

74 Abbasuddin Ahmad

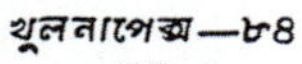

(75)

1984. Abbasuddin Ahmad (singer) Commemoration.
239 **74** 3t. multicoloured . . . . . 70 1·00

1984. "Khulnapex-84" Stamp Exhibition. No. 86 optd with T **75**.
240 **22** 2t.25 multicoloured . . . . 1·00 1·75

76 Cycling

1984. Olympic Games, Los Angeles. Multicoloured.
241 1t. Type **76** . . . . 1·75 30
242 5t. Hockey . . . . 2·50 2·25
243 10t. Volleyball . . . . 2·75 4·25

77 Farmer with Rice and Sickle

1985. 9th Annual Meeting of Islamic Development Bank, Dhaka. Multicoloured.
244 1t. Type **77** 35 15
245 5t. Citizens of four races . . 1·25 2·25

78 Mother and Baby

80 Women working at Traditional Crafts

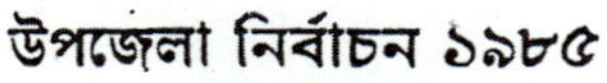

(79)

1985. Child Survival Campaign. Multicoloured.
246 1t. Type **78** 30 10
247 10t. Young child and growth graph . . . . 2·50 3·25

1985. Local Elections. Nos. 110/15 optd with T **79**.
248 40p. Type **29** 40 50
249 1t. "Cassia fistula" 50 30
250 2t.25 "Delonix regia" 70 75
251 3t.50 "Nymphaea nouchali" 80 1·25
252 4t. "Butea monosperma" . . 80 1·25
253 5t. "Anthocephalus indicus" 85 1·50

1985. U.N. Decade for Women. Multicoloured.
254 1t. Type **80** 25 10
255 10t. Women with microscope, computer terminal and in classroom . . . . 1·25 2·25

81 U.N. Building, New York, Peace Doves and Flags

1985. 40th Anniv of United Nations Organization and 11th Anniv of Bangladesh Membership. Multicoloured.
256 1t. Type **81** 10 10
257 10t. Map of world and Bangladesh flag . . . . . 80 1·40

82 Head of Youth, Flowers and Symbols of Commerce and Agriculture

83 Emblem and Seven Doves

1985. International Youth Year. Multicoloured.
258 1t. Type **82** 10 10
259 5t. Head of youth, flowers and symbols of industry . . 40 60

1985. 1st Summit Meeting of South Asian Association for Regional Co-operation, Dhaka. Multicoloured.
260 1t. Type **83** 10 10
261 5t. Flags of member nations and lotus blossom . . . . 1·50 90

84 Zainul Abedin

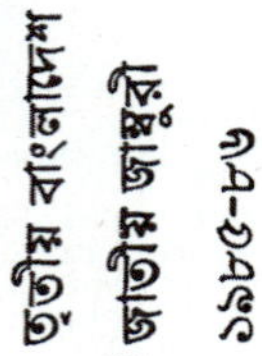

(85)

1985. 10th Death Anniv of Zainul Abedin (artist).
262 **84** 3t. multicoloured 75 30

1985. 3rd National Scout Jamboree. No. 109 optd with T **85**.
263 5t. green, blue and red . . . 2·50 3·50

86 "Fishing Net" (Safiuddin Ahmed)

1986. Bangladesh Paintings. Multicoloured.
264 1t. Type **86** 15 10
265 5t. "Happy Return" (Quamrul Hassan) 40 50
266 10t. "Levelling the Ploughed Field" (Zainul Abedin) . . 70 80

87 Two Players competing for Ball

1986. World Cup Football Championship, Mexico. Multicoloured.
267 1t. Type **87** 50 10
268 10t. Goalkeeper and ball in net . . . . 2·25 3·00
MS269 105 × 75 mm. 20t. Four players (60 × 44 mm) Imperf . . 5·50 6·50

88 General M. A. G. Osmani

90 Butterflies and Nuclear Explosion

1986. General M. A. G. Osmani (army commander-in-chief) Commemoration.
270 **88** 3t. multicoloured . . . . . 1·75 1·00

1986. South Asian Association for Regional Co-operation Seminar. No. 183 optd **SAARC SEMINAR '86**.
271 **55** 50p. multicoloured . . . . 3·00 3·50

1986. International Peace Year. Multicoloured.
272 1t. Type **90** 50 25
273 10t. Flowers and ruined buildings . . . . 2·75 4·00
MS274 109 × 80 mm. 20t. Peace dove and soldier . . . . 1·50 2·00

1987. Conference for Development. Nos. 152/3 optd **CONFERENCE FOR DEVELOPMENT '87**, No. 275 also surch **TK. 1.00**.
275 **38** 1t. on 40p. black, red and yellow 10 20
276 – 5t. gold and blue . . . . . 55 1·75

92 Demonstrators with Placards

1987. 35th Anniv of Bangla Language Movement. Multicoloured.
277 3t. Type **92** . . . . 1·40 2·50
278 3t. Martyrs' Memorial . . . 1·40 2·50
Nos. 277/8 were printed together, se-tenant, forming a composite design.

93 Nurse giving Injection

94 Pattern and Bengali Script

1987. World Health Day.
279 **93** 1t. black and blue . . . . 1·75 2·00
See also No 295.

1987. Bengali New Year Day. Multicoloured.
280 1t. Type **94** 10 10
281 10t. Bengali woman 40 60

95 Jute Shika

96 Ustad Ayet Ali Khan and Surbahar

1987. Export Products. Multicoloured.
282 1t. Type **95** 10 10
283 5t. Jute carpet (horiz) 30 35
284 10t. Cane table lamp 45 70

1987. 20th Death Anniv of Ustad Ayet Ali Khan (musician and composer).
285 **96** 5t. multicoloured . . . . . 1·50 70

97 Palanquin

1987. Transport. Multicoloured.
286 2t. Type **97** 20 15
287 3t. Bicycle rickshaw . . . . 1·00 35
288 5t. River steamer . . . . . . 1·25 65
289 7t. Express diesel train . . . 3·25 1·25
290 10t. Bullock cart . . . . . . 60 1·50

98 H. S. Suhrawardy

1987. Hossain Shadid Suhrawardy (politician) Commemoration.
291 **98** 3t. multicoloured 20 30

99 Villagers fleeing from Typhoon

1987. International Year of Shelter for the Homeless. Multicoloured.
292 5t. Type **99** 20 30
293 5t. Villagers and modern houses 20 30

100 President Ershad addressing Parliament

1987. 1st Anniv of Return to Democracy.
294 **100** 10t. multicoloured 40 60

1988. World Health Day. As T **93**.
295 25p. brown 30 20
DESIGN: 25p. Oral rehydration.

101 Woman planting Palm Saplings

1988. I.F.A.D. Seminar on Agricultural Loans for Rural Women. Multicoloured.
296 3t. Type **101** 15 20
297 5t. Village woman milking cow 20 40

102 Basketball

1988. Olympic Games, Seoul. Multicoloured.
298 5t. Type **102** . . . . 1·25 80
299 5t. Weightlifting . . . . 1·25 80
300 5t. Tennis . . . . 1·25 80
301 5t. Rifle-shooting . . . . . . 1·25 80
302 5t. Boxing . . . . 1·25 80

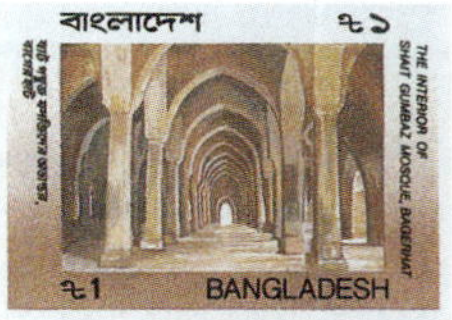

103 Interior of Shait Gumbaz Mosque, Bagerhat

1988. Historical Buildings. Multicoloured.
303 1t. Type **103** 40 10
304 4t. Paharpur Monastery . . . 80 30
305 5t. Kantanagar Temple, Dinajpur 80 30
306 10t. Lalbag Fort, Dhaka . . 1·25 1·00

104 Henri Dunant (founder), Red Cross and Crescent

105 Dr. Qudrat-i-Khuda in Laboratory

1988. 125th Anniv of International Red Cross and Red Crescent. Multicoloured.
307 5t. Type **104** . . . . 1·40 30
308 10t. Red Cross workers with patient . . . . 2·00 10

1988. Dr. Qudrat-i-Khuda (scientist) Commem.
309 **105** 5t. multicoloured 30 30

106 Wicket-keeper

107 Labourers, Factory and Technician

1988. Asia Cup Cricket. Multicoloured.
310 1t. Type **106** 80 90
311 5t. Batsman . . . . 1·00 1·00
312 10t. Bowler . . . . 1·75 2·25

1988. 32nd Meeting of Colombo Plan Consultative Committee, Dhaka.
313 **107** 3t. multicoloured 10 10
314 10t. multicoloured 40 45

108 Dhaka G.P.O. Building

1988. 25th Anniv of Dhaka G.P.O. Building. Multicoloured.
315 1t. Type **108** 15 10
316 5t. Post Office counter . . . 30 30

৫ম জাতীয় রোভার মুট
১৯৮৮-৮৯
(109)

1988. 5th National Rover Scout Moot. No. 168 optd with T **109**.
317 **47** 5t. multicoloured . . . . . 3·50 3·00

110 Bangladesh Airport

1989. Bangladesh Landmarks.
318 **110** 3t. black and blue . . . 10 10
318a – 4t. blue 10 10
710 – 5t. black and brown . . 10 15
320 – 10t. red . . . . 4·00 35
321 – 20t. multicoloured . . . 35 40
DESIGNS—VERT (22 × 33 mm): 5t. Curzon Hall. (19½ × 31½ mm): 10t. Fertiliser factory, Chittagong. HORIZ (33 × 23 mm): 4t. Chittagong port; 20t. Postal Academy, Rajshahi.

চতুর্থ দ্বিবার্ষিক এশীয়
চারুকলা প্রদর্শনী
বাংলাদেশ ১৯৮৯
(111)

1989. 4th Biennial Asian Art Exhibition. No. 266 optd with T **111**.
322 10t. "Levelling the Ploughed Field" (Zainul Abedin) . . 50 50

112 Irrigation Methods and Student with Telescope

113 Academy Logo

1989. 12th National Science and Technology Week.
323 **112** 10t. multicoloured 50 50

1989. 75th Anniv of Police Academy, Sardah.
324 **113** 10t. multicoloured 50 50

114 Rejoicing Crowds, Paris, 1789

1989. Bicentenary of French Revolution. Mult.
325 17t. Type **114** 70 75
326 17t. Storming the Bastille, 1789 . . . . 70 75
MS327 125 × 125 mm 5t. Men with pickaxes; 10t. "Liberty guiding the People" (detail) (Delacroix); 10t. Crowd with cannon. P 14 . . . 2·00 3·00
MS328 152 × 88 mm. 25t. Storming the Bastille. Imperf . . . . . 2·00 3·00
The design of No. **MS**328 incorporates the three scenes featured on No. **MS**327.

115 Sowing and Harvesting

1989. 10th Anniv of Asia–Pacific Integrated Rural Development Centre. Multicoloured.
329 5t. Type **115** 45 45
330 10t. Rural activities 55 55
Nos. 329/30 were printed together, se-tenant, forming a composite design.

116 Helper and Child playing with Baby

1989. 40th Anniv of S.O.S. International Children's Village. Multicoloured.
331 1t. Type **116** 15 10
332 10t. Foster mother with children 55 55

117 U.N. Soldier on Watch

118 Festival Emblem

1989. 1st Anniv of Bangladesh Participation in U.N. Peace-keeping Force. Multicoloured.
333 4t. Type **117** 50 30
334 10t. Two soldiers checking positions . . . . 1·00 70

1989. 2nd Asian Poetry Festival, Dhaka.
335 **118** 2t. red, deep red and green 15 10
336 – 10t. multicoloured 60 65
DESIGN: 10t. Festival emblem and hall.

119 State Security Printing Press

1989. Inauguration of State Security Printing Press, Gazipur.
337 **119** 10t. multicoloured 65 65

120 Water Lilies and T.V. Emblem

1989. 25th Anniv of Bangladesh Television. Multicoloured.
338 5t. Type **120** 35 30
339 10t. Central emblem and water lilies 65 80

121 Gharial in Shallow Water

1990. Endangered Wildlife. Gharial. Multicoloured.
340 50p. Type **121** 80 45
341 2t. Gharial feeding . . . . . 1·00 60
342 4t. Gharials basking on sand bank . . . . 1·40 70
343 10t. Two gharials resting . . 1·75 95

122 Symbolic Family

124 Boy learning Alphabet

123 Justice S. M. Murshed

1990. Population Day.
344 **122** 6t. multicoloured 55 35

1990. 10th Death Anniv of Justice Syed Mahbub Murshed.
345 **123** 5t. multicoloured . . . . 2·25 1·25

1990. International Literacy Year. Multicoloured.
346 6t. Type **124** . . . . 1·00 50
347 10t. Boy teaching girl to write 1·50 1·00

125 Penny Black with "Stamp World London 90" Exhibition Emblem

127 Mango

126 Goalkeeper and Ball

1990. 150th Anniv of the Penny Black. Multicoloured.
348 7t. Type **125** . . . . 1·50 2·00
349 10t. Penny Black, 1983 World Communications Year stamp and Bengali mail runner . . . . 1·75 2·50

1990. World Cup Football Championship, Italy. Multicoloured.
350 8t. Type **126** . . . . 1·75 1·50
351 10t. Footballer with ball . . 2·00 1·75
MS352 104 × 79 mm. 25t. Colosseum, Rome, with football. Imperf . . . . 11·00 11·00

1990. Fruit. Multicoloured.
353 1t. Type **127** 30 10
354 2t. Guava 30 10
355 3t. Water melon 35 15
356 4t. Papaya 40 25
357 5t. Bread fruit 65 50
358 10t. Carambola . . . . . . 1·25 1·25

128 Man gathering Wheat

1990. U.N. Conference on Least Developed Countries, Paris.
359 **128** 10t. multicoloured . . . . 1·25 1·00

129 Map of Asia with Stream of Letters

131 Lalan Shah

130 Canoe Racing

1990. 20th Anniv of Asia–Pacific Postal Training Centre. Multicoloured.
360 2t. Type **129** . . . . 1·75 1·75
361 6t. Map of Pacific with stream of letters . . . . . 1·50 1·50
Nos. 360/1 were printed together, se-tenant, forming a composite map design.

1990. Asian Games, Beijing. Multicoloured.
362 2t. Type **130** 80 20
363 4t. Kabaddi . . . . 1·00 25
364 8t. Wrestling . . . . 1·60 1·25
365 10t. Badminton . . . . . . 2·75 1·75

1990. 1st Death Anniv of Lalan Shah (poet).
366 **131** 6t. multicoloured . . . . 1·50 1·00

132 U.N. Logo and "40"

1990. 40th Anniv of United Nations Development Programme.
367 **132** 6t. multicoloured 80 35

133 Baby

134 "Danaus chrysippus"

1990. Immunization.

368 **133** 1t. green 10 10
369 2t. brown 10 10

1990. Butterflies. Multicoloured.

370 6t. Type **134** . . . . 1·60 1·60
371 6t. "Precis almana" . . . . . 1·60 1·60
372 10t. "Ixias pyrene" . . . . . 1·75 1·75
373 10t. "Danaus plexippus" . . 1·75 1·75

135 Drugs attacking Bangladesh

1991. U.N. Anti-drugs Decade. Multicoloured.

374 2t. Type **135** . . . . 1·25 50
375 4t. "Drug" snake around globe . . . . 1·75 1·25

136 Salimullah Hall

1991.

376 **136** 6t. blue and yellow . . . 10 15

137 Silhouetted People on Map

1991. 3rd National Census.

382 **137** 4t. multicoloured . . . . 1·25 1·50

138 "Invincible Bangla" (statue)

1991. 20th Anniv of Independence. Multicoloured.

383 4t. Type **138** . . . . 85 1·00
384 4t. "Freedom Fighter" (statue) . . . . 85 1·00
385 4t. Mujibnagar Memorial . . 85 1·00
386 4t. Eternal flame . . . . . . 85 1·00
387 4t. National Martyrs' Memorial . . . . 85 1·00

Nos. 383/7 were issued together, se-tenant, forming a composite design.

139 President Rahman Seated

141 Kaikobad

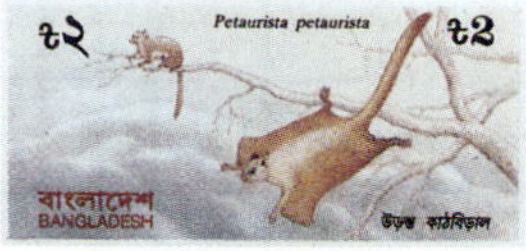

140 Red Giant Flying Squirrel

1991. 10th Death Anniv of President Ziaur Rahman. Multicoloured.

388 50p. Type **139** 25 15
389 2t. President Rahman's head in circular decoration . . . 1·00 1·10
MS390 146 × 75 mm. Nos. 388/9 (sold at 10t.) . . . . 1·60 2·50

1991. Endangered Species. Multicoloured.

391 2t. Type **140** . . . . 1·75 2·00
392 4t. Black-faced monkey (vert) 1·75 2·00
393 6t. Great Indian hornbill (vert) . . . . 1·75 2·00
394 10t. Armoured pangolin . . . 1·75 2·00

1991. 40th Death Anniv of Kaikobad (poet).

395 **141** 6t. multicoloured . . . . 1·40 1·00

142 Rabindranath Tagore and Temple

1991. 50th Death Anniv of Rabindranath Tagore (poet).

396 **142** 4t. multicoloured 80 55

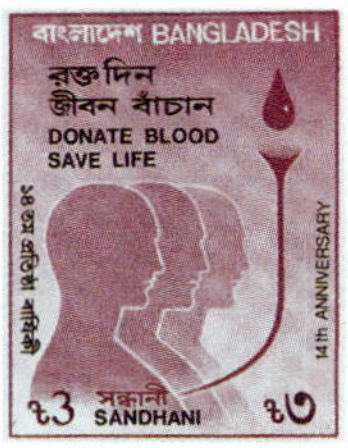

143 Voluntary Blood Programme

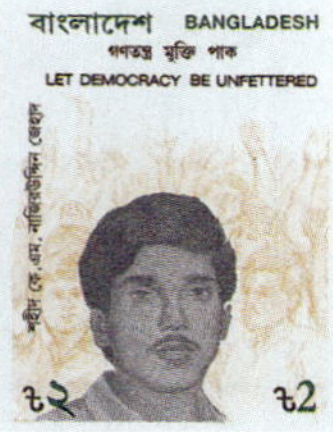

144 Shahid Naziruddin and Crowd

1991. 14th Anniv of "Sandhani" (medical students' association).

397 **143** 3t. black and red . . . . 1·00 50
398 – 5t. multicoloured . . . . 2·00 2·25

DESIGN: 5t. Blind man and eye.

1991. 1st Death Anniv of Shahid Naziruddin Jahad (democrat).

399 **144** 2t. black, green and brown . . . . 1·00 60

145 Shaheed Noor Hossain with Slogan on Chest

1991. 4th Death Anniv of Shaheed Noor Hossain (democrat).

400 **145** 2t. multicoloured . . . . 1·00 55

146 Bronze Stupa

1991. Archaeological Relics from Mainamati. Multicoloured.

401 4t. Type **146** . . . . 1·50 1·60
402 4t. Earthenware and bronze pitchers . . . . 1·50 1·60
403 4t. Remains of Salban Vihara Monastery . . . . 1·50 1·60
404 4t. Gold coins . . . . 1·50 1·60
405 4t. Terracotta plaque . . . . 1·50 1·60

147 Demostrators

1991. 1st Anniv of Mass Uprising.

406 **147** 4t. multicoloured . . . . 1·25 80

148 Munier Chowdhury

1991. 20th Anniv of Independence. Martyred Intellectuals (1st series). Each black and brown.

407 2t. Type **148** 50 55
408 2t. Ghyasuddin Ahmad . . . 50 55
409 2t. Rashidul Hasan 50 55
410 2t. Muhammad Anwar Pasha 50 55
411 2t. Dr. Muhammad Mortaza 50 55
412 2t. Shahid Saber 50 55
413 2t. Fazlur Rahman Khan . . 50 55
414 2t. Ranada Prasad Saha . . 50 55
415 2t. Adhyaksha Joges Chandra Ghose 50 55
416 2t. Santosh Chandra Bhattacharyya 50 55
417 2t. Dr. Gobinda Chandra Deb 50 55
418 2t. A. Muniruzzaman 50 55
419 2t. Mufazzal Haider Chaudhury 50 55
420 2t. Dr. Abdul Alim Choudhury 50 55
421 2t. Sirajuddin Hossain 50 55
422 2t. Shahidulla Kaiser 50 55
423 2t. Altaf Mahmud 50 55
424 2t. Dr. Jyotirmay Guha Thakurta 50 55
425 2t. Dr. Muhammad Abul Khair 50 55
426 2t. Dr. Serajul Haque Khan 50 55
427 2t. Dr. Mohammad Fazle Rabbi 50 55
428 2t. Mir Abdul Quyyum . . . 50 55
429 2t. Golam Mostafa 50 55
430 2t. Dhirendranath Dutta . . 50 55
431 2t. S. Mannan 50 55
432 2t. Nizamuddin Ahmad . . . 50 55
433 2t. Abul Bashar Chowdhury 50 55
434 2t. Selina Parveen 50 55
435 2t. Dr. Abul Kalam Azad . . 50 55
436 2t. Saidul Hassan 50 55

See also Nos. 483/92, 525/40, 568/83, 620/35, 656/71, 691/706, 731/46 and 779/94.

149 "Penaeus monodon"

1991. Shrimps. Multicoloured.

437 6t. Type **149** . . . . 2·00 2·25
438 6t. "Metapenaeus monoceros" . . . . 2·00 2·25

150 Death of Raihan Jaglu

1992. 5th Death Anniv of Shaheed Mirze Abu Raihan Jaglu.

439 **150** 2t. multicoloured . . . . 1·00 60

151 Rural and Urban Scenes

152 Nawab Sirajuddaulah

1992. World Environment Day. Multicoloured.

440 4t. Type **151** 75 25
441 10t. World Environment Day logo (horiz) . . . . 2·00 2·75

1992. 235th Death Anniv of Nawab Sirajuddaulah of Bengal.

442 **152** 10t. multicoloured . . . . 1·50 2·00

153 Syed Ismail Hossain Sirajee

1992. 61st Death Anniv of Syed Ismail Hossain Sirajee.

443 **153** 4t. multicoloured . . . . 1·00 60

154 Couple planting Seedling

1992. Plant Week. Multicoloured.

444 2t. Type **154** . . . . 1·00 80
445 4t. Birds on tree (vert) . . . 2·00 1·25

155 Canoe Racing

1992. Olympic Games, Barcelona. Multicoloured.

446 4t. Type **155** . . . . 1·40 1·75
447 6t. Hands holding torch with Olympic rings . . . . . . 1·40 1·75
448 10t. Olympic rings and doves 1·40 1·75
449 10t. Olympic rings and multiracial handshake . . . 1·40 1·75

1992. "Banglapex '92", National Philatelic Exhibition (1st issue). No. 290 optd **Banglapex '92** in English and Bengali.

450 10t. Bullock cart . . . . . . 2·25 2·75

See also Nos. 452/3.

157 Masnad-e-Ala Isa Khan

1992. 393rd Death Anniv of Masnad-e-Ala Isa Khan.

451 **157** 4t. multicoloured . . . . 1·00 60

158 Ceremonial Elephant (19th-century ivory carving)

1992. "Banglapex '92" National Philatelic Exhibition (2nd issue). Multicoloured.

452 10t. Type **158** . . . . 1·60 2·25
453 10t. Victorian pillarbox between early and modern postmen . . . . 1·60 2·25
MS454 145 × 92 mm. Nos. 452/3. Imperf (sold at 25t.) . . . . . 3·50 4·50

159 Star Mosque

1992. Star Mosque, Dhaka.

455 **159** 10t. multicoloured . . . . 2·00 2·00

160 Meer Nisar Ali Titumeer and Fort

1992. 161st Death Anniv of Meer Nisar Ali Titumeer.
456 **160** 10t. multicoloured . . . . 1·75 1·75

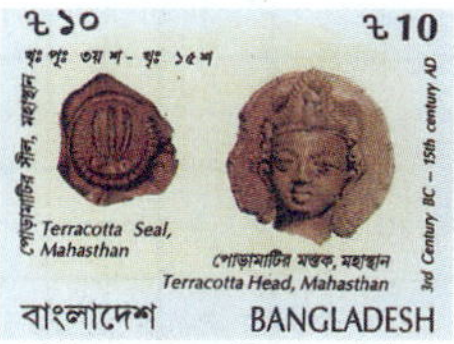
161 Terracotta Head and Seal

1992. Archaeological Relics from Mahasthangarh. Multicoloured.
457 10t. Type **161** . . . . 1·75 1·90
458 10t. Terracotta panel showing swan . . . . 1·75 1·90
459 10t. Terracotta statue of Surya . . . . 1·75 1·90
460 10t. Gupta stone column . . 1·75 1·90

162 Young Child and Food

1992. Int Conference on Nutrition, Rome.
461 **162** 4t. multicoloured . . . . 1·00 55

163 National Flags

1992. 7th South Asian Association for Regional Co-operation Summit Conference, Dhaka. Mult.
462 6t. Type **163** . . . . 1·40 75
463 10t. S.A.A.R.C. emblem . . . 1·60 2·00

164 Syed Abdus Samad

1993. Syed Abdus Samad (footballer) Commem.
464 **164** 2t. multicoloured . . . . 1·50 70

165 Haji Shariat Ullah

1993. Haji Shariat Ullah Commemoration.
465 **165** 2t. multicoloured . . . . 1·50 70

166 People digging Canal

1993. Irrigation Canals Construction Project. Mult.
466 2t. Type **166** 80 80
467 2t. Completed canal and paddy-fields 80 80

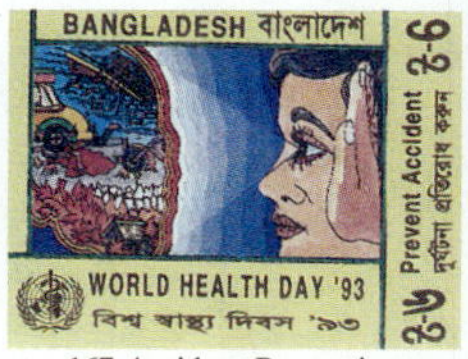
167 Accident Prevention

1993. World Health Day. Multicoloured.
468 6t. Type **167** . . . . 2·00 75
469 10t. Satellite photograph and symbols of trauma (vert) 2·25 2·75

168 National Images

1993. 1400th Year of Bengali Solar Calendar.
470 **168** 2t. multicoloured . . . . 1·00 50

169 Schoolchildren and Bengali Script

1993. Compulsory Primary Education. Mult.
471 2t. Type **169** 80 80
472 2t. Books and slate (horiz) 80 80

170 Nawab Sir Salimullah and Palace

1993. 122nd Birth Anniv of Nawab Sir Salimullah.
473 **170** 4t. multicoloured . . . . 1·25 70

171 Fish Production

1993. Fish Fortnight.
474 **171** 2t. multicoloured 50 40

172 Sunderban

1993. Natural Beauty of Bangladesh. Mult.
475 10t. Type **172** . . . . 1·00 1·40
476 10t. Kuakata beach . . . . . 1·00 1·40
477 10t. Madhabkunda waterfall (vert) . . . . 1·00 1·40
478 10t. River Piyain, Jaflang (vert) . . . . 1·00 1·40
MS479 174 × 102 mm. Nos. 475/8. Imperf (sold at 50t.) . . . . . 3·25 4·00

173 Exhibition Emblem

175 Burdwan House

174 Foy's Lake

1993. 6th Asian Art Biennale.
480 **173** 10t. multicoloured . . . . 80 1·00

1993. Tourism Month.
481 **174** 10t. multicoloured . . . . 1·00 1·25

1993. Foundation Day, Bangla Academy.
482 **175** 2t. brown and green . . . 60 40

1993. Martyred Intellectuals (2nd series). As T **148**. Each black and brown.
483 2t. Lt. Cdr. Moazzam Hussain 20 30
484 2t. Muhammad Habibur Rahman 20 30
485 2t. Khandoker Abu Taleb . . 20 30
486 2t. Moshiur Rahman 20 30
487 2t. Md. Abdul Muktadir . . 20 30
488 2t. Nutan Chandra Sinha . . 20 30
489 2t. Syed Nazmul Haque . . . 20 30
490 2t. Dr. Mohammed Amin Uddin 20 30
491 2t. Dr. Faizul Mohee 20 30
492 2t. Sukha Ranjan Somaddar 20 30

176 Throwing the Discus

1993. 6th South Asian Federation Games, Dhaka. Multicoloured.
493 2t. Type **176** 20 20
494 4t. Running (vert) 35 35

177 Tomb of Sultan Ghiyasuddin Azam Shah

1993. Muslim Monuments.
495 **177** 10t. multicoloured . . . . 75 1·00

178 Scouting Activities and Jamboree Emblem

179 Emblem and Mother giving Solution to Child

1994. 14th Asian–Pacific and 5th Bangladesh National Scout Jamboree.
496 **178** 2t. multicoloured 40 30

1994. 25th Anniv of Oral Rehydration.
497 **179** 2t. multicoloured 40 30

180 Interior of Chhota Sona Mosque, Nawabgonj

1994. Ancient Mosques. Multicoloured.
498 4t. Type **180** 40 20
499 6t. Exterior of Chhota Sona Mosque 50 65
500 6t. Exterior of Baba Adam's Mosque, Munshigonj . . . 50 65

181 Agricultural Workers and Emblem

1994. 75th Anniv of I.L.O. Multicoloured.
501 4t. Type **181** 25 20
502 10t. Worker turning cog (vert) . . . . 1·00 1·00

182 Priest releasing Peace Doves

184 Family, Globe and Logo

183 Scenes from Baishakhi Festival

1994. 1500th Year of Bengali Solar Calendar.
503 **182** 2t. multicoloured 35 25

1994. Folk Festivals. Multicoloured.
504 4t. Type **183** 35 35
505 4t. Scenes from Nabanna and Paush Parvana Festivals 35 35

1994. International Year of the Family.
506 **184** 10t. multicoloured . . . . 1·00 1·50

185 People planting Saplings

186 Player kicking Ball

1994. Tree Planting Campaign. Multicoloured.
507 4t. Type **185** 50 25
508 6t. Hands holding saplings 75 45

1994. World Cup Football Championship, U.S.A. Multicoloured.
509 20t. Type **186** . . . . 2·25 3·00
510 20t. Player heading ball . . . 2·25 3·00

187 Traffic on Bridge

1994. Inauguration of Jamuna Multi-purpose Bridge Project.
511 **187** 4t. multicoloured . . . . 1·75 55

188 Asian Black-headed Oriole

190 Nawab Faizunnessa Chowdhurani

189 Dr. Mohammad Ibrahim and Hospital

1994. Birds. Multicoloured.
512 4t. Type **188** 40 40
513 6t. Greater racquet-tailed drongo 60 80
514 6t. Indian tree pie 60 80
515 6t. Red junglefowl 60 80
MS516 165 × 110 mm. Nos. 512/15 (sold at 25t.) . . . . 2·00 2·75

1994. 5th Death Anniv of Dr. Mohammad Ibrahim (diabetes treatment pioneer).
517 **189** 2t. multicoloured 40 20

1994. 160th Birth Anniv of Nawab Faizunnessa Chowdhurani (social reformer).
518 **190** 2t. multicoloured 50 20

191 Boxing

1994. Asian Games, Hiroshima, Japan.
519 **191** 4t. multicoloured . . . . 1·25 50

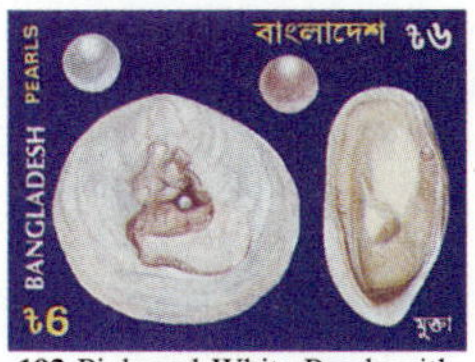
192 Pink and White Pearls with Windowpane Oysters

1994. Sea Shells. Multicoloured.
520 6t. Type **192** . . . . 1·40 1·60
521 6t. Tranquelous scallop and other shells . . . . 1·40 1·60
522 6t. Lister's conch, Asiatic Arabian cowrie, bladder moon and woodcock murex . . . . 1·40 1·60
523 6t. Spotted tun, spiny frog shell, spiral melongena and gibbous olive (vert) . . . . 1·40 1·60

193 Dr. Milon and Demonstrators

1994. 4th Death Anniv of Dr. Shamsul Alam Khan Milon (medical reformer).
524 **193** 2t. multicoloured 25 20

1994. Martyred Intellectuals (3rd series). As T **148**. Each black and brown.
525 2t. Dr. Harinath Dey 25 30
526 2t. Dr. A. F. Ziaur Rahman 25 30
527 2t. Mamun Mahmud 25 30
528 2t. Mohsin Ali Dewan . . . 25 30
529 2t. Dr. N. A. M. Jahangir . . 25 30
530 2t. Shah Abdul Majid . . . 25 30
531 2t. Muhammad Akhter . . . 25 30
532 2t. Meherunnesa 25 30
533 2t. Dr. Kasiruddin Talukder 25 30
534 2t. Fazlul Haque Choudhury 25 30
535 2t. Md. Shamsuzzaman . . . 25 30
536 2t. A. K. M. Shamsuddin . . 25 30
537 2t. Lt. Mohammad Anwarul Azim 25 30
538 2t. Nurul Amin Khan . . . 25 30
539 2t. Mohammad Sadeque . . 25 30
540 2t. Md. Araz Ali 25 30

194 "Diplazium esculentum"

1994. Vegetables. Multicoloured.
541 4t. Type **194** 70 50
542 4t. "Momordica charantia" 70 50
543 6t. "Lagenaria siceraria" . . 90 70
544 6t. "Trichosanthes dioica" . . 90 70
545 10t. "Solanum melongena" 1·40 2·00
546 10t. "Cucurbita maxima" (horiz) . . . . 1·40 2·00

195 Sonargaon

1995. 20th Anniv of World Tourism Organization.
547 **195** 10t. multicoloured . . . . 1·50 1·50

196 Exports

1995. Dhaka International Trade Fair '95. Mult.
548 4t. Type **196** 20 20
549 6t. Symbols of industry . . . 45 65

197 Soldiers of Ramgarh Battalion (1795) and of Bangladesh Rifles (1995)

1995. Bicentenary of Bangladesh Rifles. Mult.
550 2t. Type **197** 85 50
551 4t. Riflemen on patrol . . . 1·40 90

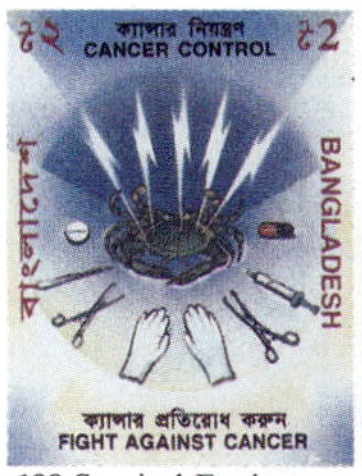
198 Surgical Equipment and Lightning attacking Crab (cancer)

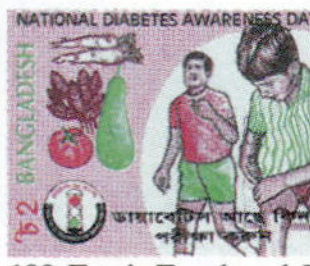
199 Fresh Food and Boy injecting Insulin

1995. Campaign against Cancer.
552 **198** 2t. multicoloured 40 25

1995. National Diabetes Awareness Day.
553 **199** 2t. multicoloured 80 25

200 Munshi Mohammad Meherullah

1995. Munshi Mohammad Meherullah (Islamic educator) Commemoration.
554 **200** 2t. multicoloured 30 25

রাজশাহীপেক্স-৯৫
(201)

1995. "Rajshahipex '95" National Philatelic Exhibition. No. 499 optd with T **201**.
555 6t. Exterior of Chhota Sona Mosque . . . . 2·00 2·25

202 "Lagerstroemia speciosa"

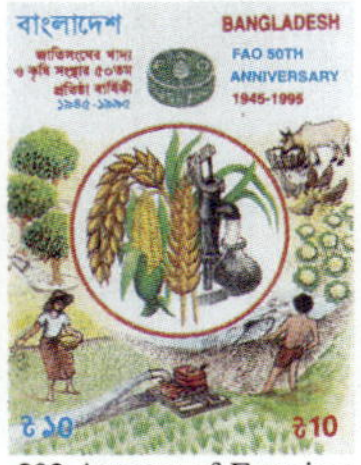
203 Aspects of Farming

1995. Flowers. Multicoloured.
556 6t. Type **202** 90 90
557 6t. "Bombax ceiba" (horiz) 90 90
558 10t. "Passiflora incarnata" . . 1·25 1·40
559 10t. "Bauhina purpurea" . . 1·25 1·40
560 10t. "Canna indica" . . . . 1·25 1·40
561 10t. "Gloriosa superba" . . . 1·25 1·40

1995. 50th Anniv of F.A.O.
562 **203** 10t. multicoloured 60 85

204 Anniversary Emblem, Peace Dove and U.N. Headquarters

1995. 50th Anniv of United Nations. Multicoloured.
563 2t. Type **204** 30 20
564 10t. Peace doves circling dates and Globe . . . . . 90 1·40
565 10t. Clasped hands and U.N. Headquarters . . . . . . 90 1·40

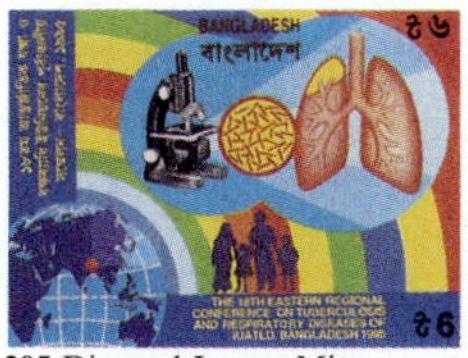
205 Diseased Lungs, Microscope, Family and Map

1995. 18th Eastern Regional Conference on Tuberculosis, Dhaka.
566 **205** 6t. multicoloured . . . . 1·50 1·00

206 Peace Doves, Emblem and National Flags

207 Aspects of COMDECA Projects

1995. 10th Anniv of South Asian Association for Regional Co-operation.
567 **206** 2t. multicoloured . . . . 1·40 55

1995. Martyred Intellectuals (4th series). As T **148**. Each black and brown.
568 2t. Abdul Ahad 25 30
569 2t. Lt. Col. Mohammad Qadir 25 30
570 2t. Mozammel Hoque Chowdhury 25 30
571 2t. Rafiqul Haider Chowdhury 25 30
572 2t. Dr. Azharul Haque . . . 25 30
573 2t. A. K. Shamsuddin . . . 25 30
574 2t. Anudwaipayan Bhattacharjee 25 30
575 2t. Lutfunnahar Helena . . . 25 30
576 2t. Shaikh Habibur Rahman . . 25 30
577 2t. Major Naimul Islam . . . 25 30
578 2t. Md. Shahidullah 25 30
579 2t. Ataur Rahman Khan Khadim 25 30
580 2t. A. B. M. Ashraful Islam Bhuiyan 25 30
581 2t. Dr. Md. Sadat Ali 25 30
582 2t. Sarafat Ali 25 30
583 2t. M. A. Sayeed 25 30

1995. 2nd Asia-Pacific Community Development Scout Camp.
584 **207** 2t. multicoloured 60 35

208 Volleyball Players

209 Man in Punjabi and Lungi

1995. Centenary of Volleyball.
585 **208** 6t. multicoloured 60 45

1995. Traditional Costumes. Multicoloured.
586 6t. Type **209** 90 90
587 6t. Woman in sari 90 90
588 10t. Christian bride and groom . . . . 1·25 1·40
589 10t. Muslim bride and groom 1·25 1·40
590 10t. Buddhist bride and groom (horiz) . . . . . . 1·25 1·40
591 10t. Hindu bride and groom (horiz) . . . . 1·25 1·40

210 Shaheed Amanullah Mohammad Asaduzzaman

211 Bowler and Map

1996. 27th Death Anniv of Shaheed Amanullah Mohammad Asaduzzaman (student leader).
592 **210** 2t. multicoloured 30 25

1996. World Cup Cricket Championship. Multicoloured.
593 4t. Type **211** . . . . 1·25 55
594 6t. Batsman and wicket keeper . . . . 1·50 80
595 10t. Match in progress (horiz) 2·00 2·25

212 Liberation Struggle, 1971

1996. 25th Anniv of Independence. Multicoloured.
596 4t. Type **212** 70 70
597 4t. National Martyrs Memorial 70 70
598 4t. Education 70 70
599 4t. Health 70 70
600 4t. Communications 70 70
601 4t. Industry 70 70

213 Michael Madhusudan Dutt

214 Gymnastics

1996. Michael Madhusudan Dutt (poet) Commemoration.
602 **213** 4t. multicoloured 50 20

1996. Olympic Games, Atlanta. Multicoloured.
603 4t. Type **214** 30 20
604 6t. Judo 40 30

605 10t. Athletics (horiz) 45 60
606 10t. High jumping (horiz) . . 45 60
MS607 165 × 110 mm. Nos. 603/6 (sold at 40t.) . . . . 1·50 2·00

1996. 25th Anniv of Bangladesh Stamps. No. **MS**234 optd "**Silver Jubilee Bangladesh Postage Stamps 1971-96**" on sheet margin.
MS608 98 × 117 mm. Nos. 232/3 (sold at 10t.) . . . . 1·10 1·40

215 Bangabandhu Sheikh Mujibur Rahman

216 Maulana Mohammad Akrum Khan

1996. 21st Death Anniv of Bangabandhu Sheikh Mujibur Rahman.
609 **215** 4t. multicoloured 40 25

1996. 28th Death Anniv of Maulana Mohammad Akrum Khan.
610 **216** 4t. multicoloured 30 20

217 Ustad Alauddin Khan

218 "Kingfisher" (Mayeesha Robbani)

1996. 24th Death Anniv of Ustad Alauddin Khan (musician).
611 **217** 4t. multicoloured 50 20

1996. Children's Paintings. Multicoloured.
612 2t. Type **218** 45 35
613 4t. "River Crossing" (Iffat Panchlais) (horiz) 55 35

219 Syed Nazrul Islam

220 Children receiving Medicine

1996. 21st Death Anniv of Jail Martyrs. Multicoloured.
614 4t. Type **219** 30 40
615 4t. Tajuddin Ahmad 30 40
616 4t. M. Monsoor Ali 30 40
617 4t. A. H. M. Quamaruzzaman 30 40

1996. 50th Anniv of UNICEF Multicoloured.
618 4t. Type **220** 50 25
619 10t. Mother and child . . . 1·10 1·40

1996. Martyred Intellectuals (5th series). As T **148**. Each black and brown.
620 2t. Dr. Jekrul Haque 45 45
621 2t. Munshi Kabiruddin Ahmed 45 45
622 2t. Md. Abdul Jabbar . . . 45 45
623 2t. Mohammad Amir 45 45
624 2t. A. K. M. Shamsul Huq Khan 45 45
625 2t. Dr. Siddique Ahmed . . . 45 45
626 2t. Dr. Soleman Khan . . . 45 45
627 2t. S. B. M. Mizanur Rahman 45 45
628 2t. Aminuddin 45 45
629 2t. Md. Nazrul Islam 45 45
630 2t. Zahirul Islam 45 45
631 2t. A. K. Lutfor Rahman . . 45 45
632 2t. Afsar Hossain 45 45
633 2t. Abul Hashem Mian . . . 45 45
634 2t. A. T. M. Alamgir 45 45
635 2t. Baser Ali 45 45

221 Celebrating Crowds

1996. 25th Anniv of Victory Day. Multicoloured.
636 4t. Type **221** 25 25
637 6t. Soldiers and statue (vert) 40 60

222 Paul P. Harris

1997. 50th Death Anniv of Paul Harris (founder of Rotary International).
638 **222** 4t. multicoloured 30 25

223 Shaikh Mujibur Rahman making Speech

1997. 25th Anniv of Shaikh Mujibur's Speech of 7 March (1996).
639 **223** 4t. multicoloured 30 25

224 Sheikh Mujibur Rahman

226 Heinrich von Stephan

225 Sheikh Mujibur Rahman and Crowd with Banners

1997. 77th Birth Anniv of Sheikh Mujibur Rahman (first President).
640 **224** 4t. multicoloured 30 25

1997. 25th Anniv (1996) of Independence.
641 **225** 4t. multicoloured 30 25

1997. Death Centenary of Heinrich von Stephan (founder of U.P.U.).
642 **226** 4t. multicoloured 30 25

227 Sheep

1997. Livestock. Multicoloured.
643 4t. Type **227** 70 70
644 4t. Goat 70 70
645 6t. Buffalo bull 90 90
646 6t. Cow 90 90

228 "Tilling the Field - 2" (S. Sultan)

1997. Bangladesh Paintings. Multicoloured.
647 6t. Type **228** 40 30
648 10t. "Three Women" (Quamrul Hassan) . . . . 60 1·25

229 Trophy, Flag and Cricket Ball

1997. 6th International Cricket Council Trophy Championship, Malaysia.
649 **229** 10t. multicoloured . . . . 2·50 2·00

230 Kusumba Mosque, Naogaon

1997. Historic Mosques. Multicoloured.
650 4t. Type **230** 65 35
651 6t. Atiya Mosque, Tangail . . 85 45
652 10t. Bagha Mosque, Rajshahi 1·25 1·75

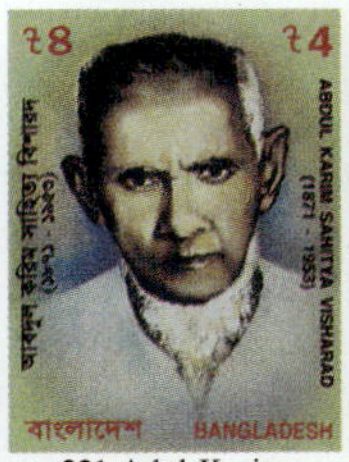

231 Adul Karim Sahitya Vishard

232 River Moot Emblem and Scouts standing on top of World

1997. 126th Birth Anniv of Abdul Karim Sahitya Vishard (scholar).
653 **231** 4t. multicoloured 30 25

1997. 9th Asia-Pacific and 7th Bangladesh Rover Moot, Lakkatura.
654 **232** 2t. multicoloured 50 25

233 Officers and Flag

1997. 25th Anniv of Armed Forces.
655 **233** 2t. multicoloured . . . . 1·50 60

1997. Martyred Intellectuals (6th series). As T **148**. Each black and brown.
656 2t. Dr. Shamsuddin Ahmed 65 65
657 2t. Mohammad Salimullah 65 65
658 2t. Mohiuddin Haider . . . 65 65
659 2t. Abdur Rahin 65 65
660 2t. Nitya Nanda Paul 65 65
661 2t. Abdel Jabber 65 65
662 2t. Dr. Humayun Kabir . . . 65 65
663 2t. Khaja Nizamuddin Bhuiyan 65 65
664 2t. Gulam Hossain 65 65
665 2t. Ali Karim 65 65
666 2t. Md. Moazzem Hossain 65 65
667 2t. Rafiqul Islam 65 65
668 2t. M. Nur Husain 65 65
669 2t. Captain Mahmood Hossain Akonda 65 65
670 2t. Abdul Wahab Talukder 65 65
671 2t. Dr. Hasimoy Hazra . . . 65 65

234 Mohammad Mansooruddin

236 Bulbul Chowdhury

235 Standard-bearer and Soldiers

1998. Professor Mohammad Mansooruddin (folklorist) Commemoration.
672 **234** 4t. multicoloured . . . . 1·40 60

1998. 50th Anniv of East Bengal Regiment.
673 **235** 2t. multicoloured 60 30

1998. Bulbul Chowdhury (traditional dancer) Commemoration.
674 **236** 4t. multicoloured 30 20

237 World Cup Trophy

239 Diana, Princess of Wales

238 Eastern Approach Road, Bangabandhu Bridge

1998. World Cup Football Championship, France. Multicoloured.
675 6t. Type **237** 50 30
676 18t. Footballer and trophy 1·50 2·25

1998. Opening of Bangabandhu Bridge. Mult.
677 4t. Type **238** 65 30
678 6t. Western approach road 75 40
679 8t. Embankment . . . . . . 95 1·40
680 10t. Main span, Bangabandhu Bridge . . . 1·25 1·60

1998. Diana, Princess of Wales Commemoration. Multicoloured.
681 8t. Type **239** . . . . 1·00 60
682 18t. Wearing pearl choker . . 1·75 1·75
683 22t. Wearing pendant necklace . . . . 1·75 2·00

240 Means of collecting Solar Energy

241 World Habitat Day Emblem and City Scene

1998. World Solar Energy Programme Summit.
684 **240** 10t. multicoloured . . . . 1·50 1·50

1998. World Habitat Day.
685 **241** 4t. multicoloured . . . . 1·25 60

242 Farmworkers, Sunflower and "20"

243 Batsman

1998. 20th Anniv of International Fund for Agricultural Development. Multicoloured.
686 6t. Type **242** 65 35
687 10t. Farmworker with baskets and harvested crops . . . 1·10 1·40

1998. Wills International Cricket Cup, Dhaka.
688 **243** 6t. multicoloured . . . . 1·75 1·25

244 Begum Rokeya

1998. Begum Rokeya (campaigner for women's education) Commemoration.
689 **244** 4t. multicoloured . . . . 1·25 60

245 Anniversary Logo

1998. 50th Anniv of Universal Declaration of Human Rights.
690 **245** 10t. multicoloured . . . . 1·25 1·25

1998. Martyred Intellectuals (7th series). As T **148**. Each black and brown.
691 2t. Md. Khorshed Ali Sarker 50 50
692 2t. Abu Yakub Mahfuz Ali 50 50
693 2t. S. M. Nural Huda 50 50
694 2t. Nazmul Hoque Sarker . . 50 50
695 2t. Md. Taslim Uddin . . . 50 50
696 2t. Gulam Mostafa 50 50
697 2t. A. H. Nural Alam 50 50
698 2t. Timir Kanti Dev 50 50
699 2t. Altaf Hossain 50 50
700 2t. Aminul Hoque 50 50
701 2t. S. M. Fazlul Hoque . . . 50 50
702 2t. Mozammel Ali 50 50
703 2t. Syed Akbar Hossain . . . 50 50
704 2t. Sk. Abdus Salam 50 50
705 2t. Abdur Rahman 50 50
706 2t. Dr. Shyamal Kanti Lala 50 50

246 Dove of Peace and U.N. Symbols

1998. 50th Anniv of U.N. Peace-keeping Operations.
707 **246** 10t. multicoloured . . . . 1·25 1·50

247 Kazi Nazrul Islam

1998. Birth Centenary (1999) of Kazi Nazrul Islam (poet).
708 **247** 6t. multicoloured . . . . 1·25 70

248 Jamboree Emblem and Scout Activities

1999. 6th Bangladesh National Scout Jamboree.
709 **248** 2t. multicoloured . . . . 1·00 50

1999. As No. 75 but redrawn. Size 35 × 22 mm.
711 10t. red 15 20
No. 711 has been redrawn so that "SIXTY-DOME MOSQUE" appears above the face value at bottom right instead of below the main inscription at top left.

249 Surjya Sen and Demonstrators

1999. Surjya Sen (revolutionary) Commemoration.
715 **249** 4t. multicoloured . . . . 1·25 60

250 Dr. Fazlur Rahman Khan and Sears Tower

251 National Team Badges

1999. 70th Birth Anniv of Dr. Fazlur Rahman Khan (architect).
716 **250** 4t. multicoloured . . . . 1·00 55

1999. Cricket World Cup, England. Multicoloured.
717 8t. Type **251** . . . . 1·75 2·00
718 10t. Bangladesh cricket team badge and flag . . . . . . 2·50 2·50
MS719 139 × 89 mm. Nos. 717/18 (sold at 30t.) . . . . 4·25 4·50

252 Mother Teresa

253 Sheikh Mujibur Rahman, New York Skyline and Dove

1999. Mother Teresa Commemoration.
720 **252** 4t. multicoloured . . . . 1·50 65

1999. 25th Anniv of Bangladesh's Admission to U.N.
721 **253** 6t. multicoloured . . . . 1·00 65

254 Shaheed Mohammad Maizuddin

255 Faces in Tree

1999. 15th Death Anniv of Shaheed Mohammad Maizuddin (politician).
722 **254** 2t. multicoloured 60 30

1999. International Year of the Elderly.
723 **255** 6t. multicoloured . . . . 1·00 60

256 Shanty Town and Modern Buildings between Hands

1999. World Habitat Day.
724 **256** 4t. multicoloured . . . . 1·00 50

257 Mobile Post Office

1999. 125th Anniv of U.P.U. Multicoloured.
725 4t. Type **257** 80 65
726 4t. Postman on motorcycle 80 65
727 6t. Postal motor launch . . . 1·00 90
728 6t. Two Bangladesh airliners 1·00 90
MS729 141 × 90 mm. Nos. 725/8 (sold at 25t.) . . . . 3·25 3·25

258 Sir Jagadis Chandra Bose

260 Cub Scouts, Globe and Flag

259 Bangladesh Flag and Monument

1999. Sir Jagadis Chandra Bose (physicist and botanist) Commemoration.
730 **258** 4t. multicoloured . . . . 1·50 60

1999. Martyred Intellectuals (8th series). As T **148**. Each black and brown.
731 2t. Dr. Mohammad Shafi . . 40 40
732 2t. Maulana Kasimuddin Ahmed 40 40
733 2t. Quazi Ali Imam 40 40
734 2t. Sultanuddin Ahmed . . . 40 40
735 2t. A. S. M. Ershadullah . . 40 40
736 2t. Mohammad Fazlur Rahman 40 40
737 2t. Captain A. K. M. Farooq 40 40
738 2t. Md. Latafot Hossain Joarder 40 40
739 2t. Ram Ranjan Bhattacharjya 40 40
740 2t. Abani Mohan Dutta . . . 40 40
741 2t. Sunawar Ali 40 40
742 2t. Abdul Kader Miah . . . 40 40
743 2t. Major Rezaur Rahman . 40 40
744 2t. Md. Shafiqul Anowar . . 40 40
745 2t. A. A. M. Mozammel Hoque 40 40
746 2t. Khandkar Abul Kashem 40 40

2000. New Millennium. Multicoloured.
747 4t. Type **259** 75 45
748 6t. Satellite, computer and dish aerial (vert) . . . . . 1·00 1·10

2000. 5th Bangladesh Cub Camporee.
749 **260** 2t. multicoloured 70 40

261 Jibanananda Das

262 Dr. Muhammad Shamsuzzoha

2000. Death Centenary (1999) of Jibanananda Das (poet).
750 **261** 4t. multicoloured 70 40

2000. 30th Death Anniv (1999) of Dr. Muhammad Shamsuzzoha.
751 **262** 4t. multicoloured 70 40

263 Shafiur Rahman

264 Meteorological Equipment

2000. International Mother Language Day. Mult.
752 4t. Type **263** 55 65
753 4t. Abul Barkat 55 65
754 4t. Abdul Jabbar 55 65
755 4t. Rafiq Uddin Ahmad . . . 55 65

2000. 50th Anniv of World Meteorological Organization.
756 **264** 10t. multicoloured . . . . 1·50 1·50

265 Cricket Week Logo and Web Site Address

266 Wasp

2000. International Cricket Week.
757 **265** 6t. multicoloured . . . . 1·50 1·00

2000. Insects. Multicoloured.
758 2t. Type **266** 40 30
759 4t. Grasshopper 55 35
760 6t. Bumble bee 70 55
761 10t. Silkworms . . . . 1·25 1·50

267 Gecko

2000. Native Fauna. Multicoloured.
762 4t. Type **267** 55 55
763 4t. Indian crested porcupine 55 55
764 6t. Indian black-tailed python 75 80
765 6t. Bengal monitor 75 80

268 Batsman

2000. Pepsi 7th Asia Cricket Cup.
766 **268** 6t. multicoloured . . . . 1·50 1·00

269 Water Cock

2000. Birds. Multicoloured.
767 4t. Type **269** 75 70
768 4t. White-breasted waterhen (*Amaurornis phoenicurus*) 75 70
769 6t. Javanese cormorant (*Phalacrocorax niger*) (vert) 1·00 90
770 6t. Indian pond heron (*Ardeola grayii*) (vert) . . . 1·00 90

270 Women's Shotput

2000. Olympic Games, Sydney. Multicoloured.
771 6t. Type **270** 80 40
772 10t. Men's Shotput 1·10 1·40

271 Clasped Hands, Landmarks and Flags

2000. 25th Anniv of Diplomatic Relations with People's Republic of China.
773 **271** 6t. multicoloured 1·25 60

272 Idrakpur Fort, Munshigonj

2000. Archaeology. Multicoloured.
774 4t. Type **272** 65 40
775 6t. Statue of Buddha, Mainamati (vert) 1·00 85

273 Year Emblem

274 Hason Raza

2000. International Volunteers' Year.
776 **273** 6t. multicoloured 1·00 55

2000. 80th Death Anniv of Hason Raza (mystic poet).
777 **274** 6t. multicoloured 1·25 65

275 U.N.H.C.R. Logo

276 Map of Faces

2000. 50th Anniv of United Nations High Commissioner for Refugees (U.N.H.C.R.).
778 **275** 10t. multicoloured 1·25 1·50

2000. Martyred Intellectuals (9th series). As T **148**. Each black and brown.
779 2t. M. A. Gofur 45 45
780 2t. Faizur Rahman Ahmed 45 45
781 2t. Muslimuddin Miah 45 45
782 2t. Sgt. Shamsul Karim Khan 45 45
783 2t. Bhikku Zinananda 45 45
784 2t. Abdul Jabber 45 45
785 2t. Sekander Hayat Chowdhury 45 45
786 2t. Chishty Shah Helalur Rahman 45 45
787 2t. Birendra Nath Sarker 45 45
788 2t. A. K. M. Nurul Haque 45 45
789 2t. Sibendra Nath Mukherjee 45 45
790 2t. Zahir Raihan 45 45
791 2t. Ferdous Dowla Bablu 45 45
792 2t. Capt A. K. M. Nurul Absur 45 45
793 2t. Mizanur Rahman Miju 45 45
794 2t. Dr. Shamshad Ali 45 45

2001. Population and Housing Census.
795 **276** 4t. multicoloured 1·25 55

277 Producing Food

2001. "Hunger-free Bangladesh" Campaign.
796 **277** 6t. multicoloured 1·25 65

278 "Peasant Women" (Rashid Chowdbury)

2001. Bangladesh Paintings.
797 **278** 10t. multicoloured 2·00 2·00

279 Lalbagh Kella Mosque

2001. Historic Buildings. Multicoloured.
798 6t. Type **279** 80 80
799 6t. Uttara Ganabhavan, Natore 80 80
800 6t. Armenian Church, Armanitola 80 80
801 6t. Panam Nagar, Sonargaon 80 80

280 Smoking Accessories, Globe and Paper People

2001. World No Tobacco Day.
802 **280** 10t. multicoloured 1·75 1·75

281 Ustad Gul Mohammad Khan

282 Begum Sufia Kamal

2001. Artists. Multicoloured.
803 6t. Type **281** 80 80
804 6t. Ustad Khadem Hossain Khan 80 80
805 6t. Gouhar Jamil 80 80
806 6t. Abdul Alim 80 80

2001. Begum Sufia Kamal (poet) Commemoration.
807 **282** 4t. multicoloured 75 40

283 Hilsa

2001. Fish. Multicoloured.
808 10t. Type **283** 90 1·00
809 10t. Tengra 90 1·00
810 10t. Punti 90 1·00
811 10t. Khalisa 90 1·00

284 Parliament House, Dhaka

2001. Completion of First Full National Parliamentary Term.
812 **284** 10t. multicoloured 2·25 2·25

285 Parliament House, Dhaka

2001. 8th Parliamentary Elections.
813 **285** 2t. multicoloured 70 45

286 "Children encircling Globe" (Urska Golob)

287 Meer Mosharraf Hossain

2001. U.N. Year of Dialogue among Civilizations.
814 **286** 10t. multicoloured 1·00 1·00
MS815 95×65 mm. **286** 10t. multicoloured (sold at 30t.) 1·50 1·75

2001. Meer Mosharraf Hossain (writer) Commemoration.
816 **287** 4t. black, red and crimson 50 30

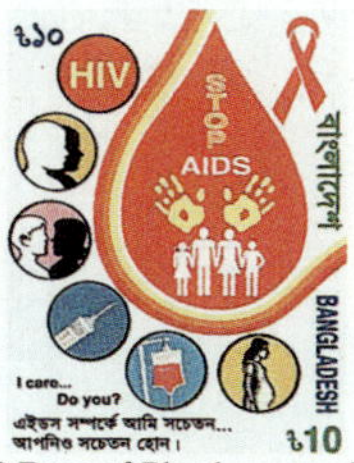

288 Drop of Blood surrounded by Images

2001. World AIDS Day.
817 **288** 10t. multicoloured 1·50 1·50

289 Sreshto Medal

2001. 30th Anniv of Independence. Gallantry Medals. Multicoloured.
818 10t. Type **289** 1·25 1·50
819 10t. Uttom medal 1·25 1·50
820 10t. Bikram medal 1·25 1·50
821 10t. Protik medal 1·25 1·50

290 Publicity Poster

2002. 10th Asian Art Biennale, Dhaka.
822 **290** 10t. multicoloured 1·00 1·00

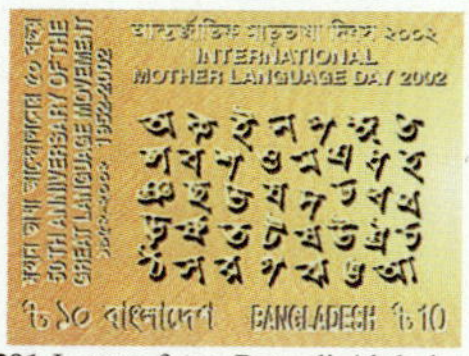

291 Letters from Bengali Alphabet

2002. 50th Anniv of Amar Ekushey (language movement). International Mother Language Day.
823 **291** 10t. black, gold and red 80 1·00
824 – 10t. black, gold and red 80 1·00
825 – 10t. black, gold and red 80 1·00
MS826 96×64 mm. 30t. multicoloured 2·00 2·25

DESIGNS—HORIZ: No. 824, Language Martyrs' Monument, Dhaka; 825, Letters from Bengali alphabet ("INTERNATIONAL MOTHER LANGUAGE DAY" inscr at right). VERT: No. **MS**826, Commemorative symbol of Martyrs' Monument.

292 Rokuon-Ji Temple, Japan

2002. 30th Anniv of Diplomatic Relations with Japan.
827 **292** 10t. multicoloured 1·00 1·00

293 Silhouetted Goats

2002. Goat Production.
828 **293** 2t. multicoloured 45 25

294 Children

2002. U.N. Special Session on Children.
829 **294** 10t. multicoloured 1·25 1·25

295 Mohammad Nasiruddin

2002. Mohammad Nasiruddin (journalist) Commemoration.
830 **295** 4t. black and brown 75 40

296 National Flags (trophy at top right)

2002. World Cup Football Championship, Japan and Korea. Multicoloured.
831 10t. Type **296** 90 1·00
832 10t. Pitch markings on world map 90 1·00
833 10t. National flags (trophy at top left) 90 1·00

297 Children tending Saplings

2002. National Tree Planting Campaign. Mult.
834 10t. Type **297** . . . . 90 1·00
835 10t. Citrus fruit . . . . . . 90 1·00
836 10t. Trees within leaf symbol (vert) . . . . 90 1·00

298 Children inside Symbolic House

299 Rural Family

2002. 30th Anniv of S.O.S. Children's Village in Bangladesh.
837 **298** 6t. multicoloured 80 45

2002. World Population Day.
838 **299** 6t. multicoloured 80 45

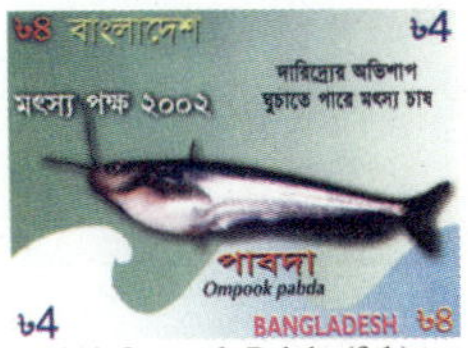

300 Ompook Pabda (fish)

2002. Fish. Multicoloured.
839 4t. Type **300** 50 50
840 4t. *Labeo gonius* 50 50

301 Bangladesh–U.K. Friendship Bridge, Bhairab

2002. Opening of Bangladesh–U.K. Friendship Bridge, Bhairab.
841 **301** 4t. multicoloured . . . . 1·00 45

302 Dhaka City Centre

2002. World Habitat Day.
842 **302** 4t. multicoloured 70 35

303 Dariabandha (Tag)

2002. Rural Games. Multicoloured.
843 4t. Type **303** 70 70
844 4t. Kanamachee (Blind-man's buff) 70 70

304 Jasimuddin

2003. Birth Centenary of Jasimuddin (poet).
845 **304** 5t. multicoloured 50 35

305 Books

306 Footballers and Flags of Participating Countries

2003. National Book Year.
846 **305** 6t. multicoloured 60 35

2003. 3rd SAFF Championship, Bangladesh.
847 **306** 10t. multicoloured . . . . 1·40 1·40

ইফাদ-এর ২৫ বছর
25 Years of IFAD
(307)

2003. 25th Anniv of International Fund for Agricultural Development. No. 687 optd with T **307**.
848 10t. Farmworker with baskets and harvested crops . . . 1·40 1·40

308 Shefa-ul-Mulk Hakim Habib-ur-Rahman

2003. 56th Death Anniv of Shefa-ul-Mulk Hakim Habib-ur-Rahman.
849 **308** 4t. multicoloured 45 25

309 Ziaur Rahman

2003. 22nd Death Anniv of Ziaur Rahman (President 1977–1981).
850 **309** 4t. multicoloured 45 25

310 Sapling in Cupped Hands and Family

2003. National Tree Plantation Campaign. Multicoloured.
851 8t. Type **310** . . . . 1·00 60
852 12t. Trees, plant, fruit and adult with children inside "petals" . . . . 1·25 1·50

311 Fruit

2003. Fruit Tree Plantation Fortnight.
853 **311** 6t. multicoloured 60 35

312 *Labeo Calbasu* (Orange-fin labeo)

2003. Fish Fortnight.
854 **312** 2t. multicoloured 45 30

313 Train on Jamuna Bridge and Signals

2003. Inauguration of Direct Train Communication between Rajshahi and Dhaka.
855 **313** 10t. multicoloured . . . . 1·50 1·50

314 Jatiya Sangsad Bhaban (Parliament House)

2003. 49th Commonwealth Parliamentary Conference.
856 **314** 10t. multicoloured 85 90

315 Mosque

316 Emblem

2003. Eid Mubarak.
857 **315** 4t. multicoloured 85 65

2003. International Centre for Diarrhoeal Disease Research, Bangladesh.
858 **316** 10t. multicoloured . . . . 1·00 1·10

317 Rajshahi University

2003. 50th Anniv of Rajshahi University.
859 **317** 4t. multicoloured 70 40

318 Books

2004. National Library Year (2003).
860 **318** 6t. multicoloured 55 35

319 Tents inside Emblem and Member Flags

2004. 7th Bangladesh and Fourth South Asian Association for Regional Co-operation Jamboree.
861 **319** 2t. multicoloured 50 30

320 Runner with Olympic Torch

2004. Sport and Environment.
862 **320** 10t. multicoloured 85 85

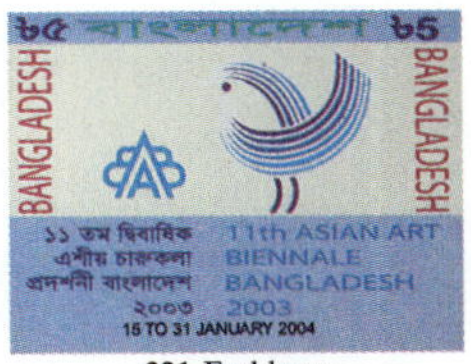

321 Emblems

2004. 11th Asian Art Biennale.
863 **321** 5t. multicoloured 45 25

322 Ziaur Rahman

2004. 33rd Anniv of Independence and National Day.
864 **322** 5t. multicoloured 45 25

323 Road and Emblems

2004. World Health Day.
865 **323** 6t. multicoloured 45 25

2004. 25th Anniv of Bangladesh National Philatelic Association. No. 843 optd *Silver Jubilee Bangladesh National Philatelic Association* and emblem.
866 4t. Type **303** 35 30

325 Stylized Tree, Fruits and Berries

2004. National Tree Plantation Campaign. Multicoloured.
867 10t. Type **325** 65 70
868 10t. Trees and saplings . . . 65 70

326 Hafez Shirazi, Iranian Flag and Banay-e Azadi (Freedom Monument), Tehran

2004. Commemoration of Diplomatic Relations with Iran. Multicoloured.

869	10t. Type **326**	65	70
870	10t. Nazrul Islam, Bangladeshi flag and War memorial, Dhaka	65	70

327 Woman Planting Tree and Fruit

2004. Fruit Tree Plantation Campaign.

871	**327**	10t. multicoloured	60	60

328 Workers carrying Rice Harvest

2004. International Year of Rice.

872	**328**	5t. multicoloured	30	25

329 Man feeding Child and Two Women

2004. World Population Day.

873	**329**	6t. multicoloured	30	25

330 UN Headquarters and Flags

2004. 30th Anniv of United Nations Membership.

874	**330**	4t. multicoloured	10	10

331 Bhasani Novo Theatre, Dhaka

2004. Bhasani Novo Theatre, Dhaka.

875	**331**	4t. multicoloured	10	10

332 Centennial Bell

2004. Centenary of Rotary International.

876	**332**	4t. multicoloured	25	20

333 *Argemone mexicana*

2004. Wild Flowers. Multicoloured.

877	5t. Type **333**	10	10
878	5t. *Cyanotis axillaries*	10	10
879	5t. *Thevetia Peruvians*	10	10
880	5t. *Pentapetes phoenicea*	10	10
881	5t. *Aegle marmelos*	10	10
882	5t. *Datura stramonium*	10	10

334 Rainbow and Emblem

2004. 13th SAARC (South Asian Association for Regional Co-operation) Summit, Dhaka (2005).

883	**334**	6t. multicoloured	10	10

335 *Sperata aor*

2004. Fish Fortnight. Multicoloured.

884	10t. Type **335**	15	20
885	10t. *Notopterus notepturus*	15	20

336 Cub in Sunflower

2004. 6th National Cub Camporee.

886	**336**	6t. multicoloured	10	15

337 Woman Farmer and Microcredit Symbol

2005. United Nations International Year of Microcredit. Multicoloured.

887	4t. Type **337**	10	10
888	10t. Woman turning lever on coin and microcredit symbol pulley	15	20

338 Beach at Sunset

2005. South Asia Tourism Year.

889	**338**	4t. multicoloured	10	10

339 Major Ziaur Rahman and War Memorial, Dhaka

2005. Independence and National Day.

890	**339**	10t. multicoloured	15	20

340 Sewing Machinist, Fish in Net, Dairy Cattle, Hens and Goats

2005. Centenary of Co-operative Movement in Bangladesh.

891	**340**	5t. multicoloured	10	10

341 Family Planting Tree

2005. National Tree Plantation Campaign. Multicoloured.

892	6t. Type **341**	60	35
893	6t. Three types of different varieties	60	35

342 G. A. Mannan (choreographer)

2005. Talented Artists. Multicoloured.

394	6t. Type **342**	60	35
895	6t. Unstad Phuljhuri Khan (musician)	60	35
896	6t. Ustad Abed Hossian Khan (musician and composer)	60	35
897	6t. Ustad Munshi Raisuddin (musician)	60	35

343 *Nandus nandus*

2005. Fish Fortnight.

898	**343**	10t. multicoloured	15	15

344 Dr. Nawab Ali

2005. Dr. Nawab Ali (physician) Commemoration.

899	**344**	8t. multicoloured	15	15

345 Books, Compass and Dividers

2006. Science Book Year (2005).

900	**345**	10t. multicoloured	15	15

346 Emblems, Globe and Computer Screen

2006. World Summit on the Information Society, Tunis (2005).

901	**346**	10t. multicoloured	15	15

347 Verwaltungssitz, Vienna and Emblem

2006. 30th Anniv of OPEC Fund for International Development (2005).

902	**347**	10t. multicoloured	15	15

348 Palace of Heavenly Peace, Beijing

2006. 30th Anniv of Bangladesh–China Diplomatic Relations (2005). Multicoloured.

903	10t. Type **348**	15	15
904	10t. Parliament Building, Dhaka	15	15
905	10t. 5th Bangladesh–China Friendship Bridge over Gabkhan River	15	15
906	10t. Great Wall of China	15	15
MS907	140 × 90 mm. Nos. 903/6	90	90

349 Major Ziaur Rahman and War Memorial, Dhaka

2006. 35th Anniversary of Independence and National Day.

908	**349**	10t. multicoloured		

350 Palm Tree

2006. National Tree Plantation Campaign and Tree Fair.

909	**350**	10t. multicoloured	15	15

351 Mother with Baby and Toddler

2006. World Health Day.

910	**351**	6t. multicoloured	1·00	1·00

352 Silhouette of Batsman

2006. ICC Under 19 Cricket World Cup (2004), Bangladesh.

911	**352**	10t. multicoloured	1·00	1·00

353 Peace Dove and Modern Buildings and Roads

2006. Five Years of Peace and Development.

912	**353**	10t. multicoloured	1·00	1·00

354 AIDS Ribbon and Globe 355 Profiles

2006. World AIDS Day.

913	**354**	10t. multicoloured	1·00	1·00

2006. International Women's Day.

914	**355**	10t. multicoloured	1·00	1·00

356 Family and Jar of Coins ('Invest in health') 357 Falling Wicket

2007. World Health Day.

915	**356**	6t. multicoloured	1·00	1·00

2007. World Cup Cricket, West Indies. Multicoloured.

916	10t. Type **357**	1·00	1·00
917	10t. Tiger, bowler and trophy (horiz)	1·00	1·00
918	10t. Bangladesh team and Cricket World Cup trophy	1·00	1·00
919	10t. Batsman and trophy (horiz)	1·00	1·00

358 House and Girls in Plantation 359 Md. Habibullah Bahar Choudhury

2007. National Tree Plantation Campaign.

920	**358**	10t. multicoloured	1·00	1·00

2007. Birth Centenary (2006) of Md. Habibullah Bahar Choudhury (politician and writer).

921	**359**	10t. multicoloured	1·00	1·00

360 Boy and Girl Scouts

2007. Centenary of World Scouting. Multicoloured.

922	10t. Type **360**	1·00	1·00
923	10t. Lord Baden-Powell (founder)	1·00	1·00

(361)

2007. 20th Anniv of Philatelic Association of Bangladesh. No. 768 optd with T **361**.

924	4t. White-breasted waterhen (*Amaurornis phoenicurus*)	1·00	1·00

OFFICIAL STAMPS

1973. Nos. 22, etc. optd **SERVICE**.

O 1	**7**	2p. black	10	1·50
O 2	–	3p. green	10	1·50
O 3	–	5p. brown	20	10
O 4	–	10p. black	20	10
O 5	–	20p. green	1·75	10
O 6	–	25p. mauve	4·00	10
O 7	–	60p. grey	4·00	2·25
O 8	–	75p. orange	1·50	30
O 9	**8**	1t. violet	14·00	5·50
O10	–	5t. blue	5·00	9·00

1974. Nos. 49/51 optd **SERVICE**.

O11	**14**	1t. violet	5·00	50
O12	–	2t. olive	7·00	2·25
O13	–	5t. blue	14·00	12·00

1976. Nos. 64/70 and 72/4 optd **SERVICE**.

O14	–	5p. green	1·50	1·00
O15	–	10p. black	2·00	1·00
O16	–	20p. green	2·25	1·00
O17	–	25p. mauve	3·25	1·00
O18	–	50p. purple	3·75	60
O19	–	60p. grey	30	2·75
O20	–	75p. olive	30	3·50
O21	**14**	1t. blue	2·75	50
O22	–	2t. green	35	2·25
O23	–	5t. blue	30	2·25

1981. Nos. 125/37 optd **SERVICE**.

O24	–	5p. brown	2·00	2·50
O25	**32**	10p. blue	2·00	2·75
O26	–	15p. orange	2·00	2·50
O27	–	20p. red	1·50	2·50
O28	–	25p. blue	80	2·50
O29	–	30p. green	3·50	3·00
O30	–	40p. purple	2·75	2·50
O31	–	50p. black	30	10
O32	–	80p. brown	2·25	50
O33	–	1t. violet	30	10
O34	–	2t. blue	35	2·75

1983. Nos. 220/9, 318a and 710 (1989) optd **Service**.

O35	**69**	5p. blue	10	10
O36	–	10p. purple	10	10
O37	–	15p. blue	10	10
O38	–	20p. black	10	10
O39	–	25p. grey	10	10
O40	–	30p. brown	10	10
O41	–	50p. brown	10	10
O42	–	1t. blue	1·75	10
O43	–	2t. green	10	10
O44	–	3t. black and blue	10	10
O45	–	4t. blue	10	15
O46	–	5t. purple	2·25	80

সার্ভিস সার্ভিস সার্ভিস

(O 5) (O 6) (O 7)

1989. Nos. 227 and 710 (1989) optd with Type O **5**.

O47		1t. blue	20	10
O48		5t. black and brown	80	90

1990. Nos. 368/9 (Immunization) optd with Type O **6**.

O49	**133**	1t. green	10	10
O50		2t. brown	10	10

1992. No. 376 optd as Type O **6** but horiz.

O51	**136**	6t. blue and yellow	10	15

1995. No. 553 (National Diabetes Awareness Day) optd as Type O **6** but horiz.

O52	**199**	2t. multicoloured	1·00	1·00

1996. Nos. 221 and 223 optd with Type O **7**.

O53	10p. purple	75	75
O54	20p. black	1·25	1·25

1999. No. 710 optd as Type O **5** but vert.

O56	5t. black and brown	10	15

BARBADOS Pt. 1

An island in the Br. West Indies, E. of the Windward Islands, attained self-government on 16 October 1961 and achieved independence within the Commonwealth on 30 November 1966.

1852. 12 pence = 1 shilling;
20 shillings = 1 pound.
1950. 100 cents = 1 West Indian, later Barbados, dollar.

1 Britannia 2

1852. Imperf.

8	**1**	(½d.) green	£170	£200
10		(1d.) blue	50·00	60·00
4a		(2d.) slate	£250	£1200
5		(4d.) red	£100	£275
11	**2**	6d. red	£750	£120
12a		1s. black	£225	75·00

1860. Perf.

21	**1**	(½d.) green	20·00	21·00
24		(1d.) blue	45·00	3·75
25		(4d.) red	£110	50·00
31	**2**	6d. red	£100	25·00
33		6d. orange	£140	40·00
35		1s. black	60·00	7·50

1873. Perf.

72	**2**	½d. green	15·00	50
74		1d. blue	95·00	2·25
63		3d. brown	£325	£110
75		3d. mauve	£130	9·00
76		4d. red	£140	11·00
79		6d. yellow	£140	2·25
81		1s. purple	£150	5·00

3 4

1873.

64	**3**	5s. red	£950	£300

1878. Half of No. 64 surch **1D**.

86	**3**	1d. on half 5s. red	£4750	£650

1882.

90	**4**	½d. green	20·00	1·50
92		1d. red	26·00	1·00
93		2½d. blue	90·00	1·50
96		3d. purple	4·50	22·00
97		4d. grey	£350	4·25
99		4d. brown	8·00	1·50
100		6d. black	75·00	45·00
102		1s. brown	29·00	21·00
103		5s. bistre	£160	£200

1892. Surch **HALF-PENNY**.

104	**4**	½d. on 4d. brown	2·25	6·00

6 Seal of Colony 7

1892.

105	**6**	¼d. grey and red	2·50	10
163		¼d. brown	9·50	30
106		½d. green	2·50	10
107		1d. red	4·75	10
108		2d. black and orange	8·00	75
166		2d. grey	7·50	15·00
139		2½d. blue	24·00	15
110		5d. olive	7·00	4·50
111		6d. mauve and red	16·00	2·00
168		6d. deep purple and purple	17·00	22·00
112		8d. orange and blue	4·00	25·00
113		10d. green and red	8·00	7·00
169		1s. black on green	13·00	14·00
114		2s.6d. black and orange	48·00	55·00
144		2s.6d. violet and green	65·00	£140

1897. Diamond Jubilee.

116	**7**	¼d. grey and red	6·00	60
117		½d. green	6·00	60
118		1d. red	6·00	60
119		2½d. blue	8·50	85
120		5d. brown	23·00	20·00
121		6d. mauve and red	30·00	25·00
122		8d. orange and blue	15·00	27·00
123		10d. green and red	48·00	55·00
124		2s.6d. black and orange	85·00	60·00

8 Nelson Monument 9 "Olive Blossom", 1650

1906. Death Centenary of Nelson.

145	**8**	¼d. black and grey	12·00	1·75
146		½d. black and green	11·00	15
147		1d. black and red	12·00	15
148		2d. black and yellow	1·75	4·50
149		2½d. black and blue	3·75	1·25
150		6d. black and mauve	18·00	26·00
151		1s. black and red	21·00	50·00

1906. Tercentenary of Annexation of Barbados.

152	**9**	1d. black, blue and green	12·00	25

1907. Surch **Kingston Relief Fund. 1d.**

153	**6**	1d. on 2d. black and orange	3·75	9·50

11 14

1912.

170	**11**	¼d. brown	1·50	1·50
171		½d. green	3·75	10
172		1d. red	11·00	10
173		2d. grey	4·50	15·00
174		2½d. blue	1·50	50
175		3d. purple on yellow	1·50	14·00
176		4d. black and red on yellow	3·00	20·00
177		6d. deep purple and purple	12·00	12·00

Larger type, with portrait at top centre.

178	1s. black on green	9·00	18·00
179	2s. purple and blue on blue	55·00	60·00
180	3s. green and violet	£110	£120

1916.

181	**14**	¼d. brown	75	40
182		½d. green	2·00	15
183a		1d. red	2·50	15
184		2d. grey	8·50	26·00
185		2½d. blue	4·75	3·25
186		3d. purple on yellow	5·00	9·50
187		4d. red on yellow	1·00	14·00
199		4d. black and red	1·00	3·75
188		6d. purple	5·50	5·00
189		1s. black on green	7·00	12·00
190		2s. purple on blue	16·00	7·50
191		3s. violet	65·00	£160
200		3s. green and violet	22·00	90·00

1917. Optd **WAR TAX**.

197	**11**	1d. red	50	15

16 18

1920. Victory. Inscr "VICTORY 1919".

201	**16**	¼d. black and brown	30	70
202		½d. black and green	1·00	15
203		1d. black and red	4·00	10
204		2d. black and grey	2·25	10·00
205		2½d. indigo and blue	2·75	22·00
206		3d. black and purple	3·00	6·50
207		4d. black and green	3·25	7·00
208		6d. black and orange	3·75	18·00
209	–	1s. black and green	12·00	38·00
210	–	2s. black and brown	38·00	50·00
211	–	3s. black and orange	40·00	70·00

The 1s. to 3s. show Victory full-face.

1921.

217	**18**	¼d. brown	25	10
219		½d. green	1·50	10
220		1d. red	80	10
221		2d. grey	1·75	20
222		2½d. blue	1·50	9·00
213		3d. purple on yellow	2·00	7·00
214		4d. red on yellow	1·75	18·00
225		6d. purple	3·50	5·50
215		1s. black on green	5·50	18·00
227		2s. purple on blue	10·00	19·00
228		3s. violet	16·00	75·00

19

21 Badge of the Colony

20 King Charles I and King George V

1925. Inscr "POSTAGE & REVENUE".

229	19	¼d. brown	25	10
230		½d. green	50	10
231		1d. red	50	10
231ca		1½d. orange	2·50	1·00
232		2d. grey	50	3·25
233		2½d. blue	50	80
234		3d. purple on yellow	1·00	45
235		4d. red on yellow	75	1·00
236		6d. purple	1·00	90
237		1s. black on green	2·00	7·50
238		2s. purple on blue	7·00	6·50
238a		2s.6d. red on blue	24·00	30·00
239		3s. violet	11·00	15·00

1927. Tercentenary of Settlement of Barbados.

240	20	1d. red	1·00	75

1935. Silver Jubilee. As T **13** of Antigua.

241	1d. blue and red	75	20
242	1½d. blue and grey	4·00	7·00
243	2½d. brown and blue	2·50	5·00
244	1s. grey and purple	20·00	24·00

1937. Coronation. As T **2** of Aden.

245	1d. red	30	15
246	1½d. brown	55	65
247	2½d. blue	1·25	75

1938. "POSTAGE & REVENUE" omitted.

248	21	½d. green	6·00	15
248c		½d. bistre	15	30
249a		1d. red	16·00	10
249c		1d. green	15	10
250		1½d. orange	15	40
250c		2d. purple	50	2·50
250d		2d. red	20	70
251		2½d. blue	50	60
252b		3d. brown	20	60
252c		3d. blue	20	1·75
253		4d. black	20	10
254		6d. violet	80	40
254a		8d. mauve	55	2·00
255a		1s. olive	1·00	10
256		2s.6d. purple	7·00	1·50
256a		5s. blue	4·50	9·00

22 Kings Charles I, George VI, Assembly Chamber and Mace

1939. Tercentenary of General Assembly.

257	22	½d. green	2·75	1·00
258		1d. red	2·75	1·25
259		1½d. orange	2·75	60
260		2½d. blue	3·25	7·00
261		3d. brown	3·50	5·50

1946. Victory. As T **9** of Aden.

262	1½d. orange	15	40
263	3d. brown	20	40

1947. Surch **ONE PENNY**.

264	17	1d. on 2d. red	2·00	3·00

1948. Silver Wedding. As T **10/11** of Aden.

265	1½d. orange	30	50
266	5s. blue	14·00	10·00

1949. U.P.U. As T **20/23** of Antigua.

267	1½d. orange	50	2·00
268	3d. blue	2·50	4·00
269	4d. grey	50	3·25
270	1s. olive	50	60

24 Dover Fort

35 Seal of Barbados

1950.

271	24	1c. indigo	35	3·75
272	–	2c. green	15	2·50
273	–	3c. brown and green	1·25	3·50
274	–	4c. red	15	40
275	–	6c. blue	15	2·25
276	–	8c. blue and brown	1·50	3·00
277	–	12c. blue and olive	1·00	1·25
278	–	24c. red and black	1·00	50
279	–	48c. violet	9·00	6·50
280	–	60c. green and lake	10·00	11·00
281	–	$1.20 red and olive	10·00	4·25
282	35	$2.40 black	23·00	29·00

DESIGNS—As Type **24**: HORIZ: 2c. Sugar cane breeding; 3c. Public buildings; 6c. Casting net; 8c. "Frances W. Smith" (schooner); 12c. Four-winged flyingfish; 24c. Old Main Guard Garrison; 60c. Careenage. VERT: 4c. Statue of Nelson; 48c. St. Michael's Cathedral; $1.20, Map and wireless mast.

1951. Inauguration of B.W.I. University College. As T **24/25** of Antigua.

283	3c. brown and blue	30	40
284	12c. blue and olive	70	2·25

36 King George VI and Stamp of 1852

1952. Centenary of Barbados Stamps.

285	36	3c. green and slate	35	40
286		4c. blue and red	35	1·00
287		12c. slate and green	35	1·00
288		24c. brown and sepia	35	55

37 Harbour Police

1953. As 1950 issue but with portrait or cypher (No. 301) of Queen Elizabeth II as in T **37**.

289	24	1c. indigo	10	80
290	–	2c. orange and turquoise	15	1·00
291	–	3c. black and green	1·00	90
292	–	4c. black and orange	20	20
293	37	5c. blue and red	1·00	60
294	–	6c. brown	1·25	60
314	–	8c. black and blue	60	35
296	–	12c. blue and olive	1·00	10
297	–	24c. red and black	60	10
317	–	48c. violet	5·00	1·50
318	–	60c. green and purple	10·00	4·00
300	–	$1.20 red and olive	19·00	4·50
319	35	$2.40 black	1·25	1·75

1953. Coronation. As T **13** of Aden.

302	4c. black and orange	75	10

1958. British Caribbean Federation. As T **28** of Antigua.

303	3c. green	35	20
304	6c. blue	50	2·25
305	12c. red	50	30

38 Deep Water Harbour, Bridgetown

1961. Opening of Deep Water Harbour.

306	38	4c. black and orange	25	50
307		8c. black and blue	25	60
308		24c. red and black	25	60

39 Scout Badge and Map of Barbados

1962. Golden Jubilee of Barbados Boy Scout Association.

309	39	4c. black and orange	70	10
310		12c. blue and brown	1·00	15
311		$1.20 red and green	1·60	3·75

1965. Centenary of I.T.U. As T **36** of Antigua.

320	2c. lilac and red	20	40
321	48c. yellow and drab	45	1·00

40 Deep Sea Coral

1965.

342	40	1c. black, pink and blue	10	20
323	–	2c. brown, yell & mve	20	15
324	–	3c. brown and orange	45	60
344	–	3c. brown and orange	30	2·75
325	–	4c. blue and green	15	10
326	–	5c. sepia, red and lilac	30	20
327	–	6c. multicoloured	45	20
328	–	8c. multicoloured	25	10
329	–	12c. multicoloured	35	10
330	–	15c. black, yellow and red	2·75	30
331	–	25c. blue and ochre	1·00	30
332	–	35c. red and green	1·50	15
333	–	50c. blue and green	2·00	40
334	–	$1 multicoloured	3·25	2·00
335	–	$2.50 multicoloured	2·75	4·25
355a	–	$5 multicoloured	16·00	9·00

DESIGNS—HORIZ: 2c. Lobster; 3c. (No. 324) Lined seahorse (wrongly inscribed "Hippocanpus"); 3c. (No. 344) (correctly inscribed "Hippocampus"); 4c. Sea urchin; 5c. Staghorn coral; 6c. Spot-finned butterflyfish; 8c. Rough file shell; 12c. Porcupinefish ("Balloon fish"); 15c Grey angel-fish; 25c. Brain coral; 35c. Brittle star; 50c. Four-winged flyingfish: $1 Queen or pink conch shell; $2.50, Fiddler crab. VERT: $5 Dolphin.

1966. Churchill Commemoration. As T **38** of Antigua.

336	1c. blue	10	2·75
337	4c. green	30	10
338	25c. brown	70	50
339	35c. violet	80	60

1966. Royal Visit. As T **39** of Antigua.

340	3c. black and blue	35	1·00
341	35c. black and mauve	1·40	1·00

54 Arms of Barbados

58 Policeman and Anchor

1966. Independence. Multicoloured.

356	4c. Type **54**	10	10
357	25c. Hilton Hotel (horiz)	15	10
358	35c. G. Sobers (Test cricketer)	1·50	65
359	50c. Pine Hill Dairy (horiz)	70	1·10

1967. 20th Anniv of U.N.E.S.C.O. As T **54/56** of Antigua.

360	4c. multicoloured	20	10
361	12c. yellow, violet and olive	45	50
362	25c. black, purple and orange	75	1·25

1967. Centenary of Harbour Police. Multicoloured.

363	4c. Type **58**	25	10
364	25c. Policeman and telescope	40	15
365	35c. "BPI" (police launch) (horiz)	45	15
366	50c. Policeman outside H.Q.	60	1·60

62 Governor-General Sir Winston Scott G.C.M.G

67 Radar Antenna

66 U.N. Building, Santiago, Chile

1967. 1st Anniv of Independence. Multicoloured.

367	4c. Type **62**	15	10
368	25c. Independence Arch (horiz)	25	10
369	35c. Treasury Building (horiz)	30	10
370	50c. Parliament Building (horiz)	40	90

1968. 20th Anniv of Economic Commission for Latin America.

371	66	15c. multicoloured	10	10

1968. World Meteorological Day. Multicoloured.

372	3c. Type **67**	10	10
373	25c. Meteorological Institute (horiz)	25	10
374	50c. Harp Gun and Coat of Arms	30	90

70 Lady Baden-Powell and Guide at Campfire

1968. Golden Jubilee of Girl Guiding in Barbados.

375	70	3c. blue, black and gold	20	60
376	–	25c. blue, black and gold	30	60
377	–	35c. yellow, black and gold	35	60

DESIGNS: 25c. Lady Baden-Powell and Pax Hill; 35c. Lady Baden-Powell and Guides' Badge.

73 Hands breaking Chain, and Human Rights Emblem

1968. Human Rights Year.

378	73	4c. violet, brown and green	10	20
379	–	25c. black, blue and yellow	10	25
380	–	35c. multicoloured	15	25

DESIGNS: 25c. Human Rights emblem and family enchained; 35c. Shadows of refugees beyond opening fence.

76 Racehorses in the Paddock

1969. Horse Racing. Multicoloured.

381	4c. Type **76**	25	15
382	25c. Starting-gate	25	15
383	35c. On the flat	30	15
384	50c. The winning-post	35	2·00
MS385	117 × 85 mm. Nos. 381/4	2·00	2·75

80 Map showing "CARIFTA" Countries

1969. 1st Anniv of "CARIFTA". Multicoloured.

386	5c. Type **80**	10	10
387	12c. "Strength in Unity" (horiz)	10	10
388	25c. Type **80**	10	10
389	50c. As 12c.	15	20

82 I.L.O. Emblem and "1919–1969"

1969. 50th Anniv of I.L.O.
390 **82** 4c. black, green and blue . . . 10 10
391 25c. black, mauve and red . . . 20 10

1969. No. 363 surch **ONE CENT**.
392 **58** 1c. on 4c. multicoloured . . 10 10

84 National Scout Badge

1969. Independence of Barbados Boy Scouts Association and 50th Anniv of Barbados Sea Scouts. Multicoloured.
393 5c. Type **84** 15 10
394 25c. Sea Scouts rowing . . . 45 10
395 35c. Scouts around campfire 55 10
396 50c. Scouts and National Scout H.Q. . . . . 80 1·25
MS397 155 × 115 mm. Nos. 393/6 14·00 13·00

1970. No. 326 surch **4**.
398 4c. on 5c. sepia, red and lilac 10 10

89 Lion at Gun Hill

1970. Multicoloured.
399 1c. Type **89** . . . . 10 1·50
400 2c. Trafalgar Fountain . . . 30 1·25
401 3c. Montefiore Drinking Fountain . . . . 10 1·00
402a 4c. St. James' Monument . . 30 10
403 5c. St. Ann's Fort 10 10
404 6c. Old Sugar Mill, Morgan Lewis . . . . 35 3·00
405 8c. The Cenotaph 10 10
406a 10c. South Point Lighthouse 1·25 15
407 12c. Barbados Museum (horiz) . . . . 1·50 10
408 15c. Sharon Moravian Church (horiz) 30 15
409 25c. George Washington House (horiz) 25 15
410 35c. Nicholas Abbey (horiz) 30 85
411 50c. Bowmanston Pumping Station (horiz) . . . . . 40 1·00
412 $1 Queen Elizabeth Hospital (horiz) . . . . 70 2·50
413 $2.50 Suger Factory (horiz) 1·50 4·00
467 $5 Seawell International Airport (horiz) . . . . . 6·50 5·50

105 Primary Schoolgirl

1970. 25th Anniv of U.N. Multicoloured.
415 4c. Type **105** 10 10
416 5c. Secondary schoolboy . . 10 10
417 25c. Technical student . . . 35 10
418 50c. University building . . . 55 1·50

106 Minnie Root

1970. Flowers of Barbados. Multicoloured.
419 1c. Barbados Easter lily (vert) 10 2·00
420 5c. Type **106** 40 10
421 10c. Eyelash orchid . . . . . 1·75 30
422 25c. Pride of Barbados (vert) 1·25 75
423 35c. Christmas hope . . . . 1·25 85
MS424 162 × 101 mm. Nos. 419/23. Imperf . . . . 2·00 6·00

107 "Via Dolorosa" Window, St. Margaret's Church, St. John

109 S. J. Prescod (politician)

108 "Sailfish" Dinghy

1971. Easter. Multicoloured.
425 4c. Type **107** 10 10
426 10c. "The Resurrection" (Benjamin West) 10 10
427 35c. Type **107** 15 10
428 50c. As 10c. . . . . 30 1·50

1971. Tourism. Multicoloured.
429 1c. Type **108** 10 50
430 5c. Tennis 40 10
431 12c. Horse-riding 60 10
432 25c. Water-skiing 40 20
433 50c. Scuba-diving 50 90

1971. Death Centenary of Samuel Jackman Prescod.
434 **109** 3c. multicoloured 10 15
435 35c. multicoloured 15 15

110 Arms of Barbados

1971. 5th Anniv of Independence. Multicoloured.
436 4c. Type **110** 20 10
437 15c. National flag and map 45 10
438 25c. Type **110** 45 10
439 50c. As 15c. . . . . 90 1·60

111 Transmitting "Then and Now"

1972. Centenary of Cable Link. Multicoloured.
440 4c. Type **111** 10 10
441 10c. Cable Ship "Stanley Angwin" 20 10
442 35c. Barbados Earth Station and "Intelsat 4" 35 20
443 50c. Mt. Misery and Tropospheric Scatter Station . . . . 50 1·75

112 Map and Badge

1972. Diamond Jubilee of Scouts. Multicoloured.
444 5c. Type **112** 15 10
445 15c. Pioneers of scouting (horiz) 15 10
446 25c. Scouts (horiz) 30 15
447 50c. Flags (horiz) . . . . . 60 1·00

113 Mobile Library

1972. Int Book Year. Multicoloured.
448 4c. Type **113** 20 10
449 15c. Bedford mobile cinema truck 25 10
450 25c. Public library 25 10
451 $1 Codrington College . . . 1·00 1·50

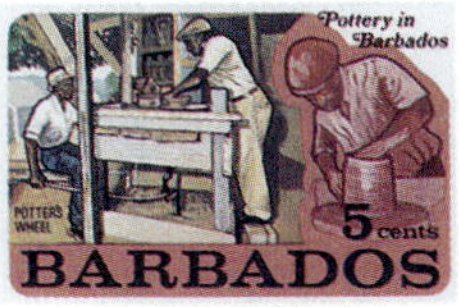

114 Potter's Wheel

1973. Pottery in Barbados. Multicoloured.
468 5c. Type **114** 10 10
469 15c. Kilns 20 10
470 25c. Finished products . . . 25 10
471 $1 Market scene . . . . . . 90 1·10

115 First Flight, 1911

1973. Aviation.
472 **115** 5c. multicoloured 30 10
473 – 15c. multicoloured 90 10
474 – 25c. blue, blk & cobalt . . 1·25 20
475 – 50c. multicoloured . . . . 2·00 1·90
DESIGNS: 15c. De Havilland Cirrus Moth on first flight to Barbados, 1928; 25c. Lockheed Super Electra, 1939; 50c. Vickers Super VC-10 airliner, 1973.

116 University Chancellor

1973. 25th Anniv of University of West Indies. Multicoloured.
476 5c. Type **116** 10 10
477 25c. Sherlock Hall 25 15
478 35c. Cave Hill Campus . . . 30 25

1974. No. 462 surch **4c.**
479 4c. on 25c. multicoloured . . 15 15

118 Old Sail Boat

1974. Fishing Boats of Barbados. Multicoloured.
480 15c. Type **118** 30 15
481 35c. Rowing-boat 55 25
482 50c. Motor fishing-boat . . . 70 70
483 $1 "Calamar" (fishing boat) 1·10 1·40
MS484 140 × 140 mm. Nos. 480/3 3·50 3·00

119 "Cattleya gaskelliana alba"

1974. Orchids. Multicoloured.
510 1c. Type **119** . . . . 15 1·25
511 2c. "Renanthera storiei" (vert) . . . . 15 1·25
512 3c. "Dendrobium" "Rose Marie" (vert) . . . . . . 15 1·00
488 4c. "Epidendrum ibaguense" (vert) . . . . 1·75 90
514 5c. "Schomburgkia humboldtii" (vert) 35 15
490 8c. "Oncidium ampliatum" (vert) . . . . 1·75 90
515 10c. "Arachnis maggie oei" (vert) 35 10
492 12c. "Dendrobium aggregatum" (vert) . . . 45 2·75
517 15c. "Paphiopedilum puddle" (vert) 70 15
493b 20c. "Spathoglottis" "The Gold" . . . . 5·00 4·75
518 25c. "Epidendrum ciliare" (Eyelash) 70 10
550 35c. "Bletia patula" (vert) 2·00 1·75
519 45c. "Phalaenopsis schilleriana" "Sunset Glow" (vert) 60 15
496 50c. As 45c. (vert) . . . . . 7·00 4·50
497 $1 "Ascocenda" "Red Gem" (vert) . . . . . . 10·00 3·25
498 $2.50 "Brassolaeliocattleya" "Nugget" . . . . 2·50 7·00
499 $5 "Caularthron bicornutum" . . . . . . 2·50 6·00
500 $10 "Vanda" "Josephine Black" (vert) . . . . . . 2·75 13·00

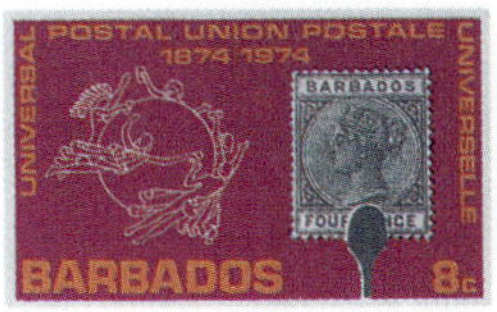

120 4d. Stamp of 1882, and U.P.U. Emblem

1974. Centenary of Universal Postal Union.
501 **120** 8c. mauve, orange & grn 10 10
502 – 35c. red, orge & brown 20 10
503 – 50c. ultram, bl & silver 25 35
504 – $1 blue, brown & black 55 1·00
MS505 126 × 101 mm. Nos. 501/4 1·75 2·50
DESIGNS: 35c. Letters encircling the globe; 50c. U.P.U. emblem and arms of Barbados; $1 Map of Barbados, sailing ship and Boeing 747 airliner.

121 Royal Yacht "Britannia"

1975. Royal Visit. Multicoloured.
506 8c. Type **121** 85 30
507 25c. Type **121** . . . . 1·40 30
508 35c. Sunset and palms . . . 60 35
509 $1 As 35c. . . . . 1·75 5·00

122 St. Michael's Cathedral

1975. 150th Anniv of Anglican Diocese. Mult.
526 5c. Type **122** 10 10
527 15c. Bishop Coleridge 15 10
528 50c. All Saints' Church . . . 45 50
529 $1 "Archangel Michael and Satan" (stained glass window, St. Michael's Cathedral, Bridgetown) . . 70 80
MS530 95 × 96 mm. Nos. 526/9 1·40 2·00

123 Pony Float

1975. Crop-over Festival. Multicoloured.
531 8c. Type **123** 10 10
532 25c. Man on stilts 10 10
533 35c. Maypole dancing . . . 15 10
534 50c. Cuban dancers 30 80
MS535 127 × 85 mm. Nos. 531/4 1·00 1·60

124 Barbados Coat of Arms

125 17th-Century Sailing Ship

1975. Coil Definitives.
536 **124** 5c. blue 15 80
537 25c. violet . . . . 25 1·10

1975. 350th Anniv of First Settlement. Multicoloured.
538 4c. Type **125** 50 20
539 10c. Bearded fig tree and fruit 30 15
540 25c. Ogilvy's 17th-century map . . . . 1·00 30
541 $1 Captain John Powell . . . 1·00 5·00
MS542 105 × 115 mm. Nos. 538/41 2·50 7·00

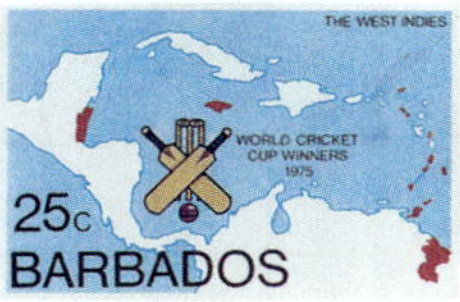

126 Map of Caribbean

1976. West Indian Victory in World Cricket Cup.
559 **126** 25c. multicoloured . . . . 1·00 1·00
560 – 45c. black and purple . . 1·00 2·00
DESIGN—VERT: 45c. The Prudential Cup.

127 Flag and Map of South Carolina

1976. Bicentenary of American Revolution. Mult.
561 15c. Type **127** 75 15
562 25c. George Washington and map of Bridgetown 75 15
563 50c. Independence Declaration . . . . 60 1·00
564 $1 Prince Hall . . . . 75 3·00

128 Early Postman

1976. 125th Anniv of Post Office Act. Multicoloured.
565 8c. Type **128** 10 10
566 35c. Modern postman . . . 25 10
567 50c. Early letter 30 75
568 $1 Delivery van . . . . . . 50 1·75

129 Coast Guard "Commander Marshall" and "T. T. Lewis" launches

1976. 10th Anniv of Independence. Multicoloured.
569 5c. Type **129** 30 20
570 15c. Reverse of currency note 30 10
571 25c. Barbados national anthem 30 20
572 $1 Independence Day parade 1·10 3·00
MS573 90 × 125 mm. Nos. 569/72 2·75 3·75

130 Arrival of Coronation Coach at Westminster Abbey

132 Maces of the House of Commons

131 Underwater Park

1977. Silver Jubilee. Multicoloured.
574 15c. Queen knighting Garfield Sobers, 1975 . . . . 30 25
575 50c. Type **130** 30 40
576 $1 Queen entering Abbey . . 30 70

1977. Natural Beauty of Barbados. Multicoloured.
577 5c. Type **131** 15 10
578 35c. Royal palms (vert) . . . 30 10
579 50c. Underwater caves . . . 40 50
580 $1 Stalagmite in Harrison's Cave (vert) . . . . 70 1·10
MS581 138 × 92 mm. Nos. 577/80 2·50 2·75

1977. 13th Regional Conference of Commonwealth Parliamentary Association.
582 **132** 10c. orange, yellow & brn 10 10
583 – 25c. green, orge & dp grn 10 10
584 – 50c. multicoloured 20 20
585 – $1 blue, orange and dp bl 55 75
DESIGNS—VERT: 25c. Speaker's Chair; 50c. Senate Chamber. HORIZ: $1 Sam Lord's Castle.

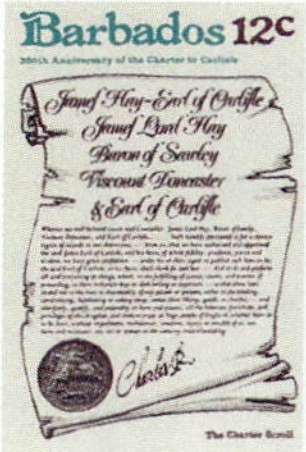

133 The Charter Scroll

135 Brown Pelican

134 Gibson's Map of Bridgtown, 1766

1977. 350th Anniv of Granting of Charter to Earl of Carlisle. Multicoloured.
586 12c. Type **133** 15 10
587 25c. The earl receiving charter 15 10
588 45c. The earl and Charles I (horiz) 30 35
589 $1 Ligon's map, 1657 (horiz) 50 1·00

1977. Royal Visit. As Nos. 574/6 but inscr "SILVER JUBILEE ROYAL VISIT".
590 15c. Garfield Sobers being knighted, 1975 . . . . . . 60 50
591 50c. Type **130** 20 75
592 $1 Queen entering Abbey . . 30 1·25

1978. 350th Anniv of Founding of Bridgetown.
593 **134** 12c. multicoloured 15 10
594 – 25c. black, green & gold 15 10
595 – 45c. multicoloured 20 15
596 – $1 multicoloured 30 60
DESIGNS: 25c. "A Prospect of Bridgetown in Barbados" (engraving by S. Copens, 1695); 45c. "Trafalgar Square, Bridgetown" (drawing by J. M. Carter, 1835); $1 The Bridges, 1978.

1978. 25th Anniv of Coronation.
597 – 50c. olive, black & blue 25 50
598 – 50c. multicoloured 25 50
599 **135** 50c. olive, black & blue 25 50
DESIGNS: No. 597, Griffin of Edward III. No. 598, Queen Elizabeth II.

136 Barbados Bridge League Logo

1978. 7th Regional Bridge Tournament, Barbados. Multicoloured.
600 5c. Type **136** 10 10
601 10c. Emblem of World Bridge Federation 15 10
602 45c. Central American and Caribbean Bridge Federation emblem . . . 25 10
603 $1 Playing cards on map of Caribbean 40 60
MS604 134 × 83 mm. Nos. 600/3 2·00 2·75

137 Camp Scene

1978. Diamond Jubilee of Guiding. Multicoloured.
605 12c. Type **137** 25 15
606 28c. Community work . . . 40 15
607 50c. Badge and "60" (vert) 55 30
608 $1 Guide badge (vert) . . . . 75 1·00

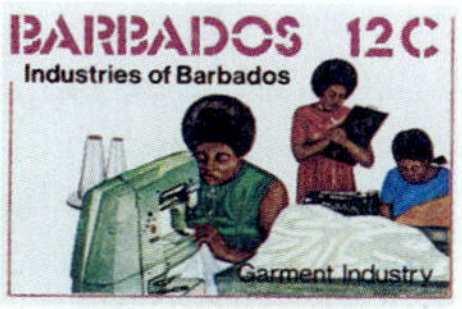

138 Garment Industry

1978. Industries of Barbados. Multicoloured.
609 12c. Type **138** 15 10
610 28c. Cooper (vert) 25 25
611 45c. Blacksmith (vert) 35 95
612 50c. Wrought iron working 40 1·50

139 "Forth" (early mail steamer)

1979. Ships. Multicoloured.
613 12c. Type **139** 35 10
614 25c. "Queen Elizabeth 2" in Deep Water Harbour . . . 55 15
615 50c. "Ra II" nearing Barbados . . . . 75 1·00
616 $1 Early mail paddle-steamer 1·00 2·50

140 1953 1c. Definitive Stamp

1979. Death Cent of Sir Rowland Hill. Mult.
617 12c. Type **140** 15 15
618 28c. 1975 350th anniv of first settlement 25c. commemorative (vert) . . . 20 30
619 45c. Penny Black with Maltese Cross postmark (vert) 30 45
MS620 137 × 90 mm. 50c. Unissued "Brittannia" blue 55 50

1979. St. Vincent Relief Fund. No. 495 surch **28c+4c ST. VINCENT RELIEF FUND.**
621 28c.+4c. on 35c. "Bletia patula" 50 60

142 Grassland Yellow Finch ("Grass Canary")

1979. Birds. Multicoloured.
622 1c. Type **142** . . . . 10 1·25
623 2c. Grey kingbird ("Rainbird") . . . . . . 10 1·25
624 5c. Lesser Antillean bullfinch ("Sparrow") . . 10 70
625 8c. Magnificent frigate bird ("Frigate Bird") . . . . 75 2·25
626 10c. Cattle egret 10 40
627 12c. Green-backed heron ("Green Gaulin") . . . . 50 1·50
627a 15c. Carib grackle ("Blackbird") . . . . 4·50 5·00
628 20c. Antillean crested hummingbird ("Humming Bird") 20 55
629 25c. Scaly-breasted ground dove ("Ground Dove") 20 60
630 28c. As 15c. . . . . 2·00 2·00
631 35c. Green-throated carib 70 70
631b 40c. Red-necked pigeon ("Ramier") . . . . 4·50 5·50
632 45c. Zenaida dove ("Wood Dove") . . . . 1·50 1·50
633 50c. As 40c. . . . . 1·50 2·00
633a 55c. American golden plover ("Black breasted Plover") 4·00 3·50
633b 60c. Bananaquit ("Yellow Breasted") . . . . 4·50 6·00
634 70c. As 60c. . . . . 2·00 3·50
635 $1 Caribbean elaenia ("Peer whistler") . . . . 2·00 1·50
636 $2.50 American redstart ("Christmas Bird") . . . 2·00 6·00
637 $5 Belted kingfisher ("Kingfisher") . . . . . 3·25 9·00
638 $10 Moorhen ("Red-seal Coot") . . . . 4·50 14·00

143 Unloading H.A.R.P. Gun on Railway Wagon at Foul Bay

1979. Space Projects Commemorations. Mult.
639 10c. Type **143** 30 10
640 12c. H.A.R.P. gun on railway wagon under tow (vert) . . 30 15
641 20c. Firing launcher (vert) . . 30 20
642 28c. Bath Earth Station and "Intelsat" 30 30
643 45c. "Intelsat" over Caribbean 35 50
644 50c. "Intelsat" over Atlantic (vert) 35 60
MS645 118 × 90 mm. $1 Lunar module descending on to Moon 1·50 1·00

144 Family

146 Private, Artillery Company, Barbados Volunteer Force, c.1909

145 Map of Barbados

1979. International Year of the Child. Multicoloured.
646 12c. Type **144** 10 10
647 28c. Ring of children and map of Barbados 15 15
648 45c. Child with teacher . . . 20 20
649 50c. Children playing 20 20
650 $1 Children and kite 35 45

1980. 75th Anniv of Rotary International. Multicoloured.
651 12c. Type **145** 15 10
652 28c. Map of Caribbean . . . 15 15
653 50c. Rotary anniversary emblem 20 35
654 $1 Paul P. Harris (founder) 30 95

1980. Barbados Regiment. Multicoloured.
655 12c. Type **146** 25 10
656 35c. Drum Major, Zouave uniform 35 15
657 50c. Sovereign's and Regimental Colours . . . 40 30
658 $1 Barbados Regiment Women's Corps 55 70

147 Early Postman

1980. "London 1980" International Stamp Exhibition. Two sheets each 122 × 125 mm containing T **147** or similar vert design. Multicoloured.
MS659 (a) 28c. × 6, Type **147**. (b) 50c. × 6, Modern postwoman and Inspector Set of 2 sheets . . . 1·00 1·25

148 Yellow-tailed Snapper

1980. Underwater Scenery. Multicoloured.
660 12c. Type **148** 20 10
661 28c. Banded butterflyfish . . 35 15

662	50c. Male and female blue-headed wrasse and princess parrotfish	45	25
663	$1 French grunt and French angelfish	70	70
MS664	136 × 110 mm. Nos. 660/3	2·50	3·75

149 Bathsheba Railway Station

1981. Early Transport. Multicoloured.

665	12c. Type **149**	30	10
666	28c. Cab stand at The Green	20	15
667	45c. Animal-drawn tram	30	30
668	70c. Horse-drawn bus	45	60
669	$1 Railway Station, Fairchild Street	70	95

150 The Blind at Work

1981. Int Year for Disabled Persons. Mult.

670	10c. Type **150**	20	10
671	25c. Sign Language (vert)	25	15
672	45c. "Be alert to the white cane" (vert)	40	25
673	$2.50 Children at play	80	3·00

151 Prince Charles dressed for Polo

152 Landship Manoeuvre

1981. Royal Wedding. Multicoloured.

674	28c. Wedding bouquet from Barbados	15	10
675	50c. Type **151**	20	15
676	$2.50 Prince Charles and Lady Diana Spencer	55	1·25

1981. Carifesta (Caribbean Festival of Arts), Barbados. Multicoloured.

677	15c. Type **152**	15	15
678	20c. Yoruba dancers	15	15
679	40c. Tuk band	20	25
680	55c. Sculpture by Frank Collymore	25	35
681	$1 Harbour scene	50	75

1981. Nos. 630, 632 and 634 surch.

682	15c. on 28c. Carib grackle	30	15
683	40c. on 45c. Zenaida dove	30	35
684	60c. on 70c. Bananaquit	30	45

154 Satellite View of Hurricane

1981. Hurricane Season.

685 **154**	35c. black and blue	35	20
686 –	50c. multicoloured	45	35
687 –	60c. multicoloured	70	50
688 –	$1 multicoloured	85	90

DESIGNS: 50c. Hurricane "Gladys" from "Apollo 7"; 60c. Police Department on hurricane watch; $1 McDonnell Banshee "hurricane chaser" aircraft.

155 Twin Falls

1981. Harrison's Cave. Multicoloured.

689	10c. Type **155**	10	10
690	20c. Stream in Rotunda Room	20	15
691	55c. Formations in Rotunda Room	25	30
692	$2.50 Cascade Pool	60	2·25

156 Black Belly Ram

1982. Black Belly Sheep. Multicoloured.

693	40c. Type **156**	15	20
694	50c. Black belly ewe	15	20
695	60c. Ewe with lambs	20	45
696	$1 Ram and ewe, with map of Barbados	35	1·50

157 Barbados Coat of Arms and Flag

1982. President Reagan's Visit. Multicoloured.

697	20c. Type **157**	40	1·25
698	20c. U.S.A. coat of arms and flag	40	1·25
699	55c. Type **157**	50	1·50
700	55c. As No. 698	50	1·50

158 Lighter

1982. Early Marine Transport. Multicoloured.

701	20c. Type **158**	20	15
702	35c. Rowing boat	35	25
703	55c. Speightstown schooner	50	40
704	$2.50 Inter-colonial schooner	1·75	2·50

159 Bride and Earl Spencer Proceeding up the Aisle

160 "To Help other People"

1982. 21st Birthday of Princess of Wales. Mult.

705	20c. Barbados coat of arms	20	15
706	60c. Princess at Llanelwedd, October, 1981	45	50
707	$1.20 Type **159**	75	1·10
708	$2.50 Formal portrait	1·25	1·90

1982. 75th Anniv of Boy Scout Movement. Mult.

709	15c. Type **160**	50	10
710	40c. "I Promise to do my Best" (horiz)	80	30
711	55c. "To do my Duty to God, the Queen and my Country" (horiz)	90	65
712	$1 National and Troop flags	1·40	1·75
MS713	119 × 93 mm. $1.50, The Scout Law	3·50	3·00

161 Arms of George Washington

1982. 250th Birth Anniv of George Washington. Multicoloured.

714	10c. Type **161**	10	10
715	55c. Washington House, Barbados	25	30
716	60c. Washington with troops	25	35
717	$2.50 Washington taking Oath	75	1·60

162 "Agraulis vanillae"

1983. Butterflies. Multicoloured.

718	20c. Type **162**	1·00	40
719	40c. "Danaus plexippus"	1·50	40
720	55c. "Hypolimnas misippus"	1·50	45
721	$2.50 "Hemiargus hanno"	3·25	3·75

163 Map of Barbados and Satellite View

1983. Commonwealth Day. Multicoloured.

722	15c. Type **163**	20	10
723	40c. Tourist beach	25	20
724	60c. Sugar cane harvesting	35	40
725	$1 Cricket match	1·25	1·10

164 U.S. Navy "M" Class Airship M-20

1983. Bicentenary of Manned Flight.

726	20c. Type **164**	35	15
727	40c. Douglas DC-3	40	40
728	55c. Vickers Viscount 837	40	50
729	$1 Lockheed TriStar 500	65	2·50

165 Nash 600, 1934 (inscr "1941")

1983. Classic Cars. Multicoloured.

730	25c. Type **165**	35	20
731	45c. Dodge D-8 coupe, 1938	40	30
732	75c. Ford Model A tourer, 1930	60	1·50
733	$2.50 Dodge Four tourer, 1918	1·25	4·50

166 Game in Progress

167 Angel playing Lute (detail "The Virgin and Child") (Masaccio)

1983. Table Tennis World Cup Competition. Multicoloured.

734	20c. Type **166**	25	20
735	65c. Map of Barbados	50	55
736	$1 World Table Tennis Cup	75	1·00

1983. Christmas. 50th Anniv of Barbados Museum.

737 **167**	10c. multicoloured	30	10
738 –	25c. multicoloured	60	20
739 –	45c. multicoloured	90	40
740 –	75c. black and gold	1·40	1·60
741 –	$2.50 multicoloured	4·50	6·00
MS742	59 × 98 mm. $2 multicoloured	1·75	2·00

DESIGNS—HORIZ: 45c. "The Barbados Museum" (Richard Day); 75c. "St. Ann's Garrison" (W. S. Hedges); $2.50, Needham's Point, Carlisle Bay. VERT: 25c., $2 Different details from "The Virgin and Child" (Masaccio).

168 Track and Field Events

1984. Olympic Games, Los Angeles.

745 **168**	50c. green, black and brown	60	45
746 –	65c. orange, blk & brn	80	60
747 –	75c. blue, black & dp bl	1·00	85
748 –	$1 brown, black and yellow	2·50	2·00
MS749	115 × 97 mm. Nos. 745/8	8·00	9·00

DESIGNS: 65c. Shooting; 75c. Sailing; $1 Cycling.

169 Global Coverage

171 Local Junior Match

170 U.P.U. 1943 3d. Stamp and Logo

1984. 250th Anniv of "Lloyd's List" (newspaper). Multicoloured.

750	45c. Type **169**	80	40
751	50c. Bridgetown harbour	90	50
752	75c. "Philosopher" (full-rigged ship), 1857	1·40	1·25
753	$1 "Sea Princess" (liner), 1984	1·40	1·60

1984. Universal Postal Union Congress, Hamburg. Sheet 90 × 75 mm.

MS754 **170**	$2 multicoloured	2·50	2·50

1984. 60th Anniv of International Chess Federation. Multicoloured.

755	25c. Type **171**	1·50	30
756	45c. Staunton and 19th-century knights	1·75	50
757	65c. Staunton queen and 18th-century queen from Macao	2·00	1·75
758	$2 Staunton and 17th-century rooks	3·75	6·50

172 Poinsettia

174 The Queen Mother at Docks

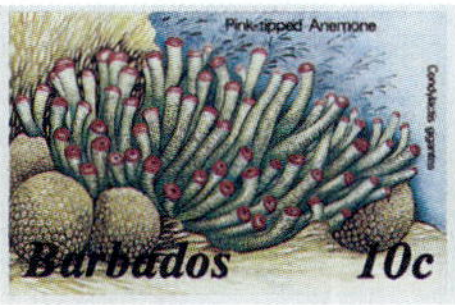

173 Pink-tipped Anemone

1984. Christmas. Flowers. Multicoloured.

759	50c. Type **172**	1·75	90
760	65c. Snow-on-the-Mountain	2·00	1·75
761	75c. Christmas Candle	2·25	3·25
762	$1 Christmas Hope	2·50	3·75

1985. Marine Life. Multicoloured.

794B	1c. Bristle worm	30	2·50
795B	2c. Spotted trunkfish	30	2·50
796A	5c. Coney	1·00	1·50
797B	10c. Type **173**	30	30
798B	20c. Christmas tree worm	30	40
799B	25c. Hermit crab	40	40
800A	35c. Animal flower	1·50	1·50
801B	40c. Vase sponge	50	50
802B	45c. Spotted moray	60	50
803B	50c. Ghost crab	60	60
804B	65c. Flamingo tongue snail	65	70
805B	75c. Sergeant major	70	75
806B	$1 Caribbean warty anemone	85	85
807B	$2.50 Green turtle	1·25	6·00
808B	$5 Rock beauty (fish)	1·50	8·00
809B	$10 Elkhorn coral	2·00	8·00

1985. Life and Times of Queen Elizabeth the Queen Mother. Multicoloured.

779	25c. In the White Drawing Room, Buckingham Palace, 1930s	50	20
780	65c. With Lady Diana Spencer at Trooping the Colour, 1981	2·50	1·00

781 75c. Type **174** 80 1·00
782 $1 With Prince Henry at his christening (from photo by Lord Snowdon) 85 1·25
MS783 91 × 73 mm. $2 In Land Rover Series I opening Syon House Garden Centre 2·50 1·50

175 Peregrine Falcon

1985. Birth Bicentenary of John J. Audubon (ornithologist). Designs showing original paintings. Multicoloured.
784 45c. Type **175** 2·25 80
785 65c. Prairie warbler (vert) 2·50 2·25
786 75c. Great blue heron (vert) 2·75 3·00
787 $1 Yellow warbler (vert) 3·00 4·00

176 Intelsat Satellite orbiting Earth

1985. 20th Anniv of Intelsat Satellite System.
788 **176** 75c. multicoloured 1·00 70

177 Traffic Policeman

1985. 150th Anniv of Royal Barbados Police. Multicoloured.
789 25c. Type **177** 80 20
790 50c. Police band on bandstand 1·40 80
791 65c. Dog handler 1·60 1·40
792 $1 Mounted policeman in ceremonial uniform 1·75 2·00
MS793 85 × 60 mm. $2 Police Band on parade (horiz.) 1·50 2·75

1986. 60th Birthday of Queen Elizabeth II. As T **110** of Ascension. Multicoloured.
810 25c. Princess Elizabeth aged two, 1928 40 20
811 50c. At University College of West Indies, Jamaica, 1953 50 40
812 65c. With Duke of Edinburgh, Barbados, 1985 70 50
813 75c. At banquet in Sao Paulo, Brazil, 1968 70 60
814 $2 At Crown Agents Head Office, London, 1983 1·10 1·50

178 Canadair DC-4M2 North Star of Trans-Canada Airlines

1986. "Expo '86" World Fair, Vancouver. Mult.
815 50c. Type **178** 75 50
816 $2.50 "Lady Nelson" (cargo liner) 2·00 2·50

1986. "Ameripex '86" International Stamp Exhibition, Chicago. As T **164** of Bahamas, showing Barbados stamps. Multicoloured.
817 45c. 1976 Bicentenary of American Revolution 25c. 70 35
818 50c. 1976 Bicentenary of American Revolution 50c. 80 55
819 65c. 1981 Hurricane Season $1 90 1·00
820 $1 1982 Visit of President Reagan 55c. 1·00 1·75
MS821 90 × 80 mm. $2 Statue of Liberty and liner "Queen Elizabeth 2" 10·00 12·00
No. **MS**821 also commemorates the Centenary of the Statue of Liberty.

1986. Royal Wedding. As T **112** of Ascension. Multicoloured.
822 45c. Prince Andrew and Miss Sarah Ferguson 75 35
823 $1 Prince Andrew in midshipman's uniform 1·25 75

179 Transporting Electricity Poles, 1923

180 "Alpinia purpurata" and Church Window

1986. 75th Anniv of Electricity in Barbados. Multicoloured.
824 10c. Type **179** 15 10
825 25c. Heathman Ladder, 1935 (vert) 25 20
826 65c. Transport fleet, 1941 60 60
827 $2 Bucket truck, 1986 (vert) 1·60 2·00

1986. Christmas. Multicoloured.
828 25c. Type **180** 20 20
829 50c. "Anthurium andraeanum" 45 45
830 75c. "Heliconia rostrata" 75 80
831 $2 "Heliconia × psittacorum" 1·50 4·25

181 Shot Putting

1987. 10th Anniv of Special Olympics. Multicoloured.
832 15c. Type **181** 25 15
833 45c. Wheelchair racing 45 30
834 65c. Long jumping 60 65
835 $2 Logo and slogan 1·25 2·50

182 Barn Swallow

183 Sea Scout saluting

1987. "Capex '87" International Stamp Exhibition, Toronto. Birds. Multicoloured.
836 25c. Type **182** 2·00 50
837 50c. Yellow warbler 2·25 1·75
838 65c. Audubon's shearwater 2·25 1·75
839 75c. Black-whiskered vireo 2·50 3·25
840 $1 Scarlet tanager 2·75 4·00

1987. 75th Anniv of Scouting in Barbados. Multicoloured.
841 10c. Type **183** 20 10
842 25c. Scout jamboree 30 20
843 65c. Scout badges 65 45
844 $2 Scout band 1·60 1·75

184 Bridgetown Synagogue

1987. Restoration of Bridgetown Synagogue. Multicoloured.
845 50c. Type **184** 2·00 1·75
846 65c. Interior of Synagogue 2·25 2·25
847 75c. Ten Commandments (vert) 2·50 2·50
848 $1 Marble laver (vert) 2·75 3·75

185 Arms and Colonial Seal

1987. 21st Anniv of Independence. Mult.
849 25c. Type **185** 50 20
850 45c. Flags of Barbados and Great Britain 1·25 35
851 65c. Silver dollar and one penny coins 1·25 55
852 $2 Colours of Barbados Regiment 2·50 2·75
MS853 94 × 56 mm. $1.50, Prime Minister E. W. Barrow (vert) 1·50 1·75

186 Herman C. Griffith

1988. West Indian Cricket. Each showing portrait, cricket equipment and early belt buckle. Multicoloured.
854 15c. E. A. (Manny) Martindale 2·50 75
855 45c. George Challenor 3·25 75
856 50c. Type **186** 3·50 2·25
857 75c. Harold Austin 3·75 3·50
858 $2 Frank Worrell 4·50 11·00

187 "Kentropyx borckianus"

188 Cycling

1988. Lizards of Barbados. Multicoloured.
859 10c. Type **187** 1·75 50
860 50c. "Hemidactylus mabouia" 3·00 70
861 65c. "Anolis extremus" 3·00 1·25
862 $2 "Gymnophthalmus underwoodii" 6·00 10·00

1988. Olympic Games, Seoul. Multicoloured.
863 25c. Type **188** 1·75 40
864 45c. Athletics 70 30
865 75c. Relay swimming 85 65
866 $2 Yachting 2·00 2·75
MS867 114 × 63 mm. Nos. 863/6 4·25 3·00

1988. 300th Anniv of Lloyd's of London. As T **123** of Ascension.
868 40c. multicoloured 55 30
869 50c. multicoloured 65 35
870 65c. multicoloured 1·50 45
871 $2 blue and red 6·50 3·00
DESIGNS—VERT: 40c. Royal Exchange, 1774; $2 Sinking of "Titanic", 1912. HORIZ: 50c. Early sugar mill; 65c. "Author" (container ship).

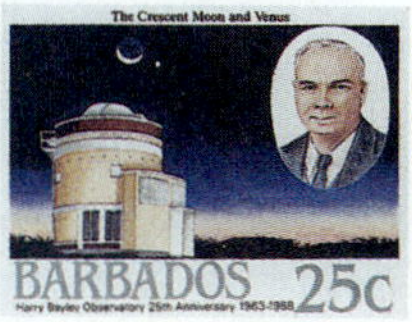

189 Harry Bayley and Observatory

1988. 25th Anniv of Harry Bayley Observatory. Multicoloured.
872 25c. Type **189** 60 20
873 65c. Observatory with North Star and Southern Cross constellations 1·40 75
874 75c. Andromeda galaxy 1·60 90
875 $2 Orion constellation 3·00 6·00

190 L.I.A.T. Hawker Siddeley H.S.748

1989. 50th Anniv of Commercial Aviation in Barbados. Multicoloured.
876 25c. Type **190** 2·50 40
877 65c. Pan Am Douglas DC-8-62 3·25 1·25
878 75c. British Airways Concorde at Grantley Adams Airport 3·75 1·75
879 $2 Caribbean Air Cargo Boeing 707-351C 6·00 9·50

191 Assembly Chamber

1989. 350th Anniv of Parliament.
880 **191** 25c. multicoloured 40 20
881 – 50c. multicoloured 60 35
882 – 75c. blue and black 1·00 50
883 – $2.50 multicoloured 2·50 2·25
DESIGNS: 50c. The Speaker; 75c. Parliament Buildings, c. 1882; $2.50, Queen Elizabeth II and Prince Philip in Parliament.

192 Brown Hare

193 Bread 'n Cheese

1989. Wildlife Preservation. Multicoloured.
884 10c. Type **192** 80 30
885 50c. Red-footed tortoise (horiz) 2·00 70
886 65c. Savanna ("Green") monkey 2·25 1·25
887 $2 "Bufo marinus" (toad) (horiz) 4·00 8·00
MS888 87 × 97 mm. $1 Small Indian mongoose 1·25 1·50

1989. 35th Commonwealth Parliamentary Conference. Square design as T **191**. Mult.
MS889 108 × 69 mm. $1 Barbados Mace 1·00 1·50

1989. Wild Plants. Multicoloured.
921 2c. Type **193** 50 1·75
891 5c. Scarlet cordia 50 1·00
892 10c. Columnar cactus 50 30
893 20c. Spiderlily 50 30
925 25c. Rock balsam 65 20
895 30c. Hollyhock 70 25
895a 35c. Red sage 1·25 1·00
927 45c. Yellow shak-shak 75 35
928 50c. Whitewood 80 40
898 55c. Bluebell 1·00 55
930 65c. Prickly sage 90 55
900 70c. Seaside samphire 1·25 1·25
901 80c. Flat-hand dildo 1·75 1·40
901a 90c. Herringbone 1·75 2·25
902 $1.10 Lent tree 1·50 2·25
934 $2.50 Rodwood 1·90 4·00
935 $5 Cowitch 3·75 7·00
936 $10 Maypole 7·00 10·00

194 Water Skiing

195 Barbados 1852 1d. Stamp

1989. "World Stamp Expo '89" International Stamp Exn., Washington. Watersports. Mult.
906 25c. Type **194** 1·50 40
907 50c. Yachting 2·50 1·00
908 65c. Scuba diving 2·50 1·75
909 $2.50 Surfing 6·50 11·00

1990. 150th Anniv of the Penny Black and "Stamp World London '90" International Stamp Exn.
910 **195** 25c. green, black and yellow 1·50 40
911 – 50c. multicoloured 2·00 1·00
912 – 65c. multicoloured 2·00 1·50
913 – $2.50 multicoloured 5·00 9·00
MS914 90 × 86 mm. 50c. multicoloured; 50c. multicoloured 1·75 2·75
DESIGNS: 50c. 1882 1d. Queen Victoria stamp; 65c. 1899 2d. stamp; $2.50, 1912 3d. stamp; miniature sheet, 50c. Great Britain Penny Black, 50c. Barbados "1906" Nelson Centenary 1s.

196 Bugler and Jockeys

1990. Horse Racing. Multicoloured.
915 25c. Type **196** 60 30
916 45c. Horse and jockey in parade ring 85 50
917 75c. At the finish 1·25 85
918 $2 Leading in the winner (vert) 2·75 6·00

1990. 90th Birthday of Queen Elizabeth the Queen Mother. As T **134** of Ascension.
919 75c. multicoloured 75 60
920 $2.50 black and green 2·25 3·25

DESIGNS—21 × 36 mm: 75c. Lady Elizabeth Bowes-Lyon, April 1923 (from painting by John Lander). 29 × 37 mm: $2.50, Lady Elizabeth Bowes-Lyon on her engagement, January 1923.

197 "Orthemis ferruginea" (dragonfly)

1990. Insects. Multicoloured.

937	50c. Type **197**	1·50	80
938	65c. "Ligyrus tumulosus" (beetle)	1·75	1·00
939	75c. "Neoconocephalus sp." (grasshopper)	2·00	1·25
940	$2 "Bostra maxwelli" (stick-insect)	3·50	5·50

1990. Visit of the Princess Royal. Nos. 925, 901 and 903 optd **VISIT OF HRH THE PRINCESS ROYAL OCTOBER 1990**.

941	25c. Rock balsam	2·25	50
942	80c. Flat-hand dildo	3·50	2·00
943	$2.50 Rodwood	8·50	12·00

199 Star

201 Sorting Daily Catch

200 Adult Male Yellow Warbler

1990. Christmas. Multicoloured.

944	20c. Type **199**	65	20
945	50c. Figures from crib	1·00	50
946	$1 Stained glass window	2·00	1·50
947	$2 Angel (statue)	3·00	5·50

1991. Endangered Species. Yellow Warbler. Multicoloured.

948	10c. Type **200**	1·40	80
949	20c. Pair feeding chicks in nest	2·00	80
950	45c. Female feeding chicks in nest	2·50	80
951	$1 Male with fledgeling	4·00	5·25

1991. Fishing in Barbados. Multicoloured.

952	5c. Type **201**	50	50
953	50c. Line fishing (horiz)	1·75	90
954	75c. Fish cleaning (horiz)	2·25	1·25
955	$2.50 Game fishing	4·50	6·50

202 Masonic Building, Bridgetown

1991. 250th Anniv of Freemasonry in Barbados (1990).

956	**202** 25c. multicoloured	1·75	50
957	– 65c. multicoloured	2·50	1·25
958	– 75c. black, yellow & brn	2·50	1·25
959	– $2.50 multicoloured	5·00	7·00

DESIGNS: 65c. Compass and square (masonic symbols); 75c. Royal Arch jewel; $2.50, Ceremonial apron, columns and badge.

203 "Battus polydamus"

1991. "Phila Nippon '91" International Stamp Exhibition, Tokyo. Butterflies. Multicoloured.

960	20c. Type **203**	1·00	40
961	50c. "Urbanus proteus" (vert)	1·50	65
962	65c. "Phoebis sennae"	1·60	95
963	$2.50 "Junonia evarete" (vert)	4·00	6·00
MS964	87 × 86 mm. $4 "Vanessa cardui"	9·00	10·00

204 School Class

1991. 25th Anniv of Independence. Multicoloured.

965	10c. Type **204**	30	20
966	25c. Barbados Workers' Union Labour College	45	30
967	65c. Building a house	1·00	90
968	75c. Sugar cane harvesting	1·00	1·00
969	$1 Health clinic	1·25	2·00
MS970	123 × 97 mm. $2.50, Gordon Greenidge and Desmond Haynes (cricketers) (vert)	12·00	12·00

205 Jesus carrying Cross

1992. Easter. Multicoloured.

971	35c. Type **205**	80	30
972	70c. Crucifixion	1·40	90
973	90c. Descent from the Cross	1·50	1·25
974	$3 Risen Christ	4·00	6·50

206 Cannon Ball

1992. Conservation. Flowering Trees. Multicoloured.

975	10c. Type **206**	60	40
976	30c. Golden shower tree	1·00	50
977	80c. Frangipani	2·25	2·50
978	$1.10 Flamboyant	2·75	3·00

207 "Epidendrum" "Costa Rica"

1992. Orchids. Multicoloured.

979	55c. Type **207**	85	65
980	65c. "Cattleya guttaca"	1·00	1·00
981	70c. "Laeliacattleya" "Splashing Around"	1·00	1·00
982	$1.40 "Phalaenopsis" "Kathy Saegert"	1·60	3·00

208 Mini Moke and Gun Hill Signal Station, St. George

1992. Transport and Tourism. Multicoloured.

983	5c. Type **208**	65	60
984	35c. Tour bus and Bathsheba Beach, St. Joseph	1·25	30
985	90c. B.W.I.A. McDonnell Douglas MD-83 over Grantley Adams Airport	3·00	2·25
986	$2 "Festivale" (liner) and Bridgetown harbour	4·25	6·50

209 Barbados Gooseberry

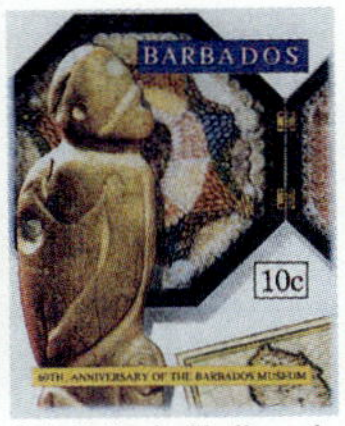

212 Sailor's Shell-work Valentine and Carved Amerindian

211 18 pdr Culverin of 1625, Denmark Fort

1993. Cacti and Succulents. Multicoloured.

987	10c. Type **209**	55	30
988	35c. Night-blooming cereus	1·25	35
989	$1.40 Aloe	3·00	3·50
990	$2 Scrunchineel	3·50	5·50

1993. 75th Anniv of Royal Air Force. As T **149** of Ascension. Multicoloured.

991	10c. Hawker Hunter F.6	75	40
992	30c. Handley Page Victor K2	1·25	40
993	70c. Hawker Typhoon IB	1·75	1·50
994	$3 Hawker Hurricane Mk I	3·75	6·50
MS995	110 × 77 mm. 50c. Armstrong Whitworth Siskin IIIA; 50c. Supermarine S6B; 50c. Supermarine Walrus Mk I; 50c. Hawker Hart	2·50	2·75

1993. 14th World Orchid Conference, Glasgow. Nos. 979/82 optd **WORLD ORCHID CONFERENCE 1993**.

996	55c. Type **207**	1·25	1·25
997	65c. "Cattleya guttaca"	1·40	1·40
998	70c. "Laeliacattleya" "Splashing Around"	1·40	1·40
999	$1.40 "Phalaenopsis" "Kathy Saegert"	2·25	3·50

1993. 17th-century English Cannon. Mult.

1000	5c. Type **211**	30	50
1001	45c. 6 pdr of 1649–60, St. Ann's Fort	85	50
1002	$1 9 pdr demi-culverin of 1691, The Main Guard	1·75	2·00
1003	$2.50 32 pdr demi–cannon of 1693–94, Charles Fort	2·75	4·50

1993. 60th Anniv of Barbados Museum. Mult.

1004	10c. Type **212**	50	50
1005	75c. "Barbados Mulatto Girl" (Agostino Brunias)	1·50	1·50
1006	90c. Morris Cup and soldier of West India Regiment, 1858	2·25	2·50
1007	$1.10 Ogilby's map of Barbados, 1679, and Ashanti gold weights	2·75	3·25

213 Plesiosaurus

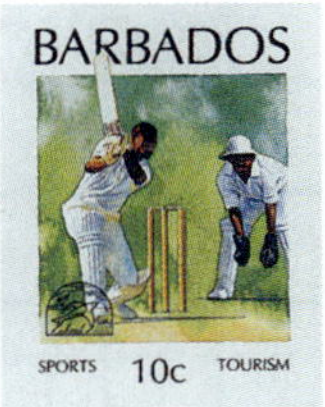

214 Cricket

1993. Prehistoric Aquatic Animals. Mult.

1008	90c. Type **213**	2·25	3·00
1009	90c. Ichthyosaurus	2·25	3·00
1010	90c. Elasmosaurus	2·25	3·00
1011	90c. Mosasaurus	2·25	3·00
1012	90c. Archelon	2·25	3·00

Nos. 1008/12 were printed together, se-tenant, with the background forming a composite design.

1994. Sports and Tourism. Multicoloured.

1013	10c. Type **214**	1·25	75
1014	35c. Rally driving	1·40	50
1015	50c. Golf	2·25	1·75
1016	70c. Long distance running	1·75	2·50
1017	$1.40 Swimming	2·00	3·50

215 Whimbrel

1994. "Hong Kong '94" Int Stamp Exhibition. Migratory Birds. Multicoloured.

1018	10c. Type **215**	50	50
1019	35c. Pacific golden plover ("American Golden Plover")	1·00	50
1020	70c. Ruddy turnstone	1·50	1·50
1021	$3 Louisiana heron ("Tricoloured Heron")	3·50	5·50

216 Bathsheba Beach and Logo

1994. 1st United Nations Conference of Small Island Developing States. Multicoloured.

1022	10c. Type **216**	25	15
1023	65c. Pico Tenneriffe	1·00	70
1024	90c. Ragged Point Lighthouse	6·00	2·50
1025	$2.50 Consett Bay	3·00	5·50

217 William Demas

219 Private, 2nd West India Regt, 1860

218 Dutch Flyut, 1695

1994. First Recipients of Order of the Caribbean Community. Multicoloured.

1026	70c. Type **217**	70	1·00
1027	70c. Sir Shridath Ramphal	70	1·00
1028	70c. Derek Walcott	70	1·00

1994. Ships. Multicoloured.

1075	5c. Type **218**	2·50	2·75
1076	10c. "Geestport" (freighter), 1994	75	50
1031B	25c. H.M.S. "Victory" (ship of the line), 1805	75	40
1078	30c. "Royal Viking Queen" (liner), 1994	50	30
1079	35c. H.M.S. "Barbados" (frigate), 1945	50	30
1080	45c. "Faraday" (cable ship), 1924	50	35
1081	50c. U.S.C.G. "Hamilton" (coastguard cutter), 1974	6·50	75
1082	65c. H.M.C.S. "Saguenay" (destroyer), 1939	75	70
1083	70c. "Inanda" (cargo liner), 1928	75	70
1084	80c. H.M.S. "Rodney" (battleship), 1944	75	70
1085	90c. U.S.S. "John F. Kennedy" (aircraft carrier), 1982	75	70
1086	$1.10 "William and John" (immigrant ship), 1627	1·00	1·00
1087	$5 U.S.C.G. "Champlain" (coastguard cutter), 1931	4·00	5·00
1042B	$10 "Artist" (full-rigged ship), 1877	7·00	9·00

1995. Bicentenary of Formation of West India Regiment. Multicoloured.

1043	30c. Type **219**	75	35
1044	50c. Light Company private, 4th West India Regt, 1795	90	55
1045	70c. Drum Major, 3rd West India Regt, 1860	1·25	1·40
1046	$1 Privates in undress and working dress, 5th West India Regt, 1815	1·40	1·50
1047	$1.10 Troops from 1st and 2nd West India Regts in Review Order, 1874	1·60	1·90

1995. 50th Anniv of End of Second World War. As T **161** of Ascension. Multicoloured.

1048	10c. Barbadian Bren gun crew	60	50
1049	35c. Avro Type 683 Lancaster bomber	90	50
1050	55c. Supermarine Spitfire	1·25	75
1051	$2.50 "Davisian" (cargo liner)	3·00	4·75
MS1052	75 × 85 mm. $2 Reverse of 1939–45 War Medal (vert)	1·50	2·25

220 Member of 1st Barbados Combermere Scout Troop, 1912

1995. 300th Anniv of Combermere School. Mult.
1053 5c. Type **220** 25 40
1054 20c. Violin and sheet of music 45 30
1055 35c. Sir Frank Worrell (cricketer) (vert) . . . . . 1·50 55
1056 $3 Painting by pupil . . . . 2·25 4·50
MS1057 174 × 105 mm. Nos. 1053/6 and 90c. 1981 Carifesta 55c. stamp. . . . . 4·00 4·75

1995. 50th Anniv of United Nations. As T **213** of Bahamas. Multicoloured.
1058 30c. Douglas C-124 Globemaster (transport), Korea, 1950–53 . . . . . 70 40
1059 45c. Royal Navy Sea King helicopter . . . . 1·00 50
1060 $1.40 Westland Wessex helicopter, Cyprus, 1964 1·50 2·00
1061 $2 Sud Aviation SA 341 Gazelle helicopter, Cyprus, 1964 . . . . . . 1·50 2·75

221 Blue Beauty

223 Football

222 Magnifying Glass, Tweezers and 1896 Colony Seal ¼d. Stamp

1995. Water Lilies. Multicoloured.
1062 10c. Type **221** 45 30
1063 65c. White water lily . . . . 1·25 60
1064 70c. Sacred lotus . . . . 1·25 60
1065 $3 Water hyacinth . . . . . 3·00 5·00

1996. Centenary of Barbados Philatelic Society. Each showing magnifying glass, tweezers and stamp. Multicoloured.
1066 10c. Type **222** 30 30
1067 55c. 1906 Tercentenary of Annexation 1d. 65 45
1068 $1.10 1920 Victory 1s. . . . . 1·25 1·40
1069 $1.40 1937 Coronation 2½d. 1·60 2·50

1996. Cent of Modern Olympic Games. Mult.
1070 20c. Type **223** 40 30
1071 30c. Relay running 45 30
1072 55c. Basketball . . . . . . 1·60 60
1073 $3 Rhythmic gymnastics . . 2·25 4·00
MS1074 68 × 89 mm. $2.50, "The Discus Thrower" (Myron) . . 2·00 3·25

224 Douglas DC-10 of Canadian Airlines

1996. "CAPEX '96" International Stamp Exhibition, Toronto. Aircraft. Multicoloured.
1089 10c. Type **224** 80 30
1090 90c. Boeing 767 of Air Canada . . . . 1·75 80
1091 $1 Airbus Industrie A320 of Air Canada . . . . . . 1·75 1·25
1092 $1.40 Boeing 767 of Canadian Airlines . . . . 2·25 3·50

225 Chattel House

1996. Chattel Houses.
1093 **225** 35c. multicoloured . . . 40 25
1094 – 70c. multicoloured . . . 70 60
1095 – $1.10 multicoloured . . 90 1·10
1096 – $2 multicoloured . . . . 1·60 3·25
DESIGNS: 70c. to $2, Different houses.

226 "Going to Church"

1996. Christmas. 50th Anniv of U.N.I.C.E.F. Children's Paintings. Multicoloured.
1097 10c. Type **226** 35 15
1098 30c. "The Tuk Band" . . . 55 25
1099 55c. "Singing carols" . . . 70 40
1100 $2.50 "Decorated house" . . 1·75 3·50

227 Doberman Pinscher

1997. "HONG KONG '97" International Stamp Exhibition. Dogs. Multicoloured.
1101 10c. Type **227** . . . . . . 1·00 50
1102 30c. German shepherd . . . 1·75 40
1103 90c. Japanese akita . . . . 2·25 1·25
1104 $3 Irish red setter . . . . . 4·75 7·00

228 Barbados Flag and State Arms

1997. Visit of President Clinton of U.S.A. Multicoloured.
1105 35c. Type **228** . . . . . . 1·00 75
1106 90c. American flag and arms 1·50 1·25

229 Measled Cowrie

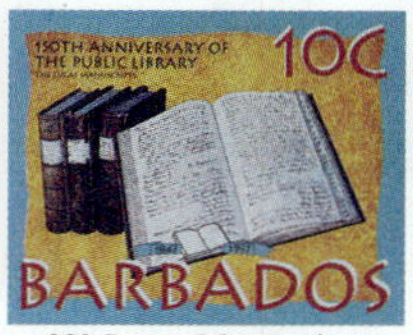

230 Lucas Manuscripts

1997. Shells. Multicoloured.
1107 5c. Type **229** 30 30
1108 35c. Trumpet triton 75 25
1109 90c. Scotch bonnet . . . . 1·40 90
1110 $2 West Indian murex . . . 2·00 3·50
MS1111 71 × 76 mm. $2.50, Underwater scene . . . . . . 2·50 3·75

1997. 150th Anniv of the Public Library Service. Multicoloured.
1112 10c. Type **230** 25 15
1113 30c. Librarian reading to children 50 25
1114 70c. Mobile library van . . 1·10 60
1115 $3 Man using computer . . 2·50 4·50

231 Barbados Cherry

1997. Local Fruits. Multicoloured.
1116 35c. Type **231** 45 30
1117 40c. Sugar apple 50 30
1118 $1.15 Soursop . . . . . . 1·10 1·25
1119 $1.70 Pawpaw . . . . . . 1·75 2·75

232 Arms of former British Caribbean Federation

1998. Birth Centenary of Sir Grantley Adams (statesman). Sheet 118 × 74 mm, containing T **232** and similar vert designs. Multicoloured.
MS1120 $1 Type **232**; $1 Sir Grantley Adams; $1 Flag of former British Caribbean Federation . . . . 6·50 7·00

1998. Diana, Princess of Wales Commemoration. Sheet 145 × 70 mm, containing vert designs as T **177** of Ascension. Multicoloured.
MS1121 $1.15, Wearing blue hat, 1985; $1.15, Wearing red jacket, 1981; $1.15, Wearing tiara, 1987; $1.15, Wearing black jacket . . 3·25 3·75

233 Environment Regeneration

1998. 50th Anniv of Organization of American States. Multicoloured.
1122 15c. Type **233** 20 15
1123 $1 Stilt dancing 70 80
1124 $2.50 Judge and figure of Justice . . . . 1·75 3·25

234 Frank Worrell Hall

1998. 50th Anniv of University of West Indies. Multicoloured.
1125 40c. Type **234** 50 30
1126 $1.15 Student graduating . . 1·25 1·25
1127 $1.40 50th anniversary plaque . . . . 1·50 2·00
1128 $1.75 Quadrangle . . . . . 2·75 4·00

235 Catamaran

236 Racing Yacht

1998. Tourism. Multicoloured.
1129 10c. Type **235** 45 30
1130 45c. "Jolly Roger" (tourist schooner) (horiz) . . . . 1·00 35
1131 70c. "Atlantis" (tourist submarine) (horiz) . . . . 1·50 1·10
1132 $2 "Harbour Master" (ferry) 3·25 4·00

1999. "Australia '99" World Stamp Exhibition, Melbourne. Sheet 90 × 90 mm.
MS1133 **236** $4 multicoloured . . 3·50 5·00

237 Juvenile Piping Plover in Shallow Water

1999. Endangered Species. Piping Plover. Mult.
1134 10c. Type **237** 20 20
1135 45c. Female with eggs . . . 55 55
1136 50c. Male and female with fledglings 55 75
1137 70c. Male in shallow water 65 1·10

1999. 30th Anniv of First Manned Landing on Moon. As T **186** of Ascension. Multicoloured.
1138 40c. Astronaut in training 55 45
1139 45c. 1st stage separation . . 55 45
1140 $1.15 Lunar landing module 1·40 1·25
1141 $1.40 Docking with service module . . . . 1·50 2·25
MS1142 90 × 80 mm. $2.50, Earth as seen from Moon (circular, 40 mm diam) . . . . 2·25 3·25

238 Hare running

1999. "China '99" International Stamp Exhibition, Beijing. Hares. Multicoloured.
1143 70c. Type **238** . . . . . . 1·40 1·50
1144 70c. Head of hare . . . . . 1·40 1·50
1145 70c. Baby hares suckling . . 1·40 1·50
1146 70c. Hares boxing . . . . . 1·40 1·50
1147 70c. Two leverets . . . . . 1·40 1·50
Nos. 1143/7 were printed together, se-tenant, forming a composite background design.

239 Horse-drawn Mail Cart

1999. 125th Anniv of U.P.U. Multicoloured.
1148 10c. Type **239** . . . . . . 1·25 35
1149 45c. Mail van . . . . 1·50 40
1150 $1.75 Sikorsky S42 flying boat . . . . 2·00 2·25
1151 $2 Computer and fax machine . . . . 2·00 2·50

240 Globe and Barbados Flag

2000. New Millennium. Sheet 90 × 80 mm.
MS1152 **240** $3 multicoloured . . 3·50 4·00

241 Drax Hall House

2000. Pride of Barbados. Multicoloured.
1153 5c. Type **241** 20 30
1154 10c. Reaping sugar cane (vert) 20 30
1155 40c. Needham's Point Lighthouse (vert) . . . . 1·50 60
1156 45c. Port St. Charles . . . 60 30
1157 65c. Interior of Jewish synagogue . . . . 1·75 1·00
1158 70c. Bridgetown Port (I) 1·50 2·00
1158a 70c. Bridgetown Port (II) 1·50 1·50
1159 90c. Harrison's Cave . . . 1·00 60
1160 $1.15 Villa Nova . . . . . 1·10 85
1161 $1.40 Cricket at Kensington Oval . . . . 2·25 1·60
1162 $1.75 Sunbury House . . . 1·50 1·75
1163 $2 Bethel Methodist Church . . . . 1·75 2·00
1164 $3 Peacock, Barbados Wildlife Reserve (vert) 2·75 3·00
1165 $5 Royal Westmoreland Golf Course (vert) . . . 6·00 6·50
1166 $10 Grantley Adams International Airport . . 9·00 10·00

Two types of 70c.:
I. Central design reversed. The bows of three of the four liners shown point to the right.
II. Design corrected. The bows of three of the four liners point to the left.

242 Sir Conrad Hunte batting

2000. West Indies Cricket Tour and 100th Test Match at Lord's. Multicoloured.
1167 45c. Type **242** 75 35
1168 90c. Malcolm Marshall bowling . . . . 1·50 75
1169 $2 Sir Garfield Sobers batting . . . . 2·50 3·00
MS1170 121 × 104 mm. $2.50, Lord's Cricket Ground (horiz) 2·75 3·25

243 Golf Clubs, Flag and Ball on Tee Peg

2000. "EXPO 2000" World Stamp Exhibition, Anaheim, U.S.A. Golf. Multicoloured.

1171	25c. Type **243**	70	35
1172	40c. Golfer teeing off on top of giant ball	90	35
1173	$1.40 Golfer on green	1·75	1·90
1174	$2 Golfer putting	2·25	3·00

244 Bentley Mk VI Drophead Coupe, 1947

2000. Vintage Cars. Multicoloured.

1175	10c. Type **244**	25	15
1176	30c. Vanden Plas Princess Limousine, 1964	50	25
1177	90c. Austin Atlantic, 1952	1·00	70
1178	$3 Bentley Special, 1950	3·00	4·00

245 Thread Snake

2001. "HONG KONG 2001" Stamp Exhibition. Sheet 125 × 80 mm.

MS1179	**245** $3 multicoloured	3·50	4·00

246 Lizardfish

2001. Deep Sea Creatures. Multicoloured.

1180	45c. Type **246**	50	60
1181	45c. Golden-tailed moray	50	60
1182	45c. Black-barred soldierfish	50	60
1183	45c. Golden zoanthid	50	60
1184	45c. Sponge brittle star	50	60
1185	45c. Magnificent feather duster	50	60
1186	45c. Bearded fireworm	50	60
1187	45c. Lima shell	50	60
1188	45c. Yellow tube sponge	50	60

247 Octagonal, Fish and Butterfly Kites

2001. "Philanippon '01" International Stamp Exhibition, Tokyo. Kites. Multicoloured.

1189	10c. Type **247**	20	15
1190	65c. Hexagonal, bird and geometric kites	60	45
1191	$1.40 Policeman, Japanese and butterfly kites	1·40	1·50
1192	$1.75 Anti-drug, geisha and eagle kites	1·60	1·75

248 George Washington on the Quay, 1751

249 Shaggy Bear(Traditional Carnival Character)

2001. 250th Anniv of George Washington's Visit to Barbados. Multicoloured.

1193	45c. Type **248**	65	40
1194	50c. George Washington in Barbados	65	40
1195	$1.15 George Washington superimposed on Declaration of Independence, 1776	1·50	1·00
1196	$2.50 Needham's Point Fort, 1750	2·50	3·25
MS1197	110 × 90 mm. $3 George Washington as President of U.S.A.	2·50	3·00

2001. 35th Anniv of Independence. Multicoloured.

1198	25c. Type **249**	40	20
1199	45c. Tuk band	70	30
1200	$1 Landship Dancers	1·25	80
1201	$2 Guitar, saxophone and words of National Anthem	2·25	2·75

2002. Golden Jubilee. As T **200** of Ascension.

1202	10c. black, violet and gold	45	20
1203	70c. multicoloured	1·00	60
1204	$1 black, violet and gold	1·25	1·00
1205	$1.40 multicoloured	1·50	2·00
MS1206	162 × 95 mm. Nos. 1202/5 and $3 multicoloured	4·75	5·50

DESIGNS—HORIZ: 10c. Princess Elizabeth; 70c. Queen Elizabeth in cerise hat; $1 Queen Elizabeth wearing Imperial State Crown, Coronation, 1953; $1.40, Queen Elizabeth in purple feathered hat. VERT (38 × 51 mm)—$3 Queen Elizabeth after Annigoni.

Designs as Nos. 1202/5 in **MS**1206 omit the gold frame around each stamp and "Golden Jubilee 1952–2002" inscription.

250 1852 (½d.) Britannia Stamp and Map

2002. 150th Anniv of Inland Postal Service. Multicoloured.

1207	10c. Type **250**	30	15
1208	45c. Early twentieth-century postman delivering letter	60	35
1209	$1.15 *Esk* (mail steamer)	1·50	1·25
1210	$2 B.W.I.A. Tri-Star airliner	2·00	2·50

251 *Alpinia purpurata*

252 Drax Hall Windmill, St. George

2002. Flowers. Multicoloured.

1211	10c. Type **251**	20	20
1212	40c. *Heliconia caribaea*	40	30
1213	$1.40 *Polianthes tuberosa* (horiz)	1·25	1·40
1214	$2.50 *Anthurium* (horiz)	2·00	2·75

2002. 375th Anniv of First Settlement.

1215	**252** 10c. brown, agate and blue	35	15
1216	– 45c. brown, agate and blue	1·00	35
1217	– $1.15 multicoloured	1·50	1·40
1218	– $3 multicoloured	3·25	4·00

DESIGNS: 45c. Donkey cart; $1.15, Cattle Mill ruins, Gibbons; $3, Morgan Lewis windmill, St. Andrew.

253 Traditional Christmas Fare

2002. Christmas. Multicoloured.

1219	45c. Type **253**	60	35
1220	$1.15 Christmas morning in the park	1·25	1·25
1221	$1.40 Nativity scene from float parade	1·40	1·50

254 AIDS Ribbon

2002. Centenary of Pan American Health Organization. Multicoloured.

1222	10c. Type **254**	40	15
1223	70c. Amateur athletes	85	50
1224	$1.15 Sir George Alleyne (Director-General of P.A.H.O.)	1·25	1·10
1225	$2 Pregnant woman	1·75	2·00

255 H.M.S. *Tartar*, 1764

2003. Royal Navy Connections. Multicoloured.

1226	10c. Type **255**	55	20
1227	70c. H.M.S. *Barbadoes*, 1803	1·10	55
1228	$1.15 H.M.S. *Valerian*, 1926	1·40	1·25
1229	$2.50 H.M.S. *Victorious*, 1941	2·50	3·25

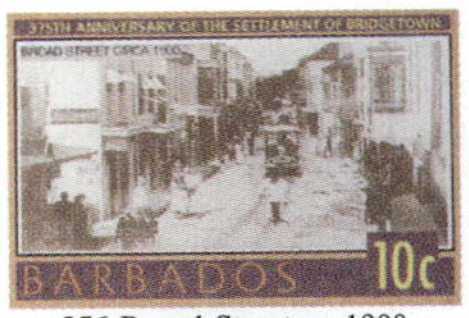

256 Broad Street, c. 1900

2003. 375th Anniv of the Settlement of Bridgetown. Multicoloured.

1230	10c. Type **256**	55	20
1231	$1.15 Swan Street, 1900	1·40	90
1232	$1.40 Roebuck Street, c. 1880	1·60	1·40
1233	$2 Chamberlain Bridge	2·25	3·00
MS1234	160 × 120 mm. Nos. 1230/3	5·50	6·00

2003. Centenary of Powered Flight. As T **209** of Ascension. Multicoloured.

1235	10c. McDonnell F2H-2P Banshee	40	20
1236	45c. Vickers Viscount 700	70	30
1237	50c. Douglas DC-9-30	80	30
1238	$1.15 Short Sunderland Mk II	1·10	70
1239	$1.40 North American P-51D Mustang	1·25	1·25
1240	$2.50 Concorde	2·75	3·50

257 Fishermen (Oistins Fish Festival)

2003. Barbados Festivals. Multicoloured.

MS1241	127 × 105 mm. 45c. Type **257**; 45c. Saxophone player (Barbados Jazz Festival); 45c. Man and woman in traditional costume (Crop Over Festival); 45c. Actresses (National Independence Festival of Creative Arts); 45c. School choir (National Independence Festival of Creative Arts); 45c. Carnival dancers (Crop Over Festival); 45c. Bass player (Barbados Jazz Festival); 45c. Competitor in fish boning competition (Oistins Fish Festival)	4·75	5·00

258 Cadet Corps Banner

2004. Centenary of the Cadet Corps. Multicoloured.

1242	10c. Type **258**	30	20
1243	25c. The Regular band marching	50	25
1244	50c. The Toy Soldier band	70	35
1245	$1 The Sea Cadets	1·00	80
1246	$3 Map reading	2·50	3·00

259 Swimming

2004. Olympic Games, Athens. Multicoloured.

1247	10c. Type **259**	35	20
1248	70c. Shooting	70	45
1249	$1.15 Running	1·10	1·10
1250	$2 Judo	2·00	2·50

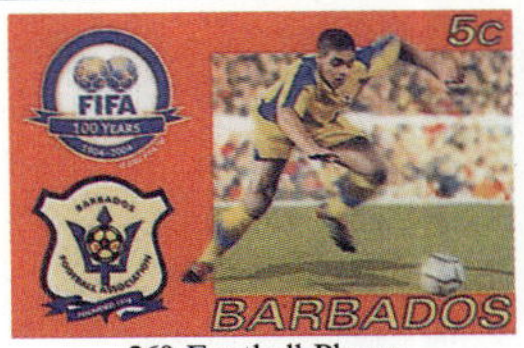

260 Football Player

2004. Centenary of FIFA (Federation Internationale de Football Association). Multicoloured.

1251	5c. Type **260**	15	30
1252	90c. Player in blue strip	1·00	70
1253	$1.40 Goal keeper	1·25	1·25
1254	$2.50 Player in yellow strip	2·00	2·50

261 Brain Coral

2004. Coral. Multicoloured.

1255	$1 Type **261**	1·40	1·50
1256	$1 Pillar coral	1·40	1·50
1257	$1 Pillar coral (different)	1·40	1·50
1258	$1 Fan coral	1·40	1·50
1259	$1 Yellow pencil coral	1·40	1·50
MS1260	85 × 85 mm. $3.50 Maze coral (36 × 36 mm)	3·50	3·75

262 White Peacock

2005. Pacific Explorer 2005 World Stamp Expo, Sydney, Australia. Butterflies. Multicoloured.

1261	50c. Type **262**	70	35
1262	$1 Great southern white	1·25	80
1263	$1.40 Orion	1·60	1·40
1264	$2.50 Mimic	2·25	3·00
MS1265	85 × 85 mm. $8 Monarch	7·00	8·00

263 Baobab

2005. Flowering Trees. Multicoloured.

1266	5c. Type **263**	15	15
1267	10c. African tulip tree	15	15
1268	25c. Rose of Sharon	25	25
1269	45c. Black willow	40	30
1270	50c. Black pearl tree	45	35
1271	75c. Seaside mahoe	70	50
1272	90c. Quickstick	80	55
1273	$1 Jerusalem Thorn	90	65
1274	$1.15 Pink cassia	1·00	70
1275	$1.40 Orchid tree	1·25	70
1276	$1.75 Yellow poui	1·50	1·50
1277	$2.10 Lignum vitae	1·90	2·10
1278	$3 Wild cinnamon	2·50	2·75
1279	$5 Pride of India	4·25	4·50
1280	$10 Immortelle	7·50	8·00

264 Firemen, c. 1955

2005. 50th Anniv of the Barbados Fire Service. Multicoloured.

1281	5c. Type **264**	40	40
1282	10c. Fire Officers marching, Fire Service Headquarters, Bridgetown, 2003	40	40
1283	90c. Rosenbauer-Panther FL 6 × 6 Airport Rescue and Fire Fighting tender	1·50	75
1284	$1.15 Fire Service parade with Dennis Pump Escape, Garrison Savannah, 1975	1·75	1·10
1285	$2.50 Scania 94G Water and Foam Tender	3·75	4·00

265 Three Anoles

2005. Extreme Anole (*Anolis extremus*). Mult.

1286	10c. Type **265**	30	15
1287	50c. Two anoles	75	35
1288	$1.75 One anole	2·25	2·50
1289	$2 Young anole hatching	2·50	3·00

266 Queen Triggerfish and Diver

2006. Endangered Species. Queen Triggerfish (*Balistes vetula*). Multicoloured.

1290	10c. Type **266**	30	30
1291	$1.15 Pair at edge of coral reef	1·25	1·00
1292	$1.40 Queen Triggerfish above sandy sea floor	1·40	1·25
1293	$2.10 Queen Triggerfish on coral reef	2·00	2·25

267 Girls reading

2006. Washington 2006 International Stamp Exhibition. "Children – they are the future". Multicoloured.

1294	10c. Type **267**	30	20
1295	50c. Wheelchair basketball	75	40
1296	$2 Three children using computer	2·00	2·25
1297	$2.50 Two children playing violins	2·25	2·50

268 Cave Shepherd, c. 1911

2006. Centenary of Cave Shepherd Store, Bridgetown. Multicoloured.

1298	10c. Type **268**	30	20
1299	50c. Cave Shepherd, c. 2000	60	35
1300	$1.75 Cave Shepherd, c. 1975	1·75	2·00
1301	$2 Cave Shepherd, c. 1920	2·00	2·25

269 Old Town Hall, Bridgetown

270 Joel 'Big Bird' Garner

2006. 175th Anniv of the Enfranchisement of Free Coloured and Black Barbadians. Multicoloured.

1302	10c. Type **269**	30	20
1303	50c. Samuel Jackman Prescod, 1806–71 (campaigner for enfranchisement)	60	35
1304	$1.40 Voting in ballot box (introduced 1885)	1·25	1·40
1305	$2.50 Sir James Lyon (Governor of Barbados, 1829–33)	2·00	2·50

2007. World Cup Cricket, West Indies. Multicoloured.

1306	$1.75 Type **270**	1·75	2·00
1307	$2.10 Old Kensington Oval, Barbados (horiz)	2·00	2·25
1308	$3 New Kensington Oval, Barbados (horiz)	2·50	2·75
MS1309	161 × 121 mm. $10 World Cup Cricket trophy	8·25	8·50

271 Emancipation (Bussa) Statue

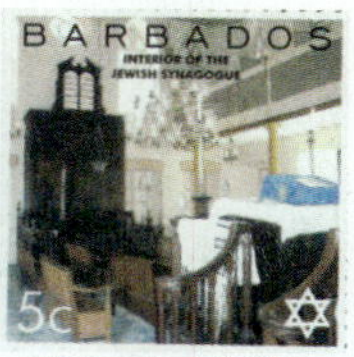

272 Interior of Nidhe Israel Synagogue, Bridgetown

2007. Bicentenary of the Abolition of the Slave Trade Act. Multicoloured (except **MS**1314).

1310	10c. Type **271**	15	10
1311	$1 William Wilberforce (abolitionist)	95	1·00
1312	$1.75 Slave hut (horiz)	1·25	1·40
1313	$2 Freedom celebrations, 1838 (horiz)	1·60	1·75
MS1314	115 × 80 mm. $3 Slave ship (black and violet)	2·50	2·75

2007. Opening of Nidhe Israel Museum, Bridgetown. Multicoloured.

1315	5c. Type **272**	10	10
1316	10c. Nidhe Israel Museum (adjacent to synagogue)	15	10
1317	$1.40 Hanukiah (candelabra)	1·00	1·10
1318	$2.50 Stained glass window in synagogue	2·00	2·25

273 Green Turtle

2007. Turtles. Multicoloured.

1319	10c. Type **273**	15	10
1320	50c. Loggerhead turtle	40	45
1321	$1 Hawksbill turtle	70	75
1322	$2.50 Leatherback turtle	2·00	2·25

POSTAGE DUE STAMPS

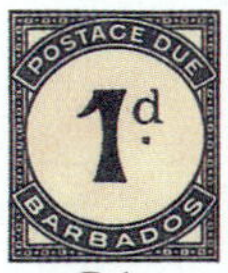

D 1

D 2

1934.

D1	D 1	½d. green	1·25	8·50
D2		1d. black	1·25	1·25
D3		3d. red	20·00	21·00

1950. Values in cents.

D4a	D 1	1c. green	30	3·00
D8		2c. black	30	5·00
D9		6c. red	50	7·00

1976.

D14a	D 2	1c. mauve and pink	10	10
D15a	–	2c. blue and light blue	10	10
D16a	–	5c. brown and yellow	10	15
D17a	–	10c. blue and lilac	15	20
D18a	–	25c. deep green and green	20	30
D19	–	$1 red and deep red	75	1·25

DESIGNS: Nos. D15/19 show different floral backgrounds.

BARBUDA Pt. 1

One of the Leeward Is., Br. W. Indies. Dependency of Antigua. Used stamps of Antigua and Leeward Is. concurrently. The issues from 1968 are also valid for use in Antigua. From 1971 to 1973 the stamps of Antigua were again used.

1922. 12 pence = 1 shilling;
20 shillings = 1 pound.
1951. 100 cents = 1 West Indian dollar.

1922. Stamps of Leeward Islands optd **BARBUDA**.

1	11	½d. green	1·50	10·00
2		1d. red	1·50	10·00
3		2d. grey	1·50	7·00
4		2½d. blue	1·50	7·50
9		3d. purple on yellow	1·75	12·00
5		6d. purple	2·00	18·00
10		1s. black on green	1·50	8·00
6		2s. purple and blue on blue	14·00	48·00
7		3s. green and violet	32·00	75·00
8		4s. black and red	40·00	75·00
11		5s. green and red on yellow	65·00	£130

2 Map of Barbuda

3 Greater Amberjack

1968.

12	2	½c. brown, black and pink	20	2·25
13		1c. orange, black and flesh	50	25
14		2c. brown, red and rose	1·25	50
15		3c. brown, yellow and lemon	50	25
16		4c. black, green & lt green	1·50	2·25
17		5c. turquoise and black	1·25	10
18		6c. black, purple and lilac	1·75	2·50
19		10c. black, blue and cobalt	60	1·00
20		15c. black, green & turq	60	2·50
20a	–	20c. multicoloured	1·50	2·00
21	3	25c. multicoloured	60	25
22	–	35c. multicoloured	2·00	25
23	–	50c. multicoloured	80	70
24	–	75c. multicoloured	80	80
25	–	$1 multicoloured	50	1·50
26	–	$2.50 multicoloured	55	3·00
27	–	$5 multicoloured	65	3·50

DESIGNS: As T **3**—20c. Great barracuda; 35c. French angelfish; 50c. Porkfish; 75c. Princess parrotfish; $1, Long-spined squirrelfish; $2.50, Bigeye; $5, Blue chromis.

10 Sprinting and Aztec Sun-stone

1968. Olympic Games. Mexico. Multicoloured.

28	25c. Type **10**	45	25
29	35c. High-jumping and Aztec statue	50	25
30	75c. Dinghy-racing and Aztec lion mask	55	45
MS31	87 × 76 mm. $1 Football and engraved plate	1·75	3·25

14 "The Ascension" (Orcagna)"

18 "Sistine Madonna" (Raphael)

15 Scout Enrolment Ceremony

1969. Easter Commemoration.

32	14	25c. black and blue	15	45
33		35c. black and red	15	50
34		75c. black and lilac	15	55

1969. 3rd Caribbean Scout Jamboree. Multicoloured.

35	25c. Type **15**	35	55
36	35c. Scouts around camp fire	45	65
37	75c. Sea Scouts rowing boat	55	85

1969. Christmas.

38	18	½c. multicoloured	10	10
39		25c. multicoloured	10	15
40		35c. multicoloured	10	20
41		75c. multicoloured	20	35

19 William I (1066–87)

21 "The Way to Calvary" (Ugolino)

1970. English Monarchs. Multicoloured.

42	35c. Type **19**	30	15
43	35c. William II (1087–1100)	10	15
44	35c. Henry I (1100–35)	10	15
45	35c. Stephen (1135–54)	10	15
46	35c. Henry II (1154–89)	10	15
47	35c. Richard I (1189–99)	10	15
48	35c. John (1199–1216)	10	15
49	35c. Henry III (1216–72)	10	15
50	35c. Edward I (1272–1307)	10	15
51	35c. Edward II (1307–27)	10	15
52	35c. Edward III (1327–77)	10	15
53	35c. Richard II (1377–99)	10	15
54	35c. Henry IV (1399–1413)	10	15
55	35c. Henry V (1413–22)	10	15
56	35c. Henry VI (1422–61)	10	15
57	35c. Edward IV (1462–83)	10	15
58	35c. Edward V (April–June 1483)	10	15
59	35c. Richard III (1483–85)	10	15
60	35c. Henry VII (1485–1509)	60	15
61	35c. Henry VIII (1509–47)	60	15
62	35c. Edward VI (1547–53)	60	15
63	35c. Lady Jane Grey (1553)	60	15
64	35c. Mary I (1553–8)	60	15
65	35c. Elizabeth I (1558–1603)	60	15
66	35c. James I (1603–25)	60	15
67	35c. Charles I (1625–49)	60	15
68	35c. Charles II (1649–1685)	60	15
69	35c. James II (1685–1688)	60	15
70	35c. William III (1689–1702)	60	15
71	35c. Mary II (1689–1694)	60	15
72	35c. Anne (1702–1714)	15	15
73	35c. George I (1714–1727)	15	15
74	35c. George II (1727–1760)	20	15
75	35c. George III (1760–1820)	20	15
76	35c. George IV (1820–1830)	20	15
77	35c. William IV (1830–1837)	20	60
78	35c. Victoria (1837–1901)	20	60

See also Nos. 710/5.

1970. No. 12 surch **20c.**

79	2	20c. on ½c. brn, blk & pink	10	20

1970. Easter. Paintings. Multicoloured.

80	25c. Type **21**	15	30
81	35c. "The Deposition from the Cross" (Ugolino)	15	30
82	75c. Crucifix (The Master of St. Francis)	15	35

22 Oliver is introduced to Fagin ("Oliver Twist")

1970. Death Centenary of Charles Dickens. Mult.

83	20c. Type **22**	20	25
84	75c. Dickens and scene from "The Old Curiosity Shop"	45	65

23 "Madonna of the Meadows" (G. Bellini)

1970. Christmas. Multicoloured.

85	20c. Type **23**	10	25
86	50c. "Madonna, Child and Angels" (from Wilton diptych)	15	30
87	75c. "The Nativity" (della Francesca)	15	35

24 Nurse with Patient in Wheelchair

25 "Angel with Vases"

1970. Centenary of British Red Cross. Multicoloured.

88		20c. Type **24**	15	30
89		35c. Nurse giving patient magazines (horiz)	20	40
90		75c. Nurse and mother weighing baby (horiz)	25	70

1971. Easter. "Mond" Crucifixion by Raphael. Multicoloured.

91		35c. Type **25**	15	85
92		50c. "Christ crucified"	15	95
93		75c. "Angel with vase"	15	1·00

26 Martello Tower

1971. Tourism. Multicoloured.

94		20c. Type **26**	15	35
95		25c. "Sailfish" dinghy	25	40
96		50c. Hotel bungalows	25	45
97		75c. Government House and Mystery Stone	25	55

27 "The Granducal Madonna" (Raphael)

1971. Christmas. Multicoloured.

98		½c. Type **27**	10	10
99		35c. "The Ansidei Madonna" (Raphael)	10	20
100		50c. "The Madonna and Child" (Botticelli)	15	25
101		75c. "The Madonna of the Trees" (Bellini)	15	30

Four stamps to commemorate the 500th Birth Anniv of Durer were prepared in late 1971, but their issue was not authorised by the Antigua Government.

1973. Royal Wedding. Nos. 370/1 of Antigua optd **BARBUDA** twice.

102	**106**	25c. multicoloured	3·25	2·00
103		$2 multicoloured	1·25	1·25

1973. Ships. Nos. 269/85 of Antigua optd **BARBUDA**.

116	**92**	½c. multicoloured	15	20
104	–	1c. multicoloured	15	30
105	–	2c. multicoloured	25	30
117	–	3c. multicoloured	25	25
106	–	4c. multicoloured	30	30
107	–	5c. multicoloured	40	40
108	–	6c. multicoloured	40	40
109	–	10c. multicoloured	45	45
118	–	15c. multicoloured	45	50
110	–	20c. multicoloured	55	60
111	–	25c. multicoloured	55	60
112	–	35c. multicoloured	55	70
113	–	50c. multicoloured	55	70
114	–	75c. multicoloured	55	70
119	–	$1 multicoloured	55	70
115	–	$2.50 multicoloured	75	1·50
121	–	$5 multicoloured	1·10	2·50

1973. Military Uniforms. Nos. 353, 355 and 357 of Antigua optd **BARBUDA**.

122		½c. multicoloured	10	10
123		20c. multicoloured	15	10
124		75c. multicoloured	40	15
MS125		127 × 145 mm. Nos. 353/7 of Antigua	2·00	3·50

1973. Carnival. Nos. 360/3 of Antigua optd **BARBUDA**.

126		20c. multicoloured	10	10
127		35c. multicoloured	10	10
128		75c. multicoloured	20	25
MS129		134 × 95 mm. Nos. 359/62 of Antigua	1·00	2·25

1973. Christmas. Nos. 364/69 of Antigua optd **BARBUDA**.

130	**105**	3c. multicoloured	10	10
131	–	5c. multicoloured	10	10
132	–	20c. multicoloured	10	10
133	–	35c. multicoloured	15	15
134	–	$1 multicoloured	30	30
MS135		130 × 128 mm. Nos. 130/4	2·25	9·00

1973. Honeymoon Visit. Nos. 373/4 of Antigua additionally optd **BARBUDA**.

136		35c. multicoloured	30	20
137		$2 multicoloured	70	60
MS138		78 × 100 mm. Nos. 136/7	1·10	1·00

1974. University of West Indies. Nos. 376/9 of Antigua optd **BARBUDA**.

139		5c. multicoloured	10	10
140		20c. multicoloured	10	10
141		35c. multicoloured	15	15
142		75c. multicoloured	15	15

1974. Military Uniforms. Nos. 380/4 of Antigua optd **BARBUDA**.

143		½c. multicoloured	10	10
144		10c. multicoloured	15	10
145		20c. multicoloured	25	10
146		35c. multicoloured	25	10
147		75c. multicoloured	45	25

1974. Centenary of U.P.U. (1st issue). Nos. 386/92 of Antigua optd with either a or b. (a) **BARBUDA 13 JULY 1992.**

148		½c. multicoloured	10	10
150		1c. multicoloured	10	10
152		2c. multicoloured	20	15
154		5c. multicoloured	50	15
156		20c. multicoloured	40	70
158		35c. multicoloured	80	1·50
160		$1 multicoloured	1·75	4·00

(b) **BARBUDA 15 SEPT. 1874 G.P.U.** ("General Postal Union").

149		½c. multicoloured	10	10
151		1c. multicoloured	10	10
153		2c. multicoloured	20	15
155		5c. multicoloured	50	15
157		20c. multicoloured	40	70
159		35c. multicoloured	80	1·50
161		$1 multicoloured	1·75	4·00
MS162		141 × 164 mm. No. **MS**393 of Antigua optd **BARBUDA**	3·50	6·00

1974. Antiguan Steel Bands. Nos. 394/98 of Antigua optd **BARBUDA**.

163		5c. deep red, red and black	10	10
164		20c. brown, lt brown & blk	10	10
165		35c. light green, green and black	10	10
166		75c. deep blue, blue and black	20	20
MS167		115 × 108 mm. Nos. 163/6	65	80

39 Footballers

1974. World Cup Football Championships (1st issue).

168	**39**	35c. multicoloured	10	10
169	–	$1.20 multicoloured	25	35
170	–	$2.50 multicoloured	35	50
MS171		70 × 128 mm. Nos. 168/70	85	90

DESIGNS: $1.20, $2.50, Footballers in action similar to Type **39**.

1974. World Cup Football Championships (2nd issue). Nos. 399/403 of Antigua optd **BARBUDA**.

172	**111**	5c. multicoloured	10	10
173	–	35c. multicoloured	20	10
174	–	75c. multicoloured	25	15
175	–	$1 multicoloured	25	25
MS176		135 × 130 mm. Nos. 172/5	75	1·25

41 Ship Letter of 1833

1974. Cent of Universal Postal Union (2nd issue). Multicoloured.

177		35c. Type **41**	10	10
178		$1.20 Stamps and postmarks of 1922	25	50
179		$2.50 Britten Norman Islander mailplane over map of Barbuda	35	75
MS180		128 × 97 mm. Nos. 177/9	1·00	2·00

42 Greater Amberjack

1974. Multicoloured.

181		½c. Oleander, Rose Bay (vert)	10	40
182		1c. Blue petrea (vert)	15	40
183		2c. Poinsettia (vert)	15	40
184		3c. Cassia tree (vert)	15	40
185		4c. Type **42**	1·75	40
186		5c. Holy Trinity School	15	15
187		6c. Snorkeling	15	30
188		10c. Pilgrim Holiness Church	15	20
189		15c. New Cottage Hospital	15	20
190		20c. Post Office and Treasury	15	20
191		25c. Island jetty and boats (vert)	30	30
192		35c. Martello Tower	30	30
193		50c. Warden's House	30	30
194		75c. Britten Norman Islander aircraft	2·50	1·00
195		$1 Tortoise	70	80
196		$2.50 Spiny lobster	80	1·75
197		$5 Magnificent frigate bird	4·00	2·50
197b		$10 Hibiscus (vert)	1·50	4·50

The 50c. to $1 are 39 × 25 mm, $2.50 and $5 45 × 29 mm, $10 34 × 48 mm.

1974. Birth Centenary of Sir Winston Churchill (1st issue). Nos. 408/12 of Antigua optd **BARBUDA**.

198	**113**	5c. multicoloured	15	10
199	–	35c. multicoloured	25	15
200	–	75c. multicoloured	40	45
201	–	$1 multicoloured	75	70
MS202		107 × 82 mm. Nos. 198/201	7·00	14·00

43 Churchill making Broadcast

1974. Birth Centenary of Sir Winston Churchill (2nd issue). Multicoloured.

203		5c. Type **43**	10	10
204		35c. Churchill and Chartwell	10	10
205		75c. Churchill painting	20	20
206		$1 Churchill making "V" sign	25	30
MS207		146 × 95 mm. Nos. 203/6	75	2·50

1974. Christmas. Nos. 413/21 of Antigua optd **BARBUDA**.

208	**114**	½c. multicoloured	10	10
209	–	1c. multicoloured	10	10
210	–	2c. multicoloured	10	10
211	–	3c. multicoloured	10	10
212	–	5c. multicoloured	10	10
213	–	20c. multicoloured	10	10
214	–	35c. multicoloured	15	15
215	–	75c. multicoloured	30	30
MS216		139 × 126 mm. Nos. 208/15	80	1·40

1975. Nelson's Dockyard. Nos. 427/32 of Antigua optd **BARBUDA**.

217	**116**	5c. multicoloured	15	15
218	–	15c. multicoloured	35	25
219	–	35c. multicoloured	40	35
220	–	50c. multicoloured	45	50
221	–	$1 multicoloured	50	80
MS222		130 × 134 mm. As Nos. 217/21, but larger format; 43 × 28 mm	1·75	2·75

45 Ships of the Line

1975. Sea Battles. Battle of the Saints, 1782. Mult.

223		35c. Type **45**	40	65
224		50c. H.M.S. "Ramillies"	40	75
225		75c. "Bonhomme Richard" (American frigate) firing broadside	50	90
226		95c. "L'Orient" (French ship of the line) burning	50	1·25

1975. "Apollo–Soyuz" Space Project. No. 197 optd **U.S.A.-U.S.S.R SPACE COOPERATION 1975** with **APOLLO** (No. 227) or **SOYUZ** (No. 228).

227		$5 multicoloured	3·25	6·00
228		$5 multicoloured	3·25	6·00

47 Officer, 65th Foot, 1763

1975. Military Uniforms. Multicoloured.

229		35c. Type **47**	60	60
230		50c. Grenadier, 27th Foot 1701–10	75	75
231		75c. Officer, 21st Foot, 1793–6	80	80
232		95c. Officer, Royal Regiment of Artillery, 1800	90	90

1975. 25th Anniv of United Nations. Nos. 203/6 optd **30TH ANNIVERSARY UNITED NATIONS 1945–1975.**

233	**43**	5c. multicoloured	10	10
234	–	35c. multicoloured	10	15
235	–	75c. multicoloured	15	20
236	–	$1 multicoloured	20	30

1975. Christmas. Nos. 457/65 of Antigua optd **BARBUDA**.

237	**121**	½c. multicoloured	10	15
238	–	1c. multicoloured	10	15
239	–	2c. multicoloured	10	15
240	–	3c. multicoloured	10	15
241	–	5c. multicoloured	10	15
242	–	10c. multicoloured	10	15
243	–	35c. multicoloured	15	20
244	–	$2 multicoloured	60	1·00
MS245		138 × 119 mm. Nos. 241/4	1·10	2·25

1975. World Cup Cricket Winners. Nos. 466/8 of Antigua optd **BARBUDA**.

246	**122**	5c. multicoloured	1·50	1·75
247	–	35c. multicoloured	2·75	2·00
248	–	$2 multicoloured	4·25	5·50

51 Surrender of Cornwallis at Yorktown (Trumbull)

1976. Bicentenary of American Revolution.

249	**51**	15c. multicoloured	10	15
250	–	15c. multicoloured	10	15
251	–	15c. multicoloured	10	15
252	–	35c. multicoloured	10	15
253	–	35c. multicoloured	10	15
254	–	35c. multicoloured	10	15
255	–	$1 multicoloured	15	25
256	–	$1 multicoloured	15	25
257	–	$1 multicoloured	15	25
258	–	$2 multicoloured	25	40
259	–	$2 multicoloured	25	40
260	–	$2 multicoloured	25	40
MS261		140 × 70 mm. Nos. 249/54 and 255/60 (two sheets)	1·40	9·00

DESIGNS—As Type **51**: Nos. 249/51; 252/4, The Battle of Princeton; 255/7, Surrender of General Burgoyne at Saratoga; 258/60, Jefferson presenting Declaration of Independence.

Type **51** shows the left-hand stamp of the 15c. design.

52 Bananaquits

1976. Birds. Multicoloured.

262		35c. Type **52**	20	25
263		50c. Blue-hooded euphonia	20	40
264		75c. Royal tern	20	50
265		95c. Killdeer plover ("Killdeer")	25	55
266		$1.25 Shiney-headed cowbird ("Glossy Cowbird")	25	70
267		$2 American purple gallinule ("Purple Gallinule")	30	85

1976. Royal Visit to the U.S.A. Nos. 249/60 additionally inscr "H.M. QUEEN ELIZABETH ROYAL VISIT 6TH JULY 1976 H.R.H. DUKE OF EDINBURGH".

268		15c. multicoloured	10	15
269		15c. multicoloured	10	15
270		15c. multicoloured	10	15
271		35c. multicoloured	10	20
272		35c. multicoloured	10	20
273		35c. multicoloured	10	20
274		$1 multicoloured	15	50
275		$1 multicoloured	15	50
276		$1 multicoloured	15	50
277		$2 multicoloured	25	70
278		$2 multicoloured	25	70
279		$2 multicoloured	25	70
MS280		143 × 81 mm. Nos. 268/73 and 274/9 (two sheets)	1·50	9·00

1976. Christmas. Nos. 514/18 of Antigua optd **BARBUDA**.

281	**128**	8c. multicoloured	10	10
282	–	10c. multicoloured	10	10
283	–	15c. multicoloured	10	10
284	–	50c. multicoloured	15	15
285	–	$1 multicoloured	25	30

1976. Olympic Games, Montreal. Nos. 495/502 of Antigua optd **BARBUDA**.

286	**125**	½c. brown, yellow and black	10	10
287	–	1c. violet and black	10	10
288	–	2c. green and black	10	10
289	–	15c. blue and black	10	10
290	–	30c. brown, yellow & blk	10	10
291	–	$1 orange, red and black	20	20
292	–	$2 red and black	35	35
MS293		88 × 138 mm. Nos. 289/92	1·75	2·40

55 P.O. Tower, Telephones and Alexander Graham Bell

1977. Cent of First Telephone Transmission. Mult.
294 75c. Type **55** 15 35
295 $1.25 T.V. transmission by satellite 20 55
296 $2 Globe showing satellite transmission scheme . . . 30 75
MS297 96 × 144 mm. Nos. 294/6 70 2·00

56 St. Margaret's Church, Westminster

1977. Silver Jubilee (1st issue). Multicoloured.
298 75c. Type **56** 10 15
299 75c. Street decorations . . . 10 15
300 75c. Westminster Abbey . . . 10 15
301 $1.25 Household Cavalry . . 15 20
302 $1.25 Coronation Coach . . 15 20
303 $1.25 Postillions 15 20
MS304 148 × 83 mm. As Nos. 298/303, but with silver borders. . . . . 75 1·50
Nos. 298/300 and 301/3 were printed together, se-tenant, forming composite designs.
See also Nos. 323/30 and 375/8.

1977. Nos. 469/86 of Antigua optd **BARBUDA**.
305 ½c. Antillean crested hummingbird 75 75
306 1c. Imperial amazon ("Imperial Parrot") 75 75
307 2c. Zenaida dove 75 75
308 3c. Loggerhead kingbird . . 75 75
309 4c. Red-necked pigeon . . . 75 75
310 5c. Rufous throated solitaire 75 75
311 6c. Orchid tree 50 50
312 10c. Bougainvillea 30 20
313 15c. Geiger tree 30 25
314 20c. Flamboyant 30 25
315 25c. Hibiscus 30 25
316 35c. Flame of the Wood . . 35 30
317 50c. Cannon at Fort James 40 40
318 75c. Premier's Office . . . 40 40
319 $1 Potworks Dam 50 60
320 $2.50 Irrigation scheme . . . 75 1·60
321 $5 Government House . . . 1·25 3·25
322 $10 Coolidge Airport . . . . 3·50 7·50

1977. Silver Jubilee (2nd issue). Nos. 526/31 of Antigua optd **BARBUDA**. (a) Ordinary gum.
323 10c. Royal Family 10 15
324 30c. Royal visit, 1966 . . . . 10 20
325 50c. The Queen enthroned . . 15 30
326 90c. The Queen after Coronation 15 40
327 $2.50 The Queen and Prince Charles . . . . 45 1·25
MS328 116 × 78 mm. $5 Queen Elizabeth and Prince Philip 80 1·25

(b) Self-adhesive.
329 50c. Queen after Coronation 40 70
330 $5 The Queen and Prince Philip . . . . 3·00 9·00

1977. Caribbean Scout Jamboree, Jamaica. Nos. 534/40 of Antigua optd **BARBUDA**.
331 ½c. Type **131** 10 10
332 1c. Hiking 10 10
333 2c. Rock-climbing 10 10
334 10c. Cutting logs 10 10
335 30c. Map and sign reading 25 40
336 50c. First aid 25 65
337 $2 Rafting . . . . 55 2·25
MS338 127 × 114 mm. Nos. 335/7 2·50 4·00

1977. 21st Anniv of Carnival. Nos. 542/47 of Antigua optd **BARBUDA**.
339 10c. Type **312** 10 10
340 30c. Carnival Queen 10 10
341 50c. Butterfly costume . . . 15 20
342 90c. Queen of the Band . . . 20 35
343 $1 Calypso King and Queen 25 45
MS344 140 × 120 mm. Nos. 339/43 1·00 1·75

61 Royal Yacht "Britannia"

1977. Royal Visit (1st issue). Multicoloured.
345 50c. Type **61** 10 20
346 $1.50 Jubilee emblem 25 35
347 $2.50 Union Jack and flag of Antigua 35 55
MS348 77 × 124 mm. Nos. 345/7 85 2·25

1977. Royal Visit (2nd issue). Nos. 548/53 of Antigua optd **BARBUDA**.
349A 10c. Royal Family 10 10
350B 30c. Queen Elizabeth and Prince Philip in car . . . 10 15
351B 50c. Queen enthroned . . . 15 20
352B 90c. Queen after Coronation 20 30
353B $2.50 The Queen and Prince Charles 45 80
MS354A 116 × 78 mm. $5 Queen and Prince Philip . . . . . . 1·75 4·00

1977. Christmas. Nos. 554/61 of Antigua optd **BARBUDA**.
355 ½c. Type **134** 10 10
356 1c. Crivelli 10 10
357 2c. Lotto 10 10
358 8c. Pontormo 10 10
359 10c. Tura (different) 10 10
360 25c. Lotto (different) 15 10
361 $2 Crivelli (different) 45 45
MS362 144 × 118 mm. Nos. 358/61 1·00 1·75

64 Airship LZ-1

1977. Special Events, 1977. Multicoloured.
363 75c. Type **64** 30 30
364 75c. German battleship and German Navy airship L-31 30 30
365 75c. "Graf Zeppelin" in hangar 30 30
366 75c. Gondola of military airship 30 30
367 95c. Sputnik 1 . . . . 35 35
368 95c. Vostok rocket 35 35
369 95c. Voskhod rocket 35 35
370 95c. Space walk 35 35
371 $1.25 Fuelling for flight . . . 40 45
372 $1.25 Leaving New York . . 40 45
373 $1.25 "Spirit of St. Louis" . . 40 45
374 $1.25 Welcome to England 40 45
375 $2 Lion of England 50 70
376 $2 Unicorn of Scotland . . . 50 70
377 $2 Yale of Beaufort 50 70
378 $2 Falcon of Plantagenets . . 50 70
379 $5 "Daniel in the Lion's Den" (Rubens) . . . . . 50 1·25
380 $5 Different detail of painting 50 1·25
381 $5 Different detail of painting 50 1·25
382 $5 Different detail of painting 50 1·25
MS383 132 × 156 mm. Nos. 362/82 6·00 17·00
EVENTS: 75c. 75th anniv of navigable airships; 95c. 20th anniv of U.S.S.R. space programme; $1.25, 50th anniv of Lindbergh's transatlantic flight; $2 Silver Jubilee of Queen Elizabeth II; $5 400th birth anniv of Rubens.
Nos. 379/82 form a composite design.

1978. 10th Anniv of Statehood. Nos. 562/7 of Antigua optd **BARBUDA**.
384 10c. Type **135** 10 10
385 15c. State flag 15 10
386 50c. Police band . . . . . . 1·25 80
387 90c. Premier V. C. Bird . . . 20 40
388 $2 State Coat of Arms . . . 40 1·00
MS389 122 × 99 mm. Nos. 385/88 7·00 4·00

66 "Pieta" (sculpture) (detail)

1978. Easter. Paintings and Sculptures by Michelangelo. Multicoloured.
390 75c. Type **66** 15 15
391 95c. "The Holy Family" . . 15 20
392 $1.25 "Libyan sibyl" (from the Sistine Chapel) . . . 15 35
393 $2 "The Flood" (from the Sistine Chapel) 20 45
MS394 117 × 85 mm. Nos. 390/3 1·90 2·00

1978. 75th Anniv of Powered Flight. Nos. 568/75 of Antigua optd **BARBUDA**.
395 ½c. Wright Glider No. III, 1902 . . . . 10 10
396 1c. Wright Flyer I, 1903 . . . 10 10
397 2c. Launch system and engine 10 10
398 10c. Orville Wright (vert) . . 10 10
399 50c. Wright Flyer III, 1905 25 20
400 90c. Wilbur Wright (vert) . . 35 25
401 $2 Wright Type B, 1910 . . . 60 45
MS402 90 × 75 mm. $2.50, Wright Flyer I on launch system . . . 1·50 2·50

1978. Sailing Week. Nos. 576/80 of Antigua optd **BARBUDA**.
403 10c. Sunfish regatta 20 10
404 50c. Fishing and work boat race 40 25
405 90c. Curtain Bluff race . . . 55 35
406 $2 Power boat rally 85 75
MS407 110 × 77 mm. $2.50, Guadeloupe–Antigua race . . 1·25 1·60

68 St. Edward's Crown

1978. 25th Anniv of Coronation (1st issue). Multicoloured.
408 75c. Type **68** 15 20
409 75c. Imperial State Crown . . 15 20
410 $1.50 Queen Mary's Crown 20 30
411 $1.50 Queen Mother's Crown 20 30
412 $2.50 Queen Consort's Crown 35 50
413 $2.50 Queen Victoria's Crown 35 50
MS414 123 × 117 mm. Nos. 408/13 1·10 1·75

1978. 25th Anniv of Coronation (2nd issue). Nos. 581/5 of Antigua optd **BARBUDA**.
415 10c. Queen Elizabeth and Prince Philip 10 10
416 30c. The Crowning 10 10
417 50c. Coronation procession 10 15
418 90c. Queen seated in St. Edward's Chair 15 20
419 $2.50 Queen wearing Imperial State Crown 30 60
MS420 114 × 103 mm. $5 Queen Elizabeth and Prince Philip . . 1·00 1·50

1978. 25th Anniv of Coronation (3rd issue). As Nos. 587/9 of Antigua, additionally inscr "BARBUDA".
421 25c. Glass Coach 30 70
422 50c. Irish State Coach 30 70
423 $5 Coronation Coach . . . . 1·00 2·25

1978. World Cup Football Championship, Argentina. Nos. 590/3 of Antigua optd **BARBUDA**.
424 10c. Player running with ball 10 10
425 15c. Players in front of goal 10 10
426 $3 Referee and player . . . . 1·00 1·25
MS427 126 × 88 mm. 25c. Player crouching with ball; 30c. Players heading ball; 50c. Players running with ball; $2 Goalkeeper diving 80 90

1978. Flowers. As Nos. 594/7 of Antigua optd **BARBUDA**.
428 25c. Petrea 15 20
429 50c. Sunflower 25 40
430 90c. Frangipani 35 45
431 $2 Passion flower 60 90
MS432 118 × 85 mm. $2.50, Hibiscus 1·00 1·50

1978. Christmas. As Nos. 599/601 of Antigua optd **BARBUDA**.
433 8c. "St. Ildefonso receiving the Chasuble from the Virgin" 10 10
434 25c. "The Flight of St. Barbara" 15 15
435 $2 "Madonna and Child, with St. Joseph, John the Baptist and Donor" . . . 60 1·25
MS436 170 × 113 mm. $4 "The Annuciation" . . . . 1·00 1·25

70 Black-barred Soldierfish

1978. Flora and Fauna. Multicoloured.
437 25c. Type **70** . . . . 55 1·50
438 50c. "Cynthia cardui" (butterfly) . . . . 80 2·25
439 75c. Dwarf poinciana . . . . 55 2·25
440 95c. "Heliconius charithonia" (butterfly) . . . . 1·00 2·50
441 $1.25 Bougainvillea . . . . . 55 2·50

71 Footballers and World Cup

72 Sir Rowland Hill

1978. Anniversaries and Events.
442 75c. Type **71** 30 30
443 95c. Wright Brothers and Flyer I (horiz) 30 40
444 $1.25 Balloon "Double Eagle II" and map of Atlantic (horiz) 40 45
445 $2 Prince Philip paying homage to the Queen . . . 40 60
MS446 122 × 90 mm. Nos. 442/5. Imperf . . . . 4·25 6·00
EVENTS: 75c. Argentina—Winners of World Cup Football Championship; 95c. 75th anniv of powered flight; $1.25, First Atlantic crossing by balloon; $2 25th anniv of Coronation.

1979. Death Centenary of Sir Rowland Hill (1st issue). Multicoloured.
447 75c. Type **72** 25 45
448 95c. Mail coach, 1840 (horiz) 25 50
449 $1.25 London's first pillar box, 1855 (horiz) 30 60
450 $2 Mail leaving St. Martin's Le Grand Post Office, London 45 85
MS451 129 × 104 mm. Nos. 447/50. Imperf . . . . 1·40 2·25

1979. Death Centenary of Sir Rowland Hill (2nd issue). Nos. 603/6 of Antigua optd **BARBUDA**.
452 25c. 1d. Stamp of 1863 . . . 15 15
453 50c. Penny Black 20 20
454 $1 Stage-coach and woman posting letter, c. 1840 . . 35 30
455 $2 Modern mail transport . . 80 60
MS456 108 × 82 mm. $2.50, Sir Rowland Hill 75 80

1979. Easter. Works of Durer. Nos. 608/11 of Antigua optd **BARBUDA**.
457 10c. multicoloured 10 10
458 50c. multicoloured 20 20
459 $4 black, mauve and yellow 90 1·10
MS460 114 × 99 mm. $2.50, multicoloured 55 75

74 Passengers alighting from British Airways Boeing 747

1979. 30th Anniv of International Civil Aviation Organization. Multicoloured.
461 75c. Type **74** 25 50
462 95c. Air traffic control . . . 25 50
463 $1.25 Ground crew-man directing Douglas DC-8 on runway 25 50

1979. International Year of the Child (1st issue). Nos. 612/15 of Antigua optd **BARBUDA**.
464 25c. Yacht 20 15
465 50c. Rocket 30 25
466 90c. Car 40 35
467 $2 Toy train 80 60
MS468 80 × 112 mm. $5 Airplane 1·10 1·10

1979. Fishes. Nos. 617/21 of Antigua optd **BARBUDA**.
469 30c. Yellow jack 20 15
470 50c. Blue-finned tuna 25 20
471 90c. Sailfish 30 30
472 $3 Wahoo . . . . 65 1·10
MS473 122 × 75 mm. $2.50, Great barracuda . . . . 1·00 1·25

1979. Death Bicentenary of Captain Cook. Nos. 622/6 of Antigua optd **BARBUDA**.
474 25c. Cook's Birthplace, Marton 25 25
475 50c. H.M.S. "Endeavour" . . 70 35
476 90c. Marine chronometer . . 70 40
477 $3 Landing at Botany Bay 1·50 1·25
MS478 110 × 85 mm. $2.50, H.M.S. "Resolution" . . . . 1·25 1·50

77 "Virgin with the Pear"

1979. International Year of the Child (2nd issue). Paintings by Durer. Multicoloured.
479 25c. Type **77** 15 15
480 50c. "Virgin with the Pink" (detail) 20 25
481 75c. "Virgin with the Pear" (different detail) 25 30
482 $1.25 "Nativity" (detail) . . . 25 40
MS483 86 × 118 mm. Nos. 479/82 1·00 1·75

1979. Christmas. Nos. 627/31 of Antigua optd **BARBUDA**.
484 8c. The Holy Family 10 10
485 25c. Mary and Jesus on donkey 15 10

486 50c. Shepherd looking at star 25 15
487 $4 The Three Kings 85 80
MS488 113 × 94 mm. $3 Angel with trumpet 80 1·10

1980. Olympic Games, Moscow. Nos. 632/6 of Antigua optd **BARBUDA**.
489 10c. Javelin 10 10
490 25c. Running 15 10
491 $1 Pole vault 35 20
492 $2 Hurdles 55 40
MS493 127 × 96 mm. $3 Boxing 70 1·10

1980. "London 1980" International Stamp Exhibition. Nos. 452/5 optd **LONDON 1980**.
494 25c. 1d. stamp of 1863 35 20
495 50c. Penny Black 45 40
496 $1 Stage-coach and woman posting letter, c. 1840 85 65
497 $2 Modern mail transport 2·75 1·50

80 "Apollo 11" Crew Badge

1980. 10th Anniv of "Apollo 11" Moon Landing. Multicoloured.
498 75c. Type **80** 60 25
499 95c. Plaque left on Moon 60 30
500 $1.25 Rejoining the mother-ship 70 50
501 $2 Lunar module 90 75
MS502 118 × 84 mm. Nos. 498/501 1·60 2·50

81 American Wigeon ("American Widgeon")

1980. Birds. Multicoloured.
503 1c. Type **81** 70 1·25
504 2c. Snowy plover 70 70
505 4c. Rose-breasted grosbeak 75 70
506 6c. Mangrove cuckoo 75 70
507 10c. Adelaide's warbler 75 70
508 15c. Scaly-breasted thrasher 80 70
509 20c. Yellow-crowned night heron 80 70
510 25c. Bridled quail dove 80 70
511 35c. Carib grackle 85 1·25
512 50c. Northern pintail 90 55
513 75c. Black-whispered vireo 1·00 55
514 $1 Blue-winged teal 1·25 80
515 $1.50 Green-throated carib (vert) 1·50 80
516 $2 Red-necked pigeon (vert) 2·25 1·25
517 $2.50 Wied's crested flycatcher ("Stolid Flycatcher") (vert) 2·75 1·50
518 $5 Yellow-bellied sapsucker (vert) 3·50 3·50
519 $7.50 Caribbean elaenia (vert) 4·00 6·00
520 $10 Great egret (vert) 4·00 5·00

1980. Famous Works of Art. Nos. 651/8 of Antigua optd **BARBUDA**.
521 10c. "David" (statue, Donatello) 10 10
522 30c. "The Birth of Venus" (painting, Sandro Botticelli) 15 15
523 50c. "Reclining Couple" (sarcophagus), Cerveteri 15 20
524 90c. "The Garden of Earthly Delights" (painting, Hieronymus Bosch) 20 25
525 $1 "Portinari Altarpiece" (painting, Hugo van der Goes) 20 25
526 $4 "Eleanora of Toledo and her Son Giovanni de'Medici" (painting, Agnolo Bronzino) 60 80
MS527 99 × 124 mm. $5 "The Holy Family" (painting, Rembrandt) 1·50 1·75

1980. 75th Anniv of Rotary International. Nos. 658/62 of Antigua optd **BARBUDA**.
528 30c. Rotary Headquarters 15 15
529 50c. Antigua Rotary banner 20 20
530 90c. Map of Antigua 25 25
531 $3 Paul P. Harris (founder) 65 65
MS532 102 × 77 mm. $5 Antigua flags and Rotary emblems 1·50 2·25

1980. 80th Birthday of the Queen Mother. Nos. 663/5 of Antigua optd **BARBUDA**.
533 10c. multicoloured 50 15
534 $2.50 multicoloured 1·25 1·50
MS535 68 × 88 mm. $3 multicoloured 2·50 1·75

1980. Birds. Nos. 666/70 of Antigua optd **BARBUDA**.
536 10c. Ringed kingfisher 3·25 1·00
537 30c. Plain pigeon 3·75 1·10
538 $1 Green-throated carib 5·00 3·00
539 $2 Black necked stilt 6·00 6·00
MS540 73 × 73 mm. $2.50, Roseate tern 5·50 2·75

1981. Sugar Cane Railway Locomotives. Nos. 681/5 of Antigua optd **BARBUDA**.
541 25c. Diesel locomotive No. 15 1·00 25
542 50c. Narrow-gauge steam locomotive 1·25 35
543 90c. Diesel locomotive Nos. 1 and 10 1·75 45
544 $3 Steam locomotive hauling sugar cane 3·25 1·40
MS545 82 × 111 mm. $2.50, Antigua sugar factory, railway yard and sheds 1·50 1·75

84 Florence Nightingale

1981. Famous Women.
546 **84** 50c. multicoloured 15 30
547 – 90c. multicoloured 40 55
548 – $1 multicoloured 35 60
549 – $4 black, brown and lilac 50 1·75
DESIGNS: 90c. Marie Curie; $1 Amy Johnson; $4 Eleanor Roosevelt.

85 Goofy in Motor-boat

1981. Walt Disney Cartoon Characters. Mult.
550 10c. Type **85** 90 15
551 20c. Donald Duck reversing car into sea 1·25 20
552 25c. Mickey Mouse asking tug-boat to take on more than it can handle 1·40 30
553 30c. Porpoise turning tables on Goofy 1·40 35
554 35c. Goofy in sailing boat 1·40 35
555 40c. Mickey Mouse and boat being lifted out of water by fish 1·40 40
556 75c. Donald Duck fishing for flying-fish with butterfly net 2·00 60
557 $1 Minnie Mouse in brightly decorated sailing boat 2·00 80
558 $2 Chip and Dale on floating ship-in-bottle 2·50 1·40
MS559 127 × 101 mm. $2.50, Donald Duck 4·50 3·00

1981. Birth Centenary of Picasso. Nos. 697/701 of Antigua optd with **BARBUDA**.
560 10c. "Pipes of Pan" 10 10
561 50c. "Seated Harlequin" 25 15
562 90c. "Paulo as Harlequin" 35 30
563 $4 "Mother and Child" 90 1·00
MS564 115 × 140 mm. $5 "Three Musicians" (detail) 1·50 1·50

87/8 Buckingham Palace (½-size illustration)

1981. Royal Wedding (1st issue). Buildings. Each printed in black on either pink, green or lilac backgrounds.
565 $1 Type **87** 25 40
566 $1 Type **88** 25 40
567 $1.50 Caernarvon Castle (right) 30 50
568 $1.50 Caernarvon Castle (left) 30 50
569 $4 Highgrove House (right) 55 90
570 $4 Highgrove House (left) 55 90
MS571 75 × 90 mm. $5 black and yellow (St. Paul's Cathedral—26 × 32 mm) 80 1·25
Same prices for any background colour. The two versions of each value form composite designs.

1981. Royal Wedding (2nd issue). Nos. 702/5 of Antigua optd **BARBUDA**.
572 25c. Prince Charles and Lady Diana Spencer 15 15
573 50c. Glamis Castle 25 25
574 $4 Prince Charles skiing 75 1·00
MS575 95 × 85 mm. $5 Glass coach 90 90

89 "Integration and Travel"

1981. International Year of Disabled Persons (1st issue).
576 **89** 50c. multicoloured 25 20
577 – 90c. black, orange and green 25 25
578 – $1 black, blue and green 30 30
579 – $4 black, yellow and brown 45 85
DESIGNS: 90c. Braille and sign language; $1 "Helping hands"; $4 "Mobility aids for disabled".
See also Nos. 603/6.

1981. Royal Wedding (3rd issue). Nos. 706/12 of Antigua optd **BARBUDA**.
580 25c. Prince of Wales at Investiture, 1969 40 70
581 25c. Prince Charles as baby, 1948 40 70
582 $1 Prince Charles at R.A.F. College, Cranwell, 1971 50 85
583 $1 Prince Charles attending Hill House School, 1956 50 85
584 $2 Prince Charles and Lady Diana Spencer 75 1·00
585 $2 Prince Charles at Trinity College, 1967 75 1·00
586 $5 Prince Charles and Lady Diana 4·25 6·50

1981. Independence. No. 686/96 of Antigua additionally optd **BARBUDA**.
587 6c. Orchid tree 50 15
588 10c. Bougainvillea 55 15
589 20c. Flamboyant 70 20
590 25c. Hibiscus 80 25
591 35c. Flame of the wood 90 30
592 50c. Cannon at Fort James 1·10 45
593 75c. Premier's Office 1·25 75
594 $1 Potworks Dam 1·50 80
595 $2.50 Irrigation scheme, Diamond Estate 2·50 2·75
596 $5 Government House and Gardens 2·75 3·75
597 $10 Coolidge International Airport 4·50 6·00

1981. 50th Anniv of Antigua Girl Guide Movement. Nos. 713/16 of Antigua optd **BARBUDA**.
598 10c. Irene Joshua (founder) 55 10
599 50c. Campfire sing-song 1·25 30
600 90c. Sailing 1·75 45
601 $2.50 Animal tending 3·00 1·40
MS602 170 × 113 mm. $4 "The Annunciation" (Rubens) 1·25 1·50

1981. International Year of Disabled Persons (2nd issue). Sport for the Disabled. Nos. 728/32 of Antigua optd **BARBUDA**.
603 10c. Swimming 15 15
604 50c. Discus throwing 20 25
605 90c. Archery 45 45
606 $2 Baseball 60 1·50
MS607 108 × 84 mm. $4 Basketball 2·00 1·75

1981. Christmas. Paintings. Nos. 723/7 of Antigua optd **BARBUDA**.
608 8c. "Holy Night" (Jacques Stella) 10 10
609 30c. "Mary with Child" (Julius Schnorr von Carolfeld) 20 20
610 $1 "Virgin and Child" (Alsono Cano) 40 40
611 $3 "Virgin and Child" (Lorenzo di Credi) 1·10 1·10
MS612 77 × 111 mm. $5 "Holy Family" (Pieter von Avon) 1·75 2·25

93 Princess of Wales

97 Vincenzo Lunardi's Balloon Flight, London, 1785

1982. Birth of Prince William of Wales (1st issue).
613 **93** $1 multicoloured 75 50
614 $2.50 multicoloured 1·00 1·10
615 $5 multicoloured 1·60 1·75
MS616 88 × 108 mm. $4 multicoloured 2·00 2·10

1982. South Atlantic Fund. Nos. 580/6 surch **S. Atlantic Fund + 50c.**
617 25c.+50c. Prince of Wales at Investiture, 1969 30 50
618 25c.+50c. Prince Charles as baby, 1948 30 50
619 $1+50c. Prince Charles at R.A.F. College, Cranwell, 1971 50 75
620 $1+50c. Prince Charles attending Hill House School, 1956 50 75
621 $2+50c. Prince Charles and Lady Diana Spencer 75 1·10
622 $2+50c. Prince Charles at Trinity College, 1967 75 1·10
623 $5+50c. Prince Charles and Lady Diana Spencer 3·00 4·25

1982. 21st Birthday of Princess of Wales (1st issue). As Nos. 613/16 but inscr "Twenty First Birthday Greetings to H.R.H. The Princess of Wales".
624 $1 multicoloured 1·50 45
625 $2.50 multicoloured 2·25 1·25
626 $5 multicoloured 3·00 2·40
MS627 88 × 108 mm. $4 multicoloured 2·75 2·25

1982. 21st Birthday of Princess of Wales (2nd issue). Nos. 748/51 of Antigua optd **BARBUDA MAIL**.
628 90c. Queen's House, Greenwich 80 45
629 $1 Prince and Princess of Wales 1·25 50
630 $4 Princess of Wales 3·00 1·50
MS631 114 × 94 mm. $3 Angel with trumpet 1·00 1·50

1982. Birth of Prince William of Wales (2nd issue). Nos. 757/60 of Antigua further optd **BARBUDA MAIL**.
632 90c. Queen's House, Greenwich 70 45
633 $1 Prince and Princess of Wales 1·25 50
634 $4 Princess of Wales 3·25 2·00
MS635 102 × 75 mm. $5 Princess of Wales (different) 4·25 2·50

1982. Birth Centenary of Franklin D. Roosevelt and 250th Birth Anniv of George Washington. Nos. 761/8 of Antigua optd **BARBUDA MAIL**.
636 10c. Roosevelt in 1940 10 10
637 25c. Washington as blacksmith 15 15
638 45c. Churchill, Roosevelt and Stalin at Yalta Conference 2·00 25
639 60c. Washington crossing Delaware 20 25
640 $1 "Roosevelt Special" train 2·00 40
641 $3 Portrait of Roosevelt 60 90
MS642 92 × 87 mm. $4 Roosevelt and wife 1·00 1·75
MS643 92 × 87 mm. $4 Portrait of Washington 1·00 1·75

1982. Christmas. Religious Paintings by Raphael. Nos. 769/73 of Antigua optd **BARBUDA MAIL**.
644 10c. "Annunciation" 10 10
645 30c. "Adoration of the Magi" 15 15
646 $1 "Presentation at the Temple" 40 40
647 $4 "Coronation of the Virgin" 1·00 1·00
MS648 95 × 142 mm. $5 "Marriage of the Virgin" 1·25 2·00

1983. 500th Birth Anniv of Raphael. Details from "Galatea" Fresco. Nos. 774/8 of Antigua optd **BARBUDA MAIL**.
649 45c. Tritons and dolphins 20 20
650 50c. Sea Nymph carried off by Triton 20 20
651 60c. Winged angel steering dolphins (horiz) 25 25
652 $4 Cupids shooting arrows 1·00 1·00
MS653 101 × 102 mm. $5 Galatea pulled along by dolphins 1·25 2·00

1983. Commonwealth Day. Nos. 779/82 of Antigua optd **BARBUDA MAIL**.
654 25c. Pineapple produce 45 55
655 45c. Carnival 50 70
656 60c. Tourism 70 1·25
657 $3 Airport 1·50 3·50

1983. World Communications Year. Nos. 783/6 of Antigua optd **BARBUDA MAIL**.
658 15c. T.V. satellite coverage of Royal Wedding 2·00 25
659 50c. Police communications 4·50 90
660 60c. House-to-diesel train telephone call 3·00 90
661 $3 Satellite earth station with planets Jupiter and Saturn 3·75 2·50
MS662 100 × 90 mm. $5 "Comsat" satellite over West Indies 1·50 2·25

1983. Bicent of Manned Flight (1st issue). Mult.
663 $1 Type **97** 25 35
664 $1.50 Montgolfier brothers' balloon flight, Paris, 1783 40 55
665 $2.50 Blanchard and Jeffries' Cross-Channel balloon flight, 1785 60 90
MS666 111 × 111 mm. $5 Maiden flight of airship LZ-127 "Graf Zeppelin", 1928 2·00 2·75
See also Nos. 672/6.

1983. Whales. Nos. 788/93 of Antigua optd **BARBUDA MAIL**.
667 15c. Bottlenose dolphin 1·25 40
668 50c. Finback whale 4·00 1·60

669 60c. Bowhead whale . . . . 4·50 1·75
670 $3 Spectacled porpoise . . . 5·50 4·25
MS671 122 × 101 mm. $5 Narwhal 6·00 4·50

1983. Bicentenary of Manned Flight (2nd issue). Nos. 811/15 of Antigua optd **BARBUDA MAIL**.
672 30c. Dornier Do-X flying boat . . . . 1·25 35
673 50c. Supermarine S6B seaplane . . . . 1·50 60
674 60c. Curtiss Sparrowhawk biplane and airship U.S.S. "Akron" . . . . 1·75 70
675 $4 Hot-air balloon "Pro-Juventute" . . . . 5·00 4·00
MS676 80 × 105 mm. $5 Airship LZ-127 "Graf Zeppelin" . . . 3·75 4·25

1983. Nos. 565/70 surch.
677 45c. on $1 Type **87** 25 45
678 45c. on $1 Type **88** 25 45
679 50c. on $1.45 Caernarvon Castle (right) 25 45
680 50c. on $1.45 Caernarvon Castle (left) 25 45
681 60c. on $4 Highgrove House (left) 25 45
682 60c. on $4 Highgrove House (right) 25 45

1983. Nos. 793/810 of Antigua optd **BARBUDA MAIL**.
683 1c. Cashew nut 10 10
684 2c. Passion fruit 15 10
685 3c. Mango 15 10
686 5c. Grapefruit 15 10
687 10c. Pawpaw 20 10
688 15c. Breadfruit 40 10
689 20c. Coconut 50 15
690 25c. Oleander 50 15
691 30c. Banana 55 20
692 40c. Pineapple 65 25
693 45c. Cordia 70 30
694 50c. Cassia 80 30
695 60c. Poui 80 30
696 $1 Frangipani . . . . 1·10 50
697 $2 Flamboyant . . . . . . 1·75 1·25
698 $2.50 Lemon . . . . 2·00 1·75
699 $5 Lignum vitae . . . . . . 3·00 2·75
700 $10 National flag and coat of arms . . . . 4·50 5·50

1983. Christmas. 500th Birth Anniv of Raphael. Nos. 816/20 of Antigua optd **BARBUDA MAIL**.
701 10c. multicoloured 10 10
702 30c. multicoloured 10 20
703 $1 multicoloured 30 50
704 $4 multicoloured . . . . . . 1·00 1·50
MS705 101 × 131 mm. $5 multicoloured . . . . 1·40 2·50

1983. Bicentenary (1984) of Methodist Church. Nos. 821/4 of Antigua optd **BARBUDA MAIL**.
706 15c. Type **181** 20 15
707 50c. Nathaniel Gilbert (founder in Antigua) . . . 30 25
708 60c. St. John Methodist Church steeple 30 30
709 $3 Ebenezer Methodist Church, St John's . . . . 80 1·00

100 Edward VII

1984. Members of British Royal Family. Mult.
710 $1 Type **100** . . . . 70 1·50
711 $1 George V . . . . 70 1·50
712 $1 George VI . . . . 70 1·50
713 $1 Elizabeth II . . . . 70 1·50
714 $1 Charles, Prince of Wales . . 70 1·50
715 $1 Prince William of Wales . . 70 1·50

1984. Olympic Games, Los Angeles (1st issue). Nos. 825/9 of Antigua optd **BARBUDA MAIL**.
716 25c. Discus 25 20
717 50c. Gymnastics 40 40
718 90c. Hurdling 50 60
719 $3 Cycling . . . . 2·75 1·50
MS720 82 × 67 mm. $5 Volleyball 2·25 3·25

1984. Ships. Nos. 830/4 of Antigua optd **BARBUDA MAIL**.
721 45c. "Booker Vanguard" (freighter) . . . . 1·50 45
722 50c. "Canberra" (liner) . . . 1·50 50
723 60c. Yachts . . . . 1·75 60
724 $4 "Fairwind" (cargo liner) . . 4·25 2·75
MS725 101 × 80 mm. $5 18th-century British man-o-war (vert) . . . . 4·50 4·25

1984. Universal Postal Union Congress, Hamburg. Nos. 835/8 of Antigua optd **BARBUDA MAIL**.
726 15c. Chenille 25 15
727 50c. Shell flower 30 30
728 60c. Anthurium 40 40
729 $3 Angels trumpet . . . . . 75 1·25
MS730 100 × 75 mm. $5 Crown of Thorns . . . . 2·00 2·50

101 Olympic Stadium, Athens, 1896

1984. Olympic Games, Los Angeles (2nd issue). Multicoloured.
731 $1.50 Type **101** 50 90
732 $2.50 Olympic stadium, Los Angeles, 1984 . . . . . . 70 1·50
733 $5 Athlete carrying Olympic torch . . . . 1·10 2·25
MS734 121 × 95 mm. No. 733 . . 1·50 2·50

1984. Presidents of the United States of America. Nos. 856/63 of Antigua optd **BARBUDA MAIL**.
735 10c. Abraham Lincoln . . . 10 10
736 20c. Harry Truman 15 15
737 30c. Dwight Eisenhower . . 20 25
738 40c. Ronald Reagan 25 30
739 90c. Gettysburg Address, 1863 . . . . 40 55
740 $1.10 Formation of N.A.T.O., 1949 . . . . . 40 65
741 $1.50 Eisenhower during Second World War 45 70
742 $2 Reagan and Caribbean Basin Initiative . . . . . 50 1·00

1984. Abolition of Slavery. Nos. 864/8 of Antigua optd **BARBUDA MAIL**.
743 40c. View of Moravian Mission 30 30
744 50c. Antigua Courthouse, 1823 . . . . 40 40
745 60c. Planting sugar-cane, Monks Hill 45 45
746 $3 Boiling house, Delaps' Estate . . . . 1·40 1·40
MS747 95 × 70 mm. $5 Loading sugar, Willoughby Bay . . . . . 2·00 2·50

1984. Songbirds. Nos. 869/74 of Antigua optd **BARBUDA MAIL**.
748 40c. Rufous-sided towhee . . 2·25 55
749 50c. Parula warbler . . . . . 2·25 70
750 60c. House wren . . . . . . 2·25 75
751 $2 Ruby-crowned kinglet . . 3·25 2·00
752 $3 Common flicker ("Yellow-shafted Flicker") . . . . . 3·50 2·75
MS753 76 × 76 mm. $5 Yellow-breasted chat . . . . 4·00 4·50

1984. 450th Death Anniv of Correggio (painter). Nos. 878/82 of Antigua optd **BARBUDA MAIL**.
754 25c. "The Virgin and Infant with Angels and Cherubs" 15 20
755 60c. "The Four Saints" . . 40 45
756 90c. "St. Catherine" 50 55
757 $3 "The Campori Madonna" 1·25 1·75
MS758 90 × 60 mm. $5 "St. John the Baptist" . . . . 1·75 3·25

1984. "Ausipex" International Stamp Exibition Melbourne. Australian Sports. Nos. 875/7 of Antigua optd **BARBUDA MAIL**.
759 $1 Grass-skiing 50 60
760 $5 Australian Football . . . 2·00 3·00
MS761 108 × 78 mm. Boomerang-throwing . . . . 2·00 3·25

1984. 150th Birth Anniv of Edgar Degas (painter). Nos. 883/7 of Antigua optd **BARBUDA MAIL**.
762 15c. "The Blue Dancers" . . 10 10
763 50c. "The Pink Dancers" . . 30 40
764 70c. "Two Dancers" 45 55
765 $4 "Dancers at the Bar" . . 1·25 3·50
MS766 90 × 60 mm. $5 "The Folk Dancers" (40 × 27 mm) . . . . 1·75 2·75

1985. Famous People. Nos. 888/96 of Antigua optd **BARBUDA MAIL**.
767 60c. Winston Churchill . . . 5·50 2·50
768 60c. Mahatma Gandhi . . . 5·50 2·50
769 60c. John F. Kennedy . . . 5·50 2·50
770 60c. Mao Tse-tung . . . . . 5·50 2·50
771 $1 Churchill with General De Gaulle, Paris, 1944 (horiz) 5·50 2·50
772 $1 Gandhi leaving London by train, 1931 (horiz) . . 5·50 2·50
773 $1 Kennedy with Chancellor Adenauer and Mayor Brandt, Berlin, 1963 (horiz) 5·50 2·50
774 $1 Mao Tse-tung with Lin Piao, Peking, 1969 (horiz) 5·50 2·50
MS775 114 × 80 mm. $5 Flags of Great Britain, India, the United States and China . . . . . . 9·00 8·00

103 Lady Elizabeth Bowes-Lyon, 1907, and Camellias

104 Roseate Tern

1985. Life and Times of Queen Elizabeth the Queen Mother. Multicoloured.
776 15c. Type **103** 35 20
777 45c. Duchess of York, 1926, and "Elizabeth of Glamis" roses 45 25
778 50c. The Queen Mother after the Coronation, 1937 . . . 45 25
779 60c. In Garter robes, 1971, and dog roses 45 30
780 90c. Attending Royal Variety Show, 1967, and red Hibiscus 60 45
781 $1 The Queen Mother in 1982, and blue plumbago 75 1·10
782 $3 Receiving 82nd birthday gifts from children, and morning glory . . . . . . 95 2·50

1985. Birth Bicentenary of John J. Audubon (ornithologist) (1st issue). Designs showing original paintings. Multicoloured.
783 45c. Type **104** 25 30
784 50c. Mangrove cuckoo . . . 25 30
785 60c. Yellow-crowned night heron 30 40
786 $5 Brown pelican . . . . . 1·00 3·50
See also Nos. 794/7 and 914/17.

1985. Centenary (1986) of Statue of Liberty (1st issue). Nos. 907/13 of Antigua optd **BARBUDA MAIL**.
787 25c. Torch from statue in Madison Square Park, 1885 . . . . 20 20
788 30c. Statue of Liberty and scaffolding ("Restoration and Renewal") (vert) . . . 20 20
789 50c. Frederic Bartholdi (sculpture) supervising construction, 1876 . . . . 30 30
790 90c. Close-up of Statue . . . 55 55
791 $1 Statue and sailing ship ("Operation Sail", 1976) (vert) 60 60
792 $3 Dedication ceremony, 1886 (vert) . . . . 1·75 1·75
MS793 110 × 80 mm. $5 Port of New York . . . . 5·75 4·75
See also Nos. 987/96.

1985. Birth Bicentenary of John J. Audubon (ornithologist) (2nd issue). Nos. 924/8 of Antigua optd **BARBUDA MAIL**.
794 90c. Slavonian grebe ("Horned Grebe") . . . . 9·00 4·25
795 $1 British storm petrel ("Least Petrel") . . . . . 9·00 4·50
796 $1.50 Great blue heron . . . 10·00 8·50
797 $3 Double-crested cormorant (white phase) . . . . . 15·00 13·00
MS798 103 × 72 mm. $5 White-tailed tropic bird (vert) . . . . . . 28·00 11·00

1985. Butterflies. Nos. 929/33 of Antigua optd **BARBUDA MAIL**.
799 25c. "Anaea cyanea" . . . . 6·50 1·25
800 60c. "Leodonta dysoni" . . . 8·50 2·00
801 90c. "Junea doraete" . . . . 9·50 2·50
802 $4 "Prepona pylene" . . . . 17·00 19·00
MS803 132 × 105 mm. $5 "Caervois gerdtrudtus" . . . . 16·00 9·00

1985. Centenary of Motorcycle. Nos. 919/23 of Antigua optd **BARBUDA MAIL**.
804 10c. Triumph 2hp "Jap", 1903 . . . . 1·00 20
805 30c. Indian "Arrow", 1949 . . 1·50 25
806 60c. BMW "R100RS", 1976 . . 2·00 55
807 $4 Harley Davidson "Model II", 1916 . . . . 5·00 4·50
MS808 90 × 93 mm. $5 Laverda "Jota", 1975 . . . . 6·00 4·00

1985. 85th Birthday of Queen Elizabeth the Queen Mother. Nos. 776/82 optd **4TH AUG 1900–1985**.
809 15c. Type **103** 75 50
810 45c. Duchess of York, 1926 and "Elizabeth of Glamis" roses . . . . 1·10 60
811 50c. The Queen Mother after the Coronation, 1937 . . . 1·10 60
812 60c. In Garter robes, 1971, and dog roses . . . . . . 1·25 1·00
813 90c. Attending Royal Variey Show, 1967, and red hibiscus . . . . 1·25 1·25
814 $2 The Queen Mother in 1982, and blue plumbago 1·40 3·75
815 $3 Receiving 82nd birthday gifts from children, and morning glory . . . . . . 1·50 3·75

1985. Native American Artefacts. Nos. 914/18 of Antigua optd **BARBUDA MAIL**.
816 15c. Arawak pot sherd and Indians making clay utensils 15 10
817 50c. Arawak body design and Arawak Indians tattooing 25 25
818 60c. Head of the god "Yocahu" and Indians harvesting manioc 35 35
819 $3 Carib war club and Carib Indians going into battle 1·25 1·50
MS820 97 × 68 mm. $5 Taino Indians worshiping stone idol 2·00 3·00

1985. 40th Anniv of International Civil Aviation Organization. Nos. 934/8 of Antigua optd **BARBUDA MAIL**.
821 30c. Cessna Skyhawk . . . . 2·50 75
822 90c. Fokker D.VII . . . . . 3·50 1·25
823 $1.50 SPAD VII . . . . . . 4·25 5·50
824 $3 Boeing 747 . . . . 6·00 8·50
MS825 97 × 83 mm. De Havilland D.H.C.6 Twin Otter . . . . . 3·25 3·50

1985. Life and Times of Queen Elizabeth the Queen Mother (2nd series). Nos. 946/9 of Antigua optd **BARBUDA MAIL**.
826 $1 The Queen Mother attending church . . . . . 6·00 2·50
827 $1.50 Watching children playing in London garden 7·00 3·00
828 $2.50 The Queen Mother in 1979 . . . . 8·00 3·50
MS829 56 × 85 mm. $5 With Prince Edward at Royal Wedding, 1981 17·00 11·00

1985. 850th Birth Anniv of Maimonides (physician philosopher and scholar). Nos. 939/40 of Antigua optd **BARBUDA MAIL**.
830 $2 green . . . . 4·50 3·75
MS831 70 × 84 mm. $5 brown . . 4·25 4·25

1985. Marine Life. Nos. 950/4 of Antigua optd **BARBUDA MAIL**.
832 15c. Magnificent frigate bird 7·00 1·25
833 45c. Brain coral . . . . . . 7·00 80
834 60c. Cushion star . . . . . 7·00 1·25
835 $3 Spotted moray . . . . . 15·00 5·50
MS836 110 × 80 mm. $5 Elkhorn coral . . . . 17·00 6·50

1986. International Youth Year. Nos. 941/5 of Antigua optd **BARBUDA MAIL**.
837 25c. Young farmers with produce 15 15
838 50c. Hotel management trainees 25 30
839 60c. Girls with goat and boys with football ("Environment") 30 35
840 $3 Windsurfing ("Leisure") 1·50 1·60
MS841 102 × 72 mm. $5 Young people with Antiguan flag . . . 2·75 3·25

1986. Royal Visit. Nos. 965/8 of Antigua optd **BARBUDA MAIL**.
842 60c. Flags of Great Britain and Antigua . . . . 3·75 50
843 $1 Queen Elizabeth II (vert) 3·00 65
844 $4 Royal Yacht "Britannia" 8·50 2·50
MS845 110 × 83 mm. $5 Map of Antigua . . . . 11·00 4·00

1986. 75th Anniv of Girl Guide Movement. Nos. 955/9 of Antigua optd **BARBUDA MAIL**.
846 15c. Girl Guides nursing . . 1·50 80
847 45c. Open-air Girl Guide meeting . . . . 2·75 1·75
848 60c. Lord and Lady Baden-Powell . . . . 2·75 2·50
849 $3 Girl Guides gathering flowers . . . . 7·50 9·50
MS850 67 × 96 mm. $5 Barn swallow (Nature study) . . . . 32·00 22·00

1986. 300th Birth Anniv of Johann Sebastian Bach (composer). Nos. 960/4 of Antigua optd **BARBUDA MAIL**.
851 25c. multicoloured . . . . . 3·50 70
852 50c. multicoloured . . . . . 3·75 1·40
853 $1 multicoloured . . . . . . 5·00 2·00
854 $3 multicoloured . . . . . . 8·50 9·00
MS855 104 × 73 mm. $5 black and grey . . . . 26·00 12·00

1986. Christmas. Religious Paintings. Nos. 985/8 of Antigua optd **BARBUDA MAIL**.
856 10c. "Madonna and Child" (De Landi) 40 30
857 25c. "Madonna and Child" (Berlinghiero) 80 50
858 60c. "The Nativity" (Fra Angelico) . . . . 1·50 1·00
859 $4 "Presentation in the Temple" (Giovanni di Paolo) . . . . 4·00 7·00
MS860 113 × 81 mm. $5 "The Nativity" (Antoniazzo Romano) 4·25 5·50

108 Queen Elizabeth II meeting Members of Legislature

1986. 60th Birthday of Queen Elizabeth II (1st issue). Multicoloured.
861 $1 Type **108** . . . . 50 1·00
862 $2 Queen with Headmistress of Liberta School . . . . 60 1·10
863 $2.50 Queen greeted by Governor-General of Antigua . . . . 60 1·25
MS864 95 × 75 mm. $5 Queen Elizabeth in 1928 and 1986 (33 × 27 mm) . . . . 6·50 8·50
See also Nos. 872/5.

109 Halley's Comet over Barbuda Beach

1986. Appearance of Halley's Comet (1st issue). Multicoloured.
865 $1 Type **109** . . . . 60 1·25
866 $2.50 Early telescope and dish aerial (vert) . . . . . 80 2·25
867 $5 Comet and world map . . 1·40 3·75
See also Nos. 886/9.

1986. 40th Anniv of United Nations Organization. Nos. 981/4 of Antigua optd **BARBUDA MAIL.**
868 40c. Benjamin Franklin and U.N. (New York) 1953 U.P.U. 5c. stamp . . . . 1·50 1·00
869 $1 George Washington Carver (agricultural chemist) and 1982 Nature Conservation 28c. stamp 2·25 2·25
870 $3 Charles Lindbergh (aviator) and 1978 I.C.A.O. 25c. stamp . . . . . . 4·00 5·00
MS871 101 × 77 mm. $5 Marc Chagell (artist) (vert) . . . . . 12·00 13·00

1986. 60th Birthday of Queen Elizabeth II (2nd issue). Nos. 1005/8 of Antigua optd **BARBUDA MAIL.**
872 60c. black and yellow . . . . 2·50 1·25
873 $1 multicoloured . . . . . . 3·00 2·00
874 $4 multicoloured . . . . . . 4·75 4·50
MS875 120 × 85 mm. $5 black and brown . . . . 8·00 9·00

1986. World Cup Football Championship, Mexico. Nos. 995/9 of Antigua optd **BARBUDA MAIL.**
876 30c. Football, boots and trophy . . . . 4·00 1·00
877 60c. Goalkeeper (vert) . . . 5·50 2·00
878 $1 Referee blowing whistle (vert) . . . . 6·00 2·25
879 $4 Ball in net . . . . 13·00 9·00
MS880 87 × 76 mm. $5 Two players competing for ball . . . . . . 23·00 15·00

1986. "Ameripex '86" International Stamp Exhibition, Chicago. Famous American Trains. Nos. 1014/18 of Antigua optd **BARBUDA MAIL.**
881 25c. "Hiawatha" express . . 2·00 1·50
882 50c. "Grand Canyon" express 2·75 2·25
883 $1 "Powhattan Arrow" express . . . . 3·50 3·00
884 $3 "Empire State" express . . 6·00 7·00
MS885 117 × 87 mm. $5 Southern Pacific "Daylight" express . . 9·00 9·50

1986. Appearance of Halley's Comet (2nd issue). Nos. 1000/4 of Antigua optd **BARBUDA MAIL.**
886 5c. Edmond Halley and Old Greenwich Observatory . . . 2·50 1·00
887 10c. Messerschmitt Me 163B Komet (fighter aircraft), 1944 . . . . 2·50 1·00
888 60c. Montezuma (Aztec Emperor) and Comet in 1517 (from "Historias de las Indias de Neuva Espana") . . . . 3·75 2·00
889 $4 Pocahontas saving Capt. John Smith and Comet in 1607 . . . . 13·00 8·00
MS890 101 × 70 mm. $5 Halley's Comet over English Harbour, Antigua . . . . 6·00 5·00

1986. Royal Wedding. Nos. 1019/22 of Antigua optd **BARBUDA MAIL.**
891 45c. Prince Andrew and Miss Sarah Ferguson 75 50
892 60c. Prince Andrew 90 65
893 $4 Prince Andrew with Prince Philip . . . . 3·50 4·00
MS894 88 × 88 mm. $5 Prince Andrew and Miss Sarah Ferguson (different) . . . . 8·00 8·00

1986. Sea Shells. Nos. 1023/7 of Antigua optd **BARBUDA MAIL.**
895 15c. Fly-specked cerith . . . 2·50 2·00
896 45c. Smooth Scotch bonnet . 2·75 2·25
897 60c. West Indian crown conch . . . . 3·50 2·75
898 $3 Criboney murex . . . . . 8·00 12·00
MS899 109 × 75 mm. $5 Colourful Atlantic moon (horiz) . . . . 20·00 18·00

1986. Flowers. Nos. 1028/36 of Antigua optd **BARBUDA MAIL.**
900 10c. "Nymphaea ampla" (water lily) 50 50
901 15c. Queen of the night . . . 60 50
902 50c. Cup of gold . . . . . . 1·00 70
903 60c. Beach morning glory . . 1·10 70
904 70c. Golden trumpet . . . . 1·25 90
905 $1 Air plant . . . . 1·50 90
906 $3 Purple wreath . . . . . . 3·00 4·00
907 $4 Zephyr lily . . . . 3·50 4·25
MS908 Two sheets, each 102 × 72 mm. (a) $4 Dozakie. (b) $5 Four o'clock flower Set of 2 sheets . . . . 27·00 24·00

1986. Mushrooms. Nos. 1042/6 of Antigua optd **BARBUDA MAIL.**
909 10c. "Hygrocybe occidentalis var scarletina" 90 50
910 50c. "Trogia buccinalis" . . 3·25 1·75
911 $1 "Collybia subpruinosa" 4·75 2·75
912 $4 "Leucocoprinus brebissonii" . . . . 9·50 8·00
MS913 102 × 82 mm. $5 Pyrrhoglossum pyrrhum . . . 25·00 14·00

1986. Birth Bicentenary of John J. Audubon (ornithologist) (3rd issue). Nos. 990/3 of Antigua optd **BARBUDA MAIL.**
914 60c. Mallard . . . . 6·50 2·50
915 90c. North American black duck ("Dusky Duck") . . 8·50 2·75
916 $1.50 American pintail ("Common Pintail") . . . 11·00 8·50
917 $3 American wigeon ("Wigeon") . . . . 16·00 14·00

1987. Local Boats. Nos. 1009/13 of Antigua optd **BARBUDA MAIL.**
918 30c. Tugboat . . . . 1·00 60
919 60c. Game fishing boat . . . 1·50 80
920 $1 Yacht . . . . 2·00 1·25
921 $4 Lugger with auxiliary sail 4·25 6·00
MS922 108 × 78 mm. $5 Boats under construction . . . . 25·00 18·00

1987. Centenary of First Benz Motor Car. Nos. 1052/60 of Antigua optd **BARBUDA MAIL.**
923 10c. Auburn "Speedster" (1933) . . . . 1·00 45
924 15c. Mercury "Sable" (1986) 1·25 50
925 50c. Cadillac (1959) . . . . 1·90 70
926 60c. Studebaker (1950) . . . 1·90 70
927 70c. Lagonda "V-12" (1939) 2·00 1·00
928 $1 Adler "Standard" (1930) 2·50 1·00
929 $3 DKW (1956) . . . . . . 3·50 4·00
930 $4 Mercedes "500K" (1936) 3·50 4·00
MS931 Two sheets, each 99 × 70 mm. (a) $5 Daimler (1896). (b) $5 Mercedes "Knight" (1921) Set of 2 sheets . . . . 27·00 15·00

1987. World Cup Football Championship Winners, Mexico. Nos. 1037/40 of Antigua optd **BARBUDA MAIL.**
932 30c. Football, boots and trophy . . . . 4·00 1·00
933 60c. Goalkeeper (vert) . . . 4·50 1·50
934 $1 Referee blowing whistle (vert) . . . . 5·50 2·25
935 $4 Ball in net . . . . 12·00 12·00

1987. America's Cup Yachting Championship. Nos. 1072/6 of Antigua optd **BARBUDA MAIL.**
936 30c. "Canada I" (1981) . . . 90 40
937 60c. "Gretel II" (1970) . . . 1·25 50
938 $1 "Sceptre" (1958) . . . . 1·60 80
939 $3 "Vigilant" (1893) . . . . 2·25 3·50
MS940 113 × 84 mm. $5 "Australia II" defeating "Liberty" (1983) (horiz) . . . . 4·50 5·00

1987. Marine Life. Nos. 1077/85 of Antigua optd **BARBUDA MAIL.**
941 15c. Bridled burrfish . . . . 6·50 1·50
942 30c. Common noddy ("Brown Noddy") . . . . 11·00 1·50
943 40c. Nassau grouper . . . . 8·00 1·50
944 50c. Laughing gull . . . . . 13·00 2·25
945 60c. French angelfish . . . . 10·00 1·75
946 $1 Porkfish . . . . 10·00 2·50
947 $2 Royal tern . . . . 21·00 10·00
948 $3 Sooty tern . . . . 21·00 11·00
MS949 Two sheets, each 120 × 94 mm. (a) $5 Banded butterflyfish. (b) $5 Brown booby Set of 2 sheets . . . . 60·00 24·00

1987. Milestones of Transportation. Nos. 1100/9 of Antigua optd **BARBUDA MAIL.**
950 10c. "Spirit of Australia" (fastest powerboat), 1978 3·25 1·50
951 15c. Werner von Siemens's electric locomotive, 1879 4·25 1·25
952 30c. U.S.S. "Triton" (first submerged circumnavigation), 1960 . . 4·25 1·25
953 50c. Trevithick's steam carriage (first passenger-carrying vehicle), 1801 . . 4·75 2·00
954 60c. U.S.S. "New Jersey" (battleship), 1942 . . . . . 5·50 2·00
955 70c. Draisine bicycle, 1818 . . 6·50 2·75
956 90c. "United States" (liner) (holder of the Blue Riband), 1952 . . . . . . 6·50 2·25
957 $1.50 Cierva C.4 (first autogyro), 1923 . . . . . 6·50 7·00
958 $2 Curtiss NC-4 flying boat (first transatlantic flight), 1919 . . . . 7·00 8·00
959 $3 "Queen Elizabeth 2" (liner), 1969 . . . . 11·00 10·00

110 Shore Crab

1987. Marine Life. Multicoloured.
960 5c. Type **110** 10 20
961 10c. Sea cucumber 10 20
962 15c. Stop-light parrotfish . . 10 20
963 25c. Banded coral shrimp . . 15 20
964 35c. Spotted drum 15 20
965 60c. Thorny starfish 20 40
966 75c. Atlantic trumpet triton 20 60
967 90c. Feather star and yellow beaker sponge 20 65
968 $1 Blue gorgonian (vert) . . 20 65
969 $1.25 Slender filefish (vert) . . 20 85
970 $5 Barred hamlet (vert) . . . 45 3·50
971 $7.50 Royal gramma ("Fairy basslet") (vert) . . . . . . 60 4·50
972 $10 Fire coral and banded butterflyfish (vert) . . . . 75 5·00

1987. Olympic Games, Seoul (1988). Nos. 1086/90 of Antigua optd **BARBUDA MAIL.**
973 10c. Handball . . . . 1·00 50
974 60c. Fencing . . . . 2·00 80
975 $1 Gymnastics . . . . 2·50 1·40
976 $3 Football . . . . 4·25 5·50
MS977 100 × 77 mm. $5 Boxing gloves . . . . 8·50 4·75

1987. Birth Centenary of Marc Chagall (artist). Nos. 1091/9 of Antigua optd **BARBUDA MAIL.**
978 10c. "The Profile" 25 40
979 30c. "Portrait of the Artist's Sister" 35 20
980 40c. "Bride with Fan" . . . 40 30
981 60c. "David in Profile" . . . 45 30
982 90c. "Fiancee with Bouquet" 60 50
983 $1 "Self Portrait with Brushes" 70 55
984 $3 "The Walk" . . . . . . 2·00 2·50
985 $4 "Three Candles" . . . . 2·25 2·75
MS986 Two sheets, each 110 × 95 mm. (a) $5 "Fall of Icarus" (104 × 89 mm). (b) $5 "Myth of Orpheus" (104 × 89 mm) Set of 2 sheets . . . . 7·00 8·00

1987. Centenary (1986) of Statue of Liberty (2nd issue). Nos. 1110/19 of Antigua optd **BARBUDA MAIL.**
987 15c. Lee Iacocoa at unveiling of restored statue 20 20
988 30c. Statue at sunset (side view) 30 20
989 45c. Aerial view of head . . 45 25
990 50c. Lee Iacocoa and torch . 50 30
991 60c. Workmen inside head of statue (horiz) 55 30
992 90c. Restoration work (horiz) 70 50
993 $1 Head of statue 80 75
994 $2 Statue at sunset (front view) . . . . 1·25 1·75
995 $3 Inspecting restoration work (horiz) . . . . 1·60 2·50
996 $5 Statue at night . . . . . 2·50 3·50

1987. Entertainers. Nos. 1120/7 of Antigua optd **BARBUDA MAIL.**
997 15c. Grace Kelly . . . . . . 2·00 70
998 30c. Marilyn Monroe . . . . 5·00 1·25
999 45c. Orson Welles . . . . . 2·00 75
1000 50c. Judy Garland . . . . . 2·00 1·00
1001 60c. John Lennon . . . . . 13·00 2·50
1002 $1 Rock Hudson . . . . . 2·75 1·75
1003 $1 John Wayne . . . . . . 4·00 3·50
1004 $3 Elvis Presley . . . . . . 24·00 11·00

1987. "Capex '87" International Stamp Exhibition, Toronto. Reptiles and Amphibians. Nos. 1133/7 of Antigua optd **BARBUDA MAIL.**
1005 30c. Whistling frog . . . . 6·00 1·75
1006 60c. Croaking lizard . . . . 7·00 1·75
1007 $1 Antiguan anole . . . . . 8·00 3·00
1008 $3 Red-footed tortoise . . . 16·00 17·00
MS1009 106 × 76 mm. $5 Ground lizard . . . . 29·00 12·00

1988. Christmas. Religious Paintings. Nos. 1144/8 of Antigua optd **BARBUDA MAIL.**
1010 45c. "Madonna and Child" (Bernardo Daddi) . . . . 2·00 30
1011 60c. St. Joseph (detail, "The Nativity" (Sano di Pietro)) . . . . 2·00 55
1012 $1 Virgin Mary (detail, "The Nativity" (Sano di Pietro)) . . . . 2·25 1·25
1013 $4 "Music-making Angel" (Melozzo da Forli) . . . 6·50 8·50
MS1014 90 × 70 mm. $5 "The Flight into Egypt" (Sano di Pietro) 9·00 6·50

1988. Salvation Army's Community Service. Nos. 1163/71 of Antigua optd **BARBUDA MAIL.**
1015 25c. First aid at daycare centre, Antigua . . . . . 2·00 1·00
1016 30c. Giving penicillin injection, Indonesia . . . 2·00 1·00
1017 40c. Children at daycare centre, Bolivia . . . . . 2·00 1·00
1018 45c. Rehabilitation of the handicapped, India . . . 2·00 1·00
1019 50c. Training blind man, Kenya . . . . 2·50 1·50
1020 60c. Weighing baby, Ghana 2·50 1·50
1021 $1 Training typist, Zambia 3·00 2·50
1022 $2 Emergency food kitchen, Sri Lanka . . . . 3·50 4·00
MS1023 152 × 83 mm. $5 General Eva Burrows . . . . 27·00 25·00

1988. Bicentenary of U.S. Constitution. Nos. 1139/43 of Antigua optd **BARBUDA MAIL.**
1024 15c. House of Burgesses, Virginia ("Freedom of Speech") 10 15
1025 45c. State Seal, Connecticut 20 25
1026 60c. State Seal, Delaware . . 25 40
1027 $4 Gouverneur Morris (Pennsylvania delegate) (vert) . . . . 1·75 3·25
MS1028 105 × 75 mm. $5 Roger Sherman (Connecticut delegate) (vert) . . . . 2·75 3·25

1988. Royal Ruby Wedding. Nos. 1149/53 of Antigua optd **BARBUDA MAIL.**
1029 25c. brown, black and blue 2·50 40
1030 60c. multicoloured . . . . . 3·00 65
1031 $2 brown, black and green 6·50 2·50
1032 $3 multicoloured . . . . . 7·50 3·00
MS1033 102 × 77 mm. $5 multicoloured . . . . 16·00 6·50

1988. Birds of Antigua. Nos. 1154/62 of Antigua optd **BARBUDA MAIL.**
1034 10c. Great blue heron . . . 3·75 1·75
1035 15c. Ringed kingfisher (horiz) . . . . 4·00 1·75
1036 50c. Bananaquit (horiz) . . 5·50 1·75
1037 60c. American purple gallinule ("Purple Gallinule") (horiz) . . . . 5·50 1·75
1038 70c. Blue-hooded euphonia (horiz) . . . . 6·00 2·75
1039 $1 Brown-throated concure ("Caribbean Parakeet") 7·00 2·75
1040 $3 Troupial (horiz) . . . . 12·00 8·50
1041 $4 Purple-throated carib (horiz) . . . . 12·00 8·50
MS1042 Two sheets, each 115 × 86 mm. (a) $5 Greater flamingo. (b) $5 Brown pelican Set of 2 sheets . . . . 38·00 19·00

1988. 500th Anniv (1992) of Discovery of America by Columbus (1st issue). Nos. 1172/80 of Antigua optd **BARBUDA MAIL.**
1043 10c. Columbus's second fleet, 1493 . . . . 3·25 1·00
1044 30c. Painos Indian village and fleet . . . . 3·25 80
1045 45c. "Santa Mariagalante" (flagship) and Painos village . . . . 4·00 80
1046 60c. Painos Indians offering Columbus fruit and vegetables . . . . 2·75 85
1047 90c. Painos Indian and Columbus with scarlet macaw . . . . 7·00 1·75
1048 $1 Columbus landing on island . . . . 5·50 1·75
1049 $3 Spanish soldier and fleet 7·00 4·50
1050 $4 Fleet under sail . . . . 7·00 4·50
MS1051 Two sheets, each 110 × 80 mm. (a) $5 Queen Isabella's cross. (b) $5 Gold coin of Ferdinand and Isabella Set of 2 sheets . . . . 15·00 13·00
See also Nos. 1112/16, 1177/85, 1285/93, 1374/80 and 1381/2.

1988. 500th Birth Anniv of Titian. Nos. 1181/9 of Antigua optd **BARBUDA MAIL.**
1052 30c. "Bust of Christ" . . . 60 20
1053 40c. "Scourging of Christ" 75 25
1054 45c. "Madonna in Glory with Saints" 80 25
1055 50c. "The Averoldi Polyptych" (detail) . . . 90 30
1056 $1 "Christ Crowned with Thorns" . . . . 1·60 55
1057 $2 "Christ Mocked" . . . . 2·50 1·50
1058 $3 "Christ and Simon of Cyrene" . . . . 3·00 2·50
1059 $4 "Crucifixion with Virgin and Saints" . . . . 3·00 3·00
MS1060 Two sheets, each 110 × 95 mm. (a) $5 "Ecce Homo" (detail). (b) $5 "Noli me Tangere" (detail) Set of 2 sheets . . . . 8·50 8·00

1988. 16th World Scout Jamboree, Australia. Nos. 1128/32 of Antigua optd **BARBUDA MAIL.**
1061 10c. Scouts around campfire and red kangaroo . . . . 2·50 1·00
1062 60c. Scouts canoeing and blue-winged kookaburra 7·50 1·50
1063 $1 Scouts on assault course and ring-tailed rock wallaby . . . . 4·00 1·75
1064 $3 Field kitchen and koala 7·50 6·50
MS1065 103 × 78 mm. $5 Flags of Antigua, Australia and Scout Movement . . . . 8·00 6·50

1988. Sailing Week. Nos. 1190/4 of Antigua optd **BARBUDA MAIL.**
1066 30c. Two yachts rounding buoy 60 35
1067 60c. Three yachts . . . . . 1·00 70
1068 $1 British yacht under way 1·25 1·10
1069 $3 Three yachts (different) 2·25 2·75
MS1070 103 × 92 mm. $5 Two yachts . . . . 7·50 4·50

1988. Flowering Trees. Nos. 1213/21 of Antigua optd **BARBUDA MAIL.**
1071 10c. Jacaranda 15 20
1072 30c. Cordia 30 20

1073 50c. Orchid tree 40 25
1074 90c. Flamboyant 60 45
1075 $1 African tulip tree 70 60
1076 $2 Potato tree . . . . . . 1·25 1·50
1077 $3 Crepe myrtle . . . . . . 1·50 2·00
1078 $4 Pitch apple . . . . . . 1·75 2·50
MS1079 Two sheets, each 106 × 76 mm. (a) $5 Cassia. (b) $5 Chinaberry Set of 2 sheets . . 6·00 6·50

1988. Olympic Games, Seoul. Nos. 1222/6 of Antigua optd **BARBUDA MAIL.**
1080 40c. Gymnastics . . . . . 1·50 40
1081 60c. Weightlifting . . . . . 1·75 55
1082 $1 Water polo (horiz) . . . 2·00 1·00
1083 $3 Boxing (horiz) . . . . . 2·75 3·00
MS1084 114 × 80 mm. $5 Runner with Olympic torch . . . . . 3·00 2·40

1988. Caribbean Butterflies. Nos. 1227/44 of Antigua optd **BARBUDA MAIL.**
1085 1c. "Danaus plexippus" . . 40 75
1086 2c. "Greta diaphanus" . . 40 75
1087 3c. "Calisto archebates" . . 50 75
1088 5c. "Hamadryas feronia" . . 50 75
1089 10c. "Mestra dorcas" . . . 60 60
1090 15c. "Hypolimnas misippus" 75 40
1091 20c. "Dione juno" 90 50
1092 25c. "Heliconius charithonia" 90 50
1093 30c. "Eurema pyro" . . . 95 50
1094 40c. "Papilio androgeus" . . 1·10 50
1095 45c. "Anteos maerula" . . 1·10 50
1096 50c. "Aphrissa orbis" . . . 1·25 75
1097 60c. "Astraptes xagua" . . 1·25 60
1098 $1 "Heliopetes arsalte" . . 1·60 1·00
1099 $2 "Polites baracoa" . . . 3·25 3·50
1100 $2.50 "Phocides pigmalion" . 3·50 4·25
1101 $5 "Prepona amphitoe" . . 5·00 6·00
1102 $10 "Oarisma nanus" . . . 8·00 9·50
1102a $20 "Parides lycimenes" . . 13·00 15·00

1989. 25th Death Anniv of John F. Kennedy (American statesman). Nos. 1245/53 of Antigua optd **BARBUDA MAIL.**
1103 1c. President Kennedy and family 10 75
1104 2c. Kennedy commanding "PT109" 10 75
1105 3c. Funeral cortege 10 75
1106 4c. In motorcade, Mexico . . 10 75
1107 30c. As 1c. . . . . 1·25 50
1108 60c. As 4c. . . . . 3·25 60
1109 $1 As 3c. . . . . 3·25 1·50
1110 $4 As 2c. . . . . 8·50 11·00
MS1111 105 × 75 mm. $5 Kennedy taking presidential oath of office 4·50 6·00

1989. 500th Anniv (1992) of Discovery of America by Columbus (2nd issue). Pre-Columbian Arawak Society. Nos. 1267/71 of Antigua optd **BARBUDA MAIL.**
1112 $1.50 Arawak warriors . . . 4·00 4·25
1113 $1.50 Whip dancers . . . . 4·00 4·25
1114 $1.50 Whip dancers and chief with pineapple . . . 4·00 4·25
1115 $1.50 Family and camp fire 4·00 4·25
MS1116 71 × 84 mm. $6 Arawak chief . . . . 5·50 6·50

1989. 50th Anniv of First Jet Flight. Nos. 1272/80 of Antigua optd **BARBUDA MAIL.**
1117 10c. Hawker Siddeley Comet 4 airliner . . . . 3·50 2·00
1118 30c. Messerschmitt Me 262 fighter . . . . 4·50 1·50
1119 40c. Boeing 707 airliner . . 4·75 1·25
1120 60c. Canadair CL-13 Sabre fighter . . . . 6·00 1·25
1121 $1 Lockheed Starfighters . . 7·00 2·50
1122 $2 Douglas DC-10 airliner 9·00 8·00
1123 $3 Boeing 747-300/400 airliner . . . . 10·00 11·00
1124 $4 McDonnell Douglas Phantom II fighter . . . 10·00 11·00
MS1125 Two sheets, each 114 × 83 mm. (a) $7 Grumman F-14 Tomcat fighter. (b) $7 Concorde airliner Set of 2 sheets 50·00 40·00

1989. Caribbean Cruise Ships. Nos. 1281/9 of Antigua optd **BARBUDA MAIL.**
1126 25c. "Festivale" . . . . . . 3·75 1·50
1127 45c. "Southward" . . . . . 4·00 1·50
1128 50c. "Sagafjord" . . . . . 4·00 1·75
1129 60c. "Daphne" . . . . . . 4·00 1·75
1130 75c. "Cunard Countess" . . 4·25 2·75
1131 90c. "Song of America" . . 4·25 2·75
1132 $3 "Island Princess" . . . . 9·50 10·00
1133 $4 "Galileo" . . . . 9·50 10·00
MS1134 (a) 113 × 87 mm. $6 "Norway". (b) 111 × 82 mm. $6 "Oceanic" Set of 2 sheets . . . 50·00 38·00

1989. Japanese Art. Paintings by Hiroshige. Nos. 1290/8 of Antigua optd **BARBUDA MAIL.**
1135 25c. "Fish swimming by Duck half-submerged in Stream" . . . . 4·00 1·00
1136 45c. "Crane and Wave" . . 4·75 1·00
1137 50c. "Sparrows and Morning Glories" . . . . 5·00 1·50
1138 60c. "Crested Blackbird and Flowering Cherry" . . . 5·00 1·50
1139 $1 "Great Knot sitting among Water Grass" . . 5·50 1·75
1140 $2 "Goose on a Bank of Water" . . . . 7·50 4·25
1141 $3 "Black Paradise Fly-catcher and Blossoms" . . 9·00 5·00
1142 $4 "Sleepy Owl perched on a Pine Branch" . . . . 10·00 5·50
MS1143 Two sheets, each 102 × 75 mm. (a) $5 "Bullfinch flying near a Clematis Branch". (b) $5 "Titmouse on a Cherry Branch" Set of 2 sheets . . . . 48·00 23·00

1989. World Cup Football Championship, Italy (1990). Nos. 1308/12 of Antigua optd **BARBUDA MAIL.**
1144 15c. Goalkeeper . . . . . . 2·00 65
1145 25c. Goalkeeper moving towards ball . . . . . . 2·00 65
1146 $1 Goalkeeper reaching for ball . . . . 5·00 2·00
1147 $4 Goalkeeper saving goal 8·00 10·00
MS1148 Two sheets, each 75 × 105 mm. (a) $5 Three players competing for ball (horiz). (b) $5 Ball and players' legs (horiz) Set of 2 sheets . . . . 38·00 32·00

1989. Christmas. Paintings by Raphael and Giotto. Nos. 1351/9 of Antigua optd **BARBUDA MAIL.**
1149 10c. "The Small Cowper Madonna" (Raphael) . . 35 30
1150 25c. "Madonna of the Goldfinch" (Raphael) . . 45 20
1151 30c. "The Alba Madonna" (Raphael) 45 20
1152 50c. Saint (detail, "Bologna Altarpiece") (Giotto) . . 70 30
1153 60c. Angel (detail, "Bologna Altarpiece") (Giotto) . . 75 45
1154 70c. Angel slaying serpent (detail, "Bologna Altarpiece") (Giotto) . . 80 60
1155 $4 Evangelist (detail, "Bologna Altarpiece") (Giotto) . . . . 2·75 4·50
1156 $5 "Madonna of Foligno" (Raphael) . . . . 2·75 4·50
MS1157 Two sheets, each 71 × 96 mm. (a) $5 "The Marriage of the Virgin" (detail) (Raphael). (b) $5 Madonna and Child (detail, "Bologna Altarpiece") (Giotto) Set of 2 sheets . . . . 12·00 14·00

1990. Fungi. Nos. 1313/21 of Antigua optd **BARBUDA MAIL.**
1158 10c. "Mycena pura" . . . . 2·50 1·50
1159 25c. Psathyrella tuberculata" (vert) . . . 2·75 65
1160 50c. "Psilocybe cubensis" . . 3·25 1·00
1161 60c. "Leptonia caeruleocapitata" (vert) 3·25 1·00
1162 75c. "Xeromphalina tenuipes" (vert) . . . . . 3·25 1·40
1163 $1 "Chlorophyllum molybdites" (vert) . . . . 3·50 1·40
1164 $3 "Marasmius haematocephalus" . . . . 6·00 7·50
1165 $4 "Cantharellus cinnabarinus" . . . . . 6·00 7·50
MS1166 Two sheets, each 88 × 62 mm. (a) $6 "Leucopaxillus gracillimus" (vert). (b) $6 "Volvariella volvacea" Set of 2 sheets . . . . 38·00 23·00

1990. Local Fauna. Nos. 1322/6 optd **BARBUDA MAIL.**
1167 25c. Desmarest's hutia . . . 1·00 60
1168 45c. Caribbean monk seal 2·50 1·25
1169 60c. Mustache bat (vert) . . 1·75 1·25
1170 $4 American manatee (vert) 4·25 6·50
MS1171 113 × 87 mm. $5 West Indian giant rice rat . . . . . 22·00 22·00

1990. 20th Anniv of First Manned Landing on Moon. Nos. 1346/50 optd **BARBUDA MAIL.**
1172 10c. Launch of "Apollo 11" 3·00 1·50
1173 45c. Aldrin on Moon . . . . 5·50 80
1174 $1 Module "Eagle" over Moon (horiz) . . . . . . 7·00 2·75
1175 $4 Recovery of "Apollo 11" crew after splashdown (horiz) . . . . 13·00 13·00
MS1176 107 × 77 mm. $5 Astronaut Neil Armstrong . . . . . . 24·00 23·00

1990. 500th Anniv (1992) of Discovery of America by Columbus (3rd issue). New World Natural History – Marine Life. Nos. 1360/8 of Antigua optd **BARBUDA MAIL.**
1177 10c. Star-eyed hermit crab 1·75 1·75
1178 20c. Spiny lobster . . . . 2·25 1·75
1179 25c. Magnificent banded fanworm . . . . 2·25 1·75
1180 45c. Cannonball jellyfish . . 3·25 1·00
1181 60c. Red-spiny sea star . . . 3·50 1·00
1182 $2 Peppermint shrimp . . . 4·75 5·00
1183 $3 Coral crab . . . . . . 5·00 6·00
1184 $4 Branching fire coral . . . 5·00 6·00
MS1185 Two sheets, each 101 × 69 mm. (a) $5 Common sea fan. (b) Portuguese man-o-war Set of 2 sheets . . . . 28·00 27·00

1990. "EXPO 90" International Gardens and Greenery Exhibition, Osaka. Orchids. Nos. 1369/77 of Antigua optd **BARBUDA MAIL.**
1186 15c. "Vanilla mexicana" . . 1·75 80
1187 45c. "Epidendrum ibaguense" . . . . 2·25 80
1188 50c. "Epidendrum secundum" . . . . 2·25 90
1189 60c. "Maxillaria conferta" 2·50 1·10
1190 $1 "Onicidium altissimum" 2·75 1·75
1191 $2 "Spiranthes lanceolata" 5·00 5·00
1192 $3 "Tonopsis utricularioides" . . . . . 5·50 6·50
1193 $5 "Epidendrum nocturnum" . . . . . . 7·00 8·50
MS1194 Two sheets, each 101 × 69 mm. (a) $6 "Octomeria graminifolia". (b) $6 "Rodriguezia lanceolata" Set of 2 sheets . . 38·00 23·00

1990. Reef Fishes. Nos. 1386/94 of Antigua optd **BARBUDA MAIL.**
1195 10c. Flamefish . . . . . . 2·50 1·75
1196 15c. Coney . . . . 2·50 1·75
1197 50c. Long-spined squirrelfish 3·50 1·50
1198 60c. Sergeant major . . . . 3·50 1·50
1199 $1 Yellow-tailed snapper . . 4·25 2·50
1200 $2 Rock beauty . . . . . . 7·00 7·00
1201 $3 Spanish hogfish . . . . 9·00 10·00
1202 $4 Striped parrotfish . . . . 9·00 10·00
MS1203 Two sheets, each 99 × 70 mm. (a) $5 Black-barred soldierfish. (b) $5 Four-eyed butterflyfish Set of 2 sheets . . 38·00 32·00

1990. 1st Anniv of Hurricane Hugo. Nos. 971/2 surch **1st Anniversary Hurricane Hugo 16th September, 1989-1990** and new value.
1204 $5 on $7.50 Fairy basslet (vert) . . . . 12·00 14·00
1205 $7.50 on $10 Fire coral and butterfly fish (vert) . . . 13·00 16·00

1990. 90th Birthday of Queen Elizabeth the Queen Mother. Nos. 1415/19 of Antigua optd **BARBUDA MAIL.**
1206 15c. multicoloured . . . . . 8·00 1·75
1207 35c. multicoloured . . . . . 11·00 1·50
1208 75c. multicoloured . . . . . 17·00 3·25
1209 $3 multicoloured . . . . . 30·00 19·00
MS1210 67 × 98 mm. $6 multicoloured . . . . 55·00 26·00

1990. Achievements in Space. Nos. 1395/414 of Antigua optd **BARBUDA MAIL.**
1211 45c. "Voyager 2" passing Saturn . . . . 3·25 2·25
1212 45c. "Pioneer 11" photographing Saturn . . 3·25 2·25
1213 45c. Astronaut in transporter . . . . 3·25 2·25
1214 45c. Space shuttle "Columbia" . . . . . . 3·25 2·25
1215 45c. "Apollo 10" command module on parachutes . . 3·25 2·25
1216 45c. "Skylab" space station 3·25 2·25
1217 45c. Astronaut Edward White in space . . . . . 3·25 2·25
1218 45c. "Apollo" spacecraft on joint mission . . . . . . 3·25 2·25
1219 45c. "Soyuz" spacecraft on joint mission . . . . . . 3·25 2·25
1220 45c. "Mariner 1" passing Venus . . . . 3·25 2·25
1221 45c. "Gemini 4" capsule . . 3·25 2·25
1222 45c. "Sputnik 1" . . . . . 3·25 2·25
1223 45c. Hubble space telescope 3·25 2·25
1224 45c. North American X-15 rocket plane . . . . . . 3·25 2·25
1225 45c. Bell XS-1 airplane . . . 3·25 2·25
1226 45c. "Apollo 17" astronaut and lunar rock formation 3·25 2·25
1227 45c. Lunar rover . . . . . 3·25 2·25
1228 45c. "Apollo 14" lunar module . . . . 3·25 2·25
1229 45c. Astronaut Buzz Aldrin on Moon . . . . 3·25 2·25
1230 45c. Soviet "Lunokhod" lunar vehicle . . . . . . 3·25 2·25

1990. Christmas. Paintings by Renaissance Masters. Nos. 1457/65 of Antigua optd **BARBUDA MAIL.**
1231 25c. "Madonna and Child with Saints" (detail, Sebastiano del Piombo) 2·25 60
1232 30c. "Virgin and Child with Angels" (detail, Grunewald) (vert) . . . . 2·25 60
1233 40c. "The Holy Family and a Shepherd" (detail, Titian) . . . . 2·25 60
1234 60c. "Virgin and Child" (detail, Lippi) (vert) . . . 3·00 1·10
1235 $1 "Jesus, St. John and Two Angels" (Rubens) . . . 3·75 1·50
1236 $2 "Adoration of the Shepherds" (detail, Vincenzo Catena) . . . . 5·50 6·00
1237 $4 "Adoration of the Magi" (detail, Giorgione) . . . . 8·50 9·50
1238 $5 "Virgin and Child adored by Warriors" (detail, Vincenzo Catena) . . . . 8·50 9·50
MS1239 Two sheets, each 71 × 101 mm. (a) $6 "Allegory of the Blessings of Jacob" (detail, Rubens) (vert). (b) $6 "Adoration of the Magi" (detail, Fra Angelico) (vert) Set of 2 sheets . . . . . 25·00 26·00

1991. 150th Anniv of the Penny Black. Nos. 1378/81 of Antigua optd **BARBUDA MAIL.**
1240 45c. green . . . . 5·00 1·00
1241 60c. mauve . . . . 5·00 1·10
1242 $5 blue . . . . 15·00 15·00
MS1243 102 × 80 mm. $6 purple 18·00 16·00

1991. "Stamp World London 90" International Stamp Exhibition. Nos. 1382/4 of Antigua optd **BARBUDA MAIL.**
1244 50c. green and red . . . . 5·00 1·00
1245 75c. brown and red . . . . 5·00 1·50
1246 $4 blue and red . . . . . . 15·00 15·00
MS1247 104 × 81 mm. $6 black and red . . . . 23·00 21·00

119 Troupial

1991. Wild Birds. Multicoloured.
1248 60c. Type **119** . . . . . . 2·25 65
1249 $2 Adelaide's warbler ("Christmas Bird") . . . 3·75 3·00
1250 $4 Rose-breasted grosbeak 5·50 6·50
1251 $7 Wied's crested flycatcher ("Stolid Flycatcher") . . 7·50 11·00

1991. Olympic Games, Barcelona (1992). Nos. 1429/33 of Antigua optd **BARBUDA MAIL.**
1252 50c. Men's 20 kilometres walk . . . . 2·75 90
1253 75c. Triple jump . . . . . 3·00 1·00
1254 $1 Men's 10,000 metres . . 3·25 1·75
1255 $5 Javelin . . . . 12·00 14·00
MS1256 100 × 70 mm. $6 Athlete lighting Olympic flame at Los Angeles Olympics . . . . . . 14·00 16·00

1991. Birds. Nos. 1448/56 of Antigua optd **BARBUDA MAIL.**
1257 10c. Pearly-eyed thrasher . . 2·75 1·50
1258 25c. Purple-throated carib 3·75 80
1259 50c. Common yellowthroat 4·50 1·00
1260 60c. American kestrel . . . 4·50 1·10
1261 $1 Yellow-bellied sapsucker 4·75 2·00
1262 $2 American purple gallinule ("Purple Gallinule") . . . 6·50 6·50
1263 $3 Yellow-crowned night heron . . . . 7·00 8·50
1264 $4 Blue-hooded euphonia 7·00 8·50
MS1265 Two sheets, each 76 × 60 mm. (a) $6 Brown pelican. (b) Magnificent frigate bird Set of 2 sheets . . . . 25·00 23·00

1991. 350th Death Anniv of Rubens. Nos. 1466/74 of Antigua optd **BARBUDA MAIL.**
1266 25c. "Rape of the Daughters of Leucippus" (detail) . . 2·25 70
1267 45c. "Bacchanal" (detail) . . 2·75 70
1268 50c. "Rape of the Sabine Women" (detail) . . . . 2·75 75
1269 60c. "Battle of the Amazons" (detail) . . . . 3·00 85
1270 $1 "Rape of the Sabine Women" (different detail) 3·50 1·75
1271 $2 "Bacchanal" (different detail) . . . . 5·50 6·00
1272 $3 "Rape of the Sabine Women" (different detail) 8·00 9·00
1273 $4 "Bacchanal" (different detail) . . . . 8·00 9·00
MS1274 Two sheets, each 111 × 71 mm. (a) $6 "Rape of Hippodameia" (detail). (b) "Battle of the Amazons" (different detail) Set of 2 sheets . . . . 28·00 30·00

1991. 50th Anniv of Second World War. Nos. 1475/88 of Antigua optd **BARBUDA MAIL.**
1275 10c. U.S. troops cross into Germany, 1944 . . . . 3·25 2·25
1276 15c. Axis surrender in North Africa, 1943 . . . . . 3·75 2·00
1277 25c. U.S. tanks invade Kwalajalein, 1944 . . . . 4·00 1·50
1278 45c. Roosevelt and Churchill meet at Casablanca, 1943 10·00 2·50
1279 50c. Marshall Badoglio, Prime Minister of Italian anti-facist government, 1943 . . . . 3·75 1·75
1280 $1 Lord Mountbatten, Supreme Allied Commander South-east Asia, 1943 . . . . 13·00 4·25
1281 $2 Greek victory at Koritza, 1940 . . . . 10·00 10·00
1282 $4 Anglo-Soviet mutual assistance pact, 1941 . . . 12·00 12·00
1283 $5 Operation Torch landings, 1942 . . . . . 12·00 12·00
MS1284 Two sheets, each 108 × 80 mm. (a) $6 Japanese attack on Pearl Harbor, 1941. (b) $6 U.S.A.A.F. daylight raid on Schweinfurt, 1943 Set of 2 sheets 55·00 38·00

1991. 500th Anniv (1992) of Discovery of America by Columbus (4th issue). History of Exploration. Nos. 1503/11 of Antigua optd **BARBUDA MAIL.**
1285 10c. multicoloured . . . . . 2·00 1·75
1286 15c. multicoloured . . . . . 2·25 1·75
1287 45c. multicoloured . . . . . 3·25 1·00
1288 60c. multicoloured . . . . . 3·50 1·25
1289 $1 multicoloured . . . . . 3·75 2·00
1290 $2 multicoloured . . . . . 5·50 5·50
1291 $4 multicoloured . . . . . 9·00 10·00
1292 $5 multicoloured . . . . . 9·00 10·00
MS1293 Two sheets, each 106 × 76 mm. (a) $6 black and red. (b) $6 black and red Set of 2 sheets 32·00 27·00

1991. Butterflies. Nos. 1494/502 of Antigua optd **BARBUDA MAIL.**
1294 10c. "Heliconius charithonia" . . . . . . 3·00 1·75
1295 35c. "Marpesia petreus" . . 4·00 1·25
1296 50c. "Anartia amathea" . . 4·50 1·40

1297 75c. "Siproeta stelenes" 5·50 2·00
1298 $1 "Battus polydamas" 5·50 2·25
1299 $2 "Historis odius" 8·00 8·00
1300 $4 "Hypolimnas misippus" 10·00 11·00
1301 $5 "Hamadryas feronia" 10·00 11·00
MS1302 Two sheets. (a) 73 × 100 mm. $6 "Vanessa cardui" (caterpillar) (vert). (b) 100 × 73 mm. $6 "Danaus plexippus" (caterpillar) (vert) Set of 2 sheets 38·00 32·00

1991. 65th Birthday of Queen Elizabeth II. Nos. 1534/8 of Antigua optd **BARBUDA MAIL.**
1303 15c. Queen Elizabeth and Prince Philip in 1976 4·00 85
1304 20c. The Queen and Prince Philip in Portugal, 1985 4·00 85
1305 $2 Queen Elizabeth II 13·00 5·50
1306 $4 The Queen and Prince Philip at Ascot, 1986 21·00 15·00
MS1307 68 × 90 mm. $4 The Queen at National Theatre, 1986 and Prince Philip 40·00 17·00

1991. 10th Wedding Anniv of Prince and Princess of Wales. Nos. 1539/43 of Antigua optd **BARBUDA MAIL.**
1308 10c. Prince and Princess of Wales at party, 1986 3·50 1·75
1309 40c. Separate portraits of Prince, Princess and sons 9·00 1·25
1310 $1 Prince Henry and Prince William 10·00 3·50
1311 $5 Princess Diana in Australia and Prince Charles in Hungary 20·00 15·00
MS1312 68 × 90 mm. $4 Prince Charles in Hackney and Princess and sons in Majorca, 1987 38·00 17·00

1991. Christmas. Religious Paintings by Fra Angelico. Nos. 1595/1602 of Antigua optd **BARBUDA MAIL.**
1313 10c. "The Annunciation" 2·25 1·00
1314 30c. "Nativity" 2·75 70
1315 40c. "Adoration of the Magi" 2·75 70
1316 60c. "Presentation in the Temple" 3·50 70
1317 $1 "Circumcision" 4·50 1·75
1318 $3 "Flight into Egypt" 7·50 8·50
1319 $4 "Massacre of the Innocents" 7·50 9·00
1320 $5 "Christ teaching in the Temple" 7·50 9·00

1992. Death Centenary (1990) of Vincent van Gogh (artist). Nos. 1512/24 of Antigua optd **BARBUDA MAIL.**
1321 5c. "Camille Roulin" 1·75 2·00
1322 10c. "Armand Roulin" 2·00 2·00
1323 15c. "Young Peasant Woman with Straw Hat sitting in the Wheat" 2·25 2·00
1324 25c. "Adeline Ravoux" 2·25 2·00
1325 30c. "The Schoolboy" 2·25 1·25
1326 40c. "Doctor Gachet" 2·50 1·50
1327 50c. "Portrait of a Man" 2·50 1·75
1328 75c. "Two Children" 4·00 2·25
1329 $2 "The Postman Joseph Roulin" 7·50 7·50
1330 $3 "The Seated Zouave" 8·50 9·00
1331 $4 "L'Arlesienne" 9·00 10·00
1332 $5 "Self-Portrait, November/December 1888" 9·00 10·00
MS1333 Three sheets, each 102 × 76 mm. (a) $5 "Farmhouse in Provence" (horiz). (b) $5 "Flowering Garden" (horiz). (c) $6 "The Bridge at Trinquetaille" (horiz). Imperf Set of 3 sheets 38·00 38·00

1992. Birth Centenary of Charles de Gaulle (French statesman). Nos. 1562/70 of Antigua optd **BARBUDA MAIL.**
1334 10c. Pres. De Gaulle and Kennedy, 1961 2·75 1·75
1335 15c. General De Gaulle with Pres. Roosevelt, 1945 (vert) 2·75 1·75
1336 45c. President De Gaulle with Chancellor Adenauer, 1962 (vert) 3·50 80
1337 60c. De Gaulle at Arc de Triomphe, Liberation of Paris, 1944 (vert) 3·75 1·00
1338 $1 General De Gaulle crossing the Rhine, 1945 4·50 2·00
1339 $2 General De Gaulle in Algiers, 1944 7·50 7·50
1340 $4 Presidents De Gaulle and Eisenhower, 1960 10·00 12·00
1341 $5 De Gaulle returning from Germany, 1968 (vert) 10·00 12·00
MS1342 Two sheets. (a) 76 × 106 mm. $6 De Gaulle with crowd. (b) 106 × 76 mm. $6 De Gaulle and Churchill at Casablanca, 1943 Set of 2 sheets 38·00 32·00

1992. Easter. Religious Paintings. Nos. 1627/35 of Antigua optd **BARBUDA MAIL.**
1343 10c. "Supper at Emmaus" (Caravaggio) 1·75 1·25
1344 15c. "The Vision of St. Peter" (Zurbaran) 2·00 1·25
1345 30c. "Christ driving the Money-changers from the Temple" (Tiepolo) 2·25 80
1346 40c. "Martyrdom of St. Bartholomew" (detail) (Ribera) 2·25 80
1347 $1 "Christ driving the Money-changers from the Temple" (detail) (Tiepolo) 4·00 2·25
1348 $2 "Crucifixion" (detail) (Altdorfer) 6·00 6·50
1349 $4 "The Deposition" (detail) (Fra Angelico) 8·50 9·50
1350 $5 "The Deposition" (different detail) (Fra Angelico) 8·50 9·50
MS1351 Two sheets. (a) 102 × 71 mm. $6 "The Last Supper" (detail) (Masip). (b) 71 × 102 mm. $6 "Crucifixion" (detail) (vert) (Altdorfer) Set of 2 sheets 25·00 25·00

1992. Anniversaries and Events. Nos. 1573/83 of Antigua optd **BARBUDA MAIL.**
1352 25c. Germans celebrating Reunification 1·00 70
1353 75c. Cubs erecting tent 2·25 1·50
1354 $1.50 "Don Giovanni" and Mozart 12·00 4·25
1355 $2 Chariot driver and Gate at night 3·00 3·50
1356 $2 Lord Baden-Powell and members of the 3rd Antigua Methodist cub pack (vert) 3·00 3·50
1357 $2 Lilienthal's signature and glider "Flugzeug Nr. 5" 3·00 3·50
1358 $2.50 Driver in Class P36 steam locomotive (vert) 9·00 4·50
1359 $3 Statues from podium 3·00 4·50
1360 $3.50 Cubs and campfire 4·50 5·50
1361 $4 St. Peter's Cathedral, Salzburg 15·00 11·00
MS1362 Two sheets. (a) 100 × 72 mm. $4 Detail of chariot and helmet. (b) 89 × 117 mm. $5 Antiguan flag and Jamboree emblem (vert) Set of 2 sheets 42·00 32·00

1992. 50th Anniv of Japanese Attack on Pearl Harbor. Nos. 1585/94 of Antigua optd **BARBUDA MAIL.**
1364 $1 "Nimitz" class carrier and "Ticonderoga" class cruiser 6·00 3·50
1365 $1 Tourist launch 6·00 3·50
1366 $1 U.S.S. "Arizona" memorial 6·00 3·50
1367 $1 Wreaths on water and aircraft 6·00 3·50
1368 $1 White tern 6·00 3·50
1369 $1 Japanese torpedo bombers over Pearl City 6·00 3·50
1370 $1 Zeros attacking 6·00 3·50
1371 $1 Battleship Row in flames 6·00 3·50
1372 $1 U.S.S. "Nevada" (battleship) underway 6·00 3·50
1373 $1 Zeros returning to carriers 6·00 3·50

1992. 500th Anniv of Discovery of America by Columbus (5th issue). World Columbian Stamp "Expo '92", Chicago. Nos. 1654/60 of Antigua optd **BARBUDA MAIL.**
1374 15c. Memorial cross and huts, San Salvador 1·25 80
1375 30c. Martin Pinzon with telescope 1·50 90
1376 40c. Christopher Columbus 2·00 90
1377 $1 "Pinta" 6·00 2·75
1378 $2 "Nina" 8·00 7·50
1379 $4 "Santa Maria" 12·00 13·00
MS1380 Two sheets, each 108 × 76 mm. (a) $6 Ship and map of West Indies. (b) $6 Sea monster Set of 2 sheets 30·00 32·00

1992. 500th Anniv of Discovery of America by Columbus (6th issue). Organization of East Caribbean States. Nos. 1670/1 of Antigua optd **BARBUDA MAIL.**
1381 $1 Columbus meeting Amerindians 3·00 2·00
1382 $2 Ships approaching island 8·00 8·00

1992. Postage Stamp Mega Event, New York. No. MS1690 of Antigua optd **BARBUDA MAIL.**
MS1383 $6 multicoloured 15·00 16·00

1992. 40th Anniv of Queen Elizabeth II's Accession. Nos. 1604/8 of Antigua optd **BARBUDA MAIL.**
1384 10c. Queen Elizabeth II and bird sanctuary 6·50 1·75
1385 30c. Nelson's Dockyard 7·50 1·25
1386 $1 Ruins on Shirley Heights 9·50 2·75
1387 $5 Beach and palm trees 19·00 15·00
MS1388 Two sheets, each 75 × 98 mm. (a) $6 Beach. (b) $6 Hillside foliage Set of 2 sheets 45·00 26·00

1992. Prehistoric Animals. Nos. 1618/26 of Antigua optd **BARBUDA MAIL.**
1389 10c. Pteranodon 2·00 1·50
1390 15c. Brachiosaurus 2·50 1·50
1391 30c. Tyrannosaurus Rex 3·00 1·25
1392 50c. Parasaurolophus 3·00 1·50
1393 $1 Deinonychus (horiz) 3·75 2·25
1394 $2 Triceratops (horiz) 6·00 5·50
1395 $4 Protoceratops hatching (horiz) 7·00 8·50
1396 $5 Stegosaurus (horiz) 7·00 8·50
MS1397 Two sheets, each 100 × 70 mm. (a) $6 Apatosaurus (horiz). (b) $6 Allosaurus (horiz) Set of 2 sheets 35·00 26·00

1992. Christmas. Nos. 1691/9 of Antigua optd **BARBUDA MAIL.**
1398 10c. "Virgin and Child with Angels" (School of Piero della Francesca) 1·75 75
1399 25c. "Madonna degli Alberelli" (Giovanni Bellini) 1·75 75
1400 30c. "Madonna and Child with St. Anthony Abbot and St. Sigismund" (Neroccio) 1·75 75
1401 40c. "Madonna and the Grand Duke" (Raphael) 2·00 75
1402 60c. "The Nativity" (Georges de la Tour) 2·25 75
1403 $1 "Holy Family" (Jacob Jordaens) 2·75 1·50
1404 $4 "Madonna and Child Enthroned" (Magaritone) 6·50 8·50
1405 $5 "Madonna and Child on a Curved Throne" (Byzantine school) 6·50 8·50
MS1406 Two sheets, each 76 × 102 mm. (a) $6 "Madonna and Child" (Domenco Ghirlando). (b) $6 "The Holy Family" (Pontormo) Set of 2 sheets 25·00 25·00

1993. Fungi. Nos. 1645/53 of Antigua optd **BARBUDA MAIL.**
1407 10c. "Amanita caesarea" 1·75 1·25
1408 15c. "Collybia fusipes" 2·00 1·25
1409 30c. "Boletus aereus" 2·25 1·50
1410 40c. "Laccaria amethystina" 2·25 1·50
1411 $1 "Russula virescens" 3·25 2·00
1412 $2 "Tricholoma equestre" ("Tricholoma auratum") 4·50 4·00
1413 $4 "Calocybe gambosa" 5·50 6·50
1414 $5 "Lentinus tigrinus" ("Panus tigrinus") 5·50 6·50
MS1415 Two sheets, each 100 × 70 mm. (a) $6 "Clavariadelphus truncatus". (b) $6 "Auricularia auricula-judae" Set of 2 sheets 26·00 24·00

1993. "Granada '92" International Stamp Exhibition, Spain. Spanish Paintings. Nos. 1636/44 of Antigua optd **BARBUDA MAIL.**
1416 10c. "The Miracle at the Well" (Alonzo Cano) 1·25 1·00
1417 15c. "The Poet Luis de Goingora y Argote" (Velazquez) 1·50 1·00
1418 30c. "The Painter Francisco Goya" (Vincente Lopez Portana) 1·75 1·00
1419 40c. "Maria de las Nieves Michaela Fourdinier" (Luis Paret y Alcazar) 1·75 1·00
1420 $1 "Carlos III eating before his Court" (Alcazar) (horiz) 3·00 2·25
1421 $2 "Rain Shower in Granada" (Antonio Munoz Degrain) (horiz) 4·75 4·75
1422 $4 "Sarah Bernhardt" (Santiago Ruisnol i Prats) 6·50 7·50
1423 $5 "The Hermitage Garden" (Joaquim Mir Trinxet) 6·50 7·50
MS1424 Two sheets, each 120 × 95 mm. (a) $6 "The Ascent of Monsieur Boucle's Montgolfier Balloon in the Gardens of Aranjuez" (Antonio Carnicero) (112 × 87 mm). (b) $6 "Olympus: Battle with the Giants" (Francisco Bayeu y Subias) (112 × 87 mm). Imperf Set of 2 sheets 19·00 22·00

1993. "Genova '92" International Thematic Stamp Exhibition. Hummingbirds and Plants. Nos. 1661/9 of Antigua optd **BARBUDA MAIL.**
1425 10c. Antillean crested hummingbird and wild plantain 2·25 1·50
1426 25c. Green mango and parrot's plantain 2·50 1·00
1427 45c. Purple-throated carib and lobster claws 2·75 1·25
1428 60c. Antillean mango and coral plant 3·00 1·50
1429 $1 Vervain hummingbird and cardinal's guard 3·50 2·25
1430 $2 Rufous-breasted hermit and heliconia 5·00 5·00
1431 $4 Blue-headed hummingbird and reed ginger 6·50 7·50
1432 $5 Green-throated carib and ornamental banana 6·50 7·50
MS1433 Two sheets, each 100 × 70 mm. (a) $6 Bee hummingbird and jungle flame. (b) $6 Western streamertail and bignonia Set of 2 sheets 30·00 22·00

1993. Inventors and Inventions. Nos. 1672/80 of Antigua optd **BARBUDA MAIL.**
1434 10c. Ts'ai Lun and paper 65 85
1435 25c. Igor Sikorsky and "Bolshoi Baltiskii" (first four-engined airplane) 3·75 80
1436 30c. Alexander Graham Bell and early telephone 1·50 80
1437 40c. Johannes Gutenberg and early printing press 1·50 80
1438 60c. James Watt and stationary steam engine 8·50 2·25
1439 $1 Anton van Leeuwenhoek and early microscope 3·50 2·75
1440 $4 Louis Braille and hands reading braille 9·00 10·00
1441 $5 Galileo and telescope 9·00 10·00
MS1442 Two sheets, each 100 × 71 mm. (a) $6 Edison and Latimer's phonograph. (b) $6 "Clermont" (first commercial paddle-steamer) Set of 2 sheets 30·00 32·00

1993. Anniversaries and Events. Nos. 900/14 of Antigua optd **BARBUDA MAIL.**
1443 10c. Russian cosmonauts 1·75 1·40
1444 40c. "Graf Zeppelin" (airship), 1929 3·00 1·00
1445 45c. Bishop Daniel Davis 80 70
1446 75c. Konrad Adenauer making speech 1·00 1·00
1447 $1 Bus Mosbacher and "Weatherly" (yacht) 2·25 1·75
1448 $1.50 Rain forest 2·50 2·50
1449 $2 Tiger 9·00 5·50
1450 $2 National flag, plant and emblem (horiz) 5·50 3·50
1451 $2 Members of Community Players company (horiz) 3·50 3·50
1452 $2.25 Women carrying pots 3·50 4·00
1453 $3 Lions Club emblem 3·75 4·25
1454 $4 Chinese rocket on launch tower 5·50 5·50
1455 $4 West German and N.A.T.O. flags 5·50 5·50
1456 $6 Hugo Eckener (airship pioneer) 6·50 7·00
MS1457 Four sheets, each 100 × 71 mm. (a) $6 Projected European space station. (b) $6 Airship LZ-129 "Hindenburg", 1936. (c) $6 Brandenburg Gate on German flag. (d) $6 "Danaus plexippus" (butterfly) Set of 4 sheets 55·00 42·00

1993. Flowers. Nos. 1733/41 of Antigua optd **BARBUDA MAIL.**
1458 15c. Cardinal's guard 1·75 1·25
1459 25c. Giant granadilla 1·90 1·10
1460 30c. Spider flower 2·00 1·25
1461 40c. Gold vine 2·25 1·40
1462 $1 Frangipani 3·50 2·25
1463 $2 Bougainvillea 4·50 4·50
1464 $4 Yellow oleander 6·00 7·00
1465 $5 Spicy jatropha 6·00 7·00
MS1466 Two sheets, each 100 × 70 mm. (a) $6 Bird lime tree. (b) $6 Fairy lily Set of 2 sheets 30·00 30·00

1993. World Bird Watch. Nos. 1248/51 optd **WORLD BIRDWATCH 9-10 OCTOBER 1993.**
1467 60c. Type **119** 4·00 1·75
1468 $2 Adelaide's warbler 7·00 4·50
1469 $4 Rose-breasted grosbeak 9·50 10·00
1470 $7 Wied's crested flycatcher 12·00 13·00

1993. Endangered Species. Nos. 1759/71 of Antigua optd **BARBUDA MAIL.**
1471 $1 St. Lucia amazon ("St. Lucia Parrot") 5·50 4·00
1472 $1 Cahow 5·50 4·00
1473 $1 Swallow-tailed kite 5·50 4·00
1474 $1 Everglade kite ("Everglades Kite") 5·50 4·00
1475 $1 Imperial amazon ("Imperial Parrot") 5·50 4·00
1476 $1 Humpback whale 5·50 4·00
1477 $1 Plain pigeon ("Puerto Rican Plain Pigeon") 5·50 4·00
1478 $1 St. Vincent amazon ("St. Vincent Parrot") 5·50 4·00
1479 $1 Puerto Rican amazon ("Puerto Rican Parrot") 5·50 4·00
1480 $1 Leatherback turtle 5·50 4·00
1481 $1 American crocodile 5·50 4·00
1482 $1 Hawksbill turtle 5·50 4·00
MS1483 Two sheets, each 100 × 70 mm. (a) $6 As No. 1476. (b) $6 West Indian manatee Set of 2 sheets. 45·00 35·00

1994. Bicentenary of the Louvre, Paris. Paintings by Peter Paul Rubens. Nos. 1742/9 and MS1758 of Antigua optd **BARBUDA MAIL.**
1484 $1 "The Destiny of Marie de' Medici" (upper detail) 4·75 3·50
1485 $1 "The Birth of Marie de' Medici" 4·75 3·50
1486 $1 "The Education of Marie de' Medici" 4·75 3·50
1487 $1 "The Destiny of Marie de' Medici" (lower detail) 4·75 3·50
1488 $1 "Henry VI receiving the Portrait of Marie" 4·75 3·50
1489 $1 "The Meeting of the King and Marie at Lyons" 4·75 3·50
1490 $1 "The Marriage by Proxy" 4·75 3·50
1491 $1 "The Birth of Louis XIII" 4·75 3·50
MS1492 70 × 100 mm. $6 "Helene Fourment with a Coach" (52 × 85 mm) 22·00 23·00

1994. World Cup Football Championship, 1994, U.S.A. (1st Issue). Nos. 1816/28 of Antigua optd **BARBUDA MAIL.**
1493 $2 Paul Gascoigne 3·50 2·50
1494 $2 David Platt 3·50 2·50
1495 $2 Martin Peters 3·50 2·50
1496 $2 John Barnes 3·50 2·50
1497 $2 Gary Lineker 3·50 2·50
1498 $2 Geoff Hurst 3·50 2·50
1499 $2 Bobby Charlton 3·50 2·50
1500 $2 Bryan Robson 3·50 2·50
1501 $2 Bobby Moore 3·50 2·50
1502 $2 Nobby Stiles 3·50 2·50

1503 $2 Gordon Banks . . . . . 3·50 2·50
1504 $2 Peter Shilton . . . . . 3·50 2·50
MS1505 Two sheets, each 135 × 109 mm. (a) $6 Bobby Moore holding World Cup. (b) $6 Gary Lineker and Bobby Robson Set of 2 sheets . . . . 28·00 23·00
See also Nos. 1573/9.

1994. Anniversaries and Events. Nos. 1829/38, 1840 and 1842/7 of Antigua optd **BARBUDA MAIL**.
1506 10c. Grand Inspector W.Heath . . . . 4·50 2·00
1507 15c. Rodnina and Oulanov (U.S.S.R.) (pairs figure skating) (horiz) . . . . . 2·00 1·50
1508 30c. Present Masonic Hall, St. John's (horiz) . . . . 5·50 1·50
1509 30c. Willy Brandt with Helmut Schmidt and George Leber (horiz) . . 1·50 1·00
1510 30c. "Cat and Bird" (Picasso) (horiz) . . . . . 1·50 1·00
1511 40c. Previous Masonic Hall, St. John's (horiz) . . . . 5·50 1·50
1512 40c. "Fish on a Newspaper" (Picasso) (horiz) . . . . . 1·50 1·00
1513 40c. Early astronomical equipment . . . . 1·50 1·00
1514 40c. Prince Naruhito and engagement photographs (horiz) . . . . 1·50 1·00
1515 60c. Grand Inspector J.Jeffery . . . . 6·50 1·75
1516 $3 Masako Owada and engagement photographs (horiz) . . . . 3·00 4·00
1517 $4 Willy Brandt and protest march (horiz) . . . . . . 4·00 4·50
1518 $4 Galaxy . . . . 4·00 4·50
1519 $5 Alberto Tomba (Italy) (giant slalom) (horiz) . . 4·00 4·50
1520 $5 "Dying Bull" (Picasso) (horiz) . . . . 4·00 4·50
1521 $5 Pres. Clinton and family (horiz) . . . . 4·00 4·50
MS1522 Six sheets. (a) 106 × 75 mm. $5 Copernicus. (b) 106 × 75 mm. $6 Womens' 1500 metre speed skating medallists (horiz). (c) 106 × 75 mm. $6 Willy Brandt at Warsaw Ghetto Memorial (horiz). (d) 106 × 75 mm. $6 "Woman with a Dog" (detail) (Picasso) (horiz). (e) 106 × 75 mm. $6 Masako Owada. (f) 106 × 75 mm. $6 Pres. Clinton taking the Oath (42½ × 57 mm) Set of 6 sheets 55·00 50·00

1994. Aviation Anniversaries. Nos. 1848/55 of Antigua optd **BARBUDA MAIL**.
1523 30c. Hugo Eckener and Dr. W. Beckers with airship "Graf Zeppelin" over Lake George, New York . . . . 3·25 1·75
1524 40c. Chicago World's Fair from "Graf Zeppelin" . . 3·25 1·75
1525 40c. Gloster Whittle E28/39, 1941 . . . . 3·25 1·75
1526 40c. George Washington writing balloon mail letter (vert) . . . . 3·25 1·75
1527 $4 Pres. Wilson and Curtiss "Jenny" . . . . 9·00 10·00
1528 $5 Airship LZ-129 "Hindenburg" over Ebbets Field baseball stadium, 1937 . . . . . 9·00 10·00
1529 $5 Gloster Meteor in dogfight . . . . 9·00 10·00
MS1530 Three sheets. (a) 86 × 105 mm. $6 Hugo Eckener (vert). (b) 105 × 86 mm. $6 Consolidated Catalina PBY-5 flying boat (57 × 42½ mm). (c) 105 × 86 mm. $6 Alexander Hamilton, Washington and John Jay watching Blanchard's balloon, 1793 (horiz) Set of 3 sheets . . 40·00 35·00

1994. Centenaries of Henry Ford's First Petrol Engine (Nos. 1531, 1533, 1533a) and Karl Benz's First Four-wheeled Car (others). Nos. 1856/60 of Antigua optd **BARBUDA MAIL**.
1531 30c. Lincoln Continental . . 2·00 1·25
1532 40c. Mercedes racing car, 1914 . . . . 2·00 1·25
1533 $4 Ford "GT40", 1966 . . . 7·00 7·50
1534 $5 Mercedes Benz "gull-wing" coupe, 1954 . . . 7·00 7·50
MS1535 Two sheets. (a) 114 × 87 mm. $6 Ford's Mustang emblem. (b) 87 × 114 mm. $6 Germany 1936 12pf. Benz and U.S.A. 1968 12c. Ford stamps Set of 2 sheets . . . . . . 23·00 21·00

1994. Famous Paintings by Rembrandt and Matisse. Nos. 1881/9 of Antigua optd **BARBUDA MAIL**.
1536 15c. "Hannah and Samuel" (Rembrandt) . . . . . . 2·25 1·75
1537 15c. "Guitarist" (Matisse) . . 2·25 1·75
1538 30c. "The Jewish Bride" (Rembrandt) . . . . . . 2·50 1·10
1539 40c. "Jacob wrestling with the Angel" (Rembrandt) 2·50 1·10
1540 60c. "Interior with a Goldfish Bowl" (Matisse) 3·00 1·25
1541 $1 "Mlle. Yvonne Landsberg" (Matisse) . . 3·75 1·75
1542 $4 "The Toboggan" (Matisse) . . . . 7·50 8·50
1543 $5 "Moses with the Tablets of the Law" (Rembrandt) 7·50 8·50
MS1544 Two sheets. (a) 124 × 99 mm. $6 "The Blinding of Samson by the Philistines" (detail) (Rembrandt). (b) 99 × 124 mm. $6 "The Three Sisters" (detail) (Matisse) Set of 2 sheets . . . 22·00 22·00

1994. "Polska '93" International Stamp Exhibition, Poznan. Nos. 1839, 1841 and MS1847f of Antigua optd **BARBUDA MAIL**.
1545 $1 "Woman Combing her Hair" (W. Slewinski) (horiz) . . . . 5·00 2·50
1546 $3 "Artist's Wife with Cat" (Konrad Kryzanowski) (horiz) . . . . 9·00 10·00
MS1547 70 × 100 mm. $6 "General Confusion" (S. I. Witkiewicz) 10·00 12·00

1994. Orchids. Nos. 1949/56 of Antigua optd **BARBUDA MAIL**.
1548 10c. "Spiranthes lanceolata" 2·75 1·75
1549 20c. "Ionopsis utricularioides" . . . . . 3·75 1·75
1550 30c. "Tetramicra canaliculata" . . . . . . 4·00 1·50
1551 50c. "Oncidium picturatum" 4·50 1·50
1552 $1 "Epidendrum difforme" 5·50 2·50
1553 $2 "Epidendrum ciliare" . . 8·00 6·50
1554 $4 "Epidendrum ibaguense" 9·00 10·00
1555 $5 "Epidendrum nocturnum" . . . . . . 9·00 10·00
MS1556 Two sheets, each 100 × 73 mm. (a) $6 "Rodriguezia lanceolata". (b) $6 "Encyclia cochleata" Set of 2 sheets . . . 35·00 32·00

1994. Centenary of Sierra Club (environmental protection society) (1992). Endangered Species. Nos. 1907/22 of Antigua optd **BARBUDA MAIL**.
1557 $1.50 Sumatran rhinoceros lying down . . . . 3·00 2·50
1558 $1.50 Sumatran rhinoceros feeding . . . . 3·00 2·50
1559 $1.50 Ring-tailed lemur on ground . . . . 3·00 2·50
1560 $1.50 Ring-tailed lemur on branch . . . . 3·00 2·50
1561 $1.50 Red-fronted brown lemur on branch . . . . 3·00 2·50
1562 $1.50 Head of red-fronted brown lemur . . . . . 3·00 2·50
1563 $1.50 Head of red-fronted brown lemur in front of trunk . . . . 3·00 2·50
1564 $1.50 Sierra Club Centennial emblem . . . . 1·75 1·60
1565 $1.50 Head of bactrian camel . . . . 3·00 2·50
1566 $1.50 Bactrian camel . . . 3·00 2·50
1567 $1.50 African elephant drinking . . . . 3·00 2·50
1568 $1.50 Head of African elephant . . . . 3·00 2·50
1569 $1.50 Leopard sitting upright . . . . 3·00 2·50
1570 $1.50 Leopard in grass (emblem at right) . . . 3·00 2·50
1571 $1.50 Leopard in grass (emblem at left) . . . . 3·00 2·50
MS1572 Four sheets. (a) 100 × 70 mm. $1.50, Sumatran rhinoceros (horiz). (b) 70 × 100 mm. $1.50, Ring-tailed lemur (horiz). (C) 70 × 100 mm. $1.50, Bactrian camel (horiz) (d) 100 × 70 mm. $1.50, African elephant (horiz) Set of 4 sheets 15·00 15·00

1995. World Cup Football Championship, U.S.A. (2nd issue). Nos. 2039/45 of Antigua optd **BARBUDA MAIL**.
1573 15c. Hugo Sanchez (Mexico) 2·25 1·25
1574 35c. Jurgen Klinsmann (Germany) . . . . 2·75 1·25
1575 65c. Antiguan player . . . 3·00 1·25
1576 $1.20 Cobi Jones (U.S.A.) . 4·00 2·75
1577 $4 Roberto Baggio (Italy) 8·00 8·50
1578 $5 Bwalya Kalusha (Zambia) . . . . 8·00 8·50
MS1579 Two sheets. (a) 72 × 105 mm. $6 Maldive Islands player (vert). (b) 107 × 78 mm. $6 World Cup trophy (vert) Set of 2 sheets . . . . 20·00 17·00

1995. Christmas. Religious Paintings. Nos. 2058/66 of Antigua optd **BARBUDA MAIL**.
1580 15c. "Virgin and Child by the Fireside" (Robert Campin) . . . . 1·75 75
1581 35c. "The Reading Madonna" (Giorgione) 2·25 70
1582 40c. "Madonna and Child" (Giovanni Bellini) . . . . 2·25 70
1583 45c. "The Little Madonna" (Da Vinci) . . . . . . 2·25 70
1584 65c. "The Virgin and Child under the Apple Tree" (Lucas Cranach the Elder) 2·75 1·00
1585 75c. "Madonna and Child" (Master of the Female Half-lengths) . . . . . 2·75 1·25
1586 $1.20 "An Allegory of the Church" (Alessandro Allori) . . . . 4·50 4·00
1587 $5 "Madonna and Child wreathed with Flowers" (Jacob Jordaens) . . . . 8·50 12·00
MS1588 Two sheets. (a) 123 × 88 mm. $6 "Madonna and Child with Commissioners" (detail) (Palma Vecchio). (b) 88 × 123 mm. $6 "The Virgin Enthroned with Child" (detail) (Bohemian master) Set of 2 sheets 16·00 16·00

1995. "Hong Kong '94" International Stamp Exhibition (1st issue). Nos. 1890/1 of Antigua optd **BARBUDA MAIL**.
1589 40c. Hong Kong 1981 $1 Fish stamp and sampans, Shau Kei Wan . . . . . 4·00 2·50
1590 40c. Antigua 1990 $2 Reef fish stamp and sampans, Shau Kei Wan . . . . . 4·00 2·50
See also Nos. 1591/6.

1995. "Hong Kong '94" International Stamp Exhibition (2nd issue). Nos. 1892/7 of Antigua optd **BARBUDA MAIL**.
1591 40c. Terracotta warriors . . 1·25 1·00
1592 40c. Cavalryman and horse 1·25 1·00
1593 40c. Warriors in armour . . 1·25 1·00
1594 40c. Painted bronze chariot and team . . . . 1·25 1·00
1595 40c. Pekingese dog . . . . 1·25 1·00
1596 40c. Warriors with horses 1·25 1·00

1995. Centenary of International Olympic Committee. Nos. 1990/2 of Antigua optd **BARBUDA MAIL**.
1597 50c. Edwin Moses (U.S.A.) (400 metres hurdles), 1984 1·00 75
1598 $1.50 Steffi Graf (Germany) (tennis), 1988 . . . . . . 8·50 4·25
MS1599 79 × 110 mm. $6 Johann Olav Koss (Norway) (500, 1500 and 10,000 metre speed skating), 1994 . . . . 9·00 10·00

1995. Dogs of the World. Chinese New Year ("Year of the Dog"). Nos. 1923/47 of Antigua optd **BARBUDA MAIL**.
1600 50c. West Highland white terrier . . . . 1·50 95
1601 50c. Beagle . . . . 1·50 95
1602 50c. Scottish terrier . . . . 1·50 95
1603 50c. Pekingese . . . . . . 1·50 95
1604 50c. Dachshund . . . . . . 1·50 95
1605 50c. Yorkshire terrier . . . 1·50 95
1606 50c. Pomeranian . . . . . 1·50 95
1607 50c. Poodle . . . . 1·50 95
1608 50c. Shetland sheepdog . . . 1·50 95
1609 50c. Pug . . . . 1·50 95
1610 50c. Shih tzu . . . . 1·50 95
1611 50c. Chihuahua . . . . . . 1·50 95
1612 50c. Mastiff . . . . 1·50 95
1613 50c. Border collie . . . . . 1·50 95
1614 50c. Samoyed . . . . 1·50 95
1615 50c. Airedale terrier . . . . 1·50 95
1616 50c. English setter . . . . . 1·50 95
1617 50c. Rough collie . . . . . 1·50 95
1618 50c. Newfoundland . . . . . 1·50 95
1619 50c. Weimarana . . . . . . 1·50 95
1620 50c. English springer spaniel 1·50 95
1621 50c. Dalmatian . . . . . . 1·50 95
1622 50c. Boxer . . . . 1·50 95
1623 50c. Old English sheepdog 1·50 95
MS1624 Two sheets, each 93 × 58 mm. (a) $6 Welsh corgi. (b) $6 Labrador retriever Set of 2 sheets . . . . 30·00 21·00

1995. Centenary of First English Cricket Tour to the West Indies (1995). Nos. 1994/7 of Antigua optd **BARBUDA MAIL**.
1625 35c. Mike Atherton (England) and Wisden Trophy . . . . 3·75 1·50
1626 75c. Viv Richards (West Indies) (vert) . . . . . 5·50 2·75
1627 $1.20 Richie Richardson (West Indies) and Wisden Trophy . . . . 7·50 4·75
MS1628 80 × 100 mm. $3 English team, 1895 (black and brown) 13·00 11·00

1995. "Philakorea '94" International Stamp Exhibition (1st issue). Nos. 1998/2009 of Antigua optd **BARBUDA MAIL**.
1629 40c. Entrance bridge, Songgwangsa Temple . . 1·00 80
1630 75c. Long-necked bottle . . 1·25 1·50
1631 75c. Punch'ong ware jar with floral decoration . . 1·25 1·50
1632 75c. Punch'ong ware jar with blue dragon pattern 1·25 1·50
1633 75c. Ewer in shape of bamboo shoot . . . . . 1·25 1·50
1634 75c. Punch'ong ware green jar . . . . 1·25 1·50
1635 75c. Pear-shaped bottle . . 1·25 1·50
1636 75c. Porcelain jar with brown dragon pattern . . 1·25 1·50
1637 75c. Porcelain jar with floral pattern . . . . 1·25 1·25
1638 90c. Song-op Folk Village, Cheju . . . . 1·25 1·25
1639 $3 Port Sogwipo . . . . . 3·00 3·75
MS1640 104 × 71 mm. $4 Ox herder playing flute (vert) . . . . . . 4·75 6·50

1995. 1st Recipients of Order of the Caribbean Community. Nos. 2046/8 of Antigua optd **BARBUDA MAIL**.
1641 65c. Sir Shridath Ramphal 60 75
1642 90c. William Demas . . . . 90 1·00
1643 $1.20 Derek Walcott . . . . 4·00 4·25

1995. 25th Anniv of First Moon Landing. Nos. 1977/89 of Antigua optd **BARBUDA MAIL**.
1644 $1.50 Edwin Aldrin (astronaut) . . . . 3·75 2·50
1645 $1.50 First lunar footprint 3·75 2·50
1646 $1.50 Neil Armstrong (astronaut) . . . . 3·75 2·50
1647 $1.50 Aldrin stepping onto Moon . . . . 3·75 2·50
1648 $1.50 Aldrin and equipment 3·75 2·50
1649 $1.50 Aldrin and U.S.A. flag 3·75 2·50
1650 $1.50 Aldrin at Tranquility Base . . . . 3·75 2·50
1651 $1.50 Moon plaque . . . . 3·75 2·50
1652 $1.50 "Eagle" leaving Moon 3·75 2·50
1653 $1.50 Command module in lunar orbit . . . . 3·75 2·50
1654 $1.50 First day cover of U.S.A. 1969 10c. First Man on Moon stamp . . 3·75 2·50
1655 $1.50 Pres. Nixon and astronauts . . . . 3·75 2·50
MS1656 72 × 102 mm. $6 Armstrong and Aldrin with postal official 21·00 16·00

1995. International Year of the Family. No. 1993 of Antigua optd **BARBUDA MAIL**.
1657 90c. Antiguan family . . . 1·75 1·50

1995. 50th Anniv of D-Day. Nos. 2010/13 of Antigua optd **BARBUDA MAIL**.
1658 40c. Short S.25 Sunderland flying boat . . . . . . 3·50 1·25
1659 $2 Lockheed P-38 Lightning fighters attacking train . . 11·00 6·00
1660 $3 Martin B-26 Marauder bombers . . . . 11·00 7·00
MS1661 108 × 78 mm. $6 Hawker Typhoon fighter bomber . . . 19·00 18·00

122 Queen Elizabeth the Queen Mother (95th birthday)

1995. Anniversaries. Multicoloured.
1662 $7.50 Type **122** . . . . . . 12·00 12·00
1663 $8 German bombers over St. Paul's Cathedral, London (horiz) (50th anniv of end of Second World War) . . . . . . 24·00 15·00
1664 $8 New York skyline with U.N. and national flags (horiz) (50th anniv of United Nations) . . . . . 15·00 16·00

1995. Hurricane Relief. Nos. 1662/4 surch **HURRICANE RELIEF** and premium.
1665 $7.50+$1 Type **122** (90th birthday) . . . . 8·00 11·00
1666 $8+$1 German bombers over St. Paul's Cathedral, London (horiz) (50th anniv of end of Second World War) . . . . . . 18·00 16·00
1667 $8+$1 New York skyline with U.N. and national flags (horiz) (50th anniv of United Nations) . . . 8·00 11·00

1996. Marine Life. Nos. 1967/76 of Antigua optd **BARBUDA MAIL**.
1668 50c. Bottlenose dolphin . . 1·40 1·40
1669 50c. Killer whale . . . . . 1·40 1·40
1670 50c. Spinner dolphin . . . . 1·40 1·40
1671 50c. Oceanic sunfish . . . . 1·40 1·40
1672 50c. Caribbean reef shark and short fin pilot whale 1·40 1·40
1673 50c. Copper-banded butterflyfish . . . . 1·40 1·40
1674 50c. Mosaic moray . . . . 1·40 1·40
1675 50c. Clown triggerfish . . . 1·40 1·40
1676 50c. Red lobster . . . . . 1·40 1·40
MS1677 Two sheets, each 106 × 76 mm. (a) $6 Seahorse. (b) $6 Swordfish ("Blue Marlin") (horiz) Set of 2 sheets . . . . 17·00 18·00

1996. Christmas. Religious Paintings. Nos. 2267/73 of Antigua optd **BARBUDA MAIL.**
1678 15c. "Rest on the Flight into Egypt" (Paolo Veronese) . . 65 40
1679 35c. "Madonna and Child" (Van Dyck) 75 40
1680 65c. "Sacred Conversation Piece" (Veronese) . . . . 1·00 55
1681 75c. "Vision of St. Anthony" (Van Dyck) 1·25 60
1682 90c. "Virgin and Child" (Van Eyck) . . . . 1·40 75
1683 $6 "The Immaculate Conception" (Giovanni Tiepolo) . . . . 4·75 7·00
MS1684 Two sheets. (a) 101 × 127 mm. $5 "Christ appearing to his Mother" (detail) (Van der Weyden). (b) 127 × 101 mm. $6 "The Infant Jesus and the Young St. John" (Murillo) Set of 2 sheets . . . 14·00 16·00

1996. Stars of Country and Western Music. Nos. 2014/38 of Antigua optd **BARBUDA MAIL.**
1685 75c. Travis Tritt 80 75
1686 75c. Dwight Yoakam . . . 80 75
1687 75c. Billy Ray Cyrus 80 75
1688 75c. Alan Jackson 80 75
1689 75c. Garth Brooks 80 75
1690 75c. Vince Gill 80 75
1691 75c. Clint Black 80 75
1692 75c. Eddie Rabbit 80 75
1693 75c. Patsy Cline 80 75
1694 75c. Tanya Tucker 80 75
1695 75c. Dolly Parton 80 75
1696 75c. Anne Murray 80 75
1697 75c. Tammy Wynette . . . 80 75
1698 75c. Loretta Lynn 80 75
1699 75c. Reba McEntire 80 75
1700 75c. Skeeter Davis 80 75
1701 75c. Hank Snow 80 75
1702 75c. Gene Autry 80 75
1703 75c. Jimmie Rodgers 80 75
1704 75c. Ernest Tubb 80 75
1705 75c. Eddy Arnold 80 75
1706 75c. Willie Nelson 80 75
1707 75c. Johnny Cash 80 75
1708 75c. George Jones 80 75
MS1709 Three sheets. (a) 100 × 70 mm. $6 Hank Williams Jr. (b) 100 × 70 mm. $6 Hank Williams Sr. (c) 70 × 100 mm. $6 Kitty Wells (horiz) Set of 3 sheets 17·00 17·00

1996. Birds. Nos. 2067/81 of Antigua optd **BARBUDA MAIL.**
1710 15c. Magnificent frigate bird 1·25 90
1711 25c. Antillean euphonia ("Blue-hooded Euphonia") . . . . . . 1·40 60
1712 35c. Eastern meadowlark ("Meadowlark") . . . . 1·50 60
1713 40c. Red-billed tropic bird 1·50 60
1714 45c. Greater flamingo . . . 1·50 60
1715 60c. Yellow-faced grassquit 1·75 1·00
1716 65c. Yellow-billed cuckoo 1·75 1·50
1717 70c. Purple-throated carib 1·75 1·50
1718 75c. Bananaquit . . . . . 1·75 1·00
1719 90c. Painted bunting . . . . 1·90 1·00
1720 $1.20 Red-legged honeycreeper . . . . . . 2·25 2·00
1721 $2 Northern jacana ("Jacana") . . . . . . 3·25 3·25
1722 $5 Greater Antillean bullfinch . . . . 5·00 6·50
1723 $10 Caribbean elaenia . . . 7·50 11·00
1724 $20 Brown trembler ("Trembler") . . . . . . 12·00 17·00

1996. Birds. Nos. 2050, 2052 and 2054/7 of Antigua optd **BARBUDA MAIL.**
1725 15c. Bridled quail dove . . 2·00 1·50
1726 40c. Purple-throated carib (vert) . . . . 2·50 1·00
1727 $1 Broad-winged hawk ("Antigua Broad-winged Hawk") (vert) . . . . . 3·75 2·50
1728 $4 Yellow warbler . . . . . 6·00 8·00
MS1729 Two sheets. (a) 70 × 100 mm. $6 Female magnificent frigate bird (vert). (b) 100 × 70 mm. $6 Black-billed whistling duck ducklings Set of 2 sheets . . . . 17·00 18·00

1996. Prehistoric Animals. Nos. 2082/100 of Antigua optd **BARBUDA MAIL.**
1730 15c. Head of pachycephalosaurus . . . . 2·00 2·00
1731 20c. Head of afrovenator . . 2·00 2·00
1732 65c. Centrosaurus . . . . . 2·00 2·00
1733 75c. Kronosaurus (horiz) . . 2·00 2·00
1734 75c. Ichthyosaurus (horiz) 2·00 2·00
1735 75c. Plesiosaurus (horiz) . . 2·00 2·00
1736 75c. Archelon (horiz) . . . 2·00 2·00
1737 75c. Pair of tyrannosaurus (horiz) . . . . 2·00 2·00
1738 75c. Tyrannosaurus (horiz) 2·00 2·00
1739 75c. Parasaurolophus (horiz) 2·00 2·00
1740 75c. Pair of parasaurolophus (horiz) . . . . 2·00 2·00
1741 75c. Oviraptor (horiz) . . . 2·00 2·00
1742 75c. Protoceratops with eggs (horiz) . . . . 2·00 2·00
1743 75c. Pteranodon and protoceratops (horiz) . . 2·00 2·00
1744 75c. Pair of protoceratops (horiz) . . . . 2·00 2·00
1745 90c. Pentaceratops drinking 2·25 1·50
1746 $1.20 Head of tarbosaurus 2·75 2·00
1747 $5 Head of styracosaurus 6·50 7·50
MS1748 Two sheets, each 101 × 70 mm. (a) $6 Head of Corythosaurus (horiz). (b) $6 Head of Carnotaurus (horiz) Set of 2 sheets . . . . 20·00 21·00

1996. Olympic Games, Atlanta (1st issue). Previous Gold Medal Winners. Nos. 2101/7 of Antigua optd **BARBUDA MAIL.**
1749 15c. Al Oerter (U.S.A.) (discus – 1956, 1960, 1964, 1968) . . . . 1·50 1·00
1750 20c. Greg Louganis (U.S.A.) (diving – 1984, 1988) . . 1·50 1·00
1751 65c. Naim Suleymanoglu (Turkey) (weightlifting – 1988) . . . . 2·00 1·00
1752 90c. Louise Ritter (U.S.A.) (high jump – 1988) . . . 2·50 1·25
1753 $1.20 Nadia Comaneci (Rumania) (gymnastics – 1976) . . . . 4·00 2·75
1754 $5 Olga Bondarenko (Russia) (10,000 m – 1988) . . . . 6·00 8·50
MS1755 Two sheets, each 106 × 76 mm. (a) $6 United States crew (eight-oared shell – 1964). (b) $6 Lutz Hessilch (Germany) (cycling – 1988) (vert) Set of 2 sheets . . . . 18·00 16·00
See also Nos. 1922/44.

1996. 18th World Scout Jamboree, Netherlands. Tents. Nos. 2203/9 of Antigua optd **BARBUDA MAIL.**
1756 $1.20 The Explorer Tent . . 1·25 1·50
1757 $1.20 Camper tent . . . . . 1·25 1·50
1758 $1.20 Wall tent . . . . . . 1·25 1·50
1759 $1.20 Trail tent . . . . . . 1·25 1·50
1760 $1.20 Miner's tent . . . . . 1·25 1·50
1761 $1.20 Voyager tent . . . . 1·25 1·50
MS1762 Two sheets, each 76 × 106 mm. (a) $6 Scout and camp fire. (b) $6 Scout with back pack Set of 2 sheets . . . . . 8·00 10·00

1996. Centenary of Nobel Prize Trust Fund. Nos. 2226/44 of Antigua optd **BARBUDA MAIL.**
1763 $1 Dag Hammarskjold (1961 Peace) . . . . . . 1·40 1·00
1764 $1 Georg Wittig (1979 Chemistry) . . . . 1·40 1·00
1765 $1 Wilhelm Ostwold (1909 Chemistry) . . . . 1·40 1·00
1766 $1 Robert Koch (1905 Medicine) . . . . 1·40 1·00
1767 $1 Karl Ziegler (1963 Chemistry) . . . . 1·40 1·00
1768 $1 Alexander Fleming (1945 Medicine) . . . . 1·40 1·00
1769 $1 Hermann Staudinger (1953 Chemistry) . . . . 1·40 1·00
1770 $1 Manfred Eigen (1967 Chemistry) . . . . 1·40 1·00
1771 $1 Arno Penzias (1978 Physics) . . . . 1·40 1·00
1772 $1 Shumal Agnon (1966 Literature) . . . . 1·40 1·00
1773 $1 Rudyard Kipling (1907 Literature) . . . . 1·40 1·00
1774 $1 Aleksandr Solzhenitsyn (1970 Literature) . . . . 1·40 1·00
1775 $1 Jack Steinburger (1988 Physics) . . . . 1·40 1·00
1776 $1 Andrei Sakharov (1975 Peace) . . . . 1·40 1·00
1777 $1 Otto Stern (1943 Physics) 1·40 1·00
1778 $1 John Steinbeck (1962 Literature) . . . . 1·40 1·00
1779 $1 Nadine Gordimer (1991 Literature) . . . . 1·40 1·00
1780 $1 William Faulkner (1949 Literature) . . . . 1·40 1·00
MS1781 Two sheets, each 100 × 70 mm. (a) $6 Elie Wiesel (1986 Peace) (vert). (b) $6 Dalai Lama (1989 Peace) (vert) Set of 2 sheets . . . . 13·00 15·00

1996. 70th Birthday of Queen Elizabeth II. Nos. 2355/8 of Antigua optd **BARBUDA MAIL.**
1782 $2 Queen Elizabeth II in blue dress . . . . 2·50 2·50
1783 $2 With bouquet . . . . . 2·50 2·50
1784 $2 In Garter robes . . . . 2·50 2·50
MS1785 96 × 111 mm. $6 Wearing white dress . . . . 7·00 6·00

1997. Christmas. Religious Paintings by Filippo Lippi. Nos. 2377/83 of Antigua optd **BARBUDA MAIL.**
1786 60c. "Madonna Enthroned" 60 35
1787 90c. "Adoration of the Child and Saints" 85 55
1788 $1 "The Annunciation" . . 1·00 80
1789 $1.20 "Birth of the Virgin" 1·25 1·10
1790 $1.60 "Adoration of the Child" . . . . 1·60 2·00
1791 $1.75 "Madonna and Child" 1·75 2·25
MS1792 Two sheets, each 76 × 106 mm. (a) $6 "Madonna and Child" (different). (b) $6 "The Circumcision" Set of 2 sheets 12·00 15·00

1997. 50th Anniv of F.A.O. Nos. 2121/4 of Antigua optd **BARBUDA MAIL.**
1793 75c. Woman buying produce from market . . . . . . 1·00 1·00
1794 90c. Women shopping . . . 1·10 1·10
1795 $1.20 Women talking . . . 1·40 1·75
MS1796 100 × 70 mm. $6 Tractor 5·50 7·00

1997. 90th Anniv of Rotary International (1995). No. 2126 of Antigua optd **BARBUDA MAIL.**
1797 $5 Beach and rotary emblem 3·25 4·25
MS1798 74 × 104 mm. $6 National flag and emblem . . . . 4·50 5·50

1997. 50th Anniv of End of Second World War in Europe and the Pacific. Nos. 2108/16 and 2132/8 of Antigua optd **BARBUDA MAIL.**
1799 $1.20 Map of Berlin showing Russian advance 90 90
1800 $1.20 Russian tank and infantry 90 90
1801 $1.20 Street fighting in Berlin 90 90
1802 $1.20 German tank exploding 90 90
1803 $1.20 Russian air raid . . . 90 90
1804 $1.20 German troops surrendering 90 90
1805 $1.20 Hoisting the Soviet flag on the Reichstag . . 90 90
1806 $1.20 Captured German standards 90 90
1807 $1.20 Gen. Chiang Kai-shek and Chinese guerrillas . . 90 90
1808 $1.20 Gen. Douglas MacArthur and beach landing 90 90
1809 $1.20 Gen. Claire Chennault and U.S. fighter aircraft 90 90
1810 $1.20 Brig. Orde Wingate and supply drop 90 90
1811 $1.20 Gen. Joseph Stilwell and U.S. supply plane . . 90 90
1812 $1.20 Field-Marshal Bill Slim and loading cow onto plane 90 90
MS1813 Two sheets, each 100 × 70 mm. (a) $3 Admiral Nimitz and aircraft carrier. (b) $6 Gen. Konev (vert) Set of 2 sheets 9·00 10·00

1997. Bees. Nos. 2172/6 of Antigua optd **BARBUDA MAIL.**
1814 90c. Mining bees . . . . . 1·00 50
1815 $1.20 Solitary bee . . . . . 1·25 80
1816 $1.65 Leaf-cutter bee . . . 1·60 1·75
1817 $1.75 Honey bees . . . . . 1·75 2·00
MS1818 110 × 80 mm. $6 Solitary mining bird . . . . 5·50 6·50

1997. Flowers. Nos. 2177/89 of Antigua optd **BARBUDA MAIL.**
1819 75c. Narcissus 75 85
1820 75c. Camellia 75 85
1821 75c. Iris 75 85
1822 75c. Tulip 75 85
1823 75c. Poppy 75 85
1824 75c. Peony 75 85
1825 75c. Magnolia 75 85
1826 75c. Oriental lily 75 85
1827 75c. Rose 75 85
1828 75c. Pansy 75 85
1829 75c. Hydrangea 75 85
1830 75c. Azaleas 75 85
MS1831 80 × 110 mm. $6 Calla lily 6·50 8·00

1997. Cats. Nos. 2190/202 of Antigua optd **BARBUDA MAIL.**
1832 45c. Somali 70 70
1833 45c. Persian and butterflies 70 70
1834 45c. Devon rex 70 70
1835 45c. Turkish angora 70 70
1836 45c. Himalayan 70 70
1837 45c. Maine coon 70 70
1838 45c. Ginger non-pedigree . . 70 70
1839 45c. American wirehair . . 70 70
1840 45c. British shorthair . . . 70 70
1841 45c. American curl 70 70
1842 45c. Black non-pedigree and butterfly 70 70
1843 45c. Birman 70 70
MS1844 104 × 74 mm. $6 Siberian kitten (vert) . . . . 8·00 9·00

1997. 95th Birthday of Queen Elizabeth the Queen Mother. Nos. 2127/31 of Antigua optd **BARBUDA MAIL.**
1845 $1.50 brown, lt brown & black . . . . 5·00 3·50
1846 $1.50 multicoloured . . . . 5·00 3·50
1847 $1.50 multicoloured . . . . 5·00 3·50
1848 $1.50 multicoloured . . . . 5·00 3·50
MS1849 102 × 27 mm. $6 multicoloured . . . . 14·00 11·00

1997. 50th Anniv of United Nations. Nos. 2117/18 of Antigua optd **BARBUDA MAIL.**
1850 75c. Signatures and Earl of Halifax 80 80
1851 90c. Virginia Gildersleeve 90 90
1852 $1.20 Harold Stassen . . . 1·25 1·50
MS1853 100 × 70 mm. $6 Pres. Franklin D. Roosevelt . . . . 4·50 6·00

1997. Trains of the World. Nos. 2210/25 of Antigua optd **BARBUDA MAIL.**
1854 35c. Trans-Gabon diesel-electric train 90 30
1855 65c. Canadian Pacific diesel-electric locomotive . . . . 1·00 40
1856 75c. Santa Fe Railway diesel-electric locomotive, U.S.A. . . . . 1·00 50
1857 90c. High Speed Train, Great Britain . . . . . . 1·00 60
1858 $1.20 TGV express train, France . . . . 1·00 1·25
1859 $1.20 Diesel-electric locomotive, Australia . . 1·00 1·25
1860 $1.20 Pendolino "ETR 450" electric train, Italy . . . . 1·00 1·25
1861 $1.20 Diesel-electric locomotive, Thailand . . 1·00 1·25
1862 $1.20 Pennsylvania Railroad Type 4 steam locomotive, U.S.A. . . . . 1·00 1·25
1863 $1.20 Beyer-Garratt steam locomotive, East African Railways . . . . 1·00 1·25
1864 $1.20 Natal Govt steam locomotive . . . . 1·00 1·25
1865 $1.20 Rail gun, American Civil War . . . . 1·00 1·25
1866 $1.20 Locomotive "Lion" (red livery), Great Britain 1·00 1·25
1867 $1.20 William Hedley's "Puffing Billy" (green livery), Great Britain . . 1·00 1·25
1868 $6 Amtrak high speed diesel locomotive, U.S.A. . . . 3·50 4·50
MS1869 Two sheets, each 110 × 80 mm. (a) $6 Locomotive "Iron Rooster", China (vert). (b) $6 "Indian-Pacific" diesel-electric locomotive, Australia (vert) Set of 2 sheets . . . . 13·00 15·00

1997. Golden Wedding of Queen Elizabeth II and Prince Philip (1st issue). Nos. 1662/3 optd **Golden Wedding of H.M. Queen Elizabeth II and Prince Philip 1947-1997.**
1870 $7.50 Type **122** . . . . . . 7·00 8·00
1871 $8 German bombers over St. Paul's Cathedral, London (horiz) . . . . . 8·00 9·00
See also Nos. 1925/30.

1997. Fungi. Nos. 2274/82 of Antigua optd **BARBUDA MAIL.**
1872 75c. "Hygrophoropsis aurantiaca" . . . . . . 1·75 1·50
1873 75c. "Hygrophorus bakerensis" . . . . 1·75 1·50
1874 75c. "Hygrophorus conicus" 1·75 1·50
1875 75c. "Hygrophorus miniatus" ("Hygrocybe miniata") . . . . 1·75 1·50
1876 75c. "Suillus brevipes" . . . 1·75 1·50
1877 75c. "Suillus luteus" . . . . 1·75 1·50
1878 75c. "Suillus granulatus" . . 1·75 1·50
1879 75c. "Suillus caerulescens" 1·75 1·50
MS1880 Two sheets, each 106 × 76 mm. (a) $6 "Conocybe filaris". (b) $6 "Hygrocybe flavescens" Set of 2 sheets . . 13·00 15·00

1997. Birds. Nos. 2140/64 of Antigua optd **BARBUDA MAIL.**
1881 75c. Purple-throated carib 70 75
1882 75c. Antillean crested hummingbird 70 75
1883 75c. Bananaquit 70 75
1884 75c. Mangrove cuckoo . . . 70 75
1885 75c. Troupial 70 75
1886 75c. Green-throated carib 70 75
1887 75c. Yellow warbler 70 75
1888 75c. Antillean euphonia ("Blue-hooded Euphonia") 70 75
1889 75c. Scaly-breasted thrasher 70 75
1890 75c. Burrowing owl 70 75
1891 75c. Carib grackle 70 75
1892 75c. Adelaide's warbler . . 70 75
1893 75c. Ring-necked duck . . . 70 75
1894 75c. Ruddy duck 70 75
1895 75c. Green-winged teal . . . 70 75
1896 75c. Wood duck 70 75
1897 75c. Hooded merganser . . 70 75
1898 75c. Lesser scaup 70 75
1899 75c. Black-billed whistling duck ("West Indian Tree Duck") 70 75
1900 75c. Fulvous whistling duck 70 75
1901 75c. Bahama pintail 70 75
1902 75c. Northern shoveler ("Shoveler") 70 75
1903 75c. Masked duck 70 75
1904 75c. American wigeon . . . 70 75
MS1905 Two sheets, each 104 × 74 mm. (a) $6 Head of purple gallinule. (b) $6 Heads of blue-winged teals Set of 2 sheets 12·00 12·00

1997. Sailing Ships. Nos. 2283/301 of Antigua optd **BARBUDA MAIL.**
1906 15c. H.M.S. "Resolution" (Cook) . . . . 1·25 1·00
1907 25c. "Mayflower" (Pilgrim Fathers) . . . . 1·00 50
1908 45c. "Santa Maria" (Columbus) . . . . 1·25 60
1909 75c. "Aemilia" (Dutch galleon) . . . . 1·00 60
1910 75c. "Sovereign of the Seas" (English galleon) . . . . 1·00 60
1911 90c. H.M.S. "Victory" (Nelson) . . . . 1·25 1·00
1912 $1.20 As No. 1909 . . . . 1·25 1·25
1913 $1.20 As No. 1910 . . . . 1·25 1·25
1914 $1.20 "Royal Louis" (French galleon) . . . . . 1·25 1·25
1915 $1.20 H.M.S. "Royal George" (ship of the line) 1·25 1·25
1916 $1.20 "Le Protecteur" (French frigate) . . . . . 1·25 1·25
1917 $1.20 As No. 1911 . . . . 1·25 1·25
1918 $1.50 As No. 1908 . . . . 1·25 1·40
1919 $1.50 "Victoria" (Magellan) 1·25 1·40
1920 $1.50 "Golden Hind" (Drake) . . . . 1·25 1·40
1921 $1.50 As No. 1907 . . . . 1·25 1·40

1922 $1.50 "Griffin" (La Salle) 1·25 1·40
1923 $1.50 As No. 1906 1·25 1·40
MS1924 (a) 102 × 72 mm. $6 U.S.S. "Constitution" (frigate). (b) 98 × 67 mm. $6 "Grande Hermine" (Cartier) Set of 2 sheets 9·00 10·00

1997. Golden Wedding of Queen Elizabeth and Prince Philip (2nd issue). Nos. 2474/80 of Antigua optd **BARBUDA MAIL.**
1925 $1 Queen Elizabeth II 2·25 2·00
1926 $1 Royal coat of arms 2·25 2·00
1927 $1 Queen Elizabeth and Prince Philip at reception 2·25 2·00
1928 $1 Queen Elizabeth and Prince Philip in landau 2·25 2·00
1929 $1 Balmoral 2·25 2·00
1930 $1 Prince Philip 2·25 2·00
MS1931 100 × 71 mm. $6 Queen Elizabeth with Prince Philip in naval uniform 13·00 13·00

1997. Christmas. Religious Paintings. Nos. 2566/72 of Antigua optd **BARBUDA MAIL.**
1932 15c. "The Angel leaving Tobias and his Family" (Rembrandt) 80 35
1933 25c. "The Resurrection" (Martin Knoller) 90 35
1934 60c. "Astronomy" (Raphael) 1·25 65
1935 75c. "Music-making Angel" (Melozzo da Forli) 1·40 1·00
1936 90c. "Amor" (Parmigianino) 1·60 1·10
1937 $1.20 "Madonna and Child with Saints" (Rosso Fiorentino) 1·75 1·90
MS1938 Two sheets, each 105 × 96 mm. (a) $6 "The Wedding of Tobias" (Gianantonio and Francesco Guardi) (horiz). (b) $6 "The Portinari Altarpiece" (Hugo van der Goes) (horiz) Set of 2 sheets 9·00 10·00

1998. Sea Birds. Nos. 2325/33 of Antigua optd **BARBUDA MAIL.**
1939 75c. Black skimmer 1·50 1·50
1940 75c. Black-capped petrel 1·50 1·50
1941 75c. Sooty tern 1·50 1·50
1942 75c. Royal tern 1·50 1·50
1943 75c. Pomarine skua ("Pomarine Jaegger") 1·50 1·50
1944 75c. White-tailed tropic bird 1·50 1·50
1945 75c. Northern gannet 1·50 1·50
1946 75c. Laughing gull 1·50 1·50
MS1947 Two sheets, each 105 × 75 mm. (a) $5 Great frigate bird. (b) $6 Brown pelican Set of 2 sheets 9·00 10·00

1998. Centenary of Radio. Entertainers. Nos. 2372/6 of Antigua optd **BARBUDA MAIL.**
1948 65c. Kate Smith 90 65
1949 75c. Dinah Shore 1·00 80
1950 90c. Rudy Vallee 1·25 90
1951 $1.20 Bing Crosby 1·50 1·75
MS1952 72 × 104 mm. $6 Jo Stafford (28 × 42 mm) 5·50 7·00

1998. Olympic Games, Atlanta (2nd issue). Previous Medal Winners. Nos. 2302/23 of Antigua optd **BARBUDA MAIL.**
1953 65c. Florence Griffith Joyner (U.S.A.) (Gold – track, 1988) 85 75
1954 75c. Olympic Stadium, Seoul (1988) (horiz) 85 75
1955 90c. Allison Jolly and Lynne Jewell (U.S.A.) (Gold – yachting, 1988) (horiz) 1·00 1·00
1956 90c. Wolfgang Nordwig (Germany) (Gold – pole vaulting, 1972) 1·00 1·00
1957 90c. Shirley Strong (Great Britain) (Silver – 100 m hurdles, 1984) 1·00 1·00
1958 90c. Sergei Bubka (Russia) (Gold – pole vault, 1988) 1·00 1·00
1959 90c. Filbert Bayi (Tanzania) (Silver – 3000 m steeplechase, 1980) 1·00 1·00
1960 90c. Victor Saneyev (Russia) (Gold – triple jump, 1968, 1972, 1976) 1·00 1·00
1961 90c. Silke Renk (Germany) (Gold – javelin, 1992) 1·00 1·00
1962 90c. Daley Thompson (Great Britain) (Gold – decathlon, 1980, 1984) 1·00 1·00
1963 90c. Robert Richards (U.S.A.) (Gold – pole vault, 1952, 1956) 1·00 1·00
1964 90c. Parry O'Brien (U.S.A.) (Gold – shot put, 1952, 1956) 1·00 1·00
1965 90c. Ingrid Kramer (Germany) (Gold – Women's platform diving, 1960) 1·00 1·00
1966 90c. Kelly McCormick (U.S.A.) (Silver – Women's springboard diving, 1984) 1·00 1·00
1967 90c. Gary Tobian (U.S.A.) (Gold – Men's springboard diving, 1960) 1·00 1·00
1968 90c. Greg Louganis (U.S.A.) (Gold – Men's diving, 1984 and 1988) 1·00 1·00
1969 90c. Michelle Mitchell (U.S.A.) (Silver – Women's platform diving, 1984 and 1988) 1·00 1·00
1970 90c. Zhou Jihong (China) (Gold – Women's platform diving, 1984) 1·00 1·00
1971 90c. Wendy Wyland (U.S.A.) (Bronze – Women's platform diving, 1984) 1·00 1·00
1972 90c. Xu Yanmei (China) (Gold – Women's platform diving, 1988) 1·00 1·00
1973 90c. Fu Mingxia (China) (Gold – Women's platform diving, 1992) 1·00 1·00
1974 $1.20 2000 m tandem cycle race (horiz) 3·25 2·50
MS1975 Two sheets, each 106 × 76 mm. (a) $5 Bill Toomey (U.S.A.) (Gold – decathlon, 1968) (horiz). (b) $6 Mark Lenzi (U.S.A.) (Gold – Men's springboard diving, 1992) Set of 2 sheets 9·00 10·00

1998. World Cup Football Championship, France. Nos. 2525/39 of Antigua optd **BARBUDA MAIL.**
1976 60c. multicoloured 75 60
1977 75c. brown 75 60
1978 90c. multicoloured 80 65
1979 $1 brown 80 80
1980 $1 brown 80 80
1981 $1 brown 80 80
1982 $1 black 80 80
1983 $1 brown 80 80
1984 $1 brown 80 80
1985 $1 brown 80 80
1986 $1 brown 80 80
1987 $1.20 multicoloured 1·00 1·10
1988 $1.65 multicoloured 1·25 1·40
1989 $1.75 multicoloured 1·40 1·60
MS1990 Two sheets, each 102 × 127 mm. (a) $6 multicoloured. (b) $6 multicoloured Set of 2 sheets 9·00 10·00

1998. Cavalry through the Ages. Nos. 2359/63 of Antigua optd **BARBUDA MAIL.**
1991 60c. Ancient Egyptian cavalryman 1·50 1·25
1992 60c. 13th-century English knight 1·50 1·25
1993 60c. 16th-century Spanish lancer 1·50 1·25
1994 60c. 18th-century Chinese cavalryman 1·50 1·25
MS1995 100 × 70 mm. $6 19th-century French cuirassier (vert) 6·50 8·00

1998. 50th Anniv of UNICEF Nos. 2364/7 of Antigua optd **BARBUDA MAIL.**
1996 75c. Girl in red sari 90 90
1997 90c. South American mother and child 1·10 1·10
1998 $1.20 Nurse with child 1·40 1·75
MS1999 114 × 74 mm. $6 Chinese child 4·75 6·00

1998. 3000th Anniv of Jerusalem. Nos. 2368/71 of Antigua optd **BARBUDA MAIL.**
2000 75c. Tomb of Zachariah and "Verbascum sinuatum" 1·75 1·00
2001 90c. Pool of Siloam and "Hyacinthus orientalis" 1·90 1·10
2002 $1.20 Hurva Synagogue and "Ranunculus asiaticus" 2·25 2·50
MS2003 66 × 80 mm. $6 Model of Herod's Temple and "Cercis siliquastrum" 6·50 6·50

1998. Diana, Princess of Wales Commemoration. Nos. 2573/85 of Antigua optd **BARBUDA MAIL.**
2004 $1.65 Diana, Princess of Wales 1·25 1·10
2005 $1.65 Wearing hoop earrings (red and black) 1·25 1·10
2006 $1.65 Carrying bouquet 1·25 1·10
2007 $1.65 Wearing floral hat 1·25 1·10
2008 $1.65 With Prince Harry 1·25 1·10
2009 $1.65 Wearing white jacket 1·25 1·10
2010 $1.65 In kitchen 1·25 1·10
2011 $1.65 Wearing black and white dress 1·25 1·10
2012 $1.65 Wearing hat (brown and black) 1·25 1·10
2013 $1.65 Wearing floral print dress (brown and black) 1·25 1·10
2014 $1.65 Dancing with John Travolta 1·25 1·10
2015 $1.65 Wearing white hat and jacket 1·25 1·10
MS2016 Two sheets, each 70 × 100 mm. (a) $6 Wearing red jumper. (b) $6 Wearing black dress for Papal audience (brown and black) Set of 2 sheets 9·00 10·00

1998. Broadway Musical Stars. Nos. 2384/93 of Antigua optd **BARBUDA MAIL.**
2017 $1 Robert Preston ("The Music Man") 1·00 1·00
2018 $1 Michael Crawford ("Phantom of the Opera") 1·00 1·00
2019 $1 Zero Mostel ("Fiddler on the Roof") 1·00 1·00
2020 $1 Patti Lupone ("Evita") 1·00 1·00
2021 $1 Raul Julia ("Threepenny Opera") 1·00 1·00
2022 $1 Mary Martin ("South Pacific") 1·00 1·00
2023 $1 Carol Channing ("Hello Dolly") 1·00 1·00
2024 $1 Yul Brynner ("The King and I") 1·00 1·00
2025 $1 Julie Andrews ("My Fair Lady") 1·00 1·00
MS2026 106 × 76 mm. $6 Mickey Rooney ("Sugar Babies") 7·00 8·00

1998. 20th Death Anniv of Charlie Chaplin (film star). Nos. 2404/13 of Antigua optd **BARBUDA MAIL.**
2027 $1 Charlie Chaplin as young man 1·25 90
2028 $1 Pulling face 1·25 90
2029 $1 Looking over shoulder 1·25 90
2030 $1 In cap 1·25 90
2031 $1 In front of star 1·25 90
2032 $1 In "The Great Dictator" 1·25 90
2033 $1 With movie camera and megaphone 1·25 90
2034 $1 Standing in front of camera lens 1·25 90
2035 $1 Putting on make-up 1·25 90
MS2036 76 × 106 mm. $6 Charlie Chaplin 9·00 9·00

1998. Butterflies. Nos. 2414/36 of Antigua optd **BARBUDA MAIL.**
2037 90c. "Charaxes porthos" 1·00 70
2038 $1.10 "Charaxes protoclea protoclea" 1·00 1·00
2039 $1.10 "Byblia ilithyia" 1·00 1·00
2040 $1.10 Black-headed tchagra (bird) 1·00 1·00
2041 $1.10 "Charaxes nobilis" 1·00 1·00
2042 $1.10 "Pseudacraea boisduvali trimeni" 1·00 1·00
2043 $1.10 "Charaxes smaragdalis" 1·00 1·00
2044 $1.10 "Charaxes lasti" 1·00 1·00
2045 $1.10 "Pseudacraea poggei" 1·00 1·00
2046 $1.10 "Graphium colonna" 1·00 1·00
2047 $1.10 Carmine bee eater (bird) 1·00 1·00
2048 $1.10 "Pseudacraea eurytus" 1·00 1·00
2049 $1.10 "Hypolimnas monteironis" 1·00 1·00
2050 $1.10 "Charaxes anticlea" 1·00 1·00
2051 $1.10 "Graphium leonidas" 1·00 1·00
2052 $1.10 "Graphium illyris" 1·00 1·00
2053 $1.10 "Nephronia argia" 1·00 1·00
2054 $1.10 "Graphium policenes" 1·00 1·00
2055 $1.10 "Papilio dardanus" 1·00 1·00
2056 $1.20 "Aethiopana honorius" 1·00 1·10
2057 $1.60 "Charaxes hadrianus" 1·25 1·40
2058 $1.75 "Precis westermanni" 1·40 1·60
MS2059 Three sheets, each 107 × 76 mm. (a) $6 "Charaxes lactincus" (horiz). (b) $6 "Eupheadra reophron". (c) "Euxantha tiberius") (horiz) Set of 3 sheets 17·00 20·00

1998. Christmas. Dogs. Nos. 2771/8 of Antigua optd **BARBUDA MAIL.**
2060 15c. Border collie 65 60
2061 25c. Dalmatian 75 60
2062 65c. Weimaraner 1·40 80
2063 75c. Scottish terrier 1·40 85
2064 90c. Long-haired dachshund 1·50 85
2065 $1.20 Golden retriever 1·75 1·75
2066 $2 Pekingese 2·25 2·75
MS2067 Two sheets, each 75 × 66 mm. (a) $6 Dalmatian. (b) $6 Jack Russell terrier Set of 2 sheets 13·00 12·00

1999. Lighthouses of the World. Nos. 2612/20 of Antigua optd **BARBUDA MAIL.**
2068 45c. Europa Point Lighthouse, Gibraltar 1·00 50
2069 65c. Tierra del Fuego, Argentina (horiz) 1·25 70
2070 75c. Point Loma, California, U.S.A. (horiz) 1·25 70
2071 90c. Groenpoint, Cape Town, South Africa 1·40 80
2072 $1 Youghal, Cork, Ireland 1·50 1·10
2073 $1.20 Launceston, Tasmania, Australia 1·60 1·25
2074 $1.65 Point Abino, Ontario, Canada (horiz) 2·00 2·50
2075 $1.75 Great Inagua, Bahamas (horiz) 2·00 2·50
MS2076 99 × 70 mm. $6 Cape Hatteras, North Carolina, U.S.A. 9·00 9·00

1999. Endangered Species. Nos. 2457/69 of Antigua optd **BARBUDA MAIL.**
2077 $1.20 Red bishop 1·75 1·50
2078 $1.20 Yellow baboon 1·75 1·50
2079 $1.20 Superb starling 1·75 1·50
2080 $1.20 Ratel 1·75 1·50
2081 $1.20 Hunting dog 1·75 1·50
2082 $1.20 Serval 1·75 1·50
2083 $1.65 Okapi 2·00 1·75
2084 $1.65 Giant forest squirrel 2·00 1·75
2085 $1.65 Lesser masked weaver 2·00 1·75
2086 $1.65 Small-spotted genet 2·00 1·75
2087 $1.65 Yellow-billed stork 2·00 1·75
2088 $1.65 Red-headed agama 2·00 1·75
MS2089 Three sheets, each 106 × 76 mm. (a) $6 South African crowned crane. (b) $6 Bat-eared fox. (c) $6 Malachite kingfisher Set of 3 sheets 16·00 18·00

1999. "Pacific 97" International Stamp Exhibition, San Francisco. Death Centenary of Heinrich von Stephan (founder of the U.P.U.). Nos. 2481/4 of Antigua optd **BARBUDA MAIL.**
2090 $1.75 blue 2·50 2·25
2091 $1.75 brown 2·50 2·25
2092 $1.75 mauve 2·50 2·25
MS2093 82 × 119 mm. $6 violet 4·50 5·50
DESIGNS: No. 2090, Kaiser Wilhelm I and Heinrich von Stephan; 2091, Von Stephan and Mercury; 2092, Carrier pigeon and loft; MS2093 Von Stephan and 15th-century Basel messenger.

1999. 175th Anniv of Brothers Grimm's Third Collection of Fairy Tales. *Cinderella*. Nos. 2485/8 of Antigua optd **BARBUDA MAIL.**
2094 $1.75 The Ugly Sisters and their Mother 2·75 2·50
2095 $1.75 Cinderella and her Fairy Godmother 2·75 2·50
2096 $1.75 Cinderella and the Prince 2·75 2·50
MS2097 124 × 96 mm. $6 Cinderella trying on slipper 6·00 7·00

1999. Orchids of the World. Nos. 2502/24 of Antigua optd **BARBUDA MAIL.**
2098 45c. *Odontoglossum cervantesii* 1·25 45
2099 65c. *Phalaenopsis* Medford Star 1·50 85
2100 75c. *Vanda* Motes Resplendent 1·50 85
2101 90c. *Odontonia* Debutante 1·75 1·00
2102 $1 *Iwanagaara* Apple Blossom 2·00 1·10
2103 $1.65 *Cattleya* Sophia Martin 2·00 2·00
2104 $1.65 Dogface Butterfly 2·00 2·00
2105 $1.65 *Laeliocattleya* Mini Purple 2·00 2·00
2106 $1.65 *Cymbidium* Showgirl 2·00 2·00
2107 $1.65 *Brassolaeliocattleya* Dorothy Bertsch 2·00 2·00
2108 $1.65 *Disa blackii* 2·00 2·00
2109 $1.65 *Paphiopedilum leeanum* 2·00 2·00
2110 $1.65 *Paphiopedilum macranthum* 2·00 2·00
2111 $1.65 *Brassocattleya* Angel Lace 2·00 2·00
2112 $1.65 *Saphrolae liocattleya* Precious Stones 2·00 2·00
2113 $1.65 Orange Theope Butterfly 2·00 2·00
2114 $1.65 *Promenaea xanthina* 2·00 2·00
2115 $1.65 *Lycasle macrobulbon* 2·00 2·00
2116 $1.65 *Amestella philippinensis* 2·00 2·00
2117 $1.65 *Masdevallia* Machu Picchu 2·00 2·00
2118 $1.65 *Phalaenopsis* Zuma Urchin 2·00 2·00
2119 $2 *Dendrobium victoria-reginae* 2·50 2·75
MS2120 Two sheets, each 76 × 106 mm. (a) $6 *Miltonia* Seine. (b) $6 *Paphiopedilum gratrixanum* Set of 2 sheets 14·00 15·00

1999. 50th Death Anniv of Paul Harris (founder of Rotary International). No. 2472/3 of Antigua optd **BARBUDA MAIL.**
2121 $1.65 Paul Harris and James Grant 2·50 3·00
MS2122 78 × 107 mm. $6 Group study exchange, New Zealand 5·00 7·00

1999. Royal Wedding. Nos. 2912/16 of Antigua optd **BARBOUDA MAIL.**
2123 $3 Sophie Rhys-Jones 2·50 2·75
2124 $3 Sophie and Prince Edward 2·50 2·75
2125 $3 Prince Edward 2·50 2·75
MS2126 108 × 78 mm. $6 Prince Edward with Sophie Rhys-Jones and Windsor Castle 6·00 7·00
All examples of Nos. 2123/5 show the incorrect country overprint as above.

1999. Fungi. Nos. 2489/501 of Antigua optd **BARBUDA MAIL.**
2127 45c. *Marasmius rotula* 1·00 35
2128 65c. *Cantharellus cibarius* 1·25 55
2129 70c. *Lepiota cristata* 1·40 60
2130 90c. *Auricularia mesenterica* 1·50 70
2131 $1 *Pholiota alnicola* 1·50 1·00
2132 $1.65 *Leccinum aurantiacum* 1·75 1·90
2133 $1.75 *Entoloma serrulatum* 1·75 1·90
2134 $1.75 *Panaeolus sphinctrinus* 1·75 1·90
2135 $1.75 *Volvariella bombycina* 1·75 1·90
2136 $1.75 *Conocybe percincta* 1·75 1·90
2137 $1.75 *Pluteus cervinus* 1·75 1·90
2138 $1.75 *Russula foetens* 1·75 1·90
MS2139 Two sheets, each 106 × 76 mm. (a) $6 *Amanita cothurnata*. (b) $6 *Panellus serotinus* Set of 2 sheets 12·00 14·00

1999. 1st Death Anniv of Diana, Princess of Wales. No. 2753 of Antigua optd **BARBUDA MAIL.**
2140 $1.20 Diana, Princess of Wales 1·50 1·50

1999. Railway Locomotives of the World. Nos. 2553/65 of Antigua optd **BARBUDA MAIL.**
2141 $1.65 Original drawing by Richard Trevithick, 1803 1·50 1·50
2142 $1.65 William Hedley's *Puffing Billy*, (1813–14) 1·50 1·50
2143 $1.65 Crampton locomotive of French Nord Railway, 1858 1·50 1·50
2144 $1.65 Lawrence Machine Shop locomotive, U.S.A., 1860 1·50 1·50
2145 $1.65 Natchez and Hamburg Railway steam locomotive *Mississippi*, U.S.A., 1834 1·50 1·50
2146 $1.65 Bury "Coppernob" locomotive, Furness Railway, 1846 1·50 1·50
2147 $1.65 David Joy's *Jenny Lind*, 1847 1·50 1·50

2148 $1.65 Schenectady Atlantic locomotive, U.S.A., 1899 . . 1·50 1·50
2149 $1.65 Kitson Class 1800 tank locomotive, Japan, 1881 . . . . 1·50 1·50
2150 $1.65 Pennsylvania Railroad express freight . . . . . 1·50 1·50
2151 $1.65 Karl Golsdorf's 4 cylinder locomotive, Austria . . . . 1·50 1·50
2152 $1.65 Series "E" locomotive, Russia, 1930 . . . . . . 1·50 1·50
MS2153 Two sheets, each 72 × 100 mm. (a) $6 George Stephenson's "Patentee" Type locomotive, 1843. (b) $6 Brunel's trestle bridge over River Lynher, Cornwall . . . . . . 9·50 10·00

1999. 175th Anniv of Cedar Hall Moravian Church. Nos. 2605/11 of Antigua optd **BARBUDA MAIL**.
2154 20c. First Church and Manse, 1822–40 . . . . . 45 35
2155 45c. Cedar Hall School, 1840 . . . . 55 30
2156 75c. Hugh A. King, minister, 1945–53 . . . . 75 45
2157 90c. Present Church building 85 50
2158 $1.20 Water tank, 1822 . . 1·25 1·25
2159 $2 Former Manse, demolished 1978 . . . . 1·75 2·50
MS2160 100 × 70 mm. $6 Present church building (different) (50 × 37 mm) . . . . 4·25 5·50

1999. Christmas. Religious Paintings. Nos. 2945/51 of Antigua optd **BARBUDA MAIL**.
2161 15c. multicoloured 35 30
2162 25c. black, stone and yellow 40 30
2163 45c. multicoloured 55 30
2164 60c. multicoloured 80 35
2165 $2 multicoloured . . . . . 1·75 2·50
2166 $4 black, stone and yellow 2·75 4·00
MS2167 76 × 106 mm. $6 multicoloured . . . . 4·25 5·50

1999. Centenary of Thomas Oliver Robinson Memorial School. Nos. 2634/40 of Antigua optd **BARBUDA MAIL**.
2168 20c. green and black 35 25
2169 45c. multicoloured 55 30
2170 65c. green and black 75 40
2171 75c. multicoloured 80 50
2172 90c. multicoloured 90 60
2173 $1.20 brown, green and black . . . . 1·10 1·25
MS2174 106 × 76 mm. $6 brown 4·25 5·50

2000. Cats and Dogs. Nos. 2540/52 of Antigua optd **BARBUDA MAIL**.
2175 $1.65 Scottish fold kitten . . 1·25 1·25
2176 $1.65 Japanese bobtail . . . 1·25 1·25
2177 $1.65 Tabby manx . . . . 1·25 1·25
2178 $1.65 Bicolor American shorthair . . . . 1·25 1·25
2179 $1.65 Sorel Abyssinian . . . 1·25 1·25
2180 $1.65 Himalayan blue point 1·25 1·25
2181 $1.65 Dachshund . . . . . 1·25 1·25
2182 $1.65 Staffordshire terrier 1·25 1·25
2183 $1.65 Shar-pei . . . . . . 1·25 1·25
2184 $1.65 Beagle . . . . . . 1·25 1·25
2185 $1.65 Norfolk terrier . . . 1·25 1·25
2186 $1.65 Golden retriever . . . 1·25 1·25
MS2187 Two sheets, each 107 × 77 mm. (a) $6 Red tabby (vert). (b) $6 Siberian husky (vert) 11·50 11·50

2000. Fishes. Nos. 2586/604 of Antigua optd **BARBUDA MAIL**.
2188 75c. Yellow damselfish . . . 75 50
2189 90c. Barred hamlet 80 55
2190 $1 Yellow-tailed damselfish ("Jewelfish") 90 70
2191 $1.20 Blue-headed wrasse . . 1·10 1·00
2192 $1.50 Queen angelfish . . . 1·25 1·25
2193 $1.65 Jackknife-fish . . . . 1·25 1·25
2194 $1.65 Spot-finned hogfish . . 1·25 1·25
2195 $1.65 Sergeant major . . . 1·25 1·25
2196 $1.65 Neon goby . . . . . 1·25 1·25
2197 $1.65 Jawfish . . . . 1·25 1·25
2198 $1.65 Flamefish . . . . . . 1·25 1·25
2199 $1.65 Rock beauty . . . . 1·25 1·25
2200 $1.65 Yellow-tailed snapper 1·25 1·25
2201 $1.65 Creole wrasse . . . . 1·25 1·25
2202 $1.65 Slender filefish . . . . 1·25 1·25
2203 $1.65 Long-spined squirrelfish . . . . . . 1·25 1·25
2204 $1.65 Royal gramma ("Fairy Basslet") . . . . 1·25 1·25
2205 $1.75 Queen triggerfish . . . 1·40 1·40
MS2206 Two sheets, each 80 × 110 mm. (a) $6 Porkfish. (b) $6 Black-capped basslet . . . 15·00 15·00

2000. Ships of the World. Nos. 2679/85 of Antigua optd **BARBUDA MAIL**.
2207 $1.75 *Savannah* (paddle-steamer) . . . . 1·25 1·25
2208 $1.75 Viking longship . . . 1·25 1·25
2209 $1.75 Greek galley . . . . 1·25 1·25
2210 $1.75 Sailing clipper . . . . 1·25 1·25
2211 $1.75 Dhow . . . . 1·25 1·25
2212 $1.75 Fishing catboat . . . 1·25 1·25
MS2213 Three sheets, each 100 × 70 mm. (a) $6 13th-century English warship (41 × 22 mm). (b) $6 Sailing dory (22 × 41 mm). (c) $6 Baltimore clipper (41 × 22 mm) 12·00 14·00

2000. Modern Aircraft. Nos. 2700/12 of Antigua optd **BARBUDA MAIL**.
2214 $1.65 Lockheed-Boeing General Dynamics Yf-22 1·25 1·25
2215 $1.65 Dassault-Breguet Rafale BO 1 . . . . . . 1·25 1·25
2216 $1.65 MiG 29 . . . . . . 1·25 1·25
2217 $1.65 Dassault-Breguet Mirage 2000D . . . . . 1·25 1·25
2218 $1.65 Rockwell B-1B "Lancer" . . . . 1·25 1·25
2219 $1.65 McDonnell-Douglas C-17A . . . . 1·25 1·25
2220 $1.65 Space Shuttle . . . . 1·25 1·25
2221 $1.65 SAAB "Grippen" . . 1·25 1·25
2222 $1.65 Eurofighter EF-2000 1·25 1·25
2223 $1.65 Sukhoi SU 27 . . . . 1·25 1·25
2224 $1.65 Northrop B-2 . . . . 1·25 1·25
2225 $1.65 Lockheed F-117 "Nighthawk" . . . . . . 1·25 1·25
MS2226 Two sheets, each 110 × 85 mm. (a) $6 F18 Hornet. (b) $6 Sukhoi SU 35 . . . . . 11·00 12·00

2000. Classic Cars. Nos. 2687/MS2699 of Antigua optd **BARBUDA MAIL**.
2227 $1.65 Ford (1896) . . . . . 1·25 1·25
2228 $1.65 Ford A (1903) . . . . 1·25 1·25
2229 $1.65 Ford T (1928) . . . . 1·25 1·25
2230 $1.65 Ford T (1922) . . . . 1·25 1·25
2231 $1.65 Ford Blackhawk (1929) . . . . 1·25 1·25
2232 $1.65 Ford Sedan (1934) . . 1·25 1·25
2233 $1.65 Torpedo (1911) . . . 1·25 1·25
2234 $1.65 Mercedes 22 (1913) . . 1·25 1·25
2235 $1.65 Rover (1920) . . . . 1·25 1·25
2236 $1.65 Mercedes Benz (1956) 1·25 1·25
2237 $1.65 Packard V-12 (1934) 1·25 1·25
2238 $1.65 Opel (1924) . . . . . 1·25 1·25
MS2239 Two sheets, each 70 × 100 mm. (a) $6 Ford (1908) (60 × 40 mm). (b) $6 Ford (1929) (60 × 40 mm) Set of 2 sheets . . 12·00 12·00

2000. 19th World Scout Jamboree, Chile. Nos. 2739/MS2742 of Antigua optd **BARBUDA MAIL**.
2240 90c. Scout handshake . . . 1·00 65
2241 $1 Scouts hiking . . . . . 1·25 90
2242 $1.20 Scout salute . . . . . 1·50 1·50
MS2243 68 × 98 mm. $6 Lord Baden-Powell . . . . 7·00 7·50

2000. 50th Anniv of Organisation of American States (1998). No. 2730 of Antigua optd **BARBUDA MAIL**.
2244 $1 Stylized Americas . . . 1·25 1·25

2000. International Year of the Ocean (1998). Nos. 2641/MS2678a/b of Antigua optd **BARBUDA MAIL**.
2245/69 40c. × 25 Spotted eagle ray; Manta ray; Hawksbill turtle; Jellyfish; Queen angelfish; Octopus; Emperor angelfish; Regal angelfish; Porkfish; Racoon butterflyfish; Atlantic barracuda; Sea horse; Nautilus; Trumpetfish; White tip shark; Sunken Spanish galleon; Black tip shark; Long-nosed butterflyfish; Green moray eel; Captain Nemo; Treasure chest; Hammerhead shark; Divers; Lionfish; Clownfish . . . . . . 14·00 15·00
2270/81 75c. × 12 Maroon-tailed conure; Cocoi heron; Common tern; Rainbow lorikeet; Saddleback butterflyfish; Goatfish and cat shark; Blue shark and stingray; Majestic snapper; Nassau grouper; Black-cap gramma and blue tang; Stingrays; Stingray and giant starfish . . . . 18·00 20·00
MS2282 Two sheets. (a) 68 × 98 mm. $6 Humpback whale. (b) 98 × 68 mm. $6 Fiddler ray Set of 2 sheets . . . . . . 13·00 13·00
Nos. 2245/69 and 2270/81 were each printed together, se-tenant, with the backgrounds forming composite designs.

2000. Olympic Games, Sydney. Nos. 3109/12 of Antigua optd **BARBUDA MAIL**.
2283 $2 Marcus Latimer Hurley (cycling), St Louis (1904) 2·25 2·25
2284 $2 Diving . . . . 2·25 2·25
2285 $2 Flaminio Stadium, Rome (1960) and Italian flag . 2·25 2·25
2286 $2 Ancient Greek javelin thrower . . . . 2·25 2·25

2000. West Indies Cricket Tour and 100th Test Match at Lord's. Nos. 3113/MS3115 of Antigua optd **BARBUDA MAIL**.
2287 90c. Richie Richardson . . 1·50 1·40
2288 $5 Viv Richards . . . . . 7·00 7·00
MS2289 121 × 104 mm. $6 Lord's Cricket Ground . . . . 8·00 8·50

2000. Satellites and Spacecraft. Nos. 2835/40 and MS2847b of Antigua optd **BARBUDA MAIL**.
2290 $1.65 "Luna 2" moon probe 1·25 1·25
2291 $1.65 "Mariner 2" space probe . . . . 1·25 1·25
2292 $1.65 Giotto space probe . . 1·25 1·25
2293 $1.65 Rosat satellite . . . . 1·25 1·25
2294 $1.65 International Ultraviolet Explorer . . . 1·25 1·25
2295 $1.65 Ulysses space probe 1·25 1·25
MS2296 106 × 76 mm. $6 "MIR" space station . . . . 7·00 7·50

2000. No. MS3233 of Antigua optd **BARBUDA MAIL**.
MS2313 Two Sheets, each 90 × 60 mm. (a) $6 Junkers 87B (dive bomber). (b) $6 Supermarine Spitfires at dusk . . . . 11·00 12·00

BARWANI Pt. 1

A State of Central India. Now uses Indian stamps.

12 pies = 1 anna; 16 annas = 1 rupee.

1 Rana Ranjit Singh

2

1921.

5	1	¼a. green	21·00	85·00
19		¼a. blue	1·50	11·00
37 B		½a. black	4·75	38·00
18		½a. pink	2·50	14·00
4		½a. blue	17·00	£180
29		½a. green	2·75	16·00
10	2	1a. red	2·50	21·00
39 B		1a. brown	15·00	28·00
11		2a. purple	2·25	25·00
41 B		2a. red	28·00	£130
31		4a. orange	80·00	£225
42Ba	–	4a. green	14·00	42·00

DESIGN: 4a. Another portrait of Rana Ranjit Singh.

4 Rana Devi Singh

5

1932.

32A	4	¼a. slate	2·50	23·00
33A		½a. green	4·00	23·00
34A		1a. brown	4·00	22·00
35A		2a. purple	3·75	42·00
36A		4a. olive	6·00	42·00

1938.

43	5	1a. brown	40·00	75·00

BASUTOLAND Pt. 1

An African territory under British protection, N.E. of Cape Province. Self-Government introduced on 1 April 1965. Attained independence on 4 October 1966, when the country was renamed Lesotho.

1933. 12 pence = 1 shilling; 20 shillings = 1 pound.
1961. 100 cents = 1 rand.

1 King George V, Nile Crocodile and Mountains

1933.

1	1	½d. green	1·00	1·75
2		1d. red	75	1·25
3		2d. purple	1·00	80
4		3d. blue	75	1·25
5		4d. grey	2·00	7·00
6		6d. yellow	2·25	1·75
7		1s. orange	2·25	4·50
8		2s.6d. brown	25·00	48·00
9		5s. violet	50·00	75·00
10		10s. olive	£150	£160

1935. Silver Jubilee. As T **13** of Antigua.

11	1d. blue and red	55	2·25
12	2d. blue and grey	65	2·25
13	3d. brown and blue	3·75	5·50
14	6d. grey and purple	3·75	5·50

1937. Coronation. As T **2** of Aden.

15	1d. red	35	1·25
16	2d. purple	50	1·25
17	3d. blue	60	1·25

1938. As T **1**, but portrait of King George VI.

18	½d. green	30	1·25
19	1d. red	50	70
20	1½d. blue	40	50
21	2d. purple	30	60
22	3d. blue	30	1·25
23	4d. grey	1·50	3·50
24	6d. yellow	1·50	1·50
25	1s. orange	1·50	1·00
26	2s.6d. brown	13·00	8·50
27	5s. violet	32·00	9·50
28	10s. olive	32·00	17·00

1945. Victory. Stamps of South Africa optd **Basutoland**. Alternate stamps inscr in English or Afrikaans.

29	**55**	1d. brown and red	50	80
30		2d. blue and violet	50	60
31		3d. blue	50	85

Prices are for bi-lingual pairs.

5 King George VI and Queen Elizabeth

1947. Royal Visit.

32	–	1d. red	10	10
33	5	2d. green	10	10
34	–	3d. blue	10	10
35	–	1s. mauve	10	10

DESIGNS—VERT: 1d. King George VI. HORIZ: 3d. Queen Elizabeth II as Princess and Princess Margaret; 1s. The Royal Family.

1948. Silver Wedding. As T **10/11** of Aden.

36	1½d. blue	20	10
37	10s. green	38·00	38·00

1949. U.P.U. As T **20/23** of Antigua.

38	1½d. blue	20	1·50
39	3d. blue	2·00	2·00
40	6d. orange	1·00	4·00
41	1s. brown	50	1·25

1953. Coronation. As T **13** of Aden.

42	2d. black and purple	40	40

8 Qiloane

9 Mohair (Shearing Goats)

1954.

43	8	½d. black and sepia	20	10
44	–	1d. black and green	20	10
45	–	2d. blue and orange	60	10
46	–	3d. sage and red	80	30
47	–	4½d. indigo and blue	70	15
48	–	6d. brown and green	1·25	15
49	–	1s. bronze and purple	1·25	30
50	–	1s.3d. brown and turquoise	22·00	6·50
51	–	2s.6d. blue and red	22·00	8·50
52	–	5s. black and red	6·00	8·50
53	9	10s. black and purple	27·00	23·00

DESIGNS—HORIZ: 1d. Orange River; 2d. Mosuto horseman; 3d. Basuto household; 4½d. Maletsunyane Falls; 6d. Herd-boy playing lesiba; 1s. Pastoral scene; 1s.3d. De Havilland Comet 1 airplane over Lancers' Gap; 2s.6d. Old Fort, Leribe; 5s. Mission cave house.

1959. No. 45 Surch ½**d.** and bar.

54	½d. on 2d. blue and orange . . .	10	15

20 "Chief Moshoeshoe I" (engraving by Delangle)

26 Basuto Household

1959. Inauguration of National Council.

55	20	3d. black and olive	40	10
56	–	1s. red and green	40	20
57	–	1s.3d. blue and orange . . .	60	45

DESIGNS: 1s. Council house; 1s.3d. Mosuto horseman.

1961. Nos. 43/53 surch.

58	8	½c. on ½d. black and sepia	10	10
59	–	1c. on 1d. black and green	10	10
60	–	2c. on 2d. blue and orange	10	10
61	–	2½c. on 3d. green and red	10	10
62	–	3½c. on 4½d. indigo and blue	10	10
63	–	5c. on 6d. brown and green	10	10
64	–	10c. on 1s. green and purple	10	10
65a	–	12½c. on 1s.3d. brown and turquoise	3·75	1·25
66	–	25c. on 2s.6d. blue and red	30	60
67	–	50c. on 5s. black and red . .	1·75	1·40
68b	9	1r. on 10s. black and purple	17·00	18·00

1961. As 1954 but value in new currency as in T **26**.

69	8	½c. black and brown	20	20
70	–	1c. black and green (as 1d.)	20	40
71	–	2c. blue and orange (as 2d.)	1·25	1·40

86 26 2½c. green and red 15 25
73 – 3½c. indigo and blue (as 4½d.) . . . . 30 1·50
88 – 5c. brown and green (as 6d.) 30 50
75 – 10c. green and purple (as 1s.) 30 40
90 – 12½c. brown & grn (as 1s.3d.) . . . . 5·00 1·50
77 – 25c. blue and red (as 2s.6d.) 6·50 6·50
92 – 50c. black and red (as 5s.) 7·25 11·00
79 9 1r. black and purple . . . . 45·00 17·00

1963. Freedom from Hunger. As T **28** of Aden.
80 12½c. violet 40 15

1963. Centenary of Red Cross. As T **33** of Antigua.
81 2½c. red and black 20 10
82 12½c. red and blue 80 60

28 Mosotho Woman and Child

1965. New Constitution. Inscr "SELF GOVERNMENT 1965". Multicoloured.
94 2½c. Type **28** 20 10
95 3½c. Maseru border post . . . 25 20
96 5c. Mountain scene 25 20
97 12½c. Legislative Buildings . . 45 70

1965. Centenary of I.T.U. As T **36** of Antigua.
98 1c. red and purple 15 10
99 20c. blue and brown 50 30

1965. I.C.Y. As T **37** of Antigua.
100 ½c. purple and turquoise . . 10 10
101 12½c. green and lavender . . 45 35

1966. Churchill Commemoration. As T **38** of Antigua.
102 1c. blue 15 70
103 2½c. green 50 10
104 10c. brown 75 30
105 22½c. violet . . . . 1·25 90

OFFICIAL STAMPS

1934. Nos. 1/3 and 6 optd **OFFICIAL**.
O1 1 ½d. green £11000 £7000
O2 1d. red £2750 £2500
O3 2d. purple £3000 £850
O4 6d. yellow £11000 £4750

POSTAGE DUE STAMPS

1933. As Type D **1** of Barbados.
D1b 1d. red . . . . 1·00 4·00
D2a 2d. violet . . . . 30 17·00

D 2

1956.
D3 D 2 1d. red . . . . 30 3·00
D4 2d. violet . . . . 30 6·00

1961. Surch.
D5 D 2 1c. on 1d. red 10 35
D6 1c. on 2d. violet . . . . . 10 1·25
D7 5c. on 2d. violet 15 45
D8 – 5c. on 2d. violet (No. D2a) . . . . 1·00 6·50

1964. As Type D **2**, but value in decimal currency.
D 9 1c. red . . . . 3·00 19·00
D10 5c. violet . . . . 3·00 19·00

For later issues see **LESOTHO**.

BATUM Pt. 1

Batum, a Russian port on the Black Sea, had been taken by Turkish troops during the First World War. Following the Armistice, British Forces occupied the town on 1 December 1918. Batum was handed over to the National Republic of Georgia on 7 July 1920.

100 kopeks = 1 rouble.

1 Aloe Tree

(2)

1919. Imperf.
1 1 5k. green . . . . 6·50 15·00
2 10k. blue . . . . 6·50 15·00
3 50k. yellow . . . . 3·75 6·00
4 1r. brown . . . . 5·50 6·00
5 3r. violet . . . . 9·50 16·00
6 5r. brown . . . . 10·00 28·00

1919. Arms types of Russia surch as T **2**. Imperf (Nos. 7/8), perf (Nos. 9/10).
7 10r. on 1k. orange . . . . . 60·00 70·00
8 10r. on 3k. red . . . . . . 24·00 29·00
9 10r. on 5k. purple £375 £400
10 10r. on 10 on 7k. blue . . . £425 £450

1919. T **1** optd **BRITISH OCCUPATION**.
11 1 5k. green . . . . 22·00 17·00
12 10k. blue . . . . 15·00 17·00
13 25k. yellow . . . . 22·00 17·00
14 1r. blue . . . . 5·50 17·00
15 2r. pink . . . . 1·00 6·00
16 3r. violet . . . . 1·00 6·00
17 5r. brown . . . . 1·25 6·00
18 7r. red . . . . 4·50 9·00

1919. Arms types of Russia surch with Russian inscr, **BRITISH OCCUPATION** and new value.
19 10r. on 3k. red . . . . . . 20·00 24·00
20a 15r. on 1k. orange . . . . . 55·00 60·00
29 25r. on 5k. purple . . . . . 42·00 55·00
30a 25r. on 10 on 7k. blue . . . 70·00 80·00
31 25r. on 20 on 14k. red and blue . . . . 75·00 90·00
32a 25r. on 25k. purple and green 95·00 £120
33a 25r. on 50k. green and purple 75·00 90·00
21 50r. on 1k. orange £475 £550
34 50r. on 2k. green £110 £140
35 50r. on 3k. red £110 £140
36 50r. on 4k. red £100 £120
37 50r. on 5k. purple . . . . . 80·00 95·00
27 50r. on 10k. blue £1800 £1900
28 50r. on 15k. blue and brown £650 £750

1920. Romanov type of Russia surch with Russian inscr, **BRITISH OCCUPATION** and new value.
41 50r. on 4k. red . . . . 70·00 90·00

1920. Nos. 11, 13 and 3 surch with new value (50r. with **BRITISH OCCUPATION** also).
42 1 25r. on 5k. green . . . . . 38·00 40·00
43 25r. on 25k. yellow . . . . 28·00 30·00
44a 50r. on 50k. yellow . . . . 17·00 18·00

1920. T **1** optd **BRITISH OCCUPATION**.
45 1 1r. brown . . . . 2·00 11·00
46 2r. blue . . . . 2·00 11·00
47 3r. pink . . . . 2·00 11·00
48 5r. black . . . . 2·00 11·00
49 7r. yellow . . . . 2·00 11·00
50 10r. green . . . . 2·00 11·00
51 15r. violet . . . . 2·50 15·00
52 25r. red . . . . 2·25 14·00
53 50r. blue . . . . 2·50 17·00

BAVARIA Pt. 7

In S. Germany. A kingdom till 1918, then a republic. Incorporated into Germany in 1920.

1849. 60 kreuzer = 1 gulden.
1874. 100 pfennig = 1 mark.

1

2 (Circle cut)

1849. Imperf.
1 1 1k. black £1100 £1600

1849. Imperf. Circle cut by labels.
3 2 3k. blue . . . . £130 3·50
23 3k. red . . . . 55·00 5·75
7 6k. brown £8000 £225

1850. Imperf. As T **2**, but circle not cut.
8a 2 1k. red . . . . £180 26·00
21 1k. yellow . . . . 95·00 21·00
11 6k. brown . . . . 48·00 7·00
25 6k. blue . . . . 80·00 22·00
16 9k. green . . . . £225 18·00
28 9k. brown . . . . £120 16·00
18 12k. red £150 £150
31 12k. green . . . . £120 70·00
19 18k. yellow £130 £225
32 18k. red £170 £550

3

6

8

1867. Imperf.
34 3 1k. green . . . . 70·00 10·50
37 3k. red . . . . 75·00 1·80
39 6k. blue . . . . 48·00 21·00
41 6k. brown . . . . 80·00 55·00
43 7k. blue . . . . £450 14·00
46 9k. brown . . . . 48·00 35·00
48 12k. mauve £400 £110
50 18k. red £150 £190
65 6 1m. mauve . . . . £700 90·00

1870. Perf.
51A 3 1k. green . . . . 35·00 5·25
69 3k. red . . . . 70 4·50
55A 6k. brown . . . . 35·00 35·00
56A 7k. blue . . . . 3·50 4·00
59A 9k. brown . . . . 4·75 4·00
60A 10k. yellow . . . . 6·25 15·00
61A 12k. mauve £1300 £5500
63A 18k. red . . . . 12·50 14·00

1876. Perf.
120 8 2pf. grey . . . . 2·20 55
103 3pf. green . . . . 11·50 2·20
121 3pf. brown 25 45
122 5pf. green 25 45
107 5pf. mauve . . . . 22·00 8·75
123 10pf. red 35 45
124 20pf. blue 35 45
114 25pf. brown . . . . 35·00 7·00
125 25pf. orange 35 70
126 30pf. olive 60 80
127 40pf. yellow . . . . 60 1·10
86 50pf. red . . . . 55·00 8·00
117 50pf. brown . . . . 65·00 4·50
128 50pf. purple . . . . 35 1·60
129 80pf. mauve . . . . 3·00 4·00
100 6 1m. mauve . . . . 5·25 2·75
101a 2m. orange . . . . 6·25 6·25
136 3m. brown . . . . 9·75 39·00
137 5m. green . . . . 9·75 48·00

11

13 Prince Luitpold

1911. Prince Regent Luitpold's 90th Birthday.
138c 11 3pf. brown on drab . . . 25 90
139c 5pf. green on green . . . 25 90
140d 10pf. red on buff 25 90
141b 20pf. blue on blue . . . . 2·20 1·40
142a 25pf. deep brown on buff 3·50 2·75
143a – 30pf. orange on buff . . . 1·80 2·10
144a – 40pf. olive on buff . . . 3·50 2·10
145a – 50pf. red on drab . . . . 3·50 3·50
146 – 60pf. green on buff . . . 3·50 3·50
147a – 80pf. violet on drab . . . 10·50 11·50
148a 13 1m. brown on drab . . . 3·00 2·50
149a 2m. green on green . . . 3·00 13·00
150a 3m. red on buff . . . . . 14·00 95·00
151 5m. blue on buff . . . . 23·00 55·00
152 10m. orange on yellow . . 40·00 90·00
153 20m. brown on yellow . . 23·00 44·00

The 30 pf. to 80 pf. values are similar to Type **11**, but larger.

14

1911. 25th Anniv of Regency of Prince Luitpold.
154 14 5pf. yellow, green & black 55 1·10
155 10pf. yellow, red & black 80 1·60

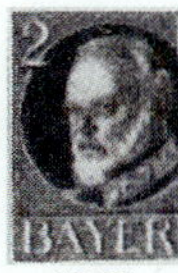
15 King Ludwig III

16

1914. Imperf or perf.
171A 15 2pf. slate . . . . 25 1·80
172A 2½ on 2pf. slate . . . . 25 1·80
173A 3pf. brown . . . . 1·10 2·20
175A 5pf. green . . . . 25 1·80
176A 7½pf. green . . . . . . 20 1·80
178A 10pf. red . . . . 30 1·80
179A 15pf. red . . . . 30 1·80
182A 20pf. blue . . . . 30 1·80
183A 25pf. grey . . . . 40 1·80
184A 30pf. orange . . . . . . 1·10 1·80
185A 40pf. olive . . . . 30 1·80
186A 50pf. brown . . . . . . 40 1·80
187A 60pf. green . . . . . . 1·10 1·80
188A 80pf. violet . . . . . . 25 1·80
189A 16 1m. brown . . . . . . 25 1·80
190A 2m. violet . . . . 25 3·00
191A 3m. red . . . . 35 6·25
192A – 5m. blue . . . . 45 22·00
193A – 10m. green . . . . . . 1·60 60·00
194A – 20m. brown . . . . . . 3·00 90·00

The 5, 10 and 20m. are larger.

1919. Peoples' State Issue. Overprinted **Volksstaat Bayern**. Imperf or perf.
195A 15 3pf. brown . . . . . . 20 1·80
196A 5pf. green . . . . 20 1·80
197A 7½pf. green . . . . . . 20 1·80
198A 10pf. lake . . . . 20 1·80
199A 15pf. red . . . . 20 1·80
200A 20pf. blue . . . . 20 1·80
201A 25pf. grey . . . . 20 1·80
202A 30pf. orange . . . . . . 20 1·80
203A 35pf. orange . . . . . . 20 2·75
204A 40pf. olive . . . . 20 1·80
205A 50pf. brown . . . . . . 20 1·80
206A 60pf. turquoise . . . . . 20 1·80
207A 75pf. brown . . . . . . 20 1·60
208A 80pf. violet . . . . . . 20 2·20
209A 16 1m. brown . . . . . . 20 1·90
210A 2m. violet . . . . 25 2·20
211A 3m. red . . . . 45 5·25
212A – 5m. blue (No. 192) . . . 1·10 11·50
213A – 10m. green (No. 193) . . 1·30 60·00
214A – 20m. brown (No. 194) . . 2·20 4·00

1919. 1st Free State Issue. Stamps of Germany (inscr "DEUTSCHES REICH") optd **Freistaat Bayern**.
215 24 2½pf. grey . . . . 20 1·60
216 10 3pf. brown . . . . 20 1·60
217 5pf. green . . . . 20 1·60
218 24 7½pf. orange . . . . . . 20 1·60
219 10 10pf. red . . . . 20 1·80
220 24 15pf. violet . . . . . . 20 1·80
221 10 20pf. blue . . . . 20 1·60
222 25pf. black & red on yell 20 1·80
223 24 35pf. brown . . . . . . 20 1·90
224 10 40pf. black and red . . . 25 1·90
225 75pf. black and green . . . 45 2·75
226 80pf. black & red on rose 45 3·25
227 12 1m. red . . . . 1·10 5·25
228 13 2m. blue . . . . 1·60 10·50
229 14 3m. black . . . . 1·60 14·00
230 15 5m. red and black . . . 1·60 14·00

1919. 2nd Free State Issue. Stamps of Bavaria overprinted **Freistaat Bayern**. Imperf or perf.
231A 15 3pf. brown . . . . . . 20 2·20
232A 5pf. green . . . . 20 2·20
233A 7½pf. green . . . . . . 20 18·00
234A 10pf. lake . . . . 20 2·20
235A 15pf. red . . . . 20 2·20
236A 20pf. blue . . . . 20 2·20
237A 25pf. grey . . . . 20 2·20
238A 30pf. orange . . . . . . 20 2·20
239A 40pf. olive . . . . 20 16·00
240A 50pf. brown . . . . . . 20 2·20
241A 60pf. turquoise . . . . . 30 16·00
242A 75pf. brown . . . . . . 45 16·00
243A 80pf. violet . . . . . . 20 4·00
244A 16 1m. brown . . . . . . 25 3·00
245A 2m. violet . . . . 25 4·50
246A 3m. red . . . . 45 8·00
247A – 5m. blue (No. 192) . . . 90 19·00
248A – 10m. green (No. 193) . . 1·80 40·00
249A – 20m. brown (No. 194) . . 2·75 65·00

1919. War Wounded. Surch **5 Pf. fur Kriegsbeschadigte Freistaat Bayern**. Perf.
250 15 10pf.+5pf. lake . . . . . 45 2·20
251 15pf.+5pf. red . . . . . . 45 2·20
252 20pf.+5pf. blue . . . . . . 45 2·75

1920. Surch **Freistaat Bayern** and value. Imperf or perf.
253A 16 1m.25pf. on 1m. green . . 25 35
254A 1m.50pf. on 1m. orange . . 25 45
255A 2m.50pf. on 1m. slate . . 45 95

1920. No. 121 surch **20** in four corners.
256 8 20 on 3pf. brown . . . . . 25 2·20

26

27

28

29

30

1920.
257 26 5pf. green . . . . 15 2·75
258 10pf. orange . . . . 15 2·75
259 15pf. red . . . . 15 2·75
260 27 20pf. violet . . . . . . 15 2·75
261 30pf. blue . . . . 15 3·50
262 40pf. brown . . . . 15 2·75
263 28 50pf. red . . . . 15 2·75
264 60pf. turquoise . . . . . . 15 2·75
265 75pf. red . . . . 15 2·75
266 29 1m. red and grey . . . . 35 2·75
267 1¼m. blue and brown . . . 45 2·75
268 1½m. green and grey . . . 45 3·50
269 2½m. black and grey . . . 50 30·00
270 30 3m. blue . . . . 1·00 16·00
271 5m. orange . . . . 95 16·00
272 10m. green . . . . 2·10 26·00
273 20m. black . . . . 2·50 37·00

OFFICIAL STAMPS

O 18

1916.
O195 **O 18** 3pf. brown 20 70
O196 5pf. green 25 70
O197 7½pf. green on green 25 55
O198 7½pf. green 25 55
O199 10pf. red 25 45
O200 15pf. red on buff . . . 45 55
O201 15pf. red 25 70
O202 20pf. blue on blue . . 1·80 2·20
O203 20pf. blue 20 45
O204 25pf. grey 25 55
O205 30pf. orange 25 55
O206 60pf. turquoise 25 55
O207 1m. purple on buff . . 80 3·00
O208 1m. purple . . . . . 2·75 £550

1919. Optd **Volksstaat Bayern**.
O215 **O 18** 3pf. brown . . . . . 20 15·00
O216 5pf. green . . . . . 20 1·90
O217 7½pf. green . . . . . 20 14·00
O218 10pf. red . . . . . 20 1·90
O219 15pf. red . . . . . 20 1·90
O220 20pf. blue . . . . . 20 1·90
O221 25pf. grey . . . . . 20 1·90
O222 30pf. orange . . . . . 20 1·90
O223 35pf. orange . . . . . 20 1·90
O224 50pf. olive . . . . . 20 1·90
O225 60pf. turquoise . . . . 20 1·90
O226 75pf. brown . . . . . 25 15·00
O227 1m. purple on buff . . 35 4·00
O228 1m. purple . . . . . 1·10 11·50

O 31

O 32

O 33

1920.
O274 **O 31** 5pf. green . . . . . . 25 7·00
O275 10pf. orange . . . . . 25 7·00
O276 15pf. red . . . . . . 25 7·00
O277 20pf. violet . . . . . 25 7·00
O278 30pf. blue . . . . . . 25 8·00
O279 40pf. brown . . . . . 25 8·00
O280 **O 32** 50pf. red . . . . . . 25 25·00
O281 60pf. green . . . . . 25 10·50
O282 70pf. lilac . . . . . . 25 32·00
O283 75pf. red . . . . . . 25 40·00
O284 80pf. blue . . . . . . 25 40·00
O285 90pf. olive . . . . . . 25 60·00
O286 **O 33** 1m. brown . . . . . . 25 55·00
O287 1¼m. green . . . . . 25 70·00
O288 1½m. red . . . . . . 25 70·00
O289 2½m. blue . . . . . . 25 80·00
O290 3m. lake 70 £110
O291 5m. green . . . . . . 6·25 £130

POSTAGE DUE STAMPS

D 6

1862. Inscr "Bayer. Posttaxe" at top. Imperf.
D34 **D 6** 3k. black £140 £350

1870. As Type **D 6**, but inscr "Bayr. Posttaxe" at top. Perf.
D65B **D 6** 1k. black . . . . . . 60·00 £1100
D66B 3k. black . . . . . . 10·50 £550

1876. Optd **Vom Empfanger zahlbar.**
D130a **8** 2pf. grey . . . . 70 2·20
D131a 3pf. grey . . . . 70 4·50
D132a 5pf. grey . . . . 1·20 4·00
D133a 10pf. grey . . . . 80 1·80

1895. No. D131a surch **2** in each corner.
D134 **8** 2 on 3pf. grey . . . . . . † £53000

RAILWAY OFFICIALS' STAMPS

1908. Stamps of 1876 optd **E**.
R133 **8** 3pf. brown . . . . 90 3·50
R134 5pf. green 25 35
R135 10pf. red 25 20
R136 20pf. blue 45 70
R137 50pf. purple . . . . 4·75 6·75

BECHUANALAND Pt. 1

A colony and protectorate in Central S. Africa. British Bechuanaland (colony) was annexed to Cape of Good Hope in 1895. Internal Self-Government in the protectorate was introduced on 1 March 1965. Attained independence on 30 September 1966, when the country was renamed Botswana.

1885. 12 pence = 1 shilling;
20 shillings = 1 pound.
1961. 100 cents = 1 rand.

A. BRITISH BECHUANALAND

1885. Stamps of Cape of Good Hope ("Hope" seated) optd **British Bechuanaland**.
4 **6** ½d. black . . . . 8·50 16·00
38 1d. red . . . . 2·25 2·25
32 2d. bistre . . . . 3·25 2·25
2 3d. red . . . . 35·00 50·00
3 4d. blue . . . . 65·00 75·00
7 6d. purple . . . . £120 38·00
8 1s. green £300 £170

1887. Stamp of Great Britain (Queen Victoria) optd **BRITISH BECHUANALAND**.
9 **71** ½d. red . . . . 1·25 1·25

3

4

1887.
10 **3** 1d. lilac and black . . . . 15·00 2·00
11a 2d. lilac and black . . . . 60·00 23·00
12 3d. lilac and black . . . . 4·00 5·50
13 4d. lilac and black . . . . 50·00 2·25
14 6d. lilac and black . . . . 60·00 2·50
15 **4** 1s. green and black . . . . 29·00 7·00
16 2s. green and black . . . . 50·00 42·00
17 2s.6d. green and black . . . 65·00 65·00
18 5s. green and black . . . . 90·00 £150
19 10s. green and black £180 £350
20 – £1 lilac and black £800 £750
21 – £5 lilac and black £3250 £1500
Nos. 20/1 are as Type **4** but larger, 23 × 39½ mm.

1888. Surch.
22 **3** "1d." on 1d. lilac and black 7·50 6·50
23 "2d." on 2d. lilac and black 29·00 3·00
25 "4d." on 4d. lilac and black £350 £450
26 "6d." on 6d. lilac and black £130 12·00
28 **4** "1s." on 1s. green and black £180 85·00

1888. Surch **ONE HALF PENNY** and bars.
29 **3** ½d. on 3d. lilac and black . . £180 £200

1891. Stamps of Great Britain (Queen Victoria) optd **BRITISH BECHUANALAND**.
33 **57** 1d. lilac . . . . 6·00 1·50
34 **73** 2d. green and red . . . . . 14·00 4·00
35 **76** 4d. green and brown . . . . 2·50 60
36 **79** 6d. purple on red . . . . . 3·75 2·00
37 **82** 1s. green . . . . 13·00 16·00

B. BECHUANALAND PROTECTORATE

1888. No. 9 to 19 optd **Protectorate** or surch also.
40 **71** ½d. red . . . . 6·00 38·00
41 **3** 1d. on 1d. lilac and black 9·00 15·00
42 2d. on 2d. lilac and black 30·00 17·00
43 3d. on 3d. lilac and black £140 £190
51 4d. on 4d. lilac and black 85·00 45·00
45 6d. on 6d. lilac and black 75·00 48·00
46 **4** 1s. green and black . . . . 95·00 55·00
47 2s. green and black £600 £950
48 2s.6s. green and black . . . £550 £850
49 5s. green and black £1200 £2000
50 10s. green and black £4000 £6000

1889. Stamp of Cape of Good Hope ("Hope" seated) optd **Bechuanaland Protectorate**.
52 **6** ½d. black . . . . 3·50 48·00

1889. No. 9 surch **Protectorate Fourpence**.
53 **71** 4d. on ½d. red . . . . . . 29·00 4·25

1897. Stamp of Cape of Good Hope ("Hope" seated) optd **BRITISH BECHUANALAND**.
56 **6** ½d. green . . . . 2·50 14·00

1897. Queen Victoria stamps of Great Britain optd **BECHUANALAND PROTECTORATE**.
59 **71** ½d. red . . . . 1·25 2·25
60 ½d. green . . . . 1·40 3·50
61 **57** 1d. lilac . . . . 4·00 75
62 **73** 2d. green and red . . . . . 5·00 3·50
63 **75** 3d. purple on yellow . . . . 5·50 8·50
64 **76** 4d. green and brown . . . . 17·00 16·00
65 **79** 6d. purple on red . . . . . 23·00 11·00

1904. King Edward VII stamps of Great Britain optd **BECHUANALAND PROTECTORATE**.
66 **83** ½d. turquoise . . . . 2·00 2·00
68 1d. red . . . . 8·00 30
69 2½d. blue . . . . 8·00 5·50
70 – 1s. green and red (No. 314) 45·00 £140

1912. King George V stamps of Great Britain optd **BECHUANALAND PROTECTORATE**.
73 **105** ½d. green . . . . 1·25 1·50
72 **102** 1d. red . . . . 2·00 60
92 **104** 1d. red . . . . 2·00 70
75 **105** 1½d. brown . . . . 5·00 3·00
93 **106** 2d. orange . . . . 1·75 1·00
78 **104** 2½d. blue . . . . 3·50 23·00
79 **106** 3d. violet . . . . 6·00 12·00
80 4d. grey . . . . 6·50 24·00
81 **107** 6d. purple . . . . 8·00 19·00
82 **108** 1s. brown . . . . 13·00 26·00
88 **109** 2s.6d. brown . . . . 85·00 £160
89 5s. red £110 £275

22 King George V, Baobab Tree and Cattle drinking

1932.
99 **22** ½d. green . . . . 1·75 30
100 1d. red . . . . 1·00 25
101 2d. brown . . . . 1·00 30
102 3d. blue . . . . 2·00 3·25
103 4d. orange . . . . 2·00 7·50
104 6d. purple . . . . 3·00 5·50
105 1s. black and olive . . . . 3·00 7·00
106 2s. black and orange . . . 24·00 48·00
107 2s.6d. black and red . . . 19·00 35·00
108 3s. black and purple . . . 35·00 48·00
109 5s. black and blue . . . . 80·00 85·00
110 10s. black and brown £150 £160

1935. Silver Jubilee. As T **13** of Antigua.
111 1d. blue and red . . . . . . 75 4·50
112 2d. blue and black . . . . . 1·25 4·50
113 3d. brown and blue . . . . . 2·75 5·00
114 6d. grey and purple . . . . 6·00 5·00

1937. Coronation. As T **2** of Aden.
115 1d. red 45 40
116 2d. brown . . . . 60 1·00
117 3d. blue . . . . 60 1·25

1938. As T **22**, but portrait of King George VI.
118 ½d. green . . . . 2·25 3·25
119 1d. red 75 50
120a 1½d. blue . . . . 1·00 1·00
121 2d. brown 75 50
122 3d. blue . . . . 1·00 2·50
123 4d. orange . . . . 2·00 3·50
124a 6d. purple . . . . 4·00 2·50
125 1s. black and olive . . . . 4·00 7·00
126 2s.6d. black and red . . . 14·00 15·00
127 5s. black and blue . . . . . 30·00 22·00
128 10s. black and brown . . . 19·00 25·00

1945. Victory. Stamps of South Africa optd **Bechuanaland**. Alternate stamps inscr in English or Afrikaans.
129 **55** 1d. brown and red . . . . 75 1·25
130 2d. blue and violet (No. 109) . . . . 50 1·25
131 3d. blue (No. 110) . . . . 50 1·50
Prices for bi-lingual pairs.

1947. Royal Visit. As Nos. 32/5 of Basutoland.
132 1d. red 10 10
133 2d. green 10 10
134 3d. blue 10 10
135 1s. mauve 10 10

1948. Silver Wedding. As T **10/11** of Aden.
136 1½d. blue 30 10
137 10s. grey . . . . 35·00 40·00

1949. U.P.U. As T **20/23** of Antigua.
138 1½d. blue . . . . 30 1·25
139 3d. blue . . . . 1·50 2·50
140 6d. mauve . . . . 60 3·00
141 1s. olive . . . . 60 1·50

1953. Coronation. As T **13** of Aden.
142 2d. black and brown . . . . 1·00 30

1955. As T **22** but portrait of Queen Elizabeth II, facing right.
143 ½d. green 50 30
144 1d. red 80 10
145 2d. brown . . . . 1·25 30
146 3d. blue . . . . 3·00 2·00
146b 4d. orange . . . . 6·50 9·00
147 4½d. blue . . . . 1·50 35
148 6d. purple . . . . 1·25 60
149 1s. black and olive . . . . 1·25 80
150 1s.3d. black and lilac . . . 14·00 9·50
151 2s.6d. black and red . . . . 12·00 9·50
152 5s. black and blue . . . . . 15·00 9·50
153 10s. black and brown . . . . 32·00 15·00

26 Queen Victoria, Queen Elizabeth II and Landscape

28 African Golden Oriole ("Golden Oriole")

1960. 75th Anniv of Protectorate.
154 **26** 1d. sepia and black . . . 40 50
155 3d. mauve and black . . . 40 30
156 6d. blue and black 40 50

1961. Stamps of 1955 surch.
157 1c. on 1d. red 30 10
158 2c. on 2d. brown 20 10
159 2½c. on 2d. brown 30 10
160 2½c. on 3d. blue . . . . . . 2·00 5·50
161d 3½c. on 4d. orange 20 60
162a 5c. on 6d. purple 20 10
163 10c. on 1s. black and olive 20 10
164 12½c. on 1s.3d. black and lilac 65 20
165 25c. on 2s.6d. black and red 1·50 50
166 50c. on 5s. black and blue 2·00 2·00
167b 1r. on 10s. black and brown 11·00 12·00

1961.
168 **28** 1c. multicoloured . . . . . 1·50 40
169 – 2c. orange, black and olive 2·00 3·75
170 – 2½c. multicoloured . . . . 1·75 10
171 – 3½c. multicoloured . . . . 2·50 3·75
172 – 5c. multicoloured . . . . . 3·25 1·00
173 – 7½c. multicoloured . . . . 2·25 2·25
174 – 10c. multicoloured . . . . 2·25 60
175 – 12½c. multicoloured . . . . 18·00 5·50
176 – 20c. brown and drab . . . 3·00 2·75
177 – 25c. sepia and lemon . . . 3·50 1·50
178 – 35c. blue and orange . . . 3·00 3·00
179 – 50c. sepia and olive . . . . 1·75 2·25
180 – 1r. black and brown . . . 6·50 2·50
181 – 2r. brown and turquoise . . 18·00 9·00
DESIGNS—VERT: 2c. Hoopoe ("African Hoopoe"); 2½c. Scarlet-chested sunbird; 3½c. Yellow-rumped bishop ("Cape Widow-bird"); 5c. Swallow-tailed bee eater; 7½c. African grey hornbill ("Grey Hornbill"); 10c. Red-headed weaver; 12½c. Brown-hooded kingfisher; 20c. Woman musician; 35c. Woman grinding maize; 1r. Lion; 2r. Police camel patrol. HORIZ: 25c. Baobab tree; 50c. Bechuana ox.

1963. Freedom from Hunger. As T **28** of Aden.
182 12½c. green 30 15

1963. Centenary of Red Cross. As T **33** of Antigua.
183 2½c. red and black 20 10
184 12½c. red and blue 40 50

1964. 400th Birth Anniv of Shakespeare. As T **34** of Antigua.
185 12½c. brown 15 15

C. BECHUANALAND

42 Map and Gaberones Dam

1965. New Constitution.
186 **42** 2½c. red and gold 20 10
187 5c. blue and gold 20 40
188 12½c. brown and gold . . . 30 40
189 25c. green and gold 40 55

1965. Centenary of I.T.U. As T **36** of Antigua.
190 2½c. red and yellow 20 10
191 12½c. mauve and brown . . . 45 30

1965. I.C.Y. As T **37** of Antigua.
192 1c. purple and turquoise . . 10 20
193 12½c. green and lavender . . 60 55

1966. Churchill Commemoration. As T **38** of Antigua.
194 1c. blue . . . . 15 1·25
195 2½c. green 35 10
196 12½c. brown 70 30
197 20c. violet 75 50

43 Haslar Smoke Generator

1966. Bechuanaland Royal Pioneer Corps.
198 **43** 2½c. blue, red and green . . 25 10
199 – 5c. brown and blue 25 20
200 – 15c. blue, red and green . . 30 25
201 – 35c. multicoloured . . . . 30 1·00
DESIGNS: 5c. Bugler; 15c. Gun-site; 35c. Regimental cap badge.

POSTAGE DUE STAMPS

1926. Postage Due stamps of Great Britain optd **BECHUANALAND PROTECTORATE**.
D1 **D 1** ½d. green . . . . 7·50 £100
D2 1d. red . . . . 7·50 60·00
D3 2d. black . . . . 7·50 85·00

D 3

1932.

D4 D 3 ½d. green . . . . 6·00 55·00
D5a 1d. red . . . . 1·50 24·00
D6c 2d. violet . . . . 1·75 20·00

1961. Surch.

D7 D 3 1c. on 1d. red 25 50
D8 2c. on 2d. violet . . . . . 25 1·50
D9 5c. on ½d. green 20 60

1961. As Type D 3 but value in decimal currency.

D10 1c. red . . . . 20 2·00
D11 2c. violet . . . . 20 2·00
D12 5c. green . . . . 40 2·00

For later issues see **BOTSWANA**.

BELARUS Pt. 10

Formerly a constituent republic of the Soviet Union, Belarus became independent in 1991.

100 kopeks = 1 rouble.

1 12th-century Cross

1992.

1 1 1r. multicoloured . . . . . . 1·30 75

2 Shyrma 3 Arms of Polotsk

1992. Birth Cent of R. R. Shyrma (composer).

2 2 20k. lt blue, blue and black . . 50 30

1992.

3 3 2r. multicoloured 80 55
See also Nos. 63 and 89/90.

4 Flag and Map (5)

1992.

4 4 5r. multicoloured . . . . . . 1·30 95
5 – 5r. black, yellow and red . . . 1·30 95
DESIGN: No. 5, State arms.

1992. Millenary of Orthodox Church in Belarus. (a) No. 1 optd with T 5.

6 1 1r. multicoloured . . . . . . 1·00 75

(b) Sheet 91 × 66 mm.

MS7 5r. multicoloured . . . . . 2·00 1·90
DESIGN: 24 × 36 mm—5r. Cross of Polotsk.

6 Kamen Tower 7 State Arms

1992. Ancient Buildings and Monuments. Mult.

8 2r. Type **6** 50 30
9 2r. Calvinist church, Zaslavl 50 30
10 2r. St. Euphrosyne's church, Polotsk 50 30
11 2r. St. Boris Gleb church, Grodno (horiz) 50 30
12 2r. Mir castle (horiz) 50 30
13 2r. Nesvizh castle (horiz) . . . 50 30

1992.

14 7 30k. blue 20 15
15 45k. green 25 15
16 50k. green 25 15
17 1r. brown 25 15
18 2r. brown 25 15
19 3r. yellow 35 20
20 5r. blue 40 20
21 10r. red 95 55
22 15r. violet 55 35
23 25r. green 80 45
24 50r. mauve 25 20
25 100r. red 55 35
26 150r. purple 80 45
27 200r. green 20 20
28 300r. red 20 20
29 600r. mauve 25 20
30 1000r. red 45 20
31 3000r. blue . . . . 1·20 65

8 Jug and Bowl

1992. Pottery. Multicoloured.

40 1r. Type **8** 40 30
41 1r. Vases and jug on jug tree 40 30
42 1r. Flagon 40 30
43 1r. Jugs 40 30

9 Chickens

1993. Corn Dollies. Multicoloured.

44 5r. Type **9** 20 10
45 10r. Woman and gunman (vert) 30 20
46 15r. Woman (vert) 50 40
47 25r. Man and woman (vert) 1·00 75

10 Harezki 11 Emblem

1993. Birth Centenary of M. I. Harezki (author).

48 10 50r. purple 60 35

1993. World Belarussian Congress, Minsk.

49 11 50r. red, gold and black . . 2·00 1·60

12 "Man Over Vitebsk"

1993. Europa. Contemporary Art. Paintings by Marc Chagall. Multicoloured.

50 1500r. Type **12** . . . . . . 8·00 7·50
51 1500r. "Promenade" (vert) . . 8·00 7·50
MS52 142 × 103 mm. 2500r. "Allegory" (50 × 37 mm) . . . 70·00 65·00

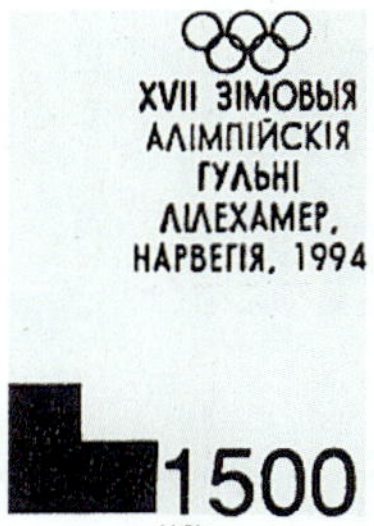

(13)

(14)

1993. Sports Events. Nos. 4/5 variously surch. (a) Winter Olympic Games, Lillehammer, Norway (1994). Surch **Winter Pre-Olympic Games Lillehammer, Norway 1500** (in capitals on No. 44) or in Cyrillic as T **13**.

53 4 1500r. on 5r. mult (in Cyrillic) . . . . 5·00 4·75
54 1500r. on 5r. mult (in English) . . . . 5·00 4·75
55 – 1500r. on 5r. black, yellow and red (in Cyrillic) . . . 5·00 4·75
56 – 1500r. on 5r. black, yellow and red (in English) . . . 5·00 4·75
MS57 Two sheets. (a) 1500r. on 5r. multicoloured (in Cyrillic); (b) 1500r. on 5r. (in English) . . . 20·00 19·00

(b) World Cup Football Championship, U.S.A. (1994). Surch **WORLD CUP USA 94 1500** or in Cyrillic as T **14**.

58 4 1500r. on 5r. mult (in Cyrillic) . . . . 5·00 4·75
59 1500r. on 5r. mult (in English) . . . . 5·00 4·75
60 – 1500r. on 5r. black, yellow and red (in Cyrillic) . . . 5·00 4·75
61 – 1500r. on 5r. black, yellow and red (in English) . . . 5·00 4·75
MS62 Two sheets. (a) 1500r. on 5r. multicoloured (in Cyrillic); (b) 1500r. on 5r. multicoloured (in English) . . . . 20·00 19·00

1993. Town Arms. As T **3**. Multicoloured.

63 25r. Minsk 50 30

15 St. Stanislav's Church, Mogilev

1993.

64 15 150r. multicoloured 80 60

16 Kastus Kalinowski (leader)

1993. 130th Anniv of Peasants' Uprising.

65 16 50r. multicoloured 40 30

17 Princess Ragneda 18 Statue of Budny

1993. 10th-century Rulers of Polotsk. Mult.

66 75r. Type **17** 50 30
67 75r. Prince Ragvalod and map 50 30

1993. 400th Death Anniv of Simon Budny (poet).

68 18 100r. multicoloured 70 65

19 Golden Eagle

1994. Birds in the Red Book. Multicoloured.

69 20r. Type **19** 20 20
70 40r. Mute swan ("Cygnus olor") 30 30
71 40r. River kingfisher ("Alcedo atthis") 30 30

1994. Nos. 14/16 surch.

72 7 15r. on 30k. blue 20 10
73 25r. on 45k. green 30 20
74 50r. on 50k. green 50 30
See also Nos. 86/8.

21 Map and Rocket Launchers (Liberation of Russia)

1994. 50th Anniv of Liberation. Multicoloured.

75 500r. Type **21** 60 45
76 500r. Map and airplanes (Ukraine) 60 45
77 500r. Map, tank and soldiers (Byelorussia) 60 45

22 Yasev Drazdovich and "Persecution"

1994. Artists and Paintings. Multicoloured.

78 300r. Type **22** 30 20
79 300r. Pyotr Sergievich and "The Path through Life" . . 30 20
80 300r. Ferdinand Rushchyts and "The Land" 30 20

23 Figure Skating 26 "Belarus"

25 Church, Synkavichai (16th-century)

1994. Winter Olympic Games, Lillehammer, Norway. Multicoloured.

81 1000r. Type **23** 40 30
82 1000r. Biathlon 40 30
83 1000r. Cross-country skiing . . 40 30
84 1000r. Speed skating 40 30
85 1000r. Ice hockey 40 30

1994. Birds in the Red Book. As Nos. 69/71 but values changed. Multicoloured.

86 300r. As Type **19** 50 30
87 400r. As No. 70 . . . . 60 40
88 400r. As No. 71 . . . . 60 40

1994. Town Arms. As T **3**. Multicoloured.

89 700r. Grodno 30 20
90 700r. Vitebsk 30 20

1994. Religious Buildings. Multicoloured.

91 700r. Type **25** 30 20
92 700r. Sts. Peter and Paul's Cathedral, Gomel (19th-century) 30 20

1994. 150th Birth Anniv of Ilya Repin (painter). Multicoloured.

93 1000r. Type **26** 50 30
94 1000r. Repin Museum 50 30
Nos. 93/4 were issued together, se-tenant, forming a composite design.

27 Tomasz Wojshezki and Battle Scene

1995. Bicentenary (1994) of Polish Insurrection. Multicoloured.

95	600r. Type **27**	45	35
96	600r. Jakub Jasinski	45	35
97	1000r. Mikhail Aginski	60	45
98	1000r. Tadeusz Kosciuszko	60	45

28 Memorial

29 Aleksandr Stepanovich Popov (radio pioneer)

1995. 50th Anniv of End of Second World War. Multicoloured.

99	180r. Type **28**	20	15
100	600r. Clouds and memorial	30	20

1995. Centenary of First Radio Transmission (by Guglielmo Marconi).

101 **29**	600r. multicoloured	50	40

30 Obelisk to the Fallen of the Red Army, Minsk

31 Cherski

1995.

102 **30**	180r. bistre and red	20	15
103	200r. green and bistre	30	20
104	280r. green and blue	40	30
107	600r. purple and bistre	50	40

1995. 150th Birth Anniv of Ivan Cherski (explorer).

115 **31**	600r. multicoloured	50	40

32 Motal

33 Head of Beaver

1995. Traditional Costumes (1st series). Mult.

116	180r. Type **32**	20	15
117	600r. Vaukavysk-Kamyanets	40	30
118	1200r. Pukhavits	70	55

See also Nos. 188/190, 256/8 and 460/1.

1995. The Eurasian Beaver. Multicoloured.

119	300r. Type **33**	30	20
120	450r. Beaver gnawing branch	40	30
121	450r. Beaver (horiz)	40	30
122	800r. Beaver swimming	75	45

34 Writer and Script

35 Arms

1995. Writers' Day.

123 **34**	600r. multicoloured	50	40

1995. National Symbols. Multicoloured.

124	600r. Type **35**	40	30
125	600r. Flag over map and arms	40	30

36 Anniversary Emblem

1995. 50th Anniv of U.N.O.

126 **36**	600r. blue, black and gold	50	40

37 Mstislavl Church

1995. Churches. Multicoloured.

127	600r. Type **37**	40	30
128	600r. Kamai Church	40	30

See also Nos. 227/8.

1995
125 год
з дня нараджэння
(**38**)

1995. 125th Birth Anniv of Ferdinand Rushchyts (artist). No. 80 optd with T **38**.

129	300r. multicoloured	1·00	95

39 Sukhoi and Aircraft

40 Red Deer (*Cervus elaphus*)

1995. Birth Centenary of P. V. Sukhoi (aircraft designer).

130 **39**	600r. multicoloured	40	30

1995. Nature. Sheet 100 × 64 mm. Imperf.

MS131 **40**	10000r. multicoloured	4·00	3·75

41 Leu Sapega (statesman)

1995. 17th-century Belarussians. Multicoloured.

132	600r. Type **41**	35	20
133	1200r. Kazimir Semyanovich (military scholar)	50	30
134	1800r. Simyaon Polatski (writer)	70	45

42 Lynx

1996. Mammals. Multicoloured.

135	1000r. Type **42**	45	30
136	2000r. Roe deer (vert)	75	45
137	2000r. Brown bear	75	45
138	3000r. Elk (vert)	95	75
139	5000r. European bison	1·50	1·30

1996. Nos. 17 and 23 optd with capital letter.

140 **7**	B (200r.) on 1r. brown	30	20
141	A (400r.) on 25r. green	30	20

44 Krapiva

1996. Birth Centenary of Kandrat Krapiva (writer).

142 **44**	1000r. multicoloured	50	30

45 Beaver

1996. The Eurasian Beaver (*Castor fiber*). Sheet 90 × 70 mm.

MS143 **45**	1200r. multicoloured	70	45

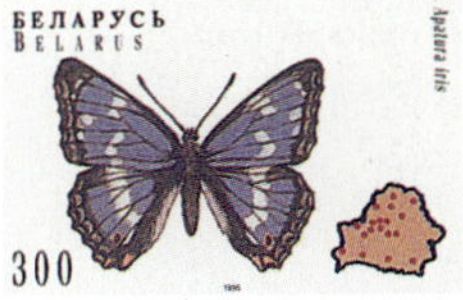

46 Purple Emperor ("Apatura iris")

1996. Butterflies and Moths. Multicoloured.

144	300r. Type **46**	1·20	95
145	300r. "Lopinga achine"	1·20	95
146	300r. Scarlet tiger moth ("Callimorpha dominula")	1·20	95
147	300r. Clifden's nonpareil ("Catocala fraxini")	1·20	95
148	300r. Swallowtail ("Papilio machaon")	1·20	95
149	300r. Apollo ("Parnassius apollo")	1·20	95
150	300r. "Ammobiota hebe"	1·20	95
151	300r. Palaeno sulphur yellow ("Colias palaeno")	1·20	95
MS152	Two sheets, each 100 × 70 mm. (a) 1000r. *Vacciniina optilete*; (b) 1000r. Willow-herb hawk moth (*Proserpinus proserpina*)	16·00	15·00

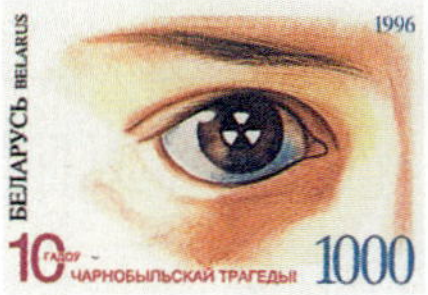

47 Radioactivity Symbol within Eye

48 State Arms

1996. 10th Anniv of Chernobyl Nuclear Disaster. Multicoloured.

153	1000r. Type **47**	30	20
154	1000r. Radioactivity symbol on diseased leaf	30	20
155	1000r. Radioactivity symbol on boarded-up window	30	20

1996. Arms and value in black, background colours given.

159 **48**	100r. blue	15	10
160	200r. grey	30	25
161	400r. brown	20	15
162	500r. green	15	10
163	600r. red	15	10
164	800r. blue	20	15
165	1000r. orange	20	10
166	1500r. mauve	25	15
167	1500r. blue	25	25
168	1800r. violet	25	15
169	2000r. green	35	30
170	2200r. mauve	30	20
171	2500r. blue	35	30
172	3000r. brown	30	30
173	3300r. yellow	40	25
174	5000r. blue	50	40
175	10000r. green	1·00	75
176	30000r. brown	3·00	2·30
177	50000r. purple	5·25	3·75

49 Russian and Belarussian Flags

1996. Russian–Belarussian Treaty.

182 **49**	1500r. multicoloured	70	45

50 Gymnastics

1996. Olympic Games, Atlanta. Multicoloured.

183	3000r. Type **50**	90	65
184	3000r. Throwing the discus	90	65
185	3000r. Weightlifting	90	65
186	3000r. Wrestling	90	65
MS187	100 × 71 mm. 5000r. Rifle-shooting. Imperf	1·50	1·10

51 Kapyl-Kletski

52 "Acorus calamus"

1996. Traditional Costumes (2nd series). Mult.

188	1800r. Type **51**	40	30
189	2200r. David-Garadots Turau	60	40
190	3300r. Kobryn	70	45
MS191	95 × 71 mm. 5000r. Naraulyanski. Imperf	1·50	1·10

See also Nos. 256/8 and 460/1.

1996. Medicinal Plants. Multicoloured.

192	1500r. Type **52**	40	30
193	1500r. "Sanguisorba officinalis"	40	30
194	2200r. "Potentilla erecta"	60	40
195	3300r. "Frangula alnus"	70	45
MS196	96 × 71 mm. 5000r. *Menyanthes trifoliate*. Imperf	1·50	1·10

53 Grey Heron ("Ardea cinerea")

1996. Birds. Multicoloured.

197	400r. Type **53**	60	40
198	400r. Black storks ("Ciconia nigra")	60	40
199	400r. Great cormorant ("Phalacrocorax carbo")	60	40
200	400r. White stork ("Ciconia ciconia")	60	40
201	400r. Black-headed gulls ("Larus ridibundus")	60	40
202	400r. Common snipe ("Gallinago gallinago")	60	40
203	400r. White-winged black tern ("Chlidonias leucopterus")	60	40
204	400r. Penduline tit ("Remiz pendulinus")	60	40
205	400r. Eurasian bittern ("Botaurus stellaris")	60	40
206	400r. Black coot ("Fulica atra")	60	40
207	400r. Little bittern ("Ixobrychus minutus")	60	40
208	400r. River kingfisher ("Alcedo atthis")	60	40
209	400r. Green-winged teals ("Anas crecca")	60	40
210	400r. Gadwalls ("Anas strepera")	60	40
211	400r. Northern pintails ("Anas acuta")	60	40
212	400r. Mallards ("Anas platyrhynchos")	60	40
213	400r. Greater scaups ("Aythya marila")	60	40
214	400r. Long-tailed duck ("Clangula hyemalis")	60	40
215	400r. Northern shovelers ("Anas clypeata")	60	40
216	400r. Garganeys ("Anas querquedula")	60	40
217	400r. European wigeon ("Anas penelope")	60	40
218	400r. Ferruginous ducks ("Aythya nyroca")	60	40
219	400r. Common goldeneyes ("Bucephala clangula")	60	40
220	400r. Goosander ("Mergus merganser")	60	40
221	400r. Smew ("Mergus albellus")	60	40
222	400r. Tufted duck ("Aythya fuligula")	60	40
223	400r. Red-breasted merganser ("Mergus serrator")	60	40
224	400r. Common pochard ("Aythya ferina")	60	40
MS225	Two sheets, each 100 × 70 mm. (a) 1000r. Common snipe (*Gallinago gallinago*); (b) 1000r. European pochards (*Aythya farina*)	10·00	9·50

54 Title Page

55 Shchakatsikhin

1996. 400th Anniv of Publication of First Belarussian Grammar.

226 **54**	1500r. multicoloured	80	55

1996. Churches. As T **37**. Multicoloured.

227	3300r. St. Nicholas's Church, Mogilev	1·00	70
228	3300r. Franciscan church, Pinsk	1·00	70

1996. Birth Centenary of Mikola Shchakatsikhin (artist).

229 **55**	2000r. multicoloured	75	45

56 Old and New Telephones

1996. Cent of Telephone Service in Minsk.
230 **56** 2000r. multicoloured . . . 75 45

57 Lukashenka

1996. President Alyaksandr Rygoravich Lukashenka.
231 **57** 2500r. multicoloured . . . 60 45

58 Kiryla Turovski (12th-century Bishop of Turov)

59 Decorated Tree, Minsk

1996. Multicoloured.
232 3000r. Type **58** 65 45
233 3000r. Mikolaj Radziwill (16th-century Chancellor of Lithuania) 65 45
234 3000r. Mikola Gusovski (15th-16th century writer) 65 45

1996. New Year. Multicoloured.
235 1500r. Type **59** 30 20
236 2000r. Winter landscape (horiz) 50 40

60 "Paraskeva"

1996. Icons in National Museum, Minsk. Multicoloured.
237 3500r. Type **60** 60 45
238 3500r. "Illya" (17th-century) 60 45
239 3500r. "Three Holy Men" (Master of Sharashov) . . 60 45
240 3500r. "Madonna of Smolensk" 60 45
MS241 70 × 100 mm. 5000r. "Birth of the Madonna" (Patr Yavseevich) . . . . 1·50 1·10

61 Zhukov

1997. Birth Cent of Marshal G. K. Zhukov.
242 **61** 2000r. black, gold and red 50 40

62 Theatre

1997. Kupala National Theatre, Minsk.
243 **62** 3500r. black and gold . . . 70 55

63 Byalnitsky-Birulya

1997. 125th Birth Anniv of W. K. Byalnitsky-Birulya (painter).
244 **63** 2000r. black and brown . . 50 40

(**64**)

1997. 105th Birth Anniv of R. R. Shyrma (composer). No. 2 surch with T **64**.
245 **2** 3500r. on 20k. light blue, blue and black 60 55

65 Salmon

1997. Fishes. Multicoloured.
246 2000r. Type **65** 40 30
247 3000r. Vimba 60 45
248 4500r. Barbel ("Barbus barbus") 80 65
249 4500r. European grayling ("Thymallus thymallus") 80 65
MS250 90 × 60 mm. 5000r. Sterlet (*Acipenser ruthenus*) . . . . . 1·50 1·10

66 "SOS" on Globe

1997. International Conference on Developing Countries, Minsk. Multicoloured.
251 3000r. Type **66** 50 40
252 4500r. Protective hand over ecosystem 70 55

Nos. 251/2 were issued together, se-tenant, with intervening label showing the Conference emblem, the whole strip forming a composite design.

67 Emblem

69 Map, National Flag and Monument to the Fallen of Second World War, Minsk

1997. 50th Anniv of Belarussian Membership of Universal Postal Union.
253 **67** 3000r. multicoloured . . . 60 45

1997. No. 18 surch **100 1997**.
254 **7** 100r. on 2r. brown 30 20

1997. Independence Day.
255 **69** 3000r. multicoloured . . . 75 55

1997. Traditional Costumes (3rd series). As T **51**. Multicoloured.
256 2000r. Dzisensk 35 35
257 3000r. Navagrydsk 60 55
258 4500r. Bykhaisk 85 80

70 Page from Skorina Bible and Vilnius

1997. 480th Anniv of Printing in Belarus. Each red, black and grey.
259 3000r. Type **70** 60 55
260 3000r. Page from Skorina Bible and Prague 60 55
261 4000r. Franzisk Skorina and Polotsk 60 55
262 7500r. Skorina and Cracow 1·30 1·20

71 Jesuit College

1997. 900th Anniv of Pinsk.
263 **71** 3000r. multicoloured . . . 60 55

72 Books and Entrance

1997. 75th Anniv of National Library.
264 **72** 3000r. multicoloured . . . 60 55

73 Dark Glasses reflecting Hands reading Braille

1997. Cent of Schools for the Blind in Belarus.
265 **73** 3000r. multicoloured . . . 50 45

74 Child in Hand "Flower"

1997. World Children's Day.
266 **74** 3000r. multicoloured . . . 60 55

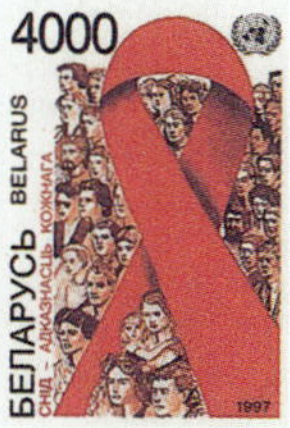

75 Red Ribbon and Crowd

1997. Red Ribbon AIDS Solidarity Campaign.
267 **75** 4000r. multicoloured . . . 70 65

76 Model 1221

1997. Belarussian Tractors. Multicoloured.
268 3300r. Type **76** 60 55
269 4400r. First Belarussian tractor, 1953 . . . . . . 75 70
270 7500r. Model 680 . . . . . 1·20 1·10
271 7500r. Model 952 . . . . . 1·20 1·10

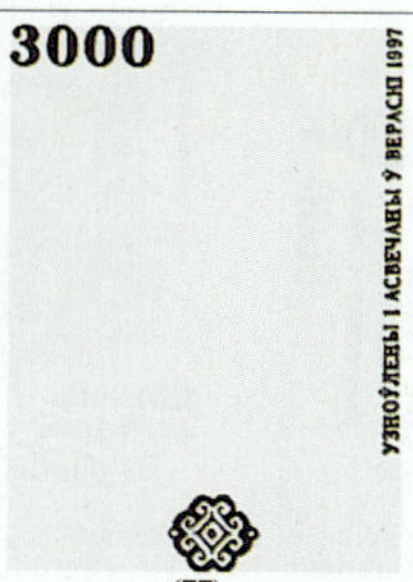

(**77**)

1997. Restoration of Cross of St. Ephrosina of Polotsk. No. 1 surch with T **77**.
272 **1** 3000r. on 1r. multicoloured 50 40

78 St. Nicholas hang-gliding over Houses (New Year)

1997. Greetings Stamps. Multicoloured.
273 1400r. Type **78** 30 20
274 4400r. Procession of musicians (Christmas) . . . 60 45

79 Cross-country Skiing

1998. Winter Olympic Games, Nagano, Japan. Multicoloured.
275 2000r. Type **79** 40 30
276 3300r. Ice hockey 50 40
277 4400r. Biathlon 70 55
278 7500r. Freestyle skiing . . . 90 75

80 Mashcherov

1998. 80th Birth Anniv of P. M. Mashcherov (writer).
279 **80** 2500r. multicoloured . . . 50 40

81 MAZ-205 Lorry, 1947

1998. Tipper Trucks. Multicoloured.
280 1400r. Type **81** 30 20
281 2000r. MAZ-503, 1968 . . . . 35 25
282 3000r. MAZ-5549, 1977 . . . 40 30
283 4400r. MAZ-5551, 1985 . . . 60 45
284 7500r. MAZ-5516, 1994 . . . 85 70

82 Entrance to Nyasvizh Castle

83 Mickiewicz

1998. Europa. National Festivals.
285 **82** 15000r. multicoloured . . . 1·00 95

1998. Birth Bicentenary of Adam Mickiewicz (political writer).
286 **83** 8600r. multicoloured . . . 65 65

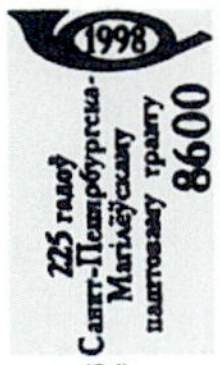

(84)

85 Bluethroat

1998. 225th Anniv of Postal Service between Mogilov and St. Petersburg. No. 64 surch with T **84**.
287 **15** 8600r. on 150r. mult . . . 65 65

1998. Birds. Multicoloured.
288 1500r. Type **85** 20 10
289 3200r. Penduline tit 30 30
290 3800r. Aquatic warbler . . . 40 35
291 5300r. Savi's warbler 50 45
292 8600r. Azure tit 85 80

86 Watermill

87 Bulldozer Model 7821

1998.
293 **86** 100r. black and green . . . 20 15
294 – 200r. black and brown . . 20 15
295 – 500r. black and blue . . . 20 15
296 – 800r. black and violet . . . 20 15
297 – 1000r. black and green . . 20 15
298 – 1500r. black and brown . . 30 30
299 – 2000r. black and blue . . . 20 15
300 – 3000r. black and yellow . . 20 20
301 – 3200r. black and green . . 30 20
302 – 5000r. black and blue . . . 25 30
303 – 5300r. black and yellow . . 30 30
304 – 10000r. black and orange . 45 40
305 **86** 30000r. black and blue . . 50 45
306 – 50000r. black, orange and deep orange 60 55
308 – 100000r. black and mauve . 80 75
309 – 500000r. black and brown 4·00 3·75

DESIGNS—VERT: 200, 50000r. Windmill; 500r. Stork; 800r. Cathedral of the Holy Trinity, Ishkold; 1000r. Bison; 1500, 3200r. Dulcimer; 2000r. Star; 3000, 5300r. Lute; 5000r. Church; 10000r. Flaming wheel; 500000r. Lyavoniha (folk dance). HORIZ: 100000r. Exhibition centre, Minsk.

1998. 50th Anniv of Belaz Truck Works. Mult.
310 1500r. Type **87** 20 15
311 3200r. Tipper Model 75131 . 25 20
312 3800r. Tipper Model 75303 . 30 25
313 5300r. Tipper Model 75483 . 35 30
314 8600r. Tipper Model 7555 . . 40 40

88 Common Morel

89 Lion's Head

1998. Fungi. Multicoloured.
315 2500r. Type **88** 20 15
316 3800r. "Morchella conica" . . 25 20
317 4600r. Shaggy parasol . . . 30 25
318 5800r. Parasol mushroom . . 35 30
319 9400r. Shaggy ink cap . . . 65 50

1998. Wood Sculptures. Multicoloured.
320 3400r. Type **89** 30 25
321 3800r. Archangel Michael . . 35 30
322 5800r. Prophet Zacharias . . 40 35
323 9400r. Madonna and Child 60 55

90 Emblem and Belarussian Stamps

1998. World Post Day.
324 **90** 5500r. multicoloured . . . 60 45

91 "Kalozha" (V. K. Tsvirka)

1998. Paintings. Multicoloured.
325 3000r. Type **91** 20 20
326 3500r. "Hotel Lounge" (S. Yu. Zhukoiski) 20 20
327 5000r. "Winter Sleep" (V. K. Byalynitski-Birulya) . . . 25 20
328 5500r. "Portrait of a Girl" (I. I. Alyashkevich) (vert) 25 20
329 10000r. "Portrait of an Unknown Woman" (I. F. Khrutski) (vert) 40 40

92 Anniversary Emblem

93 Girl, Rabbit and Fir Trees

1998. 50th Anniv of Universal Declaration of Human Rights.
330 **92** 7100r. multicoloured . . . 50 40

1998. Christmas and New Year. Multicoloured.
331 5500r. Type **93** 25 25
332 5500r. Girl, rabbit and house 25 25

94 Pushkin and Adam Mickiewicz Monument, St. Petersburg (A. Anikeichyk)

1999. Birth Bicentenary of Aleksandr Pushkin (writer).
333 **94** 15300r. multicoloured . . . 80 75

95 MAZ Model 8007 Truck and Excavator

1999. Minsk Truck and Military Works. Mult.
334 10000r. Type **95** 25 20
335 15000r. MAZ model 543M and Smerch rocket system 30 25
336 30000r. MAZ model 7907 crane 45 40
337 30000r. MAZ model 543M Rubezh missile launcher . . 45 40
MS338 175 × 120 mm. Nos. 334/7; 5000r. Model 7917 and Topol missile; 150000r. Model 74135 low-loader . . . . 6·00 5·75

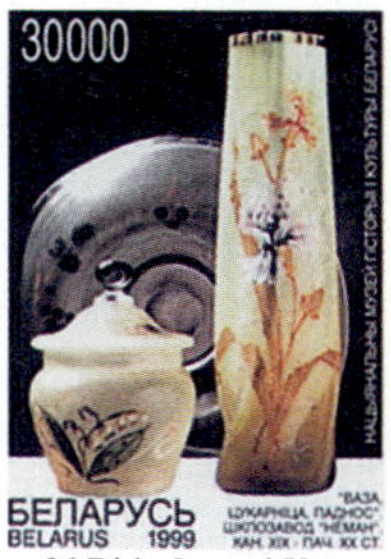

96 Dish, Jar and Vase

1999. Glasswork. Multicoloured.
339 30000r. Type **96** 50 45
340 30000r. Chalice 50 40
341 100000r. Oil lamp . . . . . 1·00 95

(97)

1999. "iBRA '99" International Stamp Exhibition, Nuremberg. No. 69 surch with T **97**.
342 150000r. on 20r. multicoloured (Type **19**) . . 2·00 1·90

98 Belavezhskaya Pushcha Reserve

1999. Europa. Parks and Gardens. Multicoloured.
345 150000r. Type **98** . . . . . 1·50 1·40
346 150000r. Beaver in Byarezinski Reserve . . . 1·50 1·40

99 Well

1999. Wooden Buildings. Multicoloured.
347 50000r. Type **99** 70 45
348 50000r. Public house 70 45
349 100000r. Windmill . . . . . 1·10 95

100 "Portrait of Yu. M. Pen" (A. M. Brazer)

1999. Vitebsk Art School. Paintings. Multicoloured.
350 30000r. Type **100** 30 20
351 60000r. "St. Anthony's Church, Vitebsk" (S. B.Yudovin) 70 45
352 100000r. "Street in Vitebsk" (Yu. M. Pen) . . . . . 1·20 85
353 100000r. "Kryvaya Street, Vitebsk" (M. P. Mikhalap) (horiz) . . . . 1·20 85
MS354 104 × 82 mm. 200000r. "The World is a River without Banks" (Marc Chagall) . . . . 2·00 1·90

101 Karvat

1999. 3rd Death Anniv of Wing Commander Karvat.
355 **101** 25000r. multicoloured . . 1·20 95

102 Main Post Office, Minsk, 1954

1999. 125th Anniv of Universal Postal Union. Mult.
356 150000r. Type **102** . . . . . 1·80 1·60
357 150000r. First post office in Minsk, 1800 . . . . 1·80 1·60

103 Golden Mushroom

1999. Fungi. Multicoloured.
358 30000r. Type **103** 30 20
359 50000r. Changeable agaric . . 55 40
360 75000r. *Lyophyllum connatum* 90 55
361 100000r. *Lyophyllum decastes* 1·20 85
MS362 97 × 79 mm. 150000r. Bootlace fungus (*Armillariella mellea*) 1·80 1·60

104 East and West Belarussians Embracing

1999. 60th Anniv of Re-unification of Republic of Byelorussia.
363 **104** 29000r. multicoloured . . 40 30

105 MAZ MA3-6430, 1998

1999. Minsk Truck and Military Works. Lorries. Multicoloured.
364 51000r. Type **105** 50 30
365 86000r. Lorry Model MAZ MA3-4370 . . . . 70 45

106 Landscape (Olya Smantser)

1999. Children's Painting Competition Winners. Mult.
366 32000r. Type **106** 30 20
367 59000r. Girl (Masha Dudarenko) (vert) 50 30

107 Teddybear in Snow (Mitya Kutas)

1999. Christmas and New Year. Children's Paintings. Multicoloured.
368 30000r. Type **107** 40 30
369 30000r. Children building snowman and ice-skating (Yulya Yakubovich) . . . 40 30

Currency Revaluation

108 Spasa-Praabrazhenskaya Church, Polatsk

110 Bison

109 Our Lady Oranta (mosaic, Spohia Catherdral, Kiev, Ukraine)

2000. Birth Bimillenary of Jesus Christ (1st issue). Mult.
370 50r. Type **108** 40 30
371 75r. St. Atsistratsiga Cathedral, Slutsk 70 45
372 100r. The Reverend Serafim Sarovskaga Church, Belaazersk 90 65

2000. Birth Bimillenary of Jesus Christ (2nd issue). Sheet 150 × 100 mm containing T **109** and similar vert designs. Multicoloured.
MS373 100r. Type **109**; 100r. Jesus Christ (fresco, Spasa-Praabrazhenskaya Church, Polatsk); 100r. Our Lady Volodimirska (icon, National Tretyakov Gallery, Moscow, Russia) . . . . 3·00 2·75

2000.
374 **110** 1r. black and green . . . 20 10
375 – 2r. black and blue 20 10
376 – 3r. black and yellow . . . 20 10
377 – 5r. black and blue 20 10
378 – 10r. black and orange . . 20 10
380 – 20r. black and mauve . . 30 15
382 – 30r. black and green . . . 40 20
383 – 50r. black and yellow . . 60 40
387 – 100r. black and mauve . . 80 55
DESIGNS—VERT: 2r. Star; 3r. Lyre; 5r. Synkovichy Church; 10r. Flaming wheel; 20r. Type **111**; 30r. Watermill; 50r. Windmill. HORIZ: 100r. Exhibition Centre.

111 Kryzhachok (folk dance)

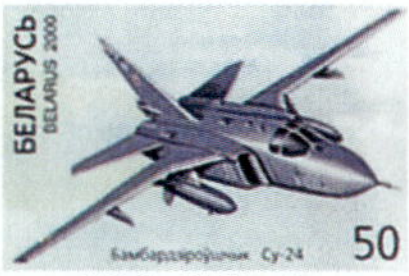

112 Su-24 Bomber

2000. Self-adhesive.
391 **111** 20r. black and red 30 15

2000. 25th Death Anniv of Pavel Sukhoi (aircraft designer). Multicoloured.
392 50r. Type **112** 80 60
393 50r. Su-27 fighter 80 60
394 50r. Su-25 battle fighter . . . 80 60
MS395 120 × 83 mm. 150r. Type **112**; 150r. As No. 394; 150r. As No. 393 . . . . 2·50 2·30

113 Kupala Holiday

114 Stone-Curlew

2000.
396 **113** A black and blue 40 30
No. 396 was for Inland Letter Post rate.

2000. Birds in the Red Book. Multicoloured.
397 50r. Type **114** 60 40
398 50r. Smew (*Mergellus albellus*) 60 40
399 75r. Willow grouse 70 45
400 100r. Lesser spotted eagle (vert) 90 65

115 "The Partisan Madonna of Minsk" (M. Savitsky)

116 "Building Europe"

2000. 55th Anniv of End of Second World War.
401 **115** 100r. multicoloured . . . 90 65

2000. Europa.
402 **116** 250r. multicoloured . . . 3·00 2·75

117 Scene from "Creation of the World"

118 Hands holding Lifebelt

2000. National Ballet Company. Multicoloured.
403 100r. Type **117** . . . . . . 1·00 75
MS404 77 × 73 mm. 150r. Scene from "Passions" . . . . . . 1·80 1·60

2000. 50th Anniv of United Nations High Commission for Refugees.
405 **118** 50r. multicoloured 45 35

119 Head of Lynx

120 People wearing National Costumes

2000. Endangered Species. The Lynx. Multicoloured.
406 100r. Type **119** 80 65
407 100r. On branch 80 65
408 150r. Walking through woodland . . . . 1·20 95
409 150r. Adult and cub . . . . 1·20 95

2000. International Year of Culture.
410 **120** 100r. multicoloured . . . 80 65

121 Rings

122 Amber

2000. Olympic Games, Sydney. Multicoloured.
411 100r. Type **121** 80 65
412 100r. Kayaking 80 65
413 100r. Rhythmic gymnastics . . 80 65
MS414 77 × 74 mm. 400r. Athletes 3·00 2·75

2000. Minerals. Multicoloured.
415 200r. Type **122** . . . . . . 1·30 1·10
416 200r. Galit . . . . 1·30 1·10
417 200r. Flint . . . . 1·30 1·10
418 200r. Silvin . . . . 1·30 1·10

123 People around decorated Tree

124 Nativity Scene

2000. New Year.
419 **123** 200r. multicoloured . . . 1·50 1·30

2000. Christmas.
420 **124** 100r. multicoloured . . . 1·20 95

125 "Connection of Times" (Roman Zabello)

2000. New Millennium. Children's Paintings. Multicoloured.
421 100r. Type **125** 80 65
422 100r. "Festival of Life" (Alena Emeliyanova) . . . 80 65

126 Euphrosiniya Polotskaya and Church

2001. 900th Birth Anniv of St. Euphrosiniya Polotskaya (Saint Euphrosyne). Imperf.
423 **126** 500r. multicoloured . . . 2·30 2·10

127 Brest

128 Runner

2001. Town Arms (1st series). Multicoloured.
424 160r. Dubrovna 50 30
424a 200r. Type **127** 60 40
425 200r. Gomel 60 40
426 200r. Borisov 60 40
427 300r. Minsk 75 45
428 300r. David-Gorodok . . . 75 45
429 350r. Kamjanets 80 55
430 460r. Slonim 90 65
431 500r. Novogrudok 95 75
432 500r. Turov 95 75
433 780r. Zaslavl . . . . 1·00 85
434 900r. Magilev . . . . 1·20 95

2001. Byelorussian Medal Winners, Olympic Games, Sydney. Sheet 78 × 75 mm.
MS435 **128** 1000r. multicoloured 4·00 3·75
No. **MS**435 is as No. **MS**414 but with face value changed and design altered to include list of winners.

129 Tupolev ANT-25 RD

2001. 25th Death Anniv of Pavel Sukhoy (aircraft designer). Multicoloured.
436 250r. Type **129** . . . . . 1·20 95
437 250r. Tupolev ANT-37 Rodina . . . . 1·20 95

2001. As T **86**.
438 1r. black and green (inscr "2002") 20 10
439 2r. black and blue (inscr "2002") 20 10
440 3r. black and yellow (inscr "2002") 20 10
441 5r. black and blue (inscr "2002") 20 10
442 10r. black and brown (inscr "2002") 20 10
442a 20r. black and mauve (inscr "2002") 30 15
442b 30r. black and green (inscr "2002") 40 20
442c 50r. black and yellow (inscr "2002") 60 40
442d 100r. black and mauve (inscr "2002") 80 55
442e 100r. black and brown (inscr "2003") 80 55
443 200r. black and green . . . 80 55
444 500r. black and brown . . . 1·80 1·40
DESIGNS: 1r. Bison; 2r. Star; 3r. Lyre; 5r. Synkovichy Church; 10r. Flaming wheel; 20r. Dancers; 50r. Windmill; 100r. Exhibition centre; 100r. (442e), Layavoniha folk dance; 200r. 18th-century town house, Vitebsk; 500r. As No. 309.

130 Stag Beetle (*Lucanus cervus*)

2001. Beetles. Multicoloured.
445 300r. Type **130** . . . . . . 1·50 1·20
446 300r. European rhinoceros beetle (*Oryctes nasicornis*) 1·50 1·20

2001. As T **110**. Self-adhesive.
447 100r. black and mauve . . . 60 40
448 200r. black and green (vert) 80 65
DESIGNS: 100r. As No. 387; 200r. As No. 438.

131 *Nymphaea alba*

132 Swans and Lake, Narochanskyi Nature Reserve

2001. Endangered Species. Flowers. Multicoloured.
455 200r. Type **131** 80 65
456 400r. *Cypripedium calceolus* 1·70 1·40

2001. Europa. Water Resources. Multicoloured.
457 400r. Geese and lake, Pripjatiskyi Nature Reserve 2·00 1·40
458 1000r. Type **132** . . . . . . 5·00 4·25

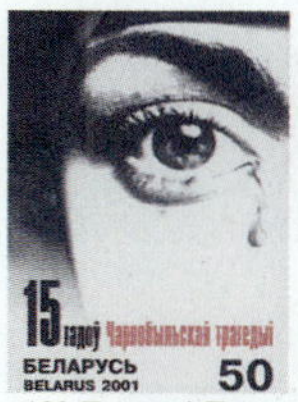

133 Eye and Tear

134 National Arms

2001. 15th Anniv of Chernobyl Nuclear Disaster.
459 **133** 50r. black and rose . . . 50 30

2001. Traditional Costumes (4th series). As T **51**. Multicoloured.
460 200r. 19th-century, Slutsk region 70 55
461 1000r. 19th-century, Pinsk region . . . . 3·50 3·25

2001. 10th Anniv of State Sovereignty.
462 **134** 500r. multicoloured . . . 2·00 1·90

135 Union Emblem

138 Figures encircling Globe

137 King and Courtier ("The blue suit made inside out")

2001. 10th Anniv of Union of Independent States.
463 **135** 195r. multicoloured . . . 80 55

2001. No. 166 surch **400**.
464 400r. on 1500r. mauve . . . 1·20 95

2001. Folk Tales. Multicoloured.
465 100r. Type **137** 50 30
466 200r. Horse-drawn coach ("Okh and the golden snuff-box") 90 65

2001. United Nations Year of Dialogue among Civilizations.
467 **138** 400r. multicoloured . . . 1·20 95

139 Otto Schmidt

141 Wind-surfer

2001. 110th Birth Anniv of Otto Yulievich Schmidt (scientist and Arctic explorer). Sheet 78 × 74 mm.
MS468 **139** 3000r. multicoloured . . . 8·00 7·50

2001. Surch.
469 400r. on 100r. blue (No. 159) 1·10 85
470 400r. on 600r. red (No. 163) 1·10 85
471 400r. on 1500r. blue (No. 167) . . . . 1·10 85
472 400r. on 3300r. yellow (No. 173) . . . . 1·10 85
473 1000r. on 100r. black and green (No. 293) . . . . . 2·50 2·10
474 1000r. on 180r. brown and red (No. 102) . . . . . . 2·50 2·10
475 1000r. on 280r. green and blue (No. 104) . . . . . . 2·50 2·10

2001. Aquatic Sports. Multicoloured.
476 200r. Type **141** 70 45
MS477 102 × 66 mm. 1000r. Water-skier . . . . 3·00 2·75

142 Arms of Francisk Skorina

144 Calligraphy

143 Building Facade

2001. Architecture and Arms. Multicoloured.
478 1000r. Type **142** . . . . . 2·20 1·90
479 2000r. City Hall, Minsk . . . 4·25 3·75
480 3000r. City Hall, Nesvizh . . 6·25 5·75
481 5000r. City Hall, Cherchersk 10·00 9·50

2001. House of Mercy (Orthodox Church humanitarian centre), Minsk.
495 **143** 200r. multicoloured . . . 70 55

2001. Christmas (496) and New Year (497). Multicoloured.
496 100r. Type **144** 50 30
497 100r. Snowy scene contained in bauble 50 30

145 E. V. Klumov

2001. 125th Birth Anniv of E. V. Klumov (surgeon and resistance worker).
498 **145** 100r. multicoloured . . . 50 30

146 Ski Slalom

2002. Winter Olympics, Salt Lake City, USA (1st issue). Multicoloured.
499 300r. Type **146** 90 65
500 300r. Figure skating 90 65
501 500r. Biathlon . . . . 1·30 1·00
502 500r. Ski jumping . . . . . 1·30 1·00
See also No. **MS**507.

147 *Formica rufa*

2002. Ants. Multicoloured.
503 200r. Type **147** 70 45
504 1000r. Grubs and worker ants (vert) . . . . 2·10 1·90
MS505 100 × 72 mm. 1000r. No. 504 plus label (vert) forming a composite design . . . . . . 2·50 1·90

148 Woman carrying Corn (Dozhinki Feast)

149 Ice Hockey Player

2002.
506 **148** B (55r.) black and yellow 30 20

2002. Winter Olympic Games, Salt Lake City, USA (2nd issue). Sheet 100 × 70 mm.
MS507 **149** 2000r. multicoloured 5·00 4·75

2002. As T **113** but inscr "2002".
508 **113** A black and blue 40 30
No. 508 was for use on inland letters.

150 Clown riding Unicycle

151 Yanka Kupala

2002. Europa. Circus. Multicoloured.
509 400r. Type **150** . . . . . . 1·50 1·40
510 500r. Horse . . . . 1·80 1·60

2002. 120th Birth Annivs of Poets. Multicoloured.
511 100r. Type **151** 30 20
512 100r. Yacub Kolas 30 20
MS513 100 × 70 mm. 500r. × 2 Nos. 511/12 . . . . 2·20 2·10

152 Church, Polotsk

153 Clover *Trifolium*

2002. No value expressed. Multicoloured.
514 H (236r.) Type **152** 60 40
515 C (314r.) Railway Station, Brest 80 55
No. 514 was for use on letters up to 20 grams to Russia, Lithuania, Latvia, Uzbekistan, Tadjikistan and Turkmenistan.
No. 515 was for use on airmail letters up to 20 grams to the same countries.

2002. Flowers. Multicoloured. Self-adhesive gum.
516 30r. Type **153** 30 15
517 50r. Matricaria 35 20
518 B (75r.) Flax (*Linium*) . . . 20 10
519 A (90r.) Cornflower (*Centaurea cyanus*) 30 20
520 100r. Pasque flower (*Pulsatilla patens*) 40 25
521 200r. Yellow water lily (Nuphar lutea) 50 30
522 H (236r.) Campanula 70 45
523 C (314r.) Rhododendron . . 70 45
524 500r. Fireweed (*Chamaenerion angustifolium*) 90 65
No. 518 was for use on post cards within Belarus.
No. 519 was for use on letters up to 20 grams within Belarus.
No. 522 was for use on letters up to 20 grams to Russia, Lithuania, Latvia, Uzbekistan, Tadjikistan and Turkmenistan.
No. 523 was for use on airmail letters up to 20 grams to Russia, Lithuania, Latvia, Uzbekistan, Tadjikistan and Turkmenistan.

154 Go-Kart

2002. Children's Activities. Multicoloured.
525 90r. Type **154** 30 15
526 239r. Model aircraft 70 45

155 White Stork (*Ciconia ciconia*)

2002. Birds. Sheet 94 × 72 mm containing T **155** and similar horiz designs. Multicoloured.
MS527 200r. Type **155**; 200r. Golden oriole (*Oriolius oriolus*); 200r. Pied wagtail (*Matacilla alba*) . . . . 1·50 1·40

156 Bridge over River Svisloch, Minsk

2002. Bridges.
528 **156** 200r. black, mauve and blue 40 30
529 – 300r. multicoloured . . . 70 55
530 – 500r. black, blue and green . . . . 1·00 85
DESIGNS: 200r. Type **156**; 300r. Bridge over River Sozh, Gomel; 500r. Bridge over River Zapadnaja Dvina, Vitebsk.

157 Lake, Braslav

2002. International Year of Eco-Tourism.
531 **157** 300r. multicoloured . . . 1·00 95

158 "By the Church" (F. Rushchits)

2002. Art. Multicoloured.
532 300r. Type **158** 75 55
533 300r. "Battle at Nemiga" (M. Philippovich) (horiz) 75 55

159 V. V. Kovalyonok and P. I. Klimuk (cosmonauts)

2002. 45th Anniv of Space Exploration. Sheet 131 × 71 mm.
MS534 **159** 3000r. multicoloured 5·50 5·25

160 Father Christmas

161 Ksimir Malevich and "Black Square"

2002. Christmas and New Year. Multicoloured.
535 300r. Type **160** 75 55
536 300r. Angel 75 55

2003. 125th Birth Anniv of Kasimir Malevich (artist). Sheet 82 × 54 mm.
MS537 **161** 3000r. multicoloured 6·00 5·75

162 Smooth Snake (*Coronella austriaca*)

163 Glass containing Land and Water

2003. Reptiles. Multicoloured.
538 300r. Type **162** 60 40
539 600r. European pond turtle (*Emys orbicularis*) . . . . 1·00 75

2003. International Year of Freshwater.
540 **163** 370r. multicoloured . . . 80 55

164 House Sparrow

165 In-line Skates

2003.
541 **164** 630r. multicoloured . . . 1·20 95

2003. Children's Sports. Multicoloured.
542 300r. Type **165** 60 40
543 300r. Scooter (vert) 60 40

166 "Europa"

2003. Europa. Poster Art. Multicoloured.
544 400r. Type **166** 80 55
545 700r. Painted wooden panels 1·30 1·00

167 Globeflower (*Trollius europaeus*)

168 Women's Costumes, Polesye

2003. Endangered Flora. Multicoloured.
546 270r. Type **167** 60 40
547 740r. Siberian iris (*Iris sibirica*) . . . . 1·30 1·00

2003. Traditional Costumes. Multicoloured.
548 380r. Type **168** 70 55
549 430r. Men and women's costumes, Mogilyov . . . 80 65
See also Nos. 636/7.

169 470 Class Sailing Dinghy

2003. Dinghy Sailing. Sheet 128 × 78 mm, containing T **169** and similar multicoloured design.
MS550 1000r. Type **169**; 1000r. Laser dinghy (vert) . . . . . 3·25 3·00

170 Bronze Age Axe Head

2003. National Museum of Natural History and Culture, Minsk. Three sheets, each 82 × 52 mm, containing T **170** and similar multicoloured designs.
MS551 (a) 1000r. Type **170**; (b) 1500r. Bronze age pot (28 × 30 mm); (c) 1500r. 14th-century bowl (28 × 30 mm) . . . 7·00 6·50

171 Horse Stall, Povitie (19th-century)

2003. Architecture. Multicoloured.
552 270r. Type **171** 50 30
553 430r. Church, Sinkevichi (1724) 80 55
554 740r. Watermill, Volma (19th-century) . . . . . . 1·10 85
MS555 97 × 112 mm. Nos. 552/4 2·50 2·30

172 Golden Retriever

173 Young Player holding Ball

2003. Dogs. Multicoloured.
556 270r. Type **172** 60 40
557 380r. Great dane 70 50
558 430r. German shepherd . . . 80 65

2003. Centenary of FIFA (Federation Internationale de Football Association). Multicoloured.
559 380r. Type **173** 70 50
560 380r. Five players (horiz) . . 70 50
561 460r. Three players (horiz) . . 80 65
562 780r. Player holding ball . . 1·30 1·00

174 Angel

2003. Christmas. Multicoloured.
563 380r. Type **174** 50 40
564 780r. Grandfather Frost . . . 1·10 85

175 "Arrival of Spring" (Pavel Maslennikov)

2004.
565 **175** 290r. multicoloured . . . 60 40

176 Blackthorn (*Prunus spinosa*)

177 Queen and King of Hearts

2004. Fruit. Multicoloured.
566 5r. Type **176** 30 15
567 10r. Lingonberry (*Vaccinium vitis idaea*) 30 15
568 20r. Bilberry (*Vaccinium myrtillus*) 30 15
569 30r. Cranberry (*Oxycoccus palustris*) 30 15
570 50r. Bog blueberry (*Vaccinium uliginosum*) . . 30 15
571 100r. Raspberry (*Rubus idaeus*) 30 15
572 B (100r.) Strawberry (*Fragaria ananassa*) 30 15
573 A (120r.) Red currant (*Ribes rubrum*) 30 15
574 200r. Dewberry (*Rubus caesius*) 30 15
575 H (290r.) Black currant (*Ribes nigrum*) 50 30
576 300r. Stone bramble (*Rubus saxatilis*) 50 30
577 C (420r.) Gooseberry (*Grossularia reclinata*) . . . 60 40
578 500r. Wild strawberry (*Fragaria*) 70 50
579 P (780r.) Sea buckthorn (*Hippophae rhamnoides*) . . 1·00 75
580 1000r. Sour cherry (*Cerasus vulgaris*) . . . . 1·30 90

2004. St. Valentine's Day.
581 **177** H (290r.) black, scarlet and yellow 75 50

178 Alder (*Alnus incana*)

179 Swallow

2004. Trees. Multicoloured. Self-adhesive gum.
582 100r. Type **178** 30 15
583 B (100r.) Birch (*Betula pendula*) 30 15
584 A (120r.) Scots pine (*Pinus sylvestris*) 30 15
585 200r. *Viburnum opulus* . . . 30 15
586 H (290r.) Ash (*Fraxinus excelsior*) 50 30
587 300r. Lime (*Tillia cordata*) . . 50 30
588 400r. Hazel (*Corylus avellana*) 60 40
589 C (420r.) Rowan (*Sorbus aucuparia*) 60 40
590 500r. Oak (*Quercus robur*) . . 75 50
591 P (780r.) Hornbeam (*Carpinus betulus*) . . . . 1·00 85
592 1000r. Elm (*Ulmus laevis*) . . 1·30 1·00

2004.
593 **179** 870r. multicoloured . . . 1·30 1·00

180 Player

181 Forest and Walker

2004. International Ice Hockey Federation World Under-18 Championships, Minsk.
594 **180** 320r. multicoloured . . . 75 50

2004. Europa. Holidays. Multicoloured.
595 320r. Type **181** 60 40
596 870r. Fisherman . . . . . . 1·40 1·10

182 Mount of Glory Monument

2004. 60th Anniv of the Liberation of Minsk. Sheet 121 × 81 mm containing T **182** and similar multicoloured design.
MS597 500r. Type **182**; 1000r. "The Parade of Partisans" (Y. Zaitsev) (52 × 30 mm) . . . . 2·30 2·10

183 Class 130 Series D Locomotive and Early 20th-century Station, Mosty

2004. Railways. Multicoloured.
598 320r. Type **183** 70 45
599 870r. Class 230 series A locomotive and 19th-century station, Vitebsk . . . . 1·20 1·00

184 *Polistes gallicus*

2004. Insects. Multicoloured.
600 320r. Type **184** 60 40
601 505r. *Bombus lucorum* 80 65
MS602 75 × 102 mm. 2000r. *Apis mellifera* (40 × 30 mm) . . . . 3·00 2·75

185 "Self Portrait"

2004. 150th Birth Anniv of Yury Pan (artist). Sheet 115 × 75 mm containing T **185** Multicoloured.
MS603 1000m. × 2, Type **185**; "Watchmaker" (horiz) . . . . 3·00 2·75

186 Cycling

2004. Olympic Games, Athens (1st issue). Multicoloured.
604 320r. Type **186** 60 40
605 505r. Hammer throwing . . . 80 65
606 870r. Tennis . . . . 1·30 1·00
See also No. **MS**611.

187 *Euphydryas matuma*

188 Yuiya Nesterenko

2004. Butterflies. Multicoloured.
607 300r. Type **187** 50 30
608 500r. *Pericallia matronula* . . 70 50
609 800r. *Zerynthia polyxena* . . 1·00 75
610 1200r. *Eudia pavonia* . . . . 1·60 1·30

2004. Olympic Games, Athens (2nd issue). Gold Medal Winners. Sheet 103 × 73 mm containing T **188** and similar vert design. Multicoloured.
MS611 500r. × 2, Type **188** (100 metres); Igor Makarov (judo) 2·00 1·90
The stamps and margin of No. **MS**611 form a composite design.

189 Byelorussian Harness Horse

2004. Horses. Sheet 120 × 100 mm containing T **189** and similar horiz designs. Multicoloured.
MS612 500r. × 4, Type **89**; Andalusian horse; Head of Byelorussian horse; Head of Andalusian horse . . . . . 3·00 2·75
The stamps and margin of No. **MS**612 form a composite design.

190 Black Persian

2004. Cats. Sheet 103 × 115 mm containing T **190** and similar horiz designs. Multicoloured.
MS613 300r. Type **190**; 500r. Siamese seal-point; 500r. Red Persian; 800r. Tortoiseshell Persian; 800r. British shorthair 4·50 4·25
The stamps and margin of No. **MS**613 form a composite design.

191 Father Christmas

193 Gerasim Bogomolov

192 Train in Station

2004. Christmas and New Year.
614 **191** 320r. multicoloured . . . 75 50

2004. Minsk Underground Railway. Multicoloured.
615 560r. Type **192** 75 55
616 560r. Locomotive, decorated pillar and passengers . . . 75 55

2005. Birth Centenary of Gerasim Vasilievich Bogomolov (hydrologist).
617 **193** 350r. black and vermilion 75 55

194 Madonna and Child (Protoierej Povnyji)

2005. 21st Century Icons. Sheet 151 × 101 mm containing T **194** and similar vert designs.
MS618 1500r. × 3, Type **194**; Nativity (George Sutulin and Olga Belaja); Archangel Michael (Andrey Kosikov) . . . . . . 6·50 6·00

195 Great Grey Owl (*Strix nebulosa*)

2005.
619 **195** 900r. multicoloured . . . 1·00 85

196 Partisans

2005. 60th Anniv of the End of World War II. Multicoloured.
620 A (160r.) Type **196** 30 15
621 H (360r.) Liberation 50 30
622 H (360r.) Woman, bells and monument, Khatyn 50 30
623 P (930r.) Victory flag . . . . 1·00 80
MS624 150 × 74 mm. 1000r. × 2, Signing treaty (40 × 30 mm); Victory parade (52 × 30 mm) 3·00 2·75

197 Greater Spotted Eagle (*Aquila clanga*)

2005. Fauna. Sheet 133 × 68 mm containing T **197** and similar horiz designs. Multicoloured.
MS625 500r. Type **197**; 500r. *Catocala sponsa*; 1000r. Beaver (*Castor fiber*); 1000r. Badger (*Meles meles*) . . . . 4·25 4·00

The stamps and margin of No. **MS**625 form a composite design. Stamps of the same design were issued by Russia.

198 Vegetables

2005. Europa. Gastronomy. Multicoloured.
626 500r. Type **198** 75 50
627 1000r. Bread and hat . . . . 1·30 95

199 Stefaniya Stanyuta

200 Hans Christian Andersen

2005. Birth Centenary of Stanyuta Stefaniya Mikhailovna (Stefaniya Stanyuta) (actress).
628 **199** 160r. black and vermilion 40 20

2005. Birth Bicentenary of Hans Christian Andersen (writer). Sheet 120 × 80 mm.
MS629 **200** 2000r. multicoloured 3·00 2·75

201 Black Stork

2005. Endangered Species. Black Stork (*Ciconia nigra*). Multicoloured.
630 500r. Type **201** 75 55
631 500r. In flight 75 55
632 1000r. Facing left . . . . . 1·30 1·00
633 1000r. Nestlings . . . . . . 1·30 1·00

202 "Harvesting" (Mikhail Sevryuk)

2005. National Art Museum. Birth Centenary of Mikhail Sevryuk (artist).
634 **202** 360r. multicoloured . . . 50 30

203 Emblem

2005. World Information Society Summit, Tunis.
635 **203** 360r. multicoloured . . . 60 40

2005. Traditional Costumes. As T **168**. Mult.
636 380r. Women, Mosty 60 40
637 570r. Women, Lepel 80 65

204 Runner and Hockey Players

2005. International Year of Sports and Physical Education.
638 **204** 570r. multicoloured . . . 80 65

205 Arms and Town

2005. Volkvoysk Millenary.
639 **205** 360r. multicoloured . . . 70 45

206 Kiril Turovsky Monument

207 Early Chess Players

2005. Turov Diocese Millenary.
640 **206** 360r. gold and vermilion 60 40

2005. Chess. Background colour given.
641 **207** 500r. multicoloured (chestnut) 70 55
642 500r. multicoloured (red) 70 55

208 Vytautas Castle

2005. Architecture. Sheet 113 × 72 mm containing T **208** and similar horiz design. Multicoloured.
MS643 500r. Type **208**; 1000r. Lida Castle . . . . 1·80 1·60

209 Tree and Town

2005. Christmas and New Year.
644 **209** 360r. silver, ultramarine and emerald 60 40

210 Snowboarding

2005. Winter Olympic Games, Turin. Multicoloured.
645 500r. Type **210** 75 55
MS646 117 × 76 mm. 2000r. Freestyle skiing (30 × 40 mm) 2·30 2·10

211 Lapwing (*Vanellus vanellus*)

2006.
647 **211** 930r. multicoloured . . . 1·30 1·00

212 Atomic Symbol and Flowers

213 Penguins (Lina Filippoch)

2006. 20th Anniv of Chernobyl Nuclear Disaster.
648 **212** 360r. multicoloured . . . 60 40

2006. Europa. Integration. Winning Designs in Children's Painting Competition. Multicoloured.
649 500r. Type **213** 75 55
650 1000r. Pegasus (Daria Buneeva) (horiz) . . . . . 1·30 1·00

214 Ivan Shamyakin

215 Wheatear

2006. 85th Birth Anniv of Ivan Shamyakin (writer).
651 **214** 360r. multicoloured . . . 60 40

2006. Birds. Multicoloured.
652 10r. Type **215** 20 10
653 20r. Blue tit 20 10
654 30r. Pied flycatcher 20 10
655 50r. Linnet 20 10
656 100r. Lesser whitethroat . . . 25 15
657 B (160r.) Robin 30 20
658 A (190r.) Black redstart . . . 35 20
659 200r. Chaffinch 40 25
660 300r. Tree sparrow 50 30
661 H (360r.) Great tit 55 35
662 500r. Greenfinch 70 50
663 1000r. Hawfinch . . . . . . 1·10 95

216 *Myotis dasycneme*

2006. Bats. Multicoloured.
664 500r. Type **216** 75 55
665 500r. *Vespertilio murinus* . . 75 55
666 500r. *Barbastella barbastellus* 75 55
MS667 97 × 115 mm. 1000r. × 3, As Nos. 664/6 . . . . 4·00 3·75

217 Silver Medals

218 Canoeists

2006. Free-style Ski Team and Dmitri Daschinski—Silver Medal Winners—Winter Olympic Games, Turin. Sheet 102 × 72 mm.
MS668 **217** 2000r. multicoloured 2·50 2·30

2006. Avgustovo Channel. Sheet 113 × 74 mm.
MS669 **218** 2000r. multicoloured 2·50 2·30

219 Series E Steam Locomotive, Railway Station, Molodechno

220 *Cephalanthera rubra*

2006. Railways. Multicoloured.
670 1000r. Type **219** . . . . . . 1·40 1·30
671 1000r. Series O steam locomotive, railway station, Brest . . . . 1·40 1·30

2006. Orchids. Multicoloured.
672 1000r. Type **220** . . . . . . 1·40 1·30
673 1000r. *Dactylorhiza majalis* 1·40 1·30
674 1000r. As Type **220** but with design reversed . . . . . 1·40 1·30

221 Wind Turbines

222 Emblem

2006. Renewable Energy. Multicoloured.
675 210r. Type **221** 30 30
676 970r. Hydro-electric dam . . 1·20 1·10

2006. 15th Anniv of Regional Concord of Communication (RCC).
677 **222** 410r. multicoloured . . . 70 65

2006. 5th National Philatelic Exhibition (BelFILA 2006). No. **MS**131 surch. Sheet 100 × 70 mm. Imperf.
MS678 3500r. on 1000r. multicoloured . . . . 4·50 4·25

224 Red Discus

2006. Fish. Discus (*Symphysodon discus*). Multicoloured.
679 500r. Type **224** 75 70
680 500r. Violet 75 70
681 500r. Green striped 75 70
682 500r. Yellow, pink striped and green 75 70

225 Decorated Tree

226 Napoleon Orda

2006. Happy New Year.
684 **225** 500r. ultramarine and blue 75 70
685 500r. blue 75 70

2007. Birth Bicentenary of Napoleon Orda (artist).
686 **226** 2000r. multicoloured . . . 5·25 5·00

2007. As T **152**. Multicoloured.
687 2000r. Minsk City Hall . . . 2·50 2·30

227 Thrush Nightingale

2007.
688 **227** 1000r. multicoloured . . . 1·30 1·20

228 Reef Knot

229 *Mustela putorius* (polecat)

230 Map of Belarus

2007. Europa. Centenary of Scouting. Multicoloured.
689 500r. Type **228** 65 40
690 1000r. Emblem . . . . . . 1·30 80

2007. Fauna. Multicoloured.
691 B (190r.) Type **229** 20 15
692 B (190r.) *Vulpes vulpes* (red fox) 20 15
693 A (220r.) *Sciurus vulgaris* (red squirrel) 35 20
694 A (220r.) *Dryomys nitedula* (forest dormouse) 35 20

2007. World Heritage. Points of Struve Geodetic Arc (points where measurements were taken to determine the shape and size of Earth) in Belarus. Sheet 112 × 79 mm.
MS695 **230** 5000r. multicoloured 6·25 6·25

231 *Gallinago media* (snipe)

2007. Cepkeliai and Kotra Nature Reserves. Multicoloured.
696 1000r. Type **231** 1·20 70
697 1000r. *Crex crex* (corncrake) 1·20 70
Nos. 696/7 were issued together, se-tenant, forming a composite design. Stamps of a similar design were issued by Lithuania.

232 *Nyctea scandiaca* (snowy owl)

2007. Owls. Multicoloured.
698 500r. Type **232** 55 35
699 500r. *Surnia ulula* (northern hawk owl) 55 35
700 1000r. *Asio flammeus* (short eared owl) 1·20 70
701 1000r. *Athene noctua* (little owl) 1·20 70

233 *Alexandra Marianna Veselovskaya* (1640)

2007. Paintings from National Art Museum. Multicoloured.
702 1050r. Type **233** 2·40 1·40
703 1050r. *Griesel Sapega* (1632) 2·40 1·40
704 1050r. *Kshishtof Veselovsky* (1636) 2·40 1·40

234 Children and Snowman

2007. Christmas and New Year. Multicoloured.
705 240r. Type **234** 40 25
706 240r. Children and parcel 40 25
707 1050r. Candle 2·10 1·30
708 1050r. Christmas tree 2·10 1·30
MS709 100 × 94 mm. 240r. As No. 705; 240r. As No. 706; 1500r. Child wearing Santa outfit; 1500r. Girl holding star 3·25 3·25
The stamps and margins of **MS**709 form a composite design.

235 Blagovest Bell (1937)

2007. Bells. Multicoloured.
710 600r. Type **235** 35 20
711 1000r. Blagovest bell (19th century) 1·40 85
712 1200r. Sub chime bell (1928) 1·75 1·00
MS713 106 × 79 mm. 2500r. Sub chime bell (18th century) 3·00 3·00
The stamps and margins of **MS**713 form a composite design.

236 Blacksmith and Armour

2007. Traditional Crafts. Multicoloured.
714 600r. Type **236** 75 45
715 600r. Weaver and cloth 75 45

237 Lamb, Sheep and Sheepdog

2007. Domestic Animals. Multicoloured.
716 240r. Type **237** 30 20
717 440r. Ram, sheep and sheepdog 60 35
718 500r. Piglets 70 40
719 1050r. Cattle 1·50 90
720 1500r. Goats 1·90 1·20

238 Medieval Falconers

239 Vincent Dunin-Marcinkevich

2008. Hunting. Multicoloured.
721 440r. Type **237** 60 35
722 1050r. Deer hunting (horiz) 1·30 80

2008. Birth Bicentenary of Vincent Dunin-Marcinkevich (writer and social activist).
723 **239** 440r. multicoloured 1·00 60

240 Konstantin Ostrozhsky

2008. 400th Death Anniv of Konstanty Wasyl Ostrogski (Konstantin Ostrozhsky) (Lithuanian prince). Sheet 93 × 78 mm.
MS724 **240** 2500r. multicoloured 1·70 1·70

241 *Egretta alba* (great white egret)

242 Symbols of Information

2008.
725 **241** 1050r. multicoloured 1·30 80

2008. TIBO International Exhibition and Congress, Minsk.
726 **242** H (440r.) multicoloured 60 35

BELGIAN CONGO Pt. 4

A Belgian colony in Central Africa. Became independent in July 1960. For later issues see Congo, Zaire, Democratic Republic of Congo, Katanga and South Kasai.

100 centimes = 1 franc.

INDEPENDENT STATE OF THE CONGO

The Independent State of the Congo was established in 1885, with King Leopold II of the Belgians as ruler.

1 Leopold II

5 Leopold II

1886. Various frames.
1 **1** 5c. green 8·25 14·50
2 10c. red 2·75 3·00
3 25c. blue 32·00 25·00
4 50c. green 5·50 6·50
5 5f. lilac £375 £190

1887. Surch **COLIS-POSTAUX Fr. 3.50.**
6 **1** 3f.50 on 5f. lilac £300 £600

1887.
7 **5** 5c. green 45 70
8 10c. red 1·00 85
9 25c. blue 90 90
10 50c. brown 40·00 14·50
11 50c. grey 2·25 11·50
12 5f. lilac £800 £300
13 5f. grey 90·00 75·00
14 10f. orange £350 £225

1887. Surch **COLIS-POSTAUX Fr. 3.50.**
15 **5** 3f.50 on 5f. violet £700 £400

1889. Surch **COLIS-POSTAUX Fr. 3.50** in frame.
16 **5** 3f.50 on 5f. violet £500 £275
17 3f.50 on 5f. grey £100 90·00

7 Port of Matadi

8 Stanley Falls

13 Oil Palms

14 Native Canoe

1894. Inscr "ETAT INDEPENDANT DU CONGO".
18 **7** 5c. black and blue 13·00 13·50
24 5c. black and brown 2·40 95
30 5c. black and green 1·25 35
19 **8** 10c. black and brown 13·00 15·00
25 10c. black and blue 1·60 95
31 10c. black and red 2·40 50
26 **13** 15c. black and brown 3·75 60
20 – 25c. black and orange 3·25 1·90
32 – 25c. black and blue 3·50 1·25
27 **14** 40c. black and green 4·75 2·10
21 – 50c. black and green 1·75 1·00
33 – 50c. black and brown 4·75 65
22 – 1f. black and violet 24·00 10·50
35 – 1f. black and red £190 4·25
28 – 3f.50 black and red £120 70·00
23 – 5f. black and red 38·00 19·00
29 – 10f. black and green £100 16·00
DESIGNS—HORIZ: 25c. Inkissi Falls; 50c. Railway Bridge over the M'pozo; 1f. African elephant hunt; 3f.50 Congo village; 10f. "Deliverance" (stern wheel paddle-steamer). VERT: 5f. Bangala Chief Morangi and wife.

BELGIAN CONGO

The Congo was annexed to Belgium in 1908 and was renamed the Belgian Congo.

1909. Nos. 23, 26/29 and 30/33 optd **CONGO BELGE.**
36A **7** 5c. black and green 2·40 1·40
37A **8** 10c. black and red 3·00 1·40
38A **13** 15c. black and brown 5·00 2·50
49 – 25c. black and blue 50 1·75
50 **14** 40c. black and green 2·40 2·10
51 – 50c. black and brown 5·00 1·75
52 – 1f. black and red 24·00 3·50
53 – 3f.50 black and red 24·00 14·50
54 – 5f. black and red 42·00 20·00
55b – 10f. black and green 85·00 21·00

1909. As 1894 issue but inscr "CONGO BELGE".
56 **7** 5c. black and green 75 85
57 **8** 10c. black and red 60 65
58 **13** 15c. black and brown 19·00 11·00
59 – 50c. black and bistre 3·25 2·75

1910. As 1894 issue but inscr "CONGO BELGE BELGISCH-CONGO" with values in French and Flemish.
60 **7** 5c. black and green 40 20
61 **8** 10c. black and red 50 15
62 **13** 15c. black and brown 35 10
63 – 25c. black and blue 1·40 25
64 **14** 40c. black and green 1·75 1·90
65 – 50c. black and bistre 3·00 1·60
66 – 1f. black and red 4·50 2·10
68 – 3f. black and red 21·00 12·50
67 – 5f. black and red 20·00 19·00
69 – 10f. black and green 32·00 18·00

32 Port of Matadi

33 Stanley Falls

34 Inkissi Falls

1915. New types as **32** to **34** (with value in words at top) and other types as 1910 all inscr "CONGO BELGE" and "BELGISCH-CONGO".
70 **32** 5c. black and green 30 15
71 **33** 10c. black and red 45 35
72b **13** 15c. black and green 55 35
73 **34** 25c. black and blue 1·00 25
74 **14** 40c. black and red 3·75 1·90
75 – 50c. black and red 7·00 1·50
76 – 1f. black and olive 2·75 65
77 – 5f. black and orange 1·90 1·00

1918. Types as before, surch with red cross and premium.
78 **32** 5c.+10c. blue and green 25 90
79 **33** 10c.+15c. blue and red 30 85
80 **13** 15c.+20c. blue and green 35 85
81 **34** 25c.+25c. blue 45 95
82 **14** 40c.+40c. blue and red 50 1·25
83 – 50c.+50c. blue and red 45 1·50
84 – 1f.+1f. blue and olive 2·25 2·50
85 – 5f.+5f. blue and orange 10·50 14·00
86 – 10f.+10f. blue and green 85·00 90·00

38 Congo Wharf

1920. Air.
87 **38** 50c. black and orange 40 10
88 – 1f. black and violet 40 10
89 – 2f. black and blue 65 35
90 – 5f. black and green 1·00 50
DESIGNS—HORIZ: 1f. District stores; 2f. Native canoes on beach. VERT: 5f. Provincial prison.

1921. Stamps of 1910 surch.
91 **14** 5c. on 40c. black and green 30 95
92 – 10c. on 5c. black and green 30 35
93 – 15c. on 50c. black and olive 30 80
94 **13** 25c. on 15c. black & yellow 1·60 95
95 **8** 30c. on 10c. black and red 30 45
96 – 50c. on 25c. black and blue 1·50 55

1921. Stamps of 1910 optd **1921.**
97 1f. black and red 1·00 75
98 3f. black and red 2·50 2·50
99 5f. black and lake 7·00 7·50
100 10f. black and green 5·75 4·00

1922. Stamps of previous issues variously surch without bars.
101 – 5c. on 50c. black and lake (No. 75) 35 60
102 **32** 10c. on 5c. black and green (No. 70) 30 25
114 **8** 0.25 on 30c. on 10c. black and red (No. 95) 13·00 13·50
115 **33** 0.25 on 30c. on 10c. black and red (No. 104) 9·50 13·00
103 **14** 25c. on 40c. black and lake (No. 74) 2·00 30

104 **33** 30c. on 10c. black and red (No. 71) 25 30
105 **34** 50c. on 25c. black and blue (No. 73) 40 25

1922. Stamps of 1915 surch with new value and two bars through old values.
108 **32** 10c. on 5c. black & green 90 95
110 – 10c. on 1f. black & olive 1·00 1·40
112 **14** 25c. on 40c. black & lake 60 60
113 – 25c. on 5f. blk & orange 1·90 2·40

46 Wood Carver

56 Native Cattle

1923.
117 A 5c. yellow 15 10
118 B 10c. green 15 10
119 C 15c. brown 15 10
120 D 20c. olive 15 10
121 E 20c. green 15 10
122 F 25c. brown 15 10
123 **46** 30c. red . . . . 45 1·40
124 30c. olive 25 45
125 35c. green . . . . 3·00 1·90
126 D 40c. purple 20 10
142 **56** 45c. purple 45 25
127 G 50c. blue 25 30
128 50c. orange 35 10
143 **56** 60c. red 30 20
129 E 75c. orange 20 20
130 75c. blue 40 85
131 **46** 75c. red 60 15
132 H 1f. brown 30 20
133 1f. blue 30 10
134 1f. red 65 10
135 D 1f.25 blue 30 35
136 1f.50 blue 30 35
137 1f.75 blue . . . . 3·25 2·75
138 I 3f. brown . . . . 4·00 2·50
139 J 5f. grey . . . . 8·25 5·00
140 K 10f. black . . . . 20·00 9·00
DESIGNS: A, Ubangi woman; B, Baluba woman; C, Babuende woman; D, Ubangi man; E, Weaver; F, Basketmaker; G, Archer; H, Potter; I, Rubber worker; J, Palm oil; K, African elephant.

55 Native Canoe

58 H. M. Stanley

1925. Great War Colonial Memorial Fund. Inscr in French or in Flemish.
141a **55** 25c.+25c. black and red 45 2·25

1927. No. 136 surch **1.75.**
144 1.75 on 1f. 50 blue 45 35

1928. 50th Anniv of Stanley's Exploration of the Congo.
145 **58** 5c. olive 10 10
146 10c. violet 10 10
147 20c. red 10 10
148 35c. green 85 95
149 40c. brown 45 40
150 60c. sepia 45 20
151 1f. red 40 10
152 1f.60 grey . . . . 4·75 5·00
153 1f.75 blue 85 55
154 2f. brown 70 40
155 2f.75 purple . . . . 3·25 35
156 3f.50 red . . . . 1·10 55
157 5f. turquoise 65 45
158 10f. blue 85 45
159 20f. red . . . . 6·50 4·00

59 Nurse weighing Children

60 Doctor and Tent Surgery

1930. Congo Natives Protection Fund.
160 **59** 10c.+5c. red . . . . 60 1·50
161 – 20c.+10c. brown . . . . 80 1·90
162 **60** 35c.+15c. green . . . . 1·90 3·00
163 – 60c.+30c. purple . . . . 1·75 3·00
164 – 1f.+50c. red . . . . . . 3·50 4·50
165 – 1f.75+75c. blue . . . . 4·75 8·00
166 – 3f.50+1f.50 red . . . . 7·25 17·00
167 – 5f.+2f.50 brown . . . . 9·00 13·00
168 – 10f.+5f. black . . . . . 11·00 18·00
DESIGNS—VERT: 20c. Missionary and child; 1f. Dispenser attending patients. HORIZ: 60c. View of local hospital; 1f.75, Nurses and patients; 3f.50, Nurse bathing baby; 5f. Operating theatre in local hospital; 10f. Children in school.

61 Native Kraal

1930. Air.
169 **61** 15f. black and sepia . . . 4·25 1·75
170 – 30f. black and purple . . . 5·75 3·75
DESIGN: 30f. Native porters.

1931. Surch.
171 40c. on 35c. grn (No. 148) . . 1·25 95
177 40c. on 35c. green (125) . . . 3·50 8·00
178 50c. on 45c. purple (142) . . . 1·90 1·25
172 1f.25 on 1f. red (151) . . . . 1·40 10
173 2f. on 1f.60 grey (152) . . . 80 25
174 2f. on 1f.75 blue (153) . . . 70 25
179 2f. on 1f.75 blue (137) . . . 7·25 9·50
175 3f.25 on 2f.75 purple (155) 2·25 1·60
180 3f.25 on 3f. brown (138) . . 6·25 7·50
176 3f.25 on 3f.50 red (156) . . . 4·25 6·00

67 Sankuru River

68 Flute Players

1931.
181 **67** 10c. brown 10 30
182 – 15c. grey 10 10
183 – 20c. mauve 15 35
184 – 25c. blue 35 10
185 **68** 40c. green 35 60
186 – 50c. violet 45 10
187 – 60c. purple 40 60
188 – 75c. red 40 15
189 – 1f. red 85 15
190 – 1f.25 brown 75 10
190b – 1f.50 black . . . . 1·00 65
191 – 2f. blue . . . . 1·00 30
191a – 2f.50 blue . . . . 1·25 1·00
192 – 3f.25 grey . . . . 1·25 1·25
193 – 4f. lilac 80 55
194 – 5f. purple . . . . 1·50 30
195 – 10f. orange . . . . 1·40 1·40
196 – 20f. sepia . . . . 2·40 2·10
DESIGNS—HORIZ: 15c., 25c. Native kraals (different views); 20c. Waterfall; 50c. Native musicians (seated); 1f.50, 2f., Riverside dwellings; 2f.50, 3f.25, Okapi; 4f. Canoes on river shore. VERT: 60c. Native musicians (standing); 75c. Mangbethu woman; 1f. Elephant transport; 1f.25., Native chief; 5f. Pressing out tapioca; 10f. Witch doctor; 20f. Woman carrying latex.

69 Fokker F.VIIb/3m over Congo

70 King Albert I

1934. Air.
197 **69** 50c. black 60 65
198 1f. red 85 30
199 1f.50 green 70 15
200 3f. brown 30 20
201 4f.50 blue 90 10
202 5f. red 95 10
203 15f. purple . . . . 2·10 85
204 30f. red . . . . 2·50 2·40
205 50f. violet . . . . 7·00 2·25

1934. Death of King Albert.
206 **70** 1f.50 black 90 55

71 The Kings of Belgium

1935. 50th Anniv of Independent State of the Congo.
207 **71** 50c. green . . . . 1·10 1·10
208 1f.25 red . . . . 1·10 15
209 1f.50 purple . . . . 1·10 15
210 2f.40 orange . . . . 2·75 3·25
211 2f.50 blue . . . . 2·75 1·75
212 4f. violet . . . . 3·00 1·90
213 5f. brown . . . . 3·00 3·25

1936. Air. Surch **3.50F.**
214 **69** 3f.50 on 3f. brown 25 10

1936. King Albert Memorial Fund. Surch **+ 50 c.**
215 **71** 1f.50+50c. purple . . . . 2·75 6·75
216 2f.50+50c. blue . . . . . 1·90 5·00

74 Queen Astrid and Congo Children

76 R. Molindi

75 Mitumba Forest

1936. Queen Astrid Fund for Congo Children.
217 **74** 1f.25+5c. brown . . . . . 70 1·25
218 1f.50+10c. red . . . . . 80 1·75
219 2f.50+25c. blue . . . . . 1·25 2·50

1937. Promotion of National Parks. (a) Sheet (140 × 111 mm) comprising block of four.
MS219a **75** 4f.50 black and red 3·75 6·25

(b) As T **76**.
220 **76** 5c. black and violet 10 15
221 – 90c. brown and red 55 75
222 – 1f.50 black and purple . . 35 20
223 – 2f.40 brown and grey . . . 20 30
224 – 2f.50 black and blue . . . 40 40
225 – 4f.50 brown and green . . 80 65
DESIGNS—VERT: 90c. Bamboo-canes; 1f.50, R. Suza; 2f.40, R. Rutshuru. HORIZ: 2f.50, Mt. Karisimbi; 4f.50, Mitumba Forest.

1938. Tourism Congress, Costermansville. Sheet 140 × 120 mm containing Nos. 220/5 but all printed in brown and blue.
MS225a 5c. to 4f.50 . . . . . . 24·00 27·00

77 Marabou Stork and Ruppels Griffon

1939. Leopoldville Zoological Gardens.
226 **77** 1f.+1f. purple . . . . . . 9·75 11·00
227 – 1f.25+1f.25 red . . . . . 8·50 11·00
228 – 1f.50+1f.50 violet . . . . 9·50 11·00
229 – 4f.50+4f.50 green . . . . 7·50 11·00
230 – 5f.+5f. brown . . . . . . 9·50 11·00
DESIGNS: 1f.25, Kob; 1f.50, Young chimpanzees; 4f.50, Crocodiles; 5f. Lioness.

78 King Albert Memorial, Leopoldville

81 "Belgium Shall Rise Again"

1941.
231 **78** 10c. grey . . . . 1·25 1·40
232 15c. brown 25 20
233 25c. blue 75 35
234 50c. lilac . . . . 1·25 30
235 75c. pink . . . . 1·60 50
236 1f.25 brown . . . . 1·10 35
237 1f.75 orange . . . . 3·00 3·00
238 2f.50 red . . . . 1·60 15
239 2f.75 blue . . . . 1·75 60
240 5f. olive . . . . 3·75 2·75
241 10f. red . . . . 4·00 2·75

1941. Surch.
242 – 5c. on 1f.50 black & purple (No. 222) (postage) . . . 15 1·10
243 **78** 75c. on 1f.75 orange . . . 1·75 2·25
244 – 2f.50 on 2f.40 brown and grey (No. 223) . . . . . 1·40 1·25
245 **69** 50c. on 1f.50 green (air) . . 90 80

1942. War Relief Fund.
246 **81** 10f.+40f. green . . . . . 2·25 2·40
247 10f.+40f. blue . . . . . 2·25 2·40

82 Oil Palms

84 Leopard

1942. (a) Inscr "BELGISCH CONGO BELGE".
248 **82** 5c. red 10 10
249 – 50f. black and blue . . . . 5·00 1·25
250 – 100f. black and red . . . . 8·75 1·60

(b) Inscr "CONGO BELGE BELGISCH CONGO", or vice versa.
251 **82** 10c. olive 10 10
252 15c. brown 10 20
253a 20c. blue 10 15
254 25c. purple 10 10
255a 30c. blue 20 10
256 50c. green 35 10
257 60c. brown 30 15
258 – 75c. black and violet . . . 50 10
259a – 1f. black and brown . . . 45 10
260 – 1f.25 black and red . . . 45 10
261 **84** 1f.75 brown . . . . 1·10 50
262 2f. yellow . . . . 1·25 10
263a 2f.50 red 80 10
264 – 3f.50 olive 60 10
265 – 5f. orange 95 10
266a – 6f. blue . . . . 1·00 10
267a – 7f. black . . . . 1·00 10
268 – 10f. brown 85 10
269a – 20f. black and red . . . . 7·00 9·50
DESIGNS—As Type **82**: 75c. to 1f.25, Head of a native woman; 3f.50 to 10f. Askari sentry. As Type **84**: 20f. Okapi; 28 × 33 mm: 50 f. Head of woman; 100f. Askari sentry.

1944. Red Cross Fund. Surch **Au profit de la Croix Rouge Ten voordeele van het Roode Kruis** (or with French and Flemish reversed) and additional value.
269aa **82** 50c.+50f. green . . . . 1·90 1·90
269b – 1f.25+100f. black and red (No. 260) . . . . 7·00 9·50
269c **84** 1f.75+100f. brown . . . 7·00 9·50
269d – 3f.50+100f. green (No. 264) . . . . . . 7·00 9·50

87 Driving Slaves to Market

88 Leopold II

1947. 50th Anniv of Abolition of Slavery in Belgian Congo.
270 **87** 1f.25 brown 40 15
270a – 1f.50 violet . . . . . . 2·25 85
270b – 3f. brown . . . . . . 2·10 10
271 – 3f.50 blue 30 10
272 **88** 10f. orange 60 20
PORTRAITS–As Type **88**: 1f.50, Lavigerie. 3f. Dhanis. 3f.50, Lambermont.

89 Seated Figure

90 Railway Train and Map

1947. Native masks and carvings as T **89**.
273 **89** 10c. orange 10 10
274 A 15c. blue 10 10
275 B 20c. blue 10 10
276 C 25c. red 20 10
277 D 40c. purple 20 10
278 **89** 50c. brown 55 10
279 A 70c. green 10 20
280 B 75c. purple 25 10
281 C 1f. purple and orange . . 1·50 10
281a A 1f.20 brown and grey . . 85 60
282 D 1f.25 purple and green . . 35 20
282a E 1f.50 red and green . . . 17·00 4·50
282b B 1f.60 blue and grey . . . 1·10 70
283 **89** 2f. red and orange . . . 80 10
283a C 2f.40 green and turquoise 1·00 20
284 A 2f.50 green and brown . . 45 10
284a E 3f. indigo and blue . . . 5·00 10
285 B 3f.50 green and blue . . . 4·00 20
286 C 5f. purple and bistre . . . 1·75 10
287 D 6f. green and orange . . . 1·60 10
287a F 6f.50 brown and red . . . 2·40 10
287b D 8f. green and blue . . . . 2·40 20
288 E 10f. brown and violet . . 12·50 10
289 F 20f. brown and red . . . 30 10
290 E 50f. black and brown . . . 4·25 25
291 F 100f. black and red . . . 6·50 85
DESIGNS: A, Seated figure (different); B, Kneeling figure; C, Double mask; D, Mask; E, Mask with tassels; F, Mask with horns.

1948. 50th Anniv of Matadi–Leopoldville Railway.
292 **90** 2f.50 green and blue . . . 1·50 25

91 Globe and 19th-century Full-rigged Ship

92 Allegorical Figure and Map

1949. 75th Anniv of U.P.U.

293	91	4f. blue	55	70

1950. 50th Anniv of "Comite Special du Katanga" (Chartered Company).

294	92	3f. slate and blue	1·90	1·25
295		6f.50 sepia and red	2·00	75

93 "Littonia"

94 St. Francis Xavier

1952. Flowers. Multicoloured.

296		10c. "Dissotis"	10	10
297		15c. "Protea"	10	10
298		20c. "Vellozia"	10	10
299		25c. Type 93	10	10
300		40c. "Ipomoea"	25	10
301		50c. "Angraecum"	25	10
302		60c. "Euphorbia"	30	20
303		75c. "Ochna"	30	10
304		1f. "Hibiscus"	55	10
305		1f.25 "Protea"	1·60	1·40
306		1f.50 "Schizoglossum"	45	10
307		2f. "Ansellia"	1·00	10
308		3f. "Costus"	95	10
309		4f. "Nymphaea"	1·25	10
310		5f. "Thunbergia"	1·60	10
311		6f.50 "Thonningia"	1·40	10
312		7f. "Gerbera"	1·60	10
313		8f. "Gloriosa"	2·75	30
314		10f. "Silene"	4·00	20
315		20f. "Aristolochia"	5·00	25
316		50f. "Eulophia"	12·50	1·00
317		100f. "Cryptosepalum"	14·50	2·50

SIZES: Nos. 296/315, 21 × 25½ mm. Nos. 316/17, 22½ × 32½ mm.

1953. 400th Death Anniv of St. Francis Xavier.

318	94	1f.50c. black and blue	1·60	50

95 Lake Kivu

1953. Kivu Festival.

319	95	3f. black and red	2·25	55
320		7f. brown and blue	2·50	30

96 Medallion

1954. 25th Anniv of Belgian Royal Colonial Institute. No. 322 has different frame.

321	96	4f.50 grey and blue	80	35
322		6f.50 brown and green	55	15

97 King Baudouin and Mountains

98 Badge and Map

1955. Inscr "CONGO BELGE . BELGISCH CONGO" or vice versa.

323	97	1f.50 black and red	9·00	1·90
324	–	3f. black and green	5·75	90
325	–	4f.50 black and blue	5·75	90
326	–	6f.50 black & purple	8·00	30

DESIGNS: 3f. Forest; 4f.50, River; 6f.50, Grassland.

1955. 5th Int Congress of African Tourism. Inscr in Flemish or French.

327	98	6f.50 blue	2·50	1·40

1956. Birth Bicentenary of Mozart. As T 316/17 of Belgium.

328	316	4f.50+1f.50 violet	4·75	5·00
329	317	6f.50+2f.50 blue	7·00	6·50

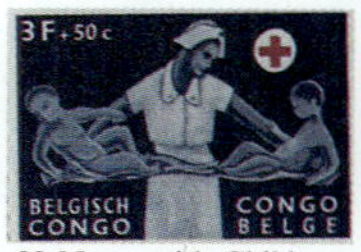

99 Nurse with Children

101 Roan Antelope

100 Belgian Monarchs

1957. Red Cross Fund. Cross in red.

330	99	3f.+50c. blue	2·10	2·25
331	–	4f.50+50c. green	2·40	2·40
332	–	6f.50+50c. brown	2·25	2·40

DESIGNS—HORIZ: 4f.50, Doctor inoculating patient; 6f.50, Nurse in tropical kit bandaging patient.

1958. 50th Anniv of Belgian Annexation of the Congo.

333	100	1f. red	40	10
334		1f.50 blue	45	10
335		3f. red	95	10
336		5f. green	1·60	60
337		6f.50 brown	1·40	25
338		10f. violet	1·40	55

1959. Wild Animals.

339	101	10c. brown, sepia & blue	10	40
340	–	20c. blue and red	10	70
341	–	40c. brown and blue	25	85
342	–	50c. multicoloured	50	60
343	–	1f. black, green & brown	55	45
344	–	1f.50 black and yellow	80	40
345	–	2f. black, brown and red	1·00	55
346	–	3f. black, purple & slate	1·00	55
347	–	5f. brown, green & sepia	1·25	50
348	–	6f.50 brn, yellow & blue	1·10	55
349	–	8f. bistre, violet & brown	1·40	80
350	–	10f. multicoloured	1·50	1·25

DESIGNS—HORIZ: 20c. White rhinoceros; 50c. Demidoff's galago; 1f.50, African buffaloes; 3f. African elephants; 6f.50, Impala; 10f. Eland and common zebras. VERT: 40c. Giraffe; 1f. Gorilla; 2f. Eastern Black and White Colobus monkey; 5f. Okapis; 8f. Giant ground pangolin.

102 Madonna and Child

103 "African Resources"

1959. Christmas.

351	102	50c. brn, ochre & chestnut	15	20
352		1f. brown, violet & blue	10	15
353		2f. brown, blue and grey	20	25

1960. 10th Anniv of African Technical Co-operation Commission. Inscr in French or Flemish.

354	103	3f. orange and grey	75	1·25

104 High Jumping

1960. Child Welfare Fund.

355	104	50c.+25c. blue and red	55	1·10
356	–	1f.50+50c. red & green	85	1·10
357	–	2f.+1f. green and red	90	1·25
358	–	3f.+1f.25 purple & bl	1·40	1·75
359	–	6f.50+3f.50 brn & red	1·60	2·25

DESIGNS: 1f.50, Hurdling; 2f. Football; 3f. Throwing the javelin; 6f.60, Throwing the discus.

POSTAGE DUE STAMPS

D 54

D 86

1923.

D141	D 54	5c. sepia	10	65
D142a		10c. red	10	60
D143		15c. violet	15	60
D144		30c. green	25	30
D145		50c. blue	35	45
D146		1f. grey	40	40

1943.

D270a	D 86	10c. olive	30	75
D271a		20c. blue	25	70
D272a		50c. green	30	55
D273a		1f. brown	25	65
D274a		2f. orange	30	50

D 99

1957.

D330	D 99	10c. brown	60	1·00
D331		20c. purple	70	1·00
D332		50c. green	1·00	1·00
D333		1f. blue	1·10	1·10
D334		2f. red	1·40	1·50
D335		4f. violet	1·50	1·75
D336		6f. blue	1·90	2·00

For later issues see **CONGO (KINSHASA), ZAIRE REPUBLIC** and **DEMOCRATIC REPUBLIC OF CONGO**.

BELGIAN OCCUPATION OF GERMANY Pt. 7

Stamps used in German territory occupied by Belgian Forces at the end of the War of 1914/18, and including the districts of Eupen and Malmedy, now incorporated in Belgium.

100 centimes = 1 Belgian franc.

1919. Stamps of Belgium optd **ALLEMAGNE DUITSCHLAND**.

1	51	1c. orange	35	55
2		2c. brown	35	55
3		3c. grey	35	2·20
4		5c. green	70	1·10
5		10c. red	1·30	2·20
6		15c. violet	70	1·10
7		20c. purple	1·10	1·30
8		25c. blue	1·30	1·80
9	63	25c. blue	4·50	9·75
10	52	35c. black and brown	1·30	1·30
11	–	40c. black and green	1·30	2·20
12	–	50c. black and red	6·50	10·50
13	–	65c. black and red	3·50	12·50
14	55	1f. violet	25·00	22·00
15	–	2f. grey	44·00	40·00
16	–	5f. blue (FRANK, No. 194)	9·75	10·50
17	–	10f. sepia	55·00	55·00

1920. Stamps of Belgium surch **EUPEN & MALMEDY** and value.

18	51	5pf. on 5c. green	25	25
19		10pf. on 10c. red	25	25
20		15pf. on 15c. violet	35	35
21		20pf. on 20c. purple	60	60
22		30pf. on 25c. blue	45	60
23	–	75pf. on 50c. black and red	18·00	18·00
24	55	1m.25 on 1f. violet	25·00	25·00

1920. Stamps of Belgium optd **Eupen**.

25	51	1c. orange	45	45
26		2c. brown	45	45
27		3c. grey	65	1·80
28		5c. green	65	1·10
29		10c. red	1·10	1·50
30		15c. violet	1·50	1·50
31		20c. purple	1·80	1·80
32		25c. blue	1·50	2·20
33	63	25c. blue	5·25	11·50
34	52	35c. black and brown	2·20	2·20
35	–	40c. black and green	2·75	2·75
36	–	50c. black and red	7·50	8·75
37	–	65c. black and red	4·00	13·00
38	55	1f. violet	29·00	22·00
39	–	2f. grey	48·00	35·00
40	–	5f. blue (FRANK, No. 194)	16·00	13·00
41	–	10f. sepia	65·00	55·00

1920. Stamps of Belgium optd **Malmedy**.

42	51	1c. orange	30	45
43		2c. brown	30	45
44		3c. grey	55	1·80
45		5c. green	75	1·10
46		10c. red	1·10	1·50
47		15c. violet	1·80	1·80
48		20c. purple	2·20	2·20
49		25c. blue	5·25	10·50
50	63	25c. blue	2·20	2·75
51	52	35c. black and brown	2·20	2·75
52	–	40c. black and green	8·75	8·75
53	–	50c. black and red	4·00	13·00
54	–	65c. black and red	4·00	13·00
55	55	1f. violet	29·00	19·00
56	–	2f. grey	48·00	35·00
57	–	5f. blue (FRANK, No. 194)	19·00	20·00
58	–	10f. sepia	65·00	65·00

POSTAGE DUE STAMPS

1920. Postage Due stamps of Belgium, 1919. (a) Optd **Eupen**.

D1		5c. green	1·10	1·30
D2		10c. red	2·20	1·30
D3		20c. green	4·50	5·25
D4		30c. blue	4·50	5·25
D5		50c. grey	22·00	18·00

(b) Optd **Malmedy**.

D 6		5c. green	2·20	1·30
D 7		10c. red	4·50	2·20
D 8		20c. green	16·00	13·00
D 9		30c. blue	8·75	9·75
D10		50c. grey	18·00	13·00

BELGIUM Pt. 4

An independent Kingdom of N.W. Europe.

1849. 100 centimes = 1 franc.
2002. 100 cents = 1 euro.

1 "Epaulettes"

3 "Medallions"

1849. Imperf.

1	1	10c. brown	£2000	75·00
2a		20c. blue	£2250	47·00

1861. Imperf.

12	3	1c. green	£150	£120
13		10c. brown	£325	9·75
14		20c. blue	£350	8·50
15		40c. red	£2500	75·00

1863. Perf.

24	3	1c. green	35·00	29·00
25		10c. brown	42·00	4·00
26		20c. blue	44·00	3·50
27		40c. red	£250	27·00

5

8

10 "Small Lion"

1865. Various frames.

34	5	10c. grey	90·00	1·90
35		20c. blue	£150	2·00
36		30c. brown	£350	9·50
37	8	40c. red	£400	18·00
38	5	1f. lilac	£1000	85·00

1866.

43	10	1c. grey	50·00	12·00
44		2c. blue	£160	85·00
45		5c. brown	£200	75·00

11

13

14

15

20

Types 13 to 20 and all later portraits to Type 38 are of Leopold II.

1869. Various frames.

46	11	1c. green	10·00	45
59a		2c. blue	23·00	3·50
60		5c. buff	65·00	1·00
49		8c. lilac	80·00	49·00
50	13	10c. green	33·00	40
51b	14	20c. blue	£150	1·20
62	15	25c. bistre	£120	3·00
53a	13	30c. buff	95·00	3·50
54b		40c. red	£140	7·50
55a	15	50c. grey	£250	10·50
56	13	1f. mauve	£475	15·00
57a	20	5f. brown	£4500	£1600

21

25

1883. Various frames.

63	21	10c. red	30·00	2·50
64	–	20c. grey	£225	9·50
65	–	25c. blue	£425	33·00
66	–	50c. violet	£400	33·00

1884. Various frames.

67	11	1c. olive	19·00	65
68		1c. grey	5·00	40
69		2c. brown	16·00	80
70		5c. green	45·00	40
71	25	10c. red	15·00	40
72	–	20c. olive	£225	1·60
73	–	25c. blue on red	20·00	90
74	–	35c. brown	22·00	2·50
75	–	50c. bistre	15·00	2·00
76	–	1f. brown on green	£900	14·00
77	–	2f. lilac	70·00	32·00

32

33

34 Arms of Antwerp

1893.

78a	32	1c. grey	75	25
79		2c. yellow	75	1·00
80		2c. brown	2·00	40
81		5c. green	11·00	55
82	33	10c. brown	3·25	30
83		10c. red	2·75	45
84		20c. olive	18·00	65
85		25c. blue	12·00	40
86a		35c. brown	25·00	1·70
87		50c. brown	65·00	18·00
88		50c. grey	75·00	2·75
89		1f. red on green	95·00	21·00
90		1f. orange	£120	6·25
91		2f. mauve	80·00	55·00

The prices for the above and all following issues with the tablet are for stamps with the tablet attached. Without tablet, the prices will be about half those quoted.

See also Nos. 106/8.

1894. Antwerp Exhibition.

93	34	5c. green on red	6·00	3·50
94		10c. red on blue	3·00	2·30
95		25c. blue on red	1·00	85

35 St. Michael encountering Satan

36

1896. Brussels Exhibition of 1897.

96	35	5c. violet	75	65
97	36	10c. red	7·50	3·75
98		10c. brown	25	25

37

38

40 St. Martin and the Beggar (from altarpiece by Van Dyck)

1905. Various frames.

99	37	10c. red	1·50	60
100		20c. olive	34·00	1·00
101		25c. blue	15·00	85
102		35c. purple	35·00	2·30
103	38	50c. grey	£120	2·10
104		1f. orange	£160	9·50
105		2f. mauve	£110	21·00

1907. As T **32** but no scroll pattern between stamps and labels.

106	1c. grey	1·80	25
107	2c. red	20·00	6·50
108	5c. green	17·00	65

1910. Brussels Exhibition. A. Unshaded background. B. Shaded background. A.

109	40	1c. (+1c.) grey	1·00	1·00
110		2c. (+2c.) purple	11·00	9·75
111		5c. (+5c.) green	3·00	2·50
112		10c. (+5c.) red	3·00	2·50

B.

113	40	1c. (+1c.) green	3·00	2·50
114		2c. (+2c.) purple	8·00	6·75
115		5c. (+5c.) green	3·00	2·50
116		10c. (+5c.) red	3·00	2·50

1911. Nos. 109/16 optd **1911.** A.

117	40	1c. (+1c.) grey	36·00	24·00
118		2c. (+2c.) purple	£180	65·00
119		5c. (+5c.) green	11·00	9·75
120		10c. (+5c.) red	11·00	9·75

B.

121	40	1c. (+1c.) green	55·00	34·00
122		2c. (+2c.) purple	85·00	31·00
123		5c. (+5c.) green	11·00	10·00
124		10c. (+5c.) red	11·00	10·00

1911. Charleroi Exhibition. Nos. 109/16 optd **CHARLEROI–1911.** A.

125	40	1c. (+1c.) grey	7·00	3·25
126		2c. (+2c.) purple	18·00	14·50
127		5c. (+5c.) green	10·00	9·50
128		10c. (+5c.) red	10·00	9·50

B.

129	40	1c. (+1c.) green	7·00	3·75
130		2c. (+2c.) purple	18·00	12·00
131		5c. (+5c.) green	10·00	9·25
132		10c. (+5c.) red	10·00	9·25

42

43

44

45 Albert I

46 (Larger head)

1912.

133	42	1c. orange	20	15
134	43	2c. brown	30	30
135	44	5c. green	20	15
136	45	10c. red	60	45
137		20c. olive	19·00	4·50
138		35c. brown	1·00	80
139		40c. green	20·00	16·00
140		50c. grey	1·00	85
141		1f. orange	4·25	3·25
142		2f. violet	22·00	20·00
143	–	5f. purple	£100	28·00

The 5f. is as Type **45** but larger (23 × 35 mm).

1912. Large head.

148	46	10c. red	20	25
145		20c. olive	30	50
150		25c. blue	30	30
147		40c. green	65	60

47 Merode Monument

48 Albert I

1914. Red Cross.

151	47	5c. (+5c.) red & green	4·00	3·75
152		10c. (+10c.) red & pink	6·00	5·75
153		20c. (+20c.) red & vio	65·00	55·00

1914. Red Cross.

154	48	5c. (+5c.) red and green	5·00	4·50
155		10c. (+10c.) red	50	50
156		20c. (+20c.) red & violet	16·00	13·50

49 Albert I

1915. Red Cross.

157	49	5c. (+5c.) red and green	11·00	2·30
158		10c. (+10c.) red and pink	32·00	12·50
159		20c. (+20c.) red & violet	60·00	18·00

51 Albert I

52 Cloth Hall, Ypres

55 Freeing of the Scheldt

1915.

170	51	1c. orange	20	15
171		2c. brown	20	15
179		3c. grey	40	30
172		5c. green	1·30	15
173		10c. red	1·20	15
174		15c. violet	1·90	30
187		20c. purple	3·00	30
176		25c. blue	50	40
188	52	35c. black and brown	50	30
189	–	40c. black and green	50	30
190	–	50c. black and red	5·50	30
191	55	1f. violet	42·00	1·00
192	–	2f. grey	27·00	2·20
193	–	5f. blue (FRANKEN)	£450	£140
194	–	5f. blue (FRANK)	1·50	1·20
195	–	10f. brown	24·00	22·00

DESIGNS: As T **52**: 40c. Dinant; 50c. Louvain. As T **55**: 2f. Annexation of the Congo; 5f. King Albert at Furnes; 10f. The Kings of Belgium.

1918. Red Cross. Surch with new value and cross. Some colours changed.

222	51	1c.+1c. orange	25	25
223		2c.+2c. brown	25	30
224		5c.+5c. green	1·50	1·10
225		10c.+10c. red	3·00	2·40
226		15c.+15c. purple	6·00	5·50
227		20c.+20c. brown	12·50	10·50
228		25c.+25c. blue	25·00	22·00
229	52	35c.+35c. black & violet	12·00	11·00
230	–	40c.+40c. black & brown	12·00	11·00
231	–	50c.+50c. black and blue	12·50	11·50
232	55	1f.+1f. grey	40·00	36·00
233	–	2f.+2f. green	85·00	75·00
234	–	5f.+5f. brn (FRANKEN)	£225	£180
235	–	10f.+10f. blue	£750	£550

63 "Perron" at Liege

64 Albert I

1919.

236a	63	25c. blue	3·00	45

1919.

237	64	1c. brown	20	25
238		2c. olive	20	25
239		5c. green	20	25
240		10c. red	30	30
241		15c. violet	40	40
242		20c. sepia	1·50	1·30
243		25c. blue	2·00	1·70
244		35c. brown	2·20	2·40
245		40c. red	8·00	7·25
246		50c. brown	13·00	12·00
247		1f. orange	55·00	46·00
248		2f. purple	£475	£350
249		5f. red	£110	90·00
250		10f. red	£150	£130

SIZES: 1c., 2c., 18½ × 21½ mm. 5c. to 2f., 22½ × 26½ mm. 5f., 10f., 27½ × 33 mm.

67 Discus thrower

68 Charioteer

1920. Olympic Games, Antwerp.

256	67	5c. (+5c.) green	2·30	1·90
257	68	10c. (+5c.) red	1·80	1·50
258	–	15c. (+5c.) brown	2·50	1·70

DESIGN—VERT: 15c. Runner.

73 Hotel de Ville, Termonde

76 Albert I

1920.

308b	73	65c. black and purple	75	35

1921. Nos. 256/8 surch **20c. 20c.**

309	67	20c. on 5c. green	75	30
310	68	20c. on 10c. red	50	30
311	–	20c. on 15c. brown	75	30

1921.

313	76	50c. blue	25	15
314		75c. red	35	30
315		75c. blue	45	20
316		1f. sepia	50	15
317		1f. blue	45	25
318		2f. green	1·00	25
319		5f. purple	16·00	15·00
320		5f. brown	10·50	11·00
321		10f. red	11·00	8·75

1921. Surch **55c 55c.**

322	73	55c. on 65c. black & pur	3·00	40

80

81 Albert I

1922. War Invalids Fund.

348	80	20c.+20c. brown	1·50	1·40

1922.

349	81	1c. orange	10	15
350		2c. olive	30	30
351		3c. brown	10	15
352		5c. slate	10	10
353		10c. green	20	20
354		15c. plum	20	20
355		20c. brown	20	20
356		25c. purple	25	30
357		25c. violet	50	20
358		30c. red	40	15
359		30c. mauve	30	15
360		35c. brown	40	35
361		35c. green	1·30	35
362		40c. red	50	25
363		50c. bistre	55	25
364		60c. olive	3·75	15
365		75c. violet	1·10	75
366		1f. yellow	50	45
367		1f. red	1·30	30
368		1f.25 blue	1·50	1·30
369		1f.50 blue	2·50	45
370		1f.75 blue	1·80	20
371		2f. blue	3·75	45
372		5f. green	50·00	2·10
373		10f. brown	90·00	9·00

83 Wounded Soldier

1923. War Invalids Fund.

374	83	20c.+20c. slate	2·50	2·20

87 Leopold I and Albert I

1925. 75th Anniv of 1st Belgian Stamps.

410	87	10c. green	9·50	8·50
411		15c. violet	4·00	4·75
412		20c. brown	4·00	4·75
413		25c. slate	4·00	3·75
414		30c. red	4·00	3·75
415		35c. blue	4·00	3·75
416		40c. sepia	4·00	3·75
417		50c. brown	4·00	3·75
418		75c. blue	4·00	3·75
419		1f. purple	8·00	7·25
420		2f. blue	5·00	4·50
421		5f. black	4·00	3·75
422		10f. red	8·50	7·50

88

90

1925. Anti-T.B. Fund.

423	88	15c.+5c. red and mauve	30	30
424		30c.+5c. red and grey	30	20
425		1f.+10c. red and blue	1·30	1·50

1926. Flood Relief. Type of 1922 surch **Inondations 30 c Watersnood.**

426	81	30c.+30c. green	1·00	85

1926. Flood Relief Fund. A. Shaded background. B. Solid background. A.

427	90	1f.+1f. blue	6·50	7·25

B.

428	90	1f.+1f. blue	1·50	1·30

91

92 Queen Elisabeth and King Albert

1926. War Tuberculosis Fund.

429	91	5c.+5c. brown	10	20
430		20c.+5c. brown	50	60
431		50c.+5c. violet	30	30
432	92	1f.50+25c. blue	70	70
433		5f.+1f. red	6·50	6·25

1927. Stamps of 1922 surch.

434	81	3c. on 2c. olive	20	15
435		10c. on 15c. plum	20	15
436		35c. on 40c. red	30	15
437		1f.75 on 1f.50 blue	1·40	85

94 Rowing Boat

1927. Anti-T.B. Fund.

438	94	25c.+10c. brown	1·00	95
439		35c.+10c. green	1·00	90
440		60c.+10c. violet	30	25
441		1f.75+25c. blue	1·30	1·20
442		5f.+1f. purple	4·50	4·25

96 Ogives

97 Ruins of Orval Abbey

1928. Orval Abbey Restoration Fund. Inscr "ORVAL 1928" or "ORVAL".

461	96	5c.+5c. red and gold	25	30
462	–	25c.+5c. violet and gold	40	40
463	–	35c.+10c. green	1·10	90
464	–	60c.+15c. brown	75	30
465	–	1f.75+25c. blue	3·00	2·20
466	–	2f.+40c. purple	25·00	18·00
467	–	3f.+1f. red	23·00	17·00
468	97	5f.+5f. lake	16·00	13·00
469	–	10f.+10f. sepia	16·00	13·00

DESIGNS—VERT: 35c., 2f. Cistercian monk stone-carving; 60c., 1f.75, 3f. Duchess Matilda retrieving her ring.

99 Mons Cathedral

101 Malines Cathedral

1928. Anti-T.B. Fund.

472	99	5c.+5c. red	30	25
473	–	25c.+15c. sepia	30	30
474	101	35c.+10c. green	1·30	1·30
475	–	60c.+15c. brown	50	45
476	–	1f.75+25c. violet	9·00	8·50
477	–	5f.+5f. purple	24·00	21·00

DESIGNS—As Type **99**: 25c. Tournai Cathedral. As Type **101**: 60c. Ghent Cathedral; 1f.75, St. Gudule Cathedral, Brussels; 5f. Louvain Library.

1929. Surch **BRUXELLES 1929 BRUSSEL 5 c** in frame.

478	81	5c. on 30c. mauve	20	15
479		5c. on 75c. violet	30	20
480		5c. on 1f.25c. blue	15	15

The above cancellation, whilst altering the original face value of the stamps, also constitutes a precancel, although stamps also come with additional ordinary postmark. The unused prices are for stamps with full gum and the used prices are for stamps without gum, with or without postmarks. We do not list precancels where there is no change in face value.

104 The Belgian Lion

105 Albert I

1929.

487	104	1c. orange	10	15
488		2c. green	50	55
489		3c. brown	10	15
490		5c. green	10	10
491		10c. bistre	10	10
492		20c. mauve	1·20	35
493		25c. red	50	15
494		35c. green	60	15
495		40c. purple	40	15
496		50c. blue	40	15
497		60c. mauve	2·50	30
498		70c. brown	1·50	15
499		75c. blue	2·50	15
500		75c. brown	7·25	15
501	105	10f. brown	20·00	4·25
502		20f. green	£100	23·00
503a		50f. purple	25·00	19·00
504a		100f. red	30·00	29·00

1929. Laying of first Stone towards Restoration of Orval Abbey. Nos. 461/9 optd with crown over ornamental letter "L" and **19-8-29**.

543	5c.+5c. red and gold	90·00	80·00
544	25c.+5c. violet and gold	90·00	80·00
545	35c.+10c. green	90·00	80·00
546	60c.+15c. brown	90·00	80·00
547	1f.75c.+25c. blue	90·00	80·00
548	2f.+40c. purple	£100	90·00
549	3f.+1f. red	90·00	80·00
550	5f.+5f. lake	90·00	80·00
551	10f.+10f. sepia	90·00	80·00

109 Canal and Belfry, Bruges

1929. Anti-T.B. Fund.

552	–	5c.+5c. brown	25	30
553	–	25c.+15c. grey	1·80	1·60
554	–	35c.+10c. green	1·50	1·20
555	–	60c.+15c. lake	50	45
556	–	1f.75+25c. blue	7·50	6·50
557	109	5f.+5f. purple	36·00	31·00

DESIGNS—HORIZ: 5c. Waterfall at Coo; 35c. Menin Gate, Ypres; 60c. Promenade d'Orleans, Spa; 1f.75, "Aquitania" and "Dinteldyk" (liners), Antwerp Harbour. VERT: 25c. Bayard Rock, Dinant.

110 Paul Rubens

111 Zenobe Gramme

1930. Antwerp and Liege Exns.

558	110	35c. green	50	20
559	111	35c. green	50	20

112 Ostend

113 "Leopold II" by Jef Lempoels

1930. Air.

560	112	50c. blue	50	25
561	–	1f.50 brown (St. Hubert)	3·00	2·50
562	–	2f. green (Namur)	2·00	90
563	–	5f. red (Brussels)	2·00	1·20
564	–	5f. violet (Brussels)	33·00	31·00

1930. Centenary of Independence.

565	–	60c. purple	30	25
566	113	1f. red	1·00	75
567	–	1f.75 blue	2·50	1·50

PORTRAITS: 60c. "Leopold I" by Lievin de Winne. 1f.75, King Albert I.

114 Antwerp City Arms

1930. International Philatelic Exhibition, Antwerp. Sheet 138 × 136 mm.

MS568	114	4f. (+6f.) green	£325	£300

1930. I.L.O. Congress. Nos. 565/7 optd **B.I.T. OCT. 1930.**

569	60c. purple	2·50	2·40
570	1f. red	10·00	8·50
571	1f.75 blue	18·00	17·00

116 Wynendaele

117 Gaesbeek

1930. Anti-T.B. Fund.

572	–	10c.+5c. mauve	40	35
573	116	25c.+15c. sepia	1·10	95
574	–	40c.+10c. purple	1·00	90
575	–	70c.+15c. slate	1·00	90
576	–	1f.+25c. red	8·50	6·25
577	–	1f.75+25c. blue	5·50	4·75
578	117	5f.+5f. green	43·00	39·00

DESIGNS: 10c. Bornhem; 40c. Beloeil; 70c. Oydonck, 1f. Ghent; 1f.75, Bouillon.

1931. Surch **2c.**

579	104	2c. on 3c. brown	15	20

1931. Surch **BELGIQUE 1931 BELGIE 10c.**

580	104	10c. on 60c. mauve	60	25

See note below No. 480.

121 Albert I

123

1931.

582	121	75c. brown (18 × 22 mm)	1·50	15
583		1f. lake (21 × 23½ mm)	30	25
584	123	1f.25 black	70	60
585		1f.50 purple	1·50	60
586		1f.75 blue	50	15
587		2f. brown	1·00	25
588		2f.45 violet	3·00	45
589		2f.50 sepia	11·50	60
590		5f. green	32·00	1·20
591		10f. red	60·00	14·50

See also No. 654.

124 Prince Leopold

1931. Disabled Soldiers' Relief Fund. Brussels National Philatelic Exhibition. Sheet 123 × 161 mm.

MS592	124	2f.45+55c. red (sold at 5f.)	£225	£200

125 Queen Elisabeth

126 Reaper

127 Mercury

1931. Anti-Tuberculosis Fund.

593	125	10c.+5c. brown	30	30
594		25c.+15c. violet	1·30	75
595		50c.+10c. green	75	60
596		75c.+15c. sepia	50	30
597		1f.+25c. lake	10·00	7·75
598		1f.75+25c. blue	7·25	4·50
599		5f.+5f. purple	65·00	55·00

1932. Surch **BELGIQUE 1932 BELGIE 10c.**

600	104	10c. on 40c. mauve	3·50	35
601		10c. on 70c. brown	3·50	30

See Note below No. 480.

1932.

602	126	2c. green	45	45
603	127	5c. red	15	15
604	126	10c. green	20	15
605	127	20c. lilac	1·30	30
606	126	25c. red	75	15
607	127	35c. green	3·00	15

129 Cardinal Mercier

132

1932. Cardinal Mercier Memorial Fund.

609	129	10c.+10c. purple	50	45
610		50c.+30c. mauve	2·50	2·40
611		75c.+25c. brown	2·50	2·30
612		1f.+2f. red	9·50	7·50
613	–	1f.75+75c. blue	75·00	75·00
614	–	2f.50+2f.50 brown	75·00	75·00
615	–	3f.+4f.50 green	75·00	75·00
616	–	5f.+20f. purple	£100	£100
617	–	10f.+40f. red	£200	£180

DESIGNS: 1f.75, 3f. Mercier protecting refugees at Malines; 2f.50, 5f. Mercier with busts of Aristotle and Thomas Aquinas; 10f. Mercier when Professor at Louvain University.

1932. Infantry Memorial.

618	132	75c.+3f.25 red	80·00	80·00
619		1f.75+4f.25 blue	80·00	80·00

133 Prof Piccard's Stratosphere Balloon "F.N.R.S.", 1931

134 Hulpe-Waterloo Sanatorium

1932. Scientific Research Fund.

621	133	75c. brown	3·00	25
622		1f.75 blue	17·00	2·10
623		2f.50 violet	20·00	14·00

1932. Anti-T.B. Fund.

624	134	10c.+5c. violet	30	30
625		25c.+15c. mauve	2·75	1·40
626		50c.+10c. red	2·50	75
627		75c.+15c. brown	1·50	30
628		1f.+25c. red	17·00	11·00
629		1f.75+25c. blue	11·00	9·00
630		5f.+5f. green	95·00	85·00

1933. Lion type surch **BELGIQUE 1933 BELGIE 10c.**

631	104	10c. on 40c. mauve	18·00	3·75
632		10c. on 70c. brown	16·00	1·30

See note below No. 480.

135 The Transept

138 Anti-T.B. Symbol

1933. Orval Abbey Restoration Fund. Inscr "ORVAL".

633	–	5c.+5c. green	65·00	60·00
634	–	10c.+15c. green	65·00	60·00
635	–	25c.+15c. brown	48·00	44·00
636	135	50c.+25c. lake	48·00	44·00
637	–	75c.+50c. green	48·00	44·00
638	–	1f.+1f.25 lake	48·00	44·00
639	–	1f.25+1f.75 sepia	48·00	44·00
640	–	1f.75+2f.75 blue	75·00	75·00
641	–	2f.+3f. mauve	75·00	75·00
642	–	2f.50+5f. brown	75·00	75·00
643	–	5f.+20f. purple	75·00	75·00
644	–	10f.+40f. blue	£300	£300

DESIGNS—VERT: 10c. Abbey Ruins; 75c. Belfry, new abbey; 1f. Fountain, new abbey. HORIZ: 5c. The old abbey; 25c. Guests' Courtyard, new abbey; 1f.25, Cloister, new abbey; 1f.75, Foundation of Orval Abbey in 1131; 2f. Restoration of the abbey, XVI and XVII centuries; 2f.50, Orval Abbey, XVIII century; 5f. Prince Leopold laying foundation stone of new abbey; 10f. The Virgin Mary (30 × 45 mm).

1933. Anti-tuberculosis Fund.

646	138	10c.+5c. grey	75	65
647		25c.+15c. mauve	3·25	3·00
648		50c.+10c. brown	2·50	2·20
649		75c.+15c. sepia	55·00	45
650		1f.+25c. red	20·00	17·00
651		1f.75+25c. blue	31·00	26·00
652		5f.+5f. purple	£140	£120

1934. Lion type surch **BELGIQUE 1934 BELGIE 10c.**

653	104	10c. on 40c. mauve	16·00	1·30

See note below No. 480.

1934. King Albert's Mourning Stamp.

654	121	75c. black	25	15

140 Peter Benoit

141 Brussels Palace

1934. Benoit Centenary Memorial Fund.

658	140	75c.+25c. brown	6·00	5·50

1934. International Exhibition, Brussels.

659	–	35c. green	75	35
660	141	1f. red	1·30	45
661	–	1f.50 brown	6·00	95
662	–	1f.75 blue	6·00	35

DESIGNS: 35c. Congo Palace; 1f.50, Old Brussels; 1f.75, Grand Palace of the Belgian section.

142 King Leopold III

143 King Leopold III

1934. War Invalids' Fund. (a) Size 18 × 22 mm. (b) Size 21 × 24 mm. (i) Exhibition Issue.

663	142	75c.+25c. green (a)	22·00	20·00
664		1f.+25c. purple (b)	22·00	18·00

(ii) Ordinary postage stamps.

665	142	75c.+25c. purple (a)	4·50	4·25
666		1f.+25c. red (b)	9·00	8·75

1934.

667	142	70c. green	40	15
668		75c. brown	60	30
669	143	1f. red	3·00	35

144 Health Crusader

1934. Anti-tuberculosis Fund. Cross in red.

670	144	10c.+5c. black	20	30
671		25c.+15c. brown	3·75	3·75
672		50c.+10c. green	2·30	2·00
673		75c.+15c. purple	1·30	1·10
674		1f.+25c. red	12·50	12·00
675		1f.75+25c. blue	10·00	9·25
676		5f.+5f. purple	£130	£120

145 The Royal Children

1935. Queen Astrid's Appeal.

680	145	35c.+15c. green	1·00	90
681		70c.+30c. purple	1·00	90
682		1f.75+50c. blue	5·00	4·25

146 "Mail-diligence"

1935. Brussels Int Exn.

683	146	10c.+10c. olive	50	60
684		25c.+25c. brown	2·30	2·00
685		35c.+25c. green	4·00	3·75

1935. Air. Surch with new value twice.

686	112	1f. on 1f.50 brown	50	50
687		4f. on 5f. red	9·50	8·75

148 Francis of Taxis

151 Queen Astrid

1935. Brussels Philatelic Exhibition (SITEB). Sheet 93 × 118 mm.

MS688	148	5f.+5f. grey	£200	£130

1935. Death of Queen Astrid. Mourning Stamp.

713	151	70c.+5c. black	20	30

1935. Anti-tuberculosis Fund. Black borders.

714	151	10c.+5c. olive	20	25
715		25c.+15c. brown	40	35
716		35c.+5c. green	30	30
717		50c.+10c. mauve	50	45
718		1f. +25c. red	1·30	1·10
719		1f.75+25c. blue	1·80	1·70
720		2f.45+55c. violet	3·50	3·25

152 State arms

153

155 King Leopold III

1936.

727	152	2c. green	10	15
728		5c. orange	10	10
729		10c. olive	10	10
730		15c. blue	10	10
731		20c. violet	10	10
732		25c. red	10	10
733		25c. yellow	10	10
734		30c. brown	10	10
735		35c. green	10	10
736		40c. lilac	20	10
737		50c. blue	50	15
738		60c. grey	20	15
739		65c. mauve	1·30	35
740		70c. green	30	30
741		75c. mauve	40	30
742		80c. green	4·75	45
743		90c. violet	30	15
744		1f. brown	40	15

1936. Various frames. (a) Size $17\frac{1}{2}$ × 22 mm.

745	153	70c. brown	25	15
746		75c. olive	25	15
747		1f. red	10	15

(b) Size 21 × 24 mm.

748	153	1f. red	30	15
749		1f.20 brown	2·30	20
750		1f.50 mauve	70	60
751		1f.75 blue	30	30
752		1f.75 red	25	15
753		2f. violet	2·00	1·70
754		2f.25 black	30	30
755		2f.50 red	9·00	35
756		3f.25 brown	30	30
757		5f. green	2·00	50

Nos. 746/7, 751/2, 754/5 and 757 are inscribed "BELGIE BELGIQUE".

1936.

760	155	1f.50 mauve	75	45
761		1f.75 blue	30	15
762		2f. violet	50	30
763		2f.25 violet	35	25
764		2f.45 black	50·00	75
765		2f.50 black	4·00	25
770		3f. brown	1·80	20
766		3f.25 brown	35	20
771		4f. blue	4·25	15
767		5f. green	3·00	60
772		6f. red	16·00	35
768		10f. purple	50	30
769		20f. red	1·00	45

See also No. 2775.

156 Borgerhout Town Hall

1936. Borgerhout Philatelic Exhibition. Sheet 95 × 119 mm.

MS775	156	70c.+30c. brown	90·00	70·00

157 Charleroi Town Hall

1936. Charleroi Philatelic Exhibition. Sheet 95 × 119 mm.

MS776	157	2f.45+55c. blue	65·00	65·00

158 Prince Baudouin

159 Queen Astrid and Prince Baudouin

1936. Anti-tuberculosis Fund.

777	158	10c.+5c. brown	10	10
778		25c.+5c. violet	25	20
779		35c.+5c. green	30	20
780		50c.+5c. brown	50	40
781		70c.+5c. olive	20	25
782		1f.+25c. red	1·50	1·30
783		1f.75+25c. blue	2·00	1·80
784		2f.45+2f.55 purple	5·50	5·75

1937. Stamp of 1929 surch **BELGIQUE 1937 BELGIE 10c.**

785	104	10c. on 40c. purple	30	30

See note below No. 480.

1937. International Stamp Day.

786	158	2f.45c.+2f.55c. slate	2·50	2·30

1937. Queen Astrid Public Utility Fund.

787	159	10c.+5c. purple	10	15
788		25c.+5c. olive	10	20
789		35c.+5c. green	10	20
790		50c.+5c. violet	50	45
791		70c.+5c. black	10	15
792		1f.+25c. red	1·50	1·30
793		1f.75c.+25c. blue	3·50	2·75
794		2f.45c.+1f.55c. brown	7·50	6·50

160 Queen Elisabeth

161 Princess Josephine Charlotte

1937. Eugene Ysaye Memorial Fund.

795	160	70c.+5c. black	30	30
796		1f.75+25c. blue	70	70
MS797		113 × 146 mm. 160 1f.50+2f.50 red (2); 2f.45+3f.55, violet (2)	40·00	17·00

See also MS1963.

1937. Anti-tuberculosis Fund.

798	161	10c.+5c. green	30	20
799		25c.+5c. brown	35	30
800		35c.+5c. green	30	30
801		50c.+5c. olive	35	30
802		70c.+5c. purple	25	20
803		1f.+25c. red	1·80	1·60
804		1f.75+25c. blue	1·70	1·50
805		2f.45+2f.55 purple	5·00	4·25

163 King Albert Memorial, Nieuport

1938. King Albert Memorial Fund. Sheet 138 × 115 mm.

MS809	163	2f.45+7f.55 red	20·00	19·00

164 King Leopold

1938. Aeronautical Propaganda.

810	164	10c.+5c. purple	30	20
811		35c.+5c. green	45	45
812		70c.+5c. black	50	55
813		1f.75+25c. blue	3·25	2·75
814		2f.45+2f.55 violet	4·50	4·00

165 Basilica of the Sacred Heart, Koekelberg

1938. Building (Completion) Fund.

815	165	10c.+5c. brown	30	30
816	–	35c.+5c. green	30	30
817	165	70c.+5c. grey	30	25
818	–	1f.+25c. red	45	45
819	165	1f.75+25c. blue	45	45
820	–	2f.45+2f.55 red	4·75	4·00
821	–	5f.+5f. green	11·00	10·50
MS822		95 × 120 mm. 5f.+5f. violet (as 821)	16·00	14·00

DESIGNS—HORIZ: 35c., 1f., 2f.45, Front view of Basilica. VERT: 5f. Interior view.

1938. Surch **2F50**.

823	155	2f.50 on 2f.45 black	12·50	30

167 Exhibition Pavilion

170 Prince Albert of Liege

1938. International Exhibition, Liege (1939). Inscr "LIEGE 1939 LUIK".

824	–	35c. green	20	25
825	167	1f. red	30	30
826	–	1f.50 brown	1·30	55
827	–	1f.75 blue	1·30	20

DESIGNS—VERT: 35c. View of Liege. HORIZ: 1f.50, R. Meuse at Liege; 1f.75, Albert Canal and King Albert.

1938. Koekelberg Basilica Completion Fund. Surch.

828	–	40c. on 35c.+5c. green (No. 816)	75	75
829	165	75c. on 70c.+5c. grey	50	45
830	–	2f.50+2f.50 on 2f.45+2f.55 red (No. 820)	6·75	6·25

1938. Anti-tuberculosis Fund.

831	170	10c.+5c. brown	30	30
832		30c.+5c. purple	30	30
833		40c.+5c. olive	30	30
834		75c.+5c. grey	30	30
835		1f.+25c. red	1·40	1·30
836		1f.75+25c. blue	1·20	1·00
837		2f.50+2f.50 green	6·25	5·50
838		5f.+5f. purple	13·50	11·50

171 King Leopold and Royal Children

1939. 5th Anniv of Int Red Cross Society.

839	–	10c.+5c. brown	25	20
840	–	30c.+5c. red	30	30
841	–	40c.+5c. olive	30	30
842	171	75c.+5c. black	30	30
843	–	1f.+25c. red	1·90	1·80
844	171	1f.75+25c. blue	1·30	1·10
845	–	2f.50+2f.50 violet	1·80	1·90
846	–	5f.+5f. green	8·00	7·25

DESIGNS—VERT: 10c. H. Dunant; 30c. Florence Nightingale; 40c. and 1f. Queen Elisabeth and Royal children; 2f.50, Queen Astrid. HORIZ: 5f. Queen Elisabeth and wounded soldier (larger).

173 Rubens's House (after engraving by Harrewijn)

175 Portrait by Memling

1939. Rubens's House Restoration Fund.

847	173	10c.+5c. brown	30	20
848	–	40c.+5c. purple	30	30
849	–	75c.+5c. green	40	50
850	–	1f.+25c. red	2·00	1·70
851	–	1f.50+25c. brown	2·50	2·20
852	–	1f.75+25c. blue	4·00	3·50

853	–	2f.50+2f.50 purple	16·00	13·50
854	–	5f.+5f. grey	20·00	18·00

DESIGNS—As Type **173**: VERT: 40c. "Rubens's Sons, Albert and Nicholas"; 1f. "Helene Fourment (2nd wife) and Children"; 1f.50, "Rubens and Isabella Brant" (1st wife); 1f.75, Rubens (after engraving by Pontius); 2f.50, "Straw Hat" (Suzanne Fourment). HORIZ: 75c. Arcade of Rubens's house. 35 × 45 mm: 5f. "The Descent from the Cross".

1939. Exn of Memling's Paintings, Bruges.

855	**175**	75c.+75c. olive	2·00	2·10

177 Orval Abbey Cloisters and Belfry

180 Thuin

1939. Orval Abbey Restoration Fund. Inscr "ORVAL".

861	–	75c.+75c. olive	4·50	4·25
862	**177**	1f.+1f. red	2·30	2·10
863	–	1f.50+1f.50 brown	2·30	2·10
864	–	1f.75+1f.75 blue	3·00	2·75
865	–	2f.50+2f.50 mauve	8·50	8·25
866	–	5f.+5f. purple	9·50	8·25

DESIGNS—As Type **177**: VERT: 75c. Monks in laboratory. HORIZ: 1f.50, Monks harvesting; 1f.75, Aerial view of Orval Abbey; 52½ × 35½ mm: 2f.50, Cardinal Van Roey, Statue of the Madonna and Abbot of Orval; 5f. Kings Albert and Leopold III and shrine.

1939. Anti-tuberculosis Fund. Belfries.

868	–	10c.+5c. olive	30	20
869	**180**	30c.+5c. brown	30	20
870	–	40c.+5c. purple	30	30
871	–	75c.+5c. grey	30	20
872	–	1f.+25c. red	1·30	1·40
873	–	1f.75+25c. blue	1·00	90
874	–	2f.50+2f.50 brown	9·50	9·00
875	–	5f.+5f. violet	11·00	10·50

DESIGNS—As Type **180**: 10c. Bruges; 40c. Lier; 75c. Mons. LARGER (21½ × 34 mm): 1f. Furnes; 1f.75, Namur; 2f.50, Alost; 5f. Tournai.

182 Arms of Mons

183 Painting

184 Monks studying Plans of Orval Abbey

1940. Winter Relief Fund.

901	**182**	10c.+5c. black, red and green	30	20
902	–	30c.+5c. multicoloured	30	20
903	–	40c.+10c. multicoloured	30	20
904	–	50c.+10c. multicoloured	30	20
905	–	75c.+15c. multicoloured	30	20
906	–	1f.+25c. multicoloured	40	40
907	–	1f.75c.+50c. mult	60	60
908	–	2f.50c.+2f.50c. olive, red and black	1·20	1·20
909	–	5f.+5f. multicoloured	1·40	1·40
MS910		103 × 145 mm. Nos. 901/9 each in first colour given, together with red	18·00	16·00

DESIGNS: 30c. to 5f. Arms of Ghent, Arlon, Bruges, Namur, Hasselt, Brussels, Antwerp and Liege, respectively.

1941. Orval Abbey Restoration Fund.

935	**183**	10c.+15c. brown	50	50
936	–	30c.+30c. grey	50	50
937	–	40c.+60c. brown	50	50
938	–	50c.+65c. violet	50	50
939	–	75c.+1f. mauve	50	50
940	–	1f.+1f.50 red	50	50
941	**183**	1f.25+1f.75 green	50	50
942	–	1f.75+2f.50 blue	50	50
943	–	2f.+3f.50 mauve	50	50
944	–	2f.50+4f.50 brown	50	50
945	–	3f.+5f. green	50	50
946	**184**	5f.+10f. brown	1·60	1·30
MS947		183 × 165 mm. 5f.+15f. blue (as 946)	10·00	9·25

DESIGNS—As Type **183**. 30c., 1f., 2f.50, Sculpture; 40c., 2f. Goldsmiths (Monks carrying candlesticks and cross); 50c., 1f.75, Stained glass (Monk at prayer); 75c., 3f. Sacred music.

1941. Surch.

955	**152**	10c. on 30c. brown	20	20
956		10c. on 40c. lilac	20	20
957	**153**	10c. on 70c. brown	20	20
958		50c. on 75c. olive	30	30
959	**155**	2f.25 on 2f.50 black	55	50

189 Maria Theresa

190 St. Martin, Dinant

1941. Soldiers' Families Relief Fund.

960	**189**	10c.+5c. black	20	15
961	–	35c.+5c. green	20	15
962	–	50c.+10c. brown	20	15
963	–	60c.+10c. violet	20	15
964	–	1f.+15c. red	20	15
965	–	1f.50+1f. mauve	30	30
966	–	1f.75+1f.75 blue	30	30
967	–	2f.25+2f.25 brown	30	30
968	–	3f.25+3f.25 brown	50	55
969	–	5f.+5f. green	90	85

PORTRAITS: 35c. to 5f. Charles of Lorraine, Margaret of Parma, Charles V, Johanna of Castile, Philip the Good, Margaret of Austria, Charles the Bold, Archduke Albert and Archduchess Isabella respectively.

1941. Winter Relief Fund. Statues.

970	**190**	10c.+5c. brown	25	20
971	–	35c.+5c. green	25	20
972	–	50c.+10c. violet	25	20
973	–	60c.+10c. brown	25	20
974	–	1f.+15c. red	25	20
975	**190**	1f.50+25c. green	30	30
976	–	1f.75+50c. blue	30	30
977	–	2f.25+2f.25 mauve	30	30
978	–	3f.25+3f.25 brown	40	35
979	–	5f.+5f. green	75	75
MS980		105 × 139 mm. 5f.+20f. purple (as 979)	23·00	19·00

DESIGNS (Statues of St. Martin in churches)—As Type **190**: 35c., 1f. Lennick, St. Quentin; 50c., 3f. Beck, Limberg; 60c., 2f.25, Dave on the Meuse; 1f.75, Hal, Brabant. 35 × 50 mm: 5f. St. Trond.

192 Concert Hall, Argenteuil

1941. Fund for Queen Elisabeth's Concert Hall. Two sheets, each 103 × 133 mm.

MS981	**192**	10f.+15f. green	7·00	5·75
MS982		As last with perforated crown and monogram with violet control number on back	7·00	6·25

193 Mercator

198 Prisoner writing Letter

1942. Anti-tuberculosis Fund. Portraits.

986	–	10c.+5c. brown	15	15
987	–	35c.+5c. green	15	15
988	–	50c.+10c. brown	15	15
989	–	60c.+10c. green	15	15
990	–	1f.+15c. red	15	15
991	**193**	1f.75+50c. blue	15	15
992	–	3f.25+3f.25 purple	15	15
993	–	5f.+5f. violet	30	30
994	–	10f.+30f. orange	1·50	1·30
MS995		77 × 59 mm. 3f.25+6f.75 green (as 968); 5f.+10f. red (as 969)	12·00	11·00

SCIENTISTS—As T **193**: 10c. Bolland. 35c. Versale. 50c. S. Stevin. 60c. Van Helmont. 1f. Dodoens. 3f.25, Oertell. 5f. Juste Lipse. 25½ × 28½ mm: 10f. Plantin.

1942. Prisoners of War Fund.

1000	**198**	5f.+45f. grey	7·50	7·75

199 St. Martin

200 St. Martin sharing his cloak

1942. Winter Relief Fund.

1001	**199**	10c.+5c. orange	20	15
1002	–	35c.+5c. green	20	15
1003	–	50c.+10c. brown	20	15
1004	–	60c.+10c. black (horiz)	20	15
1005	–	1f.+15c. red	20	15
1006	–	1f.50+25c. green	25	30
1007	–	1f.75+50c. blue	30	30
1008	–	2f.25+2f.25 brn (horiz)	30	30
1009	–	3f.25+3f.25 purple (horiz)	50	55
1010	**200**	5f.+10f. brown	1·40	1·30
1011		10f.+20f. brown & vio	1·50	1·50
1012		10f.+20f. red & violet	1·30	1·20

201 Soldiers and Vision of Home

1943. Prisoners of War Relief Fund.

1013	**201**	1f.+30f. red	3·00	2·50
1014	–	1f.+30f. brown	2·00	2·10

DESIGN: No. 1014, Soldiers emptying parcel of books and vision of home.

202 Tiler

1943. Anti-tuberculosis Fund. Trades.

1015	**202**	10c.+5c. brown	20	15
1016	–	35c.+5c. green	20	15
1017	–	50c.+10c. brown	20	15
1018	–	60c.+10c. green	20	15
1019	–	1f.+15c. red	30	25
1020	–	1f.75+75c. blue	30	25
1021	–	3f.25+3f.25 purple	50	40
1022	–	5f.+25f. violet	1·00	85

DESIGNS: 35c. Blacksmith; 50c. Coppersmith; 60c. Gunsmith; 1f. Armourer; 1f.75, Goldsmith; 3f.25, Fishmonger; 5f. Clockmaker.

203 Ornamental Letter

204 Ornamental Letters (⅔-size illustration)

1943. Orval Abbey Restoration Fund. Designs showing single letters forming "ORVAL".

1023	**203**	50c.+1f. black	40	40
1024	–	60c.+1f.90 violet	30	30
1025	–	1f.+3f. red	30	30
1026	–	1f.75+5f.25 blue	30	30
1027	–	3f.25+16f.75 green	55	55
1028	**204**	5f.+30f. brown	95	85

205 St. Leonard's Church, Leon, and St. Martin

206 Church of Notre Dame, Hal, and St. Martin

207 St. Martin and River Scheldt

1943. Winter Relief Fund.

1029	**205**	10c.+5c. brown	20	15
1030	–	35c.+5c. green	20	15
1031	–	50c.+15c. green	20	15
1032	–	60c.+20c. purple	20	15
1033	–	1f.+1f. red	30	30
1034	–	1f.75+4f.25 blue	70	80
1035	–	3f.25+11f.75 mauve	1·40	1·30
1036	**206**	5f.+25f. blue	2·10	2·00
1037	**207**	10f.+30f. green	1·60	1·50
1038	–	10f.+30f. brown	1·60	1·50

DESIGNS: (Various churches and statues of St. Martin sharing his cloak). As Type **205**: HORIZ: 35c. Dion-le-Val; 50c. Alost; 60c. Liege; 3f.25, Loppem. VERT: 1f. Courtrai; 1f.75, Angre. As Type **207**: 10f. brown Meuse landscape.

208 "Daedalus and Icarus"

209 Jan van Eyck

1944. Red Cross.

1039	**208**	35c.+1f.65 green	35	30
1040	–	50c.+2f.50 grey	35	30
1041	–	60c.+3f.40 brown	35	45
1042	–	1f.+5f. red	50	45
1043	–	1f.75+8f.25 blue	50	45
1044	–	5f.+30f. brown	80	70

DESIGNS: 50c. "The Good Samaritan" (Jacob Jordsen); 60c. "Christ healing the Paralytic" (detail); 1f. "Madonna and Child"; 1f.75, "Self-portrait"; 5f. "St. Sebastian".

Nos. 1039 and 1041/4 depict paintings by Anthony van Dyck.

1944. Prisoners of War Relief Fund.

1045	**209**	10c.+15c. violet	30	30
1046	–	35c.+15c. green	30	30
1047	–	50c.+25c. brown	30	30
1048	–	60c.+40c. olive	30	35
1049	–	1f.+50c. red	30	30
1050	–	1f.75+4f.25 blue	30	35
1051	–	2f.25+8f.25 slate	70	70
1052	–	3f.25+11f.25 brown	35	35
1053	–	5f.+35f. grey	75	75

PORTRAITS: 35c. "Godefroid de Bouillon". 50c. "Jacob van Maerlant". 60c. "Jean Joses de Dinant". 1f. "Jacob van Artevelde". 1f.75, "Charles Joseph de Ligne". 2f.25, "Andre Gretry". 3f.25, "Jan Moretus-Plantin". 5f. "Ruusbroeck".

210 "Bayard and Four Sons of Aymon", Namur

211 Lion Rampant

1944. Anti-tuberculosis Fund. Provincial legendary types.

1054	**210**	10c.+5c. brown	15	15
1055	–	35c.+5c. green	15	15
1056	–	50c.+10c. violet	15	15
1057	–	60c.+10c. brown	15	15
1058	–	1f.+15c. red	15	15
1059	–	1f.75+5f.25 blue	15	20
1060	–	3f.25+11f.75 green	30	30
1061	–	5f.+25f. blue	40	40

DESIGNS—VERT: 35c. “Brabo severing the giant’s hand”, Antwerp; 60c. “Thyl Ulenspiegel” and “Nele”, Flanders; 1f. “St. George and the Dragon”, Hainaut; 1f.75, “Genevieve of Brabant, with the Child and the Hind”, Brabant. HORIZ: 50c. “St. Hubert encounters the Hind with the Cross”, Luxemburg; 3f.25, “Tchantches wrestling with the Saracen”, Liege; 5f. “St. Gertrude rescuing the Knight with the cards”, Limburg.

1944. Inscr “BELGIQUE-BELGIE” or “BELGIE-BELGIQUE”.

1062A	**211**	5c. brown	15	15
1063A		10c. green	15	15
1064A		25c. blue	15	15
1065A		35c. brown	15	15
1066A		50c. green	15	15
1067B		75c. violet	15	20
1068B		1f. red	15	15
1069B		1f.25 brown	20	20
1070B		1f.50 orange	35	40
1071A		1f.75 blue	15	15
1072B		2f. blue	1·50	1·50
1073A		2f.75 mauve	15	15
1074B		3f. red	20	30
1075B		3f.50 grey	15	20
1076B		5f. brown	3·00	3·00
1077B		10f. black	75	75

1944. Overprinted with large **V**.

1078	**152**	2c. green	15	15
1079		15c. blue	15	15
1080		20c. violet	15	15
1081		60c. grey	15	15

213 King Leopold III and “V”

214 War Victims

215 Rebuilding Homes

1944.

1082	**213**	1f. red	15	15
1083		1f.50 mauve	15	15
1084		1f.75 blue	40	50
1085		2f. violet	50	20
1086		2f.25 green	40	50
1087		3f.25 brown	25	20
1088		5f. green	1·00	20

1945. War Victims’ Relief Fund.

1114	**214**	1f.+30f. red	1·60	1·00
1115	**215**	1¾f.+30f. blue	1·60	1·00

Nos. 1114/15 measure 50 × 35 mm.

1945. Post Office Employers’ Relief Fund.

1119	**214**	1f.+9f. red	35	25
1120	**215**	1f.+9f. red	40	25

217 Resister

218 Group of Resisters

1945. Prisoners of War Relief Fund.

1121	**217**	10c.+15c. orange	20	15
1122	–	20c.+20c. violet	20	15
1123	–	60c.+25c. brown	20	15
1124	–	70c.+30c. green	20	15
1125	**217**	75c.+50c. brown	20	15
1126	–	1f.+75c. green	25	25
1127	–	1f.50+1f. red	25	25
1128	–	3f.50+3f.50 blue	1·80	1·20
1129	**218**	5f.+40f. brown	2·30	1·20

DESIGNS—VERT: 20c., 1f. Father and child; 60c., 1f.50, Victim tied to stake. HORIZ: 70c., 3f.50, Rifleman.

219 West Flanders

224 “Marie Henriette” (paddle-steamer)

222 Douglas DC-4

1945. Anti-tuberculosis Fund.

1130	**219**	10c.+15c. green	25	15
1131	–	20c.+20c. red	25	15
1132	–	60c.+25c. brown	25	15
1133	–	70c.+30c. green	25	15
1134	–	75c.+50c. brown	25	15
1135	–	1f.+75c. violet	25	15
1136	–	1f.50+1f. red	25	25
1137	–	3f.50+1f.50 blue	65	45
1138	–	5f.+45f. mauve	3·75	2·50

ARMS DESIGNS—VERT: 20c. to 5f. Arms of Luxemburg, East Flanders, Namur, Limburg Hainaut, Antwerp, Liege and Brabant respectively.

1946. Air.

1165	**222**	6f. blue	50	25
1166		8f.50 red	65	45
1167		50f. green	6·00	85
1168		100f. grey	10·00	2·10

1946. Surch **-10%**, reducing the original value by 10%.

1171	**213**	“-10%” on 1f.50 mauve	75	20
1172		“-10%” on 2f. violet	2·00	75
1173		“-10%” on 5f. green	1·80	20

1946. Ostend–Dover Mail-boat Service Centenary.

1174a	–	1f.35 blue	20	15
1175	**224**	2f.25 green	50	30
1176	–	3f.15 grey	55	30

DESIGNS—21½ × 18½ or 21 × 17 mm: 1f.35, “Prince Baudouin” (mail steamer). As T **224**: 3f.15, “Diamant” (paddle-steamer), formerly “Le Chemin de Fer”.

225 Paratrooper

1946. Air. Bastogne Monument Fund.

1177	**225**	17f.50+62f.50 green	1·60	1·00
1178		17f.50+62f.50 purple	1·60	1·00

226 Father Damien

227 E. Vandervelde

228 Francois Bovesse

1946. Belgian Patriots. (a) Father Damien.

1179	**226**	65c.+75c. blue	2·00	1·10
1180	–	1f.35+2f. brown	2·00	1·10
1181	–	1f.75+18f. lake	2·00	1·10

DESIGNS—HORIZ: 1f.35, Molokai Leper Colony. VERT: 1f.75, Damien’s statue.

(b) Emile Vandervelde.

1182	**227**	65c.+75c. green	2·00	1·10
1183	–	1f.35+2f. blue	2·00	1·10
1184	–	1f.75+18f. red	2·00	1·10

DESIGNS—HORIZ: 1f.35, Vandervelde, miner, mother and child. VERT: 1f.75, Sower.

(c) Francois Bovesse.

1185	–	65c.+75c. violet	2·00	1·10
1186	**228**	1f.35+2f. brown	2·00	1·10
1187	–	1f.75+18f. red	2·00	1·10

DESIGNS—VERT: 65c. Symbols of Patriotism and Learning; 1f.75, Draped memorial figures holding wreath and torch.

229 Pepin d’Herstal

230 Allegory of “Flight”

1946. War Victims’ Relief Fund.

1188	**229**	75c.+25c. green	60	35
1189	–	1f.+50c. violet	75	55
1190	–	1f.50+1f. purple	75	55
1191	–	3f.50+1f.50 blue	1·00	80
1192	–	5f.+45f. mauve	13·00	11·00
1194	–	5f.+45f. orange	13·00	11·50

DESIGNS: 1f. Charlemagne; 1f.50, Godfrey of Bouillon; 3f.50, Robert of Jerusalem; 5f. Baudouin of Constantinople.

See also Nos. 1207/11, 1258/9 and 1302/6.

1946. Air.

1193	**230**	2f.+8f. violet	60	60

231 Malines

232 Joseph Plateau

1946. Anti-tuberculosis Fund. No date.

1195	**231**	65c.+35c. red	60	55
1196	–	90c.+60c. olive	70	45
1197	–	1f.35+1f.15 green	70	45
1198	–	3f.15+1f.85 blue	1·00	90
1199	–	4f.50+45f.50 brown	16·00	12·50

DESIGNS—(Arms and Industries): 90c. Dinant; 1f.35, Ostend; 3f.15, Verviers; 4f.50, Louvain.

See also Nos. 1212/16.

1947. Air. “Cipex” International Stamp Exhibition, New York. Nos. 1179/87 surch **LUCHTPOST POSTE AERIENNE** or **POSTE AERIENNE LUCHTPOST** and new value. (a) Father Damien.

1199a	1f.+2f. on 65c. +75c. blue	80	60
1199b	1f.+50+2f.50 on 1f.35+2f. brown	80	60
1199c	2f.+45f. on 1f.75+18f. red	80	60

(b) Emile Vandervelde.

1199d	1f.+2f. on 65c.+75c. green	80	60
1199e	1f.50+2f.50 on 1f.35+2f. blue	80	60
1199f	2f.+45f. on 1f.75+18f. red	80	60

(c) Francois Bovesse.

1199g	1f.+2f. on 65c.+75c. vio	80	60
1199h	1f.50+2f.50 on 1f.35+2f. brown	80	60
1199i	2f.+45f. on 1f.75+18f. red	80	60

1947. Int Film and Belgian Fine Arts Festival.

1200	**232**	3f.15 blue	1·30	20

233 Adrien de Gerlache

234 Explorers landing from “Belgica”

1947. 50th Anniv of Belgian Antarctic Expedition.

1201	**233**	1f.35 red	25	15
1202	**234**	2f.25 grey	4·00	75

1947. War Victims’ Relief Fund. Mediaeval Princes as T **229**.

1207	65c.+35c. blue	1·10	55
1208	90c.+60c. green	1·70	75
1209	1f.35+1f.15 red	3·00	1·00
1210	3f.15+1f.85 blue	3·25	1·20
1211	20f.+20f. purple	65·00	37·00

DESIGNS: 65c. John II, Duke of Brabant; 90c. Philippe of Alsace; 1f.35, William the Good; 3f.15, Notger, Bishop of Liege; 20f. Philip the Noble.

1947. Anti-Tuberculosis Fund. Arms designs as T **231**, but dated “1947”.

1212	65c.+35c. orange	70	60
1213	90c.+60c. purple	70	60
1214	1f.35+1f.15 brown	70	60
1215	3f.15+1f.85 blue	3·00	1·10
1216	20f.+20f. green	28·00	16·00

DESIGNS (Arms and Industries): 65c. Nivelles; 90c. St. Truiden; 1f.35, Charleroi; 3f.15, St. Nicholas; 20f. Bouillon.

237 Chemical Industry

240 Textile Machinery

239 Antwerp Docks

1948. National Industries.

1217	**237**	60c. blue	20	15
1218		1f.20 brown	2·50	20
1219	–	1f.35 brown	20	15
1220	–	1f.75 green	60	20
1221	–	1f.75 red	30	30
1222	**239**	2f.25 grey	1·00	60
1223	–	2f.50 mauve	8·25	50
1224	**239**	3f. purple	13·00	40
1225	**240**	3f.15 blue	1·30	60
1226		4f. blue	12·50	40
1227	–	6f. blue	25·00	50
1228	–	6f.30 purple	3·00	2·50

DESIGNS—As Type **237**: 1f.35, 1f.75 green, Woman making lace; 1f.75 red, 2f.50, Agricultural produce. As Type **239**: 6f., 6f.30, Steel works.

242 St. Benedict and King Totila

243 St. Bega and Chevremont Castle

1948. Achel Abbey Fund. Inscr “ACHEL”.

1232	**242**	65c.+65c. brown	1·00	80
1233	–	1f.35+1f.35 green	1·50	1·10
1234	–	3f.15+2f.85 blue	3·50	2·10
1235	–	10f.+10f. purple	12·00	11·00

DESIGNS—HORIZ: 1f.35, Achel Abbey. VERT: 3f.15, St. Benedict as Law-Giver; 10f. Death of St. Benedict.

1948. Chevremont Abbey Fund. Inscr “CHEVREMONT”.

1236	**243**	65c.+65c. blue	1·00	80
1237	–	1f.35+1f.35 red	1·50	90
1238	–	3f.15+2f.85 blue	3·00	1·80
1239	–	10f.+10f. brown	12·00	10·00

DESIGNS—HORIZ: 1f.35, Chevremont Basilica and Convent. VERT: 3f.15, Madonna of Chevremont and Chapel; 10f. Monk and Madonna of Mt. Carmel.

244 Statue of Anseele

245 Ghent and E. Anseele

1948. Inauguration of Edward Anseele (Socialist Leader) Statue.

1245	**244**	65c.+35c. red	2·50	1·30
1246	**245**	90c.+60c. grey	3·50	1·80
1247	–	1f.35+1f.15 brn	2·50	1·30
1248	–	3f.15+1f.85 blue	7·50	4·25
MS1249		82 × 145 mm. Nos. 1245/8	£225	90·00

DESIGNS: 1f.35, Statue and Ed. Anseele; 3f.15, Reverse side of statue.

247 “Liberty”

248 “Resistance”

1948. Antwerp and Liege Monuments Funds.

1253	**247**	10f.+10f. green	50·00	21·00
1254	**248**	10f.+10f. brown	23·00	11·00

249 Cross of Lorraine

1948. Anti-tuberculosis Fund.
1255 **249** 20c.+5c. green 25 15
1256 1f.20+30c. purple . . . 1·50 45
1257 1f.75+25c. red . . . . 1·80 65
1258 – 4f.+3f.25 blue . . . . 8·00 4·50
1259 – 20f.+20f. green . . . . . 43·00 31·00
DESIGNS—As Type **229**: 4f. Isabel of Austria; 20f. Albert, Archduke of Austria.

250 (⅓-size illustration)

1949. Social and Cultural Funds. Sheets 140 × 90 mm sold at 50f. each incl premium (a) Paintings by R. van der Weyden.
MS1260 90c. brown (T **250** "Madonna and Child"); 1f.75 purple ("Crucifixion"); 4f. blue ("Mary Magdalene") £190 £160

(b) Paintings by J. Jordaens.
MS1261 90c. violet ("Woman Reading"); 1f.75 red ("Flute-player"); 4f. blue ("Old Woman and Letter") £190 £160

1949. Surch **1-1-49** at top, **31-XII-49** and value at bottom with posthorn in between. (a) Arms type.
1262 **152** 5c. on 15c. blue 15 15
1263 5c. on 30c. brown . . . 15 15
1264 5c. on 40c. lilac 15 15
1265 20c. on 70c. green . . . 15 15
1266 20c. on 75c. mauve . . . 15 15

(b) Anseele Statue.
1267 **244** 10c. on 65c.+35c. red . . 3·75 3·75
1268 **245** 40c. on 90c.+60c. grey 2·20 2·20
1269 – 80c. on 1f.35+1f.15 brown . . . . . . 1·20 1·20
1270 – 1f.20 on 3f.15+1f.85 blue 3·00 3·00

251 King Leopold I

253 St. Madeleine from "The Baptism of Christ"

252 Forms of Postal Transport

1949. Belgian Stamp Cent.
1271 **251** 90c. green (postage) . . 65 40
1272 1f.75 brown 35 15
1273 3f. red . . . . 8·50 3·00
1274 4f. blue . . . . 7·50 85
1275 **252** 50f. brown (air) . . . . 50·00 18·00

1949. Exhibition of Paintings by Gerard David, Bruges.
1276 **253** 1f.75 brown 75 20

255 Hemispheres and Allegorical Figure

1949. 75th Anniv of U.P.U.
1295 **255** 4f. blue . . . . 4·75 2·20

256 Guido Gezelle

257 Arnica

1949. 50th Death Anniv of Gezelle (poet).
1297 **256** 1f.75+75c. green . . . . 2·00 1·30

1949. Anti-tuberculosis and other Funds. (a) Flowers.
1298 **257** 20c.+5c. black, yellow and green 25 15
1299 – 65c.+10c. black, green and buff . . . . . 1·20 55
1300 – 90c.+10c. black, blue and red . . . . . . 2·00 85
1301 – 1f.20+30c. mult . . . 2·30 95
FLOWERS: 65c. Thistle. 90c. Periwinkle. 1f.20, Poppy.

(b) Portraits as T **229**.
1302 1f.75+25c. orange . . . . . 1·00 30
1303 3f.+1f.50 red . . . . 11·00 6·25
1304 4f.+2f. blue . . . . 11·00 6·25
1305 6f.+3f. brown . . . . 19·00 10·50
1306 8f.+4f. green . . . . 22·00 12·00
PORTRAITS: 1f.75, Philip the Good. 3f. Charles V. 4f. Maria Christina. 6f. Charles of Lorraine. 8f. Maria Theresa.

260 Anglo-Belgian Monument, Hertain

261 Allegory of Saving

1950. Anglo-Belgian Union and other Funds.
1307 – 80c.+20c. green . . . . 1·40 75
1308 – 2f.50+50c. red . . . . . 6·00 3·50
1309 **260** 4f.+2f. blue . . . . . . 9·50 6·00
DESIGNS—HORIZ: 80c. Arms of Great Britain and Belgium; 2f.50, British tanks at Tournai.

1950. National Savings Bank Centenary.
1310 **261** 1f.75 sepia 55 25

262 Hurdling

263 Sikorsky S-51 Helicopter and Douglas DC-4 leaving Melsbroeck

1950. European Athletic Championships. Inscr "HEYSEL 1950".
1311 **262** 20c.+5c. green 35 20
1312 – 90c.+10c. purple . . . . 3·75 1·90
1313 – 1f.75+25c. red . . . . . 7·00 1·90
1314 – 4f.+2f. blue . . . . . . 37·00 20·00
1315 – 8f.+4f. green . . . . . 38·00 24·00
MS1316 70 × 119 mm. 1f.75+25c. (+18f.) (No. 1313) . . . . . . 75·00 49·00
DESIGNS—HORIZ: 1f.75, Relay racing. VERT: 90c. Javelin throwing; 4f. Pole vaulting; 8f. Sprinting.

1950. Air. Inauguration of Helicopter Airmail Services and Aeronautical Committee's Fund.
1317 **263** 7f.+3f. blue . . . . . . 8·00 5·00

265 Gentian

266 Sijsele Sanatorium

1950. Anti-tuberculosis and other Funds. Cross in red.
1326 **265** 20c.+5c. blue, green and purple 40 25
1327 – 65c.+10c. green and brown . . . . 1·20 45
1328 – 90c.+10c. light green and green . . . . 1·60 1·00
1329 – 1f.20+30c. blue, green and ultramarine . . . 1·80 1·00
1330 **266** 1f.75+25c. red . . . . . 2·40 1·40
1331 – 4f.+2f. blue . . . . . . 17·00 8·50
1332 – 8f.+4f. green . . . . . 29·00 18·00
DESIGNS—Flowers as Type **265**: 65c. Rushes; 90c. Foxglove; 1f.20, Sea lavender. Sanatoria as Type **266**: HORIZ: 4f. Jauche. VERT: 8f. Tombeek.

267 The Belgian Lion

268 "Science"

1951. (a) 17½ × 20½ mm.
1334 **267** 2c. brown 15 15
1335 3c. violet 15 15
1336 5c. lilac 20 15
1336a 5c. pink 15 15
1337 10c. orange 15 15
1338 15c. mauve 15 15
1333 20c. blue 15 15
1339 20c. red 15 15
1340 25c. green . . . . . . 1·80 30
1341 25c. blue 15 15
1342 30c. green 15 15
1343 40c. brown 15 15
1344a 50c. blue 20 25
1345 60c. mauve 15 15
1346 65c. purple . . . . . . 12·50 45
1347 75c. lilac 15 15
1348 80c. green 70 15
1349 90c. blue . . . . 1·00 30
1350 1f. red 15 15
1351 1f.50 grey 15 15
1353 2f. green 20 15
1354 2f.50 brown 20 15
1355 3f. mauve 20 15
1355a 4f. purple 30 15
1355b 4f.50 blue 40 15
1355c 5f. purple 35 15

(b) 20½ × 24½ mm.
1356 **267** 50c. blue 35 20
1357 60c. purple 80 60
1358a 1f. red 15 15

(c) Size 17½ × 22 mm.
1359 **267** 50c. blue 15 15
1360 1f. pink . . . . 1·50 75
1361 2f. green 50 30

1951. UNESCO Fund. Inscr "UNESCO".
1365 **268** 80c.+20c. green . . . . 1·50 55
1366 – 2f.50+50c. brown . . . 9·50 6·25
1367 – 4f.+2f. blue . . . . . . 12·50 7·25
DESIGNS—HORIZ: 2f.50, "Education". VERT: 4f. "Peace".

269 Fairey Tipsy Belfair Trainer I

1951. Air. 50th Anniv of National Aero Club.
1368 – 6f. blue . . . . 27·00 16·00
1369 **269** 7f. red . . . . 27·00 16·00
DESIGN: 6f. Arsenal Air 100 glider.

1951. Air.
1370 – 6f. brown (glider) . . . 5·25 30
1371 **269** 7f. green . . . . 5·25 80

270 Monument

272 Queen Elisabeth

1951. Political Prisoners' National Monument Fund.
1372 **270** 1f.75+25c. brown . . . 3·00 75
1373 – 4f.+2f. blue . . . . . . 27·00 15·00
1374 – 8f.+4f. green . . . . . 29·00 18·00
DESIGNS—HORIZ: 4f. Breendonk Fort. VERT: 8f. Side view of monument.

1951. Queen Elisabeth Medical Foundation Fund.
1376 **272** 90c.+10c. grey . . . . . 4·00 90
1377 1f.75+25c. red . . . . 9·00 1·90
1378 3f.+1f. green . . . . . 32·00 13·50
1379 4f.+2f. blue . . . . . 33·00 14·00
1380 8f.+4f. sepia . . . . . 42·00 18·00

273 Lorraine Cross and Dragon

274 Beersel Castle

1951. Anti-tuberculosis and other Funds.
1381 **273** 20c.+5c. red 30 15
1382 65c.+10c. blue 55 30
1383 90c.+10c. brown 70 45
1384 1f.20+30c. violet . . . 1·30 75
1385 **274** 1f.75+75c. brown . . . 4·00 1·30
1386 – 3f.+1f. green . . . . . 14·50 8·00
1387 – 4f.+2f. blue . . . . . . 16·00 9·50
1388 – 8f.+4f. black . . . . . 24·00 13·00
CASTLES—As Type **274**: VERT: 3f. Horst Castle. 8f. Veves Castle. HORIZ: 4f. Lavaux St. Anne Castle.
For stamps as Type **273** but dated "1952" see Nos. 1416/19 and for those dated "1953" see Nos. 1507/10.

276 Consecration of the Basilica

1952. 25th Anniv of Cardinalate of Primate of Belgium and Koekelberg Basilica Fund.
1389 – 1f.75+25c. brown . . . 1·30 50
1390 – 4f.+2f. blue . . . . . . 14·50 7·25
1391 **276** 8f.+4f. purple . . . . . 21·00 11·00
MS1392 120 × 72 mm. Nos. 1389/91 (10f.) £375 £190
DESIGNS—24 × 35 mm: 1f.75, Interior of Koekelberg Basilica; 4f. Exterior of Koekelberg Basilica.

277 King Baudouin

278 King Baudouin

1952.
1393 **277** 1f.50 grey . . . . 1·50 20
1394 2f. red 50 20
1395 4f. blue . . . . 6·75 40
1396a **278** 50f. purple . . . . . . 3·50 30
1397a 100f. red . . . . 5·00 30

279 Francis of Taxis

281 A. Vermeylen

1952. 13th U.P.U. Congress, Brussels. Portraits of Members of the House of Thurn and Taxis.
1398 **279** 80c. green 20 20
1399 – 1f.75 orange 20 15
1400 – 2f. brown 60 30
1401 – 2f.50 red . . . . 1·20 40
1402 – 3f. olive . . . . 1·20 30
1403 – 4f. blue . . . . 1·20 15
1404 – 5f. brown . . . . 3·25 50
1405 – 5f.75 violet . . . . . . 4·25 1·20
1406 – 8f. black . . . . 19·00 3·75
1407 – 10f. purple . . . . . . 24·00 8·25
1408 – 20f. grey . . . . £100 41·00
1409 – 40f.+10f. turquoise . . . £160 £110
DESIGNS—VERT: 1f.75, John Baptist; 2f. Leonard; 2f.50, Lamoral; 3f. Leonard Francis; 4f. Lamoral Claud; 5f. Eugene Alexander; 5f.75, Anselm Francis; 8f. Alexander Ferdinand; 10f. Charles Anselm; 20f. Charles Alexander; 40f. Beaulieu Chateau.

1952. Culture Fund. Writers.
1410 **281** 65c.+30c. lilac . . . . . 6·00 2·50
1411 – 80c.+40c. green . . . . 6·00 2·50
1412 – 90c.+45c. olive . . . . 6·00 2·50
1413 – 1f.75+75c. lake . . . . 12·50 4·25
1414 – 4f.+2f. blue . . . . . . 38·00 18·00
1415 – 8f.+4f. sepia . . . . . 41·00 19·00
PORTRAITS: 80c. K. van de Woestijne. 90c. C. de Coster. 1f.75, M. Maeterlinck. 4f. E. Verhaeren. 8f. H. Conscience.

A 4f. blue as No. 1414 and an 8f. lake as No. 1415 each se-tenant with a label showing a laurel wreath and bearing a premium "+ 9 fr." were put on sale by subscription only.

282 Arms, Malmedy

284 Dewe and Monument at Liege

1952. Anti-tuberculosis and other Funds. As T **273** but dated "1952" and designs as T **282**.
1416 **273** 20c.+5c. brown 20 15
1417 80c.+20c. green 70 45
1418 1f.20+30c. purple . . . 1·60 75
1419 1f.50+50c. olive . . . . 1·60 75
1420 **282** 2f.+75c. red . . . . . . 2·40 85
1421 – 3f.+1f.50 brown . . . . 23·00 12·50
1422 – 4f.+2f. blue . . . . . . 22·00 11·50
1423 – 8f.+4f. purple . . . . . 23·00 12·50

DESIGNS—HORIZ: 3f. Ruins, Burgreuland. VERT: 4f. Dam, Eupen; 8f. Saint and lion, St. Vith.

1953. Walthere Dewe Memorial Fund.

1435	**284**	2f.+1f. lake	2·75	1·60

285 Princess Josephine Charlotte

286 Fishing Boats "Marcel", "De Meeuw" and "Jacqueline Denise"

1953. Red Cross National Disaster Fund. Cross in red.

1436	**285**	80c.+20c. green	2·50	1·10
1437		1f.20+30c. brown	2·30	1·10
1438		2f.+50c. lake	2·30	1·10
1439		2f.50+50c. red	18·00	9·25
1440		4f.+1f. blue	16·00	8·00
1441		5f.+2f. black	16·00	8·00

1953. Tourist Propaganda and Cultural Funds.

1442	**286**	80c.+20c. green	2·00	85
1443	–	1f.20+30c. brown	5·50	2·75
1444	–	2f.+50c. sepia	5·50	2·75
1445	–	2f.50+50c. mauve	16·00	8·25
1446	–	4f.+2f. blue	24·00	13·00
1447	–	8f.+4f. green	30·00	15·00

DESIGNS—HORIZ: 1f.20, Bridge Bouillon; 2f. Antwerp. VERT: 2f.50, Namur; 4f. Ghent; 8f. Freyr Rocks and River Meuse.

289 King Baudouin

290

1953. (a) 21 × 24½ mm.

1453	**289**	1f.50 black	20	15
1454		2f. red	7·75	15
1455		2f. green	25	15
2188		2f.50 brown	30	15
1457		3f. purple	25	15
1458		3f.50 green	1·00	15
1459		4f. blue	2·50	15
2188A		4f.50 brown	65	25
1462		5f. violet	1·30	15
1463		6f. mauve	3·00	15
1464		6f.50 grey	95·00	17·00
2189		7f. blue	40	30
1466		7f.50 brown	85·00	22·00
1467		8f. blue	75	15
1468		8f.50 purple	19·00	60
1469		9f. olive	95·00	2·00
1470		12f. turquoise	1·40	20
1471		30f. orange	11·50	45

(b) 17½ × 22 mm.

1472	**289**	1f.50 black	30	30
1473		2f.50 brown	7·25	7·25
1474		3f. mauve	40	15
1475		3f.50 green	30	30
1476		4f.50 brown	2·00	85

1953. European Child Welfare Fund.

1482	**290**	80c.+20c. green	5·00	2·75
1483		2f.50+1f. red	30·00	20·00
1484		4f.+1f.50 blue	32·00	22·00

293 Ernest Malvoz

296 King Albert Statue

1953. Anti-tuberculosis and other Funds. As T **273** but dated "1953" and portraits as T **293**.

1507	**273**	20c.+5c. blue	55	30
1508		80c.+20c. purple	1·60	65
1509		1f.20+30c. brown	2·30	1·20
1510		1f.50+50c. slate	2·75	1·10
1511	**293**	2f.+75c. green	3·50	1·50
1512	–	3f.+1f.50 red	17·00	10·00
1513	–	4f.+2f. blue	19·00	11·00
1514	–	8f.+4f. brown	23·00	12·50

PORTRAITS—VERT: 3f. Carlo Forlanini. 4f. Albert Calmette. HORIZ: 8f. Robert Koch.

1954. Surch **20c** and **I-I-54** at top, **31-XII-54** at bottom and bars in between.

1515	**267**	20c. on 65c. purple	1·50	30
1516		20c. on 90c. blue	1·50	30

See note below No. 480.

1954. King Albert Memorial Fund.

1520	**296**	2f.+50c. brown	9·00	3·50
1521	–	4f.+2f. blue	30·00	13·50
1522	–	9f.+4f.50 black	27·00	13·50

DESIGNS—HORIZ: 4f. King Albert Memorial. VERT: 9f. Marche-les-Dames Rocks and medallion portrait.

298 Monument

299 Breendonk Camp and Fort

1954. Political Prisoners' National Monument Fund.

1531	**298**	2f.+1f. red	22·00	9·75
1532	**299**	4f.+2f. brown	44·00	20·00
1533	–	9f.+4f.50 green	55·00	24·00

DESIGN—VERT: 9f. As Type **298** but viewed from different angle.

300 Entrance to Beguinal House

1954. Beguinage of Bruges Restoration Fund.

1534	**300**	80c.+20c. green	1·00	60
1535	–	2f.+1f. red	14·50	7·00
1536	–	4f.+2f. violet	19·00	9·25
1537	–	7f.+3f.50 purple	36·00	20·00
1538	–	8f.+4f. brown	36·00	20·00
1539	–	9f.+4f.50 blue	65·00	31·00

DESIGNS—HORIZ: 2f. River scene. VERT: 4f. Convent Buildings; 7f. Cloisters; 8f. Doorway; 9f. Statue of our Lady of the Vineyard (larger, 35 × 53 mm).

302 Map of Europe and Rotary Symbol

1954. 50th Anniv of Rotary International and 5th Regional Conference, Ostend.

1540	**302**	20c. red	15	15
1541	–	80c. green	40	25
1542	–	4f. blue	1·60	40

DESIGNS: 80c. Mermaid, "Mercury" and Rotary symbol; 4f. Rotary symbol and hemispheres.

303 Child

304 "The Blind Man and the Paralytic" (after Anto-Carte)

1954. Anti-T.B. and other Funds.

1543	**303**	20c.+5c. green	25	30
1544		80c.+20c. black	1·00	60
1545		1f.20+30c. brown	2·30	1·20
1546		1f.50+50c. violet	4·50	2·00
1547	**304**	2f.+75c. red	7·75	3·75
1548		4f.+1f. blue	20·00	12·50

305 Begonia and the Rabot

1955. Ghent Flower Show.

1549	**305**	80c. red	40	25
1550	–	2f.50 sepia	8·50	2·40
1551	–	4f. lake	5·25	85

DESIGNS—VERT: 2f.50, Azaleas and Chateau des Comtes; 4f. Orchid and the "Three Towers".

306 "Homage to Charles V" (A. De Vriendt)

307 "Charles V" (Titian)

1955. Emperor Charles V Exhibition, Ghent.

1552	**306**	20c. red	25	10
1553	**307**	2f. green	85	10
1554	–	4f. blue	4·25	1·20

DESIGN—As Type **306**: 4f. "Abdication of Charles V" (L. Gallait).

308 Emile Verhaeren (after C. Montald)

309 "Textile Industry"

1955. Birth Centenary of Verhaeren (poet).

1555	**308**	20c. black	15	15

1955. 2nd Int Textile Exhibition, Brussels.

1556	**309**	2f. purple	1·10	25

310 "The Foolish Virgin" (R. Wouters)

311 "The Departure of the Liege Volunteers in 1830" (Soubre)

1955. 3rd Biennial Sculpture Exn, Antwerp.

1557	**310**	1f.20 green	1·10	45
1558		2f. violet	1·90	25

1955. Liege Exn. 125th Anniv of 1830 Revolution.

1559	**311**	20c. green	15	10
1560		2f. brown	75	10

312 Ernest Solvay

1955. Cultural Fund. Scientists.

1561	**312**	20c.+5c. brown	30	30
1562	–	80c.+20c. violet	1·10	45
1563	–	1f.20+30c. blue	5·75	3·00
1564	–	2f.+50c. red	6·00	2·75
1565	–	3f.+1f. green	14·00	7·75
1566	–	4f.+2f. brown	14·00	7·75

PORTRAITS—VERT: 80c. Jean-Jacques Dony. 2f. Leo H. Baekeland. 3f. Jean-Etienne Lenoir. HORIZ: 1f.20, Egide Walschaerts. 4f. Emile Fourcault and Emile Gobbe.

313 "The Joys of Spring" (E. Canneel)

314 E. Holboll (Danish postal official)

1955. Anti-T.B. and other Funds.

1567	**313**	20c.+5c. mauve	25	25
1568		80c.+20c. green	70	45
1569		1f.20+30c. brown	2·75	1·00
1570		1f.50+50c. violet	3·25	1·10
1571	**314**	2f.+50c. red	10·50	4·50
1572	–	4f.+2f. blue	26·00	12·00
1573	–	8f.+4f. sepia	26·00	14·00

PORTRAITS—As Type **314**: 4f. J. D. Rockefeller (philanthropist). 8f. Sir R. W. Philip (physician).

315 Blood Donors Emblem

316 Mozart when a Child

317 Queen Elisabeth and Mozart Sonata

1956. Blood Donors.

1574	**315**	2f. red	30	15

1956. Birth Bicentenary of Mozart. Inscr as in T **316**.

1575	–	80c.+20c. green	50	25
1576	**316**	2f.+1f. purple	3·75	2·40
1577	**317**	4f.+2f. lilac	9·00	5·25

DESIGN—As Type **316**: 80c. Palace of Charles de Lorraine, Brussels.

318

319 Queen Elisabeth Medallion (Courtens)

1956. "Scaldis" Exhibitions in Tournai, Ghent and Antwerp.

1578	**318**	2f. blue	25	15

1956. 80th Birthday of Queen Elisabeth and Foundation Fund.

1579	**319**	80c.+20c. green	50	25
1580		2f.+1f. lake	3·75	2·00
1581		4f.+2f. sepia	5·25	3·00

320

321 Electric Train Type 122 and Railway Bridge

1956. Europa.

1582	**320**	2f. green	2·30	15
1583		4f. violet	14·00	45

1956. Electrification of Brussels–Luxembourg Railway Line.

1584	**321**	2f. blue	40	25

322 E. Anseele

1956. Birth Centenary of Anseele (statesman).

1588	**322**	20c. purple	15	10

323 Medieval Ship

324 Weighing a Baby

1956. Anti-tuberculosis and other Funds.

1589	**323**	20c.+5c. brown	20	25
1590		80c.+20c. green	75	45
1591		1f.20+30c. purple	1·00	55
1592		1f.50+50c. slate	1·30	65

1593 **324** 2f.+50c. green . . . . . 3·25 1·80
1594 – 4f.+2f. purple . . . . . 14·00 8·00
1595 – 8f.+4f. red . . . . . 15·00 9·25
DESIGNS—As Type **324**: HORIZ: 4f. X-ray examination. VERT: 8f. Convalescence and rehabilitation.

325 "Atomium" and Exhibition Emblem

327 Emperor Maximilian I, with Messenger

1957. Brussels International Exhibition.
1596 **325** 2f. red 15 15
1597 2f.50 green 40 20
1598 4f. violet 60 25
1599 5f. purple . . . . . . 1·40 50

1957. Stamp Day.
1603 **327** 2f. red 30 15

328 Charles Plisnier and Albrecht Rodenbach (writers)

1957. Cultural Fund. Belgian Celebrities.
1604 **328** 20c.+5c. violet 15 15
1605 – 80c.+20c. brown 40 35
1606 – 1f.20+30c. sepia 70 50
1607 – 2f.+50c. red . . . . . . 2·10 1·30
1608 – 3f.+1f. green . . . . . 3·50 2·75
1609 – 4f.+2f. blue . . . . . . 8·50 3·25
DESIGNS: 80c. Professors Emiel Vliebergh and Maurice Wilmotte; 1f.20, Paul Pastur and Julius Hoste; 2f. Lodewijk de Raet and Jules Destree (politicians); 3f. Constantin Meunier and Constant Permeke (artists); 4f. Lieven Gevaert and Edouard Empain (industrialists).

329 Sikorsky S-58 Helicopter

1957. Conveyance of 100,000th Passenger by Belgian Helicopter Service.
1610 **329** 4f. blue, green and grey 80 45

330 Steamer entering Zeebrugge Harbour

1957. 50th Anniv of Completion of Zeebrugge Harbour.
1611 **330** 2f. blue 30 15

331 King Leopold I entering Brussels (after Simonau)

332 Scout and Guide Badges

1957. 126th Anniv of Arrival of King Leopold I in Belgium.
1612 **331** 20c. green 20 20
1613 – 2f. mauve 50 20
DESIGN—HORIZ: 2f. King Leopold I at frontier (after Wappers).

1957. 50th Anniv of Boy Scout Movement and Birth Centenary of Lord Baden-Powell.
1614 **332** 80c. brown 30 25
1615 – 4f. green . . . . 1·30 55
DESIGN—VERT: 4f. Lord Baden-Powell.

333 "Kneeling Woman" (after Lehmbruck)

334 "Agriculture and Industry"

1957. 4th Biennial Sculpture Exn, Antwerp.
1616 **333** 2f.50 green . . . . . . 1·10 70

1957. Europa.
1617 **334** 2f. purple . . . . 1·00 15
1618 4f. blue . . . . 4·25 45

335 Sledge-dog Team

1957. Belgian Antarctic Expedition, 1957–58.
1619 **335** 5f.+2f.50 orange, brown and grey . . . . . . 3·50 2·30
MS1620 115 × 83 mm. Block of four of No. 1619 in new colours, brown, red and blue £200 £130

336 General Patton's Grave at Hamm

337 Adolphe Max

1957. General Patton Memorial Issue.
1621 **336** 1f.+50c. black . . . . . 1·80 75
1622 – 2f.50+50c. green . . . . 2·75 1·10
1623 – 3f.+1f. brown . . . . . 3·75 1·90
1624 – 5f.+2f.50 slate . . . . . 8·50 5·25
1625 – 6f.+3f. red . . . . . . 11·00 7·25
DESIGNS—HORIZ: 2f.50, Patton Memorial project at Bastogne; 3f. Gen. Patton decorating Brig.-General A. MacAuliffe; 6f. (51 × 35½ mm) Tanks in action. VERT: 5f. General Patton.

1957. 18th Death Anniv of Burgomaster Adolphe Max (patriot).
1626 **337** 2f.50+1f. blue . . . . . 1·30 70

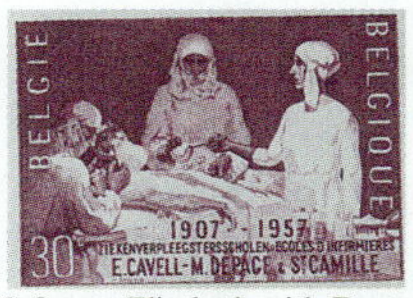

338 Queen Elisabeth with Doctors Depage and Debaisieux at a surgical operation

1957. 50th Anniv of "Edith Cavell-Marie Depage" and "St. Camille" Nursing Schools.
1627 **338** 30c. red 20 10

339 "Carnival Kings of Fosses" (Namur)

340 "Infanta Isabella with Crossbow" (Brussels)

1957. Anti-tuberculosis and other Funds. Provincial Legends.
1628 **339** 30c.+20c. pur & yell . . 25 25
1629 – 1f.+50c. sepia & blue . . 30 25
1630 – 1f.50+50c. grey & red . . 55 40
1631 – 2f.+1f. black & green . . 75 45
1632 **340** 2f.50+1f. grn & mve . . 1·90 1·20
1633 – 5f.+2f. black & blue . . 4·00 3·50
1634 – 6f.+2f.50 lake & red . . 5·00 4·25
DESIGNS: As Type **339**—HORIZ: 1f.50, "St. Remacle and the Wolf" (Liege). VERT: 1f. "Op Signoorken" (Antwerp); 2f. "The Long Man and the Pea Soup" (Limburg). As Type **340**—HORIZ: 6f. "Carnival Kings of Binche" (Hainaut). VERT: 5f. "The Virgin with the Inkwell" (West Flanders).

341 Posthorn and Postilion's Badges

1958. Postal Museum Day.
1635 **341** 2f.50 grey 20 10

342 Benelux Gate

1958. Inauguration of Brussels International Exhibition. Inscr as in T **342**.
1636 **342** 30c.+20c. sepia, brown and violet 10 10
1637 – 1f.+50c. purple, slate and green 10 10
1638 – 1f.50+50c. violet, turquoise and green 20 20
1639 – 2f.50+1f. red, blue and vermilion 30 25
1640 – 3f.+1f.50 blue, black and red 75 60
1641 – 5f.+3f. mauve, black and blue . . . . 1·50 1·20
DESIGNS—HORIZ: 1f. Civil Engineering Pavilion; 1f.50, Belgian Congo and Ruanda-Urundi Pavilion; 2f.50, "Belgium, 1900"; 3f. Atomium; 5f. (49 × 33½ mm) Telexpo Pavilion.

343 "Food and Agriculture Organization"

1958. United Nations Commemoration.
1642 – 50c. grey (postage) . . . 2·40 2·00
1643 **343** 1f. red 30 30
1644 – 1f.50 blue 35 30
1645 – 2f. purple 50 55
1646 – 2f.50 green 30 30
1647 – 3f. turquoise 55 45
1648 – 5f. mauve 35 30
1649 – 8f. brown 70 70
1650 – 11f. lilac . . . . 1·30 1·30
1651 – 20f. red . . . . 2·50 2·00
1652 – 5f. blue (air) 25 20
1653 – 6f. green 25 25
1654 – 7f.50 violet 30 30
1655 – 8f. sepia 35 35
1656 – 9f. red 50 50
1657 – 10f. brown 55 50
DESIGNS (Emblems and symbols)—HORIZ: 50c. I.L.O. 2f.50, UNESCO 3f. U.N. Pavilion, Brussels Int Exn; 6f. World Meteorological Organization; 8f. (No. 1649), Int Monetary Fund; 8f. (No. 1655), General Agreement on Tariffs and Trade; 10f. Atomic Energy Agency; 11f. W.H.O. 20f. U.P.U. VERT: 1f.50, U.N.O. 2f. World Bank; 5f. (No. 1648), I.T.U. 5f. (No. 1652), I.C.A.O. 7f.50, Protection of Refugees; 9f. UNICEF.

344 Eugene Ysaye

345 "Europa"

1958. Birth Centenary of Ysaye (violinist).
1658 **344** 30c. blue and red 15 15

1958. Europa.
1659 **345** 2f.50 blue and red . . . 2·75 20
1660 5f. red and blue . . . . 7·75 45

346 "Marguerite Van Eyck" (after Jan Van Eyck)

1958. Cultural Relief Funds. Paintings as T **346**. Frames in brown and yellow.
1661 **346** 30c.+20c. myrtle 30 25
1662 – 1f.+50c. lake 75 45
1663 – 1f.+50+50c. blue . . . . 1·30 85
1664 – 2f.50+1f. sepia . . . . . 2·50 1·70
1665 – 3f.+1f.50 red . . . . . 3·25 2·20
1666 – 5f.+3f. blue . . . . . . 6·00 4·50
PAINTINGS—HORIZ: 1f. "Carrying the Cross" (Hieronymus Bosch). 3f. "The Rower" (James Ensor). VERT: 1f.50, "St. Donatien" (Jan Gossaert). 2f.50, Self-portrait (Lambert Lombard). 5f. "Henriette with the Large Hat" (Henri Evenepoel).

347 "Hoogstraten"

348 Pax—"Creche vivante"

1958. Anti-tuberculosis and other Funds. Provincial Legends.
1667 **347** 40c.+10c. blue & grn . . 25 25
1668 – 1f.+50c. sepia & yell . . 30 25
1669 – 1f.50+50c. pur & grn . . 55 30
1670 – 2f.+1f. brown & red . . 60 40
1671 **348** 2f.50+1f. red and green 1·80 1·00
1672 – 5f.+2f. purple & blue . . 4·00 3·50
1673 – 6f.+2f. blue & red . . . 5·00 4·25
DESIGNS: As Type **347**—VERT: 1f. "Jean de Nivelles"; 1f.50, "Jeu de Saint Evermare a Russon". HORIZ: 2f. "Les penitents de Furnes". As Type **348**—HORIZ: "Marches de l'Entre Sambre et Meuse". VERT: 6f. "Pax—Vierge".

349 "Human Rights"

350 "Europe of the Heart"

1958. 10th Anniv of Human Rights Declaration.
1674 **349** 2f.50 slate 40 15

1959. "Heart of Europe". Fund for Displaced Persons.
1675 **350** 1f.+50c. purple 35 25
1676 2f.50+1f. green 85 65
1677 5f.+2f.50 brown . . . . 1·50 1·20

351 J. B. de Taxis taking the oath at the hands of Charles V (after J.-E. Van den Bussche)

352 N.A.T.O. Emblem

1959. Stamp Day.
1680 **351** 2f.50 green 50 15

1959. 10th Anniv of N.A.T.O.
1681 **352** 2f.50 blue and red . . . 40 20
1682 5f. blue and green . . . 1·10 70
On the 5f. value the French and Flemish inscriptions are transposed.
For similar design but inscr "1969", see No. 2112.

353 "Blood Transfusion"

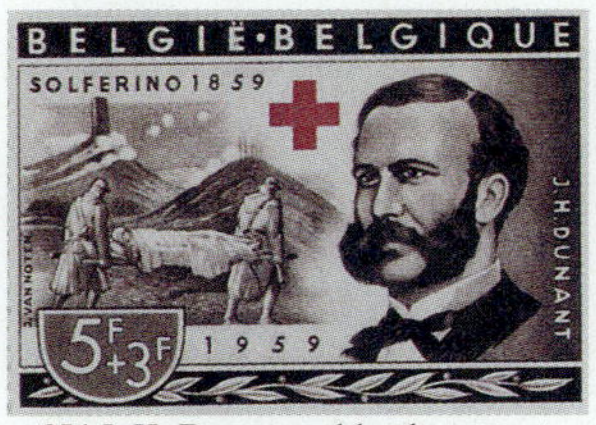

354 J. H. Dunant and battle scene at Solferino, 1859

1959. Red Cross Commem. Inscr "1859 1959".
1683 **353** 40c.+10c. red & grey . . 30 30
1684 1f.+50c. red & sepia . . 95 55
1685 1f.50+50c. red and lilac 3·00 1·60

1686 – 2f.50+1f. red & grn . . . 3·75 1·80
1687 – 3f.+1f.50 red and blue 6·75 4·00
1688 **354** 5f.+3f. red and sepia . . 13·50 7·00
DESIGN—As Type **353**—HORIZ: 2f.50, 3f. Red Cross and broken sword ("Aid for the wounded").

355 Philip the Good **356** Arms of Philip the Good

1959. Royal Library of Belgium Fund. Mult.
1689 40c.+10c. Type **355** 20 25
1690 1f.+50c. Charles the Bold 40 35
1691 1f.50+50c. Maximillian of Austria . . . . 1·30 1·10
1692 2f.50+1f. Philip the Fair . . 2·30 1·90
1693 3f.+1f.50 Charles V . . . . 4·00 2·75
1694 5f.+3f. Type **355** . . . . . 5·50 4·00

358 Town Hall, Oudenarde **359** Pope Adrian VI

1959. Oudenarde Town Hall Commem.
1699 **358** 2f.50 purple 45 15

1959. 500th Birth Anniv of Pope Adrian VI.
1700 **359** 2f.50 red 20 15
1701 5f. blue 40 35

360 "Europa" **361** Boeing 707

1959. Europa.
1702 **360** 2f.50 red 90 15
1703 5f. turquoise . . . . . . 1·60 40

1959. Inauguration of Boeing 707 Airliners by SABENA.
1704 **361** 6f. blue, grey and red . . 1·70 60

362 Antwerp fish (float) **363** Stavelot "Blancs Moussis" (carnival figures)

1959. Anti-tuberculosis and other Funds. Carnival scenes.
1705 **362** 40c.+10c. green, red and bistre 20 25
1706 – 1f.+50c. green, violet and olive 35 30
1707 – 2f.+50c. yellow, purple and brown 45 35
1708 **363** 2f.50+1f. blue, violet and grey 70 35
1709 – 3f.+1f. purple, yellow and grey . . . . . . 1·90 1·20
1710 – 6f.+2f. blue, red and olive . . . . 4·25 3·75
1711 – 7f.+3f. blk, yell, & bl . . 5·25 4·50
DESIGNS—As Type **362**—HORIZ: 1f. Mons dragon (float); 2f. Eupen and Malmedy clowns in chariot. As Type **363**—VERT: 3f. Ypres jester. HORIZ: 6f. Holy Family; 7f. Madonna and child.

364 Countess Alexandrine of Taxis (tapestry) **365** Indian Azalea

1960. Stamp Day.
1712 **364** 3f. blue 60 20

1960. Ghent Flower Show. Inscr as in T **365**.
1713 **365** 40c. red and purple . . . 15 15
1714 – 3f. yellow, red and green 55 15
1715 – 6f. red, green and blue 1·50 70
FLOWERS: 3f. Begonia. 6f. Anthurium and bromelia.

366 Refugee **367** "Labour" (after Meunier)

1960. World Refugee Year. Inscr as in T **366**.
1716 – 40c.+10c. purple 15 25
1717 **366** 3f.+1f.50 sepia 50 35
1718 – 6f.+3f. blue . . . . . . 1·50 1·10
MS1719 121 × 93 mm. Nos. 1716/18 in new colours, violet, brown and red respectively . . . . 80·00 65·00
DESIGNS: 40c. Child refugee; 6f. Woman refugee.

1960. 75th Anniv of Belgian Socialist Party. Inscr as in T **367**.
1720 **367** 40c. purple and red . . . 20 25
1721 – 3f. brown and red . . . 60 25
DESIGN—HORIZ: 3f. "Workers" (after Meunier).

369 Parachutist on ground

1960. Parachuting. Designs bearing emblem of National Parachuting Club.
1726 – 40c.+10c. black & blue 30 60
1727 – 1f.+50c. black & blue . . 1·60 1·20
1728 – 2f.+50c. black, blue and green . . . . 3·00 1·70
1729 – 2f.50+1f. black, turquoise and green 5·25 3·25
1730 **369** 3f.+1f. black, blue and green . . . . 5·50 3·25
1731 6f.+2f. black, blue and green . . . . 5·75 3·75
DESIGNS—HORIZ: 40c., 1f., Parachutists dropping from Douglas DC-4 aircraft. VERT: 2f., 2f.50, Parachutists descending.

370 Ship's Officer and Helmsman

1960. Congo Independence.
1732 **370** 10c. red 15 15
1733 – 40c. red 15 15
1734 – 1f. purple 55 25
1735 – 2f. green 55 25
1736 – 2f.50 blue 70 25
1737 – 3f. blue 70 20
1738 – 6f. violet . . . . 2·50 85
1739 – 8f. brown . . . . 8·50 6·00
DESIGNS—As Type **370**: 40c. Doctor and nurses with patient; 1f. Tree-planting; 2f. Sculptors; 2f.50, Sport (putting the shot); 3f. Broadcasting from studio. (52 × 35½ mm): 6f. Children with doll; 8f. Child with globe.

371 Refugee Airlift

1960. Congo Refugees Relief Fund.
1740 **371** 40c.+10c. turquoise . . . 20 25
1741 – 3f.+1f.50 red . . . . . 2·30 1·50
1742 – 6f.+3f. violet . . . . . 5·00 4·00
DESIGNS—As Type **371**: 3f. Mother and child. 35 × 51½ mm: 6f. Boeing 707 airplane spanning map of aircraft route.

1960. Surch.
1743 **267** 15c. on 30c. green . . . 10 10
1744 15c. on 50c. blue 10 10
1745 20c. on 30c. green . . . 10 10

373 Conference Emblem **374** Young Stamp Collectors

1960. 1st Anniv of E.P.T. Conference.
1746 **373** 3f. lake 70 20
1747 6f. green . . . . 1·70 55

1960. "Philately for the Young" Propaganda.
1748 **374** 40c. black and bistre . . 10 10

375 Pouring Milk for Child **376** Frere Orban (founder)

1960. United Nations Children's Fund.
1749 **375** 40c.+10c. yellow, green and brown 10 25
1750 – 1f.+50c. red, blue and drab 75 50
1751 – 2f.+50c. bistre, green and violet . . . . . . 2·00 1·60
1752 – 2f.50+1f. sepia, blue and red . . . . 2·30 1·70
1753 – 3f.+1f. violet, orange and turquoise . . . . . 2·75 1·90
1754 – 6f.+2f. brown, green and blue . . . . 4·25 2·75
DESIGNS: 1f. Nurse embracing children; 2f. Child carrying clothes, and ambulance; 2f.50, Nurse weighing baby; 3f. Children with linked arms; 6f. Refugee worker and child.

1960. Centenary of Credit Communal (Co-operative Bank).
1755 **376** 10c. brown and yellow 10 10
1756 40c. brown and green . . 15 10
1757 1f.50 brown and violet 90 70
1758 3f. brown and red . . . 90 20

377 Tapestry

1960. Anti-T.B. and other Funds. Arts and Crafts.
1759 **377** 40c.+10c. ochre, brown and blue 10 20
1760 – 1f.+50c. blue, brown and indigo 75 75
1761 – 2f.+50c. green, black and brown . . . . 1·60 1·00
1762 – 2f.50+1f. yellow and brown . . . . 3·00 2·00
1763 – 3f.+1f. black, brown and blue . . . . 3·25 2·40
1764 – 6f.+2f. lemon and black 5·00 3·25
DESIGNS—VERT: 1f. Crystalware; 2f. Lace. HORIZ: 2f.50, Brassware; 3f. Diamond-cutting; 6f. Ceramics.

378 King Baudouin and Queen Fabiola **379** Nicolaus Rockox (after Van Dyck)

1960. Royal Wedding.
1765 **378** 40c. sepia and green . . 20 15
1766 3f. sepia and purple . . 70 15
1767 6f. sepia and blue . . . 1·90 45

1961. Surch in figs and **1961** at top, **1962** at bottom and bars in between.
1768 **267** 15c. on 30c. green . . . 1·00 20
1769 20c. on 30c. green . . . 2·30 1·50
See note below No. 480.

1961. 400th Birth Anniv of Nicolaus Rockox (Burgomaster of Antwerp).
1770 **379** 3f. black, bistre & brn 35 15

380 Seal of Jan Bode **381** K. Kats (playwright) and Father N. Pietkin (poet)

1961. Stamp Day.
1771 **380** 3f. sepia and brown . . 35 15

1961. Cultural Funds. Portrait in purple.
1772 40c.+10c. lake and pink . . 50 30
1773 1f.+50c. lake and brown . . 2·10 1·30
1774 2f.+50c. red and yellow . . 3·75 2·75
1775 2f.50+1f. myrtle and sage 3·75 2·75
1776 3f.+1f. blue and light blue 4·25 3·00
1777 6f.+2f. blue and lavender . . 5·50 3·50
PORTRAITS: 40c. Type **381**. 1f. A. Mockel and J. F. Willems (writers). 2f. J. van Rijswick and X. Neujean (politicians). 2f.50, J. Demarteau (journalist) and A. van de Perre (politician). 3f. J. David (litterateur) and A. du Bois (writer). 6f. H. Vieuxtemps (violinist) and W. de Mol (composer).

382 White Rhinoceros **383** Cardinal A.P. de Granville (first Archbishop)

1961. Philanthropic Funds. Animals of Antwerp Zoo.
1778 40c.+10c. dp brown & brn 25 25
1779 1f.+50c. brown and green 1·20 70
1780 2f.+50c. sepia, red and black 1·70 1·30
1781 2f.50+1f. brown and red . . 2·00 1·40
1782 3f.+1f. brown and orange 2·10 1·50
1783 6f.+2f. ochre and blue . . 3·00 1·90
ANIMALS—VERT: 40c. Type **382**; 1f. Wild horse and foal; 2f. Okapi. HORIZ: 2f.50, Giraffe; 3f. Lesser panda; 6f. Elk.

1961. 400th Anniv of Archbishopric of Malines.
1784 **383** 40c.+10c. brown, red and purple 20 25
1785 – 3f.+1f.50 mult 75 70
1786 – 6f.+3f. bistre, violet and purple . . . . 1·30 1·10
DESIGNS: 3f. Cardinal's Arms; 6f. Symbols of Archbishopric and Malines.

385 "Interparliamentary Union"

1961. 50th Interparliamentary Union Conference, Brussels.
1791 **385** 3f. brown and turquoise 65 15
1792 6f. purple and red . . . 1·30 65

386 Doves

1961. Europa.
1793 **386** 3f. black and olive . . . 40 15
1794 6f. black and brown . . 70 40

387 Reactor BR 2, Mol

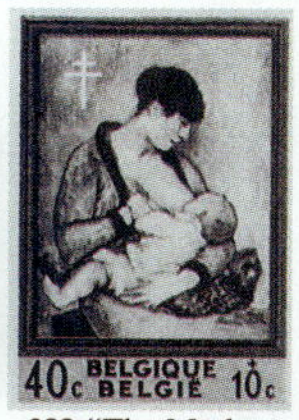

388 "The Mother and Child" (after Paulus)

1961. Euratom Commemoration.
1795 **387** 40c. green 10 10
1796 – 3f. mauve 15 10
1797 – 6f. blue 40 35
DESIGNS—VERT: 3f. Heart of reactor BR 3, Mol. HORIZ: 6f. View of reactor BR 3, Mol.

1961. Anti-T.B. and other Funds. Belgian paintings of mothers and children. Frames in gold.
1798 **388** 40c.+10c. sepia 20 25
1799 – 1f.+50c. blue 60 60
1800 – 2f.+50c. red . . . . . 1·10 1·00
1801 – 2f.50+1f. lake . . . . . 1·10 1·00
1802 – 3f.+1f. violet . . . . . 1·10 1·00
1803 – 6f.+2f. myrtle . . . . . 1·40 1·30
PAINTINGS: 1f. "Maternal Love" (Navez). 2f. "Maternity" (Permeke). 2f.50, "The Virgin and the Child" (Van der Weyden). 3f. "The Virgin with the Apple" (Memling), 6f. "The Myosotis Virgin" (Rubens).

389 Horta Museum

390 Male Castle

1962. Birth Cent of Victor Horta (architect).
1804 **389** 3f. brown 25 15

1962. Cultural and Patriotic Funds. Buildings.
1805 **390** 40c.+10c. green 20 25
1806 – 90c.+10c. mauve 30 35
1807 – 1f.+50c. lilac 60 55
1808 – 2f.+50c. violet 95 85
1809 – 2f.50+1f. brown . . . . 1·20 1·20
1810 – 3f.+1f. turquoise . . . . 1·30 1·20
1811 – 6f.+2f. red . . . . . 1·90 1·80
BUILDINGS—HORIZ: 90c. Royal Library, Brussels. 1f. Collegiate Church, Soignies. 6f. Ypres Halls. VERT: 1f. Notre-Dame Basilica, Tongres. 2f.50, Notre-Dame Church, Hanswijk, Malines. 3f. St. Denis-en-Broqueroie Abbey.

391 16th-Century Postilion

392 G. Mercator (after F. Hogenberg)

1962. Stamp Day.
1812 **391** 3f. brown and green . . 30 15
See also No. 1997.

1962. 450th Birth Anniv of Mercator (geographer).
1813 **392** 3f. sepia 30 15

393 Brother A. M. Gochet (scholar)

394 Guianan Cock of the Rock ("Coq de Roch, Rotshann")

1962. Gochet and Triest Commemoration.
1814 **393** 2f. blue 10 10
1815 – 3f. brown 30 25
PORTRAIT: 3f. Canon P.-J. Triest (benefactor of the aged).

1962. Philanthropic Funds. Birds of Antwerp Zoo. Birds, etc., in natural colours; colours of name panel and inscription given.
1816 **394** 40c.+10c. blue 20 25
1817 – 1f.+50c. blue and red . . 50 45
1818 – 2f.+50c. mauve & blk . . 80 80
1819 – 2f.50+1f. turq & red . . 1·10 1·10
1820 – 3f.+1f. brown & grn . . 1·30 1·40
1821 – 6f.+2f. blue and red . . 1·90 1·90

BIRDS: 1f. Red lory ("Rode Lori, Lori Rouge"); 2f. Green turaco ("Touracou du Senegal, Senegal Toerakoe"); 2f.50, Keel-billed toucan ("Kortbek Toecan, Toucan a Bec Court"); 3f. Greater bird of paradise ("Grand Paradijsier, Grosse Paradisvogel"); 6f. Congo peafowl ("Kongo Pauw, Paon du Congo").

395 Europa "Tree"

396 "Captive Hands" (after sculpture by Ianchelivici)

1962. Europa.
1822 **395** 3f. black, yellow & red 60 15
1823 6f. black, yellow & olive 1·10 40

1962. Concentration Camp Victims.
1824 **396** 40c. blue and black . . . 15 10

397 Reading Braille

398 "Adam" (after Michelangelo)

1962. Handicapped Children Relief Funds.
1825 **397** 40c.+10c. brown 20 25
1826 – 1f.+50c. red 40 50
1827 – 2f.+50c. mauve . . . . 1·00 1·10
1828 – 2f.50+1f. green . . . . 1·00 1·10
1829 – 3f.+1f. blue . . . . . 1·00 1·00
1830 – 6f.+2f. sepia . . . . . 1·30 1·20
DESIGNS—VERT: 1f. Girl solving puzzle; 2f.50, Crippled child with ball; 3f. Girl walking with crutches. HORIZ: 2f. Child with earphones; 6f. Crippled boys with football.

1962. "The Rights of Man".
1831 **398** 3f. sepia and green . . . 20 15
1832 6f. sepia and brown . . 40 40

399 Queen Louise-Marie

400 Menin Gate, Ypres

1962. Anti-tuberculosis and other Funds. Belgian Queens in green and gold.
1833 40c.+10c. Type **399** 10 10
1834 40c.+10c. As T **399** but inscr "ML" 10 10
1835 1f.+50c. Marie-Henriette . . 60 65
1836 2f.+1f. Elisabeth . . . . . 1·10 1·10
1837 3f.+1f.50 Astrid . . . . . 1·50 1·30
1838 8f.+2f.50 Fabiola . . . . . 1·80 1·50

1962. Ypres Millenary.
1839 **400** 1f.+50c. multicoloured 45 45
MS1840 113 × 137 mm. Block of eight . . . . 6·00 5·50

401 H. Pirenne

402 "Peace Bell"

1963. Birth Cent of Henri Pirenne (historian).
1841 **401** 3f. blue 40 15

1963. Cultural Funds and Installation of "Peace Bell" in Koekelberg Basilica. Bell in yellow; "PAX" in black.
1842 **402** 3f.+1f.50 green & bl . . 1·60 1·40
1843 6f.+3f. chestnut & brn 95 90
MS1844 82 × 116 mm. No. 1842 (block of four) . . . . . . 8·25 7·75

403 "The Sower" (after Brueghel)

404 17th-century Duel

1963. Freedom from Hunger.
1845 **403** 2f.+1f. brown, black and green 25 25
1846 – 3f.+1f. brown, black and purple 30 25
1847 – 6f.+2f. yellow, black and brown 60 60
PAINTINGS—HORIZ: 3f. "The Harvest" (Brueghel). VERT: 6f. "The Loaf" (Anto Carte).

1963. 350th Anniv of Royal Guild and Knights of St. Michael.
1848 **404** 1f. red and blue 10 10
1849 – 3f. violet and green . . . 20 10
1850 – 6f. multicoloured 50 40
DESIGNS—HORIZ: 3f. Modern fencing. VERT: 6f. Arms of the Guild.

405 19th-century Mail-coach

1963. Stamp Day.
1851 **405** 3f. black and ochre . . . 30 15
See also No. 1998.

406 Hotel des Postes, Paris, and Belgian 1c. Stamp of 1863

407 Child in Wheatfield

1963. Centenary of Paris Postal Conference.
1852 **406** 6f. sepia, mauve & grn 55 45

1963. "8th May" Peace Movement.
1853 **407** 3f. multicoloured 30 15
1854 6f. multicoloured 75 45

408 "Transport"

409 Town Seal

1963. European Transport Ministers' Conference, Brussels.
1855 **408** 6f. black and blue . . . 55 35

1963. Int Union of Towns Congress, Brussels.
1856 **409** 6f. multicoloured 45 35

410 Racing Cyclists

411 Sud Aviation SE 210 Caravelle

1963. Belgian Cycling Team's Participation in Olympic Games, Tokyo (1964).
1857 **410** 1f.+50c. multicoloured 20 30
1858 – 2f.+1f. multicoloured . . 20 30
1859 – 3f.+1f.50 mult 30 40
1860 – 6f.+3f. multicoloured . . 45 50
DESIGNS—HORIZ: 2f. Group of cyclists; 3f. Cyclists rounding bend. VERT: 6f. Cyclists being paced by motorcyclists.

1963. 40th Anniv of SABENA Airline.
1861 **411** 3f. black and turquoise 30 15

412 "Co-operation"

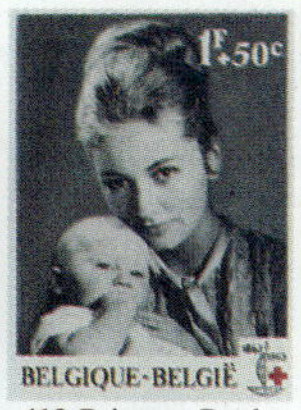

413 Princess Paola with Princess Astrid

1963. Europa.
1862 **412** 3f. black, brown & red 1·00 15
1863 6f. black, brown & blue 1·80 45
No. 1863 is inscr with "6 F" on the left, "BELGIE" at foot and "BELGIQUE" on right.

1963. Centenary of Red Cross and Belgian Red Cross Fund. Cross in red.
1864 – 40c.+10c. red & yell . . 10 10
1865 **413** 1f.+50c. grey & yellow 20 20
1866 – 2f.+50c. mauve & yell 30 30
1867 – 2f.50+1f. blue & yell . . 30 35
1868 – 3f.+1f. brown & yell . . 50 45
1869 – 3f.+1f. bronze & yell . . 2·10 2·00
1870 – 6f.+2f. green & yellow 1·30 1·30
DESIGNS—As T **413**: 40c. Prince Philippe; 2f. Princess Astrid; 2f.50, Princess Paola; 6f. Prince Albert; 46 × 35 mm: 3f. (2), Prince Albert and family.

414 J. Destree (writer)

1963. Jules Destree and H. Van de Velde Commems.
1871 **414** 1f. purple 10 10
1872 – 1f. green 10 10
DESIGN: No. 1872, H. Van de Velde (architect).

415 Bas-reliefs from Facade of Postal Cheques Office (after O. Jespars)

416 Balthasar Gerbier's Daughter

1963. 50th Anniv of Belgian Postal Cheques Office.
1873 **415** 50c. black, blue & red 10 15

1963. T.B. Relief and Other Funds. Rubens's Drawings. Background buff; inscr in black: designs colour given.
1874 **416** 50c.+10c. blue 10 10
1875 – 1f.+40c. red 25 25
1876 – 2f.+50c. violet 25 25
1877 – 2f.50+1f. green 60 60
1878 – 3f.+1f. brown 55 50
1879 – 6f.+2f. black 85 85
DRAWINGS—VERT: Rubens's children—1f. Nicolas (aged 2). 2f. Franz (aged 4). 2f.50, Nicolas (aged 6). 3f. Albert (aged 3). HORIZ: (46½ × 35½ mm): 6f. Infant Jesus, St. John and two angels.

417 Dr. G. Hansen and Laboratory

1964. Leprosy Relief Campaign.
1880 **417** 1f. black and brown . . 20 25
1881 – 2f. brown and black . . 25 30
1882 – 5f. black and brown . . 50 40
MS1883 135 × 98 mm. Nos. 1880/2 (+4f.) . . . . 2·75 2·75
DESIGNS: 2f. Leprosy hospital; 5f. Father Damien.

418 A. Vesale (anatomist) with Model of Human Arm

419 Postilion

1964. Belgian Celebrities.
1884 **418** 50c. black and green . . 10 10
1885 – 1f. black and green . . . 15 25
1886 – 2f. black and green . . . 20 25

DESIGNS—HORIZ: 1f. J. Boulvin (engineer) and internal combustion engine; 2f. H. Jaspar (statesman) and medallion.

1964. Stamp Day.
1887 **419** 3f. grey 30 15

420 Admiral Lord Gambier and U.S. Ambassador J. Q. Adams after signing treaty (from painting by Sir A. Forestier)

1964. 150th Anniv of Signing of Treaty of Ghent.
1888 **420** 6f.+3f. blue 55 60

421 Arms of Ostend

422 Ida of Bure (Calvin's wife)

1964. Millenary of Ostend.
1889 **421** 3f. multicoloured 25 15

1964. "Protestantism in Belgium".
1890 – 1f.+50c. blue 20 25
1891 **422** 3f.+1f.50 red 25 30
1892 – 6f.+3f. brown 50 55
PORTRAITS: 1f. P. Marnix of St. Aldegonde (Burgomaster of Antwerp). 6f. J. Jordaens (painter).

423 Globe, Hammer and Flame

424 Infantryman of 1918

1964. Centenary of Socialist International.
1893 **423** 50c. red and blue 10 10
1894 – 1f. red and blue 10 10
1895 – 2f. red and blue 15 25
DESIGNS: 1f. "SI" on Globe; 2f. Flames.

1964. 50th Anniv of German Invasion of Belgium. Multicoloured.
1896 1f.+50c. Type **424** 15 20
1897 2f.+1f. Colour sergeant of the Guides Regt, 1914 . . . . 15 25
1898 3f.+1f.50 Trumpeter of the Grenadiers & Drummers of the Infantry and Carabiniers, 1914 . . . . 30 35

425 Soldier at Bastogne

426 Europa "Flower"

1964. "Liberation–Resistance". Multicoloured.
1899 3f.+1f. Type **425** 25 25
1900 6f.+3f. Soldier at estuary of the Scheldt 55 55

1964. Europa.
1901 **426** 3f. grey, red and green . . 75 20
1902 6f. blue, green and red . . 2·50 45

427 "Philip the Good"

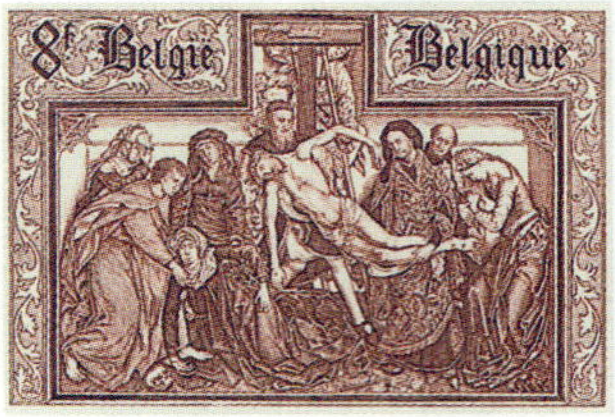

428 "Descent from the Cross"

1964. Cultural Funds. 500th Death Anniv of R. van der Weyden. Two sheets each 153 × 114 mm showing paintings by Van der Weyden.
MS1903 1f. Type **427**; 2f. "Portrait of a Lady"; 3f. "The Man with the Arrow" (+8f.) . . . . 4·25 4·25
MS1904 **428** 8f. (+8f.) brown . . 4·00 4·00

429 Pand Abbey, Ghent

1964. Pand Abbey Restoration Fund.
1905 **429** 2f.+1f. bl, turq & blk . . 25 30
1906 – 3f.+1f. brown, blue and purple 25 30
DESIGN: 3f. Waterside view of Abbey.

430 King Baudouin, Queen Juliana and Grand Duchess Charlotte

1964. 20th Anniv of "BENELUX".
1907 **430** 3f. purple, blue and olive 45 15

431 "One of Charles I's Children" (Van Dyck)

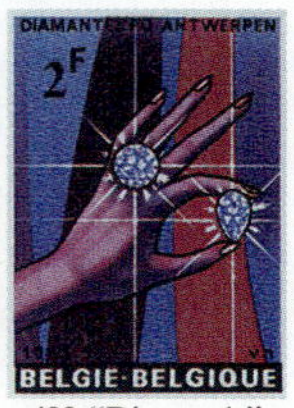

432 "Diamonds"

1964. T.B. Relief and Other Funds. Paintings of Royalty.
1908 **431** 50c.+10c. purple 15 15
1909 – 1f.+40c. red 20 25
1910 – 2f.+1f. purple 20 25
1911 – 3f.+1f. grey 30 30
1912 – 4f.+2f. violet 35 40
1913 – 6f.+3f. violet 45 50
DESIGNS—VERT: 1f. "William of Orange and his fiancee, Marie" (Van Dyck); 2f. "Portrait of a Little Boy" (E. Quellin and Jan Fyt); 3f. "Alexander Farnese at the age of 12 Years" (A. Moro); 4f. "William II, Prince of Orange" (Van Dyck). HORIZ—LARGER (46 × 35 mm): 6f. "Two Children of Cornelis De Vos" (C. de Vos).

1965. "Diamantexpo" (Diamonds Exn) Antwerp.
1914 **432** 2f. multicoloured 25 25

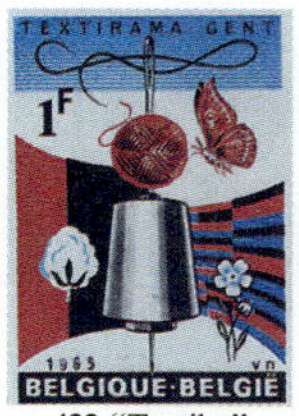

433 "Textiles"

434 Vriesia

1965. "Textirama" (Textile Exn), Ghent.
1915 **433** 1f. black, red and blue 15 15

1965. Ghent Flower Show. Inscr "FLORALIES GANTOISES", etc. Multicoloured.
1916 1f. Type **434** 10 20
1917 2f. Echinocactus 20 25
1918 3f. Stapelia 20 15

435 Paul Hymans

436 Rubens

1965. Birth Cent of Paul Hymans (statesman).
1919 **435** 1f. violet 10 10

1965. Centenary of General Savings and Pensions Funds. Painters.
1920 **436** 1f. sepia and mauve . . 20 10
1921 – 2f. sepia and turquoise 20 10
1922 – 3f. sepia and purple . . 15 10
1923 – 6f. sepia and red 40 25
1924 – 8f. sepia and blue . . . 50 45
PAINTERS: 2f. Franz Snyders. 3f. Adam van Noort. 6f. Anthony van Dyck. 8f. Jakob Jordaens.

437 "Sir Rowland Hill with Young Collectors" (detail from mural by J. Van den Bussche)

438 19th-century Postmaster

1965. "Philately for the Young".
1925 **437** 50c. green 10 10

1965. Stamp Day.
1926 **438** 3f. green 20 10

1965. U.N.W.R.A. Commemoration. Sheet 123 × 89 mm. Nos. 1916/18 in new colours.
MS1927 1f., 2f., 3f. (+14f.) . . . 2·20 2·20

439 Globe and Telephone

1965. Centenary of I.T.U.
1928 **439** 2f. black and purple . . 20 25

440 Handclasp

441 Abbey Staircase

1965. 20th Anniv of Liberation of Prison Camps.
1929 **440** 50c.+50c. purple, black and bistre 10 10
1930 – 1f.+50c. multicoloured 25 25
1931 – 3f.+1f.50 black, purple and green 30 30
1932 – 8f.+5f. multicoloured 80 80
DESIGNS—VERT: 1f. Hand reaching for barbed wire. HORIZ: 3f. Tank entering prison camp; 8f. Rose within broken wall.

1965. Affligem Abbey.
1933 **441** 1f. blue 15 15

442 St. Jean Berchmans, Birthplace and Residence

443 Toc H Lamp and Arms of Poperinge

1965. St. Jean Berchmans.
1934 **442** 2f. brown and purple . . 15 15

1965. 50th Anniv of Founding of Toc H Movement at Talbot House, Poperinge.
1935 **443** 3f. multicoloured 25 15

444 Maison Stoclet, Brussels

445 Tractor ploughing

1965. Josef Hoffman (architect) Commemoration.
1936 **444** 3f.+1f. grey and drab . . 30 30
1937 – 6f.+3f. brown 55 55
1938 – 8f.+4f. purple & drab . . 80 80
DESIGNS—Maison Stoclet: VERT: 6f. Entrance hall. HORIZ: 8f. Rear of building.

1965. 75th Anniv of Boerenbond (Belgian Farmers' Association). Multicoloured.
1939 50c. Type **445** 10 10
1940 3f. Horse-drawn plough . . 25 15

446 Europa "Sprig"

1965. Europa.
1941 **446** 1f. black and pink . . . 40 15
1942 3f. black and green . . . 55 15

447 Jackson's Chameleon

1965. Philanthropic Funds. Reptiles of Antwerp Zoo. Multicoloured.
1943 1f.+50c. Type **447** 15 30
1944 2f.+1f. Iguana 25 30
1945 3f.+1f.50 Nile lizard 30 35
1946 6f.+3f. Komodo lizard . . . 50 55
MS1947 118 × 98 mm. 8f.+4f. Soft-shelled turtle (larger) . . . . . 1·90 1·90

448 J. Lebeau (after A. Schollaert)

449 Leopold I (after 30c. and 1f. Stamps of 1865)

1965. Death Cent of Joseph Lebeau (statesman).
1948 **448** 1f. multicoloured 10 10

1965. Death Centenary of King Leopold I.
1949 **449** 3f. sepia 30 15
1950 – 6f. violet 55 40
DESIGN: 6f. As 3f. but with different portrait frame.

450 Huy

451 Guildhouse

1965. Tourist Publicity. Multicoloured.
1951 50c. Type **450** 10 10
1952 50c. Hoeilaart (vert) 10 10
See also Nos. 1995/6, 2025/6, 2083/4, 2102/3, 2123/4, 2159/60, 2240/1 and 2250/1.

1965. T.B. Relief and Other Funds. Public Buildings, Brussels.
1953 **451** 50c.+10c. blue 10 10
1954 – 1f.+40c. turquoise . . . 10 20
1955 – 2f.+1f. purple 20 20
1956 – 3f.+1f.50 violet 30 30
1957 – 10f.+4f.50 sepia and grey 80 80
BUILDINGS—HORIZ: 1f. Brewers' House; 2f. Builders' House; 3f. House of the Dukes of Brabant. VERT: (24½ × 44½ mm): 10f. Tower of Town Hall.

452 Queen Elisabeth (from medallion by A. Courtens)

453 "Peace on Earth"

1965. Queen Elisabeth Commem.
1958 **452** 3f. black 30 15

1966. 75th Anniv of "Rerum Novarum" (papal encyclical). Multicoloured.
1959 50c. Type **453** 10 10
1960 1f. "Building for Tomorrow" (family and new building) 10 10
1961 3f. Arms of Pope Paul VI (vert 24½ × 45 mm) . . . 10 10

1966. Queen Elisabeth. Sheets 82 × 116 mm incorporating old designs, each with se-tenant label showing Crown over "E". (a) In brown, blue, gold and grey.
MS1962 3f. T **125** and 3f. T **317** (sold at 20f.) . . . . 1·50 1·50
(b) In brown, myrtle and green.
MS1963 3f. T **160** and 3f. T **172** (sold at 20f.) . . . . 1·50 1·50

454 Rural Postman

455 High Diving

1966. Stamp Day.
1964 **454** 3f. black, lilac & buff . . 30 15

1966. Swimming.
1965 **455** 60c.+40c. brown, green and blue 15 15
1966 – 10f.+4f. brown, purple and green 90 75
DESIGN: 10f. Diving from block.

456 Iguanodon Fossil (Royal Institute of Natural Sciences)

457 Eurochemic Symbol

1966. National Scientific Institutions.
1967 **456** 1f. black and green . . . 25 25
1968 – 2f. black, orge & cream 15 25
1969 – 2f. multicoloured 15 25
1970 – 3f. multicoloured 10 10
1971 – 3f. gold, black and red 10 10
1972 – 6f. multicoloured 30 30
1973 – 8f. multicoloured 50 50
DESIGNS—HORIZ: No. 1968, Kasai head (Royal Central African Museum); No. 1969, Snow crystals (Royal Meteorological Institute). VERT: No. 1970, "Scholar" (Royal Library); No. 1971, Seal (General Archives); No. 1972, Arend-Roland comet and telescope (Royal Observatory); No. 1973, Satellite and rocket (Space Aeronomy Inst.).

1966. European Chemical Plant, Mol.
1974 **457** 6f. black, red and drab 45 30

458 A. Kekule

460 Rik Wouters (self-portrait)

1966. Centenary of Professor August Kekule's Benzene Formula.
1975 **458** 3f. brown, black & blue 30 15

1966. 19th World I.P.T.T. Congress, Brussels. Optd **XIXe CONGRES IPTT** and emblem.
1976 **454** 3f. black, lilac and buff 30 15

1966. 50th Death Anniv of Rik Wouters (painter).
1977 **460** 60c. multicoloured . . . 10 10

461 Minorites Convent, Liege

1966. Cultural Series.
1978 **461** 60c.+40c. purple, blue and brown 15 25
1979 – 1f.+50c. blue, purple and turquoise 15 25
1980 – 2f.+1f. red, purple and brown 15 25
1981 – 10f.+4f.50 purple, turquoise and green 75 75
DESIGNS: 1f. Val-Dieu Abbey, Aubel; 2f. Huy and town seal; 10f. Statue of Ambiorix and castle, Tongres.

463 Europa "Ship"

464 Surveying

1966. Europa.
1989 **463** 3f. green 35 15
1990 6f. purple 75 45

1966. Antarctic Expeditions.
1991 **464** 1f.+50c. green 10 10
1992 – 3f.+1f.50 violet 25 25
1993 – 6f.+3f. red 50 55
MS1994 130 × 95 mm. 10f.+5f. multicoloured . . . . 1·20 1·20
DESIGNS: 3f. Commander A. de Gerlache and "Belgica" (polar barque); 6f. "Magga Dan" (Antarctic supply ship) and meteorological operations. 52 × 35½ mm.—10f. "Magga Dan" and emperor penguins.

1966. Tourist Publicity. As T **450**. Multicoloured.
1995 2f. Bouillon 10 10
1996 2f. Lier (vert) 10 10

1966. 75th Anniv of Royal Federation of Belgian Philatelic Circles. Stamps similar to Nos. 1812 and 1851 but incorporating "1890 1996" and F.I.P. emblem.
1997 **391** 60c. purple and green . . 10 10
1998 **405** 3f. purple and ochre . . 10 10

466 Children with Hoops

467 Lions Emblem

1966. "Solidarity" (Child Welfare).
1999 – 1f.+1f. black & pink . . 10 10
2000 – 2f.+1f. black & green . . 10 10
2001 – 3f.+1f.50 black & lav . . 20 25
2002 **466** 6f.+3f. brown & flesh . . 40 40
2003 – 8f.+3f.50 brown & grn 60 60
DESIGNS—VERT: 1f. Boy with ball and dog; 2f. Girl with skipping-rope; 3f. Boy and girl blowing bubbles. HORIZ: 8f. Children and cat playing "Follow My Leader".

1967. Lions International.
2004 **467** 3f. sepia, blue and olive 25 10
2005 6f. sepia, violet and green 45 40

468 Part of Cleuter Pistol

1967. Arms Museum, Liege.
2006 **468** 2f. black, yellow & red 20 25

469 I.T.Y. Emblem

1967. International Tourist Year.
2007 **469** 6f. blue, red and black 50 30

470 Young Refugee

1967. European Refugee Campaign Fund. Sheet 110 × 77 mm comprising T **470** and similar vert designs.
MS2008 1f. black and yellow (Type **470**); 2f. black and blue; 3f. black and orange (sold at 20f.) 1·30 1·30

471 Woodland and Trientalis (flowers), Hautes Fagnes

1967. Nature Conservation. Multicoloured.
2009 1f. Type **471** 20 25
2010 1f. Dunes and eryngium (flowers), Westhoek . . . 20 25

472 Paul-Emile Janson (statesman)

473 19th-century Postman

1967. Janson Commemoration.
2011 **472** 10f. blue 65 45

1967. Stamp Day.
2012 **473** 3f. purple and red . . . 30 15

474 Cogwheels

475 Flax Plant and Shuttle

1967. Europa.
2013 **474** 3f. black, red and blue 40 20
2014 6f. black, yellow & green 85 45

1967. Belgian Linen Industry.
2015 **475** 6f. multicoloured 45 30

476 Kursaal in 19th Century

1967. 700th Anniv of Ostend's Rank as Town.
2016 **476** 2f. sepia, buff and blue 15 15

478 With F.I.T.C.E. Emblem

479 Robert Schuman (statesman)

1967. European Telecommunications Day. "Stamp Day" design of 1967 incorporating F.I.T.C.E. emblem as T **478** in green.
2021 **478** 10f. sepia and blue . . . 75 50

"F.I.T.C.E." "Federation des Ingenieurs des Telecommunications de la Communaute Europeenne."

1967. Charity.
2022 **479** 2f.+1f. green 30 30
2023 – 5f.+2f. brown, yellow and black 45 45
2024 – 10f.+5f. multicoloured 85 85
DESIGNS—HORIZ: 5f. Kongolo Memorial, Gentinnes (Congo Martyrs). VERT: 10f. "Colonial Brotherhood" emblem (Colonial Troops Memorial).

1967. Tourist Publicity. As T **450**. Mult.
2025 1f. Ypres 10 10
2026 1f. Spontin 10 15

480 "Caesar Crossing the Rubicon" (Tournai Tapestry)

481 "Jester in Pulpit" (from Erasmus's "Praise of Folly")

1967. Charles Plisnier and Lodewijk de Raet Foundations.
2028 **480** 1f. multicoloured 10 10
2029 – 1f. multicoloured 10 10
DESIGN No. 2029, "Maximilian hunting boar" (Brussels tapestry).

1967. Cultural Series. "Erasmus and His Time".
2030 1f.+50c. multicoloured . . . 10 10
2031 2f.+1f. multicoloured . . . 20 25
2032 3f.+1f.50 multicoloured . . 30 30
2033 5f.+2f. black, red & carmine 40 40
2034 6f.+3f. multicoloured . . . 60 60
DESIGNS—VERT: 1f. Type **481**. 2f. "Jester declaiming" (from Erasmus' "Praise of Folly"); 3f. Erasmus; 6f. Pierre Gilles ("Aegidius" from painting by Metzijs). HORIZ: 5f. "Sir Thomas More's Family" (Holbein).

482 "Princess Margaret of York" (from miniature)

483 Arms of Ghent University

1967. "British Week".
2035 **482** 6f. multicoloured 45 30

1967. Universities of Ghent and Liege. Mult.
2036 3f. Type **483** 25 15
2037 3f. Liege 25 15

484 Emblem of "Pro-Post" Association

1967. "Postphila" Stamp Exhibition, Brussels. Sheet 110 × 77 mm.
MS2038 **484** 10f.+5f. black, green, red and brown . . . . 1·00 1·00

485 Our Lady of Virga Jesse, Hasselt

1967. Christmas.
2039 **485** 1f. blue 10 10

486 "Children's Games" (section of Brueghel's painting)

1967. "Solidarity".

2040	**486**	1f.+50c. multicoloured	15	15
2041	–	2f.+50c. multicoloured	15	15
2042	–	3f.+1f. multicoloured . .	30	30
2043	–	6f.+3f. multicoloured . .	45	45
2044	–	10f.+4f. multicoloured	75	75
2045	–	13f.+6f. multicoloured	1·00	1·00

Nos. 2040/5 together form the complete painting.

487 Worker in Protective Hand

489 Army Postman (1916)

1968. Industrial Safety Campaign.

2046	**487**	3f. multicoloured	25	15

1968. Stamp Day.

2068	**489**	3f. purple, brown & blue	25	15

490 Belgian 1c. "Small Lion" Stamp of 1866

491 Grammont and Seal of Baudouin VI

1968. Cent of State Printing Works, Malines.

2069	**490**	1f. olive	10	10

1968. "Historical Series". Multicoloured.

2070	2f. Type **491**	30	25
2071	3f. Theux-Franchimont Castle and battle emblems	30	15
2072	6f. Archaeological discoveries, Spiennes . . .	45	30
2073	10f. Roman oil lamp and town crest, Wervik . . .	65	55

492 Europa "Key"

493 Queen Elisabeth and Dr. Depage

1968. Europa.

2074	**492**	3f. gold, black & green	65	20
2075		6f. silver, black and red	1·30	45

1968. Belgian Red Cross Fund. Cross in red.

2076	**493**	6f.+3f. sepia, black and green	60	60
2077	–	10f.+5f. sepia, black and green	85	85

DESIGN: 10f. Queen Fabiola and baby.

494 Gymnastics

495 "Explosion"

1968. Olympic Games, Mexico. Multicoloured.

2078	1f.+50c. Type **494**	10	10
2079	2f.+1f. Weightlifting	10	25
2080	3f.+1f.50 Hurdling	25	25
2081	6f.+2f. Cycling	45	40
2082	13f.+5f. Sailing (vert 24½ × 45 mm)	1·00	1·00

Each design includes the Olympic "rings" and a Mexican cultural motif.

1968. Tourist Publicity. As Type **450**.

2083	2f. multicoloured	10	10
2084	2f. black, blue and green . .	10	10

DESIGNS: No. 2083, Farm-house and windmill, Bokrijk; No. 2084, Bath-house and fountain, Spa.

1968. Belgian Disasters. Victims Fund. Mult.

2085	10f.+5f. Type **495**	90	1·00
2086	12f.+5f. "Fire"	95	1·30
2087	13f.+5f. "Typhoon"	1·00	1·00

496 St. Laurent Abbey, Liege

1968. "National Interest".

2088	**496**	2f. black, bistre & blue	15	25
2089	–	3f. brown, grey & lt brn	25	15
2090	–	6f. black, blue & dp bl	45	30
2091	–	10f. multicoloured . . .	75	45

DESIGNS: 3f. Church, Lissewege; 6f. "Mineral Seraing" and "Gand" (ore carriers), canal-lock, Zandvliet; 10f. Canal-lift, Ronquieres.

497 Undulate Triggerfish

1968. "Solidarity" and 125th Anniv of Antwerp Zoo. Designs showing fish. Multicoloured.

2092	1f.+50c. Type **497**	20	25
2093	3f.+1f.50 Ear-spotted angelfish	25	25
2094	6f.+3f. Lionfish	50	50
2095	10f.+5f. Diagonal butterflyfish	85	80

498 King Albert in Bruges (October, 1918)

499 Lighted Candle

1968. Patriotic Funds.

2096	**498**	1f.+50c. multicoloured	15	25
2097	–	3f.+1f.50 mult	20	25
2098	–	6f.+3f. multicoloured . .	45	50
2099	–	10f.+5f. multicoloured	75	80

DESIGNS—HORIZ: 3f. King Albert entering Brussels (November, 1918); 6f. King Albert in Liege (November, 1918). LARGER (46 × 35 mm): 10f. Tomb of the Unknown Soldier, Brussels.

1968. Christmas.

2100	**499**	1f. multicoloured	15	15

500 "Mineral Seraing" (ore carrier) in Ghent Canal

1968. Ghent Maritime Canal.

2101	**500**	6f. black brown, & blue	45	30

1969. Tourist Publicity. As Type **450**.

2102	1f. black, blue & pur (vert)	10	10
2103	1f. black, olive and blue . .	10	10

DESIGNS. No. 2102, Town Hall, Louvain; No. 2103, Valley of the Ourthe.

501 "Albert Magnis" (detail of wood carving by Quellin, Confessional, St. Paul's Church, Antwerp)

1969. St. Paul's Church, Antwerp, and Aulne Abbey Commemoration.

2104	**501**	2f. sepia	10	10
2105	–	3f. black and mauve . .	10	10

DESIGN: 3f. Aulne Abbey.

502 "The Travellers" (sculpture, Archaeological Museum, Arlon)

503 Broodjes Chapel, Antwerp

1969. 2,000th Anniv of Arlon.

2106	**502**	2f. purple	15	25

1969. "150 Years of Public Education in Antwerp".

2107	**503**	3f. black and grey . . .	25	10

504 Mail Train

505 Colonnade

1969. Stamp Day.

2108	**504**	3f. multicoloured	20	10

1969. Europa.

2109	**505**	3f. multicoloured	40	20
2110		6f. multicoloured	75	45

506 "The painter and the Amateur" (detail, Brueghel)

1969. "Postphila 1969" Stamp Exhibition, Brussels. Sheet 91 × 124 mm.

MS2111	**506**	10f.+5f. brown . . .	1·30	1·30

507 NATO Emblem

508 "The Builders" (F. Leger)

1969. 20th Anniv of N.A.T.O.

2112	**507**	6f. blue and brown . . .	50	40

1969. 50th Anniv of I.L.O.

2113	**508**	3f. multicoloured	30	15

509 "Houses" (I. Dimitrova)

510 Racing Cyclist

1969. UNICEF "Philanthropy" Funds. Mult.

2114	1f.+50c. Type **509**	15	25
2115	3f.+1f.50 "My Art" (C. Patric)	25	25
2116	6f.+3f. "In the Sun" (H. Rejchlova)	50	50
2117	10f.+5f. "Out for a Walk" (P. Sporn) (horiz)	80	80

1969. World Championship Cycle Races, Zolder.

2118	**510**	6f. multicoloured	50	30

511 Mgr. V. Scheppers

512 National Colours

1969. Monseigneur Victor Scheppers (founder of "Brothers of Mechlin") Commemoration.

2119	**511**	6f.+3f. purple	60	60

1969. 25th Anniv of BENELUX Customs Union.

2120	**512**	3f. multicoloured	30	15

513 Pascali Rose and Annevoie Gardens

1969. Flowers and Gardens. Multicoloured.

2121	2f. Type **513**	10	10
2122	2f. Begonia and Lochristi Gardens	10	10

1969. Tourist Publicity. As Type **450**.

2123	2f. brown, red and blue . .	10	10
2124	2f. black, green and blue . .	10	10

DESIGNS: No. 2123, Veurne Furnes; No. 2124, Vielsalm.

514 "Feats of Arms" from "History of Alexander the Great" (Tournai, 15th century)

516 Wounded Soldier

515 Astronauts and Location of Moon Landing

1969. "Cultural Works" Tapestries. Mult.

2125	1f.+50c. Type **514**	15	25
2126	3f.+1f.50 "The Violinist" from "Festival" (David Teniers II, Oudenarde, c.1700)	35	30
2127	10f.+4f. "The Paralytic", from "The Acts of the Apostles" (Brussels, c.1517)	85	85

1969. 1st Man on the Moon.

2128	**515**	6f. sepia	45	35
MS2129		95 × 130 mm. 20f.+10f. blue	2·50	2·50

DESIGN: **MS**2129 is as T **515**, but in vert format.

1969. 50th Anniv of National War Invalids Works (O.N.I.G.).

2130	**516**	1f. green	10	10

517 "The Postman" (Daniella Sainteney)

519 Count H. Carton de Wiart (from painting by G. Geleyn)

518 John F. Kennedy Motorway Tunnel, Antwerp

1969. "Philately for the Young".
2131 **517** 1f. multicoloured 10 10

1969. Completion of Belgian Road-works. Mult.
2132 3f. Type **518** 30 15
2133 6f. Loncin flyover, Wallonie motorway 45 40

1969. Birth Centenary of Count Henry Carton de Wiart (statesman).
2134 **519** 6f. sepia 45 35

520 "Barbu d'Anvers" (Cockerel)

1969. "The Poultry-yard" (poultry-breeding).
2135 **520** 10f.+5f. multicoloured 1·00 95

521 "Le Denombrement de Bethleem" (detail, Brueghel)

1969. Christmas.
2136 **521** 1f.50 multicoloured . . . 10 10

522 Emblem, "Coin" and Machinery

523 Window, St. Waudru Church, Mons

1969. 50th Anniv of National Credit Society (S.N.C.I.).
2137 **522** 3f.50 brown and blue . . 30 15

1969. "Solidarity". Musicians in Stained-glass Windows. Multicoloured.
2138 1f.50+50c. Type **523** 20 25
2139 3f.50+1f.50 's-Herenelderen Church 25 25
2140 7f.+3f. St. Jacques Church, Liege 60 65
2141 9f.+4f. Royal Museum of Art and History, Brussels 1·00 1·00
No. 2141 is larger, 36 × 52 mm.

524 Camellias

525 Beech Tree in National Botanical Gardens

1970. Ghent Flower Show. Multicoloured.
2142 1f.50 Type **524** 10 10
2143 2f.50 Water-lily 25 25
2144 3f.50 Azaleas 25 15
MS2145 122 × 92 mm. Nos. 2142/4 in slightly different shades . . 2·00 1·90

1970. Nature Conservation Year. Multicoloured.
2146 3f.50 Type **525** 30 15
2147 7f. Birch 50 35

526 Young "Postman"

1970. "Philately for the Young".
2148 **526** 1f.50 multicoloured . . . 10 10

527 New U.P.U. Headquarters Building

1970. New U.P.U. Headquarters Building.
2149 **527** 3f.50 green 30 15

528 "Flaming Sun"

1970. Europa.
2150 **528** 3f.50 cream, blk & lake 55 15
2151 7f. flesh, black and blue 1·00 45

529 Open-air Museum, Bokrijk

530 Clock-tower, Virton

1970. Cultural Works. Multicoloured.
2152 1f.50+50c. Type **529** 15 25
2153 3f.50+1f.50 Relay Post-house, Courcelles 25 25
2154 7f.+3f. "The Reaper of Trevires" (bas-relief, Virton) 50 55
2155 9f.+4f. Open-air Museum, Middelheim, (Antwerp) 75 75

1970. Historic Towns of Virton and Zelzate.
2156 **530** 2f.50 violet and ochre . . 15 25
2157 – 2f.50 black and blue . . 15 15
DESIGN—HORIZ: No. 2157, "Skaustand" (freighter), canal bridge, Zelzate.

531 Co-operative Alliance Emblem

1970. 75th Anniv of Int Co-operative Alliance.
2158 **531** 7f. black and orange . . 45 25

1970. Tourist Publicity, As Type **450**.
2159 1f.50 green, blue and black 10 10
2160 1f.50 buff, blue & deep blue 10 10
DESIGNS—HORIZ: No. 2159, Kasterlee. VERT: No. 2160, Nivelles.

532 Allegory of Resistance Movements

533 King Baudouin

1970. 25th Anniv of Prisoner of War and Concentration Camps Liberation.
2161 **532** 3f.50+1f.50 black, red and green 30 35
2162 – 7f.+3f. black, red and mauve 55 55
DESIGN: 7f. Similar to Type **532**, but inscr "LIBERATION DES CAMPS", etc.

1970. King Baudouin's 40th Birthday.
2163 **533** 3f.50 brown 25 15
See also Nos. 2207/23c and 2335/9b.

534 Fair Emblem

535 U.N. Headquarters, New York

1970. 25th International Ghent Fair.
2164 **534** 1f.50 multicoloured . . . 10 10

1970. 25th Anniv of United Nations.
2165 **535** 7f. blue and black . . . 50 30

536 Queen Fabiola

537 Angler's Rod and Reel

1970. Queen Fabiola Foundation.
2166 **536** 3f.50 black and blue . . 25 15

1970. Sports. Multicoloured.
2167 3f.50+1f.50 Type **537** . . . 35 40
2168 9f.+4f. Hockey stick and ball (vert) 70 75

538 Belgian 8c. Stamp of 1870

1970. "Belgica 72" Stamp Exhibition, Brussels (1st issue).
MS2169 1f.50+50c. violet and black; 3f.50+1f.50 lilac and black; 9f.+4f. brown and black . . . . . 3·75 3·75
DESIGNS: 3f.50, Belgian 1f. stamp of 1870; 9f. Belgian 5f. stamp of 1870.

539 "The Mason" (sculpture by G. Minne)

541 "Madonna and Child" (Jan Gossaert)

540 Man, Woman and Hillside Town

1970. 50th Anniv of National Housing Society.
2170 **539** 3f.50 brown & yell . . . 10 10

1970. 25th Anniv of Belgian Social Security.
2171 **540** 2f.50 multicoloured . . . 10 10

1970. Christmas.
2172 **541** 1f.50 brown 10 10

542 C. Huysmans (statesman)

1970. Cultural Works. Famous Belgians.
2173 **542** 1f.50+50c. brown and red 10 20
2174 – 3f.50+1f.50 brown and purple 25 25
2175 – 7f.+3f. brown & green 55 50
2176 – 9f.+4f. brown & blue . . 75 75
PORTRAITS: 3f.50, Cardinal J. Cardijn. 7f. Maria Baers (Catholic social worker). 9f. P. Pastur (social reformer).

543 Arms of Eupen, Malmedy and St. Vith

1970. 50th Anniv of Annexation of Eupen, Malmedy and St. Vith.
2177 **543** 7f. brown and sepia . . 45 45

544 "The Uneasy Town" (detail, Paul Delvaux)

545 Telephone

1970. "Solidarity". Paintings. Multicoloured.
2178 3f.50+1f.50 Type **544** . . . 35 40
2179 7f.+3f. "The Memory" (Rene Magritte) 60 60

1971. Inaug of Automatic Telephone Service.
2183 **545** 1f.50 multicoloured . . . 10 10

546 "Auto" Car

547 Touring Club Badge

1971. 50th Brussels Motor Show.
2184 **546** 2f.50 black and red . . . 15 15

1971. 75th Anniv of Royal Touring Club of Belgium.
2185 **547** 3f.50 gold, red & blue 25 15

548 Tournai Cathedral

549 "The Letter-box" (T. Lobrichon)

1971. 800th Anniv of Tournai Cathedral.
2186 **548** 7f. blue 45 45

1971. "Philately for the Young".
2187 **549** 1f.50 brown 15 15

550 Notre-Dame Abbey, Marche-les-Dames

1971. Cultural Works.
2190 **550** 3f.50+1f.50 black, green and brown 30 35
2191 – 7f.+3f. black, red and yellow 60 60
DESIGN: 7f. Convent, Turnhout.

552 King Albert I, Jules Destree and Academy

1971. 50th Anniv of Royal Academy of French Language and Literature.
2201 **552** 7f. black and grey . . . 45 45

553 Postman of 1855 (from lithograph, J. Thiriar)

554 Europa Chain

1971. Stamp Day.
2202 **553** 3f.50 multicoloured . . . 20 10

1971. Europa.
2203 **554** 3f.50 brown and black 65 20
2204 7f. green and black . . . 1·10 45

555 Satellite Earth Station

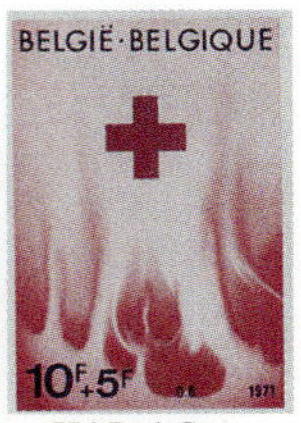

556 Red Cross

1971. World Telecommunications Day.
2205 **555** 7f. multicoloured 45 30

1971. Belgian Red Cross.
2206 **556** 10f.+5f. red & black . . 85 85

1971. As T **533**, but without dates.

2207	1f.75 green	15	25
2208	2f.25 green	25	25
2208a	2f.50 green	15	15
2209	3f. green	25	15
2209a	3f.25 plum	25	15
2210	3f.50 brown	35	15
2211	4f. blue	35	15
2212	4f.50 purple	40	15
2212a	4f.50 blue	35	15
2213	5f. violet	40	15
2214	6f. red	50	15
2214b	6f.50 violet	40	15
2215	7f. red	35	15
2215ba	7f.50 mauve	35	15
2216a	8f. black	60	15
2217	9f. sepia	70	30
2217a	9f. brown	75	15
2218a	10f. mauve	60	15
2218b	11f. sepia	85	25
2219	12f. blue	90	30
2219b	13f. blue	1·00	15
2219c	14f. green	1·20	25
2220	15f. violet	90	15
2220b	16f. green	1·40	15
2220c	17f. purple	1·20	25
2221	18f. blue	1·20	25
2221a	18f. turquoise	1·50	25
2222	20f. blue	1·30	15
2222b	22f. black	1·80	1·50
2222c	22f. turquoise	1·60	35
2222d	25f. purple	1·80	20
2223a	30f. orange	1·90	25
2223b	35f. turquoise	3·25	30
2223c	40f. blue	4·00	30
2223d	45f. brown	4·75	45

See also Nos. 2335/9.

557 Scientist, Adelie Penguins and "Erika Dan" (polar vessel)

1971. 10th Anniv of Antarctic Treaty.
2230 **557** 10f. multicoloured . . . 70 60

558 "The Discus thrower" and Munich Cathedral

559 G. Hubin (statesman)

1971. Olympic Games, Munich (1972) Publicity.
2231 **558** 7f.+3f. black & blue . . 60 60

1971. Georges Hubin Commemoration.
2232 **559** 1f.50 violet and black . . 10 10

560 Notre-Dame Abbey, Orval

561 Processional Giants, Ath

1971. 900th Anniv of Notre-Dame Abbey, Orval.
2233 **560** 2f.50 brown 10 10

1971. Historic Towns.
2234 **561** 2f.50 multicoloured . . . 10 10
2235 – 2f.50 brown 15 25
DESIGN—HORIZ: (46 × 35 mm): No. 2235, View of Ghent.

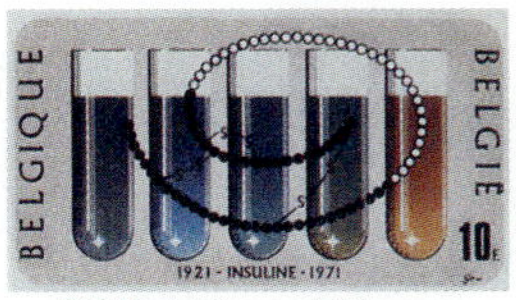

562 Test-tubes and Diagram

1971. 50th Anniv of Discovery of Insulin.
2236 **562** 10f. multicoloured . . . 65 45

563 Flemish Festival Emblem

1971. Cultural Works. Festivals. Multicoloured.
2237 3f.50+1f.50 Type **563** . . . 40 40
2238 7f.+3f. Walloon Festival emblem 65 65

564 Belgian Family and "50"

565 Dr. Jules Bordet (medical scientist)

1971. 50th Anniv of "League of Large Families".
2239 **564** 1f.50 multicoloured . . . 10 10

1971. Tourist Publicity. Designs similar to T **450**.
2240 2f.50 black, brown and blue 10 10
2241 2f.50 black, brown and blue 10 10
DESIGNS: No. 2240, St. Martin's Church, Alost; No. 2241, Town Hall and belfry, Mons.

1971. Belgian Celebrities.
2242 **565** 3f.50 green 25 10
2243 – 3f.50 brown 25 10
DESIGN: No. 2242, Type **565** (10th death anniv); No. 2243, "Stijn Streuvels" (Frank Lateur, writer, birth cent.).

566 Achaemenid Tomb, Buzpar

567 Elewijt Chateau

1971. 2500th Anniv of Persian Empire.
2244 **566** 7f. multicoloured 45 40

1971. "Belgica 72" Stamp Exhibition, Brussels (2nd issue).
2245 – 3f.50+1f.50 green 40 40
2246 **567** 7f.+3f. brown 65 60
2247 – 10f.+5f. blue 95 90
DESIGNS—HORIZ: (52 × 35½ mm): 3f. Attre Chateau; 10f. Royal Palace, Brussels.

568 F.I.B./V.B.N. Emblem

569 "The Flight into Egypt" (15th-century Dutch School)

1971. 25th Anniv of Federation of Belgian Industries.
2248 **568** 3f.50 gold, black & blue 30 15

1971. Christmas.
2249 **569** 1f.50 multicoloured . . . 10 10

1971. Tourist Publicity. Designs similar to T **450**.
2250 1f.50 blue and buff 10 10
2251 2f.50 blue and buff 20 10
DESIGNS—HORIZ: 1f.50, Town Hall, Malines. VERT: 2f.50, Basilica, St. Hubert.

570 "Actias luna"

1971. "Solidarity". Insects in Antwerp Zoo. Multicoloured.
2252 1f.50+50c. Type **570** 10 20
2253 3f.50+1f.50 "Tabanus bromius" (horiz) 35 35
2254 7f.+3f. "Polistes gallicus" (horiz) 65 60
2255 9f.+4f. "Cicindela campestris" 80 80

572 Road Signs and Traffic Signals

573 Book Year Emblem

1972. 20th Anniv of "Via Secura" Road Safety Organization.
2263 **572** 3f.50 multicoloured . . . 30 15

1972. International Book Year.
2264 **573** 7f. blue, brown & black 45 35

574 Coins of Belgium and Luxembourg

576 "Auguste Vermeylen" (I. Opsomer)

1972. 50th Anniv of Belgo–Luxembourgeoise Economic Union.
2265 **574** 1f.50 silver, black and orange 20 20

1972. Birth Centenary of Auguste Vemeylen (writer).
2267 **576** 2f.50 multicoloured . . . 15 25

577 "Belgica 72" Emblem

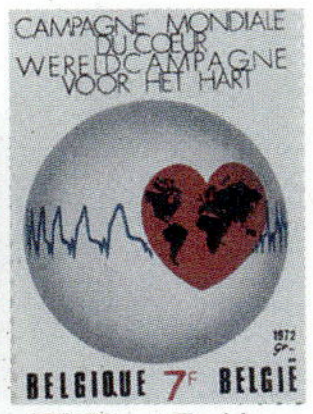

578 Heart Emblem

1972. "Belgica 72" Stamp Exn., Brussels (3rd Issue).
2268 **577** 3f.50 purple, blue & brn 35 20

1972. World Heart Month.
2269 **578** 7f. multicoloured 45 30

579 Astronaut cancelling Letter on Moon

580 "Communications"

1972. Stamp Day.
2270 **579** 3f.50 multicoloured . . . 25 10

1972. Europa.
2271 **580** 3f.50 multicoloured . . . 55 20
2272 7f. multicoloured . . . . 1·00 45

581 Quill Pen and Newspaper

582 "UIC" on Coupled Wagons

1972. "Liberty of the Press". 50th Anniv of Belga News Agency and 25th Congress of International Federation of Newspaper Editors (F.I.E.J.).
2273 **581** 2f.50 multicoloured . . . 20 10

1972. 50th Anniv of Int Railways Union (U.I.C.).
2274 **582** 7f. multicoloured 45 30
See also No. P2266.

583 Couvin

584 Leopold I 10c. "Epaulettes" Stamp of 1849

1972. Tourist Publicity.
2275 **583** 2f.50 purple, blue & grn . . 25 30
2276 – 2f.50 brown and blue . . 25 30
DESIGN—VERT: No. 2276, Aldeneik Church, Maaseik.

1972. "Belgica 72" Stamp Exn, Brussels (4th issue).
2277 **584** 1f.50+50c. brown, black and gold 25 25
2278 – 2f.+1f. red, brown and gold 30 30
2279 – 2f.50+1f. red, brown and gold 35 30
2280 – 3f.50+1f.50 lilac, black and gold 40 40
2281 – 6f.+3f. violet, black and gold 50 50
2282 – 7f.+3f. red, black and gold 60 60
2283 – 10f.+5f. blue, black and gold 90 85
2284 – 15f.+7f.50 green, turquoise and gold . . 1·40 1·40
2285 – 20f.+10f. chestnut, brown and gold . . . 1·90 1·80
DESIGNS: 2f. Leopold I 40c. "Medallion" of 1849; 2f.50, Leopold II 10c. of 1883. 3f.50, Leopold II 50c. of 1883; 6f. Albert I; 2f. "Tin Hat" of 1919; 7f. Albert I 50f. of 1929; 10f. Albert I 1f.75 of 1931; 15f. Leopold III 5f. of 1936; 20f. Baudouin 3f.50 of 1970.

585 "Beatrice" (G. de Smet)

586 Emblem of Centre

1972. "Philately for the Young".
2287 **585** 3f. multicoloured 25 25

1972. Inauguration of William Lennox Epileptic Centre, Ottignies.
2288 **586** 10f.+5f. multicoloured 1·00 90

587 Dish Aerial and "Intelstat 4" Satellite

588 Frans Masereel (wood-carver and painter)

1972. Inaug of Satellite Earth Station, Lessive.
2289 **587** 3f.50 black, silver & bl 25 10

1972. Masereel Commem.
2290 **588** 4f.50 black and green . . 35 15

589 "Adoration of the Magi" (F. Timmermans)

590 "Empress Maria Theresa" (unknown artist)

1972. Christmas.
2291 **589** 3f.50 multicoloured . . . 25 10

1972. Bicentenary of Belgian Royal Academy of Sciences, Letters and Fine Arts.
2292 **590** 2f. multicoloured 25 10

591 Greylag Goose

592 "Fire"

1972. "Solidarity". Birds from Zwin Nature Reserve. Multicoloured.
2293 2f.+1f. Type **591** 30 30
2294 4f.50+2f. Northern lapwing 45 45
2295 8f.+4f. White stork 75 75
2296 9f.+4f.50 Common kestrel (horiz) 90 90

1973. Industrial Buildings Fire Protection Campaign.
2297 **592** 2f. multicoloured 10 10

593 W.M.O. Emblem and Meteorological Equipment

595 W.H.O. Emblem as Man's "Heart"

594 Bijloke Abbey and Museum, Ghent

1973. Centenary of World Meteorological Organization.
2298 **593** 9f. multicoloured 65 45

1973. Cultural Works. Religious Buildings.
2299 **594** 2f.+1f. green 25 30
2300 – 4f.50+2f. brown 45 45
2301 – 8f.+4f. red 75 75
2302 – 9f.+4f.50 blue . . . . 1·00 90
DESIGNS: 4f.50, Collegiate Church of St. Ursmer, Lobbes; 8f. Park Abbey, Heverlee; 9f. Floreffe Abbey.

1973. 25th Anniv of W.H.O.
2303 **595** 8f. black, yellow & red 50 35

596 Ball in Hands

1973. 1st World Basketball Championships for the Handicapped, Bruges.
2304 **596** 10f.+5f. multicoloured 1·00 1·00

597 Europa "Posthorn"

598 Thurn and Taxis Courier (17th-cent)

1973. Europa.
2305 **597** 4f.50 blue, yellow & brn 80 20
2306 8f. blue, yellow & green 2·10 45

1973. Stamp Day.
2307 **598** 4f.50 brown and red . . 30 20

599 Fair Emblem

600 Arrows encircling Globe

1973. 25th International Fair, Liege.
2308 **599** 4f.50 multicoloured . . . 30 20

1973. 5th World Telecommunications Day.
2309 **600** 3f.50 multicoloured . . . 25 15

601 "Sport" (poster for Ghent Exhibition, 1913)

1973. 60th Anniv of Workers' International Sports Organization.
2310 **601** 4f.50 multicoloured . . . 30 15

602 Douglas DC-10-30CF and De Havilland D.H.9

1973. 50th Anniv of SABENA.
2311 **602** 8f. black, blue and grey 55 45

603 Ernest Tips's Biplane, 1908

1973. 35th Anniv (1972) of "Les Vieilles Tiges de Belgique" (pioneer aviators' association).
2312 **603** 10f. black, blue & green 70 45

604 15th-Century Printing-press

605 "Woman Bathing" (fresco by Lemaire)

1973. Historical Events and Anniversaries.
2313 **604** 2f.+1f. blk, brn & red . . 30 30
2314 – 3f.50+1f.50 mult 30 30
2315 – 4f.50+2f. mult 45 45
2316 – 8f.+4f. multicoloured . . 75 75
2317 – 9f.+4f.50 mult 85 85
2318 – 10f.+5f. multicoloured 1·10 1·10
DESIGNS—VERT (As Type **604**): 2f. (500th anniv of first Belgian printed book, produced by Dirk Martens); 3f.50, Head of Amon (Queen Elisabeth Egyptological Foundation. 50th anniv.); 4f.50, "Portrait of a Young Girl" (Petrus Christus, 500th death anniv). HORIZ (36 × 25 mm): 8f. Gold coins of Hadrian and Marcus Aurelius (Discovery of Roman treasure at Luttre-Liberchies); (52 × 35 mm); 9f. "Members of the Great Council" (Coessaert) (Great Council of Malines, 500th anniv.). 10f. "Jong Jacob" (East Indiaman) (Ostend Merchant Company, 250th anniv).

1973. Thermal Treatment Year.
2319 **605** 4f.50 multicoloured . . . 30 15

606 Adolphe Sax and Tenor Saxophone

607 St. Nicholas Church, Eupen

1973. Belgian Musical Instrument Industry.
2320 **606** 9f. multicoloured 60 45

1973. Tourist Publicity.
2321 **607** 2f. multicoloured 15 25
See also Nos. 2328/9, 2368/70, 2394/5, 2452/5, 2508/11, 2535/8, 2573/6, 2595/6 and 2614.

608 "Little Charles" (Evenepoel)

609 J. B. Moens (philatelist) and Perforations

1973. "Philately for the Young".
2322 **608** 3f. multicoloured 30 25

1973. 50th Anniv of Belgian Stamp Dealers Association.
2323 **609** 10f. multicoloured . . . 60 45

610 "Adoration of the Shepherds" (H. van der Goes)

611 Motorway and Emblem

1973. Christmas.
2324 **610** 4f. blue 30 20

1973. 50th Anniv of "Vlaamse Automobilistenbond" (VAB) (motoring organization).
2325 **611** 5f. multicoloured 45 20

612 L. Pierard (after sculpture by Ianchelevici)

613 Early Microphone

1973. 21st Death Anniv of Louis Pierard (politician and writer).
2326 **612** 4f. red and cream . . . 30 10

1973. 50th Anniv of Belgium Radio.
2327 **613** 4f. black and blue . . . 30 20

1973. Tourist Publicity. As T **607**.
2328 3f. grey, brown and blue . . 25 10
2329 4f. grey and green 30 25
DESIGNS—HORIZ: 3f. Town Hall, Leau; 4f. Chimay Castle.

614 F. Rops (self-portrait)

615 Jack of Diamonds

1973. 75th Death Anniv of Felicien Rops (artist and engraver).
2330 **614** 7f. black and brown . . 50 35

1973. "Solidarity". Old Playing Cards. Mult.
2331 5f.+2f.50 Type **615** 45 45
2332 5f.+2f.50 Jack of Spades . . 45 45
2333 5f.+2f.50 Queen of Hearts 45 45
2334 5f.+2f.50 King of Clubs . . 45 45

1973. As Nos. 2207/23 but smaller, 22 × 17 mm.
2335 **583** 3f. green . . . . 1·50 1·50
2336 4f. blue 40 45
2337 4f.50 blue 45 30
2338 5f. mauve 35 30
2338c 6f. red 45 40
2339 6f.50 violet 45 30
2339b 8f. grey 55 30

616 King Albert (Baron Opsomer)

617 "Blood Donation"

1974. 40th Death Anniv of King Albert I.
2340 **616** 4f. blue and black . . . 30 25

1974. Belgian Red Cross. Multicoloured.
2341 4f.+2f. Type **617** 40 40
2342 10f.+5f. "Traffic Lights" (Road Safety) . . . . . 1·00 90

618 "Protection of the Environment"

619 "Armand Jamar" (Self-portrait)

1974. Robert Schuman Association for the Protection of the Environment.
2343 **618** 3f. multicoloured 30 15

1974. Belgian Cultural Celebrities. Multicoloured.
2344 4f.+2f. Type **619** 40 40
2345 5f.+2f.50 Tony Bergmann (author) and view of Lier 45 45
2346 7f.+3f.50 Henri Vieuxtemps (violinist) and view of Verviers 60 65
2347 10f.+5f. "James Ensor" (self-portrait with masks) (35 × 52 mm) . . . . . . 1·00 1·00

620 N.A.T.O. Emblem

621 Hubert Krains (Belgian postal administrator)

1974. 25th Anniv of North Atlantic Treaty Organization.
2348 **620** 10f. blue and light blue 65 35

1974. Stamp Day.
2349 **621** 5f. black and grey . . . 30 15

622 "Destroyed Town" (O. Zadkine)

623 Heads of Boy and Girl

1974. Europa. Sculptures.
2350 **622** 5f. black and red 60 15
2351 – 10f. black and blue . . . 1·50 60
DESIGN: 10f. "Solidarity" (G. Minne).

1974. 10th Lay Youth Festival.
2352 **623** 4f. multicoloured 30 30

625 New Planetarium, Brussels

1974. Historical Buildings.
2354 **625** 3f. brown and blue . . . 20 15
2355 – 4f. brown and red . . . 30 30
2356 – 5f. brown and green . . . 35 15
2357 – 7f. brown and yellow . . 45 30
2358 – 10f. brown, orange & bl 75 35
DESIGNS—As T **625**. HORIZ: 4f. Pillory, Braine-le-Chateau. VERT: 10f. Belfry, Bruges. 45 × 25 mm: 5f. Ruins of Soleilmont Abbey; 7f. "Procession" (fountain sculpture, Ghent).

626 "BENELUX"

1974. 30th Anniv of Benelux Customs Union.
2359 **626** 5f. blue, green & lt blue 30 15

627 "Jan Vekemans at the Age of Five" (Cornelis de Vos)

628 Self-portrait and Van Gogh House, Cuesmes

1974. "Philately for the Young".
2360 **627** 3f. multicoloured 30 25

1974. Opening of Vincent Van Gogh House, Cuesmes.
2361 **628** 10f.+5f. multicoloured 1·00 90

629 Corporal Tresignies and Brule Bridge

1974. 60th Death Anniv of Corporal Leon Tresignies (war hero).
2362 **629** 4f. green and brown . . 30 25

630 Montgomery Blair and U.P.U. Emblem

631 Graph within Head

1974. Centenary of U.P.U.
2363 **630** 5f. black and green . . . 35 20
2364 – 10f. black and red . . . 70 45
DESIGN: 10f. H. von Stephan and U.P.U. Monument.

1974. 25th Anniv of Central Economic Council.
2365 **631** 7f. multicoloured 50 30

632 Rotary Emblem on Belgian Flag

633 Wild Boar

1974. 50th Anniv of Rotary Int in Belgium.
2366 **632** 10f. multicoloured . . . 70 35

1974. 40th Anniv of Granting of Colours to Ardennes Regiment of Chasseurs.
2367 **633** 3f. multicoloured 25 10

1974. Tourist Publicity. As T **607**.
2368 3f. brown and yellow . . . 30 25
2369 4f. green and blue 30 30
2370 4f. green and blue 30 30
DESIGNS—VERT: No. 2368, Aarschot. HORIZ: No. 2369, Meeting of three frontiers, Gemmenich; 2370, Nassogne.

634 "Angel" (detail, "The Mystic Lamb", Brothers Van Eyck)

635 Gentian

1974. Christmas.
2371 **634** 4f. purple 30 25

1974. "Solidarity". Flora and Fauna. Multicoloured.
2372 4f.+2f. Type **635** 45 45
2373 5f.+2f.50 Eurasian badger (horiz) 50 45
2374 7f.+3f.50 "Carabus auratus" (beetle) (horiz) 65 70
2375 10f.+5f. Spotted cat's-ear . . 1·00 1·00

636 Adolphe Quetelet (after J. Odevaere)

637 Exhibition Emblem

1974. Death Centenary of Adolphe Quetelet (scientist).
2376 **636** 10f. black and brown . . 65 40

1975. "Themabelga" Stamp Exhibition, Brussels (1st issue).
2377 **637** 6f.50 orange, blk & grn 45 15
See also Nos. 2411/16.

638 "Neoregelia carolinae"

639 Student and Young Boy

1975. Ghent Flower Show. Multicoloured.
2378 4f.50 Type **638** 30 30
2379 5f. "Tussilago petasites" . . 35 15
2380 6f.50 "Azalea japonica" . . 40 15

1975. Cent of Charles Buls Normal School.
2381 **639** 4f.50 multicoloured . . . 30 15

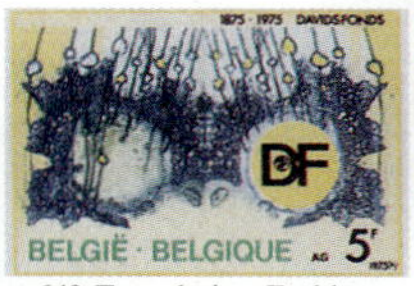

640 Foundation Emblem

641 King Albert I

1975. Centenary of Davids Foundation (Flemish cultural organisation).
2382 **640** 5f. multicoloured 40 15

1975. Birth Centenary of King Albert I.
2383 **641** 10f. black and purple . . 65 30

642 Pesaro Palace, Venice

643 "Postman of 1840" (J. Thiriar)

1975. Cultural Works.
2384 **642** 6f.50+2f.50 brown . . . 60 60
2385 – 10f.+4f.50 purple 90 90
2386 – 15f.+6f.50 blue . . . . . 1·30 1·20
DESIGNS—HORIZ: 10f. Sculpture Museum, St. Bavon Abbey, Ghent. VERT: 15f. "Virgin and Child" (Michelangelo, 500th Birth Anniv.).

1975. Stamp Day.
2387 **643** 6f.50 purple 50 20

644 "An Apostle" (detail, "The Last Supper", Dirk Bouts)

645 Prisoners' Identification Emblems

1975. Europa. Paintings.
2388 **644** 6f.50 black, blue & grn 70 20
2389 – 10f. black, red & orange 1·40 45
DESIGN: 10f. "The Suppliant's Widow" (detail, "The Justice of Otho", Dirk Bouts).

1975. 30th Anniv of Concentration Camps' Liberation.
2390 **645** 4f.50 multicoloured . . . 30 15

646 St John's Hospice, Bruges

1975. European Architectural Heritage Year.
2391 **646** 4f.50 purple 30 15
2392 – 5f. green 40 25
2393 – 10f. blue 75 40
DESIGNS—VERT: 5f. St. Loup's Church, Namur. HORIZ: 10f. Martyrs Square, Brussels.

1975. Tourist Publicity. As T **607**.
2394 4f.50 brown, buff and red 30 15
2395 5f. multicoloured 35 15
DESIGN—VERT: 4f.50, Church, Dottignies. HORIZ: 5f. Market Square, Saint Truiden.

647 G. Ryckmans and L. Cerfaux (founders), and Louvain University Library

648 "Metamorphosis" (P. Mara)

1975. 25th Anniv of Louvain Colloquium Biblicum (Biblical Scholarship Association).
2396 **647** 10f. sepia and blue . . . 70 35

1975. Queen Fabiola Foundation for the Mentally Ill.
2397 **648** 7f. multicoloured 50 30

649 Marie Popelin (women's rights pioneer) and Palace of Justice

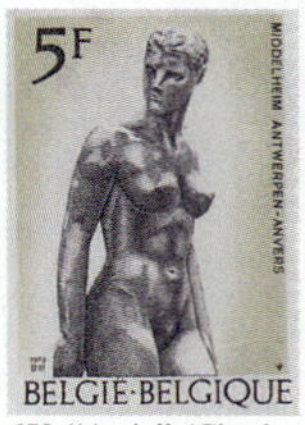

650 "Assia" (Charles Despiau)

1975. International Women's Year.
2398 **649** 6f.50 purple and green 50 20

1975. 25th Anniv of Middelheim Open-air Museum, Antwerp.
2399 **650** 5f. black and green . . . 30 15

651 Dr. Hemerijckx and Leprosy Hospital, Zaire

1975. Dr. Frans Hemerijckx (treatment of leprosy pioneer) Commemoration.
2400 **651** 20f.+10f. mult . . . . . 2·00 1·70

652 Canal Map

653 "Cornelia Vekemans at the Age of Seven" (Cornelis de Vos)

1975. Opening of Rhine–Scheldt Canal.
2401 **652** 10f. multicoloured . . . 70 40

1975. "Philately for the Young".
2402 **653** 4f.50 multicoloured . . . 35 25

654 National Bank and F. Orban (founder)

1975. 125th Anniv of Belgian National Bank.
2403 **654** 25f. multicoloured . . . 1·70 50

655 Edmond Thieffry (pilot) and "Princess Marie-Jose"

656 University Seal

1975. 50th Anniv of First Flight, Brussels–Kinshasa.
2404 **655** 7f. purple and black . . 50 25

1975. 550th Anniv of Louvain University.
2405 **656** 6f.50 black, green & bl 50 20

657 "Angels", (detail, "The Nativity", R. de le Pasture)

658 Emile Moyson (Flemish Leader)

1975. Christmas.
2406 **657** 5f. multicoloured 30 30

1975. "Solidarity".
2407 **658** 4f.50+2f. purple 50 50
2408 – 6f.50+3f. green 70 75
2409 – 10f.+5f. vio, blk & bl . . 90 85
2410 – 13f.+6f. multicoloured 1·10 1·10
DESIGNS—VERT: 6f.50, Dr. Augustin Snellaert (Flemish literature scholar); 13f. Detail of retable, St. Dymphne Church, Geel. HORIZ: 10f. Eye within hand, and Braille characters (150th anniv of introduction of Braille).

659 Cheese Seller

660 "African" Collector

1975. "Themabelga" International Thematic Stamp Exhibition, Brussels (2nd issue). Traditional Belgian Trades. Multicoloured.
2411 4f.50+1f.50 Type **659** . . . 45 45
2412 6f.50+3f. Potato seller . . . 60 60
2413 6f.50+3f. Basket-carrier . . 60 60
2414 10f.+5f. Prawn fisherman and pony (horiz) 85 75
2415 10f.+5f. Knife-grinder and cart (horiz) 85 75
2416 30f.+15f. Milk-woman with dog-cart (horiz) . . . . . 2·20 2·20

1976. Centenary of "Conservatoire Africain" (Charity Organization).
2417 **660** 10f.+5f. multicoloured 1·00 90

661 Owl Emblem and Flemish Buildings

662 Bicentennial Symbol

1976. 125th Anniv of Wilhems Foundation (Flemish cultural organization).
2418 **661** 5f. multicoloured 30 30

1976. Bicentenary of American Revolution.
2419 **662** 14f. multicoloured . . . 90 60

663 Cardinal Mercier

664 "Vlaams Ekonomisch Verbond"

1976. 50th Death Anniv of Cardinal Mercier.
2420 **663** 4f.50 purple 30 20

1976. 50th Anniv of Flemish Economic Federation.
2421 **664** 6f.50 multicoloured . . . 45 15

665 Swimming

1976. Olympic Games, Montreal. Multicoloured.
2422 4f.50+1f.50 Type **665** . . . 45 45
2423 5f.+2f. Running (vert) . . . 45 45
2424 6f.50+2f.50 Horse jumping 60 60

666 Money Centre Building, Brussels

1976. Stamp Day.
2425 **666** 6f.50 brown 50 15

667 Queen Elisabeth playing Violin

668 Basket-making

1976. 25th Anniv of Queen Elisabeth International Music Competitions.
2426 **667** 14f.+6f. red & black . . 1·20 1·20

1976. Europa. Traditional Crafts. Multicoloured.
2427 6f.50 Type **668** 65 20
2428 14f. Pottery (horiz) . . . . 1·10 45

669 Truck on Motorway

670 Queen Elisabeth

1976. 14th Congress of International Road Haulage Union, Brussels.
2429 **669** 14f. black, red & yellow 90 45

1976. Birth Centenary of Queen Elisabeth.
2430 **670** 14f. green 90 45

672 Jan Olieslagers (aviator), Bleriot XI Monoplane and club Badge

1976. 75th Anniv of Belgian Royal Aero Club. Sheet 82 × 116 mm.
MS2435 **672** 25f.+10f. black, yellow and blue . . . . 2·50 2·20

673 Ardennes Horses

1976. 50th Anniv of Ardennes Draught Horses Society.
2436 **673** 5f. multicoloured 40 30

674 King Baudouin

675 "Madonna and Child" (detail)

1976. 25th Anniv of King Baudouin's Accession. Two sheets each 110 × 62 mm containing stamps as T **674**.
MS2437 (a) 4f.50 grey; 6f.50 yellow; 10f. red (sold at 30f.). (b) 20f. green; 30f. blue (sold at 70f.) 6·50 6·25

1976. 400th Birth Anniv of Peter Paul Rubens (artist) (1st issue). Multicoloured.
2438 4f.50+1f.50 "Descent from the Cross" (detail) 50 50
2439 6f.50+3f. "Adoration of the Shepherds" (detail) (24½ × 35 mm) 60 60
2440 6f.50+3f. "Virgin of the Parrot" (detail) (24½ × 35 mm) 60 65
2441 10f.+5f. "Adoration of the Kings" (detail) (24½ × 35 mm) . . . . . 1·00 1·00
2442 10f.+5f. "Last Communion of St. Francis" (detail) (24½ × 35 mm) . . . . . 1·00 1·00
2443 30f.+15f. Type **675** . . . . 2·50 2·20
See also Nos. 2459 and 2497.

676 William the Silent, Prince of Orange

678 Underground Train

1976. 400th Anniv of Pacification of Ghent.
2444 **676** 10f. green 70 30

1976. Opening of Brussels Metro (Underground) Service.
2446 **678** 6f.50 multicoloured . . . 50 15

679 "The Young Musician" (W. C. Duyster)

680 Charles Bernard (writer, birth cent)

1976. "Philately for the Young" and Young Musicians' Movement.
2447 **679** 4f.50 multicoloured . . . 40 15

1976. Cultural Anniversaries.
2448 **680** 5f. purple 30 30
2449 – 5f. red 30 30
2450 – 6f.50 brown 40 20
2451 – 6f.50 green 40 20
DESIGNS—VERT: No. 2449, Fernand Toussaint van Boelaere (writer, birth cent 1975); No. 2450, "St. Jerome in Mountain Landscape" (J. le Patinier) (25th anniv of Charles Plisnier Foundation). HORIZ: No. 2451, "Story of the Blind" (P. Brueghel) (25th anniv of "Vereniging voor Beschaafde Omgangstaal" (Dutch language organisation)).

1976. Tourist Publicity. As T **607**.
2452 4f.50 multicoloured 30 30
2453 4f.50 multicoloured 30 30
2454 5f. brown and blue 30 30
2455 5f. brown and olive 30 30
DESIGNS—HORIZ: No. 2452, Hunnegem Priory, Grammont; No. 2454, River Lys, Sint-Martens-Latem; No. 2455, Chateau. Ham-sur-Heure. VERT: No. 2453, Remouchamps Caves.

681 "Child with Impediment" (Velasquez)

682 "The Nativity" (detail, Master of Flemalle)

1976. National Association for Aid to the Mentally Handicapped.
2456 **681** 14f.+6f. multicoloured 1·20 1·20

1976. Christmas.
2457 **682** 5f. violet 40 30

683 Monogram

1977. 400th Birth Anniv of Peter Paul Rubens (2nd issue).
2459 **683** 6f.50 black and lilac . . 50 15

684 Belgian Lion

1977. (a) Size 17 × 20 mm.
2460 **684** 50c. brown 15 15
2461 65c. red 15 15
2462 1f. mauve 15 15
2463 1f.50 grey 15 15
2464a 2f. orange 15 15
2465 2f.50 green 30 20

2466 2f.75 blue 30 30
2467a 3f. violet 20 15
2468 4f. brown 30 15
2469 4f.50 blue 40 15
2470 5f. green 30 15
2471 6f. red 40 15
2472 7f. red 50 15
2473 8f. blue 50 15
2474 9f. orange . . . . . . 1·00 25

(b) 17 × 22 mm.

2475 **684** 1f. mauve 15 20
2476 2f. orange 30 20
2477 3f. violet 30 20

685 Dr. Albert Hustin (pioneer of blood transfusion)

686 "50 Years of F.A.B.I."

1977. Belgian Red Cross.
2478 **685** 6f.50+2f.50 red and black 70 65
2479 – 14f.+7f. red, blue and black . . . . 1·20 1·10
DESIGN: 14f.+7f. Knee joint and red cross (World Rheumatism Year).

1977. 50th Anniv of Federation of Belgian Engineers.
2480 **686** 6f.50 multicoloured . . . 50 15

687 Jules Bordet School, Brussels (bicent)

688 Gulls in Flight

1977. Cultural Anniversaries.
2481 **687** 4f.50+1f. mult 30 30
2482 – 4f.50+1f. mult 30 30
2483 – 5f.+2f. multicoloured . . 45 50
2484 – 6f.50+2f. mult 55 55
2485 – 6f.50+2f. red & black . . 55 55
2486 – 10f.+5 slate 90 90
DESIGNS—VERT: 24 × 37 mm: No. 2482, Marie-Therese College, Herve (bicentenary); 2483, Detail from "La Grande Pyramide Musicale" (E. Tytgat) (50th anniv of Brussels Philharmonic Society). 35 × 45 mm: No. 2486, Camille Lemonnier (75th anniv of Society of Belgian Authors writing in French). HORIZ: 35 × 24 mm: No. 2484, Lucien van Obbergh and stage scene (50th anniv of Union of Artists). 37 × 24 mm: No. 2485, Emblem of Humanist Society (25th anniv).

1977. 25th Anniv of District 112 of Lions International.
2487 **688** 14f. multicoloured . . . 1·00 45

689 Footballers

690 Pillar Box, 1852

1977. 30th International Youth Tournament of European Football Association.
2488 **689** 10f.+5f. multicoloured . . . 1·00 90

1977. Stamp Day.
2489 **690** 6f.50 olive 50 15

691 Gileppe Dam, Jalhay

692 "Mars and Mercury Association Emblem"

1977. Europa. Multicoloured.
2490 6f.50 Type **691** 75 30
2491 14f. The Yser, Nieuport . . 1·90 60

1977. 50th Anniv of Mars and Mercury Association of Reserve and Retired Officers.
2492 **692** 5f. green, black & brown 30 15

693 De Hornes Coat of Arms

694 "Self-Portrait"

1977. Historical Anniversaries.
2493 **693** 4f.50 lilac 25 20
2494 – 5f. red 25 20
2495 – 6f.50 brown 25 20
2496 – 14f. green . . . . 1·00 60
DESIGNS AND EVENTS—VERT: 4f.50, Type **693** (300th anniv of creation of principality of Overijse under Eugene-Maximilien de Hornes); 6f.50, Miniature (600th anniv of Froissart's "Chronicles"); 14f. "The Conversion of St. Hubert" (1250th death anniv). HORIZ: (45 × 24 mm): 5f. Detail from "Oxford Chest" (675th anniv of Battle of Golden Spurs).

1977. 400th Birth Anniv of Peter Paul Rubens (3rd issue).
2497 **694** 5f. multicoloured 40 25
MS2498 100 × 152 mm. As No. 2497 but larger (24 × 37 mm) × 3 (sold at 20f.) . . . . 1·10 1·10

695 "The Mystic Lamb" (detail, Brothers Van Eyck)

1977. 50th Anniv of International Federation of Library Associations and Congress, Brussels.
2499 **695** 10f. multicoloured . . . 70 45

696 Gymnast and Footballer

1977. Sports Events and Anniversaries.
2500 **696** 4f.50 red, black & grn 30 25
2501 – 6f.50 black, violet and brown 35 15
2502 – 10f. turquoise, black and salmon 70 35
2503 – 14f. green, blk & ochre 1·00 50
DESIGNS—VERT: 4f.50, Type **696** (50th anniv of Workers' Central Sports Association); 10f. Basketball (20th European Championships); 14f. Hockey (International Hockey Cup competition). HORIZ: 6f.50, Disabled fencers (Rehabilitation through sport).

697 Festival Emblem

1977. "Europalia '77" Festival.
2504 **697** 5f. multicoloured 30 15

699 "The Egg-seller" (Gustave de Smet)

700 "The Stamp Collectors" (detail, Constant Cap)

1977. Promoting Belgian Eggs.
2506 **699** 4f.50 black and ochre . . 30 25

1977. "Philately for the Young".
2507 **700** 4f.50 sepia 30 15

1977. Tourist Publicity. As T **607**.
2508 4f.50 multicoloured 30 25
2509 4f.50 black, blue and green 30 25
2510 5f. multicoloured 30 25
2511 5f. multicoloured 30 25
DESIGNS—VERT: No. 2508, Bailiff's House, Gembloux; No. 2509, St. Aldegone's Church. HORIZ: No. 2510, View of Liege and statue of Mother and Child; No. 2511, View and statue of St. Nicholas.

701 "Nativity" (detail, R. de la Pasture)

702 Albert-Edouard Janssen (financier)

1977. Christmas.
2512 **701** 5f. red 25 25

1977. "Solidarity".
2513 **702** 5f.+2f.50 black 50 50
2514 – 5f.+2f.50 red 50 50
2515 – 10f.+5f. purple 90 85
2516 – 10f.+5f. grey 90 85
DESIGNS: No. 2514, Joseph Wauters (politician); No. 2516, Jean Capart (egyptologist); No. 2515, August de Boeck (composer).

703 Distressed Girl (Deserted Children)

704 Railway Signal as Arrows on Map of Europe

1978. Philanthropic Works. Multicoloured.
2517 4f.50+1f.50 Type **703** . . . 40 35
2518 6f.+3f. Blood pressure measurement (World Hypertension Month) . . 60 60
2519 10f.+5f. De Mick Sanatorium, Brasschaat (Anti-tuberculosis) (horiz) 85 85

1978. "European Action". Multicoloured.
2520 10f. Type **704** (25th anniv of European Conference of Transport Ministers) . . . 65 30
2521 10f. European Parliament Building, Strasbourg (first direct elections) . . . 65 30
2522 14f. Campidoglio Palace, Rome and map of EEC countries (20th anniv of Treaties of Rome) (horiz) 90 45
2523 14f. Paul Henri Spaak (Belgian Prime Minister) (horiz) 90 45

705 Grimbergen Abbey

1978. 850th Anniv of Premonstratensian Abbey, Grimbergen.
2524 **705** 4f.50 brown 40 25

706 Emblem

707 5f. Stamp of 1878

1978. 175th Anniv of Ostend Chamber of Commerce and Industry.
2525 **706** 8f. multicoloured 50 15

1978. Stamp Day.
2526 **707** 8f. brown, blk & drab 50 15

708 Antwerp Cathedral

709 Theatre and Characters from "The Brussels Street Singer"

1978. Europa. Multicoloured.
2527 8f. Type **708** . . . . 1·00 30
2528 14f. Pont des Trous, Tournai (horiz) . . . . . 2·00 60

1978. Cultural Anniversaries.
2529 **709** 6f.+3f. multicoloured . . 50 50
2530 – 6f.+3f. multicoloured . . 50 50
2531 – 8f.+4f. brown 60 60
2532 – 10f.+5f. brown 95 85
DESIGNS AND EVENTS: No. 2529, (Type **709**) (Royal Flemish Theatre Cent.); 2530, Arquebusier with standard, arms and Company Gallery, Vise (Royal Company of Crossbowmen of Vise 400th anniv); 2531, Karel van de Woestijne (poet) (birth cent); 2532, Don John of Austria (signing of Perpetual Edict, 400th anniv).

710 "Education"

711 "K.V.I."

1978. Teaching. Multicoloured.
2533 6f. Type **710** (Municipal education in Ghent, 150th anniv) 40 30
2534 8f. Paul Pastur Workers' University, Charleroi (75th anniv) 45 30

1978. Tourist Publicity. As T **607**.
2535 4f.50 sepia, buff and blue 30 30
2536 4f.50 multicoloured 30 30
2537 6f. multicoloured 40 30
2538 6f. multicoloured 40 30
DESIGNS—VERT: No. 2535, Jonathas House, Enghien. HORIZ: No. 2536, View of Wetteren and couple in local costume; 2537, Brussels tourist hostess; 2538, Carnival Prince and church tower.

1978. 50th Anniv of Royal Flemish Association of Engineers.
2539 **711** 8f. black and red 50 15

712 Young Stamp Collector

713 Mountain Scenery

1978. "Philately for the Young".
2540 **712** 4f.50 violet 30 25

1978. Olympic Games (1980) Preparation.
2541 **713** 6f.+2f.50 mult 50 50
2542 – 8f.+3f.50 green, brown and black 60 65
MS2543 150 × 100 mm. 7f. + 3f., 14f.+6f. multicoloured . . . . 2·00 2·00
DESIGNS: 7f. Ancient Greek athletes; 8f. Kremlin Towers, Moscow; 14f. Olympic flame.

714 "The Nativity" (detail, Bethlehem Door, Notre Dame, Huy)

715 Tabernacle, Brussels Synagogue (centenary)

1978. Christmas.
2544 **714** 6f. black 45 30

1978. "Solidarity". Anniversaries.
2545 **715** 6f.+2f. brown, grey and black 50 45
2546 – 8f.+3f. multicoloured . . 70 60
2547 – 14f.+7f. multicoloured 1·30 1·20

DESIGNS—HORIZ: (36 × 24 mm): 8f. Dancing figures (Catholic Students Action, 50th anniv); 14f. Father Dominique-Georges Pire and African Village (Award of Nobel Peace Prize, 20th anniv).

716 Relief Workers giving First Aid

717 "Till Eulenspiegel" (legendary character)

1978. Belgian Red Cross. Multicoloured.
2548 8f.+3f. Type **716** 70 75
2549 16f.+8f. Skull smoking, bottle and syringe ("Excess kills") . . . . . 1·40 1·30

1979. 10th Anniv of Lay Action Centres.
2550 **717** 4f.50 multicoloured . . . 35 20

718 "European Dove"

719 Millenary Emblem

1979. 1st Direct Elections to European Assembly.
2551 **718** 8f. multicoloured 50 15

1979. Brussels Millenary (1st issue).
2552 **719** 4f.50 brown, blk & red 30 25
2553 8f. turquoise, blk & grn 70 15
See also Nos. 2559/62.

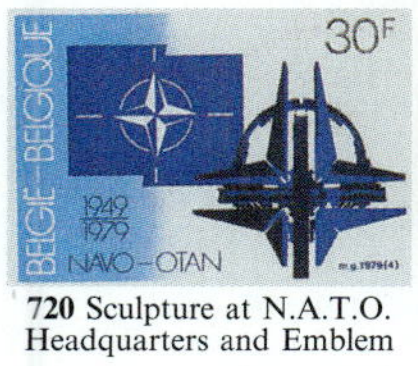

720 Sculpture at N.A.T.O. Headquarters and Emblem

721 Drawing of Monument

1979. 30th Anniv of North Atlantic Treaty Organization.
2554 **720** 30f. blue, gold and light blue . . . . 2·00 60

1979. 25th Anniv of Breendonk Monument.
2555 **721** 6f. orange and black . . 45 30

722 Railway Parcels Stamp, 1879

1979. Stamp Day.
2556 **722** 8f. multicoloured 50 15

723 Mail Coach and Renault R4 Post Van

1979. Europa. Multicoloured.
2557 8f. Type **723** . . . . 1·30 15
2558 14f. Semaphore posts, satellite and dish aerial . . 2·30 60

724 "Legend of Our Lady of Sablon" (detail of tapestry, Town Museum of Brussels)

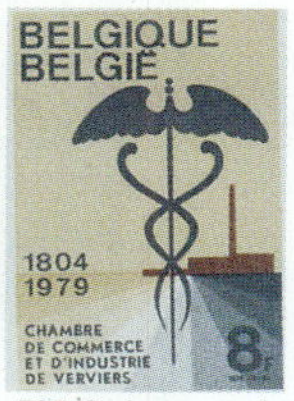

725 Caduceus and Factory

1979. Brussels Millenary (2nd issue). Multicoloured.
2559 6f.+2f. Type **724** 45 45
2560 8f.+3f. Different detail of tapestry 65 70
2561 14f.+7f. "Legend of Our Lady of Sablon" (tapestry) . . . . 1·20 1·20
2562 20f.+10f. Different detail of tapestry . . . . 1·70 1·70
MS2563 100 × 150 mm. 20f.+10f. Different detail of Town Museum tapestry (48 × 37 mm) . . . . . 1·90 1·90

The tapestry shown on Nos. 2559/60 is from Brussels Town Museum and that on Nos. 2561/2 from the Royal Museum of Art and History.

1979. 175th Anniv of Verviers Chamber of Commerce.
2564 **725** 8f. multicoloured 45 15

726 "50" and Bank Emblem

1979. 50th Anniv of Professional Credit Bank.
2565 **726** 4f.50 blue and gold . . . 30 30

727 Bas-relief

1979. 50th Anniv of Chambers of Trade and Commerce.
2566 **727** 10f. crimson, orange and red 60 30

728 Cambre Abbey

1979. Cultural Anniversaries.
2567 **728** 6f.+2f. multicoloured . . 50 45
2568 – 8f.+3f. multicoloured . . 60 60
2569 – 14f.+7f. black, orange and green . . . . . . 1·20 1·20
2570 – 20f.+10f. brown, red and grey . . . . 1·70 1·70

DESIGNS: 6f. Type **728** (50th anniv of restoration); 8f. Beauvoorde Chateau; 14f. Barthelemy Dumortier (founder) and newspaper "Courrier de L'Escaut" (150th anniv); 20f. Crypt, shrine and Collegiate Church of St. Hermes, Renaix (850th anniv of consecration).

729 "Tintin" with Dog, Stamps and Magnifier

1979. "Philately for the Young".
2571 **729** 8f. multicoloured . . . . 2·00 45

730 Le Grand-Hornu

1979. Le Grand-Hornu Industrial Archaeological Site.
2572 **730** 10f.+5f. black & grey . . 95 85

1979. Tourist Publicity. As T **607**.
2573 5f. multicoloured 30 30
2574 5f. multicoloured 30 30
2575 6f. black, turquoise & green 40 30
2576 6f. multicoloured 40 30

DESIGNS—HORIZ: No. 2573, Royal African Museum, Tervuren, and hunters with hounds; 2575, St. John's Church, Poperinge, and statue of Virgin Mary. VERT: No. 2574, Belfry, Thuin, and men carrying religious image; 2576, St. Nicholas's Church and cattle market, Ciney.

731 Francois Auguste Gevaert

732 Madonna and Child, Foy-Notre-Dame Church

1979. Music. Each brown and ochre.
2577 5f. Type **731** (150th birth anniv) 30 30
2578 6f. Emmanuel Durlet . . . 40 30
2579 14f. Grand piano and string instruments (40th anniv of Queen Elisabeth Musical Chapel) 85 45

1979. Christmas.
2580 **732** 6f. black and blue . . . 35 25

733 H. Heyman (politician, birth centenary)

734 "1830–1980"

1979. "Solidarity".
2581 **733** 8f.+3f. brown, green and black 55 55
2582 – 10f.+5f. multicoloured 75 75
2583 – 16f.+8f. black, green and yellow . . . . 1·30 1·30

DESIGNS—VERT: As Type **733**. 10f. War Invalids Organization medal (50th anniv). HORIZ: (44 × 24 mm): 16f. Child's head and International Year of the Child emblem.

1980. 150th Anniv of Independence (1st issue).
2584 **734** 9f. mauve & lt mauve . . 55 15
See also Nos. 2597/2601.

735 Frans Van Cauwelaert

736 Spring Flowers

1980. Birth Centenary of Frans Van Cauwelaert (politician).
2585 **735** 5f. black 35 15

1980. Ghent Flower Show. Multicoloured.
2586 5f. Type **736** 30 30
2587 6f.50 Summer flowers . . . 40 45
2588 9f. Autumn flowers 55 15

737 Telephone and Diagram of Satellite Orbit

1980. 50th Anniv of Telegraph and Telephone Office.
2589 **737** 10f. multicoloured . . . 65 30

738 5f. Airmail Stamp of 1930

1980. Stamp Day.
2590 **738** 9f. multicoloured 60 20

739 St. Benedict of Nursia

1980. Europa. Multicoloured.
2591 9f. Type **739** 85 20
2592 14f. Marguerite of Austria 1·90 60

740 Ivo van Damme

741 Palais de la Nation

1980. Ivo van Damme (athlete) Commemoration.
2593 **740** 20f.+10f. mult . . . . . 1·70 1·70

1980. 4th Interparliamentary Conference on European Co-operation and Security, Brussels.
2594 **741** 5f. blue, lilac and black 30 30

742 Golden Carriage, Mons

1980. Tourist Publicity. Multicoloured.
2595 6f.50 Type **742** 45 30
2596 6f.50 Damme 45 30

743 King Leopold I and Queen Louise-Marie

1980. 150th Anniv of Belgian Independence (2nd issue).
2597 **743** 6f.50+1f.50 pur & blk . . 50 50
2598 – 9f.+3f. blue & black . . 70 65
2599 – 14f.+6f. green & blk . . 1·20 1·20
2600 – 17f.+8f. orange. & blk 1·60 1·60
2601 – 25f.+10f. green & blk . . 2·20 2·20
MS2602 100 × 150 mm. 50f. black (sold at 75f.) . . . . 4·25 4·00

DESIGNS: 9f. King Leopold II and Queen Marie-Henriette; 14f. King Albert I and Queen Elisabeth; 17f. King Leopold III and Queen Astrid; 25f. King Baudouin and Queen Fabiola; 50f. Royal Mint Theatre, Brussels.

744 King Baudouin

745 "Brewer" (detail, Reliquary of St. Lambert)

1980. King Baudouin's 50th Birthday.
2603 **744** 9f. red 60 15

1980. Millenary of Liege. Multicoloured.
2604 9f.+3f. Type **745** 65 70
2605 17f.+6f. "The Miner" (sculpture by Constantin Meunier) (horiz) . . . . 1·30 1·30
2606 25f.+10f. "Seat of Wisdom" (Madonna, Collegiate Church of St. John, Liege) . . . . 2·00 2·00
MS2607 150 × 100 mm. 20f.+10f. Seal of Prince Bishop Notger (43 × 24 mm) . . . . 2·00 2·00

746 Chiny

1980. Tourist Publicity.
2608 **746** 5f. multicoloured 35 30

747 Emblem of Cardiological League of Belgium

748 Rodenbach (statue at Roulers)

1980. Heart Week.
2609 **747** 14f. light blue, red and blue 90 50

1980. Death Cent of Albrecht Rodenbach (poet).
2610 **748** 9f. brown, blue and deep blue 55 15

749 "Royal Procession" (children of Thyl Uylenspiegel Primary School)

1980. "Philately for the Young".
2611 **749** 5f. multicoloured 30 25

750 Emblem

751 "Garland of Flowers and Nativity" (attr. D. Seghers)

1980. 50th Anniv of Belgian Broadcasting Corporation.
2612 **750** 10f. black and grey . . . 70 30

1980. Christmas.
2613 **751** 6f.50 multicoloured . . . 45 30

752 Gateway, Diest

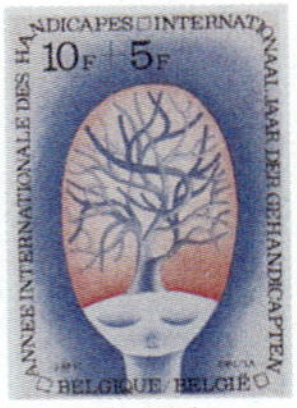

754 Brain

1980. Tourist Publicity.
2614 **752** 5f. multicoloured 30 25
See also Nos. 2648/51 and 2787/92.

1981. International Year of Disabled Persons. Multicoloured.
2637 10f.+5f. Type **754** . . . . . 1·00 1·00
2638 25f.+10f. Eye (horiz) . . . . 2·00 2·00

755 "Baron de Gerlache" (after F. J. Navez)

756 Emblem of 15th International Radiology Convention

1981. Historical Anniversaries.
2639 **755** 6f. multicoloured 35 30
2640 – 9f. multicoloured 50 15
2641 – 50f. brown & yellow . . 3·25 75
DESIGNS—As T **755**: 6f. Type **755** (1st President of Chamber of Deputies) (150th anniv of Chamber); 9f. Baron de Stassart (1st President of Senate) (after F. J. Navez) (150th anniv of Senate). 35 × 51 mm: 50f. Statue of King Leopold I by Geefs (150th anniv of royal dynasty).

1981. Belgian Red Cross.
2642 **756** 10f.+5f. bl, blk & red . . 1·00 85
2643 – 25f.+10f. blue, red and black . . . . 2·00 1·80
DESIGN: 25f. Dove and globe symbolizing international emergency assistance.

757 Tchantches and Op-Signoorke (puppets)

1981. Europa. Multicoloured.
2644 9f. Type **757** . . . . 1·00 15
2645 14f. D'Artagnan and Woltje (puppets) . . . . 1·80 75

758 Stamp Transfer-roller depicting A. de Cock (founder of Postal Museum)

759 Ovide Decroly

1981. Stamp Day.
2646 **758** 9f. multicoloured 55 15

1981. 110th Birth Anniv of Dr. Ovide Decroly (educational psychologist).
2647 **759** 35f.+15f. brown & bl . . 2·75 2·75

1981. Tourist Publicity. As T **752**. Multicoloured.
2648 6f. Statue of our Lady of Tongre 40 30
2649 6f. Egmont Castle, Zottegem 40 30
2650 6f.50 Dams on Eau d'Heure (horiz) 45 30
2651 6f.50 Tongerlo Abbey, Antwerp (horiz) 45 30

760 Footballer

761 Edouard Remouchamps (Walloon dramatist)

1981. Cent of Royal Antwerp Football Club.
2652 **760** 6f. red, brown & black 40 30

1981. 125th Anniv of Society of Walloon Language and Literature.
2653 **761** 6f.50 brown and stone 40 30

762 French Horn

1981. Centenary of De Vredekring Band, Antwerp.
2654 **762** 6f.50 blue, mve & blk . . 40 30

763 Audit Office

1981. 150th Anniv of Audit Office.
2655 **763** 10f. purple 70 30

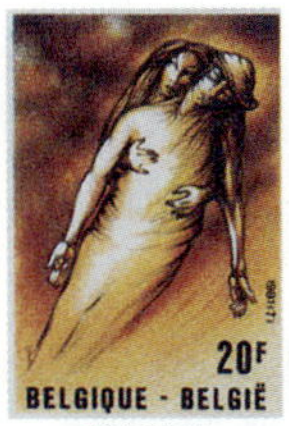

764 Pietà

1981. 25th Anniv of Bois du Cazier Mining Disaster. Sheet 150 × 100 mm.
MS2656 **764** 20f. multicoloured (sold at 30f.) . . . . 1·70 1·70

765 Tombs of Marie of Burgundy and Charles the Bold

1981. Relocation of Tombs of Marie of Burgundy and Charles the Bold in Notre-Dame Church, Bruges.
2657 **765** 50f. multicoloured . . . 3·00 75

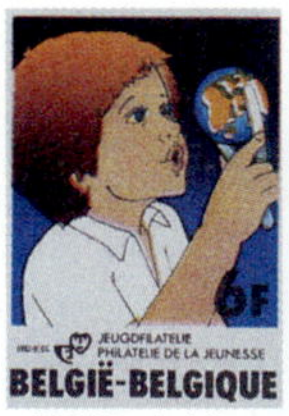

766 Boy holding Globe in Tweezers

767 King Baudouin

1981. "Philately for Youth".
2658 **766** 6f. multicoloured 35 25

1981.
2659 **767** 50f. light blue and blue 4·75 20
2660 65f. mauve and black . . 5·50 85
2661 100f. brown and blue . . 9·75 60

768 Max Waller (founder)

769 Nativity (miniature from "Missale ad usum d. Leodensis")

1981. Cultural Anniversaries.
2672 **768** 6f. multicoloured 35 15
2673 – 6f.50 multicoloured . . . 40 25
2674 – 9f. multicoloured 45 15
2675 – 10f. multicoloured . . . 55 45
2676 – 14f. lt brn & brn 90 55
DESIGNS: 6f. Type **768** (centenary of literary review "La Jeune Belgique"); 6f.50," Liqueur Drinkers" (detail, Gustave van de Woestijne (inscr "Woestyne") (birth centenary); 9f. Fernand Severin (poet, 50th death anniv); 10f. Jan van Ruusbroec (mystic, 600th death anniv); 14f. Owl (La Pensee et les Hommes organization, 25th anniv).

1981. Christmas.
2677 **769** 6f.50 brown and black 40 30

770 Mounted Gendarme, 1832

771 Cellist and Royal Conservatory of Music, Brussels

1981. "Solidarity". Multicoloured.
2678 9f.+4f. Type **770** . . . . . 85 1·00
2679 20f.+7f. Carabinier . . . . 1·70 1·70
2680 40f.+20f. Mounted Guide, 1843 . . . . 3·50 3·00

1982. 150th Anniversaries. Multicoloured.
2681 6f.50 Type **771** 35 25
2682 9f. Front of former Law Court, Brussels (anniv of judiciary) 50 15

772 Sectional View of Cyclotron

773 Billiards

1982. Science. Multicoloured.
2683 6f. Type **772** (Installation of cyclotron at National Radio-elements Institute, Fleurus) 40 30
2684 14f. Telescope and galaxy (Royal Observatory) . . . 80 45
2685 50f. Dr. Robert Koch and tubercle bacillus (centenary of discovery) 2·75 65

1982. Sports. Multicoloured.
2686 6f.+2f. Type **773** 75 75
2687 9f.+4f. Cycling . . . . . 1·00 1·00
2688 10f.+5f. Football . . . . . 1·20 1·20
2689 50f.+14f. "Treaty of Rome" (yacht) . . . . 3·50 3·00
MS2690 105 × 100 mm. 25f. multicoloured (Type **773**); 25f. brown, yellow and black (as No. 2687); 25f. red, yellow and black (as No. 2688); 25f. multicoloured (as No. 2689) . . 7·50 7·00

774 Joseph Lemaire (after Jean Maillard)

775 Voting (Universal Suffrage)

1982. Birth Centenary of Joseph Lemaire (Minister of State and social reformer).
2691 **774** 6f.50 multicoloured . . . 45 30

1982. Europa.
2692 **775** 10f. multicoloured . . . 1·80 30
2693 – 17f. green, black and grey . . . . 3·00 60
DESIGN: 17f. Portrait and signature of Emperor Joseph II (Edict of Toleration).

1982. Surch **1 F.**
2694 **684** 1f. on 5f. green 10 10

777 17th-century Postal Messenger

778 "Tower of Babel" (Brueghel the Elder)

1982. Stamp Day.
2695 **777** 10f. multicoloured . . . 65 15

1982. World Esperanto Congress, Antwerp.
2696 **778** 12f. multicoloured . . . 75 35

1982. Tourist Publicity. As T **752**.
2697 7f. blue and light blue . . . 50 30
2698 7f. black and green 50 30
2699 7f.50 brown and light brown 50 30
2700 7f.50 violet and lilac . . . 50 30
2701 7f.50 black and grey 50 30
2702 7f.50 black and pink 50 30
DESIGNS—VERT: No. 2697, Gosselies Tower; 2698, Zwijveke Abbey, Termonde; 2701, Entrance gate, Grammont Abbey; 2702, Beveren pillory. HORIZ: No. 2699, Stavelot Abbey; 2700, Abbey ruins, Villers-la-Ville.

780 Louis Paul Boon (writer)

781 Abraham Hans

1982. Cultural Anniversaries.
2707 **780** 7f. black, red and grey 40 30
2708 – 10f. multicoloured . . . 50 15
2709 – 12f. multicoloured . . . 70 35
2710 – 17f. multicoloured . . . 1·10 45
DESIGNS: 7f. Type **780** (70th birth anniv); 10f. "Adoration of the Shepherds" (detail of Portinari retable) (Hugo van der Goes, 500th death anniv); 12f. Michel de Ghelderode (dramatist, 20th death anniv); 17f. "Motherhood" (Pierre Paulus, birth centenary (1981)).

1982. Birth Centenary of Abraham Hans (writer).
2711 **781** 17f. black, turquoise and blue . . . . 1·10 35

782 Children playing Football

1982. "Philately for the Young". Scout Year.
2712 **782** 7f. multicoloured 50 30

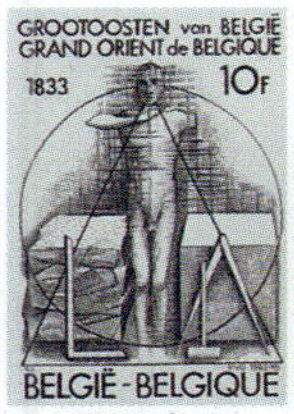
783 Masonic Emblems

784 Star over Village

1982. 150th Anniv of Belgium Grand Orient (Freemasonry Lodge).
2713 **783** 10f. yellow and black . . 60 25

1982. Christmas.
2714 **784** 10f.+1f. multicoloured 1·00 1·00

785 Cardinal Cardijn

1982. Birth Centenary of Cardinal Joseph Cardijn.
2715 **785** 10f. multicoloured . . . 70 15

786 King Baudouin

787 King Baudouin

1982.
2716 **786** 10f. blue 60 15
2717 11f. brown 75 15
2718 12f. green . . . . 1·00 15
2719 13f. red 90 15
2720 14f. black 90 15
2721 15f. red . . . . 1·80 45
2722 20f. blue . . . . 1·60 15
2723 22f. purple . . . . . . 2·50 1·40
2724 23f. green . . . . . . 2·30 60
2725 24f. grey . . . . 1·80 35
2726 25f. blue . . . . 2·00 30
2727 30f. brown . . . . . . 1·80 15
2728 40f. red . . . . 3·00 30
2729 **787** 50f. light brown, brown and black . . . . 4·00 30
2730 100f. blue, deep blue and black . . . . 12·00 30
2731 200f. light green, green and deep green . . . 27·00 1·00

788 St. Francis preaching to the Birds

789 Messenger handing Letter to King in the Field

1982. 800th Birth Anniv of St. Francis of Assisi.
2736 **788** 20f. multicoloured . . . 1·20 50

1982. "Belgica 82" Postal History Exhibition. Multicoloured.
2737 7f.+2f. Type **789** 50 50
2738 7f.50+2f.50 Messenger, Basel (vert) 60 65
2739 10f.+3f. Messenger, Nuremburg (vert) 80 80
2740 17f.+7f. Imperial courier, 1750 (vert) . . . . 1·40 1·40
2741 20f.+9f. Imperial courier, 1800 . . . . 1·60 1·60
2742 25f.+10f. Belgian postman, 1886 . . . . 2·00 1·90
MS2743 123 × 89 mm. 50f.+25f. Mail coach (48 × 37 mm) . . . 5·25 5·25

790 Emblem

791 Horse Tram

1983. 50th Anniv of Caritas Catholica Belgica.
2744 **790** 10f.+2f. red and grey . . 80 80

1983. Trams. Multicoloured.
2745 7f.50 Type **791** 60 30
2746 10f. Electric tram 75 20
2747 50f. Tram with trolley (invented by K. van de Poele) . . . . 3·25 65

792 Mountaineer

793 Brussels Buildings, Open Periodicals and Globe

1983. Belgian Red Cross. Multicoloured.
2748 12f.+3f. Type **792** . . . . . 1·00 1·00
2749 20f.+5f. Walker . . . . . . 1·50 1·50

1983. 24th International Periodical Press Federation World Congress, Brussels.
2750 **793** 20f. multicoloured . . . 1·20 40

794 Woman at Work

1983. Women.
2751 **794** 8f. multicoloured 55 30
2752 – 11f. multicoloured . . . 60 15
2753 – 20f. yellow, brown & bl 1·30 50
DESIGNS: 11f. Woman at home; 20f. Woman manager.

795 Graphic Representation of Midi Railway Station, Brussels

1983. Stamp Day. World Communications Year.
2754 **795** 11f. black, red and blue 70 25

796 Procession of the Holy Blood

1983. Procession of the Holy Blood, Bruges.
2755 **796** 8f. multicoloured 55 30

797 "The Man in the Street"

798 Hot-air Balloon over Town

1983. Europa. Paintings by Paul Delvaux. Mult.
2756 11f. Type **797** . . . . 1·50 30
2757 20f. "Night Trains" (horiz) 3·00 65

1983. Bicentenary of Manned Flight. Mult.
2758 11f. Type **798** 65 15
2759 22f. Hot-air balloon over countryside . . . . 1·50 45

799 Church of Our Lady, Hastiere

800 Milkmaid

1983. Tourist Publicity. Multicoloured.
2760 8f. Type **799** 60 30
2761 8f. Tumulus, Landen . . . 60 30
2762 8f. Park, Mouscron 60 30
2763 8f. Wijnendale Castle, Torhout 60 30

1983. Tineke Festival, Heule.
2764 **800** 8f. multicoloured 50 30

801 Plaque on Wall

802 Rainbow and Child

1983. European Small and Medium-sized Industries and Crafts Year.
2765 **801** 11f. yellow, black & red 70 15

1983. "Philately for the Young". 20th Anniv of Queen Fabiola Village No. 1 (for handicapped people).
2766 **802** 8f. multicoloured 50 20

803 Textiles

804 Conscience (after wood engraving by Nelly Degouy)

1983. Belgian Exports (1st series). Multicoloured.
2767 10f. Type **803** 70 30
2768 10f. Steel beams (metallurgy) 70 30
2769 10f. Diamonds 70 30
See also Nos. 2777/80.

1983. Death Centenary of Hendrik Conscience (writer).
2770 **804** 20f. black and green . . 1·30 35

805 "Madonna" (Jef Wauters)

806 2nd Foot Regiment

1983. Christmas.
2771 **805** 11f.+1f. multicoloured 90 85

1983. "Solidarity". Military Uniforms. Mult.
2772 8f.+2f. Type **806** 65 70
2773 11f.+2f. Lancer . . . . . . 1·10 1·10
2774 50f.+12f. Grenadier . . . . 3·75 3·50

1983. King Leopold III Commemoration.
2775 **155** 11f. black 70 10

807 Free University of Brussels

808 Albert I

1984. 150th Anniv of Free University of Brussels.
2776 **807** 11f. multicoloured . . . 75 15

1984. Belgian Exports (2nd series). As T **803**. Multicoloured.
2777 11f. Retort and test tubes (chemicals) 75 30
2778 11f. Combine harvester (agricultural produce) . . 75 30
2779 11f. Ship, coach and electric commuter train (transport) 75 30
2780 11f. Atomic emblem and computer terminal (new technology) 75 30

1984. 50th Death Anniv of King Albert I.
2781 **808** 8f. black and stone . . . 55 30

809 Judo

810 Releasing Doves

1984. Olympic Games, Los Angeles. Multicoloured.
2782 8f.+2f. Type **809** 60 60
2783 12f.+3f. Windsurfing (vert) 1·00 1·00
MS2784 125 × 90 mm. 10f. Archery; 24f. Dressage . . . . 2·30 2·20

1984. 25th Anniv of Movement without a Name.
2785 **810** 12f. multicoloured . . . 75 15

811 Clasped Hands

1984. 50th Anniv of National Lottery.
2786 **811** 12f.+3f. multicoloured 1·00 1·00

812 St. John Bosco with Children

813 Bridge

1984. 50th Anniv of Canonization of St. John Bosco (founder of Salesians).
2787 **812** 8f. multicoloured 55 15

1984. Europa. 25th Anniv of European Posts and Telecommunications Conference.
2788 **813** 12f. red and black . . . 1·40 30
2789 22f. blue and black . . . 3·50 60

814 Leopold II 1884 10c. Stamp

1984. Stamp Day.
2790 **814** 12f. multicoloured . . . 80 15

815 Dove and Pencils

1984. 2nd European Parliament Elections.
2791 **815** 12f. multicoloured . . . 95 15

816 Shako

817 Church of Our Lady of the Chapel, Brussels

1984. 150th Anniv of Royal Military School.
2792 **816** 22f. multicoloured . . . 1·40 1·00

1984. Tourist Publicity. Multicoloured.
2793 10f. Type **817** 60 25
2794 10f. St. Martin's Church and lime tree, Montigny-le-Tilleul 60 25
2795 10f. Belfry and Town Hall, Tielt (vert) 60 25

818 "Curious Masks" (detail, James Ensor)

1984. Inaug of Brussels Modern Art Museum.
2796 **818** 8f.+2f. multicoloured . . 60 65
2797 – 12f.+3f. multicoloured 1·10 1·20
2798 – 22f.+5f. multicoloured 1·60 1·60
2799 – 50f.+13f. grn, bl & blk 3·75 3·50
DESIGNS: 12f. "The Empire of Lights" (detail, Rene Magritte); 22f. "The End" (detail, Jan Cox); 50f. "Rhythm No. 6" (Jo Delahaut).

819 Symbolic Design

820 Averbode Abbey

1984. 50th Anniv of Chirojeugd (Christian youth movement).
2800 **819** 10f. yellow, violet & bl 60 30

1984. Abbeys.
2801 **820** 8f. green and brown . . 50 25
2802 – 22f. brown & dp brown 1·20 35
2803 – 24f. green & light green 1·40 50
2804 – 50f. lilac and brown . . 3·00 75
DESIGNS—VERT: 22f. Chimay; 24f. Rochefort. HORIZ: 50f. Affligem.

821 Smurf as Postman

822 Child collecting Flowers

1984. "Philately for the Young".
2805 **821** 8f. multicoloured . . . . 1·30 45

1984. Children.
2806 10f.+2f. Type **822** 80 80
2807 12f.+3f. Children with globe 90 85
2808 15f.+3f. Child on merry-go-round . . . . 1·20 1·20

823 Meulemans

824 Three Kings

1984. Birth Cent of Arthur Meulemans (composer).
2809 **823** 12f. black and orange . . 80 20

1984. Christmas.
2810 **824** 12f.+1f. multicoloured 1·00 90

825 St. Norbert

826 "Virgin of Louvain" (attr. Jan Gossaert)

1985. 850th Death Anniv of St. Norbert.
2811 **825** 22f. brown & lt brown 1·40 50

1985. "Europalia 85 Espana" Festival.
2812 **826** 12f. multicoloured . . . 80 25

827 Press Card in Hatband

828 Blood System as Tree

1985. Cent of Professional Journalists Association.
2814 **827** 9f. multicoloured 60 35

1985. Belgian Red Cross. Blood Donations.
2815 **828** 9f.+2f. multicoloured . . 80 80
2816 – 23f.+5f. red, blue and black . . . . 1·90 1·60
DESIGN: 23f. Two hearts.

829 "Sophrolaelio cattleya" "Burlingama"

830 Pope John Paul II

1985. Ghent Flower Festival. Orchids. Mult.
2817 12f. Type **829** 70 25
2818 12f. Phalaenopsis "Malibu" 70 25
2819 12f. Tapeu orchid ("Vanda coerulea") 70 25

1985. Visit of Pope John Paul II.
2820 **830** 12f. multicoloured . . . 75 25

831 Rising Sun behind Chained Gates

1985. Centenary of Belgian Workers' Party.
2821 9f. Type **831** 60 35
2822 12f. Broken wall, flag and rising sun 75 25

832 Jean de Bast (engraver)

1985. Stamp Day.
2823 **832** 12f. blue 75 20

834 Class 18 Steam Locomotive, 1896

1985. Public Transport Year. Multicoloured.
2826 9f. Type **834** 60 25
2827 12f. Locomotive "Elephant", 1835 . . . . 75 25
2828 23f. Class 23 tank engine, 1904 . . . . 1·50 55
2829 24f. Class I Pacific locomotive, 1935 . . . . 1·60 60
MS2830 150 × 100 mm. 50f. Class 27 electric locomotive, 1979 . . . 4·50 4·25

835 Cesar Franck and Score

1985. Europa. Music Year. Multicoloured.
2831 12f. Type **835** . . . . 1·50 25
2832 23f. Queen and king with viola dressed in music score (Queen Elisabeth International Music Competition) . . . 4·25 60

836 Planned Canal Lock, Strepy-Thieu

837 Church of Our Lady's Assumption, Avernas-le-Bauduin

1985. Permanent International Navigation Congress Association Centenary Congress, Brussels. Multicoloured.
2833 23f. Type **836** . . . . . . 1·50 55
2834 23f. Aerial view of Zeebrugge harbour . . . 1·50 55

1985. Tourist Publicity. Multicoloured.
2835 12f. Type **837** 80 30
2836 12f. Saint Martin's Church, Marcinelle (horiz) 80 30
2837 12f. Roman tower and Church of old beguinage, Tongres 80 30
2838 12f. House, Wachtebeke (horiz) 80 30

838 Queen Astrid

839 Baking Matton Tart, Grammont

1985. 50th Death Anniv of Queen Astrid.
2839 **838** 12f. lt brown & brown 90 15

1985. Traditional Customs. Multicoloured.
2840 12f. Type **839** 75 30
2841 24f. Young people dancing on trumpet filled with flowers (cent of Red Youths, St. Lambert Cultural Circle, Hermalle-sous-Argenteau) . . . . . 1·50 50

840 Dove and Concentration Camp

1985. 40th Anniv of Liberation. Multicoloured.
2842 9f. Type **840** 60 30
2843 23f. Battle of the Ardennes 1·50 55
2844 24f. Troops landing at Scheldt estuary . . . . . 1·50 55

841 Hawfinch ("Appelvink – Gros Bec")

842 Claes and Fictional Character

1985. Birds (1st series). Multicoloured.
2845 1f. Lesser spotted woodpecker ("Pic epeichette") 30 15
2846 2f. Eurasian tree sparrow ("Moineau friquet") . . 25 15
2847 3f. Type **841** 50 15
2847a 3f.50 European robin ("Rouge-gorge") 30 15
2848 4f. Bluethroat ("Gorge-bleue") 40 15
2848a 4f.50 Common stonechat ("Traquet patre") . . . 45 25
2849 5f. Eurasian nuthatch ("Sittelle torche-pot") . . 40 15
2850 6f. Northern bullfinch ("Bouvreuil") 60 15
2851 7f. Blue tit ("Mesange bleue") 60 20
2852 8f. River kingfisher ("Martin-pecheur") . . . 70 25
2853 9f. Eurasian goldfinch ("Chardonneret") . . . 1·00 15
2854 10f. Chaffinch ("Pinson") 75 25
See also Nos. 3073/86 and 3306/23.

1985. Birth Centenary of Ernest Claes (writer).
2855 **842** 9f. multicoloured 50 30

843 Youth

844 Trazegnies Castle

1985. "Philately for the Young". International Youth Year.
2856 **843** 9f. multicoloured 50 30

1985. "Solidarity". Castles. Multicoloured.
2857 9f.+2f. Type **844** 95 95
2858 12f.+3f. Laarne . . . . . 1·10 1·10
2859 23f.+5f. Turnhout . . . . . 1·70 1·70
2860 50f.+12f. Colonster . . . . 3·25 3·25

845 Miniature from "Book of Hours of Duc de Berry"

1985. Christmas.
2861 **845** 12f.+1f. multicoloured 90 85

846 King Baudouin and Queen Fabiola

1985. Royal Silver Wedding.
2862 **846** 12f. grey, blue and deep blue 90 25

847 Map and 1886 25c. Stamp

848 Giants and Belfry, Alost

1986. Centenary of First Independent State of Congo Stamp.
2863 **847** 10f. blue, grey & dp blue 1·00 30

1986. Carnivals. Multicoloured.
2864 9f. Type **848** 60 25
2865 12f. Clown, Binche 90 30

849 Dove as Hand holding Olive Twig

850 Emblem

1986. International Peace Year.
2866 **849** 23f. multicoloured . . . 1·50 50

1986. 10th Anniv of King Baudouin Foundation.
2867 **850** 12f.+3f. blue, light blue and grey . . . . . . 1·30 1·20

851 Virgin Mary

1986. "The Mystic Lamb" (altarpiece, Brothers Van Eyck). Multicoloured.
2868 9f.+2f. Type **851** 80 80
2869 13f.+3f. Christ in Majesty 1·20 1·20
2870 24f.+6f. St. John the Baptist 2·00 2·00
MS2871 92 × 150 mm. 50f.+12f. The Lamb (central panel) (48 × 37 mm) 8·00 8·00

852 Exhibits

1986. Stamp Day. 50th Anniv of Postal Museum, Brussels.
2872 **852** 13f. multicoloured . . . 80 20

853 Living and Dead Fish and Graph

854 Malinois Shepherd Dog

1986. Europa. Multicoloured.
2873 13f. Type **853** . . . . 1·00 30
2874 24f. Living and dead trees and graph . . . . 3·25 70

1986. Belgian Dogs. Multicoloured.
2875 9f. Type **854** 70 30
2876 13f. Tervuren shepherd dog 1·00 15
2877 24f. Groenendael cattle dog 1·80 60
2878 26f. Flanders cattle dog . . 1·90 60

855 St. Ludger Church, Zele

856 Boy, Broken Skateboard and Red Triangle

1986. Tourist Publicity.
2879 **855** 9f. brown and flesh . . . 60 30
2880 – 9f. red and pink 60 30
2881 – 13f. green & light green 85 30
2882 – 13f. black and green . . 85 30
2883 – 13f. blue and azure . . . 85 30
2884 – 13f. brown & lt brown 85 30
DESIGNS—VERT: No. 2880, Town Hall, Wavre; 2882, Chapel of Our Lady of the Dunes, Bredene. HORIZ: 2881, Water-mills, Zwalm; 2883, Chateau Licot, Viroinval; 2884, Chateau d'Eynebourg, La Calamine.

1986. "Philately for the Young". 25th International Festival of Humour, Knokke.
2885 **856** 9f. black, green & red . . 60 30

857 Constant Permeke (artist)

1986. Celebrities. Multicoloured.
2886 9f. Type **857** (birth centenary) 55 30
2887 13f. Michael Edmond de Selys-Longchamps (naturalist) 85 30
2888 24f. Felix Timmermans (writer) (birth cent) . . . 1·40 45
2889 26f. Maurice Careme (poet) 1·70 45

858 Academy Building, Ghent

1986. Centenary of Royal Academy for Dutch Language and Literature.
2890 **858** 9f. blue 60 30

859 Hops, Glass of Beer and Barley

1986. Belgian Beer.
2891 **859** 13f. multicoloured . . . 90 25

860 Symbols of Provinces and National Colours

1986. 150th Anniv of Provincial Councils.
2892 **860** 13f. multicoloured . . . 80 15

861 Lenoir Hydrocarbon Carriage, 1863

1986. "Solidarity". Cars. Multicoloured.
2893 9f.+2f. Type **861** 70 70
2894 13f.+3f. Pipe de Tourisme saloon, 1911 . . . . . . 1·20 1·10
2895 24f.+6f. Minerva 22 h.p. coupe, 1930 . . . . . . 2·00 2·00
2896 26f.+6f. FN 8 cylinder saloon, 1931 . . . . . . 2·00 2·00

862 Snow Scene

1986. Christmas.
2897 **862** 13f.+1f. multicoloured 1·00 1·00

863 Tree and "100"

1986. Centenaries. Multicoloured.
2898 9f. Type **863** (Textile Workers Christian Union) 70 30
2899 13f. Tree and "100" (Christian Unions) . . . 80 25

864 Corneel Heymans

865 Emblem

1987. Belgian Red Cross. Nobel Physiology and Medicine Prize Winners. Each black, red and stone.
2900 13f.+3f. Type **864** . . . . . 1·00 1·00
2901 24f.+6f. Albert Claude . . . 2·00 1·90

1987. "Flanders Technology International" Fair.
2902 **865** 13f. multicoloured . . . 80 20

866 Bee Orchid

868 Jakob Wiener (engraver)

867 "Waiting" (detail of mural, Gustav Klimt)

1987. European Environment Year. Multicoloured.
2903 9f.+2f. Type **866** . . . . . 1·00 1·00
2904 24f.+6f. Small horse-shoe bat . . . . 2·00 2·00
2905 26f.+6f. Peregrine falcon ("Slechtvalk–Faucan Pelerin") . . . . 2·30 2·30

1987. "Europalia 87 Austria" Festival.
2906 **867** 13f. multicoloured . . . 90 15

1987. Stamp Day.
2907 **868** 13f. deep green and green 80 15

869 Penitents' Procession, Furnes

870 Louvain-la-Neuve Church (Jean Cosse)

1987. Folklore Festivals. Multicoloured.
2908 9f. Type **869** 70 45
2909 13f. "John and Alice" (play), Wavre 80 15

1987. Europa. Architecture. Multicoloured.
2910 13f. Type **870** . . . . 1·50 30
2911 24f. St.-Maartensdal (Regional Housing Association tower block), Louvain (Braem, de Mol and Moerkerke) . . . . . 4·00 75

871 Statue of Gretry and Stage Set

872 Virelles Lake

1987. 20th Anniv of Wallonia Royal Opera.
2912 **871** 24f. multicoloured . . . 1·60 50

1987. Tourist Publicity. Multicoloured.
2913 13f. St. Christopher's Church, Racour 90 30
2914 13f. Type **872** 90 30
2915 13f. Heimolen windmill, Keerbergen 90 30
2916 13f. Boondael Chapel . . . 90 30
2917 13f. Statue of Jan Breydel and Pieter de Coninck, Bruges 90 30

873 Rowing

1987. Centenary of Royal Belgian Rowing Association (2918) and European Volleyball Championships (2919). Multicoloured.
2918 9f. Type **873** 50 30
2919 13f. Volleyball (27 × 37 mm) 80 30

874 Emblem

1987. Foreign Trade Year.
2920 **874** 13f. multicoloured . . . 80 15

875 "Leisure Time" (P. Paulus)

1987. Centenary of Belgian Social Law.
2921 **875** 26f. multicoloured . . . 1·60 50

876 Willy and Wanda (comic strip characters)

1987. "Philately for the Young".
2922 **876** 9f. multicoloured . . . . 1·60 30

878 Rixensart Castle

1987. "Solidarity". Castles. Multicoloured.
2928 9f.+2f. Type **878** 70 70
2929 13f.+3f. Westerlo . . . . . 1·10 1·10
2930 26f.+5f. Fallais . . . . . 2·00 2·00
2931 50f.+12f. Gaasbeek . . . . 3·75 3·75

879 "Madonna and Child" (Remi Lens) **880** Cross and Road

1987. Christmas.
2932 **879** 13f.+1f. multicoloured 1·00 1·00

1987. 50th Anniv of Yellow and White Cross (home nursing organization).
2933 **880** 9f.+2f. multicoloured . . 1·00 1·00

881 Newsprint ("Le Soir")

1987. Newspaper Centenaries.
2934 **881** 9f. multicoloured 65 30
2935 – 9f. black and brown . . 65 30
DESIGN—VERT: No. 2935, Type characters ("Het Laatste Nieuws" (1988)).

882 Lighthouse, "Snipe" (trawler) and Horse Rider in Sea **883** "Flanders Alive" (cultural activities campaign)

1988. The Sea. Multicoloured.
2936 10f. Type **882** 70 60
2937 10f. "Asannot" (trawler) and people playing on beach 70 60
2938 10f. Cross-channel ferry, yacht and bathing huts . . 70 60
2939 10f. Container ship, spotted redshank and oystercatcher 70 60

Nos. 2936/9 were issued together, se-tenant, forming a composite design.

1988. Regional Innovations.
2940 **883** 13f. multicoloured . . . 80 30
2941 – 13f. black, yellow & red 80 30
DESIGN: No. 2941, "Operation Athena" emblem (technological advancement in Wallonia).

884 19th-century Postman (after James Thirian) **885** "Bengale Triomphant"

1988. Stamp Day.
2942 **884** 13f. brown and cream 80 15

1988. Philatelic Promotion Fund. Illustrations from "60 Roses for a Queen" by Pierre-Joseph Redoute (1st series). Multicoloured.
2943 13f.+3f. Type **885** . . . . . 1·50 1·50
2944 24f.+6f. "Centfeuille cristata" . . . . 2·00 2·00
MS2945 150 × 100 mm. 50f.+12f. White tea rose . . . . 7·25 7·00
See also Nos. 2979/**MS**2981, 3009/**MS**3011 and **MS**3025.

886 Non-polluting Motor

1988. Europa. Transport and Communications. Multicoloured.
2946 13f. Dish aerial . . . . . . 1·80 30
2947 24f. Type **886** . . . . 4·00 75

887 Table Tennis

1988. Olympic Games, Seoul. Multicoloured.
2948 9f.+2f. Type **887** . . . . . 1·00 1·00
2949 13f.+3f. Cycling . . . . . . 1·30 1·30
MS2950 125 × 85 mm. 50f.+12f. Running . . . . 7·25 7·00

888 Amay Tower **889** Monnet

1988. Tourist Publicity.
2951 **888** 9f. black and brown . . 60 30
2952 – 9f. black and blue . . . 60 30
2953 – 9f. black, green and pink 60 30
2954 – 13f. black and pink . . . 85 25
2955 – 13f. black and grey . . . 85 25
DESIGNS—VERT: No. 2952, Lady of Hanswijk Basilica, Malines; 2954, Old Town Hall and village pump, Peer. HORIZ: No. 2953, St. Sernin's Church, Waimes; 2955, Basilica of Our Lady of Bon Secours, Peruwelz.

1988. Birth Centenary of Jean Monnet (statesman).
2956 **889** 13f. black and cream . . 75 25

890 Tapestry (detail) and Academy Building **891** Antwerp Ethnographical Museum Exhibits

1988. 50th Annivs of Royal Belgian Academy of Medicine (2957) and Royal Belgian Academy of Sciences, Literature and Fine Arts (2958). Multicoloured.
2957 9f. Type **890** 60 30
2958 9f. Symbols of Academy and building 60 30

1988. Cultural Heritage. Multicoloured.
2959 9f. Type **891** 60 30
2960 13f. Tomb of Lord Gilles Othon and Jacqueline de Lalaing, St. Martin's Church, Trazegnies . . . 80 30
2961 24f. Organ, St. Bartholomew's Church, Geraardsbergen 1·50 60
2962 26f. St. Hadelin's reliquary, St. Martin's Church, Vise 1·80 70

892 Spirou (comic strip character) and Stamp

1988. "Philately for the Young". 50th Anniv of "Spirou" (comic).
2963 **892** 9f. multicoloured . . . . 1·50 40

893 Jacques Brel (songwriter)

1988. "Solidarity". Death Anniversaries. Mult.
2964 9f.+2f. Type **893** (10th) . . 1·20 1·20
2965 13f.+3f. Jef Denyn (carillonner) (47th) . . . . 1·30 1·30
2966 26f.+6f. Fr. Ferdinand Verbiest (astronomer) (300th) . . . . 2·20 2·20

894 "75"

1988. 75th Anniv of Belgian Giro Bank.
2967 **894** 13f. multicoloured . . . 85 25

895 Winter Scene

1988. Christmas.
2968 **895** 9f. multicoloured 55 40

896 Standard Bearer and Guards of Royal Mounted Escort **897** Wooden Press, 1600

1988. 50th Anniv of Royal Mounted Escort.
2969 **896** 13f. multicoloured . . . 80 25

1988. Printing Presses.
2970 **897** 9f. black, pink and blue 60 30
2971 – 24f. brown, pink and deep brown . . . . . 1·50 60
2972 – 26f. green, pink and light green . . . . 1·60 60
DESIGNS—VERT: 24f. 18th-cent Stanhope metal letterpress. HORIZ: 26f. 19th-cent Krause lithographic press.

898 "Crucifixion of Christ" (detail, Rogier van der Weyden)

1989. Belgian Red Cross. Paintings. Mult.
2973 9f.+2f. Type **898** . . . . . 1·00 95
2974 13f.+3f. "Virgin and Child" (Gerard David) . . . . . 1·40 1·30
2975 24f.+6f. "The Good Samaritan" (detail, Denis van Alsloot) . . . . . . 2·00 2·00

899 Marche en Famenne

1989. Lace-making Towns.
2976 **899** 9f. green, black & brown 65 40
2977 – 13f. blue, black & grey 85 30
2978 – 13f. red, black & grey . . 85 30
DESIGNS: No. 2977, Bruges; 2978, Brussels.

1989. Philatelic Promotion Fund. "60 Roses for a Queen" by Pierre-Joseph Redoute (2nd series). As T **885**. Multicoloured.
2979 13f.+5f. "Centfeuille unique melee de rouge" . . . . 1·40 1·30
2980 24f.+6f. "Bengale a grandes feuilles" . . . . 2·00 2·00
MS2981 150 × 100 mm. 50f.+17f. "Aime vibere" . . . . 7·00 7·00

900 Post-chaise and Mail Coach

1989. Stamp Day.
2982 **900** 13f. yellow, black & brn 75 25

901 Marbles **902** Palette on Column

1989. Europa. Children's Games and Toys. Multicoloured.
2983 13f. Type **901** . . . . 1·40 35
2984 24f. Jumping-jack . . . . . 3·50 95

1989. 325th Anniv of Royal Academy of Fine Arts, Antwerp.
2985 **902** 13f. multicoloured . . . 80 25

903 Brussels (½-size illustration)

1989. 3rd Direct Elections to European Parliament.
2986 **903** 13f. multicoloured . . . 85 30

904 Hand (detail, "Creation of Adam", Michelangelo) **905** St. Tillo's Church, Izegem

1989. Bicentenary of French Declaration of Rights of Man.
2987 **904** 13f. black, red and blue 85 50

1989. Tourist Publicity. Multicoloured.
2988 9f. Type **905** 65 40
2989 9f. Logne Castle, Ferrieres (vert) 65 40
2990 13f. Antoing Castle (vert) 90 30
2991 13f. St. Laurentius's Church, Lokeren (vert) 90 30

906 Mallard

1989. Ducks. Multicoloured.
2992 13f. Type **906** . . . . 1·30 1·20
2993 13f. Green-winged teal ("Sarcelle d'Hiver") . . . 1·30 1·20
2994 13f. Common shoveler ("Canard Souchet") . . . 1·30 1·20
2995 13f. Pintail ("Canard Pilet") 1·30 1·20

907 "Shogun Uesugi Shigefusa" (Kamakura period wood figure)

1989. "Europalia 89 Japan" Festival.
2996 **907** 24f. multicoloured . . . 1·50 60

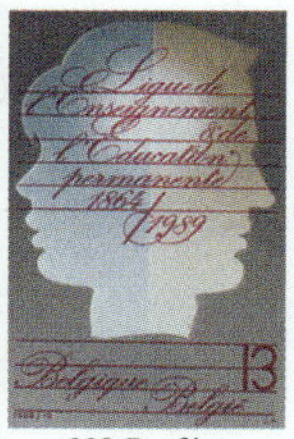

908 Profiles **909** Map

1989. 125th Anniv of League of Teaching and Permanent Education.
2997 **908** 13f. multicoloured . . . 80 25

1989. 150th Anniv of Division of Limburg between Netherlands and Belgium.
2998 **909** 13f. multicoloured . . . 80 25

910 Nibbs (comic strip character) **911** Flower Beds in Greenhouse

1989. "Philately for the Young".
2999 **910** 9f. multicoloured . . . . 1·30 45

1989. "Solidarity". Royal Greenhouses, Laeken. Multicoloured.
3000 9f.+3f. Statue and greenhouses (horiz) . . . 1·00 1·00
3001 13f.+4f. Type **911** . . . . . 1·20 1·20
3002 24f.+5f. External view of greenhouse . . . . . 1·70 1·70
3003 26f.+6f. Trees in greenhouse 2·10 2·10

912 Treble Clef

1989. 50th Anniv of Queen Elisabeth Musical Chapel, Waterloo.
3004 **912** 24f.+6f. multicoloured 2·00 2·00

913 Army Musicians

1989. Christmas. Centenary of Salvation Army in Belgium.
3005 **913** 9f. multicoloured 60 25

914 Fr. Damien and Church **915** Fr. Daens

1989. Death Cent of Fr. Damien (missionary).
3006 **914** 24f. multicoloured . . . 1·80 60

1989. 150th Birth Anniv of Fr. Adolf Daens (social reformer).
3007 **915** 9f. turquoise and green 60 25

916 "Courier" (Albrecht Durer) **917** "Iris florentina"

1990. 500th Anniv of Regular European Postal Services.
3008 **916** 14f. chocolate, buff and brown 95 25

1990. Philatelic Promotion Fund. "60 Roses for a Queen" by Pierre-Joseph Redoute (3rd series). As T **885**. Multicoloured.
3009 14f.+7f. "Bengale Desprez" 1·50 1·50
3010 25f.+12f. "Bengale Philippe" 2·50 2·50
MS3011 151 × 100 mm. 50f.+20f. "Maria Leonida" . . . . . . 7·00 7·00

1990. Ghent Flower Show. Multicoloured.
3012 10f. Type **917** 65 50
3013 14f. "Cattleya harrisoniana" 1·00 25
3014 14f. "Lilium bulbiferum" . . 1·00 25

918 Emilienne Brunfaut (women's rights activist)

1990. International Women's Day.
3015 **918** 25f. red and black . . . 1·60 60

919 Special Olympics **921** "Postman Roulin" (Vincent van Gogh)

920 Water, Tap and Heart

1990. Sporting Events. Multicoloured.
3016 10f. Type **919** 65 30
3017 14f. Football (World Cup football championship, Italy) 90 30
3018 25f. Disabled pictogram and ball (Gold Cup wheelchair basketball championship, Bruges) . . . . 1·60 65

1990. 75th Anniv of Foundation of National Water Supply Society (predecessor of present water-supply companies).
3019 **920** 14f. multicoloured . . . 1·00 30

1990. Stamp Day.
3020 **921** 14f. multicoloured . . . 1·00 30

922 Worker and Crowd **923** Liege I Post Office

1990. Centenary of Labour Day.
3021 **922** 25f. brown, pink & black 1·60 60

1990. Europa. Post Office Buildings.
3022 – 14f. black and blue . . . 1·50 30
3023 **923** 25f. black and red . . . 3·75 70
DESIGN—HORIZ: 14f. Ostend I Post Office.

924 Monument of the Lys, Courtrai

1990. 50th Anniv of the 18 Days Campaign (resistance to German invasion).
3024 **924** 14f. black, yellow & red 1·00 30

1990. "Belgica 90" International Stamp Exhibition, Brussels. "60 Roses for a Queen" by Pierre-Joseph Rerdoute (4th series). Sheet 189 × 120 mm containing vert designs as T **885**. Multicoloured.
MS3025 14f. Tricoloured rose; 14f. "Belle Rubanee"; 14f. "Mycrophylla"; 25f. "Amelie"; 25f. "Adelaide"; 25f. "Helene" (sold at 220f.) . . . . 38·00 38·00

925 Battle Scene (⅗-size illustration)

1990. 175th Anniv of Battle of Waterloo.
3026 **925** 25f. multicoloured . . . 1·70 1·70

926 Berendrecht Lock, Antwerp **927** King Baudouin

1990. Tourist Publicity. Multicoloured.
3027 10f. Type **926** 70 45
3028 10f. Procession of Bayard Steed, Termonde 70 45
3029 14f. St. Rolende's March, Gerpinnes (vert) 90 30
3030 14f. Lommel (1000th anniv) 90 30
3031 14f. St. Clement's Church, Watermael 90 30

1990.
3032 **927** 14f. multicoloured . . . 1·00 25

928 Eurasian Perch

1990. Fishes. Multicoloured.
3033 14f. Type **928** . . . . 1·80 75
3034 14f. Eurasian minnow ("Vairon") . . . . 1·80 75
3035 14f. European bitterling ("Bouviere") . . . . . . 1·80 75
3036 14f. Three-spined stickleback ("Epinoche") . . . 1·80 75

929 Orchestra and Children (½-size illustration)

1990. "Solidarity". Multicoloured.
3037 10f.+2f. Type **929** (50th anniv of Jeunesses Musicales) . . . . 1·90 1·70
3038 14f.+3f. Count of Egmont (16th-century campaigner for religious tolerance) and Beethoven (composer of "Egmont" overture) . . 2·30 2·20
3039 25f.+6f. Jozef Cantre (sculptor) and sculptures (birth centenary) . . . . 3·00 3·00

930 Lucky Luke (comic strip character)

1990. "Philately for the Young".
3040 **930** 10f. multicoloured . . . 1·30 45

931 St. Bernard

1990. 900th Birth Anniv of St. Bernard (Abbot of Clairvaux and Church mediator).
3041 **931** 25f. black and flesh . . . 1·50 60

932 "Pepingen, Winter 1977" (Jozef Lucas)

1990. Christmas.
3042 **932** 10f. multicoloured . . . 65 30

933 "Self-portrait"

1990. 300th Death Anniv of David Teniers, the Younger (painter). Multicoloured.
3043 10f. Type **933** 65 35
3044 14f. "Dancers" 90 35
3045 25f. "Peasants playing Bowls outside Village Inn" . . . 1·70 70

934 King Baudouin and Queen Fabiola (photograph by Valeer Vanbeckbergen)

1990. Royal 30th Wedding Anniversary.
3046 **934** 50f.+15f. mult . . . . . 8·00 7·75

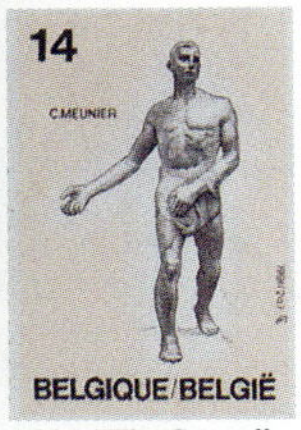

935 "Temptation of St. Anthony" (detail, Hieronymus Bosch)

936 "The Sower" (detail of "Monument to Labour", Brussels) (Constantin Meunier)

1991. Belgian Red Cross. Paintings. Mult.
3047 14f.+3f. Type **935** . . . . . 2·40 2·30
3048 25f.+6f. "The Annunciation" (detail, Dirck Bouts) . . . . . . 3·00 3·00

1991. 19th-Century Sculpture.
3049 **936** 14f. black & cinnamon 90 30
3050 – 25f. black and blue . . . 1·50 50
DESIGN: 25f. Detail of Brabo Fountain, Antwerp (Jef Lambeaux).

937 Rhythmic Gymnastics (European Youth Olympic Days, Brussels)

1991. Sports Meetings.
3051 **937** 10f. grey, mauve & blk 60 25
3052 – 10f. grey, green & black 60 25
DESIGN: No. 3052, Korfball (Third World Championship, Belgium).

938 New Stamp Printing Office, Malines (Hugo van Hoecke)

1991. Stamp Day.
3053 **938** 14f. multicoloured . . . 90 30

939 Cogwheels

1991. Centenary of Liberal Trade Union.
3054 **939** 25f. blue, light blue and deep blue . . . . . . 1·50 60

940 "Olympus 1" Communications Satellite

1991. Europa. Europe in Space. Multicoloured.
3055 14f. Type **940** . . . . 2·00 35
3056 25f. "Ariane 5" rocket carrying space shuttle "Hermes" . . . . 7·50 90

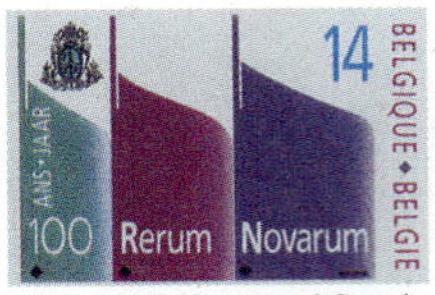

941 Leo XIII's Arms and Standard, and Christian Labour Movement Banners

1991. Centenary of "Rerum Novarum" (encyclical letter from Pope Leo XIII on workers' rights).
3057 **941** 14f. multicoloured . . . 85 25

942 "Isabella of Portugal and Philip the Good" (anon)

1991. "Europalia 91 Portugal" Festival.
3058 **942** 14f. multicoloured . . . 95 25

943 Neptune Grottoes, Couvin

1991. Tourist Publicity. Multicoloured.
3059 14f. Type **943** 85 25
3060 14f. Dieleghem Abbey, Jette 85 25
3061 14f. Niel Town Hall (vert) 85 25
3062 14f. Hautes Fagnes nature reserve 85 25
3063 14f. Giant Rolarius, Roeselare (vert) 85 25

944 King Baudouin (photograph by Dimitri Ardelean)

1991. 60th Birthday (1990) and 40th Anniv of Accession to Throne of King Baudouin.
3064 **944** 14f. multicoloured . . . 1·50 25

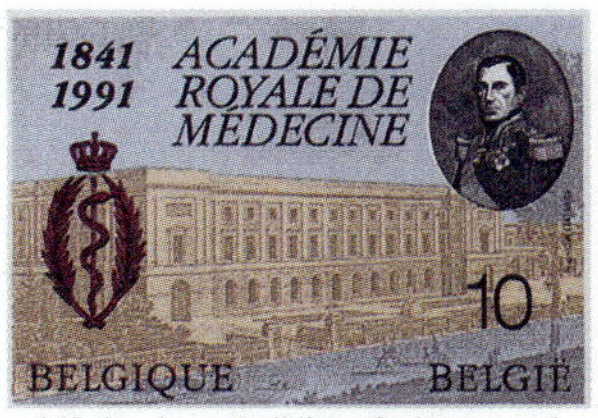

945 Academy Building, Caduceus and Leopold I

1991. 150th Anniv of Royal Academy of Medicine.
3065 **945** 10f. multicoloured . . . 60 30

946 "The English Coast at Dover"

948 Hands reaching through Bars

947 Death Cap

1991. 61st Death Anniv of Alfred Finch (painter and ceramic artist).
3066 **946** 25f. multicoloured . . . 1·50 60

1991. Fungi. Multicoloured.
3067 14f. Type **947** . . . . 1·80 1·50
3068 14f. The Blusher (inscr "Golmotte") . . . . 1·80 1·50
3069 14f. Flaky-stemmed witches' mushroom (inscr "Bolet a pied rouge") . . . . . . 1·80 1·50
3070 14f. "Hygrocybe persistens" (inscr "Hygrophore jaune conique") . . . . 1·80 1·50

1991. 30th Anniv of Amnesty International (3071) and 11th Anniv of Belgian Branch of Medecins sans Frontieres (3072). Multicoloured.
3071 25f. Type **948** . . . . 1·50 60
3072 25f. Doctor examining baby 1·50 60

1991. Birds (2nd series). As T **841**. Mult.
3073 50c. Goldcrest ("Roitelet Huppe") 15 25
3074 1f. Redpoll ("Sizerin Flamme") 20 15
3075 2f. Blackbird ("Merle Noir") 20 15
3076 3f. Reed bunting ("Bruant des Roseaux") 40 15
3077 4f. Pied wagtail ("Bergeronette Grise") 35 15
3078 5f. Barn swallow ("Hirondelle de Cheminee") 35 15
3079 5f.50 Jay ("Geai des Chenes") 50 30
3080 6f. White-throated dipper ("Cincle Plongeur") . . 50 25
3081 6f.50 Sedge-warbler ("Phragmite des Jones") 50 75
3082 7f. Golden oriole ("Loriot") 60 25
3083 8f. Great tit ("Mesange Charbonniere") 70 60
3084 9f. Song thrush ("Grive Musicienne") 70 25
3085 10f. Western greenfinch ("Verdier") 75 30
3086 11f. Winter wren ("Troglodyte Mignon") 85 25
3087 13f. House sparrow ("Moineau Domestique") 1·00 25
3088 14f. Willow warbler ("Pouillot Fitis") . . . . 1·20 40
3088a 16f. Bohemian waxwing ("Jaseur Boreal") . . . 1·30 25

949 Exhibition Emblem

1991. "Telecom 91" International Telecommunications Exhibition, Geneva.
3089 **949** 14f. multicoloured . . . 85 35

950 Blake and Mortimer in "The Yellow Mark" (Edgar P. Jacobs)

1991. "Philately for the Young". Comic Strips. Multicoloured.
3090 14f. Type **950** . . . . 1·50 1·40
3091 14f. Cori the ship boy in "The Ill-fated Voyage" (Bob de Moor) . . . . . 1·50 1·40
3092 14f. "Cities of the Fantastic" (Francois Schuiten) . . . . 1·50 1·40
3093 14f. "Boule and Bill" (Jean Roba) . . . . 1·50 1·40

951 Charles Dekeukeleire

1991. "Solidarity". Film Makers.
3094 **951** 10f.+2f. black, brown and green . . . . . . 1·00 1·00
3095 – 14f.+3f. black, orange and brown . . . . . 1·50 1·50
3096 – 25f.+6f. black, ochre and brown . . . . 2·50 2·50
DESIGNS: 14f. Jacques Ledoux; 25f. Jacques Feyder.

952 Printing Press forming "100" ("Gazet van Antwerpen")

1991. Newspaper Centenaries. Multicoloured.
3097 **952** 10f. black, lt grn & grn 60 30
3098 – 10f. yellow, blue & blk 60 30
DESIGN: No. 3098, Cancellation on "stamp" ("Het Volk").

953 "Our Lady rejoicing in the Child" (icon, Chevetogne Abbey)

955 Speed Skating

954 Mozart and Score

1991. Christmas.
3099 **953** 10f. multicoloured . . . 65 30

1991. Death Bicentenary of Wolfgang Amadeus Mozart (composer).
3100 **954** 25f. purple, bl & ultram 1·70 80

1992. Olympic Games, Albertville and Barcelona. Multicoloured.
3101 10f.+2f. Type **955** . . . . . 1·20 1·20
3102 10f.+2f. Baseball . . . . . 1·20 1·20
3103 14f.+3f. Tennis (horiz) . . . 1·50 1·50
3104 25f.+6f. Clay-pigeon shooting . . . . 2·75 2·75

956 Fire Hose and Service Emblem

957 Flames and Silhouette of Man

1992. Fire Service.
3105 **956** 14f. multicoloured . . . 80 25

1992. The Resistance.
3106 **957** 14f. yellow, black & red 80 25

958 Tapestry and Carpet

959 Belgian Pavilion and Exhibition Emblem

1992. Prestige Occupations. Multicoloured.
3107 10f. Type **958** 55 25
3108 14f. Chef's hat and cutlery (10th anniv (1991) of Association of Belgian Master Chefs) 80 30
3109 27f. Diamond and "100" (centenary (1993) of Antwerp Diamond Club) 1·80 65

1992. "Expo '92" World's Fair, Seville.
3110 **959** 14f. multicoloured . . . 80 25

960 King Baudouin

961

1992.
3111 **960** 15f. red 90 15
3115 28f. green . . . . . . 1·80 60
3120 **961** 100f. green . . . . . 7·00 75

962 Van Noten at Work

963 "White Magic No. VI"

1992. Stamp Day. 10th Death Anniv of Jean van Noten (stamp designer).
3124 **962** 15f. black and red . . . 80 25

1992. Original Art Designs for Stamps. Mult.
3125 15f. Type **963** 85 25
3126 15f. "Colours" (horiz) . . . 85 25

964 Compass Rose, Setting Sun and Harbour

1992. Europa. 500th Anniv of Discovery of America. Multicoloured.
3127 15f. Type **964** . . . . 2·00 40
3128 28f. Globe and astrolabe forming "500" . . . . . 5·50 80

965 Faces of Different Colours

1992. Anti-racism.
3129 **965** 15f. grey, black & pink 80 25

966 "The Hamlet" (Jacob Smits)

1992. Belgian Paintings in Orsay Museum, Paris. Multicoloured.
3130 11f. Type **966** 70 40
3131 15f. "The Bath" (Alfred Stevens) . . . . 1·00 25
3132 30f. "Man at the Helm" (Theo van Rysselberghe) 2·00 70

967 Proud Margaret

968 Mannekin-Pis, Brussels

1992. Folk Tales. Multicoloured.
3133 11f.+2f. Type **967** . . . . . 1·30 1·20
3134 15f.+3f. Witches ("Les Macrales") . . . . 1·80 1·90
3135 28f.+6f. Reynard the fox . . 3·25 3·00

1992. Tourist Publicity. Multicoloured.
3136 15f. Type **968** 85 30
3137 15f. Former Landcommandery of Teutonic Order, Alden Biesen (now Flemish cultural centre) (horiz) . . 85 30
3138 15f. Andenne (1300th anniv) 85 30
3139 15f. Carnival revellers on Fools' Monday, Renaix (horiz) 85 30
3140 15f. Great Procession (religious festival), Tournai (horiz) 85 30

969 European Polecat

1992. Mammals. Multicoloured.
3141 15f. Type **969** . . . . 1·50 80
3142 15f. Eurasian red squirrel 1·50 80
3143 15f. Eurasian hedgehog . . 1·50 80
3144 15f. Common dormouse . . 1·50 80

970 Henri van der Noot, Jean van der Meersch and Jean Vonck

1992. 203rd Anniv of Brabant Revolution.
3145 **970** 15f. multicoloured . . . 80 20

971 Arms of Thurn and Taxis

972 Gaston Lagaffe (cartoon character)

1992. 500th Anniv of Mention of Thurn and Taxis Postal Services in Lille Account Books.
3146 **971** 15f. multicoloured . . . 80 20

1992. "Philately for the Young".
3147 **972** 15f. multicoloured . . . 1·10 20

973 Star, "B" and Map

1992. European Single Market.
3148 **973** 15f. multicoloured . . . 90 30

974 Okapi

975 "Place Royale in Winter" (Luc de Decker)

1992. 150th Anniv of Antwerp Zoo. Mult.
3149 15f. Type **974** 80 25
3150 30f. Golden-headed tamarin 1·80 55

1992. Christmas.
3151 **975** 11f. multicoloured . . . 65 25

976 "Man with Pointed Hat" (Adriaen Brouwer)

1993. Belgian Red Cross. Paintings. Mult.
3152 15f.+3f. Type **976** . . . . . 1·90 1·90
3153 28f.+7f. "Nereid and Triton" (Peter Paul Rubens) (horiz) . . . . . 3·50 3·50

977 Council of Leptines, 743

1993. Historical Events. Multicoloured.
3154 11f. Type **977** 60 35
3155 15f. Queen Beatrix and King Matthias I Corvinus of Hungary (detail of "Missale Romanum") (77 × 24 mm) . . . . . . 1·00 30
3156 30f. Battle scene (Battles of Neerwinden, 1673 and 1773) . . . . 1·80 70
MS3157 105 × 155 mm. 28f. Illustration from Matthias I Corvinus's *Missale Romanum*, 1485 (54 × 39 mm) . . . . . 2·00 2·00

978 Town Hall

1993. Antwerp, European City of Culture. Mult.
3158 15f. Panorama of Antwerp (76 × 24 mm) . . . . . 1·00 35
3159 15f. Type **978** . . . . 1·00 30
3160 15f. "Study of Women's Heads and Male Torso" (Jacob Jordaens) . . . . 1·00 30
3161 15f. St. Job's altarpiece, Schoonbroek . . . . . 1·00 30
3162 15f. "Angels" (stained glass window by Eugeen Yoors, Mother of God Chapel, Marie-Josee Institute, Elisabethville) (vert) . . . 1·00 30

979 1893 2f. Stamp

980 "Florence 1960" (Gaston Bertrand)

1993. Stamp Day.
3163 **979** 15f. multicoloured . . . 80 25

1993. Europa. Contemporary Art. Multicoloured.
3164 15f. Type **980** 90 35
3165 28f. "The Gig" (Constant Permeke) . . . . 2·00 1·00

981 Red Admiral ("Vanessa atalanta")

1993. Butterflies. Multicoloured.
3166 15f. Type **981** 85 35
3167 15f. Purple emperor ("Apatura iris") 85 35
3168 15f. Peacock ("Inachis io") 85 35
3169 15f. Small tortoiseshell ("Aglais urticae") 85 35

982 Knot

983 Mayan Warrior (statuette)

1993. 150th Anniv of Alumni of Free University of Brussels Association.
3170 **982** 15f. blue and black . . . 80 25

1993. "Europalia 93 Mexico" Festival.
3171 **983** 15f. multicoloured . . . 80 25

984 Ommegang, Brussels

1993. Folklore Festivals. Multicoloured.
3172 11f. Type **984** 70 40
3173 15f. Royale Moncrabeau, Namur 80 25
3174 28f. Stilt-walkers, Merchtem (vert) . . . . 1·50 65

985 La Hulpe Castle

1993. Tourist Publicity.
3175 **985** 15f. black and blue . . . 85 25
3176 – 15f. black and lilac . . . 85 25
3177 – 15f. black and grey . . . 85 25
3178 – 15f. black and pink . . . 85 25
3179 – 15f. black and green . . 85 25
DESIGNS—HORIZ: No. 3176, Cortewalle Castle, Beveren; 3177, Jehay Castle; 3179, Raeren Castle. VERT: No. 3178, Arenberg Castle, Heverlee.

986 Emblem

1993. 2nd International Triennial Textile Exhibition, Tournai.
3180 **986** 15f. blue, red and black 85 25

987 Presidency Emblem

1993. Belgian Presidency of European Community Council.
3181 **987** 15f. multicoloured . . . 90 30

988 Magritte

989 King Baudouin

1993. 25th Death Anniv (1992) of Rene Magritte (artist).
3182 **988** 30f. multicoloured . . . 1·80 60

1993. King Baudouin Commemoration.
3183 **989** 15f. black and blue . . . 90 20

990 Red and White Cat

1993. Cats. Multicoloured.
3184 15f. Type **990** . . . . 1·10 65
3185 15f. Tabby and white cat standing on rock . . . . 1·10 65
3186 15f. Silver tabby lying on wall . . . . 1·10 65
3187 15f. Tortoiseshell and white cat sitting by gardening tools . . . . 1·10 65

991 Highlighted Cancer Cell

992 Frontispiece

1993. Anti-cancer Campaign.
3188 **991** 15f.+3f. multicoloured 1·50 1·50

1993. 450th Anniv of "De Humani Corporis Fabrica" (treatise on human anatomy) by Andreas Vesalius.
3189 **992** 15f. black, brown & red 80 25

993 Natacha (cartoon character)

1993. "Philately for the Young".
3190 **993** 15f. multicoloured . . . 1·00 25

994 Sun's Rays

995 "Madonna and Child" (statue, Our Lady of the Chapel, Brussels)

1993. 50th Anniv of Publication of "Le Faux Soir" (resistance newspaper).
3191 **994** 11f. multicoloured . . . 65 50

1993. Christmas.
3192 **995** 11f. multicoloured . . . 65 30

996 Child looking at Globe

1993. Children's Town Councils.
3193 **996** 15f. multicoloured . . . 85 25

997 King Albert II

998 King Albert II

1993.
3194 **997** 16f. multicoloured . . . 1·20 15
3195 16f. turquoise and blue 1·00 20
3196 20f. brown and stone . . 1·40 80
3197 30f. purple and mauve 1·50 25
3198 32f. orange and yellow 1·80 25
3199 40f. red and mauve . . . 2·40 75
3200 50f. myrtle and green . . 4·25 45
3201 **998** 100f. multicoloured . . . 6·00 45
3202 200f. multicoloured . . . 12·50 7·00

999 "Ma Toute Belle" (Serge Vandercam)

1000 Olympic Flames and Rings

1994. Painters' Designs. Multicoloured.
3210 16f. Type **999** 90 30
3211 16f. "The Malleable Darkness" (Octave Landuyt) (horiz) 90 30

1994. Sports. Multicoloured.
3212 16f.+3f. Type **1000** (cent of International Olympic Committee) . . . . . . 1·70 1·70
3213 16f.+3f. Footballers (World Cup Football Championship, U.S.A.) 1·70 1·70
3214 16f.+3f. Skater (Winter Olympic Games, Lillehammer, Norway) . . 1·70 1·70

1001 Hanriot HD-1

1002 Masthead of "Le Jour-Le Courrier" (centenary)

1994. Biplanes. Multicoloured.
3215 13f. Type **1001** 80 45
3216 15f. Spad XIII . . . . . . 1·00 30
3217 30f. Schrenck FBA.H flying boat . . . . 1·70 80
3218 32f. Stampe SV-4B . . . . 1·80 80

1994. Newspaper Anniversaries. Multicoloured.
3219 16f. Type **1002** 95 25
3220 16f. Masthead of "La Wallonie" (75th anniv) (horiz) 95 25

1003 "Fall of the Golden Calf" (detail, Fernand Allard l'Olivier)

1994. Centenary of Charter of Quaregnon (social charter).
3221 **1003** 16f. multicoloured . . . 95 25

1004 1912 5f. Stamp

1994. Stamp Day. 60th Death Anniv of King Albert I.
3222 **1004** 16f. purple, mauve & bl 95 25

1005 Reconciliation of Duke John I and Arnold, Squire of Wezemaal

1994. 700th Death Anniv of John I, Duke of Brabant. Illustrations from 15th-century "Brabantse Yeesten". Multicoloured.
3223 13f. Type **1005** 75 45
3224 16f. Tournament at wedding of his son John to Margaret of York, 1290 95 40
3225 30f. Battle of Woeringen (77 × 25 mm) . . . . . 1·90 70

1006 Georges Lemaitre (formulator of expanding Universe and of "big bang" theory)

1008 St. Peter's Church, Bertem

1007 Father Damien (missionary and leprosy worker)

1994. Europa. Discoveries and Inventions. Mult.
3226 16f. Type **1006** 90 45
3227 30f. Gerardus Mercator (inventor of Mercator projection in cartography) 1·90 85

1994. Visit of Pope John Paul II. Mult.
3228 16f. Type **1007** (beatification) 85 30
3229 16f. St. Mutien-Marie (5th anniv of canonization) . . 85 30

1994. Tourist Publicity. Multicoloured.
3230 16f. Type **1008** 85 30
3231 16f. St. Bavo's Church, Kanegem (vert) 85 30
3232 16f. Royal St. Mary's Church, Schaarbeek . . . 85 30
3233 16f. St. Gery's Church, Aubechies 85 30
3234 16f. Sts. Peter and Paul's Church, St.-Severin en Condroz (vert) 85 30

1009 Tournai Porcelain Plate from Duke of Orleans Service (Mariemont Museum)

1994. Museum Exhibits. Multicoloured.
3235 16f.+3f. Type **1009** . . . . 1·50 1·50
3236 16f.+3f. Etterbeek porcelain coffee cup and saucer (Louvain Municipal Museum) . . . . 1·50 1·50
MS3237 125 × 90 mm. 50f.+11f. Delft containers (Pharmacy Museum, Maaseik) . . . . . 7·75 7·75

1010 Guillaume Lekeu (composer)

1994. Anniversaries. Multicoloured.
3238 16f. Type **1010** (death cent) 85 40
3239 16f. Detail of painting by Hans Memling (500th death anniv) 85 40

1011 Generals Crerar, Montgomery and Bradley and Allied Troops (½-size illustration)

1994. 50th Anniv of Liberation.
3240 **1011** 16f. multicoloured . . . 1·00 80

1012 Marsh Marigold ("Caltha palustris")

1994. Flowers. Multicoloured.
3241 16f. Type **1012** . . . . . . 1·30 65
3242 16f. White helleborine ("Cephalanthera damasonium") . . . . . 1·30 65
3243 16f. Sea bindweed ("Calystegia soldanella") 1·30 65
3244 16f. Broad-leaved helleborine ("Epipactis helleborine") . . . . . . 1·30 65

1013 Cubitus (cartoon character)

1014 Simenon and Bridge of Arches, Liege

1994. "Philately for the Young".
3245 **1013** 16f. multicoloured . . . 1·10 35

1994. 5th Death Anniv of Georges Simenon (novelist).
3246 **1014** 16f. multicoloured . . . 1·10 35
The depiction of the bridge alludes to Simenon's first novel "Au Pont des Arches".

1015 Deaf Man and Butterfly

1994. "Solidarity".
3247 **1015** 16f.+3f. mult . . . . . 1·20 1·20

1016 Santa Claus on Rooftop

1994. Christmas.
3248 **1016** 13f. multicoloured . . . 75 40

1017 Field and Flax Knife (Flax Museum, Courtrai)

1995. Museums. Multicoloured.
3249 16f.+3f. Type **1017** . . . . 1·10 1·10
3250 16f.+3f. River and pump (Water and Fountain Museum, Genval) . . . . 1·10 1·10
MS3251 125 × 90 mm. 34f.+6f. Mask (International Carnival and Mask Museum, Binche) . . . . . . 3·00 3·00
The premium was for the promotion of philately.

1018 Emblem

1995. Anniversaries. Anniversary emblems.
3252 **1018** 16f. red, blue & black . . . 90 30
3253 – 16f. multicoloured . . . 90 30
3254 – 16f. multicoloured . . . 90 30
3255 – 16f. red, black & brown . . 90 30
ANNIVERSARIES: No. 3252, 50th anniv of August Vermeylen Fund; 3253, Centenary of Touring Club of Belgium; 3254, Centenary of Federation of Belgian Enterprises; 3255, 50th anniv of Social Security in Belgium.

1019 "Hibiscus rosa-sinensis"

1995. Ghent Flower Show. Multicoloured.
3256 13f. Type **1019** 75 45
3257 16f. Azalea 90 40
3258 30f. Fuchsia . . . . 1·70 75

1020 Crossword Puzzle

1021 Frans de Troyer (promoter of thematic philately)

1995. Games and Pastimes. Multicoloured.
3259 13f. Type **1020** 75 40
3260 16f. King (chess piece) . . . 90 40
3261 30f. Scrabble . . . . 1·70 1·10
3262 34f. Queen (playing cards) 1·90 1·00

1995. Post Day.
3263 **1021** 16f. black, stone & orge 90 35

1022 Watch Tower and Barbed Wire Fence

1995. Europa. Peace and Freedom. Mult.
3264 16f. Type **1022** (50th anniv of liberation of concentration camps) . . 1·80 40
3265 30f. Nuclear cloud (25th anniv of Non-Proliferation Treaty) . . . 3·00 85

1023 Soldiers of the Irish Brigade and Memorial Cross

1995. 250th Anniv of Battle of Fontenoy.
3266 **1023** 16f. multicoloured . . . 1·00 40

1024 U.N. Emblem

1995. 50th Anniv of U.N.O.
3267 **1024** 16f. multicoloured . . . 90 40

1025 "Sauvagemont, Maransart" (Pierre Alechinsky)

1995. Artists' Philatelic Creations.
3268 **1025** 16f. red, black & yellow 90 50
3269 – 16f. multicoloured . . . 90 50
DESIGN: No. 3269, "Telegram-style" (Pol Mara).

1026 Paul Cauchie (Brussels)

1995. Tourist Publicity. Art nouveau house facades by named architects. Multicoloured.
3270 16f. Type **1026** 90 55
3271 16f. Frans Smet-Verhas (Antwerp) 90 55
3272 16f. Paul Jaspar (Liege) . . 90 80

1027 Anniversary Emblem

1995. Cent of Royal Belgian Football Assn.
3273 **1027** 16f.+4f. mult . . . . . 1·30 1·20

1028 "Mercator" (Belgian cadet barque)

1995. Sailing Ships. Multicoloured.
3274 16f. Type **1028** . . . . . . 1·10 75
3275 16f. "Kruzenshtern" (Russian cadet barque) (inscr "Kruzenstern") . . . . . 1·10 75
3276 16f. "Sagres II" (Portuguese cadet barque) . . . . . . 1·10 75
3277 16f. "Amerigo Vespucci" (Italian cadet ship) . . . 1·10 75

1029 Princess Astrid and Globe

1995. Red Cross. Multicoloured.
3278 16f.+3f. Type **1029** (Chairwoman) . . . . . 1·20 1·10
3279 16f.+3f. Wilhelm Rontgen (discoverer of X-rays) and X-ray of hand . . . . . 1·20 1·10
3280 16f.+3f. Louis Pasteur (chemist) and microscope 1·20 1·10

1030 1908 Minerva

1995. Motorcycles. Multicoloured.
3281 13f. Type **1030** 75 45
3282 16f. 1913 FN (vert) 85 30
3283 30f. 1929 La Mondiale . . . 1·60 1·20
3284 32f. 1937 Gillet (vert) . . . 1·90 1·10

1031 Sammy (cartoon character)

1995. "Philately for the Young".
3285 **1031** 16f. multicoloured . . . 1·00 40

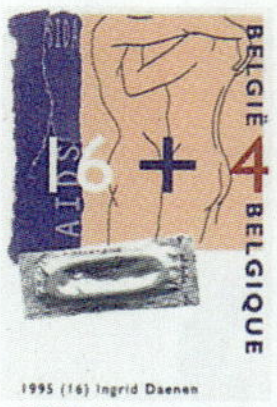

1032 Couple and Condom in Wrapper

1034 "Nativity" (from 15th-century breviary)

1033 King Albert II and Queen Paola (photograph by Christian Louis)

1995. "Solidarity". AIDS Awareness.
3286 **1032** 16f.+4f. mult . . . . . 1·10 1·10

1995. King's Day.
3287 **1033** 16f. multicoloured . . . 1·00 65

1995. Christmas.
3288 **1034** 13f. multicoloured . . . 80 40

1035 Puppets, Walloon Museum, Liege

1996. Museums. Multicoloured.
3289 16f.+4f. Type **1035** . . . . 1·10 1·10
3290 16f.+4f. National Gin Museum, Hasselt . . . . 1·10 1·10
MS3291 126 × 90 mm. 34f.+6f. "Fall of Saul" (detail of title panel), Butchers' Guild Hall Museum, Antwerp . . . . 2·75 2·75
The premium was used for the promotion of philately.

1036 "Emile Mayrisch"

1037 "LIBERALISME"

1996. 70th Death Anniv of Theo van Rysselberghe (painter). No value expressed.
3292 **1036** A (16f.) mult 90 40

1996. 150th Anniv of Liberal Party.
3293 **1037** 16f. dp blue, violet & bl 90 40

1038 Oscar Bonnevalle (stamp designer) and "Gelatenheid"

1996. Stamp Day.
3294 **1038** 16f. multicoloured . . . 90 70

1039 Dragonfly ("Sympetrum sanguineum")

1996. 150th Anniv of Royal Institute of Natural Sciences of Belgium. Insects. Multicoloured.
3295 16f. Type **1039** 85 85
3296 16f. Buff-tailed bumble bee ("Bombus terrestris") . . 85 85
3297 16f. Stag beetle ("Lucanus cervus") 85 85
3298 16f. May beetle ("Melolontha melolontha") 85 85
3299 16f. European field cricket ("Gryllus campestris") . . 85 85
3300 16f. Seven-spotted ladybird ("Coccinella septempunctata") 85 85

1040 Yvonne Nevejean (rescuer of Jewish children)

1042 King Albert II

1996. Europa. Famous Women. Multicoloured.
3301 16f. Type **1040** 90 45
3302 30f. Marie Gevers (poet) . . 1·80 85

1996. Birds (3rd series). As T **841**. Mult.
3303 1f. Crested tit ("Mesange Huppee") 15 10
3304 2f. Redwing ("Grive mauvis") 20 15
3305 3f. Eurasian skylark ("Alouette des champs") 20 20
3306 4f. Pied flycatcher ("Gore-mouche noir") 30 25
3307 5f. Common starling ("Etourneau sansonnet") 25 20
3308 6f. Spruce siskin ("Tarin des aulnes") 35 30
3309 7f. Yellow wagtail ("Bergeronnette printaniere") 30 30
3310 7f.50 Great grey shrike ("Pie-Grienche Grise") . . 35 45
3311 9f. Green woodpecker ("Pic Vert") 45 50
3312 10f. Turtle dove ("Tourterelle des Bois") 50 50
3313 15f. Willow tit ("Mesange boreale") 80 45
3314 16f. Coal tit ("Mesange noire") 80 55
3315 21f. Fieldfare ("Grive Litorne") (horiz) . . . . 1·00 85
3316 150f. Black-billed magpie ("Pie bavarde") (35 × 25 mm) . . . . . . 7·75 4·25

1996. 62nd Birthday of King Albert II.
3327 **1042** 16f. multicoloured . . . 95 55

1043 Han sur Lesse Grottoes

1996. Tourist Publicity. Multicoloured.
3328 16f. Type **1043** 90 40
3329 16f. Statue of beguine, Begijnendijk (vert) 90 40

1044 Royal Palace

1996. Brussels, Heart of Europe. Mult.
3330 16f. Type **1044** 90 40
3331 16f. St. Hubert Royal Galleries 90 40
3332 16f. Le Petit Sablon, Egmont Palace (horiz) . . 90 65
3333 16f. Jubilee Park (horiz) . . 90 40

1045 1900 Germain 6CV Voiturette

1996. Cent of Motor Racing at Spa. Mult.
3334 16f. Type **1045** 90 40
3335 16f. 1925 Alfa Romeo P2 90 40
3336 16f. 1939 Mercedes Benz W154 . . . . 90 40
3337 16f. 1967 Ferrari 330P . . . 90 40

1046 Table Tennis

1996. Olympic Games, Atlanta. Mult.
3338 16f.+4f. Type **1046** . . . . 1·10 1·10
3339 16f.+4f. Swimming . . . . 1·10 1·10
MS3340 125 × 90 mm. 34f.+6f. High jumping (41 × 34 mm) . . . . 2·75 2·75

1996.
3341 **1042** 16f. blue 95 25
3342 17f. blue . . . . . . 1·00 30
3343 18f. green . . . . . . 1·00 80
3344 19f. lilac . . . . . . 1·00 45
3344a 20f. brown . . . . . . 1·10 65
3345 25f. brown . . . . . . 1·30 80
3346 28f. brown . . . . . . 1·70 70
3347 32f. violet . . . . . . 1·60 1·20
3348 34f. blue . . . . . . 1·60 1·40
3349 36f. blue . . . . . . 1·80 1·20
3350 50f. green . . . . . . 3·00 1·60

1047 "The Straw Hat" (Peter Paul Rubens)
1048 Philip the Fair

1996. Paintings by Belgian Artists in the National Gallery, London. Multicoloured.
3351 14f. "St. Ivo" (Rogier van der Weyden) 80 55
3352 16f. Type **1047** 95 55
3353 30f. "Man in a Turban" (Jan van Eyck) . . . . . 1·90 1·20

1996. 500th Anniv of Marriage of Philip the Fair and Joanna of Castile and Procession into Brussels. Details of triptych by the Master of Affligem Abbey at Zierikzee Town Hall. Multicoloured.
3354 16f. Type **1048** 95 55
3355 16f. Joanna of Castile . . . 95 55

1049 Cloro (cartoon character)

1996. "Philately for the Young".
3356 **1049** 16f. multicoloured . . . 1·00 55

1050 Title of First Issue and Charles Letellier (founder)

1996. 150th Anniv of "Mons Almanac".
3357 **1050** 16f. black, yell & mve 95 40

1051 Arthur Grumiaux (violinist, 10th death anniv)

1996. Music and Literature Anniversaries.
3358 **1051** 16f. multicoloured . . . 95 40
3359 – 16f. multicoloured . . . 95 40
3360 – 16f. black and brown 95 40
3361 – 16f. multicoloured . . . 95 40
DESIGNS: No. 3359, Flor Peeters (organist, 10th death anniv); 3360, Christian Dotremont (poet, 5th death anniv); 3361, Paul van Ostaijen (writer, birth centenary) and cover drawing by Oscar Jespers for "Bezette Stad".

1052 Globe and Children of Different Races

1996. "Solidarity". 50th Anniv of UNICEF.
3362 **1052** 16f.+4f. mult . . . . . 1·10 1·20

1053 Christmas Trees

1996. Christmas. Sheet 185 × 145 mm containing T **1053** and similar horiz designs. Multicoloured.
MS3363 14f. Type **1053**; 14f. "Happy Christmas" in Flemish, German and French; 14f. Church; 14f. Cake stall; 14f. Stall with cribs; 14f. Meat stall; 14f. Father Christmas; 14f. Crowd including man smoking pipe; 14f. Crowd including man carrying holly 7·00 7·00

1054 Students

1997. Centenary of Catholic University, Mons.
3364 **1054** 17f. multicoloured . . . 90 40

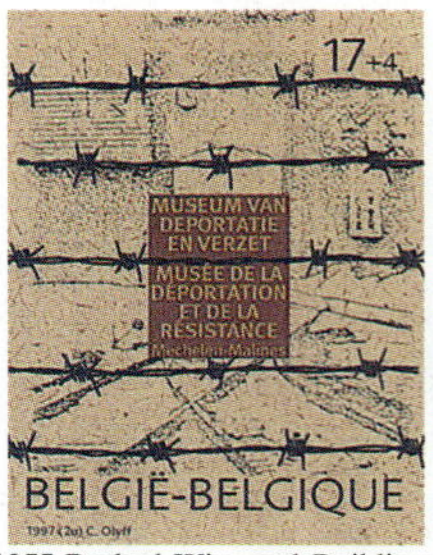

1055 Barbed Wire and Buildings

1997. Museums. Multicoloured.
3365 17f.+4f. Type **1055** (Deportation and Resistance Museum, Dossin Barracks, Malines) 1·30 1·20
3366 17f.+4f. Foundryman pouring molten metal (Fourneau Saint-Michel Iron Museum) . . . 1·30 1·20
MS3367 90 × 125 mm. 41f.+9f. Horta Museum, Saint-Giles . . 4·50 4·00
The premium was used for the promotion of philately.

1056 Deer and Landscape (½-size illustration)

1997. "Cantons of the East" (German-speaking Belgium).
3368 **1056** 17f. black and brown 90 40

1057 Marie Sasse

1997. Opera Singers. Multicoloured.
3369 17f. Type **1057** 90 70
3370 17f. Ernest van Dijck . . . 90 70
3371 17f. Hector Dufranne . . . 90 70
3372 17f. Clara Clairbert 90 70

1058 Soldier on Duty

1997. Belgian Involvement in United Nations Peacekeeping Forces.
3373 **1058** 17f. multicoloured . . . 90 40

1059 The Goat Riders

1997. Europa. Tales and Legends. Mult.
3374 17f. Type **1059** . . . . . . 1·10 75
3375 30f. Jean de Berneau . . . 2·00 1·60

1060 Spinoy working on Recess Plate

1997. Stamp Day. 4th Death Anniv of Constant Spinoy (engraver).
3376 **1060** 17f. brown, yell & blk 90 80

1061 "The Man in the Street" (detail)
1062 Flower Arrangement

1997. Birth Centenary of Paul Delvaux (artist). Multicoloured.
3377 15f. Type **1061** 75 50
3378 17f. "The Public Voice" (horiz) 95 40
3379 32f. "The Messenger of the Night" . . . . 1·80 90

1997. 2nd International Flower Show, Liege.
3380 **1062** 17f. multicoloured . . . 95 40

1063 Men's Judo

1997. Judo. Each black and red.
3381 17f.+4f. Type **1063** . . . . 1·20 1·10
3382 17f.+4f. Women's judo (showing female symbol) 1·20 1·10

1064 Queen Paola and Belvedere Villa

1997. 60th Birthday of Queen Paola.
3383 **1064** 17f. multicoloured . . . 90 40

1065 Jommeke, Flip and Filiberke (comic strip characters)

1997. "Philately for the Young".
3384 **1065** 17f. multicoloured . . . 1·00 40

1066 "Rosa damascena" "Coccinea"
1067 St. Martin's Cathedral, Hal

1997. Roses. Illustrations by Pierre-Joseph Redoute. Multicoloured.
3385 17f. Type **1066** 90 40
3386 17f. "Rosa sulfurea" 90 40
3387 17f. "Rosa centifolia" . . . 90 40

1997. Tourist Publicity. Multicoloured.
3388 17f. Type **1067** 90 70
3389 17f. Notre-Dame Church, Laeken (horiz) 90 70
3390 17f. St. Martin's Cathedral, Liege 90 70

1068 Stonecutter

1997. Trades. Multicoloured.
3391 17f. Type **1068** 90 70
3392 17f. Bricklayer 90 70
3393 17f. Carpenter 90 70
3394 17f. Blacksmith 90 70

1069 Queen amidst Workers

1997. Centenary of Apimondia (International Apicultural Association) and 35th Congress, Antwerp. Bees. Multicoloured.
3395 17f. Type **1069** 90 80
3396 17f. Development of egg . . 90 80
3397 17f. Bees emerging from cells 90 80
3398 17f. Bee collecting nectar from flower 90 80
3399 17f. Bee fanning at hive entrance and worker arriving with nectar . . . 90 80
3400 17f. Worker feeding drone 90 80

1070 "Belgica" (polar barque) ice-bound

1997. Cent of Belgian Antarctic Expedition.
3401 **1070** 17f. multicoloured . . . 90 45

1071 Mask

1073 "Fairon" (Pierre Grahame)

1997. Centenary of Royal Central Africa Museum, Tervuren. Multicoloured.
3402 17f. Type **1071** 90 40
3403 17f. Museum (74 × 24 mm) 90 40
3404 34f. Statuette . . . . 1·90 1·60

1997. Christmas.
3408 **1073** 15f. multicoloured . . . 85 50

1074 Disjointed Figure

1075 Azalea "Mrs. Haerens A"

1997. "Solidarity". Multiple Sclerosis.
3409 **1074** 17f.+4f. black & blue 1·10 1·10

1997. Willow Tit. As No. 3318 but horiz.
3410 15f. multicoloured . . . . . 90 1·10

1997. Self-adhesive.
3411 **1075** (17f.) multicoloured . . 90 35

1076 Female Symbol

1078 Gerard Walschap

1077 Thalys High Speed Train on Antoing Viaduct

1998. 50th Anniv of Women's Suffrage in Belgium.
3412 **1076** 17f. red, brown & sepia 90 50

1998. Paris–Brussels–Cologne–Amsterdam High Speed Rail Network.
3413 **1077** 17f. multicoloured . . . 90 50

1998. Writers' Birth Centenaries. Mult.
3414 17f. Type **1078** 90 55
3415 17f. Norge (Georges Mogin) 90 55

1079 King Leopold III

1080 "Black Magic"

1998. Kings of Belgium (1st series).
3416 **1079** 17f.+8f. green . . . . . 1·50 1·50
3417 – 32f.+15f. brown . . . . 2·50 2·50
MS3418 125 × 90 mm. 50f.+25f. red 5·00 4·75
KINGS: 32f. Baudouin I; 50f. Albert II.
The premium was used for the promotion of philately.

See also Nos. 3466/8 and **MS**3508.

1998. Birth Centenary of Rene-Ghislain Magritte (artist) (1st issue). Multicoloured.
3419 17f. Type **1080** 90 50
3420 17f. "The Sensitive Chord" (horiz) 90 50
3421 17f. "The Castle of the Pyrenees" 90 50
See also No. 3432.

1081 "La Foire aux Amours" (Felicien Rops)

1998. Art Anniversaries. Multicoloured.
3422 17f. Type **1081** (death cent) 90 95
3423 17f. "Hospitality for the Strangers" (Gustave van de Woestijne) (bicentenary of Museum of Fine Arts, Ghent) 90 95
3424 17f. "Man with Beard" (self-portrait of Felix de Boeck, birth centenary) 90 95
3425 17f. "black writing mixed with colours..." (Karel Appel and Christian Dotremont) (50th anniv of Cobra art movement) . . 90 95

1082 Anniversary Emblem

1998. 75th Anniv of Belgian Postage Stamp Dealers' Association.
3426 **1082** 17f. multicoloured . . . 90 50

1083 Avro RJ85 Airplane

1998. 75th Anniv of Sabena Airlines.
3427 **1083** 17f. multicoloured . . . 90 65

1084 Fox

1998. Wildlife of the Ardennes. Mult.
3428 17f. Type **1084** 90 60
3429 17f. Red deer ("Cervus elaphus") 90 60
3430 17f. Wild boar ("Sus scrofa") 90 60
3431 17f. Roe deer ("Capreolus capreolus") 90 60

1085 "The Return" (Magritte)

1998. Birth Centenary of Rene-Ghislain Magritte (artist) (2nd issue).
3432 **1085** 17f. multicoloured . . . 90 60

1086 Struyf

1088 Pelote

1087 Guitarist (Torhout and Werchter Festival)

1998. Stamp Day. 2nd Death Anniv of Edmond Struyf (founder of Pro-Post (organization for promotion of philately)).
3433 **1086** 17f. black, red & yellow 90 60

1998. Europa. National Festivals.
3434 **1087** 17f. violet and yellow 1·00 40
3435 – 17f. violet and mauve 1·00 40
DESIGN: No. 3435, Music conductor (Wallonie Festival).

1998. Sports. Multicoloured.
3436 17f.+4f. Type **1088** . . . . 1·10 1·00
3437 17f.+4f. Handball . . . . . 1·10 1·00
MS3438 123 × 88 mm. 30f.+7f. Goalkeeper (World Cup Football Championship, France) . . . . 2·30 2·30

1089 Emblem

1090 Marnix van Sint-Aldegonde

1998. European Heritage Days. Mult.
3439 17f. Type **1089** 85 65
3440 17f. Bourla Theatre, Antwerp 85 65
3441 17f. La Halle, Durbuy . . . 85 65
3442 17f. Halletoren, Kortrijk . . 85 65
3443 17f. Louvain Town Hall . . 85 65
3444 17f. Perron, Liege 85 65
3445 17f. Royal Theatre, Namur 85 65
3446 17f. Aspremont-Lynden Castle, Rekem 85 65
3447 17f. Neo-Gothic kiosk, Saint Nicolas 85 65
3448 17f. Saint-Vincent's Chapel, Tournai 85 65
3449 17f. Villers-la-Ville Abbey 85 65
3450 17f. Saint-Gilles Town Hall 85 65

1998. 400th Death Anniv of Philips van Marnix van St. Aldegonde (writer).
3451 **1090** 17f. multicoloured . . . 90 50

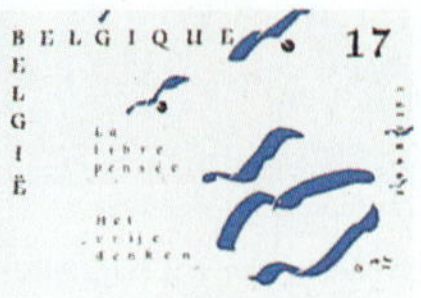

1091 Face

1998. Bicentenary of "Amis Philanthropes" (circle of free thinkers).
3452 **1091** 17f. black and blue . . 90 50

1092 Mniszech Palace

1998. Belgium Embassy, Warsaw, Poland.
3453 **1092** 17f. multicoloured . . . 90 65

1093 King Albert II

1096 Chick Bill and Ric Hochet

1094 "The Eighth Day" (dir. Jaco van Dormael)

1998.
3454 **1093** 19f. lilac . . . . 1·10 1·10
No. 3454 was for use on direct mail by large companies.

1998. 25th Anniv of Brussels and Ghent Film Festivals. Multicoloured.
3455 17f. Type **1094** 90 70
3456 17f. "Daens" (dir. Stijn Coninx) 90 70

1998. "Philately for the Young". Comic Strip Characters.
3460 **1096** 17f. multicoloured . . . 90 60

1097 "Youth and Space"

1998. 14th World Congress of Association of Space Explorers.
3461 **1097** 17f. multicoloured . . . 90 40

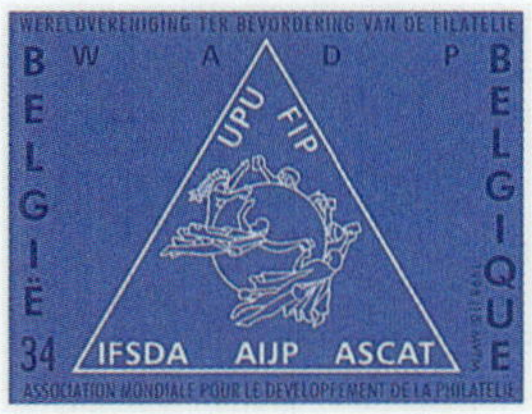

1098 Universal Postal Union Emblem

1998. World Post Day.
3462 **1098** 34f. blue & ultramarine 1·80 90

1099 "The Three Kings" (Michel Provost)

1998. Christmas. No value indicated.
3463 **1099** (17f.) multicoloured . . 90 70

1100 Detail of Triptych by Constant Dratz

1101 Blind Man with Guide Dog

1998. Cent of General Belgium Trade Union.
3464 **1100** 17f. multicoloured . . . 90 55

1998. "Solidarity". Guide Dogs for the Blind.
3465 **1101** 17f.+4f. multicoloured 1·10 1·10
The face value is embossed in Braille.

1999. Kings of Belgium (2nd series). As T **1079**.
3466 17f.+8f. deep green & green 1·40 1·30
3467 32f.+15f. black . . . . . . 2·50 2·20
MS3468 125 × 90 mm. 50f.+25f. brown and purple . . . . . . 4·50 4·25
KINGS: 17f. Albert I; 32f. Leopold II; 50f. Leopold I.
The premium was used for the promotion of philately.

1102 Candle ("Happy Birthday") **1103** Barn Owl

1999. Greetings stamps. No value expressed. Mult.
3469 (17f.) Type **1102** 85 60
3470 (17f.) Stork carrying heart ("Welcome" (new baby)) 85 60
3471 (17f.) Wristwatch ("Take your Time" (retirement)) 85 60
3472 (17f.) Four-leafed clover ("For your pleasure") . . 85 60
3473 (17f.) White doves ("Congratulations" (marriage)) 85 60
3474 (17f.) Arrow through heart ("I love you") 85 60
3475 (17f.) Woman with heart as head ("Happy Mother's Day") 85 60
3476 (17f.) Man with heart as head ("Happy Father's Day") 85 60

1999. Owls. Multicoloured.
3477 17f. Type **1103** 90 70
3478 17f. Little owl ("Athene noctua") 90 70
3479 17f. Tawny owl ("Strix aluco") 90 70
3480 17f. Long-eared owl ("Asio otus") 90 70

1104 Leopard Tank (Army)

1999. 50th Anniv of North Atlantic Treaty Organization. Multicoloured.
3481 17f. Type **1104** 90 70
3482 17f. General Dynamics F-16 jet fighters (Air Force) . . 90 70
3483 17f. "De Wandelaar" (frigate) (Navy) 90 70
3484 17f. Field hospital (Medical Service) 90 70
3485 17f. Display chart of military operations (General Staff) 90 70

1105 Envelopes and World Map

1999. 125th Anniv of U.P.U.
3486 **1105** 34f. multicoloured . . . 1·80 1·40

1106 De Bunt Nature Reserve, Hamme

1999. Europa. Parks and Gardens. Multicoloured.
3487 17f. Type **1106** . . . . . . 1·10 40
3488 17f. Harchies Marsh . . . . 1·10 40

1107 1849 10c. "Epaulettes" Stamp

1999. Stamp Day. 150th Anniv of First Belgian Postage Stamp. Multicoloured.
3489 17f. Type **1107** 85 70
3490 17f. 1849 20c. "Epaulettes" stamp 85 70

1108 Racing

1999. Sport. Belgian Motor Cycling. Multicoloured.
3491 17f.+4f. Type **1108** . . . . 1·10 1·10
3492 17f.+4f. Trial (vert) . . . . 1·10 1·10
MS3493 90 × 125 mm. 30f.+7f. Motocross (vert) . . . . 2·50 2·50

1109 "My Favourite Room"

1999. 50th Death Anniv of James Ensor (artist) (1st issue).
3494 **1109** 17f. mullticoloured . . 90 70
See also Nos. 3501/3.

1110 Giant Family, Geraardsbergen **1111** Harvesting of Cocoa Beans

1999. Tourist Publicity. Multicoloured.
3495 17f. Type **1110** 90 40
3496 17f. Members of Confrerie de la Misericorde in Car d'Or procession, Mons (horiz) 90 40

1999. Belgian Chocolate. Multicoloured.
3497 17f. Type **1111** 90 40
3498 17f. Chocolate manufacture 90 40
3499 17f. Selling product 90 40

1112 Photographs of 1959 and 1999

1999. 40th Wedding Anniv of King Albert and Queen Paola.
3500 **1112** 17f. multicoloured . . . 90 70

1113 "Woman eating Oysters"

1999. 50th Death Anniv of James Ensor (artist) (2nd issue).
3501 **1113** 17f. multicoloured . . . 85 70
3502 – 30f. black, brown and grey . . . . 1·50 1·40
3503 – 32f. multicoloured . . . 1·70 1·50
DESIGNS—30f. "Triumph of Death"; 32f. "Old Lady with Masks".

1999. "Bruphila '99" National Stamp Exhibition, Brussels. Kings of Belgium (3rd series). Sheet 191 × 121 mm containing vert designs as T **1079**. Each deep blue and blue.
MS3508 17f. As No. 3466; 17f. Type **1079**; 32f. As No. 3467; 32f. As No. 3417; 50f. As No. **MS**3468; 50f. As No. **MS**3418 . . . . . 19·00 17·00

1115 Henri la Fontaine (President of International Peace Bureau), 1913

1999. Belgian Winners of Nobel Peace Prize.
3509 **1115** 17f. red and gold . . . 85 55
3510 – 21f. blue and gold . . . 1·10 1·00
DESIGNS: 3510, Auguste Beernaert (Prime Minister 1884–94), 1909.

DENOMINATION. From No. 3511 Belgian stamps are denominated both in Belgian francs and in euros.

1116 King Albert II **1116a** King Albert II

1999.

3511	**1116**	17f. multicoloured	. .	85	35
3512		17f. blue	. . . . . .	85	45
3513		19f. purple	. . . . .	1·00	75
3514		20f. brown	. . . . .	1·00	45
3515		25f. brown	. . . . .	1·20	80
3516		30f. purple	. . . . .	1·60	1·10
3517		32f. green	. . . . .	1·60	60
3518		34f. blue	. . . . . .	1·70	1·30
3519		36f. brown	. . . . .	1·80	1·00
3520	**1116a**	50f. blue	. . . . . .	2·50	1·70
3521		200f. lilac	. . . . . .	9·75	6·00

1117 "Corentin" (Paul Cuvelier)

1999. "Philately for the Young". Comic Strips. Sheet 185 × 145 mm containing T **1117** and similar horiz designs. Multicoloured.
MS3525 17f. Type **1117**; 17f. "Jerry Spring" (Jije); 17f. "Gil Jourdan" (Maurice Tillieux); 17f. "Beaver Patrol" (Mitacq); 17f. Entrance Hall, Belgian Comic Strip Centre; 17f. "Hassan and Kadour" (Jacques Laudy); 17f. "Buck Danny" (Victor Hubinon); 17f. "Tif and Tondu" (Fernand Dineur); 17f. "Les Timour" (Sirius) . . . . 8·50 8·00

1118 Geranium "Matador" **1119** Reindeer holding Glass of Champagne

1999. Flowers. No value expressed (geranium) or inscr "ZONE A PRIOR" (tulip). Multicoloured. Self-adhesive.
3528 (17f.) Type **1118** 90 50
3529 (21f.) Tulip (21 × 26 mm) . . 1·20 60

The geranium design was for use on inland letters up to 20g. and the tulip design for letters within the European Union up to 20g.

1999. Christmas.
3530 **1119** 17f. multicoloured . . . 85 70

1120 Child bandaging Teddy Bear

1999. "Solidarity". Red Cross. Multicoloured.
3531 17f.+4f. Type **1120** . . . . 1·10 1·00
3532 17f.+4f. Child and teddy bear cleaning teeth (vert) 1·10 1·00

1121 Prince Philippe and Mathilde d'Udekem d'Acoz

1999. Engagement of Prince Philippe and Mathilde d'Udekem d'Acoz.
3533 17f. Type **1121** . . . . . . 1·20 75
MS3534 120 × 89 mm. 21f. Prince Philippe and Mathilde d'Udekem d'Acoz (different) . . . . . . 1·20 1·20

1122 Pope John Paul XXIII

1999. The Twentieth Century (1st issue). Personalities, Sports and Leisure. Sheet 166 × 200 mm containing T **1122** and similar vert designs. Multicoloured.
MS3535 17f. Type **1122**; 17f. King Baudouin; 17f. Willy Brandt (German statesman); 17f. John F. Kennedy (U.S. President, 1961–3); 17f. Mahatma Gandhi (Indian leader); 17f. Martin Luther King (civil rights leader); 17f. Vladimir Lenin (Prime Minister of Russia, 1917–24; 17f. Che Guevara (revolutionary); 17f. Golda Meir (Prime Minister of Israel, 1969–74); 17f. Nelson Mandela (Prime Minister of South Africa, 1994–99); 17f. Jesse Owens (American athlete) (modern Olympics); 17f. Football; 17f. Eddy Merckx (racing cyclist) (Tour de France); 17f. Edith Piaf (French singer); 17f. The Beatles (English pop band); 17f. Charlie Chaplin (English film actor and director); 17f. Postcards (tourism); 17f. Children around campfire (youth movements); 17f. Tintin and Snowy (comic strip); 17f. Magnifying glass over stamp (hobbies) . . . . 18·00 17·00
See also Nos. **MS**3613 and **MS**3656.

1123 Fireworks and Streamer forming "2000"

2000. New Year.
3536 **1123** 17f. multicoloured . . . 90 50

1124 Red-backed Shrike

1125 Brussels Skyline and Group of People

2000. Birds. Multicoloured.

3537	50c. Goldcrest ("Roitelet Huppe")	30	30
3538	1f. Red crossbill ("Beccroisé des Sapins")	15	15
3539	2f. Short-toed treecreeper ("Grimpereau des Jardins")	15	15
3540	3f. Meadow pipit ("Pipit Farlouse")	15	20
3541	5f. Brambling ("Pinson du Nord")	25	20
3542	7f.50 Great grey shrike ("Pie-Grieche Grise")	40	50
3543	8f. Great tit ("Mesange Charbonniere")	45	50
3544	10f. Wood warbler ("Pouillot Siffleur")	50	35
3545	16f. Type **1124**	80	55
3546	16f. Common tern ("Sterne Pierregarin")	1·60	1·00
3547	21f. Fieldfare ("Grive Litorne") (horiz)	1·00	70
3548	150f. Black-billed magpie ("Pie Bavarde") (36 × 25 mm)	7·50	4·00

2000. Brussels, European City of Culture. Mult.

3555	17f. Type **1125**	85	60
3556	17f. Toots Tielmans (jazz musician), Anne Teresa de Keersmaeker (gymnast) and skyline	85	60
3557	17f. Airplane, train and skyline	85	60

Nos. 3555/7 were issued together, se-tenant, forming a composite design showing the Brussels skyline.

1126 Queen Astrid

2000. Queens of Belgium (1st series).

3558	**1126** 17f.+8f. green and deep green	1·40	1·30
3559	– 32f.+15f. brown and black	2·50	2·40
MS3560	125 × 89 mm. 50f.+25f. deep purple and purple	3·75	3·75

DESIGNS: 32f. Queen Fabiola; 50f. Queen Paola.

The premium was used for the promotion of philately.

See also Nos. 3615/**MS**3617 and **MS**3618.

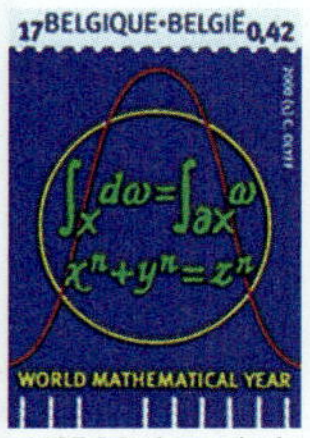

1127 Mathematical Formulae

1128 Globe and Technology (Joachim Beckers)

2000. World Mathematics Year.

3561 **1127** 17f. multicoloured . . . 85 55

2000. "Stampin' the Future". Winning Entries in Children's International Painting Competition.

3562 **1128** 17f. multicoloured . . . 85 55

1129 "Charles V as Sovereign Master of the Order of the Golden Fleece" (anon)

2000. 500th Birth Anniv of Charles V, Holy Roman Emperor. Paintings of Charles V. Multicoloured.

3563	17f. Type **1129**	80	55
3564	21f. "Charles V" (Corneille de la Haye)	1·00	1·00
MS3565	125 × 88 mm. 34f. "Charles V on Horseback" (Titian)	1·90	1·80

1130 Common Adder

2000. Amphibians and Reptiles. Multicoloured.

3566	17f. Type **1130**	90	70
3567	17f. Sand lizard (*Lacerta agilis*) (vert)	90	70
3568	17f. Common tree frog (*Hyla arborea*) (vert)	90	70
3569	17f. Spotted salamander (*Salamander salamander*)	90	70

1131 Children flying Kites

2000. Red Cross and Red Crescent Movements.

3570 **1131** 17f.+4f. multicoloured 1·20 1·40

1132 Players Celebrating

2000. European Football Championship, Belgium and The Netherlands. Multicoloured. (a) With face value. Size 26 × 38 mm.

3571	17f. Type **1132**	80	55
3572	21f. Football	95	90

(b) Size 20 × 26 mm. Self-adhesive.

3573 (17f.) As Type **1132** 90 70

Nos. 3571/3 were printed together, se-tenant, with the backgrounds forming the composite design of a crowd of spectators and the Belgian flag.

1133 Cat and Rabbit reading Book

2000. Stamp Day. Winning Entry in Stamp Design Competition.

3574 **1133** 17f. black, blue and red 85 70

1134 Francois de Tassis (detail of tapestry)

1135 *Iris spuria*

2000. "Belgica 2001" Int Stamp Exhibition, Brussels, (1st issue).

3575 **1134** 17f. multicoloured . . . 85 60

See also Nos. 3629/33.

2000. Ghent Flower Show. Multicoloured.

3576	16f. Type **1135**	90	60
3577	17f. Rhododendron (horiz)	1·00	70
3578	21f. Begonia (vert)	1·20	90

1136 Prince Philippe

2000. 2nd Anniv of Prince Philippe (cultural organization).

3579 **1136** 17f. brn, grey & sil . . 85 70

1137 Harpsichord

1139 "Building Europe"

1138 Belgium Team Emblem and Olympic Rings

2000. 250th Death Anniv of Johann Sebastian Bach. No value expressed. Multicoloured.

3580	(17f.) Type **1137**	90	80
3581	(17f.) Violin	90	80
3582	(17f.) Two tenor lutes	90	80
3583	(17f.) Treble viol	90	80
3584	(17f.) Three trumpets	90	80
3585	(17f.) Bach	90	80

2000. Olympic Games, Sydney. Multicoloured.

3586	17f. Type **1138**	80	80
3587	17f.+4f. Tae-kwon-do	1·10	1·00
3588	17f.+4f. Paralympic athlete (horiz)	1·10	1·00
MS3589	125 × 90 mm. 30f.+7f. Swimmer (horiz)	2·00	1·90

2000. Europa.

3590 **1139** 21f. multicoloured . . . 1·60 55

1140 Flemish Beguinages

2000. UNESCO World Heritage Sites in Belgium. Multicoloured.

3591	17f. Type **1140**	80	50
3592	17f. Grand-Place, Brussels	80	55
3593	17f. Four lifts, Centre Canal, Wallonia	80	55

1141 Baroque Organ, Norbertine Abbey Church, Grimbergen

2000. Tourism. Churches and Church Organs. Mult.

3594	17f. Type **1141**	85	55
3595	17f. St. Wandru Abbey, Mons	85	55
3596	17f. O.-L.-V. Hemelvaartkerk (former abbey church), Ninove	85	55
3597	17f. St. Peter's Church, Bastogne	85	55

1142 Red-backed Shrike ("Pie grieche ecorcheur")

1143 Marcel, Charlotte, Fanny and Konstantinopel

2000.

3598	**1142** 16f. multicoloured	1·60	1·10
3599	– 17f. mult (51 × 21 mm)	1·80	1·40
3600	– 23f. lilac	1·80	1·30

DESIGNS: 17f. Francois de Tassis (detail of tapestry) and Belgica 2001 emblem; 23f. King Albert II.

2000. "Philately for the Young". Kiekeboe (cartoon series created by Robert Merhottein).

3601 **1143** 17f. multicoloured . . . 80 45

1144 "Springtime"

2000. Hainaut Flower Show.

3602 **1144** 17f. multicoloured . . . 80 40

1145 Pansies

1148 Postman

1147 "Bing of the Ferro Lusto X" (Panamarenko)

2000. Flowers. No value expressed. Self-adhesive.

3603 **1145** (17f.) multicoloured . . 90 70

2000. Modern Art. Multicoloured.

3608	17f. Type **1147**	80	90
3609	17f. "Construction" (Anne-Mie van Kerckhoven) (vert)	80	90
3610	17f. "Belgique eternelle" (Jacques Charlier)	80	90
3611	17f. "Les Belles de Nuit" (Marie Jo Lafontaine)	80	90

2000. Christmas.

3612 **1148** 17f. multicoloured . . . 80 70

1149 Soldiers at Yser Front, West Flanders (First World War, 1914–18)

2000. The Twentieth Century (2nd issue). War, Peace and Art. Sheet 200 × 166 mm containing T **1149** and similar horiz designs. Multicoloured.
MS3613 17f. Type **1149**; 17f. German concentration camp and prisoners (black and scarlet); 17f. Atomic cloud and Hiroshima (atomic bomb, 1945); 17f. Winston Churchill, Franklin D. Roosevelt and Joseph Stalin (Yalta conference, 1945); 17f. Headquarters (United Nations established, 1945); 17f. Joseph Kasavubu (first President) and map of Africa (independence of Belgian Congo, 1960); 17f. American soldiers and helicopter (Vietnam War); 17f. Collapse of Berlin Wall, 1989; 17f. Campaign for Nuclear Disarmament emblem and crowd; 17f. Dome of the Rock (Middle East conflict); 17f. Rene Magritte (artist); 17f. Le Corbusier (architect) and building; 17f. Bertolt Brecht (dramatist and poet) and actors; 17f. James Joyce (novelist); 17f. Anne Teresa de Keersmaeker (choreographer); 17f. Bila Bartok (composer); 17f. Andy Warhol (artist); 17f. Maria Callas (opera singer); 17f. Henry Moore (sculptor) and sculpture; 17f. Charlie Parker (alto saxophonist and composer) and Toots Thielemans (composer and jazz musician) . . . . 18·00 17·00

1150 Stars

2000. New Year.
3614 **1150** 17f. gold, blue & blk 90 60

2001. Queens of Belgium (2nd series). As T **1126**.
3615 17f.+8f. green & dp green 1·40 1·30
3616 32f.+15f. black and green 2·50 2·40
MS3617 126 × 91 mm. 50f.+25f. deep brown and brown . . . . . . 3·75 3·75
DESIGNS: 17f. Queen Elisabeth; 32f. Queen Marie-Henriette; 50f. Queen Louise-Marie.
The premium was used for the promotion of philately.

2001. Queens of Belgium (3rd series). Vert designs as T **1126**. Each blue, deep blue and ochre.
MS3618 190 × 121 mm. 17f. As No. 3615; 17f. As Type **1126**; 32f. As No. 3616; 32f. As No. 3559; 50f. As No. **MS**3617; 50f. As No. **MS**3560 . . . . 15·00 15·00

1151 Movement of a Dynamo **1152** Virgin and Child (statue)

2001. Death Centenary of Zenobe Gramme (physicist).
3619 **1151** 17f. black, red & black 85 55

2001. 575th Anniv of Louvain Catholic University.
3620 **1152** 17f. multicoloured . . . 85 70

2001. As T **998** but with face value expressed in francs and euros.
3621 100f. multicoloured . . . . 5·00 2·00

1153 Willem Elsschot (poet)

2001. Music and Literature.
3622 **1153** 17f. brown and black 85 70
3623 – 17f. grey and black . . 85 70
MS3624 125 × 90 mm. 21f. orange and brown . . . . 1·20 1·20
DESIGNS—VERT: No. 3623, Albert Ayguesparse (poet). HORIZ: **MS**3624 21f. Queen Elisabeth and emblem (50th anniv of Queen Elisabeth International Music Competition).

1154 Boy washing Hands

2001. Europa. Water Resources.
3625 **1154** 21f. multicoloured . . . 1·30 80

1155 Type 12 Steam Locomotive

2001. 75th Anniv of National Railway Company. Multicoloured.
3626 17f. Type **1155** 90 85
3627 17f. Series 06 dual locomotive No. 671 . . . 90 85
3628 17f. Series 03 locomotive No. 328 . . . . 90 85
Nos. 3626/8 were issued together, se-tenant, forming a composite design.

1156 16th-century Postman on horseback

2001. "Belgica 2001" International Stamp Exhibition, Brussels (2nd issue). 500th Anniv of European Post. Multicoloured.
3629 17f. Type **1156** 95 75
3630 17f. 17th-century postman with walking staff (vert) 95 75
3631 17f. 18th-century postman and hand using quill (vert) 95 75
3632 17f. Steam locomotive and 19th-century postman (vert) 95 75
3633 17f. 20th-century forms of communication (vert) . . 95 75
MS3634 190 × 120 mm. 150f. Female postal worker (35 × 46 mm) . . 15·00 15·00

1157 Hassan II Mosque, Casablanca

2001. Places of Worship. Multicoloured.
3635 17f. Type **1157** 85 70
3636 34f. Koekelberg Basilica . . 1·80 1·20

1158 "Winter Landscape with Skaters" (Pieter Bruegel the Elder)

2001. Art. Multicoloured.
3637 17f. Type **1158** 85 80
3638 17f. "Heads of Negros" (Peter Paul Rubens) . . . 85 80
3639 17f. "Sunday" (Frits van den Berghe) 85 80
3640 17f. "Mussels" (Marcel Broodthaers) 85 80

1159 Pottery Vase **1160** Luc Orient

2001. Chinese Pottery. Multicoloured.
3641 17f. Type **1159** 85 75
3642 34f. Teapot . . . . 1·80 1·50

2001. "Philately for the Young". Cartoon Characters.
3643 **1160** 17f. multicoloured . . . 85 75

1161 Cyclists (World Cycling Championship, Antwerp)

2001. Sports. Multicoloured.
3644 17f.+4f. Type **1161** . . . . 1·00 1·00
3645 17f.+4f. Gymnast (World Gymnastics Championships, Ghent) 1·00 1·00

1162 Emblem

2001. Belgian Presidency of European Union.
3646 **1162** 17f. multicoloured . . . 90 50

1163 Binche

2001. Town Hall Belfries.
3647 **1163** 17f. mauve and black 85 70
3648 – 17f. blue, mauve & blk 85 70
DESIGN: No. 3648, Diksmuide.

1164 Damme

2001. Large Farmhouses. Multicoloured.
3649 17f. Type **1164** 85 70
3650 17f. Beauvechain 85 70
3651 17f. Louvain 85 70
3652 17f. Honnelles 85 70
3653 17f. Hasselt 85 70

1165 Red Cross and Doctor

2001. Red Cross.
3654 **1165** 17f.+4f. multicoloured 1·40 1·40

1166 Stam and Pilou **1167** Ovide Decroly (educational psychologist) and Road Sign

2001. Stamp Day. No value expressed. Self-adhesive.
3655 **1166** (17f.) multicoloured . . 1·00 80
No. 3655 was for use on inland standard letters up to 20g.

2001. The Twentieth Century. Science and Technology. Sheet 166 × 200 mm. Multicoloured.
MS3656 17f. Type **1167**; 17f. Dandelion and windmills (alternative energy sources); 17f. Globe, signature and map (first solo non-stop crossing of North Atlantic by Charles Lindbergh); 17f. Man with head on lap (Sigmund Freud, founder of psychoanalysis); 17f. Astronaut and foot print on moon surface (Neil Armstrong, first man on the moon, 1969); 17f. Claude Levi-Strauss (anthropologist); 17f. DNA double helix and athletes (human genetic code); 17f. Pierre Teilhard de Chardin (theologian palaeontologist and philosopher); 17f. Max Weber (sociologist) and crowd; 17f. Albert Einstein (physicist) (Theory of Relativity); 17f. Knight and jacket of pills (discovery of Penicillin, 1928); 17f. Ilya Prigogine (theoretical chemist and clock face; 17f. Text and Roland Barthes (writer and critic); 17f. Simone de Beauvoir (feminist writer); 17f. Globe and technology highway (computer science); 17f. John Maynard Keynes (economist) and folded paper; 17f. Marc Bloch (historian) and photographs; 17f. Tools and Julius Robert Oppenheimer (nuclear physicist); 17f. Marie and Pierre Curie, discoverers of radioactivity, 1896); 17f. Caricature of Ludwig Josef Wittgenstein (philosopher) 18·00 17·00

1168 Nativity

2001. Christmas.
3657 **1168** 15f. multicoloured . . . 80 40

1169 Sunset

2001. Bereavement. No value expressed.
3658 **1169** (17f.) multicoloured . . 1·00 80
See also Nos. 3732 and 3856.

1170 Daffodil **1171** Tintin

2001. Flowers. No value expressed. Self-adhesive.
(a) Without service indicator. Multicoloured.
3659 (17f.) Type **1170** 95 75

(b) Inscr "ZONE A PRIOR".
3660 (21f.) Tulip "Darwin" (vert) 1·10 85
No. 3659 was for use on inland letters up to 20g. and No. 3660 was for use on letters within the European Union up to 20g.

2001. 70th Anniv of Tintin in *Congo* (cartoon strip). Multicoloured.
3661 17f. Type **1171** 95 85
MS3662 123 × 88 mm. 34f. Tintin, Snowy and guide in car (48 × 37 mm) . . . . 2·10 2·00

New Currency. 100 cents = 1 euro.

1172 King Albert II

1173 King Albert II

2002.
3663 **1173** 7c. blue and red (postage) 20 20
3666 **1172** 42c. red 90 40
3667 47c. green . . . . . . 1·00 90
3668 **1173** 49c. red . . . . . . 1·00 85
3669 52c. blue . . . . . . 1·00 60
3670 **1172** 59c. blue . . . . . . 1·30 55
3671 60c. blue . . . . . . 1·20 90
3672 **1173** 79c. blue and red . . 1·80 1·30
3674 €4.21 brown and red . . 8·25 6·75
3674a **1172** 70c. blue (air) 85 30
3674b 60c. blue . . . . . .
3674c 80c. purple and red . .

Nos. 3663, 3668 and 3672 are inscribed "PRIOR" at left.

1174 Female Tennis Player

2002. Centenary of Royal Belgian Tennis Federation. Multicoloured.
3675 42c. Type **1174** 95 60
3676 42c. Male tennis player . . 95 60

1175 Cyclist

2002. International Cycling Events held at Circuit Zolder. Multicoloured.
3677 42c. Type **1175** (World Cyclo-Cross Championships) 95 80
3678 42c. Cyclist with hand raised (Road Cycling Championships) 95 80

1176 Dinosaur

2002. Winning Entry in Children's Stamp Design Competition at "Belgica 2001".
3679 **1176** 42c.+10c. mult . . . . 1·20 1·20

The premium was used for the promotion of philately.

1177 Antwerp from River

2002. 150th Anniv of Antwerp University.
3680 **1177** 42c. blue and black . . 90 80

1178 Buildings and Architectural Drawing

2002. "Bruges 2002", European City of Culture. Multicoloured.
3681 42c. Type **1178** 95 65
3682 42c. Organ pipes and xylophone 95 65
3683 42c. Octopus 95 65

1179 16th-century Manuscript (poem, Anna Bijns)

2002. Women and Art. Multicoloured.
3684 42c. Type **1179** 95 60
3685 84c. Woman writing (painting, Anna Boch) (vert) . . . . 1·70 1·30

1180 Fountain Pen and Writing

2002. Stamp Day.
3686 **1180** 47c. multicoloured . . . 1·00 70

1181 Papillon

2002. Centenary of Flanders Canine Society. Multicoloured.
3687 42c. Type **1181** 95 85
3688 42c. Brussels griffon 95 85
3689 42c. Bloodhounds 95 85
3690 42c. Bouvier des Ardennes 95 85
3691 42c. Schipperke 95 85

1182 Stock Dove ("Pigeon Colombin-Holenduif")

1183 Big Top, Ringmaster, Seal and Clown

2002. Birds. Multicoloured.
3692 1c. Nightingale ("Rossignol philomele-Nachtegaal") (postage) 15 15
3693 2c. Snipe ("Becassine des Marais-Watersnip") . . 30 20
3693a 3c. Marsh tit ("Mesange Nonnette-Glanskopmees") 10 10
3693b 5c. Cirl bunting ("Bruant Zizi-Cirlors") 10 10
3693c 5c. Teal ("Wintertaling-Sarcelle D'Hiver") . . . 1·00 35
3693d 6c. Little owl ('Steenuil-Chouette Cheveche') . . 1·00 35
3694 7c. Type **1182** 95 40
3694a 10c. Tengmalm's owl ("Chouette De Tengmalm-Ruigpootuil") 1·00 35
3697 20c. Mediterranean gull ("Zwarkopmeeuw-Mouette Melanocephale") 25 10
3697a 23c. Black-necked grebe ("Greb a Cou Noir - Geoorde Fuut") . . . . 1·00 35
3697b 23c. Jackdaw ("Kauw-Choucas des Tours") . . 1·00 35
3698 25c. Oystercatcher ("Scholekster-Huîtrier Pie") 55 40
3698a 30c. Corncrake ("Rale des Genets—Kwartelkoning") 40 25
3700 35c. Spotted woodpecker ("Pic Epeiche-Grote Bonte Specht") 75 65
3700a 40c. Spotted flycatcher ("Grauwe vliegenvanger-Gobemouche gris") . . . 80 70
3700b Long-eared owl ("Hibou Moyen-Duc-Ransuil") 1·50 95
3701 41c. Collared dove ("Tourterelle Turque") 95 65
3701a 44c. House martin ("Hirondelle de fenetre-Huiszwaluw") 95 70
3701b 44c. Wood pigeon ("Hourduif-Pigeon Ramier") . . . . 1·00 85
3701c 46c. Avocet ("Kluut—Avocette") . . . . 1·10 65
3701d 52c. Hoopoe ("Hop-Huppe Fasciee") 60 20
3701e 55c. Plover ("Kleine plevier-Petit gravelot") 70 15
3702 57c. Black tern ("Guifette Noire") . . . . 1·30 65
3702a 60c. Partridge ("Perdrix Crise-Patrijs") 75 20
3703 65c. Black-headed gull ("Mouette rieuse-Kapmeeuw") . . . . . . 1·30 1·10
3704 70c. Redshank ("Chevalier Gambette") . . . . . . 1·60 90
3704a 75c. Golden plover ("Goudplevier-Pluvier dore") . . . . 1·50 1·20
3704b 75c. Firecrest ("Rottelet Triple-Bandeau Vuurgoudhaatje") . . . 95 30
3704c 78c. Black-tailed godwit ("Gritto-Barge A Queue Noir") . . . . 2·50 85
3705 €1 Wheatear ("Traquet Motteux") (38 × 27 mm) 2·20 1·00
3706 €2 Ringed plover ("Grand Gravelot") (38 × 27 mm) 4·50 4·25
3707 €3.72 Moorhen ("Waterhoen-Poule d'eau") (38 × 27 mm) . . 7·75 5·50
3708 €4 Eagle owl ("Hibou grand-duc-Oehoe") (38 × 27 mm) . . . . . 8·00 6·50
3708a €4.30 Grebe ("Fuut-Grebe Huppe") . . . . 10·00 3·50
3708b Peregrine falcon (Slechtwalk-Faucon Pelerin) (38 × 28 mm) . . 13·50 9·50
3709 €5 Ruff ("Combattant Varie") (38 × 27 mm) . . 11·00 7·75
3694b 10c. Hedge sparrow (Heggemus-Accentor Maichet) (air/prior) . . . 1·00 35
3694c 15c. Spotted nutcracker (Cassenoix Mouchete-Notenkracker) (air/prior) 1·00 35

2002. Europa. Circus. Winning Entry in Children's Drawing Competition.
3710 **1183** 52c. multicoloured . . . 1·60 1·20

1184 Paramedic, Patient and Damaged Buildings

2002. Red Cross.
3711 **1184** 84c.+12c. multicoloured 2·00 2·40

1185 Abbey Buildings

2002. 850th Anniv of Leffe Abbey.
3712 **1185** 42c. multicoloured . . . 1·00 65

1186 Loppem Castle

2002. Tourism. Castles. Sheet 161 × 141 mm containing T **1186** and similar horiz designs showing castles. Multicoloured.
MS3713 42c. Type **1186**; 42c. Horst; 42c. Wissekerke; 42c. Chimay; 42c. Ecaussinnes-Lalaing; 42c. Reinhardstein; 42c. Modave; 42c. Ooidonk; 42c. Corroy-le-Chateau; 42c. Alden Biesen . . . . . . 9·50 9·50

1187 Show Jumping

2002. Horses. Designs showing equestrian events. Multicoloured.
3714 40c. Type **1187** 80 80
3715 42c. Carriage driving (vert) 90 90
MS3716 126 × 91 mm. 52c. Two Brabant draught horses' heads (Centenary of St. Paul's horse procession, Opwijk) (37 × 48 mm) 1·10 1·10

1188 Golden Spur and Battle Scene

1189 Onze-Lieve-Vrouw-Lombeek, Roosdaal

2002. 700th Anniv of Battle of the Golden Spurs (Flemish--French battle), Kortrijk. Multicoloured.
3717 42c. Type **1188** 90 60
3718 52c. Broel towers . . . . . 1·10 85
MS3719 126 × 91 mm. 57c. Flemish and French soldiers, river and knight on horseback (48 × 38 mm) 1·20 1·20

2002. Windmills. Multicoloured.
3720 42c. Type **1189** 90 85
3721 52c. Faial Island, Azores, Portugal . . . . 1·10 1·10

Stamps of a similar design were issued by Portugal.

1190 Liedekerke Lacework and Statue of Lace-maker

2002. Lace-making. Multicoloured.
3722 42c. Type **1190** 90 60
3723 74c. Pag lacework . . . . . 1·60 1·10

Stamps of a similar design were issued by Croatia.

1191 Bakelandt, Red Zita and Stagecoach

2002. "Philately for the Young". Bakelandt (comic strip created by Hec Leemans).
3724 **1191** 42c. multicoloured . . . 95 85

1192 Teddy Bear

1193 Rey

2002. "The Rights of the Child".
3725 **1192** 42c. multicoloured . . . 95 80

2002. Birth Centenary of Jean Rey (politician).
3726 **1193** 52c. blue and cobalt . . 1·20 1·10

1194 Princess Elisabeth

1195 Church, Ice Cream Van and Family

2002. 1st Birthday of Princess Elisabeth. Multicoloured.
3727 49c. Type **1194** . . . . . . 1·10 70
3728 59c. Princess Elisabeth with parents (horiz) . . . . . 1·40 65
MS3729 123 × 88 mm 84c. Princess Elisabeth (different) (59 × 38 mm) 1·90 1·80

No. 3727 was issued with a se-tenant label inscribed "PRIOR".

2002. Christmas. Sheet 166 × 40 mm containing T **1195** and similar vert designs. Multicoloured.
MS3730 41c. Type **1195**; 41c. Skier in snowy fir tree; 41c. Tobogganist and bird wearing hat; 41c. Skier wearing kilt; 41c. Skiers holding candles; 41c. Boy holding snowman-shaped ice cream; 41c. Children throwing snowballs; 41c. Children, snowman, and elderly man; 41c. Brazier, refreshment hut and people; 41c. Hut, robbers, cow and policeman . . . . 10·50 10·50

1196 Bricks

2002. The Twentieth Century. Society. Sheet 200 × 166 mm containing T **1196**.
MS3731 41c. purple, red and pink (Type **1196** (social housing)); 41c. deep purple, orange and purple ("MEI/MAI 68" and rubble (student protests)); 41c. slate, grey and green (telephone telecommunications)); 41c. red, orange and brown (slabs (gap between wealth and poverty)); 41c. brown, bistre and blue (broken crucifix (secularization of society)); 41c. multicoloured (towers of blocks (urbanization)); 41c. pink, violet and purple (combined female and male symbols (universal suffrage)); 41c. blue, orange and grey (enclosed circle (social security)); 41c. grey, green and bistre (schoolbag (equality in education)); 41c. grey, purple and deep purple (elderly man (ageing population)); 41c. blue, green and emerald ("E" (European Union)); 41c. chestnut, brown and yellow (stylized figure (declaration of Human Rights)); 41c. bistre, orange and light orange (pyramid of blocks (growth of consumer society)); 41c. blue, mauve and green (female symbol (feminism)); 41c. brown, sepia and light brown (mechanical arm (de-industrialization)); 41c. brown and green (dripping nozzle (oil crises)); 41c. multicoloured (vehicle (transportation)); 41c. lilac, brown and purple (sperm and egg (contraception)); 41c. green, red and grey (television (growth of television and radio)); 41c. pink, violet and blue (electric plug (increase in home appliances)) 18·00 18·00

1197 Sunset

2002. Bereavement. No value expressed.
3732 **1197** (49c.) multicoloured . . 1·00 90

1198 Crocus

1199 Nero and Adhemar (cartoon characters)

2002. Flowers. No value expressed. Ordinary or self-adhesive gum.
3733 **1198** (49c.) multicoloured . . 1·00 65
No. 3733 was for use on inland letters up to 50 g.

2003. 80th (2002) Birth Anniv of Marc Sleen (cartoonist). Multicoloured.
3735 49c. Type **1199** 95 80
MS3736 121 × 91 mm 82c. Nero and Marc Sleen (49 × 38 mm) . . . 2·00 1·90

1200 Firefighters, Engine and Ladders

2003. Public Services (Nos. 3737/41) and St. Valentine (3742). Multicoloured.
3737 49c. Type **1200** . . . . . . 1·00 85
3738 49c. Traffic police men and policewoman . . . . . . 1·00 85
3739 49c. Civil defence workers mending flood defences 1·00 85
3740 49c. Elderly woman wearing breathing mask, hand holding syringe and theatre nurse . . . . . . 1·00 85
3741 49c. Postman riding bicycle and obtaining signature for parcel . . . . . . 1·00 70
3742 49c. Hearts escaping from birdcage . . . . 1·00 70

1201 Van de Velde and New House, Tervuren

2003. 140th Birth Anniv of Henry van de Velde (architect). Multicoloured.
3743 49c. Type **1201** . . . . . . 1·00 80
3744 59c. Van de Velde and Belgian pavilion, Paris International Exhibition, 1937 (vert) . . . . . . 1·30 1·10
3745 59c. Van de Velde and Book Tower, Central Library, Ghent University (vert) 1·30 1·10
MS3746 91 × 125 mm 84c. Woman and Art Nouveau newel post 1·90 1·90

1202 Bowls

2003. Traditional Sports. Multicoloured.
3747 49c. Type **1202** . . . . . . 1·00 80
3748 49c. Archery . . . . 1·00 80
MS3749 91 × 126 mm. 82c. Pigeon racing . . . . 1·90 1·90

1203 Berlioz

2003. Birth Bicentenary of Hector Berlioz (composer).
3750 **1203** 59c. multicoloured . . . 1·30 1·00

1204 Statue of Men Conversing

1205 Papy Ferdinand

2003. Anniversaries. Multicoloured.
3751 49c. Type **1204** (150th anniv of engineers' association) 1·00 80
3752 49c. Statue of seated man (centenary of Solvay Business School) . . . . 1·00 80

2003. Red Cross. Cartoon characters in rescue attempt. Multicoloured.
3753 41c. + 9c. Type **1205** . . . 1·00 1·00
3754 41c. + 9c. Pilou holding light . . . . 1·00 1·00
3755 41c. + 9c. Stam running for help . . . . 1·00 1·00
Nos. 3753/5 were issued together, se-tenant, forming a composite design.

1206 Bouquet

1207 "Maigret" (film poster)

2003. 3rd International Flower Show, Liege.
3756 **1206** 49c. multicoloured . . . 1·00 75

2002. Birth Centenary of Georges Simenon (writer). Multicoloured.
3757 49c. Type **1207** . . . . . . 1·00 80
3758 59c. "Le chat" (film poster) 1·30 1·00
MS3759 91 × 126 mm. 84c. Simenon (38 × 49 mm) . . . . 1·80 1·80

1208 Bells of St. Rumbold's Cathedral, Maline

2003. 150th Anniv of Belgium–Russia Diplomatic Relations. Multicoloured.
3760 59c. Type **1208** . . . . . . 1·30 1·00
3761 59c. Bells of St. Peter and Paul's Cathedral, St. Petersburg . . . . . 1·30 1·00

1209 Eternity Symbol and "Mail Art"

2003. Stamp Day. Mail Art.
3762 **1209** 49c. multicoloured . . . 1·00 80

1210 Roland on Horseback

1212 "Belgium, The Coast" (Leo Marfut)

1211 Calcite

2003. "Philately for the Young". The Valiant Knight (comic strip created by Francois Craenhals).
3763 **1210** 49c. multicoloured . . . 1·00 80

2003. Minerals. Multicoloured.
3764 49c. Type **1211** . . . . . . 1·00 90
3765 49c. Quartz . . . . 1·00 90
3766 49c. Barytes . . . . 1·00 90
3767 49c. Galena . . . . 1·00 90
3768 49c. Turquoise . . . . . . 1·00 90

2003. Europa. Poster Art.
3769 **1212** 59c. multicoloured . . . 1·30 1·10

1213 "La Robe de Mariee" (Paul Delvaux, Koksijde)

1214 *Monument to the Seasonal Worker, Rillaar* (Jan Peirelinck)

2003. "This is Belgium" (1st series). Sheet 167 × 200 mm containing T **1213** and similar vert designs showing sites from smaller Belgian towns. Multicoloured.
MS3770 41c. Type **1213**; 41c. Mural, Town Hall, Oudenaarde; 41c. "De viust" (sculpture, Rik Poot) and Town Hall, Vilvoorde; 41c. Turnhout chateau; 41c. Ambiorix (sculpture), Gallo-Roman museum, Tongeren; 41c. Fountain (sculpture, Pol Bury), La Louviere; 41c. Town Hall, Braine; 52c. Mardasson Memorial, Bastogne; 52c. Tower and snow scene, Sankt Vith; 57c. Saxophone and Citadel, Dinant . . . . 9·50 9·50
See also Nos. **MS**3809, **MS**3943 and **MS**4033.

2003. Tourism. Statues. Multicoloured.
3771 49c. Type **1214** . . . . . . 1·00 80
3772 49c. La Tionade, Treignes (Yves and Claude Rahir) 1·00 80
3773 49c. Textile Teut, Town Hall, Hamont-Achel (Teo Groenen) . . . . 1·00 80
3774 49c. The Canal Guy, Brussels (Tom Frantzen) 1·00 80
3775 49c. The Maca, Wavre (Jean Godart) . . . . 1·00 80

1215 King Baudouin and Prince Albert

2003. 10th Anniv of the Accession of King Albert. Multicoloured.
3776 49c. Type **1215** . . . . . . 1·00 80
MS3777 90 × 125 mm. 59c. King Baudouin (38 × 48 mm); 84c. King Albert (38 × 48 mm) . . . . . 3·00 3·00

1216 "Argenteuil" (Edouard Manet)

2003. Art.
3778 **1216** 49c. multicoloured . . . 1·20 1·10
No. 3778 was issued with a se-tenant label inscribed "PRIOR".

1217 "Still Life" (Giorgio Morandi)

2003. "Europhalia 2003 Italy" Festival. Italian Presidency of European Union. Multicoloured.
3779 49c. Type **1217** . . . . . . 1·00 80
3780 79c. Cistalia 202 (1947) . . 1·20 1·10
No. 3779 was issued with a se-tenant label inscribed "PRIOR".
Stamps of the same design were issued by Italy.

1218 Elderly Couple, Family and Young People

2003. Social Cohesion.
3781 **1218** 49c. multicoloured . . . 1·00 80
No. 3781 was issued with a se-tenant label inscribed "PRIOR".

1219 St. Nichola

1220 King Albert II

2003. Christmas.
3782 **1219** 49c. multicoloured . . . 1·00 80

No. 3782 was issued with a se-tenant label inscribed "PRIOR".

2003.
3783 **1220** 49c. red . . . . 1·00 80
3784 50c. red . . . . 1·00 80
3785 79c. blue and red . . . 1·60 1·30
3786 80c. violet and red . . 1·60 1·30
Nos. 3783/6 are inscribed "PRIOR" at left.

1221 Woman holding Cat ("Jardin extraordinaire")

1222 Man leaning against Pile of Books

2003. 50th Anniv of Belgian Television. Sheet 166 × 140 mm containing T **1221** and similar vert designs. Multicoloured.
MS3795 41c. × 5 Type **1221**; Cameraman and camera; Broadcasting tower; Brothers Cassiers and Jef Burm; Scene from "Schipper naast Mathide" . . 4·50 4·00

2003. The Book. Multicoloured.
3796 49c. Type **1222** . . . . . . 1·00 80
3797 49c. Man rolling through printing machine (horiz) 1·00 80
3798 49c. Books on shelves . . . 1·00 80
Nos. 3796/8 were each issued with an attached label inscribed "Prior".

1223 Maurice Gilliams

1224 Tulip

2003. Writers.
3799 **1223** 49c. brown, sepia and light brown . . . . . 1·00 85
3800 – 59c. brown and orange 1·20 1·00
DESIGN: 59c. Marguerite Yourcenar (Maugerite de Crayencour).
No. 3799 was issued with an attached label inscribed "Prior".

2003. Flowers. No value expressed. Self-adhesive.
3801 **1224** (59c.) multicoloured . . 1·30 1·00
No. 3801 was for use on inland letters up to 50g.

1225 Herbeumont Church

2003. Christmas and New Year.
3802 **1225** 41c. multicoloured . . . 1·00 70

1226 Justin Henin Hardenne

2003. Belgian Tennis Champions. Multicoloured.
3803 49c. Type **1226** (2003 Roland Garros and U.S. Open champion) . . . . 1·00 80
3804 49c. Kim Clijsters (2002 Masters Cup and 2003 WTA No. 1 champion) (horiz) . . . . 1·00 80
Nos. 3803/4 were each issued with an attached label inscribed "Prior", either at top or bottom (vert) or left or right (horiz).

1227 XIII and Lighthouse

2004. "Philately for the Young". XIII (comic strip created by Jean van Damme and William Vance).
3805 **1227** 41c. multicoloured . . . 90 75

1228 "Portrait of Marguerite Khonopff"

1229 Carnation

2004. Fernand Khnopff (artist) Commemoration. Sheet 160 × 140 mm containing T **1228** and similar multicoloured designs.
MS3806 41c. × 4, Type **1228**; "Caresses" (55 × 24 mm); "The Abandoned City"; "Brown Eyes and a Blue Flower" (55 × 24 mm) 3·50 3·50

2004. Flowers. No value expressed. Self-adhesive.
3807 **1229** (49c.) multicoloured . . 1·00 80
No. 3807 was for use on inland letters up to 50g.

1230 Profile, Stamp and Kiss

2004. Stamp Day.
3808 **1230** 41c. multicoloured . . . 90 70

1231 Peter Piot (AIDS agency director)

1232 Herg and Models of Rocket and Tintin

2004. "This is Belgium" (2nd series). Sheet 166 × 200 mm containing T **1231** and similar vert designs showing Belgian personalities. Multicoloured.
MS3809 57c. × 10, Type **1231**; Nicole Van Goethem (film maker); Dirk Frimout and Frank de Winnie (astronaut and cosmonaut); Jaques Rogge (president, International Olympic Committee); Christian de Duve (winner, Nobel Prize for Medicine); Gabrielle Petit (war heroine); Catherine Verfaillie (director, Stem Cell Institute, Minnesota) and Christine Van Broeckhoven (director, Molecular Biology Laboratory, University of Antwerp); Jaques Stilbe (philatelist); Queen Fabiola; Adrien van der Burch (organizer, Brussels Exhibition, 1935) . . . 11·50 11·50

2004. 75th Anniv of Tintin (cartoon character created by Georges Remi (Herge)). Sheet 163 × 126 mm containing T **1232** and similar vert designs. Multicoloured.
MS3810 41c. × 5, Type **1232**; Technical sketch for Destination Moon; Tintin and Snowy (Bobbie); Tintin climbing up rocket (*Explorers on the Moon*); Tintin, Captain Haddock and Snowy on the moon (cover illustration, *Explorers on the Moon*) . . . . 4·25 4·25

1233 Sugar Beet

2004. Sugar Industry. Multicoloured.
3811 **49c.** Type **1233** . . . . . 1·00 80
3812 49c. Sugar refinery . . . 1·00 80
3813 49c. Tienen city . . . . 1·00 80
Nos. 3811/13 were each issued with a se-tenant label inscribed "Prior".

1234 Stars

2004. European Elections.
3814 **1234** 22c. cobalt, ultramarine and yellow 50 70

1235 "Temptation" (Salvador Dali)

2004. Birth Centenary of Salvador Dali (artist).
3815 **1235** 49c.+11c. multicoloured 1·30 1·20
No. 3815 was issued with a se-tenant label inscribed "Prior".

1236 Chapel, Buggenhout

2004. Tourism. Places of Pilgrimage.
3816 **1236** 49c. green . . . . . . 1·00 80
3817 – 49c. agate . . . . . . 1·00 80
3818 – 49c. purple . . . . . . 1·00 80
3819 – 49c. indigo . . . . . . 1·00 80
DESIGNS: No. 3817, Banneux; 3818, Scherpenheuvel; 3819, Beauraing (horiz).
Nos. 3816/19 were each issued with a se-tenant label inscribed "Prior".

1237 New Member's Flags and EU Emblem

2004. Enlargement of European Union (1st issue). Sheet 125 × 90 mm containing T **1237** and similar horiz designs. Multicoloured.
MS3820 50c. × 2 Type **1237** × 2; 60c. × 2 Parliament building; As No. 3814 . . . . 4·50 4·50
See also Nos. 3835/44.

1238 Le Faune Mordu (sculpture) (Jef Lambeaux), Boverie Park

2004. Liege ("Lidje todi"). Multicoloured.
3821 49c. Type **1238** 95 75
3822 49c. Bridge (Santiago Calatrava) . . . . 1·00 75
MS3823 90 × 125 mm. 75c. Blast furnace, Seraing (38 × 49 mm) 1·80 1·70

1239 Earth showing Clouds and Ozone Layer (climate and CO2)

2004. Climatology. Multicoloured.
3824 50c. Type **1239** . . . . . . 1·00 80
3825 65c. Sun and earth (earth–sun relationship) . . . . 1·30 1·10
3826 80c. Earth showing continent and viewed from space (earth) . . . . 1·60 1·40
3827 80c. Sun viewed through telescope and showing spots . . . . 1·60 1·40
Nos. 3824 and 3826 were issued with a se-tenant label inscribed "Prior".

1240 Edgar Jacobs

2004. Birth Centenary of Edgar Pierre Jacobs (creator of *Blake and Mortimer* (comic strip)). Black and yellow (60c.) or multicoloured (other).
3828 60c. Type **1240** . . . . . . 1·20 1·00
MS3829 125 × 90 mm. €1.20 Blake and Mortimer (45 × 36 mm) . . 2·75 2·75
Stamps of a similar design were issued by France.

1241 Django Reinhardt

2004. Jazz Musicians. Multicoloured.
3830 50c. Type **1241** (guitarist) 1·00 80
3831 50c. Fud Candrix (saxophonist) . . . . . . 1·00 80
3832 50c. Rene Thomas (guitarist) 1·00 80
3833 50c. Jack Sels (composer and saxophonist) . . . . 1·00 80
3834 50c. Bobby Jaspar (flautist and saxophonist) . . . . 1·00 80
Nos. 3830/4 were each issued with a se-tenant label inscribed "Prior".

1242 EU Emblem and Cyprus Flag

2004. Enlargement of European Union (2nd issue). Designs showing emblem and new member flag. Multicoloured. Self-adhesive.
3835 44c. Type **1242** 95 75
3836 44c. Estonia 95 75
3837 44c. Hungary 95 75
3838 44c. Latvia 95 75
3839 44c. Lithuania 95 75
3840 44c. Malta 95 75
3841 44c. Poland 95 75
3842 44c. Czech Republic 95 75
3843 44c. Slovakia 95 75
3844 44c. Slovenia 95 75

1243 King Albert II

2004. 70th Birthday of King Albert II. Each black and gold.
3845 50c. Type **1243** . . . . . . 1·00 80
MS3846 90 × 125 mm. 80c. As No. 3845 (38 × 48 mm) . . . . 1·70 1·70
No. 3845 was issued with a se-tenant label inscribed "Prior".

1244 Wind Break (Belgian Coast)

2004. Europa. Holidays. Winning Designs in Photographic Competition. Multicoloured.
3847 55c. Type **1244** (Muriel Vekemans) . . . . 1·20 95
3848 55c. Semois valley (Belgian Ardennes) (Freddy Deburghgraeve) . . . . . 1·20 95

1245 Female Basketball Player

2004. Olympic Games, Athens 2004. Multicoloured.
3849 50c. Type **1245** . . . . . . 1·00 80
3850 55c. Cyclist (horiz) . . . . 1·10 95
3851 60c. Pole vaulter (horiz) . . 1·20 1·00
MS3852 136 × 90 mm. 80c. Olympic flame . . . . 1·70 1·70
No. 3849 was issued with a se-tenant label inscribed "Prior".

1246 Red Cross Workers

2004. Red Cross.
3853 **1246** 50c.+11c. multicoloured 1·20 1·20
No. 3853 was issued with a se-tenant label inscribed "Prior".

1247 "L'appel"

2004. 10th Death Anniv of Idel Ianchelevici (sculptor). Multicoloured.
3854 50c. Type **1247** . . . . . . 1·00 80
3855 55c. "Perennis perdurat poeta" . . . . 1·10 90
No. 3854 was issued with a se-tenant label inscribed "Prior".
Stamps of the same design were issued by Romania.

2004. Mourning Stamp. As T **1197**.
3856 **1197** 50c. multicoloured . . . 1·00 80

1248 Squirrel and Blackcap

2004. Forest Week. Sheet 90 × 125 mm containing T **1248** and similar vert designs. Multicoloured.
MS3857 44c. × 4, Type **1248**; Nightingale, robin and red admiral butterfly; Bee, vole and weasel; Jay and peacock butterfly . . . . 3·75 3·75
The stamps and margin of **MS**3857 form a composite design of a forest scene.

1249 Volunteer Medal

2004. War Volunteers.
3858 **1249** 50c. multicoloured . . . 1·00 80

1250 Impatiens

2004. Flowers. No value expressed. Self-adhesive.
3859 **1250** (50c.) multicoloured . . 1·00 80
No. 3859 was for use on inland letters up to 50g.

1251 Foal **1252** Jack O' Lantern

2004. Belgica 2006 International Stamp Exhibition, Brussels (1st issue). Sheet 166 × 140 mm containing T **1251** and similar vert designs. Multicoloured.
MS3860 44c. × 5, Type **1251**; Robin; Cat; Puppy; Fish . . . . . . 10·00 7·50
See also Nos. 3892/**MS**3897.

2004. Halloween. Self-adhesive. Multicoloured.
3861 44c. Type **1252** 95 70
3862 44c. Witch, cat and bats . . 95 70

1253 Raymond Jean de Kramer

2004. Writers' Death Anniversaries. Multicoloured.
3863 50c. Type **1253** (writing as Jean Ray or John Flanders) (40th) . . . . . 1·00 90
3864 75c. Johan Daisne (26th) . . 1·50 1·40
3865 80c. Thomas Owen (2nd) (vert) . . . . 1·50 1·40
Nos. 3863 and 3865 were issued with a se-tenant label inscribed "Prior".

1254 Soldiers, Mother and Child on Snow-covered Street

2004. 60th Anniv of Attack on Bastogne. Multicoloured.
3866 44c. Type **1254** 95 80
3867 55c. Soldiers assisting wounded (vert) . . . . . 1·10 1·10
3868 65c. Soldiers amongst trees 1·30 1·30

1255 "Flight into Egypt"

2004. Christmas (1st issue). Paintings by Peter Paul Rubens. Multicoloured.
3869 44c. Type **1255** 90 80
3870 44c. "Adoration of the Magi" 90 80
Stamps of the same design were issued by Germany.
See also No. 3872.

1256 Rene Baeten

2004. Belgian International Motocross Champions. Sheet 151 × 166 mm containing T **1256** and similar horiz designs.
MS3871 50c. × 12, (23bis a, d, e, f, g, i, j, k and l) multicoloured; (23bis b) green and brown; (23bis c) brown, lemon and deep brown; (23bis h) blue and brown . . . 14·00 14·00
DESIGNS: Type **1256**; Jacky Martens; Georges Jobe; Joel Roberts; Eric Geboers; Roger de Coster; Stefan Everts; Gaston Rahier; Joel Smets; Harry Everts; Andre Malherbe and Steve Ramon.

The stamps of **MS**3871 were arranged around a central label, showing a motocross rider, each with a se-tenant label inscribed "Prior" attached at either left or right. The Belgium Post identification number is given in brackets to assist identification.

2004. Christmas (2nd issue). Paintings by Peter Rubens. Self-adhesive.
3872 44c. As No. 3870 (22 × 22 mm) 20 55

1257 Stylized Posthorn **1258** Woman's Legs

2005.
3873 **1257** 6c. scarlet 15 10
3874 10c. blue 15 10
3877 1 (52c.) scarlet . . . . 1·00 90

2005. Centenary of Women's Council.
3882 **1258** 50c. multicoloured . . . 1·00 90
No. 3882 was issued with a se-tenant label inscribed "Prior".

1259 Michel Vaillant

2005. "Philately for the Young". Michel Vaillant (comic strip created by Jean Graton).
3883 **1259** 50c. multicoloured . . . 1·00 90
No. 3883 was issued with a se-tenant label inscribed "Prior".

1260 "The Violinist" (Kees van Dongen) **1261** "www.175-25.be"

2005. "Promotion of Philately".
3884 **1260** 50c.+12c. multicoloured 1·30 1·50

2005. 175th Anniv of Independence (1st issue). 25th Anniv of Federal State. No value expressed. Self-adhesive.
3885 **1261** (50c.) multicoloured . . 1·00 90
See also No. **MS**3889 and **MS**3891.

1262 Johan Hendrick van Dale and "van Dale" (Dutch dictionary)

2005. Language. Multicoloured.
3886 55c. Type **1262** . . . . . 1·10 1·10
3887 55c. Maurice Grevisse and "le bon usage" (French grammar) . . . . 1·10 1·10

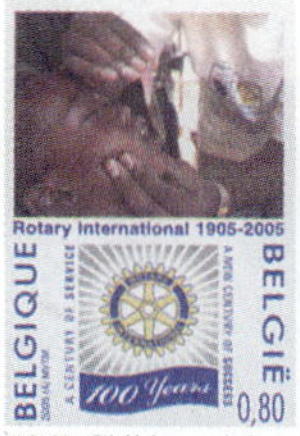

1263 Child receiving Polio Vaccine **1264** First Railway Journey from Brussels to Malines (1835)

2005. Centenary of Rotary International (charitable organization). Polio Eradication Campaign.
3888 **1263** 80c. multicoloured . . . 1·60 1·50

2005. 175th Anniv of Independence (2nd issue). Sheet 166 × 200 mm containing T **1264** and similar horiz designs. Multicoloured.
MS3889 44c. × 10, Type **1264** (transport); Bakuba dancers, Congo; Early school children (education); Factory workers (industrialization); Family (social development); Bombardment of Edingen, 1940; Brussels Expo, 1958 (trade); Rue de la Loi, Wetstraat (federalization); Berlaymont building, Brussels (Europe); "The Shadow and its Shadow" (Rene Mgritte) (art) 10·50 10·50

1265 "TSUNAMI" and Sea

2005. Red Cross. Support for Victims of Tsunami Disaster.
3890 **1265** 50c.+12c. multicoloured 1·30 1·40
No. 3890 was issued with a se-tenant label inscribed "Prior".

1266 King Albert II and Queen Paola

2005. 175th Anniv of Independence (3rd issue). Sheet 126 × 90 mm.
MS3891 **1266** 75c. multicoloured 1·80 1·80

1267 Go-Kart

2005. Belgica 2006 International Stamp Exhibition, Brussels (2nd issue). Multicoloured. (a) Self-adhesive.
3892 44c. Type **1267** 95 80
3893 44c. Motor boat 95 80
3894 44c. Train 95 80
3895 44c. Airplane 95 80
3896 44c. Spacecraft 95 80
(b) Size 27 × 39 mm. Miniature Sheet. Ordinary gum.
MS3897 166 × 131 mm. Nos. 3892/5 11·00 11·00

1268 Rose "Belinda"

2005. Ghent Flower Show. Multicoloured.
3898 44c. Type **1268** 95 80
3899 70c. Rose "Pink Iceberg" (vert) . . . . 1·40 1·40
3900 80c. Rose "Old Master" . . 1·60 1·50
Nos. 3898/3900 were impregnated with the scent of roses.
No. 3900 was issued with a se-tenant label inscribed "Prior".

1269 "The Children's Table" (Gustave van de Woestijne)

2005. Europa. Gastronomy. Multicoloured.
3901 60c. Type **1269** . . . . . . 1·30 1·20
3902 60c. "Still Life with Oysters, Fruit and Pastry" . . . . 1·30 1·20

1270 Black Stork

2005. Stamp Day.
3903 **1270** €4 multicoloured . . . 8·00 6·75

1271 Soldiers

2005. 55th Anniv of Korean War.
3904 **1271** 44c. multicoloured . . . 95 80

1272 Celebration

1273 Zimmer Tower, Lier, Flanders

2005. 60th Anniv of End of World War II. Multicoloured.
3905 44c. Type **1272** 95 80
3906 44c. Camp prisoner 95 80
3907 44c. Returning service men and prisoners 95 80

2005. Tourism. Clock Towers.
3908 **1273** 44c. black 95 80
3909 – 44c. agate 95 80
3910 – 44c. chocolate 95 80
DESIGNS: No. 3908 Type **1273**; 3909 Belfry, Mons, Wallonia; 3910 Mont des Arts Clock, Brussels.

1274 Hiker (Ardennes)

2005. Holidays. Multicoloured.
3911 50c. Type **1274** . . . . . . 1·00 85
3912 50c. Sunbather . . . . . . 1·00 85
Nos. 3911/12 were each issued with a se-tenant label inscribed "Prior".

1275 Hearts

1276 Tulip

2005. Greetings Stamps. Multicoloured. Self-adhesive.
3913 (50c.) Type **1275** . . . . . 1·00 1·30
3914 80c. Doves (wedding) . . . 1·60 1·50
3915 80c. Two rings (wedding) . . 1·60 1·50
3916 80c. Boy (birth) . . . . . . 1·60 1·50
3917 80c. Girl (birth) . . . . . . 1·60 1·50
No. 3913 was for use on inland letters up to 50g.

2005. Air. Flowers. No value expressed. Multicoloured. Self-adhesive.
3918 **1276** (70c.) multicoloured . . 1·40 95

1277 "L'humanitie assaillie par les sept Peches capiteux" (Seven Deadly Sins) (16th-century tapestry, Brussels)

2005. Carpets and Tapestries. Multicoloured.
3919 44c. Type **1277** 95 80
3920 60c. Carpet, Hereke, Turkey 1·20 1·10
Stamps of a similar design were issued by Turkey.

1278 Radio Waves

2005. 75th Anniv of Radio.
3921 **1278** 50c. magenta and black 1·00 90
No. 3921 was issued with a se-tenant label inscribed "Prior".

1279 Robert Van de Walle

2005. Belgian International Judo Champions. Sheet 100 × 167 mm containing T **1279** and similar horiz designs. Multicoloured.
MS3922 50c. × 6, Type **1279**; Ingrid Berghmans; Ulla Werbrouck; Gella Vandecaveye; Christel Deliege; Johan Laats . . . . . 6·50 6·50
The stamps of **MS**3922 were each issued with a se-tenant label inscribed "Prior" attached at either left or right.

1280 King Albert II

2005.
3923 **1280** 50c. multicoloured (postage) . . . . . 1·00 85
3923a 52c. multicoloured . . 1·00 70
3928 70c. blue and light (air) . . . . 1·40 1·30
3928a 80c. blue, grey and black 95 65
3928b 83c. multicoloured . . 1·00 70
3929 90c. blue, grey and black . . . . 1·10 95
Nos. 3923 and 3928/9 were inscribed "Prior".

1281 *Buccinum undatum*

1282 Centre for Comic Strip Art, Brussels

2005. Molluscs. Sheet 161 × 130 mm containing T **1281** and similar designs. Multicoloured. Self-adhesive.
MS3933 44c. × 6, Type **1281**; *Epitonium clathrus*; *Cepea nemoralis* and *Arion rufus*; *Donax vittatus*; *Anodonta cygnea*; *Anodonta cygnea* (different) . . 6·00 6·00

2005. Architecture. Multicoloured.
3934 44c. Type **1282** 95 80
3935 44c. Museum of Musical Instruments, Brussels . . 1·00 80
3936 65c. Bukit Pasoh Road, Singapore . . . . 1·30 1·20
3937 65c. Kandahar Street, Singapore . . . . 1·30 1·20
Stamps of the same design were issued by Singapore.

1283 Chrysanthemum

1284 "The Reaper" (Kasimir Malevich)

2005. Flowers. No value expressed. Self-adhesive.
3938 **1283** (50c.) multicoloured . . 1·00 85
No. 3938 was for use on inland letters up to 50g.

2005. "Europhalia 2005—Russia" Festival. Multicoloured.
3939 50c. Type **1284** . . . . . . 1·00 90
3940 70c. "Allegory" (Sergei Sudeikin) . . . . 1·40 1·30
No. 3939 was issued with a se-tenant label inscribed "Prior".

1285 Shrine of Our Lady, Tournai

2005. 800th Anniv of Shrine of Our Lady by Nicolas of Verdun.
3941 **1285** 75c. bronze and gold 1·50 1·30

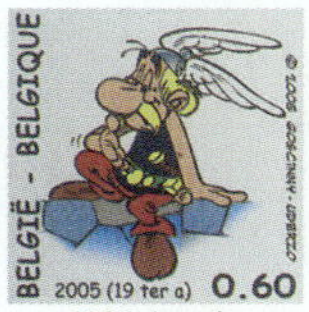

1286 Asterix

2005. Asterix (comic strip written by Rene Goscinny and illustrated by Albert Uderzo). Sheet 161 × 130 mm containing T **1286** and similar designs showing characters. Multicoloured.
MS3942 50c. × 6, Type **1286**; Cacofonix (27 × 41 mm.); Getafix (41 × 27 mm.); Obelix (41 × 27 mm.); Abraracourcix (27 × 41 mm.); Asterix feasting (39 × 34 mm.) . . . . 7·50 7·25

1287 "Objet" (Joelle Tuerlinckx)

2005. "This is Belgium" (3rd series). Art. Sheet 166 × 201 mm containing T **1287** and similar designs.
MS3943 44c. × 10, black and claret (Type **1287**); multicoloured ("ABC" (Jef Geys)); multicoloured ("La Traviata" (Lili Dujourie)); multicoloured ("Representation d'un corps rond" (Ann Veronica Janssens)); black ("Portrait of an Artist by Himself (XIII)" (Jan Vercuysse)); multicoloured ("Donderwolk" (Panamarenko)); multicoloured ("Tournus" (Marthe Wery)); multicoloured ("Figuur op de rug gezien (la nuque)" (Luc Tuymans)); black and bright carmine ("Jeu de mains" (Michel Francois)); "Mur de la montee des Anges" (Jan Fabre)) . . . . 10·00 10·00
The stamps of No. **MS**3943 form a composite design.

1288 *The Princess and the Pea*

2005. Birth Bicentenary of Hans Christian Andersen (writer). Multicoloured. (a) Ordinary gum.
3944 50c. Type **1288b** . . . . 1·00 85
3945 50c. *The Ugly Duckling* . . 1·00 85
3946 50c. *Thumbelina* . . . . . . 1·00 85
3947 50c. *The Little Mermaid* . . 1·00 85
3948 50c. *The Emperor's New Clothes* . . . . 1·00 85

(b) Size 28 × 22 mm. Self-adhesive.
3949 50c. As No. 3944 . . . . . 1·00 85
3950 50c. As No. 3945 . . . . . 1·00 85
3951 50c. As No. 3946 . . . . . 1·00 85
3952 50c. As No. 3947 . . . . . 1·00 85
3953 50c. As No. 3948 . . . . . 1·00 85
Nos. 3944/8 each have a label inscribed "Prior" attached at left.

1289 Father Christmas

1290 Maurits Sabbe

2005. Christmas. (a) Ordinary gum.
3954 **1289** 44c. multicoloured . . . 90 80

(b) Size 23 × 28 mm. Self-adhesive.
3955 **1289** 44c. multicoloured . . . 90 80

2005. Popular Literature. Writers. Multicoloured.
3956 44c. Type **1290** 90 75
3957 44c. Arthur Masson 90 75

1291 Queen Astrid

1292 Drum

2005. Birth Centenary of Queen Astrid. Each black and gold.
3958 44c. Type **1291** 90 75
MS3959 90 × 125 mm. 80c. Queen Astrid and Prince Albert (38 × 49 mm) . . . . 1·90 1·90

2005. Music. Brass Bands. Multicoloured.
3960 50c. Type **1292** . . . . . . 1·00 90
3961 50c. Cornet . . . . 1·00 90
3962 50c. Sousaphone . . . . . 1·00 90
3963 50c. Clarinet . . . . 1·00 90
3964 50c. Tuba . . . . 1·00 90
Nos. 3960/4 each have a label inscribed "Prior" attached at foot.

1293 Donkey

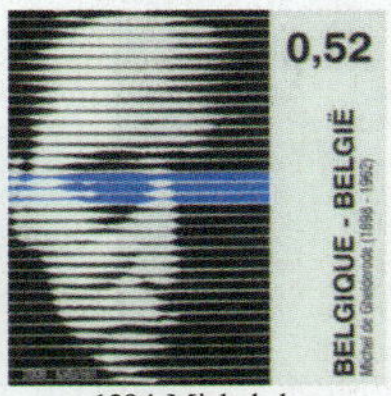

1294 Michel de Ghelderode

2006. Farm Animals. Multicoloured. Self-adhesive.
3965 46c. Type **1293** 90 85
3966 46c. Hens 90 85
3967 46c. Ducks 90 85
3968 46c. Pigs 90 85
3969 46c. Cow 90 85
3970 46c. Goat 90 85
3971 46c. Rabbits 90 85
3972 46c. Horses 90 85
3973 46c. Sheep 90 85
3974 46c. Geese 90 85

2006. Writers Commemorations.
3975 **1294** 52c. black and blue . . 1·00 90
3976 – 78c. black and magenta 1·50 1·40
DESIGN: 78c. Herman Terlinck.
No. 3975 has a label inscribed "Prior" attached at left.

1295 Guillaume Dufay and Gilles Binchois

2006. Renaissance Polyphonists (part song writers). Multicoloured.

3977	60c. Type **1295**	. . . . . .	1·20	1·00
3978	60c. Johannes Ockeghem	. .	1·20	1·00
3979	60c. Jacob Obrecht	. . . .	1·20	1·00
3980	60c. Adriaan Willaert	. . .	1·20	1·00
3981	60c. Orlandus Lassus	. . .	1·20	1·00

1296 Musical Score and Mozart

2006. 250th Birth Anniv of Wolfgang Amadeus Mozart.
3982 **1296** 70c. multicoloured . . . 1·40 1·20

1297 Cross Bowman

1298 Cross Bowman

2006. Cross Bowmen. (a) Ordinary gum.
3983 **1297** 46c. multicoloured . . . 90 85

(b) Size 24 × 32 mm. Self-adhesive gum.
3984 **1298** (52c.) multicoloured . . 1·00 85

1299 Senate

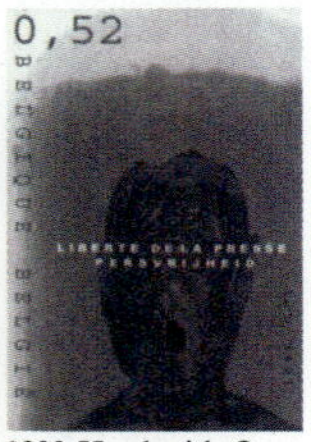

1300 Head with Open Mouth

2006. 175th Anniv of Democracy. Sheet 200 × 83 mm containing T **1299** and similar multicoloured designs.
MS3985 46c. × 3, Type **1299**; King Leopold (vert); Chamber of representatives . . . . 3·25 3·25

2006. Freedom of the Press. Sheet 197 × 100 mm containing T **1300** and similar multicoloured designs.
MS3986 52c. × 5, Type **1300** × 3; Blue sky × 2 (horiz) . . . . . 6·25 6·25
The stamps of **MS**3986 each have a label inscribed "Prior" attached at foot. The stamp depicting a blue sky shows a woman's face when tilted.

1301 Mouth and Script

1302 Mouth and Script

2006. Stamp Festival. Winning Entry in Design a Stamp Competition. (a) Ordinary gum.
3987 **1301** 46c. multicoloured . . . 50 30

(b) Size 29 × 25 mm. Self-adhesive gum.
3988 **1302** (52c.) multicoloured 55 35
3988a (52c.) As Type **1302** but design reversed 55 35
Nos. 3988/a were each issued with a se-tenant label inscribed "Prior".

1303 Justus Lipsius

1304 Winner and Trophy

2006. 400th Death Anniv of Justus Lipsius (writer and scientist).
3989 **1303** 70c. brown and cinnamon . . . . . 2·25 1·25

2006. 1st Four Stages—Giro Italia (cycle race), Wallonia.
3990 **1304** 52c. multicoloured . . . 75 45

1305 John Walker

2006. 30th Anniv of Memorial Van Damme Track and Field Event. Sheet 167 × 100 mm containing T **1305** and similar vert designs. Multicoloured.
MS3991 52c. × 5, Type **1305**; Alberto Juantorena; Ivo Van Damme; Sebastian Coe; Steve Ovett . . 8·00 8·00
The stamps of **MS**3991 were each issued with a label inscribed "Prior" at foot.

1306 Clement Van Hassel

2006. Belgian World Champions—Billiards. Sheet 153 × 167 mm containing T **1306** and similar horiz designs. Multicoloured.
MS3992 52c. × 12, Type **1306**; Tony Schrauwen; Leo Corin; Emile Wafflard; Ludo Dielis; Jos Vervest; Frederic Caudron; Laurent Boulanger; Paul Stroobants, Eddy Leppens and Peter De Backer; Raymond Ceulemans; Raymond Steylaerts; Jozef Philipoom . . . . 16·00 16·00
The stamps of **MS**3992 were each issued with a label inscribed "Prior" at either left or right.
The stamps of **MS**3992 were not for sale separately.

1307 "L'offrande de Joachim Refusee" (Lambert Lombard)

1308 Ostend Lighthouse

2006. Art. 500th Birth Anniv of Lambert Lombard (3393/4) or 150th Birth Anniv of Leon Spilliaert (3395/6). Multicoloured.

3993	65c. Type **1307**	. . . . . .	85	55
3994	65c. "August et la Sybille de Tibur" (Lambert Lombard)	. . . . . .	85	55
3995	65c. "Duizeling" (Leon Spilliaert)	. . . . . .	85	55
3996	65c. "De Dame met de Hoed" (Leon Spilliaert)		85	55

2006. Lighthouses.Multicoloured.

3997	46c. Type **1308**	. . . . . .	1·40	75
3998	46c. Blankenberge	. . . . .	1·40	75
3999	46c. Nieuwport	. . . . . .	1·40	75
4000	46c. Heist	. . . .	1·40	75

1309 Dogfish

2006. North Sea Fish. Sheet 146 × 124 mm containing T **1309** and similar multicoloured designs.
MS4001 46c. × 5, Type **1309**; Cod (47 × 26 mm); Thornback skate; Plaice (33 × 26 mm); Herring (33 × 26 mm) . . . . 7·00 7·00
The stamps and margins of **MS**4001 form a composite design.

1310 Emblem

1311 Emblem

2006. Belgica 2006 International Stamp Exhibition. (a) Ordinary Gum.
4002 **1310** 46c. multicoloured . . . 50 30

(b) Size 24 × 28 mm. Self-adhesive gum.
4003 **1311** (52c.) multicoloured . . 90 50

1312 Nurse, Patients and Bandages

1313 Nurse, Patients and Bandages

2006. Red Cross. Benjamin Secouriste (children's Red Cross certificate scheme). (a) Ordinary Gum.
4004 **1312** 52c.+12c. multicoloured 80 80

(b) Size 24 × 28 mm. Self-adhesive gum.
4005 **1313** (52c.) multicoloured 70 40
4005a (52c.) As Type **1313** but design reversed 70 40
No. 4005/a were issued with a se-tenant label inscribed "Prior".

1314 Emblem

1315 Deigne

2006. Centenary of BOIC (Belgian Olympic and Inter-federal Committee).
4006 **1314** 52c. multicoloured . . . 1·75 95
No. 4006 was issued with a se-tenant label inscribed "Prior".

2006. Tourism. Wallonia. Showing village scenes. Multicoloured.

4007	52c. Type **1315**	. . . . . .	70	40
4008	52c. Mein	. . . .	70	40
4009	52c. Celles	. . . . . .	70	40
4010	52c. Lompret	. . . . . .	70	40
4011	52c. Ny	. . . .	70	40

Nos. 4007/11 were each issued with a se-tenant label inscribed "Prior".

1316 Part of Football

2006. World Cup Football Championship, Germany. Sheet 126 × 90 mm.
MS4012 **1316** €1.30 multicoloured 4·00 4·00

1317 *Centauria*

2006. Flowers. No value expressed. Self-adhesive.
4013 **1317** (52c.) multicoloured . . 70 40
No. 4013 was for use on inland letters up to 50g.

1318 Miner

2006. 50th Anniv of Marcinelle Mine Disaster.
4014 **1318** 70c. multicoloured . . . 90 60

1319 Tulip

1320 "Oosterlinghuis" (beguinage (religious community), Bruges) (painting)

2006. Air. Flowers. No value expressed. Self-adhesive. Multicoloured.
4015 **1319** (70c.) multicoloured . . 90 60
No. 4015 was for use on letters of up to 50g. within Europe.

2006. 650th Anniv of Hanseatic League. Multicoloured.
4016 70c. Type **1320** 90 60
4017 80c. "Oosters Huis" (Bremen town hall) (painting) . . . . 1·00 65

1321 Institute Building

1322 "ABA"

2006. Centenary of the Institute of Tropical Medicine.
4018 **1321** 80c. multicoloured . . . 2·50 1·40

2006. Academie de Philatelie de Belgique.
4019 **1322** 52c. multicoloured . . . 70 40
No. 4019 was issued with a se-tenant label inscribed "Prior" attached at top.

1323 "Le Kleptomane" (Theodore Gericault)

2006. Foreign Masterpieces in Belgian Collections.
4020 **1323** 52c.+12c. multicoloured 80 80
No. 4020 was issued with a label inscribed "Prior" attached at left. The premium was for the promotion of philately.

1324 Ying Yang Symbol

2006. Belgica 2006 International Stamp Exhibition. Young Philatelist World Championship. Two sheets containing T **1324** and similar vert designs. Multicoloured.
MS4021 (a) 166 × 133 mm. 46c. × 5, Type **1324**; Tulips as wine glasses; Butterflies as four leaf clover; Tent at night; Comic page containing all designs. (b) 190 × 120 mm. €1.95 Emblem (38 × 49 mm) 13·50 13·50
Nos. **MS**4021a/b were each sold for €5, the premium for the promotion of philately.

1325 Animals (Nassira Tadmiri)

2006. Europa. Integration. Multicoloured.
4022 52c. Type **1325** . . . . . . 1·60 90
4023 52c. Children of many nations and rainbow (Lize-Maria Verhaeghe) 1·60 1·90

1326 "New Skin" (Pierre Alechinsky)

1327 "New Skin" (Pierre Alechinsky)

2006. CoBrA (artistic movement). Multicoloured. (a) Miniature sheet. Ordinary gum.
MS4024 125 × 90 mm. 46c. Type **1326**; 70c. "Untitled" (Asger Jorn) . . . . 3·40 3·40

(b) Size 28 × 25 mm. No value expressed. Self-adhesive gum.
4025 (52c.) Type **1327** . . . . . 1·60 1·90
Stamps of similar design were issued by Denmark.

1328 Rock and Roll

1329 Rock and Roll

2006. Dance. Multicoloured. (a) Miniature sheet. Ordinary gum.
MS4026 166 × 125 mm. 60c. × 5, Type **1328**; Waltz; Tango; Cha-cha-cha; Samba . . . . 4·25 4·25

(b) Size 30 × 26 mm. No value expressed. Self-adhesive gum.
4027 (52c.) Type **1329** 85 50
4028 (52c.) Waltz 85 50
4029 (52c.) Tango 85 50
4030 (52c.) Cha-cha-cha 85 50
4031 (52c.) Samba 85 50

1330 Kramikske

2006. Youth Philately. Kramikske Briochon, cartoon character created by Jean-Pol Vandenbroek.
4032 **1330** 46c. multicoloured . . . 1·50 85

1331 Tomato and Shrimps

2006. "This is Belgium" (4th series). Food. Sheet 154 × 186 mm containing T **1331** and similar multicoloured designs.
MS4033 46c. × 10, Type **1331**; Trappist beer (vert); Jenever (spirit) (vert); Chicory au gratin; Ham and sausages (vert); Waffles (vert); Stewed eels in chervil sauce; Chocolate; Mussels and fries (vert); Gueuze (beer) (vert) . . 12·00 12·00

1332 Angel playing Psaltery (detail)

1333 Angel playing Psaltery (detail)

2006. Christmas. Altarpiece by Hans Memling. Showing angel musicians. Multicoloured. (a) Ordinary gum.
4034 46c. Type **1332** 65 35
4035 46c. Tromba marina 65 35
4036 46c. Lute 65 35
4037 46c. Trumpet 65 35
4038 46c. Shawn 65 35

(b) Size 25 × 29 mm. Self-adhesive.
4039 46c. Type **1333** 65 35
4040 46c. Tromba marina 65 35
4041 46c. Lute 65 35
4042 46c. Trumpet 65 35
4043 46c. Shawn 65 35
Nos. 4034/8 were issued together, se-tenant, forming a composite design.

1334 "HAPPY BIRTHDAY TO YOU"

1335 Cycle Wheel (cyclocross)

2006. Greetings Stamps. Self-adhesive. Multicoloured. No value expressed.
4044 (52c.) Type **1334** 75 45
4045 (52c.) Birthday cake (Prior at right) 75 45
4046 (52c.) As No. 4045 (Prior at left) 75 45
4047 (52c.) As No. 4044 (Prior at right) 75 45

2007. Sport. Multicoloured. (a) Ordinary gum.
4048 46c. Type **1335** 65 35
4049 60c. Ball and skittles (bowling) 90 55
4050 65c. Club and ball (golf) . . 90 55

(b) Size 25 × 29 mm. Self-adhesive. No Value Expressed.
4051 (52c.) As Type **1335** 75 45
4052 (52c.) As No. 4049 . . . . 75 45
4053 (52c.) As No. 4050 . . . . 75 45

1336 "Nu Assis" (Amedo Modigliani)

2007. Sheet 90 × 125 mm.
MS4054 **1336** 60c.+30c. multicoloured . . . . 1·40 1·40
The premium was for the promotion of philately.

1337 Alix

2007. "Philately for the Young". Alix (comic strip created by Jacques Martin).
4055 **1337** 52c. multicoloured . . . 75 45

1338 Piano Accordion

1339 Julia Tulkens

2007. Bellows-driven Aerophones. Sheet 166 × 100 mm containing T **1338** and similar vert designs. Multicoloured.
MS4056 52c. × 5 Type **1338**; Concertina; Button accordion; Melodeon; Melodeon (different) 2·60 2·60
The stamps of **MS**4056 each have a se-tenant label inscribed "Prior" attached at foot.
The stamps of **MS**4056 were not for sale separately.

2007. Women in Literature. Sheet 166 × 100 mm containing T **1339** and similar vert designs. Multicoloured.
MS4057 52c. × 5 Type **1339**; Madeleine Bourdhouxhe; Christine d'Haen; Jacqueline Harpman; Maria Rosseels . . 7·75 7·75
The stamps of **MS**4057 each have a se-tenant label inscribed "Prior" attached at foot and form a composite background design.

1340 Hospital Librarian and Patient

1341 Hospital Librarian and Patient

2007. Red Cross. Multicoloured. (a) Self-adhesive gum.
4058 (52c.) Type **1340** . . . . . 1·25 95
4059 (52c.) As No. 4058 but with "Prior" at right . . . . . 1·25 95

(b) Size 39 × 27 mm. Ordinary gum.
4060 52c.+25c. Type **1341** . . . . 1·60 1·60
No. 4060 has a label inscribed "Prior" attached at right.

1342 "Tati l'periki" (Tati the hairdresser) (Edouard Remouchamps)

2007. Belgian Popular Theatre. Sheet 198 × 83 mm containing T **1342** and similar multicoloured designs.
MS4061 46c. × 3, Type **1342**; Romain DeConinck (vert); "Le Mariage de Melle Beulemans" (Jean-Francois Fonson and Fernand Wicheler) . . . . . . 4·25 4·25
The stamps of **MS**4061 form a composite background design.

1343 Stoclet Palace (interior) (Josef Hoffman)

1344 Robert Baden-Powell (founder)

2007. Architecture. Multicoloured.
4062 46c. Type **1343** . . . . 1·40 85
4063 80c. Stoclet Palace (exterior) 2·60 1·50
No. 4063 has a label inscribed "Prior" attached at top.
Stamps of a similar design were issued by Czech Republic.

2007. Europa. Centenary of Scouting. Multicoloured.
4064 52c. Type **1344** . . . . . . 1·60 95
MS4065 90 × 125 mm. 75c. Scouts (38 × 48 mm) . . . . 2·60 1·50
The stamp and margins of **MS**4065 form a composite background design.

1345 Country Identification Letters of Signatories (⅔-size illustration)

2007. 50th Anniv of Treaty of Rome.
4066 **1345** 80c. multicoloured . . . 2·50 1·40

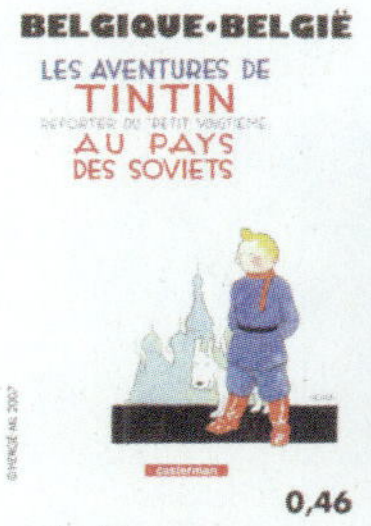

1346 'Tintin au pays de Soviets' (Tintin in the land of Soviets) (French)

1347 Dress (Museum of Fashion, Hasselt)

2007. Birth Centenary of Georges Remi (Herge) (creator of Tintin). Designs showing Tintin book covers in different languages. Multicoloured.
4067 46c. Type **1346** . . . . . 1·10 65
4068 46c. Tintin in the Congo (Danish) . . . . 1·10 65
4069 46c. Tintin in America . . . 1·10 65
4070 46c. Cigars of the Pharaoh (Luxembourg) . . . . . 1·10 65
4071 46c. The Blue Lotus (Chinese) . . . . 1·10 65
4072 46c. The Broken Ear (Portuguese) . . . . . . 1·10 65
4073 46c. The Black Island (Bengali) . . . . 1·10 65
4074 46c. King Ottokar's Sceptre (Slovakian) . . . . . . 1·10 65
4075 46c. The Crab with the Golden Claws (Russian) 1·10 65
4076 46c. The Shooting Star (Icelandic) . . . . . . 1·10 65
4077 46c. The Secret of the Unicorn (Polish) . . . . 1·10 65
4078 46c. Red Rackham's Treasure (Afrikaans) . . . 1·10 65
4079 46c. Herge . . . . 1·10 65
4080 46c. The Seven Crystal Balls (Arabic) . . . . . . 1·10 65
4081 46c. Prisoners of the Sun (Spanish) . . . . 1·10 65
4082 46c. Land of Black Gold (German) . . . . 1·10 65
4083 46c. Destination Moon (Finnish) . . . . 1·10 65
4084 46c. Explorers of the Moon (Swedish) . . . . 1·10 65
4085 46c. The Calculus Affair (Japanese) . . . . . . 1·10 65
4086 46c. The Red Sea Sharks (Turkish) . . . . 1·10 65
4087 46c. Tintin in Tibet (Tibetan) . . . . 1·10 65
4088 46c. The Castifiore Emerald (Italian) . . . . 1·10 65
4089 46c. Flight 714 (Indonesian) 1·10 65
4090 46c. Tintin and the Picaros (Greek) . . . . 1·10 65
4091 46c. Tintin and the Alph-Art (Dutch) . . . . 1·10 65

2007. Small Museums. Multicoloured.
4092 46c. Type **1347** . . . . . . 1·10 65
4093 75c. Skeleton and woman (Notre-Dame a la Rose Hospital Cultural Museum, Lessines) . . . 2·50 1·50
4094 92c. Beaker (Jewish Museum, Brussels) . . . 2·75 1·70

1348 Men carrying Canoe

1349 Men carrying Canoe

2007. Summer Stamps. No Value Expressed. Multicoloured. (a) Self-adhesive.
4095 (52c.) Type **1348** . . . . . 1·60 95
4096 (52c.) As No. 4095 but with "Prior" at left . . . . . 1·60 95
4097 (52c.) Couple with kite . . . 1·60 95
4098 (52c.) As No. 4097 but with "Prior" at left . . . . . 1·60 95

(b) Ordinary gum.
4099 52c. Type **1349** . . . . . . 1·60 95
4100 52c. As No. 4098 . . . . . 1·60 95

1350 Building

2007. 50th Anniv of King Baudouin Antarctic Base (1st Belgian Antarctic research station). Sheet 90 × 125 mm.
MS4101 **1350** 75c. multicoloured . . . 2·50 2·50

1351 Cyclists

2007. Tour de France Cycle Race.
4102 **1351** 52c. multicoloured . . . 1·75 1·00

1352 Ship in Port **1353** Ship in Port

2007. Centenary of Zeebrugge. No Value Expressed. Multicoloured. (a) Self-adhesive.
4103 (52c.) Type **1352** . . . . . 1·10 65
4104 (52c.) As No. 4103 but with 'Prior' at left . . . . . . 1·10 65

(b) Ordinary gum.
4105 €1.04 Type **1353** but with 'Prior' at left . . . . . . 2·75 1·70

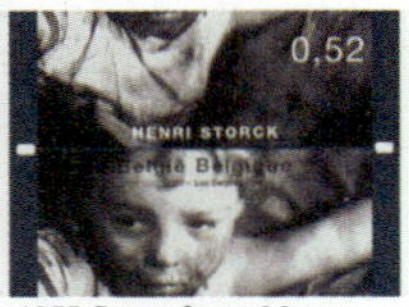

1354 Athenee Royal Francois Bovesse, Namur **1355** Scene from *Misere au Borinage* (film by Henri Storck)

2007. Tourism. Multicoloured.
4106 52c. Type **1354** . . . . . . 1·70 1·00
4107 52c. Saint Michel College, Brussels . . . . 1·70 1·00
4108 52c. Heilig Hart College . . 1·70 1·00

2007. Belgium Cinema. Birth Centenary of Henri Storck (filmmaker). Sheet 98 × 167 mm containing T **1355** and similar horiz designs. Multicoloured.
MS4109 52c. × 5, Type **1355**; Boy sleeping (*Les Fils* by Luc and Jean-Pierre Dardenne); Haircut (*L'homme au crane rase* (Man who had his hair cut short) by Andre Delvaux); Bedside scene (*Malpertius* by Harry Kumel); Seated woman (*Dust* by Marion Hansel) . . . . 8·25 8·25

1356 Tombeau du Geant, Botassart

2007. Luxembourg European Capital of Culture–2007. Multicoloured.
4110 52c. Type **1356** . . . . . . 1·70 1·00
4111 80c. Rotunda, Luxembourg Train Station . . . . . 2·50 1·50
Stamp of a similar design was issued by Luxembourg.

1357 Queen Paola **1358** King Albert II

2007. 70th Birth Anniv of Queen Paola. Sheet 125 × 90 mm.
MS4112 **1357** €1.04 multicoloured 3·50 3·50

2007.
4113 **1358** 1 (52c.) red and vermilion . . . . . 1·50 90
4114 2 (€1.04) olive, green and slate . . . . . . 2·75 1·70
4115 3 (€1.56) blue, indigo and slate . . . . . . 3·00 1·80
4116 5 (€2.60) violet, purple and slate . . . . . . 3·50 2·10
4117 7 (€3.64) brown, deep brown and slate . . . 6·25 3·75
This set is to introduce the new franking system which is in multiples of base price (currently 52c.). 1 (52c.) is for use on standard domestic mail from 0–50 grams, 2 (€1.04 (ie twice base rate of 52c.)) is for use on non-standard domestic mail from 0–100 grams, 3 (€1.56) is for use on non-standard domestic mail from 100–350 grams, 5 (€2.60) is for use on non-standard domestic mail from 350 grams–1 kilo, 7 (€3.64) is for use on non-standard domestic mail from 1–2 kilos.

1359 Pears

2007. Fruit. Multicoloured. Self-adhesive.
4118 1 (52c.) Type **1359** . . . . 1·50 90
4119 1 (52c.) Strawberries . . . . 1·50 90
4120 1 (52c.) Red currants . . . 1·50 90
4121 1 (52c.) Apples . . . . . . 1·50 90
4122 1 (52c.) Grapes . . . . . . 1·50 90
4123 1 (52c.) Cherries . . . . . 1·50 90
4124 1 (52c.) Raspberries . . . . 1·50 90
4125 1 (52c.) Peaches . . . . . 1·50 90
4126 1 (52c.) Plums . . . . . . 1·50 90
4127 1 (52c.) Blackberries . . . . 1·50 90

1360 Remington (20th-century)

1361 Remington (20th-century)

2007. Stamp Festival. Typewriters. Multicoloured. Self-adhesive.
4128 1 (52c.) Type **1360** . . . . 1·50 90
4129 1 (52c.) Royal (1925) . . . 1·50 90
4130 1 (52c.) Olympia (1950) . . 1·50 90
4131 1 (52c.) Olivetti (1972) . . . 1·50 90
4132 1 (52c.) Laptop word processor . . . . 1·50 90

(b) Ordinary gum.
MS4133 100 × 165 mm. 1 (52c.) × 5, Type **1361**; As No. 4129; As No. 4130; As No. 4131; As No. 4132 . . . . 7·50 7·50

1362 Dahlia

2007. Flowers. Multicoloured. Self-adhesive.
4134 1 (52c.) Type **1362** . . . . 1·90 1·10
4135 2 (€1.04) Petunia . . . . . 3·50 2·10

1363 Marc Van Montagu (molecular genetics)

2007. This Belgium. Science. Sheet 166 × 193 mm containing T **1363** and similar circular designs. Multicoloured. Self-adhesive.
MS4136 70c. × 9, Type **1363**; Paul Janssen (medicine); Lise Thirly (microbiology/virology); Chris Van den Wyngaert (international criminal law); Peter Carmeliet (molecular medicine); Philippe Van Parijs (social philosophy); Marie-Claire Foblets (anthropology); Andre Berger (climate studies); Pierre Rene Deligne (mathematics) . . . . 16·00 15·00

1364 Tulip 'Peach Blossom'

2007. Self-adhesive.
4137 **1364** A (80c.) multicoloured 2·75 1·60

1365 Sunset

2007. Bereavement. No value expressed.
4138 **1365** 1 (52c.) multicoloured 1·90 1·10

1366 *Les chemins de la liberte* (*Le voyage*) (Thierry Merget) **1367** Couple in Wedding Outfits

2007. Postal Art.
4139 **1366** 1 (52c.) multicoloured 1·90 1·10

2007. Greetings Stamps. Multicoloured. Self-adhesive.
4140 1 (52c.) Type **1367** . . . . 1·90 1·10
4141 1 (52c.) Father holding boy baby . . . . 1·90 1·10
4142 1 (52c.) Mother holding girl baby . . . . 1·90 1·10

2007. Belgian Billiards World Champions. Sheet 80 × 140 mm containing horiz designs as T **1306**. Multicoloured.
MS4143 1 (52c.) × 9, Piet J. Van Duppen; Albert Collette; Gustaaf Van Belle; Piet Sels; Gaston De Doncker; Theo Moons; Rene Gabriels; Victor Luypaerts; Rene Vingerhoerdt . . . . 13·50 13·50
See also **MS**3992.

1368 Christmas Tree **1369** Christmas Tree

1370 Christmas Tree

2007. Christmas and New Year. (a) Ordinary gum.
4144 **1368** 1 (52c.) multicoloured (postage) . . . . . . 1·90 1·10

(b) Self-adhesive.
4145 **1369** 1 (52c.) multicoloured 1·90 1·10

(c) Self-adhesive.
4146 **1370** A (80c.) multicoloured (air) . . . . 2·75 1·60

1371 *The Man From the Sea*

2008. Rene Magritte (artist) Commemoration. Sheet 80 × 140 mm containing T **1371** and similar multicoloured designs.
MS4147 1 (52c.) × 5, Type **1371**; *Scheherazade*; *The Midnight Marriage*; *Georgette* (32 × 41 mm); *The Ignorant Fairy* (49 × 37 mm) 9·00 9·00

1372 Give Blood

1373 Give Blood

2008. Red Cross. Give Blood Campaign. (a) Self-adhesive.
4148 **1372** 1 (52c.) multicoloured 2·50 1·50

(b) Ordinary gum.
4149 **1373** 1 (52c.)+25c. multicoloured . . . . 2·50 1·50

1374 *La Luz que se Apaga* (Jose Maria Sicilia)

2008. Art. Sheet 90 × 125 mm.
MS4150 **1374** 2 (€1.04)+40c. multicoloured . . . . 2·75 1·70

1375 Jeremiah and Kurdy Malloy

2008. 'Philately for the Young'. Jeremiah (comic strip created by Hermann Huppen (Hermann)).
4151 **1375** 1 (52c.) multicoloured 2·50 1·50

1376 Car

2008. Toys. Self-adhesive. Multicoloured.
4152 1 (52c.) Type **1376** . . . . 2·50 1·50
4153 1 (52c.) Pram . . . . 2·50 1·50
4154 1 (52c.) Doll . . . . 2·50 1·50
4155 1 (52c.) Airplane . . . . . 2·50 1·50
4156 1 (52c.) Horse . . . . . . 2·50 1·50
4157 1 (52c.) Tram . . . . . . 2·50 1·50
4158 1 (52c.) Diablo . . . . . . 2·50 1·50
4159 1 (52c.) Teddy . . . . . . 2·50 1·50
4160 1 (52c.) Top . . . . 2·50 1·50
4161 1 (52c.) Wooden scooter . . 2·50 1·50

1377 Flowers

2008. Bicentenary of Ghent Flower Show. Sheet 90 × 125 mm.

MS4162	**1377**	80c. multicoloured	2·75	2·75

1378 Suzy Delair as Mila Malou and Pierre Fresnay as Wens (scene from film *L'assassin habite au 21*)

2008. Detective Novels. Multicoloured.

4163	1	(52c.) Type **1378** (novel by Stanislas–Andre Steeman)	1·60	95
4164	1	(52c.) Jan Decleir as Angelo Ledda (scene from film *De zaak Alzheimer*) (novel by Jef Geeraerts)	1·60	95

1379 Menorah

2008. Bicentenary of Belgian Jewish Community.

4165	**1379**	90c. blue and black	2·60	1·50

EXPRESS LETTER STAMPS

E **107** Ghent

1929.

E530	–	1f.75 blue	60	25
E531	E **107**	2f.35 red	1·90	45
E581	–	2f.45 green	19·00	2·20
E532	–	3f.50 purple	15·00	10·00
E533	–	5f.25 olive	11·50	9·50

DESIGNS: 1f.75, Town Hall, Brussels; 2f.45, Eupen; 3f.50, Bishop's Palace, Liege; 5f.25, Antwerp Cathedral.

1932. No. E581 surch **2 Fr 50** and cross.

E608	2f.50 on 2f.45 green	20·00	2·20

MILITARY STAMPS

1967. As T **289** (Baudouin) but with letter "M" within oval at foot.

M2027	1f.50 green	20	15

1971. As No. 2207/8a and 2209a but with letter "M" within oval at foot.

M2224	1f.75 green	40	50
M2225	2f.25 green	35	45
M2226	2f.50 green	15	20
M2227	3f.25 plum	15	20

NEWSPAPER STAMPS

1928. Railway Parcels stamps of 1923 optd **JOURNAUX DAGBLADEN 1928**.

N443	P **84**	10c. red	50	35
N444		20c. green	50	35
N445		40c. olive	50	35
N446		60c. orange	75	40
N447		70c. brown	75	35
N448		80c. violet	1·00	50
N449		90c. slate	9·25	3·00
N450	–	1f. blue	2·00	50
N451	–	2f. olive	4·00	80
N452	–	3f. red	4·00	80
N453	–	4f. red	4·00	80
N454	–	5f. violet	4·00	90
N455	–	6f. brown	6·25	1·90
N456	–	7f. orange	18·00	3·00
N457	–	8f. brown	12·50	1·50
N458	–	9f. purple	35·00	8·50
N459	–	10f. green	12·50	2·30
N460	–	20f. pink	35·00	10·50

1929. Railway Parcels stamps of 1923 optd **JOURNAUX DAGBLADEN** only.

N505	P **84**	10c. red	75	35
N506		20c. green	50	50
N507		40c. olive	50	45
N508		60c. orange	75	60
N509		70c. brown	50	40
N510		80c. violet	1·00	85
N511		90c. slate	7·00	5·00
N512	–	1f. blue	1·50	50
N513	–	1f.10 brown	5·00	1·50
N514	–	1f.50 blue	5·00	1·50
N515	–	2f. olive	3·25	85
N516	–	2f.10 slate	15·00	10·00
N517	–	3f. red	3·25	85
N518	–	4f. red	3·25	95
N519	–	5f. violet	3·25	95
N520	–	6f. brown	7·50	1·50
N521	–	7f. orange	23·00	1·50
N522	–	8f. brown	15·00	1·50
N523	–	9f. purple	30·00	14·50
N524	–	10f. green	18·00	3·50
N525	–	20f. pink	42·00	12·50

PARCEL POST STAMPS

Stamps issued at Belgian Post Offices only.

1928. Optd **COLIS POSTAL POSTCOLLO**.

B470	**81**	4f. brown	7·50	1·50
B471		5f. bistre	7·50	1·50

B **106** G.P.O., Brussels

1929.

B526	B **106**	3f. sepia	1·30	30
B527		4f. slate	1·30	30
B528		5f. red	1·30	30
B529		6f. purple	31·00	30·00

1933. Surch **X4 4X**.

B645	B **106**	4f. on 6f. purple	28·00	30

POSTAGE DUE STAMPS

D **21**

D **35**

1870.

D63	D **21**	10c. green	4·00	2·50
D64		20c. blue	75·00	4·50

1895.

D 96a	D **35**	5c. green	20	15
D 97		10c. brown	15·00	1·70
D101		10c. red	20	15
D 98a		20c. green	20	15
D102		30c. blue	20	15
D 99		50c. brown	22·00	5·75
D103		50c. grey	40	30
D100		1f. red	19·00	12·50
D104		1f. yellow	5·00	4·50

1919. As Type **D 35**, but value in colour on white background.

D 251	D **35**	5c. green	55	30
D 323		5c. grey	15	15
D 252b		10c. red	1·50	30
D 324		10c. green	15	15
D 253b		20c. green	7·50	1·20
D 325		20c. brown	15	15
D 254		30c. blue	3·50	50
D 326		30c. red	70	55
D 327		35c. green	25	15
D 328		40c. brown	20	15
D 330		50c. grey	20	15
D 329		50c. blue	4·00	45
D 331		60c. red	30	30
D1146		65c. green	6·50	3·00
D 332		70c. brown	30	15
D 333		80c. grey	30	15
D 334		1f. violet	45	20
D 335		1f. purple	50	30
D 336		1f.20 olive	60	30
D 337		1f.40 green	55	45
D 338		1f.50 olive	60	50
D1147		1f.60 mauve	12·50	5·50
D1148		1f.80 red	14·50	5·00
D 339		2f. mauve	60	15
D1149		2f.40 lavender	8·00	3·25
D1150		3f. red	2·00	50
D 340		3f.50 blue	60	15
D1151		4f. blue	9·75	50
D1152		5f. brown	3·25	30
D1153		7f. violet	3·25	1·50
D1154		8f. purple	10·50	8·00
D1155		10f. violet	7·00	2·75

D **218**

D **462**

1945. Inscr "A PAYER" at top and "TE BETALEN" at bottom, or vice versa.

D1130A	D **218**	10c. olive	20	30
D1131A		20c. blue	20	30
D1132A		30c. red	20	30
D1133A		40c. blue	20	30
D1134A		50c. green	20	30
D1135A		1f. brown	20	30
D1136A		2f. orange	20	30

1966.

D2812	D **462**	1f. mauve	15	15
D2813		2f. green	15	15
D2814		3f. blue	25	25
D2815		4f. green	25	25
D1985ab		5f. purple	25	25
D2816		5f. lilac	25	30
D1986		6f. brown	75	30
D1987		7f. red	60	45
D2818		7f. orange	45	45
D2819		8f. grey	45	55
D2820		9f. red	50	60
D2821		10f. brown	60	65
D1988		20f. green	1·20	60
D2822		20f. green	1·00	1·20

On No. D1988 the "F" is outside the shield; on No. D2822 it is inside.

RAILWAY PARCELS STAMPS

In Belgium the parcels service is largely operated by the Belgian Railways for which the following stamps were issued.

Certain stamps under this heading were also on sale at post offices in connection with a "small parcels" service. These show a posthorn in the design except for Nos. P1116/18.

P **21**

1879.

P63	P **21**	10c. brown	75·00	6·50
P64		20c. blue	£225	20·00
P65		25c. green	£300	11·00
P66		50c. red	£1500	10·50
P67		80c. yellow	£1700	60·00
P68		1f. grey	£225	16·00

P **22**

1882.

P69	P **22**	10c. brown	24·00	1·90
P73		15c. grey	10·00	9·00
P75		20c. blue	85·00	4·25
P77		25c. green	85·00	4·25
P78		50c. red	85·00	90
P81		80c. yellow	85·00	1·30
P84		80c. brown	80·00	1·10
P86		1f. grey	£350	3·00
P87		1f. purple	£425	3·75
P88		2f. buff	£250	85·00

P **35**

1895. Numerals in black except 1f. and 2f.

P 96	P **35**	10c. brown	12·50	75
P 97		15c. slate	12·50	8·00
P 98		20c. blue	19·00	1·20
P 99		25c. green	19·00	1·40
P100		30c. orange	24·00	1·70
P101		40c. green	33·00	1·90
P102		50c. red	33·00	85
P103		60c. lilac	60·00	85
P104		70c. blue	60·00	1·30
P105		80c. yellow	60·00	1·30
P106		90c. red	90·00	1·90
P107		1f. purple	£225	2·75
P108		2f. buff	£275	14·50

P **37** Winged Railway Wheel

1902.

P109a	P **35**	10c. slate and brown	15	25
P110		15c. purple and slate	25	25
P111		20c. brown and blue	25	25
P112		25c. red and green	25	25
P113		30c. green and orange	25	25
P114		35c. green and brown	25	30
P115		40c. mauve and green	25	25
P116		50c. mauve and pink	25	25
P117		55c. blue and purple	30	30
P118		60c. red and lilac	25	25
P119		70c. red and blue	25	25
P120		80c. purple and yellow	25	25
P121		90c. green and red	25	25
P122	P **37**	1f. orange and purple	25	25
P123		1f.10 black and red	25	25
P124		2f. green and bistre	25	25
P125		3f. blue and black	25	25
P126		4f. red and green	2·00	1·70
P127		5f. green and orange	1·30	1·40
P128		10f. purple and yellow	1·30	1·10

1915. Stamps of 1912–14 optd **CHEMINS DE FER SPOORWEGEN** and Winged Railway Wheel.

P160	**44**	5c. green	£170
P161	**46**	10c. red	£200
P162		20c. green	£225
P163		25c. blue	£225
P164	**45**	35c. brown	£300
P165	**46**	40c. green	£275
P166	**45**	50c. grey	£275
P167		1f. orange	£250
P168		2f. violet	£1900
P169	–	5f. purple (No. 143)	£3750

P **59** Winged Railway Wheel

P **60** Steam Locomotive

1915.

P196	P **59**	10c. blue	1·00	55
P197		15c. olive	1·50	1·40
P198		20c. red	1·60	90
P199		25c. brown	1·60	90
P200		30c. mauve	1·60	90
P201		35c. grey	1·60	80
P202		40c. orange	2·50	2·40
P203		50c. bistre	2·40	95
P204		55c. brown	2·75	2·75
P205		60c. lilac	2·10	85
P206		70c. green	1·70	80
P207		80c. brown	1·70	80
P208		90c. blue	2·10	1·10
P209	P **60**	1f. grey	1·70	80
P210		1f.10 bl (FRANKEN)	32·00	29·00
P211		1f.10 blue (FRANK)	2·40	80
P212		2f. red	49·00	1·50
P213		3f. violet	49·00	1·50
P214		4f. green	55·00	3·00
P215		5f. brown	95·00	3·25
P216		10f. orange	£100	3·25

P **69** Winged Railway Wheel

P **70** Steam Train

1920.

P259	P **69**	10c. green	2·00	85
P280		10c. red	60	25
P281		15c. green	60	25
P261		20c. red	2·00	85
P282		20c. green	75	35
P262		25c. brown	2·50	95
P283		25c. blue	75	25
P263		30c. mauve	33·00	26·00
P284		30c. brown	75	25
P285		35c. brown	75	35
P286		40c. orange	75	25
P265		50c. bistre	9·00	1·40
P287		50c. red	1·00	25
P266		55c. brown	10·00	7·75
P288		55c. yellow	6·00	4·50
P267		60c. purple	12·00	1·20
P289		60c. red	75	25
P290		70c. green	3·50	55
P269		80c. brown	50·00	1·70
P291		80c. violet	2·50	45
P270		90c. blue	13·00	1·20
P292		90c. yellow	38·00	33·00
P293		90c. purple	7·50	45
P271	P **70**	1f. grey	90·00	1·70
P272		1f.10 blue	28·00	1·50
P273		1f.20 green	17·00	1·40
P274		1f.40 brown	17·00	1·40
P275		2f. red	£130	1·70
P276		3f. mauve	£160	1·00
P277		4f. green	£160	1·60
P278		5f. brown	£160	1·00
P279		10f. orange	£160	1·20

On Nos. P271/9 the engine has one head lamp.

1920. Three head lamps on engine.

P294	P **70**	1f. brown	7·50	30
P296		1f.10 blue	2·50	30
P297		1f.20 orange	3·25	30
P298		1f.40 yellow	19·00	3·00
P299		1f.60 green	33·00	75
P300		2f. red	35·00	30
P301		3f. red	35·00	30
P302		4f. green	35·00	30
P303		5f. violet	33·00	30
P304		10f. yellow	£180	20·00
P305		10f. brown	45·00	30
P306		15f. red	45·00	30
P307		20f. blue	£500	3·75

P 76

P 84

1921.

P312	P 76	2f. black	10·00	55
P313		3f. brown	80	55
P314		4f. green	27·00	55
P315		5f. red	27·00	55
P316		10f. brown	27·00	55
P317		15f. red	27·00	1·00
P318		20f. blue	£200	2·20

1923.

P375	P 84	5c. brown	25	25
P376		10c. red	15	15
P377		15c. blue	25	25
P378		20c. green	20	15
P379		30c. purple	20	15
P380		40c. olive	20	15
P381		50c. red	20	15
P382		60c. orange	20	15
P383		70c. brown	20	15
P384		80c. violet	20	15
P385		90c. slate	85	15

Similar type, but horiz.

P386	1f. blue	25	30
P388	1f.10 orange	2·00	65
P389	1f.50 green	2·00	40
P390	1f.70 brown	45	45
P391	1f.80 red	3·00	80
P392	2f. olive	25	25
P393	2f.10 green	5·50	95
P394	2f.40 violet	2·50	1·10
P395	2f.70 grey	35·00	85
P396	3f. red	25	20
P397	3f.30 brown	24·00	1·10
P398	4f. red	25	20
P399	5f. violet	80	20
P400	6f. brown	25	20
P401	7f. orange	50	20
P402	8f. brown	50	20
P403	9f. purple	1·80	20
P404	10f. green	75	15
P405	20f. pink	1·00	20
P406	30f. green	3·50	50
P407	40f. slate	45·00	1·20
P408	50f. bistre	6·25	50

See Nos. P911/34.

1924. No. P394 surch **2F30**.

P409	2f.30 on 2f.40 violet	5·00	60

P 139 Type 5 Steam locomotive "Goliath", 1930

P 149 Diesel Locomotive

1934.

P655	P 139	3f. green	12·50	2·50
P656		4f. mauve	5·00	25
P657		5f. red	65·00	25

1935. Centenary of Belgian Railway.

P689	P 149	10c. red	45	25
P690		20c. violet	45	25
P691		30c. brown	55	25
P692		40c. blue	60	25
P693		50c. orange	60	20
P694		60c. green	60	20
P695		70c. blue	60	25
P696		80c. black	60	25
P697		90c. red	1·00	80

Horiz type. Locomotive "Le Belge", 1835.

P698	1f. purple	75	25
P699	2f. black	2·00	25
P700	3f. orange	2·50	25
P701	4f. purple	2·50	25
P702	5f. purple	4·00	25
P703	6f. green	5·50	25
P704	7f. violet	23·00	25
P705	8f. black	23·00	35
P706	9f. blue	25·00	30
P707	10f. red	25·00	30
P708	20f. green	45·00	30
P709	30f. violet	£130	4·50
P710	40f. brown	£130	4·50
P711	50f. red	£160	4·25
P712	100f. blue	£300	55·00

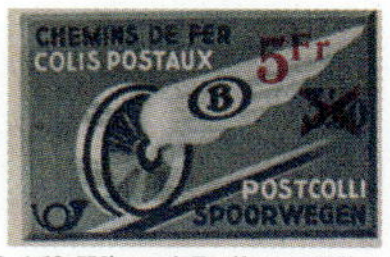

P 162 Winged Railway Wheel and Posthorn

1938.

P 806	P 162	5f. on 3f.50 green	22·00	30
P 807		5f. on 4f.50 purple	20	15
P 808		6f. on 5f.50 red	50	15
P1162		8f. on 5f.50 brown	55	20
P1163		10f. on 5f.50 blue	75	15
P1164		12f. on 5f.50 violet	1·30	25

P 176 Seal of the International Railway Congress

1939. International Railway Congress, Brussels.

P856	P 176	20c. brown	5·00	5·00
P857		50c. blue	5·00	5·00
P858		2f. red	5·00	5·00
P859		9f. green	5·00	5·00
P860		10f. purple	5·00	5·00

1939. Surch **M. 3Fr.**

P867	P 162	3f. on 5f.50 red	50	30

1940. As Nos. 399 and 404 but colours changed.

P876	5f. brown	25	35
P877	10f. black	3·50	3·50

1940. Optd **B** in oval and two vert bars.

P878	P 84	10c. red	15	20
P879		20c. green	15	20
P880		30c. purple	15	20
P881		40c. olive	15	25
P882		50c. red	15	20
P883		60c. orange	65	60
P884		70c. brown	15	25
P885		80c. violet	15	20
P886		90c. slate	25	25
P887		1f. blue	15	20
P888		2f. olive	20	20
P889		3f. red	20	25
P890		4f. red	20	25
P891		5f. violet	20	20
P892		6f. brown	30	20
P893		7f. orange	30	20
P894		8f. brown	30	20
P895		9f. purple	30	20
P896		10f. green	30	20
P897		20f. pink	65	40
P898		30f. green	85	1·20
P899		40f. slate	2·00	2·50
P900		50f. bistre	1·30	1·50

1940. As Type P 84 but colours changed.

P911	P 84	10c. olive	15	20
P912		20c. violet	15	20
P913		30c. red	15	20
P914		40c. blue	15	20
P915		50c. green	15	20
P916		60c. grey	15	20
P917		70c. green	15	20
P918		80c. orange	20	20
P919		90c. lilac	2·50	20

Similar design, but horizontal.

P920	1f. green	25	20
P921	2f. brown	30	20
P922	3f. grey	35	20
P923	4f. olive	40	20
P924	5f. lilac	50	20
P925	5f. black	75	30
P926	6f. red	75	30
P927	7f. violet	75	30
P928	8f. green	75	30
P929	9f. blue	1·00	30
P930	10f. mauve	1·00	30
P931	20f. blue	2·75	40
P932	30f. yellow	5·00	80
P933	40f. red	6·25	85
P934	50f. red	8·75	65

No. P925 was for use as a railway parcels tax stamp.

P 195 Engine Driver

P 216 Mercury

1942. Various designs.

P1090	P 195	10c. grey	30	20
P1091		20c. violet	30	20
P1092		30c. red	30	20
P1093		40c. blue	30	20
P1094		50c. blue	30	20
P1095		60c. black	30	20
P1096		70c. green	50	30
P1097		80c. orange	50	30
P1098		90c. brown	50	30
P1099	–	1f. green	30	25
P1100	–	2f. purple	30	25
P1101	–	3f. black	1·50	30
P1102	–	4f. blue	30	25
P1103	–	5f. brown	30	25
P1104	–	6f. green	1·50	55
P1105	–	7f. violet	30	25
P1106	–	8f. red	30	25
P1107	–	9f. blue	50	25
P 996	–	9f.20 red	75	70
P1108	–	10f. red	2·50	45
P1109	–	10f. brown	1·80	45
P 997	P 195	12f.30 green	75	70
P 998	–	14f.30 red	90	1·40
P1110	–	20f. green	1·00	25
P1111	–	30f. violet	1·00	30
P1112	–	40f. red	80	25
P1113	–	50f. blue	12·00	80
P 999	–	100f. blue	21·00	22·00

DESIGNS—As Type P **195**: 1f. to 9f.20, Platelayer; 10f. and 14f.30 to 50f. Railway porter; 24½ × 34½ mm: 100f. Electric train.

No. P1109 was for use as a railway parcels tax stamp.

1945. Inscribed "BELGIQUE-BELGIE" or vice-versa.

P1116A	P 216	3f. green	25	15
P1117A		5f. blue	25	15
P1118A		6f. red	25	15

P 224 Level Crossing

1947.

P1174	P 224	100f. green	6·25	35

P 230 Archer

1947.

P1193	P 230	8f. brown	1·00	40
P1194		10f. blue and black	1·00	25
P1195		12f. violet	1·50	30

1948. Surch.

P1229	P 230	9f. on 8f. brown	1·20	25
P1230		11f. on 10f. blue and black	1·20	30
P1231		13f.50 on 12f. violet	1·50	25

P 246 "Parcel Post"

1948.

P1250	P 246	9f. brown	7·00	30
P1251		11f. red	6·25	15
P1252		13f.50 black	10·50	35

P 254 Type 1 Locomotive, 1867 (dated 1862)

1949. Locomotives.

P1277	–	½f. brown	40	25
P1278	P 254	1f. red	50	25
P1279	–	2f. blue	80	20
P1280	–	3f. red (1884)	2·10	20
P1281	–	4f. green (1901)	1·30	20
P1282	–	5f. red (1902)	1·30	20
P1283	–	6f. purple (1904)	2·10	20
P1284	–	7f. green (1905)	3·25	20
P1285	–	8f. blue (1906)	4·00	20
P1286	–	9f. brown (1909)	5·00	20
P1287	–	10f. olive (1910)	7·00	20
P1288	–	10f. black and red (1905)	8·50	1·90
P1289	–	20f. orange (1920)	9·50	20
P1290	–	30f. blue (1928)	17·00	20
P1291	–	40f. red (1930)	31·00	20
P1292	–	50f. mauve (1935)	55·00	20
P1293	–	100f. red (1939)	90·00	35
P1294	–	300f. violet (1951)	£150	70

DESIGNS: 50c. Locomotive "Le Belge", 1835; 2f. Type 29 locomotive, 1875; 3f. Type 25 locomotive, 1884; 4f. Type 18 locomotive, 1901; 5f. Type 22 locomotive, 1902; 6f. Type 53 locomotive, 1904; 7f. Type 8 locomotive, 1905; 8f. Type 16 locomotive, 1906; 9f. Type 10 locomotive, 1909; 10f. (P1287) Type 36 locomotive, 1910; 10f. (P 1288) Type 38 locomotive, 1905; 20f. Type 38 locomotive, 1920; 30f. Type 48 locomotive, 1928; 40f. Type 5 locomotive, 1935; 50f. Type 1 Pacific locomotive, 1935; 100f. Type 12 locomotive, 1939; 300f. Two-car electric train, 1951.

The 300f. is larger (37½ × 25 mm).

1949. Electrification of Charleroi–Brussels Line. As Type **P254**.

P1296	60f. brown	23·00	25

DESIGN: 60f. Type 101 electric locomotive, 1945.

P 258 Loading Parcels

1950.

P1307	–	11f. orange	5·00	25
P1308	–	12f. purple	18·00	1·60
P1309	–	13f. green	5·75	20
P1310	–	15f. blue	13·50	25
P1311	P 258	16f. grey	5·00	20
P1312	–	17f. brown	6·50	25
P1313	P 258	18f. red	13·00	95
P1314	–	20f. orange	7·00	30

DESIGNS—HORIZ: 11, 12, 17f. Dispatch counter; 13, 15f. Sorting compartment.

P 271 Mercury

1951. 25th Anniv of National Belgian Railway Society.

P1375	P 271	25f. blue	14·00	11·00

1953. Nos. P1307, P1310 and P1313 surch.

P1442	–	13f. on 15f. blue	60·00	4·00
P1443	–	17f. on 11f. orange	28·00	95
P1444	P 258	20f. on 18f. red	15·00	3·00

P 288 Electric Train and Brussels Skyline

1953. Inauguration of Nord-Midi Junction.

P1451	P 288	200f. green	£225	1·10
P1452		200f. green & brown	£250	4·00

P 291 Nord Station

P 292 Central Station

1953. Brussels Railway Stations.

P1485	P 291	1f. ochre	35	20
P1486		2f. black	50	15
P1487		3f. green	65	20
P1488		4f. orange	80	15
P1489		5f. brown	2·20	20
P1490	–	5f. brown	10·00	20
P1491	P 291	6f. purple	1·10	15
P1492		7f. green	1·10	15
P1493		8f. red	1·80	15
P1494		9f. blue	2·10	15
P1495	–	10f. green	2·50	15
P1496	–	10f. black	1·30	20
P1497	–	15f. red	12·50	50
P1498	–	20f. blue	4·00	15
P1498a	–	20f. green	2·00	40
P1499	–	30f. purple	6·50	15
P1500	–	40f. mauve	8·00	15
P1501	–	50f. mauve	9·25	15
P1501a	–	50f. blue	3·00	50
P1502	–	60f. violet	20·00	15
P1503	–	80f. purple	30·00	40
P1504	P 292	100f. green	18·00	45
P1505		200f. blue	85·00	1·40
P1506		300f. mauve	£150	1·90

DESIGNS—VERT: 5f. (P1490), 10f. (P1496), 15, 20f. (P1498a), 50f. (P1501a), Congress Station; 10f. (P1495), 20f. (P1498) to 50f. (P1501), Midi Station. HORIZ: 60, 80f. Chapelle Station.

Nos. P1490, P1496/7, P1498a and P1501a were for use as railway parcels tax stamps.

P 295 Electric Train Type 121 and Nord Station, Brussels

P 326 Mercury and Railway Winged Wheel

1953.

P1517 **P 295** 13f. brown . . . . . 20·00 25
P1518 18f. blue . . . . . . 20·00 25
P1519 21f. mauve . . . . . 20·00 45

1956. Surch in figures.

P1585 **P 295** 14f. on 13f. brown 7·00 15
P1586 19f. on 18f. blue . . 7·00 15
P1587 22f. on 21f. mauve 7·00 20

1957.

P1600 **P 326** 14f. green . . . . . 7·00 20
P1601 19f. sepia . . . . . 7·00 20
P1602 22f. red . . . . . . 7·00 25

1959. Surch **20 F**.

P1678 **P 326** 20f. on 19f. sepia . . 25·00 25
P1679 20f. on 22f. red . . . 25·00 80

P 357 Brussels Nord Station, 1861–1954

1959.

P1695 **P 357** 20f. olive . . . . . . 11·50 15
P1696 – 24f. red . . . . . . 5·00 40
P1697 – 26f. blue . . . . . . 5·00 1·90
P1698 – 28f. purple . . . . . 5·00 1·40

DESIGNS—VERT: 24f. Brussels Midi station, 1869–1949. HORIZ: 26f. Antwerp Central station, 1905; 28f. Ghent St. Pieter's station.

P 368 Congress Seal, Type 202 Diesel and Type 125 Electric Locomotives

1960. 75th Anniv of Int Railway Congress Assn.

P1722 **P 368** 20f. red . . . . . . 45·00 29·00
P1723 50f. blue . . . . . . 45·00 29·00
P1724 60f. purple . . . . . 45·00 29·00
P1725 70f. green . . . . . 45·00 29·00

1961. Nos. P1695/8 surch.

P1787 **P 357** 24f. on 20f. olive . . 50·00 30
P1788 – 26f. on 24f. red . . . 5·00 25
P1789 – 28f. on 26f. blue . . 5·00 25
P1790 – 35f. on 28f. purple 5·00 30

P 477 Arlon Station

1967.

P2017 **P 477** 25f. ochre . . . . . 8·00 40
P2018 30f. green . . . . . 2·30 40
P2019 35f. blue . . . . . . 2·50 40
P2020 40f. red . . . . . . 20·00 40

P 488 Type 122 Electric Train

1968.

P2047 **P 488** 1f. bistre 25 15
P2048 2f. green 25 20
P2049 3f. green 45 15
P2050 4f. orange 45 20
P2051 5f. brown 50 20
P2052 6f. plum 45 15
P2053 7f. green 50 15
P2054 8f. red 65 15
P2055 9f. blue . . . . . . 1·10 15
P2056 – 10f. green . . . . . 2·30 15
P2057 – 20f. blue . . . . . 1·30 45
P2058 – 30f. lilac . . . . . 4·50 15
P2059 – 40f. violet . . . . . 5·00 15
P2060 – 50f. purple . . . . 6·00 20
P2061 – 60f. violet . . . . . 8·50 30
P2062 – 70f. brown . . . . 14·00 45
P2063 – 80f. purple . . . . 6·00 25
P2063a – 90f. green . . . . . 6·00 50
P2064 – 100f. green . . . . 10·00 30
P2065 – 200f. violet . . . . 13·00 60
P2066 – 300f. mauve . . . . 23·00 1·30
P2067 – 500f. yellow . . . . 35·00 2·30

DESIGNS: 10f. to 40f. Type 126 electric train; 50, 60, 70, 80, 90f. Type 160 electric train; 100, 200, 300f. Type 205 diesel-electric train; 500f. Type 210 diesel-electric train.

1970. Surch.

P2180 **P 477** 37f. on 25f. ochre . . 55·00 6·75
P2181 48f. on 35f. blue . . 5·00 4·75
P2182 53f. on 40f. red . . . 5·00 4·75

P 551 Ostend Station

1971. Figures of value in black.

P2192 **P 551** 32f. ochre . . . . . 1·80 1·20
P2193 37f. grey . . . . . . 12·50 12·00
P2194 42f. blue . . . . . . 2·00 1·50
P2195 44f. mauve . . . . . 2·00 1·50
P2196 46f. violet . . . . . 2·30 1·50
P2197 50f. red . . . . . . 2·00 1·50
P2198 52f. brown . . . . . 12·50 12·00
P2199 54f. green . . . . . 5·50 4·00
P2200 61f. blue . . . . . . 2·50 2·20

1972. Nos. P2192/5 and P2198/200 surch in figures.

P2256 **P 551** 34f. on 32f. ochre . . 2·30 1·00
P2257 40f. on 37f. grey . . 2·30 1·00
P2258 47f. on 44f. mauve . . 2·50 1·00
P2259 53f. on 42f. blue . . 3·00 1·00
P2260 56f. on 52f. brown . . 2·75 1·00
P2261 59f. on 54f. green . . 3·00 1·00
P2262 66f. on 61f. blue . . . 3·25 1·00

P 575 Emblems within Bogie Wheels

1972. 50th Anniv of Int Railways Union (U.I.C.).

P2266 **P 575** 100f. black, red and green . . . . . . 7·50 2·00

See also No. 2274.

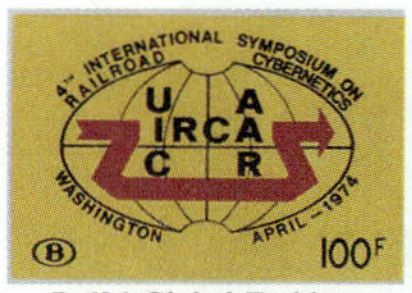

P 624 Global Emblem

1974. 4th International Symposium of Railway Cybernetics, Washington.

P2353 **P 624** 100f. black, red and yellow . . . . . . 6·50 2·00

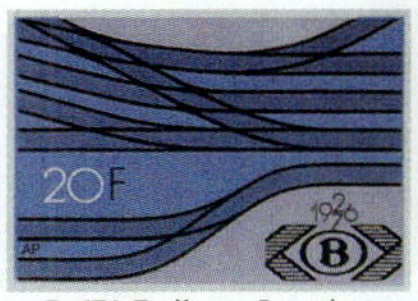

P 671 Railway Junction

P 698 Railway Station at Night

P 677 Modern Electric Train

1976.

P2431 **P 671** 20f. black, bl & lilac 1·30 1·90
P2432 50f. black, green and turquoise . . . . 2·50 1·90
P2433 100f. black & orange 4·50 2·50
P2434 150f. black, mauve and deep mauve 7·00 2·50

1976. 50th Anniv of National Belgian Railway Company.

P2445 **P 677** 6f.50 multicoloured 50 15

1977.

P2505 **P 698** 1000f. mult . . . . . 50·00 19·00

P 753 Goods Wagon, Type 2216 A8

1980. Values in black.

P2615 **P 753** 1f. ochre 15 15
P2616 2f. red 15 15
P2617 3f. blue 15 15
P2618 4f. blue 15 15
P2619 5f. brown 20 15
P2620 6f. orange 30 20
P2621 7f. violet 35 20
P2622 8f. black 35 20
P2623 9f. green 45 35
P2624 – 10f. brown 45 35
P2625 – 20f. blue . . . . . 1·10 40
P2626 – 30f. ochre . . . . . 1·90 35
P2627 – 40f. mauve . . . . 2·30 35
P2628 – 50f. purple . . . . 2·75 50
P2629 – 60f. olive . . . . . 3·25 65
P2630 – 70f. blue . . . . . 4·00 3·00
P2631 – 80f. purple . . . . 4·50 75
P2632 – 90f. mauve . . . . 5·00 3·00
P2633 – 100f. red . . . . . 5·50 1·20
P2634 – 200f. brown . . . . 11·00 1·50
P2635 – 300f. olive . . . . 18·00 2·10
P2636 – 500f. purple . . . . 30·00 4·50

DESIGNS: 10f. to 40f. Packet wagon, Type 3614 A5; 50f. to 90f. Self-discharging wagon, Type 1000 D; 100f. to 500f. Tanker wagon, Type 2000 G.

P 833 Electric Train entering Station

1985. 150th Anniv of Belgian Railways. Paintings by P. Delvaux. Multicoloured.

P2824 250f. Type **P 833** . . . . 15·00 6·50
P2825 500f. Electric trains in station . . . . 30·00 11·50

RAILWAY PARCEL TAX STAMPS

1940. As Nos. P399 and P404 but colours changed.

P876 **P 84** 5f. brown 50 45
P877 10f. black . . . . . . 5·50 5·50

P 779 Electric Locomotive at Station

P 877 Buildings and Electric Locomotive

1982.

P2703 **P 779** 10f. red & black . . 1·50 30
P2704 20f. green & blk . . 1·80 1·30
P2705 50f. brown & blk . . 3·75 75
P2706 100f. blue & blk . . 6·00 95

1987.

P2923 **P 877** 10f. red 85 60
P2924 20f. green . . . . . 1·30 1·20
P2925 50f. brown . . . . . 3·75 1·60
P2926 100f. purple . . . . 7·00 3·25
P2927 150f. brown . . . . 10·00 4·00

RAILWAY OFFICIAL STAMPS

For use on the official mail of the Railway Company.

1929. Stamps of 1922 optd with winged wheel.

O481 **81** 5c. slate 25 20
O482 10c. green 30 25
O483 35c. green 35 25
O484 60c. olive 45 20
O485 1f.50 blue . . . . . 16·00 8·25
O486 1f.75 blue . . . . . 2·00 85

1929. Stamps of 1929 optd with winged wheel.

O534 **104** 5c. green 20 10
O535 10c. bistre 20 20
O536 25c. red . . . . . . 2·10 45
O537 35c. green 65 20
O538 40c. purple 65 20
O539 50c. blue 35 20
O540 60c. mauve . . . . 18·00 9·00
O541 70c. brown . . . . 4·00 1·10
O542 75c. blue . . . . . 6·50 95

1932. Stamps of 1931–34 optd with winged wheel.

O620 **126** 10c. green 70 50
O677 **127** 35c. green . . . . . 12·50 50
O678 **142** 70c. green . . . . . 4·50 35
O679 **121** 75c. brown . . . . . 2·00 40

1936. Stamps of 1936 optd with winged wheel.

O721 **152** 10c. olive 15 15
O722 35c. green 10 10
O723 40c. lilac 20 20
O724 50c. blue 45 45
O725 **153** 70c. brown . . . . 3·75 3·75
O726 75c. olive 50 30

1941. Optd **B** in oval frame.

O948 **152** 10c. green 15 15
O949 40c. lilac 15 15
O950 50c. blue 15 15
O951 **153** 1f. red (No. 747) . . 20 15
O952a 1f. red (No. 748) . . 20 15
O953 2f.25 black 40 45
O954 **155** 2f.25 violet 30 35

1942. Nos. O722, O725 and O726 surch.

O983 **152** 10c. on 35c. green . . 15 15
O984 **153** 50c. on 70c. brown . . 15 15
O985 50c. on 75c. olive . . . 20 20

O 221

O 283

1946. Designs incorporating letter "B".

O1156 **O 221** 10c. green 15 15
O1157 20c. violet . . . . . 2·75 85
O1158 50c. blue 15 15
O1159 65c. purple . . . . 3·50 95
O1160 75c. mauve 20 20
O1161 90c. violet . . . . . 4·00 30
O1240 – 1f.35 brn (as 1219) 2·50 45
O1241 – 1f.75 green (as 1220) 5·50 45
O1242 **239** 3f. purple . . . . . 27·00 7·75
O1243 **240** 3f.15 blue . . . . . 11·00 6·25
O1244 4f. blue . . . . . . 20·00 8·75

1952.

O1424 **O 283** 10c. orange 35 10
O1425 20c. red . . . . . . 3·25 60
O1426 30c. green . . . . . 1·60 40
O1427 40c. brown 35 10
O1428 50c. blue 25 10
O1429 60c. mauve 70 20
O1430 65c. purple . . . . 28·00 22·00
O1431 80c. green . . . . . 4·75 1·10
O1432 90c. blue . . . . . 7·00 1·20
O1433 1f. red 50 15
O1433a 1f.50 grey 15 15
O1434 2f.50 brown 20 15

1954. As T **289** (King Baudouin) but with letter "B" incorporated in design.

O1523 1f.50 black 40 20
O1524 2f. red . . . . 38·00 40
O1525 2f. green 40 20
O1526 2f.50 brown . . . . 30·00 75
O1527 3f. mauve . . . . 1·80 20
O1528 3f.50 green 70 20
O1529 4f. blue . . . . 1·00 30
O1530 6f. red . . . . 1·80 50

1971. As Nos. 2209/20 but with letter "B" incorporated in design.

O2224 3f. green . . . . 1·00 75
O2225 3f.50 brown 25 10
O2226 4f. blue . . . . 1·20 50
O2227 4f.50 purple 25 20
O2228 4f.50 blue 30 20
O2229 5f. violet 30 20
O2230 6f. red 30 15
O2231 6f.50 violet 45 25
O2232a 7f. red 30 15
O2233 8f. black 45 25
O2233a 9f. brown 50 20
O2234 10f. red 50 25
O2235 15f. violet 65 35
O2236 25f. purple . . . . . . 1·30 70
O2237 30f. brown . . . . . . 1·50 75

1977. As T **684** but with letter "B" incorporated in design.

O2455 50c. brown 15 15
O2456 1f. mauve 15 15
O2457 2f. orange 20 15
O2458 4f. brown 25 15
O2459 5f. green 25 25

BELIZE Pt. 1

British Honduras was renamed Belize on 1 June 1973 and the country became independent within the Commonwealth on 21 September 1981.

100 cents = 1 dollar.

1973. Nos. 256/66 and 277/8 of British Honduras optd **BELIZE** and two stars.

347 – ½c. multicoloured 10 20
348 **63** 1c. black, brown and yellow 10 20
349 – 2c. black, green and yellow 10 20
350 – 3c. black, brown and lilac 10 10
351 – 4c. multicoloured 10 20
352 – 5c. black and red 10 20
353 – 10c. multicoloured 15 15
354 – 15c. multicoloured 20 20
355 – 25c. multicoloured 35 35
356 – 50c. multicoloured 65 75
357 – $1 multicoloured . . . . . 75 1·50
358 – $2 multicoloured . . . . . 1·25 2·75
359 – $5 multicoloured . . . . . 1·40 4·75

1973. Royal Wedding. As T **47** of Anguilla. Background colours given. Multicoloured.

360 26c. blue 15 10
361 50c. brown 15 20

82 Mozambique Mouthbrooder

1974. As Nos. 256/66 and 276/78 of British Honduras. Multicoloured.
362 ½c. Type **82** 10 50
363 1c. Spotted jewfish 10 30
364 2c. White-lipped peccary ("Waree") 10 30
365 3c. Misty grouper 10 10
366 4c. Collared anteater 10 30
367 5c. Bonefish 10 30
368 10c. Paca ("Gibnut") 15 15
369 15c. Dolphin 20 20
370 25c. Kinkajou ("Night Walker") 35 35
371 50c. Mutton snapper 60 70
372 $1 Tayra ("Bush Dog") 75 1·50
373 $2 Great barracuda 1·25 2·50
374 $5 Puma 1·50 5·50

83 Deer

1974. Mayan Artefacts (1st series). Pottery Motifs. Multicoloured.
375 3c. Type **83** 10 10
376 6c. Jaguar deity 10 10
377 16c. Sea monster 15 10
378 26c. Cormorant 25 10
379 50c. Scarlet macaw 40 40
See also Nos. 398/402.

84 "Parides arcas"

1974. Butterflies of Belize. Multicoloured.
380 ½c. Type **84** 1·00 4·50
381 1c. "Evenus regalis" 1·00 1·75
405 2c. "Colobura dirce" 50 70
406 3c. "Catonephele numilia" 1·25 70
407 4c. "Battus belus" 3·00 30
408 5c. "Callicore patelina" 3·25 30
386 10c. "Diaethria astala" 1·50 70
410 15c. "Nessaea aglaura" 75 70
388 16c. "Prepona pseudojoiceyi" 5·00 7·50
412 25c. "Papilio thoas" 6·50 40
390 26c. "Hamadryas arethusa" 2·00 4·25
413 35c. Type **84** 13·00 4·50
391 50c. "Panthiades bathildis" 3·25 65
392 $1 "Caligo uranus" 6·50 7·00
393 $2 "Heliconius sapho" 4·00 1·25
394 $5 "Eurytides philolaus" 5·50 6·00
395 $10 "Philaethria dido" 10·00 4·00

85 Churchill when Prime Minister, and Coronation Scene

1974. Birth Centenary of Sir Winston Churchill. Multicoloured.
396 50c. Type **85** 20 20
397 $1 Churchill in stetson, and Williamsburg Liberty Bell 30 30

86 The Actun Balam Vase

1975. Mayan Artefacts (2nd series). Multicoloured.
398 3c. Type **86** 10 10
399 6c. Seated figure 10 10
400 16c. Costumed priest 25 15
401 26c. Head with headdress 35 20
402 50c. Layman and priest 45 1·75

87 Musicians

1975. Christmas. Multicoloured.
435 6c. Type **87** 10 10
436 26c. Children and "crib" 20 10
437 50c. Dancer and drummers (vert) 30 55
438 $1 Family and map (vert) 55 1·60

88 William Wrigley Jr. and Chicle Tapping

1976. Bicent of American Revolution. Mult.
439 10c. Type **88** 10 10
440 35c. Charles Lindbergh 20 40
441 $1 J. L. Stephens (archaeologist) 50 1·50

89 Cycling

1976. Olympic Games, Montreal. Multicoloured.
442 35c. Type **89** 15 10
443 45c. Running 20 15
444 $1 Shooting 35 1·40

1976. No. 390 surch **20c.**
445 20c. on 26c. multicoloured 1·50 1·75

1976. West Indian Victory in World Cricket Cup. As Nos. 559/60 of Barbados.
446 35c. multicoloured 40 50
447 $1 black and purple 60 2·00

1976. No. 426 surch **5c.**
448 5c. on 15c. multicoloured 1·10 2·75

92 Queen and Bishops

1977. Silver Jubilee. Multicoloured.
449 10c. Royal Visit, 1975 10 10
450 35c. Queen and Rose Window 15 15
451 $2 Type **92** 45 90

93 Red-capped Manakin **94** Laboratory Workers

1977. Birds (1st series). Multicoloured.
452 8c. Type **93** 75 55
453 10c. Hooded oriole 90 30
454 25c. Blue-crowned motmot 1·25 55
455 35c. Slaty-breasted tinamou 1·50 75
456 45c. Ocellated turkey 1·75 1·25
457 $1 White hawk 3·00 5·50
MS458 110 × 133 mm. Nos. 452/7 8·25 11·00
See also Nos. 467/78, 488/94 and 561/7.

1977. 75th Anniv of Pan-American Health Organization. Multicoloured.
459 35c. Type **94** 20 20
460 $1 Mobile medical unit 40 65
MS461 126 × 95 mm. Nos. 459/60 85 1·40

1978. Nos. 386 and 413 optd **BELIZE DEFENCE FORCE 1ST JANUARY 1978.**
462 10c. "Diaethria astala" 75 1·50
463 35c. Type **84** 1·50 2·25

96 White Lion of Mortimer **97** "Russelia sarmentosa"

1978. 25th Anniv of Coronation.
464 **96** 75c. brown, red and silver 20 30
465 – 75c. multicoloured 20 30
466 – 75c. brown, red and silver 20 30
DESIGNS: No. 465, Queen Elizabeth II; 466, Jaguar (Maya god of Day and Night).

1978. Birds (2nd series). As T **93**. Multicoloured.
467 10c. White-capped parrot("White-crowned Parrot") 55 30
468 25c. Crimson-collared tanager 80 45
469 35c. Black-headed trogon ("Citreoline Trogon") 1·10 55
470 45c. American finfoot ("Sungrebe") 1·25 1·75
471 50c. Muscovy duck 1·40 2·50
472 $1 King vulture 2·00 6·50
MS473 111 × 133 mm. Nos. 467/72 8·00 11·00

1978. Christmas. Wild Flowers and Ferns. Mult.
474 10c. Type **97** 15 10
475 15c. "Lygodium polymorphum" 20 15
476 35c. "Heliconia aurantiaca" 20 20
477 45c. "Adiantum tetraphyllum" 20 40
478 50c. "Angelonia ciliaris" 35 50
479 $1 "Thelypteris obliterata" 50 1·25

98 Fairchild Monoplane of Internal Airmail Service, 1937

1979. Centenary of U.P.U. Membership. Mult.
480 5c. Type **98** 25 30
481 10c. "Heron H" (mail boat), 1949 25 10
482 35c. Internal mail service, 1920 (canoe) 25 20
483 45c. Steam Creek Railway mail, 1910 45 55
484 50c. Mounted mail courier, 1882 45 60
485 $1 "Eagle" (mail boat), 1856 80 2·50

1979. No. 413 surch **15c.**
487 **84** 15c. on 35c. multicoloured 2·25 1·75

1979. Birds (3rd series). As T **93**. Multicoloured.
488 10c. Boat-billed heron 65 30
489 25c. Grey-necked wood rail 90 30
490 35c. Lineated woodpecker 1·10 55
491 45c. Blue-grey tanager 1·25 70
492 50c. Laughing falcon 1·25 1·25
493 $1 Long-tailed hermit 1·60 4·50
MS494 113 × 136 mm. Nos. 488/93 4·75 6·00

101 Paslow Building, Belize G.P.O.

1979. 25th Anniv of Coronation. Multicoloured.
495 25c. Type **101** 1·50 10
496 50c. Houses of Parliament 2·00 10
497 75c. Coronation State Coach 2·50 15
498 $1 Queen on horseback (vert) 3·25 20
499 $2 Prince of Wales (vert) 3·25 35
500 $3 Queen and Duke of Edinburgh (vert) 3·25 35
501 $4 Portrait of Queen (vert) 3·25 40
502 $5 St. Edward's Crown (vert) 3·50 40
MS503 Two sheets, both 126 × 95 mm: (a) $5 Princess Anne on horseback at Montreal Olympics (vert); $10 Queen at Montreal Olympics (vert). (b) $15 As Type **101** Set of 2 sheets 25·00

102 Mortimer and Vaughan "Safety" Airplane, 1910

1979. Death Centenary of Sir Rowland Hill. 60th Anniv of I.C.A.O. (International Civil Aviation Organization), previously Int Commission for Air Navigation. Multicoloured.
504 4c. Type **102** 50 10
505 25c. Boeing 720 1·50 20
506 50c. Concorde 4·25 30
507 75c. Handley Page H.P.18 W.8b (1922) 2·00 30
508 $1 Avro Type F (1912) 2·00 30
509 $1.50 Samuel Cody's biplane (1910) 2·75 30
510 $2 A.V. Roe Triplane I (1909) 2·75 40
511 $3 Santos Dumont's biplane "14 bis" (1906) 2·75 45
512 $4 Wright Type A 3·00 65
MS513 Two sheets: (a) 115 × 95 mm. $5 Dunne D-5 (1910), $5 G.B. 1969 Concorde stamp; (b) 130 × 95 mm. $10 Boeing 720 (different) Set of 2 sheets 21·00

103 Handball

1979. Olympic Games, Moscow (1980). Mult.
514 25c. Type **103** 45 10
515 50c. Weightlifting 65 10
516 75c. Athletics 90 15
517 $1 Football 1·25 20
518 $2 Yachting 1·75 25
519 $3 Swimming 2·00 30
520 $4 Boxing 2·50 30
521 $5 Cycling 10·00 90
MS522 Two sheets: (a) 126 × 92 mm. $5 Athletics (different), $10 Boxing (different); (b) 92 × 126 mm. $15 As $5 Set of 2 sheets 16·00

104 Olympic Torch

1979. Winter Olympic Games, Lake Placid (1980). Multicoloured.
523 25c. Type **104** 20 10
524 50c. Giant slalom 45 15
525 75c. Figure-skating 65 15
526 $1 Downhill skiing 80 15
527 $2 Speed-skating 1·60 20
528 $3 Cross-country skiing 2·50 30
529 $4 Shooting 3·00 40
530 $5 Gold, Silver and Bronze medals 3·50 45
MS531 Two sheets: (a) 127 × 90 mm. $5 Lighting the Olympic Flame, $10 Gold, Silver and Bronze medals (different); (b) 90 × 127 mm. $15 Olympic Torch (different) Set of 2 sheets 20·00

105 Measled Cowrie

1980. Shells. Multicoloured.
532 1c. Type **105** 65 10
533 2c. Callico clam 80 10
534 3c. Altantic turkey wing (vert) 90 10
535 4c. Leafy jewel box (vert) 90 10
536 5c. Trochlear latirus 90 10
537 10c. Alphabet cone (vert) 1·25 10
538 15c. Cabrits murex (vert) 1·75 10

539 20c. Stiff pen shell . . . . . 1·75 10
540 25c. Little knobbed scallop (vert) . . . . 1·75 10
541 35c. Glory of the Atlantic cone (vert) . . . . 2·00 10
542 45c. Sunrise tellin (vert) . . . 2·25 10
543 50c. "Leucozonia nassa leucozonalis" . . . . . . 2·25 10
544 85c. Triangular typhis . . . 3·50 10
545 $1 Queen or pink conch (vert) . . . . 3·75 10
546 $2 Rooster-tail conch (vert) 6·00 30
547 $5 True tulip . . . . 8·50 50
548 $10 Star arene . . . . 10·00 90
MS549 Two sheets, each 125 × 90 mm. (a) Nos. 544 and 547. (b) Nos. 546 and 548 . . 40·00 15·00

106 Girl and Flower Arrangement

108 Jabiru

1980. International Year of the Child (1st issue). Multicoloured.
550 25c. Type **106** 45 10
551 50c. Boy holding football . . 70 10
552 75c. Boy with butterfly . . . 1·00 10
553 $1 Girl holding doll . . . . 1·00 10
554 $1.50 Boy carrying basket of fruit . . . . 1·50 15
555 $2 Boy holding reticulated cowrie-helmet shell . . . . 1·75 20
556 $3 Girl holding posy . . . . 2·25 25
557 $4 Boy and girl wrapped in blanket . . . . 2·50 30
MS558 130 × 95 mm. $5 Three children of different races. $5 "Madonna with Cat" (A. Dürer) (each 35 × 53 mm). . . . . . . 9·00
MS559 111 × 151 mm. $10 Children and Christmas tree (73 × 110 mm). 9·00
See also Nos. 583/91.

1980. No. 412 surch **10c**.
560 10c. on 25c. "Papilio thoas" 1·25 1·25

1980. Birds (4th series). Multicoloured.
561 10c. Type **108** . . . . 7·00 2·75
562 25c. Barred antshrike . . . . 8·00 2·75
563 35c. Northern royal flycatcher ("Royal Flycatcher") . . . . 8·00 2·75
564 45c. White-necked puffbird 8·00 3·00
565 50c. Ornate hawk-eagle . . . 8·00 3·00
566 $1 Golden-masked tanager 8·50 3·75
MS567 85 × 90 mm. $2 Type **108**, $3 As $1 . . . . 32·00 18·00

109 Speed Skating

111 Witch in Sky

1980. Winter Olympic Games, Lake Placid. Medal Winners. Multicoloured.
568 25c. Type **109** 30 15
569 50c. Ice-hockey 50 15
570 75c. Figure-skating 60 15
571 $1 Alpine-skiing 85 15
572 $1.50 Giant slalom (women) 1·25 25
573 $2 Speed-skating (women) . . 1·50 30
574 $3 Cross-country skiing . . . 2·25 40
575 $5 Giant slalom . . . . . . 3·50 55
MS576 Two sheets: (a) 126 × 91 mm. $5 Type **109**; $10 Type **109**; (b) 91 × 126 mm. $10 As 75 c. Set of 2 sheets . . . . 16·00

1980. "ESPAMER" International Stamp Exhibition, Madrid. Nos. 560/5 optd **BELIZE ESPAMER '80 MADRID 3-12 OCT 1980** and emblem (Nos. 577/9) or surch also.
577 10c. Type **107** . . . . 7·50 2·75
578 25c. Barred antshrike . . . . 8·00 3·00
579 35c. Northern royal flycatcher 8·00 3·00
580 40c. on 45c. White-necked puffbird . . . . 8·50 3·25
581 40c. on 50c. Ornate hawk eagle . . . . 8·50 3·25
582 40c. on $1 Golden-masked tanager . . . . 9·00 3·25

1980. International Year of the Child (2nd issue). "Sleeping Beauty".
583 **111** 25c. multicoloured . . . . 2·25 15
584 – 40c. multicoloured . . . . 2·50 15
585 – 50c. multicoloured . . . . 2·75 15
586 – 75c. multicoloured . . . . 3·00 20
587 – $1 multicoloured . . . . 3·00 25
588 – $1.50 multicoloured . . . 3·50 40
589 – $3 multicoloured . . . . 4·50 50
590 – $4 multicoloured . . . . 4·50 55
MS591 Two sheets: (a) 82 × 110 mm. $8 "Paumgartner Altar-piece" (Dürer); (b) 110 × 82 mm. $5 Marriage ceremony, $5 Sleeping Beauty and Prince on horseback Set of 2 sheets . . . 22·00
DESIGNS: 40c. to $4, Illustrations from the story.

112 H.M. Queen Elizabeth the Queen Mother

1980. 80th Birthday of H.M. Queen Elizabeth the Queen Mother.
592 **112** $1 multicoloured . . . . 3·00 65
MS593 82 × 110 mm, $5 As Type **112** (41 × 32 mm) . . . . 14·00 4·75

113 The Annunciation

1980. Christmas. Multicoloured.
594 25c. Type **113** 65 10
595 50c. Bethlehem . . . . 1·25 10
596 75c. The Holy Family . . . 1·50 10
597 $1 The Nativity . . . . . . 1·60 10
598 $1.50 The Flight into Egypt 1·75 15
599 $2 Shepherds following the Star . . . . 2·00 20
600 $3 Virgin, Child and Angel 2·25 25
601 $4 Adoration of the Kings 2·25 30
MS602 Two sheets, each 82 × 111 mm: (a) $5 As $1: (b) $10 As $3 Set of 2 sheets . . . . . 14·00

1981. "WIPA" International Stamp Exhibition, Vienna. Nos. 598 and 601 surch.
603 $1 on $1.50 The Flight into Egypt . . . . 9·00 1·90
604 $2 on $4 Adoration of the Kings . . . . 10·00 2·75
MS605 82 × 111 mm. $2 on $10 Virgin, Child and Angel . . . 10·00 4·50

115 Paul Harris (founder)

1981. 75th Anniv of Rotary International. Mult.
606 25c. Type **115** . . . . 2·50 25
607 50c. Emblems of Rotary activities . . . . 3·00 35
608 $1 75th Anniversary emblem 3·50 65
609 $1.50 Educational scholarship programme (horiz) . . . 4·25 1·00
610 $2 "Project Hippocrates" . . 4·75 1·40
611 $3 Emblems . . . . 6·50 2·00
612 $5 Emblems and handshake (horiz) . . . . 7·50 3·25
MS613 Two sheets: (a) 95 × 130 mm. $10 As 50c. (b) 130 × 95 mm, $5 As $1, $10 As $2 Set of 2 sheets 38·00

116 Coat of Arms of Prince of Wales

118 Athletics

1981. Royal Wedding. Mult. (a) Size 22 × 38 mm.
614 50c. Type **116** 45 50
615 $1 Prince Charles in military uniform 80 90
616 $1.50 Royal couple . . . . . 1·25 1·50

(b) Size 25 × 42 mm, with gold borders.
617 50c. Type **116** 45 30
618 $1 As No. 615 . . . . 80 50
619 $1.50 As No. 616 . . . . . 1·25 70
MS620 145 × 85 mm. $3 × 3 As Nos 614/16, but 30 × 47 mm. P 14 2·50 4·25

1981. No. 538 surch **10c**.
621 10c. on 15c. "Murex cabritii" 3·50 3·75

1981. History of the Olympics. Multicoloured.
622 85c. Type **118** . . . . 2·50 30
623 $1 Cycling . . . . 9·00 50
624 $1.50 Boxing . . . . 3·25 50
625 $2 1984 Games–Los Angeles and Sarajevo . . . . . . 4·25 50
626 $3 Baron de Coubertin . . . 5·00 60
627 $5 Olympic Flame . . . . . 6·00 70
MS628 Two sheets, each 175 × 123 mm: (a) $5 As $3, $10 As $5 (each 35 × 53 mm). P13½; (b) $15 As $2 (45 × 67 mm). P 14½. Set of 2 sheets . . . . 45·00

1981. Independence Commemoration (1st issue). Optd **Independence 21 Sept., 1981**. (a) On Nos. 532/44 and 546/8.
629 1c. Type **105** . . . . 1·00 10
630 2c. Callico clam . . . . . . 1·00 10
631 3c. Atlantic turkey wing (vert) . . . . 1·00 10
632 4c. Leafy jewel box (vert) . . 1·00 10
633 5c. Trochlear latirus . . . . 1·25 10
634 10c. Alphabet cone (vert) . . 1·50 10
635 15c. Cabrits murex (vert) . . 2·25 10
636 20c. Stiff pen shell . . . . . 2·25 15
637 25c. Little knobbed scallop (vert) . . . . 2·50 25
638 35c. Glory of the Atlantic cone . . . . 2·50 30
639 45c. Sunrise tellin (vert) . . . 3·00 40
640 50c. "Leucozonia nassa leucozonalis" . . . . . . 3·00 40
641 85c. Triangular typhis . . . 4·75 90
642 $2 Rooster-tail conch (vert) 9·00 2·50
643 $5 True tulip . . . . 11·00 5·50
644 $10 Star arene . . . . 13·00 9·50
MS645 Two sheets, each 126 × 91 mm; (a) Nos. 641 and 643; (b) Nos. 642 and 644 Set of 2 sheets . . . . 40·00

(b) On Nos. 606/12.
646 25c. Type **115** . . . . 2·75 25
647 50c. Emblems of Rotary activities . . . . 3·00 35
648 $1 75th Anniversary emblem 3·50 65
649 $1.50 Educational scholarship programme . . . . 4·25 1·25
650 $2 "Project Hippocrates" . . 5·00 1·60
651 $3 Emblems . . . . 7·00 2·50
652 $5 Emblems and hand-shake 8·00 3·75
MS653 Two sheets: (a) 95 × 130 mm. $10 As 50c.; (b) 130 × 95 mm. $5 As $1, $10 As $2 Set of 2 sheets 40·00
See also Nos. 657/63.

1981. "ESPAMER" International Stamp Exhibition, Buenos Aires. No. 609 surch **$1 ESPAMER 81 BUENOS AIRES 13-22 NOV** and emblem.
654 $1 on $1.50 Educational scholarship programme . . 11·00 3·00
MS655 95 × 130 mm. $1 on $5 75th anniversary emblem, $1 on $10 "Project Hippocrates" . . . . 16·00 8·00

(**121**)

1981. "Philatelia 81" International Stamp Exhibition, Frankfurt. No. **MS**549 surch with T **121**.
MS656 Two sheets, each 125 × 90 mm: (a) $1 on 85c. "Tripterotyphis triangularis", $1 on $5 "Fasciolaria tulipa"; (b) $1 on $2 "Strombus gallus", $1 on $10 "Arene cruentata" Set of 2 sheets . . . . 60·00

122 Black Orchid

1981. Independence Commemoration (2nd issue). Multicoloured.
657 10c. Belize Coat of Arms (horiz) . . . . 2·25 20
658 35c. Map of Belize . . . . . 5·00 40
659 50c. Type **122** . . . . 9·50 1·25
660 85c. Baird's tapir (horiz) . . 3·00 1·25
661 $1 Mahogany tree . . . . . 2·50 1·25
662 $2 Keel-billed toucan (horiz) 14·00 4·00
MS663 130 × 98 mm. $5 As 10c. 12·00 5·50

123 Uruguayan Footballer

1981. World Cup Football Championship, Spain (1st issue). Multicoloured.
664 10c. Type **123** . . . . 2·25 20
665 25c. Italian footballer . . . . 3·25 20
666 50c. German footballer . . . 4·00 45
667 $1 Brazilian footballer . . . 5·00 70
668 $1.50 Argentinian footballer 6·50 1·50
669 $2 English footballer . . . . 7·00 1·75
MS670 Two sheets: (a) 145 × 115 mm. $2 "SPAIN '82" logo; (b) 155 × 115 mm. $3 Footballer (46 × 76 mm) Set of 2 sheets . . . . 30·00 7·50
See also Nos. 721/7.

124 H.M.S. "Centurion" (frigate)

1981. Sailing Ships. Multicoloured.
671 10c. Type **124** . . . . 3·25 40
672 25c. "Madagascar" (1837) . . 4·75 50
673 35c. Brig "Whitby" (1838) . . 5·50 55
674 55c. "China" (1838) . . . . 6·00 85
675 85c. "Swiftsure" (1850) . . . 7·50 1·25
676 $2 "Windsor Castle" (1857) 11·00 3·00
MS677 110 × 87 mm. $5 Ships in battle . . . . 32·00 8·50

1982. "ESSEN '82" Int Stamp Exn, West Germany. Nos. 662 and 669 surch **$1 ESSEN 82**.
678 $1 on $2 Keel-billed toucan 10·00 2·50
679 $1 on $2 English footballer 10·00 2·50

126 Princess Diana

1982. 21st Birthday of Princess of Wales. (a) Size 22 × 38 mm.
680 **126** 50c. multicoloured . . . . 1·60 45
681 – $1 multicoloured . . . . 2·00 75
682 – $1.50 multicoloured . . . 2·00 1·50

(b) Size 25 × 43 mm.
683 **126** 50c. multicoloured . . . . 1·60 30
684 – $1 multicoloured . . . . 2·00 60
685 – $1.50 multicoloured . . . 2·00 1·10
MS686 145 × 85 mm. $3 × 3 As Nos. 680/2, but 30 × 47 mm. 2·75 3·00
DESIGNS: Portraits of Princess of Wales with different backgrounds.

127 Lighting Campfire

1982. 125th Birth Anniv of Lord Baden-Powell. Multicoloured.
687 10c. Type **127** . . . . 1·75 20
688 25c. Bird watching . . . . . 5·00 30
689 35c. Three scouts, one playing guitar . . . . . . 2·75 30
690 50c. Hiking . . . . 3·25 55
691 85c. Scouts with flag . . . . 4·50 1·00
692 $2 Saluting . . . . 5·00 2·50
MS693 Two sheets, each 85 × 115 mm: (a) $2 Scout with flag; (b) $3 Portrait of Lord Baden-Powell Set of 2 sheets 35·00 13·00

128 "Gorgonia ventalina"

1982. 1st Anniv of Independence. Marine Life. Multicoloured.

694	10c. Type **128**	2·25	20
695	35c. "Carpiuis corallinus"	3·50	20
696	50c. "Plexaura flexuasa"	4·00	45
697	85c. "Candylactis gigantea"	4·25	60
698	$1 "Stenopus hispidus"	5·50	90
699	$2 Sergeant major	6·50	1·60
MS700	130 × 98 mm. $5 "Schyllarides aequinoclialis"	29·00	10·00

1982. "BELGICA 82" International Stamp Exhibition, Brussels. Nos. 687/92 optd **BELGICA 82 INT. YEAR OF THE CHILD SIR ROWLAND HILL 1795 1879 Picasso CENTENARY OF BIRTH** and emblems.

701	10c. Type **127**	2·75	40
702	25c. Bird watching	7·00	1·25
703	35c. Three scouts, one playing guitar	3·75	1·00
704	50c. Hiking	4·25	1·50
705	85c. Scouts with flag	10·00	2·75
706	$2 Saluting	11·00	7·50

1982. Birth of Prince William of Wales (1st issue). Nos. 680/5 optd **BIRTH OF H.R.H. PRINCE WILLIAM ARTHUR PHILIP LOUIS 21ST JUNE 1982.** (a) Size 22 × 38 mm.

707	50c. multicoloured	45	45
708	$1 multicoloured	55	60
709	$1.50 multicoloured	75	85
	(b) Size 25 × 43 mm.		
710	50c. multicoloured	45	45
711	$1 multicoloured	55	60
712	$1.50 multicoloured	75	85

1982. Birth of Prince William of Wales (2nd issue). Nos. 614/19 optd **BIRTH OF H.R.H. PRINCE WILLIAM ARTHUR PHILIP LOUIS 21ST JUNE 1982.** (a) Size 22 × 38 mm.

714	50c. Type **116**	3·25	1·00
715	$1 Prince Charles in military uniform	6·00	2·00
716	$1.50 Royal couple	8·50	3·00
	(b) Size 25 × 42 mm.		
717	50c. Type **116**	50	50
718	$1 As No. 715	70	70
719	$1.50 As No. 716	1·10	1·10
MS720	145 × 85 mm. $3 × 3 As Nos. 714/16 but 30 × 47 mm	7·50	7·00

131 Scotland v New Zealand

1982. World Cup Football Championship, Spain (2nd issue). Multicoloured.

721	20c.+10c. Type **131**	2·75	1·50
722	30c.+15c. Scotland v New Zealand (different)	2·75	1·50
723	40c.+20c. Kuwait v France	3·00	1·50
724	60c.+50c. Italy v Brazil	3·50	1·75
725	$1+50c. France v Northern Ireland	4·25	2·00
726	$1.50+75c. Austria v Chile	5·00	2·50
MS727	Two sheets: (a) 91 × 137 mm. $1+50c. Germany v Italy (50 × 70 mm); (b) 122 × 116 mm. $2+$1 England v France (50 × 70 mm) Set of 2 sheets	20·00	9·50

133 Belize Cathedral

1983. Visit of Pope John Paul II.

729 **133**	50c. multicoloured	2·75	1·50
MS730	135 × 110 mm. $2.50, Pope John Paul II (30 × 47 mm.)	23·00	8·00

134 Map of Belize

1983. Commonwealth Day. Multicoloured.

731	35c. Type **134**	35	35
732	50c. "Maya Stella" from Lamanai Indian church (horiz)	40	50
733	85c. Supreme Court Building (horiz)	50	75
734	$2 University Centre, Belize (horiz)	85	2·50

1983. No. 658 surch **10c.**

735	10c. on 35c. Map of Belize	32·00	

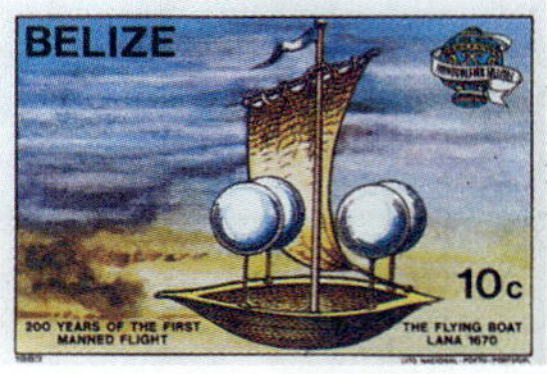

136 De Lana-Terzis "Aerial Ship", 1670

1983. Bicentenary of Manned Flight. Multicoloured.

736	10c. Type **136**	2·50	65
737	25c. De Gusmao's "La Passarole", 1709	3·25	70
738	50c. Guyton de Morveau's balloon with oars, 1784	3·50	1·00
739	85c. Airship	4·25	1·25
740	$1 Airship "Clement Bayard"	4·50	1·60
741	$1.50 Beardmore airship R-34	5·00	3·25
MS742	Two sheets: (a) 125 × 84 mm. $3 Charles Green's balloon "Royal Vauxhall"; (b) 115 × 128 mm. $3 Montgolfier balloon, 1783 (vert) Set of 2 sheets	30·00	6·00

1983. Nos. 662 and 699 surch **$1.25**.

743	$1.25 on $2 Keel-billed toucan	17·00	11·00
744	$1.25 on $2 Sergeant major	6·00	8·50

1983. No. 541 surch **10c**.

746	10c. on 35c. Glory of the Atlantic cone	38·00	

141 Altun Ha

1983. Maya Monuments. Multicoloured.

747	10c. Type **141**	10	10
748	15c. Xunantunich	10	10
749	75c. Cerros	30	40
750	$3 Lamanal	70	1·75
MS751	102 × 72 mm. $3 Xunantunich (different)	1·00	1·75

142 Belmopan Earth Station

1983. World Communications Year. Multicoloured.

752	10c. Type **142**	30	10
753	15c. "Telstar 2"	40	25
754	75c. U.P.U. logo	70	1·75
755	$2 M.V. "Heron H" mail service	1·25	4·50

143 Jaguar Cub

1983. The Jaguar. Multicoloured.

756	5c. Type **143**	30	75
757	10c. Adult jaguar	35	45
758	85c. Jaguar in river	1·40	3·00
759	$1 Jaguar on rock	1·50	3·25
MS760	102 × 72 mm. $3 Jaguar in tree (44 × 28 mm). P $13\frac{1}{2}$ × 14	1·50	2·50

144 Pope John Paul II

1983. Christmas.

761 **144**	10c. multicoloured	25	10
762	15c. multicoloured	25	10
763	75c. multicoloured	50	60
764	$2 multicoloured	80	1·40
MS765	102 × 72 mm. $3 multicoloured	1·50	4·00

145 Four-eyed Butterflyfish

1984. Marine Life from the Belize Coral Reef. Multicoloured.

766	1c. Type **145**	25	1·25
767	2c. Cushion star	30	1·00
768	3c. Flower coral	35	1·00
769	4c. Royal gramma ("Fairy basslet")	40	1·00
770	5c. Spanish hogfish	45	1·00
771	6c. Star-eyed hermit crab	45	1·25
772a	10c. Sea fans and fire sponge	50	35
773a	15c. Blue-headed wrasse	70	60
774a	25c. Blue-striped grunt	80	80
775a	50c. Coral crab	1·00	1·75
776a	60c. Tube sponge	1·00	1·75
777	75c. Brain coral	1·00	1·50
778	$1 Yellow-tailed snapper	1·00	1·25
779	$2 Common lettuce slug	1·00	55
780	$5 Three-spotted damselfish	1·25	70
781	$10 Rock beauty	1·50	1·10

1984. Visit of the Archbishop of Canterbury. Nos. 772 and 775 optd **VISIT OF THE LORD ARCHBISHOP OF CANTERBURY 8th-11th MARCH 1984.**

782	10c. Sea fans and fire sponge	1·00	50
783	50c. Coral crab	1·75	2·00

147 Shooting

1984. Olympic Games, Los Angeles. Multicoloured. (a) As T **147**.

784	25c. Type **147**	30	25
785	75c. Boxing	50	70
786	$1 Marathon	60	90
787	$2 Cycling	2·75	2·75
MS788	101 × 72 mm. $3 Statue of discus thrower	1·60	3·00
	(b) Similar designs to T **147** but Royal cypher replaced by Queen's Head.		
789	5c. Marathon	20	90
790	20c. Sprinting	25	90
791	25c. Shot-putting	25	90
792	$2 Olympic torch	35	1·25

148 British Honduras 1866 1s. Stamp

1984. "Ausipex" International Stamp Exhibition, Melbourne. Multicoloured.

793	15c. Type **148**	25	15
794	30c. British mail coach, 1784	35	25
795	65c. Sir Rowland Hill and Penny Black	65	65
796	75c. British Honduras railway locomotive, 1910	70	75
797	$2 Royal Exhibition Buildings, Melbourne (46 × 28 mm)	1·00	2·25
MS798	103 × 73 mm. $3 Australia 1932 Sydney Harbour Bridge 5s. and British Honduras 1866 1s. stamps (44 × 28 mm). P $13\frac{1}{2}$ × 14	1·10	2·00

149 Prince Albert

150 White-fronted Amazon ("White-fronted Parrot")

1984. 500th Anniv (1985) of British Royal House of Tudor. Multicoloured.

799	50c. Type **149**	25	45
800	50c. Queen Victoria	25	45
801	75c. King George VI	30	55
802	75c. Queen Elizabeth the Queen Mother	30	55
803	$1 Princess of Wales	40	75
804	$1 Prince of Wales	40	75
MS805	147 × 97 mm. $1.50, Prince Philip; $1.50, Queen Elizabeth II	1·25	2·00

1984. Parrots. Multicoloured.

806	$1 Type **150**	1·75	2·25
807	$1 White-capped parrot (horiz)	1·75	2·25
808	$1 Mealy amazon ("Mealy Parrot") (horiz)	1·75	2·25
809	$1 Red-lored amazon ("Red-lored Parrot")	1·75	2·25
MS810	102 × 73 mm. $3 Scarlet macaw	3·25	4·00

Nos. 806/9 were issued together, se-tenant, forming a composite design.

151 Effigy Censer, 1450 (Santa Rita Site)

153 White-tailed Kite

152 Governor-General inspecting Girl Guides

1984. Maya Artefacts. Multicoloured.

811	25c. Type **151**	30	25
812	75c. Vase, 675 (Actun Chapat)	60	80
813	$1 Tripod vase, 500 (Santa Rita site)	65	1·00
814	$2 Sun god Kinich Ahau, 600 (Altun Ha site)	90	2·50

1985. International Youth Year and 75th Anniv of Girl Guides Movement. Multicoloured.

815	25c. Type **152**	30	15
816	50c. Girl Guides camping	45	30
817	90c. Checking map on hike	60	45
818	$1.25 Students in laboratory	70	60
819	$2 Lady Baden-Powell (founder)	90	75

1985. Birth Bicentenary of John J. Audubon (ornithologist). Designs showing original paintings. Multicoloured.

820	10c. Type **153**	50	60
821	15c. Ruby-crowned kinglet ("Cuvier's Kinglet") (horiz)	50	60
822	25c. Painted bunting	60	60
822a	60c. As 25c.	24·00	9·00
823	75c. Belted kingfisher	60	1·40
824	$1 Common cardinal ("Northern Cardinal")	60	2·25
825	$3 Long-billed curlew (horiz)	1·00	3·00
MS826	139 × 99 mm. $5 "John James Audubon" (John Syme)	2·50	2·00

154 The Queen Mother with Princess Elizabeth, 1928

1985. Life and Times of Queen Elizabeth the Queen Mother. Multicoloured.
827 10c. Type **154** 10 10
828 15c. The Queen Mother, 1980 10 10
829 75c. Waving to the crowd, 1982 40 40
830 $5 Four generations of Royal Family at Prince William's Christening 1·50 2·75
MS831 Two sheets, each 138 × 98 mm. (a) $2 The Queen Mother with Prince Henry (from photo by Lord Snowdon) (38 × 50 mm): (b) $5 The Queen Mother, 1984 (38 × 50 mm) Set of 2 sheets 3·75 4·50

1985. Inauguration of New Government. Nos. 772/3 and 775 optd **INAUGURATION OF NEW GOVERNMENT – 21st. DECEMBER 1984**.
832 10c. Sea fans and fire sponge 1·50 60
833 15c. Blue-headed wrasse 1·50 60
834 50c. Coral crab 2·00 3·50

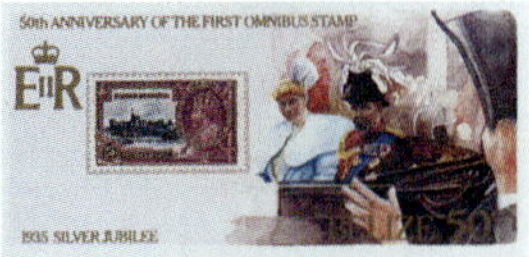

156 British Honduras 1935 Silver Jubilee 25c. stamp and King George V with Queen Mary in Carriage (½-size illustration)

1985. 50th Anniv of First Commonwealth Omnibus Issue. Designs showing British Honduras/Belize stamps. Multicoloured.
835 50c. Type **156** 55 85
836 50c. 1937 Coronation 3c., and King George VI and Queen Elizabeth in Coronation robes 55 85
837 50c. 1946 Victory 3c. and Victory celebrations 55 85
838 50c. 1948 Royal Silver Wedding 4c. and King George VI and Queen Elizabeth at Westminster Abbey service 55 85
839 50c. 1953 Coronation 4c. and Queen Elizabeth II in Coronation robes 55 85
840 50c. 1966 Churchill 25c., Sir Winston Churchill and fighter aircraft 55 85
841 50c. 1972 Royal Silver Wedding 50c. and 1948 Wedding photograph 55 85
842 50c. 1973 Royal Wedding 50c. and Princess Anne and Capt. Mark Phillips at their Wedding 55 85
843 50c. 1977 Silver Jubilee $2 and Queen Elizabeth II during tour 55 85
844 50c. 1978 25th anniversary of Coronation 75c. and Imperial Crown 55 85
MS845 138 × 98 mm. $5 Queen Elizabeth in Coronation robes (38 × 50 mm) 4·50 4·50

157 Mounted Postboy and Early Letter to Belize

1985. 350th Anniv of British Post Office. Mult.
846 10c. Type **157** 50 25
847 15c. "Hinchinbrook II" (sailing packet) engaging "Grand Turk" (American privateer) 70 25
848 25c. "Duke of Marlborough II" (sailing packet) 85 30
849 75c. "Diana" (packet) 1·40 1·50
850 $1 Falmouth packet ship 1·40 2·00
851 $3 "Conway" (mail paddle-steamer) 2·25 5·50

1985. Commonwealth Heads of Government Meeting, Nassau, Bahamas. Nos. 827/30 optd **COMMONWEALTH SUMMIT CONFERENCE, BAHAMAS 16th-22nd OCTOBER 1985**.
852 10c. Type **154** 30 30
853 15c. The Queen Mother, 1980 40 35
854 75c. Waving to the crowd, 1982 80 80
855 $4 Four generations of Royal Family at Prince William's christening 2·00 3·75
MS856 Two sheets, each 138 × 98 mm. (a) $2 The Queen Mother with Prince Henry (from photo by Lord Snowdon) (38 × 50 mm): (b) $5 The Queen Mother, 1984 (38 × 50 mm) Set of 2 sheets 2·75 3·50

1985. 80th Anniv of Rotary International. Nos. 815/19 optd **80TH ANNIVERSARY OF ROTARY INTERNATIONAL**.
857 25c. Type **152** 70 40
858 50c. Girl Guides camping 1·25 75
859 90c. Checking map on hike 1·75 2·00
860 $1.25 Students in laboratory 2·25 2·75
861 $2 Lady Baden-Powell (founder) 2·75 3·50

160 Royal Standard and Belize Flag

1985. Royal Visit. Multicoloured.
862 25c. Type **160** 1·00 95
863 75c. Queen Elizabeth II 1·25 2·00
864 $4 Royal Yacht "Britannia" (81 × 39 mm) 4·50 4·00
MS865 138 × 98 mm. $5 Queen Elizabeth II (38 × 50 mm). 5·00 5·50

161 Mountie in Canoe (Canada)

1985. Christmas. 30th Anniv of Disneyland, U.S.A. Designs showing dolls from "It's a Small World" exhibition. Multicoloured.
866 1c. Type **161** 10 15
867 2c. Indian chief and squaw (U.S.A.) 10 15
868 3c. Incas climbing Andes (South America) 10 15
869 4c. Africans beating drums (Africa) 10 15
870 5c. Snake-charmer and dancer (India and Far East) 10 15
871 6c. Boy and girl with donkey (Belize) 10 15
872 50c. Musician and dancer (Balkans) 1·75 1·50
873 $1.50 Boys with camel (Egypt and Saudi Arabia) 2·75 3·50
874 $3 Woman and girls playing with kite (Japan) 3·75 5·00
MS875 127 × 102 mm. $4 Beefeater and castle (Great Britain). P 13½ × 14 5·50 8·00

1985. World Cup Football Championship, Mexico (1986) (1st issue). Nos. 835/44 optd **PRE "WORLD CUP FOOTBALL" MEXICO 1986** and trophy.
876 50c. Type **156** 75 90
877 50c. 1937 Coronation 3c., and King George VI and Queen Elizabeth in Coronation robes 75 90
878 50c. Victory 3c., and Victory celebrations 75 90
879 50c. 1948 Royal Silver Wedding 4c., and King George VI and Queen Elizabeth at Westminster Abbey service 75 90
880 50c. 1953 Coronation 4c., and Queen Elizabeth II in Coronation robes 75 90
881 50c. 1966 Churchill 25c., Sir Winston Churchill and fighter aircraft 75 90
882 50c. 1972 Royal Silver Wedding 50c. and 1948 wedding photograph 75 90
883 50c. 1973 Royal Wedding 5c., and Princess Anne and Capt. Mark Phillips at their Wedding 75 90
884 50c. 1977 Silver Jubilee $2 and Queen Elizabeth II during tour 75 90
885 50c. 1978 25th anniv of Coronation 75c. and Imperial Crown 75 90
MS886 138 × 98 mm. $5 Queen Elizabeth II in Coronation robes 4·25 4·25
See also Nos. 936/40.

163 Indian Costume

165 Princess Elizabeth aged Three

164 Pope Pius X

1986. Costumes of Belize. Multicoloured.
887 5c. Type **163** 75 30
888 10c. Maya 80 30
889 15c. Garifuna 1·00 35
890 25c. Creole 1·25 35
891 50c. Chinese 1·75 1·25
892 75c. Lebanese 2·00 2·00
893 $1 European c. 1900 2·00 2·50
894 $2 Latin 2·75 3·75
MS895 139 × 98 mm. Amerindian (38 × 50 mm.) 6·00 7·00

1986. Easter. 20th-century Popes. Multicoloured.
896 50c. Type **164** 1·40 1·50
897 50c. Benedict XV 1·40 1·50
898 50c. Pius XI 1·40 1·50
899 50c. Pius XII 1·40 1·50
900 50c. John XXIII 1·40 1·50
901 50c. Paul VI 1·40 1·50
902 50c. John Paul I 1·40 1·50
903 50c. John Paul II 1·40 1·50
MS904 147 × 92 mm. $4 Pope John Paul II preaching (vert). 11·00 10·00

1986. 60th Birthday of Queen Elizabeth II. Mult.
905 25c. Type **165** 40 55
906 50c. Queen wearing Imperial State Crown 60 75
907 75c. At Trooping the Colour 75 85
908 $3 Queen wearing diadem 1·40 2·25
MS909 147 × 93 mm. $4 Queen Elizabeth II (37 × 50 mm) 3·25 4·50

166 Halley's Comet and Japanese "Planet A" Spacecraft

1986. Appearance of Halley's Comet. Multicoloured.
910 10c. Type **166** 55 80
911 15c. Halley's Comet, 1910 65 90
912 50c. Comet and European "Giotto" spacecraft 70 1·00
913 75c. Belize Weather Bureau 90 1·00
914 $1 Comet and U.S.A. space telescope 1·25 1·40
915 $2 Edmond Halley 1·60 1·90
MS916 147 × 93 mm. $4 Computer enhanced photograph of Comet (37 × 50 mm) 6·50 8·50

167 George Washington

1986. United States Presidents. Multicoloured.
917 10c. Type **167** 35 60
918 20c. John Adams 35 65
916 30c. Thomas Jefferson 40 70
920 50c. James Madison 50 70
921 $1.50 James Monroe 80 1·25
922 $2 John Quincy Adams 1·00 1·50
MS923 147 × 93 mm. $4 George Washington (different) 3·75 5·50

168 Auguste Bartholdi (sculptor) and Statue's Head

1986. Centenary of Statue of Liberty. Multicoloured.
924 25c. Type **168** 40 65
925 50c. Statue's head at U.S. Centennial Celebration, Philadelphia, 1876 55 85
926 75c. Unveiling ceremony, 1886 55 90
927 $4 Statue of Liberty and flags of Belize and U.S.A. 1·50 2·50
MS928 147 × 92 mm. $4 Statue of Liberty and New York skyline (37 × 50 mm.) 3·75 5·50

169 British Honduras 1866 1s. Stamp

1986. "Ameripex" International Stamp Exhibition, Chicago. Multicoloured.
929 10c. Type **169** 40 55
930 15c. 1981 Royal Wedding $1.50 stamps 55 75
931 50c. U.S.A. 1918 24c. airmail inverted centre error 75 80
932 75c. U.S.S. "Constitution" (frigate) 75 1·10
933 $1 Liberty Bell 80 1·40
934 $2 White House 90 1·60
MS935 147 × 92 mm. $4 Capitol, Washington (37 × 50 mm) 3·25 4·50

170 English and Brazilian Players

1986. World Cup Football Championship, Mexico (2nd issue). Multicoloured.
936 25c. Type **170** 1·50 1·75
937 50c. Mexican player and Maya statues 1·75 2·00
938 75c. Two Belizean players 2·00 2·25
939 $3 Aztec stone calendar 2·25 2·50
MS940 147 × 92 mm. $4 Flags of competing nations on two footballs (37 × 50 mm) 6·50 8·00

171 Miss Sarah Ferguson

1986. Royal Wedding. Multicoloured.
941 25c. Type **171** 65 40
942 75c. Prince Andrew 1·00 90
943 $3 Prince Andrew and Miss Sarah Ferguson (92 × 41 mm) 1·75 2·75
MS944 155 × 106 mm. $1 Miss Sarah Ferguson (different). $3 Prince Andrew (different) 4·25 6·00

1986. World Cup Football Championship Winners, Mexico. Nos. 936/9 optd **ARGENTINA – WINNERS 1986**.
945 25c. Type **170** 1·75 2·00
946 50c. Mexican player and Maya statues 2·00 2·25
947 75c. Two Belizean players 2·25 2·50
948 $3 Aztec stone calendar 3·25 3·50
MS949 147 × 92 mm. $4 Flags of competing nations on two footballs (37 × 50 mm) 8·00 10·00

1986. "Stockholmia '86" International Stamp Exhibition, Sweden. Nos. 929/34 optd **STOCKHOLMIA 86** and emblem.
950 10c. Type **169** 50 75
951 15c. 1981 Royal Wedding $1.50 stamp 65 90
952 50c. U.S.A. 1918 24c. airmail inverted centre error 80 1·10
953 75c. U.S.S. "Constitution" 1·00 1·50

954 $1 Liberty Bell . . . . 1·25 1·60
955 $2 White House . . . . . . 1·60 1·90
MS956 147 × 93 mm. $4 Capitol, Washington (37 × 50 mm) . . . 5·00 7·00

174 Amerindian Girl

1986. International Peace Year. Multicoloured.
957 25c. Type **174** 65 80
958 50c. European boy and girl 80 1·10
959 75c. Japanese girl . . . . . 1·00 1·60
960 $3 Indian boy and European girl . . . . 1·75 2·75
MS961 132 × 106 mm. $4 As 25c. but vert (35 × 47 mm) . . . . . . 5·50 7·00

175 "Amanita lilloi" 176 Jose Carioca

1986. Fungi and Toucans. Multicoloured.
962 5c. Type **175** . . . . 1·50 1·25
963 10c. Keel-billed toucan . . . 1·75 1·60
964 20c. "Boletellus cubensis" . . 2·00 1·75
965 25c. Collared aracari . . . . 2·00 1·75
966 75c. "Psilocybe caerulescens" 2·25 2·00
967 $1 Emerald toucanet . . . . 2·25 2·00
968 $1.25 Crimson-rumped toucanet ("Crimson-rumped Toucan") . . . . 2·50 2·25
969 $2 "Russula puiggarii" . . . 2·50 2·50

1986. Christmas. Designs showing Walt Disney cartoon characters in scenes from "Saludos Amigos". Multicoloured.
970 2c. Type **176** 20 20
971 3c. Jose Carioca, Panchito and Donald Duck 20 20
972 4c. Daisy Duck as Rio Carnival dancer 20 20
973 5c. Mickey and Minnie Mouse as musician and dancer 20 20
974 6c. Jose Carioca using umbrella as flute 20 20
975 50c. Donald Duck and Panchito . . . . 1·00 1·75
976 65c. Joe Carioca and Donald Duck playing hide and seek . . . . 1·25 2·00
977 $1.35 Donald Duck playing maracas . . . . 2·00 3·25
978 $2 Goofy as matador . . . . 2·75 3·75
MS979 131 × 111 mm. $4 Donald Duck . . . . 9·00 11·00

177 Princess Elizabeth in Wedding Dress, 1947 179 "Mother and Child"

178 "America II", 1983

1987. Royal Ruby Wedding. Multicoloured.
980 25c. Type **177** 25 20
981 75c. Queen and Duke of Edinburgh, 1972 . . . . . 45 50
982 $1 Queen on her 60th birthday 50 60
983 $4 In Garter robes . . . . . 1·00 2·00
MS984 171 × 112 mm. $6 Queen and Duke of Edinburgh (44 × 50 mm) 6·50 7·50

1987. America's Cup Yachting Championship. Multicoloured.
985 25c. Type **178** 30 25
986 75c. "Stars and Stripes", 1987 40 50
987 $1 "Australia II", 1983 . . . 50 60
988 $4 "White Crusader" . . . . 1·00 2·00
MS989 171 × 112 mm. $6 Sails of Australia II" (44 × 50 mm.) . . 5·00 7·50

1987. Wood Carvings by George Gabb. Mult.
990 25c. Type **179** 15 25
991 75c. "Standing Form" . . . 35 50
992 $1 "Love-doves" 40 60
993 $4 "Depiction of Music" . . 1·10 2·00
MS994 173 × 114 mm. $6 "African Heritage" (44 × 50 mm.) . . . 4·25 7·00

180 Black-handed Spider Monkey

1987. Primates. Multicoloured.
995 25c. Type **180** 25 20
996 75c. Black howler monkey . . 40 55
997 $1 Spider monkeys with baby 45 65
998 $4 Two black howler monkeys . . . . 1·10 2·25
MS999 171 × 112 mm. $6 Young spider monkey (44 × 50 mm.) 5·50 8·00

181 Guides on Parade

1987. 50th Anniv of Girl Guide Movement in Belize. Multicoloured.
1000 25c. Type **181** 45 20
1001 75c. Brownie camp . . . . 80 1·00
1002 $1 Guide camp . . . . . . 1·00 1·25
1003 $4 Olave, Lady Baden-Powell . . . . 3·00 5·00
MS1004 173 × 114 mm. $6 As $4 but vert (44 × 50 mm) . . . . . . 4·00 6·50

182 Indian Refugee Camp

1987. Int Year of Shelter for the Homeless. Mult.
1005 25c. Type **182** 50 25
1006 75c. Filipino family and slum 90 90
1007 $1 Family in Middle East shanty town . . . . . . 1·00 1·25
1008 $4 Building modern house in Belize . . . . 2·00 4·50

183 "Laelia euspatha"

1987. Christmas. Orchids. Illustrations from Sander's "Reichenbachia". Multicoloured.
1009 1c. Type **183** 95 95
1010 2c. "Cattleya citrina" 95 95
1011 3c. "Masdevallia backhousiana" 95 95
1012 4c. "Cypripedium tautzianum" 95 95
1013 5c. "Trichopilia suavis alba" 95 95
1014 6c. "Odontoglossum hebraicum" 95 95
1015 7c. "Cattleya trianaei schroederiana" 95 95
1016 10c. "Saccolabium giganteum" 95 95
1017 30c. "Cattleya warscewiczii" 1·25 1·25
1018 50c. "Chysis bractescens" . . 1·50 1·50
1019 70c. "Cattleya rochellensis" 1·75 1·75
1020 $1 "Laellia elegans schilleriana" . . . . . 1·90 1·90
1021 $1.50 "Laelia anceps percivaliana" . . . . . . 2·00 2·00
1022 $3 "Laelia gouldiana" . . . 2·50 2·50
MS1023 Two sheets, each 171 × 112 mm. (a) $3 "Odontoglossum roezlii" (40 × 47 mm). (b) $5 "Cattleya dowiana aurea" (40 × 47 mm) Set of 2 sheets . . . . 12·00 13·00

184 Christ condemned to Death

1988. Easter. The Stations of the Cross. Mult.
1024 40c. Type **184** 35 60
1025 40c. Christ carrying the Cross 35 60
1026 40c. Falling for the first time 35 60
1027 40c. Christ meets Mary . . 35 60
1028 40c. Simon of Cyrene helping to carry the Cross 35 60
1029 40c. Veronica wiping the face of Christ 35 60
1030 40c. Christ falling a second time 35 60
1031 40c. Consoling the women of Jerusalem 35 60
1032 40c. Falling for the third time 35 60
1033 40c. Christ being stripped 35 60
1034 40c. Christ nailed to the Cross 35 60
1035 40c. Dying on the Cross . . 35 60
1036 40c. Christ taken down from the Cross 35 60
1037 40c. Christ being laid in the sepulchre 35 60

185 Basketball

1988. Olympic Games, Seoul. Multicoloured.
1038 10c. Type **185** . . . . . . 3·00 1·00
1039 25c. Volleyball . . . . . . 1·00 30
1040 60c. Table tennis . . . . . 1·00 60
1041 75c. Diving . . . . 1·00 70
1042 $1 Judo . . . . 1·25 1·10
1043 $2 Hockey . . . . 7·00 5·00
MS1044 76 × 106 mm. $3 Gymnastics . . . . 6·00 6·50

186 Public Health Nurse, c. 1912

1988. 125th Anniv of Int Red Cross. Mult.
1045 60c. Type **186** . . . . . . 3·25 1·25
1046 75c. "Aleda E. Lutz" (hospital ship) and ambulance launch, 1937 3·50 1·50
1047 $1 Ambulance at hospital tent, 1956 . . . . 4·00 2·00
1048 $2 Auster ambulance plane, 1940 . . . . 5·50 6·00

187 Collared Anteater ("Ants Bear")

1989. Small Animals of Belize. Multicoloured.
1049 10c. Paca ("Gibnut") . . . 2·75 2·50
1050 25c. Four-eyed opossum (vert) . . . . 2·75 1·75
1051 50c. Type **187** . . . . . . 3·25 2·25
1052 60c. As 10c. . . . . 3·25 2·50
1053 75c. Red brocket . . . . . 3·25 2·50
1054 $1 Collared peccary . . . . 4·50 6·50

1989. 20th Anniv of First Manned Landing on Moon. As T **126** of Ascension. Multicoloured.
1055 25c. Docking of "Apollo 9" modules . . . . 2·00 30
1056 50c. "Apollo 9" command service module in Space (30 × 30 mm) . . . . . . 2·50 75
1057 75c. "Apollo 9" emblem (30 × 30 mm) . . . . . . 2·75 1·25
1058 $1 "Apollo 9" lunar module in space . . . . 3·00 2·25
MS1059 83 × 100 mm. $5 "Apollo II" command service module undergoing test . . . . . . 11·00 10·00

1989. No. 771 surch **5c.**
1060 5c. on 6c. Star-eyed hermit crab . . . . 11·00 2·50

1989. "World Stamp Expo '89" International Stamp Exhibition, Washington. No. **MS**1059 optd **WORLD STAMP EXPO '89, United States Postal Service Nov 17—20 and Nov 24—Dec 3. 1989 Washington Convention Center Washington, DC** and emblem.
MS1061 83 × 100 mm. $5 "Apollo II" command service module undergoing tests . . . . 9·50 10·00

190 Wesley Church 191 White-winged Tanager and "Catonephele numilia"

1989. Christmas. Belize Churches.
1062 **190** 10c. black, pink and brown 20 10
1063 – 25c. black, lilac and mauve 25 20
1064 – 60c. black, turq & bl . . 50 70
1065 – 75c. black, grn & lt grn 65 90
1066 – $1 black, lt yell & yell 80 1·25
DESIGNS: 25c. Baptist Church; 60c. St. John's Anglican Cathedral; 75c. St. Andrew's Presbyterian Church; $1 Holy Redeemer Roman Catholic Cathedral.

1990. Birds and Butterflies. Multicoloured.
1067A 5c. Type **191** 60 75
1068B 10c. Keel-billed toucan and "Nessaea aglaura" 80 80
1069A 15c. Magnificent frigate bird and "Eurytides philolaus" 80 40
1070A 25c. Jabiru and "Heliconius sapho" . . 80 40
1071A 30c. Great blue heron and "Colobura dirce" . . . 80 50
1072A 50c. Northern oriole and "Hamadryas arethusia" 1·00 60
1073A 60c. Scarlet macaw and "Evenus regalis" . . . . 1·25 70
1074A 75c. Red-legged honey-creeper and "Callicore patelina" . . . . 1·25 75
1075A $1 Spectacled owl and "Caligo uranus" . . . . 2·25 1·60
1076A $2 Green jay and "Philaethria dido" . . . 2·75 3·50
1077A $5 Turkey vulture and "Battus belus" . . . . 4·50 6·50
1078A $10 Osprey and "Papilio thoas" . . . . 8·50 11·00

1990. First Belize Dollar Coin. No. 1075 optd **FIRST DOLLAR COIN 1990.**
1079 $1 Spectacled owl and "Caligo uranus" . . . . 4·75 2·75

193 Green Turtle

1990. Turtles. Multicoloured.
1080 10c. Type **193** 65 40
1081 25c. Hawksbill turtle . . . . 1·00 40
1082 60c. Saltwater loggerhead turtle . . . . 1·50 1·50
1083 75c. Freshwater loggerhead turtle . . . . 1·60 1·60
1084 $1 Bocatora turtle . . . . . 2·00 2·00
1085 $2 Hicatee turtle . . . . . 2·75 5·00

194 Fairey Battle

1990. 50th Anniv of the Battle of Britain. Multicoloured.
1086 10c. Type **194** . . . . . . 1·00 50
1087 25c. Bristol Type 152 Beaufort . . . . 1·60 50
1088 60c. Bristol Type 142 Blenheim Mk IV . . . . 2·00 2·00
1089 75c. Armstrong-Whitworth Whitley . . . . 2·00 2·00
1090 $1 Vickers-Armstrong Wellington Mk 1c . . . . 2·00 2·00
1091 $1 Handley Page Hampden 2·50 3·50

195 "Cattleya bowringiana"

1990. Christmas. Orchids. Multicoloured.
1092 25c. Type **195** 85 20
1093 50c. "Rhyncholaelia digbyana" . . . . 1·25 50
1094 60c. "Sobralia macrantha" 1·50 1·00
1095 75c. "Chysis bractescens" 1·50 1·00
1096 $1 "Vanilla planifolia" . . . 1·75 1·75
1097 $2 "Epidendrum polyanthum" . . . . . . 2·50 4·00

196 Common Iguana

1991. Reptiles and Mammals. Multicoloured.
1098 25c. Type **196** 80 35
1099 50c. Morelet's crocodile . . 1·25 90
1100 60c. American manatee . . 1·50 1·50
1101 75c. Boa constrictor . . . . 1·75 1·75
1102 $1 Baird's tapir . . . . . . 2·00 2·00
1103 $2 Jaguar . . . . 2·75 3·75

1991. 65th Birthday of Queen Elizabeth II and 70th Birthday of Prince Philip. As T **139** of Ascension. Multicoloured.
1104 $1 Queen Elizabeth II wearing tiara . . . . . . 1·00 1·50
1105 $1 Prince Philip wearing panama . . . . 1·00 1·50

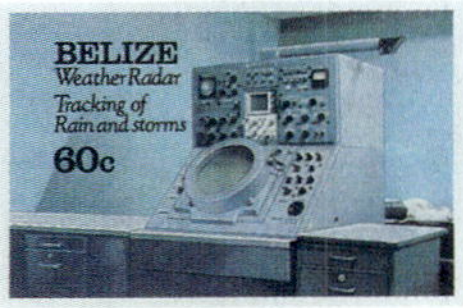

197 Weather Radar

1991. International Decade for Natural Disaster Reduction.
1106 **197** 60c. multicoloured . . . 1·50 1·25
1107 – 75c. multicoloured . . . 1·60 1·40
1108 – $1 blue and black . . . 1·75 1·75
1109 – $2 multicoloured . . . 2·50 3·25
DESIGNS: 75c. Weather station; $1 Floods in Belize after Hurricane Hattie, 1961; $2 Satellite image of Hurricane Gilbert.

198 Thomas Ramos and Demonstration

1991. 10th Anniv of Independence. Famous Belizeans (1st series). Multicoloured.
1110 25c. Type **198** 60 30
1111 60c. Sir Isaiah Morter and palm trees . . . . 1·25 1·50
1112 75c. Antonio Soberanis and political meeting . . . . 1·25 1·75
1113 $1 Santiago Ricalde and cutting sugar-cane . . . . 1·50 2·00
See also Nos. 1126/9 and 1148/51.

199 "Anansi the Spider"

1991. Christmas. Folklore. Multicoloured.
1114 25c. Type **199** . . . . . . 1·75 20
1115 60c. "Jack-o-Lantern" . . . 2·25 55
1116 60c. "Tata Duende" (vert) 2·50 1·25
1117 75c. "Xtabai" . . . . . . 2·50 1·25
1118 $1 "Warrie Massa" (vert) 2·75 2·25
1119 $2 "Old Heg" . . . . . . 4·00 7·00

200 "Gongora quinquenervis"

1992. Easter. Orchids. Multicoloured.
1120 25c. Type **200** 90 20
1121 50c. "Oncidium sphacelatum" . . . . . . 1·50 75
1122 60c. "Encyclia bratescens" 1·75 1·75
1123 75c. "Epidendrum ciliare" 1·75 1·75
1124 $1 "Psygmorchis pusilla" . . 2·00 2·25
1125 $2 "Galeandra batemanii" 2·75 4·50

1992. Famous Belizeans (2nd series). As T **198**, but inscr "EMINENT BELIZEANS" at top. Multicoloured.
1126 25c. Gwendolyn Lizarraga (politician) and High School 75 30
1127 60c. Rafael Fonseca (civil servant) and Government Offices, Belize . . . . . . 1·50 1·50
1128 75c. Vivian Seay (health worker) and nurses . . . 1·75 1·75
1129 $1 Samuel Haynes (U.N.I.A. worker) and words of National Anthem . . . . 2·00 2·25

201 Xunantunich and National Assembly

1992. 500th Anniv of Discovery of America by Columbus. Mayan sites and modern buildings. Multicoloured.
1130 25c. Type **201** . . . . . . 1·00 25
1131 60c. Altun Ha and Supreme Court . . . . 1·50 1·00
1132 75c. Santa Rita and Tower Hill Sugar Factory . . . 1·60 1·25
1133 $5 Lamanai and Citrus Company works . . . . 8·00 11·00

202 Hashishi Pampi

1992. Christmas. Folklore. Multicoloured.
1134 25c. Type **202** 30 20
1135 60c. Cadejo 60 60
1136 $1 La Sucia (vert) . . . . . 90 1·00
1137 $5 Sisimito . . . . 4·00 7·00

1993. 75th Anniv of Royal Air Force. As T **149** of Ascension. Multicoloured.
1138 25c. Sud Aviation SA 330L Puma helicopter . . . . . 1·00 60
1139 50c. Hawker Siddeley Harrier GR3 . . . . . . 1·25 80
1140 60c. De Havilland DH98 Mosquito Mk XVIII . . 1·40 1·10
1141 75c. Avro Type 683 Lancaster . . . . 1·40 1·10
1142 $1 Consolidated Liberator I 1·60 1·40
1143 $3 Short Stirling Mk I . . . 3·25 5·50

203 "Lycaste aromatica"

1993. 14th World Orchid Conference, Glasgow. Multicoloured.
1144 25c. Type **203** 40 25
1145 60c. "Sobralia decora" . . . 75 80
1146 $1 "Maxillaria alba" . . . 1·00 1·25
1147 $2 "Brassavola nodosa" . . 1·75 3·00

1993. Famous Belizeans (3rd series). As T **198**, but inscr "EMINENT BELIZEANS" at top. Multicoloured.
1148 25c. Herbert Watkin Beaumont, Post Office and postmark 40 25
1149 60c. Dr. Selvyn Walford Young and score of National Anthem 75 85
1150 75c. Cleopatra White and health centre . . . . . 90 1·25
1151 $1 Dr. Karl Heusner and early car . . . . 1·10 1·40

204 Boom and Chime Band

1993. Christmas. Local Customs. Mult.
1152 25c. Type **204** . . . . . . 1·00 20
1153 60c. John Canoe dance . . 2·00 75
1154 75c. Cortez dance . . . . . 2·00 80
1155 $2 Maya musical group . . 4·50 7·00

1994. "Hong Kong '94" International Stamp Exhibition. No. 1075 optd **HONG KONG '94** and emblem.
1156 $1 Spectacled owl and "Caligo uranus" . . . . 2·75 2·50

1994. Royal Visit. As T **202** of Bahamas. Mult.
1157 25c. Flags of Belize and Great Britain . . . . . 1·75 55
1158 60c. Queen Elizabeth II in yellow coat and hat . . . 2·25 1·25
1159 75c. Queen Elizabeth in evening dress . . . . . . 2·50 1·50
1160 $1 Queen Elizabeth, Prince Philip and Yeomen of the Guard . . . . 2·75 2·50

205 "Lonchorhina aurita" (bat)

1994. Bats. Multicoloured.
1161 25c. Type **205** 45 20
1162 60c. "Vampyrodes caraccioli" 75 65
1163 75c. "Noctilio leporinus" . . 90 80
1164 $2 "Desmodus rotundus" 2·00 3·50

1994. 75th Anniv of I.L.O. No. 1074 surch **10c** and anniversary emblem.
1165 10c. on 75c. multicoloured 2·00 1·75

207 "Cycnoches chlorochilon"

1994. Christmas. Orchids. Multicoloured.
1166 25c. Type **207** 45 20
1167 60c. "Brassavola cucullata" 75 70
1168 75c. "Sobralia mucronata" 90 90
1169 $1 "Nidema boothii" . . . 1·10 1·40

208 Ground Beetle

(209)

1995. Insects. Multicoloured.
1170A 5c. Type **208** 45 70
1171A 10c. Harlequin beetle . . . 50 70
1172A 15c. Giant water bug . . . 60 80
1173A 25c. Peanut-head bug . . . 70 20
1174A 30c. Coconut weevil . . . 70 25
1175A 50c. Mantis 85 40
1176B 60c. Tarantula wasp . . . 1·00 50
1177B 75c. Rhinoceros beetle . . 1·10 60
1178B $1 Metallic wood borer . . 1·25 1·25
1179B $2 Dobson fly . . . . . . 3·00 3·50
1180B $5 Click beetle . . . . . 4·75 6·00
1181B $10 Long-horned beetle 7·50 9·50

1995. 50th Anniv of End of Second World War. As T **161** of Ascension. Multicoloured.
1182 25c. War memorial 35 25
1183 60c. Remembrance Day parade . . . . 1·00 1·00
1184 75c. British Honduras forestry unit . . . . . . 1·10 1·10
1185 $1 Vickers-Armstrong Wellington bomber . . . 1·40 1·75

1995. "Singapore '95" International Stamp Exhibition. Nos. 1166/9 optd with T **209**.
1186 25c. Type **207** . . . . . . 1·00 30
1187 60c. "Brassavola cucullata" 1·50 90
1188 75c. "Sobralia mucronata" 1·75 1·25
1189 $1 "Nidema boothii" . . . 2·00 2·25

1995. 50th Anniv of United Nations. As T **213** of Bahamas. Multicoloured.
1190 25c. M113-light reconnaisance vehicle . . 25 20
1191 60c. Sultan armoured command vehicle 60 65
1192 75c. Leyland-Daf 8 × 4 drop truck 75 80
1193 $2 Warrior infantry combat vehicle . . . . 1·50 2·50

210 Male and Female Blue Ground Dove

1995. Christmas. Doves. Multicoloured.
1194 25c. Type **210** 35 20
1195 60c. White-fronted doves . . 70 70
1196 75c. Pair of ruddy ground doves 85 90
1197 $1 White-winged doves . . . 1·25 1·50

1996. "CHINA '96" 9th Asian International Stamp Exhibition, Peking. Nos. 1172, 1174/5 and 1179 optd **'96 CHINA** and emblem.
1198 15c. Giant water bug . . . 20 15
1199 30c. Coconut weevil 40 30
1200 50c. Mantis 55 50
1201 $2 Dobson fly . . . . . . 1·75 2·50

212 Unloading Banana Train, Commerce Bight Pier

1996. "CAPEX '96" International Stamp Exhibition, Toronto. Railways. Multicoloured.
1202 25c. Type **212** . . . . . . 1·50 55
1203 60c. Locomotive No. 1 Stann Creek station . . . 2·00 1·25
1204 75c. Locomotive No. 4 pulling mahogany log train . . . . 2·00 1·40
1205 $3 L.M.S. No. 5602 "British Honduras" locomotive . . 3·75 6·00

213 "Epidendrum stamfordianum"

214 Red Poll

1996. Christmas. Orchids. Multicoloured.
1206 25c. Type **213** 50 20
1207 60c. "Oncidium carthagenense" 80 70
1208 75c. "Oerstedella verrucosa" 90 90
1209 $1 "Coryanthes speciosa" 1·25 1·50

1997. "HONG KONG '97" International Stamp Exhibition. Chinese New Year ("Year of the Ox"). Cattle Breeds. Multicoloured.
1210 25c. Type **214** 60 25
1211 60c. Brahman . . . . 95 1·00

1212 75c. Longhorn . . . . . . 1·25 1·40
1213 $1 Charbray . . . . 1·40 1·90

215 Coral Snake

216 Adult Male Howler Monkey

1997. Snakes. Multicoloured.
1214 25c. Type **215** 45 20
1215 60c. Green vine snake . . . 70 70
1216 75c. Yellow-jawed tommygoff 80 80
1217 $1 Speckled racer . . . . . 95 1·25

1997. Endangered Species. Howler Monkey. Multicoloured.
1218 10c. Type **216** 25 25
1219 25c. Female feeding 40 25
1220 60c. Female with young . . 70 80
1221 75c. Juvenile monkey feeding . . . . 90 1·10

217 "Maxillaria elatior"

1997. Christmas. Orchids. Multicoloured.
1222 25c. Type **217** 65 25
1223 60c. "Dimmerandra emarginata" . . . . . . 1·00 75
1224 75c. "Macradenia brassavolae" . . . . . . 1·25 1·00
1225 $1 "Ornithocephalus gladiatus" . . . . 1·60 1·50

1998. Diana, Princess of Wales Commemoration. Sheet, 145 × 70 mm, containing vert designs as T **177** of Ascension. Multicoloured.
MS1226 $1 Wearing floral dress, 1988; $1 In evening dress, 1981; $1 Wearing pearl drop earrings, 1988; $1 Carrying bouquet, 1983 . . 3·00 3·50

218 School Children using the Internet

1998. 50th Anniv of Organization of American States. Multicoloured.
1227 25c. Type **218** 25 20
1228 $1 Map of Central America 1·50 1·50

219 University Arms

1998. 50th Anniv of University of West Indies.
1229 **219** $1 multicoloured . . . . 1·00 1·00

220 Baymen Gun Flats

1998. Bicentenary of Battle of St. George's Cay. Multicoloured.
1230 10c. Boat moored at quayside (vert) 30 50
1231 10c. Three sentries and cannon (vert) 30 50
1232 10c. Cannon and rowing boats (vert) 30 50
1233 25c. Type **220** 60 25
1234 60c. Baymen sloops 80 80
1235 75c. British schooners . . . 85 85
1236 $1 H.M.S. "Merlin" (sloop) 1·00 1·00
1237 $2 Spanish flagship . . . . 1·75 2·25

221 "Brassia maculata"

222 "Eucharis grandiflora"

1998. Christmas. Orchids. Multicoloured.
1238 25c. Type **221** 35 20
1239 60c. "Encyclia radiata" . . 50 40
1240 75c. "Stanhopea ecornuta" 50 55
1241 $1 "Isochilus carnosiflorus" 60 80

1999. Easter. Flowers. Multicoloured.
1242 10c. Type **222** 20 10
1243 25c. "Hippeastrum puniceum" 30 20
1244 60c. "Zephyranthes citrina" 50 50
1245 $1 "Hymenocallis littoralis" 60 80

223 Postman on Bicycle

1999. 125th Anniv of UPU. Multicoloured.
1246 25c. Type **223** 50 30
1247 60c. Postal truck 65 55
1248 75c. "Dee" (mail ship) . . . 85 80
1249 $1 Modern airliner . . . . 1·00 1·25

224 "Holy Family with Jesus and St. John" (School of Rubens)

1999. Christmas. Religious Paintings. Multicoloured.
1250 25c. Type **224** 30 20
1251 60c. "Holy Family with St. John" (unknown artist) 60 55
1252 75c. "Madonna and Child with St. John and Angel" (unknown artist) 65 70
1253 $1 "Madonna with Child and St. John" (Andrea del Salerno) . . . . 90 1·10

225 Iguana

2000. Wildlife. Multicoloured.
1254 5c. Type **225** 10 10
1255 10c. Gibnut 10 10
1256 15c. Howler monkey 10 15
1257 25c. Collared anteater . . . 15 20
1258 30c. Hawksbill turtle 15 20
1259 50c. Red brocket antelope 25 30
1260 60c. Jaguar 30 35
1261 75c. American manatee . . 40 45
1262 $1 Crocodile 55 60
1263 $2 Baird's tapir . . . . . 1·10 1·20
1264 $5 Collared peccary . . . . 2·75 3·00
1265 $10 Boa constrictor . . . . 5·50 5·75

226 Mango

2000. Fruits. Multicoloured.
1266 25c. Type **226** 35 25
1267 60c. Cashew 65 60
1268 75c. Papaya 80 75
1269 $1 Banana . . . . 1·10 1·40

227 Meeting in Battlefield Park and Supreme Court, 1950

2000. 50th Anniv of People's United Party. Mult.
1270 10c. Type **227** 20 15
1271 25c. Voters queuing, 1954 30 25
1272 60c. Legislative Council and Mace, 1964 . . . . 55 50
1273 75c. National Assembly Building (under construction and completed), Belmopan, 1967–70 . . . . 70 80
1274 $1 Belizean flag in searchlights, Independence, 1981 . . . 2·25 1·75

228 *Bletia purpurea*

2000. Christmas. Orchids. Multicoloured.
1275 25c. Type **228** 55 25
1276 60c. *Cyrtopodium punctatum* 85 50
1277 75c. *Cycnoches egertonianum* . . . . 1·00 85
1278 $1 *Catasetum integerrimum* 1·40 1·60

229 Children at Computers

2001. 20th Anniv of Independence. Multicoloured.
1279 25c. Type **229** 35 25
1280 60c. Shrimp farm 60 50
1281 75c. Privassion Cascade (vert) 75 60
1282 $2 Map of Belize (vert) . . 2·75 3·25

230 *Sobralia fragrans*

2001. Christmas. Orchids. Multicoloured.
1283 25c. Type **230** 65 25
1284 60c. *Encyclia cordigera* . . 1·00 60
1285 75c. *Maxillaria fulgens* . . 1·25 1·00
1286 $1 *Epidendrum nocturnum* 1·60 1·75

2002. Golden Jubilee. As T **200** of Ascension.
1287 25c. black, violet and gold 45 25
1288 60c. multicoloured 75 60
1289 75c. black, violet and gold 90 80
1290 $1 multicoloured . . . . . 1·10 1·25
MS1291 162 × 95 mm. Nos. 1287/90 and $5 multicoloured . . . . . 6·50 7·50
DESIGNS—Horiz: 25c. Princess Elizabeth in pantomime, Windsor, 1943; 60c. Queen Elizabeth in floral hat; 75c. Queen Elizabeth in garden with Prince Charles and Princess Anne, 1952; $1 Queen Elizabeth in South Africa, 1995. VERT (38 × 51 mm)—$5 Queen Elizabeth after Annigoni.

231 *Dichaea neglecta*

2002. Christmas. Orchids. Multicoloured.
1292 25c. Type **231** 65 25
1293 50c. *Epinendrum hawkesii* . . 80 55
1294 60c. *Encyclia belizensis* . . . 90 60
1295 75c. *Eriopsis biloba* . . . . 1·00 70
1296 $1 *Harbenaria monorrhiza* 1·25 1·50
1297 $2 *Mormodes buccinator* . . 1·75 2·75

232 B.D.F. Emblem

2003. 25th Anniv of Belize Defence Force.
1298 **232** 25c. multicoloured . . . 50 35

233 Avro Shackleton MK 3

2003. Centenary of Powered Flight. Multicoloured.
1299 25c. Type **233** 55 45
1300 60c. Lockheed L-749 Constellation 75 65
1301 75c. Sepecat Jaguar GR. 1 85 75
1302 $3 British Aerospace Harrier GR. 3 . . . . 2·25 3·00
MS1303 116 × 66 mm. $5 Ryan NYP *Spirit of St. Louis*, Belize, 1927 4·50 5·00

234 Head of Scarlet Macaw

2003. Christmas. Scarlet Macaw. Multicoloured.
1304 25c. Type **234** 80 45
1305 60c. Pair on tree . . . . . 1·25 65
1306 75c. Three macaws feeding on clay . . . . 1·40 75
1307 $5 Pair in flight . . . . . . 4·75 6·50

235 Whale Shark

2004. Whale Shark. Multicoloured.
1308 25c. Type **235** 50 30
1309 60c. Near surface of water 80 50
1310 75c. Whale shark and diver 90 55
1311 $5 Near coral reef . . . . . 4·50 5·50

2004. Wildlife. Nos. 1259/1261 surch.
1312 10c. on 50c. Red brocket antelope 30 40
1313 10c. on 60c. Jaguar 30 40
1314 15c. on 75c. American manatee 40 40

2005. No. 1300 surch.
1314a 10c. on 60c. Lockheed L-749 Constellation . . 15 15

2005. No. 1305 surch.
1314b 10c. on 60c. Pair (of scarlet macaws) on tree 15 15

237 Woolly Opossum

2005. Endangered Species. Woolly Opossum. Showing the Woolly Opossum with the country name in different colours. Multicoloured.
1315 25c. Type **237** 50 30
1316 60c. Bright new blue 80 50
1317 75c. Dull orange (horiz) . . 90 55
1318 $5 Magenta (horiz) . . . . 4·50 5·50

2005. Pope John Paul II Commemoration. As T **219** of Ascension.
1319 $1 multicoloured . . . . . 2·00 2·00

239 Blue-crowned Motmot and Flower, Guanacaste National Park, Cayo District

2005. Ecological and Cultural Heritage. Multicoloured.

1320	5c. Type **239**	15	15
1321	10c. Government House of Culture, Belize City	15	15
1322	15c. Lubaantun Archaeological Reserve and ball court warriors, Toledo District	20	20
1323	25c. Altun Ha Archaeological Reserve and jade head, Belize District	30	30
1324	30c. Nohoch Che'n Archaeological Reserve and jar, Cayo District	30	30
1325	50c. Goff's Caye, Belize District	50	50
1326	60c. Blue Hole Natural Monument and diver, Belize District	60	60
1327	75c. Lamanai Archaeological Reserve and crocodile effigy, Orange Walk District	75	75
1328	$1 Half Moon Caye, lighthouse and red footed booby (bird), Belize District	1·25	1·25
1329	$2 Beach and starfish, Placencia Peninsula, Stann Creek District	2·25	2·50
1330	$5 Museum of Belize, Belize City	5·50	6·00
1331	$10 Cerros Archaeological Reserve and Olmec jade pendant, Corozal District	9·00	9·50

240 25c. Postman on Bicycle Stamp

241 George Price (Independence negotiator and first Prime Minister)

2006. 50th Anniv of First Europa Stamp. Designs showing Belize 1999 125th Anniv of Universal Postal Union stamps. Multicoloured.

1332	25c. Type **240**	40	30
1333	75c. 60c. Postal truck stamp	85	75
1334	$3 75c. Mail ship *Dee* stamp	3·00	3·50
1335	$5 $1 Airliner stamp	5·50	6·00
MS1336	Nos. 1332/5	8·75	9·50

2006. 25th Anniv of Independence. Multicoloured.

1337	25c. Type **241**	30	30
1338	30c. Black orchid, Baird's tapir, keel-billed toucan and mahogany tree (national symbols) (horiz)	50	30
1339	60c. Map of Belize	90	60
1340	$1 1981 Independence logo	1·25	1·25
1341	$5 The Constitution of Belize (horiz)	5·50	6·00

242 Roman Goddess Diana reaching for Arrow

243 *Sleeping Giant* sculpture (George Gabb)

2006. Breast Cancer Research.

1342	**242** $1 multicoloured	1·00	1·00

A similar stamp was issued by the USA on 29 July 1998.

2007. Belizean Artists. Multicoloured.

1343	25c. Type **243**	15	10
1344	30c. *Market Scene* (Louis Belisle) (horiz)	25	20
1345	60c. *The Original Turtle Shell Band* (Pen Cayetano) (horiz)	50	45
1346	75c. *Have Some Coconut Water* (Benjamin Nicholas)	65	65
1347	$2 Woodcarving by Reuben Miguel	1·75	1·75
1348	$3 Mural of Corozal Town (Manuel Villamor)	2·40	2·50

244 Slave

2007. Bicentenary of the Abolition of the Slave Trade Act.

1349	**244** $2 multicoloured	2·10	2·25

POSTAGE DUE STAMPS

D 2

1976.

D 6	D **2** 1c. red and green	10	1·00
D 7	– 2c. purple and violet	15	1·00
D 8	– 5c. green and brown	20	1·25
D 9	– 15c. green and red	30	1·50
D10	– 25c. orange and green	40	1·75

DESIGNS: Nos. D7/10 as Type D **2** but with different frames.

BENIN Pt. 6, Pt. 12

A French possession on the W. coast of Africa incorporated, in 1899, into the colony of Dahomey.

100 centimes = 1 franc.

A. FRENCH COLONY

1892. Stamps of French Colonies. "Commerce" type, optd **BENIN**.

1	J 1c. black on blue	£120	£120
2	2c. brown on yellow	£120	£120
3	4c. brown on grey	60·00	60·00
4	5c. green on light green	18·00	14·50
5	10c. black on lilac	75·00	70·00
6	15c. blue on light blue	55·00	22·00
7	20c. red on green	£190	£170
8	25c. black on red	£110	60·00
9	30c. brown on drab	£140	£120
10	35c. black on orange	£140	£120
11	40c. red on yellow	£120	£120
12	75c. red on pink	£250	£225
13	1f. green	£275	£225

1892. Nos. 4 and 6 surch.

14	J 01 on 5c. green on lt green	£190	£170
15	40 on 15c. blue on lt blue	£130	90·00
16	75 on 15c. blue on lt blue	£600	£400

1893. "Tablet" key-type inscr "GOLFE DE BENIN" in red (1, 5, 15, 25, 75c., 1f.) or blue (others).

17	D 1c. black on blue	2·30	6·00
18	2c. brown on buff	3·00	4·25
19	4c. brown on grey	2·75	5·75
20	5c. green on light green	8·25	8·75
21	10c. black on lilac	8·00	10·50
22	15c. blue	26·00	34·00
23	20c. red on green	6·25	9·25
24	25c. black on pink	25·00	11·00
25	30c. brown on drab	11·00	10·00
26	40c. red on yellow	2·30	5·00
27	50c. red on pink	1·60	3·75
28	75c. brown on orange	10·00	19·00
29	1f. green	65·00	70·00

1894. "Tablet" key-type inscr "BENIN" in red (1, 5, 15, 25, 75c., 1f.) or blue (others).

33	D 1c. black on blue	3·00	2·50
34	2c. brown on buff	3·25	4·00
35	4c. brown on grey	2·50	3·75
36	5c. green on light green	5·75	6·25
37	10c. black on lilac	4·50	7·75
38	15c. blue	12·50	2·00
39	20c. red on green	10·00	12·50
40	25c. black on pink	11·00	3·75
41	30c. brown on drab	5·25	8·75
42	40c. red on yellow	11·50	14·00
43	50c. red on pink	18·00	27·00
44	75c. brown on orange	17·00	8·00
45	1f. green	6·00	8·50

POSTAGE DUE STAMPS

1894. Postage Due stamps of French Colonies optd **BENIN**. Imperf.

D46	U 5c. black	£120	70·00
D47	10c. black	£120	65·00
D48	20c. black	£120	70·00
D49	30c. black	£120	55·00

B. PEOPLE'S REPUBLIC

The Republic of Dahomey was renamed the People's Republic of Benin on 30 November 1975.

185 Celebrations

1976. Republic of Benin Proclamation. Mult.

603	50f. Type **185**	75	30
604	60f. President Kerekou making Proclamation	1·10	40
605	100f. Benin arms and flag	1·80	70

186 Skiing

1976. Air. Winter Olympic Games, Innsbruck. Multicoloured.

606	60f. Type **186**	1·30	70
607	150f. Bobsleighing (vert)	2·30	1·20
608	300f. Figure-skating	4·75	2·30

1976. Various Dahomey stamps surch **POPULAIRE DU BENIN** and new value (609/11) or surch only (617/18).

617	**108** 50f. on 1f. multicoloured (postage)	70	30
618	– 60f. on 2f. multicoloured (No. 415)	95	45
609	– 135f. brown, purple and blue (No. 590) (air)	2·00	90
610	– 210f. on 300f. brown, red and blue (No. 591)	2·75	1·30
611	– 380f. on 500f. brown, red and green (No. 592)	4·75	2·20

188 Alexander Graham Bell, Early Telephone and Satellite

1976. Telephone Centenary.

612	**188** 200f. red, violet & brown	3·25	1·70

189 Basketball

1976. Air. Olympic Games, Montreal. Mult.

613	60f. Long jump (horiz)	1·00	45
614	150f. Type **189**	2·00	95
615	200f. Hurdling (horiz)	2·50	1·70
MS616	150 × 120 mm. Nos. 613/15	7·50	6·75

191 Scouts and Camp-fire

1976. African Scout Jamboree, Jos, Nigeria.

619	**191** 50f. purple, brown & blk	75	35
620	– 70f. brown, green & blk	1·00	55

DESIGN: 70f. "Comradeship".

192 Konrad Adenauer

193 Benin 1c. Stamp, 1893, and Lion Cub

1976. Air. Birth Centenary of Konrad Adenauer (German statesman).

621	**192** 90f. slate, blue and red	1·50	65
622	– 250f. blue, red & lt blue	4·00	1·50

DESIGN—HORIZ: 250f. Adenauer and Cologne Cathedral.

1976. Air. "Juvarouen 76" Youth Stamp Exhibition, Rouen.

623	– 60f. blue and turquoise	1·00	50
624	**193** 210f. red, brown & olive	3·25	1·50

DESIGN—HORIZ: 60f. Dahomey 60f. Stamp of 1965, and children's silhouettes.

194 Blood Bank, Cotonou

1976. National Days of Blood Transfusion Service. Multicoloured.

625	5f. Type **194**	20	10
626	50f. Casualty and blood clinic	70	40
627	60f. Donor, patient and ambulance	1·10	55

195 Manioc

196 "Apollo" Emblem and Rocket

1976. National Products Campaign Year. Mult.

628	20f. Type **195**	50	15
629	50f. Maize cultivation	75	25
630	60f. Cocoa trees	1·00	40
631	150f. Cotton plantation	2·30	80

1976. Air. 5th Anniv of "Apollo 14" Space Mission.

632	**196** 130f. lake, brown & blue	1·50	70
633	– 270f. blue, turquoise & red	3·00	1·50

DESIGN: 270f. Landing on Moon.

197 Classroom

198 Roan Antelope

1976. 3rd Anniv of Bariba Periodical "Kparo".

634	**197** 50f. multicoloured	1·00	55

1976. Mammals in Pendjari National Park. Multicoloured.

635	10f. Type **198**	45	25
636	30f. African buffalo	80	50
637	50f. Hippopotamus (horiz)	1·60	85
638	70f. Lion	1·80	1·00

199 "Freedom" **200** "The Annunciation" (Master of Jativa)

1976. 1st Anniv of Proclamation of Republic. Multicoloured.
639 40f. Type **199** 60 25
640 150f. Maize cultivation . . . 1·80 85

1976. Air. Christmas. Multicoloured.
641 50f. Type **200** 80 40
642 60f. "The Nativity" (David) 90 50
643 270f. "Adoration of the Magi" (Dutch school) . . 3·75 1·80
644 300f. "The Flight into Egypt" (Fabriano) (horiz) . . . . 4·00 2·30

201 Table Tennis and Games Emblem

1976. West African University Games, Cotonou. Multicoloured.
645 10f. Type **201** 55 10
646 50f. Sports Hall, Cotonou . . 80 25

202 Loser with Ticket and Winner with Money

1977. Air. 10th Anniv of National Lottery.
647 **202** 50f. multicoloured 75 45

203 Douglas DC-10 crossing Globe **205** Adder

204 Chateau Sassenage, Grenoble

1977. Europafrique.
648 **203** 200f. multicoloured . . . 3·00 2·10

1977. Air. 10th Anniv of International French Language Council.
649 **204** 200f. multicoloured . . . 2·50 1·10

1977. Reptiles and Domestic Animals. Mult.
650 2f. Type **205** 45 10
651 3f. Tortoise 45 10
652 5f. Zebus 45 10
653 10f. Cats 85 25

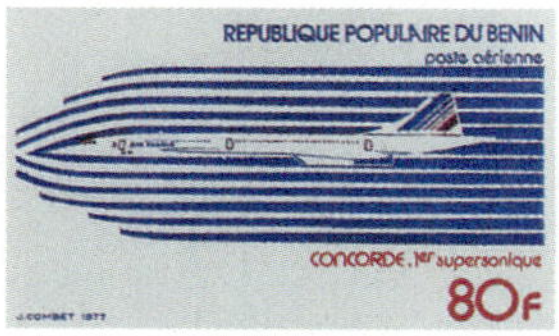

206 Concorde

1977. Air. Aviation.
654 **206** 80f. red and blue 95 40
655 – 150f. red, violet & green 2·10 90
656 – 300f. violet, red & mauve 3·00 1·60
657 – 500f. red, blue & green . . 6·25 3·25
DESIGNS: 150f. "Graf Zeppelin"; 300f. Charles Lindbergh and "Spirit of St. Louis"; 500f. Charles Nungesser and Francois Coli with "L'Oiseau".

207 Footballer heading Ball **209** Karate

208 Rheumatic Patients

1977. Air. World Football Cup Eliminators. Multicoloured.
658 60f. Type **207** 80 35
659 200f. Goalkeeper and players 2·30 1·30

1977. World Rheumatism Year.
660 **208** 100f. multicoloured . . . 1·50 75

1977. 2nd African Games, Lagos.
661 **209** 90f. multicoloured . . . . 1·40 70
662 – 100f. multicoloured . . . 1·40 90
663 – 150f. multicoloured . . . 2·30 1·10
MS664 144 × 92 mm. Nos. 661/3 6·75 6·50
DESIGNS—HORIZ: 100f. Javelin. VERT: 150f. Hurdles.

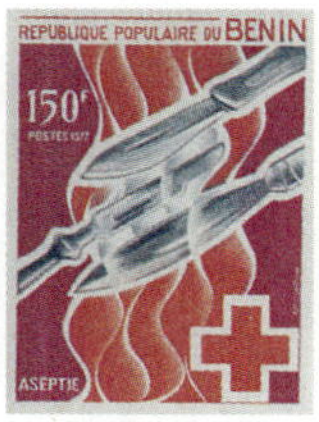

210 Mao Tse-tung **211** Sterilising Scalpels

1977. 1st Death Anniv of Mao Tse-tung.
665 **210** 100f. multicoloured . . . 2·75 1·40

1977. 150th Birth Anniv of Joseph Lister.
666 **211** 150f. grey, red & carmine 2·00 90
667 – 210f. olive, green & red 2·50 1·30
DESIGN: 210f. Lister and antiseptic spray.

212 "Miss Haverfield" (Gainsborough)

1977. Air. Paintings.
668 **212** 100f. green and brown . . 2·40 60
669 – 150f. brown, bistre & red 3·50 1·30
670 – 200f. red and bistre . . . 4·75 1·80
DESIGNS: 150f. "Self-Portrait" (Rubens); 200f. "Study of an Old Man" (da Vinci).

213 "Jarre Trouee" Emblem of King Ghezo (D'Abomey Museum) **214** Atacora Waterfall

1977. Historic Museums of Benin. Mult.
671 50f. Type **213** 75 40
672 60f. Mask (Porto-Novo Museum) (horiz) . . . . . 1·30 55
673 210f. D'Abomey Museum . . 2·75 1·20

1977. Tourism. Multicoloured.
674 50f. Type **214** 70 40
675 60f. Stilt houses, Ganvie (horiz) 95 55
676 150f. Hut village, Savalou . . 2·30 1·10
MS677 144 × 92 mm. Nos. 674/6 5·25 5·25

1977. Air. 1st Commercial Concorde Flight. Paris–New York. No. 654 optd **1er VOL COMMERCIAL 22.11.77 PARIS NEW-YORK**.
678 **206** 80f. red and blue . . . . 1·70 85

216 "Viking" on Mars ("Operation Viking", 1977)

1977. Air. Space Conquest Anniversaries.
679 **216** 100f. brown, olive & red 1·00 60
680 – 150f. blue, turq & mve . . 1·80 85
681 – 200f. brown, blue & red 2·75 1·10
682 – 500f. blue, brn & olive . . 6·50 3·00
DESIGNS AND EVENTS: 150f. Sir Isaac Newton, apple and stars (250th death anniv); 200f. Komarov and "Soyuz 2" over Moon (10th death anniv); 500f. Space dog "Laika" and rocket (20th anniv of ascent into Space).

217 Monument, Red Flag Square, Cotonou

1977. Air. 1st Anniv of Inauguration of Red Flag Square Monument.
683 **217** 500f. multicoloured . . . 6·25 2·75

218 Mother and Child with Owl of Wisdom

1977. Fight against Witchcraft. Multicoloured.
684 60f. Type **218** . . . . 1·30 55
685 150f. Felling the tree of sorcery . . . . 2·50 1·10

219 "Suzanne Fourment"

1977. Air. 400th Birth Anniv of Rubens.
686 **219** 200f. brown, red & green 3·25 1·30
687 – 380f. orange and brown 5·50 2·20
DESIGN: 380f. "Albert Rubens".

220 Battle Scene

1978. "Victory over Imperialism".
688 **220** 50f. multicoloured . . . . 1·20 45

221 Benin Houses and Map of Heads **223** Abdoulaye Issa

222 Sir Alexander Fleming, Microscope and Drugs

1978. General Population Census.
689 **221** 50f. multicoloured 80 35

1978. 50th Anniv of Discovery of Antibiotics.
690 **222** 300f. multicoloured . . . 4·50 2·10

1978. 1st Death Anniv of Abdoulaye Issa.
691 **223** 100f. multicoloured . . . 1·00 50

224 El Hadj Omar

1978. Heroes of Anti-colonial Resistance.
692 – 90f. multicoloured . . . . 1·30 45
693 **224** 100f. green, grey & blue 1·30 65
DESIGN: 90f. Samory Toure.

225 "Communications"

1978. 10th World Telecommunications Day.
694 **225** 100f. multicoloured . . . 1·50 75

226 Footballer and Stadium

1978. World Cup Football Championship, Argentina. Multicoloured.

695	200f. Type **226**	2·30	1·00
696	300f. Tackling (vert)	3·00	1·60
697	500f. Footballer and world map	5·50	2·50
MS698	190 × 121 mm. Nos. 695/7 in different colours	12·00	9·00

1978. Argentina's Victory in World Cup Football Championship. Nos. 695/7 optd.

699	**226** 200f. multicoloured	2·00	1·10
700	– 300f. multicoloured	3·00	1·90
701	– 500f. multicoloured	5·50	3·25
MS702	190 × 121 mm. Nos. 699/701 multicoloured	13·50	12·50

OPTS: 200f. **FINALE ARGENTINE: 3 HOLLANDE: 1**; 300f. **CHAMPION 1978 ARGENTINE**; 500f. **3e BRESIL 4e ITALIE**.

228 Map, Olympic Flag and Basketball Players

1978. 3rd African Games, Algiers. Multicoloured.

703	50f. Type **228**	55	25
704	60f. African map and Volleyball	95	45
705	80f. Cyclists and map of Algeria	1·00	55
MS706	208 × 80 mm. Nos. 703/5 in different colours	4·00	3·75

229 Martin Luther King

230 Bicycle Taxi (Oueme)

1978. 10th Anniv of Martin Luther King's Assassination.

707	**229** 300f. multicoloured	3·50	1·70

1978. Benin Provinces. Multicoloured.

708	50f. Type **230**	1·20	40
709	60f. Leather work (Borgou)	1·10	40
710	70f. Drums (Oueme)	1·20	45
711	100f. Calabash with burnt-work ornamentation (Zou)	1·50	55

231 "Stamps" and Magnifying Glass

1978. Philatelic Exhibition, Riccione, Italy.

712	**231** 200f. multicoloured	2·30	1·10

232 Parthenon and Frieze showing Horsemen

1978. Air. UNESCO Campaign for the Preservation of the Acropolis. Multicoloured.

713	70f. Acropolis and Frieze showing Procession	80	25
714	250f. Type **232**	2·50	1·20
715	500f. The Parthenon (horiz)	5·00	2·20

235 Turkeys

236 Post Runner and Boeing 747

1978. Domestic Poultry. Multicoloured.

722	10f. Type **235**	35	10
723	20f. Ducks	60	25
724	50f. Chickens	1·70	50
725	60f. Helmeted guineafowl	1·90	70

1978. Centenary of UPU. Paris Congress. Mult.

726	50f. Messenger of the Dahomey Kings (horiz)	1·00	40
727	60f. Pirogue oarsman, boat and post car	1·10	40
728	90f. Type **236**	1·30	55

237 Red-breasted Merganser and Baden 1851 1k. Stamp

1978. Air. "Philexafrique" Exhibition, Libreville (Gabon) (1st issue) and International Stamp Fair, Essen, West Germany. Multicoloured.

729	100f. Type **237**	4·00	1·50
730	100f. African Buffalo and Dahomey 1966 50f. African Pygmy Goose stamp	4·00	1·50

See also Nos. 747/8.

238 Raoul Follereau

1978. 1st Death Anniv of Raoul Follereau (leprosy pioneer).

731	**238** 200f. multicoloured	2·00	95

239 Wilbur and Orville Wright and Wright Flyer 1

1978. Air. 75th Anniv of First Powered Flight.

732	**239** 500f. blue, yellow & brn	6·00	3·00

240 I.Y.C. Emblem

241 Hydrangea

1979. International Year of the Child. Mult.

733	10f. Type **240**	15	10
734	20f. Children in balloon	30	10
735	50f. Children dancing around globe	45	30

1979. Flowers. Multicoloured.

736	20f. Type **241**	20	25
737	25f. Assangokan	45	25
738	30f. Geranium	70	35
739	40f. Water Lily (horiz)	90	40

242 Flags around Map of Africa

1979. OCAM Summit Meeting, Cotonou (1st series). Multicoloured.

740	50f. Type **242**	55	40
741	60f. Flags and map of Benin	85	45
742	80f. OCAM flag and map of member countries	1·20	60

See also Nos. 754/6.

1979. Various stamps surch.

743	**205** 50f. on 2f. multicoloured (postage)	£190	2·75
743a	– 50f. on 3f. multicoloured (651)	95·00	2·75
743b	– 50f. on 70f. brown, green and black (620)	95·00	2·75
744	**207** 50f. on 60f. mult (air)	95·00	2·75
745	**192** 50f. on 90f. blue, deep blue and red	95·00	2·75
746	– 50f. on 150f. mult (607)	95·00	2·75
747	**189** 50f. on 150f. mult	95·00	2·75

244 Antenna, Satellite and Wave Pattern

1979. World Telecommunications Day.

748	**244** 50f. multicoloured	80	45

245 Headquarters Building

1979. West African Savings Bank Building Opening.

749	**245** 50f. multicoloured	75	40

246 "Resolution" and "Discovery" in Karakakoa Bay, Hawaii

1979. Air. Death Bicentenary of Capt. James Cook.

750	**246** 20f. blue, green & brown	1·30	40
751	– 50f. brown, green & blue	1·00	45

DESIGN: 50f. Cook's death at Kowrowa.

247 Guelede Mask, Abomey Tapestry and Fiery-breasted Bush Shrike

1979. "Philexafrique" Stamp Exhibition, Gabon (2nd issue).

752	**247** 15f. multicoloured	1·50	55
753	– 50f. orange, yellow & turq	2·00	95

DESIGN: 50f. Lockheed Tristar 500, satellite, U.P.U. emblem and canoe post.

1979. Common African and Mauritian Organization Summit Conference, Cotonou (2nd issue). Nos. 740/2 optd **26 Au 28 Juin 1979**.

754	50f. Type **242**	80	40
755	60f. Map of Benin and flags of members	95	50
756	80f. OCAM flag and map showing member countries	1·10	55

249 Olympic Flame, Benin Flags and Pictograms

1979. Pre-Olympic Year. Multicoloured.

757	10f. Type **249**	30	10
758	50f. High jump	1·00	45

250 Roan Antelope

1979. Endangered Animals. Multicoloured.

759	5f. Type **250**	40	20
760	10f. Giraffes (vert)	55	35
761	20f. Chimpanzee	85	50
762	50f. African elephants (vert)	1·80	75

251 Emblem, Concorde and Map of Africa

1979. 20th Anniv of ASECNA (African Air Safety Organization). Multicoloured.

763	50f. Type **251**	50	25
764	60f. As No. 763 but emblem at bottom right and without dates	55	25

252 Post Offices, Antenna, Telephone and Savings Book

254 Copernicus and Planetary System

253 Rotary Emblem, Symbols of Services and Globe

1979. 20th Anniv of Posts and Telecommunications Office. Multicoloured.
765 50f. Type **252** 50 25
766 60f. Collecting, sorting and delivering mail 55 25

1980. 75th Anniv of Rotary International. Mult.
767 90f. Cotonou Rotary Club banner (vert) 95 45
768 200f. Type **253** . . . . 1·80 95

1980. 50th Anniv of Discovery of Planet Pluto. Multicoloured.
769 70f. Kepler and astrolabe . . 80 45
770 100f. Type **254** . . . . 1·20 55

255 Pharaonic Capital

1980. 20th Anniv of Nubian Monuments Preservation Campaign. Multicoloured.
771 50f. Type **255** 55 30
772 60f. Rameses II, Abu Simbel 95 45
773 150f. Temple, Abu Simbel (horiz) . . . . 1·50 85

256 Lenin in Library

1980. 110th Birth Anniv of Lenin. Mult.
774 50f. Lenin and globe 75 25
775 150f. Type **256** . . . . 2·00 85

257 Monument

1980. Martyrs Square, Cotonou.
776 **257** 50f. multicoloured 45 10
777 – 60f. multicoloured 55 25
778 – 70f. multicoloured 75 25
779 – 100f. multicoloured . . . 1·20 40
DESIGNS—HORIZ: 60f. to 100f. Different views of the monument.

258 Farmer using Telephone

259 Assan

1980. World Telecommunications Day. Mult.
780 50f. Type **258** 45 25
781 60f. Telephone 55 30

1980. Traditional Musical Instruments. Mult.
782 5f. Type **259** 25 10
783 10f. Tinbo (horiz) 25 10
784 15f. Tam-tam sato 55 25
785 20f. Kora (horiz) 55 25
786 30f. Gangan (horiz) 85 40
787 50f. Sinhoun (horiz) . . . . 1·60 55

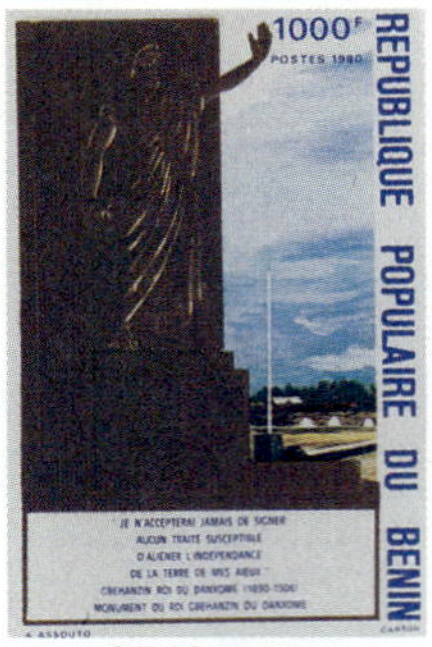

260 Monument

1980. King Gbehanzin Monument.
788 **260** 1000f. multicoloured . . . 13·00 8·50

261 Dieudonne Costes, Maurice Bellonte and "Point d'Interrogation"

1980. 50th Anniv of First Paris–New York Non-stop Flight.
789 – 90f. red, lt blue & blue . . 1·00 45
790 **261** 100f. red, blue and flesh 1·20 55
DESIGN: 90f. Airplane "Point d'Interrogation" and scenes of New York and Paris.

262 "Lunokhod I"

1980. 10th Anniv of "Lunokhod I".
791 – 90f. brown, blue and violet (postage) 95 55
792 **262** 210f. purple, blue and yellow (air) . . . . . . 2·75 1·30
DESIGN (48 × 36 mm): 90f. Rocket and "Lunokhod I".

263 Show-jumping

1980. Olympic Games, Moscow. Multicoloured.
793 50f. Olympic Flame, running track, emblem and mascot Mischa the bear (horiz) . . 50 25
794 60f. Type **263** 55 40
795 70f. Judo (horiz) 95 45
796 200f. Olympic flag and globe surrounded by sports pictogram . . . . 2·00 90
797 300f. Weightlifting . . . . . 3·00 1·50

264 OCAM Building

1980. Common African and Mauritian Organization Village, Cotonou. Multicoloured.
798 50f. Entrance to OCAM village 60 25
799 60f. View of village 75 25
800 70f. Type **264** 95 55

265 Dancers

1980. Agbadja Dance. Multicoloured.
801 30f. Type **265** 55 25
802 50f. Singer and musicians . . 95 45
803 60f. Dancers and musicians 95 55

266 Casting a Net

267 Philippines under Magnifying Glass

1980. Fishing. Multicoloured.
804 5f. Type **266** 10 10
805 10f. Fisherman with catch (vert) 30 10
806 15f. Line fishing 30 25
807 20f. Fisherman emptying eel-pot 35 25
808 50f. Hauling in a net 95 45
809 60f. Fish farm 95 45

1980. World Tourism Conference, Manila. Mult.
810 50f. Type **267** 55 25
811 60f. Conference flag on globe 95 30

268 "Othreis materna"

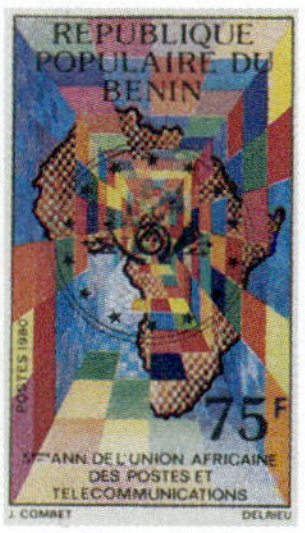

269 Map of Africa and Posthorn

1980. Insects. Multicoloured.
812 40f. Type **268** 80 35
813 50f. "Othreis fullonia" (butterfly) . . . . 1·20 45
814 200f. "Oryctes" sp. (beetle) 3·75 1·60

1980. 5th Anniv of African Posts and Telecommunications.
815 **269** 75f. multicoloured 75 25

270 Hands freed from Chains

271 "Self-portrait"

1980. 30th Anniv of Signing of Human Rights Convention. Multicoloured.
816 30f. Type **270** 30 10
817 50f. African pushing through bars 50 25
818 60f. Figure holding Human Rights flame 75 25

1980. 90th Death Anniv of Van Gogh (artist). Multicoloured.
819 100f. Type **271** . . . . 2·00 70
820 300f. "The Postman Roulin" 5·00 2·20

272 Offenbach and Scene from "Orpheus in the Underworld"

1980. Death Centenary of Jacques Offenbach (composer).
821 **272** 50f. black, red and green 1·30 50
822 – 60f. blue, brown & dp brn 1·90 75
DESIGN: 60f. Offenbach and scene from "La Vie Parisienne".

273 Kepler and Astronomical Diagram

1980. 30th Death Anniv of Johannes Kepler (astronomer).
823 **273** 50f. red, blue and grey . . 75 25
824 – 60f. blue, black and green 95 45
DESIGN: 60f. Kepler, satellite and dish aerials.

274 Footballers

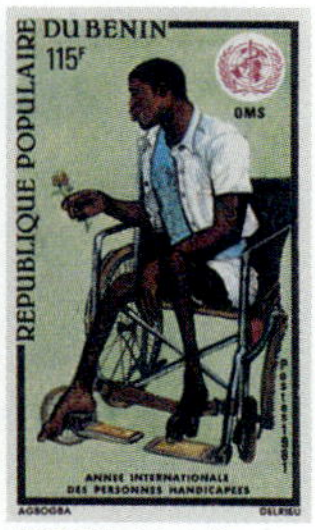

275 Disabled Person holding Flower

1981. Air. World Cup Football Championship. Multicoloured.
825 200f. Football and globe . . 1·80 70
826 500f. Type **274** . . . . 5·00 1·90

1981. International Year of Disabled People.
827 **275** 115f. multicoloured . . . 1·20 50

276 Yuri Gagarin

1981. 20th Anniv of First Man in Space.
828 **276** 500f. multicoloured . . . 5·50 2·75

277 ITU and WHO Emblems and Ribbons forming Caduceus

278 Amaryllis

1981. World Telecommunications Day.
829 **277** 115f. multicoloured . . . 1·20 45

1981. Flowers. Multicoloured.
830 10f. Type **278** 20 15
831 20f. "Eischornia crassipes" 45 30
832 80f. "Parkia biglobosa" . . . 1·50 50

279 Hotel and Map

1981. Opening of Benin Sheraton Hotel.
833 **279** 100f. multicoloured . . . 1·00 45

1981. Surch **50F.**
834 **216** 50f. on 100f. brown, green and red 85 25
835 **193** 50f. on 210f. red, brown and green 85 25

281 Prince Charles, Lady Diana Spencer and Tower Bridge

1981. Air. British Royal Wedding.
836 **281** 500f. multicoloured . . . 4·50 2·00

282 Guinea Pig

1981. Domestic Animals. Multicoloured.
837 5f. Type **282** 35 25
838 60f. Cat . . . . 1·00 45
839 80f. Dogs . . . . 1·40 70

283 Heinrich von Stephan (founder of UPU)

1981. World Universal Postal Union Day.
840 **283** 100f. slate and red 95 45

284 Heads, Quill, Paper Darts and U.P.U. Emblem

1981. International Letter Writing Week.
841 **284** 100f. blue and purple . . 95 45

285 "The Dance"

1981. Air. Birth Centenary of Pablo Picasso. Multicoloured.
842 300f. Type **285** . . . . . 3·00 1·20
843 500f. "The Three Musicians" 5·50 2·00

286 Globe, Map of Member Countries and Communication Symbols

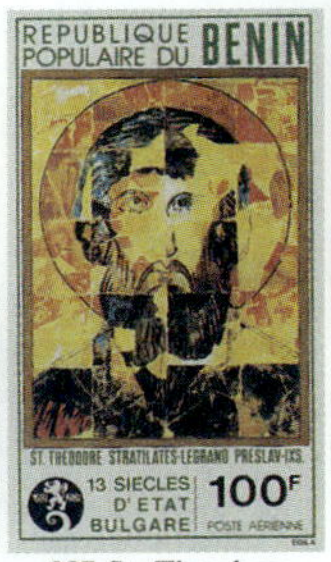

287 St. Theodore Stratilates (tile painting)

1981. 5th Anniv of ECOWAS (Economic Community of West African States).
844 **286** 60f. multicoloured 75 25

1981. Air. 1300th Anniv of Bulgarian State.
845 **287** 100f. multicoloured . . . 95 45

288 Tractor and Map

1981. 10th Anniv of West African Rice Development Association.
846 **288** 60f. multicoloured 75 25

289 Pope John Paul II

1982. Air. Papal Visit.
847 **289** 80f. multicoloured . . . . 2·00 90

290 John Glenn

1982. Air. 20th Anniv of First United States Manned Space Flight.
848 **290** 500f. multicoloured . . . 5·50 2·20

291 Dr. Robert Koch

1982. Centenary of Discovery of Tubercle Bacillus.
849 **291** 115f. multicoloured . . . 1·80 70

292 Washington, U.S. Flag and Map

1982. 250th Birth Anniv of George Washington.
850 **292** 200f. multicoloured . . . 2·30 85

1982. Red Cross. Surch **Croix Rouge 8 Mai 1982 60f.**
851 **266** 60f. on 5f. multicoloured 75 25

294 Map of Member Countries and Torch **295** Scouts round Campfire

1982. 5th Economic Community of West African States Summit, Cotonou.
852 **294** 60f. multicoloured 60 25

1982. Air. 75th Anniv of Boy Scout Movement.
853 **295** 105f. multicoloured . . . 1·20 60

296 Footballers

1982. World Cup Football Championship, Spain. Multicoloured.
854 90f. Type **296** 95 40
855 300f. Leg with sock formed from flags of participating countries and globe/ football . . . . 3·00 1·20

1982. African Posts and Telegraph Union. Surch **UAPT 1982 60f.**
856 **282** 60f. on 5f. multicoloured 75 25

298 Stamp of Map of France and Magnifying Glass

1982. "Philexfrance 82" International Stamp Exhibition, Paris.
857 **298** 90f. multicoloured 95 45

1982. World Cup Football Championship Results. Nos. 854/5 optd.
858 90f. Type **296** . . . . 1·20 45
859 300f. Leg with flags of participating countries and football "globe" . . . . . 3·75 1·30
OVERPRINTS: 90f. **COUPE 82 ITALIE bat RFA 3-1**; 300f. **COUPE 82 1 ITALIE 2 RFA 3 POLOGNE.**

1982. Riccione Stamp Exhibition. Optd **RICCIONE 1982.**
860 **231** 200f. multicoloured . . . 1·80 80

301 Laughing Kookaburra ("Dacelo Gigas") **302** World Map and Satellite

1982. Birds. Multicoloured.
861 5f. Type **301** 65 30
862 10f. Bluethroat ("La Gorge Bleue") (horiz) . . . . . . 1·00 30
863 15f. Barn swallow ("L'Hirondelle") . . . . . 1·00 35
864 20f. Woodland kingfisher ("Martin-Pecheur") and Village weaver ("Tisserin") 1·60 40
865 30f. Reed warbler ("La Rousserolle") (horiz) . . . 2·20 50
866 60f. Warbler sp. ("Faurette Commoune") (horiz) . . . 3·00 75
867 80f. Eagle owl ("Hibou Grand Doc") . . . . . . 5·50 1·40
868 100f. Sulphur-crested cockatoo ("Cacatoes") . . 6·50 1·80

1982. I.T.U. Delegates' Conference, Nairobi.
869 **302** 200f. turq, blue & blk . . 2·00 80

303 UPU Emblem and Heads

1982. UPU Day.
870 **303** 100f. green, blue & brown 1·00 45

305 "Claude Monet in his Studio"

1982. Air. 150th Birth Anniv of Edouard Manet (artist).
876 **305** 300f. multicoloured . . . 6·75 2·40

306 "Virgin and Child" (Grunewald)

1982. Air. Christmas. Multicoloured.
877 200f. Type **306** . . . . 2·20 1·10
878 300f. "Virgin and Child with Angels and Cherubins" (Correggio) . . . . 3·25 1·40

307 Pres. Mitterrand and Pres. Kerekou

1983. Visit of President Mitterrand.
879 **307** 90f. multicoloured . . . . 1·50 70

1983. Various stamps surch.
880 – 60f. on 50f. multicoloured (No. 798) (postage) . . 1·20 45
881 – 60f. on 70f. multicoloured (No. 778) . . . . . . 1·20 45
882 **279** 60f. on 100f. mult . . . . 47·00 2·75
883 – 75f. on 80f. multicoloured (No. 832) . . . . . . 1·40 55
884 – 75f. on 80f. multicoloured (No. 839) . . . . . . 1·50 85
885 **262** 75f. on 210f. red, blue and yellow (air) . . . . . . 1·50 85

309 "Tender Benin" (tug) and "Amazone" (oil rig)

1983. Seme Oilfield.
886 **309** 125f. multicoloured . . . 1·50 60

1983. Various stamps surch.
887 **267** 5f. on 50f. multicoloured 3·00 50
888 **284** 10f. on 100f. blue & pur 3·00 50
889 – 10f. on 200f. mult (No. 659) . . . . . . 3·00 50
890 – 15f. on 200f. red and bistre (No. 670) . . . . 3·00 50
891 – 15f. on 200f. mult (No. 796) . . . . . . 3·00 50
892 – 15f. on 210f. green, deep green and red (No. 667) 3·00 50
893 – 15f. on 270f. mult (No. 643) . . . . . . 3·00 50
894 **219** 20f. on 200f. brown, red and olive . . . . . . 3·00 50
895 – 25f. on 70f. mult (No. 795) . . . . . . 3·00 60
896 – 25f. on 210f. mult (No. 673) . . . . . . 3·00 60
897 – 25f. on 270f. blue, turq & red (No. 633) . . . . 3·00 50
898 – 25f. on 380f. brown and red (No. 687) . . . . . 3·00 50
899 – 30f. on 200f. brown, blue and red (No. 681) . . . 3·00 60
900 **290** 40f. on 500f. mult . . . . 3·00 60
901 **282** 75f. on 5f. multicoloured 3·25 65

902 – 75f. on 100f. red, blue and pink (No. 790) . . . . 3·25 65
903 – 75f. on 150f. mult (No. 631) . . . . 3·25 65
904 – 75f. on 150f. violet, red and green (No. 655) . . 3·25 65
905 **211** 75f. on 150f. grey, orange and red . . . . 3·25 65
906 – 75f. on 150f. dp brown, brown & red (No. 669) 3·25 65

311 WCY Emblem

1983. World Communications Year.
907 **311** 185f. multicoloured . . . 1·80 80

312 Stamps of Benin and Thailand and World Map

1983. Air. "Bangkok 1983" International Stamp Exhibition.
908 **312** 300f. multicoloured . . . 3·00 1·40

313 Hand with Tweezers and Stamp

1983. "Riccione 83" Stamp Fair, San Marino.
909 **313** 500f. multicoloured . . . 4·50 2·00

314 First Aid **315** Carved Table and Chairs

1983. 20th Anniv of Benin Red Cross.
910 **314** 105f. multicoloured . . . 1·20 60

1983. Benin Woodwork. Multicoloured.
911 75f. Type **315** . . . . . . 1·00 25
912 90f. Rustic table and chairs 1·10 40
913 200f. Monkeys holding box 2·00 75

316 Boeing 747, World Map and UPU Emblem

1983. UPU Day.
914 **316** 125f. green, blue & brown 1·20 60

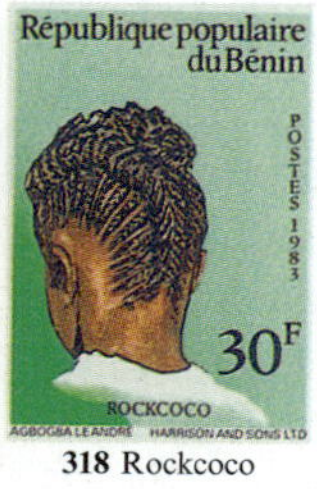

317 Egoun **318** Rockcoco

1983. Religious Cults. Multicoloured.
915 75f. Type **317** . . . . 1·00 45
916 75f. Zangbeto . . . . 1·00 45

1983. Hair-styles. Multicoloured.
917 30f. Type **318** 30 15
918 75f. Serpent 75 45
919 90f. Songas . . . . 1·30 55

319 Alfred Nobel

1983. 150th Birth Anniv of Alfred Nobel.
920 **319** 300f. multicoloured . . . 3·00 1·50

320 "Madonna of Lorette" (Raphael)

1983. Air. Christmas.
921 **320** 200f. multicoloured . . . 2·75 1·20

1984. Various stamps surch.
922 – 5f. on 150f. mult (No. 685) (postage) . . 3·25 75
923 **316** 5f. on 125f. green, blue and brown . . . . . . 3·25 75
924 **292** 10f. on 200f. mult . . . . 3·25 75
925 – 10f. on 200f. mult (No. 913) . . . . . . 3·25 75
926 – 15f. on 300f. mult (No. 820) . . . . . . 3·25 80
927 – 25f. on 300f. mult (No. 644) . . . . . . 3·25 80
928 **276** 40f. on 500f. mult . . . . 3·25 80
929 **314** 75f. on 105f. mult . . . . 3·50 1·00
930 **275** 75f. on 115f. mult . . . . 3·50 90
931 **277** 75f. on 115f. mult . . . . 3·50 90
932 **291** 75f. on 115f. mult . . . . 3·50 90
933 **311** 75f. on 185f. mult . . . . 3·50 1·00
934 **302** 75f. on 200f. turquoise, blue and black . . . . 3·50 1·00
935 **320** 15f. on 200f. mult (air) . . 3·25 75
936 **285** 15f. on 300f. mult . . . . 3·25 75
937 **312** 25f. on 300f. mult . . . . 3·25 80
938 **281** 40f. on 500f. mult . . . . 3·50 90
939 **295** 75f. on 105f. mult . . . . 3·50 90
940 **306** 90f. on 200f. mult . . . . 3·75 95
941 **305** 90f. on 300f. mult . . . . 3·75 95

322 Flags, Agriculture and Symbol of Unity and Growth **323** UPU Emblem and Magnifying Glass

1984. 25th Anniv of Council of Unity.
942 **322** 75f. multicoloured 75 25
943 90f. multicoloured 95 40

1984. 19th Universal Postal Union Congress, Hamburg.
944 **323** 90f. multicoloured 95 45

324 Abomey-Calavi Ground Station

1984. Inauguration of Abomey-Calavi Ground Station.
945 **324** 75f. multicoloured 75 45

325 Koumboro (Borgou) **326** Olympic Mascot

1984. Traditional Costumes. Multicoloured.
946 5f. Type **325** 15 10
947 10f. Taka (Borgou) 30 25
948 20f. Toko (Atacora Province) 30 25

1984. Air. Olympic Games, Los Angeles.
949 **326** 300f. multicoloured . . . 3·00 1·40

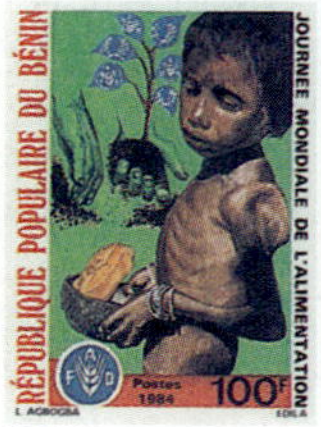

327 Plant and Starving Child **328** Anatosaurus

1984. World Food Day.
950 **327** 100f. multicoloured . . . 95 45

1984. Prehistoric Animals. Multicoloured.
951 75f. Type **328** . . . . 3·75 65
952 90f. Brontosaurus . . . . . 4·00 90

329 "Virgin and Child" (detail, Murillo)

1984. Air. Christmas.
953 **329** 500f. multicoloured . . . 5·50 2·20

1984. Various stamps surch.
954 **203** 75f. on 200f. mult (post) 6·00 1·30
955 **226** 75f. on 200f. mult . . . . 6·00 1·30
956 – 75f. on 300f. mult (No. 696) . . . . . . 6·00 1·30
957 **229** 75f. on 300f. mult . . . . 6·00 1·30
958 – 90f. on 300f. mult (No. 855) . . . . . . 6·25 1·40
959 – 90f. on 500f. mult (No. 697) . . . . . . 6·25 1·40
960 – 90f. on 500f. mult (No. 701) . . . . . . 6·75 1·40
961 **204** 75f. on 200f. mult (air) . . 4·50 1·30
962 – 75f. on 200f. mult (No. 825) . . . . . . 4·50 1·30
963 – 75f. on 300f. violet, red and mauve (No. 656) 4·50 1·30
964 – 75f. on 300f. mult (No. 878) . . . . . . 4·50 1·30
965 **239** 90f. on 500f. blue, yellow and brown . . . . . 4·50 1·40
966 – 90f. on 500f. mult (No. 715) . . . . . . 4·50 1·40
967 – 90f. on 500f. mult (No. 843) . . . . . . 4·50 1·40

331 Sidon Merchant Ship (2nd century)

1984. Air. Ships.
968 **331** 90f. black, green & blue 1·30 60
969 – 125f. multicoloured . . . 2·00 85
DESIGN—VERT: 125f. Sail merchantman "Wavertree", 1895.

332 Emblem on Globe and Hands reaching for Cultural Symbols

1985. 15th Anniv of Cultural and Technical Co-operation Agency.
970 **332** 300f. multicoloured . . . 3·25 1·20

333 Benin Arms **334** Soviet Flag, Soldier and Tank

1985. Air. Postal Convention between Benin and Sovereign Military Order of Malta. Multicoloured.
971 75f. Type **333** 75 25
972 75f. Arms of Sovereign Military Order 75 25

1985. 40th Anniv of End of Second World War.
973 **334** 100f. multicoloured . . .

335 Teke Dance, Borgou

1985. Traditional Dances. Multicoloured.
974 75f. Type **335** . . . . 1·00 40
975 100f. Tipen ti dance, Atacora 1·30 60

1985. Various Dahomey Stamps optd **POPULAIRE DU BENIN** (985/6) or **REPUBLIQUE POPULAIRE DU BENIN** (others), Nos. 976/7 and 979/85 surch also.
976 **174** 15f. on 40f. mult (post) 2·75 60
977 **182** 25f. on 40f. brown, blue and violet (air) . . . . 1·20 60
978 **115** 40f. black, purple & bl 1·30 70
978a – 75f. on 85f. brown, blue and green (No. 468) 48·00 1·60
979 – 75f. on 85f. brown, blue and green (No. 482) 3·00 75
980 **135** 75f. on 100f. purple, violet and green . . . 3·00 75
981 – 75f. on 125f. green, blue and purple (No. 509) 3·00 75
982 **127** 90f. on 20f. brown, blue and green . . . . . 3·00 80
983 – 90f. on 150f. purple, blue & brown (No. 456) . 3·00 80
984 – 90f. on 200f. green, red and blue (No. 438) . . 3·00 80
985 – 90f. on 200f. mult (No. 563) . . . . . . 3·00 80
986 – 150f. mult (No. 562) . . 3·50 1·00

338 Oil Rig

1985. Air. "Philexafrique" International Stamp Exhibition, Lome, Togo (1st issue). Mult.
987 200f. Type **338** . . . . . . 2·30 1·50
988 200f. Footballers . . . . . . 2·30 1·50
See also Nos. 999/1000.

339 Emblem

1985. International Youth Year.
989 **339** 150f. multicoloured . . . 1·40 75

340 Football between Globes

1985. World Cup Football Championship, Mexico (1986) (1st issue).
990 **340** 200f. multicoloured . . . 1·80 95
See also No. 1015.

341 Boeing 727, Map and Emblem

1985. 25th Anniv of Aerial Navigation Security Agency for Africa and Malagasy.
991 **341** 150f. multicoloured . . . 1·80 75

342 "Boletus edulis"
343 Audubon and Arctic Skua ("Labbe Parasite")

1985. Fungi. Multicoloured.
992 35f. Type **342** . . . . 1·50 45
993 40f. "Amanita phalloides" . . 1·80 75
994 100f. "Paxillus involutus" . . 4·50 1·70

1985. Birth Bicentenary of John J. Audubon (ornithologist). Multicoloured.
995 150f. Type **343** . . . . 3·00 1·50
996 300f. Audubon and oystercatcher ("Huitrier Pie") . . . . 7·00 2·20

344 Emblem, Hands and Dove

1985. 40th Anniv of United Nations Organization and 25th Anniv of Benin's Membership.
997 **344** 250f. multicoloured . . . 2·30 1·10

345 Stamps and Globe

1985. "Italia '85" International Stamp Exhibition, Rome.
998 **345** 200f. multicoloured . . . 1·80 95

1985. "Philexafrique" International Stamp Exhibition, Lome, Togo (2nd issue). As Type **338**. Multicoloured.
999 250f. Forest and hand holding tools . . . . . . 4·25 1·80
1000 250f. Magnifying glass over judo stamp . . . . 3·00 1·50

1985. Various Dahomey stamps optd **Republique Populaire du Benin**. Nos. 1001/9 and 1011 surch also.
1001 – 75f. on 35f. mult (No. 596) (postage) . . 2·50 60
1002 – 90f. on 70f. multicoloured (No. 419) . . . . . . 2·50 65
1003 – 90f. on 140f. multicoloured (No. 446) . . . . . . 2·50 65
1004 **113** 100f. on 40f. red, brown and green . . . . . . 1·90 65
1005 – 150f. on 45f. multicoloured (No. 597) . . . . . . 2·10 80
1006 – 75f. on 70f. multicoloured (No. 342) (air) . . . . 4·25 90
1007 – 75f. on 100f. multicoloured (No. 251) . . . . . . 4·25 90
1008 **59** 75f. on 200f. mult . . . 4·25 90
1009 – 90f. on 250f. multicoloured (No. 272) . . . . . . 4·25 90
1010 **110** 100f. multicoloured . . . 2·75 90
1011 – 150f. on 500f. multicoloured (No. 252) . . . . . . 2·75 90
No. 1010 is surcharged on the unoverprinted unissued stamp subsequently issued as No. 422.

349 Church, Children playing and Nativity Scene

1985. Air. Christmas.
1012 **349** 500f. multicoloured . . . 5·25 2·30

350 Emblem

1986. 10th Anniv of African Parliamentary Union and Ninth Conference, Cotonou.
1013 **350** 100f. multicoloured . . . 95 50

351 Halley, Comet and "Giotto" Space Probe

1986. Appearance of Halley's Comet.
1014 **351** 205f. multicoloured . . . 3·00 1·50

352 Footballers

1986. World Cup Football Championship, Mexico (2nd issue). Multicoloured.
1015 **352** 500f. Footballers . . . . 4·50 2·30

353 Dead and Healthy Trees
354 Amazone

1986. Anti-desertification Campaign.
1016 **353** 150f. multicoloured . . . 1·50 70

1986.
1017 **354** 100f. blue 75 30
1018 150f. purple . . . . . . 1·30 50

355 "Haemanthus"
356 "Inachis io", "Aglais urticae" and "Nymphalis antiopa"

1986. Flowers. Multicoloured.
1019 100f. Type **355** . . . . . . 1·10 70
1020 205f. "Hemerocallis" . . . 2·75 1·20

1986. Butterflies. Multicoloured.
1021 150f. Type **356** . . . . . . 3·00 1·30
1022 150f. "Anthocharis cardamines", "Papilio machaon" and "Cynthia cardui" . . . . 3·00 1·30

1986. Various stamps of Dahomey surch **Republique Populaire du Benin** and new value.
1024 – 150f. on 100f. mult (444) (postage) . . . . . . 55·00 2·75
1025 – 15f. on 85f. mult (600) (air) . . . . 33·00 2·75
1026 – 25f. on 200f. mult (432) 55·00 2·75
1027 **150** 25f. on 200f. deep green, violet and green . . . 55·00 2·75
1030 **175** 100f. purple, indigo & bl 55·00 2·75
1031 **128** 150f. on 100f. blue, violet and red . . . .

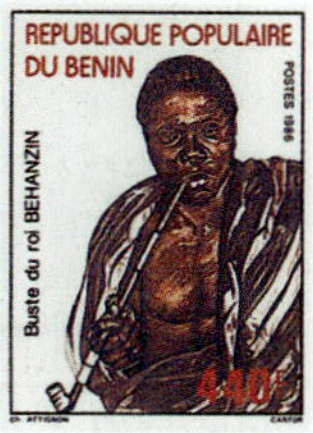
358 Statue and Buildings
359 Bust of King Behanzin

1986. Centenary of Statue of Liberty.
1032 **358** 250f. multicoloured . . . 3·00 1·20

1986. King Behanzin.
1033 **359** 440f. multicoloured . . . 5·00 2·20
For design in smaller size, see Nos. 1101/4.

360 Family with Crib, Church and Nativity Scene

1986. Air. Christmas.
1034 **360** 300f. multicoloured . . . 5·25 1·80

361 Rainbow and Douglas DC-10

1986. Air. 25th Anniv of Air Afrique.
1035 **361** 100f. multicoloured . . . 1·00 50

362 Emblem around Map in Cog

1987. Brazil Culture Week, Cotonou.
1036 **362** 150f. multicoloured . . . 1·40 65

363 Cotonou Centre for the Blind and Partially Sighted

1987. Rotary International 910 District Conference, Cotonou.
1037 **363** 300f. multicoloured . . . 3·25 1·40

1987. Various stamps of Dahomey optd **Republique Populaire du Benin**. Nos. 1038/9 and 1042/53 surch also.
1038 **129** 10f. on 65f. black, violet and red (postage) . . . . . .
1039 – 15f. on 100f. red, blue and green (434) . . . 43·00 1·80
1040 **98** 40f. green, blue and brown . . . . 55·00 2·75
1042 – 150f. on 200f. mult (560) . . . .
1043 **144** 10f. on 65f. black, yellow & purple (air)
1046 – 25f. on 150f. mult (487) 55·00 2·75
1047 – 30f. on 300f. mult (602)
1048 **140** 40f. on 15f. purple, green and blue . . . 47·00 2·75
1049 – 40f. on 100f. mult (453) 43·00 2·75
1051 – 50f. on 140f. mult (601) 55·00 2·75
1052 – 50f. on 500f. mult (252) 55·00 2·75
1053 – 70f. on 250f. mult (462)
1054 – 80f. mult (286) . . . . 55·00 2·75
1055 – 100f. mult (429) . . . . 55·00 2·75
1055a – 100f. mult (447) . . . . 55·00 2·75

365 De Dion-Bouton and Trepardoux Steam Tricycle and Ford Coupe

1987. Centenary of Motor Car. Multicoloured.
1058 150f. Type **365** . . . . . . 1·50 70
1059 300f. Daimler motor carriage, 1886 and Mercedes Benz W124 series saloon . . . . . . 3·25 1·40

366 Baptism in the Python Temple
368 G. Hansen and R. Follereau (leprosy pioneers) and Patients

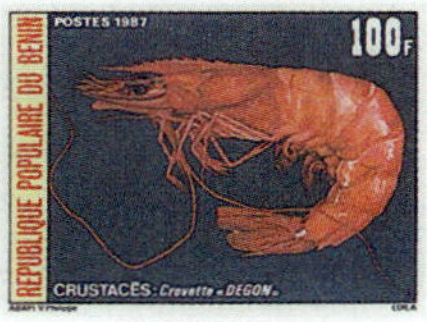
367 Shrimp

1987. Ritual Ceremonies.
1060 **366** 100f. multicoloured . . . 1·50 70

1987. Shellfish. Multicoloured.
1061 100f. Type **367** . . . . . . 1·30 75
1062 150f. Crab . . . . 2·00 1·00

1987. Anti-leprosy Campaign.
1063 **368** 200f. multicoloured . . . 2·50 1·20

369 Crop-spraying and Locusts

1987. Anti-locust Campaign.
1064 **369** 100f. multicoloured . . . 1·20 65

370 Fisherman and Farmer

1987. Air. 10th Anniv of International Agricultural Development Fund.
1065 **370** 500f. multicoloured . . . 4·50 2·40

371 Nativity Scene in Moon and Father Christmas giving Sweets to Crowd

1987. Christmas.
1066 **371** 150f. multicoloured . . . 1·50 85

372 Rally

375 Hands holding Pot Aloft

1988. 15th Anniv (1987) of Start of Benin Revolution.
1067 **372** 100f. multicoloured . . . £100 2·75

1988. Various stamps surch. (a) Stamps of Dahomey surch **Populaire du Benin** (1081c) or **Republique Populaire du Benin** (others).
1068 – 5f. on 3f. black and blue (173) (postage) 55·00 2·75
1069 – 20f. on 100f. mult (506) 55·00 2·75
1071 – 25f. on 100f. mult (576) 55·00 2·75
1073 – 50f. on 45f. mult (320) 65·00 2·75
1074 **178** 55f. on 200f. olive, brown and green . . 95·00 2·75
1075a 125f. on 100f. mult (557) . . . .
1076 **116** 10f. on 50f. black, orange and blue (air) 55·00 2·75
1077 **161** 15f. on 150f. red and black . . . . . . 55·00 2·75
1078 – 25f. on 100f. mult (526) 75·00 2·75
1079 **156** 25f. on 100f. blue, brown and violet . . 75·00 2·75
1079a **153** 40f. on 35f. mult . . . 55·00 2·75
1080 – 40f. on 100f. mult (495) 55·00
1081 **162** 40f. on 150f. red, brown and blue . . . 55·00 2·75
1081a **148** 100f. brown and green 55·00 2·75
1081b **181** 125f. on 75f. lilac, red and green . . . . 45·00 2·75
1081c – 125f. on 150f. blue and purple (541) . . . . 2·75
1082 – 125f. on 250f. mult (491) . . . . 55·00 2·75
1082a – 125f. red and brown (540) . . . . 55·00 2·75
1083 – 190f. on 250f. brown, green and red (594) 90·00
1084 – 1000f. on 150f. multicoloured (545) 55·00 2·75

(b) No. 618 of Benin surch **Republique Populaire du Benin**.
1085 – 10f. on 60f. on 2f. mult . . 55·00 2·75

(c) Stamps of Benin surch only.
1086 **359** 125f. on 440f. mult (postage) . . . . . .
1087 **338** 125f. on 200f. mult (air)
1088 – 190f. on 250f. mult (999) 90·00
1089 – 190f. on 250f. mult (1000) . . . .

1988. 25th Anniv of Organization of African Unity.
1094 **375** 125f. multicoloured . . . 1·20 50

376 Resuscitation of Man pulled from River

1988. 125th Anniv of Red Cross Movement.
1095 **376** 200f. multicoloured . . . 3·25 1·60

377 King

378 Scout and Camp

1988. 20th Death Anniv of Martin Luther King (Civil Rights leader).
1096 **377** 200f. multicoloured . . . 2·00 95

1988. 1st Benin Scout Jamboree, Savalou.
1097 **378** 125f. multicoloured . . . 1·20 55

379 Healthy Family and Health Care

1988. 40th Anniv of W.H.O. and 10th Anniv of "Health for All by 2000" Declaration.
1098 **379** 175f. multicoloured . . . 1·50 80

380 Dugout Canoes and Houses

1988. Ganvie (lake village). Multicoloured.
1099 125f. Type **380** . . . . . . 1·20 55
1100 190f. Boatman and houses 1·80 85

1988. As T **359** but smaller (17 × 24 mm).
1101 **359** 40f. black 30 15
1102 125f. red . . . . 1·00 45
1103 190f. blue . . . . 1·50 65
1104 220f. green . . . . 1·80 80

381 Adoration of the Magi

1988. Air. Christmas.
1105 **381** 500f. multicoloured . . . 4·50 2·20

382 Offering to Hebiesso, God of Thunder

384 Eiffel Tower

383 Roseate Tern

1988. Ritual Ceremony.
1106 **382** 125f. multicoloured . . . 1·20 55

1989. Endangered Animals. Roseate Tern. Mult.
1107 10f. Type **383** . . . . 1·10 70
1108 15f. Tern with fish . . . . 1·10 70
1109 50f. Tern on rocks . . . . 2·50 1·40
1110 125f. Tern flying . . . . . 5·00 2·75

1989. Centenary of Eiffel Tower.
1111 **384** 190f. multicoloured . . . 2·50 1·10

386 Tractor, Map and Pump

1989. 30th Anniv of Agriculture Development Council.
1113 **386** 75f. multicoloured . . . 95·00

387 Symbols of Revolution and France 1950 National Relief Fund Stamps

1989. Bicentenary of French Revolution and "Philexfrance 89" International Stamp Exhibition, Paris.
1114 **387** 190f. multicoloured . . . 2·50 1·50

388 Burbot

1989. Fishes. Multicoloured.
1115 125f. Type **388** . . . . . 1·30 60
1116 190f. Northern pike and Atlantic salmon . . . . . 2·00 95

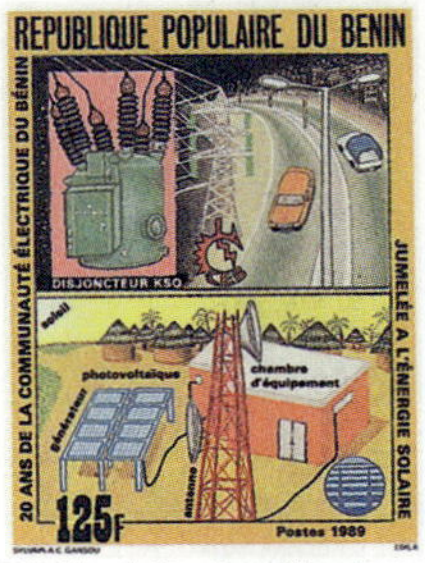

389 Circuit Breaker, Illuminated Road and Solar Energy Complex

1989. 20th Anniv of Benin Electricity Community.
1117 **389** 125f. multicoloured . . . 1·30 60

390 Lion within Wreath

1989. Death Centenary of King Glele.
1118 **390** 190f. multicoloured . . . 1·70 90

391 Nativity

1989. Christmas.
1119 **391** 200f. multicoloured . . . 1·80 95

392 Anniversary Emblem and Means of Communications

1990. Centenary of Postal and Telecommunications Ministry (1st issue).
1120 **392** 125f. multicoloured . . . 1·30 60
See also No. 1127.

393 Oranges

1990. Fruit and Flowers. Multicoloured.
1121 60f. Type **393** 75 40
1122 190f. Kaufmannia tulips (vert) . . . . 2·00 95
1123 250f. Cashew nuts (vert) . . 2·50 1·30

394 Launch of "Apollo 11" and Footprint on Moon

1990. 21st Anniv of First Manned Moon Landing.
1124 **394** 190f. multicoloured . . . 1·70 85

395 Footballers

1990. World Cup Football Championship, Italy. Multicoloured.
1125 125f. Type **395** . . . . . . 1·20 60
1126 190f. Mascot holding torch and pennant (vert) . . . 1·90 85

396 Balloons, Emblem and Means of Communication

1990. Centenary of Postal and Telecommunications Ministry (2nd issue).
1127 **396** 150f. multicoloured . . . 1·40 65

1990. World Cup Finalists. No. 1125 optd **FINALE R.F.A.-ARGENTINE 1-0**.
1128 **395** 125f. multicoloured . . . 1·20 60

398 De Gaulle

1990. Birth Centenary of Charles de Gaulle (French statesman) (1st issue).
1129 **398** 190f. multicoloured . . . 2·00 1·20
See also No. 1160.

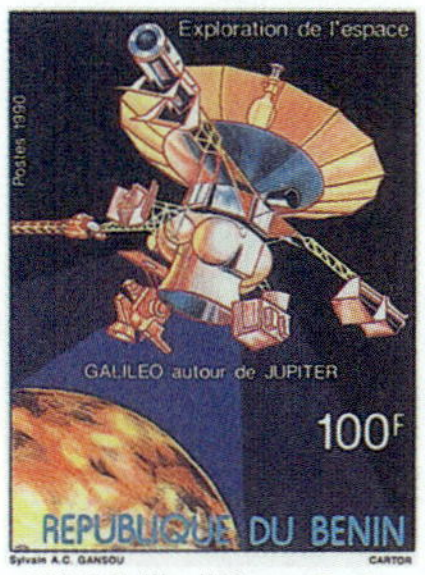

399 "Galileo" Space Probe orbiting Jupiter

1990. Space Exploration.
1130 **399** 100f. multicoloured . . . 1·00 60

400 Nativity

401 Hands pointing to Scales of Justice

1990. Christmas.
1131 **400** 200f. multicoloured . . . 1·90 1·20

1990. National Conference of Active Forces.
1132 **401** 125f. multicoloured . . .

406 Different Cultures and Emblem

1991. African Tourism Year.
1150 **406** 190f. multicoloured . . . 1·90 1·20

407 Tennis Player

408 Flag and Arms

1991. Cent of French Open Tennis Championships.
1151 **407** 125f. multicoloured . . . 1·50 95

1991. 31st Anniv of Independence.
1152 **408** 125f. multicoloured . . . 1·30 50

1991. "Riccione 91" Stamp Fair. No. 1130 optd **"Riccione 91"**.
1153 **399** 100f. multicoloured . . . 95 70

410 Adoration of the Magi

1991. Christmas.
1154 **410** 125f. multicoloured . . . 1·30 60

411 Guelede Dancer

412 Mozart

1991.
1155 **411** 190f. multicoloured . . . 2·00 80

1991. Death Bicentenary of Wolfgang Amadeus Mozart (composer).
1156 **412** 1000f. multicoloured . . 10·00 5·75

413 Slave in Chains and Route Map

1992. 500th Anniv of Discovery of America by Columbus.
1157 **413** 500f. black, brown & bl 4·50 3·00
1158 – 1000f. multicoloured . . 9·00 5·75
MS1159 133 × 93 mm. Nos. 1157/8 15·00 14·00
DESIGN—HORIZ: 1000f. Columbus landing at Guanahami, Bahamas.

1992. Birth Centenary (1990) of Charles de Gaulle (French statesman) (2nd issue). As No. 1129 but value changed.
1160 **398** 300f. multicoloured . . . 3·00 1·60

414 Child, Produce and Emblems

415 Pope John Paul II

1992. International Nutrition Conference, Rome.
1161 **414** 190f. multicoloured . . . 1·80 1·20

1993. Papal Visit.
1162 **415** 190f. multicoloured . . . 2·00 1·10

416 Emblem and Voodoo Culture

1993. "Ouidah 92" Voodoo Culture Festival.
1163 **416** 125f. multicoloured . . . 1·20 60

417 Well and Blue-throated Roller

1993. Possotome Artesian Well.
1164 **417** 125f. multicoloured . . . 2·20 1·40

418 Map, Clasped Hands and Flags of Member Countries

1993. 30th Anniv of Organization of African Unity.
1165 **418** 125f. multicoloured . . . 1·20 70

419 John F. Kennedy (President of United States, 1961–63)

1993. Death Anniversaries. Multicoloured.
1166 190f. Type **419** (30th anniv) 1·90 1·10
1167 190f. Dr. Martin Luther King (American civil rights campaigner, 25th anniv) (vert) . . . . . . 2·00 1·10

1993. Stamps of Dahomey variously optd or surch.
(a) **REPUBLIQUE DU BENIN**.
1167a **139** 5f. multicoloured (postage) . . . . . . 80·00 2·75
1170 **108** 50f. on 1f. multicoloured (617) 55·00 2·75
1171 **113** 80f. on 40f. red, brown and green . . . . . . 43·00 2·75
1173 135f. on 20f. black, green and red (190) 95·00
1175 135f. on 30f. black, brown and violet (472) . . . . . . 55·00
1177 **107** 135f. on 40f. mult . . . 38·00
1179 – 135f. on 60f. olive, red and purple (181) . . 55·00 2·75
1181 – 200f. on 100f. mult (322) . . . . . . 65·00 2·75
1186 – 15f. on 40f. mult (458) (air) . . . . . . 47·00 2·75
1190 **126** 100f. multicoloured . . 55·00 2·75
1190a **119** 125f. on 40f. mult . . . 23·00 2·75
1191 – 125f. on 65f. red and blue (552) . . . . . 55·00 2·75
1201 – 200f. on 250f. mult (569) . . . . 47·00

(b) **DU BENIN**.
1207 **60** 5f. on 1f. multicoloured (postage) . . . . . 65·00 2·75
1208 – 10f. on 3f. black and blue (173) . . . . . 55·00
1211 – 25f. multicoloured (441) 47·00 2·75
1220 – 135f. on 3f. mult (274) 80·00
1223 – 20f. on 200f. mult (451) (air) . . . . . . 55·00
1225 – 25f. on 85f. mult (600) 47·00 2·75
1227 **140** 30f. on 15f. purple, green and blue . . . . . 38·00
1231 – 125f. on 70f. mult (383) 65·00 2·75
1235 – 150f. purple, blue and brown (456) . . . . . 80·00
1236 – 150f. multicoloured (527) 55·00 2·75
1239 **150** 200f. green, violet and emerald . . . . . . 65·00 2·75
1242 – 200f. on 150f. mult (562) 95·00
1243 **179** 300f. multicoloured . . . 55·00 2·75

(c) **BENIN**.
1257 – 25f. on 500f. brown, red and green (592) (air) 47·00 2·75
1258 – 30f. on 200f. mult (528) 24·00 2·75
1260a – 100f. brown, green and blue (522) . . . . . 55·00 2·75
1261 **116** 125f. on 50f. black, orange and blue . . . 43·00 2·75
1263a – 190f. on 200f. mult (478) . . . . £190 2·75
1266 – 300f. brn, red & bl (591) . . . . 70·00 2·75

422 Conference Emblem

1994. UNESCO Conference on the Slave Route, Ouidah.
1275 **422** 300f. multicoloured . . . 47·00 2·75

423 World Map

1994. International Year of the Family.
1276 **423** 200f. multicoloured . . . 75·00 2·75

425 Water Polo

1995. Olympic Games, Atlanta (1996) (1st issue). Multicoloured.
1278 45f. Type **425** 20 20
1279 50f. Throwing the javelin (vert) 30 25
1280 75f. Weightlifting (vert) . . 45 35
1281 100f. Tennis (vert) 60 50
1282 135f. Baseball (vert) 75 55
1283 200f. Synchronised swimming (vert) . . . . . 1·30 1·00
MS1284 60 × 79 mm. 300f. Diving (31 × 39 mm) . . . . 2·40 2·20
See also Nos. 1347/**MS**1353.

426 Paddle-steamer

1995. Ships. Multicoloured.
1285 40f. Type **426** 25 15
1286 50f. "Charlotte" (paddle steamer) 30 15
1287 75f. "Citta di Catania" (Italian liner) 45 20
1288 100f. "Mountbatten" SR-N4 (hovercraft) 45 25
1289 135f. "Queen Elizabeth 2" (liner) 85 30
1290 200f. "Matsu-Nef" (Japanese nuclear-powered freighter) . . . . 1·30 60
MS1291 72 × 58 mm. 300f. "Savannah" (sail/paddle-steamer) (39 × 31 mm) . . . . 2·40 2·40

427 Chimpanzee

1995. Primates. Multicoloured.
1292 50f. Type **427** 30 15
1293 75f. Mandrill 45 20
1294 100f. Colobus 60 25
1295 135f. Barbary ape 85 30
1296 200f. Hamadryas baboon . . 1·30 70
MS1297 93 × 72 mm. 300f. Yellow baboons (31 × 39 mm) . . . . 2·50 2·10

428 Tabby Shorthair

1995. Cats. Multicoloured.
1298 40f. Type **428** 25 15
1299 50f. Sorrel Abyssinian ("Ruddy red") 30 15
1300 75f. White Persian long-hair 45 20
1301 100f. Seal colourpoint . . . 60 25
1302 135f. Tabby point 85 30
1303 200f. Black shorthair . . . 1·30 60
MS1304 82 × 86 mm. 300f. Kitten climbing out of basket (38 × 31 mm) . . . . 2·50 2·50

429 German Shepherd

1995. Dogs. Multicoloured.
1305 40f. Type **429** 25 15
1306 50f. Beagle 30 15
1307 75f. Great dane 45 20
1308 100f. Boxer 60 25
1309 135f. Pointer 85 30
1310 200f. Long-haired fox terrier 1·30 60
MS1311 80 × 70 mm. 300f. Schnauzer . . . . 2·50 2·50

430 Arms

431 Lion

1995.
1312 **430** 135f. multicoloured . . . 85 25
1313 150f. multicoloured . . . 95 55
1314 200f. multicoloured . . . 1·30 55
See also Nos. 1458 and 1480/2.

1995. Mammals. Multicoloured.
1315 50f. Type **431** 30 15
1316 75f. African buffalo 45 20
1317 100f. Chimpanzee 65 25
1318 135f. Impala 85 30
1319 200f. Cape ground squirrel (horiz) . . . . 1·30 70
MS1320 80 × 60 mm. 300f. African elephant (31 × 39 mm) . . . . 2·50 2·50

432 Hawfinches

433 "Dracunculus vulgaris"

1995. Birds and their Young. Multicoloured.
1321 40f. Type **432** 25 15
1322 50f. Spotted-necked doves 30 15
1323 75f. Peregrine falcons . . . 45 20
1324 100f. Blackburnian warblers 60 25
1325 135f. Black-headed gulls . . 80 30
1326 200f. Eastern white pelican 1·20 60

1995. Flowers. Multicoloured.
1327 40f. Type **433** 25 15
1328 50f. Daffodil 30 15
1329 75f. Amaryllis 45 20
1330 100f. Water-lily 60 25
1331 135f. "Chrysanthemum carinatum" 80 30
1332 200f. Iris . . . . 1·20 60

434 Lynx

435 "Angraecum sesquipedale"

1995. Big Cats and their Young. Mult.
1333 40f. Type **434** 25 15
1334 50f. Pumas 30 15
1335 75f. Cheetahs 45 20
1336 100f. Leopards 60 25
1337 135f. Tigers 80 30
1338 200f. Lions . . . . 1·30 60

1995. Orchids. Multicoloured.
1339 40f. Type **435** 25 15
1340 50f. "Polystachya virginea" 30 15
1341 75f. "Disa uniflora" 45 20
1342 100f. "Ansellia africana" . . 60 25
1343 135f. "Angraecum eichlerianum" 95 30
1344 200f. "Jumellea confusa" . . 1·30 60

436 Emblem

437 Diving

1995. 6th Francophone Summit, Cotonou.
1345 **436** 150f. multicoloured . . . 85 55
1346 200f. multicoloured . . . 1·10 80

1996. Olympic Games, Atlanta (2nd issue). Multicoloured.
1347 40f. Type **437** 30 25
1348 50f. Tennis 35 30
1349 75f. Running 45 35
1350 100f. Gymnastics 60 50
1351 135f. Weightlifting 90 65
1352 200f. Shooting . . . . . . 1·30 1·00
MS1353 65 × 65 mm. 1000f. Water polo (31 × 39 mm) . . . . . 5·25 4·00

438 Player with Ball

1996. World Cup Football Championship, France (1998) (1st issue).
1354 **438** 40f. multicoloured . . . 25 20
1355 – 50f. multicoloured . . . 25 20
1356 – 75f. multicoloured . . . 50 40
1357 – 100f. multicoloured . . . 60 50
1358 – 135f. multicoloured . . . 1·00 65
1359 – 200f. multicoloured . . . 1·30 1·10
MS1360 88 × 63 mm. 1000f. Tackle (31 × 39 mm) . . . . 4·75 4·00
DESIGNS: 50f. to 1000f. Different players.
See also Nos. 1614/MS1620.

439 Small Striped Swallowtail

1996. Butterflies. Multicoloured.
1361 40f. Type **439** 25 20
1362 50f. Red admiral 25 20
1363 75f. Common blue 45 35
1364 100f. African monarch . . . 55 45
1365 135f. Painted lady 95 60
1366 200f. "Argus celbulina orbitulus" . . . . 1·30 1·00
MS1367 60 × 70 mm. 1000f. Foxy charaxes ("Charaxes jasius") (31 × 39 mm) . . . . 4·50 4·00

440 Dancer

1996. "China '96" International Stamp Exhibition, Peking. Multicoloured.
1368 40f. Type **440** 35 30
1369 50f. Exhibition emblem . . 40 35
1370 75f. Water-lily 60 50
1371 100f. Temple of Heaven, Peking 85 75
Nos. 1368/71 were issued together, se-tenant, forming a composite design.

441 Emblem

1996. 15th Convention of Lions Club International, Cotonou.
1457 **441** 100f. multicoloured . . . 55 25
1372 135f. multicoloured . . . 1·10 75
1373 150f. multicoloured . . . 1·10 80
1374 200f. multicoloured . . . 1·50 1·10

442 "Holy Family of Rouvre" (Raphael)

1996. Christmas. Multicoloured.
1375 40f. Type **442** 25 20
1376 50f. "The Holy Family" (Raphael) 25 20
1377 75f. "St. John the Baptist" (Bartolome Murillo) . . . 50 40
1378 100f. "The Virgin of the Scales" (Leonardo da Vinci) 65 50
1379 135f. "The Virgin and Child" (Gerhard David) 90 65
1380 200f. "Adoration of the Magi" (Juan Mayno) . . 1·30 1·10
MS1381 99 × 74 mm. 1000f. "Rest during the Flight into Egypt" (Murillo) (39 × 31 mm) . . . . 5·25 3·75

443 "Thermopylae" (clipper) (inscr "Thermopyles")

1996. Ships. Multicoloured.
1382 40f. Type **443** 20 15
1383 50f. Barque 25 20
1384 75f. "Nightingale" (full-rigged ship) 45 30
1385 100f. Opium clipper 50 40
1386 135f. "Torrens" (full-rigged ship) 80 60
1387 200f. English tea clipper . . 1·20 1·00
MS1388 78 × 58 mm. 1000f. Opium clipper (31 × 39 mm) . . . . . 5·25 4·00

444 Serval

445 Hurdler and Gold Medal

1996. Big Cats. Multicoloured.
1389 40f. Type **444** 25 20
1390 50f. Golden cat 25 20
1391 75f. Ocelot 45 35
1392 100f. Bobcat 55 45
1393 135f. Leopard cat 95 60
1394 200f. "Felis euptilura" . . . 1·30 1·00
MS1395 80 × 64 mm. 1000f. Clouded leopard ("Neofelis nebulosa") (31 × 39 mm) . . . . 5·25 4·00

1996. Centenary of Issue by Greece of First Olympic Stamps. Multicoloured.
1396 40f. Type **445** 35 30
1397 50f. Hurdler and Olympic flames 40 35
1398 75f. Pierre de Coubertin (founder of modern Olympics) and map showing south-west U.S.A. 60 50
1399 100f. Map showing south-east U.S.A. 85 75
Nos. 1396/9 were issued together, se-tenant, forming a composite design.

446 Running

447 "Parodia subterranea"

1996. "Olymphilex '96" Olympics and Sports Stamp Exhibition, Atlanta. Multicoloured.
1400 40f. Type **446** 25 20
1401 50f. Canoeing 25 20
1402 75f. Gymnastics 50 40
1403 100f. Football 60 50
1404 135f. Tennis . . . . 1·00 65
1405 200f. Baseball . . . . . . 1·40 1·10
MS1406 65 × 95 mm. 1000f. Basketball (31 × 39 mm) . . . . 5·25 4·00

1996. Flowering Cacti. Multicoloured.
1407 40f. Type **447** 25 20
1408 50f. "Astrophytum senile" 25 20
1409 75f. "Echinocereus melanocentrus" 50 40
1410 100f. "Turbinicarpus klinkerianus" 60 50
1411 135f. "Astrophytum capricorne" . . . . . . 1·00 65
1412 200f. "Nelloydia grandiflora" . . . . . . 1·40 1·10

448 Chestnut Horse

449 Longisquama

1996. Horses. Multicoloured.
1413 40f. Type **448** 25 20
1414 50f. Horse on hillside . . . 25 20
1415 75f. Foal by fence 45 35
1416 100f. Mother and foal . . . 55 45
1417 135f. Pair of horses 95 60
1418 200f. Grey horse (horiz) . . 1·30 1·00

1996. Prehistoric Animals. Multicoloured.
1419 40f. Type **449** 25 20
1420 50f. Dimorphodon 25 20
1421 75f. Dunkleosteus (horiz) . . 45 35
1422 100f. Eryops (horiz) 55 45
1423 135f. Peloneustes (horiz) . . 85 60
1424 200f. Deinonychus (horiz) . 1·30 1·00

450 Ivory-billed Woodpecker

451 Golden Tops

1996. Birds. Multicoloured.
1425 40f. Type **450** 25 20
1426 50f. Grey-necked bald crow 25 20
1427 75f. Kakapo 45 35
1428 100f. Puerto Rican amazon 55 45
1429 135f. Japanese crested ibis 95 60
1430 200f. California condor . . 1·30 1·00
MS1431 65 × 91 mm. 1000f. Blue bird of paradise ("Paradisaea rudolphi") (31 × 39 mm) . . . 5·25 4·00

1996. Fungi. Multicoloured.
1432 40f. Type **451** 25 20
1433 50f. "Psilocybe zapotecorum" 25 20
1434 75f. "Psilocybe mexicana" 55 40
1435 100f. "Conocybe siligineoides" 65 50
1436 135f. "Psilocybe caerulescens mazatecorum" . . . . 1·00 65
1437 200f. "Psilocybe caerulescens nigripes" . . . . 1·40 1·10
MS1438 93 × 71 mm. 1000f. "Psilocybe aztecorum" (39 × 31 mm) . . . . 5·25 4·00

452 Impala

1996. Mammals. Multicoloured.
1439 40f. Type **452** 25 20
1440 50f. Waterbuck 25 20
1441 75f. African buffalo . . . 45 35
1442 100f. Blue wildebeest . . . 55 45
1443 135f. Okapi 85 60
1444 200f. Greater kudu . . . 1·30 1·00

453 White Whale

1996. Marine Mammals. Multicoloured.
1445 40f. Type **453** 25 20
1446 50f. Bottle-nosed dolphin . . 25 20
1447 75f. Blue whale 45 35
1448 100f. "Eubalaena australis" 55 45
1449 135f. "Gramphidelphis griseus" 95 60
1450 200f. Killer whale . . . . . 1·30 1·00

454 Grey Angelfish

455 Grenadier, Glassenapps Regiment

1996. Fishes. Multicoloured.
1451 50f. Type **454** 30 25
1452 75f. Sail-finned tang (horiz) 40 35
1453 100f. Golden trevally (horiz) 60 45
1454 135f. Pyramid butterflyfish (horiz) 85 60
1455 200f. Racoon butterflyfish (horiz) . . . . 1·30 1·00
MS1456 80 × 61 mm. 1000f. Parrotfish (horiz) . . . . . 5·25 4·00

1996. Arms. Dated "1996".
1458 **430** 100f. multicoloured . . . 65 25

1996. Stamps of Benin variously surch.
1469 **311** 15f. on 185f. mult (postage) . . . . . 65·00 2·75
1470 **379** 25f. on 175f. mult
1473 **359** 50f. on 220f. green (1104) . . . . . . 65·00 2·75
1479 **414** 150f. on 190f. mult . . .
1480 **415** 150f. on 190f. mult . . .
1484 **412** 250f. on 1000f. mult . . 65·00 2·75
1494 **193** 40f. on 210f. red, brown and green (air) . . . . 65·00 2·75
1495 – 40f. on 210f. purple, blue and yellow (792) . . .
1499 – 150f. on 500f. red, ultramarine and green (657) . . . .

1996. Stamps of Dahomey variously optd or surch. (a) **Republique de Benin** (1510, 1516, 1519, 1522, 1526/9, 1535, 1544, 1556, 1558 and 1568) or **REPUBLIQUE DU BENIN** (others).
1510 – 35f. on 85f. brown, orange and green (493) (postage) . . . . .
1511 – 125f. on 100f. violet, red and black (510) . . .
1516 **85** 150f. on 30f. mult . . .
1519 **113** 150f. on 40f. red, brown and green . . . . .
1522 – 150f. on 45f. mult (597)
1526 – 35f. on 100f. deep blue and blue (326) (air) . .
1527 – 35f. on 100f. on 200f. multicoloured (409) . .
1528 – 35f. on 125f. green, blue and light blue (553) . .
1529 – 35f. on 300f. brown, red and blue (591) . . . .
1535 – 150f. multicoloured (527)
1544 **112** 150f. on 40f. multicoloured . . . .
1556 – 150f. on 110f. mult (386)
1558 – 150f. on 120f. mult (404)
1568 – 200f. on 500f. mult (252)

(b) **DU BENIN**.
1578 35f. on 125f. brown and green (540) (air) . . .
1579 125f. on 65f. mult (465)
1580 **168** 135f. on 35f. mult . . .

(c) **BENIN**.
1587 **68** 150f. on 30f. mult (post) 75·00 2·75
1591 25f. on 85f. mult (600) (air) . . . .

1997. Military Uniforms. Multicoloured.
1600 135f. Type **455** 60 30
1601 150f. Officer, Von Groben's Regiment 80 35
1602 200f. Private, Dohna's Regiment . . . . 1·00 60
1603 270f. Artilleryman . . . . . 1·30 70
1604 300f. Cavalry trooper . . . 1·60 90
1605 400f. Trooper, Mollendorf's Dragoons . . . . 2·10 1·30
MS1606 90 × 108 mm. 1000f. Standard bearer (31 × 39 mm) 5·25 4·00

456 Reid Macleod Gas-turbine Locomotive, 1920

1997. Railway Locomotives. Multicoloured.
1607 135f. Type **456** 60 30
1608 150f. Class O5 steam locomotive, 1935, Germany 80 40
1609 200f. Locomotive "Silver Fox", Great Britain . . . 1·00 55
1610 270f. Class "Merchant Navy" locomotive, 1941, Great Britain . . . . . 1·30 75
1611 300f. Diesel locomotive, 1960, Denmark . . . . . 1·60 80
1612 400f. GM Type diesel locomotive, 1960 . . . . 2·10 1·10
MS1613 94 × 64 mm. 1000f. "Coronation", 1937 (39 × 31 mm) 5·25 4·00
No. 1607 is wrongly inscr "Reid Maclead 1920".

457 Footballer and Map

458 Arms

1997. World Cup Football Championship, France (1998) (2nd issue).
1614 **457** 135f. multicoloured . . . 60 30
1615 – 150f. multicoloured . . . 80 35
1616 – 200f. multicoloured . . . 1·00 60
1617 – 270f. multicoloured . . . 1·30 70
1618 – 300f. mult (horiz) . . . 1·60 90
1619 – 400f. mult (horiz) . . . 2·10 1·30
MS1620 107 × 83 mm. 1000f. multicoloured (39 × 31 mm) . . 5·25 4·00
DESIGNS: 135f. to 1000f. Each showing map of France and player.

1997. T **430** redrawn as T **458**. Dated "1997".
1621 **458** 135f. multicoloured . . . 70 25
1622 150f. multicoloured . . . 1·00 60
1623 200f. multicoloured . . . 1·20 60

459 Horse's Head

1997. Horses. Multicoloured.
1624 135f. Type **459** 70 30
1625 150f. Bay horse 80 45
1626 200f. Chestnut horse looking forward . . . . 1·00 55
1627 270f. Chestnut horse looking backwards . . . . . . 1·30 70
1628 300f. Black horse . . . . . 1·70 80
1629 400f. Profile of horse . . . 2·10 1·00
MS1630 84 × 109 mm. 1000f. Bay horse with white nose . . . . 5·25 4·00

460 Irish Setter

461 "Phalaenopsis penetrate"

1997. Dogs. Multicoloured.
1631 135f. Type **460** 60 30
1632 150f. Saluki 80 45
1633 200f. Dobermann pinscher 1·00 55
1634 270f. Siberian husky . . . . 1·60 70
1635 300f. Basenji . . . . . . 1·60 80
1636 400f. Boxer . . . . 2·30 1·00
MS1637 110 × 90 mm. 1000f. Rhodesian ridgeback (31 × 39 mm) 5·25 4·00

1997. Orchids. Multicoloured.
1638 135f. Type **461** 70 35
1639 150f. "Phalaenopsis" "Golden Sands" 80 45
1640 200f. "Phalaenopsis" "Sun Spots" . . . . 1·00 60
1641 270f. "Phalaenopsis fuscata" 1·70 70
1642 300f. "Phalaenopsis christi floyd" . . . . 1·70 85
1643 400f. "Phalaenopsis cayanne" . . . . 2·50 1·10
MS1644 99 × 99 mm. 1000f. "Phalaenopsis" "Janet Kuhn" (31 × 39 mm) . . . . 5·25 4·00

462 Buick Model C Tourer, 1905

1997. Motor Cars. Multicoloured.
1645 135f. Type **462** 70 30
1646 150f. Ford model A tonneau, 1903 . . . . . 80 45
1647 200f. Stanley steamer tourer, 1913 . . . . 1·00 60
1648 270f. Stoddar-Dayton tourer, 1911 . . . . . . 1·30 70
1649 300f. Cadillac convertible sedan, 1934 . . . . . . 1·70 85
1650 400f. Cadillac convertible sedan, 1931 . . . . . . 2·10 1·10
MS1651 112 × 85 mm. 1000f. Ford, 1928 (39 × 31 mm) . . . . . . 5·25 4·00

463 Northern Bullfinch

1997. Birds. Multicoloured.
1652 135f. Type **463** 60 30
1653 150f. Spruce siskin 80 40
1654 200f. Ring ousel . . . . . 1·00 55
1655 270f. Crested tit . . . . . 1·30 70
1656 300f. Spotted nutcracker . . 1·60 80
1657 400f. Nightingale . . . . . 2·10 1·10
MS1658 107 × 87 mm. 1000f. Yellow wagtail (31 × 39 mm) . . . . 5·25 4·00

464 "Faucaria lupina"

1997. Cacti. Multicoloured.
1659 135f. Type **464** 60 30
1660 150f. "Conophytum bilobun" 80 45
1661 200f. "Lithops aucampiae" 1·00 60
1662 270f. "Lithops helmutii" . . 1·30 75
1663 300f. "Stapelia grandiflora" 1·60 80
1664 400f. "Lithops fulviceps" . . 2·10 1·20
MS1665 109 × 90 mm. 1000f. "Pleiospilos willowmorensis" (31 × 38 mm) . . . . 5·25 4·00

465 Egyptian Merchant Ship

1997. Ancient Sailing Ships. Multicoloured.
1666 135f. Type **465** 60 30
1667 150f. Greek merchant ship 80 40
1668 200f. Phoenician galley . . . 1·00 55
1669 270f. Roman merchant ship 1·30 70
1670 300f. Norman knarr . . . . 1·60 80
1671 400f. Mediterranean sailing ship . . . . 2·10 1·00
MS1672 109 × 89 mm. 1000f. English kogge of Richard II's reign (28 × 36 mm) . . . . 5·25 4·00

466 Black-tipped Grouper

1997. Fishes. Multicoloured.
1673 135f. Type **466** 60 30
1674 150f. Cardinal fish 75 40
1675 200f. Indo-Pacific humpheaded parrotfish . . 1·00 55
1676 270f. Regal angelfish . . . . 1·30 70
1677 300f. Wrasse . . . . 1·60 80
1678 400f. Hawkfish . . . . . . 2·10 1·00
MS1679 109 × 90 mm. 1000f. Hogfish (39 × 31 mm) . . . . 5·25 4·00

467 Emblem

1997. 10th Anniv of African Petroleum Producers' Association.
1680 **467** 135f. multicoloured . . . 60 30
1681 200f. multicoloured . . . 1·00 55
1682 300f. multicoloured . . . 1·50 80
1683 500f. multicoloured . . . 2·75 1·40

468 Caesar's Mushroom

470 "Tephrocybe carbonaria"

469 "Puffing Billy", 1813

1997. Fungi. Multicoloured.
1684 135f. Type **468** 60 30
1685 150f. Slimy-banded cort . . . 80 40
1686 200f. "Amanita bisporigera" 1·00 55
1687 270f. The blusher . . . . . 1·30 70
1688 300f. Cracked green russula 1·60 80
1689 400f. Strangulated amanita 2·10 1·00
MS1690 90 × 110 mm. 1000f. Fly agaric (31 × 37 mm) . . . . . 5·25 4·00

1997. Steam Railway Locomotives. Mult.
1691 135f. Type **469** 60 30
1692 150f. "Rocket", 1829 . . . 80 40
1693 200f. "Royal George", 1827 1·00 55
1694 270f. "Novelty", 1829 . . . 1·30 70
1695 300f. "Locomotion", 1825 (vert) . . . . 1·60 80
1696 400f. "Sans Pareil", 1829 (vert) . . . . 2·10 1·00
MS1697 110 × 89 mm. 1000f. Richard Trevithick's locomotive, 1803 (39 × 31 mm) . . . . . . 5·25 4·00

1998. Fungi. Multicoloured.
1698 135f. Type **470** 55 30
1699 150f. Butter mushroom . . 75 40
1700 200f. Oyster fungus 95 55
1701 270f. "Hohenbuehelia geogenia" . . . . 1·20 70
1702 300f. Bitter bolete . . . . . 1·50 80
1703 400f. "Lepiota leucothites" 2·00 1·00
MS1704 108 × 90 mm. 1000f. "Gymnoplius junonius" . . . 4·75 3·75

471 Philadelphia or "Double Deck", 1885

1998. Fire Engines. Multicoloured.
1705 135f. Type **471** 55 30
1706 150f. "Veteran", 1850 . . . 75 40
1707 200f. Merryweather, 1894 95 55
1708 270f. 19 th-century Hippomobile . . . . 1·20 70
1709 300f. Jeep "Willy", 1948 . . 1·50 80
1710 400f. Chevrolet 6400 . . . . 2·00 1·00
MS1711 110 × 89 mm. 1000f. Foamite, 1952 (38 × 30 mm) . . 4·75 3·75

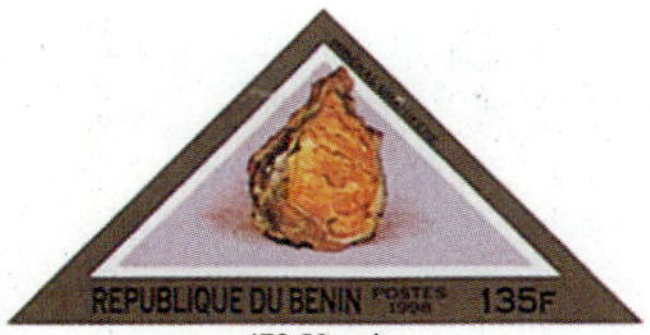

472 Uranite

1998. Minerals. Multicoloured.
1712 135f. Type **472** 55 30
1713 150f. Quartz 75 40
1714 200f. Aragonite 95 55
1715 270f. Malachite . . . . . . 1·20 70
1716 300f. Turquoise . . . . . . 1·50 80
1717 400f. Corundum . . . . . . 2·00 1·00
MS1718 89 × 109 mm. 1000f. Marble (short side as base) . . . . . 4·75 3·75

473 Locomotive

1998. Steam Railway Locomotives. Multicoloured.
1719 135f. Type **473** 55 30
1720 150f. Green locomotive . . 75 40
1721 200f. Brown locomotive . . 95 55
1722 270f. Lilac locomotive . . . 1·20 70
1723 300f. Toledo Furnace Co No. 1 . . . . 1·50 80
1724 400f. No. 1 "Helvetia" . . . 2·00 1·00
MS1725 109 × 86 mm. Shelby Steel Tube Co. Locomotive (39 × 31 mm) . . . . 4·75 3·75

474 Diana, Princess of Wales

1998. 1st Death Anniv of Diana, Princess of Wales. Multicoloured.
1726 135f. Type **474** 55 35
1727 150f. Wearing pink dress . . 75 40
1728 200f. Wearing beige jacket 95 55
1729 270f. Wearing white jacket with revers . . . . 1·20 75
1730 300f. Making speech . . . . 1·50 80
1731 400f. Wearing collarless single-breasted white jacket . . . . 2·00 1·10
1732 500f. Wearing red jacket . . 2·40 1·40
1733 600f. Wearing black jacket 2·75 1·70
1734 700f. Wearing double-breasted white jacket . . 3·25 2·00

475 Sordes

1998. Prehistoric Animals. Multicoloured.
1735 135f. Type **475** 55 35
1736 150f. Scaphognatus 70 40
1737 200f. Dsungaripterus 95 55
1738 270f. Brontosaurus . . . . 1·20 75
1739 300f. Diplodocus . . . . . 1·50 80
1740 400f. Coelurus and baryonyx . . . . 2·00 1·10
1741 500f. Kronosaurus and ichthyosaurus . . . . . . 2·40 1·40
1742 600f. Ceratosaurus . . . . 2·75 1·70
1743 700f. Yangchuansaurus . . 3·25 2·00
Nos. 1735/43 were issued together, se-tenant, forming a composite design.

476 Beagle

477 Abyssinian

1998. Dogs. Multicoloured.
1744 135f. Type **476** 55 30
1745 150f. Dalmatians 70 40
1746 200f. Dachshund 95 55
1747 270f. Cairn terrier . . . . 1·20 70
1748 300f. Shih-tzus . . . . . . 1·50 80
1749 400f. Pug . . . . 2·00 1·00
MS1750 110 × 90 mm. 1000f. Springer spaniels (39 × 31 mm) 4·75 3·75

1998. Cats. Multicoloured.
1751 135f. Type **477** 55 30
1752 150f. Striped silver tabby . . 70 40
1753 200f. Siamese 95 55
1754 270f. Red tabby (horiz) . . 1·20 70
1755 300f. Wild cat (horiz) . . . 1·50 80
1756 400f. Manx (horiz) . . . . 2·00 1·00
MS1757 110 × 89 mm. 1000f. Tortoiseshell and white (39 × 31 mm) . . . . 4·75 3·75

478 Bugatti 13 Torpedo, 1910

1998. Motor Cars. Multicoloured.
1758 135f. Type **478** 55 30
1759 150f. Clement voiturette, 1903 . . . . 70 40
1760 200f. Stutz Bearcat speedster, 1914 . . . . . 95 55
1761 270f. Darracq phaeton, 1907 1·20 70
1762 300f. Napier delivery car, 1913 . . . . 1·50 80
1763 400f. Pierce Arrow roadster, 1911 . . . . 2·00 1·00
MS1764 109 × 91 mm. 1000f. Piccolo, 1904 (31 × 39 mm) . . . 4·75 3·75

479 Apollo

1998. Butterflies. Multicoloured.
1765 135f. Type **479** 55 30
1766 150f. Orange-tip 70 40
1767 200f. Camberwell beauty . . 95 55
1768 250f. Speckled wood . . . . 1·20 70
1769 300f. Purple-edged copper 1·50 80
1770 400f. Chequered skipper . . 2·00 1·10
MS1771 106 × 76 mm. 1000f. Small tortoiseshell (39 × 31 mm) . . . 4·75 3·75

480 Gouldian Finch

1999. Birds. Multicoloured.
1772 135f. Type **480** 55 30
1773 150f. Saffron finch 70 40
1774 200f. Red-billed quelea . . . 95 55
1775 270f. Golden bishop . . . . 1·20 70
1776 300f. Red-crested cardinal 1·50 80
1777 400f. Golden-breasted bunting . . . . 2·00 1·10
MS1778 110 × 89 mm. 1000f. Green-backed twin-spot (31 × 39 mm) 4·75 3·75

481 Boat, Ceylon

1999. Sailing Boats. Multicoloured.
1779 135f. Type **481** 55 30
1780 150f. Tanka-Tim, Canton, Macao 70 40
1781 200f. Sampan, Hong Kong 95 55
1782 270f. Outrigger sailing canoe, Polynesia . . . . 1·20 70
1783 300f. Junk, Japan . . . . . 1·50 80
1784 400f. Dacca-Pulwar, Bengal 2·00 1·10
MS1785 84 × 109 mm. 1000f. Junk, China (39 × 31 mm) . . . . . 4·75 3·75

482 White Rhinoceros

1999. Mammals.
1786 **482** 50f. grey 15 10
1787 – 100f. violet 45 25
1788 – 135f. green 50 25
1789 – 135f. black 50 25
1790 – 150f. blue 65 30
1791 – 150f. green 65 30
1792 – 200f. blue 85 45
1793 – 200f. brown 85 45
1794 – 300f. brown . . . . . . 1·40 70
1795 – 300f. red . . . . 1·40 70
1796 – 400f. brown . . . . . . 1·80 90
1797 – 500f. brown . . . . . . 2·20 1·10
DESIGNS: No. 1787, Sable antelope; 1788, Warthog (*Phacochoerus aethiopicus*); 1789, Brown hyena (*Hyaena brunnea*); 1790, Eastern black-and-white colobus (*Colobus guereza*); 1791, Hippopotamus (*Hippopotamus amphibius*); 1792, Mountain zebra (*Equus zebra*); 1793, African buffalo (*Synceros caffer*) (wrongly inscr "Cyncerus"); 1794, Lion (*Panthera leo*); 1795, Cheetah (*Acinonyx jubatus*); 1796, Hunting dog; 1797, Potto.

483 Mikhail Tal

1999. Chess Players. Multicoloured.
1798 135f. Type **483** 55 30
1799 150f. Emanuel Lasker . . . 70 40
1800 200f. Jose Raul Capablanca 95 55
1801 270f. Aleksandr Alekhine . . 1·20 70
1802 300f. Max Euwe . . . . . 1·50 80
1803 400f. Mikhail Botvinnik . . 2·00 1·10
MS1804 85 × 109 mm. 1000f. Wilhelm Steinitz (29 × 36 mm) 4·75 3·75

484 *Brassocattleya cliftonii*

1999. Orchids. Multicoloured.
1805 50f. Type **484** 25 10
1806 100f. Wilsonara 45 25
1807 150f. *Cypripedium paeony* 70 40
1808 300f. *Cymbidium babylon* 1·50 80
1809 400f. Cattleya . . . . . . 2·00 1·10
1810 500f. *Miltonia minx* . . . . 2·40 1·50
MS1811 87 × 110 mm. 1000f. "Isis miltonia" (28 × 36 mm) . . . . 4·75 3·75

485 Royal Python

1999. Snakes. Multicoloured.
1812 135f. Type **485** 55 35
1813 150f. Royal python (different) 70 40
1814 200f. African rock python 95 55
1815 2000f. Head of African rock python . . . . 9·50 6·75

486 Clown Knifefish

1999. Fishes. Multicoloured.
1816 135f. Type **486** 55 30
1817 150f. Puntius filamentosus 70 40
1818 200f. *Epalzeorhynchos bicolor* 95 55
1819 270f. Spotted rasbora . . . 1·20 70
1820 300f. Tigernander . . . . . 1·50 80
1821 400f. Siamese fighting fish 2·00 1·10
MS1822 96 × 86 mm. 1000f. Three-spotted gourami (39 × 31 mm) 4·75 3·75

487 A. Murdock's Steam Tricycle, 1786

1999. Steam-powered Vehicles. Multicoloured.
1823 135f. Type **487** 55 30
1824 150f. Richard Trevithick's locomotive, 1800 . . . . 70 40
1825 200f. Trevithick's locomotive, 1803 . . . . 95 55
1826 270f. John Blenkinsop's locomotive, 1811 . . . . 1·20 70
1827 300f. Foster and Rastik's *Stourbridge Lion*, 1829 . . 1·50 80
1828 400f. Peter Cooper's *Tom Thumb*, 1829 . . . . . . 2·00 1·10
MS1829 110 × 85 mm. 1000f. Isaac Newton's locomotive, 1760 (36 × 28 mm) . . . . 4·75 3·75

488 Aesculapian Snake

1999. Snakes. Multicoloured.
1830 135f. Type **488** 55 30
1831 150f. Common pine snake 70 40
1832 200f. Grass snake 95 55
1833 270f. Green whip snake . . 1·20 70
1834 300f. Jamaica boa . . . . . 1·50 80
1835 400f. Diamond-back rattlesnake . . . . 2·00 1·10
MS1836 109 × 86 mm. 1000f. Common European adder (39 × 29 mm) . . . . 4·75 3·75

489 Testing Chinese Lantern (14th-century)

1999. "China 1999" International Stamp Exhibition, Peking. Multicoloured.

1837		50f. Type **489**	15	10
1838		100f. Satellite launching centre, Jiuquan	45	25
1839		135f. DFH-3 communications satellite	55	40
1840		150f. Satellite launch	70	45
1841		200f. Launch of *Long March* (rocket)	95	60
1842		300f. *Yuan Wang* (passenger ferry) at sea	1·50	90
1843		400f. Dish aerial	2·00	1·20
1844		500f. Items of space post	2·40	1·80

Nos. 1837/44 were issued together, se-tenant, with the backgrounds forming a composite design of the Earth.

490 Cheetah

1999. Big Cats. Multicoloured.

1845		135f. Type **490**	55	30
1846		150f. Jaguar	70	40
1847		200f. Snow leopard	95	55
1848		270f. Leopard	1·20	55
1849		300f. Puma	1·50	65
1850		400f. Tiger	2·00	90
MS1851		110 × 85 mm. 2000f. Lion	4·75	3·75

PARCEL POST STAMPS

1982. Optd or surch **Colis Postaux**.

P871	–	100f. multicoloured (No. 779) (postage)	95	50
P872	**256**	100f. on 150f. mult	95	50
P873	–	300f. mult (No. 797)	2·75	1·40
P874	**260**	1000f. multicoloured	8·25	4·00
P875	**274**	5000f. on 500f. mult (air)	41·00	19·00

1988. No. 543 of Dahomey surch **Republique Populaire du Benin colis postaux**.

P1089	**174**	5f. on 40f. multicoloured (postage)		
P1093	–	500f. on 200f. mult	5·25	2·30
P1092	–	300f. on 200f. blue, yellow & brown (air)		

POSTAGE DUE STAMPS

D 233 Pineapples

1978. Fruits. Multicoloured.

D716		10f. Type **D 233**	30	25
D717		20f. Cashew nuts (vert)	45	25
D718		40f. Oranges	95	55
D719		50f. Breadfruit	1·10	75

D 234 Village Postman on Bicycle

1978. Rural Post.

D720	**D 234**	60f. brown, grn & red	95	45
D721	–	80f. blue, brn & red	95	55

DESIGN: 80f. River village and postman in canoe.

BERGEDORF — Pt. 7

A German city on the Elbe, governed by Hamburg and Lubeck until 1867 when it was purchased by the former. In 1868 became part of North German Confederation.

16 schilling = 1 Hamburg mark.

1

1861. Various sizes. Imperf.

1	**1**	½s. black on lilac	£450	
2		½s. black on blue	48·00	£700
4		1s. black on white	44·00	£350
5		1½s. black on yellow	21·00	£1300
6		3s. black on red	£750	
7		3s. blue on red	26·00	£1800
8		4s. black on brown	26·00	£2250

BERMUDA — Pt. 1

A group of islands in the W. Atlantic, E. of N. Carolina. Usually regarded by collectors as part of the Br. W. Indies group, though this is not strictly correct.

1865. 12 pence = 1 shilling;
20 shillings = 1 pound.
1970. 100 cents = 1 dollar (U.S.).

9 Queen Victoria

13 Dry Dock

1865. Portrait. Various frames.

19	**9**	½d. stone	4·75	4·75
21a		½d. green	3·50	80
24a		1d. red	11·00	20
25		2d. blue	60·00	4·75
26a		2d. purple	3·50	1·50
27b		2½d. blue	9·00	40
10		3d. yellow	£180	60·00
28		3d. grey	22·00	7·00
20		4d. red	17·00	1·75
28a		4d. brown	35·00	60·00
7		6d. mauve	23·00	12·00
11		1s. green	12·00	£120
29b		1s. brown	13·00	16·00

1874. Surch in words.

15	**9**	1d. on 2d. blue	£700	£375
16		1d. on 3d. yellow	£450	£350
17		1d. on 1s. green	£500	£250
12		3d. on 1d. red	£18000	
14		3d. on 1s. green	£1500	£650

1901. Surch **ONE FARTHING** and bar.

30	**9**	¼d. on 1s. grey	3·25	50

1902.

34	**13**	¼d. brown and violet	1·75	1·50
31		½d. black and green	12·00	2·75
36		½d. green	16·00	3·00
32		1d. brown and red	8·00	10
38		1d. red	19·00	10
39		2d. grey and orange	7·50	10·00
40		2½d. brown and blue	22·00	7·00
41		2½d. blue	14·00	7·00
33		3d. mauve and green	3·75	2·00
42		4d. blue and brown	3·00	16·00

14 Badge of the Colony

15

1910.

44a	**14**	¼d. brown	60	1·50
77		½d. green	1·50	15
78		1d. red	15·00	80
79b		1½d. brown	9·00	35
80		2d. grey	1·50	1·50
82b		2½d. blue	1·75	70
81a		2½d. green	1·75	1·50
84		3d. purple on yellow	4·00	1·00
83		3d. blue	16·00	26·00
85		4d. red on yellow	2·00	1·00
86		6d. purple	1·00	80
51		1s. black on green	4·25	4·25
51b	**15**	2s. purple and blue on blue	20·00	50·00
52		2s.6d. black and red on blue	30·00	80·00
52b		4s. black and red	60·00	£160
53d		5s. green and red on yellow	50·00	£120
92		10s. green and red on green	£130	£250
93		12s.6d. black and orange	£250	£375
55		£1 purple and black on red	£325	£550

1918. Optd **WAR TAX**.

56	**14**	1d. red	50	1·00

18

1920. Tercentenary of Representative Institutions. (a) 1st Issue.

59	**18**	¼d. brown	3·25	23·00
60		½d. green	6·00	14·00
65		1d. red	4·00	30
61		2d. grey	14·00	48·00
66		2½d. blue	16·00	17·00
62		3d. purple on yellow	12·00	45·00
63		4d. black and red on yellow	12·00	35·00
67		6d. purple	28·00	85·00
64		1s. black on green	16·00	48·00

19

(b) 2nd Issue.

74	**19**	¼d. brown	3·00	3·75
75		½d. green	3·00	7·50
76		1d. red	4·25	35
68		2d. grey	9·00	38·00
69		2½d. blue	11·00	35·00
70		3d. purple on yellow	5·50	16·00
71		4d. red on yellow	19·00	25·00
72		6d. purple	16·00	50·00
73		1s. black on green	24·00	50·00

1935. Silver Jubilee. As T **13** of Antigua.

94		1d. blue and red	55	1·75
95		1½d. blue and grey	80	3·25
96		2½d. brown and blue	1·40	2·25
97		1s. grey and purple	17·00	32·00

20 Hamilton Harbour

22 "Lucie" (yacht)

1936.

98	**20**	½d. green	10	10
99	–	1d. black and red	50	30
100	–	1½d. black and brown	1·00	50
101	**22**	2d. black and blue	5·00	1·50
102	–	2½d. blue	1·00	25
103	–	3d. black and red	3·00	3·25
104	–	6d. red and violet	80	10
105	–	1s. green	8·00	14·00
106	**20**	1s.6d. brown	50	10

DESIGNS—HORIZ: 1d., 1½d. South Shore, near Spanish Rock; 3d. Point House, Warwick Parish. VERT: 2½d., 1s. Grape Bay, Paget Parish; 6d. House at Par-la-Ville, Hamilton.

The 1d., 1½d., 2½d. and 1s. values include a portrait of King George V.

1937. Coronation. As T **2** of Aden.

107		1d. red	70	1·25
108		1½d. brown	60	1·75
109		2½d. blue	70	1·75

26 Ships in Hamilton Harbour

28 White-tailed Tropic Bird, Arms of Bermuda and Native Flower

1938.

110	**26**	1d. black and red	1·00	20
111b		1½d. blue and brown	2·25	1·50
112	**22**	2d. blue and brown	50·00	9·00
112a		2d. blue and red	1·50	1·00
113	–	2½d. blue and deep blue	11·00	1·25
113b	–	2½d. blue and black	2·75	2·75
114	–	3d. black and red	27·00	4·00
114a	–	3d. black and blue	1·75	40
114c	**28**	7½d. black, blue and green	6·00	2·75
115	–	1s. green	2·00	50

DESIGNS—VERT: 3d. St. David's Lighthouse. The 2½d. and 1s. are as 1935, but with King George VI portrait.

1938. As T **15**, but King George VI portrait.

116c		2s. purple and blue on blue	8·00	1·50
117d		2s.6d. black and red on blue	16·00	15·00
118f		5s. green and red on yellow	28·00	24·00
119e		10s. green and red on green	42·00	45·00
120b		12s.6d. grey and orange	£100	55·00
121d		£1 purple and black on red	50·00	75·00

1940. Surch **HALF PENNY**.

122	**26**	½d. on 1d. black and red	40	2·00

1946. Victory. As T **9** of Aden.

123		1½d. brown	15	15
124		3d. blue	15	30

1948. Silver Wedding. As T **10/11** of Aden.

125		1½d. brown	30	50
126		£1 red	42·00	50·00

31 Postmaster Perot's Stamp

1949. Centenary of Postmaster Perot's Stamp.

127	**31**	2½d. blue and brown	35	35
128		3d. black and blue	35	15
129		6d. violet and green	40	15

1949. U.P.U. As T **20/23** of Antigua.

130		2½d. black	30	2·00
131		3d. blue	1·75	1·25
132		6d. purple	40	75
133		1s. green	40	1·50

1953. Coronation. As T **13** of Aden.

134		1½d. black and blue	60	30

34 Easter Lily

43 Hog Coin

1953.

135a	–	½d. olive	40	1·25
136	–	1d. black and red	2·00	50
137	**34**	1½d. green	30	10
138	–	2d. blue and red	50	40
139	–	2½d. red	2·00	50
140	–	3d. purple	30	10
141	–	4d. black and blue	55	1·25
142	–	4½d. green	1·50	1·00
143	–	6d. black and turquoise	6·00	60
156	–	6d. black and mauve	1·25	15
143a	–	8d. black and red	3·25	30
143b	–	9d. violet	9·00	2·50
144	–	1s. orange	50	15
145	–	1s.3d. blue	3·75	30
146	–	2s. brown	4·00	85
147	–	2s.6d. red	7·00	45
148	**43**	5s. red	19·00	85
149	–	10s. blue	16·00	6·00
150	–	£1 multicoloured	30·00	21·00

DESIGNS—HORIZ: ½d. Easter lilies; 1d., 4d. Postmaster Perot's stamp; 2d. "Victory II" (racing dinghy); 2½d. Sir George Somers and "Sea Venture"; 3d., 1s.3d. Map of Bermuda; 4½d. 9d. "Sea Venture" (galleon), coin and Perot stamp; 6d. (No. 143), 8d. White-tailed tropic bird; 6d. (No. 156), Perot's Post Office; 1s. Early Bermuda coins; 2s. Arms of St. George's 10s. Obverse and reverse of hog coin; £1 Arms of Bermuda. VERT: 2s.6d. Warwick Fort.

No. 156 commemorates the restoration and reopening of Perot's Post Office.

1953. Royal Visit. As No. 143a but inscr "ROYAL VISIT 1953".

151		6d. black and turquoise	60	20

1953. Three Power Talks. Nos. 140 and 145 optd **Three Power Talks December, 1953.**

152		3d. purple	10	10
153		1s.3d. blue	10	10

1956. 50th Anniv of United States-Bermuda Yacht Race. Nos. 143a and 145 optd **50TH ANNIVERSARY US – BERMUDA OCEAN RACE 1956**.

154		8d. black and red	20	45
155		1s.3d. blue	20	55

49 Arms of King James I and Queen Elizabeth II

1959. 350th Anniv of Settlement. Arms in red, yellow and blue. Frame colours given.

157	**49**	1½d. blue	25	10
158		3d. grey	30	50
159		4d. purple	35	55
160		8d. violet	35	15

161 9d. olive . . . . 35 1·25
162 1s.3d. brown 35 30

50 The Old Rectory, St George's, c.1730

1962.
163 **50** 1d. purple, black and orange 10 75
164 – 2d. multicoloured . . . . 1·00 35
165 – 3d. brown and blue 10 10
166 – 4d. brown and mauve . . . 20 40
167 – 5d. blue and red . . . . . 75 2·50
168 – 6d. blue, green & lt blue 30 30
169 – 8d. blue, green and orange 30 35
170 – 9d. blue and brown 30 60
197 – 10d. violet and ochre . . . 75 60
171 – 1s. multicoloured 30 10
172 – 1s.3d. lake, grey and bistre 75 15
173 – 1s.6d. violet and ochre . . 75 1·00
199 – 1s.6d. blue and red . . . . 1·50 50
200 – 2s. brown and orange . . . 1·50 75
175 – 2s.3d. sepia and green . . 1·00 6·50
176 – 2s.6d. sepia, green & yell 55 50
177 – 5s. purple and green . . . 1·25 1·50
178 – 10s. mauve, green and buff 4·50 7·00
179 – £1 black, olive and orange 14·00 14·00

DESIGNS: 2d. Church of St. Peter, St. George's; 3d. Government House, 1892; 4d. The Cathedral, Hamilton, 1894; 5d., 1s.6d. (No. 199) H.M. Dockyard, 1811; 6d. Perot's Post Office, 1848; 8d. G.P.O., Hamilton, 1869; 9d. Library, Par-la-Ville; 10d., 1s.6d. (No. 173) Bermuda cottage, c. 1705; 1s. Christ Church, Warwick, 1719; 1s.3d. City Hall, Hamilton, 1960; 2s. Town of St. George; 2s.3d. Bermuda house, c. 1710; 2s.6d. Bermuda house, early 18th century; 5s. Colonial Secretariat, 1833; 10s. Old Post Office, Somerset, 1890; £1 The House of Assembly, 1815.

1963. Freedom from Hunger. As T **28** of Aden.
180 1s.3d. sepia 60 40

1963. Centenary of Red Cross. As T **33** of Antigua.
181 3d. red and black 50 25
182 1s.3d. red and blue . . . . . 1·00 2·50

67 "Tsotsi in the Bundu" (Finn class yacht)

1964. Olympic Games, Tokyo.
183 **67** 3d. red, violet and blue . . 10 10

1965. Centenary of ITU. As T **36** of Antigua.
184 3d. blue and green 35 25
185 2s. yellow and blue . . . . . 65 1·25

68 Scout Badge and St. Edward's Crown

1965. 50th Anniv of Bermuda Boy Scouts Association.
186 **68** 2s. multicoloured 50 50

1965. ICY. As T **37** of Antigua.
187 4d. purple and turquoise . . 40 20
188 2s.6d. green and lavender . . 60 80

1966. Churchill Commemoration. As T **38** of Antigua.
189 3d. blue 30 20
190 6d. green . . . . 70 1·00
191 10d. brown . . . . 1·00 75
192 1s.3d. violet . . . . 1·25 2·50

1966. World Cup Football Championship. As T **40** of Antigua.
193 10d. multicoloured . . . . . 1·00 15
194 2s.6d. multicoloured . . . . 1·25 1·25

1966. 20th Anniv of UNESCO. As T **54/56** of Antigua.
201 4d. multicoloured 45 15
202 1s.3d. yellow, violet and olive 75 50
203 2s. black, purple and orange 1·00 1·10

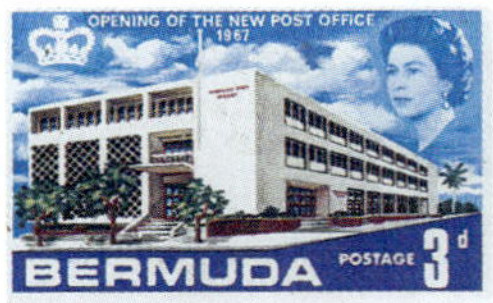

69 GPO Building

1967. Opening of New General Post Office.
204 **69** 3d. multicoloured 10 10
205 1s. multicoloured 10 10
206 1s.6d. multicoloured . . . 20 25
207 2s.6d. multicoloured . . . 20 70

70 "Mercury" (cable ship) and Chain Links

1967. Inauguration of Bermuda–Tortola Telephone Service. Multicoloured.
208 3d. Type **70** 15 10
209 1s. Map, telephone and microphone 25 10
210 1s.6d. Telecommunications media 25 25
211 2s.6d. "Mercury" (cable ship) and marine fauna 40 70

74 Human Rights Emblem and Doves

1968. Human Rights Year.
212 **74** 3d. indigo, blue and green 10 10
213 1s. brown, blue and light blue 10 10
214 1s.6d. black, blue and red 10 15
215 2s.6d. green, blue and yellow 15 25

75 Mace and Queen's Profile

1968. New Constitution.
216 **75** 3d. multicoloured 10 10
217 1s. multicoloured 10 10
218 – 1s.6d. yellow, black and blue 10 20
219 – 2s.6d. lilac, black and yellow 15 75

DESIGNS: 1s.6d., 2s.6d., Houses of Parliament, and House of Assembly, Bermuda.

77 Football, Athletics and Yachting

1968. Olympic Games, Mexico.
220 **77** 3d. multicoloured 15 10
221 1s. multicoloured 25 10
222 1s.6d. multicoloured . . . 50 30
223 2s.6d. multicoloured . . . 50 1·40

78 Brownie and Guide

1969. 50th Anniv of Girl Guides. Multicoloured.
224 3d. Type **78** 10 10
225 1s. Type **78** 20 10
226 1s.6d. Guides and Badge . . 25 40
227 2s.6d. As 1s.6d. . . . . . . 35 1·40

80 Emerald-studded Gold Cross and Seaweed

1969. Underwater Treasure. Multicoloured.
228 4d. Type **80** 20 10
229 1s.3d. Emerald-studded gold cross and sea-bed 35 15
230 2s. As Type **80** 45 90
231 2s.6d. As 1s.3d. . . . . . . 45 1·75

1970. Decimal Currency. Nos. 163/79 surch.
232 1c. on 1d. purple, black & orge . . . . 10 1·75
233 2c. on 2d. multicoloured . . 10 10
234 3c. on 3d. brown and blue . 10 30
235 4c. on 4d. brown and mauve 10 10
236 5c. on 8d. blue, green & orge 15 2·25
237 6c. on 6d. blue, green & lt blue . . . . 15 1·75
238 9c. on 9d. blue and brown . 30 2·75
239 10c. on 10d. violet and ochre 30 25
240 12c. on 1s. multicoloured . . 30 1·25
241 15c. on 1s.3d. lake, grey & bis . . . . 1·50 1·50
242 18c. on 1s.6d. blue and red 80 65
243 24c. on 2s. brown and orange 85 2·75
244 30c. on 2s.6d. sepia, grn & yell . . . . 1·00 3·00
245 36c. on 2s.3d. sepia and green 1·75 8·00
246 60c. on 5s. purple and green 2·25 4·50
247 $1.20 on 10s. mve, grn & buff . . . . 4·00 15·00
248 $2.40 on £1 black, ol & orge 5·50 19·00

83 Spathiphyllum

1970. Flowers. Multicoloured.
249 1c. Type **83** 10 20
250 2c. Bottlebrush 20 25
251 3c. Oleander (vert) 15 10
252 4c. Bermudiana 15 10
253 5c. Poinsettia 30 20
254 6c. Hibiscus 30 30
255 9c. Cereus 20 45
256 10c. Bougainvillea (vert) . . 20 15
257 12c. Jacaranda 60 60
258 15c. Passion flower . . . . 90 1·40
258a 17c. As 15c. . . . . 2·75 4·00
259 18c. Coralita . . . . 2·25 1·50
259a 20c. As 18c. . . . . 2·75 4·00
260 24c. Morning glory . . . . 1·50 4·75
260a 25c. As 24c. . . . . 2·75 4·50
261 30c. Tecoma . . . . 1·00 1·25
262 36c. Angel's trumpet . . . 1·25 1·75
262a 40c. As 36c. . . . . 2·75 5·50
263 60c. Plumbago . . . . . . 1·75 1·50
263a $1 As 60c. . . . . 3·25 6·50
264 $1.20 Bird of paradise flower . . . . 2·25 1·75
264a $2 As $1.20 . . . . 7·50 8·50
265 $2.40 Chalice cup . . . . . 6·00 4·00
265a $3 As $2.40 . . . . 11·00 11·00

84 The State House, St. George's

1970. 350th Anniv of Bermuda Parliament. Multicoloured.
266 4c. Type **84** 10 10
267 15c. The Sessions House, Hamilton 25 20
268 18c. St. Peter's Church, St. George's 25 25
269 24c. Town Hall, Hamilton . . 35 75
MS270 131 × 95 mm. Nos. 266/9 1·10 1·50

85 Street Scene, St. George's

1971. "Keep Bermuda Beautiful". Multicoloured.
271 4c. Type **85** 20 10
272 15c. Horseshoe Bay 65 65
273 18c. Gibbs Hill Lighthouse 1·50 2·25
274 24c. Hamilton Harbour . . . 1·25 2·50

86 Building of the "Deliverance"

1971. Voyage of the "Deliverance". Multicoloured.
275 4c. Type **86** 60 20
276 15c. "Deliverance" and "Patience" at Jamestown (vert) . . . . 1·50 1·75
277 18c. Wreck of the "Sea Venture" (vert) . . . . . 1·50 2·25
278 24c. "Deliverance" and "Patience" on high seas . . 1·75 2·50

87 Green overlooking Ocean View

1971. Golfing in Bermuda. Multicoloured.
279 4c. Type **87** 70 10
280 15c. Golfers at Port Royal . 1·25 65
281 18c. Castle Harbour . . . . 1·25 1·00
282 24c. Belmont . . . . 1·50 2·00

1971. Anglo-American Talks. Nos. 252, 258, 259 and 260 optd **HEATH-NIXON DECEMBER 1971**.
283 4c. Bermudiana 10 10
284 15c. Passion flower 10 20
285 18c. Coralita 15 65
286 24c. Morning glory . . . . . 20 1·00

89 Bonefish

1972. World Fishing Records. Multicoloured.
287 4c. Type **89** 30 10
288 15c. Wahoo 30 50
289 18c. Yellow-finned tuna . . . 35 75
290 24c. Greater amberjack . . . 40 1·25

1972. Silver Wedding. As T **52** of Ascension, but with "Admiralty Oar" and Mace in background.
291 4c. violet 15 10
292 15c. red 15 50

91 Palmetto

1973. Tree Planting Year. Multicoloured.
293 4c. Type **91** 25 10
294 15c. Olivewood bark 65 75
295 18c. Bermuda cedar . . . . 70 1·25
296 24c. Mahogany . . . . 75 1·60

1973. Royal Wedding. As T **47** of Anguilla, background colour given. Multicoloured.
297 15c. mauve 15 15
298 18c. blue 15 15

92 Bernard Park, Pembroke, 1973

1973. Centenary of Lawn Tennis. Multicoloured.
299 4c. Type **92** 30 10
300 15c. Clermont Court, 1873 . 40 65
301 18c. Leamington Spa Court, 1872 . . . . 45 1·75
302 24c. Staten Island Courts, 1874 . . . . 50 2·00

93 Weather Vane, City Hall

1974. 50th Anniv of Rotary in Bermuda. Mult.

320	5c. Type **93**	15	10
321	17c. St. Peter's Church, St. George's	45	35
322	20c. Somerset Bridge	50	1·50
323	25c. Map of Bermuda, 1626	60	2·25

94 Jack of Clubs and "good bridge hand"

1975. World Bridge Championships, Bermuda. Multicoloured.

324	5c. Type **94**	20	10
325	17c. Queen of Diamonds and Bermuda Bowl	35	50
326	20c. King of Hearts and Bermuda Bowl	40	1·75
327	25c. Ace of Spades and Bermuda Bowl	40	2·50

95 Queen Elizabeth II and the Duke of Edinburgh

1975. Royal Visit.

328 **95**	17c. multicoloured	60	65
329	20c. multicoloured	65	2·10

96 Short S.23 Flying Boat "Cavalier", 1937

1975. 50th Anniv of Air-mail Service to Bermuda. Multicoloured.

330	5c. Type **96**	40	10
331	17c. U.S. Navy airship "Los Angeles", 1925	1·25	85
332	20c. Lockheed Constellation, 1946	1·40	2·75
333	25c. Boeing 747-100, 1970	1·50	3·50
MS334	128 × 85 mm. Nos. 330/3	11·00	15·00

97 Supporters of American Army raiding Royal Magazine

1975. Bicentenary of Gunpowder Plot, St. George's. Multicoloured.

335	5c. Type **97**	15	10
336	17c. Setting off for raid	30	40
337	20c. Loading gunpowder aboard American ship	35	1·40
338	25c. Gunpowder on beach	35	1·50
MS339	165 × 138 mm. Nos. 335/8	2·25	7·50

98 Launching "Ready" (bathysphere)

1976. 50th Anniv of Bermuda Biological Station. Multicoloured.

357	5c. Type **98**	30	10
358	17c. View from the sea (horiz)	60	60
359	20c. H.M.S. "Challenger", 1873 (horiz)	65	2·25
360	25c. Beebe's Bathysphere descent, 1934	70	3·00

99 "Christian Radich" (cadet ship)

1976. Tall Ships Race. Multicoloured.

361	5c. Type **99**	75	20
362	12c. "Juan Sebastian de Elcano" (Spanish cadet schooner)	80	2·25
363	17c. "Eagle" (U.S. coastguard cadet ship)	80	1·50
364	20c. "Sir Winston Churchill" (cadet schooner)	80	1·75
365	40c. "Kruzenshtern" (Russian cadet barque)	1·00	2·75
366	$1 "Cutty Sark" trophy	1·25	7·00

100 Silver Trophy and Club Flags

1976. 75th Anniv of St. George's v. Somerset Cricket Cup Match. Multicoloured.

367	5c. Type **100**	30	10
368	17c. Badge and pavilion, St. George's Club	50	65
369	20c. Badge and pavilion, Somerset Club	65	2·75
370	25c. Somerset playing field	1·00	3·75

101 Royal Visit, 1975

1977. Silver Jubilee. Multicoloured.

371	5c. Type **101**	10	10
372	20c. St. Edward's Crown	15	20
373	$1 The Queen in Chair of Estate	40	1·25

102 Stockdale House, St. George's, 1784–1812

1977. Centenary of U.P.U. Membership. Mult.

374	5c. Type **102**	15	10
375	15c. Perot Post Office and stamp	25	50
376	17c. St. George's P.O. c. 1860	25	50
377	20c. Old G.P.O., Hamilton, c. 1935	30	60
378	40c. New G.P.O., Hamilton, 1967	45	1·10

103 17th-Century Ship approaching Castle Island

1977. Piloting. Multicoloured.

379	5c. Type **103**	50	10
380	15c. Pilot leaving ship, 1795	70	60
381	17c. Pilots rowing out to paddle-steamer	80	60
382	20c. Pilot gig and brig "Harvest Queen"	85	2·25
383	40c. Modern pilot cutter and R.M.S. "Queen Elizabeth 2"	1·60	3·75

104 Great Seal of Queen Elizabeth I

1978. 25th Anniv of Coronation. Multicoloured.

384	8c. Type **104**	10	10
385	50c. Great Seal of Queen Elizabeth II	30	30
386	$1 Queen Elizabeth II	60	75

105 White-tailed Tropic Bird

1978. Wildlife. Multicoloured.

387	3c. Type **105**	2·50	2·75
388	4c. White-eyed vireo	3·00	3·25
389	5c. Eastern bluebird	1·25	1·75
390	7c. Whistling frog	50	1·50
391	8c. Common cardinal ("Cardinal Redbird")	1·25	55
392	10c. Spiny lobster	20	10
393	12c. Land crab	30	70
394	15c. Lizard (Skink)	30	15
395	20c. Four-eyed butterflyfish	30	30
396	25c. Red hind	30	20
397	30c. "Danaus plexippus" (butterfly)	2·25	2·50
398	40c. Rock beauty	50	1·75
399	50c. Banded butterflyfish	55	1·50
400	$1 Blue angelfish	2·50	1·75
401	$2 Humpback whale	2·00	2·25
402	$3 Green turtle	2·50	2·50
403	$5 Cahow	5·50	5·00

106 Map by Sir George Somers, 1609

1979. Antique Maps. Multicoloured.

404	8c. Type **106**	15	10
405	15c. Map by John Seller, 1685	20	15
406	20c. Map by H. Moll, 1729–40 (vert)	25	25
407	25c. Map by Desbruslins, 1740	30	30
408	50c. Map by Speed, 1626	45	80

107 Policeman and Policewoman

1979. Centenary of Police Force. Multicoloured.

409	8c. Type **107**	30	10
410	20c. Policeman directing traffic (horiz)	50	55
411	25c. "Blue Heron" (police launch) (horiz)	60	65
412	50c. Police Morris Marina and motorcycle	80	1·50

108 1d. "Perot" Stamp of 1848 and 1840 Penny Black

1980. Death Cent of Sir Rowland Hill. Mult.

413	8c. Type **108**	20	10
414	20c. "Perot" and Sir Rowland Hill	30	25
415	25c. "Perot" and early letter	30	30
416	50c. "Perot" and "Paid 1" cancellation	35	1·00

109 Lockheed TriStar 500 approaching Bermuda

1980. "London 1980" International Stamp Exhibition. Multicoloured.

417	25c. Type **109**	30	15
418	50c. "Orduna I" (liner) at Grassy Bay, 1926	45	35
419	$1 "Delta" (screw steamer) at St. George's Harbour, 1856	85	1·10
420	$2 "Lord Sidmouth" (sailing packet) in Old Ship Channel, St. George's	1·40	2·25

110 Gina Swainson ("Miss World 1979–80")

1980. "Miss World 1979–80" Commem. Mult.

421	8c. Type **110**	15	10
422	20c. Miss Swainson after crowning ceremony	20	20
423	50c. Miss Swainson on Peacock Throne	35	35
424	$1 Miss Swainson in Bermuda carriage	70	90

111 Queen Elizabeth the Queen Mother

1980. 80th Birthday of The Queen Mother.

425 **111**	25c. multicoloured	30	1·00

112 Bermuda from Satellite

1980. Commonwealth Finance Ministers Meeting. Multicoloured.

426	8c. Type **112**	10	10
427	20c. "Camden"	20	40
428	25c. Princess Hotel, Hamilton	20	50
429	50c. Government House	35	1·25

113 Kitchen, 18th-century

1981. Heritage Week. Multicoloured.

430	8c. Type **113**	15	10
431	25c. Gathering Easter lilies, 20th-century	20	35
432	30c. Fishing, 20th-century	30	50
433	40c. Stone cutting, 19th-century	30	80
434	50c. Onion shipping, 19th-century	50	90
435	$1 Privateering, 17th-century	1·10	2·50

114 Wedding Bouquet from Bermuda

115 "Service", Hamilton

1981. Royal Wedding. Multicoloured.

436	30c. Type **114**	20	20
437	50c. Prince Charles as Royal Navy Commander	35	40
438	$1 Prince Charles and Lady Diana Spencer	55	80

1981. 25th Anniv of Duke of Edinburgh Award Scheme. Multicoloured.

439	10c. Type **115**	15	10
440	25c. "Outward Bound", Paget Island	20	20
441	30c. "Expedition", St. David's Island	20	30
442	$1 Duke of Edinburgh	55	1·25

116 Lightbourne's Cone

1982. Sea Shells. Multicoloured.

443	10c. Type **116**	30	10
444	25c. Finlay's frog shell	55	55
445	30c. Royal bonnet	60	60
446	$1 Lightbourne's murex	1·75	3·25

117 Regimental Colours and Colour Party

1982. Bermuda Regiment. Multicoloured.

447	10c. Type **117**	60	10
448	25c. Queen's Birthday Parade	80	80
449	30c. Governor inspecting Guard of Honour	1·10	1·40
450	40c. Beating the Retreat	1·25	1·75
451	50c. Ceremonial gunners	1·25	2·00
452	$1 Guard of Honour, Royal visit, 1975	1·75	3·50

118 Charles Fort

119 Arms of Sir Edwin Sandys

1982. Historic Bermuda Forts. Multicoloured.

453	10c. Type **118**	20	20
454	25c. Pembroks Fort	50	85
455	30c. Southampton Fort (horiz)	60	1·25
456	$1 Smiths Fort and Pagets Fort (horiz)	1·25	5·00

1983. Coat of Arms (1st series). Multicoloured.

457	10c. Type **119**	45	15
458	25c. Arms of the Bermuda Company	1·10	1·00
459	50c. Arms of William Herbert, Earl of Pembroke	1·90	3·75
460	$1 Arms of Sir George Somers	2·50	6·50

See also Nos. 482/5 and 499/502.

120 Early Fitted Dinghy

122 Joseph Stockdale

121 Curtiss N-9 Seaplane

1983. Fitted Dinghies. Multicoloured.

461	12c. Type **120**	45	15
462	30c. Modern dinghy inshore	60	75
463	40c. Early dinghy (different)	70	90
464	$1 Modern dinghy with red and white spinnaker	1·40	3·25

1983. Bicentenary of Manned Flight. Multicoloured.

465	12c. Type **121** (First flight over Bermuda)	60	20
466	30c. Stinson Pilot Radio seaplane (First completed flight between U.S. and Bermuda)	1·25	1·25
467	40c. S.23 Flying boat "Cavalier" (First scheduled passenger flight)	1·50	1·75
468	$1 U.S.N. "Los Angeles" (airship) moored to U.S.S. "Patoka"	2·75	5·50

1984. Bicentenary of Bermuda's First Newspaper and Postal Service. Multicoloured.

469	12c. Type **122**	30	15
470	30c. "The Bermuda Gazette"	45	80
471	40c. Stockdale's postal service (horiz)	60	1·10
472	$1 "Lady Hammond" (mail boat) (horiz)	2·00	3·25

123 Sir Thomas Gates and Sir George Somers

1984. 375th Anniv of First Settlement. Mult.

473	12c. Type **123**	20	15
474	30c. Jamestown, Virginia	50	1·25
475	40c. Wreck of "Sea Venture"	90	1·25
476	$1 Fleet leaving Plymouth, Devon	2·00	6·00
MS477	130 × 73 mm. Nos. 474 and 476	3·75	10·00

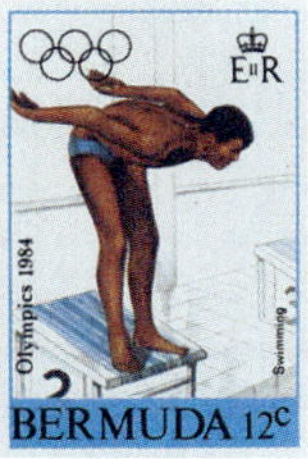

124 Swimming

125 Buttery

1984. Olympic Games, Los Angeles. Multicoloured.

478	12c. Type **124**	40	15
479	30c. Track and field events (horiz)	70	75
480	40c. Equestrian	1·10	1·25
481	$1 Sailing (horiz)	2·00	5·50

1984. Coat of Arms (2nd series). As T **119**. Mult.

482	12c. Arms of Henry Wrothesley, Earl of Southampton	50	15
483	30c. Arms of Sir Thomas Smith	1·00	85
484	40c. Arms of William Cavendish, Earl of Devonshire	1·25	1·50
485	$1 Town arms of St. George	2·75	4·50

1985. Bermuda Architecture. Multicoloured.

486	12c. Type **125**	35	15
487	30c. Limestone rooftops (horiz)	80	70
488	40c. Chimneys (horiz)	95	1·00
489	$1.50 Entrance archway	3·00	4·25

126 Osprey

127 The Queen Mother with Grandchildren, 1980

1985. Birth Bicentenary of John J. Audubon (ornithologist). Designs showing original drawings. Multicoloured.

490	12c. Type **126**	2·00	65
491	30c. Yellow-crowned night heron	2·00	95
492	40c. Great egret (horiz)	2·25	1·25
493	$1.50 Eastern bluebird ("Bluebird")	3·75	6·50

1985. Life and Times of Queen Elizabeth the Queen Mother. Multicoloured.

494	12c. Queen Consort, 1937	35	15
495	30c. Type **127**	60	50
496	40c. At Clarence House on 83rd birthday	70	60
497	$1.50 With Prince Henry at his christening (from photo by Lord Snowdon)	2·00	2·75
MS498	91 × 73 mm. $1 With Prince Charles at 80th birthday celebrations	3·75	3·50

1985. Coats of Arms (3rd series). As T **119**. Mult.

499	12c. Hamilton	75	15
500	30c. Paget	1·40	80
501	40c. Warwick	1·60	1·40
502	$1.50 City of Hamilton	3·75	4·50

128 Halley's Comet and Bermuda Archipelago

1985. Appearance of Halley's Comet. Multicoloured.

503	15c. Type **128**	85	25
504	40c. Halley's Comet, A.D. 684 (from Nuremberg Chronicles, 1493)	1·60	1·75
505	50c. "Halley's Comet, 1531" (from Peter Apian woodcut, 1532)	1·90	2·50
506	$1.50 "Halley's Comet, 1759" (Samuel Scott)	3·50	6·50

129 "Constellation" (schooner) (1943)

1986. Ships Wrecked on Bermuda. Multicoloured.

507A	3c. Type **129**	70	1·50
508A	5c. "Early Riser" (pilot boat), 1876	20	20
509A	7c. "Madiana" (screw steamer), 1903	65	2·75
510A	10c. "Curlew" (sail/steamer), 1856	30	30
511A	12c. "Warwick" (galleon), 1619	60	1·00
512A	15c. H.M.S. "Vixen" (gun-boat), 1890	40	60
512cA	18c. As 7c.	6·00	4·50
513A	20c. "San Pedro" (Spanish galleon), 1594	1·10	80
514A	25c. "Alert" (fishing sloop), 1877	60	3·00
515A	40c. "North Carolina" (barque), 1880	65	1·25
516A	50c. "Mark Antonie" (Spanish privateer), 1777	1·50	3·25
517A	60c. "Mary Celestia" (Confederate paddle-steamer), 1864	1·50	1·75
517cA	70c. "Caesar" (brig), 1818	6·50	7·00
518B	$1 "L'Herminie" (French frigate), 1839	1·50	1·60
519A	$1.50 As 70c.	4·50	6·50
520B	$2 "Lord Amherst" (transport), 1778	2·50	6·50
521B	$3 "Minerva" (sailing ship), 1849	4·25	9·00
522A	$5 "Caraquet" (cargo liner), 1923	4·75	11·00
523A	$8 H.M.S. "Pallas" (frigate), 1783	7·00	14·00

1986. 60th Birthday of Queen Elizabeth II. As T **110** of Ascension. Multicoloured.

524	15c. Princess Elizabeth aged three, 1929	45	30
525	40c. With Earl of Rosebery at Oaks May Meeting, Epsom, 1954	80	60
526	50c. With Duke of Edinburgh, Bermuda, 1975	80	75
527	60c. At British Embassy, Paris, 1972	90	90
528	$1.50 At Crown Agents Head Office, London, 1983	2·00	2·50

1986. "Ameripex '86" International Stamp Exhibition, Chicago. As T **164** of Bahamas, showing Bermuda stamps. Multicoloured.

529	15c. 1984 375th Anniv of Settlement miniature sheet	1·50	30
530	40c. 1973 Lawn Tennis Centenary, 24c.	2·25	70
531	50c. 1983 Bicentenary of Manned Flight 12c.	2·25	1·00
532	$1 1976 Tall Ships Race 17c.	3·75	3·00
MS533	80 × 80 mm. $1.50, Statue of Liberty and "Monarch of Bermuda"	7·50	7·50

No. **MS**533 also commemorates the Centenary of the Statue of Liberty.

1986. 25th Anniv of World Wildlife Fund. No. 402 surch **90c.**

534	90c. on $3 Green turtle	3·00	4·50

131 Train in Front Street, Hamilton, 1940

1987. Transport (1st series). Bermuda Railway. Multicoloured.

535	15c. Type **131**	2·00	25
536	40c. Train crossing Springfield Trestle	2·50	90
537	50c. "St. George Special" at Bailey's Bay Station	2·50	1·50
538	$1.50 Boat train at St. George	4·00	6·00

See also Nos. 557/60, 574/7 and 624/9.

132 "Bermuda Settlers", 1901

1987. Bermuda Paintings (1st series). Works by Winslow Homer. Multicoloured.

539	15c. Type **132**	60	25
540	30c. "Bermuda", 1900	85	45
541	40c. "Bermuda Landscape", 1901 (buff frame)	95	55
544	40c. Type **132**	1·00	1·75
545	40c. As No. 540	1·00	1·75
546	40c. As No. 541 (grey frame)	1·00	1·75
547	40c. As No. 542	1·00	1·75
548	40c. As No. 543	1·00	1·75
542	50c. "Inland Water", 1901	1·10	70
543	$1.50 "Salt Kettle", 1899	2·50	2·50

See also Nos. 607/10 and 630/3.

133 Sikorsky S-42B Flying Boat "Bermuda Clipper"

1987. 50th Anniv of Inauguration of Bermuda–U.S.A. Air Service. Multicoloured.

549	15c. Type **133**	2·00	15
550	40c. Short S.23 flying boat "Cavalier"	3·00	70
551	50c. "Bermuda Clipper" in flight over signpost	3·25	80
552	$1.50 "Cavalier" on apron and "Bermuda Clipper" in flight	6·00	3·50

134 19th-century Wagon carrying Telephone Poles

1987. Centenary of Bermuda Telephone Company. Multicoloured.

553 15c. Type **134** 75 15
554 40c. Early telephone exchange 1·40 60
555 50c. Early and modern telephones . . . . 1·75 70
556 $1.50 Communications satellite orbiting Earth . . 2·75 5·00

135 Mail Wagon, c. 1869

1988. Transport (2nd series). Horse-drawn Carts and Wagons. Multicoloured.

557 15c. Type **135** 25 15
558 40c. Open cart, c. 1823 . . . 55 55
559 50c. Closed cart, c. 1823 . . 65 70
560 $1.50 Two-wheeled wagon, c. 1930 . . . . . . 2·00 3·25

136 "Old Blush"

1988. Old Garden Roses (1st series). Multicoloured.

561 15c. Type **136** 85 25
562 30c. "Anna Olivier" . . . . 1·25 45
563 40c. "Rosa chinensis semperflorens" (vert) . . . 1·40 85
564 50c. "Archduke Charles" . . 1·50 1·25
565 $1.50 "Rosa chinensis viridiflora" (vert) . . . . . 3·00 6·00

See also Nos. 584/8 and, for designs with the royal cypher instead of the Queen's head, Nos. 589/98 and 683/6.

1988. 300th Anniv of Lloyd's of London. As T **123** of Ascension. Multicoloured.

566 18c. Loss of H.M.S. "Lutine" (frigate), 1799 . . . . . . 1·00 25
567 50c. "Sentinel" (cable ship) (horiz) . . . . 1·75 65
568 60c. "Bermuda" (liner), Hamilton, 1931 (horiz) . . 1·90 75
569 $2 Loss of H.M.S. "Valerian" (sloop) in hurricane, 1926 . . . . . 3·25 3·75

137 Devonshire Parish Militia, 1812

1988. Military Uniforms. Multicoloured.

570 18c. Type **137** . . . . 1·50 25
571 50c. 71 st (Highland) Regiment, 1831–34 . . . . 2·00 1·10
572 60c. Cameron Highlanders, 1942 . . . . 2·25 1·25
573 $2 Troop of horse, 1774 . . 4·75 8·00

138 "Corona" (ferry)

1989. Transport (3rd series). Ferry Services. Mult.

574 18c. Type **138** 35 25
575 50c. Rowing boat ferry . . . 75 65
576 60c. St. George's barge ferry 85 75
577 $2 "Laconia" . . . . 2·50 4·50

139 Morgan's Island

1989. 150 Years of Photography. Multicoloured.

578 18c. Type **139** 85 25
579 30c. Front Street, Hamilton 1·10 45
580 50c. Waterfront, Front Street, Hamilton . . . . 1·60 1·25
581 60c. Crow Lane from Hamilton Harbour . . . . 1·75 1·50
582 70c. Shipbuilding, Hamilton Harbour . . . . 1·90 2·25
583 $1 Dockyard . . . . 2·25 3·50

1989. Old Garden Roses (2nd series). As T **136**. Multicoloured.

584 18c. "Agrippina" (vert) . . . 90 25
585 30c. "Smith's Parish" (vert) 1·25 60
586 50c. "Champney's Pink Cluster" . . . . 1·75 1·40
587 60c. "Rosette Delizy" . . . . 1·75 1·60
588 $1.50 "Rosa bracteata" . . . 2·75 6·00

1989. Old Garden Roses (3rd series). Designs as Nos. 561/5 and 584/8, but with royal cypher at top left instead of Queen's head. Multicoloured.

589 50c. As No. 565 (vert) . . . 1·75 2·50
590 50c. As No. 563 (vert) . . . 1·75 2·50
591 50c. Type **136** . . . . . . 1·75 2·50
592 50c. As No. 562 . . . . . 1·75 2·50
593 50c. As No. 564 . . . . . 1·75 2·50
594 50c. As No. 585 (vert) . . . 1·75 2·50
595 50c. As No. 584 (vert) . . . 1·75 2·50
596 50c. As No. 586 . . . . . 1·75 2·50
597 50c. As No. 587 . . . . . 1·75 2·50
598 50c. As No. 588 . . . . . 1·75 2·50

140 Main Library, Hamilton

1989. 150th Anniv of Bermuda Library. Mult.

599 18c. Type **140** 60 25
600 50c. The Old Rectory, St. George's . . . . 1·25 65
601 60c. Somerset Library, Springfield . . . . 1·25 85
602 $2 Cabinet Building, Hamilton . . . . 3·25 4·00

141 1865 1d. Rose

1989. Commonwealth Postal Conference. Mult.

603 **141** 18c. grey, pink and red 1·50 25
604 – 50c. grey, blue & lt blue 2·00 75
605 – 60c. grey, purple and mauve . . . . 2·25 1·25
606 – $2 grey, green and emerald . . . . 3·75 5·00

DESIGNS: 50c. 1866 2d. blue; 60c. 1865 6d. purple; $2 1865 1s. green.

142 "Fairylands, c. 1890" (Ross Turner)

1990. Bermuda Paintings (2nd series). Multicoloured.

607 18c. Type **142** 75 25
608 50c. "Shinebone Alley, c. 1953" (Ogden Pleissner) . . . . 1·25 1·25
609 60c. "Salt Kettle, 1916" (Prosper Senat) . . . . . 1·25 1·50
610 $2 "St. George's, 1934" (Jack Bush) . . . . 3·25 7·00

1990. "Stamp World London 90" International Stamp Exhibition. Nos. 603/6 optd **Stamp World London 90** and logo.

611 18c. grey, pink and red . . . 1·25 25
612 50c. grey, blue and light blue 1·75 1·50
613 60c. grey, purple and mauve 2·00 1·75
614 $2 grey, green and emerald 3·50 6·00

1990. Nos. 511, 516 and 519 surch.

615 30c. on 12c. "Warwick" (galleon), (1619) . . . . . 1·50 1·25
616 55c. on 50c. "Mark Antonie" (Spanish privateer), 1777 2·00 2·25
617 80c. on $1.50 "Caesar" (brig), 1818 . . . . 2·50 4·50

145 The Halifax and Bermudas Cable Company Office, Hamilton

1990. Centenary of Cable and Wireless in Bermuda.

618 **145** 20c. brown and black . . 70 25
619 – 55c. brown and black . . 2·00 1·25
620 – 70c. multicoloured . . . . 2·00 2·75
621 – $2 multicoloured . . . . 4·75 7·50

DESIGNS: 55c. "Westmeath" (cable ship), 1890; 70c. Wireless transmitter station, St. George's, 1928; $2 "Sir Eric Sharp" (cable ship).

1991. President Bush–Prime Minister Major Talks, Bermuda. Nos. 618/19 optd **BUSH-MAJOR 16 MARCH 1991**.

622 **145** 20c. brown and black . . 2·00 1·50
623 – 55c. brown and black . . 3·00 3·50

147 Two-seater Pony Cart, 1805

1991. Transport (4th series). Horse-drawn Carriages. Multicoloured.

624 20c. Type **147** 80 30
625 30c. Varnished rockaway, 1830 . . . . 90 60
626 55c. Vis-a-Vis victoria, 1895 1·60 1·10
627 70c. Semi-formal phaeton, 1900 . . . . 2·25 2·50
628 80c. Pony runabout, 1905 . . 2·50 3·75
629 $1 Ladies phaeton, 1910 . . 2·75 4·50

148 "Bermuda, 1916" (Prosper Senat)

1991. Bermuda Paintings (3rd series). Multicoloured.

630 20c. Type **148** . . . . 1·00 30
631 55c. "Bermuda Cottage" 1930 (Frank Allison) (horiz) . . 2·00 1·40
632 70c. "Old Maid's Lane", 1934 (Jack Bush) . . . . 2·50 3·25
633 $2 "St. George's", 1953 (Ogden Pleissner) (horiz) 5·00 8·50

1991. 65th Birthday of Queen Elizabeth II and 70th Birthday of Prince Philip. As T **139** of Ascension. Multicoloured.

634 55c. Prince Philip in tropical naval uniform . . . . . . 1·25 1·75
635 70c. Queen Elizabeth II in Bermuda . . . . 1·25 1·75

149 H.M.S. "Argonaut" (cruiser) in Floating Dock

1991. 50th Anniv of Second World War. Mult.

636 20c. Type **149** . . . . 1·75 40
637 55c. Kindley Airfield . . . . 2·50 1·40
638 70c. Boeing 314A flying boat and map of Atlantic route 3·00 3·50
639 $2 Censored trans-Atlantic mail . . . . 4·75 8·50

1992. 40th Anniv of Queen Elizabeth II's Accession. As T **143** of Ascension. Multicoloured.

640 20c. Old fort on beach . . . 60 30
641 30c. Public gardens 75 55
642 55c. Cottage garden . . . . 1·25 90
643 70c. Beach and hotels . . . . 1·60 2·25
644 $1 Queen Elizabeth II . . . 1·90 2·75

150 Rings and Medallion

1992. 500th Anniv of Discovery of America by Columbus. Spanish Artifacts. Multicoloured.

645 25c. Type **150** . . . . 1·25 35
646 35c. Ink wells . . . . 1·40 75
647 60c. Gold ornaments . . . . 2·25 2·00
648 75c. Bishop buttons and crucifix . . . . 2·50 3·25
649 85c. Earrings and pearl buttons . . . . 2·75 3·75
650 $1 Jug and bowls . . . . . 3·00 4·25

151 "Wreck of 'Sea Venture' "

1992. Stained Glass Windows. Multicoloured.

651 25c. Type **151** . . . . 1·50 40
652 60c. "Birds in tree" . . . . . 2·75 2·00
653 75c. "St. Francis feeding bird" . . . . 3·25 3·00
654 $2 "Shells" . . . . 7·00 10·00

152 German Shepherd

1992. 7th World Congress of Kennel Clubs. Mult.

655 25c. Type **152** . . . . 1·25 40
656 35c. Irish setter . . . . . . 1·50 70
657 60c. Whippet (vert) . . . . . 2·25 2·25
658 75c. Border terrier (vert) . . 2·25 3·25
659 85c. Pomeranian (vert) . . . 2·50 3·75
660 $1 Schipperke (vert) . . . . 2·50 4·25

153 Policeman, Cyclist and Cruise Liner

154 "Duchesse de Brabant" and Bee

1993. Tourism Posters by Adolph Treidler. Mult.

679 25c. Type **153** . . . . 2·25 80
680 60c. Seaside golf course . . . 3·00 2·75
681 75c. Deserted beach . . . . 2·50 2·75
682 $2 Dancers in evening dress and cruise liner . . . . . 4·50 7·00

1993. Garden Roses (4th series).

683 **154** 10c. multicoloured . . . . 75 1·60
684 25c. multicoloured 75 70
685 50c. multicoloured . . . . 2·00 3·50
686 60c. multicoloured . . . . 1·10 1·90

1993. 75th Anniv of Royal Air Force. As T **149** of Ascension. Multicoloured.

687 25c. Consolidated PBY-5 Catalina 85 35
688 60c. Supermarine Spitfire Mk IX . . . . 2·00 2·00
689 75c. Bristol Type 156 Beaufighter Mk X . . . . 2·25 2·25
690 $2 Handley Page Halifax Mk III . . . . 3·75 6·00

155 Hamilton from the Sea

1993. Bicentenary of Hamilton. Mult.

691 25c. Type **155** . . . . 1·00 35
692 60c. Waterfront . . . . . . 2·00 2·00
693 75c. Barrel warehouse . . . 2·00 2·50
694 $2 Sailing ships off Hamilton 5·00 7·00

156 "Queen of Bermuda" (liner) at Hamilton

157 Queen Elizabeth II in Bermuda

1994. 75th Anniv of Furness Line's Bermuda Cruises. Adolphe Treidler Posters. Multicoloured.

695	25c. Type **156**	65	35
696	60c. "Queen of Bermuda" entering port (horiz)	1·50	1·60
697	75c. "Queen of Bermuda" and "Ocean Monarch" (liners) (horiz)	1·60	1·75
698	$2 Passengers on promenade deck at night	3·50	6·00

1994. Royal Visit. Multicoloured.

699	25c. Type **157**	1·00	35
700	60c. Queen Elizabeth and Prince Philip in open carriage	2·25	1·75
701	75c. Royal Yacht "Britannia"	4·75	3·50

158 Peach

1994. Flowering Fruits. Multicoloured.

792	5c. Type **158**	40	70
703A	7c. Fig	40	70
704A	10c. Calabash (vert)	35	35
795	15c. Natal plum	65	25
796	18c. Locust and wild honey	70	30
797	20c. Pomegranate	70	35
798	25c. Mulberry (vert)	70	40
709A	35c. Grape (vert)	70	55
710A	55c. Orange (vert)	1·00	80
711A	60c. Surinam cherry	1·25	90
802	75c. Loquat	2·00	1·75
803	90c. Sugar apple	2·25	2·00
804	$1 Prickly pear (vert)	2·50	2·75
715A	$2 Paw paw	3·50	4·50
716A	$3 Bay grape	5·00	6·50
717A	$5 Banana (vert)	7·50	8·00
718A	$8 Lemon	11·00	12·00

159 Nurse with Mother and Baby

1994. Centenary of Hospital Care. Multicoloured.

719	25c. Type **159**	1·00	35
720	60c. Patient on dialysis machine	2·00	1·90
721	75c. Casualty on emergency trolley	2·25	2·25
722	$2 Elderly patient in wheelchair with physiotherapists	4·75	7·00

160 Gombey Dancers

1994. Cultural Heritage (1st series). Multicoloured.

723	25c. Type **160**	75	35
724	60c. Christmas carol singers	1·40	1·50
725	75c. Marching band	2·50	2·00
726	$2 National Dance Group performers	4·75	7·50

See also Nos. 731/4.

161 Bermuda 1970 Flower 1c. Stamps and 1c. Coin

162 Bermuda Coat of Arms

1995. 25th Anniv of Decimal Currency. Mult.

727	25c. Type **161**	75	35
728	60c. 1970 5c. stamps and coin	1·40	1·50
729	75c. 1970 10c. stamps and coin	1·75	2·00
730	$2 1970 25c. stamps and coin	4·50	6·50

1995. Cultural Heritage (2nd series). As T **160**. Multicoloured.

731	25c. Kite flying	55	35
732	60c. Majorettes	1·50	1·50
733	75c. Portuguese dancers	1·75	2·00
734	$2 Floral float	3·75	6·00

1995. 375th Anniv of Bermuda Parliament.

735	**162** 25c. multicoloured	1·25	35
736	$1 multicoloured	2·50	3·25

For design as No. 736 but inscr "Commonwealth Finance Ministers Meeting", see No. 765.

163 U.S. Navy Ordnance Island Submarine Base

1995. Military Bases. Multicoloured.

737	20c. Type **163**	70	60
738	25c. Royal Naval Dockyard	75	35
739	60c. U.S.A.F. Fort Bell and Kindley Field	1·60	1·25
740	75c. R.A.F. Darrell's Island flying boat base	1·75	2·00
741	90c. U.S. Navy operating base	1·90	2·75
742	$1 Canadian Forces Communications Station, Daniel's Head	1·90	2·75

164 Triple Jump

1996. Olympic Games, Atlanta. Multicoloured.

743	25c. Type **164**	70	35
744	30c. Cycling	3·00	1·00
745	65c. Yachting	2·00	2·00
746	80c. Show jumping	2·00	3·00

165 Jetty and Islets, Hamilton

1996. Panoramic Paintings of Hamilton (Nos. 747/51) and St. George's (Nos. 752/6) by E. J. Holland. Multicoloured.

747	60c. Type **165**	1·60	1·90
748	60c. End of island and buildings	1·60	1·90
749	60c. Yachts and hotel	1·60	1·90
750	60c. Islet, hotel and cathedral	1·60	1·90
751	60c. Cliff and houses by shore	1·60	1·90
752	60c. Islet and end of main island	1·60	1·90
753	60c. Yacht and houses on hillside	1·60	1·90
754	60c. Yacht and St. George's Hotel on hilltop	1·60	1·90
755	60c. Shoreline and fishing boats	1·60	1·90
756	60c. Entrance to harbour channel	1·60	1·90

166 Somerset Express Mail Cart, c. 1900

1996. "CAPEX '96" International Stamp Exhibition, Toronto. Local Transport. Multicoloured.

757	25c. Type **166**	1·25	35
758	60c. Victoria carriage and railcar, 1930s	2·75	1·75
759	75c. First bus, 1946	2·75	2·00
760	$2 Sightseeing bus, c. 1947	5·00	7·50

167 Hog Fish Beacon

1996. Lighthouses. Multicoloured.

761	30c. Type **167**	1·75	50
762	65c. Gibbs Hill Lighthouse	2·25	1·25
763	80c. St. David's Lighthouse	2·75	2·00
764	$2 North Rock Beacon	4·25	8·00

See also Nos. 770/3.

1996. Commonwealth Finance Ministers' Meeting. As No. 736, but inscr "Commonwealth Finance Ministers Meeting" at top and with wider gold frame.

765	$1 multicoloured	2·50	3·00

168 Waterville

1996. Architectural Heritage. Multicoloured.

766	30c. Type **168**	1·00	45
767	65c. Bridge House	1·40	1·50
768	80c. Fannie Fox's Cottage	1·75	2·00
769	$2.50 Palmetto House	4·00	7·00

1997. "HONG KONG '97" International Stamp Exhibition. Designs as Nos. 761/4, but incorporating "HONG KONG '97" logo and with some values changed.

770	30c. As Type **167**	2·00	50
771	65c. Gibbs Hill Lighthouse	2·75	1·50
772	80c. St David's Lighthouse	3·00	2·25
773	$2.50 North Rock Beacon	6·00	8·50

169 White-tailed Tropic Bird

1997. Bird Conservation. Multicoloured.

774	30c. Type **169**	60	50
775	60c. White-tailed tropic bird and chick (vert)	1·25	1·25
776	80c. Cahow and chick (vert)	1·75	2·00
777	$2.50 Cahow	4·00	6·50

170 Queen Elizabeth II with Crowd

1997. Golden Wedding of Queen Elizabeth and Prince Philip. Multicoloured.

778	30c. Type **170**	50	40
779	$2 Queen Elizabeth and Prince Philip	3·25	4·50
MS780	90 × 56 mm. Nos. 778/9	3·75	4·50

171 Father playing with Children

1997. Education. Multicoloured.

781	30c. Type **171**	50	40
782	40c. Teacher and children with map	60	55
783	60c. Boys holding sports trophy	85	1·25
784	65c. Pupils outside Berkeley Institute	90	1·25
785	80c. Scientific experiments	1·25	2·00
786	90c. New graduates	1·40	2·50

1998. Diana, Princess of Wales Commemoration. Sheet, 145 × 170 mm, containing vert designs as T **177** of Ascension. Multicoloured.

MS787	30c. Wearing black hat, 1983; 40c. Wearing floral dress; 65c. Wearing blue evening dress, 1996; 80c. Carrying bouquets, 1993 (sold at $2.15 + 25c. charity premium)	3·50	4·00

172 "Fox's Cottage, St. Davids" (Ethel Tucker)

1998. Paintings by Catherine and Ethel Tucker. Multicoloured.

788	30c. Type **172**	1·25	40
789	40c. "East Side, Somerset"	1·40	70
790	65c. "Long Bay Road, Somerset"	2·25	1·25
791	$2 "Flatts Village"	5·00	7·00

173 Horse and Carriage

1998. Hospitality in Bermuda. Multicoloured.

809	25c. Type **173**	1·25	40
810	30c. Golf club desk	1·75	75
811	65c. Chambermaid preparing room	1·50	1·25
812	75c. Kitchen staff under training	1·50	2·00
813	80c. Waiter at beach hotel	1·75	2·25
814	90c. Nightclub bar	2·00	3·00

174 "Agave attenuata"

1998. Centenary of Botanical Gardens. Multicoloured.

815	30c. Type **174**	1·25	40
816	65c. Bermuda palmetto tree	2·25	90
817	$1 Banyan tree	2·75	2·75
818	$2 Cedar tree	4·00	7·00

175 Lizard with Fairy Lights (Claire Critchley)

1998. Christmas. Children's Paintings. Mult.

819	25c. Type **175**	1·00	35
820	40c. "Christmas stairway" (Cameron Rowling) (horiz)	1·50	1·25

176 Shelly Bay

1999. Bermuda Beaches. Multicoloured.

821	30c. Type **176**	80	40
822	60c. Catherine's Bay	1·10	1·00
823	65c. Jobson's Cove	1·25	1·10
824	$2 Warwick Long Bay	3·50	6·00

177 Tracking Station

1999. 30th Anniv of First Manned Landing on Moon. Multicoloured.

825	30c. Type **177**	1·00	40
826	60c. Mission launch (vert)	1·50	90
827	75c. Aerial view of tracking station, Bermuda	1·75	1·25
828	$2 Astronaut on Moon (vert)	3·75	6·50
MS829	90 × 80 mm. 65c. Earth as seen from Moon (circular, 40 mm diam)	2·75	3·25

178 Theodolite and Map, 1901

1999. Centenary of First Digital Map of Bermuda.

830	**178**	30c. multicoloured	1·50	40
831	–	65c. black, stone & silver	2·25	1·50
832	–	80c. multicoloured	2·75	2·75
833	–	$1 multicoloured	2·75	3·50

DESIGNS: 65c. Street map, 1901; 80c. Street plan and aerial photograph, 1999; $1 Satellite and Bermuda from Space, 1999.

179 Victorian Pillar Box and Bermuda 1865 1s. Stamp

180 Sir Henry Tucker and Meeting of House of Assembly

1999. Bermuda Postal History. Multicoloured.

834	30c. Type **179**	1·00	40
835	75c. King George V pillar box and 1920 2s. stamp	2·00	1·50
836	95c. King George VI wall box and 1938 3d. stamp	2·25	2·50
837	$1 Queen Elizabeth II pillar box and 1953 Coronation 1½d. stamp	2·25	2·50

2000. Pioneers of Progress (1st series). Each brown, black and gold.

838	30c. Type **180**	85	1·00
839	30c. Gladys Morrell and suffragettes	85	1·00
840	30c. Dr. E. F. Gordon and workers	85	1·00

See also Nos. 988/92.

181 *Amerigo Vespucci* (full-rigged ship)

182 Prince William

2000. Tall Ships Race. Multicoloured.

841	30c. Type **181**	1·25	50
842	60c. *Europa* (barque)	1·75	1·50
843	80c. *Juan Sebastian de Elcano* (schooner)	2·00	2·00

2000. Royal Birthdays. Multicoloured.

844	35c. Type **182**	1·50	45
845	40c. Duke of York	1·50	50
846	50c. Princess Royal	1·60	90
847	70c. Princess Margaret	2·00	2·50
848	$1 Queen Elizabeth the Queen Mother	2·25	3·00
MS849	169 × 90 mm. Nos. 844/8	7·00	7·50

183 Santa Claus with Smiling Vegetable (Meghan Jones)

2000. Christmas. Children's Paintings. Mult.

850	30c. Type **183**	1·00	45
851	45c. Christmas tree and presents (Carlita Lodge)	1·25	80

2001. Endangered Species. Bird Conservation. Designs as Nos. 774/7, but with different face values, inscriptions redrawn and WWF panda emblem added. Multicoloured.

852	15c. As Type **169**	75	80
853	15c. Cahow	75	80
854	20c. White-tailed tropic bird with chick (vert)	75	80
855	20c. Cahow with chick (vert)	75	80
MS856	200 × 190 mm. Nos. 852/5 each × 4	10·00	11·00

No. **MS**856 includes the "HONG KONG 2001" logo on the margin.

184 King's Castle

2001. Historic Buildings, St. George's. Mult.

857	35c. Type **184**	1·10	55
858	50c. Bridge House	1·50	75
859	55c. Whitehall	1·60	1·00
860	70c. Fort Cunningham	1·90	2·25
861	85c. St. Peter's Church	2·50	2·75
862	95c. Water Street	2·50	3·00

185 Boer Prisoners on Boat and Plough

2001. Centenary of Anglo-Boer War. Multicoloured.

863	35c. Type **185**	85	55
864	50c. Prisoners in shelter and boot	1·10	75
865	70c. Elderly Boer with children and jewellery	1·60	1·75
866	95c. Bermuda residents and illustrated envelope of 1902	2·00	3·00

186 Girl touching Underwater Environment

2001. 75th Anniv of Bermuda Aquarium. Multicoloured.

867	35c. Type **186**	90	55
868	50c. Museum exhibits (horiz)	1·25	75
869	55c. Feeding giant tortoise (horiz)	1·25	95
870	70c. Aquarium building (horiz)	1·75	1·75
871	80c. Lesson from inside tank	1·75	2·00
872	95c. Turtle	2·25	2·75

187 "Fishing Boats" (Charles Lloyd Tucker)

2001. Paintings of Charles Lloyd Tucker. Multicoloured.

873	35c. Type **187**	1·40	55
874	70c. "Bandstand and City Hall, Hamilton"	2·00	1·50
875	85c. "Hamilton Harbour"	2·25	2·25
876	$1 "Train in Front Street, Hamilton"	3·00	3·25

2002. Golden Jubilee. As T **200** of Ascension.

877	10c. black, violet and gold	60	60
878	35c. multicoloured	1·50	1·10
879	70c. black, violet and gold	2·00	1·60
880	85c. multicoloured	2·25	2·25
MS881	162 × 95 mm. Nos. 887/80 and $1 multicoloured	7·00	7·50

DESIGNS—HORIZ: 10c. Princess Elizabeth with corgi; 35c. Queen Elizabeth in evening dress, 1965; 70c. Queen Elizabeth in car, 1952; 85c. Queen Elizabeth on Merseyside, 1991. VERT (38 × 51 mm)—$2 Queen Elizabeth after Annigoni.

Designs as Nos. 877/80 in No. **MS**881 omit the gold frame around each stamp and the "Golden Jubilee 1952–2002" inscription.

188 Fantasy Cave

2002. Caves. Multicoloured.

882	35c. Type **188**	1·60	55
883	70c. Crystal Cave	2·25	1·50
884	80c. Prospero's Cave	2·50	2·25
885	$1 Cathedral Cave	3·00	3·25

189 Fielder and Somerset Club Colours

190 Slit Worm-shell

2002. Centenary of Bermuda Cup Cricket Match. Multicoloured.

886	35c. Type **189**	1·00	90
887	35c. Batsman and wicketkeeper with St. George's Club colours	1·00	90
MS888	110 × 85 mm. $1 Batsman (48 × 31 mm)	2·50	3·00

2002. Queen Elizabeth the Queen Mother Commemoration. As T **202** of Ascension.

889	30c. brown, gold and purple	1·00	45
890	$1.25 multicoloured	2·50	2·75
MS891	145 × 70 mm. Nos. 889/90	4·00	4·25

DESIGNS: 30c. Duchess of York, 1923; $1.25, Queen Mother on her birthday, 1995.

Designs as Nos. 889/90 in No. **MS**891 omit the "1900–2002" inscription and the coloured frame.

2002. Shells. Multicoloured.

892	5c. Type **190**	10	10
893	10c. Netted olive	10	15
894	20c. Angular triton (horiz)	25	30
895	25c. Frog shell (horiz)	30	35
896	30c. Colourful atlantic moon (horiz)	35	40
897	35c. Noble wentletrap	40	45
898	40c. Atlantic trumpet triton (horiz)	45	50
899	45c. Zigzag scallop	50	55
900	50c. Bermuda cone	60	65
901	75c. Very distorted distorsio (horiz)	85	90
902	80c. Purple sea snail (horiz)	90	95
903	90c. Flame helmet (horiz)	1·00	1·10
904	$1 Scotch bonnet (horiz)	1·20	1·30
905	$2 Gold mouth triton (horiz)	2·30	2·40
906	$3 Bermuda's slit shell (horiz)	3·50	3·75
907	$4 Reticulated cowrie-helmet (horiz)	4·50	4·75
908	$5 Dennison's morum (horiz)	5·75	6·00
909	$8 Sunrise tellin	9·25	9·50

191 Dove of Peace

192 Research Station and *Weatherbird II* (research ship)

2002. World Peace Day.

910	**191**	35c. multicoloured	1·00	50
911	–	70c. multicoloured	2·25	2·25

DESIGN: 70c. Dove.

2003. Centenary of Bermuda Biological Research Station. Multicoloured.

912	35c. Type **192**	1·00	50
913	70c. Spotfin butterflyfish (horiz)	1·75	1·50
914	85c. Collecting coral (horiz)	1·90	2·25
915	$1 Krill	2·00	2·40

193 Costume Dolls

2003. Heritage "Made in Bermuda". (1st Series). Multicoloured.

916	35c. Type **193**	85	40
917	70c. Model sailing ship	1·40	1·10
918	80c. Abstract sculpture in wood	1·60	1·60
919	$1 Silverware	2·00	2·50

See also Nos. 934/7, 952/5 and 980/3.

2003. 50th Anniv of Coronation. As T **206** of Ascension. Multicoloured.

920	35c. Queen in Coronation Coach	75	40
921	70c. Queen in Coronation chair, flanked by bishops of Durham and Bath & Wells	1·25	1·40
MS922	95 × 115 mm. $1.25 As 35c.; $2 As 70c.	5·00	5·50

Nos. 920/1 have red frame; stamps from **MS**922 have no frame and country name in mauve panel.

194 Red Poinsettias

2003. Christmas Greetings. Poinsettias. Mult.

925	30c. Type **194**	75	35
926	45c. White poinsettias	1·25	55
927	80c. Pink poinsettias	2·50	2·50

195 Gateway

2004. Royal Naval Dockyard, Bermuda. Multicoloured.

928	25c. Type **195**	65	50
929	35c. Fountain and Clock Tower	90	80
930	70c. Waterside seat and Clock Tower	1·75	1·50
931	85c. Marina	1·90	1·90
932	95c. Window in ramparts	2·25	2·25
933	$1 Boats moored at pontoon and Clocktower Centre	2·40	2·50

2004. Heritage "Made in Bermuda" (2nd series). As T **193**. Multicoloured.

934	35c. Carver chair	60	45
935	70c. Ceramic jug and plate	1·10	90
936	80c. Glass fish and glass plate with shell design	1·25	1·25
937	$1.25 Quilt	1·75	2·00

196 Bluefin Tuna

2004. Endangered Species. Bluefin Tuna. Multicoloured.

938	10c. Type **196**	30	30
939	35c. Five bluefin tuna	85	45
940	85c. Bluefin tuna near surface of water	1·90	1·90
941	$1.10 Bluefin tuna swimming left	2·25	2·25

197 Yellow Oncydium Orchids

2004. 50th Anniv of the Orchid Society. Multicoloured.

942	35c. Type **197**	1·00	45
943	45c. *Encyclia radiate*	1·25	55
944	85c. Purple and white orchids	2·25	2·25
945	$1.10 *Paphiopedilum spicerianum*	2·50	2·75

198 1940 Map of Bermuda and Compass

2005. 500th Anniv of Discovery of Bermuda by Juan de Bermudez (Spanish navigator). Multicoloured.

946	25c. Type **198**	80	40
947	35c. 1846 map and sextant	90	45
948	70c. 1764 map and box compass	1·50	1·10
949	$1.10 1692 map and telescope	2·25	2·25
950	$1.25 1548 map and calipers	2·25	2·50
MS951	115 × 95 mm. $5 Aerial view of Bermuda	7·50	8·00

2005. Heritage "Made in Bermuda" (3rd series). As T **193**. Multicoloured.

952	35c. Picture of Bermuda Gombey dancers	70	45
953	70c. Papier-mache sculpture of parrotfish on tube coral	1·25	1·10
954	85c. Stained glass picture of lion and lamb	1·60	1·60
955	$1 Earrings and pendant of silver, pearls and garnets	1·90	2·00

2005. Bicentenary of Battle of Trafalgar. As T **216** of Ascension but horiz. Multicoloured.

956	10c. HMS *Victory*	65	50
957	35c. HMS *Pickle* under construction in Bermuda	1·10	50
958	70c. HMS *Pickle* picking up survivors from burning *Achille*	1·75	1·40
959	85c. HMS *Pickle* racing back to England with news of victory	2·25	2·50

No. 956 contains traces of powdered wood from HMS *Victory*.

199 Ruddy Turnstone and Semipalmated Sandpiper

2005. Bermuda Habitats. Scenes from dioramas in Bermuda Natural History Museum. Multicoloured.

960	10c. Type **199**	30	30
961	25c. Least bittern in reeds	55	35
962	35c. White-tailed tropic bird	70	45
963	70c. Eastern bluebird	1·40	1·10
964	85c. Saw-whet owl	1·75	1·75
965	$1 Yellow-crowned night heron	1·90	2·00

200 Christmas Tree with Lights

2005. Christmas Greetings. Festival of Lights. Multicoloured.

966	30c. Type **200**	70	30
967	45c. Dolphin	85	40
968	80c. Snowman	1·75	2·00

201 Man working on Overhead Power Cables

2006. Centenary of the Bermuda Electric Light Company Ltd. Multicoloured.

969	35c. Type **201**	70	45
970	70c. Engineer, power lines and vehicle	1·40	1·10
971	85c. Power plant	1·75	1·75
972	$1 Office block	1·90	2·25

2006. 80th Birthday of Queen Elizabeth II. As T **223** of Ascension. Multicoloured.

973	35p. Princess Elizabeth with corgi	90	45
974	70p. Queen wearing tiara (black/white photo)	1·40	1·10
975	85p. Wearing tiara and drop earrings (colour photo)	1·75	1·75
976	$1.25 Wearing blue hat	2·75	2·50
MS977	144 × 75 mm. $1.25 As No. 974; $2 As No. 975	5·50	6·00

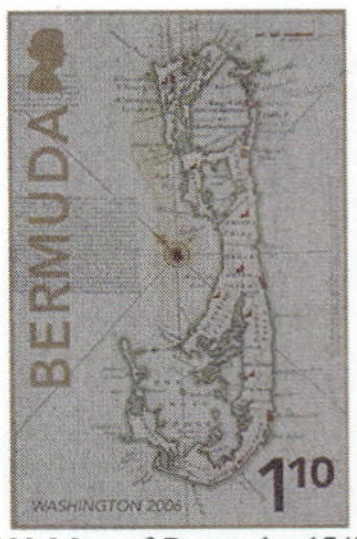

202 Map of Bermuda, 1747

2006. Washington 2006 International Stamp Exhibition.

978	**202** $1.10 multicoloured	1·90	2·00
MS979	82 × 65 mm. No. 978	1·90	2·00

2006. Heritage "Made in Bermuda" (4th series). As T **193**. Multicoloured.

980	35c. Bees, honeycomb and honey	70	45
981	70c. "Stonecutters" (detail) (Sharon Wilson)	1·40	1·10
982	85c. "I've Caught Some Whoppers" (sculpture) by Desmond Fountain	1·75	1·75
983	$1.25 Flower and perfume (Bermuda Perfumery)	2·25	2·50

203 Advent Wreath

2006. Christmas. Greetings. Advent Wreaths.

984	**203** 30c. multicoloured	70	45
985	– 35c. multicoloured	85	30
986	– 45c. multicoloured	95	40
987	– 80c. multicoloured	1·90	2·00

DESIGNS: 35c. to 80c. Showing different advent wreaths.

204 Francis L. Patton

2007. Pioneers of Progress (2nd series). Educators. Multicoloured.

988	35c. Type **204**	60	35
989	35c. Adele Tucker	60	35
990	35c. Edith and Matilda Crawford	60	35
991	35c. Millie Neversen	60	35
992	35c. May Francis	60	35

205 Hull under Construction at Rockport, Maine, USA

2007. *Spirit of Bermuda*. Sail training schooner. Multicoloured.

993	10c. Type **205**	35	15
994	35c. Close-up view	60	35
995	70c. *Spirit of Bermuda* at sea	1·10	75
996	85c. Off coast of Bermuda	1·40	80
997	$1.10 At Hamilton, Bermuda	1·60	95
998	$1.25 *Spirit of Bermuda* seen from stern	1·90	1·10

206 *Deliverance* off Building Bay

2007. 400th Anniv of Jamestown, Virginia, USA. Voyage of the *Deliverance* from Bermuda to Jamestown, 1610. Multicoloured.

999	35c. Type **206**	65	35
1000	$1.10 *Deliverance* sailing from Building Bay, St. George's, Bermuda	1·75	1·00

2007. Centenary of World Scouting. As T **281** of Bahamas. Multicoloured.

1001	35c. Bishop's Own Cubs, Government House, 22 February 1930	65	35
1002	70c. Lord Baden-Powell inspecting the Cubs, Hamilton, February 1930	1·10	75
1003	85c. Scout parade, Front Street, Hamilton, 25 February 1930	1·40	80
1004	$1.10 Dance of Kaa, Government House, 25 February 1930	1·60	95
MS1005	90 × 65 mm. $1.25 Bermuda Scouts emblem; $2 Lord Baden-Powell inspecting the Cubs, Hamilton, February 1930 (both vert)	5·25	5·25

EXPRESS LETTER STAMP

E 1 Queen Elizabeth II

1996.

E1	**E 1** $22 orange and blue	26·00	27·00

2003. As T **207** of Ascension.

E2	$25 black, blue and violet	29·00	30·00

BHOPAL Pt. 1

A state of C. India. Now uses Indian stamps.

12 pies = 1 anna; 16 annas = 1 rupee.

3

4

1876. Imperf.

5	**3** ¼a. black	8·00	16·00
2	½a. red	20·00	48·00

1878. Imperf or perf.

7	**4** ¼a. green	11·00	19·00
15	¼a. red	7·00	3·25
8	½a. red	7·00	16·00
9	½a. brown	28·00	45·00

1881. As T **3**, but larger. Imperf or perf.

29	¼a. black	2·25	2·00
37	½a. red	2·00	3·75
46	½a. black	1·50	1·75
30	1a. brown	2·25	4·75
31	2a. blue	2·00	2·25
32	4a. yellow	2·50	3·75

13

15

1884. Perf.

49	**13** ¼a. green	5·50	18·00
76	¼a. black	1·40	1·40

1884. Imperf or perf.

64	**15** ¼a. green	80	70
65	¼a. black	50	50
53	½a. black	90	3·25
56	½a. red	65	1·75

17

1890. Imperf or perf.

71	**17** 8a. greenish black	22·00	22·00

19

20 State Arms

1902. Imperf.

90	**19** ¼a. red	1·25	5·00
91	½a. black	1·25	6·00
92	1a. brown	3·00	7·50
94	2a. blue	7·00	25·00
96	4a. yellow	18·00	50·00
97	8a. lilac	55·00	£130
98	1r. red	85·00	£190

1908. Perf.

100	**20** 1a. green	3·75	4·50

OFFICIAL STAMPS

1908. As T **20** but inscr "H.H. BEGUM'S SERVICE" optd **SERVICE**.

O301	½a. green	2·25	10
O302	1a. red	4·25	40
O307	2a. blue	4·00	60
O304	4a. brown	14·00	55

O **4**

1930. Type O **4** optd **SERVICE**.

O309	O **4** ½a. green	12·00	1·75
O310	1a. red	11·00	15
O311	2a. blue	9·50	45
O312	4a. brown	10·00	90

1932. As T **20**, but inscr "POSTAGE" at left and "BHOPAL STATE" at right, optd **SERVICE**.

O313	¼a. orange	2·50	50

1932. As T **20**, but inscr "POSTAGE" at left and "BHOPAL GOVT" at right, optd **SERVICE**.

O314	½a. green	7·50	10
O315	1a. red	11·00	15
O316	2a. blue	11·00	45
O317	4a. brown	11·00	1·00

1935. Nos. O314, etc, surch.

O318	¼a. on ½a. green	32·00	14·00
O319	3p. on ½a. green	3·75	3·50
O320	¼a. on 2a. blue	29·00	20·00
O321	3p. on 2a. blue	4·50	4·50
O323	¼a. on 4a. brown	80·00	26·00
O325	3p. on 4a. brown	2·50	3·25
O326	1a. on ½a. green	5·00	1·50
O328	1a. on 2a. blue	70	2·50
O329	1a. on 4a. brown	7·00	5·00

O **8**

1935.

O330	O **8** 1a.3p. blue and red	3·50	1·50
O331	1a.6p. blue and red	2·50	1·00
O332	1a.6p. red	6·00	1·75

Nos. O331/2 are similar to Type O **8**, but inscr "BHOPAL STATE POSTAGE".

O **9**

1936. Type O **9** optd **SERVICE**.

O333	O **9** ¼a. yellow	90	60
O335	1a. red	1·50	10

O **10** The Moti Mahal

1936. As Type O **4** optd **SERVICE**.

O336d	O **10** ½a. purple and green	70	40
O337	– 2a. brown and blue	2·00	90
O338	– 2a. green and violet	12·00	30
O339	– 4a. blue and brown	3·75	50
O340	– 8a. purple and blue	5·50	2·25
O341b	– 1r. blue and purple	17·00	4·50

DESIGNS: 2a. The Moti Masjid; 4a. Taj Mahal and Be-Nazir Palaces; 8a. Ahmadabad Palace; 1r. Rait Ghat.

Nos. O336 is inscr "BHOPAL GOVT" below the arms, other values have "BHOPAL STATE".

1940. Animal designs, as Type O **10** but inscr "SERVICE" in bottom panel.
O344 ¼a. blue (Tiger) 4·75 1·75
O345 1a. purple (Spotted deer) 28·00 3·00

1941. As Type O **8** but "SERVICE" inscr instead of optd.
O346 O **8** 1a.3p. green 2·00 2·25

1944. Palaces as Type O **10** but smaller.
O347 ½a. green (Moti Mahal) 90 1·00
O348 2a. violet (Moti Masjid) 11·00 4·00
O348c 2a. purple (Moti Masjid) 3·50 3·75
O349 4a. brown (Be-Nazir) 7·00 2·25

The 2a. and 4a. are inscr "BHOPAL STATE", and the other "BHOPAL GOVT".

O **14** Arms of Bhopal

1944.
O350 O **14** 3p. blue 1·00 85
O351b 9p. brown 2·00 4·25
O352 1a. purple 5·00 1·75
O352b 1a. violet 9·00 3·25
O353 1½a. red 1·50 1·25
O354 3a. yellow 13·00 14·00
O354d 3a. brown £100 £110
O355 6a. red 19·00 50·00

1949. Surch **2 As.** and bars.
O356 O **14** 2a. on 1½a. red 2·50 7·50

1949. Surch **2 As.** and ornaments.
O357 O **14** 2a. on 1½a. red £1000 £1000

BHOR Pt. 1

A state of W. India, Bombay district. Now uses Indian stamps.

12 pies = 1 anna; 16 annas = 1 rupee.

1

3 Pandit Shankar Rao

1879. Imperf.
1 **1** ½a. red 3·75 5·00

Similar to T **1**, but rectangular.
2 1a. red 5·50 8·00

1901. Imperf.
3 **3** ½a. red 16·00 40·00

BHUTAN Pt. 21

An independent territory in treaty relations with India and bounded by India, Sikkim and Tibet.

100 chetrum = 1 ngultrum.

1 Postal Runner

2 "Uprooted Tree" Emblem and Crest of Bhutan

1962.
1 **1** 2ch. red and grey 15 15
2 – 3ch. red and blue 25 25
3 – 5ch. brown and green 80 80
4 – 15ch. yellow, black and red 15 30
5 **1** 33ch. green and violet 25 25
6 – 70ch. ultramarine and blue 50 35
7 – 1n.30 black and blue 1·40 1·40

DESIGNS—HORIZ: 3, 70ch. Archer. 5ch., 1n.30, Yak. 15ch. Map of Bhutan, Maharaja Druk Gyalpo and Paro Dzong (fortress and monastery).

1962. World Refugee Year.
8 **2** 1n. red and blue 2·75 2·75
9 2n. violet and green 2·50 2·50

3 Accoutrements of Ancient Warrior

4 "Boy filling box" (with grain)

1962. Membership of Colombo Plan.
10 **3** 33ch. multicoloured 25 25
11 70ch. multicoloured 50 50
12 1n.30 red, brown & yellow 75 75

1963. Freedom from Hunger.
13 **4** 20ch. brown, blue & yellow 25 25
14 1n.50 purple, brown & blue 65 65

1964. Winter Olympic Games, Innsbruck, and Bhutanese Winter Sports Committee Fund. Nos. 10/12 surch **INNSBRUCK 1964 +50 ch**, Olympic rings and emblem.
15 **3** 33ch.+50ch. multicoloured 2·40 2·40
16 70ch.+50ch. multicoloured 2·40 2·40
17 1n.30+50ch. multicoloured 2·40 2·40

6 Dancer with upraised hands

1964. Bhutanese Dancers. Multicoloured.
18 2ch. Standing on one leg (vert) 10 10
19 3ch. Type **6** 10 10
20 5ch. With tambourine (vert) 10 10
21 20ch. As 2ch. 10 10
22 33ch. Type **6** 10 10
23 70ch. With sword 15 15
24 1n. With tasselled hat (vert) 35 35
25 1n.30 As 5ch. 65 65
26 2n. As 70ch. 1·10 1·10

7 Bhutanese Athlete

9 Primula

8 Flags at Half-mast

1964. Olympic Games, Tokyo. Multicoloured.
27 2ch. Type **7** 15 10
28 5ch. Boxing 10 10
29 15ch. Type **7** 10 10
30 33ch. As 5ch. 15 15
31 1n. Archery 35 35
32 2n. Football 70 70
33 3n. As 1n. 1·30 1·50
MS33a 85 × 118 mm. Nos. 31/2 10·00 10·00

1964. Pres. Kennedy Commemoration.
34 **8** 33ch. multicoloured 25 25
35 1n. multicoloured 60 60
36 3n. multicoloured 90 90
MS36a 82 × 119 mm. Nos. 35/6 3·75 3·75

1965. Flowers. Multicoloured.
37 2ch. Type **9** 10 10
38 5ch. Gentian 10 10
39 15ch. Type **9** 10 10
40 33ch. As 5ch. 15 15
41 50ch. Rhododendron 25 25
42 75ch. Peony 35 35
43 1n. As 50ch. 35 35
44 2n. As 75ch. 85 85

1965. Churchill Commemoration. Optd **WINSTON CHURCHILL 1874 1965**.
45 **1** 33ch. green and violet 35 35
46 **8** 1n. multicoloured 55 55
47 – 1n. multicoloured (No. 43) 50 50
48 – 2n. multicoloured (No. 44) 85 85
49 **8** 3n. multicoloured 1·30 1·30

11 Pavilion and Skyscrapers

1965. New York World's Fair. Mult.
50 1ch. Type **11** 10 10
51 10ch. Buddha and Michelangelo's "Pieta" 10 10
52 20ch. Bhutan houses and New York skyline 10 10
53 33ch. Bhutan and New York bridges 10 10
54 1n.50 Type **11** 50 50
55 2n. As 10ch. 80 80
MS55a 120 × 86 mm. Nos. 54/5 3·50 5·50

1965. Surch.
56 **2** 5ch. on 1n. (No. 8) 28·00 28·00
57 5ch. on 2n. (No. 9) 28·00 28·00
58 – 10ch. on 70ch. (No. 23) 7·75 7·75
59 – 10ch. on 2n. (No. 26) 7·75 7·75
60 – 15ch. on 70ch. (No. 6) 6·50 6·50
61 – 15ch. on 1n.30 (No. 7) 6·50 6·50
62 – 20ch. on 1n. (No. 24) 9·25 9·25
63 – 20ch. on 1n.30 (No. 25) 9·25 9·25

13 "Telstar" and Portable Transmitter

1966. Centenary of I.T.U. Multicoloured.
64 35ch. Type **13** 15 15
65 2n. "Telstar" & morse key 40 40
66 3n. "Relay" and headphones 75 75
MS67 118 × 78 mm. Nos. 65/6 4·25 4·25

14 Asiatic Black Bear

1966. Animals. Multicoloured.
68 1ch. Type **14** 10 10
69 2ch. Snow leopard 10 10
70 4ch. Pygmy hog 10 10
71 8ch. Tiger 10 10
72 10ch. Dhole 10 10
73 75ch. As 8ch. 25 25
74 1n. Takin 40 40
75 1n.50 As 10ch. 55 55
76 2n. As 4ch. 70 70
77 3n. As 2ch. 1·00 1·00
78 4n. Type **14** 1·40 1·40
79 5n. As 1n. 2·00 2·00

15 Simtoke Dzong (fortress)

1966.
80 – 5c. brown 15 10
81 **15** 15ch. brown 15 15
82 20ch. green 25 25

DESIGN: 5ch. Rinpung Dzong (fortress).

16 King Jigme Dorji Wangchuck (obverse of 50n.p. coin)

1966. 40th Anniv of King Jigme Wangchuck's Accession (father of King Jigme Dorji Wangchuck). Circular designs, embossed on gold foil, backed with multicoloured patterned paper. Imperf. Sizes: (a) Diameter 38 mm; (b) Diameter 50 mm; (c) Diameter 63 mm. (i) 50n.p. Coin.
83 **16** 10ch. green (a) 15 15

(ii) 1r. Coin.
84 **16** 25ch. green (b) 25 25

(iii) 3r. Coin.
85 **16** 50ch. green (c) 45 45

(iv) 1 sertum Coin.
86 **16** 1n. red (a) 80 80
87 – 1n.30 red (a) 1·20 1·20

(v) 2 sertum Coin.
88 **16** 2n. red (b) 1·80 1·80
89 – 3n. red (b) 2·50 2·50

(vi) 5 sertum Coin.
90 **16** 4n. red (c) 3·25 3·25
91 – 5n. red (c) 3·75 3·75

Nos. 87, 89 and 91 show the reverse side of the coins (Symbol).

17 "Abominable Snowman"

1966. "Abominable Snowman". Various triangular designs.
92 **17** 1ch. multicoloured 10 10
93 – 2ch. multicoloured 10 10
94 – 3ch. multicoloured 10 10
95 – 4ch. multicoloured 10 10
96 – 5ch. multicoloured 10 10
97 – 15ch. multicoloured 10 10
98 – 30ch. multicoloured 10 10
99 – 40ch. multicoloured 15 15
100 – 50ch. multicoloured 15 15
101 – 1n.25 multicoloured 30 30
102 – 2n.50 multicoloured 50 50
103 – 3n. multicoloured 60 60
104 – 5n. multicoloured 85 85
105 – 6n. multicoloured 85 85
106 – 7n. multicoloured 95 95

1967. Air. Optd **AIR MAIL** and helicopter motif.
107 **6** 33ch. multicoloured 10 15
108 – 50ch. mult (No. 41) 25 25
109 – 70ch. mult (No. 23) 30 30
110 – 75ch. mult (No. 42) 25 25
111 – 1n. mult (No. 24) 35 35
112 – 1n.50 mult (No. 75) 55 55
113 – 2n. mult (No. 76) 80 80
114 – 3n. mult (No. 77) 1·20 1·20
115 **14** 4n. multicoloured 1·80 1·80
116 – 5n. mult (No. 79) 2·30 2·30

20 "Lilium sherriffiae"

1967. Flowers. Multicoloured.
117 3ch. Type **20** 10 10
118 5ch. "Meconopsis" 10 10
119 7ch. "Rhododendron dhwoju" 10 10
120 10ch. "Pleione hookeriana" 10 10
121 50ch. Type **20** 15 15
122 1n. As 5ch. 30 30
123 2n.50 As 7ch. 75 75
124 4n. As 10ch. 1·00 1·00
125 5n. "Rhododendron giganteum" 1·30 1·30

21 Scouts planting Sapling

1967. Bhutanese Boy Scouts. Multicoloured.
126 5ch. Type **21** 10 10
127 10ch. Scouts preparing meal 10 10
128 15ch. Scout mountaineering 15 15
129 50ch. Type **21** 25 25

130 1n.25. As 10ch. 70 70
131 4n. As 15ch. 1·70 1·70
MS132 93 × 93 mm. Nos. 130/1 6·25 6·25

1967. World Fair, Montreal. Nos. 53/5 optd **expo67** and emblem.
133 – 33ch. multicoloured 30 30
134 **11** 1n.50 multicoloured 40 40
135 – 2n. multicoloured 45 45
MS136 120 × 86 mm. Nos. 134/5 2·00 2·00

23 Avro Lancaster Bomber

1967. Churchill and Battle of Britain Commemoration. Multicoloured.
137 45ch. Type **23** 20 20
138 2n. Supermarine Spitfire fighter 45 45
139 4n. Hawker Hurricane Mk IIC fighter 90 90
MS140 118 × 75 mm. Nos. 138/9 2·40 2·40

1967. World Scout Jamboree, Idaho. Nos. 126/31 optd **WORLD JAMBOREE IDAHO, U.S.A. AUG. 1-9/67.**
141 **21** 5ch. multicoloured 15 15
142 – 10ch. multicoloured 20 20
143 – 15ch. multicoloured 25 25
144 – 50ch. multicoloured 35 35
145 – 1n.25 multicoloured 70 75
146 – 4n. multicoloured 1·80 1·80
MS147 93 × 93 mm. Nos. 145/6 3·75 3·75

25 Painting

1967. Bhutan Girl Scouts. Multicoloured.
148 5ch. Type **25** 10 10
149 10ch. Playing musical instrument 10 10
150 15ch. Picking fruit 10 10
151 1n.50 Type **25** 45 45
152 2n.50 As 10ch. 1·10 1·10
153 5n. As 15ch. 2·50 2·50
MS154 93 × 93 mm. Nos. 152/3 5·50 5·50

26 Astronaut in Space

1967. Space Achievements. With laminated prismatic-ribbed plastic surface. Multicoloured.
155 3ch. Type **26** (postage) 25 25
156 5ch. Space vehicle and astronaut 25 25
157 7ch. Astronaut and landing vehicle 45 45
158 10ch. Three astronauts in space 50 50
159 15ch. Type **26** 75 75
160 30ch. As 5ch. 90 90
161 50ch. As 7ch. 1·30 1·30
162 1n.25 As 10ch. 2·75 2·75
163 2n.50 Type **26** (air) 1·90 1·90
164 4n. As 5ch. 2·75 2·75
165 5n. As 7ch. 3·75 3·75
166 9n. As 10ch. 6·50 6·50
MS167 Three sheets, each 130 × 111 mm. Nos. 155/8, 159/62 and 163/6. Imperf 29·00 29·00
The laminated plastic surface gives the stamps a three-dimensional effect.

27 Tashichho Dzong

1968.
168 **27** 10ch. purple and green 20 10

28 Elephant

1968. Mythological Creatures.
169 **28** 2ch. red, blue and brown (postage) 10 10
170 – 3ch. pink, blue & green 10 10
171 – 4ch. orange, green & blue 10 10
172 – 5ch. blue, yellow & pink 10 10
173 – 15ch. green, purple & blue 10 10
174 **28** 20ch. brown, blk & orge 10 10
175 – 30ch. yellow, black & blue 15 15
176 – 50ch. bistre, green & black 15 15
177 – 1n.25 black, green & red 15 15
178 – 2n. yellow, violet & black 30 30
179 **28** 1n.50 green, purple and yellow (air) 25 25
180 – 2n.50 red, black & blue 35 35
181 – 4n. orange, green & black 60 60
182 – 5n. brown, grey & orange 80 80
183 – 10n. violet, grey & black 1·50 1·50
DESIGNS: 3, 30ch., 2n.50, Garuda; 4, 50ch., 4n. Tiger; 5ch., 1n.25, 5n. Wind horse; 15ch., 2, 10n. Snow lion.

29 Tongsa Dzong

1968.
184 **29** 50ch. green 30 15
185 – 75ch. brown and blue 35 20
186 – 1n. blue and violet 40 25
DESIGNS: 75ch. Daga Dzong; 1n. Lhuntsi Dzong.

30 Ward's Trogon

1968. Rare Birds.
187 2ch. Red-faced liocichla ("Crimson-winged Laughing Thrush") (horiz) (postage) 10 10
188 3ch. Type **30** 10 10
189 4ch. Burmese ("Grey") Peacock-pheasant (horiz) 10 10
190 5ch. Rufous-necked hornbill 10 10
191 15ch. Fire-tailed 'myzornis' ("Myzornis") (horiz) 15 15
192 20ch. As No. 187 20 20
193 30ch. Type **30** 20 20
194 50ch. As No. 189 25 25
195 1n.25 As No. 190 35 35
196 2n. As No. 191 45 45
197 1n.50 As No. 187 (air) 50 50
198 2n.50 Type **30** 60 55
199 4n. As No. 189 90 90
200 5n. As No. 190 1·20 1·20
201 10n. As No. 191 1·80 1·80

31 Mahatma Gandhi

1969. Birth Centenary of Mahatma Gandhi.
202 **31** 20ch. brown and blue 15 15
203 2n. brown and yellow 75 75

1970. Various stamps surch **5 CH** or **20 CH.**
(a) Freedom from Hunger (No. 14).
223 20ch. on 1n.50 purple, brown and blue 2·75 2·75

(b) Animals (Nos. 75/9).
224 20ch. on 1n.50 multicoloured 2·75 2·75
225 20ch. on 2n. multicoloured 2·75 2·75
204 20ch. on 3n. multicoloured 2·10 2·10
205 20ch. on 4n. multicoloured 2·10 2·10
206 20ch. on 5n. multicoloured 2·10 2·10

(c) Abominable Snowmen (Nos. 101/6).
226 20ch. on 1n.25 multicoloured 2·75 2·75
227 20ch. on 2n.50 multicoloured 2·75 2·75
207 20ch. on 3n. multicoloured 1·90 1·90
208 20ch. on 5n. multicoloured 2·10 2·10
209 20ch. on 6n. multicoloured 2·75 2·75
210 20ch. on 7n. multicoloured 2·75 2·75

(d) Flowers (Nos. 124/5).
211 20ch. on 4n. multicoloured 2·10 2·10
212 20ch. on 5n. multicoloured 2·50 2·50

(e) Boy Scouts (Nos. 130/1).
228 20ch. on 1n.25 multicoloured 2·75 2·75
213 20ch. on 4n. multicoloured 17·00 17·00

(f) Churchill (Nos. 138/9).
229 20ch. on 2n. multicoloured 2·75 2·75
230 20ch. on 4n. multicoloured 2·75 2·75

(g) 1968 Pheasants (Appendix).
231 20ch. on 2n. multicoloured 3·75 3·75
214 20ch. on 4n. multicoloured 2·10 2·10
232 20ch. on 7n. multicoloured 3·75 3·75

(h) Mythological Creatures (Nos. 175/80 and 182/3).
233 5ch. on 30ch. yellow, black and blue (postage) 85 85
234 5ch. on 50ch. bistre, green and black 85 85
235 5ch. on 1n.25 black, green and red 85 85
236 5ch. on 2n. yellow, vio & blk 85 85
215 20ch. on 2n. yellow, violet and black 3·75 3·75
237 5ch. on 1n.50 green, purple and brown (air) 85 85
238 5ch. on 2n.50 red, black and blue 85 85
216 20ch. on 5n. brown, grey and orange 2·40 2·40
217 20ch. on 10n. violet, grey and black 2·10 2·10

(i) Rare Birds (Nos. 193/201).
239 20ch. on 30ch. mult (postage) 3·75 3·75
240 20ch. on 50ch. multicoloured 3·75 3·75
241 20ch. on 1n. 25. multicoloured 3·75 3·75
218 20ch. on 2n. multicoloured 2·75 2·75
242 20ch. on 1n.50. mult (air) 3·75 3·75
219 20ch. on 2n.50. multicoloured 2·75 2·75
220 20ch. on 4n. multicoloured 2·10 2·10
221 20ch. on 5n. multicoloured 2·50 2·50
222 20ch. on 10n. multicoloured 3·50 3·50

(j) 1969 U.P.U. (Appendix).
243 20ch. on 1n.05. multicoloured 2·75 2·75
244 20ch. on 1n.40. multicoloured 2·75 2·75
245 20ch. on 4n. multicoloured 2·75 2·75
For stamps surcharged with 55 or 90ch. values, see Nos. 253/65 and for 25ch. surcharges see Nos. 385/410.

33 Wangdiphodrang Dzong and Bridge

34 Book Year Emblem

1971.
246 **33** 2ch. grey 25 10
247 3ch. mauve 35 15
248 4ch. violet 35 25
249 5ch. green 10 10
250 10ch. brown 15 10
251 15ch. blue 20 15
252 20ch. purple 30 15

1971. Various stamps surch **55 CH** or **90 CH.**
I. Dancers (Nos. 25/6).
253 55ch. on 1n.30 multicoloured 85 85
254 90ch. on 2n. multicoloured 85 85

II. Animals (Nos. 77/8).
255 55ch. on 3n. multicoloured 85 85
256 90ch. on 4n. multicoloured 85 85

III. Boy Scouts (No. 131).
257 90ch. on 4n. multicoloured 1·60 1·60

IV. 1968 Pheasants (Appendix).
258 55ch. on 5n. multicoloured 3·00 3·00
259 90ch. on 9n. multicoloured 3·00 3·00

V. Air. Mythological Creatures (No. 181).
260 55ch. on 4n. orange, green and black 55 55

VI. 1968 Mexico Olympics (Appendix).
261 90ch. on 1n.05 multicoloured 1·40 1·40

VII. Rare Birds (No. 196).
262 90ch. on 2n. multicoloured 3·00 3·00

VIII. 1969 UPU (Appendix).
263 55ch. on 60ch. multicoloured 85 85

IX. 1970 New UPU Headquarters (Appendix).
264 90ch. on 2n.50 gold and red 2·75 2·75

X. 1971 Moon Vehicles (plastic-surfaced) (Appendix).
265 90ch. on 1n.70 multicoloured 4·00 4·00

1972. International Book Year.
266 **34** 2ch. green and blue 10 10
267 3ch. brown and yellow 10 10
268 5ch. brown, orange & red 10 10
269 20ch. brown and blue 10 10

35 Dochi

1972. Dogs. Multicoloured.
270 5ch. Apsoo standing on hind legs (vert) 10 10
271 10ch. Type **35** 10 10
272 15ch. Brown and white damci 10 10
273 25ch. Black and white damci 10 10
274 55ch. Apsoo lying down 10 10
275 8n. Two damci 1·40 1·40
MS276 100 × 119 mm. Nos. 274/5 1·40 1·40

36 King and Royal Crest

1974. Coronation of King Jigme Singye Wangchuck. Multicoloured.
277 10ch. Type **36** 10 10
278 25ch. Bhutan Flag 15 15
279 1n.25 Good Luck signs 30 30
280 2n. Punakha Dzong 45 45
281 3n. Royal Crown 60 60
MS282 Two sheets, each 177 × 127 mm. (a) 5ch. As 10ch.; 5ch. As 3n.; (b) 90ch. As 1n.25; 4n. As 2n. Perf or imperf 4·75 4·75

37 Mail Delivery by Horse

1974. Centenary of UPU. Multicoloured.
283 1ch. Type **37** (postage) 10 10
284 2ch. Early and modern locomotives 10 10
285 3ch. "Hindoostan" (paddle-steamer) and "Iberia" (liner) 10 10
286 4ch. Vickers Vimy and Concorde aircraft 10 10
287 25ch. Mail runner and four-wheel drive post car 10 10
288 1n. As 25ch. (air) 20 20
289 1n.40 As 2ch. 45 45
290 2n. As 4ch. 80 80
MS291 91 × 78 mm. 10n. As 4 ch 3·75 3·75

38 Family and WPY Emblem

1974. World Population Year.
292 **38** 25ch. multicoloured 10 10
293 50ch. multicoloured 10 10
294 90ch. multicoloured 25 25
295 2n.50 multicoloured 55 55
MS296 116 × 79 mm. **38** 10n. multicoloured 2·10 2·10

39 Eastern Courtier

1975. Butterflies. Multicoloured.
297 1ch. Type **39** 10 10
298 2ch. Bamboo forester 10 10
299 3ch. Tailed labyrinth 10 10
300 4ch. Blue duchess 10 10
301 5ch. Cruiser 10 10
302 10ch. Bhutan glory 10 10

303 3n. Bi-coloured commodore . . . 65 65
304 5n. Red-breasted jezebel . . . 1·40 1·40
MS305 116×91 mm. 10n. Brown gorgon (*Dabasa gyas*) . . . . 2·75 2·75

40 King Jigme Singye Wangchuck

1976. King Jigme's 20th Birthday. Imperf.
(a) Diameter 39 mm.
306 **40** 15ch. green on gold . . . 10 10
307 1n. red on gold 25 25
308 – 1n.30 red on gold 25 25

(b) Diameter 50 mm.
309 **40** 25ch. green on gold . . . 10 10
310 2n. red on gold 45 45
311 – 3n. red on gold 70 70

(c) Diameter 63 mm.
312 **40** 90ch. green on gold . . . 75 75
313 4n. red on gold . . . . . 1·40 1·40
314 – 5n. red on gold . . . . . 1·70 1·70
DESIGN: 1n.30, 3, 5n. Decorative motif.

41 "Apollo"

1976. "Apollo"–"Soyuz" Space Link. Mult.
315 10n. Type **41** . . . . 2·40 2·40
316 10n. "Soyuz" . . . . 2·40 2·40
MS317 130×89 mm. 15n. Type **41**; 15n. As No. 316 . . . . 6·75 6·75

42 Jewellery

1976. Handicrafts and Craftsmen. Mult.
318 1ch. Type **42** 10 10
319 2ch. Coffee-pot, hand bell and sugar dish 10 10
320 3ch. Powder horns 10 10
321 4ch. Pendants and inlaid box 10 10
322 5ch. Painter 10 10
323 15ch. Silversmith 10 10
324 20ch. Wood carver with tools 10 10
325 1n.50 Textile printer 40 40
326 10n. Printer . . . . 1·90 1·90
MS327 105×79 mm. 5n. As No. 326 1·70 1·70

43 "Rhododendron cinnabarinum"
45 Dragon Mask

44 Skiing

1976. Rhododendrons. Multicoloured.
328 1ch. Type **43** 10 10
329 2ch. "R. campanulatum" . . 10 10
330 3ch. "R. fortunei" 10 10
331 4ch. "R. arboreum" 10 10
332 5ch. "R. arboreum" (different) 25 10
333 1n. "R. falconeri" 20 40
334 3n. "R. hodgsonii" 55 55
335 5n. "R. keysii" . . . . . . 1·10 1·10
MS336 105×79 mm. 10n. *R. cinnabarinum* (different) . . . . 2·75 2·75

1976. Winter Olympic Games, Innsbruck. Mult.
337 1ch. Type **44** 10 10
338 2ch. Bobsleighing 10 10
339 3ch. Ice hockey 10 10
340 4ch. Cross-country skiing . . 10 10
341 5ch. Women's figure skating 10 10
342 2n. Downhill skiing 25 25
343 4n. Speed skating 60 55
344 10n. Pairs figure skating . . 1·90 1·70
MS345 78×104 mm. 6n. Ski jumping . . . . 1·60 1·60

1976. Ceremonial Masks. Laminated prismatic-ribbed plastic surface.
346 **45** 5ch. mult (postage) 10 10
347 – 10ch. multicoloured . . . 10 10
348 – 15ch. multicoloured . . . 10 10
349 – 20ch. multicoloured . . . 10 10
350 – 25ch. multicoloured . . . 10 10
351 – 30ch. multicoloured . . . 10 10
352 – 35ch. multicoloured . . . 10 10
353 – 1n. multicoloured (air) . . 25 25
354 – 2n. multicoloured 45 45
355 – 2n.50 multicoloured . . . 75 75
356 – 3n. multicoloured 90 90
MS357 Two sheets, each 119×160 mm. (a) 5n. As No. 348; (b) 10n. As No. 351 . . . . . 4·00 4·00
DESIGNS: 10ch. to 10n. Similar Bhutanese masks.

46 Orchid

1976. Flowers. Multicoloured.
358 1ch. Type **46** 10 10
359 2ch. Orchid (different) . . . 10 10
360 3ch. Orchid (different) . . . 10 10
361 4ch. "Primula denticulata" . 10 10
362 5ch. Arum 10 10
363 2n. Orchid (different) 35 35
364 4n. "Leguminosa" 80 80
365 6n. Rhododendron . . . . . 1·20 1·20
MS366 106×80 mm. 10n. Arum (*different*) . . . . 3·75 3·75

47 Double Carp Emblem

1976. 25th Anniv of Colombo Plan.
367 3ch. Type **47** 10 10
368 4ch. Vase emblem 10 10
369 5ch. Geometric design . . . 10 10
370 25ch. Design incorporating animal's face 10 10
371 1n.25 Ornamental design . . 25 25
372 2n. Floral design 40 35
373 2n.50 Carousel design 50 45
374 3n. Wheel design 70 65

48 Bandaranaike Conference Hall

1976. 5th Non-aligned Countries Summit Conference, Colombo.
375 **48** 1n.25 multicoloured . . . 35 35
376 2n.50 multicoloured . . . 75 65

49 Liberty Bell

1978. Anniversaries and Events. Mult.
377 20n. Type **49** (bicentenary of U.S. independence) . . . . 4·00 4·00
378 20n. Alexander Graham Bell early telephone (telephone centenary) . . . . 4·00 4·00
379 20n. Archer (Olympic Games, Montreal) . . . . 4·00 4·00
380 20n. Alfred Nobel (75th anniv of Nobel Prizes) . . 4·00 4·00
381 20n. "Spirit of St. Louis" (50th anniv of Lindbergh's transatlantic flight) . . . 4·00 4·00
382 20n. Airship LZ3 (75th anniv of Zeppelin) . . . . . . 4·50 4·50
383 20n. Queen Elizabeth II (25th anniv of Coronation) . . . 4·00 4·00
MS384 Seven sheets, each 103×79 mm. (a) 25n. Flags of Bhutan and United States; (b) 25n. "Syncom II" communications satellite; (c) 25n. Shot putter; (d) 25n. Nobel medal; (e) 25n. "Spirit of St. Louis" landing at Le Bourget; (f) 25n. Airship "Viktoria Luise"; (g) 25n. Westminster Abbey . . . . 42·00 42·00

1978. Provisionals. Various stamps surch **25 Ch** (385, 394) or **25 CH** (others). I. Girl Scouts (No. 153).
385 25ch. on 5n. mult (postage) 12·50 10·00

II. Air. 1968 Mythological Creatures (Nos. 181 and 183).
386 25ch. on 4n. orange, green and black . . . . 2·50 2·10
387 25ch. on 10n. violet, grey and black . . . . 2·50 2·10

III. 1971 Admission to U.N. (Appendix).
388 25ch. on 3n. mult (postage) 2·10 1·70
389 25ch. on 5n. mult (air) . . . 2·10 1·70
390 25ch. on 6n. multicoloured 2·10 1·70

IV. Boy Scouts Anniv (Appendix).
391 25ch. on 6n. multicoloured 13·00 11·00

V. 1972 Dogs (No. 275).
392 25ch. on 8n. multicoloured 3·75 3·25

VI. 1973 Dogs (Appendix).
393 25ch. on 4n. multicoloured 3·75 3·25

VII. 1973 "Indipex 73" (Appendix).
394 25ch. on 3n. mult (postage) 3·25 3·00
395 25ch. on 5n. mult (air) . . . 3·25 3·00
396 25ch. on 6n. multicoloured 3·25 3·00

VIII. U.P.U. (Nos. 289/90).
397 25ch. on 1n. 40 multicoloured 3·00 2·50
398 25ch. on 2n. multicoloured 3·00 2·50

IX. World Population Year (No. 295).
399 25ch. on 2n.50 multicoloured 5·00 4·25

X. Butterflies (Nos. 303/4).
400 25ch. on 3n. multicoloured 5·00 4·25
401 25ch. on 5n. multicoloured 5·00 4·25

XI. "Apollo"–"Soyuz" (Nos. 315/16).
402 25ch. on 10n. mult (315) . . 12·50 10·00
403 25ch. on 10n. mult (316) . . 12·50 10·00

XII. Handicrafts (No. 326).
404 25ch. on 10n. multicoloured 2·50 2·10

XIII. Rhododendrons (No. 335).
405 25ch. on 5n. multicoloured 4·25 3·50

XIV. Winter Olympics (Nos. 343/4).
406 25ch. on 4n. multicoloured 5·75 5·00
407 25ch. on 10n. multicoloured 5·75 5·00

XV. Flowers (Nos. 364/5).
408 25ch. on 4n. multicoloured 2·10 1·80
409 25ch. on 6n. multicoloured 2·10 1·80

XVI. Colombo Plan (No. 373).
410 25ch. on 2n.50 multicoloured 2·50 2·10

50 Mother and Child

1979. International Year of the Child. Mult.
411 2n. Type **50** 50 50
412 5n. Mother carrying two children . . . . 1·10 95
413 10n. Children at school . . . 1·60 1·50
MS414 131×103 mm. Nos. 411/13 3·25 2·75

51 Conference Emblem and Dove

1979. 6th Non-Aligned Countries Summit Conference, Havana. Multicoloured.
415 25ch. Type **51** 15 15
416 10n. Emblem and Bhutanese symbols . . . . 2·50 2·20

52 Dorji (rattle)

1979. Antiquities. Multicoloured.
417 5ch. Type **52** 10 10
418 10ch. Dilbu (hand bell) (vert) 10 10
419 15ch. Jadum (cylindrical pot) (vert) 10 10
420 25ch. Jamjee (teapot) 10 10
421 1n. Kem (cylindrical container) (vert) 35 30
422 1n.25 Jamjee (different) . . . 40 40
423 1n.70 Sangphor (ornamental vessel) (vert) 60 60
424 2n. Jamjee (different) (vert) 75 70
425 3n. Yangtho (pot with lid) (vert) 95 90
426 4n. Battha (circular case) . . 1·20 1·20
427 5n. Chhap (ornamental flask) (vert) . . . . 1·70 1·60

53 Rinpiang Dzong, Bhutan Stamp and Rowland Hill Statue

1980. Death Cent of Sir Rowland Hill. Mult.
428 1n. Type **53** 45 40
429 2n. Dzong, Bhutan stamp and statue 80 75
430 5n. Ounsti Dzong, Bhutan stamp and statue . . . . . 1·30 1·20
431 10n. Lingzi Dzong and British 1912 1d. stamp . . 2·75 2·50
MS432 102×103 mm. 20n. Rope bridge, British 1d. black stamp and statue . . . . 9·50 9·50

54 Dungtse Lhakhang, Paro
55 St. Paul's Cathedral

1981. Monasteries. Multicoloured.
433 1n. Type **54** 20 15
434 2n. Kich Lhakhang, Paro (horiz) 40 35
435 2n.25 Kurjey Lhakhang (horiz) 55 50
436 3n. Tangu, Thimphu (horiz) 70 65
437 4n. Cheri, Thimphu (horiz) 95 85
438 5n. Chorten, Kora (horiz) . . 1·50 1·30
439 7n. Tak-Tsang, Paro . . . . 2·10 1·90

1981. Wedding of Prince of Wales. Multicoloured.
440 1n. Type **55** 10 10
441 5n. Type **55** 90 75
442 20n. Prince Charles and Lady Diana Spencer . . . . . 3·25 2·75
443 25n. As No. 442 . . . . . . 4·00 3·75
MS444 69×90 mm. 20n. Wedding procession . . . . 4·00 3·50

56 Orange-bellied Leafbird ("Orange-billed Chiropsis")
57 Footballers

1982. Birds. Multicoloured.
445 2n. Type **56** 70 65
446 3n. Himalayan monal pheasant ("Monal Pheasant") . . . . . . 1·00 95

447 5n. Ward's trogon . . . . . 2·00 1·80
448 10n. Mrs. Gould's sunbird . . 3·25 3·00
MS449 95 × 101 mm. 25n. Maroon oriole (*Oriolus traillii*) . . . . . 6·75 6·00

1982. World Cup Football Championship, Spain.
450 **57** 1n. multicoloured 20 15
451 – 2n. multicoloured 45 40
452 – 3n. multicoloured 65 60
453 – 20n. multicoloured . . . . 3·75 3·25
MS454 79 × 108 mm. 25n. multicoloured (horiz) . . . . . 6·75 5·25
DESIGNS: 2n. to 25n. Various football scenes.
No. **MS**454 exists in two versions, differing in the list of qualifying countries in the border.

58 St. James's Palace

59 Lord Baden-Powell (founder)

1982. 21st Birthday of Princess of Wales. Mult.
455 1n. Type **58** 40 35
456 10n. Prince and Princess of Wales . . . . 2·20 2·00
457 15n. Windsor Castle . . . . 3·75 4·00
458 25n. Princess in wedding dress . . . . 5·75 5·25
MS459 102 × 76 mm. 20n. Princess of Wales . . . . 5·00 4·50

1982. 75th Anniv of Boy Scout Movement. Multicoloured.
460 3n. Type **59** 55 50
461 5n. Scouts around campfire 1·10 95
462 15n. Map reading . . . . . 2·75 2·50
463 20n. Pitching tents . . . . . 4·00 3·75
MS464 91 × 70 mm. 25n. Scout 5·25 4·75

60 Rama finds Mowgli

1982. "The Jungle Book" (cartoon film). Mult.
465 1ch. Type **60** 10 10
466 2ch. Bagheera leading Mowgli to Man-village . . 10 10
467 3ch. Kaa planning attack on Bagheera and Mowgli . . 10 10
468 4ch. Mowgli and elephants 10 10
469 5ch. Mowgli and Baloo . . . 10 10
470 10ch. Mowgli and King Louie 10 10
471 30ch. Kaa and Shere Khan 10 10
472 2n. Mowgli, Baloo and Bagheera 45 35
473 20n. Mowgli carrying jug for girl . . . . 4·00 3·50
MS474 Two sheets, each 127 × 102 mm. (a) 20n. Mowgli and Baloo; (b) 20n. Mowgli and Baloo floating down river . . . 8·75 7·75

1982. Birth of Prince William of Wales. Nos. 455/**MS**459 optd **ROYAL BABY 21.6.82**.
475 1n. multicoloured 40 40
476 10n. multicoloured . . . . . 1·40 1·20
477 15n. multicoloured . . . . . 2·75 2·50
478 25n. multicoloured . . . . . 4·50 4·00
MS479 102 × 76 mm. 20n. multicoloured . . . . 5·00 4·75

62 Washington surveying

1982. 250th Birth Anniv of George Washington and Birth Centenary of Franklin D. Roosevelt. Mult.
480 50ch. Type **62** 10 10
481 1n. Roosevelt and Harvard University 10 10
482 2n. Washington at Valley Forge 30 30
483 3n. Roosevelt's mother and family 45 40
484 4n. Washington at Battle of Monmouth 55 50
485 5n. Roosevelt and the White House 80 75
486 15n. Washington and Mount Vernon . . . . 2·40 2·20
487 20n. Churchill, Roosevelt and Stalin at Yalta . . . . . . 3·25 3·00
MS488 Two sheets, each 102 × 73 mm. (a) 25n. Washington (vert); (b) 25n. Roosevelt (vert) 8·00 7·25

1983. "Druk Air" Bhutan Air Service. Various stamps optd **DRUK AIR** (491) or **Druk Air** (others), No. 489 surch also.
489 **42** 30ch. on 1n. multicoloued (postage) . . . . 1·30 1·30
490 – 5n. multicoloured (Scouts, Appendix) . . . . 2·40 2·10
491 – 8n. mult (No. 275) . . . . 2·50 2·20
492 – 5n. mult ("Indipex 73", Appendix) (air) . . . . 3·75 3·50
493 – 7n. mult (Munich Olympics, Appendix) . . 3·75 3·50

64 "Angelo Doni"

1983. 500th Birth Anniv of Raphael (artist). Multicoloured.
494 1n. Type **64** 15 10
495 4n. "Maddalena Doni" . . . 70 60
496 5n. "Baldassare Castiglione" 1·00 85
497 20n. "Woman with Veil" . . . 4·00 3·50
MS498 Two sheets, each 127 × 101 mm. (a) 25n. Self-portrait (detail from "Mass of Bolsena"); (b) 25n. Self-portrait (detail from "Expulsion of Heliodorus") . . . . 10·50 9·75

65 Ta-Gyad-Boom-Zu (the eight luck-bringing symbols)

1983. Religious Offerings. Multicoloured.
499 25ch. Type **65** 10 10
500 50ch. Doeyun Nga (the five sensory symbols) 15 15
501 2n. Norbu Chadun (the seven treasures) (47 × 41 mm) . . 35 35
502 3n. Wangpo Nga (the five sensory organs) 60 55
503 8n. Sha Nga (the five kinds of flesh) . . . . 1·30 1·10
504 9n. Men-Ra-Tor Sum (the sacrificial cake) (47 × 41 mm) . . . . . . 1·60 1·60
MS505 180 × 135 mm. Nos. 499/504 4·50 4·25

66 Dornier Wal Flying Boat "Boreas"

1983. Bicentenary of Manned Flight. Mult.
506 50ch. Type **66** 10 10
507 3n. Savoia-Marchetti S.66 flying boat 60 55
508 10n. Hawker Osprey biplane 2·00 1·90
509 20n. Astra airship "Ville de Paris" . . . . 4·00 3·75
MS510 106 × 80 mm. 25n. Henri Giffard's balloon "Le Grand Ballon Captif" . . . . 5·00 4·50

67 Mickey Mouse as Caveman

68 Golden Langur

1984. World Communications Year. Mult.
511 4ch. Type **67** 10 10
512 5ch. Goofy as printer 10 10
513 10ch. Chip 'n' Dale with morse key 10 10
514 20ch. Pluto talks to girlfriend on telephone 10 10
515 25ch. Minnie Mouse pulling record from bulldog . . . 10 10
516 50ch. Morty and Ferdie with microphone and loudhailers 10 10
517 1n. Huey, Dewey, and Louie listening to radio 30 30
518 5n. Donald Duck watching television on buffalo . . . 1·10 1·10
519 20n. Daisy Duck with computers and abacus . . 4·25 4·00
MS520 Two sheets, each 127 × 102 mm. (a) 20n. Mickey Mouse on television (horiz); (b) 20n. Donald Duck and satellite (horiz) . . . . 8·75 8·25

1984. Endangered Species. Multicoloured.
521 50ch. Type **68** 20 20
522 1n. Golden langur family in tree (horiz) 30 30
523 2n. Male and female Golden langurs with young (horiz) 70 70
524 4n. Group of langurs . . . . 1·40 1·30
MS525 Three sheets. (a) 88 × 121 mm. 20n. Snow leopard (horiz); (b) 121 × 88 mm. 25n. Yak; (c) 121 × 88 mm. 25n. Bharal (horiz) . . . . 14·50 12·00

69 Downhill Skiing

70 "Sans Pareil", 1829

1984. Winter Olympic Games, Sarajevo. Mult.
526 50ch. Type **69** 10 10
527 1n. Cross-country skiing . . 20 15
528 3n. Speed skating 70 65
529 20n. Four-man bobsleigh . . 3·50 3·25
MS530 108 × 76 mm. 25n. Ice hockey . . . . 4·75 4·00

1984. Railway Locomotives. Multicoloured.
531 50ch. Type **70** 10 10
532 1n. "Planet", 1830 . . . . . 15 15
533 3n. "Experiment" 1832 . . . 65 60
534 4n. "Black Hawk", 1835 . . 85 80
535 5n.50 "Jenny Lind", 1847 (horiz) . . . . 1·10 1·10
536 8n. "Bavaria", 1851 (horiz) 1·60 1·50
537 10n. Great Northern locomotive No. 1, 1870 (horiz) . . . . 2·10 1·90
538 25n. Steam locomotive Type 110, Prussia, 1880 (horiz) . . . . 5·00 4·50
MS539 Four sheets, each 92 × 65 mm. (a) 20n. Crampton's locomotive, 1846 (horiz); (b) 20n. "Erzsebet", 1870 (horiz); (c) 20n. Sondermann freight, 1896 (horiz); (d) 20n. Darjeeling–Himalaya railway (horiz) . . . . 16·00 14·50

71 Riley Sprite Sports Car, 1936

1984. Cars. Multicoloured.
540 50ch. Type **71** 10 10
541 1n. Lanchester Forty saloon, 1919 . . . . 15 15
542 3n. Itala 35/45 racer, 1907 . . 55 50
543 4n. Morris Oxford (Bullnose) tourer, 1913 . . . . . . 80 70
544 5n.50 Lagonda LG6 drophead coupe, 1939 . . 1·10 95
545 6n. Wolseley four seat tonneau, 1903 . . . . . . 1·30 1·10
546 8n. Buick Super convertible, 1952 . . . . 1·50 1·40
547 20n. Maybach Zeppelin limousine, 1933 . . . . 4·00 3·50
MS548 Two sheets, each 126 × 99 mm. (a) 25n. Renault (1901); (b) 25n. Simplex (1912) 8·00 7·25

72 Women's Archery

73 Domkhar Dzong

1984. Olympic Games, Los Angeles. Multicoloured.
549 15ch. Type **72** 10 10
550 25ch. Men's archery 15 10
551 2n. Table tennis 40 35
552 2n.25 Basketball 50 45
553 5n.50 Boxing . . . . 1·00 95
554 6n. Running . . . . 1·20 1·10
555 8n. Tennis . . . . 1·70 1·60
MS556 115 × 82 mm. 25n. Couple practising archery (72 × 43 mm) 4·50 4·00

1984. Monasteries.
557 **73** 10ch. blue 10 10
558 – 25ch. red 10 10
559 – 50ch. violet 10 10
560 – 1n. brown 20 20
561 – 2n. red 35 35
562 – 5n. green 85 85
DESIGNS: 25ch. Shemgang Dzong; 50ch. Chapcha Dzong; 1n. Tashigang Dzong; 2n. Pungthang Dzong; 5n. Dechhenphoda Dzong.

74 "Magician Mickey"

1984. 50th Anniv of Donald Duck. Scenes from films. Multicoloured.
563 4ch. Type **74** 10 10
564 5ch. "Slide, Donald, Slide" 10 10
565 10ch. "Donald's Golf Game" 10 10
566 20ch. "Mr. Duck Steps Out" 10 10
567 25ch. "Lion Around" 10 10
568 50ch. "Alpine Climbers" . . 10 10
569 1n. "Flying Jalopy" 10 10
570 5n. "Frank Duck brings 'Em Back Alive" 55 45
571 20n. "Good Scouts" . . . . 2·20 1·80
MS572 Two sheets, each 128 × 101 mm. (a) 20n. "Sea Scouts"; (b) 20n. "The Three Caballeros" . . . . 9·00 8·25

1984. Various stamps surch. (a) World Cup Football Championship, Spain (Nos. 450/3).
573 5n. on 1n. multicoloured . . 1·60 1·40
574 5n. on 2n. multicoloured . . 1·60 1·40
575 5n. on 3n. multicoloured . . 1·60 1·40
576 5n. on 20n. multicoloured . . 1·60 1·40
MS577 79 × 108 mm. 20n. on 25n. multicoloured . . . . 6·25 6·25
No. **MS**577 exists in two versions, differing in the list of qualifying countries in the border.

(b) 21st Birthday of Princess of Wales (Nos. 455/8).
578 5n. on 1n. multicoloured . . 1·40 1·30
579 5n. on 10n. multicoloured . . 1·40 1·30
580 5n. on 15n. multicoloured . . 1·40 1·30
581 40n. on 25n. multicoloured 11·00 10·00
MS582 102 × 76 mm. 25n. on 20n. multicoloured . . . . 7·50 7·50

(c) Birth of Prince William of Wales (Nos. 475/8).
583 5n. on 1n. multicoloured . . 1·30 1·30
584 5n. on 10n. multicoloured . . 1·30 1·30
585 5n. on 15n. multicoloured . . 1·30 1·30
586 40n. on 25n. multicoloured 11·00 10·50
MS587 102 × 76 mm. 25n. on 20n. multicoloured . . . . 10·00 10·00

(d) Wedding of Prince of Wales (Nos. 440/3).
588 10n. on 1n. multicoloured . . 2·40 2·20
589 10n. on 5n. multicoloured . . 2·40 2·20
590 10n. on 20n. multicoloured 2·40 2·20
591 10n. on 25n. multicoloured 2·40 2·20
MS592 69 × 90 mm. 30n. on 20n. multicoloured . . . . 10·00 10·00
On Nos. 588/**MS**592 the new value is surcharged twice.

(e) 75th Anniv of Boy Scout Movement (Nos. 460/3).
593 10n. on 3n. multicoloured . . 2·40 2·20
594 10n. on 5n. multicoloured . . 2·40 2·20
595 10n. on 15n. multicoloured 2·40 2·20
596 10n. on 20n. multicoloured 2·40 2·20
MS597 91 × 70 mm. 20n. on 25n. multicoloured . . . . 10·00 10·00

76 Shinje Choegyel

77 Bhutan and UN Flags

1985. The Judgement of Death Mask Dance. Multicoloured.

598 5ch. Type **76** 10 10
599 35ch. Raksh Lango 10 10
600 50ch. Druelgo 10 10
601 2n.50 Pago 40 35
602 3n. Telgo 55 50
603 4n. Due Nakcung 75 70
604 5n. Lha Karpo 90 85
605 5n.50 Nyalbum . . . . . 1·00 95
606 6n. Khimda Pelkyi . . . . 1·10 1·10
MS607 90 × 135 mm. Nos. 598/9 and 603/4 . . . . 2·30 2·20

1985. 40th Anniv of UNO.

608 **77** 50ch. multicoloured . . . 20 20
609 – 15n. multicoloured . . . . 2·00 1·70
610 – 20n. black and blue . . . 3·00 2·50
MS611 65 × 80 mm. 25n. black, yellow and scarlet . . . . . 3·75 3·25

DESIGNS—VERT: 15n. UN building, New York; 25n. 1945 charter; HORIZ: 20n. Veterans' War Memorial Building San Francisco (venue of signing charter, 1945).

78 Mickey Mouse tramping through Black Forest

1985. 150th Birth Anniv of Mark Twain (writer) and International Youth Year. Multicoloured.

612 50ch. Type **78** 10 10
613 2n. Mickey Mouse, Donald Duck and Goofy on steamboat trip on Lake Lucerne 35 30
614 5n. Mickey Mouse, Donald Duck and Goofy climbing Rigi-Kulm 85 75
615 9n. Mickey Mouse and Goofy rafting to Heidelberg on River Neckar . . . . 1·60 1·40
616 20n. Mickey Mouse leading Donald Duck on horse back up the Riffelberg . . 3·50 3·25
MS617 126 × 101 mm. 25n. Mickey Mouse and Goofy . . . . . . 4·75 4·25

Nos. 612/**MS**617 show scenes from "A Tramp Abroad" (cartoon film of Twain novel).

79 Prince sees Rapunzel

1985. Birth Bicentenaries (1985 and 1986) of Grimm Brothers (folklorists). Multicoloured.

618 1n. Type **79** 10 10
619 4n. Rapunzel (Minnie Mouse) in tower 50 45
620 7n. Mother Gothel calling to Rapunzel to let down her hair . . . . 1·10 95
621 8n. Prince climbing tower using Rapunzel's hair . . . 1·40 1·30
622 15n. Prince proposing to Rapunzel . . . . 2·40 2·10
MS623 126 × 101 mm. 25n. Prince riding away with Rapunzel . . 5·00 4·75

80 "Brewers Duck" (mallard)

1985. Birth Bicentenary of John J. Audubon (ornithologist). Audubon illustrations. Mult.

624 50ch. Type **80** 10 10
625 1n. "Willow Ptarmigan" (Willow/red Grouse) . . . 15 15
626 2n. "Mountain Plover" . . . 35 30
627 3n. "Red-throated Loon" (Red-throated Diver) . . . 50 50
628 4n. "Spruce Grouse" 80 70
629 5n. "Hooded Merganser" . . 95 90
630 15n. "Trumpeter Swan" (Whooper Swan) . . . . . 2·75 2·50
631 20n. Common goldeneye . . 3·75 3·25
MS632 75 × 105 mm. 25n. "Sharp-shinned Hawk" . . . . 4·50 4·00
MS633 75 × 105 mm. 25n."Tufted Titmouse" . . . . 4·50 4·00

81 Members' Flags around Buddhist Design

1985. South Asian Regional Co-operation Summit, Dhaka, Bangladesh.

634 **81** 50ch. multicoloured . . . 15 15
635 5n. multicoloured 95 85

82 Precious Wheel

85 Mandala of Phurpa (Ritual Dagger)

1986. The Precious Symbols. Multicoloured.

636 30ch. Type **82** 10 10
637 50ch. Precious Gem 10 10
638 1n.25 Precious Queen 15 15
639 2n. Precious Minister 30 30
640 4n. Precious Elephant 55 55
641 6n. Precious Horse 80 80
642 8n. Precious General . . . . 1·10 1·10

1986. Olympic Games Gold Medal Winners. Nos. 549/50 and 552/5 optd.

643 **72** 15ch. **GOLD HYANG SOON SEO SOUTH KOREA** 10 10
644 – 25ch. **GOLD DARRELL PACE USA** 10 10
645 – 2n.25 **GOLD MEDAL USA** 35 35
646 – 5n.50 **GOLD MARK BRELAND USA** 70 70
647 – 6n. **GOLD DALEY THOMPSON ENGLAND** 80 80
648 – 8n. **GOLD STEFAN EDBERG SWEDEN** . . 1·10 1·10
MS649 Two sheets, each 115 × 82 mm. (a) 25n. **HYANG SOON SEO, SOUTH KOREA;** (b) 25n. **DARRELL PACE, U.S.A.** . . . . 7·50 6·25

1986. "Ameripex 86" International Stamp Exhibition, Chicago. Various stamps optd **AMERIPEX 86**. (a) Nos. 615/**MS**617.

650 8n. multicoloured . . . . . 2·20 1·80
651 20n. multicoloured . . . . . 3·25 3·00
MS652 126 × 101 mm. 25n. multicoloured . . . . 7·50 6·25

(b) Nos. 621/**MS**623.

653 8n. multicoloured . . . . . 1·40 1·20
654 15n. multicoloured . . . . . 1·90 1·70
MS655 126 × 101 mm. 25n. multicoloured . . . . 4·00 3·50

1986. Kilkhor Mandalas of Mahayana Buddhism. Multicoloured.

656 10ch. Type **85** 10 10
657 25ch. Mandala of Amitayus in Wrathful Form 10 10
658 50ch. Mandala of Overpowering Deities . . . 10 10
659 75ch. Mandala of the Great Wrathful One 10 10
660 1n. Type **85** 15 15
661 3n. As 25ch. 45 45
662 5n. As 50ch. 65 65
663 7n. As 75ch. 85 85

1986. 75th Anniv of Girl Guides. Nos. 460/3 optd **75th ANNIVERSARY GIRL GUIDES**.

664 3n. multicoloured 40 40
665 5n. multicoloured . . . . . 1·00 1·00
666 15n. multicoloured . . . . . 3·00 3·00
667 20n. multicoloured . . . . . 4·00 4·00
MS668 91 × 70 mm. 25n. multicoloured . . . . 5·50 5·50

87 Babylonian Tablet and Comet over Noah's Ark

1986. Appearance of Halley's Comet. Mult.

669 50ch. Type **87** 10 10
670 1n. 17th-century print 10 10
671 2n. 1835 French silhouette . . 25 25
672 3n. Bayeux tapestry 40 35
673 4n. Woodblock from "Nuremburg Chronicle" 60 50
674 5n. Illustration of Revelation 6, 12–13 from 1650 Bible 80 75
675 15n. Comet in constellation of Cancer . . . . 2·30 2·10
676 20n. Decoration on Delft plate . . . . 3·25 2·75
MS677 Two sheets, each 109 × 79 mm. (a) 25n. Comet over dzong in Himalayas; (b) 25n. Comet over shrine . . . . . . 8·00 7·25

88 Statue and "Libertad" (Argentine full-rigged cadet ship)

1986. Centenary of Statue of Liberty. Multicoloured.

678 50ch. Type **88** 10 10
679 1n. "Shalom" (Israeli liner) 10 10
680 2n. "Leonardo da Vinci" (Italian liner) 25 25
681 3n. "Mircea" (Rumanian cadet barque) 40 35
682 4n. "France" (French liner) 55 50
683 5n. S.S. "United States" (American liner) 80 75
684 15n. "Queen Elizabeth 2" (British liner) . . . . . . 2·30 2·10
685 20n. "Europa" (West German liner) . . . . . . 3·25 2·75
MS686 Two sheets, each 114 × 83 mm. (a) Statue (27 × 41 mm); (b) Statue and tower blocks (27 × 41 mm) . . . . . 7·50 6·75

The descriptions of the ships on Nos. 678 and 681 were transposed in error.

89 "Santa Maria"

1987. 500th Anniv (1992) of Discovery of America by Columbus. Multicoloured.

687 20ch. Type **89** 25 30
688 25ch. Queen Isabella of Spain 25 25
689 50ch. Flying fish 25 25
690 1n. Columbus's coat of arms 50 40
691 2n. Christopher Columbus . . 85 70
692 3n. Columbus landing with Spanish soldiers . . . . 1·10 1·10
MS693 Seven sheets, each 97 × 65 mm. (a) 20ch. Pineapple; (b) 25ch. Indian hammock (horiz); (c) 50ch. Tobacco plant; (d) 1n. Greater flamingo; (e) 2n. Astrolabe; (f) 3n. Lizard (horiz); (g) 5n. Iguana (horiz) . . . . 11·50 11·50
MS694 170 × 144 mm. As Nos. 687/92 but with white backgrounds . . . . 23·00 23·00

90 Canadian National Class "U1-f" Steam Locomotive No. 6060

1987. "Capex '87" International Stamp Exhibition, Toronto. Canadian Railways. Multicoloured.

695 50ch. Type **90** 10 10
696 1n. Via Rail "L.R.C." electric locomotive No. 6903 . . . 10 10
697 2n. Canadian National GM "GF30t" diesel locomotive No. 5341 . . . . 35 30
698 3n. Canadian National steam locomotive No. 6157 . . . 45 40
699 8n. Canadian Pacific steam locomotive No. 2727 . . . 1·30 1·20
700 10n. Via Express diesel locomotive No. 6524 . . . 1·60 1·40
701 15n. Canadian National "Turbotrain" . . . . . . 2·40 2·10
702 20n. Canadian Pacific diesel-electric locomotive No. 1414 . . . . 3·00 2·75
MS703 Two sheets, each 102 × 75 mm. (a) 25n. Cab and tender of Royal Hudson steam locomotive (27 × 41 mm); (b) 25n. Canadian National steam locomotive (27 × 41 mm) . . . 7·50 6·75

91 "Two Faces" (sculpture)

1987. Birth Centenary of Marc Chagall (artist). Multicoloured.

704 50ch. Type **91** 15 15
705 1n. "At the Barber's" 25 25
706 2n. "Old Jew with Torai" . . 40 40
707 3n. "Red Maternity" 65 65
708 4n. "Eve of Yom Kippur" . . 1·00 1·00
709 5n. "The Old Musician" . . 1·20 1·20
710 6n. "The Rabbi of Vitebsk" . 1·30 1·30
711 7n. "Couple at Dusk" . . . 1·50 1·50
712 9n. "The Artistes" . . . . . 1·80 1·80
713 10n. "Moses breaking the Tablets" . . . . 2·00 2·00
714 12n. "Bouquet with Flying Lovers" . . . . 2·30 2·30
715 20n. "In the Sky of the Opera" . . . . 4·00 4·00
MS716 12 sheets, each 95 × 110 mm (e) or 110 × 95 mm (others). Imperf. (a) 25n. "The Red Gateway". (b) 25n. "Romeo and Juliet". (c) 25n. "Maternity". (d) 25n. "The Carnival for Aleko, Scene II". (e) 25n. "Magician of Paris". (f) 25n. "Visit to the Grandparents". (g) 25n. "Cow with Parasol". (h) 25n. "Russian Village". (i) 25n. "Still Life". (j) 25n. "Composition with Goat". (k) 25n. "The Smolensk Newspaper". (l) 25n. "The Concert" . . . . 47·00 47·00

92 Goofy (slalom)

1988. Winter Olympic Games, Calgary. Mult.

717 50ch. Type **92** 10 10
718 1n. Donald Duck pushing Goofy at start (downhill skiing) 15 15
719 2n. Goofy in goal (ice hockey) 25 25
720 4n. Goofy (biathlon) 55 50
721 7n. Goofy and Donald Duck (speed skating) . . . . 1·10 95
722 8n. Minnie Mouse (figure skating) . . . . 1·30 1·20
723 9n. Minnie Mouse (free-style skating) . . . . 1·50 1·30
724 20n. Goofy and Mickey Mouse (two-man bobsleigh) . . . . 3·00 2·75
MS725 Two sheets, each 127 × 101 mm. (a) 25n. Goofy (ski jumping); (b) 25n. Donald and Daisy Duck (ice skating) . . . 7·00 7·00

93 Stephenson's Railway Locomotive "Rocket", 1829

1988. Transport. Multicoloured.
726 50ch. Pullman "Pioneer" sleeper, 1985 . . . 10 10
727 1n. Type **93** . . . 15 15
728 2n. Pierre Lallement's "Velocipede", 1866 . . . 25 25
729 3n. Benz "Patent Motor Wagon", 1866 . . . 45 35
730 4n. Volkswagen Beetle . . . 55 50
731 5n. Mississippi paddle-steamers "Natchez" and "Robert E. Lee", 1870 . . 65 60
732 6n. American La France motor fire engine, 1910 . . 80 75
733 7n. Frigate U.S.S. "Constitution", 1797 (vert) 95 85
734 9n. Bell rocket belt, 1961 (vert) . . . 1·20 1·10
735 10n. Trevithick's railway locomotive, 1804 . . . 1·30 1·20
MS736 Four sheets, each 118×89 mm. (a) 25n. Steam locomotive "Mallard" (27×41 mm); (b) 25n. French "TGV" express train (41×27 mm); (c) 25n. Japanese Shinkansen "Tokaido" bullet train (41×27 mm); (d) 25n. Concorde supersonic airplane (41×27 mm) 17·00 17·00
No. 731 is wrongly inscribed "Natches" and No. 733 is wrongly dated "1787".

94 Dam and Pylon

1988. Chhukha Hydro-electric Project.
737 **94** 50ch. multicoloured . . . 30 30

1988. World Aids Day. Nos. 411/13 optd **WORLD AIDS DAY**.
738 **50** 2n. multicoloured . . . 40 35
739 – 5n. multicoloured . . . 1·00 90
740 – 10n. multicoloured . . . 2·10 1·90

96 "Diana and Actaeon" (detail)

1989. 500th Birth Anniv of Titian (painter). Multicoloured.
741 50ch. "Gentleman with a Book" . . . 10 10
742 1n. "Venus and Cupid, with a Lute Player" (detail) . . 15 15
743 2n. Type **96** . . . 30 30
744 3n. "Cardinal Ippolito dei Medici" . . . 50 45
745 4n. "Sleeping Venus" (detail) 75 70
746 5n. "Venus risen from the Waves" (detail) . . . 90 85
747 6n. "Worship of Venus" (detail) . . . 1·20 1·10
748 7n. "Fete Champetre" (detail) 1·40 1·30
749 10n. "Perseus and Andromeda" (detail) . . . 1·80 1·70
750 15n. "Danae" (detail) . . . 2·75 2·50
751 20n. "Venus at the Mirror" 3·75 3·50
752 25n. "Venus and the Organ Player" (detail) . . . 4·50 4·25
MS753 12 sheets, each 109×94 (a/d) or 94×109 mm (others). (a) 25n. "Bacchus and Ariadne"; (b) 25n. "Danae with the Shower of Gold" (horiz); (c) 25n. "The Pardo Venus" (horiz); (d) 25n. "Venus and Cupid with an Organist"; (e) 25n. "Diana and Callisto"; (f) 25n. "Mater Dolorosa with Raised Hands"; (g) 25n. "Miracle of the Irascible Son"; (h) 25n. "Portrait of Johann Friedrich"; (i) 25n. "Portrait of Laura Dianti"; (j) 25n. "St. John the Almsgiver"; (k) 25n. "Venus blindfolding Cupid"; (l) 25n. "Venus of Urbino" . . 47·00 47·00

97 Volleyball

1989. Olympic Games, Seoul (1988). Mult.
754 50ch. Gymnastics . . . 10 10
755 1n. Judo . . . 10 10
756 2n. Putting the shot . . . 25 25
757 4n. Type **97** . . . 55 50
758 7n. Basketball (vert) . . . 95 85
759 8n. Football (vert) . . . 1·10 95
760 9n. High jumping (vert) . . . 1·30 1·10
761 20n. Running (vert) . . . 2·75 2·50
MS762 Two sheets. (a) 109×79 mm. 25n. Fencing. (b) 79×109 mm. 25n. Archery (vert) . . . 7·00 7·00

1989. "Fukuoka '89" Asia-Pacific Exhibition. Nos. 598/606 optd **ASIA-PACIFIC EXPOSITION FUKUOKA '89**.
763 5ch. multicoloured . . . 10 10
764 35ch. multicoloured . . . 10 10
765 50ch. multicoloured . . . 10 10
766 2n.50 multicoloured . . . 25 25
767 3n. multicoloured . . . 40 35
768 4n. multicoloured . . . 50 45
769 5n. multicoloured . . . 60 55
770 5n.50 multicoloured . . . 75 65
771 6n. multicoloured . . . 85 80

99 Mickey Mouse

1989. 60th Anniv of Mickey Mouse. Film Posters. Multicoloured.
772 1ch. Type **99** . . . 15 15
773 2ch. "Barnyard Olympics" . . 15 15
774 3ch. "Society Dog Show" . . 15 15
775 4ch. "Fantasia" . . . 15 15
776 5ch. "The Mad Dog" . . . 15 15
777 10ch. "A Gentleman's Gentleman" . . . 15 15
778 50ch. "Symphony hour" . . 15 15
779 10n. "The Moose Hunt" . . 1·50 1·50
780 15n. "Wild Waves" . . . 2·30 2·30
781 20n. "Mickey in Arabia" . . 3·25 3·25
782 25n. "Tugboat Mickey" . . 3·75 3·75
783 30n. "Building a Building" . 4·75 4·75
MS784 12 sheets, each 127×101 mm. (a) 25n. *The Klondike Kid*; (b) 25n. "The Mad Doctoe" (c) 25n. "The Meller Drammer"; (d) 25n. "Mickey's Good Deed"; (e) 25n. "Mickey's Nightmare"; (f) 25n. "Mickey's Pal Pluto"; (g) 25n. "Steamboat Willie"; (h) 25n. "Touchdown Mickey"; (i) 25n. "Trader Mickey"; (j) 25n. "The Wayward Canary"; (k) 25n. "The Whoopee Party"; (l) 25n. "Ye Olden Days" 42·00 42·00

100 "Tricholoma pardalotum"

1989. Fungi. Multicoloured.
785 50ch. Type **100** . . . 10 10
786 1n. "Suillus placidus" . . . 10 10
787 2n. Royal boletus . . . 25 25
788 3n. "Gomphidius glutinosus" . 45 35
789 4n. Scarlet-stemmed boletus 55 50
790 5n. Elegant boletus . . . 70 65
791 6n. "Boletus appendiculatus" 85 80
792 7n. Griping toadstool . . . 1·10 95
793 10n. "Macrolepiota rhacodes" . . . 1·40 1·30
794 15n. The blusher . . . 2·10 1·90
795 20n. Death cap . . . 2·75 2·50
796 25n. False death cap . . . 3·50 3·25
MS797 12 sheets, each 97×68 mm. (a) 25n. "Boletus rhodoxanthus"; (b) 25n.Chanterelle "Chanterelle repdandum"; (c) 25n. "Dentinum repandum"; (d) 25n. Chestnut boletus ("Gyroporus castaneus"); (e) 25n. Indigo boletus ("Gyroporus cyanescens"); (f) 25n. "Hydnum imbricatum"; (g) 25n. Blue leg ("Lepista nuda"); (h) 25n. "Lepista saeva"; (i) 25n. Brown roll-rim ("Paxillus involutus"); (j) 25n. Golden russula ("Russula aurata"); (k) 25n. "Russula olivacea"; (l) 25n. Downy boletus ("Xerocomus subtomentosus") 42·00 42·00

101 "La Reale" (Spanish galley), 1680

1989. 30th Anniv of International Maritime Organization. Multicoloured.
798 50ch. Type **101** . . . 10 10
799 1n. "Turtle" (submarine), 1776 . . . 15 15
800 2n. "Charlotte Dundas" (steamship), 1802 . . . 30 30
801 3n. "Great Eastern" (paddle-steamer), 1858 . . . 50 45
802 4n. H.M.S. "Warrior" (armoured ship), 1862 . . 65 60
803 5n. Mississippi river steamer, 1884 . . . 85 75
804 6n. "Preussen" (full-rigged ship), 1902 . . . 1·00 90
805 7n. U.S.S. "Arizona" (battleship), 1915 . . . 1·20 1·10
806 10n. "Bluenose" (fishing schooner), 1921 . . . 1·60 1·50
807 15n. Steam trawler, 1925 . . 2·50 2·20
808 20n. "Liberty" freighter, 1943 3·25 3·00
809 25n. "United States" (liner), 1952 . . . 4·00 3·50
MS810 12 sheets, each 100×70 mm. (a) 25n. Chinese junk, 1988; (b) 25n. "U.S.S. Constitution" (frigate); (c) 25n. VIIC type U-boat, 1942; (d) 25n. "Cutty Sark" (clipper), 1869; (e) 25n. H.M.S. "Dreadnought" (battleship), 1906; (f) 25n. U.S.S. "Monitor" (ironclad), 1862; (g) 25n. Moran Company tug, 1950; (h) 25n. "Normandie" (French liner), 1933; (i) 25n. H.M.S. "Resolution" (Capt. Cook); (j) 25n. "Titanic" (liner), 1912; (k) 25n. H.M.S. "Victory" (ship of the line), 1805; (l) 25n. "Yamato" (Japanese battleship), 1944 . . . 42·00 42·00

102 Nehru

103 Greater Flamed-backed Woodpecker

1989. Birth Centenary of Jawaharlal Nehru (Indian statesman).
811 **102** 1n. brown . . . 30 30
No. 811 is erroneously inscribed "ch".

1989. Birds. Multicoloured.
812 50ch. Type **103** . . . 10 10
813 1n. Black-naped blue monarch ("Black–naped Monarch") . . . 15 15
814 2n. White-crested laughing thrush . . . 30 30
815 3n. Blood pheasant . . . 50 45
816 4n. Plum-headed ("Blossom-headed") parakeet . . . 65 60
817 5n. Rosy minivet . . . 85 75
818 6n. Chestnut-headed fulvetta ("Tit-Babbler") (horiz) . . 1·00 90
819 7n. Blue pitta (horiz) . . . 1·20 1·10
820 10n. Black-naped oriole (horiz) . . . 1·60 1·50
821 15n. Green magpie (horiz) . . 2·50 2·20
822 20n. Three-toed kingfisher ("Indian Three-toed Kingfisher")(horiz) . . . 3·25 3·00
823 25n. Ibis bill (horiz) . . . 4·00 3·50
MS824 12 sheets, each 76×104 mm (vert designs) or 104×76 mm (horiz). (a) 25n. Fire-tailed sunbird; (b) 25n. Crested tree swift (inscr "Indian Crested Swift"); (c) 25n. Greater (inscr "Large") racket-tailed drongo; (d) 25n. Little spider hunter; (e) 25n. Blue-backed fairy bluebird (horiz); (f) 25n. Great Indian (inscr "Pied") hornbill (horiz); (g) 25n. Red-legged (inscr "Himalayan Redbreasted") falconet (horiz); (h) 25n. Lammergeier (horiz); (i) 25n. Satyr tragopan (horiz); (j) 25n. Spotted forktail (horiz); (k) 25n. Wallcreeper (horiz); (l) 25n. White eared-pheasant (wrongly inscr "White-eared") (horiz) . . . 42·00 42·00

104 "Best Friend of Charleston", 1830, U.S.A.

105 "Charaxes harmodius"

1990. Steam Railway Locomotives. Mult.
825 50ch. Type **104** . . . 10 10
826 1n. Class U locomotive, 1948, France . . . 10 10
827 2n. Consolidation locomotive, 1866, U.S.A. . . . 25 25
828 3n. Luggage engine, 1843, Great Britain . . . 45 35
829 4n. Class 60-3 Shay locomotive No. 18, 1913, U.S.A. . . . 55 50
830 5n. "John Bull", 1831, U.S.A. . . . 70 65
831 6n. "Hercules", 1837, U.S.A. 85 80
832 7n. Locomotive No. 947, 1874, Great Britain . . . 1·10 95
833 10n. "Illinois", 1852, U.S.A. 1·40 1·30
834 15n. Class O5 locomotive, 1935, Germany . . . 2·10 1·90
835 20n. Standard locomotive, 1865, U.S.A. . . . 2·75 2·50
836 25n. Class Ps-4 locomotive, 1936, U.S.A. . . . 3·50 3·25
MS837 12 sheets, each 74×100 mm (horiz designs) or 100×74 mm (vert). (a) 25n. "The Cumberland" (U.S.A., 1845); (b) 25n. "Ariel" (U.S.A., 1877); (c) 25n. No. 22 Baldwin locomotive (U.S.A., 1873); (d) 25n. Class "A" (U.S.A., 1935) (vert); (e) 25n. Class "K-36" (U.S.A., 1923); (f) 25n. No. 999 "Empire State Express" (U.S.A., 1893); (g) 25n. "John Stevens" (U.S.A., 1849) (vert); (h) 25n. Class "A4" (Great Britain, 1935) (vert); (i) 25n. "Puffing Billy" (Great Britain, 1814) (vert); (j) 25n. "The Rocket" (Great Britain, 1829) (vert); (k) 25n. Class "P-1" (U.S.A., 1943) (vert); (l) 25n. No. 1301 Webb compound engine (Great Britain, 1889) . . . 42·00 42·00

1990. Butterflies. Multicoloured.
838 50ch. Type **105** . . . 10 10
839 1n. "Prioneris thestylis" . . . 10 10
840 2n. Eastern courtier . . . 25 25
841 3n. "Penthema lisarda" (horiz) . . . 45 35
842 4n. Golden birdwing . . . 55 50
843 5n. Great nawab . . . 70 65
844 6n. "Polyura dolon" (horiz) 85 80
845 7n. Tailed labyrinth (horiz) 1·10 95
846 10n. "Delias descombesi" . . 1·40 1·30
847 15n. "Childreni childrena" (horiz) . . . 2·10 1·90
848 20n. Leaf butterfly (horiz) . . 2·75 2·50
849 25n. "Elymnias malelas" (horiz) . . . 3·50 3·25
MS850 12 sheets, each 110×80 mm. (a) 25n. Bhutan glory; (b) 25n. Blue (inscr "Blue Banded") peacock; (c) 25n. Camberwell beauty; (d) 25n. Chequered swallowtail; (e) 25n. Chestnut tiger; (f) 25n. Common birdwing; (g) 25n. Common map butterfly; (h) 25n. Common (inscr "Great") eggfly; (i) 25n. Jungle glory; (j) 25n. Kaiser-i-hind; (k) 25n. Red lacewing; (l) 25n. Swallowtail 42·00 42·00

106 "Renanthera monachica"

107 "Plum Estate, Kameido"

1990. "Expo '90" International Garden and Greenery Exposition, Osaka. Orchids. Mult.
851 10ch. Type **106** . . . 10 10
852 50ch. "Vanda coerulea" . . . 10 10
853 1n. "Phalaenopsis violacea" 15 15
854 2n. "Dendrobium nobile" . . 30 25
855 5n. "Vandopsis lissochiloides" . . . 60 55
856 6n. "Paphiopedilum rothschildianum" . . . 85 75
857 7n. "Phalaenopsis schilleriana" . . . 1·00 90
858 9n. "Paphiopedilum insigne" 1·30 1·10
859 10n. "Paphiopedilum bellatulum" . . . 1·40 1·30
860 20n. "Doritis pulcherrima" 2·75 2·50
861 25n. "Cymbidium giganteum" 4·25 3·25
862 35n. "Phalaenopsis mariae" 5·00 4·75
MS863 12 sheets, each 111×84 mm. (a) 30n. "Dendrobium aphyllum"; (b) 30n. "Dendrobium loddigesii"; (c) 30n. "Dendrobium margaritaceum"; (d) 30n. "Paphlopedilum haynaldianum"; (e) 30n. "Paphiopedilum niveum"; (f) 30n. "Phalaenopsis amabilis"; (g) 30n. "Phalaenopsis cornu-cervi"; (h) 30n"Phalaenopsis equestris"; (i) 30n. "Vanda alpine"; (j) 30n. "Vanda coerulescens"; (k) 30n. "Vanda cristata"; (l) 30n. "Vandopsis parishi" . . . 50·00 50·00

1990. Death of Emperor Hirohito and Accession of Emperor Akihito of Japan. "100 Famous Views of Edo" by Ando Hiroshige. Multicoloured.
864 10ch. Type **107** . . . 10 10
865 20ch. "Yatsumi Bridge" . . . 10 10
866 50ch. "Ayase River and Kanegafuchi" . . . 10 10
867 75ch. "View of Shiba Coast" . . 10 10

868 1n. "Grandpa's Teahouse, Meguro" 15 15
869 2n. "Inside Kameido Tenjin Shrine" 25 25
870 6n. "Yoroi Ferry, Koami-cho" 90 80
871 7n. "Sakasai Ferry" . . . . 1·10 95
872 10n. "Fukagawa Lumberyards" . . . . . . 1·50 1·40
873 15n. "Suido Bridge and Surugadai" . . . . 2·40 2·10
874 20n. "Meguro Drum Bridge and Sunset Hill" . . . . . 3·00 2·75
875 25n. "Atagoshita and Yabu Lane" . . . . 3·75 3·25

MS876 12 sheets, each 102 × 76 mm. (a) 25n. "The City Flourishing, Tanabata Festival"; (b) 25n. "Fukagawa Susaki and Jumantsubo"; (c) 25n. "Horikiri Iris Garden"; (d) 25n. "Komakata Hall and Azuma Bridge"; (e) 25n. "Minowa, Kanasugi, Mikawashima"; (f) 25n. "New Year's Eve Foxfires at the Changing Tree, Oji"; (g) 25n. "Nihonbashi, Clearing after Snow"; (h) 25n. "Sudden Shower over Shin-Ohashi Bridge and Atake"; (i) 25n. "Suijin Shrine and Massaki on the Sumida River"; (j) 25n. "Suruga-cho"; (k) 25n. "Towboats along the Yotsugi-dori Canal"; (l) 25n. "View to the North from Asukayama" . . . 42·00 38·00

108 Thimphu Post Office

1990.
877 **108** 1n. multicoloured 15 15

109 Giant Panda

1990. Mammals. Multicoloured.
878 50ch. Type **109** 10 10
879 1n. Giant panda in tree . . . 15 15
880 2n. Giant panda with cub . . 30 30
881 3n. Giant panda (horiz) . . . 50 45
882 4n. Giant panda eating (horiz) 65 60
883 5n. Tiger (horiz) 85 75
884 6n. Giant pandas pulling up bamboo (horiz) . . . . . 1·00 90
885 7n. Giant panda and cub resting (horiz) . . . . . 1·20 1·10
886 10n. Indian elephant (horiz) 1·60 1·50
887 15n. Giant panda beside fallen tree . . . . 2·50 2·20
888 20n. Indian muntjac (inscr "Barking deer") (horiz) . . 3·25 3·00
889 25n. Snow leopard (horiz) . . 4·00 3·50

MS890 12 sheets, each 100 × 73 mm. (a) 25n. Asiatic black bear; (b) 25n. Dhole (inscr "Asiatic wild dog"); (c) 25n. Clouded leopard; (d) 25n. Gaur; (e) 25n. Giant panda; (f) 25n. Golden cat; (g) 25n. Siberian musk deer (inscr "Himalayan"); (h) 25n. Redd deer (inscr "Himalayan shou"); (i) 25n. Pygmy hog; (j) 25n. Indian rhinoceros; (k) 25n. Sloth bear; (l) 25n. Wolf . . . . 45·00 45·00

110 Roim

1990. Religious Musical Instruments. Mult.
891 10ch. Dungchen (large trumpets) 10 10
892 20ch. Dungkar (Indian chank shell) 10 10
893 30ch. Type **110** 10 10
894 50ch. Tinchag (cup cymbals) 10 10
895 1n. Dradu and drilbu (pellet drum and hand bell) . . . 10 10
896 2n. Gya-ling (oboes) 20 15
897 2n.50 Nga (drum) 30 25
898 3n.50 Kang-dung (trumpets) 35 35

MS899 Two sheets, each 92 × 135 mm. (a) Nos. 891, 893, 895 and 898; (b) Nos. 892, 894 and 896/7 . . . . 1·75 1·75

111 Penny Black and Bhutan 1962 2ch. Stamp

1990. "Stamp World London 90" International Stamp Exhibition. 150th Anniv of the Penny Black. Multicoloured.
900 50ch. Type **111** 10 10
901 1n. Oldenburg 1852 $\frac{1}{30}$th. stamp 15 15
902 2n. Bergedorf 1861 $1\frac{1}{2}$s. stamp 25 25
903 4n. German Democratic Republic 1949 50pf. stamp 50 45
904 5n. Brunswick 1852 1 sgr. stamp 60 55
905 6n. Basel 1845 $2\frac{1}{2}$r. stamp . . 85 75
906 8n. Geneva 1843 5c.+5c. stamp . . . . 1·10 1·00
907 10n. Zurich 1843 4r. stamp 1·40 1·30
908 15n. France 1849 20c. stamp 2·10 1·90
909 20n. Vatican City 1929 5c. stamp . . . . 2·75 2·50
910 25n. Israel 1948 3m. stamp 3·50 3·25
911 30n. Japan 1871 48m. stamp 4·25 3·75

MS912 12 sheets, each 106 × 76 mm. (a) 15n. Baden 1851 1k. stamp, 15n. Wurttemberg 1851 1k. stamp; (b) 15n. Germany 1872 3k. and 2g. stamps, 15n. Prussia 1850 6pf. stamp; (c) 15n. Hamburg 1859 $\frac{1}{2}$s. stamp, 15n. North German Confederation 1868 $\frac{1}{4}$g. and 1k. stamps; (d) 15n. Heligoland 1867 $\frac{1}{2}$ch. stamp, 15n. Hanover 1850 1ggr. stamp; (e) 15n. Schleswig-Holstein 1850 1s. stamp; 15n. Lubeck 1859 4s. stamp; (f) 15n. Mecklenburg-Schwerin 1856 4/4s. stamp, 15n. Mecklenburg-Strelitz 1864 $\frac{1}{3}$sgr. stamp; (g) 15n. Thurn and Taxis (Northern District) 1852 $\frac{1}{4}$sgr. stamp, 15n. Thurn and Taxis (Southern District) 1852 1k. stamp; (h) 30n. Bavaria 1849 1k. stamp; (i) 30n. West Berlin 1948 2pf. stamp; (j) 30n. Great Britain 1840 Penny Black; (k) 30n. Saxony 1850 3pf. stamp; (l) 30n. United States 1847 5c. stamp . . . . 48·00 48·00

Each value also depicts the Penny Black.
No. 901 is wrongly inscribed "Oldenberg".

112 Girls

113 Temple of Artemis, Ephesus

1990. South Asian Association for Regional Co-operation Girl Child Year. Multicoloured.
913 50ch. Type **112** 20 20
914 20n. Girl . . . . 2·75 2·40

1991. Wonders of the World. Designs featuring Walt Disney cartoon characters. Multicoloured.
915 1ch. Type **113** 10 10
916 2ch. Statue of Zeus, Olympia 10 10
917 3ch. Pyramids of Egypt . . . 10 10
918 4ch. Lighthouse of Alexandria, Egypt 10 10
919 5ch. Mausoleum, Halicarnassus 10 10
920 10ch. Colossus of Rhodes . . 10 10
921 50ch. Hanging Gardens of Babylon 10 10
922 5n. Mauna Loa Volcanoes, Hawaii (horiz) 70 65
923 6n. Carlsbad Caverns, New Mexico (horiz) 90 80
924 10n. Rainbow Bridge National Monument, Utah (horiz) . . . . 1·50 1·40
925 15n. Grand Canyon, Colorado (horiz) . . . . . 3·25 1·90
926 20n. Old Faithful, Yellowstone National Park, Wyoming (horiz) . . . . 2·75 2·50
927 25n. Sequoia National Park, California (horiz) . . . . . 3·75 3·25
928 30n. Crater Lake and Wizard Island, Oregon (horiz) . . 4·50 4·00

MS929 14 sheets, each 127 × 101 mm. (a) 25n. Alcan Highway, Alaska and Canada (horiz); (b) 25n. Catacombs of Alexandria; (c) 25n. Sears Tower, Chicago, Illinois (horiz); (d) 25n. Great Wall of China (horiz); (e) 25n. St. Sophia's Mosque, Constantinople; (f) 25n. Porcelain Tower, Nanking, China (horiz); (g) 25n. Hoover Dam, Nevada; (h) 25n. Empire State Building, New York City; (i) 25n. Panama Canal (horiz); (j) 25n. Leaning Tower of Pisa; (k) 25n. Colosseum Rome; (l) 25n. Gateway Arch, St. Louis, Missouri; (m) 25n. Golden Gate Bridge, San Francisco (horiz); (n) 25n. Stonehenge . . . . 42·00 42·00

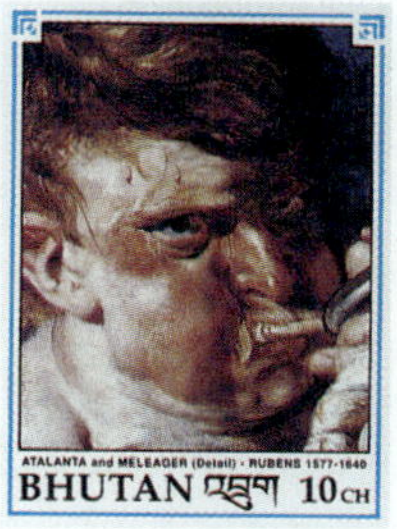

114 "Atalanta and Meleager" (detail)

1991. 350th Death Anniv (1990) of Peter Paul Rubens (painter). Multicoloured.
930 10ch. Type **114** 10 10
931 50ch. "The Fall of Phaeton" (detail) 10 10
932 1n. "Feast of Venus Verticordia" (detail) . . . 15 15
933 2n. "Achilles slaying Hector" (detail) 35 30
934 3n. "Arachne punished by Minerva" (detail) 50 35
935 4n. "Jupiter receives Psyche on Olympus" (detail) . . . 75 55
936 5n. "Atalanta and Meleager" (different detail) 90 85
937 6n. "Atalanta and Meleager" (different detail) . . . . . 1·10 1·00
938 7n. "Venus in Vulcan's Furnace" (detail) . . . . . 1·30 1·20
939 10n. "Atalanta and Meleager" (different detail) 1·70 1·60
940 20n. "Briseis returned to Achilles" (detail) . . . . . 3·50 3·25
941 30n. "Mars and Rhea Sylvia" (detail) . . . . 5·00 4·50

MS942 12 sheets, each 72 × 101 mm (a/e) or 101 × 72 mm (f/l). (a) 25n. "Atalanta and Meleager"; (b) 25n. "Feast of Venus Verticordia"; (c) 25n. "Ganymede and the Eagle"; (d) 25n. "Jupiter receives Psyche on Olympus"; (e) 25n. "Venus shivering"; (f) 25n. "Adonis and Venus" (horiz); (g) 25n. "Arachne punished by Minerva" (horiz); (h) 25n. "Briseis returned to Achilles" (horiz); (i) 25n. "The Fall of the Titans" (horiz); (j) 25n. "Hero and Leander" (horiz); (k) 25n. "Mars and Rhea Sylvia" (horiz); (l) 25n. "The Origin of the Milky Way" (horiz) . . . . 48·00 48·00

115 "Cottages, Reminiscence of the North"

1991. Death Centenary (1990) of Vincent van Gogh (painter). Multicoloured.
943 10ch. Type **115** 10 10
944 50ch. "Head of a Peasant Woman with Dark Cap" 10 10
945 1n. "Portrait of a Woman in Blue" 15 15
946 2n. "Head of an Old Woman with White Cap (the Midwife)" 45 35
947 8n. "Vase with Hollyhocks" 1·20 1·10
948 10n. "Portrait of a Man with a Skull Cap" . . . . . . 1·40 1·30
949 12n. "Agostina Segatori sitting in the Cafe du Tambourin" . . . . 1·80 1·60
950 15n. "Vase with Daisies and Anemones" . . . . 2·20 2·00
951 18n. "Fritillaries in a Copper Vase" . . . . 2·75 2·40
952 20n. "Woman sitting in the Grass" . . . . 3·00 2·75
953 25n. "On the Outskirts of Paris" (horiz) . . . . . 3·50 3·25
954 30n. "Chrysanthemums and Wild Flowers in a Vase" 4·25 3·75

MS955 12 sheets, each 76 × 101 mm (a/h) or 101 × 76 mm (i/l). (a) 30n. "Le Moulin de Blute-Fin"; (b) 30n. "Le Moulin de la Galette"; (c) 30n. "Le Moulin de la Galette" (with man in foreground); (d) 30n. "Poppies and Butterflies"; (e) 30n. "Trees in the Garden of St. Paul Hospital"; (f) 30n. "Vase with Peonies"; (g) 30n. "Vase with Red Poppies"; (h) 30n. "Vase with Zinnias"; (i) 30n. "Bowl with Sunflowers, Roses and Other Flowers" (horiz); (j) 30n. "Fishing in the Spring, Pont de Clichy" (horiz); (k) 30n. "Vase with Zinnias and Other Flowers" (horiz); (l) 30n. "Village Street in Auvers" (horiz) . . . . 48·00 48·00

116 Winning Uruguay Team, 1930

1991. World Cup Football Championship. Mult.
956 50ch. Type **116** 10 10
957 1n. Italy, 1934 . . . . 15 15
958 2n. Italy, 1938 . . . . 25 20
959 3n. Uruguay, 1950 . . . . . 45 30
960 5n. West Germany, 1954 . . 70 65
961 10n. Brazil, 1958 . . . . . . 1·40 1·30
962 20n. Brazil, 1962 . . . . . . 2·75 2·50
963 25n. England, 1966 . . . . . 3·50 3·25
964 29n. Brazil, 1970 . . . . . . 4·00 3·50
965 30n. West Germany, 1974 . . 4·25 3·75
966 31n. Argentina, 1978 . . . . 4·25 3·75
967 32n. Italy, 1982 . . . . . . 4·50 4·00
968 33n. Argentina, 1986 . . . . 4·50 4·00
969 34n. West Germany, 1990 . . 4·50 4·00
970 35n. Stadium, Los Angeles (venue for 1994 World Cup) . . . . 4·50 4·00

MS971 6 sheets, each 105 × 120 mm. (a) 30n. Roberto Baggio, Italy (vert); (b) 30n. Claudio Canniggia, Argentina (vert); (c) 30n. Paul Gascoigne, England (vert); (d) 30n. Lothar Matthaus, West Germany (vert); (e) 30n. Salvatore Schillaci, Italy (vert); (f) 30n. Peter Shilton, England . . . . . . 24·00 24·00

117 Bhutan and Japan State Flags

1991. "Phila Nippon '91" International Stamp Exhibition, Tokyo.
972 **117** 15n. multicoloured . . . 2·10 1·80

118 Teachers, Pupils and Hemisphere

1992. "Education for All by Year 2000".
973 **118** 1n. multicoloured 10 10

119 Hurdler

120 "Santa Maria"

1992. Olympic Games, Barcelona. Mult.
974 25n. Type **119** . . . . 3·25 3·25
975 25n. Body of hurdler . . . . 3·25 3·25
MS976 110 × 75 mm. 25n. Archery 4·75 4·75

Nos. 974/5 were issued together, se-tenant, forming a composite design.

1992. 500th Anniv of Discovery of America by Columbus. Multicoloured.
977 15n. Type **120** . . . . 1·10 1·10
978 20n. Columbus . . . . . . 1·40 1·40
MS979 78 × 118 mm. 25n. As No. 978 but without inscription at top (27 × 43 mm) . . . . . . 2·00 2·00

121 Brandenburg Gate and rejoicing Couple

1992. 2nd Anniv of Reunification of Germany.
980 **121** 25n. multicoloured . . . 1·80 1·80
MS981 110 × 82 mm. 25n. As No. 980 but without inscription at top (43 × 27 mm) . . . . . . 1·80 1·80

122 British Aerospace BAe 146 and Post Van

1992. 30th Anniv of Bhutan Postal Organization. Multicoloured.
982 1n. Type **122** 10 10
983 3n. Rural letter courier . . . 25 25
984 5n. Emptying post box . . . 40 40

123 Industry and Agriculture

1992. 20th Anniv of Accession of King Jigme Singye Wangchuck. Multicoloured.
985 1n. Type **123** 15 15
986 5n. British Aerospace RJ70 of National Airline 35 35
987 10n. House with water-pump 65 65
988 15n. King Jigme Singye Wangchuk . . . . . . 1·20 1·20
MS989 94 × 62 mm. 20n. King, flag and Bhutanese people (43 × 26 mm) . . . . 1·70 1·70
Nos. 985/8 were issued together, se-tenant, each horizontal pair within the block forming a composite design.

124 Dragon

1992. International Volunteer Day.
990 **124** 1n.50 multicoloured . . . 15 15
991 9n. multicoloured 65 65
992 15n. multicoloured . . . 1·20 1·20

125 "Meconopsis grandis" **127** "The Love Letter" (Jean Honore Fragonard)

1993. Medicinal Flowers. Designs showing varieties of the Asiatic Poppy. Multicoloured.
993 1n.50 Type **125** 15 15
994 7n. "Meconopsis" sp. 60 60
995 10n. "Meconopsis wallichii" 75 75
996 12n. "Meconopsis horridula" 1·00 1·00
997 20n. "Meconopsis discigera" 1·70 1·70
MS998 74 × 107 mm. 25n. "Meconopsis horridula" (different) (27 × 43 mm) . . . . 2·00 2·00

126 Rooster and Chinese Signs of the Zodiac (⅔-size illustration)

1993. New Year. Year of the Water Rooster. Sheet 89 × 89 mm.
MS999 **126** 25n. multicoloured 1·90 1·90

1993. Paintings. Multicoloured.
1000 1ch. Type **127** (postage) . . 15 15
1001 2ch. "The Writer" (Vittore Carpaccio) 15 15
1002 3ch. "Mademoiselle Lavergne" (Jean Etienne Liotard) 15 15
1003 5ch. "Portrait of Erasmus" (Hans Holbein) 15 15
1004 10ch. "Woman writing a Letter" (Gerard Terborch) 15 15
1005 15ch. Type **127** 15 15
1006 25ch. As No. 1001 . . . . 15 15
1007 50ch. As No. 1002 . . . . 15 15
1008 60ch. As No. 1003 . . . . 15 15
1009 80ch. As No. 1004 . . . . 15 15
1010 1n. Type **127** 15 15
1011 1n.25 As No. 1001 . . . . 15 15
1012 2n. As No. 1002 (air) . . . 15 15
1013 3n. As No. 1003 . . . . . 15 15
1014 6n. As No. 1004 . . . . . 15 15
MS1015 135 × 97 mm. As Nos. 1012/14 but with copper borders . . . . 1·70 1·70

128 Lesser Panda **130** Namtheo-say

1993. Environmental Protection. Multicoloured.
1016 7n. Type **128** 60 60
1017 10n. One-horned rhinoceros 85 85
1018 15n. Black-necked crane and blue poppy . . . . 1·20 1·20
1019 20n. Takin . . . . 1·50 1·50
Nos. 1016/19 were issued together, se-tenant, forming a composite design.

1993. "Taipei'93" International Stamp Exhibition, Taiwan. No. **MS**999 surch **TAIPEI'93 NU 30.**
MS1020 **126** 30n. on 25n. multicoloured . . . . 2·40 2·40

1993. Door Gods. Multicoloured.
1021 1n.50 Type **130** 10 15
1022 5n. Pha-ke-po 40 40
1023 10n. Chen-mi Jang 80 80
1024 15n. Yul-khor-sung . . . . 1·20 1·20

131 "Rhododendron mucronatum" **132** Dog

1994. Flowers. Multicoloured.
1025 1n. Type **131** 15 15
1026 1n.50 "Anemone rupicola" 15 15
1027 2n. "Polemonium coeruleum" 15 15
1028 2n.50 "Rosa marophylla" 15 15
1029 4n. "Paraquilegia microphylla" 35 35
1030 5n. "Aquilegia nivalis" . . . 40 40
1031 6n. "Geranium wallichianum" 50 50
1032 7n. "Rhododendron campanulatum" (wrongly inscr "Rhodendron") . . 60 60
1033 9n. "Viola suavis" 75 75
1034 10n. "Cyananthus lobatus" 90 90
MS1035 126 × 86 mm. 13n. Lily (horiz) . . . . 1·00 1·00

1994. New Year. Year of the Dog. "Hong Kong '94" International Stamp Exhibition.
1036 **132** 11n.50 multicoloured . . 80 80
MS1037 118 × 178 mm. **132** 20n. multicoloured . . . . 1·50 1·50

133 Trophy and Mascot

1994. World Cup Football Championship, U.S.A.
1038 **133** 15n. multicoloured . . . 80 80

134 Tagtshang Monastery (½-size illustration)

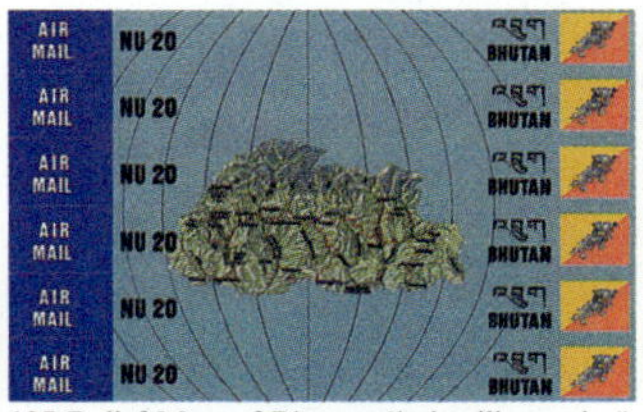

135 Relief Map of Bhutan (½-size illustration)

1994. Air. Self-adhesive.
1039 **134** 16n. multicoloured . . . 85 85
1040 **135** 20n. multicoloured . . . 1·00 1·00
The individual stamps are peeled directly from the card backing. Each card contains six different designs with the same face value forming the composite designs illustrated. Each stamp is a horizontal strip with a label indicating the main class of mail covered by the rate at the left, separated by a vertical line of roulletting. The outer edges of the cards are imperforate.

136 Tower Bridge, London (centenary)

1994. Bridges. Sheet 160 × 101 mm containing T **136** and similar horiz design. Multicoloured.
MS1041 15n. Type **136**; 16n. "Wangdur Bridge, Bhutan" (Samuel Davies) (250th anniv) 1·60 1·60

137 Astronaut on Moon

1994. 25th Anniv of First Manned Moon Landing. Sheet 114 × 57 mm containing T **137** and similar horiz design. Multicoloured.
MS1042 30n. Type **137**; 36n. Space shuttle . . . . 3·50 3·50

138 Horseman with raised Sword

1994. 350th Anniv of Victory over Tibet-Mongol Army. Multicoloured.
1043 15n. Type **138** 80 80
1044 15n. Archers and hand-to-hand sword fighting . . . 80 80
1045 15n. Horseman with insignia on helmet amongst infantry 80 80
1046 15n. Drummer, piper and troops 80 80
Nos. 1043/6 were issued together, se-tenant, forming a composite design of a battle scene and the Drugyel Dzong.

139 Paro Valley

1995. World Tourism Year. Sheet 111 × 92 mm containing T **139** and similar horiz designs. Multicoloured.
MS1047 1n.50 Type **139**; 5n. Chorton Kora; 10n. Thimphu Tshechu; 15n. Wangdue Tshechu 2·40 2·40

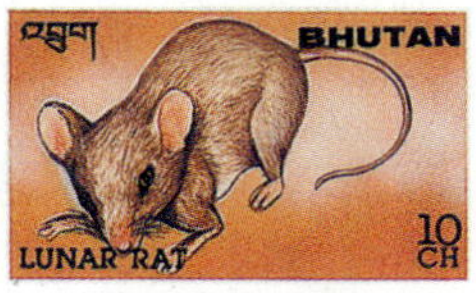

140 Lunar Rat

1995. New Year. Year of the Boar. Mult.
1048 10ch. Type **140** 15 15
1049 20ch. Lunar ox 15 15
1050 30ch. Lunar tiger 15 15
1051 40ch. Lunar rabbit 15 15
1052 1n. Lunar dragon 15 15
1053 2n. Lunar snake 15 15
1054 3n. Lunar horse 15 15
1055 4n. Lunar sheep 15 15
1056 5n. Lunar monkey 15 15
1057 7n. Lunar rooster 25 25
1058 8n. Lunar dog 35 35
1059 9n. Lunar boar 40 40
MS1060 111 × 92 mm. 10n. Wood hogs 55 55

141 "Pleione praecox" **142** Human Resources Development

1995. Flowers. Multicoloured.
1061 9n. Type **141** 50 50
1062 10n. "Primula calderina" . . 60 60
1063 16n. "Primula whitei" . . . 1·00 1·00
1064 18n. "Notholirion macrophyllum" . . . . . 1·10 1·10

1995. 50th Anniv of UNO. Multicoloured.
1065 1n.50 Type **142** 15 15
1066 5n. Transport and Communications 35 35
1067 9n. Health and Population 50 50
1068 10n. Water and Sanitation 60 60
1069 11n.50 UN in Bhutan . . . 65 65
1070 16n. Forestry and Environment 90 90
1071 18n. Peace and Security . . 1·00 1·00

143 Greater Pied Kingfisher ("Himalayan Pied Kingfisher")

144 Making Paper

1995. "Singapore '95" International Stamp Exhibition. Birds. Multicoloured.
1072 1n. Type **143** 15 15
1073 2n. Blyth's tragopan 15 15
1074 3n. Long-tailed minivets 15 15
1075 10n. Red junglefowl 60 60
1076 15n. Black-capped sibia 85 85
1077 20n. Red-billed chough 1·00 1·00
MS1078 73 × 97 mm. 20n. Black-necked crane 1·10 1·10

1995. Traditional Crafts. Multicoloured.
1079 1n. Type **144** 15 15
1080 2n. Religious painting 15 15
1081 3n. Clay sculpting 15 15
1082 10n. Weaving 60 60
1083 15n. Making boots 85 85
1084 20n. Carving wooden bowls 1·00 1·00
MS1085 121 × 82 mm. 20n. Decorative carvings on wooden buildings 1·00 1·00

145 Golden Langer

1996. New Year. Year of the Rat. Sheet 111 × 176 mm containing T **145** and similar square designs. Multicoloured.
MS1086 10n. Type **145**; 10n. Rat; 10n. Dragon 1·60 1·60

146 "The White Bird"

147 Blue Pansy

1996. Folk Tales. Multicoloured.
1087 1n. Type **146** 15 15
1088 2n. "Sing Sing Lhamo and the Moon" 15 15
1089 3n. "The Hoopoe" 15 15
1090 5n. "The Cloud Fairies" 35 35
1091 10n. "The Three Wishes" 60 60
1092 20n. "The Abominable Snowman" 1·10 1·10
MS1093 109 × 75 mm. 25n. As No. 1090 1·70 1·70

1996. Butterflies. Multicoloured.
1094 2n. Type **147** 15 15
1095 3n. Blue peacock 15 15
1096 5n. Great mormon 25 25
1097 10n. Fritillary 60 60
1098 15n. Blue duke 85 85
1099 25n. Brown gorgon 1·30 1·30
MS1100 Two sheets, each 108 × 75 mm. (a) 30n. Fivebar swordtail; (b) 30n. Xanthomelas 3·00 3·00

148 300n. Football Coin

1996. Olympic Games, Atlanta. Mult.
1101 5n. Type **148** 25 25
1102 7n. 300n. basketball coin 40 40
1103 10n. 5s. judo coin 60 60
MS1104 102 × 80 mm. 15n. Archery 85 85

149 Standard Goods Locomotive, India

1996. Trains. Multicoloured.
1105 20n. Type **149** 1·00 1·00
1106 20n. Diesel-electric locomotive, Finland 1·00 1·00
1107 20n. Shunting tank locomotive, Russia 1·00 1·00
1108 20n. Alco PA-1 diesel-electric locomotive, U.S.A. 1·00 1·00
1109 20n. Class C11 passenger tank locomotive, Japan 1·00 1·00
1110 20n. Settebello high speed electric train, Italy 1·00 1·00
1111 20n. Tank locomotive No. 191, Chile 1·00 1·00
1112 20n. Pacific locomotive, France 1·00 1·00
1113 20n. Steam locomotive No. 10, Norway 1·00 1·00
1114 20n. Atlantic express locomotive, Germany 1·00 1·00
1115 20n. Express steam locomotive, Belgium 1·00 1·00
1116 20n. Type 4 diesel-electric locomotive, Great Britain 1·00 1·00
MS1117 Two sheets, each 96 × 66 mm. (a) 70n. "Hikari" express train, Series 200, Japan; (b) Class KD steam goods locomotive, Sweden 7·25 7·25

150 Penny Black

1996.
1118 **150** 140n. gold and black 7·25 7·25

151 Vegard Ulvang, Norway

152 Bee

1997. Winter Olympic Gold Medallists. Multicoloured. (a) Without frame.
1119 10n. Type **151** (30km. cross-country skiing, 1992) 60 60
1120 15n. Kristi Yamaguchi, U.S.A. (women's figure skating, 1992) 85 85
1121 25n. Markus Wasmeier, Germany (men's super giant slalom, 1994) 1·50 1·50
1122 30n. Georg Hackl, Germany (luge, 1992) 1·70 1·70

(b) As T **151** but with black frame around design.
1123 15n. Andreas Ostler, West Germany (two-man bobsleighing, 1952) 80 80
1124 15n. East German team (four-man bobsleighing, 1984) 80 80
1125 15n. Stein Eriksen, Norway (men's giant slalom, 1952) 80 80
1126 15n. Alberto Tomba, Italy (men's giant slalom, 1988) 80 80
MS1127 Two sheets, each 106 × 76 mm. (a) 70n. Henri Oreiller, France (men's downhill skiing, 1948); (b) 70n. Swiss team (four-man bobsleighing, 1924) 7·50 7·50

1997. Insects and Arachnidae. Multicoloured.
1128 1ch. Type **152** 10 10
1129 2ch. "Neptunides polychromus" (beetle) 10 10
1130 3ch. "Conocephalus maculctus" (grasshopper) 10 10
1131 4ch. "Blattidae" sp. (beetle) 10 10
1132 5ch. Great diving beetle 10 10
1133 10ch. Hercules beetle 10 10
1134 15ch. Ladybird 10 10
1135 20ch. "Sarcophaga haemorrhoidalis" (fly) 10 10
1136 25ch. Stag beetle 10 10
1137 30ch. Caterpillar 10 10
1138 35ch. "Lycia hirtaria" (moth) 10 10
1139 40ch. "Clytarius pennatus" (beetle) 10 10
1140 45ch. "Ephemera denica" (mayfly) 10 10
1141 50ch. European field cricket 10 10
1142 60ch. Elephant hawk moth 10 10
1143 65ch. "Gerris" sp. (beetle) 10 10
1144 70ch. Banded agrion 10 10
1145 80ch. "Tachyta nana" (beetle) 10 10
1146 90ch. "Eurydema pulchra" (shieldbug) 10 10
1147 1n. "Hadrurus hirsutus" (scorpion) 10 10
1148 1n.50 "Vespa germanica" (wasp) 10 10
1149 2n. "Pyrops" sp. (beetle) 10 10
1150 2n.50 Praying mantis 10 10
1151 3n. "Araneus diadematus" (spider) 10 10
1152 3n.50 "Atrophaneura" sp. (butterfly) 10 10
MS1153 76 × 111 mm. 15n. Cockchafer ("Melolontha" sp.) 1·00 1·00

153 Polar Bears

1997. "Hong Kong '97" International Stamp Exhibition. Multicoloured.
1154 10n. Type **153** 55 55
1155 10n. Koalas ("Phascolarctos cinereus") 55 55
1156 10n. Asiatic black bear ("Selenarctos thibetanus") 55 55
1157 10n. Lesser panda ("Ailurus fulgens") 55 55
MS1158 107 × 75 mm. 20n. Giant panda ("Ailuropoda melanoleuca") 1·30 1·30

154 Rat

1997. New Year. Year of the Ox. Multicoloured.
1159 1ch. Type **154** 15 15
1160 2ch. Ox 15 15
1161 3ch. Tiger 15 15
1162 4ch. Rabbit 15 15
1163 90ch. Monkey 15 15
1164 5n. Dragon 25 25
1165 6n. Snake 35 35
1166 7n. Horse 40 40
1167 8n. Ram 50 50
1168 10n. Cock 65 65
1169 11n. Dog 75 75
1170 12n. Boar 85 85
MS1171 70 × 66 mm. 20n. Ox 2·75 2·75

155 Lynx

1997. Endangered Species. Multicoloured.
1172 10n. Type **155** 55 55
1173 10n. Lesser ("Red") panda ("Ailurus fulgens") 55 55
1174 10n. Takin ("Budorcas taxicolor") 55 55
1175 10n. Forest musk deer ("Moschus chrysogaster") 55 55
1176 10n. Snow leopard ("Panthera uncia") 55 55
1177 10n. Golden langur ("Presbytis geei") 55 55
1178 10n. Tiger ("Panthera tigris") 55 55
1179 10n. Indian muntjac ("Muntiacus muntjak") 55 55
1180 10n. Bobak marmot ("Marmota bobak") 55 55
1181 10n. Dhole ("Cuon alpinis") running 55 55
1182 10n. Dhole walking 55 55
1183 10n. Mother dhole nursing cubs 55 55
1184 10n. Two dhole 55 55
MS1185 Two sheets, each 106 × 76 mm. (a) 70n. Bharal ("Pseudois nayaur"); (b) 70n. Asiatic black bear ("Ursus thibetanus") 7·50 7·50

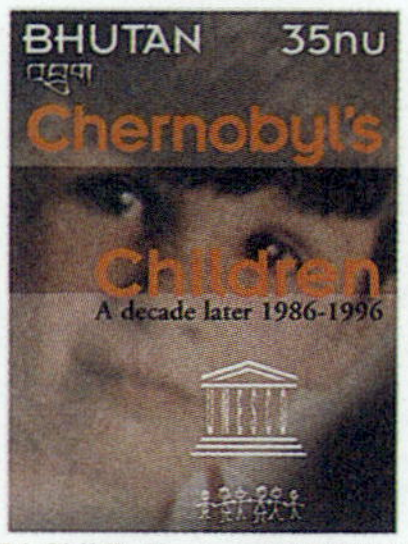

156 Child's Face and UNESCO Emblem

1997. 10th Anniv of Chernobyl Nuclear Disaster.
1186 **156** 35n. multicoloured 1·90 1·90

157 Mount Huangshah, China

1997. 50th Anniv of UNESCO World Heritage Sites. Multicoloured.
1187 10n. Type **157** 65 65
1188 10n. Statue of Emperor Qin, China 65 65
1189 10n. Imperial bronze dragon, China 65 65
1190 10n. Pyramids, Tikal National Park, Guatemala 65 65
1191 10n. Fountain, Evora, Portugal 65 65
1192 10n. Forest path, Shirakami-Sanchi, Japan 65 65
1193 10n. View from Eiffel Tower, Paris, France 65 65
1194 10n. Wooden walkway, Valley Below the Falls, Croatia 65 65
1195 15n. Bamberg Cathedral, Germany 1·00 1·00
1196 15n. Aerial view of Bamberg 1·00 1·00
1197 15n. St. Michael's Church, Hildesheim, Germany 1·00 1·00
1198 15n. Potsdam Palace, Germany 1·00 1·00
1199 15n. Church, Potsdam 1·00 1·00
1200 15n. Waterfront, Lubeck, Germany 1·00 1·00
1201 15n. Quedlinberg, Germany 1·00 1·00
1202 15n. Benedictine church, Lorsch, Germany 1·00 1·00
MS1203 Two sheets, each 126 × 102 mm. (a) 60n. House, Goslar, Germany (horiz); (b) 60n. Comenzada Cathedral, Portugal (horiz) 6·25 6·25

158 Turkish Angora

159 Stuart Pearce (England)

1997. Domestic Animals. Mult. (a) Cats.
1204 10n. Type **158** 65 65
1205 15n. Oriental shorthair 90 90
1206 15n. Japanese bobtail 85 85
1207 15n. Ceylon 85 85
1208 15n. Exotic 85 85
1209 15n. Rex 85 85
1210 15n. Ragdoll 85 85
1211 15n. Russian blue 85 85
1212 20n. British shorthair 1·20 1·20
1213 25n. Burmese 1·40 1·40

(b) Dogs.
1214 10n. Dalmatian 65 65
1215 15n. Siberian husky 90 90
1216 20n. Saluki 1·20 1·20
1217 20n. Dandie Dinmont terrier 1·20 1·20
1218 20n. Chinese crested 1·20 1·20
1219 20n. Norwich terrier 1·20 1·20
1220 20n. Basset hound 1·20 1·20
1221 20n. Cardigan Welsh corgi 1·20 1·20
1222 20n. French bulldog 1·20 1·20
1223 25n. Shar-Pei 1·40 1·40
MS1224 Two sheets, each 76 × 106 mm. (a) 60n. Tokinese (cat); (b) 60n. Hovawart (dog) 6·75 6·75

Nos. 1206/11 and 1217/22 respectively were issued together, se-tenant, forming composite designs.

1997. World Cup Football Championship, France (1998). Black (Nos. 1225, 1231, 1235, 1237, 1241, 1243) or multicoloured (others).
1225 5n. Type **159** 35 35
1226 10n. Paul Gascoigne (England) 65 65
1227 10n. Diego Maradona (Argentina 1986) (horiz) 65 65
1228 10n. Carlos Alberto (Brazil 1970) (horiz) 65 65
1229 10n. Dunga (Brazil 1994) (horiz) 65 65
1230 10n. Bobby Moore (England 1966) (horiz) 65 65
1231 10n. Fritz Walter (West Germany 1954) (horiz) . . 65 65
1232 10n. Walter Matthaus (Germany 1990) (horiz) 65 65
1233 10n. Franz Beckenbauer (West Germany 1974) (horiz) 65 65
1234 10n. Daniel Passarella (Argentina 1978) (horiz) 65 65
1235 10n. Italy team, 1938 (horiz) 65 65
1236 10n. West Germany team, 1954 (horiz) 65 65
1237 10n. Uruguay team, 1958 (horiz) 65 65
1238 10n. England team, 1966 (horiz) 65 65
1239 10n. Argentina team, 1978 (horiz) 65 65
1240 10n. Brazil team, 1962 (horiz) 65 65
1241 10n. Italy team, 1934 (horiz) 65 65
1242 10n. Brazil team, 1970 (horiz) 65 65
1243 10n. Uruguay team, 1930 (horiz) 65 65
1244 10n. David Beckham (England) . . . . 1·00 1·00
1245 20n. Steve McManaman (England) . . . . 1·20 1·20
1246 25n. Tony Adams (England) 1·50 1·50
1247 30n. Paul Ince (England) . . 1·90 1·90
MS1248 Two sheets, each 102 × 127 mm. (a) 35n. Salvatore "Toto" Schillaci (Italy) (horiz); (b) 35n. Philippe Albert (Belgium) 4·75 4·75

160 Buddha in Lotus Position

161 Jawaharlal Nehru and King Jigme Dorji Wangchuck

1997. "Indepex '97" International Stamp Exhibition, New Delhi. 50th Anniv of Independence of India. Multicoloured.
1249 3n. Type **160** 15 15
1250 7n. Mahatma Gandhi with hands together 35 35
1251 10n. Gandhi (three-quarter face portrait) 50 50
1252 15n. Buddha with feet on footstool 65 65
MS1253 Two sheets, each 75 × 106 mm. (a) 15n. Buddha with right hand raised; (b) 15n. Gandhi carrying stick . . . . 1·70 1·70

1997. Int Friendship between India and Bhutan.
1254 **161** 3n. black and pink . . . 15 15
MS1256 100 × 70 mm. 20n. multicoloured . . . . 2·30 2·30
DESIGNS: 10n. Prime Minister Rajiv Gandhi of India and King Jigme Singye Wangchuck. 76 × 34 mm—20n. President R Venkataraman of India and King Jigme Singye Wangchuck.

162 Tiger

1998. New Year. Year of the Tiger. T **162** and similar square designs. Multicoloured.
1257 3n. Type **162** 10 10
MS1258 Two sheets. (a) 95 × 95 mm. 3n. Type **162**; 5n. Lying down; 15n. Hunting; 17n. On rocky outcrop; (b) 114 × 81 mm. 20n. Head of tiger . . . . 2·75 2·75

163 Safe Motherhood and Anniversary Emblems

1998. 50th Anniv of WHO.
1259 **163** 3n. multicoloured . . . 10 10
1260 10n. multicoloured . . . 50 50
MS1261 100 × 60 mm. 15n. Safe Motherhood emblem (134 × 34 mm) 75 75

164 Mother Teresa

1998. Mother Teresa (founder of Missionaries of Charity) Commemoration. Multicoloured.
1262 10n. Type **164** 50 50
1263 10n. With Diana, Princess of Wales 50 50
1264 10n. Holding child 50 50
1265 10n. Holding baby 50 50
1266 10n. With Sisters 50 50
1267 10n. Smiling 50 50
1268 10n. Praying 50 50
1269 10n. With Pope John Paul II 50 50
1270 10n. Close-up of face . . . 50 50
MS1271 150 × 122 mm. 25n. As No. 1263 but 39 × 46 mm; 25n. As No. 1269 but different colour background and 39 × 46 mm 2·00 2·00

165 Red-billed Chough

1998. Birds. Multicoloured.
1272 10ch. Type **165** 15 15
1273 30ch. Great Indian hornbill ("Great Hornbill") . . . 15 15
1274 50ch. Western Singing bush lark ("Singing Lark") . . 15 15
1275 70ch. Chestnut-flanked white-eye 15 15
1276 90ch. Magpie robin (wrongly inscr "Megpie-robin") 15 15
1277 1n. Mrs. Gould's sunbird . . 15 15
1278 2n. Long-tailed tailor bird ("Tailorbird") 15 15
1279 3n. Mallard ("Duck") . . . 15 15
1280 5n. Great spotted cuckoo ("Spotted Cuckoo") . . . 15 15
1281 7n. Severtzov's tit warbler ("Goldcrest") 15 15
1282 9n. Common mynah 15 15
1283 10n. Green cochoa 15 15
MS1284 75 × 118 mm. 15n. Turtle dove (40 × 29 mm) 90 90

166 Rabbit

1999. New Year. Year of the Rabbit. Multicoloured.
1285 4n. Type **166** 20 20
1286 16n. Rabbit on hillock . . . 70 70
MS1287 83 × 114 mm. 20n. Rabbit beneath tree (34 × 34 mm) . . 1·00 1·00

167 Nuremberg

1999. "iBRA '99" International Stamp Exhibition, Nuremberg. Sheet 75 × 94 mm containing T **167** and similar square design. Multicoloured.
MS1288 35n. Type **167**; 40n. Exhibition emblem . . . . . . 1·00 1·00

168 King Wangchuck

1999. 25th Anniv of Coronation of King Jigme Singye Wangchuck. Multicoloured.
1289 25n. Type **168** . . . . . . 1·20 1·20
1290 25n. Facing left (yellow background) . . . . . . 1·20 1·20
1291 25n. Facing forwards (orange background) . . 1·20 1·20
1292 25n. With arm raised (green background) . . . . . . 1·20 1·20
MS1293 180 × 140 mm. 25n. King Wangchuk (magenta background) 4·25 4·25

169 Early German Steam Locomotive

1999. Trains. Multicoloured.
1294 5n. Type **169** 25 25
1295 10n. Electric locomotive . . 65 65
1296 10n. "Hikari" express train, Japan 60 60
1297 10n. Steam locomotive, South Africa, 1953 . . . 60 60
1298 10n. Super Chief locomotive, U.S.A., 1946 60 60
1299 10n. Magleus Magnet train, Japan, 1991 . . . . . . 60 60
1300 10n. *Flying Scotsman*, Great Britain, 1992 . . . . . 60 60
1301 10n. Kodama locomotive, Japan, 1958 . . . . . . 60 60
1302 10n. "Blue Train", South Africa, 1969 . . . . . 60 60
1303 10n. Intercity train, Germany, 1960 . . . . . 60 60
1304 10n. ET 403 high speed electric locomotive, Germany, 1973 . . . . . 60 60
1305 10n. 4-4-0 steam locomotive, U.S.A., 1855 . . . . . 60 60
1306 10n. Beyer-Garratt steam locomotive, South Africa, 1954 (wrongly inscr "BAYER GARRATT") 60 60
1307 10n. Settebello locomotive, Italy, 1953 . . . . . . 60 60
1308 15n. Pacific Class 01 steam locomotive, Germany . . 85 85
1309 15n. Neptune Express, Germany 85 85
1310 15n. 4-6-0 steam locomotive, Great Britain 85 85
1311 15n. Shovelnose Streamliner diesel locomotive, U.S.A. 85 85
1312 15n. Electric locomotive, Germany 85 85
1313 15n. Early steam locomotive, Germany . . 85 85
1314 15n. Union Pacific diesel locomotive, U.S.A. . . . 85 85
1315 15n. 1881 Borsig steam locomotive, Germany . . 85 85
1316 15n. Borsig 4-6-4 diesel locomotive, Germany . . 85 85
1317 15n. Diesel-electric locomotive, France . . . 85 85
1318 15n. Pennsylvania Railroad locomotive, U.S.A. . . . 85 85
1319 15n. Steam locomotive, Germany 85 85
1320 15n. Amtrak locomotive, U.S.A. 85 85
1321 15n. 2-2-2 steam locomotive, Great Britain 85 85
1322 15n. P class steam locomotive, Denmark . . 85 85
1323 15n. Electric locomotive, France 85 85
1324 15n. First Japanese locomotive 85 85
1325 15n. 2-8-2 steam locomotive, Germany 85 85
1326 20n. Steam locomotive . . . 1·20 1·20
1327 30n. Electric locomotive . . 1·70 1·70
MS1328 Two sheets, each 110 × 85 mm. (a) 80n. City of Los Angeles, U.S.A.; (b) 80n. Great Northern diesel-electric Streamliner locomotive, U.S.A 9·75 9·75

170 "Festive Dancers"

1999. 150th Death Anniv of Katsushika Hokusai (artist). Multicoloured.
1329 15n. Type **170** 75 75
1330 15n. "Drawings of Women" (woman reading) 75 75
1331 15n. "Festive Dancers" (man wearing pointed hat) 75 75
1332 15n. "Festive Dancers" (man looking up) 75 75
1333 15n. "Drawings of Women" (woman sitting on ground) 75 75
1334 15n. "Festive Dancers" (woman) 75 75
1335 15n. "Suspension Bridge between Hida and Etchu" 75 75
1336 15n. "Drawings of Women" (woman dressing hair) . . 75 75
1337 15n. "Exotic Beauty" . . . 75 75
1338 15n. "The Poet Nakamaro in China" 75 75
1339 15n. "Drawings of Women" (woman rolling up sleeve) 75 75
1340 15n. "Chinese Poet in Snow" 75 75
1341 15n. "Mount Fuji seen above Mist on the Tama River" (horiz) 75 75
1342 15n. "Mount Fuji seen from Shichirigahama" (horiz) 75 75
1343 15n. "Sea Life" (turtle) (horiz) 75 75
1344 15n. "Sea Life" (fish) (horiz) 75 75
1345 15n. "Mount Fuji reflected in a Lake" (horiz) 75 75
1346 15n. "Mount Fuji seen through the Piers of Mannenbashi" (horiz) . . 75 75
MS1347 Three sheets (a) 100 × 71 mm 80n. "Peasants leading Oxen"; (b) 71 × 100 mm 80n. "The lotus Pedestal". (c) 71 × 100 mm 870n. "Kusunoki Masahige" . . . . 15·00 15·00

171 Tyrannosaurus Rex

1999. Prehistoric Animals. Multicoloured.
1348 10n. Type **171** 60 60
1349 10n. Dimorphodon 60 60
1350 10n. Diplodocus 60 60
1351 10n. Pterodaustro 60 60
1352 10n. Tyrannosaurus Rex (different) 60 60
1353 10n. Edmontosaurus 60 60
1354 10n. Apatosaurus 60 60
1355 10n. Deinonychus 60 60
1356 10n. Hypsilophodon 60 60
1357 10n. Oviraptor 60 60
1358 10n. Stegosaurus beside lake 60 60
1359 10n. Head of Triceratops . . 60 60
1360 10n. Pterodactylus and Brachiosaurus 60 60
1361 10n. Pteranodon 60 60
1362 10n. Anurognathus and Tyrannosaurus Rex . . . 60 60
1363 10n. Brachiosaurus 60 60
1364 10n. Corythosaurus 60 60
1365 10n. Iguanodon 60 60
1366 10n. Lesothosaurus 60 60
1367 10n. Allosaurus 60 60
1368 10n. Velociraptor 60 60
1369 10n. Triceratops in water . . 60 60
1370 10n. Stegosaurus in water . . 60 60
1371 10n. Compsognathus 60 60
1372 20n. Moeritherium 90 90
1373 20n. Platybelodon 90 90
1374 20n. Woolly mammoth . . . 90 90
1375 20n. African elephant . . . 90 90
1376 20n. Deinonychus 90 90
1377 20n. Dimorphodon 90 90
1378 20n. Archaeopteryx 90 90
1379 20n. Common pheasant ("Ring-necked Pheasant") 90 90
MS1380 Four sheets, each 110 × 85 mm. (a) 80n. Hoatzin (vert); (b) 80n. Icthyosaurus (wrongly inscr "Present Day Dolphin") (vert); (c) 80n. Triceratops (vert); (d) 80n. Pteranodon (wrongly inscr "Triceratops") . . . . 18·00 18·00
Nos. 1348/59 and 1360/71 were issued together, se-tenant, with the backgrounds forming a composite design.

172 Siberian Musk Deer

1999. "China '99" World Philatelic Exhibition, Peking. Animals. Multicoloured.

1381 20n. Type **172** . . . . . . 1·00 1·00
1382 20n. Takin (*Budorcas taxicolor*) . . . . . . 1·00 1·00
1383 20n. Bharal ("Blue sheep") (*Pseudois nayur*) (wrongly inscr "nayour") . . . . . 1·00 1·00
1384 20n. Yak (*Bos gunniens*) . . 1·00 1·00
1385 20n. Common goral (*Nemorhaedus goral*) . . . 1·00 1·00

173 Sara Orange-tip

1999. Butterflies. Multicoloured.

1386 5n. Type **173** 35 35
1387 10n. Pipe-vine swallowtail 60 60
1388 15n. Longwings 85 85
1389 20n. Viceroy . . . . 1·10 1·10
1390 20n. Frosted skipper . . . . 1·20 1·20
1391 20n. Fiery skipper . . . . . 1·20 1·20
1392 20n. Banded hairstreak . . 1·20 1·20
1393 20n. Cloudless ("Clouded") sulphur . . . . 1·20 1·20
1394 20n. Milbert's tortoiseshell 1·20 1·20
1395 20n. Eastern tailed blue . . 1·20 1·20
1396 20n. Jamaican kite ("Zebra") swallowtail . . 1·20 1·20
1397 20n. Colorado hairstreak . . 1·20 1·20
1398 20n. Pink-edged sulphur . . 1·20 1·20
1399 20n. Barred sulphur (wrongly inscr "Fairy Yellow") . . . . 1·20 1·20
1400 20n. Red-spotted purple . . 1·20 1·20
1401 20n. Aphrodite . . . . . . 1·20 1·20
1402 25n. Silver-spotted skipper (vert) . . . . 1·40 1·40
1403 30n. Great spangled fritillary (vert) . . . . 1·70 1·70
1404 35n. Little copper (vert) . . 2·00 2·00
MS1405 Four sheets, each 98×68 mm. (a) 80n. Monarch (vert); (b) 80n. Checkered white; (c) 80n. Gulf fritillary (vert); (d) 80n. Grey hairstreak (vert) . . 14·50 14·50

Nos. 1390/95 and 1396/1401 were issued together, se-tenant, forming a composite design.

174 Chestnut-breasted Chlorophonia

1999. Birds. Multicoloured.

1406 15n. Type **174** 65 65
1407 15n. Yellow-faced amazon 65 65
1408 15n. White ibis 65 65
1409 15n. Parrotlet sp. ("Caique") 65 65
1410 15n. Green jay 65 65
1411 15n. Tufted coquette 65 65
1412 15n. Troupial 65 65
1413 15n. American purple gallinule ("Purple Gallinule") 65 65
1414 15n. Copper-rumped hummingbird 65 65
1415 15n. Great egret ("Common egret") 65 65
1416 15n. Rufous-browed pepper shrike 65 65
1417 15n. Glittering-throated emerald 65 65
1418 15n. Great kiskadee 65 65
1419 15n. Cuban green woodpecker 65 65
1420 15n. Scarlet ibis 65 65
1421 15n. Belted kingfisher . . . 65 65
1422 15n. Barred antshrike . . . 65 65
1423 15n. Brown-throated conure ("Caribbean Parakeet") 65 65
1424 15n. Rufous-tailed jacamar (vert) 65 65
1425 15n. Scarlet macaw (vert) . . 65 65
1426 15n. Channel-billed toucan (vert) 65 65
1427 15n. Louisiana heron ("Tricolored heron") (vert) 65 65
1428 15n. St. Vincent amazon ("St. Vincent Parrot") (vert) 65 65
1429 15n. Blue-crowned motmot (vert) 65 65
1430 15n. Horned screamer (vert) 65 65
1431 15n. Grey plover ("Black-billed Plover") (vert) . . . 65 65
1432 15n. Eastern meadowlark ("Common meadowlark") (vert) 65 65
MS1433 Three sheets, each 85×110 mm. (a) 80n. Military macaw (vert); (b) 80n. Toco toucan; (c) 80n. Red-billed scythebill (vert) . . . . . . 11·00 11·00

Nos. 1406/14, 1415/23 and 1424/32 were issued together, se-tenant, forming a composite design.

175 Yuri Gagarin (first person in space, 1961)

1999. 30th Anniv of First Manned Moon Landing. Multicoloured.

1434 20n. Type **175** 90 90
1435 20n. Alan Shepard (first American in space, 1961) 90 90
1436 20n. John Glenn (first American to orbit Earth, 1962) 90 90
1437 20n. Valentina Tereshkova (first woman in space, 1963) 90 90
1438 20n. Edward White (first American to walk in space, 1965) 90 90
1439 20n. Neil Armstrong (first person to set foot on Moon, 1969) 90 90
1440 20n. Neil Armstrong (wearing N.A.S.A. suit) 90 90
1441 20n. Michael Collins 90 90
1442 20n. Edwin (Buzz) Aldrin 90 90
1443 20n. *Columbia* (pointing upwards) 90 90
1444 20n. *Eagle* on lunar surface 90 90
1445 20n. Edwin Aldrin on lunar surface 90 90
1446 20n. N.A.S.A. X-15 rocket (1960) 90 90
1447 20n. Gemini 8 (1966) . . . 90 90
1448 20n. Saturn V rocket (1969) 90 90
1449 20n. *Columbia* (pointing downwards) 90 90
1450 20n. *Eagle* above Moon . . 90 90
1451 20n. Edwin Aldrin descending ladder 90 90
MS1452 Three sheets. (a) 111×85 mm. 80n. Neil Armstrong (different); (b) 111×85 mm. 80n. Gemini 8 docking with Agena target vehicle (56×41 mm); (c) 85×111 mm. 80n. Apollo 11 command module landing in Pacific Ocean (vert) . . . . . 11·00 11·00

Nos. 1434/9, 1440/5 and 1446/51 were issued together, se-tenant, forming a composite design.

176 Tortoiseshell Cat

1999. Animals. Multicoloured.

1453 5n. Type **176** 75 75
1454 5n. Man watching blue and white cat 75 75
1455 10n. Chinchilla golden longhair adult and kittens 1·40 1·40
1456 12n. Russian blue adult and kitten 65 65
1457 12n. Birman 65 65
1458 12n. Devon rex 65 65
1459 12n. Pewter longhair 65 65
1460 12n. Bombay 65 65
1461 12n. Sorrel somali 65 65
1462 12n. Red tabby manx . . . 65 65
1463 12n. Blue smoke longhair 65 65
1464 12n. Oriental tabby shorthair adult and kitten 65 65
1465 12n. Australian silky terrier 65 65
1466 12n. Samoyed 65 65
1467 12n. Basset bleu de Gascogne 65 65
1468 12n. Bernese mountain dog 65 65
1469 12n. Pug 65 65
1470 12n. Bergamasco 65 65
1471 12n. Basenji 65 65
1472 12n. Wetterhoun 65 65
1473 12n. Drever 65 65
1474 12n. Przewalski horse . . . 65 65
1475 12n. Shetland pony 65 65
1476 12n. Dutch gelderlander horse 65 65
1477 12n. Shire horse 65 65
1478 12n. Arab 65 65
1479 12n. Boulonnais 65 65
1480 12n. Falabella 65 65
1481 12n. Orlov trotter 65 65
1482 12n. Suffolk punch 65 65
1483 15n. Lipizzaner 65 65
1484 20n. Andalusian . . . . . 1·20 1·20
1485 25n. Weimaraner (dog) . . . 1·70 1·70
1486 30n. German shepherd dog 3·00 3·00
MS1487 Three sheets, each 115×91 mm. (a) 70n. Labrador retriever; (b) 70n. Norwegian forest cat; (c) 70n. Connemara horse . . . . 9·75 9·75

177 Bharal

1999. Animals and Birds of the Himalayas. Multicoloured. (a) Animals.

1489 20n. Type **177** 90 90
1490 20n. Lynx 90 90
1491 20n. Rat snake 90 90
1492 20n. Indian elephant 90 90
1493 20n. Langur 90 90
1494 20n. Musk deer 90 90
1495 20n. Otter 90 90
1496 20n. Tibetan wolf 90 90
1497 20n. Himalayan black bear 90 90
1498 20n. Snow leopard 90 90
1499 20n. Flying squirrel 90 90
1500 20n. Red fox 90 90
1501 20n. Ibex 90 90
1502 20n. Takin 90 90
1503 20n. Agama lizard 90 90
1504 20n. Marmot 90 90
1505 20n. Red panda 90 90
1506 20n. Leopard cat 90 90
MS1507 Three sheets, each 78×118 mm. (a) 100n. Cobra; (b) 100n. Tiger; (c) 100n. Rhinoceros (wrongly inscr "Rhinoerous") 16·00 16·00

(b) Birds.

1508 20n. Red-crested pochard 90 90
1509 20n. Satyr tragopan 90 90
1510 20n. Lammergeier ("Lammergeier Vulture") 90 90
1511 20n. Kalij pheasant 90 90
1512 20n. Great Indian hornbill 90 90
1513 20n. White stork ("Stork") 90 90
1514 20n. Rufous-necked hornbill (wrongly inscr "Rofous") 90 90
1515 20n. Black drongo ("Drongo") 90 90
1516 20n. Himalayan monal pheasant 90 90
1517 20n. Black-necked crane . . 90 90
1518 20n. Little green bee-eater 90 90
1519 20n. Oriental ibis ("Ibis") 90 90
1520 20n. Crested lark 90 90
1521 20n. Ferruginous duck . . . 90 90
1522 20n. Blood pheasant 90 90
1523 20n. White-crested laughing thrush ("Laughing Thrush") 90 90
1524 20n. Golden eagle 90 90
1525 20n. Siberian rubythroat . . 90 90
MS1526 Three sheets, each 78×118 mm. (a) 100n. Siberian rubythroat (different); (b) 100n. Black-naped monarch; (c) 100n. Mountain peacock pheasant . . 16·00 16·00

178 Elephant, Monkey, Rabbit and Bird (Four Friends)

1999. Year 2000.

1527 **178** 10n. multicoloured . . . 60 60
1528 20n. multicoloured . . . 1·10 1·10

179 Elegant Stink Horn

1999. Fungi. Multicoloured.

1529 20n. Type **179** . . . . . . 1·20 1·20
1530 20n. *Pholiota squarrosoides* 1·20 1·20
1531 20n. Scaly inky cap (*Coprinus quadrifidus*) . . 1·20 1·20
1532 20n. Golden spindles (*Clavulinopsis fusiformis*) 1·20 1·20
1533 20n. *Spathularia velutipes* 1·20 1·20
1534 20n. *Ganoderma lucidum* . . 1·20 1·20
1535 20n. *Microglossum rufum* 1·20 1·20
1536 20n. *Lactarius hygrophoroides* . . . . . 1·20 1·20
1537 20n. *Lactarius speciosus complex* . . . . 1·20 1·20
1538 20n. *Calostoma cinnabarina* 1·20 1·20
1539 20n. *Clitocybe clavipes* . . 1·20 1·20
1540 20n. *Microstoma floccosa* 1·20 1·20
1541 20n. Frost's bolete (*Boletus frostii*) . . . . 1·20 1·20
1542 20n. Common morel (*Morchella esculenta*) (wrongly inscr "estculenta") . . . . . . 1·20 1·20
1543 20n. *Hypomyces lactifluorum* 1·20 1·20
1544 20n. *Polyporus auricularius* 1·20 1·20
1545 20n. *Cantharellus lateritius* 1·20 1·20
1546 20n. *Volvariella pusilla* . . 1·20 1·20
MS1547 Three sheets, each 78×118 mm. (a) 100n. *Pholiota aurivella*; (b) 100n. *Ramarai grandis*; (c) 100n. *Oudemansiella lucidum* . . . . 16·00 16·00

180 Green Dragon with Red Flames

2000. New Year. Year of the Dragon. Multicoloured.

1548 3n. Type **180** 15 15
1549 5n. Green dragon encircling moon 25 25
1550 8n. Dragon and symbols of Chinese zodiac 50 50
1552 12n. Brown dragon encircling moon 75 75
MS1553 90×130 mm. 15n. Dragon head (29×40 mm) 85 85

181 LZ-1 (first flight), 1900

2000. Centenary of First Zeppelin Flight. Multicoloured.

1554 25n. Type **181** . . . . . . 1·30 1·30
1555 25n. LZ-2, 1906 . . . . . . 1·30 1·30
1556 25n. LZ-3 over hills (first flight, 1906) . . . . . . 1·30 1·30
1557 25n. LZ-127 *Graf Zeppelin* (first flight, 1928) . . . . 1·30 1·30
1558 25n. LZ-129 *Hindenberg* (first flight, 1936) . . . . 1·30 1·30
1559 25n. LZ-130 *Graf Zeppelin II* (first flight, 1938) . . . 1·30 1·30
1560 25n. LZ-1 over hill with tree 1·30 1·30
1561 25n. LZ-2 over mountains 1·30 1·30
1562 25n. LZ-3 against sky . . . 1·30 1·30
1563 25n. LZ-4 (first flight, 1908) 1·30 1·30
1564 25n. LZ-5 (first flight, 1909) 1·30 1·30
1565 25n. LZ-6 (formation of Deutsche Liftschiffahrts Aktien Gesallschaft (DELAG) (world's first airline), 1909) . . . . . . 1·30 1·30
1566 25n. LZ-1 over grassy hills, 1900 . . . . 1·30 1·30
1567 25n. Z11 *Ersatz*, 1913 . . . 1·30 1·30
1568 25n. LZ-6 exiting hangar, 1909 . . . . 1·30 1·30
1569 25n. LZ-10 *Schwabein* (first flight, 1911) . . . . . 1·30 1·30
1570 25n. LZ-7 *Deutschland* (inscr "Ersatz Deutschland") . . 1·30 1·30
1571 25n. LZ-11 *Viktoria Luise* 1·30 1·30
MS1572 Three sheets, each 106×80 mm. (a) 80n. Ferdinand von Zeppelin wearing white cap (vert); (b) 80n. Zeppelin wearing cap (vert); (c) 80n. Zeppelin (vert) 12·50 12·50

182 Lunix III

2000. "WORLD STAMP EXPO 2000" International Stamp Exhibition, Anaheim, California. Space. Multicoloured.

1573 25n. Type **182** . . . . . . 1·30 1·30
1574 25n. Ranger 9 . . . . 1·30 1·30
1575 25n. Lunar Orbiter . . . . 1·30 1·30
1576 25n. Lunar Prospector spacecraft . . . . 1·30 1·30
1577 25n. *Apollo 11* spacecraft . . 1·30 1·30
1578 25n. Selen satellite . . . . . 1·30 1·30
1579 25n. Space shuttle *Challenger* . . . . 1·30 1·30
1580 25n. North American X-15 experimental rocket aircraft . . . . 1·30 1·30

1581 25n. Space shuttle *Buran* . . 1·30 1·30
1582 25n. Hermes (experimental space plane) . . . . . . 1·30 1·30
1583 25n. X-33 Venturi Star (re-usable launch vehicle) . . 1·30 1·30
1584 25n. Hope (unmanned experimental spacecraft) 1·30 1·30
1585 25n. Victor Patsayev (cosmonaut) . . . . . . 1·30 1·30
1586 25n. Yladisloav Volkov (cosmonaut) . . . . . . 1·30 1·30
1587 25n. Georgi Dobrvolski (cosmonaut) . . . . . . 1·30 1·30
1588 25n. Virgil Grissom (astronaut) . . . . 1·30 1·30
1589 25n. Roger Chaffee (astronaut) . . . . 1·30 1·30
1590 25n. Edward White (astronaut) . . . . 1·30 1·30
MS1591 Three sheets. (a) 76 × 111 mm. 80n. Launch of space shuttle *Challenger* (vert); (b) 76 × 111 mm. 80n. Launch of space shuttle *Buran* (vert); (c) 116 × 85 mm. 80n. Edwin E. Aldrin on moon (first manned Moon landing, 1969) (vert) . . 31·00 31·00

183 Trashigang Dzong

2000. "EXPO 2000" World's Fair, Hanover, Germany (1st issue). Monasteries. Multicoloured.
1592 3n. Type **183** 15 15
1593 4n. Lhuentse Dzong 15 15
1594 6n. Gasa Dzong 25 25
1595 7n. Punakha Dzong 35 35
1596 10n. Trashichhoe Dzong . . 40 40
1597 20n. Paro Dzong 85 85
MS1598 157 × 98 mm. 15n. Roof (29 × 40 mm) 65 65

184 Snow Leopard

2000. "EXPO 2000" World's Fair, Hanover, Germany (2nd issue). Wildlife. Multicoloured.
1599 10n. Type **184** 40 40
1600 10n. Common raven ("Raven") 40 40
1601 10n. Golden langur 40 40
1602 10n. Rhododendron 40 40
1603 10n. Black-necked crane . . 40 40
1604 10n. Blue poppy 40 40

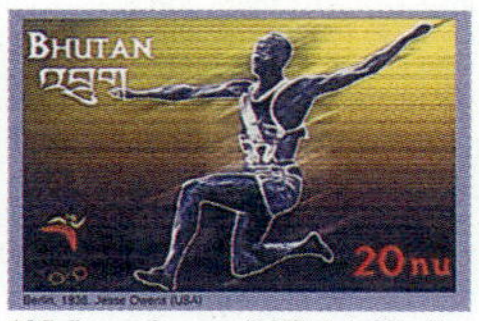

185 Jesse Owens (U.S.A.) (Berlin, 1936)

2000. Olympic Games, Sydney. Multicoloured.
1605 20n. Type **185** . . . . . . 1·00 1·00
1606 20n. Kayaking (modern games) . . . . 1·00 1·00
1607 20n. Fulton County Stadium, Atlanta, Georgia (1996 games) . . . . . 1·00 1·00
1608 20n. Ancient Greek athlete 1·00 1·00

186 G. and R. Stephenson's *Rocket* (first steam locomotive)

2000. 175th Anniv of Opening of Stockton and Darlington Railway. Multicoloured.
1609 50n. Type **186** . . . . . . 2·50 2·50
1610 50n. Steam locomotive (opening of London and Birmingham railway, 1828) . . . . 2·50 2·50
1611 50n. Northumbrian locomotive, 1825 . . . . 2·50 2·50
MS1612 118 × 79 mm. 100n. Inaugural run on Stockton and Darlington Railway, 1825 (56 × 42 mm) . . . . 4·00 4·00

187 Laird Commercial (biplane), 1929

2000. Airplanes. Multicoloured.
1613 25n. Type **187** . . . . . . 1·20 1·20
1614 25n. Ryan B-5 Brougham, 1927 (wrongly inscr "Broughm") . . . . . . 1·20 1·20
1615 25n. Cessna AW, 1928 . . . 1·20 1·20
1616 25n. Travel Air 4000 biplane, 1927 . . . . . 1·20 1·20
1617 25n. Fairchild F-71, 1927 . . 1·20 1·20
1618 25n. Command Aire biplane, 1928 . . . . . 1·20 1·20
1619 25n. Waco YMF biplane, 1935 . . . . 1·20 1·20
1620 25n. Piper J-4 Cub Coupe, 1938 . . . . 1·20 1·20
1621 25n. Ryan ST-A, 1937 . . . 1·20 1·20
1622 25n. Spartan Executive, 1939 . . . . 1·20 1·20
1623 25n. Luscombe 8, 1939 . . . 1·20 1·20
1624 25n. Stinson SR5 Reliant seaplane, 1935 . . . . 1·20 1·20
1625 25n. Cessna 195 seaplane, 1949 . . . . 1·20 1·20
1626 25n. Waco SRE biplane, 1940 . . . . 1·20 1·20
1627 25n. Erco Ercope, 1948 . . 1·20 1·20
1628 25n. Boeing Stearman biplane, 1941 . . . . . 1·20 1·20
1629 25n. Beech Staggerwing biplane, 1944 . . . . . 1·20 1·20
1630 25n. Republic Seabee, 1947 1·20 1·20
MS1631 Three sheets, each 77 × 108 mm. (a) 100n. Waco CSO seaplane, 1929; (b) 100n. Curtiss-Wright 19W, 1936; (c) 100n. Grumman G-44 Widgeon flying boat, 1941 . . . . 12·00 12·00

188 *A Kind of Loving*, 1962

190 Aquinas

189 Einstein

2000. Berlin Film Festival. Winners of Golden Bear Award. Multicoloured.
1632 25n. Type **188** . . . . . . 1·20 1·20
1633 25n. *Bushido Zankoku Monogatari*, 1963 . . . . 1·20 1·20
1634 25n. *Hobson's Choice*, 1954 1·20 1·20
1635 25n. *El Lazarillo de Tormes*, 1960 . . . . 1·20 1·20
1636 25n. *In the Name of the Father*, 1997 . . . . . 1·20 1·20
1637 25n. *Les Cousins*, 1959 . . . 1·20 1·20
MS1638 96 × 102 mm. 100n. *Die Ratten*, 1962 . . . . 4·00 4·00

2000. Albert Einstein—*Time* Magazine Man of the Century. Sheet 113 × 83 mm.
MS1639 **189** 100n. multicoloured 4·50 4·50

2000. 775th Birth Anniv of Thomas Aquinas (Catholic philosopher and theologian). Sheet 136 × 76 mm.
MS1640 **190** 25n. × 4 multicoloured 4·00 4·00

191 Pierre de Coubertin

2000. New Millennium. Multicoloured. (a) Centenary of the Modern Olympic Games.
1641 25n. Type **191** (founder of modern games) . . . . . 1·20 1·20
1642 25n. Hand holding baton (first modern Games, Athens, 1896) . . . . . 1·20 1·20
1643 25n. Jesse Owen (Berlin, 1936) . . . . 1·20 1·20
1644 25n. Handprint and white dove (Munich, 1972) . . . 1·20 1·20
1645 25n. Sydney Opera House (Sydney, 2000) . . . . . 1·20 1·20
1646 25n. Children wearing T-shirts (Greece, 2004) . . 1·20 1·20

(b) Breakthroughs in Modern Medicine.
1647 25n. Albert Calmette (bacteriologist, joint discoverer of B.C.G. vaccine) . . . . 1·20 1·20
1648 25n. Camillo Colgi and S. Ramon y Cajal (discovery of the neurone) 1·20 1·20
1649 25n. Alexander Fleming (bacteriologist, discoverer of penicillin) . . . . . 1·20 1·20
1650 25n. Jonas Salk (virologist, developer of polio vaccine) . . . . . . 1·20 1·20
1651 25n. Christiaan Barnard (surgeon, performed first human heart transplant) 1·20 1·20
1652 25n. Luc Mantagnier (A.I.D.S. research) . . . 1·20 1·20

192 Paro Taktsang

193 Christopher Columbus

2000. Sheet 86 × 49 mm.
MS1653 **192** 100n. multicoloured 4·00 4·00

2000. Explorers. Two sheets, each 66 × 83 mm. Multicoloured.
MS1654 (a) 100n. Type **193**; (b) 100n. Captain James Cook . . 8·00 8·00

194 *Crinum amoenum*

2000. Flowers of the Himalayan Mountains. Multicoloured.
1655 25n. Type **194** . . . . . . 1·20 1·20
1656 25n. *Beaumontia grandiflora* 1·20 1·20
1657 25n. *Trachelospermum lucidum* . . . . 1·20 1·20
1658 25n. *Curcuma aromatica* . . 1·20 1·20
1659 25n. *Barleria cristata* . . . 1·20 1·20
1660 25n. *Holmskioldia sanguinea* 1·20 1·20
1661 25n. *Meconopsis villosa* . . 1·20 1·20
1662 25n. *Salva hians* . . . . . 1·20 1·20
1663 25n. *Caltha palustris* . . . 1·20 1·20
1664 25n. *Anemone polyanthes* . . 1·20 1·20
1665 25n. *Cypripedium cordigerum* 1·20 1·20
1666 25n. *Cryptochilus luteus* . . 1·20 1·20
1667 25n. *Androsace globifera* . . 1·20 1·20
1668 25n. *Tanacetum atkinsonii* 1·20 1·20
1669 25n. *Aster stracheyi* . . . . 1·20 1·20
1670 25n. *Arenaria glanduligera* 1·20 1·20
1671 25n. *Sibbaldia purpurea* . . 1·20 1·20
1672 25n. *Saxifraga parnassifolia* 1·20 1·20
MS1673 Three sheets, each 68 × 98 mm. (a) 100n. *Dendrobium densiflorum* (vert); (b) 100n. *Rhododendron arboreum* (vert); (c) 100n. *Gypsophila cerastioides* . . . 14·50 14·50
Nos. 1655/60, 1661/6 and 1667/72 respectively were issued together, se-tenant, forming a composite design.

195 "The Duke and Duchess of Osuna with their Children" (detail, Francisco de Goya)

2000. "Espana 2000" International Stamp Exhibition, Madrid. Prado Museum Exhibits. Multicoloured.
1674 25n. Type **195** . . . . . 1·50 1·50
1675 25n. Young child (detail from "The Duke and Duchess of Osuna with their Children") . . . . . 1·50 1·50
1676 25n. Duke (detail from "The Duke and Duchess of Osuna with their Children") . . . . 1·50 1·50
1677 25n. "Isidoro Maiquez" (Francisco de Goya) . . . 1·50 1·50
1678 25n. "Dona Juana Galarza de Goicoechea" (Francisco de Goya) . . . 1·50 1·50
1679 25n. "Ferdinand VII in an Encampment" (Francisco de Goya) . . . . . . 1·50 1·50
1680 25n. "Portrait of an Old Man" (Joos van Cleve) 1·50 1·50
1681 25n. "Mary Tudor" (Anthonis Mor) . . . . . 1·50 1·50
1682 25n. "Portrait of a Man" (Jan van Scorel) . . . . . 1·50 1·50
1683 25n. "The Court Jester Pejeron" (Anthonis Mor) 1·50 1·50
1684 25n. "Elizabeth of France" (Frans Pourbus the Younger) . . . . 1·50 1·50
1685 25n. "King James I" (Paul van Somer) . . . . . . 1·50 1·50
1686 25n. "The Empress Isabella of Portugal" (Titian) . . . 1·50 1·50
1687 25n. "Lucrecia di Baccio del Fede, the Painter's Wife" (Andrea del Sarto) . . . 1·50 1·50
1688 25n. "Self-Portrait" (Titian) 1·50 1·50
1689 25n. "Philip II" (Sofonisba Anguisciola) . . . . . . 1·50 1·50
1690 25n. "Portrait of a Doctor" (Lucia Anguisciola) . . . 1·50 1·50
1691 25n. "Anna of Austria" (Sofonisba Anguisciola) 1·50 1·50
MS1692 Three sheets (a) 90 × 110 mm. 100n. Duchess and Duke (detail from "The Duke and Duchess of Osuna with their Children" (Francisco de Goya) (horiz); (b) 90 × 110 mm. 100n. "Charles V at Mühlberg" (Titian); (c) 110 × 90 mm. 100n. "The Relief of Genoa" (Antonio de Pereda)
Set of 3 sheets . . . . 13·50 13·50

196 Butterfly

197 Snake

2000. "Indepex Asiana 2000" International Stamp Exhibition, Calcutta. Multicoloured.
1693 5n. Type **196** 15 15
1694 8n. Red jungle fowl 40 40
1695 10n. *Zinnia elegans* 50 50
1696 12n. Tiger 60 60
MS1697 144 × 84 mm. 15n. Spotted deer (28 × 34 mm) 65 65

2001. New Year. Year of the Snake. Multicoloured.
1698 3n. Type **197** 15 15
1699 20n. Snake . . . . 1·10 1·10
MS1700 135 × 135 mm. 3, 10n. As Type **197**; 15, 20n. As No. 1699 2·00 2·00

198 Snow Leopard (*Uncia uncia*)

2001. "Hong Kong 2001" International Stamp Exhibition. Nature Protection. Sheet 195 × 138 mm containing T **198** and similar horiz designs. Multicoloured.
MS1701 15n. Type **198**; 15n. Rufous-necked hornbill (*Aceros nipalensis*); 15n. Black-necked crane (*Grus nigricollis*); 15n. Tiger (*Panthera tigris*) . . . . 2·75 2·75

199 Working in Fields

2001. International Year of Volunteers. Mult.
1702 3n. Type **199** 15 15
1703 4n. Planting crops 25 25
1704 10n. Children and bucket . . 50 50
1705 15n. Planting seeds and making compost 75 75
MS1706 170 × 120 mm. Nos. 1702/5 1·30 1·30

200 Chenrezig

2001. Buddhist Art, Taksang Monastery. Sheet 120 × 147 mm containing T **200** and similar vert designs. Multicoloured.
MS1707 10n. Type **200**; 15n. Guru Rimpoche; 20n. Sakyamuni . . 2·10 2·10

2001. Nos. 557/60 surch.

1708	4n. on 10ch. blue	40	40
1709	10n. on 25ch. red	50	50
1710	15n. on 50ch. violet	70	70
1711	20n. on 1n. brown	95	95

202 Snow Leopard's Head

203 Horse carrying Treasure Vase (Buddhist symbol)

2001. Snow Leopard (Uncia uncial). Sheet 172 × 140 mm containing T **202** and similar multicoloured design.
MS1712 10n. × 4, each × 2, Type **202**; Two adults; Three juveniles; Crouched adult . . . 4·00 4·00

2002. Year of the Horse. Multicoloured.

1713	20n. Type **203**	1·00	1·00
1714	20n. White horse	1·00	1·00
MS1715	94 × 94 mm. 25n. Horse and Dharma Wheel (horiz)	1·20	1·20

Nos. 1713/14 were issued together, se-tenant forming a composite design.

204 Teri gang

2002. International Year of Mountains. Sheet 144 × 105 mm containing T **204** and similar horiz designs. Multicoloured.
MS1716 20n. Type **204**; 20n. Tsenda gang; 20n. Jomolhari; 20n. Gangeheytag; 20n. Jitchudrake; 20n. Tse-rim Gang . . . . . . 5·75 5·75

205 *Rhomboda lanceolata*

2002. Orchids. Sheet 162 × 131 mm containing T **205** and similar vert designs. Multicoloured.
MS1717 10n. Type **205**; 10n. *Odontochilus lanceolatus*; 10n. *Zeuxine glandulosai*; 10n. *Goodyera schlechtendaliana*; 10n. *Anoectochilus lanceolatus*; 10n. *Goodyera hispida* . . . . . . 3·00 3·00

206 *Rhododendron niveum*

2002. Rhododendrons. Sheet 132 × 132 mm containing T **206** and similar square designs. Multicoloured.
MS1718 15n. Type **206**; 15n. *Rhododendron glaucophyllum*; 15n. *Rhododendron arboretum*; 15n. *Rhododendron grande*; 15n. *Rhododendron dalhousiae*; 15n. *Rhododendron barbatum* . . . 4·00 4·00

207 Kapok Tree (*Bombax ceiba*)

208 Fireman and Flags

2002. Medicinal Plants. Multicoloured.

1719	10n. Type **207**	25	25
1720	10n. Angel's trumpet (*Brugmansia suaveolens*)	25	25
1721	10n. Himalayan mayapple (*Podophyllum hexandrum*)	25	25
1722	10n. Himalayan pokeberry (*Photlacca acinosa*) . . .	25	25
MS1723	85 × 106 mm. 10n. × 4, Nos. 1719/22	1·20	1·20

2002. "United We Stand".

1724	**208** 25n. multicoloured . . .	60	60

209 Zinedine Zidane

210 Queen Elizabeth

2002. World Cup Football Championships, Japan and South Korea. Two sheets containing T **209** and similar vert designs. Multicoloured.
MS1725 (a) 167 × 118 mm. 25n. Type **209**; 25n. Michael Owen; 25n. Miyagi stadium, Japan; 25n. Cuauhtemoc Blanco (inscr "Cuahutemoc"); 25n. Gabriel Batistuta; 25n. Incheon stadium, South Korea; (b) 97 × 112 mm. 150n. Roberto Carlos . . . . 7·00 7·00

2002. Golden Jubilee of Queen Elizabeth II. Two sheets containing T **210** and similar square designs. Multicoloured.
MS1726 (a) 133 × 101 mm. 40n. Type **210**; 40n. Wearing green floral hat; 40n. With Duke of Edinburgh; 40n. Wearing white hat; (b) 79 × 108 mm. 90n. Wearing tiara . . . . 6·00 6·00

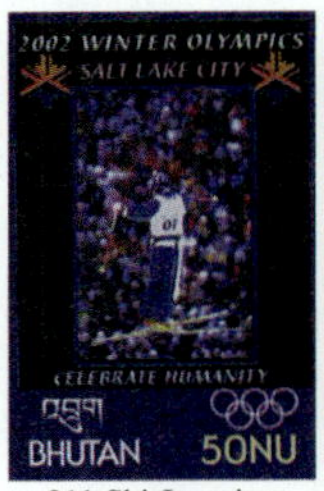

211 Ski Jumping

212 Lotus Flower

2002. Winter Olympic Games, Salt Lake City, USA. Sheet 89 × 120 mm containing T **211** and similar vert design. Multicoloured.
MS1727 50n. Type **211**; 50n. Cross country skiing . . . . 2·40 2·40

2002. United Nations Year of Eco-Tourism. Two sheets containing T **212** and similar vert designs. Multicoloured.
MS1728 (a) 117 × 75 mm. 50n. Type **212**; 50n. Northern jungle queen butterfly; 50n. Bengal tiger; (b) 72 × 95 mm. 90n. Peacock 5·75 5·75

213 Cub Scout

2002. World Scout Jamboree, Thailand. Two sheets containing T **213** and similar multicoloured designs.
MS1729 (a) 182 × 142 mm. 50n. Type **213**; 50n. Scouts of different nationalities; 50n. 1908 Scout; (b) 90 × 120 mm. 90n. Dan Beard (founder of American Boy Scouts) (vert) . . . . 5·75 5·75

214 Charles Lindbergh and *The Spirit of St Louis*

2002. 75th Anniv of First Solo Trans-Atlantic Flight. Two sheets containing T **214** and similar vert designs. Multicoloured.
MS1730 (a) 171 × 134 mm. 75n. Type **214**; 75n. Lindbergh; (b) 123 × 89 mm. 90n. Lindbergh (different) . . . . 5·75 5·75

215 Guar

2002. Flora and Fauna. Twelve sheets containing T **215** and similar horiz designs. Multicoloured.
MS1731 (a) 132 × 155 mm. 25n. Type **215**; 25n. Hog badger; 25n. Indian cobra; 25n. Leopard gecko; 25n. Gavial; 25n. Hispid hare; (b) 132 × 155 mm. 25n. Yellow-legged gull; 25n. Sand martin; 25n. Asian open-bill stork; 25n. White stork; 25n. Eurasian oystercatcher; 25n. Indian pitta; (c) 132 × 155 mm. 25n. Blue oak-leaf butterfly (inscr "Dead leaf butterfly") (Kalima horsfieldi); 25n. Golden birdwing (*Troides aeacus*); 25n. *Atrophaneura latrellei*; 25n. Kaiser-I-Hind (*Teinopalpus imperialis*); 25n. *Zeuxidia aurelius*; 25n. *Euploea dufresne*; (d) 137 × 158 mm. 25n. *Primula cawdoriana*; 25n. *Meconopsis aculeate*; 25n. *Primula wigramiana*; 25n. *Primula stuartii*; 25n. *Saxifraga andersonii*; 25n. *Rheum nobile*; (e) 133 × 153 mm. 25n. *Russula integra*; 25n. *Hydgrophorus marzuolus*; 25n. *Trichloma fulvum*; 25n. *Hypholoma fasciculare*; 25n. *Tricholoma populinum*; 25n. *Cortinarius orellanus*; (f) 136 × 161 mm. 25n. *Coelogyne rhodeana*; 25n. *Coelogyne virescens*; 25n. *Phalanopsis schilleriana*; 25n. *Angraecum eburneum*; 25n. *Dendrobium aureum*; 25n. *Dendrobium Ceasar*; (g) 89 × 92 mm. 90n. Esturine crocodile; (h) 89 × 94 mm. 90n. Mandarin duck; (i) 93 × 94 mm. 90n. *Portia philota*; (j) 103 × 101 mm. 90n. *Paris polyphylla*; (k) 101 × 101 mm. 90n. *Clathrus archeri*; (l) 99 × 100 mm. 90n. *Dendrobium chrysotoxum* 35·00 35·00

216 Elvis Presley

2003. Anniversaries in 2002. 25th Death Anniv of Elvis Presley (entertainer) (**MS**1732a/b). 85th Birth Anniv of John Fitzgerald Kennedy (president USA, 1961–1963) (**MS**1732c/d). 5th Death Anniv of Diana, Princess of Wales (**MS**1732e/f). Six sheets containing T **216** and similar vert designs. Multicoloured.
MS1732 Six sheets (a) 110 × 178 mm. 25n. × 4, Type **216**; Holding guitar at waist; Singing into microphone; Seated holding guitar to side; (b) 195 × 131 mm. 25n. × 6, Wearing shirt and kerchief; (c) 132 × 146 mm. 25n. × 6, College graduate, 1935; Walking with John F. Kennedy Jr.; As Congressman, 1946; At the White House, 1961; With Jacqueline Kennedy on tennis court; Jacqueline Kennedy and children at John F. Kennedy's funeral; (d) 76 × 108 mm. 90n. Head and shoulders; (e) 134 × 118 mm. 25n. × 4, Wearing earrings and red dress; Wearing ball-gown; Wearing jacket and blouse; Wearing tiara; (f) 65 × 98 mm. 90n. Wearing hat with feathers . . . 17·00 17·00

2003. No. 659 surch **8NU**.

1733	8n. on 75ch. multicoloured	20	20

218 Lamb

2003. Chinese New Year. ("Year of the Sheep"). Sheet 120 × 80 mm containing T **218** and similar multicoloured design.
MS1734 15n. Type **218**; 20n. Sheep's head (vert) 80 80

219 "Egret and Willow" (Suzuki Kitsu)

220 Lyonpo Sangay Ngedup

2003. Japanese Paintings. Six sheets containing T **219** and similar multicoloured designs.
MS1735 (a) 135 × 210 mm. 25n. × 6, Type **219**; "White Cranes" (Ito Jakuchu); "Cranes" (Suzuki Kitsu); "Mandarin Ducks amid Snow-covered Reeds" (Ito Jakuchu); "Rooster, Hen and Hydrangea" (Ito Jakuchu); "Hawk on Snow-covered Branch" (Shibara Zeshin); (b) 135 × 210 mm. 25n. × 6, "Beauty reading Letter" (Utagawa Kunisada); "Two Beauties" (Katsukawa Shunsho); "Beauty arranging her Hair" (Kaigetsudo Doshin); "Dancing" (Suzuki Kitsu); "Two Beauties" (Kitagawa Kikumaro); "Kambun Beauty"; (c) 159 × 140 mm. 25n. × 6, Two seated men and one lying down (38 × 51 mm); Man holding fan, man holding lute and man facing left (38 × 51 mm); Man with raised arm and woman facing left (38 × 51 mm); Two men talking and two facing left (38 × 51 mm); Man wearing blue robe facing right and bald man (38 × 51 mm); Man with beard and two women (38 × 51 mm); (d) 90 × 90 mm. 90n. "Heads of Nine Beauties in a Roundel with Plum Blossom" (Hosoda Eishi); (e) 90 × 90 mm. "Hawk carrying Monkey" (Shibata Zeshin); (f) 92 × 92 mm. "Chrysanthemums by a Stream, with Rocks" (Ito Jakuchu) . . 17·00 17·00
The stamps of No. **MS**1735c form a composite design of "Thirty six Poets".

2003. Move for Health Walk (walk by Lyonpo Sangay Ngedup (Health Minister) from Trashigang to Thimphu). Sheet 120 × 80 mm.

MS1736	**220** 50n. multicoloured	1·20	1·20

221 Girl and Parrot

222 Kalij Pheasant (*Lophura leucomelana*) (inscr "leucomelanus")

2003. Education for All. Sheet 70 × 109 mm containing T **221** and similar vert designs. Multicoloured.
MS1737 5n. Type **221**; 5n. Girl reading; 10n. Boy and girl carrying books; 20n. Girl holding football 1·00 1·00

2003. Endangered Species. Birds. Sheet 69 × 100 mm containing T **222** and similar vert designs. Multicoloured.
MS1738 2n. Type **222**; 5n. Blyth's tragopan (*Tragopan blythii*); 8n. Satyr tragopan (*Tragopan satyra*); 15n. Himalayan monal pheasant (*Lophophorus impeyanus*) (inscr "impejanus") 70 70

223 Monkey

2004. New Year. Year of the Monkey. Sheet 95 × 130 mm containing T **223** and similar vert designs. Multicoloured.
MS1739 10n. × 4, Type **223**; Facing left; With raised back legs; Family 1·00 1·00
The stamps and margin of No. **MS**1739 were issued together, se-tenant, forming a composite design.

224 Brazil World Cup Champions Team, 2002

2004. Centenary of FIFA (Federation Internationale de Football Association). Multicoloured.

1740	10n. Type **224**	25	25
1741	10n. France World Cup Champions team, 1998	25	25

2004. No. 421 surch **5n**.

1742	5n. on 1n. multicoloured	15	15

226 Traditional Ploughing

2004. 20th Anniv of Continuing Japanese Assistance with Food Production. Two sheets containing T **226** and similar multicoloured designs.
MS1743 (a) 155 × 105 mm. 5n. × 6, Type **225**; Women transplanting; Traditional threshing; Modern ploughing; Modern transplanting; Modern threshing. (b) 130 × 85 mm. 30n. King Jigme Singe Wangchuk ploughing 1·50 1·50
The stamps and margin of No. **MS**1743a were issued together, se-tenant, forming a composite design.

227 Jungle Fowl

2005. New Year. "Year of the Rooster". Sheet 155 × 110 mm containing T **227** and similar horiz design. Multicoloured.
MS1744 15n. Type **227**; 20n. Domestic fowl 85 85

228 Dancer

2005. EXPO 2005 World Exposition, Aichi, Japan. Two sheets containing T **228** and similar vert designs. Multicoloured.
MS1745 126 × 201 mm. 10n. Type **228**; 10n. Dancer wearing skull mask; 20n. Dancer holding drum; 20n. Dancer wearing horned mask 1·50 1·50
MS1746 124 × 80 mm. 30n. Buddha (25 × 35 mm) 75 75

229 Pope John Paul II

2005. Pope John Paul II Commemoration. Multicoloured.

1747	15n. Type **229**	40	40
1747a	15n. As No. 1747	40	40
1747b	15n. As No. 1747	40	40
1747c	15n. As No. 1747	40	40

230 Locomotive P36 N 0097

2005. Bicentenary of Steam Locomotives (2004). Multicoloured.

1748/51	30n. × 4, Type **230**; Diesel locomotive VIA F 40 6428; InterRegio electric train, Amtrak 464	3·00	3·00
MS1752	100 × 71 mm. 85n. Locomotive P36N0032 (vert)	2·00	2·00

231 Guido Buchwald

2005. 75th Anniv of World Cup Football Championships. Multicoloured.

1753/5	40n. × 3, Type **231**; Mario Basler; Torsten Frings	3·00	3·00
MS1756	124 × 105 mm. 85n. Fredi Bobic	2·00	2·00

232 Linked Hands and Emblem

2005. Centenary of Rotary International. Sheet 95 × 113 mm.
MS1757 **232** 85n. multicoloured 2·00 2·00

232a Wachy Zam, Wangduephodrang

2005. Bridges. Sheet 200 × 160 mm containing T **232a** and similar horiz designs. Multicoloured.
MS1758 10n. Type **232a**; 10n. Chain bridge, Doksam; 10n. Wooden cantilevered bridge, Mishi, Paro; 20n. Mo Chu bridge, Punakha; 20n. Langjo bridge, Thimphu; 20n. Punatshang Chu bridge, Wangduephodrang 2·20 2·20

233 Children from Many Nations

2005. "My Dream of Peace One Day". Winning Designs in Children's Painting Competition. Multicoloured.

1759/64	10n. × 6, Type **233**; Candle of flags; Children holding jigsaw of family; Dove and light and dark hands holding globe; Hands holding children and dark globe releasing doves; Globe holding umbrella of flags	1·50	1·50

234 King Jigme Singye Wangchuck

2005. 50th Birth Anniv of King Jigme Singye Wangchuck. Sheet 216 × 163 mm containing T **234** and similar vert designs. Multicoloured.
MS1765 20n. × 5 Type **234**; Standing on podium (inauguration) (39 × 87 mm); Speaking with microphone; Seated on throne; With women 2·60 2·60
The stamps of **MS**1765 share a composite background design.

234a Raven

2005. National Symbols. Sheet 200 × 160 mm containing T **234a** and similar square designs. Multicoloured.
MS1766 10n. Type **234a**; 10n. Takin (*Budorcas taxicolor*); 20n. Cypress tree; 20n. Blue poppy 1·30 1·30

235 St. Bernard

2006. New Year. Year of the Dog. Multicoloured.

1767	5n. Type **235**	15	15
1768	10n. Lhasa Apso (Inscr 'Apsoo')	25	25
1769	15n. Maltese terrier (inscr 'Maltese')	40	40
1770	20n. Papillion (inscr 'Papillon')	50	50
MS1771	125 × 105 mm. 5n. As No. 1767; 10n. As No. 1768; 15n. As No. 1769; 20n. As No. 1770; 25n. Husky (36 × 70 mm)	1·90	1·90

236 Jakur Dzong

2006. 50th Anniv of Europa Stamps. Multicoloured.

1772	150n. Type **236**	3·75	
1773	250n. Archery	6·25	
MS1774	100 × 72 mm. Nos. 1772/3	10·00	10·00

APPENDIX

The following stamps have either been issued in excess of postal needs or have not been available to the public in reasonable quantities at face value. Such stamps may later be given full listing if there is evidence of regular postal use.

1968.

Bhutan Pheasants. 1, 2, 4, 8, 15ch., 2, 4, 5, 7, 9n.

Winter Olympic Games, Grenoble. Optd on 1966 Abominable Snowmen issue. 40ch., 1n.25, 3, 6n.

Butterflies (plastic-surfaced). Postage 15, 50ch., 1n.25, 2n.; Air 3, 4, 5, 6n.

Paintings (relief-printed). Postage 2, 4, 5, 10, 45, 80ch., 1n.05, 1n.40, 2, 3, 4, 5n.; Air 1n.50, 2n.50, 6, 8n.

Olympic Games, Mexico. 5, 45, 60, 80ch., 1n.05, 2, 3, 5n.

Human Rights Year. Die-stamped surch on unissued "Coins". 15ch. on 50n.p., 33ch. on 1r., 9n. on 3r.75.

1969.

Flood Relief. Surch on 1968 Mexico Olympics issue. 5ch.+5ch., 80ch.+25ch., 2n.+50ch.

Fish (plastic-surfaced). Postage 15, 20, 30ch.; Air 5, 6, 7n.

Insects (plastic-surfaced). Postage 10, 75ch., 1n.25, 2n.; Air 3, 4, 5, 6n.

Admission of Bhutan to Universal Postal Union. 5, 10, 15, 45, 60ch., 1n.05, 1n.40, 4n.

5000 Years of Steel Industry. On steel foil. Postage 2, 5, 15, 45, 75ch., 1n.50, 1n.75, 2n.; Air 3, 4, 5, 6n.

Birds (plastic-surfaced). Postage 15, 50ch., 1n.25, 2n.; Air 3, 4, 5, 6n.

Buddhist Prayer Banners. On silk rayon. 15, 75ch., 2, 5, 6n.

Moon Landing of "Apollo 11" (plastic-surfaced). Postage 3, 5, 15, 20, 25, 45, 50ch., 1n.75; Air 3, 4, 5, 6n.

1970.

Famous Paintings (plastic-surfaced). Postage 5, 10, 15ch., 2n.75; Air 3, 4, 5, 6n.

New U.P.U. Headquarters Building, Berne. 3, 10, 20ch., 2n.50.

Flower Paintings (relief-printed). Postage 2, 3, 5, 10, 15, 75ch., 1n., 1n.40; Air 80, 90ch., 1n.10, 1n.40, 1n.60, 1n.70, 3n., 3n.50.

Animals (plastic-surfaced). Postage 5, 10, 20, 25, 30, 40, 65, 75, 85ch.; Air 2, 3, 4, 5n.

Conquest of Space (plastic-surfaced). Postage 2, 5, 15, 25, 30, 50, 75ch., 1n.50; Air 2, 3, 6, 7n.

1971.

History of Sculpture (plastic-moulded). Postage 10, 75ch., 1n.25, 2n.; Air 3, 4, 5, 6n.

Moon Vehicles (plastic-surfaced). Postage 10ch., 1n.70; Air 2n.50, 4n.

History of the Motor Car (plastic-surfaced). Postage 2, 5, 10, 15, 20, 30, 60, 75, 85ch., 1n., 1n.20, 1n.55, 1n.80, 2n., 2n.50; Air 4, 6, 7, 9, 10n.

Bhutan's Admission to United Nations. Postage 5, 10, 20ch., 3n.; Air 2n.50, 5, 6n.

60th Anniv of Boy Scout Movement. 10, 20, 50, 75ch., 2, 6n.

World Refugee Year. Optd on 1971 United Nations issue. Postage 5, 10, 20ch., 3n.; Air 2n.50, 5, 6n.

1972.

Famous Paintings (relief-printed). Postage 15, 20, 90ch., 2n.50; Air 1n.70, 4n.60, 5n.40, 6n.

Famous Men (plastic-moulded). Postage 10, 15, 55ch.; Air 2, 6, 8n.

Olympic Games, Munich. Postage 10, 15, 20, 30, 45ch.; Air 35ch., 1n.35, 7n.

Space Flight of "Apollo 16" (plastic-surfaced). Postage 15, 20, 90ch., 2n.50; Air 1n.70, 4n.60, 5n.40, 6n.

1973.

Dogs. 2, 3, 15, 20, 30, 99ch., 2n.50, 4n.

Roses (on scent-impregnated paper). Postage 15, 25, 30ch., 3n.; Air 6, 7n.

Moon Landing of "Apollo 17" (plastic-surfaced). Postage 10, 15, 55ch. 2n.; Air 7, 9n.

"Talking Stamps" (miniature records). Postage 10, 25ch., 1n.25, 7, 8n.; Air 3, 9n.

Death of King Jigme Dorji Wangchuck. Embossed on gold foil. Postage 10, 25ch., 3n.; Air 6, 8n.

Mushrooms. 15, 25, 30ch., 3, 6, 7n.

"Indipex 73" Stamp Exhibition, New Delhi. Postage 5, 10, 15, 25ch., 1n.25, 3n.; Air 5, 6n.

BIAFRA Pt. 1

The Eastern Region of Nigeria declared its Independence on 30 May 1967 as the Republic of Biafra. Nigerian military operations against the breakaway Republic commenced in July 1967.

The Biafran postal service continued to use Nigerian stamps when supplies of these became low. In July 1967 "Postage Paid" cachets were used pending the issue of Nos. 1/3.

12 pence = 1 shilling;
20 shillings = 1 pound.

1 Map of Republic

5 Flag and Scientist

1968. Independence. Multicoloured.

1		2d. Type **1**	10	65
2		4d. Arms, flag and date of Independence	10	65
3		1s. Mother and child (17×22 mm)	15	1·75

1968. Nos. 172/5 and 177/85 of Nigeria optd **SOVEREIGN BIAFRA** and arms.

4		½d. multicoloured (No. 172)	1·50	4·75
5		1d. multicoloured (No. 173)	2·25	7·50
6		1½d. multicoloured (No. 174)	10·00	15·00
7		2d. multicoloured (No. 175)	27·00	50·00
8		4d. multicoloured (No. 177)	17·00	50·00
9		6d. multicoloured (No. 178)	9·00	14·00
10		9d. blue and red (No. 179)	3·00	3·50
11		1s. multicoloured (No. 180)	60·00	£110
12		1s.3d. multicoloured (No. 181)	35·00	50·00
13		2s.6d. multicoloured (No. 182)	2·50	15·00
14		5s. multicoloured (No. 183)	2·50	14·00
15		10s. multicoloured (No. 184)	10·00	38·00
16		£1 multicoloured (No. 185)	10·00	38·00

The overprint on No. 15 does not include **SOVEREIGN**.

1968. 1st Anniv of Independence. Multicoloured.

17		4d. Type **5**	20	10
18		1s. Victim of atrocity	20	20
19		2s.6d. Nurse and refugees	55	3·25
20		5s. Biafran arms and banknote	60	3·75
21		10s. Orphaned child	1·00	4·25

16 Child in Chains, and Globe

17 Pope Paul VI, Africa, and Papal Arms

1969. 2nd Anniv of Independence. Multicoloured; frame colours given.

35	**16**	2d. orange	1·25	4·25
36		4d. red	1·25	4·25
37		1s. blue	1·75	7·00
38		2s.6d. green	2·00	14·00

1969. Visit of Pope Paul to Africa. Multicoloured; background colours given.

39	**17**	4d. orange	40	3·00
40	–	6d. blue	55	6·50
41	–	9d. green	75	8·50
42	–	3s. mauve	2·25	14·00

DESIGNS: Pope Paul VI, map of Africa and 6d. Arms of Vatican; 9d. St. Peter's Basilica; 3s. Statue of St. Peter.

BIJAWAR Pt. 1

A state of Central India. Now uses Indian stamps.

12 pies = 1 anna; 16 annas = 1 rupee.

1 Maharaja Sarwant Singh

2 Maharaja Sarwant Singh

1935.

6	**1**	3p. brown	6·00	6·00
2		6p. red	6·50	5·50
3		9p. violet	8·50	5·00
4		1a. blue	9·50	5·50
5		2a. green	9·00	5·00

1937.

11	**2**	4a. orange	15·00	80·00
12		6a. lemon	15·00	80·00
13		8a. green	16·00	£110
14		12a. blue	16·00	£110
15		1r. violet	42·00	£170

BOHEMIA AND MORAVIA Pt. 5

Following the proclamation of Slovak Independence on 14 March, 1939, the Czech provinces of Bohemia and Moravia became a German Protectorate. The area was liberated in 1945 and returned to Czechoslovakia.

100 haleru = 1 koruna.

1939. Stamps of Czechoslovakia optd **BOHMEN u. MAHREN CECHY a MORAVA.**

1	**34**	5h. blue	25	1·30
2		10h. brown	25	1·30
3		20h. red	25	1·30
4		25h. green	25	1·30
5		30h. purple	25	1·30
6	**59**	40h. blue	2·75	5·00
7	**77**	50h. green	25	1·30
8	**60a**	60h. violet	2·75	5·00
9	**61**	1k. purple (No. 348)	80	1·70
10		1k. purple (No. 395)	30	1·30
11	–	1k.20 purple (No. 354)	3·75	5·00
12	**64**	1k.50 red	2·75	6·00
13	–	1k.60 green (No. 355a)	2·75	6·00
14	–	2k. green (No. 356)	1·60	4·25
15	–	2k.50 blue (No. 357)	3·75	5·00
16	–	3k. brown (No. 358)	3·75	6·00
17	**65**	4k. violet	4·25	6·75
18	–	5k. green (No. 361)	4·75	10·00
19	–	10k. blue (No. 362)	6·50	15·00

2 Linden Leaves and Buds

3 Karluv Tyn Castle

5 Zlin

1939.

20	**2**	5h. blue	10	35
21		10h. brown	10	40
22		20h. red	10	35
23		25h. green	10	35
24		30h. purple	10	35
25	–	40h. blue	10	35
26	**3**	50h. green	10	35
27	–	60h. violet	10	35
28	–	1k. red	10	35
29	–	1k.20 purple	30	60
30	–	1k.50 red	10	35
31	–	2k. green	10	50
32	–	2k.50 blue	10	35
33	**5**	3k. mauve	10	35
34	–	4k. grey	10	35
35	–	5k. green	30	85
36	–	10k. blue	25	1·00
37	–	20k. brown	80	2·10

DESIGNS—As Type **3**: 40h. Svikov Castle; 60h. St. Barbara's Church, Kutna Hora; 1k. St. Vitus's Cathedral, Prague. As Type **5**—VERT: 1k.20, 1k.50, Brno Cathedral; 2k., 2k.50, Olomouc. HORIZ: 4k. Ironworks, Moravska-Ostrava; 5k., 10k., 20k. Karlsburg, Prague.

1940. As 1939 issue, but colours changed and new values.

38	**2**	30h. brown	10	35
39		40h. orange	10	15
40		50h. green	10	15
44	–	50h. green	15	15
41	**2**	60h. violet	10	35
42		80h. orange	20	25
45	–	80h. blue	15	35
43	**2**	1k. brown	20	25
46	–	1k.20 brown	35	25
47	–	1k.20 red	25	25
48	–	1k.50 pink	25	35
49	–	2k. green	15	15
50	–	2k. blue	25	35
51	–	2k.50 blue	15	15
52	–	3k. green	15	15
53	–	5k. green	20	15
54	–	6k. brown	20	50
55	–	8k. green	20	25
56	–	10k. blue	45	25
57	–	20k. brown	90	1·70

DESIGNS—As Type **3**: 50h. (No. 44), Neuhaus Castle; 80h. (No. 45), 3k. Pernstyn Castle; 1k.20 (No. 46), 2k.50, Brno Cathedral; 1k.20 (No. 47), St. Vitus's Cathedral, Prague; 1k.50 St. Barbara's Church, Kutna Hora; 2k. Pardubitz Castle. As Type **5**—HORIZ: 5k. Bridge at Beching; 6k. Samson Fountain, Budweis; 8k. Kremsier; 10k. Wallenstein Palace, Prague; 20k. Karlsburg, Prague.

6 Red Cross Nurse and Wounded Soldier

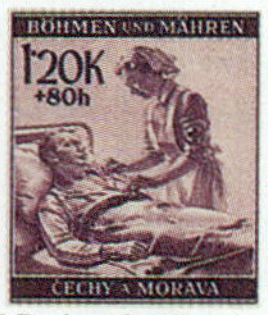

7 Patient in Hospital

1940. Red Cross Relief Fund.

58	**6**	60h.+40h. blue	60	1·20
59		1k.20+80h. plum	60	1·30

1941. Red Cross Relief Fund.

60	**7**	60h.+40h. blue	20	40
61		1k.20+80h. plum	20	40

8 Anton Dvorak

9 Harvesting

10 Blast furnace, Pilsen

1941. Birth Centenary of Dvorak (composer).

62	**8**	60h. violet	20	50
63		1k.20 brown	20	50

1941. Prague Fair.

64	**9**	30h. brown	15	35
65		60h. green	15	35
66	**10**	1k.20 plum	15	35
67		2k.50 blue	15	70

11 "Ständetheater", Prague

12 Mozart

1941. 150th Death Anniv of Mozart.

68	**11**	30h.+30h. brown	15	15
69		60h.+60h. green	15	15
70	**12**	1k.20+1k.20 red	15	25
71		2k.50+2k.50 blue	20	50

(13)

1942. 3rd Anniv of German Occupation. Optd with T **13**.

72		1k.20 red (No. 47)	35	70
73		2k.50 blue (No. 51)	40	1·00

14 Adolf Hitler

15 Adolf Hitler

1942. Hitler's 53rd Birthday.

74	**14**	30h.+20h. brown	15	15
75		60h.+40h. green	15	15
76		1k.20+80h. purple	15	15
77		2k.50+1k.50 blue	25	40

1942. Various sizes.

78	**15**	10h. black	15	25
79		30h. brown	15	25
80		40h. blue	15	25
81		50h. green	15	25
82		60h. violet	15	25
83		80h. orange	15	25
84		1k. brown	15	25
85		1k.20 red	15	35
86		1k.50 red	15	35
87		1k.60 green	15	35
88		2k. blue	15	35
89		2k.40 brown	15	35
90		2k.50 blue	15	35
91		3k. olive	15	35
92		4k. purple	15	35
93		5k. green	15	35
94		6k. brown	15	40
95		8k. blue	15	40
96		10k. green	25	85
97		20k. violet	45	85
98		30k. red	70	2·00
99		50k. blue	1·40	1·70

SIZES—17½×21½ mm: 10h. to 80h.; 18½×21 mm: 1k. to 2k.40; 19×24 mm: 2k.50 to 8k.; 24×30 mm: 10k. to 50k.

16 Nurse and Patient

17 Mounted Postman

1942. Red Cross Relief Fund.

100	**16**	60h.+40h. blue	15	25
101		1k.20+80h. red	15	25

1943. Stamp Day.

102	**17**	60h. purple	25	40

18 Peter Parler

19 Adolf Hitler

1943. Winter Relief Fund.

103	–	60h.+40h. violet	15	15
104	**18**	1k.20+80h. red	15	15
105	–	2k.50+1k.50 blue	15	15

DESIGNS: 60h. Charles IV; 2k.50, King John of Luxembourg.

1943. Hitler's 54th Birthday.

106	**19**	60h.+1k.40 violet	15	35
107		1k.20+3k.80 red	15	35

20 Scene from "The Mastersingers of Nuremberg"

21 Richard Wagner

1943. 130th Birth Anniv of Wagner.

108	**20**	60h. violet	10	15
109	**21**	1k.20 red	10	15
110	–	2k.50 blue	10	15

DESIGN: 2k.50, Blacksmith scene from "Siegfried".

22 Reinhard Heydrich

23 Arms of Bohemia and Moravia and Red Cross

1943. 1st Death Anniv of Reinhard Heydrich (German Governor).

111	**22**	60h.+4k.40 black	40	1·70

1943. Red Cross Relief Fund.

112	**23**	1k.20+8k.80 blk & red	30	50

24 National Costumes

25 Arms of Bohemia and Moravia

1944. 5th Anniv of German Occupation.

113	**24**	1k.20+3k.80 red	15	15
114	**25**	4k.20+18k.80 brown	15	15
115	**24**	10k.+20k. blue	15	25

26 Adolf Hitler

27 Smetana

1944. Hitler's 55th Birthday.

116	**26**	60h.+1k.40 brown	15	25
117		1k.20+3k.80 green	15	25

1944. 60th Death Anniv of Bedrich Smetana (composer).

118	**27**	60h.+1k.40 green	15	25
119		1k.20+3k.80 red	15	25

28 St. Vitus's Cathedral, Prague

29 Adolf Hitler

1944.

120	**28**	1k.50 purple	15	25
121		2k.50 violet	15	35

1944.

122	**29**	4k.20 green	30	50

NEWSPAPER STAMPS

N **6** Dove

N **19** Dove

1939. Imperf.

N38	N **6**	2h. brown	10	35
N39		5h. blue	10	35
N40		7h. red	10	35
N41		9h. green	10	35
N42		10h. red	10	35
N43		12h. blue	10	35
N44		20h. green	10	35
N45		50h. brown	10	40
N46		1k. green	25	85

1940. For bulk postings. No. N42 optd **GD-OT**.

N60	N **6**	10h. red	25	70

1943. Imperf.

N106	N **19**	2h. brown	10	15
N107		5h. blue	10	15
N108		7h. red	10	15
N109		9h. green	10	15
N110		10h. red	10	15
N111		12h. blue	10	15
N112		20h. green	10	15
N113		50h. brown	10	15
N114		1k. green	10	15

OFFICIAL STAMPS

O **7** Numeral and Laurel Wreath

O **19** Eagle and Numeral

1941.

O60	O **7**	30h. brown	15	15
O61		40h. blue	15	15
O62		50h. green	15	15
O63		60h. green	15	15
O64		80h. red	55	15
O65		1k. brown	25	15
O66		1k.20 red	25	15
O67		1k.50 purple	40	15
O68		2k. blue	40	15
O69		3k. green	40	15
O70		4k. purple	55	50
O71		5k. yellow	1·30	1·00

1943.

O106	O **19**	30h. brown	10	35
O107		40h. blue	10	35
O108		50h. green	10	35
O109		60h. violet	10	35
O110		80h. red	10	35
O111		1k. brown	10	35
O112		1k.20 red	10	35
O113		1k.50 brown	10	35
O114		2k. blue	10	35
O115		3k. green	10	35
O116		4k. purple	10	35
O117		5k. green	10	35

PERSONAL DELIVERY STAMPS

P **6**

1939.

P38	P **6**	50h. blue	1·30	2·10
P39		50h. red	1·80	2·50

POSTAGE DUE STAMPS

D **6**

1939.

D38	D **6**	5h. red	20	35
D39		10h. red	20	35
D40		20h. red	20	35
D41		30h. red	20	35
D42		40h. red	20	35
D43		50h. red	20	35
D44		60h. red	20	35
D45		80h. red	20	35
D46		1k. blue	20	40
D47		1k.20 blue	20	40
D48		2k. blue	65	1·30
D49		5k. blue	75	1·70
D50		10k. blue	1·10	2·10
D51		20k. blue	2·20	3·50

BOLIVAR Pt. 20

One of the states of the Granadine Confederation. A department of Colombia from 1886, now uses Colombian stamps.

1863. 100 centavos = 1 peso.

1

2

3

1863. Imperf.

1	**1**	10c. green	£350	£275
2		10c. red	20·00	20·00
3		1p. red	10·00	10·00

1872. Various frames. Imperf.

4	**2**	5c. blue	5·00	5·50
5	**3**	10c. mauve	7·00	7·50
6	–	20c. green	15·00	16·00
7	–	80c. red	38·00	30·00

6

7

8

1874. Imperf.

8	**6**	5c. blue	12·00	7·50
9	**7**	5c. blue	6·00	5·00
10	**8**	10c. mauve	2·00	2·00

9 Simon Bolivar

10 Simon Bolivar

1879. Various frames. Dated "1879". White or blue paper. Perf.

14	**9**	5c. blue	20	20
12		10c. mauve	20	20
13		20c. red	25	20

1880. Various frames. Dated "1880". White or blue paper.

19	**9**	5c. blue	15	15
20		10c. mauve	25	25
21		20c. red	25	25
22		80c. green	2·00	2·00
23		1p. orange	2·75	2·75

1882.

30	**10**	5p. red and blue	1·00	1·00
31		10p. blue and purple	1·00	1·00

11 Simon Bolivar

12 Simon Bolivar

1882. Various frames. Dated "1882".

32	**11**	5c. blue	20	20
33		10c. mauve	20	20
34		20c. red	25	35
35		80c. green	55	55
36		1p. orange	65	60

1883. Various frames. Dated "1883".

37	**11**	5c. blue	15	15
38		10c. mauve	20	20
39		20c. red	20	20
40		80c. green	45	55
41		1p. orange	55	80

1884. Various frames. Dated "1884".

42	**11**	5c. blue	40	40
43		10c. mauve	15	15
44		20c. red	15	15
45		80c. green	20	25
46		1p. orange	45	55

1885. Various frames. Dated "1885".

47	**11**	5c. blue	10	10
48		10c. mauve	10	10
49		20c. red	10	10
50		80c. green	20	25
51		1p. orange	55	35

1891.

56	**12**	1c. black	15	20
57		5c. orange	35	25
58		10c. red	55	55
59		20c. blue	65	65
60		50c. green	95	95
61		1p. violet	95	95

13 Simon Bolivar

1903. Various sizes and portraits. Imperf or perf. On paper of various colours.

63	**13**	50c. green	45	45
64		50c. blue	30	30
65		50c. violet	90	1·00
67	–	1p. red	50	50
68	–	1p. green	70	70
69	–	5p. red	35	35
70b	–	10p. blue	50	50
71	–	10p. violet	2·50	2·50

PORTRAITS: 1p. Fernandez Madrid. 5p. Rodriguez Torices. 10p. Garcia de Toledo.

20 J. M. del Castillo

23

1904. Various portraits. Imperf or perf.

77	**20**	5c. black	15	15
78	–	10c. brown (M. Anguiano)	15	15
80	–	20c. red (P.G. Ribon)	40	40

1904. Figures in various frames. Imperf.

81	**23**	½c. black	30	25
82		1c. blue (horiz)	50	50
83		2c. violet	75	70

ACKNOWLEDGEMENT OF RECEIPT STAMPS

AR 19

AR 27

1903. Imperf. On paper of various colours.

AR75	AR **19**	20c. orange	60	60
AR76		20c. blue	50	50

1904. Imperf.

AR85	AR **27**	2c. red	1·00	1·00

LATE FEE STAMPS

L 18

1903. Imperf. On paper of various colours.

L73	L **18**	20c. red	30	30
L74		20c. violet	30	30

REGISTRATION STAMPS

1879. As T **9** but additionally inscr "CERTIFICADA".

R17	**9**	40c. brown	60	60

1880. As previous issue dated "1880".

R28	**9**	40c. brown	30	35

1882. As T **11**, but additionally inscr "CERTIFICADA". Dated as shown.

R52	**11**	40c. brown ("1882")	25	40
R53		40c. brown ("1883")	40	40
R54		40c. brown ("1884")	15	15
R55		40c. brown ("1885")	35	40

R 17

1903. Imperf. On paper of various colours.

R72	R **17**	20c. orange	50	50

R 26

1904. Imperf.

R84	R **26**	5c. black	2·00	2·00

BOLIVIA Pt. 20

A republic of Central South America.

1867. 100 centavos = 1 boliviano.
1963. 100 centavos = 1 peso boliviano ($b).
1987. 100 centavos = 1 boliviano.

1 Condor

4 (9 Stars)

1867. Imperf.

3a	**1**	5c. green	2·40	3·00
10		5c. mauve	£120	90·00
7		10c. brown	£140	90·00
8		50c. yellow	12·50	19·00
11		50c. blue	£200	£160
9		100c. blue	38·00	48·00
12		100c. green	90·00	85·00

1868. Nine stars below Arms. Perf.

32	**4**	5c. green	11·00	5·50
33		10c. red	16·00	5·50
34		50c. blue	28·00	16·00
35		100c. orange	28·00	17·00
36		500c. black	£300	£225

1871. Eleven stars below Arms. Perf.

37	**4**	5c. green	6·25	4·00
38		10c. red	8·75	6·25
39		50c. blue	23·00	11·00
40		100c. orange	22·00	11·00
41		500c. black	£1100	£1100

7

11

1878. Perf.

42	**7**	5c. blue	5·75	2·50
43		10c. orange	4·75	1·90
44		20c. green	14·00	2·40
45		50c. red	70·00	7·50

1887. Eleven stars below Arms. Roul.

46	**4**	1c. red	1·50	1·40
47		2c. violet	1·50	1·40
48		5c. blue	4·50	2·00
49		10c. orange	4·50	2·00

1890. Nine stars below Arms. Perf.

50	**4**	1c. red	90	50
58		2c. violet	2·75	1·40
52		5c. blue	2·50	50
53		10c. orange	4·00	60
54		20c. green	8·00	1·00
55		50c. red	4·00	1·00
56		100c. yellow	8·00	2·00

1893. Eleven stars below Arms. Perf.

59	**4**	5c. blue	3·75	1·40

1894.

63	**11**	1c. bistre	60	60
64		2c. red	60	60

65 5c. green 60 60
66 10c. brown 60 40
67 20c. blue 2·00 85
68 50c. red 4·75 1·25
69 100c. red 11·00 4·00

12 Frias

13

1897.

77 **12** 1c. green 70 50
78 – 2c. red (Linares) 1·00 90
79 – 5c. green (Murillo) 1·40 40
80 – 10c. purple (Monteagudo) 1·60 40
81 – 20c. black and red (J. Ballivian) 3·00 70
82 – 50c. orange (Sucre) 3·00 1·40
83 – 1b. blue (Bolivar) 3·00 3·50
84 **13** 2b. multicoloured 23·00 30·00

18 Sucre

19 A. Ballivian

24

1899.

92 **18** 1c. blue 1·40 40
93 2c. red 1·00 25
94 5c. green 3·75 85
95 5c. red 1·00 50
96 10c. orange 1·40 70
97 20c. red 1·75 30
98 50c. brown 3·75 1·40
99 1b. lilac 1·00 1·00

1901.

100 **19** 1c. red 35 15
101 – 2c. green (Camacho) 40 25
102 – 5c. red (Campero) 40 25
103 – 10c. blue (J. Ballivian) 1·00 15
104 – 20c. black and purple (Santa Cruz) 45 15
105 **24** 2b. brown 2·40 1·75

25

26 Murillo

1909. Issued in La Paz. Centenary of Revolution of July, 1809. Centres in black.

110 **25** 5c. blue 5·50 3·00
111 **26** 10c. green 5·50 3·00
112 – 20c. orange (Lanza) 5·50 3·00
113 – 2b. red (Montes) 5·50 3·00

37 P. D. Murillo

F 8 Figure of Justice

1909. Centenary of Beginning of War of Independence, 1809–25.

115 – 1c. black and brown 25 15
116 – 2c. black and green 35 25
117 **37** 5c. black and red 35 10
118 – 10c. black and blue 35 10
119 – 20c. black and violet 40 25
120 – 50c. black and bistre 60 35
121 – 1b. black and brown 60 50
122 – 2b. black and brown 1·00 70

PORTRAITS: 1c. M. Betanzos. 2c. I. Warnes. 10c. B. Monteagudo. 20c. E. Arze. 50c. A. J. Sucre. 1b. S. Bolivar. 2b. M. Belgrano.

1910. Centenary of Liberation of Santa Cruz, Potosi and Cochabamba. Portraits as T **37**.

123 5c. black and green 25 10
124 10c. black and red 25 10
125 20c. black and blue 55 35

PORTRAITS: 5c. I. Warnes. 10c. M. Betanzos. 20c. E. Arze.

1911. Nos. 101 and 104 surch **5 Centavos 1911**.

127 5c. on 2c. green 40 20
128 5c. on 20c. black & purple 10·00 10·00

1912. Stamps similar to Type F **8** optd **CORREOS 1912.** or surch also.

130 F **8** 2c. green 40 25
131 5c. orange 35 35
132 10c. red 85 50
129 10c. on 1c. blue 35 15

1913. Portraits as 1901 and new types.

133 **19** 1c. pink 35 25
134 – 2c. red 35 20
135 – 5c. green 40 10
136 – 8c. yellow (Frias) 70 30
137 – 10c. grey 70 25
139 – 50c. purple (Sucre) 95 35
140 – 1b. blue (Bolivar) 1·40 85
141 **24** 2b. black 2·75 1·75

46 Monolith

47 Mt. Potosi

1916. Various sizes.

142 **46** ½c. brown 20 20
143 **47** 1c. green 25 15
144 – 2c. black and red 30 15
145 – 5c. blue 50 10
147 – 10c. blue and orange 85 10

DESIGNS—HORIZ: 2c. Lake Titicaca; 5c. Mt. Illimani; 10c. Parliament Building, La Paz.

51

54 Morane Saulnier Type P Airplane

1919.

158a **51** 1c. lake 15 10
158b 2c. violet 25 15
151 5c. green 35 10
152 10c. red 35 10
179 15c. blue 50 15
180 20c. blue 35 15
154 22c. blue 50 45
155 24c. violet 35 25
162 50c. orange 1·75 35
163 1b. brown 40 15
164 2b. brown 25 15

See also Nos. 194/206.

1923. Surch **Habilitada** and value.

165 **51** 5c. on 1c. lake 35 25
169 15c. on 10c. red 40 35
168 15c. on 22c. blue 40 35

1924. Air. Establishment of National Aviation School.

170 **54** 10c. black and red 30 25
171 15c. black and lake 1·10 70
172 25c. black and blue 55 35
173 50c. black and orange 1·10 70
174 – 1b. black and brown 1·10 1·00
175 – 2b. black and brown 2·25 2·00
176 – 5b. black and violet 3·50 3·25

Nos. 174/6 have a different view.

57 Andean Condor

1925. Centenary of Independence.

184 – 5c. red on green 50 25
185 – 10c. red on yellow 85 45
186 – 15c. red 35 10
187 **57** 25c. blue 2·00 50
188 – 50c. purple 35 10
189 – 1b. red 85 85
190 – 2b. yellow 1·25 1·25
191 – 5b. brown 1·40 1·40

DESIGNS—VERT: 5c. Torch of Freedom; 10c. Kantuta (national flower); 15c. Pres. B. Saavedra; 50c. Head of Liberty; 1b. Mounted archer; 5b. Marshal Sucre. HORIZ: 2b. Hermes.

1927. Surch **1927** and value.

192 **51** 5c. on 1c. lake 1·40 50
193 10c. on 24c. violet 1·40 85

1928.

194 **51** 2c. yellow 35 25
195 3c. pink 40 35
196 4c. red 40 35
197 20c. olive 60 25
198 25c. blue 60 35
199 30c. violet 60 50
200 40c. orange 1·00 85
201 50c. brown 1·00 50
202 1b. red 1·25 85
203 2b. purple 1·75 1·75
204 3b. green 1·75 1·60
205 4b. lake 2·75 2·40
206 5b. brown 3·25 2·75

1928. Optd **Octubre 1927** and star.

207 **51** 5c. green 25 15
208 10c. grey 35 15
209 15c. red 50 35

1928. Surch **15 cts. 1928.**

211 **51** 15c. on 20c. blue 5·50 5·50
213 15c. on 24c. violet 95 50
216 15c. on 50c. orange 70 40

66 "L.A.B." (Lloyd Aereo Boliviano)

68 Andean Condor

1928. Air.

217 **66** 15c. green 55 55
218 20c. blue 20 10
219 35c. red 35 35

1928.

221 **68** 5c. green 2·25 30
222 – 10c. blue 35 10
223 – 15c. red 35 10

DESIGNS: 10c. Pres. Siles; 15c. Map of Bolivia.

1930. Stamps of 1913 and 1916 surch **R. S. 21-4 1930** and value.

224 – 0.01c. on 2c. (No. 134) 70 70
225 – 0.03c. on 2c. (No. 144) 85 70
226 **46** 25c. on ½c. brown 70 50
227 – 25c. on 2c. (No. 144) 70 50

1930. Air. Optd **CORREO AEREO R. S. 6-V-1930** or surch **5 Cts.** also.

228 **54** 5c. on 10c. black & red 8·00 10·00
229 10c. black and red 8·00 10·00
231 15c. black and lake 8·00 10·00
232 25c. black and blue 8·00 10·00
233 50c. black and orange 8·00 10·00
235 1b. black and brown £100 £100

1930. "Graf Zeppelin" Air stamps. Stamps of 1928 surch **Z 1930** and value.

241 **66** 1b.50 on 15c. green 20·00 27·00
242 3b. on 20c. blue 20·00 27·00
243 6b. on 35c. red 35·00 45·00

75 Junkers F-13 over Bullock Cart

77 Pres. Siles

78 Map of Bolivia

79 Marshal Sucre

1930. Air.

244 **75** 5c. violet 1·60 65
245 – 15c. red 1·60 65
246 – 20c. yellow 65 40
247 **75** 35c. green 65 15
248 – 50c. blue 65 15
249 **75** 1b. brown 65 20
250 – 2b. red 65 30
251 **75** 3b. grey 3·75 1·60

DESIGN: 15, 20, 50c., 2b. Junkers F-13 seaplane over river boat.

1930.

252 **77** 1c. brown 25 25
253 – 2c. green (Potosi) 85 35
254 – 5c. blue (Illimani) 85 15
255 – 10c. red (E. Abaroa) 85 15
256 **78** 15c. violet 70 15
257 35c. red 1·40 70
258 45c. orange 1·40 70
259 **79** 50c. slate 70 50
260 – 1b. brown (Bolivar) 35 35

80 Symbols of Revolution

1931. 1st Anniv of Revolution.

263 **80** 15c. red 1·40 35
264 50c. lilac 45 50

81

1932. Air.

265 **81** 5c. blue 45 50
266 10c. grey 50 25
267 15c. red 45 35
268 25c. orange 45 35
269 30c. green 40 35
270 50c. purple 40 35
271 1b. brown 40 35

1933. Surch **Habilitada D. S. 13-7-1933** and value.

273 **51** 5c. on 1b. red 40 20
274 **78** 15c. on 35c. red 20 20
275 15c. on 45c. orange 20 20
276 **51** 15c. on 50c. brown 85 15
277 25c. on 40c. orange 40 15

83

84 M. Baptista

1933.

278 **83** 2c. green 25 15
279 5c. blue 15 10
280 10c. red 40 25
281 15c. violet 25 15
282 25c. blue 60 40

1935. Ex-President Baptista Commemoration.

283 **84** 15c. violet 50 20

85 Map of Bolivia

86 Fokker Super Universal

1935.

284 **85** 2c. blue 25 15
285 3c. yellow 25 15
286 5c. green 25 15
287 5c. red 25 15
288 10c. brown 25 15
289 15c. blue 25 15
290 15c. red 25 15
291 20c. green 25 15
292 25c. blue 35 15
293 30c. red 35 25
294 40c. orange 60 20
295 50c. violet 60 15
296 1b. yellow 60 40
297 2b. brown 60 40

1935. Air.

298 **86** 5c. brown 15 15
299 10c. green 15 15
300 20c. violet 15 15
301 30c. blue 15 15
302 50c. orange 35 15
303 1b. brown 35 30
304 1½b. yellow 1·00 15
305 2b. red 1·00 45
306 5b. green 1·25 45
307 10b. brown 2·10 85

1937. Surch **Comunicaciones D.S. 25-2-37** and value in figures.

308 **83** 5c. on 2c. green 20 20
310 15c. on 25c. blue 25 25
311 30c. on 25c. blue 40 40
312 **51** 45c. on 1b. brown 50 50
313 1b. on 2b. purple 60 60
314 **83** 2b. on 25c. blue 60 60
315 **80** 3b. on 50c. lilac 85 85
316 5b. on 50c. lilac 70 70

1937. Air. Surch **Correo Aereo D. S. 25-2-37** and value in figures.

321 **75** 5c. on 35c. green 35 35
322 **66** 20c. on 35c. red 40 25
323 50c. on 35c. red 75 40
324 1b. on 35c. red 90 50
325 **54** 2b. on 50c. black & orge 1·75 70
317 – 3b. on 50c. pur (No. 188) 90 35
318 – 4b. on 1b. red (No. 189) 75 70
319 **57** 5b. on 2b. orange 95 85
320 10b. on 5b. sepia (No. 191) 2·40 1·75
326 **54** 12b. on 10c. black & red 6·00 3·50
327 15b. on 10c. black & red 6·00 2·25

89 Native School

92 Junkers Ju52/3m over Cornfield

1938.

328	89	2c. red (postage)	10	10
329	–	10c. orange	15	10
330	–	15c. green	25	25
331	–	30c. yellow	40	35
332	–	45c. red	5·25	2·75
333	–	60c. violet	50	35
334	–	75c. blue	70	35
335	–	1b. brown	1·00	35
336	–	2b. buff	95	35

DESIGNS—VERT: 10c. Oil Wells; 15c. Industrial buildings; 30c. Pincers and torch; 75c. Indian and condor. HORIZ: 45c. Sucre-Camiri railway map; 60c. Natives and book; 1b. Machinery; 2b. Agriculture.

337	–	20c. red (air)	25	20
338	–	30c. grey	25	20
339	–	40c. yellow	25	20
340	92	50c. green	35	20
341	–	60c. blue	35	20
342	–	1b. red	50	50
343	–	2b. buff	1·25	20
344	–	3b. brown	90	20
345	–	5b. violet	6·00	1·25

DESIGNS—VERT: 20c. Mint, Potosi; 30c. Miner; 40c. Symbolical of women's suffrage; 1b. Pincers, torch and slogan; 3b. New Government emblem; 5b. Junkers aircraft over map of Bolivia. HORIZ: 60c. Airplane and monument; 2b. Airplane over river.

102 Llamas

103 Arms

1939.

346	102	2c. green	70	50
347		4c. brown	70	50
348		5c. mauve	70	35
349	–	10c. black	70	50
350	–	15c. green	70	55
351	–	20c. green	70	35
352	103	25c. yellow	60	25
353	–	30c. blue	60	35
354	–	40c. red	2·75	60
355	–	45c. black	2·50	60
356	–	60c. red	1·40	70
357	–	75c. slate	1·40	70
358	–	90c. orange	4·25	75
359	–	1b. blue	4·25	75
360	–	2b. red	5·50	75
361	–	3b. violet	6·50	1·00
362	–	4b. brown	4·00	1·40
363	–	5b. purple	5·00	1·60

DESIGNS—HORIZ: 10, 15, 20c. Vicuna; 60, 75c. Mountain viscacha; 90c., 1b. Toco toucan; 2, 3b. Andean condor; 4, 5b. Jaguar. VERT: 40, 45c. Cocoi herons.

107 Virgin of Copacabana

111 Workman

1939. Air. 2nd National Eucharistic Congress. Inscr "II° CONGRESO EUCARISTICO NACIONAL".

364	–	5c. violet	25	35
365	107	30c. green	20	20
366	–	45c. blue	60	20
367	–	60c. red	60	40
368	–	75c. red	45	40
369	–	90c. blue	30	25
370	–	2b. brown	50	25
371	–	4b. mauve	70	40
372	107	5b. blue	1·75	25
373	–	10b. yellow	3·50	25

DESIGNS—TRIANGULAR: 5c., 10b. Allegory of the Light of Religion. VERT: 45c., 4b. The "Sacred Heart of Jesus"; 75c., 90c. S. Anthony of Padua. HORIZ: 60c., 2b. Facade of St. Francis's Church, La Paz.

1939. Obligatory Tax. Workers' Home Building Fund.

374	111	5c. violet	35	10

112 Flags of 21 American Republics

1940. 50th Anniv of Pan-American Union.

375	112	9b. red, blue & yellow	70	70

114 Urns of Murillo and Sagarnaga

117 Shadow of Aeroplane on Lake Titicaca

1941. 130th Death Anniv of P. D. Murillo (patriot).

376	–	10c. purple	10	10
377	114	15c. green	15	10
378	–	45c. red	15	15
379	–	1b.05 blue	35	15

DESIGNS—VERT: 10c. Murillo statue; 1b.05 Murillo portrait. HORIZ: 45c. "Murillo dreaming in Prison".

1941. Air.

380	117	10b. green	4·00	50
381		20b. blue	4·50	85
382	–	50b. mauve	9·25	1·75
383	–	100b. brown	18·00	6·00

DESIGN: 50, 100b. Andean condor over Mt. Illimani.

119 1867 and 1941 Issues

120 "Union is Strength"

1942. 1st Students' Philatelic Exn, La Paz.

384	119	5c. mauve	65	55
385		10c. orange	65	55
386		20c. green	1·10	60
387		40c. red	1·25	65
388		90c. blue	2·50	80
389		1b. violet	3·75	2·00
390		10b. brown	12·00	7·50

1942. Air. Chancellors' Meeting, Rio de Janeiro.

391	120	40c. red	35	25
392		50c. blue	35	25
393		1b. brown	40	35
394		5b. mauve	1·40	25
395		10b. purple	1·75	1·60

121 Mt. Potosi

122 Chaquiri Dam

1943. Mining Industry.

396	121	15c. brown	25	15
397	–	45c. blue	25	15
398	–	1b.25 purple	1·40	85
399	–	1b.50 green	35	25
400	–	2b. brown	1·40	85
401	122	2b.10 blue	50	40
402	–	3b. orange	2·50	90

DESIGNS—VERT: 45c. Quechisla (at foot of Mt. Choroloque); 1b.25, Miner Drilling. HORIZ: 1b.50, Dam; 2b. Truck Convoy; 3b. Entrance to Pulacayo Mine.

125 Gen. Ballivian leading Cavalry Charge

1943. Centenary of Battle of Ingavi.

403	125	2c. green	10	10
404		3c. orange	10	10
405		25c. purple	15	10
406		45c. blue	25	15
407		3b. red	25	15
408		4b. purple	40	25
409		5b. sepia	55	35
MS409a		Two sheets each 139 × 100 mm. Nos. 403/6 and Nos. 407/9	9·00	8·00
MS409b		Do. Imperf	9·00	8·00

126 Gen. Ballivian and Trinidad Cathedral

1943. Centenary of Founding of El Beni. Centres in brown.

410	126	5c. green (postage)	10	10
411		10c. purple	15	15
412		30c. red	15	15
413		45c. blue	25	25
414		2b.10 orange	35	35
415	–	10c. violet (air)	10	10
416	–	20c. green	15	10
417	–	30c. red	20	15
418	–	3b. blue	25	20
419	–	5b. black	60	35

DESIGN: Nos. 415/19, Gen. Ballivian and mule convoy crossing bridge below airplane.

127 Trans. "Honour-Work-Law/All for the Country"

129 Allegory of "Flight"

1944. Revolution of 20th December, 1943.

420	127	20c. orange (postage)	10	10
421		20c. green	10	10
422		90c. blue	10	10
423		90c. red	10	10
424	–	1b. purple	15	10
425	–	2b.40 brown	20	15

DESIGN—VERT: 1b., 2b.40, Clasped hands and flag.

426	129	40c. mauve (air)	10	10
427	–	1b. violet	15	10
428	–	1b.50 green	15	10
429	–	2b.50 blue	35	15

DESIGN—HORIZ: 1b.50, 2b.50, Lockheed Electra airplane and sun.

131 Posthorn and Envelope

132 Douglas DC-2 and National Airways Route Map

1944. Obligatory Tax.

430	131	10c. red	1·00	25
432		10c. blue	1·00	25

Smaller Posthorn and Envelope.

469		10c. red	1·60	60
470		10c. yellow	1·40	60
471		10c. green	1·40	60
472		10c. brown	1·40	60

1945. Air. Panagra Airways, 10th Anniv of First La Paz–Tacna Flight.

433	132	10c. red	15	10
434		50c. orange	20	10
435		90c. green	30	10
436		5b. blue	45	15
437		20b. brown	1·40	45

133 Lloyd-Aereo Boliviano Air Routes

134 L. B. Vincenti and J. I. de Sanjines, Composers of National Anthem

1945. Air. 20th Anniv of First National Air Service.

438	133	20c. blue, orange & vio	10	10
439		30c. blue, orange & brn	10	10
440		50c. blue, orange & grn	10	10
441		90c. blue, orange & pur	10	10
442		2b. blue and orange	15	10
443		3b. blue, orange & red	20	15
444		4b. blue, orange & bistre	40	15

1946. Centenary of National Anthem.

445	134	5c. black and mauve	10	10
446		10c. black and blue	10	10
447		15c. black and green	10	10
448		30c. brown and red	15	15
449		90c. brown and blue	15	15
450		2b. brown and black	40	15
MS450a		Two sheets each 86 × 131 mm. (a) No. 448; (b) No. 450. Imperf. Each sold at 4b	2·25	2·25

1947. Surch **1947 Habilitada Bs. 1.40.**

451		1b.40 on 75c. blue (No. 334) (postage)	15	10
452		1b.40 on 75c. slate (No. 357)	15	10
455		1b.40 on 75c. red (No. 368) (air)	15	10

136 Seizure of Government Palace

137 Mt. Illimani

1947. Popular Revolution of 21 July 1946.

456	136	20c. green (postage)	10	10
457		50c. purple	10	10
458		1b.40 blue	10	10
459		3b.70 orange	15	10
460		4b. violet	25	15
461		10b. olive	30	30
462	137	1b. red (air)	10	10
463		1b.40 green	10	10
464		2b.50 blue	15	15
465		3b. orange	25	20
466		4b. mauve	35	20

138 Arms of Bolivia and Argentina

140 Cross and Child

1947. Meeting of Presidents of Bolivia and Argentina.

467	138	1b.40 orange (postage)	10	10
468		2b.90 blue (air)	25	25

1948. 3rd Inter-American Catholic Education Congress.

473	–	1b.40 bl & yell (postage)	35	10
474	140	2b. green and orange	50	15
475	–	3b. green and blue	55	20
476	–	5b. violet and orange	60	25
477	–	5b. brown and green	75	25
478	–	2b.50 orange & yell (air)	30	35
479	140	3b.70 red and buff	40	35
480	–	4b. mauve and blue	40	25
481	–	4b. blue and orange	40	15
482	–	13b.60 blue and green	50	25

DESIGNS: 1b.40, 2b.50, Christ the Redeemer, Monument; 3b., 4b. (No. 480), Don Bosco; 5b. (No. 476), 4b. (No. 481), Virgin of Copacabana; 5b. (No. 477), 13b.60, Pope Pius XII.

141 Map of S. America and Bolivian Auto Club Badge

142 Posthorn, Globe and Pres. G. Pacheco

1948. Pan-American Motor Race.

483	141	5b. blue & pink (postage)	1·00	20
484		10b. green & cream (air)	1·10	25

1950. 75th Anniv of U.P.U.

485	142	1b.40 blue (postage)	10	10
486		4b.20 red	10	10
487		1b.40 brown (air)	10	10
488		2b.50 orange	10	10
489		3b.30 purple	10	10

1950. Air. Surch **XV ANIVERSARIO PANAGRA 1935–1950** and value.

490	132	4b. on 10c. red	10	10
491		10b. on 20b. brown	25	20

1950. No. 379 surch **Bs. 2.- Habilitada D.S.6.VII.50.**

492		2b. on 1b.05 blue	15	10

145 Apparition at Potosi

146 Douglas DC-2

1950. 400th Anniv of Apparition at El Potosi.

493	145	20c. violet	10	10
494		30c. orange	10	10
495		50c. purple	10	10
496		1b. red	10	10
497		2b. blue	15	10
498		6b. brown	25	10

1950. Air. 25th Anniv of Lloyd Aereo Boliviano.

499	146	20c. orange	15	10
500		30c. violet	15	10

501		50c. green	15	10
502		1b. yellow	15	10
503		3b. blue	15	10
504		15b. red	50	15
505		50b. brown	1·40	40

1950. Air. Surch **Triunfo de la Democracia 24 de Sept. 49 Bs. 1.40.**

506	**137**	1b.40 on 3b. orange	15	15

148 UN Emblem and Globe

150 St. Francis Gate

149 Gate of the Sun, Tiahuanacu

1950. 5th Anniv of UNO.

507	**148**	60c. blue (postage)	70	10
508		2b. green	95	25
509		3b.60 red (air)	35	15
510		4b.70 brown	45	15

1951. 4th Centenary of Founding of La Paz. Centres in black.

511	**149**	20c. green (postage)	10	10
512	**150**	30c. orange	10	10
513	A	40c. brown	10	10
514	B	50c. red	10	10
515	C	1b. purple	10	10
516	D	1b.40 violet	15	15
517	E	2b. purple	15	15
518	F	3b. mauve	20	15
519	G	5b. red	25	15
520	H	10b. sepia	50	25
MS520a		Three sheets each 150 × 100 mm. Nos. 511/12, 520; 513, 516, 519; 514/15, 517/18	3·50	3·50
MS520b		Do. Imperf	3·50	3·50
521	**149**	20c. red (air)	15	15
522	**150**	30c. violet	15	15
523	A	40c. slate	15	15
524	B	50c. green	15	15
525	C	1b. red	20	20
526	D	2b. orange	35	35
527	E	3b. blue	35	35
528	F	4b. red	40	40
529	G	5b. green	40	40
530	H	10b. brown	45	45
MS530a		Three sheets each 150 × 100 mm. Nos. 521/2, 530; 523, 527, 529; 524/5, 526, 528	3·00	3·00
MS530b		Do. Imperf	3·00	3·00

DESIGNS—HORIZ: As Type **149**: A, Camacho Avenue; B, Consistorial Palace; C, Legislative Palace; D, G.P.O. E, Arms; F, Pedro de la Casca authorizes plans of City; G, Founding the City; H, City Arms and Captain A. de Mendoza.

151 Tennis

1951. Sports. Centres in black.

531	–	20c. blue (postage)	15	10
532	**151**	50c. red	15	10
533	–	1b. purple	20	10
534	–	1b.40 yellow	20	15
535	–	2b. red	25	15
536	–	3b. brown	55	50
537	–	4b. blue	70	50
MS537a		Two sheets each 150 × 100 mm. Nos. 531/2, 535/6; 533/4, 537	4·25	4·25
MS537b		Do. Imperf	4·25	4·25
538	–	20c. violet (air)	25	10
539	–	30c. purple	35	10
540	–	50c. orange	50	10
541	–	1b. brown	50	10
542	–	2b.50 orange	70	40
543	–	3b. sepia	70	50
544	–	5b. red	1·40	1·00
MS544a		130 × 80 mm. Nos. 741/3	9·00	7·50
MS544b		Do. Imperf	9·00	7·50

DESIGNS—Postage: 20c. Boxing; 1b. Diving; 1b.40, Football; 2b. Skiing; 3b. Pelota; 4b. Cycling. Air: 20c. Horse-jumping; 30c. Basketball; 50c. Fencing; 1b. Hurdling; 2b.50, Javelin; 3b. Relay race; 5b. La Paz Stadium.

152 Andean Condor and Flag

1951. 100th National Flag Anniv. Flag in red, yellow and green.

545	**152**	2b. green	10	10
546		3b.50c. blue	10	10
547		5b. violet	15	15
548		7b.50c. grey	35	15
549		15b. red	40	25
550		30b. brown	85	50

153 Posthorn and Envelope

154 E. Abaroa

1951. Obligatory Tax.

551	–	20c. orange	30	15
551b	–	20c. green	30	15
552	–	20c. blue	30	15
553	**153**	50c. green	40	15
553d		50c. red	40	15
553e		3b. green	40	15
553f		3b. bistre	60	45
553g		5b. violet	65	15

DESIGN: 20c. Condor over posthorn and envelope.

1952. 73rd Death Anniv of Abaroa (patriot).

554	**154**	80c. red (postage)	10	10
555		1b. orange	10	10
556		2b. green	15	10
557		5b. blue	20	15
558		10b. mauve	35	15
559		20b. brown	70	40
560		70c. red (air)	10	10
561		2b. yellow	15	15
562		3b. green	15	15
563		5b. blue	15	15
564		50b. purple	70	50
565		100b. black	75	70

155 Isabella the Catholic

156 Columbus Lighthouse

1952. 500th Birth Anniv of Isabella the Catholic.

566	**155**	2b. blue (postage)	10	10
567		6b.30 red	25	15
568		50b. green (air)	40	25
569		100b. brown	45	35

1952. Columbus Memorial Lighthouse. On tinted papers.

570	**156**	2b. blue (postage)	20	15
571		5b. red	40	20
572		9b. green	65	35
573		2b. purple (air)	15	10
574		3b.70 turquoise	15	10
575		4b.40 orange	20	10
576		20b. brown	45	10

157 Miner

159 Revolutionaries

158 Villarroel, Paz Estenssoro and Siles Zuazo

1953. Nationalization of Mining Industry.

577	**157**	2b.50c. red	10	10
578		8b. violet	15	10

1953. 1st Anniv of Revolution of April 9th, 1952.

579	**158**	50c. mauve (postage)	10	10
580		1b. red	10	10
581		2b. blue	10	10
582		3b. green	10	10
583		4b. yellow	10	10
584		5b. violet	15	10
585		3b.70 brown (air)	15	15
590	**159**	6b. mauve	15	15
586	**158**	9b. red	15	15
587		10b. turquoise	15	15
588		16b. orange	15	15
591	**159**	22b.50 brown	25	20
589	**158**	40b. grey	40	15

1953. Obligatory Tax. No. 551b and similar stamp surch **50 cts.**

592		50c. on 20c. mauve	30	30
593		50c. on 20c. green	15	15

161

162 Ear of Wheat and Map

1954. Obligatory Tax.

594	**161**	1b. lake	25	10
595		1b. brown	25	10

1954. 1st National Agronomical Congress.

596	**162**	25b. blue	15	10
597		85b. brown	35	15

163 Pres. Paz Estenssoro embracing Indian

167 Derricks

166 Refinery

1954. Air. 3rd Inter-American Indigenous Congress.

598	**163**	20b. brown	10	10
599		100b. turquoise	25	10

1954. 1st Anniv of Agrarian Reform. As T **162**, but designs inscr "REFORMA AGRARIA".

600		5b. red (postage)	10	10
601		17b. turquoise	10	10
602		27b. mauve (air)	10	15
603		30b. orange	15	10
604		45b. purple	25	10
605		300b. green	70	25

DESIGNS—5b., 17b. Cow's head and map; 27b. to 300b. Indian peasant woman.

1955. Obligatory Tax. Nos. 553e and 553f surch **Bs. 5.—D. S. 21-IV-55.**

606	**153**	5b. on 3b. green	25	10
607		5b. on 3b. bistre	25	10

1955. Development of Petroleum Industry.

608	**166**	10b. blue (postage)	10	10
609		35b. red	10	10
610		40b. green	10	10
611		50b. purple	15	10
612		80b. brown	25	10
613	**167**	55b. blue (air)	10	10
614		70b. black	20	10
615		90b. green	30	10
616		500b. mauve	45	40
617		1000b. brown	85	75

168 Control Tower

169 Douglas DC-6B Aircraft

1957. Obligatory Tax. Airport Building Fund.

618	**168**	5b. blue	50	10
620		5b. red	50	10
619	**169**	10b. green	40	10
620b		20b. brown	55	25

DESIGNS: 5b. (No. 620), Douglas DC-6B over runway; 20b. Lockheed Constellation in flight.

1957. Currency revaluation. Founding of La Paz stamps of 1951 surch. Centres in black.

621	F	50b. on 3b. mauve (post)	10	10
622	E	100b. on 2b. purple	10	10
623	C	200b. on 1b. purple	15	10
624	D	300b. on 1b.40 violet	20	10
625	**149**	350b. on 20c. green	30	10
626	A	400b. on 40c. brown	30	10
627	**150**	600b. on 30c. orange	40	10
628	B	800b. on 50c. red	45	10
629	H	1000b. on 10b. sepia	45	15
630	G	2000b. on 5b. red	50	25
631	E	100b. on 3b. blue (air)	10	10
632	D	200b. on 2b. orange	10	10
633	F	500b. on 4b. red	15	10
634	C	600b. on 1b. red	15	10
635	**149**	700b. on 20c. red	30	15
636	A	800b. on 40c. slate	40	20
637	**150**	900b. on 30c. violet	45	30
638	B	1800b. on 50c. green	45	35
639	G	3000b. on 5b. green	70	30
640	H	5000b. on 10b. brown	1·10	50

172 Congress Buildings (Santiago de Chile and La Paz)

173 "Latin America" on Globe

1957. 7th Latin-America Economic Congress, La Paz.

641	**172**	150b. bl & grey (postage)	10	10
642		350b. grey and brown	20	10
643		550b. sepia and blue	25	10
644		750b. green and red	35	10
645		900b. brown and green	50	15
646	**173**	700b. violet & lilac (air)	15	10
647		1200b. brown	25	15
648		1350b. red and mauve	40	25
649		2700b. olive and turq	75	45
650		4000b. violet and blue	95	50

174 Steam Train and Presidents of Bolivia and Argentina

1957. Yacuiba-Santa Cruz Railway Inauguration.

651	**174**	50b. orange (postage)	55	45
652		350b. blue and light blue	1·75	60
653		1000b. brown & cinna	4·25	1·25
654		600b. purple & pink (air)	1·60	60
655		700b. violet and blue	3·00	1·25
656		900b. green	4·25	75

175 Presidents and Flags of Bolivia and Mexico

1960. Visit of Mexican President to Bolivia.

657	**175**	350b. olive (postage)	15	10
658		600b. brown	25	10
659		1,500b. sepia	50	15
660		400b. red (air)	25	10
661		800b. blue	45	20
662		2,000b. green	70	40

The President's visit to Bolivia did not take place.

176 Indians and Mt. Illimani

177 "Gate of the Sun", Tiahuanacu

1960. Tourist Publicity.

663	**176**	500b. bistre (postage)	30	10
664		1000b. blue	50	15
665		2000b. sepia	1·40	35
666		4000b. green	2·50	1·75
667	**177**	3000b. grey (air)	1·25	75
668		5000b. orange	1·90	75
669		10,000b. purple	3·00	1·75
670		15,000b. violet	4·25	3·00

178 Refugees

179 "Uprooted Tree"

1960. World Refugee Year.

671	**178**	50b. brown (postage)	10	10
672		350b. purple	15	10
673		400b. blue	15	10
674		1000b. sepia	50	15
675		3000b. green	70	70
676	**179**	600b. blue (air)	35	35
677		700b. brown	35	35
678		900b. turquoise	40	35
679		1800b. violet	40	35
680		2000b. black	45	40

180 Jaime Laredo (violinist)

181 Jaime Laredo (violinist)

1960. Jaime Laredo Commem.
681 **180** 100b. green (postage) . . 10 10
682 350b. lake 20 10
683 500b. blue 25 10
684 1000b. brown 35 15
685 1500b. violet 60 60
686 5000b. black . . . . . . 2·00 2·00

687 **181** 600b. plum (air) 50 25
688 700b. olive 50 35
689 800b. brown 50 35
690 900b. blue 70 35
691 1800b. turquoise . . . . 1·00 1·00
692 4000b. grey . . . . 2·00 70

182 Rotary Emblem and Nurse with Children

183

1960. Founding of Children's Hospital by La Paz Rotary Club. Wheel in blue and yellow, foreground in yellow; background given.
693 **182** 350b. green (postage) . . 15 10
694 500b. sepia 25 10
695 600b. violet 35 10
696 1000b. grey 45 15

697 600b. brown (air) 45 25
698 1000b. olive 40 25
699 1800b. purple 70 70
700 5000b. black . . . . . . 2·00 80

1960. Air. Unissued stamp, surch as in T **183**.
701 **183** 1200b. on 10b. orange . . 2·75 1·75

184 Design from Gate of the Sun

185 Flags of Argentina and Bolivia

1960. Unissued Tiahuanacu Excavation stamps surch as in T **184**. Gold backgrounds.
702 50b. on ½c. red 30 20
703 100b. on 1c. red 35 15
704 200b. on 2c. black 50 15
705 300b. on 5c. green 25 15
706 350b. on 10c. green 25 50
707 400b. on 15c. blue 35 15
708 500b. on 20c. red 35 15
709 500b. on 50c. red 40 15
710 600b. on 22½c. green 30 25
711 600b. on 60c. violet 40 35
712 700b. on 25c. violet 50 20
713 700b. on 1b. green 85 80
714 800b. on 30c. red 40 20
715 900b. on 40c. green 30 25
716 1000b. on 2b. blue 40 35
717 1800b. on 3b. grey . . . . 3·25 2·40
718 4000b. on 4b. grey . . . . 19·00 16·00
719 5000b. on 5b. grey . . . . 5·00 4·75
DESIGNS: Various gods, motifs and ornaments. SIZES: Nos. 702/6, As Type **184**. Nos. 707/17, As Type **184** but horiz. No. 718, 49 × 23 mm. No. 719, 50 × 52½ mm.

1961. Air. Visit of Pres. Frondizi of Argentina.
720 **185** 4000b. multicoloured . . 70 60
721 – 6000b. sepia and green . . 1·00 85
DESIGN: 6000b. Presidents of Argentina and Bolivia.

186 Miguel de Cervantes (First Mayor of La Paz)

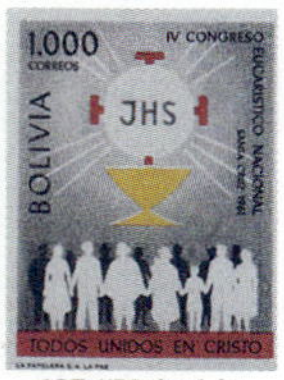

187 "United in Christ"

1961. M. de Cervantes Commem and 4th Centenary of Santa Cruz de la Sierra (1500b.).
722 **186** 600b. violet and ochre (postage) 40 10
723 – 1500b. blue and orange 60 20
724 – 1400b. brown & green (air) 60 25
DESIGNS: 1400b. Portrait as Type **186** (diamond shape, 30¼ × 30½ mm); 1500b. Nuflo de Chaves (vert: as Type **186**).
See also Nos. 755/6.

1962. 4th National Eucharistic Congress, Santa Cruz.
725 **187** 1000b. yellow, red and green (postage) 45 35
726 – 1400b. yellow, pink and brown (air) 45 35
DESIGN: 1400b. Virgin of Cotoca.

1962. Nos. 671/80 surch.
727 **178** 600b. on 50b. brown (postage) 25 15
728 900b. on 350b. purple . . 30 15
729 1000b. on 400b. blue . . 25 15
730 2000b. on 1000b. brown 25 30
731 3500b. on 3000b. green 45 45

732 **179** 1200b. on 600b. blue (air) 40 35
733 1300b. on 700b. brown 35 35
734 1400b. on 900b. green . . 40 35
735 2800b. on 1800b. violet 60 50
736 3000b. on 2000b. black 60 50

189 Hibiscus

190 Infantry

1962. Flowers in actual colours; background colours given.
737 **189** 200b. green (postage) . . 25 10
738 – 400b. brown 25 10
739 – 600b. deep blue 50 10
740 – 1000b. violet 85 20

741 – 100b. blue (air) 10 10
742 – 800b. green 40 15
743 – 1800b. violet 90 35
744 – 10,000b. deep blue . . . 4·50 2·25
MS744a 130 × 80 mm. Nos. 741/3. Imperf . . . . 4·00 4·00
FLOWERS: Nos. 738, 740 Orchids; 739, St. James' lily; 741/4, Types of Kantuta (national flowers).

1962. Armed Forces Commemoration.
745 **190** 400b. mult (postage) . . . 10 10
746 – 500b. multicoloured . . . 15 10
747 – 600b. multicoloured . . . 20 15
748 – 2000b. multicoloured . . 60 40

749 – 600b. mult (air) 35 15
750 – 1200b. multicoloured . . 45 20
751 – 2000b. multicoloured . . 65 35
752 – 5000b. multicoloured . . 1·75 85
DESIGNS: No. 746, Cavalry; 747, Artillery; 748, Engineers; 749, Parachutists and aircraft; 750, 752, "Overseas Flights" (Lockheed Super Electra airplane over oxen-cart); 751, "Aerial Survey" (Douglas DC-3 airplane photographing ground).

191 Campaign Emblem

192 Goal-Keeper diving to save Goal

1962. Malaria Eradication.
753 **191** 600b. yellow, violet and lilac (postage) 25 15
754 – 2000b. yellow, green and blue (air) 55 50
DESIGN: 2000b. As No. 753 but with laurel wreath and inscription encircling emblem.

1962. Spanish Discoverers. As T **186** but inscribed "1548–1962".
755 600b. mauve on blue (postage) 35 15
756 1200b. brown on yellow (air) 45 20
PORTRAITS: 600b. A. de Mendoza. 1200b. P. de la Gasca.

(Currency reform. 1000 (old) pesos = 1 (new) peso)

1963. 21st South American Football Championships, La Paz. Multicoloured.
757 **192** 60c. Type **192** (postage) 40 10
758 1p. Goalkeeper saving ball (vert) 60 15
759 1p.40 Andean condor on football (vert) (air) . . 2·40 1·50
760 1p.80 Ball in corner of net (vert) 70 70

193 Globe and Emblem

194 Alliance Emblem

1963. Freedom from Hunger.
761 **193** 60c. yellow, blue and indigo (postage) 25 10
762 – 1p.20 yellow, blue and myrtle (air) 50 50
DESIGN: 1p.20, Ear of wheat across Globe.

1963. Air. "Alliance for Progress".
763 **194** 1p.20 green, blue & bis 55 35

195 Oil Derrick

1963. 10th Anniv of Revolution (1962).
764 **195** 10c. grn & brn (postage) 10 10
765 – 60c. sepia and orange . . 30 10
766 – 1p. yellow, violet & green 35 15
767 – 1p.20 pink, brown and grey (air) 45 20
768 – 1p.40 green and ochre . . 55 25
769 – 2p.80 buff and slate . . . 70 50
DESIGNS: 60c. Map of Bolivia; 1p. Students; 1p.20, Ballot box and voters; 1p.40, Peasant breaking chain; 2p.80, Miners.

196 Flags of Bolivia and Peru

197 Marshal Santa Cruz

1966. Death Centenary of Marshal Santa Cruz.
770 **196** 10c. mult (postage) . . . 10 10
771 60c. multicoloured . . . 20 10
772 1p. multicoloured 35 15
773 2p. multicoloured 50 20

774 **197** 20c. blue (air) 10 10
775 60c. green 20 10
776 1p.20 brown 50 35
777 2p.80 black 65 40

198 Generals Barrientos and Ovando, Bolivian Map and Flag

199 Needy Children

1966. Co-Presidents Commemoration.
778 **198** 60c. mult (postage) . . . 20 10
779 1p. multicoloured 30 10
780 2p.80 mult (air) 95 70
781 10p. multicoloured . . . 1·10 35
MS782 136 × 83 mm. Nos. 778/81. Imperf . . . . 6·50 6·50

1966. Aid for Poor Children.
783 **199** 30c. brown, sepia and ochre (postage) 15 10
784 – 1p.40 black & blue (air) 70 45
DESIGN: 1p.40, Mother and needy children.

1966. Commemorative Issues. Various stamps surch with inscr (as given below) and value. (i) Red Cross Centenary. Surch **Centenario de la Cruz Roja Internacional**.
785 20c. on 150b. (No. 641) (post) 10 10
786 4p. on 4000b. (No. 650) (air) 95 70

(ii) General Azurduy de Padilla. Surch **Homenaje a la Generala J. Azurduy de Padilla**.
787 30c. on 550b. (No. 643) . . . 10 10
788 2p.80 on 750b. (No. 644) . . 70 35

(iii) Air. Tupiza Cent. Surch **Centenario de Tupiza**.
789 60c. on 1350b. (No. 648) . . 20 20

(iv) Air. 25th Anniv of Bolivian Motor Club. Surch **XXV Aniversario Automovil Club Boliviano**.
790 2p.80 on 2700b. (No. 649) . . 1·40 1·10

(v) Air. Cochabamba Philatelic Society Anniv. Surch **Aniversario Centro Filatelico Cochabamba**.
791 1p.20 on 800b. (No. 742) . . 35 25
792 1p.20 on 1800b. (No. 743) . . 35 25

(vi) Rotary Help for Children's Hospital. Surch with value only. (a) Postage.
793 1p.60 on 350b. (No. 693) . . 45 15
794 2p.40 on 500b. (No. 694) . . 70 25

(b) Air.
795 1p.40 on 1000b. (No. 698) . . 45 45
796 1p.40 on 1800b. (No. 699) . . 45 45

(vii) 150th Anniv of Coronilla Heroines. Surch **CL Aniversario Heroinas Coronilla**. (a) Postage.
797 60c. on 350b. (No. 682) . . . 15 10

(b) Air.
798 1p.20 on 800b. (No. 689) . . . 40 35

(viii) Air. Centenary of Hymn La Paz. Surch **Centenario Himno Paceno**.
799 1p.40 on 4000b. (No. 692) . . 40 35

(ix) Air. 12th Anniv of Agrarian Reform. Surch **XII Aniversario Reforma Agraria**.
800 10c. on 27b. (No. 602) . . . 15 15

(x) Air. 25th Anniv of Chaco Peace Settlement. Surch **XXV Aniversario Paz del Chaco**.
801 10c. on 55b. (No. 613) . . . 15 15

All the following are surch on Revenue stamps. The design shows a beach scene with palms, size 27 × 21½ mm.

(xi) Centenary of Rurrenabaque. Surch **Centenario de Rurrenabaque**.
802 1p. on 10b. brown 30 10

(xii) 25th Anniv of Busch Government. Surch **XXV Aniversario Gobierno Busch**.
803 20c. on 5b. red 10 10

(xiii) 20th Anniv of Villarroel Government. Surch **XX Aniversario Gob. Villarroel**.
804 60c. on 2b. green 15 10

(xiv) 25th Anniv of Pando Department. Surch **XXV Aniversario Dpto. Pando**. (a) Postage.
805 1p.60 on 50c. violet 45 15

(b) Air. Surch **Aereo** also.
806 1p.20 on 1b. blue 50 40

201 Sower

202 "Macheteros"

1967. 50th Anniv of Lions International. Mult.
807 **201** 70c. Type **201** (postage) 35 10
808 2p. Lions emblem and Inca obelisks (horiz) (air) 55 45
MS809 129 × 80 mm. Nos. 807/8. Imperf 90 55

1968. 9th Congress of the UPAE (Postal Union of the Americas and Spain). Bolivian Folklore. Designs showing costumed figures. Multicoloured.
810 **202** 30c. Type **202** (postage) 10 10
811 60c. "Chunchos" 15 10
812 1p. "Wiphala" 25 15
813 2p. "Diablada" 50 20

814 1p.20 "Pujllay" (air) . . . 25 15
815 1p.40 "Ujusiris" 35 20
816 2p. "Morenada" 50 25
817 3p. "Auki-aukis" 85 50
MS818 Two sheets each 132 × 80 mm. Nos. 810/13 and 814/17. Imperf . . . . 5·50 5·50

203 Arms of Tarija

204 President G. Villarroel

1968. 150th Anniv of Battle of the Tablada (1817).
819 **203** 20c. mult (postage) . . . 10 10
820 30c. multicoloured 10 10
821 40c. multicoloured 15 10
822 60c. multicoloured 20 10

823 – 1p. multicoloured (air) . . . 35 15
824 – 1p.20 multicoloured . . . 40 15
825 – 2p. multicoloured 70 35
826 – 4p. multicoloured 70 50
DESIGNS: Nos. 823/6, Moto Mendez.

1968. 400th Anniv of Cochabamba.
827 **204** 20c. brn & orge (postage) 15 10
828 30c. brown & turquoise 15 10
829 40c. brown and purple . . 15 10
830 50c. brown and green . . 15 10
831 1p. brown and bistre . . 35 10

832 – 1p.40 black & red (air) . . 35 25
833 – 3p. black and blue . . . 35 40
834 – 4p. black and red 50 50
835 – 5p. black and green . . . 60 40
836 – 10p. black and violet . . 1·10 75
DESIGN—HORIZ: 1p.40 to 10p. Similar portrait of President.

205 Painted Clay Cup

206 President J. F. Kennedy

1968. 20th Anniv of UNESCO (1966).
837 **205** 20c. mult (postage) . . . 15 10
838 60c. multicoloured 40 25

839 1p.20 black & blue (air) 40 20
840 2p.80 black and green . . 45 45
DESIGNS: Nos. 839/40, UNESCO emblem.

1968. 5th Death Anniv of John F. Kennedy (U.S. President).
841 **206** 10c. black & grn (postage) 15 10
842 4p. black and violet . . . 95 95

843 1p. black and green (air) 35 20
844 10p. black and red . . . 1·90 1·90
MS845 Two sheets each 131 × 80 mm. (a) No. 842; (b) No. 843. Imperf . . . . 7·00 7·00

207 ITU Emblem

208 Tennis Player

1968. Centenary (1965) of ITU.
846 **207** 10c. black grey and yellow (postage) 15 10
847 60c. black, orange & bistre 35 10

848 1p.20 black, grey and yellow (air) 30 10
849 1p.40 black, blue & brn 40 20

1968. South American Tennis Championships, La Paz.
850 **208** 10c. black, brown and grey (postage) 20 10
851 20c. black, brown & yell 20 10
852 30c. black, brown & blue 20 10

853 1p.40 black, brown and orange (air) 45 25
854 2p.80 black, brown & bl 50 50
MS855 Two sheets each 132 × 81 mm. (a) Nos. 850/2; (b) No. 853. Imperf . . . . 7·00 7·00

209 Unofficial 1r. Stamp of 1863

210 Rifle-shooting

1963. Stamp Centenary.
856 **209** 10c. brown, black and green (postage) 15 10
857 30c. brown, black & blue 15 10
858 2p. brown, black & drab 25 10
859 – 1p.40 green, black and yellow (air) 50 25
860 – 2p.80 green, blk & pink 70 50
861 – 3p. green, black & lilac 70 50
MS862 Two sheets each 132 × 83 mm. (a) Nos. 856/8; (b) Nos. 859/61. Imperf . . . . . 5·50 6·00
DESIGN: Nos. 859/61, First Bolivian stamp.

1969. Olympic Games, Mexico (1968).
863 **210** 40c. black, red and orange (postage) 15 10
864 – 50c. black, red and green 15 10
865 – 60c. black, blue & green 25 10

866 – 1p.20 black, green and ochre (air) 40 15
867 – 2p.80 black, red & yell . . 85 35
868 – 5p. multicoloured . . . . 1·00 1·00
MS869 Two sheets each 131 × 81 mm. (a) Nos. 863/5; (b) Nos. 866/8 . . . . 4·00 4·00
DESIGNS—HORIZ: 50c. Horse-jumping; 60c. Canoeing; 5p. Hurdling. VERT: 1p.20, Running; 2p.80, Throwing the discus.

211 F. D. Roosevelt

212 "Temensis laothoe violetta"

1969. Air. Franklin D. Roosevelt Commem.
870 **211** 5p. black, orange & brown . . . . 1·40 75

1970. Butterflies. Multicoloured.
871 5c. Type **212** (postage) . . . 35 35
872 10c. "Papilio crassus" 70 70
873 20c. "Catagramma cynosura" 70 70
874 30c. "Eunica eurota flora" . . 70 70
875 80c. "Ituna phenarete" . . . 70 70

876 1p. "Metamorpha dido wernichei" (air) 90 50
877 1p.80 "Heliconius felix" . . . 1·25 65
878 2p.80 "Morpho casica" . . . 1·75 1·75
879 3p. "Papilio yuracares" . . . 1·90 1·75
880 4p. "Heliconsus melitus" . . 2·50 2·00
MS881 Two sheets each 132 × 80 mm. (a) Nos. 871/3; (b) Nos. 876/8. Imerf . . . . . . 10·00 10·00

213 Scout mountaineering

214 President A. Ovando and Revolutionaries

1970. Bolivian Scout Movement. Multicoloured.
882 **213** 5c. Type **213** (postage) . . 15 10
883 10c. Girl-scout planting shrub 15 10
884 50c. Scout laying bricks (air) 15 10
885 1p.20 Bolivian scout badge 35 15

1970. Obligatory Tax. Revolution and National Day.
886 **214** 20c. blk & red (postage) 25 15
887 30c. black & green (air) 25 15
DESIGN: 30c. Pres. Ovando, oil derricks and laurel sprig.

1970. "Exfilca 70" Stamp Exhibition, Caracas, Venezuela. No. 706 further surch **EXFILCA 70** and new value.
888 30c. on 350b. on 10c. . . . 15 10

1970. Provisionals. Various stamps surch.
889 **178** 60c. on 900b. on 350b. (postage) 30 10
890 – 1p.20 on 1500b. (No. 723) 50 15
891 **185** 1p.20 on 4000b. (air) . . 35 15

217 Pres. G. Busch and Oil Derrick

218 "Amaryllis escobar uriae"

1971. 32nd Death Anniv of President G. Busch and 25th Death Anniv of Pres. Villarroel.
892 **217** 20c. blk & lilac (postage) 35 10
893 – 30c. black and blue (air) 30 10
DESIGN: 30c. Pres. Villarroel and oil refinery.

1971. Bolivian Flora. Multicoloured.
894 30c. Type **218** (postage) . . . 15 10
895 40c. "Amaryllis evansae" . . 15 10
896 50c. "Amaryllis yungacensis" (vert) 20 15
897 2p. "Gymnocalycium chiquitanum" (vert) . . . 55 35

898 1p.20 "Amaryllis pseudopardina" (air) . . . 45 15
899 1p.40 "Rebutia kruegeri" (vert) 60 15
900 2p.80 "Lobivia pentlandii" 95 25
901 4p. "Rebutia tunariensis" (vert) . . . . 1·60 50
MS902 Two sheets each 130 × 80 mm. (a) Nos. 894/5, 898 and 900; (b) Nos. 896/7, 899 and 901. Imperf . . . . 9·00 9·00

219 Sica Sica Cathedral

220 Pres. H. Banzer

1971. "Exfilima" Stamp Exhibition, Lima, Peru.
903 **219** 20c. multicoloured 15 10

1972. "Bolivia's Development".
904 **220** 1p.20 multicoloured . . . 35 15

221 Chiriwano de Achocalla Dance

222 "Virgin and Child" (B. Bitti)

1972. Folk Dances. Multicoloured.
905 20c. Type **221** (postage) . . . 10 10
906 40c. Rueda Chapaca 20 15
907 60c. Kena-Kena 30 15
908 1p. Waca Thokori 40 25

909 1p.20 Kusillo (air) 40 15
910 1p.40 Taquirari 45 15

1972. Bolivian Paintings. Multicoloured.
911 10c. "The Washerwoman" (M. P. Holguin) (postage) 10 10
912 50c. "Coronation of the Virgin" (G. M. Berrio) . . 20 10
913 70c. "Arquebusier" (anon.) 25 10
914 80c. "St. Peter of Alcantara" (M. P. Holguin) 25 15
915 1p. Type **222** 35 15

916 1p.40 "Chola Pacena" (G. de Rojas) (air) 40 10
917 1p.50 "Adoration of the Kings" (G. Gamarra) . . . 40 10
918 1p.60 "Pachamama Vision" (A. Borda) 40 10
919 2p. "Idol's Kiss" (G. de Rojas) 40 25

223 Tarija Cathedral

1972. "EXFILIBRA 72" Stamp Exhibition, Rio de Janeiro.
920 **223** 30c. multicoloured 15 10

224 National Arms

1972. Air.
921 **224** 4p. multicoloured 95 35

225 Santos Dumont and "14 bis"

1973. Air. Birth Centenary of Alberto Santos Dumont (aviation pioneer).
922 **225** 1p.40 black and yellow . . 1·25 45

226 "Echinocactus notocactus"

227 Power Station, Santa Isabel

1973. Cacti. Multicoloured.
923 20c. Type **226** (postage) . . . 10 10
924 40c. "Echinocactus lenninghaussii" 15 10
925 50c. "Mammillaria bocasana" 20 10
926 70c. "Echinocactus lenninghaussii" (different) 30 10

927 1p.20 "Mammillaria bocasana" (different) (air) 40 15
928 1p.90 "Opuntia cristata" . . 60 20
929 2p. "Echinocactus rebutia" 85 25

1973. Bolivian Development Multicoloured.
930 10c. Type **227** (postage) . . . 10 10
931 20c. Tin foundry 15 10
932 90c. Bismuth plant 40 10
933 1p. Gas plant 40 10

934 1p.40 Road bridge, Highways 1 and 4 (air) 50 15
935 2p. Inspection car crossing bridge, Al Beni . . . . . 8·00 2·50

228 "Cattleya nobilior"

229 Morane Saulnier Type P and Emblem

1974. Orchids. Multicoloured.
936 20c. Type **228** (postage) . . . 10 10
937 50c. "Zygopetalum bolivianum" 20 10
938 1p. "Huntleya melagris" . . 35 10
939 2p.50 "Cattleya luteola" (horiz) (air) 90 25
940 3p.80 "Stanhopaea" . . . . 1·00 35
941 4p. "Catasetum" (horiz) . . . 1·00 45
942 5p. "Maxillaria" . . . . . . 1·75 50

1974. Philatelic Exhibitions, 1975, 1976 and 1977. Four sheets each 130 × 80 mm showing reproductions of various stamps.
MS943 (a) Nos. 36, 911 and 942; (b) Nos. 36, 912 and 941; (c) Nos. 36, 914 and 939; (d) Nos. 36 and 921 6·50 6·50
See also No. **MS**954.

1974. Air. 50th Anniv of Bolivian Air Force. Multicoloured.
944 3p. Type **229** 75 50
945 3p.80 Douglas DC-3 crossing Andes . . . . 1·25 70
946 4p.50 Triplane trainer and Morane Saulnier Paris I aircraft . . . . 1·25 70
947 8p. Col. Rafael Pabon and biplane fighter . . . . . . 1·75 1·40
948 15p. Jet airliner on "50" . . 3·75 2·00

230 General Sucre (after J. Wallpher)

1974. 150th Anniv of Battle of Ayacucho.
949 **230** 5p. multicoloured 75 55

231 UPU and Exhibition Emblems

1974. Centenary of UPU and Expo UPU (Montevideo) and Prenfil UPU (Buenos Aires) Stamp Exhibitions.
950 **231** 3p.50 green, black & bl 70 45

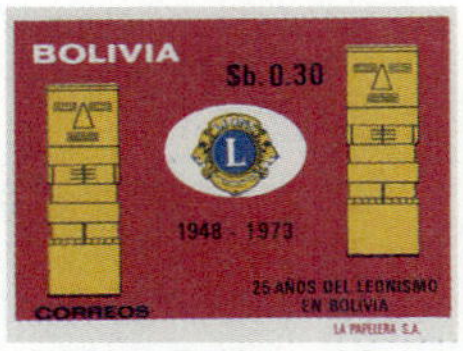

232 Lions Emblem and Steles

1975. 50th Anniv of Lions International in Bolivia.
951 **232** 30c. multicoloured 35 10

233 Exhibition Emblem

1975. "Espana 75" International Stamp Exhibition, Madrid.
952 **233** 4p.50 multicoloured . . . 55 35

234 Emblem of Meeting

1975. Cartagena Agreement. First Meeting of Postal Ministers, Quito, Ecuador.
953 **234** 2p.50 silver, violet & blk 45 30

1975. Philatelic Exhibitions 1975, 1976 and 1977. Four sheets as **MS**943.
MS954 (a) Nos. 36 and 950; (b) Nos. 36 and 951; (c) Nos. 36 and 952; (d) Nos. 36 and 953 . . . 6·50 6·50

235 Arms of Pando

237 Pres. Victor Paz Estenssoro

236 Presidents Perez and Banzer

1975. 150th Anniv of Republic (1st issue). Provincial Arms. Multicoloured.

955	20c. Type **235** (postage) . . .	10	10
956	2p. Chuzuisaca	50	35
957	3p. Cochabamba	70	50
958	20c. Beni (air)	10	10
959	30c. Tarija	10	10
960	50c. Potosi	10	10
961	1p. Oruro	4·50	1·50
962	2p.50 Santa Cruz	50	50
963	3p. La Paz	70	50

See also Nos. 965/78.

1975. Air. Visit of Pres. Perez of Venezuela.
964 **236** 3p. multicoloured 75 55

1975. 150th Anniv of Republic (2nd issue).

965	30c. Type **237** (postage) . .	10	10
966	60c. Pres. Thomas Frias . .	15	10
966a	1p. Ismael Montes	20	10
967	2p.50 Aniceto Arce	50	25
968	7p. Bautista Saavedra . . .	95	35
969	10p. Jose Manuel Pando . .	1·40	50
970	15p. Jose Maria Linares . .	1·75	1·75
971	50p. Simon Bolivar	6·25	6·25
972	50c. Rene Barrientos Ortuno (air)	15	10
973	2p. Francisco B. O'Connor	50	25
973a	3p.80 Gualberto Villaroel	70	50
974	4p.20 German Busch . . .	70	70
975	4p.50 Pres. Hugo Banzer Suarez	70	70
976	20p. Jose Ballivian	2·50	1·40
977	30p. Pres. Andres de Santa Cruz	3·25	3·25
978	40p. Pres. Antonio Jose de Sucre	4·25	4·25

Nos. 965/70, 972/4 and 976/78 are smaller, 24 × 33 mm.

238 Laurel Wreath and LAB Emblem

240 UPU Emblem

239 "EXFIVIA"

1975. Air. 50th Anniv of Lloyd-Aereo Boliviano (national airline). Multicoloured.

979	1p. Type **238**	15	10
980	1p.50 Douglas DC-9 and L.A.B. route map (horiz)	35	15
981	2p. Guillermo Kyllmann (founder) and Junkers F-13 aircraft (horiz)	45	25

1975. Obligatory Tax. As No. 893 but inscr "XXV ANIVERSARIO DE SU GOBIERNO".
982 30c. black and blue 30 10

1975. "Exfivia 75". Stamp Exhibition.
983 **239** 3p. multicoloured 70 35

1975. Air. Centenary (1974) of UPU.
984 **240** 25p. multicoloured . . . 2·00 2·00

241 Chiang Kai-shek

1976. 1st Death Anniv of President Chiang Kai-shek.
985 **241** 2p.50 multicoloured . . . 60 25

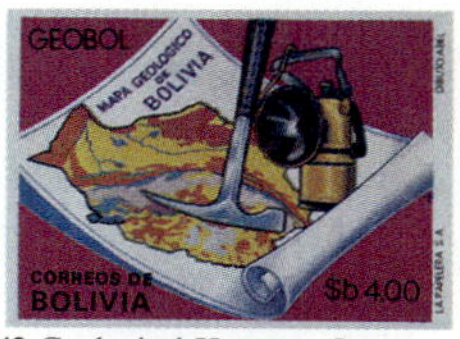

242 Geological Hammer, Lamp and Map

1976. Bolivian Geological Institute.
986 **242** 4p. multicoloured 55 55

243 Naval Insignia

1976. Navy Day.
987 **243** 50c. multicoloured 25 10

244 Douglas DC-10 and Divided Roundel

1976. 50th Anniv of Lufthansa Airline.
988 **244** 3p. multicoloured 90 35

245 Bolivian Boy Scout and Badge

247 Brother Vicente Bernedo (missionary)

246 Battle Scene

1976. 60th Anniv of Bolivian Boy Scouts.
989 **245** 1p. multicoloured 50 20

1976. Bicentenary of American Revolution.
990 **246** 4p.50 multicoloured . . . 95 45
MS991 130 × 81 mm. No. 990 . . 6·50 5·50

1976. Brother Vincente Bernedo Commemoration.
992 **247** 1p.50 multicoloured . . . 35 15

248 Rainbow over La Paz, Police Handler with Dog

249 Bolivian Family

1976. 150th Anniv of Police Service.
993 **248** 2p.50 multicoloured . . . 40 25

1976. National Census.
994 **249** 2p.50 multicoloured . . . 55 35

250 Pedro Poveda (educator)

1976. Poveda Commemoration.
995 **250** 1p.50 multicoloured . . . 35 15

251 Arms, Bolivar and Sucre

252 "Numeral"

1976. International Bolivarian Societies Congress.
996 **251** 1p.50 multicoloured . . . 55 25

1976.

997	**252**	20c. brown	10	10
998		1p. blue	25	10
999		1p.50 green	40	10

253 Boy and Girl

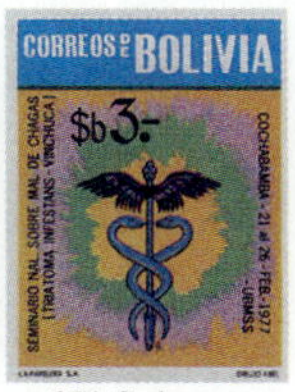

254 Caduceus

1977. Christmas 1976 and 50th Anniv of Inter-American Children's Institute.
1000 **253** 50c. multicoloured . . . 15 10

1977. National Seminar on "Chagas Disease".
1001 **254** 3p. multicoloured . . . 70 10

255 Court Buildings, La Paz

256 Tower and Map

1977. 150th Anniv of Bolivian Supreme Court. Multicoloured.

1002	2p.50 Type **255**	30	10
1003	4p. Dr. Manuel M. Urcullu, first President	45	10
1004	4p.50 Dr. Pantaleon Dalence, President, 1883–89	50	10

1977. 90th Anniv of Oruro Club.
1005 **256** 3p. multicoloured . . . 50 15

257 Newspaper Mastheads

258 Games Poster

1977. Bolivian Newspapers. Multicoloured.

1006	1p.50 Type **257**	25	10
1007	2p.50 "Ultima Hora" and Alfredo Alexander (horiz)	35	10
1008	3p. "El Diaro" and Jose Carrasco (horiz)	45	15
1009	4p. "Los Tiempos" and Demetrio Canelas	50	15
1010	5p.50 "Presencia"	70	20

1977. 8th Bolivarian Games, La Paz.
1011 **258** 5p. multicoloured . . . 70 20

259 Tin Miner and Mining Corporation Emblem

260 Miners, Globe and Chemical Symbol for Tin

1977. 25th Anniv of Bolivian Mining Corporation.
1012 **259** 3p. multicoloured . . . 4·25 2·00

1977. International Tin Symposium, La Paz.
1013 **260** 6p. multicoloured . . . 55 30

261 Map of Bolivia and Radio Masts

263 "Eye", Compass, Key and Law Book

1977. 50th Anniv of Bolivian Radio.
1014 **261** 2p.50 multicoloured . . 35 10

1977. "Exfivia 77" Philatelic Exhibition, Cochabamba. No. 719 surch **EXFIVIA — 77 $b. 5.—**.
1015 5p. on 5,000b. on $b. 5 grey and gold 85 15

1978. 50th Anniv of Audit Department.
1016 **263** 5p. multicoloured . . . 45 15

264 Aesculapius Staff and Map of Andean Countries

265 Map of the Americas

266 Mt. Illimani

1978. 5th Meeting of Andean Countries' Health Ministers.
1017 **264** 2p. orange and black . . 40 10

1978. World Rheumatism Year (1977).
1018 **265** 2p.50 blue and red . . . 35 15

1978.
1019 **266** 50c. green and blue . . . 10 10
1020 – 1p. yellow and brown . . 15 10
1021 – 1p.50 grey and red . . . 25 10
DESIGNS—HORIZ: 1p.50, Mt. Cerro de Potosi. VERT: 1p. Pre-Columbian monolith.

267 Central Bank

268 Jesus with Children

1978. 50th Anniv of Bank of Bolivia.
1022 **267** 7p. multicoloured . . . 70 25

1979. International Year of the Child.
1023 **268** 8p. multicoloured . . . 60 15

269 Antofagasta Cancellation

270 Antofagasta

1979. Centenary of Loss of Litoral Department to Chile.
1024 **269** 50c. brown and black . . 10 10
1025 – 1p. mauve and black . . 15 10
1026 – 1p.50 green and black 25 10
1027 **270** 5p.50 multicoloured . . 40 15
1028 – 6p.50 multicoloured . . 55 20
1029 – 7p. multicoloured . . . 55 20
1030 – 8p. multicoloured . . . 60 25
1031 – 10p. multicoloured . . 75 35
DESIGNS—HORIZ: 1p. La Chimba cancel; 1p.50, Mejillones cancel. VERT: (As Type **270**). 6p.50, Woman in chains; 7p. Eduardo Arbaroa; 8p. Map of Department, 1876; 10p. Arms of Litoral.

271 Map and Radio Club Emblem

272 Runner and Games Emblem

1979. Radio Club of Bolivia.
1032 **271** 3p. multicoloured . . . 40 10

1979. 1st "Southern Cross" Games. Mult.
1033 6p.50 Type **272** 55 20
1034 10p. Gymnast 75 35

273 Bulgarian Stamp of 1879

274 "Exfilmar" Emblem

1979. "Philaserdica 79" Philatelic Exhibition, Sofia, Bulgaria.
1035 **273** 2p.50 black, yellow and light yellow 30 10

1979. "Exfilmar 79" Maritime Philatelic, Exhibition, La Paz.
1036 **274** 2p. blue, black and light blue 20 20

275 OAS Emblem and Map

276 Franz Tamayo (lawyer)

1979. 9th Congress of Organization of American States, La Paz.
1037 **275** 6p. multicoloured . . . 50 20

1979. Anniversaries and Events.
1038 **276** 2p.80 light grey, black and grey 35 10
1039 – 5p. multicoloured . . . 35 20
1040 – 5p. multicoloured . . . 35 20
1041 – 6p. multicoloured . . . 45 20
1042 – 9p.50 multicoloured . . 2·00 80
DESIGNS—VERT: 2p.80, Type **276** (birth centenary); 5p. (No. 1039) U.N. emblem and delegates (18th CEPAL Sessions, La Paz); 5p. (No. 1042), Gastroenterological laboratory (Japanese health co-operation); 6p. Radio mast (50th anniv of national radio). HORIZ: 9p.50, Puerto Suarez iron ore deposits.

277 500c. Stamp of 1871, Exhibition Emblem and Flag

1980. "Exfilmar" Bolivian Maritime Stamp Exhibition, La Paz.
1043 **277** 4p. multicoloured . . . 50 15

278 Juana Azurduy de Padilla

1980. Birth Bicentenary of Juana Azurduy de Padilla (Independence heroine).
1044 **278** 4p. multicoloured . . . 55 15

279 Jean Baptiste de la Salle (founder)

1980. 300th Anniv of Brothers of Christian Schools.
1045 **279** 9p. multicoloured . . . 75 30

280 "Victory in a Chariot", Emblem and Flags

1980. "Espamer 80" International Stamp Exhibition, Madrid.
1046 **280** 14p. multicoloured . . . 1·10 45

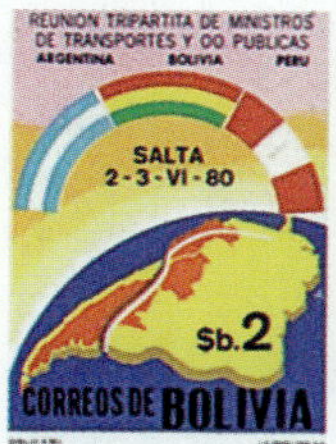
281 Flags over Map of South America

282 Diesel Locomotive

1980. Meeting of Public Works and Transport Ministers of Argentina, Bolivia and Peru.
1047 **281** 2p. multicoloured . . . 25 10

1980. Inauguration of Santa Cruz-Trinidad Railway, Third Section.
1048 **282** 3p. multicoloured . . . 90 50

283 Soldier and Citizen with Flag destroying Communism

284 Scarlet Macaw

1981. 1st Anniv of 17 July Revolution. Mult.
1049 1p. Type **283** 15 10
1050 3p. Flag shattering hammer and sickle on map 35 10
1051 40p. Flag on map of Bolivia showing provinces . . . . 3·25 85
1052 50p. Rejoicing crowd (horiz) 3·75 85

1981. Macaws. Multicoloured.
1053 4p. Type **284** 65 35
1054 7p. Green-winged macaw . . 1·00 50
1055 8p. Blue and yellow macaw 1·25 60
1056 9p. Red-fronted macaw . . 1·40 65
1057 10p. Yellow-collared macaw 1·40 65
1058 12p. Hyacinth macaw . . . 1·90 90
1059 15p. Military macaw . . . . 1·50 1·10
1060 20p. Chestnut-fronted macaw . . . . 3·00 1·25

285 Virgin and Child receiving Flower

286 Emblem

1981. Christmas.
1061 **285** 1p. pink and red 15 10
1062 – 2p. light blue and blue 30 10
DESIGN: 2p. Child and star (horiz).
See also No. 1080.

1982. 22nd American Air Force Commanders' Conference, Buenos Aires.
1063 **286** 14p. multicoloured . . . 1·10 35

287 Cobija

288 Simon Bolivar

1982. 75th Anniv of Cobija City.
1064 **287** 28p. multicoloured . . . 30 20

1982. Birth Bicentenary of Simon Bolivar.
1065 **288** 18p. multicoloured . . . 35 25

289 Dish Antenna

290 Footballers

1982. World Communication Year.
1066 **289** 26p. multicoloured . . . 30 20

1982. World Cup Football Championship, Spain. Multicoloured.
1067 4p. Type **290** 20 10
1068 100p. "The Final Number" (Picasso) . . . . 1·25 65

291 Boy playing Football

1982. Bolivian Youth. Multicoloured.
1069 16p. Type **291** 20 20
1070 20p. Girl playing piano (horiz) 25 30

292 Harvesting

1982. China-Bolivian Agricultural Co-operation.
1071 **292** 30p. multicoloured . . . 50 20

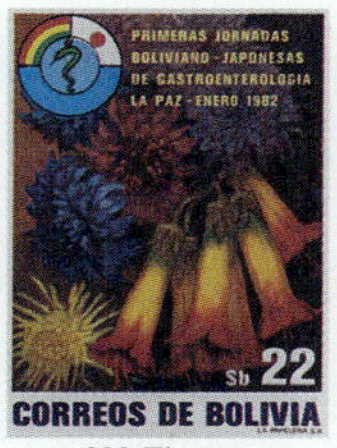
293 Flowers

1982. 1st Bolivian-Japanese Gastroenterological Days.
1072 **293** 22p. multicoloured . . . 25 20

294 Bolivian Stamps

295 Hernando Siles

1982. 10th Anniv of Bolivian Philatelic Federation.
1073 **294** 19p. multicoloured . . . 35 15

1982. Birth Centenary of Hernando Siles (former President).
1074 **295** 20p. buff and brown . . 40 20

296 Baden-Powell

297 "Liberty", Cochabamba

1982. 125th Birth Anniv of Lord Baden-Powell and 75th Anniv of Boy Scout Movement.
1075 **296** 5p. multicoloured . . . 15 10

1982. 25th Anniv of Cochabamba Philatelic Centre.
1076 **297** 3p. buff, black & blue 10 10

298 High Court, Cochabamba

299 Virgin of Copacabana

1982. 150th Anniv of High Court, Cochabamba.
1077 **298** 10p. black, red and bronze 25 10

1982. 400th Anniv of Enthronement of Virgin of Copacabana.
1078 **299** 13p. multicoloured . . . 30 15

300 Puerto Busch Naval Base

1982. Navy Day.
1079 **300** 14p. multicoloured . . . 60 20

1982. Christmas. Design as Type **285**, inscribed "NAVIDAD 1982".
1080 **285** 10p. grey and green . . 20 10

301 Footballer and Emblem

1983. 10th American Youth Football Championships.
1081 **301** 50p. multicoloured . . . 55 45

302 Sun Gate

1983. "Exfivia 83" Stamp Exhibition.
1082 **302** 150p. red 90 35

303 Presidents Figueiredo and Zuazo

1984. Visit of President of Brazil.
1083 **303** 150p. multicoloured . . 40 15

1984. Various stamps surch.
1084 **276** 40p. on 2p.80 light grey, black and grey 15 10
1085 – 60p. on 1p.50 green and black (1026) 15 10
1086 **265** 60p. on 2p.50 blue and red 15 10
1087 **274** 100p. on 2p. blue, black and light blue 30 15
1088 **174** 200p. on 350b. blue and light blue . . . . . . 2·25 90

1984. "Mladost 84" Youth Stamp Exn, Pleven, Bulgaria. No. 1035 surch.
1089 **273** 40p. on 2p.50 black, yellow and light yellow 15 10

306 "Simon Bolivar" (Mulato Gil de Quesada)
308 Pedestrian walking in Road

1984. Birth Bicentenary of Simon Bolivar. Mult.
1090 50p. Type **306** 15 10
1091 200p. "Simon Bolivar entering La Paz" (Carmen Baptista) 35 20

1984. Various stamps surch.
1092 **297** 500p. on 3p. buff, black and blue (postage) . . 45 30
1093 **290** 1000p. on 4p. mult . . 90 65
1094 **285** 2000p. on 10p. grey and green . . . . 2·00 85
1095 **296** 5000p. on 5p. mult . . . 4·75 2·00
1096 – 10000p. on 3p.80 mult (No. 940) (air) . . . . 6·25 3·75

1984. Road Safety Campaign. Multicoloured.
1097 80p. Type **308** 10 10
1098 120p. Police motorcyclist and patrol car 10 10

309 "Mendezs Birthplace" (Jorge Campos)
310 Legs and Feet on Map and Bata Emblem

1984. Birth Bicentenary of Jose Eustaquio Mendez. Multicoloured.
1099 300p. Type **309** 15 10
1100 500p. "Battle of La Tablada" (M. Villegas) . . 20 10

1984. World Footwear Festival. Mult.
1101 100p. Type **310** 10 10
1102 200p. Legs and feet on map and Power emblem . . . 10 10
1103 600p. Football and globes (World Cup, Mexico, 1986) (horiz) 15 10

311 Inca Postal Runner
312 Vicuna

1985.
1104 **311** 11000p. blue 30 15

1985. Endangered Animals.
1105 **312** 23000p. brown and deep brown 35 15
1106 – 25000p. brown, blue and orange . . . . 1·00 20
1107 – 30000p. red and green 45 20
DESIGNS—VERT: 25000p. Andean condor; 30000p. Marsh deer.

313 National Work Education Service Emblem
314 Hand with Syringe, Victim in Droplet and Campaign Emblem

1985. International Professional Education Year.
1108 **313** 2000p. blue and red . . 10 10

1985. Anti-polio Campaign.
1109 **314** 20000p. blue and violet 30 15

315 Vicenta Juaristi Eguino
316 U.N. Emblem

1985. Birth Bicentenary of Vicenta Juaristi Eguino (Independence heroine).
1110 **315** 300000p. multicoloured 30 15

1985. 40th Anniv of U.N.O.
1111 **316** 1000000p. blue and gold 45 30

317 Emblem
318 Emblem, Envelope and Posthorn

1985. 75th Anniv of "The Strongest" Football Club.
1112 **317** 200000p. multicoloured 20 10

1986. Cent of Bolivian U.P.U. Membership.
1113 **318** 800000p. multicoloured 65 30

319 Bull and Rider
321 Football as Globes

1986. 300th Anniv of Trinidad City.
1114 **319** 1400000p. multicoloured 1·00 45

1986. No. 1108 surch.
1115 **313** 200000p. on 2000p. blue and red 15 10
1116 5000000p. on 2000p. blue and red . . . . . 3·50 1·60

1986. World Cup Football Championship, Mexico.
1117 **321** 300000p. red and black 25 10
1118 – 550000p. multicoloured 45 20
1119 – 1000000p. black and green (horiz.) 80 40
1120 – 2500000p. green & yell 1·90 85
DESIGNS—VERT: 550000p. Pique (mascot); 2500000p. Trophy. HORIZ: 1000000p. Azteca Stadium, Mexico City.

322 Alfonso Subieta Viaduct
323 Envelope

1986. 25th Anniv of American Development Bank.
1121 **322** 400000p. blue 35 15

1986. 50th Anniv of Society of Postmen.
1122 **323** 2000000p. brown . . . . 1·60 70

324 Emblem and Dove
325 Emblem

1986. International Peace Year.
1123 **324** 200000p. green 15 10

1986. International Youth Year (1985).
1124 **325** 150000p. red 15 10
1125 500000p. green 45 30
1126 – 3000000p. multicoloured 2·10 1·00
DESIGNS: 3000000p. Child clutching trophy and flag (25th anniv of Enrique Happ Sports Club, Cochabamba).

326 Zampa (after F. Diaz de Ortega)
328 Refinery

327 1870 500c. Stamp

1986. 50th Death Anniv of Friar Jose Antonio Zampa.
1127 **326** 400000p. multicoloured 35 15

1986. 15th Anniv of Bolivian Philatelic Federation.
1128 **327** 600000p. brown 50 20

1986. 50th Anniv of National Petroleum Refining Corporation.
1129 **328** 1000000p. multicoloured 1·00 30

329 Demon Mask
330 Flags

1987. Centenary of 10th February Society, Oruro.
1130 **329** 20c. multicoloured . . . 10 10

1987. State Visit of President Richard von Weizsacker of German Federal Republic.
1131 **330** 30c. multicoloured . . . 15 15

331 National Arms

1987. Visit of King Juan Carlos of Spain.
1132 **331** 60c. multicoloured . . . 60 20

332 Andean ("Condor")
333 Modern View of Potosi

1987. Endangered Animals. Multicoloured.
1133 20c. Type **332** 35 25
1134 20c. Tapir 10 10
1135 30c. Vicuna (new-born) . . 15 15
1136 30c. Armadillo 15 15
1137 40c. Spectacled bear 25 20
1138 60c. Keel-billed toucans ("Tucan") . . . . 1·10 50

1987. "Exfivia 87" Stamp Exhibition, Potosi. Multicoloured.
1139 40c. Type **333** 25 20
1140 50c. 18th-century engraving of Potosi 30 25

334 "Nina" and Stern of "Santa Maria"

1987. "Espamer '87" Stamp Exhibition, La Coruna. Multicoloured.
1141 20c. Type **334** 30 15
1142 20c. "Pinta" and bow of "Santa Maria" 30 15
Nos. 1141/2 were printed together, se-tenant, forming a composite design.

335 Pan-pipes and Indian Flute

1987. Musical Instruments. Multicoloured.
1143 50c. Type **335** 30 20
1144 1b. Indian guitars . . . . . 1·00 35

336 Carabuco Church

1988. Visit of Pope John Paul II. Mult.
1145 20c. Type **336** 10 10
1146 20c. Tihuanacu church . . . 10 10
1147 20c. Cathedral of the Kings, Beni 10 10

1148 30c. St. Joseph church, Chiquitos 15 15
1149 30c. St. Francis's church, Sucre 15 15
1150 40c. Cobija chapel (vert) . . 20 15
1151 50c. Cochabamba cathedral (vert) 25 20
1152 50c. Jayu Kcota church . . 25 20
1153 60c. St. Francis's Basilica, La Paz (vert) 30 25
1154 70c. Church of Jesus, Machaca 60 30
1155 70c. St. Lawrence's church, Potosi (vert) 60 30
1156 80c. Vallegrande church . . 70 35
1157 80c. Copacabana Virgin (vert) 70 35
1158 80c. "The Holy Family" (Peter Paul Rubens) (vert) 70 35
1159 1b.30 Concepcion church . . 1·10 55
1160 1b.30 Tarija cathedral (vert) 1·10 55
1161 1b.50 Pope and Arms of John Paul II and Bolivia 1·40 65

337 Handshake and Flags

1988. Visit of President Jose Sarney of Brazil.
1162 **337** 50c. multicoloured . . . 25 20

338 St. John Bosco

339 La Paz–Beni Steam Locomotive

1988. Death Centenary of St. John Bosco (founder of Salesian Brothers).
1163 **338** 30c. multicoloured . . . 15 15

1988. Centenary of Bolivian Railways.
1164 **339** 1b. multicoloured . . . 2·25 1·10

340 Aguirre

341 "Column of the Future" (Battle of Bahia Monument)

1988. Death Cent of Nataniel Aguirre (writer).
1165 **340** 1b. black and brown . . 80 35

1988. 50th Anniv of Pando Department. Mult.
1166 40c. Type **341** 15 10
1167 60c. Rubber production . . 50 20

342 Athlete

343 Mother Rosa Gattorno

1988. Olympic Games, Seoul.
1168 **342** 1b.50 multicoloured . . 1·25 55

1988. 88th Death Anniv of Mother Rosa Gattorno (Founder of the Daughters of St. Anne).
1169 **343** 80c. multicoloured . . . 70 30

344 Bernardino de Cardenas

345 Ministry Building

1988. 220th Death Anniv of Br. Bernardino de Cardenas (first Bishop of La Paz).
1170 **344** 70c. black and brown . . 60 25

1988. Ministry of Transport and Communications.
1171 **345** 2b. black, green & red 1·60 70

346 Arms

347 Rally Car

1988. 50th Anniv of Army Communications Corps.
1172 **346** 70c. multicoloured . . . 65 25

1988. 50th Anniv of Bolivian Automobile Club.
1173 **347** 1b.50 multicoloured . . 1·00 55

348 Microphone and Emblem

1989. 50th Anniv of Radio Fides.
1174 **348** 80c. multicoloured . . . 65 30

349 Obverse and Reverse of 1852 Gold Cuartillo

1989. Coins.
1175 **349** 1b. multicoloured . . . 80 35

350 "Bulgaria 89" Stamp Exhibition Emblem and Orchid

351 Birds

1989. Events and Plants. Multicoloured.
1176 50c. Type **350** 20 15
1177 60c. "Italia '90" World Cup football championship emblem and kantuta (national flower) (horiz) 50 20
1178 70c. "Albertville 1986" emblem and "Heliconia humilis" 55 25
1179 1b. Olympic Games, Barcelona emblem and "Hoffmanseggia" 80 35
1180 2b. Olympic Games, Seoul emblem and bromeliad . . 1·60 70

1989. Bicentenary of French Revolution.
1181 **351** 70c. multicoloured . . . 60 25

352 Clock Tower and Steam Locomotive

353 Federico Ahlfeld Waterfall, River Pauserna

1989. Centenary of Uyuni.
1182 **352** 30c. grey, black & blue 75 40

1989. Noel Kempff Mercado National Park. Multicoloured.
1183 1b.50 Type **353** . . . . . . 1·25 60
1184 3b. Pampas deer . . . . . 2·40 1·00

354 Making Metal Articles

1989. America. Tiahuanacu Culture. Mult.
1185 50c. Type **354** 20 15
1186 1b. Kalasasaya Temple . . 70 35

355 Dr. Carlos Perez and Jaime Zamora

356 Cobija Arch

1989. Meeting of Presidents of Bolivia and Venezuela.
1187 **355** 2b. multicoloured . . . 1·40 70

1989. World Heritage Site, Potosi. Mult.
1188 60c. Type **356** 50 15
1189 80c. Mint 60 20

357 "Andean Lake" (Arturo Borda)

1989. Christmas. Paintings. Multicoloured.
1190 40c. Type **357** 15 10
1191 60c. "Virgin of the Roses" (anon) 45 15
1192 80c. "Conquistador" (Jorge de la Reza) 55 20
1193 1b. "Native Harmony" (Juan Rimsa) 70 25
1194 1b.50 "Woman with Pitcher" (Cecilio Guzman de Rojas) . . . . 1·10 40
1195 2b. "Flower of Tenderness" (Gil Imana) . . . . . . 1·40 55

358 Foot crushing Syringe

359 Map of Americas

1990. Anti-drugs Campaign.
1196 **358** 80c. multicoloured . . . 60 20

1990. Centenary of Organization of American States.
1197 **359** 80c. blue and deep blue 55 20

360 Colonnade

361 Penny Black, Sir Rowland Hill and Bolivian 5c. Condor Stamp

1990. 450th Anniv of White City.
1198 **360** 1b.20 multicoloured . . 85 35

1990. 150th Anniv of the Penny Black.
1199 **361** 4b. multicoloured . . . 2·75 1·25

362 Giuseppe Meaza Stadium, Milan

363 Emblem

1990. World Cup Football Championship, Italy. Multicoloured.
1200 2b. Type **362** . . . . 1·40 55
1201 6b. Match scene . . . . . 4·00 1·50

1990. Cent of Bolivian Chamber of Commerce.
1202 **363** 50c. black, blue & gold 40 10

364 Satellite, Map and Globe

366 Chipaya Village, Oruro

365 Hall

1990. Telecommunications Development Year.
1203 **364** 70c. multicoloured . . . 50 15

1990. Centenary of Cochabamba Social Club.
1204 **365** 40c. multicoloured . . . 15 10

1990. America. Multicoloured.
1205 80c. Type **366** 50 15
1206 1b. Nevado Huayna, Cordillera Real (mountain) (vert) 65 20

367 Emblem

368 Trees and Mountains

1990. "Meeting of Two Worlds. United towards Progress". 500th Anniv (1992) of Discovery of America by Columbus.
1207 **367** 2b. multicoloured . . . 1·25 40

1990. 400th Anniv of Larecaja District.
1208 **368** 1b.20 multicoloured . . . 70 25

369 Dove and German National Colours

370 Boys playing Football (Omar Espana)

1990. Unification of Germany.
1209 **369** 2b. multicoloured . . . 1·25 55

1990. Christmas. Rights of the Child.
1210 **370** 50c. multicoloured . . . 15 10

371 Arms of Bolivia and Ecuador

373 Andes

372 Flags and Andes

1990. Visit of Pres. Rodrigo Borja Cevallos of Ecuador.
1211 **371** 80c. multicoloured . . . 60 15

1990. 4th Andean Presidents' Council, La Paz.
1212 **372** 1b.50 multicoloured . . 90 30

1990. "Exfivia 90" National Stamp Exhibition.
1213 **373** 40c. blue 15 10

374 Arms of Bolivia and Mexico

376 Emblem

375 Emblem, Globe and Flags

1990. Visit of Pres. Carlos Salinas de Gortari of Mexico.
1214 **374** 60c. multicoloured . . . 50 15

1990. Express Mail Service.
1215 **375** 1b. multicoloured . . . 60 20

1991. 50th Anniv of Bolivian Radio Club.
1216 **376** 2b.40 multicoloured . . 1·40 50

377 Head of Bear

378 National Museum of Archaeology

1991. The Spectacled Bear. Multicoloured.
1217 30c. Type **377** 10 10
1218 30c. Bear on branch 10 10
1219 30c. Bear and cub at water's edge 10 10
1220 30c. Bear and cubs on branches 10 10

1991. "Espamer '91" Spain–Latin America Stamp Exhibition, Buenos Aires. Multicoloured.
1221 50c. Type **378** 15 10
1222 50c. National Art Museum 15 10
1223 1b. National Museum of Ethnography and Folklore 60 20

379 Map

380 Statue of Our Lady of La Paz and Cathedral

1991. 56th Anniv of Ending of Chaco War and Beginning of Construction of "Heroes of Chaco" Road.
1224 **379** 60c. multicoloured . . . 20 15

1991. La Paz Cathedral.
1225 **380** 1b.20 multicoloured . . 80 25

381 Presidents Lacalle and Paz Zamora

1991. Meeting of Uruguayan and Bolivian Presidents.
1226 **381** 1b. multicoloured . . . 60 20

382 Presidents Paz Zamora and Menem

1991. Meeting of Bolivian and Argentine Presidents.
1227 **382** 1b. multicoloured . . . 60 20

383 "Exfivia 83", "87" and "90" Stamps

385 Route Map, Motor Cycle and Rally Car

384 Presidents Fujimori and Paz Zamora

1991. 20th Anniv of Bolivian Philatelic Federation.
1228 **383** 70c. multicoloured . . . 45 10

1991. Presidential Summit of Bolivia and Peru.
1229 **384** 50c. multicoloured . . . 15 10

1991. Pres. Jaime Paz Zamora National Grand Prix Motor Rally, Tarija-Cobija.
1230 **385** 50c. multicoloured . . . 15 10

386 Data Retrieval Systems

1991. "Ecobol" Postal Security.
1231 **386** 1b.40 multicoloured . . 90 30

387 "First Discovery of Chuquiago" (Arturo Reque)

388 Stylized Figures and City Skyline

1991. America. Voyages of Discovery. Mult.
1232 60c. Type **387** 20 10
1233 1b.20 "Foundation of City of Our Lady of La Paz" (J. Rimsa) (vert) 80 30

1991. National Population and Housing Census.
1234 **388** 50c. multicoloured . . . 15 10

389 "Landscape" (Daniel Pena y Sarmiento)

1991. Christmas. Multicoloured.
1235 2b. Type **389** . . . . 1·00 40
1236 5b. "Fruit Seller" (Cecilio Guzman de Rojas) . . . 2·50 1·00
1237 15b. "Native Mother" (Crespo Gastelu) . . . . 7·50 3·00

390 Camp-site and Emblem

1992. 75th Anniv (1990) of Bolivian Scout Movement and Los Andes Jamboree, Cochabamba.
1238 **390** 1b.20 multicoloured . . 80 30

391 Simon Bolivar

392 Raising Flag

1992. "Exfilbo 92" National Stamp Exhibition, La Paz.
1239 **391** 1b.20 deep brown, brown and stone . . . 80 30

1992. Creation of Bolivian Free Zone in Ilo, Peru. Multicoloured.
1240 1b.20 Type **392** 65 30
1241 1b.50 Presidents Fujimori (Peru) and Paz Zamora (horiz) 80 30
1242 1b.80 Beach at Ilo (horiz) 95 35

393 Logotype of Pavilion

1992. "Expo '92" World's Fair, Seville, and "Granada '92" Int Stamp Exhibition. Mult.
1243 30c. Type **393** 10 10
1244 50c. Columbus's fleet . . . 30 10

394 Rotary International Emblem and Prize

1992. Rotary Club Miraflores District 4690 "Illimani de Oro" Prize.
1245 **394** 90c. gold, blue & black 30 20

395 School and Perez

1992. Birth Centenary of Elizardo Perez (founder of Ayllu School, Warisata).
1246 **395** 60c. blue, black & yellow 50 10

396 Government Palace

1992. UNESCO World Heritage Site, Sucre.
1247 **396** 50c. multicoloured . . . 15 10

397 Mario Martinez Guzman

398 Front Page

1992. Olympic Games, Barcelona.
1248 **397** 1b.50 multicoloured . . 80 30

1992. 25th Anniv of "Los Tiempos" (newspaper).
1249 **398** 50c. multicoloured . . . 15 10

399 Canoeing

400 Columbus leaving Palos (after Bejarano)

1992. 1st International River Bermejo Canoeing Championship.
1250 **399** 1b.20 multicoloured . . 75 30

1992. America. 500th Anniv of Discovery of America by Columbus.
1251 **400** 60c. brown and black . . 20 10
1252 – 2b. multicoloured . . . 95 40
DESIGN—HORIZ: 2b. "Columbus meeting the Caribisis Tribe" (Luis Vergara).

401 Football Match

402 "Chenopodium quinoa"

1992. World Cup Football Championship, U.S.A. (1994).
1253 **401** 1b.20 multicoloured . . 1·25 30

1992. 50th Anniv of Interamerican Institute for Agricultural Co-operation.
1254 **402** 1b.20 multicoloured . . 80 30

403 University Arms and Minerals

1992. Cent of Oruro Technical University.
1255 **403** 50c. multicoloured . . . 15 10

404 Mascots

1992. 12th Bolivarian Games, Cochabamba and Santa Cruz (1st issue).
1256 **404** 2b. multicoloured . . . 1·00 40
See also No. 1271.

405 Cayman

1992. Ecology and Conservation. Multicoloured.
1257 20c. Type **405** 10 10
1258 50c. Spotted cavy 15 10

1259 1b. Chinchilla 30 20
1260 2b. Anteater . . . . 1·00 40
1261 3b. Jaguar . . . . 1·50 65
1262 4b. Long-tailed sylph ("Picaflor") (vert) . . . . 3·50 1·60
1263 5b. Piranhas . . . . 2·50 1·10
Each stamp also bears the emblem of an anniversary or event.

406 Battle Scene

1992. 150th Anniv of Battle of Ingavi.
1264 **406** 1b.20 brown and black 65 30

407 Man following Star in Boat

1992. Christmas. Multicoloured.
1265 1b.20 Type **407** 60 20
1266 2b.50 Star over church . . . 1·40 50
1267 6b. Infant in manger and church . . . . 3·00 1·25

408 Nicolas Copernicus (450th death anniv)
409 Mother Nazaria (after Victor Eusebio Choque)

1993. Astronomy.
1268 – 50c. multicoloured . . . 15 10
1269 **408** 2b. black . . . . . . 1·00 35
DESIGN—HORIZ: 50c. Santa Ana International Astronomical Observatory, Tarija (10th anniv (1992)).

1993. Beatification (1992) of Mother Nazaria Ignacia March Meza.
1270 **409** 60c. multicoloured . . . 40 10

410 Pictograms and Flags of Ecuador, Venezuela, Peru, Bolivia, Colombia and Panama

1993. 12th Bolivarian Games, Cochabamba and Santa Cruz (2nd issue).
1271 **410** 2b.30 multicoloured . . 1·10 35

411 Bolivia 1962 10000b. Kantuta and Brazil 90r. "Bull's Eye" Stamps

1993. 150th Anniv of First Brazilian Stamps.
1272 **411** 2b.30 multicoloured . . 1·10 35

412 "Morpho sp."

1993. Butterflies. Multicoloured.
1273 60c. Type **412** 40 10
1274 60c. "Archaeoprepona demophon" 40 10
1275 80c. "Papilio sp." 45 10
1276 80c. Orion ("Historis odius") 45 10
1277 80c. Mexican fritillary ("Euptoieta hegesia") . . 45 10
1278 1b.80 "Morpho deidamia" . 1·10 30
1279 1b.80 Orange swallowtail ("Papilio thoas") . . . . 1·10 30
1280 1b.80 Monarch ("Danaus plexippus") . . . . 1·10 30
1281 2b.30 Scarlet emperor ("Anaea marthesia") . . 1·25 35
1282 2b.30 "Caligo sp." . . . . . 1·25 35
1283 2b.30 "Rothschildia sp." . . 1·25 35
1284 2b.70 "Heliconius sp." . . . 1·50 45
1285 2b.70 "Marpesia corinna" 1·50 45
1286 2b.70 "Prepona chromus" 1·50 45
1287 3b.50 Rusty-tipped page ("Siproeta epaphus") . . 1·90 60
1288 3b.50 "Heliconius sp." . . . 1·90 60

413 "Eternal Father" (wood statuette, Gaspar de la Cueva)
414 "Virgin of Urkupina"

1993.
1289 **413** 1b.80 multicoloured . . 90 30

1993. 400th Anniv of Quillacollo.
1290 **414** 50c. multicoloured . . . 15 10

415 Student, Machinery and Emblem

1993. 50th Anniv (1992) of Pedro Domingo Murillo Technical College.
1291 **415** 60c. multicoloured . . . 15 10

416 Owl (painting, Chuquisaca)
417 Common Squirrel-monkeys

1993. Cave Art. Multicoloured.
1292 80c. Type **416** 20 10
1293 80c. Animals (painting, Cochabamba) 20 10
1294 80c. Geometric patterns (engraving, Chuquisaca) (vert) 20 10
1295 80c. Sun (engraving, Beni) (vert) 20 10
1296 80c. Llama (painting, Oruro) 20 10
1297 80c. Human figure (engraving, Potosi) . . . 20 10
1298 80c. Church and tower (painting, La Paz) (vert) 20 10
1299 80c. Warrior (engraving, Tarija) (vert) 20 10
1300 80c. Religious mask (engraving, Santa Cruz) (vert) 20 10

1993. America. Endangered Animals. Mult.
1301 80c. Type **417** 20 10
1302 2b.30 Ocelot . . . . 1·00 35

418 Emblems and Map
419 Yolanda Bedregal (poet)

1993. 90th Anniv (1992) of Pan-American Health Organization. Anti-AIDS Campaign.
1303 **418** 80c. multicoloured . . . 20 10

1993. Personalities. Each brown.
1304 50c. Type **419** 15 10
1305 70c. Simon Martinic (President of Cochabamba Philatelic Centre) 20 10
1306 90c. Eugenio von Boeck (politician and President of Bolivian Philatelic Federation) 25 15
1307 1b. Marina Nunez del Prado (sculptor) 25 15

420 "Virgin with Child and Saints" (anonymous)
421 Riberalta Square

1993. Christmas. Multicoloured.
1308 2b.30 "Adoration of the Shepherds" (Leonardo Flores) 95 35
1309 3b.50 Type **420** . . . . . 1·50 60
1310 6b. "Virgin of the Milk" (Melchor Perez de Holguin) . . . . 2·50 1·00

1994. Centenary of Riberalta.
1311 **421** 2b. multicoloured . . . 85 35

422 "Population and Our World" (Mayari Rodriguez)

1994. 2nd Prize-winning Design (6–8 year group) in United Nations Fund for Population Activities International Design Contest.
1312 **422** 2b.30 multicoloured . . 1·00 35

423 Sanchez de Lozada
424 Mascot

1994. Presidency of Gonzalo Sanchez de Lozada.
1313 **423** 2b. multicoloured . . . 85 35
1314 2b.30 multicoloured . . 1·00 35

1994. World Cup Football Championship, U.S.A. Multicoloured.
1315 80c. Type **424** 20 10
1316 1b.80 Bolivia v Uruguay . . 75 30
1317 2b.30 Bolivia v Venezuela 95 35
1318 2b.50 Bolivian team (left half) . . . . 1·00 35
1319 2b.50 Bolivian team (right half) . . . . 1·00 35
1320 2b.70 Bolivia v Ecuador . . 1·10 45
1321 3b.50 Bolivia v Brazil . . . 1·50 60
Nos. 1318/19 were issued together, se-tenant, forming a composite design.

425 Child
427 "Buddleja coriacea"

426 St. Peter's Church and Mgr. Jorge Manrique Hurtado (Archbishop, 1967–87)

1994. S.O.S. Children's Villages.
1322 **425** 2b.70 multicoloured . . 1·10 45

1994. 50th Anniv (1993) of Archdiocese of La Paz. Multicoloured.
1323 1b.80 Type **426** 75 30
1324 2b. Church of the Sacred Heart of Mary and Mgr. Abel Antezana y Rojas (first Archbishop, 1943–67) (vert) 85 35
1325 3b.50 Santo Domingo Church and Mgr. Luis Sainz Hinojosa (Archbishop since 1987) (vert) . . . . 1·50 60

1994. Environmental Protection. Trees. Mult.
1326 60c. Type **427** 15 10
1327 1b.80 "Bertholletia exelsa" 50 30
1328 2b. "Schinus molle" (horiz) 80 35
1329 2b.70 "Polylepis racemosa" 1·00 45
1330 3b. "Tabebuia chrysantha" 1·25 50
1331 3b.50 "Erythrina falcata" (horiz) . . . . 1·40 60

428 Paz
429 Tramcar and Mail Van

1994. Dr. Victor Paz Estenssoro (former President).
1332 **428** 2b. multicoloured . . . 55 35

1994. America. Postal Transport. Mult.
1333 1b. Type **429** . . . . 2·25 1·50
1334 5b. Airplane and ox cart . . 1·25 80

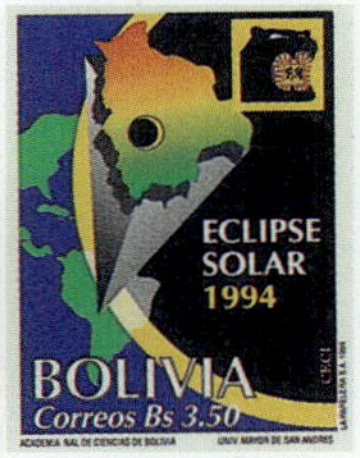

430 Coral Tree
431 Diagram of Eclipse

1994. 300th Anniv of San Borja.
1335 **430** 1b.60 multicoloured . . 40 25

1994. Solar Eclipse.
1336 **431** 3b.50 multicoloured . . 1·40 60

432 1894 100c. Stamp
433 Col. Marzana and Soldiers

1994. Centenary of Arms Issue of 1894.
1337 **432** 1b.80 multicoloured . . 50 30

1994. 62nd Anniv of Defence of Fort Boqueron.
1338 **433** 80c. multicoloured . . . 20 10

434 "Delicate Flower of Tarija"
435 Emblem

1994. Christmas. Pastels of children by Maria Susana Castillo. Multicoloured.
1339 2b. Type **434** 55 35
1340 5b. "Child of the High Plateau" . . . . 1·75 40
1341 20b. "Shoot of the Bolivian East" . . . . 6·75 2·40

1994. Pan-American Scout Jamboree, Cochabamba.
1342 **435** 1b.80 multicoloured . . 50 30

436 Sucre

437 Santa Ana Cathedral

1995. Birth Bicentenary of General Antonio Jose de Sucre. Multicoloured.
1343 1b.80 Type **436** 50 30
1344 3b.50 Sucre and national colours 90 60

1995. Centenary (1994) of Yacuma Province, Beni Department.
1345 **437** 1b.90 multicoloured . . 80 35
1346 2b.90 multicoloured . . 1·10 50

438 "Holy Virgin of Copacabana", Sanctuary and Franciscans

1995. Centenary of Franciscan Presence at Copacabana Sanctuary.
1347 **438** 60c. multicoloured . . . 15 10
1348 80c. multicoloured . . . 20 10

439 Anniversary Emblem

440 Paraguay and Bolivia Flags (Chaco Peace Treaty, 1938)

1995. 25th Anniv of Andean Development Corporation.
1349 **439** 2b.40 multicoloured . . 80 35

1995. Visit of President Juan Carlos Wasmosy of Paraguay and 169th Anniv (1994) of Republic of Bolivia.
1350 **440** 2b. multicoloured . . . 45 30

441 Montenegro

442 Digging Potatoes

1995. 50th Anniv of Publication of "Nationalism and Colonialism" by Carlos Montenegro.
1351 **441** 1b.20 black and pink . . 25 15

1995. 50th Anniv of FAO.
1352 **442** 1b. multicoloured . . . 20 10

443 Anniversary Emblem

1995. 50th Anniv of UNO.
1353 **443** 2b.90 dp blue, gold & bl 90 40

444 Andean Condor ("Condor")

1995. America. Endangered Species. Mult.
1354 5b. Type **444** . . . . 1·60 70
1355 5b. Llamas . . . . 1·60 70
Nos. 1354/5 were issued together, se-tenant, forming a composite design.

445 Airbus Industrie A320

447 Brewery Complex

446 Stone Head

1995. 50th Anniv (1994) of ICAO.
1356 **445** 50c. multicoloured . . . 10 10

1995. Archaeology. Samaipata Temple, Florida. Multicoloured.
1357 1b. Type **446** 20 10
1358 1b.90 Stone head (different) 40 25
1359 2b. Excavation and stone head 45 30
1360 2b.40 Entrance and animal-shaped vessel 55 35
Nos. 1357/60 were issued together, se-tenant, forming a composite design.

1995. Centenary of Taquina Brewery.
1361 **447** 1b. multicoloured . . . 20 10

448 "The Annunciation" (Cima da Conegliano)

449 Jose de Sanjines (lyricist)

1995. Christmas. Multicoloured.
1362 1b.20 Type **448** 25 15
1363 3b. "The Nativity" (Hans Baldung) 90 40
1364 3b.50 "Adoration of the Wise Men" (altarpiece, Rogier van der Weyden) 1·10 50

1995. 150th Anniv of National Anthem. Mult.
1365 1b. Type **449** 20 10
1366 2b. Benedetto Vincenti (composer) 45 30
Nos. 1365/6 were issued together, se-tenant, forming a composite design.

450 Flats, Villarroel, Factories, Road and Railway

452 Summit Emblem

1996. 50th Anniv of Decree for Abolition of Enforced Amerindian Labour. Mult.
1367 1b.90 Type **450** . . . . . 1·25 1·10
1368 2b.90 Pres. Gualberto Villarroel addressing Congress and freed workers . . . . 2·25 1·90
Nos. 1367/8 were issued together, se-tenant, forming a composite design.

1996. Various stamps surch.
1369 – 50c. on 3000000p. multicoloured (No. 1126) (postage) 10 10
1370 **265** 60c. on 2p.50 blue and red 10 10
1371 **313** 60c. on 5000000p. on 2000p. blue and red (No. 1116) 10 10
1372 **319** 60c. on 1400000p. mult 10 10
1373 1b. on 2500000p. green and yellow (No. 1120) 20 10
1374 **311** 1b.50 on 11000p. blue 30 20
1375 **312** 2b.50 on 23000p. brown and sepia 55 35
1376 **316** 3b. on 1000000p. blue and gold 65 40
1377 **272** 3b.50 on 6p.50 mult . . 80 50
1378 **279** 3b.50 on 9p. mult . . 80 50
1379 **323** 3b.50 on 2000000p. brown 80 50
1380 **298** 20b. on 10p. black, purple and bronze . . 5·00 2·00
1381 **299** 20b. on 13p. mult . . . 5·00 2·00
1382 – 3b.80 on 3p.80 mult (No. 945) (air) 85 55
1383 – 20b. on 3p.80 mult (No. 973a) . . . . . 5·00 2·00

1996. 10th Rio Group Summit Meeting, Cochabamba. Multicoloured.
1384 2b.50 Type **452** 55 35
1385 3b.50 Rio Group emblem 80 50

453 Summit Emblem

454 Facade

1996. Summit of the Americas on Sustainable Development, Santa Cruz de la Sierra.
1386 **453** 2b.50 multicoloured . . 55 35
1387 5b. multicoloured . . . 1·10 70

1996. National Bank.
1388 **454** 50c. black and blue . . . 10 10

455 De Lemoine

456 Family

1996. 220th Birth Anniv of Jose Joaquin de Lemoine (first postal administrator).
1389 **455** 1b. brown and stone . . 20 10

1997. CARE (Co-operative for American Relief Everywhere). Multicoloured.
1390 60c. Type **456** (20th anniv in Bolivia) 10 10
1391 70c. Hands cradling globe (50th anniv) (vert) 15 10

457 Musicians playing Piccolo and Saxophone

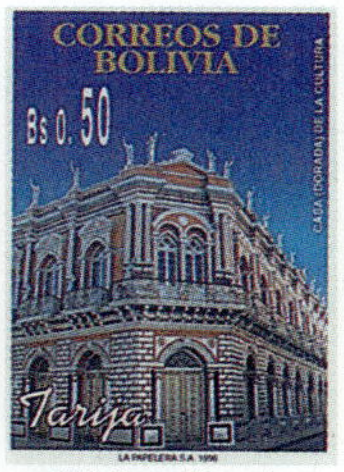

458 Casa Dorada (cultural centre)

1997. 50th Anniv of National Symphony Orchestra. "Overture" by G. Rodo Boulanger. Multicoloured.
1392 1b.50 Type **457** 30 20
1393 2b. Musicians playing violin and cello 45 30
Nos. 1392/3 were issued together, se-tenant, forming a composite design of the complete painting.

1997. Tarija. Multicoloured.
1394 50c. Type **458** 10 10
1395 60c. Entre Rios Church and musician 10 10
1396 80c. Narrows of San Luis (horiz) 15 10
1397 1b. Memorial to the Fallen of the Chaco War (territorial dispute with Paraguay) (horiz) 20 10
1398 3b. Virgin and shrine of Chaguaya (horiz) 60 40
1399 20b. Birthplace and statue of Jose Eustaquio Mendez (Independence hero), San Lorenzo (horiz) . . . . . 4·75 1·90

459 La Glorieta, Sucre

1997. Chuquisaca. Multicoloured.
1400 60c. Type **459** 10 10
1401 1b. Government Palace, Sucre (vert) 20 10
1402 1b.50 Footprints and drawing of dinosaur . . . 30 20
1403 1b.50 Interior of House of Freedom 30 20
1404 2b. Man playing traditional wind instrument (vert) . . 40 25
1405 3b. Statue of Juana Azurduy de Padilla (Independence heroine) (vert) 60 40

460 Miners' Monument

1997. Oruro. Multicoloured.
1406 50c. Type **460** 35 25
1407 60c. Demon carnival mask 10 10
1408 1b. Vigin of the Cave (statue) 20 10
1409 1b.50 Sajama (volcano) (horiz) 30 20
1410 2b.50 Chipaya child and belfry 50 30
1411 3b. Moreno (Raul Shaw) (singer and musician) (horiz) 60 40

461 Pres. Gonzalo Sanchez de Lozada of Bolivia and Pres. Chirac

1997. Visit to Bolivia of President Jacques Chirac of France.
1412 **461** 4b. multicoloured . . . 80 50

462 Children playing (Pamela G. Villarroel)

463 St. John Bosco (founder)

1997. 50th Anniv of UNICEF Children's Drawings. Multicoloured.
1413 50c. Type **462** 10 10
1414 90c. Boy leaping across clifftop (Lidia Acapa) . . 20 10
1415 1b. Children of different races on top of world (Gabriela Philco) 20 10
1416 2b.50 Children and swing (Jessica Grundy) 50 30

1997. Centenary of Salesian Brothers in Bolivia. Multicoloured.
1417 1b.50 Type **463** 30 20
1418 2b. Church and statue of Bosco with child 40 25

464 Chulumani

465 Emblem

1997. La Paz. Multicoloured.
1419 50c. Type **464** 10 10
1420 80c. Inca stone monolith . . 15 10
1421 1b.50 La Paz and Mt. Illimani 30 20
1422 2b. Gate of the Sun, Tiahuanaco (horiz) . . . 40 25
1423 2b.50 Dancers 50 30
1424 10b. "Virgin of Copacabana" and balsa raft on Lake Titicaca (horiz) . . . . 2·50 1·75

1997. Football Events. Multicoloured.
1425 3b. Type **465** (America Cup Latin-American Football Championship, Bolivia) 60 40
1426 5b. Eiffel Tower and trophy (World Cup Football Championship, France (1998) Eliminating Rounds) . . . . 1·00 65

466 Parliamentary Session and Building

467 Valley

1997. National Congress.
1427 **466** 1b. multicoloured . . . 20 10

1997. America. Traditional Costumes. Mult.
1428 5b. Type **467** . . . . 1·00 65
1429 15b. Eastern region . . . . 3·50 1·40

468 Members Flags and Southern Cross

469 "Virgin of the Hill" (anon)

1997. 6th Anniv of Mercosur (South American Common Market).
1430 **468** 3b. multicoloured . . . 60 40

1997. Christmas. Multicoloured.
1431 2b. Type **469** 40 25
1432 5b. "Virgin of the Milk" (anon) . . . . 1·00 65
1433 10b. "Holy Family" (Melchor Perez Holguin) 2·00 1·25

470 Diana, Princess of Wales

1997. Diana, Princess of Wales Commemoration. Multicoloured.
1434 2b. Type **470** 40 25
1435 3b. Diana, Princess of Wales beside minefield warning sign (horiz) 60 40

471 Presidents of Boliva and Spain

1998. State Visit of Prime Minister Jose Maria Aznar of Spain.
1436 **471** 6b. multicoloured . . . 2·00 80

472 Juan Munoz Reyes (President) and Medallion

473 Linked Arms and Globe

1998. 75th Anniv of Bolivian Engineers' Association.
1437 **472** 3b.50 multicoloured . . 60 40

1998. 70th Anniv of Rotary International in Bolivia.
1438 **473** 5b. multicoloured . . . 1·00 60

474 Delivering Letter, 1998

475 Werner Guttentag Tichauer (35th anniv of his bibliography)

1998. America. The Postman. Multicoloured.
1439 3b. Type **474** 60 40
1440 4b. Postmen on parade, 1942 (horiz) 80 50

1998. Anniversaries.
1441 **475** 1b.50 brown 20 10
1442 – 2b. green 40 25
1443 – 3b.50 black 60 40
DESIGNS—VERT: 2b. Martin Cardenas Hermosa (botanist, birth centenary (1999)); 3b. Adrian Patino Carpio (composer, 47th death anniv).

476 Amazon Water-lily

1998. Beni. Multicoloured.
1444 50c. Type **476** 10 10
1445 1b. "Callandria" sp. 20 10
1446 1b.50 White tajibo tree (vert) 20 10
1447 3b.50 Ceremonial mask . . 60 40
1448 5b. European otter . . . . 1·00 60
1449 7b. King vulture ("Tropical Condor") . . . . 1·40 90

477 River Acre

1998. Pando. Multicoloured.
1450 50c. Type **477** 10 10
1451 1b. Pale-throated sloth (vert) 20 10
1452 1b.50 Arroyo Bahia (vert) 20 10
1453 4b. Boa constrictor 80 50
1454 5b. Capybara with young 1·00 60
1455 7b. Palm trees, Cobija (vert) 1·40 90

478 Rural Activities and First Lady

1998. America. Women. Multicoloured.
1456 1b.50 Type **478** 20 10
1457 2b. First Lady, girl at blackboard and woman using computer 40 25
Nos. 1456/7 were issued together, se-tenant, forming a composite design.

479 Town Arms and Church

1998. 450th Anniv of La Paz.
1458 **479** 2b. multicoloured . . . 40 25

480 Emblem

481 Magnifying Glass and 1998 7b. Stamp

1998. 50th Anniv of Organization of American States.
1459 **480** 3b.50 blue and yellow . . 60 40

1998. "Espamer 98" Stamp Exhibition, Buenos Aires and 25th Anniv of Bolivian Philatelic Federation.
1460 **481** 2b. multicoloured . . . 40 25

482 "People going to Church" (Kathia Lucuy Saenz)

1998. Christmas. Multicoloured.
1461 2b. Type **482** 40 25
1462 6b. Pope John Paul II (vert) 1·25 80
1463 7b. Pope John Paul II with Mother Teresa (vert) . . . 1·40 90

483 U.P.U. Monument, Berne

1999. 125th Anniv of Universal Postal Union.
1464 **483** 3b.50 multicoloured . . 70 45

484 Statue of Football Player

1999. 75th Anniv of Cochabamba Football Association.
1465 **484** 5b. multicoloured . . . 1·40 65

485 Red Cross Lorries at Earthquake Site

1999. 50th Anniv of Geneva Conventions.
1466 **485** 5b. multicoloured . . . 1·00 65

486 Bernardo Guarachi and Mt. Everest

1999. 1st Ascent (1998) of Mt. Everest by a Bolivian.
1467 **486** 6b. multicoloured . . . 1·25 85

487 Winners on Podium

1999. 30th Anniv of First Special Olympics. Multicoloured.
1468 2b. Type **487** 40 25
1469 2b.50 Athletes on race track and winners on podium 50 30

488 Golden Palace

1999. Centenary of Japanese Immigration to Bolivia. Multicoloured.
1470 3b. Type **488** 60 40
1471 6b. View over lake and flags (vert) . . . . 1·25 85

489 Children dancing

1999. Anti-drugs Campaign.
1472 **489** 3b.50 multicoloured . . 70 45

490 Route Map and Presidents Hugo Banzer Suarez of Bolivia and Fernando Cardoso of Brazil

1999. Inauguration of Gas Pipeline from Santa Cruz, Bolivia, to Campinas, Brazil. Multicoloured.
1473 3b. Type **490** 60 40
1474 6b. Presidents Hugo Banzer Suarez and Fernando Cardoso embracing . . . 1·25 85

491 Village Scene

493 International Lions Emblem

492 "Hacia la Gloria" (directed Rau Duran, Mario Camacho and Jose Jimenez)

1999. 50th Anniv of SOS Children's Villages.
1475 **491** 3b.50 multicoloured . . 70 45

1999. Centenary of Motion Pictures in Bolivia. Multicoloured.
1476 50c. Type **492** 10 10
1477 50c. "Jonah and the Pink Whale" (dir. J. Carlos Valdivia) 10 10
1478 1b. "Wara Wara" (dir. Jose Velasco) 20 15
1479 1b. "Vuelve Sebastiana" (dir. Jorge Ruiz) 20 15
1480 3b. "The Chaco Campaign" (dir. Juan Penaranda, Jose Velasco and Mario Camacho) 60 40
1481 3b. "The Watershed" (dir. Jorge Ruiz) 60 40
1482 6b. "Yawar Mallku" (dir. Jorge Sanjines) . . . . . 1·25 85
1483 6b. "Mi Socio" (dir. Paolo Agazzi) . . . . 1·25 85
MS1484 180 × 80 mm. Nos. 1476/83 4·25 3·00

1999. 50th Anniv (1998) of La Paz Lions Club.
1485 **493** 3b.50 multicoloured . . 70 45

494 Mt. Tunari

1999. Cochabamba. Multicoloured.
1486 50c. Type **494** 10 10
1487 1b. Forest, Cochabamba Valley 20 15
1488 2b. Omereque vase and fertility goddess (vert) . . 40 25
1489 3b. Totora 60 40
1490 5b. Teofilo Vargas Candia (composer) and music score (vert) . . . . . . 1·00 65
1491 6b. "Christ of Harmony" (mountain-top statue) (vert) . . . . 1·25 85

495 Tarapaya Lagoon (Inca spa)

496 Globe with Children, Fish, Flower, Pencil, Heart and Stars

1999. Potosi. Multicoloured.
1492 50c. Type **495** 10 10
1493 1b. First republican coins, minted in 1827 (horiz) . . 20 10
1494 2b. Mt. Chorolque (horiz) 45 30
1495 3b. Green Lagoon (horiz) 65 40
1496 5b. "The Mestizo sitting on a Trunk" (Teofilo Loaiza) 90 60
1497 6b. Alfredo Dominguez Romeo (Tupiceno singer) 1·25 80

1999. America. A New Millennium without Arms. Multicoloured.
1498 3b.50 Type **496** 75 50
1499 3b.50 Globe emerging from flower 75 50

497 Children from S.O.S. Childrens Village

498 Ugarte

1999. Christmas. Multicoloured.
1500 2b. Type **497** 45 30
1501 6b. "The Birth of Jesus" (Gaspar Miguel de Berrios) (vert) . . . . . 1·25 80
1502 7b. "Our Family in the World" (Omar Medina) (vert) . . . . 1·50 1·00

2000. 5th Death Anniv of Victor Agustin Ugarte (football player).
1503 **498** 3b. grey, green and yellow 65 40

499 El Arenal Park

2000. Santa Cruz. Multicoloured.
1504 50c. Type **499** 10 10
1505 1b. Ox cart 20 10
1506 2b. Raul Otero Reiche, Gabriel Rene Moreno and Hernando Sanabria Fernandez (writers) . . . 45 30
1507 3b. Cotoca Virgin (statue) (vert) 65 40
1508 5b. Anthropomorphic vase (vert) . . . . 1·10 70
1509 6b. Bush dog . . . . 1·25 80

500 "The Village of Serinhaem in Brazil" (Frans Post)

2000. 500th Anniv of Discovery of Brazil.
1510 **500** 5b. multicoloured . . . 1·10 70

501 Granado

2000. Javier del Granado (poet) Commemoration.
1511 **501** 3b. grey, blue and red 65 40

502 Cyclists

503 Oriental Clay Figure

2000. "Double Copacabana" Cycle Race.
1512 **502** 1b. multicoloured . . . 20 10
1513 – 3b. multicoloured . . . 65 40
1514 – 5b. multicoloured . . . 1·10 70
1515 – 7b. multicoloured . . . 1·50 1·00
DESIGNS: 3b. to 7b. Various race scenes.

2000. National Archaeology Museum Exhibits. Each brown and gold.
1516 50c. Type **503** 10 10
1517 50c. Clay figure, Potosi . . 10 10
1518 70c. Oriental clay head, Beni 15 10
1519 90c. Clay vase, Tarija . . . 20 10
1520 1b. Clay head, Oruro . . . 20 10
1521 1b. Yampara clay urn . . . 20 10
1522 3b. Inca wood carving . . . 65 40
1523 5b. Oriental anthropomorphic vase . . 1·10 70
1524 20b. Tiwanaku clay mask 4·50 3·00

504 Male and Female Symbols in Red Vortex

2000. America. Anti-AIDS Campaign. Mult.
1525 3b.50 Type **504** 75 45
1526 3b.50 Couple walking through wall 75 45

505 Soldier's Head and Bird on Laurel Wreath

2000. Centenary of Maximiliano Parades Military School.
1527 **505** 2b.50 multicoloured . . 55 35

506 "Self-portrait"

2000. Birth Centenary of Cecilio Guzman de Rojas (artist). Showing paintings. Multicoloured.
1528 1b. Type **506** 25 15
1529 2b.50 "Triumph of Nature" (horiz) 55 35
1530 5b. "Andina" . . . . 1·10 65
1531 6b. "Students' Quarrel" (horiz) . . . . 1·25 75

507 Crowd and Brandenburg Gate

2000. 50th Anniv of German Federal Republic.
1532 **507** 6b. multicoloured . . . 1·25 75

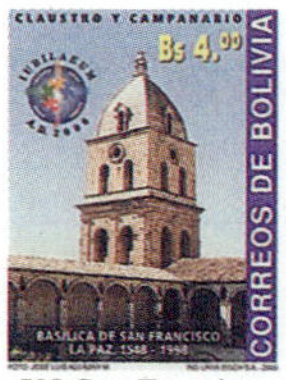

508 San Francisco Basilica, La Paz

509 Waterfall and Statue

2000. Holy Year 2000. Bolivian Episcopal Conference. Multicoloured.
1533 4b. Type **508** 90 55
1534 6b. Stalks of grain breaking through barbed-wire . . . 1·25 75

2000. New Millennium.
1535 **509** 5b. multicoloured . . . 1·10 65

510 Archangel Gabriel

511 Painting of John the Baptist and Emblem

2000. Christmas. Showing 17th-century paintings of Angels from Calamarca Church. Multicoloured.
1536 3b. Type **510** 65 40
1537 5b. Angel of Virtue . . . . 1·10 65
1538 10b. Angel with ear of corn 2·25 1·40

2000. 900th Anniv of Sovereign Military Order of St. John.
1539 **511** 6b. multicoloured . . . 1·25 75

512 Lobster Claw (*Heliconia rostrata*)

2001. Patriotic Symbols. Multicoloured.
1540 10b. Type **512** (designated national flower, 1990) . . 2·25 1·40
1541 20b. *Periphrangus dependens* (designated national flower 1924) . . . . . . 4·50 2·75
1542 30b. First Bolivian coat of arms (adopted 1825) . . . 6·50 4·00
1543 50b. Second Bolivian coat of arms (adopted 1826) . . . 11·00 6·50
1544 100b. Present day Bolivian coat of arms (adopted 1851) . . . . 20·00 12·00

513 Map and Stars of European Union and Map of Bolivia

2001. 25th Anniv of Co-operation between Bolivia and European Union.
1550 **513** 6b. multicoloured . . . 1·25 75

514 Statue of Justice, Lion and Portico

515 Temple of San Francisco, Potosi

2001. 171st Anniv of Faculty of Law and Political Sciences, Universidad de Mayor of San Andres, La Paz.
1551 **514** 6b. multicoloured . . . 1·00 60

2001. America. UNESCO World Heritage Sites. Multicoloured.
1552 1b.50 Type **515** 25 15
1553 5b. "Fraile" and "Ponce" (monoliths) (horiz) . . . 80 50

516 Man carrying Envelopes up Stairs

518 Family

517 Devil's Molar (mountain)

2001. Philately. Each green.
1554 50c. Type **516** 10 10
1555 1b. Boy with six stamps . . 15 10
1556 1b.50 Man with glasses and stamp album 25 15
1557 2b. Child wearing hat, and three stamps 35 20
1558 2b.50 Humanized stamp lying in tray 40 25

2001.
1559 **517** 1b.50 multicoloured . . 25 15

2001. National Census. Multicoloured.
1560 1b. Type **518** 15 10
1561 1b.50 People surrounding wheelchair user 25 15
1562 1b.50 Aboriginal woman and people of different races 25 15
1563 2b.50 People of different races 40 25
1564 3b. Children 50 30

519 Silver Spot (*Dione juno*)

2001. Butterflies and Insects. Multicoloured.
1565 1b. Type **519** 15 10
1566 1b. *Orthoptera* sp. 15 10

1567 1b.50 Bamboo page (*Philaethria dido*) 25 15
1568 2b.50 Jewel butterfly (*Diaethria clymena*) (inscr "Diathria clymene") . . . 40 25
1569 2b.50 *Mantis religiosa* . . . 40 25
1570 3b. *Tropidacris latreillei* . . 50 30
1571 4b. Hercules beetle (*Dynastes hercules*) (inscr "Escarabajo Hercule") . . 65 40
1572 5b. *Arctiidae* sp. 80 50
1573 5b. *Acrocinus longimanus* . . 80 50
1574 5b. *Lucanidae* sp. 80 50
1575 6b. *Morpho godarti* . . . . 1·00 60
1576 6b. *Caligo idomeneus* ("inscr idomineus") . . . . . . 1·00 60

520 Map of Americas and Emblem

2001. 21st Inter-America Scout Conference, Cochabamba.
1577 **520** 3b.50 multicoloured . . 60 35

521 Woman and Emblem

522 St. Mary Magdalen

2001. Breast Cancer Prevention Campaign.
1578 **521** 1b.50 multicoloured . . 25 15

2001. Christmas. Showing sculptures by Gaspar of La Cueva from Convent of San Francisco, Potosi. Multicoloured.
1579 3b. Type **522** 25 15
1580 5b. St. Apolonia 80 50
1581 10b. St. Teresa of Avila . . 1·75 1·00

523 Portrait and Casa La Laertad, Sucre

2001. Joaquin Gantier Valda Commemoration.
1582 **523** 4b. multicoloured . . . 65 40

524 Flags and Hands enclosing Farmer, Mother, Child and Doctor

2001. 25th Anniv of Co-operation between Bolivia and Belgium.
1583 **524** 6b. multicoloured . . . 65 40

525 Aerial Photograph and Bridge

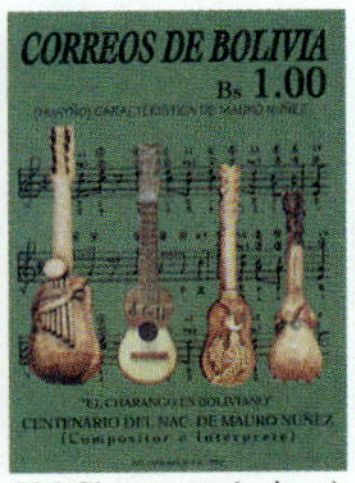
526 Charangos (guitars) and Musical Score

2002. Bolivia–Peru Presidential Summit. Multicoloured.
1584 50c. Type **525** 10 10
1585 3b. Aerial photograph and bridge (different) 40 25

2001. Birth Centenary of Mauro Nunez (musician). Multicoloured.
1586 1b. Type **526** 15 10
1587 6b. Mauro Nunez 80 50

527 Dancers with Horned Head-dresses (Diablada)

528 "El Kusillo" (folk character)

2001. Cultural Heritage. Oruro Carnival. Multicoloured.
1588 50c. Type **527** 10 10
1589 1b.50 Female dancer (Morenada) 20 15
1590 2b.50 Female dancers and man in embroidered clothes (Caporales) . . . 35 20
1591 5b. Male dancers in multicoloured head-dresses (Tobas) 70 40
1592 7b. Woman dancer in elaborate hat and yellow skirt (Suri Sikuri) (vert) 95 55
1593 7b. Dancers wearing bonnets (Pujllay) (vert) 95 55

2002. Butterflies and Insects (2nd series). As T **519**. Multicoloured.
1594 3b. White-tailed page (*Urania leilus*) 20 15
1595 3b. *Tropidacris latreilli* . . . 20 15
1596 3b. *Papilio cresphontes macho* 20 15
1597 3b. Longhorn beetle (*Acrocinus longimanus*) . . 20 15
1598 3b. *Prepona buckleyana* . . 20 15
1599 3b. *Thysannia agripyna cramer* (left wings) 20 15
1600 3b. *Thysannia agripyna cramer* (right wings) . . . 20 15
1601 3b. *Lucanus verde* (inscr "Lucano") 20 15
1602 3b. Butterfly (inscr "Nymphalidae") 20 15
1603 3b. *Escarabajo hercule* . . . 20 15
1604 3b. Butterfly (different) (inscr "Heliconinae") . . 20 15
1605 3b. Grasshopper (inscr "Orthopterdae") 20 15

Nos. 1599/1600 were issued in se-tenant pairs within the sheet, each pair forming a composite design.

2002. 3rd International Theatre Festival, La Paz.
1606 **528** 3b. multicoloured . . . 20 15

529 Mountain Viscachas (rodent), Potosi

2002. International Year of Mountains and Eco-tourism. Multicoloured.
1607 80c. Type **529** 10 10
1608 1b. Polylepis (tree), Cochabamba (vert) . . . 15 10
1609 1b.50 Huayna Potosi mountains, La Paz . . . 20 15
1610 2b.50 Payachatas mountains, Oruro 35 20
1611 2b.50 Sajama mountain, Oruro (vert) 35 20

530 Anniversary Emblem and Rainbow

2002. Centenary of Pan-American Health Organization.
1612 **530** 3b. multicoloured . . . 40 25

531 Gunnar Mendoza

2002. Dr. Gunnar Mendoza (scientist) Commemoration.
1613 **531** 4b. multicoloured . . . 55 35

532 Airliner over Mountains

2002. 50th Anniv of Military Aviation College, Germán Busch. Multicoloured.
1614 4b. Type **532** 55 35
1615 5b. Acrobatic aeroplanes (vert) 70 45
1616 6b. Three helicopters . . . 80 50

533 Orinoco Goose (*Neochen jubata*)

534 Thousand Year old Cedar Tree and Church Tower

2002. Day of Natural Resources. Multicoloured.
1617 50c. Type **533** (CEFILCO philatelic association) . . 10 10
1618 4b. Orange-breasted falcon (*Falco deiroleucus*) (30th anniv of Bolivian philatelic federation) . . . 55 35
1619 6b. Black-bodied woodpecker (*Dryocopus schulzi*) (PHILAKOREA 2002) 80 50

2002. 400th Anniv of Sucre Monastery.
1620 **534** 4b. multicoloured . . . 55 35

535 Indian Madonna

537 Couple wearing Traditional Costume

536 Potosi and Armando Alba Zambrana

2002. Twentieth-century Art. Multicoloured.
1621 70c. Type **535** (sculpture, Marina Nunez del Prado) 10 10
1622 70c. Mountain (painting, Maria Luisa Pachero) . . 10 10
1623 80c. Indian mother (sculpture, Marina Nunez del Prado) 10 10
1624 80c. "Cordillera" (painting, Maria Luisa Pachero) . . 10 10
1625 5b. Venus Negra (sculpture, Marina Nunez del Prado) 70 45
1626 5b. "Cerros" (painting, Maria Luisa Pachero) (horiz) 70 45

2002. Birth Centenary (2001) of Armando Alba Zambrana (historian).
1627 **536** 3b. multicoloured . . . 40 25

2002. Birth Bicentenary of Alcide d'Orbigny (naturalist and palaeontologist). Multicoloured.
1628 1b. Type **537** 15 10
1629 4b. Boat on river (horiz) . . 55 35
1630 6b. Alcide d'Orbigny . . . 80 50

538 Teacher and Pupils

2002. America. Education and Literacy Campaign. Multicoloured.
1631 1b. Type **538** 15 10
1632 2b.50 Indigenous children and computer 35 20

539 Mary and Jesus

2002. Christmas. Multicoloured.
1633 3b. Type **539** 40 25
1634 5b. Nativity 70 45
1635 6b. "The Adoration of the Kings" (painting, 18th-century) 80 50

540 Apolinar Camacho

541 Soldier (statue)

2003. 1st Death Anniv of Apolinar Camacho (composer).
1636 **540** 2b.50 multicoloured . . 30 15

2003. Centenary of Battle of Bahia. Multicoloured.
1637 50c. Type **541** 10 10
1638 1b. Three soldiers (statue) 15 10

542 Anniversary Emblem

543 Currency and Bank Emblem

2003. 25th Anniv of Culture of Peace Month (UN peace initiative). Bolivian Permanent Assembly of Human Rights.
1639 **542** 6b. ultramarine 80 45

2003. 75th Anniv of Central Bank.
1640 **543** 4b. multicoloured . . . 50 30

544 Court Emblem

2003. 5th Anniv of Sucre Constitutional Court.
1641 **544** 1b.50 multicoloured . . 20 10

545 Quinoa (*Chenopodium quinoa*)

2003. America. Flora and Fauna Multicoloured.
1642 50c. Type **545** 10 10
1643 1b. Llama 15 10

546 Anniversary Emblem

2003. Centenary of Panama Republic.
1644 **546** 7b. multicoloured . . . 90 50

547 Porfirio Diaz Machicao, Rosendo Villalobos and Monsignor Juan Quiros (writers)

2003. 75th Anniv of Language Academy.
1645 **547** 6b. multicoloured . . . 80 45

548 Flags and Latin America

2003. Latin American, Spanish and Portuguese Heads of Government Conference, Santa Cruz. Multicoloured.
1646 6b. Type **548** 80 45
1647 6b. Eastern globe and flags 80 45
Nos. 1646/7 were issued together, se-tenant, forming a composite design.

549 Virgin of Guadeloupe (Brother Diego de Ocana)
550 "Adoration of the Shepherds" (Leonardo Flores) (Templo de Calamarca, La Paz)

2003. 450th Anniv of La Plata Archdiocese.
1648 **549** 6b. multicoloured . . . 80 45

2003. Christmas. Multicoloured.
1649 1b.50 Type **550** 20 10
1650 6b. "Adoration of the Shepherds" (Bernardo Bitti) (Cathedral museum, Sucre) 80 45
1651 7b. "Adoration of the Shepherds" (Melchor Perez de Holguin) (Santa Teresa museum, Potosi) (horiz) 90 50

551 Pope John Paul II
552 Girl and Rainbow

2004. 25th Anniv of Pontificate of Pope John Paul II. Multicoloured.
1652 1b. Type **551** 15 10
1653 1b.50 Seated facing right (painting) 20 10
1654 5b. Giving blessing to native Bolivians 65 40
1655 6b. Wearing gold cope . . . 80 45
1656 7b. Seated facing left . . . 90 50
MS1657 150 × 110 mm. 10b. × 2, Mary of Copacabana and balsa boat on the Lake Titicaca; Santa Tersa de Avila (statue) (Gaspar de la Cueva) . . . . 2·60 2·60

2004. 10th Anniv of ARCO IRIS Foundation (street children's charitable organization).
1658 **552** 1b.80 multicoloured . . 25 10

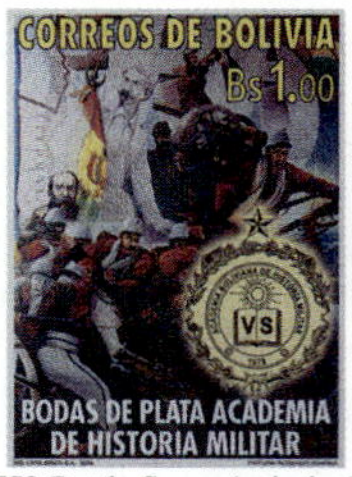

553 Battle Scene (painting)

2004. 25th Anniv of Military History Academy.
1659 **553** 1b. multicoloured . . . 15 10

554 Athens, 2004 Emblem, Rifle Shooting, Gymnastics and Judo

2004. Olympic Games, Athens. Multicoloured.
1660 1b.50 Type **554** 20 15
1661 7b. Emblem, running and swimming . . . . 1·00 55

555 Holy Family

2004. Christmas. Multicoloured.
1662 1b.50 Type **555** 20 15
1663 3b. Child praying 40 25
1664 6b. Candle 85 50

556 Typewriter on Wheels

2004. 75th Anniv of La Paz Journalists' Association.
1665 **556** 1b.50 multicoloured 2015

557 Palm

2004. America. Environmental Protection. Mult.
1666 5b. Type **557** 70 40
1667 6b. Parrots (Gilka Wara Libermann) 85 50

558 Map of Bolivia and Emblems

2005. Centenary of Rotary International (charitable organization). Multicoloured.
1668 3b. Type **558** 40 25
1669 3b. Paul Harris (founder), "100" and emblem . . . 40 25
Nos. 1668/9 were issued together, se-tenant, forming a composite design.

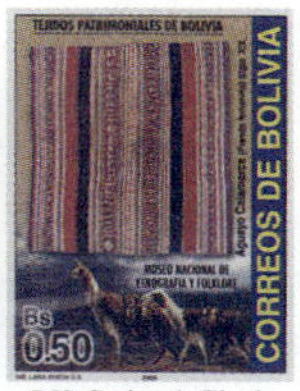

559 Water Pipe Outflow and Beach
560 Striped Cloth

2005. Environmental Projects. Multicoloured.
1670 5b. Type **559** (Pras Pando (water project)) 70 40
1671 6b. Seedling, European Union and Bolivian Flags (PRAEDAC (programme to support alternate development)) (vert) . . . 85 50

2005. Cultural Heritage. Textiles. Multicoloured.
1672 50c. Type **560** 10 10
1673 1b. Horizontal stripes and dark bands 15 10
1674 1b.50 Vertical decorated stripes and red bands . . 20 15
1675 6b. Wide black bands . . . 85 50
1676 6b. Two decorated squares (horiz) 85 50

561 Otto Felipe Braun
562 *Harpia harpyja*

2005. 80th Anniv of Colegio Mariscal Braun, La Paz.
1677 **561** 6b. multicoloured . . . 85 50

2005. Birds. Multicoloured.
1678 1b. Type **562** (Interexpo '05, Dominican Republic) . . 15 10
1679 1b.50 *Penelope dabbenei* (35th anniv of Filatelica Boliviana) 20 15
1680 7b. *Aulacorhynchus coeruleicinctus* (Washington 2006) . . . 1·00 55

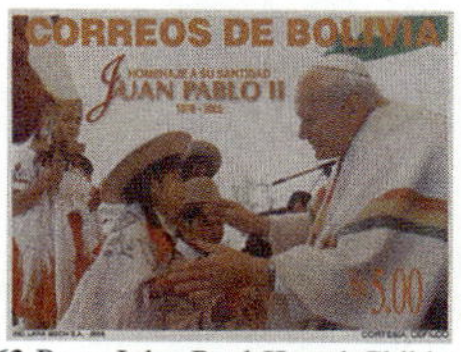

563 Pope John Paul II and Children

2005. Pope John Paul II Commemoration (1681) and Inauguration of Pope Benedict XVI (1682). Multicoloured.
1681 5b. Type **563** 70 40
1682 5b. Pope Benedict XVI (vert) 70 40

564 Sail Ship

2005. The Pacific War of 1879–1884.
1683 **564** 5b. multicoloured . . . 70 40

565 Don Quixote riding Rocinante

2005. 400th Anniv of the Publication of "Don Quixote de la Mancha" by Miguel de Cervantes.
1684 **565** 4b. multicoloured . . . 60 35

566 Mother and Child

2005. America. Struggle against Poverty. Multicoloured.
1685 6b. Type **566** 85 50
1686 7b. Fisherman and fleshless fish . . . . 1·00 55

567 Idelfonso Murguia

2005. 184th Anniv of Infanteria Colorado Regiment (presidential escort).
1687 **567** 2b. multicoloured . . . 30 20

568 Flamingos in Flight

2005. Tourism.
1688 **568** 6b. multicoloured . . . 85 50

569 Two-toed Sloth

2005. 20th Anniv of LIDEMA (conservation group).
1689 **569** 6b. multicoloured . . . 85 50

570 1863 Un-issued 2r. Stamps

2005. Stamp Day. Sheet 91 × 110 mm containing T **570** and similar horiz designs. Multicoloured.
MS1690 2r. × 3, Type **570**; 1924 5b. stamp; British 1840 Penny Black (1st stamp) and Brazil 1843 30r. ("Olho de Boi" ("Bull's Eye")) stamp; 4r. × 3, 1867 5c. stamps (1st Bolivian stamps); 1930 3b. surch on 20c. ("Graf Zeppelin") stamp; 1987 60c. stamp . . . . 5·00 5·00

571 Three Wise Men

2005. Christmas. Multicoloured.
1691 1b.50 Type **571** 20 15
1692 3b. Holy family 40 25

2006. Nos. 1119, 1115 and No. 1119 surch.
1693 1b. on 1000000p. black and green 15 10
1694 2b. on 550000 multicoloured 30 20
1695 2b.50 on 1000000 multicoloured 35 25

575 School Building, 1906

2006. Centenary of Engineering University.
1696 **575** 6b. multicoloured . . . 85 50

576 President Morales **577** Red Cross Worker

2006. Election of President Juan Evo Morales Ayma (Evo Morales) (first indigenous South American President. Multicoloured.
1697 1b.50 Type **576** 20 15
1698 5b. At inauguration 70 40
1699 6b. Wearing tribal dress . . 85 50

2006. Bolivian Red Cross.
1700 **577** 5b. multicoloured . . . 70 40

578 Inca Messenger and Envelopes **579** Boy Scouts at Exfivia 75

2006. 15th Anniv of ECOBOL.
1701 **578** 1b. green 15 10
1702 1b.50 ultramarine . . . 15 10

2006. Stamp Collectors' Day. Sheet 90 × 105 mm containing T **579** and similar horiz designs. Multicoloured.
MS1703 1b.50 Type **579**; 1b.50 Stamp album; 1b.50 Bird stamps of Bolivia and Honduras; 6b. Exfilmar 80; 6b. Ship stamps of Bolivia and Iceland; 6b. Floral stamps of Bolivia and Dominican Republic . . . . 2·75 2·75

580 Legislative Palace and Second Adapted National Flag of 1851

2006. Flags. Multicoloured.
1704 1b.50 Type **580** 20 10
1705 5b. Liberty House and first adapted national flag of 1826 . . . . 70 40
1706 6b. Liberty House and first national flag of 1825 . . . 80 50

581 Friar and Donkey

2006. 400th Anniv of Franciscan Order in Tarija. Multicoloured.
1707 2b. Type **581** 30 20
1708 2b. Early church 30 30
1709 6b. Basilica interior (vert) . . 85 50
1710 6b. "La Inmaulada" (vert) . . 85 50

582 *14-bis*

2006. Centenary of First Flight by Alberto Santos Dumont.
1711 **582** 1b.50 multicoloured . . 15 10

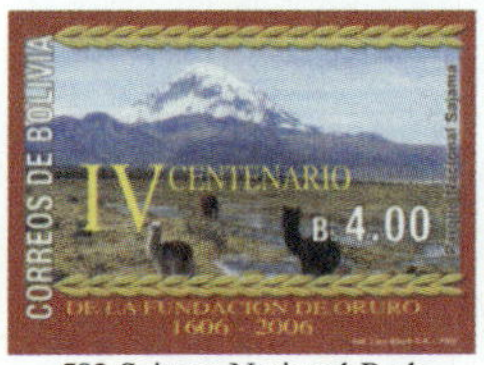

583 Sajama National Park

2006. 400th Anniv of Oruro.
1712 **583** 4b. multicoloured . . . 60 35

584 9 February Avenue

2006. Centenary of Bahia Harbour. Multicoloured.
1713 1b. Type **584** 15 10
1714 1b.50 German Busch Plaza 15 10
1715 2b.50 Tree (vert) 35 25
1716 3b. Potosi Plaza 40 25
1717 4b. Bahia Pando river . . . 60 35
1718 6b. Friendship Bridge . . . 85 50
1719 7b. Port Avenue (vert) . . . 1·00 55

585 Vicuna

2006. Endangered Species. Multicoloured.
1720 1b. Type **585** 15 10
1721 1b.50 Head of Yacare caiman (Caiman yacare) (horiz) 15 10
1722 5b. Yacare caiman (horiz) 70 40
1723 7b. Vicuna (horiz) . . . . . 1·00 55

586 Area damaged by Mining

2006. International Year of Deserts and Desertification. Multicoloured.
1724 1b.50 Type **586** 15 10
1725 2b. Erosion, Tolomosa river basin 30 20
1726 3b. Terraces 40 25
1727 4b. Erosion, Caranavi . . . 60 35

587 Low Energy Bulb as Flower **588** Virgin of Roses

2006. America. Energy Conservation. Multicoloured.
1728 3b. Type **587** 40 25
1729 4b. Light bulb containing cash 60 35

2006. Christmas. Multicoloured.
1730 4b. Type **588** 60 35
1731 5b. Adoration of the Magi 70 40
1732 6b. Adoration of the shepherds 85 50

589 Rocks (astronomical observatory)

2006. Manco Kapac. Multicoloured.
1733 5b. Type **589** 70 40
1734 6b. Copacabana Temple . . 85 50
1735 7b. Boat on lake . . . . . 1·00 55

590 Toucan

2006. Birds of Pando. Multicoloured.
1736 2b.50 Type **590** 35 25
1737 6b. Inscr "Pajaro azul" . . 85 50

591 Helmeted Curassow (inscr "Pavichi cresta azul")

2006. Birds of Santa Cruz. Multicoloured.
1738 3b.50 Type **591** 50 30
1739 7b. Harpy eagle (inscr "Aguila arpia") 85 50

592 Miniature Schnauzer

2006. Dogs. Multicoloured.
1740 1b. Type **592** 15 10
1741 2b. Husky 30 20
1742 3b. American boxer 40 25
1743 4b. Inscr "Criollo" 60 35

593 14 September Plaza

2007. 'Latin America and Caribbean Lions' Forum, Cochabamba, Bolivia.
1744 **593** 6b. multicoloured . . . 80 50

594 Map of Europe

2007. 50th Anniv of Treaty of Rome. Multicoloured.
1745 3b.50 Type **594** 50 30
1746 7b. Flag of stars 85 50
Nos. 1745/6 were issued together, se-tenant, forming a composite design.

595 Philatelic Magazines

2007. 50th Anniv of Philatelic Association. Multicoloured.
1747 50c. Type **595** 10 10
1748 1b. Arnold Glaeser (first president) and overprinted stamp 15 10
1749 2b.50 Simon Martinic and stamp catalogue 35 20
1750 3b. Franz Steimbach and Oscar Roca 40 25
1751 3b.50 Cathedral and 'Heroinas de la Coronilla' monument 50 30
1752 6b. 'Christ of the Concord' (statue) and Cathedral, Cochabamba 80 50
Nos. 1751/2 were issued together, se-tenant, forming a composite design.

596 Charango

2007. Cultural Heritage. Multicoloured.
1753 4b. Type **596** 55 35
1754 6b. Charango (different) . . 80 50

597 Emblem and '90'

2007. 90th Anniv of Bolivian Red Cross.
1755 **597** 2b.50 multicoloured . . 35 20

598 Francis Harrington (missionary and institute founder)

2007. Centenary of American Institute.
1756 **598** 7b.50 multicoloured . . 1·00 60

599 Cog, Map and Emblems

2007. 75th Anniv of Chamber of Commerce. Multicoloured.
1757 9b. Type **599** . . . . 1·20 70
1758 12b. '75 Anos', emblems and cog . . . . 1·60 95

599a *Ara ararauna* (blue and gold macaw)

2007. Birds. Multicoloured.
1758a 5b.50 Type **599a** 60 35
1758b 7b.50 *Porphyrula martinica* (purple gallinule) . . . . 1·00 60

600 Jaguar

602 Andean Condor (inscr 'Opisthocomus hoazin')

601 Emblems

2007. Santa Cruz Zoo. Multicoloured.

1759	6b. Type **600**	80	50
1760	9b. Puma	1·20	70

2007. Heads of the American Air Force Conference, Santa Cruz, Bolivia.

1761 **601**	10b.50 multicoloured	1·40	85

2007. Birds of La Paz. Multicoloured.

1762	4b. Type **602**	55	35
1763	5b.50 Andean cock-of-the rock (*Rupicola peruviana*) (inscr "Tunqui") (horiz)	75	45

603 Robert Baden Powell (founder)

2007. Centenary of World Scouting. Multicoloured.

1764	7b.50 Type **603**	1·00	60
1765	8b.50 Emblem (vert)	1·10	65

604 *Cyclarhis guyannensis*

2007. Birds. Multicoloured.

1766	3b.50 Type **604**	50	30
1767	4b. *Egretta alba* (vert)	55	30
1767a	5b.50 *Ramphastos toco*	60	35
1769	6b.50 *Bubo virgianus* (vert)	90	55
1770	6b.50 *Trogon melanurus* (vert)	90	55
1771	6b.50 *Falco sparverius*	90	55
1772	6b.50 *Hymantopus mexicanus* (vert)	90	55
1774	7b.50 *Platalea ajaja*	1·00	60
1774a	7b.50 *Opisthocomus hoazin*	1·00	60
1775	8b.50 *Sarcoramphus papa*	1·10	65
1776	8b.50 *Momotus momota*	1·10	65
1777	9b. *Tinamotis pentlandii* (vert)	1·20	70
1778	9b. *Chlorostilbon aureoventris* (vert)	1·20	70
1779	10b.50 *Ardea cocoi* (vert)	1·40	85

Nos. 1768 and 1773 have been left for stamps not yet received.

605 Signature

2007. 40th Death Anniv of Ernesto (Che) Guevara (resistance fighter). Multicoloured.

1780	30b. Type **605**	3·00	1·80
1781	50b. Images of Che Guevara (vert)	5·75	3·50

606 Aircraft on Runway

2007. 50th Anniv of Bolivian Airforce. Multicoloured.

1782	7b.50 Type **606**	1·00	60
1783	9b. Aircraft in flight	1·20	70

607 *Holy Family* (Luca Cambiasso)

2007. Christmas. Multicoloured.

1784	3b.50 Type **607**	50	30
1785	4b. *Adoration of the Shepherds* (Pieter Aersten)	55	35
1786	6b.50 *The Nativity* (Gregoria Gamarra)	90	55

POSTAGE DUE STAMPS

D 81

D 93 "Youth"

1931.

D265 **D 81**	5c. blue	70	85
D266	10c. red	70	85
D267	15c. yellow	1·00	85
D268	30c. green	1·00	85
D269	40c. violet	1·75	1·75
D270	50c. sepia	2·40	2·40

1938. Triangular designs.

D346 **D 93**	5c. red	50	50
D347 –	10c. green	50	50
D348 –	30c. blue	50	50

DESIGNS: 10c. Torch of Knowledge; 30c. Date and Symbol of 17 May 1936 Revolution.

BOPHUTHATSWANA Pt. 1

The republic of Bophuthatswana was established on 6 December 1977 as one of the "black homelands" constructed from the territory of the Republic of South Africa.

Although this independence did not receive international political recognition we are satisfied that the stamps had "de facto" acceptance as valid for the carriage of mail outside Bophuthatswana.

Bophuthatswana was formally re-incorporated into South Africa on 27 April 1994.

100 cents = 1 rand.

1 Hand releasing Dove

1977. Independence. Multicoloured.

1	4c. Type **1**	35	35
2	10c. Leopard (national emblem)	75	60
3	15c. Coat of arms	1·00	1·00
4	20c. National flag	1·25	1·40

2 African Buffalo

1977. Tribal Totems. Multicoloured.

5a	1c. Type **2**	20	15
6a	2c. Bush pig	20	15
7a	3c. Chacma baboon	20	15
8a	4c. Leopard	20	10
9a	5c. Crocodile	20	10
10	6c. Savanna monkey	20	10
11a	7c. Lion	30	15
12a	8c. Spotted hyena	20	15
13	9c. Cape porcupine	25	15
14	10c. Aardvark	25	10
15	15c. Tilapia (fish)	1·00	15
16	20c. Hunting dog	25	20
17	25c. Common duiker	40	30
18	30c. African elephant	60	35
19	50c. Python	70	40
20	1r. Hippopotamus	1·10	1·00
21	2r. Greater kudu	1·10	1·75

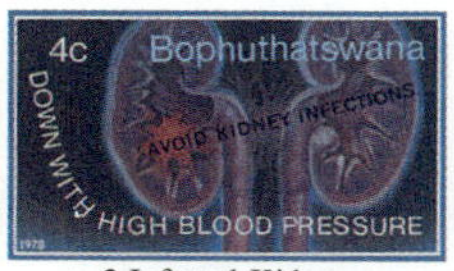

3 Infected Kidney

1978. World Hypertension Month. Multicoloured.

22	4c. Type **3**	50	25
23	10c. Heart and spoon of salt	70	70
24	15c. Spoon reflecting skull, knife and fork	1·25	1·25

4 Skull behind Steering Wheel of Car

1978. Road Safety. Multicoloured.

25	4c. Type **4**	70	40
26	10c. Child knocked off tricycle	90	80
27	15c. Pedestrian stepping in front of car	1·00	1·10
28	20c. Cyclist ignoring stop sign	1·40	1·75

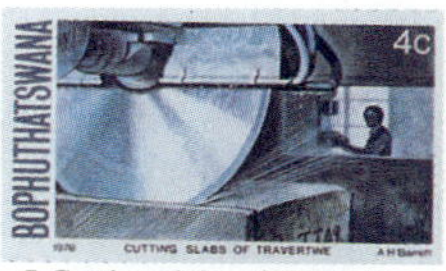

5 Cutting slabs of Travertine

1978. Semi-precious Stones. Multicoloured.

29	4c. Type **5**	65	25
30	10c. Polishing travertine	1·25	85
31	15c. Sorting semi-precious stones	1·50	1·25
32	20c. Factory at Taung	2·25	1·60

6 Wright Flyer I

1978. 75th Anniv of First Powered Flight by Wright Brothers.

33 **6**	10c. black, blue and red	1·00	1·00
34 –	15c. black, blue and red	1·40	1·50

DESIGN: 15c. Orville and Wilbur Wright.

7 Pres. Lucas M. Mangope

9 Kallie Knoetze (South Africa)

8 Drying Germinated Wheat Sorghum

1978. 1st Anniv of Independence. Multicoloured.

35	4c. Type **7**	25	20
36	15c. Full face portrait of President	75	60

1978. Sorghum Beer-making. Multicoloured.

37	4c. Type **8**	25	20
38	15c. Cooking the ground grain	65	70
39	20c. Sieving the liquid	70	75
40	25c. Drinking the beer	80	1·00

1979. Knoetze–Tate Boxing Match. Multicoloured.

41	15c. Type **9**	75	75
42	15c. John Tate (U.S.A.)	75	75

10 Emblem and Drawing of Local Fable (Hendrick Sebapo)

1979. International Year of the Child. Children's Drawings of Local Fables. Multicoloured.

43	4c. Type **10**	20	20
44	15c. Family with animals (Daisy Morapedi)	25	25
45	20c. Man's head and landscape (Peter Tladi)	35	35
46	25c. Old man, boy and donkey (Hendrick Sebapo)	45	60

11 Miner and Molten Platinum

1979. Platinum Industry.

47 **11**	4c. multicoloured	25	10
48 –	15c. multicoloured	35	30
49 –	20c. multicoloured	45	45
50 –	25c. black and grey	60	65

DESIGNS: 15c. Platinum granules and industrial use; 20c. Telecommunications satellite; 25c. Jewellery.

12 Cattle

13 Cigarettes forming Cross

1979. Agriculture. Multicoloured.

51	5c. Type **12**	20	20
52	15c. Picking cotton	25	25
53	20c. Scientist examining maize	30	30
54	25c. Catch of fish	35	35

1979. Anti-smoking Campaign.

55 **13**	5c. multicoloured	40	20

14 "Landolphia capensis"

15 Pied Babbler

1980. Edible Wild Fruits. Multicoloured.

56	5c. Type **14**	15	15
57	10c. "Vangueria infausta"	30	30
58	15c. "Bequaertiodendron magalismontanum"	40	40
59	20c. "Sclerocarya caffra"	55	55

1980. Birds. Multicoloured.

60	5c. Type **15**	30	20
61	10c. Carmine bee eater	40	35
62	15c. Shaft-tailed whydah	60	60
63	20c. Brown parrot ("Meyer's Parrot")	70	65

16 Sun City Hotel

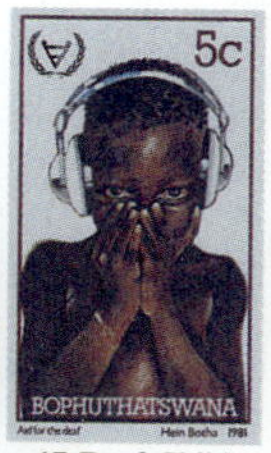

17 Deaf Child

1980. Tourism. Sun City. Multicoloured.

64	5c. Type **16**	10	15
65	10c. Gary Player Country Club	40	30
66	15c. Casino	45	50
67	20c. Extravaganza	50	70

1981. Int Year of Disabled Persons. Mult.

68	5c. Type **17**	15	10
69	15c. Blind child	30	20

70	20c. Archer in wheelchair	45	35
71	25c. Tuberculosis X-ray	60	60

18 "Behold the Lamb of God ..."

19 Siemens and Halske Wall Telephone, 1885

1981. Easter. Multicoloured.

72	5c. Type **18**	10	10
73	15c. Bread ("I am the bread of life")	25	25
74	20c. Shepherd ("I am the good shepherd")	35	35
75	25c. Wheatfield ("Unless a grain of wheat falls into the earth and dies ...")	45	45

1981. History of the Telephone (1st series). Multicoloured.

76	5c. Type **19**	10	10
77	15c. Ericsson telephone, 1895	25	25
78	20c. Hasler telephone, 1900	35	35
79	25c. Mix and Genest wall telephone, 1904	45	45

See also Nos. 92/5, 108/11 and 146/9.

20 "Themeda triandra"

21 Boy Scout

1981. Indigenous Grasses (1st series). Multicoloured.

80	5c. Type **20**	10	10
81	15c. "Rhynchelytrum repens"	20	25
82	20c. "Eragrostis capensis"	20	30
83	25c. "Monocymbium ceresiiforme"	30	45

See also Nos. 116/19.

1982. 75th Anniv of Boy Scout Movement. Multicoloured.

84	5c. Type **21**	15	10
85	15c. Mafeking siege stamps	35	35
86	20c. Original cadet	40	40
87	25c. Lord Baden-Powell	45	45

22 Jesus arriving at Bethany (John 12:1)

23 Ericsson Telephone, 1878

1982. Easter. Multicoloured.

88	15c. Type **22**	25	25
89	20c. Jesus sending disciples for donkey (Matthew 21:1,2)	30	30
90	25c. Disciples taking donkey (Mark 11:5,6)	40	40
91	30c. Disciples with donkey and foal (Matthew 21:7)	45	45

1982. History of the Telephone (2nd series). Multicoloured.

92	8c. Type **23**	15	10
93	15c. Ericsson telephone, 1885	20	20
94	20c. Ericsson telephone, 1893	20	20
95	25c. Siemens and Halske telephone, 1898	30	30

24 Old Parliament Building

1982. 5th Anniv of Independence. Multicoloured.

96	8c. Type **24**	10	10
97	15c. New government offices	20	20
98	20c. University, Mmabatho	25	25
99	25c. Civic Centre, Mmabatho	30	30

25 White Rhinoceros

1983. Pilanesberg Nature Reserve. Multicoloured.

100	8c. Type **25**	30	10
101	20c. Common zebras	40	30
102	25c. Sable antelope	40	35
103	40c. Hartebeest	60	60

26 Disciples bringing Donkeys to Jesus (Matthew 21:7)

1983. Easter. Palm Sunday. Multicoloured.

104	8c. Type **26**	10	10
105	20c. Jesus stroking colt (Mark 11:7)	30	30
106	25c. Jesus enters Jerusalem on donkey (Matthew 21:8)	35	35
107	40c. Crowd welcoming Jesus (Mark 11:9)	60	60

1983. History of the Telephone (3rd series). As T **19**. Multicoloured.

108	10c. A.T.M. table telephone c. 1920	15	10
109	20c. A/S Elektrisk wall telephone, c. 1900	30	30
110	25c. Ericsson wall telephone c. 1900	35	35
111	40c. Ericsson wall telephone c. 1900 (different)	60	60

27 Kori Bustard

1983. Birds of the Veld. Multicoloured.

112	10c. Type **27**	30	20
113	20c. Black bustard ("Black Korhaan")	45	45
114	25c. Crested bustard ("Red-crested Korhaan")	55	55
115	40c. Denhan's ("Stanley Bustard")	70	80

1984. Indigenous Grasses (2nd series). As T **20**. Multicoloured.

116	10c. "Panicum maximum"	15	10
117	20c. "Hyparrhenia dregeana"	20	20
118	25c. "Cenchrus ciliaris"	25	35
119	40c. "Urochloa brachyura"	50	70

28 Money-lenders in the Temple (Mark 11:11)

1984. Easter. Multicoloured.

120	10c. Type **28**	15	10
121	20c. Jesus driving the money-lenders from the Temple (Mark 11:15)	25	20
122	25c. Jesus and fig tree (Matthew 21:9)	35	35
123	40c. The withering of the fig tree (Matthew 21:9)	60	70

29 Car Upholstery, Ga-Rankuwa

1984. Industries. Multicoloured.

124	1c. Textile mill	10	10
125	2c. Sewing sacks, Selosesha	10	10
126	3c. Ceramic tiles, Babelegi	10	10
127	4c. Sheepskin car seat covers	10	10
128	5c. Crossbow manufacture	15	10
129	6c. Automobile parts, Babelegi	15	10
130	7c. Hosiery, Babelegi	15	10
131	8c. Specialised bicycle factory, Babelegi	30	10
132	9c. Lawn mower assembly line	30	15
133	10c. Dress factory, Thaba 'Nchu	20	10
134	11c. Molten platinum	60	20
135	12c. Type **29**	40	15
136	14c. Maize mill, Mafeking	50	15
137	15c. Plastic bags, Babelegi	25	15
137b	16c. Brick factory, Mmabatho	60	15
137c	18c. Cutlery manufacturing, Mogwase	60	15
138	20c. Men's clothing, Babelegi	25	15
138b	21c. Welding bus chassis	50	50
138c	21c. Fitting engine to bus chassis	50	50
138d	21c. Bus body construction	50	50
138e	21c. Spraying and finishing bus	50	50
138f	21c. Finished bus	50	50
139	25c. Chromium plating pram parts	30	20
140	30c. Spray painting metal beds	40	25
141	50c. Milk processing plant	50	40
142	1r. Modern printing works	60	75
143	2r. Industrial complex, Babelegi	1·00	2·50

1984. History of the Telephone (4th series). As T **19**. Multicoloured.

146	11c. Schuchhardt table telephone, 1905	15	10
147	20c. Siemens wall telephone, 1925	25	20
148	25c. Ericsson table telephone, 1900	30	30
149	30c. Oki table telephone, 1930	40	50

30 Yellow-throated Plated Lizard

1984. Lizards. Multicoloured.

150	11c. Type **30**	20	10
151	25c. Transvaal girdled lizard	30	30
152	30c. Ocellated sand lizard	35	40
153	45c. Bibron's thick-toed gecko	50	60

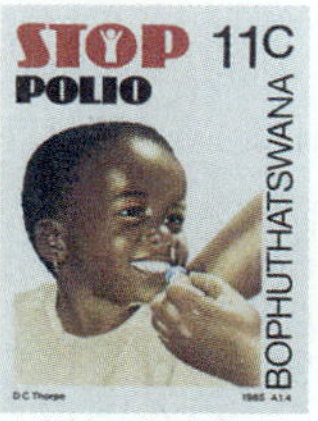

31 Giving Oral Vaccine against Polio

1985. Health. Multicoloured.

154	11c. Type **31**	40	10
155	25c. Vaccinating against measles	50	30
156	30c. Examining child for diphtheria	55	40
157	50c. Examining child for whooping cough	80	90

32 Chief Montshiwa of Barolong booRatshidi

34 "Faurea saligna" and planting Sapling

33 The Sick flock to Jesus in the Temple (Matthew, 21:41)

1985. Centenary of Mafeking.

158	**32**	11c. black, grey and orange	20	10
159	–	25c. black, grey and blue	40	30

DESIGN: 25c. Sir Charles Warren.

1985. Easter. Multicoloured.

160	12c. Type **33**	20	10
161	25c. Jesus cures the sick (Matthew 21:14)	30	20
162	30c. Children praising Jesus (Matthew 21:15)	35	30
163	50c. Community leaders discussing Jesus's acceptance of praise (Matthew 21:15, 16)	50	60

1985. Tree Conservation. Multicoloured.

164	12c. Type **34**	20	10
165	25c. "Boscia albitrunca" and kudu	25	20
166	30c. "Erythrina lysistemon" and marigua sunbird	35	30
167	50c. "Bequaertiondendron magalismontanum" and bee	55	50

35 Jesus at Mary and Martha's, Bethany (John 12:2)

1986. Easter. Multicoloured.

168	12c. Type **35**	25	10
169	20c. Mary anointing Jesus's feet (John 12:3)	30	20
170	25c. Mary drying Jesus's feet with her hair (John 12:3)	35	25
171	30c. Disciple condemns Mary for anointing Jesus's head with oil (Matthew 26:7)	45	50

36 "Wesleyan Mission Station and Residence of Moroka, Chief of the Barolong, 1834" (C. D. Bell)

1986. Paintings of Thaba 'Nchu. Multicoloured.

172	14c. Type **36**	40	15
173	20c. "James Archbell's Congregation, 1834" (Charles Davidson Bell)	60	60
174	25c. "Mission Station at Thaba 'Nchu, 1850" (Thomas Baines)	65	80

37 Farmer using Tractor (agricultural development)

1986. Temisano Development Project. Mult.

175	14c. Type **37**	20	10
176	20c. Children at school (community development)	30	20
177	25c. Repairing engine (training)	35	30
178	30c. Grain elevator (secondary industries)	50	50

38 Stewardesses and Cessna Citation II

1986. "B.O.P." Airways. Multicoloured.

179	14c. Type **38**	25	10
180	20c. Passengers disembarking from Boeing 707	40	20
181	25c. Mmabatho International Airport	50	35
182	30c. Cessna Citation II	60	50

39 Netball

40 "Berkheya zeyheri"

1987. Sports. Multicoloured.

183	14c. Type **39**	20	15
184	20c. Tennis	30	30

185 25c. Football 30 30
186 30c. Athletics 45 50

1987. Wild Flowers. Multicoloured.
187 16c. Type **40** 25 15
188 20c. "Plumbago auriculata" 35 35
189 25c. "Pterodiscus speciosus" 35 35
190 30c. "Gazania krebsiana" . . 40 50

41 E. M. Mokgoko Farmer Training Centre

1987. Tertiary Education. Multicoloured.
191 16c. Type **41** 20 15
192 20c. Main lecture block, University of Bophuthatswana 30 35
193 25c. Manpower Centre . . . 30 35
194 30c. Hotel Training School 30 50

42 Posts

1987. 10th Anniv of Independence. Communications. Multicoloured.
195 16c. Type **42** 25 15
196 30c. Telephone 35 35
197 40c. Radio 35 35
198 50c. Television 40 50

43 Jesus entering Jerusalem on Donkey (John 12:12–14)

1988. Easter. Multicoloured.
199 16c. Type **43** 25 15
200 30c. Judas negotiating with chief priests (Mark 14:10–11) 35 35
201 40c. Jesus washing the disciples' feet (John 13:5) 35 35
202 50c. Jesus handing bread to Judas (John 13:26) 40 50

44 Environment Education

1988. National Parks Board. Multicoloured.
203 16c. Type **44** 25 15
204 30c. Rhinoceros (Conservation) 40 40
205 40c. Catering workers 40 40
206 50c. Cheetahs (Tourism) . . 55 65

45 Sunflowers

1988. Crops. Multicoloured.
207 16c. Type **45** 25 15
208 30c. Peanuts 35 35
209 40c. Cotton 45 45
210 50c. Cabbages 60 60

46 Ngotwane Dam

1988. Dams. Multicoloured.
211 16c. Type **46** 30 20
212 30c. Groothoek Dam 50 50
213 40c. Sehujwane Dam 50 50
214 50c. Molatedi Dam 70 70

47 The Last Supper (Matthew 26: 26)

1989. Easter. Multicoloured.
215 16c. Type **47** 40 20
216 30c. Jesus praying in Garden of Gethsemane (Matthew 26:39) 60 55
217 40c. Judas kissing Jesus (Mark 14:45) 70 70
218 50c. Peter severing ear of High Priest's slave (John 18:10) . . . . 85 1·00

48 Cock (Thembi Atong)

1989. Children's Art. Designs depicting winning entries in National Children's Day Art Competition.
219 18c. Type **48** 30 20
220 30c. Traditional thatched hut (Muhammad Mahri) . . . 40 40
221 40c. Airplane, telephone wires and houses (Tshepo Mashokwi) 45 45
222 50c. City scene (Miles Brown) 50 60

49 Black-shouldered Kite

1989. Birds of Prey. Paintings by Claude Finch-Davies. Multicoloured.
223 18c. Type **49** . . . . 1·25 30
224 30c. Pale chanting goshawk 1·40 75
225 40c. Lesser kestrel . . . . . 1·60 1·10
226 50c. Short-toed eagle . . . . 1·75 1·50

50 Bilobial House

1989. Traditional Houses. Multicoloured.
227 18c. Type **50** 25 20
228 30c. House with courtyards at front and side 35 35
229 40c. House with conical roof 35 35
230 50c. House with rounded roof 40 50

51 Early Learning Schemes

1990. Community Services. Multicoloured.
231 18c. Type **51** 25 20
232 30c. Clinics 35 35
233 40c. Libraries 35 35
234 50c. Hospitals 40 45

52 Lesser Climbing Mouse

1990. Small Mammals. Multicoloured.
235 21c. Type **52** 30 20
236 30c. Zorilla 40 40
237 40c. Transvaal elephant shrew 60 60
238 50c. Large-toothed rock hyrax 80 85

53 Variegated Sandgrouse

1990. Sandgrouse. Paintings by Claude Finch-Davies. Multicoloured.
239 21c. Type **53** 90 30
240 35c. Double-banded sandgrouse . . . . 1·10 75
241 40c. Namaqua sandgrouse . . 1·10 90
242 50c. Yellow-throated sandgrouse . . . . 1·40 1·40

54 Basketry

1990. Traditional Crafts. Multicoloured.
243 21c. Type **54** 40 20
244 35c. Training 60 60
245 40c. Beer making 60 65
246 50c. Pottery 65 75

55 Sud Aviation Alouette II Helicopter

56 Wild Custard Apple

1990. Bophuthatswana Air Force. Multicoloured.
247 21c. Type **55** . . . . 1·40 1·10
248 21c. MBB-Kawasaki BK-117 helicopter . . . . 1·40 1·10
249 21c. Pilatus PC-7 turbo trainer . . . . 1·40 1·10
250 21c. Pilatus PC-6 . . . . . . 1·40 1·10
251 21c. CASA C-212 Aviocar . . 1·40 1·10

1991. Edible Wild Fruit. Multicoloured.
252 21c. Type **56** 50 25
253 35c. Spine-leaved monkey orange 65 70
254 40c. Sycamore fig 70 75
255 50c. Kei apple 85 95

57 Arrest of Jesus (Mark 14:46)

1991. Easter. Multicoloured.
256 21c. Type **57** 45 25
257 35c. First trial by the Sanhedrin (Mark 14:53) . . 60 55
258 40c. Assault and derision of Jesus after sentence (Mark 14:65) 70 70
259 50c. Servant girl recognizing Peter (Mark 14:67) 75 90

58 Class 7A Locomotive No. 350, 1897

59 Caneiro Chart, 1502

1991. Steam Locomotives. Multicoloured.
260 25c. Class 6A locomotive No. 194, 1897, trucks and caboose (71 × 25 mm) . . . 95 55
261 40c. Type **58** . . . . 1·25 85
262 50c. Double-boiler Class 6Z locomotives pulling Cecil Rhodes's funeral train (71 × 25 mm) . . . . . . 1·40 1·25
263 60c. Class 8 locomotive at Mafeking station, 1904 . . 1·50 1·75

1991. Old Maps (1st series). Multicoloured.
264 25c. Type **59** . . . . 1·10 40
265 40c. Cantino Chart, 1502 . . 1·50 95
266 50c. Giovanni Contarini's map, 1506 . . . . 1·75 1·40
267 60c. Martin Waldseemuller's map, 1507 . . . . 1·75 1·90
See also Nos. 268/71 and 297/300.

60 Fracanzano Map, 1508

1992. Old Maps (2nd series). Multicoloured.
268 27c. Type **60** . . . . 1·10 40
269 45c. Martin Waldseemuller's map (from edition of Ptolemy), 1513 . . . . . . 1·50 95
270 65c. Section of Waldseemuller's woodcut "Carta Marina Navigatora Portugallan Navigationes", 1516 . . . . 1·75 1·50
271 85c. Map from Laurent Fries's "Geographia", 1522 1·75 2·00

61 Delivery of Jesus to Pilate (Mark 15:1)

1992. Easter. Multicoloured.
272 27c. Type **61** 25 20
273 45c. Scourging of Jesus (Mark 15:15) 40 40
274 65c. Placing crown of thorns on Jesus's head (Mark 15: 17–18) 50 70
275 85c. Soldiers mocking Jesus (Mark 15:19) 60 90

62 Sweet Thorn

1992. Acacia Trees. Multicoloured.
276 35c. Type **62** 30 25
277 70c. Camel thorn 50 60
278 90c. Umbrella thorn 60 80
279 1r.05 Black thorn . . . . . 70 1·00

63 View of Palace across Lake

64 Light Sussex

1992. The Lost City Complex, Sun City. Mult.
280 35c. Type **63** 35 45
281 35c. Palace facade 35 45
282 35c. Palace porte cochere . . 35 45
283 35c. Palace lobby 35 45
284 35c. Tusk Bar, Palace 35 45

1993. Chickens. Multicoloured.
285 35c. Type **64** 40 25
286 70c. Rhode Island red . . . 55 50
287 90c. Brown leghorn 60 80
288 1r.05 White leghorn . . . . 70 1·10

65 Pilate offering Release of Barabbas (Luke 23:25)

1993. Easter. Multicoloured.
289 35c. Type **65** 60 30
290 70c. Jesus falling under cross (John 19:17) 95 75

291 90c. Simon of Cyrene carrying cross (Mark 15:21) 1·25 1·25
292 1r.05 Jesus being nailed to cross (Mark 15:23) 1·40 1·75

66 Mafeking Locomotive Shed, 1933 (⅔-size illustration)

1993. Steam Locomotives (2nd series). Multicoloured.
293 45c. Type **66** 65 55
294 65c. Rhodesian Railways steam locomotive No. 5, 1901 (34 × 25 mm) 75 65
295 85c. Class 16B locomotive pulling "White Train" during visit of Prince George, 1934 95 95
296 1r.05 Class 19D locomotive, 1923 (34 × 25 mm) 1·25 1·40
MS297 127 × 113 mm. Nos. 293/6 2·75 3·25

67 Sebastian Munster's Map (from edition of Ptolemy), 1540

1993. Old Maps (3rd series). Multicoloured.
298 45c. Type **67** 50 50
299 65c. Jacopo Gastaldi's map, 1564 65 65
300 85c. Map from Mercator's "Atlas", 1595 75 90
301 1r.05 Map from Ortelius's "Theatrum Orbis Terrarum", 1570 90 1·25

68 Crucifixion (Luke 23:33)

1994. Easter. Multicoloured.
302 35c. Type **68** 65 45
303 65c. Soldiers and Jews mocking Jesus (Luke 23: 35–36) 95 80
304 85c. Soldier offering Jesus vinegar (Luke 23:36) 1·10 1·25
305 1r.05 Jesus on cross and charge notice (Luke 23:38) 1·60 1·75

BOSNIA AND HERZEGOVINA
Pt. 2, Pt. 3

Turkish provinces administered by Austria from 1878 and annexed by her in 1908. In 1918 it became part of Yugoslavia.

In 1992 Bosnia and Herzegovina declared itself independent. Hostilities subsequently broke out between the Croat, Moslem and Serbian inhabitants, which ultimately led to the establishment of three de facto administrations: the mainly Moslem Bosnian government, based in Sarajevo; the Croats in Mostar; and the Serbian Republic in Pale. Under the Dayton Agreement in November 1995 the Republic was split between a Moslem-Croat Federation and the Serbian Republic.

A. AUSTRO-HUNGARIAN MILITARY POST

1879. 100 kreuzer = 1 gulden.
1900. 100 heller = 1 krone.
1993. 100 paras = 1 dinar.
2002. 100 cents = 1 euro.

1 Value at top 2 Value at bottom

1879.
106 **1** ½k. black 11·00 23·00
135 1k. grey 3·00 1·10
136 2k. yellow 1·90 50
137 3k. green 3·00 1·25
146 5k. red 4·00 55
139 10k. blue 4·00 75
140 15k. brown 3·25 3·75
141 20k. green 4·00 4·25
142 25k. purple 5·00 6·00

1900.
148 **2** 1h. black 20 15
149 2h. grey 20 15
151 3h. yellow 20 15
152 5h. green 15 10
154 6h. brown 30 15
155 10h. red 15 10
156 20h. pink £100 8·00
158 25h. blue 90 35
173 30h. brown £110 8·25
160 40h. orange £120 13·00
161 50h. purple 60 45

Larger stamps with value in each corner.
162 1k. red 80 50
163 2k. blue 1·40 1·50
164 5k. green 3·00 4·50

1901. Black figures of value.
177 **2** 20h. pink and black 60 45
178 30h. brown and black 55 45
180 35h. blue and black 1·00 65
181 40h. orange and black 70 65
182 45h. turquoise and black 80 70

4 View of Doboj

5 In the Carshija (business quarter) Sarajevo

1906.
186 **4** 1h. black 10 15
187 – 2h. violet 10 15
188 – 3h. yellow 10 15
189 – 5h. green 35 10
190 – 6h. brown 20 20
191 – 10h. red 40 10
192 – 20h. brown 65 20
193 – 25h. blue 1·40 90
194 – 30h. green 1·40 45
195 – 35h. green 1·40 45
196 – 40h. orange 1·40 45
197 – 45h. red 1·40 75
198 – 50h. brown 1·60 90
199 **5** 1k. red 4·75 3·00
200 – 2k. green 6·25 11·50
201 – 5k. blue 4·75 7·75

DESIGNS—As Type **4**: 2h. Mostar; 3h. The old castle, Jajce; 5h. Naretva pass and Prenz Planina; 6h. Valley of the Rama; 10h. Valley of the Vrbas; 20h. Old Bridge, Mostar; 25h. The Begova Djamia (Bey's Mosque), Sarajevo; 30h. Post by beast of burden; 35h. Village and lake, Jezero; 40h. Mail wagon; 45h. Bazaar at Sarajevo; 50h. Post car. As Type **5**: 2k. St. Luke's Campanile at Jajce; 5k. Emperor Francis Joseph I.
See also Nos. 359/61.

1910. 80th Birthday of Francis Joseph I. As stamps of 1906 but with date-label at foot.
343 1h. black 50 25
344 2h. violet 60 25
345 3h. yellow 60 25
346 5h. green 65 25
347 6h. brown 70 45
348 10h. red 65 15
349 20h. brown 1·60 1·40
350 25h. blue 3·00 2·50
351 30h. green 2·00 2·25
352 35h. green 2·75 2·25
353 40h. orange 3·00 2·25
354 45h. red 5·25 5·50
355 50h. brown 5·25 6·00
356 1k. red 5·25 6·25
357 2k. green 19·00 21·00
358 5k. blue 3·50 6·00

1912. As T **4** (new values and views).
359 12h. blue 4·50 5·00
360 60h. grey 3·25 4·25
361 72h. red 12·50 16·00
DESIGNS: 12h. Jajce; 60h. Konjica; 72h. Vishegrad.

25 Francis Joseph I 26 Francis Joseph I

1912. Various frames. Nos. 378/82 are larger (27 × 22 mm).
362 **25** 1h. olive 30 10
363 2h. blue 30 10
364 3h. lake 30 10
365 5h. green 30 10
366 6h. black 30 10
367 10h. red 30 10
368 12h. green 50 20
369 20h. brown 3·50 10
370 25h. blue 1·75 10
371 30h. red 1·75 10
372 **26** 35h. green 1·75 10
373 40h. violet 6·00 10
374 45h. brown 3·00 20
375 50h. blue 2·50 10
376 60h. brown 2·25 10
377 72h. blue 3·00 3·25
378 **25** 1k. brown on cream 12·00 35
379 2k. blue on blue 7·25 50
380 **26** 3k. red on green 11·00 10·00
381 5k. lilac and grey 21·00 25·00
382 10k. blue on grey 65·00 95·00

1914. Nos. 189 and 191 surch **1914.** and new value.
383 7h. on 5h. green 40 40
384 12h. on 10h. red 40 40

1915. Nos. 189 and 191 surch **1915.** and new value.
385 7h. on 5h. green 9·00 9·00
386 12h. on 10h. red 30 40

1915. Surch **1915.** and new value.
387 **25** 7h. on 5h. green 70 1·75
388 12h. on 10h. red 1·50 1·75

1916. Surch **1916.** and new value.
389 **25** 7h. on 5h. green 60 60
390 12h. on 10h. red 60 65

31

1916. War Invalids' Fund.
391 **31** 5h. (+2h.) green 85 80
392 – 10h. (+2h.) purple 1·40 1·40
DESIGN: 10h. Blind soldier and girl.
See also Nos. 434/5.

33 Francis Joseph I 34 Francis Joseph I

1916.
393 **33** 3h. black 25 25
394 5h. olive 45 50
395 6h. violet 45 50
396 10h. bistre 2·00 2·25
397 12h. grey 45 60
398 15h. red 45 25
399 20h. brown 45 60
400 25h. blue 45 60
401 30h. green 45 60
402 40h. red 45 60
403 50h. green 45 60
404 60h. lake 45 60
405 80h. brown 1·40 40
406 90h. purple 1·60 80
407 **34** 2k. red on yellow 65 1·00
408 3k. green on blue 80 2·10
409 4k. red on green 5·50 10·00
410 10k. violet on grey 28·00 20·00

1917. War Widows' Fund. Optd **WITWEN-UND WAISENWOCHE 1917.**
411 **33** 10h. (+2h.) bistre 10 20
412 15h. (+2h.) pink 10 20

36 Design for Memorial Church, Sarajevo 39 Emperor Charles

1917. Assassination of Archduke Ferdinand. Fund for Memorial Church at Sarajevo.
413 **36** 10h. (+2h.) black 10 30
414 – 15h. (+2h.) red 10 30
415 – 40h. (+2h.) blue 10 30
PORTRAITS—HORIZ: 40h. Francis Ferdinand and Sophie. VERT: 15h. Archduke Francis Ferdinand.

1917.
416 **39** 3h. grey 10 20
417 5h. olive 10 10
418 6h. violet 60 70
419 10h. brown 20 10
420 12h. blue 60 70
421 15h. red 10 10
422 20h. brown 10 10
423 25h. blue 90 65
424 30h. green 25 20
425 40h. bistre 25 20
426 50h. green 90 50
427 60h. red 90 45
428 80h. blue 20 25
429 90h. lilac 1·00 1·40
430 – 2k. red on yellow 60 35
431 – 3k. green on blue 15·00 16·00
432 – 4k. red on green 6·00 8·00
433 – 10k. violet on grey 4·00 6·25

The kronen values are larger (25 × 25 mm) and with different border.

1918. War Invalids' Fund.
434 – 10h. (+2h.) green (as No. 392) 60 70
435 **31** 15h. (+2h.) brown 60 70

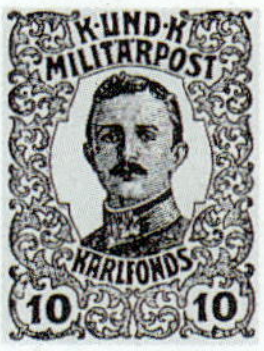

40 Emperor Charles

1918. Emperor's Welfare Fund.
436 **40** 10h. (+10h.) green 40 85
437 – 15h. (+10h.) brown 40 85
438 **40** 40h. (+10h.) purple 40 85
DESIGN—15h. Empress Zita.

1918. Optd **1918.**
439 – 2h. violet (No. 344) 50 1·00
440 **25** 2h. blue 50 1·10

NEWSPAPER STAMPS

N 27 Girl in Bosnian Costume N 35 Mercury

1913. Imperf.
N383 N **27** 2h. blue 40 40
N384 6h. mauve 1·40 1·40
N385 10h. red 1·60 1·40
N386 20h. green 2·10 1·60
For these stamps perforated see Yugoslavia, Nos. 25 to 28.

1916. For Express.
N411 N **35** 2h. red 25 25
N412 5h. green 45 45

POSTAGE DUE STAMPS

D 4 D 35

1904. Imperf. or perf.
D183 D **4** 1h. black, red & yellow 30 10
D184 2h. black, red & yellow 30 15
D185 3h. black, red & yellow 30 10
D186 4h. black, red & yellow 30 10
D187 5h. black, red & yellow 1·40 10
D188 6h. black, red & yellow 25 10
D189 7h. black, red & yellow 2·25 3·25
D190 8h. black, red & yellow 2·25 1·50
D191 10h. black, red & yellow 50 10
D192 15h. black, red & yellow 40 10
D193 20h. black, red & yellow 3·00 25
D194 50h. black, red & yellow 1·10 30
D195 200h. black, red & grn 4·00 2·25

1916.
D411 D **35** 2h. red 40 1·00
D412 4h. red 35 60
D413 5h. red 40 60
D414 6h. red 35 85
D415 10h. red 35 50
D416 15h. red 2·75 5·25
D417 20h. red 35 50
D418 25h. red 90 2·00
D419 30h. red 90 2·00
D420 40h. red 7·25 12·50
D421 50h. red 23·00 40·00
D422 1k. blue 2·50 5·25
D423 3k. blue 12·00 23·00

B. INDEPENDENT REPUBLIC
I. SARAJEVO GOVERNMENT

The following issues were used for postal purposes in those areas controlled by the Sarajevo government.

1993. 100 paras = 1 dinar.
1997. 100 fennig = 1 mark.

50 State Arms

51 Games Emblem

1993. Imperf.
450 **50** 100d. blue, lemon & yellow . . 10 10
451 500d. blue, yellow & pink . . 15 15
452 1000d. ultramarine, yellow and blue 25 25
453 5000d. blue, yellow & grn . . 75 75
454 10000d. blue, lemon & yell . . 1·50 1·50
455 20000d. blue, yellow & bis . . 3·00 3·00
456 50000d. blue, yellow & grey . . . . 7·50 7·50

1994. 10th Anniv of Winter Olympic Games, Sarajevo. Imperf.
457 **51** 50000d. black and orange . . 5·00 5·00
MS458 78 × 65 mm. 100000d. black, orange and lilac; 200000d. black, orange and lilac . . . . 10·00 10·00
DESIGNS: 45 × 27 mm—100000d. Four-man bobsleigh; 200000d. Ice hockey.

Currency Reform
10000 (old) dinars = 1 (new) dinar.

52 Koran Illustration

1995. Bairam Festival. Sheet 105 × 50 mm containing T **52** and similar horiz design. Multicoloured.
MS459 400d. Type **52**; 600d. Koran illustration (different) . . . . . 10·00 10·00

53 Facade

55 Postman and Globe

54 Historical Map, 10th–15th Centuries

1995. Sarajevo Head Post Office. Multicoloured.
460 10d. Type **53** 10 10
461 20d. Interior 15 15
462 30d. As No. 461 . . . . . . 30 30
463 35d. Before conflict 35 35
464 50d. As No. 463 . . . . . . 45 45
465 100d. Present day 90 90
466 200d. As No. 465 . . . . . 1·75 1·75

1995. Bosnian History. Multicoloured.
467 35d. Type **54** 30 30
468 100d. 15th-century Bogomil tomb, Oplicici (vert) . . . 80 80
469 200d. Arms of Kotromanic Dynasty (14th-15th centuries) (vert) . . . . . 1·60 1·60
470 300d. Charter by Ban Kulin of Bosnia, 1189 . . . . . 2·50 2·00

1995. World Post Day.
471 **55** 100d. multicoloured . . . 95 95

56 Dove with Olive Branch

1995. Europa. Peace and Freedom.
472 **56** 200d. multicoloured . . . 1·75 1·75

57 Children and Buildings (A. Softic)

1995. Children's Week.
473 **57** 100d. multicoloured . . . 95 95

58 Tramcar, 1895

59 "Simphyandra hofmannii"

1995. Centenary of Sarajevo Electric Tram System.
474 **58** 200d. multicoloured . . . 1·75 1·75

1995. Flowers. Multicoloured.
475 100d. Type **59** 95 95
476 200d. Turk's-head lily . . . . 1·90 1·90

60 Dalmatian Barbel Gudgeon

1995. Fishes. Multicoloured.
477 100d. Type **60** 95 95
478 200d. Adriatic minnow . . . 1·90 1·90

61 Kozija Bridge, Sarajevo

1995. Bridges. Multicoloured.
479 20d. Type **61** 15 15
480 30d. Arslanagica Bridge, Trebinje 25 25
481 35d. Latinska Bridge, Sarajevo 35 35
482 50d. Old bridge, Mostar . . 45 45
483 100d. Visegrad 90 90

62 Visiting Friends

1995. Christmas. Multicoloured.
484 100d. Type **62** . . . . 1·00 1·00
485 200d. Madonna and Child (vert) . . . . 2·00 2·00

63 Queen Jelena of Bosnia and Tomb (600th death anniv)

1995. Multicoloured.
486 30d. Type **63** 20 20
487 35d. Husein Kapetan Gradascevic "Dragon of Bosnia" (leader of 1831 uprising against Turkey) . . 30 30
488 100d. Mirza Safvet Basagic (125th death anniv) (horiz) 95 95

64 Places of Worship and Graveyards

1995. Religious Pluralism.
489 **64** 35d. multicoloured 35 35

65 Stadium and Sports

1995. Destruction of Olympic Stadium, Sarajevo. Multicoloured.
490 35d. Type **65** 30 30
491 100d. Stadium ablaze (vert) . . 95 95

66 Bahrija Hadzic (opera singer)

67 Child's Handprint

1996. Europa. Famous Women. Multicoloured.
492 80d. Type **66** 75 75
493 120d. Nasiha Hadzic (children's writer and radio presenter) . . . . 1·10 1·10

1996. 50th Anniv of UNICEF. Multicoloured.
494 50d. Child stepping on landmine (P. Mirna and K. Princes) 65 65
495 150d. Type **67** . . . . 1·25 1·25

68 Bobovac Castle

69 Roofed Fountain and Extract from Holy Koran

1996.
496 **68** 35d. black, blue and violet 35 35

1996. Bairam Festival.
497 **69** 80d. multicoloured 75 75

70 Town Hall

1996. Centenary of Sarajevo Town Hall.
498 **70** 80d. multicoloured 75 75

71 Hands on Computer Keyboard and Title Page of "Bosanki Prijatelj"

1996. 150th Anniv of Journalists' Association.
499 **71** 100d. multicoloured . . . 95 95

72 Essen

1996. "Essen 96" International Stamp Fair, Essen.
500 **72** 200d. multicoloured . . . 1·75 1·75

73 Running

74 "Campanula hercegovina"

1996. Centenary of Modern Olympic Games and Olympic Games, Atlanta. Multicoloured.
501 30d. Type **73** 25 25
502 35d. Games emblem 30 30
503 80d. Torch bearer and Olympic flag 75 75
504 120d. Pierre de Coubertin (founder) . . . . 1·10 1·10
Nos. 501/4 were issued together, se-tenant, with the backgrounds forming a composite design of athletes.

1996. Flowers. Multicoloured.
505 30d. Type **74** 30 30
506 35d. "Iris bosniaca" 35 35

75 Barak

1996. Dogs. Multicoloured.
507 35d. Type **75** 35 35
508 80d. Tornjak 85 85

76 Globe, Telephone and Alexander Bell

1996. Anniversaries. Multicoloured.
509 80d. Type **76** (120th anniv of Bell's invention of telephone) 80 80
510 120d. 1910 50h. stamp (cent of post car in Bosnia and Herzegovina) . . . . . . 1·10 1·10

77 Charter with Seal

1996. Granting of Privileges to Dubrovnik by Ban Stepan II Kotromanic, 1333.
511 **77** 100d. multicoloured . . . 95 95

78 Hot-air Balloons

1996. SOS Children's Village, Sarajevo.
512 **78** 100d. multicoloured . . . 95 95

79 Muslim Costume of Bjelasnice

80 Bogomil Soldier

1996. Traditional Costumes. Multicoloured.
513 50d. Type **79** 40 40
514 80d. Croatian 75 75
515 100d. Muslim costume of Sarajevo . . . . 1·10 1·10

1996. Military Uniforms. Multicoloured.
516 35d. Type **80** 30 30
517 80d. Austro-Hungarian rifleman 75 75
518 100d. Turkish light cavalryman . . . . 1·10 1·10
519 120d. Medieval Bosnian king 1·25 1·25

81 Mosque

1996. Winter Festival, Sarajevo.
520 **81** 100d. multicoloured . . . 90 90

82 Map and State Arms

1996. Bosnia Day.
521 **82** 120d. multicoloured . . . 1·00 1·00

83 Crowd around Baby Jesus

1996. Christmas.
522 **83** 100d. multicoloured . . . 90 90

84 Pope John Paul II
85 Palaeolithic Rock Carving, Badanj

1996. Papal Visit.
523 **84** 500d. multicoloured . . . 4·00 4·00

1997. Archaeological Finds. Multicoloured.
524 35d. Type **85** 30 30
525 50d. Neolithic ceramic head, Butmir 40 40
526 80d. Bronze Age "birds" wagon, Glasinac 65 65
MS527 100 × 72 mm. 100, 120d. Walls of Illyrian town of Daorson (composite design) . . . . . . 1·75 1·75

86 Ferhad Pasha Mosque, Banja Luka
87 "Clown" (Martina Nokto)

1997. Bairam Festival.
528 **86** 200d. multicoloured . . . 1·50 1·50

1997. Children's Week.
529 **87** 100d. multicoloured . . . 75 75

88 Komadina
89 Trojan Warriors and Map

1997. 72nd Death Anniv of Mujaga Komadina (developer and Mayor of Mostar).
530 **88** 100d. multicoloured . . . 75 75

1997. Europa. Tales and Legends. Mult.
531 100d. Type **89** (theory of Roberto Prays) 75 75
532 120d. Man on prayer-mat and castle ("The Miraculous Spring of Ajvatovica") 90 90

90 "Rainbow Warrior"

1997. 26th Anniv of Greenpeace (environmental organization). Designs showing the "Rainbow Warrior". Multicoloured.
533 35d. Type **90** 35 35
534 80d. inscr "Dorreboom" . . 80 65
535 100d. inscr "Beltra" . . . . 1·10 1·10
536 120d. inscr "Morgan" . . . 1·40 1·40

91 Open Air Cinema, Sarajevo

1997. 3rd International Film Festival, Sarajevo.
537 **91** 110d. multicoloured . . . 90 90

92 Games Emblem
93 Diagram of Electrons

1997. Mediterranean Games, Bari. Mult.
538 40d. Type **92** 35 35
539 130d. Boxing, basketball and kick boxing . . . . 1·10 1·10

1997. Anniversaries and Event. Mult.
540 40d. Type **93** (centenary of discovery of electrons) . . 35 35
541 110d. Vasco da Gama (navigator) and map (500th anniv of science of navigation) (vert) . . . . . 1·75 1·25
542 130d. Airmail envelope and airplane (Stamp Day) . . . 1·40 1·40
543 150d. Steam locomotive "Bosna" (125th anniv of railway in Bosnia and Herzegovina) . . . . . . 1·25 1·25

94 Vole
95 Map and Flags

1997. Flora and Fauna. Multicoloured.
544 40d. Type **94** 35 35
545 40d. "Oxytropis prenja" . . . 35 35
546 80d. Alpine newt 65 65
547 110d. "Dianthus freynii" . . 1·10 1·10

1997. International Peace Day. Mult.
548 50d. Type **95** 50 50
549 60d. Flags and right half of globe showing Europe and Africa 55 55
550 70d. Flags and left half of globe showing the Americas 60 60
551 110d. Map and flags (including U.S.A. and U.K.) . . . . 1·10 1·10
Nos. 548/51 were issued together, se-tenant, Nos. 549/50 forming a composite design.

96 House with Attic

1997. Architecture. Multicoloured.
552 40d. Type **96** 35 35
553 50d. Tiled stove and door . . 50 50
554 130d. Three-storey house . . 1·40 1·40

97 Sarajevo in 1697 and 1997

1997. 300th Anniv of Great Fire of Sarajevo.
555 **97** 110d. multicoloured . . . 1·10 1·10

98 Augustin Tin Ujevic

1997. Personalities. Multicoloured.
556 1m.30 Type **98** (lyricist and essayist) 90 90
557 2m. Zaim Imanovic (singer) (vert) . . . . 1·40 1·40

99 Sarajevo and Corps Emblem

1997. Contribution of Italian Pioneer Corps in Reconstruction of Sarajevo.
558 **99** 1m.40 multicoloured . . . 95 95

100 Diana, Princess of Wales, and Roses

1997. Diana, Princess of Wales, Commem.
559 **100** 2m.50 multicoloured . . . 1·90 1·90

101 "Gnijezdo" (Fikret Libovac)

1997. Art. Multicoloured.
560 35f. Type **101** 20 20
561 80f. "Sarajevo Library" (sculpture, Nusret Pasic) 55 55

102 Youth Builders Emblem attached to Route Map

1997. 50th Anniv of Samac-Sarajevo Railway.
562 **102** 35f. multicoloured 30 30

103 Nativity (icon)
104 Giant Slalom, Luge, Two-man Bobsleigh and Speed Skating

1997. Religious Events. Multicoloured.
563 50f. Type **103** (Orthodox Christmas) 35 35
564 1m.10 Wreath on door (Christmas) 80 80
565 1m.10 Pupils before teacher (14th-century miniature) (Haggadah) 80 80

1998. Winter Olympic Games, Nagano, Japan. Sheet 78 × 60 mm containing T **104** and similar vert design. Multicoloured.
MS566 35f. Type **104**; 1m. Games emblem 60 60

105 Mosque Fountain

1998. Bairam Festival.
567 **105** 1m. multicoloured 70 70

106 Zvornik

1998. Old Fortified Towns. Multicoloured.
568 35f. Type **106** 25 25
569 70f. Bihac 50 50
570 1m. Pocitelj 70 70
571 1m.20 Gradacac 85 85

107 Muradbegovic

1998. Birth Centenary of Ahmed Muradbegovic (dramatist and actor-director).
572 **107** 1m.50 multicoloured . . . 1·10 1·10

108 Branislav Djurdjev
109 White Storks

1998. Former Presidents of the University of Arts and Science. Multicoloured.
573 40f. Type **108** 30 30
574 70f. Alojz Benac 50 50
575 1m.30 Edhem Camo 95 95

1998. Endangered Species. The White Stork. Multicoloured.
576 70f. Type **109** 50 50
577 90f. Two storks flying 65 65
578 1m.10 Two adult storks on nest 80 80
579 1m.30 Adult stork with young 95 95

110 International Theatre Festival, Sarajevo

112 Emblem

111 Footballs

1998. Europa. National Festivals.
580 **110** 1m.10 multicoloured . . . 80 80

1998. World Cup Football Championship, France. Multicoloured.
581 50f. Type **111** 35 35
582 1m. Map of Bosnia and ball 70 70
583 1m.50 Asim Ferhatovic Hase (footballer) . . . . 1·10 1·10

1998. International League of Humanists World Congress, Sarajevo. Sheet 104 × 61 mm containing T **112** and two labels.
MS584 **112** 2m. multicoloured . . 1·25 1·25

113 Common Morel

114 Tunnel

1998. Fungi. Multicoloured.
585 50f. Type **113** 35 35
586 80f. Chanterelle 55 55
587 1m.10 Edible mushroom . . 80 80
588 1m.35 Caesar's mushroom . . 95 95

1998. 5th Anniv of Sarajevo's Supply Tunnels.
589 **114** 1m.10 multicoloured . . . 80 80

115 Eiffel Tower and Underground Train

1998. Paris Metro.
590 **115** 2m. multicoloured . . . . 1·40 1·40

116 Henri Dunant (founder of Red Cross)

118 Travnik

117 Vesna Misanovic

1998. Anti-tuberculosis Week.
591 **116** 50f. multicoloured 35 35

1998. Bosnian and Herzegovina Chess Teams. Sheet 109 × 88 mm containing T **117** and similar horiz designs. Multicoloured.
MS592 20f. Type **117** (silver medal, tenth European Team championship, Debrecen, 1992); 40f. Men's team (silver medal winners, 31st Chess Olympiad, Moscow, 1994); 60f. Women's team (32nd Chess Olympiad, Yerevan, 1996); 80f. National team (11th European Team championship, Pula, 1997) . . 1·00 1·00

1998. Old Towns.
593 **118** 5f. black and green . . . 10 10
597 – 38f. black and brown . . 25 25
DESIGN: 38f. Sarajevo.

119 Postal Workers in New Uniforms

120 Lutes

1998. World Post Day.
605 **119** 1m. multicoloured 70 70

1998. Musical Instruments.
606 **120** 80f. multicoloured 55 55

121 "The Creation of Adam" (detail of fresco on ceiling of Sistine Chapel, Michelangelo)

1998. World Disabled Day.
607 **121** 1m. multicoloured 70 70

122 Bjelasnica Mountain Range

1998.
608 **122** 1m. multicoloured 70 70

123 People

1998. 50th Anniv of Universal Declaration of Human Rights.
609 **123** 1m.35 multicoloured . . . 90 90

124 Christmas Tree (Lamija Pehilj)

1998. Christmas and New Year. Multicoloured.
610 1m. Type **124** 70 70
611 1m.50 Father Andeo Zvizdovic . . . . 1·00 1·00

125 Sarajevo University and "Proportion of Man" (Leonardo da Vinci)

127 Astronaut, Earth and Moon

126 Feral Rock Pigeons

1999. Anniversaries. Multicoloured.
612 40f. Type **125** (50th anniv) 25 25
613 40f. Sarajevo High School (120th anniv) (horiz) . . . 25 25

1999. Flora and Fauna. Multicoloured.
614 80f. Type **126** 55 55
615 1m.10 "Knautia sarajevensis" 75 75

1999. 30th Anniv of First Manned Moon Landing.
616 **127** 2m. multicoloured . . . .

128 Slapovi Une

1999. Europa. Parks and Gardens.
617 **128** 2m. multicoloured . . . . 1·40 1·40

129 Gorazde

1999.
618 **129** 40f. multicoloured 25 25

130 Children playing Football in Sun (Pranjkovic Nenad)

1999. Children's Week.
619 **130** 50f. multicoloured 35 35

131 House

1999. World Environment Day.
620 **131** 80f. multicoloured 55 55

132 Church, Mosque and Emblem

1999. "Philexfrance 99" International Stamp Exhibition, Paris, France.
621 **132** 2m. multicoloured . . . . 1·40 1·40

133 Sarajevo on Stamp

1999. 120th Anniv of First Bosnia and Herzegovina Stamps.
622 **133** 1m. multicoloured 70 70

134 Letters encircling Globe and Telephones

1999. 125th Anniv of Universal Postal Union.
623 **134** 1m.50 multicoloured . . . 1·00 1·00

135 Tuzlait from Tuoanj

1999. Minerals. Multicoloured.
624 40f. Type **135** 20 20
625 60f. Siderit from Vitez . . . 40 40
626 1m.20 Hijelofan from Busovaca 80 80
627 1m.80 Quartz from Srebrenica (vert) . . . . . 1·25 1·25

136 Dove and Cathedral

137 Kursum Medresa, Sarajevo, 1537 (site of library)

1999. Southern Europe Stability Pact, Sarajevo.
628 **136** 2m. multicoloured . . . . 1·40 1·40

1999. Gazi-Husref Library. Multicoloured.
629 1m. Type **137** 70 70
630 1m.10 Miniature from Hval Codex, 1404 . . . . 75 75

138 Koran, 1550

1999.
631 **138** 1m.50 multicoloured . . . 1·00 1·00

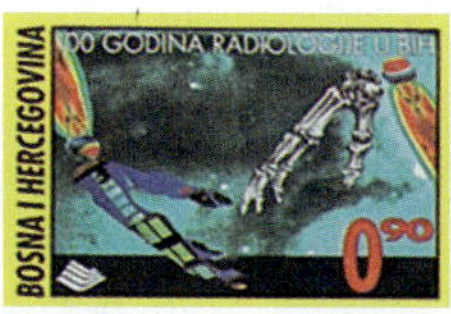
139 X-Ray and Thermal Image of Hands

1999. Centenary of Radiology in Bosnia and Herzegovina.
632 **139** 90f. multicoloured 60 60

140 Kresevljakovic

1999. 40th Death Anniv of Hamdija Kresvljakovic (historian).
633 **140** 1m.30 multicoloured . . . 90 90

141 Chess Emblems and Stars

1999. 15th European Chess Clubs Championship Final, Bugojno.
634 **141** 1m.10 multicoloured . . . 75 75

142 Twipsy (exhibition mascot)

1999. "Expo 2000" World's Fair, Hanover, Germany.
635 **142** 1m. multicoloured 60 60

143 Painting (Afan Ramic)

1999.
636 **143** 1m.20 multicoloured . . . 75 75

144 Globe and Baby

1999. Birth of World's Six Billionth Inhabitant in Sarajevo.
637 **144** 2m.50 multicoloured . . . 1·50 1·50

145 Bjelasnica Observatory

1999. 105th Anniv of Bjelsnica Meteorological Observatory. Sheet 100 × 60 mm.
MS638 **145** 1m.10 multicoloured 75 75

146 Philharmonic Orchestra Building, Sarajevo **147** Woman

1999. International Music Festival, Sarajevo.
639 **146** 40f. black and red 25 25
640 – 1m.10 multicoloured . . . 65 65
DESIGN: 1m.10, Festival poster.

2000. Bairam Festival.
641 **147** 1m.10 multicoloured . . . 65 65

148 Map of Bosnia and Herzegovina and Emblem

2000. Olympic Games, Sydney. Sheet 104 × 72 mm containing T **148** and similar horiz design. Multicoloured.
MS642 1m.30 Type **148**; 1m.70 Map of Australia and stylised sailing boats . . . . 2·25 2·25

149 Spaho **150** Morse Apparatus

2000. 60th (1999) Death Anniv of Mehmed Spaho (politician).
643 **149** 1m. multicoloured 60 60

2000. 50th Anniv of Amateur Radio in Bosnia and Herzegovina.
644 **150** 1m.50 multicoloured . . . 95 95

151 Illuminated Manuscript

2000. 50th Anniv of Institute of Oriental Studies, Sarajevo University.
645 **151** 2m. multicoloured . . . . 1·25 1·25

152 Boracko River

2000. 15th Anniv of Emerald River Nature Protection Organization. Multicoloured.
646 40f. Type **152** 25 25
647 1m. Figure of woman and river (vert) 60 60

153 Scorpionfish

2000. Greenpeace (environmental organization). Sheet 100 × 72 mm containing T **153** and similar horiz design. Multicoloured.
MS648 50f. Type **153**; 60f. Crayfish; 90f. Crimson anemone; 1m.50 Wreck of *Rainbow Warrior* (campaign ship) . . . . 1·25 1·25

154 Griffon Vulture

2000. Birds. Multicoloured.
649 1m. Type **154** 60 60
650 1m.50 White spoonbill . . . 95 95

155 "Building Europe"

2000. Europa.
651 **155** 2m. multicoloured . . . . 1·25 1·25

156 Count Ferdinand von Zeppelin and LZ-1

2000. Centenary of 1st Zeppelin Flight.
652 **156** 1m.50 multicoloured . . . 95 95

157 Zenica

2000. Towns. Multicoloured.
653 50f. Type **157** 35 35
654 1m. Mostar 65 65
655 1m.10 Bihac 75 75
656 1m.50 Tuzla (vert) . . . . . 1·00 1·00

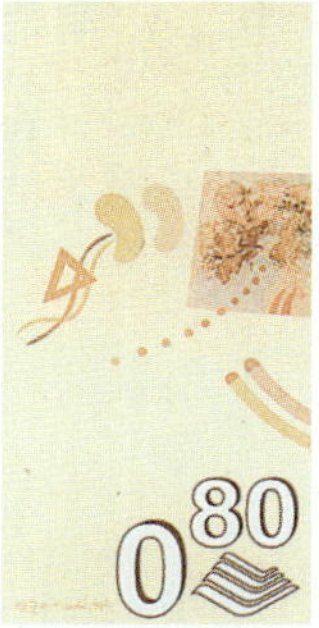

158 Millennium

2000. New Millennium. Sheet 100 × 72 mm containing T **158** and similar multicoloured design.
MS657 80f. Type **158**; 1m.20, Millennium (57 × 57 mm) . . . 80 80

159 Vranduk

2000. Towns. Multicoloured.
658 1m.30 Type **159** 90 90
659 1m.50 Franciscan Abbey, Kraljeva Sutjeska . . . . 1·00 1·00

160 Tom Sawyer, Huckleberry Finn (characters) and Twain

2000. *The Adventures of Tom Sawyer* (children's book by Mark Twain).
660 **160** 1m.50 multicoloured . . . 1·00 1·00

161 People walking (Ismet Mujezinovic)

2000. Paintings. Multicoloured.
661 60f. Type **161** 40 40
662 80f. Trees (Ivo Seremet) . . . 55 55

162 Children and Globe

2000. International Children's Week.
663 **162** 1m.60 multicoloured . . . 1·10 1·10

163 Refugees

2000. 50th Anniv of United Nations Commissioner for Refugees.
664 **163** 1m. multicoloured 65 65

164 Tesanj **165** Horse wearing Skirt

2001. Towns. Multicoloured.
665 10f. Type **164** 10 10
666 20f. Bugojno (horiz) 15 15
667 30f. Konjic (horiz) 20 20
668 35f. Zivinice (horiz) 25 25
669 2m. Cazin (horiz) . . . . . 1·20 1·20

2001. Thelma (cartoon character). Sheet 125 × 170 mm containing T **165** and similar vert designs. Multicoloured.
MS670 30f. Type **165**; 30f. Bear chased by bees; 30f. Cat and boot; 30f. Thelma wet from watering can; 30f. Roast turkey 80 80

166 Kingfisher (*Alcedo athinis*) **167** Disney

2001. Fauna. Multicoloured.
671 90f. Type **166** 60 60
672 1m.10 Bohemian waxwing (*Bombycilla garrulous*) . . 75 75
673 1m.10 Serbian work horse (*Equus caballus*) 75 75
674 1m.90 Head of Serbian horse 1·30 1·30

2001. Birth Centenary of Walt Disney (film maker).
675 **167** 1m.10 multicoloured . . . 75 75

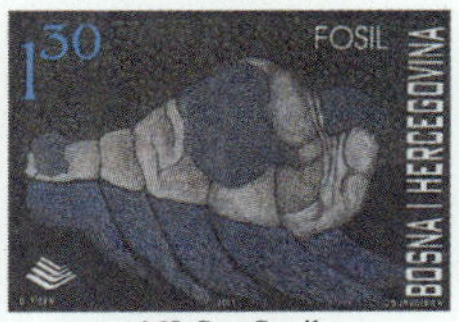

168 Sea Snail

2001. Fossils. Multicoloured.
676 1m.30 Type **168** 90 90
677 1m.80 Ammonite . . . . . . 1·30 1·30

169 Land and Sea Sports

2001. 14th Mediterranean Games, Tunis.
678 **169** 1m.30 multicoloured . . . 90 90

170 Swans on Lake

2001. Europa. Water Resources. Sheet 60 × 81 mm.
MS679 **170** 2m. multicoloured . . 1·20 1·20

2001. Adil Zulfikarpasic Foundation Bosniak Institute (inter-denominational foundation). Sheet 81 × 50 mm.
MS680 **171** 1m.10 multicoloured 75 75

172 Balic

2001. Emir Balic (bridge diving competition winner). Sheet 66 × 47 mm.
MS681 **172** 2m. multicoloured . . 1·20 1·20

173 Ferrari 625 F1 (1954)

2001. Ferrari Racing Cars. Multicoloured.

682	40f. Type **173**	25	25
683	60f. Ferrari 312 B (1970) . .	40	40
684	1m.30 Ferrari 312 T3 (1978)	90	90
685	1m.70 Ferrari 126 C3 (1983)	1·20	1·20

174 Zeljeznicar, Sarajevo Football Team

2001. National Football Champions, 2001.
686 **174** 1m. multicoloured 70 70

175 Ink Well, Quill Pen, Medal and Dove

2001. Centenary of First Nobel Prize.
687 **175** 1m.50 multicoloured . . . 1·00 1·00

176 Charlie Chaplin

2001. Charlie Chaplin Commemoration.
688 **176** 1m.60 multicoloured . . . 1·10 1·10

177 "Traces" (Edin Numankadic)

2001. Art. Multicoloured.

689	80f. Type **177**	55	55
690	2m. David (detail) (sculpture)	1·30	1·30

178 Feeding Bottle enclosed in Stop Sign and Baby at Breast

2001. International Breastfeeding Week.
691 **178** 1m.10 multicoloured . . . 75 75

179 Acropolis, Castle and Pyramid

180 Horse-drawn Tram

2001. United Nations Year of Dialogue Among Civilizations.
692 **179** 1m.30 multicoloured . . . 90 90

2001. Posteurop Plenary, Sarajevo.
693 **180** 1m.10 multicoloured . . .

181 Alija Bejtic and Monument

2001. 20th Death Anniv of Alija Bejtic (cultural historian).
694 **181** 80f. multicoloured 75 75

182 Albert Einstein and Formula

2001. 80th Anniv of Albert Einstein's Nobel Prize for Physics (photoelectric effect).
695 **182** 1m.50 multicoloured . . . 55 55

183 Davorin Popovic

2002. 1st Death Anniv of Davorin Popovic (musician).
696 **183** 38f. multicoloured 25 25

184 Bridge, Figure and Books

2002. 350th Birth Anniv of Mustafa Ejubovic (Sejh Jujo) (writer).
697 **184** 1m. multicoloured 70 70

185 Juraj Neidhardt

2002. Birth Centenary (2001) of Juraj Neidhardt (architect).
698 **185** 1m. multicoloured 70 70

186 Sevala Zidzic

187 Skier

2002. Birth Centenary (2003) of Sevala Zidzic (first female Bosnian doctor).
699 **186** 1m.30 multicoloured . . . 90 90

2002. Sarajevo's Candidacy for Winter Olympic Games, 2010.
700 **187** 1m.50 multicoloured . . . 1·00 1·00

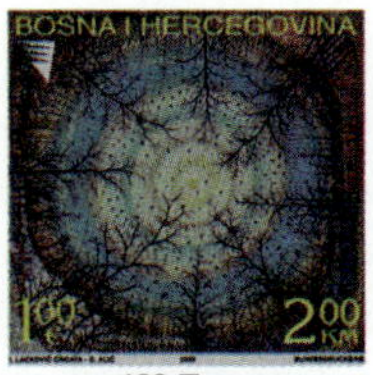

188 Trees

2002. International Earth Day.
701 **188** 2m. multicoloured . . . . 1·30 1·30

189 Scout Camp

2002. 80th Anniv of Bosnian Scouts.
702 **189** 1m. multicoloured 70 70

190 Gentian (*Gentiana dinarica*)

2002. Flora. Multicoloured.

703	1m. Type **190**	70	70
704	1m.50 Aquilegia (*Aquilegia dinarica*)	1·00	1·00

191 "War and Peace" (Asad Nuhanovic)

2002. 10th Anniv of Independence.
705 **191** 2m.50 multicoloured . . . 1·90 1·90

192 Apollo (*Parnassius Apollo*)

193 Firemen fighting Fire

2002. Butterflies. Multicoloured.

706	1m.50 Type **192**	1·00	1·00
707	2m.50 Scarce swallowtail (*Iphiclides podalirius*) . . .	1·90	1·90

2002. 120th Anniv of Sarajevo Fire Brigades. Sheet 68 × 48 mm.
MS708 **193** 2m.20 multicoloured 1·50 1·50

194 Clown

195 Boy wearing Gag

2002. Europa. Circus.
709 **194** 2m.50 multicoloured . . . 1·90 1·90

2002. Letter Writing Campaign. Sheet 120 × 105 mm containing T **195** and similar vert designs showing scenes from "Young Philatelists" (animated film). Multicoloured.
MS710 40f. Type **195**; 40f. Boy with burnt face; 40f. Boy hit by frying pan; 40f. Boy hit by hammer; 40f. Boy hit with saucepan lids . . 1·20 1·20

196 Cevapcici (traditional dish)

2002.
711 **196** 1m.10 multicoloured . . . 75 75

197 Galley

2002. Roman Ships. Sheet 90 × 54 mm containing T **197** and similar horiz design. Multicoloured.
MS712 1m.20 Type **197**; 1m.80 Galleon . . . . 2·10 2·10

198 White Water Rafting

2002. 30th Anniv of Una International Regatta.
713 **198** 1m.30 multicoloured . . . 90 90

199 Association Emblem

2002. Centenary of Napredak (Croatian cultural association).
714 **199** 1m. multicoloured 70 70

200 Mountaineer and Hut

2002. 110th Anniv of Mountaineering Association.
715 **200** 1m. multicoloured 70 70

201 Synagogue

2002. Centenary of Ashkenazi Synagogue, Sarajevo.
716 **201** 2m. multicoloured . . . . 1·20 1·20

202 Metal Worker

2002. Traditional Crafts. Sheet 110 × 75 mm containing T **202** and similar horiz designs. Multicoloured.
MS717 80f. Type **202**; 1m.10 Leather worker; 1m 20 Filigree jewellery; 1m.30 Lace work . . . . . . 3·00 3·00

203 Bosnia and Herzegovina Flag

2002.
718 **203** 1m. multicoloured 70 70

204 Coin and Map of Europe

2002. "The Euro" (European currency).
719 **204** 2m. multicoloured . . . . 1·20 1·20

205 Tvrtka I Coin (1376-1391)

2002. Old Coins.
720 **205** 20f. grey, red and black 15 15
721 – 30f. green, red and black 20 20
722 – 50f. blue, red and black 35 35
DESIGNS: 20f. Type **205**; 30f. Stepana Tomasa coin (1443-1461); 50f. Stepana Tomasevita coin (1461-1463).

206 Mother and Child Institute, Sarajevo

2002.
723 **206** 38f. multicoloured 25 25

207 Horse's Head

2002. Art. Multicoloured.
724 40f. Type **207** 30 30
725 1m.10 Portrait of a woman (25 × 42 mm) 75 75
726 1m.50 Sculpture and portrait of two women (42 × 25 mm) . . . . . . 1·00 1·00

208 Mak Dizdar **209** Emaciated Man

2002. 85th Birth Anniv of Mak Dizdar (poet).
727 **208** 1m. multicoloured 70 70

2002. Anti-Drugs Campaign.
728 **209** 1m. multicoloured 70 70

210 Josip Stadler

2003. 160th Birth Anniv of Josip Stadler (first archbishop).
729 **210** 50f. multicoloured 35 35
A stamp of the same design was issued by Bosnia and Herzegovina Croatian Posts.

211 Musician

2003. Centenary of Bosnian Cultural Union "Preporod".
730 **211** 1m. multicoloured 70 70

212 Stylized Skier

2003. European Nordic Skiing Competition, Sarajevo (2006).
731 **212** 1m. multicoloured 70 70

213 "Mother and Child"

2003. Birth Centenary of Omer Mujadzic (artist).
732 **213** 70f. multicoloured 50 50

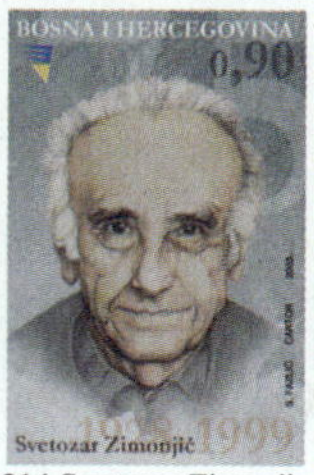

214 Svetozar Zimonjic

2003. 75th Birth Anniv of Svetozar Zimonjic (president of Sciences and Arts Academy).
733 **214** 90f. multicoloured 65 65

215 Edelweiss (*Leontopodium alpinium*)

2003. Flowers. Multicoloured.
734 90f. Type **215** 65 65
735 90f. Yellow gentian (*Gentiana symphyandra*) 65 65

216 Team Members

2003. National Volleyball Team—World Champions, 2002.
736 **216** 1m. multicoloured 70 70

217 Butterflies **219** Stylized DNA

218 Pope John Paul II and Ivan Merz

2003. Europa. Poster Art.
737 **217** 1m. multicoloured 70 70

2003. 2nd Visit of Pope John Paul II.
738 **218** 1m.50 multicoloured . . . 1·00 1·00
A stamp of the same design was issued by Bosnia and Herzegovina Croatian Posts.

2003. 50th Anniv of the Discovery of DNA (genetic material).
739 **219** 50f. multicoloured 35 35

220 Man on Rooftop **222** "Skakavac Waterfall" (Helena Skec)

221 Arches, Cekrelci Muslihudin Mosque

2003. Letter Writing Campaign. Sheet 116 × 73 mm containing T **220** and similar horiz designs showing scenes from "The Sleep of Monsters" (graphic novel by Enki Bilal). Multicoloured.
MS740 50f. × 4, Type **220**; Flying taxi; Man and woman (37 × 25 mm); Faces (37 × 25 mm) 1·40 1·40

2003. Architecture. Multicoloured.
741 1m. Type **221** 70 70
742 2m. Hajji Sinan Dervish Convent, Sarajevo (30 × 30 mm) . . . . . . 1·40 1·40

2003.
743 **222** 1m.50 multicoloured . . . 1·00 1·00

223 Children

2003. Children's Week. Ordinary gum or Self-adhesive gum.
744 **223** 50f. multicoloured 35 35

224 Alija Izetbegovic

2003. Alija Izetbegovic (first president) Commemoration. Sheet 68 × 52 mm.
MS746 **224** 2m. multicoloured . . 1·40 1·40

225 Lamps and Clock

2003. 90th Anniv of Post Building, Sarajevo. Sheet 80 × 65 mm.
MS747 **225** 3m. multicoloured . . 2·10 2·10

226 Chamois (*Rupicapra rupicapra*) **227** "Plemenitas II" (Dzevad Hozo)

2003. Fauna. Multicoloured.
748 30f. Type **226** 20 20
749 50f. Grizzly bear (*Ursus arctos*) 35 35

2003.
750 **227** 10f. multicoloured 10 10

228 Sleigh and Hands holding Present

2003. Christmas.
751 **228** 20f. multicoloured 15 15

229 Orville and Wilbur Wright and *Wright Flyer I*

2003. Centenary of Powered Flight.
752 **229** 1m. multicoloured 70 70

230 Allegorical Painting **231** Bird

2003. 65th Birth Anniv of Ibrahim Ljubovic (artist).
753 **230** 1m.50 multicoloured . . . 1·00 1·00

2004. Bayram Festival.
754 **231** 50f. multicoloured 35 35

232 Kulin on Horseback **233** Aries

2004. 800th Anniv of Reign of Kulin Ban (king).
755 **232** 50f. multicoloured 35 35

2004. Western Zodiac. Multicoloured. (a) Self-adhesive.

756	50f. Type **233**	35	35
757	50f. Taurus	35	35
758	50f. Gemini	35	35
759	50f. Cancer	35	35
760	50f. Leo	35	35
761	50f. Virgo	35	35
762	50f. Libra	35	35
763	50f. Scorpio	35	35
764	50f. Sagittarius	35	35
765	50f. Capricorn	35	35
766	50f. Aquarius	35	35
767	50f. Pisces	35	35

(b) Ordinary gum.
MS768 200 × 130 mm. 50f. × 12, Nos. 756/67 . . . . 4·25 4·25

234 Hearts

2004. St. Valentine's Day.
769 **234** 2m. multicoloured . . . . 1·40 1·40

235 Gloved Hand holding Torch **236** Jajce

2004. 20th Anniv of Winter Olympics, Sarajevo.
770 **235** 1m.50 multicoloured . . . 1·00 1·00

2004. Multicoloured.

770a	10f. Breko (horiz)	10	10
771	20f. Type **236**	15	15
771a	20f. Livno (horiz)	15	15
771b	30f. Vissoko	20	20
771c	1m. Sanski Most	70	70
772	50f. Jablanica (horiz)	35	35
773	2m. Stolac (horiz)	1·40	1·40
774	4m. Gradacac	2·75	2·75
775	5m. Fojinca (horiz)	3·50	3·50

237 *Cattleya intermedia* **238** *Aloe barbardensis*

2004. Orchids. Multicoloured.
780 1m.50 Type **237** . . . . . . 1·00 1·00
781 2m. *Brassavola* . . . . 1·40 1·40
Nos. 780/1 were issued in se-tenant pairs within the sheet and were impregnated with the scent of orchid.

2004. Succulents. Multicoloured.
782 1m.50 Type **238** . . . . . . 1·00 1·00
783 2m. *Carnegiea gigantean* . . 1·40 1·40

239 Centenary Emblem

2004. Centenary of FIFA (Federation Internationale de Football Association).
784 **239** 2m. multicoloured . . . . 1·40 1·40

240 Alarm Clock on Skis **241** Speech Bubbles

2004. Europa. Holidays. Multicoloured.
785 1m. Type **240** 70 70
786 1m.50 Alarm clocks on beach 1·00 1·00

2004. European Youth Peace Conference, Sarajevo.
787 **241** 1m.50 multicoloured . . . 1·00 1·00

242 Clown holding Balloons

2004. Greetings Stamps. Multicoloured.
788 50f. Type **242** (birthday) . . 35 35
789 1m. Bride and bridegroom (wedding) 70 70

243 Bee on Flower

2004. Bees. Sheet 100 × 50 mm containing T **243** and similar horiz design. Multicoloured.
MS790 2m. × 2, Type **243**; Flying bee 1·40 1·40

244 Old Bridge, Mostar (painting) **246** "10" in Lights

245 Athlete and Horses' Heads

2004. Reconstruction of Mostar Bridge. Multicoloured.
791 50f. Type **244** 35 35
792 100f. Bridge (different) . . . 70 70
MS793 287 × 110 mm. Nos. 791/2 1·00 1·00

2004. Olympic Games, Athens. Sheet 101 × 71 mm.
MS794 **245** 2m. multicoloured . . 70 70

2004. 10th International Film Festival, Sarajevo.
795 **246** 1m.50 vermilion, yellow and black . . . . . . 1·00 1·00

247 Abstract

2004. New Year.
796 **247** 1m. multicoloured 70 70

248 Svrzo House (18th-century Ottoman house)

2004. Cultural Heritage. Houses. Multicoloured.
797 1m. Type **248** 70 70
798 1m. Despic house (Serbian merchant's house) 70 70

249 Emblem, "50" and "

2004. 50th Anniv of European Cultural Convention.
799 **249** 1m.50 multicoloured . . . 1·00 1·00

250 "Prozori" (window) (Safet Zec)

2004. Art.
800 **250** 2m. multicoloured . . . . 1·40 1·40

251 Nikola Sop

2004. Birth Centenary of Nikola Sop (writer).
801 **251** 3m. multicoloured . . . . 2·00 2·00

252 Auditorium

2005. 50th Anniv of Chamber Theatre 55.
802 **252** 40f. multicoloured 30 30

253 Dam

2005. 50th Anniv of Jablanica Hydroelectric Power Plant.
803 **253** 60f. multicoloured 40 40

254 Electric Tram

2005. 110th Anniv of Electrification and First Electric Tram.
804 **254** 2m. multicoloured . . . . 1·40 1·40

255 Izet Sarajlic

2005. 75th Birth Anniv of Izet Sarajlic (writer).
805 **255** 1m. multicoloured 70 70

256 Hasan Kickic

2005. Birth Centenary of Hasan Kickic (writer).
806 **256** 1m.50 multicoloured . . . 1·00 1·00

257 *Rosa damascene*

2005. Roses. Multicoloured.
807 80f. Type **257** 55 55
808 1m.20 *Rosa alba* 85 85

258 Baklava

2005. Europa. Gastronomy. Multicoloured.
809 2m. Type **258** . . . . 1·40 1·40
810 2m. Sogon Dolma (stuffed onions) . . . . 1·40 1·40
MS811 115 × 88 mm. Nos. 809/10 2·75 2·75
The stamps and margin of No. **MS**811 form a composite design of a table laid with food.

259 Partridge (inscr "Tatro urogallus")

2005. Fauna. Multicoloured.
812 2m. Type **259** . . . . 1·40 1·40
813 3m. Beaver (*Castor fiber*) . . 2·10 2·10

260 Sportsmen

262 Grieving Women

261 Composers and Building Facade

2005. Mediterranean Games, Almeria.
814 **260** 1m. multicoloured . . . . 1·75 1·75

2005. 50th Anniv of Sarajevo Music Academy.
815 **261** 1m. multicoloured . . . . 1·75 1·75

2005. 10th Anniv of Srebrenica Massacre.
816 **262** 1m. multicoloured . . . . 1·75 1·75

263 Sarajevo and Doha

2005.
817 **263** 2m. multicoloured . . . . 4·75 4·75
A stamp of the same design was issued by Qatar.

264 Emblem and Post Van (EMS)

2005. Postal Service. Multicoloured.
818 10f. Type **264** 25 25
819 20f. Emblem and sorter (hybrid mail) 50 50
820 30f. Emblem and "IZBOR JE VAS!" (door to door) . . . 75 75
821 50f. Emblem and pigeons (philately) . . . . 1·00 1·00

265 *Pyrus communis*

266 Column and Garden (Hakija Kulenovic)

2005. Fruit. Multicoloured.
822 1m. Type **265** 20 20
823 1m.50 Orange (inscr "Orange carica") 25 25
824 2m. *Ficus carica* 35 35
825 2m.50 *Prunus domestica* . . . 50 50
826 5m. Cherry (inscr "Prunus avium") . . . . 1·00 1·00

2005. Birth Centenary of Hakija Kulenovic (artist).
827 **266** 2m. multicoloured . . . . 4·75 4·75

267 Dogs and Girl

268 Trade Union Building

2005. Youth Stamps. Sheet 96 × 72 mm containing T **267** and similar vert design. Multicoloured.
MS828 50f. × 2, Type **267**; Hedgehog windsurfing . . . . 2·40 2·40

2005. Centenary of Trade Unions.
829 **268** 1m. multicoloured . . . . 2·40 2·40

269 Stylized Buildings

2005. Plehan Monastery.
830 **269** 1m. multicoloured . . . . 2·40 2·40

270 Aladza Mosque, Foca

272 Decorated Salon

271 King Tvrtko Kotromanic

2005. Cultural Heritage. Multicoloured.
831 1m. Type **270** . . . . 2·40 2·40
832 1m. Zitomislici Monastery . . 2·40 2·40

2005. History. Bogomils. Multicoloured.
833 50f. Type **271** . . . . 1·20 1·20
834 50f. Kulin Ban . . . . 1·20 1·20
835 1m. Burning man (Inquisition) (stone plaque) 2·40 2·40
836 2m. Eugene IV's Papal Bull (1439) . . . . 4·75 4·75

2005. Bosnia Institute. Multicoloured.
837 70f. Type **272** . . . . 5·50 5·50
838 4m. Exhibition . . . . 5·50 5·50

273 Flowers

2005. 10th Anniv of Dayton Agreement.
839 **273** 1m.50 multicoloured . . . 3·50 3·50

274 Emblem

2005. 60th Anniv of End of World War II.
840 **274** 1m. multicoloured . . . . 2·40 2·40

275 Members Flags and Globe (left)

2005. 50th Anniv of Europa Stamps. Multicoloured.
841 3m. Type **275** . . . . . . 5·50 5·50
842 3m. Globe (right) and members flags . . . . . . 5·50 5·50
843 3m. Euro coin and map of Europe . . . . 5·50 5·50
844 3m. Stars and 1999 chess championships emblem . . 5·50 5·50
MS845 104 × 76 mm. Nos. 841/4 22·00 22·00
Nos. 841/2 were issued together, se-tenant, forming a composite design.

276 Faces

2005. World Vision. People with Special Needs Week.
846 **276** 50f. multicoloured . . . . 1·25 1·25

277 Slalom Skier

2006. Winter Olympic Games, Turin. Sheet 88 × 77 mm containing T **277** and similar horiz design. Multicoloured.
MS847 1m. Type **277**; 2m. Speed skaters . . . . 7·00 7·00

278 Treskavica Mountains, Trnovo

2006. Tourism. Multicoloured.
848 1m. Type **278** . . . . 2·40 2·40
849 1m. Rafting, Goradzde (vert) 2·40 2·40

279 Mercedes Benz 500K Cabriolet B, 1935

2006. Cars. Sheet 104 × 76 mm containing T **279** and similar horiz designs. Multicoloured.
MS850 50f. × 2 Type **279**; Dodge D11 Graber Cabriolet, 1939; 1m. Mercedes Benz SS Schwarzer, 1929; 2m. Bugatti T 57 Ventoux, 1939 . . . . 9·50 9·50

280 Crowd

2006. Europa. Integration. Multicoloured.
851 2m. Type **280** . . . . 3·50 3·50
852 2m. Crowd (different) . . . . 3·50 3·50
MS853 115 × 87 mm. 2m. × 2, As Type **280**; As No. 852 . . . . 9·50 9·50

281 *Formica rufa*

2006. Fauna and Flora. Multicoloured.
854 1m.50 Type **281** . . . . . 1·40 1·40
855 3m. *Sarcosphaera crassa* . . . 2·75 2·75

282 Prisoners and Barbed Wire

2006. Prisoner of War Day.
856 **282** 1m. multicoloured . . . . 2·40 2·40

283 Gallery Facade

2006. 60th Anniv of National Art Gallery.
857 **283** 1m. multicoloured . . . . 2·40 2·40

284 Illustration from "Zenidba nosaca Samuela"

2006. Isak Samokovlija (writer) Commemoration.
858 **284** 1m. multicoloured . . . . 2·40 2·40

284a Mohamed Kadic

2006. Birth Centenaries. Multicoloured.
858a 1m. Type **284a** . . . . . . 1·75 1·75
858b 1m. Mustafa Kamaric . . . 1·75 1·75

285 Team Members

2006. Football Event and Anniversary. Multicoloured.
859 1m. Type **285** (60th anniv of Sarajevo Football Club) . . 3·00 3·00
860 3m. Player, globe and flags (World Cup Football Championship, Germany) 6·50 6·50

286 Potatoes

2006. Vegetables. Multicoloured.
861 10f. Type **286** 25 25
862 20f. Cauliflower 45 45
863 30f. Savoy cabbage 75 75
864 40f. Green cabbage 90 90
865 1m. Carrots . . . . 2·40 2·40

286a *Lepus europaeus*

2006. Fauna. Multicoloured.
866 1m.50 Type **286a** 65 65
867 2m. *Capreolus capreolus* . . 90 90

868 2m.50 *Anas* (mallard) (horiz) 1·10 1·10
869 4m. *Vulpes vulpes* . . . . . 2·50 2·50
870 5m. *Canis lupus* (horiz) . . . 3·50 3·50

287 Emblem

2006. European Junior Table Tennis Championship.
871 **287** 1m. multicoloured . . . . 2·40 2·40

288 Basilica, Breza

2006. Cultural—Historical Heritage. Multicoloured.
872 1m. Type **288** . . . . 2·40 2·40
873 1m. Semiz Ali Pasha's Mosque, Praca (vert) . . . 2·40 2·40

289 Orange Bird

2006. Youth Philately. Sheet 115 × 88 mm containing T **289** and similar vert design. Multicoloured.
MS874 50f. × 2, Type **289**; Yellow bird . . . . 2·50 2·50

290 Girl

2006. Children's Week. Stop Violence against Children Campaign. Self-adhesive.
875 **290** 50f. multicoloured . . . . 1·00 1·00

291 School Building

2006. 300th Anniv of Muslim Secondary School, Travnik.
876 **291** 1m. multicoloured . . . . 1·75 1·75

292 Vladimir Prelog (Chemistry, 1975)

2006. Nobel Prize Winners. Multicoloured.
877 1m. Type **292** . . . . 1·75 1·75
878 2m.50 Ivo Andric (Literature, 1961) . . . . 4·25 4·25

293 Emblem

294 Museum Exhibits

2006. 30th Anniv of Tuzli University.
879 **293** 1m. multicoloured . . . . 1·75 1·75

2006.
880 **294** 1m. multicoloured . . . . 1·75 1·75

295 Steam Locomotive

2006. Railways. Multicoloured.
881 50f. Type **295** . . . . 1·00 1·00
882 1m. Modern locomotive . . . 1·75 1·75

296 Sheep

2007. Domestic Animals. Multicoloured.
883 10f. Type **296** 50 50
884 20f. Goat 50 50
885 30f. Cow 60 60
886 40f. Donkey . . . . 1·10 1·10
887 70f. Horse (42 × 35 mm) . . . 1·80 1·80
888 1m. Cat (42 × 35 mm) . . . . 2·40 2·40

297 Arms

2007. 60th Anniv of National Opera Theatre.
889 **297** 50f. multicoloured . . . . 1·00 1·00

298 Scouts

2007. Europa. Centenary of Scouting. Multicoloured.
890 2m. Type **298** . . . . 3·50 3·50
891 2m. Scouts by campfire . . . 3·50 3·50

299 Prokos Lake

2007. Tourism.
892 **299** 2m.50 multicoloured . . . 4·25 4·25

300 *Knautia travnicensis*

301 Kozarac

2007. Fauna and Flora. Multicoloured.
893 80f. Type **300** . . . . 2·10 2·10
894 1m.20 *Sciurus vulgaris* (horiz) 2·60 2·60

2007. Tourism.
895 **301** 1m. multicoloured . . . . 2·40 2·40

302 Building Facade

2007. 140th Anniv of Cazin Madrasah (Islamic school).
896 **302** 2m. multicoloured . . . . 4·75 4·75

302a Fountain, Tuzla

2007. Fountains. Multicoloured.
897 1m.50 Type **302a** . . . . . . 3·00 3·00
898 2m. Mostar . . . . 3·75 3·75
899 2m.50 Sanski Most . . . . . 4·25 4·25
900 4m. Sebilj, Sarajevo (horiz) 7·25 7·25
901 5m. Fountain, Bey's Mosque 9·75 9·75

303 Masthead

2007. Centenary of *Gajret* Periodical.
902 **303** 1m. multicoloured . . . . 2·40 2·40

304 Courtyard

2007. 30th Anniv of Islamic Science Faculty, Sarajevo.
903 **304** 2m. multicoloured . . . . 4·75 4·75

305 Front Elevation

2007. Gazi Husrev-Begova Library.
904 **305** 1m.50 multicoloured . . . 3·50 3·50

306 Landscape (Ismet Rizvic)

2007. Art. Multicoloured.
905 1m. Pocitelj Visual Art Colony . . . . 1·00 1·00
906 1m.50 Type **306** . . . . . . 1·50 1·50

307 '140' and Stylised Building

2007. 140th Anniv of Abdulah Nakas Hospital.
907 **307** 1m.50 red and silver . . . 3·50 3·50

308 Bear Figurine

2007. Museum Exhibit.
908 **308** 1m. multicoloured . . . . 2·40 2·40

309 Buildings and Karel Parik

2007. 150th Birth Anniv of Karel Parik (architect).
909 **309** 2m.50 multicoloured . . . 6·00 6·00

310 Combatants

2007. Karate.
910 **310** 1m. multicoloured . . . . 2·40 2·40

311 *Self Portrait* (Zuko Dzumhur)

2007. Zuko Dzumhur (artist, writer and caricaturist).
911 **311** 1m. multicoloured . . . .

312 Building Facade

2007. 60th Anniv of Medical Faculty of Sarajevo University.
912 **312** 1m. multicoloured . . . . 2·40 2·40

313 Joseph Blatter

2007. Honorary Ambassadors for Sport and Culture of Peace. Multicoloured.
913 2m. Type **313** . . . . 4·25 4·25
914 2m. Juan Antonio Samaranch (41 × 27 mm) . . . . . . 4·25 4·25

314 Heart (Amira Halilovic)

2007. Ecology. Children's Drawings. Multicoloured.
915 50f. Type **314** . . . . 1·00 1·00
916 50f. Couple holding globe (Maida Hasanic) . . . . . 1·00 1·00
MS916a 75 × 95 mm. Nos. 915/16 2·00 2·00

315 Fortress, Samobor

2007. Cultural Heritage.
917 **315** 1m. multicoloured . . . . 2·40 2·40

316 Meat Pie

2007. Gastronomy.
918 **316** 2m. multicoloured . . . . 4·75 4·75

317 Stegosaurus

2007. Pre-History. Dinosaurs.
919 **317** 2m. multicoloured . . . . 4·75 4·75

318 Laika

2007. 50th Anniv of Space Exploration.
920 **318** 3m. multicoloured . . . . 7·00 7·00

319 Emblem

2007. 60th Anniv of University Sports Association.
921 **319** 50f. multicoloured . . . . 1·00 1·00

II. CROATIAN POSTS

Issues made by the Croat administration in Mostar.

1993. 100 paras = 1 Croatian dinar.
1994. 100 lipa = 1 kuna.

C **1** Statue and Church

C **2** Silvije Kranjcevic (poet)

1993. Sanctuary of Our Lady Queen of Peace Shrine, Medugorje.
C1 C **1** 2000d. multicoloured . . . 50 50

1993. Multicoloured.
C2 200d. Type C **2** 10 10
C3 500d. Jajce 15 15
C4 1000d. Mostar (horiz) 20 20

C **3** Medieval Gravestone

C **4** "Madonna of the Grand Duke" (Raphael)

1993. 250th Anniv of Census in Bosnia and Herzegovina.
C5 C **3** 100d. multicoloured . . . 10 10

1993. Christmas.
C6 C **4** 6000d. multicoloured . . . 1·25 1·25

C **5** "Uplands in Bloom"

1993. Europa. Contemporary Art. Paintings by Gabrijel Jurkic. Multicoloured.
C7 3500d. Type C **5** . . . . . 1·75 1·75
C8 5000d. "Wild Poppy" . . . . 2·25 2·25

C **6** Kravica Waterfall

1993.
C9 C **6** 3000d. multicoloured . . . 60 60

C **7** Hrvoje (from "Hrvoje's Missal" by Butko)

1993. 577th Death Anniv of Hrvoje Vukcic Hrvatinic, Duke of Split, Viceroy of Dalmatia and Croatia and Grand Duke of Bosnia.
C10 C **7** 1500d. multicoloured . . 30 30

C **8** Plehan Monastery

1993.
C11 C **8** 2200d. multicoloured . . 45 45

C **9** Arms

C **11** "Campanula hercegovina"

C **10** Bronze Cross, Rama-Scit (Mile Blazevic)

1994. Proclamation (August 1993) of Croatian Community of Herceg Bosna.
C12 C **9** 10000d. multicoloured . . 2·00 2·00

1994.
C13 C **10** 2k.80 multicoloured . . 55 55

1994. Flora and Fauna. Multicoloured.
C14 3k.80 Type C **11** 75 75
C15 4k. Mountain dog 80 80

C **12** Hutova Swamp

1994.
C16 C **12** 80l. multicoloured . . . 20 20

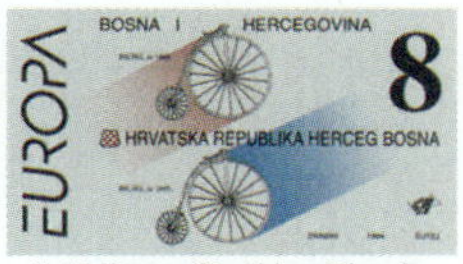

C **13** Penny Farthing Bicycles

1994. Europa. Discoveries and Inventions. Mult.
C17 8k. Type C **13** . . . . 1·50 1·50
C18 10k. Mercedes cars, 1901 . . 2·00 2·00

C **14** Views of Town and Fortress

1994. 550th Anniv of First Written Record of Ljubuski.
C19 C **14** 1k. multicoloured . . . 20 20

C **15** Hospital and Christ

C **16** Anniversary Emblem

1994. 2nd Anniv of Dr. Nikolic Franciscan Hospital, Nova Bila.
C20 C **15** 5k. multicoloured . . . 1·00 1·00

1995. 50th Anniv of UNO. Self-adhesive. Rouletted.
C21 C **16** 1k.50 blue, red & black 30 30

C **17** Crib

1995. Christmas.
C22 C **17** 5k.40 multicoloured . . 1·10 1·10

C **18** Franciscan Monastery, Kraljeva Sutjeska

C **19** Srebrenica

1995.
C23 C **18** 3k. multicoloured . . . 60 60

1995. Towns. Multicoloured.
C24 2k. Type C **19** 40 40
C25 4k. Franciscan Monastery, Mostar 80 80

C **20** Christ on the Cross

C **21** Statue and Church

1995. Europa. Peace and Freedom.
C26 C **20** 6k.50 multicoloured . . 1·25 1·25

1996. 15th Anniv of Sanctuary of Our Lady Queen of Peace Shrine, Medugorje.
C27 C **21** 10k. multicoloured . . . 2·00 2·00

C **22** Queen Katarina Kosaca Kotromanic

C **23** Monastery

1996. Europa. Famous Women.
C28 C **22** 2k.40 multicoloured . . 50 50

1996. 150th Anniv of Franciscan Monastery and Church, Siroki Brijeg.
C29 C **23** 1k.40 multicoloured . . 30 30

C **24** Virgin Mary

C **26** "Madonna and Child" (anon)

1996. Self-adhesive. Rouletted.
C30 C **24** 2k. mult (postage) . . . 40 40
C31 9k. multicoloured (air) 1·75 1·75

1996. "Taipeh '96" International Stamp Exn. Nos. C30/1 surch **1.10** and emblem.
C32 C **24** 1k.10 on 2k. mult (postage) 20 20
C33 1k.10 on 9k. mult (air) 20 20

1996. Christmas.
C34 C **26** 2k.20 multicoloured . . 45 45

C **27** St. George and the Dragon

C **28** Pope John Paul II

1997. Europa. Tales and Legends. Mult.
C35 2k. Type C **27** 40 40
C36 5k. Zeus as bull and Europa (39 × 34 mm) . . . . . . 1·00 1·00

1997. Papal Visit.
C37 C **28** 3k.60 multicoloured . . 70 70
MSC38 90 × 100 mm. No. 37 × 4 2·50 2·50

C 29 Chapel, Samatorje, Gorica

C 30 Purple Heron

1997.
C39 C **29** 1k.40 multicoloured . . 25 25

1997. Flora and Fauna. Multicoloured.
C40 1k. Type C **30** 20 20
C41 2k.40 "Symphyandra hofmannii" (orchid) . . . 45 45

C **31** "Birth of Christ" (fresco, Giotto)

1997. Christmas.
C42 C **31** 1k.40 multicoloured . . 25 25

C 32 Cats

1998. Europa. Animated Film Festival.
C43 C **32** 6k.50 multicoloured . . 1·10 1·10

C 33 Seal

C 35 "Sibiraea croatica"

C 34 Livno

1998. 550th Anniv of Herzegovina.
C44 C **33** 2k.30 red, black and gold 40 40

1998. 1100th Anniv of Livno.
C45 C **34** 1k.20 multicoloured . . 20 20

1998.
C46 C **35** 1k.40 multicoloured . . 25 25

C 36 Griffon Vulture

C 37 Adoration of the Wise Men

1998.
C47 C **36** 2k.40 multicoloured . . 40 40

1998. Christmas.
C48 C **37** 5k.40 multicoloured . . 90 90

C **38** Woman, Posavina Region

C **39** Ruins of Bobovac

1999. Regional Costumes.
C49 C **38** 40l. multicoloured . . . 10 10

1999. Old Towns.
C50 C **39** 10l. multicoloured . . . 10 10

C **40** Simic

C **41** Blidinje Nature Park

1999. Birth Centenary (1998) of Antun Simic (writer).
C51 C **40** 30l. multicoloured . . . 10 10

1999. Europa. Parks and Gardens.
C52 C **41** 1k.50 multicoloured . . 25 25

C **42** *Dianthus freynii*

1999.
C53 C **42** 80l. multicoloured . . . 50 50

C **43** Pine Marten

1999.
C54 C **43** 40l. multicoloured . . . 25 25

C **44** Gradina Osanici, Stolac

C **45** The Nativity (mosaic)

1999. Archaeology.
C55 C **44** 10l. multicoloured . . . 10 10

1999. Christmas.
C56 C **45** 30l. multicoloured . . . 20 20

C **46** Sop

C **47** Emblem

2000. 96th Birth Anniv of Nikola Sop (poet).
C57 C **46** 40l. multicoloured . . . 25 25

2000. World Health Day.
C58 C **47** 40l. multicoloured . . . 25 25

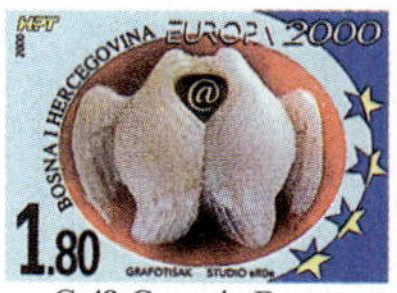

C **48** Ceramic Doves

2000. Europa.
C59 C **48** 1k.80 multicoloured . . 30 30

C **49** Chess Board and Emblem

2000. 40th Anniv of Bosnian Chess Association. Chess Events in 2000. Multicoloured.
C60 80l. Type C **49** (30th Chess Olympiad, Sarajevo) . . . 15 15
C61 80l. Octopus holding pawn and emblem (16th European Chess Club Cup, Neum) 15 15

C **50** Brother Karaula

C **51** Oak Tree (*Quercus sessilis*)

2000. Birth Bicentenary of Brother Lovro Karaula.
C62 C **50** 80l. multicoloured . . . 15 15

2000. Chestnut Oak of Siroki Brijeg.
C63 C **51** 1k.50 multicoloured . . 25 25

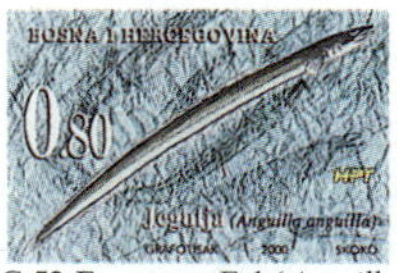

C **52** European Eel (*Anguilla anguilla*)

2000.
C64 C **52** 80l. multicoloured . . . 15 15

C **53** Franciscan Monastery, Tomislavgrad

2000.
C65 C **53** 1k.50 multicoloured . . 25 25

C **54** Woman and Patterned Cloth

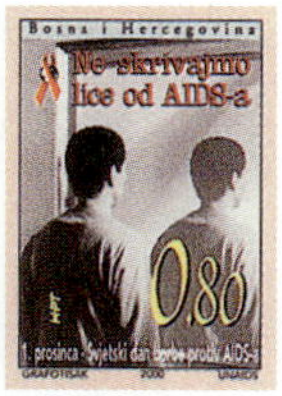

C **55** Man and Reflection

2000. Traditional Costume from Kraljeve Sutjeske.
C66 C **54** 40l. multicoloured . . . 10 10

2000. A.I.D.S. Awareness Campaign.
C67 C **55** 80l. multicoloured . . . 15 15

C **56** Nativity

C **57** *Chondrostoma phoxinus*

2000. Christmas.
C68 C **56** 40l. multicoloured . . . 10 10

2001. Fishes. Multicoloured.
C69 30l. Type C **57** 10 10
C70 1k.50 *Salmo marmoratus* . . 25 25

C **58** Tihaljina Spring

C **59** Petar Zrinski

2001. Europa. Water Resources. Multicoloured.
C71 1k.10 Type C **58** 20 20
C72 1k.80 Pliva Waterfall 30 30

2001. 330th Death Anniversaries. Multicoloured.
C73 40l. Type C **59** 10 10
C74 40l. Fran Krsto Frankopan 10 10

C **60** 16th-century Galley Ship

2001.
C75 C **60** 1k.80 multicoloured . . 30 30

C **61** Boat, Neretva River Valley

C **62** Queen of Peace of Medugorje

2001.
C76 C **61** 80l. multicoloured . . . 15 15

2001. 20th Anniv of Medugorje. Sheet 90 × 65 mm.
C77 C **62** 3k.80 multicoloured . . 65 65

C **63** Our Lady of Kondzilo (17th-century painting)

C **64** Binary Digits

2001.
C78 C **63** 80l. multicoloured . . . 10 10

2001. 50th Anniv of Computers. Each black and red.
C79 40l. Type C **64** 10 10
C80 40l. Binary forming "50" . . 10 10

C **65** Mars, Globe and Sisyphus pushing Stone

2001. Millennium.
C81 C **65** 1k.50 multicoloured . . 25 25

C **66** Father Slavko Barbaric

2001. 1st Death Anniv of Father Slavko Barbaric.
C82 C **66** 80l. multicoloured . . . 10 10

C **67** Minnie and Mickey Mouse (Danijela Nedic)

2001. Birth Centenary of Walt Disney (film maker).
C83 C **67** 1k.50 multicoloured . . 25 25

C **68** Nativity

2001. Christmas.
C84 C **68** 40l. multicoloured . . . 10 10

C **69** Alfred Nobel

2001. Centenary of the Nobel Prize.
C85 C **69** 1k.80 multicoloured . . 35 35

C **70** Skier

C **71** Vran Mountain

2002. Winter Olympic Games, Salt Lake City, U.S.A.
C86 C **70** 80l. multicoloured . . . 10 10

2002. International Year of Mountains.
C87 C **71** 40l. multicoloured . . . 10 10

C **72** Bridge over River Neretva, Mostar

2002. 550th Anniv of First Written Record of Mostar.
C88 C **72** 30l. multicoloured . . . 10 10

C **73** Clown, Lion and Mouse

C **74** Leonardo da Vinci and Designs

2002. Europa. Circus. Multicoloured.
C89 80l. Type C **73** 10 10
C90 1k.50 Big Top and clowns 25 25

2002. 550th Birth Anniv of Leonardo da Vinci (artist and designer).
C91 C **74** 40l. brown and agate . . 10 10

C **75** Players and Football

C **76** Father Bunti and Children

2002. World Cup Football Championships, Japan and South Korea.
C92 C **75** 1k.50 multicoloured . . 25 25

2002. 60th Death Anniv of Father Didak Bunti (humanitarian).
C93 C **76** 80l. multicoloured . . . 10 10

C **77** Inscribed Tablet

2002. 11th-century Inscribed Tablet, Humac.
C94 C **77** 40l. multicoloured . . . 40 40

C **78** Marilyn Monroe

C **79** Elvis Presley

2002. 40th Death Anniv of Marilyn Monroe (actor).
C95 C **78** 40l. multicoloured . . . 40 40

2002. 25th Death Anniv of Elvis Presley (entertainer).
C96 C **79** 1k.50 multicoloured . . 25 25

C **80** Transmitter Tower

C **82** 1929 Calendar

C **81** 1905 Postcard

2002. 50th Anniv of Television.
C97 C **80** 1k.50 multicoloured . . 25 25

2002. Stamp Day.
C98 C **81** 80l. multicoloured . . . 10 10

2002. Centenary of "Naprodak" (cultural association).
C99 C **82** 40l. multicoloured . . . 10 10

C **83** Stylized Player

C **84** *Viola beckiana*

2002. European Bowling Championships, Grude.
C100 C **83** 1k.50 multicoloured . . 25 25

2002. Flowers.
C101 C **84** 30l. multicoloured . . 10 10

C **85** Red Admiral (*Vanessa atalanta*)

C **86** Madonna and Child (painting, Bernardino Luini)

2002. Butterflies.
C102 C **85** 80l. multicoloured . . 10 10

2002. Christmas.
C103 C **86** 40l. multicoloured . . 10 10

C **87** School Buildings

2002. 120th Anniv of Society of Jesuits High School, Travnik.
C104 C **87** 80l. multicoloured . . 10 10

C **88** Josip Stadler

C **90** Key Box and Letter Holder

C **89** Sirokom Brijegu High School

2003. 160th Birth Anniv (first archbishop).
C105 C **88** 50l. multicoloured . . 10 10

2003.
C106 C **89** 40l. multicoloured . . 10 10

2003. Europa. Poster Art.
C107 C **90** 1k.80 multicoloured . . 30 30

C **91** Figures

2003. 800th Anniv of the Abjuration at Bilino Polje.
C108 C **91** 50l. multicoloured . . 10 10

C **92** Mary and Angels

C **94** *Oxytropis prenja*

C **93** Corkscrews

2003. 10th Anniv of HP Mostar.
C109 C **92** 980l. multicoloured . . 20 20

2003. World Wine Day.
C110 C **93** 1k.50 multicoloured . . 30 30

2003. Flora and Fauna. Multicoloured.
C111 50l. Type C **94** 10 10
C112 2k. Rock partridge (*Alectoris graeca*) 35 35

C **95** Pope John Paul II and Ivan Merz

2003. 2nd Visit of Pope John Paul II.
C113 C **95** 1k.50 multicoloured . . 30 30

C **96** Crucifix

C **97** Woman wearing Folk Costume, Rama

2003. 440th Birth Anniv of Matija Divkovic (writer).
C114 C **96** 3k.80 multicoloured . . 70 70

2003. Cultural Heritage. Multicoloured.
C115 50l. Type C **97** 10 10
C116 70l. Jewellery, Neum (horiz) 15 15

C **98** Summit Cross

C **99** Stjepan Kotromanic

2003. 70th Anniv of Summit Cross on Krizevac Mountain.
C117 C **98** 80l. multicoloured . . 15 15

2003. 650th Death Anniv of Stjepan Kotromanic (King of Bosnia).
C118 C **99** 20l. multicoloured . . 10 10

C **100** Tele-printer

2003. World Post Day.
C119 C **100** 1k.50 black and red 30 30

C **101** Quill and Inkwell

C **102** Car and Bicycle

2003. Birth Bicentenary of Alberto Fortis (writer).
C120 C **101** 50l. multicoloured . . 10 10

2003. Children.
C121 C **102** 1k. multicoloured . . 20 20

C **103** Nativity

2003. Christmas.
C122 C **103** 50l. multicoloured . . 10 10

C **104** "100"

2003. Centenary of Powered Flight.
C123 C **104** 2k. multicoloured . . 35 35

C **105** Emblem

C **106** Hearts

2004. International Investment Conference.
C124 C **105** 5k. silver 85 85

2004. St. Valentine's Day.
C125 C **106** 10l. multicoloured . . 10 10

C **107** Albert Einstein

2004. 125th Birth Anniv of Albert Einstein (physicist).
C126 C **107** 50l. multicoloured . . 10 10

C **108** Decorated Hand

2004. Tattooing.
C127 C **108** 50l. multicoloured . . 10 10

C **109** *Aquilegia dinarica*

C **110** Skis and Snow Scene

2004. Flora and Fauna. Type C **109** and similar multicoloured design. P $14\frac{1}{2}$.
C128 1k. Type C **109** 20 20
C129 1k.50 *Salamandra atra prenjensis* (horiz) 30 30

2004. Europa. Holidays. Multicoloured.
C130 1k.50 Type C **110** 30 30
C131 2k. Flippers and Beach Scene 35 35

C **111** Andrije Kacica Miosica

C **112** Ball and Boots

2004. 300th Birth Anniv of Andrije Kacica Miosica (writer and theologian).
C132 C **111** 70l. yellow and brown 10 10

2004. European Football Championship 2004, Portugal.
C133 C **112** 2k. multicoloured . . 35 35

C **113** Kocerin Tablet (carved stone), Siroki Brijeg (c.1404)

C **114** Footprint

2004.
C134 C **113** 70l. multicoloured . . 10 10

2004. 35th Anniv of First Landing on Moon.
C135 C **114** 1k. multicoloured . . 20 20

C **115** Old Bridge, Mostar

2004. Reconstruction of Mostar Bridge.
C136 C **115** 50l. multicoloured . . 10 10

C **116** Water Wheel, Buna

2004.
C137 C **116** 1k. Multicoloured . . 20 20

C **117** Envelope and Earth

2004. World Post Day.
C138 C **117** 1k.50 multicoloured 30 30

C **118** Money Box and Hippopotamus

2004. World Savings Day.
C139 C **118** 50l. multicoloured . . 10 10

C **119** Karl Friedrich Benz

2004. 160th Birth Anniv of Karl Friedrich Benz (German motor pioneer).
C140 C **119** 1k.50 multicoloured 30 30

C **120** Mary and Joseph

2004. Christmas. Multicoloured.
C141 50l. Type C **120** 10 10
C142 1k. Postman carrying present 20 20

C **121** Woman wearing Folk Costume, Kupres

C **122** *Gentiana dinarica*

2005. Cultural Heritage.
C143 C **121** 1k.50 multicoloured 30 30

2005. Flora. Multicoloured.
C144 50l. Type C **122** 10 10
C145 50l. *Petteria ramentacea* . . 10 10

C **123** Little Egret (*Egretta garzetta*)

C **124** Early Footballers

2005. Birds. Multicoloured.
C146 1k. Type C **123** 20 20
C147 1k. Black-winged stilt (*Himantopus himantopus*) 20 20
C148 1k. Kingfisher (*Alcedo atthis*) 20 20
C149 1k. European bee eater (*Merops apiaster*) 20 20

2005. Centenary of CSC Zrinjski Sports Club. Multicoloured.
C150 3k. Type C **124** 55 55
C151 3k. Modern footballers . . 55 55

C **125** Figure holding Flag

C **126** *Thumbelina* (Hans Christian Andersen)

2005. Easter.
C152 C **125** 50l. multicoloured . . 10 10

2005. Writers Anniversaries. Multicoloured.
C153 20l. Type C **126** (birth bicentenary) 10 10
C154 20l. *Tintilinic* (Ivana Brlic Mazuranic) (130th (2004) birth anniv) 10 10

C **127** Bread, Grapes, Wine, Nuts and Soft Cheese

2005. Europa. Gastronomy. Multicoloured.
C155 2k. Type C **127** 35 35
C156 2k. Bread, garlic, meats, glass and flagon 35 35

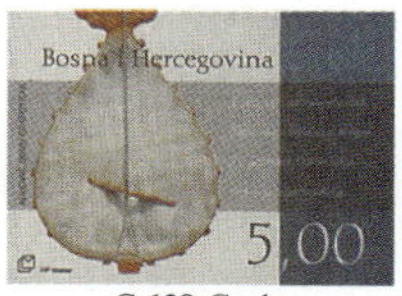

C **128** Gusle

2005. Musical Instruments.
C157 C **128** 5k. multicoloured . . 5·00 5·00

C **129** Vjetrenica Cave

2005. International Day of Water.
C158 C **129** 1k. multicoloured . . 2·50 2·50

C **130** Steam Locomotive

2005. 120th Anniv of Metkovic—Mostar Railway.
C159 C **130** 50l. multicoloured . . 1·00 1·00

C **131** Virgin Mary (statue) and Crowds

C **132** Father Grgo Martic

2005. Medjugorje Youth Festival.
C160 C **131** 1k. multicoloured . . 2·50 2·50

2005. Birth Centenary of Father Grgo Martic.
C161 C **132** 1k. multicoloured . . 2·50 2·50

C **133** Trumpet

C **134** Flowers

2005. International Music Day.
C162 C **133** 50l. multicoloured . . 1·00 1·00

2005. 10th Anniv of Dayton Agreement.
C163 C **134** 1k.50 multicoloured 3·75 3·75

C **135** Slavko Barbaric

C **136** Mary and Jesus

2005. 5th Death Anniv of Slavko Barbaric (writer).
C164 C **135** 1k. multicoloured . . 2·50 2·50

2005. Christmas. Multicoloured.
C165 50l. Type C **136** . . . . . 1·25 1·25
C166 50l. Tree . . . . 1·25 1·25

C **137** "50"

C **138** Lake and Bearded Tit

2005. 50th Anniv of Europa Stamps. Multicoloured.
C167 2k. Type C **137** . . . . . . 4·00 4·00
C168 2k. Sunflowers and envelope 4·00 4·00
C169 2k. Map and 2003 1k.80 stamp (No. C107) . . . . 4·00 4·00
C170 2k. European flags . . . . 4·00 4·00
MSC171 90 × 100 mm. Nos. 167/70 16·00 16·00

2006. International Swamp Protection Day.
C172 C **138** 1k. multicoloured . . 2·50 2·50

C **139** Faces

2006. Europa. Integration. Multicoloured.
C173 2k. Type C **139** . . . . . 4·00 4·00
C174 2k. "Integration" . . . . . 4·00 4·00

C **140** Sunflower and Globe

2006. Earth Day.
C175 C **140** 1k. multicoloured . . 2·50 2·50

C **141** Paper Birds

2006. World Press Freedom Day.
C176 C **141** 50l. multicoloured . . 1·25 1·25

C **142** Cable

2006. World Telecommunications Day.
C177 C **142** 1k. multicoloured . . 2·50 2·50

C **143** Queen of Peace (statue) and Church   C **144** Church

2006. 25th Anniv of Medugorje. Multicoloured.
C178 1k. Type C **143** . . . . . . 2·00 2·00
C179 1k. Statue with multicoloured halo amongst rocks . . . . . 2·00 2·00
C180 1k. Cross, Krizevac Hill and statue . . . . 2·00 2·00
C181 1k. Statue (detail) and church . . . . 2·00 2·00
C182 1k. Stylized church and crowd . . . . 2·00 2·20

2006. 150th Anniv of Uzdol Parish.
C183 C **144** 50l. multicoloured . . 1·25 1·25

C **145** Nikola Tesla   C **146** Archer and Stag

2006. 150th Birth Anniv of Nikola Tesla (engineer).
C184 C **145** 2k. multicoloured . . 5·00 5·00

2006. Stecci (medieval tombstones).
C185 C **146** 20l. multicoloured . . 35 35

C **147** Car   C **148** Crucifix from Woman's Rosary, Franciscan Monastery, Humac

2006. Car Free Day.
C186 C **147** 1k. black, vermilion and yellow . . . . 2·00 2·00

2006.
C187 C **148** 5k. multicoloured . . 5·00 5·00

C **149** *Upupa epops* (hoopoe)

2006. Birds of Hutovo. Multicoloured.
C188 70l. Type C **149** . . . . . 4·00 4·00
C189 70l. *Alauda arvensis* (skylark) . . . . 4·00 4·00
Nos. C190/1 have been left for additions to this set.

C **150** *Papaver kerneri*

2006. Flora. Multicoloured.
C192 20l. Type C **150** . . . . . 1·00 1·00
C193 20l. *Cerastium dinaricum* . . 1·00 1·00

C **151** Door with Wreath

2006. Christmas and New Year. Multicoloured.
C194 50l. Type C **151** . . . . . 1·25 1·25
C195 1k. Grass and candles . . . 2·50 2·50

C **152** Hearts and Birds

2007. St. Valentine's Day.
C196 C **152** 10l. multicoloured . . 1·00 1·00

C **153** Head of Dog

2007. Dogs. Tornjak. Multicoloured.
C197 70l. Type C **153** . . . . . 1·75 1·75
C198 70l. Head of dog, black markings . . . . 1·75 1·75
C199 70l. Dog with black markings . . . . 1·75 1·75
C200 70l. Dog with brown markings . . . . 1·75 1·75

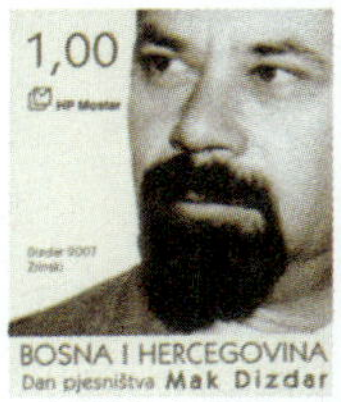

C **154** Mak Dizdar

2007. 90th Birth Anniv of Mehmedalija Mak Dizdar (poet).
C201 C **154** 1k. multicoloured . . 2·50 2·50

C **155** Clasped Hands

2007. Europa. Centenary of Scouting. Multicoloured.
C202 3k. Type C **155** . . . . . 7·00 7·00
C203 3k. Reef knot . . . . 7·00 7·00

C **156** *Sorbus domestica*

2007. Tree Day. Sheet 68 × 91 mm.
MSC204 C **156** 2k.10 multicoloured 5·25 5·25

C **157** Lion (base relief) and Map

2007. Gabela Archaeological Site, Capljina.
C205 C **157** 1k.50 multicoloured 3·75 3·75

C **158** Iris

2007. *Iris Illyrica*. Multicoloured.
C206 2k. Type C **158** . . . . . . 5·00 5·00
MSC207 61 × 80 mm. 3k. Iris and trireme (24 × 58 mm) . . . . . 7·75 7·75

C **159** Virgin Mary (statue)

2007. Medugorje. Multicoloured.
C208 1k. Type C **159** . . . . . . 2·50 2·50
C209 1k. Hands holding rosary 2·50 2·50
C210 1k. Virgin Mary and pilgrims . . . . 2·50 2·50
C211 1k. Bronze statue of Friar 2·50 2·50
C212 1k. Virgin Mary (statue) and tower . . . . 2·50 2·50

C **160** Friar Marko Dobretic

2007. 300th Birth Anniv of Friar Marko Dobretic.
C213 C **160** 60l. multicoloured . . 1·50 1·50

C **161** Duke Vlatko's Tombstone, Boljuni Necropolis

2007. Cultural Heritage Day.
C214 C **161** 20l. multicoloured . . 1·00 1·00

C **162** Emblem   C **163** Hemp and Spindle

2007. World Bowling Championship, Grude.
C215 C **162** 5k. black and scarlet 12·00 12·00

2007. Ethnological Treasures.
C216 C **163** 70l. multicoloured . . 1·75 1·75

C **164** *Fulica atra* (coot)

2007. Birds. Multicoloured.
C217 2k. Type C **164** . . . . . . 1·75 1·75
C218 2k. *Anas platyrhynchos* (mallard) . . . . 1·75 1·75
C219 2k. *Anas crecca* (common teal) . . . . 1·75 1·75
C220 2k. *Streptopella turtur* (turtle dove) . . . . . . 1·75 1·75

C **165** *Gentiana lutea*

2007. Flora of Blidinje Park. Multicoloured.
C221 3k. Type C **165** . . . . . . 7·00 7·00
MSC222 80 × 60 mm. 3k. *Vaccinium vitis-idaea* . . . . 7·00 7·00
The stamp and margins **MSC**222 form a composite design.

III. REPUBLIKA SRPSKA

Issued by the Serb administration based in Pale.

100 paras = 1 dinar.
1998. 100 fennig = 1 mark.

30 ==
Република Српска
(S **1**)

S **2** Stringed Instrument

1992. Nos. 2587/98 of Yugoslavia surch as Type S **1**.
S 1 5d. on 10p. violet and green 10 10
S 2 30d. on 3d. blue and red . . 60·00 60·00
S 3a 50d. on 40p. green & purple 50 50
S 4 60d. on 20p. red and yellow 60 60
S 5 60d. on 30p. green & orange 60 60
S 6 100d. on 1d. blue and purple . . . . 1·00 1·00
S 7a 100d. on 2d. blue and red 1·00 1·00
S 8 100d. on 3d. blue and red 1·00 1·00
S 9a 300d. on 5d. ultram & blue 3·00 3·00
S10 500d. on 50p. green & violet 5·00 5·00
S11 500d. on 60p. mauve & red 5·00 5·00

1993. Dated "1992".
S12 S **2** 10d. black and yellow . . 10 10
S13 20d. black and blue . . . 25 25
S14 30d. black and pink . . . 35 35
S15 – 50d. black and red . . . 60 60
S16 – 100d. black and red . . . 1·25 1·25
S17 – 500d. black and blue . . 6·25 6·25
DESIGNS—VERT: 50, 100d. Coat of arms. HORIZ: 500d. Monastery.

1993. Dated "1993".
S18 S **2** 5000d. black and lilac . . 10 10
S19 6000d. black and yellow 15 15
S20 10000d. black and blue . . 25 25
S21 – 20000d. black and red . . 55 55
S22 – 30000d. black and red . . 85 85
S23 – 50000d. black and lilac . . 1·40 1·40
DESIGNS—VERT: 20000, 30000d. Coat of arms. HORIZ: 50000d. Monastery.

референдум
15-16. 05. '93.
7500 ==
(S **3**)

S **4** Symbol of St. John the Evangelist

1993. Referendum. Nos. S15/16 surch as Type S **3**.

S24 7500d. on 50d. black and red 60 60
S25 7500d. on 100d. black and red 60 60
S26 9000d. on 50d. black and red 80 80

1993. No value expressed.

S27 S **4** A red 40 40

No. S27 was sold at the rate for internal letters.

Currency Reform

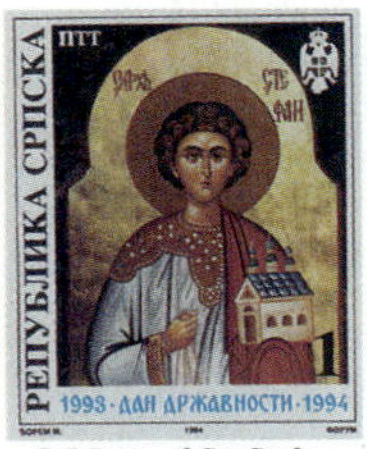

S **5** Icon of St. Stefan

1994. Republic Day.

S28 S **5** 1d. multicoloured 4·00 4·00

S **6** King Petar I

1994. 150th Birth Anniv of King Petar I of Serbia.

S29 S **6** 80p. sepia and brown 2·50 2·50

S **7** Banja Luka

1994. 500th Anniv of Banja Luka.

S30 S **7** 1d.20 multicoloured 2·00 2·50

1994. Issued at Doboj. Surch with letter. (a) On Nos. S13/16.

S31 S **2** A on 20d. black and blue
S32 R on 20d. black and blue
S33 R on 30d. black and pink
S34 – R on 50d. black and red
S35 – R on 100d. black and red

(b) On Nos. S18/19 and S21/2.

S36 S **2** R on 5000d. black and lilac
S37 R on 6000d. black and yellow
S38 – A on 20000d. black and red
S39 – R on 20000d. black and red
S40 – R on 30000d. black and red

Set of 10 65·00

Stamps surcharged "A" were sold at the current rate for internal letters and those surcharged "R" at the rate for internal registered letters. The "R" on No. S32 is reversed.

S **9** "Madonna and Child" (icon)

1994. Cajnicka Church.

S41 S **9** 1d. multicoloured 2·00 2·00

1994. Nos. S18/20 and S23 surch (Nos. 542/3 with letter).

S42 S **2** A on 5000d. black & lilac 1·10 1·10
S43 R on 6000d. black & yell 1·10 1·10
S44 40p. on 10000d. blk & bl 1·10 1·10
S45 – 2d. on 50000d. black and lilac 1·10 1·10

No. S42 was sold at the current rate for internal letters and No. S43, which shows the surcharge as the cyrillic letter resembling "P", at the rate for internal registered letters.

S **11** Tavna Monastery

1994. Monasteries. Multicoloured.

S46 60p. Type S **11** 2·00 2·00
S47 1d. Mostanica (horiz) 2·00 2·00
S48 1d.20 Zitomislic 2·25 2·25

S **12** "Aquilegia dinarica"

S **14** Relay Station, Mt. Kozara

1996. Nature Protection. Multicoloured.

S49 1d.20 Type S **12** 1·25 1·25
S50 1d.20 "Edraianthus niveus" (plant) 1·25 1·25
S51 1d.20 Shore lark 1·25 1·25
S52 1d.20 "Dinaromys bogdanovi" (dormouse) 1·25 1·25

1996. Nos. S14/16, S19 and S22 surch.

S53 S **2** 70p. on 30d. black and pink 30 30
S54 – 1d. on 100d. black & red 40 40
S55 – 2d. on 30000d. blk & red 80 80
S56 – 3d. on 50d. black and red 1·25 1·25
S57 S **2** 5d. on 6000d. black and yellow 2·25 2·25

1996.

S58 S **14** A green and bistre
S59 – R purple and brown
S60 – 1d.20 violet and blue
S61 – 2d. lilac and mauve
S62 – 5d. purple and blue
S63 – 10d. brown and sepia

Set of 6 6·50 6·50

DESIGNS—VERT: R, Kraljica relay station, Mt. Ozren; 2d. Relay station, Mt. Romanija; 5d. Stolice relay station, Mt. Maljevica. HORIZ: 1d.20, Bridge over river Drina at Srbinje; 10d. Bridge at Visegrad.

No. S58 was sold at the current rate for an internal letter and No. S59 at the rate for an internal registered letter.

S **15** Orthodox Church, Bascarsiji

1997.

S64 S **15** 2d.50 multicoloured 1·00 1·00

S **16** Pupin

S **17** "Primula kitaibeliana"

1997. 62nd Death Anniv of Michael Pupin (physicist and inventor).

S65 S **16** 2d.50 multicoloured 1·00 1·00

1997. Flowers. Multicoloured.

S66 3d.20 Type S **17** 85 85
S67 3d.20 "Pedicularis hoermanniana" 85 85
S68 3d.20 "Knautia sarajevensis" 85 85
S69 3d.20 "Oxytropis campestris" 85 85

S **18** Robert Koch

S **19** Branko Copic

1997. Obligatory Tax. Anti-tuberculosis Week. Self-adhesive.

S70 S **18** 15f. red and blue 10 10

1997. Writers. Each mauve and yellow.

S71 A (60p.) Type S **19** 25 25
S72 R (90p.) Jovan Ducic 35 35
S73 1d.50 Mesa Selimovic 35 35
S74 3d. Aleksa Santic 85 85
S75 5d. Petar Kocic 1·25 1·25
S76 10d. Ivo Andric 2·50 2·50

S **20** European Otter

S **21** Two Queens

1997. Nature Protection. Multicoloured.

S77 2d.50 Type S **20** 50 50
S78 4d.50 Roe deer 1·10 1·10
S79 6d.50 Brown bear 1·75 1·75

1997. Europa. Tales and Legends. Multicoloured.

S80 2d.50 Type S **21** 1·00 1·00
S81 6d.50 Prince on horseback 2·50 2·50

S **22** Diana, Princess of Wales

1998. Diana, Princess of Wales Commemoration.

S82 S **22** 3d.50 multicoloured ("DIANA" in Roman alphabet) 1·25 1·25
S83 3d.50 multicoloured ("DIANA" in Cyrillic alphabet) 1·25 1·25

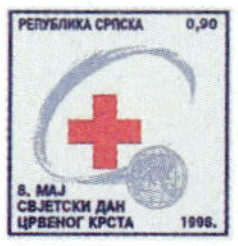

S **23** Cross and Globe

S **24** Brazil

1998. Obligatory Tax. Red Cross. Self-adhesive.

S84 S **23** 90f. red, blue and ultram 60 60

1998. World Cup Football Championship, France. Showing flags and players of countries in final rounds. Multicoloured.

S 85 90f. Type S **24** 60 60
S 86 90f. Morocco 60 60
S 87 90f. Norway 60 60
S 88 90f. Scotland 60 60
S 89 90f. Italy 60 60
S 90 90f. Chile 60 60
S 91 90f. Austria 60 60
S 92 90f. Cameroun 60 60
S 93 90f. France 60 60
S 94 90f. Saudi Arabia 60 60
S 95 90f. Denmark 60 60
S 96 90f. South Africa 60 60
S 97 90f. Spain 60 60
S 98 90f. Nigeria 60 60
S 99 90f. Paraguay 60 60
S100 90f. Bulgaria 60 60
S101 90f. Netherlands 60 60
S102 90f. Belgium 60 60
S103 90f. Mexico 60 60
S104 90f. South Korea 60 60
S105 90f. Germany 60 60
S106 90f. United States of America 60 60
S107 90f. Yugoslavia 60 60
S108 90f. Iran 60 60
S109 90f. Rumania 60 60
S110 90f. England (U.K. flag) 60 60
S111 90f. Tunisia 60 60
S112 90f. Colombia 60 60
S113 90f. Argentina 60 60
S114 90f. Jamaica 60 60
S115 90f. Croatia 60 60
S116 90f. Japan 60 60

S **25** Couple and Musical Instrument

1998. Europa. National Festivals. Multicoloured.

S117 7m.50 Type S **25** 5·00 5·00
S118 7m.50 Couple from Neretva and musical instrument 5·00 5·00

S **26** Family walking in Countryside

1998. Obligatory Tax. Anti-tuberculosis Week.

S119 S **26** 75f. multicoloured 50 50

S **27** St. Pantelejmon

S **28** Bijelijna

1998. 800th Anniv of Hilandar Monastery. Icons. Multicoloured.

S120 50f. Type S **27** 35 35
S121 70f. Jesus Christ 45 45
S122 1m.70 St. Nikola 1·10 1·10
S123 2m. St. John of Rila 1·40 1·40

1999. Towns. Multicoloured. (a) With face value.

S124 15f. Type S **28** 10 10
S125 20f. Sokolac 15 15
S126 75f. Prijedor 50 50
S127 2m. Brcko 1·40 1·40
S128 4m.50 Zvornik 3·00 3·00
S129 10m. Doboj 6·75 6·75

(b) Face value expressed by letter.

S130 A (50f.) Banja Luka 35 35
S131 R (1m.) Trebinje 70 70

No. S130 was sold at the current rate for an internal letter and No. S131 at the rate for an internal registered letter.

S **29** Airliner over Lake

1999. Founding of Air Srpska (state airline). Multicoloured.

S132 50f. Type S **29** 35 35
S133 50f. Airliner above clouds 35 35
S134 75f. Airliner over beach 50 50
S135 1m.50 Airliner over lake (different) 1·00 1·00

S **30** Table Tennis Ball as Globe

1999. International Table Tennis Championships, Belgrade. Multicoloured.

S136 1m. Type S **30** 70 70
S137 2m. Table tennis table, bat and ball 1·40 1·40

S **31** Kozara National Park

S **32** Open Hands

1999. Europa. National Parks. Multicoloured.

S138 1m.50 Type S **31** 1·00 1·00
S139 2m. Perucica National Park 1·40 1·40

1999. Obligatory Tax. Red Cross.

S140 S **32** 10f. multicoloured 10 10

S **33** Manuscript

1999. 780th Anniv of Bosnia and Herzegovina Archbishopric (S142, S144/8) and 480th Anniv of Garazole Printing Works (S141, S143). Mult.

S141 50f. Type S **33** 30 30
S142 50f. Dobrun Monastery . . 30 30
S143 50f. "G" 30 30
S144 50f. Zhitomislib Monastery 30 30
S145 50f. Gomionitsa Monastery 30 30
S146 50f. Madonna and Child with angels and prophets (icon, 1578) 30 30
S147 50f. St. Nicolas (icon) . . . 30 30
S148 50f. Wise Men (icon) . . . 30 30

S **34** Brown Trout — S **35** Lunar Module on Moon's Surface

1999. Fishes. Multicoloured.

S149 50f. Type S **34** 30 30
S150 50f. Lake trout (*Salmo trutta morpha lacustris*) 30 30
S151 75f. Huchen 45 45
S152 1m. European grayling . . . 65 65

1999. 30th Anniv of First Manned Landing on Moon. Multicoloured.

S153 1m. Type S **35** 65 65
S154 2m. Astronaut on Moon . . 1·25 1·25

S **36** Pencil and Emblem — S **37** Madonna and Child

1999. 125th Anniv of Universal Postal Union. Mult.

S155 75f. Type S **36** 45 45
S156 1m.25 Earth and emblem 75 75

NOTE: Due to the time lapse since Republika Srpska was last listed and the lack of stamps, several numbers have been left pending.

1999. Art. Icons. Multicoloured.

S157 50f. Type S **37** 30 30
S158 50f. Madonna, Cajnice . . . 30 30
S159 50f. Madonna Pelagonitisa 30 30
S160 50f. Holy Kirjak Otselnik 30 30
S161 50f. Pieta 30 30
S162 50f. Entry of Christ into Jerusalem 30 30
S163 50f. St. Jovan 30 30
S164 50f. Sava and Simeon . . . 30 30

Nos. S165/**MS**S170 and Type S **38** have been left for "New Millennium (1st series)", issued on 22 November 1999, not yet received.

Nos. S171/**MS**S172 and Type S **39** have been left for "135th Anniv of Postal Services", issued on 23 December 1999, not yet received.

Nos. S173 and Type S **40** have been left for "800th Birth Anniv of Stephan Nemanja", issued on 29 February 2000, not yet received.

Nos. S174/5 and Type S **41** have been left for "Flora", issued on 22 March 2000, not yet received.

Nos. S176/9 and Type S **42** have been left for "Drina River Bridges", issued on 12 April 2000, not yet received.

No. S180 and Type S **43** have been left for "Jovan Ducic Commemoration", issued on 26 April 2000, not yet received.

S **44** Construction of Europe — S **60** Women's Costumes, Popovo

2000. Europa. Construction of Europe. Multicoloured.

S181 1m.50 Type S **44** . . . . . 1·00 1·00
S182 2m.50 Children and stars . . 1·70 1·70

No. S183 and Type S **45** have been left for "Red Cross", issued on 8 May 2000, not yet received.

No. S184 and Type S **46** have been left for "Centenary of Banja Luka Province", issued on 26 May 2000, not yet received.

Nos. S185/6 and Type S **47** have been left for "EURO 2000", issued on 14 June 2000, not yet received.

No. S187 and Type S **48** have been left for "125th Anniv of Nevesinje Revolt", issued on 12 July 2000, not yet received.

Nos. S188/**MS**S192 and Type S **49** have been left for "Olympic Games, Sydney", issued on 6 September 2000, not yet received.

No. S193 and Type S **50** have been left for "Obligatory Tax. Anti-tuberculosis Week", issued on 14 September 2000, not yet received.

Nos. S194/5 and Type S **51** have been left for "175th Anniv of Railways", issued on 4 October 2000, not yet received.

Nos. S196/7 and Type S **52** have been left for "European Nature Conservation", issued on 31 October 2000, not yet received.

Nos. S198/**MS**S202 and Type S **53** have been left for "New Millennium (2nd series)", issued on 22 November 2000, not yet received.

Nos. S203/6 and Type S **54** have been left for "Art. Icons", issued on 20 December 2000, not yet received.

No. S207 and Type S **55** have been left for "125th Anniv of Telephony", issued on 27 February 2001, not yet received.

Nos. S208/**MS**S209 and Type S **56** have been left for "40th Anniv of First Space Flight", issued on 29 March 2001, not yet received.

No. S210 and Type S **57** have been left for "Birth Centenary of Vlado Milosevic", issued on 11 April 2001, not yet received.

Nos. S211/12 and Type S **58** have been left for "Europa. Water Conservation", issued on 4 May 2001, not yet received.

Nos. S213/16 and Type S **59** have been left for "Butterflies", issued on 19 June 2001, not yet received.

2001. Traditional Costumes. Multicoloured.

S217 50f. Type S **60** 30 30
S218 50f. Bridal costume, Zmijanje 30 30
S219 1m. Woman's costume, Bileca mountains 65 65
S220 1m. Two women, Lijevce . . 65 65

No. S221 and Type S **61** have been left for "Karate World Championship", issued on 5 September 2001, not yet received.

Nos. S222/5 and Type S **62** have been left for "Towns", issued on 5 September–23 October 2001, not yet received.

S **63** Emblem — S **64** Rastusa Cave, Teslic

2001. Obligatory Tax. Anti-Tuberculosis Week.

S226 S **63** 10f. multicoloured . . . 10 10

2001. Caves. Multicoloured.

S227 50f. Type S **64** 30 30
S228 50f. Vagan cave, Vitorog . . 30 30
S229 50f. Pavlova cave, Petrovo 30 30
S230 50f. Orlovaca cave, Pale . . 30 30
S231 50f. Ledana cave, Bobija . . 30 30
S232 50f. Hole, Podovi plateau 30 30

S **65** Alfred Nobel (founder)

2001. Centenary of Nobel Prizes. Multicoloured.

S233 1m. Type S **65** 65 65
S234 2m. Ivo Andric (winner of Nobel prize for Literature, 1961) . . . . 1·40 1·40

Nos. S235/6 and Type S **66** have been left for "European Nature Protection", issued on 15 November 2001, not yet received.

Nos. S237/40 and Type S **67** have been left for "Art", issued on 5 December 2001, not yet received.

Nos. S241 and Type S **68** have been left for "Christmas", issued on 5 December 2001, not yet received.

Nos. S242 and Type S **69** have been left for "75th Anniv of Borac Soccer Team", issued on 24 December 2001, not yet received.

Nos. S243 and Type S **70** have been left for "10th Anniv of Republic", issued on 10 January 2002, not yet received.

Nos. S244 and Type S **71** have been left for "Fight against Terrorism", issued on 29 January 2002, not yet received.

Nos. S245/6 and Type S **72** have been left for "Winter Olympic Games, Salt Lake City", issued on 13 February 2002, not yet received.

Nos. S247 and Type S **73** have been left for "Centenary of Prosvjeta", issued on 5 March 2002, not yet received.

Nos. S248/9 and Type S **74** have been left for "Towns", issued on 5 March–17 April 2002, not yet received.

NOTE: Due to the time lapse since Republika Srpska was last listed and the lack of stamps, several numbers have been left pending.

S **75** Charles Lindbergh and *Spirit of St. Louis*

2002. 75th Anniv of First Trans-Atlantic Flight.

S250 S **75** 1m. multicoloured . . . 80 80

Nos. S251/2 and Type S **76** have been left for "Europa. Circus", issued on 30 April 2002, not yet received.

Nos. S253/4 and Type S **77** have been left for "World Cup Football Championship, Japan and South Korea", issued on 31 May 2002, not yet received.

Nos. S255/60 and Type S **78** have been left for "Spas", issued on 5 July 2002, not yet received.

Nos. S261/4 and Type S **79** have been left for "Museum Exhibits", issued on 5 September 2002, not yet received.

S **80** *Boletus regius*

2002. Fungi. Multicoloured.

S265 50f. Type S **80** 35 35
S266 50f. *Macrolepiota procera* 35 35
S267 1m. *Amanita caesarea* . . . 80 80
S268 1m. *Craterellus cornucopoides* 80 80

Nos. S269 and Type S **81** have been left for "European Nature Protection", issued on 26 November 2002, not yet received.

Nos. S270/3 and Type S **82** have been left for "Art", issued on 18 December 2002, not yet received.

S **83** Vrbas Canyon (scene from film by Spiro Bocaric) (1937)

2003. Centenary of First Film shown in Republic Srpska. Sheet 92 × 73 mm.

MSS274 S **83** 3m. multicoloured 1·75 1·75

S **84** Alekse Santic — S **85** Crucifixion, Sretenje Monastery

2003. 135th Birth Anniv of Alekse Santic (writer).

S275 S **84** 1m. multicoloured . . . 80 80

2003. Easter. Multicoloured.

S276 50f. Type S **85** 35 35
S277 1m. Resurrection (painting, Altarpiece, Eisenheim by Matias Greenwald) . . . 80 80

S **86** Everest Peaks — S **87** Aviation Poster

2003. 50th Anniv of First Ascent of Mount Everest. Sheet 82 × 58 mm containing Type S **86** and similar vert design. Multicoloured.

MSS278 1m.50 Type S **86**; 1m.50 Mountaineer through magnifying glass . . . . 1·75 1·75

The stamps and margin of **MS**S278 form a composite design.

2003. Europa. Poster Art. Multicoloured.

S279 1m. Type S **87** 80 80
S280 1m.50 Naval poster . . . . 1·30 1·30

Nos. S281/4 and Type S **88** have been left for "Horses", issued on 9 June 2003, not yet received.

No. S285 and Type S **89** have been left for "Pope John Paul II", issued on 22 June 2003, not yet received.

Nos. S286/7 and Type S **90** have been left for "Medals", issued on 11 July 2003, not yet received.

No. S288 and Type S **91** have been left for "Fight against Terrorism", issued on 14 August 2003, not yet received.

No. S289 and Type S **92** have been left for "175th Birth Anniv of Leo Tolstoy", issued on 25 September 2003, not yet received.

Nos. S290/1 and Type S **93** have been left for "European Nature Protection", issued on 21 October 2003, not yet received.

Nos. S292/5 and Type S **94** have been left for "Art. Icons", issued on 19 November 2003, not yet received.

Nos. S296/7 and Type S **95** have been left for "Christmas", issued on 5 December 2003, not yet received.

Nos. S298/9 and Type S **96** have been left for "Centenary of Powered Flight", issued on 17 December 2003, not yet received.

No. **MS**S300 and Type S **97** have been left for "Bicentenary of Serbian Uprising", issued on 5 February 2004, not yet received.

No. **MS**S301 and Type S **98** have been left for "Olympic Games, Athens (1st issue)", issued on 2 March 2004, not yet received.

No. S302 and Type S **99** have been left for "125th Birth Anniv of Albert Einstein", issued on 12 March 2004, not yet received.

S **100** Risen Christ

S **101** Canoeing

2004. Easter. Multicoloured.

S303	50f. Type S **100**		35	35
S304	1m. Risen Christ (different)		80	80

2004. Europa. Holidays. Multicoloured.

S305	50f. Type S **101**		35	35
S306	1m. Hang-gliding		80	80

S **102** Hands holding Blood Droplet as Gift

S **103** Kulasi

2004. Obligatory Tax. Red Cross.

S307	S **102**	10f. multicoloured . .	10	10

2004. Spas.

S308	S **103**	20f. multicoloured . .	15	15

S **104** Milutina Milankovica

2004. 125th Birth Anniv of Milutina Milankovica.

S309	S **104**	1m. multicoloured . .	80	80

No. S310 and Type S **105** have been left for "EURO 2004", issued on 8 June 2004, not yet received.

Nos. S311/**MS**S314 and Type S **106** have been left for "Olympic Games, Athens (2nd issue)", issued on 12 July 2004, not yet received.

Nos. S315/16 and Type S **107** have been left for "European Nature Protection", issued on 27 August 2004, not yet received.

Nos. S317/20 and Type S **108** have been left for "Minerals", issued on 14 September 2004, not yet received.

Nos. S321 and Type S **109** have been left for "150th Birth Anniv of Mihalja Pupin", issued on 9 October 2004, not yet received.

Nos. S322 and Type S **110** have been left for "Fight against Terrorism", issued on 21 October 2004, not yet received.

Nos. S323/4 and Type S **111** have been left for "Spas", issued on 6 December 2004, not yet received.

Nos. S325 and Type S **112** have been left for "Christmas", issued on 7 December 2004, not yet received.

Nos. S326/7 and Type S **113** have been left for "Art", issued on 7 February 2005, not yet received.

Nos. S328 and Type S **114** have been left for "International Day of Water", issued on 22 March 2005, not yet received.

S **115** Traditional Hearth

2005. Europa. Gastronomy. Multicoloured.

S329	1m. Type S **115**	2·75	2·75
S330	1m.50 Table laid with food	4·25	4·25

Nos. S331 and Type S **116** have been left for "Easter", issued on 18 April 2005, not yet received.

S **117** Pope John Paul II

2005. Pope John Paul II Commemoration. Multicoloured.

S332	1m.50 Type S **117**	4·25	4·25
MSS333	56 × 49 mm. 5m. St. Peters Basilica and Pope John Paul II	14·00	14·00

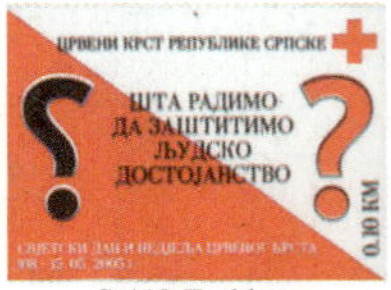

S **118** Emblem

2005. Obligatory Tax. Red Cross. Self-adhesive.

S334	S **118**	10f. vermilion and black	1·00	1·00

S **119** *Vipera berus berus*

2005. Snakes. Multicoloured.

S335	50f. Type S **119**	1·40	1·40
S336	50f. *Vipera ursinii*	1·40	1·40
S337	1m. *Vipera berus bosniensis*	2·70	2·70
S338	1m. *Vipera ammodytes* . . .	2·70	2·70

Nos. S339/40 and Type S **120** have been left for "50th Anniv of Disneyland", issued on 15 July 2005, not yet received.

S **121** Fighting Bulls, Grmec

2005. Traditions.

S341	S **121**	1m.50 multicoloured	4·25	4·25

S **122** *Prasuma Perucica*

S **123** Landscape and Lungs

2005. 50th Anniv of Europa Stamps. Multicoloured.

S342	1m.95 Type S **122**	4·00	4·00
S343	1m.95 Rafting, Odmor . . .	4·00	4·00
S344	1m.95 Mostar bridge . . .	4·00	4·00
S345	1m.95 Drina river	4·00	4·00

2005. Obligatory Tax. Anti-Tuberculosis Week.

S346	S **123**	10f. multicoloured . .	1·40	1·40

S **124** Balls and Belgrade Arena

2005. European Basketball Championship, Belgrade. Multicoloured, colour wash given.

S347	S **124**	50f. lilac	1·00	1·00
S348		50f. yellow	1·00	1·00
S349		50f. green	1·00	1·00
S350		50f. lilac	1·00	1·00
S351		50f. blue	1·00	1·00

S **125** National Museum

2005. 75th Anniversaries. Multicoloured.

S352	1m. Type S **125**	2·00	2·00
S353	1m. National Theatre (horiz)	2·00	2·00

S **126** Tunnel, Sargan

2005. Tourism. Makra Gora Railway, Visegard. Sheet 101 × 54 mm containing Type S **126** and similar vert design. Multicoloured.

MSS354 50f. Type S **126**; 1m. Station, Makra Gora . . . . . 3·00 3·00

The stamps and margin of **MS**S354 form a composite design.

S **127** *Bleriot XI*

2005. Centenary of International Aviation Federation (FAI).

S355	S **127**	1m.50 multicoloured	4·00	4·00

S **128** Flowers

S **129** Guber

2005. 10th Anniv of Dayton Agreement.

S356	S **128**	1m.50 multicoloured	4·00	4·00

2005. Spas.

S357	S **129**	50f. multicoloured . .	1·00	1·00

S **130** *Crex crex* (corncrake)

2005. European Nature Protection. Birds. Multicoloured.

S358	50f. Type S **130**	1·30	1·30
S359	1m. *Platalea leucorodia* (spoonbill)	2·60	2·60

S **131** Monument to Victims

2005. 60th Anniv of Liberation of Jasenovac Concentration Camp.

S360	S **131**	50f. multicoloured . .	1·40	1·40

S **132** Mozart

S **133** Branke Sotre

2006. 250th Birth Anniv of Wolfgang Amadeus Mozart (composer and musician).

S361	S **132**	1m.50 multicoloured	4·00	4·00

2006. Birth Centenary of Branke Sotre (artist).

S362	S **133**	1m. multicoloured . .	2·75	2·75

S **134** Biathlete

S **135** Kulasi

2006. Winter Olympic Games, Turin. Multicoloured.

S363	50f. Type S **134**	1·30	1·30
S364	1m. Alpine skier	2·60	2·60

2006. Spas.

S365	S **135**	20f. multicoloured . .	1·00	1·00

No. S365 is as No. S308 but redrawn.

S **136** Inscr "Saxifraga prenja"

2006. Flora. Multicoloured.

S366	50f. Type **136**	1·40	1·40
S367	50f. *Asperula hercegovina* . .	1·40	1·40
S368	1m. *Campanula hercegovina*	2·75	2·75
S369	1m. Inscr "Oxtropis prenja"	2·75	2·75

S **137** Basket of Eggs

2006. Easter.

S370	S **137**	70f. multicoloured . .	1·90	1·90

S **138** "Tear" (Luja Kajkut)

S **139** Emblem

2006. Europa. Integration. Multicoloured.

S371	1m. Type S **138**	2·40	2·40
S372	1m.50 "Country Dance" (Milica Popic)	7·25	7·25

2005. Obligatory Tax. Red Cross.

S373	S **139**	20f. multicoloured . .	2·75	2·75

S **140** Legs and Ball

2006. World Cup Football Championship, Germany. Multicoloured.

S374	50f. Type S **140**	1·30	1·30
S375	1m. Stadium and ball . . .	2·60	2·60
MSS376	65 × 49 mm. 3m.German player and ball	8·25	8·25

S 141 Runner

2006. 10th Anniv of Vidovdan Road Race.
S377 S **141** 1m. multicoloured . . 2·75 2·75

S 142 Nikola Tesla

2006. 150th Birth Anniv of Nikola Tesla (engineer) (1st issue). Sheet 66 × 60 mm.
MSS378 S **142** 1m.50 multicoloured 4·00 4·00
The stamps and margin of **MS**S378 form a composite design.
See also No. S385.

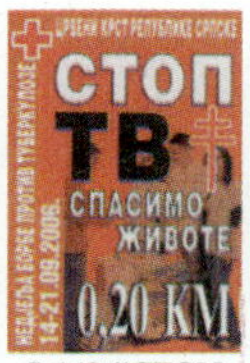
S 143 "CTON TB"

S 144 *Tetrao urogallus* (capercaille)

2006. Obligatory Tax. Anti-Tuberculosis Week.
S379 S **143** 20f. multicoloured . . 1·20 1·20

2006. European Nature Protection. Multicoloured.
S380 50f. Type S **144** . . . . . 1·40 1·40
S381 1m. *Rupicapra rupicapra* (chamois) . . . . 2·60 2·60

No. S382 and Type S **145** have been left for "50th Anniv of Children's Theatre", issued on 14 October 2006, not yet received.

S 146 Buckle

S 147 Nikola Tesla

2006. Museum Exhibits. Multicoloured.
S383 1m. Type S **146** . . . . . . 2·75 2·75
S384 1m. Curved buckle with red stones . . . . 2·75 2·75

2006. 150th Birth Anniv of Nikola Tesla (engineer) (2nd issue).
S385 S **147** 70f. multicoloured . . 1·90 1·90

S 148 Johann von Goethe

2007. 175th Birth Anniv of Johann Wolfgang von Goethe (polymath).
S386 S **148** 1m.50 multicoloured 4·00 4·00

S 149 Decorated Egg

2007. Easter.
S387 S **149** 70f. multicoloured . . 1·90 1·90

S 150 Study for Isabella d'Este

2007. 555th Birth Anniv of Leonardo da Vinci (artist and polymath). Multicoloured.
S388 70f. Type S **150** . . . . . 1·90 1·90
S389 1m. Study for The Last Supper . . . . 3·00 3·00

S 151 Campsite

S 152 Clasped Hands

2007. Europa. Centenary of Scouting. Multicoloured.
(a) 26 × 41 mm.
S390 1m. Type S **151** . . . . . . 2·20 2·20
S391 1m.50 Scouts . . . . 4·75 4·75

(b) Size 35 × 45 mm.
S392 1m. As Type S **151**, with pink upper edge . . . . 2·20 2·20
S393 1m. As Type S **151**, with pink lower edge 'EUROPA 100 JAHRE PFADFINDER-BEWEGUNG' . . . . 2·20 2·20
S394 1m. As Type S **151** with pink lower edge 'EUROPA 100 ANS DU SCOUTISME' . . . . 2·20 2·20
S395 1m.50 As No. S 391, with pink upper edge . . . . 4·75 4·75
S396 1m.50 As No. S 391, with pink upper edge 'EUROPA 100 YEARS OF SCOUTING' . . . . 4·75 4·75
S397 1m.50 As No. S 391, with pink lower edge . . . . 4·75 4·75

2007. Obligatory Tax. Red Cross.
S398 S **152** 20f. multicoloured . . 1·20 1·20

S 153 Liplje Monastery

S 154 Koarac

2007. Monasteries. Multicoloured.
S399 70f. Type S **153** . . . . . 1·90 1·90
S400 1m. Dobricevo . . . . . . 3·00 3·00

2007. Cities. Multicoloured.
S401 20f. Type S **154** . . . . . 2·20 2·20
S402 20f. Derventa . . . . 2·20 2·20
S403 20f. Prjedor . . . . 2·20 2·20
S404 20f. Laktasi . . . . 2·20 2·20
S405 20f. Foca . . . . 2·20 2·20
S406 20f. Bijelijina . . . . . . 2·20 2·20
S407 70f. Srebrenica . . . . . . 2·20 2·20
S408 1m.50 Sipovo . . . . . . 2·20 2·20
S409 1m.50 Mrkonjic Grad . . . 2·20 2·20
S410 2m. Trebinje . . . . 2·20 2·20
S411 5m. Zvornik . . . . 2·20 2·20

S 155 Serbian Tri-colour Hound

S 156 Orthodox Church and Old Post Office

2007. Dogs. Multicoloured.
S412 70f. Type S **155** . . . . . 2·00 2·00
S413 70f. Istarski Ostrodlaki gonic (rough coated scent hound) . . . . 2·00 2·00
S414 70f. Srpski odbrambeni pas (Serbian guard dog) . . . 2·00 2·00
S415 70f. Tornak (sheep dog) . . 2·00 2·00

2007. Centenary of Post Office, Obudovac.
S416 S **156** 10f. multicoloured . . 1·00 1·00

S 157 Ban Milosavljevic (statue)

S 158 Apple containing People

2007. 125th Birth Anniv of Ban Svetislav Milosavljevic (leader 1930–33).
S417 S **157** 1m.50 multicoloured 4·00 4·00

2007. Obligatory Tax. Anti-Tuberculosis Week.
S418 S **158** 20f. multicoloured . . 1·20 1·20

S 159 Early Racquet and Balls

2007. Centenary of Banja Luca Tennis Club. Sheet 83 × 58 mm containing Type S **159** and similar horiz design. Multicoloured.
MSS419 1m. × 2 Type S **159**; Modern racquet and ball . . . 5·50 5·50
The stamps and margin of **MS**S342 form a composite design.

S 160 Sputnik and Globe

S 161 *Picea abies*

2007. 50th Anniv of Space Exploration.
S420 S **160** 1m.50 multicoloured 4·00 4·00

2007. European Nature Protection. Conifers. Multicoloured.
S421 70f. Type S **161** . . . . . 1·90 1·90
S422 1m. *Picea omorica* . . . . . 3·00 3·00

BOTSWANA Pt. 1

Formerly Bechuanaland Protectorate, attained independence on 30 September 1966, and changed its name to Botswana.

1966. 100 cents = 1 rand.
1976. 100 thebe = 1 pula.

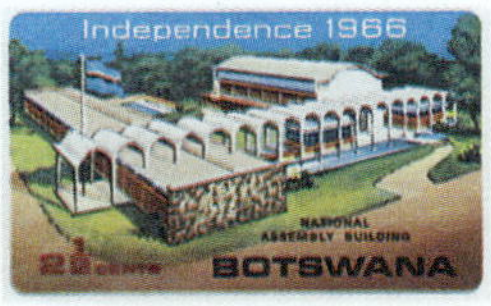
47 National Assembly Building

1966. Independence. Multicoloured.
202 2½c. Type **47** 15 10
203 5c. Abattoir, Lobatsi 20 10
204 15c. National Airways Douglas DC-3 . . . . . . 65 20
205 35c. State House, Gaberones 40 30

1966. Nos. 168/81 of Bechuanaland optd **REPUBLIC OF BOTSWANA**.
206 **28** 1c. multicoloured 25 10
207 – 2c. orange, black and olive 30 1·75
208 – 2½c. multicoloured 30 10
209 – 3½c. multicoloured . . . . 1·25 20
210 – 5c. multicoloured . . . . 1·25 1·50
211 – 7½c. multicoloured . . . . 50 1·75
212 – 10c. multicoloured . . . . 1·00 20
213 – 12½c. multicoloured . . . 2·00 2·75
214 – 20c. brown and drab . . . 20 1·00
215 – 25c. sepia and lemon . . . 20 2·00
216 – 35c. blue and orange . . . 30 2·25
217 – 50c. sepia and olive . . . 20 70
218 – 1r. black and brown . . . 40 1·25
219 – 2r. brown and turquoise 60 2·50

52 Golden Oriole

1967. Multicoloured.
220 1c. Type **52** 30 15
221 2c. Hoopoe ("African Hoopese") 60 70
222 3c. Groundscraper thrush . . 55 10
223 4c. Cordon-bleu ("Blue Waxbill") 55 10
224 5c. Secretary bird 55 10
225 7c. Southern yellow-billed hornbill ("Yellow-billed Hornbill") . . . . 60 1·00
226 10c. Burchell's gonolek ("Crimson-breasted Strike") 60 15
227 15c. Malachite kingfisher . . 7·50 3·00
228 20c. African fish eagle ("Fish Eagle") . . . . 7·50 2·00
229 25c. Go-away bird ("Grey Loerie") . . . . 4·00 1·50
230 35c. Scimitar-bill . . . . . 6·00 2·25
231 50c. Comb duck ("Knob-Billed Duck") . . . . . . 2·75 2·75
232 1r. Levaillant's barbet ("Crested Barbet") . . . . 5·00 3·50
233 2r. Didric cuckoo ("Diederick Cuckoo") . . . . 7·00 16·00

66 Students and University

1967. 1st Conferment of University Degrees.
234 **66** 3c. sepia, blue and orange 10 10
235 7c. sepia, blue and turquoise 10 10
236 15c. sepia, blue and red . . 10 10
237 35c. sepia, blue and violet 20 20

67 Bushbuck

1967. Chobe Game Reserve. Multicoloured.
238 3c. Type **67** 10 20
239 7c. Sable Antelope 15 30
240 35c. Fishing on the Chobe River . . . . 80 1·10

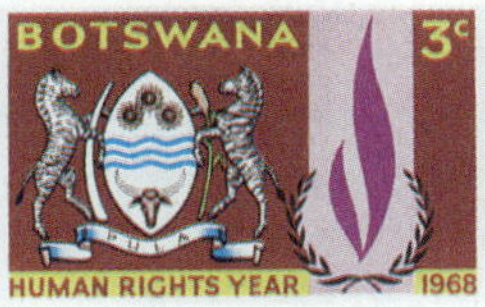
70 Arms of Botswana and Human Rights Emblem

1968. Human Rights Year.
241 **70** 3c. multicoloured 10 10
242 – 15c. multicoloured 25 45
243 – 25c. multicoloured 25 60
The designs of Nos. 242/3 are similar, but are arranged differently.

73 Eland and Giraffe Rock Paintings, Tsodilo Hills

1968. Opening of National Museum and Art Gallery. Multicoloured.
244 3c. Type **73** 20 20
245 7c. Girl wearing ceremonial beads (31 × 48 mm) 25 40
246 10c. "Baobab Trees" (Thomas Baines) 25 30
247 15c. National Museum and art gallery (72 × 19 mm) . . 40 1·50
MS248 132 × 82 mm. Nos. 244/7 1·00 2·25

77 African Family, and Star over Village

1968. Christmas.

249	77	1c. multicoloured	10	10
250		2c. multicoloured	10	10
251		5c. multicoloured	10	10
252		25c. multicoloured	15	50

78 Scout, Lion and Badge in frame

1969. 22nd World Scout Conference, Helsinki. Mult.

253	3c. Type **78**	30	30
254	15c. Scouts cooking over open fire (vert)	35	1·00
255	25c. Scouts around camp fire	35	1·00

81 Woman, Child and Christmas Star

82 Diamond Treatment Plant, Orapa

1969. Christmas.

256	81	1c. blue and brown	10	10
257		2c. olive and brown	10	10
258		4c. yellow and brown	10	10
259		35c. brown and violet	20	20
MS260		86 × 128 mm. Nos. 256/9	70	1·10

1970. Developing Botswana. Multicoloured.

261	3c. Type **82**	70	20
262	7c. Copper-nickel mining	95	20
263	10c. Copper-nickel mine, Selebi-Pikwe (horiz)	1·25	15
264	35c. Orapa Diamond mine and diamonds (horiz)	2·75	1·25

83 Mr. Micawber ("David Copperfield")

1970. Death Centenary of Charles Dickens. Mult.

265	3c. Type **83**	25	10
266	7c. Scrooge ("A Christmas Carol")	25	10
267	15c. Fagin ("Oliver Twist")	45	40
268	25c. Bill Sykes ("Oliver Twist")	70	60
MS269	114 × 81 mm. Nos. 265/8	2·75	4·00

84 U.N. Building and Emblem

1970. 25th Anniv of United Nations.

270	84	15c. blue, brown and silver	70	30

85 Crocodile

1970. Christmas. Multicoloured.

271	1c. Type **85**	10	10
272	2c. Giraffe	10	10
273	7c. Elephant	15	15
274	25c. Rhinoceros	60	80
MS275	128 × 90 mm. Nos. 271/4	1·00	3·00

86 Sorghum

1971. Important Crops. Multicoloured.

276	3c. Type **86**	15	10
277	7c. Millet	20	10
278	10c. Maize	20	10
279	35c. Groundnuts	70	1·00

87 Map and Head of Cow

88 King bringing Gift of Gold

1971. 5th Anniv of Independence.

280	87	3c. black, brown and green	10	10
281	–	4c. black, light blue and blue	10	10
282	–	7c. black and orange	20	15
283	–	10c. multicoloured	20	15
284	–	20c. multicoloured	55	2·50

DESIGNS: 4c. Map and cogs; 7c. Map and common zebra; 10c. Map and sorghum stalk crossed by tusk; 20c. Arms and map of Botswana.

1971. Christmas. Multicoloured.

285	2c. Type **88**	10	10
286	3c. King bringing frankincense	10	10
287	7c. King bringing myrrh	10	10
288	20c. Three Kings behold the star	35	65
MS289	85 × 128 mm. Nos. 285/8	1·00	3·50

89 Orion

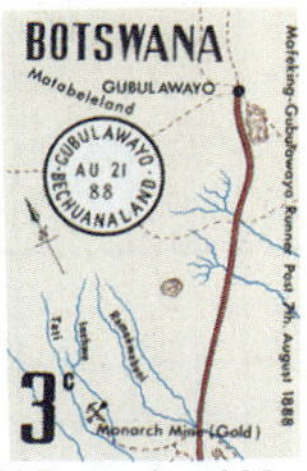

90 Postmark and Map

1972. "Night Sky".

290	89	3c. blue, black and red	75	30
291	–	7c. blue, black and yellow	1·10	80
292	–	10c. green, black and orange	1·25	85
293	–	20c. blue, black and green	1·75	3·25

CONSTELLATIONS: 7c. The Scorpion; 10c. The Centaur; 20c. The Cross.

1972. Mafeking-Gubulawayo Runner Post. Mult.

294	3c. Type **90**	30	10
295	4c. Bechuanaland stamp and map	30	35
296	7c. Runners and map	45	50
297	20c. Mafeking postmark and map	1·10	1·50
MS298	84 × 216 mm. Nos. 294/7 vertically se-tenant, forming a composite map design	11·00	15·00

For these designs with changed inscription see Nos. 652/5.

91 Cross, Map and Bells

92 Thor

1972. Christmas. Each with Cross and Map. Mult.

299	2c. Type **91**	10	75
300	3c. Cross, map and candle	10	10
301	7c. Cross, map and Christmas tree	15	25
302	20c. Cross, map, star and holly	40	85
MS303	96 × 119 mm. Nos. 299/302	1·25	3·25

1973. Centenary of I.M.O./W.M.O. Norse Myths. Multicoloured.

304	3c. Type **92**	20	10
305	4c. Sun God's chariot (horiz)	25	15
306	7c. Ymir, the frost giant	30	15
307	20c. Odin and Sleipnir (horiz)	75	70

93 Livingstone and River Scene

1973. Death Centenary of Dr. Livingstone. Mult.

308	3c. Type **93**	20	10
309	20c. Livingstone meeting Stanley	90	90

94 Donkey and Foal at Village Trough

1973. Christmas. Multicoloured.

310	3c. Type **94**	10	10
311	4c. Shepherd and flock (horiz)	10	10
312	7c. Mother and Child	10	10
313	20c. Kgotla meeting (horiz)	40	85

95 Gaborone Campus

1974. 10th Anniv of University of Botswana, Lesotho and Swaziland. Multicoloured.

314	3c. Type **95**	10	10
315	7c. Kwaluseni Campus	10	10
316	20c. Roma Campus	15	20
317	35c. Map and flags of the three countries	20	35

96 Methods of Mail Transport

1974. Centenary of U.P.U. Multicoloured.

318	2c. Type **96**	55	35
319	3c. Post Office, Palapye, circa 1889	55	35
320	7c. Bechuanaland Police Camel Post, circa 1900	95	70
321	20c. Hawker Siddeley H.S.748 and De Havilland D.H.9 mail planes of 1920 and 1974	2·75	2·50

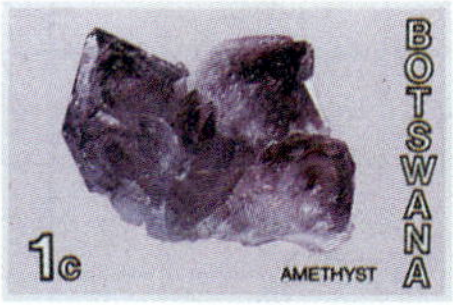

97 Amethyst

1974. Botswana Minerals. Multicoloured.

322	1c. Type **97**	60	2·00
323	2c. Agate-"Botswana Pink"	60	2·00
324	3c. Quartz	65	80
325	4c. Copper nickel	70	60
326	5c. Moss agate	70	1·00
327	7c. Agate	80	1·25
328	10c. Stilbite	1·60	65
329	15c. Moshaneng banded marble	2·00	4·00
330	20c. Gem diamonds	4·00	4·50
331	25c. Chrysotile	5·00	2·50
332	35c. Jasper	5·00	5·50
333	50c. Moss quartz	4·50	7·00
334	1r. Citrine	7·50	10·00
335	2r. Chalcopyrite	20·00	20·00

98 "Stapelia variegata"

99 President Sir Seretse Khama

1974. Christmas. Multicoloured.

336	2c. Type **98**	20	40
337	7c. "Hibiscus lunarifolius"	30	20
338	15c. "Ceratotheca triloba"	45	1·00
339	20c. "Nerine laticoma"	60	1·25
MS340	85 × 130 mm. Nos. 336/9	2·00	4·25

1975. 10th Anniv of Self-Government.

341	99	4c. multicoloured	10	10
342		10c. multicoloured	15	10
343		20c. multicoloured	25	25
344		35c. multicoloured	45	50
MS345		93 × 130 mm. Nos. 341/4	1·00	1·50

100 Ostrich

1975. Rock Paintings, Tsodilo Hills. Multicoloured.

346	4c. Type **100**	60	10
347	10c. White rhinoceros	1·00	10
348	25c. Spotted hyena	2·00	55
349	35c. Scorpion	2·00	1·10
MS350	150 × 150 mm. Nos. 346/9	12·00	7·50

101 Map of British Bechuanaland, 1885

102 "Aloe marlothii"

1975. Anniversaries. Multicoloured.

351	6c. Type **101**	30	20
352	10c. Chief Khama, 1875	40	15
353	25c. Chiefs Sebele, Bathoen and Khama, 1895 (horiz)	80	75

EVENTS: 6c. 90th anniv of Protectorate; 10c. Centenary of Khama's accession; 25c. 80th anniv of Chiefs' visit to London.

1975. Christmas. Aloes. Multicoloured.

354	3c. Type **102**	20	10
355	10c. "Aloe lutescens"	40	20
356	15c. "Aloe zebrina"	60	1·50
357	25c. "Aloe littoralis"	75	2·50

103 Drum

1976. Traditional Musical Instruments. Mult.

358	4c. Type **103**	15	10
359	10c. Hand piano	20	10
360	15c. Segankuru (violin)	25	50
361	25c. Kudu signal horn	30	1·25

104 One Pula Note

1976. 1st National Currency. Multicoloured.

362	4c. Type **104**	15	10
363	10c. Two pula note	20	10
364	15c. Five pula note	35	20
365	25c. Ten pula note	45	45
MS366	163 × 107 mm. Nos. 362/5	1·00	3·50

1976. Nos. 322/35 surch in new currency.

367	1t. on 1c. multicoloured	2·00	70
368	2t. on 2c. multicoloured	2·00	1·75
369	3t. on 3c. multicoloured	1·50	60
370	4t. on 4c. multicoloured	2·50	40
371	5t. on 5c. multicoloured	2·50	40

372	7t. on 7c. multicoloured	1·25	2·75
373	10t. on 10c. multicoloured	1·25	80
374	15t. on 15c. multicoloured	4·25	3·25
375	20t. on 20c. multicoloured	7·50	80
376	25t. on 25c. multicoloured	5·00	1·25
377	35t. on 35c. multicoloured	4·00	5·00
378	50t. on 50c. multicoloured	5·50	9·00
379	1p. on 1r. multicoloured	6·00	9·50
380	2p. on 2r. multicoloured	8·00	11·00

106 Botswana Cattle

1976. 10th Anniv of Independence. Multicoloured.

381	4t. Type **106**	15	10
382	10t. Antelope, Okavango Delta (vert)	20	10
383	15t. School and pupils	20	40
384	25t. Rural weaving (vert)	20	50
385	35t. Miner (vert)	75	85

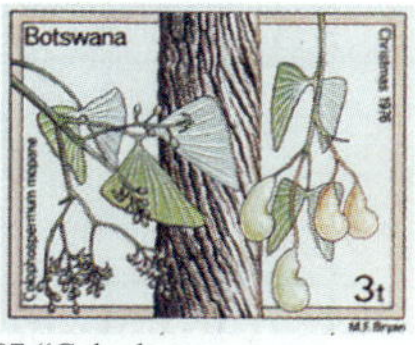

107 "Colophospermum mopane"

1976. Christmas. Trees. Multicoloured.

386	3t. Type **107**	15	10
387	4t. "Baikiaea plurijuga"	15	10
388	10t. "Sterculia rogersii"	20	10
389	25t. "Acacia nilotica"	45	50
390	40t. "Kigelia africana"	75	1·25

108 Coronation Coach

1977. Silver Jubilee. Multicoloured.

391	4t. The Queen and Sir Seretse Khama	10	10
392	25t. Type **108**	20	15
393	40t. The Recognition	35	90

109 African Clawless Otter

1977. Diminishing Species. Multicoloured.

394	3t. Type **109**	4·25	40
395	4t. Serval	4·25	40
396	10t. Bat-eared fox	4·75	40
397	25t. Temminck's ground pangolin	11·00	2·00
398	40t. Brown hyena	13·00	7·50

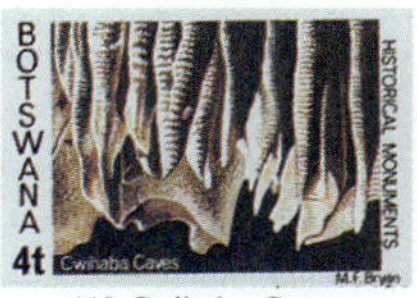

110 Cwihaba Caves

1977. Historical Monuments. Multicoloured.

399	4t. Type **110**	20	10
400	5t. Khama Memorial	20	10
401	15t. Green's Tree	30	40
402	20t. Mmajojo Ruins	30	45
403	25t. Ancient morabaraba board	30	50
404	35t. Matsieng's footprint	40	60
MS405	154 × 105 mm. Nos. 399/404	2·50	3·25

111 "Hypoxis nitida"

112 Black Bustard

1977. Christmas. Lilies. Multicoloured.

406	3t. Type **111**	15	10
407	5t. "Haemanthus magnificus"	15	10
408	10t. "Boophane disticha"	20	10
409	25t. "Vellozia retinervis"	40	55
410	40t. "Ammocharis coranica"	55	1·25

1978. Birds. Multicoloured.

411	1t. Type **112**	70	1·25
412	2t. Marabou stork	90	1·25
413	3t. Green wood hoopoe ("Red Billed Hoopoe")	70	85
414	4t. Carmine bee eater	1·00	1·00
415	5t. African jacana	1·00	40
416	7t. African paradise flycatcher ("Paradise Flycatcher)	1·00	3·00
417	10t. Bennett's woodpecker	2·00	60
418	15t. Red bishop	1·50	3·00
419	20t. Crowned plover	1·75	2·00
420	25t. Giant kingfisher	70	3·00
421	30t. White-faced whistling duck ("White-faced Duck")	70	70
422	35t. Green-backed heron	70	3·25
423	45t. Black-headed heron	1·00	3·00
424	50t. Spotted eagle owl	5·00	4·50
425	1p. Gabar goshawk	2·50	4·50
426	2p. Martial eagle	3·00	8·00
427	5p. Saddle-bill stork	6·50	16·00

113 Tawana making Kaross

1978. Okavango Delta. Multicoloured.

428	4t. Type **113**	10	30
429	5t. Tribe localities	10	10
430	15t. Bushman collecting roots	25	40
431	20t. Herero woman milking	35	70
432	25t. Yei poling "mokoro" (canoe)	40	60
433	35t. Mbukushu fishing	45	1·75
MS434	150 × 98 mm. Nos. 428/33	1·50	3·75

114 "Caralluma lutea"

115 Sip Well

1978. Christmas. Flowers. Multicoloured.

435	5t. Type **114**	35	10
436	10t. "Hoodia lugardii"	50	15
437	15t. "Ipomoea transvaalensis"	90	55
438	25t. "Ansellia gigantea"	1·10	70

1979. Water Development. Multicoloured.

439	3t. Type **115**	10	10
440	5t. Watering pit	10	10
441	10t. Hand dug well	15	10
442	22t. Windmill	20	30
443	50t. Drilling rig truck	40	55

116 Pottery

1979. Handicrafts. Multicoloured.

444	5t. Type **116**	10	10
445	10t. Clay modelling	10	10
446	25t. Basketry	20	25
447	40t. Beadwork	40	50
MS448	123 × 96 mm. Nos. 444/7	1·00	2·50

117 British Bechuanaland 1885 1d. Stamp and Sir Rowland Hill

1979. Death Centenary of Sir Rowland Hill. Mult.

449	5t. Type **117**	20	10
450	25t. Bechuanaland Protectorate 1932 2d. stamp	45	50
451	45t. 1967 Hoopoe 2c. definitive stamp	55	1·25

118 Children Playing

1979. International Year of the Child. Multicoloured.

452	5t. Type **118**	20	10
453	10t. Child playing with doll (vert)	30	20

119 "Ximenia caffra"

120 Flap-necked Chameleon

1979. Christmas. Flowers. Multicoloured.

454	5t. Type **119**	10	10
455	10t. "Sclerocarya caffra"	20	20
456	15t. "Hexalobus monopetalus"	35	35
457	25t. "Ficus soldanella"	45	45

1980. Reptiles. Multicoloured.

458	5t. Type **120**	30	10
459	10t. Leopard tortoise	30	15
460	25t. Puff adder	50	65
461	40t. White-throated monitor	60	2·50

121 Rock Breaking

1980. Early Mining. Multicoloured.

462	5t. Type **121**	25	15
463	10t. Ore hoisting	30	15
464	15t. Ore transport	70	60
465	20t. Ore crushing	75	90
466	25t. Smelting	80	90
467	35t. Tool and products	1·00	1·75

122 "Chiwele and the Giant"

1980. Folktales. Multicoloured.

468	5t. Type **122**	10	10
469	10t. "Kgori is not deceived" (vert)	15	10
470	30t. "Nyambi's wife and Crocodile" (vert)	45	45
471	45t. "Clever Hare" (horiz)	60	60

The 10t. and 30t. are 28 × 37 mm and the 45t. 44 × 27 mm.

123 Game watching, Makgadikgadi Pans

1980. World Tourism Conference, Manila.

472	**123** 5t. multicoloured	45	20

124 "Acacia gerrardii"

126 "Anax imperator" (dragonfly)

125 Heinrich von Stephan and Botswana 3d. and 3c. U.P.U. Stamps

1980. Christmas. Multicoloured.

473	6t. Type **124**	10	10
474	1t. "Acacia nilotica"	20	10
475	25t. "Acacia erubescens"	45	30
476	40t. "Dichrostachys cinerea"	70	70

1981. 150th Birth Anniv of Heinrich von Stephan (founder of Universal Postal Union). Multicoloured.

477	6t. Type **125**	50	30
478	20t.6d. and 7c. U.P.U. stamps	1·25	2·25

1981. Insects. Multicoloured.

479	6t. Type **126**	15	10
480	7t. "Sphodromantis gastrica" (mantid)	15	20
481	10t. "Zonocerus elegans" (grasshopper)	15	20
482	20t. "Kheper nigroaeneus" (beetle)	25	50
483	30t. "Papilio demodocus" (butterfly)	35	70
484	45t. "Acanthocampa belina" (moth larva)	40	1·10
MS485	180 × 89 mm. Nos. 479/84	3·00	8·50

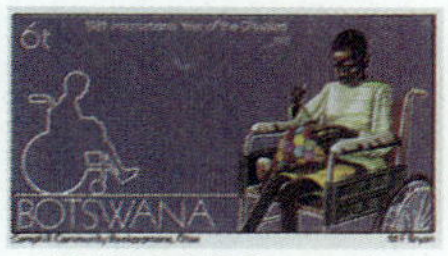

127 Camphill Community Rankoromane, Otse

1981. International Year for Disabled Persons. Multicoloured.

486	6t. Type **127**	20	10
487	20t. Resource Centre for the Blind, Mochudi	55	35
488	30t. Tlamelong Rehabilitation Centre, Tlokweng	75	45

128 Woman reading Letter

1981. Literacy Programme. Multicoloured.

489	6t. Type **128**	20	10
490	7t. Man filling in form	20	15
491	20t. Boy reading newspaper	60	35
492	30t. Child being taught to read	80	45

129 Sir Seretse Khama and Building

1981. 1st Death Anniv of Sir Seretse Khama (former President). Multicoloured.

493	6t. Type **129**	15	10
494	10t. Seretse Khama and building (different)	25	15
495	30t. Seretse Khama and Botswana flag	40	45
496	45t. Seretse Khama and building (different)	55	70

1981. Nos. 417 and 422 surch.

497	25t. on 35t. Green-backed heron	3·00	2·00
498	30t. on 10t. Bennett's woodpecker	3·00	2·00

131 Traditional Ploughing

1981. Cattle Industry. Multicoloured.

499	6t. Type **131**	10	10
500	20t. Agricultural show	30	50

501 30t. Botswana Meat Commission 35 60
502 45t. Vaccine Institute, Botswana 50 1·00

132 "Nymphaea caerulea"

1981. Christmas. Flowers. Multicoloured.
503 6t. Type **132** 20 10
504 10t. "Nymphoides indica" 25 10
505 25t. "Nymphaea lotus" 60 90
506 40t. "Ottelia kunenensis" 80 2·25

133 "Cattle Post Scene" (Boitumelo Golaakwena)

1982. Children's Art. Multicoloured.
507 6t. Type **133** 40 10
508 10t. "Kgotla Meeting" (Reginald Klinck) 50 15
509 30t. "Village Water Supply" (Keronmemang Matswiri) 1·75 1·25
510 45t. "With the Crops" (Kennedy Balemoge) 1·75 2·75

134 Common Type

1982. Traditional House. Multicoloured.
511 6t. Type **134** 40 15
512 10t. Kgatleng type 50 15
513 30t. North Eastern type 2·00 1·10
514 45t. Sarwa type 2·00 3·00

135 African Masked Weaver

136 "Coprinus comatus"

1982. Birds. Multicoloured.
515 1t. Type **135** 80 1·50
516 2t. Miombo double-collared sunbird ("Lesser double-collared Sunbird") 90 1·60
517 3t. Red-throated bee eater 1·00 1·60
518 4t. Ostrich 1·00 1·60
519 5t. Grey-headed gull 1·00 1·60
520 6t. African pygmy ("Pygmy Goose") 1·00 40
521 7t. Cattle egret 1·00 15
522 8t. Lanner falcon 2·50 1·50
523 10t. Yellow-billed stork 1·00 20
524 15t. Red-billed pintail ("Red-billed Teal") (horiz) 2·75 25
525 20t. Barn owl (horiz) 5·50 3·50
526 25t. Hammerkop ("Hammerkop") (horiz) 3·25 70
527 30t. South African stilt ("Stilt") (horiz) 3·75 90
528 35t. Blacksmith plover (horiz) 3·75 80
529 45t. Senegal wattled plover ("Watted Plover") (horiz) 3·75 1·75
530 50t. Helmeted guineafowl ("Crowned Guineafowl") (horiz) 4·75 2·50
531 1p. Cape vulture (horiz) 9·00 12·00
532 2p. Augur buzzard (horiz) 11·00 16·00

1982. Christmas. Fungi. Multicoloured.
533 7t. Type **136** 2·50 20
534 15t. "Lactarius deliciosus" 3·75 65
535 35t. "Amanita pantherina" 6·00 2·00
536 50t. "Boletus edulis" 7·50 8·00

137 President Quett Masire

1983. Commonwealth Day. Multicoloured.
537 7t. Type **137** 10 10
538 15t. Native dancers 15 20
539 35t. Melbourne conference centre 45 55
540 45t. Meeting of Heads of State, Melbourne 55 80

138 Wattled Crane

139 Wooden Spoons

1983. Endangered Species. Multicoloured.
541 7t. Type **138** 3·00 55
542 15t. "Aloe lutescens" 2·50 80
543 35t. Roan antelope 3·00 3·25
544 50t. Ivory palm 3·50 7·00

1983. Traditional Artifacts. Multicoloured.
545 7t. Type **139** 25 10
546 15t. Personal ornaments 45 30
547 35t. Ox-hide milk bag 75 65
548 50t. Decorated knives 1·00 1·10
MS549 115 × 102 mm. Nos. 545 × 8 4·25 5·00

140 "Pantala flavescens"

1983. Christmas. Dragonflies. Multicoloured.
550 6t. Type **140** 85 10
551 15t. "Anax imperator" 1·75 50
552 25t. "Trithemis arteriosa" 2·00 85
553 45t. "Chlorolestes elegans" 2·75 4·75

141 Sorting Diamonds

142 Riding Cattle

1984. Mining Industry. Multicoloured.
554 7t. Type **141** 2·00 50
555 15t. Lime kiln 2·00 75
556 35t. Copper-nickel smelter plant (vert) 3·25 3·25
557 60t. Stockpiled coal (vert) 3·75 10·00

1984. Traditional Transport. Multicoloured.
558 7t. Type **142** 20 10
559 25t. Sledge 65 60
560 35t. Wagon 85 1·50
561 50t. Two-wheeled donkey cart 1·25 4·50

143 Avro 504 Aircraft

144 "Papilio demodocus"

1984. 40th Anniv of International Civil Aviation Organization. Multicoloured.
562 7t. Type **143** 75 20
563 10t. Westland Wessex trimotor 1·00 35
564 15t. Junkers Ju 52/3m 1·40 95
565 25t. De Havilland Dominie 2·00 1·75
566 35t. Douglas DC-3 "Wenala" 2·25 3·50
567 50t. Fokker Friendship 2·50 7·00

1984. Christmas. Butterflies. Multicoloured.
568 7t. Type **144** 2·00 30
569 25t. "Byblia anvatara" 2·25 1·50
570 35t. "Danaus chrysippus" 3·50 3·00
571 50t. "Graphium taboranus" 4·75 11·00
No. 570 is incorrectly inscr "Hypolimnas misippus".

145 Seswaa (meat dish)

146 1885 British Bechuanaland Overprint on Cape of Good Hope ½d.

1985. 5th Anniv of Southern African Development Co-ordination Conference. Traditional Foods. Multicoloured.
572 7t. Type **145** 50 10
573 15t. Bogobe (cereal porridge) 75 35
574 25t. Madila (soured coagulated cow's milk) 1·00 55
575 50t. Phane (caterpillars) 1·50 2·25
MS576 117 × 103 mm. Nos. 572/5 7·00 10·00

1985. Centenary of First Bechuanaland Stamps.
577 **146** 7t. black, grey and red 1·00 20
578 – 15t. black, brown yell 1·75 50
579 – 25t. black and red 2·25 80
580 – 35t. black, blue and gold 2·50 2·00
581 – 50t. multicoloured 2·75 3·75
DESIGNS—VERT: 15t. 1897 Bechuanaland Protectorate overprint on G.B. 3d.; 25t. Bechuanaland Protectorate 1932 1d. definitive. HORIZ: 35t. Bechuanaland 1965 Internal Self-Government 5c.; 50t. Botswana 1966 Independence 2½c.

147 Bechuanaland Border Police, 1885–95

1985. Centenary of Botswana Police. Multicoloured.
582 7t. Type **147** 2·25 50
583 10t. Bechuanaland Mounted Police, 1895–1902 2·50 50
584 25t. Bechuanaland Protectorate Police, 1903–66 3·50 2·00
585 50t. Botswana Police, from 1966 5·00 7·50

148 "Cucumis metuliferus"

1985. Christmas. Edible Wild Cucumbers. Mult.
586 7t. Type **148** 1·25 10
587 15t. "Acanthosicyos naudinianus" 2·25 70
588 25t. "Coccinia sessifolia" 3·50 1·25
589 50t. "Momordica balsamina" 5·00 9·50

149 Mr. Shippard and Chief Gaseitsiwe of the Bangwaketse

150 Halley's Comet over Serowe

1985. Centenary of Declaration of Bechuanaland Protectorate. Multicoloured.
590 7t. Type **149** 35 10
591 15t. Sir Charles Warren and Chief Sechele of the Bakwena 70 45
592 25t. Revd. Mackenzie and Chief Khama of the Bamangwato 1·25 85
593 50t. Map showing Protectorate 2·75 6·50
MS594 130 × 133 mm. Nos. 590/3 12·00 14·00

1986. Appearance of Halley's Comet. Multicoloured.
595 7t. Type **150** 80 15
596 15t. Comet over Bobonong at sunset 1·50 70
597 35t. Comet over Gomare at dawn 2·00 1·50
598 50t. Comet over Thamaga and Letlhakeng 2·25 3·75

151 Milk Bag

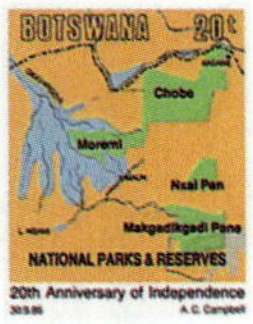

152 Map showing National Parks and Reserves

1986. Traditional Milk Containers. Multicoloured.
599 8t. Type **151** 30 10
600 15t. Clay pot and calabashes 45 30
601 35t. Wooden milk bucket 75 65
602 50t. Milk churn 1·00 1·40

1986. 20th Anniv of Independence. Sheet 100 × 120 mm. Multicoloured.
MS603 20t. Type **152**; 20t. Morupule power station; 20t. Cattle breeding in Kgalagadi; 20t. National Assembly Building 3·75 2·50

153 "Ludwigia stogonifera"

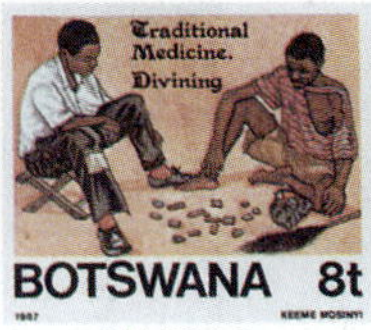

154 Divining

1986. Christmas. Flowers of Okavango. Mult.
604 8t. Type **153** 1·25 10
605 15t. "Sopubia mannii" 2·25 1·10
606 35t. "Commelina diffusa" 3·50 3·00
607 50t. "Hibiscus diversifolius" 4·00 12·00

1987. Traditional Medicine. Multicoloured.
608 8t. Type **154** 80 10
609 15t. Lightning prevention 1·50 80
610 35t. Rain making 2·25 2·50
611 50t. Blood letting 2·75 8·50

1987. Nos. 520, 523 and 530 surch.
612 3t. on 6t. African pygmy goose 1·75 60
613 5t. on 10t. Yellow-billed stork 1·75 60
614 20t. on 50t. Helmeted guineafowl (horiz) 3·25 1·40

156 Oral Rehydration Therapy

157 Cape Fox

1987. UNICEF Child Survival Campaign. Multicoloured.
615 8t. Type **156** 35 10
616 15t. Growth monitoring 60 55
617 35t. Immunization 1·25 2·00
618 50t. Breast feeding 1·50 5·00

1987. Animals of Botswana. Multicoloured.
619 1t. Type **157** 10 1·00
620 2t. Lechwe 50 1·50
621 3t. Zebra 15 1·00
622 4t. Duiker 15 1·75
623 5t. Banded mongoose 20 1·75
624 6t. Rusty-spotted genet 20 1·75
625 8t. Hedgehog 30 10
626 10t. Scrub hare 30 10
627 12t. Hippopotamus 3·00 3·50
628 15t. Suricate 2·50 2·25
629 20t. Caracal 70 65
630 25t. Steenbok 70 1·50
631 30t. Gemsbok 1·50 1·50
632 35t. Square-lipped rhinoceros 2·00 2·50
633 40t. Mountain reedbuck 1·75 1·50
634 50t. Rock dassie 90 1·75
635 1p. Giraffe 2·50 3·75
636 2p. Tsessebe 2·50 5·50
637 3p. Side-striped jackal 3·75 7·00
638 5p. Hartebeest 6·00 9·00

158 "Cyperus articulatus"

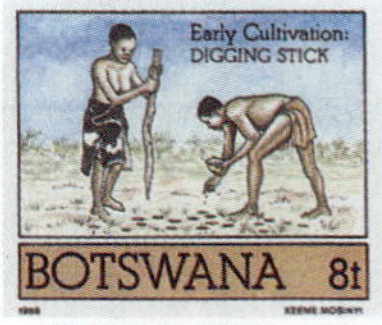

159 Planting Seeds with Digging Stick

1987. Christmas. Grasses and Sedges of Okavango. Multicoloured.

639	8t. Type **158**	40	10
640	15t. Broomgrass	60	40
641	30t. "Cyperus alopurcides"	1·25	75
642	1p. Bulrush sedge	2·50	5·75
MS643	88 × 99 mm. Nos. 639/42	4·25	5·75

1988. Early Cultivation. Multicoloured.

644	8t. Type **159**	40	10
645	15t. Using iron hoe	60	35
646	35t. Wooden ox-drawn plough	1·00	1·00
647	50t. Villagers working in lesotlas communal field	1·40	2·00

160 Red Lechwe at Water-hole

161 Gubulawayo Postmark and Route Southwards to Tati

1988. Red Lechwe. Multicoloured.

648	10t. Type **160**	90	15
649	15t. Red lechwe and early morning sun	1·75	65
650	35t. Female and calf	2·50	1·75
651	75t. Herd on the move	3·75	8·50

1988. Cent of Mafeking–Gubalawayo Runner Post. Designs as Nos. 294/7, but redrawn smaller with changed inscriptions as in T **161**. Multicoloured.

652	10t. Type **161**	35	10
653	15t. Bechuanaland 1888 6d. on 6d. stamp and route from Tati southwards	55	30
654	30t. Runners and twin routes south from Shoshong	95	75
655	60t. Mafeking postmark and routes to Bechuanaland and Transvaal	1·60	2·75
MS656	81 × 151 mm. Nos. 652/5 vertically se-tenant, forming a composite map design	6·00	6·50

162 Pope John Paul II and Outline Map of Botswana

163 National Museum and Art Gallery, Gaborone

1988. Visit of Pope John Paul II. Multicoloured.

657	10t. Type **162**	2·00	20
658	15t. Pope John Paul II	2·25	30
659	30t. Pope giving blessing and outline map	2·75	70
660	80t. Pope John Paul II (different)	3·50	2·75

1988. 20th Anniv of National Museum and Art Gallery, Gaborone. Multicoloured.

661	8t. Type **163**	15	10
662	15t. Pottery	20	25
663	30t. Blacksmith's buffalo bellows	35	40
664	60c. Children and land rover mobile museum van	70	1·00

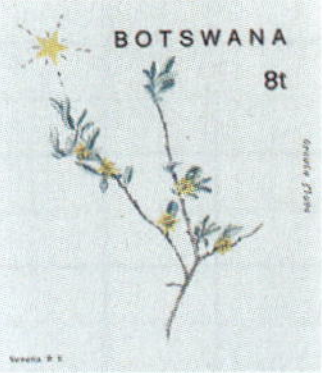

164 "Grewia flava"

165 Basket Granary

1988. Flowering Plants of South-eastern Botswana. Multicoloured.

665	8t. Type **164**	20	10
666	15t. "Cienfuegosia digitata"	30	25
667	40t. "Solanum seaforthianum"	60	55
668	75t. "Carissa bispinosa"	1·00	1·40

1989. Traditional Grain Storage. Multicoloured.

669	8t. Type **165**	75	10
670	15t. Large letlole granary	1·25	40
671	30t. Pot granary	1·75	60
672	60t. Two types of serala	2·50	2·25

166 Female with Eggs

1989. Slaty Egret. Multicoloured.

673	8t. Type **166**	55	15
674	15t. Chicks in nest	75	40
675	30t. In flight	1·00	75
676	60t. Pair building nest	1·40	1·60
MS677	119 × 89 mm. Nos. 673/6	3·25	2·75

167 "My Work at Home" (Ephraim Seeletso)

1989. Children's Paintings. Multicoloured.

678	10t. Type **167**	35	10
679	15t. "My Favourite Game" (hopscotch) (Neelma Bhatia) (vert)	50	35
680	30t. "My Favourite Toy" (clay animals) (Thabo Habana)	75	70
681	1p. "My School Day" (Thabo Olesitse)	2·00	3·25

168 "Eulophia angolensis"

171 Telephone Engineer

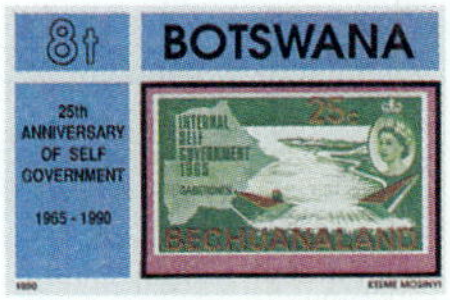

169 Bechuanaland 1965 New Constitution 25c. Stamp (25th anniv of Self-Government)

1989. Christmas. Orchids. Multicoloured.

682	8t. Type **168**	90	10
683	15t. "Eulophia hereroensis"	1·50	60
684	30t. "Eulophia speciosa"	2·00	1·00
685	60t. "Eulophia petersii"	3·50	7·00

1990. Anniversaries.

686 **169**	8t. multicoloured	70	15
687 –	15t. multicoloured	75	50
688 –	30t. multicoloured	3·75	1·60
689 –	60t. black, blue and yellow	3·75	7·00

DESIGNS: 15t. Casting vote in ballot box (25th anniv of First Elections); 30t. Outline map and flags of Southern Africa Development Co-ordination Conference countries (10th anniv); 60t. Penny Black (150th anniv of first postage stamp).

1990. Nos. 619, 624 and 627 surch.

690	10t. on 1t. Type **157**	45	20
691	20t. on 6t. Rusty-spotted genet	60	80
692	50t. on 12t. Hippopotamus	2·00	3·50

1990. "Stamp World London 90" International Stamp Exhibition. Multicoloured.

693	8t. Type **171**	35	10
694	15t. Transmission pylon	65	40
695	30t. Public telephone	1·00	75
696	2p. Testing circuit board	3·00	6·50

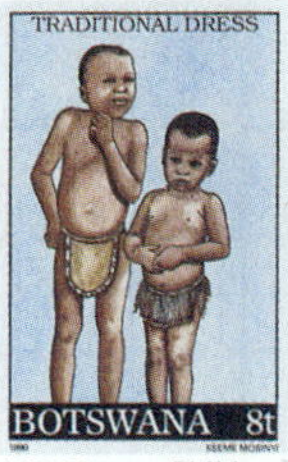

172 Young Children

173 "Acacia nigrescens"

1990. Traditional Dress. Multicoloured.

697	8t. Type **172**	35	10
698	15t. Young woman	65	40
699	30t. Adult man	1·00	70
700	2p. Adult woman	3·00	6·50
MS701	104 × 150 mm. Nos. 697/700	5·00	7·50

1990. Christmas. Flowering Trees. Multicoloured.

702	8t. Type **173**	60	10
703	15t. "Peltophorum africanum"	95	35
704	30t. "Burkea africana"	1·75	75
705	2p. "Pterocarpus angolensis"	3·75	7·50

174 Children running in front of Hatchback

1990. 1st National Road Safety Day. Multicoloured.

706	8t. Type **174**	2·50	30
707	15t. Careless overtaking	3·00	1·00
708	30t. Cattle on road	3·75	2·75

175 Cattle

176 Children

1991. Rock Paintings. Multicoloured.

709	8t. Type **175**	2·25	40
710	15t. Cattle, drying frames and tree	2·75	85
711	30t. Animal hides	3·25	1·50
712	2p. Family herding cattle	6·00	10·00

1991. National Census. Multicoloured.

713	8t. Type **176**	1·50	20
714a	15t. Village	2·00	55
715	30t. School	2·25	1·00
716	2p. Hospital	8·00	11·00

177 Tourists viewing Elephants

1991. African Tourism Year. Okavango Delta. Mult.

717	8t. Type **177**	1·50	70
718	15t. Crocodiles basking on river bank	1·75	90
719	35t. Fish eagles and De Havilland D.H.C.7 Dash Seven aircraft	3·50	3·25
720	2p. Okavango wildlife (26 × 44 mm)	5·50	9·00

178 "Harpagophytum procumbens"

179 "Cacosternum boettgeri"

1991. Christmas. Seed Pods. Multicoloured.

721	8t. Type **178**	60	10
722	15t. "Tylosema esculentum"	1·00	40
723	30t. "Abrus precatorius"	1·75	80
724	2p. "Kigelia africana"	4·50	8·50

1992. Nos. 621, 624 and 627 surch.

725	8t. on 12t. Hippopotamus	1·25	70
726	10t. on 12t. Hippopotamus	1·25	70
727	25t. on 6t. Rusty-spotted genet	1·25	1·50
728	40t. on 3t. Zebra	2·25	4·00

1992. Climbing Frogs. Multicoloured.

729	8t. Type **179**	75	30
730	10t. "Hyperolius marmoratus angolensis" (vert)	75	30
731	40t. "Bufo fenoulheti"	2·50	1·50
732	1p. "Hyperolius sp." (vert)	5·00	7·00

180 Air-conditioned Carriages

1992. Deluxe Railway Service. Multicoloured.

733	10t. Type **180**	1·50	40
734	25t. Diesel locomotive No. BD001 (vert)	2·25	80
735	40t. Carriage interior (vert)	2·50	1·25
736	2p. Diesel locomotive No. BD028	3·75	7·50
MS737	127 × 127 mm. Nos. 733/6	12·00	12·00

181 Cheetah

182 Boxing

1992. Animals. Multicoloured.

738	1t. Type **181**	30	1·75
739	2t. Spring hare	30	1·75
740	4t. Blackfooted cat	40	1·75
741	5t. Striped mouse	40	1·50
742	10t. Oribi	55	10
743	12t. Pangolin	1·00	2·50
744	15t. Aardwolf	1·00	40
745	20t. Warthog	1·00	40
746	25t. Ground squirrel	1·00	20
747	35t. Honey badger	1·25	30
748	40t. Common mole rat	1·25	30
749	45t. Wild dog	1·25	30
750	50t. Water mongoose	1·25	35
751	80t. Klipspringer	1·75	1·75
752	1p. Lesser bushbaby	1·75	1·75
753	2p. Bushveld elephant shrew	2·50	4·00
754	5p. Zorilla	4·25	7·00
755	10p. Vervet monkey	6·50	10·00

1992. Olympic Games, Barcelona. Multicoloured.

756	10t. Type **182**	60	10
757	50t. Running	1·50	50
758	1p. Boxing (different)	2·00	2·50
759	2p. Running (different)	2·50	5·00
MS760	87 × 117 mm. Nos. 756/9	5·50	8·00

183 "Adiantum incisum"

184 Helping Blind Person (Lions Club International)

1992. Christmas. Ferns. Multicoloured.

761	10t. Type **183**	40	10
762	25t. "Actiniopteris radiata"	70	35
763	40t. "Ceratopteris cornuta"	1·00	55
764	1p.50 "Pellaea calomelanos"	3·00	7·00

1993. Charitable Organizations in Botswana. Mult.

765	10t. Type **184**	80	20
766	15t. Nurse carrying child (Red Cross Society) (horiz)	90	40
767	25t. Woman watering seedling (Ecumenical Decade)	90	50
768	35t. Deaf children (Round Table) (horiz)	1·25	1·50
769	40t. Crowd of people (Rotary International)	1·25	1·75
770	50t. Hands at prayer (Botswana Christian Council) (horiz)	1·50	2·50

185 Bechuanaland Railways Class "6" Locomotive No. 1

1993. Railway Centenary. Multicoloured.

771	10t. Type **185**	75	40
772	40t. Class "19" locomotive No. 317	1·40	75
773	50t. Class "12" locomotive No. 256	1·40	90
774	1p.50 Class "7" locomotive No. 71	2·00	5·00
MS775	190 × 100 mm. Nos. 771/4	5·00	6·00

186 Long-crested Eagle

187 "Aloe zebrina"

1993. Endangered Eagles. Multicoloured.
776 10t. Type **186** 70 35
777 25t. Short-toed eagle ("Snake eagle") . . . . 1·25 65
778 50t. Bateleur ("Bateleur Eagle") . . . . 1·60 1·75
779 1p.50 Secretary bird . . . . 2·50 6·50

1993. Christmas. Flora. Multicoloured.
780 12t. Type **187** 40 10
781 25t. "Croton megalobotrys" 60 25
782 50t. "Boophane disticha" . . 85 70
783 1p. "Euphoria davyi" . . . . 1·25 3·50

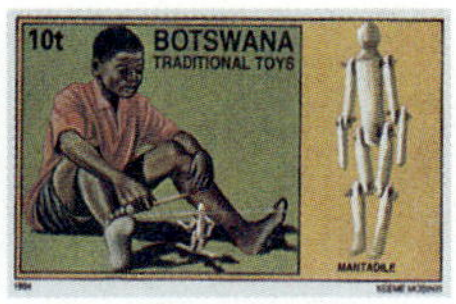

188 Boy with String Puppet

1994. Traditional Toys. Multicoloured.
784 10t. Type **188** 20 10
785 40t. Boys with clay cattle . . 45 30
786 50t. Boy with spinner 50 50
787 1p. Girls playing in make-believe houses . . . . . . 1·10 3·00

189 Interior of Control Tower, Gaborone Airport

1994. 50th Anniv of I.C.A.O. Multicoloured.
788 10t. Type **189** 40 10
789 25t. Crash fire tender 75 40
790 40t. Loading supplies onto airliner (vert) . . . . . . 1·00 85
791 50t. Control tower, Gaborone (vert) . . . . 1·00 1·75

1994. No. 743 surch **10t**.
792 10t. on 12t. Pangolin . . . . 6·50 75

191 Lesser Flamingos at Sua Pan

192 "Ziziphus mucronata"

1994. Environment Protection. Makgadikgadi Pans. Multicoloured.
793 10t. Type **191** . . . . 1·00 40
794 35t. Baobab trees (horiz) . . 50 40
795 50t. Zebra and palm trees . . 65 80
796 2p. Map of area (horiz) . . . 3·00 6·00

1994. Christmas. Edible Fruits. Multicoloured.
797 10t. Type **192** 25 10
798 25t. "Strychnos cocculoides" 40 30
799 40t. "Bauhinia petersiana" 60 70
800 50t. "Schinziphyton rautoneii" . . . . 70 1·40

193 Fisherman with Bow and Arrow

1995. Traditional Fishing. Multicoloured.
801 15t. Type **193** 35 20
802 40t. Men in canoe and boy with fishing rod 60 45
803 65t. Fisherman with net . . . 80 90
804 80t. Fisherman with basket fish trap . . . . 1·00 2·00

194 Boys watering Horses (FAO)

196 "Adenia glauca"

195 Brown Hyena

1995. 50th Anniv of United Nations. Multicoloured.
805 20t. Type **194** 20 10
806 50t. Schoolchildren queueing for soup (WFP) 35 30
807 80t. Policeman conducting census (UNDP) . . . . . 1·00 1·00
808 1p. Weighing baby (UNICEF) . . . . 70 2·00

1995. Endangered Species. Brown Hyena. Mult.
809 20t. Type **195** 45 60
810 50t. Pair of hyenas 65 75
811 80t. Hyena stealing ostrich eggs . . . . 1·10 1·50
812 1p. Adult hyena and cubs . . 1·25 2·25

198 Spears

1995. Christmas. Plants. Multicoloured.
813 20t. Type **196** 35 10
814 50t. "Pterodiscus ngamicus" 60 30
815 80t. "Sesamothamnus lugardii" . . . . 1·00 1·00
816 1p. "Fockea multiflora" . . . 1·10 2·00

1996. Nos. 738/40 surch.
817 20t. on 2t. Spring hare . . . 1·00 30
818 30t. on 1t. Type **181** . . . . 1·25 30
819 70t. on 4t. Blackfooted cat 2·00 3·25

1996. Traditional Weapons. Multicoloured.
820 20t. Type **198** 20 10
821 50t. Axes 35 30
822 80t. Shield and knobkerries 55 65
823 1p. Knives and sheaths . . . 60 1·50

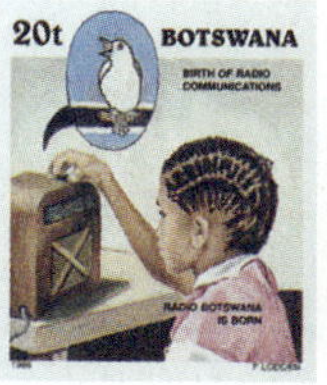

199 Child with Basic Radio

200 Olympic Flame, Rings and Wreath

1996. Centenary of Radio. Multicoloured.
824 20t. Type **199** 25 10
825 50t. Radio Botswana's mobile transmitter 40 30
826 80t. Police radio control . . . 1·50 1·10
827 1p. Listening to radio . . . . 70 1·75

1996. Centenary of Modern Olympic Games. Mult.
828 20t. Type **200** 30 10
829 50t. Pierre de Coubertin (founder of modern Olympics) 45 30
830 80t. Map of Botswana with flags and athletes 90 90
831 1p. Ruins of ancient stadium at Olympia . . . . 90 1·60

201 Family Planning Class (Botswana Family Welfare Association)

202 "Adansonia digitata" Leaf and Blossom

1996. Local Charities. Multicoloured.
832 20t. Type **201** 20 10
833 30t. Blind workers (Pudulogong Rehabilitation Centre) 20 15
834 50t. Collecting seeds (Forestry Association of Botswana) 30 30
835 70t. Secretarial class (YWCA) 40 70
836 80t. Children's day centre (Botswana Council of Women) 50 80
837 1p. Children's village, Tlokweng (S.O.S. Children's village) . . . . 60 1·50

1996. Christmas. Parts of Life Cycle for "Adansonia digitata". Multicoloured.
838 20t. Type **202** 25 10
839 50t. Fruit 40 25
840 80t. Tree in leaf 60 75
841 1p. Tree with bare branches 70 1·60

203 Tati Hotel

204 Steam Locomotive, Bechuanaland Railway, 1897

1997. Francistown Centenary. Multicoloured.
842 20t. Type **203** 15 10
843 50t. Railway Station 75 35
844 80t. Company Manager's House 60 80
845 1p. Monarch Mine . . . . . 1·00 1·60

1997. Railway Centenary. Multicoloured.
846 35t. Type **204** 40 20
847 50t. Elephants crossing railway line 60 35
848 80t. First locomotive in Bechuanaland, 1897 . . . 70 45
849 1p. Beyer-Garratt type steam locomotive No. 352 . . . 75 75
850 2p. Diesel locomotive No. BD339 . . . . 1·00 1·75
851 2p.50 Fantuzzi container stacker . . . . 1·25 2·25

205 Pel's Fishing Owl

206 "Combretum zeyheri"

1997. Birds. Multicoloured.
852 5t. Type **205** 50 75
853 10t. African harrier hawk ("Gymnogene") (horiz) . . 50 75
854 15t. Brown parrot ("Meyer's Parrot") 50 60
855 20t. Harlequin quail (horiz) 60 60
856 25t. Mariqua sunbird ("Marico Sunbird") (horiz) 60 60
857 30t. Kurrichane thrush (horiz) 65 60
858 40t. Paradise sparrow ("Redheaded Finch") . . . 70 60
859 50t. Red-billed buffalo weaver ("Buffalo Weaver") 80 40
860 60t. Sacred ibis (horiz) . . . 90 70
861 70t. Cape shoveler (horiz) . . 90 80
862 80t. Black-throated honeyguide ("Greater Honeyguide") (horiz) . . . 90 70
863 1p. Woodland kingfisher (horiz) . . . . 1·10 80
864 1p.25 Purple heron . . . . . 1·40 1·40
865 1p.50 Yellow-billed oxpecker (horiz) . . . . 1·40 1·75
866 2p. Shaft-tailed whydah . . . 1·60 2·00
867 2p.50 White stork . . . . . . 1·75 2·00
868 5p. Ovampo sparrow hawk ("Sparrowhawk") . . . . 2·25 2·75
869 10p. Spotted crake . . . . . 3·25 4·50
No. 861 is inscribed "Shoveller" in error.

1997. Golden Wedding of Queen Elizabeth and Prince Philip. As T **173** of Ascension. Multicoloured.
870 35t. Prince Philip with carriage 20 55
871 35t. Queen Elizabeth with binoculars 20 55
872 2p. Queen Elizabeth with horse team . . . . 90 1·50
873 2p. Prince Philip and horse 90 1·50
874 2p.50 Queen Elizabeth and Prince Philip . . . . . . 1·10 1·50
875 2p.50 Princess Anne and Prince Edward . . . . . . 1·10 1·50
MS876 110 × 70 mm. 10p. Queen Elizabeth and Prince Philip in landau (horiz) . . . . 4·00 5·50

1997. Christmas. Plants. Multicoloured.
877 35t. Type **206** 45 10
878 1p. "Combretum apiculatum" 1·00 35
879 2p. "Combretum molle" . . 1·75 1·90
880 2p.50 "Combretum imberbe" 2·00 2·50

207 Baobab Trees

1998. Tourism (1st series). Multicoloured.
881 35t. Type **207** 25 15
882 1p. Crocodile 50 45
883 2p. Stalactites (vert) . . . . 85 1·10
884 2p.50 Tourists and rock paintings (vert) . . . . . 1·10 1·60
See also Nos. 899/902.

1998. Diana, Princess of Wales Commemoration. As T **223a** of Bahamas. Multicoloured.
885 35t. Princess Diana, 1990 . . 25 15
886 1p. In green hat, 1992 . . . 40 35
887 2p. In white blouse, 1993 . . 75 1·10
888 2p.50 With crowd, Cambridge, 1993 . . . . . 90 1·50
MS889 145 × 70 mm. As Nos. 885/8, but each with a face value of 2p.50 3·75 4·50

208 "Village Life" (tapestry)

209 "Ficus ingens"

1998. Botswana Weavers. Multicoloured.
890 35t. Type **208** 30 15
891 55t. Weaver dyeing threads 40 20
892 1p. "African wildlife" (tapestry) . . . . 1·40 1·00
893 2p. Weaver at loom . . . . 1·50 2·25
MS894 68 × 58 mm. 2p.50, "Elephants" (tapestry) (horiz) 3·00 3·25

1998. Christmas. Plants. Multicoloured.
895 35t. Type **209** 40 10
896 55t. "Ficus pygmaea" 60 20
897 1p. "Ficus abutilifolia" . . . 1·00 55
898 2p.50 "Ficus sycomorus" . . 1·90 2·75

1999. Tourism (2nd series). As T **207**. Multicoloured.
899 35t. Rock painting of men and cattle 70 25
900 55t. Expedition at Salt Pan 1·00 30
901 1p. Rock painting of elephant and antelope (vert) . . . 1·40 1·40
902 2p. Tourists under Baobab tree (vert) . . . . 1·60 2·25

210 Road Map

1999. Southern African Development Community Day. Sheet 77 × 84 mm.
MS903 **210** 5p. multicoloured . . 3·50 3·75

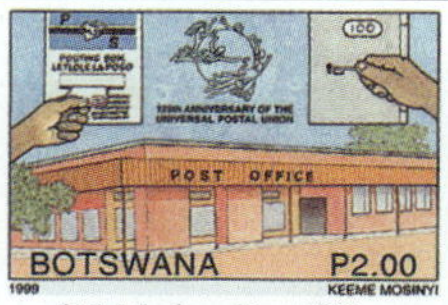

211 Modern Post Office

1999. 125th Anniv of Universal Postal Union.
904 **211** 2p. multicoloured . . . . 1·50 1·50

212 Mpule Kwelagobe winning contest

1999. Mpule Kwelagobe ("Miss Universe 1999"). Multicoloured.
905 35t. Type **212** 35 10
906 1p. In traditional dress (horiz) 75 30
907 2p. In traditional dancing costume with lion . . . . 1·10 60
908 2p.50 Wearing "Botswana" sash (horiz) . . . . . . 1·25 75
909 15p. With leopard in background (horiz) . . . . 7·00 11·00
MS910 175 × 80 mm. Nos. 905/9 9·50 12·00

213 Saddle-bill Stork and Limpopo River

2000. Scenic Rivers. Multicoloured.
911 35t. Type **213** 40 20
912 1p. Hippopotamuses in water lilies (vert) 70 60
913 2p. African skimmer and makoro (dugout canoe) . . 1·25 1·50
914 2p.50 African elephant at sunset, Chobe River (vert) 1·40 2·00

214 Mopane Moth

2000. Moths. Multicoloured.
915 35t. Type **214** 15 10
916 70t. Wild silk moth 25 20
917 1p. Crimson speckled footman ("Tiger Moth") 35 30
918 2p. African lunar moth . . . 65 60
919 15p. Speckled emperor moth 4·75 8·00
MS920 175 × 135 mm. Nos. 915/19 7·50 9·50
No. **MS**920 is in the shape of a moth.

215 Mother reading Medicine Label with Child ("Protect Your Children")

2000. United Nations Literacy Decade. Mult.
921 35t. Type **215** 20 10
922 70t. Adult literacy class ("Never Too Old To Learn") 30 20
923 2p. Man smoking next to petrol pump ("Be Aware Of Danger") . . . . 75 1·10
924 2p.50 Man at Automatic Teller Machine ("Be Independent") . . . . . 90 2·00

216 Pres. Sir Seretse Khama

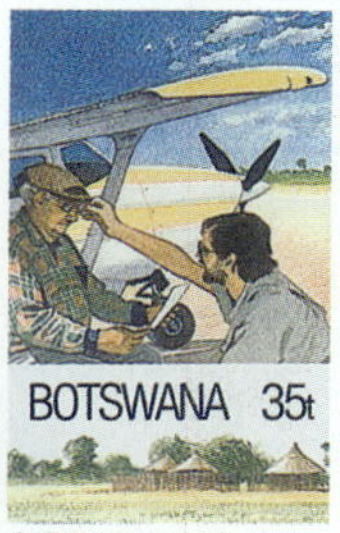

217 Doctor giving Eye Test

2000. Chiefs and Presidents.
925 **216** 35t. black, red and gold 40 10
926 – 1p. multicoloured 65 40
927 – 2p. multicoloured . . . . 1·00 1·10
928 – 2p.50 multicoloured . . . 1·25 2·00
DESIGNS—HORIZ (60 × 40 mm): 35t. Chiefs Sebele I of Bakwena, Bathoen I of Bangwaketse and Khama III of Bangato, 1895. VERT (as T **216**): 2p. Pres. Sir Ketumile Masire; 2p.50, Pres. Festus Mogae.

2000. Airborne Medical Service. Multicoloured.
929 35t. Type **217** 30 10
930 1p. Medical team and family 65 40
931 2p. Aircraft over canoes . . . 1·25 1·40
932 2p.50 Donkeys and mule cart on airstrip . . . . 1·50 2·25

218 Hippopotamus

2000. Wetlands (1st series). Okavango Delta. Mult.
933 35t. Type **218** 50 20
934 1p. Tiger fish and tilapia . . 55 30
935 1p.75 Painted reed frog and wattled crane (vert) . . . . 1·50 1·50
936 2p. Pels fishing owl and vervet monkey (vert) . . . 1·75 1·75
937 2p.50 Nile crocodile, Sitatunga and red lechwe 1·75 1·75
MS938 175 × 80 mm. Nos. 933/7 5·50 5·50
See also Nos. 958/62, 994/**MS**999 and 1009/**MS**1014.

2001. "HONG KONG 2001" Stamp Exhibition. No. **MS**938 overprinted with exhibition logo on sheet margin.
MS939 175 × 80 mm. Nos. 933/7 6·00 7·00

219 Diamonds

2001. Diamonds. Multicoloured. Self-adhesive.
940 35t. Type **219** 55 20
941 1p.75 J.C.B. in open-cast mine . . . . 1·50 1·60
942 2p. Quality inspector . . . . 1·75 1·90
943 2p.50 Diamonds in jewellery 2·00 2·25

220 African Pygmy Falcon

2001. Kgalagadi Transfrontier Wildlife Park. Joint Issue with South Africa. Multicoloured.
944 35t. Type **220** 85 35
945 1p. Leopard . . . . 1·00 70
946 2p. Gemsbok . . . . 1·40 1·60
947 2p.50 Bat-eared fox . . . . 1·60 2·25
MS948 115 × 80 mm. Nos. 945 and 947 . . . . 2·50 3·00

221 Shallow Basket

2001. Traditional Baskets. Multicoloured.
949 35t. Type **221** 20 15
950 1p. Tall basket 35 25
951 2p. Woman weaving basket 60 85
952 2p.50 Spherical basket . . . 65 95
MS953 177 × 92 mm. Nos. 949/52 2·00 3·00

222 Boys by River at Sunset

2001. Scenic Skies. Multicoloured.
954 50t. Type **222** 25 15
955 1p. Woman with baby at sunset 50 25
956 2p. Girls carrying firewood at sunset 75 75
957 10p. Traditional village at sunset near huts . . . . . 2·50 3·50

2001. Wetlands (2nd series). Chobe River. As T **218**. Multicoloured.
958 50t. Water monitor and carmine bee-eater 65 20
959 1p.75 Buffalo 75 60
960 2p. Savanna baboons (vert) 90 1·00
961 2p.50 Lion (vert) . . . . . . 1·10 1·40
962 3p. African elephants in river 2·25 2·25
MS963 175 × 80 mm. Nos. 958/62 5·00 5·00

223 Black Mamba

2002. Snakes. Multicoloured.
964 50t. Type **223** 45 15
965 1p.75 Spitting cobra (vert) . . 70 45
966 2p.50 Puff adder . . . . . . 80 1·25
967 3p. Boomslang (vert) . . . . 1·00 1·50

224 Mbukushu Pots

2002. Botswana Pottery. Multicoloured.
968 50t. Type **224** 45 10
969 2p. Sekgatla pots 80 75
970 2p.50 Setswana pots . . . . 90 1·10
971 3p. Kalanga pots . . . . . . 1·10 1·50

225 Queen Elizabeth in Evening Dress and Commonwealth Emblem

2002. Golden Jubilee. Multicoloured.
972 55t. Type **225** 65 15
973 2p.75 Queen Elizabeth with bouquet (vert) . . . . . . 1·75 2·00

226 Tree Squirrel

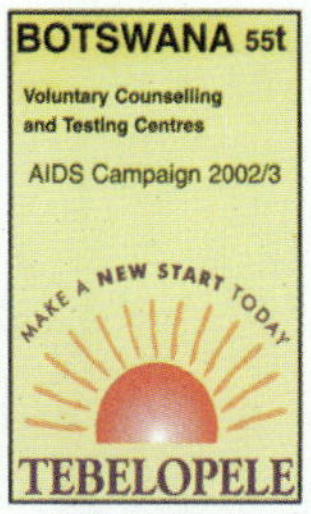

227 Tebelopele (counselling and testing centres) Symbol

2002. Mammals. Multicoloured.
974 5t. Type **226** 10 10
975 10t. Black-backed jackal . . 10 10
976 20t. African wild cat 10 10
977 30t. Slender mongoose (horiz) 15 10
978 40t. African civet (horiz) . . 15 10
979 55t. Elephant 20 15
980 90t. Reedbuck 30 25
981 1p. Kudu 35 35
982 1p.45 Waterbuck 50 50
983 1p.95 Sable (horiz) 60 65
984 2p.20 Sitatunga (horiz) . . . 70 75
985 2p.75 Porcupine (horiz) . . . 80 85
986 3p.30 Serval (horiz) . . . . . 95 1·00
987 4p. Antbear (horiz) . . . . . 1·25 1·40
988 5p. Bushpig (horiz) . . . . . 1·40 1·50
989 15p. Chakma baboon . . . . 3·50 3·75

2002. AIDS Awareness. Multicoloured.
990 55t. Type **227** 60 15
991 1p.10 AIDS ribbon and mother and baby badge . . 1·10 40
992 2p.75 Hands and male gender symbol . . . . 1·75 1·90
993 3p.30 Orphans with foster parent . . . . 1·90 2·25

2002. Wetlands (3rd series). The Makgadikgadi Pans. As T **218**. Multicoloured.
994 55t. Aardwolf 50 15
995 1p.10 Blue wildebeest and zebra 85 30
996 2p.50 Zebra (vert) . . . . . 1·40 1·40
997 2p.75 Flamingo (vert) . . . . 1·75 1·90
998 3p.30 Pelican in flight . . . . 1·90 2·25
MS999 175 × 80 mm. Nos. 994/8 5·75 5·75

228 Lentswe la Baratani ("Hill of Lovers")

2003. Natural Places of Interest. Multicoloured.
1000 55t. Type **228** 35 15
1001 2p.20 Sand dunes . . . . . 1·00 90
1002 2p.75 Moremi Waterfalls (vert) . . . . 1·50 1·50
1003 3p.30 Gcwihaba Cave . . . 1·75 1·90

229 Ngwale

2003. Beetles. Multicoloured.
1004 55t. Type **229** 40 15
1005 2p.20 Kgomo-ya-buru . . . 1·10 70
1006 2p.75 Kgomo-ya-pula . . . 1·40 1·50
1007 3p.30 Lebitse . . . . 1·75 1·90
MS1008 69 × 59 mm. 5p.50 Kgaladuwa . . . . 3·00 3·50

2003. Wetlands (4th series). The Limpopo River. As Type **218**. Multicoloured.
1009 55t. Giraffe 70 35
1010 1p.45 Black eagle and Nile crocodile (vert) . . . . . 1·50 85
1011 2p.50 Ostrich (vert) . . . . 2·00 1·50
1012 2p.75 Klipspringer . . . . 1·60 1·75
1013 3p.30 Serval cat . . . . . . 1·90 2·25
MS1014 175 × 80 mm. Nos. 1010/13 7·00 7·00

230 San People with Birds (Cg'Ose Ntcox'o)

232 Child posting Letter

231 Masimo (working the land)

2004. Kuru Art Project. Multicoloured.
1015 55t. Type **230** 35 20
1016 1p.45 Tree with gum (Nxaedom Qhomatca) . . 75 55
1017 2p.75 Tree with berries (Nxaedom Qhomatca) . . 1·10 1·40
1018 3p.30 Snake (Qgoma Ncokg'o) . . . . 1·50 1·75

2004. Traditional Life Styles. Multicoloured.
1019 80t. Type **231** 50 25
1020 2p.10 Kgotla (village meeting place) . . . . . . 1·25 85
1021 3p.90 Moraka (cattle post) 1·75 1·90
1022 4p.70 Legae (compound within village) . . . . . 2·25 2·50

2004. World Post Day. Multicoloured.
1023 80t. Type **232** 45 25
1024 2p.10 Children sharing a letter . . . . 1·00 85
1025 3p.90 Post man . . . . . . 1·60 1·90
1206 4p.70 Woman reading letter 2·00 2·50

233 Peregrine Falcon (Angola)

2004. 1st Joint Issue of Southern Africa Postal Operators Association Members. Sheet 170 × 95 mm containing T **233** and similar hexagonal designs showing national birds of Association members. Multicoloured.

MS1027 40t. Type **233**; 50t. Two African Fish Eagles in flight (Zambia); 60t. Two African fish eagles perched (Zimbabwe); 70t. Bar-tailed trogon (Malawi) (inscribed "apaloderma vittatum"); 80t. Purple-crested turaco ("Lourie") (Swaziland); 1p. African fish eagle (Namibia); 2p. Stanley ("Blue") crane (South Africa); 5p. Cattle egret (Botswana)	7·00	7·50

The 70t. value stamp is not inscribed with the country of which the bird is a national symbol.

Miniature sheets of similar designs were also issued by Namibia, Zimbabwe, Angola, Swaziland, South Africa, Malawi and Zambia.

234 *Pterodiscus speciosus*

2004. Christmas. Flowers. Multicoloured.

1028	80t. Type **234**	45	25
1029	2p.10 *Bulbine narcissifolia*	85	60
1030	3p.90 *Bulbiana hypogea*	1·60	1·90
1031	4p.70 *Hibiscus micranthus*	2·00	2·50

235 Blackbeard's Store, Phalatswe

2005. Historical Buildings. Multicoloured.

1032	80t. Type **235**	45	25
1033	2p.10 Primary School	85	60
1034	3p.90 Telegraph Office, Phalatswe	1·60	1·90
1035	4p.70 Magistrate's Court, Phalatswe	2·00	2·50

236 Cowpeas ("beans") **238** Namaqua Dove

237 Black-footed Cat with Prey

2005. Edible Crops. Multicoloured.

1036	80t. Type **236**	35	20
1037	2p.10 Pearl millet	75	55
1038	3p.90 Sorghum	1·40	1·60
1039	4p.70 Watermelon	1·75	2·00

2005. Endangered Species. Black-footed Cat (*Felis nigripes*). Multicoloured.

1040	80t. Type **237**	45	20
1041	2p.10 Black-footed cat	85	60
1042	3p.90 With cub	1·60	1·75
1043	4p.70 In close-up	2·00	2·25
MS1044	160 × 185 mm. Nos. 1040/3, × 2	7·00	7·50

2005. Christmas. Doves and Pigeons. Multicoloured.

1045	80t. Type **238**	45	20
1046	2p.10 Red-eyed dove	85	60
1047	3p.90 Laughing doves (pair)	1·60	1·75
1048	4p.70 Green pigeons (pair)	2·00	2·25

239 Nembwe

2006. Okavango Fish. Multicoloured.

1049	80t. Type **239**	25	30
1050	2p.10 Tiger fish	65	70
1051	3p.90 Pike	1·10	1·25
1052	4p.70 Spotted squeaker	1·50	1·75

240 Oxen

2006. Tswana Cattle. Multicoloured.

1053	1p.10 Type **240**	25	30
1054	2p.60 Cows and calves	70	75
1055	4p.10 Bulls	1·10	1·25
1056	4p.90 Horn shapes	1·50	1·75

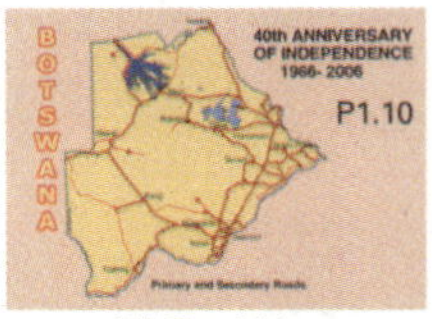

241 Road Map

2006. 40th Anniv of Independence. Showing maps of Botswana. Multicoloured.

1057	1p.10 Type **241**	25	30
1058	2p.60 Population distribution	65	70
1059	4p.10 Mines and coal resources	1·10	1·25
1060	4p.90 National parks and game reserves	1·50	1·75

242 *Hyphaene petersiana*

2006. Christmas. Trees. Multicoloured.

1062	1p.10 Type **242**	25	30
1063	2p.60 *Phoenix reclinata*	65	70
1064	4p.10 *Hyphaene petersiana*	1·10	1·25
1065	4p.90 *Phoenix reclinata*	1·50	1·75

POSTAGE DUE STAMPS

1967. Nos. D10/12 of Bechuanaland optd **REPUBLIC OF BOTSWANA**.

D13 D **1**	1c. red	15	1·75
D14	2c. violet	15	1·75
D15	5c. green	20	1·75

D **5** African Elephant D **6** Common Zebra

1971.

D16 D **5**	1c. red	1·10	3·25
D17	2c. violet	1·40	3·50
D18	6c. brown	1·75	5·50
D19	14c. green	2·00	7·50

1977.

D25a D **6**	1t. black and red	40	1·25
D26a	2t. black and green	40	1·25
D27a	4t. black and red	40	1·25
D28a	10t. black and blue	40	1·25
D29a	16t. black and brown	50	1·50

BOYACA Pt. 20

One of the states of the Granadine Confederation. A Department of Colombia from 1886, now uses Colombian stamps.

100 centavos = 1 peso.

1 Mendoza Perez

1899. Imperf or perf.

1 **1** 5c. green	60	1·50

2 **6** Battle of Boyaca Monument

1903. Imperf or perf.

3 **2**	10c. grey	15	15
4	10c. blue	60	60
12 –	10c. orange	20	15
5 **2**	20c. brown	20	20
5a	20c. lake	25	25
6 –	50c. turquoise	15	15
8 –	1p. red	20	15
9 –	1p. red	1·40	1·40
10 **6**	5p. black on red	50	35
11 –	10p. black on buff	50	40

DESIGNS—As Type **2**: 10c. orange, Building; 50c. Gen. Pinzon; 1p. Figure of value. As Type **6**: 10p. Pres. Marroquin.

BRAZIL Pt. 20

A country in the N.E. of S. America. Portuguese settlement, 1500. Kingdom, 1815. Empire, 1822. Republic from 1889.

1843. 1000 reis = 1 milreis.
1942. 100 centavos = 1 cruzeiro.
1986. 100 centavos = 1 cruzado.
1990. 100 centavos = 1 cruzeiro.
1994. 100 centavos = 1 real.

1 "Bull's Eye"

1843. Imperf.

4 **1**	30r. black	£2250	£375
5	60r. black	£600	£200
6	90r. black	£2250	£950

2 **3** **4**

1844. Imperf.

10 **2**	10r. black	£120	24·00
11	30r. black	£150	35·00
12	60r. black	£120	24·00
13	90r. black	£900	£140
14	180r. black	£3750	£1100
15	300r. black	£4750	£1400
16	600r. black	£4500	£1600

1850. Imperf.

17 **3**	10r. black	30·00	26·00
18	20r. black	90·00	£110
19	30r. black	12·00	3·50
20	60r. black	12·00	2·50
21	90r. black	95·00	12·00
22	180r. black	£120	55·00
23	300r. black	£350	70·00
24	600r. black	£450	80·00

1854. Imperf.

25 **3**	10r. blue	12·00	9·00
26	30r. blue	35·00	55·00
27 **4**	280r. red	£120	85·00
28	430r. yellow	£190	£120

5 **6**

17 Emperor Dom Pedro II

1866. Various frames, but in T **5** the Emperor has a dark beard. Perf or roul.

43 **5**	10r. red	9·00	5·25
44a **6**	20r. purple	12·00	3·00
45 **5**	50r. blue	20·00	1·75
46a	80r. purple	55·00	4·75
47a	100r. green	20·00	1·25
55 **6**	200r. black	48·00	4·75
67 **17**	300r. green and orange	90·00	24·00
56 **5**	500r. orange	£160	24·00

12 **13**

1878. Various frames, but in T **13** the Emperor's beard is white. Roulette.

57 **12**	10r. red	9·00	3·00
58 **13**	20r. mauve	12·00	2·40
59 **12**	50r. blue	18·00	1·75
60	80r. red	20·00	9·50
61	100r. green	20·00	1·25
62	200r. black	£110	15·00
63	260r. brown	60·00	20·00
64	300r. brown	60·00	6·00
65	700r. red	£130	80·00
66	1000r. grey	£140	35·00

21 **27** Pedro II

1881. Various frames. Perf.

71 **21**	10r. black	12·00	26·00
72	10r. orange	3·00	1·75
73	50r. blue	30·00	3·00
74	100r. olive	50·00	3·00
77	100r. lilac	£175	1·75
75a	200r. red	42·00	3·50

No. 77 is inscr "CORREIO".

1884.

81 **27** 100r. lilac	£175	3·50

25 **26** **29**

30 Southern Cross **31** **32**

33 Entrance to Bay of Rio de Janeiro **35** Southern Cross

1884.

78 **25**	20r. green	24·00	3·50
80 **26**	50r. blue	20·00	5·25
83 **29**	100r. lilac	48·00	1·75
84 **30**	300r. blue	£200	26·00
85a **31**	500r. olive	£110	12·00

86	32	700r. lilac	75·00	£125
87	33	1000r. blue	£225	£125

1890.

97a	35	20r. green	2·40	2·40
89		50r. green	4·75	2·40
110a		100r. purple	30·00	1·75
91		200r. violet	10·50	2·40
100		300r. slate	70·00	6·00
92		300r. blue	70·00	6·00
93		500r. buff	18·00	10·50
94		500r. grey	18·00	10·50
95		700r. brown	26·00	35·00
96		1000r. yellow	18·00	3·50

37 Head of Liberty

38 Head of Liberty

1891.

111d	37	100r. red and blue	35·00	1·75

1893.

114	38	100r. red	70·00	1·75

39 Sugar-loaf Mountain

41 Head of Liberty

43 Head of Mercury

1894.

124	39	10r. blue and red	1·90	60
125		20r. blue and orange	90	45
126		50r. blue	5·25	3·50
232		50r. green	9·00	3·75
127	41	100r. black and red	3·50	40
239		100r. red	18·00	35
128		200r. black and orange	90	35
234		200r. blue	10·50	35
129		300r. black and green	14·00	60
153		500r. black and blue	26·00	1·75
131a		700r. black and mauve	14·50	1·75
132	43	1000r. mauve and green	55·00	1·75
133		2000r. purple and grey	55·00	12·00

1897. As T **39** but inscr "REIS REIS" instead of "DEZ REIS".

165a	10r. blue and red	1·60	60

1898. Newspaper stamps of 1889 surch **1898** between value twice in figures.

168	N 34	100r. on 50r. orange	1·90	55·00
169		200r. on 100r. mauve	3·50	95
170		300r. on 200r. black	3·50	95
171		500r. on 300r. red	5·25	4·00
173		700r. on 500r. green	7·00	1·75
172		700r. on 500r. orange	7·00	18·00
174		1000r. on 700r. orange	35·00	35·00
175		1000r. on 700r. blue	25·00	18·00
176		2000r. on 1000r. orange	25·00	18·00
177		2000r. on 1000r. brown	19·00	7·00

1898. Newspaper stamp of 1890 surch **200** over **1898**.

180	N 37	200r. on 100r. mauve	14·00	9·00

1898. Newspaper stamps of 1890 surch **1898** over new value.

182	N 38	20r. on 10r. blue	1·75	3·50
183		50r. on 20r. green	9·00	10·50
184		100r. on 50r. green	18·00	21·00

1899. Postage stamps of 1890 surch **1899** over new value.

194	35	50r. on 20r. green	1·75	3·50
195		100r. on 50r. green	1·75	3·50
196		300r. on 200r. violet	9·00	18·00
190b		500r. on 300r. slate	55·00	12·50
190		500r. on 300r. blue	55·00	12·50
191		700r. on 500r. buff	35·00	10·50
192a		1,000r. on 700r. brown	25·00	10·50
193		2,000r. on 1,000r. yellow	35·00	5·25

50 Discovery of Brazil

52 Emancipation of Slaves

1900. 400th Anniv of Discovery of Brazil.

226	50	100r. red	7·00	3·50
227	–	200r. green and yellow	7·00	3·50
228	52	500r. blue	7·00	3·50
229	–	700r. green	7·00	3·50

DESIGNS—HORIZ: 200r. Declaration of Independence. VERT: 700r. Allegory of Republic.

56 Pan-American Congress

1906.

259a	56	100r. red	42·00	26·00
259b		200r. blue	90·00	8·75

57 Aristides Lobo

61 Liberty

1906.

260	57	10r. grey	90	20
261	–	20r. violet	90	20
262	–	50r. green	90	20
264	–	100r. red	1·75	20
265	–	200r. blue	1·75	20
267	–	300r. brown	3·50	60
268	–	400r. olive	26·00	1·75
269	–	500r. violet	5·25	60
272	–	600r. olive	2·75	90
273	–	700r. brown	5·25	2·75
274	61	1000r. red	28·00	90
275	–	1000r. green	3·50	35
276	–	1000r. grey	19·00	60
277	61	2000r. green	18·00	60
278		2000r. blue	9·00	90
279		5000r. pink	7·00	1·75
280	–	5000r. brown	55·00	10·50
281	–	10000r. brown	7·00	1·75

PORTRAITS: 20r. B. Constant. 50r. A. Cabral. 100r. Wandendkolk. 200r. D. da Fonseca. 300r. F. Peixoto. 400r., 600r. P. de Moraes. 500r. C. Salles. 700r., 5000r. (No. 280) R. Alves. 1000r. (Nos. 275/6) B. do Rio Branco. 10000r. N. Pecanha.

64 King Carlos and Pres. Affonso Penna and Emblems of Portuguese-Brazilian Amity

65 Emblems of Peace, Commerce and Industry

1908. Centenary of Opening of Brazilian Ports to Foreign Commerce.

282	64	100r. red	14·50	1·75

1908. National Exhibition, Rio de Janeiro.

283	65	100r. red	45·00	2·40

66 Bonifacio, San Martin, Hidalgo, Washington, O'Higgins, Bolivar

67 Cape Frio

1909. Pan-American Congress, Rio de Janeiro.

284	66	200r. blue	14·50	1·25

1915. 300th Anniv of Discovery of Cape Frio.

285	67	100r. turquoise on yellow	7·00	5·25

69 Bay of Guajara

1916. 300th Anniv of City of Belem.

286	69	100r. red	12·50	5·00

70 Revolutionary Flag

1917. Centenary of Pernambuco Revolution.

287	70	100r. blue	18·00	9·00

71 Liberty

72 Liberty

74 Inscr "BRAZIL"

1918. Various frames.

288	71	10r. brown	60	35
289		20r. violet	60	35
290		25r. grey	60	35
291		50r. green	1·75	60
292	72	100r. red	1·75	35
293		200r. blue	7·00	45
294		300r. orange	19·00	3·50
295		500r. purple	19·00	3·50
296		600r. orange	2·75	8·75
297	74	1000r. blue	7·00	35
298		2000r. brown	26·00	7·00
299		5000r. lilac	7·00	7·00
300		10,000r. red	9·00	1·00

77 Steam Locomotive

78 "Industry"

79 "Agriculture"

80 "Aviation"

81 Mercury

82 "Shipping"

1920. T 74 inscr "BRASIL".

317	77	10r. purple	60	60
387	80	10r. brown	35	35
318	77	20r. grey	60	60
388	80	20r. violet	35	35
389	78	25r. purple	35	1·10
354	79	40r. brown	60	60
306	78	50r. green	1·25	60
355		50r. brown	60	60
390	80	50r. purple	35	35
391		50r. green	35	35
308	79	80r. green	20	3·50
309	80	100r. red	3·50	60
392		100r. orange	60	35
367		100r. green	1·25	60
420		100r. yellow	1·75	35
311		150r. violet	1·75	60
312		200r. blue	5·25	60
330		200r. red	1·25	60
383		200r. green	4·75	60
405	81	300r. grey	60	35
394		300r. green	1·50	35
333		300r. red	1·25	35
406		400r. blue	1·50	35
335		400r. orange	1·25	3·50
407		500r. brown	1·75	35
385		500r. blue	2·40	60
397		600r. brown	9·00	30
422		600r. orange	5·25	35
341	82	600r. orange	1·75	60
409	81	700r. violet	3·50	35
342	82	1000r. purple	3·50	35
410	81	1000r. blue	9·00	35
362c	74	2000r. blue	10·50	1·25
411		2000r. violet	10·50	1·25
363a		5000r. brown	21·00	1·25
364		10000r. purple	21·00	1·75

93 King Albert and Pres. Pessoa

1920. Visit of King of the Belgians.

431	93	100r. red	70	50

94 Declaration of Ypiranga

97 Brazilian Army entering Bahia

1922. Centenary of Independence.

432	94	100r. blue	5·25	90
433	–	200r. red	10·50	60
434	–	300r. green	10·50	60

DESIGNS: 200r. Dom Pedro I and J. Bonifacio; 300r. National Exn. and Pres. Pessoa.

1923. Centenary of Capture of Bahia from the Portuguese.

435	97	200r. red	12·00	7·00

98 Arms of the Confederation

99 Ruy Barbosa

1924. Centenary of Confederation of the Equator.

436	98	200r. multicoloured	3·50	1·90

1927.

438b	99	1000r. red	2·40	1·25

100 "Justice"

1927. Centenary of Law Courses.

439	100	100r. blue	1·75	60
440	–	200r. red	1·25	35

DESIGN: 200r. Map and Balances.

1928. Air. Official stamps of 1913, Type O **67**, surch **SERVICO AEREO** and new value. Centres in black.

441	50r. on 10r. grey	35	35
442	200r. on 1000r. brown	2·40	4·50
443	200r. on 2000r. brown	1·25	9·50
444	200r. on 5000r. bistre	1·50	1·25
445	300r. on 500r. yellow	1·50	1·90
446	300r. on 600r. purple	90	65
447	500r. on 50r. grey	1·50	65
448	1000r. on 20r. olive	1·25	35
449	2000r. on 100r. red	2·25	1·50
450	2000r. on 200r. blue	3·00	1·60
451	2000r. on 10,000r. black	2·25	65
452	5000r. on 20,000r. blue	8·75	3·75
453	5000r. on 50,000r. green	8·75	3·75
454	5000r. on 100,000r. red	24·00	30·00
455	10,000r. on 500,000r. brown	24·00	24·00
456	10,000r. on 1,000,000r. sepia	24·00	24·00

104 Liberty holding Coffee Leaves

106 Ruy Barbosa

1928. Bicent of Introduction of the Coffee Plant.

457	104	100r. green	3·50	2·40
458		200r. red	1·75	1·25
459		300r. black	10·50	60

1928. Official stamps of 1919 surch.

460	O 77	700r. on 500r. orange	9·00	9·00
461		1000r. on 100r. red	5·25	60
462		2000r. on 200r. blue	7·00	1·25
463		5000r. on 50r. green	7·00	1·75
464		10,000r. on 10r. brown	25·00	1·75

1929.

465	106	5000r. blue	21·00	1·25

108 Santos Dumonts Airship "Ballon No. 6"

109 Santos Dumont

1929. Air.

469	–	50r. green	15	10
470	108	200r. red	1·50	15
471	–	300r. blue	2·00	15
472	–	500r. purple	2·40	15
473	–	1000r. brown	7·00	25
479	–	2000r. green	12·00	1·25
480	–	5000r. red	14·50	1·40
481	109	10,000r. grey	14·50	3·00

DESIGNS: 50r. De Gusmao's monument; 300r. A. Severo's airship "Pax"; 500r. Santos Dumont's biplane "14 bis"; 1000r. R. de Barros's flying boat "Jahu"; 2000r. De Gusmao; 5000r. A. Severo.

110

112

1930. Air.
486 **110** 3000r. violet . . . . . . 1·75 1·75

1930. 4th Pan-American Architectural Congress.
487 – 100r. turquoise . . . . . 3·50 3·50
488 **112** 200r. grey . . . . 6·00 2·40
489 – 300r. red . . . . 8·25 3·50
DESIGNS: 100r. Sun rays inscr "ARCHITECTOS"; 300r. Architrave and Southern Cross.

113 G. Vargas and J. Pessoa – "Redemption of Brazil"
114 O. Aranha – "What is the matter?"

1931. Charity. Revolution of 3 October 1930.
490 **113** 10r.+10r. blue . . . . . 15 12·00
491 20r.+20r. brown . . . . 15 9·00
492 **114** 50r.+50r. green, red and yellow 15 15
493 **113** 100r.+50r. orange . . . . 1·25 60
494 200r.+100r. green 60 60
495 – 300r.+150r. mult 60 60
496 **113** 400r.+200r. red . . . . . 1·75 1·75
497 500r.+250r. blue . . . . 1·25 90
498 600r.+300r. purple . . . 90 18·00
499 700r.+350r. mult . . . . 1·25 90
500 1$+500r. green, red and yellow . . . . 3·50 60
501 – 2$+1$ grey and red . . . 12·00 1·25
502 – 5$+2$ 500r. black & red 24·00 12·00
503 – 10$+5$ green & yellow . . 60·00 18·00
DESIGNS: 300r., 700r. as Type **113**, but portraits in circles and frames altered. Milreis values as Type **114** with different portraits and frames.

1931. No. 333 surch **1931 200 Reis**.
507 **81** 200r. on 300r. red 60 35

1931. Zeppelin Air Stamps. Surch **ZEPPELIN** and value.
508 **108** 2$500 on 200r. red (No. 470) . . . . . . 35·00 35·00
511 **106** 3$500 on 5000r. blue (No. 468b) . . . . . . 25·00 25·00
509 – 5$000 on 300r. blue (No. 471) . . . . . . 45·00 45·00
512 **74** 7$000 on 10,000r. red (No. 364) . . . . . . 28·00 28·00

1931. Air. No. 486 surch **2.500 REIS**.
510 **110** 2500r. on 3000r. violet . . 26·00 26·00

121 Brazil

1932. 400th Anniv of Colonization of Sao Vicente.
513 **121** 20r. purple 35 35
514 – 100r. black 90 90
515 – 200r. violet . . . . 1·75 35
516 – 600r. brown . . . . . . 3·00 2·75
517 – 700r. blue . . . . 3·50 3·00
DESIGNS: 100r. Natives; 200r. M. Afonso de Souza; 600r. King John III of Portugal; 700r. Founding of Sao Vicente.

125 Soldier and Flag
130 "Justice"

1932. Sao Paulo Revolutionary Government issue.
518 – 100r. brown . . . . . . 1·25 3·50
519 **125** 200r. red . . . . 60 1·25
520 – 300r. green . . . . 2·40 7·00
521 – 400r. blue . . . . 5·25 9·00
522 – 500r. sepia . . . . 7·00 9·00
523 – 600r. red . . . . 7·00 9·00
524 **125** 700r. violet . . . . 3·50 9·00
525 – 1000r. orange . . . . . . 2·40 9·00
526 – 2000r. brown . . . . . . 21·00 35·00
527 – 5000r. green . . . . . . 26·00 60·00
528 **130** 10,000r. purple . . . . . 30·00 70·00
DESIGNS—As Type **125**: 100, 500r. Map of Brazil; 300r., 600r. Symbolical of freedom, etc., 400, 1000r. Soldier in tin helmet. As Type **130**: 2000r. "LEX" and sword; 5000r. "Justice" and soldiers with bayonets.

131 Campo Bello Square and memorial. Vassouras

1933. Centenary of Vassouras.
529 **131** 200r. red . . . . 1·25 1·25

132 Flag and Dornier Wal Flying Boat

1933. Air.
532 **132** 3500r. blue, green & yell 1·75 1·75

1933. Surch **200 REIS**.
536 **81** 200r. on 300r. red 60 60

134 Flag of the Race

1933. 441st Anniv of Departure of Columbus from Polos.
537 **134** 200r. red . . . . 1·75 1·25

135 Christian Symbols
137 Faith and Energy

136 From Santos Dumont Statue, St. Cloud

1933. 1st Eucharistic Congress, Sao Salvador.
538 **135** 200r. red 70 40

1933. Obligatory Tax for Airport Fund.
539 **136** 100r. purple 60 10

1933.
540 **137** 200r. red 60 35
543 200r. violet . . . . 1·25 35

138 "Republic" and Flags
139 Santos Dumont Statue, St. Cloud

1933. Visit of Pres. Justo of Argentina.
545 **138** 200r. blue 65 60
546 400r. green . . . . 1·75 1·75
547 600r. red . . . . 5·25 7·00
548 1000r. violet . . . . . . 7·00 5·25

1934. 1st National Aviation Congress, Sao Paulo.
549 **139** 200r. blue . . . . 1·25 70

140 Exhibition Building

1934. 7th International Sample Fair, Rio de Janeiro.
550 **140** 200r. brown 65 65
551 400r. red . . . . 3·50 3·50
552 700r. blue . . . . 3·50 3·00
553 1000r. orange . . . . . . 7·00 1·75

141 Brazilian Stamp of 1844

1934. National Philatelic Exhibition, Rio. Imperf.
555 **141** 200r.+100r. purple . . . 1·25 3·00
556 300r.+100r. red . . . . 1·25 3·00
557 700r.+100r. blue . . . . 6·00 24·00
558 1000r.+100r. black . . . 6·00 24·00

142 Christ of Mt. Corcovado
145 "Brazil" and "Uruguay"

143 Jose de Anchieta

1934. Visit of Cardinal Pacelli.
559 **142** 300r. red . . . . 3·00 3·00
560 700r. blue . . . . 12·00 12·00

1934. 400th Anniv of Founding of Sao Paulo by Anchieta.
561 **143** 200r. brown . . . . . . 1·25 1·25
562 300r. violet . . . . 1·25 60
563 700c. blue . . . . 3·00 3·50
564 1000r. green . . . . . . 5·25 2·40

1935. Visit of President Terra of Uruguay.
565 – 200r. orange 65 60
566 **145** 300r. yellow . . . . . . 1·25 1·75
567 700r. blue . . . . 8·75 15·00
568 – 1000r. violet . . . . . . 18·00 10·50
DESIGN—HORIZ: 200, 1000r. Female figures as in Type **145** and bridge.

146 Town of Igarassu

1935. 400th Anniv of Founding of Pernambuco.
569 **146** 200r. brown and red . . . 1·75 1·25
570 300r. olive and violet . . 1·75 90

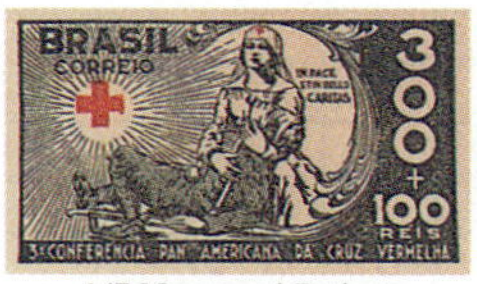

147 Nurse and Patient

1935. 3rd Pan-American Red Cross Conference.
571 **147** 200r.+100r. violet . . . . 3·00 3·00
572 300r.+100r. brown . . . 3·00 3·00
573 700r.+100r. blue . . . . 15·00 13·00

149 Gen. da Silva

1935. Cent of Farroupilha "Ragged Revolution".
574 – 200r. black . . . . 1·75 1·25
575 – 300r. red . . . . 1·25 65
576 **149** 700r. blue . . . . 4·00 10·50
577 – 1000r. violet . . . . . . 5·25 5·25
DESIGNS: 200, 300r. Mounted Gaucho; 1000r. Marshal Caxias.

151 Gavea

1935. Children's Day.
578 **151** 300r. violet and brown . . 2·40 1·60
579 300r. turquoise and black 2·40 1·60
580 300r. blue and green . . . 2·40 1·60
581 300r. black and red . . . 2·40 1·60

152 Federal District Coat of Arms

1935. 8th International Fair.
582 **152** 200r. blue . . . . 3·50 3·50

153 Coutinho's ship "Gloria", 1535

1935. 400th Anniv of Colonization of State of Espirito Santo.
583 **153** 300r. red . . . . 6·00 3·00
584 – 700r. blue . . . . 9·00 6·00
DESIGN—VERT: 700r. Arms of Coutinho.

154a Viscount Cairu
155 Cameta

1936. Death Centenary of Cairu.
585 **154a** 1200r. violet . . . . . . 14·00 9·00

1936. Tercentenary of Founding of Cameta.
586 **155** 200r. buff . . . . 2·40 2·40
587 500r. green . . . . 2·40 1·25

156 Coin Press
157 Scales of "Justice"

1936. Numismatic Congress, Sao Paulo.
588 **156** 300r. brown . . . . . . 1·75 1·75

1936. 1st National Juridical Congress, Rio.
589 **157** 300r. red . . . . 1·25 1·25

158 A. Carlos Gomes

159 "Il Guarany"

1936. Birth Centenary of C. Gomes (composer).
590 **158** 300r. red . . . . 1·25 1·25
591 300r. brown . . . . . . 1·25 1·25
592 **159** 700r. blue . . . . 3·50 1·75
593 700r. buff . . . . 4·75 3·00

1936. 9th International Sample Fair, Rio. As T **152** with inscription and date altered.
594 **152** 200r. red . . . . 1·75 1·25

160 Congress Seal
161 Botafogo Bay

1936. 2nd National Eucharistic Congress, Belo Horizonte.
595 **160** 300r. multicoloured . . . 1·75 1·25

1937. Birth Centenary of Dr. Francisco Pereira Passos.
596 **161** 700r. blue . . . . 1·25 1·25
597 700r. black . . . . 1·25 1·25

162 Esperanto Star and National Flags

1937. 9th Brazilian Esperanto Congress, Rio de Janeiro.

598	**162**	300r. green	1·75	1·25

163 Bay of Rio de Janeiro

1937. 2nd S. American Radio Conference.

599	**163**	300r. black and orange	1·25	1·25
600		700r. brown and blue	3·00	1·75

164 Globe

1937. Golden Jubilee of Esperanto.

601	**164**	300r. green	1·75	1·25

166 Iguazu Falls

1937. Tourist Propaganda.

602	–	200r. blue and brown	1·25	1·25
603	–	300r. green and orange	1·25	1·25
604	**166**	1000r. brown and sepia	3·50	2·40
605	–	2000r. red and green	15·00	16·00
606	**166**	5000r. green and black	30·00	30·00
607	–	10,000r. blue and red	60·00	60·00

DESIGNS—HORIZ: 200, 2000r. Monroe Palace, Rio. VERT: 300, 10,000r. Botanical Gardens, Rio.

168 J. Da Silva Paes **169** Eagle and Shield

1937. Bicent of Founding of Rio Grande do Sul.

608	**168**	300r. blue	1·25	60

1937. 150th Anniv of U.S. Constitution.

609	**169**	400r. blue	1·25	60

170 Coffee

1938. Coffee Propaganda.

610	**170**	1200r. multicoloured	7·00	60

171 "Grito" Memorial **173** Couto de Magalhaes

172 Arms of Olinda

1938. Commemoration of Abortive Proclamation of Republic.

611	**171**	400r. brown	1·25	60

1938. 4th Centenary of Olinda.

612	**172**	400r. violet	1·25	60

1938. Birth Centenary of De Magalhaes.

613	**173**	400r. green	90	60

174 National Archives

1938. Centenary of Founding of National Archives.

614	**174**	400r. brown	90	60

174a Rowland Hill **174b** President Vargas

1938. Brazilian International Philatelic Exhibition (BRAPEX), Rio de Janeiro. T **174a** repeated ten times in sheet together with exhibition emblem.

MS614a	117 × 118 mm. 400r. green	10·00	6·50

1938. 1st Anniv of Constitution issued by President Vargas. T **174b** repeated ten times in sheet together with star emblem.

MS614b	115 × 138 mm. 400r. blue	4·00	4·75

175 Rio de Janeiro **176** Santos

1939.

615	**175**	1200r. purple	2·40	15

1939. Centenary of Santos City.

616	**176**	400r. blue	65	60

177 Chalice-vine and Cup-of-gold Blossoms **178** Seal of Congress

1939. 1st S. American Botanical Congress, Rio.

617	**177**	400r. green	1·25	60

1939. 3rd National Eucharistic Congress, Recife.

618	**178**	400r. red	65	60

179 Duke of Caxias **180** Washington

1939. Soldiers' Day.

619	**179**	400r. blue	65	60

1939. New York World's Fair. Inscr "FEIRA MUNDIAL DE NOVA YORK".

620	**180**	400r. orange	50	25
621	–	800r. green	30	15
622	–	1200r. red	60	15
623	–	1600r. blue	60	25

DESIGNS—HORIZ: 1200r. Grover Cleveland. VERT: 800r. Dom Pedro II; 1m. Water lily; 1600r. Statue of Liberty, Rio de Janeiro; 5m. Bust of Pres. Vargas; 10m. Relief map of Brazil.

184 Benjamin Constant **188** Child and Southern Cross

1939. 50th Anniv of Constitution.

624	**184**	400r. green	90	60
625	–	800r. black	60	60
626	–	1200r. brown	1·50	60

DESIGNS—VERT: 800r. Marshal da Fonseca. HORIZ: 1200r. Marshal da Fonseca and Pres. Vargas.

1940. Child Welfare.

627	–	100r.+100r. violet	60	60
628	–	200r.+100r. blue	1·00	95
629	**188**	400r.+200r. olive	70	60
630	–	1200r.+400r. red	3·00	1·60

DESIGNS: 100r. Three Wise Men; 200r. Angel and Child; 1200r. Mother and Child.

189 Roosevelt, Vargas and American Continents **190** Map of Brazil

1940. 50th Anniv of Pan-American Union.

631	**189**	400r. blue	90	65

1940. 9th National Geographical Congress, Florianopolis.

632	**190**	400r. red	60	60

191 Water Lily **192** Map of Brazil

1940. New York World's Fair (2nd issue). No gum.

633	**191**	1m. violet	2·00	1·60
634	–	5m. red (Pres. Vargas)	8·50	4·25
635	**192**	10m. blue	8·50	2·40
MS635a		Three sheets each 127 × 147 mm. Nos. 633/5 each in block of ten	£190	£275

1940. Birth Centenary of Machado de Assis (poet and novelist). As T **173** but portrait of de Assis, dated "1839–1939".

636		400r. black	50	50

193 Two Workers **195** Brazilian Flags and Head of Liberty

194 Acclaiming King John IV of Portugal

1940. Bicentenary of Colonization of Porto Alegre.

637	**193**	400r. green	65	60

1940. Centenaries of Portugal (1140–1640–1940) (1st issue).

638	**194**	1200r. grey	3·50	60

See also Nos. 642/5.

1940. 10th Anniv of Govt. of President Vargas.

639	**195**	400r. purple	50	50

196 Date of Fifth Census **197** Globe showing Spotlight on Brazil

1941. 5th General Census.

640	**196**	400r. blue & red (postage)	30	10
641	**197**	1200r. brown (air)	5·25	90

199 Father Antonio Vieira **202** Father Jose Anchieta

1941. Centenaries of Portugal (2nd issue).

642	–	200r. pink	15	10
643	**199**	400r. blue	15	10
644	–	800r. violet	20	10
645	–	5400r. green	2·40	90

DESIGNS—VERT: 200r. Alfonso Henriques; 800r. Governor-Gen. Benevides. HORIZ: 5,400r. Carmona and Vargas.

1941. 400th Anniv of Order of Jesuits.

646	**202**	1m. violet	1·25	70

205 Oil Wells **210** Count of Porto Alegre

1941. Value in reis.

647	**205**	10r. orange	10	10
648		20r. olive	10	10
649		50r. brown	10	10
650		100r. turquoise	15	10
651	–	200r. brown	60	35
652	–	300r. red	15	10
653	–	400r. blue	20	10
654	–	500r. red	15	10
655	–	600r. violet	1·75	35
656	–	700r. red	60	35
657	–	1000r. grey	3·50	35
658	–	1200r. blue	5·25	35
659	–	2000r. purple	7·00	35
660	–	5000r. blue	9·00	60
661	**210**	10,000r. red	18·00	60
662	–	20,000r. brown	16·00	60
663	–	50m. red	26·00	26·00
664	–	100m. blue	1·25	7·00

DESIGNS: 200r. to 500r. Wheat harvesting machinery; 600r. to 1200r. Smelting works; 2000r. "Commerce"; 5000r. Marshal F. Peixoto; 20,000r. Admiral Maurity; 50m. "Armed Forces"; 100m. Pres. Vargas.

For stamps with values in centavos and cruzeiros see Nos. 751, etc.

213 Amador Bueno **214** Brazilian Air Force Emblem

1941. 300th Anniv of Amador Bueno as King of Sao Paulo.

665	**213**	400r. black	55	35

1941. Aviation Week.

666	**214**	5400r. green	5·25	2·40

1941. Air. 4th Anniv of President Vargas's New Constitution. Optd **AEREO "10 Nov." 937-941.**

667		5400r. green (No. 645)	5·25	1·75

215 Indo-Brazilian Cow **216** Bernardino de Campos

1942. 2nd Agriculture and Cattle Show, Uberaba.
668a **215** 200r. blue 90 60
669a 400r. brown 90 60

1942. Birth Centenaries of B. de Campos and P. de Morais (lawyers and statesmen).
670 **216** 1000r. red . . . . 3·50 95
671 – 1200r. blue . . . . 9·00 65
PORTRAIT: 1200r. Prudente de Morais.

217 Torch of Learning

218 Map of Brazil showing Goiania

1942. 8th National Education Congress, Goiania.
672 **217** 400r. brown 45 25

1942. Founding of Goiania City.
673 **218** 400r. violet 45 25

219 Congressional Seal

221 Tributaries of R. Amazon

1942. 4th National Eucharistic Congress, Sao Paulo.
674 **219** 400r. brown 60 40

1942. Air. 5th Anniv of President Vargas's New Constitution. No. 645 surch **AEREO "10 Nov." 937-942** and value.
675 5cr.40 on 5400r. green . . . 4·75 2·40

1943. 400th Anniv of Discovery of River Amazon.
676 **221** 40c. brown 90 60

222 Early Brazilian Stamp

223 Memorial Tablet

1943. Centenary of Petropolis.
677 **222** 40c. violet . . . . 1·25 60

1943. Air. Visit of Pres. Morinigo of Paraguay.
678 **223** 1cr.20 blue . . . . 4·75 1·25

224 Map of S. America showing Brazil and Bolivia

225 "Bulls-eye"

226

1943. Air. Visit of President Penaranda of Bolivia.
679 **224** 1cr.20 multicoloured . . . 3·50 90

1943. Centenary of 1st Brazilian Postage Stamps.
(a) Postage. Imperf.
680 **225** 30c. black . . . . 1·75 90
681 60c. black . . . . 2·40 60
682 90c. black . . . . 1·25 90
MS682a 127 × 95 mm. Nos. 680/2. No gum. Imperf . . . . 6·50 6·55

(b) Air. Perf.
683 **226** 1cr. black and yellow . . 3·50 1·25
684 2cr. black and green . . . 4·75 1·25
685 5cr. black and red . . . 6·00 1·75
MS685a 155 × 155 mm. Nos. 683/5. Imperf. No gum . . . . 24·00 24·00

227 Book of the Law

228 Ubaldino do Amaral

1943. Air. Inter-American Advocates Conference.
686 **227** 1cr.20 red and brown . . 2·40 60

1943. Birth Centenary of Ubaldino do Amaral.
687 **228** 40c. grey 60 20

229 Indo-Brazilian Cow

1943. 9th Cattle Show, Bahia.
688 **229** 40c. brown . . . . 1·50 50

230 Justice and Seal

231 Santa Casa de Misericordia Hospital

1943. Centenary of Institute of Brazilian Lawyers.
689 **230** 2cr. red . . . . 3·50 1·75

1943. 400th Anniv of Santa Casa de Misericordia de Santos.
690 **231** 1cr. blue . . . . 1·25 60

232 Barbosa Rodrigues

233 Pedro Americo

1943. Birth Centenary of B. Rodrigues (botanist).
691 **232** 40c. green 40 15

1943. Birth Cent of Americo (artist and author).
692 **233** 40c. brown 90 20

1944. Air. No. 629 surch. **AEREO** and value.
693 **188** 20c. on 400r.+200r. . . . 1·75 90
694 40c. on 400r.+200r. . . . 3·50 90
695 60c. on 400r.+200r. . . . 5·25 60
696 1cr. on 400r.+200r. . . . 5·25 90
697 1cr.20 on 400r.+200r. . . 10·50 60

235 Gen. Carneiro and Defenders of Lapa

236 Baron do Rio Branco

1944. 50th Anniv of Siege of Lapa.
698 **235** 1cr.20c. red . . . . 1·75 60

1944. Inauguration of Monument to Baron do Rio Branco.
699 **236** 1cr. blue . . . . 1·50 60

237 Duke of Caxias

238 Emblems of YMCA

1944. Centenary of Pacification of Revolutionary Uprising of 1842.
700 **237** 1cr.20 green and yellow 1·75 60

1944. Centenary of YMCA.
701 **238** 40c. blue, red and yellow 90 20

239 Rio Grande Chamber of Commerce

240 "Bartolomeo de Gusmao and the Aerostat" (Bernardino de Souza Pereira)

1944. Centenary of Founding of Rio Grande Chamber of Commerce.
702 **239** 40c. brown 90 25

1944. Air. Air Week.
703 **240** 1cr.20 red . . . . 1·25 15

241 Ribeiro de Andrada

1945. Death Cent of M. de Andrada (statesman).
704 **241** 40c. blue 90 15

242 Meeting between Caxias and Canabarro

1945. Cent of Pacification of Rio Grande do Sul.
705 **242** 40c. blue 90 15

244 L. L. Zamenhof

247 Baron do Rio Branco (statesman)

1945. 10th Brazilian Esperanto Congress, Rio de Janeiro.
706 – 40c. green (postage) . . . 90 60
707 **244** 1cr.20 brown (air) . . . . 1·25 60
DESIGN: 40c. Woman and map.

1945. Birth Centenary of Baron do Rio Branco.
708 – 40c. blue (postage) . . . 60 15
709 – 1cr.20 purple (air) . . . . 1·25 50
710 **247** 5cr. purple . . . . . . 4·75 60
DESIGNS—HORIZ: 40c. Bookplate. VERT: 1cr.20, S. America.

248 "Glory"

250 "Co-operation"

1945. Victory of Allied Nations in Europe. Roul.
711 – 20c. violet 50 10
712 **248** 40c. red 50 10
713 – 1cr. orange . . . . 1·75 60
714 – 2cr. blue . . . . 1·75 90
715 **250** 5cr. green . . . . 3·50 1·25
SYMBOLICAL DESIGNS—VERT: 20c. Tranquility (inscr "SAUDADE"). HORIZ: 1cr. "Victory" (inscr "VITORIA"); 2cr. "Peace" (inscr "PAZ").

251 F. M. da Silva

252 Bahia Institute

1945. 150th Birth Anniv of Francisco Manoel da Silva (composer of Brazilian National Anthem).
716 **251** 40c. red . . . . 1·25 60

1945. 50th Anniv of Founding of Bahia Institute of Geography and History.
717 **252** 40c. blue . . . . 1·75 15

253 Shoulder Flash

255 "V" Sign and Flashes

1945. Return of Brazilian Expeditionary Force.
718 **253** 20c. blue, red and green 50 15
719 – 40c. multicoloured 50 15
720 – 1cr. multicoloured . . . . 2·40 50
721 – 2cr. multicoloured . . . . 3·50 1·25
722 **255** 5cr. multicoloured . . . . 6·00 1·25
DESIGNS (embodying shoulder flashes) As Type **253**: 40c. B.E.F. flash. As Type **255**. HORIZ: 1cr. U.S.A. flag; 2cr. Brazilian flag.

256 Wireless Mast and Map

257 Admiral Saldanha da Gama

1945. 3rd Inter-American Radio Communication Conference.
723 **256** 1cr.20 black . . . . . . 1·25 15

1946. Birth Centenary of Admiral S. da Gama.
724 **257** 40c. grey . . . . 90 1·25

258 Princess Isabel d'Orleans-Braganza

261 P.O., Rio de Janeiro

260 Lockheed Super Electra over Bay of Rio de Janiero

1946. Birth Centenary of Princess Isabel d'Orleans-Braganza.
725 **258** 40c. black . . . . 90 1·75

1946. 5th Postal Union. Congress of the Americas and Spain.
726 – 40c. orange and black . . 50 15
727 **260** 1cr.30 orange and green 90 60
728 1cr.70 orange and red . . . 1·25 90
729 **261** 2cr. blue and slate . . . . 1·75 50
730 **260** 2cr.20 orange and blue . . 1·25 90
731 **261** 5cr. blue and brown . . . 4·75 1·25
732 10cr. blue and violet . . . 6·00 90
DESIGN (25 × 37 mm): 40c. Post-horn, V and envelope.

262 Proposed Columbus Lighthouse

1946. Construction of Columbus Lighthouse, Dominican Republic.
733 **262** 5cr. blue . . . . 9·00 2·50

263 "Liberty"

264 Orchid

1946. New Constitution.
734 **263** 40c. grey 10 10

1946. 4th National Exn of Orchids, Rio de Janeiro.
735 **264** 40c. blue, red and yellow 65 10

265 Gen. A. E. Gomes Carneiro

266 Academy of Arts

1946. Birth Cent of Gen. A. E. Gomes Carneiro.
736 **265** 40c. green 35 10

1946. 50th Anniv of Brazilian Academy of Arts.
737 **266** 40c. blue 35 10

267 Antonio de Castro Alves

268 Pres. Gonzalez

1947. Birth Centenary of Castro Alves (poet).
738 **267** 40c. turquoise 35 10

1947. Visit of Chilean President.
739 **268** 40c. brown 35 10

269 "Peace and Security"

270 "Dove of Peace"

1947. Inter-American Defence Conference, Rio de Janeiro.
740 **269** 1cr.20 blue (postage) . . . 90 10
741 **270** 2cr.20 green (air) . . . . 1·25 50

271 Pres. Truman, Map of S. America and Statue of Liberty

1947. Visit of President Truman.
742 **271** 40c. blue 50 10

272 Pres. Enrico Gaspar Dutra

273 Woman and Child

1947. Commemorating Pres. Dutra.
743 **272** 20c. green (postage) . . . 10 10
744 40c. red 15 10
745 1cr.20 blue 50 10
MS746a 130 × 75 mm. Nos. 743/5. No gum. Imperf (air) . . . . . 40·00 70·00

1947. Children's Week. 1st Brazilian Infant Welfare Convention and Paediatrics.
747 **273** 40c. blue 50 10

274 Icarus

1947. Obligatory Tax. "Week of the Wing" Aviation Fund.
748 **274** 40c.+10c. orange 50 10

275 Santos Dumont Monument, St. Cloud, France

276 Arms of Belo Horizonte

1947. Air. Homage to Santos Dumont (aviation pioneer).
749 **275** 1cr.20c. brown & green 1·25 50

1947. 50th Anniv of Founding of City of Belo Horizonte.
750 **276** 1cr.20c. red 65 10

1947. As postage stamps of 1941, but values in centavos or cruzeiros.
751 **205** 2c. olive 20 10
752 5c. brown 20 10
753 10c. turquoise 20 10
754 – 20c. brown (No. 651) . . 50 10
755 – 30c. red (No. 652) . . . . 1·25 10
756 – 40c. blue (No. 653) . . . 50 10
757 – 50c. red (No. 654) . . . . 1·25 10
758 – 60c. violet (No. 655) . . . 1·75 10
759 – 70c. red (No. 656) 60 10
760 – 1cr. grey (No. 657) . . . 3·50 10
761 – 1cr.20 blue (No. 658) . . 5·25 10
762 – 2cr. purple (No. 659) . . 9·00 10
763 – 5cr. blue (No. 660) . . . 18·00 10
764 **210** 10cr. red . . . . 14·00 10
765 – 20cr. brown (No. 662) . . 25·00 10
766 – 50cr. red (No. 663) . . . 55·00 10

277 Rio de Janeiro and Rotary Emblem

278 Globe

279 Quitandinha Hotel

1948. Air. 39th Rotary Congress Rio de Janeiro.
769 **277** 1cr.20 red . . . . 1·25 50
770 3cr.80 violet . . . . . . 3·50 60

1948. International Industrial and Commercial Exhibition, Quitandinha.
771 **278** 40c. grn & mve (postage) 15 10
772 **279** 1cr.20 brown (air) 50 15
773 3cr.80 violet . . . . . . 1·75 15

280 Arms of Paranagua

281 Girl Reading

1948. Tercentenary of Founding of Paranagua.
774 **280** 5cr. brown . . . . 4·75 1·25

1948. National Children's Campaign.
775 **281** 40c. green 15 35

282 Three Muses (after Henrique Bernardelli)

1948. Air. Centenary of National School of Music.
776 **282** 1cr.20 blue . . . . 1·25 10

283 President Berres

1948. Air. Visit of Uruguayan President.
777 **283** 1cr.70 blue 50 10

284 Merino Ram

1948. Air. International Livestock Show, Bage.
778 **284** 1cr.20 orange . . . . . . 1·75 50

285 Congress Seal

286 "Tiradentes" (trans. "Tooth-puller")

1948. Air. 5th National Eucharistic Congress, Porto Alegre.
779 **285** 1cr.20 purple 50 10

1948. Birth Bicentenary of A. J. J. da Silva Xavier (patriot).
780 **286** 40c. orange 10 10

287 Crab and Globe

288 Adult Student

1948. Anti-cancer Campaign.
781 **287** 40c. purple 50 60

1949. Campaign for Adult Education.
782 **288** 60c. purple 50 10

289 Battle of Guararapes

1949. 300th Anniv of 2nd Battle of Guararapes.
783 **289** 60c. blue (postage) . . . 2·40 50
784 – 1cr.20 pink (air) . . . . . 4·75 1·75
DESIGN: 1cr.20, View of Guararapes.

290 St. Francis of Paula Church

291 Father Nobrega

292 De Souza meeting Indians

293 Franklin D. Roosevelt

1949. Bicentenary of Ouro Fino.
785 **290** 60c. brown 50 10
MS785a 70 × 89 mm. No. 785. Imperf . . . . 35·00 45·00

1949. 4th Centenary of Founding of Bahia.
(a) Postage. Imperf.
786 **291** 60c. violet 50 10
(b) Air. Perf.
787 **292** 1cr.20 blue . . . . 1·25 15

1949. Air. Homage to Franklin D. Roosevelt. Imperf.
788 **293** 3cr.80 blue . . . . 2·40 1·75
MS788a 85 × 110 mm. No. 788 8·00 11·00

294 Douglas DC-3 and Air Force Badge

1949. Homage to Brazilian Air Force. Imperf.
789 **294** 60c. violet 50 10

295 Joaquim Nabuco

296 "Revelation"

1949. Air. Birth Centenary of J. Nabuco (lawyer and author).
790 **295** 3cr.80 purple . . . . . . 2·40 10

1949. 1st Sacerdotal Vocational Congress, Bahia.
791 **296** 60c. purple 50 10

297 Globe

1949. 75th Anniv of UPU.
792 **297** 1cr.50 blue 90 10

298 Ruy Barbosa
299 Cardinal Arcoverde

1949. Birth Cent of Ruy Barbosa (statesman).
793 **298** 1cr.20 red . . . . 1·25 15

1950. Birth Cent of Cardinal Joaquim Arcoverde.
794 **299** 60c. pink 50 10

300 "Agriculture and Industry"
301 Virgin of the Globe

1950. 75th Anniv of Arrival of Italian Immigrants.
795 **300** 60c. red 60 10

1950. Centenary of Establishment of Daughters of Charity of St. Vincent de Paul.
796 **301** 60c. blue and black . . . 50 10

302 Globe and Footballers
303 Stadium

1950. 4th World Football Championship, Rio de Janeiro.
797 **302** 60c. grey & bl (postage) 1·25 15
798 **303** 1cr.20 orange and blue (air) . . . . 1·60 50
799 – 5cr.80 yellow, green and blue . . . . 7·00 60
DESIGN—VERT: 5cr.80 Linesman and flag.

304 Three Heads, Map and Graph
305 Line of People and Map

1950. 6th Brazilian Census, 1950.
800 **304** 60c. red (postage) 50 10
801 **305** 1cr.20 brown (air) . . . . 1·25 10

306 Oswaldo Cruz
307 Blumenau and Itajai River

1950. 5th International Microbiological Congress. Rio de Janeiro.
802 **306** 60c. brown 50 10

1950. Centenary of Founding of Blumenau.
803 **307** 60c. pink 50 10

308 Government Offices
309 Arms

1950. Centenary of Amazon Province.
804 **308** 60c. red 60 10

1950. Centenary of Juiz de Fora City.
805 **309** 60c. red 60 10

310 P.O. Building, Recife

1951. Inauguration of Head Post Office, Pernambuco Province.
806 **310** 60c. red 50 10
807 1cr.20 red 60 10

311 Arms of Joinville
312 S. Romero

1951. Centenary of Founding of Joinville.
808 **311** 60c. brown 60 10

1951. Birth Centenary of Sylvio Romero (poet).
809 **312** 60c. brown 60 10

313 De La Salle
314 Heart and Flowers

1951. Birth Tricentenary of Jean-Baptiste de la Salle (educational reformer).
810 **313** 60c. blue 65 10

1951. Mothers' Day.
811 **314** 60c. purple 90 50

315 J. Caetano and Stage
316 O. A. Derby

1951. 1st Brazilian Theatrical Congress.
812 **315** 60c. blue 50 10

1951. Birth Centenary of Derby (geologist).
813 **316** 2cr. slate 65 35

317 Crucifix and Congregation
318 E. P. Martins and Map

1951. 4th Inter-American Catholic Education Congress, Rio de Janeiro.
814 **317** 60c. brown and buff . . . 65 10

1951. 29th Anniv of First Rio–New York Flight.
815 **318** 3cr.80 brown & lemon . . 3·25 50

319 Penha Convent
320 Santos Dumont and Boys with Model Aircraft

1951. 400th Anniv of Founding of Vitoria.
816 **319** 60c. brown and buff . . . 65 10

1951. "Week of the Wing" and 50th Anniv of Santos Dumont's Flight over Paris.
817 **320** 60c. brn & orge (postage) 65 15
818 – 3cr.80 violet (air) . . . . 1·90 20
DESIGN: 3cr.80, "Ballon No. 6" airship over Eiffel Tower.

321 Wheat Harvesters
322 Bible and Map

1951. Wheat Festival, Bage.
819 **321** 60c. green and grey . . . 50 50

1951. Bible Day.
820 **322** 1cr.20 brown . . . . . . 1·25 35

323 Isabella the Catholic
324 Henrique Oswald

1952. 500th Birth Anniv of Isabella the Catholic.
821 **323** 3cr.80 blue . . . . 1·90 50

1952. Birth Centenary of Oswald (composer).
822 **324** 60c. brown 65 10

325 Map and Symbol of Labour
326 Dr. L. Cardoso

1952. 5th Conf of American Members of I.L.O.
823 **325** 1cr.50 red 65 10

1952. Birth Centenary of Cardoso (scientist) and 4th Brazilian Homoeopathic Congress, Porto Alegre.
824 **326** 60c. blue 50 15

327 Gen. da Fonseca
328 L. de Albuquerque

1952. Centenary of Telegraphs in Brazil.
825 **327** 2cr.40 red 65 15
826 – 5cr. blue . . . . 3·50 15
827 – 10cr. turquoise . . . . . 3·50 15
PORTRAITS—VERT: 5cr. Baron de Capanema. 10cr. E. de Queiros.

1952. Bicentenary of Mato Grosso City.
828 **328** 1cr.20 violet 65 10

329 Olympic Flame and Athletes
330 Councillor J. A. Saraiva

1952. 50th Anniv of Fluminense Football Club.
829 **329** 1cr.20 blue . . . . 1·25 60

1952. 100th Anniv of Terezina City.
830 **330** 60c. mauve 65 10

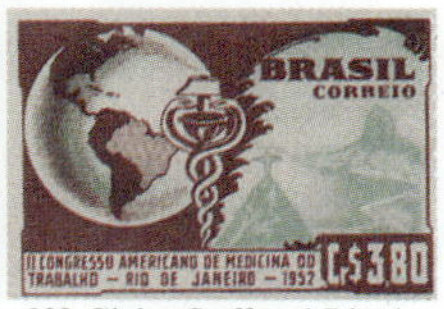

331 Emperor Dom Pedro II
332 Globe, Staff and Rio de Janeiro Bay

1952. Stamp Day and 2nd Philatelic Exhibition, Sao Paulo.
831 **331** 60c. black and blue . . . 65 10

1952. 2nd American Congress of Industrial Medicine.
832 **332** 3cr.80 green and brown 1·60 60

333 Dove, Globe and Flags

1952. United Nations Day.
833 **333** 3cr.80 blue . . . . 2·40 50

334 Compasses and Modern Buildings, Sao Paulo
335 D. A. Feijo (Statesman)

1952. City Planning Day.
834 **334** 60c. yellow, green & blue 50 10

1952. Homage to D. A. Feijo.
835 **335** 60c. brown 60 10

336 Father Damien

1952. Obligatory Tax. Leprosy Research Fund.
836 **336** 10c. brown 50 15
837 10c. green 15 10

337 R. Bernardelli

1952. Birth Centenary of Bernardelli (sculptor).
838 **337** 60c. blue 65 10

338 Arms of Sao Paulo and Settler 339 "Expansion"

1953. 400th Anniv of Sao Paulo (1st issue).
839 **338** 1cr.20 black and brown 1·75 50
840 – 2cr. green and yellow . . 3·50 50
841 – 2cr.80 brown and orange 1·90 15
842 **339** 3cr.80 brown and green 1·90 15
843 5cr.80 blue and green . . 1·50 15
DESIGNS—VERT: (Inscr as Type **339**): 2cr. Coffee blossom and berries; 2cr.80, Monk planting tree.
See also Nos. 875/9.

340 341 J. Ramalho

1953. 6th Brazilian Accountancy Congress, Port Alegre.
844 **340** 1cr.20 brown 95 10

1953. 4th Centenary of Santo Andre.
845 **341** 60c. blue 10 10

342 A. Reis and Plan of Belo Horizonte 343 "Almirante Saldanha" (cadet ship)

1953. Birth Centenary of A. Reis (engineer).
846 **342** 1cr.20 brown 15 10

1953. 4th Voyage of Circumnavigation by Training Ship "Almirante Saldanha".
847 **343** 1cr.50 blue 90 20

344 Viscount de Itaborahy 345 Lamp and Rio-Petropolis Highway

1953. Centenary of Bank of Brazil.
848 **344** 1cr.20 violet 15 10

1953. 10th Int Nursing Congress, Petropolis.
849 **345** 1cr.20 grey 15 10

346 Bay of Rio de Janeiro

1953. 4th World Conference of Young Baptists.
850 **346** 3cr.80c. turquoise 95 10

347 Ministry of Health and Education 348 Arms and Map

1953. Stamp Day and 1st National Philatelic Exhibition of Education, Rio de Janeiro.
851 **347** 1cr.20 turquoise 15 10

1953. Centenary of Jau City.
852 **348** 1cr.20 violet 15 10

349 Maria Quiteria de Jesus 350 Pres. Odria

1953. Death Centenary of Maria Quiteria de Jesus.
853 **349** 60c. blue 10 10

1953. Visit of President of Peru.
854 **350** 1cr.40 purple 15 10

351 Caxias leading Troops 352 Quill-pen and Map

1953. 150th Birth Anniv of Duke of Caxias.
855 **351** 60c. turquoise 35 15
856 – 1cr.20 purple 50 15
857 – 1cr.70 blue 50 15
858 – 3cr.80 brown . . . . . 1·60 15
859 – 5cr.80 violet 85 15
DESIGNS: 1cr.20, Tomb; 1cr.70, 5cr.80, Portrait of Caxias; 3cr.80, Coat of arms.

1953. 5th National Congress of Journalists, Curitiba.
860 **352** 60c. blue 10 10

353 H. Hora 354 President Somoza

1953. Birth Centenary of H. Hora (painter).
861 **353** 60c. purple and orange . . 35 10

1953. Visit of President Somoza of Nicaragua.
862 **354** 1cr.40 purple 20 15

355 A. de Saint-Hilaire 356 J. do Patrocinio and "Spirit of Emancipation" (after R. Amoedo)

1953. Death Centenary of A. de Saint-Hilaire (explorer and botanist).
863 **355** 1cr.20 lake 20 10

1953. Death Centenary of J. do Patrocinio (slavery abolitionist).
864 **356** 60c. slate 10 10

357 Clock Tower, Crato 358 C. de Abreu

1953. Centenary of Crato City.
865 **357** 60c. green 15 10

1953. Birth Centenary of Abreu (historian).
866 **358** 60c. blue 20 10
867 5cr. violet . . . . 1·90 20

359 "Justice" 360 Harvesting

1953. 50th Anniv of Treaty of Petropolis.
868 **359** 60c. blue 15 10
869 1cr.20 purple 15 10

1953. 3rd National Wheat Festival, Erechim.
870 **360** 60c. turquoise 15 10

361 Teacher and Pupils 362 Porters with Trays of Coffee Beans

1953. 1st National Congress of Elementary Schoolteachers, Salvador.
871 **361** 60c. red 15 10

1953. Centenary of State of Parana.
872a – 2cr. brown and black . . 1·75 60
873 **362** 5cr. orange and black . . 2·40 60
DESIGN: 2cr. Portrait of Z. de Gois e Vasconellos.

363 A. de Gusmao 364 Growth of Sao Paulo

365 Sao Paulo and Arms

1954. Death Bicent of Gusmao (statesman).
874 **363** 1cr.20 purple 50 10

1954. 400th Anniv of Sao Paulo (2nd issue).
875 **364** 1cr.20 brown . . . . . . 1·25 90
876 – 2cr. mauve . . . . . . 1·90 65
877 – 2cr.80 violet . . . . . . 3·00 55
878 **365** 3cr.80 green . . . . . . 3·00 55
879 5cr.80 red . . . . 3·00 55
DESIGNS—VERT: 2cr. Priest, pioneer and Indian; 2cr.80, J. de Anchieta.

366 J. F. Vieira, A. V. de Negreiros, A. F. Camarao and H. Dias

1954. 300th Anniv of Recovery from the Dutch of Pernambuco.
880 **366** 1cr.20 blue 50 10

367 Sao Paulo and Allegorical Figure

1954. 10th International Congress of Scientific Organization, Sao Paulo.
881 **367** 1cr.50 purple 15 10

368 Grapes and Winejar 369 Immigrants' Monument

1954. Grape Festival, Rio Grande do Sul.
882 **368** 40c. lake 15 10

1954. Immigrants' Monument, Caxias do Sul.
883 **369** 60c. violet 15 10

370 "Baronesa", 1852 (first locomotive used in Brazil) 371 Pres. Chamoun

1954. Centenary of Brazilian Railways.
884 **370** 40c. red . . . . 1·25 40

1954. Visit of President of Lebanon.
885 **371** 1cr.50 lake 20 10

372 Sao Jose College, Rio de Janeiro 373 Vel Marcelino Champagnat

1954. 50th Anniv of Marists in Brazil.
886 **372** 60c. violet 20 15
887 **373** 1cr.20 blue 20 15

374 Apolonia Pinto 375 Admiral Tamandare

1954. Birth Centenary of Apolonia Pinto (actress).
888 **374** 1cr.20 green 10 10

1954. Portraits.
889 **375** 2c. blue 15 15
890 5c. red 15 10
891 10c. green 15 10
892 – 20c. red 20 10
893 – 30c. slate 55 10
894 – 40c. red . . . . 1·25 10
895 – 50c. lilac . . . . 1·75 10
896 – 60c. turquoise 55 10
897 – 90c. salmon . . . . . . 1·50 15
904a – 1cr. brown . . . . 1·25 50
899 – 1cr.50 blue 25 10
904b – 2cr. green . . . . 1·75 50
904c – 5cr. purple . . . . . . 5·25 10
902 – 10cr. green . . . . . . 2·75 10
903 – 20cr. red . . . . 3·50 30
904 – 50cr. blue . . . . 10·50 10
PORTRAITS—20, 30, 40c. O. Cruz; 50c. to 90c. J. Murtinho; 1cr., 1cr.50, 2cr. Duke of Caxias; 5, 10cr., R. Barbosa; 20, 50cr. J. Bonifacio.

376 Boy Scout

377 B. Fernandes

1954. International Scout Encampment, Sao Paulo.
905 **376** 1cr.20 blue 95 15

1954. Tercentenary of Sorocaba City.
906 **377** 60c. red 10 10

378 Cardinal Piazza

379 Virgin and Map

1954. Visit of Cardinal Piazza (Papal Legate).
907 **378** 4cr.20 red 95 10

1954. Marian Year. Inscr "ANO MARIANO".
908 **379** 60c. lake 55 10
909 – 1cr.20 blue 65 10
DESIGN: 1cr.20, Virgin and globe.
No. 909 also commemorates the Centenary of the Proclamation of the Dogma of the Immaculate Conception.

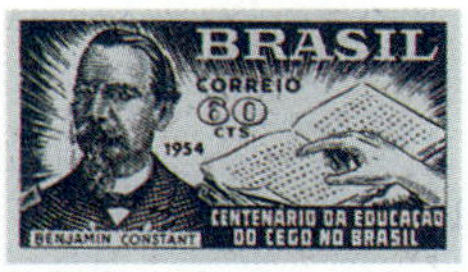

380 Benjamin Constant and Braille Book

1954. Cent of Education for the Blind in Brazil.
910 **380** 60c. green 15 10

381 River Battle of Riachuelo

382 Admiral Barroso

1954. 150th Birth Anniv of Admiral Barroso.
911 **381** 40c. brown 90 15
912 **382** 60c. violet 25 10

383 S. Hahnemann (physician)

384 Nisia Floresta (suffragist)

1954. 1st World Congress of Homoeopathy.
913 **383** 2cr.70 green 95 10

1954. Removal of Ashes of Nisia Floresta (suffragist) from France to Brazil.
914 **384** 60c. mauve 10 10

385 Ears of Wheat

386 Globe and Basketball Player

1954. 4th Wheat Festival, Carazinho.
915 **385** 60c. olive 15 10

1954. 2nd World Basketball Championship.
916 **386** 1cr.40 red 95 15

387 Girl, Torch and Spring Flowers

388 Father Bento

1954. 6th Spring Games.
917 **387** 60c. brown 50 10

1954. Obligatory Tax. Leprosy Research Fund.

918	**388**	10c. blue	15	10
919		10c. mauve	15	10
919a		10c. salmon	15	10
919b		10c. green	15	10
919c		10c. lilac	15	10
919d		10c. brown	15	10
919e		10c. slate	15	10
919f		2cr. lake	15	10
919g		2cr. lilac	15	10
919h		2cr. orange	15	10

See also Nos. 1239/40.

389 Sao Francisco Power Station

1955. Inauguration of Sao Francisco Hydro-electric Station.
920 **389** 60c. orange 15 10

390 Itutinga Power Plant

1955. Inaug of Itutinga Hydro-electric Station.
921 **390** 40c. blue 15 10

391 Rotary Symbol and Rio Bay

392 Aviation Symbols

1955. 50th Anniv of Rotary International.
922 **391** 2cr.70 green and black . . 2·40 10

1955. 3rd Aeronautical Congress, Sao Paulo.
923 **392** 60c. grey and black . . . 15 10

393 Fausto Cardoso Palace

1955. Centenary of Aracaiu.
924 **393** 40c. brown 10 10

394 Arms of Botucatu

1955. Centenary of Botucatu.
925 **394** 60c. brown 10 10
926 1cr.20 green 15 10

395 Young Athletes

396 Marshal da Fonseca

1955. 5th Children's Games, Rio de Janeiro.
927 **395** 60c. brown 50 10

1955. Birth Centenary of Marshal da Fonseca.
928 **396** 60c. violet 10 10

397 Congress Altar, Sail and Sugar-loaf Mountain

398 Cardinal Masella

1955. 36th International Eucharistic Congress.
929 **397** 1cr.40 green 10 10
930 – 2cr.70 lake (St. Pascoal) 90 90

1955. Visit of Cardinal Masella (Papal Legate) to Eucharistic Congress.
931 **398** 4cr.20 blue . . . . 1·75 15

399 Gymnasts

1955. 7th Spring Games.
932 **399** 60c. mauve 20 10

400 Monteiro Lobato

401 A. Lutz

1955. Honouring M. Lobato (author).
933 **400** 40c. green 10 10

1955. Birth Cent of Lutz (public health pioneer).
934 **401** 60c. green 15 10

402 Lt.-Col. T. C. Vilagran Cabrita

403 Salto Grande Dam

1955. Centenary of 1st Battalion of Engineers.
935 **402** 60c. blue 15 10

1956. Salto Grande Dam.
936 **403** 60c. red 15 10

404

405 Arms of Mococa

1956. 18th International Geographical Congress, Rio de Janeiro.
937 **404** 1cr.20 blue 50 10

1956. Centenary of Mococa, Sao Paulo.
938 **405** 60c. red 35 10

406 Girls Running

407 Douglas DC-3 and Map

1956. 6th Children's Games.
939 **406** 2cr.50 blue 65 10

1956. 25th Anniv of National Air Mail.
940 **407** 3cr.30 blue 95 10

408 Rescue Work

1956. Centenary of Firemen's Corps, Rio de Janeiro.
941 **408** 2cr.50 red 90 35

409 Franca Cathedral

410 Open book with Inscription and Map

1956. Centenary of City of Franca.
942 **409** 2cr.50 blue 60 10

1956. 50th Anniv of Arrival of Marist Brothers in N. Brazil.
943 **410** 2cr.50 blue (postage) . . . 50 10
944 – 3cr.30 purple (air) 15 10
DESIGN—VERT: 3cr.30, Father J. B. Marcelino Champagnat.

411 Hurdler

412 Forest and Map of Brazil

1956. 8th Spring Games.
945 **411** 2cr.50 red . . . . 1·25 35

1956. Afforestation Campaign.
946 **412** 2cr.50 green 50 10

413 Baron da Bocaina and Express Letter

414 Commemorative Stamp from Panama

1956. Birth Centenary of Baron da Bocaina.
947 **413** 2cr.50 brown 50 10

1956. Pan-American Congress. Panama.
948 **414** 3cr.30 black and green . . 95 15

415 Santos Dumont's Biplane "14 bis"

1956. Air. 50th Anniv of Dumont's First Heavier-than-air Flight.
MS948a 125 × 156 mm. **415** 3cr. red (in block of four) . . . . . . 8·00 4·50

1956. Air. Alberto Santos Dumont (aviation pioneer) Commemoration.
949 **415** 3cr. green . . . . 1·60 40
950 3cr.30 blue 20 10
951 4cr. purple . . . . 1·25 10
952 6cr.50 brown 20 10
953 11cr.50 orange . . . . . 2·50 30

416 Volta Redonda Steel Mill, and Molten Steel **417** J. E. Gomes da Silva (civil engineer)

1957. Nat Steel Company's Expansion Campaign.
955 **416** 2cr.50 brown 40 10

1957. Birth Centenary of Gomes da Silva.
956 **417** 2cr.50 green 50 10

418 Allan Kardec, Code and Globe

1957. Centenary of Spiritualism Code.
957 **418** 2cr.50 brown 15 10

419 Young Gymnast **420** Gen. Craveiro Lopes

1957. 7th Children's Games.
958 **419** 2cr.50 lake . . . . 1·25 10

1957. Visit of President of Portugal.
959 **420** 6cr.50 blue 95 10

421 Stamp of 1932 **422** Lord Baden-Powell

1957. 25th Anniv of Sao Paulo Revolutionary Government.
960 **421** 2cr.50 red 60 10

1957. Air. Birth Centenary of Lord Baden-Powell.
961 **422** 3cr.30 lake 95 10

423 Convent of Santo Antonio

1957. 300th Anniv of Emancipation of Santo Antonio Province.
962 **423** 2cr.50 purple 15 10

424 Volleyball **425** Basketball

1957. 9th Spring Games.
963 **424** 2cr.50 brown . . . . . . 1·25 10

1957. 2nd Women's World Basketball Championships.
964 **425** 3cr.30 green and brown 1·25 10

426 U.N. Emblem, Map of Suez Canal and Soldier

1957. Air. United Nations Day.
965 **426** 5cr.30 blue 15 30

427 Count of Pinhal (founder), Arms and Locomotive **428** Auguste Comte (philosopher)

1957. Centenary of City of San Carlos.
966 **427** 2cr.50 red 90 30

1957. Death Centenary of Comte.
967 **428** 2cr.50 brown 50 10

429 Sarapui Radio Station

1957. Inauguration of Sarapui Radio Station.
968 **429** 2cr.50 myrtle 50 10

430 Admiral Tamandare (founder) and "Almirante Tamandare" (cruiser) **431** Coffee Beans and Emblem

1957. 150th Anniv of Brazilian Navy.
969 **430** 2cr.50 blue 55 15
970 – 3cr.30 green 70 15
DESIGN: 3cr.30, Aircraft-carrier "Minas Gerais".

1957. Centenary of City of Ribeirao Preto.
971 **431** 2cr.50 red 60 10

432 King John VI of Portugal and Sail Merchantman

1958. 150th Anniv of Opening of Ports to Foreign Trade.
972 **432** 2cr.50 purple 60 10

433 Bugler

1958. 150th Anniv of Corps of Brazilian Marines.
973 **433** 2cr.50 red 50 10

434 Locomotive "Baronesa", 1852, and Dom Pedro II Station, Rio de Janeiro **435** High Court Building

1958. Centenary of Central Brazil Railway.
974 **434** 2cr.50 brown 85 20

1958. 150th Anniv of Military High Courts.
975 **435** 2cr.50 green 15 10

436 Brazilian Pavilion

1958. Brussels International Exhibition.
976 **436** 2cr.50 blue 10 10

437 Marshal C. M. da Silva Ronden **438** Jumping

1958. Rondon Commem and "Day of the Indian".
977 **437** 2cr.50 purple 15 10

1958. 8th Children's Games, Rio de Janeiro.
978 **438** 2cr.50 red 50 10

439 Hydro-electric Station

1958. Inaug of Salto Grande Hydro-electric Station.
979 **439** 2cr.50 purple 15 10

440 National Printing Works **441** Marshal Osorio

1958. 150th Anniv of National Printing Works.
980 **440** 2cr.50 brown 10 10

1958. 150th Birth Anniv of Marshal Osorio.
981 **441** 2cr.50 violet 10 10

442 Pres. Morales of Honduras **443** Botanical Gardens, Rio de Janeiro

1958. Visit of President of Honduras.
982 **442** 6cr.50 green . . . . . . 3·50 90

1958. 150th Anniv of Botanical Gardens, Rio de Janeiro.
983 **443** 2cr.50 green 10 10

444 Hoe, Rice and Cotton **445** Prophet Joel

1958. 50th Anniv of Japanese Immigration.
984 **444** 2cr.50 red 10 10

1958. Bicentenary of Basilica of the Good Jesus, Matosinhos.
985 **445** 2cr.50 blue 35 10

446 Brazil on Globe

1958. Int Investments Conf, Belo Horizonte.
986 **446** 2cr.50 brown 10 10

447 Tiradentes Palace, Rio de Janeiro **448** J. B. Brandao (statesman)

1958. 47th Inter-Parliamentary Union Conf.
987 **447** 2cr.50 brown 10 10

1958. Centenary of Brandao.
988 **448** 2cr.50 brown 10 10

449 Dawn Palace, Brasilia

1958. Construction of Presidential Palace.
989 **449** 2cr.50 blue 10 10

450 Freighters

1958. Govt Aid for Brazilian Merchant Navy.
990 **450** 2cr.50 blue 55 10

451 J. C. da Silva **452** Pres. Gronchi

1958. Birth Centenary of Da Silva (author).
991 **451** 2cr.50 brown 10 10

1958. Visit of President of Italy.
992 **452** 7cr. blue . . . . 1·75 10

453 Archers **454** Old People within Hour-glass

1958. 10th Spring Games, Rio de Janeiro.
993 **453** 2cr.50 orange 90 10

1958. Old People's Day.
994 **454** 2cr.50 lake 15 10

455 Machado de Assis (writer) **456** Pres. Vargas with oily Hand

1958. 50th Death Anniv of Machado de Assis.
995 **455** 2cr.50 brown 10 10

1958. 5th Anniv of State Petroleum Law.
996 **456** 2cr.50 blue 10 10

457 Globe showing Brazil and the Americas **458** Gen. L. Sodre

1958. 7th Inter-American Municipalities Congress, Rio de Janeiro.
997 **457** 2cr.50 blue 50 10

1958. Birth Centenary of Sodre.
998 **458** 3cr.30 green 10 10

459 UN Emblem **460** Footballer

1958. 10th Anniv of Human Rights Declaration.
999 **459** 2cr.50 blue 10 10

1959. World Football Cup Victory, 1958.
1000 **460** 3cr.30 brown & green . . 95 10

461 Map and Railway Line **462** Pres. Sukarno

1959. Centenary of Opening of Patos-Campina Grande Railway.
1001 **461** 2cr.50 brown 30 15

1959. Visit of President of Indonesia.
1002 **462** 2cr.50 blue 10 10

463 Basketball Player **464** King John VI of Portugal

1959. Air. World Basketball Championships 1959.
1003 **463** 3cr.30 brown & blue . . 90 10

1959.
1004 **464** 2cr.50 red 15 10

465 Polo Players

1959. Children's Games.
1005 **465** 2cr.50 brown 20 10

466 Dockside Scene **467** Church Organ, Diamantina

1959. Rehabilitation of National Ports Law.
1006 **466** 2cr.50 green 15 10

1959. Bicent of Carmelite Order in Brazil.
1007 **467** 3cr.30 lake 10 10

468 Dom J. S. de Souza (First Archbishop) **469** Sugar-loaf Mountain and Road

1959. Birth Cent of Archbishop of Diamantina.
1008 **468** 2cr.50 brown 10 10

1959. 11th International Roads Congress.
1009 **469** 3cr.30 blue and green . . 15 10

470 Londrina and Parana **471** Putting the Shot

1959. 25th Anniv of Londrina.
1010 **470** 2cr.50 green 10 10

1959. Spring Games.
1011 **471** 2cr.50 mauve 65 10

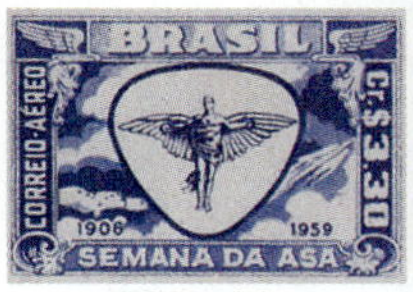

472 Daedalus **473** Globe and "Snipe" Class Yachts

1959. Air. Aviation Week.
1012 **472** 3cr.30 blue 10 10

1959. World Sailing Championships, Porto Alegre.
1013 **473** 6cr.50 green 10 10

474 Lusignan Cross and Arms of Salvador, Bahia **475** Gunpowder Factory

1959. 4th International Brazilian–Portuguese Study Conference, Bahia University.
1014 **474** 6cr.50 blue 10 10

1959. 50th Anniv of President Vargas Gunpowder Factory.
1015 **475** 3cr.30 brown 10 10

476 **477** Sud Aviation Caravelle

1959. Thanksgiving Day.
1016 **476** 2cr.50 blue 50 10

1959. Air. Inauguration of "Caravelle" Airliners by Brazilian National Airlines.
1017 **477** 6cr.50 blue 15 10

478 Burning Bush

1959. Centenary of Presbyterian Work in Brazil.
1018 **478** 3cr.30 green 10 10

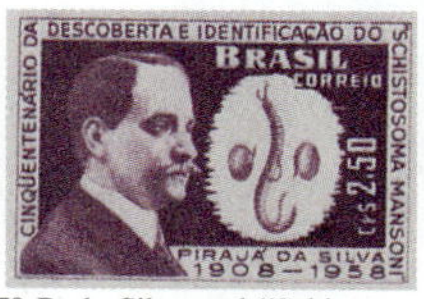

479 P. da Silva and "Schistosoma mansoni"

1959. 50th Anniv of Discovery and Identification of "Schistosoma mansoni" (fluke).
1019 **479** 2cr.50 purple 50 10

480 L. de Matos and Church **481** Pres. Lopez Mateos of Mexico

1960. Birth Centenary of Luiz de Matos (Christian evangelist).
1020 **480** 3cr.30 brown 10 10

1960. Air. Visit of Mexican President.
1021 **481** 6cr.50 brown 10 10

482 Pres. Eisenhower **483** Dr. L. Zamenhof

1960. Air. Visit of United States President.
1022 **482** 6cr.50 brown 15 10

1960. Birth Centenary of Zamenhof (inventor of Esperanto).
1023 **483** 6cr.50 green 35 10

484 Adel Pinto (engineer) **485** "Care of Refugees"

1960. Birth Centenary of Adel Pinto.
1024 **484** 11cr.50 red 25 10

1960. Air. World Refugee Year.
1025 **485** 6cr.50 blue 20 10

486 Plan of Brasilia

1960. Inauguration of Brasilia as Capital.
1026 – 2cr.50 green (postage) . . 15 10
1027 – 3cr.30 violet (air) 10 10
1028 – 4cr. blue . . . . 1·25 10
1029 – 6cr.50 mauve 10 10
1030 **486** 11cr.50 brown 15 10

1960. Miniature Sheet. Birthday of Pres. Kubitschek.
MS1031 110 × 52 mm. 27cr. Orange (postage) 80 70

DESIGNS—Outlines representing: HORIZ: 2cr.50 President's Palace of the Plateau; 3cr.30 Parliament Buildings; 4cr. Cathedral; 11cr.50, 27cr. T **486**. VERT: 6cr.50 Tower.

487 Congress Emblem

1960. Air. 7th Nat Eucharistic Congress, Curitiba.
1032 **487** 3cr.30 mauve 10 10

488 Congress Emblem, Sugar-loaf Mountain and Cross **489** Boy Scout

1960. Air. 10th Baptist World Alliance Congress, Rio de Janeiro.
1033 **488** 6cr.50 blue 10 10

1960. Air. 50th Anniv of Scouting in Brazil.
1034 **489** 3cr.30 orange 10 10

490 "Agriculture" **491** Caravel

1960. Cent of Brazilian Ministry of Agriculture.
1035 **490** 2cr.50 brown 15 10

1960. Air. 5th Death Centenary of Prince Henry the Navigator.
1036 **491** 6cr.50 black 30 10

492 P. de Frontin **493** Locomotive Piston Gear

1960. Birth Cent of Paulo de Frontin (engineer).
1037 **492** 2cr.50 orange 10 10

1960. 10th Pan-American Railways Congress.
1038 **493** 2cr.50 blue 35 10

494 Athlete **495**

1960. 12th Spring Games.
1039 **494** 2cr.50 turquoise 15 10

1960. World Volleyball Championships.
1040 **495** 11cr. blue 60 10

496 Maria Bueno in play

1960. Air. Maria Bueno's Wimbledon Tennis Victories, 1959–60.
1041 **496** 6cr. brown 15 10

497 Exhibition Emblem

1960. International Industrial and Commercial Exhibition, Rio de Janeiro.
1042 **497** 2cr.50 brown & yellow 10 10

498 War Memorial, Rio de Janeiro **499** Pylon and Map

1960. Air. Return of Ashes of World War II Heroes from Italy.
1043 **498** 3cr.30 lake 15 10

1961. Air. Inauguration of Tres Marias Hydro-electric Station.
1044 **499** 3cr.30 mauve 15 10

500 Emperor Haile Selassie **501** Sacred Book and Map of Brazil

1961. Visit of Emperor of Ethiopia.
1045 **500** 2cr.50 brown 10 10

1961. 50th Anniv of Sacre-Coeur de Marie College.
1046 **501** 2cr.50 blue 15 10

502 Map of Guanabara State **503** Arms of Academy

1961. Promulgation of Guanabara Constitution.
1047 **502** 7cr.50 brown 60 10

1961. 150th Anniv of Agulhas Negras Military Academy.
1048 **503** 2cr.50 green 20 10
1049 – 3cr.30 red 10 10
DESIGN: 3cr.30, Military cap and sabre.

504 "Spanning the Atlantic Ocean" **505** View of Ouro Preto

1961. Visit of Foreign Minister to Senegal.
1050 **504** 27cr. blue 95 10

1961. 250th Anniv of Ouro Preto.
1051 **505** 1cr. orange 35 10

506 Arsenal, Rio de Janeiro **507** Coffee Plant

1961. 150th Anniv of Rio de Janeiro Arsenal.
1052 **506** 5cr. brown 45 10

1961. Int Coffee Convention, Rio de Janeiro.
1053 **507** 20cr. brown . . . . . . 2·40 10

508 Tagore **509** 280r. Stamp of 1861 and Map of France

1960. Birth Cent of Rabindranath Tagore (poet).
1054 **508** 10cr. mauve 90 10

1961. "Goat's Eyes" Stamp Centenary.
1055 **509** 10cr. red . . . . 1·25 10
1056 – 20cr. orange . . . . . . 3·75 10
DESIGN: 20cr. 430r. stamp and map of the Netherlands.

510 Cloudburst **511** Pinnacle, Rope and Haversack

1962. World Meteorological Day.
1057 **510** 10cr. brown . . . . . . 1·25 10

1962. 50th Anniv of 1st Ascent of "Finger of God" Mountain.
1058 **511** 8cr. green 10 10

512 Dr. G. Vianna and parasites

1962. 50th Anniv of Vianna's Cure for Leishman's Disease.
1059 **512** 8cr. blue 20 10

513 Campaign Emblem **514** Henrique Dias (patriot)

1962. Air. Malaria Eradication.
1060 **513** 21cr. blue 10 10

1962. 300th Death Anniv of Dias.
1061 **514** 10cr. purple 15 10

515 Metric Measure **516** "Snipe" Sailing-boats

1962. Cent of Brazil's Adoption of Metric System.
1062 **515** 100cr. red . . . . 1·25 10

1962. 13th "Snipe" Class Sailing Championships, Rio de Janeiro.
1063 **516** 8cr. turquoise 20 10

517 J. Mesquita and Newspaper "O Estado de Sao Paulo"

1962. Birth Centenary of Mesquita (journalist and founder of "O Estado de Sao Paulo").
1064 **517** 8cr. bistre . . . . 1·25 10

518 Empress Leopoldina **520** Foundry Ladle

519 Brasilia

1962. 140th Anniv of Independence.
1065 **518** 8cr. mauve 15 10

1962. 51st Interparliamentary Conference, Brasilia.
1066 **519** 10cr. orange 40 10

1962. Inauguration of "Usiminas" (national iron and steel foundry).
1067 **520** 8cr. orange 10 10

521 UPAE Emblem

1962. 50th Anniv of Postal Union of the Americas and Spain.
1068 **521** 8cr. mauve 10 10

522 Emblems of Industry **523** Q. Bocaiuva

1962. 10th Anniv of National Bank.
1069 **522** 10cr. turquoise 15 10

1962. 50th Death Anniv of Bocaiuva (journalist and patriot).
1070 **523** 8cr. brown 10 10

524 Footballer **526** Dr. S. Neiva (first Brazilian P.M.G.)

525 Carrier Pigeon

1962. Brazil's Victory in World Football Championships, 1962.
1071 **524** 10cr. turquoise . . . . . 1·25 10

1962. Tercentenary of Brazilian Posts.
1072 **525** 8cr. multicoloured . . . 10 10
MS1072a 145 × 58 mm. **525** 100cr. multicoloured . . . . 1·00 1·25

1963.
1073 **526** 8cr. violet 50 10
1073a – 30cr. turquoise (Euclides da Cunha) 4·75 10
1073b – 50cr. brown (Prof. A. Moreira da Costa Lima) . . . . 3·50 10
1073c – 100cr. blue (G. Dias) 1·75 10
1073d – 200cr. red (Tiradentes) 7·00 10
1073e – 500cr. brown (Emperor Pedro I) . . . . . . 35·00 20
1073f – 1000cr. blue (Emperor Pedro II) . . . . . . 90·00 60

527 Rockets and "Dish" Aerial

528 Cross

1963. Int Aeronautics and Space Exn, Sao Paulo.
1074 **527** 21cr. blue 60 10

1963. Ecumenical Council, Vatican City.
1075 **528** 8cr. purple 10 10

529 "abc" Symbol

530 Basketball

1963. National Education Week.
1076 **529** 8cr. blue 10 10

1963. 4th World Basketball Championships.
1077 **530** 8cr. mauve 50 10

531 Torch Emblem

1963. 4th Pan-American Games, Sao Paulo.
1078 **531** 10cr. red 65 10

532 "OEA" and Map

533 J. B. de Andrada e Silva

1963. 15th Anniv of Organization of American States.
1079 **532** 10cr. orange 50 10

1963. Birth Bicentenary of Jose B. de Andrada e Silva ("Father of Independence").
1080 **533** 8cr. bistre 10 10

534 Campaign Emblem

1963. Freedom from Hunger.
1081 **534** 10cr. blue 50 10

535 Centenary Emblem

536 J. Caetano

1963. Red Cross Centenary.
1082 **535** 8cr. red and yellow . . . 20 10

1963. Death Centenary of Joao Caetano (actor).
1083 **536** 8cr. black 10 10

537 "Atomic" Development

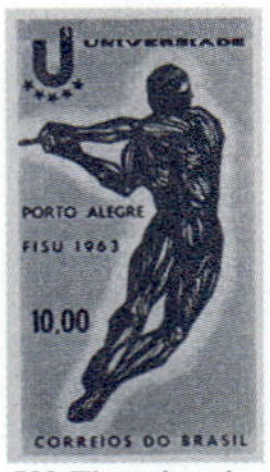

538 Throwing the Hammer

1963. 1st Anniv of National Nuclear Energy Commission.
1084 **537** 10cr. mauve 50 10

1963. International Students' Games, Porto Alegre.
1085 **538** 10cr. black and grey . . 65 10

539 Pres. Tito

540 Cross and Map

1963. Visit of President Tito of Yugoslavia.
1086 **539** 80cr. drab . . . . 2·40 10

1963. 8th Int Leprology Congress, Rio de Janeiro.
1087 **540** 8cr. turquoise 10 10

541 Petroleum Installations

543 A. Borges de Medeiros

542 "Jogos da Primavera"

1963. 10th Anniv of National Petroleum Industry.
1088 **541** 8cr. green 10 10

1963. Spring Games.
1089 **542** 8cr. yellow 10 10

1963. Birth Centenary of A. Borges de Medeiros (politician).
1090 **543** 8cr. brown 10 10

544 Bridge of Sao Joao del Rey

546 Viscount de Maua

545 Dr. A. Alvim

1963. 250th Anniv of Sao Joao del Rey.
1091 **544** 8cr. blue 10 10

1963. Birth Cent of Dr. Alvaro Alvim (scientist).
1092 **545** 8cr. slate 10 10

1963. 150th Birth Anniv of Viscount de Maua (builder of Santos–Jundiai Railway).
1093 **546** 8cr. mauve 45 20

547 Cactus

548 C. Netto

1964. 10th Anniv of North-East Bank.
1094 **547** 8cr. green 10 10

1964. Birth Centenary of Coelho Netto (author).
1095 **548** 8cr. violet 10 10

549 L. Muller

550 Child with Spoon

1964. Birth Cent of Lauro Muller (patriot).
1096 **549** 8cr. red 10 10

1964. Schoolchildren's Nourishment Week.
1097 **550** 8cr. yellow and brown . . 10 10

551 "Chalice" (carved rock), Vila Velha, Parana

552 A. Kardec (author)

1964. Tourism.
1098 **551** 80cr. red 65 10

1964. Cent of Spiritual Code, "O Evangelho".
1099 **552** 30cr. green 95 10

553 Pres. Lubke

554 Pope John XXIII

1964. Visit of Pres. Lubke of West Germany.
1100 **553** 100cr. brown . . . . . 1·25 10

1964. Pope John Commemoration.
1101 **554** 20cr. lake 60 35

555 Pres. Senghor

1964. Visit of Pres. Senghor of Senegal.
1102 **555** 20cr. sepia 15 10

556 "Visit Rio de Janeiro"

1964. 400th Anniv (1965) of Rio de Janeiro.
1103 **556** 15cr. blue and orange . . 25 10
1104 – 30cr. red and blue . . . 65 10
1105 – 30cr. black and blue . . 1·60 40
1106 – 35cr. black and orange . 15 10
1107 – 100cr. brn & grn on yell 65 10
1108 – 200cr. red and green . . 6·00 10
MS1109 Two sheets 129 × 76 mm. containing stamps similar to Nos. 1103, 1107/8 each in brown (sold at 320cr.) and 132 × 78 mm containing stamps similar to Nos. 1104/6 each in orange (sold at 100cr.) . . . . 4·00 4·00

DESIGNS: As Type **556**—HORIZ: 30cr. (No. 1105), Tramway viaduct; 200cr. Copacabana Beach. VERT: 35cr. Estacio de Sa's statue; 100cr. Church of Our Lady of the Rock. SMALLER (24½ × 37 mm): 30cr. (No. 1104), Statue of St. Sebastian.

558 Pres. De Gaulle

559 Pres. Kennedy

1964. Visit of Pres. De Gaulle.
1110 **558** 100cr. brown 95 10

1964. Pres. Kennedy Commemoration.
1111 **559** 100cr. black 15 15

560 Nahum (statue)

1964. 150th Death Anniv of A. F. Lisboa (sculptor).
1112 **560** 10cr. black 30 10

561 Cross and Sword

562 V. Brazil (scientist)

1965. 1st Anniv of Democratic Revolution.
1113 **561** 120cr. grey 15 10

1965. Birth Cent of Vital Brazil.
1114 **562** 120cr. orange . . . . . 1·25 10

563 Shah of Iran

564 Marshal Rondon and Map

1965. Visit of Shah of Iran.
1115 **563** 120cr. red 65 10

1965. Birth Cent of Marshal C. M. da S. Rondon.
1116 **564** 30cr. purple 50 10

565 Lions Emblem

566 I.T.U. Emblem and Symbols

1965. Brazilian Lions Clubs National Convention, Rio de Janeiro.
1117 **565** 35cr. black and lilac . . 15 10

1965. I.T.U. Centenary.
1118 **566** 120cr. green and yellow 65 10

567 E. Pessoa

568 Barrosos Statue

1965. Birth Centenary of Epitacio Pessoa.
1119 **567** 35cr. slate 10 10

1965. Centenary of Naval Battle of Riachuelo.
1120 **568** 30cr. blue 15 10

569 Author and Heroine

571 Scout Badge and Emblem of Rio's 400th Anniv

570 Sir Winston Churchill

1965. Centenary of Publication of Jose de Alencar's "Iracema".
1121 **569** 30cr. purple 15 10

1965. Churchill Commemoration.
1122 **570** 200cr. slate . . . . . . 1·25 10

1965. 1st Pan-American Scout Jamboree, Rio de Janeiro.
1123 **571** 30r. multicoloured . . . 1·10 10

572 ICY Emblem

1965. International Co-operation Year.
1124 **572** 120cr. black and blue . . 1·25 10

573 L. Correia

574 Exhibition Emblem

1965. Birth Centenary of Leoncia Correia (poet).
1125 **573** 35cr. green 10 10

1965. Sao Paulo Biennale (Art Exn).
1126 **574** 30cr. red 10 10

575 President Saragat

576 Grand Duke and Duchess of Luxembourg

1965. Visit of President of Italy.
1127 **575** 100cr. green on pink . . 15 10

1965. Visit of Grand Duke and Duchess of Luxembourg.
1128 **576** 100cr. brown 15 10

577 Curtiss Fledgling on Map

578 OEA Emblem

1965. Aviation Week and 3rd Philatelic Exn.
1129 **577** 35cr. blue 15 10

1965. Inter-American Conference, Rio de Janeiro.
1130 **578** 100cr. black and blue . . 45 10

579 King Baudouin and Queen Fabiola

580 Coffee Beans

1965. Visit of King and Queen of the Belgians.
1131 **579** 100cr. slate 50 10

1965. Brazilian Coffee.
1132 **580** 30cr. brown on cream 65 10

581 F. A. Varnhagen

583 Sister and Globe

582 Emblem and Map

1965. Air. 150th Birth Anniv of Francisco Varnhagen (historian).
1133 **581** 45cr. brown 15 10

1966. Air. 5th Anniv of "Alliance for Progress".
1134 **582** 120cr. blue & turquoise 95 10

1966. Air. Centenary of Dorothean Sisters Educational Work in Brazil.
1135 **583** 35cr. violet 10 10

584 Loading Ore at Quayside

585 "Steel"

1966. Inauguration of Rio Doce Iron-ore Terminal Tubarao, Espirito Santo.
1136 **584** 110cr. black and bistre 50 10

1966. Silver Jubilee of National Steel Company.
1137 **585** 30cr. black on orange . . 35 10

586 Prof. Rocha Lima

587 Battle Scene

1966. 50th Anniv of Professor Lima's Discovery of the Characteristics of "Rickettsia prowazeki" (cause of typhus fever).
1138 **586** 30cr. turquoise 65 10

1966. Centenary of Battle of Tuiuti.
1139 **587** 30cr. green 65 10

588 "The Sacred Face"

589 Mariz e Barros

1966. Air. "Concilio Vaticano II".
1140 **588** 45cr. brown 35 35

1966. Air. Death Centenary of Commander Mariz e Barros.
1141 **589** 35cr. brown 15 10

590 Decade Symbol

591 Pres. Shazar

1966. International Hydrological Decade.
1142 **590** 100cr. blue and brown 65 10

1966. Visit of President Shazar of Israel.
1143 **591** 100cr. blue 95 10

592 "Youth"

593 Imperial Academy of Fine Arts

1966. Air. Birth Centenary of Eliseu Visconti (painter).
1144 **592** 120cr. brown . . . . . 1·90 10

1966. 150th Anniv of French Art Mission's Arrival in Brazil.
1145 **593** 100cr. brown . . . . . 1·75 10

594 Military Service Emblem

595 R. Dario

1966. New Military Service Law.
1146 **594** 30cr. blue and yellow . . 15 10
MS1147 111 × 53 mm. No. 1146. No gum (sold at 100cr.) . . . . . 2·00 2·00

1966. 50th Death Anniv of Ruben Dario (Nicaraguan poet).
1148 **595** 100cr. purple 65 10

596 Santarem Candlestick

597 Arms of Santa Cruz do Sul

1966. Centenary of Goeldi Museum.
1149 **596** 30cr. brown on salmon 15 10

1966. 1st National Tobacco Exn, Santa Cruz.
1150 **597** 30cr. green 15 10

598 UNESCO Emblem

599 Capt. A. C. Pinto and Map

1966. 20th Anniv of UNESCO.
1151 **598** 120cr. black . . . . . . 1·25 35
MS1152 110 × 52 mm. No. 1151. No gum (sold at 150cr.) . . . . . 4·00 2·75

1966. Bicentenary of Arrival of Captain A. C. Pinto.
1153 **599** 30cr. red 15 10

600 Lusignan Cross and Southern Cross

601 Madonna and Child

1966. "Lubrapex 1966" Stamp Exn, Rio de Janeiro.
1154 **600** 100cr. green 95 10

1966. Christmas.
1155 **601** 30cr. green 20 10
1156 – 35cr. blue and orange . . 20 15
1157 – 150cr. pink and blue . . 3·50 3·50
DESIGN—DIAMOND(34 × 34 mm). 35cr. Madonna and child (different). VERT (46 × 103 mm). 150cr. As 35cr. insr "Pax Hominibus" but not "Brazil Correio".

602 Arms of Laguna

1967. Centenary of Laguna Postal and Telegraphic Agency.
1158 **602** 60cr. sepia 10 10

603 Grota Funda Viaduct and 1866 Viaduct

1967. Centenary of Santos–Jundiai Railway.
1159 **603** 50cr. orange . . . . . . 1·40 30

604 Polish Cross and "Black Madonna"

1967. Polish Millennium.
1160 **604** 50cr. red, blue & yellow . . . 50 10

605 Research Rocket **606** Anita Garibaldi

1967. World Meteorological Day.
1161 **605** 50cr. black and blue . . 95 10

1967.

1162	–	1c. blue	10	10
1163	–	2c. red	10	10
1164	–	3c. green	15	10
1165	**606**	5c. black	15	10
1166	–	6c. brown	15	10
1167	–	10c. green	1·40	10

PORTRAITS: 1c. Mother Angelica. 2c. Marilia de Dirceu. 3c. Dr. R. Lobato. 6c. Ana Neri. 10c. Darci Vargas.

607 "VARIG 40 Years" **608** Lions Emblem and Globes

1967. 40th Anniv of Varig Airlines.
1171 **607** 6c. black and blue . . . 15 10

1967. 50th Anniv of Lions International.
1172 **608** 6c. green 25 10
MS1173 130 × 80 mm. No. 1172. Imperf (sold at 15c.) . . . . . 1·50 1·50

609 "Madonna and Child" **610** Prince Akihito and Princess Michiko

1967. Mothers' Day.
1174 **609** 5c. violet 10 10
MS1175 130 × 76 mm. **609** 15c. violet. Imperf . . . . 1·25 1·25

1967. Visit of Crown Prince and Princess of Japan.
1176 **610** 10c. black and red . . . 15 10

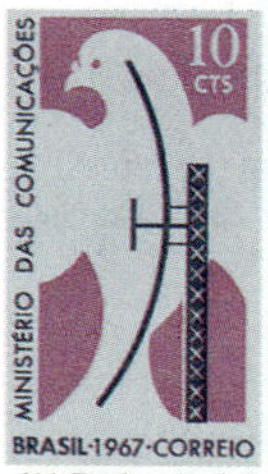

611 Radar Aerial and Pigeon **612** Brother Vicente do Salvador

1967. Inaug of Communications Ministry, Brasilia.
1177 **611** 10c. black and mauve . . 15 10

1967. 400th Birth Anniv of Brother Vicente do Salvador (founder of Franciscan Brotherhood, Rio de Janeiro).
1178 **612** 5c. brown 15 10

613 Emblem and Members **614** Mobius Symbol

1967. National 4-S ("4-H") Clubs Day.
1179 **613** 5c. green and black . . . 15 10

1967. 6th Brazilian Mathematical Congress. Rio de Janeiro.
1180 **614** 5c. black and blue . . . 15 10

615 Dorado (fish) and "Waves"

1967. Bicentenary of Piracicaba.
1181 **615** 5c. black and blue . . . 20 10

616 Papal Arms and "Golden Rose"

1967. Pope Paul's "Golden Rose" Offering to Our Lady of Fatima.
1182 **616** 20c. mauve and yellow 1·25 35

617 General A. de Sampaio

1967. Gen. Sampaio Commem.
1183 **617** 5c. blue 15 10

618 King Olav of Norway **619** Sun and Rio de Janeiro

1967. Visit of King Olav.
1184 **618** 10c. brown 15 10

1967. Meeting of International Monetary Fund, Rio de Janeiro.
1185 **619** 10c. black and red . . . 15 10

620 N. Pecanha (statesman) **621** Our Lady of the Apparition and Basilica

1967. Birth Centenary of Nilo Pecanha.
1186 **620** 5c. purple 10 10

1967. 250th Anniv of Discovery of Statue of Our Lady of the Apparition.
1187 **621** 5c. blue and ochre . . . 15 10
MS1188 80 × 130 mm. **621** 5c. and 10c. each blue and ochre. Imperf 2·00 2·00
No. **MS**1188 was issued for Christmas.

622 "Song Bird" **623** Balloon, Rocket and Airplane

1967. International Song Festival.
1189 **622** 20c. multicoloured . . . 55 35

1967. Aviation Week.
1190 **623** 10c. blue 60 10
MS1191 131 × 76 mm. **623** 15c. blue. Imperf . . . . 2·25 2·25

624 Pres. Venceslau Braz **625** Rio Carnival

1967.

1192	–	10c. blue	35	10
1193	–	20c. brown	1·75	10
1195	**624**	50c. black	12·00	10
1198	–	1cr. purple	18·00	10
1199	–	2cr. green	3·75	10

Portraits of Brazilian Presidents: 10c. Arthur Bernardes. 20c. Campos Salles. 1cr. Washington Luiz. 2cr. Castello Branco.

1967. International Tourist Year.
1200 **625** 10c. multicoloured . . . 15 10
MS1201 76 × 130 mm. **625** 15c. multicoloured. Imperf . . . . 2·00 2·00

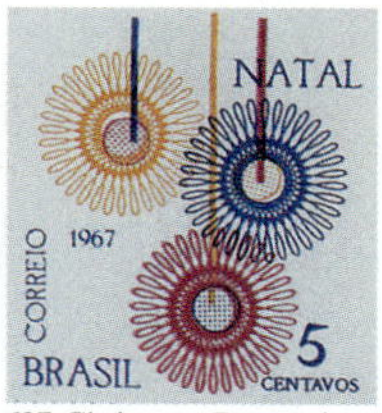

626 Sailor, Anchor and "Almirante Tamandare" (cruiser) **627** Christmas Decorations

1967. Navy Week.
1202 **626** 10c. blue 30 15

1967. Christmas.
1203 **627** 5c. multicoloured 15 10

628 O. Bilac (poet), Aircraft, Tank and Aircraft carrier "Minas Gerais" **629** J. Rodrigues de Carvalho

1967. Reservists Day.
1204 **628** 5c. blue and yellow . . . 60 15

1967. Birth Centenary of Jose Rodriques de Carvalho (jurist and writer).
1205 **629** 10c. green 10 10

630 O. Rangel

1968. Birth Cent of Orlando Rangel (chemist).
1206 **630** 5c. black and blue . . . 15 10

631 Madonna and Diver **632** Map of Free Zone

1968. 250th Anniv of Paranagua Underwater Exploration.
1207 **631** 10c. green and slate . . 20 10

1968. Manaus Free Zone.
1208 **632** 10c. red, green and yellow 15 10

633 Human Rights Emblem **634** Paul Harris

1968. 20th Anniv of Declaration of Human Rights.
1209 **633** 10c. red and blue 10 10

> GUM. All the following issues to No. 1425 are without gum, except where otherwise stated.

1968. Birth Centenary of Paul Harris (founder of Rotary International).
1210 **634** 20c. brown and green . . 1·25 60

635 College Arms

1968. Centenary of St. Luiz College. With gum.
1211 **635** 10c. gold, blue and red 25 10

636 Cabral and his Fleet, 1500

1968. 500th Birth Anniv of Pedro Cabral (discoverer of Brazil).
1212 **636** 10c. multicoloured . . . 30 15
1213 – 20c. multicoloured . . . 90 60
DESIGN: 20c. "The First Mass" (C. Portinari).

637 "Maternity" (after H. Bernardeli)

1968. Mother's Day.
1214 **637** 5c. multicoloured 20 15

638 Harpy Eagle

1968. 150th Anniv of National Museum. With gum.
1215 **638** 20c. black and blue . . . 2·50 60

639 Women of Brazil and Japan

1968. Inaug of "VARIG" Brazil–Japan Air Service.
1216 **639** 10c. multicoloured . . . 25 15

640 Horse-racing

1968. Centenary of Brazilian Jockey Club.
1217 **640** 10c. multicoloured . . . 20 10

641 Musician Wren

1968. Birds.
1218 – 10c. multicoloured . . . 50 25
1219 **641** 20c. brown, green & bl 1·50 25
1220 – 50c. multicoloured . . . 1·90 40
DESIGNS—VERT: 10c. Red-crested cardinal; 50c. Royal flycatcher.

642 Ancient Post-box

643 Marshal E. Luiz Mallet

1968. Stamp Day. With gum.
1221 **642** 5c. black, green & yellow 10 10

1968. Mallet Commemoration. With gum.
1222 **643** 10c. lilac 10 10

644 Map of South America

645 Lyceum Badge

1968. Visit of Chilean President. With gum.
1223 **644** 10c. orange 10 10

1968. Centenary of Portuguese Literacy Lyceum (High School). With gum.
1224 **645** 5c. green and pink . . . 10 10

646 Map and Telex Tape

1968. "Telex Service for 25th City (Curitiba)". With gum.
1225 **646** 20c. green and yellow . . 55 35

647 Soldiers on Medallion

648 "Cock" shaped as Treble Clef

1968. 3rd Int Song Festival, Rio de Janeiro.
1226 **647** 6c. multicoloured 25 15

1968. 8th American Armed Forces Conference.
1227 **648** 5c. black and blue . . . 15 10

649 "Petrobras" Refinery

650 Boy walking towards Rising Sun

1968. 15th Anniv of National Petroleum Industry.
1228 **649** 6c. multicoloured 50 15

1968. UNICEF.
1229 **650** 5c. black and blue . . . 20 15
1230 – 10c. black, red & blue 20 15
1231 – 20c. multicoloured . . . 50 15
DESIGNS—HORIZ: 10c. Hand protecting child. VERT: 20c. Young girl in plaits.

651 Children with Books

1968. Book Week.
1232 **651** 5c. multicoloured 15 10

652 WHO Emblem and Flags

1968. 20th Anniv of WHO.
1233 **652** 20c. multicoloured . . . 30 15

653 J. B. Debret (painter)

1968. Birth Bicentenary of Jean Baptiste Debret (1st issue).
1234 **653** 10c. black and yellow . . 20 10
See Nos. 1273/4.

654 Queen Elizabeth II

1968. State Visit of Queen Elizabeth II.
1235 **654** 70c. multicoloured . . . 1·50 90

655 Brazilian Flag

656 F. Braga and part of "Hymn of National Flag"

1968. Brazilian Flag Day.
1236 **655** 10c. multicoloured . . . 20 15

1968. Birth Cent of Francisco Braga (composer).
1237 **656** 5c. purple 25 10

657 Clasped Hands

1968. Blood Donors' Day.
1238 **657** 5c. red, black and blue 15 10

1968. Obligatory Tax. Leprosy Research Fund. Revalued currency. With gum.
1239 **388** 5c. green . . . . 5·25 1·25
1240 5c. red . . . . 2·40 60

658 Steam Locomotive No. 1 "Maria Fumaca", 1868

1968. Centenary of Sao Paulo Railway.
1241 **658** 5c. multicoloured . . . . 2·50 2·50

659 Angelus Bell

660 F.A.V. Caldas Jr

1968. Christmas. Multicoloured.
1242 5c. Type **659** 15 10
1243 6c. Father Christmas giving present 15 10

1968. Birth Centenary of Francisco Caldas Junior (founder of "Correio do Povo" newspaper).
1244 **660** 10c. black, pink & red 15 10

661 Reservists Emblem and Memorial

1968. Reservists' Day. With gum.
1245 **661** 5c. green and brown . . 15 10

662 Dish Aerial

663 Viscount do Rio Branco

1969. Inaug of Satellite Communications System.
1246 **662** 30c. black and blue . . . 90 60

1969. 150th Birth Anniv of Viscount do Rio Branco.
1247 **663** 5c. sepia and drab . . . 15 10

664 St. Gabriel

1969. St. Gabriel's Day (Patron Saint of Telecommunications).
1248 **664** 5c. multicoloured 15 10

665 Shoemaker's Last and Globe

1969. 4th Int Shoe Fair, Novo, Hamburgo.
1249 **665** 5c. multicoloured 15 10

666 Kardec and Monument

1969. Death Centenary of "Allan Kardec" (Professor H. Rivail) (French educationalist and spiritualist).
1250 **666** 5c. brown and green . . 15 10

667 Men of Three Races and Arms of Cuiaba

1969. 250th Anniv of Cuiaba (capital of Mato Grosso state).
1251 **667** 5c. multicoloured 10 10

668 Mint and Banknote Pattern

1969. Opening of New State Mint Printing Works.
1252 **668** 5c. bistre and orange . . 20 15

669 Society Emblem and Stamps

1969. 50th Anniv of Sao Paulo Philatelic Society.
1253 **669** 5c. multicoloured 10 10

670 "Our Lady of Santana" (statue)

1969. Mothers' Day.
1254 **670** 5c. multicoloured 20 15

671 ILO Emblem

1969. 50th Anniv of ILO. With gum.
1255 **671** 5c. gold and red 10 10

672 Diving Platform and Swimming Pool

673 "Mother and Child at Window" (after Di Cavalcanti)

1969. 40th Anniv of Cearense Water Sports Club, Fortaleza.
1256 **672** 20c. black, green & brn 40 15

1969. 10th Art Exhibition Biennale, Sao Paulo. Multicoloured.
1257 10c. Type **673** 60 15
1258 20c. Modern sculpture (F. Leirner) 90 30
1259 50c. "Sunset in Brasilia" (D. di Prete) . . . . . . 1·75 1·25
1260 1cr. "Angelfish" (A. Martins) . . . . . . 1·75 80
No. 1258 is square, size 33 × 33 mm and Nos. 1259/60 vertical, size 33 × 53 mm.

674 Freshwater Angelfish

675 I. O. Teles de Manezes (founder)

1969. ACAPI Fish Preservation and Development Campaign.
1261 20c. Type **674** 45 15
MS1262 134 × 100 mm. Four designs each 38 × 22 mm. 10c. Tetra; 15c. Piranha; 20c. "Megalamphodus megalopterus"; 30c. Black tetra 5·00 5·00

1969. Centenary of Spiritualist Press. With gum.
1263 **675** 50c. green and orange 1·50 90

676 Postman delivering Letter

677 General Fragoso

1969. Stamp Day. With gum.
1264 **676** 30c. blue . . . . 1·25 60

1969. Birth Centenary of General Tasso Fragoso. With gum.
1265 **677** 20c. green 90 60

678 Map of Army Bases

1969. Army Week. Multicoloured.
1266 10c. Type **678** 25 15
1267 20c. Monument and railway bridge (39 × 22 mm) . . . 1·75 60

679 Jupia Dam

1969. Inauguration of Jupia Dam.
1268 **679** 20c. multicoloured . . . 55 55

680 Mahatma Gandhi and Spinning-wheel

1969. Birth Centenary of Mahatma Gandhi.
1269 **680** 20c. black and yellow . . 1·25 60

681 Alberto Santos Dumont, "Ballon No. 6", Eiffel Tower and Moon Landing

1969. 1st Man on the Moon and Santos Dumont's Flight (1906). Commemoration.
1270 **681** 50c. multicoloured . . . 1·75 1·25

682 Smelting Plant

1969. Expansion of USIMINAS Steel Consortium.
1271 **682** 20c. multicoloured . . . 55 15

683 Steel Furnace

685 Exhibition Emblem

684 "The Water Cart" (after Debrot)

1969. 25th Anniv of ACESITA Steel Works.
1272 **683** 10c. multicoloured . . . 55 15

1969. Birth Centenary of J. B. Debret (painter) (2nd issue). Multicoloured. No. 1274 dated "1970".
1273 20c. Type **684** . . . . . . 1·25 60
1274 30c. "Street Scene" . . . . 1·00 95

1969. "Abuexpo 69" Stamp Exn.
1275 **685** 10c. multicoloured . . . 20 15

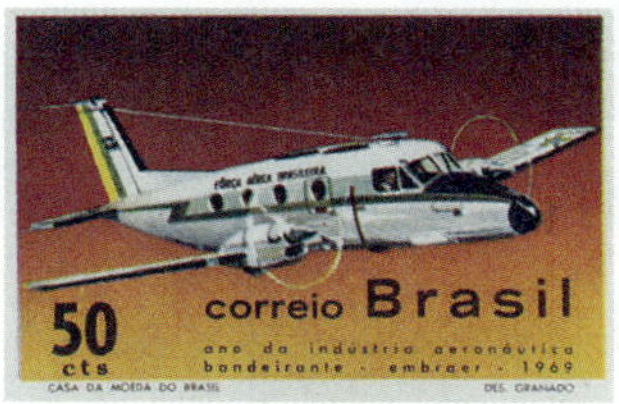

686 Embraer Bandeirante Airplane

1969. Brazilian Aeronautical Industry Expansion Year.
1276 **686** 50c. multicoloured . . . 1·75 1·25

687 Pele scoring Goal

1969. Footballer Pele's 1,000th Goal.
1277 **687** 10c. multicoloured . . . 1·25 1·75
MS1278 81 × 120 mm. **687** 75c. multicoloured. Imperf . . . . 3·00 3·25

688 "Madonna and Child" (painted panel)

1969. Christmas.
1279 **688** 10c. multicoloured . . . 55 35
MS1280 137 × 102 mm. **688** 75c. multicoloured. Imperf . . . . 4·00 4·25

689 "Pernambuco" (destroyer) and "Bahia" (submarine)

1969. Navy Day. With gum.
1281 **689** 5c. blue . . . . 1·00 15

690 Dr. H. Blumenau

1969. 150th Birth Anniv of Dr. Hermann Blumenau (German immigrant leader). With gum.
1282 **690** 20c. green 60 60

691 Carnival Dancers

1969. Carioca Carnival, Rio de Janeiro (1970). Multicoloured.
1283 5c. Type **691** 25 20
1284 10c. Samba dancers (horiz) 25 20
1285 20c. Clowns (horiz) 25 30
1286 30c. Confetti and mask . . 2·75 1·50
1287 50c. Tambourine-player . . 2·75 1·40

692 Carlos Gomes conducting

1970. Centenary of Opera "O. Guarani" by A. Carlos Gomes.
1288 **692** 20c. multicoloured . . . 60 20

693 Monastery

1970. 400th Anniv of Penha Monastery, Vilha Velha.
1289 **693** 20c. multicoloured . . . 25 15

694 National Assembly Building

1970. 10th Anniv of Brasilia. Multicoloured.
1290 20c. Type **694** 25 15
1291 50c. Reflecting Pool . . . . 1·75 1·50
1292 1cr. Presidential Palace . . . 1·75 1·50

695 Emblem on Map

1970. Rondon Project (students' practical training scheme).
1293 **695** 50c. multicoloured . . . 1·50 1·50

696 Marshal Osorio and Arms

1970. Opening of Marshal Osorio Historical Park.
1294 **696** 20c. multicoloured . . . 1·25 45

697 "Madonna and Child" (San Antonio Monastery)

698 Brasilia Cathedral (stylized)

1970. Mothers' Day.
1295 **697** 20c. multicoloured . . . 55 20

1970. 8th National Eucharistic Congress, Brasilia. With gum.
1296 **698** 20c. green 15 15

699 Census Symbol

700 Jules Rimet Cup, and Map

1970. 8th National Census.
1297 **699** 20c. yellow and green . . 55 50

1970. World Cup Football Championships Mexico.
1298 **700** 50c. black, gold & blue 50 40

701 Statue of Christ

1970. Marist Students. 6th World Congress.
1299 **701** 50c. multicoloured . . . 1·50 1·50

702 Bellini and Swedish Flag (1958)

1970. Brazil's Third Victory in World Cup Football Championships. Multicoloured.
1300 1cr. Type **702** . . . . 1·75 90
1301 2cr. Garrincha and Chilean flag (1962) . . . . 5·25 1·75
1302 3cr. Pele and Mexican flag (1970) . . . . 2·75 90

703 Pandia Calogeras

704 Brazilian Forces Badges and Map

1970. Birth Centenary of Calogeras (author and politician).
1303 **703** 20c. green . . . . 1·75 60

1970. 25th Anniv of World War II. Victory.
1304 **704** 20c. multicoloured . . . 50 15

705 "The Annunciation" (Cassio M'Boy)

1970. St. Gabriel's Day (Patron Saint of Telecommunications).
1305 **705** 20c. multicoloured . . . 90 40

706 Boy in Library

707 U.N. Emblem

1970. Book Week.
1306 **706** 20c. multicoloured . . . 90 60

1970. 25th Anniv of United Nations.
1307 **707** 50c. blue, silver & ultram 90 75

708 "Rio de Janeiro, circa 1820"

1970. 3rd Brazilian–Portuguese Stamp Exhibition "Lubrapex 70", Rio de Janeiro.
1308 **708** 20c. multicoloured . . . 60 60
1309 – 50c. brown and black . . 2·75 1·75
1310 – 1cr. multicoloured . . . 2·75 2·75
MS1311 60 × 80 mm. **708** 1cr. multicoloured. Imperf . . . . 7·00 8·00
DESIGNS: 50c. Post Office Symbol; 1cr. Rio de Janeiro (modern view).

709 "The Holy Family" (C. Portinari)

710 "Graca Aranha" (destroyer)

1970. Christmas.
1312 **709** 50c. multicoloured . . . 90 90
MS1313 107 × 52 mm. **709** 1cr. multicoloured. Imper . . . . . 8·00 9·00

1970. Navy Day.
1314 **710** 20c. multicoloured . . . 1·75 80

711 Congress Emblem

712 Links and Globe

1971. 3rd Inter-American Housing Congress, Rio de Janeiro.
1315 **711** 50c. red and black . . . 80 80

1971. Racial Equality Year.
1316 **712** 20c. multicoloured . . . 60 30

713 "Morpho melacheilus"

1971. Butterflies. Multicoloured.
1317 20c. Type **713** . . . . . . 1·25 35
1318 1cr. "Papilio thoas brasiliensis" . . . . . . 6·00 2·40

714 Madonna and Child

715 Hands reaching for Ball

1971. Mothers' Day.
1319 **714** 20c. multicoloured . . . 60 15

1971. 6th Women's Basketball World Championships.
1320 **715** 70c. multicoloured . . . 1·25 95

716 Eastern Part of Highway Map

1971. Trans-Amazon Highway Project. Mult.
1321 40c. Type **716** . . . . . . 6·25 3·75
1322 1cr. Western part of Highway Map . . . . . 6·25 5·25
Nos. 1321/2 were issued together se-tenant, forming a composite design.

717 "Head of Man" (V. M. Lima)

1971. Stamp Day. Multicoloured.
1323 40c. Type **717** . . . . . . 1·25 45
1324 1cr. "Arab Violinist" (Pedro Americo) . . . . 3·00 1·25

718 General Caxias and Map

719 Anita Garibaldi

1971. Army Week.
1325 **718** 20c. red and green . . . 50 15

1971. 150th Birth Anniv of Anita Garibaldi.
1326 **719** 20c. multicoloured . . . 20 15

720 Xavante and Santos Dumont's Biplane "14 bis"

1971. 1st Flight of Embraer Xavante Jet Fighter.
1327 **720** 40c. multicoloured . . . 1·25 45

721 Flags of Central American Republics

722 Exhibition Emblem

1971. 150th Anniv of Central American Republics' Independence.
1328 **721** 40c. multicoloured . . . 80 40

1971. "Franca 71" Industrial, Technical and Scientific Exhibition, Sao Paulo.
1329 **722** 1cr.30 multicoloured . . 1·25 90

723 "The Black Mother" (L. de Albuquerque)

724 Archangel Gabriel

1971. Centenary of Slaves Emancipation Law.
1330 **723** 40c. multicoloured . . . 40 20

1971. St. Gabriel's Day (Patron Saint of Communications).
1331 **724** 40c. multicoloured . . . 45 50

725 "Couple on Bridge" (Marisa da Silva Chaves)

1971. Children's Day. Multicoloured.
1332 35c. Type **725** 35 30
1333 45c. "Couple on Riverbank" (Mary Rosa e Silva) . . . 90 30
1334 60c. "Girl in Hat" (Teresa A. P. Ferreira) 35 30

726 "Laelia purpurata Werkhauserii superba"

727 Eunice Weaver

1971. Brazilian Orchids.
1335 **726** 40c. multicoloured . . . 1·50 50

1971. Obligatory Tax. Leprosy Research Fund.
1336 **727** 10c. green . . . . 1·25 65
1337 10c. purple 55 15

728 "25 Senac"

1971. 25th Annivs of SENAC (apprenticeship scheme) and SESC (workers' social service).
1338 **728** 20c. blue and black . . . 90 60
1339 – 40c. orange and black 90 60
DESIGN: 40c. As Type **728**, but inscribed "25 SESC".

729 "Parati" (gunboat)

1971. Navy Day.
1340 **729** 20c. multicoloured . . . 2·00 50

730 Cruciform Symbol

731 Washing Bomfim Church

1971. Christmas.
1341 **730** 20c. lilac, red and blue 30 15
1342 75c. black on silver . . . 55 1·75
1343 1cr.30 multicoloured . . 2·40 1·50

1972. Tourism. Multicoloured.
1344 20c. Type **731** . . . . . . 1·75 90
1345 40c. Cogwheel and grapes (Grape Festival, Rio Grande do Sul) . . . . . 1·75 20
1346 75c. Nazareth Festival procession, Belem . . . 1·75 1·75
1347 1cr.30 Street scene (Winter Festival of Ouro Preto) 3·50 1·75

732 Pres. Lanusse

1972. Visit of President Lanusse of Argentina.
1348 **732** 40c. multicoloured . . . 90 75

733 Presidents Castello Branco, Costa e Silva and Medici

734 Post Office Symbol

1972. 8th Anniv of 1964 Revolution.
1349 **733** 20c. multicoloured . . . 40 30

1972.
1350 **734** 20c. brown . . . . . . 1·50 10

735 Pres. Tomas

1972. Visit of Pres. Tomas of Portugal.
1351 **735** 75c. multicoloured . . . 1·25 95

736 Exploratory Borehole (C.P.R.M.)

1972. Mineral Resources. Multicoloured.
1352 20c. Type **736** 60 15
1353 40c. Oil rig (PETROBRAS) (vert) . . . . 2·75 50
1354 75c. Power station and dam (ELECTROBRAS) . . . 95 1·25
1355 1cr.30 Iron ore production (Vale do Rio Doce Co.) 3·25 1·25

737 "Female Nude" (1922 Catalogue cover by Di. Cavalcanti)

1972. 50th Anniv of 1st Modern Art Week, Sao Paulo. Sheet 79 × 111 mm. With gum.
MS1356 **737** 1cr. black and carmine 9·00 10·00

738 Postman and Map (Post Office)

1972. Communications. Multicoloured.
1357 35c. Type **738** 90 20
1358 45c. Microwave Transmitter (Telecommunications) (vert) 90 90
1359 60c. Symbol and diagram of Amazon microwave system 90 70
1360 70c. Worker and route map (Amazon Basin development) . . . . . . 1·25 70

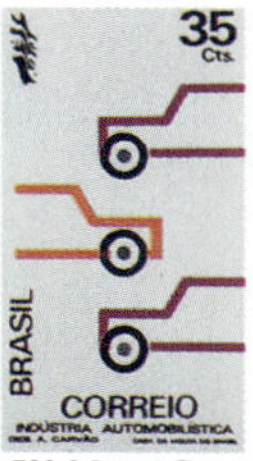

739 Motor Cars

740 Footballer (Independence Cup Championships)

1972. Major Industries.
1361 **739** 35c. orange, red & black 45 25
1362 – 45c. multicoloured . . . 45 40
1363 – 70c. multicoloured . . . 45 25
DESIGNS—HORIZ: 45c. Three hulls (Shipbuilding); 70c. Metal Blocks (Iron and Steel Industry).

1972. "Sports and Pastimes".
1364 **740** 20c. black and brown . . 40 15
1365 – 75c. black and red . . . 1·25 1·50
1366 – 1cr.30 black and blue . . 2·00 1·50
DESIGNS: 75c. Treble clef in open mouth ("Popular Music"); 1cr.30, Hand grasping plastic ("Plastic Arts").

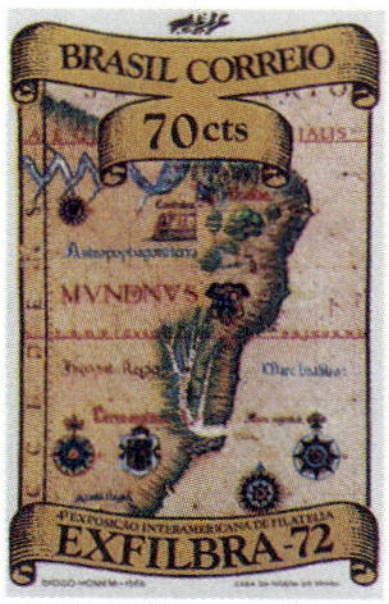

741 Diego Homem's Map of Brazil, 1568

1972. "EXFILBRA 72" 4th International Stamp Exhibition, Rio de Janeiro. Multicoloured.
1367 70c. Type **741** 60 35
1368 1cr. Nicolau Visscher's Map of Americas, c. 1652 . . . 5·25 60
1369 2cr. Lopo Homem's World Map, 1519 . . . . 2·40 90
MS1370 125 × 89 mm. 1cr. "Declaration of Ypiranga" (Pedro Americo) (horiz) . . . . 3·50 4·00

742 Figurehead, Sao Francisco River

743 "Institution of Brazilian Flag"

1972. Brazilian Folklore. Multicoloured.
1371 45c. Type **742** 45 15
1372 60c. Fandango, Rio Grande do Sul 75 75
1373 75c. Capoeira (game), Bahia 30 15
1374 1cr.15 Karaja statuette . . . 30 25
1375 1cr.30 "Bumba-Meu-Boi" (folk play) . . . . 2·50 1·00

1972. 150th Anniv of Independence.
1376 **743** 30c. green and yellow . . 1·75 1·00
1377 – 70c. mauve and pink . . 75 30
1378 – 1cr. red and brown . . . 4·00 [illegible]
1379 – 2cr. black and brown . . . 2·40 [illegible]
1380 – 3cr.50 black and grey . . 4·00 2·40
DESIGNS—HORIZ: 70c. "Proclamation of Emperor Pedro I" (lithograph after Debret); 2cr. Commemorative gold coin of Pedro I; 3cr.50, Declaration of Ypiranga monument. VERT: 1cr. "Emperor Pedro I" (H. J. da Silva).

744 Numeral and P.T.T. Symbol

747 Writing Hand and People ("Mobral" Literacy Campaign)

745 Scroll

1972.
1383 **744** 5c. orange 30 10
1384 10c. brown 40 10
1394 15c. blue 15 10
1385 20c. blue . . . . 2·40 10
1396 25c. brown 15 10
1386 30c. red . . . . 1·50 10
1387 40c. green 15 10
1388 50c. green . . . . . . 1·50 10
1398 50c. purple 60 10
1389 **745** 1cr. purple 60 10
1390 2cr. blue . . . . 1·75 10
1391 4cr. orange and lilac . . 3·50 35
1392 5cr. brown, cinnamon and red . . . . 3·50 10
1393 10cr. green, brown & blk 7·00 35
Nos. 1392/3 have a background of multiple P.T.T. symbols.

746 Fittipaldi in Racing Car

1972. Emerson Fittipaldi's Victory in Formula 1 World Motor-racing Championship. Sheet 122 × 87 mm.
MS1411 **746** 2cr. multicoloured 7·00 8·00

1972. Social Development. Multicoloured.
1412 10c. Type **747** 20 20
1413 20c. Graph and people (National Census Cent) 50 40
1414 1cr. House in hand (Pension Fund system) . . . . . . 9·00 20
1415 2cr. Workers and factory (Gross National Product) 1·25 45

748 Legislative Building, Brasilia

1972. National Congress Building, Brasilia.
1416 **748** 1cr. black, orange & bl 9·00 4·50

749 Pottery Crib

750 Farm-worker and Pension Book (Rural Social Security Scheme)

1972. Christmas.
1417 **749** 20c. black and brown . . 40 20

1972. Government Services.
1418 **750** 10c. black, orange & bl 25 20
1419 – 10c. multicoloured . . . 90 90
1420 – 70c. black, brown & red 4·50 2·00
1421 – 2cr. multicoloured . . . 5·50 2·50
DESIGNS—VERT: 70c. Dr. Oswald Cruz, public health pioneer (birth cent.). HORIZ: 10c. (No. 1419), Children and traffic lights (Transport system development); 2cr. Bull, fish and produce (Agricultural exports).

751 Brazilian Expeditionary Force Monument

1972. Armed Forces' Day.
1422 **751** 10c. black, purple & brn 1·40 85
1423 – 30c. multicoloured . . . 2·00 85
1424 – 30c. multicoloured . . . 1·40 85
1425 – 30c. black, brn & lilac 1·40 85
DESIGNS: No. 1423, Sail-training ship (Navy); No. 1424, Trooper (Army); No. 1425, Dassault Mirage IIIC jet fighter (Air Force).

GUM. All the following issues are with gum, except where otherwise stated.

752 Emblem and Cogwheels

1973. 50th Anniv of Rotary in Brazil.
1426 **752** 1cr. blue, lt blue & yell 1·75 1·00

753 Swimming

1973. Sporting Events.
1427 **753** 40c. brown and blue . . 25 20
1428 – 40c. red and green . . . 2·75 55
1429 – 40c. brown and purple 90 45
DESIGNS AND EVENTS—HORIZ: No. 1427, ("Latin Cup" Swimming Championships); No. 1428, Gymnast (Olympic Festival of Gymnastics, Rio de Janeiro). VERT: No. 1429, Volleyball player (Internation Volleyball Championships, Rio de Janeiro).

754 Paraguayan Flag

1973. Visit of Pres. Stroessner of Paraguay.
1430 **754** 70c. multicoloured . . . 1·40 80

755 "Communications"

1973. Inauguration of Ministry of Communications Building, Brasilia.
1431 **755** 70c. multicoloured . . . 90 50

756 Neptune and Map

1973. Inauguration of "Bracan I" Underwater Cable, Recife to Canary Islands.
1432 **756** 1cr. multicoloured . . . 4·25 2·40

757 Congress Emblem

758 Swallow-tailed Manakin and "Acacia decurrens"

1973. 24th Int Chamber of Commerce Congress.
1433 **757** 1cr. purple and orange 4·25 2·40

1973. Tropical Birds and Plants. Mult.
1434 20c. Type **758** 65 30
1435 20c. Troupial and "Cereus peruvianus" 65 30
1436 20c. Brazilian ruby and "Tecoma umbellata" . . 65 30

759 "Tourism"

760 "Caboclo" Festival Cart

1973. National Tourism Year.
1437 **759** 70c. multicoloured . . . 60 30

1973. Anniversaries. Multicoloured.
1438 20c. Type **760** 90 30
1439 20c. Arariboia (Indian chief) 90 30
1440 20c. Convention delegates 90 30
1441 20c. "The Graciosa Road" 90 30
EVENTS: No. 1438, 150th anniv of Liberation Day; 1439, 400th anniv of Niteroi; 1440, Cent of Itu Convention; 1441, Cent of Nhundiaquara highway.

761 "Institute of Space Research"

1973. Scientific Research Institute. Mult.
1442 20c. Type **761** 50 25
1443 70c. "Federal Engineering School", Itajuba . . . . 1·50 50
1444 1cr. "Institute for Pure and Applied Mechanics" . . . 2·00 45

762 Santos Dumont and Biplane "14 bis"

1973. Birth Centenary of Alberto Santos Dumont (aviation pioneer).
1445 **762** 20c. brown, grn & lt grn 50 20
1446 – 70c. brown, red & yellow 1·25 1·25
1447 – 2cr. brown, ultram & bl 1·60 1·25

DESIGNS: 70c. Airship "Ballon No. 6"; 2cr. Monoplane No. 20 "Demoiselle".

763 Map of the World

1973. Stamp Day.
1448 **763** 40c. black and red . . . 1·90 1·25
1449 – 40c. black and red . . . 1·90 1·25
The design of No. 1449 differs from Type **763** in that the red portion is to the top and right, instead of to the top and left.

764 G. Dias

766 Festival Banner

765 Copernicus and "Sun-god"

1973. 150th Birth Anniv of Goncalves Dias (poet).
1450 **764** 40c. black and violet . . 60 30
See also Nos. 1459 and 1477.

1973. 500th Anniv of Nicholas Copernicus (astronomer). Sheet 125 × 87 mm.
MS1451 **765** 1cr. multicoloured 2·50 3·00

1973. National Folklore Festival.
1452 **766** 40c. multicoloured . . . 60 20

767 Masonic Emblems

1973. 150th Anniv of Masonic Grand Orient Lodge of Brazil.
1453 **767** 1cr. blue . . . . 2·00 95

768 Fire Protection

1973. National Protection Campaign. Mult.
1454 40c. Type **768** 60 20
1455 40c. Cross and cornice (cultural protection) . . . 60 20
1456 40c. Winged emblem (protection in flight) . . . 60 20
1457 40c. Leaf (protection of nature) 60 20

769 St. Gabriel and Papal Bull

1973. 1st National Exhibition of Religious Philately, Rio de Janeiro. Sheet 125 × 87 mm.
MS1458 **769** 1cr. black and ochre 4·75 5·50

1973. Birth Centenary of St. Theresa of Lisieux. As T **764**.
1459 2cr. brown and orange . . . 2·75 1·40
DESIGN: Portrait of St. Theresa.

770 M. Lobato and "Emilia"

1973. Monteiro Lobato's Children's Stories. Multicoloured.
1460 40c. Type **770** 50 50
1461 40c. "Aunt Nastasia" . . . 50 50
1462 40c. "Nazarinho", "Pedrinho" and "Quindim" 50 50
1463 40c. "Visconde de Sabugosa" 50 50
1464 40c. "Dona Benta" 50 50

771 Father J. M. Nunes Garcia

1973. "The Baroque Age". Multicoloured.
1465 40c. Wood carving, Church of St. Francia, Bahia . . 60 50
1466 40c. "Prophet Isaiah" (detail, sculpture by Aleijadinho) 60 50
1467 70c. Type **771** . . . . . . 1·75 1·75
1468 1cr. Portal, Church of Conceicao da Praia . . . 5·25 2·75
1469 2cr. "Glorification of Holy Virgin", ceiling, St. Francis Assisi Church, Ouro Preto . . . . 4·25 2·75

772 Early Telephone and Modern Instruments

1973. 50th Anniv of Brazilian Telephone Company.
1470 **772** 40c. multicoloured . . . 35 15

773 "Angel" (J. Kopke)

1973. Christmas.
1471 **773** 40c. multicoloured . . . 25 10

774 "Gailora" (river steamboat)

1973. Brazilian Boats. Multicoloured.
1472 40c. Type **774** 70 50
1473 70c. "Regatao" (river trading boat) . . . . . . 1·40 1·75
1474 1cr. "Jangada" (coastal raft) 4·75 2·40
1475 2cr. "Saveiro" (passenger boat) . . . . 4·75 2·40

775 Scales of Justice

1973. Judiciary Power.
1476 **775** 40c. violet and mauve . . 30 15

1973. Birth Centenary of Placido de Castro. As T **764**.
1477 40c. black and red 55 20
DESIGN: Portrait of Castro.

776 Scarlet Ibis and "Victoria Regia" Lilies

777 Saci Perere (goblin)

1973. Brazilian Flora and Fauna. Mult.
1478 40c. Type **776** . . . . . . 1·00 50
1479 70c. Jaguar and Indian tulip 4·75 45
1480 1cr. Scarlet macaw and palm . . . . 8·50 3·75
1481 2cr. Greater rhea and mulunga plant . . . . . 8·50 3·75

1974. Brazilian Folk Tales. Multicoloured.
1482 40c. Type **777** 35 15
1483 80c. Zumbi (warrior) . . . 90 40
1484 1cr. Chico Rei (African king) . . . . 1·25 20
1485 1cr.30 Little black boy of the pasture (32 × 33 mm) 2·40 80
1486 2cr.50 Iara, queen of the waters (32 × 33 mm) . . . 9·00 4·25

778 View of Bridge

1974. Inauguration of President Costa e Silva (Rio de Janeiro–Niteroi) Bridge.
1487 **778** 40c. multicoloured . . . 35 20

779 "Press"

1974. Brazilian Communications Pioneers.
1488 **779** 40c. red, blue & bistre 30 15
1489 – 40c. brown, blue & bistre 25 15
1490 – 40c. blue, pink & brown 30 15
DESIGNS AND EVENTS: No. 1488, Birth bicentenary of Hipolito da Costa (founder of newspaper "Correio Brasiliense", 1808); 1489, "Radio waves" (Edgar R. Pinto, founder of Radio Sociedade do Rio de Janeiro, 1923); 1490, "Television screen" (F. de Assis Chateaubriand, founder of first T.V. station, Sao Paulo, 1950).

780 "Construction"

1974. 10th Anniv of March Revolution.
1491 **780** 40c. multicoloured . . . 25 20

781 Christ of the Andes

1974. Birth Cent of G. Marconi (radio pioneer).
1492 **781** 2cr.50 multicoloured . . 7·00 3·50

782 Heads of Three Races

1974. Ethnical Origins and Immigration. Mult.

1493	40c. Type **782**	25	20
1494	40c. Heads of many races	10	20
1495	2cr.50 German immigration	3·75	1·25
1496	2cr.50 Italian immigration	9·00	1·25
1497	2cr.50 Japanese immigration	2·75	1·25

783 Artwork and Stamp-printing Press

1974. State Mint.

1498	**783** 80c. multicoloured . . .	95	20

784 Sete Cidades National Park

1974. Tourism. Multicoloured.

1499	40c. Type **784**	60	25
1500	80c. Ruins of church of St. Michael of the Missions	60	25

785 Footballer

1974. World Cup Football Championship, West Germany. Sheet 125 × 87 mm.

MS1501	**785** 2cr.50 multicoloured	2·75	3·00

See also No. 1506.

786 Caraca College

1974. Bicentenary of Caraca College.

1502	**786** 40c. multicoloured . . .	20	15

787 Wave Pattern

1974. 3rd Brazilian Telecommunications Congress, Brasilia.

1503	**787** 40c. black and blue . . .	15	15

788 Fernao Dias Paes

1974. 300th Anniv of Paes Expedition.

1504	**788** 20c. multicoloured . . .	15	15

1974. Visit of President Alvarez of Mexico. As T **754**. Multicoloured.

1505	80c. Mexican Flag	1·75	1·25

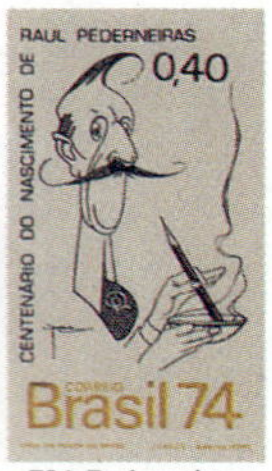

789 Flags and Crowd in Stadium

791 Pederneiras (after J. Carlos)

790 Braille "Eye" and Emblem

1974. World Cup Football Championship, West Germany (2nd issue).

1506	**789** 40c. multicoloured . . .	50	50

1974. 5th General Assembly of World Council for Welfare of the Blind. Sheet 127 × 90 mm.

MS1507	**790** 1cr.30 multicoloured	45	60

1974. Birth Centenary of Raul Pederneiras (lawyer, author and artist).

1508	**791** 40c. black & yell on brn	20	20

792 Emblem and Seascape

1974. 13th Int Union of Building Societies and Savings Associations Congress, Rio de Janeiro.

1509	**792** 1cr.30 multicoloured . .	75	60

793 "Five Women of Guaratingueta" (E di Cavalcanti)

1974. Lubrapex 74 Stamp Exhibition, Sao Paulo (1st issue). Sheet 87 × 126 mm.

MS1510	**793** 2cr. multicoloured	1·90	2·00

See also No. 1522.

794 "UPU" on World Map

1974. Centenary of UPU.

1511	**794** 2cr.50 black and blue . .	7·00	3·50

795 Aruak Hammock

1974. "Popular Culture".

1512	**795** 50c. purple	75	30
1513	– 50c. light blue and blue	1·25	30
1514	– 50c. brown, red & yellow	40	30
1515	– 50c. brown and yellow	50	30

DESIGNS—SQUARE: No. 1513, Bilro Lace. VERT: (24 × 37 mm), No. 1514, Guitar player (folk literature); 1515, Horseman (statuette by Vitalino).

796 Coffee Beans

1974. Bicentenary of City of Campinas.

1516	**796** 50c. multicoloured . . .	90	50

797 Hornless Tabapua

1974. Domestic Animals. Multicoloured.

1517	80c. Type **797**	95	60
1518	1cr.30 Creole horse	90	70
1519	2cr.50 Brazilian mastiff . .	9·00	1·75

798 Ilha Solteira Dam

799 Herald Angel

1974. Ilha Solteira Hydro-electric Power Project.

1520	**798** 50c. brown, grey & yell	65	20

1974. Christmas.

1521	**799** 50c. multicoloured . . .	30	15

800 "The Girls" (Carlos Reis)

802 Athlete

801 "Justice for Juveniles"

1974. "Lubrapex 74" Stamp Exhibition, Sao Paulo (2nd issue).

1522	**800** 1cr.30 multicoloured . .	40	25

1974. 50th Anniv of Brazilian Juvenile Court.

1523	**801** 90c. multicoloured . . .	20	20

1974. 50th Anniv of Sao Silvestre Long-distance Race.

1524	**802** 3cr.30 multicoloured . .	90	55

803 Mounted Newsvendor and Newspaper Masthead

1975. Cent of Newspaper "O Estado de S. Paulo".

1525	**803** 50c. multicoloured . . .	60	30

804 Industrial Complex, Sao Paulo

1975. Economic Resources.

1526	**804** 50c. yellow and blue . .	95	25
1527	– 1cr.40 yellow & brown	60	60
1528	– 4cr.50 yellow & black . .	3·00	25

DESIGNS: 1cr.40 Rubber industry, Acre; 4cr.50, Manganese industry, Amapa.

805 Santa Cruz Fortress, Rio de Janeiro

1975. Colonial Forts. Each brown on yellow.

1529	50c. Type **805**	10	15
1530	50c. Reis Magos Fort, Rio Grande do Norte	30	15
1531	50c. Monte Serrat Fort, Bahia	50	15
1532	90c. Nossa Senhora dos Remedios Fort, Fernando de Noronha	10	25

806 "Palafita" House, Amazonas

1975. Brazilian Architecture. Multicoloured.

1533	50c. Modern Architecture, Brasilia	1·50	1·50
1534	50c. Modern Architecture, Brasilia (yellow line at left)	16·00	8·00
1535	1cr. Type **806**	30	15
1536	1cr.40 Indian hut, Rondonia (yellow line at left)	3·00	3·00
1537	1cr.40 As No. 1536 but yellow line at right . . .	55	60
1538	3cr.30 "Enxaimel" house, Santa Catarina (yellow line at right)	95	95
1539	3cr.30 As No. 1538 but yellow line at left	4·25	4·25

807 Oscar ("Astronotus ocellatus")

1975. Freshwater Fishes. Multicoloured.

1540	50c. Type **807**	1·40	25
1541	50c. South American pufferfish ("Colomesus psitacus")	55	35
1542	50c. Tail-spot livebearer ("Phallocerus caudimaculatus")	55	40
1543	50c. Red discus ("Symphysodon discus")	85	35

808 Flags forming Serviceman's Head

809 Brazilian Pines

1975. Honouring Ex-Servicemen of Second World War.

1544	**808** 50c. multicoloured . . .	25	15

1975. Fauna and Flora Preservation. Mult.

1545	70c. Type **809**	1·60	20
1546	1cr. Giant otter (vert) . . .	1·00	40
1547	3cr.30 Marsh cayman . . .	95	40

810 Inga Carved Stone, from Paraiba

811 Statue of the Virgin Mary

1975. Archaeology. Multicoloured.

1548	70c. Type **810**	95	20
1549	1cr. Marajoara pot from Para	25	20
1550	1cr. Fossilized garfish from Ceara (horiz)	30	20

1975. Holy Year. 300th Anniv of Franciscan Province of Our Lady of the Immaculate Conception.

1551 **811**	3cr.30 multicoloured	95	60

812 Ministry of Communications Building, Rio de Janeiro

813 "Congada" Sword Dance, Minas Gerais

1975. Stamp Day.

1552 **812**	70c. red	45	15

1975. Folk Dances. Multicoloured.

1553	70c. Type **813**	25	30
1554	70c. "Frevo" umbrella dance, Pernambuco	25	30
1555	70c. "Warrior" dance, Alagoas	25	30

814 Stylized Trees

1975. Tree Festival.

1556 **814**	70c. multicoloured	25	10

815 Dish Aerial and Globe

816 Woman holding Globe

1975. Inauguration of Tangua Satellite Telecommunications Station.

1557 **815**	3cr.30 multicoloured	90	60

1975. International Women's Year.

1558 **816**	3cr.30 multicoloured	1·25	45

817 Tile, Balcony Rail and Memorial Column, Alcantara

1975. Historic Towns. Multicoloured.

1559	70c. Type **817**	40	25
1560	70c. Belfry, weather vane and jug, Goias (26 × 38 mm)	40	25
1561	70c. Sao Francisco Convent, Sao Cristovao (40 × 22 mm)	40	25

818 Crowd welcoming Walking Book

1975. Day of the Book.

1562 **818**	70c. multicoloured	20	15

819 ASTA Emblem and Arrows

1975. 45th American Society of Travel Agents Congress.

1563 **819**	70c. multicoloured	20	15

820 Two Angels

821 Aerial, and Map of America

1975. Christmas.

1564 **820**	70c. brown and red	15	10

1975. 2nd International Telecommunications Conference, Rio de Janeiro.

1565 **821**	5cr.20 multicoloured	3·50	1·75

822 Friar Nicodemus

823 People in front of Cross

1975. Obligatory Tax. Leprosy Research Fund.

1566 **822**	10c. brown	20	10

1975. Thanksgiving Day.

1567 **823**	70c. turquoise and blue	30	25

824 Emperor Pedro II in Naval Uniform (after P. P. da Silva Manuel)

825 Sal Stone Beach, Piaui

1975. 150th Birth Anniv of Emperor Pedro II.

1568 **824**	70c. brown	40	20

1975. Tourism. Multicoloured.

1569	70c. Type **825**	30	20
1570	70c. Guarapari Beach, Espirito Santo	30	20
1571	70c. Torres Cliffs Rio Grande do Sul	30	20

826 Triple Jump

1975. 7th Pan-American Games, Santo Domingo, Dominican Republic.

1572 **826**	1cr.60 turquoise & black	20	20

827 UN Emblem and HQ Building, New York

1975. 30th Anniv of United Nations.

1573 **827**	1cr.30 violet on blue	15	15

828 Light Bulbs and House

1976. "Preservation of Fuel Resources". Mult.

1574	70c. Type **828**	25	10
1575	70c. Drops of petrol and car	25	10

829 Concorde

1976. Concorde's First Commercial Flight, Paris–Rio de Janeiro.

1576 **829**	5cr.20 black and grey	1·10	40

830 Pinheiro's Nautical Map of 1776

1976. Cent of Hydrographical and Navigational Directorate. Sheet 88 × 124 mm.

MS1577 **830**	70c. multicoloured	65	80

831 Early and Modern Telephone Equipment

1976. Telephone Centenary.

1578 **831**	5cr.20 black & orange	1·25	1·25

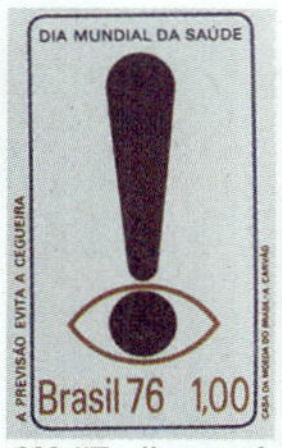

832 "Eye"-part of Exclamation Mark

833 Kaiapo Body-painting

1976. World Health Day.

1579 **832**	1cr. red, brown & violet	30	50

1976. Brazil's Indigenous Culture. Mult.

1580	1cr. Type **833**	20	10
1581	1cr. Bakairi ceremonial mask	20	10
1582	1cr. Karaja feather head-dress	20	10

834 Itamaraty Palace, Brasilia

1976. Diplomats' Day.

1583 **834**	1cr. multicoloured	35	60

835 "The Sprinkler" (3D composition by J. Tarcisio)

836 Basketball

1976. Modern Brazilian Art. Multicoloured.

1584	1cr. Type **835**	15	10
1585	1cr. "Beribboned Fingers" (P. Checcacci) (horiz)	15	10

1976. Olympic Games, Montreal.

1586 **836**	1cr. black and green	10	10
1587 –	1cr.40 black and blue	25	10
1588 –	5cr.20 black and orange	1·25	1·25

DESIGNS: 1cr.40, Olympic yachts; 5cr.20, Judo.

837 Golden Lion-Tamarin

838 Cine Camera on Screen

1976. Nature Protection. Multicoloured.

1589	1cr. Type **837**	25	20
1590	1cr. Orchid ("Acacallis cyanea")	25	30

1976. Brazilian Cinematograph Industry.

1591 **838**	1cr. multicoloured	20	10

839 Ox-cart Driver

1976.

1592 **839**	10c. red	10	10
1593 –	15c. brown	25	10
1594 –	20c. blue	20	10
1595 –	30c. red	20	10
1596 –	40c. orange	20	10
1597a –	50c. brown	25	10
1598 –	70c. black	15	10
1599 –	80c. green	1·75	10
1600a –	1cr. black	20	10
1601 –	1cr.10 purple	20	10
1602 –	1cr.30 red	20	10
1603a –	1cr.80 violet	20	10
1604a –	2cr. brown	1·50	10
1605 –	2cr.50 brown	25	10
1605a –	3cr.20 blue	25	10
1606a –	5cr. lilac	95	10
1607 –	7cr. violet	6·00	10
1608a –	10cr. green	95	10
1609 –	15cr. green	1·75	10
1610 –	20cr. blue	1·75	10
1611 –	21cr. purple	1·25	10
1612 –	27cr. brown	1·40	10

DESIGNS—HORIZ: 20c. Pirogue fisherman; 40c. Cowboy; 3cr.20, Sao Francisco boatman; 27cr. Muleteer. VERT: 15c. Bahia woman; 30c. Rubber gatherer; 50c. Gaucho; 70c. Women breaking Babacu chestnuts; 80c. Gold-washer; 1cr. Banana gatherer; 1cr.10, Grape harvester; 1cr.30, Coffee harvester; 1cr.80, Carnauba cutter; 2cr. Potter; 2cr.50, Basket maker; 5cr. Sugar-cane cutter; 7cr. Salt worker; 10cr. Fisherman; 15cr. Coconut vendor; 20cr. Lace maker; 21cr. Ramie cutter.

840 Neon Tetra ("Paracheirodon innesi")

1976. Brazilian Freshwater Fishes. Mult.

1613	1cr. Type **840**	50	45
1614	1cr. Splash tetra ("Copeina arnoldi")	50	45
1615	1cr. Prochilodus ("Prochilodus insignis")	50	45
1616	1cr. Spotted pike cichlid ("Crenicichla lepidota")	50	45
1617	1cr. Bottle-nosed catfish ("Ageneiosus sp.")	50	45
1618	1cr. Reticulated corydoras ("Corydoras reticulatus")	50	45

841 Santa Marta Lighthouse

842 Postage Stamps as Magic Carpet

1976. 300th Anniv of Laguna.

1619 **841**	1cr. blue	40	15

1976. Stamp Day.

1620 **842**	1cr. multicoloured	15	10

843 Oil Lamp and Profile

1976. 50th Anniv of Brazilian Nursing Assn.
1621 **843** 1cr. multicoloured . . . 20 10

844 Puppet Soldier **845** Winner's Medal

1976. Mamulengo Puppet Theatre. Mult.
1622 1cr. Type **844** 20 15
1623 1cr.30 Puppet girl 20 15
1624 1cr.60 Finger puppets (horiz) 20 15

1976. 27th International Military Athletics Championships, Rio de Janeiro.
1625 **845** 5cr.20 multicoloured . . 45 20

846 Family within "House" **847** Rotten Tree

1976. SESC and SENAC National Organizations for Appenticeship and Welfare.
1626 **846** 1cr. blue 15 10

1976. Conservation of the Environment.
1627 **847** 1cr. multicoloured . . . 15 10

848 Electron Orbits and Atomic Agency Emblem

1976. 20th International Atomic Energy Conference, Rio de Janeiro.
1628 **848** 5cr.20 multicoloured . . 45 25

849 Underground Train **851** School Building

850 St. Francis

1976. Inauguration of Sao Paulo Underground Railway.
1629 **849** 1cr.60 multicoloured . . 45 25

1976. 750th Death Anniv of St. Francis of Assisi.
1630 **850** 5cr.20 multicoloured . . 45 20

1976. Centenary of Ouro Preto Mining School.
1631 **851** 1cr. violet 25 30

852 "Three Kings" (J. A. da Silva)

1976. Christmas. Multicoloured.
1632 80c. Type **852** 30 20
1633 80c. "Father Christmas" (T. Onivaldo Cogo) . . . 30 20
1634 80c. "Nativity Scene" (R. Yabe) 30 20
1635 80c. "Angels" (E. Folchini) 30 20
1636 80c. "Nativity" (A.L. Cintra) 30 20

853 Section of Brazilian 30,000-reis Banknote

1976. Opening of Bank of Brazil's Thousandth Branch at Barra do Bugres. Sheet 125 × 88 mm.
MS1637 **853** 80c. multicoloured 20 30

854 "Our Lady of Monte Serrat" (Friar A. da Piedade)

1976. Brazilian Sculpture. Multicoloured.
1638 80c. Type **854** 15 10
1639 5cr. "St. Joseph" (unknown artist) (25 × 37 mm) . . . 40 20
1640 5cr.60 "The Dance" (J. Bernardelli) (square) 45 20
1641 6cr.50 "The Caravel" (B. Giorgi) (As 5cr.) . . . 35 20

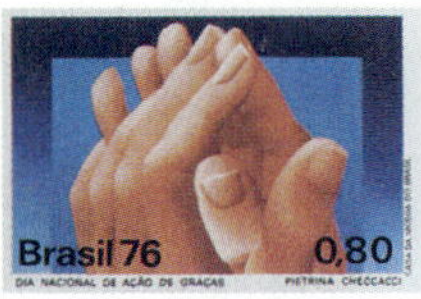

855 Hands in Prayer **856** Sailor of 1840

1976. Thanksgiving Day.
1642 **855** 80c. multicoloured . . . 15 10

1976. Brazilian Navy Commemoration. Mult.
1643 80c. Type **856** 20 10
1644 2cr. Marine of 1808 . . . . 25 15

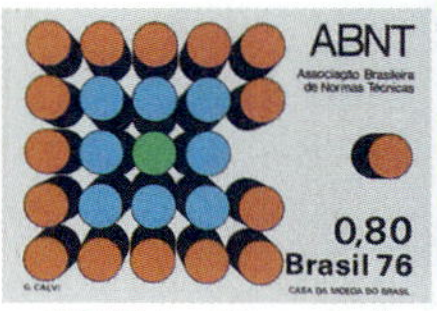

857 "Natural Resources" **858** "Wheel of Life" (wood-carving, G. T. de Oliveira)

1976. Brazilian Bureau of Standards.
1645 **857** 80c. multicoloured . . . 15 10

1977. 2nd World Black and African Festival of Arts and Culture, Lagos (Nigeria). Multicoloured.
1646 5cr. Type **858** 50 20
1647 5cr.60 "The Beggar" (wood-carving, A. dos Santos) 50 20
1648 6cr.50 Benin pectoral mask 90 20

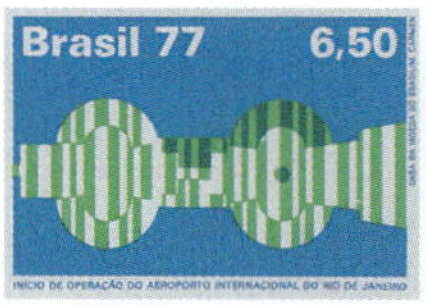

859 Airport Layout **860** Seminar Emblem

1977. Inauguration of Operation of International Airport, Rio de Janeiro.
1649 **859** 6c.50 multicoloured . . . 85 25

1977. 6th InterAmerican Budget Seminar.
1650 **860** 1cr.10 turq, bl & stone 20 10

861 Salicylic Acid Crystals **862** Emblem of Lions Clubs

1977. World Rheumatism Year.
1651 **861** 1cr.10 multicoloured . . 20 10

1977. 25th Anniv of Brazilian Lions Clubs.
1652 **862** 1cr.10 multicoloured . . 20 10

863 H. Villa-Lobos and Music

1977. Brazilian Composers. Multicoloured.
1653 1cr.10 Type **863** 25 10
1654 1cr.10 Chiquinha Gonzaga and guitar 25 10
1655 1cr.10 Noel Rosa and guitar 25 10

864 Rural and Urban Workers **865** Memorial, Porto Seguro

1977. Industrial Protection and Safety. Mult.
1656 1cr.10 Type **864** 15 10
1657 1cr.10 Laboratory vessels . . 15 10

1977. Centenary of UPU Membership. Views of Porto Seguro. Multicoloured.
1658 1cr.10 Type **865** 15 10
1659 5cr. Beach . . . . 1·25 20
1660 5cr.60 Old houses 55 20
1661 6cr.50 Post Office 50 25

866 Newspaper Title in Linotype and Print

1977. 150th Anniv of Brazilian Newspaper "Diario de Porto Allegre".
1662 **866** 1cr.10 black & purple . . 15 10

867 Blue Whale

1977. Fauna Preservation.
1663 **867** 1cr.30 multicoloured . . 55 15

868 "Cell System"

1977. 25th Anniv of National Economic Development Bank.
1664 **868** 1cr.30 multicoloured . . 15 10

869 Locomotive leaving Tunnel **870** Goliath Conch

1977. Centenary of Rio de Janeiro–Sao Paulo Railway.
1665 **869** 1c.30 black 60 25

1977. Brazilian Molluscs. Multicoloured.
1666 1cr.30 Type **870** 30 15
1667 1cr.30 Thin-bladed murex ("Murex tenuivaricosus") 30 15
1668 1cr.30 Helmet vase ("Vasum cassiforme") 30 15

871 Caduceus **872** Masonic Symbols

1977. 3rd International Congress of Odontology.
1669 **871** 1cr.30 brown, bis & orge 20 10

1977. 50th Anniv of Brazilian Grand Masonic Lodge.
1670 **872** 1cr.30 blue, dp bl & blk 25 10

873 "Sailboat" **874** Law Proclamation

1977. Stamp Day.
1671 **873** 1cr.30 multicoloured . . 15 10

1977. 150th Anniv of Juridical Courses.
1672 **874** 1cr.30 multicoloured . . 15 10

875 "Cavalhada" (horsemen) **876** Doubloon

1977. Folklore. Multicoloured.
1673 1cr.30 Type **875** 20 10
1674 1cr.30 Horseman with flag 20 10
1675 1cr.30 Jousting (horiz) . . . 20 10

1977. Brazilian Colonial Coins. Multicoloured.
1676 1cr.30 Type **876** 20 10
1677 1cr.30 Pataca 20 10
1678 1cr.30 Vintem 20 10

877 Toy Windmill **878** "Neoregelia carolinae"

1977. National Day.
1679 **877** 1cr.30 multicoloured . . 15 10

1977. Nature Conservation.
1680 **878** 1cr.30 multicoloured . . 20 10

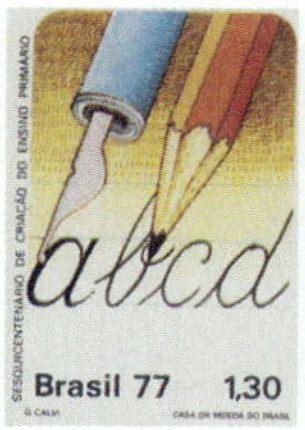

879 Pen, Pencil and Writing

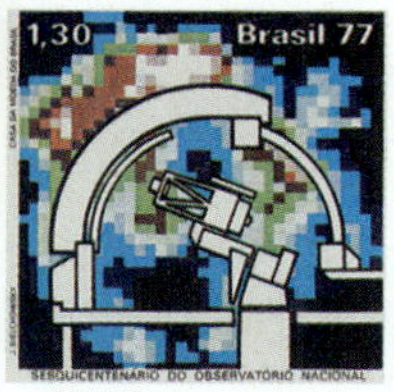

880 Observatory and Electrochromograph of Supernova

1977. 150th Anniv of Official Elementary Schooling.
1681 **879** 1cr.30 multicoloured . . 15 10

1977. 150th Anniv of National Observatory.
1682 **880** 1cr.30 multicoloured . . 20 10

881 Airship "Pax"

882 Text from "O Guarani" and Ceci

1977. Aviation Anniversaries. Multicoloured.
1683 1cr.30 Type **881** 20 10
1684 1cr.30 Savoia Marchetti flying boat "Jahu" . . . 20 10
ANNIVERSARIES: No. 1683, 75th anniv of "Pax" flight; 1684, 50th anniv of "Jahu" South Atlantic crossing.

1977. Day of the Book and Jose de Alencar Commemoration.
1685 **882** 1cr.30 multicoloured . . 15 10

883 Radio Waves

884 Nativity (in carved gourd)

1977. Amateur Radio Operators' Day.
1686 **883** 1cr.30 multicoloured . . 15 10

1977. Christmas. Multicoloured.
1687 1cr.30 Type **884** 15 10
1688 2cr. The Annunciation . . . 25 10
1689 5cr. Nativity 55 15

885 Emerald

886 Angel holding Cornucopia

1977. "Portucale 77" Thematic Stamp Exhibition. Multicoloured.
1690 1cr.30 Type **885** 20 10
1691 1cr.30 Topaz 20 10
1692 1cr.30 Aquamarine 20 10

1977. Thanksgiving Day.
1693 **886** 1cr.30 multicoloured . . 15 10

887 Curtiss Fledgling Douglas DC-3 and Badge (National Airmail Service)

1977. National Integration. Multicoloured.
1694 1cr.30 Type **887** 30 10
1695 1cr.30 Amazon River naval patrol boat and badge (Amazon Fleet) 50 10
1696 1cr.30 Train crossing bridge and badges (Engineering Corps and Railway Battalion) 75 25

888 Douglas DC-10 and Varig Airline Emblems

1977. 50th Anniv of Varig State Airline.
1697 **888** 1cr.30 black, lt bl & bl 15 10

889 Sts. Cosmus and Damian Church, Igaracu

890 Woman with Wheat Sheaf

1977. Regional Architecture, Churches. Mult.
1698 2cr.70 Type **889** 20 10
1699 7cr.50 St. Bento Monastery Church, Rio de Janeiro 60 25
1700 8cr.50 St. Francis Assisi Church, Ouro Preto . . . 65 25
1701 9cr.50 St. Anthony Convent Church, Joao Pessoa . . 80 30

1977. Diplomats' Day.
1702 **890** 1cr.30 multicoloured . . 15 10

891 Scene from "Fosca" and Carlos Gomes (composer)

1978. Bicentenary of La Scala Opera House, Milan, and Carlos Gomes Commemoration.
1703 **891** 1cr.80 multicoloured . . 30 10

892 Foot kicking Ball

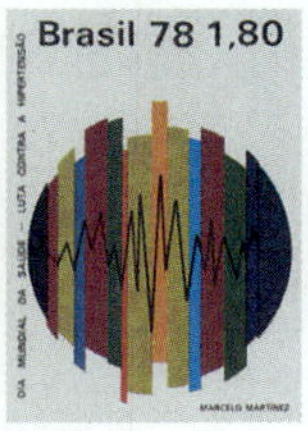

894 Electrocardiogram

893 "Postal Efficiency"

1978. World Cup Football Championship, Argentina. Multicoloured.
1704 1cr.80 Type **892** 20 10
1705 1cr.80 Ball in net 20 10
1706 1cr.80 Stylized player with cup 20 10

1978. Postal Staff College.
1707 **893** 1cr.80 multicoloured . . 15 10

1978. World Hypertension Month.
1708 **894** 1cr.80 multicoloured . . 20 10

895 World Map and Antenna

896 Saffron Finch

1978. World Telecommunications Day.
1709 **895** 1cr.80 multicoloured . . 15 10

1978. Birds. Multicoloured.
1710 7cr.50 Type **896** . . . . . . 1·25 50
1711 8cr.50 Banded cotinga . . . 1·60 60
1712 9cr.50 Seven-coloured tanager . . . . 1·90 85

897 "Discussing the Opening Speech" (G. Mondin)

1978. 85th Anniv of Union Court of Audit.
1713 **897** 1cr.80 multicoloured . . 15 10

898 Post and Telegraph Headquarters, Brasilia

1978. Opening of Post and Telegraph Headquarters.
1714 **898** 1cr.80 multicoloured . . 15 10

1978. Brapex III Third Brazilian Philatelic Exhibition. Sheet 70 × 90 mm.
MS1715 **898** 7cr. 50 multicoloured 40 55

899 President Geisel

900 Savoia Marchetti S-64 and Map

1978. President Geisel Commemoration.
1716 **899** 1cr.80 olive 20 10

1978. 50th Anniv of South Atlantic Flight by del Prete and Ferrarin.
1717 **900** 1cr.80 multicoloured . . 25 10

901 "Smallpox"

902 10r. Pedro II "White Beard" Stamp of 1878

1978. Global Eradication of Smallpox.
1718 **901** 1cr.80 multicoloured . . 20 10

1978. Stamp Day.
1719 **902** 1cr.80 multicoloured . . 15 10

903 "Jangadeiros"

1978. Birth Centenary of Helios Seelinger (painter).
1720 **903** 1cr.80 multicoloured . . 15 10

904 Musicians with Violas

1978. Folk Musicians. Multicoloured.
1721 1cr.80 Type **904** 20 10
1722 1cr.80 Two fife players . . . 20 10
1723 1cr.80 Berimbau players . . 20 10

905 Children playing Football

1978. National Week.
1724 **905** 1cr.80 multicoloured . . 20 10

906 Patio de Colegio Church

1978. Restoration of Patio de Colegio Church, Sao Paulo.
1725 **906** 1cr.80 brown 15 10

907 "Justice" (A. Ceschiatti)

1978. 150th Anniv of Federal Supreme Court.
1726 **907** 1cr.80 black and bistre 15 10

908 Ipe (flowering tree)

1978. Environment Protection. Iguacu Falls National Park. Multicoloured.
1727 1cr.80 Type **908** 25 10
1728 1cr.80 Iguacu Falls 25 10

909 Stages of "Intelsat" Assembly

1978. 3rd Assembly. Users of "Intelsat" Telecommunications Satellite.
1729 **909** 1cr.80 multicoloured . . 15 10

910 Flag of the Order of Christ

1978. "Lubrapex 78" Stamp Exhibition. Flags. Multicoloured.
1730 1cr.80 Type **910** 60 30
1731 1cr.80 Principality of Brazil 60 30
1732 1cr.80 United Kingdom of Brazil 60 30
1733 8cr.50 Empire of Brazil . . 60 30
1734 8cr.50 National Flag of Brazil 60 30

911 Postal Tramcar

1978. 18th U.P.U. Congress, Rio de Janeiro.
1735 **911** 1cr.80 brown, blk & bl 1·10 1·00
1736 – 1cr.80 brown, blk & bl 60 60
1737 – 1cr.80 grey, blk & rose 60 60
1738 – 7cr.50 grey, blk & rose 2·00 1·10
1739 – 8cr.50 brown, blk & grn 1·00 60
1740 – 9cr.50 brown, blk & grn 1·00 60
DESIGNS: No. 1736, Post container truck; 1737, Post van, 1914; 1738, Travelling post office; 1739, Mail coach; 1740, Mule caravan.

912 Gaucho

913 "Morro de Santo Antonio" (Nicolas Antoine Taunay)

1978. Day of the Book and J. Guimaraes Rosa Commemoration.
1741 **912** 1cr.80 multicoloured . . 20 10

1978. Landscape Paintings. Multicoloured.
1742 1cr.80 Type **913** 20 10
1743 1cr.80 "View of Pernambuco" (Frans Post) 20 10
1744 1cr.80 "Morro de Castelo" (Victor Meirelles) 20 10
1745 1cr.80 "Landscape at Sabara" (Alberto da Veiga Guignard) 20 10

914 Angel with Lute

915 "Thanksgiving"

1978. Christmas. Multicoloured.
1746 1cr.80 Type **914** 15 10
1747 1cr.80 Angel with lyre . . . 15 10
1748 1cr.80 Angel with trumpet 15 10

1978. Thanksgiving Day.
1749 **915** 1cr.80 ochre, blk & red 15 10

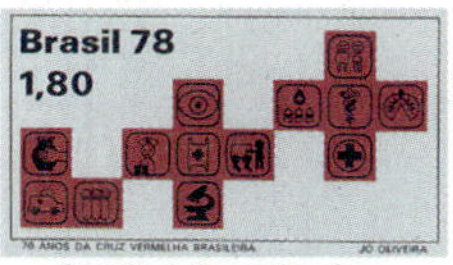

916 Red Cross Services

1978. 70th Anniv of Brazilian Red Cross.
1750 **916** 1cr.80 red and black . . 15 10

917 Peace Theatre, Belem

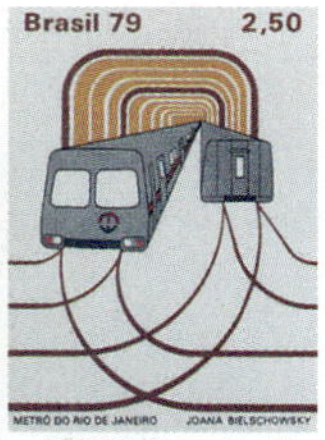

918 Underground Trains

1978. Brazilian Theatres. Multicoloured.
1751 10cr.50 Type **917** 50 15
1752 12cr. Jose de Alencar Theatre, Fortaleza 55 20
1753 12cr.50 Rio de Janeiro Municipal Theatre 60 20

1979. Inauguration of Rio de Janeiro Underground Railway.
1754 **918** 2cr.50 multicoloured . . 50 10

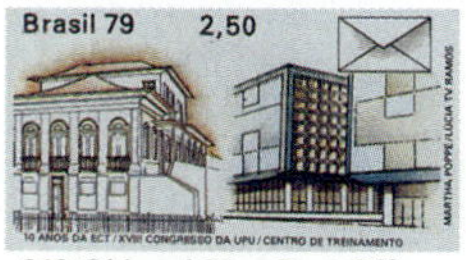

919 Old and New Post Offices

1979. 10th Anniv of Post & Telegraph Department and 18th U.P.U. Congress (2nd issue). Multicoloured.
1755 2cr.50 Type **919** 25 15
1756 2cr.50 Mail boxes 25 15
1757 2cr.50 Mail sorting 25 15
1758 2cr.50 Mail planes 25 15
1759 2cr.50 Telegraph and telex machines 25 15
1760 2cr.50 Postmen 25 15

920 "O'Day 23" Class Yacht

1979. "Brasiliana 79" 3rd World Thematic Stamp Exhibition (1st issue). Multicoloured.
1761 2cr.50 Type **920** 25 10
1762 10cr.50 "Penguin" class dinghy 55 20
1763 12cr. "Hobie Cat" class catamaran 55 20
1764 12cr.50 "Snipe" class dinghy 55 25
See Nos. 1773/6 and 1785/90.

921 Joao Bolinha (characters from children's story)

1979. Children's Book Day.
1765 **921** 2cr.50 multicoloured . . 20 10

922 "Victoria amazonica"

1979. 18th U.P.U. Congress (3rd issue). Amazon National Park. Multicoloured.
1766 10cr.50 Type **922** 60 20
1767 12cr. Amazon manatee . . . 65 25
1768 12cr.50 Tortoise 70 25

923 Bank Emblem

1979. 25th Anniv of Northeast Bank of Brazil.
1769 **923** 2cr.50 multicoloured . . 15 10

924 Physicians and Patient (15th cent woodcut)

1979. 150th Anniv of National Academy of Medicine.
1770 **924** 2cr.50 yellow and black 15 10

925 Clover with Hearts as Leaves

1979. 35th Brazilian Cardiology Congress.
1771 **925** 2cr.50 multicoloured . . 15 10

926 Hotel Nacional, Rio de Janeiro

1979. Brasiliana 79 (2nd issue). Sheet 87 × 124 mm.
MS1772 **926** 12cr.50 multicoloured 30 35

927 "Cithaerias aurora"

1979. "Brasiliana 79" (2nd issue). Butterflies. Multicoloured.
1773 2cr.50 Type **927** 30 15
1774 10cr.50 "Evenus regalis" . . 90 25
1775 12cr. "Caligo eurilochus" . . 1·00 35
1776 12cr.50 "Diaethria clymena janeira" . . . . 1·10 40

928 Embraer Xingu

929 Globe illuminating Land

1979. 10th Anniv of Brazilian Aeronautical Industry.
1777 **928** 2cr.50 dp blue and blue 15 10

1979. National Week.
1778 **929** 3cr.20 blue, green & yell 15 10

930 Our Lady Aparecida

931 Envelope and Transport

1979. 75th Anniv of Coronation of Our Lady Aparecida.
1779 **930** 2cr.50 multicoloured . . 15 10

1979. 18th UPU Congress, Rio de Janeiro (4th issue). Multicoloured.
1780 2cr.50 Type **931** 75 30
1781 2cr.50 Post Office emblems 20 10
1782 10cr.50 Globe 35 20
1783 12cr. Flags of Brazil and UPU 40 20
1784 12cr.50 UPU emblem . . . 40 20

932 "Igreja da Gloria"

933 Pyramid Fountain, Rio de Janeiro

1979. "Brasiliana 79" Third World Thematic Stamp Exhibition (3rd issue). Paintings by Leandro Joaquim. Multicoloured.
1785 2cr.50 Type **932** 15 10
1786 12cr. "Fishing on Guanabara Bay" 35 20
1787 12cr.50 "Boqueirao Lake and Carioca Arches" . . 45 25

1979. "Brasiliana 79" (4th issue). 1st International Exhibition of Classical Philately. Fountains.
1788 **933** 2cr.50 black, grn & emer 10 10
1789 – 10cr.50 black, turq & bl 35 20
1790 – 12cr. black, red and pink 40 25
DESIGNS—VERT: 12cr. Boa Vista, Recife. HORIZ: 10cr.50, Marilia Fountain, Ouro Preto.

934 World Map

935 "UPU" and Emblem

1979. 3rd World Telecommunications Exhibition, Geneva.
1791 **934** 2cr.50 multicoloured . . 15 10

1979. UPU Day.
1792 **935** 2cr.50 multicoloured . . 15 10
1793 10cr.50 multicoloured . . 35 15
1794 12cr. multicoloured . . . 35 15
1795 12cr.50 multicoloured . . 35 20

936 "Peteca" (shuttlecock)

1979. International Year of the Child. Mult.
1796 2cr.50 Type **936** 20 10
1797 3cr.20 Spinning top 20 10
1798 3cr.20 Jumping Jack 20 10
1799 3cr.20 Rag doll 20 10

937 "The Birth of Jesus"

1979. Christmas. Tiles from the Church of Our Lady of Health and Glory, Salvador. Multicoloured.
1800 3cr.20 Type **937** 15 10
1801 3cr.20 "Adoration of the Kings" 15 10
1802 3cr.20 "The Boy Jesus among the Doctors" . . . 15 10

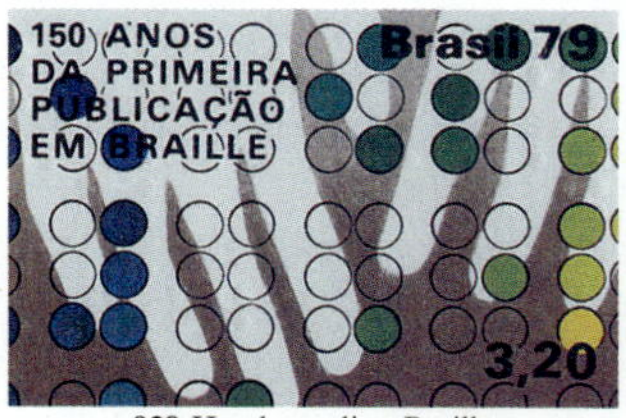

938 Hands reading Braille

1979. 150th Anniv of First Braille Publication. Sheet 127 × 88 mm.
MS1803 **938** 3cr. 20 multicoloured 30 35

939 Woman with Wheat

940 Steel Mill

1979. Thanksgiving Day.
1804 **939** 3cr.20 multicoloured . . 15 10

1979. 25th Anniv of Cosipa Steel Works, Sao Paulo.
1805 **940** 3cr.20 multicoloured . . 15 10

941 Plant within Raindrop

942 Coal Trucks

1980. Energy Conservation. Multicoloured.
1806 3cr.20 Type **941** . . 25 10
1807 17cr.+7cr. Sun and lightbulb 35 10
1808 20cr.+8cr. Windmill and lightbulb 90 55
1809 21cr.+9cr. Dam and lightbulb . . . . 1·50 30

1980. Coal Industry.
1810 **942** 4cr. black, orge & red 65 30

943 Coconuts

1980.

1811	**943**	2cr. brown	15	10
1812	–	3cr. red	15	10
1813	–	4cr. orange	15	10
1814	–	5cr. violet	15	10
1815	–	7cr. orange	35	10
1816	–	10cr. green	15	10
1817	–	12cr. green	10	10
1818	–	15cr. brown	15	10
1819	–	17cr. red	35	10
1820	–	20cr. brown	15	10
1821	–	24cr. orange	90	10
1822	–	30cr. black	90	10
1823	–	34cr. brown	5·25	1·25
1824	–	38cr. red	3·50	50
1825	–	42cr. green	7·00	1·25
1825a	–	45cr. brown	10	10
1826	–	50cr. orange	20	10
1826a	–	57cr. brown	2·40	60
1826b	–	65cr. purple	15	10
1827	–	66cr. violet	5·25	1·25
1827a	–	80cr. red	90	45
1828	–	100cr. brown	55	10
1828a	–	120cr. blue	20	10
1829	–	140cr. red	7·00	60
1829a	–	150cr. green	20	10
1830	–	200cr. green	1·75	10
1830a	–	300cr. purple	2·40	10
1831	–	500cr. brown	2·40	10
1832	–	800cr. green	1·75	10
1833	–	1000cr. olive	1·75	10
1834	–	2000cr. orange	2·40	10

DESIGNS: 3cr. Mangoes; 4cr. Corn; 5cr. Onions; 7cr. Oranges; 10cr. Passion fruit; 12cr. Pineapple; 15cr. Bananas; 17cr. Guarana; 20cr. Sugar cane; 24cr. Bee and honeycomb; 30cr. Silkworm and mulberry; 34cr. Cocoa beans; 38cr. Coffee; 42cr. Soya bean; 45cr. Manioc; 50cr. Wheat; 57cr. Peanuts; 65cr. Rubber; 66cr. Grapes; 80cr. Brazil nuts; 100cr. Cashews; 120cr. Rice; 140cr. Tomatoes; 150cr. Eucalyptus; 200cr. Castor-oil bean; 300cr. Parana pine; 500cr. Cotton; 800cr. Carnauba palm; 1000cr. Babassu palm; 2000cr. Sunflower.

944 Banknote with Development Symbols

1980. 21st Inter-American Bank of Development Directors' Annual Assembly Meeting, Rio de Janeiro.
1836 **944** 4cr. blue, brown & blk 15 10

945 Tapirape Mask

1980. Indian Art. Ritual Masks. Mult.
1837 4cr. Type **945** 20 10
1838 4cr. Tukuna mask (vert) . . 20 10
1839 4cr. Kanela mask (vert) . . 20 10

946 Geometric Head

947 Duke of Caxias (after Miranda Junior)

1980. 30th Anniv of Brazilian Television.
1840 **946** 4cr. multicoloured . . . 15 10

1980. Death Centenary of Duke de Caxias (General and statesman).
1841 **947** 4cr. multicoloured . . . 15 10

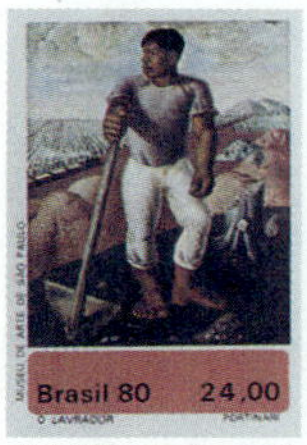

948 "The Labourer" (Candido Portinari)

1980. Art in Brazilian Museums. Mult.
1842 24cr. Type **948** 75 25
1843 28cr. "Mademoiselle Pogany" (statuette, Constantin Brancusi) . . 75 25
1844 30cr. "The Glass of Water" (A. de Figueiredo) 95 30
MUSEUMS. 24cr. Sao Paulo Museum of Art. 28cr. Rio de Janeiro Museum of Modern Art. 30cr. Rio de Janeiro Museum of Fine Art.

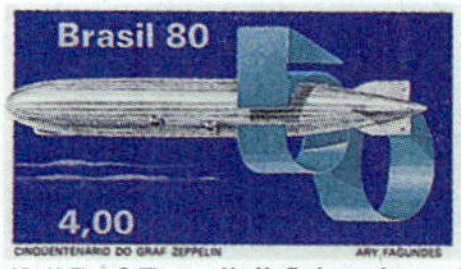

949 "Graf Zeppelin" flying through "50"

1980. 50th Annivs of "Graf Zeppelin" and First South Atlantic Air Mail Flight.
1845 **949** 4cr. black, blue & violet 20 15
1846 – 4cr. multicoloured . . . 20 15
DESIGN: No. 1846, Latecoere seaplane "Comte de la Vaulx".

950 Sail and Bone-lace "Sun"

1980. Brapex IV National Stamp Exhibition, Fortaleza. Sheet 125 × 87 mm.
MS1847 **950** 30cr. multicoloured 40 50

951 Pope John Paul II and Fortaleza Cathedral

952 Shooting

1980. Papal Visit and 10th National Eucharistic Congress. Pope John Paul II and cathedrals. Multicoloured.
1848 4cr. Type **951** 25 15
1849 4cr. St. Peter's, Rome (horiz) 25 15
1850 24cr. Apericida (horiz) . . . 65 40
1851 28cr. Rio de Janeiro (horiz) 65 20
1852 30cr. Brasilia (horiz) . . . . 1·50 25

1980. Olympic Games, Moscow. Mult.
1853 4cr. Type **952** 20 10
1854 4cr. Cycling 20 10
1855 4cr. Rowing 20 10

953 Classroom

1980. Rondon Project (voluntary student work in rural areas).
1856 **953** 4cr. multicoloured . . . 20 10

954 Helen Keller and Anne Sullivan

956 Houses and Microscope

955 Sao Francisco River Canoe

1980. Birth Centenary of Helen Keller, and 4th Brazilian Congress on Prevention of Blindness, Belo Horizonte.
1857 **954** 4cr. multicoloured . . . 20 10

1980. Stamp Day. Sheet 125 × 86 mm.
MS1858 **955** 24cr. multicoloured 1·00 1·00

1980. National Health Day. Campaign against Chagas Disease (barber bug fever).
1859 **956** 4cr. multicoloured . . . 20 10

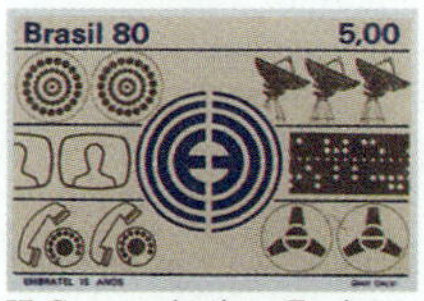

957 Communications Equipment

1980. 15th Anniv of National Telecommunications System.
1860 **957** 5cr. stone, blue & green 20 10

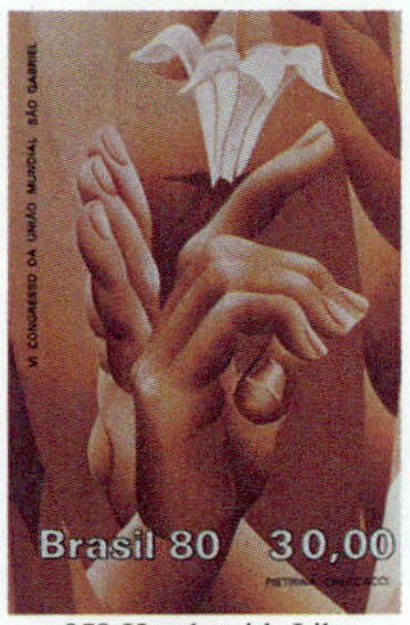

958 Hands with Lily

1980. 6th World Union of St. Gabriel (Religious Philately Federation) Congress, Sao Paulo. Sheet 124 × 86 mm.
MS1861 **958** 30cr. multicoloured 60 65

959 "Cattleya amethystoglossa"

960 Vinaceous Amazon

1980. "Espamer 80" International Stamp Exhibition, Madrid. Orchids. Multicoloured.
1862 5cr. Type **959** 30 10
1863 5cr. "Laelia cinnabarina" 30 10
1864 24cr. "Zygopetalum crinitum" . . . . 1·75 35
1865 28cr. "Laelia tenebrosa" . . 1·75 40

1980. "Lubrapex 80" Portuguese–Brazilian Stamp Exhibition, Lisbon. Parrots. Multicoloured.
1866 5cr. Type **960** 60 40
1867 5cr. Red-tailed amazon . . 60 40
1868 28cr. Red-spectacled amazon 3·00 1·00
1869 28cr. Brown backed parrotlet . . . . 3·00 1·00

961 Captain Rodrigo (fictional character)

962 Flight into Egypt

1980. Book Day and Erico Verissimo (writer). Commemoration.
1870 **961** 5cr. multicoloured . . . 20 10

1980. Christmas.
1871 **962** 5cr. multicoloured . . . 20 10

963 Wave-form

1980. Inauguration of Telecommunications Centre for Research and Development, Campanas City.
1872 **963** 5cr. multicoloured . . . 20 10

964 Carvalho Viaduct, Paranagua–Curitiba Railway Line

1980. Centenary of Engineering Club.
1873 **964** 5cr. multicoloured . . . 45 25

965 Postal Chessboard

966 Sun and Wheat

1980. Postal Chess.
1874 **965** 5cr. multicoloured . . . 55 20

1980. Thanksgiving Day.
1875 **966** 5cr. multicoloured . . . 20 15

967 Father Anchieta writing Poem in Sand

1980. Beatification of Father Jose de Anchieta.
1876 **967** 5cr. multicoloured . . . 20 10

968 Christ on the Mount of Olives

1980. 250th Birth Anniv of Antonio Lisboa (Aleijadinho) (sculptor). Wood sculptures of Christ's head. Multicoloured.
1877 5cr. Type **968** 30 30
1878 5cr. The Arrest in the Garden 30 30
1879 5cr. Flagellation 30 30
1880 5cr. Wearing Crown of Thorns 30 30
1881 5cr. Carrying the cross . . . 30 30
1882 5cr. Crucifixion 30 30

969 Agricultural Produce

1981. Agricultural Development. Mult.
1883 30cr. Type **969** . . . . . . 1·25 25
1884 35cr. Shopping 80 30
1885 40cr. Exporting 80 30

970 Scout sitting by Camp Fire

1981. 4th Pan-American Jamboree. Multicoloured.
1886 5cr. Type **970** 25 10
1887 5cr. Troop cooking 25 10
1888 5cr. Scout with totem pole 25 10

971 First-class Mailman (Empire period)

1981. 50th Anniv of Integrated Post Office and Telegraph Department (DCT). Sheet 99 × 70 mm containing T **971** and similar vert designs. Multicoloured.
MS1889 30cr. Type **971**; 35cr. DCT mailman; 40cr. Telegraph messenger (first republic) . . . 2·25 2·25

972 "The Hunter and the Jaguar"

1981. Death Centenary of Felix Emile, Baron of Tauny (artist). Sheet 70 × 90 mm.
MS1890 **972** 30cr. multicoloured 85 90

973 Lima Barreto and Rio de Janeiro Street Scene

1981. Birth Centenary of Lima Barreto (author).
1891 **973** 7cr. multicoloured . . . 60 25

974 Tupi-Guarani Ceramic Funeral Urn

1981. Artefacts from Brazilian Museums. Mult.
1892 7cr. Type **974** (Archaeology and Popular Arts Museum, Paranagua) . . 20 15
1893 7cr. Marajoara "tanga" ceramic loincloth (Emilio Goeldi Museum, Para) . . 20 15
1894 7cr. Maraca tribe funeral urn (National Museum, Rio de Janeiro) 20 15

975 Ruby-topaz Hummingbird

1981. Hummingbirds. Multicoloured.
1895 7cr. Type **975** . . . . 1·00 25
1896 7cr. Horned sungem . . . . 1·00 25
1897 7cr. Frilled coquette . . . . 1·00 25
1898 7cr. Planalto hermit . . . . 1·00 25

976 Hands and Cogwheels

1981. 72nd Int Rotary Convention, Sao Paulo.
1899 **976** 7cr. red and black . . . 15 10
1900 – 35cr. multicoloured . . . 1·50 60
DESIGN: 35cr. Head and cogwheels.

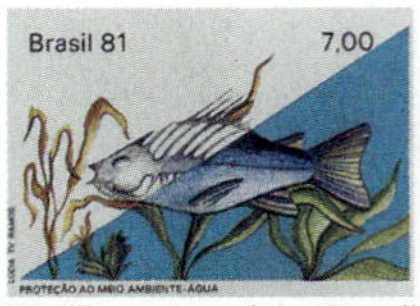

977 "Protection of the Water"

1981. Environment Protection. Multicoloured.
1901 7cr. Type **977** 25 15
1902 7cr. "Protection of the forests" 25 15
1903 7cr. "Protection of the air" 25 15
1904 7cr. "Protection of the soil" 25 15

978 Curtiss Fledgling

1981. 50th Anniv of National Air Mail Service.
1905 **978** 7cr. multicoloured . . . 20 10

979 Locomotive "Colonel Church" and Map of Railway

1981. 50th Anniv of Madeira–Mamore Railway Nationalization.
1906 **979** 7cr. multicoloured . . . 55 30

980 Esperanto Star and Arches of Alvorada Governmental Palace, Brasilia

1981. 66th World Esperanto Congress, Brasilia.
1907 **980** 7cr. green, grey & black 15 10

981 Pedro II and 50r. "Small Head" Stamp

1981. Cent of Pedro II "Small Head" Stamps.
1908 **981** 50cr. brown, blk & bl . . 1·10 25
1909 – 55cr. mauve and green 1·10 25
1910 – 60cr. blue, black & orge 95 30
DESIGNS: 55cr. Pedro II and 100r. "Small Head" stamp; 60r. Pedro II and 200r. "Small Head" stamp.

982 Military Institute of Engineering

1981. 50th Anniv of Military Institute of Engineering.
1911 **982** 12cr. multicoloured . . . 15 10

983 Caboclinhos Folkdance

1981. Festivities. Multicoloured.
1912 50cr. Type **983** 90 15
1913 55cr. Marujada folk festival 90 15
1914 60cr. Resado parade 90 20

984 Sun and Erect, Drooping, and Supported Flowers

1981. International Year of Disabled Persons.
1915 **984** 12cr. multicoloured . . . 20 10

985 "Dalechampia caperoniodes"

986 Image of Our Lady of Nazareth

1981. Flowers of the Central Plateau. Multicoloured.
1916 12cr. Type **985** 20 15
1917 12cr. "Palicourea rigida" . . 20 15
1918 12cr. "Eremanthus sphaerocephalus" (vert) 20 15
1919 12cr. "Cassia clausseni" (vert) 20 15

1981. Festival of Our Lady of Nazareth, Belem.
1920 **986** 12cr. multicoloured . . . 15 10

987 Christ the Redeemer Monument

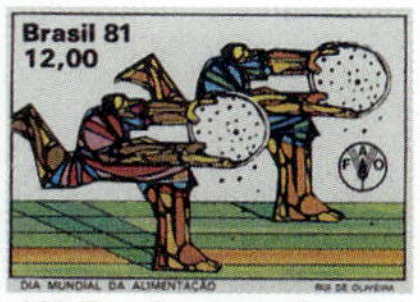

988 Farmhands seeding the Land

1981. 50th Anniv of Christ the Redeemer Monument, Rio de Janeiro.
1921 **987** 12cr. multicoloured . . . 15 10

1981. World Food Day.
1922 **988** 12cr. multicoloured . . . 15 10

989 Santos Dumont and Biplane "14 bis" landing at Paris

1981. 75th Anniv of Santos Dumont's First Powered Flight.
1923 **989** 60cr. multicoloured . . . 75 20

990 Friar Santos Rita Durao, Title Page and Scene from "Caramuru"

1981. Book Day and Bicentenary of Publication of Epic Poem "Caramuru".
1924 **990** 12cr. multicoloured . . . 15 10

991 Crib, Juazeiro de Norte (Cica)

1981. Christmas. Various designs showing Cribs. Multicoloured.
1925 12cr. Type **991** 15 10
1926 50cr. Caruaru (Vitalino Filho) 75 15
1927 55cr. Sao Jose dos Campos (Eugenia) (vert) 75 15
1928 60cr. Taubate (Candida) (vert) . . . . 1·10 20

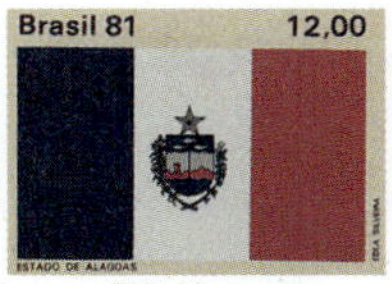

992 Alagoas

1981. State Flags (1st series). Multicoloured.
1929 12cr. Type **992** 50 50
1930 12cr. Bahia 50 50
1931 12cr. Federal District . . . 50 50
1932 12cr. Pernambuco 50 50
1933 12cr. Sergipe 50 50
See also Nos. 1988/92, 2051/5, 2113/17, 2204/7 and 3043/4.

993 Girls with Wheat

994 Heads and Symbols of Occupations

1981. Thanksgiving Day.
1934 **993** 12cr. multicoloured . . . 15 10

1981. 50th Anniv of Ministry of Labour.
1935 **994** 12cr. multicoloured . . . 15 10

995 Federal Engineering School, Itajuba

1981. Birth Centenary of Theodomiro Carneiro Santiago (founder of Federal Engineering School).
1936 **995** 15cr. green and mauve 15 10

996 Musician of Police Military Band and Headquarters

997 Army Library "Ex Libris"

1981. 150th Anniv of Sao Paulo Military Police. Multicoloured.
1937 12cr. Type **996** 25 10
1938 12cr. Lancers of Ninth of July Regiment, Mounted Police 25 10

1981. Centenary of Army Library.
1939 **997** 12cr. multicoloured . . . 15 10

998 Envelope and "Bull's Eye" Stamp

1981. 50th Anniv of Philatelic Club of Brazil. Sheet 89 × 69 mm.
MS1940 **998** 180cr. bistre, blue and black . . . . 2·25 2·50

999 Brigadier Eduardo Gomes

1982. Brigadier Eduardo Gomes Commem.
1941 **999** 12cr. blue and black . . 15 10

1000 Lage, Coal Trucks, "Ita" freighter and HL-1 Airplane

1981. Birth Cent of Henrique Lage (industrialist).
1942 **1000** 17cr. multicoloured . . 1·60 45

1001 Tackle

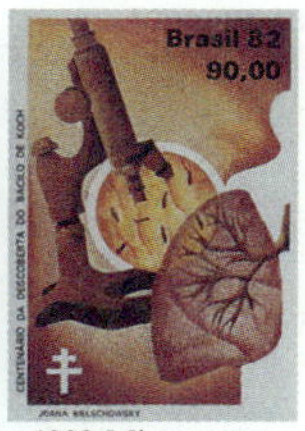

1002 Microscope, Bacillus and Lung

1982. World Cup Football Championship, Spain. Multicoloured.
1943 75cr. Type **1001** . . . . . . 1·75 50
1944 80cr. Kicking ball . . . . . 1·75 50
1945 85cr. Goalkeeper . . . . . 1·75 50
MS1946 125 × 87 mm. 100cr. × 3. As Nos. 1943/5. Imperf . . . . . 2·00 2·75

1982. Centenary of Robert Koch's Discovery of Tubercle Bacillus. Multicoloured.
1947 90cr. Type **1002** . . . . . . 4·25 1·75
1948 100cr. Flasks, tablets, syringe, bacillus and lung 4·25 1·75

1003 *Laelia purpurata*

1982. Brapex V National Stamp Exhibition, Santa Catarina. Sheet 100 × 70 mm containing T **1003** and similar vert designs showing orchids. Multicoloured.
MS1949 75cr. Type **1003**; 80cr. *Oncidium flexuosum*; 85cr. *Cleistes revolute* . . . . 4·00 4·25

1004 Oil Rig Workers

1982. Birth Centenary of Monteiro Lobato (writer).
1950 **1004** 17cr. multicoloured . . 20 10

1005 St. Vincent de Paul

1982. 400th Birth Anniv of St. Vincent de Paul.
1951 **1005** 17cr. multicoloured . . 15 10

1006 Fifth Fall

1982. Guaira's Seven Falls. Multicoloured.
1952 17cr. Type **1006** 20 10
1953 21cr. Seventh fall 25 10

1007 Envelope, Telephone, Antenna and Postcode

1982. 15th Anniv of Ministry of Communications.
1954 **1007** 21cr. multicoloured . . 15 10

1008 The Old Arsenal (National Historical Museum)

1982. 50th Anniv of Museology Course.
1955 **1008** 17cr. black and pink . . 15 10

1009 Cogwheels and Ore Mountains

1982. 40th Anniv of Vale do Rio Doce Company.
1956 **1009** 17cr. multicoloured . . 15 10

1010 Martim Afonso de Souza proclaiming Sao Vicente a Town

1982. 450th Anniv of Sao Vicente.
1957 **1010** 17cr. multicoloured . . 15 10

1011 Giant Anteater

1982. Animals. Multicoloured.
1958 17cr. Type **1011** 40 10
1959 21cr. Maned wolf 90 15
1960 30cr. Pampas deer . . . . . 1·75 25

1012 Film and "Golden Palm"

1982. 20th Anniv of "Golden Palm" Film Award to "The Given Word".
1961 **1012** 17cr. multicoloured . . 20 10

1013 Obelisk with Reliefs illustrating Verses by Guilherme de Almeida

1014 Church of Our Lady of O, Sabara

1982. 50th Anniv of Sao Paulo Revolutionary Government. Sheet 70 × 100 mm.
MS1962 **1013** 140cr. black and blue 1·40 1·50

1982. Baroque-style Architecture in Minas Gerais. Multicoloured.
1963 17cr. Type **1014** 55 10
1964 17cr. Church of Our Lady of Carmo, Mariana (horiz) 55 10
1965 17cr. Church of Our Lady of Rosary, Diamantina (horiz) 55 10

1015 St. Francis of Assisi

1016 "Large Head" Stamp of 1882

1982. 800th Birth Anniv of St. Francis of Assisi.
1966 **1015** 21cr. multicoloured . . 15 10

1982. Centenary of Pedro II "Large Head" Stamps.
1967 **1016** 21cr. yellow, brn & blk 15 10

1017 Amazon River and Hands holding Seedling, Screw and Coin

1982. Manaus Free Trade Zone.
1968 **1017** 75cr. multicoloured . . 95 20

1018 Lord Baden-Powell

1019 Xango

1982. 125th Birth Anniv of Lord Baden Powell and 75th Anniv of Boy Scout Movement. Sheet 100 × 70 mm containing T **1018** and similar vert design. Multicoloured.
MS1969 85cr. Type **1018**; 185cr. Scout saluting . . . . 2·50 2·50

1982. Orixas Religious Costumes. Mult.
1970 20cr. Type **1019** 20 10
1971 20cr. Iemanja 20 10
1972 20cr. Oxumare 20 10

1020 XII Florin

1982. 10th Anniv of Brazilian Central Bank Values Museum. Multicoloured.
1973 25cr. Type **1020** 20 10
1974 25cr. Pedro I Coronation piece 20 10

1021 "Ipiranga Cry" (Dom Pedro proclaiming independence)

1022 St. Theresa of Jesus

1982. Independence Week.
1975 **1021** 25cr. multicoloured . . 20 10

1982. 400th Death Anniv of St. Theresa of Jesus.
1976 **1022** 85cr. multicoloured . . 2·40 50

1023 Musical Instrument Maker

1024 Embraer Tucano Trainers

1982. "Lubrapex 82" Brazilian–Portuguese Stamp Exhibition, Curitiba. The Paranaense Fandango. Multicoloured.
1977 75cr. Type **1023** . . . . . . 1·75 50
1978 80cr. Dancers . . . . 1·75 50
1979 85cr. Musicians . . . . . . 1·75 50
MS1980 100 × 70 mm. Nos. 1977/9 2·25 2·25

1982. Aeronautical Industry Day.
1981 **1024** 24cr. multicoloured . . 20 25

1025 Bastos Tigre and Verse from "Saudade"

1982. Day of the Book and Birth Centenary of Bastos Tigre (poet).
1982 **1025** 24cr. multicoloured . . 15 10

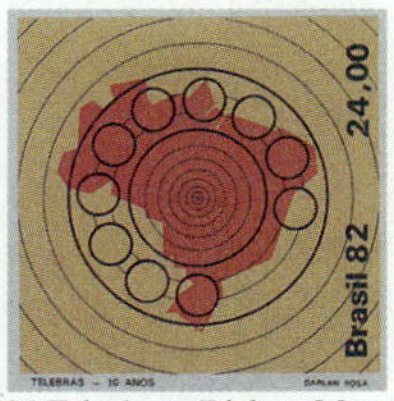

1026 Telephone Dial on Map of Brazil

1982. 10th Anniv of Telebras (Brazilian Telecommunications Corporation).
1983 **1026** 24cr. multicoloured . . 15 10

1027 "Nativity" (C.S. Miyaba)

1982. Christmas. Children's Paintings. Mult.
1984 24cr. Type **1027** . . . . . . 1·25 10
1985 24cr. "Choir of Angels" (N. N. Aleluia) . . . . . 1·25 10
1986 30cr. "Holy Family" (F. T. Filho) . . . . 1·25 15
1987 30cr. "Nativity with Angel" (N. Arand) . . . . 1·25 15

1982. State Flags (2nd series). As T **992**. Mult.
1988 24cr. Ceara . . . . 1·75 60
1989 24cr. Espirito Santo . . . . 1·75 60
1990 24cr. Paraiba . . . . 1·75 60
1991 24cr. Rio Grande do Norte 1·75 60
1992 24cr. Rondonia . . . . . . 1·75 60

1028 "Germination"

1029 "Efeta" (S. Tempel)

1982. Thanksgiving Day.
1993 **1028** 24cr. multicoloured . . 50 10

1982. The Hard of Hearing.
1994 **1029** 24cr. multicoloured . . 15 10

1030 "Benjamin Constant" (cadet ship)

1982. Bicentenary of Naval Academy. Mult.
1995 24cr. Type **1030** 85 25
1996 24cr. "Almirante Saldanha" (cadet ship) 85 25
1997 24cr. "Brasil" (training frigate) 85 25

1031 300r. Stamp of 1845

1982. Brasiliana 83 International Stamp Exhibition, Rio de Janeiro (1st issue). Sheet 99 × 69 mm.
MS1998 **1031** 200cr. black, ochre and blue . . . . 2·25 2·50
See Also Nos. 1999/2002, 2029/**MS**2032 and **MS**2033.

1032 Samba Parade Drummers

1983. "Brasiliana 83" International Stamp Exhibition, Rio de Janeiro. Carnival. Multicoloured.
1999 24cr. Type **1032** 90 35
2000 130cr. Masked clowns . . . 3·00 90
2001 140cr. Dancer . . . . . . 3·00 90
2002 150cr. Indian . . . . 3·00 90

1033 Support Ship "Barao de Teffe" in Antarctic

1983. 1st Brazilian Antarctic Expedition.
2003 **1033** 150cr. multicoloured . . 1·75 45

1034 Woman with Ballot Paper

1035 Itaipu Dam

1983. 50th Anniv of Women's Suffrage in Brazil.
2004 **1034** 130cr. multicoloured . . 1·75 50

1983. Itaipu Brazilian–Paraguayan Hydro-electric Project.
2005 **1035** 140cr. multicoloured . . 1·75 50

1036 Luther

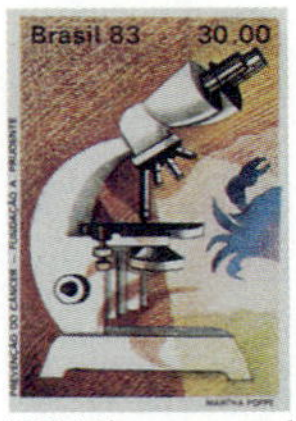

1037 Microscope and Crab

1983. 500th Birth Anniv of Martin Luther (Protestant reformer).
2006 **1036** 150cr. deep green, green and black . . . . . 2·40 50

1983. Cancer Prevention. 30th Anniv of Antonio Prudente Foundation and A.C. Camargo Hospital. Multicoloured.
2007 30cr. Type **1037** 25 20
2008 38cr. Antonio Prudente, hospital and crab 25 20

1038 Tissue Culture

1983. Agricultural Research. Multicoloured.
2009 30cr. Type **1038** 20 10
2010 30cr. Brazilian wild chestnut tree 20 10
2011 38cr. Tropical soya beans 20 10

1039 Friar Rogerio Neuhaus before Altar

1040 Council Emblem and World Map

1983. Cent of Ordination of Friar Rogerio Neuhaus.
2012 **1039** 30cr. multicoloured . . 20 10

1983. 30th Anniv of Customs Co-operation Council.
2013 **1040** 30cr. multicoloured . . 20 10

1041 Satellite

1983. World Communications Year.
2014 **1041** 250cr. multicoloured . . 3·50 1·25

1042 Toco Toucan

1983. Toucans. Multicoloured.
2015 30cr. Type **1042** 90 20
2016 185cr. Red-billed toucan . . 3·00 85
2017 205cr. Red-breasted toucan 3·00 90
2018 215cr. Channel-billed toucan 3·00 1·10

1043 "The Resurrection"

1983. 500th Birth Anniv of Raphael (artist). Sheet 70 × 90 mm.
MS2019 **1043** 250cr. multicoloured 1·75 2·00

1044 Baldwin Locomotive No. 1, 1881

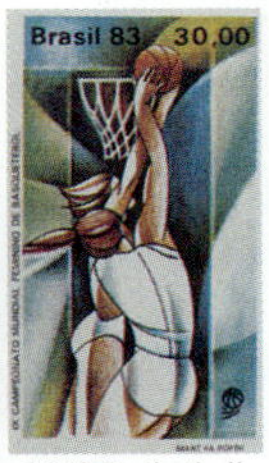

1045 Basketball Players

1983. Locomotives. Multicoloured.
2020 30cr. Type **1044** 55 30
2021 30cr. Hohenzollern locomotive No. 980, 1875 55 30
2022 38cr. Locomotive No. 1 "Maria Fumaca", 1868 55 30

1983. 9th Women's World Basketball Championship, Sao Paulo.
2023 30cr. Type **1045** 25 10
2024 30cr. Basketball players (different) 25 10

1046 Bolivar (after Tito Salas)

1983. Birth Bicentenary of Simon Bolivar.
2025 **1046** 30cr. multicoloured . . 20 10

1047 Boy with Kite and Boy waiting for Polio Vaccination

1048 Minerva and Computer Punched Tape

1983. Polio and Measles Vaccination Campaign. Multicoloured.
2026 30cr. Type **1047** 30 10
2027 30cr. Girl on bicycle and girl receiving measles vaccination 30 10

1983. 20th Anniv of Post-graduate Master's Programmes in Engineering.
2028 **1048** 30cr. light brown, blue and brown 20 10

1049 30r. "Bulls Eye" Stamp and Rio de Janeiro Bay

1983. "Brasiliana 83" International Stamp Exhibition, Rio de Janeiro. 140th Anniv of "Bull's Eye" Stamps.
2029 **1049** 185cr. black and blue 1·50 90
2030 – 205cr. black and blue 1·50 90
2031 – 215cr. black and violet 1·50 90
MS2032 100 × 70 mm. 185cr., 205cr., 215cr. each black and blue 3·50 4·00
DESIGNS: Nos. 2030/1, As Type **1049** but showing 60r. and 90r. "Bull's-Eye" stamp respectively; No. **MS**2032, "Bull's-Eye" stamp on each value as for Nos. 2029/31, and composite design of Rio de Janeiro Bay across the three.

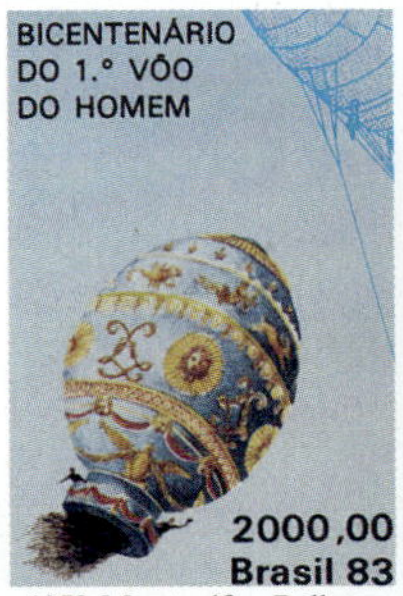

1050 Montgolfier Balloon

1051 "The First Mass in Brazil"

1983. Brasiliana 83 International Stamp Exhibition, Rio de Janeiro (4th issue). Five sheets 105 × 149 mm (a, d) or 149 × 105 mm (others), each containing design as T **1050**. Multicoloured.
MS2033 Five sheets (a) 2000cr. Type **1050** (Bicentenary of manned flight); (b) 2000cr. Racing car (Formula 1 champions 1972, 1974, 1981); (c) 2000cr. "Tornado" and "Class 470" sailing dinghies (Olympic sailing champion, 1980); (d) 2000cr. Triple jumper (Olympic triple jump champions, 1952, 1956); (e) 2000cr. World Cup and footballer (World Cup champions, 1958, 1962, 1970) . . . . . . 50·00 55·00

1983. 150th Birth Anniv (1982) of Victor Meireles (artist). Sheet 100 × 70 mm.
MS2034 **1051** 250cr. multicoloured 1·75 2·00

1983. Brazilian Aeronautics Industry.
2035 **1052** 30cr. multicoloured . . 25 10

1053 Bosco and State Departments Esplanade, Brasilia

1983. Dom Bosco's Dream of Brazil.
2036 **1053** 130cr. multicoloured . . 75 10

1054 "Council of State decides on Independence" (detail, Georgina de Albuquerque)

1983. National Week.
2037 **1054** 50cr. multicoloured . . 15 10

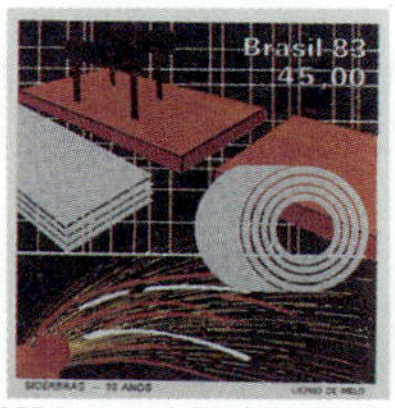

1055 Iron and Steel Production

1983. 10th Anniv of Siderbras (Brazilian Steel Corporation).
2038 **1055** 45cr. multicoloured . . 15 10

1056 "Pilosocereus gounellei"

1983. Cacti. Multicoloured.
2039 45cr. Type **1056** 95 10
2040 45cr. "Melocactus bahiensis" 95 10
2041 57cr. "Cereus jamacari" . . 95 10

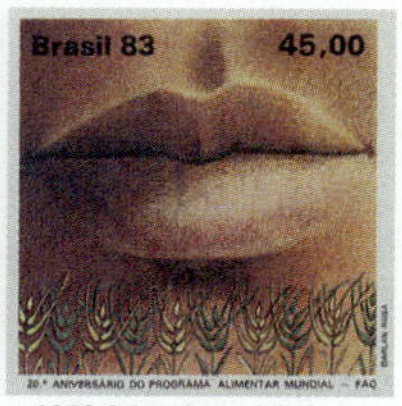

1057 Monstrance **1058** Mouth and Wheat

1983. 50th Anniv of National Eucharistic Congress.
2042 **1057** 45cr. multicoloured . . 15 10

1983. 20th Anniv of World Food Programme. Fishery Resources. Multicoloured.
2043 45cr. Type **1058** 20 15
2044 57cr. Fish and fishing pirogue 80 15

1059 Telegraph Key and Praca da Republica, Rio de Janeiro

1983. Death Centenary of Louis Breguet (telegraph pioneer). Sheet 70 × 99 mm.
MS2045 **1059** 376cr. multicoloured 1·75 1·90

1060 "Our Lady of Angels" (wood, Franisco Xavier de Brito)

1983. Christmas. Statues of the Madonna. Multicoloured.
2046 45cr. Type **1060** 90 10
2047 315cr. "Our Lady of Birth" 2·75 90
2048 335cr. "Our Lady of Joy" (fired clay, Agostinho de Jesus) . . . . 2·75 90
2049 345cr. "Our Lady of Presentation" . . . . . 2·75 90

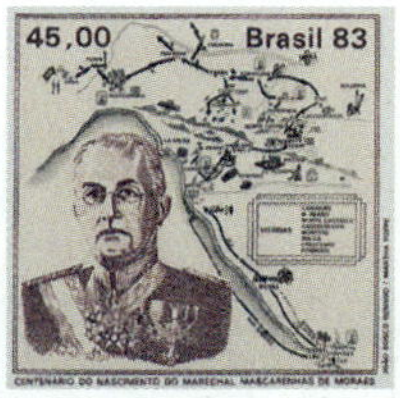

1061 Moraes and Map of Italian Campaign

1983. Birth Centenary of Marshal Mascarenhas de Moraes.
2050 **1061** 45cr. pink, green & pur 20 15

1983. State Flags (3rd series). As Type **992**. Multicoloured.
2051 45cr. Amazonas 90 55
2052 45cr. Goias 90 55
2053 45cr. Rio de Janeiro 90 55
2054 45cr. Mato Grosso do Sul 90 55
2055 45cr. Parana 90 55

1062 Praying Figure and Wheat

1983. Thanksgiving Day.
2056 **1062** 45cr. multicoloured . . 15 10

1063 Friar Vincente Borgard **1064** Montgolfier Balloon

1983. Obligatory Tax. Anti-leprosy Week.
2057 **1063** 10cr. brown . . . . . 2·75 90

1983. Bicentenary of Manned Flight.
2058 **1064** 345cr. multicoloured . . 4·25 2·40

1065 Indian, Portuguese Navigator and Negro

1984. 50th Anniv of Publication of "Masters and Slaves" by Gilberto Freyre.
2059 **1065** 45cr. multicoloured . . 60 10

1066 Crystal Palace

1984. Centenary of Crystal Palace, Petropolis.
2060 **1066** 45cr. multicoloured . . 25 10

1067 "Monument of the Flags", Sao Paulo

1984. 90th Birth Anniv of Victor Brecheret (sculptor). Sheet 100 × 70 mm.
MS2061 **1067** 805cr. multicoloured 1·10 1·25

1068 "Don Afonso" (sail/steam warship) and Figurehead

1984. Cent of Naval Oceanographic Museum.
2062 **1068** 620cr. multicoloured . . 1·25 35

1069 Manacled Hands and Beached Fishing Pirogue

1984. Centenary of Abolition of Slavery in Ceara and Amazonas. Multicoloured.
2063 585cr. Type **1069** . . . . . 1·75 90
2064 610cr. Emancipated slave . . 1·75 90

1070 King Carl XVI Gustaf and Pres. Figueiredo

1984. Visit of King of Sweden. Sheet 98 × 69 mm.
MS2065 **1070** 2105cr. mult . . . 1·75 1·75

1071 Long Jumping

1984. Olympic Games, Los Angeles. Mult.
2066 65cr. Type **1071** 90 50
2067 65cr. 100 metres 90 50
2068 65cr. Relay 90 50
2069 585cr. Pole vaulting 90 75
2070 610cr. High jumping 90 75
2071 620cr. Hurdling 90 75

1072 Oil Rigs and Blast Furnace **1073** Pedro Alvares Cabral

1984. Birth Cent (1983) of Getulio Vargas (President 1930–45 and 1951–54). Multicoloured.
2072 65cr. Type **1072** 15 10
2073 65cr. Ballot boxes and symbols of professions and trades 15 10
2074 65cr. Sugar refinery and electricity pylons 15 10

1984. "Espana 84" International Stamp Exhibition, Madrid. Explorers. Multicoloured.
2075 65cr. Type **1073** 15 10
2076 610cr. Christopher Columbus . . . . 1·75 20

1074 Heads and Map of Americas **1075** Chinese Painting

1984. 8th Pan-American Surety Association General Assembly.
2077 **1074** 65cr. multicoloured . . 15 10

1984. "Lubrapex 84" Brazilian-Portuguese Stamp Exhibition, Lisbon.
2078 **1075** 65cr. multicoloured . . 15 10
2079 – 585cr. multicoloured . . 90 50
2080 – 610cr. multicoloured . . 90 50
2081 – 620cr. multicoloured . . 90 50
DESIGNS: 585 to 620cr. Chinese paintings from Mariana Cathedral.

1076 FIFA Emblem

1984. 80th Anniv of International Federation of Football Associations. Sheet 98 × 68 mm.
MS2082 **1076** 2115cr. mult . . . 1·75 1·75

1077 Marsh Deer and Great Egret

1984. Mato Grosso Flood Plain. Multicoloured.
2083 65cr. Type **1077** 80 50
2084 65cr. Jaguar, capybara and roseate spoonbill 80 50
2085 80cr. Alligator, jabiru and red-cowled cardinals . . . 85 55

1078 "The First Letter Sent from Brazil" (Guido Mondin) **1079** Route Map and Dornier Wal Flying Boat

1984. 1st Anniv of Postal Union of the Americas and Spain H.Q., Montevideo, Uruguay.
2086 **1078** 65cr. multicoloured . . 40 15

1984. 50th Anniv of First Trans-Oceanic Air Route. Multicoloured.
2087 610cr. Type **1079** . . . . . 1·60 50
2088 620cr. Support ship "Westfalen" and Dornier Wal . . . . 2·00 45

1080 Mother and Baby **1081** Murrah Buffaloes

1984. Wildlife Preservation. Woolley Spider Monkey. Multicoloured.
2089 65cr. Type **1080** 50 10
2090 80cr. Monkey in tree 25 10

1984. Marajo Island Water Buffaloes. Designs showing different races. Multicoloured.
2091 65cr. Type **1081** 40 30
2092 65cr. Carabao buffaloes . . . 40 30
2093 65cr. Mediterranean buffaloes 30 25
Nos. 2091/3 were issued together, se-tenant, forming a composite design.

1082 Headquarters, Salvador

1984. 150th Anniv of Economic Bank.
2094 **1082** 65cr. multicoloured . . 15 10

1083 Da Luz Station, Sao Paulo **1084** Girl Guide

1984. Preservation of Historic Railway Stations. Multicoloured.
2095 65cr. Type **1083** . . . . . . 1·00 35
2096 65cr. Japeri station Rio de Janeiro . . . . 1·00 35
2097 80cr. Sao Joao del Rei station, Minas Gerais . . 1·00 35

1984. 65th Anniv of Girl Guides Movement in Brazil. Sheet 99 × 69 mm.
MS2098 **1084** 585cr. multicoloured 90 90

1085 Roof protecting Couple **1086** "Pedro I" (Solano Peixoto Machado)

1984. 20th Anniv of National Housing Bank.
2099 **1085** 65cr. multicoloured . . 10 10

1984. National Week. Designs showing children's paintings. Multicoloured.
2100 100cr. Type **1086** 15 10
2101 100cr. Girl painting word "BRASIL" (Juruce Maria Klein) 15 10
2102 100cr. Children of different races under rainbow (Priscela Barreto da Fonseca Bara) 15 10
2103 100cr. Caravels (Carlos Peixoto Mangueira) . . . 15 10

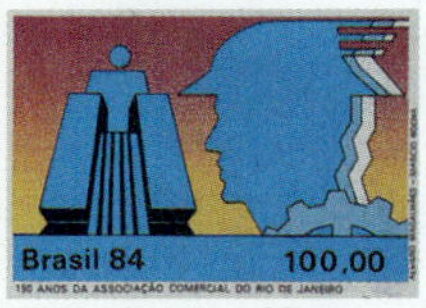

1087 Headquarters, Mercury and Cogwheel

1984. 150th Anniv of Rio de Janeiro Commercial Association.
2104 **1087** 100cr. multicoloured . . 15 10

1088 Pedro I

1984. 150th Death Anniv of Emperor Pedro I.
2105 **1088** 1000cr. multicoloured 3·50 1·75

1089 "Pycnoporus sanguineus" 1090 Child stepping from Open Book

1984. Fungi. Multicoloured.
2106 120cr. Type **1089** 40 15
2107 1050cr. "Calvatia" sp. . . . 2·75 60
2108 1080cr. "Pleurotus" sp. (horiz) . . . . 2·75 60

1984. Book Day. Children's Literature.
2109 **1090** 120cr. multicoloured . . 20 10

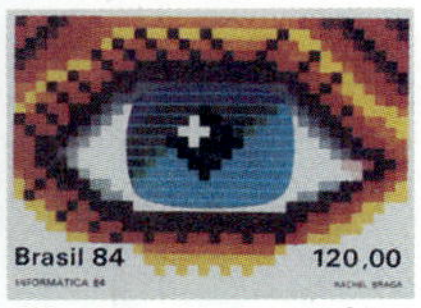

1091 New State Mint and 17th-century Minter 1092 Computer Image of Eye

1984. Inauguration of New State Mint, Santa Cruz, Rio de Janeiro.
2110 **1091** 120cr. blue & deep blue 15 10

1984. "Informatica 84" 17th National Information Congress and 4th International Informatics Fair, Rio de Janeiro.
2111 **1092** 120cr. multicoloured . . 15 10

1093 Sculpture by Bruno Giorgi and Flags 1094 Brasilia Cathedral and Wheat

1984. 14th General Assembly of Organization of American States, Brasilia.
2112 **1093** 120cr. multicoloured . . 15 10

1984. State Flags (4th series). As T **992**.
2113 120cr. red, black & buff . . 90 50
2114 120cr. multicoloured 90 50
2115 120cr. multicoloured 90 50
2116 120cr. multicoloured 90 50
2117 120cr. multicoloured 90 50
DESIGNS: No. 2113, Minas Gerais; 2114, Mato Grosso; 2115, Piaui; 2116, Maranhao; 2117, Santa Catarina.

1984. Thanksgiving Day.
2118 **1094** 120cr. multicoloured . . 15 10

1095 Father Bento Dias Pacheco 1096 "Nativity" (Djanira da Mota e Silva)

1984. Obligatory Tax. Anti-leprosy Week.
2119 **1095** 30cr. blue 50 10
See also Nos. 2208, 2263 and 2291.

1984. Christmas. Paintings from Federal Savings Bank collection. Multicoloured.
2120 120cr. Type **1096** 15 10
2121 120cr. "Virgin and Child" (Glauco Rodrigues) . . . 75 25
2122 1050cr. "Flight into Egypt" (Paul Garfunkel) . . . . 2·75 50
2123 1080cr. "Nativity" (Emiliano Augusto di Cavalcanti) . . 2·75 50

1097 Airbus Industrie A300

1984. 40th Anniv of I.C.A.O.
2124 **1097** 120cr. multicoloured . . 15 10

1098 Symbols of Agriculture and Industry on Hat

1984. 25th Anniv of North-east Development Office.
2125 **1098** 120cr. multicoloured . . 15 10

1099 "Virgin of Safe Journeys Church" (detail)

1985. 77th Death Anniv of Emilio Rouede (artist).
2126 **1099** 120cr. multicoloured . . 20 10

1100 "Brasilsat" over Brazil

1985. Launch of "Brasilsat" (first Brazilian telecommunications satellite).
2127 **1100** 150cr. multicoloured . . 25 10

1101 Electric Trains and Plan of Port Alegre Station

1985. Inauguration of Metropolitan Surface Railway, Recife and Porto Alegre.
2128 **1101** 200cr. multicoloured . . 60 20

1102 Butternut Tree 1103 Parachutist

1985. Opening of Botanical Gardens, Brasilia.
2129 **1102** 200cr. multicoloured . . 20 10

1985. 40th Anniv of Military Parachuting.
2130 **1103** 200cr. multicoloured . . 20 10

1104 Map, Temperature Graph and Weather Scenes

1985. National Climate Programme.
2131 **1104** 500cr. multicoloured . . 20 10

1105 Campolina 1107 "Polyvolume" (Mary Vieira)

1106 Ouro Preto

1985. Brazilian Horses. Multicoloured.
2132 1000cr. Type **1105** . . . . . 1·25 15
2133 1500cr. Marajoara . . . . . 1·25 15
2134 1500cr. Mangalarga pacer 1·25 15

1985. UNESCO World Heritage Sites. Multicoloured.
2135 220cr. Type **1106** 15 10
2136 220cr. Sao Miguel das Missoes 15 10
2137 220cr. Olinda 15 10

1985. 40th Anniv of Rio-Branco Institute (diplomatic training academy).
2138 **1107** 220cr. multicoloured . . 10 10

1108 National Theatre

1985. 25th Anniv of Brasilia. Multicoloured.
2139 220cr. Type **1108** 10 10
2140 220cr. Catetinho (home of former President Juscelino Keubitschek) and memorial 10 15

1109 Rondon and Morse Telegraph 1110 Fontoura and Pharmaceutical Equipment

1985. 120th Birth Anniv of Marshal Candido Mariano da Silva Rondon (military engineer and explorer).
2141 **1109** 220cr. multicoloured . . 10 10

1985. Birth Centenary of Candido Fontoura (pharmacist).
2142 **1110** 220cr. multicoloured . . 15 10

1111 Lizards 1112 Numeral

1113 Numeral

1985. Rock Paintings. Multicoloured.
2143 300cr. Type **1111** 10 10
2144 300cr. Deer 10 10
2145 2000cr. Various animals . . 75 15
MS2146 100 × 70 mm. Nos. 2143/5 75 75

Nos. **MS**2146 is inscribed for Brapex VI national stamp exhibition, Belo Horizonte.

1985.
2147 **1112** 50cr. red 10 10
2148 100cr. purple 10 10
2149 150cr. lilac 10 10
2150 200cr. blue 10 10
2151 220cr. green 50 10
2152 300cr. blue 10 10
2153 500cr. black 10 10
2154 **1113** 1000cr. brown 10 10
2155 2000cr. green 15 10
2156 3000cr. lilac 15 10
2157 5000cr. brown . . . . 1·75 10

1114 Common Noddies

1985. National Marine Park, Abrolhos. Mult.
2168 220cr. Type **1114** 55 35
2169 220cr. Magnificent frigate birds and blue-faced booby 55 35
2170 220cr. Blue-faced boobies and red-billed tropic bird 55 35
2171 2000cr. Grey plovers . . . . 2·75 65

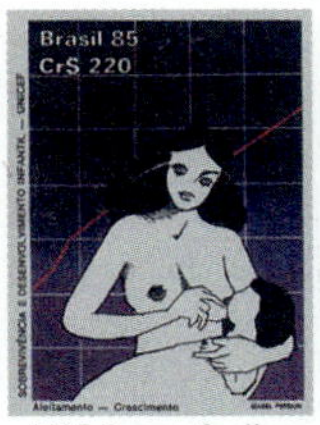

1115 Breast-feeding 1116 Bell 47J Ranger Helicopter rescuing Man, "Brasil" (corvette) and Diver

1985. United Nations Children's Fund Child Survival Campaign. Multicoloured.
2172 220cr. Type **1115** 15 10
2173 220cr. Growth chart and oral rehydration 15 10

1985. International Sea Search and Rescue Convention, Rio de Janeiro.
2174 **1116** 220cr. multicoloured . . 1·00 30

1117 World Cup and Ball

1985. World Cup Football Championship, Mexico (1986) (1st issue). Sheet 70 × 99 mm.
MS2175 **1117** 2000cr. mult . . . 2·00 2·25
See also No.**MS**2213.

1118 Children holding Hands 1119 Hands holding Host

1985. International Youth Year.
2176 **1118** 220cr. multicoloured . . 15 10

1985. 11th Nat Eucharistic Congress, Aparecida.
2177 **1119** 2000cr. multicoloured 75 50

1120 Scene from "Mineiro Blood", Camera and Mauro

1985. 60th Anniv of Humberto Mauro's Cataguases Cycle of Films.
2178 **1120** 300cr. multicoloured . . 15 10

1121 Escola e Sacro Museum

1122 Inconfidencia Museum, Ouro Preto

1985. 400th Anniv of Paraiba State.
2179 **1121** 330cr. multicoloured . . 15 10

1985. Museums. Multicoloured.
2180 300cr. Type **1122** 15 10
2181 300cr. Historical and Diplomatic Museum Itamaraty 15 10

1123 "Cabano" (Guido Mondin)

1124 Aeritalia/Aermacchi AM-X Fighter

1985. 150th Anniv of Cabanagem Insurrection, Belem City.
2182 **1123** 330cr. multicoloured . . 15 10

1985. AM-X (military airplane) Project.
2183 **1124** 330cr. multicoloured . . 15 10

1125 Captain and Crossbowman (early 16th century)

1985. Military Dress. Multicoloured.
2184 300cr. Type **1125** 15 10
2185 300cr. Arquebusier and sergeant (late 16th cent) 15 10
2186 300cr. Musketeer and pikeman (early 17th century) 15 10
2187 300cr. Mulatto fusilier and pikeman with scimitar (early 17th century) . . . 15 10

1126 "Farroupilha Rebels" (Guido Mondin)

1985. 150th Anniv of Farroupilha Revolution.
2188 **1126** 330cr. multicoloured . . 15 10

1127 Itaimbezinho Canyon

1985. Aparados da Serra National Park. Mult.
2189 3100cr. Type **1127** 95 15
2190 3320cr. Mountain range . . . 95 15
2191 3480cr. Pine forest . . . 95 15

1128 Neves and Brasilia Buildings

1985. Tancredo Neves (President-elect) Commem.
2192 **1128** 330cr. black & orange 15 10

1129 "FEB" on Envelope

1985. 40th Anniv (1984) of Brazilian Expeditionary Force Postal Service.
2193 **1129** 500cr. multicoloured . . 15 10

1130 "Especuladora", 1835

1985. 150th Anniv of Rio de Janeiro–Niteroi Ferry Service. Multicoloured.
2194 500cr. Type **1130** 70 20
2195 500cr. "Segunda", 1862 . . 70 20
2196 500cr. "Terceira", 1911 . . 70 20
2197 500cr. "Urca", 1981 . . . . 70 20

1131 Muniz M-7

1985. 50th Anniv of Muniz M-7 Biplane's Maiden Flight.
2198 **1131** 500cr. multicoloured . . 30 15

1132 Dove Emblem and Stylized Flags

1133 Front Page of First Edition

1985. 40th Anniv of UNO.
2199 **1132** 500cr. multicoloured . . 15 10

1985. 160th Anniv of "Pernambuco Daily News".
2200 **1133** 500cr. multicoloured . . 15 10

1134 Adoration

1135 Child holding Wheat

1985. Christmas. Multicoloured.
2201 500cr. Type **1134** 15 10
2202 500cr. Adoration of the Magi 15 10
2203 500cr. Flight into Egypt . . 15 10

1985. State Flags (5th series). As T **992**. Mult.
2204 500cr. Para 15 10
2205 500cr. Rio Grande do Sul 15 10
2206 500cr. Acre 15 10
2207 500cr. Sao Paulo 15 10

1985. Obligatory Tax. Anti-leprosy Week.
2208 **1095** 100cr. red 25 25

1985. Thanksgiving Day.
2209 **1135** 500cr. multicoloured . . 10 10

1136 Transport, Mined Ore and Trees

1985. Carajas Development Programme.
2210 **1136** 500cr. multicoloured . . 20 10

1137 Gusmao and Balloons

1985. 300th Birth Anniv of Bartolomeu Lourenco de Gusmao (inventor).
2211 **1137** 500cr. multicoloured . . 10 10

1138 "The Trees"

1985. Birth Centenary of Antonio Francisco da Costa e Silva (poet).
2212 **1138** 500cr. multicoloured . . 10 10

1139 Footballers

1986. World Cup Football Championship, Mexico (2nd issue) and Lubrepex 86 Brazilian—Portuguese Stamp Exhibition, Rio de Janeiro (1st issue). Sheet 69 × 99 mm.
MS2213 **1139** 10000cr. multicoloured . . . . 2·00 2·25
See also Nos. 2260/**MS**2262.

1140 Comet

1986. Appearance of Halley's Comet.
2214 **1140** 50c. multicoloured . . . 35 15

1141 Flags and Station

1142 Symbols of Industry, Agriculture and Commerce

1986. 2nd Anniv of Commander Ferraz Antarctic Station.
2215 **1141** 50c. multicoloured . . . 10 15

1986. Labour Day.
2216 **1142** 50c. multicoloured . . . 10 10

1143 "Maternity"

1144 Broken Chain Links as Birds

1986. 50th Death Anniv of Henrique Bernardelli (artist).
2217 **1143** 50c. multicoloured . . . 10 10

1986. 25th Anniv of Amnesty International.
2218 **1144** 50c. multicoloured . . . 10 10

1145 "Pyrrhopyge ruficauda"

1986. Butterflies. Multicoloured.
2219 50c. Type **1145** 85 30
2220 50c. "Pierriballia mandela molione" 85 30
2221 50c. "Prepona eugenes diluta" 85 30

1146 Gomes Peri, and Score of "O Guarani"

1147 Man in Safety Harness

1986. 150th Birth Anniv of Antonio Carlos Gomes (composer).
2222 **1146** 50c. multicoloured . . . 15 10

1986. Prevention of Industrial Accidents.
2223 **1147** 50c. multicoloured . . . 15 10

1148 "Black Beard" 10r. Stamp

1986. Stamp Day. 120th Anniv of Pedro II Black Beard Stamps and 75th Anniv of Brazilian Philatelic Society. Sheet 69 × 99 mm.
MS2224 **1148** 5cz. red and ochre 1·00 1·10

1149 Garcia D'Avilas House Chapel, Nazare de Mata

1150 Kubitschek and Alvorada Palace

1986.
2225 **1149** 10c. green 10 10
2226 – 20c. blue 10 10
2228 – 50c. orange 55 10
2230 – 1cz. brown 10 10
2231 – 2cz. red 10 10
2233 – 5cz. green 10 10
2235 – 10cz. blue 10 10
2236 – 20cz. red 10 10
2238 – 50cz. orange 15 15
2240 – 100cz. green 30 25
2241 – 200cz. blue 10 30
2242 – 500cz. brown 50 10

DESIGNS—HORIZ: 20c. Church of Our Lady of the Assumption, Anchieta; 50c. Reis Magos Fortress, Natal; 1cz. Pelourinho, Alcantara; 2cz. St. Francis's Monastery, Olinda; 5cz. St. Anthony's Chapel, Sao Roque; 10cz. St Lawrence of the Indians Church, Niteroi; 20cz. Principe da Beira Fortress, Costa Marques, Rondobua; 100cz. Church of Our Lady of Sorrows, Campanha; 200cz. Counting House, Ouro Preto; 500cz. Customs building, Belem. VERT: 50cz. Church of the Good Jesus, Matasinhos.

1986. 10th Death Anniv of Juscelino Kubitschek (President 1956–61).
2244 **1150** 50c. multicoloured . . . 25 10

1151 Mangabeira and Itamaraty Palace, Rio de Janeiro

1986. Birth Cent of Octavio Mangabeira (politician).

2245	**1151**	50c. multicoloured . . .	10	10

1152 Congress Emblem and Sao Paulo

1153 Microphone and Radio Waves

1986. 8th World Gastroenterology Congress, Sao Paulo.

2246	**1152**	50c. multicoloured . . .	10	10

1986. 50th Annivs. of National Radio and Education and Culture Ministry Radio.

2247	**1153**	50c. multicoloured . . .	10	10

1154 "Peace" (detail, Candido Portinari)

1155 "Urera mitis"

1986. International Peace Year.

2248	**1154**	50c. multicoloured . . .	10	10

1986. Flowers. Multicoloured.

2249	50c. Type **1155**	15	10
2250	6cz.50 "Couroupita guyanensis"	85	20
2251	6cz.90 Mountain ebony (horiz)	90	20

1156 Simoes Filho and Newspaper

1157 Title Page of Gregorio de Matto's MS

1986. Birth Centenary of Ernesto Simoes Filho (politician and founder of "A Tarde").

2252	**1156**	50c. multicoloured . . .	10	10

1986. Book Day. Poets' Birth Anniversaries.

2253	**1157**	50c. brown & lt brown	10	10
2254	–	50c. green and red . . .	10	10

DESIGNS: No. 2253, Type **1157** (350th anniv); 2254, Manuel Bandeira and last verse of "I'll Return to Pasargada" (centenary).

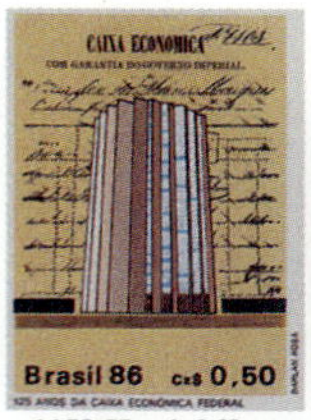

1158 Head Office, Brasilia

1159 Birds around Baby lying in Nest

1986. 125th Anniv of Federal Savings Bank.

2255	**1158**	50c. multicoloured . . .	10	10

1986. Christmas. Multicoloured.

2256	50c. Type **1159**	75	15
2257	6cz.50 Birds around tree with Christmas decorations	1·50	25
2258	7cz.30 Birds wearing Santa Claus caps	1·25	30

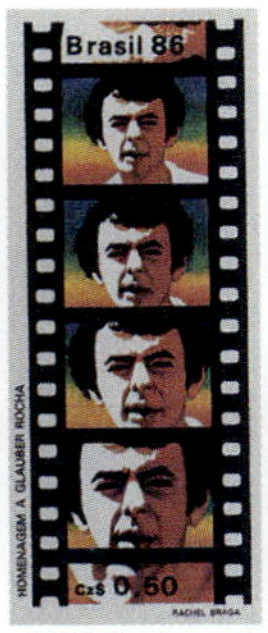

1160 Rocha on Strip of Film

1161 "History of Empress Porcina"

1986. 5th Death Anniv of Glauber Rocha (film producer).

2259	**1160**	50c. multicoloured . . .	10	10

1986. "Lubrapex 86" Brazilian–Portuguese Stamp Exhibition, Rio de Janeiro. Design showing scenes from Cordel Literature. Multicoloured.

2260	6cz.90 Type **1161**	55	40
2261	6cz.90 "Romance of the Mysterious Peacock" . .	55	40
MS2262	70 × 100 mm. Nos. 2260/2	60	60

1986. Obligatory Tax. Anti-leprosy Week.

2263	**1095**	10c. brown	10	10

1162 Lieutenant Commander, 1930

1163 "Graf Zeppelin" over Hangar

1986. Military Uniforms. Multicoloured.

2264	50c. Type **1162**	60	10
2265	50c. Military Aviation flight lieutenant, 1930	10	10

1986. 50th Anniv of Bartolomeu de Gusmao Airport, Santa Cruz.

2266	**1163**	1cz. multicoloured . . .	10	10

1164 Museum

1987. 50th Anniv of National Fine Arts Museum, Rio de Janeiro.

2267	**1164**	1cz. multicoloured . . .	10	10

1165 Villa-Lobos conducting and Musical Motifs

1167 Landscape on Open Envelope (Rural Post Office Network)

1166 Flag, Lockheed Hercules Aircraft and Antarctic Landscape

1987. Birth Cent of Heitor Villa-Lobos (composer).

2268	**1165**	1cz.50 multicoloured . .	30	10

1987. Air Force Participation in Brazilian Antarctic Programme.

2269	**1166**	1cz. multicoloured . . .	90	20

1987. Special Mail Services. Multicoloured.

2270	1cz. Type **1167**	10	10
2271	1cz. Satchel and globe (International Express Mail Service)	10	10

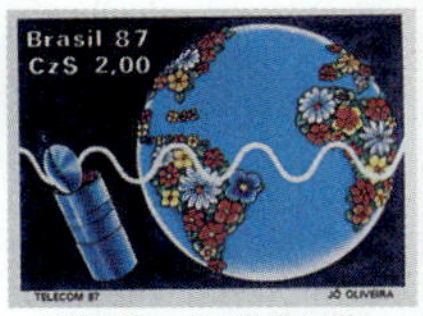

1168 "Brasilsat" Satellite, Radio Wave and Globe

1169 Modern Pentathlon

1987. "Telecom 87" World Telecommunications Exhibition, Geneva.

2272	**1168**	2cz. multicoloured . . .	10	10

1987. 10th Pan-American Games, Indianapolis, U.S.A.

2273	**1169**	18cz. multicoloured . .	1·75	50

1170 Hawksbill Turtle

1987. Endangered Animals. Multicoloured.

2274	2cz. Type **1170**	60	35
2275	2cz. Right whale	60	35

1171 Old and New Court Buildings and Symbol of Justice

1172 Arms

1987. 40th Anniv of Federal Appeal Court.

2276	**1171**	2cz. multicoloured . . .	10	10

1987. Centenary of Military Club.

2277	**1172**	3cz. multicoloured . . .	10	10

1173 Institute and Foodstuffs

1987. Centenary of Agronomic Institute, Campinas.

2278	**1173**	2cz. multicoloured . . .	10	10

1174 "Fulgora servillei"

1987. 50th Anniv of Brazilian Entomology Society. Multicoloured.

2279	3cz. Type **1174**	60	35
2280	3cz. "Zoolea lopiceps" . . .	60	35

1175 Features of Northern and North-east Regions

1176 Main Tower

1987. National Tourism Year. Multicoloured.

2281	3cz. Type **1175**	50	15
2282	3cz. Features of mid-west, south-east and south regions	10	10

1987. 150th Anniv of Royal Portuguese Reading Cabinet, Rio de Janeiro.

2283	**1176**	30cz. green and red . .	25	20

1177 International Sport Club (1975, 1976, 1979)

1987. Brazilian Football Championship Gold Cup Winners (1st series). Designs showing footballers and Club emblems.

2284	**1177**	3cz. red, black & yellow	35	10
2285	–	3cz. red, yellow & black	35	10
2286	–	3cz. multicoloured . . .	35	10
2287	–	3cz. red, black & yellow	35	10

DESIGNS: No. 2285, Sao Paulo Football Club (1977, 1986); 2286, Guarani Football Club (1978); 2287, Regatas do Flamengo Club (1980, 1982, 1983).

See also Nos. 2322/5, 2398 and 2408.

1178 St. Francis's Church and Tiled Column

1987. 400th Anniv of St. Francis's Monastery, Salvador.

2288	**1178**	4cz. multicoloured . . .	10	10

1179 Almeida and Scenes from "A Bagaceira"

1987. Birth Centenary of Jose Americo de Almeida (writer).

2289	**1179**	4cz. multicoloured . . .	10	10

1180 Barra do Picao

1987. 450th Anniv of Recife.

2290	**1180**	5cz. multicoloured . . .	30	10

1987. Obligatory Tax. Anti-leprosy Week.

2291	**1095**	30cz. green	15	15

1181 Rainbow, Dove and Open Hands

1182 Angels

1987. Thanksgiving Day.
2292 **1181** 5cz. multicoloured . . . 10 10

1987. Christmas. Multicoloured.
2293 6cz. Type **1182** 10 10
2294 6cz. Dancers on stage . . . 10 10
2295 6cz. Shepherd playing flute 10 10

1183 Bernardo Pereira de Vasconcelos (founder) and Pedro II

1987. 150th Anniv of Pedro II School, Rio de Janeiro.
2296 **1183** 6cz. yellow, blk & red 10 10

1184 "Cattleya guttata"

1987. 50th Anniv of Brazilian Orchid Growers Society. Multicoloured.
2297 6cz. Type **1184** 50 10
2298 6cz. "Laelia lobata" 50 10

1185 Statue and Fatima Basilica, Portugal

1987. Marian Year. Visit to Brazil of Statue of Our Lady of Fatima.
2299 **1185** 50cz. multicoloured . . 90 60

1186 Sousa, Indians and Fauna

1987. 400th Anniv of "Descriptive Treaties of Brazil" by Gabriel Soares de Sousa.
2300 **1186** 7cz. multicoloured . . . 40 15

1187 Page from Book of Gregorian Chants and Computer Terminal

1988. 150th Anniv of National Archives.
2301 **1187** 7cz. multicoloured . . . 10 10

1188 National Colours, Caravel and Modern Ship

1988. 180th Anniv of Opening of Brazilian Ports to Free Trade.
2302 **1188** 7cz. multicoloured . . . 10 10

1189 Microscope and Map

1988. Antarctic Research. Sheet 99 × 69 mm.
MS2303 **1189** 80cz. multicoloured 25 25

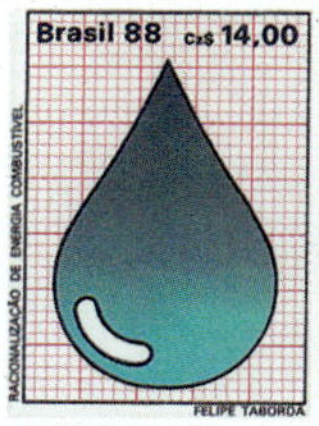

1190 Petrol Droplet

1192 Bonifacio and Emblems of his Life

1191 Williams-Honda Racing Car and Flag

1988. Energy Conservation. Multicoloured.
2304 14cz. Type **1190** 10 10
2305 14cz. Flash of electricity . . 10 10

1988. Nelson Piquet's Third Formula 1 Motor Racing World Championship Title (1987). Sheet 99 × 69 mm.
MS2306 **1191** 300cz. multicoloured 90 90

1988. 150th Death Anniv of Jose Bonifacio de Andrada e Silva (scientist, writer and "Patriarch of the Independence").
2307 **1192** 20cz. multicoloured . . 10 10

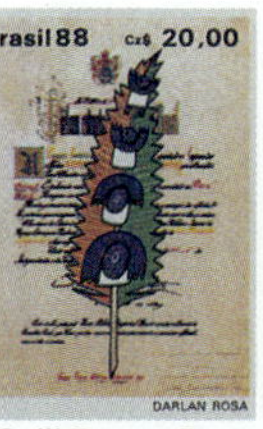

1193 Quill Pen on Page of Aurea Law

1988. Centenary of Abolition of Slavery. Mult.
2308 20cz. Type **1193** 10 10
2309 50cz. Norris map of Africa, 1773, slave ship and plan of trading routes 20 10

1194 Church of the Good Jesus de Matosinhos

1195 Concentric Circles on Map of Americas

1988. UNESCO World Heritage Sites. Mult.
2310 20cz. Type **1194** 10 10
2311 50cz. Brasilia 15 15
2312 100cz. Pelourinho, Salvador 15 15

1988. "Americas Telecom 88" Telecommunications Exhibition, Rio de Janeiro.
2313 **1195** 50cz. multicoloured . . 15 15

1196 "Kasato Maru" (first immigrant ship) and Japanese Family

1197 Postal Authority Emblem

1988. 80th Anniv of Japanese Immigration into Brazil.
2314 **1196** 100cz. multicoloured . . 55 25

1988. No value expressed.
2315 **1197** (–) blue 80 10
No. 2315 was valid for use at the current first class inland letter rate. It could not be used to pay postage to foreign countries.

1198 Judo

1199 Giant Anteater

1988. Olympic Games, Seoul.
2316 **1198** 20cz. multicoloured . . 80 10

1988. Endangered Mammals. Multicoloured.
2317 20cz. Type **1199** 50 10
2318 50cz. Thin-spined porcupine 60 15
2319 100cz. Bush dog . . . . . 1·25 25

1200 "Motherland" (Pedro Bruno)

1988. Stamp Day. Brasiliana 89 International Stamp Exhibition. Sheet 98 × 69 mm.
MS2320 **1200** 250cz. multicoloured 1·25 1·25

1201 Industrial Symbols

1988. 50th Anniv of National Confederation of Industry.
2321 **1201** 50cz. multicoloured . . 15 15

1988. Brazilian Football Championship Gold Cup Winners (2nd series). As T **1177**. Multicoloured.
2322 50cz. Sport Club do Recife (1987) 40 15
2323 50cz. Coritiba Football Club (1985) 40 15
2324 100cz. Gremio Football Porto Alegrense (1981) . . 55 25
2325 200cz. Fluminense Football Club (1984) 75 40

1202 Congress, Brasilia

1988. Promulgation of 1998 Consitution. Sheet 99 × 69 mm.
MS2326 **1202** 550cz. multicoloured 1·75 1·75

1203 Raul Pompeia and Lines from "O Ateneu"

1988. Book Day. Centenaries of Publication of "O Ateneu" and "Verses". Multicoloured.
2327 50cz. Type **1203** 15 15
2328 100cz. Olavo Bilac and lines from "Verses" 30 25

1204 Church

1205 Father Santiago Uchoa

1988. Christmas. Origami by Marcia Bloch. Multicoloured.
2329 50cz. Type **1204** 15 15
2330 100cz. Nativity 30 25
2331 200cz. Santa Claus and parcels 55 45

1988. Obligatory Tax. Anti-leprosy Week.
2332 **1205** 1cz.30 brown 50 10
See also Nos. 2614 and 2686.

1206 Mate and Rodeo Rider

1988. "Abrafex" Argentine–Brazilian Stamp Exhibition, Buenos Aires.
2333 **1206** 400cz. multicoloured . . 2·25 1·10

1207 Hatchetfish ("Gasteropelecus sp.")

1988. Freshwater Fishes. Multicoloured.
2334 55cz. Type **1207** 30 30
2335 55cz. Black arawana ("Osteoglossum ferreira") 30 30
2336 55cz. Green moenkhausia ("Moenkhausia sp.") . . 30 30
2337 55cz. Pearlfish ("Xavantei") 30 30
2338 55cz. Armoured bristlemouth catfish ("Ancistrus hoplogenys") 30 30
2339 55cz. Emerald catfish ("Brochis splendens") . . 30 30

1208 Red-tailed Amazon

1988. Brapex VII National Stamp Exhibition, Sao Paulo. Conservation of Jurelia. Sheet 99 × 68 mm containing T **1208** and similar vert designs. Multicoloured.
MS2340 100cz. Type **1208**; 250cz. "Vriesia ensiformis" (bromelia); 400cz. Great egret . . . . . . 1·50 1·50

1209 Dish Aerials

1210 "Four Arts"

1988. 10th Anniv of Ansat 10 (first Brazilian dish aerial), Macapa.
2341 **1209** 70cz. multicoloured . . 20 15

1988. Establishment of National Foundation of Scenic Arts.
2342 **1210** 70cz. multicoloured . . 20 15

1211 Court Building

1989. 380th Anniv of Bahia Court of Justice.
2343 **1211** 25c. multicoloured . . . 10 10

1212 Library Building and Detail of Main Door

1989. Public Library Year. 178th Anniv of First Public Library, Bahia.
2344 **1212** 25c. multicoloured . . . 10 10

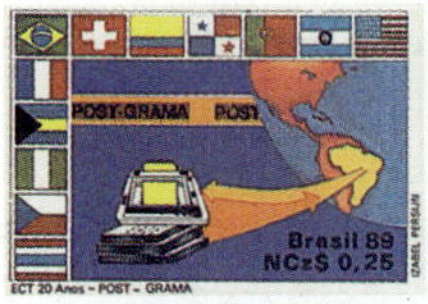

1213 Facsimile Machine

1215 Emblem

1214 Senna

1989. 20th Anniv of Post and Telegraph Department. Postal Services. Multicoloured.
2345 25c. Type **1213** 10 10
2346 25c. Hand holding parcel (Express Mail Service) . . 10 10
2347 25c. Airbus Industrie 300 airplane on runway (SEDEX express parcel service) 10 10
2348 25c. Putting coin in savings box (CEF postal savings) 10 10

1989. Aryton Senna's Formula 1 Motor Racing World Championship Title (1988). Sheet 99 × 69 mm.
MS2349 **1214** 2cz. multicoloured 10 10

1989. "Our Nature" Programme.
2350 **1215** 25c. multicoloured . . . 10 10

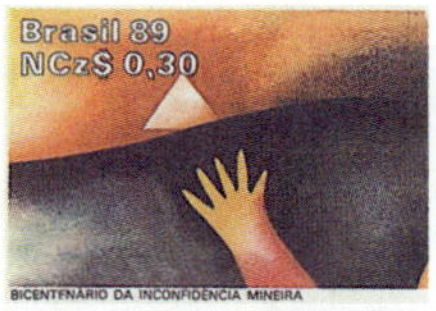

1216 Hand reaching for Symbol of Freedom

1989. Bicentenary of Inconfidencia Mineira (independence movement). Multicoloured.
2351 30c. Type **1216** 10 10
2352 30c. Man's profile and colonial buildings 10 10
2353 40c. Baroque buildings in disarray 10 10

1217 School

1989. Cent of Rio de Janeiro Military School.
2354 **1217** 50c. multicoloured . . . 10 10

1218 "Pavonia alnifolia"

1989. Endangered Plants. Multicoloured.
2355 50c. Type **1218** 90 10
2356 1cz. "Worsleya rayneri" (vert) 90 10
2357 1cz.50 "Heliconia farinosa" (vert) . . . . 1·10 10

1219 Barreto and Pedro II Square, Recife Law School

1220 "Quiabentia zehntneri"

1989. 150th Birth Anniv of Tobias Barreto (writer).
2358 **1219** 50c. multicoloured . . . 10 10

1989. Flowers. Currency expressed as "NCz $". Multicoloured.
2359 10c. "Dichorisandra" sp. . . 10 10
2360 20c. Type **1220** 10 10
2361 50c. "Bougainvillea glabra" 10 10
2363 1cz. "Impatiens" sp. 50 10
2364 2cz. "Chorisia crispiflora" (vert) 10 15
2366 5cz. "Hibiscus trilineatus" 10 10
See also Nos. 2413/24.

1221 Shooting of "Revistinha"

1989. 20th Anniv of TV Cultura.
2371 **1221** 50c. multicoloured . . . 10 10

1222 Postal Authority Emblem

1223 Brasilia T.V. Tower and Microlight

1989. No value expressed.
2372 **1222** (–) blue and orange . . 80 10
No. 2372 was sold at the current rate for first class internal postage.

1989. Aerosports and 80th Anniv of Santos Dumont's Flight in "Demoiselle". Mult.
2373 50c. Type **1223** 50 10
2374 1cz.50 Eiffel Tower and "Demoiselle" 60 10

1224 "Largo da Carioca" (detail, Nicolas Antoine Taunay)

1989. Philexfrance 89 International Stamp Exhibition, Paris and Bicentenary of French Revolution. Sheet 99 × 69 mm.
MS2375 **1224** 3cz. multicoloured 10 10

1225 Tourmaline

1989. Precious Stones. Multicoloured.
2376 50c. Type **1225** 10 10
2377 1cz.50 Amethyst 15 10

1226 Imperial Palace, Rio de Janeiro

1989. Stamp Day. Brasiliana 89 International Stamp Exhibition, Rio de Janeiro. Sheet 99 × 69 mm.
MS2378 **1226** 5cz. multicoloured 10 10

1227 Rainbow and Association H.Q. Mercury

1989. 150th Anniv of Pernambuco Trade Assn.
2379 **1227** 50c. multicoloured . . . 10 10

1228 Pioneers' Names and 19th-century to Modern Photographs

1989. International Photography Year.
2380 **1228** 1cz.50 multicoloured . . 15 10

1229 Power Station

1989. Centenary of Marmelos-o Power Station (first South American hydro-electric power station).
2381 **1229** 50c. multicoloured . . . 10 10

1230 Hebrew Volute

1231 Muiraquita

1989. Molluscs. Multicoloured.
2382 50c. Type **1230** 50 10
2383 1cz. Matthew's morum . . . 55 15
2384 1cz.50 Travasso's ancilla . . 60 20

1989. America. Pre-Columbian Artefacts. Mult.
2385 1cz. Type **1231** 80 10
2386 4cz. Caryatid vase (horiz) 80 10

1232 "Limoes" (Danilo di Prete)

1989. 20th International Biennial Art Exhibition, Sao Paulo. Sheet 99 × 79 mm containing T **1232** and similar vert designs. Multicoloured.
MS2387 2cz. Type **1232**; 3cz. "O Indio e a Suacuaoara" (sculpture, Brecheret); 5cz. Francisco Matarazzo (exhibition founder) 15 10

1233 Casimiro de Abreu

1234 Postal Authority Emblem

1989. Book Day. Writers' Birth Annivs. Mult.
2388 1cz. Type **1233** (150th anniv) 10 10
2389 1cz. Machado de Assis (150th anniv) 10 10
2390 1cz. Cora Coralina (cent) . . 10 10

1989. No value expressed. Burelage in second colour.
2391 **1234** (–) red and orange . . 3·25 35
No. 2391 was sold at the current rate for first class international postage.

1235 Police Emblem

1989. 25th Anniv of Federal Police Department.
2392 **1235** 1cz. multicoloured . . . 10 10

1236 "Deodoro presents the Flag of the Republic" (detail, anon)

1989. Centenary of Proclamation of Republic. Sheet 98 × 68 mm.
MS2393 **1236** 15cz. multicoloured 20 10

1237 Angel

1238 Candle Flame as Dove

1989. Christmas. Multicoloured.
2394 70c. Type **1237** 10 10
2395 1cz. Nativity 10 10

1989. Thanksgiving Day.
2396 **1238** 1cz. multicoloured . . . 10 10

1239 Fr. Damien de Veuster

1240 "The Yellow Man"

1989. Obligatory Tax. Anti-leprosy Week.
2397 **1239** 2c. red 10 10
See also Nos. 2458, 2509 and 2565.

1989. Football Clubs. As T **1177**. Multicoloured.
2398 50c. Bahia Sports Club . . 10 10

1989. Birth Cent of Anita Malfatti (painter).
2399 **1240** 1cz. multicoloured . . . 10 10

1241 Archive and Proclamation by Bento Goncalves

1990. Cent of Bahia State Public Archive.
2400 **1241** 2cz. multicoloured . . . 20 15

1242 "Mimosa caesalpiniifolia"

1990. 40th Anniv of Brazilian Botanical Society. Multicoloured.
2401 2cz. Type **1242** 10 10
2402 13cz. "Caesalpinia echinata" 10 10

1243 Cathedral of St. John the Baptist, Santa Cruz do Sul

1244 Sailing Barque and Modern Container Ship

1990. Churches. Multicoloured.
2403 2cz. Type **1243** 10 10
2404 3cz. Our Lady of Victory Church, Oeiras (horiz) . . 10 10
2405 5cz. Our Lady of the Rosary Church, Ouro Preto . . . 10 10

1990. Cent of Lloyd Brasileiro Navigation Company.
2406 **1244** 3cz. multicoloured . . . 30 10

1245 Chinstrap Penguins and Map

1990. Brazilian Antarctic Programme. Sheet 98 × 68 mm.
MS2407 **1245** 20cz. multicoloured 25 20

1990. Brazilian Football Clubs As T **1177**. Multicoloured.
2408 10cz. Vasco da Gama Regatas Club 15 10

1246 Collor and Newspaper Mastheads

1990. Birth Cent of Lindolfo Collor (journalist).
2409 **1246** 20cz. multicoloured . . 25 20

1247 Sarney

1249 Hearts sprouting in Flask

1248 Gold Coin, Anniversary Emblem and Bank Headquarters, Brasilia

1990. Tribute to Jose Sarney (retiring President).
2410 **1247** 20cz. blue 25 20

1990. 25th Anniv of Brazil Central Bank.
2411 **1248** 20cr. multicoloured . . 25 20

1990. World Health Day. Anti-AIDS Campaign.
2412 **1249** 20cr. multicoloured . . 25 20

1990. Flowers. As T **1220** but with currency expressed as "Cr$".
2413 1cr. "Impatiens sp" . . . 10 10
2414 2cr. "Chorisia crispiflora" (vert) 10 10
2415 5cr. "Hibiscus trilineatus" 10 10
2417 10cr. "Tibouchina granulosa" (vert) 15 10
2418 20cr. "Cassia micranthera" (vert) 25 20
2420 50cr. "Clitoria fairchildiana" (vert) . . 30 10
2421 50cr. "Tibouchina mutabilis" (vert) 75 65
2422 100cr. "Erythrina crista-galli" (vert) 65 10
2423 200cr. "Jacaranda mimosifolia" (vert) . . . 65 10
2424 500cr. "Caesalpinia peltophoroides" (vert) 65 15
2424a 1000cr. "Pachira aquatica" (vert) 15 10
2424b 2000cr. "Hibiscus pernambucensis" (vert) 25 20
2424c 5000cr. "Triplaris surinamensis" (vert) . . 90 30
2424d 10000cr. "Tabebuia heptaphylia" (vert) . . . 65 10
2424e 20000cr. "Erythrina speciosa" (vert) 65 10

1250 Amazon Post Launch

1990. River Post Network.
2425 **1250** 20cr. multicoloured . . 55 25

1251 Emperor Pedro LL and 30r. "Bull's-Eye"

1252 Map and Emblem

1990. Stamp World London 90 International Stamp Exhibition and 150th Anniv of Penny Black. Sheet 100 × 70 mm containing T **1251** and similar vert design, each black and lemon.
MS2426 20cz. Type **1251**; 100cr. Queen Victoria and Penny Black 60 60

1990. World Cup Football Championship, Italy. Sheet 69 × 99 mm.
MS2427 **1252** 120cr. multicoloured 1·30 1·30

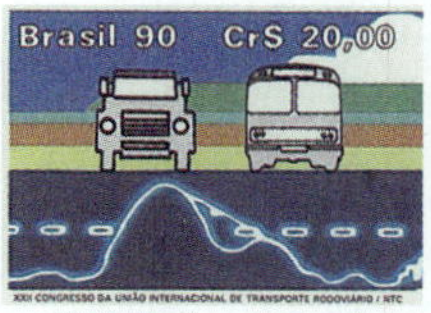

1253 Truck and Coach

1990. 22nd World Congress of Int Road Transport Union, Rio de Janeiro. Multicoloured.
2428 20cr. Type **1253** . . . . . . 1·00 55
2429 80cr. Volkswagen transporter van and car 1·25 55
Nos. 2428/29 were printed together, se-tenant, forming a composite design.

1254 Imperial Crown (Imperial Museum, Petropolis)

1990. Museum 50th Anniversaries. Multicoloured.
2430 20cr. Type **1254** 25 20
2431 20cr. "Our Lady of the Immaculate Conception" (woodcarving) (Missionary Museum, Sao Miguel das Missoes) . . . 25 20

1990. Creation of State of Tocantins. As T **992**, showing state flag.
2432 20cr. yellow, blue and black 25 20

1255 Service Building. Hildebrand Theodolite and Map of Rio de Janeiro

1990. Centenary of Army Geographic Service.
2433 **1255** 20cr. multicoloured . . 25 20

1256 Adhemar Gonzaga (producer)

1990. Brazilian Film Industry. Each maroon and purple.
2434 25cr. Type **1256** 80 25
2435 25cr. Carmen Miranda (actress) 80 25
2436 25cr. Carmen Santos (actress) 80 25
2437 25cr. Oscarito (actor) . . . 80 25

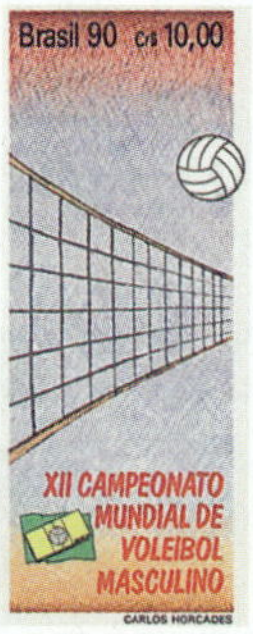

1257 Aerial View of House

1258 Ball and Net

1990. 5th Anniv of France–Brazil House, Rio de Janeiro.
2438 **1257** 50cr. multicoloured . . 60 10

1990. 12th World Men's Volleyball Championship, Brazil.
2439 **1258** 10cr. multicoloured . . 55 10

1259 Embraer/FMA Vector

1260 Globe, Pencil and Alphabet

1990. Aeronautics Industry.
2440 **1259** 10cr. multicoloured . . 15 10

1990. International Literacy Year.
2441 **1260** 10cr. multicoloured . . 15 10

1261 Institute

1990. Cent of Granbery Institute, Juiz de Fora.
2442 **1261** 13cr. multicoloured . . 15 10

1262 Map, Track and Diesel Locomotive

1990. 18th Pan-American Railways Congress, Rio de Janeiro.
2443 **1262** 95cr. multicoloured . . 1·50 1·50

1263 Satellite and Computer Communication

1990. 25th Anniv of Embratel (Telecommunications Enterprise).
2444 **1263** 13cr. multicoloured . . 15 10

1264 "Bathers" (Alfredo Ceschiatti)

1990. "Lubrapex 90" Brazilian–Portuguese Stamp Exhibition, Brasilia. Brasilia Sculptures. Mult.
2445 25cr. Type **1264** 30 25
2446 25cr. "Warriors" (Bruno Giorgi) 30 25
2447 100cr. "St. John" (Ceschiatti) . . . . 1·40 50
2448 100cr. "Justice" (Ceschiatti) 1·40 50
MS2449 150 × 89 mm. Nos. 2445/8 3·25 3·25

1265 "Bromelia antiacantha"

1990. America. 500th Anniv of Discovery of America by Columbus. Praia do Sul Nature Reserve. Multicoloured.
2450 15cr. Type **1265** 90 10
2451 105cr. Wooded shoreline of Lagoa do Sul . . . . . . 1·25 50
Nos. 2450/1 were printed together, se-tenant, forming a composite design.

1266 Oswald de Andrade (birth centenary) and Illustration from "Anthropophagic Manifesto"

1990. Book Day. Anniversaries. Mult.
2452 15cr. Type **1266** 15 10
2453 15cr. Guilherme de Almeida (birth cent) and illustration of "Greek Songs" 15 10
2454 15cr. National Library (180th anniv) and illuminated book 15 10

1267 Emblem and Tribunal Offices, Brasilia

1990. Centenary of National Accounts Tribunal.
2455 **1267** 15cr. multicoloured . . 15 10

1268 National Congress Building

1269 Fingers touching across Map of Americas

1990. Christmas. Brasilia Lights. Mult.
2456 15cr. Type **1268** 15 10
2457 15cr. Television Tower . . . 15 10

1990. Obligatory Tax. Anti-Leprosy Week. As No. 2397 but value and colour changed.
2458 **1239** 50c. blue 10 10

1990. Centenary of Organization of American States.
2459 **1269** 15cr. multicoloured . . 15 10

1270 "Nike Apache" Rocket on Launch Pad

1271 Sao Cristovao City

1990. 25th Anniv of Launch of "Nike Apache" Rocket.
2460 **1270** 15cr. multicoloured . . 15 10

1990. 400th Anniv of Colonization of Sergipe State.
2461 **1271** 15cr. multicoloured . . 15 10

1272 Gymnasts

1991. World Congress on Physical Education, Sports and Recreation, Foz do Iguacu.
2462 **1272** 17cr. multicoloured . . 20 15

1273 Cazuza

1991. "Rock in Rio" Concert. Multicoloured.
2463 25cr. Type **1273** 60 60
2464 185cr. Raul Seixas 80 80
Nos. 2463/4 were printed together, se-tenant, forming a composite design.

1274 Aeritalia/Aermacchi AM-X and Republic Thunderbolt

1991. 50th Anniv of Aeronautics Ministry.
2465 **1274** 17cr. multicoloured . . 20 15

1275 Effigies of Day Woman and Midnight Man, Olinda

1276 Antarctic Wildlife

1991. Carnival. Multicoloured.
2466 25cr. Type **1275** 10 10
2467 30cr. Electric trio on truck, Salvador 10 10
2468 280cr. Samba dancers, Rio de Janeiro 80 45

1991. Visit of President Collor to Antarctica.
2469 **1276** 300cr. multicoloured . . 3·25 2·00

1277 Hang-gliders

1991. 8th World Free Flight Championships, Governador Valadares.
2470 **1277** 36cr. multicoloured . . 15 10

1278 Yachting

1991. 11th Pan-American Games, Cuba, and Olympic Games, Barcelona (1992). Mult.
2471 36cr. Type **1278** 30 10
2472 36cr. Rowing 10 10
2473 300cr. Swimming 85 75

1279 Cross over Bottle (alcoholism)

1991. Anti-addiction Campaign. Mult.
2474 40cr. Type **1279** 10 10
2475 40cr. Cross over cigarette (smoking) 10 10
2476 40cr. Cross over syringe (drug abuse) 10 10

1280 Old and Present Offices and Mastheads

1281 Yanomami Youth in Ceremonial Paint

1991. Cent of "Jornal do Brasil" (newspaper).
2477 **1280** 40cr. multicoloured . . 10 10

1991. Indian Culture. The Yanomami. Mult.
2478 40cr. Type **1281** 10 10
2479 400cr. Hunter (horiz) . . . 80 70

1282 Orinoco Goose

1991. United Nations Conference on Environment and Development.
2480 **1282** 45cr. multicoloured . . 55 30

1283 Jararaca

1284 National Flag

1991. 90th Anniv of Butantan Institute (2481/2) and 173rd Anniv of National Museum (others). Multicoloured.
2481 45cr. Type **1283** 35 10
2482 45cr. Green tree boa 35 10
2483 45cr. Theropoda (dinosaurs) 35 10
2484 350cr. Sauropoda (dinosaurs) . . . . 1·25 60

1991. No value expressed.
2485 **1284** (–) multicoloured . . . 80 10

1285 Early Steam Pump and Santos City 6th Fire Group's Headquarters

1991. Fire Fighting.
2486 **1285** 45cr. multicoloured . . 10 10

1286 Pedra Pintada, Boa Vista, Roraima

1991. Tourism. Centenaries of Boa Vista (1990) and Teresopolis. Multicoloured.
2487 45cr. Type **1286** 10 10
2488 350cr. God's Finger, Teresopolis, Rio de Janeiro 70 60

1287 Welder, "Justice" and Farmer

1991. 50th Anniv of Labour Justice Legal System.
2489 **1287** 45cr. multicoloured . . 10 10

1288 Folklore Characters, Singers and Mota

1991. 5th International Festival of Folklore and Birth Centenary of Leonardo Mota (folklorist).
2490 **1288** 45cr. red, ochre & black 10 10

1289 Jose Basilio da Gama (poet)

1290 Pope John Paul II

1991. Writers' Birth Anniversaries. Mult.
2491 45cr. Type **1289** (250th anniv) 10 10
2492 50cr. Luis Nicolau Fagundes Varela (poet, 150th anniv) 10 10
2493 50cr. Jackson de Figueiredo (essayist and philosopher, centenary) 10 10

1991. Papal Visit and 12th National Eucharistic Congress, Natal. Multicoloured.
2494 50cr. Type **1290** 60 50
2495 400cr. Congress emblem . . 90 70
Nos. 2494/5 were issued together, se-tenant, forming a composite design.

1291 "The Constitutional Commitment" (Aurelio de Figueiredo)

1292 Exhibition Emblem and dish Aerial

1991. Centenary of 1891 Constitution.
2496 **1291** 50cr. multicoloured . . 10 10

1991. "Telecom 91" International Telecommunications Exhibition, Geneva.
2497 **1292** 50cr. multicoloured . . 10 10

1293 Ferdinand Magellan

1294 White-vented Violetear and "Cattleya warneri"

1991. America. Voyages of Discovery. Mult.
2498 50cr. Type **1293** 15 10
2499 400cr. Francisco de Orellana on River Amazon . . . . 1·25 75

1991. "Brapex 91" National Stamp Exhibition, Vitoria. Humming Birds and Orchids in Mata Atlantica Forest. Multicoloured.
2500 50cr. Type **1294** 60 15
2501 65cr. Glittering-bellied emerald and "Rodriguezia venusta" 80 35
2502 65cr. Brazilian ruby and "Zygopetalum intermedium" 80 35
MS2503 99 × 69 mm. 50cr. White-vented violetear and "Cattelya warneri"; 50cr. Glittering-bellied emerald and tree trunk; 500cr. "Rodriguezia venusta" and Brazilian ruby . . . . 6·00 6·00

1295 "Self-portrait III"

1296 Agricultural Projects

1991. Birth Cent of Lasar Segall (artist).
2504 **1295** 400cr. multicoloured . . 80 30

1991. Centenary of Bureau of Agriculture and Provision, Sao Paulo.
2505 **1296** 70cr. multicoloured . . 20 10

1297 Dr. Manuel Ferraz de Campos Salles (President, 1898–1902)

1298 Madonna and Child

1991. 150th Birth Anniversaries. Mult.
2506 70cr. Type **1297** 10 10
2507 90cr. Dr. Prudente de Moraes (President, 1894–98) and Catete Palace, Rio de Janeiro (former Executive Headquarters) 10 10
Nos. 2506/7 were issued together, se-tenant, forming a composite design.

1991. Christmas.
2508 **1298** 70cr. multicoloured . . 10 10

1991. Obligatory Tax. Anti-leprosy Week.
2509 **1239** 3cr. green 35 10

1299 Hand holding Prayer Book

1300 Pedro II

1991. Thanksgiving Day.
2510 **1299** 70cr. multicoloured . . 10 10

1991. 150th Anniv of Coronation and Death Centenary of Emperor Pedro II. Sheet 99 × 69 mm containing T **1300** and similar vert design. Multicoloured.
MS2511 80cr. Type **1300**; 800cr. Pedro II at coronation . . . . 7·00 7·00

1301 Policeman in Historic Uniform and Tobias de Aguiar Battalion Building, Sao Paulo

1991. Military Police.
2512 **1301** 80cr. multicoloured . . 10 10

1302 First Baptist Church, Niteroi (centenary)

1992. Church Anniversaries. Multicoloured.
2513 250cr. Type **1302** 20 15
2514 250cr. Presbyterian Cathedral, Rio de Janeiro (130th anniv) 20 15

1303 Afranio Costa (silver, free pistol)

1992. Olympic Games, Barcelona (1st issue). 1920 Olympics Shooting Medal Winners. Multicoloured.
2515 300cr. Type **1303** 55 20
2516 2500cr. Guilherme Paraense (gold, 30 m revolver) . . 1·75 60
See also No. 2526.

1304 Old and Modern Views of Port

1992. Centenary of Port of Santos.
2517 **1304** 300cr. multicoloured . . 50 20

1305 White-tailed Tropic Birds

1992. 2nd United Nations Conference on Environment and Development, Rio de Janeiro (1st issue). Multicoloured.
2518 400cr. Type **1305** 75 60
2519 2500cr. Spinner dolphins . . 2·00 1·90
See also Nos. 2532/5, 2536/8, 2539/42 and 2543/6.

1306 Ipe

1307 Hunting using Boleadeira

1992. No value expressed.
2520 **1306** (–) multicoloured . . . 1·25 10
No. 2520 was valid for use at the second class inland letter rate.

1992. "Abrafex '92" Argentinian–Brazilian Stamp Exhibition, Porto Alegre. Multicoloured.
2521 250cr. Type **1307** 35 35
2522 250cr. Traditional folk dancing 20 15
2523 250cr. Horse and cart . . . 20 15
2524 1000cr. Rounding-up cattle 85 75
MS2525 150 × 89 mm. 250cr. As No. 2522; 250cr. As No. 2523; 500cr. Type **1307**; 1500cr. As No. 2524 . . . . 55 55

1308 Sportsmen on Globe

1309 Tiradentes (sculpture, Bruno Giorgi)

1992. Olympic Games, Barcelona (2nd issue).
2526 **1308** 300cr. multicoloured . . 20 15

1992. Death Bicentenary of Joaquim Jose da Silvaxavier (Independence fighter). Sheet 98 × 68 mm.
MS2527 **1309** 3500cr. mult . . . 65 65

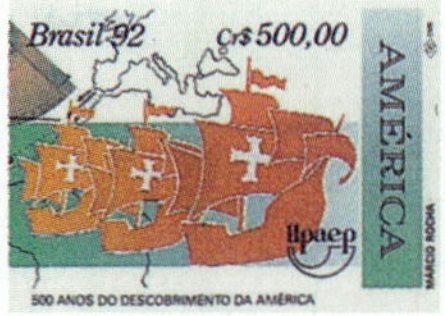

1310 Columbus's Fleet

1992. America. 500th Anniv of Discovery of America by Columbus. Multicoloured.
2528 500cr. Type **1310** 75 25
2529 3500cr. Columbus, route map and quadrant . . . 75 60
Nos. 2528/9 were issued together, se-tenant, forming a composite design.

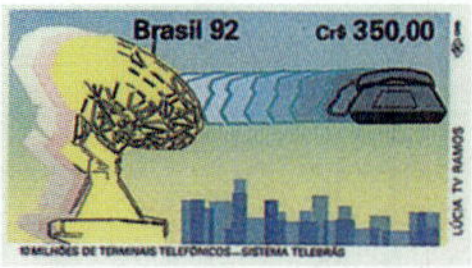

1311 Dish Aerial, Telephone and City

1992. Installation of 10,000,000th Telephone Line in Brazil.
2530 **1311** 350cr. multicoloured . . 15 10

1312 Sailing Canoes

1992. Lubrapex 92 Brazilian--Portuguese Stamp Exhibition, Lisbon. Bicentenary of "Philosophical Journey" by Alexandre Rodrigues Ferreira. Sheet 148 × 88 mm containing T **1312** and similar horiz designs.
MS2531 500cr., 1000cr., 2500cr. Composite design of watercolour by Jose Freire showing arrival of expedition's ship at Vila de Cameta 60 60

1313 Hercule Florence (botanist)

1992. 2nd UN Conference on Environment and Development (2nd issue). 170th Anniv of Langsdorff Expedition. Multicoloured.
2532 500cr. Type **1313** 20 15
2533 500cr. Aime-Adrien Taunay (ethnographer) and Amerindians 20 15
2534 500cr. Johann Moritz Rugendas (zoologist) . . 20 15
2535 3000cr. Gregory Ivanovich Langsdorff and route map 60 60

1314 Urban and Rural Symbols

1992. 2nd UN Conference on Environment and Development (3rd issue). Multicoloured.
2536 450cr. Type **1314** 20 15
2537 450cr. Flags of Sweden (host of first conference) and Brazil around globe . . . 20 15
2538 3000cr. Globe, map, flora and fauna 60 30

1315 Monica sitting by Waterfall

1992. 2nd UN Conference on Environment and Development (4th issue). Ecology. Designs showing cartoon characters. Multicoloured.
2539 500cr. Type **1315** 20 15
2540 500cr. Cebolinha in canoe 20 15
2541 500cr. Cascao photographing wildlife . . 20 15
2542 500cr. Magali picking wild fruit 20 15
Nos. 2539/42 were issued together, se-tenant, forming a composite design.

1316 "Nidularium innocentii"

1317 Humming-bird's Wings forming Flower

1992. 2nd UN Conference on Environment and Development (5th issue). 3rd Anniv of Margaret Mee Brazilian Botanical Foundation. Flower paintings by Margaret Mee. Multicoloured.
2543 600cr. Type **1316** 25 20
2544 600cr. "Canistrum exiguum" 25 20
2545 700cr. "Nidularium rubens" 25 20
2546 700cr. "Canistrum cyathiforme" 25 20

1992. National Diabetes Day.
2547 **1317** 600cr. multicoloured . . 20 15

1318 Training Tower and First Manual Pump

1319 Animals, Cave Paintings and Map of Piaui State

1992. Centenary of Joinville Volunteer Fire Service.
2548 **1318** 550cr. multicoloured . . 20 15

1992. 13th Anniv of Capivara Mountain National Park. Multicoloured.
2549 550cr. Type **1319** 20 15
2550 550cr. Canyons and map of Brazil 20 15
Nos. 2549/50 were issued together, se-tenant, forming a composite design.

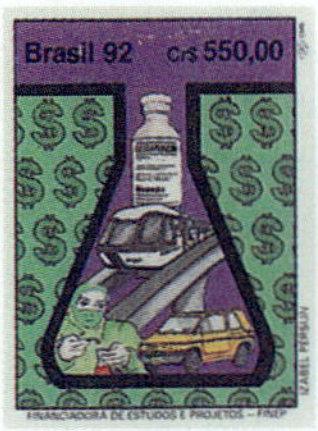

1320 Projects within Flask

1322 Santa Cruz Fortress, Anhatomirim Island

1321 Students at Work

1992. 24th Anniv of Financing Agency for Studies and Projects.
2551 **1320** 550cr. multicoloured . . 1·25 40

1992. 50th Anniv of National Industrial Training Service.
2552 **1321** 650cr. multicoloured . . 15 10

1992. Santa Catarina Fortresses. Multicoloured.
2553 650cr. Type **1322** 15 10
2554 3000cr. Santo Antonio Fort, Ratones Grande island . . 65 60

1323 Masonic Emblem and Palace, Brasilia

1324 Profiles of Child and Man forming Hourglass

1992. 170th Anniv of Grande Oriente (Federation of Brazil's Freemasonry Lodges).
2555 **1323** 650cr. multicoloured . . 10 10

1992. 50th Anniv of Brazilian Legion of Assistance.
2556 **1324** 650cr. multicoloured . . 10 10

1325 Medical Equipment and Patients

1326 Menotti del Picchia

1992. Sarah Locomotor Hospital, Brasilia.
2557 **1325** 800cr. multicoloured . . 10 10

1992. Book Day. Writers' Birth Centenaries. Multicoloured.
2558 900cr. Type **1326** 10 10
2559 900cr. Graciliano Ramos . . 10 10
2560 1000cr. Assis Chateaubriand (journalist) (horiz) 15 10

1327 Meridian Circle, Map, Cruls and Tent

1992. Centenary of Luiz Cruls's Exploration of Central Plateau.
2561 **1327** 900cr. multicoloured . . 10 10

1328 Productivity Graph on Flag

1992. 2nd Anniv of Brazilian Quality and Productivity Programme.
2562 **1328** 1200cr. multicoloured 15 10

1329 Pepino Beach, Rio de Janeiro

1992. Year of Tourism in the Americas. Sheet 70 × 100 mm containing T **1329** and similar horiz design. Multicoloured.
MS2563 1200cr. Type **1329**; 9000cr. Sugar Loaf, Rio de Janeiro . . 1·90 1·90

1330 Father Christmas

1992. Christmas. No value expressed.
2564 **1330** (–) multicoloured . . . 90 10

1992. Obligatory Tax. Anti-leprosy Week.
2565 **1239** 30cr. brown 35 10

1331 Sister Dulce, Patients and Lacerda Lift, Salvador

1993. Sister Dulce (founder of Santo Antonio Hospital and Simoes Filho Educational Centre) Commemoration.
2566 **1331** 3500cr. multicoloured 20 20

1332 Diving

1993. South American Water Sports Championships, Goiania. Sheet 69 × 99 mm containing T **1332** and similar horiz designs. Multicoloured.
MS2567a 3500cr. Type **1332**; 3500cr. Synchronized swimming; 25000cr. Water polo . . . . 3·25 3·25

1333 Tube Station, Pine Trees and Church of the Third Order of St. Francis of Assisi and Stigmata

1993. 300th Anniv of Curitiba.
2568 **1333** 4500cr. multicoloured 25 20

1334 Heart dripping Blood onto Flowers

1335 "Night with the Geniuses of Study and Love"

1993. Health and Preservation of Life. Mult.
2569 4500cr. Type **1334** (blood donation) 20 20
2570 4500cr. Crab attacking healthy cell (anti-cancer campaign) 20 20
2571 4500cr. Rainbow, head and encephalogram (mental health) 20 20

1993. 150th Birth Anniv of Pedro Americo (painter). Multicoloured.
2572 5500cr. Type **1335** 20 20
2573 36000cr. "David and Abizag" (horiz) 30 20
2574 36000cr. "A Carioca" . . . 30 20

1336 Flag

1337 "Dynastes hercules"

1993. No value expressed. Self-adhesive. Die-cut.
2575 **1336** (–) blue, yellow & grn 1·75 20

No. 2575 was valid for use at the current first class inland letter rate. It could not be used to pay postage to foreign countries.

1993. World Environment Day. Beetles. Mult.
2576 8000cr. Type **1337** 30 25
2577 55000cr. "Batus barbicornis" 90 25

1338 Map, Flags and Discussion Themes

1993. 3rd Iberian–American Summit Conference, Salvador.
2578 **1338** 12000cr. multicoloured 25 20

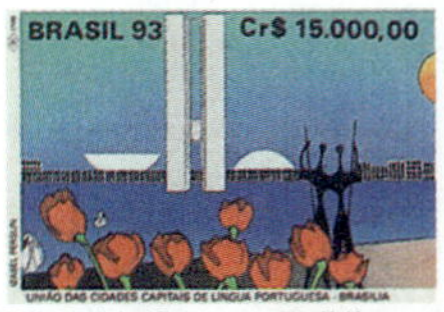

1339 Lake, Congress Building and "Os Candangos" (statue), Brasilia

1993. Union of Portuguese-speaking Capital Cities. Multicoloured.
2579 15000cr. Type **1339** 30 25
2580 71000cr. Copacabana beach and "Christ the Redeemer" (statue), Rio de Janeiro 30 25

Nos. 2579/80 were issued together, se-tenant, forming a composite design.

1340 30r. "Bulls Eye" Stamp

1993. 150th Anniv of First Brazilian Stamps (1st issue) and "Brasiliana 93" International Stamp Exhibition, Rio de Janeiro. Each black, red and yellow.
2581 30000cr. Type **1340** 90 50
2582 60000cr.60r. "Bull's Eye" stamp 90 50
2583 90000cr.90r. "Bull's Eye" stamp 90 50
MS2584 132 × 99 mm. As Nos. 2581/3 but without engraver's name and commemorative inscription . . 2·75 2·75
See also Nos. 2585/8.

1341 Cebolinha designing Stamp

1993. 150th Anniv of First Brazilian Stamps (2nd issue). No value expressed. Cartoon characters. Multicoloured.
2585 (–) Type **1341** 90 15
2586 (–) Cascao as King and 30r. "Bull's Eye" stamp . . . 90 15
2587 (–) Monica writing letter and 60r. "Bull's Eye" stamp 90 15
2588 (–) Magali receiving letter and 90r. "Bull's Eye" stamp 90 15

Nos. 2585/8 were issued together, se-tenant, forming a composite design.

Nos. 2585/8 were valid for use at the current first class inland letter rate. They could not be used to pay postage to other countries.

1342 Imperial Palace (former postal H.Q.), Rio de Janeiro

1344 Forest Mound and Tools

1343 Polytechnic School, Sao Paulo University

1993. 330th Anniv of Postal Service. Mult.
2589 20000cr. Type **1342** 40 35
2590 20000cr. Petropolis post office 40 35
2591 20000cr. Main post office, Rio de Janeiro 40 35
2592 20000cr. Niteroi post office 40 35

Currency Reform
1 (new) cruzeiro real = 1000 (old) cruzeiros.

1993. Engineering Schools. Multicoloured.
2593 17cr. Type **1343** (centenary, 1994) 30 25
2594 17cr. Old and new engineering schools, Rio de Janeiro Federal University (bicent, 1992) 30 25

1993. Preservation of Archaeological Sites. Mult.
2595 17cr. Type **1344** 20 15
2596 17cr. Coastal mound, shells and tools 20 15

1345 Guimaraes and National Congress

1993. Ulysses Guimaraes (politician).
2597 **1346** 22cr. Multicoloured. . . 25 20

1346 Hands holding Candles and Rope around Statue

1347 Hyacinth Macaw, Glaucous Macaw and Indigo Macaw

1993. Bicentenary of Procession of "Virgin of Nazareth", Belem.
2598 **1346** 22cr. multicoloured . . 25 20

1993. America. Endangered Macaws. Mult.
2599 22cr. Type **1347** 25 20
2600 130cr. Spix's macaw . . . . 1·10 90

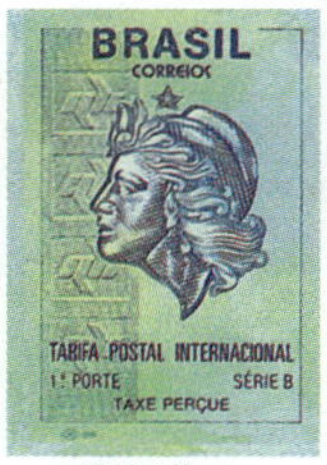

1348 Vinicius de Moraes

1349 Liberty

1993. Composers' Anniversaries. Mult.
2601 22cr. Type **1348** (80th birth anniv) 25 20
2602 22cr. Alfredo da Rocha Vianna (pseud. Pixinguinha) and score of "Carinhoso" (20th death anniv) 25 20

1993. No value expressed.
2603 **1349** (–) blue, turq & yell . . 1·75 45

No. 2603 was sold at the current rate for first class international postage.

1350 Mario de Andrade

1351 Knot

1993. Book Day. Writers' Birth Centenaries. Multicoloured.
2604 30cr. Type **1350** 30 25
2605 30cr. Alceu Amoroso Lima (pseud. Tristao de Athayde) 30 25
2606 30cr. Gilka Machado (poet) 30 25

1993. 40th Anniv of Brazil–Portugal Consultation and Friendship Treaty.
2607 **1351** 30cr. multicoloured . . 30 25

1352 Nho-Quim

1993. 2nd International Comic Strip Biennial. No value expressed. Multicoloured.
2608 (–) Type **1352** 90 30
2609 (–) Benjamin (Louneiro) . . 60 25
2610 (–) Lamparina 60 25
2611 (–) Reco-Reco, Bolao and Azeitona (Luiz Sa) . . . 60 25
See note below Nos. 2585/8.

1353 Diagram and "Tamoio" (submarine)

1993. Launch of First Brazilian-built Submarine.
2612 **1353** 240cr. multicoloured . . 1·10 70

1354 Nativity

1993. Christmas. No value expressed.
2613 **1354** (–) multicoloured . . . 80 25
See note below Nos. 2585/8.

1993. Obligatory Tax. Anti-leprosy Week.
2614 **1205** 50c. blue 20 15

1355 Republic P-47 Thunderbolt Fighters over Tarquinia Camp, Italy

1356 Flag

1993. 50th Anniv of Formation of 1st Fighter Group, Brazilian Expeditionary Force.
2615 **1355** 42cr. multicoloured . . 60 25

1994. No value expressed. Self-adhesive. Imperf.
2616 **1356** (–) blue, yellow & green 60 30
See note below Nos. 2585/8.

1357 Foundation of Republican Memory, Convent and Cloisters

1994. 340th Anniv of Convent of Merces (now Cultural Centre), Sao Luis.
2617 **1357** 58cr. multicoloured . . 40 35

1358 "Mae Menininha"

1994. Birth Centenary of Mae Menininha do Gantois (Escolastica Maria da Conceiao Nazare).
2618 **1358** 80cr. multicoloured . . 20 20

1359 Olympic Rings and Rower
1360 Blue and White Swallow

1994. Centenaries of International Olympic Committee and Rowing Federation, Rio Grande do Sul. No value expressed.
2619 **1359** (–) multicoloured . . . 1·75 90
See note below No. 2603.

1994. Birds. Multicoloured.
2620 10cr. Type **1360** 10 10
2621 20cr. Roadside hawk . . . 10 10
2622 50cr. Rufous-bellied thrush 10 10
2623 100cr. Ruddy ground dove 15 10
2624 200cr. Southern lapwing . . 30 25
2625 500cr. Rufous-collared sparrow 80 70
See after Nos. 2649/61.

1361 Map and Prince Henry

1994. 600th Birth Anniv of Prince Henry the Navigator.
2626 **1361** 635cr. multicoloured . . 1·75 90

1362 Bicycle

1994. America. Postal Vehicles. Mult.
2627 110cr. Type **1362** 15 10
2628 635cr. Post motor cycle . . 1·75 20

1363 Statue, Grain Store and Chapel of Help, Juazeiro do Norte

1994. 150th Anniv of Birth of Father Cicero Romao Batista. With service indicator.
2629 **1363** (–) multicoloured . . . 60 15
See note below Nos. 2585/8.

1364 Sabin and Children

1994. 1st Death Anniv of Albert Sabin (developer of oral polio vaccine).
2630 **1364** 160cr. multicoloured . . 25 20

1365 Castello Branco and Brasilia

1994. Carlos Castello Branco (journalist).
2631 **1365** 160cr. multicoloured . . 25 20

1366 "Euterpe oleracea"
1367 "Brazil"

1994. Birth Bicentenary of Karl Friedrich Phillip von Martius (botanist). With service indicator. Multicoloured. (a) Inscr "1. PORTE NACIONAL".
2632 (–) Type **1366** 85 15
2633 (–) "Jacaranda paucifoliolata" 85 15

(b) Inscr "1. PORTE INTERNACIONAL TAXE PERCUE".
2634 (–) "Barbacenia tomentosa" 1·50 30
Nos. 2632/3 were for use at the current first class inland letter rate and Nos. 2634 for first class international postage.

1994. With service indicator. (a) Size 21 × 28 mm. Self-adhesive. Rouletted. (i) PRINTED MATTER. Inscr "1. PORTE IMPRESSO CATEGORIA II".
2635 **1367** (–) blue 10 10

(ii) INLAND POSTAGE. Inscr "3. PORTE NACIONAL".
2636 **1367** (3rd) red 30 20

(b) INLAND POSTAGE. Inscr "PORTE NACIONAL". Size 26 × 35 mm.
2637 **1367** (4th) green 40 30
2638 (5th) red 75 30
Nos. 2635/8 were valid for internal use in the category described.

1368 Brazilian Player wearing "100"

1994. Centenary of Football in Brazil and World Cup Football Championship, U.S.A. With service indicator.
2639 **1368** (–) multicoloured . . . 2·40 90
See note below No. 2603.

1369 Emperor Tamarin ("Saguinus imperator")
1371 Pencils Crossing over Fingerprint

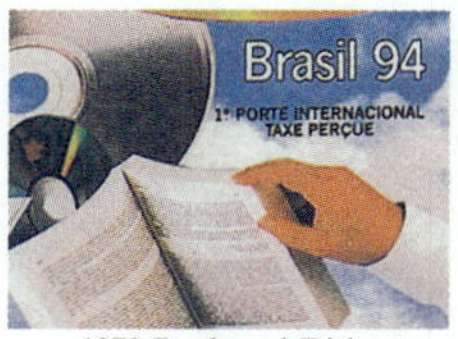

1370 Book and Disks

1994. Endangered Mammals. With service indicator. Multicoloured.
2640 (–) Type **1369** 60 15
2641 (–) Bare-faced tamarin ("Saguinus bicolor") . . . 60 15
2642 (–) Golden lion tamarin ("Leontopithecus rosalia") 60 15
See note below Nos. 2585/8.

1994. 46th International Book Fair, Frankfurt, Germany. Sheet 99 × 69 mm.
MS2643 **1370** (–) multicoloured 90 90
No. **MS**2643 was sold at the current rate for first class international postage.

1994. 10 Year Education Plan. With service indicator. Multicoloured.
2644 (–) Type **1371** (literacy campaign) 60 15
2645 (–) PRONAICA pencil and school (National Programme of Integral Care to Children and Teenagers) 60 15
2646 (–) Lecture scene and graph (increase in qualified teachers) 60 15
2647 (–) Pencil and "lecturers" on television (distance learning by video) 60 15
See note below Nos. 2585/8.

1372 Map of the Americas (Bartholomeu Velho, 1561) and Treaty Boundaries

1994. 500th Anniv of the Treaty of Tordesillas (defining Portuguese and Spanish spheres of influence). Sheet 67 × 99 mm.
MS2648 **1372** (–) multicoloured 90 90
No. **MS**2648 was sold at the current rate for first class international postage.

1994. Birds. As T **1360** but with value expressed as "R$". Multicoloured.
2649 1c. Type **1360** 10 10
2650 2c. As No. 2621 . . . . 10 10
2652 5c. As No. 2622 . . . . 10 10
2654 10c. As No. 2623 . . . . 15 10
2655 15c. Saffron finch 20 15
2656 20c. As No. 2624 . . . . 30 25
2657 22c. Fork-tailed fly-catcher 30 25
2658 50c. As No. 2625 . . . . . 75 65
2661 1r. Rufous hornero . . . . 1·50 1·25

1373 Edgard Santos (founder of Bahia University)
1374 "Petrobras X" (drilling platform), Campos Basin. Rio de Janeiro

1994. Anniversaries. With service indicator. Multicoloured.
2662 (–) Type **1373** (birth centenary) 20 15
2663 (–) Oswaldo Aranha (politician, birth centenary) 20 15
2664 (–) Otto Lara Resende (author and journalist, 2nd death anniv) 20 15
See note below Nos. 2585/8.

1994. 40th Anniv of Petrobras (state oil company).
2665 **1374** 12c. multicoloured . . . 40 15

1375 17th century Coin Production
1376 Loaf of Bread

1994. 300th Anniv of Brazilian Mint.
2666 **1375** 12c. multicoloured . . . 20 15

1994. Campaign against Famine and Misery. With service indicator.
2667 **1376** (–) multicoloured . . . 20 15
2668 – (–) black and blue . . . 20 15
DESIGN: No. 2668, Fish.
See note below Nos. 2585/8.

1377 Writing with Quill and Scales of Justice

1994. 150th Anniv of Brazilian Lawyers Institute.
2669 **1377** 12c. multicoloured . . . 20 15

1378 Family within Heart

1994. International Year of the Family.
2670 **1378** 84c. multicoloured . . . 1·25 60

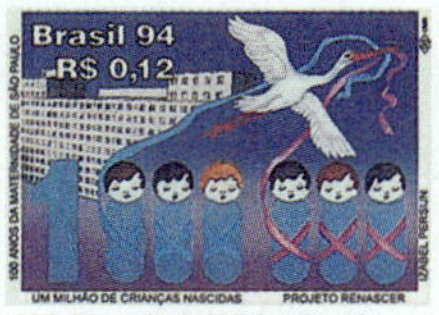

1379 Hospital, White Stork and Babies forming "1000000"

1994. Centenary of Sao Paulo Maternity Hospital. Its Millionth Birth.
2671 **1379** 12c. multicoloured . . . 20 15

1380 Celestino performing and "Maternal Heart" (record sleeve)

1994. Birth Centenary of Vicente Celestino (singer).
2672 **1380** 12c. multicoloured . . . 20 15

1381 Fernando de Azevedo (educationist)

1994. Writers' Birth Anniversaries. Mult.
2673 12c. Type **1381** (cent) . . . 20 15
2674 12c. Tomas Antonio Gonzaga (poet, 250th) . . 20 15

1382 "Joao and Maria" (Hansel and Gretel)

1994. Centenary of Publication of "Fairy Tales" by Alberto Figueiredo Pimentel (first Brazilian children's book). Multicoloured.
2675 12c. Type **1382** 20 15
2676 12c. "Dona Baratinha" (Little Mrs Cockroach) 20 15
2677 84c. "Puss in Boots" . . . 1·25 1·10
2678 84c. "Tom Thumb" . . . . 1·25 1·10

1383 St. Clare, St. Damian's Convent and Statue of St. Francis

1994. 800th Birth Anniv of St. Clare of Assisi (founder of order of Poor Clares).
2679 **1383** 12c. multicoloured . . . 20 15

1384 McLaren–Honda F1 Racing Car and Brazilian Flag

1994. Ayrton Senna (racing driver) Commemoration. Multicoloured.
2680 12c. Type **1384** 90 60
2681 12c. Senna and crowd waving farewell 90 60
2682 84c. Brazilian and chequered flags, racing cars and Senna giving victory salute . . . . 1·75 60
Nos. 2680/2 were issued together, se-tenant, forming a composite design.

1385 Books and Globe

1994. Centenary of Historical and Geographical Institute, Sao Paulo.
2683 **1385** 12c. multicoloured . . . 20 15

1386 Adoniran Barbosa and "11 o'Clock Train"

1994. Composers. Multicoloured.
2684 12c. Type **1386** 20 15
2685 12c. Score of "The Sea" (Dorival Caymmi) 20 15

1994. Obligatory Tax. Anti-Leprosy Week.
2686 **1205** 1c. purple 10 10

1387 Maggot wearing Santa Claus Hat in Apple

1994. Christmas. Multicoloured.
2687 12c. Type **1387** 20 15
2688 12c. Carol singers 20 15
2689 12c. Boy smoking pipe and letter in boot 20 15
2690 84c. Boy wearing saucepan on head and Santa Claus cloak 90 60

1388 Trophy

1994. Brazil, World Cup Football Championship (U.S.A.) Winners. Sheet 100 × 69 mm.
MS2691 **1388** 2r.14 multicoloured 2·75 2·75

1389 Pasteur

1995. Death Centenary of Louis Pasteur (chemist).
2692 **1389** 84c. multicoloured . . . 1·10 30

1390 Duke of Caxias and Soldiers

1391 Pres. Franco

1995. 150th Anniv of Peace of Ponche Verde (pacification of Farroupilha Revolution) (2693) and 50th Anniv of Battle of Monte Castello (2694). Multicoloured.
2693 12c. Type **1390** 15 10
2694 12c. Soldier, Brazilian flag and battle scene 15 10

1995. Itamar Franco (President 1992–94).
2695 **1391** 12c. multicoloured . . . 15 10

1392 Meal before Child

1393 Alexandre de Gusmao (diplomat)

1995. 50th Anniv of F.A.O.
2696 **1392** 84c. multicoloured . . . 1·10 30

1995. Birth Anniversaries. Multicoloured.
2697 12c. Type **1393** (300th anniv) 15 10
2698 12c. Visconde (Viscount) de Jequitinhonha (lawyer, bicent (1994)) 15 10
2699 15c. Barao (Baron) do Rio Branco (diplomat, 150th anniv) 20 15

1394 Guglielmo Marconi and his Transmitter

1995. Centenary of First Radio Transmission.
2700 **1394** 84c. multicoloured . . . 1·10 30

1395 Ipe-amarelo and Cherry Blossom

1396 Solitary Tinamou ("Tinamus solitarius")

1995. Centenary of Brazil–Japan Friendship Treaty.
2701 **1395** 84c. multicoloured . . . 1·10 30

1995. Birds. Multicoloured.
2702 12c. Type **1396** 15 10
2703 12c. Razor-billed curassow ("Mitu mitu") 15 10

1397 St. John's Party, Campina Grande

1995. June Festivals. Multicoloured.
2704 12c. Type **1397** 15 10
2705 12c. Country wedding, Caruaru 15 10

1398 St. Antony holding Child Jesus (painting, Vieira Lusitano)

1995. 800th Birth Anniv of St. Antony of Padua.
2706 **1398** 84c. multicoloured . . . 1·10 30

1399 Lumiere Brothers and Early Projection Equipment

1995. Centenary of Motion Pictures. Sheet 99 × 70 mm.
MS2707 **1399** 2r.14 multicoloured 2·75 2·75

1400 Laurel and "Republic"

1401 Player, Net and Anniversary Emblem

1995. 1st Anniv of Real Currency.
2708 **1400** 12c. brown, green & blk 15 10

1995. Centenary of Volleyball.
2709 **1401** 15c. multicoloured . . . 20 15

1402 "Angaturama limai"

1995. 14th Brazilian Palaeontology Society Congress, Uberaba. Dinosaurs. Multicoloured.
2710 15c. Type **1402** 20 10
2711 1r.50 Titanosaurus . . . . 2·00 1·75

1403 Crash Test Dummies in Car

1995. Road Safety Campaign. Multicoloured.
2712 12c. Type **1403** 15 10
2713 71c. Car crashing into glass of whisky 95 85

1404 "Calathea burle-marxii"

1405 Paratroopers

1995. "Singapore '95" International Stamp Exhibition. 10th Anniv of Donation to Nation by Roberto Burle Marx of his Botanical Collection. Multicoloured.
2714 15c. Type **1404** 20 15
2715 15c. "Vellozia burle-marxii" 20 15
2716 1r.50 "Heliconia aemygdiana" . . . . . . 2·00 1·75

1995. 50th Anniv of Parachutist Infantry Brigade.
2717 **1405** 15c. multicoloured . . . 20 15

1406 Paulista Museum and "Fernao Dias Paes Leme" (statue, Luigi Brizzolara)

1995. Centenary of Paulista Museum of the University of Sao Paulo.
2718 **1406** 15c. multicoloured . . . 20 15

1407 Olinda

1408 Scarlet Ibis and Stoat catching Fish

1995. Lighthouses. Multicoloured.
2719 15c. Type **1407** 35 25
2720 15c. Sao Joao 35 25
2721 15c. Santo Antonio da Barra 35 25

1995. "Lubrapex 95" Brazilian–Portuguese Stamp Exhibition, Sao Paulo. Fauna of the Tiete River Valley. Multicoloured.
2722 15c. Type **1408** 30 15
2723 84c. Great egret flying over canoe . . . . 1·10 95
MS2724 125 × 185 mm. 1r.50 × 2 Motifs as in Nos. 2722/3 forming a composite design . . . . . . 3·00 3·00

1409 X-Ray of Hand

1995. 150th Birth Anniv of Wilhelm Rontgen and Centenary of his Discovery of X-Rays.
2725 **1409** 84c. multicoloured . . . 1·10 30

1410 Arms and Crowd

1995. Centenary of Flamengo Regatta Club.
2726 **1410** 15c. multicoloured . . . 20 15

1411 Fungi and Alligator

1995. America. Environmental Protection. Mult.
2727 15c. Type **1411** 20 15
2728 84c. Black-necked swans on lake . . . . 1·10 95
Nos. 2727/8 were issued together, se-tenant, forming a composite design.

1412 Dove over World Map (left detail)

1413 Jose Maria Eca de Queiroz

1995. 50th Anniv of U.N.O. Multicoloured.
2729 1r.05 Type **1412** . . . . . 1·40 1·25
2730 1r.05 Dove over world map (right detail) . . . . . . 1·40 1·25
Nos. 2729/30 were issued together, se-tenant, forming a composite design.

1995. Book Day. Writers' Anniversaries. Mult.
2731 15c. Type **1413** (150th birth) 20 15
2732 15c. Rubem Braga (5th death) 20 15
2733 23c. Carlos Drummond de Andrade (8th death) . . . 30 25

1414 Zumbi

1995. 300th Death Anniv of Zumbi (leader of Palmares (autonomous state formed by rebelled slaves)). Sheet 100 × 69 mm.
MS2734 **1414** 1r.05 multicoloured 80 80

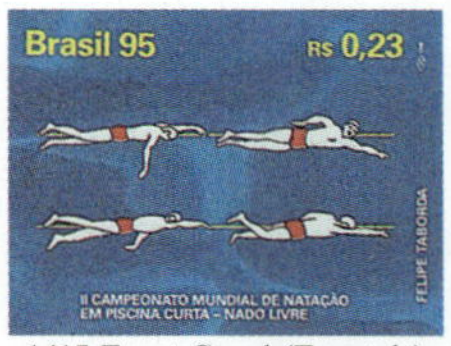

1415 Front Crawl (Freestyle)

1995. 11th World Short-course Swimming Championships, Rio de Janeiro. Multicoloured.
2735 23c. Type **1415** 30 25
2736 23c. Backstroke 30 25
2737 23c. Butterfly 30 25
2738 23c. Breaststroke 30 25
Nos. 2735/8 were issued together, se-tenant, forming a composite design of a swimming pool.

1416 Cherub

1995. Christmas. Multicoloured.
2739 15c. Type **1416** 20 15
2740 23c. Cherub (different) . . . 30 25
Nos. 2739/40 were issued together, se-tenant, forming a composite design.

1417 Flag, Former Headquarters and "Manequinho" (statue)

1995. Centenary (1994) of Botafogo Football and Regatta Club.
2741 **1417** 15c. multicoloured . . . 20 15

1418 Computer, Mouse and Masthead

1995. 170th Anniv of "Diario de Pernambuco" (newspaper).
2742 **1418** 23c. multicoloured . . . 30 25

1419 Theatre Dome

1996. Centenary of Amazon Theatre, Manaus. Sheet 98 × 69 mm.
MS2743 **1419** 1r.23 multicoloured 85 85

1420 Prestes Maia and Sao Paulo

1996. Birth Centenary of Francisco Prestes Maia (Mayor of Sao Paulo).
2744 **1420** 18c. multicoloured . . . 20 15

1421 Bornhausen and Santa Catarina

1996. Birth Centenary of Irineu Bornhausen (Governor of State of Santa Catarina).
2745 **1421** 27c. multicoloured . . . 35 30

1422 "Ouro Preto Landscape" (Alberto da Veiga Guignard)

1423 Doll

1996. Artists' Birth Centenaries. Mult.
2746 15c. Type **1422** 20 15
2747 15c. "Boat with Little Flags and Birds" (Alfredo Volpi) 20 15

1996. 50th Anniv of United Nations Children's Fund. Campaign against Sexual Abuse.
2748 **1423** 23c. multicoloured . . . 30 25

1424 Anniversary Emblem

1426 Pantanal

1425 Pinheiro da Silva and National Congress

1996. 500th Anniv (2000) of Discovery of Brazil by the Portuguese.
2749 **1424** 1r.05 multicoloured . . 1·25 1·10

1996. Birth Centenary of Israel Pinheiro da Silva (politician).
2750 **1425** 18c. multicoloured . . . 20 15

1996. Tourism. Multicoloured. Self-adhesive. Imperf (backing paper rouletted).
2751 23c. Amazon River 30 25
2752 23c. Type **1426** 30 25
2753 23c. Jangada raft 30 25
2754 23c. "The Sugarloaf", Guanabara Bay 30 25
2755 23c. Iguazu Falls 30 25

1427 Crimson Topaz

1996. "Espamer 96" Spanish and Latin-American Stamp Exhibition, Seville, Spain. Hummingbirds. Multicoloured.
2756 15c. Type **1427** 20 15
2757 1r.05 Black-breasted plover-crest . . . . 1·25 1·10
2758 1r.15 Swallow-tailed hummingbird . . . . . . 1·40 1·25

1428 Marathon Runners

1996. Cent of Modern Olympic Games. Mult.
2759 18c. Type **1428** 20 15
2760 23c. Gymnastics 30 25
2761 1r.05 Swimming . . . . . . 1·25 1·10
2762 1r.05 Beach volleyball . . . 1·25 1·10

1429 Cave Entrance

1996. National Heritage. Caverns. Sheet 99 × 68 mm.
MS2763 **1429** 2r.68 multicoloured 1·80 1·80

1430 Dish Aerial, Satellite over Earth and Sports

1996. "Americas Telecom 96" International Telecommunications Exn, Rio de Janeiro.
2764 **1430** 1r.05 multicoloured . . 1·25 25

1431 Sun and Raindrop replenishing Dry Tree

1996. World Anti-desertification Day. Sheet 70 × 96 mm.
MS2765 **1431** 1r.23 multicoloured 85 85

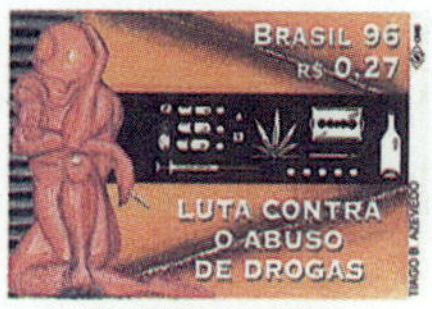

1432 Addict and Drugs

1996. Anti-drug Abuse Campaign.
2766 **1432** 27c. multicoloured . . . 35 30

1433 Coloured Pencils

1435 Gomes and Peace Theatre

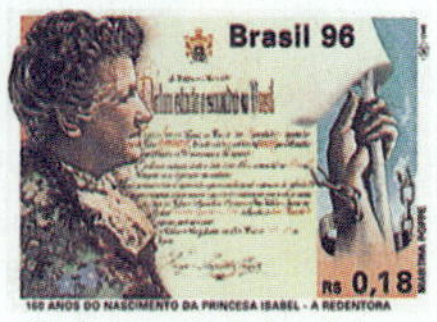

1434 Princess Isabel and Aurea Law

1996. Education Year.
2767 **1433** 23c. multicoloured . . . 30 25

1996. 150th Birth Anniv of Princess Isabel the Redeemer.
2768 **1434** 18c. multicoloured . . . 20 15
The Aurea Law abolished slavery in Brazil.

1996. Death Centenary of Carlos Gomes (opera composer).
2769 **1435** 50c. multicoloured . . . 60 50

1436 "Cattleya eldorado"

1996. 15th International Orchid Conference, Rio de Janeiro. Multicoloured.
2770 15c. Type **1436** 20 15
2771 15c. "Cattleya loddigesii" 20 15
2772 15c. "Promenaea stapellioides" 20 15

1437 Melania and Maximino and Virgin Mary

1996. 150th Anniv of Apparition of Our Lady at La Salette, France.
2773 **1437** 1r. multicoloured . . . 1·25 1·10

1438 Cuca

1996. BRAPEX 96 National Stamp Exhibition, Recife. Folk Legends. Sheet 72 × 100 mm containing T **1438** and similar horiz designs. Multicoloured.
MS2774 23c. Type **1438**; 1r.05 Boitata; 1r.15 Caipora . . . . 2·75 2·75

1439 "Marilyn Monroe" (Andy Warhol)

1996. 23rd International Biennale, Sao Paulo. Paintings. Multicoloured.
2775 55c. Type **1439** 60 50
2776 55c. "The Scream" (Edvard Munch) 60 50
2777 55c. "Mirror for the red Room" (Louise Bourgeois) 60 50
2778 55c. "Lent" (Pablo Picasso) 60 50

1440 Emblem

1996. Defenders of Nature (environmental organization).
2779 **1440** 10r. multicoloured . . . 11·00 9·50

1441 Vaqueiro

1442 Poinsettia and Lighted Candle

1996. America. Traditional Costumes. Mult.
2780 50c. Type **1441** 60 50
2781 1r. Baiana (seller of beancakes) . . . . 1·25 1·10

1996. Christmas.
2782 **1442** (–) multicoloured . . . 20 15
See second note below No. 2588.

1443 "Melindrosa" (cover of 1931 "O Cruzeiro" magazine)

1444 Ipiranga Monument

1996. 46th Death Anniv of Jose Carlos (caricaturist).
2783 **1443** (–) multicoloured . . . 20 15
See second note below No. 2588.

1996. Tourism. Multicoloured. Self-adhesive. Imperf (backing paper rouletted).
2784 (–) Type **1444** 15 10
2785 (–) Hercilio Luz Bridge . . 15 10
2786 (–) National Congress building 15 10
2787 (–) Pelourinho 15 10
2788 (–) Ver-o-Peso market . . . 15 10
Nos. 2784/8 were valid for use at the current first stage inland letter rate.

1445 Campaign Emblem and Guanabara Bay

1997. Bid by Rio de Janeiro for 2004 Olympic Games.
2789 **1445** (–) multicoloured . . . 60 50
No. 2789 was valid for use at the current first stage international letter rate.

1446 Postman and Letter Recipients

1997. America. The Postman.
2790 **1446** (–) multicoloured . . . 15 10
No. 2790 was valid for use at the current first stage inland letter rate.

1447 Alves, Flogging and Salvador Harbour

1997. 150th Birth Anniv of Antonio de Castro Alves (poet).
2791 **1447** 15c. multicoloured . . . 30 10

1448 Tamandare (after Miranda Junior) and "Rescue of 'Ocean Monarch' by Don Afonso" (Samuel Walters)

1997. Death Centenary of Marquis of Tamandare (naval reformer).
2792 **1448** 23c. multicoloured . . . 40 20

1449 "Joy. Joy"

1997. Winning Entry in "Art on Stamps" Competition.
2793 **1449** 15c. multicoloured . . . 15 10

1450 Globe in Glass of Water

1451 Embraer EMB-145

1997. World Water Day.
2794 **1450** 1r.05 multicoloured . . 1·10 95

1997. Brazilian Aircraft. Multicoloured. Self-adhesive. Imperf (backing paper rouletted).
2795 15c. Type **1451** 15 10
2796 15c. Aeritalia/Aermacchi AM-X jet fighter 15 10
2797 15c. Embraer EMB-312 H Super Tucano 15 10
2798 15c. Embraer EMB-120 Brasilia 15 10
2799 15c. Embraer EMB-312 Tucano trainer 15 10

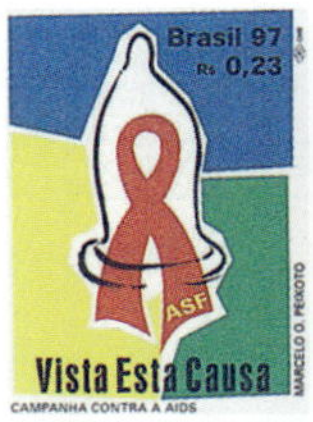

1452 Red Ribbon inside Condom

1454 Emblem

1453 Traditional Weapons and Tribesmen

1997. Family Health Association (A.S.F.) Anti-AIDS Campaign.
2810 **1452** 23c. multicoloured . . . 25 20

1997. Indian Cultures. Sheet 70 × 100 mm.
MS2811 **1453** 1r.15 multicoloured 80 80

1997. 500th Anniv (2000) of Discovery of Brazil by the Portuguese.
2812 **1454** 1r.05 multicoloured . . 1·10 95

1455 Pixinguinha

1456 Landmark

1997. Birth Centenary of Pixinguinha (musician).
2813 **1455** 15c. multicoloured . . . 15 10

1997. Centenary of Brazilian Sovereignty of Trinidade Island. Sheet 99 × 68 mm.
MS2814 **1456** 1r.23 multicoloured 85 85

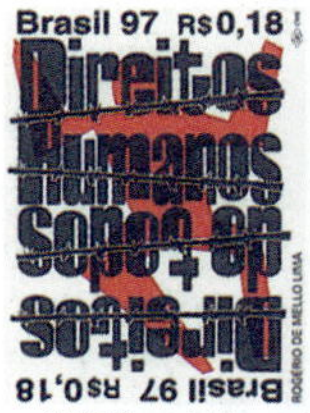

1457 Inscription

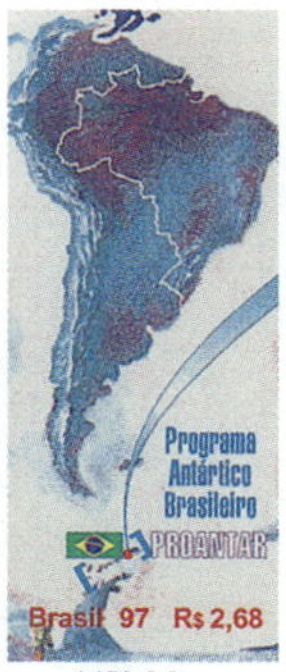

1458 Map

1997. "Human Rights, Rights of All".
2815 **1457** 18c. black and red . . . 20 15

1997. Brazilian Antarctic Programme. Sheet 69 × 99 mm.
MS2816 **1458** 2r.68 multicoloured 2·75 2·75

1459 Melon

1461 Antonio Vieira in Pulpit

1460 Mahogany ("Swietenia macropylla")

1997. Fruits. Self-adhesive. (a) Imperf (backing paper rouletted). (i) With service indicator.
2817 **1459** (–) red and green . . . 20 15

(ii) With face values.
2818 – 1c. yellow, orange & grn 10 10
2819 – 2c. yellow, brown & blk . . 10 10
2820 – 5c. orange, yellow & blk 10 10
2821 – 10c. yellow, brown & grn 10 10
2822 – 20c. yellow, red & green 20 15

(b) Die-cut wavy edge.
2823 – 1c. yellow, orange & grn 10 10
2824 – 10c. yellow, brown & grn 10 10
2825 – 20c. lt green, grn & blk . . 20 15
2826 – 22c. red, purple & green 20 15
2827 – 27c. orange, brown and green 55 50
2828 – 40c. multicoloured 40 35
2829 – 50c. multicoloured 30 25
2830 – 51c. green, lt grn & brn . . 50 45
2831 – 80c. red, green & yellow 80 70
2832 – 82c. lt grn, grn & dp grn 80 70
2833 – 1r. red, green & yellow . . 1·00 90
DESIGNS—HORIZ: Nos. 2818, 2823, Oranges; 2819, Bananas; 2820, Mango. VERT: Nos. 2821, 2824, Pineapple; 2822, Cashew nuts; 2825, Sugar-apple; 2826, Grapes; 2827, Cupuacu; 2828, Soursop; 2829, Suriname cherry ("Pitanga"); 2830, Coconut; 2831, Apples; 2832, Limes; 2833, Strawberries.
No. 2817 was valid for use at the current first stage inland letter rate.

1997. World Environment Day. Amazon Flora and Fauna. Multicoloured.
2836 27c. Type **1460** 30 25
2837 27c. Arapaima (55 × 22 mm) 30 25

1997. Death Anniversaries of Missionaries to Brazil. Multicoloured.
2838 1r.05 Type **1461** (300th) . . 1·10 95
2839 1r.05 Indian children and Jose de Auchieta (400th) 1·10 95

1462 Parnaiba Delta and Sculpture (Mestre Dezinho)

1463 Blue-black Grassquit

1997. Tourism. With service indicator. Mult.
2840 (–) Type **1462** . . . . . . 1·25 1·10
2841 (–) Lencois Maranhenses National Park and costume . . . . 1·25 1·10
Nos. 2840/1 were valid for use at the current rate for first class international postage.

1997. Birds. Multicoloured. Self-adhesive. Imperf (backing paper rouletted). (a) With service indicator.
2842 (–) Type **1463** 20 15

(b) With face value.
2843 22c. Social flycatcher ("Vermilion-crowned Flycatcher") 20 15
No. 2842 was valid for use at the current first stage inland letter rate.

1464 Academy

1998. Cent of Brazilian Literature Academy.
2850 **1464** 22c. multicoloured . . . 20 15

1465 "Gipsies" (Di Cavalcanti)

1997. Birth Centenary of Emiliano di Cavalcanti (artist).
2851 **1465** 31c. multicoloured . . . 30 25

1466 Pope John Paul II, "Christ the Redeemer" and Family

1997. 2nd World Meeting of Pope with Families, Rio de Janeiro.
2852 **1466** 1r.20 multicoloured . . 1·25 1·10

1467 Flags of Member Countries

1468 Antonio Conselheiro (religious leader)

1997. Mercosur (South American Common Market).
2853 **1467** 80c. multicoloured . . . 80 70

1997. Centenary of End of Canudos War.
2854 **1468** 22c. multicoloured . . . 20 15

1469 Mercosur Members starred on Map of South America

1997. 25th Anniv of Telebras.
2855 **1469** 80c. multicoloured . . . 80 70

1470 Lorenzo Fernandez and Score of "Sonata Breve"

1997. Composers' Birth Centenaries. Each black and gold.
2856 22c. Type **1470** 20 15
2857 22c. Francisco Mignone and score of "Second Brazilian Fantasia" 20 15

1471 "Our Good Mother" and Blackboard with Marist Motto

1997. Centenary of Marist Brothers in Brazil.
2858 **1471** 22c. multicoloured . . . 20 15

1472 Angel playing Trumpet

1473 "Equality" (Gian Calvi)

1997. Christmas.
2859 **1472** 22c. multicoloured . . . 20 15

1997. Children and Citizenship. Multicoloured.
2860 22c.+8c. Type **1473** 30 25
2861 22c.+8c. "Love and Tenderness" (Alcy Linares) 30 25
2862 22c.+8c. "Admission to School" (Ziraldo) 30 25
2863 22c.+8c. "Healthy Pregnancy" (Claudio Martins) 30 25
2864 22c.+8c. "Being Happy" (Cica Fittipaldi) 30 25
2865 22c.+8c. "Work for Parents, School for Children" (Roger Mello) 30 25
2866 22c.+8c. "Breast-feeding" (Angela Lago) 30 25
2867 22c.+8c. "Civil Registration" (Mauricio de Sousa) 30 25
2868 22c.+8c. "Integration of the Handicapped" (Nelson Cruz) 30 25
2869 22c.+8c. "Presence of Parents during Illness" (Eliardo Franca) 30 25
2870 22c.+8c. "Quality of Teaching" (Graca Lima) 30 25
2871 22c.+8c. "Safe Delivery" (Eva Furnari) 30 25
2872 22c.+8c. "Family and Community Life" (Gerson Conforti) 30 25
2873 22c.+8c. "Music playing" (Ana Raquel) 30 25
2874 22c.+8c. "Respect and Dignity" (Helena Alexandrino) 30 25
2875 22c.+8c. "Summary of Children's Statute" (Darlan Rosa) 30 25

1474 Children and Globe

1997. Education and Citizenship.
2876 **1474** 31c. blue and yellow . . 30 25

1475 Belo Horizonte at Night

1476 Outline Map and Books (Education)

1997. Centenary of Belo Horizonte.
2877 **1475** 31c. multicoloured . . . 30 25

1997. Citizens' Rights. Mult. Self-adhesive.
2878 22c. Type **1476** 20 15
2879 22c. Map and hand holding labour card (work) . . . 20 15
2880 22c. Map and fruit (agriculture) 20 15
2881 22c. Map and stethoscope (health) 20 15
2882 22c. Clapper-board and paint brush (culture) . . . 20 15

1477 Alexandrite

1998. Minerals. Multicoloured.
2883 22c. Type **1477** 15 10
2884 22c. Chrysoberyl cat's-eye 15 10
2885 22c. Indicolite 15 10

1478 Elis Regina (singer)

1998. America. Famous Women. Multicoloured.
2886 22c. Type **1478** 15 10
2887 22c. Clementina de Jesus (singer) 15 10
2888 22c. Dulcina de Moraes (actress) 15 10
2889 22c. Clarice Lispector (writer) 15 10

1479 Pupils

1998. Education. Multicoloured.
2890 31c. Type **1479** (universal schooling) 20 15
2891 31c. Teacher (teacher appraisal) 20 15
Nos. 2390/1 were issued together, se-tenant, forming a composite design of a classroom.

1480 Cruze Sousa

1998. Death Centenary of Joao da Cruze Sousa (poet).
2892 **1480** 36c. multicoloured . . . 20 15

1481 Map, 1519

1998. 500th Anniv (2000) of Discovery of Brazil by the Portuguese. Multicoloured.
2893 1r.05 Type **1481** 65 55
2894 1r.05 Galleon . . . . 1·10 90
Nos. 2893/4 were issued together, se-tenant, forming a composite design.

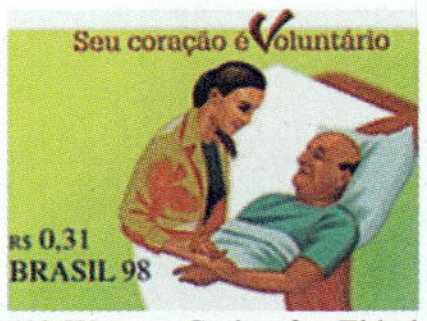
1482 Woman Caring for Elderly Man

1998. Voluntary Work. Multicoloured.
2895 31c. Type **1482** 20 15
2896 31c. Woman caring for child 20 15
2897 31c. Fighting forest fire . . 20 15
2898 31c. Adult's and child's hands 20 15
Nos. 2895/8 were issued together, se-tenant, forming a composite design.

1483 Clown

1485 Ball breaking Net (Antonio Henrique Amaral)

1484 Turtle

1998. Circus. Multicoloured.
2899 31c. Type **1483** 20 15
2900 31c. Clown resting on stick 20 15
2901 31c. Clown (left half) and outside of Big Top . . . 20 15
2902 31c. Clown (right half) and inside of Big Top 20 15
Nos. 2899/2902 were issued together, se-tenant, forming a composite design.

1998. Expo '98 World's Fair, Lisbon. International Year of the Ocean. Multicoloured.
2903 31c. Type **1484** 20 15
2904 31c. Tail of whale 20 15
2905 31c. Barracuda 20 15
2906 31c. Jellyfish and fishes . . 20 15
2907 31c. Diver and school of fishes 20 15
2908 31c. Two dolphins 20 15
2909 31c. Angelfish (brown spotted fish) 20 15
2910 31c. Two whales 20 15
2911 31c. Two long-nosed butterflyfishes (with black stripe across eye) 20 15
2912 31c. Sea perch (red and yellow fish) 20 15
2913 31c. Manatee 20 15
2914 31c. Seabream (blue, yellow and black fish) 20 15
2915 31c. Emperor angelfish and coral 20 15
2916 31c. School of snappers (blue and yellow striped fishes) 20 15
2917 31c. Flying gurnard 20 15
2918 31c. Manta ray 20 15
2919 31c. Two butterflyfishes (black and green fishes) 20 15
2920 31c. Pipefish 20 15
2921 31c. Moray eel 20 15
2922 31c. Angelfish (blue, yellow and black) and coral . . . 20 15
2923 31c. Red and yellow fish, starfish and coral 20 15
2924 31c. Crab and coral 20 15
2925 31c. Snapper and coral . . . 20 15
2926 31c. Seahorse and coral . . 20 15
Nos. 2903/26 were issued together, se-tenant, forming a composite design.

1998. World Cup Football Championship, France. Designs depicting football art by named artists. Multicoloured.
2927 22c. Type **1485** 15 10
2928 22c. Aldemir Martins . . . 15 10
2929 22c. Glauco Rodrigues . . . 15 10
2930 22c. Marcia Grostein . . . 15 10
2931 22c. Claudio Tozzi 15 10
2932 22c. Zelio Alves Pinto . . . 15 10
2933 22c. Guto Lacaz 15 10
2934 22c. Antonio Peticov . . . 15 10
2935 22c. Cildo Meireles 15 10
2936 22c. Mauricio Nogueira Lima 15 10
2937 22c. Roberto Magalhaes . . 15 10
2938 22c. Luiz Zerbine 15 10
2939 22c. Maciej Babinski (horiz) 15 10
2940 22c. Wesley Duke Lee (horiz) 15 10
2941 22c. Joao Camara (horiz) . . 15 10
2942 22c. Jose Zaragoza (horiz) 15 10
2943 22c. Mario Gruber (horiz) 15 10
2944 22c. Nelson Leirner (horiz) 15 10
2945 22c. Carlos Vergara (horiz) 15 10
2946 22c. Tomoshige Kusuno (horiz) 15 10
2947 22c. Gregorio Gruber (horiz) 15 10
2948 22c. Jose Roberto Aguilar (horiz) 15 10
2949 22c. Ivald Granato (horiz) 15 10
2950 22c. Leda Catunda (horiz) 15 10

1486 Bean Casserole and Vegetables

1998. Cultural Dishes.
2951 **1486** 31c. multicoloured . . . 20 15

1487 "Araucaria angustifolia"

1998. Environmental Protection. Multicoloured.
2952 22c. Type **1487** 15 10
2953 22c. Azure jay ("Cyanocorax caeruleus") 15 10
Nos. 2952/3 were issued together, se-tenant, forming a composite design.

1488 "Tapajo"

1998. Launching of Submarine "Tapajo".
2954 **1488** 51c. multicoloured . . . 60 35

1489 Bust of Queiroz and College Building

1998. Death Centenary of Luiz de Queiroz (founder of Agricultural College, Piracicaba).
2955 **1489** 36c. multicoloured . . . 20 15

1490 Statue of St. Benedict and Monastery

1998. 400th Anniv of St. Benedict's Monastery, Sao Paulo.
2956 **1490** 22c. multicoloured . . . 15 10

1491 Santos-Dumont and his First Balloon "Brasil"

1998. Aviation. Aircraft Designs by Alberto Santos-Dumont (aviator). Multicoloured.
2957 31c. Type **1491** 20 15
2958 31c. Santos-Dumont and Dirigible "No. 1" 20 15

1492 Early Film of Guanabara Bay

1998. Centenary (1997) of Brazilian Cinema. Multicoloured.
2959 31c. Type **1492** 20 15
2960 31c. Taciana Reis (actress) in "Limite" (dir. Mario Peixoto, 1912) 20 15
2961 31c. Grande Otela and Oscarito in "A Dupla do Barulho" (dir. Carlos Manga, 1953) (inscr "Chanchada") 20 15
2962 31c. Mazzaropi (actor) and film titles (Vera Cruz film company) 20 15
2963 31c. Glauber Rocha (director) ("New Cinema") 20 15
2964 31c. Titles of prize-winning films, 1962–98 . . . . . 20 15

1493 Andrade, Entrance to St. Antony's Church (Tiradentes) and Church of Our Lady of the Rosary (Ouro Preto)

1998. Birth Centenary of Rodrigo Melo Franco de Andrade (founder of Federal Institution for Preservation of the National Historic and Artistic Patrimony).
2965 **1493** 51c. multicoloured . . . 30 25

1494 Cascudo and Folk Characters

1998. Birth Centenary of Luis da Camara Cascudo (writer).
2966 **1494** 22c. multicoloured . . . 15 10

1495 Fencing

1998. 42nd World Aeronautical Pentathlon Championships, Natal. Multicoloured.
2967 22c. Type **1495** 15 10
2968 22c. Running 15 10
2969 22c. Swimming 15 10
2970 22c. Shooting 15 10
2971 22c. Basketball 15 10

1496 Missionary Cross and St. Michael of the Missions Church

1998. Mercosur. Missions.
2972 **1496** 80c. multicoloured . . . 50 45

1497 Untitled Work (Jose Leonilson) (Biennale emblem)

1998. 24th Art Biennale, Sao Paulo. Paintings. Mult.
2973 31c. Type **1497** 20 15
2974 31c. "Tapuia Dance" (Albert von Eckhout) . . 20 15
2975 31c. "The Schoolboy" (Vincent van Gogh) (vert) 20 15
2976 31c. "Portrait of Michel Leiris" (Francis Bacon) (vert) 20 15
2977 31c. "The King's Museum" (Rene Magritte) (vert) . . 20 15
2978 31c. "Urutu" (Tarsila do Amaral) 20 15
2979 31c. "Facade with Arcs, Circle and Fascia" (Alfredo Volpi) (vert) . . 20 15
2980 31c. "The Raft of the Medusa" (Asger Jorn) . . 20 15

1498 "Citizenship" (Erika Albuquerque)

1998. Child and Citizenship.
2981 **1498** 22c. multicoloured . . . 15 10

1499 Mail Coach and "Postilhao da America" (brigantine)

1998. Bicentenary of Reorganization of Maritime Mail Service between Portugal and Brazil.
2982 **1499** 1r.20 multicoloured . . 1·10 90

1500 "D. Pedro I" (Simplicio Rodrigues da Sa), Crown and Sceptre

1501 Mangoes and Glasses of Juice

1998. Birth Bicentenary of Emperor Pedro I.
2983 **1500** 22c. multicoloured . . . 15 10

1998. Frisco (fruit juice) Publicity Campaign. Self-adhesive.
2984 **1501** 36c. multicoloured . . . 20 15

1502 "Solanum lycocarpum"

1998. Cerrado Flowers. Multicoloured.
2985 31c. Type **1502** 20 15
2986 31c. "Cattleya walkeriana" 20 15
2987 31c. "Kielmeyera coriacea" 20 15

1503 Mother Teresa (founder of Missionaries of Charity)

1998. Peace and Fraternity. Multicoloured.
2988 31c. Type **1503** 20 15
2989 31c. Friar Galvao (first Brazilian to be beatified, 1998) 20 15
2990 31c. Betinho (Herbert Jose de Souza) 20 15
2991 31c. Friar Damiao 20 15
Nos. 2988/91 were issued together, se-tenant, forming a central composite design of the Earth.

1504 Sergio Motta and Headquarters, Brasilia

1998. 1st Anniv of National Telecommunications Agency.
2992 **1504** 31c. multicoloured . . . 20 15
Motta was Minister of Communications when the agency was established.

1505 Tiles and Church of Our Lady of Fatima, Brasilia

1998. Christmas.
2993 **1505** 22c. multicoloured . . . 15 10

1506 Moxoto Goat

1507 Man casting Winged Shadow

1998. Domestic Animals. Mult. Self-adhesive.
2994 22c. Type **1506** 15 10
2995 22c. North-eastern donkey 15 10
2996 22c. Junqueira ox 15 10
2997 22c. Brazilian terrier (vert) 15 10
2998 22c. Brazilian shorthair (vert) 15 10

1998. 50th Anniv of Universal Declaration of Human Rights.
2999 **1507** 1r.20 multicoloured . . 75 65

1508 Mother Luiza Lighthouse, Natal

1510 Stamp Vending Machines of 1940s and 1998

1509 Extent of Economic Zone, Satellite and Belmonte Lighthouse

1999. 400th Annivs of Natal (1999) and of Wise Men's Fortress (1998). Multicoloured.
3000 31c. Type **1508** 20 15
3001 31c. Wise Men's Fortress, Natal (horiz) 20 15

1999. Evaluation Programme of Sustainable Potential of Living Resources in the Exclusive Economic Zone (REVIZEE). Multicoloured.
3002 31c. Type **1509** (Sao Pedro and Sao Paulo Archipelago Research Programme) 20 15
3003 31c. Blue-faced booby on buoy 20 15
3004 31c. "Riobaldo" (research ship) 20 15
3005 31c. Turtle 20 15
3006 31c. Dolphin 20 15
3007 31c. Diver 20 15
Nos. 3002/7 were issued together, se-tenant, forming a composite design.
No. 3004 includes the emblem of "Australia 99" International Stamp Exhibition, Melbourne.

1999. 125th Anniv of Universal Postal Union. Multicoloured.
3008 31c. Type **1510** 20 15
3009 31c. Postal products vending machines of 1906 and 1998 . . . . 20 15
3010 31c. Postboxes of 1870 and 1973 . . . . 20 15
3011 31c. Brazilian Quality and Productivity Programme silver award to Rio Grande postal region, 1998 . . . . 20 15
Nos. 3008/11 were issued together, se-tenant, forming a composite design of the U.P.U. emblem.

1511 Lacerda Lift, Barra Lighthouse and Church of Our Lady of the Rosary

1999. 450th Anniv of Salvador.
3012 **1511** 1r.05 multicoloured . . 65 55

1512 Footprint, Iguanodon, Stegosaurus and Allosaurus

1999. "iBRA 99" International Stamp Exhibition, Nuremberg, Germany. Valley of the Dinosaurs, Sousa.
3013 **1512** 1r.05 multicoloured . . 65 55

1513 Fortress

1999. 415th Anniv of St. Amaro of Barra Grande Fortress, Guaruja.
3014 **1513** 22c. multicoloured . . . 15 10

1514 Children of Various Races

1516 Banner and Revellers

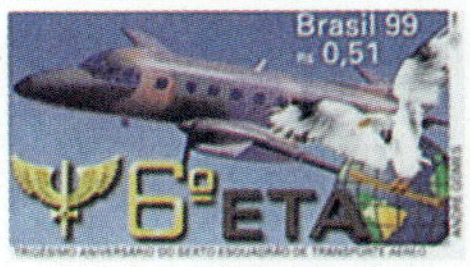

1515 Camouflaged Airplane, Emblem, Dove and Globe

1999. 500th Anniv (2000) of Discovery of Brazil (4th issue). Sheet 69 × 99 mm.
MS3015 **1514** 2r.68 multicoloured 2·75 2·75

1999. 30th Anniv of 6th Air Transportation Squadron.
3016 **1515** 51c. multicoloured . . . 30 25

1999. Feast of the Holy Spirit, Planaltina.
3017 **1516** 22c. multicoloured . . . 15 10

1517 Ouro Preto

1999. Philexfrance 99 International Stamp Exhibition. World Heritage Sites. Sheet 70 × 110 containing T **1517** and similar horiz designs. Multicoloured.
MS3018 1r.05 Type **1517**; 1r.05 Olinda; 1r.05 Sao Lius . . . . 1·90 1·90

1518 Symbols of Computer Science, Chemistry, Engineering, Metallurgy and Geology

1999. Centenary of Institute for Technological Research, Sao Paulo.
3019 **1518** 36c. multicoloured . . . 20 15

1519 Santos-Dumont and Ballon No. 3

1999. Centenary of Flight of Alberto Santos-Dumont's Airship Ballon No. 3.
3020 **1519** 1r.20 multicoloured . . 75 70

1520 Anteater and Emblem

1999. National Campaign for Prevention and Combat of Forest Fires (PREVFOGO). Mult. Self-adhesive.
3021 51c. Type **1520** 35 30
3022 51c. Flower and IBAMA emblem 35 30
3023 51c. Leaf and IBAMA emblem 35 30
3024 51c. Burnt tree trunk and PREVFOGO emblem . . 35 30
Nos. 3021/4 were issued together, se-tenant, forming a composite design of a map and flames.
Nos. 3021/4 are also impregnated with the scent of burnt wood.

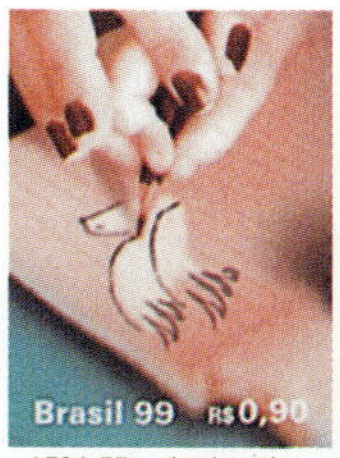

1521 Hands drawing Dove

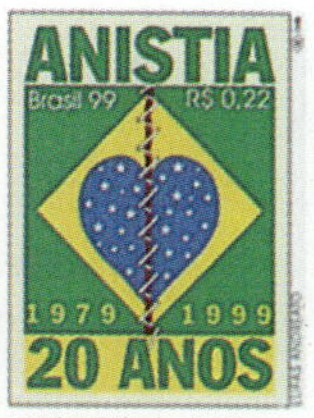

1522 Stitched Heart

1999. America. A New Millennium without Arms. Sheet 109 × 69 mm containing T **1521** and similar vert design. Multicoloured.
MS3025 90c. Type **1521**; 90c. Overturned tank . . . . 1·30 1·30

1999. 20th Anniv of Political Amnesty in Brazil.
3026 **1522** 22c. multicoloured . . . 15 10

1523 Joaquim Nabuco (politician)

1999. 150th Birth Anniversaries. Multicoloured.

3027	22c. Type **1523**	15	10
3028	31c. Rui Barbosa (politician)	20	15

1524 Dorado

1999. "China '99" International Stamp Exhibition, Peking. Fishes. Multicoloured.

3029	22c. Type **1524**	15	10
3030	31c. *Brycon microlepis*	20	15
3031	36c. *Acestrorhynchus pantaneiro*	25	20
3032	51c. Tetra "*Hyphessobrycon eques*"	35	30
3033	80c. *Rineloricaria* sp.	55	45
3034	90c. *Leporinus macrocephalus*	65	55
3035	1r.05 *Abramites* sp.	75	65
3036	1r.20 Bristle-mouthed catfish	85	75

Nos. 3029/36 were issued together, se-tenant, with the backgrounds forming a composite design.

No. 3036 also includes a hologram of the exhibition emblem.

1525 Open Book and Flags of Member Countries

1999. Mercosur. The Book.

3037 **1525**	80c. multicoloured	55	45

1526 Aguas Emendadas Ecological Station

1999. Water Resources. Multicoloured.

3038	31c. Type **1526**	20	15
3039	31c. House and jetty	20	15
3040	31c. Cedro Dam	20	15
3041	31c. Oros Dam	20	15

Nos. 3038/41 were issued together, se-tenant, forming a composite design of a whirlpool.

1527 "Ex Libris" (Eliseu Visconti)

1999. National Library, Rio de Janeiro.

3042 **1527**	22c. multicoloured	15	10

1999. State Flags (6th series). As T **992**.

3043	31c. Amapa	20	15
3044	36c. Roraima	25	20

1528 Piano and Woman

1999. 5th Death Anniv of Antonio Carlos Jobim (composer).

3045 **1528**	31c. multicoloured	20	15

1529 The Annunciation

1999. Christmas. Birth Bimillenary of Jesus Christ. Multicoloured.

3046	22c. Type **1529**	15	10
3047	22c. Adoration of the Magi	15	10
3048	22c. Presentation of Jesus in the Temple	15	10
3049	22c. Baptism of Jesus by John the Baptist	15	10
3050	22c. Jesus and the Twelve Apostles	15	10
3051	22c. Death and resurrection of Jesus	15	10

1530 Open Book and Globe

1999. New Middle School Education Programme.

3052 **1530**	31c. multicoloured	20	15

1531 Itamaraty Palace, Rio de Janeiro

1999. Centenary of Installation of Ministry of Foreign Relations Headquarters in Itamaraty Palace, Rio de Janeiro.

3053 **1531**	1r.05 brown and stone	75	65

1532 Buildings and Trees (Milena Karoline Ribeiro Reis)

2000. "Stampin the Future". Winning Entries in Children's International Painting Competition. Mult.

3054	22c.+8c. Type **1532**	20	15
3055	22c.+8c. Globe, sun, trees, children and whale (Caio Ferreira Guimaraes de Oliveira)	20	15
3056	22c.+8c. Woman with globe on dress (Clarissa Cazane)	20	15
3057	22c.+8c. Children hugging globe (Jonas Sampaio de Freitas)	20	15

1533 "2000"

2000. New Millennium.

3058 **1533**	90c. multicoloured	65	55

1534 Map of South America and Children holding Books

2000. National School Book Programme.

3059 **1534**	31c. multicoloured	20	15

1535 Ada Rogato

2000. Women Aviators. Multicoloured.

3060	22c. Type **1535**	15	10
3061	22c. Thereza de Marzo	15	10
3062	22c. Anesia Pinheiro	15	10

1536 Moqueca Capixaba

2000. Cultural Dishes. Multicoloured.

3063	1r.05 Type **1536**	75	65
3064	1r.05 Moqueca baiana	75	65

1537 Freyre and Institute Facade

2000. Birth Centenary of Gilberto Freyre (writer).

3065 **1537**	36c. multicoloured	25	15

1538 Painting and Emblem

2000. 500th Anniv of the Discovery of Brazil.

3066 **1538**	51c. multicoloured	30	25

1539 Natives

2000. 500th Anniv of the Discovery of Brazil. Multicoloured.

3067	31c. Type **1539**	15	10
3068	31c. Natives watching ships	15	10
3069	31c. Sailors in rigging	15	10
3070	31c. Ships sails and natives	15	10

1540 Sailing Ship and Brazilian Flag

2000. 500th Anniv of the Discovery of Brazil. Multicoloured.

3071	45c. Type **1540**	25	10
3072	45c. Man dressed in red suit, pineapple and telephone dial	25	10
3073	45c. Red-spectacled amazon and silhouettes of sailing ships	25	10
3074	45c. Four babies	25	10
3075	45c. Go-kart, Formula 1 racing car and Ayrton Senna	25	10
3076	45c. Sloth, Toco toucan, crocodile, penguin and tiger	25	10
3077	45c. Outline of Brazil and compass roses	25	10
3078	45c. Peace dove	25	10
3079	45c. Child with decorated face	25	10
3080	45c. "500" emblem	25	10
3081	45c. Man wearing feather headdress	25	10
3082	45c. Man in boat, sails and town (Nataly M. N. Moriya)	25	10
3083	45c. Wristwatch, balloon, Alberto Santos-Dumont and his biplane *14 bis*	25	10
3084	45c. Sailing ship and document (first report of discovery)	25	10
3085	45c. Jules Rimet Cup and World Cup trophies, player, football and year dates (Brazilian victories in World Cup Football Championship)	25	10
3086	45c. Hand writing, street lights and fireworks	25	10
3087	45c. Banners and Brazilian flag forming cow	25	10
3088	45c. Golden conure perched on branch	25	10
3089	45c. Bakairi masks	25	10
3090	45c. Globe, ship and emblem	25	10

1541 Globe and Map of Brazil

2000. 2nd Anniv of BrazilTradeNet (business information web site).

3091 **1541**	27c. multicoloured	10	10

1542 Turtle, Scarlet Macaw and Map

2000. National Coastal Management Programme (GERCO).

3092 **1542**	40c. multicoloured	20	10

1543 Waterfall and Detail of Map

2000. EXPO 2000 World's Fair, Hanover, Germany and 31st International Geologic Congress, Rio de Janeiro. Sheet 109 × 69 mm containing T **1543** and similar vert design. Multicoloured.

MS3093	1r.30 Type **1543**; 1r.30 Map of Brazil; 1r.30 Gold ingot and minerals	2·75	2·75

1544 Cruz, Students and Building Facade

2000. Centenary of the Oswaldo Cruz Foundation (medical research institution).

3094 **1544**	40c. multicoloured	20	10

1545 Mask, Musical Instruments and Jewellery

2000. Africa Day.

3095 **1545**	1r.10 multicoloured	60	20

1546 Klink in Rowing Boat and Portion of Globe showing Route

2000. Voyages by Amyr Klink (navigator). Multicoloured.

3096 1r. Type **1546** (first South Atlantic crossing by rowing boat (1984)) 55 30

3097 1r. *Paratii* (polar sailing boat) in Antarctica and portion of globe showing route (first single-handed circumnavigation of Antarctica (1999)) 55 30

Nos. 3096/7 were issued together, se-tenant, forming a composite design.

1547 Flag, Buildings, Map and City Arms

2000. 150th Anniv of Juiz de Fora.

3098 **1547** 60c. multicoloured 35 20

1548 Hang Gliding

2000. Outdoor Pursuits. Multicoloured. Self-adhesive.

3099 27c. Type **1548** 10 10
3100 27c. Surfing 10 10
3101 40c. Rock climbing 20 10
3102 40c. Skateboarding 20 10

1549 Forest

2000. Environmental Protection. Multicoloured.

3103 40c. Type **1549** 20 10
3104 40c. Oncilla standing on branch in forest 20 10
3105 40c. Vegetation, adult oncilla and head of kitten 20 10
3106 40c. Vegetation, adult oncilla and body of kitten 20 10

Nos. 3103/6 were issued together, se-tenant, forming a composite design.

1550 *Cisne Branco* (full-rigged cadet ship)

2000. Brazilian Navy. Cadet Ships. Multicoloured.

3107 27c. Type **1550** 10 10
3108 27c. *Brasil* (cadet frigate) 10 10

1551 "Oswaldo Cruz" (hospital ship) and Birds

1552 Emblem

2000. Environment Protection. Sheet 137 × 84 mm.

MS3109 **1551** 1r.50 multicoloured 90 90

2000. America. Health Campaigns. Sheet 84 × 137 mm containing T **1552** and similar vert design. Multicoloured.

MS3110 1r.10 Type **1552** (anti-AIDS); 1r.10 Glasses, pills, needles and Marijuana leaves (national anti-drugs week) 1·40 1·40

1553 Teixeira, Carneiro Ribeiro Education Center, Salvador and Pupils

2000. Birth Centenary of Anisio Teixeira (education reformer).

3111 **1553** 45c. multicoloured 25 10

1554 Child walking to School

2000. 10th Anniv of the Children and Teenagers Statute (3112) and 15th Anniv of National Movement of Street Boys and Girls (3113). Multicoloured.

3112 27c. Type **1554** 10 10
3113 40c. Rainbow with girl and boy holding star 20 10

1555 Capanema

2000. Birth Centenary of Gustavo Capanema Filho (politician).

3114 **1555** 60c. multicoloured 40 20

1556 Television and Hand writing in Notebook

2000. 5th Anniv of Telecourse 2000 (educational television programme).

3115 **1556** 27c. multicoloured 20 10

1557 Campos

2000. Birth Centenary of Milton Campos (politician and lawyer).

3116 **1557** 1r. multicoloured 70 40

1558 Hand protecting Globe

2000. World Day for Protection of the Ozone Layer.

3117 **1558** 1r.45 multicoloured 1·00 60

1559 Archery

2000. Olympic Games, Sydney. Multicoloured.

3118 40c. Type **1559** 30 15
3119 40c. Beach volleyball 30 15
3120 40c. Boxing 30 15
3121 40c. Football 30 15
3122 40c. Canoeing 30 15
3123 40c. Handball 30 15
3124 40c. Diving 30 15
3125 40c. Rhythmic gymnastics 30 15
3126 40c. Badminton 30 15
3127 40c. Swimming 30 15
3128 40c. Hurdling 30 15
3129 40c. Pentathlon 30 15
3130 40c. Basketball 30 15
3131 40c. Tennis 30 15
3132 40c. Marathon 30 15
3133 40c. High-jump 30 15
3134 40c. Long-distance running 30 15
3135 40c. Triple jump 30 15
3136 40c. Triathlon 30 15
3137 40c. Sailing 30 15
3138 40c. Pommel horse (gymnastics) 30 15
3139 40c. Weightlifting 30 15
3140 40c. Discus 30 15
3141 40c. Rings (gymnastics) 30 15
3142 40c. Athletics 30 15
3143 40c. Javelin 30 15
3144 40c. Artistic gymnastics 30 15
3145 40c. Hockey 30 15
3146 40c. Volleyball 30 15
3147 40c. Synchronized swimming 30 15
3148 40c. Judo 30 15
3149 40c. Wrestling 30 15
3150 40c. Cycling 30 15
3151 40c. Rowing 30 15
3152 40c. Parallel bars (gymnastics) 30 15
3153 40c. Horse riding 30 15
3154 40c. Pole vault 30 15
3155 40c. Fencing 30 15
3156 40c. Rifle shooting 30 15
3157 40c. Taekwondo 30 15

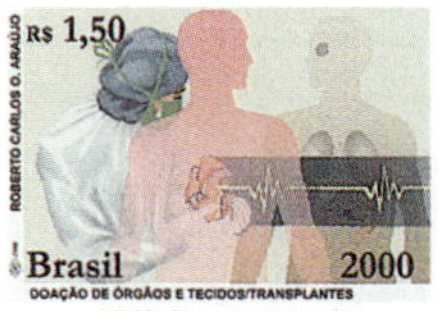

1560 Surgeon and Electrocardiogram Graph

2000. Organ Donation. Multicoloured.

3158 1r.50 Type **1560** 1·10 65
3159 1r.50 Hands holding heart 1·10 65

Nos. 3158/9 were issued together, se-tenant, each pair forming a composite design.

1561 Brazilian Clovis Mask

2000. Brazil–China Joint Issue. 25th Anniv of Diplomatic Relations between Brazil and China. Multicoloured.

3160 27c. Type **1561** 20 10
3161 27c. Chinese Monkey King puppet 20 10

1562 Chico Landi and Ferrari 125 Formula 1 Racing Car

2000. Motor Racing Personalities. Multicoloured.

3162 1r.30 Type **1562** 90 50
3163 1r.45 Ayrton Senna and Formula 1 racing car 1·00 60

1563 Embraer EMB 145 AEW

1565 Conductor's Baton and Music Score

1564 Hand reaching for Star

2000. Brazilian Aircraft. Multicoloured. Self-adhesive.

3164 27c. Type **1563** 20 10
3165 27c. Super Tucano 20 10
3166 27c. Embraer AMX-T 20 10
3167 27c. Embraer ERJ 135 20 10
3168 27c. Embraer ERJ 170 20 10
3169 27c. Embraer ERJ 145 20 10
3170 27c. Embraer ERJ 190 20 10
3171 27c. Embraer EMB 145 RS/MP 20 10
3172 27c. Embraer ERJ 140 20 10
3173 27c. Embraer EMB 120 20 10

2000. Christmas. Multicoloured.

3174 27c. Type **1564** 20 10
3175 27c. Mary and Jesus 20 10
3176 27c. Family and fishes 20 10
3177 27c. Jesus pointing to his heart 20 10
3178 27c. Trees, Globe and open hand 20 10
3179 27c. Jesus and Globe 20 10

Nos. 3174/5, 3176/7 and 3178/9 respectively were issued together, se-tenant, forming a composite design.

2000. Light and Sound Shows.

3180 **1565** 1r.30 multicoloured 90 50

1566 Maps and Baron Rio Branco

2000. Centenary of Arbitration Ruling setting Boundary between Brazil and French Guiana.

3181 **1566** 40c. multicoloured 30 15

1567 Three Wise Men, Chalice and Dove

2001. New Millennium. Multicoloured.

3182 40c. Type **1567** 30 15
3183 1r.30 Star of David, Menorah, scroll and stone tablets 90 50
3184 1r.30 Minaret, dome and Holy Kaaba 90 50

MS3185 68 × 113 mm. As Nos. 3182/4 2·10 1·25

No. **MS**3185 also has a barcode at the bottom of the sheet, separated from the miniature sheet by a line of rouletting.

1568 Map of Americas, Flags, Emblems and Waterfall

2001. 11th Pan American Scout Jamboree, Foz do Iguacu. Multicoloured.

3186 1r.10 Type **1568** 80 45
3187 1r.10 Waterfall, canoeists and emblems 80 45

Nos. 3186/7 were issued together, se-tenant, forming a composite design.

1569 Snake and Chinese Zodiac ($\frac{1}{2}$-size illustration)

2001. "HONG KONG 2001" Stamp Exhibition. New Year. Year of the Snake.

3188 **1569** 1r.45 multicoloured 1·00 60

1570 *Dirphya* sp. and Institute

2001. Centenary of Butantan Institute (vaccine research centre), Sao Paulo. Venomous Animals. Sheet 115 × 155 mm containing T **1570** and similar horiz designs showing Institute building. Multicoloured.

3189 40c. Type **1570** 30 15
3190 40c. Puss caterpillar (*Megalopyge* sp.) 30 15
3191 40c. *Phoneutria* sp. 30 15
3192 40c. Brown scorpion (*Tityus bahiensis*) 30 15
3193 40c. Brazilian rattle snake (*Crotalus durissus*) 30 15
3194 40c. Coral snake (*Micrurus corallinus*) 30 15
3195 40c. Bushmaster (*Lachesis muta*) 30 15
3196 40c. Jararaca (*Bothrops jacaraca*) 30 15

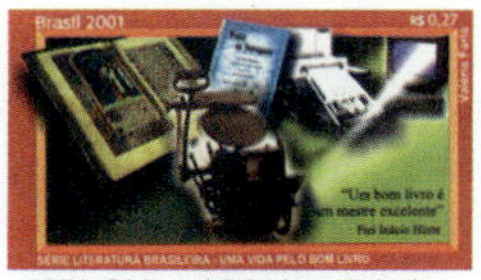

1571 Old and Modern Printing Methods

2001. Publishing.
3197 **1571** 27c. multicoloured . . . 20 10

1572 Airplane, World Map and Ship

2001. Exports.
3198 **1572** 1r.30 multicoloured . . 90 50

1573 Books and Library Facade

2001. 190th Anniv of National Library, Rio de Janeiro.
3199 **1573** 27c. multicoloured . . . 20 10

1574 Man, Microscope and Emblem

2001. Brazilian Council for Scientific and Technological Development (CNPq).
3200 **1574** 40c. blue 30 15

1575 Footballer and Emblem **1576** Children

2001. 89th Anniv of Santos Football Club.
3201 **1575** 1r. multicoloured . . . 70 40

2001. International Decade for a Culture of Peace.
3202 **1576** 1r.10 multicoloured . . 80 45

1577 Mendes and Halfeld Street

2001. Birth Centenary of Muriles Mendes (poet).
3203 **1577** 40c. multicoloured . . . 30 15

1578 Building Facade and View of Town

2001. Centenary of Minas Gerais Trade Association.
3204 **1578** 40c. multicoloured . . . 30 15

1579 Sunflower and No-Smoking Signs

2001. World No-Smoking Day.
3205 **1579** 40c. multicoloured . . . 30 15

1580 Do Rego and Illustrations from his Novels

2001. Birth Centenary of Jose Lins do Rego (writer).
3206 **1580** 60c. multicoloured . . . 40 20

1581 Hyacinth Macaw (*Anodorhynchus hyacinthinus*)

2001. Birds. Sheet 106 × 149 mm containing T **1581** and similar vert designs. Multicoloured.
MS3207 1r.30 Type **1581**; 1r.30 Sun conure (*Aratinga solititialis auricapilla*); 1r.30 Blue-throated conure (*Pyrrhura cruentata*); 1r.30 Yellow-faced amazon (*Amazona xanthops*) . . . . 2·10 2·10

1582 Sobrinho

2001. 1st Death Anniv of Alexandre Jose Barbosa Lima Sobrinho (journalist).
3208 **1582** 40c. multicoloured . . . 15 10

1583 Jericoacoara Beach, Ceara

2001. Beaches. Multicoloured.
3209 40c. Type **1583** 15 10
3210 40c. Ponta Negra beach, Rio Grande do Norte . . 15 10
3211 40c. Rosa beach, Santa Catarina 15 10

1584 Romi-Isetta, 1959 (½-size illustration)

2001. Cars. Sheet 159 × 115 mm containing T **1584** and similar horiz designs. Multicoloured.
MS3212 1r.10 Type **1584**; 1r.10 DKW-Vemag, 1965; 1r.10 Renault Gordini, 1962; 1r.10 Fusca-Volkswagen 1200, 1959; 1r.10 Simca Chambord, 1964; 1r.10 Aero Willys, 1961 . . . . 2·75 2·75

1585 Sayao

2001. Birth Centenary of Bernado Sayao (politician and construction pioneer).
3213 **1585** 60c. multicoloured . . . 25 15

1586 Eleazar de Carvalho, Musical Notation and Musicians

2001. Eleazar de Carvalho (composer and conductor) Commemoration.
3214 **1586** 45c. multicoloured . . . 15 10

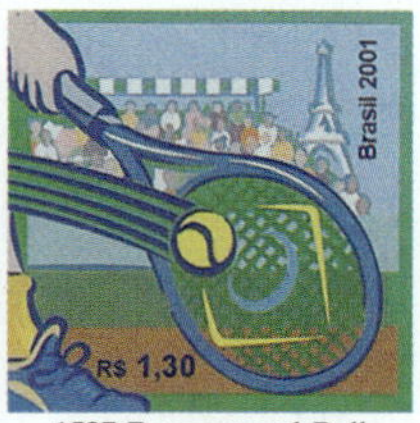

1587 Racquet and Ball

2001. Roland Garros Tennis Championship. Sheet 70 × 112 mm.
MS3215 **1587** 1r.30 multicoloured 50 30

1588 Emblem

2001. 50th Anniv of CAPES (training fund).
3216 **1588** 40c. multicoloured . . . 15 10

1589 Buildings, Symbols of Justice and Pedro Alexio

2001. Birth Centenary of Pedro Alexio (Judge and politician).
3217 **1589** 55c. multicoloured . . . 20 10

1590 Player and Ball **1592** Player and Ball

1591 Figure enclosing Map of Brazil (½-size illustration)

2001. Vasco da Gama Football Club.
3218 **1590** 70c. multicoloured . . . 25 15

2001. 5th Anniv of Solidarity Council. Multicoloured.
3219 55c. Type **1591** 20 10
3220 55c. Map enclosing figure 20 10
Nos. 3219/20 were issued together, se-tenant, forming a composite design.

2001. Palmeiras Football Club.
3221 **1592** 70c. multicoloured . . . 25 15

1593 Emblem **1594** Player and Ball

2001. World Conference on Racism, Durban, South Africa.
3222 **1593** 1r.30 multicoloured . . 50 30

2001. Gremio Football Porto Algrense (football club).
3223 **1594** 70c. multicoloured . . . 25 15

1595 Tambourine **1596** Clóvis Beviláqua

2001. Musical Instruments. Multicoloured. Self-adhesive.
3224 1c. Type **1595** 10 10
3224a 1c. Conga drum 10 10
3225 5c. Saxophone 10 10
3225a 5c. Snare drum 10 10
3226 10c. Cavaquinho (guitar) 10 10
3226a 10c. Trumpet 10 10
3227 20c. Clarinet 10 10
3228 40c. Flute 15 10
3229 45c. Mandolin 15 10
3230 50c. Fiddle 20 10
3230a 50c. Tambourine 20 10
3231 55c. Viola (guitar) 20 10
3232 60c. Zabumba 20 10
3233 70c. Viola Caipira (guitar) 25 15
3234 70c. Rattle 25 15
3235 80c. Xylophone 30 20
3236 1r. Trombone 40 20
3236a 1r. Berimbau 40 20

2001. Clóvis Beviláqua (lawyer) Commemoration.
3250 **1596** 55c. multicoloured . . . 20 10

1597 Children encircling Globe

2001. United Nations Year of Dialogue among Civilizations.
3251 **1597** 1r.30 multicoloured . . 50 30

1598 Map of Brazil and Jewish and Dutch Flags

2001. 365th Anniv of First Jewish Synagogue in Recife.
3252 **1598** 1r.30 multicoloured . . 50 30

1599 Junkers F13 Passenger Aircraft

2001. Commercial Aircraft. Sheet 107 × 149 mm containing T **1599** and similar horiz designs. Multicoloured.
MS3253 55c. Type **1599**; 55c. Douglas DC-3/C47; 55c. Dornier Do-J Wal flying boat; 55c. Lockheed Constellation; 55c. Convair CV 340; 55c. Caravelle V1 R jet airliner . . . . 1·60 1·60

1600 Cecíla Meireles

2001. Birth Centenary of Cecíla Meireles (writer).
3254 **1600** 55c. multicoloured . . . 20 10

1601 Aleijadinho (sculptor) and Bom Jesus de Matosinhos Sanctuary

2001. America. UNESCO World Heritage Sites.
3255 **1601** 1r.30 multicoloured . . 50 30

1602 Madalena Caramuru and Page

2001. Madalena Caramuru (first literate Brazilian woman) Commemoration.
3256 **1602** 55c. multicoloured . . . 20 10

1603 Face, Gavel, Book and Dove

2001. National Black Awareness Day.
3257 **1603** 40c. multicoloured . . . 15 10

1604 Caiman (*Caiman crocodilus*) and Roseate Spoonbill (*Platalea ajaja*) (inscr "*Plataleia*")

2001. Flora and Fauna. Multicoloured. Self-adhesive.
3258 55c. Type **1604** 20 10
3259 55c. American darter (*Anhinga anhinga*) 20 10
3260 55c. Cocoi heron (*Ardea cocoi*) 20 10
3261 55c. Jabiru (*Ephippiorhynchus mycteria*) (inscr "Jabiru") 20 10
3262 55c. *Pseudoplatystoma fasciatum* (fish) 20 10
3263 55c. *Leporinus macrocephalus* (fish) . . . 20 10
3264 55c. Capybara (*Hydrochoerus hydrochaeris*) (inscr "hydrochoeris") 20 10
3265 55c. Southern coati (*Nasua nasua*) 20 10
3266 55c. Water hyacinth (*Eichornia crassipes*) . . . 20 10
3267 55c. Purple gallinule (*Porphyrula martinica*) . . 20 10

1605 Three Kings and Holy Family

2001. Christmas.
3268 **1605** 40c. multicoloured . . . 15 10

1606 Emblem, Player and Football

1607 Imperial Topaz Necklace and Earrings

2001. Libertadores da America Football Championship Winners (1st issue). Flamengo Football Club (1981).
3269 **1606** 1r. multicoloured . . . 40 20
See also No. 3275.

2001. Jewellery. Sheet 101 × 70 mm containing T **1607** and similar vert design. Multicoloured.
MS3270 1r.30 Type **1607**; 1r.30 Garnet ring . . . . 1·00 1·00
No. **MS**3270 was issued with a strip containing a barcode separated by a line of rouletting.

1608 Stylized Eye, Mouth, Hand and Ear (½-size illustration)

2001. International Day of the Disabled.
3271 **1608** 1r.45 multicoloured . . 55 30

1609 Cup of Coffee and Beans

2001. Coffee.
3272 **1609** 1r.30 multicoloured . . 50 30

1610 *Copocabana*

2001. Merchant Ships. Multicoloured.
3273 55c. Type **1610** 20 10
3274 55c. *Flamengo* 20 10
Nos. 3273/4 were issued together, se-tenant, forming a composite design.

1611 Emblem, Player and Football

2001. Libertadores da America Football Championship Winners (2nd issue). Sao Paulo Football Club (1992 and 1993).
3275 **1611** 70c. multicoloured . . . 25 15

1612 Water Hyacinth (*Eichornia crassipes*)

2001. Mercosur. Flora.
3276 **1612** 1r. multicoloured . . . 40 20

1613 Chinese Zodiac and Horse (½-size illustration)

2002. New Year. Year of the Horse.
3277 **1613** 1r.45 multicoloured . . 55 30

1614 Alpine skier

2002. Winter Olympic Games, Salt Lake City, USA. Multicoloured.
3278 1r.10 Type **1614** 40 20
3279 1r.10 Cross country skier . . 40 20
3280 1r.10 Luge 40 20
3281 1r.10 Bobsled 40 20
Nos. 3278/81 were issued together, se-tenant, forming a composite design.

1615 Brasilia and Lucio Costa

2002. Birth Centenary of Lucio Costa (architect).
3282 **1615** 55c. multicoloured . . . 20 10

1616 Women encircling Globe

2002. International Women's Day.
3283 **1616** 40c. multicoloured . . . 15 10

1617 View of City from River

2002. 150th Anniv of Sao Jose do Rio Preto.
3284 **1617** 40c. multicoloured . . . 15 10

1618 Brasilia and Juscelino Kubitschek

2002. Birth Centenary of Juscelino Kubitschek (president, 1956–61).
3285 **1618** 55c. multicoloured . . . 20 10

1619 Winners' Flags and Football

2002. World Cup Football Championship, Japan and South Korea. Multicoloured.
3286 55c. Type **1619** 15 10
3287 55c. Footballer 15 10

1620 School Children and Alphabet

2002. Education. Multicoloured.
3288 40c. Type **1620** 15 10
3289 40c. Computer, globe and alphabet 15 10

1621 Josemaria Escriva

2002. Birth Centenary of Josemaria Escriva de Balaguer (founder of Opus Dei (religious organization)).
3290 **1621** 55c. multicoloured . . . 20 10

1622 North American T6

2002. Smoke Air Squadron (air force display team). Sheet 105 × 150 mm containing T **1622** and similar horiz designs. Multicoloured.
MS3291 55c. × 6, Type **1622**; T-24 Fouga Magister; Neiva T-25 Universal (inscr "T-25 Universal"); Two Embraer EMB-312 Tucano (inscr "T-27 Tucano") and plateau; T-27 Tucano and heart-shape; T-27 Tucano over forest . . . . . . 1·20 1·20

1623 Boy wearing Crown, Girls carrying Banners and Boy with Sword

2002. Cavalhadinha (children's festival). Multicoloured.
3292 40c. Type **1623** 15 10
3293 40c. Boys riding hobby horses 15 10
3294 40c. Children wearing masks 15 10
3295 40c. Musicians and drinks vendor 15 10

1624 Cannonball Tree (*Couroupita guianensis*)

2002. Self-adhesive.
3296 **1624** 55c. multicoloured . . . 20 10

1625 Coral and Fish

2002. Coral Reefs. Sheet 105 × 150 mm containing T **1625** and similar square designs. Multicoloured.
MS3297 40c. × 4, Type **1625**; Seahorse; Corals and fish; Fish and starfish 60 30

1626 Building Facade

2002. 150th Anniv of Sisterhood of Charity Hospital, Curitiba.
3298 **1626** 70c. multicoloured . . . 25 15

1627 Jules Rimet and World Cup Trophies

1629 Footballer and Emblem

1628 White-browed Guan (*Penelope jacucaca*)

2002. Brasil, Football World Cup Championship Winners (1958, 1962, 1970, 1994, 2002).
3299 **1627** 55c. multicoloured . . . 20 10

2002. Conservation of North Eastern Caatinga Region. Sheet 70 × 111 mm.
MS3300 **1628** 1r.10 multicoloured 40 20

2002. Centenary of Santos Football Club.
3301 **1629** 55c. multicoloured . . . 20 10

1630 House Facade

2002. "The Enchanted House" Museum (house of Alberto Santos Dumont (aviation pioneer)), Rio De Janeiro. Sheet containing T **1630** and similar square design. Multicoloured.
MS3302 1r. × 2, Type **1630**; Alberto Santos Dumont 40 20

1631 Radar, Airplane, Boy, Animals and Birds

2002. SIVAM (environmental monitoring of Amazon project).
3303 **1631** 1r.10 multicoloured . . 40 20

1632 Families enclosed in Wheel

2002. Crianca Esperanca (Hope of the Child) Awareness Campaign. Multicoloured.
3304 (1st Porto) Type **1632** (child development) 10 10
3305 (1st Porto) Children playing (eradication of child labour) 10 10

1633 Jorge Amado

2002. 1st Death Anniv of Jorge Amado (writer).
3306 **1633** 40c. multicoloured . . . 25 15

1634 Rio Branco Palace, Xapuri Village and Placido de Castro (revolutionary leader)

2002. Centenary of Acre River Revolution.
3307 **1634** 50c. multicoloured . . . 30 15

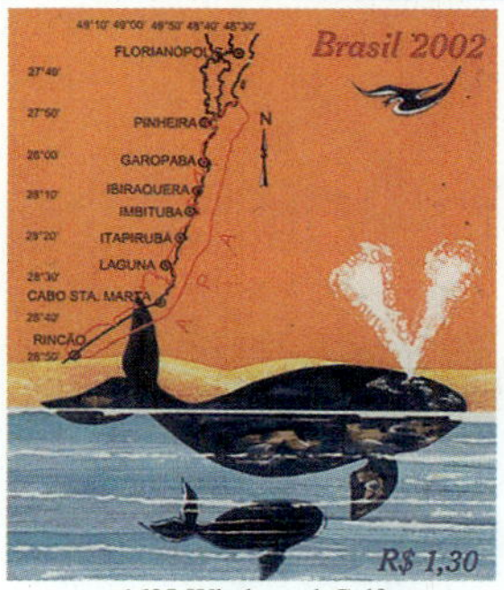

1635 Whale and Calf

2002. Southern Right Whale Habitat Protection Project. Sheet 71 × 112 mm.
MS3308 **1635** 1r.30. multicoloured 80 80

1636 Rivers

2002. Watershed of Negro and Solimoes Rivers, Manaus.
3309 **1636** 45c. multicoloured . . . 30 15

1637 Adhelmar Ferreira da Silva

2002. 1st Death Anniv of Adhelmar Ferreira da Silva (Olympic triple jump champion).
3310 **1637** 40c. multicoloured . . . 25 15

1638 Yamaha 125cc. (1974) and YZF-R1

2002. Motorcycles. Sheet 105 × 149 mm containing T **1638** and similar horiz designs. Multicoloured.
MS3311 60c. × 6 Type **1638**; Honda CB100 (1976) and CG125 Titan; Suzuki 1952 model and GSX-R1000; First Triumph model (1902) and Datona 955i; BMW R32 and R 1200C; First Harley Davidson model (1903) and V-Rod . . . . 2·10 2·10

1639 Steam Locomotive "Baroneza" (1852)

2002. Trains. Multicoloured.
3312 55c. Type **1639** 35 20
3313 55c. Locomotive "Zeze Leoni" (1922) 35 20

1640 Birds, Fish and Waterfall

2002. Mercosur (South American Common Market).
3314 **1640** 1r. multicoloured . . . 60 30

1641 Itabira, Carlos Drummond de Andrade and Rio de Janeiro

2002. Birth Centenary of Carlos Drummond de Andrade (writer).
3315 **1641** 55c. multicoloured . . . 35 20

1642 Fingerprint, Book, Globe and Figure Child

2002. America. Education and Literacy Campaign.
3316 **1642** 1r.30 multicoloured . . 80 40

1643 Map and Building

2002. National Archives.
3317 **1643** 40c. multicoloured . . . 25 10

1644 Sergio Motta (founder) and Centre Building

2002. Sergio Motta Cultural Centre.
3318 **1644** 45c. multicoloured . . . 30 15

1645 "Nativity" (Candido Portinari)

2002. Christmas.
3319 **1645** 45c. multicoloured . . . 30 15

1646 "80"

2002. 80th Anniv of Social Security.
3320 **1646** 45c. multicoloured . . . 30 15

1647 "Dancing Tapuia"

2002. Art. Paintings by Albert Eckhout. Paintings. Multicoloured.
3321 45c. Type **1647** 30 15
3322 45c. "Mameluca" 30 15
3323 45c. "Tapuia Man" 30 15
3324 45c. "Tupi Man" 30 15
3325 45c. "Negro" 30 15
3326 45c. "Tupi Woman" 30 15
3327 45c. "West African Woman and Child" 30 15
3328 45c. "Mestizo Man" 30 15

1648 Marajoara Pots, Brazil

2002. Centenary of Brazil–Iran Diplomatic Relations. Multicoloured.
3329 60c. Type **1648** 35 20
3330 60c. Iranian decorated pots 35 20
Stamps of a similar design were issued by Iran.

1649 Anniversary Emblem

1650 Salto do Itiquira, Formosa

2003. 80th Anniv of Rotary Club (charitable organization).
3331 **1649** 60c. multicoloured . . . 15 10

2003. International Day of Freshwater. Waterfalls. Multicoloured.
3332 45c. Type **1650** 30 15
3333 45c. Salto do Rio Preto, Alto Paraiso 30 15

1651 Winnowing and Building

2003. Coffee Production. Sheet 70 × 110 mm containing T **1651** and similar square design. Multicoloured.
MS3334 1r. × 2, Type **1651**; Buildings, planting and picking 1·20 1·20

1652 Flag, Hands, Dove and Map

2003. Timor Leste Independence.
3335 **1652** 1r.45 multicoloured . . 90 45

1653 *Macrosiphonia velame*

2003. America. Flora and Fauna. Sheet 107 × 150 mm containing T **1653** and similar square designs. Multicoloured.
MS3336 60c. × 6, Type **1653**; *Lychnophora ericoides*; *Lafoensia pacari*; *Tabebuia impetiginosa*; *Xylopia aromatica*; *Himatanthus obovatus* . . . . 2·10 2·10

1654 Decorated Bottles

2003. Mercosur. Recycling. Multicoloured.
3337 60c. Type **1654** 35 20
3338 60c. Paper dolls 35 20
3339 60c. Plastic flower pot . . . 35 20
3340 60c. Decorated metal box 35 20

1655 Saint Inacio, College Building and Students

2003. Centenary of St. Inacio College, Rio de Janeiro.
3341 **1655** 60c. multicoloured . . . 35 20

1656 Pluft and Maribel

2003. Pluft (cartoon character created by Maria Clara Machado).
3342 **1656** 80c. multicoloured . . . 50 25

1657 Sail Boat on Beach

2003. Centenary of Ceara State.
3343 **1657** 70c. multicoloured . . . 40 20

1658 Album, Tweezers and Stamps

2003. Philately. Sheet 110 × 71 mm containing T **1658** and similar square design. Multicoloured.
MS3344 1r.30 × 2, Type **1658**; Portuguese 25r. stamp . . . . 1·60 1·60

1659 Dolphins

2003. 500th Anniv of Fernando de Noronha Island. Sheet 69 × 100 mm.
MS3345 **1659** 2r.90 multicoloured 1·80 1·80

1660 Emblem, Buildings and Antonio Maria Zaccaria (founder)

2003. Centenary of Barnabite Priests in Brazil.
3346 **1660** 45c. multicoloured . . . 25 15

1661 Duke of Caxias and Battle Scene

2003. Birth Bicentenary of Luis Alves de Lima y Silva, Duke of Caxias.
3347 **1661** 60c. multicoloured . . . 35 20

1662 Self-Portrait

1663 Stop Sign enclosing Bottle

2003. Birth Centenary of Candido Potinari (artist).
3348 **1662** 80l. multicoloured . . . 50 25

2003. Traffic Code Awareness. Multicoloured. Self-adhesive.
3349 (50c.) Type **1663** 10 10
3350 (74c.) Triangular traffic sign enclosing dove 10 10

1664 Club Emblem

2003. Centenary of Gremio Football Porto Alegrense.
3351 **1664** 60c. multicoloured . . . 35 20

1665 Locomotive

2003. Preservation of Railways.
3352 **1665** 74c. multicoloured . . . 45 30

1666 Kite Flying

2003. Children's Games. Multicoloured.
3353 50c. Type **1666** 30 10
3354 50c. Ball games 30 15
3355 50c. Skipping 30 15
3356 50c. Hula hoop 30 15

1667 Campaign Emblem

2003. Zero Hunger Campaign.
3357 **1667** 50c. multicoloured . . . 30 15

1668 Grapes, Bridge and Mask

2003. Export Campaign. Sheet 110 × 69 mm.
MS3358 **1668** 1r.30 multicoloured 80 40

1669 Decorated Tree

2003. Christmas. T **1669** and similar triangular design. Self-adhesive.
3359 **1669** 50c. multicoloured . . . 30 15
3360 50c. multicoloured . . . 30 15

1670 Sao Paulo Art Critics Trophy and Auditing Court (building)

2003. Marcantonio Vilaca Cultural Space.
3361 **1670** 74c. multicoloured . . . 45 30

1671 Ary Barroso and Maracana Stadium

2003. Birth Centenary of Ary Barroso (conductor and sports commentator).
3362 **1671** 1r.50 multicoloured . . 90 45

1672 Palacio des Arcos, Cadeia Velha and New Congress Building, Rio de Janeiro

2003. 180th Anniv of National Congress.
3363 **1672** 74c. multicoloured . . . 45 30

1673 Para-glider over Sao Conrado, Rio de Janeiro

2003. Adventurous Sports.
3364 **1673** 75c. multicoloured . . . 45 30

1674 Cedar Lebanon

2003. 60th Anniv of Diplomatic Relations with Lebanon.
3365 **1674** 1r.75 multicoloured . . 1·00 50

1675 Heart-shaped Ribbon and Hands

2003. AIDS Awareness Campaign.
3366 **1675** 74c. multicoloured . . . 90 45

2003. Birth Centenary of Candido Potinari. Lost Paintings (1st issue). As T **1662**. Black. Self-adhesive.
3367 74c. "Menino de Brodoski" 35 20
3368 75c. "Cangaceiro" 35 20
See also Nos. 3382/6.

1676 Capistrano de Abreu

2003. 150th Birth Anniv of Capistrano de Abreu (historian and ethnographer).
3369 **1676** 50c. multicoloured . . . 30 15

1677 Fernando Henrique Cardoso

2003. Fernando Henrique Cardoso (38th president).
3370 **1677** 74c. multicoloured . . . 45 30

1678 Archangel St. Michael Chapel, Sao Paulo

2004. Cultural Heritage. Sheet 100 × 70 mm. Litho.
MS3371 **1678** 1r.50 multicoloured 90 45

1679 Faces

2004. 450th Anniv of Sao Paulo. Multicoloured.
3372 74c. Type **1679** 45 30
3373 74c. Buildings surrounding roadway 45 30
3374 74c. Park and city buildings 45 30
3375 74c. "450" 45 30

1680 Dom Vicente Scherer

2004. Birth Centenary of Cardinal Vicente Scherer.
3376 **1680** 50c. multicoloured . . . 30 15

1681 Musicians and Dancers

2004. Lapa District, Rio de Janeiro.
3377 **1681** 75c. multicoloured . . . 45 30

1682 Scarlet Ibis (*Eudocimus ruber*)

2004.
3378 **1682** 74c. multicoloured . . . 45 30

1683 Figure holding Water Droplet

2004. Mercosur. Water Conservation Campaign.
3379 **1683** 1r.20 multicoloured . . 70 35

1684 Orlando Villas Boas

2004. 90th Birth Anniv of Orlando Villas Boas (joint founder Xingu National Park and Nobel Peace Prize winner).
3380 **1684** 74c. multicoloured . . . 45 30

1685 Anniversary Emblem

2004. Centenary of FIFA (Federation Internationale de Football Association).
3381 **1685** 1r.60 multicoloured . . 95 45

2004. Birth Centenary of Candido Potinari. Lost Paintings (2nd issue). As T **1662**. Self-adhesive.
3382 55c. multicoloured 30 15
3383 80c. multicoloured 40 20
3384 95c. multicoloured 50 25
3385 1r.15 black 60 30
3386 1r.50 multicoloured 75 40
DESIGNS: 55c. "Negrinha"; 80c. "Duas Criancas"; 95c. "Menino Sentado e Carneiro"; 1r.15 "Comosicao"; 1r.50 "Marcel Gontrau".

1686 Emblem

2004. 92nd International Labour Conference (ILO).
3387 **1686** 50c. multicoloured . . . 30 15

1687 Roseate Spoonbill (*Ajaia ajaja*)

2004. Mangrove Swamps and Tidal Zones Preservation. Sheet 149 × 105 mm containing T **1687** and similar horiz designs. Multicoloured.
MS3388 1r.60 × 5, Type **1687**; Great kiskadee (*Pitangus sulphuratus*); *Chasmagnathus granulate*; *Aramides mangle*; *Goniopsis cruentata* . . . . 2·40 2·40

1688 Runner holding Olympic Torch

2004. Olympic Games, Athens. Multicoloured 2004.
3389 1r.60 Type **1688** 95 45
3390 1r.60 Athens 2004 emblem 95 45
3391 1r.60 Dinghies and catamarans 95 45
3392 1r.60 Runner 95 45

1689 Senhor Bom Jesus do Bonfim Church, Salvador

2004. Cultural Heritage.
3393 **1689** 74c. multicoloured . . . 45 30

1690 Caprichoso Bull

2004. Parintins Festival. Multicoloured.
3394 74c. Type **1690** 45 30
3395 74c. Garantido bull 45 30
Nos. 3394/5 were issued together, se-tenant, forming a composite design.

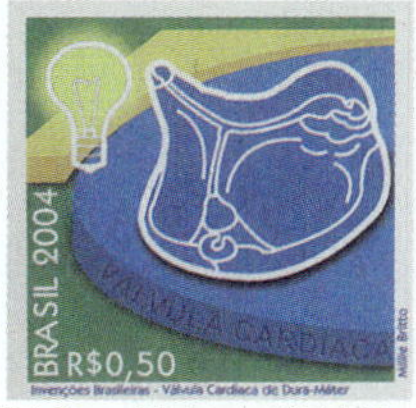

1691 Dura-Mater Artificial Heart Valve

2004. Brazilian Inventions. Multicoloured.
3396 50c. Type **1691** 30 15
3397 50c. Telephone caller identification (BINA) . . 30 15
3398 50c. Telephone cards . . . 30 15

1692 Map of South America, Satellite and Brazilian and Chinese Flags as Clasped Hands

2004. CBER-2 (Brazilian—Chinese satellite).
3399 **1692** 1r.75 multicoloured . . 1·00 55

1693 Columns, Square and Compass

2004. Masonic Philatelic Association.
3400 50c. Type **1693** 30 15
3401 50c. Stone mason 30 15
3402 50c. Jacob's ladder 30 15
3403 50c. Masonic tools 30 15

1694 Nelson Rodrigues

2004. Nelson Rodrigues (writer) Commemoration.
3404 **1694** 50c. multicoloured . . . 30 15

1695 FAB Emblem, Republic P-47 Thunderbolt and Campaign Medals

2004. World War II. Multicoloured.
3405 50c. Type **1695** (Italian air campaign) 30 15
3406 50c. Navy emblem, destroyer and campaign medals (South Atlantic campaign) 30 15
3407 50c. FEB emblem, soldiers and campaign medals (Italian land campaign) 30 15
3408 50c. Soldier reading letter 30 15

1696 Crowned Halo enclosing Statue

1698 Father Christmas

1697 Allan Kardec

2004. Centenary of Coronation of Our Lady of Immaculate Conception ("Aparecida").
3409 **1696** 74c. multicoloured . . . 45 30

2004. Birth Bicentenary of Allan Kardec (writer).
3410 **1697** 1r.60 multicoloured . . 95 45

2004. Christmas. Self-adhesive.
3411 **1698** 1st class (50c.) multicoloured 30 15
No. 3406 was for use on internal non-commercial mail weighing 20 grams or less.

1699 Post Office Building (museum)

2004. Porto Alegre Museum and Archive.
3412 **1699** 50c. multicoloured . . . 30 15

1700 *Cyperus articulatus*

2004. Aromatic Plants.
3413 **1700** 1r.60 multicoloured . . 95 45

1701 Buildings and Statue (⅔-size illustration)

2004. Pampulha Architectural Complex.
3414 **1701** 80c. multicoloured . . . 40 20

1702 Cat, Art, Textiles and Nise da Silveira

2005. Birth Centenary of Nise da Silveira (psychiatrist).
3415 **1702** 55c. multicoloured . . . 30 15

1703 Rotary Emblem and Faces

2005. Centenary of Rotary International (charitable organization).
3416 **1703** 1r.45 multicoloured . . 75 40

1704 Fruit on Tree

2005. Cupacu (*Theobrome grandiflorum*). Sheet 70 × 111 mm containing T **1704** and similar square design. Multicoloured.
MS3417 1r.90 × 2, Type **1704**; Open fruit . . . . 2·00 2·00

1705 Brazilian and Lebanese Trees and Flags

2005. Lebanese Immigration to Brazil.
3418 **1705** 1r.75 multicoloured . . 90 45

1706 Museum Building

2005. Oscar Niemeyer Museum.
3419 **1706** 80c. multicoloured . . . 40 20

1707 Pope John Paul II

1709 Dancers (contemporary dance)

1708 Circle and Arrows

2005. Pope John Paul II Commemoration.
3420 **1707** 80c. multicoloured . . . 40 20

2005. World Information Society Summit, Tunis. Sheet 86 × 128 mm containing T **1708** and similar horiz designs. Multicoloured.
MS3421 80c. × 3, Type **1708**; Figure enclosed in circle; Envelope contained in circle . . . . . 1·20 1·20
The stamps and margins of No. **MS**3421 form a composite design.

2005. Brazil Year in France. Multicoloured.
3422 80c. Type **1709** 40 20
3423 80c. Pankararu Indians (indigenous art) 40 20
3424 80c. Pato no Tucupi (gastronomy) 40 20

3425 80c. Choro musicians (music) 40 20
3426 80c. String of pages (literature) 40 20
3427 80c. Vivaldo Lima Stadium (architecture) 40 20

1710 Erico Verissimo

1711 Mario Quintana

2005. Birth Centenary of Erico Verissimo (writer).
3428 **1710** 1r.25 multicoloured . . 65 35

2005. Birth Centenary (2006) of Mario Quintana (writer).
3429 **1711** 80c. green 40 20

1712 Woman, Water Barrel, Cistern, Boy and Workmen

1713 Emblem

2005. America. Water Cisterns.
3430 **1712** 80c. multicoloured . . . 40 20

2005. 19th Congress of America, Spain and Portugal Postal Union. Self-adhesive.
3431 **1713** (80c.) multicoloured . . 40 20

1714 Gold panning, Route and Caravan

2005. Tourism. Estrada Real (road from Diamantina to Parati and Rio De Janeiro). Multicoloured.
3432 80c. Type **1714** 40 20
3433 80c. Hikers 40 20
3434 80c. Horse riders 40 20
Nos. 3432/4 were issued together, se-tenant, forming a composite design.

1715 Dancer

2005. Samba (dance).
3435 **1715** 55c. multicoloured . . . 30 15

1716 Brazilian Flag and Samba Dancers

2005. National Dances. Multicoloured.
3436 80c. Type **1716** 40 20
3437 80c. Cuban flag and Son dancers 40 20
Stamps of a similar design were issued by Cuba.

1717 Sao Francisco River

2005.
3438 **1717** 80c. multicoloured . . . 40 20

1718 School Building

1719 "ABC"

2005. Centenary of Command and General Staff School.
3439 **1718** 80c. multicoloured . . . 40 20

2005. Teachers' Day. Self-adhesive.
3440 **1719** (1st porte) multicoloured 40 20

1720 Bell

2005. Christmas (1st issue). Self-adhesive.
3441 **1720** (1st porte) multicoloured 40 20
See also No. **MS**3444.

1721 Referee and Players

2005. Women's Football.
3442 **1721** 85c. multicoloured . . . 40 20

1722 Fish Leaping (*Salminus maxillosus*)

2005. Piracema (fish reproduction). Sheet 101 × 71 mm.
MS3443 **1722** 3r.10 multicoloured 2·10 2·10

1723 "Adoration of Shepherds" (Oscar Pereira da Silva)

2005. Christmas (2nd issue). Sheet 71 × 111 mm.
MS3444 **1723** 2r.90 multicoloured 1·50 1·50

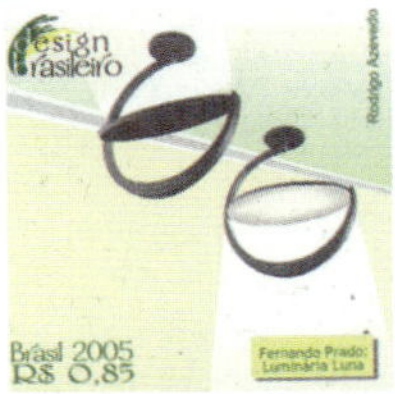

1724 Light "Luna" (Fernando Prado)

2005. Brazilian Design. Multicoloured.
3445 85c. Type **1724** 40 20
3446 85c. Ventilator "Spirit" (Indio da Costa design) 40 20
3447 85c. Chair "Corallo" (Hemberto and Fernando Corallo) 40 20
3448 85c. Table "Bandeirola" (Ivan Rezende) 40 20

1725 Hans Christian Andersen and "The Ugly Duckling"

2005. Birth Bicentenary of Hans Christian Andersen (writer).
3449 **1725** 55c. multicoloured . . . 30 15

1726 Dressmaker

1727 Sambista

2005. Professions. Multicoloured. Self-adhesive.
3450 5c. Type **1726** 10 10
3451 20c. Cobbler 10 10
3452 85c. Shoe shine 40 20

2005. Urban Art. Multicoloured.
3453 55c. Type **1727** 30 15
3454 55c. Boy in pipe 30 15
3455 55c. Graffiti artist (horiz) . . 30 15

1728 Santos-Dumont Biplane *14 bis*

2005. Centenarian Mission (Brazilian astronaut, Marcos Pontes's flight on Soyuz rocket to International Space Station). Multicoloured.
3456 85c. Type **1728** 40 20
3457 85c. "Soyuz" 40 20
3458 85c. International Space Station 40 20
Nos. 3456/8 were issued together, se-tenant, forming a composite design.

1729 Emblem

2006. World Cup Football Championship, Germany.
3459 **1729** 85c. multicoloured . . . 40 20

1730 Bidu Sayao

2006. Balduina de Oliveira Sayao (Bidu Sayao) (opera singer) Commemoration.
3460 **1730** 55c. multicoloured . . . 30 15

1731 World Map and Faces

1732 Emblem

2006. International Day of Cultural Diversity.
3461 **1731** 1r.90 multicoloured . . 55 25

2006. RIO 2007—15th Pan American Games. Self-adhesive.
3462 **1732** (1st Porte) multicoloured 40 20

1733 Stylized Athlete

2006. Brazilian Paralympics Committee.
3463 **1733** 1r.35 multicoloured . . 65 30

1734 Viola de Cocho

2006. Mercosur. Musical Instruments.
3464 **1734** 55c. multicoloured . . . 30 15

1735 Rhea, Emas National Park

2006. National Parks. Multicoloured. Self-adhesive.
3465 85c. Type **1735** 40 20
3466 85c. Uakari monkey, Sustainable Development Reserve, Mamiraua . . . 40 20
3467 85c. Maned wolf, Chapada dos Veadeiros National Park 40 20
3468 85c. Squirrel, Itatiaia National Park 40 20

2006. Urban Art (2nd issue). Sheet 111 × 70 mm containing vert designs as T **1727**. Multicoloured.
MS3468a 1r.60 × 2, As No. 3454; As No. 3455 . . . . 1·90 1·90

1735a Leaves and Fruit

2006. Cajueiro (cashew nut tree). Sheet 111 × 70 mm.
MS3468b **1735a** 2r.90 multicoloured 1·50 1·50
No. **MS**3468b was cut round in the shape of a tree.

1736 Fernando de Noronha Archipelago

2006. Tourism.
3469 **1736** 2r.50 multicoloured . . 1·20 60

1737 Santos-Dumont *14-bis*

2006. Centenary of Flight of Santos-Dumont *14-bis*.
3470 **1737** (90c.) multicoloured . . 40 20

1738 Star, House and Mail Box

2006. Christmas (1st issue). Self-adhesive.
3471 **1738** (1st Porte) multicoloured 40 20

1739 The Magi

1740 Hydro-electric Dam and Street Lighting

2006. Christmas (2nd issue). Sheet 111 × 70 mm containing T **1739** and similar multicoloured designs.
MS3472 1r.60 × 3, Type **1739** Angel (36 × 40 mm) (arched): Holy family . . . . 1·40 1·40

2006. America. Energy Conservation.
3473 **1740** 1r.75 multicoloured . . 85 40

1741 *Isurus oxyrinchus* and *Sphyrna lewini*

2006. Sharks. Sheet 70 × 111 mm containing T **1741** and similar square design. Multicoloured.
MS3474 1r.90 × 2, Type **1741** *Mustelus schmitti* . . . . . . 2·00 2·00

1742 Diving

2007. Pan American Games, Rio de Janeiro. Multicoloured. Self-adhesive.
3477 (1 Porte Carta Comercial) Type **1742** 40 20
3478 (1 Porte Carta Comercial) Swimming 40 20
3479 (1 Porte Carta Comercial) Synchronised Swimming 40 20
3480 (1 Porte Carta Comercial) Futsal 40 20
3481 (1 Porte Carta Comercial) Water polo 40 20

1743 Carimbo

2007. Dances. Multicoloured.
3482 (1 Porte Carta Comercial) Type **1743** 40 20
3483 (1 Porte Carta Comercial) Frevo 40 20

1744 Research Vessel

2007. International Polar Year. Multicoloured.
3484 (1 Porte Carta Comercial) Type **1744** 40 20
3485 (1 Porte Carta Comercial) Ferraz research station . . 40 20
3486 (1 Porte Carta Comercial) Penguin and map of Antarctica 40 20
Nos. 3484/6 were issued together, setenant, forming a composite design.

1745 First Church of Our Lady of Assumption

2007. Jose de Anchieta (Jesuit missionary) Commemoration. Multicoloured.
3487 90c. Type **1745** 55 25
3488 90c. Founding of Espirito Santo 55 25
3489 90c. Metropolitan Cathedral of Vitoria 55 25
Nos. 3487/9 were issued together, setenant, forming a composite design.

1746 Estadio Olimpico Edgard Proenca (Mangueirao), Belem

2007. Stadia. Multicoloured.
3490 60c. Type **1746** 35 15
3491 60c. Estadio Municipal Paulo Machado de Carvalho, Pacaembu . . . 35 15
3492 90c. Estadio Serra Dourada, Goiania 55 25
3493 2r.60 Estadio Jornalista Mario Filho (Maracana), Rio de Janeiro . . . . . 1·50 75

1747 JK Bridge

2007. Mercosul. National Architecture.
3494 **1747** (1 porte Carta Comercial) mult . . . 40 20

1748 Robert Baden-Powell

1749 Pope Benedict XVI

2007. Centenary of Scouting.
3495 **1748** 2r. multicoloured . . . 1·20 60

2007. Pope Benedict XVI Visit to Brazil.
3496 **1749** 90c. multicoloured . . . 55 25

1750 *Cochlespira elongate*

1751 *My New Accordion* (Napachie Pootoogook)

2007. Shells. Sheet 126 × 84 mm containing T **1750** and similar vert designs. Multicoloured.
MS3497 2r. × 3, Type **1750** *Charonia variegata*; *Chicoreus* . . . . . 3·50 3·50
The stamps and margins of **MS**3497 form a composite design of a seashore.

2007. 140th Anniv of Brazil–Canada Diplomatic Relations.
3498 **1751** 90c. multicoloured . . . 55 25

1752 *Rio Pardo* and Giuseppe Garibaldi

2007. Birth Bicentenary of Giuseppe Garibaldi (soldier and nationalist). Multicoloured.
3499 1r.40 Type **1752** 80 40
3500 1r.40 On horseback 80 40
Stamps of a similar design were issued by Uruguay.

1753 Metro Locomotive

2007. Transport. Multicoloured.
3501 1r.40 Type **1753** 80 40
3502 1r.45 Steam locomotive No. 1 *Baroneza* 85 40
3503 1r.90 Tram, Bonde Santa Teresa . . . . 1·10 55

1754 Teofilo Ottoni

2007. Birth Bicentenary of Teofilo Benedict Ottoni (politician and journalist).
3504 **1754** 60c. multicoloured . . . 35 15

1755 Children, Computers and 'abc'

2007. America. Education for All.
3505 **1755** 60c. multicoloured . . . 35 15

1756 Inscr 'High & Magic'

2007. Roses. Sheet 85 × 128 mm containing T **1756** and similar vert designs.
MS3506 2r.60 × 3, Type **1756**; Inscr 'Caballero'; Inscr 'Avalanche' 4·50 4·50

The stamps and margins of **MS**3506 form a composite design.

1757 Giraffes

1758 Candles

2007. Zoological Fauna. Multicoloured.
3507 60c. Type **1757** 35 15
3508 60c. Tiger 35 15
3509 60c. Elephant 35 15
3510 60c. Lion 35 15
3511 60c. Chimpanzees 35 15
3512 60c. Macaw 35 15

2007. Christmas. Multicoloured. Self-adhesive.
3513 1st (porte nao-Comercial) Type **1758** 40 20
3514 1st (porte Comercial) The Nativity 40 20

EXPRESS STAMP

1930. Surch **1000 REIS EXPRESSO** and bars.
E490 **66** 1000r. on 200r. blue . . . 5·25 2·40

NEWSPAPER STAMPS

N 34

N 37

1889. Roul.
N88 **N 34** 10r. orange . . . . . . 3·50 3·50
N89 20r. orange . . . . . . 9·00 9·00
N90 50r. orange . . . . . 15·00 7·00
N91 100r. orange . . . . . 6·00 3·50
N92 200r. orange . . . . . 3·50 1·75
N93 300r. orange . . . . . 4·00 1·75
N94 500r. orange . . . . . 30·00 9·00
N95 700r. orange . . . . . 4·75 15·00
N96 1000r. orange . . . . . 4·75 15·00

1889. Roul.
N 97 **N 34** 10r. green . . . . . 1·75 60
N 98 20r. green . . . . . 1·75 60
N 99 50r. buff . . . . . 2·40 1·25
N100a 100r. mauve . . . . 4·75 1·75
N101 200r. black . . . . 4·00 1·75
N102 300r. red . . . . . 18·00 15·00
N103 500r. green . . . . 70·00 90·00
N104 700r. blue . . . . 38·00 60·00
N105 1000r. brown . . . . 18·00 45·00

1890. Perf.
N111 **N 37** 10r. blue . . . . . . 18·00 15·00
N112 20r. green . . . . . 55·00 21·00
N113 100r. mauve . . . . . 18·00 18·00

N 38 Southern Cross and Sugar-loaf Mountain

1890. Perf.
N119 **N 38** 10r. blue . . . . . . 2·40 1·75
N123a 20r. green . . . . . 7·00 4·00
N127 50r. green . . . . . 18·00 15·00

OFFICIAL STAMPS

O 64 Pres. Affonso Penna

O 67 Pres. Hermes de Fonseca

O 77 Pres. Wenceslao Braz

1906. Various frames.
O282 **O 64** 10r. green & orange 90 10
O283 20r. green & orange 1·25 10
O284 50r. green & orange 1·75 10
O285 100r. green & orange 90 10
O286 200r. green & orange 1·25 35
O287 300r. green & orange 3·50 60
O288 400r. green & orange 7·00 3·00
O289 500r. green & orange 3·50 1·75
O290 700r. green & orange 4·75 4·00
O291 1000r. green & orange 4·75 1·25

O292		2000r. green & orange	5·25	2·40
O293		5000r. green & orange	10·50	1·75
O294		10000r. green & orange	10·50	1·40

1913. Various frames.

O295	O **67**	10r. black and grey	20	60
O296		20r. black and olive	20	60
O297		50r. black and grey	25	60
O298		100r. black and red	90	35
O299		200r. black and blue	1·25	35
O300		500r. black & yellow	3·00	60
O301		600r. black & purple	3·50	3·00
O302		1000r. black & brown	4·00	1·75
O303		2000r. black & brown	7·00	2·40
O304		5000r. black & bistre	9·00	3·50
O305		10000r. black	15·00	7·00
O306		20000r. black & blue	27·00	27·00
O307		50000r. black & green	48·00	48·00
O308		100000r. black & red	£140	£140
O309		500000r. black & brn	£200	£200
O310		1000000r. black & brn	£225	£225

1919.

O311	O **77**	10r. brown	25	3·50
O312		50r. green	90	1·25
O313		100r. red	1·75	60
O314		200r. blue	2·40	60
O315		500r. orange	9·00	18·00

POSTAGE DUE STAMPS

D 34

D 45

D 64

1889. Roul.

D88	D **34**	10r. red	3·50	1·25
D89		20r. red	5·25	2·40
D90		50r. red	7·00	4·75
D91		100r. red	3·50	1·75
D92		200r. red	70·00	21·00
D93		300r. red	10·50	10·50
D94		500r. red	9·00	9·00
D95		700r. red	16·00	18·00
D96		1000r. red	16·00	14·00

1890. Roul.

D 97	D **34**	10r. orange	60	35
D 98		20r. blue	60	35
D 99		50r. olive	1·25	35
D100		200r. red	7·00	1·25
D101		300r. green	3·50	1·75
D102		500r. grey	4·75	3·50
D103		700r. violet	5·25	10·50
D104		1000r. purple	7·00	7·00

1895. Perf.

D172	D **45**	10r. blue	1·75	1·25
D173		20r. green	9·00	7·00
D174		50r. green	14·00	9·00
D175		100r. red	7·00	2·40
D176b		200r. lilac	7·00	1·75
D177a		300r. blue	3·00	2·40
D178		2000r. brown	18·00	18·00

1906.

D282	D **64**	10r. slate	35	35
D283		20r. violet	35	35
D284		50r. green	40	35
D285		100r. red	1·25	60
D286		200r. blue	90	40
D287		300r. grey	60	1·25
D288		400r. green	1·25	50
D289		500r. lilac	30·00	30·00
D290		600r. purple	1·25	2·40
D291		700r. brown	26·00	26·00
D292		1000r. red	3·00	3·50
D293		2000r. green	4·75	5·25
D294		5000r. brown	1·25	38·00

D 77

1919.

D345	D **77**	5r. brown	40	40
D403		10r. mauve	35	35
D365		20r. olive	40	40
D404		20r. black	40	35
D405		50r. green	45	45
D375		100r. red	60	60
D407		200r. blue	1·75	60
D408		400r. brown	1·25	1·25
D401		600r. violet	60	60
D350		600r. orange	1·25	1·25
D409		1000r. turquoise	60	60
D439		2000r. brown	1·25	1·25
D411		5000r. blue	85	85

BREMEN — Pt. 7

A free city of the Hanseatic League, situated on the R. Weser in northern Germany. Joined the North German Confederation in 1868.

72 grote = 1 thaler (internal).
22 grote = 10 silbergroschen (overseas mail).

1

2

3

1855. Imperf.

1	**1**	3g. black on blue	£225	£450

1856. Imperf.

3	**2**	5g. black on red	£180	£350
4		7g. black on yellow	£275	£800
5	**3**	5sg. green	£140	£350

4

5

1861. Zigzag roulette or perf.

17	**4**	2g. orange	£110	£275
19	**1**	3g. black on blue	90·00	£325
20	**2**	5g. black on red	£140	£325
21		7g. black on yellow	£170	£4750
22	**5**	10g. black	£200	£1200
24	**3**	5sg. green	£550	£225

BRITISH ANTARCTIC TERRITORY — Pt. 1

Constituted in 1962 comprising territories south of latitude 60°S., from the former Falkland Island Dependencies.

1963. 12 pence = 1 shilling;
20 shillings = 1 pound.
1971. 100 (new) pence = 1 pound.

1 M.V. "Kista Dan"

1963.

1	**1**	½d. blue	1·25	1·75
2	–	1d. brown	1·25	80
3	–	1½d. red and purple	1·25	1·50
4	–	2d. purple	1·50	80
5	–	2½d. myrtle	3·25	1·25
6	–	3d. turquoise	3·75	1·50
7	–	4d. sepia	2·75	1·50
8	–	6d. olive and blue	4·75	2·50
9	–	9d. green	3·50	2·00
10	–	1s. turquoise	4·25	1·50
11	–	2s. violet and brown	20·00	10·00
12	–	2s.6d. blue	22·00	13·00
13	–	5s. orange and red	22·00	17·00
14	–	10s. blue and green	45·00	26·00
15	–	£1 black and blue	48·00	48·00
15a	–	£1 red and black	£130	£120

DESIGNS: 1d. Manhauling; 1½d. Muskeg (tractor); 2d. Skiing; 2½d. De Havilland D.H.C.2 Beaver (aircraft); 3d. R.R.S. "John Biscoe II"; 4d. Camp scene; 6d. H.M.S. "Protector"; 9d. Sledging; 1s. De Havilland D.H.C.3 Otter (aircraft); 2s. Huskies; 2s.6d. Westland Whirlwind helicopter; 5s. Snocat (tractor); 10s. R.R.S. "Shackleton"; £1 (No. 15), Antarctic map; £1 (No. 15a), H.M.S. "Endurance I".

1966. Churchill Commemoration. As T **38** of Antigua.

16		½d. blue	80	3·25
17		1d. green	3·00	3·25
18		1s. brown	21·00	6·50
19		2s. violet	24·00	7·00

17 Lemaire Channel and Icebergs

1969. 25th Anniv of Continuous Scientific Work.

20	**17**	3½d. black, blue and ultram	2·50	3·00
21	–	6d. multicoloured	1·00	2·50
22	–	1s. black, blue and red	1·00	2·00
23	–	2s. black, orange and turquoise	1·00	3·00

DESIGNS: 6d. Radio Sonde balloon; 1s. Muskeg pulling tent equipment; 2s. Surveyors with theodolite.

1971. Decimal Currency. Nos. 1/14 surch.

24		½p. on ½d. blue	60	3·00
25		1p. on 1d. brown	1·00	90
26		1½p. on 1½d. red and purple	1·25	75
27		2p. on 2d. purple	1·25	40
28		2½p. on 2½d. green	3·00	2·25
29		3p. on 3d. blue	2·50	75
30		4p. on 4d. brown	2·25	75
31		5p. on 6d. green and blue	4·75	3·50
32		6p. on 9d. green	16·00	8·00
33		7½p. on 1s. blue	18·00	8·50
34		10p. on 2s. violet and brown	18·00	12·00
35		15p. on 2s.6d. blue	18·00	12·00
36		25p. on 5s. orange and red	20·00	15·00
37		50p. on 10s. blue and green	24·00	25·00

19 Setting up Camp, Graham Land

21 James Cook and H.M.S. "Resolution"

1971. 10th Anniv of Antarctic Treaty. Multicoloured.

38		1½p. Type **19**	6·00	5·50
39		4p. Snow petrels	16·00	8·00
40		5p. Weddell seals	9·50	8·00
41		10p. Adelie penguins	22·00	9·00

Nos. 38/41 each include Antarctic map and Queen Elizabeth in their design.

1972. Royal Silver Wedding. As T **52** of Ascension, but with Kerguelen fur seals and Emperor penguins in background.

42		5p. brown	2·00	3·00
43		10p. green	2·00	3·00

1973. Multicoloured.

64a		½p. Type **21**	1·00	2·50
65		1p. Thaddeus von Bellingshausen and "Vostok"	60	2·25
66		1½p. James Weddell and "Jane"	60	2·25
67		2p. John Biscoe and "Tula"	1·50	2·50
48		2½p. J. S. C. Dumont d'Urville and "L'Astrolabe"	1·50	1·75
49		3p. James Clark Ross and H.M.S. "Erebus"	1·00	1·75
50		4p. C. A. Larsen and "Jason"	1·00	1·75
51		5p. Adrien de Gerlache and "Belgica"	1·00	1·75
52		6p. Otto Nordenskjold and "Antarctic"	1·25	2·75
53		7½p. W. S. Bruce and "Scotia"	1·25	2·75
74a		10p. Jean-Baptiste Charcot and "Pourquoi Pas?"	50	3·00
75		15p. Ernest Shackleton and "Endurance"	1·25	2·25
76		25p. Hubert Wilkins and Lockheed Vega "San Francisco"	1·00	1·50
77b		50p. Lincoln Ellsworth and Northrop Gamma "Polar Star"	85	2·75
78		£1 John Rymill and "Penola"	2·75	2·00

The 25p. and 50p. show aircraft; the rest show ships.

1973. Royal Wedding. As T **47** of Anguilla. Background colour given. Multicoloured.

59		5p. brown	40	20
60		15p. blue	70	30

22 Churchill and Churchill Peninsula, B.A.T.

1974. Birth Centenary of Sir Winston Churchill. Multicoloured.

61		5p. Type **22**	1·50	1·75
62		15p. Churchill and "Trepassey"	1·75	2·25
MS63		114 × 88 mm. Nos. 61/2	8·00	8·00

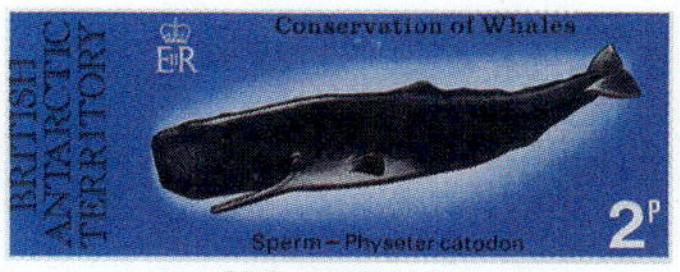

23 Sperm Whale

1977. Whale Conservation. Multicoloured.

79		2p. Type **23**	5·50	3·00
80		8p. Fin whale	6·50	3·50
81		11p. Humpback whale	7·00	3·50
82		25p. Blue whale	7·50	4·50

24 The Queen before Taking the Oath

1977. Silver Jubilee. Multicoloured.

83		6p. Prince Philip's visit, 1956/7	70	40
84		11p. The Coronation Oath	80	50
85		33p. Type **24**	1·00	65

25 Emperor Penguin

1978. 25th Anniv of Coronation.

86	–	25p. green, deep green and silver	60	1·00
87	–	25p. multicoloured	60	1·00
88	**25**	25p. green, deep green and silver	60	1·00

DESIGNS: No. 86, Black Bull of Clarence; 87, Queen Elizabeth II.

26 Macaroni Penguins

1979. Penguins. Multicoloured.

89		3p. Type **26**	9·00	10·00
90		8p. Gentoo penguins	2·00	2·75
91		11p. Adelie penguins	2·50	3·25
92		25p. Emperor penguins	3·50	4·25

27 Sir John Barrow and "Tula"

1980. 150th Anniv of Royal Geographical Society. Former Presidents. Multicoloured.

93		3p. Type **27**	15	15
94		7p. Sir Clement Markham and "Discovery"	15	25
95		11p. Lord Curzon and whaleboat "James Caird"	20	30
96		15p. Sir William Goodenough	20	35
97		22p. Sir James Wordie	25	55
98		30p. Sir Raymond Priestley	30	65

28 Map of Antarctic

1981. 20th Anniv of Antarctic Treaty.

99	**28**	10p. black, blue and light blue	30	70
100	–	13p. black, blue and green	35	80
101	–	25p. black, blue and mauve	40	90
102	–	26p. black, brown and red	40	90

DESIGNS: 13p. Conservation research ("scientific co-operation"); 25p. Satellite image mapping ("technical co-operation"); 26p. Global geophysics ("scientific co-operation").

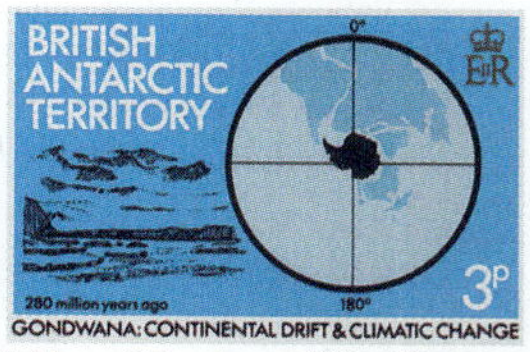

29 Map of Gondwana 280 million years ago and Contemporary Landscape Scene

1982. Gondwana – Continental Drift and Climatic Change. Maps of Gondwana showing position of continents, and contemporary landscapes. Mult.

103		3p. Type **29**	20	40
104		6p. 260 million years ago	20	50

105 10p. 230 million years ago . . 25 60
106 13p. 175 million years ago . . 30 70
107 25p. 50 million years ago . . 35 75
108 26p. Present day 35 75

30 British Antarctic Territory Coat of Arms

1982. 21st Birthday of Princess of Wales. Multicoloured.
109 5p. Type **30** 15 30
110 17p. Princess of Wales (detail of painting by Bryan Organ) 35 60
111 37p. Wedding ceremony . . . 50 90
112 50p. Formal portrait . . . . 90 1·25

31 Leopard Seal

1983. 10th Anniv of Antarctic Seal Conservation Convention. Multicoloured.
113 5p. Type **31** 25 35
114 10p. Weddell seals 30 40
115 13p. Southern elephant seals 30 45
116 17p. Kerguelen fur seals . . . 30 55
117 25p. Ross seals 30 65
118 34p. Crabeater seals 35 85

32 De Havilland Twin Otter 200/300

1983. Bicentenary of Manned Flight. Multicoloured.
119 5p. Type **32** 25 30
120 13p. De Havilland D.H.C.3 Otter 35 45
121 17p. Consolidated PBY-5A Canso amphibian 45 60
122 50p. Lockheed Vega "San Francisco" . . . . 70 1·25

33 "Corethron criophilum"

1984. Marine Life. Multicoloured.
123 1p. Type **33** . . . . 60 1·75
124 2p. "Desmonema gaudichaudi" . . . . . . 65 1·75
125 3p. "Tomopteris carpenteri" 65 1·75
126 4p. "Pareuchaeta antarctica" 70 1·75
127 5p. "Antarctomysis maxima" 70 1·75
128 6p. "Antarcturus signiensis" 70 1·75
129 7p. "Serolis cornuta" . . . . 70 1·75
130 8p. "Parathemisto gaudichaudii" . . . . . . 70 1·75
131 9p. "Bovallia gigantea" . . . 70 1·75
132 10p. "Euphausia superba" . . 70 1·75
133 15p. "Colossendeis australis" 70 1·75
134 20p. "Todarodes sagittatus" 75 1·75
135 25p. Antarctic rockcod . . . 80 1·75
136 50p. Black-finned icefish . . 1·25 2·00
137 £1 Crabeater seal . . . . . 1·75 2·50
138 £3 Antarctic marine food chain . . . . 5·00 6·50

34 M.Y. "Penola" in Stella Creek

1985. 50th Anniv of British Graham Land Expedition. Multicoloured.
139 7p. Type **34** 40 75
140 22p. Northern Base, Winter Island . . . . 70 1·40
141 27p. De Havilland Fox Moth at Southern Base, Barry Island . . . . 80 1·60
142 54p. Dog Team, near Ablation Point, George VI Sound . . . . 1·50 2·25

35 Robert McCormick and South Polar Skua

36 Dr. Edmond Halley

1985. Early Naturalists. Multicoloured.
143 7p. Type **35** . . . . 80 1·25
144 22p. Sir Joseph Dalton Hooker and "Deschampsia antarctica" . . . . . . 1·25 2·50
145 27p. Jean Rene C. Quoy and hourglass dolphin . . . . 1·25 2·50
146 54p. James Weddell and Weddell seal . . . . 1·75 3·50

1986. Appearance of Halley's Comet. Multicoloured.
147 7p. Type **36** . . . . 75 1·25
148 22p. Halley Station, Antarctica . . . . 1·00 2·25
149 27p. "Halley's Comet, 1531" (from Peter Apian woodcut, 1532) . . . . . 1·25 2·50
150 44p. "Giotto" spacecraft . . 2·25 4·50

37 Snow Crystal

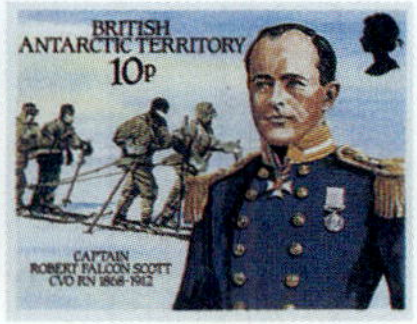

38 Captain Scott, 1904

1986. 50th Anniv of International Glaciological Society. Snow Crystals.
151 **37** 10p. light blue and blue . . 50 75
152 – 24p. green and deep green 65 1·40
153 – 29p. mauve and deep mauve . . . . 70 1·50
154 – 58p. blue and violet . . . 1·00 2·50

1987. 75th Anniv of Captain Scott's Arrival at South Pole. Multicoloured.
155 10p. Type **38** 55 95
156 24p. Hut Point and "Discovery" Ross Island, 1902–4 . . . . 90 2·00
157 29p. Cape Evans Hut, 1911–13 . . . . 1·00 2·25
158 58p. Scott's expedition at South Pole, 1912 . . . . . 1·50 3·00

39 IGY Logo

40 Aurora over South Ice Plateau Station

1987. 30th Anniv of International Geophysical Year.
159 **39** 10p. black and green . . . 30 75
160 – 24p. multicoloured . . . . 50 1·40
161 – 29p. multicoloured . . . . 60 1·75
162 – 58p. multicoloured . . . . 1·10 2·50
DESIGNS: 24p. Port Lockroy; 29p. Argentine Islands; 58p. Halley Bay.

1988. 30th Anniv of Commonwealth Trans-Antarctic Expedition. Multicoloured.
163 10p. Type **40** 30 75
164 24p. "Otter" aircraft at Theron Mountains . . . . 50 1·25
165 29p. Seismic ice-depth sounding . . . . 60 1·40
166 58p. "Sno-cat" over crevasse 1·00 2·00

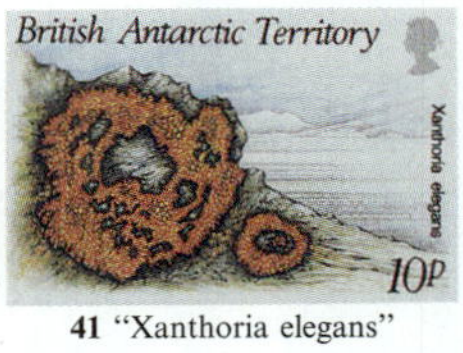

41 "Xanthoria elegans"

1989. Lichens. Multicoloured.
167 10p. Type **41** . . . . 90 1·00
168 24p. "Usnea aurantiaco-atra" 1·60 2·00
169 29p. "Cladonia chlorophaea" 1·75 2·25
170 58p. "Umbilicaria antarctica" 2·50 3·25

42 "Monocyathus" (archaeocyath)

1990. Fossils. Multicoloured.
171 1p. Type **42** . . . . 1·00 1·50
172 2p. "Lingulella" (brachiopod) 1·00 1·50
173 3p. "Triplagnoslus" (trilobite) 1·00 1·50
174 4p. "Lyriaspis" (trilobite) . . 1·25 1·50
175 5p. "Glossopteris" leaf (gymnosperm) . . . . . . 1·25 1·50
176 6p. "Gonatosorus" (fern) . . 1·25 1·60
177 7p. "Belemnopsis aucklandica" (belemnite) 1·25 1·60
178 8p. "Sanmartinoceras africanum insignicostatum" (ammonite) . . . . 1·25 1·60
179 9p. "Pinna antarctica" (mussel) . . . . 1·25 1·60
180 10p. "Aucellina andina" (mussel) . . . . 1·25 1·60
181 20p. "Pterotrigonia malagninoi" (mussel) . . . 1·75 2·25
182 25p. "Perissoptera" (conch shell) . . . . 1·75 2·25
183 50p. "Ainoceras sp." (ammonite) . . . . 2·25 3·50
184 £1 "Gunnarites zinsmeisteri" (ammonite) . . . . . . 3·50 4·75
185 £3 "Hoploparia" (crayfish) 7·00 8·50

1990. 90th Birthday of Queen Elizabeth the Queen Mother. As T **134** of Ascension.
186 26p. multicoloured . . . . . 1·50 2·25
187 £1 black and brown . . . . 3·00 4·00
DESIGNS: 29 × 36 mm: 26p. Wedding of Prince Albert and Lady Elizabeth Bowes-Lyon, 1923. 29 × 37 mm: £1 The Royal Family, 1940.

43 Late Cretaceous Forest and Southern Beech Fossil

1991. Age of the Dinosaurs. Multicoloured.
188 12p. Type **43** . . . . 1·25 1·25
189 26p. Hypsilophodont dinosaurs and skull . . . . 2·00 2·25
190 31p. Frilled sharks and tooth 2·25 2·50
191 62p. Mosasaur, plesiosaur, and mosasaur vertebra . . 3·50 4·00

44 Launching Meteorological Balloon, Halley IV Station

1991. Discovery of Antarctic Ozone Hole. Mult.
192 12p. Type **44** . . . . 90 1·75
193 26p. Measuring ozone with Dobson spectrophotometer 1·60 2·75
194 31p. Satellite map showing ozone hole . . . . 1·90 3·00
195 62p. Lockheed ER-2 aircraft and graph of chlorine monoxide and ozone levels 3·25 4·50

45 Researching Dry Valley

1991. 30th Anniv of Antarctic Treaty.
196 **45** 12p. multicoloured 90 90
197 – 26p. multicoloured . . . . 1·60 1·75
198 – 31p. black and green . . . 1·75 1·90
199 – 62p. multicoloured . . . . 3·00 3·25
DESIGNS: 26p. Relief map of ice sheet; 31p. BIOMASS logo; 62p. Ross seal.

46 "H.M.S. 'Erebus' and H.M.S. 'Terror' in the Antarctic" (J. Carmichael)

1991. Maiden Voyage of "James Clark Ross" (research ship). Multicoloured.
200 12p. Type **46** . . . . 90 1·50
201 26p. Launch of "James Clark Ross" . . . . 1·60 2·50
202 31p. "James Clark Ross" in Antarctica . . . . 1·75 2·75
203 62p. Scientific research . . . 3·00 3·75

1991. Birth Bicentenary of Michael Faraday (scientist). Nos. 200/3 additionally inscr "200th Anniversary M. Faraday 1791–1867".
204 12p. Type **46** . . . . 90 1·75
205 26p. Launch of "James Clark Ross" . . . . 1·60 2·75
206 31p. "James Clark Ross" in Antarctica . . . . 1·75 3·00
207 62p. Scientific research . . . 3·00 4·50

47 Ross Seals

1992. Endangered Species. Seals and Penguins. Multicoloured.
208 4p. Type **47** . . . . 1·00 1·25
209 5p. Adelie penguins . . . . 1·00 1·25
210 7p. Weddell seal with pup . . 1·00 1·25
211 29p. Emperor penguins with chicks . . . . 2·25 2·25
212 34p. Crabeater seals with pup 1·75 2·25
213 68p. Bearded penguins ("Chinstrap Penguin") with young . . . . 2·50 2·75

48 Sun Pillar at Faraday

1992. Lower Atmospheric Phenomena. Mult.
214 14p. Type **48** . . . . 80 1·50
215 29p. Halo over iceberg . . . 1·40 1·90
216 34p. Lee Wave cloud . . . . 1·75 2·25
217 68p. Nacreous clouds . . . . 2·75 4·00

49 "Fitzroy" (mail and supply ship)

1993. Antarctic Ships. Multicoloured.
218 1p. Type **49** . . . . 1·50 2·25
219 2p. "William Scoresby" (research ship) . . . . . 1·75 2·25
220 3p. "Eagle" (sealer) . . . . 1·75 2·25
221 4p. "Trepassey" (supply ship) 1·75 2·25
222 5p. "John Biscoe I" (research ship) . . . . 1·75 2·50
223 10p. "Norsel" (supply ship) 2·00 2·50
224 20p. H.M.S. "Protector" (ice patrol ship) . . . . . . 2·75 3·00
225 30p. "Oluf Sven" (supply ship) . . . . 3·00 3·25
226 50p. "John Biscoe II" and "Shackleton" (research ships) . . . . 3·50 4·00
227 £1 "Tottan" (supply ship) . . 4·50 5·50
228 £3 "Perla Dan" (supply ship) 8·00 10·00
229 £5 H.M.S. "Endurance I" (ice patrol ship) . . . . . 11·00 13·00

1994. "Hong Kong '94", International Stamp Exhibition. Nos. 240/5 optd **HONG KONG '94** and emblem.
230 15p. Type **51** . . . . 1·10 1·10
231 24p. De Havilland Turbo Beaver III aircraft . . . . 1·60 1·75
232 31p. De Havilland Otter aircraft and dog team . . . . 1·75 1·90
233 36p. De Havilland Twin Otter 200/300 aircraft and dog team . . . . 1·90 2·00
234 62p. De Havilland Dash Seven aircraft over landing strip, Rothera Point . . . 2·75 2·75
235 72p. De Havilland Dash Seven aircraft on runway 2·75 2·75

50 Bransfield House Post Office, Port Lockroy

1994. 50th Anniv of Operation Tabarin. Multicoloured.
236 15p. Type **50** . . . . 1·00 1·40
237 31p. Survey team, Hope Bay 1·60 1·90
238 36p. Dog team, Hope Bay . . 2·50 2·25
239 72p. "Fitzroy" (supply ship) and H.M.S. "William Scoresby" (minesweeper) 3·25 4·25

51 Huskies and Sledge

1994. Forms of Transportation. Multicoloured.
240 15p. Type **51** 70 80
241 24p. De Havilland Turbo Beaver III aircraft . . . . 90 1·00
242 31p. De Havilland Otter aircraft and dog team . . . 1·00 1·10
243 36p. De Havilland Twin Otter 200/300 aircaft and dog team . . . . 1·10 1·40
244 62p. De Havilland Dash Seven aircraft over landing strip, Rothera Point . . . 2·00 2·50
245 72p. De Havilland Dash Seven aircraft on runway 2·00 2·75

52 Capt. James Cook and H.M.S. "Resolution"

1994. Antarctic Heritage Fund. Multicoloured.
246 17p.+3p. Type **52** . . . . . 1·75 2·50
247 35p.+15p. Sir James Clark Ross with H.M.S. "Erebus" and H.M.S. "Terror" . . . . 2·00 2·75
248 40p.+10p. Capt. Robert Falcon Scott and interior of hut . . . . 2·00 2·75
249 76p.+4p. Sir Ernest Shackleton and "Endurance" . . . . . . 2·75 3·50

53 Pair of Crabeater Seals

1994. Antarctic Food Chain. Multicoloured.
250 35p. Type **53** . . . . 1·75 2·25
251 35p. Blue whale . . . . . . 1·75 2·25
252 35p. Wandering albatross . . 1·75 2·25
253 35p. Mackerel icefish . . . . 1·75 2·25
254 35p. Krill . . . . 1·75 2·25
255 35p. Seven star flying squid 1·75 2·25

54 Hauberg Mountains

1995. Geological Structures. Multicoloured.
256 17p. Type **54** . . . . 1·25 1·50
257 35p. Arrowsmith Peninsula 2·00 2·50
258 40p. Colbert Mountains . . . 2·25 2·75
259 76p. Succession Cliffs . . . . 3·50 4·50

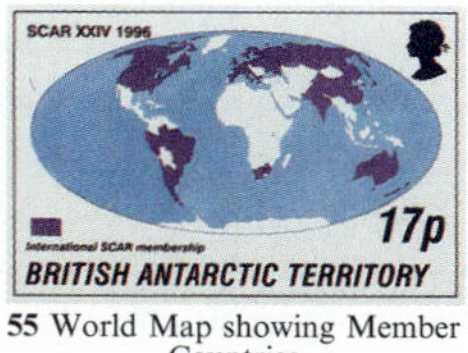

55 World Map showing Member Countries

1996. 24th Meeting of Scientific Committee on Antarctic Research. Multicoloured.
260 17p. Type **55** . . . . 1·00 1·25
261 35p. Scientist analysing ice samples . . . . 1·75 2·00
262 40p. Releasing balloon . . . 2·00 2·25
263 76p. Antarctic research ship catching marine life . . . . 2·75 3·00
MS264 100 × 90 mm. £1 S.C.A.R. logo . . . . 5·50 5·50

56 Killer Whales

1996. Whales. Multicoloured.
265 17p. Type **56** 80 75
266 35p. Sperm whales . . . . . 1·40 1·25
267 40p. Minke whales . . . . . 1·60 1·50
268 76p. Blue whale and calf . . 2·50 2·25
MS269 105 × 82 mm. £1 Humpback whale . . . . 3·50 3·75

1996. 70th Birthday of Queen Elizabeth II. As T **165** of Ascension, each incorporating a different photograph of the Queen. Mult.
270 17p. At premiere of "Chaplin", Leicester Square, 1992 . . . . . . 1·00 70
271 35p. At Buckingham Palace dinner, 1991 . . . . 1·50 1·25
272 40p. In Aberdeen, 1993 . . . 1·75 1·50
273 76p. At Royal Military School of Music, 1990 . . 2·25 2·25

1997. "HONG KONG '97" International Stamp Exhibition. Sheet 130 × 90 mm, containing design as No. 226. Multicoloured.
MS274 50p. "John Biscoe II" and "Shackleton" (research ships) 1·75 2·25

1997. Return of Hong Kong to China. Sheet 130 × 90 mm containing design as No. 227, but with "1997" imprint date.
MS275 £1 "Tottan" . . . . . . 2·75 3·25

57 Chinstrap Penguins sledging

58 Chart of South Shetland Islands (Swedish South Polar Expedition, 1902–3)

1997. Christmas. Multicoloured.
276 17p. Type **57** . . . . 1·75 90
277 35p. Emperor penguins carol singing . . . . 2·25 1·60
278 40p. Adelie penguins throwing snowballs . . . . 2·50 1·75
279 76p. Gentoo penguins ice-skating . . . . 3·25 4·00

1998. Diana, Princess of Wales Commemoration. Sheet 145 × 70 mm, containing vert designs as T **177** of Ascension. Multicoloured.
MS280 35p. Wearing sunglasses; 35p. Wearing round-necked white blouse, 1993; 35p. Wearing white blouse and jacket, 1990; 35p. Wearing green jacket, 1992 (sold at £1.40+20p. charity premium) 3·75 3·75

1998. History of Mapping in Antarctica. Multicoloured.
281 16p. Type **58** . . . . 1·75 1·50
282 30p. Map of Antarctic Peninsula (1949) . . . . . 2·25 2·00
283 35p. Map of AntarcticPeninsula (1964) 2·50 2·25
284 40p. Map of Antarctic Peninsula from Landsat (1981) . . . . 2·50 2·50
285 65p. Map of Antarctic Peninsula from satellite (1995) . . . . 3·25 3·50

59 Antarctic Explorer and H.M.S. "Erebus", 1843

1998. Antarctic Clothing. Multicoloured.
286 30p. Type **59** . . . . 1·75 1·50
287 35p. Explorer with dog, and "Discovery I", 1900 . . . 2·00 1·60
288 40p. Surveyor, and "Fitzroy", 1943 . . . . 2·25 2·00
289 65p. Scientist with Adelie penguins, and "James Clark Ross", 1998 . . . . 3·00 3·50

60 Snowy Sheathbill

1998. Antarctic Birds. Multicoloured.
290 1p. Type **60** . . . . 1·75 1·75
291 2p. Dove prion ("Antarctic Prion") . . . . 1·75 1·75
292 5p. Adelie penguin . . . . . 1·75 1·75
293 10p. Emperor penguin . . . 1·75 1·75
294 20p. Antarctic tern . . . . . 1·75 1·75
295 30p. Black-bellied storm petrel . . . . 1·75 1·75
296 35p. Southern fulmar ("Antarctic Fulmar") . . . 1·90 1·75
297 40p. Blue-eyed cormorant ("Blue-eyed Shag") . . . . 1·90 1·75
298 50p. South polar skua ("McCormick's Skua") . . 2·25 2·00
299 £1 Southern black-backed gull ("Kelp Gull") . . . . 3·75 3·50
300 £3 Wilson's storm petrel . . 8·00 8·00
301 £5 Antactic skua ("Brown Skua") . . . . 11·00 12·00

61 Mackerel Icefish

1999. Fish of the Southern Ocean. Multicoloured.
302 10p. Type **61** . . . . 1·25 1·25
303 20p. Blenny rockcod ("Toothfish") . . . . . . 1·75 1·75
304 25p. Borch . . . . 1·90 1·90
305 50p. Marbled rockcod ("Marbled notothen") . . 3·00 3·50
306 80p. Bernacchi's rockcod ("Bernach") . . . . 3·50 3·75

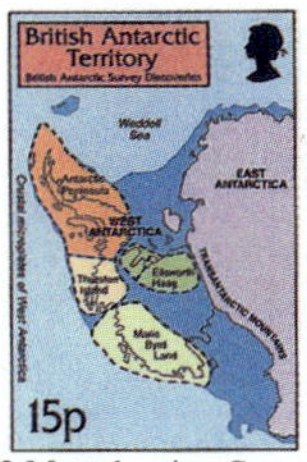

62 Map showing Crustal Microplates of West Antarctica

1999. British Antarctic Survey Discoveries. Mult.
307 15p. Type **62** . . . . 2·00 1·25
308 30p. Testing lead levels in ice 2·50 1·75
309 35p. Decolopodid sea spider (Gigantism in marine invertebrates) (horiz) . . . 2·50 1·75
310 40p. Scientist operating Dobson Spectrophotometer for testing ozone layer (horiz) . . . . 2·50 1·90
311 70p. Radar antenna (aurora electric field research) (horiz) . . . . 3·25 4·00

63 Wreck of "Endurance"

2000. Shackleton's Trans-Antarctic Expedition, 1914–17, Commemoration. Multicoloured.
312 35p. Type **63** . . . . 3·50 2·75
313 40p. Ocean Camp on ice . . 3·50 2·75
314 65p. Launching "James Caird" from Elephant Island . . . . 4·50 5·00

64 Iceberg and Opening Bars

2000. Composition of *Antarctic Symphony* by Sir Peter Maxwell Davies. Multicoloured.
315 37p. Type **64** . . . . 2·00 2·25
316 37p. Stern of *James Clark Ross* and pack ice . . . . 2·00 2·25
317 43p. Aircraft and camp on Jones Ice Self . . . . . . 2·25 2·50
318 43p. Frozen sea . . . . . . 2·25 2·50

65 Route of Commonwealth Trans-Antarctic Expedition, 1955–58

2000. "Heroic Age of Antarctica" (1st series). Commonwealth Trans-Antarctic Expedition, 1955–8. Multicoloured.
319 37p. Type **65** . . . . 3·25 2·75
320 37p. Expedition at South Pole, 1958 . . . . 3·25 2·75
321 37p. *Magga Dan* (Antarctic supply ship) . . . . 3·25 2·75
322 37p. "Sno-cat" repair camp 3·25 2·75
323 37p. "Sno-cat" over crevasse 3·25 2·75
324 37p. Seismic explosion . . . 3·25 2·75
See also Nos. 333/8 and 351/6.

66 *Bransfield* unloading "Sno-cat", Halley

2000. Survey Ships. Multicoloured.
325 20p. Type **66** . . . . 2·00 1·50
326 33p. *Ernest Shackelton* unloading supplies into *Tula* . . . . 2·75 2·00
327 37p. *Bransfield* in the ice (horiz) . . . . 2·75 2·50
328 43p. *Ernest Shackelton* with helicopter (horiz) . . . . . 3·75 3·50

67 Tourists at Port Lockroy

2001. Restoration of Port Lockroy Base. Multicoloured.
329 33p. Type **67** . . . . 1·75 1·60
330 37p. Port Lockroy and cruise ship . . . . 2·00 1·75
331 43p. Port Lockroy huts in 1945 . . . . 2·25 2·00
332 65p. Interior of Port Lockroy laboratory in 1945 . . . . 3·75 4·00

68 Map of Ross Sea Area

2001. "Heroic Age of Antarctica" (2nd series). Captain Scott's 1901–04 Expedition. Multicoloured.
333 33p. Type **68** . . . . 1·60 1·60
334 37p. Captain Robert F. Scott 1·90 1·90
335 43p. First Antarctic balloon ascent, 1902 (horiz) . . . 2·25 2·25
336 65p. "Emperor Penguin chick" (drawing by Edward Wilson) . . . . 2·75 2·75
337 70p. Shackleton, Scott and Wilson and most southerly camp, 1902 (horiz) . . . . 2·75 2·75
338 80p. *Discovery I* trapped in ice off Hut Point (horiz) 3·00 3·00

2002. Golden Jubilee. As T **200** of Ascension.
339 20p. black, mauve and gold 1·25 1·25
340 37p. multicoloured . . . . . 1·60 1·60
341 43p. black, mauve and gold 1·75 1·75
342 50p multicoloured . . . . . 2·25 2·75
MS343 162 × 95 mm. Nos. 339/42 and 50p. multicoloured . . . . 7·50 9·00

DESIGNS—HORIZ: 20p. Princess Elizabeth and Princess Margaret making radio broadcast, 1940; 37p. Queen Elizabeth in Garter robes, 1998; 43p. Queen Elizabeth at Balmoral, 1952; 50p. Queen Elizabeth in London, 1996. VERT (38 × 51 mm)—50p. Queen Elizabeth after Annigoni.

Designs as Nos. 339/42 in No. **MS**343 omit the gold frame around each stamp and the "Golden Jubilee 1952–2002" inscription.

2002. Queen Elizabeth the Queen Mother Commemoration. As T **202** of Ascension.
344 40p. black, gold and purple . . . 1·50 1·50
345 45p. multicoloured . . . . . 1·50 1·50
MS346 145 × 70 mm. 70p. black and gold; 95p. multicoloured . . . 7·50 7·50

DESIGNS: 40p. Lady Elizabeth Bowes-Lyon, 1913; 45p. Queen Mother on her birthday, 1996; 70p. Queen Elizabeth at niece's wedding, London, 1951; 95p. Queen Mother at Cheltenham Races, 1999.

Designs in No. **MS**346 omit the "1900–2002" inscription and the coloured frame.

69 Satellite and Antarctica

2002. 20th Anniv of Commission for Conservation of Antarctic Marine Living Resources (CCAMLR). Multicoloured.
347 37p. Type **69** . . . . 1·75 1·90
348 37p. Trawler and wandering albatross . . . . 1·75 1·90
349 37p. Icefish, toothfish and crabeater seal . . . . . . 1·75 1·90
350 37p. Krill and phytoplankton 1·75 1·90

2002. "Heroic Age of Antarctica" (3rd series). Scottish National Antarctic Expedition, 1902–04. As T **68** but horiz. Multicoloured.
351 30p. Map of Weddell Sea . . 2·00 2·00
352 40p. Piper Gilbert Kerr and emperor penguin (horiz) . . 2·50 2·50
353 45p. *Scotia* (expedition ship) 2·50 2·50
354 70p. Weather station and meteorologist (horiz) . . . 3·00 3·25
355 95p. William Speirs Bruce . . 3·25 3·50
356 £1 Omond House, Laurie Island (horiz) . . . . . . 3·50 3·75

2003. 50th Anniv of Coronation. As T **206** of Ascension. Multicoloured.
357 40p. Coronation Coach in procession . . . . 1·60 1·60
358 45p. Queen Elizabeth II with Prince Charles on Buckingham Palace balcony . . . . 1·75 1·75
MS359 95 × 115 mm. 95p. As 40p.; 95p. As 45p. . . . . 7·50 7·50

Nos. 357/8 have scarlet frame; stamps from **MS**359 have no frame and country name in mauve panel.

2003. As T **207** of Ascension.
360 £2 multicoloured . . . . . . 6·00 6·00

70 Blue Whale

71 Emperor Penguins

2003. Endangered Species. Blue Whale. Multicoloured.
361 40p. Type **70** . . . . 1·50 1·50
362 45p. Tail fluke . . . . 1·50 1·50
363 45p. Two blue whales . . . . 1·50 1·50
364 70p. Two blue whales at surface . . . . 2·00 2·00

2003. Penguins of the Antarctic (1st series). Multicoloured.
365 (–) Type **71** . . . . 1·50 1·50
366 (–) Head of macaroni penguin . . . . 1·50 1·50
367 (–) Gentoo penguin . . . . . 1·50 1·50
368 (–) Pair of adelie penguins . . 1·50 1·50
369 (–) Chinstrap penguin . . . . 1·50 1·50
370 (–) Gentoo penguin chick . . 1·50 1·50
371 (–) Emperor penguins (different) . . . . 1·50 1·50
372 (–) Chinstrap penguin chick 1·50 1·50
373 (–) Group of adelie penguins 1·50 1·50
374 (–) Gentoo penguin and chick 1·50 1·50
375 (–) Pair of macaroni penguins 1·50 1·50
376 (–) Emperor penguin chick 1·50 1·50

Nos. 365/76, inscribed "AIRMAIL POSTCARD", were initially sold at 40p.

See also Nos. 424/47.

72 Base G, Admiralty Bay

2003. Research Bases and Postmarks. Multicoloured.
377 1p. Type **72** 30 40
378 2p. Base B, Deception Island 40 45
379 5p. Base D, Hope Bay . . . 50 55
380 22p. Base F, Argentine Islands . . . . 1·10 1·25
381 25p. Base E, Stonington Island . . . . 1·25 1·50
382 40p. Base A, Port Lockroy 1·50 1·75
383 45p. Base H, Signy . . . . . 1·50 1·75
384 50p. Base N, Anvers Island 1·50 1·75
385 95p. Base P, Rothera . . . . 2·50 3·00
386 £1 Base T, Adelaide Island 2·50 3·00
387 £3 Base Y, Horseshoe Island 7·00 7·00
388 £5 Base Z, Halley Bay . . . 11·00 11·00

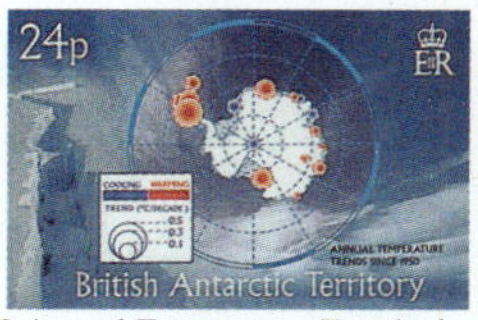

73 Annual Temperature Trends since 1950

2004. Climate Change. Multicoloured.
389 24p. Type **73** 90 90
390 24p. Larsen ice shelf 90 90
391 42p. Ice core measurements 1·50 1·50
392 42p. Ice core drilling . . . . 1·50 1·50
393 50p. Rise in air temperatures at Faraday Station . . . . 2·00 2·00
394 50p. Antarctic pearlwort . . 2·00 2·00

74 Pintado ("Cape") Petrel

2005. Birdlife International. Petrels. Multicoloured.
395 25p. Type **74** . . . . 1·25 70
396 42p. Snow petrel . . . . . . 1·90 1·25
397 75p. Wilson's storm petrel . . 3·00 2·75
398 £1 Antarctic petrel . . . . . 3·25 3·00
MS399 170 × 85 mm. 50p. × 6 Southern giant petrel and glaciers; Southern giant petrel in flight (from side); Head of Southern giant petrel; Southern giant petrel standing over chick; Southern giant petrel roosting with chick; Southern giant petrel chick . . 10·00 10·00

75 *Endurance* 1914–15 (three masted barque)

2005. *Endurance*. Multicoloured.
400 42p. Type **75** . . . . 1·40 1·40
401 50p. HMS *Endurance*, 1968–90 (ice patrol and hydrographic survey ship) 1·75 1·75
402 £1 HMS *Endurance*, 1991 (class 1A1 ice-breaker ship) 3·75 3·75

76 Deception Island from the South East

2005. 50th Anniv of FIDASE (Falkland Islands and Dependencies Aerial Survey Expedition, 1955–7). Multicoloured.
403 45p. Type **76** . . . . 1·60 1·60
404 55p. Hunting Lodge, Deception Island . . . . . 1·75 1·75
405 80p. Bell 47D helicopter with perspex bubble and flotation landing gear . . . 3·25 3·25
406 £1 Canso flying boat . . . . 3·50 3·50

77 Samson, Shakespeare and Surley

2005. Shackleton Expedition (1914—16) Dogs. Multicoloured.
407 45p. Type **77** . . . . 1·75 1·75
408 45p. Tom Crean holding puppies (vert) . . . . . . 1·75 1·75
409 55p. Dogs outside ice kennels and HMS *Endurance* . . . 1·90 1·90
410 £1 Sled dog team training on sea ice and HMS *Endurance* (vert) . . . . . 3·50 3·50

78 Faber Maunsell's Winning Concept Design

2005. Halley VI Research Station International Design Competition. Multicoloured.
411 45p. Type **78** . . . . 1·75 1·75
412 45p. Buro Happold concept design . . . . 1·75 1·75
413 55p. Hopkins concept design 1·90 1·90
414 80p. Laws building at Halley V Research Station . . . . 3·00 3·00

79 Sea and Icebergs (Erica Currie)

2006. ATCM XXIX Edinburgh (Tristan da Cunha) 2006 Stamp Design Competition. Children's Paintings. Multicoloured.
415 45p. Type **79** . . . . 1·75 1·75
416 45p. Penguins and icebergs (Meghan Joyce) . . . . . 1·75 1·75
417 55p. Icebreaker (Lorna MacDonald) . . . . 1·90 1·90
418 £1 Penguin wearing Union Jack (Danielle Dalgleish) 3·50 3·50

2006. 80th Birthday of Queen Elizabeth II. As T **223** of Ascension. Multicoloured.
419 45p. Princess Elizabeth . . . 1·50 1·50
420 55p. Queen wearing diadem, c. 1952 . . . . . 1·50 1·50
421 80p. Wearing red hat . . . . 2·25 2·25
422 £1 In evening dress . . . . . 2·75 2·75
MS423 144 × 75 mm. Nos. 420/1 4·00 4·50

Stamps from **MS**423 do not have white borders.

2006. Penguins of the Antarctic (2nd series). As T **71**. Multicoloured. (a) Ordinary gum.
424 (–) Chinstrap penguin chick 1·50 1·50
425 (–) Head of emperor penguin 1·50 1·50
426 (–) Adelie penguin with wings outstretched . . . . 1·50 1·50
427 (–) Head of chinstrap penguin 1·50 1·50
428 (–) Macaroni penguin . . . . 1·50 1·50
429 (–) Gentoo penguin feeding chick . . . . 1·50 1·50
430 (–) Emperor penguin chick 1·50 1·50
431 (–) Adelie penguin on nest . . 1·50 1·50
432 (–) Emperor penguin . . . . 1·50 1·50
433 (–) Gentoo penguin . . . . . 1·50 1·50
434 (–) Adelie penguin feeding chick . . . . 1·50 1·50
435 (–) Two emperor penguin chicks . . . . 1·50 1·50

(b) Self-adhesive. Size 24 × 29 mm.
436 (–) As No. 424 . . . . 1·50 1·50
437 (–) As No. 425 . . . . 1·50 1·50
438 (–) As No. 426 . . . . 1·50 1·50
439 (–) As No. 430 . . . . 1·50 1·50
440 (–) As No. 431 . . . . 1·50 1·50
441 (–) As No. 432 . . . . 1·50 1·50
442 (–) As No. 427 . . . . 1·50 1·50
443 (–) As No. 428 . . . . 1·50 1·50
444 (–) As No. 429 . . . . 1·50 1·50
445 (–) As No. 433 . . . . 1·50 1·50
446 (–) As No. 434 . . . . 1·50 1·50
447 (–) As No. 435 . . . . 1·50 1·50

Nos. 424/47 are inscribed "AIRMAIL POSTCARD" and were sold at 50p. each.

80 Elephant Seals

2006. Seals. Multicoloured.
448 25p. Type **80** . . . . 1·25 1·25
449 50p. Crabeater seals . . . . 1·75 1·75
450 60p. Weddell seals . . . . . 2·25 2·25
451 £1.05 Leopard seal . . . . . 3·25 3·50

81 *Marseniopsis molle* (sea lemon)

2007. Marine Invertebrates. Multicoloured.
452 25p. Type **81** 90 90
453 50p. *Isotealia antarctica* (Antarctic sea anemone) . . 1·40 1·40
454 60p. *Decolopoda australis* (sea spider) . . . . 2·10 2·10
455 £1.05 *Odontaster validus* (sea star) . . . . 3·25 3·25

82 Pinnacle Iceberg

2007. Icebergs. Multicoloured.
456 25p. Type **82** 90 90
457 50p. Pinnacle and tabular icebergs and ice floes at sunset . . . . 1·40 1·40
458 60p. Wedge iceberg . . . . . 2·10 2·10
459 £1.05 Tabular iceberg and ice floes . . . . 3·25 3·25

83 Aerial View of Antarctica

2007. International Polar Year 2007–2008. Circular sheet 97 × 97 mm.
MS460 **83** £2 multicoloured . . . 6·50 6·60

BRITISH COLUMBIA AND VANCOUVER ISLAND Pt. 1

Former British colonies, now a Western province of the Dominion of Canada, whose stamps are now used.

1860. 12 pence = 1 shilling;
20 shillings = 1 pound.
1865. 100 cents = 1 dollar.

1

1860. Imperf or perf.
2 **1** 2½d. pink £375 £180

VANCOUVER ISLAND

2

1865. Imperf or perf. Various frames.
13 **2** 5c. red £275 £160
14 – 10c. blue £225 £140

BRITISH COLUMBIA

4 Emblems of United Kingdom

1865.

22	4	3d. blue	90·00	65·00

1868. Surch in words or figures and words.

28	4	2c. brown	£160	£140
29		5c. red	£200	£150
24		10c. red	£900	£700
31		25c. yellow	£200	£150
26		50c. mauve	£750	£650
27		$1 green	£1200	£1300

BRITISH COMMONWEALTH OCCUPATION OF JAPAN Pt. 1

Stamps used by British Commonwealth Occupation Forces, 1946–49.

12 pence = 1 shilling;
20 shillings = 1 pound.

1946. Stamps of Australia optd **B.C.O.F. JAPAN 1946.**

J1	27	½d. orange	4·50	8·00
J2	46	1d. purple	3·75	4·50
J3	31	3d. brown	2·75	3·50
J4	–	6d. brown (No. 189a)	19·00	15·00
J5	–	1s. green (No. 191)	17·00	17·00
J6	1	2s. red	42·00	50·00
J7	38	5s. red	£100	£130

BRITISH EAST AFRICA Pt. 1

Now incorporated in Kenya and Uganda.

16 annas = 100 cents = 1 rupee.

1890. Stamps of Great Britain (1881) surch **BRITISH EAST AFRICA COMPANY** and value in annas.

1	57	½a. on 1d. lilac	£275	£200
2	73	1a. on 2d. green and red	£475	£275
3	78	4a. on 5d. purple and blue	£500	£300

3 Arms of the Company

11

1890. Nos. 16/19 are larger (24 × 25 mm).

4b	3	½a. brown	70	6·50
5		1a. green	6·00	8·50
6		2a. red	3·00	4·25
7c		2½a. black on yellow	4·75	5·00
8a		3a. black on red	2·00	8·50
9		4a. brown	2·50	8·50
11a		4½a. purple	2·50	17·00
29		5a. black on blue	1·25	10·00
30		7½a. black	1·25	16·00
12		8a. blue	5·50	9·50
13		8a. grey	£275	£225
14		1r. red	6·00	9·00
15		1r. grey	£225	£225
16	–	2r. red	14·00	35·00
17	–	3r. purple	10·00	50·00
18	–	4r. blue	12·00	50·00
19	–	5r. green	30·00	70·00

1891. With handstamped or pen surcharges. Initialled in black.

20	3	½a. on 2a. red	£8000	£850
31		½a. on 3a. black on red	£425	50·00
32		1a. on 3a. black on red	£12000	£3250
26		1a. on 4a. brown	£6500	£1500

1894. Surch in words and figures.

27	3	5a. on 8a. blue	70·00	85·00
28		7½a. on 1r. red	70·00	85·00

1895. Optd **BRITISH EAST AFRICA.**

33	3	½a. brown	75·00	26·00
34		1a. green	£160	£110
35		2a. red	£180	95·00
36		2½a. black on yellow	£180	55·00
37		3a. black on red	85·00	50·00
38		4a. brown	50·00	38·00
39		4½a. purple	£200	£100
40		5a. black on blue	£225	£140
41		7½a. black	£120	80·00
42		8a. blue	95·00	75·00
43		1r. red	55·00	50·00
44	–	2r. red	£450	£250
45	–	3r. purple	£225	£130
46	–	4r. blue	£200	£160
47	–	5r. green	£425	£250

1895. Surch with large 2½.

48	3	2½a. on 4½a. purple	£180	75·00

1895. Stamps of India (Queen Victoria) optd **British East Africa.**

49	23	½a. turquoise	7·00	5·50
50	–	1a. purple	6·50	6·00
51	–	1½a. brown	4·25	4·00
52	–	2a. blue	7·50	3·00
53	–	2a.6p. green	8·50	2·50
54	–	3a. orange	15·00	11·00
55a	–	4a. green (No. 96)	28·00	24·00
56	–	6a. brown (No. 80)	40·00	50·00
57c	–	8a. mauve	28·00	50·00
58	–	12a. purple on red	22·00	35·00
59	–	1r. grey (No. 101)	95·00	65·00
60	37	1r. green and red	45·00	£130
61	38	2r. red and orange	90·00	£150
62		3r. brown and green	£110	£160
63		5r. blue and violet	£130	£160

1895. No. 51 surch with small 2½.

64		2½ on 1½a. brown	95·00	50·00

1896.

65	11	½a. green	3·50	80
66		1a. red	9·50	40
67		2a. brown	7·50	5·00
68		2½a. blue	12·00	1·75
69		3a. grey	6·00	9·00
70		4a. green	7·00	3·50
71		4½a. yellow	11·00	16·00
72		5a. brown	7·50	5·00
73		7½a. mauve	7·00	22·00
74		8a. grey	7·50	5·50
75		1r. blue	60·00	25·00
76		2r. orange	65·00	29·00
77		3r. violet	65·00	32·00
78		4r. red	60·00	70·00
79		5r. brown	55·00	40·00

1897. Stamps of Zanzibar, 1896, optd **British East Africa.**

80	13	½a. green and red	55·00	45·00
81		1a. blue and red	95·00	90·00
82		2a. brown and red	38·00	21·00
83		4½a. orange and red	50·00	30·00
84		5a. brown and red	55·00	35·00
85		7½a. mauve and red	50·00	35·00

1897. As last, surch 2½.

86	13	2½ on 1a. blue and red	£110	65·00
89		2½ on 3a. grey and red	£110	55·00

1897. As Type **11**, but larger.

92a		1r. blue	80·00	40·00
93		2r. orange	95·00	95·00
94		3r. violet	£130	£140
95		4r. red	£375	£450
96		5r. brown	£325	£400
97		10r. brown	£350	£425
98		20r. green	£800	£1700
99		50r. mauve	£1600	

BRITISH FORCES IN EGYPT Pt. 1

SPECIAL SEALS AND STAMPS FOR THE USE OF BRITISH FORCES IN EGYPT

A. SEALS

A 1

1932. (a) Inscr "POSTAL SEAL".

A1	A 1	1p. blue and red	95·00	3·50

(b) Inscr "LETTER SEAL".

A2	A 1	1p. blue and red	38·00	85

A 2

1932. Christmas Seals.

A3	A 2	3m. black on blue	50·00	70·00
A4		3m. lake	7·50	50·00
A5		3m. blue	7·00	28·00
A6a		3m. red	9·50	25·00

A 3

1934.

A9	A 3	1p. red	2·75	3·25
A8		1p. green	4·00	4·00

1935. Silver Jubilee. Optd **JUBILEE COMMEMORATION 1935.**

A10	A 3	1p. blue	£250	£180

1935. Provisional Christmas Seal. Surch **Xmas 1935 3 Milliemes.**

A11	A 3	3m. on 1p. red	16·00	70·00

B. POSTAGE STAMPS

A 6 King Fuad I

A 7 King Farouk

1936.

A12	A 6	3m. green	1·00	1·50
A13		10m. red	5·50	10

1939.

A14	A 7	3m. green	4·50	7·00
A15		10m. red	6·50	10

BRITISH GUIANA Pt. 1

Situated on the N.E. coast of S. America. A British colony granted full internal self-government in August 1951. Attained independence on 26 May 1966, when the country was renamed Guyana.

100 cents = 1 dollar.

1

1850. Imperf.

1	1	2c. black on red		£170000
2		4c. black on orange		£8000
4		8c. black on green		£7000
5		12c. black on blue		£4750

Prices are for used stamps cut round. Stamps cut square are worth much more.

2

3 Seal of the Colony

1852. Imperf.

9	2	1c. black on magenta	£8500	£4250
10		4c. black on blue	£14000	£9000

1853. Imperf.

12	3	1c. red	£3750	£1300
20		4c. blue	£1100	£425

6

1856. Imperf.

23	6	1c. black on magenta	†	—
24		4c. black on magenta	—	£8500
25		4c. black on blue	£28000	£12000

7

9

1860. Perf.

29	7	1c. pink	£2000	£225
40		1c. brown	£350	95·00
85		1c. black	15·00	6·50
87		2c. orange	35·00	4·25
89		4c. blue	£100	13·00
92	9	6c. blue	£150	32·00
95	7	8c. red	£170	29·00
98		12c. lilac	£200	19·00
99		12c. grey	£200	21·00
64		24c. green	£250	50·00
79	9	24c. green	£180	13·00
82		48c. red	£275	60·00

The prices quoted for Nos. 29/82 are for fine copies with four margins. Medium specimens can be supplied at much lower rates.

10

16

1862. Various borders. Roul.

116	10	1c. black on red	£3750	£650
119		2c. black on yellow	£3750	£375
122		4c. black on blue	£4000	£750

The above prices are for stamps signed in the centre by the Postmaster. Unsigned stamps are worth considerably less.

1876.

126	16	1c. grey	2·75	1·40
171		2c. orange	27·00	15
172		4c. blue	90·00	5·00
173		6c. brown	5·00	6·50
174		8c. red	90·00	40
131		12c. violet	50·00	1·25
132		24c. green	60·00	3·00
133		48c. brown	£130	35·00
134		96c. olive	£475	£250

1878. Optd with thick horiz or horiz and vert bars.

(a) On postage stamps.

137	16	1c. on 6c. brown	38·00	£110
141	9	1c. on 6c. blue	£190	75·00

(b) On official stamps of 1875 and 1877.

138	7	1c. black	£250	75·00
139	16	1c. grey	£180	65·00
140		2c. orange	£350	65·00
144		4c. blue	£325	£100
145		6c. brown	£475	£110
146	7	8c. red	£3000	£325
148	16	8c. red	£450	£120

1881. Surch with figure. Old value barred out in ink.

(a) On postage stamps.

152	9	"1" on 48c. red	45·00	5·00
149	16	"1" on 96c. olive	3·50	6·50
150		"2" on 96c. olive	7·00	12·00

(b) On stamps optd **OFFICIAL.**

153	7	"1" on 12c. lilac	£130	70·00
154	16	"1" on 48c. brown	£170	£100
155		"2" on 12c. violet	75·00	38·00
157		"2" on 24c. green	85·00	48·00

26

30

1882.

162	26	1c. black on red	48·00	28·00
165		2c. black on yellow	80·00	50·00

Each stamp is perforated with the word "SPECIMEN".

1888. T **16** without value in bottom tablet, surch **INLAND REVENUE** and value.

175	16	1c. purple	1·50	20
176		2c. purple	1·50	85
177		3c. purple	1·00	20
178		4c. purple	10·00	30
179		6c. purple	9·00	3·75
180		8c. purple	1·50	30
181		10c. purple	6·00	2·50
182		20c. purple	20·00	16·00
183		40c. purple	22·00	25·00
184		72c. purple	50·00	60·00
185		$1 green	£425	£550
186		$2 green	£200	£250
187		$3 green	£180	£200
188		$4 green	£475	£650
189		$5 green	£300	£325

1889. No. 176 surch with additional **2.**

192	16	"2" on 2c. purple	3·00	15

1889.

193	30	1c. purple and grey	4·75	2·00
213		1c. green	75	10
194		2c. purple and orange	3·00	10
234		2c. purple and red	3·25	30
241a		2c. purple & black on red	3·50	10
253a		2c. red	8·50	10
195		4c. purple and blue	4·50	2·75
254		4c. brown and purple	2·25	60
214		5c. blue	2·75	10
243a		5c. purple & blue on blue	3·50	6·50
198		6c. purple and brown	7·00	16·00
236		6c. black and blue	6·50	11·00
256		6c. grey and black	13·00	7·00
199		8c. purple and red	12·00	2·50
215		8c. purple and black	3·00	1·10
200a		12c. purple and mauve	8·50	2·75
257		12c. orange and purple	4·00	4·50
246a		24c. purple and green	3·75	4·50
202		48c. purple and red	20·00	9·50
247a		48c. grey and brown	14·00	20·00
248a		60c. green and red	14·00	90·00
203		72c. purple and brown	28·00	40·00
205		96c. purple and red	65·00	70·00
250		96c. black & red on yellow	35·00	45·00

1890. Nos. 185/8 surch **ONE CENT.**

207	16	1 cent on $1 green	1·50	35
208		1 cent on $2 green	2·00	60
209		1 cent on $3 green	2·00	1·25
210		1 cent on $4 green	2·50	7·50

32 Mount Roraima

33 Kaieteur Falls

37

1898. Jubilee.

216	32	1c. black and red	5·50	1·75
217	33	2c. brown and blue	25·00	3·50
219w	32	5c. green and brown	48·00	4·25
220	33	10c. black and red	25·00	22·00
221	32	15c. brown and blue	30·00	19·00

1899. Nos. 219/21 surch **TWO CENTS**.

222	32	2c. on 5c. green and brown	3·25	2·00
223	33	2c. on 10c. black and red	2·50	2·25
224	32	2c. on 15c. brown and blue	2·25	1·25

1905. T **30** but inscr "REVENUE", optd **POSTAGE AND REVENUE**.

251	30	$2.40 green and violet	£160	£325

1913.

259a	37	1c. green	1·50	25
260		2c. red	1·25	10
274		2c. violet	2·50	10
261b		4c. brown and purple	3·75	25
262		5c. blue	1·75	1·00
263		6c. grey and black	2·75	1·50
276		6c. blue	3·00	30
264		12c. orange and violet	1·25	1·00
278		24c. purple and green	2·00	4·50
279		48c. grey and purple	9·50	3·50
280		60c. green and red	10·00	48·00
281		72c. purple and brown	26·00	65·00
269a		96c. black and red on yellow	22·00	48·00

1918. Optd **WAR TAX**.

271	37	2c. red	1·50	15

39 Ploughing a Rice Field

40 Indian shooting Fish

41 Kaieteur Falls

42 Public Buildings, Georgetown

1931. Centenary of County Union.

283	39	1c. green	2·50	1·25
284	40	2c. brown	2·00	10
285	41	4c. red	1·75	45
286	42	6c. blue	2·25	2·75
287	41	$1 violet	32·00	48·00

43 Ploughing a Rice Field

44 Gold Mining

53 South America

1934.

288	43	1c. green	60	1·50
289	40	2c. brown	1·50	1·00
290	44	3c. red	30	10
291	41	4c. violet	2·00	3·00
292	–	6c. blue	3·25	6·00
293	–	12c. orange	20	20
294	–	24c. purple	3·50	9·00
295	–	48c. black	7·00	8·50
296	41	50c. green	10·00	17·00
297	–	60c. brown	26·00	27·00
298	–	72c. purple	1·25	2·25
299	–	96c. black	21·00	30·00
300	–	$1 violet	32·00	32·00

DESIGNS—HORIZ: 6c. Shooting logs over falls; 12c. Stabroek Market; 24c. Sugar canes in punts; 48c. Forest road; 60c. Victoria Regia lilies; 72c. Mount Roraima; $1 Botanical Gardens. VERT: 96c. Sir Walter Raleigh and his son.

The 2c., 4c. and 50c. are without the dates shown in Types **40/44** and the 12, 48, 72 and 96c. have no portrait.

1935. Silver Jubilee. As T **13** of Antigua.

301	2c. blue and grey	20	20
302	6c. brown and blue	1·75	3·75
303	12c. green and blue	5·00	8·00
304	24c. grey and purple	9·00	11·00

1937. Coronation. As T **2** of Aden.

305	2c. brown	15	10
306	4c. grey	50	40
307	6c. blue	60	1·75

1938. Designs as for same values of 1934 issue (except where indicated) but with portrait of King George VI (as in T **53**) where portrait of King George V previously appeared.

308a	43	1c. green	30	10
309a	–	2c. violet (As 4c.)	30	10
310b	53	4c. red and black	50	15
311	–	6c. blue (As 2c.)	40	10
312a	–	24c. green	1·50	10
313	–	36c. violet (As 4c.)	2·00	20
314	–	48c. orange	60	50
315	–	60c. brown (As 6c.)	16·00	8·50
316	–	96c. purple	5·00	2·75
317	–	$1 violet	18·00	35
318	–	$2 purple (As 72c.)	7·50	22·00
319	–	$3 brown	29·00	29·00

DESIGN—HORIZ: $3 Victoria Regia lilies.

1946. Victory. As T **9** of Aden.

320	3c. red	10	40
321	6c. blue	50	85

1948. Silver Wedding. As T **10/11** of Aden.

322	3c. red	10	40
323	$3 brown	17·00	23·00

1949. UPU. As T **20/23** of Antigua.

324	4c. red	10	50
325	6c. blue	1·75	1·75
326	12c. orange	15	50
327	24c. green	15	70

1951. Inauguration of BWI University College. As T **24/25** of Antigua.

328	3c. black and red	30	50
329	6c. black and blue	30	65

1953. Coronation. As T **13** of Aden.

330	4c. black and red	30	10

55 G.P.O., Georgetown

1954.

331	55	1c. black	10	10
332	–	2c. myrtle	10	10
333	–	3c. olive and brown	3·50	20
334	–	4c. violet	75	10
335	–	5c. red and black	1·00	10
336	–	6c. green	50	10
337	–	8c. blue	30	20
338a	–	12c. black and brown	20	10
360	–	24c. black and orange	4·00	10
361	–	36c. red and black	60	60
341	–	48c. blue and brown	1·00	1·00
342	–	72c. red and green	12·00	2·75
364	–	$1 multicoloured	7·00	90
344	–	$2 mauve	20·00	7·50
345	–	$5 blue and black	18·00	28·00

DESIGNS—HORIZ: 2c. Botanical Gardens; 3c. *Victoria Regia* lilies; 5c. Map of Caribbean; 6c. Rice combine-harvester; 8c. Sugar cane entering factory; 24c. Bauxite mining; 36c. Mount Roraima; $1 Channel-billed toucan; $2 Dredging gold. VERT: 4c. Amerindian shooting fish; 12c. Felling greenheart; 48c. Kaieteur Falls; 72c. Arapaima (fish); $5 Arms of British Guiana.

70

1961. History and Culture Week.

346	70	5c. sepia and red	20	10
347		6c. sepia and green	20	15
348		30c. sepia and orange	45	45

1963. Freedom from Hunger. As T **28** of Aden.

349	20c. violet	30	10

1963. Centenary of Red Cross. As T **33** of Antigua.

350	5c. red and black	20	20
351	20c. red and blue	55	35

71 Weightlifting

1964. Olympic Games, Tokyo.

367	71	5c. orange	10	10
368		8c. blue	15	35
369		25c. mauve	25	40

1965. Centenary of ITU. As T **36** of Antigua.

370	5c. green and olive	10	15
371	25c. blue and mauve	20	15

1965. ICY. As T **37** of Antigua.

372	5c. purple and turquoise	15	10
373	25c. green and lavender	30	20

72 St George's Cathedral, Georgetown

1966. Churchill Commemoration.

374	72	5c. black, red and gold	50	10
375		25c. black, blue and gold	2·00	50

1966. Royal Visit. As T **39** of Antigua.

376	3c. black and blue	75	15
377	25c. black and mauve	1·50	60

OFFICIAL STAMPS

1875. Optd **OFFICIAL**.

O1	7	1c. black	55·00	19·00
O2		2c. orange	£180	14·00
O3		8c. red	£325	£120
O4		12c. lilac	£2500	£500
O5	9	24c. green	£1800	£225

1877. Optd **OFFICIAL**.

O 6	16	1c. grey	£250	65·00
O 7		2c. orange	£120	15·00
O 8		4c. blue	85·00	20·00
O 9		6c. brown	£5500	£600
O10		8c. red	£2000	£450

POSTAGE DUE STAMPS

1940. As Type D **1** of Barbados, but inscr "BRITISH GUIANA".

D1a	1c. green	1·50	16·00
D2a	2c. black	2·75	5·00
D3	4c. blue	30	12·00
D4	12c. red	30·00	4·50

For later issues see **GUYANA**.

BRITISH HONDURAS Pt. 1

A British colony on the East coast of Central America. Self-government was granted on 1 January 1964. The country was renamed Belize from 1 June 1973.

1866. 12 pence = 1 shilling;
20 shillings = 1 pound.
1888. 100 cents = 1 dollar.

1

8

1866.

17	1	1d. blue	55·00	15·00
18		1d. red	23·00	13·00
13		3d. brown	£140	21·00
20		4d. mauve	85·00	4·75
9		6d. red	£350	45·00
21		6d. yellow	£275	£200
16		1s. green	£275	11·00
22		1s. grey	£250	£160

1888. Surch as **2 CENTS**.

36	1	1c. on 1d. green	80	1·50
37		2c. on 1d. red	60	2·25
25		2c. on 6d. red	£160	£150
38		3c. on 3d. brown	3·25	1·40
39		6c. on 3d. blue	3·00	19·00
40		10c. on 4d. mauve	15·00	50
41		20c. on 6d. yellow	14·00	14·00
42		50c. on 1s. grey	29·00	85·00

1888. No. 42 surch **TWO**.

35	1	"TWO" on 50c. on 1s. grey	50·00	95·00

1891. No. 40 surch **6** and bar.

44	1	6c. on 10c. on 4d. mauve	1·25	1·50

1891. Nos. 38 and 39 surch.

49	1	"FIVE" on 3c. on 3d. brown	1·25	1·40
50		"15" on 6c. on 3d. blue	13·00	28·00

1891.

51	8	1c. green	2·50	1·25
52		2c. red	3·00	20
53		3c. brown	7·00	4·00
54		5c. blue	12·00	75
55		5c. black and blue on blue	17·00	2·50
56		6c. blue	9·00	2·00
57		10c. mauve and green (A)	10·00	11·00
58		10c. purple and green (B)	11·00	7·50
59		12c. lilac and green	2·50	2·25
60		24c. yellow and blue	5·50	17·00
61		25c. brown and green	80·00	£130
62		50c. green and red	25·00	60·00
63		$1 green and red	80·00	£130
64		$2 green and blue	£120	£170
65		$5 green and black	£300	£400

NOTE: 10c. (A) inscr "POSTAGE POSTAGE"; (B) inscr "POSTAGE & REVENUE".

1899. Optd **REVENUE**.

66	8	5c. blue	17·00	2·50
67		10c. mauve and green	8·00	16·00
68		25c. brown and green	2·75	35·00
69	1	50c. on 1s. grey	£180	£350

14

16

1902.

84a	14	1c. green	1·50	2·25
85a		2c. purple and black on red	1·00	20
96		2c. red	12·00	10
86		5c. black and blue on blue	1·75	20
97		5c. blue	1·75	10
87		10c. purple and green	4·00	12·00
83		20c. purple	7·50	17·00
89		25c. purple and orange	7·00	48·00
100		25c. black on green	3·25	45·00
90		50c. green and red	15·00	75·00
91		$1 green and red	55·00	85·00
92		$2 green and blue	£110	£170
93		$5 green and black	£300	£350

1913.

101	16	1c. green	3·75	1·50
102		2c. red	3·50	1·00
103		3c. orange	1·00	20
104		5c. blue	2·00	85
105		10c. purple and green	3·25	6·50
106		25c. black on green	1·25	12·00
107		50c. purple and blue on blue	17·00	15·00
108		$1 black and red	19·00	55·00
109		$2 purple and green	65·00	80·00
110		$5 purple and black on red	£250	£275

1915. Optd with pattern of wavy lines.

111a	16	1c. green	50	15·00
112		2c. red	3·50	50
113		5c. blue	30	6·00

1916. Optd **WAR**.

114	16	1c. green (No. 111a)	10	2·00
119		1c. green (No. 101)	20	30
120		3c. orange (No. 103)	80	2·50

21

1921. Peace.

121	21	2c. red	4·25	50

1921. As No. 121 but without word "PEACE".

123	4c. grey	10·00	50

22

24 Maya figures

1922.

126	22	1c. green	10·00	6·50
127		2c. brown	1·50	1·50
128		2c. red	4·50	1·50
129		3c. orange	23·00	4·00
130		4c. grey	12·00	85
131		5c. blue	1·50	55
132		10c. purple and olive	2·50	30
133		25c. black on green	1·75	8·50

134 50c. purple and blue on blue . . . . 4·75 16·00
136 $1 black and red . . . . . 9·00 26·00
137 $2 green and purple . . . 35·00 95·00
125 $5 purple and black on red £200 £250

1932. Optd **BELIZE RELIEF FUND PLUS** and value.
138 22 1c.+1c. green . . . . . . 1·00 10·00
139 2c.+2c. red . . . . 1·00 10·00
140 3c.+3c. orange . . . . . . 1·00 23·00
141 4c.+4c. grey . . . . . . 11·00 25·00
142 5c.+5c. blue . . . . . . 6·50 14·00

1935. Silver Jubilee. As T **13** of Antigua.
143 3c. blue and black . . . . . 2·00 50
144 4c. green and blue . . . . . 3·25 4·00
145 5c. brown and blue . . . . . 2·00 2·25
146 25c. grey and purple . . . . 5·00 5·50

1937. Coronation. As T **2** of Aden.
147 3c. orange 30 30
148 4c. grey 70 30
149 5c. blue . . . . 80 1·90

1938.
150 24 1c. purple and green . . . 30 1·50
151 – 2c. black and red . . . . 30 1·00
152 – 3c. purple and brown . . . 1·00 80
153 – 4c. black and green . . . 1·00 70
154 – 5c. purple and blue . . . . 2·25 1·00
155 – 10c. green and brown . . . 2·50 60
156 – 15c. brown and blue . . . 4·50 70
157 – 25c. blue and green . . . . 3·25 1·25
158 – 50c. black and purple . . . 15·00 3·50
159 – $1 red and olive . . . . . 28·00 10·00
160 – $2 blue and purple . . . . 45·00 20·00
161 – $5 red and brown . . . . 42·00 32·00
DESIGNS—VERT: 2c. Chicle tapping; 3c. Cohune palm; $1 Court House, Belize; $2 Mahogany felling; $5 Arms of Colony. HORIZ: 4c. Local products; 5c. Grapefruit; 10c. Mahogany logs in river; 15c. Sergeant's Cay; 25c. Dorey; 50c. Chicle industry.

1946. Victory. As T **9** of Aden.
162 3c. brown 10 20
163 5c. blue 10 20

1948. Silver Wedding. As T **10** and **11** of Aden.
164 4c. green 15 60
165 $5 brown . . . . 19·00 48·00

36 Island of Saint George's Cay

1949. 150th Anniv of Battle of Saint George's Cay.
166 36 1c. blue and green . . . . 10 1·25
167 3c. blue and brown . . . . 10 1·50
168 4c. olive and violet . . . . 10 1·50
169 – 5c. brown and blue . . . . 1·50 75
170 – 10c. green and brown . . . 1·50 30
171 – 15c. green and blue . . . . 1·50 30
DESIGNS: 5, 10 and 15c. H.M.S. "Merlin".

1949. U.P.U. As T **20/23** of Antigua.
172 4c. green 30 30
173 5c. blue . . . . 1·50 50
174 10c. brown . . . . 40 3·00
175 25c. blue 35 50

1951. Inauguration of B.W.I. University College. As T **24/25** of Antigua.
176 3c. violet and brown . . . . 45 1·50
177 10c. green and brown 45 30

1953. Coronation. As T **13** of Aden.
178 4c. black and green 40 30

39 Baird's Tapir

49 Mountain Orchid

1953.
179 – 1c. green and black . . . 10 40
180a 39 2c. brown and black . . . 85 20
181a – 3c. lilac and mauve . . . 10 10
182 – 4c. brown and green . . . 1·00 30
183 – 5c. olive and red 10 10
184 – 10c. slate and blue 10 10
185 – 15c. green and violet . . . 15 10
186 – 25c. blue and brown . . . 6·00 3·00
187 – 50c. brown and purple . . . 14·00 3·00
188 – $1 slate and brown . . . 6·50 5·00
189 – $2 red and grey . . . . . 6·50 4·50
190 49 $5 purple and slate . . . 42·00 15·00
DESIGNS—HORIZ: 1c. Arms of British Honduras; 3c. Mace and Legislative Council Chamber; 4c. Pine industry; 5c. Spiny lobster; 10c. Stanley Field Airport; 15c. Maya frieze, Xunantunich; 25c. "Morpho peleides" (butterfly); $1 Nine-banded armadillo; $2 Hawkesworth Bridge. VERT: 50c. Maya indian.

50 "Belize from Fort George, 1842" (C. J. Hullmandel)

1960. Post Office Centenary.
191 50 2c. green . . . . 45 1·25
192 – 10c. red 45 10
193 – 15c. blue 45 35
DESIGNS: 10c. Public seals, 1860 and 1960; 15c. Tamarind tree, Newtown Barracks.

1961. New Constitution. Stamps of 1953 optd **NEW CONSTITUTION 1960.**
194 39 2c. brown and black . . . 25 20
195 – 3c. lilac and mauve 30 20
196 – 10c. slate and blue 30 10
197 – 15c. green and violet . . . 30 20

1962. Hurricane Hattie Relief Fund. Stamps of 1953 optd **HURRICANE HATTIE.**
198 1c. green and black 10 65
199 10c. slate and blue 30 10
200 25c. blue and brown . . . . 1·75 80
201 50c. brown and purple . . . 75 1·00

55 Great Curassow

1962. Birds in natural colours; portrait and inscr in black; background colours given.
239 55 1c. yellow 10 50
240 – 2c. grey . . . . 30 1·00
204 – 3c. green . . . . 3·25 3·75
241 – 4c. grey . . . . 1·75 2·00
242 – 5c. buff 40 10
243 – 10c. stone 40 10
244 – 15c. stone 40 10
209 – 25c. slate . . . . 4·50 30
245 – 50c. grey . . . . 6·00 35
211 – $1 blue . . . . 9·00 1·00
212 – $2 stone . . . . 17·00 3·25
213 $5 grey . . . . 26·00 16·00
BIRDS: 2c. Red-legged honeycreeper; 3c. Northern jacana ("American Jacana"); 4c. Great kiskadee; 5c. Scarlet-rumped tanager; 10c. Scarlet macaw; 15c. Slaty-tailed trogon ("Massena Trogon"); 25c. Red-footed booby; 50c. Keel-billed toucan; $1 Magnificent frigate bird; $2 Rufous-tailed jacamar; $5 Montezuma oropendola.

1963. Freedom from Hunger. As T **28** of Aden.
214 22c. green 30 15

1963. Centenary of Red Cross. As T **33** of Antigua.
215 4c. red and black 20 75
216 22c. red and blue . . . . . 40 1·25

1964. New Constitution. Nos. 202, 204, 205, 207 and 209 optd **SELF GOVERNMENT 1964.**
217 55 1c. yellow 10 30
218 – 3c. green 45 30
219 – 4c. pale grey 45 30
220 – 10c. stone 45 10
221 – 25c. slate 55 30

1965. Centenary of I.T.U. As T **36** of Antigua.
222 2c. red and green 10 10
223 50c. yellow and purple . . . 35 25

1965. I.C.Y. As T **37** of Antigua.
224 1c. purple and turquoise . . 10 15
225 22c. green and lavender . . . 20 15

1966. Churchill Commemoration. As T **38** of Antigua.
226 1c. blue 10 75
227 4c. green 50 10
228 22c. brown 75 10
229 25c. violet 95 45

1966. Dedication of new Capital Site. Nos. 202, 204/5 207 and 209 optd **DEDICATION OF SITE NEW CAPITAL 9th OCTOBER 1965.**
230 55 1c. yellow 10 40
231 – 3c. green 45 40
232 – 4c. grey 45 40
233 – 10c. stone 45 10
234 – 25c. slate 55 35

58 Citrus Grove

1966. Stamp Centenary. Multicoloured.
235 5c. Type **58** 10 10
236 10c. Half Moon Cay 10 10
237 22c. Hidden Valley Falls . . 10 10
238 25c. Maya ruins, Xunantunich 15 45

59 Sailfish

1967. International Tourist Year.
246 59 5c. blue, black and yellow 15 30
247 – 10c. brown, black and red 15 10
248 – 22c. orange, black and green 30 10
249 – 25c. blue, black and yellow 30 60
DESIGNS: 10c. Red brocket; 22c. Jaguar; 25c. Atlantic tarpon.

60 "Schomburgkia tibicinis"

61 Monument Belizean Patriots

1968. 20th Anniv of Economic Commission for Latin America. Orchids. Multicoloured.
250 5c. Type **60** 20 15
251 10c. "Maxillaria tenuifolia" 25 10
252 22c. "Bletia purpurea" . . . 30 10
253 25c. "Sobralia macrantha" 40 20

1968. Human Rights Year. Multicoloured.
254 22c. Type **61** 15 10
255 50c. Monument at site of new capital 15 20

63 Spotted Jewfish

1968. Wildlife.
276 – ½c. multicoloured and blue 10 10
277 – ½c. multicoloured and yellow . . . . 2·50 1·00
256 63 1c. black, brown and yellow 30 10
257 – 2c. black, green and yellow 10 10
258 – 3c. black, brown and lilac 20 10
259 – 4c. multicoloured . . . . 15 1·25
260 – 5c. black and red . . . . 15 1·25
261 – 10c. multicoloured 15 10
262 – 15c. multicoloured . . . . 2·00 20
263 – 25c. multicoloured 30 20
264 – 50c. multicoloured . . . . 70 1·25
265 – $1 multicoloured . . . . 2·50 1·25
266 – $2 multicoloured . . . . 2·50 2·00
278 – $5 multicoloured . . . . 2·50 10·00
DESIGNS: ½c. (Nos. 276 and 277) Mozambique mouthbrooder ("Crana"); 2c. White-lipped peccary; 3c. Misty grouper; 4c. Collared anteater; 5c. Bonefish; 10c. Paca; 15c. Dolphin; 25c. Kinkajou; 50c. Mutton snapper; $1 Tayra; $2 Great barracuda; $5 Puma.

64 "Rhyncholaelia digbyana"

65 Ziricote Tree

1969. Orchids of Belize (1st series). Multicoloured.
268 5c. Type **64** 60 20
269 10c. "Cattleya bowringiana" 65 15
270 22c. "Lycaste cochleatum" 95 15
271 25c. "Coryanthes speciosum" 1·10 1·10
See also Nos. 287/90.

1969. Indigenous Hardwoods (1st series). Mult.
272 5c. Type **65** 10 20
273 10c. Rosewood 10 10
274 22c. Mayflower 20 10
275 25c. Mahogany 20 45
See also Nos. 291/4, 315/18 and 333/7.

66 "The Virgin and Child" (Bellini)

69 Santa Maria

1969. Christmas. Paintings. Multicoloured.
279 5c. Type **66** 10 10
280 15c. Type **66** 10 10
281 22c. "The Adoration of the Magi" (Veronese) 10 10
282 25c. As No. 281 . . . . . . 10 20

1970. Population Census. Nos. 260/3 optd **POPULATION CENSUS 1970.**
283 5c. multicoloured 10 10
284 10c. multicoloured 15 10
285 15c. multicoloured 20 10
286 25c. multicoloured 20 15

1970. Orchids of Belize (2nd series). As T **64**. Mult.
287 5c. Black orchid 35 15
288 15c. White butterfly orchid 50 10
289 22c. Swan orchid 70 10
290 25c. Butterfly orchid 70 40

1970. Indigenous Hardwoods (2nd series). Mult.
291 5c. Type **69** 25 10
292 15c. Nargusta 40 10
293 22c. Cedar 45 10
294 25c. Sapodilla 45 35

70 "The Nativity" (A. Hughes)

71 Legislative Assembly House

1970. Christmas. Multicoloured.
295 ½c. Type **70** 10 10
296 5c. "The Mystic Nativity" (Botticelli) 10 10
297 10c. Type **70** 10 10
298 15c. As 5c. 20 10
299 22c. Type **70** 25 10
300 50c. As 5c. 40 85

1971. Establishment of New Capital, Belmopan. Multicoloured.
301 5c. Old capital, Belize 10 10
302 10c. Government Plaza . . . 10 10
303 15c. Type **71** 10 10
304 22c. Magistrates' Court . . . 15 10
305 25c. Police H.Q 15 15
306 50c. New G.P.O 25 40
The 5c. and 10c. are larger, 60 × 22 mm.

72 "Tabebuia chrysantha"

1971. Easter. Flowers. Multicoloured.
307 ½c. Type **72** 10 10
308 5c. "Hymenocallis littoralis" 10 10
309 10c. "Hippeastrum equestre" 10 10
310 15c. Type **72** 20 10
311 22c. As 5c. 20 10
312 25c. As 10c. 20 30

1971. Racial Equality Year. Nos. 261 and 264 optd **RACIAL EQUALITY YEAR–1971.**
313 10c. multicoloured 25 10
314 50c. multicoloured 55 20

74 Tubroos

76 "Petrae volubis"

75 Hawksworth and Belcan Bridges

1971. Indigenous Hardwoods (3rd series). Mult.

315	5c. Type **74**	60	10
316	15c. Yemeri	80	30
317	26c. Billywebb	1·10	35
318	50c. Logwood	1·75	4·25
MS319	96 × 171 mm. Nos. 315/18	3·50	7·50

1971. Bridges of the World. Multicoloured.

320	½c. Type **75**	10	20
321	5c. Narrows Bridge, N.Y. and Quebec Bridge	30	15
322	26c. London Bridge (1871) and reconstructed, Arizona (1971)	80	15
323	50c. Belize Mexican Bridge and Swing Bridge	1·00	1·25

1972. Easter. Wild Flowers. Multicoloured.

324	6c. Type **76**	15	10
325	15c. Yemeri	25	30
326	26c. Mayflower	50	45
327	50c. Tiger's Claw	80	1·40

77 Seated Figure

78 Banak

1972. Mayan Artefacts. Multicoloured.

328	3c. Type **77**	25	10
329	6c. Priest in "dancing" pose	25	10
330	16c. Sun God's head (horiz)	50	15
331	26c. Priest and Sun God	70	20
332	50c. Full-front figure	1·40	3·75

1972. Indigenous Hardwoods (4th series). Mult.

333	3c. Type **78**	25	10
334	5c. Quamwood	25	10
335	16c. Waika Chewstick	55	15
336	26c. Mamee-Apple	75	25
337	50c. My Lady	1·60	3·25

1972. Royal Silver Wedding. As T **52** of Ascension, but with Orchids of Belize in background.

341	26c. green	25	10
342	50c. violet	40	65

80 Baron Bliss Day

1973. Festivals of Belize. Multicoloured.

343	3c. Type **80**	15	10
344	10c. Labour Day	15	10
345	26c. Carib Settlement Day	30	10
346	50c. Pan American Day	50	85

POSTAGE DUE STAMPS

D 1

1923.

D1	D **1** 1c. black	2·25	13·00
D4	2c. black	2·75	5·50
D5	4c. black	1·25	6·00

For later issues see **BELIZE**.

BRITISH INDIAN OCEAN TERRITORY Pt. 1

A Crown Colony, established 8 November 1965, comprising the Chagos Archipelago (previously administered by Mauritius) and Aldabra, Farquhar and Desroches, previously administered by Seychelles to which country they were returned on 29 June 1976.

The Chagos Archipelago has no indigenous population, but stamps were provided from 1990 for use by civilian workers at the U.S. Navy base on Diego Garcia.

1968. 100 cents = 1 rupee.
1990. 100 pence = 1 pound.

1968. Nos 196/200, 202/4 and 206/12 of Seychelles optd **B.I.O.T.**

1	**24** 5c. multicoloured	1·00	1·50
2	– 10c. multicoloured	10	15
3	– 15c. multicoloured	10	15
4	– 20c. multicoloured	15	15
5	– 25c. multicoloured	15	15
6	– 40c. multicoloured	20	20
7	– 45c. multicoloured	20	30
8	– 50c. multicoloured	20	30
9	– 75c. multicoloured	60	35
10	– 1r. multicoloured	70	35
11	– 1r.50 multicoloured	1·75	1·50
12	– 2r.25 multicoloured	3·00	3·75
13	– 3r.50 multicoloured	3·00	4·50
14	– 5r. multicoloured	10·00	7·50
15	– 10r. multicoloured	20·00	20·00

2 Lascar

1968. Marine Life. Multicoloured.

16	5c. Type **2**	1·00	2·00
17	10c. Smooth hammerhead (vert)	30	1·25
18	15c. Tiger shark	30	1·50
19	20c. Spotted eagle ray ("Bat ray")	30	1·00
20	25c. Yellow-finned butterflyfish and ear-spot angelfish (vert)	80	1·00
20a	30c. Robber crab	3·50	2·75
21	40c. Blue-finned trevalley ("Caranx")	2·00	40
22	45c. Crocodile needlefish ("Garfish") (vert)	2·25	2·50
23	50c. Pickhandle barracuda	2·00	30
23a	60c. Spotted pebble crab	3·50	3·25
24	75c. Indian Ocean steep-headed parrotfish	2·50	2·75
24a	85c. Rainbow runner ("Dorade")	4·50	3·50
25	1r. Giant hermit crab	1·75	35
26	1r.50 Parrotfish ("Humphead")	2·50	3·00
27	2r.25 Yellow-edged lyre-tail and Aredate grouper ("Rock cod")	12·00	10·00
28	3r.50 Black marlin	4·00	3·75
29	5r. black, green and blue (Whale shark) (vert)	15·00	11·00
30	10r. Lionfish	6·00	8·00

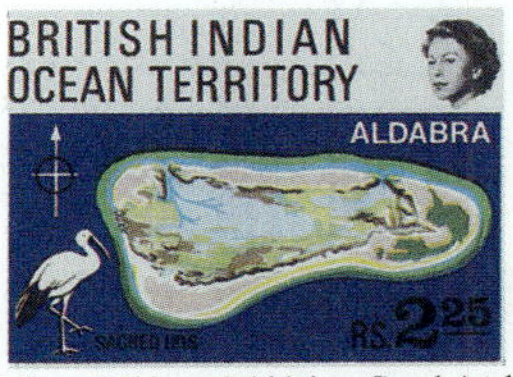

3 Sacred Ibis and Aldabra Coral Atoll

1969. Coral Atolls.

31	**3** 2r.25 multicoloured	1·75	1·00

4 Outrigger Canoe

1969. Ships of the Islands. Multicoloured.

32	45c. Type **4**	55	75
33	75c. Pirogue	55	80
34	1r. M.V. "Nordvaer"	60	90
35	1r.50 "Isle of Farquhar"	65	1·00

5 Giant Land Tortoise

1971. Aldabra Nature Reserve. Multicoloured.

36	45c. Type **5**	2·50	2·50
37	75c. Aldabra lily	3·00	2·50
38	1r. Aldabra tree snail	3·50	2·75
39	1r.50 Western reef heron ("Dimorphic Egrets")	12·00	10·00

6 Arms of Royal Society and White-throated Rail

1971. Opening of Royal Society Research Station, Aldabra.

40	**6** 3r.50 multicoloured	15·00	8·50

7 Staghorn Coral

1972. Coral. Multicoloured.

41	40c. Type **7**	3·50	4·00
42	60c. Brain coral	4·00	4·25
43	1r. Mushroom coral	4·00	4·25
44	1r.75 Organ pipe coral	5·00	6·50

1972. Royal Silver Wedding. As T **52** of Ascension, but with White-throated rail and Sacred ibis in background.

45	95c. green	50	40
46	1r.50 violet	50	40

9 "Christ on the Cross"

10 Upsidedown Jellyfish

1973. Easter. Multicoloured.

47	45c. Type **9**	20	40
48	75c. "Joseph and Nicodemus burying Jesus"	30	55
49	1r. Type **9**	30	60
50	1r.50 As 75c.	30	70
MS51	126 × 110 mm. Nos. 47/50	1·00	4·00

1973. Wildlife (1st series). Multicoloured.

53	50c. Type **10**	3·50	3·00
54	1r. "Hypolimnas misippus" and "Belenois aldabrensis" (butterflies)	4·00	3·00
55	1r.50 "Nephila madagascariensis" (spider)	4·25	3·00

See also Nos. 58/61, 77/80 and 86/9.

11 M.V. "Nordvaer"

13 Aldabra Drongo

12 Red-cloud Auger and Subulat Auger

1974. 5th Anniv of "Nordvaer" Travelling Post Office. Multicoloured.

56	85c. Type **11**	85	75
57	2r.50 "Nordvaer" off shore	1·40	1·25

1974. Wildlife (2nd series). Shells. Multicoloured.

58	45c. Type **12**	2·25	1·25
59	75c. Great green turban	2·50	1·50
60	1r. Strawberry drupe	2·75	1·75
61	1r.50 Bull-mouth helmet	3·00	2·00

1975. Birds. Multicoloured.

62	5c. Type **13**	1·25	2·75
63	10c. Black coucal ("Malagasy Coucal")	1·25	2·75
64	20c. Mascarene fody ("Red-Headed Forest Foddy")	1·25	2·75
65	25c. White tern	1·25	2·75
66	30c. Crested tern	1·25	2·75
67	40c. Brown booby	1·25	2·75
68	50c. Common noddy ("Noddy Tern") (horiz)	1·25	3·00
69	60c. Grey heron	1·25	3·00
70	65c. Blue-faced booby (horiz)	1·25	3·00
71	95c. Madagascar white eye ("Malagasy White-eye") (horiz)	1·25	3·00
72	1r. Green-backed heron (horiz)	1·25	3·00
73	1r.75 Lesser frigate bird (horiz)	2·00	5·50
74	3r.50 White-tailed tropic bird (horiz)	2·75	5·50
75	5r. Souimanga sunbird (horiz)	3·00	5·00
76	10r. Madagascar turtle dove ("Malagasy Turtle Dove") (horiz)	5·00	9·00

14 "Grewia salicifolia"

1975. Wildlife (3rd series). Seashore Plants. Multicoloured.

77	50c. Type **14**	50	1·40
78	65c. "Cassia aldabrensis"	55	1·50
79	1r. "Hypoestes aldabrensis"	65	1·60
80	1r.60 "Euphorbia pyrifolia"	80	1·75

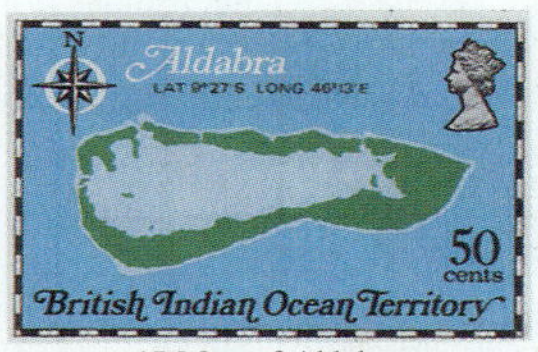

15 Map of Aldabra

1975. 10th Anniv of Territory. Maps. Multicoloured.

81	50c. Type **15**	80	65
82	1r. Desroches	95	85
83	1r.50 Farquhar	1·10	1·00
84	2r. Diego Garcia	1·25	1·25
MS85	147 × 147 mm. Nos. 81/4	7·00	14·00

16 "Utetheisa pulchella" (moth)

1976. Wildlife (4th series). Multicoloured.

86	65c. Type **16**	60	1·10
87	1r.20 "Dysdercus fasciatus" (bug)	75	1·25
88	1r.50 "Sphex torridus" (wasp)	80	1·40
89	2r. "Oryctes rhinoceros" (beetle)	85	1·40

17 White-tailed Tropic Bird

19 Territory Flag

18 1974 Wildlife 1r.50 Stamp

1990. Birds. Multicoloured.

90	15p. Type **17**	1·10	2·00
91	20p. Madagascar turtle dove ("Turtle Dove")	1·25	2·00
92	24p. Great frigate bird ("Greater Frigate")	1·40	2·00
93	30p. Green-backed heron ("Little Green Heron")	1·50	2·25
94	34p. Great sand plover ("Greater Sand Plover")	1·60	2·25
95	41p. Crab plover	1·75	2·50
96	45p. Crested tern	3·50	2·50
97	54p. Lesser crested tern	2·25	2·75

98 62p. White tern ("Fairy Tern") . . . . 2·25 2·75
99 71p. Red-footed booby . . . 2·25 3·00
100 80p. Common mynah ("Indian Mynah") . . . . 2·50 3·25
101 £1 Madagascar red fody ("Madagascar Fody") . . 3·25 3·50

1990. "Stamp World London 90" International Stamp Exhibition. Multicoloured.
102 15p. Type **18** . . . . 4·75 3·25
103 20p. 1976 Wildlife 2r. stamp 5·00 3·50
104 34p. 1975 Diego Garcia map 2r. stamp . . . . 8·50 5·50
105 54p. 1969 "Nordvaer" 1r. stamp . . . . 9·50 7·50

1990. 90th Birthday of Queen Elizabeth the Queen Mother. As T **34** of Ascension.
106 24p. multicoloured . . . . . 3·50 3·50
107 £1 black and ochre . . . . . 6·50 6·50
DESIGNS—21 × 36 mm: Lady Elizabeth Bowes-Lyon, 1923. 29 × 37 mm: £1 Queen Elizabeth and her daughters, 1940.

1990. 25th Anniv of British Indian Ocean Territory. Multicoloured.
108 20p. Type **19** . . . . 4·00 4·50
109 24p. Coat of arms . . . . . . 4·00 4·50
MS110 63 × 99 mm. £1 map of Chagos Archipelago . . . . . 9·50 12·00

20 Postman emptying Pillar Box

1991. British Indian Ocean Territory Administration. Multicoloured.
111 20p. Type **20** . . . . 1·50 2·50
112 24p. Commissioner inspecting guard of Royal Marines . . 1·75 2·50
113 34p. Policeman outside station . . . . 3·50 4·50
114 54p. Customs officers boarding yacht . . . . . 4·25 6·00

21 "Experiment" (E.I.C. survey brig), 1786

1991. Visiting Ships. Multicoloured.
115 20p. Type **21** . . . . 2·00 3·00
116 24p. "Pickering" (American brig), 1819 . . . . 2·25 3·25
117 34p. "Emden" (German cruiser), 1914 . . . . . . 3·00 4·25
118 54p. H.M.S. "Edinburgh" (destroyer), 1988 . . . . 3·75 5·50

1992. 40th Anniv of Queen Elizabeth II's Accession. As T **143** of Ascension. Multicoloured.
119 15p. Catholic chapel, Diego Garcia . . . . 1·25 1·25
120 20p. Planter's house, Diego Garcia . . . . 1·40 1·40
121 24p. Railway tracks on wharf, Diego Garcia . . . 3·00 2·00
122 34p. Three portraits of Queen Elizabeth . . . . 2·50 2·25
123 54p. Queen Elizabeth II . . . 2·50 2·50

22 R.A.F. Consolidated PBY-5 Catalina (flying boat)

1992. Visiting Aircraft. Multicoloured.
124 20p. Type **22** . . . . 1·50 2·50
125 24p. R.A.F. Hawker Siddeley Nimrod M.R.2 (maritime reconnaissance aircraft) . . 1·75 2·50
126 34p. Lockheed P-3 Orion (transport aircraft) . . . . 2·50 3·25
127 54p. U.S.A.A.F. Boeing B-52 Stratofortress (heavy bomber) . . . . 3·00 4·50

23 "The Mystical Marriage of St. Catherine" (Correggio)

1992. Christmas. Religious Paintings. Mult.
128 5p. Type **23** 70 80
129 24p. "Madonna" (anon) . . 1·25 1·60
130 34p. "Madonna" (anon) (different) . . . . 1·40 2·25
131 54p. "The Birth of Jesus" (Kaspar Jele) . . . . . . 1·75 3·50

24 Coconut Crab and Rock

1993. Endangered Species. Coconut Crab. Mult.
132 10p. Type **24** . . . . 1·25 1·25
133 10p. Crab on beach . . . . 1·25 1·25
134 10p. Two crabs . . . . . . 1·25 1·25
135 15p. Crab climbing coconut tree . . . . 1·50 1·50

1993. 75th Anniv of Royal Air Force. As T **149** of Ascension. Multicoloured.
136 20p. Vickers Virginia Mk X 1·00 1·50
137 24p. Bristol Bulldog IIA . . 1·10 1·50
138 34p. Short S.25 Sunderland Mk III . . . . 1·25 2·00
139 54p. Bristol Blenheim Mk IV 2·00 3·25
MS140 110 × 77 mm. 20p. Douglas DC-3 Dakota; 20p. Gloster G.41 Javelin; 20p. Blackburn Beverley C1; 20p. Vickers VC-10 . . . 7·50 8·00

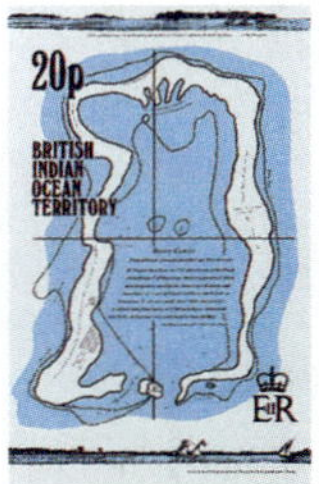

25 "Stachytarpheta urticifolia" **26** Forrest's Map of Diego Garcia, 1778

1993. Christmas. Flowers. Multicoloured.
141 20p. Type **25** . . . . 80 1·50
142 24p. "Ipomea pes-caprae" . . 80 1·50
143 34p. "Sida pusilla" . . . . . 1·10 2·25
144 54p. "Catharanthus roseus" 1·75 3·50

1994. "Hong Kong '94" International Stamp Exhibition. Nos. 92 and 101 optd **HONG KONG '94** and emblem.
145 24p. Great frigate bird ("Greater Frigate") . . . . 4·00 3·00
146 £1 Madagascar red fody ("Madagascar Fody") . . 6·00 8·00

1994. 18th-century Maps. Each black and blue.
147 20p. Type **26** . . . . 70 1·50
148 24p. Blair's plan of Diego Garcia harbour, 1786–87 75 1·60
149 34p. Blair's chart of Chagos Archipelago, 1786–87 . . 80 1·75
150 44p. Plan of part of Diego Garcia, 1774 . . . . . . 90 1·90
151 54p. Fontaine's plan of Diego Garcia, 1770 . . . . . . 1·10 2·00

27 "Junonia villida"

1994. Butterflies. Multicoloured.
152 24p. Type **27** . . . . 1·50 1·75
153 30p. "Petrelaea dana" . . . 1·75 2·50
154 56p. "Hypolimnas misippus" 2·75 4·00

28 Short-tailed Nurse Sharks

1994. Sharks. Multicoloured.
155 15p. Type **28** . . . . 3·25 3·00
156 20p. Silver-tipped sharks . . 3·25 3·00
157 24p. Black-finned reef shark 3·25 3·00
158 30p. Oceanic white-tipped sharks . . . . 3·75 3·50
159 35p. Black-tipped shark . . . 4·00 3·75
160 41p. Smooth hammerhead . . 4·00 3·75
161 46p. Sickle-finned lemon shark . . . . 4·00 3·75
162 55p. White-tipped reef shark 4·75 4·25
163 65p. Tiger sharks . . . . . 4·75 4·25
164 74p. Indian sand tiger . . . 5·00 4·50
165 80p. Great hammerhead . . . 5·00 4·50
166 £1 Great white shark . . . . 5·50 5·00

1995. 50th Anniv of End of Second World War. As T **161** of Ascension. Multicoloured.
167 20p. Military cemetery . . . 1·50 1·75
168 24p. Rusty 6-inch naval gun at Cannon Point . . . . . 1·75 1·75
169 30p. Short S.25 Sunderland flying boat . . . . 2·00 2·25
170 56p. H.M.I.S. "Clive" (sloop) 3·00 3·75
MS171 75 × 85 mm. £1 Reverse of 1939–45 War Medal (vert) . . 2·50 3·00

29 Dolphin (fish)

1995. Gamefish. Multicoloured.
172 20p. Type **29** . . . . 1·50 1·60
173 24p. Sailfish . . . . 1·60 1·60
174 30p. Wahoo . . . . 2·25 2·50
175 56p. Striped marlin . . . . . 3·25 3·75

30 "Terebra crenulata"

1996. Sea Shells. Multicoloured.
176 20p. Type **30** . . . . 1·25 1·50
177 24p. "Bursa bufonia" . . . . 1·25 1·50
178 30p. "Nassarius papillosus" 1·75 2·00
179 56p. "Lopha cristagalli" . . . 3·00 3·25

1996. 70th Birthday of Queen Elizabeth II. As T **165** of Ascension, each incorporating a different photograph of the Queen. Multicoloured.
180 20p. View of lagoon from south . . . . 75 1·00
181 24p. Manager's House, Peros Banhos . . . . 80 1·00
182 30p. Wireless hut, Peros Banhos . . . . 1·00 1·40
183 56p. Sunset . . . . 1·50 2·00
MS184 64 × 66 mm. £1 Queen Elizabeth II . . . . 2·75 3·75

31 Loggerhead Turtle

1996. Turtles. Multicoloured.
185 20p. Type **31** . . . . 1·00 1·25
186 24p. Leatherback turtle . . . 1·10 1·25
187 30p. Hawksbill turtle . . . . 1·40 1·60
188 56p. Green turtle . . . . . . 2·00 2·50

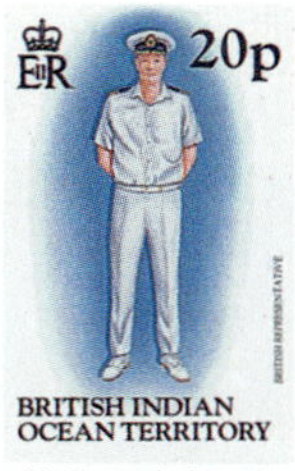

32 Commissioner's Representative (naval officer)

1996. Uniforms. Multicoloured.
189 20p. Type **32** . . . . 1·00 1·10
190 24p. Royal Marine officer . . 1·10 1·10
191 30p. Royal Marine in battle-dress . . . . 1·50 1·75
192 56p. Police officers . . . . . 2·25 2·75

1997. "HONG KONG '97" International Stamp Exhibition. Sheet 130 × 90 mm, containing design as No. 163. Multicoloured.
MS193 65p. Tiger sharks . . . . 2·00 2·75

1997. Return of Hong Kong to China. Sheet 130 × 90 mm, containing design as No. 164, but with "1997" imprint date.
MS194 74p. Indian sand tiger . . 2·75 3·50

1997. Golden Wedding of Queen Elizabeth and Prince Philip. As T **173** of Ascension. Mult.
195 20p. Queen Elizabeth at Bristol, 1994 . . . . 1·75 1·90
196 20p. Prince Philip competing in Royal Windsor Horse Show, 1996 . . . . 1·75 1·90
197 24p. Queen Elizabeth in phaeton, Trooping the Colour, 1987 . . . . . . 1·75 1·90
198 24p. Prince Philip . . . . . 1·75 1·90
199 30p. Queen Elizabeth and Prince Philip with Land Rover . . . . 1·75 1·90
200 30p. Queen Elizabeth at Balmoral . . . . 1·75 1·90
MS201 110 × 71 mm. £1.50, Queen Elizabeth and Prince Philip in landau (horiz) . . . . 10·00 10·00
Nos. 195/6, 197/8 and 199/20 respectively were printed together, se-tenant, with the backgrounds forming a compsite design.

33 H.M.S. "Richmond" (frigate) and H.M.S. "Beaver" (frigate)

1997. Exercise Ocean Wave. Multicoloured.
202 24p. Type **33** . . . . 1·50 1·60
203 24p. H.M.S. "Illustrious" (aircraft carrier) launching aircraft . . . . 1·50 1·60
204 24p. H.M.S. "Beaver" . . . 1·50 1·60
205 24p. Royal Yacht "Britannia", R.F.A. "Sir Percival" and H.M.S. "Beaver" . . . . 1·50 1·60
206 24p. Royal Yacht "Britannia" . . . . 1·50 1·60
207 24p. H.M.S. "Richmond", H.M.S. "Beaver" and H.M.S. "Gloucester" (destroyer) . . . . 1·50 1·60
208 24p. H.M.S. "Richmond" . . 1·50 1·60
209 24p. Aerial view of H.M.S. "Illustrious" . . . . . . 1·50 1·60
210 24p. H.M.S. "Gloucester" (wrongly inscr "Sheffield") 1·50 1·60
211 24p. H.M.S. "Trenchant" (submarine) and R.F.A. "Diligence" . . . . 1·50 1·60
212 24p. R.F.A. "Fort George" replenishing H.M.S. "Illustrious" and H.M.S. "Gloucester" . . . . 1·50 1·60
213 24p. Aerial view of H.M.S. "Richmond", H.M.S. "Beaver" and H.M.S. "Gloucester" . . . . . . 1·50 1·60

1998. Diana, Princess of Wales Commemoration. Sheet 145 × 70 mm, containing vert designs as T **177** of Ascension. Multicoloured.
MS214 26p. Wearing patterned jacket, 1993; 26p. Wearing heart-shaped earrings, 1988; 34p. Wearing cream jacket, 1993; 60p. Wearing blue blouse, 1982 (sold at £1.46 + 20p. charity premium) 3·25 4·00

1998. 80th Anniv of the Royal Air Force. As T **178** of Ascension. Multicoloured.
215 26p. Blackburn Iris . . . . . 1·00 1·10
216 34p. Gloster Gamecock . . . 1·25 1·40
217 60p. North American Sabre F.4 . . . . 2·25 2·50
218 80p. Avro Lincoln . . . . . 2·75 3·00
MS219 110 × 77 mm. 34p. Sopwith Baby (seaplane); 34p. Martinsyde Elephant; 34p. De Havilland Tiger Moth; 34p. North American Mustang III . . . . 6·00 7·00

34 Bryde's Whale

1998. International Year of the Ocean. Multicoloured.
220 26p. Type **34** . . . . 2·75 2·50
221 26p. Striped dolphin . . . . 2·75 2·50
222 34p. Pilot whale . . . . . . 2·75 2·50
223 34p. Spinner dolphin . . . . 2·75 2·50

35 "Westminster" (East Indiaman), 1837

1999. Ships. Multicoloured.
224 2p. Type **35** 40 75
225 15p. "Sao Cristovao" (Spanish galleon), 1589 . . 1·25 1·25
226 20p. "Sea Witch" (U.S. clipper), 1849 . . . . . . 1·25 1·25
227 26p. H.M.S. "Royal George" (ship of the line), 1778 . . 1·50 1·25

228	34p. "Cutty Sark" (clipper), 1883	2·00	1·50
229	60p. "Mentor" (East Indiaman), 1789	2·50	2·75
230	80p. H.M.S. "Trinculo" (brig), 1809	2·75	3·00
231	£1 "Enterprise" (paddle-steamer), 1825	3·00	3·50
232	£1.15 "Confiance" (French privateer), 1800	3·25	3·75
233	£2 "Kent" (East Indiaman), 1820	5·50	6·50

36 Cutty Sark (clipper)

1999. "Australia '99" World Stamp Exhibition, Melbourne. Sheet 150×75 mm, containing T **36** and similar horiz design. Multicoloured.

MS234	60p. Type **36**; 60p. "Thermopylae" (clipper)	4·75	6·00

37 Field Vole (Colin Sargent)

2000. "The Stamp Show 2000", International Stamp Exhibition, London. "Shoot a Stamp" Competition Winners. Sheet 150×100 mm, containing T **37** and similar vert designs. Multicoloured.

MS235	26p. Type **37**; 34p. Atlantic puffin (P. J. Royal); 55p. Red fox (Jim Wilson); £1 European robin ("Robin") (Harry Smith)	7·00	8·50

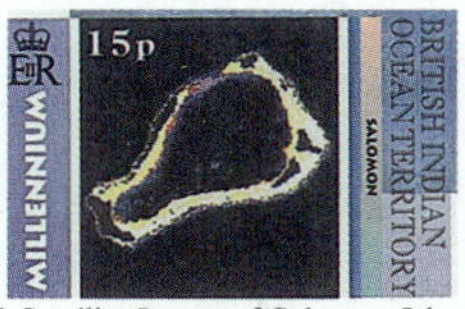

38 Satellite Image of Salomon Island

2000. New Millennium. Satellite Images of Islands. Multicoloured.

236	15p. Type **38**	1·60	1·40
237	20p. Egmont	1·75	1·50
238	60p. Blenheim Reef	2·75	2·75
239	80p. Diego Garcia	3·00	3·00

39 Queen Elizabeth the Queen Mother

40 *Delonix regia*

2000. Queen Elizabeth the Queen Mother's 100th Birthday. Multicoloured.

240	26p. Type **39**	1·40	1·40
241	34p. Wearing green hat and outfit	1·40	1·40
MS242	113×88 mm. 55p. In blue hat and outfit	4·75	5·50

2000. Christmas Flowers. Multicoloured.

243	26p. Type **40**	1·75	1·50
244	34p. *Barringtonia asiatica*	2·00	1·75
245	60p. *Zephyranthes rosea*	3·50	3·50

2000. "HONG KONG 2001" Stamp Exhibition. Sheet 150×90 mm, containing T **41** and similar design showing butterfly. Multicoloured.

MS246	26p. Type **41**; 34p. "Junonia villida chagoensis"	3·25	3·75

42 H.M.S. *Turbulent*

2001. Centenary of Royal Navy Submarine Service. Multicoloured (except Nos. 248 and 250).

247	26p. Type **42**	1·60	1·75
248	26p. H.M.S. *Churchill* (grey and black)	1·60	1·75
249	34p. H.M.S. *Resolution*	1·75	2·00
250	34p. H.M.S. *Vanguard*	1·75	2·00
251	60p. H.M.S. *Otter* (73×27 mm)	2·25	2·50
252	60p. H.M.S. *Oberon* (73×27 mm) (grey and black)	2·25	2·50

43 Cushion Star

2001. Endangered Species. Seastars. Multicoloured.

253	15p. Type **43**	1·50	1·25
254	26p. Azure sea star	2·00	1·50
255	34p. Crown-of-Thorns	2·25	1·75
256	56p. Banded bubble star	3·25	3·50

44 *Scadoxus multiflora*

2001. Plants (1st series). Flowers. Multicoloured.

257	26p. Type **44**	1·75	1·75
258	34p. *Striga asiatica*	1·75	1·75
MS259	173×78 mm. Nos. 257/8 and 10p. "Catharanthus roseus" (horiz); 60p. "Argusia argentea" (horiz); 70p. "Euphorbia cyathophora" (horiz)	5·50	6·50

In No. **MS**259 the 60p. is inscribed "argentia" in error.

45 Crab Plovers on Beach

2001. Birdlife World Bird Festival. Crab Plovers. Sheet 175×80 mm, containing T **45** and similar multicoloured designs.

MS260	50p. Type **45**; 50p. Crab plover catching crab (vert); 50p. Head of crab plover (vert); 50p. Crab plovers in flight; 50p. Crab plover standing on one leg	6·50	7·00

2002. Golden Jubilee. As T **200** of Ascension.

261	10p. brown, blue and gold	1·25	1·25
262	25p. multicoloured	1·75	1·50
263	35p. black, blue and gold	2·00	1·75
264	55p. multicoloured	2·75	3·00
MS265	162×95 mm. Nos. 261/4 and 75p. multicoloured	6·50	7·00

DESIGNS—HORIZ: 10p. Princess Elizabeth in pantomime, Windsor, 1943; 25p. Queen Elizabeth in floral hat, 1967; 35p. Princess Elizabeth and Prince Philip on their engagement, 1947; 55p. Queen Elizabeth in evening dress. VERT (38×51 mm)—75p. Queen Elizabeth after Annigoni.

Designs as Nos. 261/4 in No. **MS**265 omit the gold frame around each stamp and the "Golden Jubilee 1952–2002" inscription.

46 Adult Red-footed Booby

2002. Birdlife International. Red-footed Booby. Sheet 175×80 mm, containing T **46** and similar multicoloured designs.

MS266	50p. Type **46**; 50p. Head of dark morph red-footed booby; 50p. Adult bird in flight (vert); 50p. Dark morph on nest (vert); 50p. Fledgling on nest	9·00	9·50

2002. Queen Elizabeth the Queen Mother Commemoration. As T **202** of Ascension.

267	26p. brown, gold and purple	1·50	1·25
268	£1 multicoloured	3·00	3·25
MS269	145×70 mm. £1 black and gold; £1 multicoloured	8·00	9·00

DESIGNS: 26p. Lady Elizabeth Bowes-Lyon, 1921; £1 (No. 268) Queen Mother, 1986; £1 brownish black and gold (No. **MS**269) Queen Elizabeth at garden party, 1951; £1 multicoloured (No. **MS**269) Queen Mother at Cheltenham Races, 1994.

Designs in No. **MS**269 omit the "1900–2002" inscription and the coloured frame.

47 Microgoby

2002. 10th Anniv of Friends of Chagos (conservation association). Reef Fish. Mult.

270	2p. Type **47**	40	60
271	15p. Angel fish	85	85
272	26p. Surgeonfish	1·25	1·25
273	34p. Trunkfish	1·50	1·50
274	58p. Soldierfish	2·50	3·00
275	£1 Chagos anemonefish	4·00	4·50

48 *Halgerda tesselata*

2003. Sea Slugs. Multicoloured.

276	2p. Type **48**	40	60
277	15p. *Notodoris minor*	85	85
278	26p. *Nembrotha lineolata*	1·25	1·25
279	50p. *Chromodoris quadricolor*	2·00	2·25
280	76p. *Glossodoris cincta*	3·00	3·50
281	£1.10 *Chromodoris cf leopardus*	3·75	4·25

2003. 50th Anniv of Coronation. As T **206** of Ascension. Multicoloured.

282	£1 Queen Elizabeth II wearing Imperial State Crown in Coronation Coach	4·00	4·00
283	£2 Queen with members of Royal Family in Coronation robes	7·00	8·00
MS284	95×115 mm. £1 As No. 282; £2 As No. 283	10·00	11·00

Nos. 282/3 have red frame; stamps from **MS**284 have no frame and country name in mauve panel.

2003. As T **207** of Ascension.

285	£2.50 black, pink and red	7·00	7·50

2003. 21st Birthday of Prince William of Wales. As T **208** of Ascension. Multicoloured.

286	50p. Prince William at Cirencester Polo Club	2·25	2·25
287	£1 With Prince Charles on skiing holiday and at Cirencester Polo Club	3·75	4·00

2003. Centenary of Powered Flight. As Type **209** of Ascension. Multicoloured.

288	34p. Avro Type 683 Lancaster	1·50	1·50
289	34p. De Havilland D.H.98 Mosquito	1·50	1·50
290	58p. Hawker Hurricane	2·00	2·00
291	58p. Supermarine Spitfire	2·00	2·00
292	76p. Vickers-Armstrong Wellington	2·50	2·50
293	76p. Lockheed C-130 Hercules	2·50	2·50
MS294	233×85 mm. 26p. Boeing E-3A Sentry AWACS; 26p. Boeing B-17 Flying Fortress; 26p. Lockheed P-3 Orion; 26p. Consolidated B-24 Liberator; 26p. Lockheed C-141 StarLifter; 26p. Supermarine Walrus; 26p. Short S.25 Sunderland (flying boat); 26p. Supermarine Stranraer; 26p. PBY Catalina; 26p. Supermarine Sea Otter	9·00	10·00

49 *Pacific Marlin* (fisheries patrol ship)

2004. Fisheries Patrol. Multicoloured.

MS295	150×110 mm. 34p. Type **49**; 34p. Marlin; 58p. Skipjack tuna; 58p. Yellowfin tuna; 76p. Swordfish; 76p. Bigeye tuna	11·00	11·00

50 Madagascar Red Fody ("Madagascar Fody")

2004. Birds. Multicoloured.

296	2p. Type **50**	20	30
297	14p. Zebra dove ("Barred Ground Dove")	50	50
298	20p. Common mynah ("Indian Mynah")	70	70
299	26p. Cattle egret	80	70
300	34p. White tern ("Fairy Tern")	1·00	90
301	58p. Blue-faced booby ("Masked Booby")	1·75	1·75
302	76p. Great frigate bird	2·25	2·25
303	80p. White-tailed tropic bird	2·25	2·25
304	£1.10 Green-backed heron ("Little Green Heron")	3·25	3·50
305	£1.34 Pacific golden plover	4·00	4·25
306	£1.48 Garganey ("Garganey Teal")	4·50	4·75
307	£2.50 Bar-tailed godwit	7·00	7·50

51 Coconut Crab

2004. Crabs. Multicoloured.

308	26p. Type **51**	90	80
309	34p. Land crab	1·25	1·00
310	76p. Rock crab	2·50	2·75
311	£1.10 Ghost crab	3·75	4·00

52 Two Hawksbill Turtle Babies

2005. Turtles. Multicoloured.

312	26p. Type **52**	1·25	1·25
313	26p. Baby Green turtle	1·25	1·25
314	34p. Adult Hawksbill turtle	1·60	1·60
315	34p. Adult Green turtle	1·60	1·60
316	76p. Hawksbill turtle swimming	3·00	3·25
317	£1.10 Green turtle swimming	4·25	4·50
MS318	90×63 mm. £1.70 As No. 317	6·00	7·00

No. **MS**318 commemorates the Turtle Cove Clean-up operation sponsored by Cable and Wireless.

2005. Bicentenary of Battle of Trafalgar (1st issue). As T **216** of Ascension. Multicoloured.

319	26p. Tower Sea Service Pistol, 1796	1·10	1·10
320	26p. HMS *Phoebe*	1·10	1·10
321	34p. Boatswain RN, 1805	1·50	1·50
322	34p. HMS *Harrier*	1·50	1·50
323	76p. Portrait of Admiral Nelson	3·00	3·00
324	76p. HMS *Victory* (horiz)	3·00	3·00
MS325	120×79 mm. £1.10 HMS *Minotaur*; £1.10 HMS *Spartiate*	6·50	7·00

No. 324 contains traces of powdered wood from HMS *Victory*.

See also Nos. 344/6.

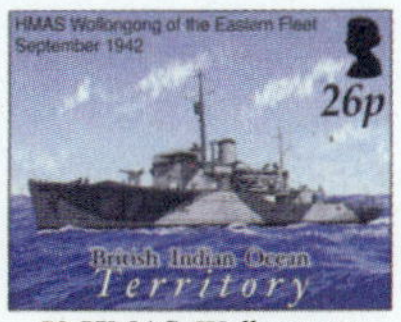

53 HMAS *Wollongong*, September 1942

2005. 60th Anniv of the End of World War II. "Route to Victory". As T **53**. Multicoloured.

326	26p. Type **53**	90	90
327	26p. *Ondina* (Dutch tanker) and HMS *Bengal* attacked by Japanese surface raiders, 11 November 1942	90	90
328	26p. HMS *Pathfinder* (arrived at Diego Garcia, 4 April 1944)	90	90
329	26p. HMS *Lossie* (rescued survivors from Australian freighter *Nellore*, 29 June 1944)	90	90
330	26p. US Liberty Ship *Jean Nicolet* (sunk by Japanese, 2 July 1944)	90	90
331	34p. General Douglas MacArthur and landing party wading ashore	1·25	1·25
332	34p. General Bernard Montgomery and tanks in North African desert	1·25	1·25
333	34p. General George Patton and tanks	1·25	1·25
334	34p. Winston Churchill and St. Paul's Cathedral	1·25	1·25
335	34p. US Pres. Franklin Roosevelt and steelworks	1·25	1·25

54 Blacktip Reef Shark

2005. Sharks and Rays. Multicoloured.

336	26p. Type **54**	90	90
337	26p. Grey reef shark	90	90
338	34p. Silvertip shark	1·25	1·25
339	34p. Tawny nurse shark	1·25	1·25
340	34p. Spotted eagle ray	1·25	1·25
341	34p. Manta ray	1·25	1·25
342	76p. Porcupine ray	2·50	2·75
343	£2 Feathertail stingray	6·00	6·50

2005. Bicentenary of the Battle of Trafalgar (2nd issue). As T **220** of Ascension. Multicoloured.

344	26p. HMS *Victory*	1·00	1·00
345	34p. Ships engaged in battle (horiz)	1·50	1·50
346	£2 Admiral Lord Nelson	6·50	6·50

55 Crab on Beach

2005. 40th Anniv of British Indian Ocean Territory. T **55** and similar vert designs. Multicoloured.

MS347 205 × 129 mm. 34p. Type **55**; 34p. Two hermit crabs on beach; 34p. Blue-faced boobies at nest; 34p. Outline map of Indian Ocean and lesser frigate bird; 34p. Pair of imperial angelfish; 34p. Pair of racoon butterflyfish; 34p. Moorish idol (fish); 34p. Outline map of British Indian Ocean Territory and turtle . . . 11·00 12·00

The stamps within No. **MS**347 form a composite background design showing a beach and coral reef.

2006. 80th Birthday of Queen Elizabeth II. As T **223** of Ascension. Multicoloured.

348	26p. Princess Elizabeth	1·25	1·25
349	34p. Queen Elizabeth II, c. 1952	1·50	1·50
350	76p. Wearing tiara	2·75	3·00
351	£1.10 Wearing headscarf	3·50	3·75
MS352	144 × 75 mm. £1 As No. 349; £1 As No. 350	7·00	7·50

56 Dusky Angelfish

2006. Marine Life (1st series). Angelfish. Sheet 205 × 129 mm containing T **56** and similar horiz designs. Multicoloured.

MS353 26p. Type **56**; 26p. Two-spined angelfish; 26p. Bicolour angelfish; 34p. Orangeback angelfish; 34p. Emperor angelfish; £2 Threespot angelfish . . . 11·00 12·00

The stamps and margins of No. **MS**353 form a composite design showing a coral reef.

See also Nos. **MS**354, **MS**356 and **MS**372.

2006. Marine Life (2nd series). Butterflyfish. Sheet 205 × 129 mm containing horiz designs as T **56**. Multicoloured.

MS354 26p. Melon butterflyfish; 26p. Raccoon butterflyfish; 26p. Scrawled butterflyfish; 34p. Longnose butterflyfish; 34p. Threadfin butterflyfish; £2 Masked bannerfish . . . 11·00 12·00

The stamps and margins of No. **MS**354 form a composite design showing a coral reef.

57 Great Frigatebird

2006. BirdLife International. Barton Point Nature Reserve. Sheet 170 × 85 mm containing T **57** and similar horiz designs. Multicoloured.

MS355 26p. Type **57**; 26p. Black-naped tern; 26p. Yellow-billed tropicbird; 26p. White tern; 26p. Brown noddy; £2 Red-footed booby . . . 10·50 11·50

The stamps within No. **MS**355 form a composite design.

2007. Marine Life (3rd series). Parrotfish. Sheet 205 × 129 mm containing horiz designs as T **56**. Multicoloured.

MS356 54p. Common parrotfish; 54p. Daisy parrotfish; 54p. Bicolour parrotfish; 54p. Bridled parrotfish; 90p. Indian Ocean steephead parrotfish; 90p. Ember parrotfish . . . 8·50 9·50

The stamps and margins of No. **MS**356 form a composite design showing a coral reef.

58 Princess Elizabeth and Lt. Philip Mountbatten, c. 1947

2007. Diamond Wedding of Queen Elizabeth II and Duke of Edinburgh. Multicoloured.

357	54p. Type **58**	1·60	1·60
358	54p. Wedding procession and crowds, 1949	1·60	1·60
359	90p. Princess Elizabeth and Lt. Philip Mountbatten arm in arm, c. 1947	3·00	3·00
360	90p. Wedding ceremony, 1949	3·00	3·00
MS361	125 × 85 mm. £2.14 Princess Elizabeth and Lt. Philip Mountbatten, c. 1947 (42 × 56 mm)	7·00	7·00

59 Charles Darwin and Beach with Tropic Bird, Terns and Turtle

2007. 125th Death Anniv of Charles Darwin. Multicoloured.

362	54p. Type **59**	1·60	1·60
363	54p. HMS *Beagle*	1·60	1·60
364	90p. Turtles	3·00	3·00
365	90p. Coral reef	3·00	3·00

60 Pomarine Skua pursuing Tropic Bird

2007. BirdLife International. Pomarine Skua (*Stercorarius pomarinus*). Multicoloured.

366	54p. Type **60**	1·75	1·75
367	54p. Pomarine skua pursuing booby	1·75	1·75
368	54p. Pair of pomarine skuas in flight	1·75	1·75
369	54p. Pair of pomarine skuas on beach	1·75	1·75
370	90p. Pomarine skua pursuing terns	3·00	3·00
371	90p. Pomarine skua on sea	3·00	3·00

2008. Marine Life (4th series). Damselfish. Sheet 205 × 129 mm containing horiz designs as T **56**. Multicoloured.

MS372 54p. *Chrysiptera unimaculata* (onespot demoiselle); 54p. *Abudefduf septemfasciatus* (banded sergeant); 54p. *Plectroglyphidodon johnstonianus* (Johnston Island damsel); 54p. *Amphiprion chagosensis* (Chagos anemonefish); 90p. *Chromis atripectoralis* (black-axil chromis); 90p. *Pomacentrus caeruleus* (caerulean damsel) . . . 9·50 9·50

The stamps and margins of No. **MS**372 form a composite design showing a coral reef.

PARCEL POST STAMPS

2002. 10th Anniv of Friends of Chagos (conservation association). Reef Fish. Sheet 115 × 95 mm, containing horiz design as T **47**. Multicoloured.

PMS1 £1.90 Parrotfish . . . 6·00 6·50

BRITISH LEVANT — Pt. 1

Stamps used at British post offices in the Turkish Empire. These offices closed in 1914. The stamps were again in use after 1918, during the British Occupation of Turkey.

Stamps of Great Britain surcharged or overprinted

A. BRITISH POST OFFICES IN TURKISH EMPIRE

I. TURKISH CURRENCY

40 paras = 1 piastre.

1885. Queen Victoria stamps surch in **PARAS** or **PIASTRES**.

7	**71**	40pa. on ½d. red	£425	£100
1	**64**	40pa. on 2½d. lilac	£110	1·25
4	**74**	40pa. on 2½d. purple on blue	6·50	10
2	**62**	80pa. on 5d. green	£200	9·50
5	**78**	80pa. on 5d. purple & blue	15·00	30
6	**81**	4pi. on 10d. purple and red	42·00	8·00
3a	**58**	12pi. on 2s.6d. lilac	48·00	24·00

1902. King Edward VII stamps surch in **PARAS** or **PIASTRES**.

29	–	30pa. on 1½d. purple & grn	6·50	55
8	**83**	40pa. on 2½d. blue	17·00	10
9	–	80pa. on 5d. purple and blue	11·00	2·50
13	**83**	1pi. on 2½d. blue	18·00	10
30	–	2pi. on 5d. purple and blue	16·00	2·25
10	–	4pi. on 10d. purple and red	15·00	4·00
21	–	5pi. on 1s. green and red	4·25	12·00
11	–	12pi. on 2s.6d. purple	35·00	35·00
12	–	24pi. on 5s. red	32·00	40·00

1906. Surch **1 Piastre**.

15	–	1pi. on 2d. green and red	£1300	£600

1909. King Edward VII stamps surch in **PIASTRE PARAS**.

17	–	1pi. 10pa. on 3d. pur on yell	12·00	40·00
18	–	1pi. 30pa. on 4d. grn & brn	5·00	17·00
19	–	1pi. 30pa. on 4d. orange	17·00	65·00
20	**83**	2pi. 20pa. on 6d. purple	23·00	65·00

1910. King Edward VII stamps surch in **PIASTRES**.

22	–	1¼pi. on 3d. purple on yellow	50	1·00
23	–	1¾pi. on 4d. orange	50	60
24	**83**	2½pi. on 6d. purple	1·40	65

1913. King George V stamps surch.

41	**105**	30pa. on ½d. green	75	13·00
35		30pa. on 1½d. brown	3·50	14·00
36a	**104**	1pi. on 2½d. blue	9·00	15
37	**106**	1¼pi. on 3d. violet	5·00	4·25
42	**104**	1¼pi. on 1d. red	1·50	1·25
38	**106**	1¾pi. on 4d. grey-green	3·00	7·50
43	**104**	3¾pi. on 2½d. blue	1·25	25
39	**108**	4pi. on 10d. blue	8·00	23·00
44	**106**	4½pi. on 3d. violet	2·00	3·75
40	**108**	5pi. on 1s. brown	40·00	60·00
45	**107**	7½pi. on 5d. brown	50	10
46	**108**	15pi. on 10d. blue	70	15
47		18¾pi. on 1s. brown	4·25	4·25
48	**109**	45pi. on 2s.6d. brown	20·00	45·00
49		90pi. on 5s. red	25·00	30·00
50		180pi. on 10s. blue	45·00	40·00

II. BRITISH CURRENCY

1905. King Edward VII stamps optd **LEVANT**.

L 1	**83**	½d. green	8·50	15
L 2		1d. red	11·00	15
L 3	–	1½d. purple and green	6·00	2·00
L 4a	–	2d. green and red	3·50	7·50
L 5	**83**	2½d. blue	8·50	20·00
L 6	–	3d. purple and yellow	6·00	12·00
L 7	–	4d. green and brown	9·50	50·00
L 8	–	5d. purple and blue	16·00	32·00
L 9	**83**	6d. purple	12·00	25·00
L10		1s. green and red	40·00	50·00

1911. King George V stamps optd **LEVANT**.

L12	**98**	½d. green	2·25	2·00
L14	**101**	½d. green	1·00	20
L16	**105**	½d. green	1·00	2·00
L13	**99**	1d. red	50	7·00
L15	**102**	1d. red	1·50	1·60
L17	**104**	1d. red	30	6·00
L18	**106**	2d. orange	2·25	32·00
L19		3d. violet	7·50	10·00
L20		4d. green	5·00	15·00
L21	**107**	5d. brown	12·00	28·00
L22a		6d. purple	26·00	8·50
L23	**108**	1s. brown	14·00	8·50
L24	**109**	2s.6d. brown	38·00	90·00

B. BRITISH FIELD OFFICE IN SALONICA

1916. King George V stamps of Great Britain optd **Levant**.

S1	**105**	½d. green	55·00	£250
S2	**104**	1d. red	55·00	£250
S3	**106**	2d. orange	£160	£375
S4		3d. violet	£130	£375
S5		4d. green	£160	£375
S6	**107**	6d. purple	90·00	£325
S7	**108**	9d. black	£325	£600
S8		1s. brown	£275	£500

The above stamps were optd at Salonica during the war of 1914–18.

BRITISH OCCUPATION OF ITALIAN COLONIES — Pt. 1

Issues for use in Italian colonies occupied by British Forces. Middle East Forces overprints were used in Cyrenaica, Dodecanese Islands, Eritrea, Italian Somaliland and Tripolitania.

MIDDLE EAST FORCES

12 pence = 1 shilling;
20 shillings = 1 pound.

1942. Stamps of Great Britain optd **M.E.F.**

M11	**128**	1d. red	1·50	10
M12		2d. orange	1·50	1·25
M13		2½d. blue	50	10
M 4		3d. violet	80	30
M 5	**129**	5d. brown	80	30
M16		6d. purple	40	10
M17	**130**	9d. olive	85	10
M18		1s. brown	50	10
M19	**131**	2s.6d. green	7·00	1·00
M20		5s. red	18·00	17·00
M21		10s. blue (No. 478a)	29·00	10·00

PRICES. Our prices for Nos. M1/21 in used condition are for stamps with identifiable postmarks of the territories in which they were issued. These stamps were also used in the United Kingdom with official sanction, from the summer of 1950 onwards, and with U.K. postmarks are worth about 25 per cent less.

POSTAGE DUE STAMPS

1942. Postage Due stamps of Great Britain optd **M.E.F.**

MD1	**D 1**	½d. green	30	13·00
MD2		1d. red	30	1·75
MD3		2d. black	1·25	1·25
MD4		3d. violet	50	4·25
MD5		1s. blue	3·75	13·00

CYRENAICA

10 milliemes = 1 piastre;
100 piastres = 1 Egyptian pound.

24 Mounted Warrior

25 Mounted Warrior

1950.

136	**24**	1m. brown	3·00	5·50
137		2m. red	3·00	5·50
138		3m. yellow	3·00	5·50
139		4m. green	3·00	5·50
140		5m. grey	3·00	3·75
141		8m. orange	3·00	2·75
142		10m. violet	3·00	2·25
143		12m. red	3·00	2·25
144		20m. blue	3·00	2·25
145	**25**	50m. blue and brown	6·00	6·50
146		100m. red and black	14·00	9·00
147		200m. violet and blue	18·00	25·00
148		500m. yellow and green	48·00	65·00

POSTAGE DUE STAMPS

D 26

1950.

D149	**D 26**	2m. brown	48·00	£100
D150		4m. green	48·00	£100
D151		8m. red	48·00	£110
D152		10m. orange	48·00	£110
D153		20m. yellow	48·00	£120
D154		40m. blue	48·00	£160
D155		100m. black	48·00	£170

ERITREA

100 cents = 1 shilling.

BRITISH MILITARY ADMINISTRATION

1948. Stamps of Great Britain surch **B.M.A. ERITREA** and value in cents or shillings.

E 1	**128**	5c. on ½d. green	1·75	65
E 2		10c. on 1d. red	1·50	2·50
E 3		20c. on 2d. orange	1·50	2·25
E 4		25c. on 2½d. blue	1·25	60
E 5		30c. on 3d. violet	1·50	4·50
E 6	**129**	40c. on 5d. brown	1·50	4·25
E 7		50c. on 6d. purple	65	1·00
E 7a	**130**	65c. on 8d. red	7·00	2·00
E 8		75c. on 9d. olive	1·75	75
E 9		1s. on 1s. brown	1·50	50
E10	**131**	2s.50 on 2s.6d. green	8·50	10·00
E11		5s. on 5s. red	8·50	17·00
E12	–	10s. on 10s. blue (No. 478a)	22·00	22·00

BRITISH ADMINISTRATION

1950. Stamps of Great Britain surch **B.A. ERITREA** and value in cents or shillings.

E13	**128**	5c. on ½d. green	1·50	8·00
E26		5c. on ½d. orange	75	75
E14		10c. on 1d. red	40	3·00
E27		10c. on 1d. blue	75	75
E15		20c. on 2d. orange	50	80
E28		20c. on 2d. brown	75	30
E16		25c. on 2½d. blue	50	60
E29		25c. on 2½d. red	75	30
E17		30c. on 3d. violet	40	2·25
E18	**129**	40c. on 5d. brown	1·00	1·75
E19		50c. on 6d. purple	40	20
E20	**130**	65c. on 8d. red	3·25	1·50
E21		75c. on 9d. olive	60	25
E22		1s. on 1s. brown	40	15
E23	**131**	2s.50 on 2s.6d. green	7·00	4·75
E24		5s. on 5s. red	7·00	12·00
E25	–	10s. on 10s. blue (No. 478a)	60·00	55·00

1951. Nos. 509/11 of Great Britain surch **B.A. ERITREA** and value in cents and shillings.

E30	**147**	2s.50 on 2s.6d. green	12·00	24·00
E31	–	5s. on 5s. red	21·00	24·00
E32	–	10s. on 10s. blue	22·00	24·00

POSTAGE DUE STAMPS

1948. Postage Due stamps of Great Britain surch **B.M.A ERITREA** and new value in cents and shillings.

ED1	**D 1**	5c. on ½d. green	9·50	22·00
ED2		10c. on 1d. red	9·50	24·00
ED3		20c. on 2d. black	13·00	16·00
ED4		30c. on 3d. violet	10·00	17·00
ED5		1s. on 1s. blue	18·00	32·00

1950. Postage Due stamps of Great Britain surch **B.A. ERITREA** and new value in cents or shillings.

ED 6	**D 1**	5c. on ½d. green	13·00	48·00
ED 7		10c. on 1d. red	13·00	18·00
ED 8		20c. on 2d. black	13·00	20·00
ED 9		30c. on 3d. violet	17·00	28·00
ED10		1s. on 1s. blue	17·00	28·00

SOMALIA
BRITISH OCCUPATION

1943. Stamps of Great Britain optd **E.A.F.** (East African Forces).

S1	**128**	1d. red	1·00	60
S2		2d. orange	1·50	1·50
S3		2½d. blue	1·25	3·50
S4		3d. violet	1·25	15
S5	**129**	5d. brown	2·00	40
S6		6d. purple	1·50	1·25
S7	**130**	9d. olive	2·00	2·25
S8		1s. brown	3·00	15
S9	**131**	2s.6d. green	17·00	8·50

PRICES. Our prices for Nos. S1/9 in used condition are for stamps with identifiable postmarks of the territories in which they were issued. These stamps were also used in the United Kingdom with official sanction, from the summer of 1950, and with U.K. postmarks are worth about 25 per cent less.

BRITISH MILITARY ADMINISTRATION

1948. Stamps of Great Britain surch **B.M.A. SOMALIA** and new value in cents and shillings.

S10	**128**	5c. on ½d. green	1·25	2·00
S11		15c. on 1½d. brown	1·75	15·00
S12		20c. on 2d. orange	3·00	4·50
S13		25c. on 2½d. blue	2·25	4·50
S14		30c. on 3d. violet	2·25	9·00
S15	**129**	40c. on 5d. brown	1·25	20
S16		50c. on 6d. purple	50	2·00
S17	**130**	75c. on 9d. olive	2·00	19·00
S18		1s. on 1s. brown	1·25	20
S19	**131**	2s.50 on 2s.6d. green	4·25	25·00
S20		5s. on 5s. red	11·00	42·00

BRITISH ADMINISTRATION

1950. Stamps of Great Britain surch **B.A. SOMALIA** and value in cents and shillings.

S21	**128**	5c. on ½d. green	20	3·00
S22		15c. on 1½d. brown	75	17·00
S23		20c. on 2d. orange	75	7·50
S24		25c. on 2½d. blue	50	8·50
S25		30c. on 3d. violet	1·25	5·00
S26	**129**	40c. on 5d. brown	55	1·00
S27		50c. on 6d. purple	50	1·00
S28	**130**	75c. on 9d. olive	2·00	7·50
S29		1s. on 1s. brown	60	1·50
S30	**131**	2s.50 on 2s.6d. green	4·00	25·00
S31		5s. on 5s. red	11·00	38·00

TRIPOLITANIA
BRITISH MILITARY ADMINISTRATION

1948. Stamps of Great Britain surch **B.M.A. TRIPOLITANIA** and value in **M.A.L.** (Military Administration lire).

T 1	**128**	1l. on ½d. green	1·00	1·75
T 2		2l. on 1d. red	50	15
T 3		3l. on 1½d. brown	50	50
T 4		4l. on 2d. orange	50	50
T 5		5l. on 2½d. blue	50	20
T 6		6l. on 3d. violet	50	40
T 7	**129**	10l. on 5d. brown	50	15
T 8		12l. on 6d. purple	50	20
T 9	**130**	18l. on 9d. olive	1·00	65
T10		24l. on 1s. brown	1·00	1·50
T11	**131**	60l. on 2s.6d. green	4·00	12·00
T12		120l. on 5s. red	16·00	24·00
T13		240l. on 10s. blue (No. 478a)	24·00	£100

BRITISH ADMINISTRATION

1950. As Nos. T1/13 but surch **B.A. TRIPOLITANIA** and value in **M.A.L.**

T14	**128**	1l. on ½d. green	3·50	13·00
T27		1l. on ½d. orange	20	6·50
T15		2l. on 1d. red	3·00	40
T28		2l. on 1d. blue	20	1·00
T16		3l. on 1½d. brown	1·75	13·00
T29		3l. on 1½d. green	30	8·00
T17		4l. on 2d. orange	2·25	4·50
T30		4l. on 2d. brown	20	1·25
T18		5l. on 2½d. blue	1·00	70
T31		5l. on 2½d. red	30	7·50
T19		6l. on 3d. violet	1·75	3·25
T20	**129**	10l. on 5d. brown	1·25	4·00
T21		12l. on 6d. purple	2·75	50
T22	**130**	18l. on 9d. olive	3·25	2·75
T23		24l. on 1s. brown	3·25	3·75
T24	**131**	60l. on 2s.6d. green	10·00	12·00
T25		120l. on 5s. red	22·00	23·00
T26	–	240l. on 10s. blue (No. 478a)	38·00	70·00

1951. Nos. 509/11 of Great Britain surch **B.A. TRIPOLITANIA** and value in **M.A.L.**

T32	**147**	60l. on 2s.6d. green	8·00	23·00
T33	–	120l. on 5s. red	9·50	27·00
T34	–	240l. on 10s. blue	40·00	60·00

POSTAGE DUE STAMPS

1948. Postage Due stamps of Great Britain surch **B.M.A. TRIPOLITANIA** and value in **M.A.L.**

TD1	**D 1**	1l. on ½d. green	5·50	55·00
TD2		2l. on 1d. red	2·50	42·00
TD3		4l. on 2d. black	11·00	42·00
TD4		6l. on 3d. violet	7·50	23·00
TD5		24l. on 1s. blue	29·00	£100

1950. As Nos. TD1/5 but surch **B.A. TRIPOLITANIA** and value in **M.A.L.**

TD 6	**D 1**	1l. on ½d. green	13·00	85·00
TD 7		2l. on 1d. red	5·50	27·00
TD 8		4l. on 2d. black	6·50	38·00
TD 9		6l. on 3d. violet	18·00	65·00
TD10		24l. on 1s. blue	48·00	£140

BRITISH POST OFFICES IN CHINA Pt. 1

Stamps for use in Wei Hai Wei, and the neighbouring islands, leased to Great Britain from 1898 to 1 October 1930, when they were returned to China. The stamps were also used in the Treaty Ports from 1917 until 1922.

100 cents = 1 dollar.

1917. Stamps of Hong Kong (King George V) optd **CHINA**.

18	**24**	1c. brown	2·50	4·25
19		2c. green	5·00	2·25
3		4c. red	7·00	30
4		6c. orange	7·00	60
5		8c. grey	15·00	1·25
6		10c. blue	15·00	30
7		12c. purple on yellow	15·00	7·00
8		20c. purple and olive	15·00	60
9		25c. purple	9·00	15·00
11		30c. purple and orange	42·00	6·50
12b		50c. black on green	42·00	5·50
13		$1 purple and blue on blue	75·00	2·50
14		$2 red and black	£225	70·00
15		$3 green and purple	£750	£225
16		$5 green and red on green	£350	£275
17		$10 purple and black on red	£950	£550

BRITISH POST OFFICES IN CRETE Pt. 1

40 paras = 1 piastre.

B 1

B 2

1898.

B1	**B 1**	20pa. violet	£425	£225

1898.

B2	**B 2**	10pa. blue	8·00	19·00
B4		10pa. brown	8·00	26·00
B3		20pa. green	14·00	17·00
B5		20pa. red	19·00	15·00

BRITISH POST OFFICES IN SIAM Pt. 1

Used at Bangkok.

100 cents = 1 dollar.

1882. Stamps of Straits Settlements optd **B** on issue of 1867.

1	**19**	32c. on 2a. yellow	£35000	

On issues of 1867 to 1883.

14	**5**	2c. brown	£475	£350
13	**9**	2c. on 32c. red (No. 60)	£3500	£3500
15	**5**	2c. red	55·00	45·00
16		4c. red	£600	£325
17		4c. brown	80·00	70·00
4	**18**	5c. brown	£375	£400
18		5c. blue	£250	£170
5	**5**	6c. lilac	£250	£120
20		8c. orange	£160	65·00
21	**19**	10c. grey	£160	85·00
8	**5**	12c. blue	£950	£475
22		12c. purple	£300	£150
9		24c. green	£700	£150
10	**8**	30c. red	£45000	£30000
11	**9**	96c. grey	£7500	£3000

BRITISH POSTAL AGENCIES IN EASTERN ARABIA Pt. 1

British stamps surcharged for use in parts of the Persian Gulf.

The stamps were used in Muscat from 1 April 1948 to 29 April 1966; in Dubai from 1 April 1948 to 6 January 1961; In Qatar: Doha from August 1950, Umm Said from February 1956 to 31 March 1957; and in Abu Dhabi from 30 March 1963 (Das Island from December 1960) to 29 March 1964.

Nos. 21/2 were placed on sale in Kuwait Post Offices in 1951 and from February to November 1953 due to shortages of stamps with "KUWAIT" overprint. Isolated examples of other values can be found commercially used from Bahrain and Kuwait.

1948. 12 pies = 1 anna; 16 annas = 1 rupee.
1957. 100 naya paise = 1 rupee.

Stamps of Great Britain surch in Indian currency.

1948. King George VI.

16	**128**	½a. on ½d. green	2·75	7·50
35		½a. on ½d. orange	70	9·00
17		1a. on 1d. red	3·00	30
36		1a. on 1d. blue	30	7·50
18		1½a. on 1½d. brown	11·00	3·75
37		1½a. on 1½d. green	11·00	26·00
19		2a. on 2d. orange	2·00	3·25
38		2a. on 2d. brown	30	8·50
20		2½a. on 2½d. blue	3·50	8·00
39		2½a. on 2½d. red	30	16·00
21		3a. on 3d. violet	3·50	10
40	**129**	4a. on 4d. blue	45	3·50
22		6a. on 6d. purple	4·00	10
23	**130**	1r. on 1s. brown	4·50	60
24	**131**	2r. on 2s.6d. green	10·00	42·00

1948. Royal Silver Wedding.

25	**137**	2½a. on 2½d. blue	2·75	3·75
26	**138**	15r. on £1 blue	25·00	35·00

1948. Olympic Games.

27	**139**	2½a. on 2½d. blue	35	2·50
28	**140**	3a. on 3d. violet	45	2·50
29	–	6a. on 6d. purple	45	2·75
30	–	1r. on 1s. brown	1·25	3·50

1949. 75th Anniv of U.P.U.

31	**143**	2½a. on 2½d. blue	50	3·00
32	**144**	3a. on 3d. violet	60	3·75
33	–	6a. on 6d. purple	60	2·75
34	–	1r. on 1s. brown	2·00	6·00

1951. Pictorial.

41	**147**	2r. on 2s.6d. green	30·00	7·00

1952. Queen Elizabeth.

42	**154**	½a. on ½d. orange	10	2·25
43		1a. on 1d. blue	10	2·25
44		1½a. on 1½d. green	10	2·25
45		2a. on 2d. brown	20	10
46	**155**	2½a. on 2½d. red	10	10
47		3a. on 3d. lilac	20	1·25
48		4a. on 4d. blue	1·50	4·00
49	**157**	6a. on 6d. purple	35	10
50	**160**	12a. on 1s.3d. green	4·75	30
51		1r. on 1s.6d. blue	2·25	10

1953. Coronation.

52	**161**	2½a. on 2½d. red	1·75	2·50
53	–	4a. on 4d. blue	1·75	1·00
54	**163**	12a. on 1s.3d. green	2·25	1·00
55	–	1r. on 1s.6d. blue	2·50	50

1955. Pictorials.

56	**166**	2r. on 2s.6d. brown	6·50	70
57	–	5r. on 5s. red	10·00	2·25

1957. Value in naye paise. Queen Elizabeth II stamps surch **NP** twice (once only on 75n.p.) and value.

79	**157**	1n.p. on 5d. brown	10	20
80	**154**	3n.p. on ½d. orange	55	80
81		5n.p. on 1d. blue	1·75	2·75
67		6n.p. on 1d. blue	20	2·75
68		9n.p. on 1½d. green	20	2·50
83		10n.p. on 1½d. green	1·00	2·75
69		12n.p. on 2d. brown	30	2·75
85	**155**	15n.p. on 2½d. red	25	10
71		20n.p. on 3d. lilac	20	10
72		25n.p. on 4d. blue	70	6·00
87		30n.p. on 4½d. brown	40	50
73	**157**	40n.p. on 6d. purple	30	10
89	**158**	50n.p. on 9d. olive	1·00	2·50
75	**160**	75n.p. on 1s.3d. green	2·00	40
91	**159**	1r. on 1s.6d. blue	22·00	5·00
92	**166**	2r. on 2s.6d. brown	12·00	40·00
93		5r. on 5s. red	24·00	55·00

DESIGN: No. 93 Caernarvon Castle.

1957. World Scout Jubilee Jamboree.

76	**170**	15n.p. on 2½d. red	25	85
77	**171**	25n.p. on 4d. blue	30	85
78	–	75n.p. on 3d. green	35	85

BRITISH VIRGIN ISLANDS Pt. 1

A group of the Leeward Islands, Br. W. Indies. Used general issues for Leeward Islands concurrently with Virgin Islands stamps until 1 July 1956. A Crown Colony.

1951. 100 cents = 1 West Indian dollar.
1962. 100 cents = 1 U.S. dollar.

1 St. Ursula

2

3

4

1866.

1	**1**	1d. green	45·00	60·00
16	**3**	4d. red	40·00	60·00
7	**2**	6d. red	60·00	90·00
11	**4**	1s. black and red	£275	£375

No. 11 has a double-lined frame.

1867. With heavy coloured border.

19	**4**	1s. black and red	65·00	75·00

6

8

1880.

26	**6**	½d. yellow	85·00	85·00
27		½d. green	6·50	11·00
24		1d. green	75·00	90·00
29		1d. red	26·00	30·00
25		2½d. brown	£100	£130
31		2½d. blue	2·75	16·00

1887.

32	**1**	1d. red	3·75	9·00
35	**3**	4d. brown	35·00	65·00
39	**2**	6d. violet	18·00	50·00
41	**4**	1s. brown	45·00	70·00

1888. No. 18 surch **4D.**

42	**4**	4d. on 1s. black and red	£130	£160

1899.

43	**8**	½d. green	3·25	55
44		1d. red	3·75	2·50
45		2½d. blue	12·00	2·75
46		4d. brown	4·00	18·00
47		6d. violet	4·50	3·00
48		7d. green	10·00	6·00
49		1s. yellow	22·00	35·00
50		5s. blue	70·00	85·00

9

11

1904.

54	**9**	½d. purple and green	1·00	40
55		1d. purple and red	2·50	35
56		2d. purple and brown	6·50	3·50
57		2½d. purple and blue	2·25	2·00
58		3d. purple and black	3·50	2·50
59		6d. purple and brown	2·75	2·50
60		1s. green and red	4·25	5·00
61		2s.6d. green and black	28·00	55·00
62		5s. green and blue	48·00	65·00

1913.

69	**11**	½d. green	2·00	4·00
70a		1d. red	2·25	14·00
71		2d. grey	4·00	26·00
72		2½d. blue	5·50	9·00

73 3d. purple on yellow . . . 2·75 6·50
74 6d. purple . . . . 5·50 13·00
75 1s. black on green . . . . 3·25 9·00
76 2s.6d. black and red on blue . . . . . . 48·00 50·00
77 5s. green and red on yellow 35·00 £110

1917. Optd **WAR STAMP**.
78c **11** 1d. red . . . . 30 3·75
79a 3d. purple on yellow . . . 3·50 15·00

14

15 King George VI and Badge of Colony

1922.
86 **14** ½d. green . . . . 85 2·75
87 1d. red 60 60
88 1d. violet . . . . 1·25 3·50
91 1½d. red . . . . 2·00 1·50
92 2d. grey . . . . 1·25 6·00
95 2½d. blue . . . . 4·50 3·50
94 2½d. orange . . . . 1·25 1·75
96 3d. purple on yellow . . . 2·25 11·00
97 5d. purple and olive . . . 5·50 45·00
98 6d. purple . . . . 1·75 6·50
83 1s. black on green . . . . 75 14·00
84 2s.6d. black and red on blue . . . . 5·50 11·00
101 5s. green and red on yellow 19·00 70·00

1935. Silver Jubilee. As T **13** of Antigua.
103 1d. blue and red . . . . . 1·25 5·00
104 1½d. blue and grey . . . . 1·25 4·50
105 2½d. brown and blue . . . 2·25 4·50
106 1s. grey and purple . . . . 14·00 23·00

1937. Coronation. As T **2** of Aden.
107 1d. red . . . . 40 3·25
108 1½d. brown . . . . 60 3·00
109 2½d. blue . . . . 50 1·50

1938.
110a **15** ½d. green . . . . 75 1·00
111a 1d. red . . . . 1·50 60
112a 1½d. brown . . . . 1·50 1·00
113a 2d. grey . . . . 1·75 90
114a 2½d. blue . . . . 2·00 2·50
115a 3d. orange . . . . 1·00 80
116a 6d. mauve . . . . 4·00 80
117a 1s. brown . . . . 1·75 70
118a 2s.6d. brown . . . . 17·00 3·00
119a 5s. red . . . . 14·00 4·00
120 10s. blue . . . . 6·00 8·00
121 £1 black . . . . 8·00 20·00

1946. Victory. As T **9** of Aden.
122 1½d. brown 10 10
123 3d. orange 10 30

1949. Silver Wedding. As T **10/11** of Aden.
124 2½d. blue 10 10
125 £1 grey . . . . 13·00 16·00

1949. 75th Anniv of U.P.U. As T **20/23** of Antigua.
126 2½d. blue . . . . 30 1·00
127 3d. orange . . . . 1·50 2·50
128 6d. mauve 45 40
129 1s. olive 35 50

1951. Inauguration of B.W.I. University College. As T **24/25** of Antigua.
130 3c. black and red . . . . . 40 2·25
131 12c. black and violet . . . 60 1·75

16 Map

1951. Restoration of Legislative Council.
132 **16** 6c. orange . . . . 50 1·50
133 12c. purple 50 50
134 24c. olive 50 50
135 $1.20 red . . . . 1·25 1·00

18 Map of Jost Van Dyke

1952.
136 – 1c. black . . . . 80 2·25
137 **18** 2c. green 70 30
138 – 3c. black and brown . . . 80 2·00
139 – 4c. red . . . . 70 2·00
140 – 5c. red and black . . . . 1·50 50
141 – 8c. blue . . . . 70 1·25
142 – 12c. violet . . . . 80 1·60
143 – 24c. brown 70 50
144 – 60c. green and blue . . . 4·50 11·00
145 – $1.20 black and blue . . 5·00 12·00
146 – $2.40 green and brown . . 11·00 16·00
147 – $4.80 blue and red . . . 12·00 17·00

DESIGNS—VERT: 1c. Sombrero lighthouse; 24c. Badge of Presidency. HORIZ—VIEWS: 3c. Sheep industry; 5c. Cattle industry; 60c. Dead Man's Chest (Is); $1.20, Sir Francis Drake Channel; $2.40, Road Town. HORIZ—MAPS: 4c. Anegada Island; 8c. Virgin Gorda Island; 12c. Tortola Island; $4.80, Virgin Islands.

1953. Coronation. As T **13** of Aden.
148 2c. black and green . . . . . 30 1·25

29 Map of Tortola

30 Virgin Island Sloop

1956.
149 **29** ½c. black and purple . . . 1·00 20
150 – 1c. turquoise and slate . . 1·50 75
151 – 2c. red and black 30 10
152 – 3c. blue and olive 30 30
153 – 4c. brown and turquoise . . 70 30
154 – 5c. black 50 10
155 – 8c. orange and blue . . . 2·00 40
156 – 12c. blue and red . . . . 4·00 75
157 – 24c. green and brown . . . 1·00 65
158 – 60c. blue and orange . . . 8·50 8·00
159 – $1.20 green and red . . . 2·00 8·00
160 **30** $2.40 yellow and purple . . 40·00 13·00
161 – $4.80 sepia and turquoise 40·00 13·00

DESIGNS—HORIZ: As Type **13**: 1c. Virgin Islands sloop; 2c. Nelthrop Red Poll bull; 3c. Road Harbour; 4c. Mountain travel; 5c. Badge of the Presidency; 8c. Beach scene; 12c. Boat launching; 24c. White cedar tree; 60c. Skipjack tuna ("Bonito"); $1.20, Treasury Square Coronation celebrations. As Type **30**: $4.80, Magnificent frigate bird ("Man-o'-War Bird").

1962. New Currency. Nos. 149/53, 155/61 surch in U.S. Currency.
162 **29** 1c. on ½c. black and purple 30 10
163 – 2c. on 1c. turq & vio . . . 1·75 10
164 – 3c. on 2c. red and black 70 10
165 – 4c. on 3c. blue and olive 30 10
166 – 5c. on 4c. brown & turq 30 10
167 – 8c. on 8c. orange and blue 30 10
168 – 10c. on 12c. blue and red 2·00 10
169 – 12c. on 24c. green & brn 30 10
170 – 25c. on 60c. blue and orange . . . . 2·75 45
171 – 70c. on $1.20 green and red 35 45
172 **30** $1.40 on $2.40 yellow and purple . . . . 9·50 4·00
173 – $2.80 on $4.80 sepia & turq . . . . 9·50 4·00

1963. Freedom from Hunger. As T **28** of Aden.
174 25c. violet 20 10

1963. Centenary of Red Cross. As T **33** of Antigua.
175 2c. red and black 15 20
176 25c. red and blue 50 20

1964. 400th Birth Anniv of Shakespeare. As T **34** of Antigua.
177 10c. blue 20 10

43 Skipjack Tuna

44 Soper's Hole

1964.
178 **43** 1c. blue and olive . . . . 30 1·75
179 – 2c. olive and red 15 30
180 3c. sepia and turquoise . . 4·75 1·25
181 – 4c. black and red . . . . 80 2·25
182 – 5c. black and green . . . 1·25 2·25
183 – 6c. black and orange . . . 30 85
184 – 8c. black and mauve . . . 30 50
185 – 10c. lake and lilac . . . 3·75 30
186 – 12c. green and blue . . . 2·00 2·75
187 – 15c. green and black . . . 35 2·75
188 – 25c. green and purple . . 11·00 1·75
189 **44** 70c. black and brown . . . 4·25 8·00
190 – $1 green and brown . . . 3·00 2·00
191 – $1.40 blue and red . . . 24·00 9·00
192 – $2.80 black and purple . . 25·00 9·00

DESIGNS—HORIZ (As Type **43**): 2c. Soper's Hole; 3c. Brown pelican; 4c. Dead Man's Chest; 5c. Road Harbour; 6c. Fallen Jerusalem; 8c. The Baths, Virgin Gorda; 10c. Map of Virgin Islands; 12c. "Youth of Tortola" (Tortola–St Thomas ferry); 15c. The Towers, Tortola; 25c. Beef Island Airfield. VERT (As Type **44**): $1 Virgin Gorda; $1.40, Yachts at anchor. (27½ × 37½ mm): $2.80, Badge of the Colony.

1965. Centenary of I.T.U. As T **36** of Antigua.
193 4c. yellow and turquoise . . 20 10
194 25c. blue and buff 45 20

1965. I.C.Y. As T **37** of Antigua.
195 1c. purple and turquoise . . 10 15
196 25c. green and lavender . . . 30 15

1966. Churchill Commemoration. As T **38** of Antigua.
197 1c. blue 10 30
198 2c. green 15 30
199 10c. brown 30 10
200 25c. violet 60 25

1966. Royal Visit. As T **39** of Antigua.
201 4c. black and blue 40 10
202 70c. black and mauve . . . . 1·40 45

58 "Atrato I" (paddle-steamer), 1866

1966. Stamp Centenary. Multicoloured.
203 5c. Type **58** 35 10
204 10c. 1d. and 6d. stamps of 1866 . . . . 35 10
205 25c. Mail transport, Beef Island, and 6d. stamp of 1866 . . . . 55 10
206 60c. Landing mail at Roadtown, 1866 and 1d. stamp of 1866 . . . . . 1·00 2·50

1966. Nos. 189 and 191/2 surch.
207 **44** 50c. on 70c. blk & brn . . 1·25 90
208 – $1.50 on $1.40 blue and red . . . . 2·25 2·00
209 – $3 on $2.80 black and purple . . . . 2·25 2·75

1966. 20th Anniv of UNESCO. As T **54/6** of Antigua.
210 2c. multicoloured 10 10
211 12c. yellow, violet and olive 25 10
212 60c. black, purple and orange 75 45

63 Map of Virgin Islands

1967. New Constitution.
213 **63** 2c. multicoloured 10 10
214 10c. multicoloured 15 10
215 25c. multicoloured 15 10
216 $1 multicoloured 55 40

64 "Mercury" (cable ship) and Bermuda–Tortola Link

1967. Inauguration of Bermuda–Tortola Telephone Service. Multicoloured.
217 4c. Type **64** 30 10
218 10c. Chalwell Telecommunications Station 20 10
219 50c. "Mercury" (cable ship) 60 30

67 Blue Marlin

1968. Game Fishing. Multicoloured.
220 2c. Type **67** 10 65
221 10c. Cobia 25 10
222 25c. Wahoo 55 10
223 40c. Fishing launch and map 85 75

1968. Human Rights Year. Nos. 185 and 188 optd **1968 INTERNATIONAL YEAR FOR HUMAN RIGHTS.**
224 10c. lake and lilac 20 10
225 25c. green and purple 30 40

72 Dr. Martin Luther King, Bible, Sword and Armour Gauntlet

1968. Martin Luther King Commemoration.
226 **72** 4c. multicoloured 25 20
227 25c. multicoloured 40 40

73 De Havilland Twin Otter 100

1968. Opening of Beef Island Airport Extension. Multicoloured.
228 2c. Type **73** . . . . 15 1·25
229 10c. Hawker Siddeley H.S.748 airliner 20 10
230 25c. De Havilland Heron 2 airplane 40 10
231 $1 Royal Engineers' cap badge . . . . 50 2·00

77 Long John Silver and Jim Hawkins

1969. 75th Death Anniv of Robert Louis Stevenson. Scenes from "Treasure Island".
232 **77** 4c. blue, yellow and red . . 20 15
233 – 10c. multicoloured 20 10
234 – 40c. brown, black and blue 25 30
235 – $1 multicoloured . . . . . 45 1·00

DESIGNS—HORIZ: 10c. Jim Hawkins escaping from the pirates; $1 Treasure trove. VERT: 40c. The fight with Israel Hands.

82 Yachts in Road Harbour, Tortola

1969. Tourism. Multicoloured.
236 2c. Tourist and yellow-finned grouper (fish) 15 50
237 10c. Type **82** 30 10
238 20c. Sun-bathing at Virgin Gorda National Park . . . 40 20
239 $1 Tourist and Pipe Organ cactus at Virgin Gorda . . 90 1·50
Nos. 236 and 239 are vert.

85 Carib Canoe

1970.
240 **85** ½c. buff, brown and sepia 10 1·50
241 – 1c. blue and green 15 30
242 – 2c. orange, brown and slate 40 1·00
243 – 3c. red, blue and sepia . . 30 1·25
244 – 4c. turquoise, blue & brn 30 50
245 – 5c. green, pink and black 30 10
246 – 6c. violet, mauve and green 40 2·00
247 – 8c. green, yellow and sepia 50 4·25
248 – 10c. blue and brown . . . 50 15
249 – 12c. yellow, red and brown 65 1·50
250 – 15c. green, orange and brown . . . . 6·00 85
251 – 25c. green, blue and purple 4·00 1·75
252 – 50c. mauve, green and brown . . . . 3·25 1·50
253 – $1 salmon, green and brown . . . . 4·00 3·75
254 – $2 buff, slate and grey . . 7·50 7·00
255 – $3 ochre, blue and sepia . 2·75 4·50
256 – $5 violet and grey . . . . 2·75 5·00

DESIGNS: 1c. "Santa Maria" (Columbus's flagship); 2c. "Elizabeth Bonaventure" (Drake's flagship); 3c. Dutch buccaneer, c. 1660; 4c. "Thetis", 1827 (after etching by E. W. Cooke); 5c. Henry Morgan's ship (17th-century); 6c. H.M.S. "Boreas" (Captain Nelson, 1784); 8c. H.M.S. "Eclair", 1804; 10c. H.M.S. "Formidable", 1782; 12c. H.M.S. "Nymph", 1778; 15c. "Windsor Castle" (sailing packet) engaging "Jeune Richard" (French brig), 1807; 25c. H.M.S. "Astrea", 1808; 50c. Wreck of R.M.S. "Rhone", 1867; $1 Tortola sloop; $2 H.M.S. "Frobisher"; $3 "Booker Viking" (cargo liner), 1967; $5 Hydrofoil "Sun Arrow".

102 "A Tale of Two Cities"

1970. Death Centenary of Charles Dickens.

257 **102**	5c. black, red and grey	10	1·00
258	– 10c. black, blue and green	20	10
259	– 25c. black, green and yellow	30	25

DESIGNS: 10c. "Oliver Twist"; 25c. "Great Expectations".

103 Hospital Visit

1970. Centenary of British Red Cross. Multicoloured.

260	4c. Type **103**	20	45
261	10c. First Aid class	20	10
262	25c. Red Cross and coat of arms	50	55

104 Mary Read

1970. Pirates. Multicoloured.

263	½c. Type **104**	10	15
264	10c. George Lowther	30	10
265	30c. Edward Teach (Blackbeard)	60	25
266	60c. Henry Morgan	80	1·00

105 Children and "UNICEF"

1971. 25th Anniv of UNICEF.

267 **105**	15c. multicoloured	10	10
268	30c. multicoloured	20	25

1972. Royal Visit of Princess Margaret. Nos 244 and 251 optd **VISIT OF H.R.H. THE PRINCESS MARGARET 1972 1972.**

269	4c. blue, light blue and brown	40	15
270	25c. green, blue and plum	60	45

107 Seaman of 1800

110 J. C. Lettsom

109 Blue Marlin

1972. "Interpex" Stamp Exhibition, New York. Naval Uniforms. Multicoloured.

271	½c. Type **107**	10	40
272	10c. Boatswain, 1787–1807	35	10
273	30c. Captain, 1795–1812	85	55
274	60c. Admiral, 1787–95	1·25	2·75

1972. Royal Silver Wedding. As T **52** of Ascension, but with sailfish and "Sir Winston Churchill" (cadet schooner) in background.

275	15c. blue	25	15
276	25c. blue	25	15

1972. Game Fish. Multicoloured.

277	½c. Type **109**	15	1·40
278	½c. Wahoo	15	1·40
279	15c. Yellow-finned tuna ("Allison tuna")	65	25
280	25c. White marlin	75	30
281	50c. Sailfish	1·25	1·50
282	$1 Dolphin	2·00	2·75
MS283	194 × 158 mm. Nos. 277/82	8·50	8·50

1973. "Interpex 1973" (Quakers). Multicoloured.

284	½c. Type **110**	10	15
285	10c. Lettsom House (horiz)	15	10
286	15c. Dr. W. Thornton	20	10
287	30c. Dr. Thornton and Capitol, Washington (horiz)	25	20
288	$1 William Penn (horiz)	60	1·10

111 Green-throated Carib and Antillean Crested Hummingbird

1973. First Issue of Coinage. Coins and local scenery. Multicoloured.

289	1c. Type **111**	10	30
290	5c. "Zenaida Dove" (5c. coin)	60	10
291	10c. "Ringed Kingfisher" (10c. coin)	75	10
292	25c. "Mangrove Cuckoo" (25c. coin)	95	15
293	50c. "Brown Pelican" (50c. coin)	1·10	1·00
294	$1 "Magnificent Frigate-bird ($1 coin)	1·40	2·00

1973. Royal Wedding. As T **47** of Anguilla. Multicoloured. Background colours given.

301	5c. brown	10	10
302	50c. blue	20	20

112 "Virgin and Child" (Pintoricchio)

113 Crest of the "Canopus" (French)

1973. Christmas. Multicoloured.

303	½c. Type **112**	10	10
304	3c. "Virgin and Child" (Lorenzo di Credi)	10	10
305	25c. "Virgin and Child" (Crivelli)	15	10
306	50c. "Virgin and Child with St. John" (Luini)	30	40

1974. "Interpex 1974". Naval Crests. Multicoloured.

307	5c. Type **113**	15	10
308	18c. U.S.S. "Saginaw"	25	25
309	25c. H.M.S. "Rothesay"	25	30
310	50c. H.M.C.S. "Ottawa"	45	60
MS311	196 × 128 mm. Nos. 307/10	1·25	4·50

114 Christopher Columbus

1974. Historical Figures.

312 **114**	5c. orange and black	20	10
313	– 10c. blue and black	20	10
314	– 25c. violet and black	25	25
315	– 40c. brown and deep brown	45	75
MS316	84 × 119 mm. Nos. 312/15	1·00	2·25

PORTRAITS: 10c. Sir Walter Raleigh; 25c. Sir Martin Frobisher; 40c. Sir Francis Drake.

115 Atlantic Trumpet Triton

1974. Seashells. Multicoloured.

317	5c. Type **115**	30	15
318	18c. West Indian murex	50	30
319	25c. Bleeding tooth	60	35
320	75c. Virgin Islands latirus	1·25	2·25
MS321	146 × 95 mm. Nos. 317/20	3·00	6·50

116 Churchill and St. Mary, Aldermanbury, London

1974. Birth Centenary of Sir Winston Churchill. Multicoloured.

322	10c. Type **116**	15	10
323	50c. St. Mary, Fulton, Missouri	35	50
MS324	141 × 108 mm. Nos. 322/3	80	1·40

117 H.M.S. "Boreas"

1975. "Interpex 1975" Stamp Exhibition, New York. Ships' Figure-heads. Multicoloured.

325	5c. Type **117**	20	10
326	18c. "Golden Hind"	40	15
327	40c. H.M.S. "Superb"	50	25
328	85c. H.M.S. "Formidable"	1·00	1·50
MS329	192 × 127 mm. Nos. 325/8	1·75	8·00

118 Rock Beauty

1975. Fishes. Multicoloured.

330	½c. Type **118**	15	50
331	1c. Long-spined squirrelfish	40	2·75
332	3c. Queen triggerfish	1·00	2·75
333	5c. Blue angelfish	30	20
334	8c. Stoplight parrotfish	30	25
335	10c. Queen angelfish	30	25
336	12c. Nassau grouper	40	30
337	13c. Blue tang	40	30
338	15c. Sergeant major	40	35
339	18c. Spotted jewfish	80	1·50
340	20c. Bluehead wrasse	60	80
341	25c. Grey angelfish	1·00	60
342	60c. Glass-eyed snapper	1·25	2·25
343	$1 Blue chromis	1·75	1·75
344	$2.50 French angelfish	2·00	4·50
345	$3 Queen parrotfish	2·50	4·50
346	$5 Four-eyed butterflyfish	2·75	6·00

119 St. George's Parish School (first meeting-place, 1950)

1975. 25th Anniv of Restoration of Legislative Council. Multicoloured.

347	5c. Type **119**	10	10
348	25c. Legislative Council Building	20	10
349	40c. Mace and gavel	25	15
350	75c. Commemorative scroll	35	65

120 Copper Mine Point

1976. Historic Sites. Multicoloured.

351	5c. Type **120**	10	10
352	18c. Pleasant Valley	20	10
353	50c. Callwood Distillery	40	30
354	75c. The Dungeon	60	65

121 Massachusetts Brig "Hazard"

1976. Bicentenary of American Revolution. Mult.

355	8c. Type **121**	30	15
356	22c. American privateer "Spy"	45	20
357	40c. "Raleigh" (American frigate)	55	60
358	75c. Frigate "Alliance" and H.M.S. "Trepassy"	80	1·25
MS359	114 × 89 mm. Nos. 355/8	2·75	11·00

122 Government House, Tortola

1976. 5th Anniv of Friendship Day with U.S. Virgin Islands. Multicoloured.

360	8c. Type **122**	10	10
361	15c. Government House, St. Croix (vert)	10	10
362	30c. Flags (vert)	15	10
363	75c. Government seals	30	40

123 Royal Visit, 1966

125 Divers checking Equipment

124 Chart of 1739

1977. Silver Jubilee. Multicoloured.

364	8c. Type **123**	10	10
365	30c. The Holy Bible	15	15
366	60c. Presentation of Holy Bible	25	40

1977. 18th-century Maps. Multicoloured.

367	8c. Type **124**	40	10
368	22c. French map, 1758	55	30

369	30c. Map from English and Danish surveys, 1775	65	65
370	75c. Map of 1779	85	1·50

1977. Royal Visit. As Nos. 364/6 inscr "SILVER JUBILEE ROYAL VISIT".

371	5c. Type **123**	10	10
372	25c. The Holy Bible	20	10
373	50c. Presentation of Holy Bible	35	25

1978. Tourism. Multicoloured.

374	½c. Type **125**	10	10
375	5c. Cup coral on wreck of "Rhone"	20	10
376	8c. Sponge formation on wreck of "Rhone"	25	10
377	22c. Cup coral and sponges	45	15
378	30c. Sponges inside cave	60	20
379	75c. Marine life	90	85

126 Fire Coral

127 Iguana

1978. Corals. Multicoloured.

380	8c. Type **126**	25	15
381	15c. Staghorn coral	40	30
382	40c. Brain coral	75	85
383	75c. Elkhorn coral	1·50	1·60

1978. 25th Anniv of Coronation.

384	– 50c. brown, green and silver	20	40
385	– 50c. multicoloured	20	40
386 **127**	50c. brown, green and silver	20	40

DESIGNS: No. 384, Plantagenet Falcon; 385, Queen Elizabeth II.

128 Lignum Vitae

1978. Flowering Trees. Multicoloured.

387	8c. Type **128**	15	10
388	22c. Ginger Thomas	20	15
389	40c. Dog almond	30	20
390	75c. White cedar	45	70
MS391	131 × 95 mm. Nos. 387/90	1·00	3·00

129 "Eurema lisa"

1978. Butterflies. Multicoloured.

392	5c. Type **129**	25	10
393	22c. "Agraulis vanillae"	40	20
394	30c. "Heliconius charithonia"	1·10	30
395	75c. "Hemiargus hanno"	1·40	1·25
MS396	159 × 113 mm. No. 392 × 6 and No. 393 × 3	2·50	5·50

130 Spiny Lobster

1978. Wildlife Conservation. Multicoloured.

397	5c. Type **130**	15	10
398	15c. Large iguana (vert)	25	10
399	22c. Hawksbill turtle	40	15
400	75c. Black coral (vert)	75	90
MS401	130 × 153 mm. Nos. 397/400	1·75	3·75

131 Strawberry Cactus

132 West Indian Girl

1979. Native Cacti. Multicoloured.

402	½c. Type **131**	10	10
403	5c. Snowy cactus	15	10
404	13c. Barrel cactus	20	20
405	22c. Tree cactus	25	35
406	30c. Prickly pear	30	40
407	75c. Dildo cactus	40	1·00

1979. International Year of the Child. Multicoloured.

408	5c. Type **132**	10	10
409	10c. African boy	10	10
410	13c. Asian girl	10	10
411	$1 European boy	50	85
MS412	91 × 114 mm. Nos. 408/11	70	1·50

133 1956 Road Harbour 3c. Definitive Stamp

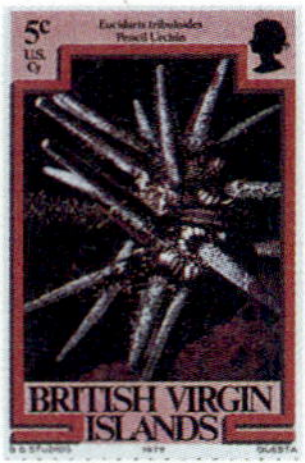

134 Pencil Urchin

1979. Death Centenary of Sir Rowland Hill.

413 **133**	5c. dp blue, blue & green	10	10
414	– 13c. blue and mauve	10	10
415	– 75c. blue and purple	45	50
MS416	37 × 91 mm. $1 blue and red	70	1·25

DESIGNS (39 × 27 mm)—13c. 1880 2½d. red-brown; 75c. Great Britain 1910 unissued 2d. Tyrian plum. (40 × 28 mm)—$1 1867 1s. "Missing Virgin" error.

1979. Marine Life. Multicoloured.

417	½c. Calcified algae	40	2·75
418	1c. Purple-tipped sea anemone	55	2·75
419	3c. Common starfish	1·25	2·75
420	5c. Type **134**	1·25	2·25
421	8c. Atlantic trumpet triton	1·25	1·75
422	10c. Christmas tree worms	30	1·25
423a	13c. Flamingo tongue snail	1·50	75
424	15c. Spider crab	40	1·00
425	18c. Sea squirts	2·00	4·25
426	20c. True tulip	55	1·50
427	25c. Rooster-tail conch	1·25	4·00
428	30c. West Indian fighting conch	2·50	1·50
429	60c. Mangrove crab	1·50	3·00
430	$1 Coral polyps	1·25	4·25
431	$2.50 Peppermint shrimp	1·25	4·00
432	$3 West Indian murex	1·25	4·50
433	$5 Carpet anemone	1·75	5·50

135 Rotary Athletics Meeting, Tortola

1980. 75th Anniv of Rotary International. Mult.

434	8c. Type **135**	10	10
435	22c. Paul P. Harris (founder)	15	10
436	60c. Mount Saga, Tortola ("Creation of National Park")	30	40
437	$1 Rotary anniversary emblem	55	75
MS438	149 × 148 mm. Nos. 434/7	1·00	3·75

136 Brown Booby

138 Sir Francis Drake

1980. "London 1980" International Stamp Exhibition. Birds. Multicoloured.

439	20c. Type **136**	20	20
440	25c. Magnificent frigate bird	25	25
441	50c. White-tailed tropic bird	40	40
442	75c. Brown pelican	55	55
MS443	152 × 130 mm. Nos. 439/42	1·25	2·25

1980. Caribbean Commonwealth Parliamentary Association Meeting, Tortola. Nos. 414/15 optd **CARIBBEAN COMMONWEALTH PARLIAMENTARY ASSOCIATION MEETING TORTOLA 11–19 JULY 1980**.

444	13c. blue and red	15	10
445	75c. deep blue and blue	40	40

1980. Sir Francis Drake Commemoration. Mult.

446	8c. Type **138**	50	10
447	15c. Queen Elizabeth I	70	15
448	30c. Drake receiving knighthood	90	30
449	75c. "Golden Hind" and coat of arms	1·75	1·25
MS450	171 × 121 mm. Nos. 446/9	3·75	6·50

139 Jost Van Dyke

1980. Island Profiles. Multicoloured.

451	2c. Type **139**	10	10
452	5c. Peter Island	10	10
453	13c. Virgin Gorda	15	10
454	22c. Anegada	20	10
455	30c. Norman Island	25	15
456	$1 Tortola	70	1·00
MS457	95 × 88 mm. No. 456	85	1·50

140 Dancing Lady

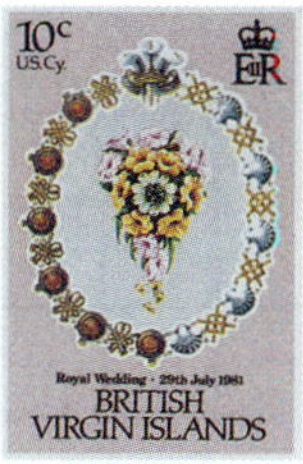

141 Wedding Bouquet from British Virgin Islands

1981. Flowers. Multicoloured.

458	5c. Type **140**	10	10
459	20c. Love in the mist	15	15
460	22c. "Pitcairnia angustifolia"	15	15
461	75c. Dutchman's pipe	35	65
462	$1 Maiden apple	35	80

1981. Royal Wedding. Multicoloured.

463	10c. Type **141**	10	10
464	35c. Prince Charles and Queen Elizabeth the Queen Mother in Garter robes	20	15
465	$1.25 Prince Charles and Lady Diana Spencer	60	80

142 Stamp Collecting

144 Detail from "The Adoration of the Shepherds" (Rubens)

143 "Development through Education"

1981. 25th Anniv of Duke of Edinburgh Award Scheme. Multicoloured.

466	10c. Type **142**	10	10
467	15c. Athletics	10	10
468	50c. Camping	25	25
469	$1 Duke of Edinburgh	40	45

1981. International Year for Disabled Persons. Multicoloured.

470	15c. Type **143**	15	15
471	20c. Fort Charlotte Children's Centre	15	20
472	30c. "Developing cultural awareness"	20	30
473	$1 Fort Charlotte Children's Centre (different)	60	1·25

1981. Christmas.

474 **144**	5c. multicoloured	15	10
475	– 15c. multicoloured	25	10
476	– 30c. multicoloured	45	15
477	– $1 multicoloured	1·10	1·10
MS478	117 × 90 mm. 50c. multicoloured (horiz)	2·00	1·00

DESIGNS: 15c. to $1 Further details from "The Adoration of the Shepherds" by Rubens.

145 Green-throated Caribs and Erythrina

147 Princess at Victoria and Albert Museum, November, 1981

146 "People caring for People"

1982. Hummingbirds. Multicoloured.

479	15c. Type **145**	50	15
480	30c. Green-throated carib and bougainvillea	60	45
481	35c. Antillean crested hummingbirds and "granadilla passiflora"	70	55
482	$1.25 Antillean crested hummingbirds and hibiscus	1·75	3·00

1982. 10th Anniv of Lions Club of Tortola. Mult.

483	10c. Type **146**	15	10
484	20c. Tortola Headquarters	20	15
485	30c. "We Serve"	25	15
486	$1.50 "Lions" symbol	60	1·00
MS487	124 × 102 mm. Nos. 483/6	1·75	4·25

1982. 21st Birthday of Princess of Wales. Mult.

488	10c. British Virgin Islands coat of arms	15	10
489	35c. Type **147**	30	15
490	50c. Bride and groom proceeding into Vestry	45	35
491	$1.50 Formal portrait	1·10	1·10

148 Douglas DC-3

1982. 10th Anniv of Air BVI. Multicoloured.

492	10c. Type **148**	45	15
493	15c. Britten Norman Islander	60	20
494	60c. Hawker Siddeley H.S.748	1·10	75
495	75c. Runway scene	1·25	90

149 Scouts raising Flag

1982. 75th Anniv of Boy Scout Movement and 50th Anniv of Scouting in B.V.I. Multicoloured.

496	8c. Type **149**	20	10
497	20c. Cub Scout	30	25
498	50c. Sea Scout	40	55
499	$1 First camp, Brownsea Island, and portrait of Lord Baden-Powell	70	1·50

150 Legislature in Session

1983. Commonwealth Day. Multicoloured.

500	10c. Type **150**	10	10
501	30c. Tourism	25	20
502	35c. Satellite view of Earth showing Virgin Islands	25	25
503	75c. B.V.I. and Commonwealth flags	70	90

151 Florence Nightingale **152** Frame Construction

1983. Nursing Week. Multicoloured.

504	10c. Type **151**	50	15
505	30c. Staff nurse and assistant nurse	90	45
506	60c. Public Health nurses testing blood pressure (horiz)	1·75	1·25
507	75c. Peebles Hospital (horiz)	1·90	1·75

1983. Traditional Boat-building. Multicoloured.

508	15c. Type **152**	25	25
509	25c. Planking	30	45
510	50c. Launching	50	80
511	$1 Maiden voyage	65	1·75
MS512	127 × 101 mm. Nos. 508/11	1·50	3·75

153 Grumman Goose Amphibian

1983. Bicentenary of Manned Flight. Multicoloured.

513	10c. Type **153**	20	15
514	30c. Riley Turbo Skyliner	45	45
515	60c. Embraer Bandeirante	65	85
516	$1.25 Hawker Siddeley H.S.748	90	1·60

154 "Madonna and Child with the Infant Baptist" **156** Port Purcell

155 Local Tournament

1983. Christmas. 500th Birth Anniv of Raphael. Multicoloured.

517	8c. Type **154**	10	10
518	15c. "La Belle Jardiniere"	20	15
519	50c. "Madonna del Granduca"	50	60
520	$1 "The Terranuova Madonna"	90	1·10
MS521	108 × 101 mm. Nos. 517/20	2·75	4·00

1984. 60th Anniv of International Chess Federation. Multicoloured.

522	10c. Type **155**	1·00	40
523	35c. Staunton king, rook and pawn (vert)	2·00	1·50
524	75c. Karpov's winning position against Jakobsen in 1980 Olympiad (vert)	3·75	4·25
525	$1 B.V.I. Gold Medal won by Bill Hook at 1980 Chess Olympiad	4·25	5·50

1984. 250th Anniv of "Lloyd's List" (newspaper). Multicoloured.

526	15c. Type **156**	25	30
527	25c. Boeing 747-100	45	50
528	50c. Wreck of "Rhone" (mail steamer), 1867	90	95
529	$1 "Booker Viking" (cargo liner)	1·50	1·60

157 Mail Ship "Boyne", Boeing 747-100 and U.P.U. Logo

1984. Universal Postal Union Congress, Hamburg. Sheet 90 × 69 mm.

MS530	**157** $1 blue and black	2·25	2·50

158 Running

1984. Olympic Games, Los Angeles. Multicoloured.

531	15c. Type **158**	40	40
532	15c. Runner	40	40
533	20c. Wind-surfing	45	45
534	20c. Surfer	45	45
535	30c. Sailing	65	65
536	30c. Yacht	65	65
MS537	97 × 69 mm. Torch-bearer	1·50	1·90

159 Steel Band

1984. 150th Anniv of Abolition of Slavery. Mult.

538	10c. Type **159**	30	35
539	10c. Dancing girls	30	35
540	10c. Men in traditional costumes	30	35
541	10c. Girl in traditional costumes	30	35
542	10c. Festival Queen	30	35
543	30c. Green and yellow dinghies	45	50
544	30c. Blue and red dinghies	45	50
545	30c. White and blue dinghies	45	50
546	30c. Red and yellow dinghies	45	50
547	30c. Blue and white dinghies	45	50

DESIGNS: Various aspects of Emancipation Festival. Nos. 543/7 form a composite design, the sail colours of the dinghies being described.

160 Sloop

1984. Boats. Multicoloured.

548	10c. Type **160**	40	20
549	35c. Fishing boat	60	65
550	60c. Schooner	75	1·25
551	75c. Cargo boat	75	1·60
MS552	125 × 90 mm. Nos. 548/51	1·50	4·00

161 One Cent Coin and Aerial View

1985. New Coinage. Coins and Local Scenery. Multicoloured.

553	1c. Type **161**	10	10
554	5c. Five cent coin and boulders on beach	10	10
555	10c. Ten cent coin and scuba diving	20	20
556	25c. Twenty-five cent coin and yachts	45	50
557	50c. Fifty cent coin and jetty	90	1·25
558	$1 One dollar coin and beach at night	1·75	2·25
MS559	103 × 159 mm. Nos. 553/8	3·00	7·00

162 Red-billed Tropic Bird **163** The Queen Mother at Festival of Remembrance

1985. Birds of the British Virgin Islands. Multicoloured.

560	1c. Type **162**	1·00	2·50
561	2c. Yellow-crowned night heron ("Night Gaulin")	1·00	2·50
562	5c. Mangrove cuckoo ("Rain Bird")	1·50	2·00
563	8c. Northern mockingbird ("Mockingbird")	1·50	2·75
564	10c. Grey kingbird ("Chinchary")	1·50	40
565	12c. Red-necked pigeon ("Wild Pigeon")	2·25	1·50
649	15c. Least bittern ("Bittlin")	2·75	1·25
567	18c. Smooth-billed ani ("Black Witch")	2·75	3·25
651	20c. Clapper rail ("Pond Shakey")	2·75	1·25
652	25c. American kestrel ("Killy-killy")	2·75	1·25
570	30c. Pearly-eyed thrasher ("Thrushie")	2·75	1·75
654	35c. Bridled quail dove ("Marmi Dove")	2·75	1·25
572	40c. Green-backed heron ("Little Gaulin")	3·00	1·75
573	50c. Scaly-breasted ground dove ("Ground Dove")	3·25	3·50
574	60c. Little blue heron ("Blue Gaulin")	3·75	5·00
658	$1 Audubon's shearwater ("Pimleco")	5·00	5·50
576	$2 Blue-faced booby ("White Booby")	5·00	8·50
577	$3 Cattle egret ("Cow Bird")	6·50	12·00
578	$5 Zenaida dove ("Turtle Dove")	8·50	14·00

1985. Life and Times of Queen Elizabeth the Queen Mother. Multicoloured.

579A	10c. Type **163**	10	20
580A	10c. At Victoria Palace Theatre, 1984	10	20
581A	25c. At the engagement of the Prince of Wales, 1981	15	40
582A	25c. Opening Celia Johnson Theatre, 1985	15	40
583A	50c. The Queen Mother on her 82nd birthday	20	70
584A	50c. At the Tate Gallery, 1983	20	70
585A	75c. At the Royal Smithfield Show, 1983	25	1·00
586A	75c. Unveiling Mountbatten Statue, 1983	25	1·00
MS587A	85 × 114 mm. $1 At Columbia University; $1 At a Wedding, St. Margaret's, Westminster, 1983	85	4·00

164 Seaside Sparrow **165** S.V. "Flying Cloud"

1985. Birth Bicentenary of John J. Audubon (ornithologist). Designs showing original paintings. Multicoloured.

588	5c. Type **164**	30	20
589	30c. Passenger pigeon	40	70
590	50c. Yellow-breasted chat	45	1·75
591	$1 American kestrel	50	2·75

1986. Visiting Cruise Ships. Multicoloured.

592	35c. Type **165**	80	85
593	50c. M.V. "Newport Clipper"	1·10	1·50
594	75c. M.V. "Cunard Countess"	1·10	2·50
595	$1 M.V. "Sea Goddess"	1·25	3·00

1986. Inaugural Flight of Miami–Beef Island Air Service. Nos 581/2 and 585/6 optd **MIAMI B.V.I. INAUGURAL FLIGHT**.

596A	25c. At the engagement of the Prince of Wales, 1981	40	50
597A	25c. Opening Celia Johnson Theatre, 1985	40	50
598A	75c. At the Royal Smithfield Show, 1983	1·25	1·50
599A	75c. Unveiling Mountbatten statue, 1983	1·25	1·50

167 Queen Elizabeth II in 1958

1986. 60th Birthday of Queen Elizabeth II. Multicoloured.

600	12c. Type **167**	15	20
601	35c. At a Maundy Service	20	45
602	$1.50 Queen Elizabeth	45	1·75
603	$2 During a visit to Canberra, 1982 (vert)	60	2·25
MS604	85 × 115 mm. $3 Queen with bouquet	3·50	6·00

168 Miss Sarah Ferguson

1986. Royal Wedding. Multicoloured.

605	35c. Type **168**	30	70
606	35c. Prince Andrew and Miss Sarah Ferguson	30	70
607	$1 Prince Andrew in morning dress (horiz)	50	1·25
608	$1 Miss Sarah Ferguson (different) (horiz)	50	1·25
MS609	115 × 85 mm. $4 Duke and Duchess of York in carriage after wedding (horiz)	2·50	6·00

169 Harvesting Sugar Cane

1986. History of Rum Making. Multicoloured.

610	12c. Type **169**	1·00	20
611	40c. Bringing sugar cane to mill	1·75	1·25
612	60c. Rum distillery	2·25	3·50
613	$1 Delivering barrels of rum to ship	5·50	5·50
MS614	115 × 84 mm. $2 Royal Navy rum issue	6·50	8·50

170 "Sentinel"

1986. 20th Anniv of Cable and Wireless Caribbean Headquarters, Tortola. Cable Ships. Multicoloured.

615	35c. Type **170**	60	80
616	35c. "Retriever" (1961)	60	80
617	60c. "Cable Enterprise" (1964)	75	1·50
618	60c. "Mercury" (1962)	75	1·50
619	75c. "Recorder" (1955)	75	1·75
620	75c. "Pacific Guardian" (1984)	75	1·75
621	$1 "Great Eastern" (1860's)	80	2·00
622	$1 "Cable Venture" (1977)	80	2·00
MS623	Four sheets, each 102 × 131 mm. (a) 40c. × 2 As 35c. (b) 50c. × 2 As 60c. (c) 80c. × 2 As 75c. (d) $1.50 × 2 As $1 Set of 4 sheets	5·00	12·00

1986. Centenary of Statue of Liberty. T **17** and similar vert views of Statue in separate miniature sheets. Multicoloured.

MS624	Nine sheets, each 85 × 115 mm. 50c.; 75c.; 90c.; $1; $1.25; $1.50; $1.75; $2; $2.50 Set of 9 sheets	5·00	13·00

172 18th-century Spanish Galleon

1987. Shipwrecks. Multicoloured.

625	12c. Type **172**	2·50	55
626	35c. H.M.S. "Astrea" (frigate), 1808	3·75	1·40
627	75c. "Rhone" (mail steamer), 1867	5·50	4·50
628	$1.50 "Captain Rokos" (freighter), 1929	8·00	11·00
MS629	85 × 65 mm. $1.50, "Volvart", 1819	16·00	15·00

173 Outline Map and Flag of Montserrat

174 Spider Lily

1987. 11th Meeting of Organization of Eastern Caribbean States. Each showing map and flag. Multicoloured.
630 10c. Type **173** 70 70
631 15c. Grenada 80 75
632 20c. Dominica 85 80
633 25c. St. Kitts-Nevis . . . . . 90 1·00
634 35c. St. Vincent and Grenadines . . . . 1·40 1·00
635 50c. British Virgin Islands . . 2·00 2·50
636 75c. Antigua and Barbuda . . 2·25 3·25
637 $1 St. Lucia . . . . 2·75 3·50

1987. Opening of Botanical Gardens. Multicoloured.
638 12c. Type **174** 80 35
639 35c. Barrel cactus . . . . . 1·75 1·00
640 $1 Wild plantain . . . . . . 2·75 3·25
641 $1.50 Little butterfly orchid 8·00 8·50
MS642 139 × 104 mm. $2.50, White cedar . . . . 3·75 6·00

175 Early Mail Packet and 1867 1s. Stamp

1987. Bicentenary of Postal Services. Multicoloured.
662 10c. Type **175** . . . . 1·75 80
663 20c. Map and 1899 1d. stamp 2·25 1·25
664 35c. Road Town Post Office and Customs House, c. 1913, and 1847 4d. stamp . . . . 2·50 1·75
665 $1.50 Piper Apache mail plane and 1964 25c. definitive . . . . 7·50 11·00
MS666 70 × 60 mm. $2.50, Mail ship, 1880's, and 1880 1d. . . . . . . 6·00 10·00

1988. 500th Birth Anniv of Titian (artist). As T **238** of Antigua. Multicoloured.
667 10c. "Salome" 65 55
668 12c. "Man with the Glove" . . 70 60
669 20c. "Fabrizio Salvaresio" . . 90 80
670 25c. "Daughter of Roberto Strozzi" . . . . 1·00 90
671 40c. "Pope Julius II" . . . . 1·60 2·00
672 50c. "Bishop Ludovico Beccadelli" . . . . 1·75 2·00
673 60c. "King Philip II" . . . . 1·90 2·50
674 $1 "Empress Isabella of Portugal" . . . . 2·50 2·75
MS675 Two sheets, each 110 × 95 mm. (a) $2 "Emperor Charles V at Muhlberg" (detail). (b) $2 "Pope Paul III and his Grandsons" (detail) Set of 2 sheets 15·00 16·00

176 De Havilland D.H.C.5 over Sir Francis Drake Channel and Staunton Pawn

1988. 1st British Virgin Islands Open Chess Tournament. Multicoloured.
676 35c. Type **176** . . . . 7·00 1·75
677 $1 Jose Capablanca (former World Champion) and Staunton king . . . . . . 11·00 8·50
MS678 109 × 81 mm. $2 Chess match . . . . 12·00 12·00

177 Hurdling

1988. Olympic Games, Seoul. Multicoloured.
679 12c. Type **177** 35 25
680 20c. Windsurfing 60 45
681 75c. Basketball . . . . 3·75 3·25
682 $1 Tennis . . . . 3·75 3·75
MS683 71 × 102 mm. $2 Athletics 3·00 4·50

178 Swimmer ("Don't Swim Alone")

1988. 125th Anniv of International Red Cross.
684 **178** 12c. black, red and blue 1·50 40
685 – 30c. black, red and blue 2·25 80
686 – 60c. black, red and blue 3·50 3·00
687 – $1 black, red and blue . . 4·25 4·00
MS688 68 × 96 mm. 50c. × 4 black and red . . . . 5·00 6·50
DESIGNS—HORIZ: 30c. Swimmers ("No swimming during electrical storms"); 60c. Beach picnic ("Don't eat before swimming"); $1 Boat and equipment ("Proper equipment for boating"). VERT: 50c. × 4 Recovery position, clearing airway, mouth-to-mouth resuscitation, cardiac massage.

179 Princess Alexandra

180 Brown Pelican in Flight

1988. Visit of Princess Alexandra. Designs showing different portraits.
689 **179** 40c. multicoloured . . . . 2·50 75
690 – $1.50 multicoloured . . . 5·50 4·75
MS691 102 × 98 mm. $2 multicoloured . . . . 5·00 6·50

1988. Wildlife (1st series). Aquatic Birds. Mult.
692 10c. Type **180** . . . . 1·60 50
693 12c. Brown pelican perched on post . . . . 1·60 55
694 15c. Brown pelican . . . . . 1·75 1·10
695 35c. Brown pelican swallowing fish . . . . . 2·75 3·00
MS696 106 × 76 mm. $2 Common shoveler (horiz) . . . . 11·00 9·00
No. **MS**696 is without the W.W.F. logo.

181 Anegada Rock Iguana

1988. Wildlife (2nd series). Endangered Species. Multicoloured.
697 20c. Type **181** . . . . 1·25 75
698 40c. Virgin Gorda dwarf gecko . . . . 1·50 1·40
699 60c. Hawksbill turtle . . . . 2·50 3·50
700 $1 Humpback whale . . . . 7·00 8·00
MS701 106 × 77 mm. $2 Trunk turtle (vert) . . . . 6·50 8·50

182 Yachts at Start

1989. Spring Regatta. Multicoloured.
702 12c. Type **182** 45 40
703 40c. Yacht tacking (horiz) . . 1·00 1·00
704 75c. Yachts at sunset . . . . 1·60 2·50
705 $1 Yachts rounding buoy (horiz) . . . . 2·00 2·75
MS706 83 × 69 mm. $2 Yacht under full sail . . . . 5·50 6·50

1989. 500th Anniv (1992) of Discovery of America by Columbus (1st issue). Pre-Columbian Arawak Society. As T **247** of Antigua. Multicoloured.
707 10c. Arawak in hammock . . 70 45
708 20c. Making fire . . . . . . 1·00 50
709 25c. Making implements . . . 1·00 60
710 $1.50 Arawak family . . . . 4·50 7·00
MS711 85 × 70 mm. $2 Religious ceremony . . . . 9·00 11·00
See also Nos. 741/5, 793/7 and 818/26.

183 "Apollo II" Emblem

1989. 20th Anniv of First Manned Landing on the Moon. Multicoloured.
712 15c. Type **183** . . . . 1·25 60
713 30c. Edwin Aldrin deploying scientific experiments . . . 2·25 1·00
714 65c. Aldrin and U.S. flag on Moon . . . . 3·00 4·00
715 $1 "Apollo II" capsule after splashdown . . . . 4·00 4·25
MS716 102 × 77 mm. $2 Neil Armstrong (38 × 50 mm) . . . 9·00 10·50

184 Black Harry and Nathaniel Gilbert preaching to Slaves

1989. Bicentenary of Methodist Church in British Virgin Islands. Multicoloured.
717 12c. Type **184** . . . . 1·00 50
718 25c. Methodist school exercise book . . . . . . 1·40 75
719 35c. East End Methodist Church, 1810 . . . . . . 1·60 85
720 $1.25 Reverend John Wesley (founder of Methodism) and church youth choir . . 3·25 6·50
MS721 100 × 69 mm. $2 Dr. Thomas Cole . . . . 4·75 9·00

185 Player tackling

1989. World Cup Football Championship, Italy, 1990. Multicoloured.
722 5c. Type **185** 80 80
723 10c. Player dribbling ball . . 80 80
724 20c. Two players chasing ball 1·50 80
725 $1.75 Goalkeeper diving for ball . . . . 7·00 7·50
MS726 100 × 70 mm. $2 British Virgin Islands team captain . . 8·50 11·00

186 Princess Alexandra and Sunset House

1990. "Stamp World London 90" International Stamp Exhibition. Royal Visitors. Multicoloured.
727 50c. Type **186** . . . . 3·50 3·50
728 50c. Princess Margaret and Government House . . . . 3·50 3·50
729 50c. Hon. Angus Ogilvy and Little Dix Bay Hotel . . . 3·50 3·50
730 50c. Princess Diana with Princes William and Henry and Necker Island Resort 3·50 3·50
MS731 89 × 80 mm. $2 Royal Yacht "Britannia" . . . . 12·00 12·00

187 Audubon's Shearwater

1990. Birds. Multicoloured.
732 5c. Type **187** . . . . 1·50 1·75
733 12c. Red-necked pigeon . . . 2·00 60
734 20c. Moorhen ("Common Gallinule") . . . . 2·25 60
735 25c. Green-backed heron ("Green Heron") . . . . . 2·25 60
736 40c. Yellow warbler . . . . 2·50 1·50
737 60c. Smooth-billed ani . . . 2·75 2·75
738 $1 Antillean crested hummingbird . . . . . . 2·75 3·25
739 $1.25 Black-faced grassquit 2·75 4·50
MS740 Two sheets, each 98 × 70 mm. (a) $2 Royal tern egg (vert) (b) $2 Red-billed tropicbird egg (vert) Set of 2 sheets . . . 9·50 7·00

1990. 500th Anniv (1992) of Discovery of America by Columbus (2nd issue). New World Natural History–Fishes. As T **260** of Antigua. Mult.
741 10c. Blue tang (horiz) . . . . 1·50 60
742 35c. Glass-eyed snapper (horiz) . . . . 2·50 70
743 50c. Slippery dick (horiz) . . 3·00 3·50
744 $1 Porkfish (horiz) . . . . . 4·50 4·75
MS745 100 × 70 mm. $2 Yellow-tailed snapper . . . . 5·00 6·50

188 Queen Elizabeth the Queen Mother

189 Footballers

1990. 90th Birthday of Queen Elizabeth the Queen Mother.
746 **188** 12c. multicoloured 50 25
747 – 25c. multicoloured 90 55
748 – 60c. multicoloured . . . . 1·75 2·25
749 – $1 multicoloured . . . . 2·00 2·50
MS750 75 × 75 mm. $2 multicoloured . . . . 2·75 2·75
DESIGNS: 25, 60c., $2 Recent photographs.

1990. World Cup Football Championship, Italy.
751 **189** 12c. multicoloured 60 40
752 – 20c. multicoloured 90 50
753 – 50c. multicoloured . . . . 1·75 2·00
754 – $1.25 multicoloured . . . 2·50 3·75
MS755 91 × 76 mm. $2 multicoloured . . . . 4·50 4·50
DESIGNS: 20, 50c., $2, Footballers.

190 Judo

1990. Olympic Games, Barcelona (1992). Mult.
756 12c. Type **190** . . . . 1·50 45
757 40c. Yachting . . . . 2·25 1·60
758 60c. Hurdling . . . . 2·75 3·75
759 $1 Show jumping . . . . . 4·00 4·50
MS760 78 × 105 mm. $2 Windsurfing 4·50 4·00

191 Tree-fern, Sage Mountain National Park

192 Haiti Haiti

1991. 30th Anniv of National Parks Trust. Multicoloured.
761 10c. Type **191** . . . . 80 1·00
762 25c. Coppermine ruins, Virgin Gorda (horiz) . . . 1·50 80
763 35c. Ruined windmill, Mt. Healthy . . . . 1·50 80
764 $2 The Baths (rock formation), Virgin Gorda (horiz) . . . . 9·00 11·00

1991. Flowers. Multicoloured.
765 1c. Type **192** . . . . 20 1·25
766 2c. Lobster claw . . . . . . 20 1·25
767 5c. Frangipani . . . . 20 1·25
887 10c. Autograph tree . . . . . 50 1·40
769 12c. Yellow allamanda 40 30
889 15c. Lantana 65 40
771 20c. Jerusalem thorn 50 30
772 25c. Turk's cap 55 40
892 30c. Swamp immortelle . . . 70 50
893 35c. White cedar 85 55
775 40c. Mahoe tree 75 65
895 45c. Pinguin 95 80
896 50c. Christmas orchid . . . . 2·25 1·75
778 70c. Lignum vitae . . . . . . 1·10 2·00
779 $1 African tulip tree . . . . 1·25 2·00
899 $2 Beach morning glory . . . 3·00 5·00
781 $3 Organ pipe cactus . . . . 4·00 7·00
901 $5 Tall ground orchid . . . . 8·50 12·00
783 $10 Ground orchid . . . . . 14·00 18·00

193 "Phoebis sennae"

194 "Agaricus bisporus"

1991. Butterflies. Multicoloured.
784 5c. Type **193** . . . . . . 90 1·25
785 10c. "Dryas iulia" . . . . 1·00 1·25
786 15c. "Junonia evarete" . . . 1·50 75
787 20c. "Dione vanillae" . . . 1·60 80
788 25c. "Battus polydamus" . . 1·60 1·00
789 30c. "Eurema lisa" . . . . 1·75 1·00
790 35c. "Heliconius charitonius" 1·75 1·10
791 $1.50 "Siproeta stelenes" . . 4·25 6·50
MS792 Two sheets. (a) 77 × 117 mm. $2 "Danaus plexippus" (horiz). (b) 117 × 77 mm. $2 "Biblis hyperia" (horiz) Set of 2 sheets . . . . 14·00 15·00

1991. 500th Anniv (1992) of Discovery of America by Columbus (3rd issue). History of Exploration. As T **277** of Antigua. Multicoloured.
793 12c. multicoloured . . . . . 1·75 50
794 50c. multicoloured . . . . . 3·25 2·00
795 75c. multicoloured . . . . . 4·00 3·25
796 $1 multicoloured . . . . . 4·50 4·00
MS797 105 × 76 mm. $2 black and orange . . . . 8·50 9·50
DESIGNS—HORIZ: 12c. "Vitoria" in Pacific (Magellan 1519–21); 50c. La Salle on the Mississippi, 1682; 75c. John Cabot landing in Nova Scotia, 1497–98; $1 Cartier discovering the St. Lawrence, 1534. VERT: $2 "Santa Maria" (woodcut).

1991. Death Centenary (1990) of Vincent Van Gogh (artist). As T **278** of Antigua. Multicoloured.
798 15c. "Cottage with Decrepit Barn and Stooping Woman" (horiz) . . . . . 1·25 50
799 30c. "Paul Gauguin's Armchair" . . . . 1·75 80
800 75c. "Breton Women" (horiz) 3·00 3·00
801 $1 "Vase with Red Gladioli" . . 3·50 3·50
MS802 103 × 81 mm. $2 "Dance Hall in Arles" (detail) (horiz) 12·00 13·00

1991. Christmas. Religious Paintings by Quinten Massys. As T **291** of Antigua. Multicoloured.
803 15c. "The Virgin and Child Enthroned" (detail) . . . . 1·25 25
804 30c. "The Virgin and Child Enthroned" (different detail) . . . . 2·00 50
805 60c. "Adoration of the Magi" (detail) . . . . 3·50 3·75
806 $1 "Virgin in Adoration" . . 3·75 4·00
MS807 Two sheets, each 102 × 127 mm. (a) $2 "The Virgin standing with Angels". (b) $2 "The Adoration of the Magi" Set of 2 sheets . . . . . . 15·00 17·00

1992. Fungi. Multicoloured.
808 12c. Type **194** . . . . 1·50 55
809 30c. "Lentinula edodes" (horiz) . . . . 2·25 85
810 45c. "Hygocybe acutoconica" 2·25 1·00
811 $1 "Gymnopilus chrysopellus" (horiz) . . . 4·00 6·00
MS812 94 × 68 mm. $2 "Pleurotous ostreatus" (horiz) . . . . . . 12·00 13·00

1992. 40th Anniv of Queen Elizabeth II's Accession. As T **288** of Antigua. Multicoloured.
813 12c. Little Dix Bay, Virgin Gorda . . . . 1·00 30
814 25c. Deadchest Bay, Peter Island . . . . 2·00 90
815 60c. Pond Bay, Virgin Gorda 2·50 2·50
816 $1 Cane Garden Bay, Tortola 2·75 3·00
MS817 75 × 97 mm. $2 Long Bay, Beef Island . . . . 9·50 10·00

195 Queen Isabella of Spain

196 Basketball

1992. 500th Anniv of Discovery of America by Columbus (4th issue). Multicoloured.
818 10c. Type **195** 80 75
819 15c. Fleet of Columbus (horiz) . . . . 1·40 90
820 20c. Arms awarded to Columbus . . . . 1·40 90
821 30c. Landing Monument, Watling Island and Columbus's signature (horiz) . . . . 1·40 1·00
822 45c. Christopher Columbus 1·90 1·40
823 50c. Landing in New World and Spanish royal standard (horiz) . . . . 1·90 1·90
824 70c. Convent at La Rabida 2·25 3·25
825 $1.50 Replica of "Santa Maria" and Caribbean Pavilion, New York World's Fair (horiz) . . . 3·50 4·75
MS826 Two sheets. (a) 116 × 86 mm. $2 Ships of second voyage at Virgin, Gorda (horiz). (b) 86 × 116 mm. $2 De la Cosa's map of New World (horiz) Set of 2 sheets . . . . 12·00 15·00

1992. Olympic Games, Barcelona. Multicoloured.
827 15c. Type **196** . . . . 2·50 75
828 30c. Tennis . . . . 2·50 90
829 60c. Volleyball . . . . 2·75 3·00
830 $1 Football . . . . 3·00 3·75
MS831 100 × 70 mm. $2 Olympic flame . . . . 11·00 13·00

197 Issuing Social Security Cheque

1993. 25th Anniv of Ministerial Government. Multicoloured.
832 12c. Type **197** 40 40
833 15c. Map of British Virgin Islands . . . . 1·25 70
834 45c. Administration building 80 70
835 $1.30 International currency abbreviations . . . . . . 2·25 4·25

198 Cruising Yacht and Swimmers, The Baths, Virgin Gorda

1993. Tourism. Multicoloured.
836 15c. Type **198** . . . . 1·75 50
837 30c. Cruising yacht under sail (vert) . . . . 2·00 60
838 60c. Scuba diving . . . . . 2·75 3·00
839 $1 Cruising yacht at anchor and snorklers (vert) . . . 3·00 3·50
MS840 79 × 108 mm. $1 "Promenade" (trimaran) (vert); $1 Scuba diving (different) (vert) 7·50 8·50

1993. 40th Anniv of Coronation. As T **307** of Antigua.
841 12c. multicoloured . . . . . 90 1·25
842 45c. multicoloured . . . . . 1·25 1·50
843 60c. grey and black . . . . . 1·40 1·75
844 $1 multicoloured . . . . . . 1·60 1·90
DESIGNS: 12c. Queen Elizabeth II at Coronation (photograph by Cecil Beaton); 45c. Orb; 60c. Queen with Prince Philip, Queen Mother and Princess Margaret, 1953; $1 Queen Elizabeth II on official visit.

200 Columbus with King Ferdinand and Queen Isabella

1993. 500th Anniv of Discovery of Virgin Islands by Columbus. Multicoloured.
846 3c. Type **200** 15 40
847 12c. Columbus's ship leaving port 40 40
848 15c. Blessing the fleet 45 45
849 25c. Arms and flag of B.V.I. 60 60
850 30c. Columbus and "Santa Maria" 70 70
851 45c. Ships of second voyage 95 95
852 60c. Columbus in ship's boat 1·50 2·25
853 $1 Landing of Columbus . . 2·00 2·50
MS854 Two sheets, each 120 × 80 mm. (a) $2 Amerindians sighting fleet. (b) $2 Christopher Columbus and ships Set of 2 sheets . . . . 11·00 13·00

201 Library Services Publications

1993. 50th Anniv of Secondary Education and Library Services. Multicoloured.
855 5c. Type **201** . . . . 60 1·00
856 10c. Secondary school sports 2·00 1·25
857 15c. Stanley Nibbs (school teacher) (vert) . . . . . 1·00 60
858 20c. Mobile library . . . . . 1·50 70
859 30c. Dr. Norwell Harrigan (adminstrator and lecturer) (vert) . . . . 1·50 70
860 35c. Children in library . . . 1·50 70
861 70c. Commemorative inscription on book . . . 2·50 3·50
862 $1 B.V.I. High School . . . 2·75 3·50

202 Anegada Ground Iguana

1994. Endangered Species. Anegada Ground Iguana.
863 **202** 5c. multicoloured 70 70
864 – 10c. multicoloured 70 70
865 – 15c. multicoloured 80 60
866 – 45c. multicoloured . . . . 1·25 1·25
MS867 106 × 77 mm. $2 multicoloured . . . . 5·00 6·00
DESIGNS: 10c. to $2 Different iguanas.
No. **MS**867 does not carry the W.W.F. Panda emblem.

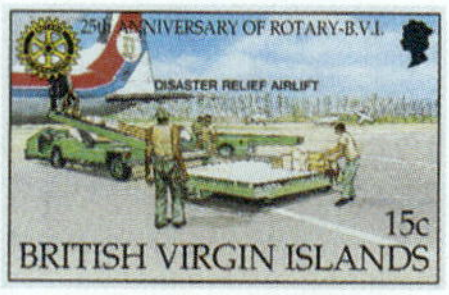

203 Loading Disaster Relief Aircraft

1994. Centenary of Rotary International in B.V.I. Multicoloured.
868 15c. Type **203** 35 35
869 45c. Training children in marine safety 85 85
870 50c. Donated operating table 90 1·00
871 90c. Paul Harris (founder) and emblem . . . . . . 1·60 2·50

1994. 25th Anniv of First Manned Moon Landing. As T **326** of Antigua. Multicoloured.
872 50c. Anniversary logo . . . . 2·00 2·25
873 50c. Lunar landing training vehicle . . . . 2·00 2·25
874 50c. Launch of "Apollo 11" 2·00 2·25
875 50c. Lunar module "Eagle" in flight . . . . 2·00 2·25
876 50c. Moon's surface . . . . . 2·00 2·25
877 50c. Neil Armstrong (astronaut) taking first step 2·00 2·25
MS878 106 × 76 mm. $2 Signatures and mission logo . . . . . . 14·00 14·00

204 Argentina v. Netherlands, 1978

205 Pair of Juvenile Greater Flamingos

1994. World Cup Football Championship, U.S.A. Previous Winners. Multicoloured.
879 15c. Type **204** . . . . 1·25 50
880 35c. Italy v. West Germany, 1982 . . . . 2·00 70
881 50c. Argentina v. West Germany, 1986 . . . . . 2·75 2·25
882 $1.30 West Germany v. Argentina, 1990 . . . . . 4·50 6·50
MS883 74 × 101 mm. $2 U.S. flag and World Cup trophy (horiz) 12·00 14·00

1995. 50th Anniv of United Nations. As T **213** of Bahamas. Multicoloured.
903 15c. Peugeot P4 all-purpose field cars 45 40
904 30c. Foden medium road tanker 75 60
905 45c. SISU all-terrain vehicle 1·00 90
906 $2 Westland Lynx AH7 helicopter . . . . 3·75 5·50

1995. Anegada Flamingos Restoration Project. Multicoloured.
907 15c. Type **205** 85 50
908 20c. Pair of adults 85 55
909 60c. Adult feeding . . . . . 1·40 2·00
910 $1.45 Adult feeding chick . . 2·50 4·00
MS911 80 × 70 mm. $2 Chicks 6·50 7·00

206 "Tortola House with Christmas Tree" (Maureen Walters)

1995. Christmas. Children's Paintings. Mult.
912 12c. Type **206** . . . . 1·75 30
913 50c. "Father Christmas in Rowing Boat" (Collin Collins) . . . . 3·00 1·40
914 70c. "Christmas Tree and Gifts" (Clare Wassell) . . 3·25 2·75
915 $1.30 "Peace Dove" (Nicholas Scott) . . . . . 4·50 6·50

207 Seine Fishing

1996. Island Profiles (1st series). Jost Van Dyke. Multicoloured.
916 15c. Type **207** . . . . 1·50 40
917 35c. Sandy Spit . . . . . . 1·75 55
918 90c. Map . . . . 4·00 3·50
919 $1.50 Foxy's Regatta . . . . 4·25 6·50
See also Nos. 1003/6 and 1105/10.

1996. 70th Birthday of Queen Elizabeth II. As T **165** of Ascension, each incorporating a different photograph of the Queen. Multicoloured.
920 10c. Government House, Tortola 30 20
921 30c. Legislative Council Building 65 55
922 45c. Liner in Road Harbour 1·50 70
923 $1.50 Map of British Virgin Islands . . . . 3·25 5·00
MS924 63 × 65 mm. $2 Queen Elizabeth II . . . . 3·00 3·75

208 Hurdling

1996. Centenary of Modern Olympic Games. Multicoloured.
925 20c. Type **208** 45 30
926 35c. Volley ball 70 60
927 50c. Swimming . . . . . . 1·10 1·75
928 $1 Yachting . . . . 2·00 2·75

209 Mercedes-Benz 500 K A, Cabriolet 1934

1996. "CAPEX '96" International Stamp Exhibition, Toronto. Early Motor Cars. Multicoloured.
929 15c. Type **209** 45 30
930 40c. Citroen 12 Traction saloon, 1934 . . . . 1·00 70
931 60c. Cadillac V-8 Sport Phaeton, 1932 . . . . . . 1·25 1·75
932 $1.35 Rolls Royce Phantom II saloon, 1934 . . . . . 2·75 4·00
MS933 79 × 62 mm. $2 Ford Sport Coupe, 1932 . . . . 3·25 4·25

210 Children with Computer

1996. 50th Anniv of UNICEF. Multicoloured.
934 10c. Type **210** 40 40
935 15c. Carnival costume . . . 50 50
936 30c. Children on Scales of Justice 80 80
937 45c. Children on beach . . . 1·25 1·25

211 Young Rainbows in Art Class

1996. 75th Anniv of Guiding in the British Virgin Islands. Multicoloured.

938	10c. Type **211**	20	20
939	15c. Brownies serving meals	30	25
940	30c. Guides around campfire	50	45
941	45c. Rangers on parade	65	60
942	$2 Lady Baden-Powell	2·75	4·00

212 Spanish Mackerel

1997. Game Fishes. Multicoloured.

943	1c. Type **212**	15	50
944	10c. Wahoo	40	40
945	15c. Great barracuda	75	35
946	20c. Tarpon	75	35
947	25c. Tiger shark	70	30
948	35c. Sailfish	1·25	65
949	40c. Dolphin	1·25	70
950	50c. Black-finned tuna	1·25	80
951	60c. Yellow-finned tuna	1·25	70
952	75c. King mackerel ("Kingfish")	1·40	85
953	$1.50 White marlin	2·50	2·00
954	$1.85 Amberjack	3·00	2·75
955	$2 Atlantic bonito	4·00	4·00
956	$5 Bonefish	7·50	8·50
957	$10 Blue marlin	13·00	14·00

1997. "HONG KONG '97" International Stamp Exhibition. Sheet 130 × 90 mm, containing design as No. 953, but with "1997" imprint date. Mult.

MS958	$1.50, White marlin	2·25	2·75

1997. Golden Wedding of Queen Elizabeth and Prince Philip. As T **173** of Ascension. Multicoloured.

959	30c. Prince Philip with horse	70	1·00
960	30c. Queen Elizabeth at Windsor, 1989	70	1·00
961	45c. Queen in phaeton, Trooping the Colour	90	1·25
962	45c. Prince Philip in Scots Guards uniform	90	1·25
963	70c. Queen Elizabeth and Prince Philip at the Derby, 1993	1·25	1·60
964	70c. Prince Charles playing polo, Mexico, 1993	1·25	1·60
MS965	110 × 70 mm. $2 Queen Elizabeth and Prince Philip in landau (horiz)	3·25	4·00

213 Fiddler Crab

1997. Crabs. Multicoloured.

966	12c. Type **213**	55	50
967	15c. Coral crab	60	50
968	35c. Blue crab	85	60
969	$1 Giant hermit crab	1·75	2·75
MS970	76 × 67 mm. $2 Arrow crab	3·50	4·50

214 "Psychilis macconnelliae"

1997. Orchids of the World. Multicoloured.

971	20c. Type **214**	80	85
972	50c. "Tolumnia prionochila"	1·25	1·10
973	60c. "Tetramicra canaliculata"	1·25	1·40
974	75c. "Liparis elata"	1·40	1·40
MS975	59 × 79 mm. $2 "Dendrobium crumenatum" (vert)	3·25	4·25

215 Sir Francis Drake and Signature

1997. 420th Anniv of Drake's Circumnavigation of the World. Multicoloured.

976	40c. Type **215**	1·40	1·40
977	40c. Drake's coat of arms	1·40	1·40
978	40c. Queen Elizabeth I and signature	1·40	1·40
979	40c. "Christopher" and "Marigold"	1·40	1·40
980	40c. "Golden Hind"	1·40	1·40
981	40c. "Swan"	1·40	1·40
982	40c. "Cacafuego" (Spanish galleon)	1·40	1·40
983	40c. "Elizabeth"	1·40	1·40
984	40c. "Maria" (Spanish merchant ship)	1·40	1·40
985	40c. Drake's astrolabe	1·40	1·40
986	40c. "Golden Hind's" figurehead	1·40	1·40
987	40c. Compass rose	1·40	1·40
MS988	96 × 76 mm. $2 "Sir Francis Drake" (ketch)	3·75	4·50

Nos. 976/87 were printed together, se-tenant, with the backgrounds forming a composite map of Drake's route.

1998. Diana, Princess of Wales Commemoration. Sheet 145 × 70 mm, containing vert designs as T **177** of Ascension. Multicoloured.

MS989	15c. Wearing pink jacket, 1992; 45c. Holding child, 1991; 70c. Laughing, 1991; $1 Wearing high-collared blouse, 1986 (sold at $2.30 + 20c. charity premium)	3·50	4·00

1998. 80th Anniv of Royal Air Force. As T **178** of Ascension. Multicoloured.

990	20c. Fairey IIIF (seaplane)	60	40
991	35c. Supermarine Scapa (flying boat)	85	50
992	50c. Westland Sea King H.A.R.3 (helicopter)	1·40	1·10
993	$1.50 BAe Harrier GR7	2·50	3·25
MS994	110 × 77 mm. 75c. Curtiss H.16 (flying boat); 75c. Curtiss JN-4A; 75c. Bell Airacobra; 75c. Boulton-Paul Defiant	6·50	7·00

216 Fingerprint Cyphoma

1998. Marine Life. Multicoloured.

995	15c. Type **216**	80	40
996	30c. Long-spined sea urchin	1·00	55
997	45c. Split crown feather duster worm	1·40	70
998	$1 Upside down jelly	2·25	3·00
MS999	77 × 56 mm. $2 Giant anemone	4·75	5·00

217 "Carnival Reveller" (Rebecca Peck)

1998. Festival. Children's Paintings. Multicoloured.

1000	30c. Type **217**	1·00	50
1001	45c. "Leader of a Troupe" (Jehiah Maduro)	1·25	65
1002	$1.30 "Steel Pans" (Rebecca McKenzie) (horiz)	3·00	3·75

218 Salt Pond

1998. Island Profiles (2nd series). Salt Island. Multicoloured.

1003	12c. Type **218**	1·25	60
1004	30c. Wreck of "Rhone" (mail steamer)	1·75	65
1005	70c. Traditional house	1·50	2·00
1006	$1.45 Salt Island from the air	3·00	4·00
MS1007	118 × 78 mm. $2 Collecting salt	6·00	7·00

219 Business Studies, Woodwork and Technology Students

1998. Anniversaries. Multicoloured.

1008	5c. Type **219**	25	50
1009	15c. Comprehensive school band	45	30
1010	30c. Chapel, Mona Campus, Jamaica	60	40
1011	45c. Anniversary plaque and University arms	75	60
1012	50c. Dr. John Coakley Lettsom and map of Little Jost Van Dyke	1·00	1·10
1013	$1 The Medical Society of London building and arms	1·60	2·25

EVENTS: 5, 15c. 30th anniv of Comprehensive Education in B.V.I.; 30, 45c. 50th anniv of University of West Indies; 50c., $1 250th anniv of Medical Society of London.

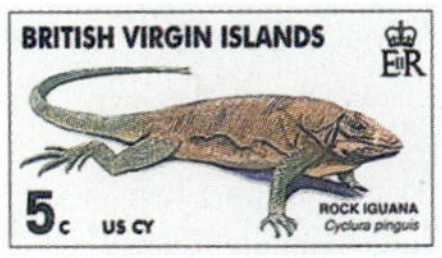

220 Rock Iguana

1999. Lizards. Multicoloured.

1014	5c. Type **220**	30	40
1015	35c. Pygmy gecko	85	45
1016	60c. Slippery back skink	1·50	1·25
1017	$1.50 Wood slave gecko	2·25	3·25
MS1018	100 × 70 mm. 75c. Doctor lizard; 75c. Yellow-bellied lizard; 75c. Man lizard; 75c. Ground lizard	5·00	6·00

1999. Royal Wedding. As T **185** of Ascension. Multicoloured.

1019	20c. Photographs of Prince Edward and Miss Sophie Rhys-Jones	1·00	40
1020	$3 Engagement photograph	4·75	6·00

1999. 30th Anniv of First Manned Landing on Moon. As T **186** of Ascension. Multicoloured.

1021	10c. "Apollo 11" on launch pad	45	35
1022	40c. Firing of second stage rockets	1·00	65
1023	50c. Lunar module on Moon	1·10	85
1024	$2 Astronauts transfer to command module	3·00	4·00
MS1025	90 × 80 mm. $2.50, Earth as seen from moon (circular, 40 mm diam)	3·75	4·50

221 Sunrise Tellin

1999. Sea Shells. Multicoloured.

1026A	5c. Type **221**	45	55
1027A	10c. King helmet	45	55
1028A	25c. Measle cowrie	65	75
1029A	35c. West Indian top shell	75	85
1030A	75c. Zigzag scallop	1·00	1·25
1031A	$1 West Indian fighting conch	1·25	1·50

Nos. 1026A/31A were printed together, se-tenant, with the backgrounds forming a composite design.

222 Zion Hill Methodist Church

1999. Christmas. Church Buildings. Multicoloured.

1032	20c. Type **222**	45	35
1033	35c. Seventh Day Adventist Church, Fat Hogs Bay, 1982	60	45
1034	50c. Ruins of St. Phillip's Anglican Church, Kingstown	85	1·00
1035	$1 St. William's Catholic Church, Road Town	1·60	2·25

223 King Henry VII

224 Duchess of York, 1920s

2000. "Stamp Show 2000" International Stamp Exhibition, London. Kings and Queens of England. Multicoloured.

1036	60c. Type **223**	1·10	1·25
1037	60c. Lady Jane Grey	1·10	1·25
1038	60c. King Charles I	1·10	1·25
1039	60c. King William III	1·10	1·25
1040	60c. King George III	1·10	1·25
1041	60c. King Edward VII	1·10	1·25

2000. 18th Birthday of Prince William. As T **191** of Ascension. Multicoloured.

1042	20c. Prince William as baby (horiz)	60	35
1043	40c. Prince William playing with ball, 1984	90	60
1044	50c. Skiing in British Columbia, 1998	1·25	1·00
1045	$1 In evening dress, 1997 (horiz)	2·00	2·50
MS1046	175 × 95 mm. 60c. Prince William in 1999 (horiz) and Nos. 1042/5	8·50	8·50

2000. 100th Birthday of Queen Elizabeth the Queen Mother. Multicoloured.

1047	15c. Type **224**	50	25
1048	35c. As Queen Mother in 1957	1·00	55
1049	70c. In evening dress, 1970	1·50	1·50
1050	$1.50 With family on 99th birthday	2·50	3·25

225 Red Hibiscus

2000. Flowers. Multicoloured.

1051	10c. Type **225**	30	30
1052	15c. Pink oleander	35	30
1053	35c. Yellow bell	75	55
1054	50c. Yellow and white frangipani	1·00	75
1055	75c. Flamboyant	1·50	2·00
1056	$2 Bougainvillea	3·25	4·50

226 Sunday Morning Well (Site of Emancipation Proclamation)

2000. New Millennium. Multicoloured.

1057	5c. Type **226**	15	25
1058	20c. Nurse Mary Louise Davies M.B.E.	45	35
1059	30c. Cheyney University, U.S.A.	60	45
1060	45c. Enid Leona Scatliffe (former chief education officer)	80	70
1061	50c. H. Lavity Stoutt Community College	90	1·00
1062	$1 Sir J. Olva Georges	1·60	2·00
MS1063	69 × 59 mm. $2 Private Samuel Hodge's Victoria Cross (vert)	3·75	4·25

227 Dr. Q. William Osborne and Arnando Scatliffe

2000. 50th Anniv of Restoration of Legislative Council. Multicoloured.

1064	10c. Type **227**	25	30
1065	15c. H. Robinson O'Neal and A. Austin Henley	35	30
1066	20c. Wilfred W. Smith and John C. Brudenell-Bruce	45	35
1067	35c. Howard R. Penn and I. G. Fonseca	65	55
1068	50c. Carlton L. de Castro and Theodolph H. Faulkner	90	90

1069 60c. Willard W. Wheatley (Chief Minister, 1971–79) . . 1·25 1·40
1070 $1 H. Lavity Stoutt (Chief Minister, 1967–71, 1979–83 and 1986–95) . . . . 1·60 2·00

2001. "HONG KONG 2001" Stamp Exhibition. Sheet 150 × 90 mm, containing T **228** and similar horiz design showing dove. Multicoloured.
MS1071 50c. Type **41**; 50c. Bar-tailed cuckoo dove . . . . . . 2·00 2·50

229 H.M.S. *Wistaria* (sloop), 1923–30

2001. Royal Navy Ships connected to British Virgin Islands (1st series). Multicoloured.
1072 35c. Type **229** . . . . . . 1·00 55
1073 50c. H.M.S. *Dundee* (sloop), 1934–35 . . . . 1·25 75
1074 60c. H.M.S. *Eurydice* (frigate), 1787 . . . . . 1·50 1·40
1075 75c. H.M.S. *Pegasus* (frigate), 1787 . . . . . 1·75 1·60
1076 $1 H.M.S. *Astrea* (frigate), 1807 . . . . 2·25 2·25
1077 $1.50 Royal Yacht *Britannia*, 1966 . . . . . 3·50 4·50
See also Nos. 1101/4.

230 Fridtjof Nansen (Peace Prize, 1922)

2001. Centenary of Nobel Prize. Multicoloured.
1078 10c. Type **230** 60 60
1079 20c. Albert Einstein (Physics Prize,1921) 70 50
1080 25c. Sir Arthur Lewis (Economic Sciences Prize, 1979) 60 50
1081 40c. Saint-John Perse (Literature Prize, 1960) . . 70 70
1082 70c. Mother Teresa (Peace Prize, 1979) . . . . . . 3·00 2·50
1083 $2 Christian Lous Lange (Peace Prize, 1921) . . . 3·25 4·00

2002. Golden Jubilee. As T **200** of Ascension.
1084 15c. brown, mauve and gold . . 70 25
1085 50c. multicoloured . . . . . 1·25 1·00
1086 60c. multicoloured . . . . . 1·25 1·40
1087 75c. multicoloured . . . . . 1·50 1·75
MS1088 162 × 95 mm. Nos. 1084/7 and $1 multicoloured . . . . . 8·00 9·00
DESIGNS—HORIZ: 15c. Princess Elizabeth in A.T.S. uniform, changing wheel; 50c. Queen Elizabeth in fur hat, 1977; 60c. Queen Elizabeth carrying bouquet; 75c. Queen Elizabeth at banquet, Prague, 1996. VERT (38 × 51 mm)—$1 Queen Elizabeth after Annigoni.
Designs as Nos. 1084/7 in No. **MS**1088 omit the gold frame around each stamp and the "Golden Jubilee 1952–2002" inscription.

231 Estuarine Crocodile

2002. Reptiles. Multicoloured.
1089 5c. Type **231** 30 50
1090 20c. Reticulated python . . 60 30
1091 30c. Komodo dragon . . . 80 45
1092 40c. Boa constrictor 95 65
1093 $1 Dwarf caiman . . . . . 2·25 2·25
1094 $2 *Sphaerodactylus parthenopion* (gecko) . . . 4·00 4·50
MS1095 89 × 68 mm. $1.50, Head of *Sphaerodactylus parthenopion* on finger . . . . 3·75 4·50

2002. Queen Elizabeth the Queen Mother Commemoration. As T **202** of Ascension.
1096 20c. brown, gold and purple . . 45 30
1097 60c. multicoloured . . . . . 1·25 1·00
1098 $2 black, gold and purple . . 3·50 3·75
1099 $3 multicoloured . . . . . 4·75 5·50
MS1100 145 × 70 mm. Nos. 1098/9 . . 8·50 9·50
DESIGNS—20c. Duchess of York, 1920s; 60c. Queen Mother at Somerset House, 2000; $2 Lady Elizabeth Bowes-Lyon, 1920; $3 Queen Mother inspecting guard of honour.

Designs as Nos. 1098/9 in No. **MS**1100 omit the "1900–2002" inscription and the coloured frame.

2002. Royal Navy Ships connected to British Virgin Islands (2nd series). As T **229**. Multicoloured.
1101 20c. H.M.S. Invincible (ship of the line) re-capturing H.M.S. *Argo* (frigate), 1783 . . . . 85 40
1102 35c. H.M.S. *Boreas* and H.M.S. *Solebay* (sailing frigates) . . . . 1·50 55
1103 50c. H.M.S. *Coventry* (frigate) . . . . 1·75 1·00
1104 $3 H.M.S. *Argyll* (frigate) . . 7·50 8·00

2002. Island Profiles (3rd series). Virgin Gorda. As T **218**. Multicoloured.
1105 5c. Spring Bay 30 50
1106 40c. Devils Bay . . . . . . 1·00 55
1107 60c. The Baths . . . . . . 1·40 1·00
1108 75c. St. Thomas Bay . . . . 1·50 1·40
1109 $1 Savannah and Pond Bay . . 1·75 1·75
1110 $2 Trunk Bay . . . . . . 3·50 4·50

232 Young West Indian Whistling Duck and Nest

2002. Birdlife International (1st series). West Indian Whistling Duck. Multicoloured.
1111 10c. Type **232** 30 40
1112 35c. Adult bird on rock (vert) 70 55
1113 40c. Adult bird landing on water (vert) 75 70
1114 70c. Two adult birds . . . . 1·25 1·75
MS1115 175 × 80 mm. Nos. 1111/14 and $2 Head of duck . . . . 6·00 7·00
See also Nos. 167/76.

233 200 Metres Race

2003. Anniversaries and Events. Multicoloured.
1116 10c. Type **233** 50 70
1117 10c. Indoor cycling 50 70
1118 35c. Laser class dinghy racing 75 75
1119 35c. Women's long-jumping . . 75 75
1120 50c. Bareboat class yachts . . 1·00 1·25
1121 50c. Racing cruiser class yachts . . . . 1·00 1·25
1122 $1.35 Carlos and Esme Downing (founders) . . . 2·00 2·25
1123 $1.35 Copies of newspaper and anniversary logo . . 2·00 2·25
ANNIVERSARIES AND EVENTS: 10c. Commonwealth Games, 2002; 35c. 20th anniv of British Virgin Islands' admission to Olympic Games; 50c. 30th anniv of Spring Regatta; $1.35, 40th anniv of *The Island Sun* (newspaper).

2003. 50th Anniv of Coronation. A T **206** of Ascension. Multicoloured.
1124 15c. Queen Elizabeth II . . 75 30
1125 $5 Queen and Royal Family on Buckingham Palace balcony . . . . 8·50 9·00
MS1126 95 × 115 mm. As Nos. 1124/5 . . . . 8·00 8·50
Nos. 1124/5 have red frame; stamps from **MS**1126 have no frame and country name in mauve panel.

2003. As T **207** of Ascension.
1127 $5 black, bistre and brown . . 5·25 5·50

2003. 21st Birthday of Prince William of Wales. As T **208** of Ascension. (a) Multicoloured.
1128 50c. Prince William at Tidworth and Beaufort Polo Clubs, 2002 . . . 1·00 75
1129 $2 Playing polo, 2002 and at Holyrood House, 2001 . . 4·00 4·25
(b) As Nos. 1128/9 but with grey frame.
1130 50c. As No. 1128 . . . . . 1·00 75
1131 $2 As No. 1129 . . . . . 4·00 4·25

2003. Centenary of Powered Flight. As T **209** of Ascension. Multicoloured.
1132 15c. Douglas DC-4 . . . . 70 40
1133 20c. Boeing Stearman "Kaydet" 75 40
1134 35c. North American B-25 J Mitchell . . . . 1·00 50
1135 40c. McDonnell Douglas F-4B Phantom . . . . . 1·10 55
1136 70c. Boeing-Vertol CH-47 Chinook helicopter . . . 2·00 1·50
1137 $2 Hughes AH-64 Apache helicopter . . . . 4·25 4·75

234 Townsmen under Arcades

235 Pomegranate

2003. Christmas. "Stories from the Life of St. Ursula: Arrival of the English Ambassadors" by Carpaccio. Multicoloured.
1138 20c. Type **234** 60 25
1139 40c. English ambassadors . . 1·00 50
1140 $2.50 King Maurus of Brittany . . . . 4·50 5·00
MS1141 172 × 87 mm. $1 King Maurus receiving English ambassadors (35 × 35 mm) and Nos. 1138/40 . . . . 7·00 7·50
Nos. 1138/40 show details of the painting and No. **MS**1141 the complete painting.

2004. Game Fish. Designs as Nos. 945/6 and 948/9. Self-adhesive. Size 23 × 19 mm.
1142 15c. Great barracuda . . . 15 20
1143 20c. Tarpon 25 30
1144 35c. Sailfish 40 45
1145 40c. Dolphin 45 50

2004. Local Fruits. Multicoloured.
1146 1c. Hog plum 10 15
1147 10c. Coco plum 15 15
1148 15c. Type **235** 25 20
1149 20c. Cashew 30 30
1150 25c. Sugar apple 40 35
1151 35c. Tamarind 60 45
1152 40c. Soursop 65 50
1153 50c. Mango 80 65
1154 60c. Papaya 90 75
1155 75c. Custard apple . . . . 1·25 90
1156 $1 Otaheite gooseberry . . . 1·60 1·75
1157 $1.50 Guava . . . . 2·50 2·25
1158 $2 Guavaberry . . . . . . 3·25 3·25
1159 $5 Mamee apple . . . . . 7·50 8·00
1160 $10 Passion fruit . . . . . 13·00 14·00

236 Festival Parade

237 Women's Football

2004. Golden Jubilee of Island Festival. Multicoloured.
1161 10c. Type **236** 30 30
1162 60c. Horse racing . . . . . 1·25 75
1163 $1 Canoeing . . . . 1·75 1·60
1164 $2 Festival queen . . . . . 3·50 4·00

2004. Centenary of FIFA (Federation Internationale de Football Association) and Olympic Games, Athens. Multicoloured.
1165 75c. Type **237** . . . . . . 1·40 1·40
1166 $1 Sprinting . . . . 1·75 1·75

238 Black and White Warbler

2005. Birdlife International (2nd series). Caribbean Endemic Bird Festival. Multicoloured.
1167 5c. Type **238** 20 25
1168 10c. Prairie warbler 20 25
1169 15c. Yellow-rumped warbler . . 30 30
1170 25c. Worm-eating warbler . . 50 50
1171 35c. Yellow warbler 70 70
1172 40c. Black-throated warbler . . 80 80
1173 50c. Prothonotary warbler . . 1·00 1·00
1174 60c. Cape May warbler . . . 1·25 1·40
1175 75c. Parula warbler (inscr "Northern Parula") . . . 1·50 1·60
1176 $2.75 Palm warbler . . . . 5·50 6·50

2005. Pope John Paul II Commemoration. As T **219** of Ascension.
1177 75c. multicoloured . . . . . 2·00 1·75

239 Virgin Islands Tree Boa

2005. Endangered Species. Virgin Islands Tree Boa (*Epicrates monensis granti*). Multicoloured.
1178 20c. Type **239** 60 40
1179 30c. Boa in plant (facing left) 80 60
1180 70c. On leafy branch . . . 2·00 1·75
1181 $1.05 In foliage (facing right) . . . . 2·75 3·00

2005. Bicentenary of the Battle of Trafalgar. As T **220** of Ascension. Multicoloured.
1182 5c. HMS *Colossus* in action before breaking the line . . . 60 60
1183 25c. HMS *Boreas* off British Virgin Islands, 1787 . . . 1·25 60
1184 75c. "HMS Victory" (Francis Smitheman) . . . 2·50 2·00
1185 $3 Admiral Lord Nelson (vert) . . . . 7·50 8·50
MS1186 120 × 79 mm. $2.50 HMS *Colossus* firing (44 × 44 mm) . . 7·00 8·00

240 Mr. Joshua Smith (first director of Social Security)

241 Decorated Century Plant

2005. Anniversaries. Multicoloured. Multicoloured.
1187 20c. Type **240** (25th anniv of Social Security) 55 40
1188 40c. Transmitter on mast and world map (40th anniv of Radio Station ZBVI) . . . . 1·00 80
1189 50c. Control tower (25th anniv of Beef Island airstrip) . . . . 1·50 1·00
1190 $1 Emblem (Centenary of Rotary International) . . 2·25 2·75

2005. Christmas. Plants and Flowers. Multicoloured.
1191 15c. Type **241** 50 30
1192 35c. Poinsettia (horiz) . . . 95 70
1193 60c. Decorated ink-berry in pot . . . . 1·60 1·25
1194 $2.50 Snow-on-the-mountain (horiz) . . . . 5·00 6·50

2006. 80th Birthday of Queen Elizabeth II. As T **223** of Ascension. Multicoloured.
1195 15c. Princess Elizabeth in Girl Guide uniform . . . 60 30
1196 75c. Queen Elizabeth II wearing white hat and green and white jacket . . 1·75 1·25
1197 $1.50 Wearing drop earrings 3·25 3·50
1198 $2 Wearing pale mauve hat and jacket . . . . . . 4·50 5·00
MS1199 144 × 75 mm. $1.50 As No. 1196; $2 As No. 1197 . . . 7·50 8·50
Stamps from **MS**1199 do not have white borders.

242 New Red Cross Headquarters, Virgin Gorda

2007. Red Cross Buildings. Multicoloured.
1200 20c. Type **242** 75 80
1201 $3 Former Red Cross building . . . . 4·50 5·00

OFFICIAL STAMPS

1985. Nos. 418/21 and 423/33 optd **OFFICIAL**.
O 1 1c. Purple-tipped sea anemone . . . . 30 1·25
O 2 3c. Common starfish . . . . 45 1·25
O 3 5c. Type **134** 45 45
O 4 8c. Triton's trumpet (shell) . . 55 60
O 5 13c. Flamingo tongue snail . . 80 75
O 6 15c. Spider crab 85 70
O 7 18c. Sea squirts . . . . . . 90 1·75
O 8 20c. True tulip (shell) . . . 90 80
O 9 25c. Rooster tail conch (shell) . . . . 1·25 2·00
O10 30c. Fighting conch (shell) . . 1·40 1·00
O11 60c. Mangrove crab . . . . 2·00 2·50
O12 $1 Coral polyps . . . . . . 3·00 3·75
O13 $2.50 Peppermint shrimp . . 4·50 9·00

O14 $3 West Indian murex (shell) 5·50 10·00
O15 $5 Carpet anemone . . . . 7·50 10·00

1986. Nos. 560/78 optd **OFFICIAL.**
O16 1c. Type **162** . . . . 40 1·50
O17 2c. Yellow-crowned night heron . . . . 40 1·50
O18 5c. Mangrove cuckoo . . . 55 1·50
O19 8c. Northern mockingbird 55 2·25
O20 10c. Grey kingbird . . . . . 70 1·50
O21 12c. Red-necked pigeon . . 70 40
O22 15c. Least bittern 70 40
O23 18c. Smooth-billed ani . . . 70 75
O24 20c. Clipper rail . . . . . . 1·00 1·00
O25 25c. American kestrel . . . 1·00 1·00
O26 30c. Pearly-eyed thrasher . . 1·25 1·00
O27 35c. Bridled quail dove . . . 1·25 1·00
O28 40c. Green-backed heron . . 1·25 1·00
O29 50c. Scaly-breasted ground dove . . . . 1·40 1·75
O30 60c. Little blue heron . . . 1·50 2·50
O31 $1 Audubon's shearwater . . 2·25 3·50
O32 $2 Blue-faced booby . . . . 2·50 4·00
O33 $3 Cattle egret . . . . . . 6·00 7·00
O34 $5 Zenaida dove . . . . . . 6·50 7·50

1991. Nos. 767/8, 771, 773/9 and 781 optd **OFFICIAL.**
O35 5c. Frangipani . . . . . . 45 1·25
O36 10c. Autograph tree . . . . 45 1·25
O37 20c. Jerusalem thorn 55 55
O38 30c. Swamp immortelle . . . 70 55
O39 35c. White cedar 70 55
O40 40c. Mahoe tree 80 70
O41 45c. Pinguin 80 75
O42 50c. Christmas orchid . . . 1·50 90
O43 70c. Lignum vitae . . . . . 1·50 2·25
O44 $1 African tulip tree . . . . 1·50 2·50
O45 $3 Organ pipe cactus . . . . 4·00 6·50

BRUNEI Pt. 1

A Sultanate on the North Coast of Borneo.

100 cents = 1 dollar.

1 Star and Local Scene

1895.
1 **1** ½c. brown . . . . 4·25 20·00
2 1c. brown . . . . 3·25 15·00
3 2c. black . . . . 4·00 16·00
4 3c. blue . . . . 3·75 14·00
5 5c. green . . . . 6·50 17·00
6 8c. purple . . . . 6·50 35·00
7 10c. red . . . . 8·00 32·00
8 25c. green . . . . 75·00 90·00
9 50c. green . . . . 20·00 £100
10 $1 green . . . . 22·00 £110

1906. Stamps of Labuan optd **BRUNEI.** or surch also.
11 **18** 1c. black and purple . . . . 35·00 55·00
12 2c. on 3c. black and brown 3·50 13·00
13 2c. on 8c. black and orange 27·00 80·00
14 3c. black and brown . . . . 35·00 85·00
15 4c. on 12c. black and yellow 5·00 5·00
16 5c. on 16c. green and brown 45·00 75·00
17 8c. black and orange . . . 10·00 32·00
18 10c. on 16c. green and brown . . . . 6·50 22·00
19 25c. on 16c. green and brown £100 £120
20 30c. on 16c. green and brown £100 £120
21 50c. on 16c. green and brown £100 £120
22 $1 on 8c. black and orange £100 £120

5 View on Brunei River

1907.
23 **5** 1c. black and green . . . . . 2·25 11·00
24 2c. black and red . . . . . 2·50 3·75
25 3c. black and brown . . . . 10·00 22·00
26 4c. black and mauve . . . . 7·50 10·00
27 5c. black and blue . . . . . 50·00 90·00
28 8c. black and orange . . . . 7·50 23·00
29 10c. black and green . . . . 4·50 5·00
30 25c. blue and brown . . . . 32·00 48·00
31 30c. violet and black . . . . 25·00 22·00
32 50c. green and brown . . . . 15·00 22·00
33 $1 red and grey . . . . . . 60·00 90·00

1908.
35 **5** 1c. green . . . . 60 2·00
60 1c. black . . . . 1·00 75
79 1c. brown . . . . 50 2·00
36 2c. black and brown . . . . 4·00 1·25
61 2c. brown . . . . 1·00 8·00
62 2c. green . . . . 2·00 1·00
80 2c. grey . . . . 60 5·00
37 3c. red . . . . 5·50 1·25
63 3c. green . . . . 1·00 6·50
64 4c. purple . . . . 1·50 1·25
65 4c. orange . . . . 2·00 1·00
40 5c. black and orange . . . . 7·00 7·00
82 5c. orange . . . . 80 1·25
67 5c. grey . . . . 19·00 12·00
68 5c. brown . . . . 19·00 1·00
41 8c. blue and indigo . . . . 7·00 11·00
71 8c. blue . . . . 6·00 5·00
72 8c. black . . . . 16·00 75
84 8c. red . . . . 50 1·00
42 10c. purple on yellow . . . . 3·00 1·75
85 10c. violet . . . . 2·00 30
86 15c. blue . . . . 1·75 70
87 25c. purple . . . . 2·75 1·00
44 30c. purple and yellow . . . 9·00 12·00
88 30c. black and orange . . . 2·50 1·00
77 50c. black on green . . . . 11·00 15·00
89 50c. black . . . . 4·00 80
46 $1 black and red on blue . . 21·00 48·00
90 $1 black and red . . . . . 10·00 75
47 $5 red on green £160 £250
91 $5 green and orange . . . . 18·00 19·00
92 $10 black and purple . . . . 75·00 30·00
48 $25 black on red £550 £1000

1922. Optd **MALAYA- BORNEO EXHIBITION. 1922.**
51 **5** 1c. green . . . . 6·00 35·00
52 2c. black and brown . . . . 6·00 42·00
53 3c. red . . . . 7·00 48·00
54 4c. red . . . . 13·00 50·00
55 5c. orange . . . . 18·00 55·00
56 10c. purple on yellow . . . . 6·50 55·00
57 25c. lilac . . . . 14·00 80·00
58 50c. black on green . . . . 45·00 £150
59 $1 black and red on blue . . 70·00 £190

7 Native Houses, Water Village

1924.
81 **7** 3c. green . . . . 1·00 5·50
83 6c. black . . . . 1·00 4·25
70 6c. red . . . . 6·00 11·00
74 12c. blue . . . . 4·50 9·00

8 Sultan Ahmed Tajudin and Water Village

1949. Silver Jubilee of H.H. the Sultan.
93 **8** 8c. black and red . . . . . 1·00 1·25
94 25c. purple and orange . . . 1·00 1·60
95 50c. black and blue . . . . 1·00 1·60

1949. 75th Anniv of UPU. As T **20/23** of Antigua.
96 8c. red . . . . 1·00 1·50
97 15c. blue . . . . 3·50 1·50
98 25c. mauve . . . . 1·00 1·50
99 50c. black . . . . 1·00 1·25

9 Sultan Omar Ali Saifuddin

1952. Dollar values as T **8**, but with arms instead of portrait inset.
100 **9** 1c. black 10 50
101 2c. black and orange . . . 10 50
102 3c. black and lake 10 30
103 4c. black and green 10 20
104 6c. black and grey 50 10
123 8c. black and red . . . . . 1·00 10
106 10c. black and sepia 15 10
125 12c. black and violet . . . . 1·50 10
126 15c. black and blue 55 10
109 25c. black and purple . . . 2·50 10
110 50c. black and blue . . . . 2·25 10
111 $1 black and green (horiz) 1·50 1·40
112 $2 black and red (horiz) . . 4·50 2·50
113 $5 black and purple (horiz) 18·00 8·50

11 Brunei Mosque and Sultan Omar

1958. Opening of the Brunei Mosque.
114 **11** 8c. black and green 20 65
115 15c. black and red 25 15
116 35c. black and lilac 30 90

12 "Protein Foods"

1963. Freedom from Hunger.
117 **12** 12c. sepia . . . . 2·75 1·00

13 ITU Emblem

1965. Centenary of ITU.
132 **13** 4c. mauve and brown . . . 35 10
133 75c. yellow and green . . . 1·00 75

14 ICY Emblem

1965. International Co-operation Year.
134 **14** 4c. purple and turquoise 20 10
135 15c. green and lavender . . 55 35

15 Sir Winston Churchill and St. Paul's Cathedral in Wartime

1966. Churchill Commemoration. Designs in black, red and gold and with backgrounds in colours given.
136 **15** 3c. blue 30 50
137 10c. green . . . . 1·50 20
138 15c. brown . . . . 1·75 35
139 75c. violet . . . . 4·25 3·00

16 Footballer's Legs, Ball and Jules Rimet Cup

1966. World Cup Football Championships.
140 **16** 4c. multicoloured 20 15
141 75c. multicoloured 80 60

17 WHO Building

1966. Inauguration of WHO Headquarters, Geneva.
142 **17** 12c. black, green and blue 40 65
143 25c. black, purple and ochre . . . . 60 1·25

18 "Education"

1966. 20th Anniv of UNESCO.
144 **18** 4c. multicoloured 35 10
145 – 15c. yellow, violet and olive 75 50
146 – 75c. black, purple and orange . . . . 2·50 6·00
DESIGNS: 15c. "Science"; 75c. "Culture".

21 Religious Headquarters Building

1967. 1400th Anniv of Revelation of the Koran.
147 **21** 4c. multicoloured 10 10
148 10c. multicoloured 15 10
149 – 25c. multicoloured 20 30
150 – 50c. multicoloured . . . . 35 1·50
Nos. 149/50 have sprigs of laurel flanking the main design (which has a smaller circle) in place of flagpoles.

22 Sultan of Brunei, Mosque and Flags

1968. Installation of Y.T.M. Seri Paduka Duli Pengiran Temenggong. Multicoloured.
151 4c. Type **22** 15 60
152 12c. Sultan of Brunei, Mosque and Flags (different) (horiz) . . . . . 40 1·50
153 25c. Type **22** . . . . 55 2·00

23 Sultan of Brunei

24 Sultan of Brunei

1968. Birthday of Sultan.
154 **23** 4c. multicoloured 10 35
155 12c. multicoloured 20 75
156 25c. multicoloured . . . . 30 1·40

1968. Coronation of Sultan of Brunei.
157 4c. multicoloured 15 25
158 12c. multicoloured 25 50
159 25c. multicoloured 40 75

25 New Building and Sultan's Portrait

1968. Opening of Hall of Language and Literature Bureau. Multicoloured.
160 10c. Type **25** . . . . 20 1·75
161 15c. New Building and Sultan's portrait (48½ × 22 mm) 20 35
162 30c. As 15c. 45 90

27 Human Rights Emblem and struggling Man

1968. Human Rights Year.
163 **27** 12c. black, yellow and green 10 20
164 25c. black, yellow and blue 15 25
165 75c. black, yellow and purple . . . . 45 1·75

28 Sultan of Brunei and WHO Emblem

1968. 20th Anniv of World Health Organization.

166	**28**	4c. yellow, black and blue	30	30
167		15c. yellow, black and violet	55	65
168		25c. yellow, black and olive	65	1·25

29 Deep Sea Oil-Rig, Sultan of Brunei and inset portrait of Pengiran Di-Gadong

1969. Installation (9th May, 1968) of Pengiran Shahbandar as Y.T.M. Seri Paduka Duli Pengiran Di-Gadong Sahibol Mal.

169	**29**	12c. multicoloured	85	50
170		40c. multicoloured	1·25	2·00
171		50c. multicoloured	1·25	2·00

30 Aerial View of Parliament Buildings

1969. Opening of Royal Audience Hall and Legislative Council Chamber.

172	**30**	12c. multicoloured	20	25
173		25c. multicoloured	30	45
174	–	50c. red and violet	60	3·25

DESIGN: 50c. Elevation of new buildings.

32 Youth Centre and Sultan's Portrait

1969. Opening of New Youth Centre.

175	**32**	6c. multicoloured	20	1·00
176		10c. multicoloured	25	10
177		30c. multicoloured	70	1·00

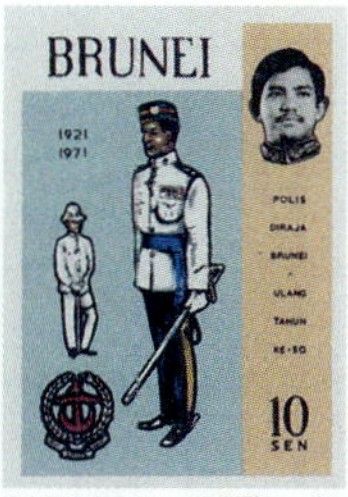

33 Soldier, Sultan and Badge

34 Badge, and Officer in Full-dress Uniform

1971. 10th Anniv of Royal Brunei Malay Regiment. Multicoloured.

178		10c. Type **33**	80	30
179		15c. Bell 205 Iroquois helicopter, Sultan and badge (horiz)	1·75	70
180		75c. "Pahlawan" (patrol boat), Sultan and badge (horiz)	3·25	7·00

1971. 50th Anniv of Royal Brunei Police Force. Multicoloured.

181		10c. Type **34**	50	30
182		15c. Badge and Patrol constable	60	90
183		50c. Badge and Traffic constable	1·10	6·00

35 Perdana Wazir, Sultan of Brunei and View of Water Village

1971. Installation of the Yang Teramat Mulia as the Perdana Wazir.

184	**35**	15c. multicoloured	40	50
185	–	25c. multicoloured	70	1·00
186	–	50c. multicoloured	1·40	5·00

Nos. 185/6 show various views of Brunei Town.

36 Pottery

1972. Opening of Brunei Museum. Mult.

187		10c. Type **36**	30	10
188		12c. Straw-work	40	20
189		15c. Leather-work	45	20
190		25c. Gold-work	1·25	1·25
191		50c. Museum Building (58 × 21 mm)	2·25	5·50

37 Modern Building, Queen Elizabeth and Sultan of Brunei

1972. Royal Visit. Each design with portrait of Queen and Sultan. Multicoloured.

192		10c. Type **37**	70	20
193		15c. Native houses	95	55
194		25c. Mosque	2·00	1·60
195		50c. Royal Assembly Hall	3·75	7·00

38 Secretariat Building

1972. Renaming of Brunei Town as Bandar Seri Begawan.

196	**38**	10c. multicoloured	20	15
197	–	15c. green, yellow and black	25	15
198	–	25c. blue, yellow and black	45	50
199	–	50c. red, blue and black	75	2·25

VIEWS: 15c. Darul Hana Palace; 25c. Old Brunei Town; 50c. Town and Water Village.

39 Blackburn Beverley C1 parachuting Supplies

1972. Opening of R.A.F. Museum, Hendon. Multicoloured.

200		25c. Type **39**	1·75	1·25
201		75c. Blackburn Beverley C1 landing	3·25	4·75

1972. Royal Silver Wedding. As T **52** of Ascension, but with girl with traditional flower-pot, and boy with bowl and pipe in background.

210		12c. red	10	10
211		75c. green	20	50

41 Interpol H.Q., Paris

1973. 50th Anniv of Interpol.

212	**41**	25c. green, purple and black	1·50	1·25
213	–	50c. blue, ultram & red	1·50	1·25

DESIGN: 50c. Different view of the H.Q.

42 Sultan, Princess Anne and Captain Phillips

1973. Royal Wedding.

214	**42**	25c. multicoloured	15	10
215		50c. multicoloured	15	25

43 Churchill Painting

44 Sultan Sir Hassanal Bolkiah Mu'izzaddin Waddaulah

1973. Opening of Churchill Memorial Building. Multicoloured.

216		12c. Type **43**	10	20
217		50c. Churchill statue	30	1·40

1975. Multicoloured. Background colours given.

218	**44**	4c. green	20	20
219		5c. blue	20	30
220		6c. green	3·25	6·50
221		10c. lilac	30	10
222		15c. brown	2·50	40
223		20c. stone	30	20
224		25c. green	40	15
225		30c. blue	40	15
226		35c. grey	40	20
227		40c. purple	40	20
228		50c. brown	40	20
229		75c. green	60	3·50
256		$1 orange	1·50	3·50
231		$2 yellow	2·25	11·00
232		$5 silver	3·00	18·00
233		$10 gold	5·00	32·00

45 Aerial View of Airport

1974. Inauguration of Brunei International Airport. Multicoloured.

234		50c. Type **45**	1·25	1·00
235		75c. Sultan in Army uniform, and airport (48 × 36 mm)	1·50	1·50

46 U.P.U. Emblem and Sultan

1974. Centenary of Universal Postal Union.

236	**46**	12c. multicoloured	20	20
237		50c. multicoloured	40	1·40
238		75c. multicoloured	50	1·75

47 Sir Winston Churchill

1974. Birth Centenary of Sir Winston Churchill.

239	**47**	12c. black, blue and gold	25	20
240	–	75c. black, green and gold	45	1·40

DESIGN: 75c. Churchill smoking cigar (profile).

48 Boeing 737 and R.B.A. Crest

1975. Inauguration of Royal Brunei Airlines. Mult.

241		12c. Type **48**	1·00	25
242		35c. Boeing 737 over Bandar Seri Begawan Mosque	1·75	1·50
243		75c. Boeing 737 in flight	2·50	3·50

1976. Surch **10 sen**.

263	**44**	10c. on 6c. brown	1·75	1·75

50 Royal Coat of Arms

51 The Moment of Crowning

1977. Silver Jubilee. Multicoloured.

264		10c. Type **50**	15	15
265		20c. Imperial State Crown	20	20
266		75c. Queen Elizabeth (portrait by Annigoni)	45	60

1978. 25th Anniv of Coronation. Multicoloured.

267		10c. Type **51**	15	10
268		20c. Queen in Coronation regalia	20	20
269		75c. Queen's departure from Abbey	55	80

52 Royal Crest

53 Human Rights Emblem and Struggling Man

1978. 10th Anniv of Coronation of Sultan.

270	**52**	10c. black, red and yellow	20	10
271	–	20c. multicoloured	40	25
272	–	75c. multicoloured	1·10	3·50
MS273		182 × 77 mm. Nos. 270/2	12·00	16·00

DESIGNS: 20c. Coronation; 75c. Sultan's Crown.

1978. Human Rights Year.

274	**53**	10c. black, yellow and red	15	10
275		20c. black, yellow and violet	20	35
276		75c. black, yellow and bistre	40	2·50

Type **53** is similar to the design used for the previous Human Rights issue in 1968.

54 Smiling Children

1979. International Year of the Child.

277	**54**	10c. multicoloured	20	10
278	–	$1 black and green	80	2·50

DESIGN: $1 I.Y.C. emblem.

55 Earth Satellite Station

1979. Telisai Earth Satellite Station. Multicoloured.

279		10c. Type **55**	20	15
280		20c. Satellite and antenna	30	40
281		75c. Television camera, telex machine and telephone	60	2·75

56 Hegira Symbol

57 Installation Ceremony

1979. Moslem Year 1400 A.H. Commemoration.
282 **56** 10c. black, yellow and green 10 15
283 20c. black, yellow and blue 15 30
284 75c. black, yellow and lilac 45 2·25
MS285 178 × 200 mm. Nos. 282/4 3·00 7·50

1980. 1st Anniv of Prince Sufri Bolkiah's Installation as First Wazir. Multicoloured. Blue borders.
286 10c. Type **57** 15 10
287 75c. Prince Sufri . . . . . . 85 2·00

1980. 1st Anniv of Prince Jefri Bolkiah's Installation as Second Wazir. Designs similar to T **57**. Multicoloured. Green borders.
288 10c. Installation ceremony . . 15 10
289 75c. Prince Jefri . . . . . . 85 2·25

58 Royal Umbrella and Sash

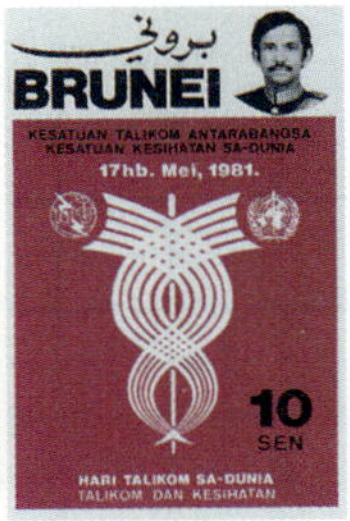
59 ITU and WHO Emblems

1981. Royal Regalia (1st series). Multicoloured.
290 10c. Type **58** 20 15
291 15c. Sword and Shield . . . 35 25
292 20c. Lance and Sheath . . . 40 40
293 30c. Betel Leaf Container . . 60 1·25
294 50c. Coronation Crown (39 × 22 mm) . . . . . . 1·25 5·00
MS295 98 × 142 mm. Nos. 290/4 5·00 8·00
See Nos. 298/303, 314/19 and 320/5.

1981. World Telecommunications and Health Day.
296 **59** 10c. black and red 50 25
297 75c. black, blue and violet 2·25 5·00

60 Shield and Broadsword

61 Prince Charles as Colonel of the Welsh Guards

1981. Royal Regalia (2nd series). Multicoloured.
298 10c. Type **60** 10 10
299 15c. Blunderbuss and Pouch 20 20
300 20c. Crossed Lances and Sash 30 30
301 30c. Sword, Shield and Sash 40 75
302 50c. Forked Lance . . . . . 60 2·50
303 75c. Royal Drum (29 × 45 mm) . . . . . . 80 4·50

1981. Royal Wedding. Multicoloured.
304 10c. Wedding bouquet from Brunei 15 15
305 $1 Type **61** . . . . 35 1·50
306 $2 Prince Charles and Lady Diana Spencer . . . . . . 50 2·50

62 Fishing

63 Blind Man and Braille Alphabet

1981. World Food Day. Multicoloured.
307 10c. Type **62** 50 15
308 $1 Farm produce and machinery . . . . 4·50 7·50

1981. International Year for Disabled Persons. Multicoloured.
309 10c. Type **63** 65 20
310 20c. Deaf people and sign language . . . . 1·50 80
311 75c. Disabled person and wheelchairs . . . . 3·00 6·75

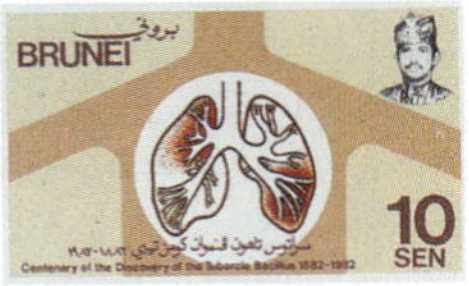
64 Drawing of Infected Lungs

1982. Centenary of Robert Koch's Discovery of Tubercle Bacillus. Multicoloured.
312 10c. Type **64** 50 25
313 75c. Magnified tubercle bacillus and microscope . . 3·00 6·50

1982. Royal Regalia (3rd series). As T **60**. Mult.
314 10c. Ceremonial Ornament 10 10
315 15c. Silver Betel Caddy . . . 20 20
316 20c. Traditional Flowerpot 25 30
317 30c. Solitary Candle 50 90
318 50c. Golden Pipe . . . . . . 70 2·50
319 75c. Royal Chin Support (28 × 45 mm) . . . . . . 90 4·00

1982. Royal Regalia (4th series). As T **60**. Mult.
320 10c. Royal Mace 25 10
321 15c. Ceremonial Shield and Spears 35 30
322 20c. Embroidered Ornament 45 40
323 30c. Golden-tasseled Cushion 75 1·50
324 50c. Ceremonial Dagger and Sheath . . . . 1·25 3·50
325 75c. Religious Mace (28 × 45 mm) . . . . . . 1·60 4·50

65 Brunei Flag

67 Football

66 "Postal Service"

1983. Commonwealth Day.
326 **65** 10c. multicoloured 15 80
327 – 20c. blue, black and buff 20 90
328 – 75c. blue, black and green 45 1·40
329 – $2 blue, black and yellow 1·10 2·00
DESIGNS: 20c. Brunei Mosque; 75c. Machinery; $2 Sultan of Brunei.

1983. World Communications Year.
330 **66** 10c. multicoloured 15 10
331 – 75c. yellow, brown and black 60 75
332 – $2 multicoloured . . . . 1·75 2·25
DESIGNS: 75c. "Telephone Service"; $2 "Communications".

1983. Official Opening of the National Hassanal Bolkiah Stadium. Multicoloured.
333 10c. Type **67** 55 15
334 75c. Athletics . . . . 2·25 1·50
335 $1 View of stadium (44 × 27 mm) . . . . 2·75 4·00

68 Fishermen and Crustacea

1983. Fishery Resources. Multicoloured.
336 10c. Type **68** . . . . 1·50 20
337 50c. Fishermen with net . . . 3·75 1·50
338 75c. Fishing trawler . . . . 4·00 4·25
339 $1 Fishing with hook and tackle . . . . 4·25 4·75

69 Royal Assembly Hall

1984. Independence.
340 **69** 10c. brown and orange . . 20 10
341 – 20c. pink and red 30 20
342 – 35c. pink and purple . . . 60 60
343 – 50c. light blue and blue . . 1·75 1·25
344 – 75c. light green and green 1·75 2·00
345 – $1 grey and brown . . . . 2·00 2·50
346 – $3 multicoloured . . . . . 7·00 10·00
MS347 150 × 120 mm. Nos. 340/6 12·00 16·00
MS348 Two sheets, each 150 × 120 mm, containing 4 stamps (34 × 69 mm). (a) 25c. × 4 grey-black and new blue (Signing of the Brunei Constitution). (b) 25c. × 4 multicoloured (Signing of Brunei–U.K. Friendship Agreement) Set of 2 sheets . . 2·25 4·50
DESIGNS—34 × 25 mm: 20c. Government Secretariat Building; 35c. New Supreme Court; 50c. Natural gas well; 75c. Omar Ali Saifuddin Mosque; $1 Sultan's Palace. 68 × 24 mm: $3 Brunei flag and map of South-East Asia.

70 Natural Forests and Enrichment Planting

1984. Forestry Resources. Multicoloured.
349 10c. Type **70** . . . . 1·00 25
350 50c. Forests and water resources . . . . 2·50 2·25
351 75c. Recreation forests . . . 3·25 4·50
352 $1 Forests and wildlife . . . 4·75 6·00

71 Sultan Omar Saiffuddin 50c. Stamp of 1952

72 United Nations Emblem

1984. "Philakorea" International Stamp Exhibition, Seoul. Multicoloured.
353 10c. Type **71** 50 15
354 75c. Brunei River view 10c.stamp of 1907 . . . . 1·50 2·25
355 $2 Star and view ½c. stamp of 1895 . . . . 2·50 6·50
MS356 Three sheets, 117 × 100 mm, each containing one stamp as Nos. 353/5 Set of 3 sheets . . . 3·75 7·00

1985. Admission of Brunei to World Organizations (1st issue).
357 **72** 50c. black, gold and blue 50 70
358 – 50c. multicoloured 50 70
359 – 50c. multicoloured 50 70
360 – 50c. multicoloured 50 70
MS361 110 × 151 mm. Nos. 357/60 4·00 4·00
DESIGNS: No. 358, Islamic Conference Organization logo; 359, Commonwealth logo; 360, A.S.E.A.N. emblem.
See also Nos. 383/7.

73 Young People and Brunei Flag

1985. International Youth Year. Multicoloured.
362 10c. Type **73** . . . . 2·00 30
363 75c. Young people at work 5·50 7·00
364 $1 Young people serving the community . . . . 6·00 7·50

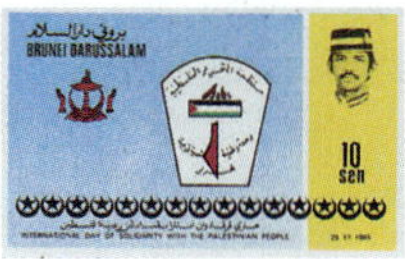
74 Palestinian Emblem

1985. International Palestinian Solidarity Day.
365 **74** 10c. multicoloured . . . . 2·25 20
366 50c. multicoloured . . . . 4·50 1·50
367 $1 multicoloured . . . . . 5·75 3·00

75 Early and Modern Scout Uniforms

76 Sultan Sir Hassanal Bolkiah Mu'izzaddin Waddaulah

1985. National Scout Jamboree. Multicoloured.
368 10c. Type **75** 60 10
369 20c. Scout on tower signalling with flag 90 40
370 $2 Jamboree emblem . . . . 2·75 3·25

1985.
371 **76** 10c. multicoloured 30 10
372 15c. multicoloured 30 10
373 20c. multicoloured 40 10
374 25c. multicoloured 40 15
375 35c. multicoloured 55 20
376 40c. multicoloured 60 25
377 50c. multicoloured 70 35
378 75c. multicoloured 90 50
379 $1 multicoloured . . . . . 1·25 70
380 $2 multicoloured . . . . . 2·75 1·75
381 $5 multicoloured . . . . . 4·25 5·00
382 $10 multicoloured . . . . 8·00 11·00
Nos. 379/82 are larger, size 32 × 39 mm.

1986. Admission of Brunei to World Organizations (2nd issue). As T **72**.
383 50c. black, gold and green . . 50 60
384 50c. black, gold and mauve 50 60
385 50c. black, gold and red . . . 50 60
386 50c. black, gold and blue . . 50 60
MS387 105 × 155 mm. Nos. 383/6 1·50 4·00
DESIGNS: No. 383, World Meteorological Organization emblem; 384, International Telecommunication Union emblem; 385, Universal Postal Union emblem; 386, International Civil Aviation Organization emblem.

78 Soldiers on Assault Course and Bell 205 Iroquois Helicopter

1986. 25th Anniv of Brunei Armed Forces. Multicoloured.
388 10c. Type **78** . . . . 4·25 4·25
389 20c. Operating computer . . 4·50 4·50
390 50c. Anti-aircraft missile, MBB-Bolkow Bo 150L helicopter and missile boat 6·00 6·00
391 75c. Army, commanders and parade . . . . 6·50 6·50
Nos. 388/91 were printed together, se-tenant, forming a composite design.

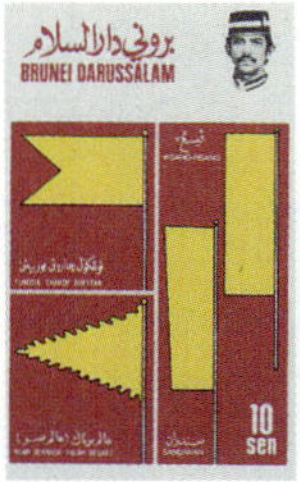
79 Tunggul Charok Buritan, Alam Bernaga (Alam Besar), Pisang-Pisang and Sandaran

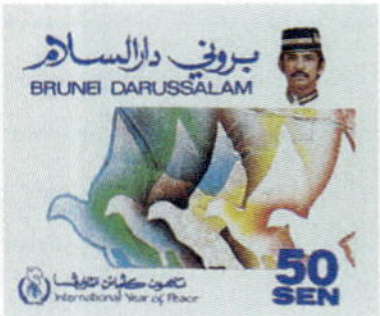
80 Stylized Peace Doves

1986. Royal Ensigns (1st series).
392 **79** 10c. black, yellow and red 30 10
393 – 75c. multicoloured . . . . 1·10 1·10
394 – $2 black, yellow and green 2·25 2·75
DESIGNS: 75c. Ula-Ula Besar, Sumbu Layang and Payong Haram; $2 Panji-Panji, Chogan Istiadat (Chogan Di-Raja) and Chogan Ugama.

1986. Royal Ensigns (2nd series). As T **79**.
395 10c. multicoloured 30 10
396 75c. black, red and yellow . . 1·10 1·10
397 $2 multicoloured . . . . . 2·25 2·75

DESIGNS: 10c. Dadap, Tunggul Kawan, Ambal, Payong Ubor-Ubor, Sapu-Sapu Ayeng and Rawai Lidah; 75c. Payong Tinggi and Payong Ubor-Ubor Tiga Ringkat; $2 Lambang Duli Yang Maha Mulia and Mahligai.

1986. International Peace Year. Multicoloured.
398 50c. Type **80** 75 75
399 75c. Stylized hands and "1986" 1·00 1·10
400 $1 International Peace Year emblem and arms of Brunei 1·25 1·50

81 Drug Addict in Cage and Syringe (poster by Othman bin Ramboh)

82 Cannon ("badil")

1987. National Anti-drug Campaign. Children's Posters. Multicoloured.
401 10c. Type **81** 1·50 35
402 75c. Drug addict and noose (Arman bin Mohd. Zaman) 3·00 4·25
403 $1 Blindfolded drug addict and noose (Abidin bin Hj. Rashid) 3·50 5·50

1987. Brassware (1st series). Multicoloured.
404 50c. Type **82** 50 50
405 50c. Lamp ("pelita") 50 50
406 50c. Betel container ("langguai") 50 50
407 50c. Water jug ("kiri") 50 50
See also Nos. 434/7.

83 Map showing Member Countries

1987. 20th Anniv of Association of South East Asian Nations. Multicoloured.
408 20c. Type **83** 35 20
409 50c. Dates and figures "20" 60 50
410 $1 Flags of member states 1·25 1·25

84 Brunei Citizens

1987. 25th Anniv (1986) of Language and Literature Bureau. Multicoloured.
411 10c. Type **84** 30 30
412 50c. Flame emblem and hands holding open book 60 60
413 $2 Scenes of village life 1·50 1·50
Nos. 411/13 were printed together, se-tenant, forming a composite design taken from a mural.

85 "Artocarpus odoratissima"

1987. Local Fruits (1st series). Multicoloured.
414 50c. Type **85** 70 70
415 50c. "Canarium odontophyllum mig" 70 70
416 50c. "Litsea garciae" 70 70
417 50c. "Mangifera foetida lour" 70 70
See also Nos. 421/4, 459/62, 480/2 and 525/8.

86 Modern House

1987. International Year of Shelter for the Homeless.
418 **86** 50c. multicoloured 40 50
419 – 75c. multicoloured 55 65
420 – $1 multicoloured 80 90
DESIGNS: 75c., $1 Modern Brunei housing projects.

1988. Local Fruits (2nd series). As T **85**. Mult.
421 50c. "Durio spp" 95 1·25
422 50c. "Durio oxleyanus" 95 1·25
423 50c. "Durio graveolens" (blue background) 95 1·25
424 50c. "Durio graveolens" (white background) 95 1·25

87 Wooden Lathe

89 Sultan reading Proclamation

88 Patterned Cloth

1988. Opening of Malay Technology Museum. Multicoloured.
425 10c. Type **87** 15 10
426 75c. Crushing sugar cane 55 70
427 $1 Bird scarer 70 85

1988. Handwoven Material (1st series). Mult.
428 10c. Type **88** 10 10
429 20c. Jong Sarat cloth 15 15
430 25c. Si Pugut cloth 20 25
431 40c. Si Pugut Bunga Berlapis cloth 30 35
432 75c. Si Lobang Bangsi Bunga Belitang Kipas cloth 55 80
MS433 105 × 204 mm. Nos. 428/32 3·00 4·50
See also Nos. 442/7.

1988. Brassware (2nd series). As T **82**. Multicoloured.
434 50c. Lidded two-handled pot ("periok") 60 75
435 50c. Candlestick ("lampong") 60 75
436 50c. Shallow circular dish with stand ("gangsa") 60 75
437 50c. Repousse box with lid ("celapa") 60 75

1988. 20th Anniv of Sultan's Coronation. Mult.
438 20c. Type **89** 45 15
439 75c. Sultan reading from Koran 1·00 60
440 $2 In Coronation robes (26 × 63 mm) 2·50 1·60
MS441 164 × 125 mm. Nos. 438/40 2·75 2·75

1988. Handwoven Material (2nd series). As T **88**. Multicoloured.
442 10c. Beragi cloth 15 10
443 20c. Bertabur cloth 20 20
444 25c. Sukma Indra cloth 25 35
445 40c. Si Pugut Bunga cloth 40 75
446 75c. Beragi Si Lobang Bangsi Bunga Cendera Kesuma cloth 75 1·40
MS447 150 × 204 mm. Nos. 442/6 3·00 4·25

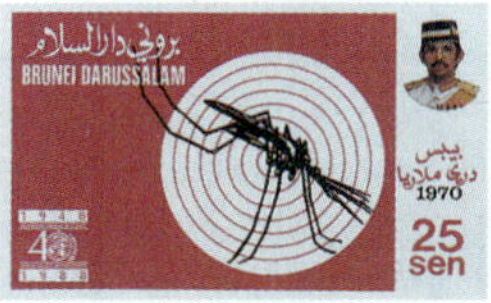
90 Malaria-carrying Mosquito

1988. 40th Anniv of WHO. Multicoloured.
448 25c. Type **90** 1·10 30
449 35c. Man with insecticide spray and sample on slide 1·25 45
450 $2 Microscope and magnified malaria cells 3·00 2·00

91 Sultan and Council of Ministers

1989. 5th Anniv of National Day. Mult.
451 20c. Type **91** 15 10
452 30c. Guard of honour 20 15
453 60c. Firework display (27 × 55 mm) 45 40
454 $2 Congregation in mosque 1·50 1·75
MS455 164 × 124 mm. Nos. 451/4 2·25 2·75

92 Dove escaping from Cage

1989. "Freedom of Palestine". Multicoloured.
456 20c. Type **92** 40 20
457 75c. Map and Palestinian flag 1·50 1·00
458 $1 Dome of the Rock, Jerusalem 2·25 1·40

1989. Local Fruits (3rd series). As T **85**. Mult.
459 60c. "Daemonorops fissa" 2·00 2·50
460 60c. "Eleiodoxa conferta" 2·00 2·50
461 60c. "Salacca zalacca" 2·00 2·50
462 60c. "Calamus ornatus" 2·00 2·50

93 Oil Pump

1989. 60th Anniv of Brunei Oil and Gas Industry. Multicoloured.
463 20c. Type **93** 2·25 30
464 60c. Loading tanker 3·75 2·25
465 90c. Oil well at sunset 4·00 3·00
466 $1 Pipe laying 4·00 3·00
467 $2 Oil terminal 7·50 8·00

94 Museum Building and Exhibits

1990. 25th Anniv of Brunei Museum. Multicoloured.
468 30c. Type **94** 1·50 70
469 60c. Official opening, 1965 2·25 2·25
470 $1 Brunei Museum 3·00 4·00

95 Letters from Malay Alphabet

1990. International Literacy Year. Multicoloured.
471 15c. Type **95** 80 40
472 90c. English alphabet 3·50 4·25
473 $1 Literacy Year emblem and letters 3·50 4·25

96 Tarsier in Tree

97 Symbolic Family

1990. Endangered Species. Western Tarsier. Multicoloured.
474 20c. Western Tarsier on branch 1·25 45
475 60c. Western Tarsier feeding 2·50 3·00
476 90c. Type **96** 3·50 4·50

1990. Worldwide Campaign against AIDS. Multicoloured.
477 20c. Type **97** 3·00 60
478 30c. Sources of infection 3·75 2·00
479 90c. "AIDS" headstone surrounded by skulls 9·50 8·00

1990. Local Fruits (4th series). As T **85**. Mult.
480 60c. "Willoughbea sp." (brown fruit) 3·00 3·75
481 60c. Ripe "Willoughbea sp." (yellow fruit) 3·00 3·75
482 60c. "Willoughbea angustifolia" 3·00 3·75

98 Proboscis Monkey on Ground

1991. Endangered Species. Proboscis Monkey. Multicoloured.
483 15c. Type **98** 1·50 60
484 20c. Head of monkey 1·60 70
485 50c. Monkey sitting on branch 3·00 3·25
486 60c. Female monkey with baby climbing tree 3·25 3·75

99 Junior School Classes

1991. Teachers' Day. Multicoloured.
487 60c. Type **99** 2·25 2·50
488 90c. Secondary school class 2·75 3·50

100 Young Brunei Beauty

1991. Fishes. Brunei Beauty. Multicoloured.
489 30c. Type **100** 1·50 85
490 60c. Female fish 2·50 4·00
491 $1 Male fish 3·00 4·75

101 Graduate with Family

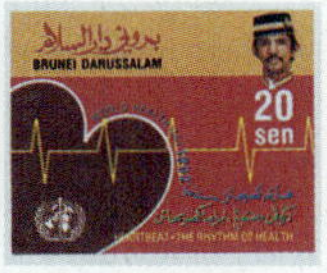
102 Symbolic Heart and Trace

1991. Happy Family Campaign. Multicoloured.
492 20c. Type **101** 70 50
493 60c. Mothers with children 1·75 2·00
494 90c. Family 2·00 3·25

1992. World Health Day.
495 **102** 20c. multicoloured 2·25 50
496 – 50c. multicoloured 3·75 2·50
497 – 75c. multicoloured 5·50 6·50
DESIGNS: 50c., 70c. (48 × 27 mm) Heart and heartbeat trace.

103 Map of Cable System

1992. Launching of Singapore–Borneo–Philippines Fibre Optic Submarine Cable System. Mult.
498 20c. Type **103** 3·00 50
499 30c. Diagram of Brunei connection 3·00 1·50
500 90c. Submarine cable 6·00 6·50

104 Modern Sculptures

1992. Visit ASEAN Year. Multicoloured.
501 20c. Type **104** . . . . 2·75 3·00
502 60c. Traditional martial arts 3·00 3·25
503 $1 Modern sculptures (different) . . . . 3·25 3·50
Nos. 501/3 were printed together, se-tenant, the backgrounds forming a composite design.

105 "ASEAN 25" and Logo

106 Sultan in Procession

1992. 25th Anniv of ASEAN (Association of South East Asian Nations). Multicoloured.
504 20c. Type **105** . . . . 1·25 65
505 60c. Headquarters building 2·75 2·75
506 90c. National landmarks . . 3·50 4·50

1992. 25th Anniv of Sultan's Accession. Mult.
507 25c. Type **106** . . . . 1·90 2·00
508 25c. Brunei International Airport . . . . 1·90 2·00
509 25c. Sultan's Palace . . . . 1·90 2·00
510 25c. Docks and Brunei University . . . . 1·90 2·00
511 25c. Mosque . . . . 1·90 2·00
Nos. 507/11 were printed together, se-tenant, forming a composite design.

107 Crested Wood Partridge

108 National Flag and "10"

1992. Birds (1st series). Multicoloured.
512 30c. Type **107** . . . . 1·00 50
513 60c. Asiatic paradise flycatcher ("Asian Paradise Flycatcher") . . . . 2·00 2·25
514 $1 Great argus pheasant . . 2·25 3·00
See also Nos. 515/17, 518/20, 575/7 and 602/5.

1993. Birds (2nd series). As T **107**. Multicoloured.
515 30c. Long-tailed parakeet . . 1·00 50
516 60c. Magpie robin . . . . . 2·00 2·25
517 $1 Blue-crowned hanging parrot ("Malay Lorikeet") 2·50 3·00

1993. Birds (3rd series). As T **107**. Multicoloured.
518 30c. Chesnut-breasted malkoha . . . . 1·25 50
519 60c. White-rumped shama . . 2·25 2·50
520 $1 Black and red broadbill (vert) . . . . 3·00 3·50

1994. 10th Anniv of National Day. Multicoloured.
521 10c. Type **108** . . . . 1·25 1·25
522 20c. Symbolic hands . . . . 1·25 85
523 30c. Previous National Day symbols . . . . 1·40 95
524 60c. Coat of arms . . . . . 1·75 1·75

1994. Local Fruits (5th issue). As T **85**, but each 36 × 26 mm. Multicoloured.
525 60c. "Nephelium mutabile" 85 1·40
526 60c. "Nephelium xerospermoides" . . . . . 85 1·40
527 60c. "Nephelium spp" . . . 85 1·40
528 60c. "Nephelium macrophyllum" . . . . . 85 1·40

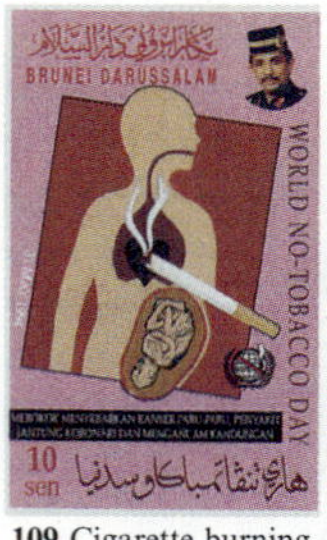

109 Cigarette burning Heart and Deformed Baby in Womb

110 Raja Isteri (wife of Sultan in Guide uniform)

1994. World No Tobacco Day. Multicoloured.
529 10c. Type **109** 40 20
530 15c. Symbols of smoking over crowd of people . . . 40 20
531 $2 Globe crushing cigarettes 3·00 5·00

1994. 40th Anniv of Brunei Girl Guides' Association. Multicoloured.
532 40c. Type **110** . . . . 2·00 2·00
533 40c. Guide receiving award 2·00 2·00
534 40c. Guide reading . . . . 2·00 2·00
535 40c. Group of guides . . . . 2·00 2·00
536 40c. Guides erecting tent . . 2·00 2·00

111 Turbo-prop Airliner on Runway

1994. 20th Anniv of Royal Brunei Airlines. Multicoloured.
537 10c. Type **111** . . . . 1·00 45
538 20c. Jet airliner on runway 1·50 45
539 $1 Jet airliner in the air . . . 3·50 4·50

112 Malay Family

1994. International Day against Drug Abuse and Trafficking. Multicoloured.
540 20c. Type **112** . . . . 1·10 1·60
541 60c. Chinese family . . . . . 1·40 1·90
542 $1 Doctor, police officers and members of youth organizations . . . . . . 1·75 2·50
Nos. 540/2 were printed together, se-tenant, forming a composite design.

113 Aerial View of City, 1970

1995. 25th Anniv of Bandar Seri Begawan. Mult.
543 30c. Type **113** . . . . 1·50 45
544 50c. City in 1980 . . . . . 2·00 1·50
545 $1 City in 1990 . . . . . . 2·75 3·50

114 United Nations General Assembly

115 Students in Laboratory

1995. 50th Anniv of United Nations. Multicoloured.
546 20c. Type **114** 40 25
547 60c. Security Council in session 75 80
548 90c. United Nations Building, New York (27 × 44 mm) 1·25 2·25

1995. 10th Anniv of University of Brunei. Mult.
549 30c. Type **115** 45 35
550 50c. University building . . . 70 70
551 90c. Sultan visiting University 1·25 2·25

116 Police Officers

117 Telephones

1996. 75th Anniv of Royal Brunei Police Force. Multicoloured.
552 25c. Type **116** . . . . 1·25 40
553 50c. Aspects of police work 1·75 1·50
554 75c. Sultan inspecting parade 2·50 3·25

1996. World Telecommunications Day. Children's Paintings. Multicoloured.
555 20c. Type **117** 85 40
556 35c. Telephone dial and aspects of telecommunications . . . . 1·40 60
557 $1 Globe and aspects of telecommunications . . . . 3·50 4·00

118 Sultan and Crowd

119 Sultan Hassanal Bolkiah Mu'izzaddin Waddaulah

1996. 50th Birthday of Sultan Hassanal Bolkiah Mu'izzaddin Waddaulah. Multicoloured.
558 50c. Type **118** . . . . 1·40 1·75
559 50c. Sultan in ceremonial dress . . . . 1·40 1·75
560 50c. Sultan receiving dignitaries at mosque . . . 1·40 1·75
561 50c. Sultan with subjects . . . 1·40 1·75
MS562 152 × 100 mm. $1 Sultan in ceremonial dress (different) . . 2·25 3·00

1996.
563 **119** 10c. multicoloured 15 10
564 15c. multicoloured 20 15
565 20c. multicoloured 20 20
566 30c. multicoloured 30 25
567 50c. multicoloured 45 40
568 60c. multicoloured 55 45
569 75c. multicoloured 65 55
570 90c. multicoloured 80 65
571 – $1 multicoloured 90 75
572 – $2 multicoloured . . . . 1·60 1·50
573 – $5 multicoloured . . . . 4·00 3·75
574 – $10 multicoloured . . . . 7·50 7·00
DESIGN—27 × 39 mm: $1 to $10 Sultan in ceremonial robes.

121 Black-naped Tern

1996. Birds (4th series). Sea Birds. Multicoloured.
575 20c. Type **121** 75 60
576 30c. Roseate tern 75 60
577 $1 Bridled tern . . . . . . 1·75 3·00
No. 576 is inscr "ROSLATE TERN" in error.

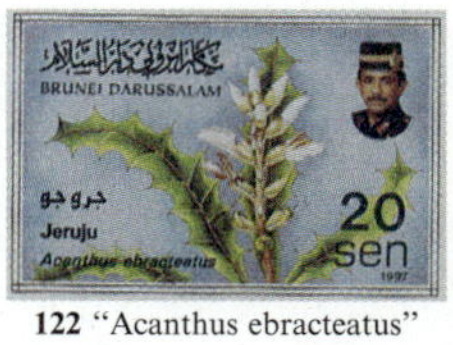

122 "Acanthus ebracteatus"

1997. Mangrove Flowers. Multicoloured.
578 20c. Type **122** 45 25
579 30c. "Lumnitzera littorea" . . 50 35
580 $1 "Nypa fruticans" . . . . 1·40 2·75

123 "Heterocentrotus mammillatus"

1997. Marine Life. Multicoloured.
581 60c. Type **123** . . . . 70 1·00
582 60c. "Linckia laevigata" (starfish) . . . . 70 1·00
583 60c. "Oxycomanthus bennetti" (plant) . . . . . 70 1·00
584 60c. "Bohadschia argus" (sea slug) . . . . 70 1·00

124 Children and Sign Language

1998. Asian and Pacific Decade of Disabled Persons, 1993–2002. Multicoloured.
585 20c. Type **124** 55 25
586 50c. Woman typing and firework display . . . . . 1·00 1·00
587 $1 Disabled athletes . . . . 1·75 2·50

125 Sultan performing Ceremonial Duties

1998. 30th Anniv of Coronation of Sultan Hassanal Bolkiah Mu'izzaddin Waddaulah. Multicoloured.
588 60c. Type **125** . . . . 1·00 65
589 90c. Sultan on Coronation throne . . . . 1·40 1·60
590 $1 Coronation parade . . . 1·50 1·60
MS591 150 × 180 mm. Nos. 588/90 3·25 4·00

126 A.S.E.A.N. Architecture and Transport

127 Crown Prince at Desk

1998. 30th Anniv of Association of South-east Asian Nations. Multicoloured.
592 30c. Type **126** . . . . 1·25 1·25
593 30c. Map of Brunei and city scenes . . . . 1·25 1·25
594 30c. Flags of member nations 1·25 1·25

1998. Proclamation of Prince Al-Muhtadee Billah as Crown Prince. Multicoloured.
595 $1 Type **127** . . . . 1·00 1·00
596 $2 Crown Prince in military uniform . . . . 1·75 2·75
597 $3 Crown Prince's emblem 2·25 3·75
MS598 175 × 153 mm. Nos. 595/7. 5·50 7·00

128 Koran, Civil Servants and Handshake

129 Blue-eared Kingfisher

1998. 5th Anniv of Civil Service Day. Multicoloured.
599 30c. Type **128** 50 30
600 60c. Symbols of progress . . 75 75
601 90c. Civil servants at work 1·10 1·60

1998. Birds (5th series). Kingfishers. Multicoloured.
602 20c. Type **129** . . . . 1·00 60
603 30c. River kingfisher ("Common Kingfisher") . . 1·25 60
604 60c. White-collared kingfisher 2·00 1·50
605 $1 Stork-billed kingfisher . . 2·50 3·00

130 Water Village, Bandar Seri Begawan

1999. 15th Anniv of National Day. Multicoloured.
606 20c. Type **130** 40 20
607 60c. Modern telecommunications and air travel . . . . 1·25 1·00
608 90c. Aspects of modern Brunei . . . . 1·40 1·75
MS609 118 × 85 mm. Nos. 606/8 2·75 3·25

131 Rifle-shooting

132 Clasped Hands and Globe

1999. 20th South-east Asia Games, Brunei. Mult.
610 20c. Type **131** 60 70
611 20c. Golf and tennis 60 70
612 20c. Boxing and judo 60 70
613 20c. Squash and table tennis 60 70
614 20c. Swimming and canoe racing 60 70
615 20c. Hockey and cycling . . 60 70
616 20c. Basketball and football 60 70
617 20c. High jumping, shot putting and running . . . 60 70
618 20c. Snooker 60 70
619 20c. Bowling 60 70
MS620 110 × 73 mm. $1 Various sports . . . . 2·50 3·00

1999. 125th Anniv of Universal Postal Union. Multicoloured.
621 20c. Type **132** 55 20
622 30c. "125" and logos 70 25
623 75c. Aspects of postal service 1·40 2·00

133 Modern Building and Children using Computer

134 Sultan Mohamed Jemal-ul-Alam and Traditional Buildings, 1901–20

2000. New Millennium. Multicoloured.
624 20c. Type **133** 75 75
625 20c. Royal Palace, tree and people using computer . . 75 75
626 20c. Aerial view of mosque and factory 75 75
627 20c. Plan of Parterre Gardens 75 75
628 20c. Container ships and airliner 75 75
629 20c. Satellite dish aerials . . 75 75
MS630 221 × 121 mm. Nos. 624/9 4·00 4·00
Nos. 624/9 were printed together, se-tenant, with the backgrounds forming a composite design.

2000. Brunei in the 20th Century. Multicoloured.
631 30c. Type **134** . . . . 1·00 1·00
632 30c. Sultan Ahmed Tajudin, oil well and Brunei police, 1921–40 . . . . 1·00 1·00
633 30c. Signing of the Constitution and Brunei Mosque, 1941–60 . . . . . 1·00 1·00
634 30c. Oil installation, satellite dish, Royal Brunei Airlines and bank note, 1961–80 . . 1·00 1·00
635 30c. Sultan on throne, international organisation emblems and crowd with trophy, 1981–99 . . . . . 1·00 1·00

135 Sultan Hashim Jalil-ul-Alam, 1885–1906

2000. The Sultans of Brunei. Multicoloured.
636 60c. Type **135** . . . . 1·40 1·40
637 60c. Sultan Mohamed Jemal-ul-Alam, 1906–24 . . . . 1·40 1·40
638 60c. Sultan Ahmed Tajudin, 1924–50 . . . . 1·40 1·40
639 60c. Sultan Omar Ali Saifuddin, 1950–67 . . . . 1·40 1·40
640 60c. Sultan Hassanal Bolkiah, 1967 . . . . 1·40 1·40
MS641 190 × 99 mm. Nos. 636/40 6·00 6·50

136 *Rafflesia pricei*

2000. Local Flowers. Multicoloured.
642 30c. Type **136** 65 30
643 50c. *Rhizanthes lowi* 95 90
644 60c. *Nepenthes rafflesiana* . . 1·25 1·40

137 Information Technology

2000. Asia–Pacific Economic Cooperation. Heads of Government Meeting. Multicoloured.
645 20c. Type **137** 60 30
646 30c. Small and medium businesses 75 35
647 60c. Tourism . . . . 1·75 2·00
MS648 150 × 108 mm. Nos. 645/7 2·75 3·00

138 Green Turtle

2000. Turtles. Multicoloured.
649 30c. Type **138** . . . . 1·00 85
650 30c. Hawksbill turtle . . . . 1·00 85
651 30c. Olive Ridley turtle . . . 1·00 85

139 Tourist Canoe on River

2001. "Visit Brunei Year" (1st series). Multicoloured.
652 20c. Type **139** . . . . 1·25 65
653 30c. Traditional water village 1·25 65
654 60c. Carved building facade 2·25 2·75
See also Nos. 669/72.

140 Sultan in Army Uniform

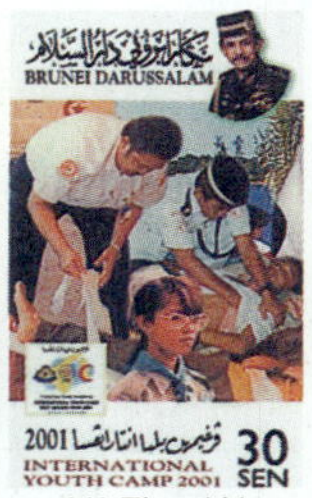

141 First Aid Demonstration

2001. 55th Birthday of Sultan Hassanal Bolkiah Muizzaddin Waddaulah. Multicoloured.
655 55c. Type **140** . . . . 1·40 1·40
656 55c. Sultan in Air Force uniform . . . . 1·40 1·40
657 55c. Sultan in traditional dress . . . . 1·40 1·40
658 55c. Sultan in Army camouflage jacket . . . . 1·40 1·40
659 55c. Sultan in Navy uniform 1·40 1·40
MS660 100 × 75 mm. 55c. Sultan and Bandar Seri Begawan (40 × 71 mm) . . . . 2·25 2·50

2001. International Youth Camp. Multicoloured.
661 30c. Type **141** 80 80
662 30c. Brunei guides and tent demonstration 80 80
663 30c. Scouts with cooking pot 80 80
MS664 110 × 77 mm. Nos. 661/3 2·25 2·75
Nos. 661/3 were printed together, se-tenant, forming a composite design.

142 Islamic Regalia

2001. 1st Islamic International Exhibition, Brunei. Multicoloured.
665 20c. Type **142** 80 80
666 20c. Exhibition centre 80 80
667 20c. Computer communications 80 80
668 20c. Opening ceremony . . . 80 80

143 Forest Walkway

2001. Visit Brunei (2nd series). Multicoloured.
669 20c. Type **143** 80 80
670 20c. Waterfall 80 80
671 20c. Jerudong Theme Park 80 80
672 20c. Footbridges across lake 80 80

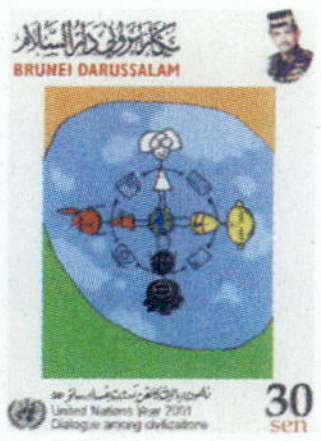

144 "Children encircling Globe" (Urska Golob)

2001. U.N. Year of Dialogue among Civilisations. Multicoloured.
673 30c. Type **144** 80 90
674 30c. Quotation marks illustrated with faces . . . 80 90
675 30c. Cubist portrait and Japanese girl 80 90
676 30c. Coloured leaves 80 90

145 Male and Female Bulwer's Pheasants

2001. Endangered Species. Bulwer's Pheasant. Mult.
677 30c. Type **145** 90 90
678 30c. Male pheasant 90 90
679 30c. Female pheasant with chicks 90 90
680 30c. Female pheasant 90 90

146 Early and Modern Telephone Systems

147 50th Anniversary Logo

2002. 50th Anniv of Department of Telecommunications (JTB). Multicoloured.
681 50c. Type **146** . . . . 1·00 1·10
682 50c. JTB Golden Jubilee emblem . . . . 1·00 1·10
683 50c. Computer networks . . 1·00 1·10

2002. 50th Anniv of Survey Department. Mult.
684 50c. Type **147** . . . . 1·00 1·10
685 50c. Survey Department Offices . . . . 1·00 1·10
686 50c. Theodolite and thermal map . . . . 1·00 1·10

148 Modern Housing, Water Village

2002. 10th Anniv of Yayasan Sultan Haji Hassanal Bolkiah Foundation. Multicoloured.
687 10c. Type **148** 50 60
688 10c. Mosque and interior . . 50 60
689 10c. School and computer class 50 60
690 10c. University of Brunei . . 50 60

149 Anti-Corruption Bureau Headquarters

2002. 20th Anniv of Anti-Corruption Bureau. Multicoloured.
691 20c. Type **149** 75 75
692 20c. Skyscrapers and mosque 75 75
693 20c. Anti-Corruption Bureau posters 75 75

150 *Melastoma malabathricum*

2003. Flowering Medicinal Plants. Multicoloured.
694 20c. Type **150** 75 75
695 20c. *Etlingera solaris* 75 75
696 20c. *Dillenia suffruticosa* . . . 75 75
697 20c. *Costus speciosus* 75 75

151 Drums and Musicians

2003. ASEAN—Japan Exchange Year. Multicoloured.
698 20c. Type **151** 60 70
699 20c. Woodworker and handicrafts 60 70
700 20c. Exchange Year logo . . 60 70

152 Sultan of Brunei and UN Emblem

2004. 20th Anniv of National Day. Multicoloured.
701 20c. Type **152** 60 70
702 20c. In military uniform . . . 60 70
703 20c. Reading speech at National Day celebration . . 60 70
704 20c. Emblem 60 70
MS705 185 × 140 mm. Nos. 701/4 2·25 2·50

153 Brunei 1895 ½c. Stamp

2004. Brunei Darussalam National Philatelic Society. Multicoloured.

706		25c. Type **153**	80	85
707		25c. Magnifying glass, perforation gauge, tweezers and stamps	80	85
708		25c. Postmarks, stamp catalogue and first day covers	80	85

154 Crown Prince Al-Muhtadee Billah Bolkiah and Sarah Salleh

2004. Royal Wedding.

709	**154**	99c. multicoloured	1·60	1·75

155 Sultan of Brunei and Jame'Asr Hassanal Bolkiah Mosque

2006. 60th Birthday of Sultan Hassanal Bolkiah Muizzaddin Waddaulah. Designs showing montage of images, all with portrait of Sultan at top right. Multicoloured (except $60), panel colours given.

710		60s. Type **155** (mauve)	70	70
711		60s. Sultan, palace and crowd with flags (red)	70	70
712		60s. Sultan and urban and agricultural scenes (yellow)	70	70
713		60s. Sultan speaking at 9th ASEAN–Japan Summit and at APEC 2000 (salmon)	70	70
714		60s. Sultan meeting woman (green)	70	70
715		60s. Sultan in military uniform (blue)	70	70
MS716		166 × 120 mm. Nos. 710/15	4·00	4·00
MS717		148 × 137 mm. $60 Montage of five black and white photographs of Sultan as young man, at Coronation, seated on throne and wearing crown and military uniform (black and grey) (99 × 90 mm)	7·00	7·00

156 General Post Office, Bandar Seri Begawan

157 Parcels and Letters travelling around Globe

2006. Centenary of Postal Services Department. Multicoloured. Litho. (a) T **156**.

718		100s. Type **156**	1·10	1·10
719		100s. Kuala Belait Post Office	1·10	1·10
720		100s. Tutong Post Office at the District Office, Tutong	1·10	1·10
721		100s. Bangar Post Office at the District Office, Temburong	1·10	1·10
MS722		115 × 115 mm. Nos. 718/21	4·50	4·50

(b) T **157** and similar vert designs showing children's drawings.

MS723		95 × 145 mm. 100s. × 6 Type **157**; Postman; Globe, letter, house and aircraft; Air mail letters, postbox and post office; Letters, globe and families in Brunei and China; Globe and national flags ('EVERYONE REACHING EVERYWHERE')	6·25	6·25

158 *Balistapus undulates* (orangestriped triggerfish)

2007. Marine Life. Multicoloured.

724		60s. Type **158**	70	70
725		60s. *Taenionotis triacanthus* (leaf scorpionfish)	70	70
MS726		100 × 70 mm. $1 *Nautilus pompilus* (chambered nautilus); $1 *Ostracion meleagris* (spotted boxfish)	2·40	2·40

Stamps in similar designs were issued by Malaysia.

159 Sultan Hassanal Bolkiah Mu'izzaddin Waddaulah

161 Public Works Department Headquarters

2007. Multicoloured.

727	**159**	10s. multicoloured	10	10
728		15s. multicoloured	20	20
729		20s. multicoloured	25	25
730		30s. multicoloured	35	35
731		50s. multicoloured	60	60
732		60s. multicoloured	70	70
733		75s. multicoloured	90	90
734		90s. multicoloured	1·10	1·10
735	–	$1 multicoloured	1·20	1·20
736	–	$2 multicoloured	2·40	2·40
737	–	$5 multicoloured	6·00	6·00
738	–	$10 multicoloured	12·00	12·00

Nos. 735/8 are as Type **159** but larger, 27 × 40 mm.

Nos. 739/**MS**742, T **160** are left for 100 Years of Bubangan, issued 23 July 2007, not yet received.

2007. Centenary (2006) of Public Works Department. Multicoloured.

743		75s. Type **161**	90	90
744		75s. Engineers Office, (PWD Headquarters), Subok, 1906	90	90
745		75s. '100' and PWD logo	90	90

162 Secretariat Building, Brunei

2007. 40th Anniv of ASEAN (Association of South-east Asian Nations). Ancient and Modern Architecture. Multicoloured.

746		20s. Type **162**	25	25
747		20s. Yangon Post Office, Myanmar	25	25
748		20s. National Museum of Cambodia	25	25
749		20s. Malacañang Palace, Philippines	25	25
750		20s. Fatahillah Museum, Jakarta, Indonesia	25	25
751		20s. National Museum of Singapore	25	25
752		20s. Lao Typical House	25	25
753		20s. Vimanmek Mansion, Bangkok, Thailand	25	25
754		20s. Malayan Railway Headquarters Building, Kuala Lumpur, Malaysia	25	25
755		20s. Presidential Palace, Hanoi, Vietnam	25	25

Similar designs were issued by the ten member countries, Indonesia, Malaysia, Philippines, Singapore, Thailand, Vietnam, Laos, Myanmar and Cambodia.

JAPANESE OCCUPATION OF BRUNEI

These stamps were valid throughout British Borneo (i.e. in Brunei, Labuan, North Borneo and Sarawak).

100 cents = 1 dollar.

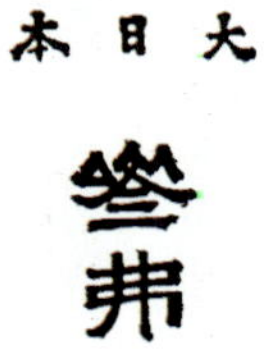

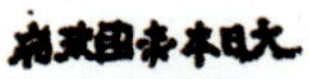

(**1**) ("Imperial Japanese Government")

(**2**) ("Imperial Japanese Postal Service $3")

1942. Stamps of Brunei optd with T **1**.

J 1	**5**	1c. black	8·00	23·00
J 2		2c. green	50·00	£110
J 3		2c. orange	4·50	9·00
J 4		3c. green	28·00	75·00
J 5		4c. orange	3·25	13·00
J 6		5c. brown	3·25	13·00
J 7	**7**	6c. grey	40·00	£225
J 8		6c. red	£550	£550
J 9	**5**	8c. black	£700	£850
J10	**7**	8c. red	6·00	12·00
J11	**5**	10c. purple on yellow	9·00	26·00
J12	**7**	12c. blue	26·00	26·00
J13		15c. blue	19·00	26·00
J14	**5**	25c. lilac	25·00	50·00
J15		30c. purple and orange	95·00	£180
J16		50c. black on green	38·00	60·00
J17		$1 black and red on blue	55·00	70·00
J18		$5 red on green	£900	£2250
J19		$25 black on red	£900	£2250

1944. No. J1 surch with T **2**.

J20	**5**	$3 on 1c. black	£7000	£7000

BRUNSWICK Pt. 7

Formerly a duchy of N. Germany. Joined North German Confederation in 1868.

30 silbergroschen = 1 thaler.

1

1852. Imperf.

1	**1**	1sg. red	£2250	£325
2		2sg. blue	£1600	£275
3		3sg. red	£1600	£275

1853. Imperf.

4	**1**	¼gg. black on brown	£900	£275
5		¼gg. black	£160	£350
15		⅓sg. black on green	26·00	£275
7		1sg. black on buff	£450	70·00
8		2sg. black on blue	£350	60·00
11		3sg. black on red	£600	£220

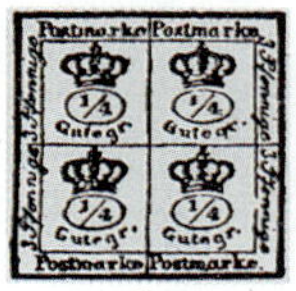

3

4

1857. Imperf.

12	**3**	$\frac{4}{4}$gg. black on brown	44·00	£110

1864. Rouletted.

22	**1**	½gg. black	£550	£2500
23		⅓sg. black on green	£200	£2750
24		1sg. black on yellow	£2750	£1400
25		1sg. yellow	£450	£150
26		2sg. black on blue	£450	£375
27		3sg. pink	£900	£550

1865. Roul.

28	**4**	½g. black	31·00	£400
29		1g. red	2·75	55·00
32		2g. blue	9·75	£140
34		3g. brown	8·00	£180

BUENOS AIRES Pt. 20

A province of the Argentine Republic. Issued its own stamps from 1858 to 1862.

8 reales = 1 peso.

P 1 Paddle Steamer

P 2 Head of Liberty

1858. Imperf.

P13	**P 1**	4r. brown	£100	80·00
P17		1 (IN) p. brown	£125	80·00
P20		1 (IN) p. blue	65·00	50·00
P25		1 (TO) p. blue	£150	£100
P 1		2p. blue	90·00	50·00
P 4		3p. green	£450	£250
P 7		4p. red	£1500	£900
P10		5p. yellow	£1500	£900

1859. Imperf.

P37	**P 2**	4r. green on blue	90·00	50·00
P38		1p. blue	12·00	7·50
P45		1p. red	60·00	30·00
P43		2p. red	£120	80·00
P48		2p. blue	£120	45·00

BULGARIA Pt. 3

Formerly a Turkish province; a principality under Turkish suzerainty from 1878 to 1908, when an independent kingdom was proclaimed. A People's Republic since 1946.

1879. 100 centimes = 1 franc.
1881. 100 stotinki = 1 lev.

1 Large Lion

2 Large Lion

1879. Value in centimes and franc.

1	**1**	5c. black and yellow	£160	36·00
3		10c. black and green	£700	£100
5		25c. black and purple	£275	26·00
7		50c. black and blue	£450	£110
8		1f. black and red	65·00	34·00

1881. Value in stotinki.

10	**2**	3s. red and grey	16·00	4·75
11		5s. black and yellow	16·00	4·50
14		10s. black and green	£100	13·50
15		15s. red and green	£100	13·50
18		25s. black and purple	£500	70·00
19		30s. blue and brown	17·00	11·50

See also No. 275/9.

A

B

C

D

1882.

46	**2**	1s. violet (Type A)	12·00	4·75
48		1s. violet (Type C)	80	20
47		2s. green (Type B)	11·00	4·75
49		2s. green (Type D)	1·00	20
21		3s. orange and yellow	1·00	45
23		5s. green	6·75	85
26		10s. red	12·00	1·40
28		15s. purple and mauve	12·00	65
31		25s. blue	5·50	1·20
33		30s. lilac and green	8·50	1·10
34		50s. blue and red	8·50	1·10
50		1l. black and red	35·00	3·25

1884. Surch with large figure of value.

38	**2**	3 on 10s. red	48·00	50·00
43		5 on 30s. blue and brown	48·00	55·00
45		15 on 25s. blue	75·00	65·00
40		50 on 1f. black and red	£300	£200

7

11 Arms of Bulgaria

13 Cherry wood Cannon used against the Turks

1889.

85	7	1s. mauve	15	15
88		2s. grey	60	40
89		3s. brown	25	25
90		5s. green	15	15
94		10s. red	40	15
96		15s. orange	30	25
100		25s. blue	40	25
58		30s. brown	7·50	45
59		50s. green	40	25
60		1l. red	40	50
83		2l. red and pink	1·90	1·40
84		3l. black and buff	3·25	3·75

1892. Surch **15**.

61	7	15 on 30s. brown	16·00	90

1895. Surch **01**.

74	2a	01 on 2s. green (No. 49)	65	25

1896. Baptism of Prince Boris.

78	11	1s. green	45	30
79		5s. blue	45	30
81		15s. violet	55	50
82		25s. red	5·00	2·20

1901. Surch in figures.

101	7	5 on 3s. brown	2·40	3·00
103		10 on 50s. green	1·90	1·00

1901. 25th Anniv of Uprising against Turkey.

104	13	5s. red	1·40	1·50
105		15s. green	1·40	1·50

14 Prince Ferdinand

16 Fighting at Shipka Pass

1901.

106	14	1s. black and purple	15	15
107		2s. blue and green	15	15
108		3s. black and orange	15	15
109		5s. brown and green	80	15
110		10s. brown and red	1·50	15
113		15s. black and lake	65	20
114		25s. black and blue	65	15
116		30s. black and brown	20·00	45
117		50s. brown and blue	95	25
118		1l. green and red	1·90	25
120		2l. black and red	4·50	1·10
123		3l. red and grey	5·50	4·00

1902. 25th Anniv of Battle of Shipka Pass.

124	16	5s. red	1·60	1·00
125		10s. green	1·60	1·00
126		15s. blue	5·75	3·50

1903. Surch.

140	15	5 on 15s. black and red	1·10	1·00
141		10 on 15s. black and red	2·40	80
143		25 on 30s. black & brown	8·50	1·30

18 Ferdinand I in 1887 and 1907

1907. 20th Anniv of Prince Ferdinand's Accession.

132	18	5s. green	8·00	1·40
134		10s. brown	13·50	1·60
137		25s. blue	27·00	2·50

1909. Optd **1909**.

146	7	1s. mauve	1·10	50
149		5s. green	1·20	55

1909. Surch **1909** and new value.

151	7	5 on 30s. brown	1·40	35
153		10 on 15s. orange	1·30	65
156		10 on 50s. green	1·50	60

1910. Surch **1910** and new value.

157	14	1 on 3s. black and orange	4·00	1·00
158		5 on 15s. black and lake	1·20	85

23 King Asen Tower

24 Tsar in General's Uniform

25 Veliko Turnovo

1911.

159	23	1s. green	15	15
182a		1s. slate	10	15
160	24	2s. black and red	15	15
161	25	3s. black and lake	80	15
162	–	5s. black and green	55	15
181	–	5s. purple and green	1·40	15
163	–	10s. black and red	80	15
181a	–	10s. sepia and brown	15	15
164	–	15s. bistre	5·50	20
183	–	15s. olive	65	15
165	–	25s. black and blue	25	15
166	–	30s. black and blue	2·40	20
182	–	30s. brown and olive	20	20
167	–	50s. black and yellow	19·00	25
168	–	1l. brown	5·50	20
169	–	2l. black and purple	95	70
170	–	3l. black and violet	8·75	2·40

DESIGNS—VERT: 5, 10, 25s., 1l. Portraits of Tsar Ferdinand. HORIZ: 15s. R. Isker; 30s. Rila Monastery; 50s. Tsars and Princes (after Ya. Veshin); 2l. Monastery of the Holy Trinity, Veliko Turnovo; 3l. Varna.

See also Nos. 229/30 and 236/7.

35 Tsar Ferdinand

1912. Tsar's Silver Jubilee.

171	35	5s. grey	2·50	1·00
172		10s. red	4·00	2·00
173		25s. blue	4·50	3·00

ОСВОБ. ВОЙНА
1912-1913
(36) "War of Liberation" 1912–13

3
СТОТИНКИ
(37a)

1913. Victory over Turks. Stamps of 1911 optd as T **36**.

174	23	1s. green	25	20
175	24	2s. black and red	25	20
176	25	3s. black and lake	80	45
177	–	5s. black and green	25	15
178	–	10s. black and red	25	15
179	–	15s. bistre	2·50	85
180	–	25s. black and blue	1·60	75

1915. No. 165 surch **10 CT.** and bar.

180a	–	10s. on 25s. blk & blue	40	20

1916. Red Cross Fund. Surch with T **37a**.

185	7	3s. on 1s. mauve	4·50	7·25

45 Veles

46 Bulgarian Ploughman

38

39 Bulgarian Peasant

1917. Liberation of Macedonia.

193	45	1s. grey	10	10
194	46	1s. green	10	10
195	–	5s. green	10	10
186	38	5s. green	50	30
187	39	15s. grey	15	20
188	–	25s. blue	15	20
189	–	30s. orange	15	25
190	–	50s. violet	50	40
191	–	2l. brown	55	50
192	–	3l. red	80	60

DESIGNS—As Type **45**: 5s. Monastery of St. John, Ohrid. As Type **38**: 25s. Soldier and Mt. Sonichka; 50s. Ohrid and Lake. As Type **39**: 30s. Nish. 2l. Demir Kapija; 3l. Gevgeli.

48 Tsar Ferdinand

1918. 30th Anniv of Tsar's Accession.

196	48	1s. slate	10	15
197		2s. brown	10	15
198		3s. blue	30	30
199		10s. red	30	30

49 Parliament Building

50 King Boris III

1919.

201	49	1s. black	10	15
202		2s. olive	10	15

1919. 1st Anniv of Enthronement of King Boris III.

203	50	3s. red	15	15
204		5s. green	15	15
205		10s. red	15	15
206		15s. violet	15	15
207		25s. blue	15	15
208		30s. brown	15	15
209		50s. brown	15	15

ЗА НАШИТЬ
ПЛЪННИЦИ
2½
(52)

ЗА НАШИТЬ
ПЛЪННИЦИ
50
(53)

1920. Prisoners of War Fund. Surch as T **52/53**.

210	49	1 on 2s. olive	15	15
211	50	2½ on 5s. green	15	15
212		5 on 10s. red	15	15
213		7½ on 15s. violet	15	15
214		12½ on 25s. blue	15	15
215		15 on 30s. brown	15	15
216		25 on 50s. brown	15	15
217	–	50 on 1l. brown (No. 168)	15	15
218	–	1 on 2l. brown (No. 191)	20	20
219	–	1½ on 3l. red (No. 192)	40	45

54 Vazov's Birthplace at Sopot and Cherry-wood Cannon

55 "The Bear-fighter", character from "Under the Yoke"

1920. 70th Birth Anniv of Ivan Vazov (writer).

220	54	30s. red	15	15
221	55	50s. green	15	15
222	–	1l. sepia	35	25
223	–	2l. brown	1·00	70
224	–	3l. violet	1·20	95
225	–	5l. blue	1·60	1·20

DESIGNS—HORIZ: 1l. Ivan Vazov in 1870 and 1920; 3l. Vazov's Houses in Plovdiv and Sofia. VERT: 2l. Vazov; 5l. Father Paisii Khilendarski (historian).

59 Aleksandr Nevski Cathedral, Sofia

62 King Boris III

1921.

226	59	10s. violet	15	15
227	–	20s. green	10	15
228	62	25s. blue	10	15
229	25	50s. orange	40	15
230		50s. blue	6·75	2·00
231	–	75s. violet	10	15
232	–	75s. blue	25	15
233	62	1l. red	25	20
234		1l. blue	15	15
235	–	2l. brown	40	15
236	–	3l. purple	40	15
237	–	5l. blue	3·50	35
238	62	10l. red	10·50	3·50

DESIGNS—HORIZ: 20s. Alexander II "The Liberator" Monument, Sofia; 75s. Shipka Pass Monastery; 5l. Rila Monastery. VERT: 2l. Harvester; 3l. King Asen Tower.

66 Tsar Ferdinand and Map

68 Mt. Shar

1921.

239	66	10s. red	10	15
240	–	10s. red	10	15
241	68	10s. red	10	15
242	–	10s. mauve	10	15
243	–	20s. blue	30	15

DESIGNS—VERT: No. 240, Tsar Ferdinand. HORIZ: No. 242, Bridge over Vardar, at Skopje; 243, St. Clement's Monastery, Ohrid.

71 Bourchier in Bulgarian Costume

72 J. D. Bourchier

73 Rila Monastery, Bourchier's Resting-place

1921. James Bourchier ("Times" Correspondent) Commemoration.

244	71	10s. red	15	20
245		20s. orange	15	20
246	72	30s. grey	15	20
247		50s. lilac	15	20
248		1l. purple	25	20
249	73	1½l. green	25	35
250		2l. green	25	25
251		3l. blue	65	35
252		5l. red	95	65

1924. Surch.

253	49	10s. on 1s. black	10	15
254	D 37	10s. on 20s. orange	10	15
255		20s. on 5s. green	6·00	6·00
256		20s. on 10s. violet	1·50	1·50
257		20s. on 30s. orange	10	10
258	50	1l. on 5s. green	15	15
259	25	3l. on 50s. blue	60	25
260	62	6l. on 1l. red	40	35

77

78

79 King Boris III

81 Aleksandr Nevski Cathedral, Sofia

82 Harvesters

83 Proposed Rest-home, Verona

1925.

261	77	10s. blue & red on rose	15	15
262		15s. orange & red on blue	15	15
263		30s. buff and black	15	15
264	78	50s. brown on green	15	15
265	79	1l. olive	35	15
266		1l. green	40	15
267	81	2l. green and buff	1·40	15

267a	79	2l. brown	50	15
268	82	4l. red and yellow	80	15

1925. Sunday Delivery Stamps.

268b	83	1l. black on green	2·75	25
268c		1l. brown	2·75	15
268d		1l. orange	4·50	25
268e		1l. pink	3·50	25
268f		1l. violet on red	4·50	25
268g	–	2l. green	50	25
268h	–	2l. violet	50	30
268i	–	5l. blue	4·75	50
268j	–	5l. red	4·75	50

DESIGN: 2, 5l., Proposed Sanatorium, Bankya.

85 St. Nedelya's Cathedral, Sofia after Bomb Outrage

86 C. Botev (poet)

1926.

269	85	50s. black	10	15

1926. Botev Commemoration.

270	86	1l. green	60	25
271		2l. blue	1·30	25
272		4l. red	1·30	1·10

87

89 King Boris III

90 Saint Clement of Ohrid

1926.

273	87	6l. olive and blue	1·50	20
274		10l. brown and sepia	5·25	1·50

1927. As T 2 in new colours.

275		10s. red and green	15	10
276		15s. black and yellow	15	15
277		30s. slate and buff	15	15
278		30s. blue and buff	15	15
279		50s. black and red	30	15

1927. Air. Various stamps optd with Albatros biplane and No. 281 surch **1l** also.

281	87	1l. on 6l. green and blue	1·20	1·60
282	79	2l. brown	1·30	1·60
283	82	4l. red and yellow	2·00	2·00
284	87	10l. orange and brown	40·00	36·00

1928.

285	89	1l. green	80	15
286		2l. brown	1·60	15

1929. 50th Anniv of Liberation of Bulgaria and Millenary of Tsar Simeon.

287	90	10s. violet	20	10
288	–	15a. purple	20	10
289	–	30s. red	20	10
290	–	50s. green	30	20
291	–	1l. red	80	20
292	–	2l. blue	1·00	20
293	–	3l. green	2·40	60
294	–	4l. brown	3·25	30
295	–	5l. brown	1·00	60
296	–	6l. blue	3·00	1·50

PORTRAITS—$23\frac{1}{2}\times33\frac{1}{2}$ mm: 15s. Konstantin Miladinov (poet and folklorist); 1l. Father Paisii Khilendarski (historian); 2l. Tsar Simeon; 4l. Vasil Levski (revolutionary); 5l. Georgi Benkovski (revolutionary); 6l. Tsar Alexander II of Russia, "The Liberator". $19\times28\frac{1}{2}$ mm: 30s. Georgi Rakovski (writer). 19×26 mm: 3l. Lyuben Karavelov (journalist).

98 Convalescent Home, Varna

1930. Sunday Delivery stamps.

297	98	1l. green and purple	4·75	15
298		1l. yellow and green	55	15
299		1l. brown and red	55	15

99

101 King Boris III

1930. Wedding of King Boris and Princess Giovanna of Italy.

300	99	1l. green	20	30
301	–	2l. purple	35	30
302	99	4l. red	35	45
303	–	6l. blue	45	45

DESIGN: 2, 6l. Portraits in separate ovals.

1931.

304a	101	1l. green (A)	25	15
305		2l. red (A)	40	15
306		4l. orange (A)	30	15
308a		4l. orange (B)	65	15
307		6l. blue (A)	40	15
308b		6l. blue (B)	80	15
308c		7l. blue (B)	25	15
308d		10l. slate (B)	10·00	50
308		12l. brown (A)	30	20
308e		14l. brown (B)	30	15
308f	–	20l. brown & pur (B)	90	65

(A) Without coloured frame-lines at top and bottom; (B) with frame-lines.

The 20l. is $24\frac{1}{2}\times33\frac{1}{2}$ mm.

103 Gymnastics

1831. Balkan Olympic Games.

309	103	1l. green	70	1·10
326		1l. turquoise	2·75	3·00
310	–	2l. red	1·30	1·20
327	–	2l. blue	3·50	3·00
311	–	4l. red	2·10	1·50
328	–	4l. purple	4·75	1·90
312	–	6l. green	5·75	3·00
329	–	6l. red	9·50	6·50
313	–	10l. orange	12·00	10·50
330	–	10l. brown	55·00	40·00
314	–	12l. blue	55·00	26·00
331	–	12l. orange	90·00	65·00
315	–	50l. brown	43·00	60·00
332	–	50l. red	£275	£275

DESIGNS—VERT (23×28 mm): 2l. Footballer; 4l. Horse-riding. As Type **103**—HORIZ: 6l. Fencing; 10l. Cycling. VERT: 12l. Diving; 50l. Spirit of Victory.

108

109 Rila Monastery

1931. Air.

316	108	1l. green	30	20
316a		1l. purple	20	15
317		2l. purple	30	20
317a		2l. green	20	15
318		6l. blue	45	30
318a		6l. red	65	25
319		12l. red	85	40
319a		12l. blue	55	30
320		20l. violet	85	60
321		30l. orange	2·00	80
322		50l. brown	2·00	1·80

1932. Air.

323	109	18l. green	60·00	32·00
324		24l. red	55·00	29·00
325		28l. blue	38·00	19·00

1934. Surch **2.**

333	101	2 on 3l. olive	4·75	45

111 Defending the Pass

113 Convalescent Home, Troyan

1934. Unveiling of Shipka Pass Memorial.

334	111	1l. green	1·20	90
340		1l. green	1·20	90
335	–	2l. red	1·20	45
341	–	2l. orange	1·20	45
336	–	3l. brown	4·00	2·75
342	–	3l. yellow	4·00	2·75
337	–	4l. red	3·25	1·00
343	–	4l. red	3·25	1·00
338	–	7l. blue	6·25	3·50
344	–	7l. light blue	6·25	3·50
339	–	14l. purple	20·00	16·00
345	–	14l. bistre	20·00	16·00

DESIGNS—VERT: 2l. Shipka Memorial; 3, 7l. Veteran standard-bearer; 14l. Widow showing memorial to orphans. HORIZ: 4l. Bulgarian veteran.

1935. Sunday Delivery stamps.

346	113	1l. red and brown	55	15
347		1l. blue and green	55	15
348	–	5l. blue and red	2·40	75

DESIGN: 5l. Convalescent Home, Bakya.

114 Capt. Georgi Mamarchef

115 Aleksandr Nevski Cathedral, Sofia

1935. Centenary of Turnovo Insurrection.

349	–	1l. blue	1·80	50
350	114	2l. purple	1·80	90

DESIGN: 1l. Velcho Atanasov Dzhamdzhiyata.

1935. 5th Balkan Football Tournament.

351	–	1l. green	3·25	3·00
352	115	2l. grey	6·00	5·00
353	–	4l. red	11·00	8·00
354	–	7l. blue	25·00	17·00
355	–	14l. orange	20·00	16·00
356	–	50l. brown	£275	£300

DESIGNS—HORIZ: 1l. Match in progress at Yunak Stadium, Sofia; 4l. Footballers. VERT: 7l. Herald and Balkan map; 14l. Footballer and trophy; 50l. Trophy.

116 Girl Gymnast

117 Janos Hunyadi

1935. 8th Bulgarian Gymnastic Tournament. Dated "12–14. VII. 1935".

357	–	1l. green	3·50	4·50
358	–	2l. blue	6·25	4·75
359	116	4l. red	12·00	11·00
360	–	7l. blue	13·00	16·00
361	–	14l. brown	13·00	13·00
362	–	50l. orange	£190	£200

DESIGNS—VERT: 1l. Parallel bars; 2l. Male gymnast in uniform; 7l. Pole vault; 50l. Athlete and lion. HORIZ: 14l. Yunak Stadium, Sofia.

1935. Unveiling of Monument to Ladislas III of Poland at Varna. Inscr "WARNEN CZYK(A)", etc.

363	117	1l. orange	1·60	60
364	–	2l. red	4·75	60
365	–	4l. red	19·00	6·25
366	–	7l. blue	3·75	2·10
367	–	14l. green	3·75	1·50

DESIGNS—VERT: 2l. King Ladislas of Hungary enthroned (22×32 mm); 7l. King Ladislas in armour (20×31 mm). HORIZ: 4l. Varna Memorial (33×24 mm); 14l. Battle scene (30×25 mm).

118 Dimitur

119

120

1935. 67th Death Anniv of Khadzhi Dimitur (revolutionary).

368	–	1l. green	3·25	65
369	118	2l. brown	4·00	1·40
370	–	4l. red	8·75	4·00
371	–	7l. blue	11·50	6·50
372	–	14l. orange	11·50	7·50

DESIGNS—VERT: 1l. Dimitur's monument at Sliven; 7l. Revolutionary group (dated 1868). HORIZ: 4l. Dimitur and Stefan Karadzha (revolutionary); 14l. Dimitur's birthplace at Sliven.

1936.

373	119	10s. red	10	15
373a		15s. green	10	15
374	120	30s. red	10	15
374a		30s. brown	15	15
374b		30s. blue	10	15
375		50s. blue	15	15
375a		50s. red	15	10
375b		50s. green	10	15

121 Nesebur

122 St. Cyril and St. Methodius

1936. Slav Geographical and Ethnographical Congress, Sofia.

376	–	1l. violet	1·60	1·80
377	–	2l. blue	1·60	1·50
378	121	7l. blue	5·25	3·00

DESIGNS—25×34 mm: 1l. Meteorological Bureau, Mt. Musala; 23×34 mm: 2l. Peasant girl.

1937. Millenary of Introduction of Cyrillic Alphabet and Slavonic Liturgy.

379	122	1l. green	60	25
380		2l. purple	60	25
381	–	4l. red	70	25
382	122	7l. blue	2·40	1·40
383	–	14l. red	2·40	1·50

DESIGN: 4., 14l. The Saints Preaching.

124 Princess Marie Louise

125 King Boris III

1937.

384	124	1l. green	40	15
385		2l. red	50	15
386		4l. red	50	30

1937. 19th Anniv of Accession.

387	125	2l. red	45	45

126 Harvesting

129 Prince Simeon

1938. Agricultural Products.

388	126	10s. orange	10	10
389		10s. red	10	10
390	–	15s. red	30	10
391	–	15s. purple	30	10
392	–	30s. brown	15	10
393	–	30s. brown	25	10
394	–	50s. blue	55	10
395	–	50s. black	55	10
396	–	1l. green	60	10
397	–	1l. green	60	10
398	–	2l. red	60	10
399	–	2l. brown	50	10
400	–	3l. purple	1·10	55
401	–	3l. purple	1·10	50
402	–	4l. brown	75	35
403	–	4l. purple	75	35
404	–	7l. violet	1·40	85
405	–	7l. blue	1·40	65
406	–	14l. brown	2·20	1·50
407	–	14l. brown	2·20	1·50

DESIGNS—VERT: 15s. Sunflower; 30s. Wheat; 50s. Chickens and eggs; 1l. Grapes; 3l. Strawberries; 4l. Girl carrying grapes; 7l. Roses; 14l. Tobacco leaves. HORIZ: 2l. "Attar of Roses".

1938. 1st Birthday of Heir Apparent.

408	129	1l. green	10	15
409		2l. red	10	15
410	–	4l. red	20	15
411	129	7l. blue	75	50
412	–	14l. brown	75	50

DESIGN: 4, 14l. Another portrait.

131 King Boris III

132 Class 01 Steam Locomotive

1938. 20th Anniv of King's Accession. Portraits of King in various uniforms.

413	131	1l. green	10	15
414	–	2l. red	70	20
415	–	4l. brown	10	20
416	–	7l. blue	30	40
417	–	14l. mauve	30	45

1939. 50th Anniv of Bulgarian State Railways. Locomotive types dated "1888–1938".

418	–	1l. green	40	35
419	132	2l. brown	40	35
420	–	4l. orange	1·60	1·10
421	–	7l. blue	5·75	5·25

DESIGNS: 1l. First Locomotive in Bulgaria, 1866; 4l. Train crossing viaduct; 7l. King Boris as engine-driver.

133 P.O. Emblem

135 Gymnast

1939. 60th Anniv of Bulgarian P.O. Inscr "1879 1939".

422	**133**	1l. green	15	10
423	–	2l. red (G.P.O., Sofia)	20	10

1939. Yunak Gymnastic Society's Rally, Sofia.

424	**135**	1l. green	40	20
425	–	2l. red	40	20
426	–	4l. brown	60	20
427	–	7l. blue	2·20	90
428	–	14l. mauve	10·00	6·75

DESIGNS: 2l. Yunak badge; 4l. "The Discus-thrower" (statue by Miron); 7l. Rhythmic dancer; 14l. Athlete holding weight aloft.

Наводнението
1939
1+1
лева
(**136**) ("Inundation 1939")

1939. Sevlievo and Turnovo Floods Relief Fund. Surch as T **136** and value.

429	**39**	1l.+1l. on 15s. grey	20	60
430	**73**	2l.+1l. on 1½l. olive	20	20
431		4l.+2l. on 2l. green	25	35
432		7l.+4l. on 3l. blue	70	80
433		14l.+7l. on 5l. red	1·40	1·40

137 Mail Plane

138 King Boris III

1940. Air.

434	**137**	1l. green	10	15
435	–	2l. red	1·10	15
436	–	4l. orange	15	15
437	–	6l. blue	15	15
438	–	10l. brown	95	30
439	–	12l. brown	55	40
440	–	16l. violet	65	50
441	–	19l. blue	80	70
442	–	30l. mauve	1·10	1·10
443	–	45l. violet	2·75	2·40
444	–	70l. red	2·75	3·00
445	–	100l. blue	9·00	8·00

DESIGNS—VERT: Aircraft over: King Asen's Tower (2l.), Bachovo Monastery (4l.), Aleksandr Nevski Cathedral, Sofia (45l.), Shipka Pass Memorial (70l.); 10l. Airplane, mail train and express motor cycle; 30l. Airplane and swallow; 100l. Airplane and Royal cypher. HORIZ: 6l. Loading mails at aerodrome. Aircraft over: Sofia Palace (12l.), Mt. El Tepe (16l.), Rila Lakes and mountains (19l.).

1940.

445a	**138**	1l. green	15	15
446		2l. red	25	15

139 First Bulgarian Postage Stamp

1940. Cent of 1st Adhesive Postage Stamp.

447	**139**	10l. olive	1·70	1·50
448	–	20l. blue	1·70	1·70

DESIGN: 20l. has scroll dated "1840–1940".

140 Grapes

142 King Boris III

141 Ploughing

1940.

449	**140**	10s. orange	15	15
450	–	15s. blue	15	15
451	**141**	30s. brown	15	15
452	–	50s. violet	15	15
452a	–	50s. green	15	15
453	**142**	1l. green	15	15
454		2l. red	15	15
455		4l. orange	15	15
456		6l. violet	30	15
457		7l. blue	15	15
458		10l. green	25	15

DESIGNS—VERT: 15s. Beehive. HORIZ: 50s. Shepherd and flock.

143 Peasant Couple and King Boris

144 King Boris and Map of Dobrudja

1940. Recovery of Dobrudja from Rumania. Designs incorporating miniature portrait of King Boris.

464	**143**	1l. green	15	15
465	–	2l. red	15	15
466	**144**	4l. brown	15	15
467		7l. blue	35	45

DESIGN—VERT: 2l. Bulgarian flags and wheat-field.

145 Bee-keeping

1940. Agricultural Scenes.

468	–	10s. purple	10	15
469	–	10s. blue	10	15
470	–	15s. green	10	15
471	–	15s. olive	10	15
472	**145**	30s. orange	15	15
473		30s. green	10	15
474	–	50s. violet	15	15
475	–	50s. purple	10	15
476	–	3l. brown	1·10	15
477	–	3l. black	1·20	95
478	–	5l. brown	65	80
479	–	5l. blue	65	65

DESIGNS: 10s. Threshing; 15s. Ploughing with oxen; 50s. Picking apples; 3l. Shepherd; 5l. Cattle.

146 Pencko Slaveikov (poet)

147 St. Ivan Rilski

1940. National Relief.

480	**146**	1l. green	10	15
481	–	2l. red	10	15
482	**147**	3l. brown	15	15
483	–	4l. orange	15	15
484	–	7l. blue	80	1·00
485	–	10l. brown	1·60	1·10

DESIGNS: 2l. Bishop Sofronii of Vratsa; 4l. Marin Drinov (historian); 7l. Chernorisets Khratur (monk); 10l. Kolo Ficheto (writer).

148 Johannes Gutenberg

149 Nikola Karastoyanov

1940. 500th Anniv of Invention of Printing and Centenary of Bulgarian Printing.

486	**148**	1l. green	10	15
487	**149**	2l. brown	15	15

150 Botev

151 Arrival in Koslodui

1941. 65th Death Anniv of Khristo Botev (poet and revolutionary).

488	**150**	1l. green	10	20
489	**151**	2l. red	10	20
490	–	3l. brown	50	65

DESIGN—VERT: 3l. Botev Memorial Cross.

152 National History Museum

1941. Buildings in Sofia.

491	**152**	14l. brown	15	15
492	–	20l. green	15	30
493	–	50l. blue	15	85

DESIGNS: 20l. Tsarita Icanna Workers' Hospital; 50l. National Bank.

153 Thasos Island

154 Ohrid

1941. Reacquisition of Macedonia.

494	–	1l. green	10	15
495	**153**	2l. orange	10	15
496	–	2l. red	10	15
497	–	4l. brown	10	15
498	**154**	7l. blue	35	40

DESIGNS—VERT: 1l. Macedonian girl. HORIZ: 2l. (No. 496) King Boris and map dated "1941"; 4l. Poganovski Monastery.

155 Children on Beach

1942. Sunday Delivery. Inscr as in T **155**.

499	–	1l. green	15	15
500	**155**	2l. orange	15	15
501	–	5l. blue	30	30

DESIGNS: 1l. St. Konstantin Sanatorium, Varna; 5l. Sun-bathing terrace, Bankya.

156 Bugler at Camp

157 Folk Dancers

1942. "Work and Joy". Inscr as at foot of T **157**.

502	–	1l. green	10	15
503	–	2l. red	15	15
504	–	4l. black	15	15
505	**156**	7l. blue	20	25
506	**157**	14l. brown	35	40

DESIGNS—VERT: 1l. Guitarist and accordion player; 2l. Camp orchestra; 4l. Hoisting the flag.

158 Wounded Soldier

159 Queen visiting Wounded

1942. War Invalids. Inscr as T **158/9**.

507	**158**	1l. green	10	10
508	–	2l. red	10	10
509	–	4l. orange	10	10
510	–	7l. blue	10	10
511	–	14l. brown	30	10
512	**159**	20l. black	25	20

DESIGNS—HORIZ: 2l. Soldier and family; 4l. First aid on battlefield; 7l. Widow and orphans at grave; 14l. Unknown Soldiers Memorial.

160 Khan Kubrat (ruled 595–642)

161 King Boris III

1942. Historical series.

513	**160**	10s. black	10	15
514	–	15s. blue	10	15
515	–	30s. mauve	10	15
516	–	50s. blue	10	15
517	–	1l. green	10	15
518	–	2l. red	10	15
519	–	3l. brown	10	15
520	–	4l. orange	10	15
521	–	5l. green	15	15
522	–	7l. blue	15	15
523	–	10l. black	15	15
524	–	14l. olive	10	15
525	–	20l. brown	40	40
526	–	30l. black	70	55

DESIGNS: 15s. Cavalry charge (Khan as parukh, 680–701); 30s. Equestrian statue of Khan Krum (803–814); 50s. Baptism of King Boris I; 1l. St. Naum's School; 2l. King Boris crowns his son, Tsar Simeon; 3l. Golden Era of Bulgarian literature; 4l. Trial of Bogomil Vasilii; 5l. Proclamation of Second Bulgarian Empire; 7l. Ivan Asen II (1214–81) at Tebizond; 10l. Expulsion of Eutimil Patriarch of Turnovo; 14l. Wandering minstrels; 20l. Father Paisii Khilendarski (historian); 30l. Shipka Pass Memorial.

1944. King Boris Mourning Issue. Portraits dated "1894–1943". Perf or imperf.

527	**161**	1l. olive	15	15
528	–	2l. brown	20	25
529	–	4l. brown	20	25
530	–	5l. violet	35	55
531	–	7l. blue	45	55

163 King Simeon II

ВСИЧКО
ЗА
ФРОНТА
(**164**)

1944.

532	**163**	3l. orange	1·00	75

1945. "All for the Front". Parcel Post stamps optd as T **164** or surch also.

533	**P 163**	1l. red	15	15
534		4l. on 1l. red	15	15
535		7l. purple	15	15
536		20l. brown	15	15
537		30l. purple	25	15
538		50l. orange	50	25
539		100l. blue	1·00	50

1945. Air. Optd with airplane or surch also.

540	**142**	1l. green	15	10
541		4l. orange	15	10
542	**P 163**	10l. on 100l. yellow	15	15
543		45l. on 100l. yellow	25	15
544		75l. on 100l. yellow	55	40
545		100l. yellow	95	60

Nos. 540/1 are perf; the rest imperf.

167

1945. Slav Congress. Perf or imperf.

546	**167**	4l. red	15	10
547		10l. blue	15	10
548		50l. red	40	30

СЪБИРАЙТЕ
ВСЪКАКВИ
ПАРЦАЛИ
(**168**) "Collect All Rags"

СЪБИРАЙТЕ
СТАРО
ЖЕЛЪЗО
(**169**) "Collect Old Iron"

СЪБИРАЙТЕ
ХАРТИЕНИ
ОТПАДЪЦИ
(**170**) "Collect Wastepaper"

1945. Salvage Campaign. Nos. 457/9 optd with T **168**/**70**.

549	**142**	1l. green	20	15
550		2l. red	60	15
551		4l. orange	40	30

Prices are the same for these stamps with any one of the overprints illustrated.

171 Lion Rampant

172

1945. Lion Rampant, in various frames.

552	–	30s. green	25	15
553	–	50s. blue	25	15
554	**171**	1l. green	25	15
555	–	2l. brown	25	15
556	–	4l. blue	25	15
557	–	5l. violet	25	15
558	**172**	9l. grey	25	15
559	–	10l. blue	15	15
560	–	15l. brown	25	15
561	–	20l. black	25	15
562	–	20l. red	25	15

173 Chain-breaker

174 "VE Day"

1945. Liberty Loan. Imperf.

563	**173**	50l. orange	20	15
564		50l. lake	20	15
565	–	100l. blue	25	15
566	–	100l. brown	25	15
567	–	150l. red	60	35
568	–	150l. green	60	35
569	–	200l. olive	95	65
570	–	200l. blue	95	65

MS570a Two blocks 88 × 123 mm, with the four values imperf (a) in brown-red and (b) in violet. Pair 10·50 13·00

DESIGNS: 100l. Hand holding coin; 150l. Water-mill; 200l. Coin and symbols of industry and agriculture.

1945. "Victory in Europe".

571	**174**	10l. green and brown	15	15
572		50l. green and red	35	15

175

176

1945. 1st Anniv of Fatherland Front Coalition.

573	**175**	1l. olive	15	15
574		4l. blue	15	15
575		5l. mauve	15	15
576	**176**	10l. blue	15	15
577		20l. red	20	15
578	**175**	50l. green	40	40
579		100l. brown	65	65

177 Refugee Children

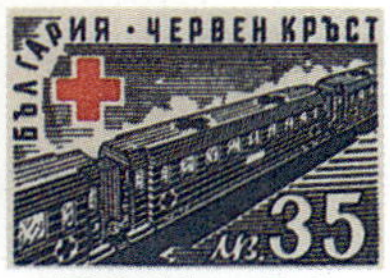

178 Red Cross Train

1946. Red Cross. Cross in red.

580	**177**	2l. olive	10	15
645d		2l. brown	10	15
581	–	4l. violet	10	15
645e	–	4l. black	10	15
582	**177**	10l. purple	10	15
645f		10l. green	15	15
583	–	20l. dark blue	15	15
645g	–	20l. light blue	20	35
584	–	30l. brown	15	25
645h	–	30l. green	30	40
585	**178**	35l. black	25	30
645i		35l. green	30	45
586	–	50l. purple	50	55
645j	–	50l. lake	65	70
587	**178**	100l. brown	1·30	90
645k		100l. blue	1·20	1·10

DESIGNS—HORIZ: 4l., 20l. Soldier on stretcher. VERT: 30l., 50l. Nurse and wounded soldier.

179 Postal Savings Emblem

180 Savings Bank-Note

1946. 50th Anniv of Savings Bank.

588	**179**	4l. red	45	30
589	**180**	10l. olive	20	15
590	–	20l. blue	20	15
591	–	50l. black	65	85

DESIGNS—VERT: 20l. Child filling money-box; 50l. Postal Savings Bank.

181 Arms of Russia and Bulgaria and Spray of Oak

182 Lion Rampant

1946. Bulgo-Russian Congress.

592	**181**	4l. red	6·00	6·00
593		4l. orange	10	15
594		20l. blue	6·00	6·00
595		20l. green	20	30

1946. Stamp Day. Imperf.

596	**182**	20l. blue	50	30

183

190

1946. Air. Inscr "PAR AVION".

597	**183**	1l. purple	25	10
598		2l. grey	25	15
599	–	4l. black	25	15
600	–	6l. blue	25	15
601	–	10l. green	25	15
602	–	12l. brown	25	15
603	–	16l. purple	25	15
604	–	19l. red	25	15
605	–	30l. orange	25	15
606	–	45l. green	30	25
607	–	75l. brown	50	30
608	**190**	100l. red	90	35
609	–	100l. grey	90	35

DESIGNS—23 × 18 mm: 4l. Bird carrying envelope; 100l. (No. 609), Airplane. 18 × 23 mm: 6l. Airplane and envelope; 10, 12, 19l. Wings and posthorn; 16l. Wings and envelope; 30l. Airplane; 45, 75l. Dove and posthorn.

192 Stamboliiski

193 Flags of Albania, Bulgaria, Yugoslavia and Rumania

1946. 23rd Death Anniv of Aleksandur Stamboliiski (Prime Minister 1919–23).

610	**192**	100l. orange	6·00	6·00

1946. Balkan Games.

611	**193**	100l. brown	1·30	1·10

196 Artillery

195 Junkers Ju87B "Stuka" Dive Bombers

1946. Military and Air Services.

612	–	2l. red	15	15
613	–	4l. grey	15	15
614	**196**	5l. red	15	10
615	**195**	6l. brown	15	10
616	–	9l. mauve	15	15
617	–	10l. violet	15	15
618	–	20l. blue	40	15
619	–	30l. orange	40	15
620	–	40l. olive	45	25
621	–	50l. green	60	45
622	–	60l. brown	90	45

DESIGNS—HORIZ: 2, 20l. Grenade thrower and machine-gunner; 9l. Building pontoon-bridge; 10, 30l. Cavalry charge; 40l. Supply column; 50l. Motor convoy; 60l. Tanks. VERT: 4l. Grenade thrower.

203 St. Ivan Rilski

208 "New Republic"

1946. Death Millenary of St. Ivan Rilski.

623	**203**	1l. brown	10	15
624	–	4l. sepia	10	15
625	–	10l. green	25	15
626	–	20l. blue	30	15
627	–	50l. red	1·40	75

DESIGNS—HORIZ: 4l. Rila Monastery; 10l. Monastery entrance; 50l. Cloistered courtyard. VERT: 20l. Aerial view of Monastery.

1946. Referendum.

628	**208**	4l. red	10	15
629		20l. blue	10	15
630		50l. brown	20	35

209 Assault

210 Ambuscade

1946. Partisan Activities.

631	**209**	1l. purple	10	15
632	**210**	4l. green	10	15
633	–	5l. brown	10	15
634	**210**	10l. red	10	15
635	**209**	20l. blue	30	15
636	–	30l. brown	30	25
637	–	50l. black	40	40

DESIGNS—VERT: 5l., 50l. Partisan riflemen; 30l. Partisan leader.

211 Nurse and Children

212a Partisans

1947. Winter Relief.

638	**211**	1l. violet	10	15
639	–	4l. red	10	15
640	–	9l. olive	10	15
641	**211**	10l. grey	10	15
642	–	20l. blue	15	15
643	–	30l. brown	15	15
644	–	40l. red	30	30
645	**211**	50l. green	50	45

DESIGNS: 4l., 9l. Child carrying gifts; 20l., 40l. Hungry child; 30l. Destitute mother and child.

1947. Anti-fascists of 1923, 1941 and 1944 Commem.

645a	–	10l. brown and orange	30	50
645b	**212a**	20l. dp blue & lt blue	30	50
645c	–	70l. brown and red	27·00	32·00

DESIGNS—HORIZ: 10l. Group of fighters; 70l. Soldier addressing crowd.

213 Olive Branch

214 Dove of Peace

1947. Peace.

646	**213**	4l. olive	10	15
647	**214**	10l. brown	10	15
648		20l. blue	20	25

"BULGARIA" is in Roman characters on the 20l.

215 "U.S.A." and "Bulgaria"

1947. Air. Stamp Day and New York International Philatelic Exhibition.

649	**215**	70l.+30l. brown	1·40	1·40

216 Esperanto Emblem and Map of Bulgaria

1947. 30th Esperanto Jubilee Congress, Sofia.

650	**216**	20l.+10l. purple & green	55	80

217 G.P.O., Sofia

218 National Theatre, Sofia

219 Parliament Building

220 President's Palace

221 G.P.O., Sofia

1947. Government Buildings. (a) T **217**.

651		1l. green	10	15
		(b) T **218**.		
652		50s. green	10	15
653		2l. red	10	15
654		4l. blue	10	15
655		9l. red	10	15
		(c) T **219**.		
656		50s. green	10	15
657		2l. blue	10	15
658		4l. blue	10	15
659		20l. blue	40	30
		(d) T **220**.		
660		1l. green	10	15
		(e) T **221**.		
661		1l. green	10	15
662		2l. red	10	15
663		4l. blue	10	15

222 Hydro-electric Power Station and Dam

223 Emblem of Industry

1947. Reconstruction.

664	**222**	4l. green	15	15
665	–	9l. brown (Miner)	15	20
666	**223**	20l. blue	20	25
667	–	40l. green (Motor plough)	65	75

224 Exhibition Building

225 Former Residence of the French Poet Lamartine

226 Rose and Grapes

227 Airplane over City

1947. Plovdiv Fair. (a) Postage.
668 **224** 4l. red 10 10
669 **225** 9l. red 10 10
670 **226** 20l. blue 20 25

(b) Air. Imperf.
671 **227** 40l. green 85 85

228 Cycle Racing

229 Basketball

231 V. E. Aprilov

1947. Balkan Games.
672 **228** 2l. lilac 35 25
673 **229** 4l. green 35 25
674 – 9l. brown 95 45
675 – 20l. blue . . . . 1·10 50
676 – 60l. red . . . . 2·75 2·10
DESIGNS—VERT: 9l. Chess; 20l. Football; 60l. Balkan flags.

1947. Death Cent of Vasil Aprilov (educationist).
678 – 4l. red 20 10
677 **231** 40l. blue 40 20
DESIGN: 4l. Another portrait of Aprilov.

233 Postman

235 Geno Kirov

1947. Postal Employees' Relief Fund.
679 **233** 4l.+2l. olive 10 15
680 – 10l.+5l. red 20 15
681 – 20l.+10l. blue 20 25
682 – 40l.+20l. brown 90 70
DESIGNS: 10l. Linesman; 20l. Telephonists; 40l. Wireless masts.

1947. Theatrical Artists' Benevolent Fund.
683 **235** 50s. brown 10 10
684 – 1l. green 10 10
685 – 2l. green 10 10
686 – 3l. blue 10 10
687 – 4l. red 10 10
688 – 5l. purple 10 10
689 – 9l.+5l. blue 15 10
690 – 10l.+6l. red 20 15
691 – 15l.+7l. violet 20 30
692 – 20l.+15l. blue 45 50
693 – 30l.+20l. purple 90 95
PORTRAITS: 1l. Zlotina Nedeva; 2l. Ivan Popov; 3l. Atanas Kirchev; 4l. Elena Snezhina; 5l. Stoyan Buchvarov; 9l. Khristo Ganchev; 10l. Adriana Budevska; 15l. Vasil Kirkov; 20l. Save Orgnyanov; 30l. Krustyn Sarafov.

236 "Rodina" (freighter)

1947. National Shipping Revival.
694 **236** 50l. blue 65 55

237 Worker and Flag

238 Worker and Globe

1948. 2nd General Workers' Union Congress.
695 **237** 4l. blue (postage) 15 10
696 **238** 60l. brown (air) 55 45

239

240

1948. Leisure and Culture.
697 **239** 4l. red 15 15
698 **240** 20l. blue 25 15
699 – 40l. green 40 30
700 – 60l. brown 65 55
DESIGNS—VERT: 40l. Workers' musical interlude; 60l. Sports girl.

241 Kikola Vaptsarov

242 Petlyakov Pe-2 Bomber over Baldwin's Tower

1948. Poets.
701 **241** 4l. red on cream 10 15
702 – 9l. brown on cream . . . 15 15
703 – 15l. purple on cream . . . 15 15
704 – 20l. blue on cream . . . 20 25
705 – 45l. green on cream . . . 70 75
PORTRAITS: 9l. Peya Yavorov; 15l. Khristo Smirnenski; 20l. Ivan Vazov; 45l. Petko Slaveikov.

1948. Air. Stamp Day.
706 **242** 50l. brown on cream . . . 1·30 1·20

243 Soldier

244 Peasants and Soldiers

1948. Soviet Army Monument.
707 **243** 4l. red on cream 10 15
708 **244** 10l. green on cream . . . 15 15
709 – 20l. blue on cream . . . 25 25
710 – 60l. olive on cream . . . 70 65
DESIGNS—HORIZ: 20l. Soldiers of 1878 and 1944. VERT: 60l. Stalin and Spassky Tower, Kremlin.

245 Malyovitsa Peak

246 Lion Emblem

1948. Bulgarian Health Resorts.
711 – 2l. red 10 15
712 – 3l. orange 10 15
713 – 4l. blue 15 15
717 **245** 5l. brown 15 15
714 – 10l. purple 20 15
718 – 15l. olive 30 15
715 **245** 20l. blue 90 50
716 – 20l. blue . . . . 1·30 50
DESIGNS: 2l. Bath, Gorna Banya; 3, 10l. Bath, Bankya; 4, 20l. (No. 716), Mineral bath, Sofia; 15l. Malyovitsa Peak.

1948.
719 **246** 50s. orange 15 15
719a 50s. brown 15 15
720 1l. green 15 15
721 9l. black 20 30

247 Dimitur Blagoev

248 Youths marching

1948. 25th Anniv of September Uprising.
722 **247** 4l. brown 10 15
723 – 9l. orange 10 15
724 – 20l. blue 30 30
725 **248** 60l. brown 75 80
DESIGNS—VERT: 9l. Gabrit Genov. HORIZ: 20l. Bishop Andrei Monument.

249 Khristo Smirnenski

250 Miner

1948. 500th Birth Anniv of Smirnenski (poet and revolutionary).
726 **249** 4l. blue 10 10
727 16l. brown 15 10

1948.
728 **250** 4l. blue 40 15

251 Battle of Grivitsa

1948. Treaty of Friendship with Rumania.
729 **251** 20l. blue (postage) 20 15
730 – 40l. black (air) 20 20
731 – 100l. mauve 90 80
DESIGNS: 40l. Parliament Buildings in Sofia and Bucharest; 100l. Projected Danube Bridge.

252 Botev's House, Kalofer

253 Botev

1948. Birth Centenary of Khristo Botev (poet and revolutionary).
732 **252** 1l. green 10 15
733 **253** 4l. brown 10 15
734 4l. purple 10 15
735 – 9l. violet 15 15
736 – 15l. brown 15 15
737a – 20l. blue 15 20
738 – 40l. brown 30 25
739 – 50l. black 40 20
DESIGNS—HORIZ: 9l. River paddle-steamer "Radetski"; 15l. Village of Kalofer; 40l. Botev's mother and verse of poem. VERT: 20l. Botev in uniform; 50l. Quill, pistol and laurel wreath.

254 Lenin

255 Road Construction

1949. 25th Death Anniv of Lenin. Inscr "1924–1949".
740 **254** 4l. brown 15 15
741 – 20l. red 35 40
DESIGN—(27 × 37 mm): 20l. Lenin as an orator.

1949. National Youth Movement.
742 **255** 4l. red 10 15
743 – 5l. brown 55 25
744 – 9l. green . . . . 1·20 30
745 – 10l. violet 25 25
746 – 20l. blue 45 50
747 – 40l. brown 90 90
DESIGNS—HORIZ: 5l. Tunnel construction; 9l. Class 10 steam locomotive; 10l. Textile workers; 20l. Girl driving tractor; 40l. Workers in lorry.

256 Lisunov Li-2 over Pleven Mausoleum

1949. Air. 7th Philatelic Congress, Pleven.
748 **256** 50l. bistre . . . . 3·25 1·60

257 G. Dimitrov

258 G. Dimitrov

1949. Death of Georgi Dimitrov (Prime Minister 1946–49).
749 **257** 4l. red 15 30
750 **258** 20l. blue 90 40

259 Hydro-electric Power Station

260 Symbols of Agriculture and Industry

1949. Five Year Industrial and Agricultural Plan.
751 **259** 4l. olive (postage) 15 15
752 – 9l. red 20 25
753 – 15l. violet 30 25
754 – 20l. blue . . . . 1·00 50
755 **260** 50l. brown (air) . . . . . 2·40 1·40
DESIGNS—VERT: 9l. Cement works; 15l. Tractors in garage. HORIZ: 20l. Tractors in field.

261 Javelin and Grenade Throwing

262 Motor-cyclist and Tractor

1949. Physical Culture Campaign.
756 **261** 4l. red 25 30
757 – 9l. olive . . . . 1·20 65
758 **262** 20l. blue . . . . 1·80 1·10
759 – 50l. red . . . . 4·50 2·75
DESIGNS—HORIZ: 9l. Hurdling and leaping barbed-wire. VERT: 50l. Two athletes marching.

263 Globe

265 Guardsman with Dog

264 Guardsman and Peasant

1949. Air. 75th Anniv of Universal Postal Union.
760 **263** 50l. blue . . . . 1·80 1·00

1949. Frontier Guards.
761 **264** 4l. brown (postage) . . . 15 20
762 – 20l. blue . . . . 1·00 50
763 **265** 60l. green (air) . . . . . 3·00 2·00
DESIGN—VERT: 20l. Guardsman on coast.

266 Georgi Dimitrov (Prime Minister 1946–49)

267 "Unanimity"

268 Zosif Stalin

1949. Fatherland Front.

764	**266**	4l. brown	15	10
765	**267**	9l. violet	20	15
766	–	20l. blue	30	20
767	–	50l. red	1·10	80

DESIGNS: 20l. Man and woman with wheelbarrow and spade; 50l. Young people marching with banners.

1949. 70th Birthday of Stalin.

768	**268**	4l. orange	20	15
769	–	40l. red	75	75

DESIGN—VERT: (25 × 37 mm): 40l. Stalin as an orator.

269 Kharalampi Stoyanov

270 Strikers and Train

1950. 30th Anniv of Railway Strike.

770	**269**	4l. brown	10	10
771	**270**	20l. blue	30	25
772	–	60l. olive	80	60

DESIGN—VERT: 60l. Two workers and flag.

271 Miner

272 Class 48 Steam Shunting Locomotive

1950.

773	**271**	1l. olive	10	10
773a		1l. violet	10	10
774	**272**	2l. black	1·90	30
774a		2l. brown	1·50	25
775	–	3l. blue	20	10
776a	–	4l. green	1·20	35
777	–	5l. red	25	10
778	–	9l. grey	25	10
779	–	10l. purple	15	10
780	–	15l. red	15	20
781	–	20l. blue	25	30

DESIGNS—VERT: 3l. Ship under construction; 10l. Power station; 15l., 20l. Woman in factory. HORIZ: 4l. Tractor; 5l., 9l. Threshing machines.

273 Kolarov

1950. Death of Vasil Kolarov (Prime Minister 1949–50). Inscr "1877–1950".

782	**273**	4l. brown	10	15
783	–	20l. blue	40	40

DESIGN—(27½ × 39½ mm): 20l. Portrait as Type **273**, but different frame.

274 Starislas Dospevski (self-portrait)

274a "In the Field" (Khristo Storclev)

1950. Painters and paintings.

784	**274**	1l. green	25	25
785	–	4l. orange	1·40	35
786	–	9l. brown	1·80	35
787	**274a**	15l. brown	2·50	65
788		20l. blue	4·00	1·80
789	–	40l. brown	4·75	2·50
790	–	60l. orange	5·25	3·75

DESIGNS—VERT: 4l. King Kaloyan and Desislava; 9l. Nikolai Pavlovich; 40l. Statue of Debeyanov (Ivan Lazarov); 60l. "Peasant" (Vladimir Dimitrov the Master).

275 Ivan Vazov and Birthplace, Sopot

276a G. Dimitrov (statesman)

1950. Birth Centenary of Ivan Vazov (poet).

791	**275**	4l. olive	15	15

1950. 1st Death Anniv of Georgi Dimitrov.

792	–	50s. brown (postage)	15	15
793	–	50s. green	15	15
794	**276a**	1l. brown	20	15
795	–	2l. slate	20	15
796	–	4l. purple	60	20
797	–	9l. red	1·00	50
798	–	10l. red	1·60	80
799	–	15l. grey	1·60	80
800	–	20l. blue	2·50	1·60
801	–	40l. brown (air)	4·75	3·00

DESIGNS—HORIZ: 50s. green, Dimitrov and birthplace, Kovachevtsi; 2l. Dimitrov's house, Sofia; 15l. Dimitrov signing new constitution; 20l. Dimitrov; 40l. Mausoleum. VERT: 50s. brown, 4, 9, 10l. Dimitrov in various poses.

277 Runners

278 Workers and Tractor

1950.

802	**277**	4l. green	60	35
803	–	9l. brown (Cycling)	75	40
804	–	20l. blue (Putting the shot)	1·00	80
805	–	40l. purple (Volleyball)	2·20	1·90

1950. 2nd National Peace Congress.

806	**278**	4l. red	10	15
807	–	20l. blue	40	40

DESIGN—VERT: 20l. Stalin on flag and three heads.

278b

279 Children on Beach

1950. Arms designs.

807a	–	2l. brown	15	15
807b	–	3l. red	15	15
807c	**278b**	5l. red	15	15
807d	–	9l. blue	25	15

Although inscribed "OFFICIAL MAIL", the above were issued as regular postage stamps.

1950. Sunday Delivery.

808	–	1l. green (Sanatorium)	20	15
809	**279**	2l. red	30	15
810	–	5l. orange (Sunbathing)	50	30
811	**279**	10l. blue	1·00	50

280 Molotov, Kolarov, Stalin and Dimitrov

281 Russian and Bulgarian Girls

1950. 2nd Anniv of Soviet–Bulgarian Treaty of Friendship.

812	**280**	4l. brown	10	15
813	–	9l. red	15	15
814	**281**	20l. blue	30	30
815	–	50l. green	1·90	90

DESIGNS—VERT: 9l. Spassky Tower and flags; 50l. Freighter and tractor.

282 Marshal Tolbukhin

284 A. S. Popov

286 Georgi Kirkov

1950. Honouring Marshal Tolbukhin.

816	**282**	4l. mauve	15	15
817	–	20l. blue	90	40

DESIGN—HORIZ: 20l. Bulgarians greeting Tolbukhin.

1951. 45th Death Anniv of Aleksandr Popov (radio pioneer).

818	**284**	4l. brown	25	15
819		20l. blue	80	40

1951. Anti-fascist Heroes.

823	–	1l. mauve	15	15
824	–	2l. plum	20	15
825	**286**	4l. red	20	15
826	–	9l. brown	55	40
827	–	15l. olive	1·60	65
828	–	20l. blue	1·60	95
829	–	50l. grey	4·00	1·40

PORTRAITS: 1l. Chankova, Adalbert Antonov-Malchika, Sasho Dimitrov and Lilyana Dimitrova; 2l. Stanke Dimitrov; 9l. Anton Ivanov; 15l. Mikhailov; 20l. Georgi Dimitrov at Leipzig; 50l. Nocho Ivanov and Acram Stoyahov.

285 First Bulgarian Truck

289 Embroidery

1951. National Occupations. (a) As T **285**.

820	–	1l. violet (Tractor)	10	10
821	–	2l. green (Steam-roller)	15	10
822	**285**	4l. brown	20	10

(b) As T **289**.

830	–	1l. brown (Tractor)	15	20
831	–	2l. violet (Steam-roller)	20	20
832	–	4l. brown (Truck)	40	45
833	**289**	9l. violet	75	40
834	–	15l. purple (Carpets)	1·40	95
835	–	20l. blue (Roses and Tobacco)	3·00	1·40
836	–	40l. green (Fruit)	4·50	2·10

The 9l. and 20l. are vert, the remainder horiz.

290 Turkish Attack

1951. 75th Anniv of April Uprising.

837	**290**	1l. brown	45	25
838	–	4l. green	45	25
839	–	9l. purple	70	55
840	–	20l. blue	1·10	90
841	–	40l. lake	1·60	1·50

DESIGNS—HORIZ: 4l. Proclamation of Uprising; 9l. Cannon and cavalry; 20l. Patriots in 1876 and 1944; 40l. Georgi Benkovsky and Georgi Dimitrov.

291 Dimitur Blagoev as Orator

1951. 60th Anniv of First Bulgarian Social Democratic Party Congress, Buzludzha.

842	**291**	1l. violet	20	15
843		4l. green	40	25
844		9l. purple	1·00	80

292 Babies in Creche

1951. Children's Day.

845	**292**	1l. brown	20	15
846	–	4l. purple	45	25
847	–	9l. green	95	40
848	–	20l. blue	1·90	1·30

DESIGNS: 4l. Children building models; 9l. Girl and children's play ground; 20l. Boy bugler and children marching.

293 Workers

294 Labour medal (Obverse)

295 Labour medal (Reverse)

1951. 3rd General Workers' Union Congress.

849	**293**	1l. black	10	15
850	–	4l. brown	15	15

DESIGN inscr "16 XII 1951"; 4l. Georgi Dimitrov and Valdo Chervenkov (Prime minister).

1952. Order of Labour.

851	**294**	1l. red	15	15
852	**295**	1l. brown	15	15
853	**294**	4l. green	15	15
854	**295**	4l. green	15	15
855	**294**	9l. violet	40	15
856	**295**	9l. blue	40	15

296 Vasil Kolarov Dam

297 G. Dimitrov and Chemical Works

1952.

857	**296**	4s. green	15	15
858		12s. violet	20	15
859		16s. brown	25	15
860		44s. red	55	15
861		80s. blue	2·75	30

1952. 70th Birth Anniv of Georgi Dimitrov (statesman). Dated "1882–1952".

862	**297**	16s. brown	35	25
863	–	44s. brown	95	50
864	–	80s. blue	1·60	95

DESIGNS—HORIZ: 44s. Georgi Dimitrov (Prime minister 1946–49) and Prime minister Vulko Chervenkov. VERT: 80s. Full-face portrait of Georgi Dimitrov.

298 Republika Power Station

299 N. Vaptsarov (revolutionary)

1952.

866	298	16s. sepia	30	15
867		44s. purple	95	15

1952. 10th Death Anniv of Nikola Vaptsarov (poet and revolutionary).

869	299	16s. lake	30	40
870	–	44s. brown	1·20	1·00
871	–	80s. sepia	2·20	1·00

PORTRAITS: 44s. Facing bayonets; 80s. Full-face.

300 Congress Delegates

1952. 40th Anniv of First Workers' Social Democratic Youth League Congress.

872	300	2s. lake	15	15
873	–	16s. violet	25	20
874	–	44s. green	1·60	40
875	–	80s. sepia	2·10	80

DESIGNS: 16s. Young partisans; 44s. Factory and guards; 80s. Dimitrov addressing young workers.

301 Attack on Winter Palace, St. Petersburg

1952. 35th Anniv of Russian Revolution. Dated "1917 1952".

876	301	4s. lake	15	15
877	–	8s. green	20	15
878	–	16s. blue	20	15
879	–	44s. sepia	60	30
880	–	80s. olive	1·40	60

DESIGNS: 8s. Volga–Don canal; 16s. Dove and globe; 44s. Lenin and Stalin; 80s. Lenin, Stalin and Himlay hydro-electric station.

302

303 Vintagers and Grapes

1952. Wood Carvings depicting National Products.

881	–	2s. brown	10	15
882	–	8s. green	10	15
883	–	12s. brown	15	15
884	–	16s. purple	30	15
885	302	28s. green	60	15
886	–	44s. brown	60	25
887	303	80s. blue	1·00	25
888		1l. violet	2·20	40
889		4l. red	3·00	2·30

DESIGNS—VERT: 2s. Numeral in carved frame. HORIZ: 8s. Gift-offering to idol; 12s. Birds and grapes; 16s. Rose-gathering; 44s. "Attar of Roses".

304 V. Levski

1953. 80th Anniv of Execution of Vasil Levski (revolutionary).

890	304	16s. brown on cream	15	15
891	–	44s. brown on cream	30	25

DESIGN: 44s. Levski addressing crowd.

305 Russian Army Crossing R. Danube

306 Mother and Children

1953. 75th Anniv of Liberation from Turkey.

892	305	8s. blue	30	15
893	–	16s. brown	25	15
894	–	44s. green	55	25
895	–	80s. lake	1·50	90
896	–	1l. black	1·90	1·50

DESIGNS—VERT: 16s. Battle of Shipka Pass. HORIZ: 44s. Peasants welcoming Russian soldiers; 80s. Bulgarians and Russians embracing; 1l. Shipka Pass memorial and Dimitrovgrad.

1953. International Women's Day.

897	306	16s. blue	15	10
898		16s. green	15	10

307 Karl Marx

308 May Day Parade

1953. 70th Death Anniv of Karl Marx.

899	307	16s. blue	15	15
900	–	44s. brown	40	30

DESIGN—VERT: 44s. Book "Das Kapital".

1953. Labour Day.

901	308	16s. red	25	15

309 Stalin

310 Goce Delcev (Macedonian revolutionary)

1953. Death of Stalin.

902	309	16s. brown	25	15
903		16s. black	25	25

1953. 50th Anniv of Ilinden–Preobrazhenie Rising.

904	310	16s. brown	10	15
905	–	44s. violet	45	30
906	–	1l. purple	60	45

DESIGNS. 44s. Insurgents and flag facing left. HORIZ: 1l. Insurgents and flag facing right.

311 Soldier and Insurgents

312 Dimitur Blagoev

1953. Army Day.

907	311	16s. red	20	15
908	–	44s. blue	50	25

DESIGN: 44s. Soldier, factories and combine-harvester.

1953. 50th Anniv of Bulgarian Workers' Social Democratic Party.

909	312	16s. brown	25	15
910	–	44s. red	55	25

DESIGN: 44s. Dimitrov and Blagoev.

313 Georgi Dimitrov and Vasil Kolarov

314 Railway Viaduct

1953. 30th Anniv of September Uprising.

911	313	8s. black	15	15
912	–	16s. brown	20	15
913	–	44s. red	65	40

DESIGNS: 16s. Insurgent and flag; 44s. Crowd of Insurgents.

1953. Bulgarian–Russian Friendship.

914	314	8s. blue	40	25
915	–	16s. slate	10	15
916	–	44s. brown	35	25
917	–	80s. orange	70	40

DESIGNS—HORIZ: 16s. Welder and industrial plant; 80s. Combine-harvester. VERT: 44s. Iron foundry.

315 Dog Rose

316 Vasil Kolarov Library

1953. Medicinal Flowers.

918	–	2s. blue	10	15
919	–	4s. orange	10	15
920	–	8s. turquoise	15	15
921	315	12s. green	15	15
922	–	12s. red	15	15
923	–	16s. blue	20	15
924	–	16s. brown	20	15
925	–	20s. red	20	15
926	–	28s. green	40	15
927	–	40s. blue	40	25
928	–	44s. brown	45	30
929	–	80s. brown	60	70
930	–	1l. brown	3·25	1·20
931	–	2l. purple	5·50	2·50

MS931a 161 × 172 mm. Twelve values as above in green (sold at 6l.) . . . 50·00 50·00

FLOWERS: 2s. Deadly nightshade; 4s. Thorn-apple; 8s. Sage; 16s. Great yellow gentian; 20s. Opium poppy; 28s. Peppermint; 40s. Bear-berry; 44s. Coltsfoot; 80s. Primula; 1l. Dandelion; 2l. Foxglove.

1953. 75th Anniv of Kolarov Library, Sofia.

932	316	44s. brown	30	30

317 Singer and Musician

318 Airplane over Mountains

1953. Amateur Theatricals.

933	317	16s. brown	10	15
934	–	44s. green	30	25

DESIGN: 44s. Folk-dancers.

1954. Air.

935	318	8s. green	10	15
936	–	12s. lake	10	15
937	–	16s. brown	15	15
938	–	20s. salmon	15	15
939	–	28s. blue	15	15
940	–	44s. purple	20	15
941	–	60s. brown	35	20
942	–	80s. green	60	30
943	–	1l. green	1·90	55
944	–	4l. blue	3·75	1·80

DESIGNS—VERT: 12s. Exhibition buildings, Plovdiv; 80s. Tirnovo; 4l. Partisans' Monument. HORIZ: 16s. Seaside promenade, Varna; 20s. Combine-harvester in cornfield; 28s. Rila Monastery; 44s. Studena hydro-electric barrage; 60s. Dimitrovgrad; 1l. Sofia University and equestrian statue.

319 Lenin and Stalin

320 Dimitur Blagoev and Crowd

1954. 30th Death Anniv of Lenin.

945	319	16s. brown	15	15
946	–	44s. lake	30	15
947	–	80s. blue	65	25
948	–	1l. green	1·10	75

DESIGNS—VERT: 44s. Lenin statue; 80s. Lenin–Stalin Mausoleum and Kremlin; 1l. Lenin.

1954. 30th Death Anniv of Blagoev.

949	320	16s. brown	15	10
950	–	44s. sepia	40	15

DESIGN: 44s. Blagoev writing at desk.

321 Dimitrov Speaking

322 Class 10 Steam Locomotive

1954. 5th Death Anniv of Dimitrov.

951	321	44s. lake	20	15
952	–	80s. brown	65	25

DESIGN—HORIZ: 80s. Dimitrov and blast-furnace.

1954. Railway Workers' Day.

953	322	44s. turquoise	1·00	30
954		44s. black	1·00	30

323 Miner Operating Machinery

324 Marching Soldiers

1954. Miners' Day.

955	323	44s. green	25	10

1954. 10th Anniv of Fatherland Front Government.

956	324	12s. lake	10	15
957	–	16s. red	10	15
958	–	28s. slate	20	15
959	–	44s. brown	25	15
960	–	80s. blue	75	40
961	–	1l. green	1·00	40

DESIGNS—VERT: 16s. Soldier and parents; 80s. Girl and boy pioneers; 1l. Dimitrov. HORIZ: 28s. Industrial plant; 44s. Dimitrov and workers.

325 Academy Building

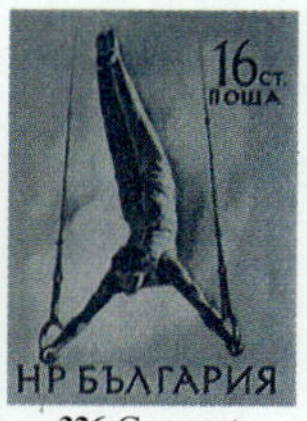

326 Gymnast

1954. 85th Anniv of Academy of Sciences.

962	325	80s. black	90	55

1954. Sports. Cream paper.

963	326	16s. green	1·00	25
964	–	44s. red	1·00	65
965	–	80s. brown	1·80	1·40
966	–	2l. blue	3·25	3·25

DESIGNS—VERT: 44s. Wrestlers; 2l. Ski-jumper. HORIZ: 80s. Horse-jumper.

327 Velingrad Rest Home

1954. 50th Anniv of Trade Union Movement.

967	327	16s. green	15	15
968	–	44s. red	15	25
969	–	80s. blue	75	50

DESIGNS—VERT: 44s. Foundryman. HORIZ: 80s. Georgi Dimitrov, Dimitur Blagoev and Georgi Kirkov.

328 Geese

329 Communist Party Building

1955.

970	328	2s. green	10	10
971	–	4s. olive	15	10
972	–	12s. brown	25	15
973	–	16s. brown	45	10
974	–	28s. blue	20	15
975	329	44s. red	7·50	1·60
976	–	80s. brown	50	25
977	–	1l. green	1·30	35

DESIGNS: 4s. Rooster and hens; 12s. Sow and piglets; 16s. Ewe and lambs; 28s. Telephone exchange; 80s. Flats; 1l. Cellulose factory.

330 Mill Girl

332 Rejoicing Crowds

1955. International Women's Day.

978	330	12s. brown	10	10
979	–	16s. green	20	10
980	–	44s. blue	65	10
981	–	44s. red	65	10

DESIGNS—HORIZ: 16s. Girl feeding cattle. VERT: 44s. Mother and baby.

1955. As Nos. 820 and 822 surch **16 CT.**

981a	–	16s. on 1l. violet	15	10
982	285	16s. on 4l. brown	70	10

1955. Labour Day.

983	332	16s. red	15	15
984	–	44s. blue	45	15

DESIGN: 44s. Three workers and globe.

333 St. Cyril and St. Methodius

334 Sergei Rumyantsev

1955. 1100th Anniv of 1st Bulgarian Literature. On cream paper.

985	333	4s. blue	10	10
986	–	8s. olive	10	10
987	–	16s. black	15	10
988	–	28s. red	20	15
989	–	44s. brown	35	25
990	–	80s. red	80	65
991	–	2l. black	2·10	1·40

DESIGNS: 8s. Monk writing; 16s. Early printing press; 28s. Khristo Botev (poet); 44s. Ivan Vazov (poet and novelist); 80s. Dimitur Blagoev (writer and editor) and books; 2l. Dimitur Blagoev Polygraphic Complex, Sofia.

1955. 30th Death Annivs of Bulgarian Poets. On cream paper.
992 **334** 12s. brown 25 15
993 – 16s. brown 35 25
994 – 44s. green 55 40
DESIGNS: 16s. Khristo Yusenov; 44s. Geo Milev.

335 F. Engels and Book

336 Mother and Children

1955. 60th Death Anniv of Engels.
995 **335** 44s. brown on cream . . 65 45

1955. World Mothers' Congress, Lausanne.
996 **336** 44s. lake on cream . . . 50 30

337 "Youth of the World"

338 Main Entrance in 1892

1955. 5th World Youth Festival, Warsaw.
997 **337** 44s. blue on cream . . . 50 30

1955. 16th International Fair, Plovdiv.
998 **338** 4s. brown on cream . . 10 15
999 – 16s. red on cream . . . 10 15
1000 – 44s. green on cream . . 20 15
1001 – 80s. cream 95 25
DESIGNS—VERT: 16s. Sculptured group; 80s. Fair poster. HORIZ: 44s. Fruit.

339 Friedrich Schiller (dramatist) (150th death anniv)

340 Industrial Plant

1955. Cultural Annivs. Writers. On cream paper.
1002 **339** 16s. brown 25 15
1003 – 44s. red 60 15
1004 – 60s. blue 70 25
1005 – 80s. black . . . . . . 1·00 30
1006 – 1l. purple . . . . 2·10 1·10
1007 – 2l. olive . . . . 2·75 2·30
PORTRAITS: 44s. Adam Mickiewicz (poet, death centenary); 60s. Hans Christian Andersen (150th birth anniv); 80s. Baron de Montesquieu (philosopher, death bicentenary); 1l. Miguel de Cervantes (350th anniv of publication of "Don Quixote"); 2l. Walt Whitman (poet) (centenary of publication of "Leaves of Grass").

1955. Bulgarian–Russian Friendship. On cream paper.
1008 **340** 2s. slate 10 15
1009 – 4s. blue 10 15
1010 – 16s. green 50 20
1011 – 44s. brown 30 15
1012 – 80s. green 60 20
1013 – 1l. black 80 40
DESIGNS—HORIZ: 4s. Dam; 16s. Friendship railway bridge over River Danube between Ruse and Giurgiu (Rumania). VERT: 44s. Monument; 80s. Ivan-Michurin (botanist); 1l. Vladimir Mayakovsky (writer).

341 Emblem

342 Quinces

1956. Centenary of Library Reading Rooms. On cream paper.
1014 **341** 12s. red 15 15
1015 – 16s. brown 15 15
1016 – 44s. myrtle 65 35

DESIGNS: 16s. K. Pshourka writing; 44s. B. Kiro reading.

1956. Fruits.
1017 **342** 4s. red . . . . 1·10 10
1017a 4s. green 15 10
1018 – 8s. green (Pears) . . . 50 15
1018a – 8s. brown (Pears) . . . 15 10
1019 – 16s. dark red (Apples) . . 1·00 15
1019a – 16s. red (Apples) . . . 30 10
1020 – 44s. violet (Grapes) . . 1·10 35
1020a – 44s. ochre (Grapes) . . 55 25

343 Artillerymen

1956. 80th Anniv of April Uprising.
1021 **343** 16s. brown 25 25
1022 – 44s. green (Cavalry charge) 30 25

344 Blagoev and Birthplace at Zagovichane

345 Cherries

1956. Birth Centenary of Dimitur Blagoev (socialist writer).
1023 **344** 44s. turquoise 50 30

1956. Fruits.
1024 **345** 2s. lake 10 10
1025 – 12s. blue (Plums) 15 10
1026 – 28s. buff (Greengages) . . 25 20
1027 – 80s. red (Strawberries) . . 75 40

346 Football

1956. Olympic Games.
1028 – 4s. blue 30 15
1029 – 12s. red 45 15
1030 – 16s. brown 50 15
1031 **346** 44s. green 90 40
1032 – 80s. brown . . . . . . 1·30 90
1033 – 1l. lake . . . . 1·90 1·30
DESIGNS—VERT: 4s. Gymnastics; 12s. Throwing the discus; 80s. Basketball. HORIZ: 16s. Pole vaulting; 1l. Boxing.

347 Tobacco and Rose

348 Gliders

1956. 17th International Fair, Plovdiv.
1034 **347** 44s. red 80 45
1035 44s. green 80 45

1956. Air. 30th Anniv of Gliding Club.
1036 – 44s. blue 20 15
1037 – 60s. violet 40 25
1038 **348** 80s. green 60 30
DESIGNS: 44s. Launching glider; 60s. Glider over hangar.

349 National Theatre

350 Wolfgang Mozart (composer, birth bicent)

1956. Centenary of National Theatre.
1039 **349** 16s. brown 10 15
1040 – 44s. turquoise 30 25

DESIGN: 44s. Dobri Voinikov and Sava Dobroplodni (dramatist).

1956. Cultural Anniversaries.
1041 – 16s. olive 20 15
1042 – 20s. brown 25 15
1043 **350** 40s. red 50 15
1044 – 44s. brown 40 15
1045 – 60s. slate 65 25
1046 – 80s. brown 75 30
1047 – 1l. green . . . . 1·30 75
1048 – 2l. green . . . . 2·40 1·50
PORTRAITS: 16s. Benjamin Franklin (journalist and statesman, 150th birth anniv); 20s. Rembrandt (artist, 350th birth anniv); 44s. Heinrich Heine (poet, death centenary); 60s. George Bernard Shaw (dramatist, birth centenary); 80s. Fyodor Dostoevsky (novelist, 75th death anniv); 1l. Henrik Ibsen (dramatist, 50th death anniv); 2l. Pierre Curie (physicist, 50th death anniv).

351 Cyclists

352 Woman with Microscope

1957. Tour of Egypt Cycle Race.
1049 **351** 80s. brown 80 45
1050 80s. turquoise 80 45

1957. International Women's Day. Inscr as in T **352**.
1051 **352** 12s. blue 10 10
1052 – 16s. brown 15 10
1053 – 44s. green 30 20
DESIGNS: 16s. Woman and children; 44s. Woman feeding poultry.

353 "New Times"

1957. 60th Anniv of "New Times" (book).
1054 **353** 16s. red 25 15

354 Lisunov Li-2 Airliner

1957. Air. 10th Anniv of Bulgarian Airways.
1055 **354** 80s. blue 80 40

355 St. Cyril and St. Methodius

356 Basketball

1957. Centenary of Canonization of Saints Cyril and Methodius (founders of Cyrillic alphabet).
1056 **355** 44s. olive and buff . . . 65 30

1957. 10th European Basketball Championships.
1057 **356** 44s. green . . . . 1·10 45

357 Girl in National Costume

358 G. Dimitrov

1957. 6th World Youth Festival, Moscow.
1058 **357** 44s. blue 40 25

1957. 75th Birth Anniv of Georgi Dimitrov (statesman).
1059 **358** 44s. red 80 25

359 V. Levski

1957. 120th Birth Anniv of Vasil Levski (revolutionary).
1060 **359** 44s. green 65 25

360 View of Turnovo and Ludwig Zamenhof (inventor)

1957. 70th Anniv of Esperanto (invented language) and 50th Anniv of Bulgarian Esperanto Association.
1061 **360** 44s. green 80 30

361 Soldiers in Battle

362 Woman Planting Tree

1957. 80th Anniv of Liberation from Turkey.
1062 – 16s. green 20 10
1063 **361** 44s. brown 50 20
DESIGN: 16s. Old and young soldiers.

1957. Reafforestation Campaign.
1064 **362** 2s. green 10 15
1065 – 12s. brown 10 15
1066 – 16s. blue 10 15
1067 – 44s. turquoise 35 25
1068 – 80s. green 80 35
DESIGNS—HORIZ: 12s. Red deer in forest; 16s Dam and trees; 44s. Polikarpov Po-2 biplane over forest; 80s. Trees and cornfield.

363 Two Hemispheres

1957. 4th World TUC, Leipzig.
1069 **363** 44s. blue 40 25

364 Lenin

1957. 40th Anniv of Russian Revolution. Inscr "1917–1957".
1070 **364** 12s. brown 45 30
1071 – 16s. turquoise . . . . . 1·20 45
1072 – 44s. blue . . . . 1·60 90
1073 – 60s. red . . . . 2·50 1·00
1074 – 80s. green . . . . 3·75 2·75
DESIGNS: 16s. Cruiser "Aurora"; 44s. Dove of Peace over Europe; 60s. Revolutionaries; 80s. Oil refinery.

365 Youth and Girl

366 Partisans

1957. 10th Anniv of Dimitrov National Youth Movement.
1075 **365** 16s. red 15 10

1957. 15th Anniv of Fatherland Front.
1076 **366** 16s. brown 15 10

367 Mikhail Glinka (composer, death centenary) **368** Hotel Vasil, Kolarov

1957. Cultural Celebrities.

1077	**367** 12s. brown	25	15
1078	– 16s. green	25	15
1079	– 40s. blue	80	30
1080	– 44s. brown	90	30
1081	– 60s. brown	1·00	50
1082	– 80s. purple	2·75	2·10

DESIGNS: 16s. Ion Comenius (educationist) (300th anniv of publication of "Didoetica Opera Omria"); 40s. Carl Linnaeus (botanist, 250th birth anniv); 44s. William Blake (writer, birth bicent); 60s. Carlo Goldoni (dramatist, 250th birth anniv); 80s. Auguste Comte (philosopher, death centenary).

1958. Holiday Resorts.

1083	– 4s. blue	10	15
1084	– 8s. brown	10	15
1085	– 12s. green	10	15
1086	**368** 16s. green	15	15
1087	– 44s. turquoise	30	15
1088	– 60s. blue	45	25
1089	– 80s. brown	55	30
1090	– 1l. brown	65	30

DESIGNS—HORIZ: 4s. Skis and Pirin Mts; 8s. Old house in Koprivshtita; 12s. Hostel at Yelingrad; 44s. Hotel at Momin-Prokhod; 60s. Seaside hotel and peninsula, Nesebur; 80s. Beach scene, Varna; 1l. Modern hotels, Varna.

369 Brown Hare **371** Wrestlers

370 Marx and Lenin

1958. Forest Animals.

1091	**369** 2s. deep green & green	20	15
1092	– 12s. brown and green	50	20
1093	– 16s. brown and green	60	25
1094	– 44s. brown and blue	95	30
1095	– 80s. brown and ochre	1·30	85
1096	– 1l. brown and blue	3·00	95

DESIGNS—VERT: 12s. Roe doe. HORIZ: 16s. Red deer; 44s. Chamois; 80s. Brown bear; 1l. Wild boar.

1958. 7th Bulgarian Communist Party Congress. Inscr as in T **370**.

1097	**370** 12s. brown	20	10
1098	– 16s. red	45	15
1099	– 44s. blue	95	15

DESIGNS: 16s. Workers marching with banners; 44s. Lenin blast furnaces.

1958. Wrestling Championships.

1100	**371** 60s. lake	1·10	90
1101	80s. sepia	1·30	1·20

372 Chessmen and "Oval Chessboard"

1958. 5th World Students' Team Chess Championship, Varna.

1102	**372** 80s. green	5·25	5·25

373 Russian Pavilion

1958. 18th International Fair, Plovdiv.

1103	**373** 44s. red	55	45

374 Swimmer

1958. Bulgarian Students' Games.

1104	**374** 16s. blue	10	15
1105	– 28s. brown	20	15
1106	– 44s. green	35	30

DESIGNS: 28s. Dancer; 44s. Volleyball players at net.

375 Onions **376** Insurgent with Rifle

1958. "Agricultural Propaganda".

1107	**375** 2s. brown	10	15
1108	– 12s. lake (Garlic)	10	15
1109	– 16s. myrtle (Peppers)	15	15
1110	– 44s. red (Tomatoes)	20	10
1111	– 80s. green (Cucumbers)	55	20
1112	– 1l. violet (Aubergines)	1·10	35

1958. 35th Anniv of September Uprising.

1113	**376** 16s. orange	20	15
1114	– 44s. lake	50	25

DESIGN—HORIZ: 44s. Insurgent helping wounded comrade.

377 Conference Emblem

1958. 1st World Trade Union's Young Workers' Conference, Prague.

1115	**377** 44s. blue	65	45

378 Exhibition Emblem

1958. Brussels International Exhibition.

1116	**378** 1l. blue and black	6·50	6·75

379 Sputnik over Globe **380** Running

1958. Air. IGY.

1117	**379** 80s. turquoise	4·00	3·50

1958. Balkan Games. Inscr "1958".

1118	**380** 16s. brown	45	10
1119	– 44s. olive	55	30
1120	– 60s. blue	80	35
1121	– 80s. green	1·30	60
1122	– 4l. lake	7·25	5·50

DESIGNS—HORIZ: 44s. Throwing the javelin; 60s. High-jumping; 80s. Hurdling. VERT: 4l. Putting the shot.

381 Young Gardeners **382** Smirnenski

1958. 4th Dimitrov National Youth Movement Congress. Inscr as in T **381**.

1123	**381** 8s. green	10	15
1124	– 12s. brown	10	10
1125	– 16s. purple	15	15
1126	– 40s. blue	30	15
1127	– 44s. red	75	30

DESIGNS—HORIZ: 12s. Farm girl with cattle; 40s. Youth with wheel-barrow. VERT: 16s. Youth with pickaxe and girl with spade; 44s. Communist Party Building.

1958. 60th Birth Anniv of Khristo Smirnenski (poet and revolutionary).

1128	**382** 16s. red	25	15

383 First Cosmic Rockets **384** Footballers

1959. Air. Launching of First Cosmic Rocket.

1129	**383** 2l. brown and blue	6·50	7·25

1959. Youth Football Games, Sofia.

1130	**384** 2l. brown on cream	1·80	1·50

385 UNESCO Headquarters, Paris

1959. Inauguration of UNESCO Headquarters Building.

1131	**385** 2l. purple on cream	1·80	1·70

386 Skier **388** Military Telegraph Linesman

1959. 40 Years of Skiing in Bulgaria.

1132	**386** 1l. blue on cream	1·30	70

1959. No. 1110 surch **45 CT**.

1133	45s. on 44s. red	80	25

1959. 80th Anniv of 1st Bulgarian Postage Stamps.

1134	**388** 12s. yellow and green	10	15
1135	– 16s. mauve and purple	25	10
1136	– 60s. yellow and brown	60	25
1137	– 80s. salmon and red	65	35
1138	– 1l. blue	80	50
1139	– 2l. brown	2·50	1·10
MS1139a	91 × 121 mm. 60s. (+41.40) yellow and black (as 1136). Imperf	50·00	50·00
MS1139b	125 × 125 mm. Remaining values in different colours (sold at 5l.) Imperf	50·00	50·00

DESIGNS—HORIZ: 16s. 19th-century mail-coach; 80s. Early postal car; 2l. Striking railway workers. VERT: 60s. Bulgarian 1879 stamp; 1l. Radio tower.

389 Great Tits **390** Cotton-picking

1959. Birds.

1140	**389** 2s. slate and yellow	10	15
1141	– 8s. green and brown	15	20
1142	– 16s. sepia and brown	60	25
1143	– 45s. myrtle and brown	95	55
1144	– 60s. grey and blue	2·10	75
1145	– 80s. drab and turquoise	3·25	1·10

DESIGNS—HORIZ: 8s. Hoopoe; 60s. Rock partridge; 80s. European cuckoo. VERT: 16s. Great spotted woodpecker; 45s. Grey partridge.

1959. Five Year Plan.

1146	– 2s. brown	10	15
1147	– 4s. bistre	15	15
1148	**390** 5s. green	15	15
1149	– 10s. brown	15	10
1150	– 12s. brown	15	15
1151	– 15s. mauve	15	15
1152	– 16s. violet	15	15
1153	– 20s. orange	25	15
1154	– 25s. blue	20	15
1155	– 28s. green	30	15
1156	– 40s. blue	35	10
1157	– 45s. brown	30	15
1158	– 60s. red	50	25
1159	– 80s. olive	1·00	25
1160	– 1l. lake	70	25
1161	– 1l.25 blue	1·90	65
1162	– 2l. red	1·00	40

DESIGNS—HORIZ: 2s. Children at play; 10s. Dairymaid milking cow; 16s. Industrial plant; 20s. Combine-harvester; 40s. Hydro-electric barrage; 60s. Furnaceman; 1l.25, Machinist. VERT: 4s. Woman doctor examining child; 12s. Tobacco harvesting; 15s. Machinist; 25s. Power linesman; 28s. Tending sunflowers; 45s. Miner; 80s. Fruit-picker; 1l. Workers with symbols of agriculture and industry; 2l. Worker with banner.

391 Patriots **392** Piper

1959. 300th Anniv of Batak.

1163	**391** 16s. brown	30	10

1959. Spartacist Games. Inscr "1958–1959".

1164	**392** 4s. olive on cream	20	15
1165	– 12s. red on yellow	20	15
1166	– 16s. lake on salmon	20	15
1167	– 20s. blue on blue	25	15
1168	– 80s. green on green	80	40
1169	– 1l. brown on orange	1·10	70

DESIGNS—VERT: 12s. Gymnastics; 1l. Urn. HORIZ: 16s. Girls exercising with hoops; 20s. Dancers leaping; 80s. Ballet dancers.

393 Soldiers in Lorry

1959. 15th Anniv of Fatherland Front Government.

1170	**393** 12s. blue and red	10	15
1171	– 16s. black and red	10	15
1172	– 45s. blue and red	20	15
1173	– 60s. green and red	25	20
1174	– 80s. brown and red	45	30
1175	– 1l.25 brown and red	95	55

DESIGNS—HORIZ: 16s. Partisans meeting Red Army soldiers; 45s. Blast furnaces; 60s. Tanks; 80s. Combine-harvester in cornfield. VERT: 1l.25, Pioneers with banner.

394 Footballer

1959. 50th Anniv of Football in Bulgaria.

1176	**394** 1l.25 green on yellow	4·75	5·25

395 Tupolev Tu-104A Jetliner and Statue of Liberty **396** Globe and Letter

1959. Air. Visit of Nikita Khrushchev (Russian Prime Minister) to U.S.A.

1177	**395** 1l. pink and blue	2·40	2·75

1959. International Correspondence Week.

1178	**396** 45s. black and green	50	15
1179	– 1l.25 red, black & blue	70	30

DESIGN: 1l.25, Pigeon and letter.

397 Parachutist **398** N. Vaptsarov

1960. 3rd Voluntary Defence Congress.
1180 **397** 1l.25 cream & turquoise 1·80 1·10

1960. 50th Birth Anniv of Nikola Vaptsarov (poet and revolutionary).
1181 **398** 80s. brown and green . . 40 30

399 Dr. L. Zamenhof

400

1960. Birth Centenary of Dr. Ludwig Zamenhof (inventor of Esperanto).
1182 **399** 1l.25 green & lt green . . 1·00 80

1960. 50th Anniv of State Opera.
1183 **400** 80s. black and green . . 55 40
1184 – 1l.25 black and red . . . 65 45
DESIGN: 1l.25, Lyre.

401 Track of Trajectory of "Lunik 3" around the Moon

1960. Flight of "Lunik 3".
1185 **401** 1l.25 green, yellow & bl 4·75 4·00

402 Skier

1960. Winter Olympic Games.
1186 **402** 2l. brown, blue & black 80 80

403 Vela Blagoeva

404 Lenin

1960. 50th Anniv of International Women's Day. Inscr "1910–1960".
1187 **403** 16s. brown and pink . . 10 15
1188 – 28s. olive and yellow . . 15 15
1189 – 45s. green and olive . . 20 15
1190 – 60s. blue and light blue 30 25
1191 – 80s. brown and red . . . 35 25
1192 – 1l.25 olive and ochre . . 70 50
PORTRAITS: 28s. Anna Maimunkowa; 45s. Vela Piskova; 60s. Rosa Luxemburg; 80s. Clara Zetkin; 1l.25, Nadezhda Krupskaya.

1960. 90th Birth Anniv of Lenin.
1193 **404** 16s. flesh and brown . . 1·30 50
1194 – 45s. black and pink . . . 2·10 60
DESIGN: 45s. "Lenin at Smolny" (writing in chair).

406 Basketball Players

407 Moon Rocket

1960. 7th European Women's Basketball Championships.
1195 **406** 1l.25 black and yellow 1·00 55

1960. Air. Landing of Russian Rocket on Moon.
1196 **407** 1l.25 black, yellow & bl 4·75 4·00

408 Parachutist

409 "Gentiana lutea"

1960. World Parachuting Championships, 1960.
1197 **408** 16s. blue and lilac . . . 40 55
1198 – 1l.25 red and blue . . . 1·90 80
DESIGN: 1l.25, Parachutes descending.

1960. Flowers.
1199 **409** 2s. orange, grn & drab 15 15
1200 – 5s. red, green and yellow 15 15
1201 – 25s. orge, grn & salmon 50 15
1202 – 45s. mauve, grn & lilac 60 25
1203 – 60s. red, green and buff 1·00 35
1204 – 80s. blue, green & drab 1·20 85
FLOWERS: 5s. "Tulipa rhodopea"; 25s. "Lilium jankae"; 45s. "Rhododendron ponticum"; 60s. "Cypripedium calceolus"; 80s. "Haberlea rhodopenis".

410 Football

1960. Olympic Games.
1205 **410** 8s. pink and brown . . . 10 15
1206 – 12s. pink and violet . . 15 15
1207 – 16s. pink & turquoise . . 40 15
1208 – 45s. pink and purple . . 50 15
1209 – 80s. pink and blue . . . 90 40
1210 – 2l. pink and green . . . 1·00 60
DESIGNS: 12s. Wrestling; 16s. Weightlifting; 45s. Gymnastics; 80s. Canoeing; 2l. Running.

411 Racing Cyclists

1960. Tour of Bulgaria Cycle Race.
1211 **411** 1l. black, yellow & red 1·20 1·10

412 Globes

1960. 15th Anniv of WFTU.
1212 **412** 1l.25 cobalt and blue . . 50 40

413 Popov

1960. Birth Centenary of Alexsandr Popov (Russian radio pioneer).
1213 **413** 90s. black and blue . . . 80 65

414 Y. Veshin

1960. Birth Centenary of Yavoslav Veshin (painter).
1214 **414** 1l. olive and yellow . . . 2·75 2·00

415 U.N. Headquarters, New York

1961. 15th Anniv of UNO.
1215 **415** 1l. cream and brown . . 1·30 1·40
MS1215a 74 × 57 mm. **415** 1l. (+1l.) pink and green. Imperf . . . . 8·00 9·50

416 Boyana Church

1961. 700th Anniv of Boyana Murals (1959).
1216 **416** 60s. black, emer & grn 60 25
1217 – 80s. grn, cream & orange 70 40
1218 – 1l.25 red, cream & green 1·20 80
DESIGNS (Frescoes of): 80s. Theodor Tiron; 1l.25, Desislava.

417 Cosmic Rocket and Dogs Belda and Strelka

1961. Russian Cosmic Rocket Flight of August, 1960.
1219 **417** 1l.25 blue and red . . . 4·75 4·75

419 Pleven Costume

420 Clock Tower, Vratsa

1961. Provincial Costumes.
1220 – 12s. yellow, green & orge 15 10
1221 **419** 16s. brown, buff & lilac 15 10
1222 – 28s. red, black, & green 20 10
1223 – 45s. blue and red 35 15
1224 – 60s. yellow, blue & turq 50 25
1225 – 80s. red, green & yellow 75 40
COSTUMES: 12s. Kyustendil; 28s. Sliven; 45s. Sofia; 60s. Rhodope; 80c. Karnobat.

1961. Museums and Monuments. Values and star in red.
1226 **420** 8s. green 10 15
1227 – 12s. violet 10 15
1228 – 16s. brown 10 15
1229 – 20s. blue 15 15
1230 – 28s. turquoise 15 15
1231 – 40s. brown 20 20
1232 – 45s. olive 20 25
1233 – 60s. slate 45 25
1234 – 80s. brown 55 25
1235 – 1l. turquoise 80 50
DESIGNS—As Type **420**. VERT: 12s. Clock Tower, Bansko; 20s. "Agushev" building, Mogilitsa (Smolensk). HORIZ: 28s. Oslekoff House, Koprivshtitsa; 40s. Pasha's House, Melnik. SQUARE (27 × 27 mm): 16s. Wine jug; 45s. Lion (bas-relief); 60s. "Horseman of Madara"; 80s. Fresco, Bachkovo Monastery; 1l. Coin of Tsar Konstantin-Asen (13th cent).

421 Dalmatian Pelican

422 "Communications and Transport"

1961. Birds.
1236 – 2s. turquoise, blk & red 20 15
1237 **421** 4s. orange, blk & grn . . 25 15
1238 – 16s. orange, brn & grn 25 25
1239 – 80s. yellow, brn & turq 3·00 55
1240 – 1l. yellow, sepia and blue 3·00 1·20
1241 – 2l. yellow, brown & blue 4·75 1·30

DESIGNS: 2s. White capercaillie; 16s. Common pheasant; 80s. Great bustard; 1l. Lammergeier; 2l. Hazel grouse.

1961. 50th Anniv of Transport Workers' Union.
1242 **422** 80s. green and black . . 55 40

423 Gagarin and Rocket

1961. World's First Manned Space Flight.
1243 **423** 4l. turquoise, blk & red 3·25 2·75

424 Shevchenko (Ukrainian poet)

1961. Death Centenary of Taras Shevchenko.
1244 **424** 1l. brown and green . . 3·50 3·25

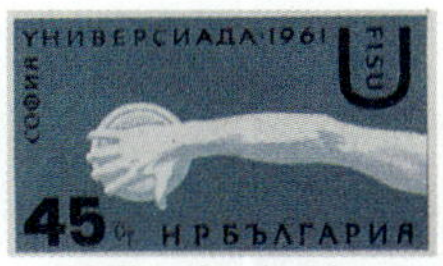

425 Throwing the Discus

1961. World Students' Games. Values and inscr in black.
1245 – 4s. blue 10 10
1246 – 5s. red 15 10
1247 – 16s. olive 20 10
1248 **425** 45s. blue 30 25
1249 – 1l.25 brown 70 40
1250 – 2l. mauve 90 65
MS1250a 66 × 66 mm. 5l. blue, yellow and green (Sports Palace and inscriptions). Imperf . . . 14·00 15·00
DESIGNS—VERT: 4s. Water polo; 2l. Basketball. HORIZ: 5s. Tennis; 16s. Fencing; 1l.25, Sports Palace, Sofia.

426 Short-snouted Seahorse

427 "Space" Dogs

1961. Black Sea Fauna.
1251 – 2s. sepia and green . . . 10 15
1252 – 12s. pink and blue . . . 15 15
1253 – 16s. violet and blue . . . 25 15
1254 **426** 45s. brown and blue . . . 90 55
1255 – 1l. blue and green . . . 1·80 95
1256 – 1l.25 brown and blue . . 2·50 1·50
DESIGNS—HORIZ: 2s. Mediterranean monk seal; 12s. Lung jellyfish; 16s. Common dolphins; 1l. Stellate sturgeons; 1l.25, Thorn-backed ray.

1961. Air. Space Exploration.
1257 **427** 2l. slate and purple . . . 2·75 2·75
1258 – 2l. blue, yellow & orange 5·25 4·50
DESIGN: No. 1258, "Venus" rocket in flight (24 × 41½ mm).

428 Dimitur Blagoev as Orator

1961. 70th Anniv of First Bulgarian Social Democratic Party Congress, Buzludzha.
1259 **428** 45s. red and cream . . . 25 15
1260 80s. blue and pink . . . 40 25
1261 2l. sepia and green . . . 1·40 55

429 Hotel

1961. Tourist issue. Inscr in black; designs green. Background colours given.

1262	**429**	4s. green	10	10
1263	–	12s. blue (Hikers)	10	10
1264	–	16s. green (Tents)	10	10
1265	–	1l.25 bistre (Climber)	60	20

Nos. 1263/5 are vert.

430 "The Golden Girl"

1961. Bulgarian Fables.

1266	**430**	2s. multicoloured	10	15
1267	–	8s. grey, black & purple	15	15
1268	–	12s. pink, black & green	20	15
1269	–	16s. multicoloured	60	25
1270	–	45s. multicoloured	1·40	40
1271	–	80s. multicoloured	1·40	60

DESIGNS: 8s. Man and woman ("The Living Water"); 12s. Archer and dragon ("The Golden Apple"); 16s. Horseman ("Krali Marko", national hero); 45s. Female archer on stag ("Samovila-Vila", fairy); 80s. "Tom Thumb" and cockerel.

431 Major Titov in Space-suit

432 "Amanita caesarea"

1961. Air. 2nd Russian Manned Space Flight.

1272	**431**	75s. flesh, blue & olive	2·40	2·00
1273	–	1l.25 pink, bl & violet	3·00	2·75

DESIGN: 1l.25, "Vostok-2" in flight.

1961. Mushrooms.

1274	**432**	2s. red, bistre & black	10	15
1275	–	4s. brown, grn & blk	10	15
1276	–	12s. brown, bistre & blk	15	15
1277	–	16s. brown, mve & blk	10	15
1278	–	45s. multicoloured	25	25
1279	–	80s. orange, sepia & blk	50	40
1280	–	1l.25 lav, brn & blk	60	50
1281	–	2l. brown, bistre & black	1·10	1·10

MUSHROOMS: 4s. "Psalliota silvatica"; 12s. "Boletus elegans"; 16s. "Boletus edulis"; 45s. "Lactarius deliciosus"; 80s. "Lepiota procera"; 1l.25, "Pleurotus ostreatus"; 2l. "Armillariella mellea".

433 Dimitur and Konstantin Miladinov (authors)

436 Isker River

1961. Publication Centenary of "Bulgarian Popular Songs".

1282	**433**	1l.25 black and olive	65	50

(Currency revaluation)

1962. Surch. (A) Surch in one line; (B) in two lines.

1283	1s. on 10s. brown (1149)	10	15
1284	1s. on 12s. brown (1150)	10	15
1285	2s. on 15s. mauve (1151)	10	15
1286	2s. on 16s. violet (1152)	10	15
1287	2s. on 20s. orange (1153) (A)	10	15
1288	2s. on 20s. orange (1153) (B)	20	15
1289	3s. on 25s. blue (1154)	15	15
1290	3s. on 28s. green (1155)	10	15
1291	5s. on 44s. green (1087)	20	15
1292	5s. on 44s. red (1110)	20	15
1293	5s. on 45s. brown (1157)	20	15
1294	10s. on 1l. red (1160)	30	20
1295	20s. on 2l. red (1162)	55	50
1296	40s. on 4l. red (889)	70	90

1962. Air.

1297	**436**	1s. blue and violet	10	15
1298	–	2s. blue and pink	15	15
1299	–	3s. brown and chestnut	15	15
1300	–	10s. black and bistre	40	15
1301	–	40s. black and green	1·40	60

DESIGNS: 2s. Yacht at Varna; 3s. Melnik; 10s. Turnovo; 40s. Pirin Mountains.

437 Freighter "Varna"

1962. Bulgarian Merchant Navy.

1302	**437**	1s. green and blue	10	10
1303	–	5s. light blue and green	35	10
1304	–	20s. violet and blue	1·00	25

SHIPS: 5s. Tanker "Komsomols"; 20s. Liner "Georgi Dimitrov".

438 Rila Mountains

1962. Views.

1305	**438**	1s. turquoise	10	15
1306	–	2s. blue	10	15
1307	–	6s. turquoise	45	15
1308	–	8s. purple	60	25
1309	–	13s. green	50	30
1310	–	1l. deep green	4·50	1·00

VIEWS: 2s. Pirin Mts; 6s. Fishing boats, Nesebur; 8s. Danube shipping; 13s. Viden Castle; 1l. Rhodope Mts.

439 Georgi Dimitrov as Typesetter

440 Pink Roses

1962. 80th Anniv of State Printing Office.

1311	**439**	2s. red, black & yellow	10	15
1312	–	13s. black, orange & yell	50	25

DESIGN: 13s. Emblem of Printing Office.

1962. Bulgarian Roses. T **440** and similar designs.

1313	1s. pink, green and violet	10	15
1314	2s. red, green and buff	10	15
1315	3s. red, green and blue	20	15
1316	4s. yellow, turquoise & grn	25	15
1317	5s. pink, green and blue	45	25
1318	6s. red, green and turquoise	60	45
1319	8s. red, green and yellow	2·10	70
1320	13s. yellow, green and blue	3·50	1·10

441 "The World United against Malaria"

1962. Malaria Eradication.

1321	**441**	5s. yellow, black & brn	40	15
1322	–	20s. yellow, green & blk	95	55

DESIGN: 20s. Campaign emblem.

442 Lenin and Front Page of "Pravda"

1962. 50th Anniv of "Pravda" Newspaper.

1323	**442**	5s. blue, red and black	80	65

443 Text-book and Blackboard

444 Footballer

1962. Bulgarian Teachers' Congress.

1324	**443**	5s. black, yellow & blue	15	10

1962. World Football Championship, Chile.

1325	**444**	13s. brown, green & blk	80	65

445 Dimitrov

1962. 80th Birth Anniv of Georgi Dimitrov (Prime Minister 1946–49).

1326	**445**	2s. green	10	15
1327		5s. blue	55	30

446 Bishop

448 Festival Emblem

1962. 15th Chess Olympiad, Varna. Inscr "1962". Inscr in black.

1328	**446**	1s. green and grey	10	15
1329	–	2s. bistre and grey	10	15
1330	–	3s. purple and grey	10	15
1331	–	13s. orange and grey	1·00	60
1332	–	20s. blue and grey	1·40	95

MS1332a 76 × 66 mm. 20s. (+30s.) red and green (Chess pieces). Imperf . . . 12·00 12·00

CHESS PIECES: 2s. Rook; 3s. Queen; 13s. Knight; 20s. Pawn.

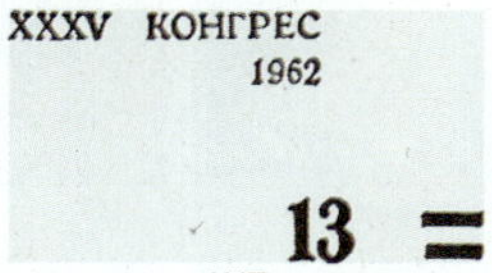

(447)

1962. 35th Esperanto Congress, Burgas. Surch as T **447**.

1333	**360**	13s. on 44s. green	2·75	2·20

1962. World Youth Festival, Helsinki. Inscr "1962".

1334	**448**	5s. blue, pink and green	15	10
1335	–	13s. blue, purple & grey	40	25

DESIGN: 13s. Girl and emblem.

449 Ilyushin Il-18 Airliner

1962. Air. 13th Anniv of TABSO Airline.

1336	**449**	13s. blue, ultram & blk	80	25

450 Apollo

1962. Butterflies and Moths. Multicoloured.

1337	1s. Type **450**	10	15
1338	2s. Eastern festoon	15	15
1339	3s. Meleager's blue	15	15
1340	4s. Camberwell beauty	20	15
1341	5s. Crimson underwing	25	20
1342	6s. Hebe tiger moth	70	20
1343	10s. Danube clouded	2·40	75
1344	13s. Cardinal	3·25	1·30

451 K. E. Tsiolkovsky (scientist)

1962. Air. 13th International Astronautics Congress. Inscr "1962".

1345	**451**	5s. drab and green	2·75	1·50
1346	–	13s. blue and yellow	1·40	75

DESIGN: 13s. Moon rocket.

452 Combine Harvester

1962. 8th Bulgarian Communist Party Congress.

1347	**452**	1s. olive and turquoise	10	15
1348	–	2s. turquoise and blue	10	30
1349	–	3s. brown and red	15	15
1350	–	13s. sepia, red & purple	75	40

DESIGNS: 2s. Electric train; 3s. Steel furnace; 13s. Blagoev and Dimitrov.

453 Cover of "History of Bulgaria"

1962. Bicentenary of Paisii Khilendarski's "History of Bulgaria".

1351	**453**	2s. black and olive	15	10
1352	–	5s. sepia and brown	30	10

DESIGN—HORIZ: 5s. Father Paisii at work on book.

454 Andrian Nikolaev and "Vostok 3"

1962. Air. 1st "Team" Manned Space Flight.

1353	**454**	1s. olive, blue and black	15	10
1354	–	2s. olive, green & black	25	15
1355	–	40s. pink, turquoise & blk	2·75	1·60

DESIGNS: 2s. Pavel Ropovich and "Vostok 4"; 40s. "Vostoks 3" and "4" in flight.

455 Parachutist

456 Aleko Konstantinov

1963.

1356	–	1s. lake	10	10
1357	–	1s. brown	10	10
1358	–	1s. turquoise	10	10
1359	–	1s. green	10	10
1360	**455**	1s. blue	10	10

DESIGNS—VERT: No. 1356, State crest. HORIZ: No. 1357, Sofia University; 1358, "Vasil Levski" Stadium, Sofia; 1359, "The Camels" (archway), Hisar.

1963. Birth Cent of Konstantinov (author).

1361	**456**	5s. green and red	25	20

457 Mars and "Mars 1" Space Probe

1963. Air. Launching of Soviet Space Station "Mars 1".

1362	**457**	5s. multicoloured	55	40
1363	–	13s. turquoise, red & blk	1·10	85

DESIGN: 13s. Release of probe from rocket.

458 Orpheus Restaurant, "Sunny Beach"

1963. Black Sea Coast Resorts.

1364	**458**	1s. blue	10	15
1365a	–	2s. red	65	15
1366	–	3s. bistre	20	15
1367	–	5s. purple	35	15
1368	–	13s. turquoise	1·00	25
1369	–	20s. green	1·40	40

VIEWS "Sunny Beach": 5s. The Dunes Restaurant; 20s. Hotel. "Golden Sands"; 2s., 3s., 13s. Various hotels.

459 V. Levski

460 Dimitrov, Boy and Girl

1963. 90th Anniv of Execution of Vasil Levski (revolutionary).
1370 **459** 13s. blue and yellow . . 80 25

1963. 10th Dimitrov Communist Youth League Congress, Sofia.
1371 **460** 2s. brown, red & black 15 15
1372 – 13s. brown, turq & blk 35 30
DESIGN: 13s. Girl and youth holding book and hammer aloft.

461 Eurasian Red Squirrel

462 Wrestling

1963. Woodland Animals.
1373 **461** 1s. brown, red and green on turquoise 10 15
1374 – 2s. blk, red & grn on yell 15 15
1375 – 3s. sep, red & ol on drab 10 15
1376 – 5s. brown, red and blue on violet 50 15
1377 – 13s. black, red and brown on pink . . . . 1·90 40
1378 – 20s. sepia, red and blue on blue . . . . . . 3·00 55
ANIMALS—HORIZ: 2s. East European hedgehog; 3s. Marbled polecat; 5s. Beech marten; 13s. Eurasian badger. VERT: 20s. European otter.

1963. 15th International Open Wrestling Championships, Sofia.
1379 **462** 5s. bistre and black . . . 15 15
1380 – 20s. brown and black . . 1·00 50
DESIGN—HORIZ: 20s. As Type **462** but different hold.

463 Congress Emblem and Allegory

1963. World Women's Congress, Moscow.
1381 **463** 20s. blue and black . . . 65 30

464 Esperanto Star and Sofia Arms

465 Rocket, Globe and Moon

1963. 48th World Esperanto Congress, Sofia.
1382 **464** 13s. multicoloured . . . 70 30

1963. Launching of Soviet Moon Rocket "Luna 4". Inscr "2.IV.1963".
1383 **465** 1s. blue 10 10
1384 – 2s. purple 10 10
1385 – 3s. turquoise 10 10
DESIGNS: 2s. Tracking equipment; 3s. Sputniks.

466 Valery Bykovsky in Spacesuit

1963. Air. 2nd "Team" Manned Space Flights. Inscr "14.VI.1963".
1386 **466** 1s. turquoise and lilac 10 10
1387 – 2s. brown and yellow . . 10 10
1388 – 5s. red and light red . . 20 10
1389 – 20s.+10s. grn & lt bl . . 1·60 75
MS1389a 79 × 68 mm. 50s. purple and brown (Spassk Tower and Globe). Imperf . . . . 3·25 2·75
DESIGNS: 2s. Valentina Tereshkova in spacesuit; 5s. Globe; 20s. Bykovsky and Tereshkova.

1963. Europa Fair, Riccione. Nos. 1314/5 and 1318 (Roses) optd **MOSTRA EUROPEISTICA.1963 RICCIONE** and sailing boat motif or additionally surch.
1390 2s. red, green and buff . . . 20 15
1391 5s. on 3s. red, green and blue 30 25
1392 13s. on 6s. red, green & turq 1·00 45

468 Relay-racing

1963. Balkan Games. Flags in red, yellow, blue, green and black.
1393 **468** 1s. green 10 10
1394 – 2s. violet 10 10
1395 – 3s. turquoise 15 10
1396 – 5s. red 40 15
1397 – 13s. brown . . . . . . 2·40 2·20
MS1397a 74 × 69 mm. 50s. black and green (as T **468**). Imperf . . . 4·75 4·75
DESIGNS: 2s. Throwing the hammer; 3s. Long jumping; 5s. High jumping; 13s. Throwing the discus. Each design includes the flags of the competing countries.

469 Slavonic Scroll

470 Insurgents

1963. 5th International Slav Congress, Sofia.
1398 **469** 5s. red, yellow & dp grn 15 10

1963. 40th Anniv of September Uprising.
1399 **470** 2s. black and red 10 10

471 "Aquilegia aurea"

472 Khristo Smirnenski

1963. Nature Protection. Flowers in natural colours; background colours given.
1400 **471** 1s. turquoise 10 15
1401 – 2s. olive 10 15
1402 – 3s. yellow 20 15
1403 – 5s. blue 45 15
1404 – 6s. purple 55 25
1405 – 8s. light grey 75 25
1406 – 10s. mauve . . . . . . 1·30 40
1407 – 13s. olive . . . . . . 2·10 65
FLOWERS: 2s. Edelweiss; 3s. "Primula deorum"; 5s. White water-lily; 6s. Tulip; 8s. "Viola delphinantha"; 10s. Alpine clematis; 13s. "Anemone narcissiflora".

1963. 65th Birth Anniv of Smirnenski (poet and revolutionary).
1408 **472** 13s. black and lilac . . . 55 30

473 Chariot Horses (wall-painting)

474 Hemispheres and Centenary Emblem

1963. Thracian Tombs, Kazanlik.
1409 **473** 1s. red, yellow and grey 10 15
1410 – 2s. violet, yellow & grey 10 15
1411 – 3s. turquoise, yell & grey 15 15
1412 – 5s. brown, yellow & grn 20 20
1413 – 13s. black, yellow & grn 45 25
1414 – 20s. red, yellow & green 1·10 65
DESIGNS (wall paintings on tombs): 2s. Chariot race; 3s. Flautists; 5s. Tray-bearer; 13s. Funeral feast; 20s. Seated woman.

1964. Centenary of Red Cross.
1415 **474** 1s. yellow, red & black 10 15
1416 – 2s. blue, red and black 10 15
1417 – 3s. multicoloured . . . 10 15
1418 – 5s. turq, red & black . . 20 15
1419 – 13s. black, red & orange 55 40
DESIGNS: 2s. Blood donation; 3s. Bandaging wrist; 5s. Nurse; 13s. Henri Dunant.

475 Speed-skating

1964. Winter Olympic Games, Innsbruck.
1420 **475** 1s. indigo, brown & blue 10 15
1421 – 2s. olive, mauve & black 10 15
1422 – 3s. green, brown & blk 10 15
1423 – 5s. multicoloured 20 20
1424 – 10s. orange, blk & grey 65 35
1425 – 13s. mauve, violet & blk 75 45
MS1425a 64 × 67 mm. 50s. red, blue and grey (Girl skater). Imperf 4·75 4·75
DESIGNS: 2s. Figure skating; 3s. Cross-country skiing; 5s. Ski jumping. Ice hockey—10s. Goalkeeper; 13s. Players.

476 Head (2nd cent)

1964. 2500 Years of Bulgarian Art. Borders in grey.
1426 **476** 1s. turquoise and red . . 10 15
1427 – 2s. sepia and red 10 15
1428 – 3s. bistre and red . . . 10 15
1429 – 5s. blue and red 20 15
1430 – 6s. brown and red . . . 25 15
1431 – 8s. brown and red . . . 40 20
1432 – 10s. olive and red . . . 45 25
1433 – 13s. olive and red . . . 85 45
DESIGNS: 2s. Horseman (1st to 4th cent); 3s. Jug (19th cent); 5s. Buckle (19th cent); 6s. Pot (19th cent); 8s. Angel (17th cent); 10s. Animals (8th to 10th cent); 13s. Peasant woman (20th cent).

477 "The Unborn Maid"

1964. Folk Tales. Multicoloured.
1434 1s. Type **477** 10 15
1435 2s. "Grandfather's Glove" 10 15
1436 3s. "The Big Turnip" . . . 10 15
1437 5s. "The Wolf and the Seven Kids" 20 15
1438 8s. "Cunning Peter" 30 20
1439 13s. "The Loaf of Corn" . . 90 25

478 Turkish Lacewing ("Ascalaphus ottomanus")

1964. Insects.
1440 **478** 1s. black, yellow & brn 10 15
1441 – 2s. black, ochre & turq 10 15
1442 – 3s. green, black & drab 15 15
1443 – 5s. violet, black & green 45 15
1444 – 13s. brown, black & vio 95 35
1445 – 20s. yellow, black & bl 1·80 45
DESIGNS—VERT: 2s. Thread lacewing fly ("Nemoptera coa"); 5s. Alpine longhorn beetle ("Rosalia alpina"); 13s. Cockchafer ("Anisoplia austriaca"). HORIZ: 3s. Cricket ("Saga natalia"); 20s. Hunting wasp ("Scolia flavitrons").

479 Football

1964. 50th Anniv of Levski Physical Culture Association.
1446 2s. Type **479** 10 10
1447 13s. Handball 60 35
MS1447a 60 × 60 mm. 60s. green and yellow (Cup and Map of Europe). Imperf . . . . 3·25 3·25

480 Title Page and Petar Beron (author)

1964. 40th Anniv of First Bulgarian Primer.
1448 **480** 20s. black and brown . . 1·20 1·60

481 Stephenson's "Rocket", 1829

1964. Railway Transport. Multicoloured.
1449 1s. Type **481** 10 15
1450 2s. Class 05 steam locomotive 10 15
1451 3s. German V.320.001 diesel locomotive 15 15
1452 5s. Electric locomotive . . . 30 15
1453 8s. Class 05 steam locomotive and train on bridge 45 30
1454 13s. Class E41 electric train emerging from tunnel . . 75 40

482 Alsatian

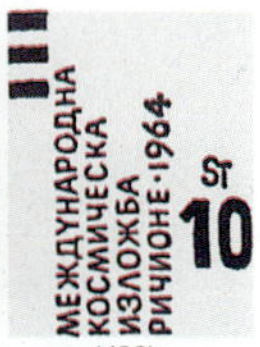

(483)

1964. Dogs. Multicoloured.
1455 1s. Type **482** 10 15
1456 2s. Setter 15 15
1457 3s. Poodle 20 15
1458 4s. Pomeranian 20 15
1459 5s. St. Bernard 25 15
1460 6s. Fox terrier 60 25
1461 10s. Pointer . . . . 2·10 80
1462 13s. Dachshund . . . . . . 2·40 1·70

1964. Air. International Cosmic Exhibition, Riccione. No. 1386 surch with T **483** and No. 1387 surch as T **483**, but in Italian.
1463 **466** 10s. on 1s. turquoise and lilac 35 25
1464 – 20s. on 2s. brown & yell 70 40

484 Partisans and Flag

1964. 20th Anniv of Fatherland. Front Government. Flag in red.
1465 **484** 1s. blue and light blue 10 15
1466 – 2s. olive and bistre . . . 10 15
1467 – 3s. lake and mauve . . . 10 15
1468 – 4s. violet and lavender 10 15
1469 – 5s. brown and orange . . 15 15
1470 – 6s. blue and light blue 20 15
1471 – 8s. green and light green 55 15
1472 – 13s. brown and salmon 75 45
DESIGNS: 2s. Greeting Soviet troops; 3s. Soviet aid—arrival of goods; 4s. Industrial plant, Kremikovtsi; 5s. Combine-harvester; 6s. "Peace" campaigners; 8s. Soldier of National Guard; 3s. Blagoev and Dimitrov. All with flag as Type **484**.

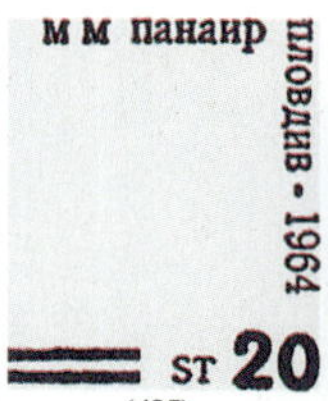

(485)

486 Transport

1964. 21st Int Fair, Plovdiv. Surch with T **485**.
1473 20s. on 44s. ochre (No. 1020a) . . . . . . 1·30 35

1964. 1st National Stamp Exn, Sofia.
1474 **486** 20s. blue . . . . 1·40 90

487 Gymnastics

488 Vratsata

1964. Olympic Games, Tokyo. Rings and values in red.

1475 **487** 1s. green and light green . . . 10 15
1476 – 2s. blue and lavender . . 10 15
1477 – 3s. blue and turquoise . . 10 15
1478 – 5s. violet and red 10 15
1479 – 13s. blue and light blue . 75 25
1480 – 20s. green and buff . . . 1·00 25
MS1480a 61 × 67 mm. 40s.+20s. ochre, red and blue (Rings, tracks etc.). Imperf . . . . 3·25 3·25

DESIGNS: 2s. Long-jump; 3s. Swimmer on starting block; 5s. Football; 13s. Volleyball; 20s. Wrestling.

1964. Landscapes.

1481 **488** 1s. green 10 15
1482 – 2s. brown 10 15
1483 – 3s. blue 15 15
1484 – 4s. brown 15 15
1485 – 5s. green 25 15
1486 – 6s. violet 65 20

DESIGNS: 2s. The Ritli; 3s. Maliovitsa; 4s. Broken Rocks; 5s. Erkyupria; 6s. Rhodope mountain pass.

489 Paper and Cellulose Factory, Bukovtsi

1964. Air. Industrial Buildings.

1487 **489** 8s. turquoise 20 10
1488 – 10s. purple 30 10
1489 – 13s. violet 30 10
1490 – 20s. blue 80 20
1491 – 40s. green . . . . . . 1·50 55

DESIGNS: 10s. Metal works, Plovdiv; 13s. Metallurgical works, Kremikovtzi; 20s. Petrol refinery, Burgas; 40s. Fertiliser factory, Stara-Zagora.

490 Rila Monastery

1964. Philatelic Exn for Franco–Bulgarian Amity.

1492 **490** 5s. black and drab . . . 20 15
1493 – 13s. black and blue . . . 65 40

DESIGN: 13s. Notre-Dame, Paris (inscr in French).

491 500-year-old Walnut

492

1964. Ancient Trees. Values and inscr in black.

1494 **491** 1s. brown 10 15
1495 – 2s. purple 10 15
1496 – 3s. sepia 15 15
1497 – 4s. blue 15 15
1498 – 10s. green 40 25
1499 – 13s. olive 70 30

TREES: 2s. Plane (1000 yrs.); 3s. Plane (600 yrs.); 4s. Poplar (800 yrs.); 10s. Oak (800 yrs.); 13s. Fir (1200 yrs.).

1964. 8th Congress of Int Union of Students, Sofia.

1500 **492** 13s. black and blue . . . 55 15

493 Bulgarian Veteran and Soviet Soldier (Sculpture by T. Zlatarev)

494 "Gold Medal"

1965. 30 Years of Bulgarian–Russian Friendship.

1501 **493** 2s. red and black 15 10

1965. Olympic Games, Tokyo (1964).

1502 **494** 20s. black, gold & brown 65 45

495 Vladimir Komarov

1965. Flight of "Voskhod 1". Multicoloured.

1503 1s. Type **495** 10 15
1504 2s. Konstantin Feoktistov . . 10 15
1505 5s. Boris Yegorov 10 15
1506 13s. The three astronauts . . 60 25
1507 20s. "Voskhod 1" 95 35

496 Corn-cob

497 "Victory against Fascism"

1965. Agricultural Products.

1508 **496** 1s. yellow 10 10
1509 – 2s. green 10 10
1510 – 3s. orange 10 10
1511 – 4s. olive 15 10
1512 – 5s. red 25 10
1513 – 10s. blue 45 20
1514 – 13s. bistre 95 25

DESIGNS: 2s. Ears of Wheat; 3s. Sunflowers; 4s. Sugar beet; 5s. Clover; 10s. Cotton; 13s. Tobacco.

1965. 20th Anniv of "Victory of 9 May, 1945".

1515 **497** 5s. black, bistre & grey 15 10
1516 – 13s. blue, black & grey 35 25

DESIGN: 13s. Globes on dove ("Peace").

498 Northern Bullfinch

499 Transport, Globe and Whale

1965. Song Birds. Multicoloured.

1517 1s. Type **498** 10 15
1518 2s. Golden oriole 10 15
1519 3s. Rock thrush 15 15
1520 5s. Barn swallows 40 15
1521 8s. European roller 65 25
1522 10s. Eurasian goldfinch . . . 2·50 40
1523 13s. Rose-coloured starling 2·50 80
1524 20s. Nightingale . . . . . . 2·75 1·80

1965. 4th International Transport Conf, Sofia.

1525 **499** 13s. multicoloured . . . 8·00 1·60

500 ICY Emblem

501 ITU Emblem and Symbols

1965. International Co-operation Year.

1526 **500** 20s. orange, olive & blk 70 40

1965. Centenary of ITU.

1527 **501** 20s. yellow, green & bl 80 25

502 Pavel Belyaev and Aleksei Leonov

1965. "Voskhod 2" Space Flight.

1528 **502** 2s. purple, grn & drab 20 60
1529 – 20s. multicoloured . . . 2·10 50

DESIGN: 20s. Leonov on space.

503 Common Stingray

1965. Fishes. Borders in grey.

1530 **503** 1s. gold, black & orange 10 10
1531 – 2s. silver, indigo & blue 10 10
1532 – 3s. gold, black & green 15 10
1533 – 5s. gold, black and red 20 10
1534 – 10s. silver, blue & turq 1·20 45
1535 – 13s. gold, black & brown 1·40 60

FISHES: 2s. Atlantic bonito; 3s. Brown scorpionfish; 5s. Tub gurnard; 10s. Mediterranean horse-mackerel; 13s. Black Sea turbot.

504 Marx and Lenin

1965. Organization of Socialist Countries' Postal Ministers' Conference, Peking.

1536 **504** 13s. brown and red . . . 90 35

505 Film and Screen

506 Quinces

1965. Balkan Film Festival. Varna.

1537 **505** 13s. black, silver & blue 55 30

1965. Fruits.

1538 **506** 1s. orange 10 10
1539 – 2s. olive (Grapes) . . . 10 10
1540 – 3s. bistre (Pears) 10 10
1541 – 4s. orange (Plums) . . . 10 10
1542 – 5s. red (Strawberries) . . 20 10
1543 – 6s. brown (Walnuts) . . 35 20

507 Ballerina

508 Dove, Emblem and Map

1965. Ballet Competitions, Varna.

1544 **507** 5s. black and mauve . . 1·10 55

1965. "Balkanphila" Stamp Exhibition, Varna.

1545 **508** 1s. silver, blue & yellow 10 10
1546 – 2s. silver, violet & yellow 10 10
1547 – 3s. gold, green & yellow 10 10
1548 – 13s. gold, red & yellow 60 65
1549 – 20s. brown, blue & silver 1·80 1·20
MS1550 71 × 62 mm. 40s. gold and blue (T **508**). Imperf . . . . 2·75 2·75

DESIGNS: 2s. Yacht emblem; 3s. Stylised fish and flowers; 13s. Stylised sun, planet and rocket. LARGER (45 × 25½ mm): 20s. Cosmonauts Pavel Belyaev and Aleksei Leonov.

509 Escapers in Boat

511 Gymnast

(510)

1965. 40th Anniv of Political Prisoners' Escape from "Bolshevik Island".

1551 **509** 2s. black and slate . . . 25 15

1965. National Folklore Competition. No. 1084 surch with T **510**.

1552 2s. on 8s. brown . . . . . 1·20 1·30

1965. Balkan Games.

1553 **511** 1s. black and red 10 15
1554 – 2s. purple and black . . 10 15
1555 – 3s. purple, black & red 10 15
1556 – 5s. brown, black & red 15 15
1557 – 10s. purple, black & mve 80 30
1558 – 13s. purple and black . . 65 30

DESIGNS: 2s. Gymnastics on bars; 3s. Weight-lifting; 5s. Rally car and building; 10s. Basketball; 13s. Rally car and map.

512 Dressage

1965. Horsemanship.

1559 **512** 1s. plum, black & blue 10 15
1560 – 2s. brown, black & ochre 10 15
1561 – 3s. red, black and purple 10 15
1562 – 5s. brown and green . . 40 15
1563 – 10s. brown, blk & grey 1·40 60
1564 – 13s. brown, grn & buff 1·50 85
MS1565 80 × 80 mm. 40s.+20s. plum and grey (as 13s.). Imperf . . . 3·50 2·75

DESIGNS: 5s. Horse-racing. Others, Horse-jumping (various).

513 Young Pioneers

515 Women of N. and S. Bulgaria

514 Junkers Ju 52/3m over Turnovo

1965. Dimitrov Septembrist Pioneers Organization.

1566 **513** 1s. green and turquoise 10 15
1567 – 2s. mauve and violet . . 10 15
1568 – 3s. bistre and olive . . . 10 15
1569 – 5s. ochre and blue . . . 15 15
1570 – 8s. orange and brown . . 40 25
1571 – 13s. violet and red . . . 75 40

DESIGNS: 2s. Admitting recruit; 3s. Camp bugler; 5s. Flying model airplane; 8s. Girls singing; 13s. Young athlete.

1965. Bulgarian Civil Aviation. Multicoloured.

1572 1s. Type **514** 10 15
1573 2s. Ilyushin Il-14M over Plovdiv 10 15
1574 3s. Mil Mi-4 helicopter over Dimitrovgrad 10 15
1575 5s. Tupolev Tu-104A over Ruse 25 15
1576 13s. Ilyushin Il-18 over Varna 95 30
1577 20s. Tupolev Tu-114 over Sofia . . . . 1·30 75

1965. 80th Anniv of Union of North and South Bulgaria.

1578 **515** 13s. black and green . . 55 45

516 I.Q.S.Y. Emblem and Earth's Radiation Zones

517 "Spring Greetings"

1965. International Quiet Sun Year.

1579 **516** 1s. yellow, green & blue 10 15
1580 – 2s. multicoloured 10 15
1581 – 13s. multicoloured . . . 70 20

DESIGNS (I.Q.S.Y. emblem and): 2s. Sun and solar flares; 13s. Total eclipse of the Sun.

1966. "Spring". National Folklore.

1582 **517** 1s. mauve, blue & drab 10 15
1583 – 2s. red, black and drab 10 15
1584 – 3s. violet, red and grey 10 15
1585 – 5s. red, violet and black 10 15

1586 – 8s. purple, brown & mve 35 20
1587 – 13s. mauve, black & bl 70 25
DESIGNS: 2s. Drummer; 3s. "Birds" (stylised); 5s. Folk dancer; 8s. Vase of flowers; 13s. Bagpiper.

518 Byala Bridge

1966. Ancient Monuments.
1588 **518** 1s. turquoise 10 15
1589 – 1s. green 10 15
1590 – 2s. green 10 15
1591 – 2s. purple 10 15
1592 – 8s. brown 30 15
1593 – 13s. blue 50 25
DESIGNS: No. 1589, Svilengrand Bridge; 1590, Fountain, Samokov; 1591, Ruins of Matochina Castle, Khaskovo; 1592, Cherven Castle, Ruse; 1593, Cafe, Bozhentsi, Gabrovo.

519 "Christ" (from fresco Boyana Church)

1966. "2,500 Years of Culture". Multicoloured.
1594 1s. Type **519** . . . . . . 3·75 4·25
1595 2s. "Destruction of the Idols" (from fresco, Boyana Church) (horiz) 20 30
1596 3s. Bachkovo Monastery . . 35 25
1597 4s. Zemen Monastery (horiz) 35 35
1598 5s. John the Baptist Church, Nesebur 45 40
1599 13s. "Nativity" (icon, Aleksandr Nevski Cathedral, Sofia) 80 85
1600 20s. "Virgin and Child" (icon, Archaeological Museum, Sofia) . . . . . 1·30 95

520 "The First Gunshot" at Koprivshtitsa

1966. 90th Anniv of April Uprising.
1601 **520** 1s. black, brown & gold 10 15
1602 – 2s. black, red and gold 10 15
1603 – 3s. black, green & gold 10 15
1604 – 5s. black, blue & gold 15 15
1605 – 10s. black, purple & gold 50 15
1606 – 13s. black, violet & gold 50 25
DESIGNS: 2s. Georgi Benkovski and Todor Kableskov; 3s. "Showing the Flag" at Panagyurishte; 5s. Vasil Petleshkov and Tsanko Dyustabanov; 10s. Landing of Khristo Botev's detachment at Kozlodui; 13s. Panyot Volov and Zlarion Dragostinov.

521 Luna reaching for the Moon

1966. Moon Landing of "Luna 9". Sheet 70 × 50 mm.
MS1607 **521** 60s. silver, black and red . . . . 3·25 3·50

522 W.H.O. Building

1966. Inaug of W.H.O. Headquarters, Geneva.
1608 **522** 13s. blue and silver . . . 65 40

523 Worker

1966. 6th Trades Union Congress, Sofia.
1609 **523** 20s. black and pink . . . 80 45

524 Indian Elephant

525 Boy and Girl holding Banners

1966. Sofia Zoo Animals. Multicoloured.
1610 1s. Type **524** 10 15
1611 2s. Tiger 10 15
1612 3s. Chimpanzee 10 15
1613 4s. Ibex 15 15
1614 5s. Polar bear 40 25
1615 8s. Lion 50 30
1616 13s. American bison . . . . 1·90 70
1617 20s. Eastern grey kangaroo 2·40 1·00

1966. 3rd Congress of Bulgarian Sports Federation.
1618 **525** 13s. blue, orge & cobalt 40 35

526 "Radetski" and Pioneer

1966. 90th Anniv of Khristo Botev's Seizure of River Paddle-steamer "Radetski".
1619 **526** 2s. multicoloured 15 10

527 Standard-bearer Simov-Kuruto

529 UNESCO Emblem

528 Federation Emblem

1966. 90th Death Anniv of Nikola Simov-Kuruto (hero of the Uprising against Turkey).
1620 **527** 5s. multicoloured 25 10

1966. 7th Int Youth Federation Assembly, Sofia.
1621 **528** 13s. blue and black . . . 50 25

1966. 20th Anniv of UNESCO.
1622 **529** 20s. ochre, red & black 55 40

530 Footballer with Ball

531 Jules Rimet Cup

1966. World Cup Football Championships, London.
(a) Showing players in action. Borders in grey.
1623 **530** 1s. black and brown . . 10 15
1624 – 2s. black and red 10 15
1625 – 5s. black and bistre . . . 15 15
1626 – 13s. black and blue . . . 55 25
1627 – 20s. black and blue . . . 80 40
(b) Sheet 60 × 65½ mm. T **531**.
MS1628 50s. gold, cerise and grey 2·75 1·60

532 Wrestling

1966. 3rd Int Wrestling Championships, Sofia.
1629 **532** 13s. sepia, green & brn 40 40

533 Throwing the Javelin

1966. 3rd Republican Spartakiade.
1630 **533** 2s. green, red & yellow 10 15
1631 – 13s. green, red & yellow 50 30
DESIGN: 13s. Running.

534 Map of Balkans, Globe and UNESCO Emblem

1966. Int Balkan Studies Congress, Sofia.
1632 **534** 13s. green, pink & blue 50 30

535 Children with Construction Toy

1966. Children's Day.
1633 **535** 1s. black, yellow & red 10 10
1634 – 2s. black, brown & grn 10 10
1635 – 3s. black, yellow & blue 15 10
1636 – 13s. black, mauve & bl 80 25
DESIGNS: 2s. Rabbit and Teddy Bear; 3s. Children as astronauts; 13s. Children with gardening equipment.

536 Yuri Gagarin and "Vostok 1"

1966. Russian Space Exploration.
1637 **536** 1s. slate and grey . . . 10 10
1638 – 2s. purple and grey . . . 10 10
1639 – 3s. brown and grey . . . 10 10
1640 – 5s. lake and grey 15 10
1641 – 8s. blue and grey 20 10
1642 – 13s. turquoise and grey 55 25
1643 – 20s.+10s. vio & grey . . 1·30 50
MS1644 70 × 62½ mm. 30s.+10s. black, red and grey. Imperf . . 2·40 1·90

DESIGNS: 2s. German Titov and "Vostok 2"; 3s. Andrian Nikolaev, Povel Popovich and "Vostok 3" and "4"; 5s. Valentina Tereshkova, Vallery Bykovsky and "Vostok 5" and "6"; 8s. Vladimir Komarov, Boris Yegorov, Konstantin Feoktistov and "Voskhod 1"; 13s. Povel Belyaev, Aleksei Leonov and "Voskhod 2"; 20s. Gagarin, Leonov and Tereshkova; 30s. Rocket and globe.

537 St. Clement (14th-cent wood-carving)

538 Metodi Shatorov

1966. 1050th Death Anniv of St. Clement of Ohrid.
1645 **537** 5s. brown, red & drab 50 30

1966. Anti-fascist Fighters. Frames in gold; value in black.
1646 **538** 2s. violet and red 10 10
1647 – 3s. brown and mauve . . 10 10
1648 – 5s. blue and red 10 10
1649 – 10s. brown and orange 25 15
1650 – 13s. brown and red . . . 55 25
PORTRAITS: 3s. Vladno Trichkov; 5s. Vulcho Ivanov; 10s. Rasko Daskalov; 13s. Gen. Vladimir Zaimov.

539 Georgi Dimitrov (statesman)

541 Bansko Hotel

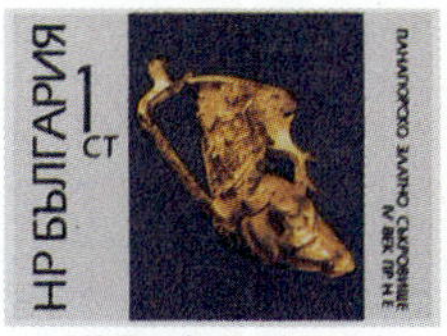

540 Deer's Head Vessel

1966. 9th Bulgarian Communist Party Congress, Sofia.
1651 **539** 2s. black and red 15 10
1652 – 20s. black, red and grey 90 25
DESIGN: 20s. Furnaceman and steelworks.

1966. The Gold Treasures of Panagyurishte. Multicoloured.
1653 1s. Type **540** 10 35
1654 2s. Amazon 15 20
1655 3s. Ram 20 15
1656 5s. Plate 20 15
1657 6s. Venus 25 15
1658 8s. Roe-buck 75 25
1659 10s. Amazon (different) . . 90 25
1660 13s. Amphora 95 30
1661 20s. Goat . . . . 1·40 65
Except for the 5s. and 13s. the designs show vessels with animal heads.

1966. Tourist Resorts.
1662 **541** 1s. blue 10 15
1663 – 2s. green (Belogradchik) 10 15
1664 – 2s. lake (Tryavna) . . . 10 15
1665 – 20s. pur (Malovitsa, Rila) 55 25

542 Christmas Tree

1966. New Year. Multicoloured.
1666 2s. Type **542** 10 15
1667 13s. Money-box 30 25

543 Percho Slaveikov (poet)

544 Dahlias

1966. Cultural Celebrities.
1668 **543** 1s. bistre, blue & orange 10 15
1669 – 2s. brown, orge & grey 10 15
1670 – 3s. blue, bistre & orange 10 15
1671 – 5s. purple, drab & orge 10 15
1672 – 8s. grey, purple & blue 40 20
1673 – 13s. violet, blue & purple 50 25
CELEBRITIES. Writers (with pen emblem): 2s. Dimcho Debelyanov (poet); 3s. Petko Todorov. Painters (with brush emblem): 5s. Dimitur Dobrovich; 8s. Ivan Murkvichka; 13s. Iliya Beshkov.

1966. Flowers. Multicoloured.
1674 1s. Type **544** 10 10
1675 1s. Clematis 10 10
1676 2s. Poet's narcissus 15 10
1677 2s. Foxgloves 15 10
1678 3s. Snowdrops 20 10
1679 5s. Petunias 20 10
1680 13s. Tiger lilies 80 25
1681 20s. Canterbury bells . . . 1·10 30

545 Common Pheasant

1967. Hunting. Multicoloured.
1682 1s. Type **545** 25 20
1683 2s. Chukar partridge 25 15
1684 3s. Grey partridge 20 15
1685 5s. Brown hare 50 20
1686 8s. Roe deer . . . . 1·40 35
1687 13s. Red deer . . . . 1·50 70

546 "Philately"

547 6th-cent B.C. Coin of Thrace

1967. 10th Bulgarian Philatelic Federation Congress, Sofia.
1688 **546** 10s. yellow, black & grn 1·20 95

1967. Ancient Bulgarian Coins. Coins in silver on black background except 13s. (gold on black). Frame colours given.
1689 **547** 1s. brown 10 15
1690 – 2s. purple 10 15
1691 – 3s. green 10 15
1692 – 5s. brown 20 15
1693 – 13s. turquoise 95 65
1694 – 20s. violet . . . . . . 1·40 1·30
COINS—SQUARE: 2s. 2nd-cent B.C. Macedonian tetradrachm; 3s. 2nd-cent B.C. Odessos (Varna) tetradrachm; 5s. 4th-cent B.C. Macedonian coin of Philip II. HORIZ: (38 × 25 mm): 13s. Obverse and reverse of 4th cent B.C. coin of King Sevt (Thrace); 20s. Obverse and reverse of 5th-cent B.C. coin of Apollonia (Sozopol).

548 Partisans listening to radio

1967. 25th Anniv of Fatherland Front. Mult.
1695 1s. Type **548** 10 15
1696 20s. Dimitrov speaking at rally 65 25

549 Nikola Kofardzhiev

550 "Cultural Development"

1967. Anti-fascist Fighters.
1697 **549** 1s. red, black & blue . . 10 15
1698 – 2s. green, black & blue 10 15
1699 – 5s. brown, black & blue 15 15
1700 – 10s. blue, black & lilac 25 15
1701 – 13s. purple, black & grey 50 25
PORTRAITS: 2s. Petko Napetov; 5s. Petko Petkov; 10s. Emil Markov; 13s. Traicho Kostov.

1967. 1st Cultural Conference, Sofia.
1702 **550** 13s. yellow, grn & gold 55 35

551 Angora Kitten

1967. Cats. Multicoloured.
1703 1s. Type **551** 10 15
1704 2s. Siamese (horiz) 15 15
1705 3s. Abyssinian 20 15
1706 5s. European black and white . . . . 1·00 15
1707 13s. Persian (horiz) . . . . 1·20 40
1708 20s. European tabby . . . . 1·90 1·00

552 "Golden Sands" Resort

1967. International Tourist Year. Multicoloured.
1709 13s. Type **552** 25 15
1710 20s. Pamporovo 60 25
1711 40s. Old Church, Nesebur 1·20 55

553 Scene from Iliev's Opera "The Master of Boyana"

1967. 3rd International Young Opera Singers' Competition, Sofia.
1712 **553** 5s. red, blue and grey . . 15 15
1713 – 13s. red, blue and grey 50 25
DESIGN—VERT: 13s. "Vocal Art" (song-bird on piano-keys).

554 G. Kirkov

1967. Birth Cent of Georgi Kirkov (patriot).
1714 **554** 2s. bistre and red . . . 15 10

555 Roses and Distillery

1967. Economic Achievements. Multicoloured.
1715 1s. Type **555** 10 15
1716 1s. Chick and incubator . . 10 15
1717 2s. Cucumber and glass-houses 10 15
1718 2s. Lamb and farm building 10 15
1719 3s. Sunflower and oil-extraction plant 10 15
1720 4s. Pigs and piggery 15 15
1721 5s. Hops and vines 15 10
1722 6s. Grain and irrigation canals 20 15
1723 8s. Grapes and "Bulgar" tractor 20 10
1724 10s. Apples and tree 35 15
1725 13s. Honey bees and honey 60 20
1726 20s. Honey bee on flower, and hives . . . . 1·10 40

556 DKMS Emblem

557 Map and Spassky Tower, Moscow Kremlin

1967. 11th Anniv of Dimitrov Communist Youth League.
1727 **556** 13s. black, red and blue 50 25

1967. 50th Anniv of October Revolution.
1728 **557** 1s. multicoloured 10 15
1729 – 2s. olive and purple . . 10 15
1730 – 3s. violet and purple . . 10 15
1731 – 5s. red and purple . . . 15 15
1732 – 13s. blue and purple . . 25 25
1733 – 20s. blue and purple . . 80 35
DESIGNS: 2s. Lenin directing revolutionaries; 3s. Revolutionaries; 5s. Marx, Engels and Lenin; 13s. Soviet oil refinery; 20s. "Molniya" satellite and Moon (Soviet space research).

558 Scenic "Fish" and Rod

560 Bogdan Peak, Sredna Mts

559 Cross-country Skiing

1967. 7th World Angling Championships, Varna.
1734 **558** 10s. multicoloured . . . 30 30

1967. Winter Olympic Games, Grenoble (1968).
1735 **559** 1s. black, red & turq . . 10 15
1736 – 2s. black, bistre & blue 10 15
1737 – 3s. black, blue & purple 10 15
1738 – 5s. black, yellow & grn 15 15
1739 – 13s. black, buff & blue 80 25
1740 – 20s.+10s. mult . . . . . 1·50 70
MS1741 98 × 98 mm. (diamond) 40s.+10s. black, ochre and blue. Imperf . . . . 2·40 1·80
DESIGNS: 2s. Ski jumping; 3s. Biathlon; 5s. Ice hockey; 13, 40s. Ice skating (pairs); 20s. Men's slalom.

1967. Tourism. Mountain Peaks.
1742 **560** 1s. green and yellow . . 10 15
1743 – 2s. sepia and blue . . . 10 15
1744 – 3s. indigo and blue . . . 10 15
1745 – 5s. green and blue . . . 15 15
1746 – 10s. brown and blue . . 25 15
1747 – 13s. black and blue . . 30 35
1748 – 20s. blue and purple . . 55 70
DESIGNS—HORIZ: 2s. Cherni Vruh, Vitosha; 5s. Persenk, Rhodopes; 10s. Botev, Stara-Planina; 20s. Vikhren, Pirin. VERT: 3s. Ruen, Osogovska Planina; 13s. Musala, Rila.

561 G. Rakovski

1967. Death Cent of G. Rakovski (revolutionary).
1749 **561** 13s. black and green . . 50 40

562 Yuri Gagarin, Valentina Tereshkova and Aleksei Leonov

1967. Space Exploration. Multicoloured.
1750 1s. Type **562** 10 15
1751 2s. John Glenn and Edward White 15 15
1752 5s. "Molniya 1" 25 15
1753 10s. "Gemini 6" and "7" . . 60 25
1754 13s. "Luna 13" 90 25
1755 20s. "Gemini 10" docking with "Agena" . . . . . 1·10 60

563 Railway Bridge over Yantra River

1967. Views of Turnovo (ancient capital).
1756 **563** 1s. black, drab and blue 10 15
1757 – 2s. multicoloured 10 15
1758 – 3s. multicoloured 10 15
1759 – 5s. black, slate and red 45 20
1760 – 13s. multicoloured . . . 45 15
1761 – 20s. black, orange & lav 65 25
DESIGNS: 2s. Hadji Nikola's Inn; 3s. Houses on hillside; 5s. Town and river; 13s. "House of the Monkeys"; 20s. Gurko street.

564 "The Ruchenitsa" (folk dance, from painting by Murkvichka)

1967. Belgian–Bulgarian "Painting and Philately" Exhibition, Brussels.
1762 **564** 20s. green and gold . . . 1·20 1·40

565 "The Shepherd" (Zlatko Boyadzhiev)

1967. Paintings in the National Gallery, Sofia. Multicoloured.
1763 1s. Type **565** 10 10
1764 2s. "The Wedding" (Vladimir Dimitrov) (vert) 10 10
1765 3s. "The Partisans" Ilya Petrov (55 × 35 mm) . . . 10 10
1766 5s. "Anastasia Penchovich" (Nikolai Pavlovich) (vert) 45 20
1767 13s. "Self-portrait" (Zakharii Zograf) (vert) 75 40
1768 20s. "Old Town of Plovdiv" (Tsanko Lavrenov) . . . 1·00 60
MS1769 65 × 85 mm. 60s. "St. Clement of Ohrid" (Anton Mitov) . . . . 2·20 45

566 Linked Satellites "Cosmos 186" and "188"

1968. "Cosmic Activities". Multicoloured.
1770 20s. Type **566** 70 25
1771 40s. "Venus 4" and orbital diagram (horiz) . . . . . 1·40 65

567 "Crossing the Danube" (Orenburgski)

1968. 90th Anniv of Liberation from Turkey. Paintings. Inscr and frames in black and gold; centre colours below.
1772 **567** 1s. green 20 15
1773 – 2s. blue 10 15
1774 – 3s. brown 10 15
1775 – 13s. blue 45 25
1776 – 20s. turquoise 75 30
DESIGNS—VERT: 2s. "Flag of Samara" (Veschin); 13s. "Battle of Orlovo Gnezdo" (Popov). HORIZ: 3s. "Battle of Pleven" (Orenburgski); 20s. "Greeting Russian Soldiers" (Goudienov).

568 Karl Marx

569 Gorky

1968. 150th Birth Anniv of Karl Marx.
1777 **568** 13s. grey, red & black . . . 50 25

1968. Birth Cent of Maksim Gorky (writer).
1778 **569** 13s. green, orange & blk . . . 50 25

570 Dancers

1968. 9th World Youth and Students' Festival. Sofia. Multicoloured.
1779 2s. Type **570** 10 15
1780 5s. Running 10 15
1781 13s. "Doves" 55 15
1782 20s. "Youth" (symbolic design) 60 35
1783 40s. Bulgarian 5c. stamp of 1879 under magnifier and Globe . . . . 1·10 70

571 "Campanula alpina" **572** "The Unknown Hero" (Ran Bosilek)

1968. Wild Flowers. Multicoloured.
1784 1s. Type **571** 10 15
1785 2s. Trumpet gentian 10 15
1786 3s. "Crocus veluchensis" . . 10 15
1787 5s. Siberian iris 15 15
1788 10s. Dog's-tooth violet . . . 20 15
1789 13s. House leek 70 15
1790 20s. Burning bush . . . . . 1·00 40

1968. Bulgarian–Danish Stamp Exhibition. Fairy Tales. Multicoloured.
1791 13s. Type **572** 35 25
1792 20s. "The Witch and the Young Men" (Hans Andersen) 45 40

573 Memorial Temple, Shipka **574** Copper Rolling-mill, Medet

1968. Bulgarian–West Berlin Stamp Exn.
1793 **573** 13s. multicoloured . . . 65 45

1968. Air.
1794 **574** 1l. red . . . . 2·00 30

575 Lake Smolyan **576** Gymnastics

1968.
1795 **575** 1s. green 10 15
1796 – 2s. myrtle 10 15
1797 – 3s. sepia 10 15
1798 – 8s. green 20 15
1799 – 10s. brown 40 15
1800 – 13s. olive 35 15
1801 – 40s. blue 95 35
1802 – 2l. brown . . . . 4·50 1·50
DESIGNS: 2s. River Ropotamo; 3s. Lomnitza Gorge, Erma River; 8s. River Isker; 10s. Cruise ship "Die Fregatte"; 13s. Cape Kaliakra; 40s. Sozopol; 2l. Mountain road, Kamchia River.

1968. Olympic Games, Mexico.
1803 **576** 1s. black and red 10 15
1804 – 2s. black, brown & grey 10 15
1805 – 3s. black and mauve . . 10 15
1806 – 10s. black, yell & turq 35 15
1807 – 13s. black, pink & blue 65 25
1808 – 20s.+10s. grey, pk & bl 1·20 55
MS1809 74×76 mm. 50s.+10s. black, grey and blue. Imperf 2·75 2·40

DESIGNS: 2s. Horse-jumping; 3s. Fencing; 10s. Boxing; 13s. Throwing the discus; 20s. Rowing; 50s. Stadium and communications satellite.

577 Dimitur on Mt. Buzludzha, 1868

1968. Centenary of Exploits of Khadzhi Dimitur and Stefan Karadzha (revolutionaries).
1810 **577** 2s. brown and silver . . 15 10
1811 – 13s. green and gold . . . 30 15
DESIGN: 13s. Dimitur and Karadzha.

578 Human Rights Emblem **579** Cinereous Black Vulture

1968. Human Rights Year.
1812 **578** 20s. gold and blue . . . 65 30

1968. 80th Anniv of Sofia Zoo.
1813 **579** 1s. black, brown & blue 35 20
1814 – 2s. black, yellow & brn 35 20
1815 – 3s. black and green . . . 20 20
1816 – 5s. black, yellow & red 35 20
1817 – 13s. black, bistre & grn 1·20 45
1818 – 20s. black, green & blue 1·90 90
DESIGNS: 2s. South African crowned crane; 3s. Common zebra; 5s. Leopard; 13s. Python; 20s. Crocodile.

580 Battle Scene

1968. 280th Anniv of Chiprovtsi Rising.
1819 **580** 13s. multicoloured . . . 50 15

581 Caterpillar-hunter **582** Flying Swans

1968. Insects.
1820 **581** 1s. green 10 10
1821 – 1s. brown 10 10
1822 – 1s. blue 10 10
1823 – 1s. brown 10 10
1824 – 1s. purple 25 10
DESIGNS—VERT: No. 1821, Stag beetle ("Lucanus cervus"); 1822, "Procerus scabrosus" (ground beetle). HORIZ: No. 1823, European rhinoceros beetle ("Oryctes nasicornis"); 1824, "Perisomena caecigena" (moth).

1968. "Co-operation with Scandinavia".
1825 – 2s. ochre and green . . . 80 85
1826 **582** 5s. blue, grey & black . . 80 70
1827 – 13s. purple and maroon 80 1·00
1828 – 20s. grey and violet . . . 80 1·00
DESIGNS: 2s. Wooden flask; 13s. Rose; 20s. "Viking ship".

583 Congress Building and Emblem

1968. International Dental Congress, Varna.
1829 **583** 20s. gold, green and red 55 15

584 Smirnenski and Verse from "Red Squadrons"

1968. 70th Birth Anniv of Khristo Smirnenski (poet).
1830 **584** 13s. black, orange & gold 40 15

585 Dove with Letter

1968. National Stamp Exhibition, Sofia and 75th Anniv of "National Philately".
1831 **585** 20s. green 90 80

586 Dalmatian Pelican

1968. Srebirna Wildlife Reservation. Birds. Mult.
1832 1s. Type **586** 10 15
1833 2s. Little egret 15 20
1834 3s. Great crested grebe . . . 15 15
1835 5s. Common tern 40 20
1836 13s. White spoonbill . . . . 1·20 65
1837 20s. Glossy ibis . . . . . . 2·20 1·10

587 Silistra Costume

1968. Provincial Costumes. Multicoloured.
1838 1s. Type **587** 10 15
1839 2s. Lovech 10 15
1840 3s. Yamboi 10 15
1841 13s. Chirpan 30 20
1842 20s. Razgrad 70 30
1843 40s. Ikhtiman . . . . 1·40 60

588 "St. Arsenius" (icon)

1968. Rila Monastery. Icons and murals. Mult.
1844 1s. Type **588** 10 15
1845 2s. "Carrying St. Ivan Rilski's Relics" (horiz) . . 10 15
1846 3s. "St. Michael torments the Rich Man's Soul" . . 10 15
1847 13s. "St. Ivan Rilski" . . . 55 25
1848 20s. "Prophet Joel" 90 40
1849 40s. "St. George" . . . . . 1·40 95
MS1850 100×74 mm. 1l. "Arrival of Relics at Rila Monastery". Imperf 4·50 4·00

589 "Matricaria chamomilla"

1968. Medicinal Plants. Multicoloured.
1851 1s. Type **589** 10 15
1852 1s. "Mespilus oxyacantha" 10 15
1853 2s. Lily of the valley . . . 10 15
1854 3s. Deadly nightshade . . . 10 15
1855 5s. Common mallow 15 15
1856 10s. Yellow peasant's eye . . 20 15
1857 13s. Common poppy . . . 45 20
1858 20s. Wild thyme 90 35

590 Silkworms and Spindles

1969. Silk Industry. Multicoloured.
1859 1s. Type **590** 10 10
1860 2s. Worm, cocoons and pattern 10 15
1861 3s. Cocoons and spinning wheel 10 10
1862 5s. Cocoons and pattern . . 10 15
1863 13s. Moth, cocoon and spindles 30 10
1864 20s. Moth, eggs and shuttle 65 20

591 "Death of Ivan Asen" **592** "Saints Cyril and Methodius" (mural, Troyan Monastery)

1969. Manasses Chronicle (1st series). Mult.
1865 1s. Type **591** 10 10
1866 2s. "Emperor Nicephorus invading Bulgaria" . . . 10 15
1867 3s. "Khan Krum's Feast" 10 15
1868 13s. "Prince Sviatoslav invading Bulgaria" . . . 60 25
1869 20s. "The Russian invasion" 80 30
1870 40s. "Jesus Christ, Tsar Ivan Alexander and Constantine Manasses" 1·50 80
See also Nos. 1911/16.

1969. Saints Cyril and Methodius Commem.
1871 **592** 28s. multicoloured . . . 95 55

593 Galleon **594** Posthorn Emblem

1969. Air. "SOFIA 1969" International Stamp Exhibition. Transport. Multicoloured.
1872 1s. Type **593** 10 15
1873 2s. Mail coach 10 15
1874 3s. Steam locomotive . . . 15 10
1875 5s. Early motor-car 10 15
1876 10s. Montgolfier's balloon and Henri Giffard's steam-powered dirigible airship 15 15
1877 13s. Early flying machines 20 15
1878 20s. Modern aircraft 65 25
1879 40s. Rocket and planets . . 1·10 65
MS1880 57×55 mm. 1l. gold and orange. Imperf . . . . 3·25 2·75
DESIGN: 1l. Postal courier.

1969. 90th Anniv of Bulgarian Postal Services.
1881 **594** 2s. yellow and green . . 10 15
1882 – 13s. multicoloured . . . 45 10
1883 – 20s. blue 60 25
DESIGNS: 13s. Bulgarian Stamps of 1879 and 1946; 20s. Post Office workers' strike, 1919.

595 I.L.O. Emblem **596** "Fox" and "Rabbit"

1969. 50th Anniv of I.L.O.
1884 **595** 13s. black and green . . 30 10

1969. Children's Book Week.
1885 **596** 2s. black, orange & grn 10 15
1886 – 2s. black, blue and red 10 15
1887 – 13s. black, olive & blue 45 20
DESIGNS: 2s. Boy with "hedgehog" and "squirrel"; 13s. "The Singing Lesson".

597 Hand with Seedling

1969. "10,000,000 Hectares of New Forests".
1888 **597** 2s. black, green & purple 15 10

598 "St. George" (14th Century)

1969. Religious Art. Multicoloured.
1889 1s. Type **598** 10 15
1890 2s. "The Virgin and St. John Bogoslov" (14th century) 10 15
1891 3s. "Archangel Michael" (17th century) 10 15
1892 5s. "Three Saints" (17th century) 20 15
1893 8s. "Jesus Christ" (17th century) 20 15
1894 13s. "St. George and St. Dimitr" (19th century) 55 20
1895 20s. "Christ the Universal" (19th century) 80 20
1896 60s. "The Forty Martyrs" (19th century) . . . . . 2·40 1·20
1897 80s. "The Transfiguration" (19th century) . . . . . 3·00 2·10
MS1898 103 × 165 mm. 40s. × 4, "St. Dimitur" (17th-century) 6·50 6·50

599 Roman Coin

600 St. George and the Dragon

1969. "SOFIA 1969" International Stamp Exhibition. "Sofia Through the Ages".
1899 **599** 1s. silver, blue and gold 10 10
1900 – 2s. silver, green & gold 10 10
1901 – 3s. silver, lake and gold 10 10
1902 – 4s. silver, violet & gold 10 10
1903 – 5s. silver, purple & gold 10 10
1904 – 13s. silver, green & gold 35 15
1905 – 20s. silver, blue & gold 70 20
1906 – 40s. silver, red & gold 1·40 40
MS1907 78 × 72 mm. 1l. multicoloured. Imperf . . . . 3·25 2·20
DESIGNS: 2s. Roman coin showing Temple of Aesculapius; 3s. Church of St. Sophia; 4s. Boyana Church; 5s. Parliament Building; 13s. National Theatre; 20s. Aleksandr Nevski Cathedral; 40s. Sofia University. 44 × 44 mm. 1l. Arms.

1969. Int Philatelic Federation Congress, Sofia.
1908 **600** 40s. black, orange & sil 1·40 50

601 St. Cyril

1969. 1,100th Death Anniv of St. Cyril.
1909 **601** 2s. green & red on silver 10 10
1910 – 28s. blue & red on silver 95 40
DESIGN: 28s. St. Cyril and procession.

1969. Manasses Chronicle (2nd series). Designs as T **591**, but all horiz. Multicoloured.
1911 1s. "Nebuchadnezzar II and Balthasar of Babylon, Cyrus and Darius of Persia" 10 10
1912 2s. "Cambyses, Gyges and Darius of Persia" 10 10
1913 5s. "Prophet David and Tsar Ivan Alexander" . . 10 10
1914 13s. "Rout of the Byzantine Army, 811" 60 15
1915 20s. "Christening of Khan Boris" . . . . 1·10 20
1916 60s. "Tsar Simeon's attack on Constantinople" . . . 2·20 95

602 Partisans

1969. 25th Anniv of Fatherland Front Government.
1917 **602** 1s. lilac, red and black 10 15
1918 – 2s. brown, red & black 10 15
1919 – 3s. green, red and black 10 15
1920 – 5s. brown, red & black 20 15
1921 – 13s. blue, red & black 25 10
1922 – 20s. multicoloured . . . 65 35
DESIGNS: 2s. Combine-harvester; 3s. Dam; 5s. Folk singers; 13s. Petroleum refinery; 20s. Lenin, Dimitrov and flags.

603 Gymnastics

1969. 3rd Republican Spartakiad. Multicoloured.
1923 2s. Type **603** 10 10
1924 20s. Wrestling 60 30

604 "Construction" and soldier

605 T. Tserkovski

1969. 25th Anniv of Army Engineers.
1925 **604** 6s. black and blue . . . 15 10

1969. Birth Cent of Tsanke Tserkovski (poet).
1926 **605** 13s. multicoloured . . . 30 15

606 "Woman" (Roman Statue)

607 Skipping-rope Exercise

1969. 1,800th Anniv of Silistra.
1927 **606** 2s. grey, blue and silver 10 15
1928 – 13s. brown, grn & silver 55 15
DESIGN—HORIZ: 13s. "Wolf" (bronze statue).

1969. World Gymnastics Competition, Varna.
1929 **607** 1s. grey, blue and green 10 15
1930 – 2s. grey and blue 10 15
1931 – 3s. grey, green and emerald 10 15
1932 – 5s. grey, purple and red 10 15
1933 – 13s.+5s. grey, bl & red 60 30
1934 – 20s.+10s. grey, green and yellow . . . . 1·00 55
DESIGNS: 2s. Hoop exercise (pair); 3s. Hoop exercise (solo); 5s. Ball exercise (pair); 13s. Ball exercise (solo); 20s. Solo gymnast.

608 Marin Drinov (founder)

1969. Cent of Bulgarian Academy of Sciences.
1935 **608** 20s. black and red . . . 40 30

609 "Neophit Rilski" (Zakharii Zograf)

1969. Paintings in National Gallery, Sofia. Mult.
1936 1s. Type **609** 10 10
1937 2s. "German's Mother" (Vasil Stoilov) 10 10
1938 3s. "Workers' Family" (Neuko Balkanski) (horiz) 15 10
1939 4s. "Woman Dressing" (Ivan Nenov) 25 10
1940 5s. "Portrait of a Woman" (Nikolai Pavlovich) . . . 25 10
1941 13s. "Krustyn Sarafov as Falstaff" (Dechko Uzunov) 70 20
1942 20s. "Artist's Wife" (N. Mikhailov) (horiz) . . 80 25
1943 20s. "Worker's Lunch" (Stoyan Sotirov) (horiz) 90 30
1944 40s. "Self-portrait" (Tseno Todorov) (horiz) . . . . 1·30 65

610 Pavel Banya

1969. Sanatoria.
1945 **610** 2s. blue 10 10
1946 – 5s. blue 10 10
1947 – 6s. green 10 10
1948 – 20s. green 50 20
SANATORIA: 5s. Khisar; 6s. Kotel; 20s. Narechen Polyclinic.

611 Deep-sea Trawler

1969. Ocean Fisheries.
1949 **611** 1s. grey and blue 15 15
1950 – 1s. green and black . . . 10 15
1951 – 2s. violet and black . . . 10 15
1952 – 3s. blue and black . . . 10 15
1953 – 5s. mauve and black . . 15 15
1954 – 10s. grey and black . . . 75 25
1955 – 13s. flesh, orange & blk 1·20 40
1956 – 20s. brown, ochre & blk 1·60 55
DESIGNS: 1s. (No. 1950), Cape hake; 2s. Atlantic horse-mackerel; 3s. South African pilchard; 5s. Large-eyed dentex; 10s. Chub mackerel; 13s. Senegal croaker; 20s. Vadigo.

612 Trapeze Act

613 V. Kubasov, Georgi Shonin and "Soyuz 6"

1969. Circus. Multicoloured.
1957 1s. Type **612** 10 10
1958 2s. Acrobats 10 10
1959 3s. Balancing act with hoops 10 10
1960 5s. Juggler, and bear on cycle 10 10
1961 13s. Equestrian act 30 20
1962 20s. Clowns 75 30

1970. Space Flights of "Soyuz 6, 7 and 8".
1963 **613** 1s. multicoloured 10 10
1964 – 2s. multicoloured 10 10
1965 – 3s. multicoloured 10 15
1966 – 28s. pink and blue . . . 1·00 30
DESIGNS: 2s. Viktor Gorbacko, Vladislav Volkov, Anatoly Filipchenko and "Soyuz 7"; 3s. Aleksei Elseev, Vladimir Shatalov and "Soyuz 8"; 28s. Three "Soyuz" spacecraft in orbit.

614 Khan Asparerch and "Old-Bulgars" crossing the Danube, 679

1970. History of Bulgaria. Multicoloured.
1967 1s. Type **614** 10 15
1968 2s. Khan Krum and defeat of Emperor Nicephorus, 811 . . . . 10 15
1969 3s. Conversion of Khan Boris I to Christianity, 865 . . . . 10 15
1970 5s. Tsar Simeon and Battle of Akhelo, 917 . . . . 15 15
1971 8s. Tsar Samuel and defeat of Byzantines, 976 . . . . 15 15
1972 10s. Tsar Kaloyan and victory over Emperor Baldwin, 1205 . . . . . 20 15
1973 13s. Tsar Ivan Assen II and defeat of Komnine of Epirus, 1230 . . . . . 60 25
1974 20s. Coronation of Tsar Ivailo, 1277 . . . . . . 95 30

615 Bulgarian Pavilion

1970. "Expo 70" World's Fair, Osaka, Japan (1st issue).
1975 **615** 20s. silver, yellow & brn 95 65
See Nos. 2009/12.

616 Footballers

1970. World Football Cup, Mexico.
1976 **616** 1s. multicoloured 10 10
1977 – 2s. multicoloured 10 10
1978 – 3s. multicoloured 10 10
1979 – 5s. multicoloured 15 10
1980 – 20s. multicoloured . . . 75 50
1981 – 40s. multicoloured . . . 1·50 65
MS1982 55 × 99 mm. 80s.+20s. multicoloured. Imperf 2·75 2·40
DESIGNS—HORIZ: 2s. to 40s. Various football scenes. VERT (45 × 69 mm.) 80s. Football and inscription.

617 Lenin

618 "Tephrocactus Alexanderi v. bruchi"

1970. Birth Cent of Lenin. Multicoloured.
1983 2s. Type **617** 10 15
1984 13s. Full-face portrait . . . 35 25
1985 20s. Lenin writing 70 35

1970. Flowering Cacti. Multicoloured.
1986 1s. Type **618** 10 15
1987 2s. "Opuntia drummondii" 10 15
1988 3s. "Hatiora cilindrica" . . 15 15
1989 5s. "Gymnocalycium vatteri" 20 15
1990 8s. "Heliantho cereus grandiflorus" 30 25
1991 10s. "Neochilenia andreaeana" . . . . 1·40 50
1992 13s. "Peireskia vargasii v. longispina" . . . . 1·40 50
1993 20s. "Neobesseya rosiflora" 1·90 70

619 Rose

620 Union Badge

1970. Bulgarian Roses.

1994	**619**	1s. multicoloured	10	15
1995	–	2s. multicoloured	10	15
1996	–	3s. multicoloured	15	15
1997	–	4s. multicoloured	20	15
1998	–	5s. multicoloured	25	15
1999	–	13s. multicoloured	40	25
2000	–	20s. multicoloured	1·20	60
2001	–	28s. multicoloured	2·10	1·10

DESIGNS: 2s. to 28s. Various roses.

1970. 70th Anniv of Agricultural Union.

2002	**620**	20s. black, gold and red	65	30

621 Gold Bowl

1970. Gold Treasures of Thrace.

2003	**621**	1s. black, blue and gold	10	15
2004	–	2s. black, lilac and gold	10	15
2005	–	3s. black, red and gold	10	15
2006	–	5s. black, green & gold	20	15
2007	–	13s. black, orge & gold	70	25
2008	–	20s. black, violet & gold	1·10	50

DESIGNS: 2s. Three small bowls; 3s. Plain lid; 5s. Pear shaped ornaments; 13s. Large lid with pattern; 20s. Vase.

622 Rose and Woman with Baskets of Produce

1970. "Expo 70" World's Fair, Osaka, Japan (2nd issue). Multicoloured.

2009		1s. Type **622**	10	15
2010		2s. Three Dancers	10	15
2011		3s. Girl in National costume	10	15
2012		28s. Dancing couples	95	40
MS2013		75 × 90 mm. 40s. Bulgarian pavilion	1·20	1·20

623 UN Emblem

1970. 25th Anniv of United Nations.

2014	**623**	20s. gold and blue	65	25

624 I. Vasov

1970. 120th Birth Anniv of Ivan Vasov (poet).

2015	**624**	13s. blue	40	25

625 Edelweiss Sanatorium, Borovets

1970. Health Resorts.

2016	**625**	1s. green	10	15
2017	–	2s. olive	10	15
2018	–	4s. blue	15	15
2019	–	8s. blue	25	15
2020	–	10s. blue	30	15

DESIGNS: 2s. Panorama Hotel, Pamporovo; 4s. Yachts, Albena; 8s. Harbour scene, Rousalka; 10s. Shtastlivetsa Hotel, Mt. Vitosha.

626 Hungarian Retriever

1970. Dogs. Multicoloured.

2021		1s. Type **626**	15	15
2022		2s. Retriever (vert)	15	15
2023		3s. Great Dane (vert)	20	15
2024		4s. Boxer (vert)	25	15
2025		5s. Cocker spaniel (vert)	35	15
2026		13s. Dobermann pinscher (vert)	90	30
2027		20s. Scottish terrier (vert)	1·50	65
2028		28s. Russian hound	1·90	95

627 Fireman with Hose

628 Congress Emblem

1970. Fire Protection.

2029	**627**	1s. grey, yellow & black	10	10
2030	–	3s. red, grey and black	15	10

DESIGN. 3s. Fire-engine.

1970. 7th World Sociological Congress, Varna.

2031	**628**	13s. multicoloured	40	15

629 Two Male Players

630 Cyclists

1970. World Volleyball Championships.

2032	**629**	2s. black and brown	10	15
2033	–	2s. orange, black & blue	10	15
2034	–	20s. yellow, black & grn	70	40
2035	–	20s. multicoloured	70	30

DESIGNS: No. 2033, Two female players; 2034, Male player; 2035, Female player.

1970. 20th Round-Bulgaria Cycle Race.

2036	**630**	20s. mauve, yellow & grn	55	30

631 Enrico Caruso and Scene from "II Pagliacci"

1970. Opera Singers. Multicoloured.

2037		1s. Type **631**	10	15
2038		2s. Khristina Morfova and "The Bartered Bride"	10	15
2039		3s. Petur Raichev and "Tosca"	10	15
2040		10s. Tsvetana Tabakova and "The Flying Dutchman"	25	20
2041		13s. Katya Popova and "The Masters of Nuremberg"	35	20
2042		20s. Fyodor Chaliapin and "Boris Godunov"	1·30	35

632 Beethoven

1970. Birth Bicentenary of Ludwig von Beethoven (composer).

2043	**632**	28s. blue and purple	1·60	95

633 Ivan Asen II Coin

1970. Bulgarian Coins of the 14th century. Multicoloured.

2044		1s. Type **633**	10	15
2045		2s. Theodor Svetoslav	10	15
2046		3s. Mikhail Shishman	10	15
2047		13s. Ivan Alexander and Mikhail Asen	35	15
2048		20s. Ivan Sratsimir	80	30
2049		28s. Ivan Shishman (initials)	1·00	40

634 "Luna 16"

1970. Moon Mission of "Luna 16". Sheet 51 × 70 mm.

MS2050	**634**	1l. red, silver and blue	4·75	4·00

635 Engels

636 Snow Crystal

1970. 150th Birth Anniv of Friedrich Engels.

2051	**635**	13s. brown and red	50	25

1970. New Year.

2052	**636**	2s. multicoloured	15	10

637 "Lunokhod 1" on Moon

1970. Moon Mission of "Lunokhod 1". Sheet 60 × 72 mm.

MS2053	**637**	80s. silver, purple and blue	4·50	2·75

638 "Girl's Head" (Zheko Spiridonov)

1971. Modern Bulgarian Sculpture.

2054	**638**	1s. violet and gold	10	15
2055	–	2s. green and gold	20	15
2056	–	3s. brown and gold	10	15
2057	–	13s. green and gold	30	15
2058	–	20s. red and gold	70	30
2059	–	28s. brown and gold	95	50
MS2060		61 × 72 mm. 1l. chestnut and gold	2·75	2·75

SCULPTURES: 2s. "Third Class Carriage" (Ivan Funev); 3s. "Elin Pelin" (Marko Markov); 13s. "Nina" (Andrei Nikolov); 20s. "Kneeling Woman" (Yavorov monument, Ivan Lazarov); 28s. "Engineer" (Ivan Funev). 36½ × 41 mm. 1l. "Refugees" (Sekul Knimov).

639 Birds and Flowers

1971. Spring.

2061	**639**	1s. multicoloured	10	10
2062	–	2s. multicoloured	10	10
2063	–	3s. multicoloured	10	10
2064	–	5s. multicoloured	10	10
2065	–	13s. multicoloured	20	10
2066	–	20s. multicoloured	75	15

DESIGNS: 2s. to 20s. Various designs of birds and flowers similar to Type **639**.

640 "Khan Asparuch crossing Danube" (Boris Angelushev)

1971. Bulgarian History. Paintings. Mult.

2067		2s. Type **640**	10	15
2068		3s. "Ivajlo in Turnovo" (Ilya Petrov)	10	15
2069		5s. "Cavalry Charge, Benkovski" (P. Morosov)	30	15
2070		8s. "Gen. Gzrko entering Sofia, 1878" (D. Gyudzhenov)	55	15
2071		28s. "Greeting Red Army" (Stefan Venev)	2·75	1·50
MS2072		137 × 131 mm. Nos. 2067/70	1·20	95

641 Running

1971. 2nd European Indoor Track and Field Championships. Multicoloured.

2073		2s. Type **641**	10	15
2074		20s. Putting the shot	1·10	20

642 School Building

1971. Foundation of First Bulgarian Secondary School, Bolgrad.

2075	**642**	2s. green, brown & sil	10	15
2076	–	20s. violet, brown & sil	65	25

DESIGN: 20s. Dimitur Mutev, Prince Bogoridi and Sava Radulov (founders).

643 Communards

1971. Centenary of Paris Commune.

2077	**643**	20s. black and red	50	30

644 Georgi Dimitrov challenging Hermann Goering

1971. 20th Anniv of "Federation Internationale des Resistants".

2078	**644**	2s. multicoloured	10	15
2079		13s. multicoloured	70	20

645 Gagarin and Space Scenes (¾-size illustration)

1971. 10th Anniv of First Manned Space Flight. Sheet 80 × 53 mm.
MS2080 **645** 40s.+20s. multicoloured 2·40 2·00

646 G. Rakovski

647 Worker and Banner ("People's Progress")

1971. 150th Birth Anniv of Georgi Rakovski (politician and Revolutionary).
2081 **646** 13s. brown, cream & grn 30 15

1971. 10th Bulgarian Communist Party Congress. Multicoloured.

2082	1s. Type **647**	10	15
2083	2s. Symbols of "Technical Progress" (horiz)	10	15
2084	12s. Men clasping hands ("Bulgarian-Soviet Friendship")	60	20

648 Pipkov and Music

1971. Birth Centenary of Panaiot Pipokov.
2085 **648** 13s. black, green & silver 50 25

649 "Three Races"

650 Mammoth

1971. Racial Equality Year.
2086 **649** 13s. multicoloured 40 25

1971. Prehistoric Animals. Multicoloured.

2087	1s. Type **650**	10	20
2088	2s. Bear (vert)	10	20
2089	3s. Hipparion	15	20
2090	13s. Mastodon	70	30
2091	20s. Dinotherium (vert)	1·10	50
2092	28s. Sabre-toothed tiger	1·50	80

651 Facade of Ancient Building

652 Weights Emblem on Map of Europe

1971. Ancient Buildings of Koprivshitsa.

2093	**651**	1s. green, brown & grn	10	10
2094	–	2s. brown, green & buff	10	10
2095	–	6s. violet, brown & blue	15	10
2096	–	13s. red, blue & orange	50	25

DESIGNS: 1s. to 13s. Different facades.

1971. 30th European Weightlifting Championships, Sofia. Multicoloured.

2097	2s. Type **652**	10	15
2098	13s. Figures supporting weights	75	25

653 Frontier Guard and Dog

654 Tweezers, Magnifying Glass and "Stamp"

1971. 25th Anniv of Frontier Guards.
2099 **653** 2s. olive, green & turq 15 10

1971. 9th Congress of Bulgarian Philatelic Federation.
2100 **654** 20s.+10s. brown, black and red 95 45

655 Congress Meeting (sculpture)

1971. 80th Anniv of Bulgarian Social Democratic Party Congress, Buzludzha.
2101 **655** 2s. green, cream and red 15 10

656 "Mother" (Ivan Nenov)

657 Factory Botevgrad

1971. Paintings from the National Art Gallery (1st series). Multicoloured.

2102	1s. Type **656**	10	15
2103	2s. "Lazorova" (Stefan Ivanov)	10	15
2104	3s. "Portrait of Yu. Kh." (Kiril Tsonev)	10	15
2105	13s. "Portrait of a Lady" (Dechko Uzunov)	50	25
2106	30s. "Young Woman from Kalotina" (Vladimir Dimitrov)	70	45
2107	40s. "Goryanin" (Stryan Venev)	1·40	80

See also Nos. 2145/50.

1971. Industrial Buildings.

2108	**657**	1s. violet	10	10
2109	–	2s. red	10	10
2110	–	10s. violet	15	10
2111	–	13s. red	20	10
2112	–	40s. brown	90	10

DESIGNS—VERT: 2s. Petro-chemical plant, Pleven. HORIZ: 10s. Chemical works, Vratsa; 13s. "Maritsa-Istok" plant, Dimitrovgrad; 40s. Electronics factory, Sofia.

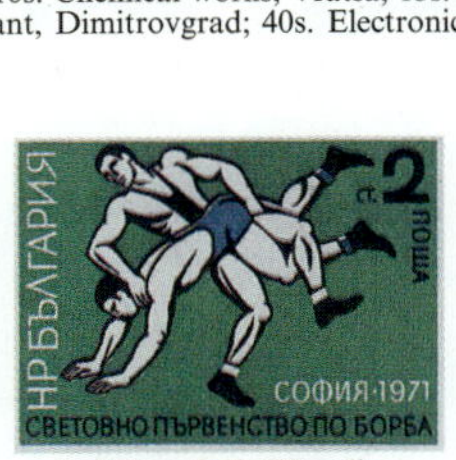

658 Free Style Wrestling

1971. European Wrestling Championships, Sofia.

2113	**658**	2s. green, black and blue	10	10
2114	–	13s. black, red and blue	60	15

DESIGN: 13s. Greco-Roman wrestling.

659 Posthorn Emblem

1971. Organization of Socialist Countries' Postal Administrations Congress.
2115 **659** 20s. gold and green 50 30

660 Entwined Ribbons

1971. 7th European Biochemical Congress, Varna.
2116 **660** 13s. red, brown & black 50 30

661 "New Republic" Statue

1971. 25th Anniv of People's Republic.

2117	**661**	2s. red, yellow and gold	10	10
2118	–	13s. green, red and gold	40	25

DESIGN: 13s. Bulgarian flag.

662 Cross-country Skiing

1971. Winter Olympic Games, Sapporo, Japan. Multicoloured.

2119	1s. Type **662**	10	15
2120	2s. Downhill skiing	10	15
2121	3s. Ski jumping	10	15
2122	4s. Figure skating	10	15
2123	13s. Ice hockey	55	35
2124	28s. Slalom skiing	95	55
MS2125	60 × 70 mm. 1l. Olympic flame and stadium	3·25	2·40

663 Brigade Members

664 UNESCO Emblem and Wreath

1971. 25th Anniv of Youth Brigades Movement.
2126 **663** 2s. blue 15 10

1971. 25th Anniv of UNESCO.
2127 **664** 20s. multicoloured 50 30

665 "The Footballer"

1971. Paintings by Kiril Tsonev. Multicoloured.

2128	1s. Type **665**	10	15
2129	2s. "Landscape" (horiz)	10	15
2130	3s. Self-portrait	10	15
2131	13s. "Lilies"	60	20
2132	20s. "Woodland Scene" (horiz)	90	40
2133	40s. "Portrait of a Young Woman"	1·50	45

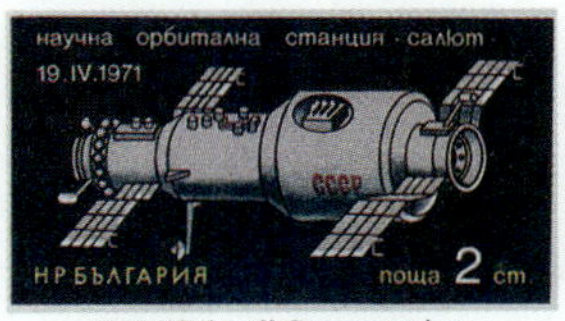

666 "Salyut" Space-station

1971. Space Flights of "Salyut" and "Soyuz 11". Multicoloured.

2134	2s. Type **666**	10	15
2135	13s. "Soyuz 11"	25	25
2136	40s. "Salyut" and "Soyuz 11" joined together	1·30	55
MS2137	70 × 74 mm. 80s. Cosmonauts G. Dobrovolsky, Vladislav Volkov and V. Patsaev (victims of "Soyuz 11" disaster). Imperf	2·40	1·60

667 "Vikhren" (ore carrier)

1972. "One Million Tons of Bulgarian Shipping".
2138 **667** 18s. lilac, red and black 80 30

668 Goce Delcev

1972. Birth Centenaries of Macedonian Revolutionaries.

2139	**668**	2s. black and red	10	10
2140	–	5s. black and green	10	10
2141	–	13s. black and yellow	40	20

PATRIOTS: 5s. Jan Sandanski (1972); 13s. Dume Gruev (1971).

669 Gymnast with Ball

1972. World Gymnastics Championships, Havana (Cuba). Multicoloured.

2142	13s. Type **669**	55	25
2143	18s. Gymnast with hoop	65	40
MS2144	61 × 74 mm. 70s. Team with hoops. Imperf	3·25	3·25

1972. Paintings in Bulgarian National Gallery (2nd series). As T **656** but horiz. Multicoloured.

2145	1s. "Melnik" (Petur Mladenov)	10	15
2146	2s. "Ploughman" (Pencho Georgiev)	10	15
2147	3s. "By the Death-bed" (Aleksandur Zhendov)	10	15
2148	13s. "Family" (Vladimir Dimitrov)	55	25
2149	20s. "Family" (Neuko Balkanski)	95	40
2150	40s. "Father Paisii" (Koyu Denchev)	1·40	60

670 Bulgarian Worker

671 "Singing Harvesters"

1972. 7th Bulgarian Trade Unions Congress.
2151 **670** 13s. multicoloured 40 15

1972. 90th Birth Anniv of Vladimir Dimitrov, the Master (painter). Multicoloured.

2152	1s. Type **671**	10	15
2153	2s. "Farm Worker"	10	15
2154	3s. "Women Cultivators" (horiz)	10	15
2155	13s. "Peasant Girl" (horiz)	55	15
2156	20s. "My Mother"	80	40
2157	40s. Self-portrait	1·50	60

672 Heart and Tree Emblem

673 St. Mark's Cathedral

1972. World Heart Month.
2158 **672** 13s. multicoloured . . . 80 45

1972. UNESCO "Save Venice" Campaign.
2159 **673** 2s. green, turquoise & bl 10 10
2160 – 13s. brown, violet & grn 55 25
DESIGN: 13s. Doge's Palace.

674 Dimitrov at Typesetting Desk

1972. 90th Birth Anniv of Georgi Dimitrov (statesman). Multicoloured.
2161 1s. Type **674** 10 15
2162 2s. Dimitrov leading uprising of 1923 . . . 10 15
2163 3s. Dimitrov at Leipzig Trial 10 15
2164 5s. Dimitrov addressing workers 10 15
2165 13s. Dimitrov with Bulgarian crowd . . . 25 25
2166 18s. Addressing young people 65 25
2167 28s. Dimitrov with children 95 40
2168 40s. Dimitrov's mausoleum 1·40 75
2169 80s. Portrait head (green and gold) . . . . . 4·00 1·70
2173 80s. As No. 2169 . . . 6·50 7·25
MS2170 87 × 84 mm. As No. 2169, but centre in red and gold. Imperf 4·75 4·00
No. 2173 has the centre in red and gold, and is imperforate.

675 "Lamp of Learning" and Quotation

1972. 250th Birth Anniv of Father Paisii Khilendurski (historian).
2171 **675** 2s. brown, green & gold 10 10
2172 – 13s. brown, grn & gold 60 25
DESIGN: 13s. Paisii writing.

676 Canoeing

1972. Olympic Games, Munich. Multicoloured.
2174 1s. Type **676** 10 15
2175 2s. Gymnastics 10 15
2176 3s. Swimming 10 15
2177 13s. Volleyball 25 20
2178 18s. Hurdling 65 30
2179 40s. Wrestling . . . . . . 1·10 80
MS2180 64 × 60 mm. 80s. Running track and sports. Imperf . . . 2·40 2·40

677 Angel Kunchev

1972. Death Cent of Angel Kunchev (patriot).
2181 **677** 2s. mauve, gold & purple 15 15

678 "Golden Sands"

1972. Black Sea Resorts. Hotels. Multicoloured.
2182 1s. Type **678** 10 15
2183 2s. Druzhba 10 15
2184 3s. "Sunny Beach" 10 15
2185 13s. Primorsko 20 15
2186 28s. Rusalka 70 40
2187 40s. Albena . . . . 1·10 50

679 Canoeing (Bronze Medal)

1972. Bulgarian Medal Winners, Olympic Games, Munich. Multicoloured.
2188 1s. Type **679** 10 15
2189 2s. Long jumping (Silver Medal) 10 15
2190 3s. Boxing (Gold Medal) . . 10 15
2191 18s. Wrestling (Gold Medal) 75 30
2192 40s. Weightlifting (Gold Medal) . . . . 1·20 55

680 Subi Dimitrov

682 "Lilium rhodopaeum"

681 Commemorative Text

1972. Resistance Heroes. Multicoloured.
2193 1s. Type **680** 10 10
2194 2s. Tsvyatko Radoinov . . 10 10
2195 3s. Iordan Lyutibrodski . . 10 10
2196 5s. Mito Ganev 10 10
2197 13s. Nedelcho Nikolov . . . 30 20

1972. 50th Anniv of U.S.S.R.
2198 **681** 13s. red, yellow & gold 40 25

1972. Protected Flowers. Multicoloured.
2199 1s. Type **682** 10 15
2200 2s. Marsh gentian 10 15
2201 3s. Sea lily 10 10
2202 4s. Globe flower 15 10
2203 18s. "Primula frondosa" . . 55 25
2204 23s. Pale pasque flower . . 75 40
2205 40s. "Fritillaria stribrnyi" . . 2·20 55

СВЕТОВЕН ПЪРВЕНЕЦ
(683)

684 Dobri Chintulov

1972. "Bulgaria, World Weightlifting Champions". No. 2192 optd with T **683**.
2206 40s. multicoloured . . . . . 1·20 55

1972. 150th Birth Anniv of Dobri Chintulov (poet).
2207 **684** 2s. multicoloured 15 10

685 Forehead Ornament (19th-century)

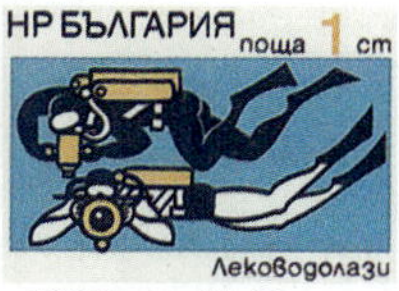

686 Divers with Cameras

1972. Antique Ornaments.
2208 **685** 1s. black and brown . . 10 15
2209 – 2s. black and green . . . 10 15
2210 – 3s. black and blue . . . 10 15
2211 – 8s. black and red . . . 20 15
2212 – 23s. black and brown . . 60 25
2213 – 40s. black and violet . . 1·20 60
DESIGNS: 2s. Belt-buckle (19th-century); 3s. Amulet (18th-century); 8s. Pendant (18th-century); 23s. Earrings (14th-century); 40s. Necklace (18th-century).

1973. Underwater Research in the Black Sea.
2214 **686** 1s. black, yellow & blue 10 20
2215 – 2s. black, yellow & blue 10 20
2216 – 18s. black, yellow & blue 50 45
2217 – 40s. black, yellow & blue 1·10 55
MS2218 118 × 98 mm. 20s. × 4. Designs as Nos. 2214/17, but background colours changed (sold at 1l.) . . . . 6·25 5·25

DESIGNS—HORIZ: 2s. Divers with underwater research vessel "Shelf 1". VERT: 18s. Diver and "NIV 100" diving bell; 40s. Lifting balloon.

687 "The Hanging of Vasil Levski" (Boris Angelushev)

688 Elhovo Mask

1973. Death Cent of Vasil Levski (patriot).
2219 **687** 2s. green and red 10 10
2220 – 20s. brown, cream & grn 95 40
DESIGN: 20s. "Vasil Levski" (Georgi Danchov).

1973. Kukeris' Festival Masks. Mult.
2221 1a. Type **688** 10 15
2222 2s. Breznik 10 15
2223 3s. Khisar 10 15
2224 13s. Radomir 30 15
2225 20s. Karnobat 35 40
2226 40s. Pernik . . . . 4·50 3·00

689 Copernicus

690 Vietnamese "Girl"

1973. 500th Birth Anniv of Copernicus.
2227 **689** 28s. purple, black & brn 1·20 90

1973. "Visit Bulgaria by Air". No. **MS**2072 surch with various airline emblems and new sheet value.
MS2228 137 × 131 mm. Nos. 2067/70 surch with new sheet value 1l. 24·00 24·00

1973. Vietnam Peace Treaty.
2229 **690** 18s. multicoloured . . . 25 25

1973. "IBRA 73" Stamp Exhibition, Munich. No. **MS**1907 optd with "IBRA" and Olympic symbols in green.
MS2230 78 × 72 mm. 1l. multicoloured £120 £120

691 Common Poppy

692 C. Botev (after T. Todorov)

1973. Wild Flowers. Multicoloured.
2231 1s. Type **691** 10 15
2232 2s. Ox-eye daisy 10 15
2233 3s. Peony 10 10
2234 13s. Cornflower 30 15
2235 18s. Corn cockle . . . . . 3·50 2·50
2236 28s. Meadow buttercup . . 95 75

1973. 125th Birth Anniv of Khristo Botev (poet and revolutionary).
2237 **692** 2s. yellow, brown & grn 10 15
2238 18s. grn, lt grn & bronze 70 70

693 Asen Khalachev and Insurgents

1973. 50th Anniv of June Uprising.
2239 **693** 1s. black, red and gold 10 10
2240 – 2s. black, orange & gold 10 10
DESIGN: 2s. "Wounded Worker" (illustration by Boris Angelushev to the poem "September" by Geo Milev).

694 Stamboliiski (from sculpture by A. Nikolov)

1973. 50th Death Anniv of Aleksandur Stamboliiski (Prime Minister 1919–23).
2241 **694** 18s. lt brn, brn & orge 25 35
2242 18s. orange . . . . . . 3·00 3·00

695 Muskrat

1973. Bulgarian Fauna. Multicoloured.
2243 1s. Type **695** 10 15
2244 2s. Racoon-dog 10 15
2245 3s. Mouflon (vert) 15 15
2246 12s. Fallow deer (vert) . . . 40 35
2247 18s. European bison . . . . 2·50 1·40
2248 40s. Elk . . . . 2·00 1·60

696 Turnovo

698 Congress Emblem

697 Insurgents on the March (Boris Angelushev)

1973. Air. Tourism. Views of Bulgarian Towns and Cities. Multicoloured.
2249 2s. Type **696** 10 15
2250 13s. Rusalka 30 15
2251 20s. Plovdiv . . . . 2·10 1·90
2252 28s. Sofia 75 65

1973. 50th Anniv of September Uprising.
2253 **697** 2s. multicoloured 10 15
2254 – 5s. violet, pink & red . . 75 45
2255 – 13s. multicoloured . . . 15 25
2256 – 18s. olive, cream & red 45 65
DESIGNS—HORIZ: 5s. "Armed Train" (Boris Angelushev). VERT: 13s. Patriotic poster by N. Mirchev. HORIZ: 18s. Georgi Dimitrov and Vasil Kolarov.

1973. 8th World Trade Union Congress, Varna.
2257 **698** 2s. multicoloured 15 15

699 "Sun" Emblem and Olympic Rings

700 "Prince Kaloyan"

1973. Olympic Congress, Varna. Multicoloured.
2258 13s. Type **699** 90 55
2259 28s. Lion Emblem of Bulgarian Olympic Committee (vert) . . . . 1·60 90
MS2260 61 × 77 mm. 80s. Footballers (40 × 25 mm) . . . 3·25 2·75

1973. Fresco Portraits, Boyana Church. Mult.
2261 1s. Type **700** 10 15
2262 2s. "Desislava" 20 15
2263 3s. "Saint" 15 15
2264 5s. "St. Eustratius" 15 15
2265 10s. "Tsar Constantine-Asen" 40 20

2266 13s. "Deacon Laurentius" 55 30
2267 18s. "Virgin Mary" 90 50
2268 20s. "St. Ephraim" 1·00 55
2269 28s. "Jesus Christ" 3·25 1·10
MS2270 56 × 76 mm. 80s. "Scribes". Imperf 6·50 6·50

701 Smirnenski and Cavalry Charge

1973. 75th Birth Anniv of Khristo Smirnenski (poet and revolutionary).
2271 **701** 1s. blue, red and gold 15 10
2272 2s. blue, red and gold 15 10

702 Human Rights Emblem

704 "Finn" One-man Dinghy

703 Tsar Todor Svetoslav meeting the Byzantine Embassy, 1307

1973. 25th Anniv of Declaration of Human Rights.
2273 **702** 13s. gold, red and blue 25 40

1973. Bulgarian History. Multicoloured.
2274 1s. Type **703** 20 15
2275 2s. Tsar Mikhail Shishman in battle against Byzantines, 1328 20 15
2276 3s. Battle of Rosokastro, 1332 and Tsar Ivan Aleksandur 20 15
2277 4s. Defence of Turnovo, 1393 and Patriarch Evtimii 20 15
2278 5s. Tsar Ivan Shisman's attack on the Turks 20 15
2279 13s. Momchil attacks Turkish ships at Umur, 1344 30 25
2280 18s. Meeting of Tsar Ivan Sratsimir and Crusaders, 1396 50 25
2281 28s. Embassy of Empress Anne of Savoy meets Boyars Balik, Teodor and Dobrotitsa 1·40 90

1973. Sailing. Various Yachts. Multicoloured.
2282 1s. Type **704** 10 15
2283 2s. "Flying Dutchman" two-man dinghy 10 15
2284 3s. "Soling" yacht 10 15
2285 13s. "Tempest" dinghy 45 25
2286 20s. "470" two-man dinghy 60 55
2287 40s. "Tornado" catamaran 2·40 2·00

705 "Balchik" (Bercho Obreshkov)

1973. 25th Anniv of National Art Gallery, Sofia and 150th Birth Anniv of Stanislav Dospevski (painter). Multicoloured.
2288 1s. Type **705** 20 20
2289 2s. "Mother and Child" (Stryan Venev) 20 20
2290 3s. "Rest" (Tsenko Boyadzhiev) 20 20
2291 13s. "Vase with Flowers" (Siruk Skitnik) (vert) 35 30
2292 18s. "Mary Kuneva" (Iliya Petrov) (vert) 55 20
2293 40s. "Winter in Plovdiv" (Zlatyn Boyadzhiev) (vert) 1·90 1·90
MS2294 100 × 95 mm. 50s. "Domnika Lambreva" (S. Dospevski) (vert); 50s. "Self-portrait" (S. Dospevski) (vert) 3·50 3·00

706 Footballers and Emblem

1973. World Cup Football Championship, Munich (1974). Sheet 62 × 94 mm.
MS2295 **706** 28s. multicoloured (sold at 1l.) 4·50 4·50

707 Old Testament Scene (Wood-carving)

1974. Wood-Carvings from Rozhen Monastery.
2296 **707** 1s. dk brn, cream & brn 15 15
2297 – 2s. dk brn, cream & brn 15 15
2298 – 3s. dk brn, cream & brn 15 15
2299 – 5s. olive, cream & green 15 15
2300 – 8s. olive, cream & green 15 15
2301 – 13s. brown, cream and chestnut 35 30
2302 – 28s. brown, cream and chestnut 55 30
DESIGNS: Nos. 2296/8, "Passover Table"; 2299/2300, "Abraham and the Angel"; 2301/2, "The Expulsion from Eden".
Nos. 2296/8, 2299/300 and 2301/2 form three composite designs.

708 "Lenin" (N. Mirchev)

1974. 50th Death Anniv of Lenin. Mult.
2303 2s. Type **708** 15 15
2304 18s. "Lenin with Workers" (W. A. Serov) 30 30

709 "Blagoev addressing Meeting" (G. Kovachev)

1974. 50th Death Anniv of D. Blagoev (founder of Bulgarian Social Democratic Party).
2305 **709** 2s. multicoloured 15 15

710 Sheep

1974. Domestic Animals.
2306 **710** 1s. brown, buff & green 15 15
2307 – 2s. purple, violet & red 15 15
2308 – 3s. brown, pink & green 15 15
2309 – 5s. brown, buff & blue 15 15
2310 – 13s. black, blue and brown 20 30
2311 – 20s. brown, pink & blue 1·50 75
DESIGNS: 2s. Goat; 3s. Pig; 5s. Cow; 13s. Buffalo; 20s. Horse.

711 Social Economic Integration Emblem

1974. 25th Anniv of Council for Mutual Economic Aid.
2312 **711** 13s. multicoloured 30 30

712 Footballers

1974. World Cup Football Championship.
2313 **712** 1s. multicoloured 10 15
2314 – 2s. multicoloured 10 15
2315 – 3s. multicoloured 10 15
2316 – 13s. multicoloured 20 15
2317 – 28s. multicoloured 40 20
2318 – 40s. multicoloured 1·60 1·20
MS2319 66 × 78 mm. 1l. multicoloured (55 × 30 mm) 3·00 3·00
DESIGNS: Nos. 2314/19, Various designs similar to Type **712**.

713 Folk-singers

1974. Amateur Arts and Sports Festival. Multicoloured.
2320 1s. Type **713** 10 15
2321 2s. Folk-dancers 10 15
2322 3s. Piper and drummer 10 15
2323 5s. Wrestling 10 15
2324 13s. Athletics 80 75
2325 18s. Gymnastics 1·00 30

714 "Cosmic Research" (Penko Barnbov)

1974. "Mladost '74" Youth Stamp Exhibition, Sofia. Multicoloured.
2326 1s. Type **714** 10 10
2327 2s. "Salt Production" (Mariana Bliznakaa) 15 10
2328 3s. "Fire-dancer" (Detelina Lalova) 65 10
2329 28s. "Friendship Train" (Vanya Boyanova) 1·90 1·20
MS2330 70 × 70 mm. 60s. "Spring" (Vladimir Kunchev) (40 × 40 mm) 2·75 2·75

715 Motor-cars

1974. World Automobile Federation's Spring Congress, Sofia.
2331 **715** 13s. multicoloured 30 30

716 Period Architecture

1974. UNESCO Executive Council's 94th Session, Varna.
2332 **716** 18s. multicoloured 30 30

717 Chinese Aster

1974. Bulgarian Flowers. Multicoloured.
2333 1s. Type **717** 10 20
2334 2s. Mallow 10 20
2335 3s. Columbine 10 20
2336 18s. Tulip 40 25
2337 20s. Marigold 50 30
2338 28s. Pansy 1·60 1·10
MS2339 80 × 60 mm. 80s. Gaillarde (44 × 33 mm) 2·00 2·00

718 19th Century Post-boy

1974. Centenary of UPU.
2340 **718** 2s. violet & blk on orge 10 15
2341 – 18s. green & blk on orge 30 20
MS2342 80 × 58 mm. 28s. blue and orange (sold at 80st.) 2·20 2·00
DESIGN: 18s. First Bulgarian mail-coach; 20s. UPU emblem.

719 Young Pioneer and Komsomol Girl

720 Communist Soldiers with Flag

1974. 30th Anniv of Dimitrov's Septembrist Pioneers Organization. Multicoloured.
2343 1s. Type **719** 10 10
2344 2s. Pioneer with doves 10 10
MS2345 60 × 84 mm. 60s. Emblem with portrait of Dimitrov (34 × 44 mm) 1·40 1·40

1974. 30th Anniv of Fatherland Front Government. Multicoloured.
2346 1s. Type **720** 15 15
2347 2s. "Soviet Liberators" 15 15
2348 5s. "Industrialisation" 15 15
2349 13s. "Modern Agriculture" 15 15
2350 18s. "Science and Technology" 40 35

721 Stockholm and Emblems

1974. "Stockholm '74" International Stamp Exhibition. Sheet 65 × 72 mm.
MS2351 **721** 40s. blue, green and yellow 5·50 5·50

722 Gymnast on Beam

723 Doves on Script

1974. 18th World Gymnastic Championships, Varna. Multicoloured.
2352 2s. Type **722** 10 10
2353 13s. Gymnast on horse . . . 30 20

1974. European Security and Co-operation Conference. Sheet 97 × 117 mm containing T **723** and similar vert designs.
MS2354 13s. yellow, blue and chestnut (T **723**); 13s. blue, mauve and chestnut (Map of Europe and script); 13s. green, blue and chestnut (Leaves on script); 13s. multicoloured (Commemorative text) (sold at 60s.) . . . . . . 3·00 3·00

724 Envelope with Arrow pointing to Postal Code

1974. Introduction of Postal Coding System (1 January 1975).
2355 **724** 2s. green, orange & blk 15 15

725 "Sourovachka" (twig decorated with coloured ribbons)

1974. New Year.
2356 **725** 2s. multicoloured 15 15

726 Icon of St. Theodor Stratilat **727** Apricot

1974. Bulgarian History.
2357 **726** 1s. multicoloured 15 15
2358 – 2s. grey, mauve & black 15 15
2359 – 3s. grey, blue and black 15 15
2360 – 5s. grey, lilac and black 15 15
2361 – 8s. black, buff and brown 15 15
2362 – 13s. grey, green & black 20 15
2363 – 18s. black, gold & red 25 25
2364 – 28s. grey, blue & black 1·00 85
DESIGNS: 2s. Bronze medallion; 3s. Carved capital; 5s. Silver bowl of Sivin Jupan; 8s. Clay goblet; 13s. Lioness (torso); 18s. Gold tray; 28s. Double-headed eagle.

1975. Fruit-tree Blossoms. Multicoloured.
2365 1s. Type **727** 15 15
2366 2s. Apple 15 15
2367 3s. Cherry 15 15
2368 19s. Pear 40 25
2369 28s. Peach 75 40

728 Peasant with Flag

1975. 75th Anniv of Bulgarian People's Agrarian Union. Sheet 104 × 95 mm containing T **728** and similar vert designs.
MS2370 2s. brown, orange and green; 5s. brown, orange and green; 13s. sepia, orange and green; 18s. chestnut, orange and green . . . . 1·00 1·00
DESIGNS: 5s. Rebels keeping watch during 1923 September uprising; 13s. Dancing; 18s. Woman harvesting fruit.

729 Spanish 6c. Stamp of 1850 and "Espana" Emblem

1975. "Espana 1975" International Stamp Exhibition, Madrid. Sheet 68 × 100 mm.
MS2371 **729** 40s. multicoloured 5·25 4·25

730 Star and Arrow **731** "Weights and Measures"

1975. 30th Anniv of "Victory in Europe" Day.
2372 **730** 2s. red, black & brown 15 15
2373 – 13s. black, brown & bl 25 20
DESIGNS: 13s. Peace dove and broken sword.

1975. Centenary of Metre Convention.
2374 **731** 13s. violet, black & silver 15 15

732 Tree and open Book

1975. 50th Anniv of Forestry School.
2375 **732** 2s. multicoloured 15 15

733 Michelangelo **734** Festival Emblem

1975. 500th Birth Anniv of Michelangelo.
2376 **733** 2s. purple and blue . . 15 15
2377 – 13s. violet and purple . . 20 20
2378 – 18s. brown and green . . 30 30
MS2379 70 × 84 mm. **733** 2s. green and red (sold at 60s.) . . . . . 1·40 1·40
DESIGNS—HORIZ: Sculptures from Giuliano de Medici's tomb: 13s. "Night"; 18s. "Day".

1975. Festival of Humour and Satire, Gabrovo.
2380 **734** 2s. multicoloured 15 15

735 Women's Head and Emblem

1975. International Women's Year.
2381 **735** 13s. multicoloured . . . 15 15

736 Vasil and Sava Kokareshkov

1975. "Young Martyrs to Fascism".
2382 **736** 1s. black, green & gold 10 10
2383 – 2s. black, mauve & gold 10 10
2384 – 5s. black, red and gold 10 10
2385 – 13s. black, blue & gold 15 20
DESIGNS—HORIZ: 2s. Mitko Palauzov and Ivan Vasilev; 5s. Nikola Nakev and Stefcho Kraichev; 13s. Ivanka Pashkolouva and Detelina Mincheva.

737 "Mother feeding Child" (Jean Millet) **738** Gabrovo Costume

1975. World Graphics Exhibition, Sofia. Celebrated Drawings and Engravings. Multicoloured.
2386 1s. Type **737** 15 15
2387 2s. "Mourning a Dead Daughter" (Goya) 15 15
2388 3s. "The Reunion" (Iliya Beshkov) 15 15
2389 13s. "Seated Nude" (Auguste Renoir) 15 15
2390 20s. "Man in a Fur Hat" (Rembrandt) 15 25
2391 40s. "The Dream" (Horore Daumier) (horiz) . . . . 1·00 55
MS2392 80 × 95 mm. 1l. "Temptation" (Albrecht Durer) (37 × 53 mm) . . . . 2·00 2·00

1975. Women's Regional Costumes. Mult.
2393 2s. Type **738** 20 15
2394 3s. Trun costume 20 15
2395 5s. Vidin costume 20 15
2396 13s. Goce Delcev costume 25 25
2397 18s. Ruse costume 70 35

739 "Bird" (manuscript illumination) **740** Ivan Vasov

1975. Original Bulgarian Manuscripts. Mult.
2398 1s. Type **739** 15 15
2399 2s. "Head" 15 15
2400 3s. Abstract design 15 15
2401 8s. "Pointing finger" 15 15
2402 13s. "Imaginary creature" 15 25
2403 18s. Abstract design 65 35

1975. 125th Anniv of Ivan Vasov (writer). Multicoloured.
2404 2s. Type **740** 15 10
2405 13s. Vasov seated 15 10

741 "Soyuz" and Aleksei Leonov

1975. "Apollo"–"Soyuz" Space Link.
2406 **741** 13s. multicoloured . . . 25 15
2407 – 18s. multicoloured . . . 40 15
2408 – 28s. multicoloured . . . 1·20 35
MS2409 76 × 84 mm. 1l. blue, grey and red . . . . 2·40 2·00
DESIGNS: 18s. "Apollo" and Thomas Stafford; 28s. The Link-up; 1l. "Apollo" and "Soyuz" after docking.

742 Ryukyu Sailing Boat, Map and Emblems

1975. International Exposition, Okinawa.
2410 **742** 13s. multicoloured . . . 25 15

743 St. Cyril and St. Methodius **744** Footballer

1975. "Balkanphila V" Stamp Exhibition, Sofia.
2411 **743** 2s. brown, lt brn & red 15 10
2412 – 13s. brown, lt brn & grn 15 10
MS2413 90 × 86 mm. 50s. sepia, brown and orange . . . . . . 1·20 1·20
DESIGNS—VERT: 13s. St. Constantine and St. Helene. HORIZ: 50s. Sophia Church, Sofia (53 × 43 mm.).

1975. 8th Inter-Toto (Football Pools) Congress, Varna.
2414 **744** 2s. multicoloured 15 15

745 Deaths-head Hawk Moth

1975. Hawk Moths. Multicoloured.
2415 1s. Type **745** 10 15
2416 2s. Oleander hawk moth . . 10 15
2417 3s. Eyed hawk moth 15 15
2418 10s. Mediterranean hawk moth 20 20
2419 13s. Elephant hawk moth 40 25
2420 18s. Broad-bordered bee hawk moth 90 40

746 UN Emblem **747** Map of Europe on Peace Dove

1975. 30th Anniv of UNO.
2421 **746** 13s. red, brown & black 25 15

1975. European Security and Co-operation Conference, Helsinki.
2422 **747** 18s. lilac, blue & yellow 50 45

748 D. Khristov

1975. Birth Cent of Dobri Khristov (composer).
2423 **748** 5s. brown, yellow & grn 15 10

749 Constantine's Rebellion against the Turks

1975. Bulgarian History. Multicoloured.
2424 1s. Type **749** 10 15
2425 2s. Vladislav III's campaign 10 15
2426 3s. Battle of Turnovo . . . 10 15
2427 10s. Battle of Chiprovtsi . . 10 15
2428 13s. 17 th-century partisans 30 20
2429 18s. Return of banished peasants 50 30

750 "First Aid"

1975. 90th Anniv of Bulgarian Red Cross.
2430 **750** 2s. brown, black and red . . . 10 10
2431 – 13s. green, black and red . . . 25 10
DESIGN: 13s. "Peace and international Co-operation".

751 Ethnographical Museum, Plovdiv

1975. European Architectural Heritage Year.
2432 **751** 80s. brown, yellow & grn . . 1·20 1·40

752 Christmas Lanterns

1975. Christmas and New Year. Multicoloured.
2433 2s. Type **752** 15 10
2434 13s. Stylized peace dove . . 15 20

753 Egyptian Galley

1975. Historic Ships (1st series). Multicoloured.
2435 1s. Type **753** 10 10
2436 2s. Phoenician galley . . . 10 10
2437 3s. Greek trireme 10 10
2438 5s. Roman galley 10 10
2439 13s. "Mora" (Norman ship) . 40 25
2440 18s. Venetian galley 70 30
See also Nos. 2597/2602, 2864/9, 3286/91 and 3372/7.

754 Modern Articulated Tramcar

1976. 75th Anniv of Sofia Tramways. Mult.
2441 2s. Type **754** 15 10
2442 13s. Early 20th-century tramcar 60 30

755 Skiing

1976. Winter Olympic Games, Innsbruck. Mult.
2443 1s. Type **755** 10 15
2444 2s. Cross-country skiing (vert) 10 15
2445 2s. Ski jumping 10 15
2446 13s. Biathlon (vert) 20 25
2447 18s. Ice hockey (vert) . . . 40 30
2448 18s. Speed skating (vert) . . 95 40
MS2449 70 × 80 mm. 80s. Ice skating (pairs) (30 × 55 mm) . . . . . 2·00 2·00

756 Stylized Bird

1976. 11th Bulgarian Communists Party Congress. Multicoloured.
2450 2s. Type **756** 10 10
2451 5s. "1956–1976, Fulfilment of the Five Year Plans" . . 10 10
2452 13s. Hammer and Sickle . . 10 10
MS2453 55 × 65 mm. 50s. Georgi Dimitrov (Prime Minister and Party secretary-general, 1945–49) (33 × 43 mm) . . . . 1·10 1·00

757 Alexander Graham Bell and early Telephone

1976. Telephone Centenary.
2454 **757** 18s. lt brown, brn & pur . . 30 25

758 Mute Swan

1976. Waterfowl. Multicoloured.
2455 1s. Type **758** 15 15
2456 2s. Ruddy shelduck 20 15
2457 3s. Common shelduck . . . 30 20
2458 5s. Garganey 45 20
2459 13s. Mallard 90 50
2460 18s. Red-crested pochard . . 1·30 1·20

759 Guerillas' Briefing

1976. Cent of April Uprising (1st issue). Mult.
2461 1s. Type **759** 10 10
2462 2s. Peasants' briefing . . . 10 10
2463 5s. Krishina, horse and guard 10 10
2464 13s. Rebels with cannon . . 20 20
See also Nos. 2529/33.

760 Kozlodui Atomic Energy Centre

1976. Modern Industrial Installations.
2465 **760** 5s. green 20 15
2466 – 8s. red 20 15
2467 – 10s. green 20 15
2468 – 13s. violet 20 20
2469 – 20s. green 35 20
DESIGNS: 8s. Bobaudol plant; 10s. Sviloza chemical works; 13s. Devaya chemical works; 20s. Sestvitro dam.

761 Guard with Patrol-dog

1976. 30th Anniv of Frontier Guards. Mult.
2470 2s. Type **761** 15 15
2471 13s. Mounted guards . . . 15 20

762 Worker with Spade

763 Botev

1976. 30th Anniv of Youth Brigades Movement.
2472 **762** 2s. multicoloured 15 15

1976. Death Cent of Khristo Botev (poet).
2473 **763** 13s. green and brown . . 25 25

764 "Martyrs of First Congress" (relief)

765 Dimitur Blagoev

1976. 85th Anniv of 1st Bulgarian Social Democratic Party Congress, Buzludzha. Multicoloured.
2474 2s. Type **764** 10 10
2475 5s. Modern memorial, Buzludzha Peak 10 10

1976. 120th Birth Anniv of Dimitur Blagoev (founder of Bulgarian Social Democratic Party).
2476 **765** 13s. black, red and gold . . 30 15

766 "Thematic Stamps"

1976. 12th Bulgarian Philatelic Federation Congress. Sheet 73 × 103 mm.
MS2477 **766** 50s. multicoloured . . 1·70 1·70

767 Children Playing

1976. Child Welfare.
2478 **767** 1s. multicoloured 15 15
2479 – 2s. multicoloured 15 15
2480 – 5s. multicoloured 15 15
2481 – 23s. multicoloured 30 30
DESIGNS: 2s. Girls with pram and boy on rocking horse; 5s. Playing ball; 23s. Dancing.

768 Wrestling

1976. Olympic Games, Montreal. Multicoloured.
2482 1s. Type **768** 10 15
2483 2s. Boxing (vert) 10 15
2484 3s. Weight-lifting (vert) . . 10 15
2485 13s. Canoeing (vert) 25 15
2486 18s. Gymnastics (vert) . . . 35 25
2487 28s. Diving (vert) 55 30
2488 40s. Athletics (vert) 75 45
MS2489 70 × 80 mm. 1l. Weightlifting (vert) . . . . . . 2·10 2·10

769 Belt Buckle, Vidin

771 Weightlifting

770 "Partisans at Night" (Petrov)

1976. Thracian Art (8th–4th Centuries B.C.). Mult.
2490 1s. Type **769** 20 15
2491 2s. Brooch, Durzhanitsa . . 20 15
2492 3s. Mirror handle, Chukarka 20 15
2493 5s. Helmet cheek guard, Gurlo 20 15
2494 13s. Gold decoration, Orizovo 20 15
2495 18s. Decorated horse-harness, Brezovo 25 15
2496 20s. Greave, Mogilanska Mogila 35 15
2497 28s. Pendant, Bukovtsi . . . 45 30

1976. Paintings by Iliya Petrov and Tsanko Lavrenov from the National Gallery. Multicoloured.
2498 2s. Type **770** 15 15
2499 5s. "Kurshum-Khan" (Lavrenov) 15 15
2500 13s. "Seated Woman" (Petrov) 25 15
2501 18s. "Boy seated in chair" (Petrov) (vert) 40 20
2502 28s. "Old Plovdiv" (Lavrenov) (vert) 65 35
MS2503 60 × 82 mm. 80s. "Self-portrait" (Petrov) (vert) . . . . . 1·80 1·80

1976. Gold Medal Winners, Montreal Olympic Games. Sheet 98 × 116 mm containing vert designs as T **771**, each with medal in red and gold.
MS2504 25s. yellow (T **771**); 25s. blue (rowing); 25s. green (running); 25s. red (wrestling) . . 2·00 2·00

772 Fish on line

1976. World Sports Fishing Congress, Varna.
2505 **772** 5s. multicoloured 15 15

773 "The Pianist"

774 St. Theodor

1976. 75th Birth Anniv of Alex Jhendov (caricaturist).
2506 **773** 2s. dp grn, cream & grn . . 10 10
2507 – 5s. dp violet, vio & lilac . . 10 10
2508 – 13s. black, pink & red . . 20 10
DESIGNS: 5s. "Trick or Treat"; 13s. "The Leader".

1976. Zemen Monastery. Frescoes. Multicoloured.
2509 2s. Type **774** 15 15
2510 3s. St. Paul and Apostle . . 15 15
2511 5s. St. Joachim 15 15
2512 13s. Prophet Melchisadek . . 15 15
2513 19s. St. Porphyrus 25 25
2514 28s. Queen Doya 40 35
MS2515 60 × 76 mm. 1l. Holy Communion . . . . 1·60 1·60

775 Legal Document

776 Horse Chestnut

1976. 25th Anniv of State Archives.
2516 **775** 5s. multicoloured 15 15

1976. Plants. Multicoloured.
2517 1s. Type **776** 10 15
2518 2s. Shrubby cinquefoil . . . 10 15
2519 5s. Holly 15 15
2520 8s. Yew 15 15
2521 13s. "Daphne pontica" . . . 25 25
2522 23s. Judas tree 65 40

777 Cloud over Sun

1976. Protection of the Environment. Mult.
2523 2s. Cloud over tree 10 15
2524 18s. Type **777** 20 20

778 Dimitur Polyanov

1976. Birth Cent of Dimitur Polyanov (poet).
2525 **778** 2s. lilac and orange . . . 15 15

779 Congress Emblem

1976. 33rd Bulgarian People's Agrarian Union Congress. Multicoloured.
2526 2s. Type **779** 15 10
2527 13s. Flags 15 20

780 Warrior with Horses (vase painting)

1976. 30th Anniv of United Nations Educational Scientific and Cultural Organization. Sheet 71 × 81 mm.
MS2528 **780** 50s. multicoloured 1·40 1·40

781 "Khristo Botev" (Zlatyu Boyadzhiev)

1976. Centenary of April Uprising (2nd issue). Multicoloured.
2529 1s. Type **781** 15 15
2530 2s. "Partisan carrying Cherrywood Cannon" (Iliya Petrov) 15 15
2531 3s. "Necklace of Immortality" (Dechko Uzunov) 15 15
2532 13s. "April 1876" (Georgi Popov) 15 15
2533 18s. "Partisans" (Stoyan Venev) 35 25
MS2534 45 × 82 mm. 60s. "The Oath" (Svetlin Rusev) . . . . 1·10 1·10

782 Tobacco Workers

1976. 70th Birth Anniv of Veselin Staikov (artist). Multicoloured.
2535 1s. Type **782** 10 10
2536 2s. "Melnik" 10 10
2537 13s. "Boat Builders" 20 20

783 "Snowflake"

1976. New Year.
2538 **783** 2s. multicoloured 15 10

784 Zakhari Stojanov

1976. 125th Birth Anniv of Zakhari Stojanov (writer).
2539 **784** 2s. brown, red and gold 15 10

785 Bronze Coin of Septimus Severus

1977. Roman Coins struck in Serdica. Mult.
2540 1s. Type **785** 15 15
2541 2s. Bronze coin of Caracalla 15 15
2542 13s. Bronze coin of Caracalla (diff.) 15 15
2543 18s. Bronze coin of Caracalla (diff.) 20 25
2544 23s. Copper coin of Diocletian 35 35

786 Championships Emblem

787 Congress Emblem

1977. World Ski-orienteering Championships.
2545 **786** 13s. blue, red & ultram 25 10

1977. 5th Congress of Bulgarian Tourist Associations.
2546 **787** 2s. multicoloured 15 10

788 "Symphyandra wanneri"

789 V. Kolarov

1977. Mountain Flowers. Multicoloured.
2547 1s. Type **788** 15 15
2548 2s. "Petcovia orphanidea" 15 15
2549 3s. "Campanula lanatre" . . 15 15
2550 13s. "Campanula scutellata" 20 20
2551 43s. Nettle-leaved bellflower 90 50

1977. Birth Centenary of Vasil Kolarov (Prime Minister 1949–50).
2552 **789** 2s. grey, black & blue . . 15 10

790 Congress Emblem

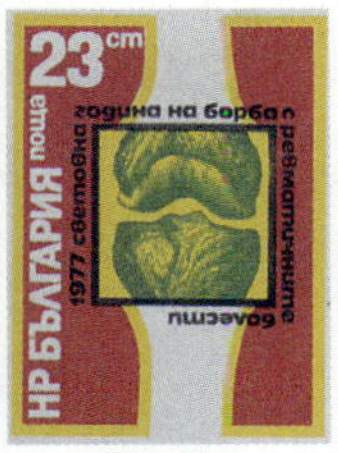

791 Joint

1977. 8th Bulgarian Trade Unions Congress.
2553 **790** 2s. multicoloured 15 10

1977. World Rheumatism Year.
2554 **791** 23s. multicoloured . . . 40 30

792 Wrestling

1977. World University Games, Sofia. Mult.
2555 2s. Type **792** 10 20
2556 13s. Running 20 20
2557 23s. Handball 45 30
2558 43s. Gymnastics 80 60

793 Ivan Vazov National Theatre

794 Congress Emblem

1977. Buildings in Sofia. Pale brown backgrounds.
2559 **793** 12s. red 15 20
2560 – 13s. brown 15 20
2561 – 23s. blue 20 25
2562 – 30s. green 25 25
2563 – 80s. violet 65 65
2564 – 1l. brown . . . . 1·10 80
DESIGNS: 13s. Party Building; 23s. People's Army Building; 30s. Clement of Ohrid University; 80s. National Art Gallery; 1l. National Assembly Building.

1977. 13th Dimitrov Communist Youth League Congress.
2565 **794** 2s. red, green and gold 15 10

795 "St. Nicholas" Nesebur

1977. Bulgarian Icons. Multicoloured.
2566 1s. Type **795** 10 15
2567 2s. "Old Testament Trinity", Sofia 10 15
2568 3s. "The Royal Gates", Veliko Turnovo 10 15
2569 5s. "Deisis", Nesebur . . . 10 15
2570 13s. "St. Nicholas", Elena 10 15
2571 23s. "The Presentation of the Blessed Virgin", Rila Monastery 35 20
2572 35s. "The Virgin Mary with Infant", Varna 45 35
2573 40s. "St. Demetrius on Horseback", Provadya . . 60 45
MS2574 100 × 99 mm. 1l. "The Twelve Festival Days", Rila Monastery. Imperf . . . . . 1·80 1·70

796 Wolf

1977. Wild Animals. Multicoloured.
2575 1s. Type **796** 10 15
2576 2s. Red fox 10 15
2577 10s. Weasel 20 15
2578 13s. Wild cat 40 25
2579 23s. Golden jackal 65 40

797 Congress Emblem

798 "Crafty Peter riding a Donkey" (drawing by Iliya Beshkov)

1977. 3rd Bulgarian Culture Congress.
2580 **797** 13s. multicoloured . . . 15 10

1977. 11th Festival of Humour and Satire, Gabrovo.
2581 **798** 2s. multicoloured 15 10

799 Congress Emblem

1977. 8th Congress of the Popular Front, Sofia.
2582 **799** 2s. multicoloured 15 10

800 Newspaper Masthead

1977. Centenary of Bulgarian Daily Press.
2583 **800** 2s. multicoloured 15 10

801 St. Cyril

1977. 1150th Birth Anniv of St. Cyril. Sheet 106 × 87 mm.
MS2584 **801** 1l. multicoloured . . 1·90 1·90

802 Conference Emblem

1977. International Writers Conference, Sofia.
2585 **802** 23s. blue, lt blue & grn 65 50

803 Map of Europe

1977. 21st Congress of European Organization for Quality Control, Varna.
2586 **803** 23s. multicoloured . . . 40 30

804 Basketball **805** Weightlifter

1977. Women's European Basketball Championships.
2587 **804** 23s. multicoloured . . . 55 30

1977. World Junior Weightlifting Championships.
2588 **805** 13s. multicoloured . . . 25 10

806 Georgi Dimitrov

1977. 95th Birth Anniv of Georgi Dimitrov (statesman).
2589 **806** 13s. brown and red . . . 15 20

807 Tail Section of Tupolev Tu-154

1977. Air. 30th Anniv of Bulgarian Airline "Balkanair".
2590 **807** 35s. multicoloured . . . 80 50

808 Games Emblem

1977. World University Games, Sofia (2nd issue). Sheet 84 × 76 mm.
MS2591 **808** 1l. multicoloured . . 1·60 1·60

809 T.V. Towers, Berlin and Sofia **810** Elin Pelin alias Dimitur Stoyanov (writer)

1977. "Sozphilex 77" Stamp Exhibition, East Berlin.
2592 **809** 25s. blue and deep blue 50 30

1977. Writers and Painters.
2593 **810** 2s. brown and gold . . . 20 20
2594 – 5s. olive and gold . . . 20 20
2595 – 13s. red and gold . . . 20 25
2596 – 23s. blue and gold . . . 45 30
DESIGNS: 5s. Peyu Yavorov (poet); 13s. Boris Angelushev (painter and illustrator); 23s. Iseno Todorov (painter).

1977. Historic Ships (2nd series). As T **753**. Multicoloured.
2597 1s. Hansa Kogge 10 15
2598 2s. "Santa Maria" 10 15
2599 3s. Drake's "Golden Hind" 10 15
2600 12s. Carrack "Santa Catherina" 25 15
2601 13s. "La Couronne" (French galleon) 25 15
2602 43s. Mediterranean galley 95 40

811 Women Canoeists

1977. World Canoe Championships.
2603 **811** 2s. blue and yellow . . . 15 15
2604 – 23s. blue and turquoise 35 20
DESIGN: 23s. Men canoeists.

812 Balloon over Plovdiv **813** Presidents Zhivkov and Brezhnev

1977. Air. 85th Anniv "Panair". International Aviation Exhibition, Plovdiv.
2605 **812** 25s. orange, yell & brn 55 30

1977. Soviet–Bulgarian Friendship.
2606 **813** 18s. brown, red & gold 30 20

814 Conference Building

1977. 64th International Parliamentary Conference, Sofia.
2607 **814** 23s. green, pink and red 40 30

815 Newspaper Mastheads **816** "The Union of Earth and Water"

1977. 50th Anniv of Official Newspaper "Rabotnichesko Delo" (Workers' Press).
2608 **815** 2s. red, green and grey 15 10

1977. 400th Birth Anniv of Rubens. Mult.
2609 13s. Type **816** 25 15
2610 23s. "Venus and Adonis" (detail) 45 30
2611 40s. "Amorous Shepherd" (detail) 80 55
MS2612 71 × 87 mm. 1l. "Portrait of a Chambermaid" . . . . . 2·20 2·00

817 Cossack with Bulgarian Child (Angelushev) **818** Albena, Black Sea

1977. Centenary of Liberation from Turkey. (1978). Posters.
2613 **817** 2s. multicoloured 25 15
2614 – 13s. green, blue & red 25 15
2615 – 23s. blue, red & green 50 30
2616 – 25s. multicoloured . . . 50 30
DESIGNS: 13s. Bugler (Cheklarov); 23s. Mars (god of war) and Russian soldiers (Petrov); 25s. Flag of Russian Imperial Army.

1977. Tourism.
2617 **818** 35s. blue, turq & brn . . 65 40
2618 – 43s. yellow, grn & blue 65 40
DESIGN: 43s. Rila Monastery.

819 Dr. Nikolai Pirogov (Russian surgeon) **821** Soviet Emblems and Decree

820 Space walking

1977. Cent of Dr. Pirogov's Visit to Bulgaria.
2619 **819** 13s. brown, buff & grn 25 25

1977. Air. 20th Anniv of First Artificial Satellite. Multicoloured.
2620 12s. Type **820** 25 20
2621 25s. Space probe over Mars 50 25
2622 35s. Space probe "Venus-4" over Venus 70 35

1977. 60th Anniv of Russian Revolution.
2623 **821** 2s. red, black & stone . . 20 15
2624 – 13s. red and purple . . . 20 15
2625 – 23s. red and violet . . . 30 20
DESIGNS: 13s. Lenin; 23s. "1977" as flame.

822 Diesel Train on Bridge

1977. 50th Anniv of Transport, Bridges and Highways Organization.
2626 **822** 13s. yellow, green & olive 50 30

1977. 150th Birth Anniv of Petko Ratshev Slaveikov (poet). As T **810**.
2627 8s. brown and gold 15 10

824 Decorative Initials of New Year Greeting

1977. New Year. Multicoloured.
2628 2s. Type **824** 15 10
2629 13s. "Fireworks" 15 10

825 Footballer

1978. World Cup Football Championship, Argentina. Multicoloured.
2630 13s. Type **825** 30 30
2631 23s. Shooting the ball . . . 50 55
MS2632 77 × 61 mm. 50s. Tackle for ball . . . . 1·40 1·40

826 Baba Vida Fortress, Vidin

1977. Air. "The Danube – European River". Mult.
2633 25s. Type **826** 30 40
2634 35s. Friendship Bridge . . . 95 1·00

827 Television Mast, Moscow **828** Shipka Monument

1978. 20th Anniv of Organization of Socialist Postal Administrations (O.S.S.).
2635 **827** 13s. multicoloured . . . 25 10

1978. Centenary of Liberation from Turkey (2nd issue). Sheet 55 × 73 mm.
MS2636 **828** 50s. multicoloured 80 90

829 Red Cross in Laurel Wreath

1978. Centenary of Bulgarian Red Cross.
2637 **829** 25s. red, brown & blue 55 30

830 "XXX" formed from Bulgarian and Russian National Colours

1978. 30th Anniv of Bulgarian–Soviet Friendship.
2638 **830** 2s. multicoloured 15 15

831 Leo Tolstoy (Russian writer) **832** Nikolai Roerich (artist)

1978. Famous Personalities.
2639 **831** 2s. green and yellow . . 25 15
2640 – 5s. brown and bistre . . 25 15
2641 – 13s. green and mauve . . 25 15
2642 – 23s. brown and grey . . 35 30
2643 – 25s. brown and green . . 35 30
2644 – 35s. violet and blue . . . 60 40

DESIGNS: 5s. Fyodor Dostoevsky (Russian writer); 13s. Ivan Turgenev (Russian writer); 23s. Vassily Vereshchagin (Russian artist); 25s. Giuseppe Garibaldi (Italian patriot); 35s. Victor Hugo (French writer).

1978. Nikolai Roerich Exhibition, Sofia.
2645 **832** 8s. brown, green & red 25 10

833 Bulgarian Flag and Red Star

1978. Communist Party National Conference, Sofia.
2646 **833** 2s. multicoloured 15 10

834 Goddess

835 "Spirit of Nature"

1978. "Philaserdica 79" International Stamp Exhibition (1st issue). Ancient Ceramics. Mult.
2647 2s. Type **834** 10 15
2648 5s. Mask with beard 10 15
2649 13s. Decorated vase 30 15
2650 23s. Vase with scallop design 50 35
2651 35s. Head of Silenus 65 50
2652 53s. Cockerel . . . . 1·40 75
See also Nos. 2674/9, 2714/18, 2721/5 and 2753/4.

1978. Birth Cent of Andrei Nikolov (sculptor).
2653 **835** 13s. blue, mauve & vio 15 10

836 Heart and Arrows

1978. World Hypertension Month.
2654 **836** 23s. red, orange & grey 40 30

837 "Kor Karoli" and Map of Route

1978. Georgi Georgiev's World Voyage.
2655 **837** 23s. blue, mauve & grn 80 50

838 Doves

1978. 11th World Youth and Students' Festival, Havana.
2656 **838** 13s. multicoloured . . . 15 10

839 "Portrait of a Young Man" (Durer)

840 "Fritillaria stribrnyi"

1978. Paintings. Multicoloured.
2657 13s. Type **839** 15 20
2658 23s. "Bathsheba at the Fountain" (Rubens) . . . 30 30
2659 25s. "Signor de Moret" (Hans Holbein the Younger) 30 30
2660 35s. "Self portrait with Saskia" (Rembrandt) . . . 45 30
2661 43s. "Lady in Mourning" (Tintoretto) 55 40
2662 60s. "Old Man with a Beard" (Rembrandt) . . . 65 55
2663 80s. "Man in Armour" (Van Dyck) 90 90

1978. Flowers. Multicoloured.
2664 1s. Type **840** 15 15
2665 2s. "Fritillaria drenovskyi" 15 15
2666 3s. "Lilium rhodopaeum" 15 15
2667 13s. "Tulipa urumoffii" . . 35 15
2668 23s. "Lilium jankae" . . . 55 30
2669 43s. "Tulipa rhodopaea" . . 95 60

841 Varna

1978. 63rd Esperanto Congress, Varna.
2670 **841** 13s. orange, red & green 30 30

842 Delcev

1978. 75th Death Anniv of Goce Delcev (Macedonian revolutionary).
2671 **842** 13s. multicoloured . . . 25 10

843 Freedom Fighters

1978. 75th Anniv of Ilinden-Preobrazhenie Rising.
2672 **843** 5s. black and red 15 10

844 "The Sleeping Venus"

1978. World Masters of Art. Sheet 71 × 71 mm. Imperf.
MS2673 **844** 1l. multicoloured . . 1·60 1·60

845 "Market" (Noiden Petkov)

1978. "Philaserdica 79" International Stamp Exhibition (2nd issue). Paintings of Sofia. Multicoloured.
2674 2s. Type **845** 10 20
2675 5s. "View of Sofia" (Euril Stoichev) 10 20
2676 13s. "View of Sofia" (Boris Ivanov) . . . . 1·20 40
2677 23s. "Tolbukhin Boulevard" (Nikola Tanev) 20 25
2678 35s. "National Theatre" (Nikola Petrov) 25 25
2679 53s. "Market" (Anton Mitov) 40 55
MS2679a 186 × 106 mm. Nos. 2674/9 4·75 4·75

846 Black Woodpecker

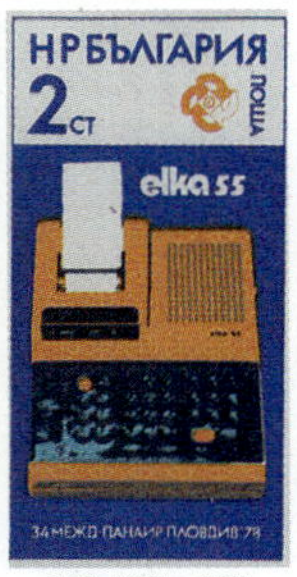

848 "Elka 55" Computer

847 Ivan Vazov National Theatre, Sofia

1978. Woodpeckers. Multicoloured.
2680 1s. Type **846** 10 15
2681 2s. Syrian woodpecker . . . 10 15
2682 3s. Three-toed woodpecker 20 15
2683 13s. Middle-spotted woodpecker 55 40
2684 23s. Lesser spotted woodpecker 95 70
2685 43s. Green woodpecker . . 1·80 1·50

1978. "Praga 78" and "Philaserdica 79" International Stamp Exhibitions. Sheet 153 × 110 mm containing T **847** and similar horiz designs. Multicoloured.
MS2686 (a) 40s. Type **847**; (b) 40s. Festival Hall, Sofia; (c) 40s. Charles Bridge, Prague; (d) 40s. Belvedere Palace, Prague . . . 2·20 2·20

1978. Plovdiv International Fair.
2687 **848** 2s. multicoloured 15 10

849 "September 1923" (Boris Angelushev)

1978. 55th Anniv of September Uprising.
2688 **849** 2s. red and brown . . . 15 10

850 Khristo Danov

1978. 150th Birth Anniv of Khristo Danov (first Bulgarian publisher).
2689 **850** 2s. orange and lake . . . 15 10

851 "The People of Vladaya" (Todor Panayotov)

1978. 60th Anniv of Vladaya Mutiny.
2690 **851** 2s. lilac, brown and red 15 10

852 Hands supporting Rainbow

854 Acrobats

853 Pipeline and Flags

1978. International Anti-apartheid Year.
2691 **852** 13s. multicoloured . . . 15 10

1978. Inauguration of Orenburg–U.S.S.R. Natural Gas Pipeline.
2692 **853** 13s. multicoloured . . . 15 10

1978. 3rd World Sports Acrobatics Championships, Sofia.
2693 **854** 13s. multicoloured . . . 15 10

855 Salvador Allende

856 Human Rights Emblem

1978. 70th Birth Anniv of Salvador Allende (Chilean politician).
2694 **855** 13s. brown and red . . . 15 10

1978. 30th Anniv of Declaration of Human Rights.
2695 **856** 23s. yellow, red & blue 55 30

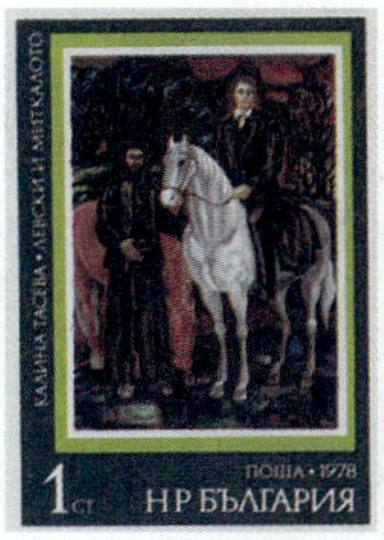

857 "Levski and Matei Mitkaloto" (Kalina Taseva)

858 Tourist Home, Plovdiv

1978. History of Bulgaria. Paintings. Multicoloured.
2696 1s. Type **857** 20 15
2697 2s. "Give Strength to my Arm" (Zlatyu Boyadzhiev) 20 15
2698 3s. "Rumena Voevoda" (Nikola Mirchev) (horiz) 20 15
2699 13s. "Kolya Ficheto" (Elza Goeva) 35 25
2700 23s. "A Family of the National Revival Period" (Naiden Petkov) 60 40

1978. European Architectural Heritage. Mult.
2701 43s. Type **858** . . . . . . 1·60 40
2702 43s. Tower of the Prince, Rila Monastery . . . . . 1·60 40

859 "Geroi Plevny" and Route Map

1978. Opening of the Varna–Ilichovsk Ferry Service.
2703 **859** 13s. blue, red & green 40 10

860 Mosaic Bird (Santa Sofia Church)

1978. "Bulgaria 78" National Stamp Exhibition, Sofia.
2704 **860** 5s. multicoloured 15 10

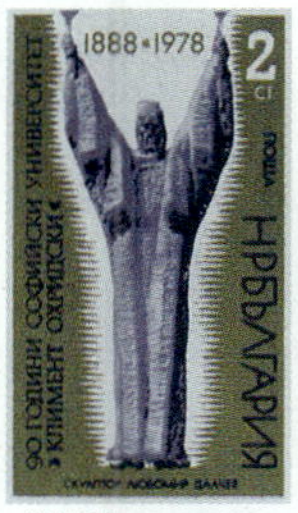

861 Monument to St. Clement of Ohrid (university patron) (Lyubemir Dalcher)

862 Nikola Karastoyanov

1978. 90th Anniv of Sofia University.
2705 **861** 2s. lilac, black & green . . . 15 10

1978. Birth Bicentenary of Nikola Karastoyanov (first Bulgarian printer).
2706 **862** 2s. brn, yell & chestnut . . . 15 10

863 Initial from 13th Century Bible Manuscript

1978. Centenary of Cyril and Methodius People's Library. Multicoloured.
2707 2s. Type **863** 20 15
2708 13s. Monk writing (from a 1567 manuscript) 20 15
2709 23s. Decorated page from 16th-century manuscript Bible 25 20
MS2710 63 × 94 mm. 80s. Seated saint with attendant (from 13th century manuscript Bible) . . . 1·30 1·30

864 Ballet Dancers

1978. 50th Anniv of Bulgarian Ballet.
2711 **864** 13s. green, mauve & lav . . . 25 25

865 Tree of Birds

1978. New Year. Multicoloured.
2712 2s. Type **865** 15 10
2713 13s. Posthorn 15 10

866 1961 Communist Congress Stamp

1978. "Philaserdica 79" International Stamp Exhibition (3rd issue) and Bulgarian Stamp Centenary (1st issue).
2714 – 2s. red and green 10 15
2715 – 13s. claret and blue . . . 20 15
2716 – 23s. green and mauve . . . 35 25
2717 **866** 35s. grey and blue . . . 50 30
2718 – 53s. green and red . . . 1·60 45
MS2719 62 × 87 mm. 1l. black, yellow and green . . . . . . 1·60 1·60
DESIGNS—HORIZ: 2s. 1901 "Cherrywood Cannon" stamp; 13s. 1946 "New Republic" stamp; 23s. 1957 Canonisation of St. Cyril and St. Methodius stamp; 1l. First Bulgarian stamp. VERT: 53s. 1962 Dimitrov stamp.
See also Nos. 2721/5 and **MS**2755.

867 Council Building, Moscow and Flags

1979. 30th Anniv of Council of Mutual Economic Aid.
2720 **867** 13s. multicoloured . . . 15 10

1979. "Philaserdica 79" Int Stamp Exn (4th issue) and Bulgarian Stamp Cent (2nd issue). As Nos. 2714/18 but inscr "1979" and colours changed.
2721 – 2s. red and blue 10 15
2722 – 13s. claret and green . . 20 15
2723 – 23s. green, yellow & red 35 25
2724 **866** 35s. grey and red 50 25
2725 – 53s. brown and violet . . 75 40

868 National Bank

868a

1979. Centenary of Bulgarian National Bank.
2726 **868** 2s. grey and yellow . . . 15 10

1979. Coil stamps.
2726a **868a** 2s. blue 10 10
2726b 5s. red 10 10
The 5s. is as T **868a** but different pattern.

869 Stamboliiski

870 Child's Head as Flower

1979. Birth Centenary of Alexandur Stamboliiski (Prime Minister 1919–23).
2727 **869** 2s. brown and yellow . . 15 10

1979. International Year of the Child.
2728 **870** 23s. multicoloured . . . 30 20

871 Profiles

872 "75" and Emblem

1979. 8th World Congress for the Deaf, Varna.
2729 **871** 13s. green and blue . . . 15 10

1979. 75th Anniv of Bulgarian Trade Unions.
2730 **872** 2s. green and orange . . 15 10

873 Soviet War Memorial

1979. Centenary of Sofia as Capital of Bulgaria. Sheet 106 × 105 mm containing T **873** and similar vert designs. Multicoloured.
MS2731 2s. Type **873**, 5s. Mother and child (sculpture); 13, 23, 25s. Bas-relief from monument to the Liberators of 1876 . . . . . . 1·60 1·60
The 13, 23 and 25s. values form a composite design.

874 Rocket

876 Running

875 Carrier Pigeon and Tupolev Tu-154 Jet

1979. Soviet–Bulgarian Space Flight. Multicoloured.
2732 2s. Georgi Ivanov (horiz) . . 20 15
2733 12s. Type **874** 20 15
2734 13s. Nikolai Rukavishnikov and Ivanov (horiz) . . . 20 15
2735 25s. Link-up with "Salyut" space station (horiz) . . . 45 30
2736 35s. Capsule descending by parachute 70 40
MS2737 67 × 86 mm. 1l. Globe and orbiting space craft (horiz) . . 2·00 2·00

1979. Centenary of Bulgarian Post and Telegraph Services. Multicoloured.
2738 2s. Type **875** 15 15
2739 5s. Old and new telephones 15 15
2740 13s. Morse key and teleprinter 15 15
2741 23s. Old radio transmitter and aerials 30 25
2742 35s. T.V. tower and satellite 50 35
MS2743 64 × 69 mm. 50s. Ground receiving station (38 × 28 mm) 1·60 1·60

1979. Olympic Games. Moscow (1980) (1st issue). Athletics. Multicoloured.
2744 2s. Type **876** 20 25
2745 13s. Pole vault (horiz) . . . 25 40
2746 25s. Discus 55 50
2747 35s. Hurdles (horiz) 70 65
2748 43s. High jump (horiz) . . . 90 80
2749 1l. Long jump . . . . . . 2·10 1·60
MS2750 90 × 65 mm. 2l. Shot put 6·25 6·25
See also Nos. 2773/**MS**2779, 2803/**MS**2809, 2816/**MS**2822, 2834/**MS**2840 and 2851/**MS**2857.

877 Thracian Gold Leaf Collar

1979. 48th International Philatelic Federation Congress, Sofia. Sheet 77 × 86 mm.
MS2751 **877** 1l. multicoloured . . 2·50 2·50

878 First Bulgarian Stamp and 1975 European Security Conference Stamp

879 Hotel Vitosha-New Otani

1979. "Philaserdica 79" International Exhibition, Sofia (5th issue). Sheet 63 × 61 mm.
MS2752 **878** 1l. multicoloured . . 5·25 5·25

1979. "Philaserdica 79" International Stamp Exhibition, Sofia (5th issue) and Bulgaria Day.
2753 **879** 2s. pink and blue 15 10

880 "Good Morning, Little Brother" (illus by Kukuliev of folktale)

1979. "Philaserdica 79" International Stamp Exhibition, Sofia (6th issue) and Bulgarian–Russian Friendship Day.
2754 **880** 2s. multicoloured 15 10

881 First Bulgarian Stamp

882 "Man on Donkey" (Boris Angelushev)

1979. Centenary of First Bulgarian Stamp (3rd issue). Sheet 91 × 121 mm.
MS2755 **881** 5s. multicoloured . . 35·00 35·00

1979. 12th Festival of Humour and Satire, Grabovo.
2756 **882** 2s. multicoloured 15 15

883 "Four Women"

1979. 450th Death Anniv of Albrecht Durer (artist). Multicoloured.
2757 13s. Type **883** 20 15
2758 23s. "Three Peasants Talking" 50 30
2759 25s. "The Cook and his Wife" 35 30
2760 35s. "Portrait of Eobanus Hessus" 50 35
MS2761 80 × 81 mm. 80s. "Rhinoceros" (horiz). Imperf 1·50 1·50

884 Clocktower, Byala Cherkva

885 Petko Todorov (birth centenary)

1979. Air. Clocktowers (1st series). Mult.
2762 13s. Type **884** 15 15
2763 23s. Botevgrad 30 20
2764 25s. Pazardzhik 35 20
2765 35s. Gabrovo 50 30
2766 53s. Tryavna 70 50
See also Nos. 2891/5.

1979. Bulgarian Writers.
2767 **885** 2s. black, brown & yell 10 20
2768 – 2s. green and yellow . . 10 20
2769 – 2s. red and yellow . . . 10 20
DESIGNS: No. 2768, Dimitur Dimov (70th birth anniv); 2769, Stefan Kostov (birth cent).

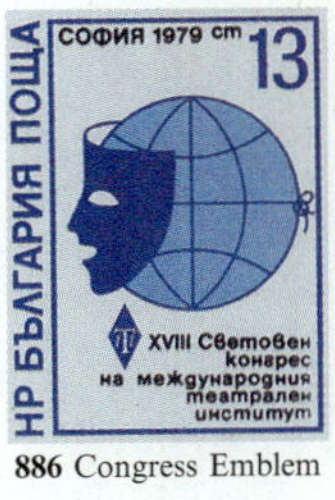

886 Congress Emblem

887 House of Journalists, Varna

1979. 18th Congress of International Theatrical Institute, Sofia.
2770 **886** 13s. cobalt, blue & black 15 10

1979. 20th Anniv of House of Journalists (holiday home), Varna.
2771 **887** 8s. orange, black & blue 15 10

888 Children of Different Races

889 Parallel Bars

1979. "Banners for Peace" Children's Meeting, Sofia.
2772 **888** 2s. multicoloured 10 10

1979. Olympic Games, Moscow (1980) (2nd issue). Gymnastics. Multicoloured.

2773	2s. Type **889**	15	25
2774	13s. Horse exercise (horiz)	20	35
2775	25s. Rings exercise	45	40
2776	35s. Beam exercise	60	55
2777	43s. Uneven bars	70	80
2778	1l. Floor exercise	1·60	1·70
MS2779	65 × 88 mm. 2l. Horizontal bars	6·25	6·25

890 "Virgin and Child" (Nesebur)

1979. Icons of the Virgin and Child. Mult.

2780	13s. Type **890**	15	20
2781	23s. Nesebur (diff)	35	25
2782	35s. Sozopol	55	25
2783	43s. Sozopol (diff)	70	40
2784	53s. Samokov	95	90

891 Anton Bezenshek

892 Mountaineer

1979. Centenary of Bulgarian Stenography.
2785 **891** 2s. yellow and grey . . . 15 10

1979. 50th Anniv of Bulgarian Alpine Club.
2786 **892** 2s. multicoloured 15 10

893 Commemorative Inscription

1979. Centenary of Bulgarian Public Health Services.
2787 **893** 2s. black, silver & green 15 20

893 Commemorative Inscription

1979. Centenary of Bulgarian Public Health Services.
2787 **893** 2s. black, silver & green 15 20

891 Anton Bezenshek

892 Mountaineer

1979. Centenary of Bulgarian Stenography.
2785 **891** 2s. yellow and grey . . . 15 10

1979. 50th Anniv of Bulgarian Alpine Club.
2786 **892** 2s. multicoloured 15 10

894 Rocket and Flowers

896 Games Emblem

895 "IZOT–0250" Computer

1979. 35th Anniv of Fatherland Front Government. Multicoloured.

2788	2s. Type **894**	10	10
2789	5s. Russian and Bulgarian flags	10	10
2790	13s. "35" in national colours	10	20

1979. 35th Plovdiv Fair.
2791 **895** 2s. multicoloured 15 10

1979. World University Games, Mexico.
2792 **896** 5s. red, yellow and blue 15 10

897 Footballer

1979. 50th Anniv of DFS Lokomotiv Football Team.
2793 **897** 2s. red and black 15 10

898 Lyuben Karavelov

899 Cross-country Skiing

1979. Death Centenary of Lyuben Karavelov (newspaper editor and President of Bulgarian Revolutionary Committee).
2794 **898** 2s. green and blue . . . 10 10

1979. Winter Olympic Games, Lake Placid (1980).

2795 **899**	2s. red, purple and black	15	15
2796 –	13s. orange, blue & blk	15	15
2797 –	23s. turquoise, blue and black	30	25
2798 –	43s. purple, turq & blk	65	40
MS2799	68 × 77 mm. 1l. green, blue and black. Imperf	2·00	2·00

DESIGNS: 13s. Speed skating; 23s. Skiing; 43s. Luge; 1l. Skiing (different).

900 "Woman from Thrace"

901 Canoeing (Canadian pairs)

1979. 80th Birth Anniv of Dechko Uzunov (artist). Multicoloured.

2800	12s. "Figure in Red" . . .	20	15
2801	13s. Type **900**	20	15
2802	23s. "Composition II" . . .	35	30

1979. Olympic Games, Moscow (1980) (3rd issue). Water Sports. Multicoloured.

2803	2s. Type **901**	20	25
2804	13s. Swimming (freestyle) . .	25	40
2805	25s. Swimming (backstroke) (horiz)	55	50
2806	35s. Kayak (horiz)	70	55
2807	43s. Diving	90	80
2808	1l. Springboard diving . . .	2·10	1·60
MS2809	64 × 88 mm. 2l. Water polo	8·00	6·75

902 Nikola Vaptsarov

1979. 70th Birth Anniv of Nikola Vaptsarov (writer).
2810 **902** 2s. pink and red 15 20

903 "Dawn in Plovdiv" (Ioan Leviev)

1979. History of Bulgaria. Paintings. Mult.

2811	2s. "The First Socialists" (Boyan Petrov) (horiz) . .	15	15
2812	13s. "Dimitur Blagoev as Editor of "Rabotnik" (Dimitur Gyvdzhenov) (horiz)	15	15
2813	25s. "Workers' Party March" (Stoyan Sotirov) (horiz)	30	30
2814	35s. Type **903**	50	50

904 Doves in a Girl's Hair

1979. New Year.
2815 **904** 13s. multicoloured . . . 15 10

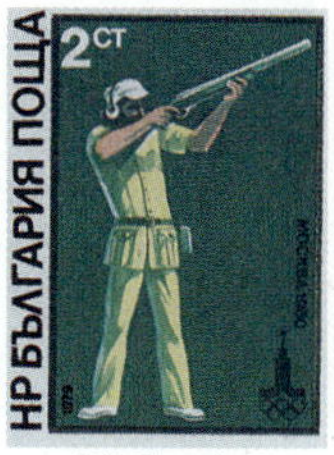
905 Shooting

1979. Olympic Games, Moscow (1980) (4th issue). Multicoloured.

2816	2s. Type **905**	20	25
2817	13s. Judo (horiz)	25	35
2818	25s. Wrestling (horiz) . . .	55	50
2819	35s. Archery	70	65
2820	43s. Fencing (horiz)	95	75
2821	1l. Fencing (different) . . .	2·20	1·40
MS2822	65 × 89 mm. 2l. Boxing	8·00	6·50

906 Procession with Relics of Saints

1979. Frescoes of Saints Cyril and Methodius in St. Clement's Basilica, Rome. Multicoloured.

2823	2s. Type **906**	20	15
2824	13s. Cyril and Methodius received by Pope Adrian II	20	15
2825	23s. Burial of Cyril the Philosopher	30	30
2826	25s. St. Cyril	40	30
2827	35s. St. Methodius	50	40

907 Television Screen showing Emblem

908 Puppet of Krali Marko (national hero)

1979. 25th Anniv of Bulgarian Television.
2828 **907** 5s. blue and deep blue 15 10

1980. 50th Anniv of International Puppet Theatre Organization (UNIMA).
2829 **908** 2s. multicoloured 15 10

909 Thracian Rider (3rd-cent votive tablet)

910 "Meeting of Lenin and Dimitrov" (Aleksandur Poplilov)

1980. Centenary of National Archaeological Museum, Sofia.

2830 **909**	2s. brown, gold & purple	15	10
2831 –	13s. brown, gold & grn	15	10

DESIGN: 13s. Grave stele of Deines (5th–6th cent).

1980. 110th Birth Anniv of Lenin.
2832 **910** 13s. multicoloured . . . 15 10

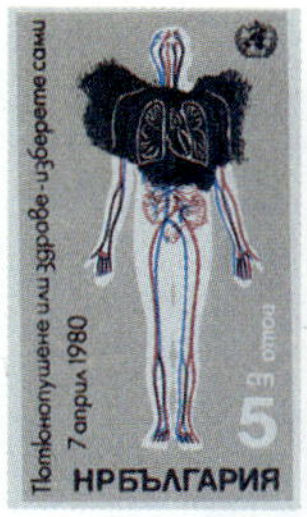
911 Diagram of Blood Circulation and Lungs obscured by Smoke

912 Basketball

1980. World Health Day. Anti-smoking Campaign.
2833 **911** 5s. multicoloured 15 10

1980. Olympic Games, Moscow (5th issue). Multicoloured.

2834	2s. Type **912**	20	25
2835	13s. Football	30	35
2836	25s. Hockey	60	40
2837	35s. Cycling	80	55
2838	43s. Handball	1·00	75
2839	1l. Volleyball	2·20	1·40
MS2840	66 × 90 mm. 2s. Weightlifting	8·00	6·50

913 Emblem, Cosmonauts and Space Station

1980. "Intercosmos" Space Programme. Sheet 111 × 102 mm.
MS2841 **913** 50s. multicoloured 1·00 1·00

914 Penyo Penev
915 Penny Black

1980. 50th Birth Anniv of Penyo Penev (poet).
2842 **914** 5s. brown, red & turq . . 15 20

1980. "London 1980" International Stamp Exhibition.
2843 **915** 25s. black and red . . . 55 40

916 Dimitur Khv. Chorbadzhuski-Chudomir (self-portrait)

1980. 90th Birth Anniv of Dimitur Khv. Chorbadzhusk-Chudomir (artist).
2844 **916** 5s. pink, brown & turq 15 10
2845 – 13s. black, blue & turq 15 20
DESIGN: 13s. "Our People".

917 Nikolai Gyaurov
918 Soviet Soldiers raising Flag on Berlin Reichstag

1980. 50th Birth Anniv of Nikolai Gyaurov (opera singer).
2846 **917** 5s. yellow, brown & grn 15 20

1980. 35th Anniv of "Victory in Europe" Day.
2847 **918** 5s. gold, brown & black 15 10
2848 – 13s. gold, brown & black 15 10
DESIGN: 13s. Soviet Army memorial, Berlin–Treptow.

919 Open Book and Sun
920 Stars representing Member Countries

1980. 75th Anniv Bulgarian Teachers' Union.
2849 **919** 5s. purple and yellow . . 15 10

1980. 25th Anniv of Warsaw Pact.
2850 **920** 13s. multicoloured . . . 15 10

921 Greek Girl with Olympic Flame
922 Ballerina

1980. Olympic Games, Moscow (6th issue). Multicoloured.
2851 2s. Type **921** 20 25
2852 13s. Spartacus monument, Sandanski 30 35
2853 25s. Liberation monument, Sofia (detail) 60 50
2854 35s. Liberation monument, Plovdiv 80 55
2855 43s. Liberation monument, Shipka Pass . . . . . . 1·00 75
2856 1l. Liberation monument, Ruse . . . . 2·20 1·40
MS2857 66 × 92 mm. 2l. Athlete with Olympic flame, Moscow . . . 8·00 6·50

1980. 10th International Ballet Competition, Varna.
2858 **922** 13s. multicoloured . . . 25 10

923 Europa Hotel, Sofia

1980. Hotels. Multicoloured.
2859 23s. Type **923** 25 25
2860 23s. Bulgaria Hotel, Burgas (vert) 25 25
2861 23s. Plovdiv Hotel, Plovdiv 25 25
2862 23s. Riga Hotel, Ruse (vert) 25 25
2863 23s. Varna Hotel, Prazhba 25 25

1980. Historic Ships (3rd series). As T **753**. Multicoloured.
2864 5s. Hansa kogge "Jesus of Lubeck" 15 15
2865 8s. Roman galley 30 15
2866 13s. Galleon "Eagle" . . . 35 15
2867 23s. "Mayflower" 60 25
2868 35s. Maltese galleon . . . 80 30
2869 53s. Galleon "Royal Louis" 1·60 45

924 Parachute Descent

1980. 15th World Parachute Championships, Kazanluk. Multicoloured.
2870 13s. Type **924** 15 15
2871 25s. Parachutist in free fall 25 25

925 Clown and Children

1980. 1st Anniv of "Banners for Peace" Children's Meeting. Multicoloured.
2872 3s. Type **925** 10 15
2873 5s. "Cosmonauts in Spaceship" (vert) 10 15
2874 8s. "Picnic" 10 15
2875 13s. "Children with Ices" . . 10 15
2876 25s. "Children with Cat" (vert) 20 20
2877 35s. "Crowd" . . . . 1·00 40
2878 43s. "Banners for Peace" monument (vert) 40 35

926 Assembly Emblem
927 Iordan Iovkov

1980. Assembly of Peoples' Parliament for Peace, Sofia.
2879 **926** 25s. multicoloured . . . 25 30

1980. Birth Centenary of Iordan Iovkov (writer).
2880 **927** 5s. multicoloured 15 20

928 Yakovlev Yak-24 Helicopter, Missile Launcher and Tank

1980. Bulgarian Armed Forces. Multicoloured.
2881 3s. Type **928** 10 10
2882 5s. Mikoyan Gurevich MiG-21 bomber, radar antennae and missile transporter 15 10
2883 8s. Mil Mi-24 helicopter, missile boat and landing ship "Ropucha" 25 15

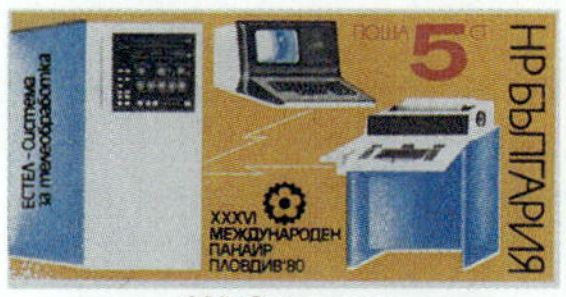

929 Computer

1980. 36th Plovdiv Fair.
2884 **929** 5s. multicoloured 15 10

930 "Virgin and Child with St. Anne"

1980. Paintings by Leonardo da Vinci. Mult.
2885 5s. Type **930** 15 15
2886 8s. Angel (detail, "The Annunciation") 15 15
2887 13s. Virgin (detail, "The Annunciation") 15 15
2888 25s. "Adoration of the Kings" (detail) 30 25
2889 35s. "Woman with Ermine" 50 30
MS2890 57 × 80 mm. 50s. "Mona Lisa". Imperf . . . . 1·20 1·00

1980. Air. Clocktowers (2nd series). As T **884**. Multicoloured.
2891 13s. Byala 15 20
2892 23s. Razgrad 25 25
2893 25s. Karnobat 30 25
2894 35s. Sevlievo 45 30
2895 53s. Berkovitsa 65 50

931 "Parodia saint-pieana"

1980. Cacti. Multicoloured.
2896 5s. Type **931** 10 15
2897 13s. "Echinopsis bridgesii" 20 15
2898 25s. "Echinocereus purpureus" 45 25
2899 35s. "Opuntia bispinosa" . . 60 30
2900 53s. "Mamillopsis senilis" 80 50

932 UN Building and Bulgarian Arms

1980. 25th Anniv of United Nations Membership. Sheet 64 × 86 mm.
MS2901 **932** 60s. multicoloured 2·40 2·40

933 Wild Horse

1980. Horses. Multicoloured.
2902 3s. Type **933** 20 30
2903 5s. Tarpan 20 30
2904 13s. Arabian 35 35
2905 23s. Anglo-Arabian 55 60
2906 35s. Draught horse 95 95

934 Vasil Stoin

1980. Birth Centenary of Vasil Stoin (collector of folk songs).
2907 **934** 5s. violet, yellow & gold 15 10

935 Armorial Lion
936 Red Star

1980. New Year. 1300th Anniv of Bulgarian State. Multicoloured.
2908 5s. Type **935** 15 10
2909 13s. Dish and dates "681–1981" 15 10

1980. 12th Bulgarian Communist Party Congress (1st issue).
2910 **936** 5s. yellow and red . . . 15 10
See also Nos. 2920/2.

937 Cross-country Skier

1981. World Ski-racing Championship, Velingrad.
2911 **937** 43s. orange, blue & blk 65 40

938 Midland Hawthorn ("Crataegus oxpacantha")
939 Skier

1981. Useful Plants. Multicoloured.
2912 3s. Type **938** 10 15
2913 5s. Perforate St. John's wort ("Hypericum perforatum") 10 15
2914 13s. Elder ("Sambucus nigra") 20 15
2915 25s. Dewberry ("Rubus caesius") 45 25

2916 35s. Lime ("Tilia argentea") 55 25
2917 43s. Dog rose ("Rosa canina") 90 40

1981. Alpine Skiing World Championships, Borovets.
2918 **939** 43s. yellow, black & blue 65 40

940 Nuclear Traces

1981. 25th Anniv of Nuclear Research Institute, Dubna, U.S.S.R.
2919 **940** 13s. black and silver . . 15 10

941 "XII" formed from Flag

1981. 12th Bulgarian Communist Party Congress (2nd issue).
2920 **941** 5s. multicoloured 20 15
2921 – 13s. red, black and blue 20 20
2922 – 23s. red, black and blue 20 30
MS2923 68 × 86 mm. 50s. multicoloured 65 70
DESIGNS: 13s. Stars; 23s. Computer tape; 50s. Georgi Dimitrov and Dimitur Blagoev.

942 Palace of Culture

1981. Opening of Palace of Culture, Sofia.
2924 **942** 5s. dp green, grn & red 15 10

943 "Self-portrait"

1981. 170th Birth Anniv (1980) of Zakharu Zograf (artist). Multicoloured.
2925 5s. Type **943** 15 15
2926 13s. "Portrait of Khristiania Zografska" 15 15
2927 23s. "The Transfiguration" (icon from Preobrazhenie Monastery) 30 25
2928 25s. "Doomsday" (detail) (horiz) 40 30
2929 35s. "Doomsday" (detail – different) (horiz) 65 40

944 Squacco Heron

1981. Birds. Multicoloured.
2930 5s. Type **944** 15 15
2931 8s. Eurasian bittern 30 15
2932 13s. Cattle egret 50 25
2933 25s. Great egret 95 45
2934 53s. Black stork . . . . . . 1·90 1·00

945 Liner "Georgi Dimitrov"

1981. Centenary of Bulgarian Shipbuilding. Mult.
2935 35s. Type **945** 70 25
2936 43s. Freighter "Petimata of RMS" 95 40
2937 53s. Tanker "Khan Asparuch" . . . . 1·20 60

946 Hofburg Palace, Vienna

1981. "WIPA 1981" International Stamp Exhibition, Vienna.
2938 **946** 35s. crimson, red & green 40 30

947 "XXXIV"

1981. 34th Bulgarian People's Agrarian Union Congress.
2939 **947** 5s. multicoloured 15 15
2940 – 8s. orange, black & blue 15 15
2941 – 13s. multicoloured . . . 15 20
DESIGNS: 8s. Flags; 13s. Bulgarian Communist Party and Agrarian Union flags.

948 Wild Cat

1981. International Hunting Exhibition, Plovdiv.
2942 **948** 5s. stone, black & brown 15 15
2943 – 13s. black, brn & stone 30 15
2944 – 23s. brown, blk & orge 50 25
2945 – 25s. black, brown & mve 55 40
2946 – 35s. lt brown, blk & brn 75 45
2947 – 53s. brown, blk & grn 1·20 60
MS2948 78 × 103 mm. 1l. brown, black and green (52 × 42 mm) 2·00 2·00
DESIGNS: 13s. Wild boar; 23s. Mouflon; 25s. Chamois; 35s. Roebuck; 53s. Fallow deer; 1l. Red deer.

949 "Crafty Peter" (sculpture, Georgi Chapkanov)

950 Bulgarian Arms and UNESCO Emblem

1981. Festival of Humour and Satire, Gabrovo.
2949 **949** 5s. multicoloured 15 10

1981. 25th Anniv of UNESCO Membership.
2950 **950** 13s. multicoloured . . . 15 10

951 Deutsche Flugzeugwerke D.F.W. C.V. Biplane

1981. Air. Aircraft. Multicoloured.
2951 5s. Type **951** 10 15
2952 12s. LAS-7 monoplane . . . 30 15
2953 25s. LAS-8 monoplane . . . 60 30
2954 35s. DAR-1 biplane 60 45
2955 45s. DAR-3 biplane 95 60
2956 55s. DAR-9 biplane . . . . 1·30 75

952 "Eye"

1981. Centenary of State Statistical Office.
2957 **952** 5s. multicoloured 15 10

953 Veliko Tirnovo Hotel

1981. Hotels.
2958 **953** 23s. multicoloured . . . 25 20

954 "Flying Figure"

1981. 90th Anniv of First Bulgarian Social Democratic Party Congress, Buzludzha. Sculptures by Velichko Minekov.
2959 **954** 5s. blue, black and green 15 15
2960 – 13s. brown, blk & orge 15 20
DESIGN: 13s. "Advancing Female".

955 Animal-shaped Dish

1981. Golden Treasure of Old St. Nicholas. Multicoloured.
2961 5s. Type **955** 15 15
2962 13s. Jug with decorated neck 15 20
2963 23s. Jug with loop pattern 25 35
2964 25s. Jug with bird pattern 30 45
2965 35s. Decorated vase 45 60
2966 53s. Decorated dish 65 85

956 Badge and Map of Bulgaria

1981. 35th Anniv of Frontier Guards.
2967 **956** 5s. multicoloured 15 10

957 Saints Cyril and Methodius (9th century)

1981. 1300th Anniv of Bulgarian State.
2968 – 5s. green and grey . . . 15 15
2969 **957** 5s. brown and yellow . . 15 15
2970 – 8s. violet and lilac . . . 15 15
2971 – 12s. mauve and purple 15 15
2972 – 13s. purple and brown 15 15
2973 – 13s. green and black . . 15 15
2974 – 16s. green & deep green 20 15
2975 – 23s. black and blue . . . 30 25
2976 – 25s. green and light green 30 25
2977 – 35s. brown and light brown 45 25
2978 – 41s. red and pink . . . 50 40
2979 – 43s. red and pink . . . 50 40
2980 – 53s. dp brown and brown 60 40
2981 – 55s. dp green and green 65 50
MS2982 Two sheets, each 83 × 74 mm. (a) 50s. grey and green; (b) 1l. brown, black and brown . . . . 2·50 2·50

DESIGNS: No. 2968, Madara horsemen (8th century); 2970, Plan of Round Church at Veliki Preslav (10th century); 2971, Four Evangelists of King Ivan, 1356; 2972, Column of Ivan Asen II (13th century); 2973, Manasiev Chronicle (14th century); 2974, Rising of April 1876; 2975, Arrival of Russian liberation troops; 2976, Foundation ceremony of Bulgarian Social Democratic Party, 1891; 2977, Rising of September 1923; 2978, Formation of Fatherland Front Government, 9 September 1944; 2979, Bulgarian Communist Party Congress, 1948; 50s. Bas-relief of lion at Stara Zagora (10th century); 2980, 10th Communist Party Congress, 1971; 2981, Kremikovski metallurgical combine; 1l. Leonid Brezhnev and Todor Yovkov.

958 Volleyball Players

959 "Pegasus" (bronze sculpture)

1981. European Volleyball Championships.
2983 **958** 13s. red, blue and black 15 10

1981. Day of the Word.
2984 **959** 5s. green 15 10

960 Loaf of Bread

961 Mask

1981. World Food Day.
2985 **960** 13s. brown, black & grn 15 15

1981. Cent of Bulgarian Professional Theatre.
2986 **961** 5s. multicoloured 15 15

962 Examples of Bulgarian Art

1981. Cultural Heritage Day.
2987 **962** 13s. green and brown . . 1·60 15

963 Footballer

1981. World Cup Football Championship, Spain (1982). Multicoloured.
2988 5s. Type **963** 10 15
2989 13s. Heading ball 20 15
2990 43s. Saving a goal 50 40
2991 53s. Running with ball . . . 60 60

964 Dove encircled by Barbed Wire

1981. Anti-apartheid Campaign.
2992 **964** 5s. red, black and yellow 15 10

1981. 13th Bulgarian Philatelic Federation Congress. Sheet 51 × 72 mm containing design as T **962** but inscr "XIII KONGRES NA SBF SOFIYA" at foot.
MS2993 60s. blue and red . . . 4·00 4·00

965 "Mother" (Lilyann Ruseva)

1981. 35th Anniv of UNICEF. Various designs showing mother and child paintings by named artists. Multicoloured.
2994 53s. Type **965** 60 25
2995 53s. "Bulgarian Madonna" (Vasil Stoilov) 60 25
2996 53s. "Village Madonna" (Ivan Milev) 60 25
2997 53s. "Mother" (Vladimir Dimitrov) 60 25

966 8th century Ceramic from Pliska

1981. New Year. Multicoloured.
2998 5s. Armorial lion 15 10
2999 13s. Type **966** 15 10

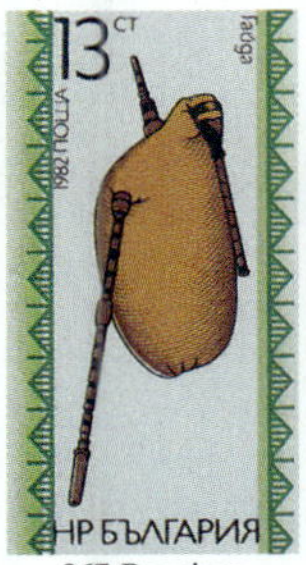

967 Bagpipes

968 Open Book

1982. Musical Instruments. Multicoloured.
3000 13s. Type **967** 15 15
3001 25s. Single and double flutes 25 20
3002 30s. Rebec 35 20
3003 35s. Flute and pipe 40 25
3004 44s. Mandolin 55 25

1982. 125th Anniv of Public Libraries.
3005 **968** 5s. green 15 10

969 "Sofia Plains"

1982. Birth Centenary of Nikola Petrov (artist).
3006 5s. Type **969** 15 15
3007 13s. "Girl Embroidering" 15 15
3008 30s. "Fields of Peshtera" . . 35 20

970 Womans' Head and Dove

1982. International Decade for Women. Sheet 66 × 76 mm.
MS3009 **970** 1l. multicoloured . . 1·50 1·50

971 "Peasant Woman"

973 Summer Snowflake

972 Georgi Dimitrov

1982. Birth Centenary of Valadimir Dimitrov (artist). Multicoloured.
3010 5s. Figures in a landscape (horiz) 15 15
3011 8s. Town and harbour (horiz) 15 15
3012 13s. Town scene (horiz) . . 15 15
3013 25s. "Reapers" 30 20
3014 30s. Woman and child . . . 30 25
3015 35s. Type **971** 35 25
MS3016 65 × 58 mm. 50s. "Self-portrait" (horiz) 95 95

1982. 9th Bulgarian Trade Unions Congress, Sofia.
3017 **972** 5s. lt brn, dp brn & brn 15 10
3018 – 5s. brown and blue . . . 15 10
DESIGN: No. 3018, Palace of Culture, Sofia.

1982. Medicinal Plants. Multicoloured.
3019 3s. Type **973** 10 15
3020 5s. Chicory 10 15
3021 8s. Rosebay willowherb . . 20 15
3022 13s. Solomon's seal 25 15
3023 25s. Sweet violet 50 25
3024 35s. "Ficaria verna" 50 40

974 Russian Space Station

1982. 25th Anniv of First Soviet Artificial Satellite.
3025 **974** 13s. multicoloured . . . 15 20

975 Georgi Dimitrov

1982. "Sozphilex '82" Stamp Exhibition, Veliko, Tirnovo. Sheet 61 × 82 mm.
MS3026 **975** 50s. red and black 1·90 1·90

976 Dimitrov and Congress Emblem

1982. 14th Dimitrov Communist Youth League Congress, Sofia.
3027 **976** 5s. blue, red & yellow . . 15 10

977 First French and Bulgarian Stamps

1982. "Philexfrance 82" International Stamp Exhibition, Paris.
3028 **977** 42s. multicoloured . . . 55 30

978 Abstract with Birds

980 Georgi Dimitrov

979 Georgi Dimitrov

1982. Alafrangi Frescoes from 19th-century Houses.
3029 **978** 5s. multicoloured 15 15
3030 – 13s. multicoloured . . . 15 15
3031 – 25s. multicoloured . . . 25 20
3032 – 30s. multicoloured . . . 25 20
3033 – 42s. multicoloured . . . 40 25
3034 – 60s. multicoloured . . . 60 40
DESIGNS: 13s. to 60s. Various flower and bird patterns.

During 1982 sets were issued for World Cup Football Championship, Spain (5, 13, 30s.), Tenth Anniv of First European Security and Co-operation Conference (5, 13, 25, 30s.), World Cup Results (5, 13, 30s.) and 10th Anniv (1983) of European Security and Co-operation Conference, Helsinki (5, 13, 25, 30s.). Supplies and distribution of these stamps were restricted and it is understood they were not available at face value.

1982. Birth Centenary of Georgi Dimitrov (statesman). Sheet 76 × 52 mm.
MS3035 **979** 50s. multicoloured 65 80

1982. 9th Fatherland Front Congress, Sofia.
3036 **980** 5s. multicoloured 15 10

981 Airplane

1982. 35th Anniv of Balkanair (state airline).
3037 **981** 42s. blue, green & red 50 40

982 Atomic Bomb Mushroom-cloud

983 Lyudmila Zhivkova

1982. Nuclear Disarmament Campaign.
3038 **982** 13s. multicoloured . . . 15 10

1982. 40th Birth Anniv of Lyudmila Zhivkova (founder of "Banners for Peace" Children's Meetings).
3039 **983** 5s. multicoloured 10 10
3040 13s. multicoloured . . . 10 10
MS3041 62 × 67 mm. **983** 1l. multicoloured . . . . 1·30 1·30

984 Emblem

1982. 10th Anniv of U.N. Environment Programme.
3042 **984** 13s. green and blue . . . 15 10

985 Wave Pattern

1982. 5th Bulgarian Painters' Association Congress.
3043 **985** 5s. multicoloured 15 20

986 Child Musicians

1982. 2nd "Banners for Peace" Children's Meeting (1st issue). Children's Paintings. Multicoloured.
3044 3s. Type **986** 10 10
3045 5s. Children skating 10 10
3046 8s. Adults, children and flowers 10 10
3047 13s. Children with flags . . 20 15
MS3048 70 × 110 mm. 50s. Children in "Sun" balloon (vert) . . . . 1·30 1·30
See also Nos. 3057/**MS**3063.

987 Moscow Park Hotel, Sofia

988 Cruiser "Aurora" and Satellite

1982. Hotels. Multicoloured.
3049 32s. Type **987** 30 20
3050 32s. Black Sea Hotel, Varna 30 20

1982. 65th Anniv of Russian October Revolution.
3051 **988** 13s. red and blue 25 25

989 Hammer and Sickle

1982. 60th Anniv of U.S.S.R.
3052 **989** 13s. red, gold & violet 15 15

990 "The Piano"

1982. Birth Cent of Pablo Picasso (artist). Mult.
3053 13s. Type **990** 20 20
3054 30s. "Portrait of Jacqueline" 50 25
3055 42s. "Maternity" 65 35
MS3056 61 × 79 mm. 1l. "Self-portrait" . . . . 1·30 1·30

991 Boy and Girl

1982. 2nd "Banners for Peace" Children's Meeting (2nd issue). Multicoloured.
3057 3s. Type **991** 15 15
3058 5s. Market place 15 15
3059 8s. Children in fancy dress (vert) 15 15
3060 13s. Chickens (vert) 20 15

3061 25s. Interlocking heads . . . 35 25
3062 30s. Lion 40 30
MS3063 70 × 109 mm. 50s. Boy and girl in garden (vert). Perf or imperf 1·10 1·10

992 Lions

1982. New Year. Multicoloured.
3064 5s. Type **992** 15 10
3065 13s. Decorated letters . . . 15 10

993 Broadcasting Tower

994 Dr. Robert Koch

1982. 60th Anniv of Avram Stoyanov Broadcasting Institute.
3066 **993** 5s. blue 15 10

1982. Cent of Discovery of Tubercle Bacillus.
3067 **994** 25s. brown and green . . 25 25

995 Simon Bolivar

996 Vasil Levski

1982. Birth Anniversaries.
3068 **995** 30s. green and grey . . . 25 30
3069 – 30s. yellow and brown 25 30
DESIGN: No. 3068, Type **995** (bicent); 3069, Rabindranath Tagore (philosopher, 120th anniv).

1983. 110th Death Anniv of Vasil Levski (revolutionary).
3070 **996** 5s. brown & green . . . 15 10

997 Skier

1983. "Universiade 83" University Games, Sofia.
3071 **997** 30s. multicoloured . . . 30 30

998 Northern Pike

1983. Freshwater Fishes. Multicoloured.
3072 3s. Type **998** 20 15
3073 5s. Beluga sturgeon 20 15
3074 13s. Chub 20 15
3075 25s. Zander 35 25
3076 30s. Wels 45 25
3077 42s. Brown trout 65 40

999 Karl Marx

1983. Death Centenary of Karl Marx.
3078 **999** 13s. red, purple & yellow 15 15

1000 Hasek and Illustrations from "The Good Soldier Schweik"

1983. Birth Centenary of Jaroslav Hasek (Czech writer).
3079 **1000** 13s. brown, grey & grn 15 15

1001 Martin Luther

1983. 500th Birth Anniv of Martin Luther (Protestant reformer).
3080 **1001** 13s. grey, black & brn 15 15

1002 Figures forming Initials

1983. 55th Anniv of Young Workers' Union.
3081 **1002** 5s. red, black & orange 15 10

1003 Khaskovo Costume

1004 Old Man feeding a Chicken

1983. Folk Costumes. Multicoloured.
3082 5s. Type **1003** 25 15
3083 8s. Pernik 25 15
3084 13s. Burgas 25 15
3085 25s. Tolbukhin 40 25
3086 30s. Blagoevgrad 55 25
3087 42s. Topolovgrad 75 40

1983. 6th International Festival of Humour and Satire, Gabrovo.
3088 **1004** 5s. multicoloured . . . 15 10

During 1983 sets were issued for European Security and Co-operation Conference, Budapest (5, 13, 25, 30s.), Olympic Games, Los Angeles (5, 13, 30, 42s.), Winter Olympic Games, Sarajevo (horiz designs, 5, 13, 30, 42s.) and European Security and Co-operation Conference, Madrid (5, 13, 30, 42s.). Supplies and distribution of these stamps were restricted, and it is understood they were not available at face value.

1005 Smirnenski

1983. 85th Birth Anniv of Khristo Smirnenski (poet).
3089 **1005** 5s. red, brown & yellow 15 10

1006 Emblem

1008 Staunton Chessmen on Map of Europe

1007 Stylized Houses

1983. 17th Int Geodesy Federation Congress.
3090 **1006** 30s. green, blue & yell 25 30

1983. "Interarch 83" World Architecture Biennale, Sofia.
3091 **1007** 30s. multicoloured . . . 25 30

1983. 8th European Chess Team Championship, Plovdiv.
3092 **1008** 13s. multicoloured . . . 25 15

1009 Brazilian and Bulgarian Football Stamps

1983. "Brasiliana 83" International Stamp Exhibition, Rio de Janeiro. Sheet 73 × 103 mm.
MS3093 **1009** 1l. green, brown and gold . . . . 1·50 1·50

1010 Valentina Tereshkova

1983. Air. 20th Anniv of First Woman in Space. Sheet 121 × 75 mm containing T **1010** and similar vert design, each blue and brown.
MS3094 50s. Type **1010**; 50s. Svetlana Savitskaya, 1982, cosmonaut . . . . 1·80 1·80

1011 Television Mast, Tolbukhin

1983. Air. World Communications Year.
3095 **1011** 5s. blue and red 15 15
3096 – 13s. mauve and red . . 20 15
3097 – 30s. yellow and red . . 30 15
DESIGNS: 13s. Postwoman; 30s. Radio tower, Mount Botev.

1012 Lenin addressing Congress

1983. 80th Anniv of 2nd Russian Social Democratic Workers' Party Congress.
3098 **1012** 5s. pur, dp pur & yell 15 10

1013 Pistol and Dagger on Book

1983. 80th Anniv of Ilinden-Preobrazhenie Rising.
3099 **1013** 5s. yellow and green . . 15 10

1014 Crystals and Hammers within Gearwheels

1983. 30th Anniv of Mining and Geology Institute, Sofia.
3100 **1014** 5s. grey, purple & blue 15 10

1015 Georgi Dimitrov and Revolution Scenes

1983. 60th Anniv of September Uprising. Mult.
3101 5s. Type **1015** 15 10
3102 13s. Wreath and revolution scenes 15 10

1016 Animated Drawings

1017 Angora

1983. 3rd Animated Film Festival, Varna.
3103 **1016** 5s. multicoloured . . . 10 10

1983. Cats. Multicoloured.
3104 5s. Type **1017** 15 20
3105 13s. Siamese 30 20
3106 20s. Abyssinian (vert) . . . 40 25
3107 25s. European 50 25
3108 30s. Persian (vert) 60 40
3109 42s. Khmer 80 60

1018 Richard Trevithick's Locomotive, 1803

1983. Locomotives (1st series). Multicoloured.
3110 5s. Type **1018** 15 10
3111 13s. John Blenkinsop's rack locomotive "Prince Royal", 1810 . . . . . . 20 10
3112 42s. William Hedley's "Puffing Billy", 1813–14 1·40 45
3113 60s. Stephenson locomotive "Adler", 1835, Germany 2·40 65
See also Nos. 3159/63.

1019 Liberation Monument, Plovdiv

1983. 90th Anniv of Bulgarian Philatelic Federation and Fourth National Stamp Exhibition, Plovdiv. Sheet 65 × 79 mm.
MS3114 **1019** 50s. grey, blue and red 90 90

1020 Mask and Laurel as Lyre **1021** Ioan Kukuzel

1983. 75th Anniv of National Opera, Sofia.
3115 **1020** 5s. red, black & gold 15 10

1983. Bulgarian Composers.
3116 **1021** 5s. yellow, brown & grn 15 15
3117 – 8s. yellow, brown & red 15 15
3118 – 13s. yellow, brown and green 15 15
3119 – 20s. yellow, brown & bl 20 25
3120 – 25s. yellow, brn & grey 25 30
3121 – 30s. yell, dp brn & brn 30 40
DESIGNS: 8s. Georgi Atanasov; 13s. Petko Stainov; 20s. Veselin Stoyanov; 25s. Lyubomir Pipkov; 30s. Pancho Vladigerov.

1022 Snowflake

1983. New Year.
3122 **1022** 5s. green, blue & gold 10 10

1023 "Angelo Donni"

1983. 500th Birth Anniv of Raphael (artist). Multicoloured.
3123 5s. Type **1023** 15 15
3124 13s. "Portrait of a Cardinal" 15 15
3125 30s. "Baldassare Castiglioni" 35 30
3126 42s. "Woman with a Veil" 50 45
MS3127 59 × 98 mm. 1l. "Sistine Madonna" 1·40 1·40

1024 Eurasian Common Shrew

1983. Protected Mammals. Multicoloured.
3128 12s. Type **1024** 35 25
3129 13s. Greater horseshoe bat 45 25
3130 20s. Common long-eared bat 70 30
3131 30s. Forest dormouse 80 35
3132 42s. Fat dormouse 1·20 60

1025 Karavelov

1984. 150th Birth Anniv of Lyuben Karavelov (poet).
3133 **1025** 5s. blue, bistre & brn 15 10

During 1984 sets were issued for European Confidence- and Security-building Measures and Disarmament Conference, Stockholm (5, 13, 30, 42s.) and Winter Olympic Games, Sarajevo (vert designs, 5, 13, 30, 42s.). Supplies and distribution of these stamps were restricted and it is understood that they were not available at face value.

1026 Mendeleev and Formulae

1984. 150th Birth Anniv of Dmitry Mendeleev (chemist).
3134 **1026** 13s. multicoloured 15 10

1027 Bulk Carrier "Gen. Vl. Zaimov"

1984. Ships. Multicoloured.
3135 5s. Type **1027** 10 10
3136 13s. Tanker "Mesta" 25 10
3137 25s. Tanker "Veleka" 55 20
3138 32s. Train ferry "Geroite na Odesa" 60 30
3139 42s. Bulk carrier "Rozhen" 80 40

1028 World Cup Stamps

1984. "Espana 84" International Stamp Exhibition, Madrid. Sheet 89 × 110 mm.
MS3140 **1028** 2l. multicoloured 4·75 4·75

1029 Pigeon with Letter over Globe **1030** Wild Cherries

1984. "Mladost '84" Youth Stamp Exhibition, Pleven (1st issue).
3141 **1029** 5s. multicoloured 15 10
See also Nos. 3171/2.

1984. Fruits. Multicoloured.
3142 5s. Type **1030** 10 15
3143 8s. Wild strawberries 15 15
3144 13s. Dewberries 25 15
3145 20s. Raspberries 30 20
3146 42s. Medlars 60 35

1031 "Vitosha Conference" (K. Buyukliiski and P. Petrov)

1984. 60th Anniv of Bulgarian Communist Party Conference, Vitosha.
3147 **1031** 5s. purple, brn & red 15 10

1032 Security Conference 1980 13s. Stamp

1984. 5th International Stamp Fair, Essen. Sheet 94 × 147 mm containing T **1032** and similar horiz design. Multicoloured.
MS3148 11.50, Type **1032**; 11.50, Security Conference 35s. stamp 7·50 7·50

1033 Athletes and Doves **1034** Mt. Everest

1984. 6th Republican Spartakiad.
3149 **1033** 13s. multicoloured 15 10

1984. Bulgarian Expedition to Mt. Everest.
3150 **1034** 5s. multicoloured 15 10

1035 Kogge

1984. Universal Postal Union Congress Philatelic Salon, Hamburg. Sheet 100 × 107 mm.
MS3151 **1035** 3l. multicoloured 6·50 6·50

1036 Drummer

1984. 6th Amateur Performers Festival.
3152 **1036** 5s. multicoloured 15 10

1037 Seal

1984. 50 Years of Bulgarian–U.S.S.R. Diplomatic Relations.
3153 **1037** 13s. multicoloured 15 10

1038 Feral Rock Pigeon **1039** Production Quality Emblem

1984. Pigeons and Doves. Multicoloured.
3154 5s. Type **1038** 10 10
3155 13s. Stock pigeon 30 15
3156 20s. Wood pigeon 40 25
3157 30s. Turtle dove 65 30
3158 42s. Domestic pigeon 90 40

1984. Locomotives (2nd series). As T **1018**. Multicoloured.
3159 13s. "Best Friend of Charleston", 1830, U.S.A. 20 15
3160 25s. "Saxonia", 1836, Saxony 35 25
3161 30s. "Lafayette", 1837, U.S.A. 45 25
3162 42s. "Borsig", 1841, Germany 90 40
3163 60s. "Philadelphia", 1843, U.S.A. 1·30 65

1984. 40th Anniv of Fatherland Front Government.
3164 **1039** 5s. red, lt green & green 15 15
3165 – 20s. red and violet 15 20
3166 – 30s. red and blue 25 20
DESIGNS: 20s. Monument to Soviet Army, Sofia; 30s. Figure nine and star.

1040 "Boy with Harmonica" **1041** Mausoleum of Russian Soldiers

1984. Paintings by Nenko Balkanski. Multicoloured.
3167 5s. Type **1040** 20 15
3168 30s. "Window in Paris" 25 20
3169 42s. "Portrait of Two Women" (horiz) 35 30
MS3170 65 × 110 mm. 1l. "Self-portrait" 1·80 1·80

1984. "Mladost '84" Youth Stamp Exhibition, Pleven (2nd issue).
3171 **1041** 5s. multicoloured 15 10
3172 – 13s. black, grn & red 15 10
DESIGN: 13s. Panorama building.

1042 Pioneers saluting

1984. 40th Anniv of Dimitrov Septembrist Pioneers Organization.
3173 **1042** 5s. multicoloured 15 10

1043 Vaptsarov (after D. Nikolov)

1984. 75th Birth Anniv of Nikola I. Vaptsarov (poet).
3174 **1043** 5s. yellow and red 15 10

1044 Goalkeeper saving Goal

1984. 75th Anniv of Bulgarian Football.
3175 **1044** 42s. multicoloured 55 35

1045 Profiles

1984. "Mladost '84" Youth Stamp Exhibition, Pleven (3rd issue). Sheet 50 × 76 mm.
MS3176 **1045** 50s. multicoloured 95 95

1046 Devil's Bridge, R. Arda

1984. Bridges. Multicoloured.
3177 5s. Type **1046** 15 20
3178 13s. Kolo Ficheto Bridge, Byala 35 25
3179 30s. Asparukhov Bridge, Varna 70 55
3180 42s. Bebresh Bridge, Botevgrad 95 90

1047 Olympic Emblem

1984. 90th Anniv of International Olympic Committee.
3181 **1047** 13s. multicoloured . . . 15 15

1048 Moon and "Luna I", "II" and "III"

1984. 25th Anniv of First Moon Rocket. Sheet 79 × 57 mm.
MS3182 **1048** 1l. multicoloured 1·90 1·90

1049 Dalmatian Pelican with Chicks

1050 Anton Ivanov

1984. Wildlife Protection. Dalmatian Pelican.
3183 **1049** 5s. multicoloured . . . 25 15
3184 – 13s. lav, blk & brn . . 60 30
3185 – 20s. multicoloured . . . 1·10 45
3186 – 32s. multicoloured . . . 1·60 85
DESIGNS: 13s. Two pelicans; 20s. Pelican on water; 32s. Pelican in flight.

1984. Birth Cent of Anton Ivanov (revolutionary).
3187 **1050** 5s. yell, brn & red . . . 15 10

1051 Girl's Profile with Text as Hair

1984. 70th Anniv of Bulgarian Women's Socialist Movement.
3188 **1051** 5s. multicoloured . . . 15 10

1052 Snezhanka Television Tower

1984. Television Towers.
3189 **1052** 5s. blue, green & mve 15 15
3190 – 1l. brown, mauve & bis 95 55
DESIGN: 1l. Orelek television tower.

1053 Birds and Posthorns

1984. New Year. Multicoloured.
3191 5s. Type **1053** 15 10
3192 13s. Decorative pattern . . 15 10

1054 "September Nights"

1984. 80th Birth Anniv of Stoyan Venev (artist). Multicoloured.
3193 5s. Type **1054** 20 15
3194 30s. "Man with Three Orders" 20 20
3195 42s. "The Hero" 35 30

1055 Peacock (butterfly)

1056 Augusto Sandino

1984. Butterflies. Multicoloured.
3196 13s. Type **1055** 20 15
3197 25s. Swallowtail 40 25
3198 30s. Great banded grayling 45 30
3199 42s. Orange-tip 70 45
3200 60s. Red admiral . . . . . 95 1·00
MS3201 75 × 60 mm. 1l. Poplar admiral (*Limenitis populi*) . . . 1·80 1·80

1984. 50th Death Anniv of Augusto Sandino (Nicaraguan revolutionary).
3202 **1056** 13s. black, red & yell 15 10

1057 Tupolev Tu-154 Jetliner

1984. 40th Anniv of ICAO.
3203 **1057** 42s. multicoloured . . . 55 35

1058 "The Three Graces" (detail)

1984. 500th Birth Anniv (1983) of Raphael (artist) (2nd issue). Multicoloured.
3204 5s. Type **1058** 15 20
3205 13s. "Cupid and the Three Graces" (detail) 20 20
3206 30s. "Original Sin" (detail) 45 30
3207 42s. "La Fornarina" . . . 65 40
MS3208 106 × 95 mm. 1l. "Galatea" (detail) . . . . 1·40 1·40

1059 "Sofia"

1984. Maiden Voyage of Danube Cruise Ship "Sofia".
3209 **1059** 13s. dp blue, blue & yell 25 15

1060 Eastern Hog-nosed Skunk

1985. Mammals.
3210 **1060** 13s. black, blue & orge 20 15
3211 – 25s. black, brown & grn 35 25
3212 – 30s. black, brown & yell 50 25
3213 – 42s. multicoloured . . . 75 30
3214 – 60s. multicoloured . . . 95 50
DESIGNS: 25s. Banded linsang; 30s. Zorilla; 42s. Banded palm civet; 60s. Broad-striped galidia.

1061 Nikolai Liliev

1985. Birth Centenary of Nikolai Liliev (poet).
3215 **1061** 30s. lt brn, brn & gold 30 30

1062 Tsvyatko Radoinov

1985. 90th Birth Anniv of Tsvyatko Radoinov (resistance fighter).
3216 **1062** 5s. brown and red . . . 10 10

1063 Asen Zlatarov

1065 Lenin Monument, Sofia

1064 Research Ship "Akademik"

1985. Birth Cent. of Asen Zlatarov (biochemist).
3217 **1063** 5s. purple, yellow & grn 10 10

1985. 13th General Assembley and 125th Anniv of Intergovernmental Oceanographic Commission. Sheet 90 × 60 mm.
MS3218 **1064** 80s. multicoloured 1·40 1·40

1985. 115th Birth Anniv of Lenin. Sheet 55 × 87 mm.
MS3219 **1065** 50s. multicoloured 75 75

1066 Olive Branch and Sword Blade

1985. 30th Anniv of Warsaw Pact.
3220 **1066** 13s. multicoloured . . . 15 10

1067 Bach

1069 St. Methodius

1068 Girl with Birds

1985. Composers.
3221 **1067** 42s. blue and red . . . 65 30
3222 – 42s. violet and green . . 65 30
3223 – 42s. yellow, brn & orge 65 30
3224 – 42s. yellow, brn & red 65 30
3225 – 42s. yellow, grn & blue 65 30
3226 – 42s. yellow, red & grn 65 30
DESIGNS: No. 3222, Mozart; 3223, Tchaikovsky; 3224, Modest Petrovich Musorgsky; 3225, Giuseppe Verdi; 3226, Filip Kutev.

1985. 3rd "Banners for Peace" Children's Meeting, Sofia. Multicoloured.
3227 5s. Type **1068** 15 15
3228 8s. Children painting . . . 15 15
3229 13s. Girl among flowers . . 15 15
3230 20s. Children at market stall 20 15
3231 25s. Circle of children . . . 30 25
3232 30s. Nurse 30 25
MS3233 70 × 110 mm. 50s. Children dancing (vert). Perf or imperf 1·60 1·60

1985. 1100th Death Anniv of St. Methodius.
3234 **1069** 13s. multicoloured . . . 40 25

1070 Soldiers and Nazi Flags

1985. 40th Anniv of V.E. ("Victory in Europe") Day. Multicoloured.
3235 5s. Type **1070** 10 15
3236 13s. 11th Infantry parade, Sofia 15 25
3237 30s. Soviet soldier with orphan 40 30
MS3238 90 × 123 mm. 50s. Soldier raising Soviet flag . . . . . . 1·00 1·00

1071 Woman carrying Child and Man on Donkey

1985. 7th International Festival of Humour and Satire, Gabrovo.
3239 **1071** 13s. black, yell & red 15 20

1072 Profiles and Flowers

1985. International Youth Year.
3240 **1072** 13s. multicoloured . . . 25 10

1073 Ivan Vazov

1985. 135th Birth Anniv of Ivan Vazov (poet).
3241 **1073** 5s. brown and stone . . 15 10

1074 Monument to Unknown Soldiers and City Arms

1985. Millenary of Khaskovo.
3242 **1074** 5s. multicoloured . . . 15 10

1075 Festival Emblem

1077 Vasil E. Aprilov (founder)

1076 Indira Gandhi

1985. 12th World Youth and Students' Festival, Moscow.
3243 **1075** 13s. multicoloured . . . 15 10

1985. Indira Gandhi (Indian Prime Minister) Commemoration.
3244 **1076** 30s. brown, orge & yell 25 20

1985. 150th Anniv of New Bulgarian School, Gabrovo.
3245 **1077** 5s. blue, purple & grn 15 10

1078 Congress Emblem

1985. 36th International Shorthand and Typing Federation Congress ("Intersteno"), Sofia.
3246 **1078** 13s. multicoloured . . . 15 10

1079 Alexandr Nevski Cathedral, Sofia

1985. Sixth General Assembly of World Tourism Organization, Sofia.
3247 **1079** 42s. green, blue & orge 40 35

1080 State Arms and UN Flag

1081 Rosa "Trakijka"

1985. 40th Anniv of UNO (3248) and 30th Anniv of Bulgaria's Membership (3249). Multicoloured.
3248 13s. Dove around UN emblem 15 15
3249 13s. Type **1080** 15 15

1985. Roses. Multicoloured.
3250 5s. "Rosa damascena" . . . 10 15
3251 13s. Type **1081** 20 15
3252 20s. "Radiman" 25 15
3253 30s. "Marista" 35 25
3254 42s. "Valentina" 50 30
3255 60s. "Maria" 70 45

1082 Peace Dove

1985. 10th Anniv of European Security and Co-operation Conference, Helsinski.
3256 **1082** 13s. multicoloured . . . 15 10

1083 Water Polo

1985. European Swimming Championships, Sofia. Multicoloured.
3257 5s. Butterfly stroke (horiz) 10 15
3258 13s. Type **1083** 20 15
3259 42s. Diving 60 30
3260 60s. Synchronized swimming (horiz) 90 40

1084 Edelweiss

1985. 90th Anniv of Bulgarian Tourist Organization.
3261 **1084** 5s. multicoloured . . . 10 10

1085 State Arms

1086 Footballers

1985. Cent of Union of E. Roumelia and Bulgaria.
3262 **1085** 5s. black, orge & green 10 10

1985. World Cup Football Championship, Mexico (1986) (1st issue).
3263 **1086** 5s. multicoloured . . . 10 15
3264 – 13s. multicoloured . . . 20 15
3265 – 30s. multicoloured . . . 45 25
3266 – 42s. multicoloured . . . 60 35
MS3267 54 × 76 mm. 1l. multicoloured (horiz) . . . . . 1·80 1·80
DESIGNS: 13s. to 1l. Various footballers.
See also Nos. 3346/**MS**3352.

1087 Computer Picture of Boy

1985. International Young Inventors' Exhibition, Plovdiv. Multicoloured.
3268 5s. Type **1087** 15 15
3269 13s. Computer picture of youth 15 15
3270 30s. Computer picture of cosmonaut 30 20

1088 St. John's Church, Nesebur

1985. 40th Anniv of UNESCO. Mult.
3271 5s. Type **1088** 15 15
3272 13s. Rila Monastery 15 15
3273 35s. Soldier (fresco, Ivanovo Rock Church) 35 25
3274 42s. Archangel Gabriel (fresco, Boyana Church) 45 25
3275 60s. Thracian woman (fresco, Kazanlak tomb) 75 45
MS3276 100 × 83 mm. 1l. Madara horseman (horiz). Imperf . . . 1·80 1·80

1089 Lyudmila Zhivkova Palace of Culture

1985. 23rd United Nations Educational, Scientific and Cultural Organization General Session, Sofia. Sheet 62 × 95 mm.
MS3277 **1089** 1l. multicoloured 1·80 1·80

1090 Colosseum, Rome

1091 "Gladiolus"

1985. "Italia '85" International Stamp Exhibition, Rome.
3278 **1090** 42s. multicoloured . . . 30 30

1985. Flowers.
3279 **1091** 5s. pink and red . . . 10 15
3280 – 5s. blue and light blue 10 15
3281 – 5s. lt violet & violet . . 10 15
3282 – 8s. light blue and blue 15 15
3283 – 8s. orange and red . . 10 15
3284 – 32s. orange and brown 40 30
DESIGNS: No. 3280, Garden iris; 3281, Dwarf morning glory; 3282, Morning glory; 3283, "Anemone coronaria"; 3284, Golden-rayed lily.

1092 St. Methodius

1093 Cologne Cathedral

1985. Cultural Congress of European Security and Co-operation Conference, Budapest. Sheet 105 × 93 mm containing T **1092** and similar vert designs. Multicoloured.
MS3285 50s. St. Cyril; 50s. Map of Europe; 50s. Type **1092** . . . 2·20 2·20

1985. Historic Ships (4th series). As T **753**. Multicoloured.
3286 5s. 17th-century Dutch fly 10 10
3287 12s. "Sovereign of the Seas" (English galleon) 20 10
3288 20s. Mediterranean polacca 35 15
3289 25s. "Prince Royal" (English warship) 30 25
3290 42s. Xebec 55 35
3291 60s. 17th-century English warship 80 50

1985. "Philatelia '85" International Stamp Exhibition, Cologne. Sheet 109 × 56 mm containing T **1093** and similar vert design, each black, blue and red.
MS3292 30s. Type **1093**; 30s. Alexandr Nevski Cathedral, Sofia 95 1·10

1094 Bacho Kiro

1095 Hands, Sword and Bible

1985. Revolutionaries.
3293 **1094** 5s. light brown, brown and blue 10 10
3294 – 5s. green, purple & brown 10 10
DESIGN: No. 3294, Georgi S. Rakovski.

1985. 150th Anniv of Turnovo Uprising.
3295 **1095** 13s. brown, blue & pur 15 15

1096 "1185 Revolution" (G. Bogdanov)

1985. 800th Anniv of Liberation from Byzantine Empire. Multicoloured.
3296 5s. Type **1096** 20 15
3297 13s. "1185 Revolution" (Al. Terziev) 20 15
3298 30s. "Battle of Klakotnitsa, 1230" (B. Grigorov and M. Ganovski) 40 30
3299 42s. "Veliko Turnovo" (Ts. Lavrenov) 60 35
MS3300 74 × 80 mm. 1l. Church of St. Dimitrius, Veliko Turnovo (38 × 28 mm). Imperf . . . . . 1·60 1·60

1097 Emblem

1985. "Bralkanfila '85" Stamp Exhibition, Vratsa. Sheet 55 × 80 mm.
MS3301 **1097** 40s. blue, black and deep blue 75 75

1098 Emblem and Globe

1985. International Development Programme for Posts and Telecommunications.
3302 **1098** 13s. multicoloured . . . 10 10

1099 Popov

1985. 70th Birth Anniv of Anton Popov (revolutionary).
3303 **1099** 5s. red 10 10

1100 Doves around Snowflake

1985. New Year. Multicoloured.
3304 5s. Type **1100** 15 10
3305 13s. Circle of stylized doves 15 10

1101 Pointer and Chukar Partridge

1985. Hunting Dogs. Multicoloured.
3306 5s. Type **1101** 25 15
3307 8s. Irish setter and common pochard 35 15
3308 13s. English setter and mallard 45 15
3309 20s. Cocker spaniel and Eurasian woodcock . . . 65 15
3310 25s. German pointer and rabbit 15 25
3311 30s. Bulgarian bloodhound and boar 15 25
3312 42s. Dachshund and fox . . 50 35

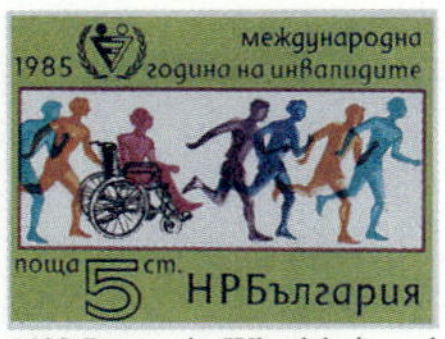

1102 Person in Wheelchair and Runners

1985. International Year of Disabled Persons (1984).
3313 **1102** 5s. multicoloured . . . 15 10

1103 Georgi Dimitrov (statesman)

1985. 50th Anniv of 7th Communist International Congress, Moscow.
3314 **1103** 13s. red 15 10

1104 Emblem within "40"

1986. 40th Anniv of UNICEF.
3315 **1104** 13s. blue, gold & black 15 10

1105 Blagoev **1106** Hands and Dove within Laurel Wreath

1986. 130th Birth Anniv of Dimitur Blagoev (founder of Bulgarian Social Democratic Party).
3316 **1105** 5s. purple and orange 15 10

1986. International Peace Year.
3317 **1106** 5s. multicoloured . . . 15 10

1107 "Dactylorhiza romana"

1986. Orchids. Multicoloured.
3318 5s. Type **1107** 10 15
3319 13s. "Epipactis palustris" . . 15 15
3320 30s. "Ophrys cornuta" . . . 30 15
3321 32s. "Limodorum abrotivum" 30 25
3322 42s. "Cypripedium calceolus" 40 30
3323 60s. "Orchis papilionacea" 1·00 40

1108 Angora Rabbit

1986. Rabbits.
3324 – 5s. grey, black & brown 10 15
3325 **1108** 25s. red and black . . . 25 15
3326 – 30s. brown, yell & blk 30 15
3327 – 32s. orange and black 30 25
3328 – 42s. red and black . . . 40 25
3329 – 60s. blue and black . . 1·10 40
DESIGNS: 5s. French grey; 30s. English lop-eared; 32s. Belgian; 42s. English spotted; 60s. Dutch black and white rabbit.

1109 Front Page and Ivan Bogorov

1986. 140th Anniv of "Bulgarian Eagle".
3330 **1109** 5s. multicoloured . . . 10 10

1110 Neptune and Comet Position, 1980

1986. Appearance of Halley's Comet. Sheet 120 × 114 mm containing T **1110** and similar horiz designs, each violet, blue and yellow.
MS3331 25s. Type **1110**; 25s. Sun, Earth, Mars, Saturn and comet postitions, 1985 and 1910/86; 25s. Uranus and comet positions, 1960, 1926, 1948 and 1970; 25s. Jupiter and comet position, 1911 . . . 1·20 1·20

1111 Bashev **1112** Wave Pattern

1986. 50th Birth Anniv (1985) of Vladimir Bashev (poet).
3332 **1111** 5s. blue & light blue . . 10 10

1986. 13th Bulgarian Communist Party Congress.
3333 **1112** 5s. blue, green and red 10 15
3334 – 8s. blue and red 10 15
3335 – 13s. blue, red & lt blue 10 15
MS3336 60 × 77 mm. 50s. multicoloured 70 70
DESIGNS: 8s. Printed circuit as tail of shooting star; 13s. Computer picture of man; 50s. Steel construction tower.

1113 "Vostok 1"

1986. 25th Anniv of First Man in Space. Sheet 105 × 100 mm containing T **1113** and similar horiz design, each deep blue and blue.
MS3337 50s. Type **1113**; 50s. Yuri Gagarin . . . . 1·40 1·40

1114 Monument, Panagyurishte **1116** Stylized Ear of Wheat

1115 Gymnast

1986. 110th Anniv of April Uprising.
3338 **1114** 5s. black, stone and green 15 10
3339 – 13s. black, stone & red 15 10
DESIGN: 13s. Statue of Khristo Botev, Vratsa.

1986. 75th Anniv of Levski-Spartak Sports Club. Sheet 81 × 65 mm. Imperf.
MS3340 **1115** 50s. multicoloured 65 65

1986. 35th Bulgarian People's Agrarian Union Congress.
3341 **1116** 5s. gold, orange & blk 10 10
3342 – 8s. gold, blue and black 10 10
3343 – 13s. multicoloured . . . 10 10
DESIGNS: 8s. Stylized ear of wheat on globe; 13s. Flags.

1117 Transport Systems **1118** Emblem

1986. Socialist Countries' Transport Ministers Conference.
3344 **1117** 13s. multicoloured . . . 15 10

1986. 17th International Book Fair, Sofia.
3345 **1118** 13s. grey, red and black 15 10

1119 Player with Ball

1986. World Cup Football Championship, Mexico (2nd issue). Multicoloured.
3346 5s. Type **1119** 15 15
3347 13s. Player tackling (horiz) 20 15
3348 20s. Player heading ball (horiz) 35 20
3349 30s. Player kicking ball (horiz) 55 25
3350 42s. Goalkeeper (horiz) . . 60 35
3351 60s. Player with trophy . . 90 50
MS3352 95 × 75 mm. 1l. Azteca Stadium (42 × 31 mm) . . . . 1·40 1·40

1120 Square Brooch

1986. Treasures of Preslav. Multicoloured.
3353 5s. Type **1120** 15 15
3354 13s. Pendant (vert) 15 15
3355 20s. Wheel-shaped pendant 25 15
3356 30s. Breast plate decorated with birds and chalice . . 30 20
3357 42s. Pear-shaped pendant (vert) 40 25
3358 60s. Enamelled cockerel on gold base 65 40

1121 Fencers with Sabres

1986. World Fencing Championships, Sofia. Mult.
3359 5s. Type **1121** 15 10
3360 13s. Fencers 15 10
3361 25s. Fencers with rapiers . . 25 20

1122 Stockholm Town Hall **1123** White Stork (*Ciconia ciconia*)

1986. "Stockholmia 86" International Stamp Exn.
3362 **1122** 42s. brn, red & dp red 40 50

1986. Nature Protection. Sheet 138 × 90 mm containing T **1123** and similar vert designs. Multicoloured.
MS3363 30s. Type **1132**; 30s. Yellow water-lily (*Nuphar lutea*); 30s. Fire salamander (*Salamandra salamandra*); 30s. White water-lily (*Nymphaea alba*) . . . . 5·50 2·40

1124 Arms and Parliament Building, Sofia

1986. 40th Anniv of People's Republic.
3364 **1124** 5s. green, red & lt grn 15 10

1125 Posthorn

1986. 15th Organization of Socialist Countries' Postal Administrations Session, Sofia.
3365 **1125** 13s. multicoloured . . . 15 10

1126 "All Pull Together" **1127** Dove and Book as Pen Nib

1986. 40th Anniv of Voluntary Brigades.
3366 **1126** 5s. multicoloured . . . 15 10

1986. 10th International Journalists Association Congress, Sofia.
3367 **1127** 13s. blue & deep blue 15 10

1128 Wrestlers

1986. 75th Anniv of Levski-Spartak Sports Club.
3368 **1128** 5s. multicoloured . . . 15 10

1129 Saints Cyril and Methodius with Disciples (fresco)

1986. 1100th Anniv of Arrival in Bulgaria of Pupils of Saints Cyril and Methodius.
3369 **1129** 13s. brown and buff . . 15 10

1130 Old and Modern Telephones

1986. Centenary of Telephone in Bulgaria.
3370 **1130** 5s. multicoloured . . . 15 10

1131 Weightlifter

1986. World Weightlifting Championships, Sofia.
3371 **1131** 13s. multicoloured . . . 15 10

1986. Historic Ships (5th series). 18th-century ships. As T **753**. Multicoloured.

3372	5s. "King of Prussia" . . .	10	10
3373	13s. Indiaman	15	10
3374	25s. Xebec	30	20
3375	30s. "Sv. Paul"	40	30
3376	32s. Topsail schooner . . .	40	30
3377	42s. "Victory"	50	40

1132 (½-size illustration)

1986. European Security and Co-operation Conference Review Meeting, Vienna. Sheet 109 × 86 mm containing T **1132** and similar vert designs.
MS3378 50s. olive, orange and green; 50s. green, orange and blue (Vienna Town Hall); 50s. multicoloured (United Nations Centre, Vienna) . . . . 2·75 2·75

1133 Silver Jug decorated with Seated Woman

1986. 14th Congress of Bulgarian Philatelic Federation and 60th Anniv of International Philatelic Federation. Repousse work found at Rogozen.
3379 **1133** 10s. grey, black & bl 15 15
3380 – 10s. green, blk & red 15 15
DESIGN: No. 3380, Silver jug decorated with sphinx.

1134 Doves between Pine Branches

1986. New Year.
3381 **1134** 5s. red, green and blue 10 10
3382 – 13s. mauve, blue & vio 15 10
DESIGN: 13s. Fireworks and snowflakes.

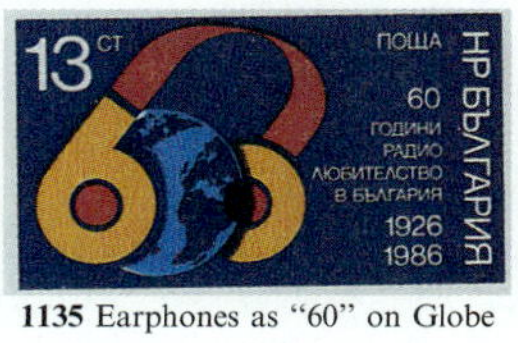

1135 Earphones as "60" on Globe

1986. 60th Anniv of Bulgarian Amateur Radio.
3383 **1135** 13s. multicoloured . . . 15 10

1136 "The Walnut Tree" (Danail Dechev)

1986. 90th Anniv of Sofia Art Academy. Modern Paintings. Sheet 146 × 102 mm containing T **1136** and similar horiz designs. Multicoloured.
MS3384 25s. Type **1136**; 25s. "Resistance Fighters and Soldiers" (Iliya Beshkov); 30s. "Melnik" (Veselin Staikov); 30s. "The Olive Grove" (Kiril Tsonev) . . . . 2·00 2·00

1137 Gen. Augusto Sandino and Flag

1988. 25th Anniv of Sandinista National Liberation Front of Nicaragua.
3385 **1137** 13s. multicoloured . . . 15 10

1138 Dimitur and Konstantin Miladinov (authors)

1139 Pencho Slaveikov (poet)

1986. 125th Anniv of "Bulgarian Popular Songs".
3386 **1138** 10s. blue, brn & red . . 15 10

1986. Writers' Birth Annivs. Multicoloured.

3387	5s. Type **1139** (125th anniv)	15	10
3388	5s. Stoyan Mikhailovski (130th anniv)	15	10
3389	8s. Nikola Atanasov (dramatist) (centenary) . .	15	10
3390	8s. Ran Bosilek (children's author) (centenary) . . .	15	10

1140 Raiko Daskalov

1141 "Girl with Fruit"

1986. Birth Cent of Raiko Daskalov (politician).
3391 **1140** 5s. brown 15 10

1986. 500th Birth Anniv of Titian (painter). Multicoloured.

3392	5s. Type **1141**	10	15
3393	13s. "Flora"	15	15
3394	20s. "Lucretia and Tarquin"	20	15
3395	30s. Caiphas and Mary Magdalene	35	15
3396	32s. "Toilette of Venus" (detail)	35	25
3397	42s. "Self-portrait"	75	30
MS3398	105 × 75 mm. 1l. "Danae" (32 × 54 mm)	2·40	1·50

1142 Fiat, 1905

1986. Racing Cars.

3399	**1142**	5s. brown, red & black	10	15
3400	–	10s. red, orange & blk	15	15
3401	–	25s. green, red & black	30	15
3402	–	32s. brown, red & blk	40	25
3403	–	40s. violet, red & blk	50	25
3404	–	42s. grey, black and red	90	35

DESIGNS: 10s. Bugatti, 1928; 25s. Mercedes, 1936; 32s. Ferrari, 1952; 40s. Lotus, 1985; 42s. Maclaren, 1986.

1143 Steam Locomotive

1987. 120th Anniv of Ruse–Varna Railway.
3405 **1143** 5s. multicoloured . . . 15 30

1144 Debelyanov

1987. Birth Cent of Dimcho Debelyanov (poet).
3406 **1144** 5s. dp blue, yellow & bl 15 10

1145 Lazarus Ludwig Zamenhof (inventor)

1987. Centenary of Esperanto (invented language).
3407 **1145** 13s. blue, yellow & grn 15 10

1146 The Blusher

1147 Worker

1987. Edible Fungi. Multicoloured.

3408	5s. Type **1146**	10	15
3409	20s. Royal boletus	20	15
3410	30s. Red-capped scaber stalk	35	30
3411	32s. Shaggy ink cap	45	30
3412	40s. Bare-toothed russula . .	55	35
3413	60s. Chanterelle	70	65

1987. 10th Trade Unions Congress, Sofia.
3414 **1147** 5s. violet and red . . . 15 10

1148 Silver-gilt Plate with Design of Hercules and Auge

1987. Treasure of Rogozen. Multicoloured.

3415	5s. Type **1148**	10	15
3416	8s. Silver-gilt jug with design of lioness attacking stag	10	15
3417	20s. Silver-gilt plate with quatrefoil design	15	15
3418	30s. Silver-gilt jug with design of horse rider . . .	20	25
3419	32s. Silver-gilt pot with palm design	25	25
3420	42s. Silver jug with chariot and horses design	40	20

1149 Ludmila Zhivkova Feativai Complex, Varna

1987. Modern Architecture. Sheet 107 × 100 mm containing T **1149** and similar horiz designs. Multicoloured.
MS3421 30s. Type **1149**; 30s. Ministry of Foreign Affairs building, Sofia; 30s. Interpred building, Sofia; 30s. Hotel, Sandanski . . . . 1·40 1·40

1150 Wrestlers

1152 "X" and Flags

1151 Totem Pole

1987. 30th European Freestyle Wrestling Championships, Turnovo.
3422 **1150** 5s. lilac, red and violet 10 10
3423 – 13s. dp blue, red & blue 15 10
DESIGNS: 13st. Wrestlers (different).

1987. "Capex '87" International Stamp Exhibition, Toronto.
3424 **1151** 42s. multicoloured . . . 50 30

1987. 10th Fatherland Front Congress.
3425 **1152** 5s. green, orange & bl 15 10

1153 Georgi Dimitrov and Profiles

1987. 15th Dimitrov Communist Youth League Congress.
3426 **1153** 5s. purple, green & red 15 10

1154 Mask

1156 Mariya Gigova

1155 Mastheads

1987. 8th International Festival of Humour and Satire, Gabrovo.
3427 **1154** 13s. multicoloured . . . 15 10

1987. 60th Anniv of "Rabotnichesko Delo" (newspaper).
3428 **1155** 5s. red and black . . . 15 10

1987. 13th World Rhythmic Gymnastics Championships, Varna.

3429	**1156**	5s. blue and yellow . .	10	15
3430	–	8s. red and yellow . . .	10	15
3431	–	13s. blue and stone . .	15	15
3432	–	25s. red and yellow . .	25	15
3433	–	30s. black and yellow	25	20
3434	–	42s. mauve and yellow	40	25
MS3435		78 × 87 mm. 1l. violet and ochre	95	95

DESIGNS: 8s. Iliana Raeva; 13s. Aneliya Ralenkova; 25s. Dilyana Georgieva; 30s. Liliya Ignatova; 42s. Bianka Panova; 1l. Neshka Robeva.

1157 Man breaking Chains around Globe and Kolarov

1987. 110th Birth Anniv of Vasil Kolarov (Prime Minister 1949–50).
3436 **1157** 5s. multicoloured . . . 15 10

1158 Stela Blagoeva

1160 Roe Deer

1159 Levski

1987. Birth Centenary of Stela Blagoeva.
3437 **1158** 5s. brown and pink . . 15 35

1987. 150th Birth Anniv of Vasil Levski (revolutionary).
3438 **1159** 5s. brown and green . . 10 10
3439 – 13s. green and brown 15 10
DESIGN: 13s. Levski and Bulgarian Revolutionary Central Committee emblem.

1987. Stags. Multicoloured.
3440 5s. Type **1160** 10 15
3441 10s. Elk (horiz) 10 15
3442 32s. Fallow deer 30 25
3443 40s. Sika deer 40 25
3444 42s. Red deer (horiz) . . . 40 25
3445 60s. Reindeer 60 25
MS3445a 145 × 131 mm. Nos. 3340/5. Imperf . . . . . 1·80 1·80

1161 Barbed Wire as Dove

1987. International Namibia Day.
3446 **1161** 13s. black, red & orge 15 10

1162 Kirkov

1163 "Phacelia tanacetifolia"

1987. 120th Birth Anniv of Georgi Kirkov (pseudonym Maistora) (politician).
3447 **1162** 5s. red and pink . . . 15 10

1987. Flowers. Multicoloured.
3448 5s. Type **1163** 10 15
3449 10s. Sunflower 10 15
3450 30s. False acacia 25 20
3451 32s. Dutch lavender 30 25
3452 42s. Small-leaved lime . . . 35 25
3453 60s. "Onobrychis sativa" . . 55 40

1164 Mil Mi-8 Helicopter, Tupolev Tu-154 and Antonov An-12 Aircraft

1987. 40th Anniv of Balkanair.
3454 **1164** 25s. multicoloured . . . 30 10

1165 1879 5c. Stamp

1987. "Bulgaria '89" International Stamp Exhibition, Sofia (1st issue).
3455 **1165** 13s. multicoloured . . . 15 10
See also Nos. 3569, 3579/82 and 3602/5.

1166 Copenhagen Town Hall

1167 "Portrait of Girl" (Stefan Ivanov)

1987. "Hafnia '87" International Stamp Exhibition, Copenhagen.
3456 **1166** 42s. multicoloured . . . 30 40

1987. Paintings in Sofia National Gallery. Mult.
3457 5s. Type **1167** 10 15
3458 8s. "Woman carrying Grapes" (Bencho Obreshkov) 10 15
3459 20s. "Portrait of a Woman wearing a Straw Hat" (David Perez) 20 15
3460 25s. "Women listening to Marimba" (Kiril Tsonev) 25 15
3461 32s. "Boy with Harmonica" (Nenko Balkanski) . . . 30 30
3462 60s. "Rumyana" (Vasil Stoilov) 55 50

1168 Battle Scene

1987. 75th Anniv of Balkan War.
3463 **1168** 5s. black, stone and red 15 10

1169 Emblem

1987. 30th Anniv of International Atomic Energy Agency.
3464 **1169** 13s. blue, green and red 15 10

1170 Mastheads

1987. 95th Anniv of "Rabotnik", 90th Anniv of "Rabotnicheski Vestnik" and 60th Anniv of "Rabotnichesko Delo" (newspapers).
3465 **1170** 5s. red, blue and gold 15 10

1171 Winter Wren

1987. Birds. Multicoloured.
3466 5s. Type **1171** 10 15
3467 13s. Yellowhammer 20 15
3468 20s. Eurasian nuthatch . . . 25 15
3469 30s. Blackbird 40 25
3470 42s. Hawfinch 60 25
3471 60s. White-throated dipper 80 35

1172 "Vega" Automatic Space Station

1987. 30th Anniv of Soviet Space Exploration. Sheet 98 × 98 mm containing T **1172** and similar horiz design.
MS3472 50s. blue, orange and purple (Type **1172**); 50s. deep blue, blue and purple ("Soyuz" spacecraft docking with "Mir" space station) 1·60 1·60

1173 Lenin and Revolutionary

1987. 70th Anniv of Russian Revolution.
3473 **1173** 5s. purple and red . . . 10 10
3474 – 13s. blue and red . . . 15 10
DESIGN: 13s. Lenin and cosmonaut.

1174 Biathlon

1987. Winter Olympic Games, Calgary. Mult.
3475 5s. Type **1174** 10 15
3476 13s. Slalom 15 15
3477 30s. Figure skating (women's) 35 30
3478 42s. Four-man bobsleigh . . 55 40
MS3479 65 × 87 mm. 1l. Ice hockey 95 95

1175 "Socfilex" Emblem within Folk-design Ornament

1987. New Year. Multicoloured.
3480 5s. Type **1175** 10 10
3481 13s. Emblem within flower ornament 15 10

1176 Helsinki Conference Centre

1987. European Security and Co-operation Conference Review Meeting, Vienna. Sheet 140 × 100 mm containing T **1176** and similar vert designs.
MS3482 50s. lavender, brown and red; 50s. multicoloured (Map of Europe); 50s. multicoloured (Vienna Conference Centre) . . 3·25 3·25

1177 Kabakchiev

1178 "Scilla bythynica"

1988. 110th Birth Anniv of Khristo Kabakchiev (Communist Party official).
3483 **1177** 5s. multicoloured . . . 15 10

1988. Marsh Flowers. Multicoloured.
3484 5s. Type **1178** 10 10
3485 10s. "Geum rhodopaeum" 15 10
3486 13s. "Caltha polypetala" . . 20 10
3487 25s. Fringed water-lily . . . 35 15
3488 30s. "Cortusa matthioli" . . 40 25
3489 42s. Water soldier 60 25

1179 Commander on Horseback

1988. 110th Anniv of Liberation from Turkey. Multicoloured.
3490 5s. Type **1179** 10 10
3491 13s. Soldiers 15 10

1180 Emblem

1988. Public Sector Workers' 8th International Congress, Sofia.
3492 **1180** 13s. multicoloured . . . 15 10

1181 "Yantra", 1888

1988. Centenary of State Railways. Locomotives. Multicoloured.
3493 5s. Type **1181** 15 10
3494 13s. "Khristo Botev", 1905 20 10
3495 25s. Steam locomotive No. 807, 1918 . . . . . 25 15
3496 32s. Class 46 steam locomotive, 1943 . . . . 35 15
3497 42s. Diesel locomotive, 1964 60 25
3498 60s. Electric locomotive, 1979 . . . . 80 30

1182 Ivan Nedyalkov (Shablin)

1183 Traikov

1988. Post Office Anti-fascist Heroes.
3499 **1182** 5s. light brown and brown 10 10
3500 – 8s. grey and blue . . . 10 10
3501 – 10s. green and olive . . 10 10
3502 – 13s. pink and red . . . 20 20
DESIGNS: 8s. Delcho Spasov; 10s. Nikola Ganchev (Gudzho); 13s. Ganka Rasheva (Boika).

1988. 90th Birth Anniv of Georgi Traikov (politician).
3503 **1183** 5s. orange and brown 15 10

1184 Red Cross, Red Crescent and Globe

1185 Girl

1988. 125th Anniv of International Red Cross.
3504 **1184** 13s. multicoloured . . . 15 10

1988. 4th "Banners for Peace" Children's Meeting, Sofia. Children's paintings. Multicoloured.
3505 5s. Type **1185** 10 10
3506 8s. Artist at work 10 10
3507 13s. Circus (horiz) 15 10
3508 20s. Kite flying (horiz) . . . 20 15
3509 32s. Accordion player . . . 30 25
3510 42s. Cosmonaut 45 25
MS3511 86 × 90 mm. 50s. Emblem with film frame (Youth Film Festival) (horiz) 70 75

1186 Marx

1988. 170th Birth Anniv of Karl Marx.
3512 **1186** 13s. red, black & yellow . . . 15 10

1187 Herring Gull

1189 "Soyuz TM" Spacecraft, Flags and Globe

1188 African Elephant

1988. Birds. Multicoloured.
3513 5s. Type **1187** 25 10
3514 5s. White stork 25 10
3515 8s. Grey heron 45 10
3516 8s. Carrion crow 45 10
3517 10s. Northern goshawk . . . 60 10
3518 42s. Eagle owl . . . . . . 1·20 15

1988. Centenary of Sofia Zoo. Multicoloured.
3519 5s. Type **1188** 10 10
3520 13s. White rhinoceros . . . 10 10
3521 25s. Hunting dog 15 15
3522 30s. Eastern white pelican 25 30
3523 32s. Abyssinian ground hornbill 30 40
3524 42s. Snowy owl 65 60

1988. 2nd Soviet–Bulgarian Space Flight. Mult.
3525 5s. Type **1189** 10 10
3526 13s. Rocket on globe . . . 15 10

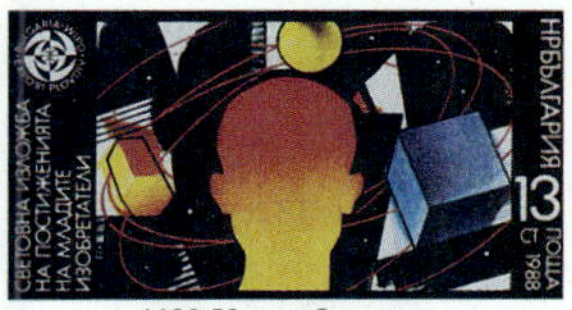
1190 Young Inventor

1988. International Young Inventors' Exhibition, Plovdiv.
3527 **1190** 13s. multicoloured . . . 15 10

1191 1856 Handstamp of Russian Duchy of Finland

1988. "Finlandia '88" International Stamp Exhibition, Helsinki.
3528 **1191** 30s. blue and red . . . 30 30

1192 Player taking Corner Kick

1193 "Portrait of Child"

1988. 8th European Football Championship, West Germany. Multicoloured.
3529 5s. Type **1192** 10 10
3530 13s. Goalkeeper and player 15 10
3531 30s. Referee and player . . 30 20
3532 42s. Player with trophy . . 45 25
MS3533 90 × 69 mm. 1l. Stadium (horiz) . . . . 1·20 1·20

1988. 2nd Death Anniv of Dechko Uzunov (painter). Multicoloured.
3534 5s. Type **1193** 10 10
3535 13s. "Portrait of Mariya Vasileva" 15 10
3536 30s. "Self-portrait" 30 15

1194 Valentina Tereshkova

1988. 25th Anniv of First Woman in Space. Sheet 87 × 56 mm.
MS3537 **1194** 1l. pink and blue 1·20 1·20

1195 "St. John"

1196 High Jumping

1988. Icons from Kurdzhali. Multicoloured.
3538 5s. Type **1195** 15 10
3539 8s. "St. George and Dragon" 15 10

1988. Olympic Games, Seoul. Multicoloured.
3540 5s. Type **1196** 10 10
3541 13s. Weightlifting 15 10
3542 30s. Wrestling 30 25
3543 42s. Gymnastics 50 25
MS3544 115 × 75 mm. 1l. Volleyball 1·10 1·10

1197 Dimitur and Karadzha

1988. 120th Death Anniv of Khadzhi Dimitur and Stefan Karadzha (revolutionaries).
3545 **1197** 5s. green, black & brn 15 10

1198 Magazines

1988. 30th Anniv of "Problems of Peace and Socialism" (magazine).
3546 **1198** 13s. multicoloured . . . 15 10

1199 "The Dead Tree" (Roland Udo)

1988. Paintings in Lyudmila Zhivkova Art Gallery. Multicoloured.
3547 30s. Type **1199** 30 25
3548 30s. "Algiers Harbour" (Albert Marque) 30 25
3549 30s. "Portrait of Hermine David" (Jule Pasquin) . . 30 25
3550 30s. "Madonna and Child with two Saints" (Giovanni Rosso) 30 25

1200 University Building

1988. Centenary of St. Clement of Ohrid University, Sofia.
3551 **1200** 5s. black, yellow & grn 15 10

1201 Czechoslovakia 1918 Stamp Design

1988. "Praga '88" International Stamp Exhibition, Prague.
3552 **1201** 25s. red and blue . . . 30 30

1202 Korea 1884 5m. Stamp

1988. "Olymphilex '88" Olympic Stamps Exhibition, Seoul.
3553 **1202** 62s. red and green . . . 70 70

1203 Anniversary Emblem

1204 Parliament Building, Sofia, and Map

1988. 25th Anniv of Kremikovtsi Steel Mills.
3554 **1203** 5s. violet, red and blue 15 10

1988. 80th Interparliamentary Conference, Sofia.
3555 **1204** 13s. blue and red . . . 15 10

1205 Chalice, Glinena

1988. Kurdzhali Culture. Multicoloured.
3556 5s. Type **1205** 15 10
3557 8s. Part of ruined fortifications, Perperikon (vert) 15 10

1206 Soldiers

1988. 300th Anniv of Chiprovtsi Rising.
3558 **1206** 5s. multicoloured . . . 15 10

1207 Brown Bear

1988. Bears. Multicoloured.
3559 5s. Type **1207** 10 10
3560 8s. Polar bear 10 10
3561 13s. Sloth bear 20 10
3562 20s. Sun bear 30 15
3563 32s. Asiatic black bear . . . 40 25
3564 42s. Spectacled bear 55 25

1208 Emblem

1988. 80th Council of Mutual Economic Aid Transport Commission Meeting, Sofia.
3565 **1208** 13s. red and black . . . 15 10

1209 Emblem

1988. World Ecoforum.
3566 **1209** 20s. multicoloured . . . 25 10

1210 Amphitheatre, Plovdiv

1988. "Plovdiv '88" National Stamp Exhibition.
3567 **1210** 5s. multicoloured . . . 15 10

1211 Transmission Towers

1988. 25th Anniv of Radio and Television.
3568 **1211** 5s. green, blue & brown 15 10

1212 1879 5c. Stamp

1988. "Bulgaria '89" International Stamp Exhibition (2nd issue).
3569 **1212** 42s. orange, blk & mve 40 45

1213 "Ruse" (river boat)

1988. 40th Anniv of Danube Commission. Sheet 104 × 124 mm containing T **1213** and similar horiz design. Multicoloured.
MS3570 1l. Type **1213**; 1l. *Al. Stamboliiski* (river cruiser) . . 2·40 2·40

1214 Children and Cars

1988. Road Safety Campaign.
3571 **1214** 5s. multicoloured . . . 15 10

1215 Rila Hotel, Borovets

1988. Hotels. Multicoloured.
3572 5s. Type **1215** 10 15
3573 8s. Pirin Hotel, Bansko . . 10 15

3574 13s. Shtastlivetsa Hotel, Vitosha 15 15
3575 30s. Perelik Hotel, Pamporovo 45 25

1216 Tree Decoration

1988. New Year. Multicoloured.
3576 5s. Type **1216** 10 10
3577 13s. "Bulgaria '89" emblem, tree and decorations . . . 15 10

1217 Space Shuttle "Buran"

1988. Energiya--Buran Space Flight. Sheet 102 × 67 mm.
MS3578 **1217** 1l. blue . . . . . 1·20 1·10

1218 Mail Coach

1988. "Bulgaria '89" International Stamp Exhibition, Sofia (3rd issue). Mail Transport. Multicoloured.
3579 25s. Type **1218** 30 15
3580 25s. Paddle-steamer 30 10
3581 25s. Lorry 30 15
3582 25s. Biplane 30 10

1219 India 1947 1½a. Independence Stamp

1989. "India 89" International Stamp Exhibition, New Delhi.
3583 **1219** 62s. green and orange 65 70

1220 France 1850 10c. Ceres Stamp

1989. "Philexfrance '89" International Stamp Exhibition, Paris.
3584 **1220** 42s. brown and blue . . 50 45

1221 Slalom

1989. "Sofia '89" University Winter Games, Sofia. Sheet 84 × 142 mm containing T **1221** and similar vert designs. Multicoloured. Imperf.
MS3585 25s. Type **1221**; 25s. Ice hockey; 25s. Biathlon; 25s. Speed skating . . . . 1·30 1·20

1222 Don Quixote (sculpture, House of Humour and Satire) **1223** "Ramonda serbica"

1989. International Festival of Humour and Satire, Gabrovo.
3586 **1222** 13s. multicoloured . . . 15 10

1989. Flowers. Multicoloured.
3587 5s. Type **1223** 10 10
3588 10s. "Paeonia maskula" . . 10 10
3589 25s. "Viola perinensis" . . . 25 15
3590 30s. "Dracunculus vulgaris" 35 25
3591 42s. "Tulipa splendens" . . 45 30
3592 60s. "Rindera umbellata" 65 40

1224 Common Noctule Bat

1989. Bats. Multicoloured.
3593 5s. Type **1224** 10 15
3594 13s. Greater horseshoe bat 25 15
3595 30s. Large mouse-eared bat 60 30
3596 42s. Particoloured frosted bat 90 40

1225 Stamboliiski

1989. 110th Birth Anniv of Aleksandur Stamboliiski (Prime Minister 1919–23).
3597 **1225** 5s. black and orange . . 15 10

1226 Launch of "Soyuz 33"

1989. 10th Anniv of Soviet–Bulgarian Space Flight. Sheet 130 × 90 mm containing T **1226** and similar vert design. Multicoloured.
MS3598 50s. Type **1226**; 50s. Cosmonauts Nicolai Rukavishnikov and Georgi Ivanov 1·60 1·30

1227 Young Inventor

1989. International Young Inventors' Exhibition, Plovdiv.
3599 **1227** 5s. multicoloured . . . 15 10

1228 Stanke Dimitrov-Marek (Party activist) **1229** "John the Baptist" (Toma Vishanov)

1989. Birth Centenaries.
3600 **1228** 5s. red and black . . . 15 10
3601 – 5s. red and black . . . 15 10
DESIGN: No. 3601, Petko Yenev (revolutionary).

1989. "Bulgaria '89" International Stamp Exhibition, Sofia (4th issue). Icons. Multicoloured.
3602 30s. Type **1229** 30 15
3603 30s. "St. Dimitur" (Ivan Terziev) 30 15
3604 30s. "Archangel Michael" (Dimitur Molerov) . . . 30 15
3605 30s. "Madonna and Child" (Toma Vishanov) 30 15

1230 Fax Machine and Woman reading letter

1989. 110th Anniv of Bulgarian Post and Telegraph Services. Multicoloured.
3606 5s. Type **1230** 10 20
3607 8s. Telex machine and old telegraph machine 10 20
3608 35s. Modern and old telephones 30 30
3609 42s. Dish aerial and old radio 40 40

1231 "Nike in Quadriga" (relief)

1989. 58th International Philatelic Federation Congress, Sofia. Sheet 87 × 120 mm.
MS3610 **1231** 1l. multicoloured 1·20 1·20

1232 A. P. Aleksandrov, A. Ya. Solovov and V. P. Savinikh

1989. Air. "Soyuz TM5" Soviet-Bulgarian Space Flight.
3611 **1232** 13s. multicoloured . . . 25 10

1233 Party Programme **1234** Sofronii Vrachanski (250th anniv)

1989. 70th Anniv of First Bulgarian Communist Party Congress, Sofia.
3612 **1233** 5s. blk, red & dp red 15 10

1989. Writers' Birth Anniversaries.
3613 **1234** 5s. green, brown & blk 15 10
3614 – 5s. green, brown & blk 15 10
DESIGN: No. 3614, Iliya Bluskov (150th anniv).

1235 Birds

1989. Bicentenary of French Revolution. Each black, red and blue.
3615 13s. Type **1235** 20 15
3616 30s. Jean-Paul Marat . . . 35 15
3617 42s. Robespierre 45 20

1236 Gymnastics

1989. 7th Friendly Armies Summer Spartakiad. Multicoloured.
3618 5s. Type **1236** 10 10
3619 13s. Show jumping 20 10
3620 30s. Long jumping 35 15
3621 42s. Shooting 45 20

1237 Aprilov **1238** Zagorchinov

1989. Birth Bicent of Vasil Aprilov (educationist).
3622 **1237** 8s. lt blue, blue & blk 15 10

1989. Birth Centenary of Stoyan Zagorchinov (writer).
3623 **1238** 10s. turq, brown & blk 15 10

1239 Woman in Kayak

1989. Canoeing and Kayak Championships, Plovdiv. Multicoloured.
3624 13s. Type **1239** 20 15
3625 30s. Man in kayak 40 25

1240 Felix Nadar taking Photograph from his Balloon "Le Geant" (1863) and Airship "Graf Zeppelin" over Alexsandr Nevski Cathedral, Sofia

1989. 150th Anniv of Photography.
3626 **1240** 42s. black, stone & yell 55 25

1241 Lammergeier and Lynx

1989. Centenary of Natural History Museum.
3627 **1241** 13s. multicoloured . . . 30 25

1242 Soldiers

1243 Lyubomir Dardzhikov

1989. 45th Anniv of Fatherland Front Government. Multicoloured.

3628 5s. Type **1242** 10 10
3629 8s. Welcoming officers . . . 10 10
3630 13s. Crowd of youths . . . 15 10

1989. 48th Death Anniversaries of Post Office War Heroes. Multicoloured.

3631 5s. Type **1243** 10 10
3632 8s. Ivan Bankov Dobrev . . 10 10
3633 13s. Nestor Antonov . . . 10 10

1244 Yasenov

1246 Nehru

1245 Lorry leaving Weighbridge

1989. Birth Cent of Khisto Yasenov (writer).

3634 **1244** 8s. grey, brown & blk 15 10

1989. 21st Transport Congress, Sofia.

3635 **1245** 42s. blue & deep blue 55 40

1989. Birth Centenary of Jawaharlal Nehru (Indian statesman).

3636 **1246** 13s. yellow, brn & blk 15 10

1247 Cranes flying

1989. Ecology Congress of European Security and Co-operation Conference, Sofia. Sheet 130 × 85 mm containing T **1247** and similar vert design. Multicoloured.

MS3637 50s. Type **1247**; 1l. Cranes flying (different) . . . . 2·40 2·40

1248 Javelin Sand Boa

1989. Snakes. Multicoloured.

3638 5s. Type **1248** 10 10
3639 10s. Aesculapian snake . . . 10 10
3640 25s. Leopard snake 30 10
3641 30s. Four-lined rat snake . . 45 25
3642 42s. Cat snake 55 30
3643 60s. Whip snake 90 45

1249 Tiger and Balloon of Flags

1250 Boy on Skateboard

1989. Young Inventors' Exhibition, Plovdiv.

3644 **1249** 13s. multicoloured . . . 15 10

1989. Children's Games. Sheet 100 × 120 mm containing T **1250** and similar vert designs. Multicoloured.

MS3645 30s.+15s. Type **1250**; 30s.+15s. Girl with ball and doll; 30s.+15s. Girl jumping over ropes; 30s.+15s. Boy with toy train 2·20 2·30

1251 Goalkeeper saving Ball

1989. World Cup Football Championship, Italy (1990) (1st issue). Multicoloured.

3646 5s. Type **1251** 10 10
3647 13s. Player tackling 15 10
3648 30s. Player heading ball . . 40 20
3649 42s. Player kicking ball . . 60 30
MS3650 109 × 54 mm. 50s. Player tackling; 50s. Players . . . . . 1·30 1·00

See also Nos. 3675/**MS**3679.

1252 Gliders

1989. 82nd International Airsports Federation General Conference, Varna. Aerial Sports. Mult.

3651 5s. Type **1252** 10 10
3652 13s. Hang gliding 25 20
3653 30s. Parachutist landing . . 45 25
3654 42s. Free falling parachutist 70 35

1253 Children on Road Crossing

1989. Road Safety.

3655 **1253** 5s. multicoloured . . . 15 10

1254 Santa Claus's Sleigh

1255 European Shorthair

1989. New Year. Multicoloured.

3656 5s. Type **1254** 15 10
3657 13s. Snowman 20 10

1989. Cats.

3658 **1255** 5s. black and yellow . . 15 15
3659 – 5s. black and grey . . . 15 15
3660 – 8s. black and yellow . . 15 15
3661 – 10s. black & brown . . 20 15
3662 – 10s. black and blue . . 20 15
3663 – 13s. black and red . . 30 20

DESIGNS—HORIZ: No. 3659, Persian; 3660, European shorthair (different); 3662, Persian (different). VERT: No. 3661, Persian (different); 3663, Siamese.

1256 Christopher Columbus and "Santa Maria"

1990. Navigators and their Ships. Multicoloured.

3664 5s. Type **1256** 20 20
3665 8s. Vasco da Gama and "Sao Gabriel" 20 20
3666 13s. Ferdinand Magellan and "Vitoria" 20 20
3667 32s. Francis Drake and "Golden Hind" 35 30
3668 42s. Henry Hudson and "Discoverie" 45 45
3669 60s. James Cook and H.M.S. "Endeavour" . . 60 55

1257 Banner

1990. Centenary of Esperanto (invented language) in Bulgaria.

3670 **1257** 10s. stone, green & blk 15 10

1258 "Portrait of Madeleine Rono" (Maurice Brianchon)

1990. Paintings. Multicoloured.

3671 30s. Type **1258** 40 25
3672 30s. "Still Life" (Suzanne Valadon) 40 25
3673 30s. "Portrait of a Woman" (Moise Kisling) 40 25
3674 30s. "Portrait of a Woman" (Giovanni Boltraffio) . . 40 25

1259 Players

1990. World Cup Football Championship, Italy.

3675 **1259** 5s. multicoloured . . . 10 15
3676 – 13s. multicoloured . . . 15 10
3677 – 30s. multicoloured . . . 40 20
3678 – 42s. multicoloured . . . 65 30
MS3679 80 × 125 mm. 2 × 50s. multicoloured . . . . 1·30 1·00

DESIGNS: 13 to 50s. Various match scenes.

1260 Bavaria 1849 1k. Stamp

1990. "Essen 90" International Stamp Fair.

3680 **1260** 42s. black and red . . . 55 60

1261 Penny Black

1990. "Stamp World London 90" International Stamp Exhibition. Sheet 90 × 140 mm containing T **1261** and similar horiz design.

MS3681 50s. black and blue (Type **1261**); 50s. black and red (Sir Rowland Hill (instigator of postage stamps)) . . . . 1·60 1·40

1262 "100" and Rainbow

1990. Centenary of Co-operative Farming.

3682 **1262** 5s. multicoloured . . . 15 10

1263 "Elderly Couple at Rest"

1990. Birth Centenary of Dimitur Chorbadzhiiski-Chudomir (artist).

3683 **1263** 5s. multicoloured . . . 15 10

1264 Map

1990. Centenary of Labour Day.

3684 **1264** 10s. multicoloured . . . 15 10

1265 Emblem

1990. 125th Anniv of ITU.

3685 **1265** 20s. blue, red & black 30 20

1266 Belgium 1849 10c. "Epaulettes" Stamp

1990. "Belgica 90" International Stamp Exhibition, Brussels.

3686 **1266** 30s. brown and green 50 40

1267 Lamartine and his House

1990. Birth Bicentenary of Alphonse de Lamartine (poet).

3687 **1267** 20s. multicoloured . . . 30 25

1268 Brontosaurus

1990. Prehistoric Animals. Multicoloured.

3688 5s. Type **1268** 10 15
3689 8s. Stegosaurus 15 15
3690 13s. Edaphosaurus 20 15
3691 25s. Rhamphorhynchus . . . 45 30
3692 32s. Protoceratops 60 45
3693 42s. Triceratops 80 65

1269 Swimming

1990. Olympic Games, Barcelona (1992) (1st issue). Multicoloured.

3694	5s. Type **1269**	10	10
3695	13s. Handball	20	10
3696	30s. Hurdling	45	30
3697	42s. Cycling	70	35
MS3698	77 × 117 mm. 50s. Tennis player serving; 50s. Tennis player waiting to receive ball	1·20	1·20

See also Nos. 3840/**MS**3844.

1270 Southern Festoon

1990. Butterflies and Moths. Multicoloured.

3699	5s. Type **1270**	10	15
3700	10s. Jersey tiger moth	15	15
3701	20s. Willow-herb hawk moth	20	15
3702	30s. Striped hawk moth	55	25
3703	42s. "Thecla betulae"	75	40
3704	60s. Cynthia's fritillary	1·00	60

1271 Airbus Industrie A310 Jetliner

1990. Aircraft. Multicoloured.

3705	5s. Type **1271**	10	15
3706	10s. Tupolev Tu-204	15	15
3707	25s. Concorde	40	25
3708	30s. Douglas DC-9	45	30
3709	42s. Ilyushin Il-86	60	35
3710	60s. Boeing 747-300/400	95	50

No. 3705 is wrongly inscribed Airbus "A300".

1272 Iosif I

1274 Putting the Shot

1273 Road and UN Emblem within Triangles

1990. 150th Birth Anniv of Exarch Iosif I.

3711	**1272**	5s. mauve, black & grn	15	10

1990. International Road Safety Year.

3712	**1273**	5s. multicoloured	15	10

1990. "Olymphilex '90" Olympic Stamps Exhibition, Varna. Multicoloured.

3713	5s. Type **1274**	10	30
3714	13s. Throwing the discus	20	10
3715	42s. Throwing the hammer	65	40
3716	60s. Throwing the javelin	90	60

1275 "Sputnik" (first artificial satellite, 1957)

1990. Space Research. Multicoloured.

3717	5s. Type **1275**	10	10
3718	8s. "Vostok" and Yuri Gagarin (first manned flight, 1961)	10	15
3719	10s. Aleksei Leonov spacewalking from "Voskhod 2" (first spacewalk, 1965)	20	10
3720	20s. "Soyuz"–"Apollo" link, 1975	35	20
3721	42s. Space shuttle "Columbia", 1981	70	40
3722	60s. Space probe "Galileo"	1·00	55
MS3723	90 × 71 mm. 1l. Neil Armstrong from "Apollo 11" on lunar surface (first manned moon landing, 1969) (28 × 53 mm)	1·40	1·10

1276 St. Clement of Ohrid

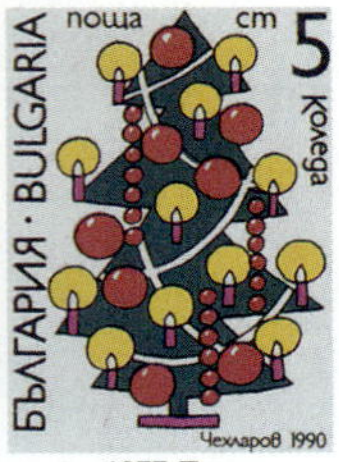

1277 Tree

1990. 1150th Birth Anniv of St. Clement of Ohrid.

3724	**1276**	5s. brown, black & grn	15	10

1990. Christmas. Multicoloured.

3725	5s. Type **1277**	15	10
3726	20s. Father Christmas	20	10

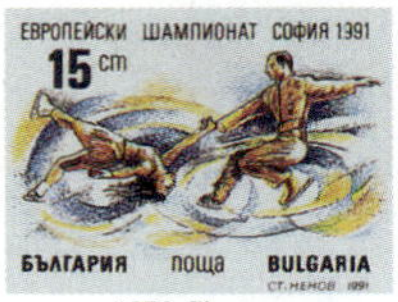

1278 Skaters

1991. European Figure Skating Championships, Sofia.

3727	**1278**	15s. multicoloured	25	10

1279 Chicken

1281 "Good Day" (Paul Gauguin)

1280 Death Cap

1991. Farm Animals.

3728	–	20s. brown and black	15	10
3729	–	25s. blue and black	15	10
3730	**1279**	30s. brown and black	15	10
3731	–	40s. brown and black	20	15
3732	–	62s. green and black	40	25
3733	–	86s. red and black	45	25
3734	–	95s. mauve and black	55	25
3735	–	1l. brown and black	60	30
3736	–	2l. green and black	95	55
3737	–	5l. violet and black	2·20	1·60
3738	–	10l. blue and black	2·75	2·30

DESIGNS: 20s. Sheep; 25s. Goose; 40s. Horse; 62, 95s. Billy goat; 86s. Sow; 1l. Donkey; 2l. Bull; 5l. Common turkey; 10l. Cow.

1991. Fungi. Multicoloured.

3746	5s. Type **1280**	10	40
3747	10s. "Amanita verna"	15	40
3748	20s. Panther cap	30	55
3749	32s. Fly agaric	50	55
3750	42s. Beefsteak morel	65	25
3751	60s. Satan's mushroom	1·00	35

1991. Paintings. Multicoloured.

3752	20s. Type **1281**	10	15
3753	43s. "Madame Dobini" (Edgar Degas)	10	25
3754	62s. "Peasant Woman" (Camille Pissarro)	30	25
3755	67s. "Woman with Black hair" (Edouard Manet)	45	25
3756	80s. "Blue Vase" (Paul Cezanne)	55	30
3757	2l. "Madame Samari" (Pierre Auguste Renoir)	1·20	75
MS3758	65 × 90 mm. 3l. "Self-portrait" (Vincent van Gogh)	1·80	1·80

1282 Map

1991. 700th Anniv of Swiss Confederation.

3759	**1282**	62s. red and violet	40	25

1283 Postman on Bicycle, Envelopes and Paper

1991. 100 Years of Philatelic Publications in Bulgaria.

3760	**1283**	30s. multicoloured	15	10

1284 "Meteosat" Weather Satellite

1991. Europa. Europe in Space. Multicoloured.

3761	43s. Type **1284**	15	25
3762	62s. "Ariane" rocket	65	30

1285 Przewalski's Horse

1991. Horses. Multicoloured.

3763	5s. Type **1285**	10	20
3764	10s. Tarpan	10	20
3765	25s. Black arab	15	20
3766	35s. White arab	20	30
3767	42s. Shetland pony	40	30
3768	60s. Draught horse	65	40

1286 "Expo '91"

1991. "Expo '91" Exhibition, Plovdiv.

3769	**1286**	30s. multicoloured	15	10

1287 Mozart

1991. Death Bicentenary of Wolfgang Amadeus Mozart (composer).

3770	**1287**	62s. multicoloured	40	30

1288 Astronaut and Rear of Space Shuttle "Columbia"

1991. Space Shuttles. Multicoloured.

3771	12s. Type **1288**	10	10
3772	32s. Satellite and "Challenger"	10	15
3773	50s. "Discovery" and satellite	30	15
3774	86s. Satellite and "Atlantis" (vert)	40	20
3775	1l.50 Launch of "Buran" (vert)	70	30
3776	2l. Satellite and "Atlantis" (vert)	1·10	45
MS3777	86 × 74 mm. 3l. Earth, "Atlantis" and Moon	1·70	1·70

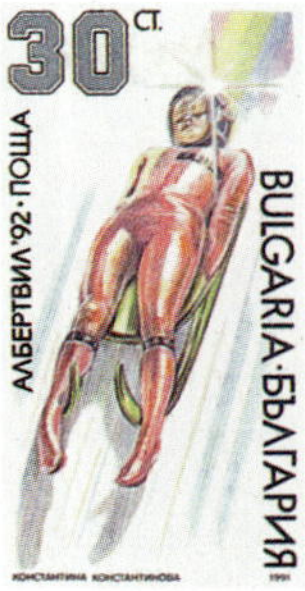

1289 Luge

1291 Japanese Chin

1290 Sheraton Hotel Balkan, Sofia

1991. Winter Olympic Games, Albertville (1992). Multicoloured.

3778	30s. Type **1289**	15	20
3779	43s. Skiing	30	20
3780	67s. Ski jumping	45	20
3781	2l. Biathlon	1·10	70
MS3782	128 × 86 mm. 3l. Two-man bobsleigh	1·60	1·60

1991.

3783	**1290**	62s. multicoloured	30	30

1991. Dogs. Multicoloured.

3784	30s. Type **1291**	10	25
3785	43s. Chihuahua	10	25
3786	62s. Miniature pinscher	20	25
3787	80s. Yorkshire terrier	45	25
3788	1l. Mexican hairless	55	40
3789	3l. Pug	1·60	1·20

1292 Arms

1991. "Philatelia '91" Stamp Fair, Cologne.

3790	**1292**	86s. multicoloured	50	40

1293 Brandenburg Gate

1991. Bicentenary of Brandenburg Gate, Berlin. Sheet 90 × 70 mm.

MS3791	**1293**	4l. green and blue	2·00	1·80

1294 Japan 1871 48mon "Dragon" Stamp

1991. "Phila Nippon '91" International Stamp Exhibition, Tokyo.
3792 **1294** 62s. black, brown & bl . . . 25 20

1295 Early Steam Locomotive and Tender

1991. 125th Anniv of the Railway in Bulgaria. Multicoloured.
3793 30s. Type **1295** 20 10
3794 30s. Early six-wheeled carriage 20 10

1296 Ball ascending to Basket 1297 "Christ carrying the Cross"

1991. Centenary of Basketball. Multicoloured.
3795 43s. Type **1296** 10 15
3796 62s. Ball level with basket mouth 10 15
3797 90s. Ball entering basket . . 45 15
3798 1l. Ball in basket 45 20

1991. 450th Birth Anniv of El Greco (painter). Multicoloured.
3799 43s. Type **1297** 15 15
3800 50s. "Holy Family with St. Anna" 15 15
3801 60s. "St. John of the Cross and St. John the Evangelist" 20 15
3802 62s. "St. Andrew and St. Francis" 20 15
3803 1l. "Holy Family with Magdalene" 40 25
3804 2l. "Cardinal Fernando Nino de Guevara" . . . 90 40
MS3805 68 × 86 mm. 3l. Detail of "Holy Family with St. Anna" (different) (39 × 50 mm) . . . . 1·10 70

1298 Snowman, Moon, Candle, Bell and Heart

1991. Christmas. Multicoloured.
3806 30s. Type **1298** 15 10
3807 62s. Star, clover, angel, house and Christmas tree 15 10

1299 Small Pasque Flower

1991. Medicinal Plants. Multicoloured.
3808 30s.(+15s.) Pale pasque flower 10 10
3809 40s. Type **1299** 10 10
3810 55s. "Pulsatilla halleri" . . . 15 10
3811 60s. "Aquilegia nigricans" . . 15 10
3812 1l. Sea buckthorn 35 15
3813 2l. Blackcurrant 90 45
No. 3808 includes a se-tenant premium-carrying label for 15s. inscribed "ACTION 2000. For Environment Protection".

1300 Greenland Seals

1991. Marine Mammals. Multicoloured.
3814 30s. Type **1300** 10 10
3815 43s. Killer whales 10 10
3816 62s. Walruses 15 15
3817 68s. Bottle-nosed dolphins . 15 10
3818 1l. Mediterranean monk seals 35 25
3819 2l. Common porpoises . . . 90 40

1301 Synagogue

1992. 500th Anniv of Jewish Settlement in Bulgaria.
3820 **1301** 1l. multicoloured . . . 30 10

1302 Rossini, "The Barber of Seville" and Figaro

1992. Birth Bicentenary of Gioacchino Rossini (composer).
3821 **1302** 50s. multicoloured . . . 15 10

1303 Plan of Fair

1992. Centenary of Plovdiv Fair.
3822 **1303** 1l. black and stone . . 30 15

1304 Volvo "740"

1992. Motor Cars. Multicoloured.
3823 30s. Type **1304** 10 10
3824 45s. Ford "Escort" 10 10
3825 50s. Fiat "Croma" 15 10
3826 50s. Mercedes Benz "600" . . 15 10
3827 1l. Peugeot "605" 40 20
3828 2l. B.M.W. "316" 95 25

1305 Amerigo Vespucci

1992. Explorers. Multicoloured.
3829 50s. Type **1305** 15 15
3830 50s. Francisco de Orellana . . 15 15
3831 1l. Ferdinand Magellan . . 30 15
3832 1l. Jimenez de Quesada . . 30 15
3833 2l. Sir Francis Drake . . 70 35
3834 3l. Pedro de Valdivia . . . 1·00 50
MS3835 121 × 83 mm. 4l. Christopher Columbus . . . . 1·60 1·30

1306 Granada

1992. "Granada '92" Int Stamp Exhibition.
3836 **1306** 62s. multicoloured . . . 25 20

1307 "Santa Maria"

1992. Europa. 500th Anniv of Discovery of America by Columbus. Multicoloured.
3837 1l. Type **1307** 55 25
3838 2l. Christopher Columbus . 1·00 55
Nos. 3837/8 were issued together, se-tenant, forming a composite design.

1308 House

1992. S.O.S. Children's Village.
3839 **1308** 1l. multicoloured . . . 40 15

1309 Long Jumping

1992. Olympic Games, Barcelona (2nd issue). Multicoloured.
3840 50s. Type **1309** 15 15
3841 50s. Swimming 15 15
3842 1l. High jumping 40 25
3843 3l. Gymnastics . . . . . . 1·20 50
MS3844 52 × 75 mm. 4l. Olympic Torch (vert) . . . . 1·40 1·20

1310 1902 Laurin and Klement Motor Cycle

1992. Motor Cycles. Multicoloured.
3845 30s. Type **1310** 10 10
3846 50s. 1928 Puch "200 Luxus" 10 10
3847 50s. 1931 Norton "CS 1" . . 10 10
3848 70s. 1950 Harley Davidson . 15 10
3849 1l. 1986 Gilera "SP 01" . . 35 20
3850 2l. 1990 BMW "K 1" . . . 90 30

1311 Genoa

1992. "Genova '92" International Thematic Stamp Exhibition.
3851 **1311** 1l. multicoloured . . . 40 15

1312 Grasshopper 1313 Silhouette of Head on Town Plan

1992. Insects. Multicoloured.
3852 1l. Four-spotted libellula . . 10 10
3853 2l. "Raphidia notata" . . . 20 10
3854 3l. Type **1312** 40 10
3855 4l. Stag beetle 50 10
3856 5l. Fire bug 70 10
3857 7l. Ant . . . . 1·40 50
3858 20l. Wasp . . . . 1·90 1·40
3859 50l. Praying mantis . . . . 7·25 2·50

1992. 50th Anniv of Institute of Architecture and Building.
3862 **1313** 1l. red and black . . . 30 15

1314 Oak

1992. Trees. Multicoloured.
3863 50s. Type **1314** 10 15
3864 50s. Horse chestnut 10 15
3865 1l. Oak 40 15
3866 1l. Macedonian pine 40 15
3867 2l. Maple 75 30
3868 3l. Pear . . . . 1·20 45

1315 Embroidered Flower

1992. Centenary of Folk Museum, Sofia.
3869 **1315** 1l. multicoloured . . . 40 10

1316 "Bulgaria" (freighter)

1992. Centenary of National Shipping Fleet. Multicoloured.
3870 30s. Type **1316** 10 10
3871 50s. "Kastor" (tanker) . . . 20 10
3872 1l. "Geroite na Sebastopol" (train ferry) 40 15
3873 2l. "Aleko Konstantinov" (tanker) 60 25
3874 2l. "Bulgaria" (tanker) . . . 75 30
3875 3l. "Varna" (container ship) 1·20 35

1317 Council Emblem

1992. Admission to Council of Europe.
3876 **1317** 7l. multicoloured . . . 2·75 95

1318 Family exercising on Beach

1992. 4th World Sport for All Congress, Varna. Sheet 58 × 75 mm.

MS3877	**1318** 4l. multicoloured	1·60	1·50

1319 "Santa Claus" (Ani Bacheva)

1992. Christmas. Children's Drawings. Mult.

3878	1l. Type **1319**	30	10
3879	7l. "Madonna and Child" (Georgi Petkov)	1·90	70

1320 Leopard

1322 Tengmalm's Owl

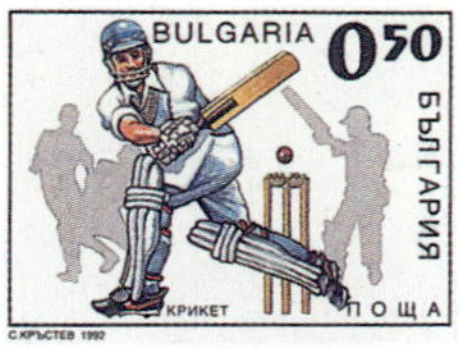

1321 Cricket

1992. Big Cats. Multicoloured.

3880	50s. Type **1320**	15	10
3881	50s. Cheetah	15	10
3882	1l. Jaguar	35	15
3883	2l. Puma	75	30
3884	2l. Tiger	75	30
3885	3l. Lion	1·20	45

1992. Sport. Multicoloured.

3886	50s. Type **1321**	10	15
3887	50s. Baseball	10	15
3888	1l. Pony and trap racing	40	15
3889	1l. Polo	40	15
3890	2l. Hockey	90	25
3891	3l. American football	1·30	50

1992. Owls. Multicoloured.

3892	30s. Type **1322**	15	15
3893	50s. Tawny owl (horiz)	15	15
3894	1l. Long-eared owl	40	15
3895	2l. Short-eared owl	80	40
3896	2l. Eurasian scops owl (horiz)	80	40
3897	3l. Barn owl	1·30	55

1323 "Khan Kubrat" (Dimitur Gyudzhenov)

1992. Historical Paintings. Multicoloured.

3898	50s. Type **1323**	15	15
3899	1l. "Khan Asparukh (Nikolai Pavlovich)	40	15
3900	2l. "Khan Terval at Tsarigrad" (Dimitur Panchev)	80	30
3901	3l. "Prince Boris" (Nikolai Pavlovich)	1·20	45
MS3902	75 × 90 mm. 4l. "The Warrior" (Mito Ganovski) (vert)	1·40	1·40

1324 Sculpted Head

1325 Shooting

1993. Centenary of National Archaeological Museum, Sofia.

3903	**1324** 1l. multicoloured	50	15

1993. "Borovets '93" Biathlon Championship. Multicoloured.

3904	1l. Type **1325**	50	20
3905	7l. Cross-country skiing	3·25	1·10

1326 Rilski

1327 "Morning" (sculpture, Georgi Chapkunov)

1993. Birth Bicentenary of Neofit Rilski (compiler of Bulgarian grammar and dictionary).

3906	**1326** 1l. bistre and red	50	15

1993. Europa. Contemporary Art. Multicoloured.

3907	3l. Type **1327**	50	35
3908	8l. "Composition" (D. Buyukliiski)	1·30	70

1328 Veil-tailed Goldfish

1993. Fishes. Multicoloured.

3909	1l. Type **1328**	15	15
3910	2l. Yucatan sail-finned molly	20	15
3911	3l. Two-striped lyretail	20	15
3912	3l. Freshwater angelfish	40	15
3913	4l. Red discus	65	25
3914	8l. Pearl gourami	1·10	45

1329 Apple

1330 Monteverdi

1993. Fruits. Multicoloured.

3915	1l. Type **1329**	15	10
3916	2l. Peach	25	10
3917	2l. Pear	25	10
3918	3l. Quince	50	15
3919	5l. Pomegranate	90	25
3920	7l. Fig	1·50	45

1993. 350th Death Anniv of Claudio Monteverdi (composer).

3921	**1330** 1l. green, yellow & red	25	10

1331 High Jumping

1993. Int Games for the Deaf, Sofia. Mult.

3922	1l. Type **1331**	20	10
3923	2l. Swimming	35	10
3924	3l. Cycling	45	25
3925	4l. Tennis	65	25
MS3926	86 × 75 mm. 5l. Football	65	70

1332 Baptism (from Manasses Chronicle)

1993. 1100th Anniv of Preslav and Introduction of Cyrillic Script. Sheet 113 × 110 mm containing T **1332** and similar horiz designs. Multicoloured.

MS3927	5l. Type **1332**; 5l. Prince Boris I (after Dimitur Gyudzhenov); 5l. Tsar Simeon I (after Dimitur Gyudzhenov); 5l. Cavalry charge (after Manasses Chronicle)	2·40	2·40

1333 Prince Alexander

1334 Tchaikovsky

1993. Death Centenary of Prince Alexander I.

3928	**1333** 3l. multicoloured	55	15

1993. Death Centenary of Pyotr Tchaikovsky (composer).

3929	**1334** 3l. multicoloured	55	15

1335 Crossbow

1336 Newton

1993. Weapons. Multicoloured.

3930	1l. Type **1335**	15	15
3931	2l. 18th-century flintlock pistol	20	15
3932	3l. Revolver	45	15
3933	3l. Luger pistol	45	15
3934	5l. Mauser rifle	70	35
3935	7l. Kalashnikov assault rifle	1·20	55

1993. 350th Birth Anniv of Sir Isaac Newton (mathematician).

3936	**1336** 1l. multicoloured	15	10

1337 "100" on Stamps and Globe

1993. Centenary of Bulgarian Philately.

3937	**1337** 1l. multicoloured	15	10

1338 "Ecology" in Cyrillic Script

1993. Ecology. Multicoloured.

3938	1l. Type **1338**	15	10
3939	7l. "Ecology" in English	80	40

1339 Mallard

1993. Hunting. Multicoloured.

3940	1l. Type **1339**	15	10
3941	1l. Common pheasant	15	10
3942	2l. Red fox	20	15
3943	3l. Roe deer	40	15
3944	6l. European brown hare	75	30
3945	8l. Wild boar	1·10	45

1340 "Taurus", "Gemini" and "Cancer"

1341 Sofia Costume

1993. Christmas. Signs of the Zodiac. Mult.

3946	1l. Type **1340**	10	10
3947	1l. "Leo", "Virgo" and "Libra"	10	10
3948	7l. "Aquarius", "Pisces" and "Aries"	65	40
3949	7l. "Scorpio", "Sagittarius" and "Capricorn"	65	40

Nos. 3946/7 and 3948/9 were each issued together, se-tenant; when placed together the four stamps form a composite design.

1993. Costumes. Multicoloured.

3950	1l. Type **1341**	15	10
3951	1l. Plovdiv	15	10
3952	2l. Belograd	20	10
3953	3l. Oryakhovo	30	15
3954	3l. Shumen	30	15
3955	8l. Kurdzhali	1·00	35

1342 Freestyle Skiing

1343 "Self-portrait" and "Tsar Simeon"

1994. Winter Olympic Games, Lillehammer, Norway. Multicoloured.

3956	1l. Type **1342**	10	10
3957	2l. Speed skating	20	10
3958	3l. Two-man luge	40	10
3959	4l. Ice hockey	60	20
MS3960	59 × 90 mm. 3l. multicoloured	65	65

1994. Death Centenary of Nikolai Pavlovich (artist).

3961	**1343** 3l. multicoloured	30	15

1344 Plesiosaurus

1994. Prehistoric Animals. Multicoloured.

3962	2l. Type **1344**	20	10
3963	3l. Archaeopteryx	30	15
3964	3l. Iguanodon	30	10
3965	4l. Edmontonia	45	15
3966	5l. Styracosaurus	55	20
3967	7l. Tyrannosaurus	60	25

1345 Players (Chile, 1962)

1994. World Cup Football Championship, U.S.A. Multicoloured.

3968	3l. Type **1345**	35	15
3969	6l. Players (England, 1966)	70	40
3970	7l. Goalkeeper making save (Mexico, 1970)	80	50
3971	9l. Player kicking (West Germany, 1974)	1·00	70
MS3972	90 × 123 mm. 5l. Player punching air (Mexico, 1986) (vert); 5l. Player tackling (U.S.A., 1994)	1·20	1·30

1346 Photoelectric Analysis (Georgi Nadzhakov)

1994. Europa. Discoveries. Multicoloured.

3973	3l. Type **1346**	30	10
3974	15l. Cardiogram and heart (Prof. Ivan Mitev)	1·60	1·00

1347 Khristov

1994. 80th Birth Anniv of Boris Khristov (actor).

3975 **1347**	3l. multicoloured	30	15

1348 Sleeping Hamster

1349 Space Shuttle, Satellite and Dish Aerial

1994. The Common Hamster. Multicoloured.

3976	3l. Type **1348**	35	10
3977	7l. Hamster looking out of burrow	75	35
3978	10l. Hamster sitting up in grass	95	45
3979	15l. Hamster approaching berry	1·50	65

1994. North Atlantic Co-operation Council (North Atlantic Treaty Organization and Warsaw Pact members).

3980 **1349**	3l. multicoloured	30	15

1350 Baron Pierre de Coubertin (founder of modern games)

1351 "Christ Pantocrator"

1994. Cent of International Olympic Committee.

3981 **1350**	3l. multicoloured	40	15

1994. Icons. Multicoloured.

3982	2l. Type **1351**	25	10
3983	3l. "Raising of Lazarus"	40	10
3984	5l. "Passion of Christ"	65	20
3985	7l. "Archangel Michael"	90	35
3986	8l. "Sts. Cyril and Methodius"	95	45
3987	15l. "Madonna Enthroned"	1·80	65

1352 Vechernik

1994. Christmas. Breads. Multicoloured.

3988	3l. Type **1352**	30	10
3989	15l. Bogovitsa	1·60	65

1353 "Golden Showers"

(1354)

1994. Roses. Multicoloured.

3990	2l. Type **1353**	25	10
3991	3l. "Caen Peace Monument"	35	10
3992	5l. "Theresa of Lisieux"	60	25
3993	7l. "Zambra 93"	80	40
3994	10l. "Gustave Courbet"	1·30	45
3995	15l. "Honore de Balzac"	1·90	70

1994. Bulgaria's Fourth Place in World Cup Football Championship. No. **MS**3972 overprinted with T **1354** in margin.

MS3996	90 × 123 mm. 5l. multicoloured; 5l. multicoloured	9·25	8·00

1355 "AM/ASES", 1912

1994. Trams. Multicoloured.

3997	1l. Type **1355**	10	10
3998	2l. "AM/ASES", 1928	20	10
3999	3l. "M.A.N./AEG", 1931	30	15
4000	5l. "D.T.O.", 1942	45	20
4001	8l. Republika, 1951	1·00	40
4002	10l. Kosmonavt articulated tramcar set, 1961	1·10	50

1356 Petleshkov and Flag

1995. 150th Birth Anniv of Vasil Petleshkov (leader of 1876 April uprising).

4003 **1356**	3l. multicoloured	30	15

1357 Daisy growing through Cracked Helmet

1995. Europa. Peace and Freedom. Mult.

4004	3l. Type **1357**	45	50
4005	15l. Dove with olive branch on rifle barrel	2·10	1·40

1358 Player

1995. Centenary of Volleyball. Sheet 92 × 75 mm containing T **1358** and similar multicoloured design.

MS4006	10l. Type **1358**; 15l. Player hitting ball (vert)	2·40	2·40

1359 Sea Lily (*Pancratium martimum*)

1995. European Nature Conservation Year. Sheet 70 × 99 mm containing T **1359** and similar horiz design. Multicoloured.

MS4007	10l. Type **1359**; 15l. Imperial Eagle (*Aquila heliaca*)	2·40	2·40

1360 Emperor Penguin

1995. Antarctic Animals. Multicoloured.

4008	1l. Shrimp (horiz)	15	10
4009	2l. Ice fish (horiz)	20	10
4010	3l. Sperm whale (horiz)	35	20
4011	5l. Weddell's seal (horiz)	55	25
4012	8l. South polar skua (horiz)	55	40
4013	10l. Type **1360**	1·10	50

1361 Stambolov

1995. Death Cent of Stefan Stambolov (politician).

4014 **1361**	3l. multicoloured	30	15

1362 Pole Vaulting

1995. Olympic Games, Atlanta (1996) (1st issue). Multicoloured.

4015	3l. Type **1362**	35	10
4016	7l. High jumping	80	30
4017	10l. Long jumping	1·10	45
4018	15l. Triple jumping	1·80	70

See also Nos. 4083/6.

1363 Pea

1365 "Ivan Nikolov-Zograf"

1364 "100"

1995. Food Plants. Multicoloured.

4019	2l. Type **1363**	25	10
4020	3l. Chickpea	30	15
4021	3l. Soya bean	30	15
4022	4l. Spinach	45	15
4023	5l. Peanut	55	25
4024	15l. Lentil	1·60	70

1995. Centenary of Organized Tourism.

4025 **1364**	1l. multicoloured	30	15

1995. Birth Centenary of Vasil Zakhariev (painter).

4026 **1365**	2l. multicoloured	25	10
4027 –	3l. multicoloured	30	15
4028 –	5l. black, brown & grn	55	25
4029 –	10l. multicoloured	1·10	45

DESIGNS: 3l. "Rila Monastery"; 5l. "Self-portrait"; 10l. "Raspberry Collectors".

1366 "Dove-Hands" holding Globe

1995. 50th Anniv of UNO.

4030 **1366**	3l. multicoloured	30	15

1367 Polikarpov Po-2 Biplane

1995. Aircraft. Multicoloured.

4031	3l. Type **1367**	35	20
4032	5l. Lisunov Li-2 airliner	55	25
4033	7l. Junkers Ju 52	75	35
4034	10l. Focke Wulf Fw 58	1·00	45

1368 Charlie Chaplin and Mickey Mouse

1995. Centenary of Motion Pictures. Mult.

4035	2l. Type **1368**	20	10
4036	3l. Marilyn Monroe and Marlene Dietrich	35	15
4037	5l. Nikolai Cherkasov and Humphrey Bogart	55	25
4038	8l. Sophia Loren and Liza Minelli	80	35
4039	10l. Gerard Philipe and Toshiro Mifune	1·00	45
4040	15l. Katya Paskaleva and Nevena Kokanova	1·60	70

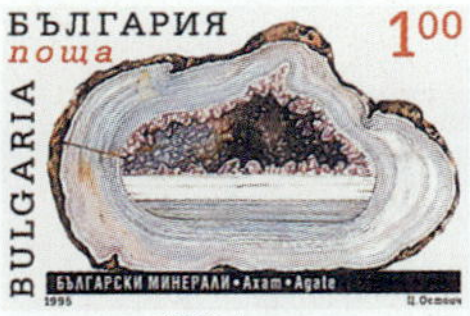
1369 Agate

1995. Minerals. Multicoloured.

4041	1l. Type **1369**	10	10
4042	2l. Sphalerite	20	10
4043	5l. Calcite	55	25
4044	7l. Quartz	75	30
4045	8l. Pyromorphite	90	35
4046	10l. Almandine	1·00	45

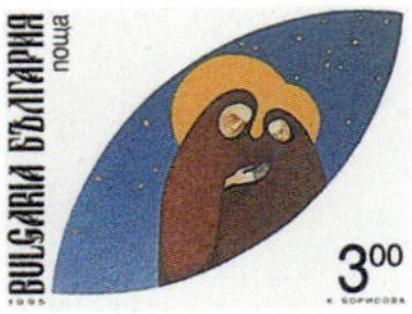
1370 Mary and Joseph

1995. Christmas. Multicoloured.
4047 3l. Type **1370** 30 15
4048 15l. Three wise men approaching stable . . . 1·50 60

1371 "Polynesian Woman with Fruit"

1996. Birth Centenary of Kiril Tsonev (painter).
4049 **1371** 3l. multicoloured . . . 30 15

1372 Luther (after Lucas Cranach the elder)

1996. 450th Death Anniv of Martin Luther (Protestant reformer).
4050 **1372** 3l. multicoloured . . . 30 15

1373 Preobrazhenie

1374 Bulgarian National Bank

1996. Monasteries.
4051 **1373** 3l. green 15 10
4052 – 5l. red 20 10
4053 – 10l. blue 45 20
4054 – 20l. orange 90 35
4055 – 25l. brown . . . . . . 1·10 45
4056 – 40l. purple . . . . . . 1·80 70
DESIGNS: 5l. Arapov; 10l. Dryanovo; 20l. Bachkov; 25l. Troyan; 40l. Zograf.

1996. 5th Anniv of European Reconstruction and Development Bank.
4063 **1374** 7l. green, red and blue 25 15
4064 – 30l. blue, red & purple 1·10 55
DESIGN: 30l. Palace of Culture, Sofia.

1375 Yew

1996. Conifers. Multicoloured.
4065 5l. Type **1375** 20 10
4066 8l. Silver fir 35 15
4067 10l. Norway spruce 45 20
4068 20l. Scots pine 80 30
4069 25l. "Pinus heldreichii" . . 1·00 40
4070 40l. Juniper . . . . 1·80 75

1376 Battle Scene and Mourning Women

1377 Modern Officer's Parade Uniform

1996. 120th Anniversaries. Multicoloured.
4071 10l. Type **1376** (April uprising) 40 20
4072 40l. Khristo Botev and script (poet, death anniv) (horiz) . . . . 1·60 80

1996. Military Uniforms. Multicoloured.
4073 5l. Type **1377** 20 10
4074 8l. Second World War combat uniform 35 15
4075 10l. Balkan War uniform . . 40 20
4076 20l. Guard officer's ceremonial uniform . . . 80 35
4077 25l. Serbo-Bulgarian War officer's uniform . . . . 1·00 40
4078 40l. Russo-Turkish War soldier's uniform . . . . 1·80 1·00

1378 Monument

1996. 50th Anniv of the Republic.
4079 **1378** 10l. multicoloured . . . 50 15

1379 Elisaveta Bagryana (poet)

1996. Europa. Famous Women. Multicoloured.
4080 10l. Type **1379** 40 65
4081 40l. Katya Popova (opera singer) . . . . 1·60 2·00

1380 Player

1381 Nikola Stanchev (wrestling, Melbourne 1956)

1996. European Football Championship, England. Sheet 71 × 86 mm containing T **1380** and similar vert design. Multicoloured.
MS4082 10l. Type **1380**; 15l. Player (different) 80 70

1996. Olympic Games, Atlanta (2nd issue). Bulgarian Medal Winners. Multicoloured.
4083 5l. Type **1381** 15 10
4084 8l. Boris Georgiev (boxing, Helsinki 1952) 30 10
4085 10l. Ivanka Khristova (putting the shot, Montreal 1976) 30 15
4086 25l. Z. Iordanova and S. Otsetova (double sculls, Montreal 1976) 80 30
MS4087 89 × 68 mm. 15l. Olympic Stadium, Athens, 1896 . . . . 50 50

1382 "The Letter" (detail)

1384 St. Ivan

1383 Water Flea

1996. 250th Birth Anniv of Francisco Goya (painter). Multicoloured.
4088 5l. Detail of fresco 15 10
4089 8l. Type **1382** 30 10
4090 26l. "3rd of May 1808 in Madrid" (detail) 90 40
4091 40l. "Neighbours on a Balcony" (detail) . . . . 1·40 65
MS4092 99 × 73 mm. 10l. "Clothed Maja" (50 × 26 mm); 15l. "Naked Maja" (50 × 26 mm) 80 80

1996. Aquatic Life. Multicoloured.
4093 5l. Type **1383** 15 10
4094 10l. Common water louse 35 15
4095 12l. European river crayfish 40 20
4096 25l. Prawn 90 20
4097 30l. "Cumella limicola" . . 95 40
4098 40l. Mediterranean shore crab . . . . 1·40 60

1996. 1050th Death Anniv of Ivan Rilski (founder of Rila Monastery). Sheet 56 × 87 mm.
MS4099 **1384** 10l. multicoloured 40 30

1385 Tryavna

1996. Houses.
4100 **1385** 10l. brown and stone 20 10
4101 – 15l. red and yellow . . 30 15
4102 – 30l. green and yellow 60 30
4103 – 50l. violet and mauve 1·00 50
4104 – 60l. green and lt green 1·20 55
4105 – 100l. ultramarine & bl 2·10 1·00
DESIGNS: 15l. Nesebur; 30l. Tryavna (different); 50l. Koprivshtitsa; 60l. Plovdiv; 100l. Koprivshtitsa (different).

1386 "Philadelphia", 1836

1996. Steam Locomotives. Multicoloured.
4106 5l. Type **1386** 15 20
4107 10l. "Jenny Lind", 1847 . . 30 20
4108 12l. "Liverpool", 1848 . . . 35 25
4109 26l. "Anglet", 1876 . . . . 90 55

1387 Anniversary Emblem and Academy

1996. Centenary of National Arts Academy.
4110 **1387** 15l. black and yellow 40 25

1388 Sword and Miniature from "Chronicle of Ivan Skilitsa"

1996. 1100th Anniv of Tsar Simeon's Victory over the Turks. Multicoloured.
4111 10l. Type **1388** 25 20
4112 40l. Dagger and right-hand detail of miniature . . . . 1·10 75
Nos. 4111/12 were issued together, se-tenant, forming a composite design.

1389 Fishes and Diver (Dilyana Lokmadzhieva)

1996. 50th Anniv of UNICEF. Children's Paintings. Multicoloured.
4113 7l. Type **1389** 25 20
4114 15l. Circus (Velislava Dimitrova) 50 25
4115 20l. Man and artist's pallet (Miglena Nikolova) . . . 65 35
4116 60l. Family meal (Darena Dencheva) . . . . 1·90 1·20

1390 Christmas Tree

1391 "Zograf Monastery"

1996. Christmas. Multicoloured.
4117 15l. Type **1390** 45 30
4118 60l. Star over basilica and Christmas tree . . . . . 1·80 1·20

1996. Birth Centenary of Tsanko Lavrenov (painter).
4119 **1391** 15l. multicoloured . . . 40 25

1392 Pointer

1997. Puppies. Multicoloured.
4120 5l. Type **1392** 15 20
4121 7l. Chow chow 20 20
4122 25l. Carakachan dog 65 50
4123 50l. Basset hound . . . . . 1·30 95

1393 Bell

1997. 150th Birth Anniv of Alexander Graham Bell (telephone pioneer).
4124 **1393** 30l. multicoloured . . . 50 25

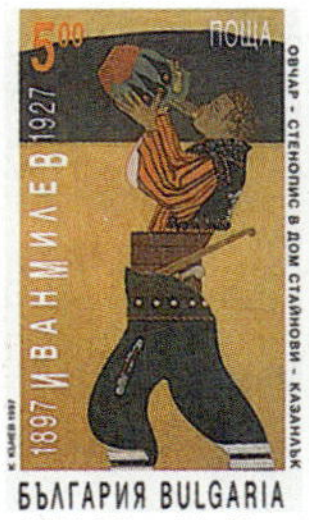
1394 Man drinking

1395 Lady March (symbol of spring)

1997. Birth Centenary of Ivan Milev (painter). Murals from Kazaluk. Multicoloured.
4125 5l. Type **1394** 15 15
4126 15l. Woman praying 30 15
4127 30l. Reaper 60 25
4128 60l. Mother and child . . . 1·20 50

1997. Europa. Tales and Legends. Mult.
4129 120l. Type **1395** 30 40
4130 600l. St. George (national symbol) . . . . 1·00 1·30

1396 Kisimov in Character

1997. Birth Cent of Konstantin Kisimov (actor).
4131 **1396** 120l. multicoloured . . 15 15

1397 Von Stephan

1398 Old Town, Nesebur

1997. Death Centenary of Heinrich von Stephan (founder of U.P.U.).
4132 **1397** 60l. multicoloured . . . 15 15

1997. Historic Sights.
4133 **1398** 80l. brown and black 15 15
4134 – 200l. violet and black 20 15
4135 – 300l. yellow and black 25 15
4136 – 500l. green and black 40 15
4137 – 600l. yellow and black 55 30
4138 – 1000l. orange and black 90 30
DESIGNS: 200l. Sculpture, Ivanovski Church; 300l. Christ (detail of icon), Boyana Church; 500l. Horseman (stone relief), Madara; 600l. Figure of woman (carving from sarcophagus), Sveshary; 1000l. Tomb decoration, Kazanlak.

1399 Gaetano Donizetti

1997. Composers' Anniversaries. Multicoloured.
4139 120l. Type **1399** (birth bicentenary) 40 25
4140 120l. Franz Schubert (birth bicentenary) 40 25
4141 120l. Felix Mendelssohn-Bartholdy (150th death anniv) 40 25
4142 120l. Johannes Brahms (death centenary) 40 25

1400 "Trifolium rubens"

1997. Flowers in the Red Book. Multicoloured.
4143 80l. Type **1400** 10 10
4144 100l. "Tulipa hageri" . . . 20 10
4145 120l. "Inula spiraeifolia" . . 35 15
4146 200l. Thin-leafed peony . . 45 25

1401 Anniversary Emblem

1402 Georgiev

1997. 50th Anniv of Civil Aviation.
4147 **1401** 120l. multicoloured . . 25 15

1997. Death Centenary of Evlogii Georgiev.
4148 **1402** 120l. multicoloured . . 25 15

1403 Show Jumping and Running

1997. World Modern Pentathlon Championship, Sofia. Multicoloured.
4149 60l. Type **1403** 10 10
4150 80l. Fencing and swimming 20 10
4151 100l. Running and fencing 30 10
4152 120l. Shooting and swimming 45 15
4153 200l. Show jumping and shooting 70 25

1404 St. Basil's Cathedral

1997. 850th Anniv of Moscow and "Moskva 97" International Stamp Exhibition. Sheet 87 × 96 mm.
MS4154 **1404** 120l. multicoloured 1·20 1·20

1405 D 2500 M Boat Engine

1997. Centenary of Diesel Engine. Multicoloured.
4155 80l. Type **1405** 20 15
4156 100l. D 2900 T tractor engine 30 15
4157 120l. D 3900 A truck engine 50 15
4158 200l. D 2500 K fork-lift truck engine 65 20

1406 Goddess with Mural Crown

1997. 43rd General Assembly of Atlantic Club, Sofia.
4159 **1406** 120l. mve, bl & ultram 30 15
4160 – 120l. grn, bl & ultram 30 15
4161 – 120l. brn, bl & ultram 30 15
4162 – 120l. vio, bl & ultram 30 15
DESIGNS: No. 4160, Eagle on globe; 4161, Venue; 4162, Venue (different).

1407 Cervantes and Don Quixote with Sancho

1997. 450th Birth Anniv of Miguel de Cervantes (writer).
4163 **1407** 120l. multicoloured . . 30 15

1408 Raztsvetnikov

1997. Birth Centenary of Asen Raztsvetnikov (writer and translator).
4164 **1408** 120l. multicoloured . . 25 10

1409 Fragment of Tombstone

1997. Millenary of Coronation of Tsar Samuel. Multicoloured.
4165 120l. Type **1409** 25 15
4166 600l. Tsar Samuel and knights in battle . . . . 1·40 60

1410 Star and Houses forming Christmas Tree

1997. Christmas. Multicoloured.
4167 120l. Type **1410** 20 15
4168 600l. Stable with Christmas tree roof . . . . 1·40 50

1411 Speed Skating

1997. Winter Olympic Games, Nagano, Japan (1998). Multicoloured.
4169 60l. Type **1411** 10 10
4170 80l. Skiing 20 10
4171 120l. Shooting (biathlon) . . 30 10
4172 600l. Ice skating . . . . . 1·40 45

1412 Radiometric System R-400

1997. 25th Anniv of Bulgarian Space Experiments. Sheet 87 × 68 mm.
MS4173 **1412** 120l. multicoloured 50 30

1413 State Arms

1997.
4174 **1413** 120l. multicoloured . . 30 15

1414 Botev (after B. Petrov)

1415 Brecht

1998. 150th Birth and 120th Death (1996) Anniv of Khristo Botev (poet and revolutionary).
4175 **1414** 120l. multicoloured . . 25 15

1998. Birth Cent of Bertolt Brecht (playwright).
4176 **1415** 120l. multicoloured . . 25 15

1416 Arrows

1998. Cent of Bulgarian Telegraph Agency.
4177 **1416** 120l. multicoloured . . 25 15

1417 Barn Swallow at Window

1998. 120th Birth Anniv of Aleksandur Bozhinov (children's illustrator). Multicoloured.
4178 120l. Type **1417** 35 10
4179 120l. Blackbird with backpack on branch . . . 35 10
4180 120l. Father Frost and children 35 10
4181 120l. Maiden Rositsa in field holding hands up to rain 35 10

1418 Tsar Alexander II

1419 Christ ascending and Hare pulling Cart of Eggs

1998. 120th Anniv of Liberation from Turkey. Multicoloured.
4182 120l. Type **1418** 20 10
4183 600l. Independence monument, Ruse . . . . 1·10 40

1998. Easter.
4184 **1419** 120l. multicoloured . . 25 15

1420 Torch Bearer

1998. 75th Anniv of Bulgarian Olympic Committee.
4185 **1420** 120l. multicoloured . . 25 15

1421 Map of Participating Countries

1998. Phare International Programme for Telecommunications and Post.
4186 **1421** 120l. multicoloured . . 25 15

1422 Girls in Folk Costumes

1998. Europa. National Festivals. Multicoloured.
4187 120l. Type **1422** 15 20
4188 600l. Boys wearing dance masks . . . . 1·40 75

ПЪРВИ
ЗЛАТЕН МЕДАЛ
ЗА БЪЛГАРИЯ
Е. ДАФОВСКА
(1423)

1424 "Dante and Virgil in Hell"

1998. Winning of Gold Medal in 15km Biathlon by Ekaterina Dafovska at Winter Olympic Games, Nagano. No. 4171 optd with T **1423**.
4189 120l. multicoloured . . . . 1·40 1·10

1998. Birth Bicentenary of Eugene Delacroix (artist).
4190 **1424** 120l. multicoloured . . 25 15

1425 Footballer and Club Badge

1426 European Tabby

1998. 50th Anniv of TsSKA Football Club.
4191 **1425** 120l. multicoloured . . 25 15

1998. Cats. Multicoloured.
4192 60l. Type **1426** 15 10
4193 80l. Siamese 20 10
4194 120l. Exotic shorthair . . . 30 10
4195 600l. Birman . . . . 1·40 35

1427 "Oh, You are Jealous!"

1998. 150th Birth Anniv of Paul Gauguin (artist).
4196 **1427** 120l. multicoloured . . 25 15

1428 Khilendarski-Bozveli

1998. 150th Death Anniv of Neofit Khilendarski-Bozveli (priest and writer).
4197 **1428** 120l. multicoloured . . 25 15

1429 Tackling

1998. World Cup Football Championship, France. Multicoloured.
4198 60l. Type **1429** 15 10
4199 80l. Players competing for ball 20 10
4200 120l. Players and ball . . . 30 10
4201 600l. Goalkeeper . . . . . 1·40 35
MS4202 68 × 91 mm. 120l. Lion, ball and Eiffel Tower 40 25

1430 A. Aleksandrov

1998. 10th Anniv of Second Soviet–Bulgarian Space Flight.
4203 **1430** 120l. multicoloured . . 25 15

1431 Vasco da Gama

1998. "Expo '98" World's Fair, Lisbon. 500th Anniv of Vasco da Gama's Voyage to India. Multicoloured.
4204 600l. Type **1431** . . . . . . 1·00 40
4205 600l. "Sao Gabriel" (Vasco da Gama's ship) . . . . 1·40 55
Nos. 4204/5 were issued together, se-tenant, forming a composite design.

1432 Focke Wolf FW 61, 1937

1998. Helicopters. Multicoloured.
4206 80l. Type **1432** 20 15
4207 100l. Sikorsky R-4, 1943 . . 20 15
4208 120l. Mil Mi-V12, 1970 . . 30 15
4209 200l. McDonnell-Douglas MD-900, 1995 . . . . . 70 15

1433 Mediterranean Monk Seal (*Monachus monachus*)

1998. International Year of the Ocean. Sheet 67 × 88 mm.
MS4210 **1433** 120l. multicoloured 65 25

1434 Talev

1998. Birth Centenary of Dimitur Talev (writer).
4211 **1434** 180l. multicoloured . . 50 25

1435 Aleksandur Malinov (Prime Minister, 1931)

1436 "Limenitis redukta" and "Ligularia sibirica"

1998. 90th Anniv of Independence.
4212 **1435** 180l. black, blue & yell 50 15

1998. Butterflies and Flowers. Multicoloured.
4213 60l. Type **1436** 20 20
4214 180l. Painted lady and "Anthemis macrantha" 40 20
4215 200l. Red admiral and "Trachelium jacquinii" . . 40 20
4216 600l. "Anthocharis gruneri" and "Geranium tuberosum" . . . . . . 1·60 75

1437 Smirnenski

1998. Birth Cent of Khristo Smirnenski (writer).
4217 **1437** 180l. multicoloured . . 50 25

1438 Silhouette of Man

1998. 50th Anniv of Universal Declaration of Human Rights.
4218 **1438** 180l. multicoloured . . 50 25

1439 Bruno

1998. 450th Birth Anniv of Giordano Bruno (scholar).
4219 **1439** 180l. multicoloured . . 50 25

1440 Man diving through Heart ("I Love You")

1998. Greetings Stamps. Multicoloured.
4220 180l. Type **1440** 50 20
4221 180l. Making wine (holiday) (vert) 50 20
4222 180l. Man in chalice (birthday) (vert) 50 20
4223 180l. Waiter serving wine (name day) (vert) 50 20

1441 Madonna and Child

1998. Christmas.
4224 **1441** 180l. multicoloured . . 40 15

1442 Geshov

1999. 150th Birth Anniv of Ivan Evstratiev Geshov (politician).
4225 **1442** 180l. multicoloured . . 50 15

1443 National Assembly Building, Sofia

1999. 120th Anniv of Third Bulgarian State. Mult.
4226 180l. Type **1443** 40 20
4227 180l. Council of Ministers 40 20
4228 180l. Statue of Justice (Supreme Court of Appeal) 40 20
4229 180l. Coins (National Bank) 40 20
4230 180l. Army 40 20
4231 180l. Lion emblem of Sofia and lamp post 40 20

1444 Georgi Karakashev (stage designer) and Set of "Kismet"

1999. Birth Centenaries. Multicoloured.
4232 180l. Type **1444** 50 20
4233 200l. Bencho Obreshkov (artist) and "Lodki" . . . 50 20
4234 300l. Score and Asen Naidenov (conductor of Sofia Opera) 70 30
4235 600l. Pancho Vladigerov (composer) and score of "Vardar" . . . . 1·50 60

1445 Rainbow Lory (*Trichoglossus haematodus*)

1999. "Bulgaria '99" European Stamp Exhibition. Parrots. Sheet 100 × 110 mm containing T **1445** and similar vert designs. Multicoloured.
MS4236 600l. Type **1445**; 600l. Eastern rosella; 600l. Budgerigar; 600l. Green-winged macaw . . 7·50 6·50

1446 Sun and Emblem

1999. 50th Anniv of North Atlantic Treaty Organization.
4237 **1446** 180l. multicoloured . . 40 15

1447 Decorated Eggs

1999. Easter.
4238 **1447** 180l. multicoloured . . 50 15

1448 Red-crested Pochard and Ropotamo Reserve

1999. Europa. Parks and Gardens. Multicoloured.
4239 180l. Type **1448** 65 40
4240 600l. Central Balkan National Park . . . . . 1·90 1·20

1449 Albrecht Durer (self-portrait) and Nuremberg

1999. "iBRA '99" International Stamp Exhibition, Nuremberg, Germany.
4241 **1449** 600l. multicoloured . . 1·60 65

1450 Anniversary Emblem

1999. 50th Anniv of Council of Europe.
4242 **1450** 180l. multicoloured . . 40 15

1451 Honore de Balzac (novelist)

1999. Birth Anniversaries. Multicoloured.
4243 180l. Type **1451** (bicentenary) 60 15
4244 200l. Johann Wolfgang von Goethe (poet and playwright) (250th anniv) 60 15
4245 300l. Aleksandr Pushkin (poet) (bicentenary) . . . 80 20
4246 600l. Diego de Silva Velazquez (painter) (400th anniv) . . . . 1·80 40

1452 Penny Farthing

1999. Bicycles. Multicoloured.
4247 180l. Type **1452** 50 20
4248 200l. Road racing bicycles 50 20
4249 300l. Track racing bicycles 70 25
4250 600l. Mountain bike . . . . 1·50 55

1453 St. Cyril and Methodius

1999. "Bulgaria '99" European Stamp Exhibition, Sofia. 19th-century Icons of Sts. Cyril and Methodius. Sheet 100 × 110 mm containing T **1453** and similar vert designs. Multicoloured.
MS4251 600l. Type **1453**; 600l. St. Cyril with scroll and staff and St. Methodius; 600l. Sts. Cyril and Methodius with scrolls; 600l. St. Cyril with crucifix, St. Methodius and Christ . . . 8·00 6·50

1454 Sopot Monastery Fountain

1456 Cracked Green Russula

1455 *Oxytropis urumovii*

1999. Fountains.
4252 **1454** 1st. light brown 10 10
4254 – 8st. green and black . . 15 10
4255 – 10st. deep brown 25 15
4257 – 18st. light blue 50 20
4258 – 20st. bright blue . . . 60 20
4260 – 60st. brown and black 1·80 40
DESIGNS: 8st. Peacock Fountain, Karlovo; 10st. Peev Fountain, Kopivshtitsa; 18st. Sandanski Fountain; 20st. Eagle Owl Fountain, Karlovo; 60st. Fountain, Sokolski Monastery.

1999. "Bulgaria '99" European Stamp Exhibition, Sofia (2nd issue). Flowers in Pirin National Park. Sheet 109 × 100 mm containing T **1455** and similar horiz designs. Multicoloured.
MS4265 60st. Type **1455**; 60st. Bellflower; 60st. Iris; 60st. Spotted gentian . . . . 9·25 6·50

1999. Fungi. Multicoloured.
4266 10st. Type **1456** 25 15
4267 18st. Field mushroom . . . 60 30
4268 20st. "Hygrophorus russula" 70 30
4269 60st. Wood blewit . . . . . 1·90 95

1457 Diagram of path of Eclipse

1458 Four-leaved Clover

1999. Solar Eclipse (11 Aug 1999). Sheet 90 × 90 mm.
MS4270 **1457** 20st. multicoloured 1·60 90

1999. Centenary of Organized Peasant Movement.
4271 **1458** 18st. multicoloured . . 50 15

1459 1884 25st. Postage Due Stamp

1460 Lesser Grey Shrike

1999. "Bulgaria '99" European Stamp Exhibition, Sofia (3rd issue). 125th Anniv of Universal Postal Union. Sheet 110 × 102 mm containing T **1459** and similar vert deisgns. Multicoloured.
MS4272 60st. Type **1459**; 60st. Dove and hand with letter; 60st. Globe and left half of messenger; 60st. Right half of messenger with letter and globe . . . . 6·50 4·00

1999. Song Birds and their Eggs. Multicoloured.
4273 8st. Type **1460** 25 25
4274 18st. Mistle thrush 60 55
4275 20st. Dunnock 70 55
4276 60st. Ortolan bunting . . . 2·10 1·60

1461 Greek Tortoise

1999. Reptiles. Multicoloured.
4277 10st. Type **1461** 25 10
4278 18st. Swamp turtle 70 20
4279 30st. Hermann's tortoise . . 80 25
4280 60st. Caspian turtle . . . . 1·90 60

1462 Boxing (16 medals)

1999. Bulgarian Olympic Medal Winning Sports. Multicoloured.
4281 10st. Type **1462** 25 10
4282 20st. High jumping (17 medals) 70 20
4283 30st. Weightlifting (31 medals) 80 25
4284 60st. Wrestling (60 medals) 1·90 55

1463 Police Light and Emblem

1999. 10th European Police Conference.
4285 **1463** 18st. multicoloured . . 50 15

1464 Jug

1465 Virgin and Child

1999. Gold Artefacts from Panagyurishte.
4286 **1464** 2st. brown and green 25 20
4287 – 3st. brown and green 25 15
4288 – 5st. brown and blue . . 25 15
4289 – 30st. brown and violet 50 20
4290 – 1l. brown and red . . . 2·20 60
DESIGNS: 3st. Human figures around top of drinking horn; 5st. Bottom of chamois-shaped drinking horn; 30st. Decorated handle and spout; 1l. Head-shaped jug.

1999. Christmas. Religious Icons. Multicoloured.
4291 18st. Type **1465** 35 15
4292 60st. Jesus Christ . . . . . 1·90 45

1466 Scout beside Fire

1999. Scouts. Multicoloured.
4293 10st. Type **1466** 25 20
4294 18st. Scout helping child . . 40 20
4295 30st. Scout saluting 80 20
4296 60st. Girl and boy scouts . . 2·20 55

1467 Emblem

1469 White Stork (*Ciconia ciconia*)

1468 Emblem and Flag

1999. "Expo 2005" World's Fair, Aichi, Japan.
4297 **1467** 18st. multicoloured . . 50 15

2000. Bulgarian Membership of European Union.
4298 **1468** 18st. multicoloured . . 30 15

2000. Endangered Species. Sheet 80 × 60 mm.
MS4299 **1469** 60st. multicoloured 1·40 95

1470 Peter Beron and Scientific Instruments

2000. Birth Anniversaries. Multicoloured.
4300 10st. Type **1470** (scientist, bicentenary) 30 10
4301 20st. Zakhari Stoyanov (writer, 150th anniv) . . . 45 10
4302 50st. Kolyo Ficheto (architect, bicentenary) . . 90 35

1471 Madonna and Child with Circuit Board

2000. Europa. Multicoloured.
4303 18st. Type **1471** 40 10
4304 60st. Madonna and Child (Leonardo da Vinci) with circuit board . . . . . . 1·60 40

1472 Judo

2000. Olympic Games, Sydney. Multicoloured.
4305 10st. Type **1472** 30 10
4306 18st. Tennis 30 10
4307 20st. Pistol shooting 50 15
4308 60st. Long jump . . . . . 1·30 40

1473 *Puss in Boots* (Charles Perrault)

2000. Children's Fairytales. Multicoloured.
4309 18st. Type **1473** 70 15
4310 18st. *Little Red Riding Hood* (Brothers Grimm) 70 15
4311 18st. *Thumbelina* (Hans Christian Andersen) . . . 70 15

1474 "Friends" (detail) (Assen Vasiliev)

2000. Artists Birth Centenaries. Art. Multicoloured.
4312 18st. Type **1474** 70 15
4313 18st. "All Soul's Day" (detail) (Pencho Georgiev) 70 15
4314 18st. "Veliko Tunovo" (detail) (Ivan Khristov) 70 15
4315 18st. "At the Fountain" (sculpture) (detail) (Ivan Funev) 70 15

1475 Roman Mosaic (detail), Stara Zagora

2000. "EXPO 2000" World's Fair, Hanover, Germany.
4316 **1475** 60st. multicoloured . . 1·40 80

1476 Johannes Gutenberg (inventor of printing) and Printed Characters

2000. Anniversaries. Multicoloured.
4317 10st. Type **1476** (600th birth anniv) 30 10
4318 18st. Johann Sebastian Bach (composer, 250th death anniv) 30 10
4319 20st. Guy de Maupassant (writer, 150th birth anniv) 40 10
4320 60st. Antoine de Saint-Exupery (writer and aviator, birth centenary) 1·10 30

1477 *La Jeune* (Lebardy-Juillot airship) and Eiffel Tower, 1903

2000. Centenary of First Zeppelin Flight. Airship Development. Multicoloured.
4321 10st. Type **1477** 25 10
4322 18st. LZ-13 *Hansa* (Zeppelin airship) over Cologne . . 25 15
4323 20st. N-1 *Norge* over Rome 40 15
4324 60st. *Graf Zeppelin* over Sofia . . . . 1·00 45

1478 Vazov and Text

2000. 150th Birth Anniv of Ivan Vazov (writer).
4325 **1478** 18st. multicoloured . . 50 15

1479 Letter "e" with Hands

2000. 25th Anniv of Organization for Security and Co-operation in Europe. Helsinki Final Act (establishing governing principles). Sheet 68 × 72 mm containing T **1479** and similar horiz design. Multicoloured.
MS4326 20st. Type **1479**; 20st. Three "e's" . . . . 1·20 95

1480 St. Atanasii Church, Startsevo

2000. Churches.
4327 **1480** 22st. black and blue . . 45 30
4328 – 24st. black and mauve 45 30
4329 – 50st. black and yellow 90 30
4330 – 65st. black and green 1·20 40
4331 – 3l. black and orange . . 6·00 1·20
4332 – 5l. black and rose . . . 8·75 2·20

DESIGNS: 24st. St. Clement of Orhid, Sofia; 50st. Mary of the Ascension, Sofia; 65st. St. Nedelya, Nedelino; 3l. Mary of the Ascension, Sofia (different), Sofia; 5l. Mary of the Ascension, Pamporovo.

1481 Ibex (*Capra ibex*)

2000. Animals. Multicoloured.
4333 10st. Type **1481** 25 10
4334 22st. Argali (*Ovis ammon*) 40 10
4335 30st. European bison (*Bison bonasus*) 55 15
4336 65st. Yak (*Bos grunniens*) . . 55 35

1482 Field Gladiolus (*Gladiolus segetum*)

1484 Order of Gallantry, 1880

1483 Crowd and Emblem

2000. Spring Flowers. Multicoloured.
4337 10st. Type **1482** 15 10
4338 22st. Liverwort (*Hepatica nobilis*) 20 10
4339 30st. Pheasant's eye (*Adonis vernalis*) 30 15
4340 65st. Peacock anemone (*Anemone pavonina*) . . . 60 35

2000. 50th Anniv of European Convention on Human Rights.
4341 **1483** 65st. multicoloured . . 1·10 30

2000. Medals. Multicoloured.
4342 12st. Type **1484** 30 10
4343 22st. Order of St. Aleksandu, 1882 . . . 45 10
4344 30st. Order of Merit, 1891 60 15
4345 65st. Order of Cyril and Methodius, 1909 . . . . 1·20 35

1485 Prince Boris-Mihail

2000. Bimillenary of Christianity. Multicoloured.
4346 22st. Type **1485** 50 35
4347 22st. St. Sofroni Vrachanski 50 35
4348 65st. Mary and Child (detail) . . . . 1·30 1·10
4349 65st. Antim I . . . . 1·30 1·10

1486 Seal

2000. 120th Anniv of Supreme Audit Office.
4350 **1486** 22st. multicoloured . . 40 25

1487 Microchip, Planets and "The Proportions of Man" (Leonardo DaVinci)

2001. New Millennium.
4351 **1487** 22st. multicoloured . . 50 15

1488 Tram

2001. Centenary of the Electrification of Bulgarian Transport. Multicoloured.
4352 22st. Type **1488** 40 35
4353 65st. Train carriages . . . . 1·20 1·00

1489 Muscat Grapes and Evsinograd Palace

2001. Viticulture. Multicoloured.
4354 12st. Type **1489** 30 10
4355 22st. Gumza grapes and Baba Vida Fortress . . . 50 10
4356 30st. Shiroka Melnishka Loza grapes and Melnik Winery 65 15
4357 65st. Mavrud grapes and Asenova Krepost Fortress 1·40 30

1490 " " and Microcircuits

2001. Information Technology. Sheet 82 × 95 mm containing T **1490** and similar horiz design. Multicoloured.
MS4358 Type **1490**; 65st. John Atanasoff (computer pioneer) and ABC . . . . 1·90 1·60

1491 Southern Europe and Emblem

2001. 10th Anniv of the Atlantic Club of Bulgaria. Sheet 87 × 67 mm.
MS4359 **1491** 65st. multicoloured 1·40 1·00

1492 Eagle and Lakes, Rila

2001. Europa. Water Resources. Multicoloured.
4360 22st. Type **1492** . . . . . . 1·90 50
4361 65st. Cave and waterfall, Rhodope . . . . 6·00 1·40

1493 Building, Bridge and Kableschkov

2001. 125th Anniv of the April Uprising and 150th Birth Anniv of Todor Kableschkov (revolutionary leader).
4362 **1493** 22st. multicoloured . . 40 15

1494 Juvenile Egyptian Vulture in Flight

2001. Endangered Species. Egyptian Vulture (*Neophron percnopterus*). Multicoloured.
4363 12st. Type **1494** 30 10
4364 22st. Juvenile landing . . . 45 20
4365 30st. Adult and chick . . . 60 25
4366 65st. Adult and eggs . . . . 1·50 60

1495 Georgi (Gundy) Asparuchov (footballer)

2001. Sportsmen. Multicoloured.
4367 22st. Type **1495** 45 35
4368 30st. Dancho (Dan) Kolev (wrestler) 60 50
4369 65st. Gen. Krum Lekarski (equestrian) . . . . 1·40 1·10

1496 Rainbow and People

2001. 50th Anniv United Nations High Commissioner for Refugees.
4370 **1496** 65st. multicoloured . . 1·40 25

1497 Alexander Zhendov

2001. Artists Birth Centenaries. Multicoloured.
4371 22st. Type **1497** 50 10
4372 65st. Ilya Beshkov . . . . . 1·40 25

1498 Court Seal

2001. 10th Anniv of Constitutional Court.
4373 **1498** 25st. multicoloured . . 50 15

1499 Flags

2001. North Atlantic Treaty Organization Summit, Sofia. Sheet 116 × 111 mm containing T **1499** and similar horiz designs.
MS4374 12st. Type **1499**; 24st. Streamer of flags; 25st. Flags in upper right semi-circle; 65st. Flags in upper left semi-circle . . . . 3·00 2·00

1500 Children encircling Globe

2001. United Nations Year of Dialogue among Civilizations.
4375 **1500** 65st. multicoloured . . 1·10 25

1501 Black Sea Turbot (*Scopthalmus maeoticus*)

2001. International Day for the Protection of the Black Sea. Sheet 73 × 91 mm.
MS4376 **1501** 65st. multicoloured 1·30 1·10

1502 The Nativity

1503 Cape Shabla Lighthouse

2001. Christmas.
4377 **1502** 25st. multicoloured . . 50 15

2001. Lighthouses.
4378 **1503** 25st. red and green . . 50 15
4379 – 32st. blue and yellow 65 15
DESIGN: 32st. Kaliakra Cape lighthouse.

1504 Monastery Buildings

2001. Zographu Monastery, Mount Athos. Sheet 85 × 105 mm containing T **1504** and similar horiz design. Multicoloured.
MS4380 25st. Type **1504**; 65st. Icon 1·60 1·40

1505 Father Christmas (from film by Al. Zahariev)

2001. Bulgarian Animation.
4381 **1505** 25c. multicoloured . . . 50 40

1506 Vincenzo Bellini

2001. Birth Bicentenary of Vincenzo Bellini (composer).
4382 **1506** 25st. multicoloured . . 50 40

1507 Crowd and Ancient Calendar

2001. Founders of Bulgarian State (1st series). Multicoloured.
4383 10st. Type **1507** 30 15
4384 25st. Khans, Kubrat and Asparuh 60 30
4385 30st. Khans, Krum and Omurtag 60 35
4386 65st. King Boris and Tsar Simeon . . . . 1·40 80
See also Nos. 4427/7, 4456/9, 4511/14, 4559/62 and 4610/13.

1508 "€" Symbol and Stars

2002. The Euro (European currency).
4387 **1508** 65st. multicoloured . . 1·00 80

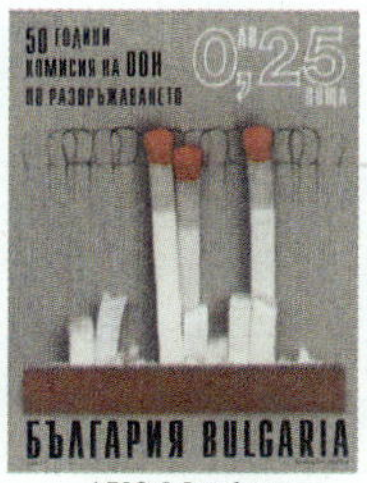

1509 Matches

2002. 50th Anniv of United Nations Disarmament Commission.
4388 **1509** 25st. multicoloured . . 50 15

1510 Limestone Arch

2002. "BALKANMAX '02" International Stamp Exhibition. Sheet 95 × 87 mm containing T **1510** and similar vert design. Multicoloured.
MS4389 25st. Type **1510**; 65st. Long-legged buzzard (*Buteo rufinus*) 9·25 6·50

1511 Figure Skater

2002. Winter Olympic Games, Salt Lake City. Multicoloured.
4390 25st. Type **1511** 40 30
4391 65st. Speed skater . . . . . 1·20 80

1512 Station Building and Bearded Penguins

2002. 10th National Antarctic Expedition.
4392 **1512** 25st. multicoloured . . 1·30 1·30

1513 Performing Elephant

2002. Europa. Circus. Multicoloured.
4393 25st. Type **1513** 40 30
4394 65st. Clown . . . . 1·20 90

1514 Veselin Stojano

2002. Birth Centenaries. Multicoloured.
4395 25st. Type **514** (composer) 25 25
4396 65st. Angel Karaliechev (writer) 80 75

1515 "Illustrated Landscape" (Vasil Barakov)

2002. Art. Multicoloured.
4397 10st. Type **1515** 25 10
4398 25st. Book illustration from "Under the Yoke" (novel by Ivan Vazov) (Boris Angulshev) (horiz) 40 25
4399 65st. "The Balcony and Canary" (Ivan Nenov) . . 1·10 75

1516 Stefan Kanchev

2002. 1st Death Annivs of Stamp Designers. Multicoloured.
4400 25st. Type **1516** 55 25
4401 65st. Alex Popilov . . . . . 1·60 75

1517 Melon (*Cucumis melo*)

2002. Fruits. Multicoloured.
4402 10st. Type **1517** 25 10
4403 25st. Watermelon (*Citrullus lanatus*) 35 20
4404 27st. Pumpkin (*Cucurbita pepo*) 50 30
4405 65st. Calabash (*Lagenaria siceraria*) . . . . 1·10 55

1518 Cock Bird

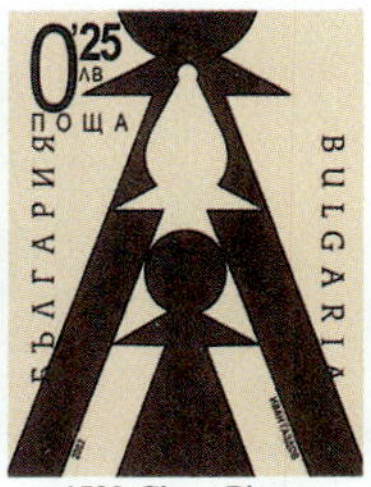

1520 Chess Pieces

1519 Pope John Paul II and Monument to Cyril & Methodius

2002. Poultry. Multicoloured.
4406 10st. Type **1518** 20 10
4407 20st. Leghorn pair (horiz) . . 25 20
4408 25st. Two cocks fighting (horiz) 25 25
4409 65st. Plymouth rock pair (inscr "Plimouth Rock") 1·20 55

2002. Pope John Paul II's Visit to Bulgaria.
4410 **1519** 65st. multicoloured . . 1·10 55

2002. Sheet 91 × 71 mm containing T **1520** and similar vert design.
MS4411 25st. brown, cinnamon and black (Type **1520**); 65st. multicoloured (Hand holding pawn) . . . . 1·60 1·60

1521 Flag and Stars

2002. 10th Anniv of Bulgaria's Admission to Council of Europe.
4412 **1521** 25st. multicoloured . . 50 15

1522 Rabbit

2002. Woodcarvings by Peter Kuschlev.
4413 **1522** 6st. brown and black 35 10
4414 – 12st. orange and black 35 10
4415 – 36st. green and black 90 40
4416 – 44st. pink and black . . 1·10 45
DESIGNS: 12st. Deer; 36st. Bird; 44st. Boar.

1523 *Marie-Luisa* (1st ocean-going liner)

2002. Merchant Ships. Multicoloured.
4417 12st. Type **1523** 25 10
4418 36st. *Persenk* (cargo ship) 65 40
4419 49st. *Kaliakra* (sail training ship) 90 50
4420 65st. *Sofia* (container ship) 1·10 55

1524 Father Christmas and Sun

2002. Christmas.
4421 **1524** 36st. multicoloured . . 65 40

1525 Flag and NATO Emblem

2002. Bulgaria's Participation in NATO Conference, Prague. Sheet 85 × 65 mm.
MS4422 **1525** 65st. multicoloured 4·00 3·25

1526 Paper Bird

2002. 30th Anniv of Security and Co-operation in Europe Conference. Sheet 85 × 60 mm.
MS4423 **1526** 65st. multicoloured 4·00 3·25

1527 Tsar Samuil

2002. Founders of Bulgarian State (2nd series). Multicoloured.
4424 18st. Type **1527** 25 20
4425 36st. Tsars Peter II and Assen 65 40
4426 49st. Tsar Kaloyan 90 50
4427 65st. Tsar Ivan Assen II . . 1·20 55

1528 Exhibition Emblem

2003. Europalia Cultural Exhibition, Belgium.
4428 **1528** 65st. multicoloured . . 1·30 55

1529 "Rose Pickers" (Stoyan Sotirov)

2003. Artists' Birth Centenaries. Multicoloured.
4429 18st. Type **1529** 30 15
4430 36st. "The Blind Fiddler" (Illya Petrov) 70 40
4431 65st. "Swineherd" (Zlatyo Boyadjiev) . . . . 1·30 60

1530 Space Construction surrounding Earth

1531 Statue of Russian and Bulgarian Soldiers

2003. Space Exploration. Sheet 104 × 85 mm.
MS4432 **1530** 65st. multicoloured 2·20 2·20

2003. 125th Anniv of Bulgarian State.
4433 **1531** 36st. multicoloured . . 70 40

1532 Exarch Stefan I, Menorah Candlestick and Dimitar Peshev

2003. 60th Anniv of Rescue of Bulgarian Jews.
4434 **1532** 36st. multicoloured . . 70 40

1533 Silhouettes of Birds and Woman

2003. Europa. Poster Art. Multicoloured.
4435 36st. Type **1533** 70 40
4436 65st. Chicken, legs and farm animals . . . . 1·30 55

1534 "Vase with Fifteen Sunflowers"

2003. 150th Birth Anniv of Vincent van Gogh (artist). Sheet 70 × 90 mm.
MS4437 **1534** 65st. multicoloured 1·30 1·30

1535 Pterodactylus

2003. Dinosaurs. Multicoloured.
4438 30st. Type **1535** 50 35
4439 36st. Gorgosaurus 60 40
4440 49st. Mesosaurus 90 50
4441 65st. Monoclonius . . . . . 1·10 60

1536 *Nymphoides Peltata*

2003. Water Plants (1st issue). Multicoloured.
4442 **1536** 36st. multicoloured . . 70 40
See also Nos. 4447/50.

1537 Honey Bee (*Apis mellifera*)

2003. Bees. Multicoloured.
4443 20st. Type **1537** 40 20
4444 30st. *Anthidium manicatum* 55 35
4445 36st. Bumble bee (*Bombus subterraneus*) 70 40
4446 65st. Blue carpenter bee (*Xylocopa violacea*) . . . 1·30 55

1538 *Butomus umbellatus*

2003. Water Plants (2nd issue). Multicoloured.
4447 20st. Type **1538** 45 20
4448 36st. *Sagirraria sagittifolia* 45 40
4449 50st. *Menyanthes trifoliate* 1·00 50
4450 65st. *Iris pseudoacorus* . . . 1·40 60

1539 Gotze Delchev

2003. Death Centenary of Gotze Delchev (revolutionary). Centenary of Macedonian Uprising.
4451 **1539** 36st. multicoloured . . 70 40

1540 Mountains

2003. International Year of Mountains.
4452 **1540** 65st. multicoloured . . 1·40 60

1541 Bulgarian and USA Flags as Bowtie

2003. Centenary of Bulgaria—USA Diplomatic Relations.
4453 **1541** 65st. multicoloured . . 1·30 60

1542 John Atanasoff

1543 Pawn and Buildings

2003. Birth Centenary of John Atanasoff (computer pioneer).
4454 **1542** 65st. multicoloured . . 1·30 60

2003. European Chess Championship, Plovdiv.
4455 **1543** 65st. multicoloured . . 1·30 60

1544 Tsar Ivan Alexander

2003. Founders of Bulgarian State (3rd series). Multicoloured.
4456 30st. Type **1544** 60 30
4457 45st. Despot Dobrotitsa . . 75 45
4458 65st. Tsar Ivan Shishman 1·20 60
4459 89st. Tsar Ivan Sratsimir . . 1·40 75

1545 Taekwondo

1546 Father Christmas

2003. 80th Anniv of National Olympic Committee. Multicoloured.
4460 20st. Type **1545** 40 20
4461 36st. Mountain biking . . . 65 40
4462 50st. Softball 95 50
4463 65st. Canoe slalom . . . . 1·20 60

2003. Christmas.
4464 **1546** 65st. multicoloured . . 1·30 95

1547 Carriage and Man wearing Top Hat

2003. Carriages. Multicoloured.
4465 30st. Type **1547** 60 30
4466 36st. Closed carriage with woman passenger 70 40
4467 50st. State coach, woman and dog . . . . 1·00 50
4468 65st. Couple and large carriage . . . . 1·30 55

1548 FIFA Centenary Emblem

2003. Centenary of FIFA (Federation Internationale de Football Association). Multicoloured.
4469 20st. Type **1548** 45 20
4470 25st. Early players 45 25
4471 36st. Early players and rules 70 40
4472 50st. FIFA fair play trophy (vert) . . . . 1·00 50
4473 65st. FIFA world player trophy (vert) . . . . . . 1·30 60

1549 Eye, Square, Compass and Statue

1550 *Noctua tertia*

2003. 10th Anniv of Re-establishment of Masonic Activity in Bulgaria.
4474 **1549** 80st. multicoloured . . 1·60 75

2004. Moths. Multicoloured.
4475 40st. Type **1550** 70 40
4476 45st. *Rethera komarovi* . . 90 45
4477 55st. *Symtomis marjana* . . 1·00 50
4478 80st. *Arctia caja* . . . . . 1·60 75

1551 Mask

2004. SERVA, International Masquerade Festival, Pernik.
4479 **1551** 80st. multicoloured . . 1·50 75

1552 OSCE Emblem and Bridge

2004. Bulgaria, Chair of Organization for Security and Co-operation in Europe.
4480 **1552** 80st. multicoloured . . 1·60 75

1553 Theatre Facade

2004. Centenary of Ivan Vazov National Theatre, Sofia.
4481 **1553** 45st. multicoloured . . 90 45

1554 Atanas Dalchev

2004. Birth Centenaries. Multicoloured.
4482 45st. Type **1554** (poet) . . . 90 45
4483 80st. Lubomir Pipkov (composer) . . . . 1·50 75

1555 NATO Emblem and National Colours

2004. Accession to Full Membership of NATO.
4484 **1555** 80st. multicoloured . . 1·50 75

1556 Georgi Ivanov

2004. 25th Anniv of First Bulgarian in Space. Sheet 84 × 68 mm.
MS4485 **1556** 80st. multicoloured 1·50 1·50

1557 Cover of Document

1558 Globe surmounted by Mortar Board

2004. 125th Anniv of Turnovska Constitution and Restoration of Bulgarian State. Sheet 86 × 67 mm.
MS4486 **1557** 45st. multicoloured 90 90

2004. "Bulgarian Dream" (graduate assistance) Programme.
4487 **1558** 45st. multicoloured . . 80 45

1559 Salvador Dali (sculpture)

2004. Birth Centenary of Salvador Dali (artist). Sheet 85 × 65 mm.
MS4488 **1559** 80st. multicoloured 1·50 75

1560 Luben Dimitrov (sculptor) and Boris Ivanov (cinema director)

2004. Birth Centenaries. Multicoloured.
4489 45st. Type **1560** 90 70
4490 80st. Vassil Stoilov and Stoyan Venev (artists) . . 1·50 1·20

1561 Mountains and Skiers

2004. Europa. Holidays. Multicoloured.
4491 45st. Type **1561** 90 70
4492 80st. Beach scene . . . . . 1·50 1·20

1562 Christo Stoychkov

2004. Bulgarian Footballers. Multicoloured.

4493 45st. Type **1562** 90 40
4494 45st. Georgi Asparuchov . . 90 40
4495 45st. Krassimir Balakov . . 90 40
4496 45st. Nikola Kotkov 90 40

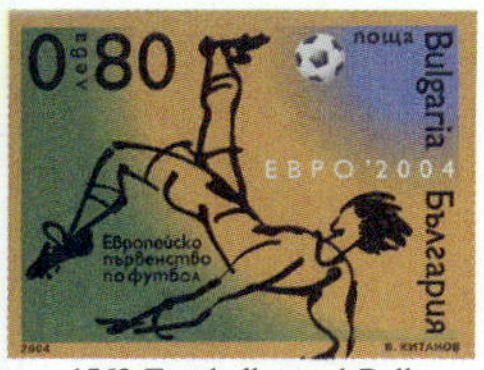
1563 Footballer and Ball

2004. European Football Championship 2004, Portugal. Sheet 85 × 67 mm.

MS4497 **1563** 80st. multicoloured 1·50 1·50

1564 Seal

2004. 125th Anniv of Bulgaria—Austria Diplomatic Relations.

4498 **1564** 80st. multicoloured . . 1·50 70

1565 Lion (statue), Flag and Document

2004. 125th Anniv of Ministry of Interior.

4499 **1565** 45st. multicoloured . . 90 45

1566a De Dion Button Post Car (1905)

2004. 125th Anniv of Postal Service. Sheet 93 × 80 mm.

MS4500 **1566a** 45st. multicoloured 90 90

No. **MS**4500 contains a se-tenant stamps size label, which with the stamp forms a composite design.

1567 Red Kite (*Milvus milvus*)

2004. Endangered Species. Preservation of the Black Sea. Sheet 86 × 86 mm containing T **1567** and similar horiz design. Multicoloured.

MS4501 45st. Type **1567**; 80st. *Blennius ocellaris* . . . . . 2·40 2·40

1568 Runner holding Torch and Olympic Flame (Berlin, 1936)

2004. Olympic Games, Athens 2004. Designs showing runner and Olympic flame. Multicoloured.

4502 10st. Type **1568** 20 10
4503 20st. Munich, 1972 . . . . 40 20
4504 45st. Moscow, 1980 . . . . 90 45
4505 80st. Athens, 2004 . . . . . 1·50 70

1569 *Krum* (steamer)

2004. 125th Anniv of Bulgarian Navy. Multicoloured.

4506 10st. Type **1569** 20 10
4507 25st. *Druski* (torpedo boat) 50 30
4508 45st. *Christo Botev* (mine-sweeper) 90 45
4509 80st. *Smeli* (frigate) . . . . 1·50 70

1570 Square and Compass

2004. 125th Anniv of Bulgarian Masonic Movement.

4510 **1570** 45st. multicoloured . . 90 45

1571 Patriarch Ephtimius Turnovski

2004. Founders of Bulgarian State (4th series). Multicoloured.

4511 10st. Type **1571** 20 10
4512 20st. Kniaz Fruzhin and Kniaz Constantine . . . 40 20
4513 45st. Georgi Peyachevich and Peter Partchevich . . 90 45
4514 80st. Piessii Hilendarski . . 1·50 70

1572 *Polyporus squamosus*

2004. Fungi. Sheet 125 × 93 mm containing T **1572** and similar horiz designs. Multicoloured.

MS4515 10st. Type **1572**; 20st. *Fomes fomentarius*; 45st. *Piptoporus betulinus*; 80st. *Laetiporus sulphurous* . . . . . 3·00 3·00

1573 Two Sturgeon

2004. Sturgeon (*Huso huso*). Multicoloured.

4516 80st. Type **1573** . . . . . . 1·50 70
4517 80st. From below . . . . . 1·50 70
4518 80st. Looking down . . . . 1·50 70
4519 80st. Eating . . . . 1·50 70

1574 Father Christmas

2004. Christmas.

4520 **1574** 45st. multicoloured . . 90 45

1575 Hands

2004. 12th Organization for Security and Co-operation in Europe (OSCE) Council, Sofia. Sheet 84 × 67 mm.

MS4521 **1575** 80st. multicoloured 1·50 70

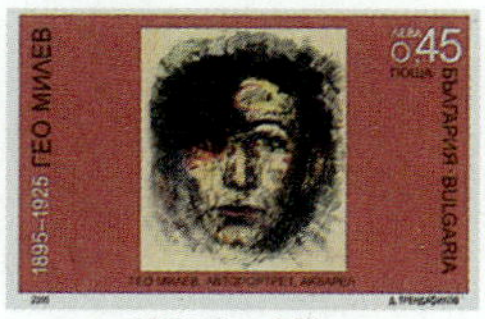
1576 Geo Milev

2005. Birth Centenary of Georghi Milev Kassabov (Geo Milev) (writer and revolutionary).

4522 **1576** 45st. multicoloured . . 90 45

1577 Emblem

1578 Charlie Chaplin in "Gold Rush" (1925)

2005. Centenary of Rotary International (charitable organization).

4523 **1577** 80st. multicoloured . . 1·50 70

2005. History of Cinema. Sheet 88 × 118 mm containing T **1578** and similar vert designs. Multicoloured.

MS4524 10st. Type **1578**; 20st. Scene from "Battleship Potemkin (Bronenoset Potemkin)" (1925); 45st. Marlene Dietrich in "Blue Angel (Der Blaue Engel)" (1930); 80st. Vassil Ghendov in "Bulgarian is a Gallant Man" (first Bulgarian film) . . . . . 3·00 3·00

1579 "The Monument" (lithograph) (Nickolai Pavlovitch)

2005. 135th Anniv of Exarchate (independent Bulgarian ecclesiastical organisation). Sheet 68 × 88 mm.

MS4525 **1579** 45st. multicoloured 90 45

1580 European Stars and Bulgarian Flag

1581 Panayot Hitov and Philip Totyo

2005. Volunteers for Europe (educational campaign).

4526 **1580** 80st. multicoloured . . 1·50 70

2005. 175th Birth Anniv of Panayot Hitov and Philip Totyo (revolutionaries).

4527 **1581** 45st. multicoloured . . 90 45

1582 Robert Peary

2005. Polar Explorers. Sheet 64 × 95 mm containing T **1582** and similar horiz design. Multicoloured.

MS4528 45st. Type **1582** (American) (North Pole, 1909); 80st. Rual Admundsen (Norwegian) (South Pole, 1911) . . . . 2·40 2·40

1583 Peugeot (1936)

2005. Fire Engines. Sheet 136 × 77 mm containing T **1583** and similar horiz design. Multicoloured.

MS4529 10st. Type **1583**; 20st. Mercedes (1935); 45st. Magirus (1934); 80st. Renault (1925) . . 50 25

1584 Hans Christian Andersen

2005. Birth Bicentenary of Hans Christian Andersen (writer). Sheet 87 × 78 mm.

MS4530 **1584** 80st. multicoloured 55 30

1585 Hand holding Scroll

2005. Cyrillic Alphabet. Sheet 88 × 59 mm.

MS4531 **1585** 80st. multicoloured 55 30

1586 Electric Locomotive 46

2005. Railways. Multicoloured.

4532 45st. Type **1586** 30 15
4533 80st. Modern locomotive DMV 10 . . . . 55 30

1587 *Radetski* (revolutionary ship) (Georgi Dimov)

2005. Children's Painting.

4534 **1587** 45st. multicoloured . . 30 15

1588 Blinis

2005. Europa. Gastronomy. Multicoloured.
4535 45st. Type **1588** 30 15
4536 80st. Bread, kebab and tomatoes 85 45

1589 Stylized Figures

1590 *Cordulegaster bidentata*

2005. 50th Anniv of Europa—CEPT Postage Stamps.
4537 **1589** 45st. violet, green and black 30 15
4538 – 80st. blue, magenta and black 85 45
DESIGNS: 45st. Type **1589**; 80st. Square of figures.

2005. Dragonflies. Multicoloured.
4539 10st. Type **1590** 10 10
4540 20st. *Erythromma najas* (horiz) 15 10
4541 45st. *Sympetrum pedemontanum* (horiz) . . 30 15
4542 80st. *Brachytron pratense* . . 85 45

1591 Elias Canetti

2005. Birth Centenary of Elias Canetti (writter).
4543 **1591** 80st. multicoloured . . 85 45

1592 *Synema globosum*

1593 Flag as Tree Bark

2005. Spiders. Multicoloured.
4544 10st. Type **1592** 10 10
4545 20st. *Argiope bruennichi* . . 15 10
4546 45st. *Eresus cinnaberinus* . . 30 15
4547 80st. *Araneus diadematus* . . 85 45

2005. 110th Anniv of Organized Tourism.
4548 **1593** 45st. multicoloured . . 30 15

1594 Map

2005. 120th Anniv of Unification of Bulgaria.
4549 **1594** 45st. multicoloured . . 30 15

1595 Girl wearing Traditional Costume, Sofia

1596 Stamen Grigoroff (discoverer)

2005. Women's Traditional Costumes. Mult.
4550 20st. Type **1595** 15 10
4551 25st. Pleven 15 10
4552 45st. Sliven 30 15
4553 80st. Stara Zagora 85 45

2005. Centenary of Discovery of *Lactobacillus bulgaricus Grigoroff* (yoghurt bacilli) (1st issue). Sheet 94 × 81 mm.
MS4554 **1596** 80st. multicoloured 85 85
See also **MS**4557.

1597 Chess Board and Antoaneta Steffanova (Women's World Chess Champion)

2005. Chess.
4555 **1597** 80st. multicoloured . . 85 45

1598 Virgin and Child

2005. Christmas.
4556 **1598** 45st. multicoloured . . 30 15

1599 Stamen Grigoroff (discoverer)

2005. Centenary of Discovery of Lactobacillus bulgaricus Grigoroff (yoghurt bacilli) (2nd issue). Sheet 94 × 81 mm. Imperf.
MS4557 **1599** 80st. multicoloured 85 85
The design of **MS**4557 is as Type **1596** with the addition of an owl in the top right corner. The sheets include a perforated number.

1600 Stylized Couple

2005. 50th Anniv of Membership of United Nations. Sheet 86 × 88 mm.
4558 **1600** 80st. multicoloured . . 85 85

1601 Patriarchs Illarion Makariopolski and Antim I

2005. Founders of Bulgarian State (5th series).
4559 **1601** 10st. chocolate and green 10 10
4560 – 20st. brown and green 15 10
4561 – 45st. claret and green 30 15
4562 – 80st. purple and green 85 40
DESIGNS: 10st. Type **1601**; 20st. Georgi Rakovski and Vassil Levski; 45st. Luben Karavelov and Christo Botev; 80st. Panayot Volov and Pavel Bobekov.

1602 *Rosa pendulina*

1603 Mozart

2006. Roses. Multicoloured.
4563 54st. Type **1602** 70 35
4564 1l.50 *Rosa gallica* . . . . . 1·00 50
4565 2l. *Rosa spinosissima* . . . . 1·30 65
4566 10l. *Rosa arvensis* . . . . . 12·50 6·25

2006. 250th Birth Anniv of Wolfgang Amadeus Mozart.
4567 **1603** 1l. multicoloured . . . 1·00 65

1604 Ellin Pellin (writer)

2006. 115th Anniv of National Philatelic Press. Bulgarian Philatelists. Multicoloured.
4568 35st. Type **1604** 30 15
4569 55st. Lazar Dobritch (circus artiste) 70 35
4570 60st. Boris Christov (opera singer) 85 45
4571 1l. Bogomil Nonev (writer) 1·40 70

1605 Snowboarder

2006. Winter Olympic Games, Turin. Sheet 86 × 118 mm containing T **1605** and similar vert design. Multicoloured.
MS4572 55st. Type **1605**; 1l. Ice dancers . . . . 2·00 2·00

1606 Sextant

2006. 10th Anniv of Bulgarian Antarctic Cartography. Sheet 86 × 69 mm.
MS4573 **1606** 1l. multicoloured 1·30 65

1607 Ship (15th Century manuscript)

2006. 610th Anniv of Battle at Nikopol.
4574 **1607** 1l.50 multicoloured . . 2·00 1·00

1608 *Martes martes*

2006. Ecology. Sheet 86 × 118 mm containing T **1608** and similar horiz design. Multicoloured.
MS4575 55st. Type **1608**; 1l.50 *Ursus arctos* . . . . 2·60 2·60

1609 Stylized Figure and Stars

2006. Europa. Integration. Multicoloured.
4576 55st. Type **1609** 70 35
4577 1l. Star as flower . . . . . 1·40 70

1610 Emblem

2006. Meeting of NATO Foreign Ministers, Sofia. Sheet 87 × 70 mm.
MS4578 **1610** 1l.50 multicoloured 2·00 2·00

1611 Mastheads

2006. 70th Anniv of "Trud" Newspaper.
4579 **1611** 55st. multicoloured . . 70 35

1612 Vesselin Topalov

2006. Vesselin Topalov—World Chess Champion. Sheet 87 × 71 mm.
MS4580 **1612** 1l.50 multicoloured 2·00 2·00
No. **MS**4580 also exist imperforate.

1613 Building Facade

2006. 25th Anniv of National Palace of Culture.
4581 **1613** 55st. multicoloured . . 35 20

1614 *Circus aeruginosus*

2006. Raptors. Multicoloured.
4582 10st. Type **1614** 15 10
4583 35st. *Circus cyaneus* 45 25
4584 55st. *Circus macrourus* . . . 75 40
4585 1l. *Circus pygargus* . . . . 1·50 75

1615 Building Facade, Ship and Sailor

2006. 125th Anniv of Nikola Vaptsarov Naval Academy, Varna.
4586 **1615** 55st. multicoloured . . 70 35

1616 Players

2006. World Cup Football Championship, Germany. Sheet 87 × 87 mm.
MS4587 **1616** 1l. multicoloured 1·40 1·40

1617 Emblem

2006. 50th Anniv of Bulgaria in UNESCO.
4588 **1617** 1l. multicoloured . . . 1·40 70

1618 Gena Dimitrova

1619 *Saponaria strajensis*

2006. 65th Birth Anniv and First Death Anniv of Gena Dimitrova (opera singer).
4589 **1618** 1l. multicoloured . . . 1·40 70

2006. Flora. Multicoloured.
4590 10st. Type **1619** 15 10
4591 35st. *Trachystemon orientalis* 45 25
4592 55st. *Hypericum calycinum* 75 40
4593 1l. *Rhododendron ponticum* 1·50 75

1620 Rover Maestro

2006. Bulgaria Automobile Industry. Multicoloured.
4594 10st. Type **1620** 15 10
4595 35st. Moskovitch 45 25
4596 55st. Bulgaralpine 75 40
4597 1l. Bulgarrnault . . . . . . 1·50 75

1621 "Return of the Prodigal Son"

2006. 400th Birth Anniv of Rembrandt Harmenszoon van Rijn. Sheet 65 × 84 mm.
MS4598 **1621** 1l. multicoloured 1·40 1·40

1622 "All Soul's Day" (Ivan Murkvitchka)

2006. Art Anniversaries. Multicoloured.
4599 10st. Type **1622** (150th birth anniv) 15 10
4600 35st. "Sozopol—Houses" (Vesselin Statkov) (birth centenary) 45 25
4601 55st. "Sofia in Winter" (Nikola Petrov) (90th death anniv) 75 40
4602 1l. "T. Popova" (John Popov) (birth centenary) 1·50 75

1623 Competitors

2006. World Sambo Championship, Sofia.
4603 **1623** 55st. multicoloured . . 75 40

1624 Post Van

2006. Post Europ. Sheet 85 × 75 mm.
MS4604 **1624** 1l. multicoloured 1·40 1·40

1625 Angel

2006. Christmas.
4605 **1625** 55st. multicoloured . . 75 40

1626 Ballot Box and Flags

2006. Bulgaria and Romania's Membership of European Union. Multicoloured.
4606 55st. Type **1626** 75 35
4607 1l. "EU" . . . . 1·40 70
MS4608 97 × 87 mm. Nos. 4606/7 2·10 2·10
Stamps of a similar design were issued by Romania.

1627 Peter Dimkov

2006. 120th Birth Anniv of Peter Dimkov (naturopath).
4609 **1627** 55st. multicoloured . . 75 40

1628 Generals Danail Nikolaev and Racho Petrov

2006. Founders of Bulgarian State (6th series). Multicoloured.
4610 10st. Type **1628** 15 10
4611 35st. Petko Karavelov and Marin Drinov 45 25
4612 55st. Konstantin Stoylov and Stephan Stambolov 75 40
4613 1l. Prince Albert I of Bulgaria . . . . 1·40 1·40

1629 Aircraft and Terminal Building

2006. New Airport Terminal, Sofia. Sheet 87 × 72 mm.
MS4614 **1629** 55st. multicoloured 75 40

1631 Emilian Stanev

2007. Birth Centenary of Nikola Stoyanov Stanev (Emilian Stanev) (writer).
4616 **1631** 55st. multicoloured . . 75 40

1632 Flags as Stars

2007. 50th Anniv of Treaty of Rome.
4617 **1632** 1l. multicoloured . . . 1·40 70

1633 Ivan Dimov

2007. Theatre Personalities. Multicoloured.
4618 10st. Type **1633** 15 10
4619 55st. Sava Ognyanov . . . 75 40
4620 1l. Krustyo Sarfov . . . . 1·40 70

1634 Sputnik

2007. 50th Anniv of First Manmade Satellite. Sheet 87 × 56 mm.
MS4621 **1634** 1l. multicoloured 1·40 70

1635 Campfire

2007. Europa. Centenary of Scouting. Multicoloured.
(a) Size 39 × 28 mm.
4622 55st. Type **1635** 75 40
4623 1l.50 Route finding . . . . 2·00 1·00

(b) Size 31 × 23 mm.
4624 1l. As Type **1635** . . . . . 1·40 70
4625 1l. As No. 4623 . . . . . . 1·40 70

1636 DAR-3 Garvan II(1937)

2007. Military Aircraft. Multicoloured.
4626 10st. Type **1636** 15 10
4627 35st. DAR-9 Siniger (1939) 45 25
4628 55st. Kaproni Bulgarski KB-6 Papagal(1939) . . . 70 40
4629 1l. Kaproni Bulgarski KB-11A Fanzan . . . . 1·40 70

1637 Boris I

2007. 1100th Death Anniv of Knyaz (Prince) Boris I (Michael).
4630 **1637** 55st. multicoloured . . 70 40

1637a Basilica and Saint Cyril

2007. 150th Anniv of Excavation of San Clement Basilica, Rome.
4630a **1637a** 1l. multicoloured . . 1·20 60

1638 Dimcho Debelyanov

1639 St. Spass Monastery, Lozenski

2007. Birth Anniversaries. Multicoloured.
4631 10st. Type **1638** (poet) (120th) 15 10
4632 35st. Nenko Balkanski (artist) (centenary) 45 25
4633 55st. Vera Lukova (artist) (centenary) 65 35
4634 1l. Theodor Trayanov (poet) (125th) . . . . 1·20 60

2007. Monasteries. Multicoloured.
4635 63st. Type **1639** 80 40
4636 75st. St. Mina, Obradovski 90 45
4637 1l.20 St. George the Victor, Kremikovski . . . . . . 1·50 75
4638 2l.20 Three Saints, Chepinski . . . . 2·70 1·40

1640 Symbols of Transport

2007. International Transport Forum, Sofia.
4639 **1640** 1l. multicoloured . . . 1·20 60

1641 Presidents of Bulgaria and Azerbaijan

2007. 15th Anniv of Bulgaria–Azerbaijan Diplomatic Relations. Sheet 86 × 64 mm.
MS4640 **1641** 1l. multicoloured 1·20 60

1642 *Onosma thracica*

1643 Vassal Levski

2007. Flora. Multicoloured.
4641 10st. Type **1642** 15 10
4642 45st. *Astracantha aitosensis* 55 30
4643 55st. *Veronica krumovii* . . 65 35
4644 1l. *Verbascum adrianopolitanum* . . . . 1·20 60

2007. 170th Birth Anniv of Vassal Levski (revolutionary leader).
4645 **1643** 55st. multicoloured . . 65 35

1644 Sailor

2007. Junior World Sailing Championship–Olympian Class 470, Burgas.

4646	**1644**	1l. multicoloured	1·20	60

1645 Lt. Colonel Pavel Kalitin (painting) and 'Battle at Stara Zagora' (Nikola Kozhuharov)

2007. 130th Anniv of Battle at Stara Zagora.

4647	**1645**	55st. multicoloured	65	35

1646 Players

2007. Rugby. 50th (2005) Anniv of Locomotiv Rugby Club, Sofia. World Rugby Championship–2007, France.

4648	**1646**	55st. multicoloured	65	35

1647 *Lutra lutra* (otter)

2007. Ecology. 15th Anniv of Ropotamo Reserve. Sheet 85 × 85 mm containing T **1647** and similar horiz design. Multicoloured.

MS4649 55st. Type **1647**; 1l. *Haliaeetus albicilla* (white tailed eagle) . . . 1·90 1·90

The stamps and margins of **MS**4549 form a composite design.

1648 *Alcedo atthis* (kingfisher)

2007. Endangered Species. Birds. Sheet 97 × 130 mm containing T **1648** and similar horiz design. Multicoloured.

MS4650 10st. Type **1648**; 35st. *Tichodroma muraria* (wall creeper); 55st. *Bombycilla garrulous* (waxwing); 1l. *Phoenicopterus ruber* (flamingo) . . . 2·40 2·40

1649 Emblem

2007. 10th Anniv Grand Lodge of the Ancient Freemasons.

4651	**1649**	55st. multicoloured	65	35

1650 Centre Building

2007. Inauguration of Exchange and Sorting Centre, Sofia. Sheet 87 × 63 mm.

MS4652 **1650** 55st. multicoloured 65 35

1651 Ivan Hadjiski

1652 Woman holding Offerings

2007. Birth Centenary of Ivan Hadjiski (social psychologist).

4653	**1651**	55st. multicoloured	65	35

2007. Christmas.

4654	**1652**	55st. multicoloured	65	35

1653 Rumyana Neykova (European 2000m. skiff rowing champion)

2007. Women Sports Personalities. Multicoloured.

4655	10st. Type **1653**	15	10
4656	35st. Stanka Zlateva (World freestyle wrestling champion)	45	25
4657	1l. Stefka Kostadinova (World record high jump (30.8.1987))	1·20	60

1654 '100' and Soldier

2007. Centenary of Military Reconnaissance.

4658	**1654**	55st. multicoloured	65	35

1655 Hristo Botev

2008. Birth Centenary of Hristo Botev (poet and revolutionary).

4659	**1655**	55st. multicoloured	65	35

1656 Polar Bear

2008. International Polar Year. 20th Anniv of Bulgarian Antarctic Expedition. Sheet 115 × 85 mm containing T **1656** and similar horiz design. Multicoloured.

MS4660 55st. Type **1656**; 1l. Skua stealing penguin chick . . . 1·90 1·90

The stamps and margins of **MS**4660 form a composite design.

1657 Volleyball Player

1658 Arms of Bulgaria

2008. Olympic Games, Beijing. Sheet 88 × 109 mm containing T **1657** and similar vert design. Multicoloured.

MS4661 55st. Type **1657**; 1l. Two players . . . 1·90 1·90

The stamps of **MS**4661 form a composite design of a volley ball match.

2008. 130th Anniv of San Stefano Peace Treaty (treaty between Russia and the Ottoman Empire at the end of the Russo-Turkish War (setting up an autonomous self-governing tributary principality of Bulgaria)).

4662	**1658**	55st. multicoloured	65	35

EXPRESS STAMPS

E 137 Express Delivery Van

1939.

E429	–	5l. blue	50	30
E430	**E 137**	6l. brown	35	30
E431	–	7l. brown	40	30
E432	**E 137**	8l. red	65	30
E433	–	20l. red	1·20	70

DESIGNS—VERT: 5l., 20l. Bicycle messenger; 7l. Motor-cyclist and sidecar.

OFFICIAL STAMPS

O 158

O 177

1942.

O507	**O 158**	10s. green	10	10
O508		30s. orange	10	10
O509		50s. brown	10	15
O510	–	1l. blue	10	10
O511	–	2l. green	10	10
O534	–	2l. red	10	10
O512	–	3l. mauve	10	15
O513	–	4l. pink	10	10
O514	–	5l. red	15	15

The 1l. to 5l. are larger (19 × 23 mm).

1945. Arms designs. Imperf or perf.

O580	–	1l. mauve	15	15
O581	**O 177**	2l. green	15	15
O582	–	3l. brown	15	10
O583	–	4l. blue	15	15
O584	–	5l. red	15	15

PARCEL POST STAMPS

P 153 Weighing Machine

P 154 Loading Motor Lorry

1941.

P494	**P 153**	1l. green	15	10
P495	A	2l. red	15	10
P496	**P 154**	3l. brown	15	10
P497	B	4l. orange	15	10
P498	**P 153**	5l. blue	15	10
P506		5l. green	15	15
P499	B	6l. purple	15	15
P507		6l. brown	15	15
P500	**P 153**	7l. blue	15	15
P508		7l. sepia	15	15
P501	**P 154**	8l. turquoise	15	10
P509		8l. green	15	10
P502	A	9l. olive	40	15
P503	B	10l. orange	30	15
P504	**P 154**	20l. violet	40	15
P505	A	30l. black	1·60	15

DESIGNS—HORIZ: A, Loading mall coach; B, Motor-cycle combination.

P 163

1944. Imperf.

P532	**P 163**	1l. red	15	15
P533		3l. green	15	10
P534		5l. green	15	10
P535		7l. mauve	15	10
P536		10l. blue	15	10
P537		20l. brown	15	10
P538		30l. purple	15	10
P539		50l. orange	40	25
P540		100l. blue	70	40

POSTAGE DUE STAMPS

D 7

D 12

D 16

1884. Perf.

D75	**D 7**	5s. orange	30·00	4·75
D54		25s. lake	6·50	3·00
D55		50s. blue	4·00	9·25

1886. Imperf.

D50	**D 7**	5s. orange	£120	9·75
D51		25s. lake	£200	8·75
D52a		50s. blue	12·00	8·75

1893. Surch with bar and **30.**

D78d	**D 7**	30s. on 50s. blue (perf)	14·50	8·00
D79		30s. on 50s. blue (imperf)	18·00	7·25

1896. Perf.

D83	**D 12**	5s. orange	8·00	1·70
D84		10s. violet	6·00	1·60
D85		30s. green	3·75	1·20

1901.

D124	**D 16**	5s. red	35	30
D125		10s. green	65	30
D126		20s. blue	6·75	30
D127		30s. red	65	30
D128		50s. orange	9·25	8·00

D 37

D 110

1915.

D200	**D 37**	5s. green	20	15
D240		10s. violet	15	15
D202		20s. red	15	15
D241		20s. orange	15	15
D203a		30s. red	15	15
D242		50s. blue	15	15
D243		1l. green	15	15
D244		2l. red	15	15
D245		3l. brown	30	15

1932.

D326	**D 110**	1l. bistre	50	70
D327		2l. red	50	70
D328		6l. purple	1·40	95

D 111

D 112

D 293

1933.

D333	**D 111**	20s. sepia	10	10
D334		40s. blue	10	15
D335		80s. red	10	15
D336	**D 112**	1l. brown	30	40
D337		2l. olive	40	1·10
D338		6l. violet	25	30
D339		14l. blue	35	50

1947. As Type **D 112**, but larger (18 × 24 mm).

D646	1l. brown	15	15
D647	2l. red	30	30
D648	8l. orange	20	15
D649	20l. blue	70	30

1951.

D849	**D 293**	1l. brown	15	15
D850		2l. purple	15	15
D851		8l. orange	50	30
D852		20l. blue	1·20	95

BULGARIAN OCCUPATION OF RUMANIA Pt. 3

(DOBRUJA DISTRICT)

100 stotinki = 1 leva.

(1)

1916. Bulgarian stamps of 1911 optd with T **1**.

1	**23**	1s. grey	10	10
2	–	5s. brown and green	1·50	1·25
3	–	10s. sepia and brown	15	10
4	–	25s. black and blue	15	10

BUNDI Pt. 1

A state of Rajasthan, India. Now uses Indian stamps.

12 pies = 1 anna; 16 annas = 1 rupee.

3 Native Dagger

11 Raja protecting Sacred Cows

1894. Imperf.

12	**3**	½a. grey	4·75	4·75
13		1a. red	3·75	3·75
14		2a. green	13·00	17·00
8		4a. green	70·00	95·00
15		8a. red	14·00	18·00
16a		1r. yellow on blue	16·00	27·00

1898. As T **3**, but with dagger point to left.

17a	**3**	4a. green	18·00	25·00

1914. Roul or perf.

26	**11**	¼a. blue	1·90	4·25
38		½a. black	1·90	4·50
28		1a. red	3·75	12·00
20a		2a. green	4·50	9·00
30		2½a. yellow	7·50	27·00
31		3a. brown	8·50	45·00
32		4a. green	3·50	42·00
33		6a. blue	14·00	£110
42		8a. orange	9·00	70·00
43		10a. olive	16·00	£100
44		12a. green	13·00	95·00
25		1r. lilac	27·00	£120
46		2r. brown and black	85·00	£225
47		3r. blue and brown	£130	£300
48		4r. green and red	£275	£375
49		5r. red and green	£275	£375

20

21 Maharao Rajah Bahadur Singh

1941. Perf.

79	**20**	3p. blue	2·75	5·00
80		6p. blue	4·25	8·50
81		1a. red	6·50	10·00
82		2a. brown	8·50	18·00
83		4a. green	15·00	55·00
84		8a. green	20·00	£200
85		1r. blue	42·00	£300

1947.

86	**21**	¼a. green	2·25	38·00
87		½a. violet	2·00	32·00
88		1a. green	2·00	32·00
89	–	2a. red	1·90	65·00
90	–	4a. orange	2·25	90·00
91	–	8a. blue	3·00	
92	–	1r. brown	15·00	

DESIGNS: 2, 4a. Rajah in Indian dress; 8a., 1r. View of Bundi.

OFFICIAL STAMPS

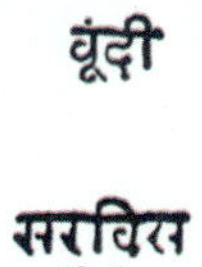

(O 1)

1915. Optd as Type O 1.

O 6A	¼a. blue	1·60	
O16A	½a. black	10·00	
O 8A	1a. red	4·00	
O18A	2a. green	6·50	
O 2A	2½a. yellow	4·00	
O 3A	3a. brown	3·75	
O19A	4a. green	12·00	
O11A	6a. blue	14·00	
O20A	8a. orange	15·00	
O21A	10a. olive	65·00	
O22A	12a. green	50·00	
O 5A	1r. lilac	60·00	
O24A	2r. brown and black	£400	
O25A	3r. blue and brown	£350	
O26A	4r green and red	£300	
O27A	5r. red and green	£325	

1915. Optd **BUNDI SERVICE**.

O 6B	**11**	¼a. blue	1·75	
O16 B		½a. black	3·00	
O 8bB		1a. red	16·00	
O18 B		2a. green	19·00	
O 2 B		2½a. yellow	20·00	
O 3 B		3a. brown	23·00	
O19 B		4a. green	80·00	
O11 B		6a. blue	30·00	
O20 B		8a. orange	35·00	
O21 B		10a. olive	95·00	
O22 B		12a. green	£120	
O 5 B		1r. lilac	55·00	
O24 B		2r. brown and black	£190	
O25 B		3r. blue and brown	£225	
O26 B		4r. green and red	£300	
O27 B		5r. red and green	£325	

Prices for Nos. O2/27 are for unused examples. Used examples are generally worth a small premium over the prices quoted.

1941. Optd **SERVICE**.

O53	**20**	3p. blue	6·00	16·00
O54		6p. blue	16·00	16·00
O55		1a. red	15·00	11·00
O56		2a. brown	16·00	13·00
O57		4a. green	48·00	£110
O58	**20**	8a. green	£180	£550
O59		1r. blue	£250	£650

For later issues see **RAJASTHAN**.

BURKINA FASO Pt. 12

A country in W. Africa, formerly known as Upper Volta. The name was changed in August 1984.

100 centimes = 1 franc.

249 "Graphium pylades"

1984. Air. Butterflies. Multicoloured.

738	10f. Type **249**	30	10
739	120f. "Hyploimnas misippus"	1·30	55
740	400f. "Danaus chrysippus"	4·25	2·10
741	450f. "Papilio demodocus"	5·00	2·30

250 Soldier with Gun

253 Footballers and Statue

252 National Flag

1984. 1st Anniv of Captain Thomas Sankara's Presidency. Multicoloured.

742	90f. Type **250**	39·00	
743	120f. Capt. Sankara and crowd	55·00	

1984. Aid for the Sahel. No. 682 of Upper Volta optd **BURKINA FASO Aide au Sahel 84**.

743a	100f. multicoloured		

1985. Nos. 716/21 of Upper Volta optd **BURKINA FASO**.

744	25f. Type **246** (postage)	45	20
745	185f. "Pterocarpus lucens"	2·75	1·50
746	200f. "Phlebopus colossus sudanicus"	3·75	1·70
747	250f. "Cosmos sulphureus"	4·50	2·10
748	300f. "Trametes versicolor" (air)	4·75	2·40
749	400f. "Ganoderma lucidum"	6·50	3·25

1985. National Symbols. Multicoloured.

750	5f. Type **252** (postage)	40	20
751	15f. National arms (vert)	45	25
752	90f. Maps of Africa and Burkina Faso	1·80	90
753	120f. Type **252** (air)	1·60	80
754	150f. As No. 751	2·20	1·00
755	185f. As No. 752	2·50	1·20

1985. World Cup Football Championship, Mexico.

756	**253**	25f. mult. (postage)	40	10
757	–	45f. multicoloured	55	20
758	–	90f. multicoloured	1·10	35
759	–	100f. multicoloured (air)	1·20	30
760	–	150f. multicoloured	1·40	55
761	–	200f. mult (horiz)	1·90	85
762	–	250f. mult (horiz)	2·50	1·10
MS763		78 × 77 mm. 500f. multicoloured (horiz)	5·50	1·30

DESIGNS: 45f. to 500f. Mexican statues and various footballing scenes.

254 Children playing and Boy

1985. Air "Philexafrique" International Stamp Exhibition, Lome, Togo (1st issue). Multicoloured.

764	200f. Type **254**	2·00	1·20
765	200f. Solar panels, transmission mast, windmill, dish aerial and tree	2·00	1·20

See also Nos. 839/40.

255 G. A. Long's Steam Tricycle

1985. Centenary of Motor Cycle. Multicoloured.

766	50f. Type **255** (postage)	90	20
767	75f. Pope	1·10	25
768	80f. Manet	1·60	35
769	100f. Ducati (air)	95	30
770	150f. Jawa	1·60	55
771	200f. Honda	2·20	85
772	250f. B.M.W.	2·75	1·10

256 "Chamaeleon dilepis"

1985. Reptiles and Amphibians. Multicoloured.

773	5f. Type **256** (postage)	25	15
774	15f. "Agama stellio"	70	15
775	33f. "Lacerta lepida" (horiz)	1·10	15
776	85f. "Hiperolius marmoratus" (horiz)	1·70	30
777	100f. "Echis leucogaster" (horiz) (air)	1·40	30
778	150f. "Kinixys erosa" (horiz)	2·10	50
779	250f. "Python regius" (horiz)	3·25	70

257 Benz "Victoria", 1893

1985. Motor Cars and Aircraft. Multicoloured.

780	5f. Type **257** (postage)	20	10
781	25f. Peugeot "174", 1927	45	10
782	45f. Bleriot XI airplane	60	10
783	50f. Breguet 14T biplane	60	10
784	500f. Bugatti "Napoleon T41 Royale" (air)	5·25	1·30
785	500f. Airbus Industrie A300	4·25	1·30
786	600f. Mercedes-Benz "540 K", 1938	5·25	1·70
787	600f. Airbus Industrie A300	5·25	1·70
MS788	100 × 68 mm. 1000f. Louis Bleriot and airplanes, Karl Benz and early Benz motor car	8·50	3·50

258 Wood Duck

1985. Birth Bicentenary of John J. Audubon (ornithologist). Multicoloured.

789	60f. Type **258** (postage)	60	20
790	100f. Northern mockingbird	90	40
791	300f. Northern oriole	3·00	90
792	400f. White-breasted nuthatch	3·50	1·20
793	500f. Common flicker (air)	4·25	1·30
794	600f. Rough-legged buzzard	5·25	1·60
MS795	73 × 83 mm. 1000f. White-crowned pigeon	9·00	3·50

259 Young Lady Elizabeth Bowes-Lyon on Pony

1985. 85th Birthday of Queen Elizabeth the Queen Mother. Multicoloured.

796	75f. Type **259** (postage)	80	35
797	85f. Marriage of Lady Elizabeth Bowes-Lyon and Albert, Duke of York	80	35
798	500f. Duke and Duchess of York with Princess Elizabeth (air)	4·00	1·30
799	600f. Royal family in Coronation robes	5·25	1·60
MS800	104 × 64 mm. 1000f. Queen Elizabeth the Queen Mother at christening of Prince William of Wales	8·50	3·50

260 Gaucho on Piebald Horse

1985. "Argentina '85" International Stamp Exhibition, Buenos Aires. Horses. Multicoloured.

801	25f. Type **260** (postage)	45	10
802	45f. Gaucho on horse	75	25
803	90f. Rodeo rider	1·30	40
804	100f. Rider hunting gazelle (air)	1·00	35
805	150f. Horses and gauchos at camp fire	1·50	55
806	200f. Horse and man sitting on steps	2·10	85
807	250f. Riding contest	2·75	1·10
MS808	100 × 89 mm. 500f. Foal (39 × 31 mm)	7·50	3·00

261 Electric Locomotive No. 105-30 and Tank Wagon

1985. Trains. Multicoloured.

809	50f. Type **261** (postage)	80	10
810	75f. Diesel shunting locomotive	1·00	25
811	80f. Diesel passenger locomotive	1·30	25
812	100f. Diesel railcar (air)	1·10	10
813	150f. Diesel locomotive No. 6093	1·60	30
814	200f. Diesel railcar No. 105	2·10	40
815	250f. Diesel locomotive pulling passenger train	2·75	55

262 Pot (Tikare)

263 "Pholiota mutabilis"

1985. Handicrafts. Multicoloured.
816 10f. Type **262** (postage) . . . 25 10
817 40f. Pot with lid decorated with birds (P. Bazega) . . 70 20
818 90f. Bronze statuette of mother with child (Ouagadougou) . . . . . 1·40 35
819 120f. Bronze statuette of drummer (Ouagadougou) (air) . . . . 2·10 50

1985. Fungi. Multicoloured.
820 15f. Type **263** (postage) . . . 20 10
821 20f. "Hypholoma (nematoloma) fasciculare" 20 10
822 30f. "Ixocomus granulatus" 40 20
823 60f. "Agaricus campestris" 90 15
824 80f. "Trachypus scaber" . . 1·40 50
825 250f. "Marasmius scorodonius" . . . . . . 3·75 1·50
826 150f. "Armillaria mellea" (air) . . . . 2·75 70

264 "Virgin and Child"

1985. "Italia '85" International Stamp Exhibition, Rome. Paintings by Botticelli.
827 25f. Type **264** (postage) . . . 50 10
828 45f. "Portrait of an Unknown Man" 90 20
829 90f. "Mars and Venus" . . . 1·60 40
830 100f. "Birth of Venus" (air) 1·20 50
831 150f. "Allegory of Calumny" 1·40 65
832 200f. "Pallas and the Centaur" . . . . 2·50 85
833 250f. "Allegory of Spring" 3·25 1·10
MS834 71 × 91 mm. 500f. "Virgin of the Pomegranate" (31 × 39 mm) 5·00 2·00

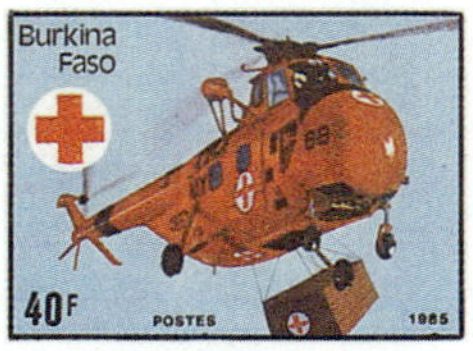

265 Sikorsky S-55 Helicopter

1985. Red Cross. Multicoloured.
835 40f. Type **265** (postage) . . . 1·70 35
836 85f. Ambulance . . . . . . 3·00 50
837 150f. Henri Dunant (founder) (vert) (air) . . . . . . 2·30 65
838 250f. Nurse attending patient (vert) . . . . 3·75 1·10

266 Transport and Communications (development)

1985. Air. "Philexafrique" International Stamp Exhibition, Lome, Togo (2nd issue). Mult.
839 250f. Type **266** . . . . . . 3·50 1·50
840 250f. Youth activities (youth) 3·50 1·50

267 Girls drumming and clapping

1986. Dodo Carnival. Multicoloured.
841 20f. Type **267** 10 10
842 25f. Masked lion dancers . . 25 10
843 40f. Masked stick dancers and drummers 45 15
844 45f. Stick dancers with elaborate headdresses . . . 55 20
845 90f. Masked elephant dancer 1·20 45
846 90f. Animal dancers . . . . 1·20 45

268 Mother breast-feeding Baby

1986. Child Survival Campaign.
847 **268** 90f. multicoloured . . . . 1·10 50

269 Couple carrying Rail

1986. Railway Construction. Multicoloured.
848 90f. Type **269** (postage) . . . 85 35
849 120f. Laying tracks . . . . . 1·00 45
850 185f. Workers waving to passing train . . . . . . 1·50 65
851 500f. "Inauguration of First German Railway" (Heim) (air) . . . . 4·25 2·00
MS852 90 × 68 mm. 1000f. Experimental inter-city train and diesel locomotive series 290 . . 8·50 3·50
Nos. 851/**MS**852 commemorate the 150th Anniv of German railways.

270 Columbus before King of Portugal, and "Nina"

271 Village and First Aid Post

1986. 480th Death Anniv of Christopher Columbus (explorer). Multicoloured.
853 250f. Type **270** (postage) . . 2·50 70
854 300f. "Santa Maria" and Columbus with astrolabe 2·75 90
855 400f. Columbus imprisoned and "Santa Maria" . . . . 3·75 1·10
856 450f. Landing at San Salvador and "Pinta" (air) 4·25 1·80
MS857 90 × 68 mm. 1000f. Fleet leaving Palos . . . . 8·50 2·10

1986. "Health For All by Year 2000". Mult.
858 90f. Type **271** 95 35
859 100f. Man receiving first aid (26 × 36 mm) 95 45
860 120f. People queuing for vaccinations (26 × 36 mm) 1·30 50

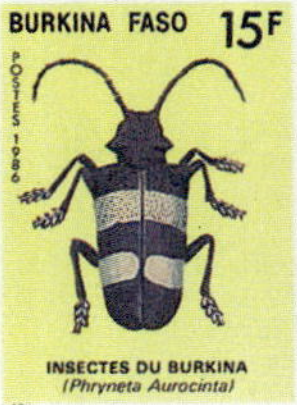

272 "Phryneta aurocinta"

273 Woman feeding Child and Fresh Foods

1986. Insects. Multicoloured.
861 15f. Type **272** 25 10
862 20f. "Sternocera interrupta" 35 10
863 40f. "Prosoprocera lactator" 80 30
864 45f. "Gonimbrasia hecate" 90 35
865 85f. "Charaxes epijasius" . . 1·40 60

1986. Gobi Health Strategy. Multicoloured.
866 30f. Type **273** 40 10
867 60f. Ingredients of oral rehydration therapy . . . 70 30
868 90f. Mother holding child for vaccination . . . . 1·00 45
869 120f. Doctor weighing child 1·50 55

274 UPU Emblem on Dove

275 Emblem

1986. World Post Day.
870 **274** 120f. multicoloured . . . 1·30 55

1986. International Peace Year.
871 **275** 90f. blue . . . . 1·20 55

276 Namende Dancers

277 Warthog

1986. National Bobo Culture Week. Mult.
872 10f. Type **276** 25 10
873 25f. Mouhoun dancers . . . 50 10
874 90f. Houet dancer . . . . . 1·10 45
875 105f. Seno musicians . . . . 1·10 50
876 120f. Ganzourgou dancers . . 1·70 60

1986. Wildlife. Multicoloured.
877 50f. Type **277** 70 20
878 65f. Spotted hyena 80 30
879 90f. Antelope . . . . 1·20 35
880 100f. Red-fronted gazelle . . 1·20 45
881 120f. Harnessed antelope . . 1·30 55
882 145f. Hartebeest . . . . . . 1·80 65
883 500f. Kob . . . . 5·75 2·20

278 Peul

279 Charlie Chaplin within Film Frame (10th death anniv)

1986. Traditional Hairstyles. Multicoloured.
884 35f. Type **278** 35 10
885 75f. Dafing 80 35
886 90f. Peul (different) . . . . 1·30 45
887 120f. Mossi . . . . 1·60 60
888 185f. Peul (different) . . . . 2·30 90

1987. 10th Fespaco Film Festival.
889 – 90f. mauve, black & brn 1·10 60
890 – 120f. multicoloured . . . 2·20 85
891 **279** 185f. multicoloured . . . 3·25 1·40
DESIGNS: 90f. Camera on map in film frame; 120f. Cameraman and soundman (60th anniv of first talking film "The Jazz Singer").

280 Woman trimming Rug

281 "Calotripis procera"

1987. International Women's Day.
892 **280** 90f. multicoloured . . . . 1·00 45

1987. Flowers. Multicoloured.
893 70f. Type **281** 80 30
894 75f. "Acacia seyal" 80 30
895 85f. "Parkia biglobosa" . . . 1·00 50
896 90f. "Sterospernum kunthianum" . . . . . . 1·00 50
897 100f. "Dichrostachys cinerea" 1·40 55
898 300f. "Combretum paniculatum" . . . . . . 3·50 1·30

282 High Jumping

1987. Olympic Games, Seoul (1988). 50th Death Anniv of Pierre de Coubertin (founder of modern Olympic Games). Multicoloured.
899 75f. Type **282** 80 40
900 85f. Tennis (vert) 90 40
901 90f. Ski jumping 95 55
902 100f. Football . . . . 1·00 55
903 145f. Running . . . . 1·40 70
904 350f. Pierre de Coubertin and tennis game (vert) . . . . 3·50 1·70

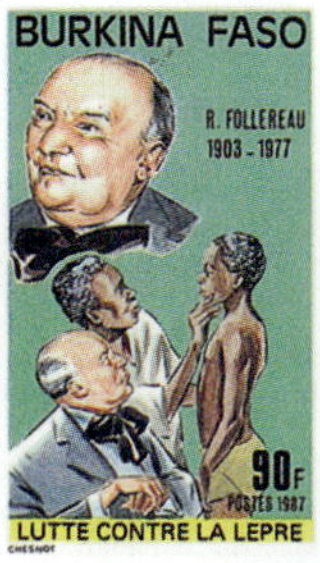

283 Follereau and Doctor treating Patient

285 Globe in Envelope

284 Woman sweeping

1987. Anti-leprosy Campaign. 10th Death Anniv of Raoul Follereau (pioneer). Multicoloured.
905 90f. Type **283** . . . . 1·10 45
906 100f. Laboratory technicians 1·30 45
907 120f. Gerhard Hansen (discoverer of bacillus) . . 1·50 55
908 300f. Follereau kissing patient 3·50 1·50

1987. World Environment Day. Multicoloured.
909 90f. Type **284** . . . . 1·00 60
910 145f. Emblem . . . . 1·50 75

1987. World Post Day.
911 **285** 90f. multicoloured . . . . 1·00 55

286 Luthuli and Open Book

1987. Anti-Apartheid Campaign. 20th Death Anniv of Albert John Luthuli (anti-apartheid campaigner). Multicoloured.
912 90f. Barbed wire and apartheid victims . . . . . 1·00 45
913 100f. Type **286** . . . . . . 1·10 45

287 Dagari

288 Balafon (16 key xylophone)

1987. Traditional Costumes. Multicoloured.
914 10f. Type **287** 10 10
915 30f. Peul 25 10
916 90f. Mossi (female) 85 45

917 200f. Senoufo . . . . 1·60 90
918 500f. Mossi (male) . . . . . 5·00 2·30

1987. Traditional Music Instruments. Multicoloured.
919 20f. Type **288** 25 10
920 25f. Kunde en more (3 stringed lute) (vert) 25 20
921 35f. Tiahoun en bwaba (zither) 40 25
922 90f. Jembe en dioula (conical drum) 90 45
923 1000f. Bendre en more (calabash drum) (vert) . . 9·75 4·50

289 Dwellings

1987. International Year of Shelter for the Homeless.
924 **289** 90f. multicoloured . . . . 1·00 45

290 Small Industrial Units

291 People with Candles

1987. Five Year Plan for Popular Development. Multicoloured.
925 40f. Type **290** 35 10
926 55f. Management of dams . . 60 25
927 60f. Village community building primary school . . 60 25
928 90f. Bus (Transport and communications) . . . . . 1·00 35
929 100f. National education: literacy campaign . . . . 1·00 55
930 120f. Intensive cattle farming 1·30 55

1988. 40th Anniv of WHO.
931 **291** 120f. multicoloured . . . 1·30 45

292 Exhibition Emblem and Games Mascot

293 Houet "Sparrow Hawk" Mask

1988. Olympic Games, Seoul, and "Olymphilex '88" Olympic Stamps Exhibition, Rome (932). Multicoloured.
932 30f. Type **292** 30 10
933 160f. Olympic flame (vert) . . 1·50 60
934 175f. Football . . . . 1·70 70
935 235f. Volleyball (vert) . . . 2·30 1·10
936 450f. Basketball (vert) . . . 4·25 2·00
MS937 115 × 100 mm. 500f. 1500 metres race (36 × 48 mm) . . . 5·75 5·25

1988. Masks. Multicoloured.
938 10f. Type **293** 10 10
939 20f. Ouillo "Young Girls" mask 30 25
940 30f. Houet "Hartebeest" mask 40 25
941 40f. Mouhoun "Blacksmith" mask 45 25
942 120f. Ouri "Nanny" mask . . 1·30 45
943 175f. Ouri "Bat" mask (horiz) . . . . 1·80 75

294 Kieriba Jug

295 Envelopes forming Map

1988. Handicrafts. Multicoloured.
944 5f. Type **294** 10 10
945 15f. Mossi basket (horiz) . . 10 10
946 25f. Gurunsi chair (horiz) . . 25 10
947 30f. Bissa basket (horiz) . . . 25 20
948 45f. Ouagadougou hide box (horiz) 45 20
949 85f. Ouagadougou bronze statuette 75 40
950 120f. Ouagadougou hide travelling bag (horiz) . . . 1·10 55

1988. World Post Day.
951 **295** 120f. blue, black & yellow 1·10 45

296 White-collared Kingfisher

1988. Aquatic Wildlife. Multicoloured.
952 70f. Type **296** 60 25
953 100f. Elephantfish . . . . . 1·00 40
954 120f. Frog . . . . 1·40 45
955 160f. White-faced whistling duck . . . . 1·60 70

297 Mohammed Ali Jinnah (first Pakistan Governor-General)

298 Shepherds adoring Child

1988. Death Anniversaries. Multicoloured.
956 80f. Type **297** (40th anniv) (postage) 75 40
957 120f. Mahatma Gandhi (Indian human rights activist, 40th anniv) . . . 1·10 55
958 160f. John Fitzgerald Kennedy (U.S. President, 25th anniv) . . . . . . 1·70 70
959 235f. Martin Luther King (human rights activist, 20th anniv) (air) . . . . . . 2·10 1·10

1988. Christmas. Stained Glass Windows. Mult.
960 120f. Type **298** . . . . . . 1·20 40
961 160f. Wise men presenting gifts to Child . . . . . 1·40 70
962 450f. Virgin and Child . . . 4·00 1·80
963 1000f. Flight into Egypt . . . 8·50 4·50

299 Satellite and Globe

300 WHO and Aids Emblems

1989. 20th Anniv of FESPACO Film Festival. Multicoloured.
964 75f. Type **299** (postage) . . . 1·70 40
965 500f. Ababacar Samb Makharam (air) . . . . . 6·25 2·75
966 500f. Jean Michel Tchissoukou . . . . 6·25 2·75
967 500f. Paulin Soumanou Vieyra . . . . 6·25 2·75
MS968 114 × 85 mm. As Nos. 965/7 but with anniversary inscriptions and values in gold . . . . . . 21·00 19·00

1989. Campaign against AIDS.
969 **300** 120f. multicoloured . . . 1·10 55

301 "Oath of the Tennis Court" (Jacques Louis David) (½-size illustration)

1989. Air. "Philexfrance 89" International Stamp Exhibition, Paris, and Bicentenary of French Revolution. Multicoloured.
970 150f. Type **301** . . . . 1·40 80
971 200f. "Storming of the Bastille" (Thevenin) . . . 2·00 1·20
972 600f. "Rouget de Lisle singing La Marseillaise" (Pils) . . . . 6·25 3·50

302 Map and Tractor

1989. 30th Anniv of Council of Unity.
973 **302** 75f. multicoloured 75 40

303 "Striga generioides"

304 Sahel Dog

1989. Parasitic Plants. Multicoloured.
974 20f. Type **303** 25 10
975 50f. "Striga hermonthica" . . 45 25
976 235f. "Striga aspera" . . . . 2·10 1·10
977 450f. "Alectra vogelii" . . . 4·00 1·80

1989. Dogs. Multicoloured.
978 35f. Type **304** 45 25
979 50f. Young dog 55 25
980 60f. Hunting dog 80 35
981 350f. Guard dog . . . . . . 3·50 1·80

305 Statue

307 Pilgrims at Shrine of Our Lady of Yagma

1989. Solidarity with Palestinian People.
982 **305** 120f. multicoloured . . . 1·20 45

1989. Nos. 647/9 of Upper Volta optd **BURKINA FASO.**
983 **229** 90f. multicoloured 80 30
984 120f. multicoloured . . . 1·00 40
985 170f. multicoloured . . . 1·50 60

1990. Visit of Pope John Paul II. Multicoloured.
986 120f. Type **307** . . . . 1·20 55
987 160f. Pope and crowd . . . . 1·70 90

308 Mail Steamer, Globe and Penny Black

309 Goalkeeper catching Ball

1990. 150th Anniv of Penny Black and "Stamp World London 90" International Stamp exhibition. Multicoloured.
988 120f. Type **308** . . . . 1·20 55
MS989 70 × 80 mm. 500f. Penny Black and early mail steamers (vert) . . . . 4·25 4·00

1990. World Cup Football Championship, Italy. Multicoloured.
990 30f. Type **309** 35 25
991 150f. Footballers . . . . . . 1·60 70
MS992 72 × 65 mm. 1000f. Footballers and "1990" . . . . 8·50 8·25

310 "Cantharellus cibarius"

311 Open Book

1990. Fungi. Multicoloured.
993 10f. Type **310** 20 20
994 15f. "Psalliota bispora" . . . 25 20
995 60f. "Amanita caesarea" . . 85 60
996 190f. "Boletus badius" . . . 2·75 1·50
MS997 77 × 108 mm. 75f. × 4 As Nos. 993/6 . . . . 4·75 4·00

1990. International Literacy Year.
998 **311** 40f. multicoloured 45 20
999 130f. multicoloured . . . 1·20 55

312 Maps, Emblem and Native Artefacts

313 De Gaulle

1990. 2nd International Salon of Arts and Crafts, Ouagadougou. Multicoloured.
1000 35f. Type **312** 25 20
1001 45f. Pottery (horiz) 40 20
1002 270f. Cane chair . . . . . 2·20 1·10

1990. Birth Centenary of Charles de Gaulle (French statesman).
1003 **313** 200f. multicoloured . . . 2·00 90

314 Quartz

315 Hand Holding Cigarette, Syringe and Tablets

1991. Rocks. Multicoloured.
1004 20f. Type **314** 25 10
1005 50f. Granite 70 40
1006 280f. Amphibolite . . . . . 2·75 1·70

1991. Anti-drugs Campaign.
1007 **315** 130f. multicoloured . . . 1·10 65

316 Film and Landscape

318 Traditional Hairstyle

317 Morse and Key

1991. 12th "Fepaco 91" Pan-African Cinema and Television Festival. Multicoloured.
1008 150f. Type **316** . . . . . . 1·70 90
MS1009 77 × 108 mm. 1000f. "Stallion of Yennenga" (Festival Grand Prix statuette) . . . . . 12·00 12·00

1991. Birth Bicentenary of Samuel Morse (inventor of signalling system).
1010 **317** 200f. multicoloured . . . 1·80 1·10

1991.
1011 **318** 5f. multicoloured 10 10
1012 10f. multicoloured 10 10
1013 25f. multicoloured 10 10
1014 50f. multicoloured 20 10
1018 130f. multicoloured . . . 1·10 25
1019 150f. multicoloured . . . 1·40 60
1020 200f. multicoloured . . . 1·70 85
1021 330f. multicoloured . . . 2·20 75

319 "Grewia tenax"

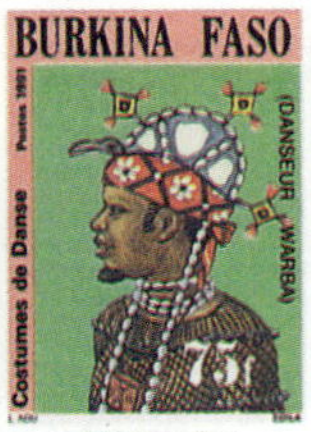

320 Warba

1991. Flowers. Multicoloured.

1025	5f. Type **319**	10	10
1026	15f. "Hymenocardia acide"	10	10
1027	60f. "Cassia sieberiana" (vert)	70	30
1028	100f. "Adenium obesum"	90	55
1029	300f. "Mitragyna inermis"	2·75	1·60

1991. Dance Costumes. Multicoloured.

1030	75f. Type **320**	85	40
1031	130f. Wiskamba	1·20	70
1032	280f. Pa-Zenin	3·00	1·60

321 Pillar Box and Globe

322 Cake Tin

1991. World Post Day.

1033	**321** 130f. multicoloured	1·20	55

1992. Cooking Utensils.

1034	45f. Type **322**	70	65
1035	130f. Cooking pot (vert)	1·40	70
1036	310f. Pestle and mortar (vert)	2·75	1·40
1037	500f. Ladle and bowl	4·75	2·10

323 Yousouf Fofana

325 Child and Cardiograph

324 Disabled Man at Potter's Wheel

1992. African Nations Cup Football Championship, Senegal. Multicoloured.

1038	50f. Type **323**	50	30
1039	100f. Francois-Jules Bocande	1·00	70
MS1040	98 × 93 mm. 500f. Stadium and trophy	4·75	4·50

1992. U.N. Decade of the Handicapped.

1041	**324** 100f. multicoloured	90	55

1992. World Health Day. "Health in Rhythm with the Heart".

1042	**325** 330f. multicoloured	3·50	1·80

326 Columbus and "Santa Maria"

1992. "Genova '92" International Thematic Stamp Exhibition and 500th Anniv of Discovery of America by Columbus. Multicoloured.

1043	50f. Type **326**	70	30
1044	150f. Amerindians watching Columbus's fleet off San Salvador	2·10	90
MS1045	129 × 91 mm. 350f. Route map of first voyage (51 × 30 mm)	4·75	3·50

327 "Dysdercus voelkeri" (fire bug) on Cotton Boll

328 Crib

1992. Insects. Multicoloured.

1046	20f. Type **327**	25	10
1047	40f. "Rhizopertha dominica" (beetle) on leaf	50	30
1048	85f. "Orthetrum microstigma" (dragonfly) on stem	1·20	50
1049	500f. Honey bee on flower	5·25	2·50

1992. Christmas. Multicoloured.

1050	10f. Type **328**	10	10
1051	130f. Children decorating crib	1·30	65
1052	1000f. Boy with Christmas card	9·50	5·25

329 Film Makers' Monument

330 Yellow-billed Stork

1993. 13th "Fespaco" Pan-African Film Festival, Ouagadougou. Multicoloured.

1053	250f. Type **329**	2·50	1·50
1054	750f. Douta Seck (comedian) (horiz)	7·50	4·50

1993. Birds. Multicoloured.

1055	100f. Type **330**	95	60
1056	200f. Marabou stork	2·00	1·20
1057	500f. Saddle-bill stork	5·00	2·75
MS1058	120 × 82 mm. Nos. 1046/8 (sold at 1200f.)	14·50	11·00

331 Statue of Liberty, Globe and Ball

1993. World Cup Football Championship, U.S.A. (1994). Multicoloured.

1059	500f. Type **331**	5·00	2·50
1060	1000f. Players, map of world and U.S. flag	9·75	5·50

332 Peterbilt Canadian Hauler and Diesel Locomotive Type BB 852, France

333 "Saba senegalensis"

1993. Centenary of Invention of Diesel Engine.

1061	**332** 1000f. multicoloured	9·50	5·25

1993. Wild Fruits. Multicoloured.

1062	150f. Type **333**	1·60	80
1063	300f. Karite (horiz)	3·00	1·60
1064	600f. Baobab	6·50	3·25

334 Flowers, "Stamps" and Sights of Paris

1993. 1st European Stamp Salon, Flower Gardens, Paris (1994). Multicoloured.

1065	400f. Type **334**	4·50	2·30
1066	650f. "Stamps", sights of Paris, daffodils and irises	5·75	3·75

335 Peulh Copper Hair Ornament

1993. Jewellery. Multicoloured.

1067	200f. Type **335**	1·80	1·10
1068	250f. Mossi agate necklace (vert)	2·20	1·30
1069	500f. Gourounsi copper bracelet	4·50	2·50

336 Gazelle

1993. The Red-fronted Gazelle. Multicoloured.

1070	30f. Type **336**	1·00	35
1071	40f. Two gazelle	1·00	40
1072	60f. Two gazelle (different)	2·00	75
1073	100f. Gazelle	4·00	1·30
MS1074	110 × 89 mm. Nos. 1061/4 (sold at 400f.)	6·25	6·00

337 Woodland Kingfisher

1994. Kingfishers.

1075	600f. Type **337**	4·75	2·75
1076	1200f. Striped kingfisher	9·50	5·50
MS1077	84 × 72 mm. 2000f. African pygmy kingfisher	15·00	13·50

338 Players

1994. World Cup Football Championship, United States. Multicoloured.

1078	1000f. Type **338**	6·00	2·75
1079	1800f. Goalkeeper saving ball	9·00	4·50
MS1080	84 × 72 mm. No. 1079 (sold at 2000f.)	9·75	9·25

339 Dog with Puppy

1994. 1st European Stamp Salon, Flower Gardens, Paris, France.

1081	**339** 1500f. multicoloured	6·75	4·00
MS1082	82 × 80 mm. No. 1081 (sold at 2000f.)	9·75	9·25

340 Astronaut planting Flag on Moon

341 Guinea Sorrel

1994. 25th Anniv of First Manned Moon Landing. Multicoloured.

1083	750f. Type **340**	3·75	2·10
1084	750f. Landing module on Moon	3·75	2·10

Nos. 1083/4 were issued together, se-tenant, forming a composite design.

1994. Vegetables. Multicoloured.

1085	40f. Type **341**	35	10
1086	45f. Aubergine	35	10
1087	75f. Aubergine	35	20
1088	100f. Okra	60	30

342 Pig

343 Pierre de Coubertin (founder) and Anniversary Emblem

1994. Domestic Animals. Multicoloured.

1089	150f. Type **342**	80	45
1090	1000f. Goat (vert)	4·75	2·75
1091	1500f. Sheep	7·00	3·00

1994. Centenary of Int Olympic Committee.

1092	**343** 320f. multicoloured	1·60	90

344 Donkey Rider

345 Crocodile

1995. 20th Anniv of World Tourism Organization. Multicoloured.

1093	150f. Type **344**	80	65
1094	350f. Bobo-Dioulasso railway station (horiz)	1·50	90
1095	450f. Great Mosque, Bani (horiz)	2·00	1·20
1096	650f. Roan antelope and map (horiz)	2·75	1·70

1995. Multicoloured, colour of frame given.

1097	**345** 10f. brown	10	10
1098	20f. mauve	10	10
1099	25f. brown	10	10
1100	30f. green	10	10
1101	40f. purple	10	10
1102	50f. grey	10	10
1103	75f. purple	25	10
1104	100f. brown	40	10
1105	150f. green	55	35
1106	175f. blue	75	40
1107	250f. brown	90	60
1108	400f. green	1·40	1·00

346 "Rabi" (dir. Gaston Kabore)

1995. "Fespaco 95" Pan-African Film Festival and Centenary of Motion Pictures. Multicoloured.

1109	150f. Type **346**	80	50
1110	250f. "Tila" (Idrissa Ouedraogo)	95	65

347 Elvis Presley in "Loving You"

1995. Entertainers. Multicoloured.

1111	300f. Type **347**	1·40	80
1112	400f. Marilyn Monroe	1·80	1·10
1113	500f. Elvis Presley in "Jailhouse Rock"	2·30	1·40
1114	650f. Marilyn Monroe in "Asphalt Jungle"	2·75	1·80
1115	750f. Marilyn Monroe in "Niagara"	3·00	2·10
1116	1000f. Elvis Presley in "Blue Hawaii"	4·50	3·00
MS1117	Two sheets. (a) 123 × 95 mm. 1500f. Marilyn Monroe in "The Seven Year Itch" (41 × 48 mm). (b) 137 × 89 mm. 1500f. Marilyn Monroe and Elvis Presley (60th birth anniv of Presley (50 × 41 mm)) Set of 2 sheets	13·00	12·50

348 Common Gonolek

1995. Birds. Multicoloured.

1118	450f. Type **348**	2·00	1·00
1119	600f. Red-cheeked cordon-bleu	3·00	1·50
1120	750f. Golden bishop	3·50	2·10
MS1121	80 × 120 mm. Nos. 1118/20 (sold at 2000f.)	8·75	8·25

349 Hissing Sand Snake

1995. Reptiles. Multicoloured.

1122	450f. Type **349**	2·50	1·50
1123	500f. Sand python	2·50	1·60
1124	1500f. Tortoise	7·50	4·50

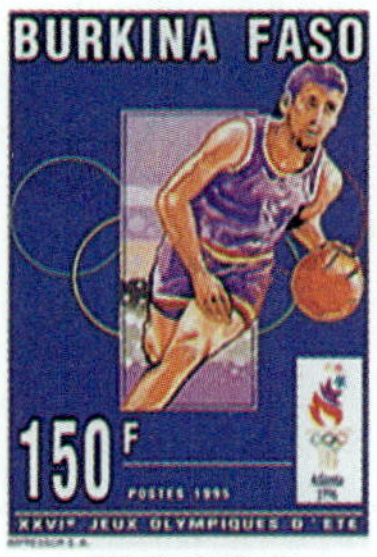

350 Basketball

1995. Olympic Games, Atlanta (1996). Mult.

1125	150f. Type **350**	55	30
1126	250f. Baseball	95	55
1127	650f. Tennis	2·20	1·40
1128	750f. Table tennis	3·25	1·80
MS1129	127 × 89 mm. 1500f. Dressage (35 × 50 mm)	6·50	6·25

351 Juan Manuel Fangio (racing driver)

1995. Sportsmen. Multicoloured.

1130	300f. Type **351**	3·75	95
1131	400f. Andre Agassi (tennis player)	1·40	90
1132	500f. Ayrton Senna (racing driver)	2·00	1·10
1133	1000f. Michael Schumacher (racing driver)	3·75	2·10
MS1134	146 × 112 mm. 1500f. Enzo Ferrari, Formula 1 racing car and Ferrari F40 sports car (56 × 48 mm)	13·00	8·75

352 Children and Christmas Tree

1995. Christmas. Multicoloured.

1135	150f. Type **352**	75	55
1136	450f. Grotto, Yagma	2·20	1·50
1137	500f. Flight into Egypt	2·50	1·60
1138	1000f. Adoration of the Wise Men	4·50	3·00

353 Headquarters Building, New York

1995. 50th Anniv of United Nations. Multicoloured.

1139	500f. Type **353**	2·20	1·70
1140	1000f. Village council under tree with superimposed U.N. emblem (vert)	4·25	3·00

354 Mossi Type

1995. Traditional Houses. Multicoloured.

1141	70f. Type **354**	25	10
1142	100f. Kassena type	45	25
1143	200f. Roro type	90	35
1144	250f. Peulh type	1·10	55

APPENDIX

The following stamps have either been issued in excess of postal needs or have not been available to the public in reasonable quantities at face value. Such stamps may later be given full listing if there is evidence of regular postal use.

1985.

85th Birthday of Queen Elizabeth the Queen Mother. 1500f.

BURMA   Pt. 1, Pt. 21

A territory in the east of India, which was granted independence by the British in 1948. From May 1990 it was known as Myanmar.

1937. 12 pies = 1 anna; 16 annas = 1 rupee.
1953. 100 pyas = 1 kyat.

1937. Stamps of India (King George V) optd **BURMA**.

1	**55**	3p. grey	1·00	10
2	**79**	½a. green	1·00	10
3	**80**	9p. green	1·00	10
4	**81**	1a. brown	2·50	10
5	**59**	2a. red	75	10
6	**61**	2½a. orange	60	10
7	**62**	3a. red	3·25	30
8	**83**	3½a. blue	3·50	10
9	**63**	4a. olive	1·00	10
10	**64**	6a. bistre	1·00	35
11	**65**	8a. mauve	2·00	10
12	**66**	12a. red	7·00	1·75
13	**67**	1r. brown and green	32·00	3·75
14		2r. red and orange	32·00	18·00
15		5r. blue and violet	38·00	23·00
16		10r. green and red	£120	70·00
17		15r. blue and olive	£450	£130
18		25r. orange and blue	£850	£325

2 King George VI and "Chinthes"

3 King George VI and "Nagas"

4 "Karaweik" (royal barge)

8 King George VI and Peacock

1938. King George VI.

18a	**2**	1p. orange	3·00	1·00
19		3p. violet	20	2·00
20		6p. blue	20	10
21		9p. green	1·00	1·50
22	**3**	1a. brown	20	10
23		1½a. green	20	2·50
24		2a. red	1·00	50
25	**4**	2a.6p. red	14·00	2·50
26	–	3a. mauve	14·00	3·00
27	–	3a.6p. blue	2·50	6·50
28	**3**	4a. blue	1·75	10
29	–	8a. green	4·00	55
30	**8**	1r. purple and blue	4·00	55
31		2r. brown and purple	16·00	3·50
32	–	5r. violet and red	55·00	35·00
33	–	10r. brown and green	60·00	65·00

DESIGNS—HORIZ: As Type **4**: 3a. Burma teak; 3a.6p. Burma rice; 8a. River Irrawaddy. VERT: As Type **3**: 5, 10r. King George VI and "Nats".

1940. Cent of First Adhesive Postage Stamp. Surch **COMMEMORATION POSTAGE STAMP 6th MAY 1840 ONE ANNA 1A** and value in native characters.

34	**4**	1a. on 2a.6p. red	4·00	2·00

For Japanese issues see "Japanese Occupation of Burma".

1945. British Military Administration. Stamps of 1938 optd **MILY ADMN**.

35	**2**	1p. orange	10	10
36		3p. violet	10	1·25
37		6p. blue	10	30
38		9p. green	30	1·25
39	**3**	1a. brown	10	10
40		1½a. green	10	15
41		2a. red	10	15
42	**4**	2a.6p. red	2·00	2·25
43	–	3a. mauve	1·50	20
44	–	3a.6p. blue	10	70
45	**3**	4a. blue	10	70
46	–	8a. green	10	1·25
47	**8**	1r. purple and blue	40	50
48		2r. brown and purple	40	1·25
49	–	5r. violet and red	40	1·25
50	–	10r. brown and green	40	1·25

1946. British Civil Administration. As 1938, but colours changed.

51	**2**	3p. brown	10	3·00
52		6p. violet	10	30
53		9p. green	15	4·50
54	**3**	1a. blue	15	20
55		1½a. orange	15	10
56		2a. red	15	50
57	**4**	2a.6p. blue	2·75	5·50
57a	–	3a. blue	6·50	7·00
57b	–	3a.6p. black and blue	1·50	3·25
58	**3**	4a. purple	50	60
59	–	8a. mauve	1·75	4·75
60	**8**	1r. violet and mauve	1·25	2·00
61		2r. brown and orange	6·50	5·00
62	–	5r. green and brown	7·00	22·00
63	–	10r. red and violet	16·00	30·00

14 Burman

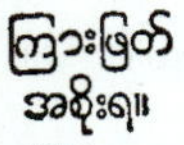

(**18** Trans. "Interim Government")

1946. Victory.

64	**14**	9p. green	20	20
65	–	1½a. violet (Burmese woman)	20	10
66	–	2a. red (Chinthe)	20	10
67	–	3a.6p. (Elephant)	50	20

1947. Stamps of 1946 opt with T **18** or with larger opt on large stamps.

68	**2**	3p. brown	1·25	70
69		6p. violet	10	30
70		9p. green	10	30
71	**3**	1a. blue	10	30
72		1½a. orange	1·75	10
73		2a. red	30	15
74	**4**	2a.6p. blue	1·75	1·00
75	–	3a. blue	2·50	1·75
76	–	3a.6p. black and blue	1·25	2·25
77	**3**	4a. purple	1·75	30
78	–	8a. mauve	1·75	2·75
79	**8**	1r. violet and mauve	5·50	2·25
80		2r. brown and orange	5·50	6·00
81	–	5r. green and brown	5·50	5·50
82	–	10r. red and violet	3·75	5·50

20 Gen. Aung San, Chinthe and Map of Burma

21 Martyrs' Memorial

1948. Independence Day.

83	**20**	½a. green	10	10
84		1a. pink	10	10
85		2a. red	20	15
86		3½a. blue	25	15
87		8a. brown	25	25

1948. 1st Anniv of Murder of Aung San and his Ministers.

88	**21**	3p. blue	10	10
89		6p. green	10	10
90		9p. red	10	10
91		1a. violet	10	10
92		2a. mauve	10	10
93		3½a. green	10	10
94		4a. brown	20	10
95		8a. red	20	15
96		12a. purple	25	15
97		1r. green	45	25
98		2r. blue	90	50
99		5r. brown	2·00	1·30

22 Playing Cane-ball

25 Bell, Mingun Pagoda

27 Transplanting Rice

28 Lion Throne

1949. 1st Anniv of Independence.

100	**22**	3p. blue	1·10	25
120		3p. orange	20	10
101	–	6p. green	20	10
121	–	6p. purple	10	10
102	–	9p. red	20	10
122	–	9p. blue	10	10
103	**25**	1a. red	20	10
123		1a. blue	10	10
104	–	2a. orange	20	10
124	–	2a. green	35	15
105	**27**	2a.6p. mauve	20	15
125		2a.6p. green	35	15
106	–	3a. violet	20	15
126	–	3a. red	20	15
107	–	3a.6p. green	25	15
127	–	3a.6p. orange	20	15
108	–	4a. brown	25	15
128	–	4a. red	20	15
109	–	8a. red	35	15
129	–	8a. blue	35	20
110	**28**	1r. green	65	15
130		1r. violet	50	55
111		2r. blue	1·50	45
131		2r. green	1·10	60
112		5r. brown	3·00	1·40
132		5r. blue	3·25	1·70
113		10r. orange	5·50	2·20
133		10r. blue	6·25	4·25

DESIGNS—As Type **22**: 6p. Dancer; 9p. Girl playing saunggaut (string instrument); 2a. Hintha (legendary bird). As Type **25**: 4a. Elephant hauling log. As Type **27**: 3a. Girl weaving; 3a.6p. Royal Palace; 8a. Ploughing paddy field with oxen.

See also Nos. 137/50.

29 UPU Monument, Berne

30 Independence Monument, Rangoon, and Map

1949. 75th Anniv of UPU.

114	**29**	2a. orange	25	25
115		3½a. green	25	15
116		6a. violet	35	25
117		8a. red	45	45
118		12½a. blue	90	60
119		1r. green	1·10	85

1953. 5th Anniv of Independence.

134	**30**	14p. green (22 × 18 mm)	20	10
135		20p. red (36½ × 26½ mm)	25	15
136		25p. blue (36½ × 26½ mm)	45	15

1954. New Currency. As 1949 issue but values in pyas and kyats.

137	**22**	1p. orange	70	10
138	–	2p. purple (as 6p.)	10	10
139	–	3p. blue (as 9p.)	10	10
140	**25**	5p. blue	10	10
141	**27**	10p. green	10	10
142	–	15p. green (as 2a.)	25	10
143	–	20p. red (as 3a.)	20	10
144	–	25p. orange (as 3a.6p.)	20	15
145	–	30p. red (as 4a.)	25	15
146	–	50p. blue (as 8a.)	25	15
147	**28**	1k. violet	80	25
148		2k. green	1·50	45
149		5k. blue	4·25	80
150		10k. blue	7·75	1·40

31 Sangiti Mahapasana Rock Cave in Grounds of Kaba-Aye Pagoda

1954. 6th Buddhist Council, Rangoon.
151 – 10p. blue 10 10
152 – 15p. purple 15 15
153 **31** 35p. brown 25 25
154 – 50p. green 45 25
155 – 1k. red 95 50
156 – 2k. violet . . . . 1·60 1·10
DESIGNS: 10p. Rock caves and Songha of Cambodia; 15p. Buddhist priests and Kuthodaw Pagoda, Mandalay; 50p. Rock cave and Songha of Thailand; 1k. Rock cave and Songha of Ceylon; 2k. Rock cave and Songha of Laos.

32 Fifth Buddhist Council Monuments

1956. Buddha Jayanti.
157 **32** 20p. green and blue . . . 15 15
158 – 40p. green and blue . . . 35 25
159 – 60p. yellow and green . . . 45 35
160 – 1k.25 blue and yellow . . . 95 80
DESIGNS: 40p. Thatbyinnyu Pagoda, Pagan; 60p. Shwedagan Pagoda, Rangoon; 1k.25, Sangiti Mahapasana Rock Cave and Kaba-Aye Pagoda, Rangoon (venue of 6th Buddhist Council).

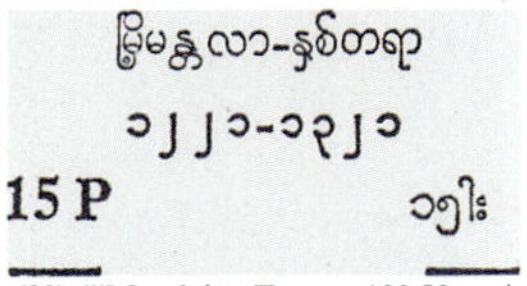
(**33**) ("Mandalay Town—100 Years/ 1221–1321")

1959. Centenary of Mandalay. No. 144 surch with T **33** and Nos. 147/8 with two-line opt only.
161 – 15p. on 25p. orange . . . 25 15
162 **28** 1k. violet 85 80
163 2k. green . . . . 1·70 1·20

1961. No. 134 surch as right-hand characters in third line of T **33**.
164 **30** 15p. on 14p. green 60 25

35 Torch-bearer in Rangoon

1961. 2nd South-East Asia Peninsula Games, Rangoon.
165 **35** 15p. blue and red 15 15
166 – 25p. green and brown . . . 25 15
167 – 50p. mauve and blue . . . 70 25
168 – 1k. yellow and green . . . 1·00 80
DESIGNS—VERT: 25p. Contestants; 50p. Women sprinting in Aung San Stadium, Rangoon. HORIZ: 1k. Contestants.

36 Children at Play

1961. 15th Anniv of UNICEF.
169 **36** 15p. red and pink 35 10

37 Flag and Map

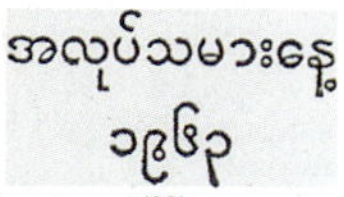
(**39**)

1963. 1st Anniv of Military Coup by General Ne Win.
170 **37** 15p. red 35 15

1963. Freedom from Hunger. Nos. 141 and 146 optd **FREEDOM FROM HUNGER**.
171 **27** 10p. green 45 35
172 – 50p. blue 85 70

1963. Labour Day. No. 143 optd with T **39**.
173 20p. red 35 15

40 White-browed Fantail

41 ITU Emblem and Symbols

1964. Burmese Birds (1st series).
174 **40** 1p. black 25 15
175 2p. red 25 15
176 3p. green 25 15
177 – 5p. blue 35 25
178 – 10p. brown 45 25
179 – 15p. green 45 25
180 – 20p. brown and red . . . 70 35
181 – 25p. brown and yellow . . 85 35
182 – 50p. blue and red . . . 1·30 45
183 – 1k. blue, yellow & grey . . 4·00 1·10
184 – 2k. blue, green and red . . 7·75 3·00
185 – 5k. multicoloured . . . . 16·00 7·50
BIRDS—22 × 26 mm: 5 to 15p. Indian roller. 27 × 37 mm: 25p. Crested serpent eagle. 50p. Sarus crane. 1k. Indian pied hornbill. 5k. Green peafowl. 35½ × 25 mm: 20p. Red-whiskered bulbul. 37 × 27 mm: 2k. Kalij pheasant.
See also Nos. 195/206.

1965. Centenary of ITU.
186 **41** 20p. mauve 15 15
187 50p. green (34 × 24½ mm) . . . 45 45

42 ICY Emblem

43 Harvesting

1965. International Co-operation Year.
188 **42** 5p. blue 15 10
189 10p. brown 15 10
190 15p. olive 25 15

1966. Peasants' Day.
191 **43** 15p. multicoloured 25 15

44 Cogwheel and Hammer

45 Aung San and Agricultural Cultivation

1967. May Day.
192 **44** 15p. yellow, black & blue 25 15

1968. 20th Anniv of Independence.
193 **45** 15p. multicoloured 25 15

46 Burma Pearls

47 Spike of Paddy

1968. Burmese Gems, Jades and Pearls Emporium, Rangoon.
194 **46** 15p. ultram, blue & yell . . 45 15

1968. Burmese Birds (2nd series). Designs and colours as Nos. 174/85 but formats and sizes changed.
195 **40** 1p. black 25 25
196 2p. red 25 25
197 3p. green 35 35
198 – 5p. blue 35 35
199 – 10p. brown 45 45
200 – 15p. yellow 50 50
201 – 20p. brown and red . . . 50 50
202 – 25p. brown and yellow . . 60 50
203 – 50p. blue and red . . . . 1·30 1·00
204 – 1k. blue, yellow & grey . . 11·00 1·00
205 – 2k. blue, green and red . . 8·75 2·50
206 – 5k. multicoloured . . . . 19·00 10·50
NEW SIZES—21 × 17 mm: 1, 2, 3p. 39 × 21 mm: 20p., 2k. 23 × 28 mm: 5, 10, 15p. 21 × 39 mm: 25, 50p., 1, 5k.

1969. Peasants' Day.
218 **47** 15p. yellow, blue & green 25 10

48 ILO Emblem

49 Football

1969. 50th Anniv of ILO.
219 **48** 15p. gold and green . . . 15 15
220 50p. gold and red 45 25

1969. 5th South-East Asian Peninsula Games, Rangoon.
221 **49** 15p. multicoloured 15 15
222 – 25p. multicoloured 25 15
223 – 50p. multicoloured 50 15
224 – 1k. black, green & blue . . 1·30 50
DESIGNS—HORIZ: 25p. Running. VERT: 50p. Weightlifting; 1k. Volleyball.

50 Marchers with Independence, Resistance and Union Flags

1970. 25th Anniv of Burmese Armed Forces.
225 **50** 15p. multicoloured 25 15

51 "Peace and Progress"

1970. 25th Anniv of United Nations.
226 **51** 15p. multicoloured 25 10

52 Boycott Declaration and Marchers

1970. National Day and 50th Anniv of University Boycott. Multicoloured.
227 15p. Type **52** 15 10
228 25p. Students on boycott march 15 10
229 50p. Banner and demonstrators 45 25

53 Burmese Workers

1971. 1st Burmese Socialist Programme Party Congress. Multicoloured.
230 5p. Type **53** 15 10
231 15p. Burmese races and flags 15 10
232 25p. Hands holding scroll . . 25 15
233 50p. Party flag 50 35
MS234 179 × 127 mm. Nos. 230/3. Imperf . . . . 11·50 11·50

54 Child drinking Milk

1971. 25th Anniv of UNICEF. Multicoloured.
235 15p. Type **54** 25 10
236 50p. Marionettes 60 45

55 Aung San and Independence Monument, Panglong

1972. 25th Anniv of Independence. Multicoloured.
237 15p. Type **55** 15 10
238 50p. Aung San and Burmese in national costumes . . . 25 15
239 1k. Flag and map (vert) . . . 60 35

56 Burmese and Stars

1972. 10th Anniv of Revolutionary Council.
240 **56** 15p. multicoloured 15 10

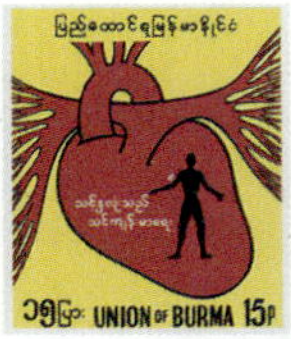
57 Human Heart

59 Casting Vote

58 Ethnic Groups

1972. World Health Day.
241 **57** 15p. red, black & yellow 15 15

1973. National Census.
242 **58** 15p. multicoloured 25 15

1973. National Constitutional Referendum.
243 **59** 5p. red and black 15 10
244 – 10p. multicoloured 15 10
245 – 15p. multicoloured 15 10
DESIGNS—HORIZ: 10p. Voter supporting map. VERT: 15p. Burmese with ballot papers.

60 Open-air Meeting

1974. Opening of 1st Pyithu Hluttaw (People's Assembly). Multicoloured.
246 15p. Burmese flags, 1752–1974 (80 × 26 mm) 15 15
247 50p. Type **60** 45 25
248 1k. Burmese badge 85 60

61 UPU Emblem and Carrier Pigeon

1974. Centenary of Universal Postal Union. Mult.
249 15p. Type **61** 15 10
250 20p. Woman reading letter (vert) 25 15
251 50p. UPU emblem on "stamps" (vert) 50 25
252 1k. Stylized doll (vert) . . . 80 45
253 2k. Postman delivering letter to family . . . . 2·10 85

62 Kachin Couple

63 Bamar Couple

1974. Burmese Costumes. Inscr "SOCIALIST REPUBLIC OF THE UNION OF BURMA".
254 **62** 1p. mauve 10 10
255 3p. brown and mauve . . . 10 10
256 5p. violet and mauve . . . 10 10
257 10p. blue 15 10
258 15p. green and light green 10 10
259 **63** 20p. black, brown & blue 15 10
260 – 50p. violet, brown & ochre 45 25
261 – 1k. violet, mauve & black 1·30 70
262 – 5k. multicoloured . . . . 4·25 2·50
DESIGNS—As Type **62**: 3p. Kayah girl; 5p. Kayin couple and bronze drum; 15p. Chin couple. As Type **63**: 50p. Mon woman; 1k. Rakhine woman; 5k. Musician.

For 15, 50p. and 1k. stamps in these designs, but inscr "UNION OF BURMA", see Nos. 309/11.

64 Woman on Globe and IWY Emblem

1975. International Women's Year.
263 **64** 50p. black and green . . . 35 25
264 – 2k. black and blue . . . . 1·50 1·10
DESIGN—VERT: 2k. Globe on flower and IWY emblem.

65 Burmese and Flag **66** Emblem and Burmese Learning Alphabet

1976. Constitution Day.
265 **65** 20p. black and blue . . . 15 15
266 – 50p. brown and blue . . . 35 25
267 – 1k. multicoloured . . . . 1·00 60
DESIGNS—As Type **65**: 50p. Burmese with banners and flag. 57 × 21 mm: 1k. Map of Burma, Burmese and flag.

1976. International Literacy Year.
268 **66** 10p. brown and red . . . 10 10
269 – 15p. turquoise, grn & blk 10 10
270 – 50p. blue, orange & black 45 25
271 – 1k. multicoloured 85 60
DESIGNS—HORIZ: 15p. Abacus and open books. 50p. Emblem. VERT: 1k. Emblem, open book and globe.

67 Early Train and Ox-cart

1977. Centenary of Railway.
272 – 15p. green, black & mauve 4·00 1·00
273 **67** 20p. multicoloured . . . . 1·10 35
274 – 25p. multicoloured . . . . 1·70 45
275 – 50p. multicoloured . . . . 2·40 80
276 – 1k. multicoloured . . . . 5·25 1·60
DESIGNS—26 × 17 mm: 15p. Early steam locomotive. As Type **67**—HORIZ: 25p. Diesel locomotive DD1517, steam train and railway station; 50p. Ava railway bridge over River Irrawaddy. VERT: Diesel train emerging from tunnel.

68 Karaweik Hall

1978.
277 **68** 50p. brown 50 35
278 – 1k. multicoloured 85 60
DESIGN—79½ × 25 mm: 1k. Side view of Karaweik Hall.

69 Jade Naga and Gem

1979. 16th Gem Emporium.
279 **69** 15p. green and turquoise 15 10
280 – 20p. blue, yellow & mauve 35 15
281 – 50p. blue, brown & green 70 45
282 – 1k. multicoloured . . . . 1·40 80
DESIGNS—As T **69**: 20p. Hintha (legendary bird) holding pearl in beak; 50p. Hand holding pearl and amethyst pendant. 55 × 20 mm: 1k. Gold jewel-studded dragon.

70 "Intelsat IV" Satellite over Burma

1979. Introduction of Satellite Communications System.
283 **70** 25p. multicoloured 25 15

71 IYC Emblem on Map of Burma **72** Weather Balloon

1979. International Year of the Child.
284 **71** 25p. orange and blue . . . 50 25
285 50p. red and violet . . . . 1·00 45

1980. World Meteorological Day.
286 **72** 25p. blue, yellow & black 35 15
287 – 50p. green, black and red 50 45
DESIGN: 50p. Meteorological satellite and WMO emblem.

73 Weightlifting

1980. Olympic Games, Moscow.
288 **73** 20p. green, orange & blk 15 10
289 – 50p. black, orange and red 50 25
290 – 1k. black, orange and blue 1·00 60
DESIGNS: 50p. Boxing; 1k. Football.

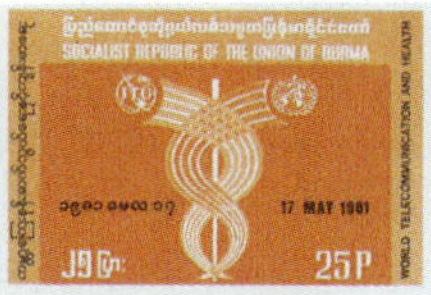

74 ITU and WHO Emblems with Ribbons forming Caduceus

1981. World Telecommunications Day.
291 **74** 25p. orange and black . . 25 15

75 Livestock and Vegetables

1981. World Food Day. Multicoloured.
292 25p. Type **75** 45 15
293 50p. Farm produce and farmer holding wheat . . . 60 20
294 1k. Globe and stylized bird 85 50

76 Athletes and Person in Wheelchair

1981. International Year of Disabled Persons.
295 **76** 25p. multicoloured 25 25

77 Telephone, Satellite and Antenna

1983. World Communications Year.
296 **77** 15p. blue and black . . . 15 10
297 25p. mauve and black . . 25 15
298 50p. green, black and red 50 35
299 1k. brown, black & green 1·40 80

78 Fish and Globe

1983. World Food Day.
300 **78** 15p. yellow, blue & black 15 10
301 25p. orange, green & black 25 15
302 50p. green, yellow & black 70 70
303 1k. blue, yellow and black 2·10 1·60

79 Globe and Log

1984. World Food Day.
304 **79** 15p. blue, yellow & black 10 10
305 25p. violet, yellow & black 15 10
306 50p. green, pink and black 50 45
307 1k. mauve, yellow & black 1·30 1·00

80 Potted Plant

1985. International Youth Year.
308 **80** 15p. multicoloured 25 15

1989. As Nos. 258/9 and 260/1 but inscr "UNION OF BURMA".
309 **62** 15p. dp green & green 25 15
310 – 50p. violet and brown . . 60 35
311 – 1k. violet, mauve & black 95 70

Examples of No. 309a, which have been prepared several years earlier but not issued, were inadvertently supplied to Shan State post office in July 1995. Subsequently a limited quantity were sold to philatelists in Yangon.

OFFICIAL STAMPS

1937. Stamps of India (King George V) optd **BURMA SERVICE.**
O 1 **55** 3p. grey . . . . 3·50 10
O 2 **79** ½a. green . . . . 14·00 10
O 3 **80** 9p. green . . . . 5·00 1·00
O 4 **81** 1a. brown . . . . 7·00 10
O 5 **59** 2a. red . . . . 15·00 45
O 6 **61** 2½a. orange . . . . . . 7·00 2·50
O 7 **63** 4a. olive . . . . 7·00 10
O 8 **64** 6a. bistre . . . . 7·00 12·00
O 9 **65** 8a. mauve . . . . 7·00 2·50
O10 **66** 12a. red . . . . 7·00 10·00
O11 **67** 1r. brown and green . . . 20·00 7·00
O12 2r. red and orange . . . 40·00 55·00
O13 5r. blue and violet . . . £130 60·00
O14 10r. green and red £375 £180

1939. Stamps of 1938 optd **SERVICE.**
O15 **2** 3p. violet 15 20
O16 6p. blue 15 20
O17 9p. green . . . . 4·00 5·00
O18 **3** 1a. brown 15 15
O19 1½a. green . . . . 3·50 2·25
O20 2a. red . . . . 1·25 20
O21 **4** 2a.6p. red . . . . 21·00 18·00
O22 **3** 4a. blue . . . . 4·50 1·25
O23 – 8a. green (No. 29) . . . 15·00 4·00
O24 **8** 1r. purple and blue . . . 16·00 5·50
O25 2r. brown and purple . . . 30·00 16·00
O26 – 5r. violet and red (No. 32) 25·00 32·00
O27 – 10r. brown and green (No. 33) . . . . £130 38·00

1946. Stamps of 1946 optd **SERVICE.**
O28 **2** 3p. brown . . . . 3·00 4·50
O29 6p. violet . . . . 2·25 2·25
O30 9p. green . . . . 65 4·50
O31 **3** 1a. blue . . . . 20 2·00
O32 1½a. orange 20 20
O33 2a. red . . . . 20 2·00
O34 **4** 2a.6p. blue . . . . 2·00 9·00
O35 **3** 4a. purple 20 70
O36 – 8a. mauve (No. 59) . . . 3·75 5·00
O37 **8** 1r. violet and mauve . . . 80 7·50
O38 2r. brown and orange . . . 8·00 45·00
O39 – 5r. green and brown (No. 62) . . . . 15·00 55·00
O40 – 10r. red and violet (No. 63) 17·00 65·00

1947. Interim Government. Nos. O28 etc., optd with T **18** or with large overprint on larger stamps.
O41 **2** 3p. brown . . . . 1·00 40
O42 6p. violet . . . . 3·75 10
O43 9p. green . . . . 5·00 90
O44 **3** 1a. blue . . . . 5·00 80
O45 1½a. orange . . . . 8·50 30
O46 2a. red . . . . 5·00 15
O47 **4** 2a.6p. blue . . . . 29·00 13·00
O48 **3** 4a. purple . . . . 18·00 40
O49 – 8a. mauve . . . . 18·00 4·00
O50 **8** 1r. violet and mauve . . . 15·00 2·25
O51 2r. brown and orange . . . 15·00 20·00
O52 – 5r. green and brown . . . 15·00 20·00
O53 – 10r. red and violet . . . 15·00 30·00

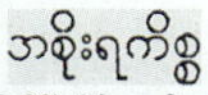

(O **29**) (size of opt varies)

1949. 1st Anniv of Independence. Nos. 100/4 and 107/113 optd as Type O **29**.
O114 **22** 3p. blue 55 15
O115 – 6p. green 10 10
O116 – 9p. red 10 10
O117 **25** 1a. red 10 10
O118 – 2a. orange 20 15
O119 – 3a.6p. green 20 15
O120 – 4a. brown 20 15
O121 – 8a. red 20 15
O122 **28** 1r. green 55 25
O123 2r. blue 90 45
O124 5r. brown . . . . 2·40 1·70
O125 10r. orange . . . . 6·00 4·25

1954. Nos. 137/40 and 142/50 optd as Type O **29**.
O151 **22** 1p. orange 55 15
O152 – 2p. purple 20 15
O153 – 3p. blue 20 15
O154 **25** 5p. blue 20 15
O155 – 15p. green 20 15
O156 – 20p. red 20 15
O157 – 25p. orange 20 15
O158 – 30p. red 20 15
O159 – 50p. blue 20 15
O160 **28** 1k. violet 65 15
O161 2k. green . . . . 1·50 35
O162 5k. blue . . . . 3·00 95
O163 10k. blue . . . . 6·50 3·00

1964. No. 139 optd **Service.**
O174 – 3p. blue . . . . 10·50 7·00

1965. Nos. 174/7 and 179/85 optd as Type O **29**.
O196 **40** 1p. black 15 15
O197 2p. red 25 25
O198 3p. green 25 25
O199 – 5p. blue 35 25
O200 – 15p. green 35 25
O201 – 20p. brown and red . . . 70 60
O202 – 25p. brown and yellow 80 70
O203 – 50p. blue and red . . . . 1·40 85
O204 – 1k. blue, yellow & grey 4·00 1·10
O205 – 2k. blue, green & red . . 5·25 1·90
O206 – 5k. multicoloured . . . . 15·00 13·00

1968. Nos. 195/8 and 200/6 optd as Type O **29**.
O207 1p. black 15 15
O208 2p. red 15 15
O209 3p. green 15 15
O210 5p. blue 25 15
O211 15p. green 25 15
O212 20p. brown and red 25 15
O213 25p. brown and yellow . . 45 15
O214 50p. blue and red 85 45
O215 1k. blue, yellow and grey 1·30 1·10
O216 2k. blue, green and red . . 2·75 2·30
O217 5k. multicoloured . . . . 6·50 5·75

For later issues see **MYANMAR**.

JAPANESE OCCUPATION OF BURMA

1942. 12 pies = 1 anna; 16 annas = 1 rupee.
1942. 100 cents = 1 rupee.

(1) (3)

Note.—There are various types of the Peacock overprint. Our prices, as usual in this Catalogue, are for the cheapest type.

1942. Postage stamps of Burma of 1937 (India types) optd as T **1**.
J22 **55** 3p. grey . . . . 3·75 22·00
J23 **80** 9p. green . . . . 26·00 65·00
J24 **59** 2a. red £110 £190
J 2 **83** 3½a. blue . . . . 70·00

1942. Official stamp of Burma of 1937 (India type) optd as T **1**.
J3 **64** 6a. bistre . . . . 80·00

1942. Postage stamps of Burma, 1938, optd as T **1** or with T **3** (rupee values).
J25 **1** 1p. orange £225 £325
J12 3p. violet . . . . 18·00 75·00
J27 6p. blue . . . . 25·00 55·00

J14		9p. green	22·00	70·00
J29	3	1a. brown	9·00	42·00
J30		1½a. green	22·00	70·00
J16		2a. red	25·00	85·00
J17		4a. blue	50·00	£110
J18	8	1r. purple and blue	£325	£500
J19		2r. brown and purple	£180	£375

1942. Official stamps of Burma of 1939 optd with T **1**.

J 7	1	3p. violet	30·00	90·00
J 8		6p. blue	21·00	65·00
J 9	3	1a. brown	22·00	55·00
J35		1½a. green	£180	£325
J10		2a. red	28·00	£100
J11		4a. blue	28·00	80·00

(6a) ("Yon Thon" = "Office Use")

1942. Official stamp of Burma of 1939 optd with T **6a**.

J44		8a. green (No. O23)	95·00	

7

8 Farmer

1942. Yano Seal.

J45	7	(1a.) red	42·00	70·00

1942.

J46	8	1a. red	20·00	20·00

1942. Stamps of Japan surch in annas or rupees.

J47	–	¼a. on 1s. brown (No. 314)	38·00	45·00
J48	83	½a. on 2s. red	45·00	48·00
J49	–	¾ a on 3s. green (No. 316)	70·00	75·00
J50	–	1a. on 5s. purple (No. 396)	70·00	60·00
J51	–	3a. on 7s. green (No. 320)	£110	£130
J52	–	4a. on 4s. green (No. 317)	55·00	60·00
J53	–	8a. on 8s. violet (No. 321)	£150	£150
J54	–	1r. on 10s. red (No. 322)	23·00	26·00
J55	–	2r. on 20s. blue (No. 325)	50·00	50·00
J56	–	5r. on 30s. blue (No. 327)	13·00	27·00

1942. No. 386 of Japan commemorating the fall of Singapore, surch in figures.

J56g	–	4a. on 4s.+2s. green and red	£160	£170

1942. Handstamped **5 C.**

J57	5	5c. on 1a. red (No. J46)	18·00	22·00

1942. Nos. J47/53 with anna surcharges obliterated, and handstamped with new values in figures.

J58	–	1c. on ¼a. on 1s. brown	50·00	50·00
J59	84	2c. on ½a. on 2s. red	50·00	50·00
J60	–	3c. on ¾a. on 3s. green	55·00	55·00
J61	–	5c. on 1a. on 5s. red	75·00	65·00
J62	–	10c. on 3a. on 7s. green	£140	£130
J63	–	15c. on 4a. on 4s. green	48·00	50·00
J64	–	20c. on 8a. on 8s. violet	£700	£600

1942. Stamps of Japan surch in cents.

J65	–	1c. on 1s. brown (No. 314)	28·00	20·00
J66	83	2c. on 2s. red	55·00	35·00
J67	–	3c. on 3s. green (No. 316)	80·00	55·00
J68	–	5c. on 5s. purple (No. 396)	85·00	50·00
J69	–	10c. on 7s. green (No. 320)	£100	70·00
J70	–	15c. on 4s. green (No. 317)	22·00	23·00
J71	–	20c. on 8s. violet (No. 321)	£180	85·00

14 Burma State Crest

15 Farmer

1943. Perf or imperf.

J72	14	5c. red	22·00	26·00

1943.

J73a	15	1c. orange	3·00	6·50
J74		2c. green	60	1·00
J75		3c. blue	3·25	1·00
J77		5c. red	3·25	5·00
J78		10c. brown	6·50	6·00
J79		15c. mauve	30	3·00
J80		20c. lilac	30	1·00
J81		30c. green	30	1·50

16 Soldier carving word "Independence"

17 Rejoicing Peasant

18 Boy with National Flag

1943. Independence Day. Perf or roul.

J85	16	1c. orange	1·25	1·75
J86	17	3c. blue	2·50	2·75
J87	18	5c. red	2·50	3·00

19 Burmese Woman

20 Elephant carrying Log

21 Watch Tower Mandalay

1943.

J88	19	1c. orange	20·00	15·00
J89		2c. green	50	2·00
J90		3c. violet	50	2·25
J91	20	5c. red	65	60
J92		10c. blue	1·75	1·10
J93		15c. orange	1·00	3·00
J94		20c. green	1·00	1·75
J95		30c. brown	1·00	2·00
J96	21	1r. orange	30	2·00
J97		2r. violet	30	2·25

22 Bullock Cart

23 Shan Woman

1943. Shan States issue.

J 98	22	1c. brown	30·00	38·00
J 99		2c. green	35·00	38·00
J100		3c. violet	4·75	10·00
J101		5c. blue	2·25	6·50
J102	23	10c. blue	14·00	18·00
J103		20c. red	32·00	18·00
J104		30c. brown	21·00	50·00

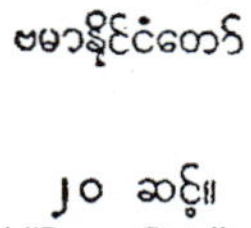
(24 "Burma State" and value)

1944. Optd with T **24**.

J105	22	1c. brown	3·50	6·00
J106		2c. green	50	3·25
J107		3c. violet	2·25	7·00
J108		5c. blue	1·25	2·25
J109	23	10c. blue	3·25	2·00
J110		20c. red	50	1·50
J111		30c. brown	50	1·75

BURUNDI Pt. 12

Once part of the Belgian territory, Ruanda-Urundi. Independent on 1 July 1962, when a monarchy was established. After a revolution in 1967 Burundi became a republic.

100 centimes = 1 franc.

1962. Stamps of Ruanda-Urundi optd **Royaume du Burundi** and bar or surch also. (a) Flowers. (Nos. 178 etc.)

1		25c. multicoloured	25	20
2		40c. multicoloured	25	20
3		60c. multicoloured	35	35
4		1f.25 multicoloured	16·00	16·00
5		1f.50 multicoloured	60	60
6		5f. multicoloured	1·10	90
7		7f. multicoloured	1·75	1·40
8		10f. multicoloured	2·50	2·25

(b) Animals (Nos. 203/14).

9		10c. black, red and brown	10	10
10		20c. black and green	10	10
11		40c. black, olive and mauve	10	10
12		50c. brown, yellow & green	10	10
13		1f. black, blue and brown	10	10
14		1f.50 black and orange	10	10
15		2f. black, brown and turq	10	10
16		3f. black, red and brown	10	10
17		3f.50 on 3f. black, red & brn	10	10
18a		4f. on 10f. multicoloured	20	20
19		5f. multicoloured	20	20
20		6f.50 brown, yellow and red	20	20
21		8f. black, mauve and blue	35	25
23		10f. multicoloured	50	30

(c) Animals (Nos. 229/30).

24	25	20f. multicoloured	1·60	60
25	–	50f. multicoloured	1·90	1·10

10 King Mwambutsa IV and Royal Drummers

1962. Independence. Inscr "1.7.1962".

26	10	50c. sepia and lake	10	10
27	A	1f. green, red & deep green	10	10
28	B	2f. sepia and olive	10	10
29	10	3f. sepia and red	10	10
30	A	4f. green, red and blue	15	10
31	B	8f. sepia and violet	30	15
32	10	10f. sepia and green	40	15
33	A	20f. green, red and sepia	45	20
34	B	50f. sepia and mauve	1·25	45

DESIGNS—VERT: A, Burundi flag and arms. HORIZ: B, King and outline map of Burundi.

1962. Dag Hammarskjold Commem. No. 222 of Ruanda-Urundi surch **HOMMAGE A DAG HAMMARSKJOLD ROYAUME DU BURUNDI** and new value. U.N. emblem and wavy pattern at foot. Inscr in French or Flemish.

35		3f.50 on 3f. salmon and blue	35	35
36		6f.50 on 3f. salmon and blue	65	45
37		10f. on 3f. salmon and blue	1·25	1·10

1962. Malaria Eradication. As Nos. 31 and 34 but colours changed and with campaign emblem superimposed on map.

38	B	8f. sepia, turquoise & bistre	55	35
39		50f. sepia, turquoise & olive	1·40	35

12 Prince Louis Rwagasore

13 "Sowing"

1963. Prince Rwagasore Memorial and Stadium Fund.

40	12	50c.+25c. violet	10	10
41	–	1f.+50c. blue and orange	10	10
42	–	1f.50+75c. vio & bistre	10	10
43	12	3f.50+1f.50 mauve	20	10
44	–	5f.+2f. blue and pink	20	10
45	–	6f.50+3f. violet & olive	25	10

DESIGNS—HORIZ: 1f., 5f. Prince and stadium; 1f.50, 6f.50 Prince and memorial.

1963. Freedom from Hunger.

46	13	4f. purple and olive	15	15
47		8f. purple and olive	20	15
48		15f. purple and green	35	15

1963. "Peaceful Uses of Outer Space" Nos. 28 and 34 optd **UTILISATIONS PACIFIQUES DE L'ESPACE** around globe encircled by rocket.

49	B	2f. sepia and olive	2·25	2·25
50		50f. sepia and mauve	3·50	3·50

1963. 1st Anniv of Independence. Nos. 30/3 but with colours changed and optd **Premier Anniversaire**.

51	A	4f. green, red and olive	20	10
52	B	8f. sepia and orange	30	10
53	10	10f. sepia and mauve	40	20
54	A	20f. green, red and grey	90	30

1963. Nos. 27 and 33 surch.

55	A	6f.50 on 1f. green, red and deep green	55	10
56		15f. on 20f. grn, red & sepia	85	35

17 Globe and Red Cross Flag

1963. Centenary of Red Cross.

57	17	4f. green, red and grey	20	10
58		8f. brown, red and grey	40	20
59		10f. blue, red and grey	50	20
60		20f. violet, red and grey	1·10	40
MS60a		90×140 mm. Nos. 57/60 in new colours, each with +2f. surcharge in black. Imperf	3·50	3·50

IMPERF STAMPS. Many Burundi stamps from No. 61 onwards exist imperf from limited printings and/or miniature sheets.

18 "1962" and UNESCO Emblem

1963. 1st Anniv of Admission to UNO. Emblems and values in black.

61	18	4f. olive and yellow	15	10
62	–	8f. blue and lilac	25	10
63	–	10f. violet and blue	40	10
64	–	20f. green and yellow	65	20
65	–	50f. brown and ochre	1·75	35
MS65a		111×74 mm. Nos. 64/5 but with emblems changed. Imperf	4·25	4·25

EMBLEMS: 8f. ITU; 10f. WMO; 20f. UPU, 50f. FAO; **MS**65a 20f. FAO; 50f. WMO.

19 UNESCO Emblem and Scales of Justice

1963. 15th Anniv of Declaration of Human Rights.

66	19	50c. blk, blue and pink	10	10
67	–	1f.50 black, blue & orange	10	10
68	–	3f.50 black, green & brown	15	10
69	–	6f.50 black, green and lilac	25	10
70	–	10f. black, bistre and blue	40	15
71	–	20f. multicoloured	70	25

DESIGNS: 3f.50, 6f.50, Scroll; 10f., 20f. Lincoln.

20 Ice-hockey

22 Burundi Dancer

21 Hippopotamus

1964. Winter Olympic Games, Innsbruck.

72	20	50c. black, gold and olive	15	10
73	–	3f.50 black, gold & brown	20	10
74	–	6f.50 black, gold and grey	45	20
75	–	10f. black, gold and grey	90	35
76	–	20f. black, gold and bistre	2·10	65
MS76a		122×85 mm. 10f.+5f. and 20f.+5f. (as Nos. 75/6 but in new colours). Perf or imperf	4·25	1·30

DESIGNS: 3f.50, Figure-skating; 6f.50, Olympic flame; 10f. Speed-skating; 20f. Skiing (slalom).

1964. Burundi Animals. Multicoloured. (i) Postage. (a) Size as T **21**.

77		50c. Impala	10	10
78		1f. Type **21**	10	10
79		1f.50 Giraffe	10	10
80		2f. African buffalo	20	10
81		3f. Common zebra	20	10
82		3f.50 Waterbuck	20	10

(b) Size 16×42½ mm or 42½×26 mm.

83		4f. Impala	25	10
84		5f. Hippopotamus	30	10
85		6f.50 Common zebra	30	10

86 8f. African buffalo 55 20
87 10f. Giraffe 60 20
88 15f. Waterbuck 85 30

(c) Size 53½ × 33½ mm.

89 20f. Cheetah 1·50 40
90 50f. African elephant 4·00 65
91 100f. Lion 6·50 1·10

(ii) Air. Inscr "POSTE AERIENNE" and optd with gold border. (a) Size 26 × 42½ mm or 42½ × 26 mm.

92 6f. Common zebra 35 10
93 8f. African buffalo 60 10
94 10f. Impala 70 10
95 14f. Hippopotamus 85 15
96 15f. Waterbuck 1·40 35

(b) Size 53½ × 33½ mm.

97 20f. Cheetah 1·75 40
98 50f. African elephant 4·00 90

The impala, giraffe and waterbuck stamps are all vert. designs, and the remainder are horiz.

1964. World's Fair, New York (1st series). Gold backgrounds.

99 **22** 50c. multicoloured 10 10
100 – 1f. multicoloured 10 10
101 – 4f. multicoloured 15 10
102 – 6f.50 multicoloured 20 10
103 – 10f. multicoloured 40 15
104 – 15f. multicoloured 70 20
105 – 20f. multicoloured 90 30
MS105a 120 × 100 mm. Nos. 103/5. Perf or imperf 3·50 3·50

DESIGNS: 1f. to 20f. Various dancers and drummers as Type **22**.

See also Nos. 175/**MS**81a.

23 Pope Paul and King Mwambutsa IV

1964. Canonization of 22 African Martyrs. Inscriptions in gold.

106 **23** 50c. lake and blue 15 10
107 – 1f. blue and purple 15 10
108 – 4f. sepia and mauve 25 10
109 – 8f. brown and red 40 15
110 – 14f. brown and turquoise 40 20
111 **23** 20f. green and red 65 40

DESIGNS—VERT: 1f., 8f. Group of martyrs. HORIZ: 4f., 14f., Pope John XXIII and King Mwambutsa IV.

24 Putting the Shot

1964. Olympic Games, Tokyo. Inscr "TOKYO 1964". Multicoloured.

112 50c. Type **24** 10 10
113 1f. Throwing the discus 10 10
114 3f. Swimming (horiz) 10 10
115 4f. Relay-racing 10 10
116 6f.50 Throwing the javelin 30 20
117 8f. Hurdling (horiz) 35 20
118 10f. Long-jumping (horiz) 40 20
119 14f. High-diving 55 20
120 18f. High-jumping (horiz) 65 35
121 20f. Gymnastics (horiz) 85 35
MS121a 115 × 71 mm. 18f.+2f. and 20f.+5f. (as Nos. 120/1). Perf or imperf 3·25 3·25

25 Scientist, Map and Emblem

1965. Anti-T.B. Campaign. Country name, values and Lorraine Cross in red.

122 **25** 2f.+50c. sepia and drab 10 10
123 4f.+1f.50 green & pink 25 10
124 5f.+2f.50 violet & buff 30 15
125 8f.+3f. blue and grey 40 20
126 10f.+5f. red and green 55 30
MS126a 100 × 71 mm. 10f.+10f. sepia and olive. Perf or imperf 1·10 1·10

26 Purple Swamphen

27 "Relay" Satellite and Telegraph Key

1965. Birds. Multicoloured. (i) Postage. (a) Size as T **26**.

127 50c. Type **26** 10 10
128 1f. Little bee eater 10 10
129 1f.50 Secretary bird 10 10
130 2f. Painted stork 20 10
131 3f. Congo peafowl 25 10
132 3f.50 African darter 30 10

(b) Size 26 × 42½ mm.

133 4f. Type **26** 40 10
134 5f. Little bee eater 50 15
135 6f.50 Secretary bird 60 15
136 8f. Painted stork 60 15
137 10f. Congo peafowl 70 15
138 15f. African darter 85 25

(c) Size 33½ × 53 mm.

139 20f. Saddle-bill stork 1·25 25
140 50f. Abyssinian ground hornbill 2·40 50
141 100f. South African crowned crane 4·00 90

(ii) Air. Inscr "POSTE AERIENNE". Optd with gold border. (a) Size 26 × 42½ mm.

142 6f. Secretary bird 50 10
143 8f. African darter 60 15
144 10f. Congo peafowl 70 15
145 14f. Little bee eater 75 20
146 15f. Painted stork 85 20

(b) Size 33½ × 53 mm.

147 20f. Saddle-bill stork 1·25 30
148 50f. Abyssinian ground hornbill 2·25 80
149 75f. Martial eagle 2·50 1·00
150 130f. Lesser flamingo 4·75 1·60

1965. Centenary of ITU. Multicoloured.

151 1f. Type **27** 10 10
152 3f. "Telstar 1" and hand telephone 10 10
153 4f. "Lunik 3" and wall telephone 10 10
154 6f.50 Weather satellite and tracking station 15 10
155 8f. "Telstar 2" and headphones 15 15
156 10f. "Sputnik" and radar scanner 20 15
157 14f. "Syncom" and aerial 30 20
158 20f. "Pioneer 5" space probe and radio aerial 35 30
MS158a 121 × 85 mm. Nos. 156 and 158. Perf or imperf 2·50 2·50

28 Arms (reverse of 10f. coin)

1965. 1st Independence Anniv Gold Coinage Commem. Circular designs on gold foil, backed with multicoloured patterned paper. Imperf. (i) Postage. (a) 10f. coin. Diameter 1½ in.

159 **28** 2f.+50c. red & yellow 15 15
160 – 4f.+50c. blue & red 20 20

(b) 25f. coin. Diameter 1¾ in.

161 **28** 6f.+50c. orange & grey 50 30
162 – 8f.+50c. blue & purple 60 60

(c) 50f. coin. Diameter 2½ in.

163 **28** 12f.+50c. green & purple 60 60
164 – 15f.+50c. green & lilac 65 65

(d) 100f. coin. Diameter 2⅜in.

165 **28** 25f.+50c. blue and flesh 1·25 1·25
166 – 40f.+50c. mauve & brn 1·75 1·75

(ii) Air. (a) 10f. coin. Diameter 1½ in.

167 **28** 3f.+1f. violet & lavender 30 30
168 – 5f.+1f. red & turquoise 40 40

(b) 25f. coin. Diameter 1¾ in.

169 **28** 11f.+1f. purple & yellow 60 60
170 – 14f.+1f. green and red 60 60

(c) 50f. coin. Diameter 2½ in.

171 **28** 20f.+1f. black and blue 85 85
172 – 30f.+1f. red and orange 1·10 1·10

(d) 100f. coin. Diameter 2¾ in.

173 **28** 50f.+1f. violet and blue 1·25 1·25
174 – 100f.+1f. purple & mve 3·00 3·00

DESIGNS: The 4, 5, 8, 14, 15, 30, 40 and 100f. each show the obverse side of the coin (King Mwambutsa IV).

1965. Worlds Fair, New York (2nd series). As Nos. 99/105, but with silver backgrounds.

175 **22** 50c. multicoloured 10 10
176 – 1f. multicoloured 10 10
177 – 4f. multicoloured 15 10
178 – 6f.50 multicoloured 25 10
179 – 10f. multicoloured 45 20
180 – 15f. multicoloured 55 30
181 – 20f. multicoloured 70 35
MS181a 120 × 100 mm. Nos. 179/81. perf or imperf 2·50 2·50

29 Globe and ICY Emblem

1965. International Co-operation Year. Mult.

182 1f. Type **29** 10 10
183 4f. Map of Africa and cogwheel emblem of UN Science and Technology Conference 15 10
184 8f. Map of South-East Asia and Colombo Plan emblem 20 10
185 10f. Globe and UN emblem 25 10
186 18f. Map of Americas and "Alliance for Progress" emblem 40 10
187 25f. Map of Europe and CEPT emblems 60 30
188 40f. Space map and satellite (UN—"Peaceful Uses of Outer Space") 1·00 50
MS188a 100 × 100 mm. 18f. (Map of Africa and UN emblem); 25f. and 40f. (similar to Nos. 187/8). Perf or imperf 2·60 2·60

30 Prince Rwagasore and Memorial

1966. Prince Rwagasore and Pres. Kennedy Commemoration.

189 **30** 4f.+1f. brown and blue 20 10
190 – 10f.+1f. blue, brn & grn 30 10
191 – 20f.+2f. green and lilac 65 15
192 – 40f.+2f. brown & green 75 30
MS193 75 × 90 mm. 20f.+5f. and 40f.+5f. (as Nos. 189 and 191). Perf or imperf 2·25 2·50

DESIGNS—HORIZ: 10f. Prince Rwagasore and Pres. Kennedy; 20f. Pres. Kennedy and memorial library. VERT: 40f. King Mwambutsa at Pres. Kennedy's grave.

31 Protea

1966. Flowers. Multicoloured. (i) Postage. (a) Size as T **31**.

194 50c. Type **31** 15 10
195 1f. Crossandra 15 10
196 1f.50 Ansellia 15 10
197 2f. Thunbergia 15 10
198 3f. Schizoglossum 25 10
199 3f.50 Dissotis 25 10

(b) Size 41 × 41 mm.

200 4f. Type **31** 25 10
201 5f. Crossandra 35 10
202 6f.50 Ansellia 45 10
203 8f. Thunbergia 65 10
204 10f. Schizoglossum 70 10
205 15f. Dissotis 85 10

(c) Size 50 × 50 mm.

206 20f. Type **31** 1·10 15
207 50f. Gazania 2·50 35
208 100f. Hibiscus 4·00 55
209 150f. Markhamia 6·25 75

(ii) Air. (a) Size 41 × 41 mm.

210 6f. Dissotis 25 15
211 8f. Crossandra 35 15
212 10f. Ansellia 35 15
213 14f. Thunbergia 40 15
214 15f. Schizoglossum 40 15

(b) Size 50 × 50 mm.

215 20f. Gazania 65 20
216 50f. Type **31** 1·75 40
217 75f. Hibiscus 2·50 1·00
218 130f. Markhamia 3·75 1·40

32 UNESCO

33

1966. 20th Anniv of UNESCO.

MS219 Three sheets, each 201 × 127 mm, each containing single stamps (Type **32**) with se-tenant label inscribed in English or French and an adjoining block of six stamps (3 × 2) as Type **33**, forming a composite design of the mural tapestry hanging in the U.N. General Assembly building, New York. (a) Postage: Two sheets 1f.50 × 7 and 4f. × 7. (b) Air. One sheet 14f. × 7 multicoloured Set of 3 sheets 6·00

1967. 4th Anniv of Independence (1966).

MS220 Four unissued sheets, diamond-shaped, 200 × 200 mm, each containing eight "Flower" stamps as Type **31** but with values and corresponding designs changed, and centre se-tenant label showing "Flag", "Map", "Arms" or "Flower" emblem. Values: 6, 7, 8, 10, 14, 15, 20 and 50f. Multicoloured. Stamps and sheet margins have the original inscriptions obliterated by the overprint **REPUBLIQUE DU BURUNDI** in black on gold panels Set of 4 sheets 11·00

1967. Various stamps optd. (i) Nos. 127, etc. (Birds) optd **REPUBLIQUE DU BURUNDI** and bar. (a) Postage.

221 50c. multicoloured 1·60 25
222 1f.50 multicoloured 35 25
223 3f.50 multicoloured 45 35
224 5f. multicoloured 60 45
225 6f.50 multicoloured 60 65
226 8f. multicoloured 70 80
227 10f. multicoloured 80 80
228 15f. multicoloured 1·10 1·25
229 20f. multicoloured 2·75 1·75
230 50f. multicoloured 5·25 3·75
231 100f. multicoloured 8·50 7·00

(b) Air.

232 6f. multicoloured 55 25
233 8f. multicoloured 70 40
234 10f. multicoloured 85 65
235 14f. multicoloured 1·10 65
236 15f. multicoloured 1·25 80
237 20f. multicoloured 1·75 95
238 50f. multicoloured 6·25 2·75
239 75f. multicoloured 8·50 3·50
240 130f. multicoloured 12·00 5·75

(ii) Nos. 194, etc. (Flowers) optd as Nos. 221, etc., but with two bars. (a) Postage.

241 50c. multicoloured 15 15
242 1f. multicoloured 15 15
243 1f.50 multicoloured 15 15
244 2f. multicoloured 15 15
245 3f. multicoloured 20 15
246 3f.50 multicoloured 30 15
247 4f. multicoloured 1·90 15
248 5f. multicoloured 50 20
249 6f.50 multicoloured 45 30
250 8f. multicoloured 45 30
251 10f. multicoloured 60 40
252 15f. multicoloured 75 45
253 50f. multicoloured 3·75 65
254 100f. multicoloured 9·00 2·50
255 150f. multicoloured 8·50 9·25

(b) Air.

256 6f. multicoloured 20 15
257 8f. multicoloured 30 15
258 10f. multicoloured 35 15
259 14f. multicoloured 45 30
260 15f. multicoloured 55 30
261 20f. multicoloured 1·75 40
262 50f. multicoloured 3·75 65
263 75f. multicoloured 5·75 90
264 130f. multicoloured 5·75 1·50

35 Sir Winston Churchill and St. Paul's Cathedral

1967. Churchill Commemoration. Multicoloured.

265	4f.+1f. Type **35** (postage)	30	10
266	15f.+2f. Churchill and Tower of London	50	25
267	20f.+3f. Big Ben and Boadicea Statue, Westminster	60	35
MS268	80×80 mm. 50f.+5f. Sir Winston Churchill (57×57 mm) (air). Perf or imperf	3·00	3·00

36 Egyptian Mouthbrooder

1967. Fishes. Multicoloured. (a) Postage. (i) Size as T **36**.

269	50c. Type **36**	15	20
270	1f. Spotted climbing-perch	15	20
271	1f.50 Six-banded lyretail	15	20
272	2f. Congo tetra	15	20
273	3f. Jewel cichlid	15	20
274	3f.50 Spotted mouthbrooder	15	20
	(ii) Size 53½×27 mm.		
275	4f. Type **36**	50	20
276	5f. As 1f.	50	20
277	6f.50. As 1f.50	65	20
278	8f. As 2f.	65	20
279	10f. As 3f.	1·00	20
280	15f. As 3f.50	1·10	20
	(iii) Size 63½×31½ mm.		
281	20f. Type **36**	1·90	30
282	50f. Dusky snakehead	3·50	50
283	100f. Red-tailed notho	7·50	75
284	150f. African tetra	7·50	1·10
	(b) Air. (i) Size 50×23 mm.		
285	6f. Type **36**	30	20
286	8f. As 1f.	45	20
287	10f. As 1f.50	55	20
288	14f. As 2f.	65	20
289	15f. As 3f.	80	20
	(ii) Size 59×27 mm.		
290	20f. As 3f.50	95	20
291	50f. As 50f. (No. 282)	4·75	30
292	75f. As 100f.	6·00	50
293	130f. As 150f.	11·00	1·00

37 Baule Ancestral Figures

1967. "African Art". Multicoloured.

294	50c. Type **37** (postage)	10	10
295	1f. "Master of Buli's" carved seat	10	10
296	1f.50 Karumba antelope's head	10	10
297	2f. Bobo buffalo's head	10	10
298	4f. Guma-Goffa funeral figures	15	10
299	10f. Bakoutou "spirit" (carving) (air)	30	20
300	14f. Bamum sultan's throne	40	20
301	17f. Bebin bronze head	45	20
302	24f. Statue of 109th Bakouba king	55	30
303	26f. Burundi basketwork and lances	60	35

1967. 50th Anniv of Lions International. Nos. 265/**MS**268 optd **1917 1967** and emblem.

304	4f.+1f. multicoloured	50	20
305	15f.+2f. multicoloured	80	35
306	20f.+3f. multicoloured	95	35
MS307	80×80 mm. 50f.+5f. multicoloured (air) Perf or imperf	4·25	4·25

39 Lord Baden-Powell (founder)

1967. 60th Anniv of Scout Movement and World Scout Jamboree, Idaho.

308	50c. Scouts climbing (postage)	20	10
309	1f. Scouts preparing meal	20	10
310	1f.50 Type **39**	20	10
311	2f. Two scouts	20	10
312	4f. Giving first aid	30	10
313	10f. As 50c. (air)	60	15
314	14f. As 1f.	70	15
315	17f. Type **39**	85	15
316	24f. As 2f.	1·10	35
317	26f. As 4f.	1·25	40

40 "The Gleaners" (Millet)

1967. World Fair, Montreal. Multicoloured.

318	4f. Type **40**	15	10
319	8f. "The Water-carrier of Seville" (Velasquez)	15	10
320	14f. "The Triumph of Neptune and Amphitrite" (Poussin)	35	15
321	18f. "Acrobat with a ball" (Picasso)	35	15
322	25f. "Margaret van Eyck" (Van Eyck)	95	25
323	40f. "St. Peter denying Christ" (Rembrandt)	1·10	50
MS324	105×105 mm. Nos. 322/3. Perf or imperf	3·25	3·25

41 Boeing 707

1967. Air. Opening of Bujumbura Airport. Aircraft and inscr in black and silver.

325	**41**	10f. green	40	10
326	–	14f. yellow	65	20
327	–	17f. blue	95	20
328	–	26f. purple	1·60	30

AIRCRAFT: 14f. Boeing 727 over lakes. 17f. Vickers Super VC-10 over lake. 26f. Boeing 727 over Bujumbura Airport.

42 Pres. Micombero and Flag

1967. 1st Anniv of Republic. Multicoloured.

329	5f. Type **42**	25	10
330	14f. Memorial and Arms	35	15
331	20f. View of Bujumbura and Arms	50	20
332	30f. "Place de la Revolution" and President Micombero	90	30

43 "The Adoration of the Shepherds" (J. B. Mayno)

1967. Christmas. Religious Paintings. Mult.

333	1f. Type **43**	10	10
334	4f. "The Holy Family" (A. van Dyck)	15	10
335	14f. "The Nativity" (Maitre de Moulins)	40	20
336	26f. "Madonna and Child" (C. Crivelli)	75	30
MS337	120×120 mm. Nos. 333/6	4·25	4·25

44 Burundi Scouts

1968. Air. 20th Anniv of Burundi Scouts and 60th Anniv of Scout Movement. Diamond-shaped sheet containing T **44** and similar design. Multicoloured.

MS338	142×142 mm. 24f. and 26f. with two se-tenant labels depicting Lord Baden-Powell and scouting activities	2·25	2·25

DESIGN: 26f. Burundi scouts practising first-aid.

45 Downhill Skiing

1968. Winter Olympic Games, Grenoble. Mult.

339	5f. Type **45**	20	10
340	10f. Ice-hockey	25	10
341	14f. Figure-skating	40	10
342	17f. Bobsleighing	50	10
343	26f. Ski-jumping	65	10
344	40f. Speed-skating	1·10	25
345	60f. Olympic torch	1·75	30
MS346	129×82 mm. Nos. 344/5. Perf or imperf	2·75	2·75

46 "Portrait of a Young Man" (Botticelli)

1968. Famous Paintings. Multicoloured.

347	1f.50 Type **46** (postage)	10	10
348	2f. "La Maja Vestida" (Goya) (horiz)	10	10
349	4f. "The Lacemaker" (Vermeer)	15	10
350	17f. "Woman and Cat" (Renoir) (air)	40	20
351	24f. "The Jewish Bride" (Rembrandt) (horiz)	55	30
352	26f. "Pope Innocent X" (Velasquez)	80	40

47 Module landing on Moon

1968. Space Exploration. Multicoloured.

353	4f. Type **47** (postage)	20	10
354	6f. Russian cosmonaut in Space	30	10
355	8f. Weather satellite	30	10
356	10f. American astronaut in Space	45	15
357	14f. Type **47** (air)	40	15
358	18f. As 6f.	50	15
359	25f. As 8f.	80	25
360	40f. As 10f.	1·10	40
MS361	109×82 mm. 25f. Type **47**; 40f. Weather satellite. Perf or imperf	2·40	2·40

48 "Salamis aethiops"

1968. Butterflies. Multicoloured. (a) Postage. (i) Size 30½×34 mm.

362	50c. Type **48**	15	15
363	1f. "Graphium ridleyanus"	20	15
364	1f.50 "Cymothoe"	25	15
365	2f. "Charaxes eupale"	35	15
366	3f. "Papilio bromius"	40	15
367	3f.50 "Teracolus annae"	50	15
	(ii) Size 34×38 mm.		
368	4f. Type **48**	50	15
369	5f. As 1f.	50	15
370	6f.50 As 1f.50	60	15
371	8f. As 2f.	90	20
372	10f. As 3f.	1·10	20
373	15f. As 3f.50	1·40	25
	(iii) Size 41×46 mm.		
374	20f. Type **48**	2·50	30
375	50f. "Papilio zenobia"	4·50	75
376	100f. "Danais chrysippus"	8·25	1·25
377	150f. "Salamis temora"	14·00	2·10
	(b) Air. With gold frames. (i) Size 33×37 mm.		
378	6f. As 3f.50	50	15
379	8f. As 1f.	55	15
380	10f. As 1f.50	60	15
381	14f. As 2f.	70	20
382	15f. As 3f.	1·00	20
	(ii) Size 39×44 mm.		
383	20f. As 50f. (No. 375)	2·40	25
384	50f. Type **48**	5·50	50
385	75f. As 100f.	6·75	90
386	130f. As 150f.	12·50	1·10

49 "Woman by the Manzanares" (Goya)

1968. International Letter-writing Week. Mult.

387	4f. Type **49** (postage)	25	10
388	7f. "Reading a Letter" (De Hooch)	35	10
389	11f. "Woman reading a Letter" (Terborch)	40	10
390	14f. "Man writing a Letter" (Metsu)	45	10
391	17f. "The Letter" (Fragonard) (air)	60	10
392	26f. "Young Woman reading Letter" (Vermeer)	80	20
393	40f. "Folding a Letter" (Vigee-Lebrun)	90	25
394	50f. "Mademoiselle Lavergne" (Liotard)	95	35
MS395	103×120 mm. Nos. 393/4 (without "POSTE AERIENNE" inscr). Perf or imperf	2·00	2·00

50 Football

1968. Olympic Games, Mexico. Multicoloured.
396 4f. Type **50** (postage) 25 10
397 7f. Basketball 30 10
398 13f. High jumping 35 10
399 24f. Relay racing 55 20
400 40f. Throwing the javelin . . 1·25 40
401 10f. Putting the shot (air) . . 25 15
402 17f. Running 45 15
403 26f. Throwing the hammer . . 70 25
404 50f. Hurdling . . . . . . 1·40 45
405 75f. Long jumping . . . . . 2·25 60
MS406 95 × 85 mm. Nos. 404/5 (without "POSTE AERIENNE" inscr). Perf or imperf . . . . . 6·00 6·00

51 "Virgin and Child" (Lippi)

1968. Christmas. Paintings. Multicoloured.
407 3f. Type **51** (postage) 20 10
408 5f. "The Magnificat" (Botticelli) 25 10
409 6f. "Virgin and Child" (Durer) 40 10
410 11f. "Virgin and Child" (Raphael) 40 10
411 10f. "Madonna" (Correggio) (air) 25 10
412 14f. "The Nativity" (Baroccio) 35 15
413 17f. "The Holy Family" (El Greco) 55 20
414 26f. "Adoration of the Magi" (Maino) 75 35
MS415 Two sheets each 120 × 120 mm. (a) Nos. 407/10; (b) Nos. 411/14. Perf or imperf . . 2·75 2·75

52 WHO Emblem and Map

1969. 20th Anniv of World Health Organization Operation in Africa.
416 **52** 5f. multicoloured 15 10
417 6f. multicoloured 20 10
418 11f. multicoloured 25 15

53 Hand holding Flame

1969. Air. Human Rights Year.
419 **53** 10f. multicoloured 35 10
420 14f. multicoloured 45 10
421 26f. multicoloured 65 25

1969. Space Flight of "Apollo 8". Nos. 407/14 optd ***VOL DE NOEL APOLLO 8*** and space module.
422 3f. multicoloured (postage) 15 10
423 5f. multicoloured 25 10
424 6f. multicoloured 40 10
425 11f. multicoloured 50 20
426 10f. multicoloured (air) . . . 30 15
427 14f. multicoloured 35 20
428 17f. multicoloured 55 25
429 26f. multicoloured 70 35

55 Map showing African Members

1969. 5th Anniv of Yaounde Agreement between Common Market Countries and African-Malagasy Economic Community. Multicoloured.
430 5f. Type **55** 20 10
431 14f. Ploughing with tractor 40 15
432 17f. Teacher and pupil . . . 55 20
433 26f. Maps of Africa and Europe (horiz) 75 25

56 "Resurrection" (Isenmann)

1969. Easter. Multicoloured.
434 11f. Type **56** 30 10
435 14f. "Resurrection" (Caron) 40 15
436 17f. "Noli me Tangere" (Schongauer) 45 20
437 26f. "Resurrection" (El Greco) 75 30
MS438 102 × 125 mm. Nos. 434/7. Perf or imperf . . . . 1·50 1·60

57 Potter

1969. 50th Anniv of ILO. Multicoloured.
439 3f. Type **57** 10 10
440 5f. Farm workers 10 10
441 7f. Foundry worker 25 10
442 10f. Harvester 25 15

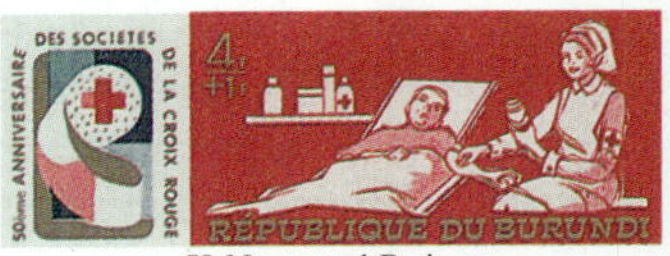

58 Nurse and Patient

1969. 50th Anniv of League of Red Cross Societies. Multicoloured.
443 4f.+1f. Type **58** (postage) . . 15 10
444 7f.+1f. Stretcher bearers . . 35 10
445 11f.+1f. Operating theatre . . 50 15
446 17f.+1f. Blood bank 60 25
447 26f.+3f. Laboratory (air) . . 75 25
448 40f.+3f. Red Cross truck in African village . . . . . . 1·10 45
449 50f.+3f. Nurse and woman patient . . . . 1·60 50
MS450 90 × 97 mm. Nos. 447/9 (without "POSTE AERIENNE" inscr). Perf or imperf . . . . . 3·50 3·50

59 Steel Works

1969. 5th Anniv of African Development Bank. Multicoloured.
451 10f. Type **59** 30 30
452 17f. Broadcaster 50 50
453 30f. Language laboratory . . . 70 70
454 50f. Tractor and harrow . . 1·25 1·25
MS455 103 × 125 mm. Nos. 451/4. Perf or imperf . . . . 2·50 2·50

60 Pope Paul VI

1969. 1st Papal Visit to Africa. Multicoloured.
456 3f.+2f. Type **60** 15 10
457 5f.+2f. Pope Paul and map of Africa (horiz) 30 10
458 10f.+2f. Pope Paul and African flags (horiz) . . . 30 10
459 14f.+2f. Pope Paul and the Vatican (horiz) 55 10
460 17f.+2f. Type **60** 60 10
461 40f.+2f. Pope Paul and Uganda Martyrs (horiz) . . 1·25 30
462 50f.+2f. Pope Paul enthroned (horiz) . . . . 1·60 35
MS463 80 × 103 mm. As Nos. 461/2 but face values 40f.+5f. and 50f.+5f. Perf or imperf . . . . 2·75 2·75

61 "Girl reading Letter" (Vermeer)

1969. International Letter-writing Week. Mult.
464 4f. Type **61** 15 10
465 7f. "Graziella" (Renoir) . . . 20 10
466 14f. "Woman writing a Letter" (Terborch) 30 10
467 26f. "Galileo" (unknown painter) 55 15
468 40f. "Beethoven" (unknown painter) . . . . 1·10 35
MS469 133 × 75 mm. Nos. 467/8. Perf or imperf . . . . 2·10 2·10

62 Blast-off

63 "Adoration of the Magi" (detail, Rubens)

1969. 1st Man on the Moon. Multicoloured.
470 4f. Type **62** (postage) 30 10
471 6f.50 Rocket in Space 40 10
472 7f. Separation of lunar module 50 10
473 14f. Module landing on Moon 80 15
474 17f. Command module in orbit . . . . 1·10 25
475 26f. Astronaut descending ladder (air) . . . . . . 1·25 20
476 40f. Astronaut on Moon's surface . . . . 2·00 25
477 50f. Module in sea . . . . . 3·00 45
MS478 140 × 90 mm. 26f. As 14f.; 40f. As 26f.; 50f. As 40f. Perf or imperf . . . . 6·25 6·25

1969. Christmas. Multicoloured.
479 5f. Type **63** (postage) 15 10
480 6f. "Virgin and Child with St. John" (Romano) . . . 15 10
481 10f. "Madonna of the Magnificat" (Botticelli) . . 40 15
482 17f. "Virgin and Child" (Garofalo) (horiz) (air) . . 60 15
483 26f. "Madonna and Child" (Negretti) (horiz) 80 20
484 50f. "Virgin and Child" (Barbarelli) (horiz) . . . . 1·60 35
MS485 Two sheets (a) 110 × 85 mm. Nos. 479/81; (b) 85 × 110 mm. Nos. 482/4. Perf or imperf Set of 2 sheets . . . . 3·75 1·10

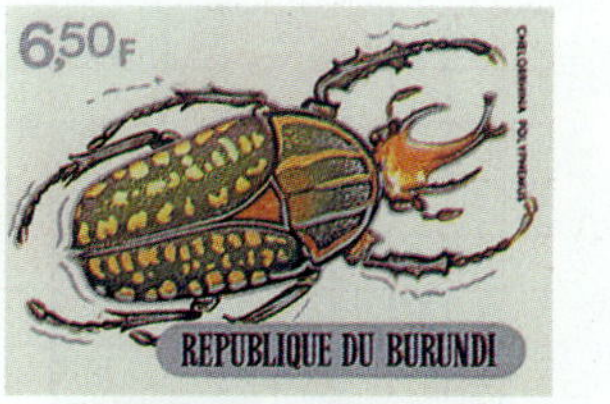

64 "Chelorrhina polyphemus"

1970. Beetles. Multicoloured. (a) Postage. (i) Size 39 × 28 mm.
486 50c. "Sternotomis bohemani" 20 10
487 1f. "Tetralobus flabellicornis" 20 10
488 1f.50 Type **64** 20 10
489 2f. "Brachytritus hieroglyphicus" 20 10
490 3f. "Goliathus goliathus" . . 20 10
491 3f.50 "Homoderus mellyi" . . 30 10

(ii) Size 46 × 32 mm.
492 4f. As 50c. 45 10
493 5f. As 1f. 65 10
494 6f. Type **64** 65 10
495 8f. As 2f. 65 10
496 10f. As 3f. 70 10
497 15f. As 3f.50 . . . . 1·10 15

(iii) Size 62 × 36 mm.
498 20f. As 50c. . . . . 1·50 30
499 50f. "Stephanorrhina guttata" 4·00 40
500 100f. "Phyllocnema viridocostata" . . . . . . 6·75 85
501 150f. "Mecynorrhina oberthueri" . . . . 8·25 1·60

(b) Air. (i) Size 46 × 32 mm.
502 6f. As 3f.50 . . . . 35 10
503 8f. As 1f. 45 10
504 10f. Type **64** 60 15
505 14f. As 2f. 70 15
506 15f. As 3f. 75 20

(ii) Size 52 × 36 mm.
507 20f. As 50f. (No. 499) . . . . 1·25 25
508 50f. As 50c. . . . . 4·00 35
509 75f. As 100f. . . . . 5·00 55
510 130f. As 150f. . . . . 8·00 80

65 "Jesus Condemned to Death"

1970. Easter. "The Stations of the Cross" (Carredano). Multicoloured.
511 1f. Type **65** (postage) 10 10
512 1f.50 "Carrying the Cross" 10 10
513 2f. "Jesus falls for the First Time" 10 10
514 3f. "Jesus meets His Mother" 10 10
515 3f.50 "Simon of Cyrene takes the Cross" 15 10
516 4f. "Veronica wipes the face of Christ" 15 10
517 5f. "Jesus falls for the Second Time" 15 10
518 8f. "The Women of Jerusalem" (air) 20 10
519 10f. "Jesus falls for the Third Time" 25 15
520 14f. "Christ stripped" 30 25
521 15f. "Jesus nailed to the Cross" 40 25
522 18f. "The Crucifixion" . . . 40 30
523 20f. "Descent from the Cross" 50 30
524 50f. "Christ laid in the Tomb" . . . . 1·25 45
MS525 Two sheets each 155 × 125 mm. (a) Nos. 511/17; (b) Nos. 518/24 . . . . 4·00 2·50

66 Japanese Parade

1970. World Fair, Osaka, Japan (EXPO '70). Multicoloured.
526 4f. Type **66** 15 10
527 6f.50 Exhibition site from the air 75 15

528	7f. African pavilions	20	10
529	14f. Pagoda (vert)	30	10
530	26f. Recording pavilion and pool	60	15
531	40f. Tower of the Sun (vert)	1·00	30
532	50f. National flags (vert)	1·25	35
MS533	105×80 mm. As Nos. 531/2 with additional "POSTE AERIENNE" inscr. Perf or imperf	2·25	65

67 Burundi Cow

1970. Source of the Nile. Multicoloured.

534	7f. Any design (postage)	95	30
535	14f. Any design (air)	1·25	30

Nos. 534 and 535 were each issued in se-tenant sheets of 18 stamps as Type **67**, showing map sections, animals and birds, forming a map of the Nile from Cairo to Burundi.

68 Common Redstart

1970. Birds. Multicoloured. (a) Postage. Size 44×33 mm or 33×44 mm.

536	2f. Great grey shrike (vert)	25	10
537	2f. Common starling (vert)	25	10
538	2f. Yellow wagtail (vert)	25	10
539	2f. Sand martin (vert)	25	10
540	3f. Winter wren	60	10
541	3f. Firecrest	60	10
542	3f. Eurasian sky lark	60	10
543	3f. Crested lark	60	10
544	3f.50 Woodchat shrike (vert)	65	10
545	3f.50 Rock thrush (vert)	65	10
546	3f.50 Black redstarts (vert)	65	10
547	3f.50 Ring ousel (vert)	65	10
548	4f. Type **68**	95	10
549	4f. Dunnock	95	10
550	4f. Grey wagtail	95	10
551	4f. Meadow pipit	95	10
552	5f. Hoopoe (vert)	1·25	15
553	5f. Pied flycatcher (vert)	1·25	15
554	5f. Great reed warbler (vert)	1·25	15
555	5f. River kingfisher (vert)	1·25	15
556	6f.50 House martin	1·40	20
557	6f.50 Sedge warbler	1·40	20
558	6f.50 Fieldfare	1·40	20
559	6f.50 Golden oriole	1·40	20

(b) Air. Size 52×44 mm or 44×52 mm.

560	8f. As No. 536	1·50	20
561	8f. As No. 537	1·50	20
562	8f. As No. 538	1·50	20
563	8f. As No. 539	1·50	20
564	10f. As No. 540	1·75	25
565	10f. As No. 541	1·75	25
566	10f. As No. 542	1·75	25
567	10f. As No. 543	1·75	25
568	14f. As No. 544	1·75	25
569	14f. As No. 545	1·75	25
570	14f. As No. 546	1·75	25
571	14f. As No. 547	1·75	25
572	20f. Type **68**	2·10	30
573	20f. As No. 549	2·10	30
574	20f. As No. 550	2·10	30
575	20f. As No. 551	2·10	30
576	30f. As No. 552	2·25	30
577	30f. As No. 553	2·25	30
578	30f. As No. 554	2·25	30
579	30f. As No. 555	2·25	30
580	50f. As No. 556	3·75	30
581	50f. As No. 557	3·75	30
582	50f. As No. 558	3·75	30
583	50f. As No. 559	3·75	30

69 Library

1970. International Educational Year. Mult.

584	3f. Type **69**	10	10
585	5f. Examination	15	10
586	7f. Experiments in the laboratory	25	10
587	10f. Students with electron microscope	30	10

70 United Nations Building, New York

1970. Air. 25th Anniv of United Nations. Mult.

588	7f. Type **70**	25	10
589	11f. Security Council in session	30	10
590	26f. Paul VI and U Thant	70	20
591	40f. U.N. and National flags	1·00	30
MS592	125×80 mm. As Nos. 590/1 but without "POSTE AERIENNE" inscr. Perf or imperf	1·70	50

71 Pres. Micombero and Wife

1970. 4th Anniv of Republic.

593	4f. Type **71**	10	10
594	7f. Pres. Micombero and flag	25	10
595	11f. Revolution Memorial	35	15
MS596	125×142 mm. Nos. 593/5 (air). Perf or imperf	70	35

72 King Baudouin and Queen Fabiola

1970. Air. Visit of King and Queen of the Belgians. Each brown, purple and gold.

597	6f. Type **72**	65	15
598	20f. Pres. Micombero and King Baudouin	1·50	40
599	40f. Pres. Micombero in evening dress	3·00	70
MS600	143×117 mm. As Nos. 597/9 but with "POSTE AERIENNE" inscr omitted. Perf or imperf	5·00	1·25

73 "Adoration of the Magi" (Durer)

1970. Christmas. Multicoloured.

601	6f.50+1f. Type **73** (postage)	50	15
602	11f.+1f. "The Virgin of the Eucharist" (Botticelli)	60	25
603	20f.+1f. "The Holy Family" (El Greco)	90	30
604	14f.+3f. "The Adoration of the Magi" (Velasquez) (air)	50	25
605	26f.+3f. "The Holy Family" (Van Cleve)	85	40
606	40f.+3f. "Virgin and Child" (Van der Weyden)	1·40	60
MS607	Two sheets each 135×75 mm. (a) Nos. 601/3; (b) Nos. 604/6. Perf or imperf	4·75	2·00

74 Lenin in Discussion

76 "The Resurrection" (Il Sodoma)

75 Lion

1970. Birth Cent of Lenin. Each brown and gold.

608	3f.50 Type **74**	20	15
609	5f. Lenin addressing Soviet	30	15
610	6f.50 Lenin with soldier and sailor	40	15
611	15f. Lenin speaking to crowd	60	25
612	50f. Lenin	2·00	55

1971. African Animals (1st series). Multicoloured. (a) Postage. Size 38×38 mm.

613	1f. Type **75**	35	10
614	1f. African buffalo	35	10
615	1f. Hippopotamus	35	10
616	1f. Giraffe	35	10
617	2f. Topi	50	15
618	2f. Black rhinoceros	50	15
619	2f. Common zebra	50	15
620	2f. Leopard	50	15
621	3f. Grant's gazelle	85	25
622	3f. Cheetah	85	25
623	3f. African white-backed vultures	85	25
624	3f. Okapi	85	25
625	5f. Chimpanzee	1·00	25
626	5f. African elephant	1·00	25
627	5f. Spotted hyena	1·00	25
628	5f. Gemsbok	1·00	25
629	6f. Gorilla	1·40	25
630	6f. Blue wildebeest	1·40	25
631	6f. Warthog	1·40	25
632	6f. Hunting dog	1·40	25
633	11f. Sable antelope	2·25	30
634	11f. Caracal	2·25	30
635	11f. Ostriches	2·25	30
636	11f. Bongo	2·25	30

(b) Air. Size 44×44 mm.

637	10f. Type **75**	70	35
638	10f. As No. 614	70	35
639	10f. As No. 615	70	35
640	10f. As No. 616	70	35
641	14f. As No. 617	80	40
642	14f. As No. 618	80	40
643	14f. As No. 619	80	40
644	14f. As No. 620	80	40
645	17f. As No. 621	90	40
646	17f. As No. 622	90	40
647	17f. As No. 623	90	40
648	17f. As No. 624	90	40
649	24f. As No. 625	1·50	55
650	24f. As No. 626	1·50	55
651	24f. As No. 627	1·50	55
652	24f. As No. 628	1·50	55
653	26f. As No. 629	1·50	55
654	26f. As No. 630	1·50	55
655	26f. As No. 631	1·50	55
656	26f. As No. 632	1·50	55
657	31f. As No. 633	1·60	70
658	31f. As No. 634	1·60	70
659	31f. As No. 635	1·60	70
660	31f. As No. 636	1·60	70

See also Nos. 1028/75, 1178/1225 and 1385/97.

1971. Easter. Multicoloured.

661	3f. Type **76** (postage)	15	10
662	6f. "The Resurrection" (Del Castagno)	30	10
663	11f. "Noli Me Tangere" (Correggio)	45	15
664	14f. "The Resurrection" (Borrassa) (air)	50	20
665	17f. "The Resurrection" (Della Francesca)	65	20
666	26f. "The Resurrection" (Pleydenwyurff)	85	30
MS667	Two sheets each 117×84 mm. (a) Nos. 661/3; (b) Nos. 664/6. Colours changed. Perf or imperf	3·00	1·10

1971. Air. United Nations Campaigns. Nos. 637/48 optd or surch. (a) Optd **LUTTE CONTRE LE RACISME ET LA DISCRIMINATION RACIALE** and Racial Equality Year emblem.

668	10f. multicoloured	90	15
669	10f. multicoloured	90	15
670	10f. multicoloured	90	15
671	10f. multicoloured	90	15

(b) Surch **LUTTE CONTRE L'ANALPHABETISME**, UNESCO emblem and premium (Campaign against Illiteracy).

672	14f.+2f. multicoloured	1·40	25
673	14f.+2f. multicoloured	1·40	25
674	14f.+2f. multicoloured	1·40	25
675	14f.+2f. multicoloured	1·40	25

(c) Surch **AIDE INTERNATIONALE AUX REFUGIES**, emblem and premium (Int Help for Refugees).

676	17f.+1f. multicoloured	2·25	40
677	17f.+1f. multicoloured	2·25	40
678	17f.+1f. multicoloured	2·25	40
679	17f.+1f. multicoloured	2·25	40

1971. Air. Olympic Commems. Nos. 653/56 surch. (a) Surch **75eme ANNIVERSAIRE DES JEUX OLYMPIQUES MODERNES (1896–1971)**, Olympic rings and premium.

680	26f.+1f. multicoloured	1·25	35
681	26f.+1f. multicoloured	1·25	35
682	26f.+1f. multicoloured	1·25	35
683	26f.+1f. multicoloured	1·25	35

(b) Surch **JEUX PRE-OLYMPIQUES MUNICH 1972**, rings and premium (Olympic Games, Munich (1972)).

684	31f.+1f. multicoloured	2·25	1·10
685	31f.+1f. multicoloured	2·25	1·10
686	31f.+1f. multicoloured	2·25	1·10
687	31f.+1f. multicoloured	2·25	1·10

79 "Venetian Girl"

81 "The Virgin and Child" (Il Perugino)

1971. International Letter-writing Week. Paintings by Durer. Multicoloured.

688	6f. Type **79**	30	30
689	11f. "Jerome Holzschuhers"	35	35
690	14f. "Emperor Maximilian"	40	40
691	17f. Altar painting, Paumgartner	65	65
692	26f. "The Halle Madonna"	80	80
693	31f. Self-portrait	1·00	1·00
MS694	137×80 mm. As Nos. 692/3 (air). Perf or imperf	1·80	1·80

1971. 6th Congress of International Institute of French Law, Bujumbura. Nos. 668/693 optd **VIeme CONGRES DE L'INSTITUT INTERNATIONAL DE DROIT D'EXPRESSION FRANCAISE**.

695	6f. multicoloured	30	10
696	11f. multicoloured	35	10
697	14f. multicoloured	45	20
698	17f. multicoloured	65	20
699	26f. multicoloured	75	25
700	31f. multicoloured	1·00	25
MS701	137×80 mm. No. **MS**694. Perf or imperf	1·50	1·50

1971. Christmas. Paintings of "Virgin and Child" by following artists. Multicoloured.

702	3f. Type **81** (postage)	15	10
703	5f. Del Sarto	25	10
704	6f. Morales	50	10
705	14f. Da Conegliano (air)	55	15
706	17f. Lippi	60	20
707	31f. Leonardo da Vinci	1·10	45
MS708	Two sheets each 125×80 mm. (a) Nos. 702/4; (b) Nos. 705/7	3·00	1·10

1971. 25th Anniv of UNICEF. Nos. 702/7 surch **UNICEF XXVe ANNIVERSAIRE 1946–1971**, emblem and premium.

709	3f.+1f. mult (postage)	30	10
710	5f.+1f. multicoloured	50	20
711	6f.+1f. multicoloured	60	30
712	14f.+1f. mult (air)	40	20
713	17f.+1f. multicoloured	95	25
714	31f.+1f. multicoloured	1·50	45
MS715	Two sheets each 125×80 mm. No. **MS**708 surch with 2f. premium on each stamp in the sheets	3·00	3·00

83 "Archangel Michael" (icon, St. Mark's)

1971. UNESCO "Save Venice" Campaign. Multicoloured.

716 3f.+1f. Type **83** (postage) . . 25 10
717 5f.+1f. "La Polenta" (Longhi) 35 15
718 6f.+1f. "Gossip" (Longhi) . . 35 15
719 11f.+1f. "Diana's Bath" (Pittoni) 45 25

720 10f.+1f. Casa d'Oro (air) . . 45 10
721 17f.+1f. Doge's Palace . . . 65 15
722 24f.+1f. St. John and St. Paul Church 90 25
723 31f.+1f. "Doge's Palace and Piazzetta" (Canaletto) . . . 2·00 40
MS724 Two sheets each 115 × 132 mm. (a) Nos. 716/19; (b) Nos. 720/3. Each design in sheet has a 2f. premium. Perf or imperf 5·25 1·50

84 "Lunar Orbiter"

1972. Conquest of Space. Multicoloured.

725 6f. Type **84** 15 15
726 11f. "Vostok" spaceship . . . 40 15
727 14f. "Luna 1" 45 30
728 17f. First Man on Moon . . 65 30
729 26f. "Soyuz 11" space flight 80 40
730 40f. "Lunar Rover" . . . . 1·60 95

MS731 135 × 135 mm. Nos. 725/30 with additional inscr (air) . . . 4·00 2·25

85 Slalom skiing

1972. Winter Olympic Games, Sapporo, Japan. Multicoloured.

732 5f. Type **85** 15 10
733 6f. Pair skating 20 10
734 11f. Figure-skating 35 10
735 14f. Ski-jumping 35 20
736 17f. Ice-hockey 50 20
737 24f. Speed skating 60 25
738 26f. Ski-bobbing 60 25
739 31f. Downhill skiing 75 25
740 50f. Bobsleighing . . . . . 1·50 35

MS741 107 × 127 mm. As Nos. 738/40. Perf or imperf (air) 2·75 85

86 "Ecce Homo" (Metzys)

1972. Easter. Paintings. Multicoloured.

742 3f.50 Type **86** 20 10
743 6f.50 "The Crucifixion" (Rubens) 30 10
744 10f. "The Descent from the Cross" (Portormo) . . . 40 10
745 18f. "Pieta" (Gallegos) . . . 70 15
746 27f. "The Trinity" (El Greco) 1·40 30
MS747 111 × 160 mm. Nos. 742/6. Perf or imperf . . . . 3·00 75

87 Gymnastics

1972. Olympic Games. Munich. Multicoloured.

748 5f. Type **87** (postage) 20 10
749 6f. Throwing the javelin . . . 20 10
750 11f. Fencing 35 15
751 14f. Cycling 50 20
752 17f. Pole-vaulting 75 20

753 24f. Weightlifting (air) . . . 65 25
754 26f. Hurdling 90 25
755 31f. Throwing the discus . . 1·40 40
756 40f. Football . . . . 1·50 50
MS757 123 × 75 mm. Nos. 755/6 without "POSTE AERIENNE" inscr . . . . 3·00 90

88 Prince Rwagasore, Pres. Micombero and Drummers

1972. 10th Anniv of Independence. Multicoloured.

758 5f. Type **88** (postage) . . . 15 10
759 7f. Rwagasore, Micombero and map 25 10
760 13f. Pres. Micombero and Burundi flag 40 15

761 15f. Type **65** (air) 30 15
762 18f. As 7f. 35 15
763 27f. As 13f. 60 30
MS764 Two sheets each 147 × 80 mm. (a) Nos. 758/60; (b) Nos. 761/3 . . . . 2·10 95

89 "Madonna and Child" (A. Solario)

1972. Christmas. "Madonna and Child" paintings by artists given below. Multicoloured.

765 5f. Type **89** (postage) 30 10
766 10f. Raphael 50 10
767 15f. Botticelli 75 15

768 18f. S. Mainardi (air) 50 15
769 27f. H. Memling . . . . . . 1·00 25
770 40f. Lotto . . . . 1·50 40
MS771 Two sheets each 128 × 82 mm. (a) Nos. 765/7; (b) Nos. 768/70 . . . . 4·50 1·10

90 "Platycoryne crocea"

1972. Orchids. Multicoloured.

772 50c. Type **90** (postage) . . . 30 15
773 1f. "Cattleya trianaei" . . . 30 15
774 2f. "Eulophia cucullata" . . 30 15
775 3f. "Cymbidium hamsey" . . 30 15
776 4f. "Thelymitra pauciflora" 30 15
777 5f. "Miltassia" 30 15
778 6f. "Miltonia" . . . . . . 1·25 15
779 7f. Type **90** . . . . 1·25 15
780 8f. As 1f. . . . . 1·40 15
781 9f. As 2f. . . . . 1·40 20
782 10f. As 3f. . . . . 1·90 20

783 13f. As 4f. (air) . . . . . . 1·25 15
784 14f. As 5f. . . . . 1·25 15
785 15f. As 6f. . . . . 1·60 20
786 18f. Type **90** . . . . 1·60 20
787 20f. As 1f. . . . . 1·60 25
788 27f. As 2f. . . . . 2·75 30
789 36f. As 3f. . . . . 4·50 40
Nos. 779/89 are size 53 × 53 mm.

1972. Christmas Charity. Nos. 765/770 surch.

790 5f.+1f. mult (postage) . . . 35 15
791 10f.+1f. multicoloured . . . 65 20
792 15f.+1f. multicoloured . . . 75 25

793 18f.+1f. multicoloured (air) 60 20
794 27f.+1f. multicoloured . . . 90 25
795 40f.+1f. multicoloured . . . 1·50 45
MS796 Two sheets as **MS**771 with 2f. premium surch on each stamp 4·50 1·10

92 H. M. Stanley

1973. Centenary of Stanley/Livingstone African Exploration. Multicoloured.

797 5f. Type **92** (postage) 20 10
798 7f. Expedition bearers 25 10
799 13f. Stanley directing foray 45 15

800 15f. Dr. Livingstone (air) . . 35 20
801 18f. Stanley meets Livingstone 55 20
802 27f. Stanley conferring with Livingstone . . . . 1·00 30
MS803 100 × 141 mm. Nos. 800/2. Perf or imperf . . . . 1·90 70

93 "The Scourging" (Caravaggio)

1973. Easter. Multicoloured.

804 5f. Type **93** (postage) 15 10
805 7f. "Crucifixion" (Van der Weyden) 25 10
806 13f. "The Deposition" (Raphael) 50 15

807 15f. "Christ bound to the Pillar" (Guido Reni) (air) 45 25
808 18f. "Crucifixion" (M. Grunewald) 70 25
809 27f. "The Descent from the Cross" (Caravaggio) . . . 1·10 30
MS810 Two sheets each 121 × 74 mm. (a) Nos. 804/6; (b) Nos. 807/9 . . . . 3·00 1·10

94 Interpol Emblem

1973. 50th Anniv of Interpol. Multicoloured.

811 5f. Type **94** (postage) 25 10
812 10f. Burundi flag 40 10
813 18f. Interpol H.Q., Paris . . 60 15

814 27f. As 5f. (air) 75 25
815 40f. As 10f. . . . . 1·25 35

95 Capricorn, Aquarius and Pisces

1973. 500th Birth Anniv of Copernicus.

816 **95** 3f. gold, red and black (postage) 20 10
817 – 3f. gold, red and black . . 20 10
818 – 3f. gold, red and black . . 20 10
819 – 3f. gold, red and black . . 20 10
820 – 5f. multicoloured 30 10
821 – 5f. multicoloured 30 10
822 – 5f. multicoloured 30 10
823 – 5f. multicoloured 30 10
824 – 7f. multicoloured 40 10
825 – 7f. multicoloured 40 10
826 – 7f. multicoloured 40 10
827 – 7f. multicoloured 40 10
828 – 13f. multicoloured 60 10
829 – 13f. multicoloured 60 10
830 – 13f. multicoloured 60 10
831 – 13f. multicoloured 60 10

832 – 15f. multicoloured (air) . . 40 15
833 – 15f. multicoloured 40 15
834 – 15f. multicoloured 40 15
835 – 15f. multicoloured 40 15
836 – 18f. multicoloured 55 15
837 – 18f. multicoloured 55 15
838 – 18f. multicoloured 55 15
839 – 18f. multicoloured 55 15
840 – 27f. multicoloured 95 25
841 – 27f. multicoloured 95 25
842 – 27f. multicoloured 95 25
843 – 27f. multicoloured 95 25
844 – 36f. multicoloured . . . . 2·10 40
845 – 36f. multicoloured . . . . 2·10 40
846 – 36f. multicoloured . . . . 2·10 40
847 – 36f. multicoloured . . . . 2·10 40
MS848 Two sheets each 137 × 147 mm. (a) Nos. 816/31; (b) Nos. 832/47 . . . . 20·00 10·00

DESIGNS: No. 816, Type **95**; 817, Aries, Taurus and Gemini; 818, Cancer, Leo and Virgo; 819, Libra, Scorpio and Sagittarius; 820/23, Greek and Roman Gods; 824/7, Ptolemy and Ptolemaic System; 828/31, Copernicus and Solar System; 823/5, Copernicus, Earth, Pluto and Jupiter; 836/39, Copernicus, Venus, Saturn and Mars; 840/43, Copernicus, Uranus, Neptune and Mercury; 844/7, Earth and spacecraft.

The four designs of each value were issued se-tenant in blocks of four within the sheet, forming composite designs.

96 "Protea cynaroides"

1973. Flora and Butterflies. Multicoloured.

849 1f. Type **96** (postage) 70 15
850 1f. "Precis octavia" 70 15
851 1f. "Epiphora bauhiniae" . . 70 15
852 1f. "Gazania longiscapa" . . 70 15
853 2f. "Kniphofia" – "Royal Standard" 70 15
854 2f. "Cymothoe coccinata hew" . . . . 1·00 20
855 2f. "Nudaurelia zambesina" 1·00 20
856 2f. "Freesia refracta" . . . . 1·00 15
857 3f. "Calotis eupompe" . . . 1·00 20
858 3f. Narcissus . . . . 1·00 15
859 3f. "Cineraria hybrida" . . . 1·00 15
860 3f. "Cyrestis camillus" . . . 1·00 20
861 5f. "Iris tingitana" . . . . . 1·40 15
862 5f. "Papilio demodocus" . . . 2·10 20
863 5f. "Catopsilia avelaneda" . . 2·10 20
864 5f. "Nerine sarniensis" . . . 1·40 15
865 6f. "Hypolimnas dexithea" . . 2·10 20
866 6f. "Zantedeschia tropicalis" 1·40 15
867 6f. "Sandersonia aurantiaca" 1·40 15
868 6f. "Drurya antimachus" . . 2·10 20
869 11f. "Nymphaea capensis" . . 1·75 20
870 11f. "Pandoriana pandora" . 2·75 25
871 11f. "Precis orythia" . . . . 2·75 25
872 11f. "Pelargonium domesticum"–"Aztec" . . 1·75 20

873 10f. Type **96** (air) 50 10
874 10f. As No. 850 . . . . . . 90 10
875 10f. As No. 851 . . . . . . 90 10
876 10f. As No. 852 . . . . . . 50 10
877 14f. As No. 853 . . . . . . 60 10
878 14f. As No. 854 . . . . . . 1·00 20
879 14f. As No. 855 . . . . . . 1·00 20
880 14f. As No. 856 . . . . . . 40 15
881 17f. As No. 857 . . . . . . 1·25 25
882 17f. As No. 858 . . . . . . 90 20
883 17f. As No. 859 . . . . . . 90 20
884 17f. As No. 860 . . . . . . 1·25 25
885 24f. As No. 861 . . . . . . 1·40 25
886 24f. As No. 862 . . . . . . 1·75 30
887 24f. As No. 863 . . . . . . 1·75 30
888 24f. As No. 864 . . . . . . 1·10 25
889 26f. As No. 865 . . . . . . 1·75 30
890 26f. As No. 866 . . . . . . 1·10 30
891 26f. As No. 867 . . . . . . 1·10 30
892 26f. As No. 868 . . . . . . 1·75 30
893 31f. As No. 869 . . . . . . 1·25 35
894 31f. As No. 870 . . . . . . 1·90 45
895 31f. As No. 871 . . . . . . 1·90 45
896 31f. As No. 872 . . . . . . 1·25 35

Nos. 849, 852/3, 856, 858/9, 861, 864, 866/7, 869, 872, 876/7, 880, 882/3, 885, 888, 890/1, 893 and 896 depict flora and the remainder butterflies.

The four designs of each value were issued se-tenant in blocks of four within the sheet, forming composite designs.

97 "Virgin and Child" (G. Bellini)

1973. Christmas. Various paintings of "The Virgin and Child" by artists listed below. Multicoloured.
897 5f. Type **97** (postage) 45 10
898 10f. Van Eyck 55 15
899 15f. G. A. Boltraffio 75 20
900 18f. Raphael (air) 35 10
901 27f. P. Perugino . . . . . . 1·10 30
902 40f. Titian . . . . 1·60 40
MS903 Two sheets each 144 × 78 mm. (a) Nos. 897/9; (b) Nos. 900/2 . . . . 4·75 1·25

1973. Christmas Charity. Nos. 897/902 surch.
904 **97** 5f.+1f. mult (postage) . . . 50 15
905 – 10f.+1f. multicoloured . . 80 20
906 – 15f.+1f. multicoloured . . 95 25
907 – 18f.+1f. mult (air) 70 15
908 – 27f.+1f. multicoloured . . 1·10 35
909 – 40f.+1f. multicoloured . . 1·60 50
MS910 Two sheets as **MS**903 with 2f. premium surch on each stamp 4·75 1·25

98 "The Pieta" (Veronese)

1974. Easter. Religious Paintings. Multicoloured.
911 5f. Type **98** 15 10
912 10f. "The Virgin and St. John" (Van der Weyden) 30 15
913 18f. "The Crucifixion" (Van der Weyden) 60 20
914 27f. "The Entombment" (Titian) 85 30
915 40f. "The Pieta" (El Greco) 2·10 50
MS916 145 × 120 mm. Nos. 911/15 4·00 1·25

99 Egyptian Mouthbrooder ("Haplochromis multicolor")

1974. Fishes. Multicoloured.
917 1f. Type **99** (postage) 55 10
918 1f. Spotted mouthbrooder ("Tropheus duboisi") . . . 55 10
919 1f. Freshwater butterfly-fish ("Pantodon buchholzi") . . 55 10
920 1f. Six-banded distichodus ("Distichodus sexfasciatus") 55 10
921 2f. Rainbow krib ("Pelmatochromis kribensis") 55 10
922 2f. African leaf-fish ("Polycentropsis abbreviata") 55 10
923 2f. Three-lined tetra ("Nannaethiops tritaeniatus") 55 10
924 2f. Jewel cichlid ("Hemichromis bimaculatus") 55 10
925 3f. Spotted climbing-perch ("Ctenopoma acutirostre") 55 10
926 3f. African mouthbrooder ("Tilapia melanopleura") 55 10
927 3f. Angel squeaker ("Synodontis angelicus") 55 10
928 3f. Two-striped lyretail ("Aphyosemion bivittatum") 55 10
929 5f. Diamond fingerfish ("Monodactylus argenteus") 90 10
930 5f. Regal angelfish ("Pygoplites diacanthus") 90 10
931 5f. Moorish idol ("Zanclus canescens") 90 10
932 5f. Peacock hind ("Cephalopholis argus") and surgeonfish 90 10
933 6f. Bigeye ("Priacanthus arenatus") . . . . 2·75 10
934 6f. Rainbow parrotfish ("Scarus guacamaia") and French angelfish . . . . . 2·75 10
935 6f. French angelfish ("Pomacanthus arcuatus") 2·75 10
936 6f. John dory ("Zeus faber") 2·75 10
937 11f. Scribbled cowfish ("Lactophrys quadricornis") . . . . . . 3·00 20
938 11f. Ocean surgeonfish ("Acanthurus bahianus") 3·00 20
939 11f. Queen triggerfish ("Balistes vetula") . . . . 3·00 20
940 11f. Queen angelfish ("Holocanthus ciliaris") . . 3·00 20
941 10f. Type **99** (air) 45 10
942 10f. As No. 918 . . . . . . 45 10
943 10f. As No. 919 . . . . . . 45 10
944 10f. As No. 920 . . . . . . 45 10
945 14f. As No. 921 . . . . . . 95 10
946 14f. As No. 922 . . . . . . 95 10
947 14f. As No. 923 . . . . . . 95 10
948 14f. As No. 924 . . . . . . 95 10
949 17f. As No. 925 . . . . . . 95 10
950 17f. As No. 926 . . . . . . 95 10
951 17f. As No. 927 . . . . . . 95 10
952 17f. As No. 928 . . . . . . 95 10
953 24f. As No. 929 . . . . . . 2·10 10
954 24f. As No. 930 . . . . . . 2·10 10
955 24f. As No. 931 . . . . . . 2·10 10
956 24f. As No. 932 . . . . . . 2·10 10
957 26f. As No. 933 . . . . . . 3·00 20
958 26f. As No. 934 . . . . . . 3·00 20
959 26f. As No. 935 . . . . . . 3·00 20
960 26f. As No. 936 . . . . . . 3·00 20
961 31f. As No. 937 . . . . . . 3·75 30
962 31f. As No. 938 . . . . . . 3·75 30
963 31f. As No. 939 . . . . . . 3·75 30
964 31f. As No. 940 . . . . . . 3·75 30
The four designs of each value are arranged together in se-tenant blocks of four within the sheet, forming composite designs.

100 Footballers and World Cup Trophy

1974. World Cup Football Championships.
965 **100** 5f. mult (postage) 25 10
966 – 6f. multicoloured 30 10
967 – 11f. multicoloured 40 20
968 – 14f. multicoloured 50 25
969 – 17f. multicoloured 55 25
970 – 20f. multicoloured (air) . . 70 35
971 – 26f. multicoloured 90 45
972 – 40f. multicoloured . . . . 1·40 60
MS973 88 × 142 mm. As Nos. 970/2 but without airmail inscriptions 3·00 1·40
DESIGNS: Nos. 966/72, Football scenes as Type **100**.

101 Burundi Flag

1974. Centenary of UPU. Multicoloured.
974 6f. Type **101** (postage) . . . 20 10
975 6f. Burundi P.T.T. Building 20 10
976 11f. Postmen carrying letters 30 10
977 11f. Postmen carrying letters 30 10
978 14f. UPU Monument . . . . 1·25 70
979 14f. Mail transport . . . . 1·25 70
980 17f. Burundi on map 55 10
981 17f. Dove and letter 55 10
982 24f. Type **101** (air) 80 20
983 24f. As No. 975 . . . . . . 80 20
984 26f. As No. 976 . . . . . . 1·10 30
985 26f. As No. 977 . . . . . . 1·10 30
986 31f. As No. 978 . . . . . . 2·75 1·10
987 31f. As No. 979 . . . . . . 2·75 1·10
988 40f. As No. 980 . . . . . . 3·50 45
989 40f. As No. 981 . . . . . . 3·50 45
MS990 Two sheets each 96 × 164 mm. (a) Nos. 974/81; (b) Nos. 982/9 . . . . 20·00 6·00
The two designs in each denomination were arranged together in se-tenant pairs within the sheet, each pair forming a composite design.

102 "St. Ildefonse writing a letter" (El Greco)

1974. International Letter-writing Week. Mult.
991 6f. Type **102** 30 15
992 11f. "Lady sealing a letter" (Chardin) 50 20
993 14f. "Titus at desk" (Rembrandt) 55 30
994 17f. "The Love-letter" (Vermeer) 60 30
995 26f. "The Merchant G. Gisze" (Holbein) . . . 65 50
996 31f. "A. Lenoir" (David) . . 90 55
MS997 95 × 105 mm. Nos. 955/6 1·50 1·00

103 "Virgin and Child". (Van Orley)

1974. Christmas. Showing "Virgin and Child" paintings by artists named. Multicoloured.
998 5f. Type **103** (postage) . . . 25 10
999 10f. Hans Memling 45 15
1000 15f. Botticelli . . . . 1·00 20
1001 18f. Hans Memling (different) (air) 35 20
1002 27f. F. Lippi . . . . 1·10 35
1003 40f. L. di Gredi . . . . . 1·50 45
MS1004 Two sheets each 126 × 89 mm. (a) Nos. 998/1000; (b) Nos. 1001/3 . . . . 4·50 1·50

1974. Christmas Charity. Nos. 998/1003 surch.
1005 **103** 5f.+1f. mult (postage) . . 30 10
1006 – 10f.+1f. multicoloured 40 25
1007 – 15f.+1f. multicoloured 1·10 30
1008 – 18f.+1f. mult (air) . . . 55 20
1009 – 27f.+1f. multicoloured 85 35
1010 – 40f.+1f. multicoloured 1·60 45
MS1011 Two sheets as **MS**1004 with 2f. premium on each stamp . . 4·50 1·50

104 "Apollo" Spacecraft with Docking Tunnel

1975. "Apollo–Soyuz" Space Project.
1012 26f. Type **104** (postage) . . 45 30
1013 26f. Leonov and Kubasov 45 30
1014 26f. "Soyuz" Spacecraft . . 45 30
1015 26f. Slayton, Brand and Stafford 45 30
1016 31f. "Soyuz" launch 55 40
1017 31f. "Apollo" and "Soyuz" spacecraft 55 40
1018 31f. "Apollo" third stage separation 55 40
1019 31f. Slayton, Brand, Stafford, Leonov and Kubasov 55 40
1020 27f. Type **104** (air) 60 45
1021 27f. As No. 1012 . . . . . 60 45
1022 27f. As No. 1013 . . . . . 60 45
1023 27f. As No. 1014 . . . . . 60 45
1024 40f. As No. 1015 . . . . . 80 60
1025 40f. As No. 1016 . . . . . 80 60
1026 40f. As No. 1017 . . . . . 80 60
1027 40f. As No. 1018 . . . . . 80 60
The four designs in each value were issued together in se-tenant blocks of four within the sheet.

105 Addax

1975. African Animals (2nd series). Multicoloured.
1028 1f. Type **105** (postage) . . . 40 15
1029 1f. Roan antelope 40 15
1030 1f. Nyala 40 15
1031 1f. White rhinoceros 40 15
1032 2f. Mandrill 40 15
1033 2f. Eland 40 15
1034 2f. Salt's dik-dik 40 15
1035 2f. Thomson's gazelles . . . 40 15
1036 3f. African claw-less otter 55 15
1037 3f. Bohar reedbuck 55 15
1038 3f. African civet 55 15
1039 3f. African buffalo 55 15
1040 5f. Black wildebeest 55 15
1041 5f. African asses 55 15
1042 5f. Angolan black and white colobus 55 15
1043 5f. Gerenuk 55 15
1044 6f. Addra gazelle 95 20
1045 6f. Black-backed jackal . . . 95 20
1046 6f. Sitatungas 95 20
1047 6f. Banded duiker 95 20
1048 11f. Fennec fox . . . . . . 1·40 20
1049 11f. Lesser kudus . . . . . 1·40 20
1050 11f. Blesbok . . . . 1·40 20
1051 11f. Serval . . . . 1·40 20
1052 10f. Type **105** (air) 60 10
1053 10f. As No. 1029 . . . . . 60 10
1054 10f. As No. 1030 . . . . . 60 10
1055 10f. As No. 1031 . . . . . 60 10
1056 14f. As No. 1032 . . . . . 70 15
1057 14f. As No. 1033 . . . . . 70 15
1058 14f. As No. 1034 . . . . . 70 15
1059 14f. As No. 1035 . . . . . 70 15
1060 17f. As No. 1036 . . . . . 1·10 15
1061 17f. As No. 1037 . . . . . 1·10 15
1062 17f. As No. 1038 . . . . . 1·10 15
1063 17f. As No. 1039 . . . . . 1·10 15
1064 24f. As No. 1040 . . . . . 1·75 20
1065 24f. As No. 1041 . . . . . 1·75 20
1066 24f. As No. 1042 . . . . . 1·75 20
1067 24f. As No. 1043 . . . . . 1·75 20
1068 26f. As No. 1044 . . . . . 1·90 20
1069 26f. As No. 1045 . . . . . 1·90 20
1070 26f. As No. 1046 . . . . . 1·90 20
1071 26f. As No. 1047 . . . . . 1·90 20
1072 31f. As No. 1048 . . . . . 2·25 25
1073 31f. As No. 1049 . . . . . 2·25 25
1074 31f. As No. 1050 . . . . . 2·25 25
1075 31f. As No. 1051 . . . . . 2·25 25
The four designs in each value were issued together in horiz. se-tenant strips within the sheet, forming composite designs.

1975. Air. International Women's Year. Nos. 1052/9 optd **ANNEE INTERNATIONALE DE LA FEMME**.
1076 **105** 10f. multicoloured . . . 80 50
1077 – 10f. multicoloured . . . 80 50
1078 – 10f. multicoloured . . . 80 50
1079 – 10f. multicoloured . . . 80 50
1080 – 14f. multicoloured . . . 1·40 60
1081 – 14f. multicoloured . . . 1·40 60
1082 – 14f. multicoloured . . . 1·40 60
1083 – 14f. multicoloured . . . 1·40 60

1975. Air. 30th Anniv of United Nations. Nos. 1068/75 optd **30eme ANNIVERSAIRE DES NATIONS UNIES**.
1084 26f. multicoloured . . . . . 1·40 1·25
1085 26f. multicoloured . . . . . 1·40 1·25
1086 26f. multicoloured . . . . . 1·40 1·25
1087 26f. multicoloured . . . . . 1·40 1·25
1088 31f. multicoloured . . . . . 2·25 2·00
1089 31f. multicoloured . . . . . 2·25 2·00
1090 31f. multicoloured . . . . . 2·25 2·00
1091 31f. multicoloured . . . . . 2·25 2·00

108 "Jonah"

1975. Christmas. 500th Birth Anniv of Michaelangelo. Multicoloured.
1092 5f. Type **108** (postage) . . . 25 10
1093 5f. "Libyan Sibyl" 25 10
1094 13f. "Daniel" 90 10
1095 13f. "Cumaean Sybil" . . . 90 10
1096 27f. "Isaiah" . . . . 1·25 15
1097 27f. "Delphic Sybil" (different) . . . . 1·25 15
1098 18f. "Zachariah" (air) . . . 90 10
1099 18f. "Joel" 90 10
1100 31f. "Erythraean Sybil" . . 1·60 30
1101 31f. "Ezekiel" . . . . 1·60 30
1102 40f. "Persian Sybil" . . . . 2·00 35
1103 40f. "Jeremiah" . . . . . . 2·00 35
MS1104 Two sheets each 138 × 111 mm. (a) Nos. 1092/7; (b) Nos. 1098/1103 . . . . 14·00 2·25

1975. Christmas Charity. Nos. 1092/1103 surch **+1F**.
1105 **108** 5f.+1f. mult (postage) . . 45 10
1106 – 5f.+1f. multicoloured . . 45 10

1107 – 13f.+1f. multicoloured 75 10
1108 – 13f.+1f. multicoloured 75 10
1109 – 27f.+1f. multicoloured 1·25 15
1110 – 27f.+1f. multicoloured 1·25 15

1111 – 18f.+1f. mult (air) 1·00 10
1112 – 18f.+1f. multicoloured 1·00 10
1113 – 31f.+1f. multicoloured 1·60 30
1114 – 31f.+1f. multicoloured 1·60 30
1115 – 40f.+1f. multicoloured 1·90 35
1116 – 40f.+1f. multicoloured 1·90 35
MS1117 Two sheets as **MS**1104 with 2f. premium on each stamp 14·00 2·25

110 Speed Skating

111 Basketball

1976. Winter Olympic Games, Innsbruck. Mult.
1118 17f. Type **110** (postage) 45 20
1119 24f. Figure-skating 50 20
1120 26f. Two-man bobsleigh 60 20
1121 31f. Cross-country skiing 70 30

1122 18f. Ski-jumping (air) 40 25
1123 36f. Skiing (slalom) 1·50 40
1124 50f. Ice-hockey 1·60 60
MS1125 Two sheets (a) 101 × 101 mm. Nos. 1118/21; (b) 131 × 131 mm. Nos. 1122/4 5·75 2·10

1976. Olympic Games, Montreal. Multicoloured.
1126 14f. Type **111** (postage) 40 30
1127 14f. Pole-vaulting 40 30
1128 17f. Running 60 45
1129 17f. Football 60 45
1130 28f. As No. 1127 90 65
1131 28f. As No. 1128 90 65
1132 40f. As No. 1129 1·50 1·10
1133 40f. Type **111** 1·50 1·10

1134 27f. Hurdling (air) 90 65
1135 27f. High-jumping (horiz) 90 65
1136 31f. Gymnastics (horiz) 1·25 90
1137 31f. As No. 1134 (horiz) 1·25 90
1138 50f. As No. 1135 (horiz) 1·90 1·40
1139 50f. As No. 1136 (horiz) 1·90 1·40
MS1140 Two sheets. (a) 115 × 120 mm. 14f. Football; 17f. Pole vault; 28f. Basketball; 40f. Running (postage). (b) 99 × 120 mm. 27f. Gymnastics; 31f. High jump; 50f. Hurdles (air) 7·00 5·50

112 "Battle of Bunker Hill" (detail, John Trumbull)

113 "Virgin and Child" (Dirk Bouts)

1976. Air. Bicent of American Revolution. Mult.
1141 18f. Type **112** 55 15
1142 18f. As Type **112** 55 15
1143 26f. Franklin, Jefferson and John Adams 75 25
1144 26f. As No. 1143 75 25
1145 36f. "Signing of Declaration of Independence" (Trumbull) 1·25 35
1146 36f. As No. 1145 1·25 35
MS1147 101 × 148 mm. Nos. 1141/6 5·00 1·50
The two designs of each value form composite pictures. Type **112** is the left-hand portion of the painting.

1976. Christmas. Multicoloured.
1148 5f. Type **113** (postage) 35 10
1149 13f. "Virgin of the Trees" (Bellini) 65 10
1150 27f. "Virgin and Child" (C. Crivelli) 1·00 25
1151 18f. "Virgin and Child" with St. Anne" (Leonardo) (air) 80 30
1152 31f. "Holy Family with Lamb" (Raphael) 1·10 60
1153 40f. "Virgin with Basket" (Correggio) 1·60 70
MS1154 Two sheets each 122 × 80 mm. (a) Nos. 1148/50; (b) Nos. 1151/3 5·50 2·00

1976. Christmas Charity. Nos. 1148/53 surch **+1F.**
1155 **113** 5f.+1f. mult (postage) 25 10
1156 – 13f.+1f. multicoloured 70 30
1157 – 27f.+1f. multicoloured 1·10 50
1158 – 18f.+1f. mult (air) 60 30
1159 – 31f.+1f. multicoloured 1·00 45
1160 – 40f.+1f. multicoloured 1·90 65
MS1161 Two sheets as **MS**1154 with 2f. premium on each stamp 5·50 2·00

115 "The Ascent of Calvary" (Rubens)

1977. Easter. 400th Birth Anniv of Peter Paul Rubens. Multicoloured.
1162 10f. Type **115** 35 25
1163 21f. "Christ Crucified" 95 70
1164 27f. "The Descent from the Cross" 1·10 80
1165 35f. "The Deposition" 1·50 1·10
MS1166 111 × 85 mm. As Nos. 1162/5 (air) 4·00 2·70

116 Alexander Graham Bell

117 Kobs

1977. Telephone Centenary and World Telecommunications Day. Multicoloured.
1167 10f. Type **116** (postage) 25 15
1168 10f. Satellite, Globe and telephones 25 15
1169 17f. Switchboard operator and wall telephone 45 30
1170 17f. Satellite transmitting to Earth 45 30
1171 26f. A. G. Bell and first telephone 80 60
1172 26f. Satellites circling Globe, and videophone 80 60

1173 18f. Type **116** (air) 40 30
1174 18f. As No. 1172 40 30
1175 36f. As No. 1169 1·10 80
1176 36f. As No. 1168 1·10 80
MS1177 120 × 135 mm. 10f. As No. 1171; 17f. Type **116**; 26f. As No. 1168; 18f. As No. 1170; 36f. As No. 1172 3·25 2·00

1977. African Animals (3rd series). Multicoloured.
1178 2f. Type **117** (postage) 75 20
1179 2f. Marabou storks 75 20
1180 2f. Blue wildebeest 75 20
1181 2f. Bush pig 75 20
1182 5f. Grevy's zebras 85 20
1183 5f. Whale-headed stork 85 20
1184 5f. Striped hyenas 85 20
1185 5f. Pygmy chimpanzee 85 20
1186 8f. Greater flamingoes 95 20
1187 8f. Nile crocodiles 95 20
1188 8f. Green tree snake 95 20
1189 8f. Greater kudus 95 20
1190 11f. Large-toothed rock hyrax 1·00 20
1191 11f. Cobra 1·00 20
1192 11f. Golden jackals 1·00 20
1193 11f. Verreaux eagles 1·00 20
1194 21f. Ratel 1·25 30
1195 21f. Bushbuck 1·25 30
1196 21f. Secretary bird 1·25 30
1197 21f. Klipspringer 1·25 30
1198 27f. Bat-eared fox 1·60 30
1199 27f. African elephants 1·60 30
1200 27f. Vulturine guineafowl 1·60 30
1201 27f. Impalas 1·60 30

1202 9f. Type **117** (air) 60 25
1203 9f. As No. 1179 60 25
1204 9f. As No. 1180 60 25
1205 9f. As No. 1181 60 25
1206 13f. As No. 1182 85 30
1207 13f. As No. 1183 85 30
1208 13f. As No. 1184 85 30
1209 13f. As No. 1185 85 30
1210 30f. As No. 1186 1·25 50
1211 30f. As No. 1187 1·25 50
1212 30f. As No. 1188 1·25 50
1213 30f. As No. 1189 1·25 50
1214 35f. As No. 1190 1·40 60
1215 35f. As No. 1191 1·40 60
1216 35f. As No. 1192 1·40 60
1217 35f. As No. 1193 1·40 60
1218 54f. As No. 1194 2·40 70
1219 54f. As No. 1195 2·40 70
1220 54f. As No. 1196 2·40 70
1221 54f. As No. 1197 2·40 70
1222 70f. As No. 1198 3·25 85
1223 70f. As No. 1199 3·25 85
1224 70f. As No. 1200 3·25 85
1225 70f. As No. 1201 3·25 85
The four designs in each value were issued together se-tenant in horizontal strips within the sheet, forming composite designs.

118 "The Man of Iron" (Grimm)

119 UN General Assembly and UN 3c. Stamp, 1954

1977. Fairy Tales. Multicoloured.
1226 5f. Type **118** 20 10
1227 5f. "Snow White and Rose Red" (Grimm) 20 10
1228 5f. "The Goose Girl" (Grimm) 20 10
1229 5f. "The Two Wanderers" (Grimm) 20 10
1230 11f. "The Hermit and the Bear" (Aesop) 60 10
1231 11f. "The Fox and the Stork" (Aesop) 60 10
1232 11f. "The Litigious Cats" (Aesop) 60 10
1233 11f. "The Blind and the Lame" (Aesop) 60 10
1234 14f. "The Ice Maiden" (Andersen) 70 10
1235 14f. "The Old House" (Andersen) 70 10
1236 14f. "The Princess and the Pea" (Andersen) 70 10
1237 14f. "The Elder Tree Mother" (Andersen) 70 10
1238 17f. "Hen with the Golden Eggs" (La Fontaine) 80 15
1239 17f. "The Wolf Turned Shepherd" (La Fontaine) 80 15
1240 17f. "The Oyster and Litigants" (La Fontaine) 80 15
1241 17f. "The Wolf and the Lamb" (La Fontaine) 80 15
1242 26f. "Jack and the Beanstalk" (traditional) 1·60 25
1243 26f. "Alice in Wonderland) (Lewis Carroll) 1·60 25
1244 26f. "Three Heads in the Well" (traditional) 1·60 25
1245 26f. "Tales of Mother Goose" (traditional) 1·60 25

1977. 25th Anniv of United Nations Postal Administration. Multicoloured.
1246 8f. Type **119** (postage) 40 30
1247 8f. UN 4c. stamp, 1957 40 30
1248 8f. UN 3c. stamp, 1954 (FAO) 40 30
1249 8f. UN 1½c. stamp, 1951 40 30
1250 10f. Security Council and UN 8c. red, 1954 50 35
1251 10f. UN 8c. green, 1956 50 35
1252 10f. UN 8c. black, 1955 50 35
1253 10f. UN 7c. stamp, 1959 50 35
1254 21f. Meeting hall and UN 3c. grey, 1956 80 60
1255 21f. UN 8c. stamp, 1956 80 60
1256 21f. UN 3c. brown, 1953 80 60
1257 21f. UN 3c. green, 1952 80 60

1258 24f. Building by night and UN 4c. red, 1957 (air) 80 60
1259 24f. UN 8c. brn & grn, 1960 80 60
1260 24f. UN 8c. green, 1955 80 60
1261 24f. UN 8c. red, 1955 80 60
1262 27f. Aerial view of UN 8c. red, 1957 90 65
1263 27f. UN 3c. stamp, 1953 90 65
1264 27f. UN 8c. green, 1954 90 65
1265 27f. UN 8c. brown, 1956 90 65
1266 35f. UN Building by day and UN 5c. stamp, 1959 1·40 1·00
1267 35f. UN 3c. stamp, 1962 1·40 1·00
1268 35f. UN 3c. bl & pur, 1951 1·40 1·00
1269 35f. UN 1c. stamp, 1951 1·40 1·00
MS1270 Two sheets each 127 × 76 mm. (a) 8f. As No. 1253; 10f. As No. 1255; 21f. As No. 1248. (b) 24f. As No. 1263; 27f. As No. 1266; 35f. As No. 1260 4·75 3·30
The four designs in each value were issued together in se-tenant blocks of four, each design in the block having the same background.

120 "Virgin and Child" (Jean Lambardos)

121 Cruiser "Aurora" and Russian 5r. Stamp, 1922

1977. Christmas. Paintings of Virgin and Child by artists named. Multicoloured.
1271 5f. Type **120** (postage) 15 10
1272 13f. Melides Toscano 65 50
1273 27f. Emmanuel Tzanes 95 70

1274 18f. Master of Moulins (air) 50 35
1275 31f. Lorenzo di Credi 1·00 75
1276 40f. Palma the Elder 1·25 90
MS1277 Two sheets each 130 × 72 mm. (a) Nos. 1271/3. (b) Nos. 1274/6 4·50 3·25

1977. 60th Anniv of Russian Revolution. Mult.
1278 5f. Type **121** 40 10
1279 5f. Russia S.G. 455 40 10
1280 5f. Russia S.G. 1392 40 10
1281 5f. Russia S.G. 199 40 10
1282 8f. Decemberists' Square, Leningrad and Russia S.G. 983 25 10
1283 8f. Russia S.G. 2122 25 10
1284 8f. Russia S.G. 1041 25 10
1285 8f. Russia S.G. 2653 25 10
1286 11f. Pokrovski Cathedral, Moscow and Russia S.G. 3929 45 10
1287 11f. Russia S.G. 3540 45 10
1288 11f. Russia S.G. 3468 45 10
1289 11f. Russia S.G. 3921 45 10
1290 13f. May Day celebrations, Moscow and Russia S.G. 4518 60 15
1291 13f. Russia S.G. 3585 60 15
1292 13f. Russia S.G. 3024 60 15
1293 13f. Russia S.G. 2471 60 15
The four designs in each value were issued in se-tenant blocks of four, each design in the block having the same background.

122 Tanker Unloading (Commerce)

1977. 15th Anniv of Independence. Mult.
1294 1f. Type **122** 20 15
1295 5f. Assembling electric armatures (Economy) 20 15
1296 11f. Native dancers (Tourism) 30 20
1297 14f. Picking coffee (Agriculture) 45 30
1298 17f. National Palace, Bujumbura 55 40

1977. Christmas Charity. Nos. 1271/6 surch **+1F.**
1299 **120** 5f.+1f. mult (postage) 30 15
1300 – 13f.+1f. multicoloured 65 20
1301 – 27f.+1f. multicoloured 95 45

1302 – 18f.+1f. mult (air) 65 25
1303 – 31f.+1f. multicoloured 1·00 45
1304 – 40f.+1f. multicoloured 1·60 60
MS1305 Two sheets as **MS**1277 with 2f. premium on each stamp 4·75 3·50

123 "Madonna and Child" (Solario)

124 Abyssinian Ground Hornbill

1979. Christmas (1978). Paintings of Virgin and Child by named artists. Multicoloured.
1306 13f. Rubens 85 85
1307 17f. Type **123** 90 90
1308 27f. Tiepolo 1·40 1·40
1309 31f. Gerard David 1·60 1·60
1310 40f. Bellini 2·00 2·00
MS1311 114 × 120 mm. Nos. 1306/10 (air) 6·75 6·75

1979. Christmas Charity. Nos. 1306/10 surch **+1F.**
1312 – 13f.+1f. multicoloured 85 85
1313 **123** 17f.+1f. multicoloured 90 90
1314 – 27f.+1f. multicoloured 1·40 1·40
1315 – 31f.+1f. multicoloured 1·60 1·60
1316 – 40f.+1f. multicoloured 2·00 2·00
MS1317 As **MS**1311 with 2f. premium on each stamp 6·75 6·75

1979. Birds. Multicoloured.
1318 1f. Type **124** (postage) 1·10 60
1319 2f. African darter 1·10 60
1320 3f. Little bee eater 1·10 60
1321 5f. Lesser flamingo 1·50 80
1322 8f. Congo peafowl 1·90 1·10
1323 10f. Purple swamphen 2·10 1·25
1324 20f. Martial eagle 2·40 1·40
1325 27f. Painted stork 3·00 1·75
1326 50f. Saddle-bill stork 4·75 2·50

1327 6f. Type **124** (air) 1·75 1·00
1328 13f. As No. 1319 2·10 1·25
1329 18f. As No. 1320 2·40 1·40
1330 26f. As No. 1321 2·75 1·60
1331 31f. As No. 1322 3·00 1·60
1332 36f. As No. 1323 3·00 1·75
1333 40f. As No. 1324 3·75 2·10
1334 54f. As No. 1325 4·00 2·40
1335 70f. As No. 1326 5·25 3·00

125 Mother and Child

1979. International Year of the Child. Mult.

1336	10f. Type **125**	90	90
1337	20f. Baby	1·40	1·40
1338	27f. Child with doll	1·50	1·50
1339	50f. S.O.S. village, Gitega	2·00	2·00
MS1340	131 × 85 mm. Nos. 1336/9 additionally inscr "+ 2f."	6·25	6·25

126 "Virgin and Child" (Raffaellino Del Garbo)

127 Sir Rowland Hill and Penny Black

1979. Christmas. "Virgin and Child" paintings by named artists. Multicoloured.

1341	20f. Type **126**	90	90
1342	27f. Giovanni Penni	1·10	1·10
1343	31f. Giulio Romano	1·25	1·25
1344	50f. Detail of "Adoration of the Shepherds" (Jacopo Bassano)	1·75	1·75
MS1345	85 × 110 mm. Nos. 1341/4 (air)	5·00	5·00

1979. Death Centenary of Sir Rowland Hill. Mult.

1346	20f. Type **127**	80	80
1347	27f. German East Africa 25p. stamp and Ruanda-Urundi 5c. stamp	95	95
1348	31f. Burundi 1f.25 and 50f. stamps of 1962	1·10	1·10
1349	40f. 4f. (1962) and 14f. (1969) stamps of Burundi	1·25	1·25
1350	60f. Heinrich von Stephan (founder of UPU) and Burundi 14f. UPU stamps of 1974	6·75	3·00
MS1351	110 × 105 mm. Nos. 1346/50	11·00	7·00

1979. Christmas Charity. Nos. 1341/4 additionally inscr with premium.

1352	20f.+1f. multicoloured	65	65
1353	27f.+1f. multicoloured	1·40	1·40
1354	31f.+1f. multicoloured	1·60	1·60
1355	50f.+1f. multicoloured	2·10	2·10
MS1356	85 × 110 mm. As **MS**1345 with 2f. premium on each stamp (air)	11·00	7·00

1980. As Nos. 1318/19 and 1321/3 but new values.

(a) With copper frames.

1356a	5f. Abyssinian ground hornbill		
1356b	10f. African darter		
1356c	40f. Lesser flamingo		
1356d	45f. Congo peafowl		
1356e	50f. Purple swamphen		

(b) With grey-green frames.

1356f	5f. As No. 1356a		
1356g	10f. As No. 1356b		
1356h	40f. As No. 1356c		
1356i	45f. As No. 1356d		
1356j	50f. As No. 1356e		

128 Approaching Hurdle (110 m Hurdles, Thomas Munkelt)

130 Congress Emblem

129 "The Virgin and Child" (Sebastiano Mainardi)

1980. Olympic Medal Winners. Multicoloured.

1357	20f. Type **128**	95	95
1358	20f. Jumping hurdle	95	95
1359	20f. Completing jump	95	95
1360	30f. Discus—beginning to throw	1·40	1·40
1361	30f. Continuing throw	1·40	1·40
1362	30f. Releasing discus	1·40	1·40
1363	40f. Football—running for goal (Czechoslovakia)	1·50	1·50
1364	40f. Kicking ball	1·50	1·50
1365	40f. Saving ball	1·50	1·50
MS1366	145 × 111 mm. As Nos. 1357/65	8·75	8·75

1980. Christmas. Multicoloured.

1367	10f. Type **129**	90	90
1368	30f. "Doni Tondo" (Michelangelo)	1·50	1·50
1369	40f. "The Virgin and Child" (Piero di Cosimo)	2·10	2·10
1370	45f. "The Holy Family" (Fra Bartolomeo)	2·25	2·25
MS1371	134 × 103 mm. As Nos. 1367/70 (air)	6·75	6·75

1980. 1st National Party Congress, Uprona.

1372 **130**	10f. multicoloured	30	30
1373	40f. multicoloured	1·50	1·50
1374	45f. multicoloured	1·60	1·60
MS1375	108 × 68 mm. As Nos. 1372/4 (air)	3·25	3·25

1981. Christmas Charity. Nos. 1367/70 additionally inscr with premium.

1376	10f.+1f. multicoloured	75	75
1377	30f.+1f. multicoloured	1·75	1·75
1378	40f.+1f. multicoloured	2·25	2·25
1379	50f.+1f. multicoloured	2·50	2·50
MS1380	134 × 103 mm. As Nos. 1376/9 but each stamp with 2f. premium (air)	7·25	7·25

131 Kepler and Dish Aerial

1981. 350th Death Anniv of Johannes Kepler (astronomer). First Earth Satellite Station in Burundi. Multicoloured.

1381	10f. Type **131**	60	60
1382	40f. Satellite and antenna	1·50	1·50
1383	45f. Satellite (different) and antenna	1·90	1·90
MS1384	78 × 108 mm. Nos. 1381/3	3·50	3·50

132 Giraffes

1982. African Animals (4th series). Multicoloured.

1385	2f. Lion	4·75	2·10
1386	3f. Type **132**	4·75	2·10
1387	5f. Black rhinoceros	4·75	2·10
1388	10f. African buffalo	15·00	6·75
1389	20f. African elephant	23·00	11·50
1390	25f. Hippopotamus	26·00	12·50
1391	30f. Common zebra	30·00	14·50
1392	50f. Warthog	55·00	26·00
1393	60f. Eland	70·00	32·00
1394	65f. Black-backed jackal	85·00	40·00
1395	70f. Cheetah	95·00	45·00
1396	75f. Blue Wildebeest	£100	48·00
1397	85f. Spotted hyena	£120	60·00

1983. Animal Protection Year. Nos. 1385/97 optd with World Wildlife Fund Emblem.

1398	2f. Type **131**	5·00	4·25
1399	3f. Giraffe	5·00	4·25
1400	5f. Black rhinoceros	5·00	4·25
1401	10f. African buffalo	14·00	13·00
1402	20f. African elephant	23·00	20·00
1403	25f. Hippopotamus	26·00	24·00
1404	30f. Common zebra	28·00	25·00
1405	50f. Warthog	55·00	48·00
1406	60f. Eland	70·00	60·00
1407	65f. Jackal ("Canis mesomelas")	80·00	75·00
1408	70f. Cheetah	95·00	80·00
1409	75f. Blue wildebeest	£100	90·00
1410	85f. Spotted Hyena	£120	£110

133 Flag and National Party Emblem

1983. 20th Anniv (1982) of Independence. Multicoloured.

1411	10f. Type **133**	65	65
1412	25f. Flag and arms	1·00	1·00
1413	30f. Flag and map of Africa	1·10	1·10
1414	50f. Flag and emblem	1·50	1·50
1415	65f. Flag and President Bagaza	2·00	2·00

134 "Virgin and Child" (Lucas Signorelli)

1983. Christmas. Multicoloured.

1416	10f. Type **134**	1·10	1·10
1417	25f. E. Murillo	1·50	1·50
1418	30f. Carlo Crivelli	1·75	1·75
1419	50f. Nicolas Poussin	2·40	2·40
MS1420	106 × 151 mm. Nos. 1416/19, but with green backgrounds	6·75	6·75

DESIGNS: Virgin and Child paintings by named artists.

1983. Christmas Charity. Nos. 1416/19 additionally inscr with premium.

1421	10f.+1f. multicoloured	1·10	1·10
1422	25f.+1f. multicoloured	1·50	1·50
1423	30f.+1f. multicoloured	1·75	1·75
1424	50f.+1f. multicoloured	2·40	2·40
MS1425	106 × 151 mm. As **MS**1420 with 2f. premium on each stamp (air)	6·75	6·75

Nos. 1421/4 have green backgrounds; stamps on **MS**1425 have carmine backgrounds.

135 "Papilio zalmoxis"

1984. Butterflies. Multicoloured.

1426	5f. Type **135**	2·00	85
1427	5f. "Cymothoe coccinata"	2·00	85
1428	10f. "Papilio antimachus"	4·75	2·10
1429	10f. "Asterope pechueli"	4·75	2·10
1430	30f. "Bebearia mardania"	9·25	4·00
1431	30f. "Papilio hesperus"	9·25	4·00
1432	35f. "Euphaedra perseis"	12·00	5·25
1433	35f. "Euphaedra neophron"	12·00	5·25
1434	65f. "Pseudacraea striata"	22·00	9·75
1435	65f. "Euphaedra imperialis"	22·00	9·75

136 Stamps of German East Africa and Belgian Occupation

1984. 19th U.P.U. Congress, Hamburg. Mult.

1436	10f. Type **136**	65	65
1437	30f. 1962 Burundi overprinted stamps	1·10	1·10
1438	35f. 1969 14f. Letter-writing Week and 1982 30f. Zebra stamps	1·25	1·25
1439	65f. Heinrich von Stephan (founder of UPU) and 1974 14f. UPU Centenary stamps	18·00	11·50
MS1440	147 × 84 mm. As Nos. 1436/9 but each 39 × 31 mm (air)	21·00	15·00

137 Jesse Owens (runner)

1984. Olympic Games, Los Angeles. Mult.

1441	10f. Type **137**	1·10	1·10
1442	30f. Rafer Johnson (discus thrower)	1·60	1·60
1443	35f. Bob Beamon (long jumper)	1·75	1·75
1444	65f. K. Keino (sprinter)	2·25	2·25
MS1445	119 × 99 mm. As Nos. 1441/4 but some colours changed (air)	6·75	6·75

138 "Virgin and Child" (Botticelli)

1984. Christmas. Multicoloured.

1446	10f. "Rest on the Flight into Egypt" (Murillo)	30	30
1447	25f. "Virgin and Child" (R. del Garbo)	1·10	1·10
1448	30f. Type **138**	1·60	1·60
1449	50f. "Adoration of the Shepherds" (J. Bassano)	2·00	2·00
MS1450	125 × 92 mm. As Nos. 1446/9 but some colours changed. Olive border	5·00	5·00

1984. Christmas Charity. As Nos. 1446/49 but with additional premium.

1451	10f.+1f. multicoloured	30	30
1452	25f.+1f. multicoloured	1·10	1·10
1453	30f.+1f. multicoloured	1·60	1·60
1454	50f.+1f. multicoloured	2·00	2·00
MS1455	125 × 92 mm. As No. **MS**1450 with 2f. premium on each stamp (air)	5·00	5·00

139 Thunbergia

140 Bombs as Flats

1986. Flowers. Multicoloured.

1456	2f. Type **139** (postage)	1·40	80
1457	3f. African violets	1·40	80
1458	5f. "Clivia"	1·40	80
1459	10f. "Cassia"	1·40	80
1460	20f. Bird of Paradise flower	2·50	1·60
1461	35f. "Gloriosa"	4·50	3·00
1462	70f. Type **139** (air)	2·50	2·10
1463	75f. As No. 1457	2·75	2·25
1464	80f. As No. 1458	2·75	2·40
1465	85f. As No. 1459	3·25	2·75
1466	100f. As No. 1460	3·50	2·75
1467	150f. As No. 1461	6·00	5·00

1987. International Peace Year (1986). Mult.

1468	10f. Type **140**	20	20
1469	20f. Molecular diagrams as flower	40	40
1470	30f. Clasped hands across globe	1·10	1·10
1471	40f. Chicks in split globe	1·25	1·25
MS1472	85 × 120 mm. Nos. 1468/71	3·00	3·00

141 Map, Airplane and Emblem

1987. 10th Anniv of Great Lakes Countries Economic Community. Multicoloured.

1473	5f. Type **141**	55	55
1474	10f. Map, ear of wheat, cogwheel and emblem	65	65
1475	15f. Map, factory and emblem	75	75
1476	25f. Map, electricity pylons and emblem	1·60	1·60
1477	35f. Map, flags and emblem	2·25	2·25
MS1478	117 × 114 mm. Nos. 1473/7 plus label	5·75	5·75

142 Leaves and Sticks Shelter

1988. International Year of Shelter for the Homeless (1987). Multicoloured.

1479	10f. Type **142**	55	55
1480	20f. People living in concrete pipes	70	70
1481	80f. Boys mixing mortar	1·50	1·50
1482	150f. Boys with model house	3·00	3·00
MS1483	124 × 100 mm. Nos. 1479/82	5·75	5·75

143 Skull between Cigarettes

144 Pope John Paul II

1989. Anti-smoking Campaign. Multicoloured.
1484 5f. Type **143** 70 70
1485 20f. Cigarettes, lungs and skull . . . . 1·40 1·40
1486 80f. Cigarettes piercing skull 2·25 2·25
MS1487 120 × 80 mm. Nos. 1484/6 4·25 4·25
No. **MS**1487 also shows World Health Organization 40th Anniv emblem.

1989. Various stamps surch.
1487b 20f. on 3f. mult (No. 1457) 70 70
1487c 80f. on 30f. mult (No. 1430) . . . . . 2·00 2·00
1487d 80f. on 30f. mult (No. 1431) . . . . . 2·00 2·00
1487e 80f. on 35f. mult (No. 1432) . . . . . 2·00 2·00
1487f 80f. on 35f. mult (No. 1433) . . . . . 2·00 2·00
1487g 85f. on 65f. mult (No. 1435) . . . . .

1990. Papal Visit.
1488 **144** 5f. multicoloured . . . 45 45
1489 10f. multicoloured . . . 45 45
1490 20f. multicoloured . . . 70 70
1491 30f. multicoloured . . . 70 70
1492 50f. multicoloured . . . 1·40 1·40
1493 80f. multicoloured . . . 2·00 2·00

145 Hippopotamus

1991. Animals. Multicoloured.
1495 5f. Type **145** . . . . . . 1·10 75
1496 10f. Hen and cockerel . . . 1·10 75
1497 20f. Lion . . . . 1·10 75
1498 30f. Elephant . . . . . . 1·10 1·10
1499 50f. Helmet guineafowl ("Pintade") . . . . . . 3·00 2·25
1500 80f. Crocodile . . . . . . 4·50 3·25
MS1501 109 × 123 mm. Nos. 1495/1500 . . . . . . 16·00 8·75

146 Drummer

147 "Impatiens petersiana"

1992. Traditional Dancing. Multicoloured.
1502 15f. Type **146** 25 25
1503 30f. Men dancing 40 40
1504 115f. Group of drummers (horiz) . . . . 1·90 1·90
1505 200f. Men dancing in fields (horiz) . . . . 3·25 3·25
MS1506 120 × 105 mm. Nos. 1502/5 5·75 5·75

1992. Flowers. Multicoloured.
1507 15f. Type **147** 90 65
1508 20f. "Lachenalia aloides" "Nelsonii" 90 65
1509 30f. Egyptian lotus . . . . 1·40 1·00
1510 50f. Kaffir lily . . . . . . 3·00 2·25
MS1511 105 × 120 mm. Nos. 1507/10 6·25 4·50

148 Pigtail Macaque

1992. Air. Animals. Multicoloured.
1512 100f. Type **148** . . . . . 2·40 1·75
1513 115f. Grevy's zebra . . . . 2·75 2·10
1514 200f. Ox . . . . 4·00 3·00
1515 220f. Eastern white pelican . 5·00 3·75
MS1516 105 × 120 mm. Nos. 1512/15 14·00 10·00

149 People holding Hands and Flag

1992. 30th Anniv of Independence. Multicoloured.
1517 30f. Type **149** 20 20
1518 85f. State flag 80 80
1519 110f. Independence monument (vert) . . . . 1·10 1·10
1520 115f. As No. 1518 . . . . 1·10 1·10
1521 120f. Map (vert) . . . . . 1·40 1·40
1522 140f. Type **149** . . . . . 1·50 1·50
1523 200f. As No. 1519 . . . . 2·10 2·10
1524 250f. As No. 1521 . . . . 2·75 2·75

150 "Russula ingens"

1992. Fungi. Multicoloured.
1525 10f. Type **150** 15 15
1526 15f. "Russula brunneorigida" 20 20
1527 20f. "Amanita zambiana" 25 30
1528 30f. "Russula subfistulosa" 40 45
1529 75f. "Russula meleagris" . . 90 95
1530 85f. As No. 1529 . . . . . 1·00 1·10
1531 100f. "Russula immaculata" 1·25 1·25
1532 110f. Type **150** . . . . . . 1·40 1·40
1533 115f. As No. 1526 . . . . . 1·40 1·40
1534 120f. "Russula sejuncta" . . 1·40 1·60
1535 130f. As No. 1534 . . . . . 1·50 1·60
1536 250f. "Afroboletus luteolus" 3·00 3·25

151 Columbus's Fleet, Treasure and Globes

1992. 500th Anniv of Discovery of America by Columbus. Multicoloured.
1541 200f. Type **151** . . . . . . 2·00 2·00
1542 400f. American produce, globes and Columbus's fleet . . . . 4·25 4·25

152 Serval

1992. The Serval. Multicoloured.
1543 30f. Type **152** 60 50
1544 130f. Pair sitting and crouching . . . . 2·40 2·00
1545 200f. Pair, one standing over the other . . . . 3·75 3·00
1546 220f. Heads of pair . . . . 4·00 3·50

153 Running

154 Emblems

1992. Olympic Games, Barcelona. Multicoloured.
1547 130f. Type **153** . . . . . . 1·50 1·50
1548 500f. Hurdling . . . . . . 5·25 5·25

1992. International Nutrition Conference, Rome. Multicoloured.
1549 200f. Type **154** . . . . . . 2·00 2·00
1550 220f. Woman's face made from vegetables (G. Arcimbolo) . . . . . 2·40 2·40

155 Horsemen

156 Flags of Member Countries and European Community Emblem

1992. Christmas. Details of "Adoration of the Magi" by Gentile da Fabriano. Multicoloured.
1551 100f. Type **155** 90 90
1552 130f. Three Kings . . . . . 1·10 1·10
1553 250f. Holy family . . . . . 2·50 2·50
MS1554 109 × 91 mm. Nos. 1551/3 (sold at 580f.) . . . . 4·50 4·50

1993. European Single Market. Multicoloured.
1555 130f. Type **156** . . . . . . 1·25 1·25
1556 500f. Europe shaking hands with Africa . . . . 5·00 5·00

157 Indonongo

1993. Musical Instruments. Multicoloured.
1557 200f. Type **157** . . . . . . 2·00 2·00
1558 220f. Ingoma (drum) . . . 2·25 2·25
1559 250f. Ikembe (xylophone) 2·50 2·50
1560 300f. Umuduri (musical bow) . . . . 3·25 3·25

158 Broad Blue-banded Swallowtail

159 Players, Stadium, United States Flag and Statue of Liberty

1993. Butterflies. Multicoloured.
1561 130f. Type **158** . . . . . . 1·50 1·25
1562 200f. Green charaxes . . . 2·40 2·10
1563 250f. Migratory glider . . . 3·00 2·50
1564 300f. Red swallowtail . . . 3·75 3·50
MS1565 84 × 123 mm. Nos. 1561/4 (sold at 980f.) . . . . 10·00 9·00

1993. World Cup Football Championship, U.S.A. (1994). Multicoloured.
1566 130f. Type **159** . . . . . . 1·25 1·25
1567 200f. Players, stadium, United States flag and Golden Gate Bridge . . . 2·50 2·50

160 Cattle

161 Woman with Baby and Two Men

1993. Domestic Animals. Multicoloured.
1568 100f. Type **160** . . . . . . 1·00 1·00
1569 120f. Sheep . . . . 1·10 1·10
1570 130f. Pigs . . . . 1·25 1·25
1571 250f. Goats . . . . 2·50 2·50

1993. Christmas. Each orange and black.
1572 100f. Type **161** . . . . . . 1·25 1·25
1573 130f. Nativity . . . . 1·50 1·50
1574 250f. Woman with baby and three men . . . . 3·00 3·00
MS1575 127 × 82 mm. Nos. 1572/4 (sold at 580f.) . . . . 5·75 5·75

162 Elvis Presley

163 "The Discus Thrower" (statue)

1994. Entertainers. Multicoloured.
1576 60f. Type **162** 30 30
1577 115f. Mick Jagger 55 55
1578 120f. John Lennon 60 60
1579 200f. Michael Jackson . . . 1·00 1·00
MS1580 80 × 114 mm. Nos. 1576/9 2·40 2·40

1994. Cent of International Olympic Committee.
1581 **163** 150f. multicoloured . . . 75 75

164 Pres. Buyoya handing over Baton of Power to Pres. Ndadaye

165 Madonna, China

1994. 1st Anniv of First Multi-party Elections in Burundi. Multicoloured.
1582 30f.+10f. Type **164** 20 20
1583 110f.+10f. Pres. Ndadaye (first elected President) giving inauguration speech 60 60
1584 115f.+10f. Arms on map . . 60 60
1585 120f.+10f. Warrior on map 65 65

1994. Christmas. Multicoloured.
1586 115f. Type **165** 55 55
1587 120f. Madonna, Japan . . . 60 60
1588 250f. Black Virgin, Poland 1·25 1·25
MS1589 80 × 118 mm. No. 1588 1·25 1·25

166 Emblem and Earth

167 "Cassia didymobotrya"

1995. 50th Anniversaries. Multicoloured.
1590 115f. Type **166** (FAO) . . . 55 55
1591 120f. UNO emblems and dove 60 60

1995. Flowers. Multicoloured.
1592 15f. Type **167** 15 15
1593 20f. "Mitragyna rubrostipulosa" 15 15
1594 30f. "Phytolacca dodecandra" 25 20
1595 85f. "Acanthus pubescens" 65 60
1596 100f. "Bulbophyllum comatum" 80 75
1597 110f. "Angraecum evrardianum" 90 80
1598 115f. "Eulophia burundiensis" 90 80
1599 120f. "Habenaria adolphii" 1·00 90

168 Otraca Bus

169 Boy with Panga

1995. Transport. Multicoloured.
1600 30f. Type **168** 15 15
1601 115f. Transintra lorry . . . 65 65
1602 120f. Lake ferry 90 70
1603 250f. Air Burundi airplane 1·40 1·40

1995. Christmas. Multicoloured.
1604 100f. Type **169** 55 55
1605 130f. Boy with sheaf of wheat 75 75

1606 250f. Mother and children 1·40 1·40
MS1607 126 × 82 mm. Nos. 1604/6 (sold at 580f.) 5·75 5·75

170 Venuste Niyongabo

1996. Olympic Games, Atlanta. Runners. Mult.
1608 130f. Type **170** (5000 m gold medal winner) 40 40
1609 500f. Arthemon Hatungimana 1·50 1·50

171 Hadada Ibis

1996. Birds. Multicoloured.
1610 15f. Type **171** 25 25
1611 20f. Egyptian goose 25 25
1612 30f. African fish eagle 25 25
1613 120f. Goliath heron 75 75
1614 165f. South African crowned crane 1·00 1·00
1615 220f. African jacana 1·40 1·40

172 Marlier's Julie

1996. Fishes of Lake Tanganyika. Multicoloured.
1616 30f. Type **172** 25 20
1617 115f. "Cyphotilapia frontosa" 75 60
1618 120f. "Lamprologus brichardi" 75 60
1619 250f. Stone squeaker 1·50 1·25
MS1620 108 × 108 mm. Nos. 1616/19 (sold at 615f.) 6·00 6·00

173 Children

1998. 50th Anniv of S.O.S Children's Villages. Multicoloured.
1621 100f. Type **173** 25 25
1622 250f. Flags, "50" and children waving 65 65
1623 270f. Children dancing around flag 70 70

174 Madonna and Child

175 Diana, Princess of Wales

1999. Christmas (1996–98). Multicoloured.
1624 100f. Type **174** (1996) 25 25
1625 130f. Madonna and Child (different) (1997) 30 30
1626 250f. Madonna and Child (different) (1998) 65 65
MS1627 125 × 82 mm. Nos. 1624/6 (sold at 580f.) 5·75 5·75

1999. 2nd Death Anniv of Diana, Princess of Wales.
1628 **175** 100f. multicoloured 20 20
1629 250f. multicoloured 20 20
1630 300f. multicoloured 50 50

176 Danny Kaye (entertainer) holding African Baby

2000. New Millennium. "A World Free from Hunger".
1631 **176** 350f. multicoloured 60 60

BUSHIRE Pt. 1

An Iranian seaport. Stamps issued during the British occupation in the 1914–18 War.

20 chahis = 1 kran, 10 krans = 1 toman.

1915. Portrait stamps of Iran (1911) optd **BUSHIRE Under British Occupation.**
1 **57** 1ch. orange and green 55·00 60·00
2 2ch. brown and red 55·00 50·00
3 3ch. green and grey 70·00 70·00
4 5ch. red and brown £375 £350
5 6ch. lake and green 50·00 38·00
6 9ch. lilac and brown 50·00 65·00
7 10ch. brown and red 50·00 65·00
8 12ch. blue and green 70·00 70·00
9 24ch. green and purple £120 75·00
10 1kr. red and blue £110 42·00
11 2kr. red and green £325 £200
12 3kr. black and lilac £250 £250
13 5kr. blue and red £170 £150
14 10kr. red and brown £150 £130

1915. Coronation issue of Iran optd **BUSHIRE Under British Occupation.**
15 **66** 1ch. blue and red £475 £425
16 2ch. red and blue £8500 £9000
17 3ch. green £650 £600
18 5ch. red £7500 £7500
19 6ch. red and green £6500 £6500
20 9ch. violet and brown £900 £850
21 10ch. brown and green £1400 £1400
22 12ch. blue £1700 £1700
23 24ch. black and brown £650 £500
24 **67** 1kr. black, brown and silver £650 £650
25 2kr. red, blue and silver £650 £650
26 3kr. black, lilac and silver £750 £750
27 5kr. slate, brown and silver £700 £750
28 – 1t. black, violet and gold £650 £650
29 – 3t. red, lake and gold £4750 £4750

BUSSAHIR (BASHAHR) Pt. 1

A state in the Punjab, India. Now uses Indian stamps.

12 pies = 1 anna; 16 annas = 1 rupee.

1

1895. Various frames. Imperf, perf or roul.
9 **1** ¼a. pink 70·00 £100
10 ½a. grey 23·00 £140
11 1a. red 24·00 95·00
12 2a. yellow 32·00 95·00
13 4a. violet 25·00 95·00
14 8a. brown 24·00 £110
15 12a. green 80·00 £130
16 1r. blue 45·00 £120

1896. Similar types, but inscriptions on white ground and inscr "POSTAGE" instead of "STAMP".
27 **1** ¼a. violet 21·00 19·00
37 ¼a. red 4·25 11·00
25 ½a. blue 10·00 19·00
26 1a. olive 18·00 42·00
32 1a. red 4·75 16·00
41 2a. yellow 50·00 80·00
36 4a. red 55·00 £110

CAICOS ISLANDS Pt. 1

Separate issues for these islands, part of the Turks and Caicos Islands group, appeared from 1981 to 1985.

100 cents = 1 dollar.

1981. Nos. 514, 518, 520, 523 and 525/7 of Turks and Caicos Islands optd **CAICOS ISLANDS.**
1 1c. Indigo hamlet 15 15
2 5c. Spanish grunt 20 20
3 8c. Four-eyed butterflyfish 20 20
4 20c. Queen angelfish 35 30
5 50c. Royal gramma ("Fairy Basslet") 40 1·00
6 $1 Fin-spot wrasse 60 1·75
7 $2 Stoplight parrotfish 1·10 3·25

1981. Royal Wedding. Nos. 653/6 of Turks and Caicos Islands optd. (A) **Caicos Islands.**
8A 35c. Prince Charles and Lady Diana Spencer 20 25
9A 65c. Kensington Palace 30 40
10A 90c. Prince Charles as Colonel of the Welsh Guards 40 50
MS11A 96 × 82 mm. $2 Glass Coach 1·00 2·00

(B) **CAICOS ISLANDS.**
8B 35c. Prince Charles and Lady Diana Spencer 30 70
9B 65c. Kensington Palace 40 1·00
10B 90c. Prince Charles as Colonel of the Welsh Guards 50 1·50
MS11B 96 × 82 mm. $2 Glass Coach 1·00 2·50

1981. Royal Wedding. As Nos. 657/9 of Turks and Caicos Islands, but each inscr "Caicos Islands". Mult. Self-adhesive.
12 20c. Lady Diana Spencer 30 40
13 $1 Prince Charles 80 1·25
14 $2 Prince Charles and Lady Diana Spencer 4·00 5·50

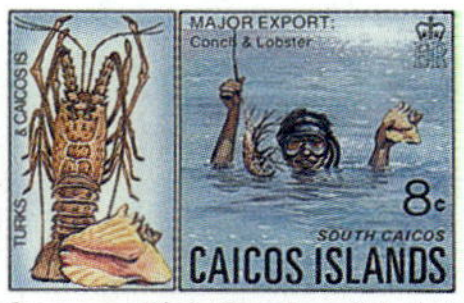

4 Queen or Pink Conch and Lobster Fishing, South Caicos

1983. Multicoloured.
15 8c. Type **4** 1·50 85
16 10c. Hawksbill turtle, East Caicos 1·75 1·00
17 20c. Arawak Indians and idol, Middle Caicos 1·75 1·00
18 35c. Boat-building, North Caicos 2·00 1·50
19 50c. Marine biologist at work, Pine Cay 3·00 2·25
20 95c. Boeing 707 airliner at new airport, Providenciales 5·50 3·00
21 $1.10 Columbus's "Pinta", West Caicos 5·50 3·00
22 $2 Fort George Cay 3·75 4·75
23 $3 Pirates Anne Bonny and Calico Jack at Parrot Cay 6·00 4·75

5 Goofy and Patch

1983. Christmas. Multicoloured.
30 1c. Type **5** 10 30
31 1c. Chip and Dale 10 30
32 2c. Morty 10 30
33 2c. Morty and Ferdie 10 30
34 3c. Goofy and Louie 10 30
35 3c. Donald Duck, Huey, Dewey and Louie 10 30
36 50c. Uncle Scrooge 4·00 3·25
37 70c. Mickey Mouse and Ferdie 4·25 3·75
38 $1.10 Pinocchio, Jiminy Cricket and Figaro 5·00 4·50
MS39 126 × 101 mm. $2 Morty and Ferdie 3·75 3·50

6 "Leda and the Swan"

7 High Jumping

1984. 500th Birth Anniv of Raphael. Mult.
40 35c. Type **6** 75 50
41 50c. "Study of Apollo for Parnassus" 1·00 70
42 95c. "Study of two figures for the battle of Ostia" 2·00 1·25
43 $1.10 "Study for the Madonna of the Goldfinch" 2·00 1·50
MS44 71 × 100 mm. $2.50, "The Garvagh Madonna" 3·00 3·25

1984. Olympic Games, Los Angeles.
45 **7** 4c. multicoloured 10 10
46 – 25c. multicoloured 30 20
47 – 65c. black, deep blue and blue 1·75 50
48 – $1.10 multicoloured 1·25 85
MS49 105 × 75 mm. $2 multicoloured 2·25 3·00
DESIGNS—VERT: 25c. Archery; 65c. Cycling; $1.10, Football. HORIZ: $2.50, Show jumping.

8 Horace Horsecollar and Clarabelle Cow

1984. Easter. Walt Disney Cartoon Characters. Multicoloured.
50 35c. Type **8** 1·40 60
51 45c. Mickey and Minnie Mouse, and Chip 1·50 75
52 75c. Gyro Gearloose, Chip 'n Dale 1·90 1·25
53 85c. Mickey Mouse, Chip 'n Dale 1·90 1·40
MS54 127 × 101 mm. $2.20, Donald Duck 5·50 3·75

1984. Universal Postal Union Congress Hamburg. Nos. 20/1 optd **UNIVERSAL POSTAL UNION 1874–1984** and emblem.
55 95c. Boeing 707 airliner at new airport, Providenciales 1·00 1·25
56 $1.10 Columbus's "Pinta", West Caicos 1·25 1·50

1984. "Ausipex" International Stamp Exhibition, Melbourne. No. 22 optd **AUSIPEX 1984.**
57 $2 Fort George Cay 2·40 2·50

11 Seamen sighting American Manatees

1984. 492nd Anniv of Columbus's First Landfall. Multicoloured.
58 10c. Type **11** 1·00 80
59 70c. Columbus's fleet 3·75 3·25
60 $1 First landing in the West Indies 4·25 3·75
MS61 99 × 69 mm. $2 Fleet of Columbus (different) 2·75 3·00

12 Donald Duck and Mickey Mouse with Father Christmas

1984. Christmas. Walt Disney Cartoon Characters. Multicoloured.
62 20c. Type **12** 1·50 85
63 35c. Donald Duck opening refrigerator 1·75 1·00
64 50c. Mickey Mouse, Donald Duck and toy train 2·50 2·25
65 75c. Donald Duck and parcels 3·00 3·00
66 $1.10 Donald Duck and carol singers 3·25 3·25
MS67 127 × 102 mm. $2 Donald Duck as Christmas tree 3·75 4·00

13 Thick-billed Vireo

1985. Birth Bicentenary of John J. Audubon (ornithologist). Multicoloured.

68		20c. Type **13**	1·75	70
69		35c. Black-faced grassquit	2·00	95
70		50c. Pearly-eyed thrasher	2·25	1·50
71		$1 Greater Antillean bullfinch	2·75	2·50
MS72		100 × 70 mm. $2 Striped-headed tanager	3·50	3·50

14 Two Children learning to Read and Write (Education)

16 The Queen Mother visiting Foundation for the Disabled, Leatherhead

15 Douglas DC-3 on Ground

1985. International Youth Year. 40th Anniv of United Nations. Multicoloured.

73		16c. Type **14**	20	25
74		35c. Two children on playground swings (Health)	50	55
75		70c. Boy and girl (Love)	1·00	1·10
76		90c. Three children (Peace)	1·25	1·40
MS77		101 × 71 mm. $2 Child, dove carrying ears of wheat and map of the Americas	2·75	3·25

1985. 40th Anniv of International Civil Aviation Organization. Multicoloured.

78		35c. Type **15**	3·00	55
79		75c. Convair CV 440 Metropolitan	4·00	1·40
80		90c. Britten Norman Islander	4·00	1·60
MS81		100 × 70 mm. $2.20, Hand-gliding over the Caicos Islands	3·00	3·25

1985. Life and Times of Queen Elizabeth the Queen Mother. Multicoloured.

82		35c. Type **16**	1·25	55
83		65c. With Princess Anne (horiz)	1·75	95
84		95c. At Epsom, 1961	2·25	1·60
MS85		56 × 85 mm. $2 Visiting Royal Hospital, Chelsea	4·75	3·00

1985. 150th Birth Anniv of Mark Twain (author). Designs as T **118** of Anguilla, showing Walt Disney cartoon characters in scenes from "Tom Sawyer, Detective". Multicoloured.

86		8c. Huckleberry Finn (Goofy) and Tom Sawyer (Mickey Mouse) reading reward notice	60	20
87		35c. Huck and Tom meeting Jake Dunlap	1·75	65
88		95c. Huck and Tom spying on Jubiter Dunlap	3·25	2·00
89		$1.10 Huck and Tom with hound (Pluto)	3·25	2·25
MS90		127 × 101 mm. Tom unmasking Jubiter Dunlap	4·75	4·25

1985. Birth Bicentenaries of Grimm Brothers (folklorists). Designs as T **119** of Anguilla, showing Walt Disney cartoon characters in scenes from "Six Soldiers of Fortune". Multicoloured.

91		16c. The Soldier (Donald Duck) with his meagre pay	1·75	30
92		25c. The Soldier meeting the Strong Man (Horace Horsecollar)	2·00	45
93		65c. The Soldier meeting the Marksman (Mickey Mouse)	3·50	1·25
94		$1.35 The Fast Runner (Goofy) winning the race against the Princess (Daisy Duck)	4·25	2·25
MS95		126 × 101 mm. $2 The Soldier and the Strong Man with sack of gold	4·75	4·00

CAMBODIA Pt. 21

A kingdom in south-east Asia.

From 1887 Cambodia was part of the Union of Indo-China. In 1949 it became an Associated State of the French Union, in 1953 it attained sovereign independence and in 1955 it left the Union.

Following the introduction of a republican constitution in 1970 the name of the country was changed to Khmer Republic and in 1975 to Kampuchea.

In 1989 it reverted to the name of Cambodia. Under a new constitution in 1993 it became a parliamentary monarchy.

1951. 100 cents = 1 piastre.
1955. 100 cents = 1 riel.

1 "Apsara" or Dancing Nymph

2 Throne Room, Phnom-Penh

3 King Norodom Sihanouk

5 "Kinnari"

1951.

1	**1**	10c. green and deep green	50	3·50
2		20c. brown and red	45	1·50
3		30c. blue and violet	55	60
4		40c. blue and ultramarine	1·10	90
5	**2**	50c. green and deep green	95	85
6	**3**	80c. green and blue	1·70	4·25
7	**2**	1p. violet and blue	1·30	45
8	**3**	1p.10 red and lake	2·10	4·25
9	**1**	1p.50 red and lake	2·00	1·40
10	**2**	1p.50 blue and indigo	2·10	2·30
11	**3**	1p.50 brown and chocolate	2·10	1·80
12		1p.90 blue and indigo	3·75	6·00
13	**2**	2p. brown and red	2·75	75
14	**3**	3p. brown and red	4·25	2·30
15	**1**	5p. violet and blue	12·50	5·75
16	**2**	10p. blue and violet	13·50	10·50
17	**3**	15p. violet and deep violet	28·00	45·00
MS17a		Three sheets, each 130 × 90 mm. Nos. 15/17. Price for 3 sheets	£120	£100

1952. Students' Aid Fund. Surch **AIDE A L'ETUDIANT** and premium.

18	**3**	1p.10+40c. red and lake	3·50	13·00
19		1p.90+60c. blue & indigo	3·50	13·00
20		3p.+1p. brown and red	3·50	13·00
21	**1**	5p.+2p. violet and blue	3·75	13·00

1953. Air.

22	**5**	50c. green	1·10	2·10
23		3p. red	2·00	1·80
24		3p.30 violet	2·50	5·25
25		4p. blue and brown	2·75	1·20
26		5p.10 ochre, red and brown	4·00	6·75
27		6p.50 purple and brown	3·75	8·75
28		9p. green and mauve	5·00	13·00
29		11p.50 multicoloured	9·75	18·00
30		30p. ochre, brown and green	16·00	26·00
MS30a		Three sheets, each 129 × 100 mm. Nos. 22, 24, 26 and 30 (sold at 50p.); Nos. 23, 25 and 29 (sold at 25p.); Nos. 27/8 (sold at 20p.) Price for 3 sheets	£180	£160

6 Arms of Cambodia

7 "Postal Transport"

1954.

31	–	10c. red	1·20	1·80
32	–	20c. green	1·40	50
33	–	30c. blue	1·40	2·10
34	–	40c. violet	1·40	85
35	–	50c. purple	1·40	25
36	–	70c. brown	1·60	3·25
37	–	1p. violet	1·70	1·80
38	–	1p.50 red	1·70	60
39	**6**	2p. red	1·30	45
40		2p.50 green	1·60	60
41	**7**	2p.50 green	2·50	2·10
42	**6**	3p. blue	2·10	1·70
43	**7**	4p. sepia	3·25	2·75
44	**6**	4p.50 violet	2·75	1·80
45	**7**	5p. red	3·50	2·50
46	**6**	6p. brown	3·00	2·50
47	**7**	10p. violet	4·00	2·75
48		15p. blue	5·00	5·00
49	–	20p. blue	11·50	5·75
50	–	30p. green	18·00	9·75
MS50a		Three sheets, each 120 × 20 mm. Nos. 31/5 (sold at 2p.); Nos. 39/40, 42, 44 and 46 (sold at 20p.); Nos. 41, 43, 45 and 47/8 (sold at 40p.) and one sheet 160 × 92 mm containing Nos. 36/8 and 49/50 (sold at 60p.) Price for 4 sheets	£150	£140

DESIGNS—VERT: 10c. to 50c. View of Phnom Daun Penah. HORIZ: 70c. 1, 1p.50, 20, 30p. East Gate, Temple of Angkor.

8 King Norodom Suramarit

9 King and Queen of Cambodia

1955.

51	–	50c. blue	25	20
52	**8**	50c. violet	35	30
53		1r. red	40	30
54		2r. blue	70	45
55	–	2r.50 brown	1·00	35
56	–	4r. green	1·40	45
57	–	6r. lake	1·90	1·20
58	**8**	7r. brown	2·30	1·40
59	–	15r. lilac	3·25	1·20
60	**8**	20r. green	4·75	4·25

PORTRAIT: Nos. 51, 55/7 and 59, Queen Kossamak.

For stamps as Nos. 58 and 60, but with black border, see Nos. 101/2.

1955. Coronation (1st issue).

61	**9**	1r.50 sepia and brown	75	45
62		2r. black and blue	75	55
63		3r. red and orange	95	30
64		5r. black and green	1·50	55
65		10r. purple and violet	2·50	55

See Nos. 66/71.

10 King Norodom Suramarit

11 Prince Sihanouk, Flags and Globe

1956. Coronation (2nd issue).

66	**10**	2r. red	1·10	2·30
67	–	3r. blue	1·60	3·25
68	–	5r. green	2·40	4·50
69	**10**	10r. green	6·25	9·25
70	–	30r. violet	13·00	22·00
71	–	50r. purple	25·00	25·00

PORTRAIT—VERT: 3, 5, 50r. Queen of Cambodia.

1957. 1st Anniv of Admission of Cambodia to UNO.

72	**11**	2r. red, blue and green	1·20	90
73		4r.50 blue	1·20	90
74		8r.50 red	1·20	90

12

13 Mythological Bird

1957. 2,500th Anniv of Buddhism. (a) With premiums.

75	**12**	1r.50+50c. bis, red & bl	1·40	1·80
76		6r.50+1r.50 bis, red & pur	2·10	2·75
77		8r.+2r. bistre, red & blue	3·50	4·50

(b) Colours changed and premiums omitted.

78	**12**	1r.50 red	1·30	1·00
79		6r.50 violet	1·50	1·20
80		8r. green	1·50	1·50

1957. Air.

81	**13**	50c. lake	35	10
82		1r. green	60	10
83		4r. blue	1·80	45
84		50r. red	7·50	2·75
85		100r. red, green and blue	13·00	5·00
MS85a		160 × 92 mm. Nos. 81/5 (sold at 160r.)	13·00	28·00

14 King Ang Duong

15 King Norodom I

1958. King Ang Duong Commemoration.

86	**14**	1r.50 brown and violet	55	45
87		5r. bistre and black	70	65
88		10r. sepia and purple	1·40	90
MS88a		156 × 92 mm. Nos. 86/8 (sold at 25r.)	6·00	5·00

1958. King Norodom I Commemoration.

89	**15**	2r. brown and blue	60	35
90		6r. green and orange	85	55
91		15r. brown and green	1·70	1·10
MS91a		156 × 92 mm. Nos. 89/91 (sold at 32r.)	6·00	4·50

16 Children

1959. Children's World Friendship.

92	**16**	20c. purple	25	35
93		50c. blue	45	45
94		80c. red	90	85

1959. Red Cross Fund. Nos. 92/4 surch with red cross and premium.

95	**16**	20c.+20c. purple	30	45
96		50c.+30c. blue	65	65
97		80c.+50c. red	1·30	1·20

18 Prince Sihanouk, Plan of Port and Freighter

19 Sacred Plough in Procession

1960. Inauguration of Sihanoukville Port.

98	**18**	2r. sepia and red	55	55
99		5r. brown and blue	55	65
100		20r. blue and violet	2·00	2·00

1960. King Norodom Suramarit Mourning issue. Nos. 58 and 60 reissued with black border.

101	**8**	7r. brown and black	3·00	4·25
102		20r. green and black	3·00	4·25

1960. Festival of the Sacred Furrow.

103	**19**	1r. purple	60	45
104		2r. brown	75	65
105		3r. green	1·20	90

20 Child and Book ("Education")

21 Flag and Dove of Peace

1960. "Works of the Five Year Plan".

106	**20**	2r. brown, blue and green	50	30
107	–	3r. green and brown	65	35
108	–	4r. violet, green and pink	65	45
109	–	6r. brown, orange & green	75	55
110	–	10r. blue, green and bistre	1·80	1·10
111	–	25r. red and lake	3·75	2·20
MS111a		Two sheets, each 150 × 100 mm. Nos. 106, 109 and 111 (sold at 42r.); Nos. 107/8 and 110 (sold at 23r.) Price for 2 sheets	5·25	6·50

DESIGNS—HORIZ: 3r. Chhouksar Barrage ("Irrigation"); 6r. Carpenter and huts ("Construction"); 10r. Rice-field ("Agriculture"). VERT: 4r. Industrial scene and books ("National balance-sheet"); 25r. Anointing children ("Child welfare").

1961. Peace. Flag in red and blue.

112	**21**	1r.50 green and brown	30	45
113		5r. red	45	65
114		7r. blue and green	60	90
MS114a		147 × 93 mm. Nos. 112/14 (sold at 16r.)	20·00	11·00
MS114b		as **MS**114a but stamps in new colours (sold at 20r.)	4·00	11·00

23 Frangipani

24 "Rama" (from temple door, Baphoun)

1961. Cambodian Flowers.
115 **23** 2r. yellow, green & mauve . . 50 55
116 – 5r. mauve, green and blue . . 80 1·10
117 – 10r. red, green and blue . . 2·30 2·00
MS117a 130 × 100 mm. Nos. 115/17 (sold at 20r.) . . . . 7·00 7·00
FLOWERS: 5r. Oleander. 10r. Amaryllis.

1961. Cambodian Soldiers Commemoration.
118 **24** 1r. mauve 50 20
118a 2r. blue . . . . 1·90 1·80
119 3r. green 85 30
120 6r. orange . . . . 1·00 45
MS120a 150 × 85 mm. Nos. 118/20 (sold at 12r.) . . . . 3·25 3·25

25 Prince Norodom Sihanouk and Independence Monument

1961. Independence Monument.
121 **25** 2r. green (postage) 80 35
122 4r. sepia 80 45
123 7r. multicoloured (air) . . 75 75
124 30r. red, blue and green . . 2·30 2·30
125 50r. multicoloured . . . . 3·50 3·75
MS125a Two sheets, each 150 × 85 mm. Nos. 121/2 (sold at 10r.); Nos. 123/5 (sold at 100r.). Price for 2 sheets . . . . . . 15·00 11·00

1961. 6th World Buddhist Conference. Optd **VIe CONFERENCE MONDIALE BOUDDHIQUE 12-11-1961.**
126 **6** 2p.50 (2r.50) green 90 55
127 4p.50 (4r.50) violet . . . . 1·40 85

27 Power Station (Czech Aid)

28 Campaign Emblem

1962. Foreign Aid Programme.
128 **27** 2r. lake and red 30 20
129 – 3r. brown, green and blue . . 35 20
130 – 4r. brown, red and blue . . 35 30
131 – 5r. purple and green . . . 55 35
132 – 6r. brown and blue . . . . 1·00 35
MS132a 150 × 85 mm. Nos. 128/32 (sold at 25r.) . . . . 7·50 5·00
DESIGNS: 3r. Motorway (American Aid); 4r. Textile Factory (Chinese Aid); 5r. Friendship Hospital (Soviet Aid); 6r. Airport (French Aid).

1962. Malaria Eradication.
133 **28** 2r. purple and brown . . . 35 30
134 4r. green and brown . . . 40 35
135 6r. violet and bistre 35 45

29 Curucmas

1962. Cambodian Fruits (1st issue).
136 **29** 2r. yellow and brown . . . 45 45
137 – 4r. green and turquoise . . 65 55
138 – 6r. red, green and blue . . 75 85
MS138a 150 × 85 mm. Nos. 136/8 (sold at 15r.) . . . . 6·00 3·75
FRUITS: 4r. Lychees. 6r. Mangosteens.

1962. Cambodian Fruits (2nd issue).
139 2r. brown and green 75 35
140 5r. green and brown . . . . 1·10 55
141 9r. brown and green . . . . 1·30 75
DESIGNS—VERT: 2r. Pineapples. 5r. Sugar-cane. 9r. "Bread" trees.

1962. Surch.
142 **16** 50c. on 80c. red 55 35
150 – 3r. on 2r.50 brn (No. 55) . . 75 45

1962. Inauguration of Independence Monument. Surch **INAUGURATION DU MONUMENT** and new value.
143 **25** 3r. on 2r. green (postage) . . 55 35
144 12r. on 7r. mult (air) . . . 1·50 1·00

32 Campaign Emblem, Corn and Maize

33 Temple Preah Vihear

1963. Freedom from Hunger.
145 **32** 3r. chestnut, brown & blue 50 45
146 6r. chestnut, brown & blue 50 45

1963. Reunification of Preah Vihear Temple with Cambodia.
147 **33** 3r. brown, purple & green 40 35
148 6r. green, orange and blue 70 55
149 15r. brown, blue & green 1·10 90

35 Kep sur Mer

1963. Cambodian Resorts. Multicoloured.
151 3r. Koh Tonsay (vert) . . . 40 30
152 7r. Popokvil (waterfall) (vert) 65 35
153 20r. Type **35** . . . . 2·10 90

1963. Red Cross Centenary. Surch **1863 1963 CENTENAIRE DE LA CROIX-ROUGE** and premium.
154 **28** 4r.+40c. green & brown . . 65 75
155 6r.+60c. violet & bistre . . 1·00 1·10

37 Scales of Justice

1963. 15th Anniv of Declaration of Human Rights.
156 **37** 1r. green, red and blue . . 40 45
157 3r. red, blue and green . . 70 55
158 12r. blue, green and red . . 1·30 1·30

38 Kouprey

39 Black-billed Magpie

1964. Wild Animal Protection.
159 **38** 50c. brown, green & chest 85 35
160 3r. brown, chestnut & grn 1·20 55
161 6r. brown, blue and green 1·80 1·10

1964. Birds.
162 **39** 3r. blue, green and indigo 1·10 65
163 – 6r. orange, purple & blue 1·80 1·00
164 – 12r. green and purple . . . 3·25 2·00
BIRDS: 6r. River kingfisher. 12r. Grey heron.

40 "Hanuman"

42 Airline Emblem

1964. Air.
165 **40** 5r. mauve, brown & blue 65 45
166 10r. bistre, mauve & green 1·00 55
167 20r. bistre, violet and blue 1·70 1·10
168 40r. bistre, blue and red . . 3·75 2·00
169 80r. orange, green & purple 6·00 5·00

1964. Air Olympic Games, Tokyo. Surch **JEUX OLYMPIQUES TOKYO-1964**, Olympic rings and value.
170 **40** 3r. on 5r. mve, brn and bl 60 35
171 6r. on 10r. bis, mve & grn 1·00 55
172 9r. on 20r. bistre, vio & bl 1·10 90
173 12r. on 40r. bis, bl & red 2·30 1·40

1964. 8th Anniv of Royal Air Cambodia.
174 **42** 1r.50 red and violet 25 20
175 3r. red and blue 45 30
176 7r.50 red and blue 90 45

43 Prince Norodom Sihanouk

44 Weaving

1964. 10th Anniv of Foundation of Sangkum (Popular Socialist Community).
177 **43** 2r. violet 45 30
178 3r. brown 60 35
179 10r. blue . . . . 1·20 75

1965. Native Handicrafts.
180 **44** 1r. violet, brown & bistre 30 30
181 – 3r. brown, green & purple 55 35
182 – 5r. red, purple and green 85 75
DESIGNS: 3r. Engraving. 5r. Basket-making.

1965. Indo-Chinese People's Conference. Nos. 178/9 optd **CONFERENCE DES PEUPLES INDOCHINOIS.**
183 **43** 3r. brown 45 45
184 10r. blue 70 65

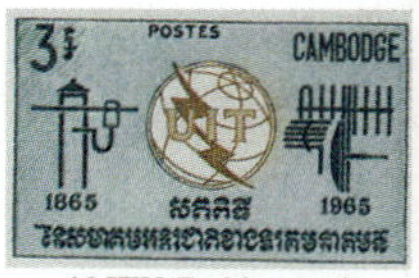

46 ITU Emblem and Symbols

47 Cotton

1965. Centenary of ITU.
185 **46** 3r. bistre and green 35 35
186 4r. blue and red 45 55
187 10r. purple and violet . . . 75 75

1965. Industrial Plants. Multicoloured.
188 1r.50 Type **47** 45 30
189 3r. Groundnuts 70 35
190 7r.50 Coconut palms . . . . 1·10 75

48 Preah Ko

1966. Cambodian Temples.
191 **48** 3r. green, turquoise & brn 75 45
192 – 5r. brown, green & purple 95 55
193 – 7r. brown, green & ochre 1·30 65
194 – 9r. purple, green and blue 2·20 90
195 – 12r. red, green & verm . . 2·75 1·60
TEMPLES: 5r. Baksei Chamkrong, 7r. Banteay Srei, 9r. Angkor Vat. 12r. Bayon.

49 WHO Building

1966. Inaug of WHO Headquarters, Geneva.
196 **49** 2r. multicoloured 30 20
197 3r. multicoloured 35 30
198 5r. multicoloured 60 45

50 Tree-planting

51 UNESCO Emblem

1966. Tree Day.
199 **50** 1r. brown, green & dp brn 25 30
200 3r. brown, green & orange 40 35
201 7r. brown, green and grey 70 45

1966. 20th Anniv of UNESCO.
202 **51** 3r. multicoloured 35 30
203 7r. multicoloured 45 55

52 Stadium

1966. "Ganefo" Games, Phnom Penh.
204 **52** 3r. blue 15 20
205 – 4r. green 20 35
206 – 7r. red 30 55
207 – 10r. brown 40 75
DESIGNS: 4r., 7r., 10r. Various bas-reliefs of ancient sports from Angkor Vat.

53 Wild Boar

56 Ballet Dancer

1967. Fauna.
208 **53** 3r. black, green and blue 70 45
209 – 5r. multicoloured 80 75
210 – 7r. multicoloured . . . . . 1·30 1·10
FAUNA—VERT: 5r. Hog-deer. HORIZ: 7r. Indian elephant.

1967. International Tourist Year. Nos. 191/2, 194/5 and 149 optd **ANNEE INTERNATIONALE DU TOURISME 1967.**
211 **48** 3r. green, turquoise & brn 65 45
212 5r. brown, green & purple 75 45
213 – 9r. purple, green and blue 1·10 75
214 – 12r. red, green & verm . . 1·30 90
215 **33** 15r. brown, blue & green 1·60 1·10

1967. Millenary of Banteay Srei Temple. No. 193 optd **MILLENAIRE DE BANTEAY SREI 967–1967.**
216 7r. brown, green and ochre 1·10 45

1967. Cambodian Royal Ballet. Designs showing ballet dancers.
217 **56** 1r. orange 30 35
218 – 3r. blue 65 35
219 – 5r. blue 85 45
220 – 7r. red . . . . 1·30 65
221 – 10r. multicoloured . . . . 1·70 90

1967. Int Literacy Day. Surch **Journee Internationale de l'Alphabetisation 8-9-67** and new value.
222 **37** 6r. on 12r. blue, grn & red 70 35
223 **15** 7r. on 15r. brown & green 85 55

58 Decade Emblem

59 Royal University of Kompong-Cham

1967. International Hydrological Decade.
224 **58** 1r. orange, blue and black 20 20
225 6r. orange, blue and violet 40 35
226 10r. orange, lt green & grn 60 55

1968. Cambodian Universities and Institutes.
227 **59** 4r. purple, blue & brown 40 30
228 – 6r. brown, green and blue 55 35
229 – 9r. brown, green and blue 75 45
DESIGNS: 6r. "Khmero-Soviet Friendship" Higher Technical Institute; 9r. Sangkum Reaster Niyum University Centre.

60 Doctor tending child

1968. 20th Anniv of WHO.
230 **60** 3r. blue 45 30
231 – 7r. blue 65 45
DESIGN: 7r. Man using insecticide.

61 Stadium

1968. Olympic Games, Mexico.
232 **61** 1r. brown, green and red . . . 40 30
233 – 2r. brown, red and blue . . 45 35
234 – 3r. brown, blue and purple 55 35
235 – 5r. violet 60 35
236 – 7r.50 brown, green & red 85 45
DESIGNS—HORIZ: 2r. Wrestling; 3r. Cycling. VERT: 5r. Boxing; 7r.50, Runner with torch.

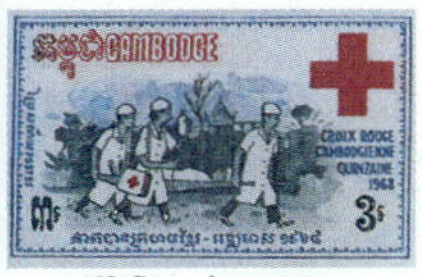
62 Stretcher-party

1968. Cambodian Red Cross Fortnight.
237 **62** 3r. red, green and blue . . 70 30

63 Prince Norodom Sihanouk

1968. 15th Anniv of Independence.
238 **63** 7r. violet, green and blue 45 45
239 – 8r. brown, green and blue 45 65
DESIGN: 8r. Soldiers wading through stream.

64 Human Rights Emblem and Prince Norodom Sihanouk

1968. Human Rights Year.
240 **64** 3r. blue 30 20
241 5r. purple 65 30
242 7r. black, orange & green 95 45

65 ILO Emblem

1969. 50th Anniv of ILO.
243 **65** 3r. blue 25 20
244 6r. red 40 30
245 9r. green 65 45

66 Red Cross Emblems around Globe

1969. 50th Anniv of League of Red Cross Societies.
246 **66** 1r. multicoloured 30 20
247 3r. multicoloured 40 30
248 10r. multicoloured 85 45

67 Golden Birdwing

1969. Butterflies.
249 **67** 3r. black, yellow & violet 1·40 55
250 – 4r. black, green & verm . . 1·40 85
251 – 8r. black, orange & green 1·80 1·40
DESIGNS: 4r. Tailed jay. 8r. Orange tiger.

68 Diesel Train and Route Map

1969. Opening of Phnom Penh–Sihanoukville Railway.
252 **68** 3r. multicoloured 30 30
253 – 6r. brown, black & green 45 30
254 – 8r. black 75 35
255 – 9r. blue, turquoise & grn 85 45
DESIGNS: 6r. Phnom Penh Station; 8r. Diesel locomotive and Kampor Station; 9r. Steam locomotive at Sihanoukville Station.

69 Siamese Tigerfish

1970. Fishes. Multicoloured.
256 3r. Type **69** 75 65
257 7r. Marbled sleeper . . . . . 1·50 1·10
258 9r. Chevron snakehead . . . 2·40 1·50

70 Vat Tepthidaram

71 Dish Aerial and Open Book

1970. Buddhist Monasteries in Cambodia. Mult.
259 2r. Type **70** 40 30
260 3r. Vat Maniratanaram (horiz) 45 30
261 6r. Vat Patumavati (horiz) . . 85 35
262 8r. Vat Unnalom (horiz) . . 1·60 45

1970. World Telecommunications Day.
263 **71** 3r. multicoloured 15 20
264 4r. multicoloured 25 20
265 9r. multicoloured 40 35

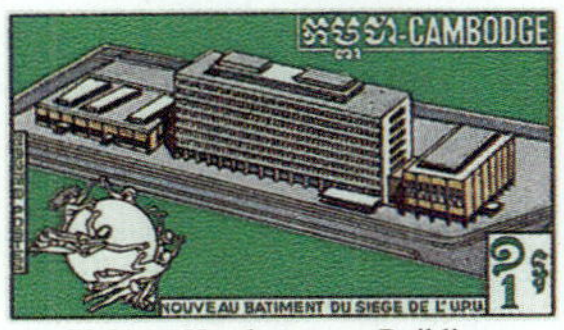
72 New Headquarters Building

1970. Opening of New UPU Headquarters Building, Berne.
266 **72** 1r. multicoloured 20 10
267 3r. multicoloured 30 10
268 4r. multicoloured 55 10
269 10r. multicoloured . . . . 1·10 35

73 "Nelumbium speciosum"

1970. Aquatic Plants. Multicoloured.
270 3r. Type **73** 40 55
271 4r. "Eichhornia crassipes" . . 60 55
272 13r. "Nymphea lotus" . . . 1·10 85

74 "Banteay-srei" (bas-relief)

1970. World Meteorological Day.
273 **74** 3r. red and green 30 10
274 4r. red, green and blue . . 45 30
275 7r. green, blue and black 60 55

75 Rocket, Dove and Globe

1970. 25th Anniv of United Nations.
276 **75** 3r. multicoloured 25 20
277 5r. multicoloured 45 35
278 10r. multicoloured 65 55

76 IEY Emblem

1970. International Education Year.
279 **76** 1r. blue 15 10
280 3r. purple 20 10
281 8r. green 50 35

77 Samdech Chuon Nath

1971. 2nd Death Anniv of Samdech Chuon-Nath (Khmer language scholar).
282 **77** 3r. multicoloured 25 10
283 8r. multicoloured 60 30
284 9r. multicoloured 75 45

For issues between 1971 and 1989 see under KHMER REPUBLIC and KAMPUCHEA in volume 3.

203 17th-century Coach

1989. Coaches. Multicoloured.
1020 2r. Type **203** 10 10
1021 3r. Paris–Lyon coach, 1720 15 10
1022 5r. Mail coach, 1793 . . . . 25 10
1023 10r. Light mail coach, 1805 55 20
1024 15r. Royal mail coach . . . 80 30
1025 20r. Russian mail coach . . 95 35
1026 35r. Paris–Lille coupe, 1837 (vert) . . . . 1·90 55
MS1027 60 × 84 mm. 45r. Royal messenger coach, 1815 (31 × 39 mm) . . . . 4·25 90
No. **MS**1027 commemorates "Philexfrance '89" International Stamp Exhibition, Paris.

204 "Papilio zagreus"

1989. "Brasiliana 89" International Stamp Exhibition, Rio de Janeiro. Butterflies. Multicoloured.
1028 2r. Type **204** 10 10
1029 3r. "Morpho catenarius" . . 15 10
1030 5r. "Morpho aega" 25 10
1031 10r. "Callithea sapphira" ("wrongly inscr "saphhira") 50 10
1032 15r. "Catagramma sorana" 75 20
1033 20r. "Pierella nereis" . . . 95 20
1034 35r. "Papilio brasiliensis" 1·90 20
MS1035 100 × 66 mm. 45r. *Thecla marsyas* (39 × 31 mm) . . . . 5·25 90

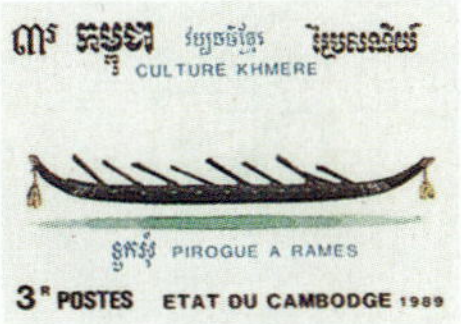
205 Pirogue

1989. Khmer Culture. Multicoloured.
1036 3r. Type **205** 20 10
1037 12r. Pirogue (two sets of oars) 80 35
1038 30r. Pirogue with cabin . . 2·10 90

206 Youth

207 Goalkeeper

1989. National Development. Multicoloured.
1039 3r. Type **206** 20 10
1040 12r. Trade unions emblem (horiz) 60 20
1041 30r. National Front emblem (horiz) . . . . 1·70 75

1990. World Cup Football Championship, Italy. Multicoloured.
1042 2r. Type **207** 10 10
1043 3r. Dribbling ball 15 10
1044 5r. Controlling ball with thigh 25 10
1045 10r. Running with ball . . . 55 10
1046 15r. Shooting 80 20
1047 20r. Tackling 95 20
1048 35r. Tackling (different) . . 1·90 20
MS1049 94 × 75 mm. 45r. Players (31 × 39 mm) . . . . 4·25 90

208 Two-horse Postal Van

1990. "Stamp World London 90" International Stamp Exhibition. Royal Mail Horse-drawn Transport. Multicoloured.
1050 2r. Type **208** 10 10
1051 3r. One-horse cart 10 10
1052 5r. Rural post office cart . . 15 10
1053 10r. Rural post office van 25 10
1054 15r. Local post office van 40 20
1055 20r. Parcel-post cart 55 20
1056 35r. Two-horse wagon . . . 1·10 20
MS1057 69 × 80 mm. 45r. Rural one-horse van (39 × 31 mm) . . . . 4·25 90

209 Rice Grains

210 Shooting

1990. Cultivation of Rice. Multicoloured.
1058 3r. Type **209** 20 10
1059 12r. Transporting rice (horiz) 80 35
1060 30r. Threshing rice . . . . 2·10 90

1990. Olympic Games, Barcelona (1992) (1st issue). Multicoloured.
1061 2r. Type **210** 10 10
1062 3r. Putting the shot 15 10
1063 5r. Weightlifting 25 10
1064 10r. Boxing 55 10
1065 15r. Pole vaulting 80 20
1066 20r. Basketball . . . . . . 1·10 20
1067 35r. Fencing . . . . 1·90 20
MS1068 83 × 70 mm. 45r. Gymnastics (31 × 37 mm) . . . 4·25 90
See also Nos. 1163/**MS**1170, 1208/**MS**1213 and 1241/**MS**1246.

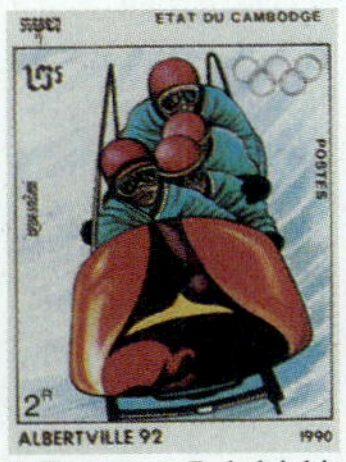
211 Four-man Bobsleighing

1990. Winter Olympic Games, Albertville (1992) (1st issue). Multicoloured.
1069 2r. Type **211** 10 10
1070 3r. Speed skating 15 10
1071 5r. Figure skating 20 10
1072 10r. Ice hockey 45 10
1073 15r. Biathlon 70 20
1074 20r. Lugeing 90 20
1075 35r. Ski jumping . . . . . 1·70 20
MS1076 64 × 104 mm. Ice hockey goalkeeper (31 × 38 mm) . . . 4·25 90
See also Nos. 1152/**MS**1159.

212 Facade of Banteay Srei

1990. Khmer Culture. Multicoloured.

1077 3r. Type **212** 20 10
1078 12r. Ox-carts (12th-century relief) 80 35
1079 30r. Banon ruins (36 × 21 mm) . . . . . . 2·10 90

213 "Zizina oxleyi"

1990. "New Zealand 1990" International Stamp Exhibition, Auckland. Butterflies. Multicoloured.

1080 2r. Type **213** 10 10
1081 3r. "Cupha prosope" 10 10
1082 5r. "Heteronympha merope" . 15 10
1083 10r. "Dodonidia helmsi" . . 30 20
1084 15r. "Argirophenga antipodum" 55 20
1085 20r. "Tysonotis danis" 80 20
1086 35r. "Pyrameis gonnarilla" 1·20 30
MS1087 76 × 65 mm. 45r. "Pyrameis itea" (39 × 31 mm) . . . . . . 5·75 1·10

214 "Vostok"

1990. Spacecraft. Multicoloured.

1088 2r. Type **214** 10 10
1089 3r. "Soyuz" 10 10
1090 5r. Satellite 15 10
1091 10r. "Luna 10" 35 20
1092 15r. "Mars 1" 55 30
1093 20r. "Venus 3" 70 35
1094 35r. "Mir" space station . . 1·10 75
MS1095 92 × 72 mm. 45r. "Energiya" and space shuttle "Burn" (31 × 39 mm) . . . . 5·25 90

215 Poodle

1990. Dogs. Multicoloured.

1096 20c. Type **215** 20 10
1097 80c. Shetland sheepdog . . 20 10
1098 3r. Samoyede 45 10
1099 6r. Springer spaniel 85 10
1100 10r. Wire-haired fox terrier 1·10 20
1101 15r. Afghan hound . . . . 1·70 20
1102 25r. Dalmatian . . . . . . 2·30 20
MS1103 95 × 83 mm. Burmese mountain dog (39 × 31 mm) . . . 4·25 90

216 "Cereus hexagonus"

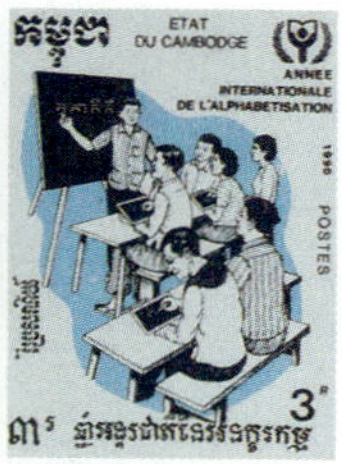
217 Learning to Write

1990. Cacti. Multicoloured.

1104 20c. Type **216** 10 10
1105 80c. "Arthrocereus rondonianus" 10 10
1106 3r. "Matucana multicolor" 15 10
1107 6r. "Hildewintera aureispina" 25 10
1108 10r. "Opuntia retrosa" . . . 50 20
1109 15r. "Erdisia tenuicula" . . 75 20
1110 25r. "Mamillaria yaquensis" 1·10 20

1990. International Literacy Year.

1111 **217** 3r. black and blue . . . 15 10
1112 12r. black and yellow . . 1·10 35
1113 30r. black and pink . . . 3·50 90

218 English Nef, 1200

1990. Ships. Multicoloured.

1114 20c. Type **218** 20 10
1115 80c. 16th-century Spanish galleon 30 10
1116 3r. Dutch jacht, 1627 . . . . 45 10
1117 6r. "La Couronne" (French galleon), 1638 . . . . . . 85 10
1118 10r. Dumont d'Urville's ship "L'Astrolabe", 1826 . . . 1·10 20
1119 15r. "Louisiane" (steamer), 1864 . . . . 1·90 20
1120 25r. Clipper, 1900 (vert) . . 2·30 20
MS1121 97 × 80 mm. 45r. 19th-century merchant brig (31 × 39 mm) . . . . 4·75 90
No. 1118 is wrongly inscribed "d'Uville".

219 Phnom-Penh–Kampong Som Railway

1990. National Development. Multicoloured.

1122 3r. Type **219** 30 10
1123 12r. Port, Kampong Som 1·30 35
1124 30r. Fishing boats, Kampong Som . . . . . 3·75 90

220 Sacre-Coeur de Montmartre and White Bishop

221 Columbus

1990. "Paris '90" World Chess Championship, Paris. Multicoloured.

1125 2r. Type **220** 20 10
1126 3r. "The Horse Trainer" (statue) and white knight 30 10
1127 5r. "Victory of Samothrace" (statue) and white queen 45 10
1128 10r. Azay-le-Rideau Chateau and white rook 95 20
1129 15r. "The Dance" (statue) and white pawn . . . . . 1·40 30
1130 20r. Eiffel Tower and white king . . . . 1·90 35
1131 35r. Arc de Triomphe and black chessmen . . . . . 3·25 55
MS1132 91 × 58 mm. 45r. White chessmen (39 × 31 mm) . . . . 5·25 1·10

1990. 500th Anniv (1992) of Discovery of America by Columbus (1st issue). Multicoloured.

1133 2r. Type **221** 30 10
1134 3r. Queen Isabella's jewel-chest 45 10
1135 5r. Queen Isabella the Catholic 55 10
1136 10r. "Santa Maria" (flagship) 95 10
1137 15r. Juan de la Cosa . . . . 1·40 10
1138 20r. Monument to Columbus . . . . 1·90 20
1139 35r. Devin Pyramid, Yucatan . . . . 3·50 20
MS1140 79 × 60 mm. 45r. Christopher Columbus (31 × 39 mm) . . . . 5·25 90
See also Nos. 1186/**MS**1193.

222 Tyre Factory

1991. National Festival. Multicoloured.

1141 100r. Type **222** 55 20
1142 300r. Rural hospital . . . . 2·10 90
1143 500r. Freshwater fishing (27 × 40 mm) . . . . . . 3·25 1·20

223 Tackle

224 Speed Skating

1991. World Cup Football Championship, U.S.A. (1994) (1st issue).

1144 **223** 5r. multicoloured 15 10
1145 – 25r. multicoloured . . . 15 10
1146 – 70r. multicoloured . . . 35 10
1147 – 100r. multicoloured . . . 40 10
1148 – 200r. multicoloured . . . 75 20
1149 – 400r. multicoloured . . . 1·50 20
1150 – 1000r. multicoloured . . . 3·50 20
MS1151 85 × 93 mm. 900r. multicoloured . . . . 5·25 90
DESIGNS: 25r. to 1000r. Different footballing scenes.
See also Nos. 1220/**MS**1225, 1317/**MS**1322 and 1381/**MS**1386.

1991. Winter Olympic Games, Albertville (1992) (2nd issue). Multicoloured.

1152 5r. Type **224** 20 10
1153 25r. Slalom skiing 30 10
1154 70r. Ice hockey 55 10
1155 100r. Bobsleighing 65 10
1156 200r. Freestyle skiing . . . 1·30 20
1157 400r. Ice skating . . . . . 2·50 20
1158 1000r. Downhill skiing . . . 3·75 20
MS1159 87 × 62 mm. 900r. Ski jumping (31 × 39 mm) . . . . 5·25 90

225 "Torso of Vishnu Reclining" (11th cent)

1991. Sculpture. Multicoloured.

1160 100r. "Garuda" (Koh Ker, 10th century) 35 20
1161 300r. Type **225** . . . . . . 1·10 90
1162 500r. "Reclining Nandin" (7th century) . . . . . . 1·90 1·10

226 Pole Vaulting

1991. Olympic Games, Barcelona (1992) (2nd issue). Multicoloured.

1163 5r. Type **226** 20 10
1164 25r. Table tennis 30 10
1165 70r. Running 45 10
1166 100r. Wrestling 55 10
1167 200r. Gymnastics (bars) . . 95 20
1168 400r. Tennis . . . . 1·80 20
1169 1000r. Boxing . . . . . . 4·25 20
MS1170 78 × 73 mm. 900r. Gymnastics (beam) (31 × 39 mm) 5·25 90

227 Douglas DC-10-30

1991. Airplanes. Multicoloured.

1171 5r. Type **227** 15 10
1172 25r. McDonnell Douglas MD-11 . . . . 20 10
1173 70r. Ilyushin Il-96-300 . . . 30 10
1174 100r. Airbus Industrie A310 40 10
1175 200r. Yakovlev Yak-42 . . 80 20
1176 400r. Tupolev Tu-154 . . . 1·50 20
1177 1000r. Douglas DC-9 . . . 3·75 20

228 Diaguita Funerary Urn, Catamarca

1991. "Espamer '91" Iberia–Latin America Stamp Exhibition, Buenos Aires. Multicoloured.

1178 5r. Bareales glass pot, Catamarca (horiz) 15 10
1179 25r. Type **228** 20 10
1180 70r. Quiroga urn, Tucuman 30 10
1181 100r. Round glass pot, Santiago del Estero (horiz) 45 10
1182 200r. Pitcher, Santiago del Estero (horiz) 85 20
1183 400r. Diaguita funerary urn, Tucuman . . . . 1·60 20
1184 1000r. Bareales funerary urn, Catamarca (horiz) . . 4·00 20
MS1185 80 × 65 mm. 900r. Funerary urn, Catamarce (36 × 27 mm) 5·25 90

229 "Pinta"

1991. 500th Anniv (1992) of Discovery of America by Columbus (2nd issue). Each brown, stone and black.

1186 5r. Type **229** 20 10
1187 25r. "Nina" 30 10
1188 70r. "Santa Maria" 55 10
1189 100r. Landing at Guanahani, 1492 (horiz) 65 10
1190 200r. Meeting of two cultures (horiz) . . . . . 1·30 20
1191 400r. La Navidad (first European settlement in America) (horiz) . . . . 2·50 20
1192 1000r. Amerindian village (horiz) . . . . 5·75 20
MS1193 84 × 59 mm. Columbus (39 × 31 mm) . . . . 5·75 90

230 "Neptis pryeri"

1991. "Phila Nippon '91" International Stamp Exhibition, Tokyo. Butterflies. Multicoloured.

1194 5r. Type **230** 15 10
1195 25r. "Papilio xuthus" . . . 15 10
1196 70r. Common map butterfly 10 10
1197 100r. "Argynnis anadiomene" 40 10
1198 200r. "Lethe marginalis" . . 75 20
1199 400r. "Artopoetes pryeri" . . 95 20
1200 1000r. African monarch . . 3·50 20
MS1201 73 × 57 mm 900r. "Ochlodes subhyalina" (39 × 31 mm) . . . . 5·25 1·10

231 Coastal Fishing Port

1991. National Development. Food Industry. Multicoloured.

1202 100r. Type **231** 50 45
1203 300r. Preparing palm sugar (29 × 40 mm) . . . . . . 1·40 90
1204 500r. Picking peppers . . . 2·40 1·20

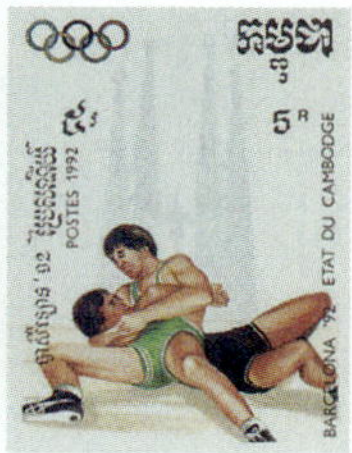

232 Chakdomuk Costumes

233 Wrestling

1992. National Festival. Traditional Costumes. Multicoloured.

1205	150r. Type **232**	50	20
1206	350r. Longvek	1·40	30
1207	1000r. Angkor	2·50	45

1992. Olympic Games, Barcelona (3rd issue). Multicoloured.

1208	5r. Type **233**	15	10
1209	15r. Football	15	10
1210	80r. Weightlifting	20	10
1211	400r. Archery	1·00	30
1212	1500r. Gymnastics	3·50	35
MS1213	79 × 59 mm. 1000r. show jumping (31 × 39 mm)	4·25	90

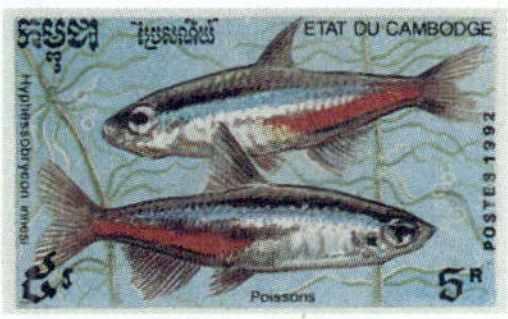

234 Neon Tetra

1992. Fishes. Multicoloured.

1214	5r. Type **234**	15	10
1215	15r. Siamese fighting fish	15	10
1216	80r. Kaiser tetra	20	10
1217	400r. Dwarf gourami	1·00	30
1218	1500r. Port hoplo	3·50	35
MS1219	80 × 65 mm. 1000r. Freshwater angelfish (39 × 31 mm)	4·25	90

235 Germany v. Columbia

236 Monument

1992. World Cup Football Championship, U.S.A. (1994) (2nd issue). Multicoloured.

1220	5r. Type **235**	15	10
1221	15r. Netherlands player (horiz)	15	10
1222	80r. Uruguay v. C.I.S. (ex-Soviet states)	20	10
1223	400r. Cameroun v. Yugoslavia	1·00	30
1224	1500r. Italy v. Sweden	3·50	35
MS1225	75 × 51 mm. 1000r. Shot at goal (39 × 31 mm)	4·25	90

1992. Khmer Culture. 19th-century Architecture. Multicoloured.

1226	150r. Type **236**	55	35
1227	350r. Stupa	1·30	85
1228	1000r. Mandapa library	3·50	2·00

237 Motor Car

1992. 540th Birth Anniv (1992) of Leonardo da Vinci (artist and inventor). Multicoloured.

1229	5r. Type **237**	20	10
1230	15r. Container ship	20	10
1231	80r. Helicopter	30	10
1232	400r. Scuba diver	1·50	30
1233	1500r. Parachutists (vert)	4·75	35
MS1234	79 × 59 mm. 1000r. Da Vinci and drawing of "Flying Man" (31 × 39 mm)	4·75	90

238 Juan de la Cierva and Autogyro

1992. "Expo '92" World's Fair, Seville. Inventors. Multicoloured (except **MS**1240).

1235	5r. Type **238**	20	10
1236	15r. Thomas Edison and electric light bulb	20	10
1237	80r. Samuel Morse and Morse telegraph	30	10
1238	400r. Narciso Monturiol and "Ictineo" (early submarine)	1·40	30
1239	1500r. Alexander Graham Bell and early telephone	2·75	35
MS1240	83 × 62 mm. 1000r. pink and black (Robert Fulton (steamship)) (31 × 39 mm)	4·75	90

239 Weightlifting

1992. Olympic Games, Barcelona (4th issue). Multicoloured.

1241	5r. Type **239**	20	10
1242	15r. Boxing	20	10
1243	80r. Basketball	30	10
1244	400r. Running	1·40	30
1245	1500r. Water polo	4·75	35
MS1246	71 × 75 mm. 1000r. Gymnastics (39 × 31 mm)	4·50	90

240 Palm Trees

1992. Environmental Protection. Multicoloured.

1247	5r. Couple on riverside	20	10
1248	15r. Pagoda	20	10
1249	80r. Type **240**	30	10
1250	400r. Boy riding water buffalo	1·40	30
1251	1500r. Swimming in river	4·75	35
MS1252	100 × 71 mm. 1000r. Angkor Wat (39 × 31 mm)	4·50	90

241 Louis de Bougainville and "La Boudeuse"

242 "Albatrellus confluens"

1992. "Genova '92" International Thematic Stamp Exhibition, Genoa. Multicoloured.

1253	5r. Type **241**	20	10
1254	15r. James Cook and H.M.S. "Endeavour"	30	10
1255	80r. Charles Darwin and H.M.S. "Beagle"	45	10
1256	400r. Jacques Cousteau and "Calypso"	1·50	30
1257	1500r. "Kon Tiki" (replica of balsa raft)	5·25	35
MS1258	80 × 65 mm. 1000r. Christopher Columbus (28 × 36 mm)	4·50	90

1992. Fungi. Multicoloured.

1259	5r. Type **242**	15	10
1260	15r. Scarlet-stemmed boletus	20	10
1261	80r. Verdigris agaric	25	10
1262	400r. "Telamonia armillata"	1·00	30
1263	1500r. Goaty smell cortinarius	3·75	35

243 Bellanca Pacemaker Seaplane, 1930

1992. Aircraft. Multicoloured.

1264	5r. Type **243**	20	10
1265	15r. Canadair CL-215 fire-fighting amphibian, 1965	20	10
1266	80r. Grumman G-21 Goose amphibian, 1937	30	10
1267	400r. Grumman SA-6 Sealand flying boat, 1947	1·30	30
1268	1500r. Short S.23 Empire "C" Class flying boat, 1936	4·50	35
MS1269	80 × 60 mm. Grumman G-44 Widgeon, 1940 (31 × 39 mm)	4·50	90

244 Dish Aerial

1992. National Development. Multicoloured.

1270	150r. Type **244**	55	20
1271	350r. Dish aerial, flags and satellite	1·30	30
1272	1000r. Hotel Cambodiana	4·00	45

245 Sociological Institute

1993. National Festival. Multicoloured.

1273	50r. Type **245**	45	20
1274	450r. Motel Cambodiana	1·40	30
1275	1000r. Theatre, Bassac	4·00	45

246 Bottle-nosed Dolphin and Submarine

1993. Wildlife and Technology. Multicoloured.

1276	150r. Type **246**	55	10
1277	200r. Supersonic jet airplane and peregrine falcon	65	20
1278	250r. Eurasian beaver and dam	75	20
1279	500r. Satellite and natterer's bat	2·00	20
1280	900r. Rufous humming-bird and helicopter	3·00	30

247 "Datura suaveolens"

1993. Wild Flowers. Multicoloured.

1281	150r. Type **247**	55	10
1282	200r. "Convolvulus tricolor"	65	20
1283	250r. "Hippeastrum" hybrid	75	20
1284	500r. "Camellia" hybrid	1·90	20
1285	900r. "Lilium speciosum"	3·00	30
MS1286	75 × 50 mm. 1000t. Various flowers (31 × 39 mm)	4·50	1·10

248 Vihear Temple

1993. Khmer Culture. Multicoloured.

1287	50r. Sculpture of ox	45	20
1288	450r. Type **248**	1·30	75
1289	1000r. Offering to Buddha	3·75	1·70

249 Philippine Flying Lemur

1993. Animals. Multicoloured.

1290	150r. Type **249**	55	20
1291	200r. Red giant flying squirrel	65	20
1292	250r. Fringed gecko	75	30
1293	500r. Wallace's flying frog	2·00	35
1294	900r. Flying lizard	3·00	65

250 "Symbrenthia hypselis"

1993. "Brasiliana '93" International Stamp Exhibition, Rio de Janeiro. Butterflies. Mult.

1295	250r. Type **250**	75	20
1296	350r. "Sithon nedymond"	1·30	20
1297	600r. "Geitoneura minyas"	1·90	30
1298	800r. "Argyreus hyperbius"	2·40	35
1299	1000r. "Argyrophenga antipodum"	3·25	65
MS1300	82 × 52 mm. 1500r. "Parage schakra" (39 × 31 mm)	5·75	1·10

251 Armed Cambodians reporting to U.N. Base

253 Santos-Dumont, Eiffel Tower and "Ballon No. 6", 1901

252 Venetian Felucca

1993. United Nations Transitional Authority in Cambodia Pacification Programme. Each black and blue.

1301	150r. Type **251**	55	10
1302	200r. Military camp	65	20
1303	250r. Surrender of arms	75	20
1304	500r. Vocational training	1·70	20
1305	900r. Liberation	2·75	30
MS1306	54 × 84 mm. 1000r. Return to homes (31 × 39 mm)	4·75	1·10

1993. Sailing Ships. Multicoloured.

1307	150r. Type **252**	40	10
1308	200r. Phoenician galley	50	20
1309	250r. Egyptian merchantman	65	20
1310	500r. Genoese merchantman	1·50	20
1311	900r. English merchantman	2·40	30

1993. 120th Birth Anniv of Alberto Santos-Dumont (aviator). Multicoloured.

1312	150r. Type **253**	55	10
1313	200r. "14 bis" (biplane), 1906 (horiz)	65	20
1314	250r. "Demoiselle" (monoplane), 1909 (horiz)	75	20
1315	500r. Embraer EMB-201 A (horiz)	2·00	20
1316	900r. Embraer EMB-111 (horiz)	3·00	30

254 Footballer

1993. World Cup Football Championship, U.S.A. (1994) (3rd issue).

1317 **254**	250r. multicoloured	75	10
1318 –	350r. multicoloured	1·30	20
1319 –	600r. multicoloured	1·90	20
1320 –	800r. multicoloured	2·40	20
1321 –	1000r. mult (vert)	3·25	30
MS1322	60 × 85 mm. 1500r. multicoloured (39 × 31 mm)	5·75	1·10

DESIGNS: 350r. to 1500r. Various footballing scenes.

255 European Wigeon

1993. "Bangkok 1993" International Stamp Exhibition, Thailand. Ducks. Multicoloured.
1323 250r. Type **255** 75 20
1324 350r. Baikal teal . . . . . 1·30 30
1325 600r. Mandarin . . . . . . 1·90 35
1326 800r. Wood duck . . . . . 2·40 65
1327 1000r. Harlequin duck . . . 3·25 85
MS1328 63 × 89 mm. 1500tr. Head of mandarin (39 × 31 mm) . . 5·75 90

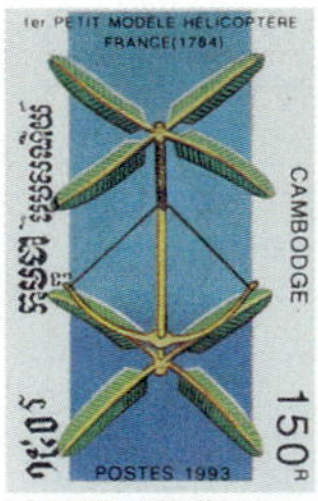

256 First Helicopter Model, France, 1784 **257** "Cnaphalocrosis medinalis"

1993. Vertical Take-off Aircraft. Multicoloured.
1329 150r. Type **256** 55 10
1330 200r. Model of steam helicopter, 1863 . . . . . 65 20
1331 250r. New York–Atlanta–Miami autogyro flight, 1927 (horiz) 75 20
1332 500r. Sikorsky helicopter, 1943 (horiz) . . . . . . 1·70 20
1333 900r. French vertical take-off jet . . . . 3·00 30
MS1334 90 × 49 mm. 1000r. Juan de la Clerva's C.4, 1923 (first practical autogyro) . . . . . 4·75 90

1993. National Development. Harmful Insects. Multicoloured.
1335 50r. Type **257** 30 20
1336 450r. Brown leaf-hopper . . 1·50 20
1337 500r. "Scirpophaga incertulas" . . . . 1·70 30
1338 1000r. Stalk-eyed fly . . . . 3·50 30
MS1339 89 × 90 mm. 1000r. "Leptocorisa oratorius" (31 × 39 mm) . . . . 4·75 90

258 Ministry of Posts and Telecommunications

1993. 40th Anniv of Independence.
1340 **258** 300r. multicoloured . . . 1·10 30
1341 – 500r. multicoloured . . . 1·70 65
1342 – 700r. blue. red & black . 2·50 90
DESIGNS—VERT: 500r. Independence monument. HORIZ: 700r. National flag.

259 Boy with Pony **260** Figure Skating

1993. Figurines by M. J. Hummel. Multicoloured.
1343 50r. Type **259** 20 10
1344 100r. Girl and pram 55 10
1345 150r. Girl bathing doll . . . 75 10
1346 200r. Girl holding doll . . . 95 20
1347 250r. Boys playing . . . . 1·20 20
1348 300r. Girls pulling boy in cart . . . . 1·50 30
1349 350r. Girls playing ring-o-roses . . . . 1·70 35
1350 600r. Boys with stick and drum . . . . 2·75 55

1994. Winter Olympic Games, Lillehammer, Norway. Multicoloured.
1351 150r. Type **260** 45 10
1352 250r. Two-man luge (horiz) 75 20
1353 400r. Skiing (horiz) . . . . 1·30 20
1354 700r. Biathlon (horiz) . . . 2·30 20
1355 1000r. Speed skating . . . . 3·25 30
MS1356 85 × 60 mm. 1500r. Curling (31 × 39 mm) . . . . 5·75 90

261 Opel 4/12 Laubfrosch two-seater, 1924

1994. Motor Cars. Multicoloured.
1357 150r. Type **261** 55 10
1358 200r. Mercedes 35 h.p. four-seater, 1901 . . . . . . 65 20
1359 250r. Ford Model "T" Tudor sedan, 1927 . . . 75 20
1360 500r. Rolls Royce 40/50 Silver Ghost tourer, 1907 1·70 20
1361 900r. Hutton racing car, 1908 . . . . 2·75 30
MS1362 80 × 60 mm 1000r. Duesenberg model J phaeton, 1931 (31 × 39 mm) . . . . . . 4·50 90

262 Gymnastics **263** Siva and Uma (10th century, Banteay Srei)

1994. Olympic Games, Atlanta (1996) (1st issue). Multicoloured.
1363 150r. Type **262** 45 10
1364 200r. Football 65 10
1365 250r. Throwing the javelin 75 20
1366 300r. Canoeing 85 20
1367 600r. Running . . . . . . 1·90 20
1368 1000r. Diving (horiz) . . . 3·50 20
MS1369 79 × 63 mm. 1500r. Show jumping (31 × 39 mm) . . . . 5·75 90
See also Nos. 1437/**MS**1442 and 1495/**MS**1501.

1994. Khmer Culture. Statues. Multicoloured.
1370 300r. Type **263** . . . . . . 1·10 55
1371 500r. Vishnu (6th cent, Tvol Dai-Buon) . . . . 1·90 90
1372 700r. King Jayavarman VII (12th–13th century, Krol Romeas Angkor) . . . . 2·75 1·30

264 Olympic Flag

1994. Centenary of International Olympic Committee. Multicoloured.
1373 100r. Type **264** 30 10
1374 300r. Flag and torch . . . . 1·10 45
1375 600r. Flag and Pierre de Coubertin (reviver of modern Olympic Games) 2·30 85

265 Mesonyx

1994. Prehistoric Animals. Multicoloured.
1376 150r. Type **265** 55 20
1377 250r. Doedicurus 85 30
1378 400r. Mylodon . . . . . . 1·50 45
1379 700r. Uintatherium . . . . 2·50 55
1380 1000r. Hyrachyus . . . . . 3·50 85

266 Players **267** "Soldiers in Combat"

1994. World Cup Football Championship, U.S.A. (4th issue).
1381 **266** 150r. multicoloured . . . 45 10
1382 – 250r. multicoloured . . . 75 20
1383 – 400r. multicoloured . . . 1·30 20
1384 – 700r. multicoloured . . . 2·30 20
1385 – 1000r. multicoloured . . 3·25 30
MS1386 58 × 78 mm. 1500r. multicoloured . . . . 5·75 90
DESIGNS: 250r. to 1500r. Various footballing scenes.

1994. Tourism. Statues in Public Gardens. Mult.
1387 300r. "Stag and Hind" . . . 1·30 45
1388 500r. Type **267** . . . . . . 1·90 90
1389 700r. "Lions" . . . . 2·75 1·40

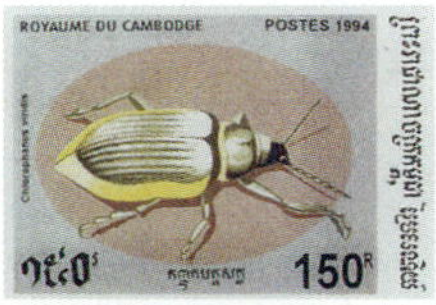

268 "Chlorophanus viridis"

1994. Beetles. Multicoloured.
1390 150r. Type **268** 55 10
1391 200r. "Chrysochroa fulgidissima" 65 20
1392 250r. "Lytta vesicatoria" . . 75 20
1393 500r. "Purpuricenus kaehleri" . . . . 2·00 45
1394 900r. Herculese beetle . . . 3·00 75
MS1395 69 × 50 mm. "Timarcha tenebricosa" (31 × 39 mm) . . 4·75 90

269 Halley's Diving-bell, 1690

1994. Submarines. Multicoloured.
1396 150r. Type **269** 55 10
1397 200r. "Gimnote", 1886 (horiz) 65 20
1398 250r. "Peral" (Spain), 1888 (horiz) 75 20
1399 500r. "Nautilus" (first nuclear-powered submarine), 1954 (horiz) 2·00 20
1400 900r. "Trieste" (bathyscaphe), 1953 (horiz) . . . . 3·00 30
MS1401 80 × 70 mm. 1000r. Narciso Monturiol's submarine "Ictineo", 1885 (39 × 31 mm) . . . . . . 4·75 90

270 Francois-Andre Philidor, 1795

1994. Chess Champions. Multicoloured.
1402 150r. Type **270** 55 10
1403 200r. Mahe de la Bourdonnais, 1821 . . . 65 20
1404 250r. Karl Anderssen, 1851 75 20
1405 500r. Paul Morphy, 1858 . . 2·00 45
1406 900r. Wilhelm Steinitz, 1866 3·00 75
MS1407 90 × 50 mm. 1000r. Emanual Lasker, 1894 (31 × 38 mm) . . . . 4·50 1·10

271 Sikorsky S-42 Flying Boat

1994. Aircraft. Multicoloured.
1408 150r. Type **271** 55 10
1409 200r. Vought-Sikorsky VS-300A helicopter prototype 65 20
1410 250r. Sikorsky S-37 biplane 75 20
1411 500r. Sikorsky S-35 biplane 2·00 20
1412 900r. Sikorsky S-43 amphibian . . . . 3·00 30
MS1413 80 × 50 mm. 1500r. Sikorsky Ilya Muromets (80th Anniv of first multi-engined airplane) (39 × 31 mm) . . . . 4·50 90

272 Penduline Tit

1994. Birds. Multicoloured.
1414 150r. Type **272** 45 10
1415 250r. Bearded reedling . . . 75 20
1416 400r. Little bunting . . . . 1·40 20
1417 700r. Cirl bunting . . . . . 2·40 45
1418 1000r. Goldcrest . . . . . . 3·50 75
MS1419 60 × 90 mm. 1500r. African pitta (31 × 39) . . . . 5·75 1·40

273 Postal Service Float

1994. National Independence Festival. Mult.
1420 300r. Type **273** . . . . . . 1·10 45
1421 500r. Soldiers marching . . 1·60 90
1422 700r. Women's army units on parade . . . . 2·50 1·40

274 Chruoi Changwar Bridge

1994. National Development. Multicoloured.
1423 300r. Type **274** 85 30
1424 500r. Olympique Commercial Centre . . . 1·50 45
1425 700r. Sakyamony Chedei Temple . . . . 1·90 65

275 Psittacosaurus

1995. Prehistoric Animals. Multicoloured.
1426 100r. Type **275** 20 10
1427 200r. Protoceratops 45 20
1428 300r. Montanoceraptors . . 65 20
1429 400r. Centrosaurus . . . . 1·40 30
1430 700r. Styracosaurus . . . . 2·30 35
1431 800r. Triceratops . . . . . 3·00 55

276 Orange-tip **278** Death Cap

277 Swimming

1995. Butterflies. Multicoloured.
1432 100r. Type **276** 20 10
1433 200r. Scarce swallowtail . . 65 20
1434 300r. Dark green fritillary 95 20
1435 600r. Red admiral . . . . . 1·40 20
1436 800r. Peacock . . . . 2·10 30

1995. Olympic Games, Atlanta (1996) (2nd issue). Multicoloured.
1437 100r. Type **277** 30 10
1438 200r. Callisthenics (vert) . . 65 20
1439 400r. Basketball (vert) . . . 1·20 20
1440 800r. Football (vert) . . . . 2·75 20
1441 1000r. Cycling (vert) . . . . 3·25 30
MS1442 48 × 69 mm. 1500r. Running (31 × 39 mm) . . . . 3·75 90

1995. Fungi. Multicoloured.
1443 100r. Type **278** 30 10
1444 200r. Chanterelle 75 20
1445 300r. Honey fungus . . . . 1·10 20
1446 600r. Field mushroom . . . 1·80 20
1447 800r. Fly agaric . . . . . . 2·40 30

279 Kneeling Ascetic

281 Black-capped Lory

280 Gaur

1995. Khmer Culture. Statues. Multicoloured.
1448 300r. Type **279** 85 30
1449 500r. Parasurama . . . . . 1·50 45
1450 700r. Shiva . . . . 1·90 65

1995. Protected Animals. Multicoloured.
1451 300r. Type **280** 85 20
1452 500r. Kouprey (vert) . . . . 1·50 30
1453 700r. Saurus crane (vert) . . 1·90 45

1995. Parrot Family. Multicoloured.
1454 100r. Type **281** 30 10
1455 200r. Princess parrot 65 20
1456 400r. Eclectus parrot . . . 1·20 20
1457 800r. Scarlet macaw . . . . 2·75 20
1458 1000r. Budgerigar . . . . . 3·25 30
MS1459 52 × 81 mm. 1500r. Yellow-headed amazon (30 × 38 mm) 4·75 90

282 Bird (sculpture)

1995. Tourism. Public Gardens. Multicoloured.
1460 300r. Type **282** 85 30
1461 500r. Water feature . . . . 1·50 45
1462 700r. Mythical figures (sculpture) . . . . 1·60 65

283 Richard Trevithick's Locomotive, 1804

1995. Steam Locomotives. Multicoloured.
1463 100r. Type **283** 20 10
1464 200r. G. and R. Stephenson's "Rocket", 1829 . . . . . 75 20
1465 300r. George Stephenson's "Locomotion", 1825 . . . 1·10 20
1466 600r. "Lafayette", 1837 . . 1·70 45
1467 800r. "Best Friend of Charleston", 1830 . . . . 2·10 75
MS1468 74 × 59 mm. 1000r. George Stephenson (inventor of steam locomotive) (31 × 38 mm) . . . 3·25 1·50

284 Bristol Type 142 Blenheim Mk II Bomber

1995. Second World War Planes. Multicoloured.
1469 100r. Type **284** 20 10
1470 200r. North American B-25B Mitchell bomber (horiz) 75 20
1471 300r. Avro Type 652 Anson Mk I general purpose plane (horiz) . . . . . 1·10 20
1472 600r. Avro Manchester bomber (horiz) . . . . . 1·70 20
1473 800r. Consolidated B-24 Liberator bomber (horiz) 2·10 30
MS1474 81 × 49 mm. 1000r. Boeing B-17 Flying Fortress bomber (31 × 38 mm) . . . . 3·25 90

285 Gathering Crops

1995. 50th Anniv of FAO. Multicoloured.
1475 300r. Type **285** 55 30
1476 500r. Transplanting crops . 1·10 45
1477 700r. Paddy field . . . . . 1·60 65

286 Bridge

1995. 50th Anniv of UNO. Preah Kunlorng Bridge. Multicoloured.
1478 300r. Type **286** 55 30
1479 500r. People on bridge . . . 1·10 45
1480 700r. Closer view of bridge 1·60 65

287 Queen Monineath

1995. National Independence. Multicoloured.
1481 700r. Type **287** . . . . . . 2·10 65
1482 800r. King Norodom Sihanouk . . . . 2·75 75

288 Pennant Coralfish

1995. Fishes. Multicoloured.
1483 100r. Type **288** 30 10
1484 200r. Copper-banded butterflyfish 65 20
1485 400r. Crown anemonefish 1·20 20
1486 800r. Palette surgeonfish . 2·75 20
1487 1000r. Queen angelfish . . . 2·10 30
MS1488 85 × 50 mm. win-spotted wrasse . . . . 4·75 90

289 Post Office Building

1995. Cent of Head Post Office, Phnom Penh.
1489 **289** 300r. multicoloured . . . 85 30
1490 500r. multicoloured . . . 1·60 45
1491 700r. multicoloured . . . 2·30 65

290 Independence Monument

1995. 40th Anniv of Admission of Cambodia to United Nations Organization. Multicoloured.
1492 300r. Type **290** 55 30
1493 400r. Angkor Wat . . . . . 1·10 45
1494 800r. U.N. emblem and national flag (vert) . . . 1·60 65

291 Tennis

292 Kep State Chalet

1996. Olympic Games, Atlanta (3rd issue). Mult.
1495 100r. Type **291** 10 10
1496 200r. Volleyball 25 10
1497 300r. Football 45 20
1498 500r. Running 60 20
1499 900r. Baseball . . . . 1·10 20
1500 1000r. Basketball . . . . . 1·10 20
MS1501 64 × 94 mm. 1500r. Windsurfing (28 × 38 mm) . . . 3·25 90

1996.
1502 **292** 50r. blue and black . . . 20 10
1503 – 100r. red and black . . . 20 10
1504 – 200r. yellow and black 20 10
1505 – 500r. blue and black . . 55 20
1506 – 800r. mauve and black 95 30
1507 – 1000r. yellow and black 1·30 45
1508 – 1500r. green and black 1·80 65
DESIGNS—HORIZ: 100r. Power station; 200r. Wheelchair; 500r. Handicapped basketball team; 1000r. Kep beach; 1500r. Serpent Island. VERT: 800r. Man making crutches.

293 European Wild Cat

1996. Wild Cats. Multicoloured.
1509 100r. "Felis libyca" (vert) 20 10
1510 200r. Type **293** 35 10
1511 300r. Caracal 50 20
1512 500r. Geoffroy's cat 80 20
1513 900r. Black-footed cat . . 1·20 20
1514 1000r. Flat-headed cat . . . 1·40 20

294 Player dribbling Ball

295 Tusmukh

1996. World Cup Football Championship, France (1998) (1st issue). Multicoloured.
1515 **294** 100r. multicoloured . . . 30 10
1516 – 200r. multicoloured . . . 45 10
1517 – 300r. multicoloured . . . 75 20
1518 – 500r. multicoloured . . . 1·30 20
1519 – 900r. multicoloured . . . 2·30 20
1520 – 1000r. mult (horiz) . . . 2·75 20
MS1521 65 × 79 mm. 1500r. multicoloured (31 × 38 mm) . . 4·75 90
DESIGNS: 200r. to 1500r. Different players.
See also Nos. 1613/**MS**1619 and 1726/**MS**1732.

1996. Khmer Culture. Multicoloured.
1522 100r. Type **295** 20 10
1523 300r. Ream Iso . . . . . . 1·30 45
1524 900r. Isei . . . . 2·20 85

296 Pacific Steam Locomotive No. 620, Finland

1996. Railway Locomotives. Multicoloured.
1525 100r. Type **296** 10 10
1526 200r. GNR steam locomotive No. 261, Great Britain 10 10
1527 300r. Steam tank locomotive, 1930 . . . . 30 20
1528 500r. Steam tank locomotive No. 1362, 1914 . . . . . 40 20
1529 900r. LMS Turbomotive No. 6202, 1930, Great Britain 55 20
1530 1000r. Locomotive "Snake", 1884, New Zealand . . . 75 20
MS1531 80 × 55 mm. 1500r. Canadian Pacific train with Vistadome observation car (39 × 31 mm) . . . . 4·75 90
No. **MS**1531 commemorates "CEPEX '96" International Stamp Exhibition, Toronto.

297 White-rumped Shama

1996. Birds. Multicoloured.
1532 100r. Type **297** 30 10
1533 200r. Pekin robin 45 10
1534 300r. Varied tit 75 20
1535 500r. Black-naped oriole . . 1·30 20
1536 900r. Japanese bush warbler 2·30 20
1537 1000r. Blue and white flycatcher . . . . 2·75 20

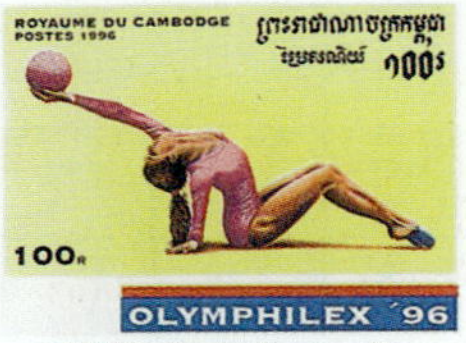

298 Rhythmic Gymnastics

1996. "Olymphilex '96" Olympic Stamps Exhibition, Atlanta, U.S.A. Multicoloured.
1538 100r. Type **298** 20 10
1539 200r. Judo 30 10
1540 300r. High jumping 55 20
1541 500r. Wrestling . . . . . . 1·10 20
1542 900r. Weightlifting . . . . 1·90 20
1543 1000r. Football . . . . . . 2·30 20
MS1544 84 × 55 mm. 1500r. Diving (31 × 39 mm) . . . . 3·75 90

299 Douglas M-2, 1926

1996. Biplanes. Multicoloured.
1545 100r. Type **299** 30 10
1546 200r. Pitcairn PS-5 Mailwing, 1926 . . . . . 45 10
1547 300r. Boeing 40-B, 1928 . . . 75 20
1548 500r. Potez 25, 1925 . . . . 1·30 20
1549 900r. Stearman C-3MB, 1927 . . . . 2·30 20
1550 1000r. De Havilland D.H.4, 1918 . . . . 2·75 20
MS1551 80 × 60 mm. 1500r. Standar JR-1B, 1918 (39 × 30 mm) . . 4·75 90

300 Aspara

302 Jose Raul Capablanca (1921–27)

301 Coelophysis

1996. Tonle Bati Temple Ruins.

1552 **300**	50r. black and yellow	20	10
1553 –	100r. black and blue	20	10
1554 –	200r. black and brown	45	10
1555 –	500r. black and blue	75	20
1556 –	800r. black and green	1·10	30
1557 –	1000r. black and green	1·40	45
1558 –	1500r. black and bistre	2·30	65

DESIGNS—VERT: 100r. Aspara (different); 200r. Aspara (different); 800r. Taprum Temple; 1000r. Grandmother Peou Temple. HORIZ: 500r. Reliefs on wall; 1500r. Overall view of Tonle Bati.

1996. Prehistoric Animals. Multicoloured.

1559	50r. Type **301**	10	10
1560	100r. Euparkeria	10	10
1561	150r. Plateosaurus	30	10
1562	200r. Herrerasaurus	50	10
1563	250r. Dilophosaurus	55	10
1564	300r. Tuojiangosaurus	70	10
1565	350r. Camarasaurus	1·10	20
1566	400r. Ceratosaurus	1·30	20
1567	500r. Espinosaurio	1·50	30
1568	700r. Ouranosaurus	2·00	35
1569	800r. Avimimus	2·50	55
1570	1200r. Deinonychus	3·50	65

Nos. 1559/62, 1563/6 and 1567/70 respectively were issued together, se-tenant, each sheetlet containing a composite design of a globe.

1996. World Chess Champions. Multicoloured.

1571	100r. Type **302**	30	10
1572	200r. Aleksandr Alekhine (1927–35, 1937–46)	45	10
1573	300r. Vasily Vasilevich Smyslov (1957–58)	75	20
1574	500r. Mikhail Nekhemyevich Tal (1960–61)	1·30	20
1575	900r. Robert Fischer (1972–75)	2·30	20
1576	1000r. Anatoly Karpov (1975–85)	2·75	20
MS1577	70 × 87 mm. 1500r. Garry Kasparov (1985–2000) (31 × 38 mm)	4·75	90

303 Brown Bear

1996. Mammals and their Young. Multicoloured.

1578	100r. Type **303**	30	10
1579	200r. Lion	45	10
1580	300r. Malayan tapir	65	20
1581	500r. Bactrian camel	1·30	20
1582	900r. Ibex (vert)	2·10	20
1583	1000r. Californian sealion (vert)	2·75	20

304 Rough Collie

1996. Dogs. Multicoloured.

1584	200r. Type **304**	45	10
1585	300r. Labrador retriever	65	20
1586	500r. Dobermann pinscher	1·30	20
1587	900r. German shepherd	2·10	20
1588	1000r. Boxer	2·40	30

305 Chinese Junk

1996. Ships. Multicoloured.

1589	200r. Type **305**	45	10
1590	300r. Phoenician warship, 1500–1000 B.C.	65	20
1591	500r. Roman war galley, 264–241 B.C.	1·30	20
1592	900r. 19th-century full-rigged ship	2·10	20
1593	1000r. "Sirius" (paddle-steamer), 1838	2·40	30
MS1594	90 × 60 mm. 1500r. "Great Eastern" (cable ship and paddle-steamer), 1858 (39 × 31 mm)	4·75	90

306 Silver Pagoda, Phnom Penh

1996. 45th Anniv of Cambodian Membership of Universal Postal Union.

1595 **306**	200r. multicoloured	55	20
1596	400r. multicoloured	1·10	35
1597	900r. multicoloured	2·10	85

307 Environmental Vessel and Helicopter

1996. 25th Anniv of Greenpeace (environmental organization). Multicoloured.

1598	200r. Type **307**	75	10
1599	300r. Float-helicopter hovering over motor launch	1·40	20
1600	500r. Helicopter on deck and motor launches	2·10	30
1601	900r. Helicopter with two barrels suspended beneath	3·75	35
MS1602	111 × 90 mm. 10000r. Float-helicopter (31 × 39 mm)	4·75	90

308 Ox

1996. New Year. Year of the Ox. Details of painting by Han Huang. Multicoloured.

1603	500r. Type **308**	65	20
1604	500r. Ox with head turned to right (upright horns)	65	20
1605	500r. Brown and white ox with head up ("handlebar" horns)	65	20
1606	500r. Ox with head in bush ("ram's" horns)	65	20

309 Dam, Phnom Kaun Sat

1996. 10th International United Nations Volunteers Day. Multicoloured.

1607	100r. Type **309**	30	10
1608	500r. Canal, O Angkrung	1·40	45
1609	900r. Canal, Chrey Krem	2·50	85

310 Architect's Model of Reservoir

1996. 43rd Anniv of Independence. Water Management. Multicoloured.

1610	100r. Type **310**	30	10
1611	500r. Reservoir	1·40	45
1612	900r. Reservoir (different)	2·50	85

311 Players

1997. World Cup Football Championship, France (1998) (2nd issue).

1613 **311**	100r. multicoloured	30	10
1614 –	200r. multicoloured	45	10
1615 –	300r. multicoloured	75	20
1616 –	500r. multicoloured	1·30	20
1617 –	900r. multicoloured	2·30	20
1618 –	1000r. multicoloured	2·75	20
MS1619	99 × 68 mm. 2000r. multicoloured (39 × 31 mm)	4·75	90

DESIGNS: 200r. to 2000r. Different footballing scenes.

312 Two Elephants

1997. The Indian Elephant. Multicoloured.

1620	300r. Type **312**	30	10
1621	500r. Group of three	55	20
1622	900r. Elephants fighting	1·10	30
1623	1000r. Adult and calf	1·30	35

314 Horse-drawn Water Pump, 1731

315 Statue on Plinth

1997. Fire Engines. Multicoloured.

1630	200r. Type **314**	30	10
1631	500r. Putnam horse-drawn water pump, 1863	45	10
1632	900r. Merryweather horse-drawn engine, 1894	65	20
1633	1000r. Shand Mason Co horse-drawn water pump, 1901	85	20
1634	1500r. Maxin Motor Co automatic pump, 1949	1·30	20
1635	4000r. Merryweather exhaust pump, 1950	3·50	20
MS1636	106 × 87 mm. 5400r. Mack Truck Co. mechanical ladder, 1953 (39 × 31 mm)	4·75	90

1997. Angkor Wat.

1637 **315**	300r. black and red	30	10
1638 –	300r. black and blue	30	10
1639 –	800r. black and green	65	10
1640 –	1500r. black & brown	1·30	10
1641 –	1700r. black & orange	1·50	20
1642 –	2500r. black and blue	1·90	20
1643 –	3000r. black & green	2·50	20

DESIGNS—VERT: No. 1638, Statue in wall recess; 1639, Walled courtyard; 1640, Decorative panel with two figures. HORIZ: No. 1641, Rectangular gateway; 1642, Statues and arched gateway; 1643, Stupa and ruins.

316 Steller's Eider

1997. Aquatic Birds. Multicoloured.

1644	200r. Type **316**	10	10
1645	500r. Egyptian goose	25	10
1646	900r. American wigeon	40	20
1647	1000r. Falcated teal	45	20
1648	1500r. Surf scoter	65	20
1649	4000r. Blue-winged teal	1·90	20
MS1650	95 × 75 mm. 5400r. Baikal teal (31 × 39 mm)	4·75	90

317 Von Stephan

318 Main Entrance

1997. Death Centenary of Heinrich von Stephan (founder of UPU).

1651 **317**	500r. blue & dp blue	45	20
1652	1500r. green and olive	1·30	30
1653	2000r. yellow & green	1·80	45

1997. Khmer Culture. Banteay Srei Temple. Multicoloured.

1654	500r. Type **318**	45	20
1655	1500r. Main and side entrances	1·30	30
1656	2000r. Courtyard	1·80	45

319 Birman

1997. Cats. Multicoloured.

1657	200r. Type **319**	30	10
1658	500r. Exotic shorthair	45	10
1659	900r. Persian	65	20
1660	1000r. Turkish van	85	20
1661	1500r. American shorthair	1·30	20
1662	4000r. Scottish fold	3·50	20
MS1663	90 × 70 mm. 5400r. Sphinx (31 × 39 mm)	3·75	90

320 No. 488

1997. Steam Railway Locomotives. Multicoloured.

1664	200r. Type **320**	30	10
1665	500r. "Frederick Smith"	45	10
1666	900r. No. 3131	65	20
1667	1000r. London Transport No. L44, Great Britain	85	20
1668	1500r. LNER No. 1711, Great Britain	1·30	20
1669	4000r. No. 60523 "Chateau du Soleil"	3·50	20
MS1670	76 × 60 mm. 5400r. LNER No. 2006, Great Britain	4·25	90

321 Shar-pei

1997. Dogs. Multicoloured.

1671	200r. Type **321**	30	10
1672	500r. Chin-chin	45	10
1673	900r. Pekingese	55	20
1674	1000r. Chow-chow (vert)	65	20
1675	1500r. Pug (vert)	1·30	20
1676	4000r. Akita (vert)	3·50	20
MS1677	111 × 88 mm. 5400r. Chinese crested (vert)	3·75	90

322 Qunalom Temple

1997. 30th Anniv of Association of South East Asian Nations. Multicoloured.
1678 500r. Type **322** 45 20
1679 1500r. Royal Palace . . . . 1·30 30
1680 2000r. National Museum . . . . 1·80 45

323 15th-century Caravelle

1997. Sailing Ships. Multicoloured.
1681 200r. Type **323** 30 10
1682 500r. Spanish galleon 45 10
1683 900r. "Great Harry" (British galleon) 65 20
1684 1000r. "La Couronne" (French galleon) 85 20
1685 1500r. 18th-century East Indiaman . . . . 1·30 20
1686 4000r. 19th-century clipper 3·50 20
MS1687 94 × 68 mm. 5400r. H.M.S. "Victory" (Nelson) . . . . . . 4·25 90

324 Public Garden **325** Satan's Mushroom

1997. Public Gardens (Nos. 1688/91) and Tuk Chha Canal (others).
1688 **324** 300r. green and black . . 30 10
1689 – 300r. red and black . . . 30 10
1690 – 800r. yellow and black 65 10
1691 – 1500r. orange and black 1·30 10
1692 – 1700r. pink and black . . 1·50 20
1693 – 2500r. blue and black . . 1·90 20
1694 – 3000r. blue and black . . 2·50 20
DESIGNS—HORIZ: 300r. Statue at intersection of paths; 300r. Hedging in triangular bed; 1500r. Tree and statue of lion; 1700r. View along canal; 2500r. View across canal; 3000r. Closed lock gates. VERT: 800r. Mounted bowl.

1997. Fungi. Multicoloured.
1695 200r. Type **325** 30 10
1696 500r. "Amanita regalis" . . 45 10
1697 900r. "Morchella semilibera" 65 20
1698 1000r. "Gomphus clavatus" . 85 20
1699 1500r. "Hygrophorus hypothejus" . . . . 1·30 20
1700 4000r. "Albatrellus confluens" . . . . 3·50 20
MS1701 110 × 89 mm. 5400r. Red-cracked boletus . . . . 4·75 90

326 Peaceful Fightingfish ("Betta imbellis") and Siamese Fightingfish ("Betta splendens")

1997. Fishes. Multicoloured.
1702 200r. Type **326** 20 10
1703 500r. Banded gourami . . . 25 10
1704 900r. Rosy barbs 40 20
1705 1000r. Paradise fish 55 20
1706 1500r. "Epalzeorhynchos frenatus" . . . . 1·00 20
1707 4000r. "Capoeta tetrazona" 2·10 20
MS1708 96 × 72 mm. 5400r. Harlequin fish . . . . 4·75 90

327 Kampot Post Office

1997. 44th Anniv of Independence. Multicoloured.
1709 1000r. Type **327** 85 30
1710 3000r. Prey Veng Post Office 2·75 65

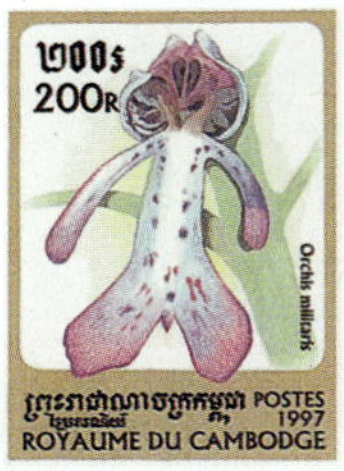

328 "Orchis militaris" **329** In black Jacket

1997. Orchids. Multicoloured.
1711 200r. Type **328** 20 10
1712 500r. "Orchiaceras bivonae" 30 10
1713 900r. "Orchiaceras spuria" 50 20
1714 1000r. "Gymnadenia conopsea" 60 20
1715 1500r. "Serapias neglecta" 1·30 20
1716 4000r. "Pseudorhiza bruniana" . . . . 2·75 20
MS1717 70 × 90 mm. 5400r. "Dactylodenia wintonii" . . . 4·75 90

1997. Diana, Princess of Wales Commemoration. Multicoloured.
1718 100r. Type **329** 15 10
1719 200r. In black dress 15 10
1720 300r. In blue jacket 15 10
1721 500r. Close-up of Princess in visor 30 10
1722 1000r. In mine-protection clothing 50 10
1723 1500r. With Elizabeth Dole 85 10
1724 2000r. Holding landmine . . 1·20 20
1725 2500r. With Mother Teresa and Sisters of Charity . . 1·40 20

330 Player with Ball **331** Suorprat Gateway

1998. World Cup Football Championship, France (3rd issue).
1726 **330** 200r. multicoloured . . . 15 10
1727 – 500r. multicoloured . . . 25 10
1728 – 900r. multicoloured . . . 45 20
1729 – 1000r. multicoloured . . 55 20
1730 – 1500r. multicoloured . . 80 20
1731 – 4000r. multicoloured . . 2·30 20
MS1732 110 × 90 mm. 5400r. multicoloured (39 × 31 mm) . . 3·25 90
DESIGNS: 500r. to 5400r. Different footballing scenes.

1998. Temple Ruins.
1733 **331** 300r. orange and black 20 10
1734 – 500r. pink and black . . 30 10
1735 – 1200r. orange and black 45 10
1736 – 1500r. orange and black 65 10
1737 – 1700r. blue and black . . 75 20
1738 – 2000r. green and black 95 20
1739 – 3000r. lilac and black . . 1·50 20
DESIGNS—HORIZ: No. 1734, Kumlung wall; 1735, Bapuon entrance; 1737, Prerup; 1738, Preah Khan. VERT: No. 1736, Palilai; 1739, Bayon.

332 Tiger Cub **334** Rottweiler

333 Oakland, Antioch and Eastern Electric Locomotive No. 105

1998. New Year. Year of the Tiger. Multicoloured.
1740 200r. Type **332** 20 10
1741 500r. Tiger and cubs 30 10
1742 990r. Tiger on alert 45 20
1743 1000r. Tiger washing itself (horiz) 55 20
1744 1500r. Tiger lying in grass (horiz) 80 20
1745 4000r. Tiger snarling (horiz) 2·30 20
MS1746 120 × 90 mm. 5400r. Tiger on rock (31 × 30 mm) . . . . 3·25 90

1998. Railway Locomotives. Multicoloured.
1747 200r. Type **333** 20 10
1748 500r. New York, Westchester and electric locomotive No. 1 . . . . 45 10
1749 900r. Spokane and Inland electric locomotive No. MII 55 20
1750 1000r. International Railway electric locomotive 75 20
1751 1500r. British Columbia Electric Railway locomotive No. 823 . . . 1·10 20
1752 4000r. Southern Pacific electric locomotive No. 200 . . . . 3·00 20
MS1753 88 × 94 mm. Storage battery locomotive (vert triangle) . . . 3·75 90

1998. Dogs. Multicoloured.
1754 200r. Type **334** 15 10
1755 500r. Beauceron 35 10
1756 900r. Boxer 50 20
1757 1000r. Siberian husky . . . 60 20
1758 1500r. Welsh Pembroke corgi 85 20
1759 4000r. Basset hound . . . . 2·30 20
MS1760 110 × 89 mm. Schnauzer (28 × 37½ mm) . . . . 3·75 90

335 Stag Beetle

1998. Beetles. Multicoloured.
1761 200r. Type **335** 20 10
1762 500r. "Carabus auronitens" (ground beetle) 45 10
1763 900r. Alpine longhorn beetle 65 20
1764 1000r. "Geotrupes" (dor beetle) 75 20
1765 1500r. "Megasoma elephas" 1·10 20
1766 4000r. "Chalcosoma" . . . 2·75 20
MS1767 110 × 90 mm. 5400r. "Leptura rubra" (longhorn beetle) 3·75 90

336 Prerup Temple

1998. Khmer Culture. Multicoloured.
1768 500r. Type **336** 30 20
1769 1500r. Bayon Temple 75 30
1770 2000r. Angkor Vat . . . . 1·10 45

337 Cutter

1998. Ships. Multicoloured.
1771 200r. Type **337** 20 10
1772 500r. "Britannia" (mail paddle-steamer, 1840) . . 45 10
1773 900r. Viking longship, Gokstad 65 20
1774 1000r. "Great Britain" (steam/sail) 75 20
1775 1500r. Medieval coasting nau . . . . 1·10 20
1776 4000r. Full-rigged ship (inscr "Fregate") . . . . . . 2·75 20
MS1777 110 × 91 mm. 5400r. "Tartane" (fishing boat) (39 × 31 mm) . . . . 3·75 90

338 Scottish Fold

1998. Domestic Cats. Multicoloured.
1778 200r. Type **338** 15 10
1779 500r. Ragdoll 35 10
1780 900r. Cymric 50 20
1781 1000r. Devon rex 60 20
1782 1500r. American curl . . . 85 20
1783 4000r. Sphinx . . . . 2·30 20
MS1784 90 × 108 mm. 5400r. Japanese bobtail (39 × 31 mm) 3·75 90

339 "Petasites japonica"

1998. Flowers. Multicoloured.
1785 200r. Type **339** 15 10
1786 500r. "Gentiana triflora" . . 30 10
1787 900r. "Doronicum cordatum" 50 20
1788 1000r. "Scabiosa japonica" 55 20
1789 1500r. "Magnolia sieboldii" 75 20
1790 4000r. "Erythronium japonica" . . . . 2·30 20
MS1791 90 × 101 mm. China aster (30 × 36 mm) . . . . 3·25 90

340 "Baptism of Christ" (Gerard David)

1998. "Italia 98" International Stamp Exhibition, Milan. Paintings. Multicoloured.
1792 200r. Type **340** 20 10
1793 500r. "Madonna of Martin van Niuwenhoven" (Hans Memling) 30 10
1794 900r. "Baptism of Christ" (Hendrich Holtzius) . . . 55 20
1795 1000r. "Christ with the Cross" (Luis de Morales) 65 20
1796 1500r. "Elias in the Desert" (Dirk Bouts) 95 20
1797 4000r. "The Virgin" (Petrus Christus) . . . . 2·75 20
MS1798 87 × 107 mm. "The Immaculate Conception" (Bartolome Murillo) (39 × 31 mm) 3·75 90
There are errors of spelling in some of the inscriptions.

341 "Phyciodes tharos"

1998. Butterflies. Multicoloured.
1799 200r. Type **341** 20 10
1800 500r. "Pararge megera" . . 30 10
1801 900r. Monarch 55 20
1802 1000r. Apollo 65 20
1803 1500r. Swallowtail 95 20
1804 4000r. "Eumenis semele" . . 2·75 20
MS1805 91 × 110 mm. 5400r. Blue morpho (39 × 31 mm) . . . . 3·75 90

342 Post Box, 1997

1998. World Post Day. Multicoloured.
1806 1000r. Type **342** 55 30
1807 3000r. Wall-mounted post box, 1951 . . . . 1·40 65

343 Big-Headed Turtle

1998. Tortoise and Turtles. Multicoloured.
1808 200r. Type **343** 15 10
1809 500r. Green turtle 25 10
1810 900r. American soft-shelled turtle 40 20
1811 1000r. Hawksbill turtle 50 20
1812 1500r. Aldabra tortoise 70 20
1813 4000r. Leatherback sea turtle 2·00 20
MS1814 5400r. Matamata turtle (39 × 31 mm) 3·25 90

344 Bayon Dance

1998. 45th Anniv of Independence. Multicoloured.
1815 500r. Type **344** 35 20
1816 1500r. Bayon dance (different) 85 30
1817 2000r. Bayon dance (different) 1·20 45

345 Cheetah

1998. Big Cats. Multicoloured.
1818 200r. Type **345** 15 10
1819 500r. Snow leopard 25 10
1820 900r. Ocelot 40 20
1821 1000r. Leopard 50 20
1822 1500r. Serval 70 20
1823 4000r. Jaguar 2·00 20
MS1824 90 × 109 mm. 5400r. Tiger (31 × 39 mm) 3·25 90

346 Rabbit

1999. New Year. Year of the Rabbit. Multicoloured. Showing rabbits.
1825 200r. Type **346** 30 10
1826 500r. Facing left 45 10
1827 900r. Sitting in bush 75 20
1828 1000r. Sitting on rock 85 20
1829 1500r. Sitting upright 1·40 20
1830 4000r. Head looking out from grass (vert) 3·75 20
MS1831 110 × 84 mm. 5400r. Rabbit (39 × 31 mm) 3·75 90

347 Foster and Rastik's "Stourbridge Lion", 1829, U.S.A.

1999. Steam Railway Locomotives. Multicoloured.
1832 200r. Type **347** 20 10
1833 500r. "Atlantic", 1832 30 10
1834 900r. No. 035, 1934 45 20
1835 1000r. Daniel Gooch's "Iron Duke", 1847, Great Britain 60 20
1836 1500r. "4-6-0" 95 20
1837 4000r. "4-4-2" 2·50 20
MS1838 84 × 109 mm. 5400r. "Fire Fly", 1840, "Great Britain" (39 × 31 mm) 3·75 90

348 Aquamarine

349 Alsatian

1999. Minerals. Multicoloured.
1839 200r. Type **348** 10 10
1840 500r. Cat's eye 20 10
1841 900r. Malachite 35 20
1842 1000r. Emerald 45 20
1843 1500r. Turquoise 65 20
1844 4000r. Ruby 1·80 20
MS1845 107 × 88 mm. 5400r. Diamond (39 × 31 mm) 3·75 90

1999. Dogs. Multicoloured.
1846 200r. Type **349** 20 10
1847 500r. Shih tzu (horiz) 30 10
1848 900r. Tibetan spaniel (horiz) 50 20
1849 1000r. Ainu-ken 55 20
1850 1500r. Lhassa apso (horiz) 90 20
1851 4000r. Tibetan terrier (horiz) 2·50 20
MS1852 109 × 88 mm. 5400r. Tosa inu (31 × 39 mm) 3·75 90

350 La Rapide steam carriage, 1881

1999. Cars. Multicoloured.
1853 200r. Type **350** 15 10
1854 500r. Duryea motor buggy, 1895 25 10
1855 900r. Marius Barbarou voiturette, 1898 40 20
1856 1000r. Panhard and Levassor voiturette, 1898 50 20
1857 1500r. Mercedes-Benz Tonneau, 1901 70 20
1858 4000r. Ford model sedan, 1915 2·00 20
MS1859 108 × 86 mm. 5400r. Marcus, 1875 (39 × 31 mm) 3·75 90

351 Ragdoll

353 *Araschnia levana*

352 Dragon Bridge

1999. Cats. Multicoloured.
1860 200r. Type **351** 20 10
1861 500r. Russian blue 25 10
1862 900r. Bombay 50 20
1863 1000r. Siamese 55 20
1864 1500r. Oriental shorthair 95 20
1865 4000r. Somali 2·50 20
MS1866 84 × 109 mm. 5400r. Egyptian mau (31 × 38 mm) 3·75 90

1999. Khmer Culture. Multicoloured.
1867 500r. Type **352** 25 20
1868 1500r. Temple of 100 Columns, Kratie 80 30
1869 2000r. Krapum Chhouk, Kratie 1·20 45

1999. Butterflies. Multicoloured.
1870 200r. Type **353** 20 10
1871 500r. Painted lady (horiz) 25 10
1872 900r. *Clossiana euphrosyne* 50 20
1873 1000r. *Coenonympha hero* 55 20
1874 1500r. Apollo (horiz) 90 20
1875 4000r. *Plebejus argus* 2·50 20
MS1876 109 × 90 mm. 5400r. Purple-edged copper (31 × 39 mm) 3·75 90

354 Saurornitholestes

1999. Prehistoric Animals. Multicoloured.
1877 200r. Type **354** 15 10
1878 500r. Prenocephale 20 10
1879 900r. Wuerhosaurus 40 20
1880 1000r. Muttaburrasaurus 45 20
1881 1500r. Shantungosaurus 70 20
1882 4000r. Microceratops 2·10 20
MS1883 111 × 84 mm. 5400r. Daspletosaurus 3·75 90

355 *Flabellina affinis*

357 Prasat Neak Poan

356 "Flowers in a Vase" (Henri Fantin-Latour)

1999. Molluscs. Multicoloured.
1884 200r. Type **355** 20 10
1885 500r. *Octopus macropus* 30 10
1886 900r. *Helix hortensis* 55 20
1887 1000r. *Lima hians* 65 20
1888 1500r. *Arion empiricorum* 95 20
1889 4000r. Swan mussel 2·75 20
MS1890 110 × 84 mm. 5400r. *Eledone aldrovandii* 3·75 90

1999. "Philexfrance 99" International Stamp Exhibition, Paris. Paintings. Multicoloured.
1891 200r. Type **356** 30 10
1892 500r. "Fruit" (Paul Cezanne) 45 10
1893 900r. "Table and Chairs" (Andre Derain) 75 20
1894 1000r. "Vase on a Table" (Henri Matisse) 85 20
1895 1500r. "Tulips and Marquerites" (Othon Friesz) 1·40 20
1896 4000r. "Still Life with Tapestry" (Matisse) 3·75 20
MS1897 107 × 84 mm. 5400r. "Still Life with Tapestry" (detail) (Cezanne) 3·75 90

1999. Temples.
1898 **357** 100r. blue and black 20 10
1899 – 300r. red and black 20 10
1900 – 500r. grn & blk (vert) 30 10
1901 – 1400r. green and black 85 10
1902 – 1600r. mauve and black 95 20
1903 – 1800r. vio & blk (vert) 1·10 20
1904 – 1900r. brown and black 1·20 20
DESIGNS: 300r. Statue, Neak Poan; 500r. Banteay Srey; 1400r. Banteay Samre; 1600r. Banteay Srey; 1800r. Bas-relief, Angkor Vat; 1900r. Brasat Takeo.

358 Pagoda, Tongzhou

359 *Cymbidium insigne*

1999. "China 1999" International Stamp Exhibition, Peking. Multicoloured.
1905 200r. Type **358** 20 10
1906 500r. Pagoda, Tianning Temple 30 10
1907 900r. Pagoda, Summer Palace 75 10
1908 900r. Pagoda, Blue Cloud Temple 75 10
1909 1000r. White pagoda, Bei Hai 75 10
1910 1000r. Pagoda, Scented Hill 75 10
1911 1500r. Pagoda, Yunju Temple 1·30 20
1912 4000r. White pagoda, Miaoying Temple 3·25 20

1999. Orchids. Multicoloured.
1913 200r. Type **359** 20 10
1914 500r. *Papilionanthe teres* 30 10
1915 900r. *Panisea uniflora* 55 20
1916 1000r. *Euanthe sanderiana* 65 20
1917 1500r. *Dendrobium trigonopus* 95 20
1918 4000r. *Vanda coerulea* 2·75 20
MS1919 109 × 80 mm. 5400r. *Paphiopedilum callosum* (26 × 36 mm) 3·75 90

360 Northern Bullfinch

1999. Birds. Multicoloured.
1920 200r. Type **360** 30 10
1921 500r. Hawfinch 45 10
1922 900r. Western greenfinch 75 20
1923 1000r. Yellow warbler 85 20
1924 1500r. Great grey shrike 1·40 20
1925 4000r. Blue tit 3·75 20
MS1926 109 × 85 mm. 5400r. European robin (39 × 30 mm) 3·75 90

361 Emblem

1999. 46th Anniv of Independence. Multicoloured.
1927 500r. Type **361** 30 20
1928 1500r. People with symbols of transport and industry 75 30
1929 2000r. People queueing to vote 1·10 45

362 Tiger Barbs

1999. Fishes. Multicoloured.
1930 200r. Type **362** 30 10
1931 500r. Rainbow shark minnow 45 10
1932 900r. Clown rasbora 75 20
1933 1000r. Orange-spotted cichlid 85 20
1934 1500r. Crescent betta 1·40 20
1935 4000r. Honey gourami 3·75 20
MS1936 109 × 84 mm. Eyespot pufferfish (39 × 31 mm) 3·75 90

363 Harpy Eagle

1999. Birds of Prey. Multicoloured.
1937 200r. Type **363** 30 10
1938 500r. Bateleur (vert) 45 10
1939 900r. Egyptian vulture (vert) 75 20
1940 1000r. Peregrine falcon (vert) 85 20
1941 1500r. Red-tailed hawk (vert) 1·40 20
1942 4000r. American bald eagle 3·75 20
MS1943 109 × 85 mm. 5400r. Red kite (31 × 39 mm) 3·75 90

364 Mail Carriage and Globe

1999. 125th Anniv of Universal Postal Union.
1944 **364** 1600r. multicoloured 1·60 90

365 Giant Panda

1999. Mammals. Multicoloured.
1945 200r. Type **365** 20 10
1946 500r. Yak 30 10
1947 900r. Chinese water deer . . 55 20
1948 1000r. Eurasian water shrew (horiz) 65 20
1949 1500r. European otter (horiz) 95 20
1950 4000r. Tiger (horiz) . . . . 2·75 20
MS1951 110×81 mm. 5400r. Pere David's deer (39×31 mm) . . 3·75 90

366 Coral Snake

1999. Snakes. Multicoloured.
1952 200r. Type **366** 30 10
1953 500r. Rainbow boa 45 10
1954 900r. Yellow anaconda . . . 75 20
1955 1000r. Southern ring-necked snake 85 20
1956 1500r. Harlequin snake . . . 1·40 20
1957 4000r. Eastern tiger snake . . 3·75 20
MS1958 107×81 mm. 5400r. Green python (36×28 mm) . . . . . 3·75 90

367 Dragon

2000. New Year. Year of the Dragon.
1959 **367** 200r. multicoloured . . . 30 10
1960 – 500r. red, buff and black . 45 10
1961 – 900r. multicoloured . . . 75 20
1962 – 1000r. multicoloured . . 85 20
1963 – 1500r. multicoloured . . 1·40 20
1964 – 4000r. multicoloured . . 3·75 20
MS1965 - 86×110 mm. 4500r. multicoloured . . . . 3·25 90
DESIGNS: 500r. Dragon enclosed in circle; 900r. Green dragon with red flames; 1000r. Heraldic dragon; 1500r. Red dragon with blue extremities; 4000r. Blue dragon with yellow flames; 4500r. Dragon's head (32×40 mm).

368 Iguanodon (½-size illustration)

2000. Dinosaurs. Multicoloured.
1966 200r. Type **368** 20 10
1967 500r. Euoplocepalus 30 10
1968 900r. Diplosaurus 55 20
1969 1000r. Diplodocus 65 20
1970 1500r. Stegoceras 95 20
1971 4000r. Stegosaurus . . . . 2·75 20
MS1972 110×85 mm. 4500r. Brachiosaurus (32×40 mm) . . 3·75 90

369 Ground Beetle (*Calosoma sycophanta*)

2000. Insects. Multicoloured.
1973 200r. Type **369** 30 10
1974 500r. European rhinoceros beetle (*Oryctes nasicornis*) 45 10
1975 900r. *Diochrysa fastuosa* . . 75 20
1976 1000r. *Blaps gigas* 85 20
1977 1500r. Green tiger beetle (*Cincindela campestris*) . . 1·40 20
1978 4000r. *Cissistes cephalotes* 3·75 20
MS1979 107×85 mm. 4500r. Scarab beetle (*Scarabaeus aegyptiorum*) (40×32 mm) . . . . 3·25 90

370 Box Turtle (*Cuora amboinensis*)

2000. "Bangkok 2000" International Stamp Exhibition. Turtles and Tortoise. Multicoloured.
1980 200r. Type **370** 30 10
1981 500r. Yellow box turtle (*Cuora flavomarginata*) . . 45 10
1982 900r. Black-breasted leaf turtle (*Geoemyda spengleri*) (horiz) 75 20
1983 1000r. Impressed tortoise (*Manouria (Geochelone) impressa*) (horiz) 85 20
1984 1500r. Reeves' turtle (*Chinemys reevesi*) (horiz) 1·40 20
1985 4000r. Spiny turtle (*Heosemys spinosa*) (horiz) 3·75 20
MS1986 111×86 mm. 4500r. Annadal's turtle (*Hieremys annandalei*) (horiz) (40×32 mm) 3·25 90

371 Ox-cart carrying Rice

2000. Rice Cultivation.
1987 **371** 100r. green and black . . 20 10
1988 – 300r. blue and black . . 30 10
1989 – 500r. mauve and black 45 10
1990 – 1400r. blue and black . . 1·10 10
1991 – 1600r. brown and black 1·50 20
1992 – 1900r. brown and black 1·80 20
1993 – 2200r. red and black . . 2·10 20
DESIGNS: 300r. Harrowing; 500r. Threshing; 1400r. Winnowing; 1600r. Planting; 1900r. Ploughing; 2200r. Binding sheaves.

372 *Jules Petiet* Steam Locomotive

2000. Locomotives. "WIPA 2000" International Stamp Exhibition, Vienna (**MS**2000). Multicoloured.
1994 200r. Type **372** 30 10
1995 500r. *Longue Chaudiere* steam locomotive, 1891 45 10
1996 900r. *Glehn du Busquet* steam locomotive, 1891 65 20
1997 1000r. *Le Grand Chocolats* steam locomotive 85 20
1998 1500r. *Le Pendule Francais* diesel locomotive . . . . 1·30 20
1999 4000r. TGV 001 locomotive, 1976 . . . . 3·50 20
MS2000 110×86 mm. 4500r. "Le Shuttle" in tunnel (80×32 mm) 3·25 90

373 Fly Agaric (*Amanita muscaria*)

2000. Fungi. Multicoloured.
2001 200r. Type **373** 20 10
2002 500r. Panther cap (*Amanita pantherina*) 30 10
2003 900r. *Clitocybe olearia* . . . 55 20
2004 1000r. *Lactarius scrobiculatus* 65 20
2005 1500r. *Scleroderma vulgare* 95 20
2006 4000r. *Amanita verna* . . . 2·75 20
MS2007 110×86 mm. 4500r. Death cap (*Amanita phalloides*) (32×40 mm) . . . . 3·75 90

374 *Betta unimaculata* and *Betta pugnax* (½-size illustration)

2000. Fighting Fish. Multicoloured.
2008 200r. Type **374** 10 10
2009 500r. *Betta macrostoma* and *Betta taeniata* 30 10
2010 900r. *Betta foerschi* and *Betta imbellis* 65 20
2011 1000r. *Betta tessyae* and *Betta picta* 65 20
2012 1500r. *Betta edithae* and *Betta bellica* 95 20
2013 4000r. *Betta smaragdina* . . 2·75 20
MS2014 110×85 mm. 4500r. Siamese fighting fish (*Betta splendens*) (40×32 mm) . . . . 3·25 90

375 Woman in Arched Alcove (stone carving)

2000. Khmer Cultural Heritage. Each brown and black.
2015 500r. Type **375** 30 20
2016 1000r. Woman in flowered head-dress in rectangula bas-relief 75 30
2017 2000r. Woman with right arm raised in arche bas-relief . . . . 1·10 45

376 Galapagos Albatross (*Diomedea irrorata*)

2000. Sea Birds. Multicoloured.
2018 200r. Type **376** 30 10
2019 500r. Kentish plover (*Charadrius alexandrinus*) (*vert*) 45 10
2020 900r. Blue-footed booby (*Sula nebouxii*) 65 20
2021 1000r. Common tern (*Sterna hirundo*) 85 20
2022 1500r. Herring gull (*Larus argentatus*) (*vert*) . . . 1·30 20
2023 4000r. Whiskered tern (*Chlidonias hybrida*) . . . 3·50 20
MS2024 108×83 mm. 4500r. Gannet (*Sula (Morus) bassana*) 3·25 90

377 *Cypripedium macranthum*

2000. Orchids. Multicoloured.
2025 200r. Type **377** 30 10
2026 500r. *Vandopsis gigantean* 45 10
2027 900r. *Calypso bulbosa* . . . 65 20
2028 1000r. *Vanda luzonica* . . . 85 20
2029 1500r. *Paphiopedilum villosum* . . . . 1·30 20
2030 4000r. *Vanda merrillii* . . . 3·50 20
MS2031 81×107 mm. 4500r. *Paphiopedilum Victoria* . . . . 3·25 90

378 Rowers in Large Canoe

2000. Tourism. Multicoloured.
2032 500r. Type **378** 30 20
2033 1500r. Front of decorated canoe 75 30
2034 2000r. Temple, elephant and dancer . . . . 1·10 45

379 Weightlifting

2000. Sports. Multicoloured.
2035 200r. Type **379** 20 10
2036 500r. Gymnastics 45 10
2037 900r. Baseball 55 20
2038 1000r. Tennis 65 20
2039 1500r. Basketball . . . . . 1·10 20
2040 4000r. High jump . . . . . 2·75 20
MS2041 110×85 mm. 4500r. Running . . . . 3·00 90

380 Metz DLK 23-6

2000. Fire Engines. Multicoloured.
2042 200r. Type **380** 20 20
2043 500r. Iveco-Magirus SLF 24/100 . . . . 45 35
2044 900r. Metz SLF 7000 WS 55 45
2045 1000r. Iveco-Magirus TLF 24/50 . . . . 65 55
2046 1500r. Saval-Konenburg RFF-11.000 . . . . . . 1·10 90
2047 4000r. Metz TLF 24/50 . . . 2·75 2·30
MS2048 110×85 mm. 4500r. Metz TLF 16/25 . . . . 6·50 5·50

381 Smooth Haired Dachshund

2000. Dachshunds. Multicoloured.
2049 200r. Type **381** 20 10
2050 500r. Wire haired 45 10
2051 900r. Long haired 55 20
2052 1000r. Two smooth haired 65 20
2053 1500r. Mother and pups . . 1·10 20
2054 4000r. Two puppies . . . . 2·75 20
MS2055 117×86 mm. 4500r. Head of wire haired (32×40 mm) . . 3·00 90

382 Rover 12 C (1912)

2000. Cars. Espana 2000 International Stamp Exhibition, Madrid. Multicoloured.
2056 200r. Type **382** 20 10
2057 500r. Austin 30 CV (1907) 45 10
2058 900r. Rolls-Royce Silver Ghost (1909) 55 20
2059 1000r. Graham Paige (1929) 65 20
2060 1500r. Austin 12 (1937) . . 1·10 20
2061 4000r. Mercedes-Benz 300SL (1957) . . . . 2·75 20
MS2062 110×86 mm. 4500r. MG (1936) (40×32 mm) . . . . . 3·00 90

383 18th-century Korean Painting and Two Kittens

2000. Cats. Multicoloured.
2063 200r. Type **383** 20 10
2064 500r. 18th-century Portuguese tiles and tabby cat 45 10

2065 900r. Satsuma ceramic cat and two cats 55 20
2066 1000r. Goddess Basset (Egyptian) and mother cat and kittens 65 20
2067 1500r. Goddess Freya (engraving) and tortoiseshell cat . . . . . 1·10 20
2068 4000r. Japanese painting and Manx cat . . . . . 2·75 20
MS2069 110 × 86 mm. 4500r. Leaping cat (40 × 32 mm) . . . 3·00 90

384 Flowers, Monument and Flag

2000. 47th Anniv of Independence. Multicoloured.
2070 500r. Type **384** 30 20
2071 1500r. Dove, monument and flag 75 30
2072 2000r. Flag, monument and crowd . . . . 1·10 45

385 The Courageous Little Tailor

2000. Children's Stories. Multicoloured.
2073 200r. Type **385** 20 10
2074 500r. Tom Thumb 45 10
2075 900r. Thumbelina 50 20
2076 1000r. Pinocchio (*horiz*) . . 65 20
2077 1500r. The Crayfish (*horiz*) 1·10 20
2078 4000r. Peter Pan (*horiz*) . . 2·75 20
MS2079 110 × 85 mm. 4500r. Pied Piper of Hamelin (32 × 40 mm) 3·00 90

386 Wattled Starling (*Creatophora cinera*)

2000. Birds. Multicoloured.
2080 200r. Type **386** 20 10
2081 500r. Common starling (*Sturnus vulgaris*) 45 10
2082 900r. Pekin robin (*Leiothrix lutea*) 55 20
2083 1000r. Guianian cock of the rock (*Rupicola rupicola*) 85 20
2084 1500r. Alpine accentor (*Prunella collaris*) . . . . 1·10 20
2085 4000r. Bearded reedling (*Panurus biarmicus*) (inscr "biarnicus") . . . . . . 2·75 20
MS2086 85 × 110 mm. 4500r. Inscr "Muscicapula pallipes" (32 × 40 mm) . . . . 3·00 90

387 Johannes Gutenberg (invention of printing press)

2001. Millennium. Multicoloured.
2087 200r. Type **387** 20 10
2088 500r. Michael Faraday (discovery of electricity) 45 10
2089 900r. Samuel Morse (invention of Morse code) 55 20
2090 1000r. Alexander Bell (invention of telephone) 65 20
2091 1500r. Enrico Fermi (discovery of nuclear fission) . . . . 1·10 20
2092 4000r. Edward Roberts (invention of personal computer) . . . . 2·75 20
MS2093 86 × 112 mm. 5400r. Christopher Columbus (discovery of America) (40 × 32 mm); 5400r. Neil Armstrong (first moon walk) (40 × 32 mm) . . . . 7·50 90

388 Snake Head

2001. Year of the Snake. Multicoloured.
2094 200r. Type **388** 20 10
2095 500r. Two snakes entwined 45 10
2096 900r. Snake entwined with moon 55 20
2097 1000r. Entwined snakes (*different*) 65 20
2098 1500r. Snake encircling moon . . . . 1·10 20
2099 4000r. Three snakes' heads 2·75 20
MS2100 110 × 86 mm. 5400r. Snake head (*different*) (40 × 32 mm) 3·75 90

389 Sandou Ladder Transport (1910)

2001. Fire Engines. Multicoloured.
2101 200r. Type **389** 20 10
2102 500r. Gallo ladder transport (1899) 45 10
2103 900r. Merry Weather appliance (1950) 55 20
2104 1000r. Merry Weather ambulance (1940) 65 20
2105 1500r. Man-Metz appliance (1972) . . . . 1·10 20
2106 4000r. Roman diesel appliance (1970) . . . . 2·75 20
MS2107 111 × 87 mm. 5400r. Metropolitan steam engine (1898) (40 × 32 mm). . . . . 3·75 90

390 Puff Ball (*Lycoperdon perlatum*)

2001. Fungi. Multicoloured.
2108 200r. Type **390** 20 10
2109 500r. *Trametes versicolor* . . 45 10
2110 900r. *Hypholoma sublaterium* (inscr "Hipholoma") . . . 55 20
2111 1000r. Fly agaric (*Amanita muscaria*) 65 20
2112 1500r. *Lycoperdon umbrinum* 1·10 20
2113 4000r. *Cortinarius orellanus* 2·75 20
MS2114 111 × 84 mm. 5400r. Death cap (*Amanita phalloides*) (32 × 40 mm) . . . . 3·75 90

391 Preah Vihear

2001. Temples.
2115 **391** 200r. blue and black . . 20 10
2116 – 300r. red and black . . 30 10
2117 – 600r. green and black . . 45 10
2118 – 1000r. orange and black 65 10
2119 – 1500r. green and black 95 20
2120 – 1700r. violet and black 1·20 20
2121 – 2200r. brown and black 1·40 20

DESIGNS: 300r. Thonmanom; 600r. Tasom; 1000r. Kravan; 1500r. Takeo; 1700r. Mebon; 2200r. Banteay Kdei.

392 Angkor Wat

2001. 3rd Anniv of Day of Khmer Culture. Showing bas-reliefs. Multicoloured.
2122 500r. Type **392** 30 20
2123 1500r. Bayon Temple . . . 1·10 30
2124 2000r. Bayon Temple (different) . . . . 1·40 45

393 Large Tortoiseshell (*Nymphalis polychloros*)

2001. Butterflies. Belgica 2001 International Stamp Exhibition, Brussels. Multicoloured.
2125 200r. Type **393** 20 10
2126 500r. *Cethosia hypsea* . . . 45 10
2127 900r. *Papilio palinurus* . . . 55 20
2128 1000r. Lesser purple emperor (*Apatua ilia*) . . 65 20
2129 1500r. Clipper (*Parthenos Sylvia*) . . . . 1·10 20
2130 4000r. *Morpho grandensis* 2·75 20
MS2131 111 × 85 mm. 5400r. *Heliconius melpomene* (40 × 32 mm) . . . . 3·75 90

394 Gary Cooper

2001. Cinema Actors. Multicoloured.
2132 200r. Type **394** 20 10
2133 500r. Marlene Dietrich . . . 45 10
2134 900r. Walt Disney 55 20
2135 1000r. Clark Gable 65 20
2136 1500r. Jeanette Macdonald 1·10 20
2137 4000r. Melvyn Souglas . . . 2·75 20
MS2138 86 × 111 mm. 5400r. Rudolf Valentino (32 × 40 mm); 5400r. Marilyn Monroe (32 × 40 mm) 7·50 90

395 TVR M series (1972)

2001. Cars. Multicoloured.
2139 200r. Type **395** 20 10
2140 500r. Ferrari 410 (1956) . . 45 10
2141 900r. Peugeot 405 (1995) . . 55 20
2142 1000r. Fiat 8VZ (1953) . . . 65 20
2143 1500r. Citroen Xsara (1997) 1·10 20
2144 4000r. Renault Espace (1997) . . . . 2·75 20
MS2145 111 × 85 mm. 5400r. Ferrari 250 GT (1963) (40 × 32 mm) 3·75 90

396 Bayon Temple

2001. Tourism. Bayon Temple. Multicoloured.
2146 500r. Type **396** 30 30
2147 1500r. Faces and monument 1·10 90
2148 2000r. Face and trees . . . 1·40 1·20

397 Steam Locomotive 4-6-0

2001. Trains. Philanippon '01 International Stamp Exhibition, Tokyo. Multicoloured.
2149 200r. Type **397** 20 20
2150 500r. Steam locomotive 4-6-4 . . . . 45 35
2151 900r. Steam locomotive 4-4-0 . . . . 55 45
2152 1000r. Steam locomotive 4-6-4 . . . . 65 55
2153 1500r. Locomotive 4-6-2 . . 1·10 90
2154 4000r. Locomotive 4-8-2 . . 2·75 2·30
MS2155 110 × 84 mm. 5400r. Steam locomotive 2-8-2 (40 × 32 mm). 3·75 3·25

398 Emperor Penguin (*Aptenodytes forsteri*)

2001. Penguins. Multicoloured.
2156 200r. Type **398** 20 20
2157 500r. Jackass penguin (*Spheniscus demersus*) . . 45 35
2158 900r. Humboldt penguin (*Spheniscus humboldti*) . . 55 45
2159 1000r. Rockhopper penguin (*Eudypes crestatus*) (inscr "cristatus") 65 55
2160 1500r. King penguin (*Aptenodytes patagonica*) 1·10 90
2161 4000r. Bearded penguin (*Pygocelis Antarctica*) . . 2·75 2·30
MS2162 108 × 83 mm. 5400r. Gentoo penguin (*Pygoscelis papua*) (40 × 32 mm) . . . . . 3·75 3·25

399 Singapura

2001. Cats. Multicoloured.
2163 200r. Type **399** 10 10
2164 500r. Cymric 30 30
2165 900r. Exotic short haired (inscr "shirthair") 65 55
2166 1000r. Ragdoll 65 55
2167 1500r. Manx . . . . 1·10 90
2168 4000r. Somali . . . . 2·75 2·40
MS2169 110 × 85 mm. 5400r. Egyptian mau (40 × 32 mm) . . 3·75 3·25

400 Khleng Chak

2001. Traditional Kites. Multicoloured.
2170 300r. Type **400** 20 20
2171 500r. Khleng Kanton . . . 30 30
2172 1000r. Khleng Phnong . . . 55 45
2173 1500r. Khleng KaunMorn 1·10 90
2174 3000r. Khleng Me Ambao 2·10 1·80

401 *Parodia cintiensis*

2001. Cacti. Multicoloured.
2175 200r. Type **401** 10 10
2176 500r. *Astrophytum asterias* 30 30
2177 900r. *Parodia faustiana* . . . 65 55
2178 1000r. *Coryphantha sulcolanata* 65 55
2179 1500r. *Neochilenia hankena* 1·10 90
2180 4000r. *Mammillaria boolii* (inscr "Mamillaria") . . . 2·75 2·40
MS2181 110 × 85 mm. 5400r. *Mammillaria* inscr "Mamilleria swinglei" (32 × 40 mm) . . . . 3·75 3·25

402 Fishing Dance

2001. Dances. Multicoloured.
2182 500r. Type **402** 30 30
2183 1500r. Red fish dance . . . 1·10 90
2184 2000r. Dance of Apsara . . 1·50 1·30

403 Timber Wolf (*Canis occidentalis*)

2001. Wolves and Foxes. Multicoloured.

2185	200r. Type **403**	20	20
2186	500r. Alaska tundra wolf (*Canis tundrorum*)	45	30
2187	900r. Fox (inscr "Vulpes fulvas")	55	45
2188	1000r. Coyote (*Canis latrans*)	65	55
2189	1500r. Fennec fox (*Vulpes zerda*)	1·10	90
2190	4000r. Arctic fox (*Alopex lagopus*)	2·75	2·30
MS2191	112×87 mm. 5400r. Iberian wolf (*Canis signatus*) (40×32 mm)	3·75	3·25

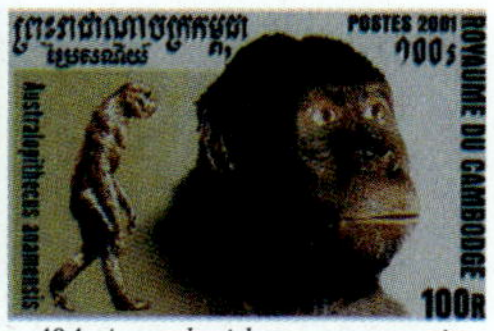

404 *Australopithecus anamensis*

2001. Prehistoric Man. Multicoloured.

2192	100r. Type **404**	10	10
2193	200r. *Australopithecus afarensis*	20	20
2194	300r. *Australopithecus africanus*	20	20
2195	500r. *Australopithecus rudolfensis*	30	30
2196	500r. *Australopithecus boisei*	30	30
2197	1000r. *Homo habilis*	65	55
2198	1500r. *Homo erectus*	1·10	90
2199	4000r. *Homo sapiens neanderthalensis* (inscr "nesnderthalensis")	2·75	2·40
MS2200	110×85 mm. 5400r. *Homo sapiens sapiens* (40×32 mm)	3·75	3·25

404a World Cup Champions (1934)

2001. Italian Football. Multicoloured.

2200a	200r. Type **404a**	20	15
2200b	500r. World Cup champions (1938)	30	25
2200c	900r. European Cup champions (1968)	55	45
2200d	1000r. World Cup champions (1982)	65	50
2200e	1500r. World Cup qualifying team (2002)	1·10	90
2200f	4000r. Federazione Italiana Giuoco Calcio emblem	2·75	2·40

404b Castle (18th-century)

2001. Chess. Multicoloured.

2200g	200r. Type **404b**	20	15
2200h	500r. Pawn (19th-century)	30	25
2200i	900r. King (19th-century)	55	45
2200j	1000r. Bishop (17th-century)	65	50
2200k	1500r. Queen (17th-century)	1·10	90
2200l	4000r. Knight (20th-century) 2.74		2·40
MS2200m	112×87 mm. 5400r. King (16th-century) (40×32 mm)	3·75	3·25

405 Preah Vihear Temple

2002. 10th Anniv of ASEAN (Association of South East Asian Nations) Post. Temples. Multicoloured.

2201	500r. Type **405**	30	25
2202	1000r. Preah Ko	55	40
2203	1500r. Banteay Srei	1·10	85
2204	2500r. Bayon	1·80	1·40
2205	3500r. Ankor Wat	2·20	1·70

406 Bridge No. 26, Route 6A

2003. Japanese Grant Aid. Multicoloured.

2206	100r. Type **406**	15	10
2207	200r. Bridge No. 25, Route 6A	30	25
2208	400r. Chroy Changvar bridge	45	35
2209	800r. Kazuna bridge	60	45
2210	3500r. Monument	3·00	2·40

407 Ox Cart carrying supplies

2003. 140th Anniv of Red Cross and Red Crescent. Multicoloured.

2211	100r. Type **407**	25	20
2212	200r. Red Cross worker (vert)	25	20
2213	300r. Queen Norodom Monineath Sihanouk and young men	30	25
2214	400r. Queen greeting young woman in crowd	30	25
2215	500r. Queen and man	30	25
2216	700r. Queen greeting older woman in crowd	40	30
2217	800r. Queen presenting cloth	65	45
2218	1000r. Woman with shaved head and Queen	65	45
2219	1900r. Queen and M. Bun Rany Hun Sen (pres. of Cambodian Red Cross) (vert)	1·20	95
2220	2100r. M. Bun Rany Hun Sen and Red Cross worker (vert)	1·20	95
2221	4000r. Queen and M. Bun Rany Hun Sen holding baby	2·50	2·00

408 Sugar Palm Tree

410 Conference Emblem

409 Ankor Wat, Cambodia

2003. Sugar Palm. Multicoloured.

2222	300r. Type **408**	30	25
2223	500r. Female flower	30	25
2224	700r. Male flower	40	30
2225	1500r. Fruit	1·10	85

2003. 50th Anniv of China–Cambodia Diplomatic Relations. Multicoloured.

2226	2000r. Type **409**	1·20	95
2227	2000r. Great Wall, China	1·20	95

2003. 36th ASEAN Ministerial Meeting and Tenth ASEAN Regional Forum, Phnom Penh. Multicoloured.

2228	400r. Type **410**	40	30
2229	500r. Dancer (Apsara dance)	50	40
2230	600r. Seated dancer	55	45
2231	1600r. Two seated dancers	1·30	1·00
2232	1900r. Two dancers (Temonorom dance)	1·50	1·20

411 King Norodom Sihanouk and Map

2003. 50th Anniv of Independence. King Norodom Sihanouk. Multicoloured.

2233	200r. Type **411**	25	20
2234	400r. With soldiers (vert)	40	30
2235	500r. Seated (vert)	50	40
2236	800r. With arm extended (vert)	55	45
2237	1000r. Saluting (vert)	65	50
2238	2000r. Independence monument and King Norodom Sihanouk (vert)	1·20	95
2239	5000r. Wearing suit	3·50	2·70

412 Scoop-shaped Fishing Basket

2004. Fishing Tools. Multicoloured.

2240	100r. Type **412**	20	10
2241	200r. Narrow basket	30	20
2242	800r. Cylindrical basket	40	25
2243	1700r. Goblet-shaped basket (vert)	90	55
2244	2200r. Cylindrical basket with baffles (vert)	1·10	70
MS2245	85×110 mm. 2000r. Child and basket (vert)	1·10	1·10

413 Bayon Sculpture

2004. Day of Khmer Culture. Multicoloured.

2246	100r. Type **413**	20	10
2247	200r. Banteay Srei sculpture	30	20
2248	400r. Banteay Srei sculpture (detail)	40	25
2249	800r. Bayon sculpture (different) (vert)	55	35
2250	3500r. Banteay Srei sculpture (detail) (different) (vert)	1·50	90
MS2251	110×85 mm. 2000r. As No. 2250 with design enlarged (vert)	1·10	1·10

414 Waterwheel

2004. Tourism. Landscapes. Multicoloured.

2252	600r. Type **414**	30	20
2253	900r. Paddy fields	50	30
2254	2000r. River and palms	1·10	70
MS2255	110×85 mm. 2000r. Ox cart	1·10	1·10

415 Two Dancers

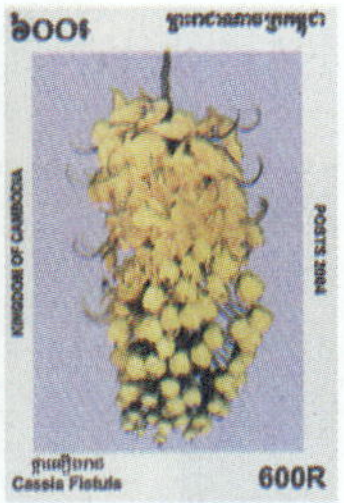

416 *Cassia fistula*

2004. Tepmonorum Dance. Multicoloured.

2256	400r. Type **415**	40	30
2257	1000r. Two dancers wearing blue outfits	65	50
2258	2100r. Two female dancers	1·30	1·00
MS2259	110×85 mm. 2000r. As No. 2259 with design enlarged	1·20	1·20

2004. Flowers. Multicoloured.

2260	600r. Type **416**	35	25
2261	700r. *Butea monosperma*	40	30
2262	900r. *Couroupita quianensis*	55	40
2263	1000r. *Delonix regia* (horiz)	65	50
2264	1800r. *Lagerstroemia floribunda*	1·00	80
MS2265	110×85 mm. 2000r. *Lagerstroemia floribunda* (horiz)	1·20	1·20

417 Preah Khan

2004. Tourism. Temples. Multicoloured.

2266	200r. Type **417**	20	10
2267	500r. Pre Rup	25	15
2268	600r. Banteay Samre	30	20
2269	1600r. Bayon	80	50
2270	1900r. Ankor Wat	90	55
MS2271	110×85 mm. 2000r. Stone head, Bayon (vert)	1·10	1·10

418 King Norodom Sihamoni

2004. Coronation of King Norodom Sihamoni. Multicoloured.

2272	100r. Type **418**	20	10
2273	400r. With monks	30	20
2274	500r. Planting tree	35	20
2275	600r. King Norodom Sihamoni (portrait)	40	25
2276	700r. With crowd, greeting child (horiz)	45	30
2277	900r. Greeting men in uniform (horiz)	50	35
2278	2100r. Releasing dove (horiz)	95	55
2279	2200r. With young men (horiz)	1·10	70
2280	4000r. King Norodom Sihamoni and temple (horiz)	1·70	1·10

419 Anniversary Emblem

420 Aspara Dance

2005. 50th Anniv of Cambodian Red Cross Society. Multicoloured.

2281	400r. Type **419**	15	10
2282	700r. Signing book (horiz)	30	20
2283	800r. Lok Chumteav Bun Rany Hun Sen (president) dispensing aid (horiz)	35	20
2284	1900r. Queen Mother Norodom Monineath Sihanouk dispensing aid (horiz)	1·00	60
2285	2100r. Lok Chumteav Bun Rany Hun Sen presenting certificate to volunteer (horiz)	1·10	65
2286	2200r. King Norodom Sihamoni and Queen Mother Norodom Monineath Sihanouk on dais (horiz)	1·20	70

2005. Traditional Dance. Aspara Dance. Mult.

2287	800r. Type **420**	35	20
2288	900r. Gold skirt, facing right	40	30
2289	1400r. Blue skirt, facing left	55	35
2290	1600r. Cream skirt, leg raised	95	55
2291	2000r. Chequered skirt, facing left	1·10	65

421 Banteay Kdei

2005. Cultural Heritage. Multicoloured.

2292		500r. Type **421**	20	10
2293		700r. Elephant terrace, Angkor Thom	30	20
2294		1000r. Thommanon temple, Angkor	50	30
2295		2000r. Ta Prohm temple, Angkor	1·10	65
2296		2500r. Angkor Wat	1·30	80

EXPRESS MAIL STAMPS

E 313 Bohemian Waxwing

1997. Birds. Multicoloured.

E1624		600r. Type E **313**	1·10	45
E1625		900r. Great grey shrike	1·30	65
E1626		1000r. Eurasian tree sparrow	1·80	75
E1627		2000r. Black redstart	3·50	1·70
E1628		2500r. Reed bunting	4·75	2·00
E1629		3000r. Ortolan bunting	5·25	2·50

POSTAGE DUE STAMPS

D 13

1957.

D81	D 13	10c. red, blue & black	20	20
D82		50c. red, blue & black	55	45
D83		1r. red, blue & black	85	75
D84		3r. red, blue & black	1·10	90
D85		5r. red, blue & black	1·80	1·60

CAMEROON Pt. 1

12 pence = 1 shilling;
20 shillings = 1 pound.

Former German colony occupied by British and French troops during 1914–16. The territory was divided between them and the two areas were administered under League of Nations mandates from 1922, converted into United Nations trusteeships in 1946.

The British section was administered as part of Nigeria until 1960, when a plebiscite was held. The northern area voted to join Nigeria and the southern part joined the newly-independent Cameroun Republic (formerly the French trust territory). In November 1995 this republic joined the Commonwealth.

I. CAMEROONS EXPEDITIONARY FORCE

1915. "Yacht" key-types of German Kamerun surch **C.E.F.** and value in English currency.

B 1	N	$\frac{1}{2}$d. on 3pf. brown	13·00	42·00
B 2		$\frac{1}{2}$d. on 5pf. green	3·25	9·50
B 3		1d. on 10pf. red	1·25	9·50
B 4		2d. on 20pf. blue	3·50	22·00
B 5		$2\frac{1}{2}$d. on 25pf. black and red on yellow	12·00	50·00
B 6		3d. on 30pf. black and orange on buff	12·00	55·00
B 7		4d. on 40pf. black and red	12·00	55·00
B 8		6d. on 50pf. black and purple on buff	12·00	55·00
B 9		8d. on 80pf. black and red on rose	12·00	55·00
B10	O	1s. on 1m. red	£180	£750
B11		2s. on 2m. blue	£180	£750
B12		3s. on 3m. black	£180	£750
B13		5s. on 5m. red and black	£250	£800

II. CAMEROONS TRUST TERRITORY

Issue used in the British trusteeship from October 1960 until June 1961 in the northern area and until September 1961 in the southern area, when they joined with Nigeria and the Cameroun Republic respectively.

1960. Stamps of Nigeria of 1953 optd **CAMEROONS U.K.T.T.**

T1	**18**	$\frac{1}{2}$d. black and orange	10	1·50
T2	–	1d. black and green	10	70
T3	–	$1\frac{1}{2}$d. green	10	20
T4c	–	2d. grey	70	1·25
T5	–	3d. black and lilac	15	10
T6	–	4d. black and blue	10	1·75
T7	–	6d. brown and black	30	20
T8	–	1s. black and purple	15	10
T9	**26**	2s.6d. black and green	1·50	1·00
T10	–	5s. black and orange	2·00	3·50
T11	–	10s. black and brown	2·75	6·50
T12	**29**	£1 black and violet	9·50	23·00

III. REPUBLIC OF CAMEROON

The Republic of Cameroon joined the Commonwealth on 1 November 1995 and issues from that date will be listed below, when examples and information have been received.

CAMEROUN Pt. 7, Pt. 6, Pt. 12

Territory in western Africa which became a German Protectorate in 1884. During 1914–16 it was occupied by Allied troops and in 1922 Britain and France were granted separate United Nations mandates.

In 1960 the French trust territory became an independent republic and, following a plebiscite, in September 1961 the southern part of the area under British control joined the Cameroun Republic. In November 1995 the republic joined the Commonwealth.

A. GERMAN COLONY OF KAMERUN

100 pfennig = 1 mark.

1897. Stamps of Germany optd **Kamerun**.

K1a	**8**	3pf. brown	11·00	17·00
K2		5pf. green	6·50	8·50
K3	**9**	10pf. red	4·50	5·00
K4		20pf. blue	4·50	7·50
K5		25pf. orange	20·00	42·00
K6a		50pf. brown	16·00	27·00

1900. "Yacht" key-types inscr "KAMERUN".

K 7	N	3pf. brown	1·50	1·70
K21		5pf. green	90	1·70
K22		10pf. red	2·75	1·70
K10		20pf. blue	26·00	2·40
K11		25pf. black & red on yell	1·60	5·50
K12		30pf. black & orge on buff	2·20	4·75
K13		40pf. black and red	2·20	4·25
K14		50pf. black & pur on buff	2·20	6·25
K15		80pf. black & red on rose	2·75	11·00
K16	O	1m. red	75·00	75·00
K17		2m. blue	6·00	75·00
K18		3m. black	6·00	£120
K19		5m. red and black	£170	£500

B. FRENCH ADMINISTRATION OF CAMEROUN

100 centimes = 1 franc.

1915. Stamps of Gabon with inscription "AFRIQUE EQUATORIALE-GABON" optd **Corps Expeditionnaire Franco-Anglais CAMEROUN.**

1	**7**	1c. brown and orange	80·00	50·00
2		2c. black and brown	£120	£120
3		4c. violet and blue	£120	£120
4		5c. olive and green	32·00	34·00
5		10c. red and lake (on No. 37 of Gabon)	32·00	18·00
6		20c. brown and violet	£120	£130
7	**8**	25c. brown and blue	60·00	50·00
8		30c. red and grey	£120	£120
9		35c. green and violet	60·00	48·00
10		40c. blue and brown	£120	£120
11		45c. violet and red	£120	£120
12		50c. grey and green	£120	£120
13		75c. brown and orange	£170	£130
14	**9**	1f. yellow and brown	£180	£130
15		2f. brown and red	£190	£170

1916. Optd **Occupation Francaise du Cameroun.**

(a) On stamps of Middle Congo.

16	**1**	1c. olive and brown	80·00	85·00
17		2c. violet and brown	85·00	85·00
18		4c. blue and brown	85·00	80·00
19		5c. green and blue	46·00	46·00
20	**2**	35c. brown and blue	£110	55·00
21		45c. violet and orange	90·00	85·00

(b) On stamps of French Congo.

22	**6**	15c. violet and green	95·00	95·00
23	**8**	20c. green and red	£100	90·00
24		30c. red and yellow	80·00	75·00
25		40c. brown and green	55·00	80·00
26		50c. violet and lilac	95·00	80·00
27		75c. purple and orange	95·00	70·00
28	–	1f. drab and grey (48)	£110	£110
29	–	2f. red and brown (49)	£110	£110

1916. Stamps of Middle Congo optd **CAMEROUN Occupation Francaise.**

30	**1**	1c. olive and brown	30	3·25
31		2c. violet and brown	65	3·00
32		4c. blue and brown	65	3·25
33		5c. green and blue	80	2·30
34		10c. red and blue	75	2·75
34a		15c. purple and red	2·75	4·25
35		20c. brown and blue	1·50	3·50
36	**2**	25c. blue and green	1·00	1·30
37		30c. pink and green	2·00	2·75
38		35c. brown and blue	1·60	3·00
39		40c. green and brown	1·70	4·50
40		45c. violet and orange	2·30	4·50
41		50c. green and orange	2·75	4·50
42		75c. brown and blue	2·30	5·75
43	**3**	1f. green and violet	2·30	3·50
44		2f. violet and green	7·50	13·00
45		5f. blue and pink	10·00	25·00

1921. Stamps of Middle Congo (colours changed) optd **CAMEROUN.**

46	**1**	1c. orange and green	10	4·25
47		2c. red and brown	10	4·50
48		4c. green and grey	15	4·75
49		5c. orange and red	10	3·00
50		10c. light green and green	55	3·50
51		15c. orange and blue	1·10	4·75
52		20c. grey and purple	1·90	4·75
53	**2**	25c. orange and grey	1·40	1·90
54		30c. red and carmine	1·40	4·75
55		35c. blue and grey	1·80	4·75
56		40c. orange and green	1·70	4·75
57		45c. red and brown	1·30	4·00
58		50c. ultramarine and blue	80	3·25
59		75c. green and purple	95	5·00
60	**3**	1f. orange and grey	3·00	5·50
61		2f. red and green	7·25	17·00
62		5f. grey and red	7·25	25·00

1924. Stamps of 1921 surch.

63	**1**	25c. on 15c. orange & blue	40	5·50
64	**3**	25c. on 2f. red and green	1·80	5·50
65		25c. on 5f. grey and red	1·30	6·00
66	**2**	"65" on 45c. red and brown	1·90	6·50
67		"85" on 75c. green & red	2·75	6·75

5 Cattle fording River

1925.

68	**5**	1c. mauve and olive	10	3·00
69		2c. green & red on green	35	2·30
70		4c. black and blue	45	3·00
71		5c. mauve and yellow	40	40
72		10c. orange & pur on yell	1·30	80
73		15c. green	2·50	4·25
88		15c. red and lilac	1·00	3·00
74	A	20c. brown and olive	1·50	4·50
89		20c. green	1·10	3·25
90		20c. brown and red	55	15
75		25c. black and green	1·00	10
76		30c. red and green	1·10	1·20
91		30c. green and olive	1·10	1·30
77		35c. black and brown	1·80	5·00
91a		35c. green	3·75	4·00
78		40c. violet and orange	3·50	3·50
79		45c. red	95	4·75
92		45c. brown and mauve	3·25	3·50
80		50c. red and green	2·75	20
93		55c. red and blue	4·25	6·00
81		60c. black and mauve	2·50	4·25
94		60c. red	1·30	4·25
82		65c. brown and blue	2·75	65
83		75c. blue	1·40	3·00
95		75c. mauve and brown	95	1·10
95a		80c. brown and red	1·70	5·25
84		85c. blue and red	1·20	3·00
96		90c. red	3·25	3·50
85	B	1f. brown and blue	1·40	5·00
97		1f. blue	1·20	1·30
98		1f. mauve and brown	1·60	2·50
99		1f. brown and green	3·50	1·90
100		1f.10 brown and red	3·50	9·25
100a		1f.25 blue and brown	11·00	9·25
101		1f.50 blue	3·00	95
101a		1f.75 red and brown	1·70	1·90
101b		1f.75 blue	10·00	11·50
86		2f. orange and olive	4·00	30
102		3f. mauve and brown	4·50	2·50
87		5f. black & brown on bl	4·50	1·00
103		10f. mauve and orange	10·50	8·50
104		20f. green and red	24·00	19·50

DESIGNS—VERT: A, Tapping rubber-trees. HORIZ: B, Liana suspension bridge.

1926. Surch with new value.

105	B	1f.25 on 1f. blue	1·10	4·50

1931. "Colonial Exhibition" key-types inscribed "CAMEROUN".

106	E	40c. green	4·25	7·75
107	F	50c. mauve	4·75	7·50
108	G	90c. orange	5·25	7·25
109	H	1f.50 blue	5·25	6·00

14 Sailing Ships

1937. Paris International Exhibition. Inscr "EXPOSITION INTERNATIONALE PARIS 1937".

110	–	20c. violet	2·25	5·25
111	**14**	30c. green	2·50	5·00
112	–	40c. red	1·70	4·75
113	–	50c. brown & deep brown	2·30	3·25
114	–	90c. red	2·00	4·50
115	–	1f.50 blue	1·80	4·75
MS115a		120 × 100 mm. 163f. red and agate	8·75	21·00

DESIGNS—VERT: 20c. Allegory of Commerce; 50c. Allegory of Agriculture. HORIZ: 40c. Berber, Negress and Annamite; 90c. France extends torch of Civilization; 1f.50, Diane de Poitiers.

19 Pierre and Marie Curie

1938. International Anti-cancer Fund.

116	**19**	1f.75+50c. blue	8·00	24·00

20

21 Lamido Woman

1939. New York World's Fair.

117	**20**	1f.25 red	2·30	5·50
118		2f.25 blue	2·75	5·50

1939.

119	**21**	2c. black	20	4·25
120		3c. mauve	40	4·00
121		4c. blue	75	4·25
122		5c. brown	60	4·25
123		10c. green	65	3·75
124		15c. red	90	4·75
125		20c. purple	95	4·75
126	A	25c. black	1·40	3·75
127		30c. orange	75	5·00
128		40c. blue	85	4·75
129		45c. green	1·90	7·00
130		50c. brown	1·00	3·75
131		60c. blue	1·40	5·25
132		70c. purple	2·50	7·00
133	B	80c. blue	3·25	7·50
134		90c. blue	1·80	2·30
135		1f. red	2·75	3·75
135a		1f. brown	1·80	3·00
136		1f.25 red	4·50	11·50
137		1f.40 orange	2·30	5·75
138		1f.50 brown	1·40	2·50
139		1f.60 brown	2·50	7·00
140		1f.75 blue	1·80	3·75
141		2f. green	1·90	2·30
142		2f.25 blue	2·00	3·75
143		2f.50 purple	2·50	3·25
144		3f. violet	1·50	2·50
145	C	5f. brown	2·00	2·75
146		10f. purple	1·90	4·75
147		20f. green	4·00	6·50

DESIGNS—VERT: A, Banyo Waterfall; C, African boatman. HORIZ: B, African elephants.

25 Storming the Bastille

1939. 150th Anniv of Revolution.

148	**25**	45c.+25c. green	8·00	17·00
149		70c.+30c. brown	5·75	16·00
150		90c.+35c. orange	7·00	20·00
151		1f.25+1f. red	7·00	21·00
152		2f.25+2f. blue	11·50	25·00

1940. Adherence to General de Gaulle. Optd **CAMEROUN FRANCAIS 27-8-40.**

153	**21**	2c. black	85	90
154		3c. mauve	90	2·30
155		4c. blue	55	1·20
156		5c. brown	6·00	5·75
157		10c. green	65	90
158		15c. red	1·40	4·25
159		20c. purple	19·00	17·00
160	A	25c. black	1·10	55
161		30c. orange	16·00	18·00
162		40c. blue	4·75	2·00
163		45c. green	1·80	90
164	–	50c. red & green (No. 80)	75	60
165	A	60c. blue	5·75	6·75
166		70c. purple	2·30	1·50
167	B	80c. blue	6·25	2·50
168		90c. blue	55	25
169	**20**	1f.25 red	4·00	2·30
170	B	1f.25 red	85	65
171		1f.40 orange	1·60	1·60
172		1f.50 brown	65	35
173		1f.60 brown	1·70	65
174		1f.75 blue	95	60
175	**20**	2f.25 blue	3·75	2·30
176	B	2f.25 blue	60	55
177		2f.50 purple	85	30
178	–	5f. black and brown on blue (No. 87)	25·00	4·00
179	C	5f. brown	23·00	3·50
180	–	10f. mve & orge (No. 103)	26·00	4·00
181	C	10f. purple	70·00	60·00
182	–	20f. green & red (No. 104)	60·00	7·50
183	C	20f. green	£140	£180

1940. War Relief Fund. Nos. 100a, 101a and 86 surch **OEUVRES DE GUERRE** and premium.

184		1f.25+2f. blue and brown	30·00	32·00
185		1f.75+3f. red and brown	29·00	34·00
186		2f.+5f. orange and olive	22·00	21·00

1940. Spitfire Fund. Nos. 126, 129, 131/2 surch **+5 Frs. SPITFIRE.**

187	A	25c.+5f. black	£110	£120
188		45c.+5f. green	£120	£120
189		60c.+5f. blue	£120	£120
190		70c.+5f. purple	£120	£120

1941. Spitfire Fund. Surch **SPITFIRE +10 fr. General de GAULLE.**

190a	**20**	1f.25+10f. red	£110	£120
190b		2f.25+10f. blue	£110	£120

29b Sikorsky S-43 over Map

29c Sikorsky S-43 Amphibian

1941. Air.
190c **29b** 25c. red 65 5·00
190d 50c. green 45 5·00
190e 1f. purple 2·50 5·00
190f **29c** 2f. olive 1·50 3·50
190g 3f. brown 1·70 3·75
190h 4f. blue 1·20 3·75
190i 6f. myrtle 1·50 3·25
190j 7f. purple 1·40 3·25
190k 12f. orange 7·25 11·50
190l 20f. red 3·75 5·75
190m – 50f. blue 4·25 5·75
DESIGN: 50f. Latecoere 631 flying boat over harbour.

1941. Laquintinie Hospital Fund. Surch **+10 Frs. AMBULANCE LAQUINTINIE.**
191 **20** 1f.25+10f. red 34·00 36·00
192 2f.25+10f. blue 48·00 34·00

31 Cross of Lorraine, Sword and Shield

32 Fairey FC-1

1942. Free French Issue.
193 **31** 5c. brown (postage) 10 1·90
194 10c. blue 10 10
195 25c. green 10 40
196 30c. red 10 30
197 40c. green 50 25
198 80c. purple 60 95
199 1f. mauve 85 20
200 1f.50 red 80 10
201 2f. black 65 10
202 2f.50 blue 55 45
203 4f. violet 50 75
204 5f. yellow 80 80
205 10f. brown 65 30
206 20f. green 85 90
207 **32** 1f. orange (air) 1·30 3·75
208 1f.50 red 2·00 4·50
209 5f. purple 1·20 4·50
210 10f. black 1·10 4·75
211 25f. blue 1·90 4·75
212 50f. green 2·75 3·25
213 100f. red 2·25 3·00

1943. Surch **Valmy +100 frs.**
213a – 1f.25+100f. blue and brown (No. 100a) 13·00 52·00
213b **20** 1f.25+100f. red 10·50 52·00
213c – 1f.25+100f. red (No. 136) 32·00 52·00
213d – 1f.50+100f. brown (No. 138) 20·00 52·00
213e **20** 2f.25+100f. blue 18·50 52·00

33

34 Felix Eboue

1944. Mutual Aid and Red Cross Funds.
214 **33** 5f.+20f. red 55 7·50

1945. Surch.
215 **31** 50c. on 5c. brown 1·30 4·75
216 60c. on 5c. brown 55 4·75
217 70c. on 5c. brown 65 5·00
218 1f.20 on 5c. brown 95 5·00
219 2f.40 on 25c. green 95 2·25
220 3f. on 25c. green 1·00 2·50
221 4f.50 on 25c. green 1·60 6·00
222 15f. on 2f.50 blue 1·40 5·75

1945.
223 **34** 2f. black 10 2·25
224 25f. green 70 4·50

35 "Victory"

1946. Air. Victory.
225 **35** 8f. purple 65 2·25

36 Chad

1946. Air. From Chad to the Rhine. Inscr "DU TCHAD AU RHIN".
226 **36** 5f. blue 2·75 6·00
227 – 10f. purple 1·90 5·50
228 – 15f. red 2·25 5·50
229 – 20f. blue 2·25 5·75
230 – 25f. brown 5·25 6·00
231 – 50f. black 1·90 6·00
DESIGNS: 10f. Koufra; 15f. Mareth; 20f. Normandy; 25f. Paris; 50f. Strasbourg.

37 Zebu and Herdsman

45 Aeroplane, African and Mask

1946.
232 **37** 10c. green (postage) 10 1·50
233 30c. orange 10 3·00
234 40c. blue 10 4·50
235 – 50c. sepia 70 1·40
236 – 60c. purple 75 4·00
237 – 80c. brown 75 4·50
238 – 1f. orange 1·10 10
239 – 1f.20 green 1·10 5·00
240 – 1f.50 red 2·00 2·30
241 – 2f. black 60 10
242 – 3f. red 2·30 10
243 – 3f.60 red 1·70 5·00
244 – 4f. blue 1·10 10
245 – 5f. red 2·00 10
246 – 6f. blue 2·00 10
247 – 10f. green 1·60 10
248 – 15f. blue 2·30 50
249 – 20f. green 2·30 65
250 – 25f. black 2·00 1·40
251 – 50f. green (air) 2·30 70
252 – 100f. brown 2·50 2·50
253 **45** 200f. olive 5·25 4·75
DESIGNS—VERT: 50c. to 80c. Tikar women; 1f. to 1f.50, Africans carrying bananas; 2f. to 4f. Bowman; 5f. to 10f. Lamido horsemen; 15f. to 25f. Native head. HORIZ: 50f. Birds over mountains; 100f. African horsemen and Dewoitine D-333 trimotor airplane.

46 People of Five Races, Lockheed Constellation Airplane and Globe

1949. Air. 75th Anniv of UPU.
254 **46** 25f. multicoloured 3·25 7·25

47 Doctor and Patient

1950. Colonial Welfare Fund.
255 **47** 10f.+2f. green & turq 5·25 12·50

48 Military Medal

49 Porters Carrying Bananas

50 Transporting Logs

1952. Military Medal Centenary.
256 **48** 15f. red, yellow and green 5·50 5·00

1953.
257 **49** 8f. violet, orange and purple (postage) 25 10
258 15f. brown, yellow & red 2·30 45
259 – 40f. brown, pink & choc 1·50 65
260 **50** 50f. ol, brn & sep (air) 4·00 70
261 – 100f. sepia, brown & turq 11·00 1·50
262 – 200f. brown, blue & grn 12·50 6·75
262a – 500f. indigo, blue and lilac 20·00 16·00
DESIGNS—As Type **49**: 40f. Woman gathering coffee. As Type **50**: HORIZ: 100f. Airplane over giraffes; 200f. Freighters, Douala Port. VERT: 500f. Sud Ouest Corse II over Piton d'Humsiki.

51 Edea Barrage

1953. Air. Opening of Edea Barrage.
263 **51** 15f. blue, lake and brown 1·00 90

52 "D-Day"

1954. Air. 10th Anniv of Liberation.
264 **52** 15f. green and turquoise 6·25 4·75

53 Dr. Jamot and Students

1954. Air. 75th Birthday of Dr. Jamot (physician).
265 **53** 15f. brown, blue & green 4·50 6·50

54 Native Cattle

1956. Economic and Social Development Fund. Inscr "F.I.D.E.S.".
266 **54** 5f. brown and sepia 30 20
267 – 15f. turq, blue & black 1·40 25
268 – 20f. turquoise and blue 1·20 60
269 – 25f. blue 1·70 60
DESIGNS: 15f. R. Wouri bridge; 20f. Technical education; 25f. Mobile medical unit.

55 Coffee

1956.
270 **55** 15f. vermilion and red 30 10

56 Woman, Child and Flag

57 "Human Rights"

1958. 1st Anniv of First Cameroun Govt.
271 **56** 20f. multicoloured 25 15

1958. 30th Anniv of Declaration of Human Rights.
272 **57** 20f. brown and red 1·00 2·75

58 "Randia malleifera"

60 Prime Minister A. Ahidjo

59 Loading Bananas on Ship at Douala

1958. Tropical Flora.
273 **58** 20f. multicoloured 1·10 40

1959.
274 **59** 20f. multicoloured 90 30
275 – 25f. green, brn & pur 1·10 65
DESIGN—VERT: 25f. Bunch of bananas and native bearers in jungle path.

C. INDEPENDENT REPUBLIC

1960. Proclamation of Independence. Inscr "1 ER JANVIER 1960".
276 – 20f. multicoloured 80 25
277 **60** 25f. green, bistre & black 80 25
DESIGN: 20f. Cameroun flag and map.

61 "Uprooted Tree"

62 CCTA Emblem

1960. World Refugee Year.
278 **61** 30f. green, blue and brown 1·10 55

1960. 10th Anniv of African Technical Co-operation Commission.
279 **62** 50f. black and purple 1·60 80

63 Map and Flag

64 U.N. Headquarters, Emblem and Cameroun Flag

1961. Red Cross Fund. Flag in green, red and yellow; cross in red; background colours given.
280 **63** 20f.+5f. green and red 1·20 95
281 25f.+10f. red and green 1·50 1·20
282 30f.+15f. red and green 2·10 1·60

1961. Admission to UNO. Flag in green, red and yellow; emblem in blue, buildings and inscr in colours given.
283 **64** 15f. brown and green 50 30
284 25f. green and blue 75 40
285 85f. purple, blue and red 2·30 1·40

1961. Surch **REPUBLIQUE FEDERALE** and value in Sterling currency.
286 – ½d. on 1f. orange (238) (postage) 45 25
287 – 1d. on 2f. black (241) 45 40
288 **54** 1½d. on 5f. brown & sepia 55 45
289 – 2d. on 10f. green (247) 1·00 70
290 – 3d. on 15f. turquoise, indigo and black (267) 1·30 70
291 – 4d. on 15f. vermilion and red (270) 1·50 90
292 – 6d. on 20f. mult (274) 2·10 1·30
293 **60** 1s. on 25f. grn, bis & blk 3·00 2·20
294a **61** 2s.6d. on 30f. green, blue and brown 5·50 5·00
295a – 5s. on 100r. sepia, brown and turquoise (264) (air) 10·00 9·50
296a – 10s. on 200f. brown, blue and green (265) 20·00 19·00
297a – £1 on 500f. indigo, blue and lilac (253a) 34·00 32·00

The above were for use in the former British Cameroon Trust Territory pending the introduction of the Cameroun franc.

66 Pres. Ahidjo and Prime Minister Foncha

1962. Reunification. (a) T **66**.
298 20f. brown and violet
299 25f. brown and green
300 60f. green and red
Set of 3 . . . 60·00 50·00

(b) T **66** surch in Sterling currency.
301 3d. on 20f. brown & violet
302 6d. on 25f. brown and green
303 2s.6d. on 60f. green and red
Set of 3 . . . £500 £475

68 Lions International Badge, Doctor and Leper

1962. World Leprosy Day. Lions International Relief Fund.
304 **68** 20f.+5f. purple & brown 75 70
305 25f.+10f. purple & blue 95 90
306 50f.+15f. purple & green 1·80 1·60

69 European, African and Boeing 707 Airliners

1962. Air. Foundation of "Air Afrique" Airline.
307 **69** 25f. purple, violet & grn 1·00 50

70 Campaign Emblem

71 Giraffes and Waza Camp

1962. Malaria Eradication.
308 **70** 25f.+5f. mauve . . . 1·00 80

1962. (a) Postage. Animals.
309 A 50c. sepia, blue & turquoise 10 10
310 B 1f. black, turquoise & orge 10 10
311 C 1f.50 brown, sage & blk 20 10
312 D 2f. black, blue and green 20 20
313 C 3f. brown, orange & purple 20 20
314 B 4f. sepia, green & turq 25 20
315 D 5f. purple, green & brown 35 20
316 A 6f. sepia, blue and lemon 45 25
317 E 8f. blue, red and green 95 70
318 F 10f. black, orange & blue 75 25
319 A 15f. brown, blue & turq 1·40 45
320 **71** 20f. brown and grey 95 45
321 F 25f. brown, yellow & grn 2·75 1·00
322 E 30f. black, blue & brown 3·00 1·10
323 **71** 40f. lake and green 6·50 2·10

(b) Air.
324 – 50f. brown, myrtle & blue 95 70
325 – 100f. multicoloured 4·75 1·50
326 – 200f. black, brn & turq 8·00 2·40
327 – 500f. buff, purple and blue 11·00 3·75

DESIGNS—HORIZ: As Type **71**: A, Moustached monkey; B, African elephant and Ntem Falls; C, Kob, Dschang; D, Hippopotamus, Hippo Camp; E, African manatee, Lake Ossa; F, Buffalo, Batoun Region. (48 × 27 mm): 50f. Cocotiers Hotel, Douala; 100f. "Cymothoe sangaris" (butterfly); 200f. Ostriches; 500f. Kapsikis, Mokolo (landscape).

72 Union Flag

1962. 1st Anniv of Union of African and Malagasy States. Flag in green, red and gold.
328 **72** 30f. brown . . . 2·00 90

73 Map and View

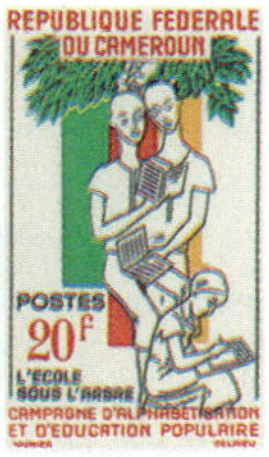

74 "The School Under the Tree"

1962. 1st Anniv of Reunification.
329 **73** 9f. bistre, violet & brown 35 25
330 18f. red, green and blue 45 40
331 – 20f. bistre, blue and purple 60 40
332 – 25f. orange, sepia & blue 60 45
333 – 50f. blue, sepia and red 1·50 90

DESIGNS: 20f., 25f. Sunrise over Cameroun; 50f. Commemorative scroll.

1962. Literacy and Popular Education Plan.
334 **74** 20f. red, yellow and green 1·00 50

75 Globe and "Telstar"

1963. 1st Trans-Atlantic Television Satellite Link.
335 **75** 1f. ol, vio & blue (postage) 20 10
336 2f. lake, green and blue 30 25
337 3f. olive, purple and green 30 25
338 25f. blue and green 1·00 1·00
339 100f. brown and green (air) (48 × 27 mm) 2·30 1·40

76 Globe and Emblem

77 VHF Station, Mt. Bankolo, Yaounde

1963. Freedom from Hunger.
340 **76** 18f.+5f. blue, brn & grn 90 50
341 25f.+5f. green & brown 1·30 60

1963. Inauguration of Doala–Yaounde VHF Radio Service.
342 **77** 15f. mult (postage) 45 30
343 – 20f. multicoloured 60 45
344 – 100f. multicoloured (air) 2·30 1·40

DESIGNS: 20f. Aerials and control panel; 100f. Edea relay station (26 × 44 mm).

78 "Centre regional ..."

80 Pres. Ahidjo

1963. Inauguration of UNESCO Regional Schoolbooks Production Centre, Yaounde.
345 **78** 20f. red, black and green 45 25
346 25f. red, black and orange 55 25
347 100f. red, black and gold 2·00 1·10

1963. Air. African and Malagasian Posts and Telecommunications Union. As T **18** of Central African Republic.
348 85f. multicoloured . . . 2·20 1·50

1963. 2nd Anniv of Reunification. Multicoloured.
349 9f. Type **80** 40 30
350 18f. Map and flag 60 30
351 20f. Type **80** 75 40

1963. Air. Inauguration of "DC-8" Service. As T **11** of Congo Republic.
352 50f. multicoloured . . . 1·30 60

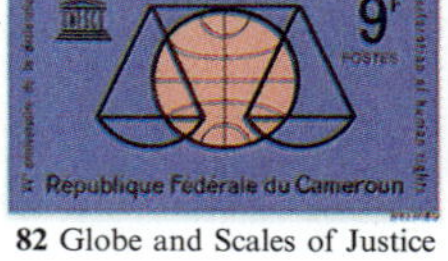

82 Globe and Scales of Justice

1963. 15th Anniv of Declaration of Human Rights.
353 **82** 9f. brown, black and blue 40 25
354 18f. red, black and green 55 25
355 25f. green, black & red 75 35
356 75f. blue, black & yellow 1·80 95

83 Lion

1964. Waza National Park.
357 **83** 10f. bistre green & brown 1·40 45
358 25f. bistre and green 2·00 85

84 Football Stadium, Yaounde

1964. Tropics Cup. Inscr as in T **84**.
359 **84** 10f. brown, turquoise & grn 45 25
360 – 18f. green, red and violet 60 40
361 – 30f. blue, brown and black 1·00 60

DESIGNS: 18f. Sports Equipment; 30f. Stadium Entrance. Yaounde.

85 Palace of Justice, Yaounde

1964. 1st Anniv of European–African Economic Convention. Multicoloured.
362 15f. Type **85** 1·20 70
363 40f. Sun, moon and economic emblems (vert) 2·30 1·40

86 Olympic Flame and Hurdling

1964. Olympic Games, Toyko.
364 **86** 9f. red, blk & grn (postage) 1·70 1·40
365 – 10f. brown, violet and red 2·20 1·40
366 – 300f. turquoise, brown and red (air) 8·25 4·75

MS366a 168 × 100 mm. Nos. 364/66 (air) 14·50 14·50

DESIGNS—VERT: 10f. Running. HORIZ: 300f. Wrestling.

87 Ntem Falls

88 Co-operation

1964. Folklore and Tourism.
367 – 9f. red, blue & grn (postage) 55 25
368 – 18f. blue, brown and red 75 45
369 **87** 20f. drab, green and red 90 45
370 – 25f. red, brown & orange 1·40 75
371 – 50f. brown, grn & bl (air) 1·20 70
372 – 250f. sepia, grn & brn 11·00 3·75

DESIGNS—As Type **87**. VERT: 9f. Bamileke dance costume; 18f. Bamenda dance mask. HORIZ: 25f. Fulani horseman. LARGER (43 × 27½ mm): 50f. View of Kribi and Longji; 250f. Black rhinoceros.

1964. French, African and Malagasy Co-operation.
373 **88** 18f. brown, green and blue 95 40
374 30f. brown, turq & brn 1·40 55

89 Pres. Kennedy

1964. Air. Pres. Kennedy Commem.
375 **89** 100f. sepia, grn & apple 2·30 2·20
MS375a **89** 129 × 90 mm. Block of four 9·00 9·00

90 Inscription recording laying of First Rail

1965. Opening of Mbanga–Kumba Railway.
376 **90** 12f. indigo, green and blue 95 50
377 – 20f. yellow, green and red 2·50 1·00

DESIGN—HORIZ: (36 × 22 mm): 20f. Series BB500 diesel locomotive.

91 Abraham Lincoln

1965. Air. Death Centenary of Abraham Lincoln.
378 **91** 100f. multicoloured 2·30 1·60

92 Ambulance and First Aid Post

1965. Cameroun Red Cross.
379 **92** 25f. yellow, green and red 75 30
380 – 50f. brown, red and grey 1·50 55

DESIGN—VERT: 50f. Nurse and child.

93 "Syncom" and ITU Emblem

1965. Air. Centenary of ITU.
381 **93** 70f. black, blue and red 1·60 85

94 Churchill giving "V" Sign

95 "Map" Savings Bank

1965. Air. Churchill Commem. Multicoloured.
382 12f. Type **94** 1·20 70
383 18f. Churchill, oak spray and cruiser "De Grasse" 1·20 70

1965. Federal Postal Savings Bank.
384 **95** 9f. yellow, red and green 40 25
385 – 15f. brown, green & blue 55 25
386 – 20f. brown, chest & turq 60 40

DESIGNS—HORIZ: (48 × 27 mm): 15f. Savings Bank building. VERT: (27 × 48 mm): 20f. "Cocoa-bean" savings bank.

96 Africa Cup and Players

1965. Winning of Africa Cup by Oryx Football Club.
387 **96** 9f. brown, yellow and red 75 35
388 20f. blue, yellow and red 1·50 55

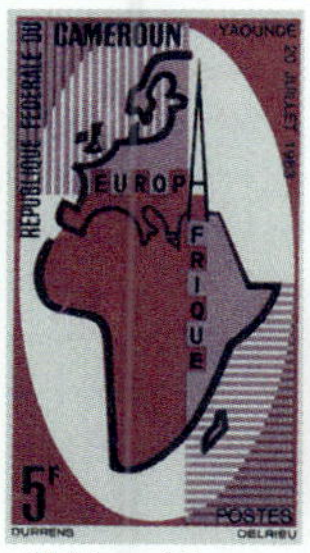

97 Map of Europe and Africa
98 UPU Monument, Berne and Doves

1965. "Europafrique".
389 **97** 5f. red, lilac and black . . 30 25
390 – 40f. multicoloured . . . . 1·30 80
DESIGN: 40f. Yaounde Conference.

1965. 5th Anniv of Admission to UPU.
391 **98** 30f. purple and red 80 60

99 ICY Emblem

1965. International Co-operation Year.
392 **99** 10f. red & blue (postage) 45 35
393 100f. blue and red (air) . . 2·30 1·00

100 Pres. Ahidjo and Government House

1965. Re-election of Pres. Ahidjo. Multicoloured.
394 9f. Pres. Ahidjo wearing hat, and Government House (vert) 30 10
395 18f. Type **100** 45 20
396 20f. As 9f. 55 25
397 25f. Type **100** 85 45

101 Musgum Huts, Pouss

1965. Folklore and Tourism.
398 **101** 9f. green, brown and red (postage) 40 25
399 – 18f. brown, green & blue 45 25
400 – 20f. brown and blue . . . 95 40
401 – 25f. grey, lake and green 95 40
402 – 50f. brown, blue and green (48 × 27 mm) (air) 2·20 80
DESIGNS—HORIZ: 18f. Great Calao's dance (N. Cameroons); 25f. National Tourist office, Yaounde; 50f. Racing pirogue on Sanaga River, Edea. VERT: 20f. Sultan's palace gate Foumban.

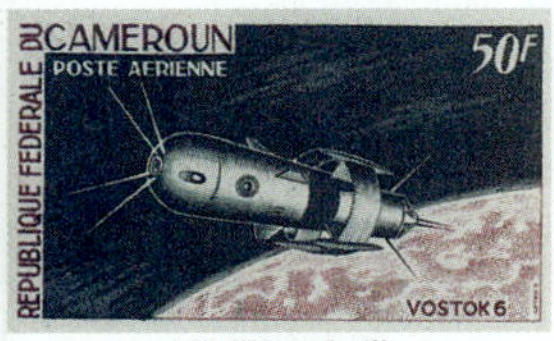

102 "Vostok 6"

1966. Air. Spacecraft.
403 **102** 50f. green and red 95 55
404 – 100f. blue and purple . . 2·10 90
405 – 200f. violet and blue . . . 3·75 2·20
406 – 500f. blue and indigo . . 8·75 4·50
DESIGNS: 100f. "Gemini 4", and White in space; 200f. "Gemini 5"; 500f. "Gemini 6" and "Gemini 7" making rendezvous.

103 Mountain's Hotel, Buea

1966. Cameroun Hotels.
407 **103** 9f. bistre, green and red (postage) 35 25
408 – 20f. black, green & blue 45 25
409 – 35f. red, brown & green 95 55
410 **103** 18f. black, grn & bl (air) 45 25
411 – 25f. indigo, red and blue 65 45
412 – 50f. brown, orange & grn 2·40 1·10
413 – 60f. brown, green & blue 1·40 75
414 – 85f. blue, red and green 1·80 85
415 – 100f. purple, blue & grn 2·75 1·20
416 – 150f. orange, brn & blue 3·50 1·60
HOTELS—HORIZ: 20f. Deputies, Yaounde. 25f. Akwa Palace, Douala. 35f. Dschang. 50f. Terminus, Yaounde. 60f. Imperial, Yaounde. 85f. Independence, Yaounde. 150f. Huts, Waza Camp. VERT: 100f. Hunting Lodge, Mora.

104 Foumban Bas-relief

1966. World Festival of Negro Arts, Dakar.
417 **104** 9f. black and red 75 25
418 – 18f. purple, brn and grn 75 30
419 – 20f. brown, blue & violet 1·00 40
420 – 25f. brown and plum . . 1·20 40
DESIGNS—VERT: 18f. Ekoi mask; 20f. Bamileke statue. HORIZ: 25f. Bamoun stool.

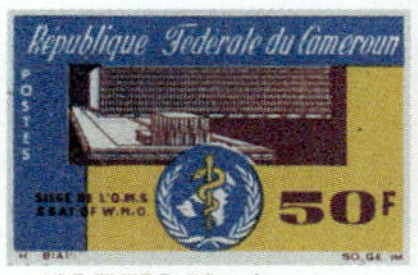

105 WHO Headquarters, Geneva
106 "Phaeomeria magnifica"

1966. U.N. Agency Buildings.
421 **105** 50f. lake, blue and yellow 1·20 70
422 – 50f. yellow, blue & green 55 25
DESIGN: No. 422, ITU Headquarters, Geneva.

1966. Flowers. Multicoloured. (a) Postage. Size as T **106**.
423 9f. Type **106** 60 25
424 15f. "Strelitzia reginae" . . . 95 25
425 18f. "Hibiscus schizopetalus x rosa-sinensis" 75 25
426 20f. "Antigonon leptopus" 75 25

(b) Air. Size 26 × 45½ mm.
427 25f. "Hibiscus mutabilis" ("Caprice des dames") . . 75 25
428 50f. "Delonix regia" . . . . 1·50 30
429 100f. "Bougainvillea glabra" 3·00 60
430 200f. "Thevetia peruviana" 4·50 1·60
431 250f. "Hippeastrum equestre" 5·50 2·10
For stamps as Type **106** but showing fruits, see Nos. 463/71.

107 Mobile Gendarmerie

1966. Air. Cameroun Armed Forces.
432 **107** 20f. blue, brown & plum 55 25
433 – 25f. green, violet & brown 55 25
434 – 60f. indigo, green & blue 1·80 80
435 – 100f. blue, red & purple 2·75 1·20
DESIGNS: 25f. Paratrooper; 60f. Gunboat "Vigilant"; 100f. Dassault MD-315 Flamant airplane.

108 Wembley Stadium

1966. Air. World Cup Football Championship.
436 **108** 50f. green, blue and red 1·40 55
437 – 200f. red, blue and green 4·50 2·20
DESIGN: 200f. Footballers.

109 Douglas DC-8F Jet Trader and "Air Afrique" Emblem

1966. Air. Inauguration of DC-8 Air Service.
438 **109** 25f. grey, black & purple 80 45

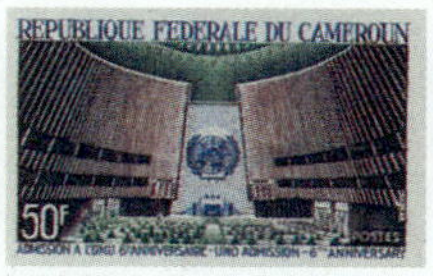

110 U.N. General Assembly

1966. 6th Anniv of Admission to U.N.
439 **110** 50f. purple, green & blue 90 25
440 – 100f. blue, brown & green 1·90 85
DESIGN—VERT: 100f. Africans encircling U.N. emblem within figure "6".

111 1st Minister's Residency, Buea (side view)

1966. 5th Anniv of Cameroun's Reunification. Multicoloured.
441 9f. Type **111** 40 25
442 18f. Prime Minister's Residency, Yaounde (front view) 50 25
443 20f. As 18f. but side view . . 55 45
444 25f. As Type **111** but front view 85 45

112 Learning to Write

1966. 20th Anniv of UNESCO and UNICEF.
445 **112** 50f. brown, purple & blue 1·30 60
446 – 50f. black, blue & purple 1·30 60
DESIGN: No. 446. Cameroun children.

113 Buea Cathedral

1966. Air. Religious Buildings.
447 **113** 18f. purple, blue & green 45 25
448 – 25f. violet, brown & green 55 25
449 – 30f. lake, green & purple 75 40
450 – 60f. green, red & turquoise . . . . 1·40 70
BUILDINGS: 25f. Yaounde Cathedral. 30f. Orthodox Church, Yaounde. 60f. Garoua Mosque.

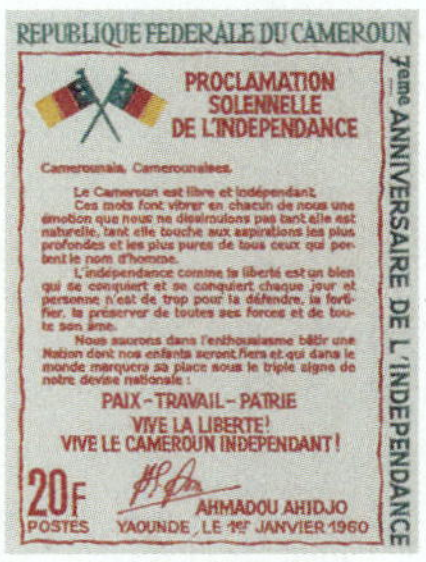

114 Proclamation

1967. 7th Anniv of Independence.
451 **114** 20f. red, green & yellow 2·00 1·10

115 Map of Africa, Railway Lines and Signals
117 Aircraft and ICAO Emblem

116 Lions Emblem and Jungle

1967. 5th African and Malagasy Railway Technicians Conference, Yaounde. Multicoloured.
452 20f. Type **115** . . . . 2·30 1·00
453 20f. Map of Africa and diesel train . . . . 3·25 1·40

1967. 50th Anniv of Lions International. Mult.
454 50f. Type **116** 95 55
455 100f. Lions emblem and palms . . . . 2·00 1·20

1967. International Civil Aviation Organization.
456 **117** 50f. multicoloured . . . . 1·30 60

118 Dove and IAEA Emblem

1967. International Atomic Energy Agency.
457 **118** 50f. blue and green . . . 1·30 60

119 Rotary Banner and Emblem

1967. 10th Anniv of Cameroun Branch, Rotary Int.
458 **119** 25f. red, gold and blue . . 1·20 55

120 "Pioneer A"

1967. Air. "Conquest of the Moon".
459 **120** 25f. green, brown & blue 45 25
460 – 50f. violet, purple & grn 90 40
461 – 100f. purple, brown & bl 2·30 90
462 – 250f. purple, grey and brown . . . . 5·00 2·75
DESIGNS: 50f. "Ranger 6"; 100f. "Luna 9"; 250f. "Luna 10".

121 Grapefruit
122 Sanaga Waterfalls

1967. Fruits. Multicoloured.
463 1f. Type **121** 10 10
464 2f. Papaw 10 10
465 3f. Custard-apple 25 25
466 4f. Breadfruit 25 25
467 5f. Coconut 35 25
468 6f. Mango 45 25
469 8f. Avocado 95 30
470 10f. Pineapple . . . . 1·50 45
471 30f. Bananas . . . . 3·50 1·50

1967. International Tourist Year.
472 **122** 30f. multicoloured 80 35

123 Map, Letters and Pylons

1967. Air. 5th Anniv of African and Malagasy Posts and Telecommunications Union (UAMPT).
473 **123** 100f. pur, lake & turq . . 2·20 95

124 Harvesting Coconuts (carved box)

1967. Cameroun Art.
474 **124** 10f. brown, red and blue 35 25
475 – 20f. brown, green & yell 50 30
476 – 30f. brown, red & green 90 45
477 – 100f. brown, red & grn 2·30 95
DESIGNS (Carved boxes): 20f. Lion-hunting; 30f. Harvesting coconuts (different); 100f. Carved chest.

125 Crossed Skis

1967. Air. Winter Olympic Games, Grenoble.
478 **125** 30f. brown and blue . . . 1·50 85

126 Cameroun Exhibit

1967. Air. World Fair, Montreal.
479 **126** 50f. brown, chest & pur 95 40
480 – 100f. brown, purple & grn 3·00 1·10
481 – 200f. green, purple & brn 4·25 2·20
DESIGNS: 100f. Totem poles; 200f. African pavilion.
For No. 481 optd **PREMIER HOMME SUR LA LUNE 20 JUILLET 1969/FIRST MAN LANDING ON MOON 20 JULY 1969** see note below Nos. 512/17.

127 Chancellor Adenauer and Cologne Cathedral

128 Arms of the Republic

1967. Air. Adenauer Commem. Multicoloured.
482 30f. Type **127** 95 40
483 70f. Adenauer and Chancellor's residence, Bonn . . . . 2·00 70

1968. 8th Anniv of Independence.
484 **128** 30f. multicoloured . . . . 1·00 50

129 Pres. Ahidjo and King Faisal of Saudi Arabia

1968. Air. Pres. Ahidjo's Pilgrimage to Mecca and Visit to the Vatican. Multicoloured.
485 30f. Type **129** 85 45
486 60f. Pope Paul VI greeting Pres. Ahidjo . . . . 2·10 70

130 "Explorer VI" (televised picture of Earth)

1968. Air. Telecommunications Satellites.
487 **130** 20f. grey, red and blue . . 50 25
488 – 30f. blue, indigo and red 80 45
489 – 40f. green, red & plum . . 1·10 50
DESIGNS: 30f. "Molnya"; 40f. "Molnya" (televised picture of Earth).

131 Douala Port

1968. Air. Five-year Development Plan.
490 – 20f. blue, red and green 55 30
491 – 30f. blue, green & brown 4·50 1·80
492 – 30f. blue, brown & green 1·00 50
493 – 40f. brown, green & turq 1·00 40
494 **131** 60f. purple, indigo & blue 2·50 1·00
DESIGNS—VERT: 20f. Steel forge; 30f. (No. 491), "Transcamerounais" express train leaving tunnel; 30f. (No. 492), Tea-harvesting; 40f. Rubber-tapping.

132 Spiny Lobster

1968. Fishes and Crustaceans.
495 **132** 5f. green, brown & violet 20 20
496 – 10f. slate, brown & blue 30 20
497 – 15f. brown, chest & pur 65 20
498 – 20f. brown and blue . . . 75 20
499 – 25f. blue, brown and green . . . . 1·10 55
500 – 30f. brown, blue and red 1·50 55
501 – 40f. blue, brown & orge 1·70 70
502 – 50f. red, slate and green 2·50 85
503 – 55f. purple, brown & blue 3·25 1·20
504 – 60f. blue, purple & green 5·25 1·60
DESIGNS—HORIZ: 10f. Freshwater crayfish; 15f. Nile mouthbrooder; 20f. Sole. 25f. Northern pike; 30f. Swimming crab; 55f. Dusky snakehead; 60f. Capitaine threadfin. VERT: 40f. African spadefish; 50f. Prawn.

133 Refinery and Tanker

1968. Inauguration of Petroleum Refinery, Port Gentil, Gabon.
505 **133** 30f. multicoloured . . . . 1·20 45

134 Boxing

136 Mahatma Gandhi and Map of India

135 Human Rights Emblem

1968. Air. Olympic Games, Mexico.
506 **134** 30f. brown, green & emer 75 35
507 – 50f. brown, red & green 1·30 60
508 – 60f. brown, blue & green 1·50 70
MS509 131 × 101 mm. Nos. 506/8 4·50 4·50
DESIGNS: 50f. Long-jumping; 60f. Gymnastics.

1968. Human Rights Year.
510 **135** 15f. blue & orge (postage) 60 25
511 30f. green & purple (air) 75 40

1968. Air. "Apostles of Peace".
512 **136** 30f. black, yellow & blue 55 45
513 – 30f. black and blue . . . 55 45
514 – 40f. black and pink . . . 95 75
515 – 60f. black and lilac . . . 1·20 75
516 – 70f. black, blue & buff . . 1·30 90
517 – 70f. black and green . . . 1·30 90
MS518 122 × 162 mm. Nos. 512, 514/15 and 517 . . . . . . 7·50 7·50
PORTRAITS: No. 513, Martin Luther King. No. 514, J. F. Kennedy. No. 515, R. F. Kennedy. No. 516, Gandhi (full-face). No. 517, Martin Luther King (half-length).

During 1969, Nos. 481 and 512/17 were issued optd **PREMIER HOMME SUR LA LUNE 20 JUILLET 1969/FIRST MAN LANDING ON MOON 20 JULY 1969** in very limited quantities.

137 "The Letter" (A. Cambon)

1968. Air. "Philexafrique" Stamp Exhibition, Abidjan (in 1969). (1st issue).
519 **137** 100f. multicoloured . . . 3·25 2·50

138 Wouri Bridge and 1f. stamp of 1925

1969. Air. "Philexafrique" Stamp Exhibition, Abidjan, Ivory Coast (2nd issue).
520 **138** 50f. blue, olive and green 3·25 2·10

139 President Ahidjo

1969. 9th Anniv of Independence.
521 **139** 30f. multicoloured 80 30

140 Vat of Chocolate

1969. Chocolate Industry Development.
522 **140** 15f. blue, brown and red 45 25
523 – 30f. brown, choc & grn 75 40
524 – 50f. red, green & bistre 1·00 55
DESIGNS—HORIZ: 30f. Chocolate factory. VERT 50f. Making confectionery.

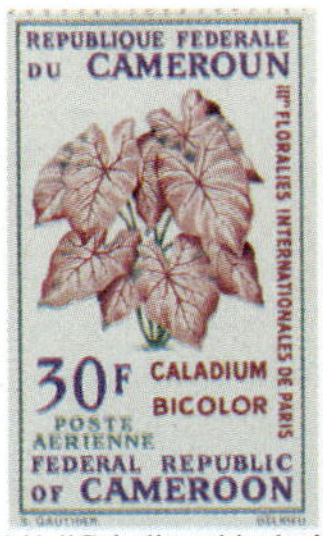

141 "Caladium bicolor"

142 Reproduction Symbol

1969. Air. 3rd Int Flower Show, Paris. Mult.
525 30f. Type **141** 80 55
526 50f. "Aristolochia elegans" 1·70 80
527 100f. "Gloriosa simplex" . . 3·50 1·50

1969. Abbia Arts and Folklore.
528 **142** 5f. purple, turq & blue . . 30 20
529 – 10f. orange, olive & blue 45 20
530 – 15f. indigo, red & blue . . 45 25
531 – 30f. green, brown & blue 95 40
532 – 70f. red, green and blue 1·70 85
DESIGNS—HORIZ: 10f. "Two Toucans"; 30f. "Vulture attacking Monkey". VERT: 15f. Forest Symbol; 70f. Oliphant-player.

143 Post Office, Douala

1969. Air. New Post Office Buildings.
533 **143** 30f. brown, blue & green 55 25
534 – 50f. red, slate & turquoise 95 45
535 – 100f. brown and turquoise 1·80 85
DESIGNS: 50f. G.P.O., Buea; 100f. G.P.O., Bafoussam.

144 "Coronation of Napoleon" (David)

1969. Air. Birth Bicent of Napoleon Bonaparte.
536 **144** 30f. multicoloured . . . . 1·20 70
537 – 1,000f. gold . . . . . . 42·00 40·00
DESIGN: 1,000f. "Napoleon crossing the Alps". No. 537 is embossed on gold foil.

145 Kumba Station

146 Bank Emblem

1969. Opening of Mbanga–Kumba Railway. Mult.
538 30f. Type **145** . . . . 1·10 55
539 50f. Diesel train on bridge over River Mungo (vert) 2·75 1·00

1969. 5th Anniv of African Development Bank.
540 **146** 30f. brown, green & vio 80 40

1969. Air. Negro Writers. Portrait designs as T **136**.
541 15f. brown and blue 45 25
542 30f. brown and purple . . . 75 25
543 30f. brown and yellow . . . 75 25
544 50f. brown and green 95 45
545 50f. brown and agate 95 45
546 100f. brown and yellow . . . 1·90 1·10
MS547 115 × 125 mm. Nos. 541/6 7·25 7·25

DESIGNS—VERT: No. 541, Dr. P. Mars (Haiti); No. 542, W. Dubois (U.S.A.); No. 543, A. Cesaire (Martinique); No. 544, M. Garvey (Jamaica); No. 545, L. Hughes (U.S.A.); No. 546, R. Maran (Martinique).

148 I.L.O. Emblem

1969. Air. 50th Anniv of I.L.O.
548 **148** 30f. black and turquoise . . 70 40
549 50f. black and mauve . . 1·30 60

149 Astronauts and "Apollo 11" in Sea

1969. Air. 1st Man on the Moon. Multicoloured.
550 200f. Type **149** . . . . 4·75 2·20
551 500f. Astronaut and module on Moon . . . . 11·50 4·50

150 Airplane, Map and Airport

1969. 10th Anniv of Aerial Navigation Security Agency for Africa and Madagascar (ASECNA).
552 **150** 100f. green . . . . 1·80 85

151 President Ahidjo, Arms and Map

1970. Air. 10th Anniv of Independence.
553 **151** 1,000f. gold & mult . . . 25·00 23·00
No. 553 is embossed on gold foil.

152 Mont Febe Hotel, Yaounde

1970. Air. Tourism.
554 **152** 30f. grey, green & brn . . 80 30

153 Lenin **154** "Lantana camara"

1970. Air. Birth Centenary of Lenin.
555 **153** 50f. brown and yellow . . 1·90 75

1970. African Climbing Plants. Multicoloured.
556 15f. Type **154** (postage) . . . 45 25
557 30f. "Passiflora quadrangularis" . . . . . 1·00 40
558 50f. "Cleome speciosa" (air) 1·50 70
559 100f. "Mussaenda erythrophylla" . . . . . . 3·00 1·40

155 Lions' Emblem and Map of Africa

1970. Air. 13th Congress of Lions International District 403, Yaounde.
560 **155** 100f. multicoloured . . . 2·20 95

156 New UPU HQ.

1970. New UPU Headquarters Building, Berne.
561 **156** 30f. green, violet & blue 90 25
562 50f. blue, red and grey . . 1·30 40

157 U.N. Emblem and Stylized Doves

1970. Air. 25th Anniv of United Nations.
563 **157** 30f. brown and orange . . 90 45
564 – 50f. indigo and blue . . . 1·30 65
DESIGN—VERT: 50f. U.N. emblem and stylized dove.

158 Fermenting Vats

1970. Brewing Industry.
565 **158** 15f. brown, green & grey 45 25
566 – 30f. red, brown and blue 90 40
DESIGN: 30f. Storage tanks.

159 Japanese Pavilion

1970. Air. Expo 70.
567 **159** 50f. blue, red and green 95 55
568 – 100f. red, blue and green 2·00 90
569 – 150f. brown, slate & blue 3·50 1·60
DESIGNS—VERT: 100f. Expo Emblem and Map of Japan. HORIZ: 150f. Australian Pavilion.

160 Gen. De Gaulle in Tropical Kit **162** Dancers

161 Aztec Stadium, Mexico City

1970. Air. "Homage to General De Gaulle".
570 **160** 100f. brown, blue & grn 3·00 1·60
571 – 200f. blue, green & brn 5·50 2·50
DESIGN: 200f. Gen. De Gaulle in military uniform.

Nos. 570/1 were issued together as a triptych, separated by a stamp-size label showing maps of France and Cameroun.

1970. Air. World Cup Football Championship, Mexico. Multicoloured.
572 50f. Type **161** 95 55
573 100f. Mexican team . . . . 2·00 1·10
574 200f. Pele and Brazilian team with World Cup (vert) . . 3·50 1·90

1970. Ozila Dancers.
575 **162** 30f. red, orange & grn . . 1·20 45
576 50f. red, brown & scar . . 2·40 95

163 Doll in National Costume **164** Beethoven (after Stieler)

1970. Cameroun Dolls.
577 **163** 10f. green, black & red . . 65 45
578 15f. red, green & yellow 75 55
579 30f. brown, green & blk 1·60 70

1970. Air. Birth Bicent of Beethoven.
580 **164** 250f. multicoloured . . . 5·25 2·75

1970. Air. Rembrandt Paintings. As T **144**. Mult.
581 70f. "Christ at Emmaus" . . 1·50 60
582 150f. "The Anatomy Lesson" 2·50 1·30

166 "Industry and Agriculture" **167** Bust of Dickens

1970. "Europafrique" Economic Community.
583 **166** 30f. multicoloured 80 40

1970. Air. Death Centenary of Charles Dickens.
584 **167** 40f. brown and red . . . 95 35
585 – 50f. multicoloured . . . . 1·10 55
586 – 100f. multicoloured . . . 1·90 1·10
DESIGNS: 50f. Characters from David Copperfield; 100f. Dickens writing.

1971. Air. De Gaulle Memorial Issue. Nos. 570/1 optd **IN MEMORIAM 1890-1970**.
587 **160** 100f. brown, blue & grn 3·00 1·40
588 – 200f. blue, green & brn 5·50 2·30

169 University Buildings

1971. Inauguration of Federal University, Yaounde.
589 **169** 50f. green, blue & brown 1·00 45

170 Presidents Ahidjo and Pompidou

1971. Visit of Pres. Pompidou of France.
590 **170** 30f. multicoloured . . . . 1·50 70

171 "Cameroun Youth"

1971. 5th National Youth Festival.
591 **171** 30f. multicoloured 80 45

172 Timber Yard, Douala

1971. Air. Industrial Expansion.
592 **172** 40f. brown, green & red 55 25
593 – 70f. brown, green and blue . . . . 1·20 50
594 – 100f. red, blue & green . . 1·60 70
DESIGNS—VERT: 70f. "Alucam" aluminium plant, Edea. HORIZ: 100f. Mbakaou Dam.

173 "Gerbera hybrida" **174** "World Races"

1971. Flowers. Multicoloured.
595 20f. Type **173** 65 40
596 40f. "Opuntia polyantha" . . 1·50 55
597 50f. "Hemerocallis hybrida" 1·90 70
For similar designs inscr "United Republic of Cameroon" etc., see Nos. 648/52.

1971. Racial Equality Year. Multicoloured.
598 20f. Type **174** 50 25
599 30f. Hands of four races clasping globe 75 25

175 Crowned Cranes, Camp de Waza

1971. Landscapes.
600 **175** 10f. blue, red and green 1·70 45
601 – 20f. red, brown & green 1·10 45
602 – 30f. green, blue & brown 1·10 45
DESIGNS: 20f. African pirogue; 30f. Sanaga River.

176 Relay-racing

1971. Air. 75th Anniv of Modern Olympic Games.
603 **176** 30f. blue, red and brown 60 30
604 – 50f. purple and blue . . . 85 40
605 – 100f. black, green & red 1·70 70
DESIGNS—VERT: 50f. Olympic runner with torch. HORIZ: 100f. Throwing the discus.

177 "Villalba" (deep-sea trawler)

1971. Air. Fishing Industry.
606 **177** 30f. brown, green & blue 95 50
607 – 40f. purple, blue & green 1·00 70
608 – 70f. brown, red and blue 1·90 90
609 – 150f. multicoloured . . . 4·75 1·90
DESIGNS: 40f. Traditional fishing method, Northern Cameroun; 70f. Fish quay, Douala; 150f. Shrimp-boats, Douala.

178 Peace Palace, The Hague

1971. 25th Anniv of International Court of Justice, The Hague.
610 **178** 50f. brown, blue & green 90 35

179 1916 French Occupation 20c. and 1914–18 War Memorial, Yaounde

1971. Air. "Philatecam 71" Stamp Exhibition, Yaounde (1st issue).
611 **179** 20f. brown, ochre & grn 50 25
612 – 25f. brown, green & blue 60 25
613 – 40f. green, grey & brown 95 25
614 – 50f. multicoloured 1·10 45
615 – 100f. green, brown & orge 2·10 85
DESIGNS: 25f. 1954 15f. Jamot stamp and memorial; 40f. 1965 25f. Tourist Office stamp and public buildings, Yaounde; 50f. German stamp and Imperial German postal emblem; 100f. 1915 Expeditionary Force optd, error, and Expeditionary Force memorial.
See also No. 620.

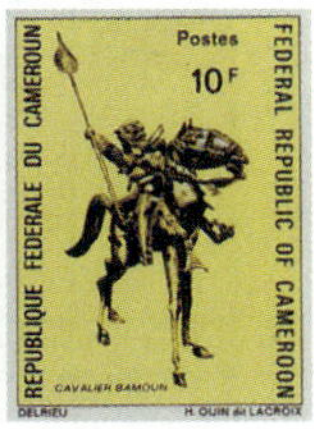

180 Rope Bridge **181** Bamoun Horseman (carving)

1971. "Rural Life". Multicoloured.
616 40f. Type **180** 1·40 45
617 45f. Local market (horiz) 1·40 45

1971. Cameroun Carving.
618 **181** 10f. brown and yellow 45 20
619 – 15f. brown and yellow 45 25
DESIGN: 15f. Fetish statuette.

182 Pres. Ahidjo, Flag and "Reunification" Road

1971. Air. "Philatecam 71" Stamp Exhibition, Yaounde (2nd issue).
620 **182** 250f. multicoloured 6·00 4·25

183 Satellite and Globe

1971. Pan-African Telecommunications Network.
621 **183** 40f. multicoloured 80 50

184 UAMPT Headquarters, Brazzaville and Carved Stool

1971. Air. 10th Anniv of African and Malagasy Posts and Telecommunications Union.
622 **184** 100f. multicoloured 1·90 85

185 Children acclaiming Emblem

1971. 25th Anniv of UNICEF.
623 **185** 40f. purple, blue & slate 85 25
624 – 50f. red, green and blue 1·00 50
DESIGN—VERT: 50f. Ear of Wheat and Emblem.

186 "The Annunciation" (Fra Angelico)

1971. Air. Christmas. Paintings. Multicoloured.
625 40f. Type **186** 55 25
626 45f. "Virgin and Child" (Del Sarto) 80 45
627 150f. "The Holy Family with the Lamb" (detail Raphael) (vert) 3·25 1·20

187 Cabin, South-Central Region

1972. Traditional Cameroun Houses. Mult.
628 10f. Type **187** 30 25
629 15f. Adamaoua round house 50 25

188 Airline Emblem

1972. Air. Cameroun Airlines' Inaugural Flight.
630 **188** 50f. multicoloured 80 25

189 Giraffe and Palm Tree **190** Africa Cup

1972. Festival of Youth. Multicoloured.
631 2f. Type **189** 30 10
632 5f. Domestic scene 30 10
633 10f. Blacksmith (horiz) 30 20
634 15f. Women 30 20

1972. African Football Cup Championship. Mult.
635 20f. Type **190** 65 25
636 40f. Players with ball (horiz) 85 40
637 45f. Team captains 1·40 55

191 "St. Mark's Square and Doge's Palace" (detail-Caffi)

1972. Air. UNESCO "Save Venice" Campaign. Multicoloured.
638 40f. Type **191** 75 40
639 100f. "Regatta on the Grand Canal" (detail – Canaletto) 2·00 70
640 200f. "Regatta on the Grand Canal" (detail – Canaletto) (different) 4·00 1·40

192 Assembly Building, Yaounde

1972. 110th Session of Inter-Parliamentary Council, Yaounde.
641 **192** 40f. multicoloured 80 40

193 Horseman, North Cameroun

1972. Traditional Life and Folklore. Mult.
642 15f. Type **193** 40 20
643 20f. Bororo woman (vert) 50 20
644 40f. Wouri River and Mt. Cameroun 1·80 55

194 Pataiev, Dobrovolsky and Volkov

1972. Air. "Soyuz 11" Cosmonauts. Memorial Issue.
645 **194** 50f. multicoloured 90 50

195 U.N. Building, New York, Gate of Heavenly Peace, Peking and Chinese Flag

1972. Air. Admission of Chinese People's Republic to U.N.
646 **195** 50f. multicoloured 2·75 70

196 Chemistry Laboratory, Federal University

1972. Pres. Ahidjo Prize.
647 **196** 40f. red, green & purple 80 50

1972. Flowers. As T **173**, but inscr "UNITED REPUBLIC OF CAMEROON", etc. Mult.
648 40f. "Solanum macranthum" 85 30
649 40f. "Kaempferia aethiopica" 1·00 25
650 45f. "Hoya carnosa" 1·00 50
651 45f. "Cassia alata" 1·20 30
652 50f. "Crinum sanderianum" 1·50 40

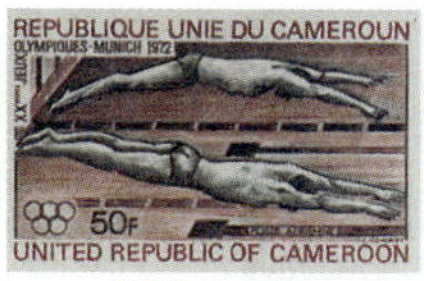

197 Swimming

1972. Air. Olympic Games, Munich.
653 **197** 50f. green, brown & lake 95 45
654 – 50f. brown, blue and sepia 95 45
655 – 200f. lake, grey & purple 3·75 1·70
MS656 140 × 100 mm. As Nos. 653/5 but colours changed; 50f. brown, violet and blue; 50f. brown, blue and purple; 200f. brown and blue 6·50 6·50
DESIGNS—HORIZ: No. 655, Horse-jumping. VERT: No. 654, Boxing.

198 "Charaxes ameliae" **201** Great Blue Turacos

1972. Butterflies. Multicoloured.
657 40f. Type **198** 3·00 90
658 45f. "Papiliotynderaeus" 4·25 1·30

1972. No. 471 surch.
659 40f. on 30f. multicoloured 1·00 50

1972. Air. Olympic Gold Medal Winners. Nos. 653/5 optd as listed below.
660 50f. green, brown and red 95 45
661 50f. brown, blue and sepia 95 45
662 200f. lake, grey and purple 3·75 1·70
OVERPRINTS: No. 660, **NATATION MARK SPITZ 7 MEDAILLES D'OR**. No. 661, **SUPER-WELTER KOTTYSCH MEDAILLE D'OR**. No. 662, **CONCOURS COMPLET MEADE MEDAILLE D'OR**.

1972. Birds. Multicoloured.
663 10f. Type **201** 1·20 45
664 45f. Red-faced lovebirds (horiz) 2·75 1·10

202 "The Virgin with Angels" (Cimabue) **203** St. Theresa

1972. Air. Christmas. Multicoloured.
665 45f. Type **202** 1·00 45
666 140f. "The Madonna of the Rose Arbour" (S. Lochner) 2·75 1·60

1973. Air. Birth Centenary of St. Theresa of Lisieux.
667 **203** 45f. blue, brown & violet 75 25
668 – 100f. mauve, brown, & bl 1·70 70
DESIGN: 100f. Lisieux Basilica.

204 Emperor Haile Selassie and "Africa Hall", Addis Ababa

1973. Air. 80th Birthday of Emperor Haile Selassie of Ethiopia.
669 **204** 45f. multicoloured 90 50

205 Cotton Cultivation, North Cameroun **207** Human Hearts

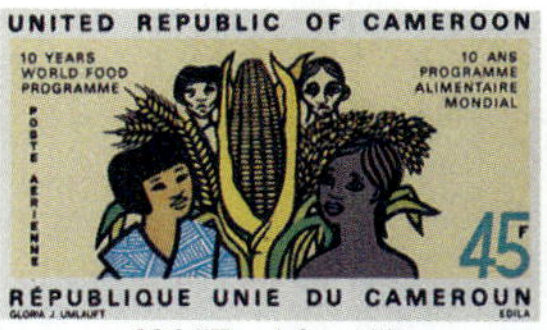

206 "Food for All"

1973. 3rd Five Year Plan. Multicoloured.
670 5f. Type **205** 20 10
671 10f. Cacao pods, South-central region 30 10
672 15f. Forestry, South-eastern area 50 20
673 20f. Coffee plant, West Cameroun 1·00 25
674 45f. Tea-picking, West Cameroun 2·20 40

1973. Air. 10th Anniv of World Food Programme.
675 **206** 45f. multicoloured 80 45

1973. Air. 25th Anniv of W.H.O.
676 **207** 50f. red and blue 90 45

208 Pres. Ahidjo, Map, Flag and Cameroun Stamp

1973. 1st Anniv of United Republic. Mult.
677 10f. Type **208** (postage) . . . 65 25
678 20f. Pres. Ahidjo, proclamation and stamp 1·00 50
679 45f. Pres. Ahidjo, map of Cameroun rivers and stamp (air) 85 25
680 70f. Significant dates on Cameroun flag . . . . . . 1·10 65

209 Mask **210** Dr. G. A. Hansen

1973. Bamoun Masks.
681 **209** 5f. black, brown & green 10 10
682 – 10f. brown, black & purple 30 10
683 – 45f. brown, black & red 75 40
684 – 100f. brown, black & blue 1·90 70
DESIGNS: 10f., 45f., 100f., as Type **209**, but different masks.

1973. Centenary of Hansen's Identification of Leprosy Bacillus.
685 **210** 45f. blue, lt blue & brown 1·70 70

211 Scout Emblem and Flags **213** Folk-dancers

1973. Air. Admission of Cameroun to 24th World Scout Conference.
686 **211** 40f. multicoloured 85 35
687 45f. multicoloured . . . . 1·20 50
688 100f. multicoloured . . . 2·50 80

1973. African Solidarity "Drought Relief". No. 670 surch **100F. SECHERESSE SOLIDARITE AFRICAINE.**
689 **205** 100f. on 5f. multicoloured 1·70 1·20

1973. Folklore Dances of South-west Cameroun. Multicoloured.
690 10f. Type **213** 20 10
691 25f. Dancer in plumed hat . . 55 20
692 45f. Dancers with "totem" 1·10 30

214 WMO Emblem

1973. Centenary of WMO.
693 **214** 45f. blue and green . . . 1·50 40

215 Garoua Party H.Q. Building

1973. 7th Anniv of Cameroun National Union.
694 **215** 40f. multicoloured 80 45

216 Crane with Letter and Telecommunications Emblem

1973. 12th Anniv of UAMPT.
695 **216** 100f. blue, lt blue & green 1·70 75

217 African Mask and Old Town Hall, Brussels **218** Avocado

1973. Air. African Fortnight, Brussels.
696 **217** 40f. brown and purple . . 80 45

1973. Cameroun Fruits. Multicoloured.
697 10f. Type **218** 60 25
698 20f. Mango 75 30
699 45f. Plum . . . . 1·70 65
700 50f. Custard-apple . . . . . 2·10 80

219 Map of Africa

1973. Air. Aid for Handicapped Children.
701 **219** 40f. red, brown & green 80 50

220 Kirdi Village

1973. Cameroun Villages.
702 **220** 15f. black, green & brown 35 20
703 – 45f. brown, red & orange 85 45
704 – 50f. black, green & orange 1·00 55
DESIGNS: 45f. Mabas village. 50f. Fishing village.

221 Earth Station

1973. Air. Inauguration of Satellite Earth Station, Zamengoe.
705 **221** 100f. brown, blue & grn 1·40 75

222 "The Madonna with Chancellor Rolin" (Van Eyck) **223** Handclasp on Map of Africa

1973. Air. Christmas. Multicoloured.
706 45f. Type **222** . . . . 1·00 55
707 140f. "The Nativity" (Federico Fiori–Il Barocci) 2·75 1·70

1974. 10th Anniv of Organization of African Unity.
708 **223** 40f. blue, red and green 55 25
709 45f. green, blue and red 65 25

224 Mill-worker

1974. C.I.C.A.M. Industrial Complex.
710 **224** 45f. brown, green & red 80 25

225 Bilinga Carved Panel (detail)

1974. Cameroun Art.
711 **225** 10f. brown and green . . 30 25
712 – 40f. brown and red . . 85 25
713 – 45f. red and blue . . . . 1·00 45
DESIGNS: 40f. Tubinga carving (detail); 45f. Acajou Ngollon carved panel (detail).

1974. No. 469 surch.
714 40f. on 8f. multicoloured . . 80 35

227 Cameroun Cow **228** Route-map and Track

1974. Cattle-raising in North Cameroun. Mult.
715 40f. Type **227** (postage) . . . 1·20 50
716 45f. Cattle in pen (air) . . . 1·20 50

1974. Trans-Cameroun Railway. Inauguration of Yaounde–Ngaoundere Line.
717 **228** 5f. brown, blue & green 45 25
718 – 20f. brown, blue & violet 95 40
719 – 40f. red, blue & green . . 1·80 80
720 – 100f. green, blue & brown 3·00 1·40
DESIGNS—HORIZ: 20f. Laying track; 100f. Railway bridge over Djerem River. VERT: 40f. Welding rails.

229 Sir Winston Churchill

1974. Air. Birth Cent of Sir Winston Churchill.
721 **229** 100f. black, red & blue . . 1·60 75

230 Footballer and City Crests

1974. Air. World Cup Football Championship.
722 **230** 45f. orange, slate & grey 80 25
723 – 100f. orange, slate & grey 1·40 70
724 – 200f. blue, orange & blk 3·00 1·70
DESIGNS: 100f. Goalkeeper and city crests; 200f. World Cup.

1974. Air. West Germany's Victory in World Cup Football Championship. Nos. 722/4 optd **7th JULY 1974 R.F.A. 2 HOLLANDE 1 7 JUILLET 1974.**
725 **230** 45f. orange, slate & grey 75 25
726 – 100f. orange, slate & grey 1·30 70
727 – 200f. blue, orange & blk 2·75 1·70

232 UPU Emblem and Hands with Letters

1974. Centenary of Universal Postal Union.
728 **232** 40f. red, blue and green (postage) 90 45
729 – 100f. green, vio & bl (air) 1·70 85
730 – 200f. green, red and blue 2·75 1·70
DESIGNS: 100f. Cameroun UPU headquarters stamps of 1970; 200f. Cameroun UPU 75th anniv stamps of 1949.

233 Copernicus and Solar System

1974. Air. 500th Birth Anniv (1973) of Copernicus.
731 **233** 250f. blue, red & brown 4·00 2·30

234 Modern Chess Pieces

1974. Air. Chess Olympics, Nice.
732 **234** 100f. multicoloured . . . 4·00 1·60

235 African Mask and "Arphila" Emblem

1974. Air. "Arphila 75" Stamp Exhibition, Paris.
733 **235** 50f. brown and red . . . 60 45

236 African Leaders, UDEAC HQ and Flags

1974. 10th Anniv of Central African Customs and Economics Union.
734 **236** 40f. mult (postage) . . . 1·40 70
735 – 100f. multicoloured (air) 1·80 75
DESIGN: 100f. Similar to Type **236**.

1974. No. 717 surch **100F 10 DECEMBRE 1974.**
736 **228** 100f. on 5f. brn, bl & grn 1·90 1·10

238 "Apollo" Emblem, Astronaut, Module and Astronaut's Boots

1974. Air. 5th Anniv of 1st Landing on Moon.
737 **238** 200f. brown, red & blue 3·25 1·70

1974. Christmas. As T **222**. Multicoloured.
738 40f. "Virgin of Autumn" (15th-century sculpture) . . 95 45
739 45f. "Virgin and Child" (Luis de Morales) . . . . 1·20 60

239 De Gaulle and Eboue

1975. Air. 30th Anniv of Felix Eboue ("Free French" leader).
740 **239** 45f. multicoloured . . . . 1·70 70
741 200f. multicoloured . . . 6·00 2·75

240 "Celosia cristata"

242 Afo Akom Statue

241 Fish and Fishing-boat

1975. Flowers of North Cameroun. Mult.
742 5f. Type **240** 20 20
743 40f. "Costus spectabilis" . . 1·20 40
744 45f. "Mussaenda erythrophylla" . . . . . . 1·40 50

1975. Offshore Fishing.
745 **241** 40f. brown, blue & choc 1·90 70
746 – 45f. brown, bistre & blue 1·90 70
DESIGN: 45f. Fishing-boat and fish in net.

1975.
747 **242** 40f. multicoloured 50 25
748 45f. multicoloured . . . 75 45
749 200f. multicoloured . . . 2·50 1·60

243 "Polypore" (fungus)

245 Presbyterian Church, Elat

244 View of Building

1975. Natural History. Multicoloured.
750 15f. Type **243** . . . . 75·00 2·10
751 40f. "Nymphalis Chrysalis" 45·00 95

1975. Inaug of New Ministry of Posts Building.
752 **244** 40f. blue, green & brown 65 25
753 45f. brown, green & blue 90 50

1975. Churches and Mosque.
754 **245** 40f. brown, blue & black 45 25
755 – 40f. brown, blue & slate 45 25
756 – 45f. brown, green & blk 55 25
DESIGNS: No. 755, Foumban Mosque; No. 756, Catholic Church, Ngaoundere.

246 Marquis de Lafayette (after Chappel) and Naval Battle

247 Harvesting Maize

1975. Air. Bicent (1976) of American Revolution.
757 **246** 100f. blue, turq & brn . . 2·10 1·10
758 – 140f. blue, brown & green 2·30 1·10
759 – 500f. green, brown & blue 7·25 2·50
DESIGNS: 140f. George Washington (after Stuart) and Continental Infantry (after Ogden); 500f. Benjamin Franklin (after Peale and Nee) and Boston.

1975. "Green Revolution". Multicoloured.
760 40f. Type **247** 75 25
761 40f. Ploughing with oxen (horiz) 75 25

248 "The Burning Bush" (N. Froment)

1975. Air. Christmas. Multicoloured.
762 50f. Type **248** 85 50
763 500f. "Adoration of the Magi" (Gentile da Fabriano) (horiz) . . . . . 7·25 5·25

249 Tracking Aerial

1976. Inauguration of Satellite Monitoring Station, Zamengoe. Multicoloured.
764 40f. Type **249** 50 25
765 100f. Close-up of tracking aerial (vert) . . . . 1·20 50

250 Porcelain Rose

252 Masked Dancer

251 Concorde

1976. Flowers. Multicoloured.
766 40f. Type **250** 90 25
767 50f. Flower of North Cameroun . . . . 1·40 35

1976. Air. Concorde's First Commercial Flight, Paris to Rio de Janeiro.
768 **251** 500f. multicoloured . . . 5·25 2·75
MS769 130 × 93 mm. No. 768 . . 7·75 7·75

1976. Cameroun Dances. Multicoloured.
770 40f. Type **252** (postage) . . . 80 50
771 50f. Drummers and two dancers (air) 60 25
772 100f. Female dancer . . . . 1·20 50

253 Telephone Exchange

255 Dr. Adenauer and Cologne Cathedral

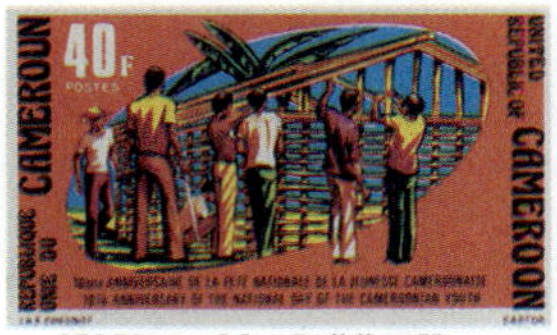

254 Young Men Building House

1976. Air. Telephone Centenary.
773 **253** 50f. multicoloured 85 55

1976. 10th Anniv of National Youth Day. Multicoloured.
774 40f. Type **254** 45 25
775 45f. Gathering palm leaves 50 25

1976. Birth Centenary of Dr. Konrad Adenauer (Statesman).
776 **255** 100f. multicoloured . . . 95 45

256 "Adoration of the Shepherds" (Charles Le Brun)

1976. Air. Christmas.
777 30f. Type **256** 80 35
778 60f. "Adoration of the Magi" (Rubens) . . . . 1·00 45
779 70f. "Virgin and Child" (Bellini) . . . . 1·30 60
780 500f. "The New-born" (G. de la Tour) . . . . 8·50 4·75
MS781 149 × 119 mm. Nos. 777/80 12·50 12·50

257 Pres. Ahidjo and Douala Party H.Q.

1976. 10th Anniv of Cameroun National Union. Multicoloured.
782 50f. Type **257** 45 20
783 50f. Pres. Ahidjo and Yaounde Party H.Q. . . . 45 20

258 Bamoun Copper Pipe

259 Crowned Cranes ("Crown-Cranes")

1977. 2nd World Festival of Negro Arts, Nigeria. Multicoloured.
784 50f. Type **258** (postage) . . . 75 30
785 60f. Traditional chief on throne (sculpture) (air) . . 1·10 45

1977. Cameroun Birds. Multicoloured.
786 30f. Ostrich . . . . 2·50 70
787 50f. Type **259** . . . . 2·75 80

260 "Christ on the Cross" (Issenheim Altarpiece, Mathias Grunewald)

1977. Air. Easter. Multicoloured.
788 50f. Type **260** 95 30
789 125f. "Christ on the Cross" (Veslasquez) (vert) . . . . 1·50 75
790 150f. "The Entombment" (Titian) . . . . 2·50 1·10
MS791 210 × 115 mm. Nos. 788/90 7·00 7·00

261 Lions Club Emblem

262 Rotary Club Emblem, Mountain and Road

1977. Air. 19th Congress of Douala Lions Club.
792 **261** 250f. multicoloured . . . 3·50 2·10

1977. Air. 20th Anniv of Douala Rotary Club.
793 **262** 60f. red and blue 75 45

263 Jean Mermoz and Seaplane "Comte de la Vaulx"

1977. Air. History of Aviation.
794 **263** 50f. blue, orange & brown 95 40
795 – 60f. purple and orange . . 95 55
796 – 80f. lake and blue . . . . 1·20 55
797 – 100f. green and yellow . . 1·60 80
798 – 300f. blue, red & purple 5·25 2·50
799 – 500f. purple, grn & plum 7·75 4·50
MS800 Two sheets (a) 170 × 100 mm. Nos. 794/6; (b) 190 × 100 mm. Nos. 797/9 . . . 20·00 20·00
DESIGNS—VERT: 60f. Antoine de Saint-Exupery and Latecoere 2b. HORIZ: 80f. Maryse Bastie and Caudron C-635 Simoun; 100f. Sikorski S-43 amphibian (1st airmail, Marignane–Douala, 1937); 300f. Concorde; 500f. Charles Lindbergh and "Spirit of St. Louis".

1977. Air. 10th Anniv of International French Language Council. As T **204** of Benin.
801 70f. multicoloured . . . . . 1·40 1·10

264 Cameroun 40f. and Basle 2½r. Stamps

1977. "Jufilex" Stamp Exhibition, Berne.
802 **264** 50f. multicoloured 95 45
803 – 70f. green, black & brown 1·30 60
804 – 100f. multicoloured . . . 2·10 95
DESIGNS: 70f. Zurich 4r. and Kamerun 1m. stamps; 100f. Geneva 5+5c. and Cameroun 20f. stamps.

265 Stafford and "Apollo" Rocket

1977. U.S.A.–U.S.S.R. Space Co-operation. Mult.
805 40f. Type **265** (postage) . . . 45 25
806 60f. Leonov and "Soyuz" rocket 65 25
807 100f. Brand and "Apollo" space vehicle (air) 95 45

808 250f. "Apollo–Soyuz" link-up 2·30 1·10
809 350f. Kubasov and "Soyuz" vehicle 3·25 1·50
MS810 120 × 81 mm. 500f. Slayton and space handshake 5·00 5·00

266 Luge Sledging

1977. Winter Olympics. Innsbruck. Multicoloured.
811 40f. Type **266** (postage) 1·10 45
812 50f. Ski-jumping 1·70 45
813 140f. Ski-marathon (air) 1·20 60
814 200f. Ice-hockey 1·80 85
815 350f. Figure-skating 3·25 1·50
MS816 116 × 77 mm. 500f. Slalom 5·00 5·00

1977. Palestinian Welfare. No. 765 optd **Au bien-etre des familles des martyrs et des combattants pour la liberte de la Palestine. To the Welfare of the families of martyrs and freedom fighters of Palestine**.
817 100f. multicoloured 95 55

268 Mao Tse-tung and Great Wall of China

1977. 1st Death Anniv of Mao Tse-tung.
818 **268** 100f. brown and green 2·75 90

269 Knee Joint

1977. Air. World Rheumatism Year.
819 **269** 70f. brown, red & blue 75 30

1977. Air. 1st Paris–New York Commercial Flight of Concorde. Nos. 798 and 768 optd **PREMIER VOL PARIS-NEW YORK FIRST FLIGHT PARIS-NEW YORK 22 nov. 1977 — 22nd Nov. 1977.**
820 – 300f. blue, red & purple 3·25 1·60
821 **251** 500f. multicoloured 5·00 2·50

271 "The Nativity" (Albrecht Altdorfer)

1977. Christmas. Multicoloured.
822 30f. Type **271** (postage) 55 25
823 50f. "Madonna of the Grand Duke" (Raphael) 1·10 40
824 60f. "Virgin and Child with Four Saints" (Bellini) (horiz) (air) 1·00 45
825 400f. "Adoration of the Shepherds" (G. de la Tour) (horiz) 5·00 2·50

272 Club Flag and Rotary Emblem

273 Pres. Ahidjo, Flag and Map

1978. 20th Anniv of Yaounde Rotary Club.
826 **272** 50f. multicoloured 75 30

1978. New Cameroun Flag. Multicoloured.
827 50f. Type **273** (postage) 90 30
828 60f. President, Flag and arms (air) 75 30

274 "Cardioglossa escalerae"

1978. Cameroun Frogs. Multicoloured.
829 50f. Type **274** (postage) 1·40 55
830 60f. "Cardioglossa elegans" 2·10 80
831 100f. "Cardioglossa trifasciata" (air) 3·00 1·20

275 "L'Arlesienne" (Van Gogh)

1978. Air. Paintings. Multicoloured.
832 200f. Type **275** 4·50 1·80
833 200f. "Deposition of Christ" (Durer) 3·50 1·10

276 Raoul Follereau and Leprosy Distribution Map

1978. Air. World Leprosy Day.
834 **276** 100f. multicoloured 1·20 55

277 Capt. Cook and the Siege of Quebec

1978. Air. 250th Birth Anniv of Capt. James Cook.
835 **277** 100f. green, blue & lilac 2·10 90
836 – 250f. brown, red and lilac 4·75 2·00
DESIGN: 250f. Capt. Cook, H.M.S. "Adventure" and H.M.S. "Resolution".

278 Footballers

1978. Air. World Cup Football Championship, Argentina. Multicoloured.
837 100f. Argentinian Team (horiz) 1·00 45
838 200f. Type **278** 2·00 95
839 1000f. Football illuminating globe 10·00 5·50

279 Jules Verne and scene from "From the Earth to the Moon"

1978. 150th Birth Anniv of Jules Verne (novelist). Multicoloured.
840 250f. Type **279** (postage) 2·30 80
841 400f. Portrait and "20,000 Leagues under the Sea" (horiz) (air) 4·00 1·60

280 "Hypolimnas salmacis"

1978. Butterflies. Multicoloured.
842 20f. Type **280** 1·40 65
843 25f. "Euxanthe trajanus" 1·80 65
844 30f. "Euphaedra cyparissa" 2·50 65

281 Planting Trees

282 Carved Bamoun Drum

1978. Protection against Saharan Encroachment.
845 **281** 10f. multicoloured 30 10
846 15f. multicoloured 35 10

1978. Musical Instruments. Multicoloured.
847 50f. Type **282** (postage) 45 25
848 60f. Gueguerou (horiz) 80 40
849 100f. Mvet Zither (air) 1·20 50

283 Presidents of Cameroun and France with Independence Monument, Douala

1978. Visit of President Giscard d'Estaing.
850 **283** 60f. multicoloured 1·40 80

284 African, Human Rights Charter and Emblem

1979. 30th Anniv of Declaration of Human Rights.
851 **284** 5f. mult (postage) 30 10
852 500f. multicoloured (air) 6·00 2·75
See also No. 1070.

285 Lions Emblem and Map of Cameroun

286 Globe, Emblem and Waving Children

1979. Air. Lions International Congress.
853 **285** 60f. multicoloured 75 40

1979. International Year of the Child.
854 **286** 50f. multicoloured 75 25

287 Penny Black, Rowland Hill and German Cameroun 10pf. Stamp

1979. Air. Death Cent of Sir Rowland Hill.
855 **287** 100f. black, red & turq 1·20 60

288 Black Rhinoceros

289 "Telecom 79"

1979. Endangered Animals (1st series). Mult.
856 50f. Type **288** 1·30 35
857 60f. Giraffe (vert) 1·70 45
858 60f. Gorilla 1·70 45
859 100f. African elephant (vert) 2·75 65
860 100f. Leopard 2·75 65
See also Nos. 891/2, 904/6, 975/7, 939/40 and 1007/8.

1979. Air. 3rd World Telecommunications Exhibition, Geneva.
861 **289** 100f. orange, blue & grey 1·20 60

290 Pope John Paul II

291 Dr. Jamot, Map and "Glossina palpalis"

1979. Air. Popes.
862 **290** 100f. blue, violet & grn 2·30 80
863 – 100f. brown, red & green 2·30 80
864 – 100f. chestnut, olive & grn 2·30 80
DESIGNS: No. 863, Pope John Paul I. No. 864, Pope Paul VI.

1979. Birth Centenary of Dr. Eugene Jamot (discoverer of sleeping sickness cure).
865 **291** 50f. brown, blue and red 2·75 70

292 "The Annunciation" (Fra Filippo Lippi)

1979. Christmas. Multicoloured.
866 10f. Type **292** 10 10
867 50f. "Rest during the Flight into Egypt" (Antwerp Master) 45 10
868 60f. "The Nativity" (Kalkar) 80 25

869 60f. "The Flight into Egypt" (Kalkar) 80 25
870 100f. "The Nativity" (Boticelli) . . . . 1·60 45

293 "Double Eagle II" and Balloonists

1979. Air. 1st Atlantic Crossing by Balloon. Multicoloured.
871 500f. Type **293** . . . . 5·25 2·00
872 500f. "Double Eagle II" over Atlantic and balloonists in basket . . . . 5·25 2·00

294 "Piper capense"

1979. Medicinal Plants. Multicoloured.
873 50f. Type **294** . . . . 1·10 25
874 60f. "Pteridium aquilinum" 1·30 25

295 Pres. Ahidjo, Map, Independence Stamp and Arms

1980. 20th Anniv of Independence.
875 **295** 50f. multicoloured 60 25

296 Congress Building

1980. 3rd Ordinary Congress of Cameroun National Union, Bafoussam.
876 **296** 50f. multicoloured 60 25

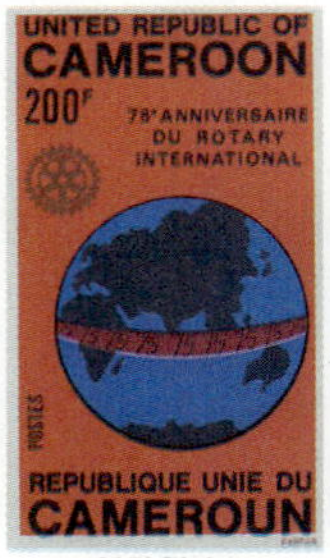

297 Globe

299 "Dissotis perkinsiae"

298 Voacanga Fruit and Seeds

1980. 75th Anniv of Rotary International. Mult.
877 200f. Type **297** . . . . 2·20 90
878 200f. Map of Cameroun . . 2·20 90
MS879 179 × 140 mm. Nos. 877/8 plus 8 labels . . . . 5·00 5·00

1980. Medicinal Plants. Multicoloured.
880 50f. Type **298** 65 10
881 60f. Voacanga tree 75 10
882 100f. Voacanga flowers . . . 1·10 25

1980. Flowers. Multicoloured.
883 50f. Type **299** 70 10
884 60f. "Brillantaisia" sp. . . . 1·00 20
885 100f. "Clerodendron splendens" . . . . 1·70 45

300 Ka'aba, Mecca

1980. 1350th Anniv of Mohammed's Occupation of Mecca.
886 **300** 50f. multicoloured 95 40

301 Ice Skating

1980. Air. Olympic Games, Moscow and Lake Placid.
887 – 100f. brown and ochre . . 95 45
888 **301** 150f. brown and blue . . 1·30 60
889 – 200f. brown and green . . 2·00 75
890 – 300f. brown and red . . . 2·50 1·30
DESIGNS: 100f. Running; 200f. Throwing the Javelin; 300f. Wrestling.

302 Crocodile

1980. Endangered Animals (2nd series). Mult.
891 200f. Type **302** . . . . 3·00 80
892 300f. Kob . . . . 4·00 1·30

303 Bororo Girls and Roumsiki Peak

1980. Tourism. Multicoloured.
893 50f. Type **303** 55 25
894 60f. Dschang tourist centre 55 25

304 Banana Trees

1981. Bertona Agricultural Research Station. Multicoloured.
895 50f. Type **304** 65 10
896 60f. Cattle in watering hole 85 25

305 Girl on Crutches

1981. Int Year of Disabled People. Multicoloured.
897 60f. Type **305** 55 25
898 150f. Boy in wheelchair . . . 1·40 65

306 Camair Headquarters, Douala

1981. 10th Anniv of Cameroun Airlines. Mult.
899 100f. Type **306** 95 35
900 200f. Boeing 747 "Mount Cameroun" . . . . 2·00 75
901 300f. Douala International Airport . . . . 3·00 1·10

307 Presentation African Club Champions Cup

308 African Buffalo

1981. Football Victories of Cameroun Clubs. Multicoloured.
902 60f. Type **307** 95 45
903 60f. Cup presentation (African Cup Winner's Cup) 95 45

1981. Endangered Animals (3rd series). Mult.
904 50f. Type **308** . . . . 1·50 45
905 50f. Cameroun tortoise . . . 1·50 45
906 100f. Long-tailed pangolin . . 3·00 50

309 Prince Charles, Lady Diana Spencer and St. Paul's Cathedral

1981. Wedding of Prince of Wales. Multicoloured.
907 500f. Type **309** . . . . 4·50 1·90
908 500f. Prince Charles, Lady Diana and Royal Coach 4·50 1·90
MS909 145 × 94 mm. Nos. 907/8 10·00 10·00

310 Bafoussam–Bamenda Road

1981. Tourism.
910 **310** 50f. multicoloured 55 25

311 Yuri Gagarin and "Vostok 1"

1981. 20th Anniv of 1st Men in Space. Mult.
911 500f. Type **311** . . . . . . 5·00 1·70
912 500f. Alan Shepard and "Freedom 7" . . . . . . 5·00 1·70

312 "Cam Iroko" (freighter) in Harbour

1981. Cameroun Shipping Lines.
913 **312** 60f. multicoloured 95 40

313 Scout Salute and Badge within Knotted Rope, and National Flag

1981. Air. 4th African Scouting Conference, Abidjan. Multicoloured.
914 100f. Type **313** 95 40
915 500f. Saluting Girl Guide . . 4·50 1·80

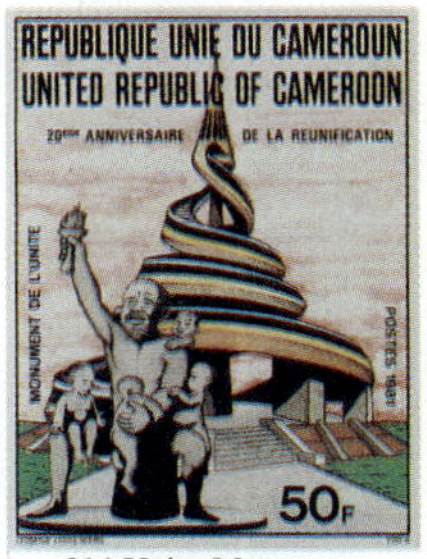

314 Unity Monument

1981. 20th Anniv of Reunification.
916 **314** 50f. multicoloured 60 25

315 "L'Estaque" (Cezanne)

1981. Air. Paintings. Multicoloured.
917 500f. Type **315** . . . . 6·00 1·80
918 500f. "Guernica" (detail) (Picasso) . . . . 6·00 1·80

316 "Virgin and Child" (detail of San Zeno altarpiece, Mantegna)

1981. Air. Christmas. Paintings. Multicoloured.
919 50f. "Virgin and Child" (detail, "The Burning Bush") (Nicholas Froment) 45 10
920 60f. Type **316** 60 25
921 400f. "The Flight into Egypt" (Giotto) (horiz) . . . . . 3·50 1·30
MS922 190 × 111 mm. Nos. 919/21 7·75 7·75

317 "Voacanga thouarsii"

1981. Medicinal Plants. Multicoloured.
923 60f. Type **317** . . . . 1·00 35
924 70f. "Cassia alata" . . . . . 1·30 50

318 "Descent from the Cross" (detail, Giotto)

1982. Easter. Paintings. Multicoloured.
925 100f. "Christ in the Garden of Olives" (Eugene Delacroix) . . . . 1·00 30
926 200f. Type **318** . . . . 1·90 70
927 250f. "Pieta in the Countryside" (Bellini) . . . 2·30 80

319 Carving, Giraffes and Map

1982. "Philexfrance 82" International Stamp Exhibition, Paris.
928 **319** 90f. multicoloured . . . . 1·50 35

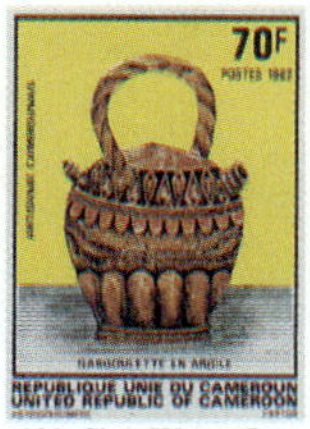

320 Clay Water Jug

1982. Local Handicrafts. Multicoloured.
929 60f. Python-skin handbag . . 60 25
930 70f. Type **320** 80 25

321 Pres. Ahidjo, Map and Arms

1982. 10th Anniv of United Republic.
931 **321** 500f. multicoloured . . . 5·25 1·70

322 Douala Town Hall

1982. Town Halls. Multicoloured.
932 40f. Type **322** 45 10
933 60f. Yaounde town hall . . . 60 25
See also No. 1139.

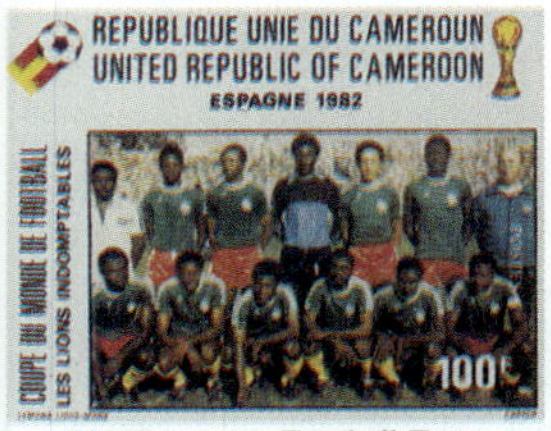

323 Cameroun Football Team

1982. World Cup Football Championship, Spain. Multicoloured.
934 100f. Type **323** . . . . 1·50 45
935 200f. Cameroun and Algerian teams . . . . 3·00 75
936 300f. Nkono Thomas, Cameroun goalkeeper . . . 4·50 1·00
937 400f. Cameroun team (different) . . . . 6·00 1·50
MS938 216 × 95 mm. No. 937 × 2 15·00 15·00

324 Bongo

325 Cameroun Mountain Francolin ("Perdrix")

1982. Endangered Animals (4th series). Mult.
939 200f. Type **324** . . . . 3·00 80
940 300f. Black colobus . . . . . 4·25 1·30

1982. Birds. Multicoloured.
941 10f. Type **325** . . . . 1·80 35
942 15f. Red-eyed dove ("Tourterelle") . . . . 2·10 60
943 20f. Barn swallow ("Hirondelle") . . . . . . 3·00 80
See also No. 1071.

326 Scouts round Campfire

1982. 75th Anniv of Boy Scout Movement. Multicoloured.
944 200f. Type **326** . . . . 2·30 80
945 400f. Lord Baden-Powell . . 4·00 1·60

327 ITU Emblem

328 Nyasoso Chapel

1982. ITU Delegates' Conference, Nairobi.
946 **327** 70f. multicoloured 75 25

1982. 25th Anniv of Presbyterian Church. Multicoloured.
947 45f. Buea Chapel 50 25
948 60f. Type **328** 75 25

329 World Cup, Footballers and Globe

1982. World Cup Football Championship Result.
949 **329** 500f. multicoloured . . . 5·25 2·20
950 1000f. multicoloured . . . 10·50 3·50

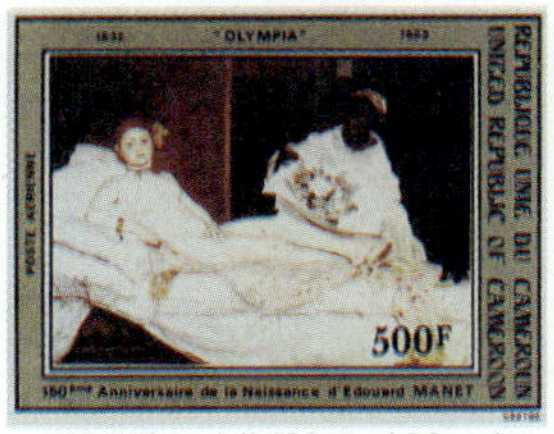

330 "Olympia" (Edouard Manet)

1982. Air. Artists' Anniversaries. Multicoloured.
951 500f. Type **330** (150th birth anniv) . . . . 5·50 2·10
952 500f. "Still-life" (Georges Braque, birth centenary) 5·50 2·10

331 Council Headquarters, Brussels

333 Pres. Kennedy

332 Yaounde University Hospital

1983. 30th Anniv of Customs Co-operation Council. Multicoloured.
953 250f. Type **331** . . . . 2·30 1·10
954 250f. Council emblem . . . . 2·30 1·10

1983. Second Yaounde Medical Days.
955 **332** 60f. multicoloured 75 25
956 70f. multicoloured 95 25

1983. Air. 20th Death Anniv of John F. Kennedy (U.S. President).
957 **333** 500f. multicoloured . . . 5·00 2·20

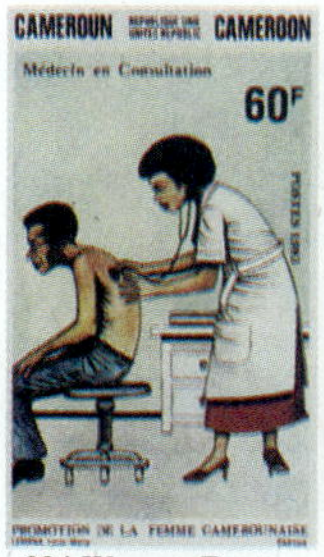

334 Woman Doctor

335 Lions Emblem and Map

1983. Cameroun Women. Multicoloured.
958 60f. Type **334** 75 25
959 70f. Woman lawyer 75 25

1983. Air. District 403 of Lions International Convention, Douala.
960 **335** 70f. multicoloured 65 25
961 150f. multicoloured . . . 1·10 65

336 Bafoussam Town Hall

1983. Town Halls. Multicoloured.
962 60f. Type **336** 65 25
963 70f. Garoua town hall . . . 75 25

337 President Biya and National Flag

1983. 11th Anniv of United Republic. Mult.
964 60f. Type **337** 55 20
965 70f. Pres. Biya and national arms 75 25

338 Container Ship and Buoy

1983. 25th Anniv of IMO.
966 **338** 500f. multicoloured . . . 5·00 2·10

339 Martial Eagle ("L'Aigle Martial")

340 Bread Mask ("Wery-Nwen-Nto")

1983. Birds. Multicoloured.
967 25f. Type **339** . . . . 1·10 45
968 30f. Rufous-breasted sparrow hawk ("L'Epervier") . . . 1·50 60
969 50f. Purple heron ("Le Heron Pourpre") . . . . 2·75 80
See also Nos. 1157 and 1169.

1983. Cameroun Artists. Multicoloured.
970 60f. Type **340** 75 20
971 70f. Basket with lid ("Chechia Bamoun") . . . 95 25

341 Mobile Rural Post Office

1983. World Communications Year. Multicoloured.
972 90f. Type **341** 95 30
973 150f. Radio operator with morse key . . . . 1·50 50
974 250f. Tom-tom drums . . . 2·75 85

342 African Civet

1983. Endangered Animals (5th series). Mult.
975 200f. Type **342** . . . . 2·75 75
976 200f. Gorilla . . . . 2·75 75
977 350f. Guinea-pig (vert) . . . 4·50 1·50
See also No. 1170.

343 "Jeanne d'Aragon" (Raphael)

1983. Air. Paintings. Multicoloured.
978 500f. Type **343** . . . . 5·50 1·90
979 500f. "Massacre of Scio" (Delacroix) . . . . 5·50 1·90

344 Lake Tizon

1983. Landscapes. Multicoloured.
980 60f. Type **344** 55 20
981 70f. Mount Cameroun in eruption 75 25

345 Boy and Girl holding Hands

346 Christmas Tree

1983. 35th Anniv of Declaration of Human Rights.
982 **345** 60f. multicoloured 55 20
983 70f. multicoloured 75 20

1983. Christmas. Multicoloured.
984 60f. Type **346** 50 20
985 200f. Stained-glass window, Yaounde Cathedral . . . . 1·80 75
986 500f. Statue of angel, Reims Cathedral . . . . 4·75 1·70
987 500f. "The Rest on the Flight into Egypt" (Philipp Otto Runge) (horiz) . . . . . . 4·75 1·70
MS988 140 × 89 mm. Nos. 985/7 12·00 12·00

348 "Pieta" (G. Hernandez)

1984. Air. Easter. Multicoloured.
992 200f. Type **348** . . . . 2·00 75
993 500f. "Martyrdom of St. John the Evangelist" (C. le Brun) . . . . 5·00 2·20
MS994 160 × 104 mm. Nos. 992/3 8·25 8·25

349 Urban Council Building, Bamenda

1984. Town Halls. Multicoloured.
995 60f. Type **349** 60 25
996 70f. Mbalmayo 75 35

350 High Jump

351 Running with Ball

1984. Air. Olympic Games, Los Angeles. Mult.
997 100f. Type **350** 95 40
998 150f. Volleyball . . . . . . 1·40 60
999 250f. Basketball . . . . . . 2·30 90
1000 500f. Cycling . . . . 4·50 1·80

1984. Air. European Football Championship. Multicoloured.
1001 250f. Type **351** . . . . . . 2·30 90
1002 250f. Heading ball . . . . . 2·30 45
1003 500f. Tackle . . . . 4·50 1·80
MS1004 130 × 85 mm. As Nos. 1001/3, but with the background colours different 11·00 11·00

352 Catholic Church, Zoetele

1984. Churches. Multicoloured.
1005 60f. Type **352** 55 25
1006 70f. Marie Gocker Protestant Church, Yaounde 75 40

353 Antelope

1984. Endangered Animals (6th series). Mult.
1007 250f. Type **353** . . . . 3·50 1·10
1008 250f. Wild boar . . . . . . 3·50 1·10

354 Pres. Biya and Arms

1984. Air. President's Oath-taking Ceremony.
(a) Inscr in French.
1009 **354** 60f. multicoloured . . . 45 25
1010 70f. multicoloured . . . 55 25
1011 200f. multicoloured . . . 2·00 70

(b) Inscr in English.
1012 **354** 60f. multicoloured . . . 50 25
1013 70f. multicoloured . . . 75 25
1014 200f. multicoloured . . . 2·00 70

355 "Diana Bathing" (Watteau)

1984. Air. Anniversaries. Multicoloured.
1015 500f. Type **355** (300th birth anniv) (wrongly inscr "1624") . . . . 5·75 1·90
1016 500f. Diderot (encyclopaedist, death bicentenary) . . . . . . 5·75 1·90

1984. Air. Olympic Games Medal Winners. Nos. 997/1000 optd.
1017 100f. **MOEGENBURG (R.F.A.) 11-08-84** 95 50
1018 150f. **U.S.A. 11-08-84** . . . 1·40 70
1019 250f. **YOUGOSLAVIE 9-08-84** . . . . 2·30 1·10
1020 500f. **GORSKI (U.S.A.) 3-08-84** . . . . 4·50 2·20

357 Nightingale ("Le Rossignol")

358 Neil Armstrong

1984. Birds. Multicoloured.
1021 60f. Type **357** . . . . 3·00 80
1022 60f. Ruppell's griffon ("Le Vautour") . . . . 3·00 80
See also No. 1158.

1984. Air. 15th Anniv of 1st Man on the Moon. Multicoloured.
1023 500f. Type **358** . . . . . . 5·00 1·90
1024 500f. Launching of "Apollo 12" . . . . . . 5·00 1·90

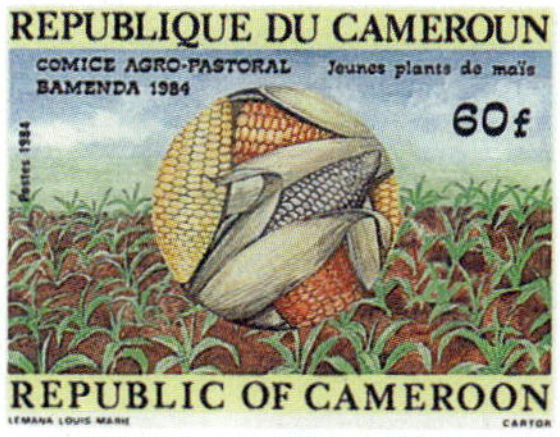

359 Maize and Young Plants

1984. Agro-pastoral Fair. Bamenda. Mult.
1025 60f. Type **359** 65 25
1026 70f. Zebus 75 30
1027 300f. Potatoes . . . . 3·50 1·30

360 Anniversary Emblem

362 Balafons (xylophone)

361 Wrestling

1984. 40th Anniv of ICAO.
1028 – 200f. multicoloured . . . 1·90 90
1029 **360** 200f. blue & deep blue 1·90 90
1030 – 300f. multicoloured . . . 2·75 1·40
1031 – 300f. multicoloured . . . 3·50 1·50
DESIGNS: No. 1028, "Icarus" (Hans Herni); 1030, Cameroun Airlines Boeing 737; 1031, "Solar Princess" (Sadiou Diouf).

1985. "Olymphilex '85" International Thematic Stamps Exhibition, Lausanne.
1032 **361** 150f. multicoloured . . . 1·50 70

1985. Musical Instruments. Multicoloured.
1033 60f. Type **362** 65 20
1034 70f. Mvet (stringed instrument) 85 30
1035 100f. Flute . . . . 1·40 40

363 Intelcam Headquarters, Yaounde

1985. 20th Anniv of Int Telecommunications Satellite Consortium.
1036 – 125f. black, orange & bl 1·70 60
1037 **363** 200f. multicoloured . . . 2·20 90
DESIGN: 125f. "Intelsat V" satellite.

365 U.N. Emblem and Headquarters

1985. 40th Anniv of UNO.
1038 **365** 250f. multicoloured . . . 2·50 1·00
1039 500f. multicoloured . . . 5·00 2·00

366 French and Cameroun Flags and Presidents

1985. President Mitterrand of France's Visit to Cameroun. (a) Inscr "Mitterand" in error.
1040 **366** 60f. multicoloured . . .
1041 70f. multicoloured . . .

(b) Inscr corrected to "Mitterrand".
1041a **366** 60f. multicoloured . . . 1·40 45
1041b 70f. multicoloured . . . 1·40 45

367 UNICEF Emblem

1985. Child Survival Campaign.
1042 **367** 60f. black, blue & yell 65 25
1043 – 300f. multicoloured . . . 3·00 1·30
DESIGN: Doctor inoculating babies.

368 Lake Barumbi, Kumba

1985. Landscapes. Multicoloured.
1044 60f. Type **368** 80 25
1045 70f. Pygmy village, Bonando 80 30
1046 150f. River Cameroun . . . 1·60 65

369 Ebolowa Town Hall

1985. Town Halls. Multicoloured.
1047 60f. Type **369** 55 25
1048 60f. Ngaoundere town hall 55 25

370 Pope John Paul II

371 Porcupine

1985. Papal Visit to Cameroun. Multicoloured.
1049 60f. Type **370** . . . . 1·00 40
1050 70f. Pope John Paul II holding crucifix . . . . . . 1·30 70
1051 200f. Pres. Biya and Pope John Paul II . . . . . . 3·50 1·70
MS1052 137 × 100 mm. Nos. 1049/51 6·75 6·75

1985. Animals. Multicoloured.
1053 125f. Type **371** . . . . . . 1·40 55
1054 200f. Squirrel . . . . 2·20 90
1055 350f. Greater cane rat . . . 3·75 1·60

372 Wooden Mask

374 Yellow-casqued Hornbill ("Le Toucan")

373 "Tomb of Henri Claude d'Harcourt" (detail)

1985. Cameroun Art (1st series). Multicoloured.
1056 60f. Type **372** 65 20
1057 70f. Wooden mask (different) 80 30
1058 100f. Men using pestle and mortar (wooden bas-relief) 1·40 75
See also Nos. 1081/3.

1985. Air. Death Anniversaries. Multicoloured.
1059 500f. Type **373** (bicentenary Jean Baptiste Pigalle (sculptor)) . . . . 5·75 2·30
1060 500f. Louis Pasteur (bacteriologist, 90th anniv) (after Edelfelt) . . 5·75 2·30

1985. Birds. Multicoloured.
1061 140f. Type **374** . . . . 2·00 70
1062 150f. Cock . . . . 2·10 70
1063 200f. European robins ("Le Rouge-gorge") . . . . . 3·00 1·10
See also No. 1156.

375 Child's Toys

1985. Air. Christmas. Multicoloured.
1064 250f. Type **375** . . . . . . 2·30 1·00
1065 300f. Akono church . . . . 2·75 1·30
1066 400f. Christmas crib . . . . 3·25 1·70
1067 500f. "The Virgin of the Blue Diadem" (Raphael) 5·00 2·30

376 Emblem, Flag and Volunteers

1986. 25th Anniv of American Peace Corps in Cameroun.
1068 **376** 70f. multicoloured . . . 75 30
1069 100f. multicoloured . . . 1·00 45

1986. As Nos. 851 and 941 but inscr "Republique du Cameroun/Republic of Cameroon".
1070 **284** 5f. multicoloured 25 10
1071 **325** 10f. multicoloured . . . 45 10

377 "Virgin Mary" (Pierre Prud'hon)

1986. Easter. Multicoloured.
1072 210f. Type **377** . . . . . . 2·00 95
1073 350f. "Stoning of St. Stephen" (Van Scorel) 3·00 1·50

378 "Anax sp."

1986. Insects. Multicoloured.
1074 70f. Type **378** . . . . 1·20 45
1075 70f. Bee on flower (vert) . . 1·30 50
1076 100f. Grasshopper . . . . . 1·90 70

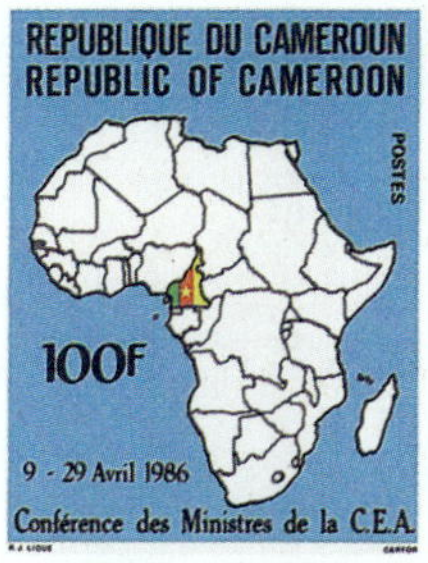

379 Map of Africa

1986. Economic Commission for Africa Ministers' Conference. Multicoloured.
1077 100f. Type **379** . . . . . . 1·00 55
1078 175f. Members' flags . . . . 2·10 85

380 Azteca Stadium

1986. Air. World Cup Football Championship, Mexico. Multicoloured.
1079 300f. Type **380** . . . . . . 2·75 1·40
1080 400f. Mexico team . . . . 3·75 1·70

1986. Cameroun Art (2nd series). As T **372**. Multicoloured.
1081 70f. Copper Statuette . . . 65 30
1082 100f. Wooden ash-tray . . . 95 35
1083 130f. Wooden horseman . . 1·70 55

381 Queen Elizabeth

1986. 60th Birthday of Queen Elizabeth II. Multicoloured.
1084 100f. Type **381** . . . . . . 1·10 50
1085 175f. Queen and President Biya . . . . 1·60 80
1086 210f. Queen Elizabeth (different) . . . . 2·10 1·00

382 President Biya

1986. 1st Anniv of Cameroun Republic Democratic Party. Multicoloured.
1087 70f. Type **382** 80 30
1088 70f. Bamenda Party headquarters (horiz) . . . 80 30
1089 100f. President Biya making speech . . . . 1·00 40

383 Argentine Team

1986. Air. World Cup Football Championship Winners.
1090 **383** 250f. multicoloured . . . 3·00 1·40

384 Mask Dancer with Sword **386** Bishop Desmond Tutu (Nobel Peace Prize Winner)

385 Cheetah

1986. Traditional Dances of North-west Kwem. Multicoloured.
1091 100f. Type **384** . . . . . . 1·00 55
1092 130f. Mask dancer with rattle . . . . 1·40 70

1986. Endangered Animals (7th series). Mult.
1093 300f. Type **385** . . . . . . 3·25 1·50
1094 300f. Varan . . . . 3·25 1·50

1986. International Peace Year. Multicoloured.
1095 175f. Type **386** . . . . . . 1·90 80
1096 200f. Type **386** . . . . . . 2·10 95
1097 250f. I.P.Y. and U.N. emblems . . . . 2·40 1·20

387 Pierre Curie (physicist)

1986. Air. Death Anniversaries. Multicoloured.
1098 500f. Type **387** (80th anniv) 6·75 2·50
1099 500f. Jean Mermoz and "Arc en Ciel" (aviation pioneer, 50th anniv) . . . 6·75 2·50

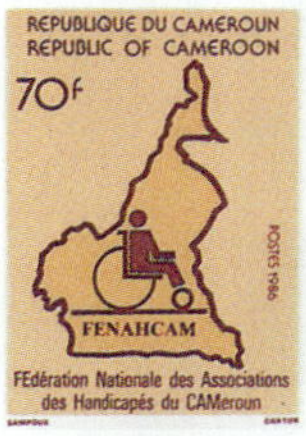

388 Emblem **389** Man holding Syringe and National Flag "Umbrella" over Woman and Child

1986. National Federation of Cameroun Handicapped Associations.
1100 **388** 70f. yellow and red . . . 70 25

1986. African Vaccination Year.
1101 70f. Type **389** 85 30
1102 100f. Flag behind woman holding child being immunised . . . . 1·00 45

390 Trees on Map **391** Loading Palm Nuts onto Trailer at Dibombari

1986. National Tree Day.
1103 70f. Type **390** 85 30
1104 100f. Hands holding clump of earth and seedling . . 1·00 45

1986. Agricultural Development. Multicoloured.
1105 70f. Type **391** 85 30
1106 70f. Payment for produce harvested 85 30
1107 200f. Pineapple plantation 1·90 90

392 "Antestiopsis lineaticollis intricata"

1987. Harmful Insects. Multicoloured.
1108 70f. Type **392** . . . . 1·10 45
1109 100f. "Distantiella theobroma" . . . . . . 1·60 65

393 Millet

1987. Agricultural Show, Maroua. Multicoloured.
1110 70f. Type **393** 85 30
1111 100f. Cotton . . . . 1·00 45
1112 150f. Cattle . . . . 1·50 80

394 Shot-putting

1987. 4th All-Africa Games, Kenya. Mult.
1113 100f. Type **394** 95 40
1114 140f. Pole-vaulting . . . . . 1·40 60

395 Drill Baboon

1988. Endangered Mammals. Drill Baboon. Multicoloured.
1115 30f. Type **395** . . . . 1·80 80
1116 40f. Adult baboons . . . . 2·00 90
1117 70f. Young baboon . . . . 2·50 1·50
1118 100f. Mother with baby . . 4·75 2·10

396 National Assembly Building

1989. Centenary of Interparliamentary Union.
1119 **396** 50f. multicoloured . . . 55 15

397 Cameroun and Argentine Players

1990. World Cup Football Championship, Italy. Multicoloured.

1120		200f. Type **397**	1·80	75
1121		250f. Cameroun player and match scene	2·20	1·10
1122		250f. Cameroun winning goal	2·20	1·10
1123		300f. Cameroun first eleven	2·75	1·40
MS1124		108 × 77 mm. Nos. 1120/3	10·00	10·00

1990. Nos. 1062 and 1093 surch.

1125	–	20f. on 150f. mult	1·90	20
1126	**385**	70f. on 300f. mult	6·25	35

399 Milla and Match Scene

1990. Roger Milla, 4th Best Player in World Cup.

1127	**399**	500f. multicoloured	5·25	2·75
MS1128		108 × 76 mm. No. 1125	8·50	8·50

400 Anniversary Emblem

1990. 40th Anniv of United Nations Development Programme.

1129	**400**	50f. multicoloured	55	25

401 UNESCO and ILY Emblems

1990. International Literacy Year.

1130	**401**	200f. black, lt blue & bl	1·90	80

402 Arms and Pres. Paul Biya

1991. 30th Anniv (1990) of Independence. Multicoloured.

1131		150f. Type **402**	1·60	70
1132		1000f. Flag, city and 1960 20f. Independence stamp	9·75	4·50
MS1133		164 × 99 mm. Nos. 1131/2	12·00	12·00

403 Treating Cacao Plantation

1991. Unissued stamps (for Ebolowa Agricultural Show) with bars over inscr and surch **125F.** Multicoloured.

1134		125f. on 70f. Type **403**	95	45
1135		125f. on 100f. Sheep	1·30	75

The stamps without surcharge were sold only by the Paris agency.

405 Snake on National Colours and Map

407 Serle's Bush Shrike ("La Pie Grieche du Mont-kupe")

406 Oribi

1991. Anti-AIDS Campaign. Multicoloured.

1137		15f. Type **405**	10	10
1138		25f. Youth pushing back "AIDS" in French and English (horiz)	40	10

See also Nos. 1171/2.

1991. As No. 932 but inscr "Republic du Cameroun / Republic of Cameroun".

1139	**322**	40f. multicoloured	45	10

1991. Sovereign Military Order of Malta Child Survival Project. Antelopes. Multicoloured.

1140		125f.+10f. Type **406**	1·80	1·10
1141		250f.+20f. Waterbucks	2·75	2·20
MS1142		144 × 90 mm. Nos. 1140/1	6·25	6·25

1991. Birds. Multicoloured.

1143		70f. Type **407**	75	45
1144		70f. Grey-necked bald crow ("Le Picathartes Chauve") (horiz)	75	45
1145		300f. As No. 1144	2·75	1·60
1146		350f. Type **407**	3·50	1·60
MS1147		108 × 80 mm. Nos. 144/5	7·75	7·75

408 African Elephant

1991. Animals. Multicoloured.

1148		125f. Type **408**	1·50	70
1149		250f. Buffalo	2·75	1·60
MS1150		120 × 80 mm. Nos. 1148/9	6·25	6·25

409 Mvolye Church

1991. Centenary (1990) of Catholic Church in Cameroun. Multicoloured.

1151		125f. Type **409**	1·40	70
1152		250f. Akono church	2·40	1·50
MS1153		108 × 80 mm. Nos. 1151/2	4·00	4·00

410 Emblems

1991. 7th African Group Meeting of Int Savings Banks Institute, Yaounde.

1154	**410**	250f. multicoloured	2·40	1·20
MS1155		107 × 80 mm. No. 1154	2·75	2·75

1992. Birds. As previous designs but with values changed. Multicoloured.

1156		125f. As No. 1063	1·40	50
1157		200f. As No. 968	2·00	85
1158		350f. Type **357**	3·50	1·50

411 Columbus's Fleet

412 Mbappe Lepe (footballer)

1992. 500th Anniv of Discovery of America by Columbus. Multicoloured.

1159		125f. Type **411**	1·40	70
1160		250f. Columbus kneeling on beach	2·50	1·40
1161		400f. Meeting Amerindians	3·75	2·10
1162		500f. Fleet crossing the Atlantic	5·25	3·00

1992. Cameroun Football. Multicoloured.

1163		125f. Type **412**	1·30	70
1164		250f. League emblem	2·50	1·50
1165		400f. National Football Federation emblem (horiz)	3·75	2·10
1166		500f. Ahmadou Ahidjo Stadium, Yaounde (horiz)	5·50	3·00

See also Nos. 1173/5.

413 Crocodile

1993. Endangered Animals. Mult. Self-adhesive.

1167		125f. Type **413**	1·40	70
1168		250f. Kob (vert)	2·40	1·40

1993. As Nos. 967 and 975 but inscr "REPUBLIQUE DU CAMEROUN REPUBLIC OF CAMEROON" and with values changed.

1169	**339**	370f. multicoloured	3·50	1·80
1170	**342**	410f. multicoloured	4·25	2·10

1993. Anti-AIDS Campaign. As Nos. 1137/8 but values changed. Multicoloured.

1171		100f. Type **405**	1·00	60
1172		175f. As No. 1138	1·90	1·00

1993. As Nos. 1163/5 but values changed.

1173		10f. As No. 1165		
1174		25f. As No. 1164		
1175		50f. Type **412**		

414 President Biya holding Football and Lion (national team mascot)

1994. World Cup Football Championship, United States. Multicoloured.

1176		125f. Type **414**	85	45
1177		250f. Emblem, lion, player and map of Cameroun	1·40	75
1178		450f. Players, ball showing world map, national flag and trophy	2·50	1·50
1179		500f. Eagle and lion supporting ball	3·00	1·70
MS1180		120 × 100 mm. Nos. 1176/9	13·00	13·00

415 Grey Parrot

417 Anniversary Emblem and Dove carrying Branch

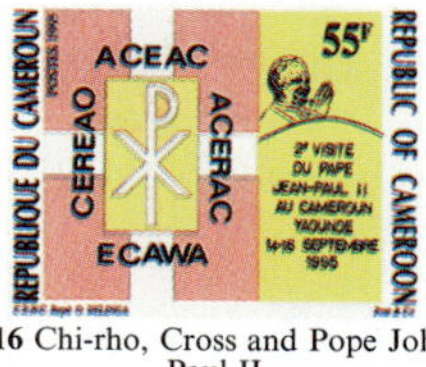

416 Chi-rho, Cross and Pope John Paul II

1995.

1181	**415**	125f. multicoloured	1·30	45

1995. 2nd Papal Visit.

1182	**416**	55f. black, pink & yell	35	25
1183	–	125f. multicoloured	85	35

DESIGN: 125f. Pope and open book.

1995. 50th Anniv of UNO Multicoloured.

1184		200f. Type **417**	1·20	55
1185		250f. Anniversary emblem and figures joining hands	1·50	75

Cameroun joined the Commonwealth on 1 November 1995.

MILITARY FRANK STAMP

M 78 Arms and Crossed Swords

1963. No value indicated.

M1	M **78**	(–) lake	3·00	3·25

POSTAGE DUE STAMPS

D 8 Felling Mahogany Tree

D 25 African Idols

1925.

D 88	D **8**	2c. black and blue	35	3·75
D 89		4c. purple and olive	30	3·00
D 90		5c. black and lilac	70	3·75
D 91		10c. black and red	70	4·50
D 92		15c. black and grey	1·00	4·25
D 93		20c. black and olive	1·70	4·75
D 94		25c. black and yellow	1·30	5·75
D 95		30c. orange and blue	1·50	5·75
D 96		50c. black and brown	1·50	5·75
D 97		60c. red and green	1·60	6·50
D 98		1f. green & red on grn	1·60	1·70
D 99		2f. mauve and red	2·75	8·25
D100		3f. blue and brown	5·50	10·50

1939.

D148	D **25**	5c. purple	35	4·50
D149		10c. blue	10	5·00
D150		15c. red	10	4·50
D151		20c. brown	10	4·50
D152		30c. blue	10	3·25
D153		50c. green	15	4·50
D154		60c. purple	15	4·50
D155		1f. violet	75	3·25
D156		2f. orange	35	5·00
D157		3f. blue	40	6·00

D 46

1947.

D254	D **46**	10c. red	10	4·50
D255		30c. orange	10	4·75
D256		50c. black	10	4·75
D257		1f. red	75	4·50
D258		2f. green	2·30	5·00
D259		3f. mauve	2·30	5·25
D260		4f. blue	2·00	4·25
D261		5f. brown	1·80	4·75
D262		10f. blue	2·00	3·00
D263		20f. sepia	2·75	4·50

D 77 "Hibiscus rosa sinensis"

1963. Flowers. Multicoloured.

D342		50c. Type D **77**	10	50
D343		50c. "Erythrine"	10	50
D344		1f. "Plumeria lutea"	10	50
D345		1f. "Ipomoea sp."	10	50
D346		1f.50 "Grinum sp."	10	50
D347		1f.50 "Hoodia gordonii"	10	50
D348		2f. "Ochna"	20	60
D349		2f. "Gloriosa"	20	60
D350		5f. "Costus spectabilis"	20	60
D351		5f. "Bougainvillea spectabilis"	20	60
D352		10f. "Delonix regia"	55	55

D353		10f. "Haemanthus"	55	55
D354		20f. "Titanopsis"	1·30	1·20
D355		20f. "Ophthalmophyllum"	1·30	1·20
D356		40f. "Zingiberacee"	2·00	1·80
D357		40f. "Amorphophalus"	2·00	1·80

CANADA Pt. 1

A British dominion consisting of the former province of Canada with British Columbia, New Brunswick, Newfoundland, Nova Scotia and Prince Edward Island.

1851. 12 pence = 1 shilling (Canadian).
1859. 100 cents = 1 dollar.

COLONY OF CANADA

1 Beaver

2 Prince Albert

3

4

5

6 Jacques Cartier

1851. Imperf.

17	4	½d. red	£800	£500
5	1	3d. red	£1600	£170
9	2	6d. purple	£21000	£950
12	5	7½d. green	£9000	£1700
14	6	10d. blue	£8500	£1200
4	3	12d. black	£130000	£60000

1858. Perf.

25	4	½d. red	£3000	£700
26	1	3d. red	£3750	£300
27a	2	6d. purple	£11000	£2750

1859. Values in cents. Perf.

29	4	1c. red	£325	38·00
44		2c. red	£500	£160
31	1	5c. red	£350	16·00
38	2	10c. purple	£1000	60·00
36		10c. brown	£950	60·00
40	5	12½c. green	£850	55·00
42	6	17c. blue	£1100	75·00

DOMINION OF CANADA

13

14

1868. Various frames.

54	13	½c. black	60·00	60·00
55	14	1c. brown	£350	45·00
56a		1c. yellow	£850	80·00
57		2c. green	£450	38·00
49		3c. red	£950	28·00
63		5c. green	£750	75·00
59b		6c. brown	£950	45·00
60		12½c. blue	£700	48·00
70		15c. purple	65·00	19·00
69		15c. blue	£160	32·00

27

21

28

1870. Various frames.

101	27	½c. black	15·00	9·00
75	21	1c. yellow	30·00	1·25
104		2c. green	40·00	2·50
105		3c. red	38·00	80
106		5c. grey	70·00	1·75
107		6c. brown	38·00	11·00
117	–	8c. grey	£120	6·50
120	–	8c. purple	85·00	6·50
111	21	10c. pink	£225	28·00

On 8c. head is to left.

1893.

115	28	20c. red	£225	48·00
116		50c. blue	£250	35·00

30

31

1897. Jubilee.

121	30	½c. black	50·00	50·00
122		1c. orange	10·00	4·50
124		2c. green	20·00	9·00
126		3c. red	12·00	2·25
128		5c. blue	40·00	14·00
129		6c. brown	90·00	90·00
130		8c. violet	32·00	30·00
131		10c. purple	55·00	48·00
132		15c. slate	90·00	90·00
133		20c. red	90·00	90·00
134		50c. blue	£130	95·00
136		$1 lake	£450	£450
137		$2 violet	£750	£350
138		$3 bistre	£950	£700
139		$4 violet	£900	£600
140		$5 green	£900	£600

1897. Maple-leaves in four corners.

141	31	½c. black	7·50	5·00
143		1c. green	19·00	90
144		2c. violet	18·00	1·50
145		3c. red	30·00	1·50
146		5c. blue	65·00	2·75
147		6c. brown	60·00	26·00
148		8c. orange	80·00	7·00
149		10c. purple	£130	55·00

1898. As T **31** but figures in lower corners.

150		½c. black	5·00	1·10
151		1c. green	26·00	50
154		2c. purple	24·00	30
155		2c. red	38·00	30
156		3c. red	60·00	1·00
157		5c. blue	£110	3·00
159		6c. brown	95·00	55·00
160		7c. yellow	65·00	18·00
162		8c. orange	£110	32·00
163		10c. purple	£170	14·00
165		20c. green	£300	50·00

33

35 King Edward VII

1898. Imperial Penny Postage.

168	33	2c. black, red and blue	27·00	5·50

1899. Surch **2 CENTS**.

171		2c. on 3c. red (No. 145)	17·00	8·00
172		2c. on 3c. red (No. 156)	17·00	4·25

1903.

175	35	1c. green	25·00	50
176		2c. red	20·00	50
178		5c. blue	80·00	2·50
180		7c. olive	65·00	2·75
182		10c. purple	£130	16·00
185		20c. olive	£225	25·00
187		50c. violet	£350	85·00

36 King George V and Queen Mary, when Prince and Princess of Wales

44

1908. Tercentenary of Quebec. Dated "1608 1908".

188	36	½c. brown	3·75	3·50
189	–	1c. green	16·00	2·75
190	–	2c. red	19·00	1·00
191	–	5c. blue	48·00	26·00
192	–	7c. olive	65·00	48·00
193	–	10c. violet	70·00	55·00
194	–	15c. orange	85·00	70·00
195	–	20c. brown	£120	£100

DESIGNS: 1c. Cartier and Champlain; 2c. King Edward VII and Queen Alexandra; 5c. Champlain's House in Quebec; 7c. Generals Montcalm and Wolfe; 10c. Quebec in 1700; 15c. Champlain's departure for the West; 20c. Cartier's arrival before Quebec.

1912.

196	44	1c. green	6·00	50
200		2c. red	5·50	50
205		3c. brown	5·50	50
205b		5c. blue	60·00	75
209		7c. yellow	20·00	3·00
210		10c. purple	90·00	2·75
212		20c. olive	32·00	1·50
215		50c. sepia	50·00	3·75

See also Nos. 246/55.

1915. Optd **WAR TAX** diagonally.

225	44	5c. blue	£110	£200
226		20c. olive	55·00	£100
227		50c. sepia	£110	£160

46

47

1915.

228	46	1c. green	8·00	50
229		2c. red	17·00	1·50

1916.

233	47	2c.+1c. red	30·00	1·25
239		2c.+1c. brown	4·25	50

48 Quebec Conference, 1864, from painting "The Fathers of the Confederation" by Robert Harris

1917. 50th Anniv of Confederation.

244	48	3c. brown	18·00	2·50

1922.

246	44	1c. yellow	2·50	60
247		2c. green	2·25	10
248		3c. red	3·75	10
249		4c. yellow	8·00	3·50
250		5c. violet	5·00	1·75
251		7c. brown	12·00	7·50
252		8c. blue	19·00	11·00
253		10c. blue	17·00	3·25
254		10c. brown	19·00	3·25
255		$1 orange	55·00	8·00

1926. Surch **2 CENTS** in one line.

264	44	2c. on 3c. red	50·00	60·00

1926. Surch **2 CENTS** in two lines.

265	44	2c. on 3c. red	16·00	25·00

51 Sir J. A. Macdonald

52 "The Fathers of the Confederation"

1927. 60th Anniv of Confederation. I. Commemoration Issue. Dated "1867–1927".

266	51	1c. orange	2·50	1·50
267	52	2c. green	2·25	30
268	–	3c. red	7·50	5·00
269	–	5c. violet	4·00	3·50
270	–	12c. blue	24·00	5·00

DESIGNS—HORIZ: As Type **52**: 3c. Parliament Buildings, Ottawa; 12c. Map of Canada, 1867–1927. VERT: As Type **51**: 5c. Sir W. Laurier.

56 Darcy McGee

57 Sir W. Laurier and Sir J. A. Macdonald

II. Historical Issue.

271	56	5c. violet	3·00	2·50
272	57	12c. green	17·00	4·50
273	–	20c. red	17·00	12·00

DESIGN—As Type **57**: 20c. R. Baldwin and L. H. Lafontaine.

59

1928. Air.

274	59	5c. brown	6·50	4·25

60 King George V

61 Mount Hurd and Indian Totem Poles

1928.

275	60	1c. orange	2·75	1·50
276		2c. green	1·25	20
277		3c. lake	17·00	18·00
278		4c. bistre	13·00	8·00
279		5c. violet	6·50	4·25
280		8c. blue	7·50	6·00
281	61	10c. green	8·50	1·50
282	–	12c. black	23·00	13·00
283	–	20c. lake	28·00	14·00
284	–	50c. blue	£130	42·00
285	–	$1 olive	£120	70·00

DESIGNS—HORIZ: 12c. Quebec Bridge; 20c. Harvesting with horses; 50c. "Bluenose" (fishing schooner); $1 Parliament Buildings, Ottawa.

66

67 Parliamentary Library, Ottawa

68 The Old Citadel, Quebec

1930.

288	66	1c. orange	1·75	1·00
289		1c. green	1·50	10
290		2c. green	1·75	10
291		2c. red	1·50	2·25
292b		2c. brown	1·25	10
293		3c. red	1·00	10
294		4c. yellow	7·00	4·50
295		5c. violet	2·75	5·00
296		5c. blue	5·50	20
297		8c. blue	11·00	16·00
298		8c. orange	7·50	5·50
299	67	10c. olive	17·00	1·00
300	68	12c. black	14·00	5·50
325		13c. violet	50·00	2·25
301	–	20c. red	22·00	1·25
302	–	50c. blue	80·00	17·00
303	–	$1 olive	£100	27·00

DESIGNS—HORIZ: 20c. Harvesting with tractor; 50c. Acadian Memorial Church, Grand Pre, Nova Scotia; $1 Mount Edith Cavell.

72 Mercury and Western Hemisphere

73 Sir Georges Etienne Cartier

1930. Air.

310	72	5c. brown	19·00	18·00

1931.

312	73	10c. green	10·00	20

1932. Air. Surch **6** and bars.

313	59	6c. on 5c. brown	3·00	2·50

1932. Surch **3** between bars.

314a	66	3c. on 2c. red	1·00	60

76 King George V

77 Duke of Windsor when Prince of Wales

78 Allegory of British Empire

80 King George V

1932. Ottawa Conference. (a) Postage.

315	**76**	3c. red	70	80
316	**77**	5c. blue	9·50	5·00
317	**78**	13c. green	9·50	6·00

(b) Air. Surch **6 6 OTTAWA CONFERENCE 1932**.

318	**72**	6c. on 5c. brown	10·00	15·00

1932.

319	**80**	1c. green	60	10
320		2c. brown	70	10
321b		3c. red	85	10
322		4c. brown	35·00	9·00
323		5c. blue	10·00	10
324		8c. orange	26·00	4·25

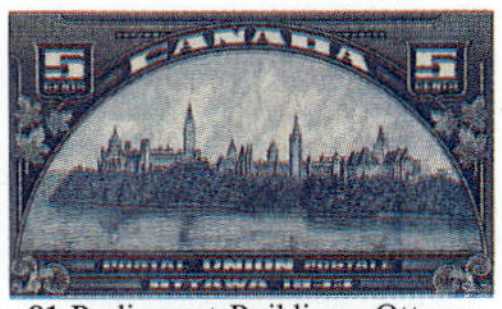

81 Parliament Buildings, Ottawa

1933. UPU Congress (Preliminary Meeting).

329	**81**	5c. blue	7·50	3·00

1933. Optd **WORLD'S GRAIN EXHIBITION & CONFERENCE REGINA 1933**.

330	–	20c. red (No. 295)	16·00	7·00

83 S.S. "Royal William" (after S. Skillett)

1933. Cent of 1st Transatlantic Steamboat Crossing.

331	**83**	5c. blue	15·00	3·25

84 Jacques Cartier approaching Land

1934. 4th-century of Discovery of Canada.

332	**84**	3c. blue	4·00	1·50

85 U.E.L. Statue, Hamilton

1934. 150th Anniv of Arrival of United Empire Loyalists.

333	**85**	10c. olive	8·50	6·00

86 Seal of New Brunswick

1934. 150th Anniv of New Brunswick.

334	**86**	2c. brown	1·50	2·50

87 Queen Elizabeth II when Princess

88 King George VI when Duke of York

89 King George V and Queen Mary

1935. Silver Jubilee. Dated "1910–1935".

335	**87**	1c. green	60	80
336	**88**	2c. brown	60	80
337	**89**	3c. red	2·00	80
338	–	5c. blue	5·50	7·00
339	–	10c. green	6·00	7·00
340	–	13c. blue	6·50	7·00

DESIGNS—VERT: 5c. Duke of Windsor when Prince of Wales. HORIZ: 10c. Windsor Castle; 13c. Royal Yacht "Britannia".

93 King George V

94 Royal Canadian Mounted Policeman

1935.

341	**93**	1c. green	1·75	10
342		2c. brown	1·75	10
343		3c. red	1·75	10
344		4c. yellow	3·50	2·00
345		5c. blue	3·50	10
346		8c. orange	4·25	4·25
347	**94**	10c. red	6·50	50
348	–	13c. purple	7·50	65
349	–	20c. green	21·00	70
350	–	50c. violet	25·00	5·50
351	–	$1 blue	40·00	11·00

DESIGNS—HORIZ: 13c. Confederation, Charlottetown, 1864; 20c. Niagara Falls; 50c. Parliament Buildings, Victoria, B.C.; $1 Champlain Monument, Quebec.

99 Daedalus

1935. Air.

355	**99**	6c. brown	3·00	1·00

100 King George VI and Queen Elizabeth

1937. Coronation.

356	**100**	3c. red	1·75	1·50

101 King George VI

102 Memorial Chamber Parliament Buildings, Ottawa

104 Fort Garry Gate, Winnipeg

1937.

357	**101**	1c. green	1·50	10
358		2c. brown	1·75	10
359		3c. red	1·75	10
360		4c. yellow	5·50	1·75
361		5c. blue	5·50	10
362		8c. orange	5·50	3·00
363	**102**	10c. red	5·00	30
364	–	13c. blue	22·00	2·00
365	**104**	20c. brown	22·00	2·00
366	–	50c. green	48·00	13·00
367	–	$1 violet	60·00	13·00

DESIGNS—HORIZ: 13c. Halifax Harbour; 50c. Vancouver Harbour; $1 Chateau de Ramezay, Montreal.

107 Fairchild 45-80 Sekani Seaplane over "Distributor" on Mackenzie River

1938. Air.

371	**107**	6c. blue	13·00	1·50

108 Queen Elizabeth II when Princess and Princess Margaret

1939. Royal Visit.

372	**108**	1c. black and green	2·00	20
373	–	2c. black and brown	2·00	1·25
374	–	3c. black and red	1·50	20

DESIGNS—HORIZ: 3c. King George VI and Queen Elizabeth. VERT: 2c. National War Memorial, Ottawa.

111 King George VI in Naval Uniform

112 King George VI in Military Uniform

114 Grain Elevator

115 Farm Scene

121 Air Training Camp

1942. War Effort.

375	**111**	1c. green (postage)	1·50	10
376	**112**	2c. brown	1·75	10
377	–	3c. red	1·25	60
378	–	3c. purple	90	10
379	**114**	4c. grey	5·50	1·50
380	**112**	4c. red	70	10
381	**111**	5c. blue	3·00	10
382	**115**	8c. brown	5·50	75
383	–	10c. brown	9·50	10
384	–	13c. green	7·50	8·50
385	–	14c. green	22·00	1·00
386	–	20c. brown	18·00	45
387	–	50c. violet	26·00	5·50
388	–	$1 blue	42·00	8·00
399	**121**	6c. blue (air)	26·00	9·50
400		7c. blue	4·00	20

DESIGNS—As Type **112**: 3c. King George VI. As Type **121**. VERT: 10c. Parliament Buildings. HORIZ: 13, 14c. Ram tank; 20c. Corvette; 50c. Munitions factory; $1 H.M.S. "Cossack" (destroyer).

122 Ontario Farm Scene

1946. Re-conversion to Peace.

401	**122**	8c. brown (postage)	1·25	2·50
402	–	10c. green	2·00	10
403	–	14c. sepia	4·25	2·25
404	–	20c. grey	3·00	10
405	–	50c. green	16·00	4·25
406	–	$1 purple	25·00	4·25
407	–	7c. blue (air)	5·00	2·00

DESIGNS: 10c. Great Bear Lake; 14c. St. Maurice River power station; 20c. Combine harvester; 50c. Lumbering in British Columbia; $1 "Abegweit" (train ferry); 7c. Canada geese in flight.

129 Alexander Graham Bell and "Fame"

130 "Canadian Citizenship"

1947. Birth Centenary of Graham Bell (inventor of the telephone).

408	**129**	4c. blue	15	30

1947. Advent of Canadian Citizenship and 80th Anniv of Confederation.

409	**130**	4c. blue	10	25

131 Queen Elizabeth II when Princess

132 Queen Victoria. Parliament Building, Ottawa, and King George VI

1948. Princess Elizabeth's Wedding.

410	**131**	4c. blue	10	15

1948. Centenary of Responsible Government.

411	**132**	4c. grey	10	10

133 Cabot's Ship "Matthew"

1949. Entry of Newfoundland into Canadian Confederation.

412	**133**	4c. green	30	10

134 "Founding of Halifax, 1749" (after C. W. Jeffries)

135 King George VI

1949. Halifax Bicentenary.

413	**134**	4c. violet	30	10

1949. Portraits of King George VI.

414	**135**	1c. green	25	10
415	–	2c. sepia	1·75	45
415a	–	2c. green	1·50	10
416	–	3c. purple	30	10
417	–	4c. red	20	10
418	–	5c. blue	2·00	40

1950. As Nos. 414 and 416/18 but without "POSTES POSTAGE".

424	1c. green	50	65
425	2c. sepia	50	3·50
426	3c. purple	50	65
427	4c. red	50	20
428	5c. blue	50	1·50

142 Drying Furs

141 Oil Wells in Alberta

145 Mackenzie King

1950.

432	**142**	10c. purple	3·75	10
441	–	20c. grey	2·00	10
431	**141**	50c. green	6·00	1·00
433	–	$1 blue	38·00	5·00

DESIGNS: 20c. Forestry products; $1 Fisherman.

1951. Canadian Prime Ministers.

434	–	3c. green (Borden)	10	75
444	–	3c. purple (Abbott)	25	65
435	**145**	4c. red	10	10
445	–	4c. red (A. Mackenzie)	25	25
475	–	4c. violet (Thompson)	15	35
483	–	4c. violet (Bennett)	10	40
476	–	5c. blue (Bowell)	15	20
484	–	5c. blue (Tupper)	10	10

146 Mail Trains, 1851 and 1951

149 Reproduction of 3d., 1851

1951. Centenary of First Canadian Postage Stamp. Dated "1851 1951".

436	**146**	4c. black	50	10
437	–	5c. violet	1·00	2·00
438	–	7c. blue	50	1·25
439	**149**	15c. red	1·60	10

DESIGNS—As Type **146**: 5c. "City of Toronto" and S.S. "Prince George"; 7c. Mail coach and Canadair DC-4M North Star airplane.

150 Queen Elizabeth II when Princess and Duke of Edinburgh

1951. Royal Visit.
440 **150** 4c. violet 25 15

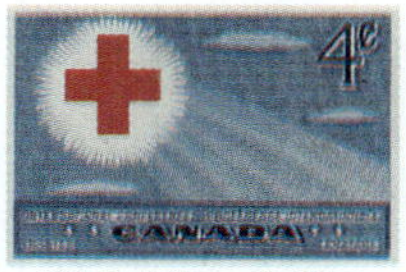

152 Red Cross Emblem

1952. 18th Int Red Cross Conf, Toronto.
442 **152** 4c. red and blue 15 10

153 Canada Goose

1952.
443 **153** 7c. blue . . . . 1·25 10

165 Eskimo Hunter **164** Northern Gannet

160 Textile Industry

154 Pacific Coast Indian House and Totem Pole

1953.
477 **165** 10c. brown 50 10
474 **164** 15c. black . . . . 1·00 10
488 – 20c. green 60 10
489 – 25c. red 70 10
462 **160** 50c. green . . . . 1·50 10
446 **154** $1 black . . . . 3·25 20
DESIGNS (As Type **160**)—HORIZ: 20c. Pulp and paper industry. VERT: 25c. Chemical industry.

155 Polar Bear

158 Queen Elizabeth II

1953. National Wild Life Week.
447 **155** 2c. blue 10 10
448 – 3c. sepia (Elk) 10 60
449 – 4c. slate (American bighorn) 15 10

1953.
450 **158** 1c. brown 10 10
451 2c. green 15 10
452 3c. red 15 15
453 4c. violet 20 10
454 5c. blue 20 10

159 Queen Elizabeth II

161

1953. Coronation.
461 **159** 4c. violet 10 10

1954.
463 **161** 1c. brown 10 10
464 2c. green 20 10
465 3c. red 70 10
466 4c. violet 30 10
467 5c. blue 30 10
468 6c. orange . . . . 1·50 55

1954. National Wild Life Week. As T **155**.
472 4c. slate (Walrus) 35 20
473 5c. blue (American beaver) 35 10

166 Musk-ox

168 Dove and Torch

167 Whooping Cranes

1955. National Wild Life Week.
478 **166** 4c. violet 30 10
479 **167** 5c. blue . . . . 1·00 20

1955. 10th Anniv of ICAO.
480 **168** 5c. blue 20 20

169 Pioneer Settlers

1955. 50th Anniv of Alberta and Saskatchewan Provinces.
481 **169** 5c. blue 15 20

170 Scout Badge and Globe

1955. 8th World Scout Jamboree.
482 **170** 5c. brown and green . . . 25 10

173 Ice-hockey Players

1956. Ice-hockey Commemoration.
485 **173** 5c. blue 20 20

1956. National Wild Life Week. As T **155**.
486 4c. violet (Reindeer) 20 15
487 5c. blue (Mountain goat) . . 20 10

178

179 Fishing

1956. Fire Prevention Week.
490 **178** 5c. red and black 30 10

1957. Outdoor Recreation.
491 **179** 5c. blue 25 10
492 – 5c. blue 25 10
493 – 5c. blue 25 10
494 – 5c. blue 25 10
DESIGNS: No. 492, Swimming; 493, Hunting; 494, Skiing.

183 White-billed Diver

1957. National Wild Life Week.
495 **183** 5c. black 50 20

184 Thompson with Sextant, and North American Map

185 Parliament Buildings, Ottawa

1957. Death Cent of David Thompson (explorer).
496 **184** 5c. blue 25 30

1957. 14th UPU Congress, Ottawa.
497 **185** 5c. slate 15 10
498 – 15c. slate . . . . 55 1·75
DESIGNS—HORIZ ($33\frac{1}{2} \times 22$ mm): 15c. Globe within posthorn.

187 Miner

188 Queen Elizabeth II and Duke of Edinburgh

1957. Mining Industry.
499 **187** 5c. black 35 20

1957. Royal Visit.
500 **188** 5c. black 30 10

189 "A Free Press"

190 Microscope

1958. The Canadian Press.
501 **189** 5c. black 15 70

1958. International Geophysical Year.
502 **190** 5c. blue 20 10

191 Miner panning for Gold

1958. Centenary of British Columbia.
503 **191** 5c. turquoise 20 10

192 La Verendrye statue

1958. La Verendrye (explorer) Commemoration.
504 **192** 5c. blue 15 10

193 Samuel de Champlain and Heights of Quebec

194 Nurse

1958. 350th Anniv of Founding of Quebec by Samuel de Champlain.
505 **193** 5c. brown and green . . . 30 10

1958. National Health.
506 **194** 5c. purple 30 10

195 "Petroleum 1858–1958"

196 Speaker's Chair and Mace

1958. Centenary of Canadian Oil Industry.
507 **195** 5c. red and olive 30 10

1958. Bicentenary of First Elected Assembly.
508 **196** 5c. slate 30 10

197 John McCurdy's Biplane "Silver Dart" **198** Globe showing NATO Countries

1959. 50th Anniv of First Flight of the "Silver Dart" in Canada.
509 **197** 5c. black and blue 30 10

1959. 10th Anniv of NATO.
510 **198** 5c. blue 40 10

199

200 Queen Elizabeth II

1959. "Associated Country Women of the World" Commemoration.
511 **199** 5c. black and olive . . . 15 10

1959. Royal Visit.
512 **200** 5c. red 30 10

201 Maple Leaf linked with American Eagle

1959. Opening of St. Lawrence Seaway.
513 **201** 5c. blue and red 20 10

202 Maple Leaves

203 Girl Guides Badge

1959. Bicentenary of Battle of Quebec.
514 **202** 5c. green and red 30 10

1960. Golden Jubilee of Canadian Girl Guides Movement.
515 **203** 5c. blue and brown . . . 20 10

204 Dollard des Ormeaux

205 Surveyor, Bulldozer and Compass Rose

1960. Tercent of Battle of Long Sault.
516 **204** 5c. blue and brown . . . 20 10

1961. Northern Development.
517 **205** 5c. green and red 15 10

206 E. Pauline Johnson **207** Arthur Meighen (statesman)

1961. Birth Centenary of E. Pauline Johnson (Mohawk poetess).
518 **206** 5c. green and red 15 10

1961. Arthur Meighen Commemoration.
519 **207** 5c. blue 15 10

208 Engineers and Dam

1961. Colombo Plan.
520 **208** 5c. brown and blue . . . 30 10

209 "Resources for Tomorrow" **210** "Education"

1961. Natural Resources.
521 **209** 5c. green and brown . . . 15 10

1962. Education Year.
522 **210** 5c. black and brown . . . 15 10

211 Lord Selkirk and Farmer **212** Talon bestowing Gifts on Married Couple

1962. 150th Anniv of Red River Settlement.
523 **211** 5c. brown and green . . . 20 10

1962. Jean Talon Commemoration.
524 **212** 5c. blue 20 10

213 British Columbia and Vancouver Island 2½d. Stamp of 1860, and Parliament Buildings, B.C. **214** Highway (map version) and Provincial Arms

1962. Centenary of Victoria, B.C.
525 **213** 5c. red and black 30 10

1962. Opening of Trans-Canada Highway.
526 **214** 5c. black and brown . . . 15 10

215 Queen Elizabeth II and Wheat (agriculture) Symbol **216** Sir Casimir Gzowski

1962. Different symbols in top left corner.
527 **215** 1c. brown 10 10
528 – 2c. green 15 10
529 – 3c. violet 15 10
530 – 4c. red 15 10
531 – 5c. blue 15 10
SYMBOLS: 1c. Crystals (Mining); 2c. Tree (Forestry); 3c. Fish (Fisheries); 4c. Electricity pylon (Industrial power); 5c. Wheat (Agriculture).

1963. 150th Birth Anniv of Sir Casimir Gzowski (engineer).
535 **216** 5c. purple 10 10

217 "Export Trade" **218** Frobisher and barque "Gabriel"

1963.
536 **217** $1 red . . . . 4·75 2·00

1963. Sir Martin Frobisher Commemoration.
537 **218** 5c. blue 20 10

219 Horseman and Map

1963. Bicent of Quebec–Trois-Rivieres–Montreal Postal Service.
538 **219** 5c. brown and green . . . 15 10

220 Canada Geese **221** Douglas DC-9 Airliner and Uplands Airport, Ottawa

1963.
540 **221** 7c. blue 35 70
540a 8c. blue 50 50
539 **220** 15c. blue . . . . 1·00 10

222 "Peace on Earth" **223** Maple Leaves

1964. "Peace".
541 **222** 5c. ochre, blue & turq . . 15 10

1964. "Canadian Unity".
542 **223** 5c. lake and blue 10 10

224 White Trillium and Arms of Ontario

1964. Provincial Badges.
543 **224** 5c. green, brown and orange 40 20
544 – 5c. green, brown and yellow 40 20
545 – 5c. red, green and violet 30 20
546 – 5c. blue, red and green . . 30 20
547 – 5c. purple, green and brown 30 20
548 – 5c. brown, green and mauve 30 20
549 – 5c. lilac, green and purple 50 20
550 – 5c. green, yellow and red 30 20
551 – 5c. sepia, orange and green 30 20
552 – 5c. black, red and green 30 20
553 – 5c. drab, green and yellow 30 20
554 – 5c. blue, green and red . . 30 20
555 – 5c. red and blue 30 20
FLOWERS AND ARMS OF: No. 544, Madonna Lily, Quebec; 545, Purple Violet, New Brunswick; 546, Mayflower, Nova Scotia; 547, Dogwood, British Columbia; 548, Prairie Crocus, Manitoba; 549, Lady's Slipper, Prince Edward Island; 550, Wild Rose, Alberta; 551, Prairie Lily, Saskatchewan; 552, Pitcher Plant, Newfoundland; 553, Mountain Avens, Northwest Territories; 554, Fireweed, Yukon Territory; 555, Maple Leaf, Canada.

1964. Surch **8**.
556 **221** 8c. on 7c. blue 15 15

238 Fathers of the Confederation Memorial, Charlottetown

1964. Centenary of Charlottetown Conference.
557 **238** 5c. black 10 10

239 Maple Leaf and Hand with Quill Pen

1964. Centenary of Quebec Conference.
558 **239** 5c. red and brown 15 10

240 Queen Elizabeth II **241** "Canadian Family"

1964. Royal Visit.
559 **240** 5c. purple 15 10

1964. Christmas.
560 **241** 3c. red 10 10
561 5c. blue 10 10

242 "Co-operation"

1965. International Co-operation Year.
562 **242** 5c. green 35 10

243 Sir W. Grenfell

1965. Birth Centenary of Sir Wilfred Grenfell (missionary).
563 **243** 5c. green 20 10

244 National Flag

1965. Inauguration of National Flag.
564 **244** 5c. red and blue 15 10

245 Sir Winston Churchill **246** Peace Tower, Parliament Buildings, Ottawa

1965. Churchill Commemoration.
565 **245** 5c. brown 15 10

1965. Inter-Parliamentary Union Conference, Ottawa.
566 **246** 5c. green 10 10

247 Parliament Buildings, Ottawa, 1865 **248** "Gold, Frankincense and Myrrh"

1965. Centenary of Proclamation of Ottawa as Capital.
567 **247** 5c. brown 10 10

1965. Christmas.
568 **248** 3c. green 10 10
569 5c. blue 10 10

249 "Alouette 2" over Canada **250** La Salle

1966. Launching of Canadian Satellite, "Alouette 2".
570 **249** 5c. blue 15 10

1966. 300th Anniv of La Salle's Arrival in Canada.
571 **250** 5c. green 15 10

251 Road Signs **252** Canadian Delegation and Houses of Parliament

1966. Highway Safety.
572 **251** 5c. yellow, blue and black 15 10

1966. Centenary of London Conference.
573 **252** 5c. brown 10 10

253 Douglas Point Nuclear Power Station **254** Parliamentary Library, Ottawa

1966. Peaceful Uses of Atomic Energy.
574 **253** 5c. blue 10 10

1966. Commonwealth Parliamentary Association Conference, Ottawa.
575 **254** 5c. purple 10 10

255 "Praying Hands", after Durer **256** Flags and Canada on Globe

1966. Christmas.
576 **255** 3c. red 10 10
577 5c. orange 10 10

1967. Canadian Centennial.
578 **256** 5c. red and blue 10 10

257 Queen Elizabeth, Northern Lights and Dog-team **262** "Alaska Highway" (A. Y. Jackson)

1967.
579 **257** 1c. brown 10 10
580 – 2c. green 10 10
581 – 3c. purple 30 20
582 – 4c. red 20 10
583 – 5c. blue 20 10
601 – 6c. red 45 10
607 – 6c. black 30 10
609 – 7c. green 30 20
584 **262** 8c. purple 25 80
610 – 8c. black 30 10
585 – 10c. olive 25 10
586 – 15c. purple 30 10
587 – 20c. blue . . . . 1·40 10
588 – 25c. green 75 10
589 – 50c. brown . . . . . . 1·50 10
590 – $1 red . . . . 1·50 65
DESIGNS—As Type **257**: 2c. Totem pole; 3c. Combine-harvester and oil derrick; 4c. Ship in lock; 5c., Harbour scene; 6c., 7c. "Transport"; 8c. (No. 610), Library of Parliament. As Type **262**: 10c. "The Jack Pine" (T. Thomson); 15c. "Bylot Island" (L. Harris); 20c. "Quebec Ferry" (J. W. Morrice); 25c. "The Solemn Land" (J. E. H. MacDonald); 50c. "Summer's Stores" (Grain elevators, J. Ensor); $1 "Oilfield" (near Edmonton, H. G. Glyde).

269 Canadian Pavilion

270 Allegory of "Womanhood" on Ballot-box

1967. World Fair, Montreal.
611 **269** 5c. blue and red 10 10

1967. 50th Anniv of Women's Franchise.
612 **270** 5c. purple and black . . . 10 10

271 Queen Elizabeth II and Centennial Emblem

272 Athlete

1967. Royal Visit.
613 **271** 5c. plum and brown . . . 15 10

1967. Pan-American Games, Winnipeg.
614 **272** 5c. red 10 10

273 "World News"

1967. 50th Anniv of Canadian Press.
615 **273** 5c. blue 10 10

274 Governor-General Vanier

1967. Vanier Commemoration.
616 **274** 5c. black 10 10

275 People of 1867, and Toronto, 1967

276 Carol Singers

1967. Cent of Toronto as Capital City of Ontario.
617 **275** 5c. green and red 10 10

1967. Christmas.
618 **276** 3c. red 10 10
619 5c. green 10 10

277 Grey Jays

278 Weather Map and Instruments

1968. Wild Life.
620 **277** 5c. multicoloured 30 10
See also Nos. 638/40.

1968. 20th Anniv of First Meteorological Readings.
621 **278** 5c. multicoloured 15 10

279 Narwhal

1968. Wild Life.
622 **279** 5c. multicoloured 15 10

280 Globe, Maple Leaf and Rain Gauge

1968. International Hydrological Decade.
623 **280** 5c. multicoloured 15 10

281 The "Nonsuch"

1968. 300th Anniv of Voyage of the "Nonsuch".
624 **281** 5c. multicoloured 20 10

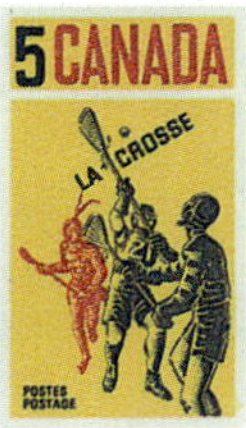

282 Lacrosse Players

283 Front Page of "The Globe", George Brown and Legislative Building

1968. Lacrosse.
625 **282** 5c. multicoloured 15 10

1968. 150th Birth Anniv of George Brown (politician and journalist).
626 **283** 5c. multicoloured 10 10

284 H. Bourassa (politician and journalist)

286 Armistice Monument, Vimy

285 John McCrae, Battlefield and First Lines of "In Flanders Fields"

1968. Birth Centenary of Henri Bourassa.
627 **284** 5c. black, red and cream 10 10

1968. 50th Death Anniv of John McCrae (soldier and poet).
628 **285** 5c. multicoloured 10 10

1968. 50th Anniv of 1918 Armistice.
629 **286** 15c. black 30 40

287 Eskimo Family (carving)

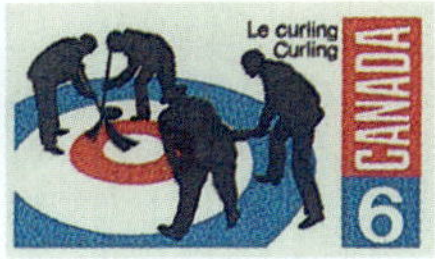

289 Curling

1968. Christmas.
630 **287** 5c. black and blue . . . 10 10
631 – 6c. black and ochre . . . 10 10
DESIGN: 6c. "Mother and Child" (carving).

1969. Curling.
632 **289** 6c. black, blue and red . . 15 10

290 Vincent Massey

292 Globe and Tools

291 "Return from the Harvest Field" (Suzor-Cote)

1969. Vincent Massey, First Canadian-born Governor-General.
633 **290** 6c. sepia and ochre . . . 10 10

1969. Birth Centenary of Marc Aurele de Foy Suzor-Cote (painter).
634 **291** 50c. multicoloured . . . . 70 2·00

1969. 50th Anniv of I.L.O.
635 **292** 6c. green 10 10

293 Vickers Vimy Aircraft over Atlantic Ocean

1969. 50th Anniv of 1st Non-stop Transatlantic Flight.
636 **293** 15c. brown, green and blue 40 55

294 "Sir William Osler" (J. S. Sargent)

295 White-throated Sparrow

1969. 50th Death Anniv of Sir William Osler (physician).
637 **294** 6c. blue and brown . . . 20 10

1969. Birds. Multicoloured.
638 6c. Type **295** 25 10
639 10c. Savannah sparrow ("Ipswich Sparrow") (horiz) . . . . 35 1·10
640 25c. Hermit thrush (horiz) . . 1·10 3·50

298 Flags of Winter and Summer Games

300 Sir Isaac Brock and Memorial Column

299 Outline of Prince Edward Island showing Charlottetown

1969. Canadian Games.
641 **298** 6c. green, red and blue . . 10 10

1969. Bicentenary of Charlottetown as Capital of Prince Edward Island.
642 **299** 6c. brown, black and blue 20 20

1969. Birth Bicentenary of Sir Isaac Brock.
643 **300** 6c. orange, bistre and brown 10 10

301 Children of the World in Prayer

302 Stephen Butler Leacock, Mask and "Mariposa"

1969. Christmas.
644 **301** 5c. multicoloured 10 10
645 6c. multicoloured 10 10

1969. Birth Centenary of Stephen Butler Leacock (humorist).
646 **302** 6c. multicoloured 10 10

303 Symbolic Cross-roads

1970. Centenary of Manitoba.
647 **303** 6c. blue, yellow and red 15 10

304 "Enchanted Owl" (Kenojuak)

1970. Centenary of Northwest Territories.
648 **304** 6c. red and black 10 10

305 Microscopic View of Inside of Leaf

1970. International Biological Programme.
649 **305** 6c. green, yellow and blue 15 10

306 Expo 67 Emblem and stylized Cherry Blossom

1970. World Fair, Osaka. Multicoloured.
650 25c. Type **306** (red) . . . . . 1·50 2·25
651 25c. Dogwood (violet) . . . 1·50 2·25
652 25c. White trillium (green) . . 1·50 2·25
653 25c. White garden lily (blue) 1·50 2·25
NOTE: Each stamp shows a stylized cherry blossom, in a different colour, given above in brackets.

310 Henry Kelsey

1970. 300th Birth Anniv of Henry Kelsey (explorer).
654 **310** 6c. multicoloured 10 10

311 "Towards Unification"

1970. 25th Anniv of UNO.
655 **311** 10c. blue 75 75
656 15c. mauve and lilac . . . 75 50

312 Louis Riel (Metis leader)

313 Mackenzie's Inscription, Dean Channel

1970. Louis Riel Commemoration.
657 **312** 6c. blue and red 10 10

1970. Sir Alexander Mackenzie (explorer).
658 **313** 6c. brown 15 10

314 Sir Oliver Mowat (statesman)

1970. Sir Oliver Mowat Commemoration.
659 **314** 6c. red and black 10 10

315 "Isles of Spruce" (A. Lismer)

1970. 50th Anniv of "Group of Seven" (artists).
660 **315** 6c. multicoloured 10 10

316 "Horse-drawn Sleigh" (D. Niskala)

328 Sir Donald A. Smith

1970. Christmas. Children's Drawings. Mult.
661 5c. Type **316** 50 20
662 5c. "Stable and Star of Bethlehem" (L. Wilson) . . 50 20
663 5c. "Snowmen" (M. Lecompte) 50 20
664 5c. "Skiing" (D. Durham) . . 50 20
665 5c. "Santa Claus" (A. Martin) 50 20
666 6c. "Santa Claus" (E. Bhattacharya) 50 20
667 6c. "Christ in Manger" (J. McKinney) 50 20
668 6c. "Toy Shop" (N. Whateley) 50 20
669 6c. "Christmas Tree" (J. Pomperleau) 50 20
670 6c. "Church" (J. McMillan) 50 20
671 10c. "Christ in Manger" (C. Fortier) (37 × 20 mm) 30 30
672 15c. "Trees and Sledge" (J. Dojcak) (37 × 20 mm) 45 60

1970. 150th Birth Anniv of Sir Donald Alexander Smith.
673 **328** 6c. yellow, brown and green 15 10

329 "Big Raven" (E. Carr)

1971. Birth Centenary of Emily Carr (painter).
674 **329** 6c. multicoloured 20 30

330 Laboratory Equipment

332 Maple "Keys"

331 "The Atom"

1971. 50th Anniv of Discovery of Insulin.
675 **330** 6c. multicoloured 30 30

1971. Birth Centenary of Lord Rutherford (scientist).
676 **331** 6c. yellow, red and brown 20 20

1971. "The Maple Leaf in Four Seasons". Mult.
677 6c. Type **332** (spring) 20 20
678 6c. Green leaves (summer) . . 20 20
679 7c. Autumn leaves 20 20
680 7c. Withered leaves and snow (winter) 20 20

333 Louis Papineau

334 Chart of Coppermine River

1971. Death Centenary of Louis-Joseph Papineau (politician).
681 **333** 6c. multicoloured 15 20

1971. Bicentenary of Samuel Hearne's Expedition to the Coppermine River.
682 **334** 6c. red, brown and buff 40 40

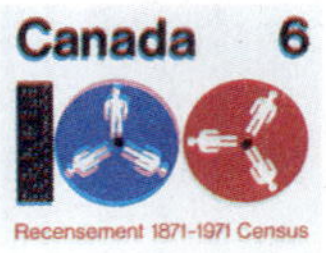

335 "People" and Computer Tapes

1971. Centenary of 1st Canadian Census.
683 **335** 6c. blue, red and black . . 30 20

336 Maple Leaves

1971. Radio Canada International.
684 **336** 15c. red, yellow and black 50 1·50

337 "B. C."

1971. Centenary of British Columbia's Entry into the Confederation.
685 **337** 7c. multicoloured 15 10

338 "Indian Encampment on Lake Huron" (Kane)

339 "Snowflake"

1971. Death Centenary of Paul Kane (painter).
686 **338** 7c. multicoloured 20 10

1971. Christmas.
687 **339** 6c. blue 10 10
688 7c. green 15 10
689 – 10c. silver and red . . . . 50 1·25
690 – 15c. silver, purple and lavender . . . . 65 2·00
DESIGN: 10c., 15c. "Snowflake" design similar to Type **339** but square (26 × 26 mm).

340 Pierre Laporte (Quebec Cabinet Minister)

341 Skaters

1971. 1st Anniv of Assassination of Pierre Laporte.
691 **340** 7c. black on buff 15 10

1972. World Figure Skating Championships, Calgary.
692 **341** 8c. purple 15 10

342 J. A. MacDonald

343 Forest, Central Canada

344 Vancouver

1972.
693 **342** 1c. orange 10 30
694 – 2c. green 10 10
695 – 3c. brown 10 50
696 – 4c. black 10 50
697 – 5c. mauve 10 10
698 – 6c. red 10 50
699 – 7c. brown 40 50
700 – 8c. blue 15 10
701 – 10c. red 75 10
702a **343** 10c. green, turquoise and orange 40 15
703b – 15c. blue and brown . . 1·00 10
704a – 20c. orange, violet and blue . . . . 1·00 10
705b – 25c. ultram and blue . . 1·00 10
706 – 50c. green, blue and brown . . . . 1·00 30
709a **344** $1 multicoloured 85 70
708 – $2 multicoloured . . . . 1·50 2·00
DESIGNS—As Type **342** (1 to 7c. show Canadian Prime Ministers): 2c. W. Laurier; 3c. R. Borden; 4c. W. L. Mackenzie King; 5c. R. B. Bennett; 6c. L. B. Pearson; 7c. Louis St. Laurent; 8, 10c. Queen Elizabeth II. As Type **343**: 15c. American bighorn; 20c. Prairie landscape from the air; 25c. Polar bears; 50c. Seashore, Eastern Canada. As Type **344**: $2 Quebec.

345 Heart

1972. World Health Day.
719 **345** 8c. red 30 10

346 Frontenac and Fort Saint-Louis, Quebec

1972. 300th Anniv of Governor Frontenac's Appointment to New France.
720 **346** 8c. red, brown and blue 15 15

347 Plains Indians' Artefacts

347a Buffalo Chase

348 Thunderbird and Tribal Pattern

348a Dancer in Ceremonial Costume

1972. Canadian Indians. (a) Horiz designs showing Artefacts as T **347** or Scenes from Indian Life as T **347a**.
721 **347** 8c. multicoloured 40 10
722 **347a** 8c. brown, yellow & blk 40 10
723 – 8c. multicoloured 40 10
724 – 8c. multicoloured 40 10
725 – 8c. multicoloured 40 10
726 – 8c. brown, yellow & blk 40 10
727 – 8c. multicoloured 40 10
728 – 8c. multicoloured 40 10
729 – 10c. multicoloured . . . 40 20
730 – 10c. red, brown and black 40 20
TRIBES: Nos. 721/2, Plains Indians; Nos. 723/4, Algonkians; Nos. 725/6, Pacific Coast Indians; Nos. 727/8, Subarctic Indians; Nos. 729/30, Iroquoians.

(b) Vert designs showing Thunderbird and pattern as T **348** or Costumes as T **348a**.
731 **348** 8c. orange, red and black 40 15
732 **348a** 8c. multicoloured 40 15
733 – 8c. red, violet and black 40 10
734 – 8c. green, brown and black 40 10
735 – 8c. red and black 40 10
736 – 8c. multicoloured 40 10
737 – 8c. green, brown and black 40 10
738 – 8c. multicoloured 40 10
739 – 10c. brown, orange & blk 40 20
740 – 10c. multicoloured . . . 40 20
TRIBES: Nos. 731/2, Plains Indians; Nos. 733/4, Algonkians; Nos. 735/6, Pacific Coast Indians; Nos. 737/8, Subarctic Indians; Nos. 739/40, Iroquoians.

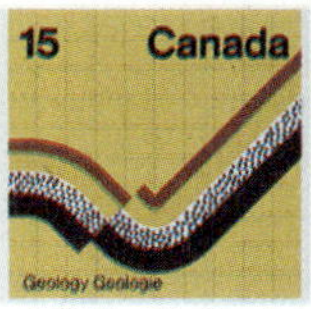

349 Earth's Crust

350 Candles

1972. Earth Sciences.
741 – 15c. multicoloured . . . . 1·10 1·90
742 – 15c. grey, blue and black 1·10 1·90
743 **349** 15c. multicoloured . . . . 1·10 1·90
744 – 15c. green, orange and black . . . . 1·10 1·90
DESIGNS AND EVENTS: No. 741 Photogrammetric surveying (12th Congress of International Society of Photogrammetry); No. 742 "Siegfried" lines (6th Conference of Int Cartographic Association); No. 743 (24th International Geological Congress); No. 744 Diagram of village at road-intersection (22nd Int Geographical Congress).

1972. Christmas. Multicoloured.
745 6c. Type **350** 15 10
746 8c. Type **350** 15 10
747 10c. Candles with fruits and pine boughs (horiz) . . . . 50 1·25
748 15c. Candles with prayer-book, caskets and vase (horiz) . . . . 60 1·75
Nos. 747/8 are size 36 × 20 mm.

351 "The Blacksmith's Shop" (Krieghoff)

352 F. de Montmorency-Laval

1972. Death Centenary of Cornelius Krieghoff (painter).
749 **351** 8c. multicoloured 30 15

1973. 350th Birth Anniv of Monsignor de Laval (1st Bishop of Quebec).
750 **352** 8c. blue, gold and silver 20 40

353 Commissioner French and Route of the March West

1973. Centenary of Royal Canadian Mounted Police.

751	**353**	8c. brown, orange and red	35	20
752	–	10c. multicoloured	1·00	1·25
753	–	15c. multicoloured	2·25	2·00

DESIGNS: 10c. Spectrograph; 15c. Mounted policeman.

354 Jeanne Mance

1973. 300th Death Anniv of Jeanne Mance (nurse).

754	**354**	8c. multicoloured	20	40

355 Joseph Howe

356 "Mist Fantasy" (MacDonald)

1973. Death Centenary of Joseph Howe (Nova Scotian politician).

755	**355**	8c. gold and black	20	40

1973. Birth Cent of J. E. H. MacDonald (artist).

756	**356**	15c. multicoloured	30	55

357 Oaks and Harbour

1973. Centenary of Prince Edward Island's Entry into the Confederation.

757	**357**	8c. orange and red	20	30

358 Scottish Settlers

1973. Bicentenary of Arrival of Scottish Settlers at Pictou, Nova Scotia.

758	**358**	8c. multicoloured	25	20

359 Queen Elizabeth II

1973. Royal Visit and Commonwealth Heads of Government Meeting, Ottawa.

759	**359**	8c. multicoloured	25	20
760		15c. multicoloured	80	1·50

360 Nellie McClung

361 Emblem of 1976 Olympics

1973. Birth Centenary of Nellie McClung (feminist).

761	**360**	8c. multicoloured	20	50

1973. 1976 Olympic Games, Montreal (1st issue).

762	**361**	8c. multicoloured	25	15
763		15c. multicoloured	45	1·25

See also Nos. 768/71, 772/4, 786/9, 798/802, 809/11, 814/16, 829/32, 833/7 and 842/4.

362 Ice-skate

363 Diving

1973. Christmas. Multicoloured.

764	6c. Type **362**	15	10
765	8c. Bird decoration	20	10
766	10c. Santa Claus (20 × 36 mm)	70	1·40
767	15c. Shepherd (20 × 36 mm)	80	1·75

1974. 1976 Olympic Games, Montreal. (2nd issue). "Summer Activities". Each blue.

768	8c. Type **363**	30	50
769	8c. "Jogging"	30	50
770	8c. Cycling	30	50
771	8c. Hiking	30	50

1974. 1976 Olympic Games, Montreal. (3rd issue). As T **361** but smaller (20 × 36½ mm).

772	**361**	8c.+2c. multicoloured	25	45
773		10c.+5c. multicoloured	40	1·00
774		15c.+5c. multicoloured	45	1·40

364 Winnipeg Signpost, 1872

1974. Winnipeg Centennial.

775	**364**	8c. multicoloured	20	15

365 Postmaster and Customer

366 "Canada's Contribution to Agriculture"

1974. Centenary of Canadian Letter Carrier Delivery Service. Multicoloured.

776	8c. Type **365**	50	80
777	8c. Postman collecting mail	50	80
778	8c. Mail handler	50	80
779	8c. Mail sorters	50	80
780	8c. Postman making delivery	50	80
781	8c. Rural delivery by car	50	80

1974. Centenary of "Agricultural Education". Ontario Agricultural College.

782	**366**	8c. multicoloured	20	20

367 Telephone Development

1974. Centenary of Invention of Telephone by Alexander Graham Bell.

783	**367**	8c. multicoloured	20	20

368 Bicycle Wheel

1974. World Cycling Championships, Montreal.

784	**368**	8c. black, red and silver	20	30

369 Mennonite Settlers

1974. Centenary of Arrival of Mennonites in Manitoba.

785	**369**	8c. multicoloured	20	20

1974. 1976 Olympic Games, Montreal (4th issue). "Winter Activities". As T **363**. Each red.

786	8c. Snow-shoeing	55	60
787	8c. Skiing	55	60
788	8c. Skating	55	60
789	8c. Curling	55	60

370 Mercury, Winged Horses and UPU Emblem

1974. Centenary of UPU.

790	**370**	8c. violet, red and blue	15	15
791		15c. red, violet and blue	50	1·50

371 "The Nativity" (J. P. Lemieux)

1974. Christmas. Multicoloured.

792	6c. Type **371**	10	10
793	8c. "Skaters in Hull" (H. Masson) (34 × 31 mm)	10	10
794	10c. "The Ice Cone, Montmorency Falls" (R. C. Todd)	30	75
795	15c. "Village in the Laurentian Mountains" (C. A. Gagnon)	35	1·10

372 Marconi and St. John's Harbour, Newfoundland

1974. Birth Centenary of Guglielmo Marconi (radio pioneer).

796	**372**	8c. multicoloured	20	20

373 Merritt and Welland Canal

1974. William Merritt Commemoration.

797	**373**	8c. multicoloured	20	30

374 Swimming

376 "Anne of Green Gables" (Lucy Maud Montgomery)

375 "The Sprinter"

1975. 1976 Olympic Games, Montreal (5th issue). Multicoloured.

798	8c.+2c. Type **374**	45	65
799	10c.+5c. Rowing	60	1·25
800	15c.+5c. Sailing	70	1·40

1975. 1976 Olympic Games, Montreal (6th issue). Multicoloured.

801	$1 Type **375**	1·25	2·00
802	$2 "The Diver" (vert)	1·75	3·50

1975. Canadian Writers (1st series). Multicoloured.

803	8c. Type **376**	30	10
804	8c. "Maria Chapdelaine" (Louis Hemon)	30	10

See also Nos. 846/7, 940/1 and 1085/6.

377 Marguerite Bourgeoys (founder of the Order of Notre Dame)

378 S. D. Chown (founder of United Church of Canada)

1975. Canadian Celebrities.

805	**377**	8c. multicoloured	60	40
806	–	8c. multicoloured	60	40
807	**378**	8c. multicoloured	30	75
808	–	8c. multicoloured	30	75

DESIGNS—As Type **377**: No. 806, Alphonse Desjardins (leader of Credit Union movement). As Type **378**: No. 808, Dr. J. Cook (first moderator of Presbyterian Church in Canada).

379 Pole-vaulting

380 "Untamed" (photo by Walt Petrigo)

1975. 1976 Olympics (7th issue). Multicoloured.

809	20c. Type **379**	40	50
810	25c. Marathon-running	55	80
811	50c. Hurdling	70	1·25

1975. Centenary of Calgary.

812	**380**	8c. multicoloured	30	30

381 I. W. Y. Symbol

382 Fencing

1975. International Women's Year.

813	**381**	8c. grey, brown and black	30	30

1975. Olympic Games, Montreal (1976) (8th issue). Multicoloured.

814	8c.+2c. Type **382**	35	75
815	10c.+5c. Boxing	45	1·50
816	15c.+5c. Judo	55	1·75

383 "Justice-Justitia" (statue by W. S. Allward)

385 "Santa Claus" (G. Kelly)

384 "William D. Lawrence" (full-rigged ship)

1975. Centenary of Canadian Supreme Court.

817	**383**	8c. multicoloured	20	30

1975. Canadian Ships (1st series). Coastal Vessels.

818	**384**	8c. brown and black . . .	70	75
819	–	8c. green and black . . .	70	75
820	–	8c. green and black . . .	70	75
821	–	8c. brown and black . . .	70	75

DESIGNS: No. 819, "Neptune" (steamer); 820, "Beaver" (paddle-steamer); 821, "Quadra" (steamer).

See also Nos. 851/4, 902/5 and 931/4.

1975. Christmas. Multicoloured.

822	6c. Type **385**	15	10
823	6c. "Skater" (B. Cawsey) . .	15	10
824	8c. "Child" (D. Hebert) . . .	15	10
825	8c. "Family" (L. Caldwell)	15	10
826	10c. "Gift" (D. Lovely) . . .	30	50
827	15c. "Trees" (R. Kowalski) (horiz)	40	75

386 Text, Badge and Bugle

387 Basketball

1975. 50th Anniv of Royal Canadian Legion.

828	**386**	8c. multicoloured	20	20

1976. Olympic Games, Montreal (9th issue). Mult.

829	8c.+2c. Type **387**	1·50	1·00
830	10c.+5c. Gymnastics	60	1·40
831	20c.+5c. Soccer	70	1·60

388 Games Symbol and Snow Crystal

389 "Communications Arts"

1976. 12th Winter Olympic Games, Innsbruck.

832	**388**	20c. multicoloured	20	40

1976. Olympic Games, Montreal (10th issue). Multicoloured.

833	20c. Type **389**	40	25
834	25c. Handicrafts	65	75
835	50c. Performing Arts	95	1·60

390 Place Ville Marie and Notre-Dame Church

1976. Olympic Games, Montreal (11th issue). Multicoloured.

836	$1 Type **390**	2·25	4·50
837	$2 Olympic stadium and flags	2·75	5·50

391 Flower and Urban Sprawl

1976. HABITAT. U.N. Conference on Human Settlements, Vancouver.

838	**391**	20c. multicoloured	20	30

392 Benjamin Franklin and Map

1976. Bicentenary of American Revolution.

839	**392**	10c. multicoloured	20	35

393 Wing Parade before Mackenzie Building

394 Transfer of Olympic Flame by Satellite

1976. Centenary of Royal Military College. Mult.

840	8c. Colour party and Memorial Arch	15	20
841	8c. Type **393**	15	20

1976. Olympic Games, Montreal (12th issue). Multicoloured.

842	8c. Type **394**	20	10
843	20c. Carrying the Olympic flag	45	60
844	25c. Athletes with medals . .	45	85

395 Archer

1976. Disabled Olympics.

845	**395**	20c. multicoloured	20	30

396 "Sam McGee" (Robert W. Service)

397 "Nativity" (F. Mayer)

1976. Canadian Writers (2nd series). Mult.

846	8c. Type **396**	15	40
847	8c. "Le Survenant" (Germaine Guevremont)	15	40

1976. Christmas. Stained-glass Windows. Mult.

848	8c. Type **397**	10	10
849	10c. "Nativity" (G. Maile & Son)	10	10
850	20c. "Nativity" (Yvonne Williams)	20	60

398 "Northcote" (paddle-steamer)

1976. Canadian Ships (2nd series). Inland Vessels.

851	**398**	10c. lt brown, brn & blk	45	60
852	–	10c. blue and black . . .	45	60
853	–	10c. blue and black . . .	45	60
854	–	10c. lt green, green & blk	45	60

DESIGNS: No. 852, "Passport" (paddle-steamer); 853, "Chicora" (paddle-steamer); 854, "Athabasca" (steamer).

399 Queen Elizabeth II

1977. Silver Jubilee.

855	**399**	25c. multicoloured	30	50

400 Bottle Gentian

401 Queen Elizabeth II (bas-relief by J. Huta)

402 Houses of Parliament

403 Trembling Aspen

404 Prairie Town Main Street

405 Fundy National Park

1977.

856	**400**	1c. multicoloured . . .	10	20
870	**402**	1c. blue	1·25	2·75
857	–	2c. multicoloured . . .	10	10
858	–	3c. multicoloured . . .	10	10
859	–	4c. multicoloured . . .	10	10
860	–	5c. multicoloured . . .	10	10
871	**402**	5c. lilac	65	1·00
861	–	10c. multicoloured . . .	15	10
867	**401**	12c. blue, grey and black	15	10
872	**402**	12c. blue	70	30
866	–	12c. multicoloured . . .	15	60
868	**401**	14c. red, grey and black	20	10
873	**402**	14c. red	15	10
875	**403**	15c. multicoloured . . .	15	10
866a	–	15c. multicoloured . . .	15	15
869	**401**	17c. black, grey and green	50	10
874	**402**	17c. green	30	10
876	–	20c. multicoloured . . .	15	10
877	–	25c. multicoloured . . .	15	10
878	–	30c. multicoloured . . .	20	10
869b	**401**	30c. dp pur, grey & pur	70	1·00
869c		32c. black, grey and blue	50	85
879	–	35c. multicoloured . . .	25	10
883	**404**	50c. multicoloured . . .	85	1·00
883a	–	60c. multicoloured . . .	65	80
881	–	75c. multicoloured . . .	85	1·50
882	–	80c. multicoloured . . .	85	1·25
884	**405**	$1 multicoloured . . .	70	50
884b	–	$1 multicoloured	85	45
884c	–	$1.50 multicoloured . .	1·75	2·75
885	–	$2 multicoloured	1·00	45
885c	–	$2 multicoloured	3·75	1·50
885d	–	$5 multicoloured	3·00	2·50
885e	–	$5 multicoloured	7·00	4·00

DESIGN—As Type **400**: 2c. Red columbine; 3c. Canada lily; 4c. Hepatica; 5c. Shooting star; 10c. Franklin's lady's slipper orchid. 12c. Jewel-weed; 15c. (No. 866a) Canada violet. As Type **403**: 20c. Douglas fir; 25c. Sugar maple; 30c. Red oak; 35c. White pine. As Type **404**: 60c. Ontario City street; 75c. Eastern City street; 80c. Maritimes street. As Type **405**: $1 Glacier; $1.50, Waterton Lakes; $2 (No. 885) Kluane; $2 (No. 885c) Banff; $5 (No. 885d) Point Pelee; $5 (No. 885e) La Maurice.

406 Puma

407 "April in Algonquin Park"

1977. Endangered Wildlife (1st series).

886	**406**	12c. multicoloured	20	20

See also Nos. 906, 936/7, 976/7 and 1006/7.

1977. Birth Centenary of Tom Thomson (painter). Multicoloured.

887	12c. Type **407**	15	20
888	12c. "Autumn Birches" . . .	15	20

408 Crown and Lion

1977. Anniversaries. Multicoloured.

889	12c. Type **408**	15	25
890	12c. Order of Canada	15	25

EVENTS: No. 889, 25th anniv of First Canadian-born Governor-General; No. 890, 10th anniv of Order of Canada.

409 Peace Bridge, Niagara River

1977. 50th Anniv of Opening of Peace Bridge.

891	**409**	12c. multicoloured	15	15

410 Sir Sandford Fleming (engineer)

1977. Famous Canadians.

892	**410**	12c. blue	30	30
893	–	12c. brown	30	30

DESIGN: No. 893, Joseph E. Bernier (explorer) and "Arctic" (survey ship).

411 Peace Tower, Parliament Buildings, Ottawa

1977. 23rd Commonwealth Parliamentary Conference.

894	**411**	25c. multicoloured	20	30

412 Hunter Braves following Star

1977. Christmas. Canada's first carol "Jesous Ahatonhia". Multicoloured.

895	10c. Type **412**	10	10
896	12c. Angelic choir	10	10
897	25c. Christ Child and "Chiefs from afar"	20	45

413 Seal Hunter (soapstone sculpture)

1977. Canadian Eskimos ("Inuits") (1st series). Hunting. Multicoloured.

898	12c. Type **413**	35	35
899	12c. Fishing with spear . . .	35	35
900	12c. Disguised archer	35	35
901	12c. Walrus hunting	35	35

See also Nos. 924/7, 958/61 and 989/92.

414 Pinky (fishing boat)

1977. Canadian Ships (3rd series). Sailing Craft. Multicoloured.

902	12c. Type **414**	20	35
903	12c. "Malahat" (schooner)	20	35
904	12c. Tern schooner	20	35
905	12c. Mackinaw boat	20	35

415 Peregrine Falcon

1978. Endangered Wildlife (2nd series).
906 **415** 12c. multicoloured 30 20

416 Pair of 1851 12d. Black Stamps

1978. "CAPEX '78" International Philatelic Exhibition, Toronto.
907 **416** 12c. black and sepia . . . 10 10
914 – 14c. blue, lt grey & grey 15 10
915 – 30c. red, lt grey and grey 25 40
916 – $1.25 violet, lt grey & grey . . . . 70 1·50
MS917 101 × 96 mm. Nos. 914/16 1·00 2·50
DESIGNS: 14c. Pair of 1855 10d. Cartier stamps; 30c. Pair of 1857 ½d. red stamps; $1.25, Pair of 1851 6d. Prince Albert stamps.

417 Games Emblem

1978. 11th Commonwealth Games, Edmonton (1st issue). Multicoloured.
908 14c. Type **417** 10 10
909 30c. Badminton 20 60
See also Nos. 918/21.

418 "Captain Cook" (Nathaniel Dance)

419 Hardrock Silver Mine, Cobalt, Ontario

1978. Bicentenary of Cook's 3rd Voyage. Mult.
910 14c. Type **418** 20 20
911 14c. "Nootka Sound" (J. Webber) 20 20

1978. Resources Development. Multicoloured.
912 14c. Type **419** 15 20
913 14c. Giant excavators, Athabasca Tar Sands . . . 15 20

1978. 11th Commonwealth Games, Edmonton (2nd issue). As T **417**. Multicoloured.
918 14c. Games stadium 20 20
919 14c. Running 20 20
920 30c. Alberta legislature building 50 50
921 30c. Bowls 50 50

420 Princes' Gate (Exhibition entrance)

421 Marguerite d'Youville

1978. Centenary of National Exhibition.
922 **420** 14c. multicoloured 15 30

1978. Marguerite d'Youville (founder of Grey Nuns) Commemoration.
923 **421** 14c. multicoloured 15 30

1978. Canadian Eskimos ("Inuits") (2nd series). Travel. As T **413**. Multicoloured.
924 14c. Woman on foot (painting by Pitseolak) . . 30 40
925 14c. "Migration" (soapstone sculpture of sailing umiak by Joe Talurinili) 30 40
926 14c. Aeroplane (stonecut and stencil print by Pudlo) . . 30 40
927 14c. Dogteam and dogsled (ivory sculpture by Abraham Kingmeatook) 30 40

422 "Madonna of the Flowering Pea" (Cologne School)

423 "Chief Justice Robinson" (paddle-steamer)

1978. Christmas. Paintings. Multicoloured.
928 12c. Type **422** 10 10
929 14c. "The Virgin and Child with St. Anthony and Donor" (detail, Hans Memling) 10 10
930 30c. "The Virgin and Child" (Jacopo di Cione) 25 90

1978. Canadian Ships (4th series). Ice Vessels. Multicoloured.
931 14c. Type **423** 45 65
932 14c. "St. Roch" (steamer) . . 45 65
933 14c. "Northern Light" (steamer) 45 65
934 14c. "Labrador" (steamer) . . 45 65

424 Carnival Revellers

425 Eastern Spiny Soft-shelled Turtle

1978. Quebec Carnival.
935 **424** 14c. multicoloured 20 20

1979. Endangered Wildlife (3rd series). Multicoloured.
936 17c. Type **425** 20 10
937 35c. Bowhead whale 90 90

426 Knotted Ribbon round Woman's Finger

427 Scene from "Fruits of the Earth" by Frederick Philip Grove

1979. Postal Code Publicity. Multicoloured.
938 17c. Type **426** 20 15
939 17c. Knotted string around man's finger 20 15

1979. Canadian Writers (3rd series). Multicoloured.
940 17c. Type **427** 15 15
941 17c. Scene from "Le Vaisseau d'Or" by Emile Nelligan 15 15

428 Charles-Michel de Salaberry (military hero)

429 Ontario

1979. Famous Canadians. Multicoloured.
942 17c. Type **428** 25 15
943 17c. John By (engineer) . . . 25 15

1979. Canada Day. Flags. Multicoloured.
944a 17c. Type **429** 25 40
944b 17c. Quebec 25 40
944c 17c. Nova Scotia 25 40
944d 17c. New Brunswick 25 40
944e 17c. Manitoba 25 40
944f 17c. British Columbia . . . 25 40
944g 17c. Prince Edward Island 25 40
944h 17c. Saskatchewan 25 40
944i 17c. Alberta 25 40
944j 17c. Newfoundland 25 40
944k 17c. Northwest Territories 25 40
944l 17c. Yukon Territory . . . 25 40

430 Paddling Kayak

1979. Canoe-Kayak Championships.
956 **430** 17c. multicoloured 15 30

431 Hockey Players

1979. Women's Field Hockey Championships, Vancouver.
957 **431** 17c. black, yellow and green 15 30

1979. Canadian Eskimos (3rd series). Shelter and the Community. As T **413**. Multicoloured.
958 17c. "Summer Tent" (print by Kiakshuk) 15 40
959 17c. "Five Eskimos building an Igloo" (soapstone sculpture by Abraham) . . 15 40
960 17c. "The Dance" (print by Kalvak) 15 40
961 17c. "Inuit drum dance" (soapstone sculptures by Madeleine Isserkut and Jean Mapsalak) 15 40

432 Toy Train

1979. Christmas. Multicoloured.
962 15c. Type **432** 10 10
963 17c. Hobby-horse 10 10
964 35c. Rag doll (vert) . . . . 25 1·00

433 Child watering Tree of Life (painting by Marie-Annick Viatour)

1979. International Year of the Child.
965 **433** 17c. multicoloured 15 30

434 Canadair CL-215

1979. Canadian Aircraft (1st series). Flying Boats. Multicoloured.
966 17c. Type **434** 25 20
967 17c. Curtiss HS-2L 25 20
968 35c. Vickers Vedette 65 65
969 35c. Consolidated Canso . . . 65 65
See also Nos. 996/9, 1026/9 and 1050/3.

435 Map of Arctic Islands

1980. Centenary of Arctic Islands Acquisition.
970 **435** 17c. multicoloured 15 30

436 Skier

1980. Winter Olympic Games, Lake Placid.
971 **436** 35c. multicoloured 55 85

437 "A Meeting of the School Trustees" (Robert Harris)

1980. Centenary of Royal Canadian Academy of Arts. Multicoloured.
972 17c. Type **437** 25 20
973 17c. "Inspiration" (Philippe Hebert) 25 20
974 35c. "Sunrise on the Saguenay" (Lucius O'Brien) 50 55
975 35c. Thomas Fuller's design sketch for the original Parliament Buildings . . . 50 55

438 Canadian Whitefish

439 Garden Flowers

1980. Endangered Wildlife (4th series). Multicoloured.
976 17c. Type **438** 30 15
977 17c. Prairie chicken 30 15

1980. International Flower Show, Montreal.
978 **439** 17c. multicoloured 15 20

440 "Helping Hand"

441 Opening Bars of "O Canada"

1980. Rehabilitation.
979 **440** 17c. gold and blue 15 20

1980. Centenary of "O Canada" (national song). Multicoloured.
980 17c. Type **441** 15 15
981 17c. Calixa Lavallee (composer), Adolphe-Basile Routhier (original writer) and Robert Stanley Weir (writer of English version) 15 15

442 John G. Diefenbaker (statesman)

443 Emma Albani (singer)

1980. John G. Diefenbaker Commemoration.
982 **442** 17c. blue 15 20

1980. Famous Canadians. Multicoloured.
983 17c. Type **443** 15 25
984 17c. Healey Willan (composer) 15 25
985 17c. Ned Hanlan (oarsman) (horiz) 15 15

444 Alberta

1980. 75th Anniv of Alberta and Saskatchewan Provinces. Multicoloured.
986 17c. Type **444** 15 15
987 17c. Saskatchewan 15 15

445 Uraninite Molecular Structure

446 "Christmas Morning" (J. S. Hallam)

1980. Uranium Resources.

988	**445**	35c. multicoloured	30	30

1980. Canadian Eskimos ("Inuits") (4th series). Spirits. As T **413**. Multicoloured.

989	17c. "Return of the Sun" (print, Kenojouak)	20	15
990	17c. "Sedna" (sculpture, Ashoona Kiawak)	20	15
991	35c. "Shaman" (print, Simon Tookoome)	35	55
992	35c. "Bird Spirit" (sculpture, Doris Hagiolok)	35	55

1980. Christmas. Multicoloured.

993	15c. Type **446**	10	10
994	17c. "Sleigh Ride" (Frank Hennessy)	15	10
995	35c. "McGill Cab Stand" (Kathleen Morris)	30	1·40

447 Avro (Canada) CF-100 Canuck Mk 5

1980. Canadian Aircraft (2nd series). Multicoloured.

996	17c. Type **447**	40	20
997	17c. Avro Type 683 Lancaster	40	20
998	35c. Curtiss JN-4 Canuck biplane	60	65
999	35c. Hawker Hurricane Mk I	60	65

448 Emmanuel-Persillier Lachapelle

449 Mandora (18th century)

1980. Dr. E.-P. Lachapelle (founder, Notre-Dame Hospital, Montreal) Commemoration.

1000	**448**	17c. brown, deep brown and blue	15	15

1981. "The Look of Music" Exhibition, Vancouver.

1001	**449**	17c. multicoloured	15	15

450 Henrietta Edwards

1981. Feminists. Multicoloured.

1002	17c. Type **450**	30	30
1003	17c. Louise McKinney	30	30
1004	17c. Idola Saint-Jean	30	30
1005	17c. Emily Stowe	30	30

451 Vancouver Marmot

1981. Endangered Wildlife (5th series). Multicoloured.

1006	17c. Type **451**	15	10
1007	35c. American bison	35	30

452 Kateri Tekakwitha

453 "Self Portrait" (Frederick H. Varley)

1981. 17th-century Canadian Women. Statues by Emile Brunet.

1008	**452**	17c. brown and green	15	20
1009	–	17c. deep blue and blue	15	20

DESIGN: No. 1009, Marie de l'Incarnation.

1981. Canadian Paintings. Multicoloured.

1010	17c. Type **453**	20	10
1011	17c. "At Baie Saint-Paul" (Marc-Aurele Fortin) (horiz)	20	10
1012	35c. "Untitled No 6" (Paul-Emile Borduas)	40	45

454 Canada in 1867

1981. Canada Day. Maps showing evolution of Canada from Confederation to present day. Multicoloured.

1013	17c. Type **454**	15	20
1014	17c. Canada in 1873	15	20
1015	17c. Canada in 1905	15	20
1016	17c. Canada since 1949	15	20

455 Frere Marie-Victorin

456 The Montreal Rose

1981. Canadian Botanists. Multicoloured.

1017	17c. Type **455**	20	30
1018	17c. John Macoun	20	30

1981. Montreal Flower Show.

1019	**456**	17c. multicoloured	15	20

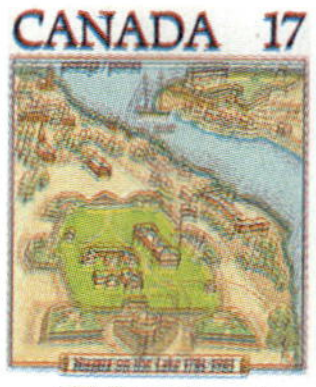

457 Drawing of Niagara-on-the-Lake

458 Acadian Community

1981. Bicentenary of Niagara-on-the-Lake (town).

1020	**457**	17c. multicoloured	15	20

1981. Centenary of First Acadia (community) Convention.

1021	**458**	17c. multicoloured	15	20

459 Aaron R. Mosher

460 Christmas Tree, 1781

1981. Birth Centenary of Aaron R. Mosher (founder of Canadian Labour Congress).

1022	**459**	17c. multicoloured	15	20

1981. Christmas. Bicentenary of First Illuminated Christmas Tree in Canada.

1023	15c. Type **460**	20	15
1024	15c. Christmas Tree, 1881	20	15
1025	15c. Christmas Tree, 1981	20	15

461 De Havilland Tiger Moth

462 Canadian Maple Leaf Emblem

1981. Canadian Aircraft (3rd series). Multicoloured.

1026	17c. Type **461**	20	15
1027	17c. Canadair CL-41 Tutor jet trainer	20	15
1028	35c. Avro (Canada) CF-102 jet airliner	35	40
1029	35c. De Havilland D.H.C.7 Dash 7	35	40

1981.

1030a	**462**	A (30c.) red	20	40

No. 1030a was printed before a new first class domestic letter rate had been agreed, "A" representing the face value of the stamp, later decided to be 30c.

1982. As T **462** but including face values.

1033	**462**	5c. purple	10	20
1033d		8c. blue	1·75	2·50
1034		10c. green	1·50	2·25
1036		30c. red	35	30
1032		30c. red, grey and blue	30	50
1036b		32c. red	1·50	2·50
1032b		32c. red, brown and stone	45	45

463 1851 3d. Stamp

1982. "Canada 82" International Philatelic Youth Exhibition, Toronto. Stamps on Stamps. Mult.

1037	30c. Type **463**	30	30
1038	30c. 1908 Centenary of Quebec 15c. commemorative	30	30
1039	35c. 1935 10c. R.C.M.P	30	50
1040	35c. 1928 10c.	30	50
1041	60c. 1929 50c.	60	1·00
MS1042	159 × 108 mm. Nos. 1037/41	2·25	3·75

464 Jules Leger

465 Stylized drawing of Terry Fox

1982. Jules Leger (politician) Commemoration.

1043	**464**	30c. multicoloured	20	20

1982. Cancer victim Terry Fox's "Marathon of Hope" (Trans-Canada fund-raising run) Commemoration.

1044	**465**	30c. multicoloured	20	20

466 Stylized Open Book

1982. Patriation of Constitution.

1045	**466**	30c. multicoloured	20	20

467 Male and Female Salvationists with Street Scene

1982. Centenary of Salvation Army in Canada.

1046	**467**	30c. multicoloured	20	20

468 "The Highway near Kluane Lake" (Yukon Territory) (Jackson)

1982. Canada Day. Paintings of Canadian Landscapes. Multicoloured.

1047a	30c. Type **468**	35	40
1047b	30c. "Street Scene, Montreal" (Quebec) (Hebert)	35	40
1047c	30c. "Breakwater" (Newfoundland) (Pratt)	35	40
1047d	30c. "Along Great Slave Lake" (Northwest Territories) (Richard)	35	40
1047e	30c. "Till Hill" (Prince Edward Island) (Lamb)	35	40
1047f	30c. "Family and Rainstorm" (Nova Scotia) (Colville)	35	40
1047g	30c. "Brown Shadows" (Saskatchewan) (Knowles)	35	40
1047h	30c. "The Red Brick House" (Ontario) (Milne)	35	40
1047i	30c. "Campus Gates" (New Brunswick) (Bobak)	35	40
1047j	30c. "Prairie Town—Early Morning" (Alberta) (Kerr)	35	40
1047k	30c. "Totems at Ninstints" (British Columbia) (Plaskett)	35	40
1047l	30c. "Doc Snider's House" (Manitoba) (Fitzgerald)	35	40

469 Regina Legislative Building

1982. Centenary of Regina.

1048	**469**	30c. multicoloured	20	20

470 Finish of Race

1982. Centenary of Royal Canadian Henley Regatta.

1049	**470**	30c. multicoloured	20	25

471 Fairchild FC-2W1

1982. Canadian Aircraft (4th series). Bush Aircraft. Multicoloured.

1050	30c. Type **471**	35	20
1051	30c. De Havilland D.H.C.2 Beaver	35	20
1052	60c. Fokker Super Universal	65	85
1053	60c. Noorduyn Norseman	65	85

472 Decoy

475 Mary, Joseph and Baby Jesus

1982. Heritage Artefacts.

1054	**472**	1c. black, lt brn and brn	10	10
1055	–	2c. black, blue and green	10	10
1056	–	3c. black and deep blue	10	10
1057	–	5c. black, pink and brown	10	10
1058	–	10c. black, blue & turq	10	10
1059	–	20c. black, lt brn & brn	20	10
1060	–	25c. multicoloured	60	10
1061	–	37c. black, grn & dp grn	60	50
1062	–	39c. black, grey and violet	1·75	1·75
1063	–	42c. multicoloured	1·75	30
1064	–	48c. dp brn, brn & pink	50	40
1065	–	50c. black, lt blue & blue	1·75	20
1066	–	55c. multicoloured	1·50	30
1067	–	64c. dp grey, blk & grey	60	35
1068	–	68c. black, lt brn & brn	1·75	50
1069	–	72c. multicoloured	1·50	35

DESIGNS—VERT: 2c. Fishing spear; 3c. Stable lantern; 5c. Bucket; 10c. Weathercock; 20c. Skates; 25c. Butter stamp. HORIZ: 37c. Plough; 39c. Settle-bed; 42c. Linen chest; 48c. Cradle; 50c. Sleigh; 55c. Iron kettle; 64c. Kitchen stove; 68c. Spinning wheel; 72c. Hand-drawn cart.

1982. Christmas. Nativity Scenes.
1080 30c. Type **475** 20 10
1081 35c. The Shepherds 25 60
1082 60c. The Three Wise Men 45 1·50

476 Globes forming Symbolic Designs

478 Scene from Novel "Angeline de Montbrun" by "Laure Conan" (Felicite Angers)

477 Map of World showing Canada

1983. World Communications Year.
1083 **476** 32c. multicoloured . . . 30 30

1983. Commonwealth Day.
1084 **477** $2 multicoloured . . . . 2·00 3·25

1983. Canadian Writers (4th series).
1085 32c. Type **478** 40 90
1086 32c. Woodcut illustrating "Sea-gulls" (poem by E. J. Pratt) 40 90

479 St. John Ambulance Badge and "100"

480 Victory Pictogram

1983. Centenary of St. John Ambulance in Canada.
1087 **479** 32c. red, yellow and brown 30 30

1983. "Universiade 83" World University Games, Edmonton.
1088 **480** 32c. multicoloured . . . 25 15
1089 64c. multicoloured . . . 50 70

481 Fort William, Ontario

1983. Canada Day. Forts (1st series). Multicoloured.
1090 32c. Fort Henry, Ontario (44 × 22 mm) 65 80
1091 32c. Type **481** 65 80
1092 32c. Fort Rodd Hill, British Columbia 65 80
1093 32c. Fort Wellington, Ontario (28 × 22 mm) . . 65 80
1094 32c. Fort Prince of Wales, Manitoba (28 × 22 mm) 65 80
1095 32c. Halifax Citadel, Nova Scotia (44 × 22 mm) . . . 65 80
1096 32c. Fort Chambly, Quebec 65 80
1097 32c. Fort No. 1, Point Levis, Quebec 65 80
1098 32c. Coteau-du-Lac Fort, Quebec (28 × 22 mm) . . 65 80
1099 32c. Fort Beausejour, New Brunswick (28 × 22 mm) 65 80
See also Nos. 1163/72.

482 Scouting Poster by Marc Fournier (aged 21)

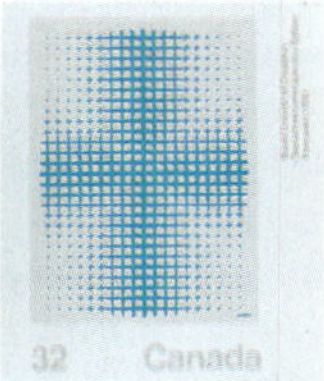

483 Cross Symbol

1983. Scouting in Canada (75th Anniv) and 15th World Scout Jamboree, Alberta.
1100 **482** 32c. multicoloured . . . 30 30

1983. 6th Assembly of the World Council of Churches, Vancouver.
1101 **483** 32c. green and lilac . . . 30 20

484 Sir Humphrey Gilbert (founder)

485 "NICKEL" Deposits

1983. 400th Anniv of Newfoundland.
1102 **484** 32c. multicoloured . . . 30 30

1983. Cent of Discovery of Sudbury Nickel Deposits.
1103 **485** 32c. multicoloured . . . 30 30

486 Josiah Henson and Escaping Slaves

1983. 19th-century Social Reformers. Multicoloured.
1104 32c. Type **486** 35 50
1105 32c. Father Antoine Labelle and rural village (32 × 26 mm) 35 50

487 Robert Stephenson's Locomotive "Dorchester", 1836

1983. Railway Locomotives (1st series). Mult.
1106 32c. Type **487** . . . . . . 90 1·00
1107 32c. Locomotive "Toronto", 1853 . . . . 90 1·00
1108 37c. Timothy Hackworth's locomotive "Samson", 1838 . . . . 90 1·00
1109 64c. Western Canadian Railway locomotive "Adam Brown", 1855 . . 1·40 2·25
See also Nos. 1132/5, 1185/8 and 1223/6.

488 School Coat of Arms

1983. Centenary of Dalhousie Law School.
1110 **488** 32c. multicoloured . . . 30 40

489 City Church

1983. Christmas. Churches. Multicoloured.
1111 32c. Type **489** 30 10
1112 37c. Family walking to church 40 90
1113 64c. Country chapel . . . . 1·00 2·00

490 Royal Canadian Regiment and British Columbia Regiment

491 Gold Mine in Prospecting Pan

1983. Canadian Army Regiments. Multicoloured.
1114 32c. Type **490** . . . . . . 75 1·25
1115 32c. Royal Winnipeg Rifles and Royal Canadian Dragoons . . . . 75 1·25

1984. 50th Anniv of Yellowknife.
1116 **491** 32c. multicoloured . . . 30 30

492 Montreal Symphony Orchestra

1983. 50th Anniv of Montreal Symphony Orchestra.
1117 **492** 32c. multicoloured . . . 35 30

493 Jacques Cartier

494 U.S.C.S. "Eagle"

1984. 450th Anniv of Jacques Cartier's Voyage to Canada.
1118 **493** 32c. multicoloured . . . 40 30

1984. Tall Ships Visit.
1119 **494** 32c. multicoloured . . . 35 30

495 Service Medal

496 Oared Galleys

1984. 75th Anniv of Canadian Red Cross Society.
1120 **495** 32c. multicoloured . . . 35 40

1984. Bicentenary of New Brunswick.
1121 **496** 32c. multicoloured . . . 35 30

497 St. Lawrence Seaway

1984. 25th Anniv of St. Lawrence Seaway.
1122 **497** 32c. multicoloured . . . 45 30

498 New Brunswick

1984. Canada Day. Paintings by Jean Paul Lemieux. Multicoloured.
1123a 32c. Type **498** 50 60
1123b 32c. British Columbia . . . 50 60
1123c 32c. Northwest Territories 50 60
1123d 32c. Quebec 50 60
1123e 32c. Manitoba 50 60
1123f 32c. Alberta 50 60
1123g 32c. Prince Edward Island 50 60
1123h 32c. Saskatchewan 50 60
1123i 32c. Nova Scotia (vert) . . 50 60
1123j 32c. Yukon Territory . . . 50 60
1123k 32c. Newfoundland 50 60
1123l 32c. Ontario (vert) 50 60
The captions on the Northwest Territories and Yukon Territory paintings were transposed at the design stage.

499 Loyalists of 1784

1984. Bicentenary of Arrival of United Empire Loyalists.
1124 **499** 32c. multicoloured . . . 30 30

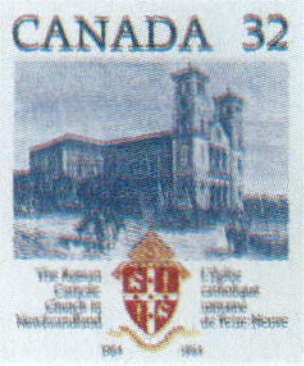

500 St. John's Basilica

501 Coat of Arms of Pope John Paul II

1984. Bicentenary of Roman Catholic Church in Newfoundland.
1125 **500** 32c. multicoloured . . . 30 25

1984. Papal Visit.
1126 **501** 32c. multicoloured . . . 40 20
1127 64c. multicoloured . . . 85 1·10

502 Louisbourg Lighthouse, 1734

1984. Canadian Lighthouse (1st series). Mult.
1128 32c. Type **502** . . . . . . 1·75 1·75
1129 32c. Fisgard Lighthouse, 1860 . . . . 1·75 1·75
1130 32c. Ile Verte Lighthouse, 1809 . . . . 1·75 1·75
1131 32c. Gibraltar Point Lighthouse, 1808 . . . . 1·75 1·75
See also Nos. 1176/9.

503 Great Western Railway Locomotive "Scotia", 1860

1984. Railway Locomotives (2nd series). Mult.
1132 32c. Type **503** . . . . . . 1·40 1·40
1133 32c. Northern Pacific Railroad locomotive "Countess of Dufferin", 1872 . . . . 1·40 1·40
1134 37c. Grand Trunk Railway Class E3 locomotive, 1886 1·40 1·60
1135 64c. Canadian Pacific Class D10a steam locomotive 2·00 2·75
MS1136 153 × 104 mm. As Nos. 1132/5, but with background colour changed from green to blue 5·50 7·00
No. **MS**1136 commemorates "CANADA '84" National Stamp Exhibition, Montreal.
See also Nos. 1185/8 and 1223/6.

504 "The Annunciation" (Jean Dallaire)

505 Pilots of 1914–18, 1939–45 and 1984

1984. Christmas. Religious Paintings. Multicoloured.
1137 32c. Type **504** 40 10
1138 37c. "The Three Kings" (Simone Bouchard) . . . 70 1·00
1139 64c. "Snow in Bethlehem" (David Milne) . . . . . 90 1·75

1984. 60th Anniv of Royal Canadian Air Force.
1140 **505** 32c. multicoloured . . . 35 30

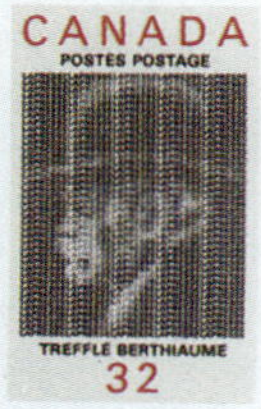

506 Treffle Berthiaume (editor)

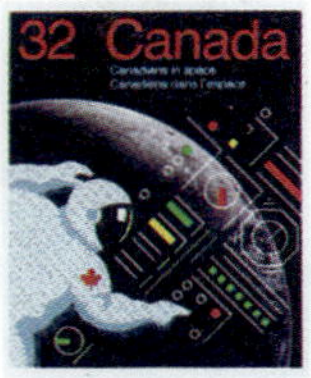

508 Astronaut in Space, and Planet Earth

507 Heart and Arrow

1984. Centenary of "La Presse" (newspaper).
1141 **506** 32c. brown, red & lt brn . . . 35 30

1985. International Youth Year.
1142 **507** 32c. multicoloured . . . 30 30

1985. Canadian Space Programme.
1143 **508** 32c. multicoloured . . . 40 30

509 Emily Murphy

1985. Women's Rights Activists. Multicoloured.
1144 32c. Type **509** 40 90
1145 32c. Therese Casgrain . . . 40 90

510 Gabriel Dumont (Metis leader) and Battle of Batoche, 1885

1985. Centenary of the North-West Rebellion.
1146 **510** 32c. blue, red and grey . . . 30 30

511 Rear View, Parliament Building, Ottawa

512 Queen Elizabeth II

512a Queen Elizabeth II in 1984 (from photo by Karsh)

1985.

1147b	–	1c. green	70	80
1148	–	2c. green	20	1·25
1149	–	5c. brown	55	1·40
1150a	–	6c. brown	50	30
1150b	–	6c. purple	2·00	1·00
1151	**511**	34c. black	1·75	2·25
1155		34c. multicoloured . .	60	10
1158		34c. brown	2·25	3·00
1161	**512**	34c. black and blue . .	1·40	30
1152	**511**	36c. purple	3·75	4·00
1156a		36c. multicoloured . .	30	45
1159		36c. red	1·50	55
1162	**512**	36c. purple	2·75	1·10
1153	**511**	37c. blue	1·25	30
1157	–	37c. multicoloured . .	85	10
1162a	**512a**	37c. multicoloured . .	3·00	10
1154	**511**	38c. blue	2·25	1·25
1157c	–	38c. multicoloured . .	50	10
1160b	**511**	38c. green	50	30
1162b	**512a**	38c. multicoloured . .	1·00	20
1162c		39c. multicoloured . .	1·00	20
1162d		40c. multicoloured . .	1·00	20
1162e		42c. multicoloured . .	1·00	40
1162f		43c. multicoloured . .	1·25	65
1162g		45c. multicoloured . .	1·50	80
1162h		46c. multicoloured . .	1·00	45
1162i		47c. multicoloured . .	1·00	45

DESIGNS: 1, 5, 6c. (1150b) East Block, Parliament Building; 2, 6c. (1150a) West Block, Parliament Building; 37c. (1157) Front view, Parliament Building; 38c. (1157c) Side view, Parliament Building.

1985. Canada Day. Forts (2nd series). As T **481**. Multicoloured.
1163 34c. Lower Fort Garry, Manitoba 50 60
1164 34c. Fort Anne, Nova Scotia 50 60
1165 34c. Fort York, Ontario . . 50 60
1166 34c. Castle Hill, Newfoundland 50 60
1167 34c. Fort Whoop Up, Alberta 50 60
1168 34c. Fort Erie, Ontario . . 50 60
1169 34c. Fort Walsh, Saskatchewan 50 60
1170 34c. Fort Lennox, Quebec 50 60
1171 34c. York Redoubt, Nova Scotia 50 60
1172 34c. Fort Frederick, Ontario 50 60
Nos. 1163 and 1168 measure 44 × 22 mm and Nos. 1166/7 and 1171/2 28 × 22 mm.

513 Louis Hebert (apothecary)

514 Parliament Buildings and Map of World

1985. 45th International Pharmaceutical Sciences Congress of Pharmaceutical Federation, Montreal.
1173 **513** 34c. multicoloured . . . 45 35

1985. 74th Conference of Inter-Parliamentary Union, Ottawa.
1174 **514** 34c. multicoloured . . . 45 35

515 Guide and Brownie Saluting

516 Sisters Islets Lighthouse

1985. 75th Anniv of Girl Guide Movement.
1175 **515** 34c. multicoloured . . . 45 35

1985. Canadian Lighthouses (2nd series). Multicoloured.
1176 34c. Type **516** . . . . . . 2·00 2·00
1177 34c. Pelee Passage Lighthouse . . . . 2·00 2·00
1178 34c. Haut-fond Prince Lighthouse . . . . 2·00 2·00
1179 34c. Rose Blanche Lighthouse, Cains Island 2·00 2·00
MS1180 190 × 90 mm. Nos. 1176/9 7·50 8·00
No. **MS**1180 publicises "Capex 87" International Stamp Exhibition, Toronto.

517 Santa Claus in Reindeer-drawn Sleigh

518 Naval Personnel of 1910, 1939–45 and 1985

1985. Christmas. Santa Claus Parade. Multicoloured.
1181 32c. Canada Post's parade float . . . . 80 1·10
1182 34c. Type **517** 70 20
1183 39c. Acrobats and horse-drawn carriage . . . . . 80 1·25
1184 68c. Christmas tree, pudding and goose on float . . . 1·75 2·25

1985. Steam Railway Locomotives (3rd series). As T **503**. Multicoloured.
1185 34c. Grand Trunk Railway Class K2 . . . . 1·00 1·40
1186 34c. Canadian Pacific Class P2a . . . . 1·00 1·40
1187 39c. Canadian Northern Class O10a . . . . . . 1·25 1·50
1188 68c. Canadian Govt Railway Class H4D . . . 2·00 2·50

1985. 75th Anniv of Royal Canadian Navy.
1189 **518** 34c. multicoloured . . . 65 65

519 "The Old Holton House, Montreal" (James Wilson Morrice)

1985. 125th Anniv of Montreal Museum of Fine Arts.
1190 **519** 34c. multicoloured . . . 40 50

520 Map of Alberta showing Olympic Sites

1986. Winter Olympic Games, Calgary (1988) (1st issue).
1191 **520** 34c. multicoloured . . . 40 50
See also Nos. 1216/17, 1236/7, 1258/9 and 1281/4.

521 Canada Pavilion

1986. "Expo '86" World Fair, Vancouver (1st issue). Multicoloured.
1192 34p. Type **521** . . . . . . 1·25 50
1193 39p. Early telephone, dish aerial and satellite . . . . 2·00 2·75
See also Nos. 1196/7.

522 Molly Brant

523 Aubert de Gaspe and Scene from "Les Anciens Canadiens"

1986. 250th Birth Anniv of Molly Brant (Iroquois leader).
1194 **522** 34c. multicoloured . . . 40 50

1986. Birth Bicentenary of Philippe Aubert de Gaspe (author).
1195 **523** 34c. multicoloured . . . 40 50

1986. "Expo '86" World Fair, Vancouver (2nd issue). As T **521**. Multicoloured.
1196 34c. Expo Centre, Vancouver (vert) 70 50
1197 68c. Early and modern trains . . . . 1·40 2·75

524 Canadian Field Post Office and Cancellation, 1944

1986. 75th Anniv of Canadian Forces Postal Service.
1198 **524** 34c. multicoloured . . . 85 60

525 Great Blue Heron

526 Railway Rotary Snowplough

1986. Birds of Canada. Multicoloured.
1199 34c. Type **525** . . . . . . 1·50 1·75
1200 34c. Snow goose . . . . . 1·50 1·75
1201 34c. Great horned owl . . . 1·50 1·75
1202 34c. Spruce grouse . . . . 1·50 1·75

1986. Canada Day. Science and Technology. Canadian Inventions (1st series). Multicoloured.
1203 34c. Type **526** . . . . . . 1·10 1·75
1204 34c. Space shuttle "Challenger" launching satellite with Canadarm 1·10 1·75
1205 34c. Pilot wearing anti-gravity flight suit and Supermarine Spitfire . . . 1·10 1·75
1206 34c. Variable-pitch propeller and Avro 504 airplane . . 1·10 1·75
See also Nos. 1241/4 and 1292/5.

527 C.B.C. Logos over Map of Canada

1986. 50th Anniv of Canadian Broadcasting Corporation.
1207 **527** 34c. multicoloured . . . 40 50

528 Ice Age Artefacts, Tools and Settlement

1986. Exploration of Canada (1st series). Discoverers. Multicoloured.
1208 34c. Type **528** . . . . . . 1·25 1·75
1209 34c. Viking ships . . . . . 1·25 1·75
1210 34c. John Cabot's "Matthew", 1497, compass and Arctic char (fish) . . . . 1·25 1·75
1211 34c. Henry Hudson cast adrift, 1611 . . . . 1·25 1·75
MS1212 119 × 84 mm. Nos. 1208/11 5·50 6·50
No. **MS**1212 publicises "Capex '87" International Stamp Exhibition, Toronto.
See also Nos. 1232/5, 1285/8 and 1319/22.

529 Crowfoot (Blackfoot Chief) and Indian Village

1986. Founders of the Canadian West. Multicoloured.
1213 34c. Type **529** . . . . . . 1·00 1·00
1214 34c. James Macleod of the North West Mounted Police and Fort Macleod 1·00 1·00

530 Peace Dove and Globe

1986. International Peace Year.
1215 **530** 34c. multicoloured . . . 60 60

531 Ice Hockey

532 Angel with Crown

1986. Winter Olympic Games, Calgary (1988) (2nd issue). Multicoloured.
1216 34c. Type **531** . . . . . . 1·75 1·75
1217 34c. Biathlon . . . . 1·75 1·75

1986. Christmas. Multicoloured.
1218 29c. Angel singing carol (36 × 22 mm) 65 35
1219 34c. Type **532** 60 25
1220 39c. Angel playing lute . . . 1·00 1·60
1221 68c. Angel with ribbon . . . 1·50 2·75

533 John Molson with Theatre Royal, Montreal, "Accomodation" (paddle-steamer) and Railway Train

1986. 150th Death Anniv of John Molson (businessman).
1222 **533** 34c. multicoloured . . . 1·00 50

1986. Railway Locomotives (4th series). As T **503** but size 60 × 22 mm. Multicoloured.
1223 34c. Canadian National Class V-1-a diesel locomotive No. 9000 . . 1·75 1·75
1224 34c. Canadian Pacific Class T1a steam locomotive No. 9000 . . . . 1·75 1·75
1225 39c. Canadian National Class U-2-a steam locomotive . . . . 1·75 1·00
1226 68c. Canadian Pacific Class H1c steam locomotive No. 2850 . . . . 2·50 3·25

534 Toronto's First Post Office

1987. "Capex '87" International Stamp Exhibition, Toronto. Post Offices.
1227 34c. Type **534** 60 20
1228 36c. Nelson-Miramichi, New Brunswick 65 45
1229 42c. Saint-Ours, Quebec . . 70 65
1230 72c. Battleford, Saskatchewan . . . . . . 1·00 1·25
MS1231 155 × 92 mm. 36c. As No. 1227 and Nos. 1228/30, but main inscr in green . . . . . 3·25 2·75

535 Etienne Brule exploring Lake Superior

1987. Exploration of Canada (2nd series). Pioneers of New France. Multicoloured.
1232 34c. Type **535** . . . . . . 1·25 1·40
1233 34c. Radisson and Des Groseilliers with British and French flags . . . . 1·25 1·40
1234 34c. Jolliet and Father Marquette on the Mississippi . . . . 1·25 1·40
1235 34c. Jesuit missionary preaching to Indians . . . 1·25 1·40

1987. Winter Olympic Games, Calgary (1988) (3rd issue). As T **531**. Multicoloured.
1236 36c. Speed skating 50 40
1237 42c. Bobsleighing 75 60

536 Volunteer Activities

1987. National Volunteer Week.
1238 **536** 36c. multicoloured . . . 30 35

537 Canadian Coat of Arms

539 R. A. Fessenden (AM Radio)

538 Steel Girder, Gear Wheel and Microchip

1987. 5th Anniv of Canadian Charter of Rights and Freedoms.
1239 **537** 36c. multicoloured . . . 75 35

1987. Centenary of Engineering Institute of Canada.
1240 **538** 36c. multicoloured . . . 65 40

1987. Canada Day. Science and Technology. Canadian Inventors (2nd series). Multicoloured.
1241 36c. Type **539** . . . . . . 1·25 1·50
1242 36c. C. Fenerty (newsprint pulp) . . . . 1·25 1·50
1243 36c. G.-E. Desbarats and W. Leggo (half-tone engraving) . . . . . . 1·25 1·50
1244 36c. F. N. Gisborne (first North American undersea telegraph) . . . . . . 1·25 1·50

540 "Segwun"

1987. Canadian Steamships. Multicoloured.
1245 36c. Type **540** . . . . . . 1·75 2·50
1246 36c. "Princess Marguerite" (52 × 22 mm) . . . . . . 1·75 2·50

541 Figurehead from "Hamilton", 1813

1987. Historic Shipwrecks. Multicoloured.
1247 36c. Type **541** . . . . . . 1·25 1·50
1248 36c. Hull of "San Juan", 1565 . . . . 1·25 1·50
1249 36c. Wheel from "Breadalbane", 1853 . . . 1·25 1·50
1250 36c. Bell from "Ericsson", 1892 . . . . 1·25 1·50

542 Air Canada Boeing 767-200 and Globe

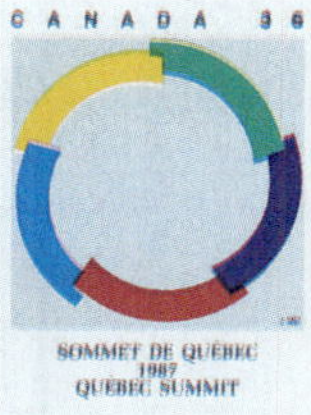

543 Summit Symbol

1987. 50th Anniv of Air Canada.
1251 **542** 36c. multicoloured . . . 1·00 35

1987. 2nd Int Francophone Summit, Quebec.
1252 **543** 36c. multicoloured . . . 30 35

544 Commonwealth Symbol

545 Poinsettia

1987. Commonwealth Heads of Government Meeting, Vancouver.
1253 **544** 36c. multicoloured . . . 35 40

1987. Christmas. Christmas Plants. Multicoloured.
1254 31c. Decorated Christmas tree and presents (36 × 20 mm) 70 35
1255 36c. Type **545** 40 40
1256 42c. Holly wreath . . . . . 1·00 50
1257 72c. Mistletoe and decorated tree . . . . 1·25 80

1987. Winter Olympic Games, Calgary (1988) (4th issue). As T **531**. Multicoloured.
1258 36c. Cross-country skiing . . 90 75
1259 36c. Ski-jumping 90 75

546 Football, Grey Cup and Spectators

547 Flying Squirrel

548a Runnymede Library, Toronto

1987. 75th Grey Cup Final (Canadian football championship), Vancouver.
1260 **546** 36c. multicoloured . . . 35 40

1988. Canadian Mammals and Architecture. Multicoloured. (a) As T **547**.
1261 1c. Type **547** 10 10
1262 2c. Porcupine 10 10
1263 3c. Muskrat 10 10
1264 5c. Varying hare 10 10
1265 6c. Red fox 10 10
1266 10c. Striped skunk 10 10
1267 25c. American beaver . . . 30 15
1268 43c. Lynx (26 × 20 mm) . . . 1·40 1·00
1269 44c. Walrus (27 × 21 mm) . . 1·40 20
1270 45c. Pronghorn (27 × 21 mm) 50 40
1270c 46c. Wolverine (27 × 21 mm) . . . . . 1·50 1·00
1271 57c. Killer whale (26 × 20 mm) . . . . . 2·00 55
1272 59c. Musk ox (27 × 21 mm) 3·00 2·00
1273 61c. Wolf (27 × 21 mm) . . 70 1·00
1273b 63c. Harbour porpoise (27 × 21 mm) . . . . . 2·00 2·50
1274 74c. Wapiti (26 × 20 mm) . 1·60 50
1275 76c. Brown bear (27 × 21 mm) . . . . . 2·00 50
1276 78c. White whale (27 × 21 mm) . . . . . 1·00 55
1276c 80c. Peary caribou (27 × 21 mm) . . . . . 1·00 60

(b) As T **548a**.
1277 $1 Type **548a** . . . . 1·50 30
1278 $2 McAdam Railway Station, New Brunswick 2·25 50
1279 $5 Bonsecours Market, Montreal . . . . 4·75 4·00

1988. Winter Olympic Games, Calgary (5th issue). As T **531**. Multicoloured.
1281 37c. Slalom skiing 85 50
1282 37c. Curling 85 50
1283 43c. Figure skating 85 45
1284 74c. Luge . . . . 1·40 80

549 Trade Goods, Blackfoot Encampment and Page from Anthony Henday's Journal

1988. Exploration of Canada (3rd series). Explorers of the West. Multicoloured.
1285 37c. Type **549** . . . . . . 1·00 70
1286 37c. Discovery and map of George Vancouver's voyage . . . . 1·00 70
1287 37c. Simon Fraser's expedition portaging canoes . . . . 1·00 70
1288 37c. John Palliser's surveying equipment and view of prairie . . . . . 1·00 70

550 "The Young Reader" (Ozias Leduc)

1988. Canadian Art (1st series).
1289 **550** 50c. multicoloured . . . 70 70
See also Nos. 1327, 1384, 1421, 1504, 1539, 1589, 1629, 1681, 1721, 1825, 1912, 2011, 2097 and 2133.

551 Mallard landing on Marsh

552 Kerosene Lamp and Diagram of Distillation Plant

1988. Wildlife and Habitat Conservation. Mult.
1290 37c. Type **551** . . . . . . 1·00 50
1291 37c. Moose feeding in marsh 1·00 50

1988. Canada Day. Science and Technology. Canadian Inventions (3rd series). Multicoloured.
1292 37c. Type **552** . . . . . . 1·00 1·00
1293 37c. Ears of Marquis wheat 1·00 1·00
1294 37c. Electron microscope and magnified image . . . 1·00 1·00
1295 37c. Patient under "Cobalt 60" cancer therapy . . . 1·00 1·00

553 "Papilio brevicauda"

1988. Canadian Butterflies. Multicoloured.
1296 37c. Type **553** . . . . . 80 1·00
1297 37c. "Lycaeides idas" . . . 80 1·00
1298 37c. "Oeneis macounii" . . 80 1·00
1299 37c. "Papilio glaucus" . . . 80 1·00

554 St. John's Harbour Entrance and Skyline

1988. Centenary of Incorporation of St. John's, Newfoundland.
1300 **554** 37c. multicoloured . . . 35 40

555 Club Members working on Forestry Project and Rural Scene

1988. 75th Anniv of 4-H Clubs.
1301 **555** 37c. multicoloured . . . 35 40

556 Saint-Maurice Ironworks

557 Tahltan Bear Dog

1988. 250th Anniv of Saint-Maurice Ironworks, Quebec.
1302 **556** 37c. black, orange & brn 40 40

1988. Canadian Dogs. Multicoloured.
1303 37c. Type **557** . . . . . . 1·00 1·25
1304 37c. Nova Scotia duck tolling retriever . . . . . 1·00 1·25
1305 37c. Canadian eskimo dog 1·00 1·25
1306 37c. Newfoundland . . . . 1·00 1·25

558 Baseball, Glove and Pitch

559 Virgin with Inset of Holy Child

1988. 150th Anniv of Baseball in Canada. Multicoloured.
1307 **558** 37c. multicoloured . . . 35 40

1988. Christmas. Icons. Multicoloured.
1308 32c. Holy Family (36 × 21 mm) 45 35
1309 37c. Type **559** 45 40
1310 43c. Virgin and Child . . . 50 45
1311 74c. Virgin and Child (different) 90 75

On No. 1308 the left-hand third of the design area is taken up by the bar code.

No. 1309 also commemorates the millennium of Ukrainian Christianity.

560 Bishop Inglis and Nova Scotia Church

1988. Bicentenary of Consecration of Charles Inglis (first Canadian Anglican bishop) (1987).
1312 **560** 37c. multicoloured . . . 35 40

561 Frances Ann Hopkins and "Canoe manned by Voyageurs"

1988. 150th Birth Anniv of Frances Anne Hopkins (artist).
1313 **561** 37c. multicoloured . . . 35 40

562 Angus Walters and "Bluenose" (yacht)

563 Chipewyan Canoe

1988. 20th Death Anniv of Angus Walters (yachtsman).
1314 **562** 37c. multicoloured . . . 40 40

1989. Small Craft of Canada (1st series). Native Canoes. Multicoloured.
1315 38c. Type **563** 85 70
1316 38c. Haida canoe 85 70
1317 38c. Inuit kayak 85 70
1318 38c. Micmac canoe 85 70

See also Nos. 1377/80 and 1428/31.

564 Matonabbee and Hearne's Expedition

1989. Exploration of Canada (4th issue). Explorers of the North. Multicoloured.
1319 38c. Type **564** . . . . . . 1·25 75
1320 38c. Relics of Franklin's expedition and White Ensign . . . . 1·25 75
1321 38c. Joseph Tyrell's compass, hammer and fossil . . . . 1·25 75
1322 38c. Vilhjalmur Stefansson, camera on tripod and sledge dog team . . . . 1·25 75

565 Construction of Victoria Bridge, Montreal and William Notman

1989. Canada Day. "150 Years of Canadian Photography". Designs showing early photographs and photographers. Multicoloured.
1323 38c. Type **565** 85 85
1324 38c. Plains Indian village and W. Hanson Boorne 85 85
1325 38c. Horse-drawn sleigh and Alexander Henderson . . 85 85
1326 38c. Quebec street scene and Jules-Ernest Livernois . . 85 85

566 Tsimshian Ceremonial Frontlet, c. 1900

1989. Canadian Art (2nd series).
1327 **566** 50c. multicoloured . . . 80 60

567 Canadian Flag and Forest

1989. Self-adhesive. Multicoloured.
1328 38c. Type **567** . . . . . . 1·50 2·25
1328b 39c. Canadian flag and prairie . . . . 1·50 2·25
1328c 40c. Canadian flag and sea 1·25 1·25
1328d 42c. Canadian flag over mountains . . . . 2·00 2·50
1328e 43c. Canadian flag over lake . . . . 1·40 2·00

568 Archibald Lampman

569 "Clavulinopsis fusiformis"

1989. Canadian Poets. Multicoloured.
1329 38c. Type **568** . . . . . . 1·10 1·40
1330 38c. Louis-Honore Frechette 1·10 1·40

1989. Mushrooms. Multicoloured.
1331 38c. Type **569** . . . . . . 70 1·00
1332 38c. "Boletus mirabilis" . . 70 1·00
1333 38c. "Cantharellus cinnabarinus" . . . . . 70 1·00
1334 38c. "Morchella esculenta" 70 1·00

570 Night Patrol, Korea

1989. 75th Anniv of Canadian Regiments. Mult.
1335 38c. Type **570** (Princess Patricia's Canadian Light Infantry) . . . . 1·50 1·50
1336 38c. Trench raid, France, 1914–18 (Royal 22e Regiment) . . . . 1·50 1·50

571 Globe in Box

572 Film Director

1989. Canada Export Trade Month.
1337 **571** 38c. multicoloured . . . 40 45

1989. Arts and Entertainment.
1338 **572** 38c. brown, dp brn & vio . . . . 1·00 1·25
1339 – 38c. brown, dp brn & grn . . . . 1·00 1·25
1340 – 38c. brown, dp brn & mve . . . . 1·00 1·25
1341 – 38c. brown, dp brn & bl 1·00 1·25

DESIGNS: No. 1339, Actors; No. 1340, Dancers; No. 1341, Musicians.

573 "Snow II" (Lawren S. Harris)

1989. Christmas. Paintings of Winter Landscapes. Multicoloured.
1342 33c. "Champ-de-Mars, Winter" (William Brymner) (35 × 21 mm) 1·00 55
1343 38c. "Bend in the Gosselin River" (Marc-Aurele Suzor-Cote) (21 × 35 mm) 40 35
1344 44c. Type **573** 65 50
1345 76c. "Ste. Agnes" (A. H. Robinson) . . . . 1·40 85

On No. 1342 the left-hand third of the design area is taken up by a bar code.

574 Canadians listening to Declaration of War, 1939

1989. 50th Anniv of Outbreak of Second World War (1st issue).
1346 **574** 38c. black, silver & pur 1·10 1·25
1347 – 38c. black, silver and grey . . . . 1·10 1·25
1348 – 38c. black, silver and green . . . . 1·10 1·25
1349 – 38c. black, silver and blue . . . . 1·10 1·25

DESIGNS: No. 1347, Army mobilization; No. 1348, British Commonwealth air crew training; No. 1349, North Atlantic convoy.

See also Nos. 1409/12, 1456/9, 1521/4, 1576/9, 1621/4, and 1625/8.

575 Canadian Flag

576

1989.
1350 **575** 1c. multicoloured . . . 20 1·00
1351 – 5c. multicoloured . . . 40 30
1352 – 39c. multicoloured . . 2·25 2·25
1354 **576** 39c. multicoloured . . 70 10
1360 – 39c. purple 60 75
1353 – 40c. multicoloured . . 2·00 2·50
1355 – 40c. multicoloured . . 80 10
1361 – 40c. blue 40 50
1356 – 42c. multicoloured . . 90 15
1362 – 42c. red 40 50
1357 – 43c. multicoloured . . 1·00 1·00
1363 – 43c. green . . . . . . 1·50 2·00
1358d – 45c. multicoloured . . 60 65
1364 – 45c. green 65 65
1359 – 46c. multicoloured . . 70 45
1365 – 46c. red 50 50
1367 – 47c. multicoloured . . 70 75
1368 – 48c. multicoloured . . 70 45
1369 49c. multicoloured . . 75 60
1370 – 50c. multicoloured . . 65 70
1371 – 50c. multicoloured . . 65 70
1372 – 50c. multicoloured . . 65 70
1373 – 50c. multicoloured . . 65 70
1374 – 50c. multicoloured . . 65 70
1374a – 51c. multicoloured . . 65 70
1374b – 51c. multicoloured . . 65 70
1374c – 51c. multicoloured . . 65 70
1374d – 51c. multicoloured . . 65 70
1374e – 51c. multicoloured . . 65 70

DESIGNS: Nos. 1351/3, 1360/5, As T **575** but different folds in flag. As T **576**: No. 1355, Flag over forest; 1356, Flag over mountains; 1357, Flag over prairie; 1358d, Flag and skyscraper; 1359, Flag and iceberg; 1367, Flag and inukshuk (Inuit cairn); 1368, Flag in front of Canada Post Headquarters, Ottawa, Flag and Edmonton; 1370, Broadway Bridge, Saskatoon; 1371, Durrell, South Twillingate Island; 1372, Shannon Falls, Squamish; 1373, Church of Saint-Hilaire, Quebec; 1374, Cruise boat and skyline, Toronto; 1374a, Winter scene near New Glasgow, Prince Edward Island; 1374b, Bridge, Bouctouche, New Brunswick; 1374c, Wind turbines, Pincher Creek, Alberta; 1374d, Southwest bastion, Lower Fort Garry National Historic Site, Manitoba; 1374e, Dogsled, St. Elias Mountains, Yukon.

No. 1359 comes with ordinary or self-adhesive gum and 1367/9 and 1370/4e are self-adhesive.

577 Norman Bethune in 1937 and performing Operation, Montreal

1990. Birth Centenary of Dr. Norman Bethune (surgeon). Multicoloured.
1375 39c. Type **577** . . . . . . 1·75 1·75
1376 39c. Bethune in 1939, and treating wounded Chinese soldiers . . . . 1·75 1·75

1990. Small Craft of Canada (2nd series). Early Work Boats. As T **563**. Multicoloured.
1377 39c. Fishing dory . . . . . 1·10 1·40
1378 39c. Logging pointer . . . . 1·10 1·40
1379 39c. York boat . . . . . . 1·10 1·40
1380 39c. North canoe . . . . . 1·10 1·40

578 Maple Leaf Mosaic

1990. Multiculturalism.
1381 **578** 39c. multicoloured . . . 35 40

579 Mail Van (facing left)

580 Amerindian and Inuit Dolls

1990. "Moving the Mail". Multicoloured.
1382 39c. Type **579** 75 75
1383 39c. Mail van (facing right) 75 75

1990. Canadian Art (3rd series). As T **550**. Multicoloured.
1384 50c. "The West Wind" (Tom Thomson) 55 65

1990. Dolls. Multicoloured.
1385 39c. Type **580** . . . . . . 1·25 1·40
1386 39c. 19th-century settlers' dolls . . . . 1·25 1·40
1387 39c. Commercial dolls, 1917–36 . . . . 1·25 1·40
1388 39c. Commercial dolls, 1940–60 . . . . 1·25 1·40

581 Canadian Flag and Fireworks

582 "Stromatolites" (fossil algae)

1990. Canada Day.
1389 **581** 39c. multicoloured . . . 50 50

1990. Prehistoric Canada (1st series). Primitive Life. Multicoloured.
1390 39c. Type **582** . . . . . . 1·25 1·40
1391 39c. "Opabinia regalis" (soft invertebrate) . . . . . 1·25 1·40
1392 39c. "Paradoxides davidis" (trilobite) . . . . . . 1·25 1·40
1393 39c. "Eurypterus remipes" (sea scorpion) . . . . . . 1·25 1·40

See also Nos. 1417/20, 1568/71 and 1613/16.

583 Acadian Forest

1990. Canadian Forests. Multicoloured.
1394 39c. Type **583** 80 70
1395 39c. Great Lakes–St. Lawrence forest . . . 80 70
1396 39c. Pacific Coast forest . . 80 70
1397 39c. Boreal forest 80 70

584 Clouds and Rainbow

1990. 150th Anniv of Weather Observing in Canada.
1398 **584** 39c. multicoloured . . . 60 50

585 "Alphabet" Bird

1990. International Literacy Year.
1399 **585** 39c. multicoloured . . . 40 50

586 Sasquatch

1990. Legendary Creatures. Multicoloured.
1400 39c. Type **586** . . . . . . 1·25 1·50
1401 39c. Kraken . . . . . . 1·25 1·50
1402 39c. Werewolf . . . . . . 1·25 1·50
1403 39c. Ogopogo . . . . . . 1·25 1·50

587 Agnes Macphail

588 "Virgin Mary with Christ Child and St. John the Baptist" (Norval Morrisseau)

1990. Birth Centenary of Agnes Macphail (first woman elected to Parliament).
1404 **587** 39c. multicoloured . . . 40 50

1990. Christmas. Native Art.
1405 – 34c. multicoloured . . . 50 35
1406 **588** 39c. multicoloured . . . 40 40
1407 – 45c. multicoloured . . . 40 45
1408 – 78c. black, red and grey 70 75
DESIGNS—35 × 21 mm: 34c. "Rebirth" (Jackson Beardy). As T **588**: 45c. "Mother and Child" (Inuit sculpture, Cape Dorset); 78c. "Children of the Raven" (Bill Reid).
No. 1405 includes a bar code in the design.

1990. 50th Anniv of Second World War (2nd issue). As T **574**.
1409 39c. black, silver and green 2·00 2·00
1410 39c. black, silver and brown 2·00 2·00
1411 39c. black, silver and brown 2·00 2·00
1412 39c. black, silver and mauve 2·00 2·00
DESIGNS: No. 1409, Canadian family at home, 1940; 1410, Packing parcels for the troops; 1411, Harvesting; 1412, Testing anti-gravity flying suit.

589 Jennie Trout (first woman physician) and Women's Medical College, Kingston

590 Blue Poppies and Butchart Gardens, Victoria

1991. Medical Pioneers. Multicoloured.
1413 40c. Type **589** . . . . . . 1·10 90
1414 40c. Wilder Penfield (neurosurgeon) and Montreal Neurological Institute . . . . 1·10 90
1415 40c. Frederick Banting (discoverer of insulin) and University of Toronto medical faculty . . . . . 1·10 90
1416 40c. Harold Griffith (anesthesiologist) and Queen Elizabeth Hospital, Montreal . . . . 1·10 90

1991. Prehistoric Canada (2nd series). Primitive Vertebrates. As T **582**. Multicoloured.
1417 40c. Foord's crossopt ("Eusthenopteron foordi") (fish fossil) . . . . 2·00 1·75
1418 40c. "Hylonomus lyelli" (land reptile) . . . . . 2·00 1·75
1419 40c. Fossil conodonts (fossil teeth) . . . . 2·00 1·75
1420 40c. "Archaeopteris halliana" (early tree) . . . 2·00 1·75

1991. Canadian Art (4th series). As T **550**. Multicoloured.
1421 50c. "Forest, British Columbia" (Emily Carr) 1·25 1·50

1991. Public Gardens. Multicoloured.
1422 40c. Type **590** 70 70
1423 40c. Marigolds and International Peace Garden, Boissevain . . . 70 70
1424 40c. Lilac and Royal Botanical Gardens, Hamilton 70 70
1425 40c. Roses and Montreal Botanical Gardens . . . 70 70
1426 40c. Rhododendrons and Halifax Public Gardens 70 70

591 Maple Leaf

592 South Nahanni River

1991. Canada Day.
1427 **591** 40c. multicoloured . . . 50 60

1991. Small Craft of Canada (3rd series). As T **563**. Multicoloured.
1428 40c. Verchere rowboat . . . 1·40 1·40
1429 40c. Touring kayak . . . . 1·40 1·40
1430 40c. Sailing dinghy . . . . 1·40 1·40
1431 40c. Cedar strip canoe . . . 1·40 1·40

1991. Canadian Rivers (1st series). Multicoloured.
1432 40c. Type **592** . . . . . . 1·00 1·40
1433 40c. Athabasca River . . . 1·00 1·40
1434 40c. Boundary Waters, Voyageur Waterway . . . 1·00 1·40
1435 40c. Jacques-Cartier River 1·00 1·40
1436 40c. Main River . . . . . 1·00 1·40
See also Nos. 1492/6, 1558/62 and 1584/8.

593 "Leaving Europe"

594 Ski Patrol rescuing Climber

1991. Centenary of Ukrainian Immigration. Panels from "The Ukrainian Pioneer" by William Kurelek. Multicoloured.
1437 40c. Type **593** 80 85
1438 40c. "Canadian Winter" . . 80 85
1439 40c. "Clearing the Land" . . 80 85
1440 40c. "Harvest" 80 85

1991. Emergency Services. Multicoloured.
1441 40c. Type **594** . . . . . . 2·00 1·75
1442 40c. Police at road traffic accident . . . . 2·00 1·75
1443 40c. Firemen on extending ladder . . . . 2·00 1·75
1444 40c. Boeing-Vertol Chinook rescue helicopter and "Spindrift" (lifeboat) . . 2·00 1·75

595 "The Witched Canoe"

596 Grant Hall Tower

1991. Canadian Folktales. Multicoloured.
1445 40c. Type **595** . . . . . . 1·25 95
1446 40c. "The Orphan Boy" . . 1·25 95
1447 40c. "Chinook" . . . . . 1·25 95
1448 40c. "Buried Treasure" . . 1·25 95

1991. 150th Anniv of Queen's University, Kingston.
1449 **596** 40c. multicoloured . . . 1·10 1·00

597 North American Santa Claus

598 Players jumping for Ball

1991. Christmas. Multicoloured.
1450 35c. British Father Christmas (35 × 21 mm) 1·00 55
1451 40c. Type **597** . . . . . . 1·00 20
1452 46c. French Bonhomme Noel . . . . 1·25 1·50
1453 80c. Dutch Sinterklaas . . . 2·00 3·25

1991. Basketball Centenary. Multicoloured.
1454 40c. Type **598** . . . . . . 1·50 75
MS1455 155 × 90 mm. 40c. Type **598**, but with shorter inscr below face value; 46c. Player taking shot; 80c. Player challenging opponent . . . . 6·50 6·00

1991. 50th Anniv of Second World War (3rd issue). As T **574**.
1456 40c. black, silver and blue 1·75 1·25
1457 40c. black, silver and brown 1·75 1·25
1458 40c. black, silver and lilac 1·75 1·25
1459 40c. black, silver and brown 1·75 1·25
DESIGNS: No. 1456, Women's services, 1941; 1457, Armament factory; 1458, Cadets and veterans, 1459, Defence of Hong Kong.

599 Blueberry

600 McIntosh Apple

600a Court House, Yorktown

1991. Multicoloured. (a) Edible Berries. As T **599**.
1460 1c. Type **599** 10 10
1461 2c. Wild strawberry 10 10
1462 3c. Black crowberry 50 10
1463 5c. Rose hip 10 10
1464 6c. Black raspberry 10 10
1465 10c. Kinnikinnick 10 10
1466 25c. Saskatoon berry 25 25

(b) Fruit and Nut Trees. As T **600**.
1467 48c. Type **600** 50 35
1468 49c. Delicious apple . . . . 2·50 1·00
1469 50c. Snow apple . . . . . 1·50 1·00
1470 52c. Gravenstein apple . . . 1·10 50
1471 65c. Black walnut . . . . . 1·25 50
1472 67c. Beaked hazelnut . . . . 1·00 1·25
1473 69c. Shagbark hickory . . . 2·50 1·25
1474 71c. American chestnut . . 2·25 1·00
1475 84c. Stanley plum . . . . . 1·00 75
1476 86c. Bartlett pear . . . . . 1·50 1·00
1477 88c. Westcot apricot . . . . 1·75 1·60
1478 90c. Elberta peach . . . . . 1·00 1·00

(c) Architecture. As T **600a**.
1479a $1 Type **600a** . . . . . . 2·25 80
1480a $2 Provincial Normal School, Truro . . . . . 3·00 1·60
1481 $5 Public Library, Victoria 5·50 4·75

601 Ski Jumping

1992. Winter Olympic Games, Albertville. Mult.
1482 42c. Type **601** . . . . . . 1·25 1·25
1483 42c. Figure skating . . . . 1·25 1·25
1484 42c. Ice hockey . . . . . . 1·25 1·25
1485 42c. Bobsleighing . . . . . 1·25 1·25
1486 42c. Alpine skiing . . . . . 1·25 1·25

602 Ville-Marie in 17th Century

1992. "CANADA 92" International Youth Stamp Exhibition, Montreal. Multicoloured.
1487 42c. Type **602** . . . . . . 1·00 1·25
1488 42c. Modern Montreal . . . 1·00 1·25
1489 48c. Compass rose, snow shoe and crow's nest of Cartier's ship "Grande Hermine" . . . . 1·75 1·00
1490 84c. Atlantic map, Aztec "calendar stone" and navigational instrument 2·50 2·50
MS1491 181 × 120 mm. Nos. 1487/90 7·00 7·00

1992. Canadian Rivers (2nd series). As T **592** but horiz. Multicoloured.
1492 42c. Margaree River . . . . 1·25 1·25
1493 42c. West (Eliot) River . . . 1·25 1·25
1494 42c. Ottawa River . . . . . 1·25 1·25
1495 42c. Niagara River . . . . 1·25 1·25
1496 42c. South Saskatchewan River . . . . 1·25 1·25

603 Road Bed Construction and Route Map

605 Jerry Potts (scout)

604 "Quebec, Patrimoine Mondial" (A. Dumas)

1992. 50th Anniv of Alaska Highway.
1497 **603** 42c. multicoloured . . . 1·10 70

1992. Olympic Games, Barcelona. As T **601**. Multicoloured.
1498 42c. Gymnastics . . . . . 1·10 1·25
1499 42c. Athletics . . . . 1·10 1·25
1500 42c. Diving . . . . 1·10 1·25
1501 42c. Cycling . . . . 1·10 1·25
1502 42c. Swimming . . . . . . 1·10 1·25

1992. Canada Day. Paintings. Multicoloured.
1503a 42c. Type **604** . . . . . . 1·30 1·40
1503b 42c. "Christie Passage, Hurst Island, British Columbia" (E. J. Hughes) . . . . 1·30 1·40
1503c 42c. "Toronto, Landmarks of Time" (Ontario) (V. McIndoe) . . . . . 1·30 1·40
1503d 42c. "Near the Forks" (Manitoba) (S. Gouthro) 1·30 1·40
1503e 42c. "Off Cape St. Francis" (Newfoundland) (R. Shepherd) . . . . . 1·30 1·40
1503f 42c. "Crowd at City Hall" (New Brunswick) (Molly Bobak) . . . . 1·30 1·40
1503g 42c. "Across the Tracks to Shop" (Alberta) (Janet Mitchell) . . . . 1·30 1·40
1503h 42c. "Cove Scene" (Nova Scotia) (J. Norris) . . . 1·30 1·40
1503i 42c. "Untitled" (Saskatchewan) (D. Thauberger) . . . . 1·30 1·40

1503j 42c. "Town Life" (Yukon) (T. Harrison) . . . . . 1·30 1·40
1503k 42c. "Country Scene" (Prince Edward Island) (Erica Rutherford) . . . 1·30 1·40
1503l 42c. "Playing on an Igloo" (Northwest Territories) (Agnes Nanogak) . . . 1·30 1·40

1992. Canadian Art (5th series). As T **550**. Multicoloured.
1504 50c. "Red Nasturtiums" (David Milne) . . . . . 1·25 1·40

1992. Folk Heroes. Multicoloured.
1505 42c. Type **605** . . . . . . 1·25 1·40
1506 42c. Capt. William Jackman and wreck of "Sea Clipper", 1867 . . . . . 1·25 1·40
1507 42c. Laura Secord (messenger) . . . . 1·25 1·40
1508 42c. Jos Montferrand (lumberjack) . . . . . . 1·25 1·40

606 Copper

1992. 150th Anniv of Geological Survey of Canada. Minerals. Multicoloured.
1509 42c. Type **606** . . . . . . 1·50 1·60
1510 42c. Sodalite . . . . 1·50 1·60
1511 42c. Gold . . . . 1·50 1·60
1512 42c. Galena . . . . 1·50 1·60
1513 42c. Grossular . . . . . . 1·50 1·60

607 Satellite and Photographs from Space

1992. Canadian Space Programme. Multicoloured.
1514 42c. Type **607** . . . . . . 1·25 1·75
1515 42c. Space shuttle over Canada (hologram) (32 × 26 mm) . . . . . . 1·25 1·75

608 Babe Siebert, Skates and Stick

609 Companion of the Order of Canada Insignia

1992. 75th Anniv of National Ice Hockey League. Multicoloured.
1516 42c. Type **608** . . . . . . 1·60 1·60
1517 42c. Claude Provost, Terry Sawchuck and team badges . . . . 1·60 1·60
1518 42c. Hockey mask, gloves and modern player . . . 1·60 1·60

1992. 25th Anniv of the Order of Canada and Daniel Roland Michener (former Governor-General) Commemoration. Multicoloured.
1519 42c. Type **609** . . . . . . 1·40 1·60
1520 42c. Daniel Roland Michener . . . . 1·40 1·60

1992. 50th Anniv of Second World War (4th issue). As T **574**.
1521 42c. black, silver & brown 1·60 1·90
1522 42c. black, silver & green . . 1·60 1·90
1523 42c. black, silver & brown 1·60 1·90
1524 42c. black, silver and blue 1·60 1·90
DESIGNS: No. 1521, Reporters and soldier, 1942; 1522, Consolidated Liberator bombers over Newfoundland; 1523 Dieppe raid; 1524, U-boat sinking merchant ship.

610 Estonian Jouluvana

611 Adelaide Hoodless (women's movement pioneer)

1992. Christmas. Multicoloured.
1525 37c. North American Santa Claus (35 × 21 mm) . . . 90 80
1526 42c. Type **610** 40 20
1527 48c. Italian La Befana . . . 1·75 2·00
1528 84c. German Weihnachtsmann . . . . 2·25 3·00

1993. Prominent Canadian Women. Multicoloured.
1529 43c. Type **611** . . . . . . 1·10 1·40
1530 43c. Marie-Josephine Gerin-Lajoie (social reformer) 1·10 1·40
1531 43c. Pitseolak Ashoona (Inuit artist) . . . . . . 1·10 1·40
1532 43c. Helen Kinnear (lawyer) 1·10 1·40

612 Ice Hockey Players with Cup

613 Coverlet, New Brunswick

1993. Centenary of Stanley Cup.
1533 **612** 43c. multicoloured . . . 75 60

1993. Hand-crafted Textiles. Multicoloured.
1534 43c. Type **613** . . . . . . 1·10 1·40
1535 43c. Pieced quilt, Ontario 1·10 1·40
1536 43c. Doukhobor bedcover, Saskatchewan . . . . . . 1·10 1·40
1537 43c. Ceremonial robe, Kwakwaka'wakw . . . . 1·10 1·40
1538 43c. Boutonne coverlet, Quebec . . . . 1·10 1·40

1993. Canadian Art (6th series). As T **550**. Multicoloured.
1539 86c. "The Owl" (Kenojuak Ashevak) . . . . 2·25 2·75

614 Empress Hotel, Victoria

1993. Historic Hotels. Multicoloured.
1540 43c. Type **614** . . . . . . 70 1·10
1541 43c. Banff Springs Hotel . . 70 1·10
1542 43c. Royal York Hotel, Toronto . . . . . . 70 1·10
1543 43c. Le Chateau Frontenac, Quebec . . . . 70 1·10
1544 43c. Algonquin Hotel, St. Andrews . . . . . . 70 1·10

615 Algonquin Park, Ontario

616 Toronto Skyscrapers

1993. Canada Day. Provincial and Territorial Parks. Multicoloured.
1545 43c. Type **615** 70 80
1546 43c. De La Gaspesie Park, Quebec 70 80
1547 43c. Cedar Dunes Park, Prince Edward Island . . 70 80
1548 43c. Cape St. Mary's Seabird Reserve, Newfoundland 70 80
1549 43c. Mount Robson Park, British Columbia 70 80
1550 43c. Writing-on-Stone Park, Alberta 70 80
1551 43c. Spruce Woods Park, Manitoba 70 80
1552 43c. Herschel Island Park, Yukon 70 80
1553 43c. Cypress Hills Park, Saskatchewan 70 80
1554 43c. The Rocks Park, New Brunswick 70 80
1555 43c. Blomidon Park, Nova Scotia 70 80
1556 43c. Katannilik Park, Northwest Territories . . 70 80

1993. Bicentenary of Toronto.
1557 **616** 43c. multicoloured . . . 1·00 70

1993. Canadian Rivers (3rd series). As T **592**. Multicoloured.
1558 43c. Fraser River . . . . . 1·00 1·10
1559 43c. Yukon River . . . . . 1·00 1·10
1560 43c. Red River . . . . . . 1·00 1·10
1561 43c. St. Lawrence River . . 1·00 1·10
1562 43c. St. John River . . . . 1·00 1·10

617 Taylor's Steam Buggy, 1867

1993. Historic Automobiles (1st issue). Sheet 177 × 125 mm, containing T **617** and similar horiz designs. Multicoloured.
MS1563 43c. Type **617**; 43c. Russel Model L touring car, 1908; 49c. Ford Model T touring car, 1914 (43 × 22 mm); 49c. Studebaker Champion Deluxe Starlight coupe, 1950 (43 × 22 mm); 86c. McLaughlin-Buick 28–496 special, 1928 (43 × 22 mm); 86c. Gray-Dort 25 SM luxury sedan, 1923 (43 × 22 mm) . . . . 7·50 8·00
See also Nos. **MS**1611, **MS**1636 and **MS**1683/4.

618 "The Alberta Homesteader"

1993. Folk Songs. Multicoloured.
1564 43c. Type **618** . . . . . . 70 1·00
1565 43c. "Les Raftmans" (Quebec) . . . . 70 1·00
1566 43c. "I'se the B'y that Builds the Boat" (Newfoundland) . . . . . 70 1·00
1567 43c. "Onkwa:ri Tenhanonniahkwe" (Mohawk Indian) . . . . 70 1·00

1993. Prehistoric Canada (3rd series). Dinosaurs. As T **582** but 40 × 28 mm. Multicoloured.
1568 43c. Massospondylus . . . 80 80
1569 43c. Stryacosaurus 80 80
1570 43c. Albertosaurus 80 80
1571 43c. Platecarpus 80 80

619 Polish Swiety Mikolaj

1993. Christmas. Multicoloured.
1572 38c. North American Santa Claus (35 × 22 mm) . . . 90 90
1573 43c. Type **619** 55 20
1574 49c. Russian Ded Moroz . . 1·10 1·40
1575 86c. Australian Father Christmas . . . . 1·90 2·75

1993. 50th Anniv of Second World War (5th issue). As T **574**.
1576 43c. black, silver and green 1·50 1·75
1577 43c. black, silver and blue 1·50 1·75
1578 43c. black, silver and blue 1·50 1·75
1579 43c. black, silver and brown 1·50 1·75
DESIGNS: No. 1576, Loading munitions for Russia, 1943; No. 1577, Loading bombs on Avro Lancaster; No. 1578, Escorts attacking U-boat; No. 1579, Infantry advancing, Italy.

620 (face value at right)

1994. Self-adhesive Greetings stamps. Mult.
1580 43c. Type **620** . . . . . . 1·00 1·00
1581 43c. As Type **620** but face value at left . . . . . 1·00 1·00
It was intended that the sender should insert an appropriate greetings label into the circular space on each stamp before use.
For 45c. values in this design see Nos. 1654/5.

621 Jeanne Sauve

1994. Jeanne Sauve (former Governor-General) Commemoration.
1582 **621** 43c. multicoloured . . . 60 60

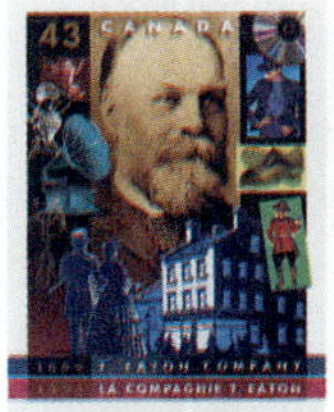

622 Timothy Eaton, Toronto Store of 1869 and Merchandise

1994. 125th Anniv of T. Eaton Company Ltd (department store group).
1583 **622** 43c. multicoloured . . . 55 75

1994. Canadian Rivers (4th series). As T **592**, but horiz. Multicoloured.
1584 43c. Saguenay River 80 90
1585 43c. French River 80 90
1586 43c. Mackenzie River . . . 80 90
1587 43c. Churchill River 80 90
1588 43c. Columbia River 80 90

1994. Canadian Art (7th series). As T **550**. Multicoloured.
1589 88c. "Vera" (detail) (Frederick Varley) . . . . 1·50 2·00

623 Lawn Bowls

1994. 15th Commonwealth Games, Victoria. Multicoloured.
1590 43c. Type **623** 50 55
1591 43c. Lacrosse 50 55
1592 43c. Wheelchair race 50 55
1593 43c. High jumping 50 55
1594 50c. Diving 50 70
1595 88c. Cycling . . . . 1·50 1·60

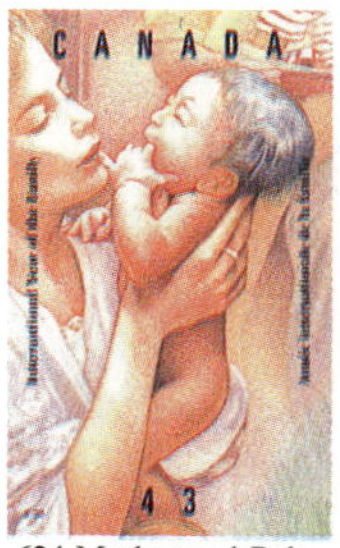

624 Mother and Baby

1994. International Year of the Family. Sheet 178 × 134 mm, containing T **624** and similar vert designs. Multicoloured.
MS1596 43c. Type **624**; 43c. Family outing; 43c. Grandmother and granddaughter; 43c. Computer class; 43c. Play group, nurse with patient and female lawyer . . . 3·00 3·50

625 Big Leaf Maple Tree

1994. Canada Day. Maple Trees. Multicoloured.
1597 43c. Type **625** 75 90
1598 43c. Sugar maple 75 90
1599 43c. Silver maple 75 90
1600 43c. Striped maple 75 90
1601 43c. Norway maple 75 90
1602 43c. Manitoba maple . . . 75 90
1603 43c. Black maple 75 90
1604 43c. Douglas maple 75 90
1605 43c. Mountain maple . . . 75 90
1606 43c. Vine maple 75 90
1607 43c. Hedge maple 75 90
1608 43c. Red maple 75 90

626 Billy Bishop (fighter ace) and Nieuport 17

627 Symbolic Aircraft, Radar Screen and Clouds

1994. Birth Centenaries. Multicoloured.
1609 43c. Type **626** . . . . . . 1·00 1·25
1610 43c. Mary Travers ("La Bolduc") (singer) and musicians . . . . 1·00 1·25

1994. Historic Automobiles (2nd issue). Sheet 177×125 mm, containing horiz designs as T **617**. Multicoloured.
MS1611 43c. Ford Model F60L-AMB military ambulance, 1942–43; 43c. Winnipeg police wagon, 1925; 50c. Sicard snowblower, 1927 (43×22 mm); 50c. Bickle Chieftain fire engine, 1936 (43×22 mm); 88c. St. John Railway Company tramcar No. 40, 1894 (51×22 mm), 88c. Motor Coach Industries Courier 50 Skyview coach, 1950 (51×22 mm) . . . . 9·00 9·50
No. **MS**1611 was sold in a protective pack.

1994. 50th Anniv of ICAO.
1612 **627** 43c. multicoloured . . . 1·00 70

1994. Prehistoric Canada (4th series). Mammals. As T **582**, but 40×28 mm. Multicoloured.
1613 43c. Coryphodon . . . . . 1·75 1·75
1614 43c. Megacerops . . . . . 1·75 1·75
1615 43c. Arctodus simus (bear) 1·75 1·75
1616 43c. Mammuthus primigenius (mammoth) 1·75 1·75

628 Carol Singing around Christmas Tree

629 Flag and Lake

1994. Christmas. Multicoloured.
1617 (–)c. Carol singer (35×21 mm) 80 90
1618 43c. Type **628** 50 20
1619 50c. Choir (vert) . . . . . 1·00 1·40
1620 88c. Couple carol singing in snow (vert) . . . . 2·25 3·00
No. 1617 is without face value, but was intended for use as a 38c. on internal greetings cards posted before 31 January 1995. The design shows a barcode at left.

1994. 50th Anniv of Second World War (6th issue). As T **574**.
1621 43c. black, silver and green 1·75 1·75
1622 43c. black, silver and red . . 1·75 1·75
1623 43c. black, silver and blue 1·75 1·75
1624 43c. black, silver and grey 1·75 1·75
DESIGNS: No. 1621, D-Day landings, Normandy; No. 1622, Canadian artillery, Normandy; No. 1623, Hawker Typhoons on patrol; No. 1624, Canadian infantry and disabled German self-propelled gun, Walcheren.

1995. 50th Anniv of Second World War (7th issue). As T **574**.
1625 43c. black, silver and purple 2·00 1·75
1626 43c. black, silver and brown 2·00 1·75
1627 43c. black, silver and green 2·00 1·75
1628 43c. black, silver and blue 2·00 1·75
DESIGNS: No. 1625, Returning troop ship; 1626, Canadian P.O.W.s celebrating freedom; 1627, Canadian tank liberating Dutch town; 1628, Parachute drop in support of Rhine Crossing.

1995. Canadian Art (8th series). As T **550**. Multicoloured.
1629 88c. "Floraison" (Alfred Pellan) . . . . 1·50 2·00

1995. 30th Anniv of National Flag. No face value.
1630 **629** (43c.) multicoloured . . 1·00 50

630 Louisbourg Harbour

1995. 275th Anniv of Fortress of Louisbourg. Multicoloured.
1631 (43c.) Type **630** 70 80
1632 (43c.) Barracks (32×29 mm) 70 80
1633 (43c.) King's Bastion (40×29 mm) 70 80
1634 (43c.) Site of King's Garden, convent and hospital (56×29 mm) 70 80
1635 (43c.) Site of coastal fortifications 70 80

1995. Historic Automobiles (3rd issue). Sheet 177×125 mm, containing horiz designs as T **617**. Multicoloured.
MS1636 43c. Cockshutt "30" farm tractor, 1950; 43c. Bombadier "Ski-Doo Olympique 335" snowmobile, 1970; 50c. Bombadier "B-12 CS" multi-passenger snowmobile, 1948 (43×22 mm); 50c. Gotfredson "Model 20" farm truck, 1924 (43×22 mm); 88c. Robin-Nodwell "RN 110" tracked carrier, 1962 (43×22 mm); 88c. Massey-Harris "No. 21" self-propelled combine-harvester, 1942 (43×22 mm) . . . . 7·00 7·50
No. **MS**1636 was sold in a protective pack.

631 Banff Springs Golf Club, Alberta

1995. Centenaries of Canadian Amateur Golf Championship and of the Royal Canadian Golf Association. Multicoloured.
1637 43c. Type **631** 80 80
1638 43c. Riverside Country Club, New Brunswick . . . 80 80
1639 43c. Glen Abbey Golf Club, Ontario 80 80
1640 43c. Victoria Golf Club, British Columbia 80 80
1641 43c. Royal Montreal Golf Club, Quebec 80 80

632 "October Gold" (Franklin Carmichael)

1995. Canada Day. 75th Anniv of "Group of Seven" (artists). Miniature sheets, each 180×80 mm, containing square designs as T **632**. Multicoloured.
MS1642a 43c. Type **632**; 43c. "From the North Shore, Lake Superior" (Lawren Harris); 43c. "Evening, Les Eboulements, Quebec" (A. Jackson) . . . . 3·00 3·50
MS1642b 43c. "Serenity, Lake of the Woods" (Frank Johnston); 43c. "A September Gale, Georgian Bay" (Arthur Lismer); 43c. "Falls, Montreal River" (J. E. H. MacDonald); 43c. "Open Window" (Frederick Varley) 3·00 3·50
MS1642c 43c. "Mill Houses" (Alfred Casson); 43c. "Pembina Valley" (Lionel FitzGerald); 43c. "The Lumberjack" (Edwin Holgate) 3·00 3·50
The three sheets were sold together in an envelope which also includes a small descriptive booklet.

633 Academy Building and Ship Plan

634 Aspects of Manitoba

1995. Centenary of Lunenburg Academy.
1643 **633** 43c. multicoloured . . . 50 45

1995. 125th Anniv of Manitoba as Canadian Province.
1644 **634** 43c. multicoloured . . . 50 45

635 Monarch Butterfly

1995. Migratory Wildlife. Multicoloured.
1645 45c. Type **635** . . . . . 1·10 1·40
1646 45c. Belted kingfisher* . . . 1·10 1·40
1647 45c. Belted kingfisher* . . . 1·10 1·40
1648 45c. Pintail . . . . 1·10 1·40
1649 45c. Hoary bat . . . . . . 1·10 1·40
*No. 1646: Inscr "aune migratrice" in error. No. 1647: Inscr corrected to "faune migratrice".

636 Quebec Railway Bridge

1995. 20th World Road Congress, Montreal. Bridges. Multicoloured.
1650 45c. Type **636** . . . . . . 2·00 1·90
1651 45c. 401-403-410 Interchange, Mississauga 2·00 1·90
1652 45c. Hartland Bridge, New Brunswick . . . . 2·00 1·90
1653 45c. Alex Fraser Bridge, British Columbia . . . . 2·00 1·90

1995. Self-adhesive Greetings stamps. As T **620**. Multicoloured. Imperf.
1654 45c. Face value at right . . 60 75
1655 45c. Face value at left . . . 60 75
It is intended the sender should insert an appropriate greetings label into the circular space on each stamp before use.

637 Mountain, Baffin Island, Polar Bear and Caribou

1995. 50th Anniv of Arctic Institute of North America. Multicoloured.
1656 45c. Type **637** . . . . . . 1·00 1·25
1657 45c. Arctic poppy, Auyuittuq National Park and cargo canoe . . . . 1·00 1·25
1658 45c. Inuk man and igloo . . 1·00 1·25
1659 45c. Ogilvie Mountains, dog team and ski-equipped airplane . . . . 1·00 1·25
1660 45c. Inuit children . . . . . 1·00 1·25

638 Superman

640 "The Nativity"

639 Prime Minister MacKenzie King signing U.N. Charter, 1945

1995. Comic Book Superheroes. Multicoloured.
1661 45c. Type **638** 75 85
1662 45c. Johnny Canuck 75 85
1663 45c. Nelvana 75 85
1664 45c. Captain Canuck 75 85
1665 45c. Fleur de Lys 75 85

1995. 50th Anniv of United Nations.
1666 **639** 45c. multicoloured . . . 75 50

1995. Christmas. Sculptured Capitals from Ste.-Anne-de-Beaupre Basilica designed by Emile Brunet (Nos. 1668/70). Multicoloured.
1667 40c. Sprig of holly (35×22 mm) 85 70
1668 45c. Type **640** 50 20
1669 52c. "The Annunciation" . . 1·60 1·60
1670 90c. "The Flight to Egypt" 2·25 2·75

641 World Map and Emblem

1995. 25th Anniv of La Francophonie and The Agency for Cultural and Technical Co-operation.
1671 **641** 45c. multicoloured . . . 60 50

642 Concentration Camp Victims, Uniform and Identity Card

1995. 50th Anniv of the End of The Holocaust.
1672 **642** 45c. multicoloured . . . 70 50

643 American Kestrel

1996. Birds (1st series). Multicoloured.
1673 45c. Type **643** . . . . . . 1·90 1·75
1674 45c. Atlantic puffin . . . . 1·90 1·75
1675 45c. Pileated woodpecker . . 1·90 1·75
1676 45c. Ruby-throated hummingbird . . . . . . 1·90 1·75
See also Nos. 1717/20, 1779/82, 1865/8, 1974/7 and 2058/61.

644 "Louis R. Desmarais" (tanker), Three-dimensional Map and Radar Screen

1996. High Technology Industries. Multicoloured.
1677 45c. Type **644** . . . . . . 75 1·00
1678 45c. Canadair Challenger 601-3R, jet engine and navigational aid . . . . . 75 1·00
1679 45c. Map of North America and eye . . . . 75 1·00
1680 45c. Genetic engineering experiment and Canola (plant) . . . . 75 1·00

1996. Canadian Art (9th series). As T **550**. Multicoloured.
1681 90c. "The Spirit of Haida Gwaii" (sculpture) (Bill Reid) . . . . 1·40 2·00

645 "One World, One Hope" (Joe Average)

1996. 11th International Conference on AIDS, Vancouver.
1682 **645** 45c. multicoloured . . . 70 70

1996. Historic Automobiles (4th issue). Sheet 177×125 mm, containing horiz designs as T **617**. Multicoloured.
MS1683 45c. Still Motor Co electric van, 1899; 45c. Waterous Engine Works steam roller, 1914; 52c. International D.35 delivery truck, 1938; 52c. Champion road grader, 1936; 90c. White Model WA 122 articulated lorry, 1947 (51×22 mm); 90c. Hayes HDX 45-115 logging truck, 1975 (51×22 mm) . . . . 7·50 8·00

No. MS1683 also includes the "CAPEX '96" International Stamp Exhibition logo on the sheet margin and was sold in a protective pack.

1996. "CAPEX '96" International Stamp Exhibitiion, Toronto. Sheet 368 × 182 mm, containing horiz designs as Nos. MS1563, MS1611, MS1636 and MS1683, but with different face values, and one new design (45c.).

MS1684 5c. Bombadier "Ski–Doo Olympique 335" snowmobile, 1970; 5c. Cockshutt "30" farm tractor, 1950; 5c. Type **617**; 5c. Ford "Model F160L-AMB" military ambulance, 1942; 5c. Still Motor Co electric van, 1895; 5c. International "D.35" delivery truck, 1936; 5c. Russel "Model L" touring car, 1908; 5c. Winnipeg police wagon, 1925; 5c. Waterous Engine Works steam roller, 1914; 5c. Champion road grader, 1936; 10c. White "Model WA 122" articulated lorry, 1947 (51 × 22 mm); 10c. St. John Railway Company tramcar, 1894 (51 × 22 mm); 10c. Hayes "HDX 45-115" logging truck, 1975 (51 × 22 mm); 10c. Motor Couch Industries "Courier 50 Skyview" coach, 1950 (51 × 22 mm); 20c. Ford "Model T" touring car, 1914 (43 × 22 mm); 20c. McLaughlin-Buick "28-496 special", 1928 (43 × 22 mm); 20c. Bombadier "B-12 CS" multi-passenger snowmobile, 1948 (43 × 22 mm); 20c. Robin-Nodwell "RN 110" tracked carrier, 1962 (43 × 22 mm); 20c. Studebaker "Champion Deluxe Starlight" coupe, 1950 (43 × 22 mm); 20c. Gray-Dort "25 SM" luxury sedan, 1923 (43 × 22 mm); 20c. Gotfredson "Model 20" farm truck, 1924 (43 × 22 mm); 20c. Massey-Harris "No. 21" self-propelled combine-harvester, 1942 (43 × 22 mm); 20c. Bickle "Chieftain" fire engine, 1936 (43 × 22 mm); 20c. Sicard snowblower, 1927 (43 × 22 mm); 45c. Bricklin "SV-1" sports car, 1975 (51 × 22 mm) . . . . . 8·00 9·00

The price quoted for No. MS1684 is for a folded example.

646 Skookum Jim Mason and Bonanza Creek

1996. Centenary of Yukon Gold Rush. Multicoloured.

1685 45c. Type **646** . . . . . . 80 1·00
1686 45c. Prospector and boats on Lake Laberge . . . . 80 1·00
1687 45c. Superintendent Sam Steele (N.W.M.P.) and U.S.A.–Canada border . . 80 1·00
1688 45c. Dawson saloon . . . . 80 1·00
1689 45c. Miner with rocker box and sluice . . . . 80 1·00

647 Patchwork Quilt Maple Leaf

648 Ethel Catherwood (high jump), 1928

1996. Canada Day. Self-adhesive. Imperf.

1690 **647** 45c. multicoloured . . . 1·00 60

1996. Canadian Olympic Gold Medal Winners. Multicoloured.

1691 45c. Type **648** 85 85
1692 45c. Etienne Desmarteau (56lb weight throw), 1904 85 85
1693 45c. Fanny Rosenfeld (400 m relay), 1928 . . . 85 85
1694 45c. Gerald Ouellette (small bore rifle, prone), 1956 . . 85 85
1695 45c. Percy Williams (100 and 200 m), 1928 . . . . 85 85

649 Indian Totems, City Skyline, Forest and Mountains

650 Canadian Heraldic Symbols

1996. 125th Anniv of British Columbia.

1696 **649** 45c. multicoloured . . . 50 50

1996. 22nd International Congress of Genealogical and Heraldic Sciences, Ottawa.

1697 **650** 45c. multicoloured . . . 50 50

651 "L'Arivee d'un Train en Gare" (1896)

1996. Centenary of Cinema. Two sheets, each 180 × 100 mm, containing T **651** and similar vert designs. Multicoloured. Self-adhesive.

MS1698a 45c. Type **651**; 45c. "God's Country" (1919); 45c. "Hen Hop" (1942); 45c."Pour la Suite du Monde" (1963); 45c. "Goin' Down the Road" (1970). . . . 4·25 4·75
MS1698b 45c. "Mon Oncle Antoine" (1971); 45c. "The Apprenticeship of Duddy Kravitz" (1974); 45c. "Les Ordres" (1974); 45c. "Les Bons Debarras" (1980); 45c. "The Grey Fox" (1982) 4·25 4·75

The two sheets were sold together in an envelope with a descriptive booklet.

652 Interlocking Jigsaw Pieces and Hands

1996. Literacy Campaign.

1699 **652** 45c.+5c. mult . . . . . 85 1·00

653 Edouard Montpetit and Montreal University

1996. Edouard Montpetit (academic) Commem.

1700 **653** 45c. multicoloured . . . 50 50

654 Winnie and Lt. Colebourn, 1914

1996. Stamp Collecting Month. Winnie the Pooh. Multicoloured.

1701 45c. Type **654** . . . . . . 1·75 1·50
1702 45c. Christopher Robin Milne and teddy bear, 1925 . . . . 1·75 1·50
1703 45c. Illustration from "Winnie the Pooh", 1926 1·75 1·50
1704 45c. Winnie the Pooh at Walt Disney World, 1996 1·75 1·50
MS1705 152 × 112 mm. Nos 1701/4 5·50 5·50

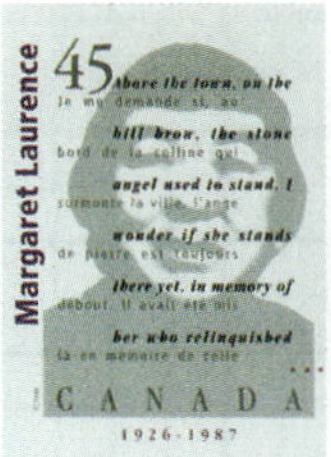

655 Margaret Laurence

656 Children tobogganing

1996. Canadian Authors.

1706 **655** 45c. multicoloured . . . 1·10 1·40
1707 – 45c. black, grey and red 1·10 1·40
1708 – 45c. multicoloured . . . 1·10 1·40
1709 – 45c. multicoloured . . . 1·10 1·40
1710 – 45c. multicoloured . . . 1·10 1·40

DESIGNS: No. 1707, Donald G. Creighton; 1708, Gabrielle Roy; 1709, Felix-Antoine Savard; 1710, Thomas C. Haliburton.

1996. Christmas. 50th Anniv of UNICEF. Multicoloured.

1711 45c. Type **656** 50 20
1712 52c. Father Christmas skiing . . . . 80 1·00
1713a 90c. Couple ice-skating . . 1·25 2·00

657 Head of Ox

659 Abbe Charles-Emile Gadbois

658 Man and Boy with Bike, and A. J. and J. W. Billes (company founders)

1997. Chinese New Year ("Year of the Ox").

1714 **657** 45c. multicoloured . . . 85 90
MS1715 155 × 75 mm. No. 1714 × 2 2·00 2·50

No. MS1715 is an extended fan shape with overall measurements as quoted.

1997. "HONG KONG '97" International Stamp Exhibition. As No. MS1715, but with exhibition logo added to the sheet margin in gold.

MS1716 155 × 75 mm. No. 1714 × 2 6·00 6·50

1997. Birds (2nd series). As T **643**. Multicoloured.

1717 45c. Mountain bluebird . . 1·25 1·40
1718 45c. Western grebe . . . . 1·25 1·40
1719 45c. Northern gannet . . . 1·25 1·40
1720 45c. Scarlet tanager . . . . 1·25 1·40

1997. Canadian Art (10th series). As T **550**. Multicoloured.

1721 90c. "York Boat on Lake Winnipeg, 1930" (Walter Phillips) . . . . 1·50 2·00

1997. 75th Anniv of the Canadian Tire Corporation.

1722 **658** 45c. multicoloured . . . 80 50

1997. Abbe Charles-Emile Gadbois (musicologist) Commemoration.

1723 **659** 45c. multicoloured . . . 60 50

660 Blue Poppy

662 Osgoode Hall and Seal of Law School

661 Nurse attending Patient

1997. "Quebec in Bloom" International Floral Festival.

1724 **660** 45c. multicoloured . . . 60 55

1997. Centenary of Victorian Order of Nurses.

1725 **661** 45c. multicoloured . . . 1·00 50

1997. Bicentenary of Law Society of Upper Canada.

1726 **662** 45c. multicoloured . . . 75 50

663 Great White Shark

1997. Ocean Fishes. Multicoloured.

1727 45c. Type **663** . . . . . . 1·00 1·25
1728 45c. Pacific halibut . . . . 1·00 1·25
1729 45c. Common sturgeon . . 1·00 1·25
1730 45c. Blue-finned tuna . . . 1·00 1·25

664 Lighthouse and Confederation Bridge

1997. Opening of Confederation Bridge, Northumberland Strait. Multicoloured.

1731 45c. Type **664** . . . . . . 1·40 1·00
1732 45c. Confederation Bridge and great blue heron . . 1·40 1·00

665 Gilles Villeneuve in Ferrari T-3

1997. 15th Death Anniv of Gilles Villeneuve (racing car driver). Multicoloured.

1733 45c. Type **665** . . . . . . 1·00 60
1734 90c. Villeneuve in Ferrari T-4 . . . . 2·00 2·25
MS1735 203 × 115 mm. Nos. 1733/4 each × 4 . . . . 8·00 8·00

666 Globe and the "Matthew"

1997. 500th Anniv of John Cabot's Discovery of North America.

1736 **666** 45c. multicoloured . . . 1·00 55

667 Sea to Sky Highway, British Columbia, and Skier

1997. Scenic Highways (1st series). Multicoloured.

1737 45c. Type **667** . . . . . . 1·25 1·40
1738 45c. Cabot Trail, Nova Scotia, and rug-making 1·25 1·40
1739 45c. Wine route, Ontario, and glasses of wine . . . 1·25 1·40
1740 45c. Highway 34, Saskatchewan, and cowboy . . . . 1·25 1·40

See also Nos. 1810/13 and 1876/9.

668 Kettle, Ski-bike, Lounger and Plastic Cases

1997. 20th Congress of International Council of Societies for Industrial Design.

1741 **668** 45c. multicoloured . . . 60 50

669 Caber Thrower, Bagpiper, Drummer and Highland Dancer

1997. 50th Anniv of Glengarry Highland Games, Ontario.
1742 **669** 45c. multicoloured . . . 1·00 50

670 Knights of Columbus Emblem

1997. Centenary of Knights of Columbus (welfare charity) in Canada.
1743 **670** 45c. multicoloured . . . 50 50

671 Postal and Telephone Workers with PTTI Emblem

1997. 28th World Congress of Postal, Telegraph and Telephone International Staff Federation, Montreal.
1744 **671** 45c. multicoloured . . . 50 50

672 CYAP Logo

1997. Canada's Year of Asia Pacific.
1745 **672** 45c. multicoloured . . . 1·00 50

673 Paul Henderson celebrating Goal

1997. 25th Anniv of Canada–U.S.S.R. Ice Hockey Series. Multicoloured.
1746 45c. Type **673** . . . . . . 1·25 1·25
1747 45c. Canadian team celebrating . . . . . . 1·25 1·25

674 Martha Black

1997. Federal Politicians. Multicoloured.
1748 45c. Type **674** . . . . . . 70 1·00
1749 45c. Lionel Chevrier . . . . 70 1·00
1750 45c. Judy LaMarsh . . . . 70 1·00
1751 45c. Real Caouette . . . . 70 1·00

675 Vampire and Bat

1997. The Supernatural. Centenary of Publication of Bram Stoker's "Dracula". Multicoloured.
1752 45c. Type **675** 65 85
1753 45c. Werewolf 65 85
1754 45c. Ghost 65 85
1755 45c. Goblin 65 85

676 Grizzly Bear

1997. Mammals. Multicoloured.
1756 $1 Great northern diver ("Loon") (47 × 39 mm) 85 90
1757 $1 White-tailed deer (47 × 39 mm) 85 90
1758 $1 Atlantic walrus (47 × 39 mm) 85 90
1759 $2 Polar bear (47 × 39 mm) 1·70 1·80
1760 $2 Peregrine falcon (47 × 39 mm) . . . . . 1·70 1·80
1761 $2 Sable Island horse (mare and foal) (47 × 39 mm) . . . . . 1·70 1·80
1762 $5 Moose . . . . 7·00 7·00
1762a $8 Type **676** . . . . 9·00 9·00
MS1762b Two sheets, each 155 × 130 mm. (a) Nos. 1757/8, each × 2. (b) Nos. 1760/1, each × 2 . . . . 10·00 10·50

677 "Our Lady of the Rosary" (detail, Holy Rosary Cathedral, Vancouver)

1997. Christmas. Stained Glass Windows. Multicoloured.
1763a 45c. Type **677** 45 20
1764 52c. "Nativity" (detail, Leith United Church, Ontario) 65 65
1765 90c. "Life of the Blessed Virgin" (detail, St. Stephen's Ukrainian Catholic Church, Calgary) . . . . 1·10 1·50

678 Livestock and Produce

1997. 75th Anniv of Royal Agricultural Winter Fair, Toronto.
1766 **678** 45c. multicoloured . . . 1·25 55

679 Tiger

1998. Chinese New Year ("Year of the Tiger").
1767 **679** 45c. multicoloured . . . 60 50
MS1768 130 × 110 mm. As No. 1767 × 2 . . . . 1·25 1·50
No. **MS**1768 is diamond-shaped with overall measurements as quoted.

680 John Robarts (Ontario, 1961–71)

681 Maple Leaf

1998. Canadian Provincial Premiers. Multicoloured.
1769 45c. Type **680** 65 75
1770 45c. Jean Lesage (Quebec, 1960–66) 65 75
1771 45c. John McNair (New Brunswick, 1940–52) . . . 65 75
1772 45c. Tommy Douglas (Saskatchewan, 1944–61) 65 75
1773 45c. Joseph Smallwood (Newfoundland, 1949–72) 65 75
1774 45c. Angus MacDonald (Nova Scotia, 1933–40, 1945–54) 65 75
1775 45c. W. A. C. Bennett (British Columbia, 1960–66) 65 75
1776 45c. Ernest Manning (Alberta, 1943–68) 65 75
1777 45c. John Bracken (Manitoba, 1922–43) . . . 65 75
1778 45c. J. Walter Jones (Prince Edward Island, 1943–53) 65 75

1998. Birds (3rd series). As T **643**. Multicoloured.
1779 45c. Hairy woodpecker . . 1·40 1·25
1780 45c. Great crested flycatcher 1·40 1·25
1781 45c. Eastern screech owl . . 1·40 1·25
1782 45c. Rosy finch ("Gray-crowned Rosy-finch") . . 1·40 1·25

1998. Self-adhesive Automatic Cash Machine Stamps. Imperf.
1783 **681** 45c. multicoloured . . . 45 40
For stamps in this design, but without "POSTAGE POSTES" at top left see Nos. 1836/40.

682 Coquihalla Orange Fly

1998. Fishing Flies. Multicoloured.
1784 45c. Type **682** 90 90
1785 45c. Steelhead Bee 90 90
1786 45c. Dark Montreal 90 90
1787 45c. Lady Amherst 90 90
1788 45c. Coho Blue 90 90
1789 45c. Cosseboom Special . . 90 90

683 Mineral Excavation, Oil Rig and Pickaxe

684 1898 2c. Imperial Penny Postage Stamp and Postmaster General Sir William Mulock

1998. Centenary of Canadian Institute of Mining, Metallurgy and Petroleum.
1790 **683** 45c. multicoloured . . . 70 50

1998. Centenary of Imperial Penny Postage.
1791 **684** 45c. multicoloured . . . 1·00 55

685 Two Sumo Wrestlers

1998. 1st Canadian Sumo Basho (tournament), Vancouver. Multicoloured.
1792 45c. Type **685** 65 75
1793 45c. Sumo wrestler in ceremonial ritual 65 75
MS1794 84 × 152 mm. Nos. 1792/3 1·25 1·50

686 St. Peters Canal, Nova Scotia

687 Staff of Aesculapius and Cross

1998. Canadian Canals. Multicoloured.
1795 45c. Type **686** . . . . . . 1·25 1·25
1796 45c. St. Ours Canal, Quebec 1·25 1·25
1797 45c. Port Carling Lock, Ontario . . . . 1·25 1·25
1798 45c. Lock on Rideau Canal, Ontario . . . . 1·25 1·25
1799 45c. Towers and platform of Peterborough Lift Lock, Trent–Severn Waterway, Ontario . . . . 1·25 1·25
1800 45c. Chambly Canal, Quebec . . . . 1·25 1·25
1801 45c. Lachine Canal, Quebec 1·25 1·25
1802 45c. Rideau Canal in winter, Ontario . . . . 1·25 1·25
1803 45c. Boat on Big Chute incline railway, Trent–Severn Waterway, Ontario 1·25 1·25
1804 45c. Sault Ste. Marie Canal, Ontario . . . . 1·25 1·25

1998. Canadian Health Professionals.
1805 **687** 45c. multicoloured . . . 1·00 55

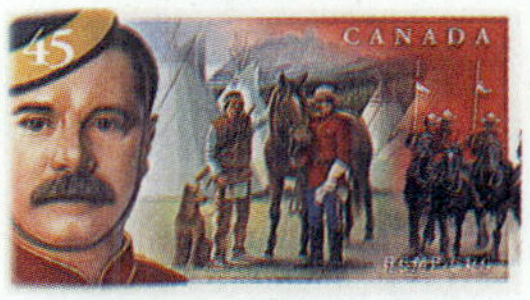

688 Policeman of 1873 and Visit to Indian Village

1998. 125th Anniv of Royal Canadian Mounted Police. Multicoloured.
1806 45c. Type **688** 90 75
1807 45c. Policewoman of 1998 and aspects of modern law enforcement 90 75
MS1808 160 × 102 mm. Nos. 1806/7 1·75 1·90

689 William J. Roue (designer) and "Bluenose" (schooner)

1998. William James Roue (naval architect) Commemoration.
1809 **689** 45c. multicoloured . . . 70 50

1998. Scenic Highways (2nd series). As T **667**. Multicoloured.
1810 45c. Dempster Highway, Yukon, and caribou . . . 65 75
1811 45c. Dinosaur Trail, Alberta, and skeleton . . 65 75
1812 45c. River Valley Drive, New Brunswick, and fern 65 75
1813 45c. Blue Heron Route, Prince Edward Island, and lobster 65 75

690 "Painting" (Jean-Paul Riopelle)

1998. 50th Anniv of "Refus Global" (manifesto of The Automatistes group of artists). Multicoloured. Self-adhesive. Imperf.
1814 45c. Type **690** . . . . . . 1·10 1·10
1815 45c. "La derniere campagne de Napoleon" (Fernand Leduc) (37 × 31½ mm) . . 1·10 1·10
1816 45c. "Jet fuligineux sur noir torture" (Jean-Paul Mousseau) . . . . 1·10 1·10
1817 45c. "Le fond du garde-robe" (Pierre Gauvreau) (29½ × 42 mm) . . . . . 1·10 1·10
1818 45c. "Joie lacustre" (Paul-Emile Borduas) . . . . . 1·10 1·10
1819 45c. "Seafarers Union" (Marcelle Ferron) (36 × 34 mm) . . . . . . 1·10 1·10
1820 45c. "Le tumulte a la machoire crispee" (Marcel Barbeau) (36 × 34 mm) . . 1·10 1·10

691 Napoleon-Alexandre Comeau (naturalist)

1998. Legendary Canadians. Multicoloured.
1821 45c. Type **691** 55 75
1822 45c. Phyllis Munday (mountaineer) 55 75

1823 45c. Bill Mason (film-maker) 55 75
1824 45c. Harry Red Foster (sports commentator) . . 55 75

1998. Canadian Art (11th series). As T **550**. Multicoloured.
1825 90c. "The Farmer's Family" (Bruno Bobak) . . . . . 1·00 1·40

692 Indian Wigwam

1998. Canadian Houses. Multicoloured.
1826 45c. Type **692** 50 60
1827 45c. Settler sod hut 50 60
1828 45c. Maison Saint-Gabriel (17th-century farmhouse), Quebec 50 60
1829 45c. Queen Anne style brick house, Ontario 50 60
1830 45c. Terrace of town houses 50 60
1831 45c. Prefabricated house . . 50 60
1832 45c. Veterans' houses . . . 50 60
1833 45c. Modern bungalow . . 50 60
1834 45c. Healthy House, Toronto 50 60

693 University of Ottawa

1998. 150th Anniv of University of Ottawa.
1835 **693** 45c. multicoloured . . . 50 50

1998. As T **681**, but without "POSTAGE POSTES" at top left. Self-adhesive gum, imperf (46c.) or ordinary gum, perf (others).
1839 **681** 45c. multicoloured . . . 1·25 1·25
1840 46c. multicoloured . . . 1·00 1·00
1836 55c. multicoloured . . . 1·25 1·25
1837 73c. multicoloured . . . 1·25 1·40
1838 95c. multicoloured . . . 1·75 2·00

694 Performing Animals

1998. Canadian Circus. Multicoloured.
1851 45c. Type **694** . . . . . . 1·10 1·10
1852 45c. Flying trapeze and acrobat on horseback . . 1·10 1·10
1853 45c. Lion tamer . . . . . . 1·10 1·10
1854 45c. Acrobats and trapeze artists . . . . 1·10 1·10
MS1855 133 × 133 mm. Nos. 1851/4 3·50 4·00

695 John Peters Humphrey (author of original Declaration draft)

1998. 50th Anniv of Universal Declaration of Human Rights.
1856 **695** 45c. multicoloured . . . 50 50

696 H.M.C.S. "Sackville" (corvette)

1998. 75th Anniv of Canadian Naval Reserve. Multicoloured.
1857 45c. Type **696** 80 90
1858 45c. H.M.C.S. "Shawinigan" (coastal defence vessel) . . 80 90

697 Angel blowing Trumpet

698 Rabbit

1998. Christmas. Statues of Angels. Multicoloured.
1859 45c. Type **697** 60 20
1860b 52c. Adoring Angel . . . 70 55
1861b 90c. Angel at prayer . . . 1·40 2·00

1999. Chinese New Year ("Year of the Rabbit").
1862 **698** 46c. multicoloured . . . 50 50
MS1863 Circular 100 mm diam. **698** 95c. mult (40 × 40 mm) . . . . 1·75 1·50
No. **MS**1863 also exists with the "CHINA '99" World Stamp Exhibition, Beijing, logo overprinted in gold on the top of the margin.

699 Stylized Mask and Curtain

701 "Marco Polo" (full-rigged ship)

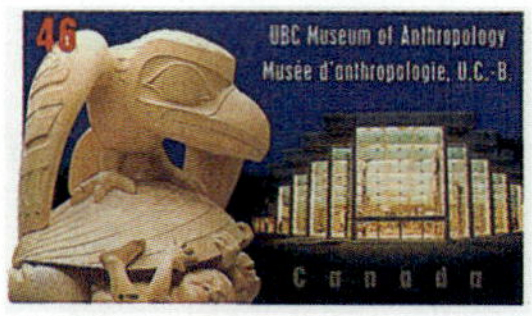

700 "The Raven and the First Men" (B. Reid) and The Great Hall

1999. 50th Anniv of Le Theatre du Rideau Vert.
1864 **699** 46c. multicoloured . . . 50 50

1999. Birds (4th series). As T **643**. Multicoloured. Ordinary or self-adhesive gum.
1865 46c. Northern goshawk . . 85 85
1866 46c. Red-winged blackbird 85 85
1867 46c. American goldfinch . . 85 85
1868 46c. Sandhill crane 85 85

1999. 50th Anniv of University of British Columbia Museum of Anthropology.
1873 **700** 46c. multicoloured . . . 50 50

1999. Canada–Australia Joint Issue. "Marco Polo" (emigrant ship).
1874 **701** 46c. multicoloured . . . 50 50
MS1875 160 × 95 mm. 85c. As No. 1728 of Australia. 46c. Type **701**. (No. **MS**1875 was sold at $1.25 in Canada) . . . . . 1·75 1·75
No. **MS**1875 includes the "Australia '99" emblem on the sheet margin and was postally valid in Canada to the value of 46c.
The same miniature sheet was also available in Australia.

1999. Scenic Highways (3rd series). As T **667**. Multicoloured.
1876 46c. Route 132, Quebec, and hang-glider 75 80
1877 46c. Yellowhead Highway, Manitoba, and bison . . 75 80
1878 46c. Dempster Highway, Northwest Territories, and Indian village elder . . . 75 80
1879 46c. The Discovery Trail, Newfoundland, and whale's tailfin 75 80

702 Inuit Children and Landscape

1999. Creation of Nunavut Territory.
1880 **702** 46c. multicoloured . . . 50 50

703 Elderly Couple on Country Path

1999. International Year of Older Persons.
1881 **703** 46c. multicoloured . . . 50 50

704 Khanda (Sikh symbol)

705 "Arethusa bulbosa" (orchid)

1999. Centenary of Sikhs in Canada.
1882 **704** 46c. multicoloured . . . 50 50

1999. 16th World Orchid Conference, Vancouver. Multicoloured.
1883 46c. Type **705** 75 75
1884 46c. "Amerorchis rotundifolia" 75 75
1885 46c. "Cypripedium pubescens" 75 75
1886 46c. "Platanthera psycodes" 75 75

706 Bookbinding

707 "Northern Dancer" (racehorse)

1999. Traditional Trades. Multicoloured.
(a) Ordinary gum.
1887 1c. Type **706** 10 10
1888 2c. Decorative ironwork . . 10 10
1889 3c. Glass-blowing 10 10
1890 4c. Oyster farming 10 10
1891 5c. Weaving 10 10
1892 9c. Quilting 10 10
1893 10c. Wood carving 10 15
1894 25c. Leatherworking 20 25

(b) Self-adhesive.
1895 65c. Jewellery making (horiz) 50 55
1896 77c. Basket weaving (horiz) 60 65
1897 $1.25 Wood-carving (horiz) 1·00 1·10

1999. Canadian Horses. Multicoloured. Ordinary or self-adhesive gum.
1903 46c. Type **707** 80 80
1904 46c. "Kingsway Skoal" (rodeo horse) 80 80
1905 46c. "Big Ben" (show jumper) 80 80
1906 46c. "Armbro Flight" (trotter) 80 80

708 Logo engraved on Limestone

709 Athletics

1999. 150th Anniv of Barreau du Quebec (Quebec lawyers' association).
1911 **708** 46c. multicoloured . . . 50 50

1999. Canadian Art (12th series). As T **550**. Mult.
1912 95c. "Coq licorne" (Jean Dallaire) . . . . 1·25 1·50

1999. 13th Pan-American Games, Winnipeg. Mult.
1913 46c. Type **709** 85 80
1914 46c. Cycling 85 80
1915 46c. Swimming 85 80
1916 46c. Football 85 80

1999. "China '99" International Stamp Exhibition, Beijing. Sheet 78 × 133 mm, containing Nos. 1883/6. Multicoloured.
MS1917 46c. Type **705**; 46c. Amerorchis rotundifolia; 46c. Cypripedium pubescens; 46c. Platanthera psycodes . . . . . 2·25 2·75

710 Female Rower

1999. 23rd World Rowing Championships, St. Catharines.
1918 **710** 46c. multicoloured . . . 50 50

711 UPU Emblem and World Map

1999. 125th Anniv of Universal Postal Union.
1919 **711** 46c. multicoloured . . . 65 50

712 De Havilland Mosquito F.B. VI

1999. 75th Anniv of Canadian Air Force. Mult.
1920 46c. Type **712** 65 70
1921 46c. Sopwith F.1 Camel . . 65 70
1922 46c. De Havilland Canada DHC-3 Otter 65 70
1923 46c. De Havilland Canada CC-108 Caribou 65 70
1924 46c. Canadair CL-28 Argus Mk 2 . . . . 65 70
1925 46c. Canadair (North American) F-86 Sabre 6 65 70
1926 46c. McDonnell Douglas CF-18 . . . . 65 70
1927 46c. Sopwith 5.F.1 Dolphin 65 70
1928 46c. Armstrong Whitworth Siskin IIIA 65 70
1929 46c. Canadian Vickers (Northrop) Delta II . . . 65 70
1930 46c. Sikorsky CH-124A Sea King helicopter 65 70
1931 46c. Vickers-Armstrong Wellington Mk II 65 70
1932 46c. Avro Anson Mk I . . 65 70
1933 46c. Canadair (Lockheed) CF-104G Starfighter . . . 65 70
1934 46c. Burgess-Dunne 65 70
1935 46c. Avro 504K 65 70

713 Fokker DR-1

1999. 50th Anniv of Canadian International Air Show. Multicoloured.
1936 46c. Type **713** 75 75
1937 46c. H101 Salto glider . . . 75 75
1938 46c. De Havilland DH100 Vampire Mk III 75 75
1939 46c. Wing walker on Stearman A-75 . . . . . 75 75
Nos. 1936/9 were printed together, se-tenant, forming a composite design which includes a nine-plane Snowbird formation of Canadair CT114 Tutor in the background.

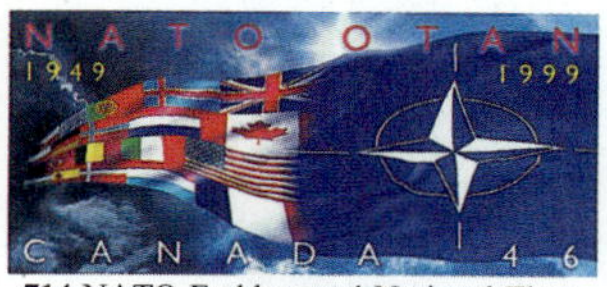

714 NATO Emblem and National Flags

1999. 50th Anniv of North Atlantic Treaty Organization.
1940 **714** 46c. multicoloured . . . 70 50

715 Man ploughing on Book

1999. Centenary of Frontier College (workers' education organization).
1941 **715** 46c. multicoloured . . . 50 50

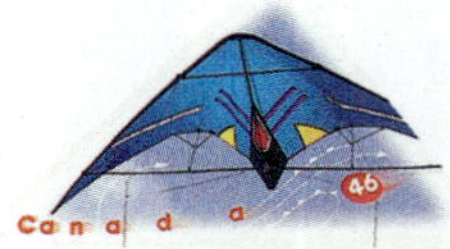

716 Master Control Sports Kite

1999. Stamp Collecting Month. Kites. Mult.
1942 46c. Type **716** 55 60
1943 46c. Indian Garden Flying Carpet (irregular rectangle, 35½ × 32 mm) 55 60

1944 46c. Gibson Girl box kite (horiz, $38\frac{1}{2}\times25$ mm) . . . 55 60
1945 46c. Dragon Centipede (oval, 39 × 29 mm) . . . 55 60

717 Boy holding Dove

1999. New Millennium. Three sheets, each 108 × 108 mm, containing T **717** and similar square designs in blocks of 4. Self-adhesive.
MS1946 – 46c. × 4 multicoloured 2·00 2·50
MS1947 **717** 55c. × 4 multicoloured 4·50 4·75
MS1948 – 95c. × 4 brown . . . . 3·75 4·50
DESIGNS: 46c. Holographic image of dove in flight; 95c. Dove with olive branch.

718 Angel playing Drum

1999. Christmas. Victorian Angels. Multicoloured.
1949 46c. Type **718** 60 20
1950 55c. Angel with toys 70 50
1951 95c. Angel with star . . . . 1·40 2·25

719 Portia White (singer)

1999. Millennium Collection (1st series). Entertainment and Arts. Miniature sheets, each 108 × 112 mm, containing T **719** and similar vert designs. Multicoloured.
MS1952 46c. Type **719**; 46c. Glenn Gould (pianist); 46c. Guy Lombardo (conductor of "Royal Canadians"); 46c. Félix Leclerc (musician, playwright and actor) 2·25 2·75
MS1953 46c. Artists looking at painting (Royal Canadian Academy of Arts); 46c. Cloud, stave and pencil marks (The Canada Council); 46c. Man with video camera (National Film Board of Canada); 46c. Newsreader (Canadian Broadcasting Corporation) . . 2·25 2·75
MS1954 46c. Calgary Stampede; 46c. Circus performers; 46c. Ice hockey (Hockey Night); 46c. Goalkeeper (Ice hockey live from The Forum) 2·25 2·75
MS1955 46c. IMAX cinema; 46c. Computer image (Softimage); 46c. Ted Rogers Sr ("Plugging in the Radio"); 46c. Sir William Stephenson (inventor of radio facsimile system) . . . . . . 2·25 2·75
MS1952/5 Set of 4 sheets . . . . 8·00 10·00
See also Nos. **MS**1959/62, **MS**1969/73 and **MS**1982/5.

720 Millennium Partnership Programme Logo

2000. Canada Millennium Partnership Programme.
1956 **720** 46c. red, green and blue 50 50

721 Chinese Dragon

2000. Chinese New Year ("Year of the Dragon").
1957 **721** 46c. multicoloured . . . 50 50
MS1958 150 × 85 mm. **721** 90c. multicoloured . . . . 1·25 1·50

2000. Millennium Collection (2nd series). Charities, Medical Pioneers, Peacekeepers and Social Reforms. Miniature sheets, each 108 × 112 mm, containing vert designs as T **719**. Multicoloured.
MS1959 46c. Providing equipment (Canadian International Development Agency); 46c. Dr. Lucille Teasdale (medical missionary); 46c. Terry Fox (Marathon of Hope); 46c. Delivering meal (Meals on Wheels) . . . . 2·25 2·50
MS1960 46c. Sir Frederick Banting (discovery of insulin); 46c. Armand Frappier (developer of BCG vaccine); 46c. Dr. Hans Selye (research into stress); 46c. "Dr. Maude Abbott" (pathologist) (M. Bell Eastlake) . . . . . . 2·25 2·50
MS1961 46c. Senator Raoul Dandurand (diplomat); 46c. Pauline Vanier and Elizabeth Smellie (nursing pioneers); 46c. Lester B. Pearson (diplomat); 46c. One-legged man (Ottawa Convention on Banning Landmines) . . . . 2·25 2·50
MS1962 46c. Nun and surgeon (medical care); 46c. "Women are persons" (sculpture by Barbara Paterson) (Appointment of women senators); 46c. Alphonse and Dorimène Desjardins (People's bank movement); 46c. Father Moses Coady (Adult education pioneer) . . . . 2·25 2·50
MS1959/62 Set of 4 sheets . . . 8·00 9·00

722 Wayne Gretzky (ice-hockey player)

2000. 50th National Hockey League All-Star Game. Multicoloured.
1963 46c. Type **722** 80 80
1964 46c. Gordie Howe (No. 9 in white jersey) 80 80
1965 46c. Maurice Richard (No. 9 in blue and red jersey) . . 80 80
1966 46c. Doug Harvey (No. 2) 80 80
1967 46c. Bobby Orr (No. 4) . . 80 80
1968 46c. Jacques Plante (No. 1) 80 80
See also Nos. 2052/7, 2118/23, 2178/3, 2250/5 and 2316/27.

2000. Millennium Collection (3rd series). First Inhabitants, Great Thinkers, Culture and Literary Legends, and Charitable Foundations. Miniature sheets, each 108 × 112 mm, containing vert designs as T **719**. Multicoloured.
MS1969 46c. Pontiac (Ottawa chief); 46c. Tom Longboat (long-distance runner); 46c. "Inuit Shaman" (sculpture by Paul Toolooktook); 46c. Shaman and patient (Indian medicine) . . . . 2·25 2·50
MS1970 46c. Prof. Marshall McLuhan (media philosopher); 46c. Northrop Frye (literary critic); 46c. Roger Lemelin (novelist); 46c. Prof. Hilda Marion Neatby (educator) . . . . . . 2·25 2·50
MS1971 46c. Bow of Viking longship (L'Anse aux Meadows World Heritage Site); 46c. Immigrant family (Pier 21 monument); 46c. Neptune mask (Neptune Theatre, Halifax); 46c. Auditorium and actor (The Stratford Festival) . . . . . . 2·25 2·50
MS1972 46c. W. O. Mitchell (writer); 46c. Gratien Gélinas (actor, producer and playwright); 46c. Text and fountain pen (Cercle du Livre de France); 46c. Harlequin and roses (Harlequin Books) 2·25 2·50
MS1973 46c. Hart Massey (Massey Foundation); 46c. Izaak Walton Killam and Dorothy Killam; 46f. Eric Lafferty Harvie (Glenbow Foundation); 46c. Macdonald Stewart Foundation . . . . . 2·25 2·50
MS1969/73 Set of 5 sheets . . . 10·00 11·00

2000. Birds (5th series). As T **643**. Multicoloured. Ordinary or self-adhesive gum.
1974 46c. Canadian warbler . . . 85 80
1975 46c. Osprey 85 80
1976 46c. Pacific diver ("Pacific Loon") 85 80
1977 46c. Blue jay 85 80

2000. Millennium Collection (4th series). Canadian Agriculture, Commerce and Technology. Miniature sheets, each 108 × 112 mm, containing vert designs as T **719**. Multicoloured.
MS1982 46c. Sir Charles Saunders (developer of Marquis wheat); 46c. Baby (Pablum baby food); 46c. Dr. Archibald Gowanlock Huntsman (frozen fish pioneer); 46c. Oven chips and field of potatoes (McCain Frozen Foods) 2·25 2·50
MS1983 46c. Early trader and Indian (Hudson's Bay Company); 46c. Satellite over earth (Bell Canada Enterprises); 46c. Jos. Louis biscuits and Vachon family (Vachon Family Bakery); 46c. Bread and eggs (George Weston Limited) . . . . 2·25 2·50
MS1984 46c. George Klein and cog wheels (inventor of electric wheelchair and micro-surgical staple gun); 46c. Abraham Gesner (developer of kerosene); 46c. Alexander Graham Bell (inventor of telephone); 46c. Joseph-Armand Bombadier (inventor of snowmobile) . . . . 2·25 2·50
MS1985 46c. Workers and steam locomotive (Rogers Pass rail tunnel); 46c. Manic 5 dam (Manicouagan River hydro-electric project); 46c. Mobile Servicing System for International Space Station (Canadian Space Program); 46c. CN Tower (World's tallest building) . . . 2·25 2·50
MS1982/5 Set of 4 sheets . . . . 8·00 9·00

723 Judges and Supreme Court Building

2000. 125th Anniv of Supreme Court of Canada.
1986 **723** 46c. multicoloured . . . 50 50

724 Lethbridge Bridge, Synthetic Rubber Plant, X-ray of Heart Pacemaker and Microwave Radio System

2000. 75th Anniv of Ceremony for Calling of an Engineer.
1987 **724** 46c. multicoloured . . . 50 50
Each vertical pair completes the engineer's ring as shown on Type **274**.

725

2000. "Picture Postage" Greetings Stamps. Self-adhesive.
1988 **725** 46c. multicoloured . . . 50 50
No. 1988 was issued to include appropriate greetings labels which could be inserted into the rectangular space on each stamp.
See also Nos. 2045 and 2099.

726 Coastal-style Mailboxes in Autumn

2000. Traditional Rural Mailboxes. Multicoloured.
1989 46c. Type **726** 75 75
1990 46c. House and cow-shaped mailboxes in springtime . . 75 75
1991 46c. Tractor-shaped mailbox in summertime 75 75
1992 46c. Barn and duck-shaped mailboxes in winter . . . 75 75

727 Gorge and Fir Tree

2000. Canadian Rivers and Lakes. Multicoloured. Self-adhesive.
1993 55c. Type **727** 60 65
1994 55c. Lake and water lilies 60 65
1995 55c. Glacier and reflected mountains 60 65
1996 55c. Estuary and aerial view 60 65
1997 55c. Waterfall and forest edge 60 65
1998 95c. Iceberg and mountain river . . . . 95 1·10
1999 95c. Rapids and waterfall 95 1·10
2000 95c. Moraine and river . . . 95 1·10
2001 95c. Shallows and waves on lake . . . . 95 1·10
2002 95c. Forest sloping to waters edge and tree . . . . . . 95 1·10

728 Queen Elizabeth the Queen Mother with Roses
729 Teenager with Two Children

2000. Queen Elizabeth the Queen Mother's 100th Birthday.
2003 **728** 95c. multicoloured . . . 1·40 1·40

2000. Centenary of Boys and Girls Clubs of Canada.
2004 **729** 46c. multicoloured . . . 50 50

730 Clouds over Rockies and Symbol

2000. 57th General Conference Session of Seventh-day Adventist Church, Toronto.
2005 **730** 46c. multicoloured . . . 50 50

731 "Space Travellers and Canadian Flag" (Rosalie Anne Nardelli)

2000. "Stampin' the Future" (children's stamp design competition). Multicoloured.
2006 46c. Type **731** 60 60
2007 46c. "Travelling to the Moon" (Sarah Lutgen) . . 60 60
2008 46c. "Astronauts in shuttle" (Andrew Wright) 60 60
2009 46c. "Children completing Canada as jigsaw" (Christine Weera) 60 60
MS2010 114 × 90 mm. Nos. 2006/9 1·90 2·25

2000. Canadian Art (13th series). As T **550**. Mult.
2011 95c. "The Artist at Niagara, 1858" (Cornelius Krieghoff) . . . . 1·25 1·40

732 Tall Ships, Halifax Harbour

2000. Tall Ships Race. Multicoloured. Self-adhesive.
2012 46c. Type **732** 75 85
2013 46c. Tall ships, Halifax Harbour (face value top right) 75 85
Nos. 2012/13 are arranged as five se-tenant pairs on a background photograph of Halifax Harbour.

733 Workers, Factory and Transport

2000. Centenary of Department of Labour.
2014 **733** 46c. multicoloured . . . 50 50

734 Petro-Canada Sign, Oil Rig and Consumers

2000. 25th Anniv of Petro-Canada (oil company). Self-adhesive.
2015 **734** 46c. multicoloured . . . 75 50

735 Narwhal

2000. Whales. Multicoloured.
2016 46c. Type **735** . . . . . . 1·00 1·00
2017 46c. Blue whale (*Balaenoptera musculus*) 1·00 1·00
2018 46c. Bowhead whale (*Balaena mysticetus*) . . . 1·00 1·00
2019 46c. White whales (*Delphinapterus leucas*) . . 1·00 1·00
Nos. 2016/19 were printed together, se-tenant, with the backgrounds forming an overall composite design.

736

2000. "Picture Postage" Christmas Greetings. Self-adhesive.
2020 **736** 46c. multicoloured . . . 50 50
See also Nos. 2045/9 and 2099/103.

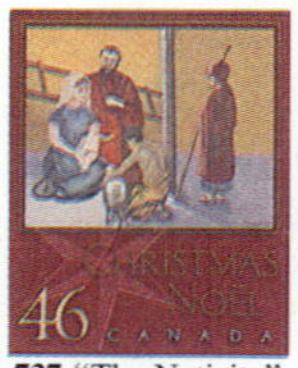

737 "The Nativity" (Susie Matthias)

738 Lieut.-Col. Sam Steele, Lord Strathcona's Horse

2000. Christmas. Religious Paintings by Mouth and Foot Artists. Multicoloured.
2021 46c. Type **737** 50 20
2022 55c. "The Nativity and Christmas Star" (Michael Guillemette) 65 60
2023 95c. "Mary and Joseph journeying to Bethlehem" (David Allan Carter) . . 1·25 1·90

2000. Canadian Regiments. Multicoloured.
2024 46c. Type **738** 75 75
2025 46c. Drummer, Voltigeurs de Quebec 75 75

739 Red Fox

740 Maple Leaves

740a Maple Leaves and Key

740b Red Maple Leaf and Stem

2000. Wildlife. Multicoloured.
2026 60c. Type **739** 65 70
2027 75c. Grey wolf 80 95
2028 $1.05 White-tailed deer . . . 1·10 1·25

2000. Self-adhesive coil stamp.
2029 **740** 47c. multicoloured . . . 1·00 1·00
2030 48c. multicoloured . . . 80 80
2031 **740a** 49c. multicoloured . . . 70 70
2032 **740b** 80c. multicoloured . . . 1·10 1·10
2036 $1.40 multicoloured (green leaf) . . . . . 1·90 1·90

2000. "Picture Postage" Greetings Stamps. As T **725** and **736**. Multicoloured. Self-adhesive.
2045 47c. Type **725** 55 55
2046 47c. Type **736** 55 55
2047 47c. Roses frame 55 55
2048 47c. Mahogany frame . . . 55 55
2049 47c. Silver frame 55 55

741 Green Jade Snake

2001. Chinese New Year. ("Year of the Snake").
2050 **741** 47c. multicoloured . . . 50 50
MS2051 112 × 75 mm. $1.05, Brown jade snake . . . . 1·25 1·60

2001. National Hockey League. All-Star Game Players (2nd series). As T **722**. Multicoloured.
2052 47c. Jean Beliveau (wearing No. 4) 75 75
2053 47c. Terry Sawchuk (on one knee) 75 75
2054 47c. Eddie Shore (wearing No. 2) 75 75
2055 47c. Denis Potvin (wearing No. 5) 75 75
2056 47c. Bobby Hull (wearing No. 9) 75 75
2057 47c. Syl Apps (in Toronto jersey) 75 75
See also Nos. 2118/23 and 2178/83.

2001. Birds (6th series). As T **643**. Multicoloured. Ordinary or self-adhesive gum.
2058 47c. Golden eagle 75 75
2059 47c. Arctic tern 75 75
2060 47c. Rock ptarmigan . . . 75 75
2061 47c. Lapland bunting ("Lapland Longspur") . . 75 75

742 Highjumping

2001. 4th Francophonie Games. Multicoloured.
2066 47c. Type **742** 70 70
2067 47c. Folk dancing 70 70

743 Ice Dancing

2001. World Figure Skating Championships, Vancouver. Multicoloured.
2068 47c. Type **743** 80 80
2069 47c. Pairs 80 80
2070 47c. Men's singles 80 80
2071 47c. Women's singles . . . 80 80

744 3d. Beaver Stamp of 1851

2001. 150th Anniv of the Canadian Postal Service.
2072 **744** 47c. multicoloured . . . 70 50

745 Toronto Blue Jay Emblem, Maple Leaf and Baseball

2001. 25th Season of the Toronto Blue Jays (baseball team). Self-adhesive.
2073 **745** 47c. multicoloured . . . 60 50

746 North and South America on Globe

748 Christ on Palm Sunday and Khachkar (stone cross)

747 Butchart Gardens, British Columbia

2001. Summit of the Americas, Quebec.
2074 **746** 47c. multicoloured . . . 1·00 50

2001. Tourist Attractions (1st series). Multicoloured. Self-adhesive.
2075 60c. Type **747** 70 75
2076 60c. Apple Blossom Festival, Nova Scotia 70 75
2077 60c. White Pass and Yukon Route 70 75
2078 60c. Sugar Bushes, Quebec 70 75
2079 60c. Court House, Niagra-on-the-Lake, Ontario . . 70 75
2080 $1.05 The Forks, Winnipeg, Manitoba . . . . 1·25 1·40
2081 $1.05 Barkerville, British Colombia . . . . 1·25 1·40
2082 $1.05 Canadian Tulip Festival, Ontario . . . . 1·25 1·40
2083 $1.05 Auyuittuq National Park, Nunavut . . . . . 1·25 1·40
2084 $1.05 Signal Hill, St. John's, Newfoundland . . . . . 1·25 1·40
See also Nos. 2143/52, 2205/14 and 2257/61.

2001. 1700th Anniv of Armenian Church.
2085 **748** 47c. multicoloured . . . 60 45

749 Cadets, Mackenzie Building and Military Equipment

2001. 125th Anniv of Royal Military College of Canada.
2086 **749** 47c. multicoloured . . . 70 45

750 Pole-vaulting

751 "Pierre Trudeau" (Myfanwy Pavelic)

2001. 8th International Amateur Athletic Federation World Championships, Edmonton. Multicoloured.
2087 47c. Type **750** 65 65
2088 47c. Sprinting 65 65

2001. Pierre Trudeau (former Prime Minister) Commemoration.
2089 **751** 47c. multicoloured . . . 60 45
MS2090 128 × 155 mm. No. 2090 × 4 2·00 2·25

752 "Morden Centennial" Rose (⅔-size illustration)

2001. Canadian Roses. Multicoloured. Self-adhesive.
2091 47c. Type **752** 75 75
2092 47c. "Agnes" 75 75
2093 47c. "Champlain" 75 75
2094 47c. "Canadian White Star" 75 75
MS2095 145 × 90 mm. Nos. 2091/4 2·75 3·00

753 Ottawa Chief Hassaki addressing Peace Delegates

2001. 300th Anniv of Great Peace Treaty of Montreal between American Indians and New France.
2096 **753** 47c. multicoloured . . . 60 45

2001. Canadian Art (14th series). As T **550**. Multicoloured.
2097 $1.05 "The Space Between Columns 21 (Italian)" (Jack Shadbolt) . . . . . 1·40 1·60

754 Clown juggling with Crutches and Handicapped Boy

2001. The Shriners (charitable organization) Commemoration.
2098 **754** 47c. multicoloured . . . 60 45

755 Toys and Flowers

2001. "Picture Postage" Greetings Stamps. Frames as Nos. 2045/7 and 2049, but each inscr "Domestic Lettermail Postes-lettres du regime interieur". Multicoloured. Self-adhesive.
2099 As Type **725** 60 60
2100 As Type **736** 60 60
2101 Type **755** 60 60
2102 Roses frame 60 60
2103 Silver frame 60 60

756 Jean Gascon and Jean-Louis Roux (founders of Theatre du Nouveau Monde, Montreal)

2001. Theatre Anniversaries. Multicoloured.
2104 47c. Type **756** (50th anniv) 65 65
2105 47c. Ambrose Small (founder of Grand Theatre, London, Ontario) (centenary) . . . 65 65

757 Hot Air Balloons

2001. Stamp Collecting Month. Hot Air Balloons. Multicoloured, background colours given below. Self-adhesive.
2106 47c. Type **757** (green background) 80 80
2107 47c. Balloons with lavender background 80 80
2108 47c. Balloons with mauve background 80 80
2109 47c. Balloons with bistre background 80 80

758 Horse-drawn Sleigh and Christmas Lights

2001. Christmas. Festive Lights. Multicoloured.
2110 47c. Type **758** 70 20
2111 60c. Ice skaters and Christmas lights . . . . . 1·00 1·00
2112 $1.05 Children with snowman and Christmas lights . . . . 1·40 1·90

759 Pattern of Ys Logo

2001. 150th Anniv of YMCA in Canada.
2113 **759** 47c. multicoloured . . . 60 45

760 Statues from Canadian War Memorial, Ottawa and Badge

2001. 75th Anniv of Royal Canadian Legion.
2114 **760** 47c. multicoloured . . . 70 45

761 Queen Elizabeth II and Maple Leaf

2002. Golden Jubilee.
2115 **761** 48c. multicoloured . . . 70 45

762 Horse and Bamboo Leaves **763** Speed Skating

2002. Chinese New Year ("Year of the Horse"). Multicoloured.
2116 **762** 48c. multicoloured . . . 60 45
MS2117 102 × 102 mm. $1.25, Horse and peach blossom . . . . . 1·40 1·60

2002. National Hockey League. All-Star Game Players (3rd series). As T **722**. Multicoloured.
2118 48c. Tim Horton (wearing Maple Leaf No. 7 jersey) 75 75
2119 48c. Guy Lafleur (wearing Canadiens No. 10 jersey) 75 75
2120 48c. Howie Morenz (wearing Canadiens jersey and brown gloves) 75 75
2121 48c. Glenn Hall (wearing Chicago Blackhawks jersey) 75 75
2122 48c. Red Kelly (wearing Maple Leaf No. 4 jersey) 75 75
2123 48c. Phil Esposito (wearing Boston Bruins No. 7 jersey) 75 75

2002. Winter Olympic Games, Salt Lake City. Multicoloured.
2124 48c. Type **763** 75 75
2125 48c. Curling 75 75
2126 48c. Aerial skiing 75 75
2127 48c. Women's ice hockey . . 75 75

764 Lion Symbol of Governor General and Rideau Hall, Ottawa

2002. 50th Anniv of First Canadian Governor-General.
2128 **764** 48c. multicoloured . . . 60 45

765 University of Manitoba (125th Anniv)

2002. Canadian Universities' Anniversaries (1st issue). Multicoloured.
2129 48c. Type **765** 75 75
2130 48c. Universite Laval, Quebec (150th anniv of charter) 75 75
2131 48c. Trinity College, Toronto (150th anniv of foundation) 75 75
2132 48c. Saint Mary's University, Halifax (bicent) 75 75
See also Nos. 2190/1, 2271/2, 2333/7, 2419, 2487 and 2544/5.

2002. Canadian Art (15th series). As T **550**. Multicoloured.
2133 $1.25 "Church and Horse" (Alex Colville) . . . . . 1·40 1·60

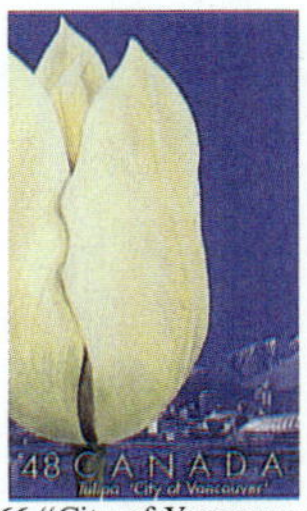

766 "City of Vancouver" Tulip and Vancouver Skyline

2002. 50th Canadian Tulip Festival, Ottawa. Tulips. Multicoloured. Self-adhesive.
2134 48c. Type **766** 70 75
2135 48c. "Monte Carlo" and Dows Lake tulip beds . . 70 75
2136 48c. "Ottawa" and National War Memorial 70 75
2137 48c. "The Bishop" and Ottawa Hospital 70 75

767 *Dendronepthea gigantea* and *Dendronepthea* (coral)

2002. Canada–Hong Kong Joint Issue. Corals. Multicoloured.
2138 48c. Type **767** 70 75
2139 48c. *Tubastrea*, *Echinogorgia* and island 70 75
2140 48c. North Atlantic pink tree coral, Pacific orange cup and North Pacific horn coral 70 75
2141 48c. North Atlantic giant orange tree coral and black coral 70 75
MS2142 161 × 87 mm. Nos. 2138/41 2·25 2·50

2002. Tourist Attractions (2nd series). As T **747**. Multicoloured. Self-adhesive.
2143 65c. Yukon Quest Sled Dog Race 85 90
2144 65c. Icefields Parkway, Alberta 85 90
2145 65c. Train in Agawa Canyon, Northern Ontario 85 90
2146 65c. Old Port, Montreal . . 85 90
2147 65c. Saw mill, Kings Landing, New Brunswick 85 90
2148 $1.25 Northern Lights, Northwest Territories . . 1·40 1·60
2149 $1.25 Stanley Park, British Columbia . . . . . . 1·40 1·60
2150 $1.25 Head-Smashed-In Buffalo Jump, Alberta . . 1·40 1·60
2151 $1.25 Saguenay Fjord, Quebec . . . . 1·40 1·60
2152 $1.25 Lighthouse, Peggy's Cove, Nova Scotia . . . 1·40 1·60

768 "Embacle" (Charles Daudelin)

2002. Sculptures. Multicoloured.
2153 48c. Type **768** 60 65
2154 48c. "Lumberjacks" (Leo Mol) 60 65

769 1899 Queen Victoria 2c. Stamp, Stonewall Post Office and Postmark

2002. Centenary of Canadian Postmasters and Assistants Association.
2155 **769** 48c. multicoloured . . . 60 45

770 World Youth Day Logo

2002. 17th World Youth Day, Toronto. Self-adhesive.
2156 **770** 48c. multicoloured . . . 60 45

2002. "Amphilex 2002" International Stamp Exhibition, Amsterdam. Ordinary gum.
MS2157 160 × 97 mm. As Nos. 2134/7 . . . . 2·25 2·50

771 Hands gripping Rope and P.S.I. Logo

2002. Public Services International World Congress, Ottawa.
2158 **771** 48c. multicoloured . . . 60 45

772 Tree in Four Seasons

2002. 75th Anniv of Public Pensions.
2159 **772** 48c. multicoloured . . . 60 45

773 Mount Elbrus, Russia

2002. International Year of Mountains. Multicoloured. Self-adhesive.
2160 48c. Type **773** 70 70
2161 48c. Puncak Jaya, Indonesia 70 70
2162 48c. Mount Everest, Nepal 70 70
2163 48c. Mount Kilimanjaro, Tanzania 70 70
2164 48c. Vinson Massif, Antarctica 70 70
2165 48c. Mount Aconcagua, Argentina 70 70
2166 48c. Mount McKinley, U.S.A. 70 70
2167 48c. Mount Logan, Canada 70 70

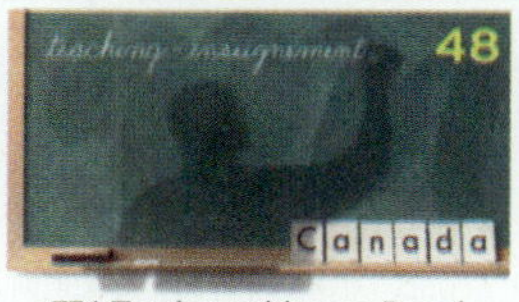

774 Teacher writing on Board

2002. World Teachers' Day.
2168 **774** 48c. multicoloured . . . 60 45

775 Frieze from Toronto Stock Exchange and Globe

2002. 150th Anniv of Toronto Stock Exchange.
2169 **775** 48c. multicoloured . . . 60 45

776 Sir Sandford Fleming, Map of Canada and *Iris* (cable ship)

2002. Communications Centenaries. Multicoloured.
2170 48c. Type **776** (opening of Pacific Cable) 65 65
2171 48c. Guglielmo Marconi, Map of Canada and wireless equipment (first Transatlantic radio message) 65 65

777 "Genesis" (painting by Daphne Odjig)

2002. Christmas. Aboriginal Art. Multicoloured.
2172 48c. Type **777** 55 20
2173 65c. "Winter Travel" (painting by Cecil Youngfox) 70 70
2174 $1.25 "Mary and Child" (sculpture by Irene Katak Angutitaq) . . . . 1·25 1·50

778 Conductor's Hands and Original Orchestra

2002. Centenary of Quebec Symphony Orchestra.
2175 **778** 48c. multicoloured . . . 1·00 45

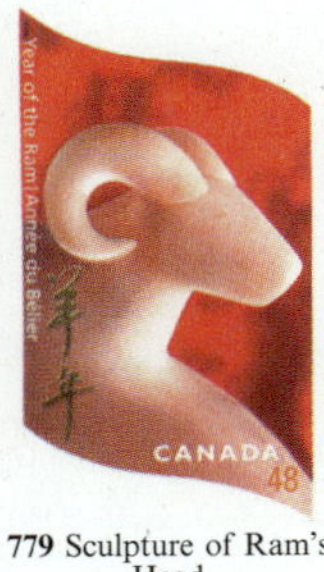

779 Sculpture of Ram's Head

2003. Chinese New Year ("Year of the Ram"). Multicoloured.
2176 48c. Type **779** 60 45
MS2177 125 × 103 mm. $1.25 Sculpture of goat's head (33 × 57 mm) . . . . 1·25 1·50

2003. National Hockey League. All-Star Game Players (4th series). As T **722**. Multicoloured. Ordinary or self-adhesive.
2178 48c. Frank Mahovlich (wearing Maple Leaf No. 27 jersey) 70 75
2179 48c. Raymond Bourque (wearing Boston Bruins No. 77 jersey) 70 75
2180 48c. Serge Savard (wearing Canadiens No. 18 jersey) 70 75
2181 48c. Stan Mikita (wearing Chicago Blackhawks No. 21 jersey) 70 75
2182 48c. Mike Bossy (wearing New York Islanders No. 22 jersey) 70 75
2183 48c. Bill Durnan (wearing Canadiens jersey and brown gloves) 70 75

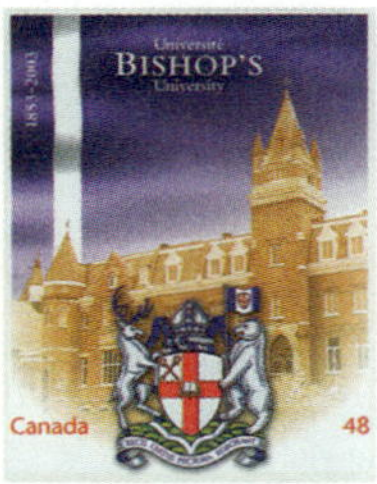

779a Bishop's University, Quebec (150th anniv of university status)

2003. Canadian Universities' Anniversaries (2nd issue). Multicoloured.
2190 48c. Bishop's University, Quebec (150th anniv of university status) 65 65
2191 48c. University of Western Ontario, London (125th anniv) 65 65
2192 48c. St. Francis Xavier University, Nova Scotia (150th Anniv) 65 65
2193 48c. Macdonald Institute, University of Guelph, Ontana (centenary) . . . 65 65
2194 48c. Universite de Montreal (125th anniv) 65 65

780 Leach's Storm Petrel

2003. Bird Paintings by John Audubon (1st series). Multicoloured. Ordinary gum.
2195 48c. Type **780** 85 85
2196 48c. Brent goose ("Brant") 85 85
2197 48c. Great cormorant . . . 85 85
2198 48c. Common murre 85 85

(b) Self-adhesive.
2199 65c. Gyrfalcon (vert) . . . . 1·60 1·75
See also Nos. 2274/8 and 2340/4.

781 Ranger looking through Binoculars

2003. 60th Anniv of Canadian Rangers.
2200 **781** 48c. multicoloured . . . 70 45

782 Greek Figure with Dove

2003. 75th Anniv of American Hellenic Educational Progressive Association in Canada.
2201 **782** 48c. multicoloured . . . 70 45

783 Firefighter carrying Boy and Burning Buildings

2003. Volunteer Firefighters.
2202 **783** 48c. multicoloured . . . 1·00 65

784 Queen Elizabeth II

2003. 50th Anniv of Coronation.
2203 **784** 48c. multicoloured . . . 70 55

785 Quebec City (c. 1703) Seal and Excerpt from Letter

2003. Pedro da Silva (first official courier of New France).
2204 **785** 48c. multicoloured . . . 70 55

2003. Tourist Attractions (3rd series). As T **747**. Multicoloured. Self-adhesive.
2205 65c. Wilberforce Falls, Nunavut . . . . 95 1·10
2206 65c. Inside Passage, British Columbia . . . . 95 1·10
2207 65c. Royal Canadian Mounted Police Depot Division, Regina, Saskatchewan . . . . . . 95 1·10
2208 65c. Casa Loma, Toronto 95 1·10
2209 65c. Gatineau Park, Quebec 95 1·10
2210 $1.25 Dragon boat race, Vancouver . . . . 1·75 1·90
2211 $1.25 Polar bear, Churchill, Manitoba . . . . 1·75 1·90
2212 $1.25 Niagara Falls, Ontario 1·75 1·90
2213 $1.25 Magdalen Islands, Quebec . . . . 1·75 1·90
2214 $1.25 Province House, Charlottetown, Prince Edward Island . . . . . 1·75 1·90

2003. Vancouver's Successful Bid for Winter Olympic Games, 2010. No. 1368 (Canadian flag definitive) optd **VANCOUVER 2010**.
2215 48c. multicoloured 80 65

787 Mountains and Sea

2003. Canada–Alaska Cruise "Picture Postage". Multicoloured. Self-adhesive.
2216 (–) Type **787** . . . . . . 3·00 3·25
2217 (–) Tail fin of whale, mountains and sea . . . 3·00 3·25

788 Assembly Logo

2003. 10th Lutheran World Federation Assembly, Winnipeg.
2218 **788** 48c. multicoloured . . . 70 55

789 Canadian F-86 Sabre Fighter Plane, Sailors and Infantrymen

2003. 50th Anniv of Signing of Korea Armistice.
2219 **789** 48c. multicoloured . . . 70 55

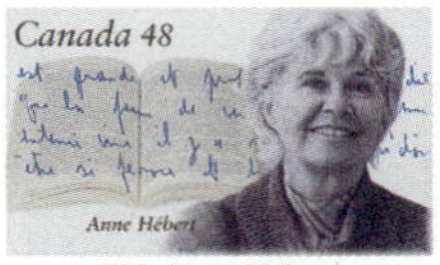

790 Anne Hebert

2003. 50th Anniv of National Library of Canada. Showing authors and portions of their handwritten text. Multicoloured.
2220 48c. Type **790** 80 85
2221 48c. Hector de Saint-Denys Garneau 80 85
2222 48c. Morley Callaghan . . . 80 85
2223 48c. Susanna Moodie and Catharine Parr Traill . . 80 85

791 Cyclists in Road Race

2003. World Road Cycling Championships, Hamilton, Ontario.
2224 **791** 48c. multicoloured . . . 1·00 70

792 Marc Garneau

2003. Stamp Collecting Month. Canadian Astronauts. Multicoloured. Self-adhesive.
2225 48c. Type **792** 85 85
2226 48c. Roberta Bondar . . . 85 85
2227 48c. Steve MacLean 85 85
2228 48c. Chris Hadfield 85 85
2229 48c. Robert Thirsk 85 85
2230 48c. Bjarni Tryggvason . . 85 85
2231 48c. Dave Williams 85 85
2232 48c. Julie Payette 85 85

793 Maple Leaves, Canada

795 Ice Skates and Wrapped Presents

794 White Birds

2003. National Emblems. Multicoloured.
2233 48c. Type **793** 70 70
2234 48c. Cassis fistula flowers, Thailand 70 70
MS2235 120 × 96 mm. Nos. 2233/4 1·40 1·40
No. **MS**2235 commemorates Bangkok 2003 International Stamp Exhibition, Thailand.

Stamps of the same designs were issued by Thailand.

2003. 80th Birth Anniv of Jean-Paul Riopelle (painter and sculptor). T **794** and similar horiz designs showing details from fresco "L'Hommage a Rosa Luxemburg". Multicoloured.
MS2236 178 × 244 mm. 48c. Type **794**; 48c. Two white herons and white birds; 48c. Flying bird, flower and three white birds in cameo; 48c. Grouse on moor, white bird and sun; 48c. Two flying white birds in cameo and silhouette of falcon; 48c. Two white birds and cameo of flying duck . . . . 3·50 4·00
MS2237 159 × 95 mm. $1.25 Eggs and bird silhouette . . . . . . 2·00 2·25

2003. Christmas. Multicoloured.
2238 48c. Type **795** 70 55
2239 65c. Teddy bear and wrapped presents . . . . 1·25 1·10
2240 $1.25 Toy duck on wheels and wrapped presents . . 1·90 2·25

796 Queen Elizabeth II, 2002

797 Monkey King on Cloud

2003. Self-adhesive.
2241 **796** 49c. black, mauve and scarlet 70 70
2242 50c. multicoloured . . . 70 70

2004. Chinese New Year ("Year of the Monkey"). Showing scenes from "Journey to the West" by Wu Ch'eng-en. Multicoloured.
2247 49c. Type **797** 70 70
MS2248 115 × 82 mm. $1.40 Monkey on road to India . . . 1·90 1·90

2004. Hong Kong 2004 International Stamp Exhibition. No. **MS**2248 optd **Hong Kong Stamp Expo 2004** and exhibition emblem in gold on sheet margin.
MS2249 115 × 82 mm. $1.40 Monkey on road to India . . . 1·90 1·90

2004. National Hockey League. All-Star Players (5th series). As T **722**. Multicoloured. Ordinary or self-adhesive gum.
2250 49c. Larry Robinson (wearing Canadiens jersey) 1·00 1·00
2251 49c. Marcel Dionne (wearing Los Angeles Kings jersey) . . . . . . 1·00 1·00
2252 49c. Ted Lindsay (wearing Detroit Red Wings jersey) 1·00 1·00
2253 49c. Johnny Bower (wearing Toronto Maple Leafs goal keeper kit) . . . . 1·00 1·00
2254 49c. Brad Park (wearing New York Rangers jersey) 1·00 1·00
2255 49c. Milt Schmidt (wearing Boston Bruins jersey) . . 1·00 1·00

798 Bonhomme (Snowman), Quebec Winter Carnival

2004. Tourist Attractions (4th series). Multicoloured. Self-adhesive. Imperf.
2257 49c. Type **798** . . . . . . 1·00 1·00
2258 49c. St. Joseph's Oratory . . 1·00 1·00
2259 49c. Audience at International Jazz Festival, Montreal . . . . 1·00 1·00
2260 49c. People watching Traversee Internationale du Lac St-Jean . . . . . 1·00 1·00
2261 49c. People at Canadian National Exhibition and Prince's Gate . . . . . . 1·00 1·00

799 Governor General Ramon Hnatyshyn

800 *Fram* (polar research ship)

2004. 70th Birth Anniv of Governor General Ramon Hnatyshyn.
2262 **799** 49c. multicoloured . . . 70 70

2004. 150th Birth Anniv of Otto Sverdrup (polar explorer). Each purple and buff.
2263 49c. Type **800** . . . . . . 1·00 70
MS2264 166 × 60 mm. $1.40 As No. 2263 plus two labels . . . 1·90 1·90
Stamps of similar designs were issued by Greenland and Norway.

801 Silhouettes of Cadets

2004. 125th Anniv of Royal Canadian Army Cadets. Self-adhesive. Imperf.
2265 **801** 49c. multicoloured . . . 1·00 70

802 Subway Train, Toronto

2004. Light Rail Urban Transit. Multicoloured.
2266 49c. Type **802** . . . . . . 1·00 1·00
2267 49c. TransLink SkyTrain, Vancouver . . . . 1·00 1·00
2268 49c. Metro train, Montreal 1·00 1·00
2269 49c. CTrain, Calgary . . . 1·00 1·00

803 Canadian Map and Employee

2004. 40th Anniv of Home Hardware (co-operative business). Self-adhesive.
2270 **803** 49c. multicoloured . . . 65 65

2004. Canadian Universities Anniversaries (3rd series). As T **779a**. Multicoloured.
2271 49c. University of Sherbrooke (50th anniv) 70 70
2272 49c. University of Prince Edward Island (bicent) . . 70 70

804 Teddy Bears

2004. Centenary of Montreal Children's Hospital. Self-adhesive.
2273 **804** 49c. multicoloured . . . 85 70

805 Ruby-crowned kinglet

2004. Bird Paintings by John Audubon (2nd series). Multicoloured. (a) Ordinary gum.
2274 49c. Type **805** 85 85
2275 49c. White-winged crossbill 85 85
2276 49c. Bohemian waxwing . . 85 85
2277 49c. Boreal chickadee . . 85 85

(b) Self-adhesive. Imperf.
2278 80c. Lincoln's sparrow . . . 1·40 1·50

806 Sir Samuel Cunard

2004. Sir Samuel Cunard and Sir Hugh Allan (founders of transatlantic mail service) Commemorations. Multicoloured. Self-adhesive.
2279 49c. Type **806** 80 80
2280 49c. Sir Hugh Allan 80 80
Nos. 2279/80 were printed together, se-tenant, forming a composite design.

806a Butterfly on Flower

2004. "Write me...Ring me" Greetings Stamps. Multicoloured.
2280a Type **806a** 60 60
2280b Two young children at beach 60 60
2280c Red rose 60 60
2280d Pug (dog) 60 60
Nos. 2280a/d are inscribed "Domestic Lettermail" (initial value was 49c.).

807 Soldiers storming Juno Beach, Normandy

2004. 60th Anniv of D-Day Landings.
2281 **807** 49c. multicoloured . . . 1·00 80

808 Pierre Dugua de Mons

2004. 400th Anniv of First French Settlement in Acadia, St. Croix Island (1st issue).
2282 **808** 49c. ochre, blue and orange 80 70
See also No. 2361, 2400 and 2508.

809 Spyros Louis (Greek athlete) and Marathon Runner

2004. Olympic Games, Athens, Greece. Multicoloured.
2283 49c. Type **809** 95 95
2284 49c. Girls playing football 95 95

810 Golfer and Trophy from Early Tournament

2004. Canadian Open Golf Championship. Multicoloured. Self-adhesive.
2285 49c. Type **810** . . . . . . 1·00 90
2286 49c. Golfer and trophy from modern tournament . . . 1·00 90

811 Segmented Heart

2004. 50th Anniv of Montreal Heart Institute. Self-adhesive.
2287 **811** 49c. multicoloured . . . 80 70

812 Goldfish in Bowl

2004. Pets. Multicoloured. Self-adhesive. Imperf.
2288 49c. Type **812** . . . . . . 1·00 1·00
2289 49c. Two cats on chair . . . 1·00 1·00
2290 49c. Child with rabbit . . . 1·00 1·00
2291 49c. Child with dog . . . . 1·00 1·00

813 Gerhard Herzberg (Chemistry, 1971)

2004. Nobel Chemistry Prize Winners. Mult.
2292 49c. Type **813** 90 90
2293 49c. Michael Smith (Chemistry, 1993) 90 90

814 Maple Leaf in Photo Album Frame

2004. Picture Postage. Multicoloured. Self-adhesive.
2294 (49c.) Type **814** 90 90
2295 (49c.) Maple leaf in silver frame 90 90
Nos. 2294/2295 were both inscribed "Domestic Postage Paid" and sold for 49c.

815 Victoria Cross (embossed)

2004. 150th Anniv of First Canadian Recipient of the Victoria Cross. Multicoloured.
2296 49c. Type **815** . . . . . . 1·10 1·10
2297 49c. Victoria Cross and signature of Queen Elizabeth II . . . . . . 1·10 1·10
Nos. 2296/7 were printed together as sheetlets of 16 around a central illustration and the names of 94 Canadians who have received the Victoria Cross.

816 "Self-portrait", 1974

2004. "Art Canada". Birth Centenary of Jean Paul Lemieux (artist). Multicoloured.
2298 49c. Type **816** . . . . . . 1·00 85
MS2299 150 × 86 mm. 49c. Type **815**; 80c. "A June Wedding", 1972 (53 × 34 mm); $1.40 "Summer", 1959 (64 × 31 mm) 4·50 4·50

817 Santa in his Sleigh and Reindeer

2004. Christmas. Multicoloured. Self-adhesive.
2300 49c. Type **817** 90 45
2301 80c. Santa sitting in a Cadillac and towing a house . . . . 1·60 1·60
2302 $1.40 Santa driving a train 2·50 2·75

818 Red Calla Lily

819 Rooster facing East (right)

2004. Flowers. Multicoloured. (1st series) Self-adhesive.
2303 50c. Type **818** 40 45
2304 51c. Red bergamot 40 45
2305 85c. Yellow calla lily . . . 70 75
2306 89c. Lady's slipper orchids 75 80
2307 $1.05 Pink fairy slipper orchids . . . . 1·30 1·40
2308 $1.45 purple Dutch iris . . 1·20 1·30
2309 $1.49 Himalayan blue poppies . . . . 1·40 1·50
Nos. 2305/9 come imperf.
See also Nos. 2470/**MS**2477 and 2530/**MS**2537.

2005. Chinese New Year ("Year of the Rooster"). 35th Anniv of Diplomatic Relations with China (**MS**2315b). T **819** and similar multicoloured designs.
2314 50c. Type **819** 60 45
MS2315 Two sheets, each 105 × 82 mm. (a) $1.45 Rooster facing west (left) (40 × 41 mm). (b) $1.45 As No. **MS**2315a. . . . 2·20 2·20
Nos. **MS**2315a/b both have a barcode tab attached at foot.

2004. National Hockey League. All-Star Game Players (6th series). As T **722**. Multicoloured. Ordinary or self-adhesive gum.
2316 50c. Henri Richard (wearing Habs jersey) 70 70
2317 50c. Grant Fuhr (wearing Oilers goal keeper kit) . . 70 70
2318 50c. Allan Stanley (wearing Toronto Maple Leafs jersey) 70 70
2319 50c. Pierre Pilote (wearing Chicago Black Hawks jersey) 70 70
2320 50c. Bryan Trottier (wearing New York Islanders jersey) 70 70
2321 50c. John Bucyk (wearing Boston Bruins jersey) . . 70 70

820 Alevin Fishing Fly

2005. Fishing Flies. Multicoloured. (a) Ordinary gum.
MS2328 190 × 112 mm. 50c. × 4 Type **820**; Jock Scott; P.E.I. Fly; Mickey Finn . . . . 2·25 2·50

(b) Self-adhesive.
2329 50c. Type **820** 60 65
2330 50c. Jock Scott 60 65
2331 50c. Mickey Finn 60 65
2332 50c. P.E.I. Fly 60 65

2005. Canadian Universities Anniversaries (4th series). As T **779a** (No. 2190). Multicoloured.
2333 50c. Nova Scotia Agricultural College . . . 70 50

821 Inukshuk of Five Rocks

822 Yellow Daffodils

2005. Expo 2005 International Exhibition, Aichi, Japan.
2335 **821** 50c. multicoloured . . . 70 50

2005. Daffodils. Multicoloured. (a) Self-adhesive.
2336 50c. Type **822** 65 65
2337 50c. White daffodils with yellow trumpets 65 65

(b) Ordinary gum.
MS2338 120 × 80 mm. Nos. 2336/7 1·25 1·40

No. **MS**2338 also commemorates Pacific Explorer 2005 World Stamp Expo Exhibition, Sydney, Australia.

823 TD Bank Building of c.1900, Cashier and TD Tower, Toronto

2005. 150th Anniv of TD Bank Financial Group. Self-adhesive.
2339 **823** 50c. multicoloured . . . 60 50

824 Horned Lark

2005. Bird Paintings by John Audubon (3rd series). Multicoloured. (a) Ordinary gum.
2340 50c. Type **824** 65 70
2341 50c. Piping plover 65 70
2342 50c. Stilt sandpiper 65 70
2343 50c. Willow ptarmigan . . . 65 70

(b) Size 45 × 35 mm. Self-adhesive. Imperf.
2344 85c. Double-crested cormorant . . . . 1·10 1·25

825 Jacques Cartier Bridge, Montreal, Quebec

2005. Bridges. Multicoloured. Self-adhesive.
2345 50c. Type **825** 65 70
2346 50c. Souris Swinging Bridge, Manitoba 65 70
2347 50c. Angus L. Macdonald Bridge, Halifax, Nova Scotia 65 70
2348 50c. Canso Causeway, Nova Scotia 65 70

826 Magazine Covers of 1911, 1954, 1962 and 1917

2005. Centenary of *Maclean's* Magazine.
2349 **826** 50c. multicoloured . . . 60 50

827 Saskatoon Berries and Osprey, Waterton Lakes National Park, Alberta, Canada

2005. Biosphere Reserves. Multicoloured.
2350 50c. Type **827** 70 65
2351 50c. Red Deer stags, Killarney National Park, Ireland 70 65
MS2352 120 × 70 mm. Nos. 2350/1 1·40 1·40

Stamps in similar designs were issued by Ireland.

828 Sailor Lookout, Canadian Navy Corvette and Survivors in Lifeboat

2005. 60th Anniv of Battle of the Atlantic.
2353 **828** 50c. multicoloured . . . 60 50

829 Candle, Silhouettes, Memorial Cross GRV and New Museum Building

2005. Opening of New Canadian War Museum Building, Ottawa. Self-adhesive.
2354 **829** 50c. multicoloured . . . 60 50

830 "Down in the Laurentides"

2005. "Art Canada". 150th Birth Anniv of Homer Watson (artist). Paintings. Multicoloured.
2355 50c. Type **830** 60 50
MS2356 150 × 87 mm. 50c. Type **830**; 85c. "The Flood Gate" (53 × 39 mm) . . . . 1·10 1·20

No. **MS**2356 also commemorates the 125th anniversary of the National Gallery of Canada.

831 Volunteer with Search Dog, Crashed Aircraft and Satellite

832 Ellen Fairclough and Parliament Buildings, Ottawa

2005. Search and Rescue. Sheet 260 × 170 mm containing T **831** and similar vert designs. Multicoloured.
MS2357 50c. × 2 Type **831**; 50c. × 2 Rescuers, crew in life raft and sinking ship; 50c. × 2 Seaman winched into helicopter and float plane; 50c. × 2 Mountain rescue team with stretcher and satellite 4·50 4·50

2005. Birth Centenary of Ellen Fairclough (first woman federal cabinet minister).
2358 **832** 50c. multicoloured . . . 45 45

833 Diver spinning in mid-air

834 Port-Royal, 1605 (from drawing by Samuel de Champlain)

2005. 11th FINA (Federation Internationale de Natation) World Championships, Montreal. Multicoloured.
2359 50c. Type **833** 65 65
2360 50c. Swimmer in butterfly stroke 65 65

2005. French Settlement in North America (2nd issue). 400th Anniv of Founding of Port-Royal, Nova Scotia.
2361 **834** 50c. multicoloured . . . 60 50

835 Chemicals Plant, Calgary Skyline, Mount Grassi and Railway Line

2005. Centenary of Alberta Province. Self-adhesive.
2362 **835** 50c. multicoloured . . . 60 50

The backing paper is illustrated with four different scenes, each running across two stamps: Calgary Stampede; Jasper Avenue, Edmonton, 1963; Lake Minnewanka, Banff; and oil refinery of c. 1912.

836 Woman with Arms outstretched, Sunflowers and Legislature Building, Regina

2005. Centenary of Saskatchewan.
2363 **836** 50c. multicoloured . . . 60 50

837 1930 50c. Acadian Memorial Church Stamp and Acadian Flag

2005. 250th Anniv of Deportation of French Settlers from Acadia (Nova Scotia) to British Colonies of North America.
2364 **837** 50c. multicoloured . . . 60 50

838 Oscar Peterson

2005. 80th Birthday of Oscar Peterson (jazz composer and musician).
2365 **838** 50c. multicoloured . . . 60 50
MS2366 112 × 116 mm. No. 2365 × 4 2·40 2·00

839 Children playing and discarded Leg Braces

2005. 50th Anniv of Mass Polio Vaccination in Canada.
2367 **839** 50c. multicoloured . . . 60 50

840 Wall climbing

2005. Youth Sports. Multicoloured. Self-adhesive.
2368 50c. Type **840** 60 50
2369 50c. Skateboarding 60 50
2370 50c. Mountain biking . . . 60 50
2371 50c. Snowboarding 60 50

841 *Puma concolor* (cougar)

2005. 35th Anniv of Canada—China Diplomatic Relations. Carnivores. Multicoloured.
2372 50c. Type **841** 60 50
2373 50c. *Panthera pardus orientalis* (Amur leopard) 60 50
MS2374 108 × 58 mm. Nos. 2372/3 1·20 1·10

Stamps of the same design were issued by China (People's Republic).

842 Snowman

843 Creche by Michel Forest

2005. Christmas (1st issue). Self-adhesive.
2375 **842** 50c. multicoloured . . . 60 50

2005. Christmas (2nd issue). Showing Christmas creches. Multicoloured. Self-adhesive.
2376 50c. Type **843** 60 50
2377 85c. Creche with aboriginal figures by Keena (31 × 39 mm) . . . . . . 1·10 1·25
2378 $1.45 Creche by Sylvia Daoust (27 × 40 mm) . . 1·80 1·60

844 Chow

845 Queen Elizabeth II, Ottawa, 2002

2006. Chinese New Year ("Year of the Dog"). Multicoloured.
2379 51c. Type **844** 60 50
MS2380 129 × 106 mm. $1.49 Chow with puppy . . . . 1·80 1·60

2006. 80th Birthday of Queen Elizabeth II (1st issue). Self-adhesive.
2381 **845** 51c. multicoloured . . . 60 50

See also No. **MS**2392.

846 Team Pursuit Speed Skating

2006. Winter Olympic Games, Turin, Italy. Multicoloured.
2382 51c. Type **846** 60 50
2383 51c. Skeleton (sled) 60 50

847 Trilliums and Black-throated Blue Warbler (Shade Garden)

848 Balloons

2006. Gardens. Multicoloured. Self-adhesive.

2384	51c. Type **847**	60	50
2385	51c. Purple coneflowers and American painted lady butterfly (flower garden)	60	50
2386	51c. Water lilies and green darner dragonfly	60	50
2387	51c. Rock garden and blue-spotted salamander	60	50

2006. Greetings Stamp. Self-adhesive.

2388	**848**	51c. multicoloured	60	50

849 "The Field of Rapeseed"

2006. "Art Canada". Paintings by Dorothy Knowles. Multicoloured.

2389	51c. Type **849**	60	50
MS2390	150 × 87 mm. 51c. Type **849**; 89c. "North Saskatchewan River" (42 × 51 mm)	1·40	1·60

850 Hands enclosing Globe

851 Colophon emerging from Book

2006. 50th Anniv of Canadian Labour Congress.

2391	**850**	51c. multicoloured	60	50

2006. 80th Birthday of Queen Elizabeth II (2nd issue). Sheet 125 × 75 mm. Multicoloured.

MS2392	$1.49 × 2 As Type **845** but 39 × 31 mm	3·50	3·75

2006. Centenary of McClelland & Stewart (publishing house). Self-adhesive.

2393	**851**	51c. blue and silver	60	50

852 Mid 19th-Century Transformation Mask and Other Exhibits

2006. 150th Anniv of Canadian Museum of Civilization, Gatineau, Quebec. Self-adhesive.

2394	**852**	89c. multicoloured	1·25	1·40

853 Lorne Greene

2006. Canadians in Hollywood. Multicoloured.

(a) Self-adhesive.

2395	51c. Type **853**	60	50
2396	51c. Fay Wray	60	50
2397	51c. Mary Pickford	60	50
2398	51c. John Candy	60	50

(b) Ordinary gum.

MS2399	180 × 63 mm. As Nos. 2395/8	2·25	2·50

854 Champlain's Ship

2006. French Settlement in North America (3rd issue). 400th Anniv of Samuel de Champlain's Survey of East Coast of North America.

2400	51c. × 2 Type **854**	60	50
MS2401	204 × 146 mm. 51c. Type **854**; 39c. × 2, As Type **2879** of USA	1·00	1·25

No. **MS**2401 also commemorates Washington 2006 International Stamp Exhibition.

A self-adhesive stamp in the same design and an identical miniature sheet were also issued by the United States.

855 Girl watching Beluga Whale

2006. 50th Anniv of Vancouver Aquarium. Self-adhesive.

2402	**855**	51c. multicoloured	60	50

856 Pilot and Snowbirds

2006. 35th Anniv of Snowbirds Demonstration Team (431 Squadron). Multicoloured.

2403	51c. Type **856**	60	50
2404	51c. Snowbirds and emblem	60	50
MS2405	130 × 65 mm. Nos. 2403/4	1·10	1·25

857 James White (Chief Geographer), Proportional Dividers and Modern Map

2006. Centenary of "The Atlas of Canada".

2406	**857**	51c. multicoloured	60	50

858 Player and Event Tickets

2006. World Lacrosse Championships, London, Ontario. Self-adhesive.

2407	**858**	51c. multicoloured	60	50

859 Early and Modern Climbers

861 "g" as Beaver enclosing "50"

860 Barrow's Goldeneye

2006. Centenary of the Alpine Club of Canada. Self-adhesive.

2408	**859**	51c. multicoloured	60	50

2006. Duck Decoys. Multicoloured.

2409	51c. Type **860**	60	50
2410	51c. Mallard (decoy with white ring around neck)	60	50
2411	51c. Black duck (plain brown decoy)	60	50
2412	51c. Red-breasted merganser (black and white decoy with red bill)	60	50
MS2413	130 × 145 mm. Nos. 2409/12	2·25	2·50

2006. 50th Anniv of the Society of Graphic Designers of Canada.

2414	**861**	51c. multicoloured	60	50

862 Glasses of Wine

2006. Canadian Wine and Cheese. Multicoloured. Self-adhesive.

2415	51c. Type **862**	60	50
2416	51c. Wine taster (horiz as Type **862**)	60	50
2417	51c. Canadian cheeses (wedge-shaped, 36 × 38 mm)	60	50
2418	51c. Serving cheese platter at fromagerie (wedge-shaped, 36 × 38 mm)	60	50

2006. Canadian Universities Anniversaries (5th series). Vert design as T **779a** (No. 2190). Multicoloured.

2419	51c. Macdonald College, Sainte-Anne-de-Bellevue, Quebec (centenary)	60	50

863 Newfoundland Marten

2006. Endangered Species (1st series). Multicoloured.

(a) Self-adhesive.

2420	51c. Type **863**	60	50
2421	51c. Blotched tiger salamander	60	50
2422	51c. Blue racer	60	50
2423	51c. Swift fox	60	50

(b) Ordinary gum. Size 48 × 24 mm.

MS2424	160 × 74 mm. Nos. 2420/3	2·25	2·50

See also Nos. 2511/**MS**2515.

864 Maureen Forrester and Place des Arts, Montréal

2006. Canadian Opera Singers. Multicoloured.

2425	51c. Type **864**	60	50
2426	51c. Raoul Jobin and Palais Garnier, Paris	60	50
2427	51c. Leopold Simoneau, Pierrette Alarie and Opera-Comique, France	60	50
2428	51c. Jon Vickers and La Scala, Milan	60	50
2429	51c. Edward Johnson and Metropolitan Opera Company, New York	60	50

865 "Madonna and Child" (detail) (Antoine-Sebastien Falardeau)

866 "Snowman" (Yvonne McKague Housser)

2006. Christmas (1st issue). Self-adhesive.

2430	**865**	51c. multicoloured	60	50

2006. Christmas (2nd issue). Showing Christmas cards from 1931 "Painters of Canada" series. Multicoloured. Self-adhesive.

2431	51c. Type **866**	60	50
2432	89c. "Winter Joys" (J. E. Sampson)	1·10	70
2433	$1.49 "Contemplation" (Edwin Holgate)	1·75	2·00

867 Ice Fields and Fjord, Sirmilik National Park, Nunavut

868 Queen Elizabeth II, 2005

2006. Self-adhesive stamps inscr "P" instead of face value. Each showing Canadian flag. Multicoloured.

2434	(51c.) Type **867**	60	60
2435	(51c.) Coast and ancient trees, Chemainus, British Columbia	60	60
2436	(51c.) Polar bears, Churchill, Manitoba	60	60
2437	(51c.) Lighthouse at Bras d'Or Lake, Nova Scotia	60	60
2438	(51c.) Tuktut Nogait National Park, Northwest Territories	60	60
2439	(51c.) Sambra Island lighthouse, Nove Scotia	60	60
2440	(51c.) Point Clark lighthouse, Ontario	60	60
2441	(51c.) Cap-des-Rosiers lighthouse, Quebec	60	60
2442	(51c.) Warren Landing lighthouse, Manitoba	60	60
2443	(51c.) Pachena Point lighthouse, British Coloumbia	60	60

Nos. 2434/8 were inscribed "P" and initially sold for 51c. each and Nos. 2439/43 were inscribed 'P' and initially sold for 52c. each.

2006. Self-adhesive. Multicoloured.

2464	(51c.) Type **868**	60	60
2465	(52c.) Queen Elizabeth II, Saskatoon, 2005	60	60

No. 2464 was inscribed 'P' and initially sols for 51c., and No. 2465 was inscribed 'P' and initially sold for 52c.

869 Spotted coralroot

871 Ribbons and Confetti

870 Pig

2006. Flowers (2nd series). Multicoloured. Self-adhesive.

2470	**869**	(51c.) Spotted coralroot	60	15
2471		93c. Flat-leaved bladderwort	1·10	85
2472		$1.10 Marsh skullcap	1·25	1·25
2473		$1.55 Little larkspur	1·75	2·00

(b) Self-adhesive.

2474	93c. Flat-leaved bladderwort	1·10	1·00
2475	$1.10 Marsh skullcap	1·25	1·40
2476	$1.55 Little larkspur	1·75	2·00

(c) Ordinary gum.

MS2477	120 × 72 mm. As Nos. 2470/3	4·25	5·50

No. 2470 was inscribed "P" and initially sold for 51c. each.

2007. Chinese New Year ("Year of the Pig"). Multicoloured.
2478 52c. Type **870** 60 50
MS2479 98 × 97 mm. $1.55 Pig (running to right) . . . . . . 1·75 2·00
No. 2479 is cut in a lantern shape.

2007. Greetings Stamp. Self-adhesive.
2480 **871** 52c. multicoloured . . . 60 50

872 King Eider (*Somateria spectabilis*)

2007. International Polar Year. Multicoloured.
2481 52c. Type **872** 60 50
2482 52c. *Crossota millsaeare* (deep-sea jellyfish) 60 50
MS2483 105 × 70 mm. Nos. 2481/2 1·50 1·50

873 *Syringa vulgaris* "Princess Alexandra"

2007. Lilacs. Multicoloured. (a) Self-adhesive.
2484 52c. Type **873** 60 50
2485 52c. *Syringa × prestoniae* "Isabella" 60 50

(b) Ordinary gum.
MS2486 128 × 80 mm. As Nos. 2484/5 . . . . 1·25 1·10

2007. Canadian Universities' Anniversaries (6th issue). As T **779a** (No. 2190). Multicoloured. Self-adhesive.
2487 52c. HEC (Ecole des hautes etudes commerciales), Montreal (centenary) . . 60 50
2488 52c. University of Saskatchewan 60 50

874 "Jelly Shelf"

2007. "Art Canada". Paintings by Mary Pratt. Multicoloured.
2489 52c. Type **874** 60 50
MS2490 150 × 87 mm. 52c. Type **874**; $1.55 "Iceberg in the North Atlantic" (62 × 40 mm) 2·40 2·50

875 Parliament Buildings, Ottawa, 2007 and Lumberers Regatta, 1860

2007. 150th Anniv of Ottawa as Capital of Canada. Self-adhesive.
2491 **875** 52c. multicoloured . . . 1·00 85

(b) Ordinary gum.
MS2492 102 × 102 mm. 52c. As No. 2491; $1.55 As No. 2491 3·50 3·00

876 University of Lethbridge (Arthur Erickson), 1971

2007. Centenary of Royal Architectural Institute of Canada. Multicoloured.
2493 52c. Type **876** . . . . . . 1·00 85
2494 52c. St. Mary's Church (Douglas Cardinal), 1969 1·00 85
2495 52c. Ontario Science Centre (Raymond Moriyama), 1969 . . . . 1·00 85
2496 52c. National Gallery of Canada (Moshe Safdie), 1988 . . . . 1·00 85

877 Capt. George Vancouver

879 Gordon Lightfoot

878 Official U-20 World Cup Football and Canadian Team in Action

2007. 250th Birth Anniv of Captain George Vancouver (explorer of west coast of North America).
2497 **877** $1.55 multicoloured . . 2·50 2·00
MS2498 70 × 120 mm. **877** $1.55 multicoloured . . . . 2·50 2·00

2007. FIFA U-20 World Cup, Canada.
2499 **878** 52c. multicoloured . . . 1·00 85

2007. Canadian Recording Artists. Multicoloured. (a) Self-adhesive.
2500 52c. Type **879** . . . . . . 1·00 85
2501 52c. Joni Mitchell . . . . . 1·00 85
2502 52c. Anne Murray . . . . . 1·00 85
2503 52c. Paul Anka . . . . . . 1·00 85

(b) Ordinary gum.
MS2504 Circular 105 × 105 mm. As Nos. 2500/3 . . . . 3·25 2·75

880 Sunrise over Alexander Bay, Terra Nova National Park, Newfoundland

2007. 50th Anniv of Terra Nova National Park, Newfoundland. Self-adhesive.
2505 **880** 52c. multicoloured . . . 1·00 85

881 Jasper National Park

2007. Centenary of Jasper National Park, Alberta. Self-adhesive.
2506 **881** 52c. multicoloured . . . 1·00 85

882 Scouts forming Emblem

2007. Centenary of Scouting. Self-adhesive.
2507 **882** 52c. multicoloured . . . 1·00 85

883 Membertou (Grand Chief of the Mi'kmaq) and French Settlement, Port Royal

2007. French Settlement in North America (4th issue). Chief Membertou.
2508 **883** 52c. multicoloured . . . 1·00 85

884 Founding Members and Registry Roll

2007. Centenary of the Law Society of Saskatchewan.
2509 **884** 52c. multicoloured . . . 1·00 85

885 Books, Photograph of James Muir Gavel (first President)

886 *Hippodamia convergens* and (convergent lady beetle)

2007. Centenary of the Law Society of Alberta.
2510 **885** 52c. multicoloured . . . 1·00 85

2007. Endangered Species (2nd series). As T **863**. Multicoloured. (a) Self-adhesive.
2511 52c. North Atlantic right whale . . . . 1·00 85
2512 52c. Northern cricket frog 1·00 85
2513 52c. White sturgeon . . . . 1·00 85
2514 52c. Leatherback turtle . . . 1·00 85

(b) Ordinary gum. Size 48 × 24 mm.
MS2515 160 × 75 mm. As Nos. 2511/14 . . . . 3·50 3·00

2007. Beneficial Insects. Multicoloured.
2516 1c. Type **886** 10 10
2517 3c. *Chrysopa oculata* (golden-eyed lacewing) . . 10 10
2518 5c. *Bombus polaris* (northern bumblebee) 10 10
2519 10c. *Aeshna canadensis* (Canada darner dragonfly) 15 10
2520 25c. *Hyalophora cecropia* (cecropia moth) 50 40
MS2521 133 × 58 mm. Nos. 2516/20 1·00 85

887 Reindeer

888 Nativity ('HOPE')

2007. Christmas (1st issue). Self-adhesive.
2526 **887** (52c.) multicoloured . . 1·00 85
No. 2526 was inscribed 'P' and initially sold for 52c.

2007. Christmas (2nd issue). Multicoloured. Self-adhesive.
2527 (52c.) Type **888** . . . . . . 1·00 85
2528 93c. Angel playing trumpet ('JOY') . . . . 1·70 1·50
2529 $1.55 Dove ('PEACE') . . 2·50 2·00
No. 2527 was inscribed 'P' and initially sold for 52c.

889 *Odontioda* Island Red

890 Rat Bride

2007. Flowers (3rd series). Canadian Hybrid Orchids. Multicoloured. (a) Self-adhesive.
2530 (52c.) Type **889** . . . . . . 1·00 85
2531 96c. *Potinara* Janet Elizabeth 'Fire Dancer' 1·70 1·50
2532 $1.15 *Laeliocattleya* Memoria Evelyn Light . . 1·90 1·60
2533 $1.60 *Masdevallia* Kaleidoscope 'Conni' . . 2·75 2·25

(b) Ordinary gum.
MS2537 120 × 72 mm. As Nos. 2530/3 . . . . 7·50 7·75
No. 2530 was inscribed 'P' and sold for 52c.

2008. Chinese New Year ('Year of the Rat'). Multicoloured.
2538 52c. Type **890** . . . . . . 1·00 85
MS2539 130 × 100 mm. $1.60 Rat groom . . . . 2·75 1·25

891 Fireworks

2008. Greetings Stamp. Self-adhesive.
2540 **891** (52c.) multicoloured . . 1·00 85
No. 2540 was inscribed 'P' and initially sold for 52c.

892 *Paeonia lactiflora* 'Elgin'

2008. Peonies. Multicoloured. (a) Self-adhesive.
2541 52c. Type **892** . . . . . . 1·00 85
2542 52c. *Paeonia lactiflora* 'Coral 'n Gold' . . . . . . 1·00 85

(b) Ordinary gum.
MS2543 120 × 84 mm. As Nos. 2541/2 . . . . 2·00 1·70

893 Dentistry Building, University of Alberta (centenary)

2008. Canadian Universities' Anniversaries (7th issue). Multicoloured. Self-adhesive.
2544 52c. Type **893** . . . . . . 1·00 85
2545 52c. Walter C. Koerner Library, University of British Columbia (centenary) . . . . . . 1·00 85

OFFICIAL STAMPS

1949. Optd **O.H.M.S.**
O162 **111** 1c. green (postage) . . . 3·75 3·50
O163 **112** 2c. brown . . . . 12·00 12·00
O164 – 3c. purple (No. 378) . . 2·00 2·50
O165 **112** 4c. red . . . . 3·00 2·50
O166 – 10c. green (No. 402) . . 4·50 15
O167 – 14c. sepia (No. 403) . . 6·50 3·75
O168 – 20c. grey (No. 404) . . 12·00 60
O169 – 50c. green (No. 405) . . £160 £120
O170 – $1 purple (No. 406) . . 45·00 48·00

O171 – 7c. blue (No. 407) (air) 24·00 7·00

1949. Optd **O.H.M.S.**
O172 **135** 1c. green . . . . 3·25 1·50
O173 – 2c. sepia (No. 415) . . . 3·50 1·50
O174 – 3c. purple (No. 416) . . 2·75 1·50
O175 – 4c. red (No. 417) . . . 2·75 15
O176 – 5c. blue (No. 418) . . . 6·00 2·00
O177 **141** 50c. green . . . . . . 32·00 28·00

1950. Optd **G.**
O178 **135** 1c. green (postage) . . . 1·50 10
O179 – 2c. sepia (No. 415) . . . 3·00 3·75
O180 – 2c. green (No. 415a) . . 1·75 10
O181 – 3c. purple (No. 416) . . 2·25 10
O183 – 4c. red (No. 417) . . . 3·00 60
O184 – 5c. blue (No. 418) . . . 3·50 1·75
O193 **153** 7c. blue . . . . 2·00 2·75
O185 – 10c. green (No. 402) . . 3·00 10
O191 **142** 10c. purple . . . . . . 4·00 30
O186 – 14c. sepia (No. 403) . . 19·00 8·00
O187 – 20c. grey (No. 404) . . 35·00 30
O194 – 20c. grey (No. 441) . . 2·00 10
O188 **141** 50c. green . . . . . . 15·00 16·00
O189 – $1 purple (No. 406) . . 75·00 75·00
O192 – $1 blue (No. 433) . . . 65·00 75·00

O190 – 7c. blue (No. 407) (air) 24·00 15·00

1953. First Queen Elizabeth II stamps optd **G.**
O196 **158** 1c. brown 15 10
O197 2c. green 20 10
O198 3c. red 20 10
O199 4c. violet 30 10
O200 5c. blue 30 10

1953. Pictorial stamps optd **G.**
O206 **165** 10c. brown 70 20
O207 – 20c. green (No. 488) . . 2·50 20
O201 **160** 50c. green . . . . . . 3·00 3·00
O195 **154** $1 black . . . . 10·00 13·00

1955. Second Queen Elizabeth II stamps optd **G.**
O202 **161** 1c. brown 65 20
O203 2c. green 15 10
O204 4c. violet 40 10
O205 5c. blue 15 10

1963. Third Queen Elizabeth II stamps optd **G.**
O208 **215** 1c. brown . . . . . . 40 4·25
O209 2c. green . . . . 40 4·00
O210 4c. red . . . . 40 2·25
O211 5c. blue . . . . 40 1·75

OFFICIAL SPECIAL DELIVERY STAMPS

1950. Optd **O.H.M.S.**

OS20		10c. green (No. S15)	17·00	26·00

1950. Optd **G.**

OS21		10c. green (No. S15)	26·00	30·00

POSTAGE DUE STAMPS

D 1

D 2

1906.

D1	D 1	1c. violet	10·00	2·75
D3		2c. violet	25·00	1·00
D5		4c. violet	45·00	50·00
D7		5c. violet	32·00	4·00
D8		10c. violet	32·00	20·00

1930.

D 9	D 2	1c. violet	8·50	11·00
D10		2c. violet	7·50	1·90
D11		4c. violet	15·00	6·50
D12		5c. violet	16·00	32·00
D13		10c. violet	65·00	32·00

D 3

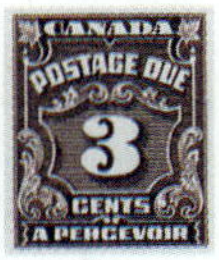
D 4

1933.

D14	D 3	1c. violet	9·50	16·00
D15		2c. violet	7·50	4·75
D16		4c. violet	12·00	15·00
D17		10c. violet	24·00	40·00

1935.

D18	D 4	1c. violet	80	10
D19		2c. violet	3·50	10
D20		3c. violet	6·00	5·00
D21		4c. violet	1·50	10
D22		5c. violet	6·00	3·75
D23		6c. violet	2·00	3·00
D24		10c. violet	70	10

D 5

1967. (a) Size 21 × 17½ mm.

D25	D 5	1c. red	1·75	4·00
D26		2c. red	1·00	1·00
D27		3c. red	1·00	4·25
D28		4c. red	2·75	1·25
D29		5c. red	4·25	4·75
D30		6c. red	1·60	3·75
D31		10c. red	2·00	2·50

(b) Size 19½ × 16 mm.

D32	D 5	1c. red	30	30
D33		2c. red	1·00	3·00
D34		3c. red	2·50	3·50
D35		4c. red	30	60
D36a		5c. red	30	2·00
D37		6c. red	2·75	3·75
D38		8c. red	30	45
D39		10c. red	40	45
D40		12c. red	30	50
D41		16c. red	3·00	4·00
D42		20c. red	30	1·25
D43		24c. red	30	1·75
D44		50c. red	40	2·25

REGISTRATION STAMPS

R 1

1875.

R1	R 1	2c. orange	60·00	1·00
R6		5c. green	85·00	1·25
R9		8c. blue	£350	£250

SPECIAL DELIVERY STAMPS

S 1

1898.

S2	S 1	10c. green	50·00	9·00

S 2

1922.

S4	S 2	20c. red	35·00	6·50

S 3 Mail-carrying, 1867 and 1927

1927. 60th Anniv of Confederation.

S5	S 3	20c. orange	11·00	10·00

S 4

1930.

S6	S 4	20c. red	42·00	7·00

1932. As Type S 4, but inscr "CENTS" instead of "TWENTY CENTS".

S7		20c. red	45·00	17·00

S 5 Allegory of Progress

1935.

S8	S 5	20c. red	3·75	3·50

S 6 Canadian Coat of Arms

1938.

S 9	S 6	10c. green	21·00	4·00
S10		20c. red	40·00	28·00

1939. Surch **10 10** and bars.

S11	S 6	10c. on 20c. red	10·00	14·00

S 8 Coat of Arms and Flags

S 9 Lockheed L.18 Lodestar

1942.

S12	S 8	10c. green (postage)	8·00	30
S13	S 9	16c. blue (air)	6·00	45
S14		17c. blue	4·50	55

1946.

S15		10c. green (postage)	5·00	30
S16		17c. blue (air)	4·50	6·50

DESIGNS: 10c. As Type S 8 but with wreath of leaves; 17c. As Type S 9 but with Canadair DC-4M North Star airplane.

CANAL ZONE Pt. 22

Territory adjacent to the Panama Canal leased by the U.S.A. from the Republic of Panama. The U.S. Canal Zone postal service closed on 30 September 1979.

1904. 100 centavos = 1 peso.
1906. 100 centesimos = 1 balboa.
1924. 100 cents = 1 dollar (U.S.).

1904. Stamps of Panama (with **PANAMA** optd twice) optd **CANAL ZONE** horiz in one line.

1	5	2c. red (No. 54)	£375	£275
2		5c. blue (No. 55)	£200	£130
3		10c. orange (No. 56)	£275	£190

1904. Stamps of the United States of 1902 optd **CANAL ZONE PANAMA**.

4	103	1c. green	24·00	14·50
5	117	2c. red	22·00	22·00
6	107	5c. blue	70·00	50·00
7	109	8c. violet	£160	95·00
8	110	10c. brown	£130	65·00

Stamps of Panama overprinted.

1904. 1905 stamps optd **CANAL ZONE** in two lines.

9	38	1c. green	3·00	1·90
10		2c. red	4·75	2·50

1904. Stamps with **PANAMA** optd twice, optd **CANAL ZONE** in two lines or surch also.

11	5	2c. red (No. 54)	5·00	4·25
12		5c. blue (No. 55)	4·00	3·50
14		8c. on 50c. brown (No. 65)	25·00	18·00
13		10c. orange (No. 56)	16·00	8·00

1906. 1892 stamps surch **PANAMA** on both sides and **CANAL ZONE** and new value in centre between bars.

19	5	1c. on 20c. violet (No. 64)	1·50	1·20
22		2c. on 1p. red (No. 66)	2·50	2·75

1906. 1906 stamps optd **CANAL ZONE** vert.

26	42	1c. black and green	1·80	1·10
27	43	2c. black and red	2·10	1·00
28	45	5c. black and blue	5·00	2·20
29	46	8c. black and purple	17·00	7·25
30	47	10c. black and violet	15·00	7·25

1909. 1909 stamps optd **CANAL ZONE** vert.

35	48	1c. black and green	3·00	1·40
36	49	2c. black and red	3·75	1·50
37	51	5c. black and blue	12·50	3·25
38	52	8c. black and purple	7·75	4·50
43	53	10c. black and purple	36·00	4·75

1911. Surch **CANAL ZONE 10 cts.**

53	38	10c. on 13c. grey	6·00	2·20

1914. Optd **CANAL ZONE** vert.

54	38	10c. grey	39·00	10·00

1915. 1915 and 1918 stamps optd **CANAL ZONE** vert.

55		1c. black and green (No. 162)	15·00	5·75
56		2c. black and red (No. 163)	7·50	3·50
57		5c. black and blue (No. 166)	7·50	5·00
58		10c. black & orange (No. 167)	15·00	11·50
59		12c. black & violet (No. 178)	12·00	4·00
60		15c. black & blue (No. 179)	46·00	16·00
61		24c. black & brown (No. 180)	42·00	9·75
62		50c. black & orange (No. 181)	£275	£140
63		1b. black & violet (No. 182)	£170	50·00

1921. 1921 stamps optd **CANAL ZONE** vert.

64	65	1c. green	3·50	1·10
65	–	2c. red (No. 186)	2·50	1·30
66	68	5c. blue	9·00	3·50
67	–	10c. violet (No. 191)	12·00	5·50
68	–	15c. blue (No. 192)	35·00	13·50
69	–	24c. sepia (No. 194)	47·00	18·00
70	–	50c. black (No. 195)	£120	80·00

1924. 1924 stamps optd **CANAL ZONE** vert.

72	72	1c. green	11·00	3·50
73		2c. red	7·50	2·20

1924. Stamps of the United States of 1922 optd **CANAL ZONE** horiz.

74		½c. sepia (No. 559)	1·90	70
75		1c. green (No. 602)	2·30	70
76		1½c. brown (No. 603)	3·00	1·30
103		2c. red (No. 604)	2·75	1·60
87		3c. violet (No. 638a)	4·00	2·50
88		5c. blue (No. 640)	5·50	2·30
106		10c. orange (No. 645)	18·00	8·00
90		12c. purple (No. 693)	24·00	9·00
141		14c. blue (No. 695)	3·75	2·75
92		15c. grey (No. 696)	7·75	2·50
93		17c. black (No. 697)	5·00	2·50
94		20c. red (No. 698)	6·00	2·50
95		30c. sepia (No. 700)	5·25	3·25
84		50c. mauve (No. 701)	90·00	43·00
97		$1 brown (No. 579)	£150	34·00

1926. Liberty Bell stamp of United States optd **CANAL ZONE**.

101	177	2c. red	6·00	5·00

22 Gen. Gorgas

24 Panama Canal under Construction

1928.

107	22	1c. green	25	10
108	–	2c. red	25	10
109	24	5c. blue	95	30
110	–	10c. orange	25	15
111	–	12c. purple	80	50
112	–	14c. blue	90	70
113	–	15c. grey	45	30
114	–	20c. brown	65	15
115	–	30c. black	90	60
116	–	50c. mauve	1·50	50

PORTRAITS: 2c. Gen. Goethals. 10c. H. F. Hodges. 12c. Col. Gaillard. 14c. Gen. Sibert. 15c. Jackson Smith. 20c. Admiral Rousseau. 30c. Col. S. B. Williamson. 50c. Governor Blackburn.

1929. Air. Stamps of 1928 surch **AIR MAIL** and value.

124	–	10c. on 50c. mauve	7·00	5·25
117	22	15c. on 1c. green	8·00	4·50
125	–	20c. on 2c. red	5·25	1·40
119	–	25c. on 2c. red	3·75	1·60

36 Steamer, Panama Canal

1931. Air.

126	36	4c. purple	55	55
127		5c. green	45	35
128		6c. brown	55	30
129		10c. orange	70	30
130		15c. blue	90	30
131		20c. violet	1·40	30
132		30c. red	2·50	80
133		40c. yellow	2·50	85
134		$1 black	6·50	1·50

1933. No. 720 of United States optd **CANAL ZONE**.

140		3c. violet	2·50	30

38 Gen. Goethals

45 Balboa (before construction)

1934. 20th Anniv of Opening of Panama Canal.

142	38	3c. violet	25	15

1939. 25th Anniv of Opening of Panama Canal and 10th Anniv of Canal Zone Airmail Service. (a) Postage. As T **45**. Inscr "25TH ANNIVERSARY 1939 OPENING PANAMA CANAL 1914".

149	45	1c. green	55	30
150	–	2c. red	55	30
151	–	3c. violet	55	25
152	–	5c. blue	1·20	90
153	–	6c. orange	2·30	2·30
154	–	7c. black	2·50	2·40
155	–	8c. green	3·50	2·75
156	–	10c. blue	3·50	3·00
157	–	11c. green	6·00	6·75
158	–	12c. purple	6·00	6·25
159	–	14c. violet	6·00	6·25
160	–	15c. olive	8·75	5·50
161	–	18c. red	7·75	7·25
162	–	20c. brown	11·00	6·25
163	–	25c. orange	15·00	14·00
164	–	50c. purple	19·00	5·50

DESIGNS: 2c. Balboa (after construction); 3c., 5c. Gaillard Cut; 6c., 7c. Bas Obispo; 8c., 10c. Gatun Locks; 11c., 12c. Canal Channel; 14c., 15c. Gamboa; 18c., 20c. Pedro Miguel Locks; 25c.50c. Gatun Spillway.

(b) Air. Inscr "TENTH ANNIVERSARY AIR MAIL" and "25TH ANNIVERSARY OPENING PANAMA CANAL".

143		5c. black	3·00	1·80
144		10c. violet	2·50	1·60
145		15c. brown	3·75	90
146		25c. blue	11·00	6·50
147		30c. red	11·00	4·75
148		$1 green	30·00	16·00

DESIGNS—HORIZ: As Type **45**: 5c. Douglas DC-3 airplane over Sosa Hill; 10c. Douglas DC-3 airplane, Sikorsky S-42A flying boat and map of Central America; 15c. Sikorsky S-42A and Fort Amador; 25c. Sikorsky S-42A at Cristobal Harbour, Manzanillo Island; 30c. Sikorsky S-42A over Culebra Cut. $1 Sikorsky S-42A and palm trees.

1939. Stamps of United States (1938) optd **CANAL ZONE**.

165	276	½c. orange	15	10
166	–	1½c. brown (No. 801)	15	10

67 John F. Stevens

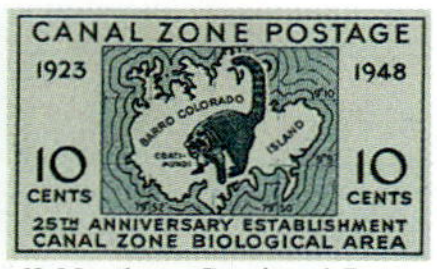

69 Northern Coati and Barro Colorado Island

1946. Portraits.

188	–	½c. red (Davis)	35	20
189	–	1½c. brown (Magoon)	35	20
190	–	2c. red (Theodore Roosevelt)	15	15
191	67	5c. blue	35	15
192	–	25c. green (Wallace)	70	50

1948. 25th Anniv of Establishment of Canal Zone Biological Area.

194	69	10c. black	1·10	75

70 "Arriving at Chagres on the Atlantic Side."

74 Western Hemisphere

1949. Centenary of the Gold Rush.

195	70	3c. blue	40	20
196	–	6c. violet	50	25
197	–	12c. green	90	75
198	–	18c. mauve	1·60	1·20

DESIGNS: 6c. "Up the Chagres River to Las Cruces"; 12c. "Las Cruces Trail to Panama"; 18c. "Leaving Panama for San Francisco".

1951. Air.

199	74	4c. purple	60	30
200		5c. green	80	50
201		6c. brown	40	25
202		7c. olive	80	45
210		8c. red	30	25
203		10c. orange	75	30
204		15c. purple	3·00	2·30
205		21c. blue	6·00	3·25
206		25c. yellow	8·25	2·40
207		31c. red	6·00	2·50
208		35c. blue	5·00	2·50
209		80c. black	3·75	1·40

75 Labourers in Gaillard Cut

76 Locomotive "Nueva Granada", 1852

1951. West Indian Panama Canal Labourers.

211	75	10c. red	1·80	1·20

1955. Centenary of Panama Railway.

212	76	3c. violet	60	45

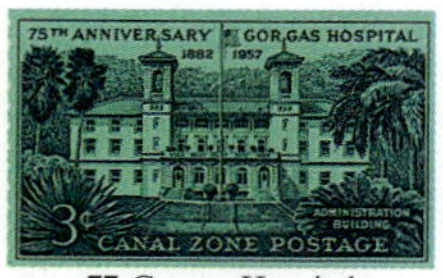

77 Gorgas Hospital

1957. 75th Anniv of Gorgas Hospital.

213	77	3c. black on green	40	30

78 "Ancon II" (liner)

80 "First Class" Scout Badge

79 Roosevelt Medal and Map of Canal Zone

1958.

214	78	4c. turquoise	30	25

1958. Birth Centenary of Theodore Roosevelt.

215	79	4c. brown	40	25

1960. 50th Anniv of American Boy Scout Movement.

216	80	4c. ochre, red and blue	40	30

81 Administration Building, Balboa

82 U.S. Army Caribbean School Crest

1960.

217	81	4c. purple	20	15

1961. Air.

221	82	15c. blue and red	1·10	60

83 Girl Scout Badge and Camp on Lake Gatun

1962. 50th Anniv of U.S. Girl Scout Movement.

222	83	4c. ochre, green and blue	45	25

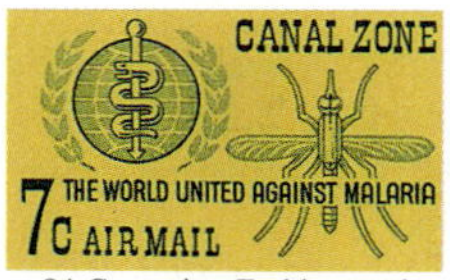

84 Campaign Emblem and Mosquito

1962. Air. Malaria Eradication.

223	84	7c. black on yellow	35	35

85 Thatcher Ferry Bridge

1962. Opening of Thatcher Ferry Bridge.

224	85	4c. black and silver	20	20

86 Torch of Progress

1963. Air. "Alliance for Progress".

225	86	15c. blue, green and black	90	70

87 Cristobal

1964. Air. 50th Anniv of Panama Canal.

226	87	6c. black and green	40	30
227	–	8c. black and red	40	30
228	–	15c. black and blue	90	60
229	–	20c. black and purple	1·40	80
230	–	30c. black and brown	2·00	1·80
231	–	80c. black and bistre	3·50	2·40

DESIGNS: 8c. Gatun Locks; 15c. Madden Dam; 20c. Gaillard Cut; 30c. Miraflores Locks; 80c. Balboa.

93 Seal and Jetliner

1965. Air.

232	93	6c. black and green	30	30
233		8c. black and red	25	10
234		10c. black and orange	25	15
235		11c. black and green	25	15
236		13c. black and green	70	20
237		15c. black and blue	45	15
238		20c. black and violet	50	25
239		22c. black and violet	70	1·60
240		25c. black and green	55	55
241		30c. black and brown	70	25
242		35c. black and red	80	1·60
243		80c. black and ochre	1·80	60

94 Goethal's Memorial, Balboa

96 Dredger "Cascadas"

1968.

244	94	6c. blue and green	25	25
245	–	8c. multicoloured	30	20

DESIGN: 8c. Fort San Lorenzo.

1976.

249	96	13c. black, green & blue	30	15

97 Electric Towing Locomotive

1978.

251	97	15c. green and deep green	45	15

OFFICIAL STAMPS

1941. Air. Optd **OFFICIAL PANAMA CANAL.**

O167	36	5c. green	4·50	1·50
O168		6c. brown	10·50	4·75
O169		10c. orange	9·00	3·50
O170		15c. blue	12·50	4·25
O171		20c. violet	12·50	6·50
O172		30c. red	15·00	8·50
O173		40c. yellow	14·50	7·50
O174		$1 black	17·00	10·00

1941. Optd **OFFICIAL PANAMA CANAL.**

O180	22	1c. green	1·80	40
O181	38	3c. violet	3·50	75
O182	24	5c. blue	£850	45·00
O183	–	10c. orange	6·00	2·00
O184	–	15c. grey (No. 113)	11·50	2·75
O185	–	20c. brown (No. 114)	14·00	3·25
O186	–	50c. mauve (No. 116)	34·00	8·75

1947. No. 192 optd **OFFICIAL PANAMA CANAL.**

O193	67	5c. blue	7·75	2·75

POSTAGE DUE STAMPS

1914. Postage Due stamps of United States of 1894 optd **CANAL ZONE** diag.

D55	D 87	1c. red	65·00	18·00
D56		2c. red	£190	43·00
D57		10c. red	£650	29·00

1915. Postage Due stamps of Panama of 1915 optd **CANAL ZONE** vert.

D59	D 58	1c. brown	9·00	5·00
D60	–	2c. brown	£160	13·00
D61	–	10c. brown	38·00	9·50

1915. Postage Due stamps of Panama of 1915 surch **CANAL ZONE** vert and value in figures.

D62	D 58	1c. on 1c. brown	85·00	15·00
D63	–	2c. on 2c. brown	23·00	5·50
D66	–	4c. on 4c. brown	30·00	9·75
D64	–	10c. on 10c. brown	17·00	3·50

1925. Postage Due stamps of United States of 1894 optd **CANAL ZONE** horiz in two lines.

D92	D 87	1c. red	9·00	3·00
D93		2c. red	12·00	3·50
D94		10c. red	£120	17·00

1925. Stamps of Canal Zone of 1924 optd **POSTAGE DUE.**

D89	1c. green (No. 75)	75·00	11·50
D90	2c. red (No. 103)	19·00	5·75
D91	10c. orange (No. 106)	42·00	8·75

1929. No. 109 surch **POSTAGE DUE** and value and bars.

D120	24	1c. on 5c. blue	5·25	2·75
D121		2c. on 5c. blue	9·00	3·50
D122		5c. on 5c. blue	9·00	3·75
D123		10c. on 5c. blue	9·00	3·75

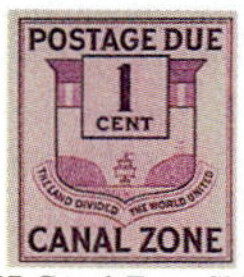

D 37 Canal Zone Shield

1932.

D135	D 37	1c. red	20	15
D136		2c. red	20	15
D137		5c. red	35	20
D138		10c. red	1·40	1·10
D139		15c. red	1·10	70

CANTON Pt. 17

A treaty port in S. China. Stamps issued at the French Indo-Chinese P.O., which was closed in 1922.

1901. 100 centimes = 1 franc.
1919. 100 cents = 1 piastre.

Stamps of Indo-China overprinted or surcharged.

CANTON
州廣
(1)

1901. "Tablet" key-type, optd with T **1**. The Chinese characters represent "Canton" and are therefore the same on every value.

1	D	1c. black and blue	1·00	80
2		2c. brown on yellow	1·80	2·30
3		4c. brown on grey	3·25	2·50
4		5c. green	90	1·20
6		10c. black on lilac	3·75	9·00
7		15c. blue	1·90	3·75
8		15c. grey	5·25	4·75
9		20c. red on green	12·50	18·00
10		25c. black on pink	11·00	10·00
11		30c. brown on drab	17·00	50·00
12		40c. red on yellow	42·00	55·00
13		50c. red on rose	27·00	50·00
14		75c. brown on orange	36·00	75·00
15		1f. green	55·00	60·00
16		5f. mauve on lilac	£190	£190

1903. "Tablet" key-type, surch. as T **1**. The Chinese characters indicate the value and therefore differ for each value.

17	D	1c. black on blue	2·30	7·25
18		2c. brown on yellow	4·25	5·50
19		4c. brown on grey	2·50	6·25
20		5c. green	2·00	6·25
21		10c. red	2·75	6·25
22		15c. grey	2·50	5·75
23		20c. red on green	10·00	28·00
24		25c. blue	7·00	9·25
25		25c. black on pink	9·50	10·00
26		30c. brown on drab	40·00	40·00
27		40c. red on yellow	70·00	65·00
28		50c. red on rose	£275	£225
29		50c. brown on blue	75·00	75·00
30		75c. brown on orange	90·00	75·00
31		1f. green	70·00	75·00
32		5f. mauve on lilac	90·00	75·00

1906. Surch **CANTON** (letters without serifs) and value in Chinese.

33	8	1c. green	1·00	4·50
34		2c. purple on yellow	1·10	3·25
35		4c. mauve on blue	85	2·30
36		5c. green	1·90	3·00
37		10c. red	3·75	4·25
38		15c. brown on blue	3·00	7·75
39		20c. red on green	3·00	6·25
40		25c. blue	3·50	3·00
41		30c. brown on cream	5·50	3·25
42		35c. black on yellow	2·50	6·00
43		40c. black on grey	6·75	11·00
44		50c. brown on cream	8·25	12·00
45	D	75c. brown on orange	65·00	75·00
46	8	1f. green	16·00	25·00
47		2f. brown on yellow	30·00	60·00
48	D	5f. mauve on lilac	85·00	£110
49	8	10f. red on green	75·00	£120

1908. 1907 stamps surch **CANTON** and value in Chinese.

50	10	1c. black and brown	60	40
51		2c. black and brown	35	60
52		4c. black and blue	70	1·80
53		5c. black and green	1·30	25
54		10c. black and red	2·75	50
55		15c. black and violet	3·00	3·00
56	11	20c. black and violet	4·00	4·25
57		25c. black and blue	6·50	35
58		30c. black and brown	8·00	6·75
59		35c. black and green	11·00	6·50
60		40c. black and brown	17·00	7·25
61		50c. black and red	19·00	3·75
62	12	75c. black and orange	17·00	10·50
63	–	1f. black and red	28·00	20·00
64	–	2f. black and green	60·00	55·00
65	–	5f. black and blue	65·00	60·00
66	–	10f. black and violet	£120	95·00

1919. As last, but additionally surch.

67	10	⅖c. on 1c. black and brown	75	3·75
68		⅘c. on 2c. black and brown	65	1·90
69		1⅗c. on 4c. black and blue	1·50	3·25
70		2c. on 5c. black and green	2·30	95
71		4c. on 10c. black and red	1·90	1·30
72		6c. on 15c. black & violet	3·00	1·60
73	11	8c. on 20c. black & violet	3·25	2·50
74		10c. on 25c. black & blue	5·00	30
75		12c. on 30c. black & brown	5·25	3·25
76		14c. on 35c. black & green	1·20	90
77		16c. on 40c. black & brown	3·00	1·10
78		20c. on 50c. black and red	5·00	40
79	12	30c. on 75c. black & orange	3·75	95
80	–	40c. on 1f. black and red	18·00	10·00
81	–	80c. on 2f. black and green	21·00	20·00
82	–	2p. on 5f. black and blue	20·00	27·00
83	–	4p. on 10f. black & violet	13·00	30·00

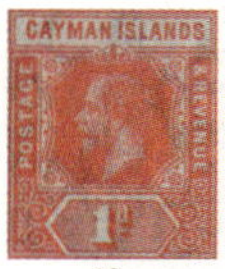## CAPE JUBY — Pt. 9

Former Spanish possession on the N.W. coast of Africa, ceded to Morocco in 1958.

100 centimos = 1 peseta.

1916. Stamps of Rio de Oro surch **CABO JUBI** and value.

1a	12	5c. on 4p. red	90·00	26·00
2		10c. on 10p. violet	33·00	16·00
3		15c. on 50c. brown	33·00	16·00
4		40c. on 1p. lilac	55·00	22·00

1919. Stamps of Spain optd **CABO JUBY.**

5	38a	¼c. green	15	15
18	66	1c. green (imperf)	18·00	11·50
6	64	2c. brown	15	15
7		5c. green	40	25
8		10c. red	50	30
9		15c. yellow	2·20	1·70
10		20c. green	14·00	11·00
19		20c. violet	80·00	30·00
11		25c. blue	2·10	70
12		30c. green	2·10	80
13		40c. orange	2·10	80
14		50c. blue	2·50	2·20
15		1p. red	7·25	6·00
16		4p. purple	29·00	25·00
17		10p. orange	42·00	39·00

1925. Stamps of Spain optd **CABO JUBY.**

19a	68	2c. green	£225	55·00
20		5c. purple	3·50	2·75
21		10c. green	9·75	2·75
22		20c. violet	20·00	9·00

1926. As Red Cross stamps of Spain of 1926 optd **CABO-JUBY.**

23	70	1c. orange	10·00	10·00
24	–	2c. red	10·00	10·00
25	–	5c. brown	2·50	2·50
26	–	10c. green	1·30	1·30
27	70	15c. violet	90	90
28	–	20c. purple	90	90
29	71	25c. red	90	90
30	70	30c. green	90	90
31	–	40c. blue	30	30
32	–	50c. red	30	30
33	–	1p. red	30	30
34	–	4p. bistre	1·20	1·20
35	71	10p. violet	2·75	2·75

1929. Seville and Barcelona Exhibition stamps of Spain (Nos. 504/14) optd **CABO JUBY.**

36	–	5c. red	30	45
37	–	10c. green	30	45
38	83	15c. blue	30	45
39	84	20c. violet	30	45
40	83	25c. red	30	45
41	–	30c. brown	30	45
42	–	40c. blue	30	45
43	84	50c. orange	35	55
44	–	1p. grey	15·00	22·00
45	–	4p. red	22·00	33·00
46	–	10p. brown	22·00	33·00

1934. Stamps of Spanish Morocco optd **Cabo Juby.**

(a) Stamps of 1928.

47	11	1c. red	1·50	1·30
48		2c. violet	3·25	1·60
49		5c. blue	3·25	1·60
50		10c. green	7·50	4·50
51		15c. brown	17·00	11·00
52	12	25c. red	3·25	3·25
53	–	1p. green	30·00	24·00
54	–	2p.50 purple	70·00	48·00
55	–	4p. blue	90·00	65·00

(b) Stamps of 1933.

56	14	1c. red	35	35
57	–	10c. green	2·20	2·30
58	14	20c. black	6·50	6·00
59	–	30c. red	6·50	6·00
60	15	40c. blue	23·00	21·00
61		50c. orange	44·00	36·00

1935. Stamps of Spanish Morocco of 1933 optd **CABO JUBY.**

62	14	1c. red	15	15
63	–	2c. green	50	40
64	–	5c. mauve	1·90	60
65	–	10c. green	11·50	6·00
66	–	15c. yellow	4·50	3·00
67	14	20c. black	4·25	3·50
68	–	25c. red	48·00	35·00
73	–	25c. violet	3·00	3·00
74	–	30c. red	3·00	3·00
75	–	40c. orange	4·25	4·25
76	–	50c. blue	8·25	8·25
77	–	60c. green	10·50	10·50
69	–	1p. grey	7·00	6·50
78	–	2p. brown	55·00	55·00
70	–	2p.50 brown	28·00	20·00
71	–	4p. green	45·00	30·00
72	–	5p. black	37·00	32·00

1937. 1st Anniv of Civil War. Nos. 184/99 of Spanish Morocco optd **CABO JUBY.**

79	1c. blue	30	30
80	2c. brown	30	30
81	5c. mauve	30	30
82	10c. green	30	30
83	15c. blue	30	30
84	20c. purple	30	30
85	25c. mauve	30	30
86	30c. red	30	30
87	40c. orange	90	90
88	50c. blue	90	90
89	60c. green	90	90
90	1p. violet	90	90
91	2p. blue	60·00	60·00
92	2p.50 black	60·00	60·00
93	4p. brown	60·00	60·00
94	10p. black	60·00	60·00

1938. Air. Nos. 203/12 of Spanish Morocco optd **CABO JUBY.**

95	5c. brown	10	10
96	10c. green	10	30
97	25c. red	10	10
98	40c. blue	1·50	1·50
99	50c. mauve	10	10
100	75c. blue	10	15
101	1p. brown	10	15
102	1p.50 violet	3·00	90
103	2p. red	2·10	2·10
104	3p. black	5·50	5·50

1939. As Nos. 213/16 of Spanish Morocco optd **CABO JUBY.**

105	5c. red	35	35
106	10c. green	35	35
107	15c. purple	35	35
108	20c. blue	35	35

1940. Nos. 217/32 of Spanish Morocco, but without "ZONA" on back, optd **CABO JUBY.**

109	1c. brown	10	10
110	2c. green	10	10
111	5c. blue	10	10
112	10c. mauve	10	10
113	15c. green	10	10
114	20c. violet	10	10
115	25c. brown	10	10
116	30c. green	10	10
117	40c. green	45	45
118	45c. red	45	45
119	50c. brown	45	45
120	75c. blue	1·40	1·00
121	1p. brown and blue	2·75	1·90
122	2p.50 green and brown	7·75	5·25
123	5p. brown and purple	7·75	5·25
124	10p. brown & deep brown	23·00	19·00

1942. Air. Nos. 258/62 of Spanish Morocco, but without "Z" opt and inscr "CABO JUBY".

125	5c. blue	10	10
126	10c. brown	10	10
127	15c. green	10	10
128	90c. pink	35	35
129	5p. black	1·30	1·30

1944. Nos. 269/82 (agricultural scenes) of Spanish Morocco optd **CABO JUBY.**

130	–	1c. blue and brown	10	10
131	–	2c. light green & green	10	10
132	26	5c. green and brown	10	10
133	–	10c. orange and blue	10	10
134	–	15c. light green & green	10	10
135	–	20c. black and purple	10	10
136	–	25c. brown and blue	10	10
137	–	30c. blue and green	10	10
138	–	40c. purple and brown	10	10
139	26	50c. brown and blue	10	10
140	–	75c. blue and green	95	95
141	–	1p. brown and blue	95	95
142	–	2p.50 blue and black	2·75	2·75
143	–	10p. black and orange	19·00	17·00

1946. Nos. 285/94 (craftsmen) of Spanish Morocco optd **CABO JUBY.**

144	–	1c. brown and purple	10	10
145	27	2c. violet and green	10	10
146	–	10c. blue and orange	10	10
147	27	15c. green and blue	10	10
148	–	25c. blue and green	10	10
149	–	40c. brown and blue	10	10
150	27	45c. red and black	20	20
151	–	1p. blue and green	1·20	1·20
152	–	2p.50 green and orange	3·50	3·50
153	–	10p. grey and blue	10·00	10·00

1948. Nos. 307/17 (transport and commerce) of Spanish Morocco, but without "Z" on back, optd **CABO JUBY.**

154	30	2c. brown and violet	25	80
155	–	5c. violet and purple	10	10
156	–	15c. green and blue	10	10
157	–	25c. green and black	10	10
158	–	35c. black and blue	10	10
159	–	50c. violet and red	10	10
160	–	70c. blue and green	10	10
161	–	90c. green and mauve	10	10
162	–	1p. violet and blue	25	20
163	30	2p.50 green and purple	7·75	8·25
164	–	10p. blue and black	3·25	3·25

EXPRESS LETTER STAMPS

1919. Express letter stamp of Spain optd **CABO JUBY.**

E18	E 53	20c. red	2·75	2·75

1926. Red Cross stamp. As Express letter stamp of Spain optd **CABO-JUBY.**

E36	E 77	20c. black and blue	2·75	2·75

1934. Stamp of Spanish Morocco optd **Cabo Juby.**

E62	E 12	20c. black	2·00	2·00

1935. Stamp of Spanish Morocco optd **CABO JUBY.**

E79	E 16	20c. red	3·00	3·00

1937. No. E200 of Spanish Morocco optd **CABO JUBY.**

E95	E 19	20c. red	90	90

1940. No. E233 of Spanish Morocco optd **CABO JUBY.**

E125	E 21	25c. red	35	35

CAPE OF GOOD HOPE — Pt. 1

Formerly a British Colony, later the southern-most province of the Union of South Africa.

12 pence = 1 shilling;
20 shillings = 1 pound.

1 "Hope"

1853. Imperf.

18	1	1d. red	£180	£225
19		4d. blue	£180	60·00
20		6d. lilac	£250	£450
8b		1s. green	£275	£300

3

1861. Imperf.

13	3	1d. red	£14000	£2250
14		4d. blue	£21000	£1700

4 "Hope" seated, with vine and ram (with outer frame-line)

6 (No outer frame-line)

1864. With outer frame line. Perf.

23a	4	1d. red	85·00	26·00
24		4d. blue	£120	3·75
52a		6d. purple	12·00	20
53a		1s. green	£100	50

1868. Surch.

32	4	1d. on 6d. violet	£550	£100
33		1d. on 1s. green	95·00	60·00
34	6	3d. on 4d. blue	£110	2·00
27	4	4d. on 6d. violet	£300	16·00

1880. No outer frame line.

48	6	½d. black	6·00	10
49		1d. red	7·50	10
36		3d. pink	£200	27·00
43		3d. purple	8·00	1·25
51		4d. blue	14·00	50
54		5s. orange	£100	6·50

1880. Surch **THREEPENCE.**

35	6	3d. on 4d. pink	75·00	2·25

1880. Surch **3.**

37	6	"3" on 3d. pink	85·00	1·75

1882. Surch **One Half-penny.**

47	6	½d. on 3d. purple	35·00	4·25

1882.

61	6	½d. green	1·50	50
62		2d. brown	2·00	1·25
63		2½d. olive	15·00	10
63a		2½d. blue	7·00	10
64		3d. mauve	11·00	1·00
65		4d. olive	5·50	2·75
66		1s. green	70·00	5·50
67		1s. yellow	12·00	2·00

On the 2½d. stamps the value is in a white square at upper right-hand corner as well as at foot.

1891. Surch **2½d.**

55a	6	2½d. on 3d. mauve	4·50	20

1893. Surch **ONE PENNY.**

57a	6	1d. on 2d. brown	3·75	50

17 "Hope" standing. Table Bay in background

18 Table Mountain and Bay and Arms of the Colony

19

1893.

58	17	½d. green	4·00	10
59a		1d. red	1·50	10
60		3d. mauve	4·00	1·75

1900.

69	18	1d. red	4·00	10

1902. Various frames.

70	19	½d. green	2·25	10
71		1d. red	2·00	10
72		2d. brown	14·00	80
73		2½d. blue	2·75	7·00
74		3d. purple	9·00	1·00
75		4d. green	12·00	65
76		6d. mauve	19·00	30
77		1s. yellow	15·00	80
78		5s. orange	£100	21·00

CAPE VERDE ISLANDS — Pt. 9, Pt. 12

Islands in the Atlantic. Formerly Portuguese; became independent on 5 July 1975.

1877. 1000 reis = 1 milreis.
1913. 100 centavos = 1 escudo.

1877. "Crown" key-type inscr "CABO VERDE".

1	P	5r. black	2·50	1·70
2a		10r. yellow	15·00	10·50
18		10r. green	2·20	1·70
3		20r. bistre	1·50	1·20
19		20r. red	4·50	3·00
4		25r. pink	1·90	80
20		25r. lilac	3·25	2·40
5		40r. blue	75·00	45·00
21		40r. yellow	1·90	1·40
15		50r. green	£120	65·00
22		50r. blue	5·50	3·50
7b		100r. lilac	6·75	2·75
8		200r. orange	4·00	3·00
9b		300r. brown	4·75	4·25

1886. "Embossed" key-type inscr "PROVINCIA DE CABO-VERDE".

33	Q	5r. black	3·75	2·50
34		10r. green	5·50	2·40
35		20r. red	6·75	4·25
26		25r. mauve	6·75	4·50
27		40r. brown	6·75	2·75
28		50r. blue	6·75	2·75
29		100r. brown	6·75	3·75
30		200r. lilac	15·00	8·50
31		300r. orange	17·00	3·50

1894. "Figures" key-type inscr "CABO-VERDE".

37	R	5r. orange	1·30	1·00
38		10r. mauve	1·30	1·00
39		15r. brown	3·25	2·10
40		20r. lilac	3·25	2·10
41		25r. green	2·75	1·70
42		50r. blue	2·75	1·70
51		75r. red	9·25	4·75
43		80r. green	10·00	5·25
44		100r. brown on buff	7·50	4·25
58		150r. red on rose	26·00	22·00
59		200r. blue on blue	26·00	22·00
46		300r. blue on buff	30·00	14·00

1898. "King Carlos" key-type inscr "CABO VERDE".

60	S	2½r. grey	30	25
61		5r. orange	40	25
62		10r. green	40	25
63		15r. brown	4·50	1·60
111		15r. green	1·50	1·00
64		20r. lilac	1·30	75
65		25r. green	2·75	1·00
112		25r. red	80	30
66		50r. blue	2·75	1·20
113		50r. brown	3·00	1·90
114		65r. blue	19·00	12·00
67		75r. red	7·00	2·75
115		75r. purple	2·75	1·70
68		80r. mauve	7·00	2·75
69		100r. blue on blue	2·75	1·50
116		115r. brown on pink	12·00	8·00
117		130r. brown on yellow	12·50	8·00
70		150r. brown on yellow	2·20	1·20
71		200r. purple on pink	3·25	2·40
72		300r. blue on pink	8·25	4·00
118		400r. blue on yellow	13·00	8·50
73		500r. black on blue	8·25	4·00
74		700r. mauve on yellow	23·00	14·50

1902. Key-types of Cape Verde Is. surch.

119	S	50r. on 65r. blue	3·25	2·40
75	Q	65r. on 5r. black	4·50	3·00
78	R	65r. on 10r. mauve	5·50	3·00
79		65r. on 20r. lilac	5·50	3·00
80		65r. on 100r. brn on buff	7·00	4·25
76	Q	65r. on 200r. lilac	4·50	3·00
77		65r. on 300r. orange	4·50	3·00
85	R	115r. on 5r. orange	3·25	2·40
82	Q	115r. on 10r. green	4·50	3·00
83		115r. on 20r. red	4·50	3·00
87	R	115r. on 25r. green	2·30	1·70
88		115r. on 150r. red on rose	6·75	5·25
90	Q	130r. on 50r. blue	4·50	3·00
93	R	130r. on 75r. red	3·25	2·40
96		130r. on 80r. green	2·75	1·60
92	Q	130r. on 100r. brown	4·50	3·00
97	R	130r. on 200r. blue on blue	3·00	2·10
106	V	400r. on 2½r. brown	1·30	1·20
98	Q	400r. on 25r. mauve	2·20	2·10
99		400r. on 40r. brown	4·50	3·00

101 R 400r. on 50r. blue . . . . 4·50 2·40
103 400r. on 300r. blue on buff 2·00 1·40

1902. "King Carlos" key-type of Cape Verde Is. optd **PROVISORIO.**
107 S 15r. brown . . . . 1·50 1·00
108 25r. green . . . . 1·50 1·00
109 50r. blue . . . . 1·50 1·00
110 75r. red . . . . 3·00 2·10

1911. "King Carlos" key-type of Cape Verde Is. optd **REPUBLICA.**
120 S 2½r. grey 20 20
121 5r. orange 20 20
122 10r. green 80 65
123 15r. green 70 35
124 20r. lilac . . . . 1·20 65
125 25r. red 70 35
126 50r. brown . . . . 7·00 4·75
127 75r. purple . . . . 1·10 65
128 100r. blue on blue . . . . 1·10 65
129 115r. brown on pink . . . 1·10 65
130 130r. brown on yellow . . . 1·10 65
131 200r. purple on pink . . . 5·25 3·25
132 400r. blue on yellow . . . 2·75 95
133 500r. black on blue . . . 2·75 95
134 700r. mauve on yellow . . . 2·75 1·10

1912. "King Manoel" key-type inscr "CABO VERDE" and optd **REPUBLICA.**
135 T 2½r. lilac 15 15
136 5r. black 15 15
137 10r. green 35 30
138 20r. red . . . . 1·90 1·10
139 25r. brown 35 15
140 50r. blue . . . . 3·75 2·75
141 75r. brown 90 80
142 100r. brown on green . . . 90 80
143 200r. green on pink . . . 1·40 80
144 300r. black on blue . . . 1·40 80
145 400r. blue and black . . . 3·00 2·40
146 500r. brown and olive . . . 3·00 2·40

1913. Surch. **REPUBLICA CABO VERDE** and new value on "Vasco da Gama" issues of (a) Portuguese Colonies.
147 ¼c. on 2½r. green . . . . . 1·10 50
148 ½c. on 5r. red . . . . . 1·10 50
149 1c. on 10r. purple . . . . 1·10 50
150 2½c. on 25r. green . . . . 1·10 50
151 5c. on 50r. blue . . . . . 1·50 1·20
152 7½c. on 75r. brown . . . . 3·00 2·30
153 10c. on 100r. brown . . . . 1·50 1·50
154 15c. on 150r. bistre . . . . 2·00 2·00

(b) Macao.
155 ¼c. on ½a. green . . . . . 1·10 70
156 ½c. on 1a. red . . . . . 1·10 70
157 1c. on 2a. purple . . . . . 1·10 70
158 2½c. on 4a. green . . . . . 1·10 70
159 5c. on 8a. blue . . . . . 5·75 5·00
160 7½c. on 12a. brown . . . . 4·75 2·00
161 10c. on 16a. brown . . . . 1·70 1·30
162 15c. on 24a. bistre . . . . 4·75 2·75

(c) Timor.
163 ¼c. on ½a. green . . . . . 1·10 70
164 ½c. on 1a. red . . . . . 1·10 70
165 1c. on 2a. purple . . . . . 1·10 70
166 2½c. on 4a. green . . . . . 1·00 70
167 5c. on 8a. blue . . . . . 5·75 4·50
168 7½c. on 12a. brown . . . . 4·50 2·50
169 10c. on 16a. brown . . . . 1·80 1·50
170 15c. on 24a. bistre . . . . 3·75 1·90

1913. Stamps of 1902 optd **REPUBLICA.**
171 S 75r. red (No. 110) . . . . 4·50 3·00
192 R 115r. on 5r. (No. 85) . . . 1·10 60
193 Q 115r. on 10r. (No. 82) . . . 2·00 1·20
195 115r. on 20r. (No. 83) . . . 2·20 1·40
198 R 115r. on 25r. (No. 87) . . . 2·00 1·40
200 115r. on 150r. (No. 88) . . . 65 60
201 Q 130r. on 50r. (No. 90) . . . 2·00 1·00
202 R 130r. on 75r. (No. 93) . . . 2·00 80
204 130r. on 80r. (No. 96) . . . 2·00 80
206 Q 130r. on 100r. (No. 92) . . . 1·30 80
208 R 130r. on 200r. (No. 97) . . . 1·30 80

1914. "Ceres" key-type inscr "CABO VERDE". Name and value in black.
219 U ¼c. green 60 45
220 ½c. black 60 45
221 1c. green 60 45
222 1½c. brown 60 45
223 2c. red . . . . 1·00 55
224 2c. grey 25 20
180 2½c. violet 50 45
214 2½c. mauve 20 20
215 3c. orange . . . . 2·10 1·90
216 4c. red 20 15
228 4½c. grey 30 30
229 5c. blue 75 65
230 6c. mauve 30 30
231 7c. blue 30 30
232 7½c. brown 30 25
233 8c. grey 50 40
234 10c. red 30 30
235 12c. green 50 45
236 15c. pink 30 25
237 20c. green 30 25
238 24c. blue 90 70
239 25c. brown 90 70
188 30c. brown on green . . . 3·75 2·50
240 30c. green 40 40
189 40c. brown on pink . . . . 2·20 1·90
241 40c. turquoise 40 40
190 50c. orange on orange . . . 2·75 1·90
242 50c. mauve 75 60
243 60c. blue . . . . 1·00 70
244 60c. red . . . . 1·10 70
245 80c. red . . . . 3·50 1·00
191 1e. green on blue . . . . 2·75 2·10
246 1e. pink . . . . 4·25 2·20
247 1e. blue . . . . 4·50 2·75
248 2e. purple . . . . 4·25 2·20
249 5e. brown . . . . 7·50 5·25
250 10e. pink . . . . 17·00 10·50
251 20e. green . . . . 48·00 35·00

1921. Nos. 153/4 surch.
252 2c. on 15c. on 150r. brown 1·80 1·20
253 4c. on 10c. on 100r. brown 2·20 2·10

1921. No. 69 surch **6 c. REPUBLICA.**
254 S 6c. on 100r. blue on blue . . 2·20 1·70

1921. Charity Tax stamp of Portuguese Colonies (General issues) optd **CABO VERDE CORREIOS** or surch also.
255 ¼ on 1c. green 45 30
256 ½c. on 1c. green 55 40
257 1c. green 50 40

1922. Provisionals of 1913 surch **$04.**
260 R 4c. on 130r. on 75r. red (No. 202) 80 60
262 4c. on 130r. on 80r. green (No. 204) 80 60
265 4c. on 130r. on 200r. blue (No. 208) 80 65

1925. Provisional stamps of 1902 surch **Republica 40 C.**
267 V 40c. on 400r. on 2½r. brown (No. 106) 80 65
268 R 40c. on 400r. on 300r. blue on buff (No. 103) 80 60

1931. No. 245 surch **70 C.**
269 U 70c. on 80c. red . . . . . 21·00 8·25

1934. As T **17** of Angola (new "Ceres" type).
270 **17** 1c. brown 15 10
271 5c. sepia 15 10
272 10c. mauve 15 10
273 15c. black 20 20
274 20c. grey 20 20
275 30c. green 20 20
276 40c. red 20 20
277 45c. blue . . . . 1·60 70
278 50c. brown 75 45
279 60c. olive 75 45
280 70c. brown 75 45
281 80c. green 75 45
282 85c. red . . . . 3·25 2·10
283 1e. red . . . . 2·20 40
284 1e.40 blue . . . . 3·00 2·50
285 2e. mauve . . . . 3·75 2·10
286 5e. green . . . . 17·00 4·00
287 10e. brown . . . . 26·00 15·00
288 20e. orange . . . . 50·00 20·00

1938. As Nos. 383/409 of Angola.
289 1c. olive (postage) 15 10
290 5c. brown 15 10
291 10c. red 15 10
292 15c. purple 80 70
293 20c. slate 40 20
294 30c. purple 40 20
295 35c. green 40 20
296 40c. brown 40 20
297 50c. mauve 40 20
298 60c. black 40 20
299 70c. violet 40 20
300 80c. orange 35 20
301 1e. red 55 20
302 1e.75 blue . . . . 1·50 55
303 2e. green . . . . 2·75 1·60
304 5e. olive . . . . 6·50 1·60
305 10e. blue . . . . 10·50 2·10
306 20e. brown . . . . 35·00 4·25
307 10c. red (air) 65 50
308 20c. violet 65 50
309 50c. orange 65 50
310 1e. blue 65 50
311 2e. red . . . . 1·50 80
312 3e. green . . . . 2·00 1·40
313 5e. brown . . . . 5·75 2·00
314 9e. red . . . . 9·50 3·50
315 10e. mauve . . . . 10·50 4·50

14 Route of President's Tour

16 Machado Point, Sao Vicente

17 Ribeira Brava, Sao Nicolau

1939. Pres. Carmona's 2nd Colonial Tour.
316 **14** 80c. violet on mauve . . . 4·50 3·00
317 1e.75 blue on blue . . . . 37·00 27·00
318 20e. brown on cream . . . 75·00 25·00

1948. Nos. 276 and 294 surch.
319 10c. on 30c. purple . . . . . 1·80 1·00
320 25c. on 40c. red . . . . . . 1·90 1·00

1948.
321 **16** 5c. purple and bistre . . . 40 30
322 – 10c. green and light green 40 30
323 **17** 50c. purple and lilac . . . 75 30
324 – 1e. purple . . . . 2·75 1·10
325 – 1e.75 blue and green . . . 3·25 1·70
326 – 2e. brown and ochre . . . 7·50 2·10
327 – 5e. green and yellow . . . 15·00 4·00
328 – 10e. red and orange . . . 24·00 14·00
329 – 20e. violet and buff . . . 60·00 26·00
DESIGNS—VERT: 10c. Ribeira Grande. HORIZ: 1e. Porto Grande, Sao Vicente; 1e.75, 5e. Mindelo, Sao Vicente; 2e. Joao de Evora beach, Sao Vicente; 10e. Volcano, Fogo; 20e. Paul.

1948. Honouring the Statue of Our Lady of Fatima. As T **33** of Angola.
330 50c. blue . . . . 8·75 3·75

1949. 75th Anniv of U.P.U. As T **39** of Angola.
331 1e. mauve . . . . 7·00 3·50

1950. Holy Year. As T **41/2** of Angola.
332 1e. brown 85 45
333 2e. blue . . . . 3·50 1·70

1951. Surch with figures and bars over old value.
334 10c. on 35c. (No. 295) . . . 45 40
335 20c. on 70c. (No. 299) . . . 60 45
336 40c. on 70c. (No. 299) . . . 70 45
337 50c. on 80c. (No. 300) . . . 70 45
338 1e. on 1e.75 (No. 302) . . . 75 45
339 2e. on 10e. (No. 305) . . . 1·40 1·50

1951. Termination of Holy Year. As T **44** of Angola.
340 2e. violet and mauve . . . . 1·00 80

1952. No. 302 surch with figures and cross over old values.
341 10c. on 1e.75 blue . . . . . 1·10 95
342 20c. on 1e.75 blue . . . . . 1·10 95
343 50c. on 1e.75 blue . . . . . 4·75 4·25
344 1e. on 1e.75 blue 60 15
345 1e.50 on 1e.75 blue 60 15

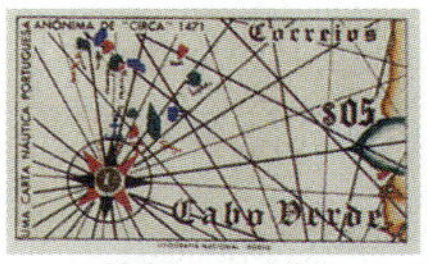

20 Map, c. 1471

21 V. Dias and G. de Cintra

1952. Portuguese Navigators as T **20/21.** Mult.
346 5c. Type **20** 10 10
347 10c. Type **21** 10 10
348 30c. D. Afonso and A. Fernandes 15 10
349 50c. Lancarote and S. da Costa 15 10
350 1e. D. Gomes and A. da Nola 15 10
351 2e. Princes Fernando and Henry the Navigator . . . 1·10 10
352 3e. A. Goncalves and D. Dias 9·50 1·30
353 5e. A. Goncalves Baldaia and J. Fernandes . . . . . 3·25 65
354 10e. D. Fanes da Gra and A. de Freitas . . . . . . 6·25 1·60
355 20e. Map, 1502 . . . . . . 11·50 2·10

22 Doctor giving Injection

23 Facade of Monastery

1952. 1st Tropical Medicine Congress, Lisbon.
356 **22** 20c. black and green . . . 55 40

1953. Missionary Art Exhibition.
357 **23** 10c. brown and olive . . . 10 10
358 50c. violet and salmon . . 70 35
359 1e. green and orange . . . 1·70 1·00

1953. Portuguese Stamp Centenary. As T **48** of Angola.
360 50c. multicoloured . . . . . 1·40 90

1954. 4th Cent of Sao Paulo. As T **49** of Angola.
361 1e. black, green and buff . . 55 45

24 Arms of Cape Verde Is. and Portuguese Guinea

26 Prince Henry the Navigator

25 Arms of Praia

1955. Presidential Visit.
362 **24** 1e. multicoloured 40 20
363 1e.60c. multicoloured . . . 60 55

1958. Centenary of City of Praia. Multicoloured.
364 **25** 1e. on yellow 50 40
365 2e.50 on salmon . . . . . 1·00 80

1958. Brussels International Exn. As T **55** of Angola.
366 2e. multicoloured 65 30

1958. 6th International Congress of Tropical Medicine. As T **56** of Angola. Multicoloured.
367 3c. "Aloe vera" (plant) . . . 1·70 1·90

1960. 500th Death Anniv of Prince Henry the Navigator.
368 **26** 2e. multicoloured 40 20

27 Antonio da Nola

28 "Education"

1960. 500th Anniv of Colonization of Cape Verde Islands. Multicoloured.
369 1e. Type **27** 60 40
370 2e.50 Diogo Gomes . . . . 1·70 90

1960. 10th Anniv of African Technical Co-operation Commission.
371 **28** 2e.50 multicoloured . . . . 1·10 60

29 Arms of Praia

30 Militia Regiment Drummer, 1806

1961. Urban Arms. As T **29.** Arms multicoloured; inscriptions in red and green; background colours given.
372 5c. buff 20 15
373 15c. blue 20 15
374 20c. yellow 20 15
375 30c. lilac 20 15
376 1e. green 65 15
377 2e. lemon 65 15
378 2e.50 pink 95 15
379 3e. brown . . . . 1·50 45
380 5e. blue . . . . 1·50 45
381 7e.50 olive . . . . 1·60 80
382 15e. mauve . . . . 2·30 80
383 30e. yellow . . . . 6·00 2·30
ARMS: 15c. Nova Sintra. 20c. Ribeira Brava. 30c. Assomada. 1e. Maio. 2e. Mindelo. 2e.50 Santa Maria. 3e. Pombas. 5e. Sal-Rei. 7e.50, Tarrafal. 15e. Maria Pia. 30e. San Felipe.

1962. Sports. As T **62** of Angola. Multicoloured.
384 50c. Throwing the javelin . . 25 20
385 1e. Discus thrower 85 20
386 1e.50 Batsman (cricket) . . . 60 30
387 2e.50 Boxing 85 35
388 4e.50 Hurdler . . . . 1·40 95
389 12e.50 Golfers . . . . 2·75 1·90

1962. Malaria Eradication. Mosquito design as T **63** of Angola. Multicoloured.
390 2e.50 "Anopheles pretoriensis" . . . . 1·20 85

1963. 10th Anniv of T.A.P. Airline. As T **69** of Angola.
391 2e.50 multicoloured 90 60

1964. Centenary of National Overseas Bank. As T **71** of Angola but portrait of J. da S. M. Leal.
392 1e.50 multicoloured 85 65

1965. Centenary of I.T.U. As T **73** of Angola.
393 2e.50 multicoloured . . . . . 1·70 1·20

1965. Portuguese Military Uniforms. Mult.
394 50c. Type **30** 25 20
395 1e. Militiaman, 1806 . . . . 45 20
396 1e.50 Infantry Grenadiers officers, 1833 . . . . . . 60 35
397 2e.50 Infantry grenadier, 1833 1·10 30
398 3e. Cavalry officer, 1834 . . 2·30 45
399 4e. Infantry grenadier, 1835 1·10 45

400 5e. Artillery officer, 1848 . . 1·20 45
401 10e. Infantry drum-major, 1856 . . . . 2·50 1·50

1966. 40th Anniv of National Revolution. As T **77** of Angola, but showing different building. Multicoloured.
402 1e. Dr A. Moreira's Academy and Public Assistance Building 50 40

1967. Centenary of Military Naval Association. As T **79** of Angola. Multicoloured.
403 1e. F. da Costa and gunboat "Mandovy" 60 45
404 1e. 50 C. Araujo and minesweeper "Augusto Castilho" . . . . 1·00 75

1967. 50th Anniv of Fatima Apparitions. As T **80** of Angola. Multicoloured.
405 1e. Image of Virgin Mary . . 25 20

33 President Tomas

34 Port of Sao Vicente

1968. Visit of President Tomas of Portugal.
406 **33** 1e. multicoloured 25 20

1968. 500th Birth Anniv of Pedro Cabral (explorer). As T **84** of Angola. Multicoloured.
407 1e. Cantino's map, 1502 . . . 65 60
408 1e.50 Pedro Alvares Cabral (vert) . . . . 1·10 65

1968. "Produce of Cape Verde Islands". Mult.
409 50c. Type **34** 20 15
410 1e. "Purgueira" (Tatrophus curcus) (vert) 35 20
411 1e.50 Groundnuts (vert) . . . 35 20
412 2e.50 Castor-oil plant (vert) 35 20
413 3e.50 "Inhame" (Dioscorea alata) (vert) 40 20
414 4e. Date palm (vert) 40 20
415 4e.50 "Goiabeira" (Psidium guajava) (vert) 65 20
416 5e. Tamarind (vert) 95 25
417 10e. Manioc (vert) . . . . . 1·20 50
418 30e. Girl of Cape Verde (vert) 3·00 2·10

1969. Birth Centenary of Admiral Gago Coutinho. As T **86** of Angola. Multicoloured.
419 30c. Fairey IIID seaplane "Lusitania" and map of Lisbon-Rio flight (vert) . . 15 15

1969. 500th Birth Anniv of Vasco da Gama (explorer). Multicoloured. As T **87** of Angola.
420 1e.50 Vasco da Gama (vert) 30 25

1969. Centenary of Overseas Administrative Reforms. As T **88** of Angola.
421 2e. multicoloured 30 20

1969. 500th Birth Anniv of King Manoel I. As T **89** of Angola. Multicoloured.
422 3e. Manoel I 40 30

1970. Birth Centenary of Marshal Carmona. As T **91** of Angola. Multicoloured.
423 2e.50 Half-length portrait . . 40 30

35 Desalination Installation

37 Cabral, Flag and People

1971. Inauguration of Desalination Plant, Mindelo.
424 **35** 4e. multicoloured . . . . . 1·00 70

1972. 400th Anniv of Camoens' "Lusiad" (epic poem). As T **96** of Angola. Multicoloured.
425 5e. Galleons at Cape Verde 50 25

1972. Olympic Games, Munich. As T **97** of Angola. Multicoloured.
426 4e. Basketball and boxing . . 50 25

1972. 50th Anniv of 1st Flight Lisbon–Rio de Janeiro. As T **98** of Angola. Multicoloured.
427 3e.50 Fairey IIID seaplane "Lusitania" near Sao Vicente 50 25

1973. Centenary of I.M.O./W.M.O. As Type **99** of Angola.
428 2e.50 multicoloured 50 25

1975. Independence. No. 407 optd **INDEPENDENCIA 5-Julho-75.**
430 1e. multicoloured 15 10

1975. 3rd Anniv of Amilcar Cabral's Assassination.
431 **37** 5e. multicoloured 20 15

38 Islanders with Broken Shackles

1976. 1st Anniv of Independence.
432 **38** 50c. multicoloured 10 10
433 3e. multicoloured 15 10
434 15e. multicoloured 40 20
435 50e. multicoloured . . . . 1·25 65
MS436 150 × 110 mm. Nos. 432/5 1·90 1·00

1976. Nos. 428, 424 and 415 optd **REPUBLICA DE.**
437 2e.50 multicoloured (No. 428) 15 10
438 4e. multicoloured (No. 424) 11·00 1·75
439 4e.50 multicoloured (No. 415) 1·00 1·00

40 Cabral and Map

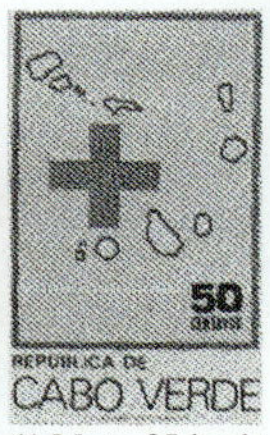

41 Map of Islands

1976. 20th Anniv of PAIGC (Revolutionary Party).
440 **40** 1e. multicoloured 10 10

1977. Red Cross.
441 **41** 50c. multicoloured 10 10

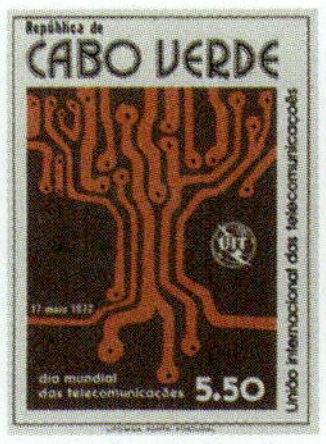

42 Printed Circuit

43 Ashtray on Stand

1977. International Telecommunications Day.
442 **42** 5e.50 orange, brown & blk 15 10

1977. Craftsmanship in Coconut. Multicoloured.
443 20c. Type **43** 10 10
444 30c. Ornamental bell 10 10
445 50c. Lamp 10 10
446 1e. Nativity 10 10
447 1e.50 Desk lamp 10 10
448 5e. Storage jar 15 10
449 10e. Container with hinged lid 35 15
450 20e. Tobacco jar 65 20
451 30e. Stringed instrument . . 1·10 35

44 5r. Stamp, 1877

45 Congress Emblem

1977. Centenary of First Cape Verde Stamps.
452 **44** 4e. multicoloured 15 10
453 8e. multicoloured 25 10

1977. 3rd PAIGC Congress, Bissau.
454 **45** 3e.50 multicoloured 15 10

1978. No. 419 surch **3$00.**
455 3e. on 30c. multicoloured . . 15 10

47 Microwave Antenna

1978. 10th World Telecommunications Day.
456 **47** 3e.50 multicoloured 15 10

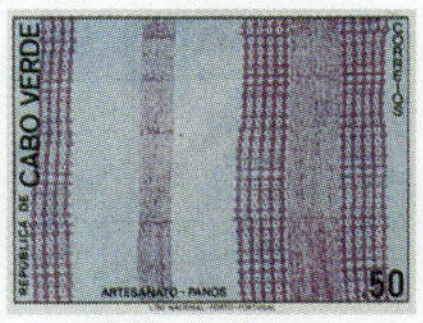

48 Textile Pattern

1978. Handicrafts. Multicoloured.
457 50c. Type **48** 10 10
458 1e.50 Carpet runner and map of Islands 10 10
459 2e. Woven ribbon and map of Islands 10 10
460 3e. Shoulder bag and map of Islands 10 10
461 10e. Woven Cushions (vert) 30 20

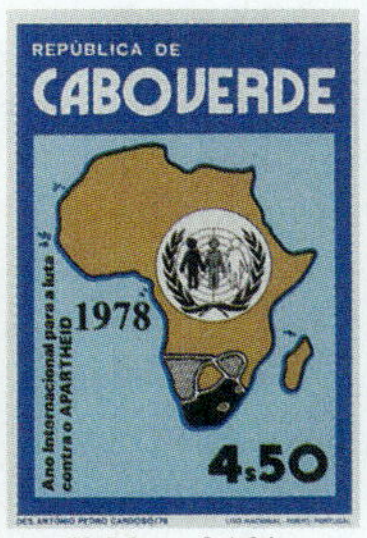

49 Map of Africa

51 Human Rights Emblem

50 Freighter "Cabo Verde"

1978. International Anti-Apartheid Year.
462 **49** 4e.50 multicoloured 15 10

1978. 1st Cape Verde Merchant Ship.
463 **50** 1e. multicoloured 50 10

1978. 30th Anniv of Declaration of Human Rights.
464 **51** 1e.50 multicoloured 10 10
465 2e. multicoloured 10 10

52 Children with Flowers

1979. International Year of the Child. Mult.
466 1e.50 Children with balloons and flags 10 10
467 3e.50 Type **52** 10 10

53 Monument

54 Poster

1979. 20th Anniv of Pindjiguiti Massacre.
468 **53** 4e.50 multicoloured 15 10

1979. 1st National Youth Week.
469 **54** 3e.50 multicoloured 15 10

55 Mindelo

1980. Centenary of Mindelo City.
470 **55** 4e. multicoloured 55 15

56 Family, Graph and Map

57 National Flag

1980. 1st Population and Housing Census.
471 **56** 3e.50 multicoloured 10 10
472 4e.50 multicoloured 15 10

1980. 5th Anniv of Independence (1st issue).
473 **57** 4e. multicoloured 10 10
See also Nos. 481/3.

58 Running

59 Stylized Bird

1980. Olympic Games, Moscow. Multicoloured.
474 1e. Type **58** 10 10
475 2e.50 Boxing 10 10
476 3e. Basketball 10 10
477 4e. Volleyball 10 10
478 20e. Swimming 55 25
479 50e. Tennis . . . . 1·25 50
MS480 98 × 67 mm. 30e. Football (horiz) . . . . 2·35 1·25

1980. 5th Anniv of Independence (2nd issue).
481 **59** 4e. multicoloured 10 10
482 7e. multicoloured 15 10
483 11e. multicoloured 25 15

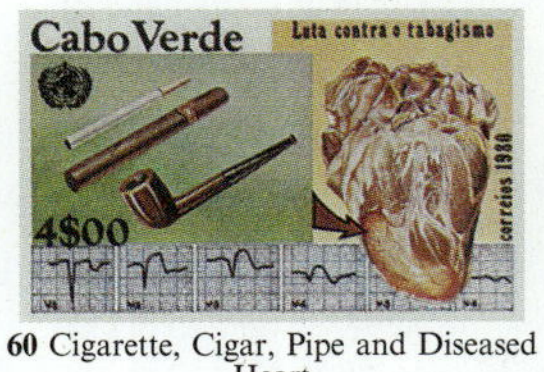

60 Cigarette, Cigar, Pipe and Diseased Heart

1980. World Health Day. Anti-smoking Campaign. Multicoloured.
484 4e. Type **60** 10 10
485 7e. Healthy lungs plus smoking equals diseased lungs 20 10

61 Albacore

1980. Marine Life. Multicoloured.
486 50c. Type **61** 10 10
487 4e.50 Atlantic horse-mackerel 15 10
488 8e. Mediterranean moray . . 40 15
489 10e. Brown meagre 40 15
490 12e. Skipjack tuna 50 20
491 50e. Blue shark . . . . . . 1·50 70

62 "Area Verdel"

1980. Freighters. Multicoloured.
492 3e. Type **62** 25 15
493 5e.50 "Ilha do Maio" 30 20
494 7e.50 "Ilha de Komo" . . . 65 25
495 9e. "Boa Vista" 65 25
496 12e. "Santo Antao" 75 35
497 30e. "Santiago" . . . . . . 1·75 75

63 "Lochnera rosea"

1980. Flowers. Multicoloured.
498 50c. Type **63** 10 10
499 4e.50 "Poinciana regia Bojer" 10 10
500 8e. "Mirabilis jalapa" 25 10
501 10e. "Nerium oleander" . . . 25 10
502 12e. "Bougainvillea litoralis" 30 10
503 30e. "Hibiscus rosa sinenis" 70 30

64 Desert Scene and Hands holding plant

1981. Desert Erosion Prevention. Multicoloured.
504 4e.50 Type **64** 15 10
505 10e.50 Hands caring for plant and river scene 25 15

65 Map, Flag, and "Official Bulletin" announcing Constitution

67 Antenna

66 Austrian Winter Olympics Stamps of 1975

1981. 6th Anniv of Constitution.
506 **65** 4e.50 multicoloured 15 10

1981. WIPA 1981 International Stamp Exhibition, Vienna. Sheet 107 × 62 mm.
MS507 **66** 50e. multicoloured . . 1·25 1·25

1981. Telecommunications. Multicoloured.
508 4e.50 Type **67** 10 10
509 8e. Dish antenna 25 10
510 20e. Dish antenna and satellite 50 30

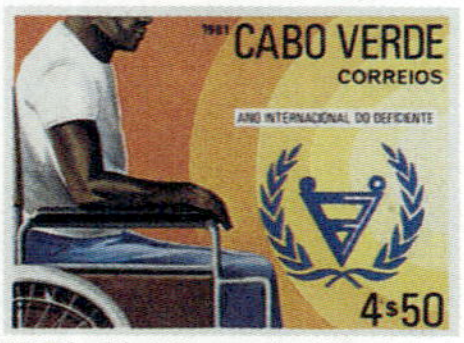

68 Disabled Person in Wheelchair and IYDP Emblem

1981. International Year of Disabled Persons.
511 **68** 4e.50 multicoloured 15 10

69 Moorhens

1981. Birds. Multicoloured.
512 1e. Little egret (vert) 25 10
513 4e.50 Barn owl (vert) 40 20
514 8e. Grey-headed kingfisher (vert) 90 30
515 10e. Type **69** . . . . 1·90 40
516 12e. Helmet guineafowls . . 2·60 40
MS517 79 × 54 mm. 50e. Raza Island lark (Alauda razae) (vert) . . . 1·40 1·40

70 Map showing Member States

1982. CILSS Congress, Praia.
518 **70** 11e.50 multicoloured . . . 30 10

71 Tackle

1982. "Amilcar Cabral" Football Cup Competition. Multicoloured.
519 4e.50 Type **71** 15 10
520 7e.50 Running with ball . . . 20 10
521 11e.50 Goalmouth scene . . . 30 10

72 Militiawomen

1982. 1st Anniv of Cape Verde Women's Organization. Multicoloured.
522 4e.50 Type **72** 15 10
523 8e. Women farmers 20 10
524 12e. Nursery teacher 30 10

73 Footballers

1982. World Cup Football Championship, Spain.
525 **73** 1e.50 multicoloured 10 10
526 – 4e.50 multicoloured 15 10
527 – 8e. multicoloured 20 10
528 – 10e.50 multicoloured . . . 25 10
529 – 12e. multicoloured 30 10
530 – 20e. multicoloured 50 30
MS531 82 × 96 mm. 50e. multicoloured (29 × 37 mm) . . 1·40 1·40
DESIGNS: 4e.50 to 50e. Various footballing scenes.

74 "Morrissey-Ernestina"

1982. Return of Schooner "Morrissey-Ernestina".
532 **74** 12e. multicoloured . . . . 1·50 45

75 San Vicente Shipyard

1982. 7th Anniv of Independence.
533 **75** 10e.50 multicoloured . . . 1·25 45

76 "Hypolimnas misippus"

1982. Butterflies. Multicoloured.
534 2e. Type **76** 15 10
535 4e.50 "Melanitis lede" . . . 25 15
536 8e. "Catopsilia florella" . . . 40 20
537 10e.50 "Colias electo" . . . 55 20
538 11e.50 "Danaus chrysippus" 65 20
539 12e. "Papilio demodecus" . . 65 20

77 Amilcar Cabral

1983. Amilcar Cabral Symposium.
540 **77** 7e. multicoloured 15 10
541 10e.50 multicoloured . . . 20 10

78 Francisco Xavier de Cruz (composer)

1983. Composers and Poets. Multicoloured.
543 7e. Type **78** 15 10
544 14e. Eugenio Tavares (poet) 30 10

79 "World Communications Network"

1983. World Communications Year.
545 **79** 13e. multicoloured 20 10

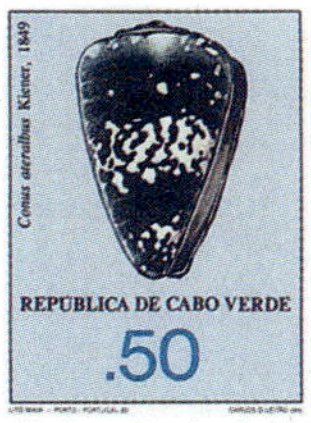

80 Cape Verde Cone

81 Arch and Cross

1983. Shells. Multicoloured.
546 50c. Type **80** 10 10
547 1e. "Conus decoratus" . . . 10 10
548 3e. "Conus salreiensis" . . . 15 10
549 10e. "Conus verdensis" . . . 30 20
550 50e. "Conus cuneolus" . . . 1·40 90

1983. 450th Anniv of Christianity in Cape Verde Islands.
551 **81** 7e. multicoloured 15 10

82 Auster D5/160 Husky

1984. 40th Anniv of ICAO. Multicoloured.
552 50c. Type **82** 10 10
553 2e. De Havilland Dove . . . 10 10
554 10e. Hawker Siddeley HS748 25 15
555 13e. De Havilland Dragon Rapide 25 15
556 20e. De Havilland Twin Otter 50 30
557 50e. Britten-Norman Islander 1·10 65

83 Families, Houses and Emblems as Balloons

84 Figure rising from Nautilus Shell

1984. National Solidarity Campaign.
558 **83** 6e.50 multicoloured 10 10
559 13e.50 multicoloured . . . 20 10

1985. 2nd Cape Verde Womens' Organization Conference.
560 **84** 8e. multicoloured 25 15

85 Emblem

87 "Steamer"

1985. 10th Anniv of Independence.
561 **85** 8e. multicoloured 15 10
562 12e. multicoloured 20 10

1985.
564 **87** 30e. on 10c. multicoloured 40 40
MS565 Three sheets, each 190 × 260 mm. (a) 50e. As No. 564 but ship upper structure red; (b) 50e. As No. 564 but ship upper structure yellow; (c) 50e. As No. 564 but ship upper structure green . . . . 4·00 4·00

88 "Mabuya vaillanti"

89 Food in Pot over Fire

1986. Endangered Reptiles. Multicoloured.
566 8e. Type **88** 30 10
567 10e. "Tarentola gigas brancoensis" 35 10
568 15e. "Tarentola gigas gigas" 45 10
569 30e. "Hemidactylus bouvieri" 90 20
MS570 130 × 60 mm. 50e. Type **88**; 50e. As No. 569 . . . . 2·25 2·25

1986. World Food Day. Multicoloured.
571 8e. Type **89** 15 10
572 12e. Women pounding food in mortar 15 10
573 15e. Woman rolling flat bread with stone 20 10

90 Dove and Olive Branch

1986. International Peace Year.
574 **90** 12e. multicoloured 15 10
575 30e. multicoloured 40 20

91 Family Planning and Child Health Centre, Praia, and Woman breast-feeding Baby

1987. Child Survival Campaign. Multicoloured.
576 8e. Type **91** 15 10
577 10e. Assomada SOS children's village 15 10
578 12e. Family planning clinic, Mindelo, and nurse with child 15 10
579 16e. Children's home, Mindelo, and nurse with baby 25 10
580 100e. Calouste Gulbenkian kindergarten, Praia, and child writing . . . . 1·40 1·25

92 Mindelo City

1987. Tourism. Multicoloured.
581 1e. Type **92** 10 10
582 2e.50 Santo Antao island . . 10 10
583 5e. Fogo island 10 10
584 8e. Pillory, Velha City . . . 15 10
585 10e. Boa Entrada valley, Santiago island 15 10
586 12e. Fishing boats, Santiago 50 15
587 100e. Furna harbour, Brava island . . . . 1·40 65

93 "Carvalho" (schooner)

1987. Sailing Ships. Multicoloured.
588 **93** 12e. black, mauve & blue 45 20
589 – 16e. black, blue & mauve 45 20
590 – 50e. black, blue & dp blue 1·90 70
MS591 105 × 105 mm 60e. × 2, black, brown and violet . . . . . . 4·00 4·00
DESIGNS: 16e. "Nauta"; 50e. "Maria Sony"; 60e. "Madalan".

94 Emblem

1987. 2nd National Development Plan.
592 **94** 8e. multicoloured 15 10

95 Moths on Stem

1988. Crop Protection. Multicoloured.
593 50c. Type **95** 10 10
594 2e. Caterpillars on plant treated with bio-insecticides 10 10
595 9e. Use of imported predators 20 10
596 13e. Use of imported predatorial insects 30 15
597 16e. Locust on stem 35 15
598 19e. Damaged wood 45 20
MS599 115 × 70 mm. 50e. Agricultural Research Institute (41 × 30 mm) . . . . 1·40 1·40

96 17th-century Dutch Map

1988. Antique Maps of Cape Verde Islands. Multicoloured.
600 1e.50 Type **96** 10 10
601 2e.50 18th-cent Belgian map 10 10
602 4e.50 18th-cent French map 10 10
603 9e.50 18th-cent English map 15 10
604 19e.50 19th-cent English map 30 15
605 20e. 18th-cent French map (vert) 30 15

97 Church of the Abbot of the Holy Shelter, Tarrafal, Santiago

1988. Churches. Multicoloured.
606 5e. Type **97** 10 10
607 8e. Church of Our Lady of Light, Maio 15 10
608 10e. Church of the Nazarene, Praia, Santiago 15 10
609 12e. Church of Our Lady of the Rosary, Sao Nicolau 20 10
610 15e. Church of the Nazarene, Mindelo, Sao Vicente . . . 25 15
611 20e. Church of Our Lady of Grace, Praia, Santiago . . 30 15

98 Boy filling Tin with Water

1988. Water Economy Campaign.
612 **98** 12e. multicoloured 20 10

99 Red Cross Workers

1988. 125th Anniv of Red Cross Movement.
613 **99** 7e. multicoloured 10 10

100 Group of Youths and Pres. Pereira

1988. 3rd Congress of African Party for the Independence of Cape Verde. Multicoloured.
614 7e. Type **100** 10 10
615 10e.50 Pres. Pereira and Perez de Cuellar (U.N. Secretary-General) 15 10
616 30e. Emblem and Pres. Pereira 50 25
MS617 130 × 90 mm. 100e. As No. 616 . . . . 1·40 1·40

101 Handball

1988. Olympic Games, Seoul. Multicoloured.
618 12e. Type **101** 20 10
619 15e. Tennis 25 15
620 20e. Football 30 15
621 30e. Boxing 50 25
MS622 130 × 90 mm. 50e. Long jump 70 70

102 Hot-air Balloon "Pro Juventute"

1989. 2nd Pro Juventute Congress.
623 **102** 30e. multicoloured . . . 45 25

103 Silva

1989. Death Centenary of Roberto Duarte Silva (chemist).
624 **103** 12e.50 multicoloured . . 20 10

104 "Liberty guiding the People" (Eugene Delacroix)

1989. Bicentenary of French Revolution.
625 **104** 20e. multicoloured . . . 30 15
626 24e. multicoloured . . . 35 20
627 25e. multicoloured . . . 40 20
MS628 120 × 76 mm. 100e. multicoloured . . . . 1·40 1·40
DESIGNS: 29 × 37 mm. 100e. Detail of Arc de Triomphe, Paris.
No. **MS**628 also commemorates "Philexfrance 89" International Stamp Exhibition.

105 Anniversary Emblem

1989. Centenary of Interparliamentary Union. Mult.
629 2e. Type **105** 10 10
630 4e. Dove 10 10
631 13e. National Assembly building 20 10

106 Fonte Lima Women firing Pots

1989. Traditional Pottery. Multicoloured.
632 13e. Type **106** 20 10
633 20e. Terra di Monti women and children arranging pots to bake in sun (vert) . . . 30 15
634 24e. Terra di Monti woman shaping pot 35 20
635 25e. Fonte Lima women kneading clay (vert) . . . 40 20

107 Boy and Truck

108 Pope John Paul II

1989. Christmas. Home-made Toys. Mult.
636 1e. Type **107** 10 10
637 6e. Boy with car on waste ground 10 10
638 8e. Boy with truck on pavement 15 10
639 11e.50 Boys with various vehicles 15 10
640 18e. Boys and sit-on scooter 30 15
641 100e. Boy with boat . . . . 1·50 75

1990. Papal Visit.
642 **108** 13e. multicoloured 20 10
643 20e. multicoloured 30 15
MS644 110 mm. 200e. multicoloured 3·00 3·00
DESIGN: 200e. Pope wearing mitre.

109 Green Turtles

1990. Turtles. Multicoloured.
645 50c. Type **109** 10 10
646 1e. Leatherback turtles . . . 10 10
647 5e. Olive ridley turtles . . . 10 10
648 10e. Loggerhead turtles . . . 15 10
649 42e. Hawksbill turtles 65 35

110 Footballers

1990. World Cup Football Championship, Italy.
650 **110** 4e. multicoloured 10 10
651 – 7e.50 multicoloured . . . 15 10
652 – 8e. multicoloured 15 10
653 – 100e. multicoloured . . . 1·60 80
MS654 87 × 54 mm. 100e. multicoloured . . . . 1·40 1·40
DESIGNS: 7e.50 to 100e. Different footballing scenes.

111 Face

1990. 1st Congress of Cape Verde Women's Movement.
655 **111** 9e. multicoloured 15 10

112 Teacher helping Boy to Read

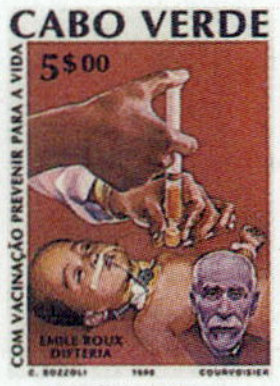

113 Diphtheria Treatment and Emile Roux (pioneer of antitoxic method)

1990. International Literacy Year. Multicoloured.
656 2e. Type **112** 10 10
657 3e. Teacher with adult class 10 10
658 15e. Teacher with flash-card 25 15
659 19e. Adult student pointing to letters on blackboard . . 30 15

1990. Vaccination Campaign. Multicoloured.
660 5e. Type **113** 10 10
661 13e. Tuberculosis vaccination and Robert Koch (discoverer of tubercle bacillus) 20 10
662 20e. Tetanus vaccination and Gaston Ramon 30 15
663 24e. Poliomyelitis oral vaccination and Jonas Edward Salk (discoverer of vaccine) 40 20

114 Musician on Bull's Back

1990. Traditional Stories. Multicoloured.
664 50c. Type **114** 10 10
665 2e.50 Fisherman and mermaid ("Joao Piquinote") 10 10
666 12e. Girl and snake 20 10
667 25e. Couple and eggs ("Ti Lobo, Ti Lobo") 40 20

115 World Map and Beam destroying AIDS Virus

1991. Anti-AIDS Campaign. Multicoloured.

668	13e. Type **115**	20	10
669	24e. Beam, AIDS virus and "SIDA"	40	20

116 Fishing Boat at Sea and Fishermen on Shore

1991. Fishing Industry. Multicoloured.

670	10e. Type **116**	20	15
671	24e. Fisherman removing hook from fish	70	30
672	25e. Fishing boats	55	30
673	50e. Fishermen taking in lines	1·10	65

117 Our Lady of the Rosary Church

1991. Tourism. Ruins of Ribeira Grande, Santiago Island. Multicoloured.

674	12e.50 Type **117**	20	10
675	15e. Se Cathedral	25	15
676	20e. Sao Filipe fortress	30	15
677	30e. St. Francis's Convent	45	20
MS678	81 × 79 mm. 100e. Pillory (vert)	1·40	1·40

118 "Lavandula rotundifolia" 119 Guitar

1991. Medicinal Plants. Multicoloured.

679	10e. Type **118**	15	10
680	15e. "Micromeria forbesii"	25	15
681	21e. "Sarcostemma daltonii"	30	15
682	24e. "Periploca chevalieri"	40	20
683	30e. "Echium hypertropicum"	45	20
684	35e. "Erysimum caboverdeanum"	55	25

1991. Musical Instruments. Multicoloured.

685	10e. Type **119**	25	15
686	20e. Violin	50	35
687	29e. Guitar with five double strings	80	40
688	47e. Cimboa	1·25	75

120 Crib (Tito Livio Goncalves)

1991. Christmas. Multicoloured.

690	31e. Type **120**	50	25
691	50e. Fonte-Lima crib	80	40

121 Rose Apples

1992. Tropical Fruits. Multicoloured.

692	16e. Type **121**	35	15
693	25e. Mangoes	50	25
694	31e. Cashews	65	30
695	32e. Avocados	70	35

122 Ships anchored in Bay

1992. 500th Anniv of Discovery of America by Columbus. Columbus's Landings in Cape Verde Islands. Multicoloured.

696	40e. Type **122**	1·10	70
697	40e. Caravel	1·10	70
MS698	130 × 63 mm. Nos. 696/7 (sold at 150e.)	4·00	4·00

123 Alhambra, Granada

1992. Granada 92 International Stamp Exhibition, Spain. Sheet 135 × 95 mm.

MS699	**123** 50e. multicoloured (sold at 150e.)	4·00	4·00

124 Throwing the Javelin

1992. Olympic Games, Barcelona. Multicoloured.

700	16e. Type **124**	35	15
701	20e. Weightlifting	40	20
702	32e. Pole vaulting	70	35
703	40e. Putting the shot	85	40
MS704	98 × 71 mm. 100e. Gymnastics (26 × 32 mm)	1·40	1·40

125 Oxen and Sugar Cane

1992. Production of Molasses. Multicoloured.

705	19e. Type **125**	35	15
706	20e. Crushing cane	35	15
707	37e. Feeding cane into mill	70	35
708	38e. Cooking molasses	70	35

126 Cat

1992. Domestic Animals. Multicoloured.

709	16e. Type **126**	30	15
710	31e. Chickens	55	25
711	32e. Dog (vert)	60	30
712	50e. Horse	90	45

127 "Tubastrea aurea"

1993. Corals. Multicoloured.

713	5e. Type **127**	10	10
714	31e. "Corallium rubrum"	55	25
715	37e. "Porites porites"	65	30
716	50e. "Millepora alcicornis"	90	45

128 "Praia Harbour, Santiago Island, 1806"

1993. Brasilliana 93 International Stamp Exhibition, Rio de Janeiro, and union of Portuguese-speaking Capital Cities. Sheet 118 × 75 mm.

MS717	**128** 100e. multicoloured	1·80	1·80

129 King Ferdinand and Queen Isabella of Spain and Pope Alexander VI

1993. 500th Annivs of Pope Alexander VI's Bulls (on Portuguese and Spanish spheres of influence) and of Treaty of Tordesillas. Multicoloured.

718	37e. Type **129**	65	30
719	37e. King Joao II of Portugal and Pope Julius II	65	30
720	38e. Astrolabe, quill and left-half of globe	70	35
721	38e. Map of Iberian Peninsula and right-half of globe with Cape Verde Islands highlighted	70	35

Stamps of the same value were issued together in se-tenant pairs, each pair forming a composite design.

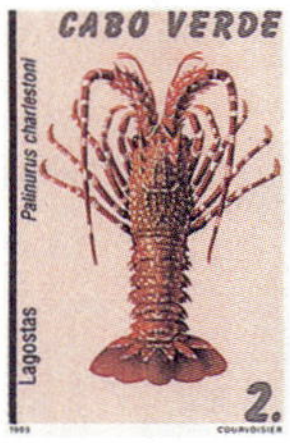

130 "Palinurus charlestoni"

1993. Lobsters. Multicoloured.

722	2e. Type **130**	10	10
723	10e. Brown lobster	20	10
724	17e. Royal lobster	30	15
725	38e. Stone lobster	70	35
MS726	110 × 70 mm.100e. Royal lobster on seabed (51 × 36 mm)	1·80	1·80

131 Cory's Shearwater

1993. Nature Reserves. Multicoloured.

727	10e. Type **131** (Branco and Raso Islets)	25	15
728	30e. Brown booby (De Cima and Raso Islets)	80	25
729	40e. Magnificent frigate bird (Curral Velho and Baluarte Islets)	1·50	35
730	41e. Red-billed tropic bird (Raso and De Cima Islets)	1·90	40

132 Rose

1993. Flowers. Multicoloured.

731	5e. Type **132**	10	10
732	30e. Bird of Paradise flower	55	25
733	37e. Sweet William	65	30
734	50e. Cactus dahlia	90	45

1994. Hong Kong 94 International Stamp Exhibition,. Sheet 110 × 70 mm. Multicoloured.

MS735	No. 729 (sold at 150e.)	4·00	4·00

133 Map and Prince Henry (½-size illustration)

1994. 600th Birth Anniv of Prince Henry the Navigator.

736	**133** 37e. multicoloured	55	25

134 Players and Giants Stadium, New York

1994. World Cup Football Championship, U.S.A. Multicoloured.

737	1e. Type **134**	10	10
738	20e. Referee showing red card and Rose Bowl, Los Angeles	30	15
739	37e. Scoring goal and Foxboro Stadium, Boston	55	25
740	38e. Linesman raising flag and Silverdome, Detroit	55	25
MS741	110 × 70 mm. 100e. Tackle and RFK Stadium, Washington D.C	1·80	1·80

135 Sand Tiger 136 "Prata" Bananas

1994. Sharks. Multicoloured.

742	21e. Type **135**	45	15
743	27e. Black-tipped shark	60	25
744	37e. Whale shark	1·00	50
745	38e. Velvet belly	1·00	50

1994. Bananas. Multicoloured.

746	12e. Type **136**	20	10
747	16e. "Pao" bananas (horiz)	25	10
748	30e. "Ana roberta" bananas	45	20
749	40e. "Roxa" bananas	60	30
MS750	64 × 82 mm. 100e. "Prata" bananas on tree (27 × 40 mm) (sold at 150e.)	1·80	1·80

No. **MS**750 commemorates Philakorea 1994 International and Singpex 94 stamp exhibitions.

137 Fontes Pereira de Melo

1994. Lighthouses. Multicoloured.

751	2e. Type **137**	10	10
752	37e. Morro Negro	60	30
753	38e. D. Amelia (vert)	60	30
754	50e. D. Maria Pia (vert)	80	40

138 X-Ray Tube and Dates

1995. Centenary of Discovery of X-Rays by Wilhelm Rontgen.

755	**138** 20e. multicoloured	30	15
756	37e. multicoloured	60	30
MS757	Sheet 142 × 95 mm. Nos. 755/6 (sold at 100e.)	1·80	1·80

139 Child with Tuna 141 Communications

140 Wire-haired Fox Terrier and "Two Foxhounds and Fox Terrier" (John Emms)

1995. 50th Anniv of FAO. Multicoloured.

758	37e. Type **139**	70	30
759	38e. Globe and wheat ear	60	30

1995. Dogs. Heads of dogs and paintings. Mult.

760	1e. Type **140**	10	10
761	10e. Cavalier King Charles and "Shooting Over Dogs" (Richard Ansdell)	15	10
762	40e. German shepherd and rough collies	65	30
763	50e. Bearded collie and "Hounds at Full Cry" (Thomas Blinks)	80	40

1995. 20th Anniv of Independence.

764 **141**	37e. multicoloured	1·00	40

142 Sweet William ("Dianthus barbatus")

1995. Singapore 95 International Stamp Exhibition. Sheet 110 × 70 mm.

MS765 **142**	37e. multicoloured (sold at 150e.)	4·00	4·00

143 Horse Race

1995. St. Philip's Flag Festival, Fogo. Mult.

766	2e. Type **143**	10	10
767	10e. Preparing for horse race	15	10
768	37e. Preparing food and clapping to music	55	25
769	40e. Crowd watching final horse race	60	30

144 Grasshopper playing Guitar

1995. Childrens' Stories. 300th Death Anniv of Jean de La Fontaine (writer). Scenes from "The Ant and the Grasshopper". Multicoloured.

770	10e. Type **144**	15	10
771	25e. Grasshopper in snowstorm looking through ants' window	40	20
772	38e. Ant laying-in supplies for winter	55	25
773	45e. Ants welcoming grasshopper into their home	70	35

145 "Sonchus daltonii"

1996. Endangered Flowers. Multicoloured.

774	20e. Type **145**	30	15
775	37e. "Echium vulcanorum"	55	25
776	38e. "Nauplius smithii"	55	25
777	50e. "Campanula jacobaea"	75	35

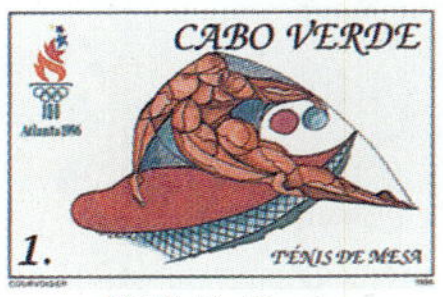

146 Table Tennis

1996. Olympic Games, Atlanta. Multicoloured.

778	1e. Type **146**	10	10
779	37e. Gymnastics	55	25
780	100e. Athletics	1·50	75

147 Student (Education of Girls) **148** Deep Sea Fishing

1996. 50th Anniv of UNICEF. Multicoloured.

781	20e. Type **147**	25	10
782	40e. Mother kissing child (Right to Love)	50	25

1996. Water Sports. Multicoloured.

783	2e.50 Type **148**	10	10
784	10e. Sailboard	20	10
785	22e.50 Jet skiing	30	15
786	100e. Surfing (horiz)	1·25	60
MS787	155 × 110 mm. 100e. Fish (scuba diving) (78 × 60 mm)	1·80	1·80

1997. Nos. 582 and 650/1 surch.

788	3e. on 2e.50 multicoloured	10	10
789	37e. on 4e. multicoloured	50	25
790	38e. on 7e.50 multicoloured	55	25

150 State Arms

1997. National Symbols. Multicoloured.

791	25e. Type **150**	30	15
792	37e. National anthem	40	20
793	50e. State flag	60	30

151 Small-toothed Sawfish

1997. The Small-toothed Sawfish. Multicoloured.

794	15e. Type **151**	20	10
795	15e. Underside of sawfish	20	10
796	15e. Sawfish and school of fishes	20	10
797	15e. Two sawfishes	20	10

152 Fish and Dolphins

1997. Oceans. Multicoloured.

798	45e. Type **152**	55	25
799	45e. Mermaid and merman	55	25
800	45e. Fishes, eel, coral and sunken gate	55	25

Nos. 798/800 were issued together, se-tenant, forming a composite design.

153 Yellow-finned Tuna

1997. Tuna. Multicoloured.

801	13e. Type **153**	15	10
802	21e. Big-eyed tuna	25	10
803	41e. Little tuna	50	25
804	45e. Skipjack tuna	55	25

154 Players chasing Ball

1998. World Cup Football Championship, France. Multicoloured.

805	10e. Type **154**	10	10
806	30e. Ball in net (vert)	45	20
807	45e. Player with ball (vert)	55	25
808	50e. Globe, football and trophy	60	30

155 Fish Dish

1998. Local Cuisine.

809 **155**	5e. multicoloured	10	10
810 –	25e. multicoloured	30	15
811 –	35e. multicoloured	40	20
812 –	40e. multicoloured	45	20

DESIGNS: 25e. to 40e. Different food dishes.

156 Navigators reading Books and Banana Tree

1998. 500th Anniv (1997) of Vasco da Gama's Expedition to India. Multicoloured.

813	50e. Type **156**	60	30
814	50e. Seaman with sword and couple	60	30
815	50e. Compass rose and Portuguese galleon in harbour	1·00	40

Nos. 813/15 were issued together, se-tenant, forming a composite design.

157 Brava Island Costume **158** "Byblia ilithyia"

1998. Local Women's Costumes. Multicoloured.

816	10e. Type **157**	10	10
817	18e. Fogo Island	20	10
818	30e. Boa Vista Island	35	15
819	50e. Santiago Island	60	30

1999. Butterflies and Moths. Multicoloured.

820	5e. Type **158**	10	10
821	10e. "Aganais speciosa"	10	10
822	20e. Crimson-speckled moth	25	10
823	30e. Painted lady	35	15
824	50e. Cabbage looper	60	30
825	100e. "Grammodes congenita"	1·25	60
MS826	114 × 68 mm. No. 822/3	60	60

159 Concorde in Flight

1999. 30th Anniv of Concorde (supersonic airplane). Multicoloured.

827	30e. Type **159**	35	15
828	50e. Concorde on airport apron	60	30

160 Alain Gerbault (solo yachtsman) and Mindelo Harbour

1999. "Philexfrance 99" International Stamp Exhibition, Paris, France. Multicoloured.

829	30e. Type **160**	40	20
830	50e. Roberto Duarte Silva (chemist) and Eiffel Tower, Paris	60	30
MS831	155 × 79 mm. Nos. 829/30 (sold at 100e.)	1·80	1·90

161 Globe in Envelope and UPU Emblem

1999. 125th Anniv of Universal Postal Union. Mult.

832	30e. Type **161**	40	20
833	50e. Paper airplanes	60	30

Nos. 832/3 are not inscribed with the country name.

162 Cola Sanjon Dance **163** Globe, Open Book and Hourglass

1999. Local Dances. Multicoloured.

834	10e. Type **162**	10	10
835	30e. Contradanca	30	15
836	50e. Desfile de Tabanca (horiz)	50	25
837	100e. Batuque (horiz)	1·00	50

2000. New Millennium. Multicoloured.

838	40e. Type **163**	40	20
839	50e. "2000" (horiz)	50	25

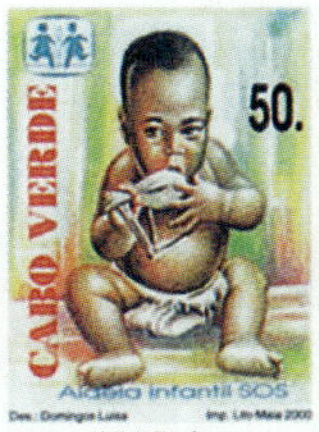

164 Baby

2000. 50th Anniv (1999) of S.O.S. Children's Villages. Multicoloured.

840	50e. Type **164**	50	25
841	100e. Child and emblem (horiz)	1·00	50

165 "25" and Emblem

2000. 25th Anniv of Independence.

842 **165**	50e. multicoloured	50	25

166 Gymnastics

2000. Olympic Games, Sydney. Multicoloured.

843	10e. Type **166**	10	10
844	40e. Taekwondo	40	20
845	50e. Athletics	50	25
MS846	70 × 120 mm. Nos. 843/5	1·00	1·00

167 Dragon Tree **168** Students (left-hand detail)

2000. Dragon Tree.
847 **167** 5e. green 10 10
848 40e. red 50 25
849 60e. brown 70 35

2000. 134th Anniv of the Liceu de Sao Nicolau Seminary. Multicoloured.
850 60e. Type **168** 70 35
851 60e. Students (right-hand detail) 70 35
852 60e. Jose Alves Feio, Jose Julio Dias (co-founders) and Antonio Jose de Oliveira Boucas (Principal) (56 × 26 mm) 70 35
Nos. 850/2 were issued together, se-tenant, forming a composite design.

169 White Sea Bream (*Diplodus sargus*)

2001. Fish. Multicoloured.
853 10e. Type **169** 10 10
854 22e. *Diplodus prayensis* . . . 20 10
855 28e. Marmora sea bream (*Lithognathus mormyrus*) 25 15
856 48e. *Diplodus fasciatus* . . . 45 20
857 60e. *Diplodus puntazzo* . . . 55 25

170 *Thomisus onustus*

2001. Spiders. Multicoloured.
858 13e. Type **170** 10 10
859 16e. *Scytodes velutina* 15 10
860 40e. *Hersiliola simony* 35 15
861 100e. *Loxosceles rufescens* . . 95 45

171 *Acacia albida*

2001. Trees. Multicoloured.
862 50e. Type **171** 45 20
863 60e. *Ficus sycomorus* 55 25

172 Grand Place, Brussels and Fountain

2001. "Belgica 2001" International Stamp Exhibition, Brussels. Sheet 116 × 86 mm.
MS864 **172** 100e. multicoloured 95 45

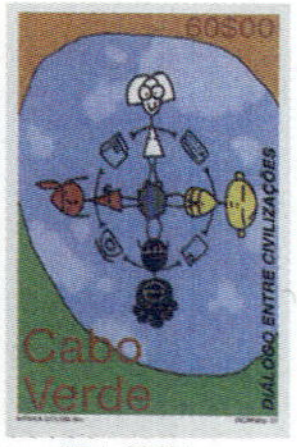

173 Artemisia gorgonum (inscr "Artimisia") **174** Children encircling Globe

2001. Plants (1st series). Multicoloured.
865 20e. Type **173** 20 10
866 27e. *Globularia amygdalifolia* 25 15
867 47e.50 *Sidereoxylon marginata* (*horiz*) 45 25
868 50e. *Umbilicus schmidtii* (*horiz*) 45 20
869 60e. *Verbascum cystolithicum* 55 25
870 100e. *Limonium lobinii* . . . 95 45
See also Nos. 873/6.

2001. United Nations Year of Dialogue among Civilizations.
871 **174** 60e. multicoloured 55 25

175 Antonio Goncalves

2001. Birth Centenary of Antonio Aurelio Goncalves (writer).
872 **175** 100e. multicoloured . . . 95 45

2002. Plants (2nd series). As T **173**. Multicoloured.
873 10e. *Euphorbia tuckeyana* (inscr "tuckeyna") (*horiz*) 10 10
874 50e. *Limonium* 45 20
875 60e. *Aeonium gorgoneum* . . 55 25
876 100e. *Polycarpaea gayi* . . . 95 45

176 Player heading Ball into Goal

2002. World Cup Football Championship, Japan and South Korea. Multicoloured.
877 60e. Type **176** 55 25
878 100e. Player kicking ball towards goal 95 45

177 Two Adult Turtles

2002. Marine Turtles (*Caretta caretta*). Multicoloured.
879 10e. Type **177** 10 10
880 20e. Laying eggs 20 10
881 30e. Young emerging from sand 30 15
882 60e. Young crawling towards sea 55 25
883 100e. Adult swimming . . . 95 45
MS884 150 × 110 mm. 100e. Adult on beach (80 × 61 mm) 95 45

178 Basket from St. Nicholas Island

2002. Traditional Baskets. Multicoloured.
885 20e. Type **178** 20 10
886 33e. From St. Anthony Island 30 15
887 60e. From Santiago Island 55 25
888 100e. From Boa Vista Island 95 45

179 Carlos Alberto Silva Martins (Katchass) (musician)

2003. Poets and Musicians. Multicoloured.
889 12e. Type **179** 10 10
890 20e. Jorge Monteiro (Jotamonte) (composer) . . 20 10
891 32e. Luís Rendall (composer) 30 15
892 47e.50 Jorge Barbosa (poet) 45 20
893 60e. Januario Leite (poet) . . 55 25
894 100e. Jose Lopes (poet) . . . 95 45

180 Cesaria Evora

2003. Cesaria Evora (singer) Commemoration. Multicoloured.
895 60e. Type **180** 55 25
896 100e. Cesaria Evora (different) 95 45
MS897 85 × 115 mm. 200e. Cesaria Evora's legs (51 × 38 mm) . . . . 1·90 1·90
MS897 forms a composite design of Cesaria Evora singing.

181 Purple Heron (*Ardea purpurea boumei*)

2003. Herons and Egrets. Multicoloured.
898 10e. Type **181** 10 10
899 27e. Grey heron (*Ardea cinerea*) 25 10
900 42e. Cattle egret (*Bubulcus ibis*) 40 20
901 60e. Little egret (*Egretta garzeta*) 55 25

182 Scout

2003. Scouting. Multicoloured.
902 60e. Type **182** (13th anniv of Scouts Association) 75 30
903 100e. Scout with raised hand (3rd anniv of Catholic Scouts Corps) . . . . . . 1·20 60

183 Blue Whale (Balaenoptera musculus)

2003. Marine Mammals. Multicoloured.
904 10e. Type **183** 15 10
905 20e. Sperm whale (Physeter macrocephalus) 25 10
906 50e. Humpback whale (Megaptera novaeangliae) 30 15
907 60e. Pilot whale (Globicephala macrorhynchus) 75 30

184 CAMS 51-F (biplane flying boat) at Calheta de Sao Martinho

2003. 75th Anniv of First Postal Hydroplane Base, Calheta de Sao Martinho. Multicoloured.
908 10e. Type **184** 15 10
909 42e. Paulin Paris (1st pilot) and route 50 25
910 60e. Route and CAMS 51-F 75 30
MS911 100 × 54 mm. 100e. As No. 908 but with design enlarged (57 × 33 mm) . . . . 1·20 1·20

185 Pope John Paul II and Child **186** Mahogany (*Khaya senegalensis*)

2003. 25th Anniv of the Pontificate of Pope John Paul II. Multicoloured.
912 30e. Type **185** 25 10
913 60e. Pope John Paul II and ships (horiz) 75 30
MS914 83 × 64 mm. 100e. Pope John Paul II blessing crucifix . . . . 1·20 1·20

2004. Trees. Multicoloured.
915 20e. Type **186** 25 10
916 27e. Black thorn (*Acacia nilotica*) 35 15
917 60e. Ceiba (*Ceiba pentandra*) 75 30
918 100e. Palm (*Phoenix atlantica*) . . . . 1·20 60

187 Windmill **188** Taekwondo

2004. Ecological Energy Production.
919 **187** 20e. blue 25 10
920 60e. magenta 75 30
921 100e. green . . . . 1·20 60

2004. Olympic Games, Athens. Multicoloured.
922 10e. Type **188** 15 10
923 60e. Gymnastics 75 30
924 100e. Boxing (horiz) . . . . 1·20 60

189 Ponta Barril, Sao Nicolau

2004. Lighthouses. Multicoloured.
925 10e. Type **189** 15 10
926 30e. Ponta Jalunga, Brava . . 35 20
927 40e. Dom Luis, Sao Vicente (horiz) 50 30
928 50e. Ponta Preta, Santiago (horiz) 70 35

190 House with Veranda

2004. Fogo Island's Historic Houses. Multicoloured.
929 20e. Type **190** 25 10
930 40e. House with veranda, bay window and wall with gate 50 30
931 50e. Three storied house . . 60 35
932 60e. Pink house 75 45

191 Wall-mounted Telephone

2004. Twentieth-century Telephones. Multicoloured.
933 10e. Type **191** 15 10
934 40e. Early windup handset 50 30
935 60e. Candlestick telephone . . 75 45
936 100e. Bakelite telephone . . . 1·20 75

192 "storia storia"

2005. Stories. Multicoloured.
937 10e. Type **192** 15 10
938 20e. "era um vez!" 25 10
939 30e. "sapatinha ribera baxu" 35 20
940 60e. "Quem ki sabi mas conta midjor" 75 45

193 Amilcar Cabral (freedom fighter)

2005. 30th Anniv of Independence.
941 **193** 60e. multicoloured 75 45

194 *Conus evorai*

2005. Shells. Multicoloured.

942	30e. Type **194**	35	20
943	40e. *Harpa doris*	50	30
944	50e. Strombus lotus	60	20
945	60e. *Phyllonotus duplex*	75	45

195 *Passer iagoensis*

2005. Birds. Multicoloured.

946	19e. Type **195**	25	10
947	42e. *Estrilda astrid*	55	35
948	44e. *Passer domesticus*	55	35
949	55e. *Acrocephalus brevipennis*	70	40

196 Emblem

2005. World Information Society Summit, Tunis.

950	**196** 60e. multicoloured	75	45

197 Tobacco Pipes

2005. Artefacts. Multicoloured.

951	5e. Type **197**	10	10
952	10e. Spy glass, ornate stand and decorated box	15	10
953	30e. Cannon	40	25
954	60e. Astrolabe	85	50
MS955	115 × 85 mm. 100e. Shackles (80 × 60 mm)	1·40	85

CHARITY TAX STAMPS

Used on certain days of the year as an additional postal tax on internal letters. Other values in some of the types were for use on telegrams only. The proceeds were devoted to public charities. If one was not affixed in addition to the ordinary postage, postage due stamps were used to collect the deficiency and the fine.

1925. As Marquis de Pombal issue of Portugal but inscr "CABO VERDE".

C266	**C 73** 15c. violet	1·10	1·10
C267	– 15c. violet	1·10	1·10
C268	**C 75** 15c. violet	1·10	1·10

C **16** St. Isabel

C **31**

C **32**

1948.

C321	**C 16** 50c. green	2·30	1·40
C322	1e. red	3·25	1·60

1959. Surch.

C368	**C 16** 50c. on 1e. red	90	70

1959. Colours changed.

C369	**C 16** 50c. mauve	1·60	90
C370	1e. blue	1·60	90

1967.

C406	**C 31** 30c. multicoloured	35	35
C407	50c. mult (purple panel)	70	70
C408	50c. mult (red panel)	30	30
C409	1e. mult (brown panel)	70	70
C410	1e. mult (purple panel)	70	70

1968. Pharmaceutical Tax stamps surch as in Type C **32**.

C411a	**C 32** 50c. on 1c. black, orange and green	1·20	90
C412c	50c. on 2c. black, orange and green	70	40
C413	50c. on 3c. black, orange and green	85	60
C414	50c. on 5c. black, orange and green	85	60
C415	50c. on 10c. black, orange and green	90	80
C416	1e. on 1c. black, orange and green	1·80	1·40
C417a	1e. on 2c. black, orange and green	1·40	1·10

NEWSPAPER STAMP

1893. "Newspaper" key-type inscr "CABO VERDE".

N37	V 2½r. brown	75	50

POSTAGE DUE STAMPS

1904. "Due" key-type inscr "CABO VERDE".

D119	W 5r. green	30	30
D120	10r. grey	30	30
D121	20r. brown	30	30
D122	30r. orange	65	35
D123	50r. brown	40	30
D124	60r. brown	3·75	2·40
D125	100r. mauve	1·10	80
D126	130r. blue	1·10	80
D127	200r. red	1·00	85
D128	500r. lilac	2·40	1·80

1911. Nos. D119/28 optd **REPUBLICA**.

D135	W 5r. green	20	20
D136	10r. grey	20	20
D137	20r. brown	20	20
D138	30r. orange	20	20
D139	50r. brown	20	20
D140	60r. brown	40	30
D141	100r. mauve	40	30
D142	130r. blue	50	40
D143	200r. red	1·00	85
D144	500r. lilac	1·30	1·00

1921. "Due" key-type inscr "CABO VERDE" with currency in centavos.

D252	W ½c. green	15	15
D253	1c. slate	15	15
D254	2c. brown	15	15
D255	3c. orange	15	15
D256	5c. brown	15	15
D257	6c. brown	15	15
D258	10c. mauve	15	15
D259	13c. blue	55	40
D260	20c. red	55	40
D261	50c. grey	75	55

1925. As Nos. C266/8, optd **MULTA**.

D266	**C 73** 30c. violet	45	45
D267	– 30c. violet	45	45
D268	**C 75** 30c. violet	45	45

1952. As Type D **45** of Angola, but inscr "CABO VERDE". Numerals in red; name in black.

D356	10c. brown and grey	15	15
D357	30c. black, blue & mauve	15	15
D358	50c. blue, green & yellow	15	15
D359	1e. blue and pale blue	15	15
D360	2e. brown and orange	30	30
D361	5e. green and grey	60	60

CAROLINE ISLANDS Pt. 7

A group of islands in the Pacific Ocean, formerly a German protectorate; under Japanese mandate after 1918. Now under United States trusteeship.

100 pfennig = 1 mark.

1899. Stamps of Germany optd **Karolinen**.

7	**8** 3pf. brown	13·00	12·50
8	5pf. green	18·00	17·00
9	**9** 10pf. red	18·00	19·00
10	20pf. blue	24·00	27·00
11	25pf. orange	55·00	60·00
12	50pf. brown	55·00	60·00

1901. "Yacht" key-types inscr "KAROLINEN".

13	N 3pf. brown	1·10	1·70
14	5pf. green	1·10	2·00
15	10pf. red	1·10	4·75
16	20pf. blue	1·30	8·50
17	25pf. black & red on yellow	1·60	13·50
18	30pf. black & orge on buff	1·60	13·50
19	40pf. black and red	1·60	15·00
20	50pf. black & pur on buff	2·00	21·00
21	80pf. black & red on rose	3·00	24·00
22	O 1m. red	4·50	60·00
23	2m. blue	7·25	85·00
24	3m. black	10·00	£140
25	5m. red and black	£160	£500

1910. No. 13 surch **5 Pf.**

26	N 5pf. on 3pf. brown		£6000

CASTELROSSO Pt. 3

One of the Aegean Is. Occupied by the French Navy on 27 December 1915. The French withdrew in August 1921 and, after a period of Italian Naval administration, the island was included in the Dodecanese territory.

A. FRENCH OCCUPATION

100 centimes = 1 franc = 4 piastres.

1920. Stamps of 1902–20 of French Post Offices in Turkish Empire optd **B. N. F. CASTELLORIZO**.

F 1	A 1c. grey	29·00	29·00
F 2	2c. purple	29·00	29·00
F 3	3c. red	29·00	29·00
F 4	5c. green	34·00	34·00
F 5	B 10c. red	40·00	40·00
F 6	15c. red	60·00	60·00
F 7	20c. brown	65·00	65·00
F 8	1pi. on 20c. blue	65·00	65·00
F 9	30c. lilac	70·00	70·00
F10	C 40c. red and blue	£120	£120
F11	2pi. on 50c. brown & lilac	£130	£130
F12	4pi. on 1f. red & green	£170	£170
F13	20pi. on 5f. blue & brown	£475	£475

1920. Optd **O. N. F. Castellorizo**. (a) On stamps of 1902–20 of French Post Offices in Turkish Empire.

F14	A 1c. grey	16·00	16·00
F15	2c. purple	16·00	16·00
F16	3c. red	19·00	19·00
F17	5c. green	19·00	19·00
F18	B 10c. red	19·00	19·00
F19	15c. red	25·00	25·00
F20	20c. brown	44·00	44·00
F21	1pi. on 25c. blue	44·00	44·00
F22	30c. lilac	40·00	40·00
F23	C 40c. red and blue	42·00	42·00
F24	2pi. on 50c. brown & lilac	50·00	50·00
F25	4pi. on 1f. red and green	50·00	50·00
F26	20pi. on 5f. blue & brown	£275	£275

(b) On Nos. 334 and 341 of France.

F27	**18** 10c. red	22·00	14·00
F28	25c. blue	22·00	14·00

1920. Stamps of France optd **O F CASTELLORISO**.

F29	**18** 5c. green	£120	£120
F30	10c. red	£120	£120
F31	20c. red	£120	£120
F32	25c. blue	£120	£120
F33	**13** 50c. brown and lilac	£700	£700
F34	1f. red and green	£700	£700

B. ITALIAN OCCUPATION

100 centesimi = 1 lira.

1922. Stamps of Italy optd **CASTELROSSO**.

15	**37** 5c. green	90	15·00
16	10c. red	90	15·00
17	15c. grey	90	18·00
18	**41** 20c. orange	90	18·00
19	**39** 25c. blue	90	15·00
20	40c. brown	90	15·00
21	50c. violet	90	17·00
22	60c. red	90	21·00
23	85c. brown	90	26·00
24	**34** 1l. brown and green	90	26·00

2

1923.

10	**2** 5c. green	1·90	11·00
11	10c. red	1·90	11·00
12	25c. blue	1·90	11·00
13	50c. purple	1·90	11·00
14	1l. brown	1·90	11·00

1930. Ferrucci stamps of Italy optd **CASTELROSSO**.

25	**114** 20c. violet	4·25	3·25
26	– 25c. green (No. 283)	4·25	6·00
27	– 50c. black (as No. 284)	4·25	3·25
28	– 1l.25 blue (No. 285)	4·25	8·00
29	– 5l.+2l. red (as No. 286)	15·00	35·00

1932. Garibaldi stamps of Italy optd **CASTELROSSO**.

30	– 10c. brown	15·00	25·00
31	**128** 20c. brown	15·00	25·00
32	– 25c. green	15·00	25·00
33	**128** 30c. blue	15·00	25·00
34	– 50c. purple	15·00	25·00
35	– 75c. red	15·00	25·00
36	– 1l.25 blue	15·00	25·00
37	– 1l.75+25c. brown	15·00	25·00
38	– 2l.55+50c. red	15·00	25·00
39	– 5l.+1l. violet	15·00	25·00

CAUCA Pt. 20

A State of Colombia, reduced to a Department in 1886, now uses Colombian stamps.

100 centavos = 1 peso.

2

1902. Imperf.

2	**2** 10c. black on red	1·00	1·00
3	20c. black on orange	85	85

CAVALLA (KAVALLA) Pt. 16

French P.O. in a former Turkish port, now closed.

100 centimes = 1 franc.
40 paras = 1 piastre.

1893. Stamps of France optd **Cavalle** or surch also in figures and words.

41	**10** 5c. green	14·00	24·00
43	10c. black on lilac	8·50	14·00
45	15c. blue	40·00	25·00
46	1pi. on 25c. black on pink	19·00	3·75
47	2pi. on 50c. red	80·00	30·00
48	4pi. on 1f. green	85·00	60·00
49	8pi. on 2f. brown on blue	95·00	£120

1902. "Blanc", "Mouchon" and "Merson" key-types inscr "CAVALLE". The four higher values surch also.

50	A 5c. green	2·00	2·30
51	B 10c. red	3·50	2·50
52	15c. red	13·00	11·50
53	15c. orange	3·75	3·00
54	1pi. on 25c. blue	3·75	2·75
55	C 2pi. on 50c. brown & lilac	5·75	3·75
56	4pi. on 1f. red and green	6·75	5·75
57	8pi. on 2f. lilac and brown	19·00	13·00

CAYES OF BELIZE Pt. 1

A chain of several hundred islands, coral atolls, reefs and sandbanks stretching along the eastern seaboard of Belize.

The following issues for the Cayes of Belize fall outside the criteria for full listing as detailed on page viii.

100 cents = 1 dollar.

APPENDIX

1984.

Marine Life, Map and Views, 1, 2, 5, 10, 15, 25, 75c., $3, $5.

250th Anniv of "Lloyd's List" (newspaper). 25, 75c., $1, $2.

Olympic Games, Los Angeles. 10, 15, 75c., $2.

90th Anniv of "Caye Service" Local Stamps. 10, 15, 75c., $2.

1985.

Birth Bicent of John J. Audubon (ornithologist). 25, 75c., $1, $3.

Shipwrecks. $1 × 4.

CAYMAN ISLANDS Pt. 1

A group of islands in the British West Indies. A dependency of Jamaica until August 1962, when it became a Crown Colony.

1900. 12 pence = 1 shilling;
20 shillings = 1 pound.
1969. 100 cents = 1 Jamaican dollar.

1

2

1900.

1a	**1** ½d. green	8·00	16·00
2	1d. red	8·00	2·25

1902.

8	**2** ½d. green	7·00	9·50
4	1d. red	10·00	9·00
10	2½d. blue	7·00	3·25
13	4d. brown and blue	32·00	60·00
11	6d. brown	16·00	38·00
14	6d. olive and red	32·00	70·00

12		1s. orange	32·00	48·00
15		1s. violet and green	55·00	80·00
16		5s. orange and green	£190	£300

1907. Surch **One Halfpenny.**

17	2	½d. on 1d. red	50·00	80·00

1907. Surch.

18	2	½d. on 5s. orange and green	£275	£425
19		1d. on 5s. orange and green	£250	£375
35		2½d. on 4d. brown and blue	£1700	£3000

11

8

1907.

38	11	¼d. brown	3·00	50
25	8	½d. green	2·50	4·00
26		1d. red	1·50	75
27		2½d. blue	3·50	3·50
28		3d. purple on yellow	3·25	5·50
29		4d. black and red on yellow	55·00	70·00
30		6d. purple	12·00	35·00
31		1s. black on green	8·50	22·00
32		5s. green and red on yellow	38·00	65·00
34		10s. green and red on green	£170	£225

12

19

1912.

40	12	¼d. brown	1·00	40
41		½d. green	2·75	5·00
42		1d. red	3·25	2·50
43		2d. grey	1·00	10·00
44		2½d. blue	7·00	11·00
45a		3d. purple on yellow	3·50	8·00
46		4d. black and red on yellow	1·00	10·00
47		6d. purple	3·75	7·50
48b		1s. black on green	3·50	3·50
49		2s. purple and blue on blue	12·00	50·00
50		3s. green and violet	19·00	65·00
51		5s. green and red on yellow	75·00	£170
52b		10s. green and red on green	90·00	£160

1917. Surch **1½d** with **WAR STAMP.** in two lines.

54	12	1½d. on 2½d. blue	1·75	6·00

1917. Optd or surch as last, but with **WAR STAMP** in one line and without full point.

57	12	½d. green	60	2·50
58		1½d. on 2d. grey	2·50	7·00
56		1½d. on 2½d. blue	30	60
59		1½d. on 2½d. orange	80	1·25

1921.

69	19	¼d. brown	50	1·50
70		½d. green	50	30
71		1d. red	1·40	85
72		1½d. brown	1·75	30
73		2d. grey	1·75	4·00
74		2½d. blue	50	50
75		3d. purple on yellow	1·25	4·00
62		4d. red on yellow	1·00	4·00
76		4½d. green	2·75	3·00
77		6d. red	5·50	32·00
63		1s. black on green	1·25	9·50
80		2s. violet on blue	14·00	24·00
81		3s. violet	23·00	16·00
82		5s. green on yellow	24·00	45·00
83		10s. red on green	60·00	85·00

20 Kings William IV and George V

1932. Centenary of "Assembly of Justices and Vestry".

84	20	¼d. brown	1·50	1·00
85		½d. green	2·75	8·00
86		1d. red	2·75	11·00
87		1½d. orange	2·75	2·75
88		2d. grey	2·75	3·50
89		2½d. blue	2·75	1·50
90		3d. green	4·00	5·00
91		6d. purple	9·50	23·00
92		1s. black and brown	17·00	32·00
93		2s. black and blue	45·00	75·00
94		5s. black and green	85·00	£120
95		10s. black and red	£275	£350

21 Cayman Islands

1935.

96	21	¼d. black and brown	50	1·00
97	–	½d. blue and green	1·00	1·00
98	–	1d. blue and red	4·00	2·25
99	–	1½d. black and orange	1·50	1·75
100	–	2d. blue and purple	3·75	1·10
101	–	2½d. blue and black	3·25	1·25
102	21	3d. black and green	2·50	3·00
103	–	6d. purple and black	8·50	4·00
104	–	1s. blue and orange	6·00	6·50
105	–	2s. blue and black	45·00	35·00
106	–	5s. green and black	50·00	50·00
107	–	10s. black and red	85·00	95·00

DESIGNS—HORIZ: ½, 2d., 1s. Cat boat; 1d., 2s. Red-footed boobys ("Booby-birds"); 2½, 6d., 5s. Hawksbill turtles. VERT: 1½d., 10s. Queen or pink conch shells and coconut palms.

1935. Silver Jubilee. As T **13** of Antigua.

108		½d. black and green	15	1·00
109		2½d. brown and blue	2·50	1·00
110		6d. blue and olive	1·50	5·50
111		1s. grey and purple	8·00	8·00

1937. Coronation. As T **2** of Aden.

112		½d. green	30	1·90
113		1d. red	50	20
114		2½d. blue	95	40

26 Beach View

29 Hawksbill Turtles

1938.

115a	26	¼d. orange	10	65
116	–	½d. green	1·00	55
117	–	1d. red	30	75
118	26	1½d. black	30	10
119a	29	2d. violet	60	30
120	–	2½d. blue	40	20
120a	–	2½d. orange	3·00	50
121	–	3d. orange	40	15
121a	–	3d. blue	3·00	30
122a	29	6d. olive	3·00	1·50
123a	–	1s. brown	5·00	2·00
124a	26	2s. green	25·00	9·00
125	–	5s. red	32·00	15·00
126	29	10s. brown	25·00	9·00

DESIGNS—HORIZ: ½d., 1s. Caribbean dolphin; 1d., 3d. Map of Islands; 2½d., 5s. "Rembro" (schooner).

1946. Victory. As T **9** of Aden.

127		1½d. black	30	20
128		3d. yellow	30	20

1948. Silver Wedding. As T **10/11** of Aden.

129		½d. green	10	1·00
130		10s. blue	18·00	23·00

1949. U.P.U. As T **20/25** of Antigua.

131		2½d. orange	30	1·00
132		3d. blue	1·50	2·25
133		6d. olive	60	2·25
134		1s. brown	60	50

31 Cat Boat

44 South Sound Lighthouse, Grand Cayman

1950.

135	31	¼d. blue and red	15	60
136	–	½d. violet and green	15	1·25
137	–	1d. olive and blue	60	75
138	–	1½d. green and brown	40	75
139	–	2d. violet and red	1·25	1·50
140	–	2½d. blue and black	1·25	60
141	–	3d. green and blue	1·40	1·50
142	–	6d. brown and blue	2·00	1·25
143	–	9d. red and green	11·00	2·00
144	–	1s. brown and orange	3·25	2·75
145	–	2s. violet and purple	11·00	11·00
146	–	5s. olive and violet	18·00	7·00
147	–	10s. black and red	21·00	16·00

DESIGNS: ½d. Coconut grove, Cayman Brac; 1d. Green turtle; 1½d. Making thatch rope; 2d. Cayman seamen; 2½d. Map; 3d. Parrotfish; 6d. Bluff, Cayman Brac; 9d. Georgetown Harbour. 1s. Turtle in "crawl"; 2s. "Ziroma" (schooner); 5s. Boat-building; 10s. Government offices, Grand Cayman.

1953. As 1950 issue but with portrait of Queen Elizabeth II as in T **44**.

148		¼d. blue and red	1·00	50
149		½d. violet and green	75	50
150		1d. olive and blue	70	40
151		1½d. green and brown	60	20
152		2d. violet and red	3·00	85
153		2½d. blue and black	3·50	80
154		3d. green and blue	4·00	60
155		4d. black and blue	2·00	40
156		6d. brown and blue	1·75	30
157		9d. red and green	7·50	30
158		1s. brown and orange	3·75	20
159		2s. violet and purple	13·00	8·00
160		5s. olive and violet	15·00	7·00
161		10s. black and red	18·00	7·50
161a		£1 blue	32·00	10·00

Portrait faces right on ½d., 2d., 2½d., 4d., 1s. and 10s. values and left on others. The £1 shows a larger portrait of the Queen (vert).

1953. Coronation. As T **13** of Aden.

162		1d. black and green	30	2·00

46 Arms of the Cayman Islands

1959. New Constitution.

163	46	2½d. black and blue	45	2·50
164		1s. black and orange	55	50

48 Cat Boat

1962. Portraits as in T **48**.

165	–	¼d. green and red	55	1·00
166	48	1d. black and olive	80	20
167	–	1½d. yellow and purple	2·75	80
168	–	2d. blue and brown	1·00	30
169	–	2½d. violet and turquoise	85	1·00
170	–	3d. blue and red	30	10
171	–	4d. green and purple	2·25	60
172	–	6d. turquoise and sepia	3·25	30
173	48	9d. blue and purple	3·50	40
174	–	1s. sepia and red	1·25	10
175	–	1s.3d. turquoise and brown	4·50	2·25
176	–	1s.9d. turquoise and violet	18·00	1·25
177	–	5s. plum and green	11·00	11·00
178	–	10s. olive and blue	20·00	9·50
179	–	£1 red and black	20·00	21·00

DESIGNS—VERT: ¼d. Cuban amazon ("Cayman Parrot"); 9d. Angler with king mackerel; 10s. Arms; £1 Queen Elizabeth II. HORIZ: 1½d. "Schomburgkia thomsoniana" (orchid); 2d. Cayman Islands map; 2½d. Fisherman casting net; 3d. West Bay Beach; 4d. Green turtle; 6d. "Lydia E. Wilson" (schooner), 1s Iguana; 1s.3d. Swimming pool, Cayman Brac; 1s.9d. Water sports; 5s. Fort George.

1963. Freedom from Hunger. As T **28** of Aden.

180		1s.9d. red	30	15

1963. Centenary of Red Cross. As T **33** of Antigua.

181		1d. red and black	30	75
182		1s.9d. red and blue	70	1·75

1964. 400th Birth Anniv of Shakespeare. As T **34** of Antigua.

183		6d. purple	20	10

1965. Centenary of ITU. As T **36** of Antigua.

184		1d. blue and purple	15	10
185		1s.3d. purple and green	55	45

1965. ICY. As T **37** of Antigua.

186		1d. purple and turquoise	15	10
187		1s. green and lavender	50	25

1966. Churchill Commemoration. As T **38** of Antigua.

188		¼d. blue	10	1·75
189		1d. green	60	15
190		1s. brown	1·50	15
191		1s.9d. violet	1·60	75

1966. Royal Visit. As T **39** of Antigua.

192		1d. black and blue	75	35
193		1s.9d. black and mauve	2·50	1·25

1966. World Cup Football Championship. As T **40** of Antigua.

194		1½d. multicoloured	15	10
195		1s.9d. multicoloured	50	25

1966. Inauguration of WHO Headquarters, Geneva. As T **41** of Antigua.

196		2d. black, green and blue	60	15
197		1s.3d. black, purple and ochre	1·40	60

62 Telephone and Map

1966. International Telephone Links.

198	62	4d. multicoloured	20	20
199		9d. multicoloured	20	30

1966. 20th Anniv of UNESCO. As T **54/6** of Antigua.

200		1d. multicoloured	15	10
201		1s.9d. yellow, violet and olive	60	10
202		5s. black, purple and orange	1·50	70

63 B.A.C One Eleven 200/400 Airliner over "Ziroma" (Cayman schooner)

1966. Opening of Cayman Jet Service.

203	63	1s. black, blue and green	35	30
204		1s.9d. purple, blue and green	40	35

64 Water-skiing

1967. International Tourist Year. Multicoloured.

205		4d. Type **64**	35	10
206		6d. Skin diving	35	30
207		1s. Sport fishing	35	30
208		1s.9d. Sailing	40	75

68 Former Slaves and Emblem

1968. Human Rights Year.

209	68	3d. green, black and gold	10	10
210		9d. brown, gold and green	10	10
211		5s. ultram, gold and green	30	90

69 Long-jumping

1968. Olympic Games, Mexico. Multicoloured.

212		1s. Type **69**	15	10
213		1s.3d. High-jumping	20	25
214		2s. Pole-vaulting	20	75

72 "The Adoration of the Shepherds" (Fabritius)

1968. Christmas. Multicoloured.

215		¼d. Type **72***	10	20
221		¼d. Type **72***	10	20
216		1d. "The Adoration of the Shepherds" (Rembrandt)	10	10
217		6d. Type **72**	15	10
218		8d. As 1d.	15	15
219		1s.3d. Type **72**	20	25
220		2s. As 1d.	25	35

*No. 215 has a brown background and No. 221 a bright purple one.

74 Grand Cayman Thrush ("Cayman Thrush")

1969. Multicoloured.
222 ½d. Type **74** 10 75
223 1d. Brahmin cattle 10 10
224 2d. Blowholes on the coast 10 10
225 2½d. Map of Grand Cayman 15 10
226 3d. Georgetown scene . . . 10 10
227 4d. Royal "Poinciana" . . . 15 10
228 6d. Cayman Brac and Little Cayman on chart 20 10
229 8d. Motor vessels at berth . . 25 10
230 1s. Basket-making 15 10
231 1s.3d. Beach scene . . . . . 35 1·00
232 1s.6d. Straw-rope making . . 35 1·00
233 2s. Great barracuda . . . . 1·25 80
234 4s. Government House . . . 35 80
235 10s. Arms of the Cayman Islands (vert) . . . . . . 1·00 1·50
236 £1 black, ochre and red (Queen Elizabeth II) (vert) 1·25 2·00

1969. Decimal Currency. Nos. 222/36 surch **C-DAY 8th September 1969**. Multicoloured.
238 **74** ¼c. on ½d. 10 75
239 – 1c. on 1d. 10 10
240 – 2c. on 2d. 10 10
241 – 3c. on 4d. 10 10
242 – 4c. on 2½d. 10 10
243 – 5c. on 6d. 10 10
244 – 7c. on 8d. 10 10
245 – 8c. on 3d. 15 10
246 – 10c. on 1s. 25 10
247 – 12c. on 1s.3d. . . . . . 35 1·75
248 – 15c. on 1s.6d. . . . . . 45 1·50
249 – 20c. on 2s. . . . . 1·25 1·75
250 – 40c. on 4s. 45 85
251 – $1 on 10s. . . . . 1·00 2·50
252 – $2 on £1 . . . . 1·50 3·25

90 "Madonna and Child" (Vivarini) **92** "Noli me tangere" (Titian)

1969. Christmas. Multicoloured. Background colours given.
253 **90** ¼c. red 10 10
254 ¼c. mauve 10 10
255 ¼c. green 10 10
256 ¼c. blue 10 10
257 – 1c. blue 10 10
258 **90** 5c. red 10 10
259 – 7c. green 10 10
260 **90** 12c. green 15 15
261 – 20c. purple 20 25
DESIGNS: 1c., 7c., 20c. "The Adoration of the Kings" (Gossaert).

1970. Easter. Multicoloured; frame colours given.
262 **92** ¼c. red 10 10
263 ¼c. green 10 10
264 ¼c. brown 10 10
265 ¼c. violet 10 10
266 10c. blue 35 10
267 12c. brown 40 10
268 40c. plum 55 60

93 Barnaby (*Barnaby Rudge*)

1970. Death Centenary of Charles Dickens.
269 **93** 1c. black, green and yellow 10 10
270 – 12c. black, brown and red 35 10
271 – 20c. black, brown and gold 40 10
272 – 40c. black, ultram & blue 45 25
DESIGNS: 12c. Sairey Gamp ("Martin Chuzzlewit"); 20c. Mr. Micawber and David ("David Copperfield"); 40c. The "Marchioness" ("The Old Curiosity Shop").

97 Grand Cayman Thrush ("Cayman Thrush")

1970. Decimal Currency. Designs as Nos. 222/36, but with values inscribed in decimal currency as in T **97**.
273 ¼c. multicoloured 65 30
274 1c. multicoloured 10 10
275 2c. multicoloured 10 10
276 3c. multicoloured 20 10
277 4c. multicoloured 20 10
278 5c. multicoloured 35 10
279 7c. multicoloured 30 10
280 8c. multicoloured 30 10
281 10c. multicoloured 30 10
282 12c. multicoloured . . . . . 90 1·00
283 15c. multicoloured . . . . . 1·25 4·00
284 20c. multicoloured . . . . . 3·25 1·25
285 40c. multicoloured 85 75
286 $1 multicoloured . . . . . . 1·25 4·75
287 $2 black, ochre and red . . . 2·00 4·75

98 The Three Wise Men

1970. Christmas.
288 **98** ¼c. green, grey and emerald 10 10
289 – 1c. black, yellow and green 10 10
290 **98** 5c. grey, orange and red 10 10
291 – 10c. black, yellow and red 10 10
292 **98** 12c. grey, green and blue 15 10
293 – 20c. black, yellow and green 20 15
DESIGN: 1, 10, 20c. Nativity scene and Globe.

100 Grand Cayman Terrapin

1971. Turtles. Multicoloured.
294 5c. Type **100** 30 25
295 7c. Green turtle 35 25
296 12c. Hawksbill turtle 55 30
297 20c. Turtle farm . . . . . . 1·00 1·40

101 "Dendrophylax fawcettii" **102** "Adoration of the Kings" (French 15th century)

1971. Orchids. Multicoloured.
298 ¼c. Type **101** . . . . 10 1·25
299 2c. "Schomburgkia thomsoniana" 60 90
300 10c. "Vanilla claviculata" . . 2·00 50
301 40c. "Oncidium variegatum" 4·00 3·50

1971. Christmas. Multicoloured.
302 ¼c. Type **102** 10 10
303 1c. "The Nativity" (Parisian, 14th century) 10 10
304 5c. "Adoration of the Magi" (Burgundian, 15th century) 10 10
305 12c. Type **102** 20 15
306 15c. As 1c. 20 25
307 20c. As 5c. 25 35
MS308 113 × 115 mm. Nos. 302/7 1·25 2·25

103 Turtle and Telephone Cable

1972. Co-axial Telephone Cable.
309 **103** 2c. multicoloured 10 10
310 10c. multicoloured 15 10
311 40c. multicoloured 30 40

104 Court House Building

1972. New Government Buildings. Multicoloured.
312 5c. Type **104** 10 10
313 15c. Legislative Assembly Building 10 10
314 25c. Type **104** 15 15
315 40c. As 15c. 20 30
MS316 121 × 108 mm. Nos. 312/15 50 2·00

1972. Royal Silver Wedding. As T **52** of Ascension but with Hawksbill Turtle and Queen or Pink Conch in background.
317 12c. violet 15 10
318 30c. green 15 20

106 $1 Coin and Note

1972. First Issue of Currency. Multicoloured.
319 3c. Type **106** 20 10
320 6c. $5 Coin and note 20 70
321 15c. $10 Coin and note . . . 60 30
322 25c. $25 Coin and note . . . 80 45
MS323 128 × 107 mm. Nos. 319/22 3·50 3·25

107 "The Way of Sorrow"

1973. Easter. Stained-glass Windows. Multicoloured.
324 10c. Type **107** 15 10
325 12c. "Christ Resurrected" . . 20 10
326 20c. "The Last Supper" (horiz) 25 15
327 30c. "Christ on the Cross" (horiz) 30 25
MS328 122 × 105 mm. Nos. 324/7 (imperf) . . . . 1·00 1·60

108 "The Nativity" (Sforza Book of Hours) **109** White-winged Dove

1973. Christmas.
329 **108** 3c. multicoloured 10 10
330 – 5c. multicoloured 10 10
331 **108** 9c. multicoloured 15 10
332 – 12c. multicoloured 15 10
333 **108** 15c. multicoloured 15 15
334 – 25c. multicoloured 20 25
DESIGN: 5, 12, 25c. "The Adoration of the Magi" (Breviary of Queen Isabella).

1973. Royal Wedding. As T **47** of Anguilla. Background colour given. Multicoloured.
335 10c. green 10 10
336 30c. mauve 15 10

1974. Birds (1st series). Multicoloured.
337 3c. Type **109** . . . . 2·00 30
338 10c. Vitelline warbler . . . . 2·75 30
339 12c. Antillean grackle ("Greater Antillian Grackle") . . . . 2·75 30
340 20c. Great red-bellied woodpecker ("West Indian Red-bellied Woodpecker") 4·25 80
341 30c. Stripe-headed tanager . . 5·50 1·50
342 50c. Yucatan vireo . . . . . 7·00 5·50
See also Nos. 383/8.

110 Old School Building

1974. 25th Anniv of University of West Indies. Multicoloured.
343 12c. Type **110** 10 15
344 20c. New Comprehensive School 15 20
345 30c. Creative Arts Centre, Mona 15 60

111 Hermit Crab and Staghorn Coral

1974. Size 41½ × 27 mm or 27 × 41½ mm. Mult.
346 1c. Type **111** . . . . 3·50 1·25
347 3c. Treasure-chest and lion's paw . . . . 3·50 75
348 4c. Treasure and spotted scorpionfish 50 70
349 5c. Flintlock pistol and brain coral . . . . 3·00 75
350 6c. Blackbeard and green turtle . . . . 35 2·25
366 8c. As 9c. . . . . 2·50 8·50
351 9c. Jewelled pomander and porkfish . . . . 4·00 11·00
352 10c. Spiny lobster and treasure . . . . 4·50 80
353 12c. Jewelled sword and dagger and sea-fan . . . . 35 2·00
354 15c. Cabrit's murex and treasure . . . . 45 1·25
417 20c. Queen or pink conch and treasure . . . . . . 3·50 3·00
356 25c. Hogfish and treasure . . 45 70
357 40c. Gold chalice and seawhip . . . . 4·00 1·25
358 $1 Coat of arms (vert) . . . 2·75 3·25
419 $2 Queen Elizabeth II (vert) 8·50 6·50
For smaller designs see Nos. 445/52.

112 Sea Captain and Ship (Shipbuilding)

1974. Local Industries. Multicoloured.
360 8c. Type **112** 30 10
361 12c. Thatcher and cottage . . 25 10
362 20c. Farmer and plantation 25 20
MS363 92 × 132 mm. Nos. 360/2 1·50 3·25

113 Arms of Cinque Ports and Lord Warden's Flag **114** "The Crucifixion"

1974. Birth Centenary of Sir Winston Churchill. Multicoloured.
380 12c. Type **113** 15 10
381 50c. Churchill's coat of arms 45 70
MS382 98 × 86 mm. Nos. 380/1 60 1·60

1975. Birds (2nd series). As T **109**. Multicoloured.
383 3c. Common flicker ("Yellow-shafted Flicker") 70 50
384 10c. Black-billed whistling duck ("West Indian Tree Duck") . . . . 1·25 50
385 12c. Yellow warbler . . . . 1·40 65
386 20c. White-bellied dove . . . 2·00 2·00
387 30c. Magnificent frigate bird 3·25 4·25
388 50c. Cuban amazon ("Cayman Amazon") . . . 3·75 12·00

1975. Easter. French Pastoral Staffs.
389 **114** 15c. multicoloured 10 20
390 – 35c. multicoloured 20 45
MS391 128 × 98 mm. Nos, 389/90 65 2·75
DESIGN: 35c. Pastoral staff similar to Type **114**.

115 Israel Hands

1975. Pirates. Multicoloured.
392 10c. Type **115** 30 15
393 12c. John Fenn 30 30
394 20c. Thomas Anstis 50 50
395 30c. Edward Low . . . . . . 60 1·50

1975. Christmas. "Virgin and Child with Angels". As T **114**.
396 12c. multicoloured 10 10
397 50c. multicoloured 30 30
MS398 113 × 85 mm. Nos. 396/7 1·00 3·00

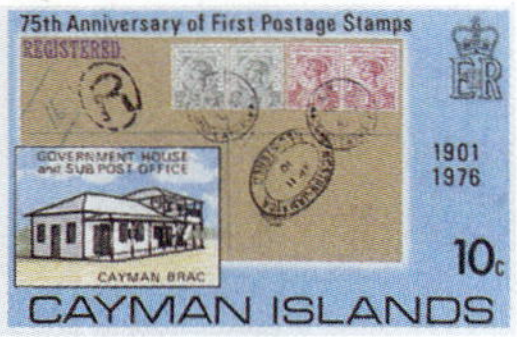

116 Registered Cover, Government House and Sub-Post Office

1975. 75th Anniv of First Cayman Islands Postage Stamp. Multicoloured.

399	10c. Type **116**	15	10
400	20c. ½d. stamp and 1890–94 postmark	20	15
401	30c. 1d. stamp and 1908 surcharge	30	25
402	50c. ½d. and 1d. stamps	45	65
MS403	117 × 147 mm. Nos. 399/402	2·50	3·00

117 Seals of Georgia, Delaware and New Hampshire

1976. Bicentenary of American Revolution. Mult.

404	10c. Type **117**	40	15
405	15c. Carolina, New Jersey and Maryland seals	55	20
406	20c. Virginia, Rhode Island and Massachusetts seals	65	25
407	25c. New York, Connecticut and North Carolina seals	65	35
408	30c. Pennsylvania seal, Liberty Bell and U.S. Great Seal	70	40
MS409	166 × 124 mm. Nos. 404/8	4·00	8·50

118 "470" Dinghies

119 Queen Elizabeth II and Westminster Abbey

1976. Olympic Games, Montreal. Multicoloured.

410	20c. Type **118**	40	10
411	50c. Racing dinghy	70	50

1977. Silver Jubilee. Multicoloured.

427	8c. The Prince of Wales' visit, 1973	10	20
428	30c. Type **119**	15	40
429	50c. Preparation for the Anointing (horiz)	30	75

120 Scuba Diving

1977. Tourism. Multicoloured.

430	5c. Type **120**	10	10
431	10c. Exploring a wreck	15	10
432	20c. Royal gramma ("Fairy basslet") (fish)	45	20
433	25c. Sergeant major (fish)	55	35
MS434	146 × 89 mm. Nos. 430/3	2·25	4·50

121 "Composia fidelissima" (moth)

1977. Butterflies and Moth. Multicoloured.

435	5c. Type **121**	75	20
436	8c. "Heliconius charithonia"	85	20
437	10c. "Danaus gilippus"	85	20
438	15c. "Agraulis vanillae"	1·25	45
439	20c. "Junonia evarete"	1·25	45
440	30c. "Anartia jatrophae"	1·50	70

122 Cruise Liner "Southward"

1978. New Harbour and Cruise Ships. Multicoloured.

441	3c. Type **122**	40	10
442	5c. Cruise liner "Renaissance"	40	10
443	30c. New harbour (vert)	90	25
444	50c. Cruise liner "Daphne" (vert)	1·25	65

1978. As Nos. 346/7, 349, 352, 417, 357/8 and 419, but designs smaller, 40 × 26 mm or 26 × 40 mm.

445	1c. Type **111**	1·00	1·25
446	3c. Treasure chest and lion's paw	80	50
447	5c. Flintlock pistol and brain coral	1·50	2·00
448	10c. Spiny lobster and treasure	1·25	60
449	20c. Queen or pink conch and treasure	2·25	1·00
450	40c. Gold chalice and seawhip	13·00	18·00
451	$1 Coat of arms (vert)	21·00	5·50
452	$2 Queen Elizabeth II (vert)	4·00	18·00

123 "The Crucifixion" (Durer)

1978. Easter and 450th Death Anniv of Durer.

459 **123**	10c. mauve and black	30	10
460 –	15c. yellow and black	40	15
461 –	20c. turquoise and black	50	20
462 –	30c. lilac and black	60	35
MS463	120 × 108 mm. Nos. 459/62	4·00	5·50

DESIGNS: 15c. "Christ at Emmaus"; 20c. "The Entry into Jerusalem"; 30c. "Christ washing Peter's Feet".

124 "Explorers" Singing Game

125 Yale of Beaufort

1978. 3rd International Council Meeting of Girls' Brigade. Multicoloured.

464	3c. Type **124**	20	10
465	10c. Colour party	25	10
466	20c. Girls and Duke of Edinburgh Award interests	40	20
467	50c. Girls using domestic skills	70	80

1978. 25th Anniv of Coronation.

468 **125**	30c. green, mauve and silver	20	25
469 –	30c. multicoloured	20	25
470 –	30c. green, mauve and silver	20	25

DESIGNS: No. 469, Queen Elizabeth II; 470, Barn owl.

126 Four-eyed Butterflyfish

1978. Fish (1st series). Multicoloured.

471	3c. Type **126**	25	10
472	5c. Grey angelfish	30	10
473	10c. Squirrelfish	45	10
474	15c. Queen parrotfish	60	30
475	20c. Spanish hogfish	70	35
476	30c. Queen angelfish	80	50

127 Lockheed L.18 Lodestar

1979. 25th Anniv of Owen Roberts Airfield. Mult.

477	3c. Type **127**	30	15
478	5c. Consolidated PBY-5A Catalina amphibian	30	15
479	10c. Vickers Viking 1B	35	15
480	15c. B.A.C. One Eleven 455 on tarmac	65	25
481	20c. Piper PA-31 Cheyenne II, Bell 47G Trooper helicopter and Hawker Siddeley H.S.125	75	35
482	30c. B.A.C. One Eleven 475 over airfield	1·00	50

128 Trumpetfish

1979. Fishes (2nd series). Multicoloured.

483	1c. Type **128**	10	10
484	3c. Nassau grouper	25	10
485	5c. French angelfish	25	10
486	10c. Schoolmaster snapper	35	10
487	20c. Banded butterflyfish	55	25
488	50c. Black-barred soldierfish	1·00	70

129 1900 1d. Stamp

1979. Death Centenary of Sir Rowland Hill.

489 **129**	5c. black, carmine and blue	10	10
490 –	10c. multicoloured	15	10
491 –	20c. multicoloured	20	25
MS492	138 × 90 mm. 50c. mult	55	65

DESIGNS: 10c. Great Britain 1902 3d. purple on lemon; 20c. 1955 £1 blue.

130 The Holy Family and Angels

1979. Christmas. Multicoloured.

493	10c. Type **130**	15	10
494	20c. Angels appearing to Shepherds	25	10
495	30c. Nativity	30	20
496	40c. The Magi	40	30

131 Local Rotary Project

1980. 75th Anniv of Rotary International.

497 **131**	20c. blue, black and yellow	20	15
498 –	30c. blue, black and yellow	25	20
499 –	50c. blue, yellow and black	35	30

DESIGNS—VERT: 30c. Paul P. Harris (founder); 50c. Rotary anniversary emblem.

132 Walking Mail Carrier

1980. "London 1980" International Stamp Exhibition. Multicoloured.

500	5c. Type **132**	10	10
501	10c. Delivering mail by cat boat	15	10
502	15c. Mounted mail carrier	20	10
503	30c. Horse-drawn wagonette	25	15
504	40c. Postman on bicycle	35	15
505	$1 Motor transport	45	55

133 Queen Elizabeth the Queen Mother at the Derby, 1976

1980. 80th Birthday of the Queen Mother.

506 **133**	20c. multicoloured	20	25

134 American Thorny Oyster

1980. Shells (1st series). Multicoloured.

507	5c. Type **134**	30	10
508	10c. West Indian murex	30	10
509	30c. Angular triton	45	40
510	50c. Caribbean vase	70	80

See also Nos. 565/8 and 582/5.

135 Lantana

1980. Flowers (1st series). Multicoloured.

511	5c. Type **135**	15	10
512	15c. "Bauhinia"	20	10
513	30c. "Hibiscus Rosa"	25	10
514	$1 "Milk and Wine Lily"	50	90

See also Nos. 541/4.

136 Juvenile Tarpon and Fire Sponge

137 Eucharist

1980. Multicoloured.

515A	3c. Type **136**	1·00	2·00
516B	5c. Flat tree or mangrove-root oyster	1·25	80
517A	10c. Mangrove crab	50	1·50
518A	15c. Lizard and "Phyciodes phaon" (butterfly)	1·00	1·75
519A	20c. Louisiana heron ("Tricoloured Heron")	1·50	2·25
520A	30c. Red mangrove flower	70	1·00
521A	40c. Red mangrove seeds	75	1·50
522A	50c. Waterhouse's leaf-nosed bat	1·25	1·50
523A	$1 Black-crowned night heron	4·75	5·00
524A	$2 Coat of arms	1·25	3·75
525A	$4 Queen Elizabeth II	2·00	4·75

1981. Easter. Multicoloured.

526	3c. Type **137**	10	10
527	10c. Crown of thorns	10	10
528	20c. Crucifix	15	10
529	$1 Lord Jesus Christ	50	60

138 Wood Slave

1981. Reptiles and Amphibians. Multicoloured.

530	20c. Type **138**	25	20
531	30c. Cayman iguana	30	35
532	40c. Lion lizard	40	45
533	50c. Terrapin ("Hickatee")	45	55

139 Prince Charles

1981. Royal Wedding. Multicoloured.

534	20c. Wedding bouquet from Cayman Islands	15	10
535	30c. Type **139**	20	10
536	$1 Prince Charles and Lady Diana Spencer	50	75

140 Disabled Scuba Divers

1981. Int Year for Disabled Persons. Mult.

537	5c. Type **140**	10	10
538	15c. Old school for the handicapped	25	20
539	20c. New school for the handicapped	30	25
540	$1 Disabled people in wheelchairs by the sea	1·25	85

1981. Flowers (2nd series). As T **135**. Multicoloured.

541	3c. Bougainvillea	10	10
542	10c. Morning Glory	15	10
543	20c. Wild amaryllis	25	25
544	$1 Cordia	1·00	1·75

141 Dr. Robert Koch and Microscope

1982. Centenary of Robert Koch's Discovery of Tubercle Bacillus. Multicoloured.

545	15c. Type **141**	25	25
546	30c. Koch looking through microscope (vert)	45	45
547	40c. Microscope (vert)	70	70
548	50c. Dr. Robert Koch (vert)	80	80

142 Bride and Groom walking down Aisle

144 "Madonna and Child with the Infant Baptist"

143 Pitching Tent

1982. 21st Birthday of Princess of Wales. Mult.

549	20c. Cayman Islands coat of arms	20	25
550	30c. Lady Diana Spencer in London, June, 1981	60	45
551	40c. Type **142**	60	65
552	50c. Formal portrait	2·25	1·00

1982. 75th Anniv of Boy Scout Movement. Mult.

553	3c. Type **143**	15	10
554	20c. Scouts camping	40	40
555	30c. Cub Scouts and Leaders	60	55
556	50c. Boating skills	80	85

1982. Christmas. Raphael Paintings. Multicoloured.

557	3c. Type **144**	10	10
558	10c. "Madonna of the Tower"	20	20
559	20c. "Ansidei Madonna"	35	35
560	30c. "Madonna and Child"	50	50

145 Mace

1982. 150th Anniv of Representative Government. Multicoloured.

561	3c. Type **145**	10	30
562	10c. Old Courthouse	20	30
563	20c. Commonwealth Parliamentary Association coat of arms	35	50
564	30c. Legislative Assembly building	50	90

1983. Shells (2nd series). As T **134**. Multicoloured.

565	5c. Colourful Atlantic moon	15	30
566	10c. King helmet	25	30
567	20c. Rooster-tail conch	30	40
568	$1 Reticulated cowrie-helmet	50	4·00

146 Legislative Building, Cayman Brac

1983. Royal Visit. Multicoloured.

569	20c. Type **146**	45	35
570	30c. Legislative Building, Grand Cayman	60	50
571	50c. Duke of Edinburgh (vert)	1·25	90
572	$1 Queen Elizabeth II (vert)	2·00	2·00
MS573	113 × 94 mm. Nos. 569/72	4·25	3·25

147 Satellite View of Earth

1983. Commonwealth Day. Multicoloured.

574	3c. Type **147**	15	10
575	15c. Cayman Islands and Commonwealth flags	35	30
576	20c. Fishing	40	35
577	40c. Portrait of Queen Elizabeth II	65	65

148 MRCU Cessna Ag Wagon

1983. Bicentenary of Manned Flight. Multicoloured.

578	3c. Type **148**	60	50
579	10c. Consolidated PBY-5A Catalina amphibian	65	50
580	20c. Boeing 727-200	1·25	1·50
581	40c. Hawker Siddeley H.S.748	1·75	3·75

1984. Shells (3rd series). As T **134**. Multicoloured.

582	3c. Florida moon	70	40
583	10c. Austin's cone	80	40
584	30c. Leaning dwarf triton	2·25	2·75
585	50c. Filose or threaded turban	2·50	4·75

149 "Song of Norway" (cruise liner)

152 Couple on Beach at Sunset

151 Snowy Egret

1984. 250th Anniv of "Lloyd's List" (newspaper). Multicoloured.

586	5c. Type **149**	45	20
587	10c. View of old harbour	50	25
588	25c. Wreck of "Ridgefield" (freighter)	1·00	1·00
589	50c. "Goldfield" (schooner)	2·00	2·50
MS590	105 × 75 mm. $1 "Goldfield" (schooner) (different)	2·10	2·25

1984. Universal Postal Union Congress, Hamburg. No. 589 optd **UPU CONGRESS HAMBURG 1984**.

591	50c. Schooner "Goldfield"	1·00	1·50

1984. Birds of the Cayman Islands (1st series). Multicoloured.

592	5c. Type **151**	1·00	75
593	10c. Bananaquit	1·00	75
594	35c. Belted kingfisher ("Kingfisher")	3·25	2·50
595	$1 Brown booby	6·00	11·00

See also Nos. 627/30.

1984. Christmas. Local Festivities. Multicoloured.

596	5c. Type **152**	85	1·50
597	5c. Family and schooner	85	1·50
598	5c. Carol singers	85	1·50
599	5c. East End bonfire	85	1·50
600	25c. Yachts	1·25	1·50
601	25c. Father Christmas in power-boat	1·25	1·50
602	25c. Children on beach	1·25	1·50
603	25c. Beach party	1·25	1·50
MS604	59 × 79 mm. $1 As No. 599, but larger 27 × 41 mm	3·75	3·00

Nos. 596/9 and 600/3 were each printed together, se-tenant, the four designs of each value forming a composite picture of a beach scene at night (5c.) or in the daytime (25c.).

153 "Schomburgkia thomsoniana" (var. minor)

154 Freighter Aground

1985. Orchids. Multicoloured.

605	5c. Type **153**	1·00	30
606	10c. "Schomburgkia thomsoniana"	1·00	30
607	25c. "Encyclia plicata"	2·50	1·00
608	50c. "Dendrophylax fawcettii"	3·75	3·00

1985. Shipwrecks. Multicoloured.

609	5c. Type **154**	90	50
610	25c. Submerged sailing ship	2·75	1·25
611	35c. Wrecked trawler	3·00	2·50
612	40c. Submerged wreck on its side	3·25	3·50

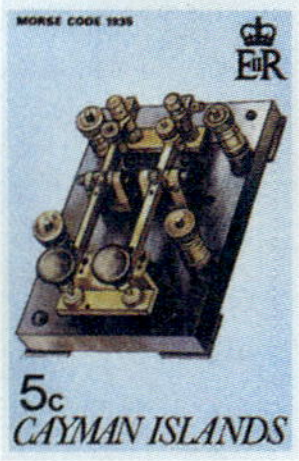

155 Athletics

156 Morse Key (1935)

1985. International Youth Year. Multicoloured.

613	5c. Type **155**	20	40
614	15c. Students in library	35	30
615	25c. Football (vert)	65	55
616	50c. Netball (vert)	1·25	2·25

1985. 50th Anniv of Telecommunications System. Multicoloured.

617	5c. Type **156**	45	70
618	10c. Hand cranked telephone	50	70
619	25c. Tropospheric scatter dish (1966)	1·50	80
620	50c. Earth station dish aerial (1979)	2·50	5·00

1986. 60th Birthday of Queen Elizabeth II. As T **110** of Ascension. Multicoloured.

621	5c. Princess Elizabeth at wedding of Lady May Cambridge, 1931	10	30
622	10c. In Norway, 1955	15	30
623	25c. Queen inspecting Royal Cayman Islands Police, 1983	1·50	75
624	50c. During Gulf tour, 1979	75	2·00
625	$1 At Crown Agents Head Office, London, 1983	1·10	2·75

157 Magnificent Frigate Bird

1986. Birds of the Cayman Islands (2nd series). Multicoloured.

627	10c. Type **157**	1·75	1·00
628	25c. Black-billed whistling duck ("West Indian Whistling Duck") (vert)	2·25	1·40
629	35c. La Sagra's flycatcher (vert)	2·50	2·50
630	40c. Yellow-faced grassquit	3·50	5·00

1986. Royal Wedding. As T **112** of Ascension. Multicoloured.

633	5c. Prince Andrew and Miss Sarah Ferguson	40	25
634	50c. Prince Andrew aboard H.M.S. "Brazen"	1·60	2·00

158 Red Coral Shrimp

159 Golf

1986. Marine Life. Multicoloured.

635	5c. Type **158**	40	1·00
636	10c. Yellow crinoid	40	50
637	15c. Hermit crab	35	60
638	20c. Tube dwelling anemone	35	1·75
639	25c. Christmas tree worm	45	2·50
640	35c. Porcupinefish	70	2·75
641	50c. Orangeball anenome	80	4·50
642	60c. Basket starfish	3·50	9·00
643	75c. Flamingo tongue	10·00	11·00
644	$1 Sea anenome	1·10	2·50
645	$2 Diamond blenny	1·25	4·50
646	$4 Rough file shell	2·00	6·50

1987. Tourism. Multicoloured.

647	10c. Type **159**	2·25	1·25
648	15c. Sailing	2·25	1·25
649	25c. Snorkelling	2·25	1·50
650	35c. Paragliding	2·50	2·00
651	$1 Game fishing	5·00	10·00

160 Ackee

162 Poinsettia

161 Lion Lizard

1987. Cayman Islands Fruits. Multicoloured.

652	5c. Type **160**	75	1·25
653	25c. Breadfruit	2·00	55
654	35c. Pawpaw	2·00	70
655	$1 Soursop	4·50	8·00

1987. Lizards. Multicoloured.

656	10c. Type **161**	2·00	75
657	50c. Iguana	4·00	3·75
658	$1 Anole	5·00	6·50

1987. Flowers. Multicoloured.

659	5c. Type **162**	90	80
660	25c. Periwinkle	2·25	75
661	35c. Yellow allamanda	2·25	1·10
662	75c. Blood lily	3·50	5·00

163 "Hemiargus ammon" and "Strymon martialis" **164** Green-backed Heron

1988. Butterflies. Multicoloured.

663	5c. Type **163**	1·25	65
664	25c. "Phocides pigmalion"	2·50	85
665	50c. "Anaea troglodyta"	4·00	3·75
666	$1 "Papilio andraemon"	4·00	6·50

1988. Herons. Multicoloured.

667	5c. Type **164**	1·25	65
668	25c. Louisiana heron	2·25	85
669	50c. Yellow-crowned night heron	3·00	3·00
670	$1 Little blue heron	3·50	4·25

165 Cycling **166** Princess Alexandra

1988. Olympic Games, Seoul. Multicoloured.

671	10c. Type **165**	3·50	1·00
672	50c. Cayman Airways Boeing 727 airliner and national team	4·50	3·25
673	$1 "470" dinghy	4·50	4·25
MS674	53 × 60 mm. $1 Tennis	4·00	3·00

1988. Visit of Princess Alexandra. Multicoloured.

675	5c. Type **166**	1·75	1·00
676	$1 Princess Alexandra in evening dress	7·50	6·50

167 George Town Post Office, and Cayman Postmark on Jamaica 1d., 1889

1989. Centenary of Cayman Islands Postal Service. Multicoloured.

677 **167**	5c. multicoloured	85	1·00
678 –	25c. green, black and blue	2·00	1·00
679 –	35c. multicoloured	2·00	1·25
680 –	$1 multicoloured	8·00	9·50

DESIGNS: 25c. "Orinoco" (mail steamer) and 1900 ½d. stamp; 35c. G.P.O., Grand Cayman and "London 1980" $1 stamp; $1 Cayman Airways B.A.C. One Eleven 200/400 airplane and 1966 1s. Jet Service stamp.

168 Captain Bligh ashore in West Indies **169** Panton House

1989. Captain Bligh's Second Breadfruit Voyage, 1791–93. Multicoloured.

681	50c. Type **168**	4·50	4·50
682	50c. H.M.S. "Providence" (sloop) at anchor	4·50	4·50
683	50c. Breadfruit in tubs and H.M.S. "Assistant" (transport)	4·50	4·50
684	50c. Sailors moving tubs of breadfruit	4·50	4·50
685	50c. Midshipman and stores	4·50	4·50

Nos. 681/5 were printed together, se-tenant, forming a composite design.

1989. Architecture. Designs showing George Town buildings. Multicoloured.

686	5c. Type **169**	75	90
687	10c. Town hall and clock tower	75	90
688	25c. Old Court House	1·40	55
689	35c. Elmslie Memorial Church	1·60	75
690	$1 Post Office	3·50	6·50

170 Map of Grand Cayman, 1773, and Surveying Instruments

1989. Island Maps and Survey Ships. Multicoloured.

691	5c. Type **170**	1·75	1·50
692	25c. Map of Cayman Islands, 1956, and surveying instruments	4·00	1·25
693	50c. H.M.S. "Mutine", 1914	5·50	5·00
694	$1 H.M.S. "Vidal", 1956	8·50	10·00

171 French Angelfish

1990. Angelfishes. Multicoloured.

707	10c. Type **171**	1·25	70
708	25c. Grey angelfish	2·25	90
709	50c. Queen angelfish	3·50	4·25
710	$1 Rock beauty	5·50	8·00

1990. 90th Birthday of Queen Elizabeth the Queen Mother. As T **134** of Ascension.

711	50c. multicoloured	1·25	2·25
712	$1 black and blue	2·75	4·00

DESIGNS—21 × 36 mm: 50c. Silver Wedding photograph, 1948. 29 × 37 mm: $1 King George VI and Queen Elizabeth with Winston Churchill, 1940.

172 "Danaus eresimus"

1990. "Expo 90" International Garden and Greenery Exhibition, Osaka. Butterflies. Multicoloured.

713	5c. Type **172**	65	60
714	25c. "Brephidium exilis"	1·50	1·10
715	35c. "Phyciodes phaon"	1·75	1·25
716	$1 "Agraulis vanillae"	4·00	6·50

173 Goes Weather Satellite

1991. International Decade for Natural Disaster Reduction. Multicoloured.

717	5c. Type **173**	80	75
718	30c. Meteorologist tracking hurricane	2·00	1·10
719	40c. Damaged buildings	2·25	1·25
720	$1 U.S. Dept of Commerce weather reconnaisance Lockheed WP-3D Orion	5·00	8·00

174 Angels and "Datura candida"

1991. Christmas. Multicoloured.

721	5c. Type **174**	90	90
722	30c. Mary and Joseph going to Bethlehem and "Allamanda cathartica"	2·25	60
723	40c. Adoration of the Kings and "Euphorbia pulcherrima"	2·50	1·10
724	60c. Holy Family and "Guaiacum officinale"	3·50	6·00

175 Coconut Palm **177** Woman and Donkey with Panniers

176 Single Cyclist

1991. Island Scenes. Multicoloured.

725	5c. Type **175**	50	30
726	15c. Beach scene (horiz)	1·75	30
727	20c. Poincianas in bloom (horiz)	70	35
728	30c. Blowholes (horiz)	1·75	50
729	40c. Police band (horiz)	2·50	1·40
730	50c. "Song of Norway" (liner) at George Town	2·00	1·40
731	60c. The Bluff, Cayman Brac (horiz)	1·75	2·25
732	80c. Coat of arms	1·50	2·50
733	90c. View of Hell (horiz)	1·60	2·50
734	$1 Game fishing (horiz)	3·25	2·50
735	$2 "Nieuw Amsterdam" (1983) and "Holiday" (liners) in harbour	8·00	7·50
736	$8 Queen Elizabeth II	16·00	19·00

1992. 40th Anniv of Queen Elizabeth II's Accession. As T **143** of Ascension. Multicoloured.

737	5c. Caymans' house	30	30
738	20c. Sunset over islands	1·00	50
739	30c. Beach	1·10	65
740	40c. Three portraits of Queen Elizabeth	1·10	1·00
741	$1 Queen Elizabeth II	2·00	3·50

1992. Olympic Games, Barcelona. Cycling. Mult.

742	15c. Type **176**	1·75	65
743	40c. Two cyclists	2·50	1·50
744	60c. Cyclist's legs	3·00	3·25
745	$1 Two pursuit cyclists	3·75	4·50

1992. Island Heritage. Multicoloured.

746	5c. Type **177**	50	50
747	30c. Fisherman weaving net	1·25	85
748	40c. Maypole dancing	1·50	1·10
749	60c. Basket making	2·50	3·50
750	$1 Cooking on caboose	3·00	4·50

178 Yellow Stingray

1993. Rays. Multicoloured.

751	5c. Type **178**	70	60
752	30c. Southern stingray	1·75	1·25
753	40c. Spotted eagle-ray	2·00	1·50
754	$1 Manta	4·25	5·50

179 Turtle and Sailing Dinghies **180** Cuban Amazon with Wings spread

1993. Tourism. Multicoloured.

755	15c. Type **179**	1·50	1·75
756	15c. Tourist boat, fishing launch and scuba diver	1·50	1·75
757	15c. Golf	1·50	1·75
758	15c. Tennis	1·50	1·75
759	15c. Pirates and ship	1·50	1·75
760	30c. Liner, tourist launch and yacht	1·75	1·90
761	30c. George Town street	1·75	1·90
762	30c. Tourist submarine	1·75	1·90
763	30c. Motor scooter riders and cyclist	1·75	1·90
764	30c. Cayman Airways Boeing 737 airliners	1·75	1·90

1993. Endangered Species. Cuban Amazon ("Grand Cayman Parrot"). Multicoloured.

765	5c. Type **180**	85	1·50
766	5c. On branch with wings folded	85	1·50
767	30c. Head of parrot	2·25	2·50
768	30c. Pair of parrots	2·25	2·50

181 "Ionopsis utricularioides" and Manger

1993. Christmas. Orchids. Multicoloured.

769	5c. Type **181**	1·50	75
770	40c. "Encyclia cochleata" and shepherd	3·00	85
771	60c. "Vanilla pompona" and wise men	4·00	4·00
772	$1 "Oncidium caymanense" and Virgin Mary	5·50	8·00

182 Queen Angelfish

1994. "Hong Kong '94" International Stamp Exhibition. Reef Life. Sheet 121 × 85 mm, containing T **182** and similar vert designs. Multicoloured.

MS773	60c. Type **182**; 60c. Diver with porkfish and short-finned hogfish; 60c. Rock beauty and Royal gramma; 60c. French angelfish and Banded butterflyfish	9·50	12·00

183 Flags of Great Britain and Cayman Islands **184** Black-billed Whistling Duck

1994. Royal Visit. Multicoloured.

774	5c. Type **183**	2·00	1·25
775	15c. Royal Yacht "Britannia"	3·00	1·00
776	30c. Queen Elizabeth II	3·00	1·10
777	$2 Queen Elizabeth and Prince Philip disembarking	8·50	11·00

1994. Black-billed Whistling Duck ("West Indian Whistling Duck"). Multicoloured.

778	5c. Type **184**	1·50	1·00
779	15c. Duck landing on water (horiz)	2·25	75
780	20c. Duck preening (horiz)	2·25	80
781	80c. Duck flapping wings	4·50	5·50
782	$1 Adult and duckling	5·00	6·50
MS783	71 × 45 mm. $1 As No. 782, but including Cayman Islands National Trust symbol	8·00	9·00

185 "Electrostrymon angelia" **186** H.M.S. "Convert" (frigate)

1994. Butterflies. Multicoloured.

784	10c. Type **185**	1·00	1·50
785	10c. "Eumaeus atala"	1·00	1·50
786	$1 "Eurema daira"	4·75	5·00
787	$1 "Urbanus dorantes"	4·75	5·00

1994. Bicentenary of Wreck of Ten Sail off Grand Cayman. Multicoloured.

788	10c. Type **186**	55	55
789	10c. Merchant brig and full-rigged ship	55	55
790	15c. Full-rigged ship near rock	75	50
791	20c. Long boat leaving full-rigged ship	85	55
792	$2 Merchant brig	4·50	7·50

187 Young Green Turtles

1995. Sea Turtles. Multicoloured.
793 10c. Type **187** 55 45
794 20c. Kemp's ridley turtle . . 80 55
795 25c. Hawksbill turtle 90 60
796 30c. Leatherback turtle . . . 95 70
797 $1.30 Loggerhead turtle . . . 3·50 4·75
798 $2 Pacific ridley turtles . . . 4·50 6·00
MS799 167 × 94 mm. Nos. 793/8 10·00 12·00

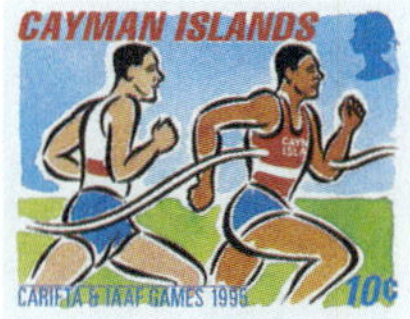
188 Running

1995. CARIFTA and IAAF Games, George Town. Multicoloured.
800 10c. Type **188** 60 40
801 20c. High jumping 90 70
802 30c. Javelin throwing . . . . 1·25 80
803 $1.30 Yachting . . . . . 4·25 6·00
MS804 100 × 70 mm. $2 Athletes with medals . . . . 6·50 7·50

1995. 50th Anniv of End of Second World War. As T **161** of Ascension. Multicoloured.
805 10c. Members of Cayman Home Guard 70 55
806 25c. "Comayagua" (freighter) 1·75 85
807 40c. U-boat "U125" . . . . 2·00 1·50
808 $1 U.S. Navy L-3 airship . . 3·75 6·00
MS809 75 × 85 mm. $1.30, Reverse of 1939–45 War Medal (vert) 2·50 3·00

189 Queen Elizabeth the Queen Mother

1995. 95th Birthday of Queen Elizabeth the Queen Mother. Sheet 70 × 90 mm.
MS810 **189 189** $4 multicoloured 8·50 9·50

190 Ox and Christ Child

191 Sea Grape

1995. Christmas. Nativity Animals. Multicoloured.
811 10c. Type **190** 70 30
812 20c. Sheep and lamb . . . . 1·25 45
813 30c. Donkey . . . . 2·25 60
814 $2 Camels . . . . 8·50 11·00
MS815 160 × 75 mm. Nos. 811/14 8·75 11·00

1996. Wild Fruit. Multicoloured.
816 10c. Type **191** 50 40
817 25c. Guava . . . . 1·00 50
818 40c. West Indian cherry . . . 1·50 80
819 $1 Tamarind . . . . 2·75 4·50

192 "Laser" Dinghy

193 Guitar and Score of National Song

1996. Centenary of Modern Olympic Games. Multicoloured.
820 10c. Type **192** 55 40
821 20c. Sailboarding 85 60
822 30c. "Finn" dinghy . . . . . 1·00 80
823 $2 Running . . . . 4·25 7·00

1996. National Identity. Multicoloured.
824 10c. Type **193** 35 30
825 20c. Cayman Airways Boeing 737-200 . . . . 1·25 55
826 25c. Queen Elizabeth opening Legislative Assembly . . . 75 50
827 30c. Seven Mile Beach . . . 75 55
828 40c. Scuba diver and stingrays . . . . 1·00 75
829 60c. Children at turtle farm 2·00 1·10
830 80c. Cuban amazon ("Cayman Parrot") (national bird) . . . . . . 3·00 2·00
831 90c. Silver thatch palm (national tree) . . . . . . 1·75 2·00
832 $1 Cayman Islands flag . . . 3·75 2·25
833 $2 Wild Banana Orchid (national flower) . . . . 5·50 5·50
834 $4 Cayman Islands coat of arms . . . . 9·00 12·00
835 $6 Cayman Islands currency 11·00 14·00

194 "Christmas Time on North Church Street" (Joanne Sibley)

1996. Christmas. Paintings. Multicoloured.
836 10c. Type **194** 40 30
837 25c. "Gone Fishing" (Lois Brezinsky) 70 50
838 30c. "Claus Encounters" (John Doak) 80 70
839 $2 "A Caymanian Christmas" (Debbie van der Bol) . . . . 4·00 7·00

1997. "HONG KONG '97" International Stamp Exhibition. Sheet 130 × 90 mm, containing design as No. 830 with "1997" imprint date. Multicoloured.
MS840 80c. Cuban amazon ("Cayman Parrot") . . . . . 1·75 2·00

1997. Golden Wedding of Queen Elizabeth and Prince Philip. As T **173** of Ascension. Multicoloured.
841 10c. Queen Elizabeth . . . . 1·10 1·40
842 10c. Prince Philip and Prince Charles at Trooping the Colour . . . . 1·10 1·40
843 30c. Prince William horse riding, 1989 . . . . . . 1·75 1·90
844 30c. Queen Elizabeth and Prince Philip at Royal Ascot . . . . 1·75 1·90
845 40c. Prince Philip at the Brighton Driving Trials . . 1·90 2·00
846 40c. Queen Elizabeth at Windsor Horse Show, 1993 1·90 2·00
MS847 110 × 70 mm. $1 Queen Elizabeth and Prince Philip in landau (horiz) . . . . 5·50 5·50

195 Children accessing Internet

196 Santa in Hammock

1997. Telecommunications. Multicoloured.
848 10c. Type **195** 35 25
849 25c. Cable & Wireless cable ship 70 45
850 30c. New area code "345" on children's T-shirts 75 60
851 60c. Satellite dish . . . . . 1·50 2·50

1997. Christmas. Multicoloured.
852 10c. Type **196** 35 25
853 30c. Santa with children on the Bluff 65 45
854 40c. Santa playing golf . . . 1·50 80
855 $1 Santa scuba diving . . . 2·00 3·50

1998. Diana, Princess of Wales Commemoration. As T **91** of Kiribati. Multicoloured.
856 10c. Wearing gold earrings, 1997 . . . . 40 40
857 20c. Wearing black hat . . . 70 90
MS858 145 × 70 mm. 10c. As No. 856; 20c. As No. 857; 40c. With bouquet, 1995; $1 Wearing black and white blouse, 1983 (sold at $1.70 + 30c. charity premium) 3·50 4·00

1998. 80th Anniv of the Royal Air Force. As T **178** of Ascension. Multicoloured.
859 10c. Hawker Horsley 60 70
860 20c. Fairey Hendon 75 80
861 25c. Hawker Siddeley Gnat 85 90
862 30c. Hawker Siddeley Dominie . . . . 95 1·00
MS863 110 × 77 mm. 40c. Airco D.H.9; 60c. Spad 13 Scout; 80c. Airspeed Oxford; $1 Martin Baltimore . . . . 5·50 6·50

197 Black-billed Whistling Duck ("West Indian Whistling Duck")

198 Santa at the Blowholes

1998. Birds. Multicoloured.
864 10c. Type **197** . . . . 1·00 60
865 20c. Magnificent frigate bird ("Magnificant Frigatbird") 1·50 60
866 60c. Red-footed booby . . . 2·50 3·00
867 $1 Cuban amazon ("Grand Cayman Parrot") . . . . 3·25 4·25

1998. Christmas. Multicoloured.
868 10c. Type **198** 30 30
869 30c. Santa diving on wreck of "Capt. Keith Tibbetts" . . 75 60
870 40c. Santa at Pedro Castle . . 90 75
871 60c. Santa arriving on Little Cayman . . . . 1·75 2·50

199 "They Rolled the Stone Away" (Miss Lassie)

1999. Easter. Paintings by Miss Lassie (Gladwyn Bush). Multicoloured.
884 10c. Type **199** 30 30
885 20c. "Ascension" (vert) . . . 60 60
886 30c. "The World Praying for Peace" 75 75
887 40c. "Calvary" (vert) 95 95

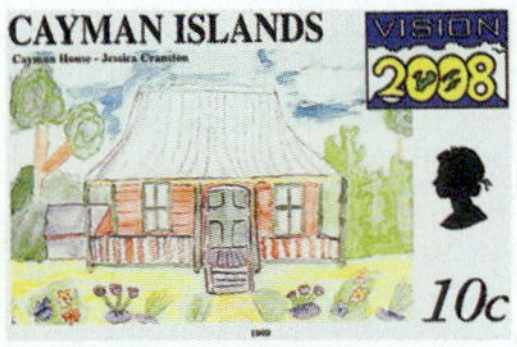
200 "Cayman House" (Jessica Cranston)

1999. Vision 2008 Project. Children's Paintings. Multicoloured.
888 10c. Type **200** 40 20
889 30c. "Coral Reef" (Sarah Hetley) . . . . 1·00 55
890 40c. "Fisherman on North Sound" (Sarah Cuff) . . . 1·10 70
891 $2 "Three Fish and a Turtle" (Ryan Martinez) . . . . . 4·25 6·00

1999. Royal Wedding. As T **185** of Ascension. Multicoloured.
892 10c. Photographs of Prince Edward and Miss Sophie Rhys-Jones 50 30
893 $2 Engagement photograph 3·75 4·75

1999. 30th Anniv of First Manned Landing on Moon. As T **186** of Ascension. Multicoloured.
894 10c. Coastguard cutter on patrol during launch . . . 45 35
895 25c. Firing of third stage rockets 80 60
896 30c. Buzz Aldrin descending to Moon's surface 85 65
897 60c. Jettisoning of lunar module . . . . 1·40 2·25
MS898 90 × 80 mm. $1.50, Earth as seen from Moon (circular, 40 mm diam) . . . . 3·00 4·00

1999. "Queen Elizabeth the Queen Mother's Century". As T **187** of Ascension. Multicoloured.
899 10c. Visiting anti-aircraft battery, London, 1940 . . 45 30
900 20c. With children on her 94th birthday, 1994 . . . 65 55
901 30c. With Prince Charles and Prince William, 1997 . . . 80 80
902 40c. Reviewing Chelsea Pensioners, 1986 . . . . . 90 90
MS903 145 × 70 mm. $1.50, Duchess of York with Princess Elizabeth, 1926, and Royal Wedding, 1923 2·75 3·50

201 1969 Christmas ¼c. Stamp

1999. Christmas. Designs showing previous Christmas stamps. Multicoloured.
904 10c. Type **201** 40 25
905 30c. 1984 Christmas 5c. . . . 70 50
906 40c. 1997 Christmas 10c. . . 85 65
907 $1 1979 Christmas 20c. (horiz) . . . . 1·90 2·50
MS908 111 × 100 mm. Nos. 904/7 3·00 4·25

2000. "Stamp Show 2000" International Stamp Exhibition, London. Kings and Queens of England. As T **223** of British Virgin Islands. Multicoloured.
909 10c. King Henry VII 45 60
910 40c. King Henry VIII . . . . 1·25 1·60
911 40c. Queen Mary I . . . . . 1·25 1·60
912 40c. King Charles II . . . . 1·25 1·60
913 40c. Queen Anne . . . . . . 1·25 1·60
914 40c. King George IV . . . . 1·25 1·60
915 40c. King George V . . . . 1·25 1·60

202 Ernie fishing from Rubber Ring

2000. "Sesame Street" (children's T.V. programme). Multicoloured.
916 10c. Type **202** 25 25
917 20c. Grover flying 40 50
918 20c. Zoe in airplane 40 50
919 20c. Oscar the Grouch in balloon 40 50
920 20c. The Count on motorbike 40 50
921 20c. Big Bird rollerskating . . 40 50
922 20c. Cookie Monster heading for Cookie Factory 40 50
923 20c. Type **202** 40 50
924 20c. Bert in rowing boat . . 40 50
925 20c. Elmo snorkeling 40 50
926 30c. As No. 920 . . . . . . 55 55
MS927 139 × 86 mm. 20c. Elmo with stamps . . . . 70 1·00
Nos. 917/25 were printed together, se-tenant, with the backgrounds forming a composite design.

2000. 18th Birthday of Prince William. As T **191** of Ascension. Multicoloured.
928 10c. Prince William in 1999 (horiz) 50 35
929 20c. In evening dress, 1997 (horiz) 75 55
930 30c. At Muick Falls, 1997 . . 1·10 70
931 40c. In uniform of Parachute Regiment, 1986 . . . . . 1·40 1·25
MS932 175 × 95 mm. $1 As baby with toy mouse (horiz) and Nos. 928/31 . . . . 7·50 7·50

203 Green Turtle

2000. Marine Life. Multicoloured.
933 10c. Type **203** 55 45
934 20c. Queen angel fish 80 45
935 30c. Sleeping parrotfish . . . 1·10 65
936 $1 Green moray eel . . . . 3·50 4·50

204 Boy thinking about Drugs and Fitness

2000. National Drugs Council. Multicoloured.
937 10c. Type **204** 60 35
938 15c. Rainbow, sun, clouds and "ez2B Drug Free" . . 85 35
939 30c. Musicians dancing . . . 1·40 65
940 $2 Hammock between two palm trees . . . . 5·00 7·50

205 Children on Beach ("Backing Sand")

206 Woman on Beach

2000. Christmas. Traditional Customs. Mult.
941 10c. Type **205** 80 40
942 30c. Christmas dinner . . . . 2·00 70
943 40c. Yard dance . . . . . . 2·25 85
944 60c. Conch shell borders . . 2·75 3·25

2001. United Nations Women's Human Rights Campaign.
945 **206** 10c. multicoloured 75 75

207 Red Mangrove Cay

2001. Cayman Brac Tourism Project. Mult.
946 15c. Type **207** . . . . 1·00 75
947 20c. Peter's Cave (vert) . . . 1·10 80
948 25c. Bight Road steps (vert) . . 1·25 90
949 30c. Westerly Ponds . . . . 1·40 1·00
950 40c. Aerial view of Spot Bay . . 1·40 1·40
951 60c. The Marshes . . . . . 2·50 3·50

208 Work of National Council of Voluntary Organizations

2001. Non-Profit Organizations. Multicoloured.
952 15c. Type **208** 80 65
953 20c. Pet welfare (Cayman Humane Society) . . . . . 1·50 90
954 25c. Stick figures (Red Cross and Red Crescent) . . . . 1·60 1·40
955 30c. Pink flowers (Cayman Islands Cancer Society) (vert) . . . . 1·60 1·40
956 40c. Women's silhouettes and insignia (Lions Club Breast Cancer Awareness Campaign) (vert) . . . . . 1·75 1·60
MS957 145 × 95 mm. Nos. 952/6 (sold at $1.80) . . . . 6·00 7·00
No. **MS**957 was sold at $1.80 which included a 50c. donation to the featured organisations.

209 Children walking Home

2001. Transportation. Multicoloured.
958 15c. Type **209** 50 40
959 15c. Boy on donkey 50 40
960 20c. Bananas by canoe . . . 50 30
961 25c. Horse and buggy 60 40
962 30c. Catboats fishing 60 45
963 40c. Schooner 90 60
964 60c. Police cyclist (vert) . . . 2·75 1·25
965 80c. Lady drivers . . . . . 1·50 1·40
966 90c. Launching *Cimboco* (motor coaster) (vert) . . . 2·00 1·75
967 $1 Amphibian aircraft . . . 2·50 1·75
968 $4 Container ship . . . . . 8·00 8·50
969 $10 Boeing 767 airliner . . . 17·00 19·00

210 Father Christmas on Scooter with Children, Cayman Brac

2001. Christmas. Multicoloured.
970 15c. Type **210** 75 40
971 30c. Father Christmas on eagle ray, Little Cayman . . 1·25 55
972 40c. Father Christmas in catboat, Grand Cayman . . 1·40 90
973 60c. Father Christmas parasailing over Grand Cayman . . . . 1·75 2·50

211 Statue of Liberty, U.S. and Cayman Flags

2002. In Remembrance. Victims of Terrorist Attacks on U.S.A. (11 September 2001).
974 **211** $1 multicoloured . . . . 2·50 3·25

2002. Golden Jubilee. As T **200** of Ascension.
975 15c. grey, blue and gold . . . 60 40
976 20c. multicoloured 75 40
977 30c. black, blue and gold . . 90 60
978 80c. multicoloured . . . . . 2·25 2·50
MS979 162 × 95 mm. Nos. 975/8 and $1 multicoloured . . . . 7·50 7·50
DESIGNS—HORIZ: 15c. Princess Elizabeth as young child; 20c. Queen Elizabeth in evening dress, 1976; 30c. Princess Elizabeth and Princess Margaret as Girl Guides, 1942; 80c. Queen Elizabeth at Newbury, 1996. VERT (38 × 51 mm)—$1 Queen Elizabeth after Annigoni.
Designs as Nos. 975/8 in No. **MS**979 omit the gold frame around each stamp and the "Golden Jubilee 1952–2002" inscription.

212 Snoopy painting Woodstock at Cayman Brac Bluff

2002. "A Cayman Vacation". Peanuts (cartoon characters by Charles Schulz). Multicoloured.
980 15c. Type **212** 60 50
981 20c. Charlie Brown and Sally at Hell Post Office, Grand Cayman 65 50
982 25c. Peppermint Patty and Marcie on beach, Little Cayman 70 60
983 30c. Snoopy as Red Baron and Boeing 737-200 over Grand Cayman . . . . . 1·25 70
984 40c. Linus and Snoopy at Point of Sand, Little Cayman . . . . 1·25 85
985 60c. Charlie Brown playing golf at The Links, Grand Cayman . . . . 2·50 3·00
MS986 230 × 160 mm. Nos. 980/5 6·50 7·50
No. **MS**986 is die-cut in the shape of a suitcase.

213 Cayman Islands Footballers

2002. World Cup Football Championship, Japan and Korea and 35th Anniv of Cayman Islands Football Association.
987 **213** 30c. multicoloured . . . . 1·50 1·25
988 40c. multicoloured . . . . 1·50 1·25

2002. Queen Elizabeth the Queen Mother Commemoration. As T **202** of Ascension.
989 15c. black, gold and purple 80 30
990 30c. multicoloured . . . . . 1·25 60
991 40c. black, gold and purple 1·50 1·00
992 $1 multicoloured . . . . . 2·75 3·25
MS993 145 × 70 mm. Nos. 991/2 5·50 7·00
DESIGNS: 15c. Queen Elizabeth at Red Corss and St. John's summer fair, London, 1943; 30c. Queen Mother at Royal Caledonian School, Bushey; 40c. Duchess of York in 1936; $1 Queen Mother at film premiere in 1989.
Designs in No. **MS**993 omit the "1900–2002" inscription and the coloured frame.

214 Angel Gabriel appearing to Virgin Mary

2002. Christmas. Multicoloured.
994 15c. Type **214** 50 45
995 20c. Mary and Joseph travelling to Bethlehem . . 60 45
996 30c. The Holy Family . . . 75 50
997 40c. Angel appearing to shepherds 90 70
998 60c. Three Wise Men . . . . 1·50 2·25
MS999 234 × 195 mm. Nos. 994/8 4·25 4·75

215 Catalina Flying Boat, North Sound, Grand Cayman

2002. 50th Anniv of Cayman Islands. Aviation. Multicoloured.
1000 15c. Type **215** 90 70
1001 20c. Grand Cayman Airport, 1952 . . . . . . 1·00 70
1002 25c. Cayman Brac Airways AC 50 . . . . 1·10 70
1003 30c. Cayman Airways Boeing 737 . . . . 1·25 70
1004 40c. British Airways Concorde at Grand Cayman, 1984 . . . . . . 1·75 1·25
1005 $1.30 Island Air DHC 6 Twin Otter on Little Cayman . . . . 3·75 4·75

216 Skipping

2003. Children's Games. Multicoloured.
1006 15c. Type **216** 80 60
1007 20c. Maypole dancing . . . 90 60
1008 25c. Gig . . . . 1·00 65
1009 30c. Hopscotch . . . . 1·10 70
1010 $1 Marbles . . . . 3·00 3·50

2003. 50th Anniv of Coronation. As T **206** of Ascension. Multicoloured.
1011 15c. Queen Elizabeth II wearing Imperial State Crown . . . . 1·00 35
1012 $2 Newly crowned Queen flanked by Bishops of Durham and Bath & Wells . . . . 4·50 5·00
MS1013 95 × 115 mm. 20c. As 15c.; $4 As $2 . . . . 6·50 7·50
Nos. 1011/12 have red frames; stamps from **MS**1013 have no frame and country name in mauve panel.

2003. As T **207** of Ascension.
1014 $4 black, red and violet . . 8·00 8·50

2003. 21st Birthday of Prince William of Wales. As T **208** of Ascension. Multicoloured.
1015 15c. Prince William at Tidworth Polo Club, 2002 and on Raleigh International Expedition, 2000 . . . . 80 35
1016 40c. At Golden Jubilee church service, 2002 and Queen Mother's 101st birthday, 2001 . . . . 1·50 60
1017 80c. At Queen Mother's 101st birthday and at Holyrood House, 2001 . . 2·50 2·75
1018 $1 At Eton College and at Christmas Day church service in 2000 . . . . . 2·50 2·75

217 Turtles hatching

2003. 500th Anniv of Discovery of Cayman Islands. Multicoloured.
1019 15c. Type **217** 65 55
1020 20c. Old waterfront, George Town, 1975 . . . . . . 75 65
1021 20c. *Santa Maria* (Columbus) and turtle . . 90 70
1022 25c. Nassau grouper (fish) and corals . . . . 1·00 70
1023 30c. *Kirk-B* (Cayman Brac schooner) . . . . 1·10 75
1024 40c. George Town harbour 1·25 75
1025 60c. Musical instruments . . 1·25 1·25
1026 80c. Smokewood tree and ghost orchids . . . . . . 2·00 2·00
1027 90c. Little Cayman Baptist Church . . . . 2·00 2·25
1028 $1 Loading thatch rope onto *Caymania* . . . . 2·50 2·75
1029 $1.30 Children's dance troupe . . . . 3·00 4·00
1030 $2 Cayman Parliament in session . . . . 4·00 4·50
MS1031 216 × 151 mm. Nos. 1019/30 18·00 20·00

218 Bell and "Merry Christmas"

2003. Christmas. Multicoloured.
1032 15c. Type **218** 85 55
1033 20c. Christmas wreath and "Celebrate with Family" 95 55
1034 30c. Gold star, angel and "Happy New Year" . . . 1·25 60
1035 40c. Christmas lights and "Happy Holidays" . . . 1·60 70
1036 60c. Poinsettias and "Seasons Greetings" . . . 2·25 2·75

219 Female and Calf

2003. Endangered Species. Short-finned Pilot Whale. Multicoloured.
1037 15c. Type **219** . . . . . . 1·00 75
1038 20c. Four pilot whales . . . 1·25 80
1039 30c. Two pilot whales at surface . . . . 1·60 1·10
1040 40c. Short-finned pilot whale 1·90 1·50

220 *Lady Slater*

2004. Centenary of Shipping Registry. Multicoloured.
1041 15c. Type **220** . . . . . . 1·00 55
1042 20c. *Seanostrum* . . . . . . 1·25 60
1043 30c. *Kirk Pride* . . . . . . 1·60 1·00
1044 $1 *Boadicea* . . . . 4·50 5·00

221 "Jesus carrying His Cross" (Carole Mayer)

222 Swimming

2004. Easter. Multicoloured.
1045 15c. Type **221** . . . . . . 1·00 50
1046 30c. "The Ascension" (Natasha Claire Kozaily) 1·50 1·25

2004. Olympic Games, Athens, Greece. Multicoloured.
1047 15c. Type **222** 65 40
1048 40c. Sprinting . . . . 1·25 75
1049 60c. Long jump . . . . . . 1·50 1·50
1050 80c. Two Cayman Islands swimmers . . . . 1·90 2·25

223 Blue Iguana

2004. Blue Iguana. Multicoloured.

1051	15c. Type **223**	65	55
1052	20c. Baby iguana hatching from egg	70	55
1053	25c. Four iguanas	80	60
1054	30c. Baby iguana on finger	90	65
1055	40c. Iguana with open mouth	1·10	75
1056	90c. Eye of iguana	2·50	3·00
MS1057	104 × 58 mm. 60c. Iguana on rock facing right; 80c. Iguana on rock facing left	4·25	4·50

2005. Bicentenary of Battle of Trafalgar. As T **216** of Ascension. Multicoloured.

1058	15c. HMS *Victory* (horiz)	70	55
1059	20c. HMS *Tonnant* tangling into bow of *Algesiras* (horiz)	70	55
1060	25c. Flint cannon lock and linstock (horiz)	70	55
1061	60c. Boatswain's Mate RN (horiz)	1·25	1·25
1062	$1 Portrait of Admiral Nelson	2·25	2·50
1063	$2 HMS *Orion* in action against *Intrepide* (horiz)	4·00	5·00
MS1064	120 × 79 mm. 60c. Pluton; $2 HMS *Tonnant*	6·00	6·50

No. 1058 contains traces of powdered wood from HMS *Victory*.

224 Rotary Emblem

2005. Centenary of Rotary International.

1065 **224**	15c. multicoloured	50	40
1066 –	30c. ultramarine, black and grey	90	85

DESIGN: 30c. Polio Plus and Rotary emblems.

225 *Myrmecophila purpurea*

2005. Orchids. Multicoloured.

1067	15c. Type **225**	50	40
1068	20c. *Prosthechea boothiana*	50	40
1069	30c. *Tolumnia calochila* (vert)	70	60
1070	40c. *Encyclia Phoenicia*	90	70
1071	80c. *Prosthechea cochleata* (vert)	1·75	1·90
MS1072	80 × 52 mm. $1.50 *Encyclia kingsii*	3·25	3·50

2005. Pope John Paul II Commemoration. As T **219** of Ascension.

1073	30c. multicoloured	1·25	1·00

226 The Queen (butterfly)

2005. Butterflies. Multicoloured. (a) Ordinary gum.

1074	15c. Type **226**	60	50
1075	20c. Mexican fritillary	60	50
1076	25c. Malachite	65	50
1077	30c. Cayman crescent spot	75	60
1078	40c. Cloudless sulphur	95	75
1079	90c. Swallowtail	2·00	2·75

(b) Self-adhesive. Size 29 × 24 mm.

1080	15c. Type **226**	70	80
1081	20c. Mexican fritillary	70	80
1082	30c. Cayman crescent spot	80	90

227 Angels

228 Wash Wood (*Jacquinia keyensis*)

2005. Christmas. Multicoloured.

1083	15c. Type **227**	60	40
1084	30c. Three Wise Men (horiz)	90	50
1085	40c. Holy Family	1·25	80
1086	60c. Shepherds (horiz)	1·50	1·75
MS1087	156 × 106 mm. Nos. 1083/6	3·75	4·00

2006. Trees. Multicoloured.

1088	15c. Type **228**	50	40
1089	20c. Red mangrove (*Rhizophora mangle*)	55	50
1090	30c. Ironwood (*Chionanthus caymanensis*)	70	50
1091	60c. West Indian cedar (*Cedrela odorata*)	1·40	1·25
1092	$2 Spanish elm (*Cordia gerascanthus*)	3·75	4·50

2006. 80th Birthday of Queen Elizabeth II. As T **223** of Ascension. Multicoloured.

1093	15c. Princess Elizabeth as young child	70	40
1094	40c. Queen Elizabeth in uniform, c. 1952	1·25	80
1095	$1 Wearing tiara	2·00	2·25
1096	$2 Wearing white blouse	3·75	4·25
MS1097	144 × 75 mm. As Nos. 1094/5, but without white borders	7·00	7·50

229 Hawksbill Turtle

2006. Cayman's Aquatic Treasures. Multicoloured. (a) Ordinary gum.

1098	25c. Type **229**	80	80
1099	25c. Grey angelfish	80	80
1100	60c. Queen angelfish (vert)	1·50	1·50
1101	75c. Diamond blenny	1·75	2·00
1102	$1 Spotted drum (juvenile) (vert)	3·75	4·25
MS1103	145 × 95 mm. As Nos. 1098/102	6·25	6·50

(b) Size 29 × 24 mm. Self-adhesive.

1104	25c. As Type **229**	80	85
1105	25c. As No. 1099	80	85
1106	60c. As No. 1100	1·50	1·60
1107	75c. As No. 1101	1·75	2·00

Stamps from **MS**1103 do not have white borders.

230 Bananaquit

2006. Birds (1st series). Multicoloured.

1108	25c. Type **230**	75	15
1109	50c. Vitelline warbler	1·40	90
1110	75c. Cuban Amazon ("Grand Cayman Parrot")	1·75	1·25
1111	80c. White-bellied dove ("Caribbean Dove")	1·75	1·25
1112	$1 Caribbean elaenia	2·00	1·75
1113	$1.50 Great red-bellied woodpecker ("West Indian Woodpecker")	3·00	3·00
1114	$1.60 Thick-billed vireo	3·25	3·25
1115	$2 Common flicker ("Northern Flicker")	4·00	4·25
1116	$4 Cuban bullfinch	8·00	8·50
1117	$5 Stripe-headed tanager ("Western spindalis")	9·00	9·50
1118	$10 Loggerhead kingbird	17·00	18·00
1119	$20 Red-legged thrush	30·00	32·00

See also Nos. 1124/6

231 "Faith" and the Three Magi

2006. Christmas. Multicoloured.

1120	25c. Type **231**	75	30
1121	75c. "Hope" and prophet speaking of the Messiah	1·75	1·75
1122	80c. "Joy" and angel	1·75	1·75
1123	$1 "Love" and Mary with baby Jesus	2·00	2·25

232 Bananaquit

2007. Birds (2nd series). Designs as Nos. 1108, and 1110/11 but each 30 × 25 mm with redrawn inscriptions. Self-adhesive.

1124	25c. Type **232**	85	90
1125	75c. Cuban amazon ('GRAND CAYMAN PARROT')	1·90	1·90
1126	80c. White-bellied dove ('CARIBBEAN DOVE')	1·90	1·90

233 Brac Reef Dock

2007. Cayman Islands Scenes. Multicoloured.

1127	20c. Type **233**	35	40
1128	25c. Waterfront, Hog Sty Bay, George Town, Grand Cayman	40	45
1129	30c. East End blowholes, Grand Cayman Island (vert)	50	55
1130	40c. Man lying in hammock on beach at sunset (vert)	65	70
1131	75c. Poinciana flowers	1·60	1·75
1132	$1 Driftwood on shore, Little Cayman Island	2·10	2·25

2007. Centenary of Scouting. As T **281** of Bahamas. Multicoloured.

1133	25c. Early Wolf Cubs with their flag	35	45
1134	75c. Modern Cub Scouts after Remembrance Day Parade, 2006	1·50	1·60
1135	80c. Scouts camping	1·60	1·75
1136	$1 Drill team, Remembrance Day Parade, 2005	1·75	1·90
MS1137	90 × 65 mm. 50c. Cayman Islands scouts in opening ceremony of 13th Caribbean Scout Jamboree, Jamaica, 2006 (vert); $1.50 Lord Baden-Powell (vert)	3·75	4·00

2007. Diamond Wedding of Queen Elizabeth II and Duke of Edinburgh. As T **58** of British Indian Ocean Territory. Multicoloured.

1138	50c. Princess Elizabeth alighting from car and Lt. Philip Mountbatten, c. 1949	90	95
1139	75c. Princess Elizabeth wearing tiara and wedding veil, 1949	1·50	1·60
1140	80c. Queen Elizabeth the Queen Mother and Princesses Elizabeth and Margaret	1·60	1·75
1141	$1 Princess Elizabeth and Duke of Edinburgh in procession down Westminster Abbey aisle on wedding day, 1949	1·75	2·00
MS1142	125 × 85 mm. $2 Princess Elizabeth and Lt. Philip Mountbatten, c. 1949 (42 × 56 mm)	3·75	4·00

234 Nativity

2007. Christmas. Stained glass windows. Mult.

1143	25c. Type **234**	45	50
1144	50c. Jesus Christ	95	1·00
1145	75c. Jesus with disciples	1·40	1·40
1146	80c. Peace dove	1·75	1·90
1147	$1 The Cross	2·00	2·10
1148	$1.50 Shepherd with lamb	2·75	3·00

235 Beach at Sunset and Turtles ('Hello')

2008. Greetings Stamps. Multicoloured. (a) Ordinary gum.

1149	20c. Type **235**	35	40
1150	20c. Crossed fingers and horseshoes ('Good Luck')	35	40
1151	20c. Balloons and stars ('Congratulations')	35	40
1152	20c. Invitation and fireworks ('You're Invited')	35	40
1153	20c. Fountain pen and flowers ('Best Wishes')	35	40
1154	20c. Cupid and hearts ('Love')	35	40
1155	25c. Type **235**	40	45
1156	25c. As No. 1150	40	45
1157	25c. As No. 1151	40	45
1158	25c. As No. 1152	40	45
1159	25c. As No. 1153	40	45
1160	25c. As No. 1154	40	45
1161	50c. Type **235**	80	85
1162	50c. As No. 1150	80	85
1163	50c. As No. 1151	80	85
1164	50c. As No. 1152	80	85
1165	50c. As No. 1153	80	85
1166	50c. As No. 1154	80	85
1167	75c. Type **235**	1·50	1·60
1168	75c. As No. 1150	1·50	1·60
1169	75c. As No. 1151	1·50	1·60
1170	75c. As No. 1152	1·50	1·60
1171	75c. As No. 1153	1·50	1·60
1172	75c. As No. 1154	1·50	1·60
1173	80c. Type **235**	1·60	1·75
1174	80c. As No. 1150	1·60	1·75
1175	80c. As No. 1151	1·60	1·75
1176	80c. As No. 1152	1·60	1·75
1177	80c. As No. 1153	1·60	1·75
1178	80c. As No. 1154	1·60	1·75
1179	$1 Type **235**	1·75	1·90
1180	$1 As No. 1150	1·75	1·90
1181	$1 As No. 1151	1·75	1·90
1182	$1 As No. 1152	1·75	1·90
1183	$1 As No. 1153	1·75	1·90
1184	$1 As No. 1154	1·75	1·90

(b) Self-adhesive. Size 30 × 25 mm.

1185	20c. As Type **235**	35	40
1186	25c. As No. 1151	40	45
1187	25c. As No. 1152	40	45
1188	25c. As No. 1154	40	45

CENTRAL AFRICAN EMPIRE

Pt. 12

Central African Republic was renamed Central African Empire on 4 December 1976, when Pres. Bokassa became Emperor.

The country reverted to Central African Republic on his overthrow in 1979.

100 centimes = 1 franc.

1977. Various stamps of Central African Republic optd **EMPIRE CENTRAFRICAIN**.

439 **150**	3f. mult (postage)	55	50
444 **167**	10f. multicoloured	30	25
457 –	10f. red and blue (386)	30	25
459 **172**	10f. multicoloured	45	40
460 –	15f. multicoloured (391)	75	75
465 –	15f. brown, grn & bl (397)	30	25
445 –	20f. multicoloured (366)	45	40
461 –	20f. multicoloured (392)	55	50
446 –	25f. multicoloured (367)	35	30
451 –	25f. multicoloured (376)	35	30
449 **168**	30f. multicoloured	30	25
452 –	30f. multicoloured (377)	55	55
462 –	30f. multicoloured (393)	30	25
447 –	40f. multicoloured (370)	45	40
450 –	40f. multicoloured (373)	45	40
453 –	40f. multicoloured (378)	45	40
454 –	40f. multicoloured (380)	55	55
455 **170**	40f. multicoloured	45	40
456 –	40f. multicoloured (384)	40	25
458 –	40f. multicoloured (389)	75	75
482 –	40f. multicoloured (423)	40	25
466 –	50f. blue, brn & grn (398)	75	75
440 **163**	100f. multicoloured	1·70	1·60
441 **164**	100f. grn, red & brn	1·80	1·80
442 **165**	100f. brn, grn & blue	1·70	1·60
468 **179**	100f. black and yellow	1·70	1·60
469 **180**	100f. purple, blue & grn	1·80	1·90
491 **185**	100f. multicoloured	1·80	1·90
483 –	50f. mult (424) (air)	45	25
448 –	100f. multicoloured (371)	95	90
463 **173**	100f. red and blue	95	90
467 **178**	100f. multicoloured	95	90
484 –	100f. multicoloured (425)	95	90
464 **174**	200f. multicoloured	4·25	2·10
443 **166**	500f. red, green & brown	8·50	8·25

1977. "Apollo–Soyuz" Space Link. Nos. 410/**MS**415 of Central African Republic optd **EMPIRE CENTRAFRICAIN**.

470 **181**	40f. mult (postage)	50	25
471 –	50f. multicoloured	75	40
472 –	100f. multicoloured (air)	95	55
473 –	200f. multicoloured	1·90	90
474 –	300f. multicoloured	3·00	1·30
MS475	103 × 78 mm. 500f. multicoloured	5·25	3·50

1977. Air. Bicentenary of American Revolution. Nos. 416/**MS**421 of Central African Republic optd **EMPIRE CENTRAFRICAIN**.

476 **182**	100f. multicoloured	1·00	70
477 –	125f. multicoloured	1·40	1·10
478 –	150f. multicoloured	1·60	1·30
479 –	200f. multicoloured	2·30	1·80
480 –	250f. multicoloured	2·50	2·00
MS481	119 × 81 mm. 450f. multicoloured	5·25	5·25

1977. Winners of Winter Olympic Games, Innsbruck. Nos. 426/**MS**430 of Central African Republic optd **EMPIRE CENTRAFRICAIN.**

485	– 40f. mult (postage)	55	50
486	– 60f. multicoloured	75	65
487	**184** 100f. multicoloured (air)	1·00	80
488	– 200f. multicoloured	2·20	1·70
489	– 300f. multicoloured	3·25	2·40
MS490	103 × 78 mm. 500f. multicoloured	5·25	5·00

1977. "Viking" Space Mission. Nos. 433/**MS**438 of Central African Republic optd **EMPIRE CENTRAFRICAIN.**

492	**186** 40f. mult (postage)	55	50
493	– 60f. multicoloured	75	65
494	– 100f. multicoloured (air)	1·00	1·00
495	– 200f. multicoloured	2·30	2·20
496	– 300f. multicoloured	3·50	3·50
MS497	102 × 78 mm. 500f. multicoloured	5·25	5·00

189 Pierre and Marie Curie (Physics, 1903)

1977. Nobel Prize-winners. Multicoloured.

503	40f. Type **189** (postage)	1·00	40
504	60f. W. C. Rontgen (Physics, 1901)	90	45
505	100f. Rudyard Kipling (Literature, 1907) (air)	1·80	50
506	200f. Ernest Hemingway (Literature, 1954)	3·50	85
507	300f. L. Pirandello (Literature, 1934)	3·50	1·00
MS508	118 × 80 mm. 500f. Rabindranath Tagore (Literature, 1913)	5·25	1·90

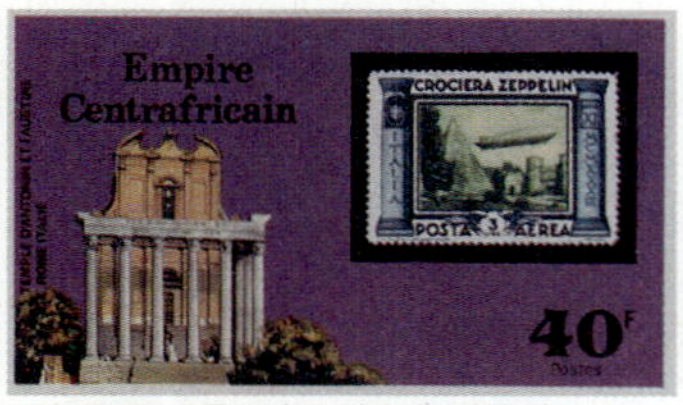

190 Roman Temple and Italy 1933 3l. stamp

1977. "Graf Zeppelin" Flights. Multicoloured.

509	40f. Type **190** (postage)	85	25
510	60f. St. Basil's Cathedral, Moscow, and Russia 1930 40k. stamp	1·00	45
511	100f. North Pole and Germany 1931 "Polarfahrt" stamp (air)	1·40	40
512	200f. Museum of Science and Industry, Chicago, and Germany 1933 "Chicagofahrt" stamp	2·50	75
513	300f. Brandenburg Gate, Berlin, and German 1931 stamp	3·75	1·00
MS514	129 × 90 mm. 500f. Capitol, Washington, and US $1.30 stamp, 1930	5·50	2·20

191 Charles Lindbergh and "Spirit of St. Louis"

1977. History of Aviation. Multicoloured.

515	50f. Type **191**	50	25
516	60f. Alberto Santos-Dumont and "14 bis" biplane	75	25
517	100f. Louis Bleriot and Bleriot XI	1·40	45
518	200f. Roald Amundsen and Dornier Wal flying boat	2·10	60
519	300f. Concorde	4·00	1·40
MS520	117 × 91 mm. 500f. Lindbergh and his arrival in Paris	5·00	1·80

192 Lily

193 Group of Africans and Rotary Emblem

1977. Flowers. Multicoloured.

521	5f. Type **192**	45	30
522	10f. Hibiscus	90	70

1977. 20th Anniv of Bangui Rotary Club.

523	**193** 60f. multicoloured	3·50	1·80

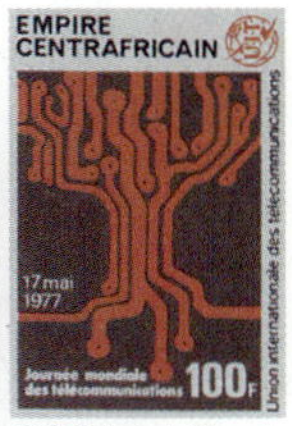

194 Africans queueing beside Bible **195** Printed Circuit

1977. Bible Week.

524	**194** 40f. multicoloured	5·75	1·40

1977. World Telecommunications Day.

525	**195** 100f. orange, brown & blk	3·00	2·10

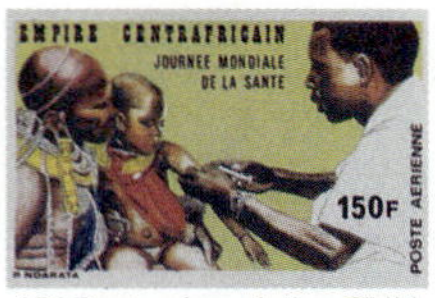

196 Doctor inoculating Child

1977. Air. World Health Day.

526	**196** 150f. multicoloured	3·50	1·80

197 Goalkeeper

1977. World Cup Football Championship (1978). Multicoloured.

527	50f. Type **197**	50	25
528	60f. Goalmouth melee	60	25
529	100f. Mid-field play	1·00	30
530	200f. World Cup poster	2·10	60
531	300f. Mario Jorge Lobo Zagalo (Argentine trainer) and Buenos Aires stadium	3·75	1·30
MS532	120 × 81 mm. 500f. Ferenc Puskas (Hungarian player)	6·25	2·20

198 Emperor Bokassa I

1977. Coronation of Emperor Bokassa.

533	**198** 40f. mult (postage)	35	15
534	60f. multicoloured	50	25
535	100f. multicoloured	1·00	55
536	150f. multicoloured	1·40	70
537	200f. mult (air)	1·90	85
538	300f. multicoloured	2·50	1·40
MS539	102 × 80 mm. 500f. Emperor Bokassa, inscription and furled flag (48 × 39 mm)	5·25	2·50

199 Bangui Telephone Exchange

1978. Opening of Automatic Telephone Exchange, Bangui. Multicoloured.

541	40f. Type **199**	45	25
542	60f. Bangui Telephone Exchange (different)	60	35

200 Bokassa Sports Palace

1978. Bokassa Sports Palace. Multicoloured.

543	40f. Type **200**	45	25
544	60f. Sports Palace (different)	60	35

201 "The Holy Family"

1978. 400th Birth Anniv of Rubens. Mult.

545	60f. Type **201**	75	25
546	150f. "Marie de Medici"	1·30	45
547	200f. "The Artist's Sons"	2·00	65
548	300f. "Neptune" (horiz)	3·25	85
MS549	90 × 116 mm. 500f. "Marie de Medici" (different) (37 × 49 mm)	5·75	2·00

202 Black Rhinoceros

1978. Endangered Animals. Multicoloured.

550	40f. Type **202**	1·10	25
551	50f. Crocodile	1·70	30
552	60f. Leopard (vert)	1·90	45
553	100f. Giraffe (vert)	3·00	65
554	200f. African elephant	7·75	90
555	300f. Gorilla (vert)	9·25	1·50

203 Mail Coach and Satellite

1978. 100 Years of Progress in Posts and Telecommunications. Multicoloured.

556	40f. Type **203** (postage)	45	25
557	50f. Steam locomotive and space communications	1·80	85
558	60f. Paddle-steamer and ship-to-shore communications	55	25
559	80f. Renault car and "Pioneer" satellite	75	25
560	100f. Mail balloon and "Apollo"–"Soyuz" link-up (air)	1·00	40
561	200f. Seaplane "Comte da la Vaulx" and Concorde	1·80	70
MS562	104 × 70 mm. 500f. Tom-toms and Zeppelin (53 × 35 mm)	6·75	1·90

205 H.M.S. "Endeavour" under Repair (after W. Byrne)

1978. 250th Birth Anniv of Captain Cook. Mult.

578	60f. Type **205**	75	25
579	80f. Cook on board "Endeavour" (vert)	1·00	40
580	200f. Landing party in New Hebrides	2·75	75
581	350f. Masked paddlers in canoe (after Webber)	4·50	1·50

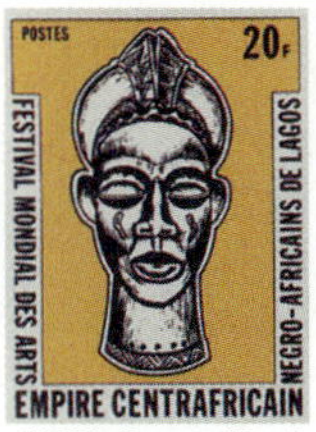

206 Ife Bronze Head

1978. 2nd World Festival of Negro Arts, Lagos.

582	**206** 20f. black and yellow	30	25
583	– 30f. black and blue	30	25
584	– 60f. multicoloured	70	40
585	– 100f. multicoloured	1·20	70

DESIGNS—VERT: 30f. Carved mask. HORIZ: 60f. Dancers; 100f. Dancers with musical instruments.

207 Clement Ader and "Avion III"

1978. Air. Aviation Pioneers. Multicoloured.

586	40f. Type **207**	50	25
587	50f. Wright Brothers and glider No. III	50	25
588	60f. Alcock, Brown and Vickers Vimy	60	40
589	100f. Sir Alan Cobham and De Havilland D.H.50	1·20	40
590	150f. Dr. Claude Dornier and Dornier Gs1 flying boat	1·80	70
MS591	117 × 80 mm. 500f. Wright Brothers and "Flyer"	5·50	1·80

208 "Self-portrait"

1978. 450th Death Anniv of Albrecht Durer (artist). Multicoloured.

592	60f. Type **208**	60	25
593	80f. "The Four Apostles"	1·00	25
594	200f. "The Virgin and Child"	2·40	90
595	350f. "The Emperor Maximilian I"	4·00	1·50

1978. Air. "Philexafrique" Stamp Exhibition, Gabon (1st issue) and International Stamp Fair, Essen. As T **237** of Benin. Multicoloured.

596	100f. Red crossbills and Mecklenberg-Schwerin 1856 ¼s. stamp	2·20	1·40
597	100f. Crocodile and Central African Republic 1960 500f. stamp	2·20	1·40

See also Nos. 647/8.

209 Third Mummiform Coffin

1978. Treasures of Tutankhamun. Mult.

598	40f. Type **209**	70	30
599	60f. Tutankhamun and Ankhesenamun (back of gilt throne)	95	35
600	80f. Ecclesiastical throne	1·40	50
601	100f. Head of Tutankhamun (wooden statuette)	1·50	50
602	120f. Lion's head (funerary bedhead)	2·00	65
603	150f. Life-size statue of Tutankhamun	2·50	70
604	180f. Gilt throne	3·25	85
605	250f. Canopic coffin	4·00	1·10

210 Lenin speaking at the Smolny Institute

211 Catherine Bokassa

1978. 60th Anniv of Russian Revolution.

606	**210**	40f. multicoloured	50	30
607	–	60f. multicoloured	60	45
608	–	100f. black, grey and gold	1·00	50
609	–	150f. red, black and gold	1·90	80
610	–	200f. multicoloured	2·50	1·00
611	–	300f. multicoloured	3·25	1·50
MS612		78 × 110 mm. 500f. multicoloured	5·25	4·00

DESIGNS—VERT: 60f. Lenin addressing crowd in Red Square; 200f. Lenin in Smolny Institute; 300f. Lenin and banner; 500f. Cruiser "Aurora" and Order of Lenin. HORIZ: 100f. Lenin, Kurpskaya and family; 150f. Lenin, cruiser "Aurora", banner and revolutionaries.

1978. 1st Anniv of Emperor Bokassa's Coronation. Multicoloured.

613	40f. Type **211** (postage)	50	25
614	60f. Emperor Bokassa	70	30
615	150f. The Emperor and Empress (horiz) (air)	1·70	75
MS616	Two sheets. (a) 101 × 82 mm. 250f. Coronation ceremony (horiz); (b) 76 × 100 mm. 1000f. Emperor and eagle	12·00	5·50

212 Rowland Hill, Letter-weighing Scale and Penny Black

1978. Death Centenary of Sir Rowland Hill (1st issue). Multicoloured.

617	40f. Type **212** (postage)	55	25
618	50f. Postman on bicycle and U.S. 5c. stamp, 1847	55	25
619	60f. Danish postman and Austrian newspaper stamp, 1856	80	35
620	80f. Postilion, mail coach and Geneva 5+5c. stamp, 1843	95	45
621	100f. Postman, mail train and Tuscan 3l. stamp, 1860 (air)	2·40	1·00
622	200f. Mail balloon and French 10c. stamp, 1850	1·70	70
MS623	81 × 85 mm. 500f. First Central African Republic stamps, 1959 (37 × 38 mm)	5·50	1·80

See also Nos. 671/**MS**675.

1978. Argentina's Victory in World Cup Football Championship. Nos. 527/31 optd **VAINQUEUR ARGENTINE**.

625	50f. Type **197**	55	35
626	60f. Goalmouth melee	60	40
627	100f. Midfield play	95	60
628	200f. World Cup poster	2·00	1·10
629	300f. Mario Jorge Lobo Zagalo and Buenos Aires Stadium	3·00	1·40
MS630	120 × 81 mm. 500f. multicoloured, optd **ARGENTINE-PAYS BAS 3-1/25 juin 1978**	5·25	5·25

214 Children painting and Dutch Master

1979. International Year of the Child (1st issue). Multicoloured.

631	40f. Type **214** (postage)	50	10
632	50f. Eskimo children and skier	65	20
633	60f. Benz automobile and children with toy car	85	25
634	80f. Satellite and children launching rocket	1·20	25
635	100f. Dornier Do-X flying boat and Chinese child flying kite (air)	1·30	45
636	200f. Hurdler and children playing leap-frog	2·50	70
MS637	109 × 79 mm. 500f. Albert Einstein and child with abacus (55 × 32 mm)	5·50	1·80

See also Nos. 666/70.

215 High Jump

1979. Pre-Olympic Year (1st issue). Mult.

639	40f. Type **215** (postage)	50	10
640	50f. Cycling	55	20
641	60f. Weightlifting	65	25
642	80f. Judo	90	30
643	100f. Hurdles (air)	1·00	40
644	200f. Long jump	1·90	70
MS645	110 × 79 mm. 500f. Pole vault (55 × 37 mm)	5·00	1·70

See also Nos. 676/80 and 700/**MS**706.

216 Co-operation Monument, "Aurivillius arata" and Hibiscus

1979. "Philexafrique" Exhibition (2nd issue). Mult.

647	60f. Type **216**	2·40	1·20
648	150f. Envelopes, van, canoeist and UPU emblem	4·25	2·30

217 School Teacher

1979. 50th Anniv of International Bureau of Education.

649	**217**	70f. multicoloured	85	45

218 "Madonna seated on a Bench" (woodcut)

1979. 450th Death Anniv (1978) of Albrecht Durer (artist) (2nd issue). Sheet 90 × 115 mm.

MS650	**218**	500f. green and lake	5·50	1·80

219 Chicken

1979. National Association of Farmers. Mult.

651	10f. Type **219** (postage)	1·80	1·10
652	20f. Bullock	1·80	1·10
653	40f. Sheep	3·75	2·20
654	60f. Horse (air)	5·50	2·10

OFFICIAL STAMPS

1977. Official stamps of Central African Republic optd **EMPIRE CENTRAFRICAIN**.

O498	O **109**	5f. multicoloured	25	10
O499		40f. multicoloured	45	25
O500		100f. multicoloured	1·20	40
O501		140f. multicoloured	1·50	80
O502		200f. multicoloured	2·50	1·10

O **204** Coat of Arms

1978.

O564	O **204**	1f. multicoloured	10	10
O565		2f. multicoloured	10	10
O566		5f. multicoloured	10	10
O567		10f. multicoloured	25	10
O568		15f. multicoloured	25	10
O569		20f. multicoloured	25	10
O570		30f. multicoloured	45	25
O571		40f. multicoloured	45	25
O572		50f. multicoloured	70	55
O673		60f. multicoloured	65	45
O574		100f. multicoloured	1·10	90
O575		130f. multicoloured	1·40	1·50
O576		140f. multicoloured	1·70	1·30
O577		200f. multicoloured	3·25	1·60

CENTRAL AFRICAN REPUBLIC

Pt. 12

Formerly Ubangi-Shari. An independent republic within the French Community.

100 centimes = 1 franc.

1 President Boganda

3 "Dactyloceras widenmanni"

4 Abyssinian Roller

1959. Republic. 1st Anniv. Centres multicoloured. Frame colours given.

1	**1**	15f. blue	35	25
2	–	25f. red	50	25

DESIGN—HORIZ: 25f. As Type **1** but flag behind portrait.

1960. 10th Anniv of African Technical Co-operation Commission. As T **62** of Cameroun.

3	50f. blue and green	1·70	95

1960.

4	–	50c. brn, red & turq (postage)	10	10
5	–	1f. myrtle, brown & violet	10	10
6	–	2f. myrtle, brown and green	10	20
7	–	3f. brown, red and olive	45	20
8	**3**	5f. brown and green	45	25
9	–	10f. blue, black and green	95	55
10	–	20f. red, black and green	2·30	80
11	–	85f. red, black and green	7·25	1·70
12	–	50f. turq, red & green (air)	1·90	60
13	**4**	100f. violet, brown & green	2·40	90
14	–	200f. multicoloured	4·50	2·20
15	–	250f. multicoloured	6·75	2·50
16	–	500f. brown, blue and green	13·00	5·25

BUTTERFLIES—As Type **3**: 50c., 3f. "Cymothoe sangaris"; 1f., 2f. "Charaxe mobilis"; 10f. "Charaxes ameliae"; 20f. "Charaxes zingha"; 85f. "Drurya antimachus". BIRDS—As Type **4**: 50f. Great blue turaco; 200f. Green turaco; 250f. Red-faced lovebirds; 500f. African fish eagle.

See also Nos. 42/5.

1960. National Festival. No. 2 optd **FETE NATIONALE 1-12-1960.**

17	25f. multicoloured	1·40	1·30

1960. Air. Olympic Games. No. 276 of French Equatorial Africa optd with Olympic rings, **XVIIe OLYMPIADE 1960 REPUBLIQUE CENTRAFRICAINE** and surch **250F** and bars.

18	250f. on 500f. blue, blk & grn	8·75	8·25

7 Pasteur Institute, Bangui

1961. Opening of Pasteur Institute, Bangui.

19	**7**	20f. multicoloured	1·00	80

8 U.N. Emblem, Map and Flag

1961. Admission into UNO.

20	**8**	15f. multicoloured	40	30
21		25f. multicoloured	50	30
22		85f. multicoloured	1·50	1·00

1961. National Festival. Optd with star and **FETE NATIONALE 1-12-01.**

23	**8**	25f. multicoloured	2·00	1·90

1962. Air. "Air Afrique" Airline. As T **69** of Cameroun.

24	50f. violet, brown and green	95	70

1962. Union of African States and Madagascar Conference, Bangui. Surch **U.A.M. CONFERENCE DE BANGUI 25-27 MARS 1962 50F.**

25	**8**	50f. on 85f. multicoloured	1·70	1·60

1962. Malaria Eradication. As T **70** of Cameroun.

26	25f.+5f. slate	1·10	1·10

12 Hurdling

13 Pres. Dacko

1962. Sports.

27	**12**	20f. sep, yell & grn (postage)	45	30
28	–	50f. sepia, yellow and green	1·30	80
29	–	100f. sep, yell & grn (air)	2·20	1·50

DESIGNS—As Type **12**: 50f. Cycling. VERT: (26 × 47 mm): 100f. Pole-vaulting.

1962.

30	**13**	20f. multicoloured	35	20
31		25f. multicoloured	45	25

1962. 1st Anniv of Union of African and Malagasy States. As T **72** of Cameroun.

32	30f. green	1·20	95

15 Athlete

17 "National Army"

18 "Posts and Telecommunications"

1962. Air. "Coupe des Tropiques" Games, Bangui.
33 **15** 100f. brown, turquoise & red . . . . 2·40 1·60

1963. Freedom from Hunger. As T **76** of Cameroun.
34 25f.+5f. turquoise, brn & bis 1·00 1·00

1963. 3rd Anniv of Proclamation of Republic.
35 **17** 20f. multicoloured 65 45

1963. Air. African and Malagasy Posts and Telecommunications Union.
36 **18** 85f. multicoloured . . . . . 1·80 90

19 "Telecommunications"

1963. Space Telecommunications.
37 **19** 25f. green and purple . . . 75 60
38 – 100f. green, orange & blue 1·80 1·60
DESIGN: 100f. Radio waves and globe.

20 "Young Pioneers"

21 Boali Falls

1963. Young Pioneers.
39 **20** 30f. brown, blue & turquoise 85 50

1963.
40 **21** 30f. purple, green and blue 85 50

22 Map of Africa and Sun

1963. Air. "African Unity".
41 **22** 25f. ultramarine, yellow & bl 65 45

23 "Colotis evippe"

1963. Butterflies. Multicoloured.
42 1f Type **23** 20 20
43 3f "Papilio dardanus" 55 25
44 4f "Papilio lormieri" 80 35
45 60f. "Papilio zalmoxis" . . . 5·00 3·00

24 "Europafrique"

25 ABJ-6 Diesel Railcar

1963. Air. European–African Economic Convention.
46 **24** 50f. multicoloured . . . . . 2·75 2·10

1963. Air. Bangui–Douala Railway Project.
47 – 20f. green, purple & brown 65 50
48 **25** 25f. chocolate, blue & brn 95 60
49 – 50f. violet, purple & brown 2·50 1·90
50 – 100f. purple, turquoise and brown . . . . 3·75 2·75
MS50a 190 × 98 mm. Nos. 47/50 8·00 8·00
DESIGNS: (Diesel rolling stock)—HORIZ: 20f. ABJ-6 railcar; 100f. Diesel locomotive. VERT: 50f. Series BB500 diesel shunter.

26 UNESCO Emblem, Scales of Justice and Tree

1963. 15th Anniv of Declaration of Human Rights.
51 **26** 25f. bistre, green and brown 85 60

27 Bangui Cathedral

1964. Air.
52 **27** 100f. brown, green & blue 2·00 1·10

28 Cleopatra, Temple of Kalabsha

30 "Tree" and Sun Emblem

29 Radar Scanner

1964. Air. Nubian Monuments Preservation.
53 **28** 25f.+10f. mauve, bl & grn 1·30 1·20
54 50f.+10f. brn, grn & turq . . 2·20 2·10
55 100f.+10f. pur, vio & grn 3·50 3·25

1964. Air. World Meteorological Day.
56 **29** 50f. violet, brown and blue 1·00 1·00

1964. International Quiet Sun Years.
57 **30** 25f. orange, ochre & turq 1·30 85

31 Map and African Heads of State

33 Pres. Kennedy

32 Throwing the Javelin

1964. Air. 5th Anniv of Equatorial African Heads of State Conference.
58 **31** 100f. multicoloured . . . . 1·80 90

1964. Air. Olympic Games, Tokyo.
59 **32** 25f. brown, green and blue 45 30
60 – 50f. red, black and green . . 95 55
61 – 100f. brown, blue and green 2·20 1·30
62 – 250f. black, green and red 6·50 3·00
MS62a 130 × 100 mm. Nos. 59/62 16·00 15·00
DESIGNS: 50f. Basketball; 100f. Running; 250f. Diving and swimming.

1964. Air. Pres. Kennedy Memorial Issue.
63 **33** 100f. brown, black & violet 2·40 1·70
MS63a 90 × 130 mm. No. 63 in block of four . . . . 10·50 10·00

34 African Child

35 Silhouettes of European and African

1964. Child Welfare. Different portraits of children. As T **34**.
64 **34** 20f. brown, green & purple 45 25
65 – 25f. brown, blue and red . . 45 30
66 – 40f. brown, purple & green 60 45
67 – 50f. brown, green and red 80 60
MS67a 144 × 100 mm. Nos. 64/7 3·25 3·00

1964. French, African and Malagasy Co-operation. As T **88** of Cameroun.
68 25f. brown, red and green . . 85 50

1964. National Unity.
69 **35** 25f. multicoloured 85 50

36 "Economic Co-operation"

1964. Air. "Europafrique".
70 **36** 50f. green, red and yellow 1·20 85

37 Handclasp

1965. Air. International Co-operation Year.
71 **37** 100f. multicoloured . . . . 1·80 90

38 Weather Satellite

1965. Air. World Meteorological Day.
72 **38** 100f. blue and brown . . . 1·80 90

39 Abraham Lincoln

1965. Air. Death Centenary of Abraham Lincoln.
73 **39** 100f. flesh, blue & green . . 1·80 90

40 Team of Oxen

1965. Harnessed Animals in Agriculture.
74 **40** 25f. red, brown and green 50 30
75 – 50f. purple, green and blue 95 55
76 – 85f. brown, green and blue 1·30 80
77 – 100f. multicoloured . . . . 1·70 90
DESIGNS: 50f. Ploughing with bullock; 85f. Ploughing with oxen; 100f. Oxen with hay cart.

41 Pouget-Maisonneuve Telegraph Instrument

1965. Centenary of ITU.
78 **41** 25f. blue, red & grn (post) 55 45
79 – 30f. lake and green 60 55
80 – 50f. red and violet . . . . . 1·00 70
81 – 85f. blue and purple . . . . 1·80 1·20
82 – 100f. brown, blue & green (48½ × 27 mm) (air) . . . 2·00 1·20
DESIGNS—VERT: 30f. Chappe's telegraph instrument; 50f. Doignon regulator for Hughes telegraph. HORIZ: 85f. Pouillet's telegraph apparatus; 100f. "Relay" satellite and ITU emblem.

42 Women and Loom ("To Clothe")

43 Coffee Plant, Hammer Grubs and "Epicampoptera strandi"

1965. "MESAN" Welfare Campaign. Designs depicting "Five Aims".
83 **42** 25f. green, brown and blue (postage) 45 30
84 – 50f. brown, blue and green 80 55
85 – 60f. brown, blue and green 1·00 65
86 – 85f. multicoloured . . . . . 1·40 70
87 – 100f. blue, brown and green (48 × 27 mm) (air) . . . . 1·80 1·10
DESIGNS: 50f. Doctor examining child, and hospital ("To care for"); 60f. Student and school ("To instruct"); 85f. Women and child, and harvesting scene ("To nourish"); 100f. Village houses ("To house"). "MESAN—Mouvement Evolution Social Afrique Noire".

1965. Plant Protection.
88 **43** 2f. purple, red and green . . 30 10
89 – 3f. red, green and black . . 75 20
90 – 30f. purple, green and red 4·50 90
DESIGNS—HORIZ: 3f. Coffee plant, caterpillar and hawk-moth. VERT: 30f. Cotton plant caterpillar and rose-moth.

1965. Surch.
91 – 2f. on 3f. (No. 43) . . . . . 4·25 4·00
92 **1** 5f. on 15f. . . . . 3·75 3·00
93 – 5f. on 85f. (No. 76) 35 30
94 **13** 10f. on 20f. . . . . 4·50 4·25
95 – 10f. on 100f. (No. 77) . . . 55 55

45 Camp Fire

47 "Industry and Agriculture"

46 U.N. and Campaign Emblems

1965. Scouting.
96 **45** 25f. red, purple and blue . . 75 25
97 – 50f. brown and blue (Boy Scout) . . . . 1·30 65

1965. Freedom from Hunger.
98 **46** 50f. brown, blue and green 1·10 75

1965. Air. "Europafrique".
99 **47** 50f. multicoloured . . . . . 1·00 75

48 Mercury (statue after Coysevox)

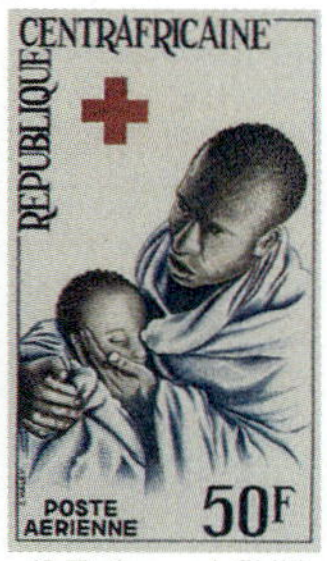

49 Father and Child

1965. Air. 5th Anniv of Admission to UPU.
100 **48** 100f. black, blue & red . . 2·30 1·30

1965. Air. Red Cross.
101 **49** 50f. black, blue and red . . 1·20 55
102 – 100f. brown, green and red (Mother and Child) . . 2·50 1·20

50 Grading Diamonds

51 Mbaka Porter

1966. National Diamond Industry.
103 **50** 25f. brown, violet and red 1·00 50

1966. World Festival of Negro Arts, Dakar.
104 **51** 25f. multicoloured 85 50

52 WHO Building

53 "Eulophia cucullata"

1966. WHO Headquarters, Geneva. Inaug.
105 **52** 25f. violet, blue & yellow 85 50

1966. Flowers. Multicoloured.
106 2f. Type **53** 25 10
107 5f. "Lissochilus horsfalii" . . 45 10
108 10f. "Tridactyle bicaudata" . . 45 25
109 15f. "Polystachya" 95 50
110 20f. "Eulophia alta" . . . . 1·40 60
111 25f. "Microcelia macrorrhynchium" . . . . 2·00 95

54 Douglas DC-8F Aircraft and "Air Afrique" Emblem

1966. Air. Inaug of "DC-8" Air Services.
112 **54** 25f. multicoloured 85 45

55 Congo Forest Mouse

1966. Rodents. Multicoloured.
113 5f. Type **55** 55 30
114 10f. Black-striped mouse . . . 1·00 50
115 20f. Dollman's tree mouse . . 1·70 80

56 "Luna 9"

1966. Air. "Conquest of the Moon". Mult.
116 130f. Type **56** . . . . 1·70 1·00
117 130f. "Surveyor" . . . . . . 1·70 1·00
118 200f. "From the Earth to the Moon" (Jules Verne) . . . 3·25 1·80
MS119 132 × 160 mm. Nos. 116/18 8·25 7·75

57 Cernan

59 UNESCO Emblem

58 Satellite "D 1" and Rocket "Diamant"

1966. Air. Astronauts. Multicoloured.
120 50f. Type **57** . . . . 1·10 60
121 50f. Popovich . . . . 1·10 60

1966. Air. Launching of Satellite "D 1".
122 **58** 100f. purple and brown . . 1·80 95

1966. 20th Anniv of UNESCO.
123 **59** 30f. multicoloured 60 45

60 Symbols of Industry and Agriculture

61 Pres. Bokassa

1966. Air. Europafrique.
124 **60** 50f. multicoloured . . . . 1·20 95

1967.
125 **61** 30f. black, ochre & green 60 35

1967. Provisional Stamps. (a) Postage. No. 111 surch **XX** and value.
126 10f. on 25f. multicoloured . . 50 25

(b) Air. No. 112 with face value altered by obliteration of figure "2" in "25".
127 **54** 5f. multicoloured 45 25

63 Douglas DC-8 over Bangui M'Poko Airport

1967. Air.
128 **63** 100f. blue, green & brown 2·30 1·10

64 Aerial View of Fair

1967. Air. World Fair, Montreal.
129 **64** 100f. brown, ultram & bl 2·00 80

65 Central Market, Bangui

1967. Multicoloured.
130 30f. Type **65** 85 45
131 30f. Safari Hotel, Bangui . . 85 35

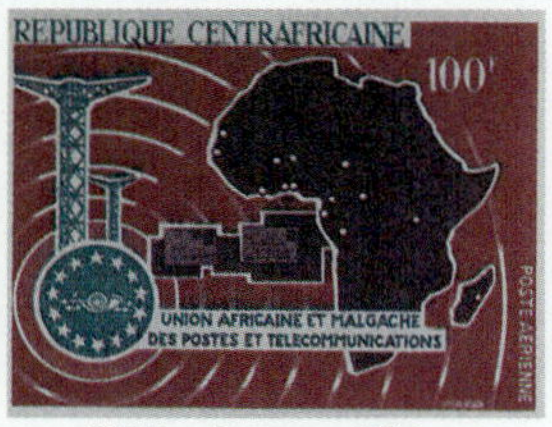

66 Map, Letters and Pylons

1967. Air. 5th Anniv of African and Malagasy Posts and Telecommunications Union (UAMPT).
132 **66** 100f. purple, grn & red . . 2·00 85

67 "Leucocoprinus africanus"

68 Projector, Africans and Map

1967. Mushrooms. Multicoloured.
133 5f. Type **67** . . . . 5·25 60
134 10f. "Synpodia arborescens" 8·25 1·00
135 15f. "Phlebopus sudanicus" 9·25 1·30
136 30f. "Termitomyces schimperi" . . . . . . 26·00 3·25
137 50f. "Psalliota sebedulis" . . . 42·00 5·00

1967. "Radiovision" Service.
138 **68** 30f. blue, green and brown 85 50

69 Coiffure

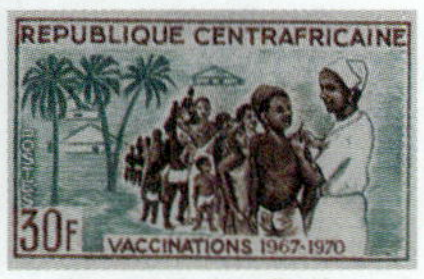

70 Inoculation Session

1967. Female Coiffures. Showing different hairstyles.
139 **69** 5f. brown and blue 30 15
140 – 10f. brown, choc & red . . 45 25
141 – 15f. brown, choc & grn . . 75 45
142 – 20f. brown, choc & orge 95 55
143 – 30f. brown, choc & purple 1·30 70

1967. Vaccination Programme, 1967–70.
144 **70** 30f. brown, green & red . . 85 60

71 Douglas DC-3

1967. Aircraft.
145 **71** 1f. grey, grn & brn (post) 10 10
146 – 2f. black, blue and purple 10 10
147 – 5f. black, green and blue 30 10
148 – 100f. brown, grn & bl (air) 2·00 85
149 – 200f. blue, brown and green . . . . 4·75 1·80
150 – 500f. slate, red and blue . . 12·50 4·75

DESIGNS—As T **71**: 2f. Beechcraft Baron; 5f. Douglas DC-4. 48 × 27 mm: 100f. Potez 25-TOE; 200f. Junkers 52/3m; 500f. Sud Aviation Caravelle.

72 Presidents Boganda and Bokassa

1967. Air. 9th Anniv of Republic.
151 **72** 130f. multicoloured . . . . 2·00 1·30

73 Primitive Shelter, Toulou

1967. 6th Pan-African Prehistory Congress, Dakar.
152 **73** 30f. blue, purple and red 75 40
153 – 50f. bistre, ochre & green 1·50 80
154 – 100f. purple, brown & blue 2·75 1·10
155 – 130f. red, green & brown 3·00 1·10

DESIGNS—VERT: 50f. Kwe perforated stone; 100f. Megaliths, Bouar. HORIZ: 130f. Rock drawings, Toulou.

74 Pres. Bokassa

1968. Air.
156 **74** 30f. multicoloured 85 50

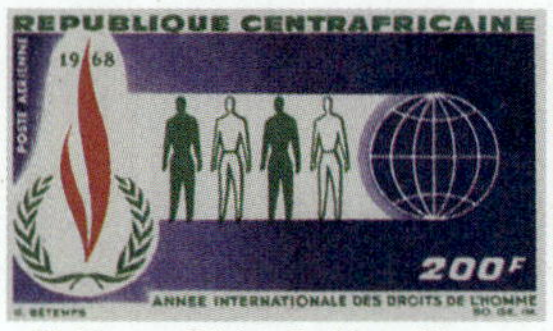

75 Human Rights Emblem, Human Figures and Globe

1968. Air. Human Rights Year.
157 **75** 200f. red, green and violet 3·50 1·70

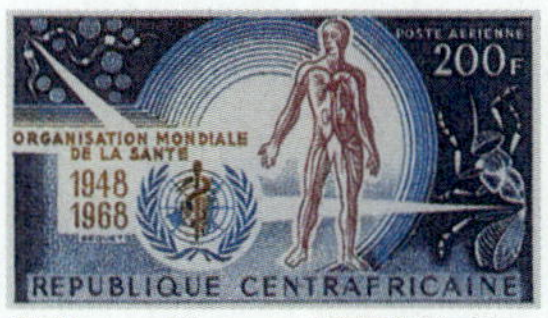

76 Human Figure and WHO Emblem

1968. Air. 20th Anniv of WHO.
158 **76** 200f. red, blue & brown . . 3·75 2·10

77 Alpine Skiing

78 Parachute-landing on Venus

1968. Air. Olympic Games, Grenoble and Mexico.
159 **77** 200f. brown, blue and red 5·00 3·25
160 – 200f. brown, blue and red 5·00 3·25
DESIGN: No. 160, Throwing the javelin.

1968. Air. "Venus 4". Exploration of planet Venus.
161 **78** 100f. blue, turquoise & grn 1·80 95

79 Marie Curie and impaled Crab (of Cancer)

1968. Air. Marie Curie Commem.
162 **79** 100f. brown, violet & blue 2·40 1·20

80 Refinery and Tanker

1968. Inauguration of Petroleum Refinery, Port Gentil, Gabon.
163 **80** 30f. multicoloured 85 40

1968. Air. Surch. Nos. 165/6 are obliterated with digit.
164 **56** 5f. on 130f. (No. 116) . . . 10 10
165 – 10f. (100f. No. 148) . . . 30 10
166 – 20f. (200f. No. 149) . . . 45 30
167 – 50f. on 130f. (No. 117) . . 1·00 60

82 "CD-8" Bulldozer

1968. Bokassa Project.
168 **82** 5f. brown, black & green 35 15
169 – 10f. black, brown & green 65 30
170 – 20f. green, yellow & brown 75 40
171 – 30f. blue, drab and brown 1·20 55
172 – 30f. red, blue and green . . 1·20 60
DESIGNS: 10f. Baoule cattle; 20f. Spinning-machine; 30f. (No. 171), Automatic looms; 30f. (No. 172), "D4-C" bulldozer.

83 Bangui Mosque

1968. 2nd Anniv of Bangui Mosque.
173 **83** 30f. flesh, green and blue 80 45

84 Za Throwing-knife

1968. Hunting Weapons.
174 **84** 10f. blue and bistre 45 25
175 – 20f. green, brown & blue 60 40
176 – 30f. green, orange & blue 95 45
DESIGNS: 20f. Kpinga-Gbengue throwing-knife; 30f. Mbano cross-bow.

85 "Ville de Bangui" (1958)

1968. River Craft.
177 **85** 10f. blue, green and purple (postage) 60 40
178 – 30f. brown, blue & green 1·10 55
179 – 50f. black, brown & grn . . 1·90 90
180 – 100f. brown, grn & bl (air) 2·40 1·10
181 – 130f. blue, green & purple 2·75 1·40
DESIGNS: 30f. "J. B. Gouandjia" (1968); 50f. "Lamblin" (1944). LARGER (48 × 27 mm): 100f. "Pie X" (Bangui, 1894); 130f. "Ballay" (Bangui, 1891).

86 "Madame de Sevigne" (French School, 17th century)

1968. Air. "Philexafrique" Stamp Exhibition, Abidjan, Ivory Coast (1969) (1st issue).
182 **86** 100f. multicoloured . . . . 3·00 2·50

87 President Bokassa, Cotton Plantation, and Ubangui Chari stamp of 1930

1969. Air. "Philexafrique" Stamp Exhibition, Abidjan, Ivory Coast (2nd issue).
183 **87** 50f. black, green & brown 1·80 1·70

88 "Holocerina angulata"

1969. Air. Butterflies. Multicoloured.
184 10f. Type **88** 75 30
185 20f. "Nudaurelia dione" . . 1·20 55
186 30f. "Eustera troglophylla" (vert) . . . . 2·75 85
187 50f. "Aurivillius aratus" . . . 4·50 2·20
188 100f. "Epiphora albida" . . . 7·50 3·50

89 Throwing the Javelin

90 Miner and Emblems

1969. Sports. Multicoloured.
189 5f. Type **89** (postage) 20 10
190 10f. Start of race 30 15
191 15f. Football 45 20
192 50f. Boxing (air) . . . . . . 1·00 40
193 100f. Basketball . . . . . . 2·10 70
Nos. 192/3 are 48 × 28 mm.

1969. 50th Anniv of I.L.O.
194 **90** 30f. multicoloured 90 40
195 50f. multicoloured . . . . 1·40 65

91 "Apollo 8" over Moon's Surface

1969. Air. Flight of "Apollo 8" Around Moon.
196 **91** 200f. multicoloured . . . . 3·50 1·80

92 Nuremberg Spire and Toys

1969. Air. International Toy Fair, Nuremberg.
197 **92** 100f. black, purple & grn 1·90 1·10

1969. Air. Birth Bicentenary of Napoleon Bonaparte. As T **144** of Cameroun. Multicoloured.
198 100f. "Napoleon as First Consul" (Girodet-Trioson) (vert) . . . . 2·30 1·40
199 130f. "Meeting of Napoleon and Francis II of Austria" (Gros) . . . . 3·25 1·60
200 200f. "Marriage of Napoleon and Marie-Louise" (Rouget) . . . . 4·75 3·00

93 President Bokassa in Military Uniform

94 Pres. Bokassa, Flag and Map

1969.
201 **93** 30f. multicoloured 60 30

1969. 10th Anniv of ASECNA. As T **151** of Cameroun.
202 100f. blue . . . . 1·80 85

1970. Air. Die-stamped on gold foil.
203 **94** 2000f. gold . . . . 37·00 35·00

95 Garayah

97 F. D. Roosevelt (25th Death Anniv)

96 Flour Storage Depot

1970. Musical Instruments.
204 **95** 10f. brown, sepia & green 60 25
205 – 15f. brown and green . . . 65 25
206 – 30f. brown, lake & yellow 1·00 50
207 – 50f. blue and red . . . . . 1·50 55
208 – 130f. brown, olive & blue 5·00 1·30
DESIGNS—VERT: 130f. Gatta and Babylon. HORIZ: 15f. Ngombi; 30f. Xylophone; 50f. Nadla.

1970. Societie Industrielle Centrafricaine des Produits Alimentaires et Derives (SICPAD) Project. Multicoloured.
209 25f. Type **96** . . . . 11·50 80
210 50f. Mill machinery . . . . 24·00 1·60
211 100f. View of flour mill . . . 36·00 2·50

1970. Air. World Leaders. Multicoloured.
212 100f. Lenin (birth centenary) 3·50 1·50
213 100f. Type **97** . . . . 1·90 1·00

1970. New UPU Headquarters Building, Berne. As T **156** of Cameroun.
214 100f. vermilion, red and blue 1·70 75

1970. Air. Moon Landing of "Apollo 12". No. 196 optd **ATTERRISSAGE d'APOLLO 12 19 novembre 1969**.
215 **91** 200f. multicoloured . . . . 15·00 10·50

99 Pres. Bokassa

101 Silkworm

100 Cheese Factory, Sarki

1970.
216 **99** 30f. multicoloured . . . . 7·25 4·50
217 40f. multicoloured . . . . 8·25 4·75

1970. "Operation Bokassa" Development Projects. Multicoloured.
218 5f. Type **100** (postage) . . . 45 25
219 10f. M'Bali Ranch . . . . . 5·50 4·00
220 20f. Zebu bull and herdsman (vert) 75 40
221 40f. Type **101** . . . . 2·20 70
222 140f. Type **101** (air) . . . . 2·20 90

102 African Dancer

1970. Air. "Knokphila 70" Stamp Exhibition, Knokke, Belgium. Multicoloured.
223 100f. Type **102** . . . . 1·80 60
224 100f. African produce . . . . 2·00 60

103 Footballer

1970. Air. World Cup Football Championship, Mexico.
225 **103** 200f. multicoloured . . . 3·75 1·70

104 Central African Republic's Pavilion

1970. Air. "EXPO 70", Osaka, Japan.
226 **104** 200f. multicoloured . . . 4·00 1·90

105 Dove and Cogwheel

1970. Air. 25th Anniv of UNO.
227 **105** 200f. black, yellow & bl 3·75 1·70

106 Presidents Mobutu, Bokassa and Tombalbaye

1970. Air. Reconciliation with Chad and Zaire.
228 **106** 140f. multicoloured . . . 2·75 1·10

107 Scaly Francolin and Helmeted Guineafowl

1971. Wildlife. Multicoloured.
229 5f.+5f. Type **107** . . . . . . 4·75 2·20
230 10f.+5f. Common duiker and true achatina (snail) . . . 6·25 3·00
231 20f.+5f. Hippopotamus, African elephant and tortoise in tug-of-war . . . 7·75 3·25
232 30f.+10f. Tortoise and Senegal coucal . . . . . . 10·50 7·75
233 50f.+20f. Monkey and leopard . . . . 18·00 12·50

108 Lengue Dancer

1971. Traditional Dances. Multicoloured.
234 20f.+5f. Type **108** 55 25
235 40f.+10f. Lengue (diff) . . . 95 45

236 100f.+40f. Teke . . . . . . 2·75 1·30
237 140f.+40f. Englabolo . . . . 3·25 1·60

110 Monteir's Mormyrid

1971. Fishes. Multicoloured.
244 10f. Type **110** 35 25
245 20f. Trunk-nosed mormyrid 75 30
246 30f. Wilverth's mormyrid . . 1·20 65
247 40f. Elephant-nosed mormyrid . . . . 2·30 75
248 50f. Curve-nosed mormyrid 3·00 1·30

111 Satellite and Globe

1971. Air. World Telecommunications Day.
249 **111** 100f. multicoloured . . . 1·90 90

112 Berberati Cathedral

1971. Consecration of Roman Catholic Cathedral, Berberati.
250 **112** 5f. multicoloured 45 20

113 Gen. De Gaulle

114 Lesser Bushbaby

1971. 1st Death Anniv of De Gaulle.
251 **113** 100f. multicoloured . . . 3·50 2·10

1971. Animals: Primates. Multicoloured.
252 30f. Type **114** 85 65
253 40f. Western needle-clawed bushbaby . . . . 1·20 75
254 100f. Angwantibo (horiz) . . 2·75 1·70
255 150f. Potto (horiz) . . . . . 4·75 2·50
256 200f. Red colobus (horiz) . . 6·50 3·75

1971. Air. 10th Anniv of African and Malagasy Posts and Telecommunications Union. Similar to T **184** of Cameroun. Multicoloured.
257 100f. Headquarters and carved head . . . . 1·90 90

115 Shepard in Capsule

1971. Space Achievements. Multicoloured.
258 40f. Type **115** 55 40
259 40f. Gagarin in helmet . . . 55 40
260 100f. Aldrin in Space . . . 1·40 55
261 100f. Leonov in Space . . . 1·40 55
262 200f. Armstrong on Moon 2·50 1·20
263 200f. "Lunokhod 1" on Moon . . . . 2·50 1·20

116 Crab Emblem

117 "Operation Bokassa"

1971. Air. Anti-cancer Campaign.
264 **116** 100f. multicoloured . . . 2·40 1·20

1971. 12th Year of Independence.
265 **117** 40f. multicoloured 80 50

118 Racial Equality Year Emblem

1971. Racial Equality Year.
266 **118** 50f. multicoloured 80 50

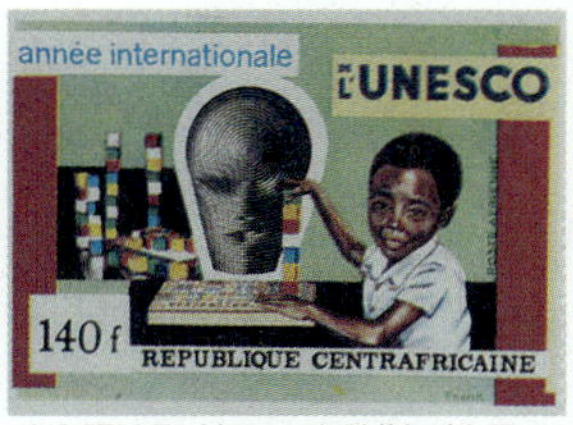
119 IEY Emblem and Child with Toy Bricks

1971. Air. 25th Anniv of UNESCO.
267 **119** 140f. multicoloured . . . 1·90 85

120 African Children

1971. Air. 25th Anniv of UNICEF.
268 **120** 140f.+50f. mult . . . . . 3·00 1·80

121 Arms and Parade

122 Pres. G. Nasser

1972. Bokassa Military School.
269 **121** 30f. multicoloured 80 50

1972. Air. Nasser Commemoration.
270 **122** 100f. ochre, brown & red 2·10 95

123 Book Year Emblem

124 Heart Emblem

1972. International Book Year.
271 **123** 100f. gold, yellow & brn 3·00 1·30

1972. World Heart Month.
272 **124** 100f. red, black & yellow 1·80 95

125 First-Aid Post

126 Global Emblem

1972. Red Cross Day.
273 **125** 150f. multicoloured . . . 3·25 1·60

1972. World Telecommunications Day.
274 **126** 50f. black, yellow & red 95 60

127 Boxing

1972. Air. Olympic Games, Munich.
275 **127** 100f. bistre and brown . . 1·70 1·10
276 – 100f. violet and green . . 1·70 1·10
MS277 130 × 100 mm. Designs as Nos. 275/6, but colours changed: 100f. emerald and purple; 100f. purple and brown . . . . . . 4·50 4·25
DESIGN—VERT: No. 276 Long jump.

128 Pres. Bokassa and Family

1972. Mothers' Day.
278 **128** 30f. multicoloured 60 40

129 Pres. Bokassa planting Cotton Bush

130 Savings Bank Building

1972. "Operation Bokassa" Cotton Development.
279 **129** 40f. multicoloured 95 45

1972. Opening of New Postal Cheques and Savings Bank Building.
280 **130** 30f. multicoloured 95 45

131 "Le Pacifique" Hotel

1972. "Operation Bokassa" Completion of "Le Pacifique" Hotel.
281 **131** 30f. blue, red and green 55 25

132 Giraffe and Monkeys

133 Postal Runner

134 Tiling's Postal Rocket, 1931

1972. Clock-faces from Central African HORCEN Factory. Multicoloured.
282 5f. Rhinoceros chasing African 30 25
283 10f. Camp fire and Native warriors 45 25
284 20f. Fishermen 45 30
285 30f. Type **132** 75 55
286 40f. Warriors fighting . . . . 1·20 70

1972. "CENTRAPHILEX" Stamp Exhibition, Bangui.
287 **133** 10f. mult (postage) . . . 30 20
288 – 20f. multicoloured 45 25
289 **134** 40f. orange, blue and slate (air) 70 45
290 – 50f. blue, slate & orange 80 70
291 – 150f. grey, orange & brn 2·30 1·50
292 – 200f. blue, orange & brn 3·25 2·30
MS293 201 × 100 mm. Nos. 289/92 8·75 8·50
DESIGNS—AS Type **133**: HORIZ: Protestant Youth Centre. As Type **134**: VERT: 50f. Douglas DC-3 and camel postman; 150f. "Sirio" satellite and rocket. HORIZ: 200f. "Intelsat 4" satellite and rocket.

135 University Buildings

1972. Inauguration of Bokassa University.
294 **135** 40f. grey, blue and red . . 80 45

136 Mail Van

1972. World UPU Day.
295 **136** 100f. multicoloured . . . 2·00 80

137 Paddy Field

1972. Bokassa Plan. State Farms. Multicoloured.
296 5f. Type **137** 65 20
297 25f. Rice cultivation . . . . 1·30 25

138 Four Linked Arrows

140 Hotel Swimming Pool

1972. Air. "Europafrique".
298 **138** 100f. multicoloured . . . 1·60 85

1972. Air. Munich Olympic Gold Medal Winners. Nos. 275/6 optd as listed below.
299 **127** 100f. bistre and brown . . 1·60 95
300 – 100f. violet and green . . 1·60 95
MS301 130 × 100 mm. **MS**277 with opts as Nos. 299/300 . . . . . 3·75 3·50
OVERPRINTS: No. 299, **POIDS-MOYEN LEMECHEV MEDAILLE D'OR**. No. 300, **LONGUEUR WILLIAMS MEDAILLE D'OR**.

1972. Opening of Hotel St. Sylvestre.
302 **140** 30f. brown, turq & grn 45 30
303 – 40f. purple, green & blue 50 35
DESIGN: 40f. Facade of Hotel.

141 Landing Module and Lunar Rover on Moon

1972. Air. Moon Flight of "Apollo 16".
304 **141** 100f. green, blue & grey . . . 1·60 80

142 "Virgin and Child" (F. Pesellino)

1972. Air. Christmas. Multicoloured.
305 100f. Type **142** . . . . 1·80 1·10
306 150f. "Adoration of the Child" (F. Lippi) . . . . . 2·75 1·50

143 Learning to Write

1972. "Central African Mothers". Multicoloured.
307 5f. Type **143** 10 10
308 10f. Baby-care 30 10
309 15f. Dressing hair 40 25
310 20f. Learning to read 45 25
311 180f. Suckling baby . . . . 2·50 1·30
312 190f. Learning to walk . . . 2·50 1·50

144 Louys (marathon), Athens, 1896

1972. Air. 75th Anniv of Revival of Olympic Games.
313 **144** 30f. purple, brown & grn . . 35 25
314 – 40f. green, blue & brown . . 45 25
315 – 50f. violet, blue and red . . 55 45
316 – 100f. purple, brn & grey . . 1·20 55
317 – 150f. black, blue & purple . 1·70 1·30
DESIGNS: 40f. Barrelet (sculling), Paris, 1900; 50f. Prinstein (triple-jump), St. Louis, U.S.A., 1904; 100f. Taylor (400 m freestyle swimming), London, 1908; 150f. Johansson (Greco-Roman wrestling), Stockholm, 1912.

145 WHO Emblem, Doctor and Nurse

1973. Air. 25th Anniv of WHO.
318 **145** 100f. multicoloured . . . 1·60 85

146 "Telecommunications"

1973. World Telecommunications Day.
319 **146** 200f. orange, blue & black 2·40 1·20

147 Harvesting

1973. 10th Anniv of World Food Programme.
320 **147** 50f. multicoloured 80 50

148 "Garcinia punctata"

1973. "Flora". Multicoloured.
321 10f. Type **148** 45 20
322 20f. "Bertiera racemosa" . . 65 25
323 30f. "Coryanthe pachyceras" 90 50
324 40f. "Combretodendron africanum" . . . . . . 1·30 60
325 50f. "Xylopia villosa" . . . . 1·70 25

149 Pygmy Chameleon

1973.
326 **149** 15f. multicoloured . . . . 1·50 40

150 "Mboyo Ndili"

1973. Caterpillars. Multicoloured.
327 3f. Type **150** 75 25
328 5f. "Piwili" . . . . 1·20 45
329 25f. "Loulia Konga" . . . . 2·50 65

1973. African Solidarity "Drought Relief". No. 321 surch **SECHERESSE SOLIDARITE AFRICAINE** and value.
330 **148** 100f. on 10f. mult . . . . 1·60 1·10

1973. UAMPT. As Type **216** of Cameroun.
331 100f. red, brown and olive . . 1·10 70

1973. Air. African Fortnight, Brussels. As T **217** of Cameroun.
332 100f. brown and violet . . . 1·30 75

152 African and Symbolic Map

1973. Air. Europafrique.
333 **152** 100f. red, green & brown 1·60 85

153 Bird with Letter

1973. Air. World UPU Day.
334 **153** 200f. multicoloured . . . 2·30 1·40

154 Weather Map

1973. Air. Centenary of IMO/WMO.
335 **154** 150f. multicoloured . . . 2·40 1·00

155 Copernicus

1973. Air. 500th Birth Anniv of Copernicus.
336 **155** 100f. multicoloured . . . 2·75 1·80

156 Pres. Bokassa

158 Launch

1973.
337 **156** 1f. mult (postage) 10 10
338 2f. multicoloured 10 10
339 3f. multicoloured 10 10
340 5f. multicoloured 10 10
341 10f. multicoloured 35 10
342 15f. multicoloured 35 20
343 20f. multicoloured 45 25
344 30f. multicoloured 45 30
345 40f. multicoloured 60 35
346 – 50f. multicoloured (air) 65 35
347 – 100f. multicoloured . . . 1·30 70
DESIGNS—SQUARE (35 × 35 mm): 50f. Pres. Bokassa facing left. VERT (26 × 47 mm): 100f. Pres. Bokassa in military uniform.

1973. Air. Moon Flight of "Apollo 17".
348 **158** 50f. red, green & brown 55 30
349 – 65f. green, red & purple 75 45
350 – 100f. blue, brown & red 1·20 70
351 – 150f. green, brown & red 1·70 85
352 – 200f. green, red and blue 2·20 1·30
DESIGNS—HORIZ: 65f. Surveying lunar surfaces; 100f. Descent on Moon. VERT: 150f. Astronauts on Moon's surface; 200f. Splashdown.

159 Interpol Emblem within "Eye"

1973. 50th Anniv of Interpol.
353 **159** 50f. multicoloured 80 55

160 St. Theresa

1973. Air. Birth Centenary of St. Theresa of Lisieux.
354 **160** 500f. blue and light blue 6·25 4·00

161 Main Entrance

1974. Opening of "Catherine Bokassa" Mother-and-Child Centre.
355 **161** 30f. brown, red and blue 35 25
356 – 40f. brown, blue and red 45 40
DESIGN: 40f. General view of Centre.

162 Cigarette-packing Machine

1974. "Centra" Cigarette Factory.
357 **162** 5f. purple, green & red . . 10 10
358 – 10f. blue, green & brown 35 20
359 – 30f. blue, green and red 45 25
DESIGNS: 10f. Administration block and factory building; 30f. Tobacco warehouse.

163 "Telecommunications"

165 Mother and Baby

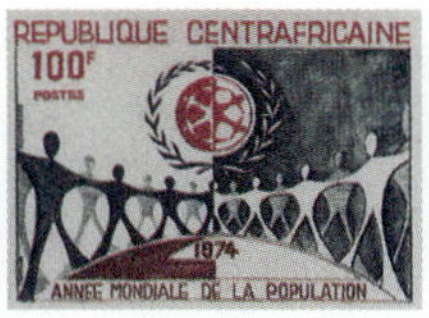

164 "Peoples of the World"

1974. World Telecommunications Day.
360 **163** 100f. multicoloured . . . 1·50 85

1974. World Population Year.
361 **164** 100f. green, red & brown 1·20 70

1974. 26th Anniv of WHO.
362 **165** 100f. brown, blue & grn 1·70 75

166 Letter and UPU Emblem

168 Modern Building

167 Battle Scene

1974. Centenary of UPU.
363 **166** 500f. red, green & brown 7·00 4·25

1974. "Activities of Forces' Veterans". Mult.
364 10f. Type **167** 10 10
365 15f. "Today" (Peace-time activities) 20 10
366 20f. Planting rice 30 10
367 25f. Cattle-shed 35 20
368 30f. Workers hoeing 35 25
369 40f. Veterans' houses 55 25

1974. 10th Anniv of Central African Customs and Economics Union. As Nos. 734/5 of Cameroun.
370 40f. multicoloured (postage) 60 35
371 100f. multicoloured (air) . . 1·30 80

1975. "OCAM City" Project.
372 **168** 30f. multicoloured 35 10
373 – 40f. multicoloured 45 25
374 – 50f. multicoloured 55 40
375 – 100f. multicoloured . . . 1·00 55
DESIGNS: Nos. 373/5, Various views similar to Type **150**.

1975. "J. B. Bokassa Pilot Village Project". As T **168**, but inscr "VILLAGE PILOTE J. B. BOKASSA".
376 25f. multicoloured 30 10
377 30f. multicoloured 35 25
378 40f. multicoloured 45 30
DESIGNS: Nos. 376/8, Various views similar to Type **168**.

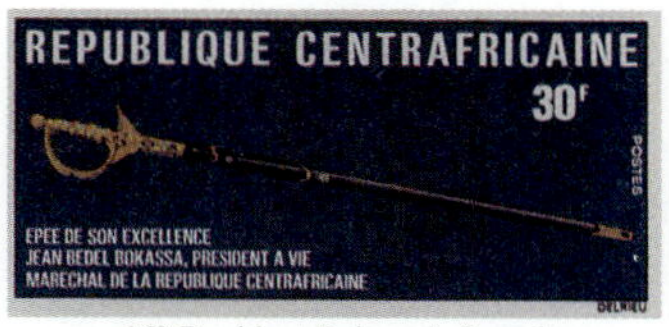

169 President Bokassa's Sword

1975. "Homage to President Bokassa". Mult.
379 30f. Type **169** (postage) . . . 45 30
380 40f. President Bokassa's baton 55 25
381 50f. Pres. Bokassa in uniform (vert, 36 × 49 mm) (air) . . 60 35
382 100f. Pres. Bokassa in cap and cape (vert, 36 × 49 mm) . . . . 1·30 55

170 Foreign Minister and Ministry

1975. Government Buildings. Multicoloured.
383 40f. Type **170** 55 35
384 40f. Television Centre (36 × 23 mm) 55 35

171 "No Entry"

1975. Road Signs.
385 **171** 5f. red and blue 10 10
386 – 10f. red and blue 10 10
387 – 20f. red and blue 30 10
388 – 30f. multicoloured . . . 45 25
389 – 40f. multicoloured . . . 75 30
SIGNS: 10f. "Stop"; 20f. "No stopping"; 30f. "School"; 40f. "Crossroads".

172 Kob

1975. Wild Animals. Multicoloured.
390 10f. Type **172** 45 10
391 15f. Warthog 90 25
392 20f. Waterbuck . . . . . . 1·20 25
393 30f. Lion . . . . 1·30 40

173 Carved Wooden Mask

1975. Air. "Arphila" International Stamp Exhibition. Paris.
394 **173** 100f. red, rose and blue 1·30 70

174 Dr. Schweitzer and Dug-out Canoe **175** Forest Scene

1975. Air. Birth Centenary of Dr. Albert Schweitzer.
395 **174** 200f. black, blue & brown 3·75 2·00

1975. Central African Woods.
396 **175** 10f. brown, green & red 10 10
397 – 15f. brown, green & blue 30 10
398 – 50f. blue, brown & green 55 25
399 – 100f. brown, blue & grn 1·20 60
400 – 150f. blue, brown & grn 1·60 1·00
401 – 200f. brown, red & green 2·10 1·40
DESIGNS—VERT: 15f. Cutting sapeles. HORIZ: 50f. Mobile crane; 100f. Log stack; 150f. Floating logs; 200f. Timber-sorting yard.

176 Women's Heads and Women Working

1975. International Women's Year.
402 **176** 40f. multicoloured 45 25
403 100f. multicoloured . . . 1·30 65

177 River Vessel "Jean Bedel Bokassa"

1976. Air. Multicoloured.
404 30f. Type **177** 60 30
405 40f. Frontal view of "Jean Bedel Bokassa" 85 50

178 Co-operation Monument

1976. Air. Central African–French Co-operation and Visit of President Giscard d'Estaing. Mult.
406 100f. Type **178** . . . . 1·30 85
407 200f. Flags and Presidents Giscard d'Estaing and Bokassa . . . . 2·75 1·40

179 Alexander Graham Bell

1976. Telephone Centenary.
408 **179** 100f. black and yellow . . 1·70 1·00

180 Telecommunications Satellite

1976. World Telecommunications Day.
409 **180** 100f. purple, blue & grn 1·70 1·10

181 Rocket on Launch-pad

1976. Apollo–Soyuz Space Link. Multicoloured.
410 40f. Type **181** (postage) . . . 60 30
411 50f. Blast-off 75 40
412 100f. "Soyuz" in flight (air) 1·00 25
413 200f. "Apollo" in flight . . . 1·90 65
414 300f. Crew meeting in space 3·00 1·00
MS415 103 × 78 mm. 500f. Space link . . . . 5·00 1·90

182 French Hussar

1976. Air. American Revolution Bicent. Mult.
416 100f. Type **182** 85 40
417 125f. Black Watch soldier . . 1·20 50
418 150f. German Dragoons' officer . . . . 1·20 55
419 200f. British Grenadiers' officer . . . . 2·20 60
420 250f. American Ranger . . . 2·50 95
MS421 119 × 81 mm. 450f. American dragoon . . . . 7·25 2·10

183 "Drurya antimachus"

1976. Butterflies. Multicoloured.
422 30f. Type **183** (postage) . . . 5·25 1·10
423 40f. "Argema mittrei" (vert) 7·50 1·10
424 50f. "Acherontia atropos" and "Saturnia pyri" (air) 4·75 1·10
425 100f. "Papilio nireus" and "Heniocha marnois" . . . 9·50 1·60

184 Dorothy Hamill of U.S.A. (figure skating)

1976. Medal Winners, Winter Olympic Games, Innsbruck. Multicoloured.
426 40f. Piero Gros of Italy (slalom) (horiz) (postage) 50 25
427 60f. Karl Schnabl and Toni Innauer of Austria (ski-jumping) (horiz) 75 40
428 100f. Type **184** (air) 95 45
429 200f. Alexandre Gorshkov and Ludmilla Pakhomova (figure-skating, pairs) (horiz) . . . . 1·90 75
430 300f. John Curry of Great Britain (figure-skating) . . 3·00 1·10
MS431 103 × 78 mm. 500f. Rosi Mittermaier of West Germany (skiing) . . . . 6·00 1·90

185 UPU Emblem, Letters, and Types of Mail Transport

1976. World UPU Day.
432 **185** 100f. multicoloured . . . 1·60 90

186 Assembly of "Viking"

1976. "Viking" Space Mission to Mars. Multicoloured.
433 40f. Type **186** (postage) . . . 50 25
434 60f. Launch of "Viking" . . 75 40
435 100f. Parachute descent on Mars (air) 95 45
436 200f. "Viking" on Mars (horiz) . . . . 1·90 70
437 300f. "Viking" operating gravel scoop . . . . 3·00 1·00
MS438 102 × 78 mm. 500f. "Viking" in flight (horiz) . . . . 5·00 1·90

Issues between 1977 and 1979 are listed under **CENTRAL AFRICAN EMPIRE**.

220 Ski Jump

1979. Air. Winter Olympic Games, Lake Placid (1980). Multicoloured.
655 60f. Type **220** 60 25
656 100f. Downhill skiing . . . . 1·00 45
657 200f. Ice hockey . . . . . . 2·10 90
658 300f. Skiing (slalom) . . . . 3·00 1·40
MS659 103 × 77 mm. 500f. Two-man bobsleigh . . . . 5·50 1·80

1979. "Apollo 11" Moon Landing. 10th Anniv. Nos. 433/7 optd **ALUNISSAGE APOLLO XI JUILLET 1969** and lunar module.
660 **186** 40f. mult (postage) . . . 50 30
661 – 60f. multicoloured . . . 65 45
662 – 100f. multicoloured (air) 95 60
663 – 200f. multicoloured . . . 1·80 95
664 – 300f. multicoloured . . . 2·75 1·40
MS665 102 × 78 mm. 500f. multicoloured . . . . 5·50 5·00

222 Thumbellina (Andersen) **224** Basketball

223 Steam Locomotive, U.S.A. Stamp and Hill

1979. International Year of the Child (2nd issue). Multicoloured.
666 30f. Type **222** 30 10
667 40f. Sleeping Beauty (horiz) 40 10
668 60f. Hansel and Gretel . . . 55 25
669 200f. The Match Girl (horiz) 2·10 75
670 250f. The Little Mermaid . . 2·50 85

1979. Death Centenary of Sir Rowland Hill (2nd issue). Multicoloured.
671 60f. Type **223** 55 25
672 100f. Locomotive "Champion" (1882, U.S.A.), French stamp and Hill . . . . 1·00 35
673 150f. Steam locomotive, German stamp and Hill . . 1·70 55
674 250f. Steam locomotive, British stamp and Hill . . 2·75 1·10
MS675 115 × 78 mm. 500f. Locomotive, Central African Republic stamps and Hill . . . 6·00 2·10

1979. Olympic Games, Moscow (2nd issue). Basketball.
676 **224** 50f. multicoloured 45 10
677 – 125f. multicoloured . . . 1·20 45
678 – 200f. multicoloured . . . 2·00 60
679 – 300f. multicoloured . . . 3·00 95
680 – 500f. multicoloured . . . 4·50 1·50
DESIGNS: 125f. to 500f. Views of different basketball matches.

1980. Various stamps, including one unissued, of Central African Empire optd **REPUBLIQUE CENTRAFRICAINE**.
681 **192** 5f. multicoloured 20 20
682 – 10f. mult (No. 522) . . . 20 25
683 – 20f. multicoloured (Balambo (stand)) . . . 20 10
684 **206** 20f. black and yellow . . 20 10
685 – 30f. black and blue (No. 583) 40 20

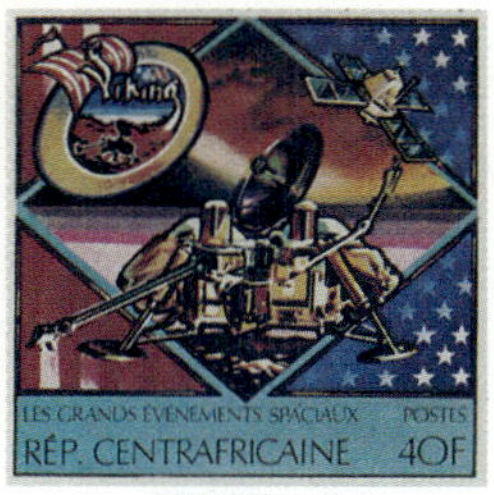

226 "Viking"

1980. Space Exploration. Multicoloured.
686 40f. Type **226** (postage) . . . 45 10
687 50f. "Apollo"–"Soyuz" link 55 15
688 60f. "Voyager" 65 20
689 100f. European Space Agency 1·10 30

690 150f. Early satellites (air) . . 1·50 40
691 200f. Space shuttle . . . . . 2·00 55
MS692 85 × 58 mm. 500f. Neil Armstrong (50 × 41 mm) . . . 5·25 1·60

1980. Air. Winter Olympic Medal Winners. Nos. 655/8 optd as listed below.
693 **220** 60f. multicoloured 55 25
694 – 100f. multicoloured . . . 95 45
695 – 200f. multicoloured . . . 1·80 90
696 – 300f. multicoloured . . . 2·75 1·40
MS697 103 × 77 mm. 500f. multicoloured . . . . 5·50 3·25
DESIGNS: 60f. **VAINQUEUR INNAVER AUTRICHE**; 100f. **VAINQUEUR MOSER-PROELL AUTRICHE**; 200f. **VAINQUEUR ETATS-UNIS**; 300f. **VAINQUEUR STENMARK SUEDE**; 500f. **VAINQUEURS / SCHAERER-BENZ / SUISSE**.

228 Telephone and Sun

1980. World Telecommunications Day. Mult.
698 100f. Type **228** . . . . 1·00 60
699 150f. Telephone and sun (different) . . . . 1·50 85

229 Walking

1980. Olympic Games, Moscow (3rd issue). Mult.
700 30f. Type **229** (postage) . . . 40 10
701 40f. Women's relay 50 10
702 70f. Running 75 25
703 80f. Women's high jump . . 75 25

704 100f. Boxing (air) 95 25
705 150f. Hurdles . . . . 1·50 45
MS706 87 × 84 mm. 250f. Long jump (39 × 36 mm) . . . . 5·25 1·60

229a Fruit

1980.
706a **229a** 40f. multicoloured . . .

230 Agriculture

232 "Foligne Madonna" (detail)

1980. European-African Co-operation. Mult.
707 30f. Type **230** (postage) . . . 35 10
708 40f. Industry 45 10
709 70f. Communications 80 25
710 100f. Building construction and rocket . . . . 1·40 40
711 150f. Meteorological satellite (air) . . . . 1·50 50
712 200f. Space shuttle . . . . . 1·80 65
MS713 89 × 64 mm. 500f. Concorde (41 × 29 mm) . . . . 5·25 1·70

1980. Olympic Medal Winners. Nos. 676/80 optd.
717 50f. **MEDAILLE OR YOUGOSLAVIE** 50 25
718 125f. **MEDAILLE OR URSS** 1·20 45
719 200f. **MEDAILLE OR URSS** 1·80 70
720 300f. **MEDAILLE ARGEN TITALIE** . . . . 3·00 1·10
721 500f. **MEDAILLE BRONZE URSS** . . . . 4·50 1·70

1980. Christmas. Multicoloured.
722 60f. Type **232** 60 25
723 150f. "Virgin and Saints" . . 1·50 65
724 250f. "Conestabile Madonna" 2·75 1·10

1980. 5th Anniv of African Posts and Telecommunications Union. As T **269** of Benin.
725 70f. multicoloured 75 40

233 Peruvian Football Team

1981. World Cup Football Championship, Spain (1982). Multicoloured.
726 10f. Type **233** (postage) . . . 10 10
727 15f. Scottish team 20 10
728 20f. Mexican team 30 10
729 25f. Swedish team 30 10
730 30f. Austrian team 45 10
731 40f. Polish team 45 25
732 50f. French team 75 25
733 60f. Italian team 75 25
734 70f. West German team . . . 95 35
735 80f. Brazilian team 95 40

736 100f. Dutch team (air) . . . 95 25
737 200f. Spanish team . . . . . 1·80 45
MS738 119 × 87 mm. 500f. Argentina team . . . . 6·00 1·70

234 "Fight between Jacob and the Angel"

236 ITU and WHO Emblems and Ribbons forming Caduceus

1981. Air. 375th Birth Anniv of Rembrandt. Multicoloured.
739 60f. Type **234** 55 25
740 90f. "Christ in the Tempest" 95 25
741 150f. "Jeremiah mourning the Destruction of Jerusalem" 1·70 70
742 250f. "Anna accused by Tobit of Theft of a Goat" 2·75 80
MS743 104 × 80 mm. 500f. "Belshazzar's Feast" (horiz) . . 5·50 1·80

1981. Olympic Games Medal Winners. Nos. 700/**MS**706 optd.
744 30f. **50 K.M. MARCHE HARTWIG GAUDER–G.D.R.** (postage) 30 10
745 40f. **4 × 400 M. DAMES–U.R.S.S** 45 25
746 70f. **100 M. COURSE HOMMES ALAN WELLS–G.B.R** 75 30
747 80f. **SAUT EN HAUTEUR DAMES SARA SIMEONI–ITALIE** . . . 75 45
748 100f. **BOXE–71 KG ARMANDO MARTINEZ–CUBA** (air) . . . . 1·00 35
749 150f. **110 M. HAIES HOMMES THOMAS MUNKELT–G.D.R** . . . 1·50 65
MS750 87 × 84 mm. 250f. **SAUT LONGUEUR / LUTZ DOMBROWSKI–G.D.R** . . . 5·50 5·00

1981. World Telecommunications Day.
751 **236** 150f. multicoloured . . . 1·40 75

237 Boeing 747 carrying Space Shuttle "Enterprise"

1981. Conquest of Space. Multicoloured.
752 100f. "Apollo 15" and jeep on the Moon 95 40
753 150f. Type **237** . . . . . . 1·40 45
754 200f. Space Shuttle launch . . 1·80 65
755 300f. Space Shuttle performing experiment in space . . . . 3·00 1·00
MS756 103 × 78 mm. 500f. Space shuttle approaching landing strip 6·00 1·70

238 "Family of Acrobats with a Monkey"

1981. Birth Bicentenary of Pablo Picasso. Mult.
757 40f. Type **238** (postage) . . . 45 10
758 50f. "The Balcony" 75 25
759 80f. "The Artist's Son as Pierrot" . . . . 1·20 40
760 100f. "The Three Dancers" 1·70 45

761 150f. "Woman and Mirror with Self-portrait" (air) . . 2·10 50
762 200f. "Sleeping Woman, the Dream" . . . . 5·00 1·40
MS763 78 × 113 mm. 500f. "Portrait of Maria" (40 × 50 mm) . . . 5·50 1·60

239 Tractor and Plough breaking Chain

1981. 1st Anniv of Zimbabwe's Independence.
764 **239** 100f. multicoloured . . . 1·00 45
765 150f. multicoloured . . . 1·40 60
766 200f. multicoloured . . . 2·00 80

240 Prince Charles

1981. Royal Wedding (1st issue). Multicoloured.
767 75f. Type **240** 55 25
768 100f. Lady Diana Spencer . . 95 30
769 150f. St. Paul's Cathedral . . 1·40 65
770 175f. Couple and Prince's personal Standard . . . . 1·80 65
MS771 69 × 91 mm. 500f. Prince and Lady Diana . . . . 7·75 1·80
See also Nos. 772/**MS**778.

241 Lady Diana Spencer with Children

1981. Royal Wedding (2nd issue). Multicoloured.
772 40f. Type **241** (postage) . . . 45 10
773 50f. Investiture of the Prince of Wales 55 25
774 80f. Lady Diana Spencer at Althorp House 75 25
775 100f. Prince Charles in naval uniform . . . . 1·20 40
776 150f. Prince of Wales's feathers (air) . . . . 2·30 55
777 200f. Highgrove House . . . 3·50 1·00
MS778 120 × 70 mm. 500f. St. Paul's Cathedral (57 × 33 mm) . . . . 5·25 1·80

242 C. V. Rietschoten

1981. Navigators. Multicoloured.
779 40f. Type **242** (postage) . . . 45 25
780 50f. M. Pajot 45 30
781 60f. L. Jaworski 65 45
782 80f. M. Birch 85 55

783 100f. O. Kersauson (air) . . 1·20 60
784 200f. Sir Francis Chichester 2·20 1·10
MS785 100 × 80 mm. 500f. A. Colas 6·00 1·60

243 Renault, 1906

1981. 75th Anniv of French Grand Prix Motor Race. Multicoloured.
786 20f. Type **243** 45 10
787 40f. Mercedes-Benz, 1937 . . 45 10
788 50f. Matra-Ford, 1969 . . . 65 25
789 110f. Tazio Nuvolari . . . . 1·40 45
790 150f. Jackie Stewart . . . . 2·00 70
MS791 104 × 80 mm. 450f. Racing car, 1914 . . . . 7·75 4·00

244 Emperor's Crown pierced by Bayonet

1981. Overthrow of the Empire. Multicoloured.
792 5f. Type **244** 10 10
793 10f. Type **244** 25 10
794 25f. Axe splitting crown, and angel holding map 30 10
795 60f. As 25f. 65 25
796 90f. Emperor Bokassa's statue being toppled and map of Republic . . . . . 1·00 45
797 500f. As 90f. . . . . 4·50 2·00

245 FAO Emblem

1981. World Food Day.
798 **245** 90f. green, brown & yell 95 30
799 110f. green, brown & bl 1·10 45

246 Lizard

247 Plumed Guineafowl ("Komba")

1981. Air. Reptiles. Multicoloured.
800 30f. Type **246** 80 20
801 60f. Snake . . . . 1·00 30
802 110f. Crocodile . . . . . . 1·80 50

1981. Birds. Multicoloured.
803 50f. Type **247** 65 25
804 90f. Schlegel's francolin ("Dodoro") . . . . 1·30 25
805 140f. Black-headed bunting and ortolan bunting ("Kaya") . . . . 2·10 40

248 Bank Building

1981. Central African States' Bank.
806 **248** 90f. multicoloured 95 30
807 110f. multicoloured . . . 1·10 45

249 "Madonna and Child" (Fra Angelico)

1981. Christmas. Various paintings showing Virgin and Child by named artists. Multicoloured.
808 50f. Type **249** (postage) . . . 65 25
809 60f. Cosme-Tura 85 35
810 90f. Bramantino . . . . . . 1·30 50
811 110f. Memling . . . . 1·70 70
812 140f. Correge (air) . . . . . 1·80 45
813 200f. Gentileschi . . . . . . 3·00 70
MS814 81 × 98 mm. 500f. "The Holy Family" (Cranach) (41 × 50 mm) 6·25 1·90

250 Scouts with Packs

1982. 75th Anniv of Boy Scout Movement. Mult.
815 100f. Type **250** . . . . 1·10 45
816 150f. Three scouts (horiz) . . 1·60 60
817 200f. Scouts admiring mountain view (horiz) . . 2·30 85
818 300f. Scouts taking oath . . 3·25 1·40
MS819 84 × 113 mm. 500f. Lord Baden-Powell, scout and totem 5·75 1·70

251 African Elephant

1982. Animals. Multicoloured.
820 60f. Type **251** (postage) . . . 70 10
821 90f. Giraffe . . . . 1·00 30
822 100f. Addax . . . . 1·20 40
823 110f. Okapi . . . . 1·40 55
824 300f. Mandrill (air) . . . . . 3·00 70
825 500f. Lion . . . . 5·00 1·50
MS826 100 × 80 mm. 600f. Nile crocodile (47 × 38 mm) . . . . 6·50 1·80

252 "Grandfather Snowman"

1982. Norman Rockwell Illustrations. Mult.
827 30f. Type **252** 30 10
828 60f. "Croquet Players" . . . 80 25
829 110f. "Women talking" . . . 1·20 45
830 150f. "Searching" . . . . . 1·70 60

253 Vickers Valentia biplane, 1928

1982. Transport. Multicoloured.
831 5f. Astra Torres AT-16 airship, 1919 (postage) . . 10 10
832 10f. Beyer-Garrat 1 locomotive 10 10
833 20f. Bugatti "Royale" car, 1926 . . . . 30 25
834 110f. Type **253** . . . . 1·30 45
835 300f. Nuclear-powered freighter "Savannah" (air) 3·75 70
836 500f. Space shuttle . . . . 5·25 1·50
MS837 100 × 81 mm. 600f. Man with winged horse (38 × 48 mm) . . 5·25 1·60

254 George Washington

1982. Anniversaries. Multicoloured.
838 200f. "Le Jardin de Bellevue" (E. Manet) (150th birth anniv) (horiz) . . . . . . 3·00 90
839 300f. Type **254** (250th birth anniv) . . . . 2·75 1·00
840 400f. Goethe (150th death anniv) . . . . 3·75 1·50
841 500f. Princess of Wales (21st Birthday) . . . . 4·50 2·30
MS842 80 × 104 mm. 500f. Princess of Wales (different) . . . . . 5·25 1·60

255 Edward VII and Lady Diana Spencer with her Brother

1982. 21st Birthday of Princess of Wales. Mult.
843 5f. George II and portrait of Lady Diana as child (postage) 10 10
844 10f. Type **255** 10 10
845 20f. Charles I and Lady Diana with guinea pig . . 30 10
846 110f. George V and Lady Diana as student in Switzerland . . . . 1·20 25
847 300f. Charles II and Lady Diana in skiing clothes (air) . . . . 3·00 70
848 500f. George IV and Lady Diana as nursery teacher 4·75 1·50
MS849 120 × 74 mm. 600f. Prince and Princess of Wales on wedding day (56 × 33 mm) . . . . 5·75 1·60

256 Football

1982. Olympic Games, Los Angeles. (1984). Multicoloured.
850 5f. Type **256** (postage) . . . 10 10
851 10f. Boxing 10 10
852 20f. Running 30 10
853 110f. Hurdling . . . . 1·00 25
854 300f. Diving (air) . . . . . 2·75 70
855 500f. Show jumping . . . 4·50 1·50
MS856 80 × 108 mm. 600f. Basketball (38 × 56 mm) . . . 5·50 1·70

257 Weather Satellite

259 Pestle and Mortar, Chopping Board and Dish

1982. Space Resources. Multicoloured.
857 5f. Space shuttle and scientist (Food resources) (postage) 10 10
858 10f. Type **257** 10 10
859 20f. Space laboratory (Industrial use) 30 10
860 110f. Astronaut on Moon (Lunar resources) . . . . 1·00 25
861 300f. Satellite and energy map (Planetary energy) (air) . . . . 2·75 75
862 500f. Satellite and solar panels (Solar energy) . . . 4·50 1·50
MS863 104 × 67 mm. 600f. Kohoutek, Halley's comet and satellites (Energy from comets) 5·50 1·60

1982. Birth of Prince William of Wales. Nos. 767/70 optd **NAISSANCE ROYALE 1982**.
864 **240** 75f. multicoloured 55 25
865 – 100f. multicoloured . . . 75 45
866 – 150f. multicoloured . . . 1·30 60
867 – 175f. multicoloured . . . 1·90 85
MS868 69 × 91 mm. 500f. multicoloured . . . . 4·75 3·75

1982. Utensils. Multicoloured.
869 5f. Basket of vegetables (horiz) 10 10
870 10f. As. No. 869 . . . . . . 10 10
871 25f. Flagon made from decorated gourd 30 10
872 60f. As No. 871 . . . . . . 75 25
873 120f. Clay jars (horiz) . . . . 1·40 45
874 175f. Decorated bowls (horiz) 1·80 65
875 300f. Type **259** . . . . 3·75 1·30

260 Footballers

1982. World Cup Football Championship Results. Unissued stamps optd as T **260**. Multicoloured.
876 60f. **ITALIE 1er ALLEMAGNE 2e (R.F.A.)** 80 25
877 150f. **POLOGNE 3e** . . . . 1·60 60
878 300f. **FRANCE 4e** . . . . . 3·25 1·30
MS879 104 × 81 mm. 500f. **ITALIE 1er** . . . . 5·25 1·60

261 Jean Tubind

262 Globe and UPU Emblem

1982. Painters. Multicoloured.
880 40f. Type **261** 55 25
881 70f. Pierre Ndarata and 10f. stamp 85 35
882 90f. As No. 881 . . . . . . 1·10 45
883 140f. Type **261** . . . . 1·70 75

1982. UPU Day.
884 **262** 60f. violet, blue and red 55 25
885 120f. violet, yellow & red 1·20 50

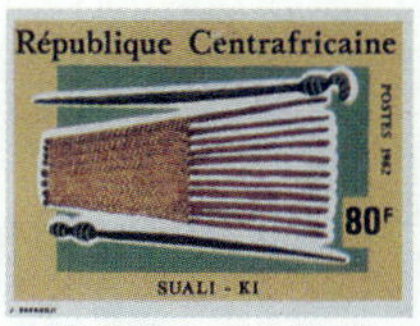

263 Hairpins and Comb

1983. Hair Accessories.
886 **263** 20f. multicoloured 10 10
887 30f. multicoloured 35 20
888 70f. multicoloured 65 30
889 80f. multicoloured 95 45
890 120f. multicoloured . . . 1·30 50

264 Koch and Microscope

1982. Centenary of Discovery of Tubercle Bacillus by Dr. Robert Koch.
891 **264** 100f. mauve and black . . 1·20 30
892 120f. red and black . . . 1·50 50
893 175f. blue and black . . . 2·00 80

265 Emblem

1982. 10th Anniv of United Nations Environment Programme.
894 **265** 120f. blue, orange & blk 1·20 35
895 150f. blue, yellow & blk 1·30 55
896 300f. blue, green & black 2·75 1·10

266 Granary

1982.
897 **266** 60f. multicoloured 55 25
898 80f. multicoloured 95 40
899 120f. multicoloured . . . 1·30 60
900 200f. multicoloured . . . 2·20 1·10

267 "The Beautiful Gardener"

268 Stylized Transmitter

1982. Air. Christmas. Paintings by Raphael. Multicoloured.
901 150f. Type **267** . . . . 2·00 45
902 500f. "The Holy Family" . . 5·00 1·50

1983. I.T.U. Delegates' Conference, Nairobi (1982).
903 **268** 100f. multicoloured . . . 95 40
904 120f. multicoloured . . . 1·30 55

269 Steinitz

1983. Chess Masters. Multicoloured.

905	5f. Type **269** (postage)	10	10
906	10f. Aaron Niemsovich	10	10
907	20f. Aleksandr Alekhine	30	10
908	110f. Botvinnik	1·40	25
909	300f. Boris Spassky (air)	3·50	80
910	500f. Bobby Fischer	5·00	1·40
MS911	116 × 72 mm. 600f. Korchnoi and Karpov (55 × 52 mm)	6·75	2·10

270 George Washington

271 Telephone, Satellite and Globe

1983. Celebrities. Multicoloured.

912	20f. Type **270** (postage)	10	10
913	110f. Pres. Tito of Yugoslavia	1·10	30
914	500f. Princess of Wales with Prince William (air)	5·00	1·60
MS915	120 × 70 mm. 600f. Prince and Princess of Wales with Prince William	5·00	3·00

1983. U.N. Decade for African Transport and Communications. Multicoloured.

916	5f. Type **271**	10	10
917	60f. Type **271**	75	25
918	120f. Radar screen and map of Africa	1·20	45
919	175f. As No. 918	1·70	60

272 Billy Hamilton and Bruno Pezzey

1983. World Cup Football Championship, Spain. Multicoloured.

920	5f. Type **272** (postage)	10	10
921	10f. Sergeij Borovski and Zbigniew Boniek	10	10
922	20f. Pierre Littbarski and Jesus Maria Zamora	35	25
923	110f. Zico and Alberto Pajsarella	1·30	30
924	300f. Paolo Rossi and Smolarek (air)	2·75	75
925	500f. Rummenigge and Alain Giresse	5·00	1·30
MS926	101 × 81 mm. 600f. Paolo Rossi and Karl Heinz Rummenigge	5·50	3·00

273 "Entombment"

1983. Easter. Paintings by Rembrandt. Mult.

927	100f. Type **273**	95	45
928	300f. "Christ on the Cross"	2·75	1·30
929	400f. "Descent from the Cross"	3·75	1·80

274 J. and L. Robert and Colin Hullin's Balloon, 1784

1983. Air. Bicentenary of Manned Flight. Mult.

930	65f. Type **274**	85	25
931	130f. John Wise and "Atlantic", 1859	1·40	35
932	350f. "Ville d'Orleans", Paris, 1870	3·75	1·10
933	400f. Modern advertising balloon	4·25	1·40
MS934	116 × 91 mm. 500f. Montgolfier balloon, 1783	6·00	1·60

275 Emile Levassor, Rene Panhard and Panhard-Levassor Car, 1895

276 IMO Emblem

1983. Car Manufacturers. Multicoloured.

935	10f. Type **275** (postage)	10	10
936	20f. Henry Ford and first Ford car, 1896	10	10
937	30f. Louis Renault and first Renault car, 1899	30	25
938	80f. Ettore Bugatti and Bugatti "Type 37", 1925	95	30
939	400f. Enzo Ferrari and Ferrari "815 Sport", 1940 (air)	4·25	1·00
940	500f. Ferdinand Porsche and Porsche "356 Coupe", 1951	4·75	1·20
MS941	77 × 88 mm. 600f. Karl Benz and first petrol-driven car, 1886	5·75	1·60

1983. 25th Anniv of Int Maritime Organization.

942	**276**	40f. blue, lt blue & turq	45	10
943		100f. multicoloured	95	45

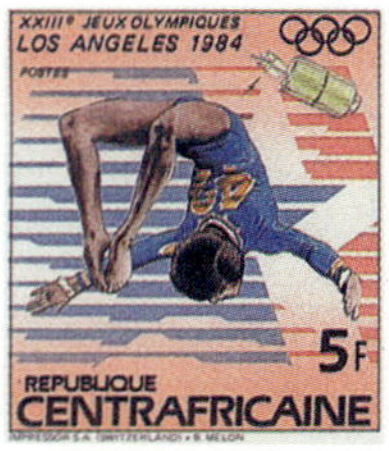

277 Gymnastics

1983. Olympic Games, Los Angeles. Mult.

944	5f. Type **277** (postage)	10	10
945	40f. Javelin	45	10
946	60f. High jump	60	25
947	120f. Fencing	1·50	30
948	200f. Cycling (air)	2·00	45
949	300f. Sailing	3·00	75
MS950	108 × 80 mm. 600f. Ball games (horiz 50 × 41 mm)	5·50	1·60

278 WCY Emblem and Satellite

1983. World Communications Year. Mult.

951	50f. Type **278**	40	25
952	130f. WCY emblem and satellite (different)	1·30	50

279 Horse Jumping

1983. Air. Pre-Olympic Year. Multicoloured.

953	100f. Type **279**	95	40
954	200f. Dressage	2·00	80
955	300f. Jumping double jump	3·00	90
956	400f. Trotting	4·00	1·30
MS957	104 × 79 mm. 500f. Horse jumping (different)	5·75	1·60

280 Andre Kolingba

281 Antenna, Bangui M'Poko Earth Station

1983. 2nd Anniv of Military Committee for National Recovery.

958	**280**	65f. multicoloured	55	25
959		130f. multicoloured	1·40	40

1983. Bangui M'Poko Earth Station.

960	**281**	130f. multicoloured	1·40	60

282 Flower and Broken Chain on Map of Africa

1983. Namibia Day.

961	**282**	100f. green, lt grn & red	1·30	45
962		200f. multicoloured	1·80	85

283 J. Montgolfier and Balloon

1983. Bicentenary of Manned Flight. Mult.

963	50f. Type **283** (postage)	45	10
964	100f. J. Blanchard and Channel crossing, 1785	1·00	25
965	200f. Joseph Gay-Lussac and ascent to 4000 m, 1804	2·20	65
966	300f. Henri Giffard and steam-powered dirigible airship, 1852	3·00	1·00
967	400f. Santos-Dumont and airship "Ballon No. 6", Paris, 1901 (air)	4·00	1·30
968	500f. A. Laquot and captive observation balloon, 1914	5·00	1·70
MS969	79 × 85 mm. 600f. J. Charles and hydrogen balloon and G. Tissandier and dirigible	6·00	1·60

284 "Global Communications"

1983. World Communications Year. UPU Day.

970	**284**	205f. multicoloured	2·00	1·00

285 Black Rhinoceros

1983. Endangered Animals. Multicoloured.

971	10f. Type **285** (postage)	40	10
972	40f. Two rhinoceros	1·10	20
973	70f. Black rhinoceros (different)	1·80	35
974	180f. Black rhinoceros and young	5·00	65
975	400f. Rangers attending sick rhinoceros (air)	5·25	1·20
976	500f. Wild animals and flag	6·50	1·40
MS977	111 × 75 mm. 600f. Cheetah (47 × 32 mm)	5·75	1·70

286 Handicapped Person and Old Man

1983. National Day of the Handicapped and Old.

978	**286**	65f. orange and mauve	55	30
979		130f. orange and blue	1·20	55
980		250f. orange and green	1·80	85

287 Fish Pond

1983. Fishery Resources. Multicoloured.

981	25f. Type **287**	20	10
982	65f. Net fishing	80	25
983	100f. Traditional fishing	1·00	45
984	130f. Butter catfish, eel and cichlids on plate	2·00	70
985	205f. Weir basket	2·40	75

288 "The Annunciation" (Leonardo da Vinci)

1984. Air. Christmas. Multicoloured.

986	130f. Type **288**	1·20	40
987	205f. "The Virgin of the Rocks" (Leonardo da Vinci)	2·00	55
988	350f. "Adoration of the Shepherds" (Rubens)	3·50	1·10
989	500f. "A. Goubeau before the Virgin" (Rubens)	4·75	1·40

289 Bush Fire

1984. Nature Protection. Multicoloured.

990	30f. Type **289**	2·10	40
991	130f. Soldiers protecting wildlife from hunters	3·00	1·00

290 Goethe and Scene from "Faust"

1984. Celebrities. Multicoloured.

992	50f. Type **290** (postage)	45	10
993	100f. Henri Dunant and battle scene	95	10
994	200f. Alfred Nobel	1·60	40
995	300f. Lord Baden-Powell and scout camp	2·50	70
996	400f. President Kennedy and first foot-print on Moon (air)	4·25	1·10
997	500f. Prince and Princess of Wales	4·75	1·30
MS998	101 × 72 mm. 600f. Prince and Princess of Wales	5·25	1·60

291 Fixed Bar

1984. Air. Olympic Games, Los Angeles. Gymnastics. Multicoloured.

999 65f. Type **291** 55 25
1000 100f. Parallel bars . . . . . 1·00 25
1001 130f. Ribbon (horiz) . . . . 1·40 40
1002 205f. Cord . . . . 2·20 70
1003 350f. Hoop . . . . 3·75 1·10
MS1004 102 × 78 mm. 500f. Rhythmic team gymnastics (horiz) . . . . 5·25 1·60

292 "Madonna and Child" (Raphael)

1984. Paintings. Multicoloured.

1005 50f. Type **292** (postage) . . 50 10
1006 100f. "The Madonna of the Pear" (Durer) . . . . . 1·00 20
1007 200f. "Aldobrandini Madonna" (Raphael) . . 2·20 50
1008 300f. "Madonna of the Pink" (Durer) . . . . . 3·00 85
1009 400f. "Virgin and Child" (Correggio) (air) . . . . 4·00 1·60
1010 500f. "The Bohemian" (Modigliani) . . . . . . 5·50 2·10
MS1011 80 × 111 mm. 600f. "Madonna and Child on the Throne" (Raphael) (vert 29 × 58 mm) . . . . 6·00 1·60

293 "Le Pericles" (mail ship)

1984. Transport. Multicoloured. (a) Ships.

1012 65f. Type **293** 80 30
1013 120f. "Pereire" (steamer) . . 1·30 55
1014 250f. "Admella" (passenger steamer) . . . . 2·50 1·10
1015 400f. "Royal William" (paddle-steamer) . . . . 4·50 1·90
1016 500f. "Great Britain" (steam/sail) . . . . . . 5·50 2·50

(b) Locomotives.

1017 110f. CC-1500 ch . . . . . 1·20 45
1018 240f. Series 210, 1968 . . . 2·50 95
1019 350f. 231-726, 1937 . . . 3·75 1·30
1020 440f. Pacific Series S3/6, 1908 . . . . 5·00 1·50
1021 500f. Henschel 151 Series 45, 1937 . . . . 5·75 3·25

Nos. 1017/21 each include an inset portrait of George Stephenson in the design.

294 Forest

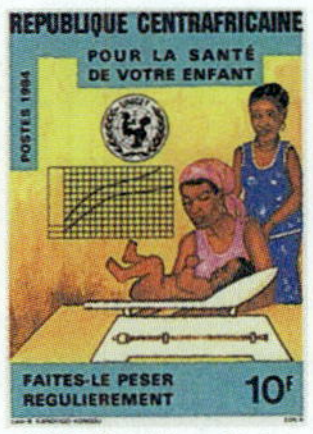

295 Weighing Baby and Emblem

1984. Forest Resources. Multicoloured.

1022 70f. Type **294** 85 30
1023 130f. Log cabin and timber 1·70 65

1984. Infant Survival Campaign. Multicoloured.

1024 10f. Type **295** 10 10
1025 30f. Vaccinating baby . . . 45 25
1026 65f. Feeding dehydrated baby 55 40
1027 100f. Mother, healthy baby and foodstuffs . . . . . 1·10 60

296 Bangui-Kette Conical Trap

1984. Fish Traps. Multicoloured.

1028 50f. Type **296** 75 30
1029 80f. Mbres fish trap . . . . 1·00 60
1030 150f. Bangui-Kette round fish trap . . . . 2·20 80

297 Galileo and "Ariane" Rocket **298** "Leptoporus lignosus"

1984. Space Technology. Multicoloured.

1031 20f. Type **297** (postage) . . 30 10
1032 70f. Auguste Piccard and stratosphere balloon "F.N.R.S." 70 25
1033 150f. Hermann Oberth and satellite . . . . 1·50 50
1034 205f. Albert Einstein and "Giotto" satellite . . . . 2·00 65
1035 300f. Marie Curie and "Viking I" and "II" (air) 3·50 90
1036 500f. Dr. U. Merbold and "Navette" space laboratory . . . . 4·50 1·10
MS1037 75 × 59 mm. 600f. Neil Armstrong and "Apollo II" (41 × 34 mm) . . . . 5·25 1·60

1984. Fungi. Multicoloured.

1038 5f. Type **298** (postage) . . . 10 10
1039 10f. "Phlebopus sudanicus" 10 10
1040 40f. "Termitomyces letestui" 60 25
1041 130f. "Lepiota esculenta" 1·50 30
1042 300f. "Termitomyces aurantiacus" (air) . . . 3·25 85
1043 500f. "Termitomyces robustus" . . . . 6·00 1·30
MS1044 68 × 90 mm. 600f. "Tricholoma lobayensis" (34 × 40 mm) . . . . 6·00 1·80

299 Hibiscus **300** G. Boucher (speed skating)

1984. Flowers. Multicoloured.

1045 65f. Type **299** 90 45
1046 130f. Canna . . . . 1·60 75
1047 205f. Water Hyacinth . . . 2·50 1·00

1984. Winter Olympic Gold Medallists. Mult.

1048 30f. Type **300** (postage) . . 30 10
1049 90f. W. Hoppe, R. Wetzig, D. Schauerhammer and A. Kirchner (bobsleigh) 95 30
1050 140f. P. Magoni (ladies' slalom) . . . . 1·40 45
1051 200f. J. Torvill and C. Dean (ice skating) . . . . . 2·00 60
1052 400f. M. Nykanen (90 m ski jump) (air) . . . . 4·00 1·00
1053 400f. Russia (ice hockey) . . 4·75 1·30
MS1054 79 × 58 mm. 600f. W.D. Johnson (men's downhill skiing) 5·50 1·60

301 Workers sowing Cotton Seeds

1984. Economic Campaign. Multicoloured.

1055 25f. Type **301** 35 20
1056 40f. Selling cotton 55 45
1057 130f. Cotton market . . . . 1·60 65

302 Woman picking corn

1984. World Food Day.

1058 **302** 205f. multicoloured . . . 2·50 1·00

303 Abraham Lincoln

1984. Celebrities. Multicoloured.

1059 50f. Type **303** (postage) . . 50 90
1060 90f. Auguste Piccard (undersea explorer) . . . 95 30
1061 120f. Gottlieb Daimler (automobile designer) . . 1·50 45
1062 200f. Louis Bleriot (pilot) 2·30 60
1063 350f. A. Karpov (chess champion) (air) . . . . 3·75 90
1064 400f. Henri Dunant (founder of Red Cross) . . . . . 4·25 1·10
MS1065 79 × 114 mm. 600f. Queen Elizabeth, the Queen Mother (85th birthday, 1985) (35 × 50 mm) 5·25 1·60

304 Profile, Water and Emblem

1984. Bangui Rotary Club and Water.

1066 **304** 130f. multicoloured . . . 1·70 50
1067 205f. multicoloured . . . 2·50 80

305 United States (4 × 400 m relay)

1985. Air Olympic Games Gold Medallists. Multicoloured.

1068 60f. Type **305** 55 20
1069 140f. E. Moses (400 m hurdles) . . . . . 1·60 45
1070 300f. S. Aouita (5000 m) . . 3·50 90
1071 440f. D. Thompson (decathlon) . . . . 4·25 1·20
MS1072 102 × 76 mm. 500f. J. Cruz (800 metres) (horiz) . . . . . 5·50 3·00

306 "Virgin and Infant Jesus" (Titian)

1985. Air. Christmas (1984). Multicoloured.

1073 130f. Type **306** . . . . . 1·20 60
1074 350f. "Virgin with Rabbit" (Titian) . . . . 3·25 1·30
1075 400f. "Virgin and Child" (Titian) . . . . 3·75 1·50

307 Eastern Screech Owls

1985. Air. Birth Bicentenary of John J. Audubon (ornithologist) (1st issue). Multicoloured.

1076 60f. Type **307** 60 20
1077 110f. Mangrove cuckoo (vert) . . . . 1·20 50
1078 200f. Mourning doves (vert) 2·00 1·00
1079 500f. Wood ducks . . . . . 5·25 2·20

See also Nos. 1099/1104.

1985. International Exhibitions. Nos. 1014/15, 1019/20 and **MS**1004 optd.

1083 250f. multicoloured (postage) . . . . 2·40 1·50
1084 350f. multicoloured . . . . 3·50 1·80
1085 400f. multicoloured . . . . 4·25 2·30
1086 440f. multicoloured . . . . 5·25 2·75
MS1087 102 × 78 mm. 500f. multicoloured (air) . . . . . . 4·75 4·50

DESIGNS: 250f. **ARGENTINA '85 BUENOS AIRES**; 350f. **TSUKUBA EXPO '85**; 400f **Italia '85 ROME** and emblem; 440f. **MOPHILA HAMBOURG**; 500f. **OLYMPICPHILEX '85 LUSANNE** and emblem.

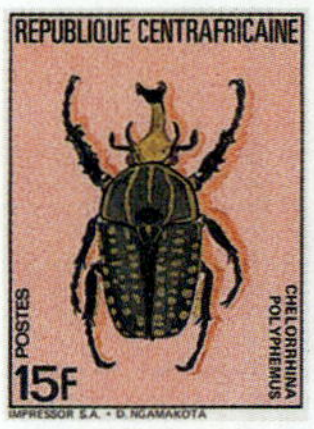

310 "Chelorrhina polyphemus" **312** Blue Jay

311 Olympic Games Poster and Stockholm

1985. Beetles. Multicoloured.

1088 15f. Type **310** . . . . 1·70 25
1089 20f. "Fornasinius russus" 2·10 35
1090 25f. "Goliathus giganteus" 2·50 45
1091 65f. "Goliathus meleagris" 6·25 75

1985. "Olymphilex '85" Olympic Stamps Exhibition, Lausanne. Multicoloured.

1092 5f. Type **311** (postage) . . . 15 10
1093 10f. Olympic Games poster and Paris 15 10
1094 20f. Olympic Games poster and London 30 15
1095 100f. Olympic Games poster and Tokyo . . . . . . 3·00 75
1096 400f. Olympic Games poster and Mexico (air) . . . . 4·00 90
1097 500f. Olympic Games poster and Munich . . . . . . 4·50 1·10
MS1098 107 × 68 mm. 600f. Baron Pierre de Coubertin (55 × 25 mm) 5·50 1·60

1985. Birth Bicentenary of John J. Audubon (ornithologist) (2nd issue). Multicoloured.

1099 40f. Type **312** (postage) . . 65 15
1100 80f. Chuck Will's widow . . 1·00 20
1101 130f. Ivory-billed woodpecker . . . . . . 1·70 40
1102 250f. Collie's magpie-jay . . 2·75 60
1103 300f. Mangrove cuckoo (horiz) (air) . . . . 3·00 70
1104 500f. Barn swallow (horiz) 5·25 1·30
MS1105 69 × 103 mm. 600f. Pileated woodpeckers . . . . 6·25 1·70

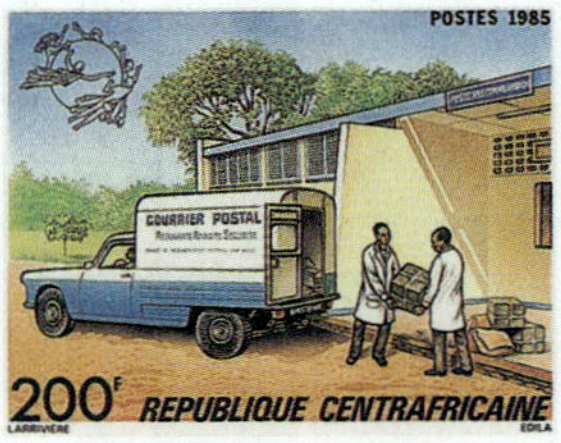

313 Delivering Post by Van

1985. "Philexafrique" Stamp Exhibition, Lome, Togo (1st issue). Multicoloured.

1106 200f. Type **313** . . . . . 2·30 1·10
1107 200f. Scouts and flag . . . 2·30 1·10

See also Nos. 1154/5.

314 Tiger and Rudyard Kipling

1985. Int Youth Year (1st issue). Multicoloured.

1108	100f. Type **314**	1·20	40
1109	200f. Men on horseback and Joseph Kessel	2·20	80
1110	300f. Submarine gripped by octopus and Jules Verne	2·75	1·20
1111	400f. Mississippi stern-wheeler, Huckleberry Finn and Mark Twain	3·75	1·70

See also Nos. 1163/**MS**1169.

315 Louis Pasteur

1985. Anniversaries. Multicoloured.

1112	150f. Type **315** (centenary of discovery of anti-rabies vaccine) (postage)	2·20	60
1113	200f. Henri Dunant (founder of Red Cross) and 125th anniv of Battle of Solferino (horiz)	2·50	80
1114	300f. Girl guides (75th anniv of Girl Guide Movement) (air)	2·20	1·20
1115	450f. Queen Elizabeth the Queen Mother (85th birthday)	4·00	2·00
1116	500f. Statue of Liberty (cent)	5·00	2·40

316 Pele and Footballers

1985. World Cup Football Championship, Mexico. Multicoloured.

1117	5f. Type **316** (postage)	10	10
1118	10f. Harald "Tony" Schumacher	10	10
1119	20f. Paolo Rossi	10	15
1120	350f. Kevin Keegan (wrongly inscr "Kervin")	3·25	1·00
1121	400f. Michel Platini (air)	4·00	1·00
1122	500f. Karl Heinz Rummenigge	4·50	1·20
MS1123	94 × 64 mm. 600f. Diego Armando Maradona	5·25	1·50

317 La Kotto Waterfalls **318** Pope with Hand raised in Blessing

1985.

1124	**317**	65f. multicoloured	95	35
1125		90f. multicoloured	1·10	45
1126		130f. multicoloured	1·70	75

1985. Papal Visit. Multicoloured.

1127	65f. Type **318**	1·00	35
1128	130f. Pope John Paul II in Communion robes	1·90	75

319 Soldier using Ox-drawn Plough

1985. Economic Campaign. Multicoloured.

1129	5f. Type **319**	15	10
1130	60f. Soldier sowing cotton	60	30
1131	130f. Soldier sowing cotton (different)	1·30	50

320 As Young Girl with her Brother

1985. 85th Birthday of Queen Elizabeth the Queen Mother. Multicoloured.

1132	100f. Type **320** (postage)	80	25
1133	200f. Queen Mary with Duke and Duchess of York	1·90	45
1134	300f. Duchess of York inspecting Irish Guards	3·00	85
1135	350f. Duke and Duchess of York with the young Princesses	3·25	95
1136	400f. In the Golden State Coach at Coronation of King George VI (air)	4·00	1·00
1137	500f. At the service for her Silver Wedding	5·00	1·30
MS1138	75 × 87 mm. 600f. Holding Prince Charles at his christening	5·25	1·50

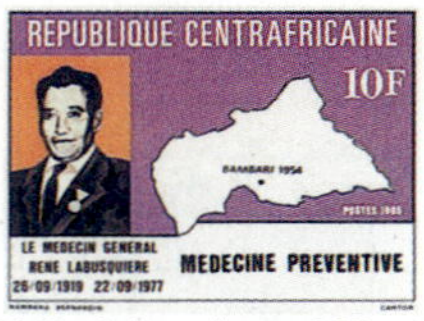

321 Dr. Labusquiere and Map of Republic

1985. 8th Death Anniv of General Doctor Labusquiere. Multicoloured.

1139	**321**	10f. multicoloured	15	10
1140		45f. multicoloured	45	25
1141		110f. multicoloured	95	50

322 Mail Van delivering Parcels to Local Post Office

1985. Postal Service. Multicoloured.

1142	15f. Type **322**	15	10
1143	60f. Van collecting mail from local post office	60	25
1144	150f. Vans at main post office	1·50	75

323 Gagarin, Korolev and Space Station Complex

1985. Space Research. Multicoloured.

1145	40f. Type **323** (postage)	30	10
1146	110f. Copernicus and "Cassini" space probe	1·00	40
1147	240f. Galileo and "Viking" orbiter	2·20	70
1148	300f. T. von Karman and astronaut recovering satellite	2·75	80
1149	450f. Percival Lowell and "Viking" space probe (air)	4·75	1·00
1150	500f. Dr. U. Merbold and "Columbus" space station	5·00	1·20
MS1151	96 × 68 mm. 600f. "Apollo II" capsule and astronaut	5·50	1·50

324 Damara Solar Energy Plant

1985.

1152	**324**	65f. multicoloured	80	30
1153		130f. multicoloured	1·40	65

325 Ouaka Sugar Refinery

1985. "Philexafrique" Stamp Exhibition, Lome, Togo (2nd issue). Multicoloured.

1154	250f. Nature studies	3·50	1·60
1155	250f. Type **325**	3·50	1·60

326 Pres. Mitterrand, Gen. Kolingba and Flags

1985. Visit of President Mitterrand of France.

1156	**326**	65f. multicoloured	65	25
1157		130f. multicoloured	1·30	50
1158		160f. multicoloured	1·90	80

327 Map and U.N. Emblem **328** "Virgin and Angels" (Master of Burgo de Osma)

1985. 40th Anniv of UNO and 25th Anniv of Central African Republic Membership.

1159	**327**	140f. multicoloured	1·30	60

1985. Air. Christmas. Multicoloured.

1160	100f. Type **328**	1·00	35
1161	200f. "Nativity" (Louis Le Nain)	2·20	85
1162	400f. "Virgin and Child with Dove" (Piero di Cosimo)	4·00	1·60

329 Leonardo da Vinci and "Madonna of the Eyelet"

1985. Int Youth Year (2nd issue). Multicoloured.

1163	40f. Type **329** (postage)	55	10
1164	80f. Johann Sebastian Bach	95	25
1165	100f. Diego Velasquez and "St. John of Patmos"	1·20	40
1166	250f. Franz Schubert and illustration of "King of Aulnes"	2·50	60
1167	400f. Francisco Goya and "Vicente Osario de Moscoso" (air)	4·25	1·00
1168	500f. Wolfang Amadeus Mozart	4·75	1·20
MS1169	79 × 79 mm. 600f. Pablo Picasso and "Woman in Plumed Hat"	6·50	1·80

330 Halley and "Comet"

1985. Appearance of Halley's Comet (1st issue). Multicoloured.

1170	100f. Type **330** (postage)	75	25
1171	200f. Newton's telescope	1·80	45
1172	300f. Halley and Newton observing comet	2·75	80
1173	350f. American space probe and comet	3·25	1·00
1174	400f. Sun, Russian space probe and diagram of comet trajectory (air)	3·75	95
1175	500f. Infra-red picture of comet	4·75	1·20
MS1176	70 × 100 mm. 600f. American space probe, Earth, sun and comet	5·50	1·60

See also No. 1184/8.

331 Columbus with Globe

1986. 480th Death Anniv of Christopher Columbus (explorer). Multicoloured.

1177	90f. Type **331** (postage)	95	25
1178	110f. Receiving blessing	1·20	40
1179	240f. Crew going ashore in rowing boat	2·40	1·00
1180	300f. Columbus with American Indians	3·00	80
1181	400f. Ships at sea in storm (air)	4·25	1·60
1182	500f. Sun breaking through clouds over fleet	5·00	1·90
MS1183	71 × 100 mm. 600f. Columbus	5·25	1·50

332 Halley and Comet

1986. Air. Appearance of Halley's Comet (2nd issue). Multicoloured.

1184	110f. Type **332**	95	25
1185	130f. "Giotto" space probe	1·30	25
1186	200f. Comet and globe	2·00	55
1187	300f. "Vega" space probe	2·75	75
1188	400f. Space shuttle	4·00	1·00

1986. Nos. 874/5 surch.

1188a	–	30f. on 175f. mult		
1188b	**259**	65f. on 300f. mult		

333 Spiky Hair Style **334** Communications

1986. Traditional Hair Styles. Multicoloured.

1189	20f. Type **333**	35	10
1190	30f. Braids around head	40	20
1191	65f. Plaits	55	35
1192	160f. Braids from front to back of head	2·20	70

1986. Franco-Central African Week. Mult.

1193	40f. Type **334**	45	15
1194	60f. Youth	55	25
1195	100f. Basket weaver (craft)	1·20	45
1196	130f. Cyclists (sport)	1·70	60

335 "Allamanda neriifolia"

1986. Flora and Fauna. Multicoloured.
1197 25f. Type **335** (postage) . . 30 15
1198 65f. Bongo (horiz) 85 25
1199 160f. "Plumieria acuminata" 1·80 40
1200 300f. Cheetah (horiz) . . . 3·50 85
1201 400f. "Eulophia erthoplata" (air) . . . . 4·00 1·00
1202 500f. Leopard (horiz) . . . 5·25 1·20
MS1203 100 × 69 mm. 600f. Giant eland and "Eulophia cucllata" (50 × 29) . . . . 5·50 1·70

336 Palm Tree and Bossongo Oil Refinery

1986. Centrapalm. Multicoloured.
1204 25f. Type **336** 30 20
1205 65f. Type **336** 75 45
1206 120f. Palm tree and Bossongo agro-industrial complex . . . . 1·30 75
1207 160f. As No. 1206 . . . . . 1·70 90

337 Pointer

1986. Dogs and Cats. Multicoloured.
1208 10f. Type **337** (postage) . . 20 15
1209 20f. Egyptian mau 45 25
1210 200f. Newfoundland . . . . 2·50 70
1211 300f. Borzoi (air) . . . . . 3·25 70
1212 400f. Persian red . . . . . 4·75 1·10
MS1213 95 × 60 mm. 500f. Spaniel and Burmese . . . . 5·50 1·60

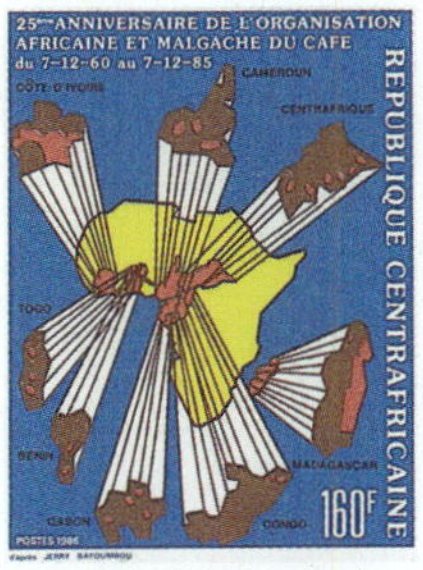

338 Map of Africa showing Member Countries

1986. 25th Anniv of African and Malagasy Coffee Producers Organization.
1214 **338** 160f. multicoloured . . . 1·70 70

339 Trophy, Brazilian flag, L.-A. Muller and Socrates

1986. World Cup Football Championship, Mexico. Multicoloured.
1215 30f. Type **339** (postage) . . 30 15
1216 110f. Trophy, Belgian flag, V. Scifo and F. Ceulemans . . . . . . 1·00 45
1217 160f. Trophy, French flag, Y. Stopyra and M. Platini 1·50 55
1218 350f. Trophy, West German flag, A. Brehme and H. Schumacher . . . . . 3·25 90
1219 450f. Trophy, Argentinian flag and Diego Maradona (air) . . . . 4·25 1·20
MS1220 110 × 68 mm. 500f. Hands holding trophy, H. Schumacher and J. L. Burruehaga (50 × 35 mm) 5·25 1·70

340 Judith Resnik and Astronaut
341 People around Globe within Emblem

1986. Anniversaries and "Challenger" Astronauts Commemoration. Multicoloured.
1221 15f. Type **340** (postage) . . 20 10
1222 25f. Frederic Bartholdi and torch (centenary of Statue of Liberty) 35 10
1223 70f. Elvis Presley (9th death anniv) . . . . 1·30 25
1224 300f. Ronald MacNair and man watching astronaut on screen . . . . . . 3·00 80
1225 485f. on 70f. No. 1223 . . . 6·75 1·40
1226 450f. Christa McAuliffe and Shuttle lifting off (air) . . 4·25 1·50
MS1227 86 × 86 mm. 500f. "Challenger" crew (50 × 41 mm) 4·50 1·50

1986. International Peace Year.
1228 **341** 160f. multicoloured . . . 1·60 65

342 Globe, Douglas DC-10 and "25"
343 Emblem and Flag as Map

1986. 25th Anniv of Air Afrique.
1229 **342** 200f. multicoloured . . . 1·80 85

1986. UNICEF Child Survival Campaign. Multicoloured.
1230 15f. Type **343** 10 10
1231 130f. Doctor vaccinating child . . . . 1·30 60
1232 160f. Basket of fruit and boy holding fish on map 1·50 75

344 "Nativity" (detail, Giotto)

1986. Air. Christmas. Multicoloured.
1233 250f. Type **344** . . . . . . 2·30 1·10
1234 440f. "Adoration of the Magi" (detail, Sandro Botticelli) (vert) . . . . . 4·25 1·60
1235 500f. "Nativity" (detail, Giotto) (different) . . . . 5·00 2·00

345 Transmission Mast, People with Radios and Baskets of Produce

1986. African Telecommunications Day. Telecommunications and Agriculture. Mult.
1236 170f. Type **345** (Rural Radio Agriculture Project) . . . 1·90 95
1237 265f. Lorry, satellite, men using telephones and sacks of produce . . . . 2·75 1·40

346 Steam Locomotive Class "DH 2 Green Elephant" and Alfred de Glehn

1986. 150th Anniv of German Railways. Mult.
1238 40f. Type **346** (postage) . . 50 10
1239 70f. Rudolf Diesel (engineer) and steam locomotive No. 1829 Rheingold . . . 75 45
1240 160f. Electric locomotive Type 103 Rapide and Carl Golsdorf . . . . . 1·90 55
1241 300f. Wilhelm Schmidt and Beyer-Garratt type steam locomotive . . . . . . 3·25 90
1242 400f. De Bousquet and compound locomotive Class 3500 (air) . . . . . 4·00 1·20
MS1243 83 × 67 mm. 500f. Werner von Siemens (electrical engineer) and electric locomotive . . . . 5·00 1·50

347 Player returning Ball

1986. Air. Olympic Games, Seoul (1988) (1st issue). Tennis. Multicoloured.
1244 150f. Type **347** . . . . . . 1·70 55
1245 250f. Player serving (vert) 2·75 75
1246 440f. Right-handed player returning to left-handed player (vert) . . . . . . 4·25 1·40
1247 600f. Left-handed player returning to right-handed player . . . . 6·00 1·60
See also Nos. 1261/4, 1310/13 and 1315/18.

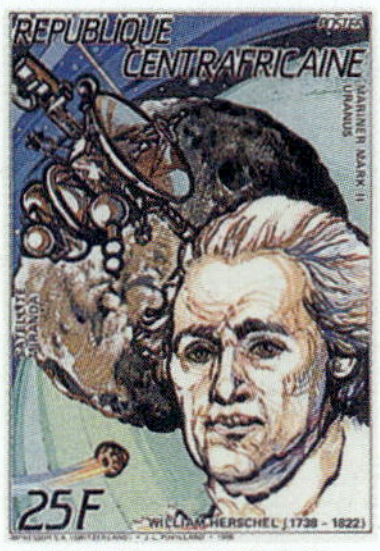

348 "Miranda" Satellite, Uranus, "Mariner II" and William Herschel (astronomer)

1987. Space Research. Multicoloured.
1248 25f. Type **348** (postage) . . 30 10
1249 65f. Mars Rover vehicle and Werner von Braun (rocket pioneer) 70 20
1250 160f. "Mariner II", Titan and Rudolf Hanel . . . . 1·50 40
1251 300f. Space ship "Hermes", space platform "Eureka" and Patrick Baudry . . . 2·75 80
1252 400f. Halley's Comet, "Giotto" space probe and Dr. U. Keller (air) . . . . 3·50 1·10
1253 500f. European space station "Columbus", Wubbo Ockels and Ulf Merbold 4·50 1·20

349 Footballer and "Woman with Umbrella" Fountain

1987. Olympic Games, Barcelona (1992). Mult.
1255 30f. Type **349** (postage) . . 35 15
1256 150f. Judo competitors and Barcelona Cathedral . . 1·30 50
1257 265f. Cyclist and Church of the Holy Family . . . . 2·50 80
1258 350f. Diver and Christopher Columbus's tomb (air) . . 3·25 1·00
1259 495f. Runner and human tower . . . . 4·75 1·50

350 Triple Jumping

1987. Air. Olympic Games, Seoul (1988) (2nd issue). Multicoloured.
1261 100f. Type **350** 95 35
1262 200f. High jumping (horiz) 1·80 75
1263 300f. Long jumping (horiz) 2·75 1·10
1264 400f. Pole vaulting . . . . 3·50 1·50
MS1265 104 × 86 mm. 500f. High jumping (different) (horiz) . . 4·50 2·50

351 Two-man Luge
352 Peace Medal

1987. Winter Olympic Games, Calgary (1988) (1st issue). Multicoloured.
1266 20f. Type **351** (postage) . . 30 10
1267 140f. Cross-country skiing 1·40 55
1268 250f. Figure skating . . . . 2·30 70
1269 300f. Ice hockey (air) . . . 2·75 90
1270 400f. Slalom . . . . 3·75 1·20
MS1271 130 × 77 mm. 500f. Downhill skiing . . . . . . 4·50 1·50
See also Nos. 1320/**MS**1324.

1987. International Peace Year (1986).
1272 **352** 50f. brown, blue & blk 45 25
1273 160f. brown, grn & blk 1·50 1·30

1987. 10th Death Anniv of Elvis Presley (singer). Nos. 1223 and 1225 optd **Elvis Presley 1977–1987**.
1274 70f. multicoloured 95 25
1275 485f. on 70f. multicoloured 5·75 1·70

354 Woman at Village Pump

1987. International Decade of Drinkable Water. Multicoloured.
1276 5f. Type **354** . . . . 33·00
1277 10f. Woman at village pump (different) . . . . 33·00
1278 200f. Three women at village pump . . . . . . 38·00

355 "Charaxes candiope"

1987. Butterflies. Multicoloured.
1279 100f. Type **355** . . . . . 1·50 65
1280 120f. "Graphium leonidas" 2·00 75
1281 130f. "Charaxes brutus" . . 2·20 80
1282 160f. "Salamis aetiops" . . 2·50 1·00

356 Nola Football Team

1987. Campaign for Integration of Pygmies.
1283 **356** 90f. multicoloured . . . 1·50 80
1284 160f. multicoloured . . . 2·00 1·20

357 James Madison (U.S. President, 1809–17)

1987. Anniversaries and Celebrities. Mult.

1285 40f. Type **357** (bicent of U.S. constitution) (postage) 45 15
1286 160f. Queen Elizabeth II and Prince Philip (40th wedding anniv) . . . . . 1·50 25
1287 200f. Steffi Graf (tennis player) . . . . 2·00 55
1288 300f. Gary Kasparov (chess champion) and "The Chess Players" (after Honore Daumier) (air) . . 3·00 85
1289 400f. Boris Becker (tennis player) . . . . 3·75 1·30
MS1290 86 × 86 mm. 500f. Scene from "Orpheus" (opera) and Christoph Wilibald Gluck (composer, death bicent) (50 × 35 mm) . . . . 5·50 1·50

358 Brontosaurus

1988. Prehistoric Animals. Multicoloured.

1291 50f. Type **358** 50 15
1292 65f. Triceratops 65 20
1293 100f. Ankylosaurus . . . . 1·00 35
1294 160f. Stegosaurus . . . . . 1·60 55
1295 200f. Tyrannosaurus rex (vert) . . . . 2·00 75
1296 240f. Corythosaurus (vert) 2·40 85
1297 300f. Allosaurus (vert) . . . 3·00 1·10
1298 350f. Brachiosaurus (vert) 3·75 1·40

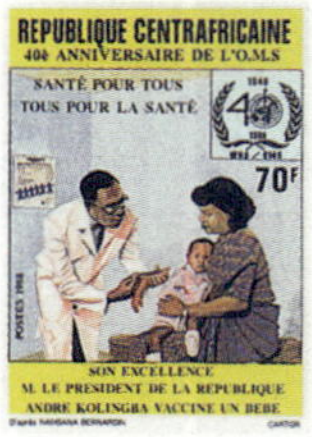

359 Pres. Kolingba vaccinating Baby

360 Carmine Bee Eater

1988. 40th Anniv of WHO.

1299 **359** 70f. multicoloured . . . 75 45
1300 120f. multicoloured . . . 1·20 65

1988. Scouts and Birds. Multicoloured.

1301 25f. Type **360** (postage) . . 30 15
1302 170f. Red-crowned bishop 1·50 60
1303 300f. Lesser pied kingfisher 3·00 1·40
1304 400f. Red-cheeked cordon-bleu (air) . . . . 2·75 1·60
1305 450f. Lizard buzzard . . . . 3·25 2·10
MS1306 90 × 70 mm. 500f. Splendid glossy starling . . . . 5·25 1·70

361 Schools replanting Campaign

1988. National Tree Day. Multicoloured.

1307 50f. Type **361** 45 25
1308 100f. Type **361** 95 60
1309 130f. Felling tree and planting saplings . . . . 1·50 75

362 1972 100f. Stamp and Beam Exercise

1988. Air. Olympic Games, Seoul (3rd issue). Gymnastics. Multicoloured.

1310 90f. Type **362** 95 35
1311 200f. 1964 50f. stamp and beam exercise (horiz) . . . 1·80 65
1312 300f. 1964 100f. stamp and vault exercise (horiz) . . . 2·75 1·10
1313 400f. 1964 250f. stamp and parallel bars exercise (horiz) . . . . 3·50 1·50
MS1314 105 × 85 mm. 500f. 1972 100f. stamp and ring exercise (horiz) . . . . 4·50 2·30

363 Running

364 Cross-country Skiing

1988. Olympic Games, Seoul (4th issue). Mult.

1315 150f. Type **363** (postage) . . 1·50 25
1316 300f. Judo . . . . 2·75 80
1317 400f. Football (air) . . . . 3·00 1·00
1318 450f. Tennis . . . . 4·50 1·40
MS1319 70 × 100 mm. 500f. Boxing (horiz) . . . . 4·50 1·50

1988. Winter Olympic Games, Calgary (2nd issue). Multicoloured.

1320 170f. Type **364** (postage) . . 1·50 45
1321 350f. Ice hockey . . . . . 3·00 80
1322 400f. Downhill skiing (air) 2·75 80
1323 450f. Slalom . . . . 3·75 1·20
MS1324 122 × 85 mm. 500f. Slalom (horiz) . . . . 4·50 1·40

1988. Nos. 1302/5 surch.

1325 30f. on 170f. mult (postage) 40 20
1326 70f. on 300f. mult . . . . . 1·10 65
1327 160f. on 400f. mult (air) . . 1·90 1·00
1328 200f. on 450f. mult . . . . 2·75 1·40

366 Hospital and Grounds

1988. 1st Anniv of L'Amitie Hospital. Mult.

1329 5f. Type **366** 45 25
1330 60f. Aerial view of hospital complex 95 55
1331 160f. Hospital entrance . . 1·50 80

367 Buildings Complex

1988. 30th Anniv of Republic. Multicoloured.

1332 65f. Family on map, flags and dove . . . . 50·00
1334 240f. Type **367** . . . . . . 50·00

368 Kristine Otto (East Germany)

369 Hebmuller and Volkswagen Cabriolet, 1953

1989. Olympic Games, Seoul, Gold Medal Winners. Multicoloured.

1335 150f. Type **368** (100 m butterfly and 100 m backstroke) (postage) . . . . 1·80 55
1336 240f. Matt Biondi (100 m freestyle) . . . . 2·75 80
1337 300f. Florence Griffith-Joyner (U.S.A.) (100 and 200 m sprints) . . . . . 3·50 90
1338 450f. Pierre Durand (France) (show jumping) (air) . . . . 5·50 1·30
MS1339 98 × 68 mm. 600f. Carl Lewis (USA) (100m., 200m., long jump relay) . . . . 6·25 1·80

1989. Transport. Multicoloured.

1340 20f. Type **369** (postage) . . 30 10
1341 205f. Werner von Siemens and his first electric locomotive, 1879 . . . . 2·00 70
1342 300f. Dennis Conner and "Stars and Stripes" (winner of Americas Cup yacht races) . . . . . . 2·75 80
1343 400f. Andre Citroen and "16 Six" car, 1955 . . . . . 3·75 1·40
1344 450f. Mare Seguin and Decauville Mallet locomotive, 1895 (air) . . 4·00 1·40
MS1345 80 × 75 mm. 750f. Duesenberg brothers and "J" Phaeton, 1929 (41 × 29 mm) . . 6·75 2·10

370 Allegory in Honour of Liberty

1989. Bicentenary of French Revolution and "Philexfrance 89" International Stamp Exhibition, Paris (1st issue). Multicoloured.

1346 200f. Type **370** . . . . . . 2·50 80
1347 300f. Declaration of Rights of Man . . . . 3·00 1·50
MS1348 113 × 80 mm. 500f. Demolition of the Bastille (51 × 40 mm) . . . . 5·00 3·25

See also Nos. 1366/**MS**1370.

371 Statue of Liberty at Night

1989. Centenary of Statue of Liberty. Mult.

1349 150f. Type **371** . . . . . 1·50 70
1350 150f. Maintenance worker 1·50 70
1351 150f. Close-up of face . . . 1·50 80
1352 200f. Maintenance worker (different) . . . . 1·80 1·10
1353 200f. Colour party in front of statue . . . . 1·80 1·10
1354 200f. Close-up of head at night . . . . 1·80 1·10

373 "Apollo 11" Astronaut on Moon

1989. Air. 20th Anniv of First Manned Landing on Moon. Multicoloured.

1355 40f. Type **373** 35 20
1356 80f. "Apollo 15" astronaut and moon buggy 75 30
1357 130f. "Apollo 16" module landing in sea . . . . . 1·50 55
1358 1000f. "Apollo 17" astronaut on Moon . . . 9·00 2·75

374 Champagnat, Map and "Madonna and Child"

1989. Birth Bicentenary of Marcelino Champagnat (founder of Marist Brothers). Multicoloured.

1359 15f. Type **374** 10 10
1360 50f. Champagnat, cross, globe and emblem 45 25
1361 160f. Champagnat and flags (horiz) . . . . 1·60 1·20

375 Food Products

1989. Bambari Harvest Festival. Multicoloured.

1362 100f. Type **375** . . . . . . 1·00 60
1363 160f. Ploughing with oxen 1·60 75

376 Raising of Livestock

1989. World Food Day. Multicoloured.

1364 60f. Type **376** 55 40
1365 240f. Soldiers catching poachers . . . . 2·40 1·20

377 Gen. Kellermann and Battle of Valmy

1989. Bicentenary of French Revolution and "Philexfrance 89" International Stamp Exhibition, Paris (2nd issue). Multicoloured.

1366 160f. Type **377** (postage) . . 1·80 40
1367 200f. Gen. Dumouriez and Battle of Jemappes (wrongly inscr "JEMMAPES") . . . . 2·40 60
1368 500f. Gen. Pichegru and capture of Dutch fleet (air) . . . . 5·50 1·30
1369 600f. Gen. Hoche and Royalist landing at Quiberon . . . . 6·50 1·20
MS1370 160 × 107 mm. 1000f. Napoleon Bonaparte and Battle of Rivoli (60 × 50 mm) . . . . . 14·50 3·75

378 Players and Trophy

1989. Victory in 1987 African Basketball Championships, Tunis (1st issue). Multicoloured.
1371 160f. Type **378** . . . . . . 1·50 70
1372 240f. National team with medals and trophy (horiz) 2·00 95
1373 500f. Type **378** . . . . . . 5·00 2·10
See also Nos. 1383/4.

379 Governor's Palace, 1906

1989. Centenary of Bangui. Multicoloured.
1374 100f. Type **379** . . . . . . 1·00 45
1375 160f. Bangui post office . . 1·70 95
1376 200f. A. Dosilie (founder of Bangui post office) (vert) 2·10 1·00
1377 1000f. Michel Dolisie and Chief Gbembo agreeing peace pact (vert) . . . . 9·75 4·50

380 Footballer and Palermo Cathedral Belltower

381 Trophy and Map of Africa

1989. World Cup Football Championship, Italy (1990) (1st issue). Multicoloured.
1378 20f. Type **380** (postage) . . 15 20
1379 160f. Footballer and St. Francis's church, Bologna . . . . 1·50 45
1380 200f. Footballer and Old Palace, Florence . . . . 2·00 70
1381 120f. Footballer and Church of Trinita dei Monti, Rome (air) . . . . 1·20 55
MS1382 83 × 84 mm. 1000f. Footballer and Milan cathedral (30 × 42 mm) . . . . 10·00 2·30
See also Nos. 1405/8.

1990. Victory in 1987 African Basketball Championships, Tunis (2nd issue).
1383 **381** 100f. multicoloured . . . 95 45
1384 130f. multicoloured . . . 1·30 70

382 Tree with Map as Foliage

383 Speed Skating

1990. Inauguration (1989) of Forest Conservation Organization.
1385 **382** 160f. multicoloured . . . 1·70 70

1990. Winter Olympic Games, Albertville (1992). Multicoloured.
1386 10f. Type **383** (postage) . . 15 15
1387 60f. Cross-country skiing . . 55 40
1388 500f. Slalom skiing (air) . . 4·50 1·10
1389 750f. Ice dancing . . . . . 6·75 1·60
MS1390 105 × 71 mm. 1000f. Skiing 8·75 2·10

384 "Euphaera eusemoides"

1990. Scouts and Butterflies. Multicoloured.
1391 25f. Type **384** 30 15
1392 65f. Becker's glider 55 25
1393 160f. "Pseudacraea clarki" 1·50 40
1394 250f. Giant charaxes . . . . 2·40 70
1395 300f. "Euphaedra gausape" 2·75 75
1396 500f. Red swallowtail . . . 4·50 1·10
MS1397 131 × 103 mm. 1000f. "Euphaedra edwardsi" . . . . 9·50 2·20

385 Throwing the Javelin

1990. Olympic Games, Barcelona (1992). Mult.
1398 10f. Type **385** (postage) . . 15 15
1399 40f. Running 40 25
1400 130f. Tennis . . . . 1·20 40
1401 240f. Hurdling (horiz) . . . 2·20 55
1402 400f. Yachting (horiz) (air) 3·75 1·00
1403 500f. Football (horiz) . . . 4·75 1·30
MS1404 95 × 68 mm. 1000f. Boxing (38 × 27 mm) . . . . 8·75 2·10

386 Footballers and Globe

1990. Air. World Cup Football Championship, Italy (2nd issue).
1405 **386** 5f. multicoloured 20 10
1406 – 30f. multicoloured . . . 30 15
1407 – 500f. multicoloured . . . 5·00 1·10
1408 – 1000f. multicoloured . . 8·75 2·10
DESIGNS: 30 to 1000f. Various footballing scenes.

387 Pres. Gorbachev of U.S.S.R., Map of Malta and Pres. Bush of U.S.A.

1990. Anniversaries and Events. Multicoloured.
1409 120f. Type **387** (summit conference, Malta) (postage) 95 25
1410 130f. Sir Rowland Hill and Penny Black (150th anniv of first postage stamps) 1·20 25
1411 160f. Galileo space probe and planet Jupiter . . . . 1·30 25
1412 200f. Pres. Gorbachev meeting Pope John Paul II, statue of Saturn and dove . . . . 1·80 40
1413 240f. Neil Armstrong and eagle (21st anniv of first manned landing on Moon) . . . . 2·20 55
1414 250f. Concorde, German experimental Maglev train and Rotary International emblem . . . . 2·40 70
1415 300f. Don Mattingly (baseball player) and New York Yankees club badge (air) . . . . 2·75 70
1416 500f. Charles de Gaulle (French statesman, birth centenary) . . . . . . 4·75 1·10
MS1417 82 × 112 mm. 1000f. Astronauts and rocket (35 × 50 mm) . . . . 8·75 2·10

388 AIDS Information on Radio, Television and Leaflets

1991. Anti-AIDS Campaign. Multicoloured.
1418 5f. Type **388** 25 10
1419 70f. Type **388** . . . . 1·00 50
1420 120f. Lecture on AIDS (vert) . . . . 1·50 75

389 Demonstrators

1991. Protection of Animals. Multicoloured.
1421 15f. Type **389** 40 10
1422 60f. Type **389** . . . . 1·50 35
1423 100f. Decrease in elephant population, 1945–2045 (vert) . . . . 2·20 50

390 Butter Catfish

1991. Fishes. Multicoloured.
1424 50f. Type **390** 85 25
1425 160f. Type **390** . . . . . . 2·00 80
1426 240f. Distichodus . . . . . 3·00 1·40

391 President Kolingba

1992. 10th Anniv (1991) of Assumption of Power by Military Committee under Andre Kolingba.
1427 **391** 160f. multicoloured . . . 1·50 65

392 Count Ferdinand von Zeppelin (airship pioneer)

1992. Celebrities, Anniversaries and Events. Multicoloured.
1428 80f. Type **392** (75th death anniv) (postage) 80 20
1429 140f. Henri Dunant (founder of Red Cross) . . . . . 1·50 45
1430 160f. Michael Schumacher (racing driver) . . . . . 1·80 70
1431 350f. Brandenburg Gate (bicent) and Konrad Adenauer (German Federal Republic Chancellor) signing 1949 constitution . . . . . . 4·25 1·20
1432 500f. Pope John Paul II (tour of West Africa) (air) 5·50 1·20
1433 600f. Wolfgang Amadeus Mozart (composer, death bicent (1991)) . . . . . . 6·50 1·40
MS1434 81 × 105 mm. 1000f. Christopher Columbus, "Santa Maria" and 15th-cent view of La Cartuja de las Cuevas (Expo' 92 World's Fair, Seville) . . . . . 9·50 2·10

393 Dam

395 Breastfeeding

394 Compass Rose and Organization Emblem

1993. River M'Bali Dam. Multicoloured.
1435 160f. Type **393** . . . . . . 1·50 70
1436 200f. People fishing near dam (self-sufficiency in food) . . . . 2·00 90

1993. International Customs Day and 40th Anniv of Customs Co-operation Council.
1437 **394** 240f. multicoloured . . . 2·30 1·40

1993. International Nutrition Conference, Rome (1992). Multicoloured.
1438 90f. Type **395** 75 40
1439 140f. Foodstuffs . . . . . 1·30 70

396 Bangui University

1993.
1440 **396** 100f. multicoloured . . . 95 40

397 Masako Owada as Baby

1993. Wedding of Crown Prince Naruhito of Japan and Masako Owada. Multicoloured.
1441 50f. Type **397** (postage) . . 40 25
1442 65f. Prince Naruhito as child with parents 60 25
1443 160f. Masako Owada at Harvard University, U.S.A. . . . . 1·60 55
1444 450f. Prince Naruhito at Oxford University (air) . . 4·25 1·20
MS1445 184 × 83 mm. 750f. Prince Naruhito and Masako Owada 6·75 1·80

398 Presley singing "Heartbreak Hotel" (1956)

1993. 16th Death Anniv of Elvis Presley (entertainer). Multicoloured.
1446 200f. Type **398** . . . . . . 2·10 55
1447 300f. "Love Me Tender", 1957 . . . . 3·00 80
1448 400f. "Jailhouse Rock", 1957 . . . . 3·75 1·40
1449 600f. "Harum Scarum", 1965 (air) . . . . . . 5·50 1·40
MS1450 98 × 69 mm. 1000f Elvis performing (35 × 50 mm) . . . 8·75 2·30

399 First World Cup Final, 1928, and Uruguay v. Argentina, 1930

1993. World Cup Football Championship, U.S.A. (1994). History of the World Cup. Multicoloured.

1451 40f. Type **399** 35 10
1452 50f. Italy v. Czechoslovakia, 1934, and Italy v. Hungary, 1938 . . . . . 45 10
1453 60f. Uruguay v. Brazil, 1950, and Germany v. Hungary, 1954 . . . . . 55 25
1454 80f. Brazil v. Sweden, 1958, and Brazil v. Czechoslovakia, 1962 . . 75 25
1455 160f. England v. West Germany, 1966, and Brazil v. Italy, 1970 . . . 1·50 25
1456 200f. West Germany v. The Netherlands, 1974, and Argentina v. The Netherlands, 1978 . . . . 1·80 40
1457 400f. Italy v. West Germany, 1982, and Argentina v. West Germany, 1986 . . . . . 3·50 70
1458 500f. West Germany v. Argentina, 1990, and 1994 Championship emblem and player . . . . 4·50 1·20
MS1459 101 × 85 mm. 1000f. West Germany and Argentina teams (59 × 29 mm) . . . . 8·75 2·10

400 Baron Pierre de Coubertin (founder of modern games)

1993. Centenary (1996) of Modern Olympic Games. Multicoloured.

1460 90f. Ancient Greek athlete 75 30
1461 90f. Type **400** 75 30
1462 90f. Charles Bennett (running), Paris, 1900 . . 75 30
1463 90f. Etienne Desmarteau (stone throwing), St. Louis, 1904 . . . . . 75 30
1464 90f. Harry Porter (high jump), London, 1908 . . 75 30
1465 90f. Patrick MacDonald (putting the shot), Stockholm, 1912 . . . . 75 30
1466 90f. Coloured and black Olympic rings (1916) . . 75 30
1467 90f. Frank Loomis (400 m hurdles), Antwerp, 1920 . . . . 75 30
1468 90f. Albert White (diving), Paris, 1924 . . . . 95 35
1469 100f. El Ouafi (marathon), Amsterdam, 1928 . . . . 95 35
1470 100f. Eddie Tolan (100 m), Los Angeles, 1932 . . . . 95 35
1471 100f. Jesse Owens (100 m, long jump and 200 m hurdles), Berlin, 1936 . . . . 95 35
1472 100f. Coloured and black Olympic rings (1940) . . 95 35
1473 100f. Coloured and black Olympic rings (1944) . . 95 35
1474 100f. Tapio Rautavaara (throwing the javelin), London, 1948 . . . . . 95 35
1475 100f. Jean Boiteux (400 m freestyle swimming), Helsinki, 1952 95 35
1476 100f. Petrus Kasterman (three-day equestrian event), Melbourne, 1956 95 35
1477 100f. Sante Gaiardoni (cycling), Rome, 1960 . . 95 35
1478 160f. Anton Geesink (judo), Tokyo, 1964 . . . . . . 1·50 45
1479 160f. Bob Beamon (long jump), Mexico, 1968 . . . 1·50 45
1480 160f. Mark Spitz (swimming), Munich, 1972 1·50 45
1481 160f. Nadia Comaneci (gymnastics (beam)), Montreal, 1976 . . . . . 1·50 45
1482 160f. Aleksandre Ditjatin (gymnastics (rings) and dressage), Moscow, 1980 1·50 45
1483 160f. J. F. Lamour (sabre), Los Angeles, 1984 . . . . 1·50 45
1484 160f. Pierre Durand (show jumping), Seoul, 1988 . . 1·50 45
1485 160f. Michael Jordan (basketball), Barcelona, 1992 . . . . 1·50 45
1486 160f. Footballer and Games emblem, Atlanta, 1996 . . 1·50 45

401 Man planting Sapling, and Animals

402 Woman selling Foodstuffs

1993. Biodiversity. Multicoloured.

1487 100f. Type **401** . . . . . . 1·50 70
1488 130f. Man amongst flora and fauna (vert) . . . . 2·10 90

1993. The Environment and Sustainable Development. Multicoloured.

1489 160f. Type **402** . . . . . . 1·50 70
1490 240f. Woman tending cooking pot . . . . . . 2·50 1·40

403 Saltoposuchus

1993. Prehistoric Animals. Multicoloured.

1491 25f. Type **403** 35 10
1492 25f. Rhamphorhynchus . . 35 10
1493 25f. Dimorphodon 35 10
1494 25f. Archaeopteryx 35 10
1495 30f. "Compsognathos longipes" 35 10
1496 30f. "Cryptocleidus oxoniensis" 35 10
1497 30f. Stegosaurus 35 10
1498 30f. Cetiosaurus 35 10
1499 50f. Brontosaurus 45 20
1500 50f. "Corythosaurus casuarius" 45 20
1501 50f. Styracosaurus 45 20
1502 50f. Gorgosaurus 45 20
1503 500f. Scolosaurus . . . . . 4·75 1·00
1504 500f. Trachodon . . . . . 4·75 1·00
1505 500f. Struthiomimus . . . . 4·75 1·00
1506 500f. "Tarbosaurus bataar" 4·75 1·00
MS1507 120 × 170 mm. 1000f Tylosaur (50 × 59 mm) (air) . . 10·00 2·30

Nos. 1491/1506 were issued together, se-tenant, forming a composite design of a volcanic landscape.

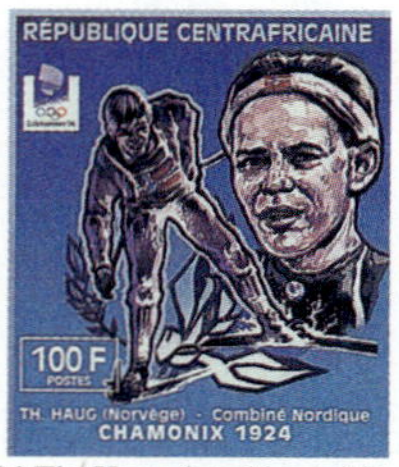

404 Th. Haug (combined skiing, Chamonix, 1924)

1994. Winter Olympic Games, Lillehammer, Norway. Previous Medal Winners. Multicoloured.

1508 100f. Type **404** . . . . . . 1·00 25
1509 100f. J. Heaton (luge, St. Moritz, 1928) . . . . 1·00 25
1510 100f. B. Ruud (ski jumping, Lake Placid, 1932) . . . 1·00 25
1511 100f. I. Ballangrud (speed skating, Garmisch-Partenkirchen, 1936) . . . 1·00 25
1512 100f. G. Fraser (slalom, St. Moritz, 1948) . . . 1·00 25
1513 100f. West German 4-man bobsleigh team (Oslo, 1952) . . . . 1·00 25
1514 100f. U.S.S.R. ice hockey team (Cortina d'Ampezzo, 1956) . . . . 1·00 25
1515 100f. J. Vuarnet (downhill skiing, Squaw Valley, 1960) . . . . 1·00 25
1516 200f. M. Goitschel (giant slalom, Innsbruck, 1964) 1·70 45
1517 200f. Jean-Claud Killy (special slalom, Grenoble, 1968) . . . . 1·70 45
1518 200f. U. Wehling (cross-country skiing, Sapporo, 1972) . . . . 1·70 45
1519 200f. Irina Rodnina and Aleksandr Zaitsev (figure skating, Innsbruck, 1976) 1·70 45
1520 200f. E. Heiden (speed skating, Lake Placid, 1980) . . . . 1·70 45
1521 200f. Katarina Witt (figure skating, Sarajevo, 1984) 1·70 45
1522 200f. J. Mueller (single luge, Calgary, 1988) . . . . . 1·70 45
1523 200f. E. Grospiron (acrobatic skiing, Albertville, 1992) . . . . 1·70 45
1524 200f. Speed skiing, Lillehammer, 1994 . . . . 1·70 45

405 "Ansellia africa"

1994. Flowers, Vegetables, Fruit and Fungi. Multicoloured.

1525 25f. Type **405** 10 10
1526 30f. Yams 30 10
1527 40f. Oranges 30 10
1528 50f. Termite mushroom . . 40 10
1529 60f. "Polystachia bella" (flower) 45 10
1530 65f. Manioc 55 10
1531 70f. Banana 55 10
1532 80f. "Synpodia arborescens" (wrongly inscr "Sympodia") (fungi) . . . 75 10
1533 90f. "Aerangis rhodosticta" (flower) 75 10
1534 100f. Maize 85 10
1535 160f. Mango . . . . 1·40 25
1536 200f. "Phlebopus sudanicus" (fungi) . . . . 1·70 25
1537 300f. Coffee beans . . . . 2·75 45
1538 400f. Sweet potato . . . . 3·75 55
1539 500f. "Angraecum eburneum" (flower) . . . 4·50 75
1540 600f. "Leucocoprinus africanus" (fungi) . . . . 5·25 90

Nos. 1525/40 were issued together, se-tenant, the backgrounds forming a composite design.

MILITARY FRANK STAMPS

1963. Optd **FM**. No. M1 also has the value obliterated with two bars. Centre multicoloured; frame colour given.

M35 **1** (–) on 15f. blue . . . . . 14·50
M36 15f. blue . . . . 15·00

OFFICIAL STAMPS

O 41 Arms

O 109 Arms

1965.

O78 **O 41** 1f. multicoloured . . . 10 10
O79 2f. multicoloured . . . 10 10
O80 5f. multicoloured . . . 10 10
O81 10f. multicoloured . . . 30 10
O82 20f. multicoloured . . . 50 25
O83 30f. multicoloured . . . 90 55
O84 50f. multicoloured . . . 1·00 80
O85 100f. multicoloured . . 2·50 1·20
O86 130f. multicoloured . . 4·00 2·30
O87 200f. multicoloured . . 6·00 3·00

1971.

O238 **O 109** 5f. multicoloured . . 10 10
O239 30f. multicoloured . . 50 25
O240 40f. multicoloured . . 85 25
O241 100f. multicoloured 1·50 55
O242 140f. multicoloured 2·20 80
O243 200f. multicoloured 3·50 1·40

POSTAGE DUE STAMPS

D 15 "Sternotomis gama" (Beetle)

1962. Beetles.

D33 50c. brown and turquoise . . 10 10
D34 50c. turquoise and brown . . 10 10
D35 1f. brown and green 20 20
D36 1f. green and brown 20 20
D37 2f. pink and black 25 25
D38 2f. green, black and pink . . 25 25
D39 5f. green and brown 45 40
D40 5f. green and brown 45 40
D41 10f. green, black and drab 75 75
D42 10f. drab, black and green 75 75
D43 25f. brown, black and green 2·00 1·90
D44 25f. brown, green and black 2·00 1·90

DESIGNS: No. D33, Type D **15**; D34, "Sternotomis virescens"; D35, "Augosoma centaurus"; D36, "Phosphorus virescens" and "Ceroplesis carabarica"; D37, "Ceroplesis S.P."; D38, "Cetoine scaraboidae"; D39, "Cetoine scaraboidae"; D40, "Macrorhina S.P."; D41, "Taurina longiceps"; D42, "Phryneta leprosa"; D43, "Monohamus griseoplagiatus"; D44, "Jambonus trifasciatus".

D **308** Giant Pangolin ("Manis gigantea")

1985.

D1080 D **308** 5f. multicoloured . . 40 35
D1081 20f. multicoloured 70 70
D1082 30f. multicoloured 80 80

APPENDIX

The following stamps have either been issued in excess of postal needs or have not been availble to the public in reasonable quantities at face value. Such stamps may later be given full listing if there is evidence of regular postal use.

All the stamps listed below are embossed on gold foil.

1977.

Coronation of Emperor Bokassa. Air 2500f.

1978.

100 Years of Progress in Posts and Telecommunications. Air 1500f.

Death Centenary of Sir Rowland Hill. Air 1500f.

1979.

International Year of the Child. Air 1500f.

Olympic Games, Moscow. Air 1500f. ("The Discus-thrower")

Space Exploration. Air 1500f.

1980.

Olympic Games, Moscow. Air 1500f. (Relay)

European-African Co-operation. Air 1500f.

World Cup Football Championship, Spain. Air 1500f.

1981.

Olympic Games Medal Winners. 1980 Olympic Games issue optd. Air 1500f.

Birth Centenary of Pablo Picasso. Air 1500f.

Wedding of Prince of Wales. Air 1500f.

Navigators. Air 1500f.

Christmas. Air 1500f.

1982.

Animals and Rotary International. Air 1500f.

Transport. Air 1500f.

21st Birthday of Princess of Wales. Air 1500f.

Olympic Games, Los Angeles.Air 1500f. (horiz)

Space Resources. Air 1500f.

1983.

Chess Masters. Air 1500f.

World Cup Football Championship, Spain. Air 1500f.

Car Manufacturers. Air 1500f.

Olympic Games, Los Angeles. Air 1500f. (vert)

Bicentenary of manned flight. Air 1500f.

1984.

Winter Olympic Gold Medalists. Air 1500f.

Celebrities. Air 1500f.

1985.

85th Birthday of Queen Elizabeth the Queen Mother. Air 1500f.

Appearence of Halley's Comet. Air 1500f.

480th Death Anniv of Christopher Columbus. Air 1500f.

1988.

Olympic Games, Seoul. Air 1500f.

Scouts and Birds. Air 1500f.

1989.

Olympic Games, Seoul, Gold Medal Winner. Air 1500f.

Bicentenary of French Revolution. Air 1500f.

World Cup Football Championship, Italy. Air 1500f.

1990.

Winter Olympic Games, Albertville (1992). Air 1500f.

Scouts and Butterflies. Air 1500f.

Birth Centenary of Charles de Gaulle. Air 1500f.

1993.

Wedding of Crown Prince Naruhito of Japan and Masako Owada. Air 1500f.

16th Death Anniv of Elvis Presley. Air 1500f.

World Cup Football Championship, U.S.A. (1994). Air 1500f.

Visit of Pope John Paul II to Africa. Air 1500f.

1994.

Winter Olympic Games, Lillehammer. Air 1500f.

CENTRAL LITHUANIA Pt. 10

Became temporarily independent in 1918 and was subsequently absorbed by Poland.

POLISH OCCUPATION

100 fenigi = 1 mark.

1

3 Girl

1920. Imperf or perf.

1	1	25f. red	10	10
20		25f. green	20	30
2		1m. blue	10	10
21		1m. brown	20	30
3		2m. violet	15	15
22		2m. yellow	20	30

1920. Stamps of Lithuania of 1919 surch **SRODKOWA LITWA POCZTA**, new value and Arms of Poland and Lithuania. Perf.

4	5	2m. on 15s. violet	6·50	8·00
5		4m. on 10s. red	4·00	5·00
6		4m. on 20s. blue	6·00	8·00
7		4m. on 30s. orange	5·00	6·00
8	6	6m. on 50s. green	6·00	7·00
9		6m. on 60s. red and violet	6·00	8·00
10		6m. on 75s. red & yellow	6·00	8·00
11	7	10m. on 1a. red & grey	12·00	14·00
12		10m. on 3a. red & brown	£450	£550
13		10m. on 5a. red and green	£450	£550

1920. Imperf or perf. Inscr "LITWA SRODKOWA".

14	3	25f. grey	15	15
15	–	1m. orange	20	15
16	–	2m. red	40	50
17	–	4m. olive and yellow	60	75
18	–	6m. grey and red	1·00	1·25
19	–	10m. yellow and brown	1·50	2·00

DESIGNS: 1m. Warrior; 2m. Ostrabrama Gate, Vilnius; 4m. St. Stanislaus Cathedral and Tower, Vilnius; 6m. Rector's insignia; 10m. Gen. Zeligowski.

1921. Fund for Polish Participation in Plebiscite for Upper Silesia. Surch **NA SLASK** and new value. Imperf or perf.

23	1	25f.+2m. red	50	60
24		25f.+2m. green	50	60
25		1m.+2m. blue	60	80
26		1m.+2m. brown	60	80
27		2m.+2m. violet	70	1·10
28		2m.+2m. yellow	70	1·10

1921. Red Cross Fund. Nos. 16/17 surch with cross and value. Imperf or perf.

29		2m.+1m. red	50	65
30		4m.+1m. green and yellow	50	65

1921. White Cross Fund. As Nos. 16, 17 and 19, but with cross and value in white added. Imperf or perf.

31		2m.+1m. purple	30	30
32		4m.+1m. green and buff	30	30
33		10m.+2m. yellow and brown	30	30

13 St. Nicholas Cathedral

14 St. Stanislaus Cathedral

1921. Imperf or perf.

34	13	1m. yellow and slate	30	40
35	14	2m. green and red	30	40
36	–	3m. green	40	50
37	–	4m. brown	40	60
38	–	5m. brown	40	60
39	–	6m. buff and green	40	60
40	–	10m. buff and purple	60	80
41	–	20m. buff and brown	60	90

DESIGNS—HORIZ: 4m. Queen Jadwiga and King Wladislaw Jagiello; 6m. Poczobut Observatory, Vilnius University; 10m. Union of Lithuania and Poland, 1569; 20m. Kosciuszko and Mickiewicz. VERT: 3m. Arms (Eagle); 5m. Arms (Shield).

21 Entry into Vilnius

22 General Zeligowski

1921. 1st Anniv of Entry of Gen. Zeligowski into Vilnius. Imperf or perf.

42	21	100m. blue and bistre	1·75	1·75
43	22	150m. green and brown	2·25	2·25

24 Arms

1922. Opening of National Parliament. Inscr "SEJM—WILNIE". Imperf or perf.

44	–	10m. brown	1·50	1·75
45	24	25m. red and buff	1·75	1·90
46	–	50m. blue	2·75	3·00
47	–	75m. lilac	4·00	4·50

DESIGNS—HORIZ: 50m. National Assembly, Vilnius. VERT: 10m. Agriculture; 75m. Industry.

POSTAGE DUE STAMPS

D 9 Government Offices

1921. Inscr "DOPLATA". Imperf or perf.

D23	D 9	50f. red	50	60
D24	–	1m. green	50	60
D25	–	2m. purple	50	60
D26	–	3m. purple	75	90
D27	–	5m. purple	75	90
D28	–	20m. red	1·00	1·25

DESIGNS—HORIZ: 2m. Castle on Troki Island. VERT: 1m. Castle Hill, Vilnius; 3m. Ostrabrama Gate, Vilnius; 5m. St. Stanislaus Cathedral; 20m. (larger) St. Nicholas Cathedral.

CEYLON Pt. 1

An island to the south of India formerly under British administration, then a self-governing Dominion. The island became a Republic within the Commonwealth on 22 May 1972 and was renamed Sri Lanka (q.v.).

1857. 12 pence = 1 shilling;
20 shillings = 1 pound.
1872. 100 cents = 1 rupee.

1

2

4

8

1857. Imperf.

17	4	½d. lilac	£180	£225
2	1	1d. blue	£750	38·00
3		2d. green	£170	60·00
4	2	4d. red	£65000	£4500
5	1	5d. brown	£1500	£150
6		6d. brown	£2000	£140
7	2	8d. brown	£28000	£1500
8		9d. brown	£45000	£900
9	1	10d. orange	£800	£300
10		1s. violet	£4750	£200
11	2	1s.9d. green	£800	£800
12		2s. blue	£6000	£1200

The prices of these imperf stamps vary greatly according to condition. The above prices are for fine copies with four margins. Poor to medium specimens are worth much less.

1861. Perf.

48c	4	½d. lilac	40·00	40·00
49	1	1d. blue	£140	7·00
50		2d. green	80·00	13·00
64b		2d. yellow	70·00	8·00
65b	2	4d. red	65·00	19·00
22	1	5d. brown	90·00	8·00
66c		5d. green	42·00	50·00
67b		6d. brown	42·00	35·00
56	2	8d. brown	£120	55·00
69b		9d. brown	55·00	6·00
70b	1	10d. orange	60·00	16·00
71b		1s. violet	95·00	8·50
72b	2	2s. blue	£140	14·00

1866. The 3d. has portrait in circle.

61	8	1d. blue	23·00	10·00
62	–	3d. red	85·00	45·00

9

10

30

1872. Various frames.

256	9	2c. brown	3·50	30
147		2c. green	2·50	15
122	10	4c. grey	40·00	1·50
148		4c. purple	4·00	30
149		4c. red	4·75	12·00
258		4c. yellow	3·00	2·75
150a	–	8c. yellow	4·00	8·50
126	–	16c. violet	95·00	2·75
127	–	24c. green	60·00	2·00
128	–	32c. grey	£150	15·00
129	–	36c. blue	£160	24·00
130	–	48c. red	80·00	7·50
131	–	64c. brown	£300	70·00
132	–	96c. grey	£225	26·00
201	30	1r.12 red	28·00	25·00
138		2r.50 red	£550	£300
249		2r.50 purple on red	32·00	50·00

1882. Nos. 127 and 131 surch in words and figures.

142		16c. on 24c. green	27·00	7·00
143		20c. on 64c. brown	11·00	7·00

1885. As Nos. 148/132 surch **Postage & Revenue** and value in words.

178		5c. on 4c. red	28·00	4·50
179		5c. on 8c. yellow	80·00	9·00
180		5c. on 16c. violet	£130	14·00
154		5c. on 24c. green	£3250	£110
182		5c. on 24c. purple	—	£500
155		5c. on 32c. grey	65·00	15·00
156		5c. on 36c. blue	£300	13·00
157		5c. on 48c. red	£1600	60·00
158		5c. on 64c. brown	£120	9·00
159		5c. on 96c. grey	£500	70·00

1885. As Nos. 126/249 surch with new value in words.

184		10c. on 16c. violet	£7000	£1500
162		10c. on 24c. green	£450	£120
185		10c. on 24c. purple	15·00	8·00
163		10c. on 36c. blue	£375	£200
174		10c. on 64c. brown	70·00	£130
186		15c. on 16c. violet	12·00	9·00
165		20c. on 24c. green	60·00	19·00
166		20c. on 32c. grey	75·00	60·00
167		25c. on 32c. grey	20·00	5·00
168		28c. on 48c. red	40·00	8·00
169x		30c. on 36c. blue	12·00	9·00
170		56c. on 96c. grey	26·00	22·00
176		1r.12 on 2r.50 red	£110	45·00

1885. Surch **REVENUE AND POSTAGE 5 CENTS.**

187		5c. on 8c. lilac (as No. 150a)	21·00	1·50

1885. As Nos. 126/32 surch in words and figures.

188		10c. on 24c. purple	11·00	8·50
189		15c. on 16c. yellow	60·00	13·00
190		28c. on 32c. grey	26·00	2·50
191		30c. on 36c. olive	28·00	15·00
192		56c. on 96c. grey	50·00	16·00

1885. Surch **1 R. 12 C.**

193	30	1r.12 on 2r.50 red	50·00	£110

39

28

43

1886.

245	39	3c. brown and green	4·00	45
257		3c. green	3·50	55
195	28	5c. purple	2·75	10
259	39	6c. red and black	1·75	45
260		12c. olive and red	4·00	7·50
196		15c. olive	7·00	1·80
261		15c. blue	6·00	1·25
198		25c. brown	4·50	1·10
199		28c. grey	22·00	1·40
247		30c. mauve and brown	4·25	2·50
262		75c. black and brown	6·50	7·50
263	43	1r.50 red	26·00	42·00
264		2r.25 blue	35·00	42·00

1887. Nos. 148/9 surch. A. Surch **TWO CENTS**.

202	10	2c. on 4c. purple	1·40	80
203		2c. on 4c. red	2·25	30

B. Surch **TWO.**

204	10	2c. on 4c. purple	75	30
205		2c. on 4c. red	7·00	20

C. Surch **2 Cents** and bar.

206	10	2c. on 4c. purple	70·00	32·00
207		2c. on 4c. red	2·75	75

D. Surch **Two Cents** and bar.

208	10	2c. on 4c. purple	55·00	25·00
209		2c. on 4c. red	2·50	1·10

E. Surch **2 Cents** without bar.

210	10	2c. on 4c. purple	60·00	32·00
211		2c. on 4c. red	11·00	1·00

1890. Surch **POSTAGE Five Cents REVENUE**.

233	39	5c. on 15c. olive	3·25	2·00

1891. Surch **FIFTEEN CENTS.**

239	39	15c. on 25c. brown	15·00	14·00
240		15c. on 28c. grey	17·00	8·50

1892. Surch **3 Cents** and bar.

241	10	3c. on 4c. purple	1·00	3·25
242		3c. on 4c. red	5·50	8·50
243	39	3c. on 28c. grey	4·75	4·50

1898. Surch **Six Cents.**

250	39	6c. on 15c. green	1·00	75

1898. Surch with new value.

254	30	1r.50 on 2r.50 grey	20·00	48·00
255		2r.25 on 2r.50 yellow	38·00	80·00

44

45

1903. Various frames.

277	44	2c. brown	1·50	10
278	45	3c. green (A)	1·50	15
293		3c. green (B)	1·00	75
279		4c. orange and blue	2·50	1·50
268	–	5c. purple	1·50	60
289	–	5c. purple	3·75	10
281	–	6c. red	3·00	15
291	–	6c. red	1·50	10
294	45	10c. olive and red	2·50	2·50
282		12c. olive and red	1·50	1·75
283		15c. blue	2·75	60
284		25c. brown	6·00	3·75
295		25c. grey	2·50	2·00
285		30c. violet and green	2·50	3·00
296		50c. brown	4·00	7·50
286		75c. blue and orange	5·25	8·00
297		1r. purple on yellow	7·50	10·00
287		1r.50 grey	28·00	10·00
298		2r. red on yellow	15·00	28·00
288		2r.25 brown and green	22·00	30·00
299		5r. black on green	38·00	75·00
300		10r. black on red	90·00	£190

(A) has value in shaded tablet; (B) in white tablet as in Type **45**.

Nos. 268 and 281 have the value in words; Nos. 289 and 291 in figures.

52

57

1912.

301	52	1c. brown	1·00	10
307a		2c. orange	30	20
339		3c. green	3·50	75
340		3c. grey	75	20
341		5c. purple	60	15
342		6c. red	2·25	75
343		6c. violet	1·50	15
345		9c. red on yellow	1·25	30
346		10c. olive	1·40	40
347a		12c. red	1·00	2·25
311a		15c. blue	1·75	1·25
349a		15c. green on yellow	3·00	1·00
350b		20c. blue	3·50	45
351		25c. yellow and blue	2·00	1·90
352a		30c. green and violet	4·50	1·25
353		50c. black and red	1·75	80
315		1r. purple on yellow	4·50	3·50
355		2r. black and red on yellow	7·00	9·00
317		5r. black on green	18·00	32·00

318 10r. purple & blk on red 70·00 90·00
319 20r. black and red on blue £150 £160

Large type, As Bermuda T 15.
358 50r. purple £550 £950
359 100r. black £1900
360 100r. purple and blue £1400

1918. Optd **WAR STAMP**, No. 335 surch **ONE CENT** and bar also.
335 **52** 1c. on 5c. purple 50 40
330 2c. orange 20 40
332 3c. green 20 50
333 5c. purple 50 30

1918. Surch **ONE CENT** and bar.
337 **52** 1c. on 5c. purple 15 25

1926. Surch with new value and bar.
361 **52** 2c. on 3c. grey 1·00 1·00
362 5c. on 6c. violet 50 40

1927.
363 **57** 1r. purple 2·50 1·25
364 2r. green and red 3·75 2·75
365 5r. green and purple 14·00 21·00
366 10r. green and orange 42·00 90·00
367 20r. purple and blue £140 £250

59 Adam's Peak

1935. King George V.
368 – 2c. black and red 30 40
369 **59** 3c. black and green 35 40
370 – 6c. black and blue 30 30
371 – 9c. green and orange 1·00 65
372 – 10c. black and purple 1·25 2·75
373 – 15c. brown and green 1·00 50
374 – 20c. black and blue 1·75 3·00
375 – 25c. blue and brown 1·40 1·25
376 – 30c. red and green 2·25 3·25
377 – 50c. black and violet 13·00 1·75
378 – 1r. violet and brown 24·00 18·00
DESIGNS—VERT: 2c. Tapping rubber; 6c. Colombo Harbour; 9c. Plucking tea; 20c. Coconut palms. HORIZ: 10c. Hill paddy (rice); 15c. River scene; 25c. Temple of the Tooth, Kandy; 30c. Ancient irrigation tank; 50c. Indian elephants; 1r. Trincomalee.

1935. Silver Jubilee. As T **13** of Antigua.
379 6c. blue and grey 75 30
380 9c. green and blue 75 2·25
381 20c. brown and blue 4·25 2·75
382 50c. grey and purple 5·25 12·00

1937. Coronation. As T **2** of Aden.
383 6c. red 65 1·00
384 9c. green 2·50 4·50
385 20c. blue 3·50 4·00

70 Sigiriya (Lion Rock)

1938. As 1935 issue but with portrait of King George VI, and "POSTAGE & REVENUE" omitted.
386b – 2c. black and red 2·00 10
387d **59** 3c. black and green 80 10
387f – 5c. green and orange 30 10
388 – 6c. black and blue 30 10
389 **70** 10c. black and blue 3·25 10
390 – 15c. green and brown 2·00 10
391 – 20c. black and blue 3·25 10
392a – 25c. blue and brown 4·25 10
393 – 30c. red and green 12·00 3·00
394e – 50c. black and violet 5·00 20
395 – 1r. blue and brown 17·00 1·25
396 – 2r. black and red 13·00 3·00
396b – 2r. black and violet 2·25 2·25
DESIGNS—VERT: 5c. Coconut palms; 20c. Plucking tea; 2r. Ancient guard-stone, Anuradhapura. Others, same as for corresponding values of 1935 issue.

1938. As T **57**, but head of King George VI to right.
397a 5r. green and purple 18·00 5·50

1940. Surch with new value and bars.
398 3c. on 6c. blk & bl (No. 388) 65 10
399 3c. on 20c. blk & bl (No. 391) 4·00 2·00

1946. Victory. As T **9** of Aden.
400 6c. blue 30 35
401 15c. brown 30 1·75

75 Parliament Building

1947. New Constitution.
402 **75** 6c. black and blue 20 15
403 – 10c. black, orange and red 25 40
404 – 15c. green and purple 25 80
405 – 25c. yellow and green 25 1·75
DESIGNS—VERT: 10c. Adam's Peak; 25c. Anuradhapura. HORIZ: 15c. Temple of the Tooth.

79 Lion Flag of Dominion

80 D. S. Senanayake

1949. 1st Anniv of Independence.
406 **79** 4c. red, yellow and brown 20 20
407 **80** 5c. brown and green 10 10
408 **79** 15c. red, yellow and orange 1·00 40
409 **80** 25c. brown and blue 15 1·00
No. 408 is larger, 28 × 22 mm.

82 Globe and Forms of Transport

1949. 75th Anniv of UPU. Inscr as in T **82**. Designs showing globe.
410 **82** 5c. brown and green 75 10
411 – 15c. black and red (horiz) 1·10 2·75
412 – 25c. black and blue (vert) 1·10 1·10

85 Kandyan Dancer

88 Sigiriya (Lion Rock)

90 Ruins at Madirigiriya

1950.
413 **85** 4c. purple and red 10 10
414 – 5c. green 10 10
415 – 15c. green and violet 2·50 50
416 **88** 30c. red and yellow 30 70
417 – 75c. blue and orange 7·50 20
418 **90** 1r. blue and brown 1·75 30
DESIGNS—VERT (As Types **85** and **88**): 5c. Kiri Vehera, Polonnaruwa; 15c. Vesak orchid. (As Type **90**): 75c. Octagon Library, Temple of the Tooth.

94 Coconut Trees

99 Tea Plantation

1951.
419 – 2c. brown and turquoise 10 1·25
420 – 3c. black and violet 10 1·00
421 – 6c. sepia and green 10 30
422 **94** 10c. green and grey 1·00 65
423 – 25c. orange and blue 10 20
424 – 35c. red and green 1·50 1·50
425 – 40c. brown 5·00 1·00
426 – 50c. slate 30 10
427 **99** 85c. black and turquoise 75 30
428 – 2r. blue and brown 7·50 1·25
429 – 5r. brown and orange 5·00 1·40
430 – 10r. brown and buff 50·00 16·00
DESIGNS—VERT (As Type **94**): 2c. Sambars, Ruhuna National Park; 3c. Ancient guardstone, Anuradhapura; 6c. Harvesting rice; 25c. Sigiriya fresco; 35c. Star orchid. (As Type **99**): 5r. Bas-relief, Anuradhapura; 10r. Harvesting rice. HORIZ (As Type **94**): 40c. Rubber plantation; 50c. Outrigger canoe. (As Type **99**): 2r. River Gal Dam.

103 Ceylon, Mace and Symbols of Progress

104 Queen Elizabeth II

1952. Colombo Plan Exhibition.
431 **103** 5c. green 10 30
432 15c. blue 10 60

1953. Coronation.
433 **104** 5c. green 1·25 10

105 Ceremonial Procession

106 King Coconuts

1954. Royal Visit.
434 **105** 10c. blue 1·00 10

1954.
435 **106** 10c. orange, brown and buff 10 10

107 Farm Produce

1955. Royal Agricultural and Food Exhibition.
436 **107** 10c. brown and orange 10 10

108 Sir John Kotelawala and House of Representatives

1956. Prime Minister's 25 Years of Public Service.
437 **108** 10c. green 10 10

109 Arrival of Vijaya in Ceylon

110 Lampstand and Dharmachakra

1956. Buddha Jayanti. Inscr "2500".
438 **109** 3c. blue and grey 15 15
439 **110** 4c.+2c. yellow and blue 20 75
440 – 10c.+5c. red, yell & grey 20 1·00
441 – 15c. blue 25 10
DESIGNS—VERT: 10c. Hand of Peace and Dharmachakra. HORIZ: 15c. Dharmachakra encircling the globe.

113 Mail Transport

114 Stamp of 1857

1957. Stamp Centenary.
442 **113** 4c. red and turquoise 75 50
443 10c. red and blue 75 10
444 **114** 35c. brown, yellow and blue 30 50
445 85c. brown, yellow & grn 80 1·60

1958. Nos. 439/40 with premium obliterated with bars.
446 **110** 4c. yellow and blue 10 10
447 – 10c. red, yellow and grey 10 10

117 Kandyan Dancer

118 "Human Rights"

1958. As Nos. 413 and 419 etc, and 435, but with inscriptions changed as in T **117**.
448 2c. brown and turquoise 10 50
449 3c. black and violet 10 70
450 4c. purple and red 10 10
451 5c. green 10 1·60
452 6c. sepia and green 10 65
453 10c. orange, brown and buff 10 10
454 15c. green and violet 3·50 80
455 25c. orange and blue 15 10
456 30c. red and yellow 20 1·40
457 35c. red and green 6·50 30
459 50c. slate 30 10
460a 75c. blue and orange 9·00 2·25
461 85c. black and turquoise 3·75 7·00
462 1r. blue and brown 60 10
463 2r. blue and brown 1·75 30
464 5r. brown and orange 7·50 30
465 10r. brown and buff 10·00 1·00

1958. 10th Anniv of Declaration of Human Rights.
466 **118** 10c. red, brown and purple 10 10
467 85c. red, turq & grn 30 55

119 Portraits of Founders and University Buildings

1959. Institution of Pirivena Universities.
468 **119** 10c. orange and blue 10 10

120 "Uprooted Tree"

121 S. W. R. D. Bandaranaike

1960. World Refugee Year.
469 **120** 4c. brown and gold 10 85
470 25c. violet and gold 10 15

1961. Prime Minister Bandaranaike Commemoration.
471 **121** 10c. blue and turquoise 10 10
See also Nos. 479 and 481.

122 Ceylon Scout Badge

123 Campaign Emblem

1962. Golden Jubilee of Ceylon Boy Scouts Association.
472 **122** 35c. buff and blue 15 10

1962. Malaria Eradication.
473 **123** 25c. red and drab 10 10

124 De Havilland Leopard Moth and Hawker Siddeley Comet 4

1963. 25th Anniv of Airmail Services.
474 **124** 50c. black and blue 50 50

125 "Produce" and Campaign Emblem

(126)

1963. Freedom from Hunger.
475 **125** 5c. red and blue 75 2·00
476 25c. brown and olive 3·00 30

1963. No. 450 surch with T **126**.
477 2c. on 4c. purple and red 10 10

127 "Rural Life"

131 Anagarika Dharmapala (Buddhist missionary)

129 Terrain, Indian Elephant and Tree

1963. Golden Jubilee of Ceylon Co-operative Movement (1962).
478 **127** 60c. red and black . . . . 2·00 50

1963. Design as T **121**, but smaller (21 × 26 mm) and with inscription rearranged at top.
479 10c. blue 10 10
481 10c. violet and grey 10 10
No. 481 has a decorative pattern at foot instead of the inscription.

1963. National Conservation Week.
480 **129** 5c. sepia and blue 60 40

1964. Birth Centenary of A. Dharmapala (founder of Maha Bodhi Society).
482 **131** 25c. sepia and yellow . . 10 10

135 D. S. Senanayake

143 Ceylon Jungle Fowl

138 Ruins at Madirigiriya

1964.
485 – 5c. multicoloured . . . . 2·00 1·00
486 **135** 10c. green 80 10
487 – 10c. green 10 10
488 – 15c. multicoloured . . . . 3·00 30
489 **138** 20c. purple and buff . . . 20 25
494 **143** 60c. multicoloured . . . . 4·00 1·25
495 – 75c. multicoloured . . . . 2·75 70
497 – 1r. brown and green . . . 1·00 30
499 – 5r. multicoloured . . . . 6·00 6·50
500 – 10r. multicoloured . . . . 22·00 3·50
MS500a 148 × 174 mm. As Nos. 485, 488, 494 and 495 (imperf) . . . 7·00 14·00
DESIGNS—HORIZ (As Type **143**): 5c. Southern grackle ("Grackle"); 15c. Common peafowl ("Peacock"); 75c. Asian black-headed oriole ("Oriole"). (As Type **138**): 5r. Girls transplanting rice. VERT (As Type **135**): 10c. (No. 487) Similar portrait, but large head and smaller inscriptions. (21 × 35 mm): 1r. Tea plantation. (23 × 36 mm): 10r. Map of Ceylon.

150 Exhibition Buildings and Cogwheels

1964. Industrial Exhibition.
501 – 5c. multicoloured 10 75
502 **150** 5c. multicoloured 10 75
No. 501 is inscribed "INDUSTRIAL EXHIBITION" in Sinhala and Tamil, No. 502 in Sinhala and English.

151 Trains of 1864 and 1964

1964. Centenary of Ceylon Railways.
503 – 60c. blue, purple and green . . . . 2·75 40
504 **151** 60c. blue, purple and green . . . . 2·75 40
No. 503 is inscribed "RAILWAY CENTENARY" in Sinhala and Tamil, No. 504 in Sinhala and English.

152 ITU Emblem and Symbols

1965. Centenary of ITU.
505 **152** 2c. blue and red . . . . 1·00 1·10
506 30c. brown and red . . . 3·00 45

153 ICY Emblem

1965. International Co-operation Year.
507 **153** 3c. blue and red . . . . 1·25 1·00
508 50c. black, red and gold 3·25 50

154 Town Hall, Colombo

1965. Centenary of Colombo Municipal Council.
509 **154** 25c. green and sepia . . . 20 20

1965. No. 481 surch **5**.
510 5c. on 10c. violet and grey . . 10 1·00

157 Kandy and Council Crest

1966. Centenary of Kandy Municipal Council.
512 **157** 25c. multicoloured 20 20

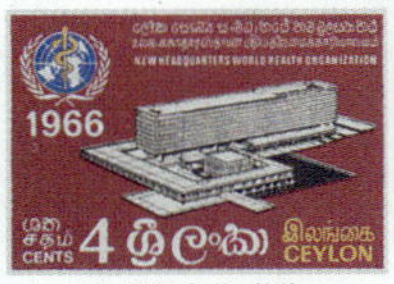
158 WHO Building

159 Rice Paddy and Map of Ceylon

1966. Inauguration of WHO Headquarters, Geneva.
513 **158** 4c. multicoloured . . . . 1·75 3·00
514 1r. multicoloured . . . . 6·75 1·50

1966. International Rice Year. Multicoloured.
515 6c. Type **159** 20 75
516 30c. Rice paddy and globe 30 15

161 UNESCO Emblem

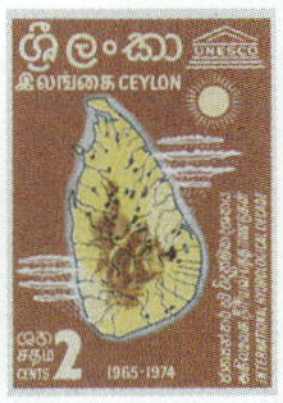
162 Water-resources Map

1966. 20th Anniv of UNESCO.
517 **161** 3c. multicoloured . . . . 2·75 3·75
518 50c. multicoloured . . . . 8·00 50

1966. International Hydrological Decade.
519 **162** 2c. brown, yellow and blue 30 85
520 2r. multicoloured . . . . 1·50 2·25

163 Devotees at Buddhist Temple

1967. Poya Holiday System. Multicoloured.
521 5c. Type **163** 15 60
522 20c. Mihintale 15 10
523 35c. Sacred Bo-tree, Anuradhapura 15 15
524 60c. Adam's Peak 15 10

167 Galle Fort and Clock Tower

1967. Centenary of Galle Municipal Council.
525 **167** 25c. multicoloured 70 20

168 Field Research

1967. Centenary of Ceylon Tea Industry. Mult.
526 4c. Type **168** 60 80
527 40c. Tea-tasting equipment 1·75 1·50
528 50c. Leaves and bud . . . . 1·75 20
529 1r. Shipping tea . . . . . . 1·75 10

169 Elephant Ride

1967. International Tourist Year.
530 **169** 45c. multicoloured . . . . 2·25 80

1967. 1st National Stamp Exhibition. No. **MS**500a optd "**FIRST NATIONAL STAMP EXHIBITION 1967**".
MS531 148 × 174 mm. Nos. 485, 488, 494/5. Imperf . . . . 8·50 9·00

170 Ranger, Jubilee Emblem and Flag

1967. Golden Jubilee of Ceylon Girl Guides' Association.
532 **170** 3c. multicoloured 50 20
533 25c. multicoloured 75 10

171 Colonel Olcott and Buddhist Flag

1967. 60th Death Anniv of Colonel Olcott (theosophist).
534 **171** 15c. multicoloured 30 20

172 Independence Hall

174 Sir D. B. Jayatilleke

1968. 20th Anniv of Independence. Multicoloured.
535 5c. Type **172** 10 55
536 1r. Lion flag and sceptre . . 50 10

1968. Birth Centenary of Sir Baron Jayatilleke (scholar and statesman).
537 **174** 25c. brown 10 10

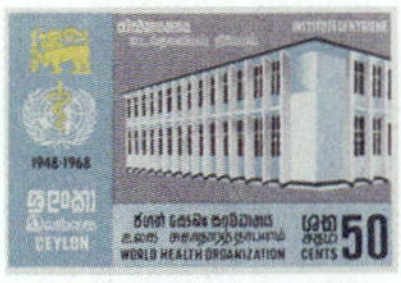
175 Institute of Hygiene

1968. 20th Anniv of World Health Organization.
538 **175** 50c. multicoloured 10 10

176 Vickers Super VC-10 over Terminal Building

1968. Opening of Colombo Airport.
539 **176** 60c. multicoloured . . . . 1·00 10

177 Open Koran and "1400"

1968. 1400th Anniv of Koran.
541 **177** 25c. multicoloured 10 10

178 Human Rights Emblem

1968. Human Rights Year.
542 **178** 2c. multicoloured 10 15
543 20c. multicoloured 10 10
544 40c. multicoloured 10 10
545 2r. multicoloured . . . . 70 4·00

179 All-Ceylon Buddhist Congress Headquarters

1968. Golden Jubilee of All-Ceylon Buddhist Congress.
546 **179** 5c. multicoloured 10 50

180 E. W. Perera (patriot)

181 Symbols of Strength in Savings

1969. Perera Commemoration.
547 **180** 60c. brown 10 30

1969. Silver Jubilee of National Savings Movement.
548 **181** 3c. multicoloured 10 30

182 Seat of Enlightenment under Sacred Bodhi Tree

184 A. E. Goonesinghe

1969. Vesak Day. Inscr "Wesak".
549 **182** 4c. multicoloured 10 50
550 – 6c. multicoloured 10 50
551 **182** 35c. multicoloured 10 10
DESIGN: 6c. Buduresmala (six-fold Buddha-rays).

1969. Goonesinghe Commemoration.
552 **184** 15c. multicoloured 10 10

185 ILO Emblem

1969. 50th Anniv of ILO.

553	**185**	5c. black and blue	10	10
554		25c. black and red	10	10

186 Convocation Hall, University of Ceylon

188 Ath Pana (Elephant Lamp)

1969. Educational Centenary. Multicoloured.

555	4c. Type **186**	10	80
556	35c. Lamp of learning, globe and flags (horiz)	20	10
557	50c. Uranium atom	20	10
558	60c. Symbols of scientific education	30	10

1969. Archaeological Centenary. Multicoloured.

559	6c. Type **188**	25	1·50
560	1r. Rock fortress of Sigiriya	25	10

190 Leopard

1970. Wild Life Conservation. Multicoloured.

561	5c. Water buffalo	1·25	1·25
562	15c. Slender loris	2·00	75
563	50c. Spotted deer	1·40	1·25
564	1r. Type **190**	1·40	1·75

191 Emblem and Symbols

1970. Asian Productivity Year.

565	**191**	60c. multicoloured	10	10

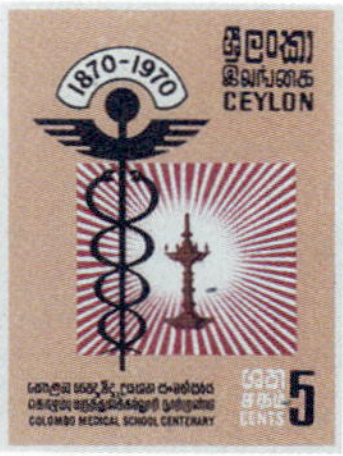

192 New UPU HQ Building

193 Oil Lamp and Caduceus

1970. New UPU Headquarters Building.

566	**192**	50c. orange, black and blue	50	10
567		1r.10 red, black and blue	4·50	40

1970. Centenary of Colombo Medical School.

568	**193**	5c. multicoloured	1·25	80
569		45c. multicoloured	1·50	60

194 Victory March and S. W. R. D. Bandaranaike

1970. Establishment of United Front Government.

570	**194**	10c. multicoloured	10	10

195 U.N. Emblem and Dove of Peace

196 Keppetipola Dissawa

1970. 25th Anniv of United Nations.

571	**195**	2r. multicoloured	2·00	3·50

1970. 152nd Death Anniv of Keppetipola Dissawa (Kandyan patriot).

572	**196**	25c. multicoloured	10	10

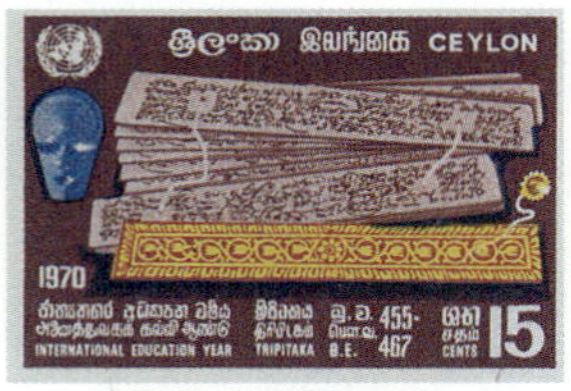

197 Ola Leaf Manuscript

1970. International Education Year.

573	**197**	15c. multicoloured	2·75	1·25

198 C. H. de Soysa

199 D. E. H. Pedris (patriot)

1971. 135th Birth Anniv of C. H. de Soysa (philanthropist).

574	**198**	20c. multicoloured	15	50

1971. D. E. H. Pedris Commemoration.

575	**199**	25c. multicoloured	15	50

200 Lenin

201 Ananda Rajakaruna

1971. Lenin Commemoration.

576	**200**	40c. multicoloured	15	50

1971. Poets and Philosophers.

577	**201**	5c. blue	10	15
578	–	5c. brown	10	15
579	–	5c. orange	10	15
580	–	5c. blue	10	15
581	–	5c. brown	10	15

PORTRAITS: No. 578, Arumuga Navalar; 579, Rev. S. Mahinda; 580, Ananda Coomaraswamy; 581, Cumaratunga Munidasa.

1971. Surch in figures.

582	**182**	5c. on 4c. multicoloured	6·50	1·75
583	**186**	5c. on 4c. multicoloured	10	1·25
584	**194**	15c. on 10c. multicoloured	10	30
585	–	25c. on 6c. mult (No. 550)	30	60
586	**188**	25c. on 6c. multicoloured	30	2·25

203 Colombo Plan Emblem and Ceylon

1971. 20th Anniv of Colombo Plan.

587	**203**	20c. multicoloured	15	30

204 Globe and CARE Package

1971. 20th Anniv of Co-operative for American Relief Everywhere.

588	**204**	50c. blue, violet and lilac	35	30

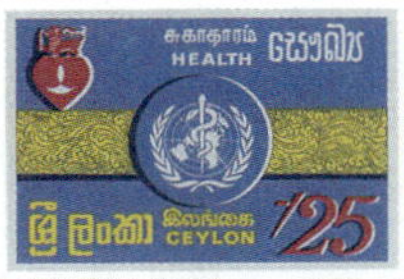

205 WHO Emblem and Heart

1972. World Health Day.

589	**205**	25c. multicoloured	2·50	60

206 Map of Asia and U.N. Emblem

1972. 25th Anniv of ECAFE.

590	**206**	85c. multicoloured	4·75	2·75

OFFICIAL STAMPS

1895. Stamps of Queen Victoria optd **On Service**.

O11	**9**	2c. green	12·00	60
O18		2c. brown	9·00	60
O12	**39**	3c. brown and green	10·00	1·50
O19		3c. green	10·00	3·50
O13	**28**	5c. purple	4·00	30
O14	**39**	15c. olive	16·00	50
O20		15c. blue	20·00	60
O15		25c. brown	11·00	2·00
O16		30c. mauve and brown	13·00	60
O21		75c. black and brown	6·00	7·00
O17	**30**	1r.12 red	90·00	60·00

1903. Stamps of King Edward VII optd **On Service**.

O22	**44**	2c. brown	16·00	1·00
O23	**45**	3c. green	10·00	2·00
O24	–	5c. purple (No. 268)	23·00	1·50
O25	**45**	15c. blue	32·00	2·50
O26		25c. brown	26·00	18·00
O27		30c. violet and green	15·00	1·50

For later issues see **SRI LANKA**.

CHAD — Pt. 6, Pt. 12

Formerly a dependency of Ubangi-Shari. Became one of the separate colonies of Fr. Equatorial Africa in 1937. In 1958 became a republic within the French Community.

100 centimes = 1 franc.

1922. Stamps of Middle Congo, colours changed, optd **TCHAD**.

1	**1**	1c. pink and violet	50	4·50
2		2c. brown and pink	1·30	4·50
3		4c. blue and violet	1·80	5·00
4		5c. brown and green	2·50	5·25
5		10c. green and turquoise	4·25	6·00
6		15c. violet and pink	4·00	6·50
7		20c. green and violet	8·00	12·50
8	**2**	25c. brown and chocolate	9·50	23·00
9		30c. red	2·75	5·50
10		35c. blue and pink	3·00	7·25
11		40c. brown and green	3·00	7·75
12		45c. violet and green	3·50	7·75
13		50c. blue and light blue	2·00	7·50
14		60 on 75c. violet on pink	4·50	11·00
15		75c. pink and violet	4·00	7·25
16	**3**	1f. blue and pink	17·00	27·00
17		2f. blue and violet	22·00	40·00
18		5f. blue and brown	18·00	36·00

1924. Stamps of 1922 and similar stamps further optd **AFRIQUE EQUATORIALE FRANCAISE**.

19	**1**	1c. pink and violet	25	4·00
20		2c. brown and pink	10	4·25
21		4c. blue and violet	60	4·50
22		5c. brown and green	60	4·25
23		10c. green and turquoise	2·30	5·00
24		10c. red and grey	1·00	4·50
25		15c. violet and red	95	4·50
26		20c. green and violet	1·80	4·75
27	**2**	25c. brown and chocolate	1·80	4·75
28		30c. red	1·10	4·75
29		30c. grey and blue	85	4·00
30		30c. olive and green	1·90	5·50
31		35c. blue and pink	95	4·75
32		40c. brown and green	2·00	4·50
33		45c. violet and green	1·70	5·25
34		50c. blue and light blue	85	4·75
35		50c. green and purple	2·30	2·00
36		60 on 75c. violet on pink	55	4·75
37		65c. brown and blue	3·00	7·00
38		75c. pink and violet	1·30	4·25
39		75c. blue and light blue	2·00	4·25
40		75c. purple and brown	3·25	6·75
41		90c. carmine and red	4·25	17·00
42	**3**	1f. blue and pink	2·75	4·00
43		1f.10 green and blue	2·75	7·25
44		1f.25 brown and blue	10·50	20·00
45		1f.50 ultramarine and blue	4·25	20·00
46		1f.75 brown and mauve	48·00	80·00
47		2f. blue and violet	3·00	4·00
48		3f. mauve on pink	6·50	26·00
49		5f. blue and brown	3·50	6·75

1925. Stamps of Middle Congo optd **TCHAD** and **AFRIQUE EQUATORIALE FRANCAISE** and surch also.

50	**3**	65 on 1f. brown and green	2·00	5·75
51		85 on 1f. brown and green	5·25	5·75
52	**2**	90 on 75c. red and pink	2·50	6·00
53	**3**	1f.25 on 1f. blue & ultram	1·30	4·25
54		1f.50 on 1f. blue & ultram	2·75	6·00
55		3f. on 5f. brown and red	5·00	11·00
56		10f. on 5f. green and red	13·00	24·00
57a		20f. on 5f. violet & orange	40·00	55·00

1931. "Colonial Exhibition" key-types inscr "TCHAD".

58	E	40c. green	3·50	12·00
59	F	50c. mauve	4·00	11·50
60	G	90c. red	3·00	9·25
61	H	1f.50 blue	6·00	10·50

2 "Birth of the Republic"

3 Flag, Map and U.N. Emblem

1959. Ist Anniv of Republic.

62	**2**	15f. multicoloured	3·50	2·75
63	–	25f. lake and myrtle	65	45

DESIGN: 25f. Map and birds.

1960. 10th African Technical Co-operation Commission. As T **62** of Cameroun.

64	50f. violet and purple	1·90	3·25

1960. Air. Olympic Games. No. 276 of French Equatorial Africa surch with Olympic rings and **XVIIe OLYMPIADE 1960 REPUBLIQUE DU TCHAD 250F**.

65	250f. on 500f. blue, black & grn	9·50	9·50

1961. Admission into U.N.

66	**3**	15f. multicoloured	45	20
67		25f. multicoloured	50	25
68		85f. multicoloured	1·60	80

4 Shari Bridge and Hippopotamus

1961.

69	–	50c. green and black	10	10
70	–	1f. green and black	10	10
71	–	2f. brown and black	10	10
72	–	3f. orange and green	10	10
73	–	4f. red and black	10	10
74	**4**	5f. lemon and black	20	15
75	–	10f. pink and black	20	20
76	–	15f. violet and black	45	20
77	–	20f. red and black	55	30
78	–	25f. blue and black	60	30
79	–	30f. blue and black	70	45
80	–	60f. yellow and black	1·40	65
81	–	85f. orange and black	1·60	95

DESIGNS (with animal silhouettes)—VERT: 50c. Biltine and Dorcas gazelle; 1f. Logone and elephant; 2f. Batha and lion; 3f. Salamat and buffalo; 4f. Ouaddai and greater kudu; 10f. Abtouyour and bullock; 15f. Bessada and Derby's eland; 20f. Tibesti and moufflon; 25f. Tikem Rocks and hartebeest; 30f. Kanem and cheetah; 60f. Borkou and oryx; 85f. Guelta D'Archei and addax.

5 Red Bishops

1961. Air.

82	**5**	50f. black, red and green	3·00	1·10
83	–	100f. multicoloured	6·75	2·00
84	–	200f. multicoloured	12·00	3·75
85	–	250f. blue, orange and green	15·00	5·25
86	–	500f. multicoloured	30·00	11·00

BIRDS: 100f. Scarlet-chested sunbird; 200f. African paradise flycatcher; 250f. Malachite kingfisher; 500f. Carmine bee eater.

1962. Air. "Air Afrique" Airline. As T **69** of Cameroun.
87 25f. blue, brown and black . . 60 25

1962. Malaria Eradication. As T **70** of Cameroun.
88 25f.+5f. orange 75 75

1962. Sports. As T **12** of Central African Republic. Multicoloured.
89 20f. Relay-racing (horiz) (postage) 45 30
90 50f. High-jumping (horiz) . . 1·10 55
91 100f. Throwing the discus (air) 2·50 1·25
The 100f. is 26 × 47 mm.

1962. 1st Anniv of Union of African and Malagasy States. As No. 328 of Cameroun.
92 **72** 30f. blue 70 40

1963. Freedom from Hunger. As T **76** of Cameroun.
93 25f.+5f. blue, brown & green 80 80

6 Pres. Tombalbaye

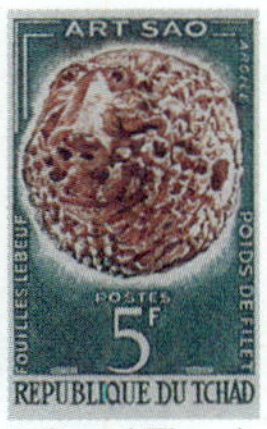

7 Carved Thread-weight

1963.
94 **6** 20f. multicoloured 45 20
95 85f. multicoloured . . . . . 1·10 55

1963. Air. African and Malagasy Posts and Telecommunications Union. As T **11** of Central African Republic.
96 85f. multicoloured . . . . . . 1·25 55

1963. Space Telecommunications. As Nos. 37/8 of Central African Republic.
97 25f. violet, emerald and green 50 35
98 100f. blue and pink . . . . . 2·00 1·25

1963. Air. 1st Anniv of "Air Afrique" and Inauguration of "DC-8" Service. As T **11** of Congo Republic.
99 50f. multicoloured . . . . . . 1·50 75

1963. Air. European–African Economic Convention. As T **24** of Central African Republic.
100 50f. multicoloured . . . . . 1·00 60

1963. Sao Art.
101 **7** 5f. orange and turquoise . . 10 10
102 – 15f. purple, slate and red . . 30 25
103 – 25f. brown and blue 60 35
104 – 60f. bronze and brown . . . 1·40 60
105 – 80f. bronze and brown . . . 1·60 80
DESIGNS: 15f. Ancestral mask; 25f. Ancestral statuette; 60f. Gazelle's-head pendant; 80f. Pectoral.

1963. 15th Anniv of Declaration of Human Rights. As Central African Republic T **26**.
106 25f. purple and green 65 35

8 Broussard Monoplane

1963. Air.
107 **8** 100f. blue, green & brown 2·25 1·25

9 Pottery

1964. Sao Handicrafts.
108 **9** 10f. black, orange & blue 30 20
109 – 30f. red, black and yellow 55 30
110 – 50f. black, red and green . . 1·00 45
111 – 85f. black, yellow & purple 1·25 65
DESIGNS: 30f. Canoe-building; 50f. Carpet-weaving; 85f. Blacksmith working iron.

10 Rameses II in War Chariot, Abu Simbel

1964. Air. Nubian Monuments Preservation Fund.
112 **10** 10f.+5f. violet, grn & red 60 35
113 25f.+5f. purple, grn & red 95 50
114 50f.+5f. turq, grn & red . . 1·90 1·40

1964. World Meteorological Day. As T **14** of Congo Republic.
115 50f. violet, blue and purple 1·00 50

11 Cotton

1964. Multicoloured.
116 20f. Type **11** 95 50
117 25f. Flamboyant tree . . . . 1·10 55

1964. Air. 5th Anniv of Equatorial African Heads of State Conf. As T **31** of Central African Republic.
118 100f. multicoloured . . . . . 1·50 75

12 Globe, Chimneys and Ears of Wheat

1964. Air. Europafrique.
119 **12** 50f. orange, purple & brn 1·00 55

13 Football

1964. Air. Olympic Games. Tokyo.
120 **13** 25f. green, lt green & brn 75 45
121 – 50f. brown, indigo & blue 1·00 55
122 – 100f. black, green and red 2·00 1·10
123 – 200f. black, bistre and red 4·25 2·10
MS123a 191 × 100 mm. Nos. 120/3 6·25 3·25
DESIGNS—VERT: 50f. Throwing the javelin; 100f. High-jumping. HORIZ: 200f. Running.

1964. Air. Pan-African and Malagasy Post and Telecommunications Congress, Cairo. As T **23** of Congo Republic.
124 25f. sepia, red and mauve . . 60 25

1964. French, African and Malagasy Co-operation. As T **88** of Cameroun.
125 25f. brown, blue and red . . 60 30

14 Pres. Kennedy

15 National Guard

1964. Air. Pres. Kennedy Commem.
126 **14** 100f. multicoloured . . . . 1·75 1·10
MS126a 90 × 129 mm. No. 126 (× 4) 2·40 1·20

1964. Chad Army. Multicoloured.
127 20f. Type **15** 50 20
128 25f. Standard-bearer and troops of Land Forces . . 55 25

16 Barbary Sheep

1964. Fauna. Protection. Multicoloured.
129 5f. Type **16** 25 15
130 10f. Addax 35 20
131 20f. Scimitar oryx 65 30
132 25f. Giant eland (vert) . . . 95 35
133 30f. Giraffe, African buffalo and lion (Zakouma Park)(vert) . . . . . . 1·25 50
134 85f. Greater kudu (vert) . . . 3·00 1·10

17 Perforator of Olsen's Telegraph Apparatus

1965. I.T.U. Centenary.
135 **17** 30f. brown, red and green 55 25
136 – 60f. green, red and brown 1·00 45
137 – 100f. green, brown & red 1·90 80
DESIGNS—VERT: 60f. Milde's telephone. HORIZ: 100f. Distributor of Baudot's telegraph apparatus.

18 Badge and Mobile Gendarmes

1965. National Gendarmerie.
138 **18** 25f. multicoloured 60 35

19 ICY Emblem

1965. Air. International Co-operation Year.
139 **19** 100f. multicoloured . . . . 1·25 70

20 Abraham Lincoln

1965. Air. Death Centenary of Abraham Lincoln.
140 **20** 100f. multicoloured . . . . 1·75 75

21 Guitar

1965. Native Musical Instruments.
141 – 1f. brown & grn (postage) 10 10
142 **21** 2f. brown, purple and red 10 10
143 – 3f. lake, black and brown 20 15
144 – 15f. green, orange and red 50 25
145 – 60f. green and lake . . . . 1·60 80
146 – 100f. ultram, brn & bl (48½ × 27 mm) (air) . . . . . 1·90 1·25
DESIGNS—VERT: 1f. Drum and seat; 3f. Shoulder drum; 60f. Harp. HORIZ: 15f. Viol; 100f. Xylophone.

22 Sir Winston Churchill

1965. Air. Churchill Commemoration.
147 **22** 50f. black and green . . . 1·00 50

23 Dr. Albert Schweitzer (philosopher and missionary) and "Appealing Hands"

1966. Air. Schweitzer Commemoration.
148 **23** 100f. multicoloured . . . . 1·90 95

24 Mask in Mortar

26 WHO Building

1966. World Festival of Negro Arts, Dakar.
149 **24** 15f. purple, bistre & blue 35 20
150 – 20f. brown, red and green 50 25
151 – 60f. purple, blue and red 1·40 55
152 – 80f. green, brown & violet 2·10 85
DESIGNS—Sao Art: 20f. Mask; 60f. Mask (different) (All from J. Courtin's excavations at Bouta Kebira); 80f. Armband (from INTSH excavations, Gawi).

1966. No. 94 surch.
153 **6** 25f. on 20f. multicoloured 60 30

1966. Inaug of WHO Headquarters, Geneva.
154 **26** 25f. blue, yellow and red 45 20
155 32f. blue, yellow & green 50 25

27 Caduceus and Map of Africa

28 Footballer

1966. Central African Customs and Economic Union.
156 **27** 30f. multicoloured 60 30

1966. World Cup Football Championship.
157 **28** 30f. red, green and emerald 50 25
158 – 60f. red, black and blue . . 1·25 50
DESIGN—VERT: 60f. Footballer (different).

29 Youths, Flag and Arms

1966. Youth Movement.
159 **29** 25f. multicoloured 60 30

30 Columns

31 Skull of Lake Chad Man ("Tchadanthropus uxoris")

1966. 20th Anniv of UNESCO.
160 **30** 32f. blue, violet and red . . 65 50

1966. Air. Inauguration of "DC-8" Air Services. As T **54** of Central African Republic.
161 30f. grey, black and green . . 60 25

1966. Archaeological Excavation.
162 **31** 30f. slate, yellow and red 1·60 75

32 White-throated Bee Eater

1966. Air. Birds. Multicoloured.

163	50f. Greater blue-eared glossy starling	3·50	1·40
164	100f. Type **32**	4·50	2·40
165	200f. African pigmy kingfisher	8·50	2·50
166	250f. Red-throated bee eater	12·50	3·25
167	500f. Little green bee eater	18·00	7·00

33 Battle-axe

35 Sportsmen and Dais on Map

34 Congress Palace

1966. Prehistoric Implements.

168	**33**	25f. brown, blue and red	35	25
169	–	30f. black, brown & blue	45	25
170	–	85f. brown, red and blue	1·50	60
171	–	100f. brown, turq & sepia	1·75	85
MS172		129 × 99 mm. Nos. 168/71	4·00	2·00

DESIGNS: 30f. Arrowhead; 85f. Harpoon; 100f. Sandstone grindstone and pounder. From Tchad National Museum.

1967. Air.

173 **34** 25f. multicoloured 55 25

1967. Sports Day.

174 **35** 25f. multicoloured 60 35

36 "Colotis protomedia klug"

1967. Butterflies. Multicoloured.

175	5f. Type **36**	20	15
176	10f. "Charaxes jasius epijasius L"	35	20
177	20f. "Junonia cebrene trim"	1·00	50
178	130f. "Danaida petiverana H.D."	3·25	1·40

37 Lions Emblem

39 H.Q. Building

38 Dagnaux's Breguet "19" Aircraft

1967. Air. 50th Anniv of Lions International.

179 **37** 50f.+10f. multicoloured . . 1·25 65

1967. Air. 1st Anniv of Air Chad Airline.

180	**38**	25f. green, blue & brown	55	40
181	–	30f. indigo, green and blue	75	40
182	–	50f. brown, green & blue	1·25	75
183	–	100f. red, blue and green	2·50	1·10

DESIGNS: 30f. Latecoere "631" flying-boat; 50f. Douglas "DC-3"; 100f. Piper Cherokee "6".

1967. Air. 5th Anniv of UAMPT. As T **66** of Central African Republic.

184 100f. brown, bistre & mve . . 1·25 75

1967. Opening of WHO Regional Headquarters, Brazzaville.

185 **39** 30f. multicoloured 60 30

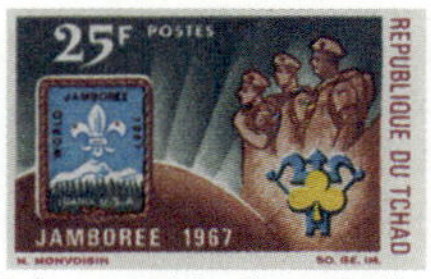

40 Scouts and Jamboree Emblem

1967. World Scout Jamboree, Idaho. Multicoloured.

186	25f. Type **40**	45	20
187	32f. Scout and Jamboree emblem	65	25

41 Flour Mills

1967. Economic Development.

188	**41**	25f. slate, brown and blue	45	20
189	–	30f. blue, brown & green	55	30

DESIGN: 30f. Land reclamation, Lake Bol.

42 Woman and Harpist

43 Emblem of Rotary International

1967. Bailloud Mission in the Ennedi. Rock paintings.

190	–	2f. choc, brn & red (post)	20	15
191	–	10f. red, brown and violet	45	25
192	**42**	15f. lake, brown and blue	55	25
193	–	20f. red, brown and green	1·25	50
194	–	25f. red, brown and blue	1·60	60
195	–	30f. lake, brown and blue	1·00	50
196	–	50f. lake, brown and green	1·90	80
197	–	100f. red, brn & grn (air)	3·00	1·40
198	–	125f. lake, brown & blue	4·25	2·10

DESIGNS: 2f. Archers; 10f. Male and female costumes; 20f. Funeral vigil; 25f. "Dispute"; 30f. Giraffes; 50f. Cameleer pursuing ostrich. (48 × 27 mm): 100f. Masked dancers; 125f. Hunters and hare.

1968. 10th Anniv of Rotary Club, Fort Lamy.

199 **43** 50f. multicoloured 95 45

44 Downhill Skiing

1968. Air. Winter Olympic Games, Grenoble.

200	**44**	30f. brown, green & purple	95	35
201	–	100f. blue, green & turq	2·50	1·10

DESIGN—VERT: 100f. Ski-jumping.

45 Chancellor Adenauer

46 "Health Services"

1968. Air. Adenauer Commemoration.

202	**45**	52f. brown, lilac and green	1·00	50
MS203		120 × 170 mm. No. 202 × 4	4·00	2·00

1968. Air. Anniv of WHO.

204	**46**	25f. multicoloured	45	20
205		32f. multicoloured	55	25

47 Allegory of Irrigation

1968. International Hydrological Decade.

206 **47** 50f. blue, brown & green 75 30

48 "The Snake-charmer"

1968. Air. Paintings by Henri Rousseau. Mult.

207	100f. Type **48**	2·50	1·60
208	130f. "The War" (49 × 35 mm)	3·75	2·25

49 College Building, Student and Emblem

1968. National College of Administration.

209 **49** 25f. purple, blue and red 45 25

50 Child writing and Blackboard

52 "Utetheisa pulchella"

51 Harvesting Cotton

1968. Literacy Day.

210 **50** 60f. black, blue & brown 80 35

1968. Cotton Industry.

211	**51**	25f. purple, green & blue	50	20
212	–	30f. brown, blue & green	50	20

DESIGN—VERT: 30f. Loom, Fort Archambault Mill.

1968. Butterflies and Moths. Multicoloured.

213	25f. Type **52**	1·10	35
214	30f. "Ophideres materna"	1·40	35
215	50f. "Gynanisa maja"	2·75	70
216	100f. "Epiphora bauhiniae"	3·75	1·25

53 Hurdling

1968. Air. Olympic Games, Mexico.

217	**53**	32f. chocolate, grn & brn	80	50
218	–	80f. purple, blue and red	1·75	75

DESIGN: 80f. Relay-racing.

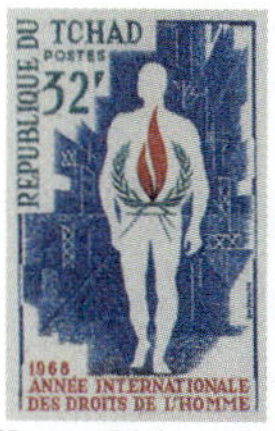

54 Human Rights Emblem within Man

1968. Human Rights Year.

219 **54** 32f. red, green and blue . . 60 25

1969. Air. "Philexafrique" Stamp Exn, Abidjan, Ivory Coast (1st issue). As T **137** of Cameroun. Multicoloured.

220 100f. "The actor Wolf, called Bernard" (J. L. David) . . 2·75 2·75

1969. Air. "Philexafrique" Stamp Exn, Abidjan, Ivory Coast (2nd issue). As T **138** of Cameroun. Multicoloured.

221 50f. Moundangs dancers and Chad postage due stamp of 1930 . . . . 1·90 1·90

55 G. Nachtigal and Tibesti landscape, 1869

1969. Air. Chad Explorers.

222	–	100f. violet, green & blue	1·75	75
223	**55**	100f. purple, blue & brown	1·75	75

DESIGN: No. 222, H. Barth (portrait) and aboard canoe, Lake Region, 1851.

56 "Apollo 8" circling Moon

1969. Air. Flight of "Apollo 8" around the Moon.

224 **56** 100f. black, blue & orange 1·75 75

57 St. Bartholomew

1969. Jubilee Year of Catholic Church. Mult.

225	50c. St. Paul	10	10
226	1f. St. Peter	10	10
227	2f. St. Thomas	10	10
228	5f. St. John the Evangelist	10	10
229	10f. Type **57**	10	10
230	20f. St. Matthew	25	15
231	25f. St. James the Less	25	15
232	30f. St. Andrew	30	20
233	40f. St. Jude	35	20
234	50f. St. James the Greater	45	25
235	85f. St. Philip	70	45
236	100f. St. Simon	80	55

58 Mahatma Gandhi

59 Motor Vehicles and ILO Emblem

1969. Air. "Apostles of Peace".

237	**58**	50f. brown and green	95	45
238	–	50f. sepia and agate	95	45
239	–	50f. brown and pink	95	45
240	–	50f. brown and blue	95	45
MS241		120 × 160 mm. Nos. 237/40	3·75	1·75

DESIGNS: No. 238, President Kennedy; No. 239, Martin Luther King; No. 240, Robert F. Kennedy.

1969. 50th Anniv of ILO.

242 **59** 32f. blue, purple & green 60 30

60 Cipolla, Baran and Sambo (pair with cox)

61 "African Woman" (Bezombes)

1969. "World Solidarity". Multicoloured. (a) Gold Medal Winners, Mexico Olympics.

243 1f. Type **60** 25 25
244 1f. R. Beamon (long-jump) 25 25
245 1f. I. Becker (women's pentathlon) 25 25
246 1f. C. Besson (women's 400 m) 25 25
247 1f. W. Davenport (110 m hurdles) 25 25
248 1f. K. Dibiasi (diving) . . . 25 25
249 1f. R. Fosbury (high-jump) 25 25
250 1f. M. Gamoudi (5000 m) . . 25 25
251 1f. Great Britain (sailing) . . 25 25
252 1f. J. Guyon (cross-country riding) 25 25
253 1f. D. Hemery (400 m hurdles) 25 25
254 1f. S. Kato (gymnastics) . . . 25 25
255 1f. B. Klinger (small bore rifle shooting) 25 25
256 1f. R. Matson (shot put) . . 25 25
257 1f. R. Matthes (100 m backstroke) 25 25
258 1f. D. Meyer (women's 200 m freestyle) 25 25
259 1f. Morelon and Trentin (tandem cycle) 25 25
260 1f. D. Rebillard (4000 m cycle pursuit) . . 25 25
261 1f. T. Smith (200 m) 25 25
262 1f. P. Trentin (1000 m cycle) 25 25
263 1f. F. Vianelli (196 km cycle race) 25 25
264 1f. West Germany (dressage) 25 25
265 1f. M. Wolke (welterweight boxing) 25 25
266 1f. Zimmermann and Esser (women's kayak pair) . . . 25 25

(b) Paintings.

267 1f. Type **61** 25 25
268 1f. "Mother and Child" (Gauguin) 25 25
269 1f. "Holy Family" (Murillo) (horiz) 25 25
270 1f. "Adoration of the Kings" (Rubens) 25 25
271 1f. "Three Negroes" (Rubens) 25 25
272 1f. "Woman with Flowers" (Veneto) 25 25

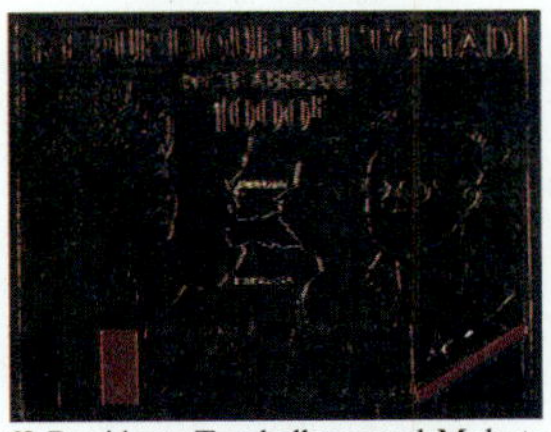
62 Presidents Tombalbaye and Mobutu

1969. Air. 1st Anniv of Central African States Union.
273 **62** 1000f. gold, red and blue 20·00 20·00
This stamp is embossed in gold foil; colours of flags enamelled.

63 "Cochlospermum tinctorium"

1969. Flowers. Multicoloured.
274 1f. Type **63** 10 10
275 4f. "Parkia biglobosa" 20 15
276 10f. "Pancratium trianthum" 30 20
277 15f. "Ipomoea aquatica" . . 45 20

1969. Air. Birth Bicentenary of Napoleon Bonaparte. Multicoloured. As T **144** of Cameroun.
278 30f. "Napoleon visiting the Hotel des Invalides" (Veron-Bellecourt) 95 50
279 85f. "The Battle of Wagram" (H. Vernet) . . . . 1·90 1·00
280 130f. "The Battle of Austerlitz" (Gerard) . . . 3·50 1·90

64 Frozen Carcases

1969. Frozen Meat Industry.
281 **64** 25f. red, green and orange 35 20
282 – 30f. brown, slate & green 50 25
DESIGN: 30f. Cattle and refrigerated abattoir, Farcha.

1969. 5th Anniv of African Development Bank. As T **146** of Cameroun.
283 30f. brown, green and red . . 45 25

66 Astronaut and Lunar Module

1969. Air. 1st Man on the Moon. Embossed on gold foil.
289 **66** 1000f. gold . . . . 22·00 22·00

67 Nile Mouthbrooder

68 President Tombalbaye

1969. Fishes.
290 **67** 2f. purple, grey and green 20 10
291 – 3f. grey, red and blue . . . 30 25
292 – 5f. blue, yellow and ochre 55 25
293 – 20f. blue, green and red . . 1·75 60
FISHES: 3f. Deep-sided citharinid; 5f. Nile pufferfish; 20f. Lesser tigerfish.

1969. 10th Anniv of ASECNA. As T **150** of Cameroun.
294 30f. orange 55 30

1970. President Tombalbaye.
295 **68** 25f. multicoloured 45 20

69 "Village Life" (G. Narcisse)

1970. Air. African Paintings. Multicoloured.
296 100f. Type **69** . . . . 2·10 1·00
297 250f. "Market Woman" (I. N'Diaye) . . . . 4·00 1·60
298 250f. "Flower-seller" (I. N'Diaye) (vert) . . . . 4·00 1·60

70 Lenin

72 Osaka Print

71 Class and Torchbearers

1970. Birth Centenary of Lenin.
299 **70** 150f. black, cream & gold 2·50 1·25

1970. New U.P.U. Headquarters Building, Berne, As T **156** of Cameroun.
300 30f. brown, violet and red . . 55 30

1970. International Education Year.
301 **71** 100f. multicoloured . . . . 1·50 80

1970. Air. World Fair "EXPO 70", Osaka, Japan.
302 **72** 50f. green, blue and red . . 45 30
303 – 100f. blue, green and red 75 45
304 – 125f. slate. brown & red 1·00 55
DESIGNS: 100f. Tower of the Sun; 125f. Osaka print (different).

1970. Air. "Apollo" Moon Flights. Nos. 164/6 surch with new value, and optd with various inscriptions and diagrams concerning space flights.
305 **32** 50f. on 100f. mult ("Apollo 11") . . . . . 1·50 1·00
306 – 100f. on 200f. mult ("Apollo 12") . . . . . 2·75 1·40
307 – 125f. on 250f. mult ("Apollo 13") . . . . . 4·25 2·25

74 Meteorological Equipment and "Agriculture"

76 Ahmed Mangue (Minister of Education)

75 "DC-8-63" over Airport

1970. World Meteorological Day.
308 **74** 50f. grey, green & orange 75 30

1970. Air. "Air Afrique" DC-8 "Fort Lamy".
309 **75** 30f. multicoloured 75 35

1970. Ahmed Mangue (air crash victim) Commem.
310 **76** 100f. black, red and gold 1·10 50

77 Tanning

1970. Trades and Handicrafts.
311 **77** 1f. bistre, brown and blue 10 10
312 – 2f. brown, blue and green 15 10
313 – 3f. violet, brown & mauve 20 15
314 – 4f. brown, bistre & green 25 15
315 – 5f. brown, green and red 35 35
DESIGNS—VERT: 2f. Dyeing; 4f. Water-carrying. HORIZ: 3f. Milling palm-nuts for oil; 5f. Copper-founding.

78 U.N. Emblem and Dove

79 "The Visitation" (Venetian School, 15th cent)

1970. 25th Anniv of United Nations.
316 **78** 32f. multicoloured 60 35

1970. Air. Christmas. Multicoloured.
317 20f. Type **79** 50 30
318 25f. "The Nativity" (Venetian School, 15th cent) 75 35
319 30f. "Virgin and Child" (Veneziano) 95 45

80 Map and OCAM Building

1971. OCAM (Organization Commune Africaine et Malgache) Conference, Fort Lamy.
320 **80** 30f. multicoloured 60 30

81 Maritius "Post Office" 2d. of 1847

1971. Air. "PHILEXOCAM" Stamp Exhibition, Fort-Lamy.
321 **81** 10f. slate, brown & turq . . 30 20
322 – 20f. brown, black & turq 45 20
323 – 30f. brown, black and red 55 30
324 – 60f. black, brown & purple 80 50
325 – 80f. slate, brown and blue 1·25 70
326 – 100f. brown, slate & blue 1·60 95
MS327 160 × 130 mm. Nos. 321/6 5·00 2·75
DESIGNS—20f. Tuscany 3 lire of 1860; 30f. France 1f. of 1849; 30f., 60f. U.S.A. 10c. of 1847; 80f. Japan 5 sen of 1872; 100f. Saxony 3pf. of 1850.

82 Pres. Nasser

83 "Racial Harmony" Tree

1971. Air. 1st Death Anniv of Gamal Abdel Nasser (Egypt).
328 **82** 75f. multicoloured 80 35

1971. Racial Equality Year.
329 **83** 40f. red, green and blue . . 75 30

1971. Air. Reconciliation with Central African Republic and Zaire. As T **106** of Central African Republic.
330 100f. multicoloured . . . . . 1·50 75

84 Map and Dish Aerial

1971. World Telecommunications Day.
331 **84** 5f. orge, red & bl (postage) 20 15
332 – 40f. green, brown & pur 55 25
333 – 50f. black, brown & red . . 75 30
334 – 125f. red, green & blue (air) . . . . 1·90 85
DESIGNS: 40f. Map and communications tower; 50f. Map and satellite. (48 × 27 mm): 125f. Map and telecommunications symbols.

85 Scouts by Camp-fire

1971. Air. World Scout Jamboree, Asagiri, Japan.
335 **85** 250f. multicoloured . . . . 3·75 1·90

86 Great Egret

1971. Air.
336 **86** 1000f. multicoloured 29·00 16·00

87 Ancient Marathon Race

1971. Air. 75th Anniv of Modern Olympic Games. Multicoloured.
337 40f. Type **87** 55 30
338 45f. Ancient stadium, Olympia 80 35
339 75f. Ancient wrestling 1·00 50
340 130f. Athens Stadium, 1896 Games 1·75 85

88 Sidney Bechet **89** Gen. de Gaulle

1971. Air. Famous American Black Musicians. Multicoloured.
341 50f. Type **88** 1·25 50
342 75f. Duke Ellington 1·60 75
343 100f. Louis Armstrong 2·50 1·25

1971. Air. 1st Death Anniv of De Gaulle.
344 – 200f. gold, blue and light blue 6·25 6·25
345 **89** 200f. gold, green & yellow 6·25 6·25
MS346 110 × 70 mm. Nos. 344/5 and central stamp-sized label with inscr 12·00 12·00
DESIGN: No. 344, Governor-General Felix Eboue.

1971. Air. 10th Anniv of African and Malagasy Posts and Telecommunications Union. As T **184** of Cameroun. Multicoloured.
347 100f. Headquarters building and Sao carved animal head 1·25 60

90 Children's Heads

1971. 25th Anniv of UNICEF.
348 **90** 50f. blue, green & purple 85 35
On the above stamp, "24e" has been obliterated and "25e" inserted in the commemorative inscription.

91 Gorane Nangara Dancers

1971. Chad Dancers. Multicoloured.
349 10f. Type **91** 30 20
350 15f. Yondo initiates 45 25
351 30f. M'Boum (vert) 80 35
352 40f. Sara Kaba (vert) 1·25 55

93 Presidents Pompidou and Tombalbaye

1972. Visit of French President.
354 **93** 40f. multicoloured 1·25 60

94 Bobsleighing

1972. Air. Winter Olympic Games, Sapporo, Japan.
355 **94** 50f. red and blue 70 40
356 – 100f. green and purple 1·50 60
DESIGN: 100f. Slalom.

95 Human Heart **96** "Gorrizia dubiosa"

1972. World Heart Month.
357 **95** 100f. red, blue and violet 1·50 75

1972. Insects. Multicoloured.
358 1f. Type **96** 10 10
359 2f. "Argiope sector" 20 15
360 3f. "Nephila senegalense" 25 15
361 4f. "Oryctes boas" 35 25
362 5f. "Hemistigma albipunctata" 45 25
363 25f. "Dinothrombium tinctorium" 45 30
364 30f. "Bupreste sternocera H." 50 30
365 40f. "Hyperechia bomboides" 60 35
366 50f. "Chrysis" (Hymenoptere) 95 50
367 100f. "Tithoes confinis" (Longicore) 2·50 85
368 130f. "Galeodes araba" (Solifuge) 3·75 1·40

1972. Air. UNESCO "Save Venice" Campaign. As T **191** of Cameroun. Multicoloured.
369 40f. "Harbour Panorama" (detail, Caffi) 95 50
370 45f. "Venice Panorama" (detail, Caffi) (horiz) 1·25 60
371 140f. "Grand Canal" (detail, Caffi) 3·00 1·40

97 Hurdling

1972. Olympic Games, Munich. Multicoloured.
372 50f. Type **97** 75 35
373 130f. Gymnastics 1·50 75
374 150f. Swimming 1·90 85
MS375 102 × 86 mm. 300f. Cycling 3·75 1·70

98 Alphonse Daudet and Scene from "Tartarin de Tarascon"

1972. Air. International Book Year.
376 **98** 100f. brown, red & purple 1·50 75

99 Dromedary

1972. Domestic Animals.
377 **99** 25f. brown and violet 45 20
378 – 30f. blue and mauve 50 25
379 – 40f. brown and green 70 30
380 – 45f. brown and blue 85 35
DESIGNS: 30f. Horse; 40f. Saluki hound; 45f. Goat.

100 "Luna 16" and Moon Probe

1972. Air. Russian Moon Exploration.
381 **100** 100f. violet, brown & blue 1·40 70
382 – 150f. brown, blue & purple 2·10 80
DESIGN—HORIZ: 150f. "Lunokhod 1" Moon vehicle.

101 Tobacco Production

1972. Economic Development.
383 **101** 40f. green, red & brown 50 25
384 – 50f. brown, green & blue 75 35
DESIGN: 50f. Ploughing with oxen.

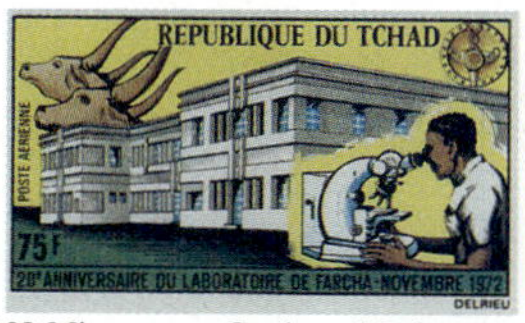

102 Microscope, Cattle and Laboratory

1972. Air. 20th Anniv of Farcha Veterinary Laboratory.
385 **102** 75f. multicoloured 80 35

103 Massa Warrior

1972. Chad Warriors. Multicoloured.
386 15f. Type **103** 55 25
387 20f. Moudang archer 70 35

104 King Faisal and Pres. Tombalbaye

1972. Visit of King Faisal of Saudi Arabia. Multicoloured.
388 100f. Type **104** (postage) 1·90 95
389 75f. King Faisal and Ka'aba, Mecca (air) 1·00 50

105 Gen. Gowon, Pres. Tombalbaye and Map

1972. Visit of Gen. Gowon, Nigerian Head-of-State.
390 **105** 70f. multicoloured 75 30

106 "Madonna and Child" (G. Bellini)

1972. Air. Christmas. Paintings. Multicoloured.
391 40f. Type **106** 45 25
392 75f. "Virgin and Child" (bas-relief, Da Santivo, Dall' Occhio) 80 45
393 80f. "Nativity" (B. Angelico) (horiz) 1·25 65
394 90f. "Adoration of the Magi" (P. Perugino) 1·60 80

107 Commemorative Scroll

1972. 50th Anniv of U.S.S.R.
395 **107** 150f. multicoloured 1·50 55

108 High-jumping

1973. 2nd African Games, Lagos. Multicoloured.
396 50f. Type **108** 75 35
397 125f. Running 1·40 60
398 200f. Putting the shot 2·00 1·00
MS399 103 × 86 mm. 250f. Throwing the discus 2·75 1·30

109 Copernicus and Planetary System Diagram

1973. Air. 500th Birth Anniv of Nicholas Copernicus.
400 **109** 250f. grey, brown & mve 4·00 1·90

1973. African Solidarity. "Drought Relief". No. 377 surch **SECHERESSE SOLIDARITE AFRICAINE 100F.**
401 **99** 100f. on 25f. brown & vio 1·60 90

1973. UAMPT. As Type **216** of Cameroun.
402 100f. green, red & brown 1·50 75

111 "Skylab" over Globe

1974. Air. "Skylab" Exploits.
403 **111** 100f. brown, red & blue 1·25 55
404 – 150f. turquoise, blue & brn 1·90 80
DESIGN: 150f. Close-up of "Skylab".

112 Chad Mother and Children

1974. 1st Anniv of Chad Red Cross.

405	**112**	30f.+10f. multicoloured	60	60

113 Football Players

1974. Air. World Cup Football Championship, West Germany.

406	**113**	50f. brown and red . . .	50	30
407	–	125f. green and red (vert)	1·40	60
408	–	150f. red and green . . .	1·90	95

DESIGNS: Nos. 407/8, Footballers in action similar to Type **113**.

114 Chad Family

116 Rotary Emblem

115 U.P.C. Emblem and Mail Canoe

1974. Air. World Population Year.

409	**114**	250f. brown, green & bl	3·00	1·60

1974. Air. Centenary of U.P.U.

410	**115**	30f. brown, red & green	50	25
411	–	40f. black and blue . .	2·75	1·50
412	–	100f. blue, brown & blk	1·60	70
413	–	150f. violet, green & turq	2·25	75

DESIGNS—U.P.U. Emblem and: 40f. Electric train; 100f. Jet airliner; 150f. Satellite.

1975. 70th Anniv of Rotary International.

414	**116**	50f. multicoloured	75	35

117 Heads of Women of Four Races

1975. Air. International Women's Year.

415	**117**	250f. multicoloured . . .	3·75	1·90

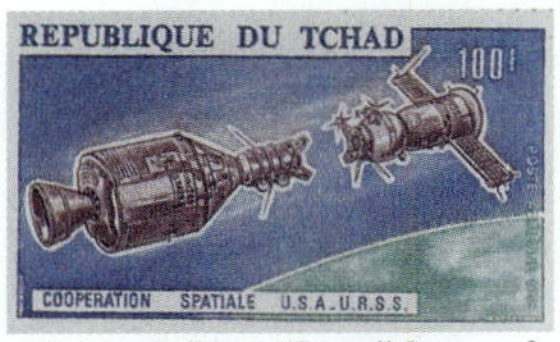

118 "Apollo" and "Soyuz" Spacecraft about to dock

1975. Air. "Apollo–Soyuz" Test Project.

416	**118**	100f. brown, blue & green	1·10	50
417	–	130f. brown, blue & green	1·40	75

DESIGN: 130f. "Apollo" and "Soyuz" spacecraft docked.

119 "Craterostigma plantagineum"

1975. Flowers. Multicoloured.

418	5f. Type **119**	10	10
419	10f. "Tapinanthus globiferus"	20	15
420	15f. "Commelina forsalaei" (vert)	30	15
421	20f. "Adenium obasum" . .	35	15
422	25f. "Hibiscus esulenus" . .	60	20
423	30f. "Hibiscus sabdariffa" . .	75	25
424	40f. "Kigelia africana" . . .	1·10	30

120 Football

1975. Air. Olympic Games, Montreal (1976).

425	**120**	75f. green and red	80	30
426	–	100f. brown, blue & red	1·25	55
427	–	125f. blue and brown . .	1·40	80

DESIGNS: 100f. Throwing the discus; 125f. Running.

1975. Air. Successful Rendezvous of "Apollo–Soyuz" Mission. Optd **JONCTION 17 JUILLET 1975**.

428	**118**	100f. brown, blue & grn	1·10	70
429	–	130f. brown, blue & grn	1·40	90

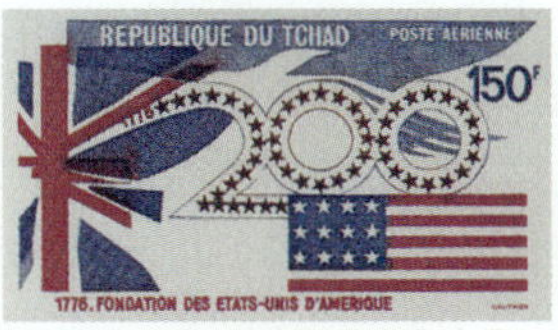

122 Stylized British and American Flags

1975. Air. Bicentenary of American Revolution.

430	**122**	150f. blue, red & brown	1·90	95

123 "Adoration of the Shepherds" (Murillo)

1975. Air. Christmas. Religious Paintings. Mult.

431	40f. Type **123**	55	35
432	75f. "Adoration of the Shepherds" (G. de la Tour)	1·00	55
433	80f. "Virgin of the Bible" (R. van der Weyden) (vert) . .	1·25	60
434	100f. "Holy Family with the Lamb" (attrib. Raphael) (vert)	1·90	95

124 Alexander Graham Bell and Satellite

1976. Telephone Centenary.

435	**124**	100f. multicoloured . . .	1·00	50
436		125f. multicoloured . . .	1·50	75

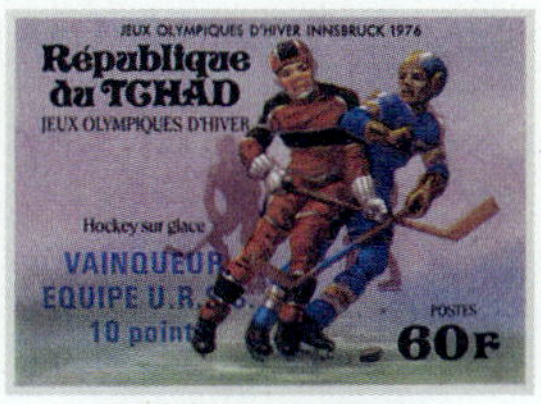

125 U.S.S.R. (ice hockey)

1976. Winter Olympics. Medal-winners, Innsbruck. Multicoloured.

437	60f. Type **125** (postage) . . .	75	35
438	90f. Ski-jumping (K. Schnabl, Austria)	95	40
439	250f. Bobsleighing (West Germany) (air)	2·25	75
440	300f. Speed-skating (J. E. Storholt, Norway)	2·75	1·10
MS441	103 × 78 mm. 500f. F. Klamner of Austria (downhill skiing)	4·75	1·75

These stamps were not issued without overprints.

126 Paul Revere (after Copley) and his Night Ride

1976. Air. Bicentenary of American Revolution.

442	100f. Type **126**	80	25
443	125f. Washington (after Stuart) and "Washington crossing the Delaware" (detail, Leutze)	95	35
444	150f. Lafayette offering his services to America	1·25	45
445	200f. Rochambeau and detail "Siege of Yorktown" (Couder)	1·60	70
446	250f. Franklin (after Duplessis) and "Declaration of Independence" (detail, Trumball)	2·25	80
MS447	103 × 78 mm. 400f. De Grasse (after Mauzaisse) and "Battle of Virginia Capes" (detail, Zveg)	3·00	1·40

127 Hurdles

1976. Olympic Games, Montreal. Multicoloured.

448	45f. Type **127** (postage) . . .	60	25
449	100f. Boxing (air)	95	35
450	200f. Pole vaulting	1·90	55
451	300f. Putting the shot	2·75	95
MS452	103 × 77 mm. 500f. Sprint	5·50	1·40

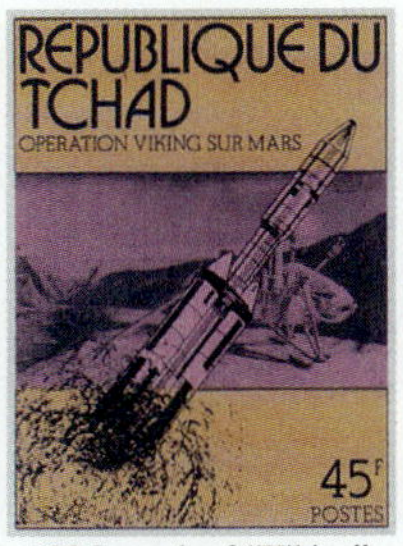

128 Launch of "Viking"

1976. "Viking" landing on Mars. Mult.

453	45f. Type **128** (postage) . . .	45	20
454	90f. Trajectory of flight . . .	80	30
455	100f. Descent to Mars (air)	85	35
456	200f. "Viking" in flight . . .	1·60	50
457	250f. "Viking" on landing approach	1·90	75
MS458	114 × 89 mm. 450f. "Viking" on Mars	3·25	1·10

129 Flag and Clasped Hands on Map of Chad

1976. National Reconciliation. Mult.

459	30f. Type **129**	35	25
460	60f. Type **129**	85	30
461	120f. Map, people and various occupations . . .	1·60	70

130 Release of Political Prisoners

1976. 1st Anniv of April 1st Revolution. Mult.

462	30f. Type **130**	25	20
463	60f. Officer-cadets on parade	50	30
464	120f. Type **130**	1·10	55

131 Concorde

1976. Air. Concorde's First Commercial Flight.

465	**131**	250f. blue, red & black . .	4·25	2·75

132 Gourd and Ladle

1976. Pyrograved Gourds.

466	**132**	30f. multicoloured	30	20
467	–	60f. multicoloured	60	25
468	–	120f. multicoloured . . .	1·25	60

DESIGNS: 60f., 120f. Gourds with different decorations.

1976. Nobel Prizewinners. As T **189** of Central African Empire. Multicoloured.

469	45f. Robert Koch (Medicine, 1905)	95	35
470	90f. Anatole France (Literature, 1921)	1·25	60
471	100f. Albert Einstein (Physics, 1921) (air)	1·25	30
472	200f. Dag Hammarskjold (Peace, 1961)	1·90	50
473	300f. Dr. S. Tomonaga (Physics, 1965)	2·75	75
MS474	116 × 79 mm. 500f. Alexander Fleming (Medicine, 1945)	4·25	1·10

133 "The Nativity" (Hans Holbein)

1976. Air. Christmas. Multicoloured.

475	30f. "The Nativity" (Altdorfer)	30	20
476	60f. Type **133**	55	30

477 120f. "Adoration of the Shepherds" (Honthorst) (horiz) . . . . 1·00 60
478 150f. "Adoration of the Magi" (David) (horiz) . . 1·60 95

134 "Lesdiguieres Bridge"

1976. Air. Centenary of Impressionism. Paintings by Johan Bathold Jongkind. Multicoloured.
479 100f. Type **134** . . . . 1·40 70
480 120f. "Warship" . . . . . . 3·00 1·10

1977. Zeppelin Flights. As T **190** of Central African Empire. Multicoloured.
481 100f. Friedrichshafen and German 50pf. stamp, 1936 (postage) . . . . 1·25 50
482 125f. Polar scene and German 1m. stamp, 1931 (air) . . . . 1·10 30
483 150f. Chicago store and German 4m. stamp, 1933 2·00 45
484 175f. New York, London and German 2m. stamp, 1928 4·00 75
485 200f. New York and U.S. $2.60 stamp, 1930 . . . . 2·75 85
MS486 130 × 92 mm. 500f. As No. 485 . . . . 5·50 1·70

1977. Air. 10th Anniv of International French Language Council. As T **204** of Benin.
487 100f. multicoloured 85 50

135 Simon Bolivar

1977. Great Personalities. Multicoloured.
488 150f. Type **135** . . . . 1·25 50
489 175f. Joseph J. Roberts . . . 1·50 50
490 200f. Queen Wilhelmina . . . 1·75 60
491 200f. General de Gaulle . . . 2·50 85
492 325f. King Baudouin and Queen Fabiola . . . . . . 2·75 95
493 250f. Coronation of Queen Elizabeth II (horiz) . . . . 2·50 90

136 Queen Elizabeth II

1977. 25th Anniv of Queen Elizabeth II's Accession to Throne Multicoloured.
493 250f. Type **136** . . . . . . 2·50 90
MS494 110 × 91 mm. 450f. Queen Elizabeth and Prince Philip . . 4·75 1·90

137 Lafayette and Arrival in America

1977. Air. Bicentenary of American Independence. Multicoloured.
495 100f. Type **137** . . . . . . 1·10 50
496 120f. Abraham Lincoln . . . 1·25 60
497 150f. F. J. Madison . . . . 1·75 75

138 Radio Aerial, Sound Waves and Map

1977. Posts and Telecommunications Emblems.
498 – 30f. black and yellow . . 35 20
499 **138** 60f. multicoloured 70 25
500 – 120f. multicoloured . . . 1·25 60
DESIGNS—HORIZ (47 × 26 mm): 30f. Posthorn and initials "ONPT". VERT (26 × 36 mm): 120f. Telecommunications skyline and initials "TIT".

139 Concorde

1977. Air. "North Atlantic"—Concorde and Lindbergh Commemorations.
501 **139** 100f. blue, red & lt blue 75 45
502 – 120f. brown, blue & grn 85 50
503 – 150f. violet, red & green 1·10 65
504 – 200f. orange, pur & brn 1·60 85
505 – 300f. blue, purple & blk 2·50 1·25
DESIGNS: 120f. to 300f. Various portraits of Lindbergh with "Spirit of St. Louis" against different backgrounds.

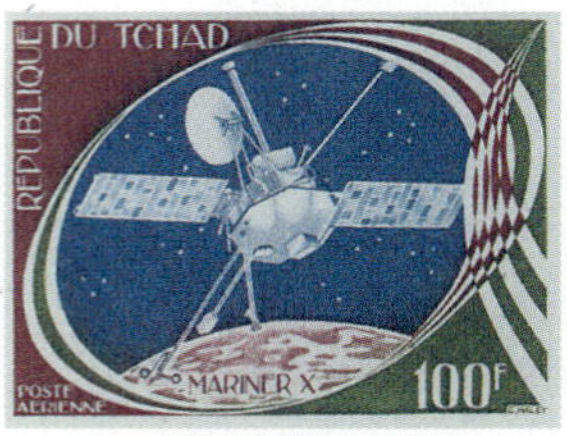

140 "Mariner 10"

1977. Air. Space Research.
506 **140** 100f. blue, olive & green 80 50
507 – 200f. brown, green & red 1·75 1·00
508 – 300f. brown, grn & bistre 2·50 1·25
DESIGNS: 200f. "Luna 21"; 300f. "Viking".

141 Running

142 "Back Pain"

1977. Air. Sports.
509 **141** 30f. brown, red & blue . . 30 20
510 – 60f. brown, blue & orge 55 30
511 – 120f. multicoloured . . . 1·00 50
512 – 125f. mauve, violet & grn 1·25 60
DESIGNS: 60f. Volleyball; 120f. Football; 125f. Basketball.

1977. World Rheumatism Year.
513 **142** 30f. red, green and violet 35 20
514 – 60f. red, violet and green 55 25
515 – 120f. blue, red & lt blue 1·25 60
DESIGNS—HORIZ: 60f. "Neck pain". VERT: 120f. "Knee pain".

1977. Air. 1st Commercial Paris–New York Flight of Concorde. Optd **PARIS NEW-YORK 22.11.77.**
516 **139** 100f. blue, red & lt blue 2·25 1·25

144 Saving a Goal

1977. World Football Cup Championship. Mult.
517 40f. Type **144** 35 15
518 60f. Heading the ball 55 20
519 100f. Referee 95 30
520 200f. Foot kicking ball . . . 1·90 60
521 300f. Pele (Brazilian player) 3·00 95
MS522 118 × 80 mm. 500f. Helmut Schoen and stadium . . . . . 4·75 1·60

145 "Christ in the Manger" (detail)

1977. Air. Christmas. Paintings by Rubens. Mult.
523 30f. Type **145** 45 25
524 60f. "Virgin and Child with Two Donors" 75 35
525 100f. "The Adoration of the Shepherds" . . . . . . 1·25 60
526 125f. "The Adoration of the Magi" (detail) . . . . . . 1·60 80

1978. Coronation of Queen Elizabeth II. No. 493 **MS**494 optd **ANNIVERSAIRE DU COURONNEMENT 1953–1978.**
527 250f. multicoloured . . . . . 2·50 1·50
MS528 111 × 92 mm. 450f. multicoloured . . . . 4·25 2·75

147 Antoine de Saint-Exupery

1978. Air. History of Aviation. Multicoloured.
529 40f. Type **147** 50 20
530 50f. Wright Brothers and aircraft in flight 60 25
531 80f. Hugo Junkers 85 45
532 100f. Italo Balbo . . . . . . 1·10 55
533 120f. "Concorde" . . . . . 1·25 75
MS534 104 × 98 mm. 500f. Wright Brothers and aircraft on ground 4·75 2·50

1978. Air. "Philexafrique" Stamp Exhibition, Gabon (1st issue), and International Stamp Fair, Essen. As T **237** of Benin. Multicoloured.
535 100f. Grey heron and Mecklenburg-Strelitz, ¼sgr. stamp, 1864 . . . . . . 2·75 1·90
536 100f. Black rhinoceros and Chad 500f. stamp, 1961 . . 2·75 1·90

148 "Portrait"

150 Head and Unhealthy and Healthy Villages

149 "Helene Fourment"

1978. 450th Death Anniv of Albrecht Durer (artist). Multicoloured.
537 60f. Type **148** 50 15
538 150f. "Jacob Muffel" . . . . 1·40 30
539 250f. "Young Girl" . . . . 2·25 60
540 350f. "Oswolt Krel" . . . . 3·50 80

1978. 400th Birth Anniv of Peter Paul Rubens (artist). Multicoloured.
541 60f. "Abraham and Melchisedek" (horiz) . . . 60 15
542 120f. Type **149** . . . . 1·10 25
543 200f. "David and the Elders of Israel" (horiz) . . . . 1·90 60
544 300f. "Anne of Austria" . . . 3·25 85
MS545 78 × 104 mm. 500f. "Marie de Medici" . . . . 4·75 1·40

1978. National Health Day.
546 **150** 60f. multicoloured 60 35

1978. World Cup Football Championship Finalists. Nos. 517/21 optd with teams and scores of past finals.
547 **144** 40f. multicoloured 35 20
548 – 60f. multicoloured . . . 50 30
549 – 100f. multicoloured . . . 85 50
550 – 200f. multicoloured . . . 1·90 95
551 – 300f. multicoloured . . . 3·00 1·50
MS552 118 × 80 mm. 500f. multicoloured . . . . 4·75 2·50
OPTS: 40f. **1962 BRESIL-TCHECOSLOVAQUE 3-1**; 60f. **1966 GRANDE BRETAGNE ALLEMAGNE (RFA) 4-2**; 100f. **1970 BRESIL-ITALIE 4-1**; 200f. **1974 ALLEMAGNE (RFA)-PAYS BAS 2-1**; 300f. **1978 ARGENTINE-PAYS BAS 3-1**; 500f. **ARGENTINE-PAYS BAS 3-1**.

152 Camel Riders, Satellites and UPU Emblem

1978. "Philexafrique 2" Exhibition, Libreville, Gabon (2nd issue).
553 **152** 60f. red, mauve & blue . . 1·60 95
554 – 150f. multicoloured . . . 3·00 2·25
DESIGN: 150f. Mother and child, native village and hibiscus.

153 Sand Gazelle

1979. Endangered Animals. Multicoloured.
555 40f. Type **153** 45 15
556 50f. Addax 50 15
557 60f. Scimitar oryx 60 20
558 100f. Cheetah . . . . 1·00 40
559 150f. African ass . . . . . . 1·60 50
560 300f. Black rhinoceros . . . 3·25 90

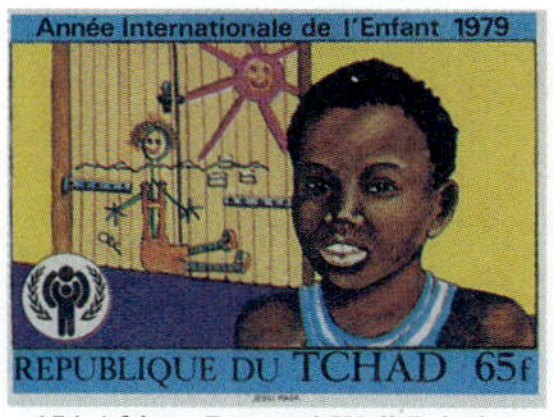

154 African Boy and Wall Painting

1979. International Year of the Child. Mult.
561 65f. Type **154** 50 20
562 75f. Asian girl 55 25
563 100f. European child and doves 80 30
564 150f. African boys and drawing of boats . . . . 1·25 50
MS565 103 × 77 mm. 250f. Pencil and drawing of hands . . . . 1·90 75

155 "The Holy Family with There Hares" (woodcut)

1979. 450th Death Anniv (1978) of Albrecht Durer (artist). Sheet 90 × 115 mm.
MS566 **155** 500f. lake and brown 3·75 1·75

1979. 10th Anniv of "Apollo 11" Moon Landing. Nos. 453/7 optd with lunar module and **ALUNISSAGE APOLLO XI JUILLET 1969**.
567 45f. Type **128** (postage) . . . 35 25
568 90f. Trajectory of flight . . . 80 35
569 100f. Descent on Mars (air) 75 50
570 200f. "Viking" in flight . . . 1·50 85
571 250f. "Viking" on landing approach . . . . 1·90 1·10
MS572 114 × 89 mm. 450f. multicoloured . . . . 3·25 1·90

157 Hurdles

1979. Air. Olympic Games, Moscow 1980. Mult.
573 15f. Type **157** 20 15
574 30f. Hockey 30 20
575 250f. Swimming . . . . . . 1·90 70
576 350f. Running . . . . 2·50 90
MS577 117 × 80 mm. 500f. Yachting 3·75 1·75

158 Reed Canoe and Austrian 10k. stamp, 1910

1979. Air. Death Centenary of Sir Rowland Hill. Multicoloured.
578 65f. Type **158** 50 15
579 100f. Sailing canoe and U.S. $1 stamp of 1894 . . . . . 85 30
580 200f. "Curacao" (paddle-steamer) and French 1f. stamp of 1853 . . . . . . 1·75 60
581 300f. "Calypso" (liner) and Holstein 1¼s. stamp of 1864 . . . . 2·25 1·10
MS582 103 × 91 mm. 500f. Liner and Chad 10c. Postage Due stamps of 1930 . . . . 3·75 1·75

159 Slalom

160 "Concorde" and Map of Africa

1979. Winter Olympic Games, Lake Placid (1980). Multicoloured.
583 20f. Type **159** 20 15
584 40f. Biathlon 35 15
585 60f. Ski jump (horiz) 40 15
586 150f. Women's giant slalom 1·10 35
587 350f. Cross-country skiing (horiz) . . . . 2·50 80
588 500f. Downhill skiing (horiz) 3·75 1·25

1980. 20th Anniv of African Air Safety Organization (ASECNA).
589 **160** 15f. multicoloured 30 10
590 30f. multicoloured 45 25
591 60f. multicoloured 90 50

1981. Various stamps optd **POSTES 1981** or surch also.
592 **157** 30f. on 15f. multicoloured 75 60
593 – 30f. mult (No. 574) . . . 75 60
594 **158** 60f. on 65f. multicoloured 1·50 1·00
595 – 60f. on 100f. mult (No. 579) . . . . . . 1·50 1·00

162 Footballer

1982. World Cup Football Championship, Spain. Multicoloured.
596 30f. Hungary (postage) . . . 25 15
597 40f. Type **162** 30 15
598 50f. Algeria 35 20
599 60f. Argentina 45 20
600 80f. Brazil (air) 55 20
601 300f. West Germany . . . . 2·25 70
MS602 77 × 100 mm. 500f. Spain (38 × 48 mm) . . . . 3·75 1·75
DESIGNS: As T **162** but each value showing different team's footballer.

163 Lady Diana and her Brother (1967)

1982. 21st Birthday of Princess of Wales. Mult.
603 30f. Lady Diana in christening robe (1961) (postage) 30 15
604 40f. Portrait of Lady Diana (1965) 35 15
605 50f. Type **163** 45 20
606 60f. Lady Diana and her pony (1975) 55 20
607 80f. Lady Diana in Switzerland (1977) (air) . . 60 20
608 300f. Lady Diana as nursery teacher (1980) . . . . . 2·50 70
MS609 78 × 75 mm. 500f. Princess of Wales (39 × 36 mm) . . . . . 3·75 1·75

164 West German Scouts

1982. 75th Anniv of Scout Movement. Mult.
610 30f. Type **164** (postage) . . . 35 15
611 40f. Upper Volta scouts . . . 35 15
612 50f. Mali scouts and African dancers 50 20
613 60f. Scottish scout, piper and dancer 60 20
614 80f. Kuwait scouts (air) . . . 55 20
615 300f. Chad cub scout . . . . 2·25 70
MS616 110 × 74 mm. 500f. Chad scouts (53 × 35 mm) . . . . . 3·75 1·75

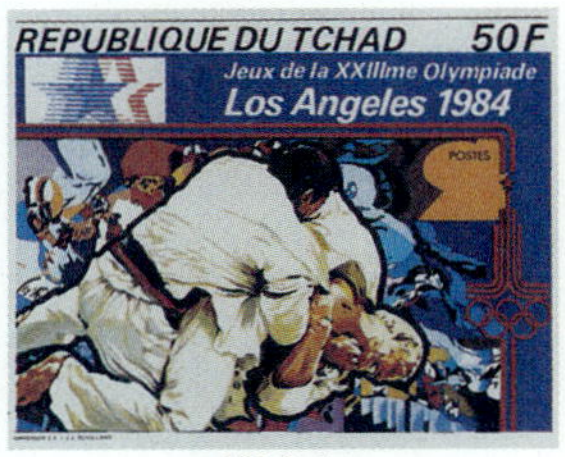

165 Judo

1982. Olympic Games, Los Angeles (1984) (1st issue). Multicoloured.
617 30f. Gymnastics (horse exercise) (postage) 30 15
618 40f. Show jumping 30 15
619 50f. Type **165** 35 20
620 60f. High jumping 60 20
621 80f. Hurdling (air) 55 20
622 300f. Gymnastics (floor exercise) . . . . 2·25 70
MS623 110 × 82 mm. 500f. Relay (56 × 38 mm) . . . . 3·75 1·75
See also Nos. 678/MS684 and 735/MS739.

1982. Birth of Prince William of Wales. Nos. 603/8 optd **21 JUIN 1982 WILLIAM ARTHUR PHILIP LOUIS PRINCE DE GALLES**.
624 30f. Type **163** (postage) . . . 30 15
625 40f. Portrait of Lady Diana as a young girl 35 15
626 50f. Lady Diana and her brother 45 20
627 60f. Lady Diana with her pony 50 20
628 80f. Lady Diana in Switzerland (air) 60 20
629 300f. Lady Diana with children . . . . 2·50 70
MS630 78 × 75 mm. 500f. Portrait (39 × 36 mm) . . . . 3·75 1·75

167 Marco Tardelli (Italy) and Passarella (Argentine)

1983. World Cup Football Championship Results. Multicoloured.
631 30f. Type **167** (postage) . . . 25 10
632 40f. Paolo Rossi (Italy) and Zico (Brazil) 30 15
633 50f. Pierre Littbarski (West Germany) and Platini (France) 35 20
634 60f. Gabriele Oriali (Italy) and Smolarek (Poland) . . 45 20
635 70f. Boniek (Poland) and Alain Giresse (France) (air) 55 20
636 300f. Bruno Conti (Italy) and Paul Breitner (West Germany) . . . . 2·25 70
MS637 110 × 79 mm. 500f. Rummenigge (West Germany) and Paolo Rossi (Italy) (56 × 32 mm) 3·75 1·75

168 Philidor and 19th-century European Rook

1982. Chess Grand Masters. Multicoloured.
638 30f. Type **168** (postage) . . . 35 15
639 40f. Paul Morphy and 19th-century Chinese knight 50 15
640 50f. Howard Staunton and Lewis knight 60 25
641 60f. Jean-Paul Capablanca and African knight 75 25
642 80f. Boris Spassky and Staunton knight (air) . . . 1·25 25
643 300f. Anatoly Karpov and 19th-century Chinese knight . . . . 3·00 1·00
MS644 98 × 80 mm. 500f. Victor Kortschnoi and modern chess pieces (53 × 35 mm) . . . . . 3·75 1·75

169 K. E. Tsiolkovski and "Soyuz"

1983. Exploitation of Space. Multicoloured.
645 30f. Type **169** (postage) . . . 25 10
646 40f. R. H. Goddard and space telescope 30 15
647 50f. Korolev and ultra-violet telescope 35 20
648 60f. Von Braun and Space Shuttle 45 20
649 80f. Esnault Pelterie and "Ariane" rocket and "Symphonie" satellite (air) 55 25
650 300f. H. Oberth and construction of orbiting space station . . . . . . 2·25 70
MS651 85 × 85 mm. 500f. J.F.Kennedy and first man on the Moon (vert 41 × 50 mm) . . . 3·75 1·75

170 Charles and Robert Balloon, 1783

1983. Air. Balloons. Multicoloured.
652 100f. Type **170** 95 50
653 200f. Blanchard balloon, Berlin, 1788 . . . . 1·90 95
654 300f. Charles Green balloon, London, 1837 (horiz) . . . 2·50 1·75
655 400f. Modern advertising airship (horiz) . . . . . . 3·25 1·75
MS656 79 × 98 mm. 500f. Montgolfiere balloon, 1783 . . 3·75 1·75

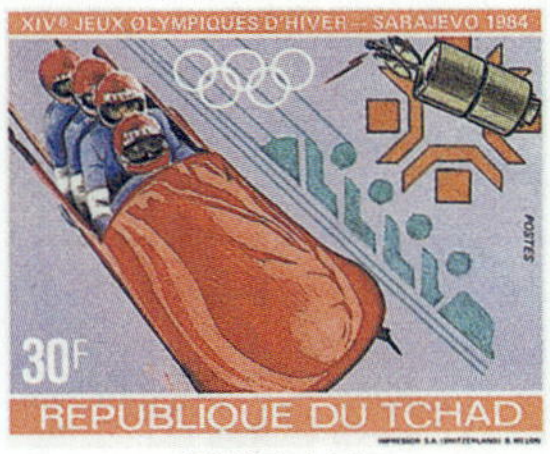

171 Bobsleigh

1983. Winter Olympic Games, Sarajevo. Mult.
657 30f. Type **171** (postage) . . . 25 10
658 40f. Speed skating 30 15
659 50f. Cross-country skiing . . 30 20
660 60f. Ice hockey 35 20
661 80f. Ski jump (air) 55 20
662 300f. Downhill skiing . . . . 2·25 70
MS663 100 × 80 mm. 500f. Ice dancing . . . . 3·75 1·75

172 Montgolfier Brothers and "Le Martial" Balloon, 1783

1983. Bicentenary of Manned Flight. Multicoloured.
664 25f. Type **172** (postage) . . . 20 15
665 45f. Pilatre de Rozier and first manned flight, 1783 35 20
666 50f. Jacques Garnerin and balloon (first parachute descent, 1797) 35 20
667 60f. J. P. Blanchard and balloon at Chelsea, 1784 45 30
668 80f. H. Giffard and steam-powered dirigible, 1852 (air) 75 40
669 250f. Zeppelin and airship "L 21", 1900 . . . . 2·10 1·25
MS670 57 × 95 mm. 300f. Montgolfier Brothers and ascent of La Flesselles (41 × 38 mm) 3·75 1·75

173 Gottlieb Daimler, Karl Benz and Mercedes "Type S," 1927

1983. Car Manufacturers. Multicoloured.
671 25f. Type **173** (postage) . . . 30 10
672 35f. Friedrich von Martini and Torpedo, Martini "Type GC 32", 1913 . . . 45 15
673 50f. Walter P. Chrysler and Chrysler "70", 1926 . . . 70 20
674 60f. Nicola Romeo and Alfa Romeo "6 C 1750 Grand Sport", 1929 . . . . . . 75 20
675 80f. Stewart Rolls, Henry Royce and "Phantom II Continental", 1934 (air) . . 95 20
676 250f. Lord Shrewsbury and Talbot-Lago "Record", 1948 . . . . 2·50 70
MS677 109 × 68 mm. 300f. Ettore Bugatti and Royale Coupe de Ville "41", 1926–33 . . . . 3·75 1·75

174 Kayak

1983. Olympic Games, Los Angeles (2nd issue). Multicoloured.
678 25f. Type **174** (postage) . . . 20 10
679 45f. Long jumping 30 15
680 50f. Boxing 35 15
681 60f. Discus-throwing 45 20
682 80f. Relay race (air) 60 20
683 350f. Horse jumping . . . . 2·50 70
MS684 90 × 93 mm. 500f. Gymnastics (horiz 50 × 41 mm) 3·75 1·75

175 Dove on Map

1983. Peace and Reconciliation. Multicoloured.
685 50f. Type **175** (postage) . . . 35 15
686 50f. Foodstuffs on map . . . 45 20
687 50f. President Habre 35 15
688 60f. As No. 687 . . . . . . 45 15
689 80f. Type **175** 65 25
690 80f. As No. 686 . . . . . . 80 30
691 80f. As No. 687 . . . . . . 65 25
692 100f. As No. 687 . . . . . . 75 25
693 150f. Type **175** (air) . . . . 1·00 30
694 150f. As No. 686 . . . . . . 1·40 50
695 200f. Type **175** . . . . . . 1·25 45
696 200f. As No. 686 . . . . . . 1·75 65

1983. 15th World Scout Jamboree, Canada. Nos. 610/15 optd **XV WORLD JAMBOREE MONDIAL ALBERTA CANADA 1983.**
697 30f. multicoloured (postage) 25 15
698 40f. multicoloured 30 15
699 50f. multicoloured 35 20
700 60f. multicoloured 45 20
701 80f. multicoloured (air) . . . 55 20
702 300f. multicoloured . . . . . 2·25 70

1983. 60th Anniv of Int Chess Federation. Nos. 638/43 optd **60e ANNIVERSAIRE FEDERATION MONDIAL D'ECHECS 1924–1984.**
704 30f. multicoloured (postage) 50 20
705 40f. multicoloured 60 20
706 50f. multicoloured 60 25
707 60f. multicoloured 75 25
708 80f. multicoloured (air) . . . 1·25 45
709 300f. multicoloured . . . . . 3·75 1·25
MS710 98 × 80 mm. 500f. multicoloured . . . . 5·75 1·75

178 Chad Martyrs

1984. Celebrities. Multicoloured.
711 50f. Type **178** (postage) . . . 35 15
712 200f. P. Harris and Rotary Headquarters, U.S.A. . . . 1·50 35
713 300f. Alfred Nobel and will 2·50 60
714 350f. Raphael and "Virgin with the Infant and St. John the Baptist" . . . 3·75 75
715 400f. Rembrandt and "The Holy Family" (air) . . . . 3·75 85
716 500f. Goethe and Scenes from "Faust" . . . . 4·25 1·00
MS717 78 × 86 mm. 600f. Rubens and "Helene Fourment and two of her Children" . . . . 4·50 1·90

179 Martyrs Memorial

1984. Martyrs Memorial.
718 **179** 50f. mult (postage) . . . 35 15
719 80f. multicoloured 60 25
720 120f. multicoloured 85 25
721 200f. multicoloured (air) 1·60 50
722 250f. multicoloured . . . 2·25 75

180 Durer and Painting

1984. Celebrities and Events. Multicoloured.
723 50f. Type **180** (postage) . . . 75 15
724 200f. Henri Dunant and battle scene . . . . 1·75 35
725 300f. Early telephone and satellite receiving station, Goonhilly Downs . . . . 2·25 60
726 350f. President Kennedy and first foot-print on Moon 2·75 75
727 400f. Infra-red satellite picture (Europe–Africa co-operation) (air) . . . . . 2·50 75
728 500f. Prince and Princess of Wales . . . . 3·75 1·00
MS729 60 × 110 mm. 600f. Wedding of Prince and Princess of Wales 4·50 1·90

181 "Communications"

1984. World Communications Year.
730 **181** 50f. mult (postage) . . . 45 15
731 60f. multicoloured 50 35
732 70f. multicoloured 50 35
733 125f. multicoloured (air) 1·00 55
734 250f. multicoloured . . . 1·90 1·10

182 Two-man Kayak

1984. Air. Olympic Games, Los Angeles (3rd issue). Multicoloured.
735 100f. Type **182** 75 25
736 200f. Kayaks (close-up) . . . 1·50 50
737 300f. One-man kayak . . . . 2·25 75
738 400f. Coxed fours . . . . . 3·00 1·00
MS739 104 × 80 mm. 500f. Coxless four . . . . 3·75 1·75

183 Class 13 Kitson Steam Locomotive

1984. Historic Transport. Multicoloured.
740 50f. Type **183** (postage) . . . 1·50 1·00
741 200f. Sailing boat on Lake Chad . . . . 1·75 65
742 300f. Graf Zeppelin (airship) 3·00 1·25
743 350f. Six-wheel Renault automobile, 1930 . . . . . 2·75 1·25
744 400f. Bloch "120" airplane (air) . . . . 2·50 1·50
745 500f. Douglas "DC-8" airplane . . . . 3·75 2·00
MS746 84 × 109 mm. 600f. Ariane space rocket and "Intelsat V" communications satellite . . . 4·50 1·90

184 African with broken Manacles

185 Pres. Hissein Habre

1984. 2nd Anniv of Entrance of Government Forces in N'Djamena.
747 **184** 50f. multicoloured 50 25

1984.
748 **185** 125f. black, blue & yellow 1·25 50

186 British East Indiaman

1984. Transport. Multicoloured. (a) Ships.
749 90f. Type **186** 95 45
750 125f. "Vera Cruz" (steamer) 1·25 55
751 200f. "Carlisle Castle" (sail merchantman) . . . . . . 2·25 75
752 300f. "Britannia" (steamer) 2·75 1·25

(b) Locomotives.
753 100f. Series 701, 1885, France 1·25 15
754 150f. "Columbia", 1888, Belgium . . . . 1·90 25
755 250f. Mediterranean locomotive, 1900, Italy . . 3·00 40
756 350f. MAV 114 . . . . . . 4·50 55

187 Virgin and Child

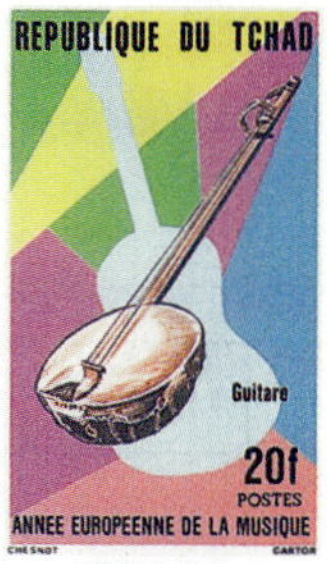

188 Guitars

1984. Christmas.
757 **187** 50f. brown and blue . . . 45 15
758 60f. brown and orange . . 50 20
759 80f. brown and green . . 65 25
760 85f. brown and purple . . 70 25
761 100f. brown and orange 85 30
762 135f. brown and blue . . 1·25 45

1985. European Music Year. Multicoloured.
763 20f. Type **188** 20 10
764 25f. Harps 25 15
765 30f. Xylophones 30 15
766 50f. Drums 45 20
767 70f. As No. 766 . . . . . . 55 20
768 80f. As No. 764 . . . . . . 75 30
769 100f. Type **188** 90 45
770 250f. As No. 765 . . . . . 2·25 85

189 "Chlorophyllum molybdites"

1985. Fungi. Multicoloured.
771 25f. Type **189** 55 30
772 30f. "Tulostoma volvulatum" 70 35
773 50f. "Lentinus tuberregium" 1·00 45
774 70f. As No. 773 . . . . . . 1·40 60
775 80f. "Podaxis pistillaris" . . 1·75 65
776 100f. Type **189** . . . . . . 2·50 1·00

190 Stylized Tree and Scout

1985. Air. "Philexafrique" Stamp Exhibition, Lome, Togo (1st issue). Multicoloured.
777 200f. Type **190** . . . . 1·90 1·50
778 200f. Fokker "27" airplane 1·90 1·50
See also Nos. 808/9.

191 Abraham Lincoln

1985. Celebrities. Multicoloured.
779 25f. Type **191** (postage) . . . 20 10
780 45f. Henri Dunant (founder of Red Cross) 45 15
781 50f. Gottlieb Daimler (automobile designer) . . . 60 15
782 60f. Louis Bleriot (pilot) (air) 55 30
783 80f. Paul Harris (founder of Rotary International) . . . 55 20
784 350f. Auguste Piccard (undersea explorer) . . . . 3·75 1·60
MS785 78 × 75 mm. 600f. Anatoly Karpov (chess champion) . . . 4·50 1·90

192 Figures within Geometric Pattern

193 Sun and Hands breaking through Darkness

1985. International Youth Year. Multicoloured.
786 70f. Type **192** 50 25
787 200f. Figures on ribbon around globe . . . . . . 1·50 75

1985. 3rd Anniv of Entrance of Government Forces in N'DJamena. Multicoloured.
788 70f. Type **193** 55 25
789 70f. Claw attacking hand . . 55 25
790 70f. Pres. Hissein Habre (36 × 48 mm) 25 20
791 110f. Type **193** 80 35
792 110f. As No. 789 . . . . . . 80 35
793 110f. As No. 790 . . . . . 1·10 35

194 Saddle-bill Stork ("Jabiru")

196 Sitatunga

195 Fokker Friendship, Farman M.F.11 and Emblem

1985. Birth Bicentenary of John J. Audubon (ornithologist).
794 **194** 70f. black, blue & brown 1·40 85
795 – 110f. olive, green & brown . . . . 2·00 1·25

796 – 150f. blue, red and olive . . . 3·00 1·90
797 – 200f. dp blue, mauve & bl . . . 3·50 2·10
MS798 129 × 100 mm. 500f. sepia, brown and olive . . . 3·75 1·90
DESIGNS: 110f. Ostrich; 150f. Marabou stork; 200, 500f. Crested serpent eagle.

1985. Air. 25th Anniv of ASECNA (navigation agency). Multicoloured.
799 70f. Type **195** 50 30
800 110f. Fokker "F.27" "Friendship" and "Spirit of St. Louis" 75 50
801 250f. Fokker "F.27" "Friendship" and Vickers Vimy . . . . 1·90 1·25

1985. Mammals.
802 **196** 50f. brown, bl & dp brn . . 55 35
803 – 70f. brown, green and red . . 70 50
804 – 250f. multicoloured . . . 2·50 1·60
MS805 130 × 100 mm. 500f. black, red and turquoise . . . . . 3·75 1·75
DESIGNS—HORIZ: 70f. Greater kudus; 500f. White rhinoceros. VERT: 250f. Bearded mouflons.

197 U.N. Emblem on Peace Dove and Girl with Flowers

1985. 40th Anniv of UNO and 25th Anniv of U.N. Membership.
806 **197** 200f. blue, red & brown . . 1·50 1·00
807 – 300f. blue, red & yellow . . 2·25 1·50
DESIGN: 300f. U.N. emblem as flower with peace doves forming stalk.

198 Girl with Posy, Youth Ceremony and IYY Emblem

1985. Air. "Philexafrique" Stamp Exhibition, Lome, Togo (2nd issue). Multicoloured.
808 250f. Type **198** (International Youth Year) . . . . 2·25 1·90
809 250f. Computer terminal, liner, airplane, diesel freight train, rocket and UPU emblem . . . . 4·25 1·00

199 Hugo

1985. Air. Death Centenary of Victor Hugo (writer).
810 **199** 70f. blue, sepia and brown . . 50 35
811 110f. brown, green & red . . 75 50
812 250f. black, red & orange . . 1·90 1·00
813 300f. purple, blue and red . . 2·25 1·25

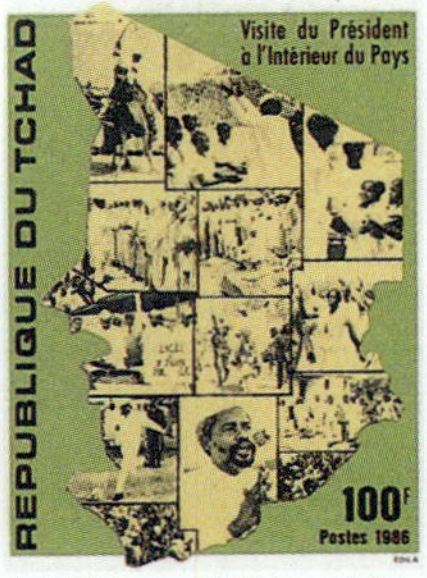

200 Nativity **201** Pictures of Visit on Map

1985. Air. Christmas.
814 **200** 250f. multicoloured . . . 1·90 75

1986. Visit of President to Interior.
815 **201** 100f. yellow, black & grn . . 95 50
816 170f. yellow, black & pink . . 1·90 75
817 200f. yellow, black & grn . . 2·25 1·25

1987. Various stamps surch.
818 – 170f. on 300f. mult (725) (postage) 70 60
819 – 230f. on 300f. blue, red and yellow (807) . . . 1·00 85
820 – 240f. on 300f. mult (742) . . 1·00 85
822 **175** 100f. on 200f. mult (air) . . 70 55
823 – 100f. on 200f. mult (696) . . 60 60
824 – 100f. on 250f. mult (669) . . 70 55
825 – 100f. on 300f. mult (643) . . 40 30
826 – 100f. on 300f. mult (662) . . 40 30
827 **179** 170f. on 200f. mult . . . 70 60
828 **181** 170f. on 250f. mult . . . 1·10 90
829 – 170f. on 300f. mult (601) . . 70 60
830 – 170f. on 300f. mult (622) . . 70 60
831 – 240f. on 300f. mult (636) . . 1·00 90

203 Fada

1987. Liberation of Fada.
832 **203** 40f. multicoloured . . . .

204 Boy suffering from Trachoma

1987. Lions Club Anti-trachoma Campaign. Mult.
835 30f. Type **204** . . . .
837 100f. Type **204** . . . .
838 120f. Healthy boy and afflicted boys (horiz) . . .
840 200f. Doctor examining boy (horiz) . . . .

205 400 m Hurdles

1988. Air. Olympic Games, Seoul. Multicoloured.
841 100f. Type **205** 75 25
842 170f. 5000 m (horiz) . . . . 1·25 35
843 200f. Long jump (horiz) . . . 1·50 50
844 600f. Triple jump . . . . . 4·50 1·40
MS845 105 × 80 mm. 750f. 10,000 metres . . . . 7·50 3·50

206 Barbary Sheep

1988. Endangered Animals. Barbary Sheep. Mult.
846 25f. Type **206** 25 20
847 45f. Mother and lamb . . . 50 25
848 70f. Two sheep 75 30
849 100f. Two adults with lamb . . 1·00 50

207 President and Crowd on Map **208** Boy posting Letter

1989. "Liberation".
850 **207** 20f. multicoloured 25 15
851 25f. multicoloured 25 15
852 40f. multicoloured 35 20
853 100f. multicoloured . . . 1·00 30
854 170f. multicoloured . . . 1·60 50

1989. World Post Day.
855 **208** 100f. multicoloured . . .
856 120f. multicoloured . . .
857 170f. multicoloured . . .
858 250f. multicoloured . . .

209 N'Djamena Cathedral and Pope with Crucifix

1990. Visit of Pope John Paul II. Multicoloured.
859 20f. Type **209** 25 10
860 80f. Cathedral and Pope (different) 70 35
861 100f. Type **209** 95 60
862 170f. As No. 860 . . . . . . 1·60 1·10

210 Traditional Hairstyle

1990.
863 **210** 100f. multicoloured . . . 45 25
864 120f. multicoloured . . . 55 30
865 170f. multicoloured . . . 80 45
866 250f. multicoloured . . . 1·10 65

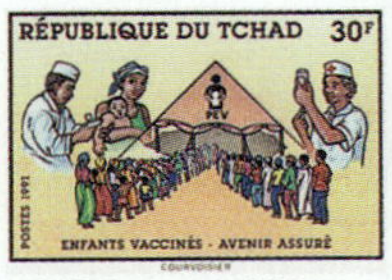

215 Queues and Nurse vaccinating Child **216** Torch, Hands with Broken Manacles and Ballot Box

1991. "Child Vaccination—Assured Future".
880 **215** 30f. multicoloured 25 20
881 100f. multicoloured . . . 75 45
882 170f. multicoloured . . . 1·25 75
883 180f. multicoloured . . . 1·25 75
884 200f. multicoloured . . . 1·50 1·00

1991. Day of Freedom and Democracy.
885 **216** 10f. multicoloured 10 10
886 20f. multicoloured 20 15
887 40f. multicoloured 30 20
888 70f. multicoloured 50 30
889 130f. multicoloured . . . 95 60
890 200f. multicoloured . . . 1·50 80

217 Mother and Child **219** Mother and Child, Globe and Cereals

218 Class

1992. 20th Anniv of Medecins sans Frontieres (medical relief organization).
891 **217** 20f. multicoloured 20 10
892 45f. multicoloured 30 20
893 85f. multicoloured 70 35
894 170f. multicoloured . . . 1·25 70
895 300f. multicoloured . . . 2·25 1·10

1992. Literacy Campaign.
896 **218** 25f. multicoloured 20 10
897 40f. multicoloured 30 20
898 70f. multicoloured 50 25
899 100f. multicoloured . . . 75 35
900 180f. multicoloured . . . 1·25 60
901 200f. multicoloured . . . 1·50 95

1992. International Nutrition Conference, Rome.
902 **219** 10f. multicoloured 15 10
903 60f. multicoloured 45 25
904 120f. multicoloured . . . 95 55
905 500f. multicoloured . . . 3·50 1·60

220 Stone Heads, Easter Island

2000. Wonders of the World. Multicoloured.
906 50f. Type **220** . . . .
907 150f. Stonehenge . . . . . .
908 300f. Jericho . . . .
909 400f. Machu Picchu . . . .
910 500f. Valley of statues . . .
911 700f. Chichen Itza . . . . .
912 900f. Persepolis . . . . . .

221 Mastiff ("Matin Espagnol")

2000. Dogs. Multicoloured.
915 400f. Type **221** . . . .
916 500f. Kuvasz . . . .
917 700f. Beauceron . . . . . .
918 900f. Rough collie . . . . .

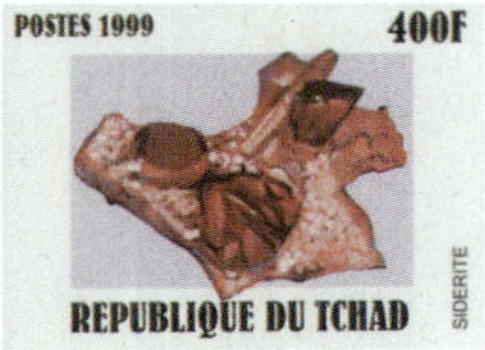

222 Siderite

2000. Minerals. Multicoloured.
921 400f. Type **222** . . . .
922 500f. Dolomite and quartz . .
923 700f. Azurite . . . .
924 900f. Calcite . . . .

223 Renault (1906)

2000. Vintage Cars. Multicoloured.
927 400f. Type **223** . . . .
928 500f. Pierce Arrow (1919) . .
929 700f. Citroen (1919) . . . .
930 900f. Ford (1928) . . . . .

224 Green Locomotive 0-6-0

2000. Trains. Multicoloured.
933 400f. Type **224** . . . .
934 500f. Brown locomotive . . .
935 700f. Blue locomotive . . . .
936 900f. Purple locomotive with red stripe . . . .

225 Betty Boop

2000. Betty Boop (cartoon character). Multicoloured.

937 250f. Type **225**
938 250f. As cheer leader
939 250f. Wearing fur coat
940 250f. At soda bar
941 250f. Wearing short leotard and leggings
942 250f. Wearing cap and shorts
943 250f. Wearing cap and leggings
944 250f. Seated
945 250f. Wearing ragged shorts and boots
MS946 89 × 140 mm. 1500f. Riding bicycle
MS947 140 × 94 mm. 2000f. Roller skating

Nos. 937/8 and 940/5 have a composite background design.

226 Larry and Curly

2000. Three Stooges (comedy act) (1st issue). Multicoloured.

948 250f. Type **226**
949 250f. As cowboys
950 250f. As cowboys on horseback
951 250f. Larry with raised arm
952 250f. Moe having hair pulled
953 250f. Moe holding hammer
954 250f. As cowboys, Curly kneeling
955 250f. Larry and Moe leading man by nose
956 250f. Moe and patient
MS957 130 × 92 mm. 1500f. As No. 956 (42 × 51 mm)
MS958 122 × 92 mm. 2000f. As No. 954 (42 × 51 mm)

See also Nos. 969/**MS**978.

227 Lucy

2000. "I love Lucy" (TV show starring Lucille Ball). Multicoloured.

959 225f. Type **227**
960 225f. Crouched wearing tutu
961 225f. Dressed as clown
962 225f. Wearing tutu and wings
963 225f. With leg raised
964 225f. Falling backwards
965 225f. With bent knees
966 225f. Wearing clown outfit being sprayed with water
967 225f. Wearing tutu with leg on barre
MS968 Two sheets, each 122 × 88 mm. (a) 1500f. As clown (51 × 36 mm). (b) 2000f. As clown jumping

228 Larry and Moe

2000. Three Stooges (comedy act) (2nd issue). Multicoloured.

969 300f. Type **228**
970 300f. Larry and Moe wearing suits holding diplomas
971 300f. Moe
972 300f. Larry
973 300f. Three Stooges
974 300f. Shemp facing left
975 300f. Shemp facing right
976 300f. Shemp and Larry
977 300f. Moe and Larry
MS978 Two sheets, each 130 × 92 mm. (a) 1500f. Moe as troubadour (42 × 51 mm). (b) 2000f. Larry holding fiddle (42 × 51 mm)

229 Emblem

2000. Centenary of Fort Lamy N'Djamena.

980 **229** 300f. multicoloured
981 475f. multicoloured

230 Giraffes (*Giraffa camelopardalis*)

2000. Fauna. Multicoloured.

982 150f. Type **230**
983 150f. Two giraffes
984 150f. Three giraffes
985 150f. Two giraffes (different)
986 200f. Gazelle (*Gazella granti*)
987 200f. Facing right
988 200f. Eating
989 200f. Drinking
990 250f. Addax (*Addax nasomaculatus*)
991 250f. Laying down
992 250f. Facing left
993 250f. Grazing
994 300f. Barbary sheep(*Ammotragus lervia*)
995 300f. Barbary sheep's head
996 300f. Facing left
997 300f. Facing front
998 375f. Black rhinoceros (*Diceros bicornis*)
999 375f. Facing right
1000 375f. Facing left
1001 375f. Amongst herbage
1002 400f. Leopard (*Panthera pardus*)
1003 400f. Laying down
1004 400f. Facing left
1005 400f. Leopard's head
1006 450f. Hippopotamus (*Hippopotamus amphibius*)
1007 450f. Two laying down
1008 450f. Group
1009 450f. Drinking
1010 450f. Gelada baboon (*Theropithecus gelada*)
1011 450f. Vervet monkey (*Cercopithecus aethiops*)
1012 450f. Olive baboon (Papio anubis)
1013 450f. Gelada baboon mother and baby
1014 475f. Scimitar-horned oryx (*Oryx dammah*)
1015 475f. Facing right
1016 475f. Grazing
1017 475f. Two scimitar-horned oryx
1018 500f. Two lions (*Panthera leo*)
1019 500f. Drinking
1020 500f. Mother and cub
1021 500f. Laying down
1022 600f. Elephant (Loxodonta africana)
1023 600f. Grazing
1024 600f. Facing front
1025 600f. Elephant's head
1026 750f. African buffalo cow and calf (*Syncerus caffer*)
1027 750f. African buffalo
1028 750f. Laying down
1029 750f. African buffalo's head
MS1030 Three sheets, each 130 × 90 mm. (a) 1000f. Two hippopotami (42 × 51 mm). (b) 1000f. Two rhinoceros (42 × 51 mm). (b) 1500f. Lion eating (42 × 51 mm)

MILITARY FRANK STAMPS

1965. No. 77 optd **F.M.**

M148	20f. red and black	£250	£250

M 24 Soldier with Standard

M 92 Shoulder Flash of 1st Regiment

1966. No value indicated.

M149 **M 24**	(–) multicoloured	1·50	1·00

1972. No value indicated.

M353 **M 92**	(–) multicoloured	75	35

OFFICIAL STAMPS

O 23 Flag and Map

1966. Flag in blue, yellow and red.

O148 **O 23**	1f. blue	10	10
O149	2f. grey	10	10
O150	5f. black	15	10
O151	10f. blue	25	10
O152	25f. orange	25	15
O153	30f. turquoise	40	20
O154	40f. red	45	20
O155	50f. purple	55	25
O156	85f. green	85	45
O157	100f. brown	1·40	50
O158	200f. red	2·50	95

POSTAGE DUE STAMPS

1928. Postage Due type of France optd **TCHAD A. E. F.**

D58 **D 11**	5c. blue	10	4·50
D59	10c. brown	35	4·50
D60	20c. olive	75	4·75
D61	25c. red	85	5·25
D62	30c. red	70	5·00
D63	45c. green	1·00	5·75
D64	50c. purple	85	6·00
D65	60c. brown on cream	1·10	6·50
D66	1f. red on cream	1·00	6·50
D67	2f. red	1·50	11·00
D68	3f. violet	90	7·00

D 3 Village of Straw Huts

D 4 Pirogue on Lake Chad

1930.

D69 **D 3**	5c. olive and blue	10	4·75
D70	10c. brown and red	65	5·00
D71	20c. brown and green	1·80	5·25
D72	25c. brown and blue	2·00	5·50
D73	30c. green and brown	2·00	5·50
D74	45c. olive and green	1·90	6·00
D75	50c. brown & mauve	2·50	6·75
D76	60c. black and lilac	3·25	8·50
D77 **D 4**	1f. black and brown	4·25	9·00
D78	2f. brown and mauve	3·50	14·00
D79	3f. brown and red	13·50	70·00

D 6 Gonoa Hippopotamus

1962.

D 89	50c. bistre	10	10
D 90	50c. brown	10	10
D 91	1f. blue	10	10
D 92	1f. green	10	10
D 93	2f. red	15	15
D 94	2f. red	15	15
D 95	5f. myrtle	30	30
D 96	5f. violet	30	30
D 97	10f. brown	75	75
D 98	10f. brown	75	75
D 99	25f. purple	1·75	1·75
D100	25f. violet	1·75	1·75

DESIGNS (rock-paintings): No. D89, Type **D 6**; D90, Gonoa kudu; D91, Two Gonoa antelopes; D92, Three Gonoa antelopes; D93, Gonoa antelope; D94, Tibestiram; D95, Tibestiox; D96, Oudingueur boar; D97, Gonoa elephant; D98, Gira-Gira rhinoceros; D99, Bardai warrior; D100, Gonoa masked archer. The two designs in each value are arranged in tete-beche pairs throughout the sheet.

D 65 Kanem Puppet

1969. Native Puppets.

D284 **D 65**	1f. brown, red & grn	10	10
D285	– 2f. brown, grn & red	10	10
D286	– 5f. green and brown	10	10
D287	– 10f. brown, pur & grn	20	20
D288	– 25f. brown, pur & grn	45	25

DESIGNS: 2f. Kotoko doll; 5f. Copper doll; 10f. Kotoko (diff); 25f. Guera doll.

APPENDIX

The following stamps have either been issued in excess of postal needs or have not been available to the public in reasonable quantities at face value. Such stamps may later be given full listing if there is evidence of regular postal use.

1970.

"Apollo programme". Postage 40f.; Air 15, 25f.

Birth Bicent of Napoleon. Air. 10, 25, 32f.

World Cup Football Championship, Mexico. Air 5f.

World Cup. Previous Winners. 1, 4f., 5f. × 2.

"Expo 70" World Fair, Osaka, Japan. Japanese Paintings. 50c., 1, 2f.

Christmas. Paintings. Postage 3, 25f.; Air 32f.

Past Olympic Venues. Postage 3, 8, 20f.; Air 10, 35f.

1971.

Space Exploration. 8, 10, 35f.

Winter Olympic Games, Sapporo, Japan. Japanese Paintings. 50c., 1, 2f.

Kings and Queens of France. Postage 25f. × 2, 30, 32, 35f., 40f. × 2, 50f. × 4, 60f.; Air 40, 50, 60, 70, 75, 80f., 100f. × 5, 150f., 200f. × 4.

150th Death Anniv of Napoleon. Air. 10f.

Famous Paintings. 1, 4, 5f.

Past Olympic Venues. Postage 15, 20f.; Air 25, 50f.

Winter Olympic Games, Sapporo, Japan. Optd on 1970 "Expo 70" issue 50c., 1, 2f.

Olympic Games Munich. World Cup Previous Winners issue (1970) optd **1f.**

1972.

Moon Flight of "Apollo 15". Air 40, 80, 150, 250, 300, 500f.

"Soyuz 11" Disaster. Air 30, 50, 100, 200, 300, 400f.

Pres. Tombalbaye. Postage 30, 40f.; Air 70, 80f.

Winter Olympic Games, Sapporo, Japan. Postage 25, 75, 150f.; Air 130, 200f.

13th World Scout Jamboree, Asagiri, Japan (1971). Postage 30, 70, 80f.; Air 100, 200f.

Medal Winners, Sapporo Winter Olympics. Postage 25, 75, 100, 130f.; Air 150, 200f.

Olympic Games, Munich. Postage 20, 40, 60f.; Air 100, 120, 150f.

African Animals. Air 20, 30, 100, 130, 150f.

Medal Winners, Munich Olympics (1st series). Postage 10, 20, 40, 60f.; Air 150, 250f.

Medal Winners, Munich Olympics (2nd series). Gold frames, Postage 20, 30, 50f.; Air 150, 250f.

1973.

Locomotives. 10, 40, 50, 150, 200f.

Domestic Animals (2nd issue). Postage 20, 30f.; Air 100, 130, 150f.

Horses. 20, 60, 100, 120f.

Airplanes. Air 5, 25, 70, 150, 200f.

Christmas. Postage 30, 40, 55f.; Air 60, 250f.

Other issues exist which were prepared by various agencies, but it is uncertain whether these were placed on sale in Chad. They include further values in the "Kings and Queens of France" series.

All the stamps below are on gold foil.

1982.

World Cup Football Championship, Spain. Air 1500f.

21st Birthday of Princess of Wales. Air 1500f.

75th Anniv of Scout Movement. Air 1500f.

Olympic Games, Los Angeles. Air 1500f.

Birth of Prince William of Wales. 21st Birthday of Princess of Wales stamp optd. Air 1500f.

1983.

World Cup Football Championship Results. Air 1500f.

Chess Grand Masters. Air 1500f.

Exploitation of Space. Air 1500f.

Winter Olympic Games, Sarajevo. Air 1500f.

Bicentary of Manned Flight. Air 1500f.

Olympic Games, Los Angeles. Air 1500f.

1993.

30th Anniv of the Organisation for African Unity. 15f.; 30f.; 110f.; 190f.

Death Centenary of Victor Schoelcher. 55; 105; 125; 300f.

1994.

Inauguration of Bank of Central African States 20; 30; 105; 190f.

1995.

Traditional Grain Stores. 75; 150; 300; 450f.

1996.

Fungi. 150; 170; 200; 350; 450; 800f.
Marilyn Monroe Commemoration. 170; 200; 300; 1000f.
Singers and Entertainers. 170; 350; 500; 700f.
The Beatles. 300f. × 9.
John Lennon Commemoration. 100f. × 9.
Elvis Presley Commemoration. 500f. × 9.
Jacqueline Kennedy Commemoration. 200f. × 9.
Marilyn Monroe Commemoration. 250f. × 9.
Olympic Games, Nagano. 250f. × 4; 300f. × 4.
Sumo Wrestlers. 400f. × 4.
Michael Schumacher. 700f. × 4.
Rotary International. Ungulates. 170; 350; 500; 600f.
Rotary International. Ungulates. Overprinted for Calgary '96. 170; 350; 500; 600f.

1997.

Deng Xiaoping Commemoration. 75f. × 6
Bruce Lee commemoration. 125f. × 6.
Jacqueline Kennedy Commemoration. 150f. × 9.
Traditional Housework. 50f.; 100f.; 150; 300; 450; 500f.
Diana, Princess of Wales. 250f. × 9; 300f. × 9; 450f. × 9.
John f. Kennedy Commemoration. 250f. × 9.
20th Death Anniv of Elvis Presley. 600f. × 9.
Marilyn Monroe Commemoration. 500f. × 9.
Aircraft. 150f. × 6; 200f. × 6; 250f. × 6; 475f. × 6.
150th Anniv of Swiss Railways. 350f. × 6.
Trains. 600f. × 6.

1998.

Personalities. 100; 150; 300; 450; 475; 500; 600; 800; 1000f.
50th Anniv of Diplomatic relations with India. 150f. × 3.
Dogs and Cats. 330f. × 2; 450f. × 2; 475f. × 2; 500f. × 2.
Wild Animals. 150f. × 2; 550f. × 2; 600f. × 2.
Traditional Hairstyles. 50; 100; 150; 300; 400f.
Fauna. 150f. × 6; 250f. × 6; 300f. × 12; 350f. × 6.
Butterflies. 660f. × 6
Ostrich. Surcharged. 300f. × 4 on 220f. × 4
Kofi Annan. 150f. × 9.
American Railway Pioneers. 200f. × 9.
Bela Lugosi Commemoration. 250f. × 9.
Pope John Paul II. 300f. × 9.
Ronald Reagan. 450f. × 9.
John Glenn. 500f. × 9.
Fossils and Pre-History. 150f. × 9.
Dinosaurs. 400f. × 6; 450f. × 6.
Historical Vehicles. 50; 150; 200; 300; 400; 500f.

1999.

African Birds. 75; 150; 200; 300; 400; 475f.
Diana, Princess of Wales Commemoration. 250f. × 9.
Football. 300f. × 4; 400f. × 4; 500f. × 4.
Chess. 375f. × 6; 500f. × 6.
Betty Boop. 450f. × 9.
Carl Benz Commemoration. 250f. × 6.
Elvis Presley Commemoration. 300f. × 9.
Napoleon Bonaparte. 300 × 6.
Pope John Paul II. 475f. × 6.
Space Exploration. 500f. × 6.

CHAMBA Pt. 1

An Indian "convention" state of the Punjab. Stamps of India overprinted.

12 pies = 1 anna; 16 annas = 1 rupee.

1886. Queen Victoria. Optd **CHAMBA STATE** in two lines.
1 **23** ½a. turquoise 1·00 1·25
2 – 1a. purple 2·50 2·50
4 – 1a.6p. brown 3·00 14·00
6 – 2a. blue 1·25 2·25
7 – 2a.6p. green 35·00 £100
9 – 3a. orange 3·00 6·00
11 – 4a. green (No. 96) 4·50 8·00
12 – 6a. brown (No. 80) 5·50 22·00
14 – 8a. mauve 9·00 12·00
16 – 12a. purple on red 7·00 16·00
17 – 1r. grey (No. 101) 48·00 £150
18 **37** 1r. green and red 9·50 17·00
19 **38** 2r. red and brown £100 £400
20 3r. brown and green £120 £350
21 5r. blue and violet £130 £550

1900. Queen Victoria. Optd **CHAMBA STATE** in two lines.
22 **40** 3p. red 60 90
23 3p. grey 60 2·25
25 **23** ½a. green 75 1·75
26 – 1a. red 75 40
27 – 2a. lilac 11·00 35·00

1903. King Edward VII. Optd **CHAMBA STATE** in two lines.
28 **41** 3p. grey 25 1·60
30 – ½a. green (No. 122) 80 60
31 – 1a. red (No. 123) 1·60 90
33 – 2a. lilac 1·90 3·50
34 – 3a. orange 4·75 6·00
35 – 4a. olive 7·00 22·00
36 – 6a. bistre 4·50 24·00
37 – 8a. mauve 6·00 24·00
39 – 12a. purple on red 8·00 32·00
40 – 1r. green and red 8·50 24·00

1907. King Edward VII. Optd **CHAMBA STATE** in two lines.
41 – ½a. green (No. 149) 2·50 4·00
42 – 1a. red (No. 150) 2·50 4·00

1913. King George V. Optd **CHAMBA STATE** in two lines.
43 **55** 3p. grey 40 1·25
44 **56** ½a. green 1·00 1·25
45a **57** 1a. red 2·00 4·00
55 1a. brown 3·50 5·50
56 **58** 1½a. brown (No. 163) 27·00 £130
57 1½a. brown (No. 165) 2·50 6·50
58 1½a. red 90 24·00
47 **59** 2a. purple 4·00 12·00
59 **61** 2a.6p. blue 60 4·25
60 2a.6p. orange 2·75 23·00
48 **62** 3a. orange 4·75 9·00
61 3a. blue 4·25 23·00
49 **63** 4a. olive 4·00 5·50
50 **64** 6a. bistre 4·50 7·50
51 **65** 8a. mauve 6·00 16·00
52 **66** 12a. red 5·50 13·00
53b **67** 1r. brown and green 18·00 30·00

1921. No. 192 of India optd **CHAMBA**.
54 **57** 9p. on 1a. red 1·00 18·00

1927. Stamps of India (King George V) optd **CHAMBA STATE** in one line.
62 **55** 3p. grey 20 1·75
63 **56** ½a. green 30 2·50
76 **79** ½a. green 1·10 11·00
64 **80** 9p. green 5·00 22·00
65 **57** 1a. brown 1·75 1·50
77 **81** 1a. brown 2·25 1·25
66 **82** 1a.3p. mauve 1·40 6·50
67 **58** 1½a. red 6·50 7·50
68 **70** 2a. lilac 2·25 4·00
78 **59** 2a. red 1·25 25·00
69 **61** 2a.6p. orange 3·25 20·00
70 **62** 3a. blue 1·25 22·00
80 3a. red 2·25 12·00
71 **71** 4a. green 1·25 7·00
81 **63** 4a. olive 5·50 17·00
72 **64** 6a. bistre 26·00 £170
73 **65** 8a. mauve 1·60 12·00
74 **66** 12a. red 1·60 16·00
75 **67** 1r. brown and green 12·00 30·00

1938. Stamps of India (King George VI Nos. 247/64) optd **CHAMBA STATE**.
82 **91** 3p. slate 11·00 22·00
83 ½a. brown 1·60 14·00
84 9p. green 10·00 38·00
85 1a. red 2·00 3·75
86 **92** 2a. red 8·00 16·00
87 – 2a.6p. violet 8·50 32·00
88 – 3a. green 9·00 29·00
89 – 3a.6p. blue 9·00 30·00
90 – 4a. brown 23·00 30·00
91 – 6a. green 26·00 70·00
92 – 8a. violet 24·00 65·00
93 – 12a. red 18·00 65·00
94 **93** 1r. slate and brown 35·00 75·00
95 2r. purple and brown 60·00 £350
96 5r. green and blue 95·00 £475
97 10r. purple and red £150 £750
98 15r. brown and green £160 £1000
99 25r. slate and purple £225 £1100

1942. Stamps of India (King George VI) optd **CHAMBA**. (a) On issue of 1938.
100 **91** ½a. brown 50·00 45·00
101 1a. red 75·00 60·00
102 **93** 1r. slate and brown 21·00 65·00
103 2r. purple and brown 24·00 £275
104 5r. green and blue 45·00 £300
105 10r. purple and red 70·00 £475
106 15r. brown and green £150 £850
107 25r. slate and purple £140 £850

(b) On issue of 1940.
108 **100a** 3p. slate 1·25 5·50
109 ½a. mauve 70 6·50
110 9p. green 1·10 20·00
111 1a. red 1·75 5·50
112 **101** 1½a. violet 2·00 14·00
113 2a. red 8·50 16·00
114 3a. violet 21·00 48·00
115 3½a. blue 11·00 45·00
116 **102** 4a. brown 15·00 15·00
117 6a. green 17·00 42·00
118 8a. violet 18·00 50·00
119 12a. purple 24·00 65·00
120 – 14a. purple (No. 277) 14·00 3·00

OFFICIAL STAMPS

Stamps of India overprinted.

1886. Queen Victoria. Optd **SERVICE CHAMBA STATE**.
O 1 **23** ½a. turquoise 75 20
O 3 – 1a. purple 2·75 30
O 5 – 2a. blue 2·50 2·50
O 7 – 3a. orange 2·50 13·00
O 8 – 4a. green (No. 96) 3·75 8·00
O10 – 6a. brown (No. 80) 5·00 15·00
O13 – 8a. mauve 3·75 3·00
O14 – 12a. purple on red 10·00 48·00
O15 – 1r. grey (No. 101) 15·00 £150
O16 **37** 1r. green and red 6·00 42·00

1902. Queen Victoria. Optd **SERVICE CHAMBA STATE**.
O17 **40** 3p. grey 60 80
O18 **23** ½a. green 1·25 4·00
O20 – 1a. red 1·50 60
O21 – 2a. lilac 12·00 35·00

1903. King Edward VII. Optd **SERVICE CHAMBA STATE**.
O22 **41** 3p. grey 35 15
O24 ½a. green (No. 122) 25 10
O25 1a. red (No. 123) 1·25 30
O27 – 2a. lilac 1·25 1·50
O28 – 4a. olive 3·50 20·00
O29 – 8a. mauve 8·50 20·00
O31 – 1r. green and red 1·75 14·00

1907. King Edward VII. Optd **SERVICE CHAMBA STATE**.
O32 – ½a. green (No. 149) 40 75
O33 – 1a. red (No. 150) 2·25 2·50

1913. King George V Official stamps optd **CHAMBA STATE**.
O34 **55** 3p. grey 20 40
O36 **56** ½a. green 20 60
O38 **57** 1a. red 20 10
O47 1a. brown 4·50 70
O40 **59** 2a. lilac (No. O83) 1·10 15·00
O41 **63** 4a. olive (No. O86) 1·10 20·00
O42 **65** 8a. mauve 1·75 21·00
O43 **67** 1r. brown and green 5·50 32·00

1914. King George V Postage stamps optd **SERVICE CHAMBA STATE**.
O44 **59** 2a. lilac (No. 166) 15·00
O45 **63** 4a. olive (No. 210) 13·00

1921. No O97 of India optd **CHAMBA**.
O46 **57** 9p. on 1a. red 15 8·50

1927. King George V Postage stamps optd **CHAMBA STATE SERVICE**.
O48 **55** 3p. grey 50 40
O49 **56** ½a. green 35 15
O61 **79** ½a. green 5·50 50
O50 **80** 9p. green 4·00 11·00
O51 **57** 1a. brown 20 10
O62 **81** 1a. brown 2·75 45
O52 **82** 1¼a. mauve 6·00 1·00
O53 **70** 2a. lilac 2·50 60
O63 **59** 2a. red 5·50 1·25
O54 **71** 4a. olive 1·50 2·75
O65 **63** 4a. green 8·00 7·50
O55 **65** 8a. mauve 8·00 11·00
O56 **66** 12a. red 5·00 26·00
O57 **67** 1r. brown and green 15·00 48·00
O58 2r. red and orange 24·00 £250
O59 5r. blue and violet 42·00 £300
O60 1r. green and red 65·00 £300

1938. King George VI Postage stamps of India optd **CHAMBA STATE SERVICE**.
O66 **91** 9p. green 25·00 70·00
O67 1a. red 30·00 6·00
O68 **93** 1r. slate and brown £225 £750
O69 2r. purple and brown 42·00 £400
O70 5r. green and blue 60·00 £450
O71 10r. purple and red 85·00 £800

1940. Official stamps of India optd **CHAMBA**.
O72 **O 20** 3p. grey 70 1·25
O73 ½a. brown 30·00 3·75
O74 ½a. purple 70 3·75
O75 9p. green 7·00 12·00
O76 1a. red 1·00 3·00
O77 1a.3p. brown 85·00 22·00
O78 1½a. violet 7·50 8·50
O79 2a. orange 7·50 8·50
O80 2½a. violet 4·50 24·00
O81 4a. brown 7·50 18·00
O82w 8a. violet 17·00 70·00

1942. King George VI Postage stamps of India optd **CHAMBA SERVICE**.
O83 **93** 1r. slate and brown 20·00 2·25
O84 2r. purple and brown 35·00 £300
O85 5r. green and blue 65·00 £425
O86 10r. purple and red 75·00 £750

CHARKHARI Pt. 1

A state of Central India. Now uses Indian stamps.

12 pies = 1 anna; 16 annas = 1 rupee.

1

2

1894. Imperf. No gum.
10 **1** ¼a. purple 1·75 2·50
6a ½a. purple 2·50 3·00
7a 1a. green 4·50 6·50
8a 2a. green 7·00 8·50
9a 4a. green 7·50 14·00

1909. Perf or imperf.
15a **2** 1p. brown 4·75 38·00
16 1p. blue 60 45
33 1p. violet 21·00 £160
32 1p. green 60·00 £225
25 ½a. red 2·25 1·60
34 ½a. olive 2·50 14·00
35 ½a. brown 6·00 25·00
36 ½a. black 60·00 £190
18a 1a. green 2·50 1·60
40 1a. brown 13·00 26·00
41 1a. red £130 70·00
19 2a. blue 3·25 3·25
43 2a. grey 60·00 80·00
20 4a. green 4·25 5·50
44 4a. red 3·00 20·00
21 8a. red 7·50 20·00
22 1r. brown 13·00 42·00

4

7 Imlia Palace

5

1912. Imperf.
28 **4** 1p. violet 7·00 5·00

1922. Imperf.
29 **5** 1a. violet 80·00 85·00

1931. Perf.
45 – ½a. green 2·25 10
46 **7** 1a. sepia 1·60 10
47 – 2a. violet 1·75 10
48 – 4a. olive 1·50 15
49 – 8a. mauve 2·00 10
50 – 1r. green and red 2·75 20
51 – 2r. red and brown 4·00 25
52 – 3r. brown and green 15·00 40
53 – 5r. blue and lilac 9·50 50

DESIGNS—HORIZ: ½a. The Lake; 2a. Industrial school; 4a. Bird's-eye view of city; 8a. Fort; 1r. Guest House; 2r. Palace Gate; 3r. Temples at Rainpur; 5r. Goverdhan Temple.

1940. Nos. 21/2 surch.
54 **2** ½a. on 8a. red 35·00 £130
55 1a. on 1r. brown £120 £425
56 "1 ANNA" on 1r. brown £1100 £1000

CHILE Pt. 20

A republic on the W. coast of S. America.

1853. 100 centavos = 1 peso.
1960. 10 milesimos = 1 centesimo; 100 centesimos = 1 escudo.
1975. 100 centavos = 1 peso.

1 Columbus

9

10

1853. Imperf.
29 **1** 1c. yellow 18·00 20·00
17 5c. brown £100 11·00
37 5c. red 23·00 6·50
32 10c. blue 32·00 5·00
33 20c. green 35·00 28·00

1867. Perf.
41 **9** 1c. orange 12·50 1·25
43 2c. black 17·00 2·75
45 5c. red 13·00 90

46		10c. blue	13·00	1·10
48		20c. green	22·00	2·00

1877. Roul.

49	**10**	1c. slate	2·00	75
50		2c. orange	9·00	1·50
51		5c. lake	11·50	50
52		10c. blue	10·00	1·60
53		20c. green	13·00	2·50

12

15

1878. Roul.

55	**12**	1c. green	1·00	15
57		2c. red	1·00	15
58		5c. red	5·00	25
59a		5c. blue	1·50	50
60a		10c. orange	2·25	10
61		15c. green	2·50	15
62		20c. grey	2·50	35
63		25c. brown	2·50	15
64		30c. red	5·00	2·00
65a		50c. violet	2·50	1·00
66	**15**	1p. black and brown	13·50	2·00

16

18

1900. Roul.

82	**16**	1c. green	75	10
83		2c. red	75	10
84a		5c. blue	3·50	25
85		10c. lilac	4·00	35
79		20c. grey	4·00	1·25
80		30c. brown	4·50	1·25
81		50c. brown	5·50	1·50

1900. Surch **5**.

86	**12**	5c. on 30c. red	1·00	20

1901. Perf.

87	**18**	1c. green	25	15
88		2c. red	35	15
89		5c. blue	1·10	15
90		10c. black and red	2·10	25
91		30c. black and violet	6·75	65
92		50c. black and red	6·50	1·75

1903. Surch **Diez CENTAVOS**.

93	**16**	10c. on 30c. brown	1·60	95

20 Huemul (mountain deer)

24 Pedro Valdivia

1904. Animal supporting shield at left without mane and tail. Optd **CORREOS** in frame.

94	**20**	2c. brown	25	15
95		5c. red	40	15
96		10c. olive	1·40	40

1904. As T **20**, but animal with mane and tail optd **CORREOS** in frame and the 1p. also surch **CENTAVOS 3 3**.

97	**20**	2c. brown	5·00	
98		3c. on 1p. brown	35	20
99		5c. red	6·00	
100		10c. green	12·00	

1904. Surch **CORREOS** in frame and new value.

101	**24**	1c. on 20c. blue	25	15
102		3c. on 5c. red	40·00	40·00
103		12c. on 5c. red	85	35

26 Christopher Columbus

28 Christopher Columbus

27 Christopher Columbus

1905.

104	**26**	1c. green	25	15
105		2c. red	25	15
106		3c. brown	60	25
107		5c. blue	60	15
108	**27**	10c. black and grey	1·25	15
109		12c. black and lake	5·25	2·00
110		15c. black and lilac	1·25	15
111		20c. black and brown	2·50	15
112		30c. black and green	3·50	25
113		50c. black and blue	3·50	25
114	**28**	1p. grey and green	12·50	8·50

1910. Optd **ISLAS DE JUAN FERNANDEZ** or surch also.

115	**27**	5c. on 12c. black & red	40	30
116	**28**	10c. on 1p. grey & green	1·10	65
117		20c. on 1p. grey & green	1·75	1·00
118		1p. grey and green	3·50	2·40

31 Battle of Chacabuco

33 San Martin Monument

1910. Centenary of Independence. Centres in black.

119	–	1c. green	25	15
120	**31**	2c. lake	25	15
121	–	3c. brown	1·00	65
122	–	5c. blue	35	10
123	–	10c. brown	1·50	25
124	–	12c. red	3·00	90
125	–	15c. slate	1·60	65
126	–	20c. orange	2·50	1·00
127	–	25c. blue	3·50	2·40
128	–	30c. mauve	3·25	1·40
129	–	50c. olive	6·75	1·50
130	**33**	1p. yellow	13·50	4·50
131	–	2p. red	13·50	3·75
132	–	5p. green	35·00	17·00
133	–	10p. purple	30·00	13·50

DESIGNS—HORIZ: 1c. Oath of Independence; 3c. Battle of Roble; 5c. Battle of Maipu; 10c. Fight between frigates "Lautaro" and "Esmeralda"; 12c. Capture of the "Maria Isabella"; 15c. First sortie of the liberating forces; 20c. Abdication of O'Higgins; 25c. First Chilean Congress. VERT: 30c. O'Higgins Monument; 50c. Carrera Monument; 2p. General Blanco; 5p. General Zenteno; 10p. Admiral Cochrane.

46 Columbus

47 Valdivia

49 O'Higgins

64 Admiral Cochrane

50 Freire

52 Prieto

65 M. Rengifo

57 A. Pinto

1911. Inscr "CHILE CORREOS".

135	**46**	1c. green	15	10
136	**47**	2c. red	15	10
150	**46**	2c. red	15	10
137	–	3c. sepia	50	35
151	–	4c. sepia	20	10
138	**49**	5c. blue	15	10
161	**64**	5c. blue	35	15
152	–	8c. grey	70	30
139	**50**	10c. black and grey	50	30
153	**49**	10c. black and blue	70	10
140	–	12c. black and red	85	30
154	–	14c. black and red	70	10
141	**52**	15c. black and purple	70	30
142	–	20c. black and orange	1·40	15
167	–	25c. black and blue	50	15
168	–	30c. black and brown	1·50	15
155	**52**	40c. black and purple	4·50	65
186	**65**	40c. black and violet	40	15
170	–	50c. black and green	1·50	15
156	–	60c. black and blue	8·50	1·60
171	–	80c. black and sepia	1·90	55
188	**57**	1p. black and green	70	10
189	–	2p. black and red	3·25	30
190	–	5p. black and olive	8·00	70
190a	–	10p. black and orange	8·00	1·00

PORTRAITS: 3c., 4c. Toro Z. 8c. Freire. 12, 14c. F. A. Pinto. 20c. Bulnes. 25c., 60c. Montt. 30c. Perez. 50c. Errazuriz Z. 80c. Admiral Latorre. 2p. Santa Maria. 5p. Balmaceda. 10p. Errazuriz E.

61 Columbus

62 Valdivia

63 Columbus

1915. Larger Stars.

157	**61**	1c. green	20	10
158	**62**	2c. red	20	10
160	**61**	4c. brown (small head)	30	10
159	**63**	4c. brown (large head)	25	10

67 Chilean Congress Building

67a O'Higgins

1923. Pan-American Conference.

176	**67**	2c. red	15	10
177		4c. brown	15	10
178		10c. black and blue	15	10
179		20c. black and orange	40	15
180		40c. black and mauve	70	20
181		1p. black and green	85	35
182		2p. black and red	3·00	40
183		5p. black and green	10·00	2·25

1927. Air. Unissued stamp surch **Correo Aereo** and value.

184	**67a**	40c. on 10c. blue & brn	£200	30·00
184a		80c. on 10c. blue & brn	£200	42·00
184b		1p.20 on 10c. bl & brn	£200	50·00
184c		1p.60 on 10c. bl & brn	£200	50·00
184d		2p. on 10c. blue & brn	£200	50·00

1928. Air. Optd **CORREO AEREO** and bird or surch also.

191	–	20c. blk & orge (No. 141)	35	15
199	**65**	40c. black and violet	40	20
200	**57**	1p. black and green	1·10	35
194	–	2p. black & red (No. 189)	1·60	25
201	**64**	3p. on 5c. blue	40·00	30·00
195	–	5p. black & ol (No. 190)	2·75	70
196	**49**	6p. on 10c. black & blue	50·00	30·00
198	–	10p. blk & orge (No. 190a)	9·00	2·75

1928. As Types of 1911, but inscr "CORREOS DE CHILE".

205	**64**	5c. blue	50	10
206		5c. green	50	10
204	**49**	10c. black and blue	75	25
208	**52**	15c. black and purple	1·75	10
209	–	20c. black and orange (As No. 142)	4·00	15
210	–	25c. black and blue (As No. 167)	75	10
211	–	30c. black and brown (As No. 168)	55	20
212	–	50c. black and green (As No. 170)	50	10

1929. Air. Nos. 209/12 optd **CORREO AEREO** and bird.

213a		20c. black and orange	25	15
214		25c. black and blue	40	15
215		30c. black and brown	25	15
216		50c. black and green	35	15

71 Winged Wheel

72 Sower

1930. Centenary of Nitrate Industry.

217	**71**	5c. green	35	15
218		10c. brown	35	15
219		15c. violet	35	15
220	–	25c. slate (Girl harvester)	1·40	15
221	**72**	70c. blue	3·25	1·00
222		1p. green (24½ × 30 mm)	2·50	50

73 Andean Condor and Fokker Super Universal Airplane

75 Ford 4AT Trimotor over Los Cerrillos Airport

1931. Air. Inscr "LINEA AEREA NACIONAL".

223	**73**	5c. green	40	25
224		10c. brown	40	25
225		20c. red	40	10
226a	–	50c. sepia	40	25
227	**75**	50c. blue	1·75	85
228	–	1p. violet	55	30
229	–	2p. slate	1·50	25
230	**75**	5p. red	3·50	60

DESIGN: 50c. (No. 226a), 1p., 2p. Fokker Super Universal airplane.

76 O'Higgins

79 Mariano Egana

1931.

231	**76**	10c. blue	1·00	10
232	–	20c. brown (Bulnes)	85	10
233	–	30c. mauve (Perez)	1·40	10

1934. Centenary of Constitution of 1833.

234	**79**	30c. mauve	50	25
235	–	1p.20 blue	90	25

PORTRAIT: 1p.20, Joaquin Tocornal (24½ × 29 mm).

83 Fokker Super Universal Aircraft over Globe

87 Diego de Almagro

1934. Air. As T **83**.

236		10c. green	15	10
237		15c. green	25	20
238		20c. blue	20	15
239		30c. black	20	15
239a		40c. blue	20	15
240		50c. brown	20	15
241		60c. black	20	15
356a		70c. blue	30	20
243		80c. green	20	15
244		1p. grey	20	15
245		2p. blue	20	15
360		3p. brown	25	15
361		4p. brown	25	15
248		5p. red	20	10
249		6p. brown	35	15
250		8p. green	30	10
251		10p. purple	35	15
252		20p. olive	35	15
253		30p. grey	35	10
254		40p. violet	70	20
255a		50p. purple	85	40

DESIGNS—21 × 25 mm: 10, 15, 20c. Fokker Super Universal over Santiago; 30, 40, 50c. Junkers G.24 over landscape; 60c. Condor in flight; 70c. Airplane and star; 80c. Condor and statue of Caupolican; 25 × 29 mm: 1, 2p. Type **83**; 3, 4, 5p. Stinson Faucett F.19 seaplane in flight; 6, 8, 10p. Northrop Alpha monoplane and rainbow; 20, 30p. Stylized Dornier Wal flying boat and compass; 40, 50p. Airplane riding a storm.

1936. 400th Anniv of Discovery of Chile.

256	–	5c. red	35	15
257	–	10c. violet	15	10
258	–	20c. mauve	20	10
259	–	25c. blue	2·00	55
260	–	30c. green	20	10
261	–	40c. black	2·00	50
262	–	50c. blue	1·10	20
263	–	1p. green	1·50	35
264	–	1p.20 blue	1·25	45
265	**87**	2p. brown	1·25	55
266	–	5p. red	3·50	1·40
267	–	10p. purple	9·00	7·00

DESIGNS: 5c. Atacama desert; 10c. Fishing boats; 20c. Coquito palms; 25c. Sheep. 30c. Coal mines; 40c. Lonquimay forests; 50c. Lota coal port; 1p. "Orduna" (liner), Valparaiso; 1p.20. Mt. Puntiaguda; 5p. Cattle; 10p. Shovelling nitrate.

88 Laja Waterfall

90 "Calbuco" (fishing boat)

1938.

268	**88**	5c. purple	15	10
269	–	10c. red	15	10
269a	–	15c. red	15	10
270	–	20c. blue	45	10
271	–	30c. pink	15	10
272	–	40c. green	15	10
273	–	50c. violet	15	10
274	**90**	1p. orange	15	10
275	–	1p.80 blue	85	20
338h	–	2p. red	50	10
278	–	5p. green	35	10
338j	–	10p. purple	1·10	10

DESIGNS—As Type **88**: 10c. Rural landscape; 15c. Boldo tree; 20c. Nitrate works; 30c. Mineral spas; 40c. Copper mine; 50c. Petroleum tanks. As Type **90**: 1p.80, Osorno Volcano; 2p. "Conte de Biancamano" (freighter) and "Ponderoso" (tug); 5p. Lake Villarrica; 10p. Steam locomotive No. 908.

92 "Abtao" (armed steamer) and Policarpo Toro

1940. 50th Anniv of Occupation of Easter Island and Local Hospital Fund.
279 **92** 80c.+2p.20 red & green . . 2·00 1·40
280 – 3p.60+6p.40 green and red 2·00 1·40
DESIGN: 3p.60, "Abtao" and E. Eyraud.

93 Western Hemisphere

1940. 50th Anniv of Pan-American Union.
281 **93** 40c. green 20 10

1940. Air. Surch with winged device above new values.
282 **73** 80c. on 20c. red 45 25
283 **75** 1p.60 on 5p. red . . . . . 3·25 85
284 – 5p.10 on 2p. slate (No. 229) . . . . 2·50 1·00

96 Fray Camilo Henriquez

97 Founding of Santiago

1941. 400th Anniv of Santiago.
285 **96** 10c. red 30 15
286 – 40c. green 40 10
287 – 1p.10 red . . . . 1·00 85
288 **97** 1p.80 blue . . . . 1·00 50
289 – 3p.60 blue . . . . 3·25 1·60
PORTRAITS—As Type **96**: 40c. P. Valdivia. 1p.10, B. V. MacKenna. 3p.60, D. B. Arana.

98 Potez 56 and Globe

99 Sikorsky S-43 Amphibian and Galleon

1941. Air. No. 304 is dated "1541–1941" and commemorates the 4th Centenary of Santiago.
290 – 10c. olive 30 10
291 – 10c. mauve 30 10
316 – 10c. blue 20 10
292 **98** 20c. red 30 10
318 20c. green 20 10
294 20c. brown 20 10
295 – 30c. violet 30 10
295a – 30c. olive 20 10
296 – 40c. brown 30 10
297 – 40c. blue 20 10
324 – 50c. red 30 10
325 – 50c. orange 30 10
299a – 60c. green 20 15
326 – 60c. orange 30 10
300 – 70c. red 60 20
301 – 80c. blue . . . . 3·00 35
302 – 80c. olive 20 15
303a – 90c. brown 30 10
304 **99** 1p. blue 60 20
304a 1p. green and blue . . . 30 10
305 – 1p.60 violet 30 15
306 – 1p.80 violet 30 10
307 – 2p. lake 85 25
308 – 2p. brown 60 10
309 – 3p. green . . . . 1·25 45
310a – 3p. violet and yellow . . 2·50 25
334 – 3p. violet and orange . . 85 15
311 – 4p. violet and brown . . 2·00 55
335 – 4p. green 85 30
336a – 5p. brown 35 20
336 – 5p. red 35 25
314 – 10p. green and blue . . . 9·50 4·00
337 – 10p. blue 85 25
DESIGNS: (each incorporating a different type of airplane): 10c. Steeple; 30c. Flag; 40c. Stars; 50c. Mountains; 60c. Tree; 70c. Estuary; 80c. Shore; 90c. Sun rays; 1p.60, 1p.80, Wireless mast; 2p. Compass; 3p. Telegraph wires; 4p. Rainbow; 5p. Factory; 10p. Snow-capped mountain.

See also Nos. 395 etc.

101 V. Letelier

102 University of Chile

103 Coat of arms and Aeroplane

1942. Centenary of Santiago de Chile University.
339 **101** 30c. red (postage) 20 10
340 – 40c. green 20 10
341 – 90c. violet . . . . 1·50 70
342 **102** 1p. brown . . . . 1·00 40
343 – 1p.80 blue . . . . 2·50 1·40
344 **103** 100p. red (air) . . . . . 30·00 20·00
DESIGNS—As Type **101**: 40c. A. Bello; 90c. M. Bulnes; 1p.80, M. Montt.

104 Manuel Bulnes

105 Straits of Magellan

1944. Centenary of Occupation of Magellan Straits.
345 **104** 15c. black 15 10
346 – 30c. red 15 10
347 – 40c. green 15 10
348 – 1p. brown 85 25
349 **105** 1p.80 blue . . . . 1·25 70
PORTRAITS: 30c. J. W. Wilson. 40c. D. D. Almeida. 1p. Jose de los Santos Mardones.

106 "Lamp of Life"

1944. International Red Cross.
350 **106** 40c. black, red and green 50 10
351 – 1p.80 red and blue . . . 1·00 50
DESIGN: 1p.80, Serpent and chalice symbol of Hygiene.

107 O'Higgins (after J. G. de Castro)

108 Battle of Rancagua (after Subercaseaux)

1944. Death Centenary of Bernardo O'Higgins.
367 **107** 15c. black and red 15 10
368 – 30c. black and brown . . 25 10
369 – 40c. black and green . . 25 10
370 **108** 1p.80 black and blue . . 1·25 80
DESIGNS—As Type **108**: 30c. Battle of the Maipu; 40c. Abdication of O'Higgins.

109 Columbus Lighthouse, Dominican Republic

110 Andres Bello

1945. 450th Anniv of Discovery of America by Columbus.
371 **109** 40c. green 30 15

1946. 80th Death Anniv of Andres Bello (educationist).
372 **110** 40c. green 15 10
373 1p.80 blue 15 10

111 Antarctic Territory

113 Miguel de Cervantes

112 Eusebio Lillo and Ramon Carnicer

1947.
374 **111** 40c. red 40 15
375 2p.50 blue . . . . 1·25 30

1947. Centenary of National Anthem.
376 **112** 40c. green 15 10

1947. 400th Birth Anniv of Cervantes.
377 **113** 40c. red 15 10

114 Arturo Prat and "Esmeralda" (sail corvette)

1948. Birth Centenary of Arturo Prat.
378 **114** 40c. blue 35 10

115 O'Higgins

119 "Chiasognathus granti"

1948.
379 **115** 60c. black 10 10

1948. No. 272 surch **VEINTE CTS**. and bar.
380 20c. on 40c. green 10 10

1948. Centenary of Publication on Chilean Flora and Fauna. Botanical and zoological designs, as T **119** inscr "CENTENARIO DEL LIBRO DE GAY 1844–1944".
381a/y 60c. blue (postage) 80 35
382a/y 2p.60 green . . . . 1·50 90
383a/y 3p. red (air) . . . . 1·60 1·10
Each value in 25 different designs.
Prices are for individual stamps.

120 Airline Badge

121 B. V. Mackenna

1949. Air. 20th Anniv of National Airline.
384 **120** 2p. blue 15 25

1949. Vicuna Mackenna Museum.
385 **121** 60c. blue (postage) . . . 10 10
386 3p. red (air) 15 10

122 Wheel and Lamp

1949. Cent of School of Arts and Crafts, Santiago.
387 **122** 60c. mauve (postage) . . 15 10
388 – 2p.60 blue 30 20
389 – 5p. green (air) 45 30
390 – 10p. brown 75 40
DESIGNS: 2p.60, Shield and book; 5p. Shield, book and factory; 10p. Wheel and column.

123 Heinrich von Stephan

124 Douglas DC-6B and Globe

1950. 75th Anniv of UPU.
391 **123** 60c. red (postage) 10 10
392 2p.50 blue 45 20
393 **124** 5p. green (air) 30 20
394 10p. brown 60 35

1950. Air. As T **98/99**.
395 20c. brown 15 10
396 40c. violet 15 10
404c 60c. blue 25 10
398 1p. green 15 10
399 2p. brown 15 10
404f 3p. blue 15 10
401 4p. orange 30 10
402 5p. violet 15 10
403 10p. green 20 10
480 20p. brown 30 10
481 50p. green 35 10
482 100p. red 75 10
483 200p. blue 80 10
DESIGNS (each including an aeroplane): 20c. Mountains; 40c. Coastline; 60c. Fishing vessel; 1p. Araucanian pine tree; 2p. Chilean flag; 3p. Dock crane; 4p. River; 5p. Industrial plant; 10p. Landscape; 20p. Aerial railway; 50p. Mountainous coastline; 100p. Antarctic map; 200p. Rock "bridge" in sea.

126 Crossing the Andes (after Y. Prades)

1951. Death Centenary of Gen. San Martin.
405 – 60c. blue (postage) . . . 10 10
406 **126** 5p. purple (air) 50 15
PORTRAIT (25 × 29 mm): 60c. San Martin.

1951. Air. No. 303a surch **UN PESO**.
407 1p. on 90c. brown 15 10

128 Issabella the Catholic

1952. 500th Birth Anniv of Issabella the Catholic.
408 **128** 60c. blue (postage) . . . 10 10
409 10p. red (air) 40 20

1952. Surch **40 Ctvs.**
410 **115** 40c. on 60c. black 10 10

1952. Air. No. 302 surch **40 Centavos**.
411 40c. on 80c. olive 15 10

116 M. de Toro y Zambrano

131 Arms of Valdivia

132 Old Spanish Watch-tower

1952.
379b **116** 80c. green 15 10
379c – 1p. turquoise (O'Higgins) 10 10
446 – 2p. lilac (Carrera) . . . 10 10
447 – 3p. blue (R. Freire) . . . 10 10
448 – 5p. sepia (M. Bulnes) . . 10 10
449 – 10p. violet (F. A. Pinto) 10 10
450 – 50p. red (M. Montt) . . 35 10

1953. 400th Anniv of Valdivia.
414 **131** 1p. blue (postage) 15 10
415 – 2p. violet 15 10
416 – 3p. green 35 10
417 – 5p. brown 45 10
418 **132** 10p. red (air) . . . . . . 1·25 20
DESIGNS—As Type **132**: 2p. Ancient cannons, Corral Fort; 3p. Valdivia from the river; 5p. Street scene (after old engraving).

133 J. Toribio Medina

134 Stamp of 1853

1953. Birth Centenary of Toribio Medina.
419 **133** 1p. brown 15 10
420 2p.50 blue 25 10

1953. Chilean Stamp Centenary.
421 **134** 1p. brown (postage) . . . 15 10
422 100p. turquoise (air) . . . 3·00 1·75

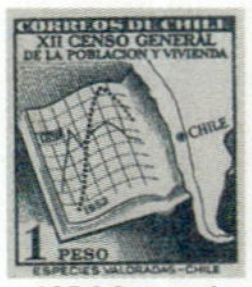

135 Map and Graph

136 Aircraft of 1929 and 1954

1953. 12th National Census.
423 **135** 1p. green 10 10
424 2p.50 blue 15 10
425 3p. brown 25 15
426 4p. red 35 15

1954. Air. 25th Anniv of National Air Line.
427 **136** 3p. blue 10 10

137 Arms of Angol

138 I. Domeyko

1954. 400th Anniv of Angol City.
428 **137** 2p. red 10 15

1954. 150th Birth Anniv of Domeyko (educationist and mineralogist).
429 **138** 1p. blue (postage) 15 10
430 5p. brown (air) 15 10

139 Locomotive "Tiger", 1856

1954. Centenary of Chilean Railways.
431 **139** 1p. red (postage) 20 25
432 10p. purple (air) . . . . 90 1·25

140 Arturo Prat

141 Arms of Vina del Mar

1954. 75th Anniv of Naval Battle of Iquique.
433 **140** 2p. violet 15 10

1955. Int Philatelic Exhibition, Valparaiso.
434 **141** 1p. blue 15 10
435 – 2p. red 15 10
DESIGN: 2p. Arms of Valparaiso.

142 Dr. A. del Rio

143 Christ of the Andes

1955. 14th Pan-American Sanitary Conference.
436 **142** 2p. blue 10 10

1955. Exchange of Visits between Argentine and Chilean Presidents.
437 **143** 1p. blue (postage) 15 10
438 100p. red (air) . . . . . 1·90 75

144 De Havilland Comet 1

145 M. Rengifo

1955. Air.
441a **144** 100p. green 75 15
441b – 200p. blue . . . . . . 4·50 75
441c – 500p. red . . . . . . 6·00 75
AIRCRAFT: 200p. Morane Saulnier Paris I. 500p. Douglas DC-6B.

1955. Death Centenary of Joaquin Prieto (President, 1833–41).
442 **145** 3p. blue 10 10
443 – 5p. red (Egana) 10 10
444 – 50p. purple (Portales) . . 1·40 25
For 15p. in similar design see under Compulsory Tax Stamps.

147 Bell Trooper Helicopter and Bridge

148 F. Santa Maria

149 Atomic Symbol and Cogwheels

1956. Air.
451 – 1p. red 20 10
452 **147** 2p. sepia 20 10
455 – 5p. violet 20 10
456 – 10p. green 15 10
456a – 20p. blue 15 10
456b – 50p. red 20 10
DESIGNS: 1p. De Havilland Venom FB.4; 5p. Diesel locomotive and Douglas DC-6B; 10p. Oil derricks and Douglas DC-6B; 20p. De Havilland Venom FB.4 and Easter Island monolith; 50p. Douglas DC-2 and control tower.
See also Nos. 524/7.

1956. 25th Anniv of Santa Maria Technical University, Valparaiso.
457 **148** 5p. brown (postage) . . . 15 10
458 **149** 20p. green (air) 25 15
459 – 100p. violet 70 40
DESIGN—As Type **149**: 100p. Aerial view of University.

150 Gabriela Mistral

151 Arms of Osorno

1958. Gabriela Mistral (poetess, Nobel Prize Winner).
460 **150** 10p. brown (postage) . . 15 10
461 100p. green (air) 30 10

1958. 400th Anniv of Osorno.
462 **151** 10p. red (postage) 15 10
463 – 50p. green 35 10
464 – 100p. blue (air) 65 25
PORTRAITS: 50p. G. H. de Mendoza. 100p. O'Higgins.

152 "La Araucana" (poem) and Antarctic Map

153 Arms of Santiago de Chile

1958. Antarctic issue.
465 **152** 10p. blue (postage) . . . 20 10
466 – 200p. purple . . . . . . 3·25 1·25
467 **152** 20p. violet (air) 45 10
468 – 500p. blue . . . . 5·50 1·75
DESIGN: 200p., 500p. Chilean map of 1588.

1958. National Philatelic Exhibition, Santiago.
469 **153** 10p. purple (postage) . . 15 10
470 50p. green (air) 25 10

154

155 Antarctic Territory

1958. Cent of Chilean Civil Servants' Savings Bank.
471 **154** 10p. blue (postage) . . . 10 10
472 50p. brown (air) 25 10

1958. I.G.Y.
473 **155** 40p. red (postage) 40 10
474 50p. green (air) 50 15

156 Religious Emblems

1959. Air. Human Rights Day.
475 **156** 50p. red . . . . 65 1·00

157 Bridge, Valdivia

1959. Centenary of German School, Valdivia and Philatelic Exhibition.
476 **157** 40p. green (postage) . . . 20 10
477 – 20p. red (air) 15 15
DESIGN—VERT: 20p. A. C. Anwandter (founder).

158 Expedition Map

159 D. Barros-Arana

1959. 400th Anniv of Juan Ladrillero's Expedition of 1557.
484 **158** 10p. violet (postage) . . . 25 10
485 50p. green (air) 35 10

1959. 50th Death Anniv of D. Barros-Arana (historian).
486 **159** 40p. blue (postage) . . . 15 10
487 100p. lilac (air) 40 20

160 J. H. Dunant (founder)

1959. Red Cross Commemoration.
488 **160** 20p. lake & red (postage) 20 10
489 50p. black & red (air) . . 25 10

161 F. A. Pinto

162 Choshuenco Volcano

1960. (a) Portraits as T **161**.
490 – 5m. turquoise 10 10
491 **161** 1c. red 10 10
493 – 5c. blue 10 10

(b) Views as T **162**.
492 **162** 2c. blue 10 10
492a 2c. blue (23½ × 18 mm) 10 10
494 – 10c. green 20 10
495 – 20c. blue 35 10
496 – 1E. turquoise 40 15
DESIGNS—As Type **161**: 5m. M. Bulnes; 5c. M. Montt. As Type **162**: 10c. R. Maule Valley; 20c., 1E. Inca Lake.

163 Martin 4-0-4 Airplane and Dock Crane

164 Refugee Family

1960. Air (Inland).
497 – 1m. orange 10 10
498 – 2m. green 10 10
499 **163** 3m. violet 10 10
500 – 4m. olive 10 10
501 – 5m. turquoise 10 10
502 – 1c. blue 10 10
503 – 2c. brown 25 10
504 – 5c. green . . . . 1·90 15
505 – 10c. red 45 10
506 – 20c. blue 60 10
DESIGNS: Airplane over—1m. Araucanian pine; 2m. Chilean flag; 4m. River; 5m. Industrial plant; 1c. Landscape; 2c. Aerial railway; 5c. Mountainous coastline; 10c. Antarctic map; 20c. Rock "bridge" in sea.

1960. World Refugee Year.
507 **164** 1c. green (postage) . . . 35 10
508 10c. violet (air) 60 10

165 Arms of Chile

1960. 150th Anniv of 1st National Government (1st issue).
509 **165** 1c. brn & red (postage) 15 10
510 10c. chestnut & brn (air) 20 10
See also Nos. 512/23.

166 Rotary Emblem and Map

1960. Air. Rotary International S. American Regional Conference, Santiago.
511 **166** 10c. blue 25 10

167 J. M. Carrera **168** "Population"

1960. 150th Anniv of 1st National Government (2nd issue). (a) Postage.
512 – 1c. red and brown 15 10
513 – 5c. turquoise & green . . 15 10
514 – 10c. purple and brown . . 15 10
515 – 20c. green and blue . . . 15 10
516 – 50c. red and brown . . . 50 10
517 **167** 1E. brown and green . . 1·40 40
DESIGNS—HORIZ: 1c. Palace of Justice; 10c. M. de Toro y Zambrano and M. de Rozas; 20c. M. de Salas and Juan Egana; 50c. M. Rodriguez and J. Mackenna. VERT: 5c. Temple of the National Vow.

(b) Air.
518 – 2c. violet and red 10 10
519 – 5c. purple and blue 15 10
520 – 10c. bistre and brown . . . 15 10
521 – 20c. violet and blue 25 10
522 – 50c. blue and green 45 20
523 – 1E. brown and red . . . . 1·40 40
DESIGNS—HORIZ: 2c. Palace of Justice; 10c. J. G. Martin and J. G. Argomedo; 20c. J. A. Eyzaguirre and J. M. Infante; 50c. Bishop J. I. Cienfuegos and Fray C. Henriquez. VERT: 5c. Temple of the National Vow. 1E. O'Higgins.

1961. Air (Foreign). As T **147** or **144** (10c. and 50c.), but values in new currency.
524 5m. brown 15 10
525 1c. blue 10 10
526 2c. blue 10 10
527 5c. red 10 10
528 10c. blue 10 10
529 20c. red 10 10
530 50c. turquoise 10 10
DESIGNS: 5m. Diesel locomotive and Douglas DC-6B; 1c. Oil derricks and Douglas DC-6B; 2c. De Havilland Venom FB.4 and monolith; 5c. Douglas DC-2 and control tower; 10c. De Havilland Comet 1; 20c. Morane Saulnier Paris I; 50c. Douglas DC-6B.

1961. National Census. 13th Population Census (5c.); 2nd Housing Census (10c.).
531 **168** 5c. green 40 10
532 – 10c. violet (buildings) . . 40 10

169 Pedro de Valdivia **170** Congress Building

1961. Earthquake Relief Fund. Inscr "ESPANA A CHILE".
533 **169** 5c.+5c. green and pink (postage) . . . . 1·00 15
534 – 10c.+10c. violet & buff . . 1·00 15
535 – 10c.+10c. brown and orange (air) . . . . . 1·00 20
536 – 20c.+20c. red and blue . . 1·00 20
PORTRAITS: No. 534, J. T. Medina. No. 535, A. de Ercilla. No. 536, Gabriela Mistral.

1961. 150th Anniv of 1st National Congress.
537 **170** 2c. brown (postage) . . . 40 10
538 10c. green (air) . . . . . 1·10 70

171 Footballers and Globe

1962. World Football Championships, Chile.
539 **171** 2c. blue (postage) 10 10
540 – 5c. green 15 10
541 – 5c. purple (air) 15 10
542 **171** 10c. lake 25 10
DESIGN—HORIZ: Nos. 540/1, Goalkeeper and stadium.

172 Mother and Child

1963. Freedom from Hunger.
543 **172** 3c. purple (postage) . . . 10 10
544 – 20c. green (air) 15 10
DESIGN—HORIZ: 20c. Mother holding out food bowl.

173 Centenary Emblem **174** Fire Brigade Monument

1963. Red Cross Centenary.
545 **173** 3c. red & grey (postage) 10 10
546 – 20c. red and grey (air) . . 15 10
DESIGN—HORIZ: 20c. Centenary emblem and silhouette of aircraft.

1963. Centenary of Santiago Fire Brigade.
547 **174** 3c. violet (postage) . . . 10 10
548 – 30c. red (air) 30 15
DESIGN—HORIZ: (39 × 30 mm): 30c. Fire engine of 1863.

175 Band encircling Globe **176** Enrique Molina

1964. Air. "Alliance for Progress" and Pres. Kennedy Commemoration.
549 **175** 4c. blue 10 10

1964. Molina Commemoration (founder of Concepcion University).
550 **176** 4c. bistre (postage) . . . 10 10
551 60c. violet (air) 10 10

1965. Casanueva Commemoration. As T **176** but portrait of Mons. Carlos Casanueva, Rector of Catholic University.
552 4c. purple (postage) 10 10
553 60c. green (air) 10 10

177 Battle Scene (after Subercaseaux)

1965. Air. 150th Anniv of Battle of Rancagua.
554 **177** 5c. brown and green . . . 10 10

178 Monolith **179** ITU Emblem and Symbols

1965. Easter Island Discoveries.
555 **178** 6c. purple 10 10
556 10c. mauve 15 10

1965. Air. Centenary of ITU.
557 **179** 40c. purple and red . . . 15 10

180 Crusoe on Juan Fernandez **181** Skier descending slope

1965. Robinson Crusoe Commemoration.
558 **180** 30c. red 15 10

1965. World Skiing Championships.
559 **181** 4c. green (postage) . . . 15 10
560 – 20c. blue (air) 10 10
DESIGN—HORIZ: 20c. Skier crossing slope.

182 Angelmo Harbour **183** Aviators, Monument

1965. Air.
561 **182** 40c. brown 30 10
562 **183** 1E. red 20 10

184 Copihue (National Flower) **185** A. Bello

1965.
563 **184** 15c. red and green . . . 15 10
563a 20c. red and green . . . 15 10

1965. Air. Death Centenary of Andres Bello (poet).
564 **185** 10c. red 10 10

186 Dr. L. Sazie **187** Skiers

1966. Death Centenary of Dr. L. Sazie.
565 **186** 1E. green . . . . 1·25 10

1966. Air. World Skiing Championships.
566 – 75c. red and lilac 20 10
567 – 3E. ultramarine and blue 40 10
568 **187** 4E. brown and blue . . . 85 25
MS568a 110 × 140 mm. Nos. 566/7. Imperf. No gum . . . . 1·90
DESIGN—HORIZ: (38 × 25 mm): 75c., 3E. Skier in slalom race.

188 Ball and Basket **189** J. Montt

1966. Air. World Basketball Championships.
569 **188** 13c. red 15 10

1966.
570 **189** 30c. violet 10 10
571 – 50c. brown (G. Riesco) . . 10 10

190 W. Wheelwright and Paddle-steamers "Chile" and "Peru"

1966. 125th Anniv (1965) of Arrival of Paddle-steamers "Chile" and "Peru".
572 **190** 10c. ultram & bl (postage) 40 10
573 70c. blue and green (air) 60 10

191 "Learning" **193** Chilean Flag and Ships

192 ICY Emblem

1966. Education Campaign.
574 **191** 10c. purple 10 10

1966. International Co-operation Year (1965).
575 **192** 1E. brn & green (postage) 1·75 10
576 3E. red and blue (air) . . 60 20
MS576a 111 × 140 mm. Nos. 757/6. Imperf. No gum . . . . 1·75

1966. Air. Antofagasta Centenary.
577 **193** 13c. purple 10 10

194 Capt. Pardo and "Yelcho" (coastguard vessel)

1967. 50th Anniv of Pardo's Rescue of Shackleton Expedition.
578 **194** 20c. turquoise (postage) 1·40 10
579 – 40c. blue (air) 30 15
DESIGN: 40c. Capt. Pardo and Antarctic sectoral map.

195 Chilean Family **197** Pine Forest

196 R. Dario (poet)

1967. 8th International Family Planning Congress.
580 **195** 10c. black and purple (postage) 10 10
581 80c. black and blue (air) 20 10

1967. Air. Birth Centenary of Ruben Dario (Nicaraguan poet).
582 **196** 10c. blue 15 10

1967. National Afforestation Campaign.
583 **197** 10c. green & bl (postage) 10 10
584 75c. green & brown (air) 20 10

198 Lions Emblem

1967. 50th Anniv of Lions International.
585 **198** 20c. blue & brn (postage) 15 10
586 1E. violet & yellow (air) 15 10
587 5E. blue and yellow . . . 1·40 50

199 Chilean Flag

1967. 150th Anniv of National Flag.
588 **199** 80c. red & blue (post) . . 20 10
589 50c. red and blue (air) . . 15 10

200 ITY Emblem

1967. Air. International Tourist Year.
590 **200** 30c. black and blue . . . 10 10

201 Cardinal Caro **203** Farmer and Wife

202 San Martin and O'Higgins

1967. Birth Centenary of Cardinal Caro.
591 **201** 20c. lake (postage) . . . 35 20
592 40c. violet (air) 75 15

1968. 150th Anniv of Battles of Chacabuco and Maipu.
593 **202** 3E. blue (postage) 10 10
594 2E. violet (air) 10 10
MS594a 140 × 109 mm. Nos. 593/4. Imperf . . . . 2·50

1968. Agrarian Reform.
595 **203** 20c. black, green and orange (postage) . . . 15 10
596 50c. black, green and orange (air) 15 10

204 Juan I. Molina (scientist) and "Lamp of Learning" **205** Hand supporting Cogwheel

1968. Molina Commemoration.
597 **204** 2E. purple (postage) . . . 10 10
598 – 1E. green (air) 10 10
DESIGN: 1E. Molina and books.

1968. 4th Manufacturing Census.
599 **205** 30c. red 15 10

206 Map, "San Sebastian" (galleon) and "Alonso de Erckla" (ferry)

1968. "Five Towns" Centenaries.
600 **206** 30c. blue (postage) . . . 50 10
601 – 1E. purple (air) 15 10
DESIGN—VERT: 1E. Map of Chiloe Province.

207 Club Emblem

1968. 40th Anniv of Chilean Automobile Club.
602 **207** 1E. red (postage) 20 10
603 5E. blue (air) 15 15

208 Chilean Arms

1968. Air. State Visit of Queen Elizabeth II.
604 **208** 50c. brown and green . . 15 10
605 – 3E. brown and blue . . . 15 10
606 – 5E. purple and plum . . . 25 15
MS607 124 × 189 mm. Nos. 604/6. Imperf. No gum . . . . . . 6·00
DESIGN—HORIZ: 3E. Royal arms of Great Britain. VERT: 5E. St. Edward's Crown on map of South America.

209 Don Francisco Garcia Huidobro (founder)

1968. 225th Anniv of Chilean Mint.
608 **209** 2E. blue & red (postage) 10 10
609 – 5E. brown and green . . 20 10
610 – 50c. purple & yell (air) . . 10 10
611 – 1E. red and blue 15 15
MS612 150 × 120 mm. Nos. 608/11. Imperf. No gum (sold at 12e.) 1·60
DESIGNS: 50c. First Chilean coin and press; 1E. First Chilean stamp printed by the mint (1915); 5E. Philip V of Spain.

210 Satellite and Dish Aerial

1969. Inauguration of "ENTEL-CHILE" Satellite Communications Ground Station, Longovilo (1st issue).
613 **210** 30c. blue (postage) . . . 10 10
614 2E. purple (air) 20 10
See also Nos. 668/9.

211 Red Cross Symbols

1969. 50th Anniv of League of Red Cross Societies.
615 **211** 2E. red & violet (postage) 15 10
616 5E. red and black (air) . . 15 10

212 Rapel Dam

1969. Rapel Hydro-electric Project.
617 **212** 40c. green (postage) . . . 10 10
618 3E. blue (air) 15 10

213 Rodriguez Memorial

1969. 150th Death Anniv of Col. Manuel Rodriguez.
619 **213** 2E. red (postage) 10 10
620 30c. brown (air) 10 10

214 Open Bible

1969. 400th Anniv of Spanish Translation of Bible.
621 **214** 40c. brown (postage) . . 10 10
622 1E. green (air) 15 10

215 Hemispheres and ILO Emblem

1969. 50th Anniv of ILO.
623 **215** 1E. grn & blk (postage) 10 10
624 2E. purple & black (air) 10 10

216 Human Rights Emblem **217** "EXPO" Emblem

1969. Human Rights Year (1968).
625 **216** 4E. red and blue (postage) 35 25
626 4E. red and brown (air) 45 25
MS627 119 × 140 mm. Nos. 625/6. Imperf. No gum (sold at 12e.) 2·00

1969. World Fair "EXPO 70", Osaka, Japan.
628 **217** 3E. blue (postage) 10 10
629 5E. red (air) 15 10

218 Mint, Santiago (18th cent)

1970. Spanish Colonization of Chile.
630 **218** 2E. purple 20 10
631 – 3E. red 15 10
632 – 4E. blue 15 10
633 – 5E. brown 15 10
634 – 10E. green 15 10
MS635 110 × 140 mm. Nos. 631, 633/4. Imperf. No gum (sold at 25e.) . . . . 2·00
DESIGNS—HORIZ: 5E. Cal y Canto Bridge. VERT: 3E. Pedro de Valdivia; 4E. Santo Domingo Church, Santiago; 10E. Ambrosio O'Higgins.

219 Policarpo Toro and Map

1970. 80th Anniv of Seizure of Easter Island.
636 **219** 5E. violet (postage) . . . 25 10
637 50c. turquoise (air) . . . 35 10

221 Chilean Schooner and Arms

1970. 150th Anniv of Capture of Valdivia by Lord Cochrane.
640 **221** 40c. lake (postage) . . . 45 10
641 2E. blue (air) 90 10

222 Paul Harris **223** Mahatma Gandhi

1970. Birth Centenary of Paul Harris (founder of Rotary International).
642 **222** 10E. blue (postage) . . . 90 20
643 1E. red (air) 30 15

1970. Birth Centenary of Gandhi.
644 **223** 40c. green (postage) . . . 2·50 20
645 1E. brown (air) 30 15

225 Education Year Emblem **226** "Virgin and Child"

1970. International Education Year.
648 **225** 2E. red (postage) 10 10
649 4E. brown (air) 15 10

1970. O'Higgins National Shrine, Maipu.
650 **226** 40c. green (postage) . . . 10 10
651 1E. blue (air) 15 15

227 Snake and Torch Emblem **228** Chilean Arms and Copper Symbol

1970. 10th Int Cancer Congress, Houston, U.S.A.
652 **227** 40c. purple & bl (postage) 80 10
653 2E. brown and green (air) 50 10

1970. Copper Mines Nationalization.
654 **228** 40c. red & brn (postage) 15 10
655 3E. green & brown (air) 25 10

229 Globe, Dove and Cogwheel

1970. 25th Anniv of United Nations.
656 **229** 3E. vio & red (postage) 10 10
657 5E. green and red (air) . . 20 10

1970. Nos. 613/14 surch.
658 **210** 52c. on 30c. blue (postage) 30 10
659 52c. on 2E. purple (air) 50 15

231 Freighter "Lago Maihue" and Ship's Wheel

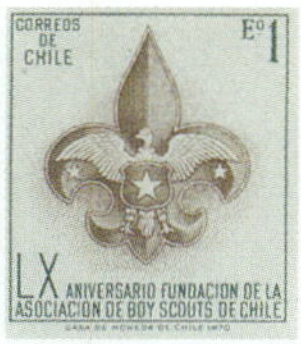

233 Scout Badge

232 Bernardo O'Higgins and Fleet

1971. State Maritime Corporation.
660 **231** 52c. red (postage) 30 10
661 5E. brown (air) 50 10

1971. 150th Anniv of Peruvian Liberation Expedition.
662 **232** 5E. grn & blue (postage) 35 10
663 1E. purple & blue (air) . . 50 10

1971. 60th Anniv of Chilean Scouting Association.
664 **233** 1E. brn & grn (postage) 20 10
665 5c. green & lake (air) . . 20 10

234 Young People and U.N. Emblem

1971. 1st Latin-American Meeting of UNICEF Executive Council, Santiago (1969).
666 **234** 52c. brn & blue (postage) 10 10
667 2E. green & blue (air) . . 15 10

1971. Longovilo Satellite Communications Ground Station (2nd issue). As T **210**, but with "LONGOVILO" added to centre inscr and wording at foot of design changed to "PRIMERA ESTACION LATINOAMERICANA".
668 40c. green (postage) 30 10
669 2E. brown (air) 50 15

235 Diver with Harpoon Gun

1971. 10th World Underwater Fishing Championships, Iquique.
670 **235** 1E.15 myrtle and green 65 10
671 2E.35 ultramarine & blue 15 10

239 Magellan and Caravel

1971. 450th Anniv of Discovery of Magellan Straits.
676 **239** 35c. plum and blue . . . 30 10

240 Dagoberto Godoy and Bristol Monoplane over Andes

1971. 1st Trans-Andes Flight (1918) Commem.
677 **240** 1E.15 green and blue . . 20 10

241 Statue of the Virgin, San Cristobal

1971. 10th Postal Union of the Americas and Spain Congress, Santiago.
678 **241** 1E.15 blue 75 10
679 – 2E.35 blue and red . . . 45 10
680 – 4E.35 red 45 10
681 – 9E.35 lilac 45 10
682 – 18E.35 mauve 60 10
DESIGNS—VERT: 4E.35, St. Francis's Church, Santiago. HORIZ: 2E.35, U.P.A.E. emblem; 9E.35, Central Post Office, Santiago; 18E.35, Corregidor Inn.

242 Cerro el Tololo Observatory

1972. Inauguration of Astronomical Observatory, Cerro el Tololo.
683 **242** 1E.95 blue & dp blue . . 20 10

243 Boeing 707 over Tahiti

1972. 1st Air Service Santiago–Easter Island–Tahiti.
684 **243** 2E.35 purple and ochre 30 10

244 Alonso de Ercilla y Zuniga

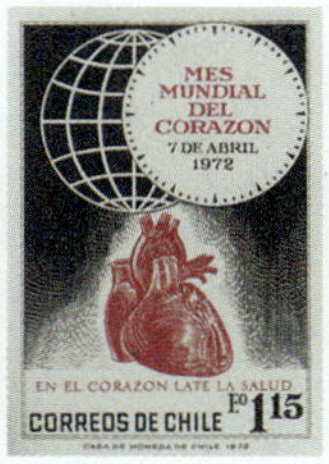

246 Human Heart

245 Antarctic Map and Dog-sledge

1972. 400th Anniv (1969) of "La Araucana" (epic poem by de Ercilla y Zungia).
685 **244** 1E. brown (postage) . . . 15 10
686 2E. blue (air) 20 15

1972. 10th Anniv of Antarctic Treaty.
687 **245** 1E.15 black and blue . . 80 15
688 3E.50 blue and green . . 55 10

1972. World Heart Month.
689 **246** 1E.15 red and black . . . 20 10

247 Text of Speech by Pres. Allende

1972. 3rd United Nations Conference on Trade and Development, Santiago.
690 **247** 35c. green and brown . . 25 15
691 – 1E.15 violet and blue . . 10 10
692 **247** 4E. violet and pink . . . 50 25
693 – 6E. blue and orange . . . 20 10
DESIGNS: 1E.15, 6E. Conference Hall Santiago.
Nos. 690 and 692 each include a se-tenant label showing Chilean workers and inscr "CORREOS DE CHILE". The stamp was only valid for postage with the label attached.

248 Soldier and Crest

1972. 150th Anniv of O'Higgins Military Academy.
694 **248** 1E.15 yellow and blue . . 15 10

249 Copper Miner

250 Barquentine "Esmeralda"

1972. Copper Mines Nationalization Law (1971).
695 **249** 1E.15 blue and red . . . 15 10
696 5E. black, blue and red 30 10

1972. 150th Anniv of Arturo Prat Naval College.
697 **250** 1E.15 purple . . . . . . 1·00 20

251 Observatory and Telescope

1972. Inauguration of Cerro Calan Observatory.
698 **251** 50c. blue 20 10

252 Dove with Letter

1972. International Correspondence Week.
699 **252** 1E.15 violet & mauve . . 15 10

253 Gen. Schneider, Flag and Quotation

1972. 2nd Death Anniv of General Rene Schneider.
700 **253** 2E.30 multicoloured . . . 30 20

254 Book and Students

1972. International Book Year.
701 **254** 50c. black and red 15 10

255 Folklore and Handicrafts

1972. Tourist Year of the Americas.
702 **255** 1E.15 black and red . . . 15 10
703 – 2E.65 purple and blue . . 40 10
704 – 3E.50 brown and red . . 15 10
DESIGNS—HORIZ: 2E.65, Natural produce. VERT: 3E.50, Stove and rug.

256 Carrera in Prison

257 Antarctic Map

1973. 150th Death Anniv of General J. M. Carrera.
705 **256** 2E.30 blue 20 10

1973. 25th Anniv of General Bernardo O'Higgins Antarctic Base.
706 **257** 10E. red and blue 35 15

258 "Latorre" (cruiser) and Emblem

259 Telescope

1973. 50 Years of Chilean Naval Aviation.
707 **258** 20E. blue and brown . . 55 10

1973. Inaug of La Silla Astronomical Observatory.
708 **259** 2E.30 black and blue . . 20 10

260 Interpol Emblem

261 Bunch of Grapes

1973. 50th Anniv of Interpol.
709 **260** 30E. blue, black & brown 1·40 20
710 – 50E. black and red . . . 1·40 25
DESIGN: 50E. Fingerprint superimposed on globe.

1973. Chilean Wine Exports. Multicoloured.
711 20E. Type **261** 50 10
712 100E. Inscribed globe . . . . 1·00 20

1974. Centenary of World Meteorological Organization. No. 668 surch **"Centenario de la Organizacion Meteorologica Mundial IMO-W-MO 1973"** and value.
713 27E.+3E. on 40c. green . . . 15 10

263 UPU Headquarters Building, Berne

1974. Centenary of UPU. Unissued stamp surch.
714 **263** 500E. on 45c. green . . . 85 20

264 Bernardo O'Higgins and Emblems

1974. Chilean Armed Forces.
715 **264** 30E. yellow and red . . . 20 10
716 – 30E. lake and red 20 10
717 – 30E. blue and light blue 20 10
718 – 30E. blue and lilac 20 10
719 – 30E. emerald and green 20 10

DESIGNS: No. 716, Soldiers with mortar; No. 717, Naval gunners; No. 718, Air Force pilot; No. 719, Mounted policeman.

1974. 500th Birth Anniv (1973) of Copernicus. No. 683 surch **"V Centenario del Nacimiento de Copernico 1473 - 1973"** and value.
720 **242** 27E.+3E. on 1E.95 blue and deep blue 30 10

1974. Centenary of Vina del Mar. No. 496 surch **"Centenario de la ciudad de Vina del Mar 1874 - 1974"** and value.
721 27E.+3E. on 1E. turquoise 15 10

267 Football and Globe

269 Police and Gloved Hand

1974. World Cup Football Championships, West Germany.
722 **267** 500E. orange and red . . 20 10
723 – 1000E. blue & dp blue . . 1·00 15
DESIGN—HORIZ: 1000E. Football on stylized stadium.

1974. Various stamps surch.
724 **212** 47E.+3E. on 40c. green 15 10
725 **228** 67E.+3E. on 40c. red and brown 15 10
726 **214** 97E.+3E. on 40c. brown 15 10
727 **223** 100E. on 40c. green . . . 20 10
728 – 300E. on 50c. brown (No. 571) 20 10

1974. Campaign for Prevention of Traffic Accidents.
729 **269** 30E. brown and green . . 25 10

270 Manutara and Part of Globe

271 Core of Globe

1974. Inaugural LAN Flight to Tahiti, Fiji and Australia. Each green and brown.
730 200E. Type **270** 40 15
731 200E. Tahitian dancer and part of Globe 40 15
732 200E. Map of Fiji and part of Globe 40 15
733 200E. Eastern grey kangaroo and part of Globe 40 15

1974. International Symposium of Volcanology, Santiago de Chile.
734 **271** 500E. orange & brown . . 60 10

1974. Inauguration of Votive Temple. No. 650 surch **24 OCTUBRE 1974 INAUGURACION TEMPLO VOTIVO** and value.
735 **226** 100E. on 40c. green . . . 15 10

273 Map of Robinson Crusoe Island

275 F. Vidal Gormaz and Seal

274 O'Higgins and Bolivar

1974. 400th Anniv of Discovery of Juan Fernandez Archipelago. Each brown and blue.
736 200E. Type **273** 85 20
737 200E. Chontas (hardwood palm-trees) 40 20
738 200E. Mountain goat 40 20
739 200E. Spiny lobster 40 20

1974. 150th Anniv of Battles of Junin and Ayacucho.
740 **274** 100E. brown and buff . . 20 10

1975. Centenary of Naval Hydrographic Institute.
741 **275** 100E. blue and mauve . . 20 10

1975. Surch **Revalorizada 1975** and value.
742 **228** 70c. on 40c. red & brown 15 10

277 Dr. Schweitzer

278 Lighthouse

1975. Birth Centenary of Dr. Albert Schweitzer (missionary).
743 **277** 500E. brown and yellow 35 10

1975. 50th Anniv of Valparaiso Lifeboat Service. Each blue and green.
744 150E. Type **278** 55 20
745 150E. Wreck of "Teotopoulis" 75 25
746 150E. "Cap Christiansen" (lifeboat) 75 25
747 150E. Survivor in water . . . 55 20
MS748 110 × 150 mm. Nos. 744/7. Imperf . . . . 1·75 1·75

279 Sail/steam Corvette "Baquedano"

1975. 30th Anniv of Shipwreck of Sail Frigate "Lautaro".
749 **279** 500E. black and green . . 75 20
750 – 500E. black and green . . 75 20
751 – 500E. black and green . . 75 20
752 – 500E. black and green . . 75 20
753 **279** 800E. black and brown 1·00 25
754 – 800E. black and brown 1·00 25
755 – 800E. black and brown 1·00 25
756 – 800E. black and brown 1·00 25
757 **279** 1000E. black and blue . . 1·25 25
758 – 1000E. black and blue . . 1·25 25
759 – 1000E. black and blue . . 1·25 25
760 – 1000E. black and blue . . 1·25 25
DESIGNS: Nos. 750, 754, 758, Sail frigate "Lautaro"; Nos. 751, 755, 759, Cruiser "Chacabuco"; Nos. 752, 756, 760, Cadet barquentine "Esmeralda".

280 "The Happy Mother" (A. Valenzuela)

281 Diego Portales (politician)

1975. International Women's Year. Chilean Paintings. Multicoloured.
761 50c. Type **280** 65 15
762 50c. "Girl" (F. J. Mandiola) 65 15
763 50c. "Lucia Guzman" (P. L. Rencoret) 65 15
764 50c. "Unknown Woman" (Magdalena M. Mena) . . 65 15

1975. Inscr "D. PORTALES".
765 **281** 10c. green 20 10
765a 20c. lilac 10 10
765b 30c. orange 10 10
766 50c. brown 15 10
767 1p. blue 15 10
767a 1p.50 brown 15 10
767b 2p. black 15 10
767c 2p.50 brown 15 10
767d 3p.50 red 15 10
768 5p. mauve 15 15
For this design inscr "DIEGO PORTALES", see Nos. 901 etc.

282 Lord Cochrane and Fleet, 1820

1975. Birth Bicentenary of Lord Thomas Cochrane. Multicoloured.
769 1p. Type **282** 80 25
770 1p. Cochrane's capture of Valdivia, 1820 . . . . . 80 25
771 1p. Capture of "Esmeralda", 1820 . . . . 80 25
772 1p. Cruiser "Cochrane", 1874 80 25
773 1p. Destroyer "Cochrane", 1962 . . . . 80 25

283 Flags of Chile and Bolivia

1976. 150th Anniv of Bolivia's Independence.
774 **283** 1p.50 multicoloured . . . 1·75 10

284 Lake of the Incas

1976. 6th General Assembly of Organization of American States.
775 **284** 1p.50 multicoloured . . . 1·40 10

285 George Washington

1976. Bicentenary of American Revolution.
776 **285** 5p. multicoloured . . . . 1·50 15

286 Minerva and Academy Emblem

1976. 50th Anniv of Polytechnic Military Academy.
777 **286** 2p.50 multicoloured . . . 1·00 10

287 Indian Warrior

1976. 3rd Anniv of Military Junta. Multicoloured.
778 1p. Type **287** 25 15
779 2p. Andean condor with broken chain . . . . . . 2·50 1·00
780 3p. Winged woman ("Rebirth of the Country") 25 15

288 Chilean Base, Antarctica

1977. Presidential Visit to Antarctica.
781 **288** 2p. multicoloured . . . . 5·25 25

289 College Emblem and Cultivated Field

290 Statue of Justice

1977. Cent of Advanced Agricultural Education.
782 **289** 2p. multicoloured . . . . 1·40 15

1977. 150th Anniv of Supreme Court.
783 **290** 2p. brown and grey . . . 1·40 10

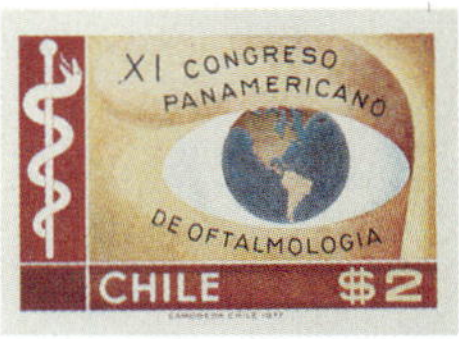

291 Globe within "Eye"

1977. 11th Pan-American Ophthalmological Congress.
784 **291** 2p. multicoloured . . . . 2·00 10

292 Police Emblem and Activities

1977. 50th Anniv of Chilean Police Force. Multicoloured.
785 2p. Type **292** 60 10
786 2p. Mounted carabinero (vert) 25 10
787 2p. Policewoman with children (vert) 25 10
788 2p. Torres del Paine and Osorno Volcano (vert) . . 25 10

293 "Intelsat" Satellite and Globe

1977. World Telecommunications Day.
789 **293** 2p. multicoloured 25 10

294 Front Page, Press and Schooner

1977. 150th Anniv of Newspaper "El Mercurio de Valparaiso".
790 **294** 2p. multicoloured 20 15

295 St. Francis of Assisi

296 "Science and Technology"

1977. 750th Death Anniv of St. Francis of Assisi.
791 **295** 5p. multicoloured . . . . 1·00 15

1977. Council for Science and Technology.
792 **296** 4p. multicoloured 40 15

297 Weaving (Mothers' Centres)

298 Diego de Almagro (discoverer of Chile)

1977. 4th Anniv of Government Junta. Welfare Facilities. Multicoloured.
793 5p. Type **297** 55 10
794 5p. Nurse with cripple (Care of the Disabled) 55 10
795 10p. Children dancing (Protection of Minors) (horiz) . . . . 1·00 15
796 10p. Elderly man (Care for the Aged) (horiz) . . . . . 1·00 15

1977. Columbus Day.
797 **298** 5p. brown 45 10

299 Boy, Christmas Bell and Post Box

1977. Christmas.
798 **299** 2p.50 multicoloured . . . 15 15

300 Freighter loading Timber

1978. Timber Export. Multicoloured.
799 10p. Type **300** . . . . 1·00 25
800 20p. As T **300** but inscr "CORREOS" and with ship flying Chilean flag . . 1·50 35

301 Papal Arms and Globe

1978. World Peace Day.
801 **301** 10p. multicoloured . . . 80 15

302 University

1978. 50th Anniv of Catholic University, Valparaiso.
802 **302** 25p. multicoloured . . . 2·50 60

303 "Bernardo O'Higgins" (Gil de Castro)

1978. Birth Bicentenary of Bernardo O'Higgins (1st issue).
803 **303** 10p. multicoloured . . . 1·00 15
See also Nos. 804, 806/8 and 816.

304 Chacabuco Victory Monument

1978. Birth Bicentenary of Bernardo O'Higgins (2nd issue), and 5th Anniv of Military Junta.
804 **304** 10p. multicoloured . . . 1·00 15

305 Teacher writing on Blackboard

1978. 10th Anniv and 9th Meeting of Inter-American Council for Education, Science and Culture.
805 **305** 15p. multicoloured . . . 60 15

306 "The Last Moments at Rancagua" (Pedro Subercaseaux)

1978. Birth Bicentenary of Bernardo O'Higgins (3rd issue).
806 **306** 30p. multicoloured . . . 2·00 65

307 "First National Naval Squadron" (Thomas Somerscales)

1978. Birth Bicentenary of Bernardo O'Higgins (4th issue).
807 **307** 20p. multicoloured . . . 1·75 80

308 Medallion

1978. Birth Bicentenaries of O'Higgins (5th issue) and San Martin.
808 **308** 7p. multicoloured 30 10

309 Council Emblem

310 Three Kings

1978. 30th Anniv of International Council of Military Sports.
809 **309** 50p. multicoloured . . . 3·50 1·00

1978. Christmas. Multicoloured.
810 3p. Type **310** 65 15
811 11p. Virgin and Child . . . . 1·25 20

311 Bernardo and Rodulfo Philippi

1978. The Philippi Brothers (scientists and travellers).
812 **311** 3p.50 multicoloured . . . 20 10

1979. No. 765 surch **$ 3.50**.
813 **281** 3p.50 on 10c. green . . . 15 10

313 Flowers and Flags of Chile and Salvation Army

1979. 70th Anniv of Salvation Army in Chile.
814 **313** 10p. multicoloured . . . 55 25

314 Pope Paul VI

1979. Pope Paul VI Commemoration.
815 **314** 11p. multicoloured . . . 80 25

315 Battle of Maipu Monument

1979. Birth Bicentenary of Bernardo O'Higgins (6th issue).
816 **315** 8p.50 multicoloured . . . 55 20

316 "Battle of Iquique" (Thomas Somerscales)

1979. Naval Battle Centenaries. Multicoloured.
817 3p.50 Type **316** 75 25
818 3p.50 "Battle of Punta Gruesa" (Alvaro Casanova Zenteno) 75 25
819 3p.50 "Battle of Angamos" (Alvaro Casanova Zenteno) 75 25

317 Diego Portales

319 Monument at Puntas Arenas (Miodrag Zivkovic)

318 Horse-drawn Ambulance

1979.
820 **317** 1p.50 brown 15 10
821 2p. grey 10 10
822 3p.50 red 10 10
823 4p.50 blue 20 10
824 5p. red 20 10
825 6p. green 20 10
826 7p. yellow 20 10
827 10p. blue 25 10
828 12p. orange 10 10

The 1p.50, 3p.50, 5p. and 6p. are inscribed "D. PORTALES" and have the imprint "CAMONEDA CHILE". The 2p., 4p.50, 7p. and 10p. are inscribed "DIEGO PORTALES" and have the imprint "CASA DE MONEDA DE CHILE".

1979. 75th Anniv of Chilean Red Cross.
831 **318** 25p. multicoloured . . . 2·75 60

1979. Centenary of Yugoslav Immigration.
832 **319** 10p. multicoloured . . . 45 15

320 Children in Playground (Kiochi Kayano Gomez)

1979. International Year of the Child. Mult.
833 9p.50 Type **320** 45 30
834 11p. Running girl (Carmed Pizarro Toto) (vert) . . . 55 35
835 12p. Children dancing in circle (Ana Pizarro Munizaga) . . . . 1·00 50

321 Laveredo and Arms of Coyhaique

1979. 50th Anniv of Coyhaique.
836 **321** 20p. multicoloured . . . 80 40

322 Exhibition Emblem and Posthorn

1979. 3rd World Telecommunications Exhibition, Geneva.
837 **322** 15p. grey, blue & orange 70 30

323 Canal

1979. 25th Anniv of Puerto Williams, Navirino Island.
838 **323** 3p.50 multicoloured . . . 70 15

324 Chileans adoring Child Jesus

325 Rafael Sotomayor (Minister of War)

1979. Christmas.
839 **324** 3p.50 multicoloured . . . 1·10 20

1979. Military Heroes. Each ochre and brown.
840 3p.50 Type **325** 50 10
841 3p.50 General Erasmo Escala (Commander in Chief of Army) 50 10

842 3p.50 Colonel (later General) Emilio Sotomayor (Commander of troops at Battle of Dolores) 50 10
843 3p.50 Colonel Eleuterio Ramirez (Commander of 2nd Line Regiment) . . . 50 10

326 Bell Model 205 Iroquois Rescue Helicopter at Tinguiririca Volcano

1980. 50th Anniv of Chilean Air Force. Mult.
844 3p.50 Type **326** 40 15
845 3p.50 Consolidated Catalina Skua amphibian in Antarctic 40 15
846 3p.50 Northrop Tiger II jet fighter in Andes 40 15

327 Rotary Emblem and Globe

1980. 75th Anniv of Rotary International.
847 **327** 10p. multicoloured . . . 80 25

328 "The Death of Bueras" (Pedro Leon Carmona)

329 "Gen. Manuel Gaquedano" (after Pedro Subercaseaux)

1980. Cavalry Charge led by Colonel Santiago Bueras at Battle of Maipu, 1818.
848 **328** 12p. multicoloured . . . 65 30

1980. Centenary of Battle of Arica Head. Mult.
849 3p.50 Type **329** 25 10
850 3p.50 Gen. Pedro Largos (43 × 26 mm) 25 10
851 3p.50 Col. Juan Jose San Martin (43 × 26 mm) . . . 25 10

330 Freire and Bars of "Ay, Ay, Ay!"

1980. Birth Centenary of Osman Perez Freire (composer).
852 **330** 6p. multicoloured 35 15

331 Mt. Gasherbrum II, Chilean flag and Ice-pick

1980. Chilean Himalayan Expedition (1979).
853 **331** 15p. multicoloured . . . 1·00 35

332 "St Vincent de Paul" (stained glass window, former Mother House)

334 Mummy of Inca Child

333 Andean Condor

1980. 125th Anniv of Sisters of Charity in Chile.
854 **332** 10p. multicoloured . . . 50 25

1980. 7th Anniv of Military Government.
855 **333** 3p.50 multicoloured . . . 40 20

1980. 150th Anniv of National History Museum. Multicoloured.
856 5p. Type **334** 55 15
857 5p. Claudio Gay (founder) (after Alejandro Laemlein) 55 15

335 "Pablo Burchard" (Pedro Lira)

336 Emblem and Buildings

1980. Centenary of National Museum of Fine Arts.
858 **335** 3p.50 multicoloured . . . 20 10

1980. "Fisa '80" International Fair, Santiago.
859 **336** 3p.50 multicoloured . . . 20 10

337 "Family and Angels" (Sara Hinojosa Orellana)

338 Infantryman

1980. Christmas. Multicoloured.
860 3p.50 Type **337** 85 10
861 10p.50 "The Holy Family" (Catalina Imboden Fernandez) . . . . 1·10 20

1980. Army Uniforms of 1879 (1st series). Multicoloured.
862 3p.50 Type **338** 55 15
863 3p.50 Cavalry officer (parade uniform) 55 15
864 3p.50 Artillery officer 55 15
865 3p.50 Colonel of Engineers (parade uniform) 55 15
See also Nos. 887/90.

339 Congress Emblem

340 Cattle

1980. 23rd International Congress of Military Medicine and Pharmacy, Santiago.
866 **339** 11p.50 multicoloured . . 55 30

1981. Eradication of Foot and Mouth Disease from Chile.
867 **340** 9p.50 multicoloured . . . 45 20

341 Robinson Crusoe Island

1981. Tourism. Multicoloured.
868 3p.50 Type **341** 25 15
869 3p.50 Easter Island monoliths 60 15
870 10p.50 Gentoo penguins, Antarctica . . . . 1·75 50

342 "Javiera Carrera" (after D. M. Pizarro) and Flag

1981. Birth Bicentenary of Javiera Carrera (creator of first national flag).
871 **342** 3p.50 multicoloured . . . 20 10

343 UPU Emblem

1981. Centenary of UPU Membership.
872 **343** 3p. multicoloured 25 15

344 Unloading Cargo from Lockheed Hercules

1981. 1st Anniv of Lieutenant Marsh Antarctic Air Force Base.
873 **344** 3p.50 multicoloured . . . 50 15

345 ITU and W.H.O. Emblems and Ribbons forming Caduceus

1981. World Telecommunications Day.
874 **345** 3p.50 multicoloured . . . 20 15

346 Arturo Prat Antarctic Naval Base

1981. 20th Anniv of Antarctic Treaty.
875 **346** 3p.50 multicoloured . . . 1·00 20

347 Capt. Jose Luis Araneda

1981. Centenary of Battle of Sangrar.
876 **347** 3p.50 multicoloured . . . 25 15

348 Philatelic Society Yearbook and Medal

1981. 92nd Anniv of Philatelic Society of Chile.
877 **348** 4p.50 multicoloured . . . 25 15

349 "Exchange of Speeches between Minister Recabarren and Indian Chief Conuepan at the Nielol Hill" (Hector Robles Acuna)

1981. Centenary of Temuco City.
878 **349** 4p.50 multicoloured . . . 25 15

350 Exports (embroidery by J.L. Gutierrez)

1981. Exports.
879 **350** 14p. multicoloured . . . 65 20

351 Moneda Palace (seat of Government)

1981. 8th Anniv of Military Government.
880 **351** 4p.50 multicoloured . . . 25 15

352 St. Vincent de Paul

1981. 400th Birth Anniv of St. Vincent de Paul (founder of Sisters of Charity).
881 **352** 4p.50 multicoloured . . . 25 15

353 Medallion by Rene Thenot, Quill and Law Code

1981. Birth Bicentenary of Andres Bello (statesman, lawyer, and founder of Chile University). Multicoloured.

882 4p.50 Type **353** 25 15
883 9p.50 Profile of Bello and three of his books 40 20
884 11p.50 University of Chile arms and Nicanor Plaza's statue of Bello 45 20

354 Flag on Map of South America and Police Badge

1981. 2nd South American Uniformed Police Congress, Santiago.

885 **354** 4p.50 multicoloured . . . 30 15

355 FAO and U.N. Emblems

1981. World Food Day.

886 **355** 5p.50 multicoloured . . . 30 15

1981. Army Uniforms of 1879 (2nd series). As T **338**. Multicoloured.

887 5p.50 Infantryman 55 20
888 5p.50 Military School cadet 55 20
889 5p.50 Cavalryman 55 20
890 5p.50 Artilleryman 55 20

356 Mother and Child

1981. International Year of Disabled Persons.

891 **356** 5p.50 multicoloured . . . 30 15

357 "Nativity" (Ruth Tatiana Aguero Eguiliz)

1981. Christmas. Multicoloured.

892 5p.50 Type **357** 75 10
893 11p.50 "The Three Kings" (Ignacio Jorge Manriquez Gonzalez) 95 20

358 Dario Salas

1981. Birth Cent of Dario Salas (educationist).

894 **358** 5p.50 multicoloured . . . 25 15

359 Main Buildings of University

1981. 50th Anniv of Federico Santa Maria Technical University, Valparaiso.

895 **359** 5p.50 multicoloured . . . 25 15

360 Fair Emblem

1982. "Fida '82" International Air Fair.

896 **360** 4p.50 multicoloured . . . 30 15

361 Cardinal Caro and Chilean Family

1982. 1st Anniv of New Constitution. Mult.

897 4p.50 Type **361** 25 15
898 11p. Diego Portales and national arms 45 20
899 30p. Bernardo O'Higgins and national arms 65 40

362 Globe on Chilean Flag

363 Pedro Montt (President, 1906–10)

1982. 12th Panamerican Institute of Geography and History General Assembly.

900 **362** 4p.50 multicoloured . . . 25 15

1982. As T **281** but inscr "DIEGO PORTALES" and designs as T **363**.

901 **281** 1p. blue 60 10
902 – 1p. blue 10 10
903 **281** 1p.50 orange 10 10
904 2p. grey 10 10
905 – 2p. lilac 10 10
906 **281** 2p.50 yellow 10 10
907 **363** 4p.50 mauve 30 10
908 – 5p. red 10 10
909 **281** 5p. mauve 60 10
910 – 7p. blue 25 10
911 – 10p. black 15 10

DESIGNS: Nos. 902, 905, 908, 910, 911, Ramon Barros Luco (President, 1911–15).

364 Dassault Mirage IIIC Airplane and Chilean Air Force and American Air Forces Co-operation System Badges

1982. American Air Forces Co-operation System.

916 **364** 4p.50 multicoloured . . . 50 15

365 Trawler and Map

367 Capt. Ignacio Carrera Pinto

366 Scout Emblems and Brownsea Island

1982. Fisheries Exports.

917 **365** 20p. multicoloured . . . 2·00 80

1982. 75th Anniv of Boy Scout Movement and 125th Birth Anniv of Lord Baden-Powell (founder). Multicoloured.

918 4p.50 Type **366** 75 15
919 4p.50 Lord Baden-Powell and Brownsea Island 75 15

Nos. 918/19 were printed together, se-tenant, forming a composite design.

1982. Centenary of Battle of Concepcion. Mult.

920 4p.50 Type **367** 25 20
921 4p.50 Sub-lieutenant Arturo Perez Canto 25 20
922 4p.50 Sub-lieutenant Julio Montt Salamanca 25 20
923 4p.50 Sub-lieutenant Luis Cruz Martinez 25 20

368 Old Man at Window

1982. World Assembly on Ageing, Vienna.

924 **368** 4p.50 multicoloured . . . 25 15

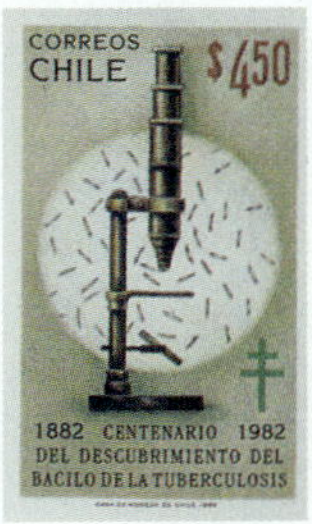

369 Microscope and Bacillus

1982. Centenary of Discovery of Tubercle Bacillus.

925 **369** 4p.50 multicoloured . . . 30 15

370 National Flag and Flame of Freedom

1982. 9th Anniv of Military Government.

926 **370** 4p.50 multicoloured . . . 25 15

1982. Nos. 688/9 surch.

927 **245** 1p. on 3E.50 blue & grn 30 10
928 **246** 2p. on 1E.15 red & black 35 10

372 "Nativity" (Mariela Espinoza Fuetes)

1982. Christmas. Multicoloured.

929 10p. Type **372** 25 10
930 25p. "Adoration of the Shepherds" (Jared Jeria Abarca) (vert) . . . . . . 1·25 40

373 "Virgin Mary and Marcellus" (stained-glass window, Sacred Heart of Jesus Church, Barcelona)

374 "El Sur", Quill and Printing Press

1982. 9th World Union of Former Marist Alumni Congress.

931 **373** 7p. multicoloured . . . . 1·60 40

1982. Cent of Concepcion's Newspaper "El Sur".

932 **374** 7p. multicoloured 25 15

375 "Steamship Copiapo" (W. Yorke)

1982. 110th Anniv of South American Steamship Company.

933 **375** 7p. multicoloured . . . . 1·50 30

376 Club Badge, Radio Aerial, Dove and Globe

1982. 60th Anniv of Radio Club of Chile.

934 **376** 7p. multicoloured 25 10

377 Arms of Sovereign Military Order

1983. Postal Agreement with Sovereign Military Order of Malta. Multicoloured.

935 25p. Type **377** 65 40
936 50p. Arms of Chile . . . . . 1·00 55

378 Badge

380 Child watching Railway

379 Cardinal Samore

1983. 50th Anniv of Criminal Investigation Bureau.
937 **378** 20p. multicoloured . . . 65 20

1983. Cardinal Antonio Samore Commem.
938 **379** 30p. multicoloured . . . 80 25

1983. Centenary of Valparaiso Incline Railway.
939 **380** 40p. multicoloured . . . 1·25 65

381 Puoko Tangata (carved head from Easter Island)

383 General Francisco Morazan

382 Winged Girl with Broken Chains

1983. Tourism. Multicoloured.
940 7p. Type **381** 25 15
941 7p. Ruins of Pucar de Quitor, San Pedro de Atacama . . 25 15
942 7p. Rock painting, Rio Ibanez, Aisen 25 15
943 7p. Diaguita pot 25 15

1983. 10th Anniv of Military Government. Mult.
944 7p. Type **382** 50 15
945 7p. Young couple with flag 50 15
946 10p. Family with torch . . . 55 15
947 40p. National arms . . . . . 1·10 40

1983. Famous Hondurans. Multicoloured.
948 7p. Type **383** 20 10
949 7p. Sabio Jose Cecilio del Valle 20 10

384 Central Post Office, Santiago

385 "Holy Family" (Lucrecia Cardenas Gomez)

1983. World Communications Year. Mult.
950 7p. Type **384** 55 10
951 7p. Space Shuttle "Challenger" 55 10

Nos. 950/1 were printed together in se-tenant pairs within the sheet forming a composite design.

1983. Christmas. Children's Paintings. Mult.
952 10p. "Nativity" (Hanny Chacon Scheel) 25 10
953 30p. Type **385** 90 25

386 Presidential Coach, 1911

1984. Railway Centenary. Multicoloured.
954 9p. Type **386** . . . . 1·40 60
955 9p. Service car and tender . . 1·40 60
956 9p. Class 80 steam locomotive, 1929 . . . . . 1·40 60

Nos. 954/6 were printed together, se-tenant, forming a composite design.

387 Juan Luis Sanfuentes

1984. (a) Inscr "CORREOS CHILE".
989 **387** 5p. red 10 10
958 9p. green 15 10
959 10p. grey 15 10
960 15p. blue 15 10

(b) Inscr "D.S. No. 20 CHILE".
961 **387** 9p. brown 15 10
962 15p. blue 15 10
963 20p. yellow 20 10

388 Piper Pillan Trainer and Flags

1984. 3rd International Aeronautical Fair.
966 **388** 9p. multicoloured 85 10

389 Agriculture, Industry and Science

1984. 20th Anniv of Chilean Nuclear Energy Commission.
967 **389** 9p. multicoloured 25 10

1984. Nos. 944/5 surch.
968 9p. on 7p. Type **382** 65 10
969 9p. on 7p. Young couple with flag 65 10

391 Chilean Women's Antarctic Expedition

1984. Chile's Antarctic Territories. Mult.
970 15p. Type **391** 90 50
971 15p. Villa Las Estrellas Antarctic settlement . . . 75 30
972 15p. Scouts visiting Antarctic, 1983 . . . . 75 30

392 Parinacota Church (Tarapaca Region)

1984. 10th Anniv of Regionalization. Mult.
973 9p. Type **392** 50 20
974 9p. El Tatio geyser (Antofagasta Region) . . . 50 20
975 9p. Copper miners (Atacama Region) 50 20
976 9p. El Tololo observatory (Coquimbo Region) . . . 50 20
977 9p. Valparaiso harbour (Valparaiso Region) . . . 75 20
978 9p. Stone images (Easter Island Province) 50 20
979 9p. St. Francis's Church (Santiago Metropolitan Region) 50 20
980 9p. El Huique Hacienda (Libertador General Bernardo O'Higgins Region) 50 20
981 9p. Hydro-electric dam and reservoir, Machicura (Maule Region) 50 20
982 9p. Sta. Juana de Gaudalcazar Fort (Bio Bio Region) 50 20
983 9p. Araucana woman (Araucania Region) 50 20
984 9p. Church, Guar Island (Los Lagos Region) 50 20
985 9p. South Highway (Aisen del General Carlos Ibanez del Campo Region) 50 20
986 9p. Shepherd (Magallanes Region) 50 20
987 9p. Villa Las Estrellas (Chile Antarctic Territories) . . . 75 30

393 Pedro Sarmiento de Gamboa and Map

1984. 400th Anniv of Spanish Settlements on Straits of Magellan.
988 **393** 100p. multicoloured . . . 2·25 80

394 Antonio Varas de la Barra (founder) and Coin

1984. Centenary of State Savings Bank.
990 **394** 35p. multicoloured . . . 50 20

395 Flame and Bernardo O'Higgins Monument

1984. 11th Anniv of Military Government.
991 **395** 20p. multicoloured . . . 30 15

396 Clown

1984. Centenary of Circus in Chile.
992 **396** 45p. multicoloured . . . 80 25

397 Blue Whale

1984. Endangered Animals. Multicoloured.
993 9p. Type **397** 70 20
994 9p. Juan Fernandez fur seal 70 20
995 9p. Chilean guemal 70 20
996 9p. Long-tailed chinchilla . . 70 20

398 "Shepherds following Star" (Ruth M. Flores Rival)

1984. Christmas. Multicoloured.
997 9p. Type **398** 15 10
998 40p. "Bethlehem" (Vianka Pastrian Navea) 95 30

399 Satellite and Planetarium

1984. Inaug of Santiago University Planetarium.
999 **399** 10p. multicoloured . . . 30 15

400 Andean Hog-nosed Skunk

401 Flags and Emblem

1985. Flora and Fauna. Multicoloured.
1000 10p. Type **400** 60 25
1001 10p. "Leucocoryne purpurea" 60 25
1002 10p. Black-winged stilt . . . 90 30
1003 10p. Marine otter 60 25
1004 10p. "Balbisia peduncularis" 60 25
1005 10p. Patagonian conure . . 90 30
1006 10p. Southern pudu 60 25
1007 10p. "Fuchsia magellanica" 60 25
1008 10p. Common diuca finch 90 30
1009 10p. Argentine grey fox . . 60 25
1010 10p. "Alstroemeria sierrae" 60 25
1011 10p. Austral pygmy owl . . 90 30

1985. 25th Anniv (1986) of American Air forces Co-operation System.
1012 **401** 45p. multicoloured . . . 1·50 1·00

402 Chile and Argentina Flags and Papal Arms

1985. Chilean–Argentinian Peace Treaty.
1013 **402** 20p. multicoloured . . . 45 25

403 Kentenich and Schoenstatt Sanctuary, La Florida

1985. Birth Centenary of Father Jose Kentenich (founder of Schoenstatt Movement).
1014 **403** 40p. multicoloured . . . 75 40

404 Landscape and Shrimp

1985. Antarctic Territories and 25th Anniv of Antarctic Treaty. Multicoloured.
1015 15p. Type **404** 50 30
1016 20p. Seismological Station, O'Higgins Base 65 40
1017 35p. Earth receiving station, Anvers Island . . . . . . 1·10 70

405 "Canis fulvipes"

1985. Endangered Animals. Multicoloured.
1018 20p. Type **405** 70 30
1019 20p. James's flamingo . . . 1·90 40
1020 20p. Giant coot . . . . . . 1·90 40
1021 20p. Huidobria otter 70 30

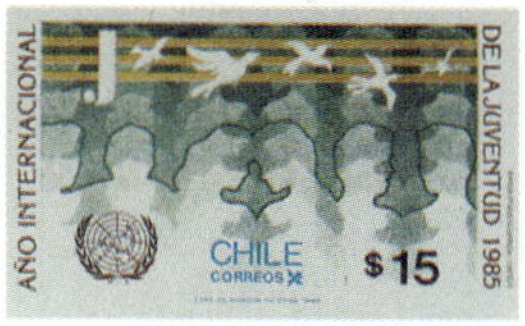

406 Doves and "J"

1985. International Youth Year (1022) and 40th Anniv of UNO (1023). Multicoloured.
1022 15p. Type **406** 20 15
1023 15p. U.N. emblem 20 15

407 Farmer with Haycart

1985. Occupations. Each in brown.
1024 10p. Type **407** 10 15
1025 10p. Photographer with plate camera 10 15
1026 10p. Street entertainer . . . 10 15
1027 10p. Basket maker 10 15

408 Carrera and Statue

1985. Birth Bicentenary of Gen. Jose Miguel Carrera (Independence leader and first President).
1028 **408** 40p. multicoloured . . . 75 30

409 "Holy Family"

411 Escort of Light Infantry, 1818

410 "Nativity" (Jennifer Gomez)

1985. Chilean Art.
1029 **409** 10p. brown and ochre . . . 10 15

1985. Christmas. Multicoloured.
1030 15p. Type **410** 20 10
1031 100p. Man with donkey (Esteban Morales Medina) (vert) . . . . 2·00 90

1985. 16th American Armies Conference. Mult.
1032 20p. Type **411** 35 20
1033 35p. Officer of the Hussars of the Grand Guard, 1813 . . 75 30

412 Moon, Earth and Comet

1985. Appearance of Halley's Comet.
1034 **412** 45p. multicoloured . . . 35 20
MS1035 90 × 105 mm. No. 1034 (sold at 180p.) 90 90

413 Living Trees and Flame

414 Saltpetre

1985. Forest Fires Prevention. Multicoloured.
1036 40p. Type **413** 65 20
1037 40p. Burnt trees and flame . . 70 20

1986. Exports. Each brown and blue.
1038 12p. Type **414** 15 10
1039 12p. Iron 15 10
1040 12p. Copper 15 10
1041 12p. Molybdenum 15 10

415 Dungeness Point Lighthouse

1986. Chilean Lighthouses. Multicoloured.
1042 45p. Type **415** 45 25
1043 45p. Evangelistas lighthouse in storm 45 25

416 St. Lucia Hill, Santiago

1986. Death Centenary of Benjamin Vicuna Mackenna (Municipal Superintendent).
1044 **416** 30p. multicoloured . . . 30 20

417 Diego Portales

1986. Unissued stamp surch.
1045 **417** 12p. on 3p.50 mult . . . 70 10

418 National Stadium, Chile, 1962

1986. World Cup Football Championship, Mexico. Multicoloured.
1046 15p. Type **418** 15 10
1047 20p. Azteca Stadium, Mexico, 1970 . . . . . . 20 15
1048 35p. Maracana Stadium, Brazil, 1950 . . . . . . 35 25
1049 50p. Wembley Stadium, England, 1966 . . . . . 50 40

419 Birds flying above City

1986. Environmental Protection. Mult.
1050 20p. Type **419** 20 10
1051 20p. Fish 30 10
1052 20p. Full litter bin in forest 20 10

420 "Santiaguillo" (caravel) and flags

421 Emblem

1986. 450th Anniv of Valparaiso.
1053 **420** 40p. multicoloured . . . 85 30

1986. 25th Anniv of Inter-American Development Bank.
1054 **421** 45p. multicoloured . . . 40 20

422 St. Rosa and Pelequen Sanctuary

1986. 400th Birth Anniv of St. Rosa of Lima.
1055 **422** 15p. multicoloured . . . 15 10

423 Stone Head on Raraku Volcano

1986. Easter Island. Multicoloured.
1056 60p. Type **423** . . . . . . 1·00 25
1057 100p. Tongariki ruins . . . 1·60 45
MS1058 Two sheets. (a) 90 × 104 mm. No. 1056; (b) 104 × 90 mm. No. 1057 (sold at 420p.) . . . . 2·00 2·50

424 Flags, Stamps in Album, Magnifying Glass and Tweezers

1986. "Ameripex '86" International Stamp Exhibition, Chicago.
1059 **424** 100p. multicoloured . . 1·40 50

425 Schooner "Ancud"

1986. Naval Traditions. Multicoloured.
1060 35p. Type **425** 80 45
1061 35p. Brigantine "Aguila" . . 80 45
1062 35p. Sail corvette "Esmeralda" 80 45
1063 35p. Sail frigate "O'Higgins" 80 45

426 "Gate of Serenity"

1986. Paintings by Juan F. Gonzalez. Mult.
1064 30p. "Rushes and Chrysanthemums" 25 15
1065 30p. Type **426** 25 15

427 Antarctic Terns

1986. Antarctic Fauna. Sea Birds. Mult.
1066 40p. Type **427** . . . . . . 1·40 55
1067 40p. Blue-eyed cormorants 1·40 55
1068 40p. Emperor penguins . . 1·40 55
1069 40p. Antarctic skuas . . . . 1·40 55

428 Pedro de Ona (poet)

1986. Chilean Literature. Multicoloured.
1070 20p. Type **428** 15 15
1071 20p. Vicente Huidobro . . . 15 15

429 Major-General, 1878

1986. Centenary of Military Academy. Mult.
1072 45p. Type **429** 65 20
1073 45p. Major, 1950 . . . . . 65 20

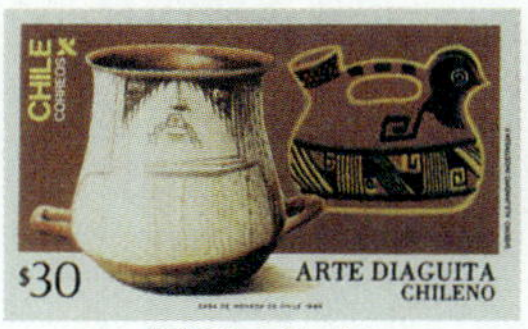

430 Diaguita Art

1986. Indian Art. Multicoloured.
1074 30p. Type **430** 20 15
1075 30p. Mapuche art 20 15

431 "Nativity" (Begona Andrea Orrego Castro)

1986. Christmas. Multicoloured.
1076 15p. Type **431** 15 10
1077 105p. "Shrine and Mountains" (Andrea Maribel Riquelme Labarde) . . . . 1·60 80

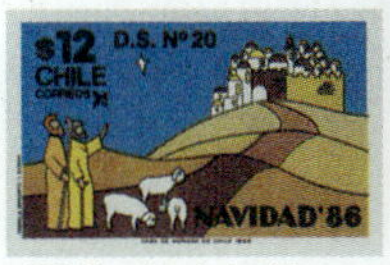

432 Shepherds looking at Hill Town

433 Emblem and Globe

1986. Christmas.
1078 **432** 12p. multicoloured . . . 20 10

1986. International Peace Year.
1079 **433** 85p. multicoloured . . . 1·00 50

1986. No. 1029 surch.
1080 **409** 12p. on 10p. brown and ochre 15 10

1986. Nos. 1024/7 surch.
1081 12p. on 10p. Farmer with haycart 25 10
1082 12p. on 10p. Photographer with plate camera 25 10
1083 12p. on 10p. Street entertainer 25 10
1084 12p. on 10p. Basket maker 25 10
1085 15p. on 10p. Farmer with haycart 25 10
1086 15p. on 10p. Photographer with plate camera 25 10
1087 15p. on 10p. Street entertainer 25 10
1088 15p. on 10p. Basket maker 25 10

436 Profiles and Flag

1986. Women's Voluntary Organization.
1089 **436** 15p. multicoloured . . . 15 10

437 Virgin of Carmelites

439 "The Guitarist of Quinchamali"

438 Kitson Meyer Steam Locomotive No. 59

1986. 60th Anniv of Coronation of Virgin of the Carmelites.
1090 **437** 25p. multicoloured . . . 40 15

1987. Railways.
1091 **438** 95p. multicoloured . . . 1·75 80

1987. Folk Tales. (a) As T **439**.
1092 **439** 15p. green 20 10
1093 – 15p. blue 40 10
1094 – 15p. brown 20 10
1095 – 15p. mauve 20 10

(b) Discount stamps. Inscr "D/S No 20" in colour of stamp in right-hand margin and dated "1992".
1092C 15p. As Type **439** 10 10
1093C 15p. As No. 1093 . . . . 10 10
1094C 15p. As No. 1094 . . . . 10 10
1095C 15p. As No. 1095 . . . . 10 10
DESIGNS: No. 1093, "El Caleuche"; 1094, "El Pihuychen"; 1095, "La Lola".

440 Rowing Boat and Storage Tanks

1987. 40th Anniv of Capt. Arturo Prat Antarctic Naval Base. Multicoloured.
1096 100p. Type **440** . . . . . . 2·50 1·10
1097 100p. Buildings and rowing boat at jetty . . . . . . 2·50 1·10
Nos. 1096/7 were printed together, se-tenant, forming a composite design.

441 Pope and "Christ the Redeemer" Statue

1987. Visit of Pope John Paul II. Mult.
1098 20p. Type **441** 10 10
1099 25p. Votive Temple, Maipu 35 10
1100 90p. "Cross of the Seas", Magellan Straits . . . . 1·10 50
1101 115p. "Virgin of the Hill" statue, Santiago . . . . 1·60 80
MS1102 104 × 90 mm. No. 1101 (sold at 250p.) . . . . 1·40 1·40

442 Horse-riding Display

443 Players and Ball

1987. 60th Anniv of Carabineers. Mult.
1103 50p. Type **442** 65 15
1104 50p. Sea rescue by Air Police 65 15

1987. World Youth Football Cup. Mult.
1105 45p. Type **443** 50 15
1106 45p. Player and Concepcion stadium 50 15
1107 45p. Player and Antofagasta stadium 50 15
1108 45p. Player and Valparaiso stadium 50 15
MS1109 89 × 105 mm. 45p. No. 1105 (sold at 150p.) 80 80

444 Battleship "Almirante Latorre"

1987. Naval Tradition. Multicoloured.
1110 60p. Type **444** 95 45
1111 60p. Cruiser "O'Higgins" . . 95 45

445 Portales and "El Vigia" Newspaper

1987. 150th Death Anniv of Diego Portales (statesman).
1112 **445** 30p. multicoloured . . . 40 10

446 Works Projects

1987. Centenary of Ministry of Public Works.
1113 **446** 25p. multicoloured . . . 1·00 30

447 School Entrance

1987. Centenary of Infantry School. Mult.
1114 50p. Type **447** 25 10
1115 100p. Soldiers and national flag 80 40

448 "Chiasognathus granti"

449 Family

1987. Flora and Fauna. Multicoloured.
1116 25p. Type **448** 40 25
1117 25p. Sanderling 50 30
1118 25p. Peruvian guemal . . . 40 25
1119 25p. Chilean palm 40 25
1120 25p. "Colias vauthieri" (butterfly) 50 25
1121 25p. Osprey 50 30
1122 25p. Commerson's dolphin 50 25
1123 25p. Mountain cypress . . . 40 25
1124 25p. San Fernandez Island spiny lobster 40 25
1125 25p. Fernandez firecrown 50 30
1126 25p. Vicuna 50 25
1127 25p. Arboreal fern 40 25
1128 25p. Spider-crab 45 25
1129 25p. Lesser rhea 50 30
1130 25p. Mountain viscacha . . 50 25
1131 25p. Giant cactus 40 25

1987. International Year of Shelter for the Homeless.
1132 **449** 40p. multicoloured . . . 45 10

450 Emblem

452 "Holy Family" (Ximena Soledad Rosales Opazo)

451 Condell, Battle of Iquique and Statue

1987. "fisa'87", 25th International Santiago Fair.
1133 **450** 20p. multicoloured . . . 10 15

1987. Death Centenary of Admiral Carlos Condell.
1134 **451** 50p. multicoloured . . . 1·00 60

1987. Christmas. Multicoloured.
1135 30p. Type **452** 35 10
1136 100p. "Star over Bethlehem" (Marcelo Bordones Meneses) . . . . 1·00 60

453 Casting

454 "Nativity"

1987. "Cobre '87" International Copper Conference, Vina del Mar.
1137 **453** 40p. multicoloured . . . 20 10
MS1138 88 × 103 mm. No. 1137 (sold at 150p.) 80 80

1987. Christmas. (a) Non-discount.
1139 **454** 15p. blue and orange . . 20 10

(b) Discount stamps. Additionally inscr "D.S. No. 20".
1140 **454** 15p. blue and orange . . 20 10

455 Non-smokers inhaling Smoke

457 Freire

456 "Capitan Luis Alcazar" (supply ship) and Antarctic Landscape

1987. Anti-smoking Campaign.
1141 **455** 15p. blue and orange . . 20 10

1987. 25th Anniv of National Antarctic Research Commission.
1142 **456** 45p. multicoloured . . . 1·25 40

1987. Birth Bicentenary of General Ramon Freire Serrano (Director, 1823–27).
1143 **457** 20p. red and purple . . 25 20

458 Violin and Frutillar Church and Lake

1988. 20th Music Weeks, Frutillar.
1144 **458** 30p. multicoloured . . . 15 10

459 St. John with Boy (after C. Di Girolamo)

460 Bird, Da Vinci's Glider, Wright's Flyer 1, Junkers Ju 52/3m, De Havilland Vampire and Grumman Tomcat

1988. Death Centenary of St. John Bosco (founder of Salesian Brothers).
1145 **459** 40p. multicoloured . . . 45 10

1988. "Fida'88" 5th International Air Fair.
1146 **460** 60p. blue and deep blue 75 25

461 Shot Putting, Pole Vaulting and Javelin Throwing

1988. Olympic Games, Seoul. Multicoloured.
1147 50p. Type **461** 60 45
1148 100p. Swimming, cycling and running . . . . . . 1·25 1·00
MS1149 90 × 105 mm. Nos. 1147/8 (sold at 250p.) . . . . 1·40 1·40

1988. Discount stamp. No. 958 surch **$20 D.S.No 20.**
1150 **387** 20p. on 9p. green . . . 10 20

463 Kava-Kava Head

1988. Easter Island. (a) Inscr "CORREOS" only.
1151 **463** 20p. black and pink . . 25 15
1152 – 20p. black and pink . . 25 15

(b) Discount stamps. As T **463** but additionally inscr "D.S.No 20".
1153 **463** 20p. black and yellow . . 25 15
1154 – 20p. black and yellow . . 25 15
DESIGN: Nos. 1152, 1154, Tangata Manu bird-man (petroglyph).

464 Medal, Scientist, Bull and Farm Workers

1988. 150th Anniv of National Agricultural Society.
1155 **464** 45p. multicoloured . . . 25 15

465 Tending Accident Victim

1988. 125th Anniv of Red Cross.
1156 **465** 150p. multicoloured . . 2·25 2·00

466 Gipsy Moth, Boeing 767, Mirage 50 and Merino

1988. Birth Centenary of Commodore Arturo Merino Benitez (air pioneer).
1157 **466** 35p. multicoloured . . . 45 10

467 Cadet Barquentine "Esmeralda"

1988. Naval Tradition. Multicoloured.
1158 50p. Type **467** 75 45
1159 50p. "Capt. Arturo Prat" (stained glass window, Valparaiso Naval Museum) 75 45

468 Vatican City and University Arms

1988. Centenary of Pontifical Catholic University of Chile.
1160 **468** 40p. multicoloured . . . 45 10

469 Esslingen Locomotive No. 3331

1988. Railway Anniversaries. Multicoloured.
1161 60p. Type **469** (75th anniv of Arica–La Paz railway) 2·40 1·25
1162 60p. North British locomotive No. 45 (cent of Antofagasta–Bolivia railway) 35 25
MS1163 104 × 88 mm. Nos. 1161/2 (sold at 180p.) . . . . 1·10 1·10

470 Chemistry Student

1988. 175th Anniv of Jose Miguel Carrera National Institute.
1164 **470** 45p. multicoloured . . . 25 15

471 "Chloraea chrysantha"

1988. Flowers. Multicoloured.
1165 30p. Type **471** 45 10
1166 30p. "Lapogeria rosea" . . 45 10
1167 30p. "Nolana paradoxa" . . 45 10
1168 30p. "Rhodophiala advena" . 45 10
1169 30p. "Schizanthus hookeri" 45 10
1170 30p. "Acacia caven" . . . 45 10
1171 30p. "Cordia decanda" . . 45 10
1172 30p. "Leontochir ovallei" 45 10
1173 30p. "Alstroemeria pelegrina" 45 10
1174 30p. "Copiapoa cinerea" . . 45 10
1175 30p. "Salpiglossis sinuata" 45 10
1176 30p. "Leucocoryne coquimbensis" 45 10
1177 30p. "Eucryphia glutinosa" 45 10
1178 30p. "Calandrinia longiscapa" 45 10
1179 30p. "Desfontainia spinosa" 45 10
1180 30p. "Sophora macrocarpa" 45 10

472 Commander Policarpo Toro and "Angamos"

1988. Centenary of Incorporation of Easter Island into Chile. Multicoloured.
1181 50p. Type **472** 75 20
1182 50p. Map of Easter Island and globe 55 20
1183 100p. Dancers 90 50
1184 100p. Petroglyphs of bird-men 90 50
MS1185 105 × 89 mm. Nos. 1181/4 (sold at 450p.) . . . . 4·00 4·00

473 Bleriot XI over Town

1988. 70th Anniv of First National Airmail Service.
1186 **473** 150p. multicoloured . . 90 60

474 Pottery

1988. 15th Anniv of Centre for Education of Women. Traditional Crafts. Multicoloured.
1187 25p. Type **474** 10 10
1188 25p. Embroidery 10 10

475 Policeman and Brigade Members

1988. Schools' Security Brigade.
1189 **475** 45p. multicoloured . . . 20 10

476 "Nativity" (Paulette Thiers)

477 Cancelled 1881 2c. Stamp

1988. Christmas. Multicoloured.
1190 35p. Type **476** 15 10
1191 100p. "Family going to church" (Jose M. Lamas) 70 35

1988. Centenary of Chile Philatelic Society.
1192 **477** 40p. multicoloured . . . 45 10

478 Child in Manger

479 Manuel Bulnes and Battle of Yungay, 1839

1988. Christmas. (a) Non-discount.
1193 **478** 20p. purple and yellow 10 10
(b) Discount stamps. As T **478** but additionally inscr "D.S. No. 20".
1194 **478** 20p. purple and yellow 10 10

1989. Historic Heroes. Multicoloured.
1195 50p. Type **479** 20 10
1196 50p. Soldier and battle scene 20 10
1197 100p. Roberto Simpson and Battle of Casma, 1839 . . 1·25 55
1198 100p. Sailor and battle scene 1·25 55

480 St. Ambrose's Church, Vallenar (bicentenary)

483 Sister Teresa of the Andes

1989. Town Anniversaries. Multicoloured.
1199 30p. Type **480** 10 10
1200 35p. Craftsman, Combarbala (bicent) . . . 15 10
1201 45p. Laja Falls, Los Angeles (250th anniv) 20 10
See also No. 1306.

1989. Various stamps surch. (a) Surch **$25** only.
1202 25p. on 15p. green (1092) 10 10
1203 25p. on 15p. blue (1093) . . 30 10
1204 25p. on 15p. brown (1094) 10 10
1205 25p. on 15p. mauve (1095) 10 10
1206 25p. on 20p. black and pink (1151) 10 10
1207 25p. on 20p. black and pink (1152) 10 10
1208 25p. on 20p. black and yellow (1153) 10 10
1209 25p. on 20p. black and yellow (1154) 10 10

(b) Surch **D.S. No 20 $25**.
1210 25p. on 20p. black and pink (1151) 10 10
1211 25p. on 20p. black and pink (1152) 10 10

1989. Beatifications. Multicoloured.
1212 40p. Type **483** 20 10
1213 40p. Laura Vicuna 20 10

484 Christopher Columbus

1989. "Exfina '89" Stamp Exhibition, Santiago. Multicoloured.
1214 100p. Type **484** 70 35
1215 100p. "Nina", "Santa Maria" and "Pinta" . . . 95 40
MS1216 90 × 105 mm. Nos. 1214/15 1·60 1·60

485 Container Ship and Trawler

1989. 50th Anniv of Energy Production Corporation. Multicoloured.
1217 60p. Type **485** 90 20
1218 60p. Tree trunks on trailer and factory 25 15
1219 60p. Telephone tower and pylon 25 15
1220 60p. Coal wagons and colliery 25 15

486 Town and Sketch

1989. Birth Centenary of Gabriela Mistral (writer). Multicoloured.
1221 30p. Type **486** 15 10
1222 30p. Mistral with children 15 10
1223 30p. Mistral writing 15 10
1224 30p. Mistral receiving Nobel Prize 15 10

487 Grapes

1989. Exports. (a) Inscr as T **487**.
1225 **487** 5p. blue 15 10
1226 – 5p. red and blue 15 10
1227 **487** 10p. deep blue & blue 15 10
1228 – 10p. red and blue . . . 15 10
1229 **487** 25p. blue and green . . 10 10
1230 – 25p. red and green . . . 10 10
1350 **487** 45p. blue and mauve . . 15 10
1351 – 45p. red and mauve . . 15 10
(b) Discount stamps. As T **487** but additionally inscr "D.S. No. 20".
1231 **487** 25p. blue and yellow . . 10 10
1232 – 25p. red and yellow . . 10 10
1352 **487** 45p. blue and yellow . . 15 15
1353 – 45p. red and yellow . . 15 15
DESIGNS: Nos. 1226, 1228, 1230, 1232, 1351, 1353, Apple.

488 Battle Scene, Soldiers and "Justice"

1989. 150th Anniv of Army Court of Justice.
1233 **488** 50p. multicoloured . . . 20 10

489 Monument

490 Victoria, Vina del Mar

1989. Frontier Guards' Martyrs' Monument.
1234 **489** 35p. multicoloured . . . 15 10

1989. Transport.
1235 **490** 30p. black and orange 15 10
1236 – 35p. black and blue . . 35 10
1237 – 40p. black and green . . 20 10
1238 – 45p. black and green . . 55 10
1239 – 50p. black and red . . . 55 10
1240 – 60p. black and bistre . . 45 15
1241 – 100p. black and green 65 35
DESIGNS—VERT: 35p. Scow, Chiloe Archipelago. HORIZ: 40p. Ox-cart, Cautin; 45p. Raft ferry, Rio Palena; 50p. Lighters, Gen. Carrera Lake; 60p. Valparaiso incline railway; 100p. Santiago funicular.
See also Nos. 1346 and 1458.

491 Scientist and Bearded Penguins

1989. 25th Anniv of Chilean Antarctic Institute.
1245 **491** 150p. multicoloured . . 2·10 1·00

492 Present Naval Engineers School and "Chacabuco" (first school)

1989. Centenary of Naval Engineering. Mult.
1246 45p. Type **492** 40 10
1247 45p. Sailors in engine room 40 10
1248 45p. Destroyer, Aerospatiale Dauphin 2 helicopter and submarine 40 10
1249 45p. Launch of "Aquiles" (patrol boat) 40 10

493 Globes, Polar Bear and Gentoo Penguins

494 Atacamena Culture

1989. "World Stamp Expo '89" International Stamp Exhibition, Washington D.C.
1250 **493** 250p. multicoloured . . 3·00 1·75
MS1251 90 × 104 mm. No. 1250 3·00 3·00

1989. America. Pre-Columbian Cultures. Mult.
1252 30p. Type **494** 40 10
1253 150p. Selk'nam and Onas cultures . . . . 1·25 60

495 Balls

497 Vicuna, Lauca

496 "Rowing to Church" (Cristina Lopez)

1989. Christmas. (a) As T **495**.
1254 **495** 25p. yellow and green . . 10 10
1255 – 25p. yellow and green . . 10 10

(b) Discount stamps. Additionally inscr "D.S. No 20".
1256 **495** 25p. red and green . . . 10 10
1257 – 25p. red and green . . . 10 10
DESIGN: Nos. 1255, 1257, Bells.

1989. Christmas.
1258 **496** 100p. multicoloured . . 80 40

1990. National Parks. Multicoloured.
1259 35p. Type **497** 30 10
1260 35p. Chilian flamingo, Salar de Surire 50 20
1261 35p. Cactus, La Chimba . . 30 10
1262 35p. Guanaco, Pan de Azucar 30 10
1263 35p. Long-tailed meadowlark, Fray Jorge 50 20
1264 35p. Sooty tern, Rapa Nui 50 20
1265 35p. Lesser grison, La Campana 30 10
1266 35p. Torrent duck, Rio Clarillo 50 20
1267 35p. Mountain cypress, Rio de los Cipreses 30 10
1268 35p. Black-necked swan, Laguna de Torca 50 20
1269 35p. Puma, Laguna del Laja 40 20
1270 35p. Araucaria, Villarrica 30 10
1271 35p. "Philesia magellanica", Vicente Perez Rosales . . 30 10
1272 35p. "Nothofagus pumilio", Dos Lagunas 30 10
1273 35p. Leopard seal, Laguna San Rafael 40 20
1274 35p. Lesser rhea, Torres del Paine 50 20

498 Boot

1990. World Cup Football Championship, Italy. Multicoloured.
1275 50p. Type **498** 20 10
1276 50p. Hand 20 10
1277 50p. Ball in net 20 10
1278 50p. Player 20 10

499 Vickers Wibault I Biplane, 1927–37

1990. Chilean Airforce Airplanes. Multicoloured.
1279 40p. Type **499** 25 10
1280 40p. Curtiss O1E Falcon, 1928–40 . . . . 25 10
1281 40p. Pitts S-2A (Falcons aerobatic team, 1981–90) 25 10
1282 40p. Extra 33 (Falcons aerobatic team, 1990) . . 25 10
MS1283 120 × 115 mm. Nos. 1279/82 1·00 1·00
No. 1282 is inscribed "EXTRA 300". And **MS**1283 is also inscribed for "Fidae'90" international air fair.

500 Inca

1990. 500th Anniv of Discovery of America by Columbus. Multicoloured.
1284 60p. Type **500** 20 10
1285 60p. Spanish officer 20 10

501 Valparaiso

1990. Ports. Multicoloured.
1286 40p. Type **501** 15 10
1287 40p. San Vicente 15 10

502 "Piloto Pardo" (Antarctic supply ship)

1990. Naval Tradition. Multicoloured.
1288 50p. Type **502** 70 30
1289 50p. "Yelcho" (survey ship) 70 30

503 "Sunrise in Chile"

1990. "Democracy in Chile". Multicoloured.
1290 20p. Type **503** 10 10
1291 30p. Dove ("Peace in Chile") 10 10
1292 60p. "ChiLe" ("Rejoicing in Chile") 45 10
1293 100p. Star ("Thus Chile pleases me") 70 25
MS1294 115 × 120 mm. Nos. 1290/3 1·30 1·30

504 Child and Slogan

1990. "One Chile for All Chileans".
1295 **504** 45p. multicoloured . . . 15 10
MS1296 90 × 105 mm. No. 1295 15 15

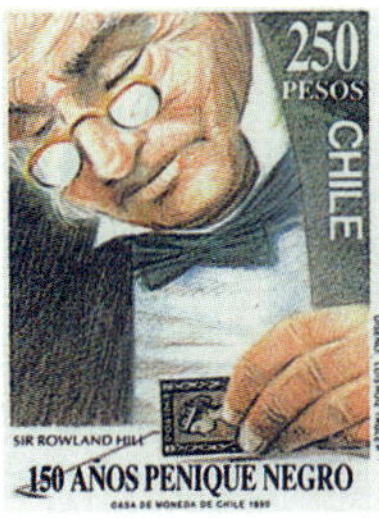

505 Sir Rowland Hill

506 Flags

1990. 150th Anniv of the Penny Black.
1297 **505** 250p. multicoloured . . 1·50 75
MS1298 105 × 90 mm. No. 1297 1·50 1·50

1990. Centenary of Organization of American States.
1299 **506** 150p. multicoloured . . 95 40

507 Purplish Scallop and Diver with Net

1990. Fishing. Multicoloured.
1300 40p. Type **507** 25 15
1301 40p. Giant wedge clam and man with net 25 15
1302 40p. Swordfish ("Albacora") and harpooner on "San Antonio" (fishing boat) 40 15
1303 40p. Marine spider crab and fishing boat raising catch 40 15
1304 40p. Chilean hake ("Merluza") and trawler 40 15
1305 40p. Women baiting hooks 40 15

1990. Town Anniversaries. 250th Anniv of San Felipe. As T **480**. Multicoloured.
1306 50p. Curimon Convent . . . 20 10

508 Aerosol

509 Salvador Allende

1990. Environmental Protection. Each red and black. (a) As T **508**.
1307 35p. Type **508** 15 10
1308 35p. Tree and tree stumps 15 10
1309 35p. Factory chimneys emitting smoke 15 10
1310 35p. Oil tanker polluting wildlife and sea 40 10
1311 35p. Deer escaping from burning forest 15 10

(b) Discount stamps. Additionally inscr "D.S. No 20".
1312 35p. Type **508** 15 10
1313 35p. As No. 1308 . . . . . 15 10
1314 35p. As No. 1309 . . . . . 15 10
1315 35p. As No. 1310 . . . . . 40 10
1316 35p. As No. 1311 . . . . . 15 10
See also Nos. 1421/30.

1990. Presidents.
1317 **509** 35p. black and blue . . 15 10
1318 – 35p. black and blue . . 15 10
1319 – 40p. black and green . . 15 10
1320 – 45p. black and green . . 15 10
1321 – 50p. black and red . . . 20 10
1322 – 60p. black and red . . . 20 10
1323 – 70p. black and blue . . 25 15
1324 – 80p. black and blue . . 30 20
1325 – 90p. black and brown . . 30 20
1326 – 100p. black & brown . . 35 25
DESIGNS: No. 1318, Eduardo Frei; 1319, Jorge Alessandri; 1320, Gabriel Gonzalez; 1321, Juan Antonio Rios: 1322, Pedro Aguirre Cerda; 1323, Juan E. Montero; 1324, Carlos Ibanez; 1325, Emiliano Figueroa; 1326, Arturo Alessandri.

510 Opening Ceremony

1990. Rodeo. Multicoloured.
1327 45p. Type **510** 15 10
1328 45p. Riders saluting crowd 15 10
1329 45p. Rider reining in . . . 15 10
1330 45p. Two riders cornering steer 15 10

511 Chilean Flamingoes

1990. America. The Natural World. Mult.
1331 30p. Type **511** 85 20
1332 150p. South American fur seals . . . . 1·40 40

512 Chilean State Arms and Spanish Royal Arms

1990. State Visit by King Juan Carlos and Queen Sofia of Spain. Multicoloured.
1333 100p. Type **512** 70 25
1334 100p. Spanish and Chilean (at right) State Arms . . 70 25

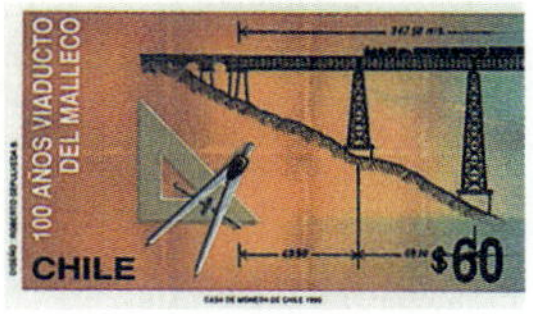

513 Construction Diagram of Viaduct

1990. Centenary of Malleco Viaduct. Mult.
1335 60p. Type **513** 55 20
1336 60p. Boy waving to steam train on completed viaduct 55 20
Nos. 1335/6 were printed together, se-tenant, forming a composite design.

514 Antarctic Skua, Whale and Supply Ship

1990. 50th Anniv of Chilean Antarctic Territory. Multicoloured.
1337 250p. Type **514** . . . . . 1·25 85
1338 250p. Adelie penguins, Bell Model 206 jet helicopters and tents . . . . 2·00 80
MS1339 104 × 89 mm. Nos. 1337/8 3·25 3·25

515 Children decorating Tree

1990. Christmas. (a) As T **515**.
1340 **515** 35p. green & emerald . . 10 10

(b) Discount stamps. Additionally inscr "D.S. No 20".
1341 **515** 35p. green and orange 10 10

516 Santa Claus in Space (Carla Levill)

1990. Christmas. Children's drawings. Mult.
1342 35p. Type **516** 10 10
1343 150p. Television on sea bed (Jose M. Lamas) 70 35

517 Assembly Hall

1990. National Congress. Multicoloured.
1344 100p. Type **517** 75 25
1345 100p. Painting above dais 75 25

1991. Discount stamp. As No. 1238 but colour changed and additionally inscr "D.S. No 20".
1346 45p. black and yellow . . . 40 10

518 Casa Colorada

1991. 450th Anniv of Santiago. Multicoloured.
1347 100p. Type **518** 75 25
1348 100p. City landmarks . . . 75 25
MS1349 89 × 104 mm. Nos. 1347/8 1·50 1·50

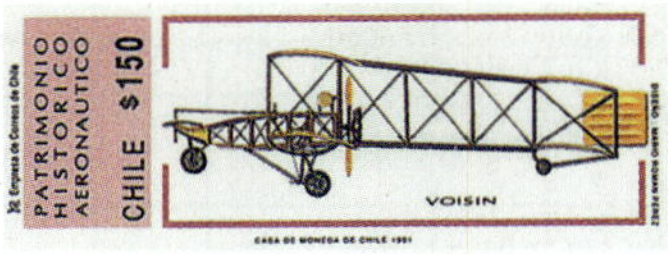

519 Voisin "Boxkite"

1991. Aviation History. Multicoloured.
1354 150p. Type **519** 90 45
1355 150p. Royal Aircraft Factory S.E.5A 90 45
1356 150p. Morane Saulnier MS 35 . . . . 90 45
1357 150p. Consolidated PBY-5A/OA-10 Catalina amphibian 90 45

520 Map, Player and Left Half of Ball

1991. America Cup Football Championship. Mult.
1358 100p. Type **520** 75 25
1359 100p. Right half of ball and goalkeeper 75 25
Nos. 1358/9 were printed together, se-tenant, forming a composite design.

521 Drill and Miner

1991. Coal Mining. Multicoloured.
1360 200p. Type **521** . . . . . . 1·60 45
1361 200p. Miners emptying truck 1·90 45

522 Youths and Emblem

525 Santiago Cathedral

523 Dish and Hanging Ornaments

1991. Centenary of Scientific Society.
1362 **522** 45p. black and green . . 15 10

1991. Traditional Crafts. Multicoloured.
1363 90p. Type **523** 55 25
1364 90p. Carvings and ceramics 55 25

1991. Various stamps surch.
1365 **463** 45p. on 20p. black and yellow 15 10
1366 – 45p. on 20p. black and yellow (1154) 15 10
1367 **487** 45p. on 25p. blue & yell 15 10
1368 – 45p. on 25p. red and yellow (1232) 15 10

1991. National Monuments.
1369 **525** 300p. black, pink & brn 1·90 70

526 Dish Aerial and Transmission Masts

1991. World Telecommunications Day.
1370 **526** 90p. multicoloured . . . 65 25

527 Pope Leo XIII and Factory Line

528 Capt. L. Pardo and Sir Ernest Shackleton

1991. Centenary of "Rerum Novarum" (papal encyclical on workers' rights).
1371 **527** 100p. multicoloured . . 65 25

1991. Naval Tradition. 75th Anniv of Pardo's Rescue of Shackleton Expedition. Multicoloured.
1372 50p. Type **528** 40 10
1373 50p. "Yelcho" (coast-guard vessel) 75 25
1374 50p. Chilean sailor sighting stranded men on Elephant Island 40 10
1375 50p. "Endurance" 75 25
MS1376 89 × 109 mm. Nos. 1372/5 2·20 2·20

529 Flags and Globe

531 "Maipo" (container ship)

530 Building and Police Officers

1991. 21st General Assembly of Organization of American States, Santiago.
1377 **529** 70p. multicoloured . . . 80 15

1991. Opening of New Police School.
1378 **530** 50p. Multicoloured . . . 15 10

1991. National Merchant Navy Day.
1379 **531** 45p. black and red . . . 45 10

532 Opening Ceremony

1991. 11th Pan-American Games, Havana. Mult.
1380 100p. Type **532** 60 25
1381 100p. Cycling, running and basketball competitors . . 60 25

533 Carriage and Building

1991. Bicentenary of Los Andes.
1382 **533** 100p. multicoloured . . 60 25

534 Common Octopus

536 "Woman in Red" (Pedro Reszka)

535 Nitrate Processing and Jose Balmaceda (President, 1886–91)

1991. Marine Life. Multicoloured.
1383 50p. Type **534** 30 15
1384 50p. "Durvillaea antarctica" 30 15
1385 50p. Lenguado 45 15
1386 50p. "Austromegabalanus psittacus" 30 15
1387 50p. Barnacle rock shell ("Concholepas concholepas") 30 15
1388 50p. Crab ("Cancer setosus") 30 15
1389 50p. "Lessonia nigrescens" 30 15
1390 50p. Sea-urchin 30 15
1391 50p. Crab ("Homalaspis plana") 30 15
1392 50p. "Porphyra columbina" 30 15
1393 50p. Loro knife-jaw 45 15
1394 50p. "Chorus giganteus" . . 30 15
1395 50p. Rock shrimp 30 15
1396 50p. Peruvian anchovy . . . 45 15
1397 50p. "Gracilaria sp." . . . 30 15
1398 50p. "Pyura chilensis" . . . 30 15

1991. Centenary of 1891 Revolution. Pre-Revolution Events. Multicoloured.
1399 100p. Type **535** 90 25
1400 100p. Education and Balmaceda 60 25

1991. Paintings. Multicoloured.
1401 50p. Type **536** 40 10
1402 70p. "The Traveller" (Camilo Mori) . . . . . 1·25 30
1403 200p. "Head of Child" (Benito Rebolledo) . . . 90 45
1404 300p. "Child in Fez" (A. Valenzuela Puelma) 2·00 70

537 Map of South American Interests in Antartica

1991. 30th Anniv of Antarctica Treaty. Mult.
1405 80p. Type **537** 70 20
1406 80p. Wildlife 90 45

538 Globe in Envelope (Guillermo Suarez)

1991. International Letter Writing Week. Children's drawings. Multicoloured.
1407 45p. Type **538** 45 10
1408 70p. Human figures in envelope (Jorge Vargas) 60 15

539 Amerindians watching Columbus's Fleet

1991. America. Voyages of Discovery. Mult.
1409 50p. Type **539** 30 15
1410 150p. Columbus's fleet and navigator . . . . 1·40 65

540 Line Drawing of Neruda

541 Boy and Stars

1991. 20th Anniv of Award of Nobel Prize for Literature to Pablo Neruda. Multicoloured, colour of cap given.
1411 **540** 45p. blue 15 10
1412 45p. red 15 10
MS1413 90 × 105 mm. Nos. 1411/12 30 30
Nos. 1411/12 were issued together, se-tenant, the backgrounds of the stamps forming a composite design of one of Neruda's manuscripts.

1991. Christmas. Multicoloured.
1414 45p. Type **541** 15 10
1415 100p. Girl and stars 30 25

542 Postman making Delivery

544 Houses and Figures

1991. Christmas. (a) As T **542**.
1416 **542** 45p. mauve and violet 15 10
1417 – 45p. mauve and violet 30 10

(b) Discount stamps. Additionally inscr "D.S. No 20" in left-hand margin.
1418 **542** 45p. mauve and violet 15 10
1419 – 45p. mauve and violet 30 20
DESIGN: Nos. 1417, 1419, Starlit town.

1992. No. 1238 surch **$60**.
1420 60p. on 45p. black & green 40 15

1992. Environmental Protection. As Nos. 1307/16 but values and colours changed. (a) As T **508**, each yellow and green.
1421 60p. Type **508** 20 15
1422 60p. As No. 1308 . . . . . 20 15
1423 60p. As No. 1309 . . . . . 20 15
1424 60p. As No. 1310 . . . . . 40 15
1425 60p. As No. 1311 . . . . . 20 15

(b) Discount stamps. Additionally inscr "D.S. No 20". Each orange and green.
1426 60p. Type **508** 20 15
1427 60p. As No. 1308 . . . . . 20 15
1428 60p. As No. 1309 . . . . . 20 15
1429 60p. As No. 1310 . . . . . 40 15
1430 60p. As No. 1311 . . . . . 20 15

1992. 16th Population and Housing Census.
1431 **544** 60p. blue, orange & blk 20 15

545 Score and Mozart

1992. Death Bicentenary of Wolfgang Amadeus Mozart (composer). Multicoloured.
1432 60p. Type **545** 50 15
1433 200p. Mozart playing harpsichord . . . . . . 1·10 50
MS1434 90 × 104 mm. Nos. 1432/3 1·60 1·60

546 Stylized Jet Fighter

1992. "Fidae '92" International Air and Space Fair.
1435 **546** 60p. multicoloured . . . 20 15

547 Arms and Church, San Jose de Maipo

1992. 200th (80p.) or 250th (others) Anniversaries of Cities. Multicoloured.
1436 80p. Type **547** 50 20
1437 90p. Pottery (Melipilla) . . 55 25
1438 100p. Lircunlauta House (San Fernando) 60 25
1439 150p. Fruits and woodsman (Cauquenes) 75 35
1440 250p. Huilquilemu Cultural Villa (Talca) . . . . . . 1·25 60

548 Chilean Pavilion

1992. "Expo '92" World's Fair, Seville. Mult.
1441 150p. Type **548** 90 35
1442 200p. Iceberg . . . . 1·10 50
MS1443 105 × 90 mm. Nos. 1441/2 2·00 2·00

549 "Morula praecipua", Maculated Conch and Dragon's-head Cowrie

1992. Marine Flora and Fauna of Easter Island. Multicoloured.
1444 60p. Type **549** 35 20
1445 60p. "Codium pocockiae" 35 20
1446 60p. Easter Island swordfish ("Myripristis tiki") . . . 50 20
1447 60p. Seaweed 35 20
1448 60p. Fuentes' wrasse ("Pseudolabrus fuentesi") 50 20
1449 60p. Coral 35 20
1450 60p. Spiny lobster 35 20
1451 60p. Sea urchin 35 20

550 Statues, Liner and Launch

1992. Easter Island Tourism. Multicoloured.
1452 200p. Type **550** 85 50
1453 200p. Airplane, dancers and hill-carving 85 50
Nos. 1452/3 were issued together, se-tenant, forming a composite design.

551 Sun shining through Doorway and Handicapped People

552 Flags and Emblem

1992. National Council for the Handicapped.
1454 **551** 60p. multicoloured . . . 20 15

1992. 50th Anniv of National Defence Staff.
1455 **552** 60p. multicoloured . . . 45 15

553 "Simpson" (submarine)

1992. 75th Anniv of Chilean Submarine Fleet. Multicoloured.
1456 150p. Type **553** 90 35
1457 250p. Officer using periscope 1·40 60

1992. Discount stamp. As No. 1240 but additionally inscr "D/S No 20".
1458 60p. black and bistre . . . 1·10 30

1992. Nos. 1350/3 surch **$60**.
1459 **487** 60p. on 45p. blue & mve 20 15
1460 – 60p. on 45p. red & mve 20 15
1461 **487** 60p. on 45p. blue & yell 20 15
1462 – 60p. on 45p. red & yell 20 15

1992. Nos. 1416/19 surch **$60**.
1463 **542** 60p. on 45p. mauve and violet (1416) 20 15
1464 – 60p. on 45p. mauve and violet (1417) 35 15
1465 **542** 60p. on 45p. mauve and violet (1418) 20 15
1466 – 60p. on 45p. mauve and violet (1419) 35 15

556 Emperor Penguin

1992. The Emperor Penguin. Multicoloured.
1467 200p. Type **556** . . . . . . 1·40 50
1468 250p. Adult and chick . . . 1·75 60
MS1469 104 × 90 mm. Nos. 1467/8 3·00 3·00

557 Santiago Central Post Office

1992. National Monuments.
1470 **557** 200p. multicoloured . . 1·25 50

558 Columbus and Navigation Instruments

1992. America. 500th Anniv of Discovery of America by Columbus. Multicoloured.
1471 200p. Type **558** . . . . . . 1·25 50
1472 250p. Church, map of Americas and "Santa Maria" . . . . 1·10 70

559 Presenter at Microphone

560 O'Higgins, Flag and Monument

1992. 70th Anniv of Chilean Radio.
1473 **559** 250p. multicoloured . . 1·40 60

1992. 150th Death Anniv of Bernardo O'Higgins.
1474 **560** 60p. multicoloured . . . 20 15

561 Arrau as a Child

1992. Claudio Arrau (pianist). Multicoloured.
1475 150p. Type **561** 80 35
1476 200p. Arrau playing piano 1·10 50
MS1477 105 × 90 mm. Nos. 1475/6 1·90 1·90

562 Statue

563 Nativity

1992. 150th Anniv of University of Chile. Mult.
1478 200p. Type **562** . . . . . 1·00 50
1479 200p. Coat of arms, statues and clock . . . . 1·00 50
Nos. 1478/9 were issued together, se-tenant, forming a composite design.

1992. Christmas. (a) As T **563**.
1480 **563** 60p. brown and stone . . 20 15
1481 – 60p. brown and stone . . 20 15

(b) Discount stamps. Additionally inscr "DS/20" in right-hand margin.
1482 **563** 60p. red and stone . . . 20 15
1483 – 60p. red and stone . . . 20 15
DESIGN: Nos. 1481, 1483, Nativity (different).

564 Dam

1992. 23rd Ministerial Meeting of Latin-American Energy Organization.
1484 **564** 70p. black and yellow . . 25 20

565 Hands and Stars

1992. National Human Rights Day.
1485 **565** 100p. multicoloured . . 55 25

566 Achao Church

567 St. Ignatius de Loyola (founder)

1993. Churches. (a) As T **566**.
1487 **566** 70p. black and pink . . 25 20
1488 – 70p. black and pink . . 25 20

(b) Discount stamps. Additionally inscr "DS/20" in left-hand margin.
1489 **566** 70p. black and yellow . . 25 20
1490 – 70p. black and yellow . . 25 20
DESIGN: Nos. 1488, 1490, Castro church.
See also Nos. 1507/15.

1993. 400th Anniv of Jesuits' Arrival in Chile.
1491 **567** 200p. multicoloured . . 1·25 75
MS1492 105 × 90 mm. No. 1491 1·25 1·25

568 St. Teresa

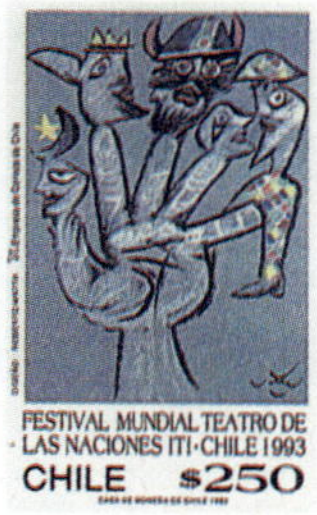

569 Finger-Puppets

1993. Canonization of St. Teresa of the Andes.
1493 **568** 300p. multicoloured . . 1·50 70

1993. International Theatre Festival.
1494 **569** 250p. multicoloured . . 1·10 60

570 Satellite in Orbit

1993. 2nd Pan-American Space Conference.
1495 **570** 150p. multicoloured . . 80 35
MS1496 105 × 89 mm. No. 1495 80 80

571 Clotario Blest (Trade Union leader)

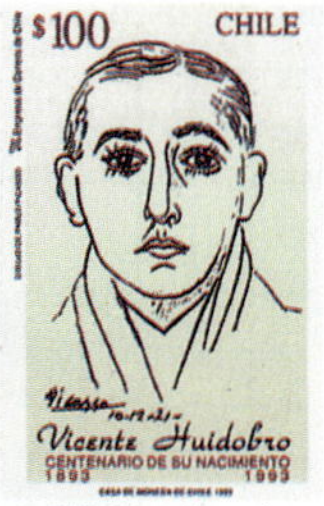

572 Drawing of Huidobro by Picasso

1993. Labour Day.
1497 **571** 70p. multicoloured . . . 50 20

1993. Birth Centenary of Vicente Huidobro (poet). Each black, stone and red.
1498 100p. Type **572** 30 25
1499 100p. Drawing of Huidobro by Juan Gris 30 25

573 Watterous, 1902

1993. Fire Engines (1st series). Multicoloured.
1500 100p. Type **573** 60 25
1501 100p. Merryweather, 1872 60 25
MS1502 105 × 89 mm. Nos. 1500/1 1·20 1·20
See also Nos. 1577/80.

574 Douglas B-26 Invader

1993. Aviation and Space. Multicoloured.

1503	100p. Type **574**	60	25
1504	100p. Mirage M 50 Pantera	60	25
1505	100p. Sanchez Besa biplane	60	25
1506	100p. Bell-47 Dl helicopter	60	25

1993. Churches. (a) As T **566**.

1507	10p. black and green	10	10
1508	20p. black and brown	10	10
1509	30p. black and orange	10	10
1510	40p. black and blue	10	10
1511	50p. black and green	15	10
1512	80p. black and buff	25	20
1513	90p. black and green	25	20
1514	100p. black and grey	30	25

(b) Discount stamp. Additionally inscr "DS/20" at left.

1515	80p. black and lilac	25	20
1516	90p. black and red	25	20
1517	100p. black and yellow	30	25

CHURCHES: 10p. Chonchi; 20p. Vilupulli; 30p. Llau-Llao; 40p. Dalcahue; 50p. Tenaun; 80p. Quinchao; 90p. Quehui; 100p. Nercon.

575 Nortina

577 Early Coin Production

576 "Late Dawn" (Mario Carreno)

1993. Regional Variations of La Cueca (national dance). Multicoloured.

1525	70p. Type **575**	45	15
1526	70p. Central	45	15
1527	70p. Chilota	45	15

1993. Santiago, Iberian-American City of Culture 1993. Paintings. Multicoloured.

1528	80p. Type **576**	50	20
1529	90p. "Summer" (Gracia Barrios)	50	20
1530	150p. "Protection" (Roser Bru) (vert)	70	35
1531	200p. "Tango, Valparaiso" (Nemesio Antunez)	1·00	45

1993. 250th Anniv of Chilean Mint.

1532 **577**	250p. multicoloured	1·25	55
MS1533	105 × 90 mm. No. 1523	1·25	1·25

578 Patagonian Conure

579 Underground Train

1993. America. Endangered Animals. Mult.

1534	150p. Type **578**	90	35
1535	200p. Chilean guemal	1·40	45

1993. 25th Anniv of Chilean Metro.

1536 **579**	80p. multicoloured	45	20

580 "Ancud" (schooner) off Santa Ana Point

1993. 150th Anniv of Chilean Possession of Strait of Magellan.

1537 **580**	100p. multicoloured	40	25

581 Marines in Inflatable Assault Boats

1993. Naval Tradition. Multicoloured.

1538	80p. Type **581** (175th anniv of Marines)	25	20
1539	80p. Sailors making fast patrol boat (125th anniv of Alejandro Navarette Training School)	25	20
1540	80p. "Esmeralda" (cadet barquentine) and cadets in traditional "unloading the cannon" exercise (175th anniv of Arturo Prat Naval College)	25	20
1541	80p. "Sailing of First Squadron" (175th anniv) (painting, Alvaro Casanova Zenteno)	25	20

582 Carved Figures

1993. International Year of Indigenous Peoples.

1542 **582**	100p. multicoloured	60	25

583 Holy Family

584 Adelie Penguins

1993. Christmas. (a) Sold at face value.

1543 **583**	70p. lilac and stone	20	15

(b) Discount stamp. Additionally inscribed "DS/20" in right-hand margin.

1544 **583**	70p. blue and green	20	15

1993. Chilean Antarctic Territory. Mult.

1545	200p. Type **584**	1·40	45
1546	250p. Adelie penguin with young	1·60	55
MS1547	105 × 89 mm. Nos. 1545/6	3·00	3·00

585 Plaza de Armas, Ancud

1993. City Anniversaries. Multicoloured.

1548	80p. Type **585** (225th)	35	20
1549	80p. Matriz church, Curico (250th)	35	20
1550	80p. Corner Pillar House, Rancagua (250th)	35	20

586 Hands

1994. International Year of the Family.

1551 **586**	100p. multicoloured	55	25

587 Violin

1994. 26th Music Weeks, Frutillar. Mult.

1552	150p. Type **587**	90	35
1553	150p. Cello	90	35

Nos. 1552/3 were issued together, se-tenant, forming a composite design.

588 Sukhoi Su-30 Flanker

1994. "Fidae '94" International Air and Space Fair. Multicoloured.

1554	300p. Type **588**	1·60	65
1555	300p. Vought Sikorsky OS2U3 Kingfisher seaplane	1·60	65
1556	300p. Lockheed F-117A Stealth	1·60	65
1557	300p. Northrop F-5E Tiger III	1·60	65

589 Ears of Grain

1994. 50th Anniv of Chile Agronomical Engineers' College.

1558 **589**	220p. multicoloured	1·50	45

1994. Nos. 1092/5 surch **$80**.

1559	80p. on 15p. green	25	20
1560	80p. on 15p. blue	35	20
1561	80p. on 15p. brown	25	20
1562	80p. on 15p. mauve	25	20

591 Skeletons buried under Cactus

1994. 75th Anniv of Concepcion University. Details of "Latin American Presence" (mural by Jorge Gonzalez Camarena). Multicoloured.

1563	250p. Type **591**	1·50	55
1564	250p. Faces	1·50	55
1565	250p. Building pyramid from spare parts	1·50	55
1566	250p. Cablework in building	1·50	55

Nos. 1563/6 were issued together, se-tenant, forming a composite design.

592 Gentoo Penguins and Harbour

1994. 30th Anniv of Chilean Antarctic Institute. Multicoloured.

1567	300p. Type **592**	1·90	65
1568	300p. Antarctic base	1·90	65

Nos. 1567/8 were issued together, se-tenant, forming a composite design.

593 "Vanessa terpsichore"

1994. Butterflies. Multicoloured.

1569	100p. Type **593**	60	25
1570	100p. "Hypsochila wagenknechti"	60	25
1571	100p. Polydamas swallowtail ("Battus polydamas")	60	25
1572	100p. "Polythysana apollina"	60	25
1573	100p. "Satyridae"	60	25
1574	100p. "Tetraphloebia stellygera"	60	25
1575	100p. "Eroessa chilensis"	60	25
1576	100p. Cloudless sulphur ("Phoebis sennae")	60	25

594 Merryweather Steam Fire Engine, 1869

1994. Fire Engines (2nd series). Mult.

1577	150p. Type **594**	80	35
1578	150p. Poniente steam fire engine, 1863	80	35
1579	150p. Mieusset steam fire engine, 1905	80	35
1580	150p. Merryweather motor fire engine, 1903	80	35

595 Bust and Banner

1994. Centenary of Javiera Carrera School for Girls, Santiago.

1581 **595**	200p. multicoloured	85	45

596 Door Panels, Porvenir (centenary)

1994. Town Anniversaries. Multicoloured.

1582	90p. Type **596**	50	20
1583	100p. Railway station, Villa Alemana (cent)	1·00	25
1584	150p. Church, Constitucion (bicentenary)	70	35
1585	200p. Fountain and church, Linares (bicent)	90	45
1586	250p. Steam locomotive and statue, Copiapo (250th)	2·25	55
1587	300p. La Serena (450th)	1·60	65

597 Painting by Carlos Maturana

600 Fr. Hurtado

599 First Chilean Mail Van

1994. 20th International Very Large Data Bases Conference, Santiago.
1588 **597** 100p. multicoloured . . 30 25

1994. Nos. 1487/8 and 1544 surch **$80**.
1589 **566** 80p. on 70p. blk & pink 25 20
1590 – 80p. on 70p. blk & pink 25 20
1591 **583** 80p. on 70p. blue & grn 25 20

1994. America. Postal Transport. Mult.
1592 80p. Type **599** 50 20
1593 220p. De Havilland D.H.60G Gipsy Moth (first Chilean mail plane) 1·10 50

1994. Beatification of Fr. Alberto Hurtado.
1594 **600** 300p. blue, green & blk 1·40 70

601 Madonna and Child

603 "Almirante Williams" (destroyer)

602 Star

1994. Christmas. (a) Sold at face value.
1595 **601** 80p. multicoloured . . . 25 20
(b) Discount stamp. Additionally inscribed "DS/20" at foot.
1596 **601** 80p. multicoloured . . . 25 20

1995. International Women's Day. Mult.
1597 90p. Type **602** 55 25
1598 90p. Moon and sun 55 25
1599 90p. Dove 55 25
1600 90p. Earth 55 25

1995. Naval Tradition.
1601 **603** 100p. multicoloured . . 30 25

604 Emblem

605 Arms

1995. United Nations World Summit for Social Development, Copenhagen.
1602 **604** 150p. multicoloured . . 75 35

1995. 150th Anniv of Conciliar Seminary of Ancud.
1603 **605** 200p. multicoloured . . 90 45

606 Stained Glass Window, Santiago Cathedral

1995. 400th Anniv of Augustinian Order in Chile.
1604 **606** 250p. multicoloured . . 1·10 60

607 Religious Mask, Limari

1995. Rock Paintings. Multicoloured.
1605 150p. Type **607** 75 35
1606 150p. Herdsmen and llamas, Taira 75 35
1607 150p. Whale, Tal-tal 75 35
1608 150p. Masks, Encanto Valley 75 35

608 Camera and Director's Chair

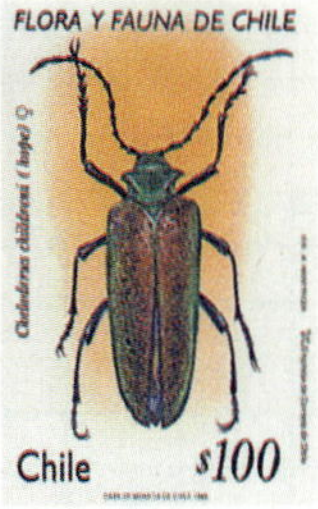

610 "Cheloderus childreni"

609 Arms and Express Steam Train

1995. Centenary of Motion Pictures. Mult.
1609 100p. Type **608** 55 25
1610 100p. Advertising poster for "The Kid" 55 25
1611 100p. Early cinema advertising poster 55 25
1612 100p. Advertising poster for "Valparaiso Mi Amor" 55 25

1995. Bicentenary of Parral.
1613 **609** 200p. multicoloured . . 1·00 50

1995. Flora and Fauna. Multicoloured.
1614 100p. Type **610** 55 25
1615 100p. "Eulychnia acida" (cactus) 55 25
1616 100p. "Chiasognathus grantii" (stag beetle) . . . 55 25
1617 100p. "Browningia candelaris" (cactus) . . . 55 25
1618 100p. "Capiapoa dealbata" (cactus) 55 25
1619 100p. "Acanthinodera cummingi" (beetle) . . . 55 25
1620 100p. "Neoporteria subgibbosa" (cactus) . . . 55 25
1621 100p. "Semiotus luteipennis" (beetle) 55 25

611 Congress Emblem

1995. 2nd World Police Congress, Santiago.
1622 **611** 200p. multicoloured . . 90 45

612 "Tower of Babel V" (Mario Toral)

1995. 30th Anniv of Ministry of Housing and Town-planning.
1623 **612** 200p. multicoloured . . 90 45

613 Bello

614 Open Book and Emblem

1995. 25th Anniv of Andres Bello Agreement (South American co-operation in education. science and culture).
1624 **613** 250p. purple and black 1·10 60

1995. 50th Anniversaries. Multicoloured.
1625 100p. Type **614** (UNESCO) 30 25
1626 100p. Globes and handshake (UNO) 30 25
1627 100p. Seedling in hand (FAO) 30 25
Nos. 1625/7 were issued together, se-tenant, forming a composite design.

615 Farming (M. Cruces)

616 Sailing Ship and Cape Horn

1995. America. Environmental Protection. Children's Paintings. Multicoloured.
1628 100p. Type **615** 55 25
1629 250p. Forestry (E. Munoz) (horiz) . . . . 1·00 55

1995. 51st World Congress of Cape Horn Captains.
1630 **616** 250p. multicoloured . . 90 55

617 Crib and Inhabitants of North Chile

618 Carlos Dittborn (trainer) and Arica Stadium

1995. Christmas. (a) Sold at face value.
1631 **617** 90p. blue and violet . . 25 20
1632 – 90p. blue and violet . . 25 20
(b) Discount stamps. Additionally inscr "DS/20".
1633 **617** 90p. green and purple . . 25 20
1634 – 90p. green and purple . . 25 20
DESIGNS: Nos. 1632, 1634, Crib and people of South Chile.

1995. Centenary of Chile Football Federation. Mult.
1635 100p. Type **618** 55 25
1636 100p. Hugo Lepe (player) 55 25
1637 100p. Eladio Rojas (player) 55 25
1638 100p. Honorino Landa (player) 55 25

619 Mistral

1995. 50th Anniv of Award of Nobel Prize for Literature to Gabriela Mistral.
1639 **619** 300p. blue and black . . 1·25 65

620 Penguins

1995. Chilean Antarctic Territory. The Macaroni Penguin. Multicoloured.
1640 100p. Type **620** 60 25
1641 250p. Penguins (different) 1·50 55
MS1642 105 × 90 mm. Nos. 1640/1 2·10 2·10

621 Kiwi Fruit and Container Ship

1995. 60th Anniv of Chilean Exports Association. Fruit. Multicoloured.
1643 100p. Type **621** 40 25
1644 100p. Grapes and container ship 40 25
1645 100p. Peaches and container ship 40 25
1646 100p. Apples and container ship 40 25
1647 100p. Soft fruit and airplane 40 25

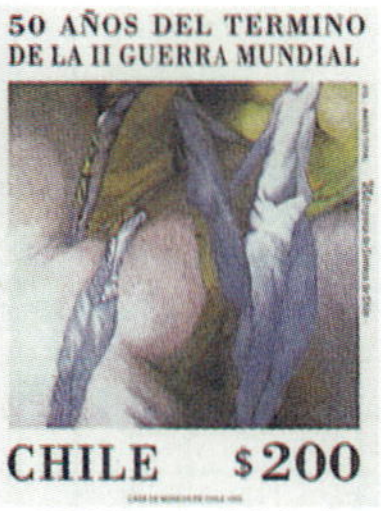

622 "Reunion" (Mario Toral)

623 Oil Rig

1995. 50th Anniv of End of Second World War.
1648 **622** 200p. multicoloured . . 90 45

1995. 50th Anniv of Discovery of Oil in Chile. Multicoloured.
1649 100p. Type **623** 40 25
1650 100p. Concon Refinery (grass in foreground) . . 40 25
1651 100p. Concepcion Refinery 40 25
1652 100p. Rig (different) 40 25

624 Embraer EMB-145

1996. "FIDAE '96" International Air and Space Fair, Santiago. Aircraft. Multicoloured.
1653 400p. Type **624** . . . . . 2·50 90
1654 400p. Mirage M5M Elkan 2·50 90
1655 400p. De Havilland D.H.C. 6 Twin Otter . . . . . . 2·50 90
1656 400p. Saab JAS-39 Gripen 2·50 90

625 School

1996. 175th Anniv of Serena Boys' School.
1657 **625** 100p. multicoloured . . 75 25

626 Old Cordoba Rail Station, Seville

1996. "Espamer" and "Aviation and Space" Spanish and Latin American Stamp Exhibitions, Seville, Spain. Multicoloured.
1658 200p. Type **626** . . . . . . 1·10 25
1659 200p. Lope de Vega Theatre, Seville 85 45

627 Extinguish Matches Properly

629 "Weather Rose" (Ricardo Mesa)

628 "Esmeralda" (cadet barquentine) in Dry-dock

1996. Safety Precautions. Multicoloured.
(a) Accidents in the Home.

1660 50p. Type **627** 15 10
1661 50p. Do not leave boiling water unattended 15 10
1662 50p. Keep sharp objects away from children 15 10
1663 50p. Protect electrical sockets 15 10
1664 50p. Do not improvise electrical connections 15 10
1665 50p. Do not play the television or radio too loud 15 10
1666 50p. Check gas connections regularly 15 10
1667 50p. Do not overload electrical circuits 15 10
1668 50p. Keep inflammable materials away from fire 15 10
1669 50p. Do not leave toys lying around on the floor 15 10

(b) Road Safety.

1670 50p. Use crossings 15 10
1671 50p. Obey the instructions of the traffic police 15 10
1672 50p. Only cross on the green light 15 10
1673 50p. Wait on the pavement for buses 15 10
1674 50p. Do not cross the road between vehicles 15 10
1675 50p. Do not travel on the step of buses 15 10
1676 50p. Walk on the side of the road facing on-coming traffic 15 10
1677 50p. Look out for drains 15 10
1678 50p. Do not play ball in the road 15 10
1679 50p. Bicyclists should obey the Highway Code 15 10

(c) Safety at School.

1680 50p. Do not panic in emergencies 15 10
1681 50p. Do not run around corners 15 10
1682 50p. Do not play practical jokes 15 10
1683 50p. Do not sit on banisters or railings 15 10
1684 50p. Do not run on the stairs 15 10
1685 50p. Do not drink while walking 15 10
1686 50p. Do not swing on your chair 15 10
1687 50p. Do not play with pointed or sharp objects 15 10
1688 50p. Do not open doors sharply 15 10
1689 50p. Go straight home after school and do not stop to talk to strangers 15 10

(d) Safety in the Workplace.

1690 50p. Wear protective clothing 15 10
1691 50p. Do not work with tools in bad condition 15 10
1692 50p. Keep your attention on your work (man at lathe) 15 10
1693 50p. Always use the proper tools 15 10
1694 50p. Work carefully (man at filing cabinet) 15 10
1695 50p. Do not leave objects on the stairs 15 10
1696 50p. Do not carry so much that you cannot see where you are going 15 10
1697 50p. Check ladders are safe 15 10
1698 50p. Always keep the workplace clean and tidy 15 10
1699 50p. Remove old nails first 15 10

(e) Enjoy Leisure Safely.

1700 50p. Only swim in the permitted areas 15 10
1701 50p. Do not put any part of the body out of the window of a moving vehicle 15 10
1702 50p. Avoid excessive exposure to the sun 15 10
1703 50p. Do not contaminate swimming water with detergents 15 10
1704 50p. Do not throw litter 15 10
1705 50p. Always put out fires before leaving them 15 10
1706 50p. Do not play pranks in water 15 10
1707 50p. Check safety precautions 15 10
1708 50p. Do not fly kites near overhead electrical lines 15 10
1709 50p. Do not run by the side of swimming pools 15 10

(f) Alcohol and Drugs Awareness.

1710 50p. Do not drink and drive 15 10
1711 50p. Do not drink if you are pregnant 15 10
1712 50p. Do not give in to peer pressure 15 10
1713 50p. Being under the influence of alcohol is irresponsible in the workplace 15 10
1714 50p. Do not destroy your family through alcohol 15 10
1715 50p. You do not need drugs to have a good time 15 10
1716 50p. You do not need drugs to succeed 15 10
1717 50p. You do not need drugs to entertain 15 10
1718 50p. Do not abandon your friends and family for drugs 15 10
1719 50p. Without drugs you are free and safe 15 10

1996. Centenary of Dry-dock No. 1, Talcahuano.
1720 **628** 200p. multicoloured 70 45

1996. Modern Sculpture. Multicoloured.
1721 150p. Type **629** 70 35
1722 150p. "Friendship" (Francisca Cerda) 70 35
1723 200p. "Memory" (Fernando Undurraga) (horiz) 70 35
1724 200p. "Andean Airs" (Benito Rojo) (horiz) 70 35

630 Addict and Syringe full of Pills

1996. International Day against Drug Abuse.
1725 **630** 250p. multicoloured 75 55

631 Boxing Glove

1996. Centenary of National Olympic Committee and Modern Olympic Games. Olympic Games, Atlanta. Multicoloured.
1726 450p. Type **631** 2·25 1·00
1727 450p. Running shoe 2·25 1·00
1728 450p. Rollerblade 2·25 1·00
1729 450p. Ball 2·25 1·00

632 School

1996. 150th Anniv of San Fernando School.
1730 **632** 200p. multicoloured 85 45

633 Polluted Forest

1996. 4th International Congress on Earth Sciences. Multicoloured.
1731 200p. Type **633** 95 45
1732 200p. Industrial pollution 95 45
1733 200p. Deforestation 95 45
1734 200p. Map, camera and cracked earth 95 45

Nos. 1731/4 were issued together, se-tenant, forming a composite design.

634 Crookesite and Open-cast Mine

1996. Mining. Multicoloured.
1735 150p. Type **634** 70 35
1736 150p. Lapis lazuli and pendant 70 35
1737 150p. Bornite and calcium and crates 70 35
1738 150p. Azurite and atacamite 70 35

635 St. John Leonardi (founder)

1996. 50th Anniv of Order of Mother of God in Chile.
1739 **635** 200p. multicoloured 90 45

636 German-style Wooden house and Mt. Osorno

1996. 150th Anniv of German Immigration. Multicoloured.
1740 250p. Type **636** 1·00 50
1741 300p. "German Fountain" (monument) 1·10 60

637 King Penguins

1996. Chilean Antarctic Territory. Mult.
1742 250p. Type **637** 1·40 50
1743 300p. Adult and young king penguins 1·75 60
MS1744 105 × 90 mm. Nos. 1742/3 3·00 3·00

638 Lancia Fire Engine, 1937

1996. Centenary of Castro Fire Service. Mult.
1745 200p. Type **638** 90 40
1746 200p. Ford V8 fire engine, 1940 90 40
1747 200p. Gorlitz G. A. Fischer 4-speed motor pump, 1930s 90 40
1748 200p. Lever-action pump, 1907 90 40

639 Rafting, Vicente Perez Rosales National Park

1996. National Parks. Multicoloured.
1749 100p. Type **639** 55 25
1750 100p. Horse riding, Torres del Paine National Park 55 25
1751 100p. Cross-country skiing, Puyehue National Park 55 25
1752 100p. Walking, Pan de Azucar National Park 55 25

640 Latorre and "Almirante Latorre" (destroyer)

641 Women with Child

1996. 150th Birth Anniv of Admiral Juan Jose Latorre.
1753 **640** 200p. multicoloured 70 40

1996. America. Costumes. Multicoloured.
1754 100p. Type **641** 55 25
1755 100p. Men with horse 55 25
1756 250p. Men on horseback 95 50

642 "Visual History of a Nation" (Mario Toral) (left-hand detail)

644 The Three Kings

643 Beach, Arms and Cathedral, Arica

1996. 6th Ibero-Latin American Heads of State Summit, Santiago. Multicoloured.
1757 110p. Type **642** 55 25
1758 110p. Right-hand detail of painting 55 25

Nos. 1757/8 were issued together, se-tenant, forming a composite design.

1996. Cities. 1st Anniv of Arica Law. Multicoloured.
1759 100p. Type **643** 55 25
1760 150p. Llamas and Chilean flamingoes, Parinacota Province 65 30

1996. Christmas. (a) Face value in black.
1761 **644** 100p. multicoloured 30 25

(b) Discount stamp. Additionally inscribed "DS/20" at foot and with face value in orange.
1762 **644** 100p. multicoloured 30 25

645 Pablo Neruda (poet), Gabriela Mistral (writer) and Nobel Prize Medal

1996. Visit of King and Queen of Sweden.
1763 **645** 300p. multicoloured 1·40 60

646 Children, Star and Globe

1996. 50th Anniv of UNICEF.
1764 **646** 200p. multicoloured 80 40

647 Church

1997. Centenary of Frontera Region. Mult.
1765 110p. Type **647** (centenary of Christian and Missionary Church Alliance) 60 25
1766 110p. Mountain valley (cent of Lonquimay Municipality) 60 25

648 Base Camp **649** La Pincoya

1997. 50th Anniv of Arturo Prat Antarctic Naval Base.
1767 250p. Type **648** . . . . . . 1·00 50
1768 300p. Monument and flags (horiz) . . . . 1·25 60

1997. Mythology. (a) As T **649**.
1769 40p. black and blue 10 10
1770 110p. black and orange . . 30 25

(b) Discount stamp. Additionally inscr "DS/20".
1778 110p. black and green . . . 30 25
DESIGN: Nos. 1770, 1778, La Fiura.

650 "Justice" and National Flag

1997. 70th Anniv of Controller General.
1781 **650** 110p. multicoloured . . 55 25

651 Underground Train in Station

1997. Inauguration of Metro Line No. 5.
1782 **651** 200p. multicoloured . . 1·25 60

652 Masonic Symbols and Flags

1997. 50th Anniv of Interamerican Masonic Confederation and 17th Grand General Assembly, Santiago.
1783 250p. Type **652** . . . . . 1·00 50
MS1784 85 × 105 mm. 1200p. Dividers, set-square and book (48 × 59 mm) . . . . 3·00 3·00

653 Von Stephan

1997. Death Centenary of Heinrich von Stephan (founder of Universal Postal Union).
1785 **653** 250p. multicoloured . . 1·00 50

654 Books

1997. World Books and Copyright Day.
1786 **654** 110p. multicoloured . . 55 25

655 "Death to the Invader, Chile"

1997. Birth Centenary of David Alfaro Siqueiros (painter). Designs showing details of his murals in the Mexican School, Chillan, Chile. Multicoloured.
1787 150p. Type **655** 70 30
1788 200p. "Death to the Invader, Mexico" 95 40
MS1789 Two sheets each 120 × 100 mm. (a) 1000p. Detail as in Type **655** (47 × 35 mm); (b) 1000p. Detail as in No. 1788 (47 × 35 mm) . . . . 3·50 3·50

656 Arms and Town Hall

1997. Centenary of Providencia.
1790 **656** 250p. multicoloured . . 1·10 50

657 Pacific Ocean and Mt. Osorno (after Hokusai Katsushika) **658** Award, National Flag and "Thumbs-up" Sign

1997. Centenary of Chile–Japan Relations.
1791 **657** 300p. multicoloured . . 1·10 60

1997. National Centre for Productivity and Quality.
1792 **658** 110p. multicoloured . . 75 25

659 Transmission from University of Chile to "El Mercurio" (newspaper) Offices

1997. 75th Anniv of First Radio Broadcast in Chile.
1793 **659** 110p. multicoloured . . 80 25

660 Postman on Bicycle, 1997

1997. America. The Postman. Multicoloured.
1794 110p. Type **660** 55 25
1795 250p. Late 19th-century mounted postman 95 50

661 Carlo Morelli in "Rigoletto" **662** Jack-in-a-Box and Baubles on Tree

1997. Opera Singers. Multicoloured.
1796 120p. Type **661** 35 25
1797 200p. Pedro Navia in "La Boheme" 55 40
1798 250p. Renato Zanelli in "Faust" 70 50
1799 300p. Rayen Quitral in "The Magic Flute" . . . . . . 1·10 60
1800 500p. Ramon Vinay in "Othello" . . . . 1·60 70

1997. Christmas. (a) "NAVIDAD '97" in blue.
1801 **662** 110p. multicoloured . . 30 25

(b) Discount stamp. "NAVIDAD '97" in orange and additionally inscr "D/S 20" below face value.
1802 **662** 110p. multicoloured . . 30 25

663 Cancelling Letters **664** Great Dane

1997. 250th Anniv of Postal Service in Chile. Multicoloured.
1803 120p. Type **663** 85 25
1804 300p. Man posting letter . . 1·60 60

1998. Dogs. Multicoloured. (a) As T **664**.
1805 120p. Type **664** 25 20
1806 120p. Dalmatian 25 20

(b) Discount stamps. Additionally inscr "DS/20".
1807 120p. Type **664** 25 20
1808 120p. As No. 1806 . . . . 25 20

665 Prat and "Esmeralda" (sail corvette) **666** Summit Emblem

1998. 150th Birth Anniv of Captain Arturo Prat Chacon.
1809 **665** 120p. multicoloured . . 40 25

1998. 2nd Summit of the Americas, Santiago. Mult.
1810 150p. Type **666** 35 25
MS1811 114 × 88 mm. 1000p. Summit emblem (26 × 41 mm) 1·50 1·50

667 Vets treating Horse

1998. Centenary of Army Veterinary Service. Mult.
1812 250p. Type **667** 55 40
1813 350p. Vet using stethoscope on horse 80 55

668 "Los Zambos de Calama" (Mauricio Moran)

1998. Paintings. Multicoloured.
1814 350p. Type **668** 80 55
1815 400p. "Soaking Watermelon" (Roser Bru) 90 65

669 Monk writing in Book

1998. 150th Anniv of Capuchin Order in Chile. Multicoloured.
1816 150p. Type **669** 35 25
1817 250p. Monk treating man's leg 55 40

670 Players

1998. World Cup Football Championship, France. Multicoloured.
1818 250p. Type **670** 55 40
1819 350p. Players and trophy . . 80 55
1820 500p. Players and map of France . . . . 1·10 75
1821 700p. Attacker and goalkeeper . . . . 1·50 1·10
MS1822 114 × 89 mm. 1500p. Player with ball (vert) . . . . 1·60 1·60

671 Bearded Penguin and Emblem

1998. 25th Meeting of Scientific Committee on Antarctic Research (1823) and 10th Meeting of Council of Managers of National Antarctic Programmes (1824), Concepcion. Multicoloured.
1823 250p. Type **671** 55 40
1824 350p. Two Gentoo penguins on map of Antarctica and emblem 80 55

672 Lighthouse

1998. International Year of the Ocean (1st issue). 150th Anniv of General Office for Territorial Waters and the Merchant Navy.
1825 **672** 500p. multicoloured . . 1·10 85

673 Iceberg and Ocean

1998. International Year of the Ocean (2nd issue).
1826 **673** 400p. blue, violet and black 90 60
1827 – 400p. blue, violet and black 90 60
1828 – 500p. multicoloured . . 1·10 75
DESIGNS: No. 1827, Compass rose, map of South Chile and ocean; 1828, Easter Island monolith and ocean.

674 Clara Solovera

1998. Composers and Folk Singers. Multicoloured.
1829 200p. Type **674** 45 30
1830 250p. Francisco Flores del Campo 55 40
1831 300p. Victor Jara 65 45
1832 350p. Violeta Parra 80 55

675 Delivery to Letter Box and Dog

1998. World Stamp Day.
1833 **675** 250p. multicoloured . . 55 40

676 Bilbao

1998. 175th Birth Anniv of Francisco Bilbao (writer).
1834 **676** 250p. purple, blue and orange 55 40

677 Amanda Labarca (educationist)

1998. America. Famous Women.
1835 **677** 120p. mauve, blue and black 25 20
1836 – 250p. yellow, mauve and black 55 40
DESIGN: 250p. Marta Brunet (writer).

678 "Self-portrait" (Augusto Eguiluz)

1998. Paintings. Multicoloured.
1837 300p. Type **678** 65 45
1838 450p. "Solitary Tree" (Agustin Abarca) (horiz) 1·00 70
MS1839 105 × 90 mm. 1500p. "Two Nudes" (Henriette Petit) . . . 1·60 1·60

679 Arms and University

680 Rufous-collared Sparrow

1998. 70th Anniv of Valparaiso Catholic University.
1840 **679** 130p. multicoloured . . 30 20

1998. Birds. Multicoloured.
1841 10p. Type **680** 10 10
1842 20p. Austral blackbird . . . 10 10
1845 50p Magellanic woodpecker (vert) 10 10
1849 100p Peregrine falcon (vert) 25 20

681 Children and Tents

1998. 19th World Scout Jamboree, Picarquin. Mult.
1856 120p. Type **681** 25 20
1857 200p. Lord Baden-Powell (founder of Scout movement) 40 30
1858 250p. Tents and doves . . . 55 40
1859 300p. Scout, tents and globe 65 45
1860 1000p. Emblem and singsong (vert) . . . . . 2·25 1·50
MS1861 127 × 105 mm. 3000p. Jamboree emblems and layout of camp . . . . 3·25 3·25

682 Capt. Alberto Larraguibel and Horse

1999. 50th Anniv of World Equestrian High Jump Record.
1862 **682** 200p. multicoloured . . 45 35

683 Fire Engine, 1990

1999. Centenary of Temuco Fire Department. Mult.
1863 140p. Type **683** 35 25
1864 200p. Ford fire engine, 1929 45 35
1865 300p. Ford K 1800 fire engine, 1955 . . . . . . 70 50
1866 350p. Mercedes Benz fire engine, 1967 . . . . . . 75 55
MS1867 119 × 100 mm. 1500p. Fireman with boy (vert) . . . 1·50 1·50

684 Chamber

1999. 1000th Session of Chilean Chamber of Deputies.
1868 **684** 140p. multicoloured . . 35 25

685 Facade

1999. 150th Anniv of Sagrados College.
1869 **685** 250p. multicoloured . . 60 45

686 Pedro Aguirre Cerda (Chilean President, 1938–41)

1999. 60th Anniv of Economic Development Corporation.
1870 **686** 140p. multicoloured . . 35 25

687 Man with Sphere on Shoulder

1999. Centenary of Chilean Insurance Association.
1871 **687** 140p. multicoloured . . 35 25

688 Footballer and Club Emblem

1999. Centenary of Barcelona Football Club. Sheet 103 × 88 mm.
MS1872 **688** 1000p. multicoloured 1·50 1·50

689 Weddell Seal and Blue-eyed Cormorants

1999. Antarctica. Multicoloured.
1873 360p. Type **689** 85 60
1874 450p. Bearded penguin . . . 1·10 80
MS1875 89 × 105 mm. 1500p. Kerguelen fur seal (35 × 47 mm) 1·60 1·60

690 Easter Island, Dancers, Ship and Figures

1999. Easter Island.
1876 **690** 360p. multicoloured . . 85 60

691 Business and Arts School

1999. 150th Anniv of Santiago University. Mult.
1877 140p. Type **691** 35 25
1878 250p. State Technical University 60 45
1879 300p. Woman using microscope, computer and building 70 50

692 J. L. Molina (naturalist), Statue of Humboldt, Mountains and Llamas

1999. Bicentenary of Alexander von Humboldt's Exploration of South America. Multicoloured.
1880 300p. Type **692** 70 50
1881 360p. Rodulfo A. Philippi (medical doctor and naturalist), statue of Humboldt and humboldt penguins 85 60

693 Cardinal Silva and Crucifix

1999. Cardinal Raul Silva Henrique Commemoration. Multicoloured.
1882 140p. Type **693** 35 25
1883 200p. Silva and image of Christ 45 35

694 Chinese and Chilean Flags with Pagoda

1999. "China 1999" International Stamp Exhibition, Peking. Multicoloured.
1884 140p. Type **694** 35 25
1885 450p. Chinese and Chilean Flags with junk . . . . . 1·10 80
MS1886 120 × 100 mm. 1500p. Great Wall, China (59 × 47 mm) . . . 1·60 1·60

695 Our Lady of the Rosary Church Tower, Train and Arms

696 Nurse and Donor

1999. Centenary of Quilpue City.
1887 **695** 250p. multicoloured . . 60 45

1999. Red Cross Blood Donation Campaign.
1888 **696** 140p. multicoloured . . 35 25

697 People in Glass Ball

1999. 75th Anniv of Employment Legislation.
1889 **697** 320p. multicoloured . . 75 55

698 Emblem

1999. 42nd International Congress of Confederation of Authors' and Composers' Societies, Santiago.
1890 **698** 170p. multicoloured . . 40 30

699 Elderly Couple watching Children

1999. International Year of Elderly Persons.
1891 **699** 250p. multicoloured . . 60 45

700 Post Box, 1854

1999. 125th Anniv of Universal Postal Union. Multicoloured.
1892 300p. Type **700** 70 50
1893 360p. Gold coloured post box, 1900 . . . . 85 60

701 Bomb releasing Doves

1999. America. A New Millennium without Arms. Multicoloured.
1894 140p. Type **701** 35 25
1895 320p. Broken bomb 75 55

702 Felipe Herrera Lane (first President, 1960–71) and Projects

1999. 40th Anniv of Inter-American Development Bank.
1896 **702** 360p. multicoloured . . 85 60

703 Globe and Chilean Flag

1999. Holy Year 2000.
1897 **703** 450p. multicoloured . . 1·10 80

704 Clock Face, "2000" and Fireworks (½-size illustration)

1999. New Millennium. Multicoloured. (a) As T **704**.
1898 170p. Type **704** 40 30

(b) Discount stamps. Additionally inscr "D.S. 20".
1899 170p. Type **704** 40 30

Nos. 1898/9 each include the prize draw coupons shown in T **704**.

705 Recabarren and Blest

1999. Trade Union Leaders. Multicoloured.
1900 200p. Type **705** 45 35
1901 200p. Jimenez and Bustos 45 35

Nos. 1900/1 were issued together, se-tenant, forming a composite design.

706 Mountains and Map of Islands

2000. Discovery of Juan Fernandez Archipelago. Multicoloured.
1902 360p. Type **706** 85 60
1903 360p. Mountains and map of islands (different) . . . 85 60
1904 360p. Fernandez firecrown and mountains 85 60
1905 360p. *Rhaphythamnus venustus* (plant) 85 60
1906 360p. Lobster 85 60
1907 360p. Antennae of lobster and anchored boat . . . 85 60
1908 360p. Plant and boat . . . 85 60
1909 360p. *Gavilea insularis* (orchid) 85 60

Nos. 1902/9 were issued together, se-tenant, forming a composite design.

707 Condorito celebrating

2000. 50th Anniv (1999) of Condorito (cartoon character) by Rene Rios. Multicoloured.
1910 150p. Type **707** 35 25
1911 260p. Playing football . . . 60 45
1912 480p. As a fireman . . . . 1·10 80
1913 980p. On horseback . . . . 2·40 1·75
MS1914 120 × 100 mm. 2000p. With other characters (47 × 35 mm) 3·00 3·00

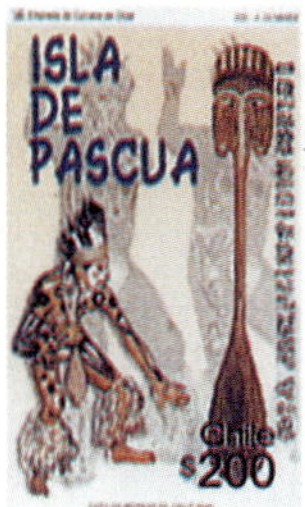

708 Dancer and Local Crafts

2000. Easter Island. Multicoloured.
1915 200p. Type **708** 50 45
1916 260p. Statue and rock carving 60 45
1917 340p. Statue and man wearing headdress 80 60
1918 480p. Dancer and text . . . 1·10 80

709 Steam Locomotive and Pot

2000. Centenary of Carahue. Multicoloured.
1919 220p. Type **709** 55 40
1920 220p. Potato tubers and plant 55 40

Nos. 1919/20 were issued together, se-tenant, forming a composite design.

710 Iguanodon

2000. Discount stamps. Prehistoric Animals. Mult.
1921 150p. Type **710** 35 25
1922 150p. Plesiosaur 35 25
1923 150p. Titanosaurus 35 25
1924 150p. Milodon 35 25

711 Emblem, Printing Press and Office

2000. Centenary of *El Mercurio* (newspaper).
1925 **711** 370p. multicoloured . . 90 65

712 Emblems

2000. 4th National Masonic Lodge Congress.
1926 **712** 460p. multicoloured . . 1·10 80

713 *Quillaja saponaria*

2000. Medicinal Plants. Multicoloured.
1927 200p. Type **713** 40 25
1928 360p. *Fabiana imbricata* . . 70 45

714 Map and Butterfly

2000. 500th Anniv of Discovery of Brazil. Mult.
1929 260p. Type **714** 50 30
MS1930 89 × 99 mm. 1500p. Monkey, child's face and parrots (47 × 35 mm) . . . . 1·60 1·60

715 Man wearing Costume (Bailarin de Diablada Festival, La Tirana)

2000. Religious Festivals. Multicoloured.
1931 150p. Type **715** 30 20
1932 200p. Girl wearing costume (San Pedro de Atacama fiesta) 40 25
1933 370p. Men dancing (La Candelaria Copiapo fiesta) 75 45
1934 460p. Drummer (Chinese Dance of Andacollo) . . 90 55

716 San Martin

2000. 150th Death Anniv of General Jose de San Martin.
1935 **716** 320p. multicoloured . . 65 40

717 Emblem, Globe and Weather Symbols

718 Magellanic Penguin (*Spheniscus magellanicus*)

2000. 50th Anniv of World Meteorological Organization.
1936 **717** 320p. multicoloured . . 65 40

2000. Antarctica. Multicoloured.
1937 450p. Type **718** 90 55
1938 650p. Humpback whales (*Megaptera novaeangliae*) (horiz) . . . . 1·25 1·40
1939 940p. Killer whale (*Orcinus orca*) (horiz) . . . . . . 1·90 2·00
MS1940 89 × 104 mm. 2000p. Southern elephant seal (35 × 47 mm) . . . . 3·00 3·00

No. 1937 is inscribed "Sphenis" in error.

719 Tennis, Football, Athletics and Sydney Opera House

2000. Olympic Games, Sydney. Multicoloured.
1941 290p. Type **719** 60 40
1942 290p. Archery, high jumping, cycling and Australian flag 60 40

Nos. 1941/2 were issued together, se-tenant, forming a composite design.

720 Native Chileans with Axe and Bow

2000. 450th Anniv of City of Concepcion. Depicting paintings by G. de la Fuente Riojas. Multicoloured.

1943 250p. Type **720** 50 30
1944 250p. Chileans and Spanish Conquistadors 50 30
1945 250p. Hand and scenes of destruction 50 30
1946 250p. Seated woman with shield 50 30
1947 250p. Horse, locomotive and coal truck 50 30
1948 250p. Modern Chileans and child 50 30

Nos. 1943/8 were issued together, se-tenant, forming a composite design.

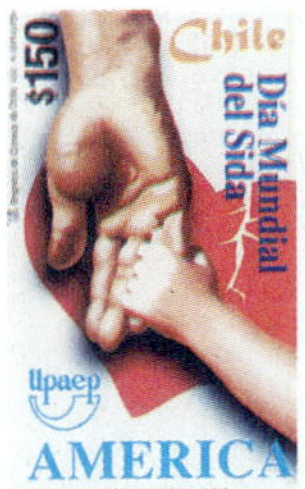

721 Child's Hand holding Adult's Hand

2000. America. AIDS Awareness Campaign. Multicoloured.

1949 150p. Type **721** 30 20
1950 220p. Joined hands showing bones 45 30

722 Documents and Courtroom

2000. Penal Reform. Multicoloured.

1951 150p. Type **722** 30 20
MS1952 119 × 98 mm. 2000p. Smiling faces and door . . . . 3·00 3·00

723 Star

2000. Christmas. Multicoloured. (a) As T **723**.

1953 150p. Type **723** 30 20
1954 150p. Silhouette of sleigh and reindeer above church 30 20
1955 150p. The Three Wise Men 30 20
1956 150p. Star on Christmas tree 30 20
1957 150p. Boy posting letter . . 30 20
1958 150p. Boy asleep 30 20
1959 150p. Man with bowl of fish and hindquarters of oxen 30 20
1960 150p. Jesus in manger . . . 30 20
1961 150p. Mary and Joseph . . 30 20
1962 150p. Girl decorating tree 30 20

(b) Discount stamps. As Nos. 1953/62 additionally inscr "D S/20" above (Nos. 1963/7) or below (Nos. 1968/72) face value.

1963 150p. As No. 1953 . . . . 30 20
1964 150p. As No. 1954 . . . . 30 20
1965 150p. As No. 1955 . . . . 30 20
1966 150p. As No. 1956 . . . . 30 20
1967 150p. As No. 1957 . . . . 30 20
1968 150p. As No. 1958 . . . . 30 20
1969 150p. As No. 1959 . . . . 30 20
1970 150p. As No. 1960 . . . . 30 20
1971 150p. As No. 1961 . . . . 30 20
1972 150p. As No. 1962 . . . . 30 20

Nos. 1953/62 and Nos. 1963/72 respectively were issued together, se-tenant, forming a composite design.

724 Wild Cat, Gibbon and Ostrich

2001. 75th Anniv of Santiago National Zoo. Multicoloured.

1973 160p. Type **724** 30 20
1974 160p. Lion, elephant and bird 30 20
1975 160p. Polar bears 30 20
1976 160p. Hippopotamus, chameleon and fox . . . 30 20

Nos. 1973/6 were issued together, se-tenant, forming a composite design.

725 Antiguo de Yumbel Church and Statue

2001. San Sebastian de Yumbel Festival.

1977 **725** 210p. multicoloured . . 35 20

726 Hurtado sweeping and Car

727 Slender-billed Conure (*Enicognathus leptorhynchus*)

2001. Birth Centenary of Fr. Alberto Hurtado. Multicoloured.

1978 160p. Type **726** 30 20
1979 340p. Hurtado and children 30 20

2001. Discount Stamps. Birds. Multicoloured. Inscr "D/S No. 20".

1980 160p. Type **727** 30 20
1981 160p. Moustached turaka (*Pteroptochos megapodius*) 30 20
1982 160p. Chilean mockingbird (*Mimus thenca*) 30 20
1983 160p. Fernandez firecrown (*Sephanoides fernandensis*) 30 20

728 Flag, Globe and Industries

2001. 42nd Annual Reunion of the Governors of Inter-American Development Bank and Inter-American Investments Corporation.

1984 **728** 230p. multicoloured . . 80 50

729 Lockheed C-130 Hercules (transport)

2001. Chilean Airforce Anniversaries. Mult.

1985 260p. Type **729** (50th anniv of Chilean Air Force in Antarctica) 45 30
1986 260p. Flugzeugbau Extra-300 (20th anniv of High Acrobatics Squadron) 45 30
1987 260p. North American AT-6 Texan (75th anniv of No. 1 Aviation Group) 45 30
1988 260p. Consolidated PBY-5A/OA-10 Catalina (amphibian) (50th Anniv of first flight to Easter Island) 45 30

730 Mine, Products and Molten Copper

2001. 30th Anniv of Nationalization of Copper Industry. Multicoloured.

1989 **730** 400p. multicoloured . . 70 40
MS1990 118 × 97 mm. 2000p. Miner and digger . . . . 3·50 3·50

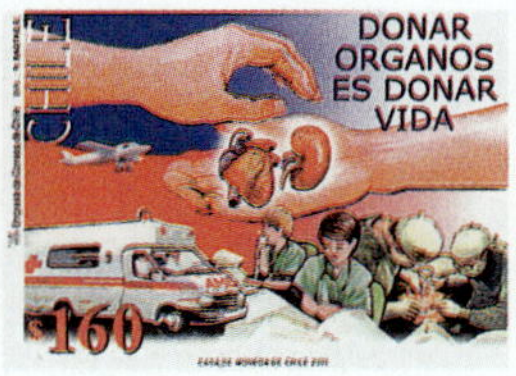

731 Ambulance, Organs and Medical Staff

2001. Organ Donation Campaign.

1991 **731** 160p. multicoloured . . 30 20

732 Pampas Cat (*Lynchailurus colocolo*)

2001. Endangered Species.

1992 **732** 100p. multicoloured . . 10 10

See also Nos. 2046/7.

733 Carved Rocks, Head and Island

2001. Easter Island. Multicoloured.

1993 260p. Type **733** 50 30
1994 260p. Island, seagull, aboriginal and statue . . 50 30
MS1995 90 × 100 mm. 2000p. Carved figure and island . . . 2·60 1·50

Nos. 1993/4 were issued together, se-tenant, forming a composite design.

734 Manuel Blanco Encalada (first president), Elderly Firemen and Traditional Appliance

2001. 150th Anniv of Valpariso Fire Brigade. Multicoloured.

1996 160p. Type **734** 30 15
1997 260p. Traditional appliance, burning building, fireman and modern appliance . . 50 30
1998 350p. 1887 firemen 65 35
1999 490p. Helicopter, modern fire-fighters and tanker lorry 90 50
MS2000 90 × 106 mm. 2000p. Fireman, appliance and helicopter 2·60 1·50

735 *Laccata ohiensis*

2001. Fungi. Multicoloured.

2001 300p. Type **735** 55 30
2002 400p. *Macrolepiota rhacodes* 75 45

736 Flags, Badge and Soldiers

2001. 24th American Armies Conference.

2003 **736** 350p. multicoloured . . 65 35

737 Bernardo O'Higgins and First National Congress

2001. Bernardo O'Higgins Commemoration. 190th Anniv of First National Congress.

2004 **737** 260p. multicoloured . . 50 30

738 Scientist and Weddell seal

2001. Antarctica. Multicoloured.

2005 350p. Type **738** 65 35
2006 700p. Scientists holding Giant petrel . . . . . . 1·30 75
MS2007 105 × 90 mm. 2000p. Snowy sheathbill . . . . 2·60 1·50

739 Quinchao Church

2001. America. Cultural Heritage. Multicoloured.

2008 160p. Type **739** 30 15
2009 230p. Tenuan Church . . . 40 20

740 "La Araucana" (detail)

2001. 90th Birth Anniv of Roberto Matta (artist).

2010 **740** 300p. multicoloured . . 55 30

741 Caldera Station Buildings

2001. 150th Anniv of Chilean Railways. Multicoloured.

2011 200p. Type **741** 35 20
2012 200p. Steam locomotive and Copiapo station 35 20
2013 220p. Electric locomotive (45 × 33 mm) 35 20

Nos. 2011/12 were issued together, se-tenant, forming a composite design.

742 Schooner

2001. Cape Horn.

2014 **742** 220p. multicoloured . . 40 20

743 Three Shepherds

2001. Christmas. Multicoloured. (a) As T **743**.
2015 160p. Type **743** 30 15
2016 160p. Shepherd and cow . . 30 15
2017 160p. Mary and Joseph . . 30 15
2018 160p. Donkey and King . . 30 15
2019 160p. Cow and two Kings 30 15
2020 160p. Shepherd with raised hands 30 15
2021 160p. Sheep 30 15
2022 160p. Jesus in manger . . . 30 15
2023 160p. Bearded man with staff 30 15
2024 160p. Sheep facing left . . . 30 15

(b) Discount stamps. As Nos. 2015/24 additionally inscr "D S/20".
2025 160p. As No. 2015 . . . . 30 15
2026 160p. As No. 2016 . . . . 30 15
2027 160p. As No. 2017 . . . . 30 15
2028 160p. As No. 2018 . . . . 30 15
2029 160p. As No. 2019 . . . . 30 15
2030 160p. As No. 2020 . . . . 30 15
2031 160p. As No. 2021 . . . . 30 15
2032 160p. As No. 2022 . . . . 30 15
2033 160p. As No. 2023 . . . . 30 15
2034 160p. As No. 2024 . . . . 30 15

Nos. 2015/24 and 2025/34 respectively were issued together, se-tenant, forming a composite design.

744 Globe, Map of Chile and Monument

2001. Tropic of Capricorn. 75th Anniv of Rotary Club (charitable organization).
2035 **744** 240p. multicoloured . . 45 25

745 Austral Thrush (*Turdus falcklandii*)

2002. Discount Stamps. Birds. Multicoloured. Inscr "D/S No. 20".
2036 10p. Type **745** 10 10
2037 20p. Long-tailed meadow lark (*Sturnella loyca*) . . 10 10

746 Department Emblem

2002. Centenary of Internal Revenue Services.
2038 **746** 180p. multicoloured . . 30 15

747 Scull, Black-necked Swans and Spanish Turret

2002. 450th Anniv of Valdivia.
2039 **747** 260p. multicoloured . . 45 25

748 Police Officers and Vehicles

2002. 75th Anniv of Police Force.
2040 **748** 250p. multicoloured . . 40 20

749 Domeyko and Santiago University, Chile

2002. Birth Bicentenary of Ignacego Domeyko (scientist).
2041 **749** 290p. multicoloured . . 50 25
A stamp of the same design was issued by Poland.

750 Town Hall, Arms and Cathedral

2002. 450th Anniv of Villarrica.
2042 **750** 290p. multicoloured . . 50 25

751 Town Arms, Road, Peninsula and Church

2002. 400th Anniv of Calbuco.
2043 **751** 230p. multicoloured . . 40 20

752 Arms, School Building and Diego Barros Arana (founder)

753 Flag and Hand signing Document

2002. Centenary of Barros Arana National Boarding School, Santiago.
2044 **752** 250p. multicoloured . . 40 20

2002. 1st Anniv of Abolition of the Death Penalty.
2045 **753** 240p. multicoloured . . 40 20

2002. Endangered Species. As T **732**. Multicoloured.
2046 10p. Andean mountain cat (*Oreailurus jacobita*) . . . 10 10
2047 20p. Geoffroy's cat (*Oncifelis geoffroyi* (inscr "geoffrovi")) 10 10

754 Moai, Island and Sophora toromiro (extinct tree)

2002. Easter Island. Multicoloured.
2048 250p. Type **754** 40 20
2049 450p. Common dicua finch, island and man wearing native dress 75 35
MS2050 89 × 104 mm. 2000p. *Sophora toromiro*, island and common dicua finch (48 × 48 mm) 3·25 3·25

755 Achao Church, Chiloe

2002. UNESCO World Heritage Sites. Churches. Multicoloured.
2051 230p. Type **755** 40 20
2052 290p. Dalcahue, Chiloe . . 50 25

756 Adults and Teacher

2002. America. Education and Literacy Campaign. Multicoloured.
2053 230p. Type **756** 40 20
2054 450p. Child reading, teacher, computer and boy 75 35

757 Toy Windmills

2002. Traditional Games. Multicoloured.
2055 290p. Type **757** 50 25
2056 380p. Kite flying (vert) . . . 65 30

758 Cerro Tololo Observatory

2002. Observatories. Multicoloured.
2057 450p. Type **758** 75 35
2058 550p. Paranal 95 45
MS2059 90 × 104 mm. 2000p. Cerro Tololo (different) (48 × 48 mm) 3·25 3·25

759 Hospital Building, Baby, MRI Scanner, Theatre and Doctor

2002. 50th Anniv of University of Chile Clinical Hospital.
2060 **759** 250p. multicoloured . . 40 20

760 Trees and Students

2002. 50th Anniv of Forestry Education.
2061 **760** 250p. multicoloured . . 40 20

761 Flamingo (*Phoenicoparru andinus*)

2002. 12th Convention on International Trade in Endangered Species (CITIES) Conference, Santiago, Chile. Multicoloured.
2062 300p. Type **761** 50 25
2063 450p. Vicuna (*Vicugna vicugna*) 75 35
MS2064 90 × 104 mm. 2000p. Chinchilla (*Chinchilla lanigera*) (48 × 48 mm) . . . . 3·25 3·25

762 Southern Right Whale (*Eubalaena australis*)

2002. Whales. Multicoloured.
2065 250p. Type **762** 40 20
2066 500p. Minke whale (*Balaenoptera acutorostrata*) 85 40
MS2067 90 × 104 mm. 2000p. Sperm whale (Physeter macrocephalus) (48 × 48 mm) . . . . 3·25 3·25

763 Justice

2002. Campaign to end Violence Against Women.
2068 **763** 230p. multicoloured . . 40 20

764 Church, Rose, Chilean and German Flags and Town Emblem

2002. 150th Anniv of Puerto Varas.
2069 **764** 190p. multicoloured . . 30 15

765 Magellanic Woodpecker (*Campephilus magellanicus*)

2003. Discount Stamps. Birds. Multicoloured. Inscr "D/S No. 20".
2070 500p. Type **765** 90 45
2071 1000p. Peregrine falcon (*Falco peregrinus*) . . . . 1·80 90

766 "Angelmo" (Hardy Wistuba)

2003. 150th Anniv of Puerto Montt.
2072 **766** 240p. multicoloured . . 45 20

767 Claudio Arrau

2003. Birth Centenary of Claudio Arrau (musician).
2073 **767** 200p. multicoloured . . 35 15

768 1853 5c. Stamp and Postal Building

2003. 150th Anniv of First Stamp. Multicoloured.
2074 300p. Type **768** 55 25
2075 300p. 1853 10c. stamp and building 55 25
MS2076 119 × 100 mm. 2000p. Building facade and stamp (detail) 3·50 3·50
Nos. 2074/5 were issued together, se-tenant, forming a composite design.

769 Trees, Cacti and Flowers

2003. America. Flora and Fauna. Multicoloured.
2077 240p. Type **769** 45 20
2078 300p. Frog, butterfly, pudu, fox and parrot 55 25

770 Decorated Window and Building FaÇade

2003. 180th Anniv of Supreme Court.
2079 **770** 200p. multicoloured . . 35 15

771 Supporters, Nurse and Early Vehicles

2003. Centenary of Chile Red Cross Society.
2080 **771** 200p. black and vermilion 35 15

772 Nativity

2003. Christmas.
2081 **772** 190p. multicoloured . . 35 15

773 Bristol M1C, Wright Flyer, Dagoberto Godoy (Chilean aviation pioneer) and Wright Brothers

2003. Centenary of Powered Flight.
2083 **773** 200p. multicoloured . . 35 15

774 Cristo Redentor

2004. Centenary of Cristo Redentor (Christ the Redeemer) (statue commemorating the delineation of Brazil–Chile border).
2084 **774** 200p. multicoloured . . 35 15

775 Globe and Emblem

2004. World Conference of Grand Lodges, Santiago.
2085 **775** 190p. multicoloured . . 35 15

776 Pablo Neruda

2004. Birth Centenary of Neftali Ricardo Reyes Basoalto (Pablo Neruda) (writer and politician).
2086 **776** 300p. multicoloured . . 55 25

777 Flag and People

2004. 80th Anniv of Social Security.
2087 **777** 190p. multicoloured . . 35 15

778 Damaged Environment, Lynx and Healthy Environment

2004. America. Environmental Protection. Mult.
2088 100p. Type **778** 20 10
2089 600p. Fox in healthy environment, trucks and chimneys . . . . 1·00 45

779 School Buildings, Pupils and Mountain

2004. 150th Anniv of German School, Osorno.
2090 **779** 250p. multicoloured . . 45 20

780 Magnifying Glass, Tweezers and Stamps

2004. Tematica 2004, National Stamp Exhibition.
2091 **780** 310p. multicoloured . . 55 25

781 Ships, Satellite Dish and Flag

2004. Centenary of Naval Communications.
2092 **781** 400p. multicoloured . . 70 30

782 Symbols of Power Generation

2004. Cent of Electricity and Power Generation.
2093 **782** 240p. multicoloured . . 45 20

783 Emblem and Aircraft (½-size illustration)

2005. 75th Anniv of National Air Force.
2094 **783** 230p. multicoloured . . 55 25

784 Document and Building

2005. Introduction of Law No. 20,000 (anti-drugs law).
2095 **784** 220p. multicoloured . . 50 25

785 Pope John Paul II and Child

2005. Pope John Paul II Commemoration. Multicoloured.
2096 230p. Type **785** 55 25
2097 230p. Holding staff 55 25
2098 230p. With raised arm . . . 55 25

786 Building Facade

2005. Bicentenary of Currency Bureau.
2099 **786** 230p. multicoloured . . 55 25

787 Emblem and Mountains

2005. Centenary of Rotary International.
2100 **787** 230p. multicoloured . . 55 25

788 Don Quixote

2005. 400th Anniv of "Don Quixote de la Mancha" (novel by Miguel de Cervantes). 120th Anniv of Language Academy (1st series). Each grey.
2101 10p. Type **788** 10 10
2102 10p. Windmill 10 10
2103 20p. Three windmills . . . 10 10
2104 20p. Miguel de Cervantes 10 10
See also Nos. 2126/9.

789 Early and Modern Miners

2005. Centenary of CODELCO El Teniente (copper mine).
2105 **789** 390p. multicoloured . . 85 40

790 Emblem (½-size illustration)

2005. 75th Anniv of Aviation Secretariat.
2106 **790** 400p. multicoloured . . 80 40

791 Building Facade

2005. 150th Anniv of Custom House, Valparaiso.
2107 **791** 390p. multicoloured . . 75 35

792 Fountains

2005. Bicentenary of Fuente Provincial Municipality, Santiago.
2108 **792** 230p. multicoloured . . 55 25

793 Outstretched Hand and Man

2005. America. Struggle against Poverty. Mult.
2109 250p. Type **793** 60 30
2110 250p. Child and hand . . . 60 30
Nos. 2109/10 were issued together, se-tenant, forming a composite design.

794 Alberto Hurtado

2005. Canonization of Father Alberto Hurtado Cruchaga.
2111 **794** 390p. multicoloured . . 85 40

795 Globe, Map, Flags, Perforations and Emblem

2005. EXPO Austral 2005 Stamp Exhibition, Punta Arenas, Magallanes.
2112 **795** 390p. multicoloured . . 85 40

796 Linked Hands

798 Post Office Building

797 Nurses, Operating Theatre and Building

2005. Civil Wedding Law.
2113 **796** 260p. multicoloured . . 50 25

2005. Centenary of Chile-Germany Cooperation. German Clinic.
2114 **797** 230p. multicoloured . . 45 20

2005. Restoration of Central Post Office.
2115 **798** 230p. multicoloured . . 45 20

799 Constitution and Assembly

2005. Political Constitution.
2116 **799** 230p. multicoloured . . 45 20

800 Uniformed Women

2006. International Woman's Day.
2117 **800** 390p. multicoloured . . 75 35

801 "100" and Emblems

2006. Centenary of Departments of Education, Sport and Recreation.
2118 **801** 230p. multicoloured . . 45 20

802 Castle, Seabirds and Sea

2006. Centenary of Castle Wulff, Vina del Mar. Multicoloured.
2119 230p. Type **802** 45 20
2120 390p. Arms, windmill and buildings 75 35

803 Moro de Arica

2006. Tourism. Each black.
2121 230p. Type **803** 45 30
2122 230p. Heads, Easter Island 45 30
2123 230p. Palafitos, Castro . . . 45 30
2124 230p. Torres del Paine . . . 45 30
2125 230p. Penguins, Chilean Antarctic 45 30

2006. 400th Anniv of "Don Quixote de la Mancha" (novel by Miguel de Cervantes). 120th Anniv of Language Academy (2nd series). As T **788**. Each grey.
2126 10p. Castle 10 10
2127 10p. Two windmills 10 10
2128 10p. Windmill 10 10
2129 10p. Don Quixote and Sancho Panza 10 10

804 Stone Bridge and Students

2006. 50th Anniv of Catolica del Norte University. Multicoloured.
2130 230p. Type **804** 45 30
2131 230p. Students and building 45 30

805 Buildings and Pool

2006. Bicentenary of Plaza de la Ciudadania.
2132 **805** 390p. multicoloured . . 75 35

806 Buildings

2006. International Forum on Quality. Mult.
2133 230p. Type **806** 45 30
2134 230p. Flag 45 30
Nos. 2133/4 were issued together, se-tenant, forming a composite background.

807 River Valley and Sun (upper left quadrant)

808 Inscr "Pua IX Region (1906)

2006. America. Energy Conservation. Multicoloured.
2135 390p. Type **807** 75 35
2136 390p. Lake and sun (upper right quadrant) 75 35
2137 390p. Oil installation and sun (lower left quadrant) 75 35
2138 390p. Wind turbines and sun (lower right quadrant) 75 35

2006. Centenary of Adventist University of Chile. Multicoloured.
2139 250p. Type **808** 45 25
2140 250p. "Chillan VIII Region (1922)" 45 25
2141 250p. "Chillan VIII Region (1960–70)" 45 25
2142 250p. "Chillan VIII Region (2006)" 45 25

809 *Balaenoptera acutorostrata*

2006. Antarctica. Multicoloured.
2143 500p. Type **809** . . . . . . 1·20 50
2144 500p. *Aptenodytes forsteri* 1·20 50
Stamps of a similar design were issued by Estonia.

810 Map

2006. 160th Anniv of Magellan Straits and Fort Bulnes. Multicoloured.
2145 250p. Type **810** 60 30
2146 250p. Tower, Fort Bulnes 60 30

811 Federico Santa María (founder) and Building Facade

2006. 75th Anniv of Federico Santa Maria Technical University, Valparaiso.
2147 **811** 250p. multicoloured . . 60 30

812 Factory, San Borja

2006. 150th Anniv of GASCO (gas company). Multicoloured.
2148 250p. Type **812** 60 30
2149 250p. GASCO building facade 60 30

813 Carabinieros

2007. 80th Anniv of Carabinieros (national military police). Multicoloured.
2150 250p. Type **813** 60 30
2151 250p. Family and mounted police 60 30

814 Valle de la Luna

2007. Tourism. Multicoloured.
2152 390p. Type **814** 90 40
2153 390p. Heads, Easter Island 90 40
2154 390p. Villarrica-Pucon volcano 90 40
2155 390p. Penguin, Chilean Antarctic 90 40

815 Parinacota Church

2007. Church Centenaries. Multicoloured.
2156 250p. Type **815** 60 30
2157 250p. San Pedro de Atacama 60 30

816 Cardinal Silva Henriquez

2007. Birth Centenary of Cardinal Raul Silva Henriquez (Archbishop of Santiago). Multicoloured.
2158 250p. Type **816** 60 30
2159 250p. As older man with young men 60 30
2160 250p. In procession behind horse 60 30
2161 250p. Addressing crowd . . 60 30

817 Marta Colvin and Sculpture

2007. Birth Centenary of Marta Colvin (artist). Multicoloured.
2162 250p. Type **817** 60 30
2163 250p. Wooden figure . . . 60 30
2164 250p. Stone abstract 60 30
2165 250p. Metal abstract 60 30

818 Buildings at Night

2007. Las Condes Commune.
2166 **818** 330p. multicoloured . . 80 35

819 Artequin (interactive museum)

2007. Museums.
2167 **819** 10p. green 10 10
2168 – 20p. black 10 10
2169 – 30p. lilac 10 10
2170 – 50p. vermilion 15 10
DESIGNS: 10p. Type **819**; 20p. Museum of Fine Arts; 30p. Natural History Museum; 50p. Santiago Museum.

820 Ranco Lake

2007. Inauguration of Los Rios Region. Multicoloured.
2171 390p. Type **820** 90 40
2172 390p. Huilo Huilo waterfall 90 40
2173 390p. Pedro de Valdivia bridge 90 40
2174 390p. Choshuenco volcano 90 40

821 Morro de Arica

2007. Inauguration of Arica y Parinacota Region. Multicoloured.
2175 250p. Type **821** 60 30
2176 250p. Parinacota volcano . . 60 30
2177 250p. Anzota caves 60 30
2178 250p. Vicunas 60 30

822 Post Office, 1747

2007. 260th Anniv of Post in Chile. Multicoloured.
2179 390p. Type **822** 90 40
2180 390p. Modern Post Office 90 40
2181 390p. Outline of early and modern buildings 90 40
MS2182 100 × 100 mm. 3000p. Cyclist (statue) . . . . 6·75 6·75

823 Building Facade

2007. 80th Anniv of Naval Comptroller. Multicoloured.
2183 390p. Type **823** 90 40
2184 390p. Modern headquarters 90 40
Nos. 2183/4 were issued together, se-tenant, forming a composite design.

824 Children and Computer

2007. America. Education for All. Multicoloured.
2185 250p. Type **824** 60 30
2186 250p. Chemistry students . . 60 30
2187 250p. Runners 60 30
2188 250p. Musicians 60 30
2189 250p. Child and globe . . . 60 30
Nos. 2185/9 were issued together, se-tenant, forming a composite design.

825 Santa, Dog and Fan

2007. Christmas. Multicoloured.
2190 250p. Type **825** 60 30
2191 250p. Santa and sleigh . . . 60 30
2192 250p. Santa in horned car 60 30
2193 250p. Santa in chimney . . 60 30

826 Sunset

2007. Centenary of Malleco National Reserve. Multicoloured.
2194 250p. Type **826** 60 30
2195 250p. Conifer and puma . . 60 30
2196 250p. Waterfall 60 30
2197 250p. Forest and coyote . . 60 30

ACKNOWLEDGEMENT OF RECEIPT STAMP

1894. Portrait of Columbus. Inscr "A.R.". Perf or Imperf.
AR77 5c. brown . . . . 1·40 1·40

COMPULSORY TAX STAMPS

T **100** Arms of Talca

T **224** Chilean Arms

1942. Talca Bicentenary.
T338 T **100** 10c. blue 10 10

1955. Death Centenary of Pres. Prieto. As T **145**.
T445 15p. green 15 10
PORTRAIT: 15p. Pres. Prieto.

1970. Postal Tax. No. 492a and 555 surch **E° 0,10 Art. 77 LEY 17272.**
T638 **162** 10c. on 2c. blue 10 10
T639 **178** 10c. on 6c. purple . . . 10 10

1971. Postal Modernization.
T646 T **224** 10c. blue 15 10
T647 15c. red 15 10

1971. Postal Modernization. Nos. T646/7 surch.
T673 T **224** 15c. on 10c. blue . . 10 10
T674 20c. on 15c. red . . 10 10
T675 50c. on 15c. red . . 10 10

OFFICIAL STAMPS

1928. Stamps of 1911 inscr "CHILE CORREOS" optd **Servicio del ESTADO.**
O190 **49** 10c. black and blue . . . 3·75 1·00
O191 – 20c. (No. 142) . . . . . 1·60 50
O192 – 25c. (No. 167) . . . . . 4·25 50
O193 – 50c. (No. 170) . . . . . 1·75 50
O194 **57** 1p. black and green . . . 2·75 70

1930. Stamps inscr "CORREOS DE CHILE" optd **Servicio del ESTADO.**
O217 **49** 10c. (No. 204) . . . . . 2·00 70
O234 **76** 10c. blue . . . . 1·60 35
O219 – 20c. (No. 209) 90 25
O235 – 20c. brown (No. 232) . . 1·10 25
O220 – 25c. (No. 210) 90 25
O221 – 50c. (No. 212) . . . . . 1·10 35

1934. Stamps inscr "CORREOS DE CHILE" optd **OFICIAL.**
O236 **64** 5c. green (No. 206) . . . 70 35
O237 **76** 10c. blue 70 35
O238 – 20c. brown (No. 232) . . . 4·50 35

1939. Optd **Servicio del ESTADO.**
O279 – 50c. violet (No. 273) . . 4·50 2·00
O280 **90** 1p. orange . . . . . . 3·75 2·50

1941. Nos. 269/338j optd **OFICIAL.**
O281 – 10c. red . . . . 1·75 1·00
O282 – 15c. red 95 25
O283 – 20c. blue . . . . 4·50 2·75
O284 – 30c. red 45 25
O285 – 40c. green 45 25
O286 – 50c. violet . . . . 3·00 50
O339 **90** 1p. orange . . . . 2·00 80
O288 – 1p.80 blue . . . . 8·00 4·75
O442 – 2p. red . . . . 1·60 1·00
O383 – 5p. green . . . . 3·00 1·25
O443 – 10p. purple . . . . . . 10·00 5·00

1953. No. 379c optd **OFICIAL.**
O386 1p. turquoise 85 35

1956. Nos. 446/450 optd **OFICIAL.**
O451 2p. lilac . . . . 2·40 50
O452 3p. blue . . . . 8·00 4·00
O453 5p. sepia . . . . 1·50 40
O454a 10p. violet . . . . 1·25 40
O455 50p. red . . . . 5·00 1·40

1958. Optd **OFICIAL.**
O469 **152** 10p. blue . . . . £140 35·00

1960. No. 493 optd **OFICIAL.**
O507 5c. blue . . . . 3·75 1·25

POSTAGE DUE STAMPS

D **18**

D **19**

D **68**

1895.
D 98 D **18** 1c. red on yellow . . . 1·25 40
D 99 2c. red on yellow . . . 1·25 40
D100 4c. red on yellow . . . 1·25 40
D101 6c. red on yellow . . . 1·25 40
D102 8c. red on yellow . . . 1·25 40
D103 10c. red on yellow . . 1·25 40
D104 20c. red on yellow . . 1·25 40
D 93 40c. red on yellow . . 3·00 90
D 94 50c. red on yellow . . 4·00 1·00
D 95 60c. red on yellow . . 6·00 1·50
D 96 80c. red on yellow . . 7·00 3·00
D109 100c. red on yellow . . 20·00 11·50
D 97 1p. red on yellow . . 12·00 6·00

1898.
D110 D **19** 1c. red 60 50
D111 2c. red 75 60
D112 4c. red . . . . 1·75 1·25
D113 10c. red 60 60
D114 20c. red 60 60

1924.
D184 D **68** 2c. red and blue . . . 1·25 1·00
D185 4c. red and blue . . . 1·25 1·00
D186 8c. red and blue . . . 1·25 1·00
D187 10c. red and blue . . . 1·25 1·00
D188 20c. red and blue . . . 1·25 1·00
D189 40c. red and blue . . . 1·25 1·00
D190 60c. red and blue . . . 1·25 1·00
D191 80c. red and blue . . . 1·25 1·00
D192 1p. red and blue . . . 1·40 2·50
D193 2p. red and blue . . . 2·00 4·00
D194 5p. red and blue . . . 2·50 4·00

CHINA Pt. 17

People's Republic in Eastern Asia, formerly an Empire.

CHINESE CHARACTERS

Simple	Formal	
半	半	= ½
一	壹	= 1
二	貳	= 2
三	叁	= 3
四	肆	= 4
五	伍	= 5
六	陸	= 6
七	柒	= 7
八	捌	= 8
九	玖	= 9
十	拾	= 10
百	佰	= 100
千	仟	= 1,000
萬	萬	= 10,000

分	= cent
圓	= dollar

Examples:

十五	= 15
五十	= 50
叁佰圓	= 300 dollars
伍仟圓	= 5,000 dollars

CHINESE EMPIRE

1878. 100 candarins = 1 tael.
1897. 100 cents = 1 dollar.

1 Dragon

2

1878.
7 **1** 1ca. green £170 £130
2 3ca. red £250 £100
3 5ca. orange £475 £120

1885.
13 **2** 1ca. green . . . . 23·00 19·00
14 3ca. mauve . . . . 60·00 6·50
15 5ca. yellow . . . . £110 22·00

4

10

1894. Dowager Empress's 60th Birthday.
16 **4** 1ca. orange . . . . 10·00 12·50
17 – 2ca. green . . . . 17·00 10·00
18 – 3ca. yellow . . . . 12·50 4·50
19 – 4ca. pink . . . . 45·00 45·00
20 **4** 5ca. orange £100 £100
21 – 6ca. brown . . . . 18·00 8·25
22 **10** 9ca. green . . . . 50·00 14·00
23 12ca. orange . . . . £100 75·00
24 – 24ca. red . . . . £170 65·00
DESIGNS—VERT: (as Type **4**): 2ca. to 4ca. and 6ca. Dragon. HORIZ: (as Type **10**): 24ca. Junks.

1897. Surch in English and Chinese characters.
78 – ½c. on 3ca. yellow (No. 18) 5·00 4·00
34 **2** 1c. on 1ca. green . . . . . 20·00 25·00
79 **4** 1c. on 1ca. orange . . . . . 7·00 4·25
80 – 2c. on 2ca. green (No. 17) 8·25 2·75
35 **2** 2c. on 3ca. mauve . . . . . £110 50·00
40 – 4c. on 4ca. pink (No. 19) . . 10·00 5·75
36 **2** 5c. on 5ca. yellow . . . . . 50·00 16·00
41 – 5c. on 5ca. orange (No. 20) 12·50 6·75
42 – 8c. on 6ca. brown (No. 21) 14·00 8·25
43 – 10c. on 6ca. brown (No. 21) 50·00 75·00
63 **10** 10c. on 9ca. green . . . . . 65·00 39·00
64 10c. on 12ca. orange . . . . £130 45·00
46 – 30c. on 24ca. red (No. 24) £190 £150

17

24

30 Carp

31 Bean Goose

1897. Surch in English and Chinese characters.
88 **17** 1c. on 3c. red . . . . £150 85·00
89 2c. on 3c. red £150 £100
90 4c. on 3c. red £275 £150
91 $1 on 3c. red £1300 £850
92 $5 on 3c. red £6500 £6000

1897. Inscr "IMPERIAL CHINESE POST".
96 **24** ½c. purple . . . . 2·20 2·30
97 1c. yellow . . . . 2·50 1·40
98 2c. orange . . . . 2·50 95
99 4c. brown . . . . 4·75 1·80
100 5c. red . . . . 5·00 2·00
101 10c. green . . . . 11·50 2·20
102 **30** 20c. lake . . . . 30·00 7·00
103 30c. red . . . . 50·00 16·00
104 50c. green . . . . 46·00 30·00
105 **31** $1 red £190 £130
106 $2 orange and yellow . . . £1000 £1000
107 $5 green and red £500 £500

32 Dragon

33 Carp

34 Bean Goose

1898. Inscr "CHINESE IMPERIAL POST".
121 **32** ½c. brown 20 20
122 1c. buff 20 20
123 2c. red . . . . 1·90 85
151 2c. green . . . . 1·60 1·20
152 3c. green . . . . 1·90 85
124 4c. brown . . . . 2·40 85
153 4c. red . . . . 2·40 1·20
112 5c. pink . . . . 7·00 1·30

126		5c. orange	11·50	3·50
154		5c. mauve	4·50	85
155		7c. red	7·00	4·00
127		10c. green	9·00	85
156		10c. blue	8·50	85
157	**33**	16c. green	28·00	7·00
128		20c. purple	14·00	95
115		30c. red	19·00	6·00
130		50c. green	24·00	2·50
131	**34**	$1 red and orange	70·00	8·50
132		$2 purple and yellow	£170	22·00
119		$5 green and orange	£400	£130

36 Temple of Heaven

1909. 1st Year of Reign of Emperor Hsuan T'ung.

165	**36**	2c. green and orange	2·75	2·50
166		3c. blue and orange	4·00	3·25
167		7c. purple and orange	6·00	4·25

POSTAGE DUE STAMPS

1904. Stamps of 1898 optd **POSTAGE DUE** in English and Chinese characters.

D137	**32**	½c. brown	6·75	4·00
D138		1c. buff	7·75	4·00
D139a		2c. red	8·50	4·00
D140		4c. brown	8·25	6·25
D141		5c. red	18·00	11·00
D142		10c. green	29·00	14·50

D 37

1904.

D143	**D 37**	½c. blue	2·75	90
D144		1c. blue	4·25	80
D168		1c. brown	5·50	2·50
D145		2c. blue	3·50	80
D169		2c. brown	11·00	12·00
D146		4c. blue	6·25	95
D147		5c. blue	7·00	1·30
D148		10c. blue	6·50	1·90
D149		20c. blue	24·00	4·75
D150		30c. blue	32·00	32·00

CHINESE REPUBLIC

1912. 100 cents = 1 dollar.
1948. 100 cents = 1 gold yuan.
1949. 100 cents = 1 silver yuan.

1912. Optd vert with four Chinese characters signifying "Republic of China".

192	**32**	½c. brown	70	50
193		1c. buff	1·10	50
194		2c. green	1·10	50
221		3c. green	1·60	65
196		4c. red	2·20	65
197		5c. mauve	3·25	40
198		7c. lake	4·25	1·50
225		10c. blue	8·50	1·40
200	**33**	16c. olive	11·00	5·00
227		20c. red	22·00	2·50
202		30c. red	11·00	4·00
203		50c. green	18·00	3·00
204	**34**	$1 red and salmon	£130	12·50
205		$2 red and yellow	£110	29·00
232		$5 green and salmon	£350	£350

41 Dr. Sun Yat-sen

1912. Revolution Commemoration.

242	**41**	1c. orange	1·60	2·50
243		2c. green	1·70	2·50
244		3c. blue	1·70	2·50
245		5c. mauve	2·75	1·80
246		8c. sepia	3·00	2·75
247		10c. blue	3·00	2·75
248		16c. olive	8·25	8·00
249		20c. lake	12·50	6·00
250		50c. green	30·00	19·00
251		$1 red	£100	31·00
252		$2 brown	£250	£190
253		$5 slate	85·00	£130

1912. As T **41** but portrait of Pres. Yuan Shih-kai, inscr "Commemoration of the Republic".

254		1c. orange	90	90
255		2c. green	90	90
256		3c. blue	90	90
257		5c. mauve	90	1·00
258		8c. sepia	4·00	2·30
259		10c. blue	2·75	1·40
260		16c. olive	4·00	4·25
261		20c. lake	3·00	3·00
262		50c. green	19·00	12·00
263		$1 red	60·00	31·00
264		$2 brown	70·00	34·00
265		$5 slate	£225	£190

43 Junk

44 Reaper

45 Entrance Hall of Classics, Peking

1913.

287	**43**	½c. sepia	45	20
269		1c. orange	40	20
289a		1½c. purple	1·70	40
270		2c. green	1·40	20
271		3c. green	3·50	20
292		4c. red	9·50	20
314		4c. grey	10·50	65
315		4c. olive	1·60	35
293		5c. mauve	4·00	20
294		6c. grey	9·50	25
317		6c. red	3·25	40
318		6c. brown	22·00	2·75
295		7c. violet	11·50	3·25
296		8c. orange	6·75	25
297		10c. blue	7·25	45
298	**44**	13c. brown	4·25	45
278		15c. brown	18·00	4·00
323		15c. blue	4·00	50
324		16c. olive	4·50	50
325		20c. lake	4·00	30
326		30c. purple	12·00	30
282		50c. green	36·00	2·50
304	**45**	$1 black and yellow	65·00	55
328		$1 sepia and brown	23·00	50
305		$2 black and blue	£150	2·30
329		$2 brown and blue	32·00	90
306		$5 black and red	£350	23·00
330		$5 green and red	55·00	4·75
307		$10 black and green	£550	£160
331		$10 mauve and green	£275	33·00
308		$20 black and orange	£1800	£1700
332		$20 blue and purple	£500	£100

1920. Flood Relief Fund. Surch with new value in English and Chinese characters.

349	**43**	1c. on 2c. green	4·50	1·50
361		2c. on 3c. green	3·25	40
350		3c. on 4c. red	6·25	2·30
351		5c. on 6c. grey	9·25	4·00

47 Curtiss JN-4 "Jenny" over Great Wall of China

I

II

1921. Air. Tail fin of aeroplane as Type I.

352	**47**	15c. black and green	28·00	30·00
353		30c. black and red	28·00	30·00
354		45c. black and purple	28·00	20·00
355		60c. black and blue	33·00	35·00
356		90c. black and olive	45·00	48·00

For similar stamps in this type but with tail fin as Type II, see Nos. 384a/8.

48 Yen Kung-cho, Pres. Hsu Shih-chang and Chin Yung-peng

53 Temple of Heaven

1921. 25th Anniv of Chinese National Postal Service.

357	**48**	1c. orange	4·50	1·20
358		3c. turquoise	4·50	1·10
359		6c. grey	5·25	2·50
360		10c. blue	5·50	2·00

1923. Adoption of the Constitution.

362	**53**	1c. orange	3·50	80
363		3c. turquoise	3·50	1·60
364		4c. red	7·75	1·90
365		10c. blue	11·50	2·30

1925. Surch in English and Chinese characters.

366	**43**	1c. on 2c. green	2·20	20
367		1c. on 3c. green	1·60	85
369		1c. on 4c. olive	1·50	30
370		3c. on 4c. grey	2·40	20

The figures in this surcharge are at the top and are smaller than for the 1920 provisionals.

55 Marshal Chang Tso-lin

56 General Chiang Kai-shek

1928. Assumption of Title of Marshal of the Army and Navy by Chang Tso-lin.

372	**55**	1c. orange	1·10	1·00
373		4c. olive	2·20	2·20
374		10c. blue	6·00	4·75
375		$1 red	38·00	50·00

1929. Unification of China under Gen. Chiang Kai-shek.

376	**56**	1c. orange	1·50	50
377		4c. olive	3·00	65
378		10c. blue	13·00	1·20
379		$1 red	75·00	42·00

57 Mausoleum at Nanking

58 Dr. Sun Yat-sen

1929. State Burial of Dr. Sun Yat-sen.

380	**57**	1c. orange	1·00	60
381		4c. olive	1·50	90
382		10c. blue	5·75	1·90
383		$1 red	55·00	24·00

1929. Air. As T **47**, but tail fin of airplane as Type II.

384a	**47**	15c. black and green	3·00	55
385		30c. black and red	7·00	2·30
386		45c. black and purple	14·00	6·50
387		60c. black and blue	17·00	8·50
388		90c. black and olive	14·00	14·50

1931.

389	**58**	1c. orange	45	20
396		2c. olive	35	10
391		4c. green	90	20
398		5c. green	35	10
399		15c. green	3·75	1·10
400		15c. red	40	10
401		20c. blue	70	20
402		25c. blue	40	10
403a		$1 sepia and brown	9·25	35
735		$1 violet	35	1·50
404a		$2 brown and blue	15·00	75
736		$2 olive	35	3·00
405a		$5 black and red	25·00	3·50
737		$20 green	1·00	60
738		$30 brown	35	55
739		$50 orange	35	55

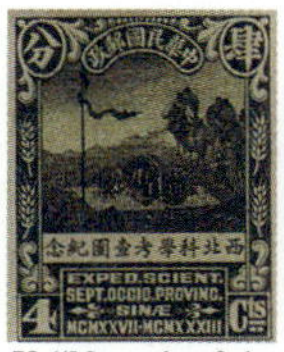

59 "Nomads of the Desert"

60 General Teng K'eng

1932. North-West China Scientific Expedition.

406	**59**	1c. orange	23·00	29·00
407		4c. olive	23·00	29·00
408		5c. red	23·00	29·00
409		10c. blue	23·00	29·00

1932. Martyrs of the Revolution.

410	**60**	½c. brown	20	10
508	–	1c. orange	20	20
509	–	2c. blue	20	20
412	**60**	2½c. purple	20	20
511	–	3c. brown	20	20
512	**60**	4c. lilac	20	20
513	–	5c. orange	20	45
514	–	8c. orange	20	20
515	–	10c. purple	2·75	30
516	–	13c. green	20	45
517	–	15c. purple	30	40
417	–	17c. green	40	10
418	–	20c. red	85	10
519	–	20c. blue	25	20
520	–	21c. brown	35	25
521	–	25c. purple	25	35
541	–	28c. green	30	60
542	–	30c. purple	45	25
543	–	40c. orange	30	25
544	–	50c. green	30	10

DESIGNS: 1, 25, 50c. Ch'en Ying-shih; 2, 10, 17, 28c. Shung Chiao-jen; 3, 5, 15, 30c. Liao Chung-k'ai; 8, 13, 21c. Chu Chih-hsin; 20, 40c. Gen. Huang Hsing.

61 Junkers F-13 over Great Wall

1932. Air.

422	**61**	15c. green	35	40
556		25c. orange	40	55
557		30c. red	40	55
558		45c. purple	40	85
559		50c. brown	40	55
560		60c. blue	40	80
561		90c. green	40	85
562		$1 green	55	65
563		$2 brown	1·40	1·40
564		$5 red	1·10	1·10

62 Tan Yen-kai

63

1933. Tan Yen-kai Memorial.

440	**62**	2c. olive	2·10	65
441		5c. green	2·75	30
442		25c. blue	7·25	1·10
443		$1 red	55·00	21·00

1936. "New Life" Movement. Symbolic designs as T **63**.

444	**63**	2c. olive	1·10	30
445		5c. green	1·30	20
446	–	20c. blue (various emblems)	5·00	60
447	–	$1 red (Lighthouse)	26·00	5·50

66 "Postal Communications."

72 Dr. Sun Yat-sen

1936. 40th Anniv of Chinese National Postal Service.

448	**66**	2c. orange	1·30	45
449	–	5c. green	95	20
450	–	25c. blue	3·75	35
451	–	100c. red	22·00	5·25

DESIGNS: 5c. The Bund, Shanghai; 25c. G.P.O., Shanghai; 100c. Ministry of Communications, Nanking.

1936. Surch in figures and Chinese characters.

452	**44**	5c. on 15c. blue	1·20	35
453		5c. on 16c. olive	2·75	70

1937. Surch in figures and Chinese characters.

454	**58**	1 on 4c. green	1·00	30
455	–	8 on 40c. orange (No. 543)	1·50	55
456	**58**	10 on 25c. blue	1·00	20

1938.

462	**72**	2c. green	20	20
464		3c. red	20	20
489B		5c. green	15	15
492A		8c. green	50	20
469		10c. green	20	20
470		15c. red	1·30	1·50
471		16c. brown	1·10	40
472		25c. blue	85	65
494B		30c. red	15	15
495B		50c. blue	40	15
496A		$1 sepia and brown	2·20	20
497A		$2 brown and blue	90	30
498A		$5 green and red	90	45
499A		$10 violet and green	3·75	1·50
500A		$20 blue and purple	12·00	3·25

For dollar values in single colours, see Nos. 666 etc.

For 15c. brown see Japanese Occupation of China: IV Shanghai and Nanking No. 12.

74 Chinese and U.S. Flags and Map of China

1939. 150th Anniv of U.S. Constitution. Flags in red and blue.

501	**74**	5c. green	95	35
502		25c. blue	1·00	70
503		50c. brown	2·30	1·30
504		$1 red	3·75	2·40

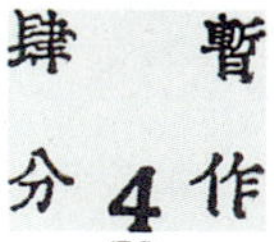

(76)

1940. Surch as T **76**.

577	**72**	3c. on 5c. green	60	1·60
582		4c. on 5c. green	55	55
619		7c. on 8c. green	90	1·00

77 Dr. Sun Yat-sen

78 Industry

1941.

583 **77** $\frac{1}{2}$c. brown 15 25
584 1c. orange 20 20
585 2c. blue 20 20
586 5c. green 20 20
587 8c. orange 50 55
588 8c. green 35 20
589 10c. green 15 20
590 17c. green . . . . 4·25 11·50
591 25c. purple 25 60
592 30c. red 25 30
593 50c. blue 35 20
594 $1 black and brown . . . 45 20
595 $2 black and blue . . . 55 20
596 $5 black and red 95 35
597 $10 black and green . . . 3·50 2·00
598 $20 black and purple . . . 3·00 3·75

1941. Thrift Movement.
599 **78** 8c. green 35 55
600 21c. brown 45 65
601 28c. olive 55 75
602 33c. red . . . . 1·00 1·30
603 50c. blue . . . . 1·20 1·10
604 $1 purple . . . . 1·50 1·40
MS605 155 × 171 mm. Nos. 599/604 in slightly different colours. Imperf. No gum . . . . 38·00 42·00

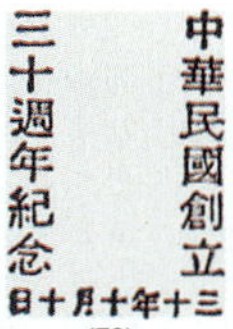

(79)

(81)

82 Dr. Sun Yat-sen

1941. 30th Anniv of Republic. Optd with T **79**.
606 – 1c. orange (No. 508) . . . 75 1·10
607 **72** 2c. green . . . . 75 1·10
608 **60** 4c. lilac . . . . 75 1·10
609 **72** 8c. green . . . . 75 1·10
610 10c. green . . . . 75 1·10
611 16c. brown . . . . 75 1·10
612 – 21c. brown (No. 520) . . . 75 1·10
613 – 28c. green (No. 541) . . . 90 1·70
614 **72** 30c. red . . . . 95 3·25
615 $1 sepia and brown . . . 3·25 4·00

1942. Provincial surcharges. Surch as T **81**.
622 **60** 1c. on $\frac{1}{2}$c. brown . . . . 40 1·50
624 **77** 1c. on $\frac{1}{2}$c. brown . . . . 50 2·20
690g – 20c. on 13c. green (516) 2·50 7·00
691i **72** 20c. on 16c. brown . . . 1·70 6·75
693e – 20c. on 17c. green (417) 3·75 8·00
694f – 20c. on 21c. brown (520) 1·40 6·00
695e – 20c. on 28c. green (541) 1·00 6·75
625 **72** 40c. on 50c. blue . . . . 1·40 3·75
627 **77** 40c. on 50c. blue . . . . 3·50 5·75
626 – 40c. on 50c. green (544) 4·00 5·25
689a 50c. on 16c. brown . . . 1·50 1·70

1942.

628A **82** 10c. green . . . . 20 1·10
629A 16c. olive . . . . 16·00 42·00
630A 20c. olive . . . . 20 1·00
631A 25c. purple . . . . 20 1·40
632A 30c. red 20 80
642 30c. brown . . . . 35 11·00
633A 40c. brown . . . . 20 1·00
634A 50c. green 20 20
635A $1 red 50 20
636A $1 olive 30 30
637A $1.50 blue 30 40
638A $2 green 30 30
645 $2 blue . . . . 5·00 6·00
646 $2 purple 20 20
639A $3 yellow 30 30
640A $4 brown 30 30
641A $5 red 30 30
650 $6 violet 40 45
651 $10 brown 20 20
652 $20 blue 20 20
653 $50 green . . . . 4·00 20
654 $70 violet . . . . 5·00 35
655 $100 brown 20 30

1942. As T **72** but emblem at top redrawn with solid background. Perf, imperf or roul.
666 **72** $4 blue 60 85
667 $5 grey . . . . 1·20 1·10
656 $10 brown . . . . 1·20 85
657 $20 green . . . . 1·20 70
658 $20 red . . . . 30·00 20·00
659 $30 purple 90 70
660 $40 red 95 70
661 $50 blue . . . . 1·50 95
662 $100 brown . . . . 5·25 3·50

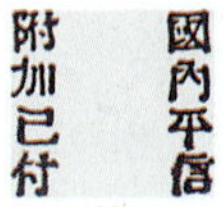

(83)

(83a)

(T **83** Trans. "Surcharge for Domestic Postage Paid")

1942. Surch as T **83**.
688e **82** 16c. olive . . . . 55·00 43·00

1943. No 688e surch as T **83a**.
701e **82** 50c. on 16c. olive . . . . 3·25 5·00

89 Dr. Sun Yat-sen

91 Savings Bank and Money Box

90 War Refugees

1944.

702 **89** 40c. red . . . . 30 5·50
703 $2 brown 30 30
704 $3 red 20 20
705 $3 brown 75 50
706 $6 grey 30 35
707 $10 red 30 30
708 $20 pink 30 30
709 $50 brown . . . . 3·25 45
710 $70 violet 45 45

1944. War Refugees' Relief Fund. Various frames.
724 **90** $2+$2 on 50c.+50c. blue 1·00 2·50
725 $4+$4 on 8c.+8c. green . . 1·00 2·50
726 $5+$5 on 21c.+21c. brn . . 1·40 2·50
727 $6+$6 on 28c.+28c. olive 2·30 2·75
728 $10+$10 on 33c.+33c. red 3·25 3·25
729 $20+$20 on $1+$1 violet 4·25 4·25
MS730 190 × 100 mm. Nos. 724/9 40·00 40·00

1944.

731 **91** $40 slate 25 45
732 $50 green 25 20
733 $100 brown 25 20
734 $200 green 25 20

92 Dr. Sun Yat-sen

93 Dr. Sun Yat-sen

1944. 50th Anniv of Kuomintang.
740 **92** $2 green . . . . 1·00 2·00
741 $5 brown . . . . 1·20 2·10
742 $6 purple . . . . 1·80 4·00
743 $10 blue . . . . 2·50 5·00
744 $20 red . . . . 4·25 7·50

1945. 20th Death Anniv of Dr. Sun Yat-sen.
746 **93** $2 green . . . . 35 1·30
747 $5 brown . . . . 45 1·30
748 $6 blue . . . . 50 1·90
749 $10 blue . . . . 80 1·50
750 $20 red . . . . 1·10 3·25
751 $30 buff . . . . 1·70 4·00

94 Dr. Sun Yat-sen

96 Pres. Lin Sen

95 Gen. Chiang Kai-shek

1945.

758 **94** $2 green 30 55
759 $5 green 30 35
760 $10 blue 30 35
761 $20 red 25 35

1945. Equal Treaties with Great Britain and U.S.A., abolishing Foreign Concessions. Flags in national colours.
762 **95** $1 blue . . . . 65 1·10
763 $2 green . . . . 65 1·20
764 $5 olive . . . . 65 1·20
765 $6 brown . . . . 90 1·30
766 $10 red . . . . 4·00 6·50
767 $20 red . . . . 4·25 7·00

1945. In Memory of President Lin Sen.
768 **96** $1 black and blue . . . . 80 1·70
769 $2 black and green . . . . 80 1·70
770 $5 black and red . . . . 80 1·70
771 $6 black and violet . . . . 1·20 1·90
772 $10 black and brown . . . 3·00 3·50
773 $20 black and olive . . . 4·25 5·50

(97)

(98)

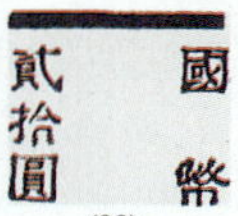

(99)

1945. Chinese National Currency (C.N.C.). Various issues surch as T **97** (for Japanese controlled Government at Shanghai and Nanking) and further surch as T **98**.
774 **72** 10c. on $20 on 3c. red . . 20 1·10
775 – 15c. on $30 on 2c. blue (509) . . . . 20 1·20
776 **77** 25c. on $50 on 1c. orange 20 95
777 **72** 50c. on $100 on 3c. red . . 20 40
778 **60** $1 on $200 on 1c. orange (508) 20 20
779 **72** $2 on $400 on 3c. red . . . 20 30
780 **77** $5 on $1000 on 1c. orange 20 20

1945. Kaifeng provisionals. C.N.C. surcharges. Stamps of Japanese Occupation of North China surch as T **99**.
781 **60** $10 on 20c. lake (No. 166) 8·50 10·50
782 $20 on 40c. orge (No. 168) 22·00 25·00
783 $50 on 30c. red (No. 167) 15·00 19·00

100 Pres. Chiang Kai-shek

101 Pres. Chiang Kai-shek

1945. Inauguration of Pres. Chiang Kai-shek. Flag in blue and red.
784 **100** $2 green 50 90
785 $4 blue 70 90
786 $5 olive . . . . 70 1·10
787 $6 brown . . . . 1·60 2·20
788 $10 grey . . . . 4·25 5·50
789 $20 red . . . . 4·75 5·75

1945. Victory. Flag in red.
790 **101** $20 green and blue . . . 30 20
791 $50 brown and blue . . . 55 50
792 $100 blue 45 35
793 $300 red and blue 45 35

(102)

103 Dr. Sun Yat-sen

1945. C.N.C. surcharges. Nos. 410, 412, 514, 516/17, 519/20 and 541 surch as T **102** (value tablet at top).
794 $3 on 2$\frac{1}{2}$c. purple . . . . . 10·00 13·00
795 $10 on 15c. purple 20 20
796 $20 on 8c. orange 20 20
797 $20 on 20c. blue 30 60
798 $30 on $\frac{1}{2}$c. brown 30 70
799 $50 on 21c. brown 30 70
801 $70 on 13c. green 20 20
802 $100 on 28c. green 35 65

1945. No gum.
808 **103** $20 red 15 15
809 $30 blue 15 20
810 $40 orange 50 45
811 $50 green 80 30
812 $100 brown 20 20
813 $200 brown 20 20

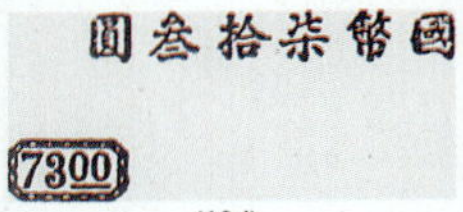

(104)

(108)

1946. Air. C.N.C. surcharges. Surch as T **104**.
820 **61** $23 on 30c. red 20 85
821 $53 on 15c. green 20 85
822 $73 on 25c. orange . . . . . 20 1·00
823 $100 on $2 brown 20 30
824 $200 on $5 red 20 30

1946. C.N.C. surcharges. Surch as T **108** (octagonal value tablet at bottom).
898 – $10 on 1c. orange (508) . . 20 55
903 **77** $10 on 1c. orange . . . . 40 2·10
896 **72** $20 on 2c. green 20 95
904 **77** $20 on 2c. blue . . . . . 30 1·40
899 – $20 on 3c. brown (511) . . 30 1·40
897 **72** $20 on 3c. red 20 80
879 – $20 on 8c. orange (514) . . 30 1·90
869 **72** $20 on 8c. green . . . . . 2·10 2·10
882 **77** $20 on 8c. orange . . . . . 1·10 5·75
883 **77** $20 on 8c. green . . . . . 30 1·10
900 **60** $30 on 4c. lilac 30 65
880 – $50 on 5c. orange (513) . . 30 30
876 **72** $50 on 5c. green 40 30
884 **77** $50 on 5c. green . . . . . 1·10 30

(105)

107 Dr. Sun Yat-sen

1946. C.N.C. surcharges. Surch as T **105** (rectangular value tablet at bottom). (a) Box with chequered pattern.
831 **72** $20 on 3c. red . . . . . 20 1·10
846 – $20 on 8c. orange (514) 20 80
832 **72** $50 on 3c. red 20 40
833 $50 on 5c. green 20 50
847 – $50 on 5c. orange (513) 20 25
851 **77** $50 on 5c. green . . . . 65 1·30
854 **82** $50 on $1 green 20 20
848 – $100 on 1c. orange (508) 20 20
834 **72** $100 on 3c. red 20 20
842 $100 on 8c. green 45 30
852 **77** $100 on 8c. green 40 25
860 **58** $100 on $1 purple 40 20
868 **107** $100 on $20 red 45 35
837 **72** $200 on 10c. green 85 35
861 **58** $200 on $4 blue 55 25
855 **82** $250 on $1.50 blue . . . 40 1·50
862 **58** $250 on $2 green 55 30
863 $250 on $5 red 55 25
838 **72** $300 on 10c. green 20 20
853 **77** $300 on 10c. green 20 75
839 **72** $500 on 3c. red 55 25
864 **58** $500 on $20 green 20 20
865 $800 on $30 brown . . . 20 2·20
830 $1000 on 2c. green 90 35
856 **82** $1000 on $2 green 30 25
857 $1000 on $2 blue . . . . 25 1·50
858 $1000 on $2 brown . . . 45 40
866 **94** $1000 on $2 green . . . . 20 1·80
859 **82** $2000 on $5 red 35 40
867 **94** $2000 on $5 green 15 40

(b) Box with diamond pattern.
978 **58** $500 on $20 green 20 20
979 **107** $1250 on $70 orange . . . 20 3·50
980 **118** $1800 on $350 buff . . . 20 3·50
974 **82** $2000 on $3 yellow . . . 40 35
976 **89** $2000 on $3 red 20 20
975 **82** $3000 on $3 yellow . . . 20 20
977 **89** $3000 on $3 brown . . . 20 75

1946.

885 **107** $20 red . . . . 5·50 25
886 $30 blue 25 20
887 $50 violet 20 15
888 $70 orange . . . . 14·50 2·00
889 $100 red 15 15
890 $200 green 15 15
891 $500 green 25 15
892 $700 brown . . . . 15 1·10
893 $10000 purple 30 25
894 $3000 blue 85 25
895 $5000 red and green 85 25

109 Douglas DC-4 over Mausoleum of Dr. Sun Yat-sen

110 Pres. Chiang Kai-shek

1946. Air. No gum.
905 **109** $27 blue . . . . 30 1·00

1946. President's 60th Birthday.
906A **110** $20 red 40 55
907A $30 green 40 70
908A $50 orange 40 60
909A $100 green 55 85
910A $200 yellow 70 75
911A $300 red 70 55

For stamps of this type, but additionally inscribed with four characters around head, see Taiwan Nos. 30/5, or North Eastern Provinces, Nos. 48/53.

111 National Assembly House, Nanking

112 Entrance to Dr. Sun Yat-sen Mausoleum

1946. Opening of National Assembly, Nanking. No gum.
912 **111** $20 green 65 35
913 $30 blue 65 35

914		$50 brown	65	35
915		$100 red	65	35

1947. 1st Anniv of Return of Government to Nanking.

942	112	$100 green	40	35
943		$200 blue	40	35
944		$250 red	40	60
945		$350 brown	40	60
946		$400 purple	45	45

For stamps of this type but additionally inscribed with four characters above numeral of value, see Taiwan, Nos. 36/40, or North Eastern Provinces, Nos. 65/70.

113 Dr. Sun Yat-sen

114 Confucius

115 Confucius's Lecture School

116 Tomb of Confucius

118 Dr. Sun Yat-sen and Plum Blossoms

1947.

947	113	$500 olive	30	20
948		$1,000 red and green	40	20
949		$2,000 lake and blue	45	20
950		$5,000 black and orange	45	20

1947. Confucius Commem. No gum.

951	114	$500 red	50	50
952	115	$800 brown	45	65
953	116	$1,250 green	45	85
954		$1,800 blue	45	1·10

DESIGN—HORIZ: $1,800, Confucian Temple.

1947. (a) With noughts for cents. No gum.

955	118	$150 blue	20	18·00
956		$250 violet	30	3·50
957		$500 green	20	10
958		$1,000 red	20	10
959		$2,000 orange	20	10
960		$3,000 blue	20	10
961		$4,000 grey	20	20
962		$5,000 brown	20	10
963		$6,000 purple	20	20
964		$7,000 brown	20	20
965		$10,000 red and blue	30	10
966		$20,000 green and red	1·00	10
967		$50,000 blue and green	1·10	10
968		$100,000 green & orange	3·00	15
969		$200,000 blue and purple	3·00	30
970		$300,000 orange & brown	3·50	45
971		$500,000 brown & green	4·00	45

(b) Without noughts for cents.

1032	118	$20,000 red	40	25
1033		$30,000 brown	20	15
1034		$40,000 green	20	15
1035		$50,000 blue	20	15
1036		$100,000 olive	20	15
1037		$200,000 purple	65	15
1038		$300,000 green	2·00	70
1039		$500,000 mauve	1·00	20
1040		$1,000,000 red	65	20
1041		$2,000,000 orange	85	20
1042		$3,000,000 bistre	2·75	45
1043		$5,000,000 blue	5·00	75

119 Map of Taiwan and Chinese Flag

122 Postal Kiosk

1947. Restoration of Taiwan (Formosa) (1st issue).

972	119	$500 red	30	80
973		$1,250 green	30	80

See also Nos. 1003/4.

1947. Progress of the Postal Service.

981	–	$500 red	30	40
982	122	$1,000 violet	30	40
983		$1,250 green	30	60
984	–	$1,800 blue	30	80

DESIGN: $500, $1,800, Mobile Post Office.

123 Air, Sea and Rail Transport

124 Postboy and Motor Van

1947. 50th Anniv of Directorate General of Posts.

985	123	$100 violet	30	70
986	124	$200 green	30	70
987		$300 lake	30	70
988	–	$400 red	30	70
989	–	$500 blue	30	70

DESIGN—As T **123**: $400, $500, Junk and airplane.

126 Book of the Constitution and National Assembly Building

1947. Adoption of the Constitution.

990	126	$2,000 red	45	50
991		$3,000 blue	45	50
992		$5,000 green	45	50

127 Reproductions of 1947 and 1912 Stamps

1948. Perf or imperf. (a) Nanking Philatelic Exn.

1001	127	$5,000 red	70	2·50

(b) Shanghai Philatelic Exhibition.

1002	127	$5,000 green	70	2·50

128 Sun Yat-sen Memorial Hall

1948. Restoration of Taiwan (Formosa) to Chinese Rule (2nd issue).

1003	128	$5,000 lilac	40	1·10
1004		$10,000 red	40	1·10

(130)

(129)

(133)

1948. "Re-valuation" surcharges. (a) Surch as T **130**.

1012	118	$4,000 on $100 red	20	22·00
1013		$5,000 on $100 red	20	10
1014		$8,000 on $700 brown	25	80

(b) Surch as T **129**.

1005	82	$5,000 on $1 green	20	20
1007		$5,000 on $2 green	20	20
1008	103	$10,000 on $20 red	20	20
1018	82	$15,000 on 10c. green	20	40
1015		$15,000 on 50c. green	20	60
1019		$15,000 on $4 purple	20	60
1020		$15,000 on $6 blue	30	40
1009		$20,000 on 10c. green	20	20
1010		$20,000 on 50c. green	20	30
1011		$30,000 on 30c. red	20	30
1016		$40,000 on 20c. olive	20	60
1017		$60,000 on $4 brown	25	30

(c) Air. Surch as T **133**.

1022	61	$10,000 on 30c. red	20	60
1028	109	$10,000 on $27 blue	35	1·30
1023	61	$20,000 on 25c. orange	20	80
1024		$30,000 on 90c. olive	20	80
1025		$50,000 on 60c. blue	20	80
1026		$50,000 on $1 green	20	70

On No. 1028 the Chinese characters read vertically.

135 Great Wall of China

137 "Hai Tien" (freighter) and "Eton" (steamer) of 1872

138 "Kiang Ya" (freighter)

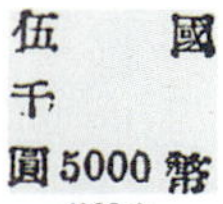
(138a)

1948. Tuberculosis Relief Fund. Cross in red. Perf or imperf. No gum.

1029	135	$5,000+$2,000 violet	20	2·20
1030		$10,000+$2,000 brown	20	2·20
1031		$15,000+$2,000 grey	20	2·20

1948. 75th Anniv of China Merchants' Steam Navigation Company. No gum.

1044	137	$20,000 blue	40	1·50
1045		$30,000 mauve	40	1·50
1046	138	$40,000 brown	40	2·10
1047		$60,000 red	40	2·10

1948. C.N.C. surcharge. Surch with T **138a**.

1048	107	$5,000 on $100 claret	8·00	55·00

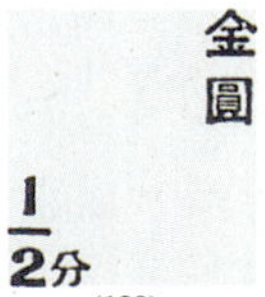
(139)

(140)

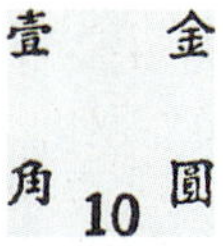
(141)

1948. Gold Yuan surcharges. (a) Surch as T **139** or **140**.

1049	82	½c. on 30c. brown	20	5·00
1050	118	½c. on $500 green	20	20
1051	107	1c. on $20 red	20	1·50
1052	82	2c. on $1.50 blue	20	2·10
1053		3c. on $5 red	20	2·10
1054		4c. on $1 red	20	2·10
1055		5c. on 50c. green	20	35

(b) Surch as T **141**.

1056	89	5c. on $20 red	20	75
1057	103	5c. on $30 blue	20	95
1058	72	10c. on 2c. green	20	1·10
1059	60	10c. on 2½c. purple	20	75
1061	82	10c. on 25c. brown	20	1·00
1062	89	10c. on 40c. red	20	95
1063	82	10c. on $1 green	20	20
1065	89	10c. on $2 brown	20	20
1066	82	10c. on $20 blue	20	20
1067	89	10c. on $20 red	£200	£200
1068	94	10c. on $20 red	20	45
1069	107	10c. on $20 red	75	2·75
1070	103	10c. on $30 blue	20	1·20
1071	89	10c. on $70 violet	20	45
1072	118	10c. on $7,000 brown	1·50	95
1073		10c. on $20,000 red	20	3·00
1074	89	20c. on $6 purple	20	30
1075	58	20c. on $30 brown	40	3·25
1076	107	20c. on $30 blue	45	2·50
1077		20c. on $100 red	20	2·50
1079	60	50c. on ½c. brown	20	45
1081	82	50c. on 20c. green	20	40
1082		50c. on 30c. red	20	95
1083		50c. on 40c. brown	20	60
1084	89	50c. on 40c. red	20	75
1085a	82	50c. on $4 purple	20	1·30
1086		50c. on $20 blue	20	20
1087	94	50c. on $20 red	40	1·10
1088	107	50c. on $20 red	20	95
1089	82	50c. on $70 lilac	25	25
1090a	118	50c. on $6,000 purple	20	95
1091	82	$1 on 30c. brown	20	20
1092		$1 on 40c. brown	20	20
1093		$1 on $1 red	40	1·30
1094		$1 on $5 red	45	30
1095	89	$2 on $2 brown	20	20
1096	102	$2 on $20 red	20	20
1097	107	$2 on $100 red	20	20
1098	–	$5 on 17c. green (417)	60	60
1099	89	$5 on $2 brown	20	20
1100	118	$5 on $30,000 blue	20	95
1101	–	$8 on 20c. blue (519)	40	40
1102	118	$8 on $30,000 brown	20	1·50
1103	–	$10 on 40c. orange (543)	95	75
1104	89	$10 on $2 brown	20	25
1105		$20 on $2 brown	15	15
1106	107	$20 on $20 red	3·75	2·50
1107	82	$50 on 30c. red	20	25
1108	89	$50 on $2 brown	25	20
1109	107	$80 on $20 red	20	75
1110	82	$100 on $1 green	20	75
1111	89	$100 on $2 brown	30	25
1112	118	$20,000 on $40,000 green	13·00	15·00
1113		$50,000 on $20,000 red	1·20	40
1114		$50,000 on $30,000 brown	14·00	11·00
1115		$100,000 on $20,000 red	14·00	12·00
1116		$100,000 on $30,000 brown	2·40	30
1117		$200,000 on $40,000 green	14·00	15·00
1118		$200,000 on $50,000 blue	13·00	16·00

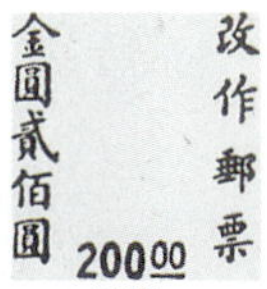
(142)

143 Liner, Train and Airplane

(144)

145 Dr. Sun Yat-sen

1949. Gold Yuan surcharges. Parcels Post stamps surch as T **142**.

1119	P 104	$200 on $3,000 orange	75	45
1120		$500 on $5,000 blue	85	35
1121		$1,000 on $10,000 vio	1·30	45

1949. Gold Yuan surcharges. Revenue stamps surch. (a) As T **144**.

1136	143	50c. on $20 brown	20	45
1137		$1 on $15 orange	20	6·50
1127		$2 on $50 blue	20	95
1144		$3 on $50 blue	20	60
1138		$5 on $500 brown	20	35
1129		$10 on $30 mauve	20	45
1140		$15 on $20 brown	20	35
1141		$25 on $20 brown	20	35
1145		$50 on $50 blue	20	35
1147		$50 on $300 green	20	45
1130		$80 on $50 blue	20	95
1146		$100 on $50 blue	40	2·00
1124		$200 on $50 blue	60	75
1142		$200 on $500 brown	40	50
1125		$300 on $50 blue	85	95
1143		$500 on $15 orange	1·00	3·00
1134		$500 on $30 mauve	50	2·10
1135		$1,000 on $50 blue	8·25	7·00
1148		$1,000 on $100 olive	2·30	4·00
1126		$1,500 on $50 blue	1·00	2·75
1151		$2,000 on $300 green	40	55

(b) As T **144** but with key pattern inverted at top and bottom.

1183	143	$50 on $10 green	8·75	11·50
1184		$100 on $10 green	2·00	13·50
1185		$500 on $10 green	1·25	5·00
1186		$1,000 on $10 green	1·00	7·75
1187		$5,000 on $20 brown	25·00	19·00
1188		$10,000 on $20 brown	14·50	11·50
1189		$50,000 on $20 brown	17·00	19·00
1190		$100,000 on $20 brown	21·00	19·00
1191		$500,000 on $20 brown	£300	£190
1192		$2,000,000 on $20 brn	£750	£275
1193		$5,000,000 on $20 brn	£1300	£550

1949.

1152	145	$1 orange	20	60
1153		$10 green	30	60
1154		$20 purple	10	60
1155		$50 green	10	60
1156		$100 brown	10	60
1157		$200 red	10	60
1158		$500 mauve	10	60
1159		$800 red	10	2·10
1160		$1,000 blue	20	60
1168		$2,000 violet	20	1·10
1169		$5,000 blue	20	35
1177		$5,000 red	55	1·10
1170		$10,000 brown	20	35
1171		$20,000 green	20	1·10
1179		$20,000 orange	1·20	1·50
1172		$50,000 pink	20	35
1180		$50,000 blue	2·20	2·75
1173		$80,000 brown	40	3·00
1174		$100,000 green	35	35
1181		$200,000 blue	4·00	3·25
1182		$500,000 purple	5·25	2·30

For stamps of Type **145** in Silver Yuan currency see Nos. 1348/56.

146 Steam Locomotive

147 Douglas DC-4

148 Postman on Motor Cycle

149 Mountains

1949. No value indicated. Perf or roul.

1211A	146	Orange (Ord. postage)	3·50	1·90
1212A	147	Green (Air Mail)	6·50	17·00
1213A	148	Mauve (Express)	6·50	16·00
1214A	149	Red (Registration)	7·00	8·75

Owing to the collapse of the Gold Yuan the above were sold at the rate for the day for the service indicated.

(154)

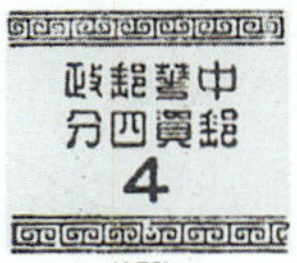
(159)

1949. Gold Yuan currency. Revenue stamps optd as T **154**. No gum.

1232	143	$10 green (B)	23·00	29·00
1233		$30 mauve (A)	95·00	90·00
1234		$50 blue (C)	25·00	25·00
1235		$100 olive (D)	45·00	60·00
1236		$200 purple (A)	15·00	9·75
1237		$500 green (A)	18·00	16·00

Opt. translation: (A) Domestic Letter Fee. (B) Express Letter Fee. (C) Registered Letter Fee. (D) Air Mail Fee.

1949. Silver Yuan surcharges. Revenue stamps surch as T **159**. No gum.

1312	143	1c. on $20 brown	55·00	55·00
1284		1c. on $5,000 brown	5·00	4·25
1285		4c. on $100 olive	3·00	2·20
1286		4c. on $3,000 orange	3·00	1·10
1313		10c. on $20 brown	55·00	55·00
1287		10c. on $50 blue	4·50	1·80
1288		10c. on $1,000 red	4·75	2·00
1289		20c. on $1,000 red	5·00	2·50
1290		50c. on $30 mauve	15·00	4·25
1291		50c. on $50 blue	22·00	1·80
1292		$1 on $50 blue	16·00	21·00

On Nos. 1312 and 1313 the key pattern is inverted at top and bottom.

169 Tundra Swans over Globe

170 Globe and Doves

1949. No gum.

1344	169	$1 orange	8·25	11·50
1345		$2 blue	43·00	17·00
1346		$5 red	43·00	21·00
1347		$10 green	43·00	47·00

1949. Silver Yuan currency.

1348	145	1c. green	25·00	9·00
1349		2c. orange	4·00	18·00
1350		4c. green	10	1·10
1351		10c. lilac	30	1·10
1352		16c. red	60	11·50
1353		20c. blue	35	4·00
1354		50c. brown	1·50	22·00
1355		100c. blue	£325	£375
1356		500c. red	£400	£425

1949. 75th Anniv of UPU. Value optd in black. Imperf. No gum.

1357	170	$1 orange	5·00	10·00

171 Buddha's Tower, Peking

172 Bronze Bull

1949. Value optd. Roul.

1358	171	15c. green and brown	7·00	8·00
1359	172	40c. red and green	8·00	8·00

(173)

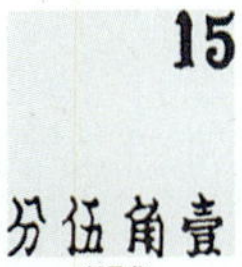
(174)

1949. Silver Yuan surcharges. (a) Chungking issue. Surch as T **173**.

1360	145	2½c. on $50 green	1·20	1·50
1361		2½c. on $50,000 blue	3·50	1·50
1362		5c. on $1,000 blue	2·75	1·50
1363		5c. on $20,000 orange	1·70	1·30
1364		5c. on $200,000 blue	2·75	1·30
1365		5c. on $500,000 purple	1·70	1·30
1366		10c. on $5,000 red	5·00	3·25
1367		10c. on $10,000 brown	5·00	3·25
1368		15c. on $200 red	6·25	10·00
1369		25c. on $100 brown	10·00	16·00

(b) Canton issue. Surch as T **174**.

1371	145	1c. on $100 brown	7·00	7·75
1372		2½c. on $500 mauve	8·50	8·50
1374		15c. on $10 green	13·50	19·00
1375		15c. on $20 purple	19·00	25·00

EXPRESS DELIVERY STAMP

E 80

1941. Perf. No gum.

E616	E 80	(No value) red & yellow	32·00	23·00

This stamp was sold at $2, which included ordinary postage.

MILITARY POST STAMPS

(M 85)

M 93 Entrenched Soldiers

1942. Optd variously as Type M **85**.

M682	72	8c. olive	4·50	7·75
M684	77	8c. green	5·75	10·00
M676		8c. orange	£450	
M683	72	16c. olive	42·00	60·00
M677	82	16c. olive	5·25	9·75
M678		50c. green	4·50	8·50
M679		$1 red	4·25	7·75
M680		$1 olive	4·25	7·75
M681		$2 green	5·00	10·50
M687		$2 purple	75·00	£100

1945.

M745	M 93	(No value) red	60	10·00

PARCELS POST STAMPS

P 90

P 104

P 112

1944.

P711	P 90	$500 green	—	1·00
P712		$1,000 blue	—	1·00
P713		$3,000 red	—	1·00
P714		$5,000 brown	—	48·00
P715		$10,000 purple	—	90·00

1946.

P814	P 104	$3,000 orange	—	50
P815		$5,000 blue	—	50
P816		$10,000 violet	—	2·50
P817		$20,000 red	—	4·75

1947. Type P **112** and similar design.

P925	$1,000 yellow	—	1·20
P926	$3,000 green	—	1·20
P927	$5,000 red	—	1·20
P928	$7,000 blue	—	1·20
P929	$10,000 red	—	1·20
P930	$30,000 olive	—	1·40
P931	$50,000 black	—	1·40
P932	$70,000 brown	—	1·60
P933	$100,000 purple	—	1·80
P934	$200,000 green	—	2·00
P935	$300,000 pink	—	2·20
P936	$500,000 plum	—	2·50
P937	$3,000,000 blue	—	4·00
P938	$5,000,000 lilac	—	4·00
P939	$6,000,000 grey	—	5·00
P940	$8,000,000 red	—	5·25
P941	$10,000,000 olive	—	6·25

(P 146)

1949. Gold Yuan surcharges. 1947 issue surch as Type P **146**.

P1194	$10 on $3,000 green	—	1·50
P1195	$20 on $5,000 red	—	1·50
P1196	$50 on $10,000 red	—	1·50
P1197	$100 on $3,000,000 blue	—	1·80
P1198	$200 on $5,000,000 lilac	—	1·80
P1199	$500 on $1,000 yellow	—	2·20
P1200	$1,000 on $7,000 blue	—	2·20

Parcels post stamps were not on sale in unused condition; those now on the market were probably stocks seized by the Communists.

POSTAGE DUE STAMPS

1912. Chinese Empire Postage Due Stamps optd with vertical row of Chinese characters.

D207	D 37	½c. blue	60	35
D208		1c. brown	80	40
D209		2c. brown	1·20	50
D210		4c. blue	3·50	2·75
D211		5c. blue	£110	£110
D212		5c. brown	4·00	1·60
D213		10c. blue	5·00	2·40
D214		20c. blue	8·50	7·25
D215		30c. blue	12·00	15·00

(D 41)

D 46

D 62

1912. Optd with Type D **41**.

D233	D 37	½c. blue	6·25	3·25
D234		½c. brown	1·25	55
D235		1c. brown	1·25	75
D236		2c. brown	3·00	6·00
D237		4c. blue	5·00	7·75
D238		5c. brown	10·00	9·75
D239		10c. blue	11·50	22·00
D240		20c. brown	28·00	36·00
D241		30c. blue	60·00	49·00

1913.

D341	D 46	½c. blue	55	75
D342		1c. blue	1·30	25
D343		2c. blue	1·30	30
D344		4c. blue	1·80	45
D345		5c. blue	2·50	65
D346		10c. blue	3·00	90
D347		20c. blue	8·50	1·50
D340		30c. blue	20·00	6·50

1932.

D432	D 62	½c. orange	20	25
D433		1c. orange	20	25
D434		2c. orange	20	25
D435		4c. orange	40	25
D569		5c. orange	80	40
D570		10c. orange	25	40
D571		20c. orange	25	40
D572		30c. orange	25	40
D573		50c. orange	45	55
D574		$1 orange	45	85
D575		$2 orange	85	85

(D 75) ("Temporary-use Postage Due")

1940. Optd with Type D **75**.

D545	72	$1 brown and red	4·25	11·00
D546		$2 brown and blue	3·50	5·00

D 90

D 94

D 112

1944. No gum.

D717	D 90	10c. green	25	1·60
D718		20c. blue	25	1·60
D719		40c. red	25	1·60
D720		50c. green	25	1·60
D721		60c. blue	25	1·70
D722		$1 red	25	1·60
D723		$2 purple	25	1·60

1945.

D752	D 94	$2 red	25	1·20
D753		$6 red	25	1·20
D754		$8 red	25	1·50
D755		$10 red	25	1·60
D756		$20 red	25	1·60
D757		$30 red	55	1·60

1947.

D916	D 112	$50 purple	25	1·60
D917		$80 purple	25	1·60
D918		$100 purple	25	1·60
D919		$160 purple	25	1·60
D920		$200 purple	25	1·60
D921		$400 purple	25	1·60
D922		$500 purple	25	1·60
D923		$800 purple	25	1·60
D924		$2,000 purple	25	1·60

(D 127)

(D 146)

1948. Surch as Type D **127**.

D 993	D 94	$1,000 on $20 purple	10	2·30
D 994		$2,000 on $30 purple	10	1·60
D 995		$3,000 on $50 purple	10	1·60
D 996		$4,000 on $100 pur	10	2·30
D 997		$5,000 on $200 pur	10	1·40
D 998		$10,000 on $300 pur	10	60
D 999		$20,000 on $500 pur	10	60
D1000		$30,000 on $1,000 pur	10	50

1949. Gold Yuan surcharges. Surch as Type D **146**.

D1201	102	1c. on $40 orange	25	7·25
D1202		2c. on $40 orange	25	7·25
D1203		5c. on $40 orange	25	7·25
D1204		10c. on $40 orange	25	7·25
D1205		20c. on $40 orange	25	7·25
D1206		50c. on $40 orange	25	7·25
D1207		$1 on $40 orange	25	5·75
D1208		$2 on $40 orange	25	5·75
D1209		$5 on $40 orange	35	6·00
D1210		$10 on $40 orange	40	3·75

REGISTRATION STAMP

1941. Roul. No gum.

R617	E 80	(No value) grn & buff	23·00	18·00

This stamp was sold at $1.50 which included ordinary postage.

CHINESE PROVINCES

Manchuria

A. KIRIN AND HEILUNGKIANG

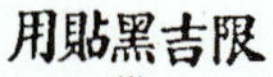
(1)

(2)

Stamps of China optd

1927. Stamps of 1913 optd with T **1**.

1	43	½c. sepia	1·30	25
2		1c. orange	1·30	25
3		1½c. purple	1·80	1·40
4		2c. green	1·80	35
5		3c. green	1·40	65
6		4c. olive	1·20	25
7		5c. mauve	1·70	25
8		6c. red	1·80	1·30
9		7c. violet	3·50	1·90
10		8c. orange	3·00	1·50
11		10c. blue	2·50	40
12	44	13c. brown	3·50	3·00
13		15c. blue	3·50	2·10
14		16c. olive	4·00	2·75
15		20c. lake	4·25	2·30
16		30c. purple	6·50	2·50
17		50c. green	10·50	3·00
18	45	$1 sepia and brown	26·00	6·25
19		$2 brown and blue	49·00	13·00
20		$5 green and red	£225	£225

1928. Chang Tso-lin stamps optd with T **2**.

21	55	1c. orange	2·10	1·40
22		4c. olive	1·50	1·50
23		10c. blue	3·75	3·75
24		$1 red	36·00	33·00

1929. Unification stamps optd as T **2**.

25	56	1c. orange	1·60	1·60
26		4c. olive	2·75	2·50
27		10c. blue	10·00	9·25
28		$1 red	80·00	75·00

1929. Sun Yat-sen Memorial stamps optd as T **2**.

29	57	1c. orange	1·70	2·00
30		4c. olive	2·10	2·30
31		10c. blue	6·50	4·00
32		$1 red	65·00	49·00

B. NORTH-EASTERN PROVINCES

Issues made by the Chinese Nationalist Government of Chiang Kai-shek.

1 Dr. Sun Yat-sen

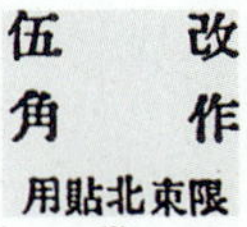
(2)

1946. Surch as T **2**.

1	1	50c. on $5 red	25	2·30
2		50c. on $10 green	60	2·50
3		$1 on $10 green	25	1·70
4		$2 on $20 purple	25	1·30
5		$4 on $50 brown	25	1·10

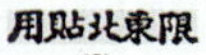
(3)

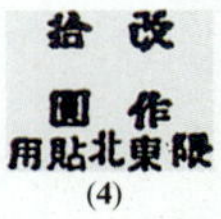
(4)

1946. Stamps of China optd with T **3** (= "Limited for use in North East").

6	–	1c. orange (508)	25	3·25
7	–	3c. brown (511)	25	3·00
8	–	5c. orange (513)	25	2·50
9	72	10c. green	25	2·75
11		20c. blue	25	3·00

1946. Stamps of China surch as T **4** but larger.

14	–	$5 on $50 on 21c. brown (No. 799)	70·00	75·00
15	–	$10 on $100 on 28c. green (No. 802)	75·00	90·00
16	91	$20 on $200 green	70·00	75·00

5 Dr. Sun Yat-sen

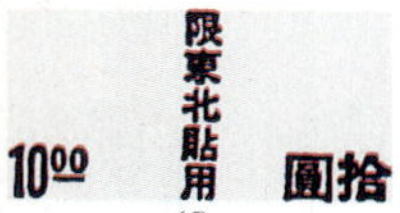

(6)

1946.

17 **5** 5c. lake 25 2·20
18 10c. orange 25 2·10
19 20c. green 25 3·00
20 25c. brown 25 2·30
21 50c. orange 25 1·80
22 $1 blue 25 1·40
23 $2 purple 25 1·60
24 $2.50 blue 25 2·30
25 $3 brown 25 1·70
26 $4 brown 25 2·20
27 $5 green 25 1·70
28 $10 red 25 1·10
29 $20 olive 25 90
34 $22 black 55·00 85·00
35 $44 red 30·00 42·00
36 $50 violet 55 1·00
37 $65 green 60·00 £100
38 $100 green 25 50
39 $109 green 65·00 £100
40 $200 brown 25 90
41 $300 green 25 1·80
42 $500 red 25 50
43 $1,000 orange 25 45

1946. Nanking National Assembly stamps of China surch as T **6**.
44 **111** $2 on $20 green 35 1·90
45 $3 on $30 blue 35 2·30
46 $5 on $50 brown 35 2·00
47 $10 on $100 red 35 2·00

7 Pres. Chiang Kai-shek (note characters to right of head)

(8)

1947. President's 60th Birthday.
54 **7** $2 red 45 2·50
55 $3 green 70 2·50
56 $5 red 70 2·50
57 $10 green 75 2·50
58 $20 orange 95 2·50
59 $30 red 95 2·50

For other stamps as Types **7** and **9** but with different Chinese characters, see China–Taiwan Types **4** and **5**.

1947. Stamps of China surch as T **8**.
60 **107** $100 on $1,000 purple 65 2·50
61 $300 on $3,000 blue 65 2·50
62 **58** $500 on $30 brown 40 3·00
63 **107** $500 on $5,000 red & green 90 2·75

9 Entrance to Dr. Sun Yat-sen Mausoleum (note characters above face value)

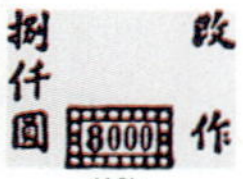

(10)

1947. 1st Anniv of Return of Govt. to Nanking.
64 **9** $2 green 40 1·20
65 $4 blue 40 1·20
66 $6 red 40 1·20
67 $10 brown 40 1·20
68 $20 purple 40 1·20

1948. Surch as T **10**.
70 **5** $1,500 on 20c. green 65 3·25
71 $3,000 on $1 blue 30 2·75
72 $4,000 on 25c. brown 30 2·20
73 $8,000 on 50c. orange 30 2·00
74 $10,000 on 10c. orange 25 1·80
75 $50,000 on $109 green 70 4·50
76 $100,000 on $65 green 65 4·50
77 $500,000 on $22 black 1·10 4·50

No. 70 has five characters on the left side of the surcharge and No. 77 four characters.

MILITARY POST STAMPS

1946. Military Post stamp of China optd as T **3** but larger.
M13 **M 93** (No value) red 1·70 13·00

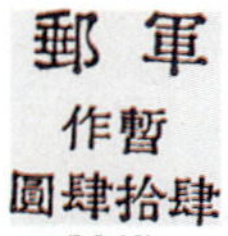

(M 10)

1947. Surch with Type M **10**.
M69 **5** $44 on 50c. orange 7·25 25·00

PARCELS POST STAMPS

P 11

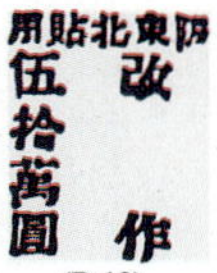

(P 12)

1948.
P78 **P 11** $500 red 28·00
P79 $1,000 red 55·00
P80 $3,000 olive 70·00
P81 $5,000 blue £110
P82 $10,000 green £140
P83 $20,000 blue £140

1948. Parcels Post stamp of China surch with Type P **12**.
P84 $500,000 on $5,000,000 lilac (No. P938) — £120

Parcels Post stamps were not on sale unused.

POSTAGE DUE STAMPS

D 7

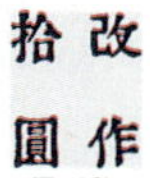

(D 13)

1947.
D48 **D 7** 10c. blue 35 5·50
D49 20c. blue 35 5·50
D50 50c. blue 35 4·25
D51 $1 blue 15 3·00
D52 $2 blue 15 4·00
D53 $5 blue 15 3·50

1948. Surch as Type D **13**.
D85 **D 7** $10 on 10c. blue 25 6·00
D86 $20 on 20c. blue 25 6·00
D87 $50 on 50c. blue 25 6·00

Sinkiang (Chinese Turkestan)

A province between Tibet and Mongolia. Issued distinguishing stamps because of its debased currency.

The following are all optd on stamps of China.

(1)

(3)

1915. 1913 issue optd with T **1**.
17 **43** ½c. sepia 1·60 1·80
2 1c. orange 1·30 55
49 1½c. purple 2·00 3·50
3 2c. green 1·80 1·00
4 3c. green 1·80 45
5 4c. red 3·50 85
52 4c. grey 3·00 5·00
53 4c. olive 3·75 3·00
6 5c. mauve 2·75 70
7 6c. grey 5·00 2·10
55 6c. red 5·50 2·00
56 6c. brown 14·00 14·50
8 7c. violet 5·00 6·50
9 8c. orange 4·25 4·25
10 10c. blue 4·25 2·10
60 **44** 13c. brown 5·00 6·25
11 15c. brown 5·00 2·75
61 15c. blue 6·50 5·00
12 16c. olive 9·75 7·00
63 20c. lake 6·25 4·50
14 30c. purple 11·00 8·50
65 50c. green 9·00 5·00
34 **45** $1 black and yellow 22·00 8·50
66 $1 sepia and brown 18·00 6·25
35 $2 black and blue 29·00 11·00
67 $2 brown and blue 27·00 8·50
36 $5 black and red 85·00 29·00
68 $5 green and red 65·00 23·00
37 $10 black and green £200 £140
69 $10 mauve and green £200 £120
38 $20 black and yellow £1100 £650
70 $20 blue and purple £300 £225

1921. 25th Anniv of Chinese National Postal Service stamps optd with T **3**.
39 **48** 1c. orange 1·30 1·30
40 3c. turquoise 2·30 2·30
41 6c. grey 6·75 5·75
42 10c. blue 48·00 43·00

(4)

1923. Adoption of the Constitution stamps optd with T **4**.
43 **53** 1c. orange 4·50 4·50
44 3c. turquoise 5·25 5·25
45 4c. red 7·75 7·75
46 10c. blue 21·00 21·00

(5)

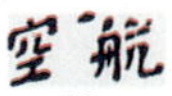

(6)

1928. Assumption of Title of Marshal of the Army and Navy by Chang Tso-lin. Optd with T **5**.
71 **55** 1c. orange 1·30 1·30
72 4c. olive 2·10 2·10
73 10c. blue 5·00 5·00
74 $1 red 42·00 36·00

1929. Unification of China. Optd as T **5**.
75 **56** 1c. orange 2·75 2·30
76 4c. olive 3·50 3·50
77 10c. blue 8·50 8·50
78 $1 red 65·00 55·00

1929. Sun Yat-sen State Burial. Optd as T **5**.
79 **57** 1c. orange 1·40 1·30
80 4c. olive 2·20 2·10
81 10c. blue 5·25 5·00
82 $1 red 60·00 46·00

1932. Air. Handstamped on Sinkiang issues as T **6** ("By Air Mail").
83 **43** 5c. mauve (No. 6) £250 £180
84 10c. blue (No. 10) £250 £140
85 **44** 15c. blue (No. 61) £1700 £475
86 30c. purple (No. 14) £750 £600

1932. Dr. Sun Yat-sen stamps optd as T **3**.
87 **58** 1c. orange 1·20 2·75
95 2c. olive 1·60 1·60
103 4c. green 1·40 3·75
104 5c. green 1·60 3·75
105 15c. green 2·30 4·50
114 15c. red 3·25 2·50
115 20c. blue 2·50 1·00
107 25c. blue 2·75 2·50
108 $1 sepia and brown 8·75 10·00
100 $2 brown and blue 24·00 25·00
101 $5 black and red 30·00 50·00

1933. Tan Yen-kai Memorial. Optd as T **5**.
117 **62** 2c. olive 3·00 3·00
118 5c. green 3·50 3·50
119 25c. blue 11·50 11·50
120 $1 red 60·00 49·00

1933. Martyrs' issue optd as T **3**.
121 **60** ½c. sepia 35 2·20
122 – 1c. orange 1·80 2·50
167 – 2c. blue 1·60 1·80
123 **60** 2½c. mauve 45 2·30
124 – 3c. brown 45 2·75
169 **60** 4c. lilac 20 2·10
125 – 8c. orange 1·30 2·75
126 – 10c. purple 45 2·75
171 – 13c. green 35 2·50
172 – 15c. purple 20 2·50
173 – 17c. olive 50 2·50
137 – 20c. lake 25 5·50
174 – 20c. blue 20 2·40
175 – 21c. sepia 65 2·75
185 – 25c. purple 1·20 4·25
176 – 28c. olive 80 2·75
130 – 30c. red 65 4·25
131 – 40c. orange 1·00 4·50
132 – 50c. green 1·10 4·25

1940. Dr. Sun Yat-sen stamps optd as T **3**.
139 **72** 2c. olive 1·00 2·00
140 3c. red 25 2·00
141 5c. green 25 1·80
143 8c. olive 25 1·60
144 10c. green 35 1·30
145 15c. red 90 3·00
146 16c. olive 85 2·75
147 25c. blue 1·10 3·25
156 30c. red 75 2·75
158 50c. blue 1·10 2·50
160 $1 brown and red 1·30 4·25
161 $2 brown and blue 1·30 4·75
162 $5 green and red 1·40 6·50
163 $10 violet and green 2·30 6·00
164 $20 blue and red 4·25 9·25

(8)

(9)

1942. Air. Air stamps optd with T **8** or larger.
187 **61** 15c. green 5·25 6·50
197 25c. orange 4·50 7·75
198 30c. red 5·00 8·25
190 45c. purple 7·75 13·00
199 50c. brown 6·50 9·75
192 60c. blue 7·75 16·00
193 90c. olive 42·00 60·00
194 $1 green 8·50 14·00
200 $2 brown 31·00 31·00
201 $5 red 31·00 31·00

1942. Thrift stamps optd as T **8**.
221 **78** 8c. green 6·75 13·50
215 21c. brown 6·75 13·50
216 28c. olive 6·75 13·50
223 33c. red 8·75 13·50
218 50c. blue 10·00 13·50
225 $1 purple 13·50 20·00
MS220 155×171 mm. China No. **MS**605 £550 £350

1943. Dr. Sun Yat-sen stamps optd as T **3**.
227 **82** 10c. green 1·30 5·00
228 20c. olive 1·60 4·75
229 25c. purple 25 8·00
230 30c. red 70 5·50
231 40c. brown 25 5·00
232 50c. green 25 4·50
233 $1 red 3·00 4·25
234 $1 olive 30 4·50
235 $1.50 blue 30 6·50
236 $2 green 1·90 5·25
237 $3 yellow 40 6·00
238 $5 red 2·00 5·75

1943. Stamps optd with T **9**.
239 **72** 10c. green 18·00 36·00
240 – 20c. blue (No. 519) 18·00 36·00
241 **72** 50c. blue 18·00 36·00

1944. Dr. Sun Yat-sen stamps optd as T **3**.
248 **77** $4 blue 1·10 8·25
249 $5 grey 1·90 8·50
250 $10 brown 1·90 8·50
251 $20 green 1·30 6·50
243 $20 red 4·00 11·50
253 $30 purple 2·50 10·50
245 $40 red 3·25 11·50
255 $50 blue 2·75 12·00
247 $100 brown 8·25 14·50

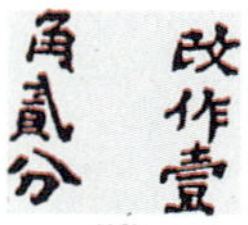

(10)

1944. Nos. 227 and 229 of Sinkiang surch as T **10**.
257 **82** 12c. on 10c. green 5·00 15·00
258 24c. on 25c. purple 5·25 15·00

1945. Stamps optd as T **3**.
259 **89** 40c. red 35 10·00
260 $3 red 35 9·25

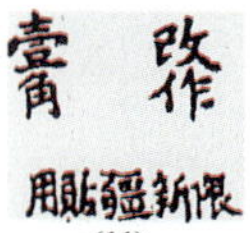

(11)

1949. Silver Yuan surcharges. Sun Yat-sen issues of China surch as T **11**.
261 **107** 1c. on $100 red (No. 889) 14·00 14·00
262 3c. on $200 green (No. 890) 14·00 17·00
263 5c. on $500 green (No. 891) 14·00 17·00
264 **136** 10c. on $20,000 red (No. 1032) 12·00 15·00
265 50c. on $4,000 grey (No. 961) 46·00 46·00
266 $1 on $6,000 purple (No. 963) 55·00 55·00

Szechwan

A province of China. Issued distinguishing stamps because of its debased currency.

(1)

Stamps of China optd with T **1**.

1933. Issue of 1913.
1 **43** 1c. orange 7·75 70
2 5c. mauve 7·75 1·00
3 **44** 50c. green 21·00 5·00

1933. Dr. Sun Yat-sen issue.
4 **58** 2c. olive 1·20 70
5 5c. green 17·00 1·70
6 15c. green 5·50 2·50
7 15c. red 6·00 8·50
8 25c. blue 5·25 1·30
9 $1 sepia and brown 16·00 3·00
10 $2 brown and blue 38·00 5·00
11 $5 black and red 90·00 27·00

1933. Martyrs issue (Nos. 410 etc).
12 **60** ½c. sepia 55 60
13 – 1c. orange 90 40
14 **60** 2½c. mauve 2·40 2·75
15 – 3c. brown 2·10 2·10
16 – 8c. orange 1·30 1·10
17 – 10c. purple 3·25 40
18 – 13c. green 3·50 70
19 – 17c. olive 4·00 1·00
20 – 20c. lake 6·25 70
21 – 30c. red 5·00 70
22 – 40c. orange 12·00 95
23 – 50c. green 27·00 1·60

Yunnan

A province of China which issued distinguishing stamps because of its debased currency.

(1)

(2)

(3)

Stamps of China optd.

1926. Issue of 1913, optd with T **1**.
1 **43** ½c. sepia 60 35
2 1c. orange 1·20 25
3 1½c. purple 1·70 3·00
4 2c. green 2·00 45
5 3c. green 1·80 35
6 4c. olive 2·00 40
7 5c. mauve 3·00 40
8 6c. red 3·75 1·10
9 7c. violet 4·50 2·00

10		8c. orange	4·75	1·70
11		10c. blue	3·00	25
12	44	13c. brown	4·00	3·25
13		15c. blue	3·75	2·20
14		16c. olive	4·75	2·50
15		20c. lake	5·50	2·30
16		30c. purple	11·00	8·50
17		50c. green	6·75	4·50
18	45	$1 sepia and brown	19·00	9·75
19		$2 brown and blue	38·00	12·00
20		$5 green and red	£150	£180

1929. Unification of China. Optd with T **2**.

21	56	1c. orange	1·50	1·40
22		4c. olive	2·75	4·25
23		10c. blue	7·50	6·50
24		$1 red	85·00	65·00

1929. Sun Yat-sen State Burial. Optd as T **2**.

25	57	1c. orange	1·50	1·30
26		4c. olive	1·50	2·75
27		10c. blue	5·75	6·25
28		$1 red	55·00	49·00

1932. Dr. Sun Yat-sen stamps optd with T **3**.

29	58	1c. orange	3·00	2·10
30		2c. olive	3·50	4·25
44		4c. green	8·25	5·25
45		5c. green	7·50	5·00
46		15c. green	4·00	4·25
47		15c. red	4·50	4·75
32		20c. blue	2·75	2·75
48		25c. blue	5·25	5·50
33		$1 sepia and brown	36·00	42·00
34		$2 brown and blue	60·00	65·00
35		$5 black and red	£180	£225

1933. Tan Yen-kai Memorial. Optd with T **2**.

52	62	2c. olive	1·50	1·90
53		5c. green	2·30	1·80
54		25c. blue	5·00	4·25
55		$1 red	60·00	47·00

1933. Martyrs issue optd as T **3**.

56	60	½c. sepia	1·20	1·10
57	–	1c. orange	2·50	1·80
58	60	2½c. mauve	2·75	3·00
59	–	3c. brown	4·25	2·50
60	–	8c. orange	6·00	6·00
61	–	10c. purple	3·25	3·25
62	–	13c. green	3·00	2·75
63	–	17c. olive	8·50	8·50
64	–	20c. lake	3·25	2·00
65	–	30c. red	7·50	6·50
66	–	40c. orange	31·00	31·00
67	–	50c. green	31·00	31·00

COMMUNIST CHINA

Issues were made by various Communist administrations from 1930 onwards. These had limited local availability and are outside the scope of this catalogue. For details of such issues see Part 17.

In 1946 (North East China) and 1949 these local issues were consolidated into Regional People's Post stamps for those local administrations listed below.

A. East China People's Post

EC **105** Methods of Transport

1949. 7th Anniv of Shandong Communist Postal Administration.

EC322	EC 105	$1 green	25	20
EC323		$2 green	25	20
EC324		$3 red	25	20
EC325		$5 brown	25	20
EC326		$10 blue	25	20
EC327		$13 violet	25	20
EC328		$18 blue	25	20
EC329		$21 red	25	20
EC330		$30 green	25	30
EC331		$50 red	35	50
EC332		$100 green	10·00	8·75

The $5 has an overprinted character obliterating a Japanese flag on the tower.

EC **106** Steam Train and Postal Runner

EC **107** Victorious Troops and Map of Battle

1949. Dated "1949.2.7".

EC333	EC 106	$1 green	20	50
EC334		$2 green	20	40
EC335		$3 red	20	40
EC336		$5 brown	25	40
EC337		$10 blue	40	70
EC338		$13 violet	25	60
EC339		$18 blue	25	70
EC340		$21 red	25	1·00
EC341		$30 green	30	1·10
EC342		$50 red	30	1·60
EC343		$100 green	65	65

For stamps as Type EC **106**, but dated "1949", see Nos. EC364/71.

1949. Victory in Huaihai Campaign.

EC344	EC 107	$1 green	20	20
EC345		$2 green	20	20
EC346		$3 red	20	20
EC347		$5 brown	20	20
EC348		$10 blue	25	20
EC349		$13 violet	25	25
EC350		$18 blue	25	25
EC351		$21 red	25	25
EC352		$30 green	25	25
EC353		$50 red	25	25
EC354		$100 green	2·10	2·10

EC **108** Maps of Shanghai and Nanjing

1949. Liberation of Nanjing and Shanghai.

EC355	EC 108	$1 red	20	30
EC356		$2 green	20	30
EC357		$3 violet	25	25
EC358		$5 brown	25	25
EC359		$10 blue	25	25
EC360		$30 green	25	30
EC361		$50 red	25	55
EC362		$100 green	25	40
EC363		$500 orange	2·75	2·10

1949. As Type EC **106** but dated "1949".

EC364		$10 blue	25	25
EC365a		$15 red	45	30
EC366		$30 green	25	25
EC367		$50 red	25	45
EC368		$60 green	25	65
EC369		$100 green	4·50	45
EC370		$1,600 violet	1·30	2·10
EC371		$2,000 purple	1·40	2·10

EC **111** Zhu De, Mao Tse-tung and Troops

EC **112** Mao Tse-tung

1949. 22nd Anniv of Chinese People's Liberation Army.

EC378	EC 111	$70 orange	20	25
EC379		$270 red	20	25
EC380		$370 green	30	25
EC381		$470 purple	50	40
EC382		$570 blue	25	35

For other values in this design with only three characters in bottom panel, see South West China Nos. SW9/19.

1949.

EC383	EC 112	$10 blue	2·10	2·75
EC384		$15 red	2·50	3·00
EC385		$70 brown	25	20
EC386		$100 purple	25	20
EC387		$150 orange	25	25
EC388		$200 green	25	25
EC389		$500 blue	25	25
EC390		$1,000 red	25	25
EC391		$2,000 green	25	25

(EC **113**) ("Chinese People's Postal Service East China Region")

1949. Stamps of Nationalist China surch as Type EC **113**.

EC392	145	$400 on $200 red	21·00	1·10
EC393		$1,000 on $50 green	2·10	65
EC394		$1,200 on $100 brown	30	1·10
EC395		$1,600 on $20,000 grn	30	1·80
EC396		$2,000 on $1,000 blue	30	70

PARCELS POST STAMPS

Stamps of Nationalist China surch.

(ECP **110**)

1949. No. 1347 surch as Type ECP **110**.

ECP372	169	$200 on $10 green	55·00	28·00
ECP373		$500 on $10 green	55·00	28·00
ECP374		$1,000 on $10 green	55·00	28·00
ECP375		$2,000 on $10 green	55·00	28·00
ECP376		$5,000 on $10 green	55·00	28·00
ECP377		$10,000 on $10 green	£140	28·00

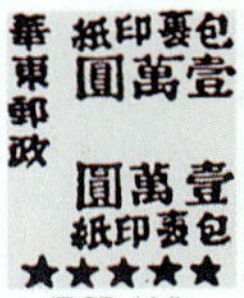

(ECP **114**)

(ECP **115**)

1949. Nos. 1344/6 and unissued 10c. surch as Type ECP **114**.

ECP397	169	$5,000 on 10c. blue	60·00	40·00
ECP398		$10,000 on $1 orange	70·00	45·00
ECP399		$20,000 on $2 blue	90·00	60·00
ECP400		$50,000 on $5 red	£200	75·00

1949. Nos. P711/2 and P926/7 surch as Type ECP **115**.

ECP401	P 90	$5,000 on $500 green	55	50·00
ECP402		$10,000 on $1 blue	£120	50·00
ECP403	P 112	$20,000 on $3 green	£120	50·00
ECP404		$50,000 on $5 red	8·75	50·00

B. North China People's Post

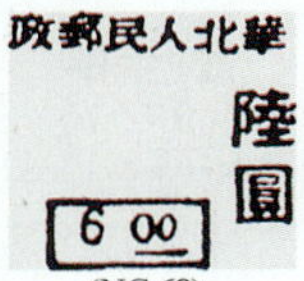

(NC **68**)

(NC **69**)

(NC **70**)

1949. Surch "North China People's Postal Administration". (a) Surch as Type NC **68**.

NC258		$5 on $500 orange	25·00	19·00
NC259		$6 on $500 orange	30·00	25·00
NC260		$12 on $200 red	5·00	6·25

(b) Surch as Type NC **69**.

NC261		$3 on 2 (20c.) brown	£250	£150
NC262		$3 on 5 (50c.) blue	19·00	12·50
NC263		$5 on 2 (20c.) brown	16·00	12·50
NC264		$5 on 5 (50c.) blue	£325	£190

(c) Surch as Type NC **70**.

NC265		$1 on $60 red	23·00	20·00
NC266		$5 on $80 purple	17·00	15·00
NC267		$6 on $2 brown	80·00	55·00
NC268		$6 on $40 brown	19·00	12·50
NC269		$6 on $80 purple	£400	£300

NC **71** Infantry

NC **72** Industry

1948. Imperf.

NC270	NC 71	50c. purple	1·00	1·00
NC271		$1 blue	4·50	4·50
NC272		$2 green	1·00	1·00
NC273		$3 violet	1·00	1·00
NC274		$5 brown	1·00	1·00
NC275	NC 72	$6 purple	1·00	1·00
NC276	NC 71	$10 green	1·10	1·10
NC277		$12 red	7·50	1·10

The 50c. and $6 have value in Chinese characters only.

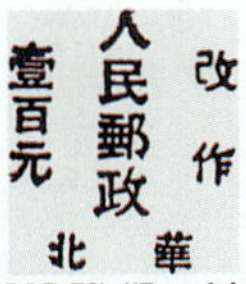

(NC **73**) "People's Postal Service North China"

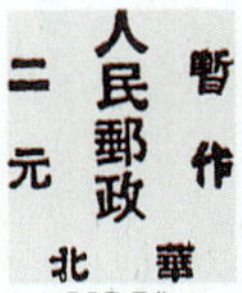

(NC **74**)

1949. Surch as Type NC **73**. (a) On stamp of Nationalist China.

NC278		$100* on $100 red	17·00	60

(b) On stamps of North Eastern Provinces.

NC279	5	50c. on 5c. red	40	2·20
NC280		$1 on 10c. orange	40	1·70
NC281		$2 on 20c. green	39·00	21·00
NC282		$3 on 50c. orange	40	1·40
NC283		$4 on $5 green	4·25	1·70
NC284		$6 on $10 red	1·40	1·70
NC285		$10 on $300 green	2·75	3·50
NC286		$12 on $1 blue	1·10	2·75
NC287		$18 on $3 brown	1·10	1·30
NC288		$20* on 50c. orange	1·40	1·10
NC290		$20 on $20 green	2·75	3·50
NC291		$30 on $2.50 blue	4·25	5·25
NC292		$40 on 25c. brown	8·75	7·00
NC293		$50 on $109 green	11·50	3·75
NC294		$80* on $1 blue	14·50	7·00
NC295		$100 on $65 green	18·00	2·50

1949. Surch as Type NC **74**. (a) On stamps of Nationalist China.

NC296	107	$100* on $100 red	48·00	28·00
NC297		$300* on $700 brown	10·00	10·00
NC298	118	$500* on $500 green	7·25	3·50
NC299		$3,000* on $3,000 blue	11·00	7·00

(b) On stamps of North Eastern Provinces.

NC300a	5	$1* on 25c. brown	50	80
NC301		$2 on 20c. green	1·40	2·50
NC302		$3 on 50c. orange	70	1·70
NC303		$4 on $5 green	5·50	3·50
NC305		$6 on $10 red	4·00	3·50
NC306		$10* on $300 green	8·75	7·50
NC307		$12 on $1 blue	1·40	1·40
NC308		$20* on 50c. orange	17·00	12·00
NC309		$20* on $20 green	6·00	3·50
NC310		$40* on 25c. brown	6·00	4·25
NC311		$50* on $109 green	8·75	10·50
NC312		$80* on $1 blue	6·00	5·25

*On these stamps the bottom character in the left-hand column of overprints is square in shape.

NC **75**

1949. Labour Day. Perf or imperf.

NC313A	NC 75	$20 red	1·60	1·20
NC314A		$40 blue	1·60	1·20
NC315A		$60 brown	1·60	1·40
NC316A		$80 green	2·00	1·50
NC317A		$100 violet	2·50	1·50

NC **79** Mao Tse-tung

NC **80**

1949. 28th Anniv of Chinese Communist Party. Perf or imperf.

NC327A	NC 79	$10 red	75	55
NC328A	NC 80	$20 blue	75	55
NC329A	NC 79	$50 orange	4·50	55
NC330A	NC 80	$80 green	90	90
NC331A	NC 79	$100 violet	4·50	90
NC332A	NC 80	$120 green	65	90
NC333A	NC 79	$140 purple	4·50	90

(NC **81**) ("People's Postal Service North China")

1949. Surch as Type NC **81**. (a) On stamp of Nationalist China.

NC334	118	$10 on $7,000 brown	10·00	7·00

(b) On stamps of North Eastern Provinces.

NC336	5	$10 on $10 red	6·00	2·75
NC337		$30 on 20c. green	6·00	1·70
NC338		$50 on $44 red	6·00	90
NC339		$100 on $3 brown	11·00	3·50
NC341		$200 on $4 brown	28·00	17·00

NC **83** Gate of Heavenly Peace, Peking

NC **84** Field Workers and Factory

1949.

NC349	NC 83	$50 orange	1·90	3·25
NC350		$100 red	30	90
NC351		$200 green	65	90
NC352		$300 purple	8·25	2·10
NC353		$400 blue	8·25	2·10
NC354		$500 brown	8·25	1·10
NC355		$700 violet	3·00	3·25

1949.

NC356	NC 84	$1,000 orange	2·50	1·40
NC357		$3,000 blue	30	1·10
NC358		$5,000 red	30	2·20
NC359		$10,000 brown	30	4·25

PARCELS POST STAMPS

Stamps of Nationalist China surch.

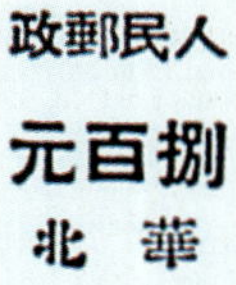

(NCP **76**)

1949. Surch as Type NCP **76**.

NCP318	P 112	$300 on $6,000,000 grey	—	50·00
NCP319		$400 on $8,000,000 red	—	50·00

NCP320		$500 on $10,000,000 green	—	50·00
NCP321		$800 on $5,000,000 lilac	—	50·00
NCP322		$1 on $3,000,000 blue	—	70·00

NC 77 Pagoda

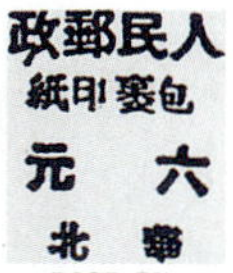
(NCP 78)

1949. Money Order stamps. Type NC 77 surch as Type NCP 78. No gum.

NCP323	$6 on $5 red	10·00	3·25
NCP324	$6 on $50 grey	10·00	3·25
NCP325	$50 on $20 purple	10·00	3·25
NCP326	$100 on $10 green	10·00	6·50

NCP 82 Steam Train

1949.

NCP342	NCP 82	$500 red	8·25	12·00
NCP343		$1,000 blue	60·00	21·00
NCP344		$2,000 green	60·00	30·00
NCP345		$5,000 green	90·00	65·00
NCP346		$10,000 orange	£160	£120
NCP347		$20,000 red	£325	£300
NCP348		$50,000 purple	£700	£550

C. Port Arthur and Dairen

The Soviet Union obtained facilities in these two ports by treaty in 1945. The Chinese Communists retained the civil administration, but a separate postal authority was established.

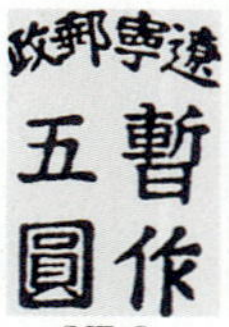
(NE 6)

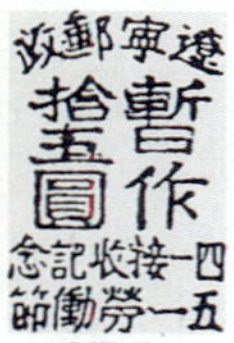
(NE 7)

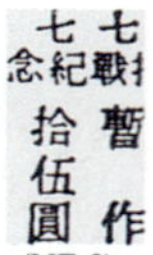
(NE 8)

1946. Stamps of Japan handstamped "Liaoning Posts" and new value at Type NE **6**.

NE 8	20c. on 3s. green (No. 316)	18·00	19·00
NE 9	$1 on 17s. violet (No. 402)	14·50	17·00
NE11	$5 on 6s. red (No. 242)	27·00	25·00
NE12	$5 on 6s. orange (No. 319)	20·00	18·00
NE13	$15 on 40s. purple (No. 406)	£100	£110

1946. Transfer of Administration on 1 April and Labour Day. Stamps of Manchukuo handstamped as Type NE 7.

NE14	19	$1 on 1f. red	17·00	22·00
NE15	–	$5 on 4f. green (No. 84)	22·00	30·00
NE16	20	$15 on 30f. brown	48·00	55·00

1946. 9th Anniv of Outbreak of War with Japan. Stamps of Manchukuo surch as Type NE 8.

NE17	$1 on 6f. red (No. 86)	10·50	18·00
NE18	$5 on 2f. green (No. 82)	48·00	80·00
NE19	$15 on 12f. orange (No. 90)	£100	£100

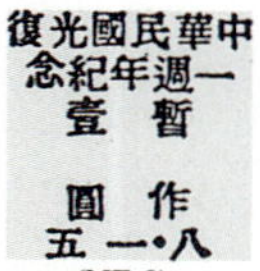
(NE 9)

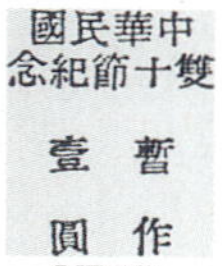
(NE 10)

1946. 1st Anniv of Japanese Surrender. Stamps of Manchukuo surch as Type NE 9.

NE20	–	$1 on 12f. orange (No. 90)	21·00	25·00
NE21	19	$5 on 1f. red	48·00	46·00
NE22	13	$15 on 5f. black	£100	90·00

1946. 35th Anniv of Chinese Revolution. Stamps of Manchukuo surch as Type NE 10.

NE23	$1 on 6f. red (No. 86)	30·00	28·00
NE24	$5 on 12f. orange (No. 90)	55·00	46·00
NE25	$15 on 2f. green (No. 82)	£100	90·00

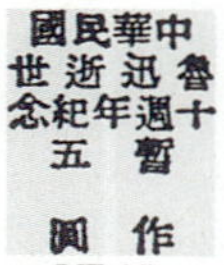
(NE 11)

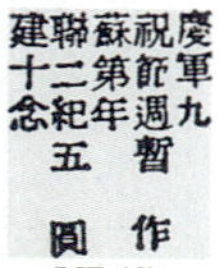
(NE 12)

1946. 10th Death Anniv of Lu Xun (author). Stamps of Manchukuo surch as Type NE 11.

NE26	19	$1 on 1f. red	44·00	41·00
NE27	–	$5 on 6f. red (No. 86)	80·00	80·00
NE28	–	$15 on 12f. orange (No. 90)	£110	£110

1947. 29th Anniv of Red Army. Stamps of Manchukuo surch as Type NE 12.

NE29	–	$1 on 2f. green (No. 82)	75·00	70·00
NE30	–	$5 on 6f. red (No. 86)	£150	£140
NE31	13	$15 on 13f. brown	£300	£275

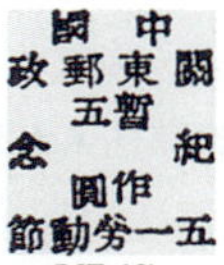
(NE 13)

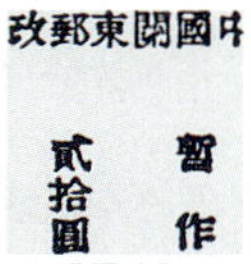
(NE 14)

1947. Labour Day. Stamps of Manchukuo surch as Type NE 13.

NE32	–	$1 on 2f. green (No. 82)	22·00	22·00
NE33	–	$5 on 6f. red (No. 86)	60·00	60·00
NE34	20	$15 on 30f. brown	£100	90·00

1947. Stamps of Manchukuo surch. "Guandong Postal Service, China" and new value as Type NE 14.

NE35	–	$5 on 2f. green (No. 82)	37·00	37·00
NE36	–	$15 on 4f. green (No. 84)	60·00	55·00
NE37	20	$20 on 30f. brown	90·00	85·00

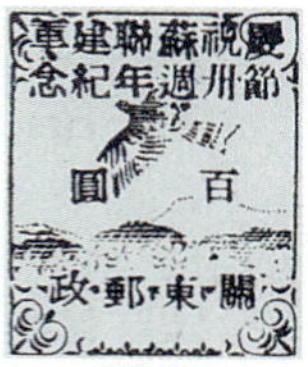
NE 15

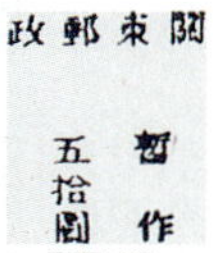
(NE 16)

1948. 30th Anniv of Red Army. Surch as on Type NE 15. (a) On stamps of Manchukuo.

NE39	$10 on 2f. green (No. 82)	£130	£130
NE40	$20 on 6f. red (No. 86)	£160	£160

(b) On label (Type NE 15) commemorating 2,600th Anniv of Japanese Empire.

NE41	$100 on (no value) blue and brown	£650	£650

1948. Stamps of Manchukuo surch "Guangdong Postal Administration" and new value as Type NE 16.

NE42	$20 on 2f. green (No. 82)	£450	£450
NE43	$50 on 4f. green (No. 84)	£650	£550
NE44	$100 on 20f. brown (No. 152)	£650	£550

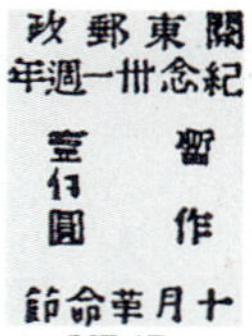
(NE 17)

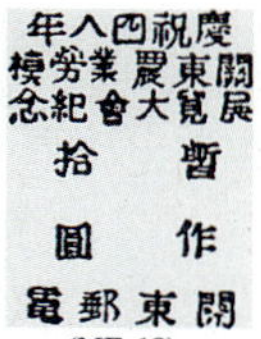
(NE 18)

1948. 31st Anniv of Russian October Revolution. Stamps of Manchukuo surch as Type NE 17.

NE45	19	$10 on 1f. red	£225	£325
NE46	–	$50 on 2f. green (No. 82)	£425	£550
NE47	–	$100 on 4f. green (No. 84)	£1000	£550

1948. Guangdong Agricultural and Industrial Exhibition Stamps of Manchukuo surch as Type NE 18.

NE48	$10 on 2f. green (No. 82)	£950	£950
NE49	$50 on 20f. brown (No. 95)	£1100	£1100

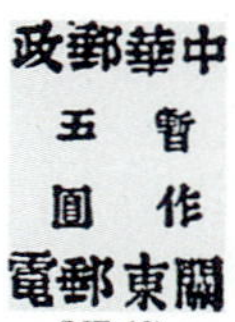
(NE 19)

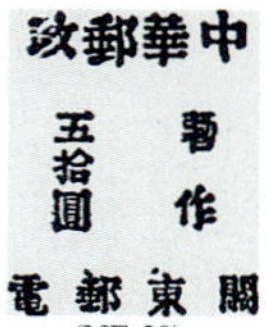
(NE 20)

1948. Stamps of Japan and Manchukuo surch "Chinese Postal Administration: Guangdong Posts and Telegraphs" and new values. (a) No. 316 of Japan surch with Type NE 19.

NE50	$5 on 3s. green	£110	£110

(b) Stamps of Manchukuo surch as Type NE 19.

NE51	$10 on 1f. red (No. 80)	£200	£225
NE52	$50 on 2f. green (No. 82)	£450	£425
NE53	$100 on 4f. green (No. 84)	£800	£850

(c) Stamps of Manchukuo surch as Type NE 20.

NE54	$10 on 2f. green (No. 82)	£275	£200
NE55	$50 on 1f. red (No. 80)	£325	£275

NE 21 Peasant and Artisan

NE 23 Dalian Port

1949.

NE56	NE 21	$5 green	2·10	6·00
NE57	–	$10 orange	18·00	18·00
NE58	NE 23	$50 red	16·00	14·50

DESIGN—VERT: $10, "Transport".

For designs as Type NE 23 but with different character in bottom panel, see No. NE62.

NE 24 "Labour"

NE 25 Mao Tse-tung

1949. Labour Day.

NE59	NE 24	$10 red	16·00	17·00

1949. 28th Anniv of Chinese Communist Party.

NE61	NE 25	$50 red	30·00	32·00

1949. Bottom panel inscr "Lushuan and Dalian Post and Telegraphic Administration".

NE62	NE 23	$50 red	22·00	22·00

NE 27 Heroes' Monument, Dalian

1949. 4th Anniv of Victory over Japan and Opening of Dalian Industrial Fair.

NE63	NE 27	$10 red, blue & lt bl	90·00	80·00
NE64		$10 red, blue & green	14·50	12·00

(NE 28)

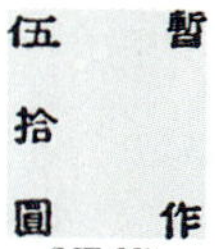
(NE 29)

(NE 30)

1949. Nos. NE56/7 surch as Types NE 28/30.

NE65	NE 28	$7 on $5 green	34·00	30·00
NE66	NE 29	$50 on $5 green	85·00	55·00
NE67		$100 on $10 orange	£425	£325
NE68	NE 30	$500 on $5 green	£600	
NE69	NE 29	$500 on $10 orge	£1200	£1300
NE70	NE 30	$500 on $10 orge	£550	£375

NE 31 Acclamation of Mao Tse-tung

1949. Founding of Chinese People's Republic.

NE71	NE 31	$35 red, yellow & bl	18·00	18·00

NE 32 Stalin and Lenin

1949. 32nd Anniv of Russian October Revolution.

NE72	NE 32	$10 green	11·00	11·00

NE 33 Josef Stalin

NE 34 Gate of Heavenly Peace, Peking

1949. Stalin's 70th Birthday.

NE73	NE 33	$20 purple	20·00	23·00
NE74		$35 red	20·00	23·00

1950.

NE75	NE 34	$10 blue	8·00	5·50
NE76		$20 green	38·00	18·00
NE77		$35 red	1·50	4·25
NE78		$50 lilac	2·50	4·25
NE79		$100 mauve	1·60	12·00

All Soviet forces were withdrawn by 26 May 1955 and the stamps of the Chinese People's Republic are now in use.

D. North-East China People's Post

NE 48 Mao Tse-tung

NE 49 Mao Tse-tung

1946.

NE133	NE 48	$1 violet	18·00	9·25
NE134	NE 49	$2 red	1·40	90
NE135		$5 orange	1·60	90
NE136		$10 blue	1·80	1·10

NE 50 Map of China with Communist Lion, Japanese Wolf and Chiang Kai-shek

NE 51 Railwaymen

1946. 10th Anniv of Seizure of Chiang Kai-shek at Xi'an.

NE137	NE 50	$1 violet	1·80	1·40
NE138		$2 orange	1·80	1·40
NE139		$5 brown	6·50	6·50
NE140		$10 green	9·25	9·25

1947. 24th Anniv of Massacre of Strikers at Zhengzhou Station.

NE141	NE 51	$1 red	90	2·00
NE142		$2 green	90	2·00
NE143		$5 red	1·60	2·50
NE144		$10 green	3·50	5·00

NE 52 Women Cheering

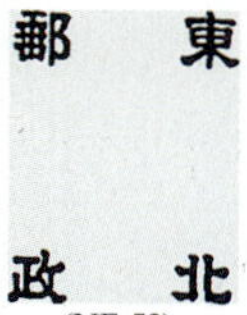
(NE 53)

1947. International Women's Day.

NE145	NE 52	$5 red	90	2·20
NE146		$10 brown	90	2·20

1947. Optd with Type NE 53 ("North East Postal Service").

NE147	NE 53	$5 red	2·75	4·25
NE148		$10 brown	2·75	4·25

NE 54 Children's Troop-comforts Unit

NE 55 Peasant and Workman

1947. Children's Day.

NE149	NE 54	$5 red	1·40	2·10
NE150		$10 green	3·00	2·75
NE151		$30 orange	4·50	3·75

1947. Labour Day.

NE152	NE 55	$10 red	1·40	1·40
NE153		$30 blue	1·80	1·80
NE154		$50 green	3·25	3·25

NE 56 "Freedom"

伍 改
拾
圓 作
5000
(NE 57)

1947. 28th Anniv of Students' Rebellion, Peking University.

NE155	NE 56	$10 green	2·30	2·30
NE156		$30 brown	2·30	2·30
NE157		$50 violet	2·75	2·75

1947. Surch as Type NE 57.

NE158	NE 48	$50 on $1 violet	22·00	23·00
NE159	NE 49	$50 on $2 red	22·00	23·00
NE160b	NE 48	$100 on $1 violet	22·00	23·00
NE161	NE 49	$100 on $2 red	22·00	23·00

NE 58 Youths with Banner

1947. 22nd Anniv of Nanjing Road Incident, Shanghai.

NE162	NE 58	$2 red and mauve	1·10	2·75
NE163		$5 red and green	1·10	2·75
NE164		$10 red & yellow	1·80	2·75
NE165		$20 red & violet	1·80	2·75
NE166		$30 red & brown	2·40	2·75
NE167		$50 red and blue	4·25	2·75
NE168		$100 red & brown	5·25	2·75
MSNE169 218 × 160 mm. Nos. NE162/8. Imperf			£140	£110

NE 59 Mao Tse-tung

1947. 26th Anniv of Chinese Communist Party.

NE170	NE 59	$10 red	8·75	10·00
NE171		$30 mauve	8·75	10·00
NE172		$50 purple	18·00	24·00
NE173		$100 red	23·00	27·00

NE 60 Hand grasping rifle

NE 61 Mountains and River

1947. 10th Anniv of Outbreak of War with Japan.

NE174	NE 60	$10 orange	4·00	4·25
NE175		$30 green	2·75	4·25
NE176		$50 blue	5·00	4·25
NE177		$100 brown	6·50	4·25
MSNE178 150 × 110 mm. Nos. NE174/7. Imperf			£150	£160

1947. 2nd Anniv of Japanese Surrender.

NE179	NE 61	$10 brown	4·25	10·50
NE180		$30 green	4·25	10·50
NE181		$50 green	8·75	10·50
NE182		$100 brown	11·50	10·50

拾 改
圓 作
1000
(NE 62)

NE 63 Map of Manchuria

1947. Surch as Type NE 62.

NE183	NE 48	$5 on $1 violet	21·00	21·00
NE184	NE 49	$10 on $2 red	21·00	21·00

1947. 16th Anniv of Japanese Attack on Manchuria.

NE185	NE 63	$10 green	4·25	8·00
NE186		$20 mauve	4·25	8·00
NE187		$30 brown	8·00	8·00
NE188		$50 red	8·00	8·00

NE 64 Mao Tse-tung

NE 65 Offices of N.E. Political Council

1947.

NE189	NE 64	$1 purple	1·40	3·75
NE190		$5 green	2·40	3·75
NE191		$10 green	7·25	9·50
NE192		$15 violet	7·25	7·25
NE193		$20 red	75	2·00
NE194		$30 green	75	2·50
NE195		$50 brown	14·00	11·00
NE213		$50 green	90	1·70
NE196		$90 blue	4·25	7·00
NE197		$100 red	65	3·75
NE215		$150 red	2·10	3·00
NE214		$250 lilac	85	2·75
NE228		$300 green	48·00	25·00
NE198		$500 orange	18·00	14·50
NE229		$1,000 yellow	1·40	1·40

For stamps as Type NE 64 but with "YUAN" in top right tablet, see Nos. NE236/40.

1947. 35th Anniv of Chinese Republic.

NE199	NE 65	$10 yellow	28·00	28·00
NE200		$20 red	28·00	28·00
NE201		$100 brown	70·00	70·00

NE 66

NE 67 Tomb of Gen. Li Zhaolin

1947. 11th Anniv of Seizure of Chiang Kai-shek at Xi'an.

NE202	NE 66	$30 red	5·50	9·00
NE203		$90 blue	7·25	10·00
NE204		$150 green	11·00	10·00

1948. 2nd Death Anniv of Gen. Li Zhaolin.

NE205A	NE 67	$30 green	11·00	11·00
NE206A		$150 lilac	11·00	11·00

NE 68 Flag and Globe

NE 69 Youth with Torch

1948. Labour Day.

NE207	NE 68	$50 red	7·25	11·00
NE208		$150 green	2·75	17·00
NE209		$250 violet	2·75	32·00

1948. Youth Day.

NE210	NE 69	$50 green	7·25	6·50
NE211		$150 brown	7·25	10·00
NE212		$250 red	14·00	16·00

壹 改
佰
圓 作
10000
(NE 70)

NE 71 Crane Operator

1948. Surch as Type NE 70.

NE217a	NE 64	$100 on $1 purple	46·00	46·00
NE218		$100 on $15 violet	17·00	16·00
NE219		$300 on $5 green	50·00	23·00
NE220		$300 on $30 green	5·50	9·25
NE221		$300 on $90 blue	5·50	9·25
NE230	NE 49	$500 on $2 red	5·50	3·75
NE222	NE 64	$500 on $50 green	25·00	18·00
NE231	NE 49	$1,500 on $5 orge	5·50	7·00
NE223	NE 64	$1,500 on $150 red	21·00	14·00
NE232	NE 49	$2,500 on $10 blue	7·00	8·25
NE224	NE 64	$2,500 on $300 grn	8·25	11·00

1948. All-China Labour Conference.

NE225	NE 71	$100 red & pink	70	1·50
NE226		$300 brown & yell	2·00	3·00
NE227		$500 blue & green	1·40	1·40

NE 72 Workman, Soldier and Peasant

NE 74 "Production in Field and Industry"

1948. Liberation of the North East.

NE233	NE 72	$500 red	5·50	5·50
NE234		$1,500 green	8·25	8·25
NE235		$2,500 brown	14·50	14·50

1949. As Type NE 64 but "YUAN" at top right.

NE236		$300 green	1·00	2·20
NE237		$500 orange	1·40	1·60
NE238		$1,500 green	45	1·70
NE239		$4,500 brown	45	1·80
NE240		$6,500 blue	45	2·10

1949.

NE241	NE 74	$5,000 blue	4·25	3·00
NE242		$10,000 orange	30	2·75
NE243		$50,000 green	40	3·75
NE244		$100,000 violet	85	11·00

NE 75 Workers and Banners

NE 76 Workers' Procession

1949. Labour Day.

NE245	NE 75	$1,000 red and blue	30	1·00
NE246		$1,500 red and blue	30	1·00
NE247		$4,500 red & brown	45	1·10
NE248		$6,500 brown & grn	45	1·10
NE249		$10,000 purple & bl	55	1·30

1949. 28th Anniv of Chinese Communist Party.

NE250	NE 76	$1,500 red, vio & bl	45	1·00
NE251		$4,500 red, brn & bl	45	1·00
NE252		$6,500 red, pink & bl	85	1·10

NE 77 North-East Heroes, Monument

NE 78 Factory

1949. 4th Anniv of Japanese Surrender.

NE253	NE 77	$1,500 red	85	1·10
NE254		$4,500 green	85	1·10
NE255		$6,500 blue	1·20	1·10

REPRINTS. The note above No. 1401 of China also refers here to Nos. NE257/60, 261/3, 271/4, 286/89 and 312/4.

1949.

NE256	NE 78	$1,500 red	85	1·10

1949. 1st Session of Chinese People's Political Conference. As T 181 of People's Republic but with additional inscr.

NE257		$1,000 blue	3·75	6·00
NE258		$1,500 red	3·75	6·00
NE259		$3,000 green	5·50	6·00
NE260		$4,500 purple	6·50	7·00

1949. World Federation of Trade Unions, Asiatic and Australasian Conference, Peking. As T 182 of People's Republic but with additional inscr.

NE261		$5,000 red	£140	55·00
NE262		$20,000 green	£225	65·00
NE263		$35,000 blue	£325	85·00

貳 改
仟
圓 作
2000
(NE 79)

1949. Surch as T NE 79.

NE264	NE 64	$2,000 on $300 green	21·00	4·00
NE265		$2,000 on $4,500 brown	44·00	30·00
NE266		$2,500 on $1,500 green	65	4·50
NE267		$2,500 on $6,500 blue	22·00	30·00
NE268	NE 78	$5,000 on $1,500 red	55	1·60
NE269	NE 64	$20,000 on $4,500 brown	35	4·50
NE270		$35,000 on $300 green	45	6·25

1950. Chinese People's Political Conference. As T 183/4 of People's Republic but with additional inscr.

NE271		$1,000 red	9·25	12·00
NE272		$1,500 blue	9·25	12·00
NE273		$5,000 purple	18·00	13·00
NE274		$20,000 green	18·00	18·00

1950. As T 185 of People's Republic but with additional four-character inscr.

NE303	NE 34	$250 brown	85	3·25
NE275		$500 green	1·40	1·30
NE276		$1,000 orange	1·60	50
NE277		$1,000 mauve	3·75	1·30
NE306		$2,000 green	1·80	2·30
NE307		$2,500 yellow	85	2·30
NE300		$5,000 orange	5·50	5·75
NE309		$10,000 brown	1·50	2·30
NE310		$12,500 purple	85	4·00
NE283		$20,000 purple	1·10	1·30
NE301		$30,000 red	2·10	14·00
NE284		$35,000 blue	1·10	2·50
NE285		$50,000 green	18·00	2·50
NE302		$100,000 violet	9·25	14·50

1950. Foundation of People's Republic. Additional inscr at left.

NE286	188	$5,000 red, yell & grn	55·00	48·00
NE287		$10,000 red, yell & brn	65·00	48·00
NE288		$20,000 red, yell & pur	75·00	48·00
NE289		$30,000 red, yell & bl	£100	65·00

1950. Peace Campaign. Additional characters below olive branch.

NE290	191	$2,500 brown	9·25	17·00
NE291		$5,000 green	14·00	17·00
NE292		$20,000 blue	18·00	17·00

1950. 1st Anniv of People's Republic. Additional characters at left. Flag in red, yellow and brown.

NE293	193	$1,000 violet	32·00	25·00
NE294		$2,500 brown	48·00	32·00
NE295		$5,000 green (44 × 53 mm)	55·00	41·00
NE296		$10,000 green	75·00	41·00
NE297		$20,000 blue	£110	65·00

1950. 1st All-China Postal Conference. Additional characters at right.

NE298	194	$2,500 orange & green	11·00	8·75
NE299		$5,000 green and red	11·00	8·75

1950. Sino-Soviet Treaty. Additional characters in top right-hand coner.

NE312	195	$2,500 red	18·00	9·25
NE313		$5,000 green	23·00	9·25
NE314		$20,000 blue	23·00	9·25

PARCELS POST STAMPS

NEP 82

1951.

NEP315A	NEP 82	$1,000,000 violet	£180	—
NEP316B		$300,000 purple	£375	—
NEP317B		$500,000 green	£650	—
NEP318B		$1,000,000 red	£1000	—

E. North-West China People's Post

NW 25 Mao Tse-tung

NW 26 Great Wall

1949. Imperf.

NW 97	NW 25	$50 pink	1·60	2·30
NW 98	NW 26	$100 blue	90	1·00
NW 99	NW 25	$200 orange	2·50	3·75
NW100	NW 26	$400 brown	3·25	3·75

F. South-West China People's Post

SW 3 Zhu De, Mao Tse-tung and Troops

SW 4 Map of China with Flag in S.W.

1949.

SW 9	SW 3	$10 blue	6·25	4·50
SW10		$20 purple	25	2·75
SW11		$30 orange	25	1·25
SW12		$50 green	60	95
SW13		$100 red	30	75
SW14		$200 blue	2·20	95
SW15		$300 violet	6·25	1·50
SW16		$500 grey	9·50	4·00
SW17		$1,000 purple	12·50	9·25
SW18		$2,000 green	23·00	19·00
SW19		$5,000 orange	25·00	25·00

For other values in this design see East China, Nos. EC378/82.

1950. Liberation of the South West.

SW20	SW 4	$20 blue	30	1·30
SW21		$30 green	2·00	2·75
SW22		$50 red	40	1·60
SW23		$100 brown	95	1·60

(SW 5) ($3,000)

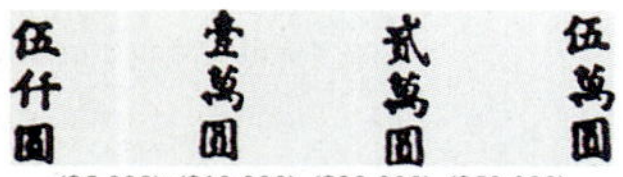
($5,000) ($10,000) ($20,000) ($50,000)

1950. Surch as Type SW **5** (characters in left-hand column of surcharge differ as indicated in illustrations and footnote).

SW24	SW 4	$60 on $30 green	19·00	15·00
SW25		$150 on $30 green	18·00	13·00
SW26		$300 on $20 blue	1·50	2·75
SW27		$300 on $100 brown	19·00	7·50
SW28		$1,500 on $100 brown	19·00	12·50
SW29		$3,000 on $50 red	10·50	9·00
SW30		$5,000 on $50 red	5·00	7·00
SW31		$10,000 on $50 red	50·00	25·00
SW32		$20,000 on $50 red	3·75	25·00
SW33		$50,000 on $50 red	5·00	50·00

Nos. SW24 and SW26/7 have three characters in left-hand column; Nos. SW25 and SW28 have five.

G. Chinese People's Republic

1949. Yuans.
1955. 100 fen = 1 yuan.

GUM or NO GUM. Nos. 1401/1891 were issued without gum (except Nos. 1843/5 and 1850/7). From No. 1892 onwards all postage stamps were issued with gum, unless otherwise stated. From 1965 some issues seem to have no gum, though in fact they bear an adhesive substance.

SERIAL MARKINGS. Issues other than definitive issues are divided into two categories: "commemorative" and "special". Figures below the design of each stamp of such issues indicate: (a) serial number of the issue; (b) number of stamps in the issue; (c) number of stamps within the issue; and (d) year of issue (from No. 1557 on). Neither chronological order of issue nor sequence of value is always strictly followed. From No. 2343 these serial markings were omitted until No. 2433.

REPRINTS were later made in replacement of exhausted stocks by the Chinese Postal Administration for sale to stamp collectors and were not available for postal purposes. Nos. 1401/11, 1432/5, 1456/8, 1464/73, 1507/9, 1524/37 and 1543/52. Our prices are for originals. For notes describing the distinguishing features of the reprints, see Stanley Gibbons Part 17 (China) Catalogue.

For other values in the following types see North East China.

181 Celebrations at Gate of Heavenly Peace, Peking

182 Globe, Fist and Banner

1949. Celebration of First Session of Chinese People's Political Conference.

1401	181	$30 blue	2·10	1·30
1402		$50 red	2·10	1·70
1403		$100 green	2·10	1·70
1404		$200 purple	2·10	1·70

1949. World Federation of Trade Unions. Asiatic and Australasian Congress, Peking.

1405	182	$100 red	6·25	5·00
1406		$300 green	6·25	5·00
1407		$500 blue	6·25	5·00

183 Conference Hall

184 Mao Tse-tung

1950. Chinese People's Political Conference.

1408	183	$50 red	2·75	2·50
1409		$100 blue	2·75	2·50
1410	184	$300 purple	2·75	2·30
1411		$500 green	2·75	2·30

185 Gate of Heavenly Peace, Peking

1950.

1412	185	$200 green	12·50	1·50
1413		$300 lake	60	90
1414		$500 red	60	35
1415		$800 orange	55·00	60
1420a		$1,000 lilac	95	15
1417		$2,000 olive	13·50	2·00
1420b		$3,000 brown	95	15
1418		$5,000 pink	60	1·40
1419		$8,000 blue	60	11·50
1420c		$10,000 brown	95	15

See also Nos. 1481a/7 and 1493/8.

(186)

187 Harvesters and Ox

1950. Surch as T **186**. Perf or roul.

1427	148	$100 on (–) mauve	65	1·70
1428	149	$200 on (–) red	2·40	1·30
1429	147	$300 on (–) green	35	90
1424	146	$500 on (–) orange	60	40
1430		$800 on (–) orange	3·25	35
1426		$1,000 on (–) orange	60	60

1950. Unissued stamp of East China surch.

1431	187	$20,000 on $10,000 red	£500	47·00

188 Mao Tse-tung, Flag and Parade

1950. Foundation of People's Republic on 1 October 1949.

1432	188	$800 red, yellow & green	18·00	9·00
1433		$1,000 red, yellow & brn	15·00	10·50
1434		$2,000 red, yellow & pur	27·00	10·50
1435		$3,000 red, yellow & blue	36·00	13·00

(189)

(190)

1950. Stamps of North Eastern Provinces surch as T **189**.

1436	5	$50 on 20c. green	3·75	5·00
1437		$50 on 25c. brown	4·00	2·40
1438		$50 on 50c. orange	85	2·00
1439		$100 on $2.50 blue	1·90	2·00
1440		$100 on $3 brown	2·50	2·00
1441		$100 on $4 brown	1·50	7·25
1442		$100 on $5 green	2·30	1·50
1443		$100 on $10 red	30·00	10·50
1444		$400 on $20 green	70·00	29·00
1445		$400 on $44 red	1·20	4·75
1446		$400 on $65 green	£110	46·00
1447		$400 on $100 green	26·00	6·50
1448		$400 on $200 brown	£120	11·50
1449		$400 on $300 green	£120	15·00

1950. Nos. 1344/7 and unissued values of Nationalist China (Whistling Swans) surch as T **190**.

1450	169	$50 on 10c. blue	20	35
1451		$100 on 16c. green	15	40
1452		$100 on 50c. green	20	35
1453		$200 on $1 orange	25	25
1453a		$200 on $2 blue	6·25	70
1454		$400 on $5 red	35	35
1455		$400 on $10 green	35	85
1455a		$400 on $20 purple	95	2·30

Nos. 1451/2 are imperf.

191 "Peace" (after Picasso)

192 Gate of Heavenly Peace, Peking

1950. Peace Campaign (1st issue).

1456	191	$400 brown	9·75	5·50
1457		$800 green	9·75	5·50
1458		$2,000 blue	9·75	5·50

See also Nos. 1510/12 and 1590/2.

1950. Clouds redrawn.

1481a	192	$100 blue	1·00	1·00
1482		$200 green	6·50	2·75
1483		$300 lake	55	3·50
1483a		$400 green	6·00	1·10
1484		$500 red	60	1·30
1462		$800 orange	12·50	75
1485a		$1,000 violet	75	1·00
1463		$2,000 olive	3·75	1·50
1486a		$3,000 brown	60	5·00
1487		$5,000 pink	60	7·00

193 Flag of People's Republic

194 "Communications"

1950. 1st Anniv of People's Republic. Flag in red, yellow and brown.

1464	193	$100 violet	14·00	5·25
1465		$400 brown	20·00	6·75
1466		$800 green (44 × 53 mm)	20·00	5·25
1467		$1,000 olive	28·00	10·50
1468		$2,000 blue	40·00	13·00

1950. 1st All-China Postal Conference.

1469	194	$400 brown and green	10·50	4·00
1470		$800 green and red	10·50	4·00

195 Stalin greets Mao Tse-tung

1950. Sino-Soviet Treaty.

1471	195	$400 red	12·00	7·00
1472		$800 green	12·00	6·75
1473		$2,000 blue	14·00	7·00

(196)

(197)

1950. Nos. EC364/5a, EC367 and EC370/1 of East China People's Post surch as T **196**.

1474		$50 on $10 blue	25	25
1475		$100 on $15 red	25	25
1476		$300 on $50 red	1·40	70
1477		$400 on $1,600 purple	2·20	1·00
1478		$400 on $2,000 lilac	95	55

1950. Stamps of East China surch as T **197**.

1479	EC 112	$50 on $10 blue	20	20
1480		$400 on $15 red	40	20
1481		$400 on $2,000 green	2·00	1·00

198 Temple of Heaven and Ilyushin Il-18

1951. Air.

1488	198	$1,000 red	25	50
1489		$3,000 green	35	30
1490		$5,000 orange	30	30
1491		$10,000 green and purple	50	50
1492		$30,000 brn and blue	6·75	2·50

1951. Pink network background.

1493	185	$10,000 brown	1·40	10·50
1494		$20,000 olive	1·40	8·75
1495		$30,000 green	£140	43·00
1496		$50,000 violet	90·00	22·00
1497		$100,000 red	£2750	£200
1498		$200,000 blue	£2750	£200

(200)

201 Mao Tse-tung

1951. Surch as T **200**. Perf or roul.

1503	148	$5 on (–) mauve	2·10	1·60
1500	147	$10 on (–) green	65	65
1501	149	$15 on (–) red	35	65
1506	146	$25 on (–) orange	50	1·00

1951. 30th Anniv of Chinese Communist Party.

1507	201	$400 brown	5·50	3·75
1508		$500 green	5·50	3·75
1509		$800 red	5·50	3·75

202 Dove of Peace, after Picasso

1951. Peace Campaign (2nd issue).

1510	202	$400 brown	13·00	3·75
1511		$800 green	13·00	3·50
1512		$1,000 violet	13·00	5·00

(203)

204 National Emblem

1951. Money Order stamps as North China, Type NC **77**, surch with T **203**. Perf or roul.

1513		$50 on $2 green	3·25	3·25
1515		$50 on $5 orange	85	1·10
1517		$50 on $50 grey	85	80

1951. National Emblem Issue. Yellow network background.

1519	204	$100 blue	5·75	4·25
1520		$200 brown	5·75	4·25
1521		$400 orange	5·75	4·50
1522		$500 green	5·75	3·50
1523		$800 red	5·75	3·50

205 Lu Hsun

1951. 15th Death Anniv of Lu Hsun (author).

1524	205	$400 violet	4·25	3·50
1525		$800 green	6·25	2·75

206 Rebels at Chintien

1951. Centenary of Taiping Rebellion.

1526	206	$400 green	6·50	4·75
1527		$800 red	6·50	4·00
1528	–	$800 orange	6·50	4·25
1529	–	$1,000 blue	6·50	4·00

DESIGN: Nos. 1528/9, Coin and Documents of Taiping "Heavenly Kingdom of Great Peace".

207 Peasants and Tractor

1952. Agrarian Reform.

1530	**207**	$100 red	4·25	2·75
1531		$200 blue	4·25	2·75
1532		$400 brown	4·25	1·80
1533		$800 green	4·25	1·80

208 The Potala, Lhasa

209 "Child Protection"

1952. Liberation of Tibet.

1534	**208**	$400 red	6·00	3·75
1535	–	$800 green	6·00	3·75
1536	**208**	$800 red	6·00	3·25
1537	–	$1,000 violet	6·00	3·25

DESIGN: Nos. 1535, 1537 Tibetan ploughing with yaks.

1952. Int Child Protection Conference, Vienna.

1538	**209**	$400 green	50	30
1539		$800 blue	60	35

210 Hammer and Sickle

211 Gymnast

1952. Labour Day. Dated "1952".

1540	**210**	$800 red	35	20
1541	–	$800 green	25	15
1542	–	$800 brown	35	20

DESIGNS: No. 1541, Hand and dove; No. 1542, Hammer, dove and ear of corn.

1952. Gymnastics by Radio. As T **211**.

1543	$400 red (14–17)	3·25	2·30
1544	$400 deep blue (18–21)	3·25	2·30
1545	$400 purple (22–25)	3·25	2·30
1546	$400 green (26–29)	3·25	2·30
1547	$400 red (30–33)	3·25	2·30
1548	$400 blue (34–37)	3·25	2·30
1549	$400 orange (38–41)	3·25	2·30
1550	$400 violet (42–45)	3·25	2·30
1551	$400 bistre (46–49)	3·25	2·30
1552	$400 pale blue (50–53)	3·25	2·30

DESIGNS: Various gymnastic exercises, the stamps in each colour being arranged in blocks of four throughout the sheet, each block showing four stages of the exercise depicted. Where two stages are the same, the stamps differ only in the serial number in brackets, in the right-hand corner of the bottom margin of the stamp. The serial numbers are shown above after the colours of the stamps.

Prices are for single stamps.

212 "A Winter Hunt" (A.D. 386–580)

1952. "Glorious Mother Country" (1st issue). Tun Huang Mural Paintings.

1553	**212**	$800 sepia	50	25
1554	–	$800 brown	50	25
1555	–	$800 slate	50	25
1556	–	$800 purple	50	25

PAINTINGS: No. 1554, "Benefactor" (A.D. 581–617). No. 1555, "Celestial Flight" (A.D. 618–906). No. 1556, "Tiger" (A.D. 618–906).

See also Nos. 1565/8, 1593/96, 1601/4 and 1628/31.

213 Marco Polo Bridge, Lukouchiao

1952. 15th Anniv of War with Japan.

1557	**213**	$800 blue	45	30
1558	–	$800 green	70	45
1559	–	$800 plum	45	30
1560	–	$800 red	60	25

DESIGNS (dated "1937–1952"): No. 1558, Victory at Pinghsingkwan; No. 1559, Departure of New Fourth Army from Central China; No. 1560, Mao Tse-tung and Chu The.

214 Airman, Sailor and Soldier

217 Dove of Peace over Pacific Ocean

216 Huai River Barrage

1952. 25th Anniv of People's Liberation Army.

1561	**214**	$800 red	35	25
1562	–	$800 green	50	30
1563	–	$800 violet	35	25
1564	–	$800 brown	35	15

DESIGNS—HORIZ: No. 1562, Soldier, tanks and guns; 1563, Sailor and destroyers; 1564, Pilot, Ilyushin Il-4 DB-3 bomber and Mikoyan Gurevich MiG-15 jet fighters.

1952. "Glorious Mother Country" (2nd issue).

1565	**216**	$800 violet	30	15
1566	–	$800 red	30	15
1567	–	$800 purple	30	25
1568	–	$800 green	30	25

DESIGNS: No. 1566, Chungking–Chengtu railway viaduct; 1567, Oil refinery; 1568, Tractor, disc harrows and combine drill.

1952. Asia and Pacific Ocean Peace Conference.

1569	**217**	$400 purple	35	25
1570	–	$800 orange	35	25
1571	**217**	$800 red	35	25
1572	–	$2,500 green	35	25

DESIGNS—HORIZ: Nos. 1570 and 1572, Doves and globe.

218 Peasants collecting food for the Front

1952. 2nd Anniv of Chinese Volunteer Force in Korea.

1573	–	$800 blue	35	20
1574	**218**	$800 red	35	20
1575	–	$800 violet	35	20
1576	–	$800 brown	35	20

DESIGNS (dated "1950–1952"): HORIZ: No. 1573, Marching troops. No. 1575, Infantry attack. No. 1576, Meeting of Chinese and North Korean soldiers.

220 Textile Worker

1953. International Women's Day.

1578	**220**	$800 red	50	25
1579	–	$800 green	50	25

DESIGN: No. 1579, Woman harvesting grain.

221 Shepherdess

222 Karl Marx

1953.

1580	–	$50 purple	80	20
1581	**221**	$200 green	1·20	25
1582	–	$250 blue	7·00	1·80
1583	–	$800 turquoise	60	20
1584	–	$1,600 grey	80	40
1585	–	$2,000 orange	1·40	25

DESIGNS: $50, Mill girl; $250, Carved lion; $800, Lathe-operator; $1,600, Miners; $2, Old Palace, Peking.

1953. 135th Birth Anniv of Karl Marx.

1586	**222**	$400 brown	65	25
1587		$800 green	60	25

223 Workers and Flags

224 Dove of Peace

1953. 7th National Labour Union Conference.

1588	**223**	$400 blue	60	25
1589		$800 red	45	25

1953. Peace Campaign (3rd issue).

1590	**224**	$250 green	70	20
1591		$400 brown	55	15
1592		$800 violet	80	15

225 Horseman and Steed (A.D. 386–580)

1953. "Glorious Mother Country" (3rd issue).

1593	**225**	$800 green	75	25
1594	–	$800 orange	40	25
1595	–	$800 blue	45	25
1596	–	$800 red	40	25

PAINTINGS: No. 1594, Court players (A.D. 386–580). No. 1595, Battle scene (A.D. 581–617). No. 1596, Ox-drawn palanquin (A.D. 618–906).

226 Mao Tse-tung and Stalin at Kremlin

1953. 35th Anniv of Russian Revolution.

1597	**226**	$800 green	80	35
1598	–	$800 red	55	25
1599	–	$800 blue	70	25
1600	–	$800 brown	65	25

DESIGNS—HORIZ: No. 1598, Lenin addressing revolutionaries. VERT: No. 1599, Statue of Stalin; No. 1600, Stalin making speech.

227 Compass (300 B.C.)

228 Rabelais (writer)

1953. "Glorious Mother Country" (4th issue). Scientific instruments.

1601	**227**	$800 black	50	25
1602	–	$800 green	35	25
1603	–	$800 slate	40	25
1604	–	$800 brown	40	25

DESIGNS: No. 1602, Seismoscope (A.D. 132); 1603, Drum cart for measuring distances (A.D. 300); 1604, Armillary sphere (A.D. 1437).

1953. Famous Men.

1605	**228**	$250 green	50	25
1606	–	$400 purple	50	30
1607	–	$800 blue	50	25
1608	–	$2,200 brown	50	25

PORTRAITS: $400, Jose Marti (Cuban revolutionary). $800, Chu Yuan (poet). $2,200, Copernicus (astronomer).

229 Flax Mill, Harbin

1954. Industrial Development.

1609	**229**	$100 brown	30	20
1610	–	$200 green	30	20
1611	–	$250 violet	30	20
1612	–	$400 sepia	30	20
1613	–	$800 purple	30	20
1614	–	$800 blue	35	20
1615	–	$2,000 red	30	20
1616	–	$3,200 brown	40	25

DESIGNS: No. 1610, Tangku Harbour; 1611, Tienshui–Lanchow Railway; 1612, Heavy machine works; 1613, Blast furnace; 1614, Open-cast mines, Fuhsin; 1615, North-East Electric power station; 1616, Geological survey team.

230 Gate of Heavenly Peace, Peking

231 Statue of Lenin and Stalin at Gorki

232 Lenin Speaking

233 Painted Pottery (c. 2000 B.C.)

1954.

1617	**230**	$50 red	25	20
1618		$100 blue	25	20
1619		$200 green	25	20
1620		$250 blue	3·25	55
1621		$400 green	30	20
1622		$800 orange	25	20
1623		$1,600 grey	25	70
1624		$2,000 olive	25	35

1954. 30th Death Anniv of Lenin.

1625	**231**	$400 green	90	30
1626	–	$800 brown	70	30
1627	**232**	$2,000 red	1·70	40

DESIGN: (25 × 37 mm) $800, Lenin (full-face portrait).

1954. "Glorious Mother Country" (5th issue).

1628	**233**	$800 brown	45	25
1629	–	$800 black	45	25
1630	–	$800 turquoise	45	25
1631	–	$800 lake	45	25

DESIGNS—As Type **233**: No. 1629, Musical stone (1200 B.C.); 1630, Bronze basin (816 B.C.); 1631, Lacquered wine cup and cosmetic tray (403–221 B.C.).

234 Heavy Rolling Mill

235 Statue of Stalin

1954. Anshan Steel Works.

1632	–	$400 turquoise	60	35
1633	**234**	$800 purple	60	35

DESIGN: $400, Seamless steel-tubing mill.

1954. 1st Death Anniv of Stalin.

1634	**235**	$400 black	1·00	30
1635	–	$800 sepia	55	25
1636	–	$2,000 red	1·00	35

DESIGNS—VERT: $800, Full-face portrait of Stalin (26 × 37 mm). HORIZ: $2, Stalin and hydro-electric station ($42\frac{1}{2}$ × 25 mm).

236 Exhibition Building

1954. Russian Economic and Cultural Exn, Peking.

1637	**236**	$800 brown on yellow	10·00	4·75

237 The Universal Fixture

1954. Workers' Inventions.
1638 **237** $400 green 45 20
1639 – $800 red 45 20
DESIGN: $800, The reverse repeater.

238 Woman Worker

239 Rejoicing Crowds

1954. 1st Session of National Congress.
1640 **238** $400 purple 25 20
1641 **239** $800 red 75 25

240 "New Constitution"

1954. Constitution Commemoration.
1642 **240** $400 brown on buff . . 45 20
1643 $800 red on yellow . . . 55 25

241 Pylons

242 Nurse and Red Cross Worker

1955. Development of Overhead Transmission of Electricity.
1644 **241** $800 blue . . . . 1·10 35

1955. 50th Anniv of Chinese Red Cross.
1645 **242** 8f. red and green . . . . 8·75 1·60

243 Miner

244 Gate of Heavenly Peace, Peking

1955.
1646 **243** ½f. brown . . . . . . 2·10 20
1647 – 1f. purple . . . . . . 2·10 20
1648 – 2f. green . . . . . . 2·75 20
1648a – 2½f. blue . . . . . . 2·40 20
1649 – 4f. green . . . . . . 2·40 30
1650 – 8f. red . . . . 3·25 45
1650b – 10f. red . . . . . . 19·00 20
1651 – 20f. blue . . . . . . 7·50 25
1652 – 50f. grey . . . . . . 7·00 30
1653 **244** 1y. red . . . . 1·10 25
1654 2y. brown . . . . . . 1·80 25
1655 5y. grey . . . . 3·25 45
1656 10y. red . . . . 6·50 4·50
1657 20y. violet . . . . . . 10·00 15·00
DESIGNS—As Type **243**: 1f. Lathe operator; 2f. Airman; 2½f. Nurse; 4f. Soldier; 8f. Foundry worker; 10f. Chemist; 20f. Farm girl; 50f. Sailor.

246 Workmen and Industrial Plant

247 Chang-Heng (A.D. 78–139, astronomer)

1955. 5th Anniv of Sino–Russian Treaty.
1658 – 8f. brown . . . . 5·75 75
1659 **246** 20f. olive . . . . 6·50 1·30
DESIGN—HORIZ: (37 × 32 mm): 8f. Stalin and Mao Tse-tung.

1955. Scientists of Ancient China.
1660 **247** 8f. sepia on buff . . . . 2·40 40
1661 – 8f. blue on buff . . . . 2·40 40
1662 – 8f. black on buff . . . . 2·40 40
1663 – 8f. purple on buff . . . 2·40 40
MS1663a Four sheets, each 63 × 90 mm. Nos. 1660/3 but printed on white paper. Imperf 95·00 29·00
PORTRAITS: No. 1661, Tsu Chung-chi (429–500, mathematician). No. 1662, Chang-Sui (683–727, astronomer). No. 1663, Li-Shih-chen (1518–1593, pharmacologist).

248 Foundry

1955. Five Year Plan. Frames in black.
1664 **248** 8f. red and orange . . . 80 20
1665 – 8f. brown and yellow . . 80 20
1666 – 8f. yellow and black . . 80 20
1667 – 8f. violet and blue . . . 80 20
1668 – 8f. yellow and brown . . 80 20
1669 – 8f. yellow and red . . . 80 20
1670 – 8f. grey and blue 80 20
1671 – 8f. orange and black . . 80 20
1672 – 8f. yellow and brown . . 80 20
1673 – 8f. red and orange . . . 80 20
1674 – 8f. yellow and green . . 80 20
1675 – 8f. red and yellow . . . 80 20
1676 – 8f. yellow and grey . . . 80 20
1677 – 8f. yellow and blue . . . 80 20
1678 – 8f. orange and blue . . . 80 20
1679 – 8f. yellow and brown . . 80 20
1680 – 8f. red and brown . . . 80 20
1681 – 8f. yellow and brown . . 80 20
DESIGNS—No. 1665, Electricity pylons; No. 1666, Mining machinery; No. 1667, Oil tankers and derricks; No. 1668, Heavy machinery workshop; No. 1669, Factory guard and industrial plant; No. 1670, Textile machinery; No. 1671, Factory workers; No. 1672, Combine-harvester; No. 1673, Dairy herd and farm girl; No. 1674, Dam; No. 1675, Artists decorating pottery; No. 1676, Lorry; No. 1677, Freighter and wharf; No. 1678, Surveyors; No. 1679, Students; No. 1680, Man, woman and child; No. 1681, Workers' rest home.

249 Lenin

1955. 85th Birth Anniv of Lenin.
1682 **249** 8f. blue . . . . 7·50 40
1683 20f. lake . . . . 7·50 2·00

250 Engels

1955. 60th Death Anniv of Engels.
1684 **250** 8f. red . . . . 7·50 40
1685 20f. sepia . . . . 7·50 2·00

251 Capture of Lu Ting Bridge

1955. 20th Anniv of Long March by Communist Army.
1686 **251** 8f. red . . . . 7·50 45
1687 – 8f. blue . . . . 7·50 1·90
DESIGN—VERT: (28 × 46 mm): No. 1687, Crossing the Ta Hsueh Mountains.

252 Convoy of Lorries

1956. Opening of Sikang–Tibet and Tsinghai–Tibet Highways.
1688 **252** 4f. blue 40 20
1689 – 8f. brown 40 20
1690 – 8f. red 40 25
DESIGNS—VERT: (21 × 42 mm): No. 1689, Suspension bridge: Tatu River. HORIZ: As T **252**: No. 1690, Opening ceremony, Lhasa.

254 Gate of Heavenly Peace

1956. Views of Peking.
1691 – 4f. red . . . . 2·50 25
1692 – 4f. green . . . . 2·50 25
1693 **254** 8f. red . . . . 2·50 25
1694 – 8f. blue . . . . 2·50 25
1695 – 8f. brown . . . . 2·50 25
VIEWS: No. 1691, Summer Palace; 1692, Peihai Park; 1694, Temple of Heaven; 1695, Great Throne Hall, Tai Ho Palace.

255 Salt Production

1956. Archaeological Discoveries at Chengtu.
1696 **255** 4f. green 35 25
1697 – 4f. black 35 25
1698 – 8f. sepia 35 25
1699 – 8f. sepia 35 25
DESIGNS—HORIZ: (Brick carvings of Tung Han Dynasty, A.D. 25–200): No. 1697, Residence; No. 1698, Hunting and farming; No. 1699, Carriage crossing bridge.

256

257 Gate of Heavenly Peace, Peking

1956. National Savings.
1700 **256** 4f. buff . . . . 5·00 55
1701 8f. red . . . . 5·75 55

1956. 8th National Communist Party Congress.
1702 **257** 4f. green . . . . 4·75 40
1703 8f. red . . . . 5·00 40
1704 16f. red . . . . 5·25 75

258 Dr. Sun Yat-sen

259 Putting the Shot

1956. 90th Birth Anniv of Dr. Sun Yat-sen.
1705 **258** 4f. brown . . . . 8·00 25
1706 8f. blue . . . . 7·00 1·30

1955. 1st Chinese Workers' Athletic Meeting, 1955. Inscr "1955". Flower in red and green; inscr in brown.
1707 **259** 4f. lake . . . . 1·30 25
1708 – 4f. purple (Weightlifting) 1·30 25
1709 – 8f. green (Sprinting) . . 1·30 25
1710 – 8f. blue (Football) . . . 1·30 25
1711 – 8f. brown (Cycling) . . . 1·30 25

260 Assembly Line

1957. Lorry Production.
1712 – 4f. brown 50 25
1713 **260** 8f. blue 60 25
DESIGN: 4f. Changchun motor plant.

261 Nanchang Revolutionaries

1957. 30th Anniv of People's Liberation Army.
1714 **261** 4f. violet . . . . 8·75 80
1715 – 4f. green . . . . 8·75 1·00
1716 – 8f. brown . . . . 8·75 70
1717 – 8f. blue . . . . 8·75 70
DESIGNS: No. 1715, Meeting of Red Armies at Chinkangshan; No. 1716, Liberation Army crossing the Yellow River; No. 1717, Liberation of Nanking.

262 Congress Emblem

263 Yangtse River Bridge

1957. 4th WFTU Congress, Leipzig.
1718 **262** 8f. brown . . . . 3·75 40
1719 22f. blue . . . . 3·75 55

1957. Opening of Yangtse River Bridge, Wuhan.
1720 **263** 8f. red 50 25
1721 – 20f. blue 50 20
DESIGN: 20f. Aerial view of bridge.

264 Fireworks over Kremlin

265 Airport Scene

1957. 40th Anniv of Russian Revolution.
1722 **264** 4f. red . . . . 6·25 35
1723 – 8f. sepia . . . . 6·25 35
1724 – 20f. green . . . . . . 6·25 35
1725 – 22f. brown . . . . . . 6·25 35
1726 – 32f. blue . . . . 6·25 1·10
DESIGNS: 8f. Soviet emblem, globe and broken chains; 20f. Dove of Peace and plant; 22f. Hands supporting book bearing portraits of Marx and Lenin; 32f. Electricity power pylon.

1957. Air.
1727 **265** 16f. blue . . . . 10·50 35
1728 – 28f. olive . . . . 10·50 35
1729 – 35f. black . . . . 10·50 2·40
1730 – 52f. blue . . . . 10·50 85
DESIGNS—Lisunov Li-2 over: 28f. mountain highway; 35f. railway tracks; 52f. collier at station.

266 Yellow River Dam and Power Station

1957. Harnessing of the Yellow River.
1731 – 4f. orange . . . . 8·75 1·30
1732 **266** 4f. blue . . . . 8·75 1·80
1733 – 8f. lake . . . . 8·75 60
1734 – 8f. green . . . . 8·75 60

DESIGNS: No. 1731, Map of Yellow River; No. 1733, Yellow River ferry; No. 1734, Aerial view of irrigation on Yellow River.

267 Ploughing

1957. Co-operative Agriculture. Multicoloured.
1735 8f. Farmer enrolling for farm 50 25
1736 8f. Type **267** 50 25
1737 8f. Tree-planting 50 25
1738 8f. Harvesting 50 25

268 "Peaceful Construction"

269 High Peak Pagoda, Tenfeng

1958. Completion of First Five Year Plan.
1739 **268** 4f. green and cream . . 35 25
1740 – 8f. red and cream . . . 35 25
1741 – 16f. blue and cream . . 35 25
DESIGNS: 8f. "Industry and Agriculture" (grapple and wheat-sheaves); 16f. "Communications and Transport" (steam train on viaduct and ship).

1958. Ancient Chinese Pagodas.
1742 **269** 8f. brown . . . . 1·20 25
1743 – 8f. blue . . . . 1·20 25
1744 – 8f. brown . . . . 1·20 25
1745 – 8f. green . . . . 1·20 25
DESIGNS: No. 1743, One Thousand League Pagoda, Tali; No. 1744, Buddha Pagoda, Yinghsien; No. 1745, Flying Rainbow Pagoda, Hungchao.

270 Trilobite of Hao Li Shan

271

1958. Chinese Fossils.
1746 **270** 4f. blue 70 25
1747 – 8f. sepia 70 25
1748 – 16f. green 70 25
DESIGNS: 8f. Dinosaur of Lufeng; 16f. "Sinomegaceros pachyosteus" (deer).

1958. Unveiling of People's Heroes Monument, Peking.
1749 **271** 8f. red . . . . 15·00 1·50
MS1749a 137 × 87 mm. No. 1749. Imperf . . . . £110 50·00

272 Karl Marx (after Zhukov)

273 Cogwheels of Industry

1958. 140th Birth Anniv of Karl Marx.
1750 **272** 8f. brown . . . . 7·75 95
1751 – 22f. myrtle . . . . . . 7·75 1·90
DESIGN: 22f. Marx addressing German workers' Educational Association, London.

1958. 8th All-China Trade Union Congress, Peking.
1752 **273** 4f. blue . . . . 7·00 2·10
1753 8f. purple . . . . 7·00 1·30

274 Federation Emblem

275 Mother and Child

1958. 4th International Democratic Women's Federation Congress, Vienna.
1754 **274** 8f. blue . . . . 6·50 25
1755 20f. green . . . . 6·50 3·00

1958. Chinese Children. Multicoloured.
1756 8f. Type **275** . . . . 10·50 1·60
1757 8f. Watering sunflowers . . 10·50 1·60
1758 8f. "Hide and seek" . . . . 10·50 1·60
1759 8f. Children sailing boat . . 10·50 1·60

276 Kuan Han-ching (playwright)

277 Peking Planetarium

1958. 700th Anniv of Works of Kuan Han-ching.
1760 – 4f. green on cream . . . 8·50 3·25
1761 **276** 8f. purple on cream . . 8·50 55
1762 – 20f. black on cream . . 8·50 85
MS1762a 100 × 128 mm. Nos. 1760/2 but printed on white paper. Imperf £180 70·00
DESIGNS: Scenes from Han-ching's comedies: 4f. "The Butterfly Dream"; 20f. "The Riverside Pavilion".

1958. Peking Planetarium.
1763 **277** 8f. green . . . . 4·25 75
1764 – 20f. blue . . . . 4·25 1·50
DESIGN: 20f. Planetarium in operation.

278 Marx and Engels

279 Tundra Swan and Radio Pylon

1958. 110th Anniv of "Communist Manifesto".
1765 **278** 4f. purple . . . . 7·25 3·50
1766 – 8f. blue . . . . 7·25 25
DESIGN: 8f. Front cover of first German "Communist Manifesto".

1958. Organization of Socialist Countries' Postal Administrations Conference, Moscow.
1767 **279** 4f. blue . . . . 6·00 75
1768 8f. green . . . . 6·00 2·20

280 Peony and Doves

281 Chang Heng's Weather-cock

1958. International Disarmament Conf, Stockholm.
1769 **280** 4f. red . . . . 8·75 80
1770 – 8f. green . . . . 8·75 5·25
1771 – 22f. brown . . . . . . 8·75 2·40
DESIGNS: 8f. Olive branch; 22f. Atomic symbol and factory plant.

1958. Chinese Meteorology.
1772 **281** 8f. black on yellow . . . 60 25
1773 – 8f. black on blue 60 25
1774 – 8f. black on green . . . 60 25
DESIGNS: No. 1773. Meteorological balloon; No. 1774, Typhoon signal-tower.

282 Union Emblem within figure "5"

283 Chrysanthemum

1958. 5th International Students' Union Congress, Peking.
1775 **282** 8f. purple . . . . 6·00 65
1776 22f. green . . . . 6·00 90

1958. Flowers.
1777 – 1½f. mauve (Peony) . . . 6·00 60
1778 – 3f. green (Lotus) . . . . 6·00 1·90
1779 **283** 5f. orange . . . . 6·00 45

284 Telegraph Building, Peking

1958. Opening of Peking Telegraph Building.
1780 **284** 4f. olive . . . . 1·80 25
1781 8f. red . . . . 1·80 25

285 Exhibition Emblem and Symbols

1958. National Exhibition of Industry and Communications.
1782 **285** 8f. green . . . . 5·25 65
1783 – 8f. red . . . . 5·25 65
1784 – 8f. brown . . . . 5·25 2·40
DESIGNS: No. 1783, Chinese dragon riding the waves; No. 1784, Horses in the sky.

286 Labourer on Reservoir Site

1958. Inauguration of Ming Tombs Reservoir.
1785 **286** 4f. brown 60 25
1786 – 8f. blue 60 25
DESIGN: 8f. Ming Tombs Reservoir.

287 Sputnik and ancient Theodolite

1958. Russian Sputnik Commemoration.
1787 **287** 4f. red . . . . 2·75 30
1788 – 8f. violet . . . . 2·75 30
1789 – 10f. green . . . . 2·75 1·50
DESIGNS: 8f. Third Russian sputnik encircling globe; 10f. Three Russian sputniks encircling globe.

288 Chinese and Korean Soldiers

1958. Return of Chinese People's Volunteers from Korea.
1790 **288** 8f. purple . . . . 1·10 25
1791 – 8f. brown . . . . 1·10 25
1792 – 8f. red . . . . 1·10 25
DESIGNS: No. 1791, Chinese soldier embracing Korean woman; No. 1792, Girl presenting bouquet to Chinese soldier.

289 Forest Landscape

1958. Afforestation Campaign.
1793 **289** 8f. green . . . . 2·20 1·00
1794 – 8f. slate . . . . 2·20 40
1795 – 8f. violet . . . . 2·20 40
1796 – 8f. blue . . . . 2·20 65
DESIGNS—VERT: No. 1794, Forest patrol. HORIZ: No. 1795, Tree-felling by power-saw. No. 1796, Tree planting.

290 Atomic Reactor

1958. Inauguration of China's First Atomic Reactor.
1797 **290** 8f. blue . . . . 6·00 2·75
1798 – 20f. brown . . . . . . 6·00 1·50
DESIGN: 20f. Cyclotron in action.

291 Children with Model Aircraft

292 Rooster

1958. Aviation Sports.
1799 **291** 4f. red 85 25
1800 – 8f. myrtle 85 25
1801 – 10f. sepia 85 25
1802 – 20f. slate . . . . 1·50 25
DESIGNS: 8f. Gliders. 10f. Parachutists; 20f. Yakovlev Yak-18U trainers.

1959. Chinese Folk Paper-cuts.
1803 – 8f. black on violet . . . 6·25 20
1804 – 8f. black on green . . . 6·25 50
1805 **292** 8f. black on red . . . . 6·25 1·20
1806 – 8f. black on blue . . . . 6·25 50
DESIGNS: No. 1803, Camel. 1804, Pomegranate; 1806, Actress on stage.

293 Mao Tse-tung and Steel Workers

294 Chinese Women

1959. Steel Production Progress. Inscr "1958".
1807 **293** 4f. red . . . . 5·25 1·40
1808 – 8f. purple . . . . 5·25 1·40
1809 – 10f. red . . . . 5·25 1·40
DESIGNS: 8f. Battery of steel furnaces; 10f. Steel "blowers" and workers.

1959. International Women's Day.
1810 **294** 8f. green on cream . . . 70 30
1811 – 22f. mauve on cream . . 70 20
DESIGN: 22f. Russian and Chinese women.

295 Natural History Museum, Peking

296 Barley

1959. Opening of Natural History Museum, Peking.
1812 **295** 4f. turquoise 60 25
1813 8f. sepia 60 25

1959. Successful Harvest, 1958.
1814 8f. red (Type **296**) . . . . . 1·60 30
1815 8f. red (Rice) . . . . 1·60 30
1816 8f. red (Cotton) . . . . . . 1·60 30
1817 8f. red (Soya beans, groundnuts and rape) . . 1·60 30

297 Workers with Marx–Lenin Banner

298 Airport Building

1959. Labour Day. Inscr "1889–1959".
1818 **297** 4f. blue . . . . 4·75 1·50
1819 – 8f. red . . . . 4·75 1·50
1820 – 22f. green . . . . 4·75 1·50
DESIGNS: 8f. Hands clasping Red Flag; 22f. "5.1" and workers.

1959. Inauguration of Peking Airport.
1821 **298** 8f. black on lilac . . . . 8·75 1·10
1822 – 10f. black on green . . . 8·75 50
DESIGN: 10f. Ilyushin Il-14P at airport.

299 Students with Banners

300 F. Joliot-Curie (first President)

1959. 40th Anniv of "May 4th" Students' Rising.

1823	**299**	4f. red, brown and olive	19·00	5·25
1824	–	8f. red, brown & bistre	19·00	5·25

DESIGN: 8f. Workers with banners.

1959. 10th Anniv of World Peace Council.

1825	**300**	8f. purple	6·50	3·25
1826	–	22f. violet	6·50	25

DESIGN: 22f. Silhouettes of European, Chinese and Negro.

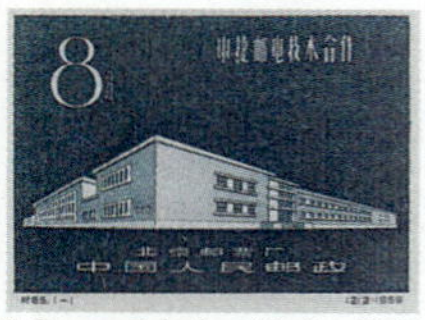
301 Stamp Printing Works, Peking

1959. Sino-Czech Co-operation in Postage Stamp Production.

1827	**301**	8f. myrtle	7·75	2·20

302

1959. World Table Tennis Championships, Dortmund.

1828	**302**	4f. blue and black	2·30	45
1829		8f. red and black	2·50	30

303 Moon Rocket

304 "Prologue"

1959. Launching of First Lunar Rocket.

1830	**303**	8f. red, blue & black	10·50	2·30

1959. 1st Anniv of People's Communes.

1831	**304**	8f. red	70	25
1832	–	8f. dull purple	70	25
1833	–	8f. orange	70	25
1834	–	8f. green	70	25
1835	–	8f. blue	70	25
1836	–	8f. olive	70	25
1837	–	8f. blue	70	25
1838	–	8f. mauve	70	25
1839	–	8f. black	70	25
1840	–	8f. green	70	25
1841	–	8f. violet	70	25
1842	–	8f. red	70	25

DESIGNS: No. 1832, Steel worker ("Rural Industries"); No. 1833, Farm girl ("Agriculture"); No. 1834, Salesgirl ("Trade"); No. 1835, Peasant ("Study"); No. 1836, Militiaman ("Militia"); No. 1837, Cook with tray of food ("Community Meals"); No. 1838, Child watering flowers ("Nursery"); No. 1839, Old man with pipe ("Old People's Homes"); No. 1840, Health worker ("Public Health"); No. 1841, Young flautist ("Recreation and Entertainment"); No. 1842, Star-shaped flower ("Epilogue").

305 Mao Tse-tung and Gate of Heavenly Peace, Peking

306 Republican Emblem

1959. 10th Anniv of People's Republic. (a) 1st issue. Inscr "1949–1959". With gum.

1843	**305**	8f. red and brown	11·00	5·25
1844	–	8f. red and blue	11·00	1·70
1845	–	22f. red and green	11·00	1·10

DESIGNS: No. 1844, Marx, Lenin and Kremlin; No. 1845, Dove of peace and globe.

(b) 2nd issue. Emblem in red and yellow; inscriptions in yellow; background colours given.

1846	**306**	4f. turquoise	8·50	4·50
1847		8f. lilac	8·50	45
1848		10f. blue	8·50	45
1849		20f. buff	8·50	2·75

307 Steel Plant

(c) 3rd issue. Inscr "1949–1959". Frames in purple; centre colours given. With gum.

1850	**307**	8f. red	90	50
1851	–	8f. drab	90	50
1852	–	8f. bistre	90	50
1853	–	8f. blue	90	50
1854	–	8f. salmon	90	50
1855	–	8f. green	90	50
1856	–	8f. turquoise	90	50
1857	–	8f. lilac	90	50

DESIGNS: No. 1851, Coal-mine. No. 1852, Steelmill; No. 1853, Double-decked bridge; No. 1854, Combine-harvester; No. 1855, Dam construction; No. 1856, Textile mill; No. 1857, Chemical works.

308 Rejoicing Populace

(d) 4th Issue. Multicoloured.

1858	8f. Type **308**	4·50	1·50
1859	10f. Rejoicing people and industrial plant (vert)	4·50	1·50
1860	20f. Tree, banners and people carrying wheat and flowers (vert)	4·50	1·50

309 Mao Tse-tung proclaiming Republic

(e) 5th issue.

1861	**309**	20f. lake	25·00	11·00

310 Boy Bugler ("Summer Camps")

311 Exhibition Emblem and Symbols of Communication

1959. 10th Anniv of Chinese Youth Pioneers.

1862	–	4f. yellow, red & black	3·25	50
1863	**310**	4f. red and blue	3·25	50
1864	–	8f. red and brown	3·25	50
1865	–	8f. red and blue	3·25	50
1866	–	8f. red and green	3·25	50
1867	–	8f. red and purple	3·25	50

DESIGNS: No. 1862, Pioneers' emblem; No. 1864, Schoolgirl with flowers and satchel ("Study"); No. 1865, Girl with rain gauge ("Science"); No. 1866, Boy with sapling ("Forestry"); No. 1867, Girl skater ("Athletic Sports").

1959. National Exhibition of Industry and Communications, Peking. Inscr "1949–1959".

1868	**311**	4f. blue	50	25
1869	–	8f. red	50	25

DESIGN: 8f. Exn emblem and symbols of industry.

312 Cultural Palace of the Nationalities

313 "Statue of Sport"

1959. Inauguration of Cultural Palace of the Nationalities. Peking.

1870	**312**	4f. black and red	3·50	50
1871		8f. black and green	3·50	60

1959. 1st National Games, Peking. Multicoloured.

1872	8f. Type **313**	1·50	25
1873	8f. Parachuting	1·50	25
1874	8f. Pistol-shooting	1·50	25
1875	8f. Diving	1·50	25
1876	8f. Table tennis	1·50	25
1877	8f. Weightlifting	1·50	25
1878	8f. High jumping	1·50	25
1879	8f. Rowing	1·50	25
1880	8f. Running	1·50	25
1881	8f. Basketball	1·50	25
1882	8f. Fencing	1·50	25
1883	8f. Motor cycling	1·50	25
1884	8f. Gymnastics	1·50	25
1885	8f. Cycling	1·50	25
1886	8f. Horse-racing	1·50	25
1887	8f. Football	1·50	25

314 Wheat (Main Pavilion)

1960. Opening of National Agricultural Exhibition Hall, Peking.

1888	**314**	4f. black, red & orange	60	20
1889	–	8f. black and blue	60	20
1890	–	10f. black and brown	60	20
1891	–	20f. black and turquoise	60	20

DESIGNS: 8f. Meteorological symbols (Meteorological Pavilion); 10f. Cattle (Animal Husbandry Pavilion); 20f. Fishes (Aquatic Products Pavilion).

315 Crossing the Chinsha River

1960. 25th Anniv of Conference during the Long March, Tsunyi, Kweichow.

1892	–	4f. blue	9·75	80
1893	–	8f. turquoise	9·75	2·50
1894	**315**	10f. green	13·00	1·00

DESIGNS: 4f. Conference Hall, Tsunyi; 8f. Mao Tse-tung and flags.

316 Clara Zetkin (founder)

317 Chinese and Soviet Workers

1960. 50th Anniv of International Women's Day. Frame and inscriptions black. Centre colours given.

1895	**316**	4f. blue, black & flesh	1·60	35
1896	–	8f. multicoloured	1·60	50
1897	–	10f. multicoloured	1·60	50
1898	–	22f. multicoloured	2·30	35

DESIGNS: 8f. Mother, child and dove; 10f. Woman tractor-driver; 22f. Women of three races.

1960. 10th Anniv of Sino-Soviet Treaty.

1899	**317**	4f. brown	5·75	1·70
1900	–	8f. black, yellow & red	5·75	1·70
1901	–	10f. blue	5·75	1·90

DESIGNS: 8f. Flowers and Sino-Soviet emblems; 10f. Chinese and Soviet soldiers.

318 Flags of Hungary and China

1960. 15th Anniv of Hungarian Liberation.

1902	**318**	8f. multicoloured	10·00	1·80
1903	–	8f. red, black and blue	10·00	5·00

DESIGN: No. 1903, Parliament Building, Budapest.

319 Lenin Speaking

320 "Lunik 2"

1960. 90th Birth Anniv of Lenin.

1904	**319**	4f. lilac	5·25	1·00
1905	–	8f. black and red	9·50	4·25
1906	–	20f. brown	18·00	2·10

DESIGNS: 8f. Lenin (portrait); 20f. Lenin talking with Red Guards (after Vasilyev).

1960. Lunar Rocket Flights.

1907	**320**	8f. red	3·00	95
1908	–	10f. green ("Lunik 3")	3·25	95

321 View of Prague

1960. 15th Anniv of Liberation of Czechoslovakia.

1909	–	8f. multicoloured	8·25	1·90
1910	**321**	8f. green	8·25	2·50

DESIGN—VERT: No. 1909, Child pioneers and flags of China and Czechoslovakia.

SERIAL NUMBERS. In this and many later multicoloured sets containing several stamps of the same denomination, the serial number is quoted in brackets to assist identification. This is the last figure in the bottom left corner of the stamp.

322 Narial Bouquet Goldfish

1960. Chinese Goldfish. Multicoloured.

1911	4f. (1) Type **322**	23·00	4·00
1912	4f. (2) Black-backed telescopic-eyed goldfish	24·00	4·00
1913	4f. (3) Bubble-eyed goldfish	24·00	4·00
1914	4f. (4) Ranchu goldfish	16·00	2·40
1915	8f. (5) Pearl-scaled goldfish	29·00	4·25
1916	8f. (6) Black moor goldfish	16·00	3·25
1917	8f. (7) Celestial goldfish	16·00	2·20
1918	8f. (8) Oranda goldfish	16·00	2·20
1919	8f. (9) Purple oranda goldfish	16·00	5·00
1920	8f. (10) Red-capped goldfish	16·00	5·00
1921	8f. (11) Red-capped oranda goldfish	24·00	4·25
1922	8f. (12) Red veil-tailed goldfish	24·00	4·25

323 Sow with Litter

1960. Pig-breeding.

1923	**323**	8f. black and red	14·00	1·20
1924	–	8f. black and green	14·00	1·20
1925	–	8f. black and mauve	14·00	1·20
1926	–	8f. black and olive	14·00	1·20
1927	–	8f. black and orange	16·00	5·50

DESIGNS: No. 1924, Pig being inoculated; No. 1925, Group of pigs; No. 1926, Pig and feeding pens; No. 1927, Pig and crop-bales.

324 "Serving the Workers"

325 N. Korean and Chinese Flags, and Flowers

1960. 3rd National Literary and Art Workers' Congress, Peking. Inscr "1960".
1928 **324** 4f. red, sepia and green 6·75 2·00
1929 – 8f. red, bistre & turq . . 7·75 2·50
DESIGN: 8f. Inscribed stone seal.

1960. 15th Anniv of Liberation of Korea.
1930 **325** 8f. red, yellow and green 11·50 3·25
1931 – 8f. red, indigo and blue 11·50 4·00
DESIGN: No. 1931, "Flying Horse" of Korea.

326 Peking Railway Station

1960. Opening of New Peking Railway Station.
1932 **326** 8f. multicoloured . . . . 10·50 3·50
1933 – 10f. blue, cream & turq 12·50 3·75
DESIGN: 10f. Steam train arriving at station.

327 Chinese and N. Vietnamese Flags, and Children

328 Worker and Spray Fan

1960. 15th Anniv of N. Vietnam Republic.
1934 **327** 8f. red, yellow & black 3·50 1·60
1935 – 8f. multicoloured . . . . 3·50 2·00
DESIGN—VERT: No. 1935, "Lake of the Returning Sword", Hanoi.

1960. Public Health Campaign.
1936 **328** 8f. black and orange . . 1·40 35
1937 – 8f. green and blue . . . 1·40 35
1938 – 8f. brown and blue . . . 1·40 35
1939 – 8f. lake and brown . . . 1·40 35
1940 – 8f. blue and turquoise 1·40 35
DESIGNS: No. 1937, Spraying insecticide; No. 1938, Cleaning windows; No. 1939, Medical examination of child; No. 1940, "Tai Chi Chuan" (Chinese physical drill).

329 Facade of Great Hall

1960. Completion of "Great Hall of the People". Multicoloured.
1941 8f. Type **329** . . . . 11·00 2·75
1942 10f. Interior of Great Hall 13·00 2·75

330 Dr. N. Bethune operating on Soldier

331 Friedrich Engels

1960. 70th Birth Anniv of Dr. Norman Bethune (Canadian surgeon with 8th Route Army).
1943 **330** 8f. grey, black and red 3·00 75
1944 – 8f. brown . . . . 3·00 50
PORTRAIT. No. 1943 Dr. N. Bethune.

1960. 140th Birth Anniv of Engels.
1945 – 8f. brown . . . . 6·75 1·80
1946 **331** 10f. orange and blue 7·75 2·50
DESIGN: 8f. Engels addressing congress at The Hague.

332 Big "Ju-I"

333 "Yue Jin"

1960. Chrysanthemums. Background colours given. Multicoloured.
1947 – 4f. blue . . . . 16·00 3·25
1948 – 4f. pink . . . . 20·00 3·25
1949 – 8f. grey . . . . 13·00 1·80
1950 **332** 8f. blue . . . . 13·00 1·80
1951 – 8f. green . . . . 15·00 1·80
1952 – 8f. violet . . . . 15·00 1·80
1953 – 8f. olive . . . . 15·00 1·80
1954 – 8f. turquoise . . . . . . 15·00 1·80
1955 – 10f. grey . . . . 16·00 1·80
1956 – 10f. brown . . . . . . 13·00 1·50
1957 – 20f. blue . . . . 15·00 1·80
1958 – 20f. red . . . . 23·00 2·75
1959 – 22f. brown . . . . . . 20·00 5·75
1960 – 22f. red . . . . 35·00 8·00
1961 – 30f. green . . . . 22·00 5·00
1962 – 30f. mauve . . . . . . 18·00 4·75
1963 – 35f. green . . . . 23·00 5·00
1964 – 52f. purple . . . . . . 20·00 7·00
CHRYSANTHEMUMS: No. 1947, "Hwang Shih Pa". No. 1948, "Green Peony". No. 1949, "Er Chiao". No. 1951, "Ju-I" with Golden Hooks. No. 1952, "Golden Peony". No. 1953, "Generalissimo's Banner". No. 1954, "Willow Thread". No. 1955, "Cassia on Salver of Hibiscus". No. 1956, "Pearls on Jade Salver". No. 1957, "Red Gold Lion". No. 1958, "Milky White Jade". No. 1959, "Purple Jade with Fragrant Beads". No. 1960, "Cassia on Ice Salver". No. 1961, "Inky Black Lotus". No. 1962, "Jade Bamboo Shoot of Superior Class". No. 1963, "Smiling Face". No. 1964, "Swan Ballet".

1960. 1st Chinese-built Freighter. Launching. No gum.
1965 **333** 8f. blue . . . . 3·50 1·40

334 Pantheon, Paris

336 Chan Tien-yu

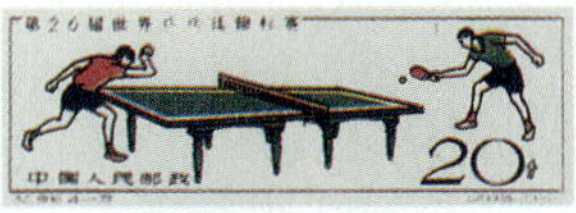
335 Table Tennis Match

1961. 90th Anniv of Paris Commune.
1966 **334** 8f. black and red . . . . 6·25 1·30
1967 – 8f. sepia and red . . . . 6·25 1·30
DESIGN: No. 1967, Proclamation of Commune.

1961. 26th World Table Tennis Championships, Peking. Multicoloured.
1968 8f. Championship emblem and jasmine . . . . . . 1·10 75
1969 10f. Table tennis bat and ball and Temple of Heaven . . . . 1·30 90
1970 20f. Type **335** . . . . 1·70 90
1971 22f. Peking Workers Gymnasium . . . . 2·30 1·50
MS1971a 150 × 100 mm. Nos. 1968/71. No gum £450 £275

1961. Birth Centenary of Chan Tien-yu (railway construction engineer).
1972 **336** 8f. black and sage . . . 2·75 1·10
1973 – 10f. brown and sepia . . 3·50 1·60
DESIGN: 10f. Steam train on Peking-Changchow Railway.

337 Congress Building, Shanghai

1961. 40th Anniv of Chinese Communist Party. Flags, red; frames, gold.
1974 **337** 4f. purple . . . . 12·50 1·20
1975 – 8f. green . . . . 12·50 1·80
1976 – 10f. brown . . . . . . 12·50 4·00
1977 – 20f. blue . . . . 16·00 1·20
1978 – 30f. red . . . . 21·00 1·90
DESIGNS: 8f. "August 1" Building, Nanchang; 10f. Provisional Central Govt. Building, Juichin; 20f. Pagoda Hill, Yenan; 30f. Gate of Heavenly Peace, Peking.

338 Flags of China and Mongolia

339 "August 1" Building, Nanchang

1961. 40th Anniv of Mongolian People's Revolution.
1979 **338** 8f. red, blue & yellow . . 15·00 1·40
1980 – 10f. orange, yellow & grn . . . . 20·00 6·25
DESIGN: 10f. Mongolian Government Building.

1961. Size 24 × 16½ mm. No gum.
1981 **339** 1f. blue . . . . 7·25 30
1982 1½f. red . . . . 14·00 30
1983 2f. green . . . . 7·75 80
1984 A 3f. violet . . . . . . 23·00 1·40
1985 4f. green . . . . 2·75 50
1986 5f. green . . . . 2·00 20
1987 B 8f. green . . . . 2·00 20
1988 10f. purple . . . . . . 4·75 20
1989 20f. blue . . . . 2·00 20
1990 C 22f. brown 95 20
1991 30f. blue . . . . 2·00 20
1992 50f. red . . . . 2·00 20
DESIGNS: A, Tree and Sha Chow Pa Building, Juichin; B, Yenan Pagoda; C, Gate of Heavenly Peace, Peking.
For redrawn, smaller, designs see Nos. 2010/21.

340 Military Museum

1961. People's Revolutionary Military Museum.
1993 **340** 8f. brown, green & blue 18·00 1·00
1994 10f. black, green & brn 19·00 1·90

341 Uprising at Wuhan

1961. 50th Anniv of Revolution of 1911.
1995 **341** 8f. black and grey . . . 9·25 2·20
1996 – 10f. black and brown . . 11·00 1·00
DESIGN—VERT: 10f. Dr. Sun Yat-sen.

342 Donkey

343 Tibetans Rejoicing

1961. Tang Dynasty Pottery (618–907 A.D.). Centres multicoloured. Background colours given.
1997 **342** 4f. blue . . . . 5·75 80
1998 – 8f. green . . . . 5·75 80
1999 – 8f. purple . . . . 5·75 80
2000 – 10f. blue . . . . 5·75 80
2001 – 20f. olive . . . . 7·25 1·60
2002 – 22f. turquoise . . . . . 11·50 2·75
2003 – 30f. red . . . . 13·50 9·25
2004 – 50f. slate . . . . 13·50 4·25
DESIGNS: No. 1998, Donkey; Nos. 1999/2002, Various horses; Nos. 2003/4, Various camels.

1961. "Rebirth of the Tibetan People".
2005 **343** 4f. brown and buff . . . 3·75 85
2006 – 8f. brown and turquoise 3·75 85
2007 – 10f. brown and yellow 18·00 1·70
2008 – 20f. brown and pink . . 27·00 2·50
2009 – 30f. brown and blue . . 44·00 3·75
DESIGNS: 8f. Sower; 10f. Tibetan celebrating "bumper crop"; 20f. "Responsible Citizens"; 30f. Tibetan children.

343a "August 1" Building, Nanchang

344 Lu Hsun (after Hsieh Chia-seng)

1962. Size 20½ × 16½ mm. No gum.
2010 **343a** 1f. blue 40 15
2011 2f. green 50 15
2013 A 3f. violet 40 20
2014 **343a** 3f. brown . . . . . . 1·60 1·10
2015 A 4f. green 65 20
2016 B 4f. red . . . . 1·60 1·10
2017 C 8f. green . . . . 1·00 20
2018 10f. purple . . . . . . 1·50 25
2019 20f. blue . . . . 1·50 40
2020 B 30f. blue . . . . 2·40 55
2021 52f. red . . . . 1·10 1·10
DESIGNS: A, Tree and Sha Chow Pa Building, Juichin; B, Gate of Heavenly Peace, Peking; C, Yenan Pagoda.

1962. 80th Birth Anniv of Lu Hsun (writer).
2022 **344** 8f. black and red . . . . 1·60 35

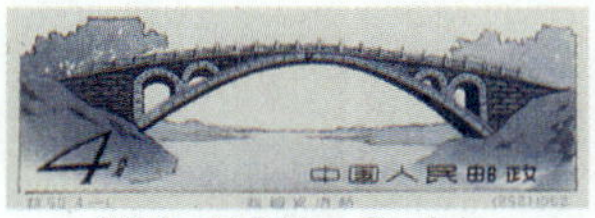
345 Anchi Bridge, Chaohsien

1962. Ancient Chinese Bridges.
2023 **345** 4f. violet and lavender 1·60 25
2024 – 8f. slate and green . . . 1·60 25
2025 – 10f. sepia and bistre . . 1·90 40
2026 – 20f. blue and turquoise 3·00 60
BRIDGES: 8f. Paotai, Soochow. 10f. Chupu, Kuanhsien. 20f. Chenyang, Sankiang.

346 Tu Fu

347 Manchurian Cranes and Trees

1962. 1250th Birth Anniv of Tu Fu (poet).
2027 – 4f. black and bistre . . . 11·50 85
2028 **346** 8f. black and turquoise 11·50 2·00
DESIGN: 4f. Tu Fu's Memorial, Chengtu.

1962. "The Sacred Crane". Paintings by Chen Chi-fo. Multicoloured.
2029 8f. Type **347** . . . . 10·00 2·40
2030 10f. Two cranes in flight . . 12·00 3·50
2031 20f. Crane on rock . . . . 28·00 3·75

348 Cuban Soldier

1962. "Support for Cuba".
2032 **348** 8f. black and lake . . . 26·00 5·50
2033 – 10f. black and green . . 33·00 2·20
2034 – 22f. black and blue . . 55·00 15·00
DESIGNS: 10f. Sugar-cane planter; 22f. Militiaman and woman.

349 Torch and Map

1961. "Support for Algeria".
2035 **349** 8f. orange and brown . . 65 60
2036 – 22f. brown and ochre . . 1·30 90
DESIGN: 22f. Algerian patriots.

350 Mei Lan-fang (actor)

351 Han "Flower Drum" Dance

1962. "Stage Art of Mei Lan-fang". Multicoloured. Each showing Lan-fang in stage costume with items given below.
2037 4f. Type **350** . . . . £110 4·50
2038 8f. Drum . . . . 25·00 2·75
2039 8f. Fan . . . . 25·00 2·75
2040 10f. Swords . . . . 25·00 5·75
2041 20f. Bag . . . . 25·00 7·50
2042 22f. Ribbons (horiz) . . . . 45·00 9·50
2043 30f. Loom (horiz) . . . . . 65·00 29·00
2044 50f. Long sleeves (horiz) 70·00 25·00
MS2044a 108 × 147 mm 3y. multicoloured £2250 £1200

1962. Chinese Folk Dances (1st issue). Multicoloured. No gum.
2045 4f. Type **351** 70 30
2046 8f. Mongolian "Ordos" . . 95 30

2047 10f. Chuang "Catching shrimp" . . . . 1·00 35
2048 20f. Tibetan "Fiddle" . . . 1·60 75
2049 30f. Yi "Friend" . . . . . . 2·30 75
2050 50f. Uighur "Tambourine" 3·50 1·20
See also Nos. 2104/15.

352 Soldiers storming the Winter Palace, Petrograd

1962. 45th Anniv of Russian Revolution.
2051 – 8f. brown and red . . . 16·00 75
2052 **352** 20f. bronze and red . . . 24·00 1·80
DESIGN—VERT: 8f. Lenin leading soldiers.

353 Revolutionary Statue and Map

354 Tsai Lun (A.D. ?–121, inventor of paper making process)

1962. 50th Anniv of Albanian Independence.
2053 **353** 8f. sepia and blue . . . 1·80 55
2054 – 10f. multicoloured . . . 2·10 85
DESIGN: 10f. Albanian flag and girl pioneer.

1962. Scientists of Ancient China. Multicoloured.
2055 4f. Type **354** . . . . . . 4·50 35
2056 4f. Paper-making . . . . . 3·25 30
2057 8f. Sun Szu-miao (581–682, physician) . . . . 3·25 30
2058 8f. Preparing medical treatise . . . . 3·25 40
2059 10f. Shen Ko (1031–1095, geologist) . . . . 3·25 30
2060 10f. Making field notes . . 4·75 45
2061 20f. Ku Shou-chin (1231–1316, astronomer) . . . . 7·25 75
2062 20f. Astronomical equipment 7·25 75

355 Tank Monument, Havana

1963. 4th Anniv of Cuban Revolution.
2063 **355** 4f. sepia and red . . . . 25·00 1·60
2064 – 4f. black and green . . . 21·00 1·60
2065 – 8f. lake and brown . . . 21·00 1·90
2066 – 8f. lake and brown . . . 55·00 9·50
2067 – 10f. black and buff . . . 55·00 6·50
2068 – 10f. sepia, red and blue 55·00 22·00
DESIGNS—As Type **355**: No. 2064, Cuban revolutionaries; No. 2067, Cuban soldier; No. 2068, Castro and Cuban flag. LARGER (48½ × 27 mm) No. 2065, Crowd in Havana (value on left); No. 2066, Crowd in Peking (value on right).

356 Tibetan Clouded Yellow

357 Marx and Engels

1963. Butterflies. Multicoloured. No gum.
2069 4f. (1) Type **356** . . . . . 9·50 4·00
2070 4f. (2) Tritailed glory . . . 9·50 1·00
2071 4f. (3) Neumogeni jungle queen . . . . 9·50 1·00
2072 4f. (4) Washan swordtail . . 9·50 1·00
2073 4f. (5) Striped ringlet . . . 9·50 1·00
2074 8f. (6) Green dragontail . . 10·50 75
2075 8f. (7) Dilunuleted peacock 10·50 75
2076 8f. (8) Yamfly . . . . . . 10·50 75
2077 8f. (9) Golden kaiser-i-hind 10·50 75
2078 8f. (10) Mushaell hair-streak 10·50 75
2079 10f. (11) Yellow orange-tip 10·50 1·20
2080 10f. (12) Great jay . . . . 10·50 1·20
2081 10f. (13) Striped punch . . 10·50 1·20
2082 10f. (14) Beck butterfly . . 10·50 1·20
2083 10f. (15) Omei skipper . . 10·50 2·00
2084 20f. (16) Philippine birdwing 9·50 2·75
2085 20f. (17) Keeled apollo . . . 9·50 3·00
2086 22f. (18) Blue-banded king crow . . . . 9·50 4·00
2087 30f. (19) Solskyi copper . . 10·00 3·50
2088 50f. (20) Clipper . . . . . 15·00 5·00

1963. 145th Birth Anniv of Karl Marx. No. gum.
2089 – 8f. black, pink & gold 5·25 2·00
2090 – 8f. red and gold . . . . 5·25 2·00
2091 **357** 8f. brown and gold . . . 5·25 2·00
DESIGNS: No. 2089, Marx; No. 2090, Slogan "Workers of the World Unite" over cover of 1st edition of "Communist Manifesto".

358 Child with Top

359 Giant Panda eating Apples

1963. Children. Multicoloured, background colours given. No gum.
2092 **358** 4f. turquoise 70 25
2093 – 4f. brown 70 25
2094 – 8f. grey 70 25
2095 – 8f. blue 70 25
2096 – 8f. beige 70 25
2097 – 8f. slate 70 25
2098 – 8f. green 70 25
2099 – 8f. grey 70 25
2100 – 10f. green . . . . 1·50 50
2101 – 10f. violet . . . . 1·50 50
2102 – 20f. drab . . . . 3·00 1·20
2103 – 20f. green . . . . 3·00 1·20
DESIGNS (each shows a child): No. 2093, Eating candied hawberries; No. 2094, As "traffic policeman"; No. 2095, With toy windmill; No. 2096, Listening to caged cricket; No. 2097, With toy sword; No 2098, Embroidering; No. 2099, With umbrella; No. 2100, Playing with sand; No. 2101, Playing table tennis; No. 2102, Doing sums; No. 2103, Flying kite.

1963. Chinese Folk Dances (2nd issue). As T **351** but inscr "(261) 1962" to "(266) 1962" in bottom right corner. Multicoloured. No gum.
2104 4f. Puyi "Weaving Cloth" 85 30
2105 8f. Kazakh 80 30
2106 10f. Olunchun 95 35
2107 20f. Kaochan "Labour" . . 1·10 50
2108 30f. Miao "Reed-pipe" . . . 1·50 65
2109 50f. Korean "Fan" . . . . 2·30 90

1963. Chinese Folk Dances (3rd issue). As T **351** but inscr "(279) 1963" to "(284) 1963" in bottom right corner. Multicoloured. No gum.
2110 4f. Yu "Wedding Ceremony" 65 30
2111 8f. Pai "Encircling Mountain Forest" 90 30
2112 10f. Yao "Long Drum" . . 1·20 35
2113 20f. Li "Third Day of Third Month" . . . . 1·40 50
2114 30f. Kava "Knife" . . . . 2·30 70
2115 50f. Tai "Peacock" . . . . 4·25 1·00

1963. Giant Panda. Perf or imperf.
2116 **359** 8f. black and blue . . . 27·00 1·80
2117 – 8f. black and green . . 27·00 6·75
2118 – 10f. black and drab . . 30·00 3·25
DESIGNS—As Type **278**. No. 2117, Giant panda eating bamboo shoots. HORIZ: (52 × 31 mm): No. 2118, Two giant pandas.

360 Table Tennis Player

361 Snub-nosed Monkey

1963. 27th World Table-Tennis Championships.
2119 **360** 8f. grey . . . . 11·50 1·70
2120 – 8f. brown . . . . 11·50 90
DESIGN: No. 2120, Trophies won by Chinese team.

1963. Snub-nosed Monkeys. Multicoloured.
2121 8f. Type **361** . . . . 7·50 1·30
2122 10f. Two monkeys . . . . 8·50 1·30
2123 22f. Two monkeys on branch of tree . . . . . . 14·50 5·50

362 Old Pines of Hwangshan

1963. Hwangshan Landscapes. Multicoloured.
2124 4f. (1) Mount of The Green Jade Screen (vert) . . . . 13·00 1·20
2125 4f. (2) The Guest-welcoming Pines (vert) . . . . . . 13·00 1·20
2126 4f. (3) Pines and rocks behind the lake (vert) . . 13·00 1·40
2127 4f. (4) Terrace of Keeping Cool (vert) . . . . 14·50 1·40
2128 8f. (5) Mount of the Heavenly Capital (vert) 19·00 1·50
2129 8f. (6) Mount of Scissors (vert) . . . . 19·00 1·50
2130 8f. (7) Forest of Ten Thousand Pines (vert) . . 19·00 1·50
2131 8f. (8) The Flowering Bush in a Dream (vert) . . . 20·00 1·50
2132 10f. (9) Mount of the Lotus Flower . . . . 22·00 1·50
2133 10f. (10) Cumulus Flood Wave of the Eastern Lake 24·00 1·50
2134 10f. (11) Type **362** . . . . . 26·00 1·50
2135 10f. (12) Cumulus on the Eastern Lake . . . . . . 29·00 1·50
2136 20f. (13) The Stalagmite Mountain Range . . . . 32·00 5·25
2137 22f. (14) The Apes of the Stone watch the lake below . . . . 34·00 8·25
2138 30f. (15) The Forest of Lions . . . . 90·00 49·00
2139 50f. (16) The Fairy Isles of Peng Lai . . . . 90·00 20·00

363 Football

364 Clay Rooster and Goat

1963. "GANEFO" Athletic Games, Jakarta, Indonesia.
2140 **363** 8f. red & black on lav 12·00 85
2141 – 8f. blue & black on buff 12·00 85
2142 – 8f. brown & blk on blue 12·00 85
2143 – 8f. purple & blk on mve 12·00 85
2144 – 10f. multicoloured . . . 12·00 3·50
DESIGNS—As Type **282**: No. 2141, Throwing the discus; No. 2142, Diving; No. 2143, Gymnastics. HORIZ: (48½ × 27½ mm). No. 2144, Athletes on parade.

1963. Chinese Folk Toys. Multicoloured. No. gum.
2145 4f. (1) Type **364** 70 25
2146 4f. (4) Cloth camel 70 25
2147 4f. (7) Cloth tigers 70 25
2148 8f. (2) Clay ox and rider . . 70 25
2149 8f. (5) Cloth rabbit, wooden figure and clay cock . . . 70 25
2150 8f. (8) Straw cock 70 25
2151 10f. (3) Cloth donkey and clay bird 70 25
2152 10f. (6) Clay lion 70 25
2153 10f. (9) Clay-paper tumbler and cloth tiger . . . . . 1·10 25

365 Vietnamese Family

366 Cuban and Chinese Flags

1963. "Liberation of South Vietnam". Mult.
2154 8f. Type **365** . . . . 3·00 95
2155 8f. Vietnamese with flag . . 3·00 1·60

1964. 5th Anniv of Cuban Revolution. Mult.
2156 8f. Type **366** . . . . 10·50 75
2157 8f. Boy waving flag . . . . 15·00 4·25

367 Woman driving Tractor

1964. "Women of the People's Commune". Multicoloured.
2158 8f. (1) Type **367** 75 25
2159 8f. (2) Harvesting 75 25
2160 8f. (3) Picking cotton . . . 75 25
2161 8f. (4) Picking fruit 80 25
2162 8f. (5) Reading book . . . 80 25
2163 8f. (6) Holding rifle 80 25

368 "Sino-African Friendship"

370 History Museum

369 Marx, Engels, Lenin and Stalin

1964. African Freedom Day.
2164 **368** 8f. multicoloured 90 35
2165 – 8f. brown and black . . 90 35
DESIGN: No. 2165, African beating drum.

1964. Labour Day.
2166 **369** 8f. black, red & gold . . 13·50 2·00
2167 – 8f. black, red & gold . . 6·50 1·60
DESIGN: No. 2167, Workers and banners.

1964. No gum.
2168 **370** 1f. brown 25 25
2169 A 1½f. purple 25 55
2170 B 2f. green 25 25
2171 C 3f. green 25 25
2172 **370** 4f. blue 25 25
2172a A 5f. purple 60 25
2173 B 8f. red 60 25
2174 C 10f. drab 85 25
2175 **370** 20f. violet 85 25
2176 A 22f. orange . . . . . . 1·70 25
2177 B 30f. green . . . . . . 2·75 35
2177a C 50f. blue . . . . 8·00 2·20
DESIGNS: A, Gate of Heavenly Peace; B, Great Hall of the People; C, Military Museum.

371 Date Orchard, Yenan

372 Map of Vietnam and Flag

1964. "Yenan-Shrine of the Chinese Revolution". Yenan buildings. Multicoloured.
2178 8f. (1) Type **371** . . . . . 14·50 80
2179 8f. (2) Central Auditorium, Yang Chia Ling . . . . 5·50 60
2180 8f. (3) Mao Tse-tung's Office and Residence at Date Orchard, Yenan . . . . 5·50 60
2181 8f. (4) Auditorium, Wang Chia Ping . . . . 5·50 60
2182 8f. (5) Border Region Assembly Hall . . . . 15·00 80
2183 52f. (6) Pagoda Hill . . . . 18·00 3·25

1964. South Vietnam Victory Campaign.
2184 **372** 8f. multicoloured . . . . 13·50 3·50

373 "The Alchemist's Glowing Crucible" (peony) **374** "Chueh" (wine cup)

1964. Chinese Peonies. Multicoloured.

2185	4f. (1) Type **373**	9·50	1·20
2186	4f. (2) Night-shining Jade	9·50	1·20
2187	8f. (3) Purple Kuo's Cap	9·50	1·20
2188	8f. (4) Chao Pinks	9·50	1·20
2189	8f. (5) Yao Yellows	9·50	1·20
2190	8f. (6) Twin Beauties	10·00	1·20
2191	8f. (7) Ice-veiled Rubies	10·00	1·40
2192	10f. (8) Gold-sprinkled Chinese Ink	11·00	1·90
2193	10f. (9) Cinnabar Jar	11·00	1·90
2194	10f. (10) Lantien Jade	16·00	2·75
2195	10f. (11) Imperial Robe Yellow	16·00	2·75
2196	10f. (12) Hu Reds	16·00	2·75
2197	20f. (13) Pea Green	22·00	5·50
2198	43f. (14) Wei Purples	33·00	19·00
2199	52f. (15) Intoxicated Celestial Peach	46·00	23·00
MS2199a	77 × 136 mm. 2y. Glorious Crimson and Great Gold Pink (48 × 59 mm)	£950	£450

1964. Bronze Vessels of the Yin Dynasty (before 1050 B.C.).

2200	**374**	4f. (1) black, grn & yell	4·50	95
2201	–	4f. (2) black, grn & yell	4·50	95
2202	–	8f. (3) black, grn & yell	7·50	95
2203	–	8f. (4) black, blue & grn	8·50	95
2204	–	10f. (5) black and drab	8·50	95
2205	–	10f. (6) black, grn & yell	8·50	95
2206	–	20f. (7) black and grey	9·25	3·75
2207	–	20f. (8) black, bl & yell	9·25	3·75

DESIGNS: No. 2201, "Ku" (beaker); 2202, "Kuang" (wine urn); 2203, "Chia" (wine cup); 2204, "Tsun" (wine vessel); 2205, "Yu" (wine urn); 2206, "Tsun" (wine vessel); 2207, "Ting" (ceremonial cauldron).

375 "Harvesting" **376** Marx, Engels and Trafalgar Square, London (vicinity of old St. Martin's Hall)

1964. Agricultural Students. Multicoloured.

2208	8f. (1) Type **375**	1·50	25
2209	8f. (2) "Sapling planting"	1·50	25
2210	8f. (3) "Study"	1·50	25
2211	8f. (4) "Scientific experiment"	1·50	25

1964. Centenary of "First International".

2212	**376**	8f. red, brown and gold	36·00	16·00

377 Rejoicing People **378** Oil Derrick

1964. 15th Anniv of People's Republic. Mult.

2213	8f. (1) Type **377**	22·00	2·75
2214	8f. (2) Chinese flag	22·00	2·75
2215	8f. (3) As T **377** in reverse	22·00	2·75
MS2215a	150 × 114 mm. Nos. 2213/14 forming a composite design without dividing perfs	£1500	£600

Nos. 2213/5 were issued in the form of a triptych, in sheets.

1964. Petroleum Industry. Multicoloured.

2216	4f. Geological surveyors and van (horiz)	40·00	5·00
2217	8f. Type **378**	21·00	2·20
2218	8f. Oil-extraction equipment	21·00	2·20
2219	10f. Refinery	49·00	2·20
2220	20f. Railway petroleum trucks (horiz)	95·00	12·50

379 Albanian and Chinese Flags and Plants

1964. 20th Anniv of Liberation of Albania.

2221	**379**	8f. multicoloured	11·50	1·70
2222	–	10f. black, red & yellow	13·50	8·75

DESIGN: 10f. Enver Hoxha and Albanian arms.

380 Dam under Construction

1964. Hsinankiang Hydro-electric Power Station. Multicoloured.

2223	4f. Type **380**	60·00	2·50
2224	8f. Installation of turbo-generator rotor	19·00	90
2225	8f. Main dam	45·00	1·60
2226	20f. Pylon	95·00	9·00

381 Fertilisers

1964. Chemical Industry. Main design and inscr in black; background colours given.

2227	**381**	8f. (1) red	2·10	35
2228	–	8f. (2) green	2·10	35
2229	–	8f. (3) brown	2·10	35
2230	–	8f. (4) mauve	2·10	35
2231	–	8f. (5) blue	2·10	35
2232	–	8f. (6) orange	2·10	35
2233	–	8f. (7) violet	2·10	35
2234	–	8f. (8) turquoise	2·10	35

DESIGNS: (2), Plastics; (3), Medicinal drugs; (4), Rubber; (5), Insecticides; (6), Acids; (7), Alkalis; (8), Synthetic fibres.

382 Mao Tse-tung standing in Room

1965. 30th Anniv of Tsunyi Conference. Mult.

2235	8f. (1) Type **382**	31·00	5·00
2236	8f. (2) Mao Tse-tung (vert) (26½ × 36 mm)	26·00	4·25
2237	8f. (3) "Victory at Loushan Pass"	23·00	5·00

383 Conference Hall **384** Lenin

1965. 10th Anniv of Bandung Conference. Mult.

2238	8f. Type **383**	90	25
2239	8f. Rejoicing Africans and Asians	90	25

1965. 95th Birth Anniv of Lenin.

2240	**384**	8f. multicoloured	12·50	5·00

385 Table Tennis Player **386** All China T.U. Federation Team scaling Mt. Minya Konka

1965. World Table Tennis Championships, Peking.

2241	**385**	8f. (1) multicoloured	55	25
2242	–	8f. (2) multicoloured	55	25
2243	–	8f. (3) multicoloured	55	25
2244	–	8f. (4) multicoloured	55	25

DESIGNS: Nos. 2242/4 each show different views of table tennis players.

1965. Chinese Mountaineering Achievements. Each black, yellow and blue.

2245	8f. (1) Type **386**	4·25	95
2246	8f. (2) Men and women's mixed team on slopes of Muztagh Ata	4·25	95
2247	8f. (3) Climbers on Mt. Jolmo Lungma	4·25	95
2248	8f. (4) Women's team camping on Kongur Tiubie Tagh	4·25	95
2249	8f. (5) Climbers on Shishma Pangma	4·75	1·80

387 Marx and Lenin

1965. Organization of Socialist Countries' Postal Administrations Conference, Peking.

2250	**387**	8f. multicoloured	12·00	5·25

388 Tseping

1965. "Chingkang Mountains – Cradle of the Chinese Revolution". Multicoloured.

2251	4f. (1) Type **388**	8·25	45
2252	8f. (2) Sanwantsun	8·25	45
2253	8f. (3) Octagonal Building, Maoping	8·25	45
2254	8f. (4) River and bridge at Lungshih	14·00	1·20
2255	8f. (5) Tachingtsun	11·50	1·20
2256	10f. (6) Bridge at Lungyuankou	19·00	60
2257	10f. (7) Hwangyangchieh	18·00	85
2258	52f. (8) Chingkang peaks	40·00	8·50

389 Soldiers with Texts

1965. People's Liberation Army. Mult.

2259	8f. (1) Type **389**	17·00	4·75
2260	8f. (2) Soldiers reading book	17·00	4·75
2261	8f. (3) Soldier with grenade-thrower	15·00	1·90
2262	8f. (4) Giving tuition in firing rifle	15·00	1·90
2263	8f. (5) Soldiers at rest (vert)	15·00	1·90
2264	8f. (6) Bayonet charge (vert)	15·00	1·90
2265	8f. (7) Soldier with banners (vert)	31·00	7·25
2266	8f. (8) Military band (vert)	23·00	2·50

390 "Welcome to Peking" **391** Soldier firing Weapon

1965. Chinese–Japanese. Youth Meeting, Peking. Multicoloured.

2267	4f. (1) Type **390**	1·40	20
2268	8f. (2) Chinese and Japanese youths with linked arms	1·40	25
2269	8f. (3) Chinese and Japanese girls	1·40	25
2270	10f. (4) Musical entertainment	1·60	25
2271	22f. (5) Emblem of Meeting	2·30	50

1965. "Vietnamese People's Struggle".

2272	**391**	8f. (1) brown and red	1·20	35
2273	–	8f. (2) olive and red	1·20	35
2274	–	8f. (3) purple and red	1·20	35
2275	–	8f. (4) black and red	1·20	35

DESIGNS—VERT: (2) Soldier with captured weapons; (3) Soldier giving victory salute. HORIZ: (48½ × 26 mm): (4) "Peoples of the world".

392 "Victory" **393** Football

1965. 20th Anniv of Victory over Japanese.

2276	–	8f. (1) multicoloured	22·00	6·75
2277	–	8f. (2) green and red	13·00	90
2278	**392**	8f. (3) sepia and red	13·00	90
2279	–	8f. (4) green and red	13·00	90

DESIGNS—HORIZ: (50½ × 36 mm): (1) Mao Tse-tung writing. As Type **392**—HORIZ: (2) Soldiers crossing Yellow River. (4) Recruits in cart.

1965. 2nd National Games. Multicoloured.

2280	4f. (1) Type **393**	8·75	75
2281	4f. (2) Archery	8·75	75
2282	8f. (3) Throwing the javelin	11·00	75
2283	8f. (4) Gymnastics	11·00	75
2284	8f. (5) Volleyball	11·00	75
2285	10f. (6) Opening ceremony (horiz) (56 × 35½ mm)	26·00	75
2286	10f. (7) Cycling	49·00	75
2287	20f. (8) Diving	55·00	1·50
2288	22f. (9) Hurdling	10·50	2·00
2289	30f. (10) Weightlifting	10·50	4·00
2290	43f. (11) Basketball	15·00	7·00

394 Textile Workers

1965. Women in Industry. Multicoloured.

2291	8f. (1) Type **394**	7·00	60
2292	8f. (2) Machine building	7·00	60
2293	8f. (3) Building construction	7·00	60
2294	8f. (4) Studying	7·00	60
2295	8f. (5) Militia guard	7·00	3·75

395 Children playing with Ball

1966. Children's Games. Multicoloured.

2296	4f. (1) Type **395**	40	20
2297	4f. (2) Racing	40	20
2298	8f. (3) Tobogganing	40	20
2299	8f. (4) Exercising	40	25
2300	8f. (5) Swimming	50	25
2301	8f. (6) Shooting	50	25
2302	10f. (7) Jumping with rope	1·00	35
2303	52f. (8) Playing table tennis	1·80	1·20

396 Mobile Transformer

1966. New Industrial Machines.
2304 **396** 4f. (1) black and yellow . . 11·00 75
2305 – 8f. (2) black and blue . . 12·50 75
2306 – 8f. (3) black and pink . . 12·50 75
2307 – 8f. (4) black and olive . . 12·50 75
2308 – 8f. (5) black and purple . . 12·50 75
2309 – 10f. (6) black and grey . . 14·00 2·50
2310 – 10f. (7) black & turq . . 14·00 3·75
2311 – 22f. (8) black and lilac . . 23·00 4·75
DESIGNS—VERT: (2), Electron microscope; (4), Vertical boring and turning machine; (6), Hydraulic press; (8), Electron accelerator. HORIZ: (3), Lathe; (5), Gear-grinding machine; (7), Milling machine.

397 Women of Military and Other Services

1966. Women in Public Service. Mult.
2312 8f. (1) Type **397** 60 25
2313 8f. (2) Train conductress . . 60 25
2314 8f. (3) Red Cross worker . . 60 25
2315 8f. (4) Kindergarten teacher 60 25
2316 8f. (5) Roadsweeper 60 25
2317 8f. (6) Hairdresser 60 25
2318 8f. (7) Bus conductress . . . 60 25
2319 8f. (8) Travelling saleswoman 60 25
2320 8f. (9) Canteen worker . . . 60 25
2321 8f. (10) Rural postwoman 60 25

398 "Thunderstorm" (sculpture)

399 Dr. Sun Yat-sen

1966. Afro-Asian Writers' Meeting.
2322 **398** 8f. black and red . . . . 3·25 65
2323 – 22f. gold, yellow & red 6·00 95
DESIGN: 22f. Meeting emblem.

1966. Birth Centenary of Dr. Sun Yat-sen.
2324 **399** 8f. sepia and buff . . . 26·00 9·00

400 Athletes with Mao Tse-tung's Portrait

1966. "Cultural Revolution" Games. Multicoloured.
2325 8f. (1) Type **400** . . . . . . 23·00 7·00
2326 8f. (2) Athletes with linked arms hold Mao texts . . 23·00 7·00
2327 8f. (3) Two women athletes with Mao texts . . . . 23·00 5·75
2328 8f. (4) Athletes reading Mao texts . . . . 23·00 5·75
SIZES: No. 2326, As Type **400**, but vert; Nos. 2327/8, 36½ × 25 mm.

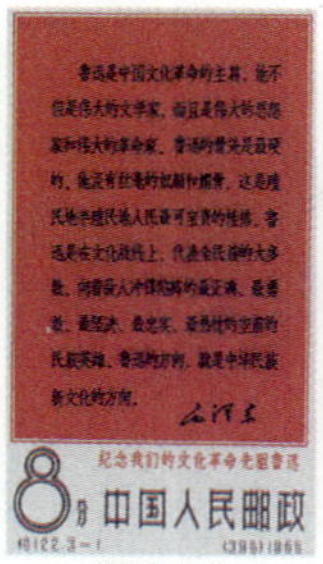
401 Mao's Appreciation of Lu Hsun (patriot and writer)

402 "Be Resolute ..." (Mao Tse-tung)

1966. 30th Death Anniv of Lu Hsun.
2329 **401** 8f. (1) black & orange 60·00 20·00
2330 – 8f. (2) black, flesh & red 20·00 12·00
2331 – 8f. (3) black & orange 40·00 12·00
DESIGNS: (2) Lu Hsun; (3) Lu Hsun's manuscript.

1967. Heroic Oilwell Firefighters.
2332 **402** 8f. (1) gold, red & black 25·00 10·00
2333 – 8f. (2) black and red . . 27·00 10·00
2334 – 8f. (3) black and red . . 27·00 10·00
DESIGNS—HORIZ: (48 × 27 mm): (2) Drilling Team No. 32111 fighting flames. VERT: (3) Smothering flames with tarpaulins.

403 Liu Ying-chun (military hero)

1967. Liu Ying-chun Commem. Multicoloured.
2335 8f. (1) Type **403** . . . . . . 23·00 8·00
2336 8f. (2) Liu Ying-chun holding book of Mao texts . . . . 23·00 8·00
2337 8f. (3) Liu Ying-chun holding horse's bridle . . 23·00 8·00
2338 8f. (4) Liu Ying-chun looking at film slide . . . 23·00 8·00
2339 8f. (5) Liu Ying-chun lecturing . . . . 23·00 8·00
2340 8f. (6) Liu Ying-chun making fatal attempt to stop bolting horse . . . . 23·00 8·00

404 Soldier, Nurse, Workers and Banners

1967. 3rd Five-Year Plan. Multicoloured.
2341 8f. (1) Type **404** . . . . . . 34·00 7·25
2342 8f. (2) Armed woman, peasants and banners . . 34·00 7·25

405 Mao Tse-tung

406 Mao Text (39 characters)

1967. "Thoughts of Mao Tse-tung" (1st issue). Similar designs showing Mao texts each gold and red. To assist identification of Nos. 2344/53 the total number of Chinese characters within the frames are given. (a) Type **405**.
2343 8f. multicoloured . . . . . 75·00 16·00

(b) As Type **406**. Red outer frames.
2344 8f. Type **406** . . . . 70·00 14·50
2345 8f. (50 characters) . . . . . 70·00 14·50
2346 8f. (39–in six lines) . . . . 70·00 14·50
2347 8f. (53) . . . . 70·00 14·50
2348 8f. (46) . . . . 70·00 14·50

(c) As Type **406**. Gold outer frames.
2349 8f. (41) . . . . 75·00 16·00
2350 8f. (49) . . . . 75·00 16·00
2351 8f. (35) . . . . 75·00 16·00
2352 8f. (22) . . . . 75·00 16·00
2353 8f. (29) . . . . 75·00 16·00
See also No. 2405.

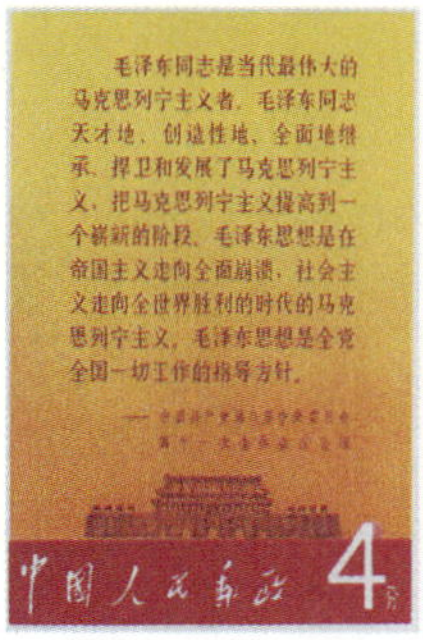
407 Text praising Mao

1967. Labour Day.
2354 **407** 4f. multicoloured . . . . 55·00 10·50
2355 – 8f. multicoloured . . . . 55·00 10·50
2356 – 8f. multicoloured . . . . 55·00 10·50
2357 – 8f. multicoloured . . . . 55·00 10·50
2358 – 8f. multicoloured . . . . 75·00 10·50
DESIGNS (Mao Tse-tung and): No. 2355, Poem; No. 2356, Multi-racial crowd with texts; No. 2357, Red Guards. (36 × 50½ mm): Mao with hand raised in greeting.
For stamps similar to No. 2358, see Nos. 2367/9.

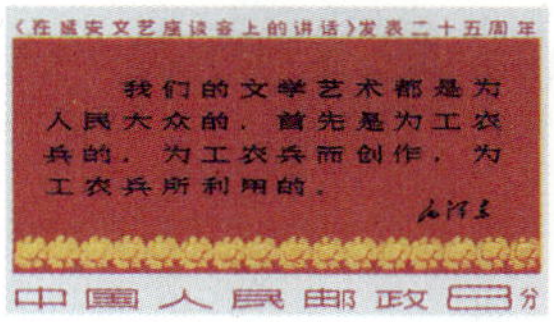
408 Mao Text

1967. 25th Anniv of Mao Tse-tung's "Talks on Literature and Art".
2359 **408** 8f. black, red & yellow £150 30·00
2360 – 8f. black, red & yellow £150 30·00
2361 – 8f. multicoloured . . . £180 45·00
DESIGNS: No. 2360, As Type **408** but different text. (50 × 36½ mm): No. 2361, Mao supporters in procession.

409 Mao Tse-tung

410 Mao Tse-tung and Lin Piao

1967. 46th Anniv of Chinese Communist Party.
2362 **409** 4f. red . . . . 50·00 10·00
2363 8f. red . . . . £140 8·75
2364 35f. brown . . . . . . 40·00 20·00
2365 43f. red . . . . 45·00 20·00
2366 52f. red . . . . 60·00 20·00

1967. "Our Great Teacher". Multicoloured.
2367 8f. Type **410** . . . . £190 50·00
2368 8f. Mao Tse-tung (horiz) . . 55·00 25·00
2369 10f. Mao Tse-tung conferring with Lin Piao (horiz) . . . . £225 50·00
For 8f. stamp showing Mao with hand raised in greeting, see No. 2358.

411 Mao Tse-tung as "Sun"

1967. 18th Anniv of People's Republic. Mult.
2370 8f. Type **411** . . . . 40·00 12·00
2371 8f. Mao Tse-tung with representatives of Communist countries . . 33·00 10·00

412 "Mount Liupan" (½-size illustration)

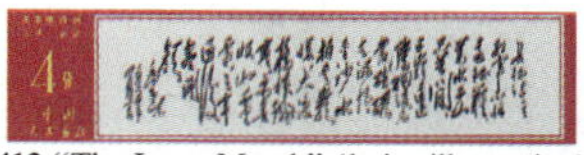
413 "The Long March" (½-size illustration)

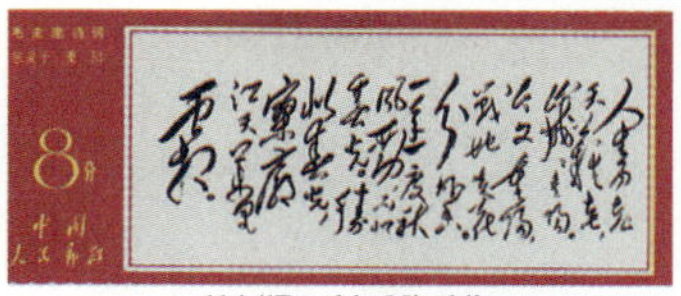
414 "Double Ninth"

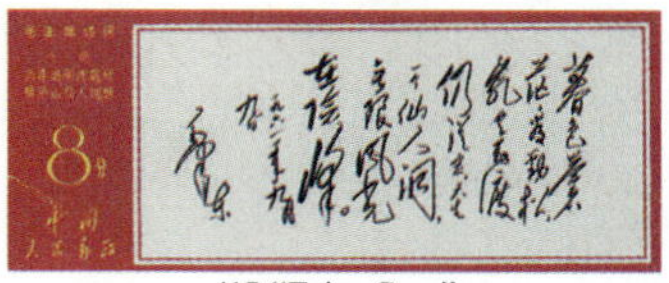
415 "Fairy Cave"

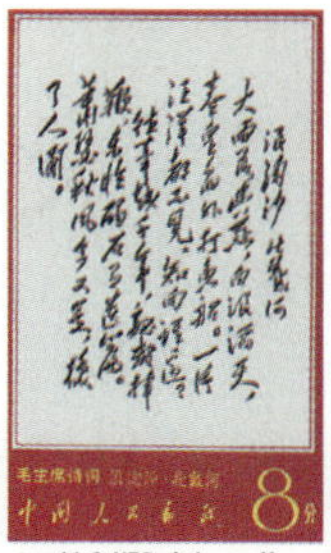
416 "Huichang"

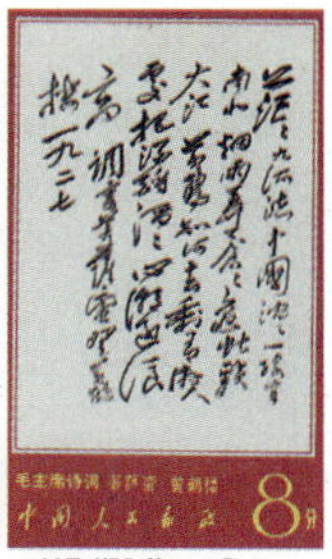
417 "Yellow Crane Pavilion"

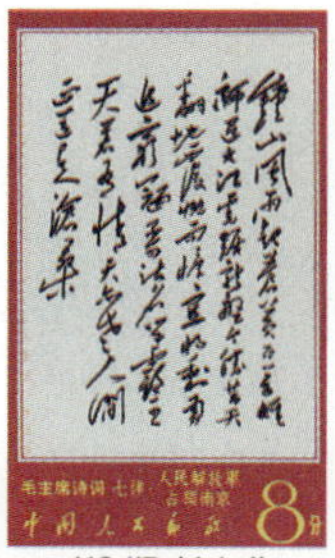
418 "Beidahe"

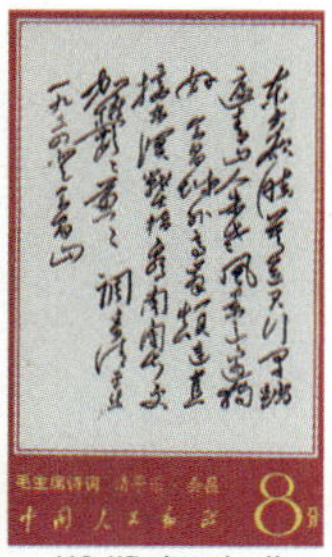
419 "Swimming"

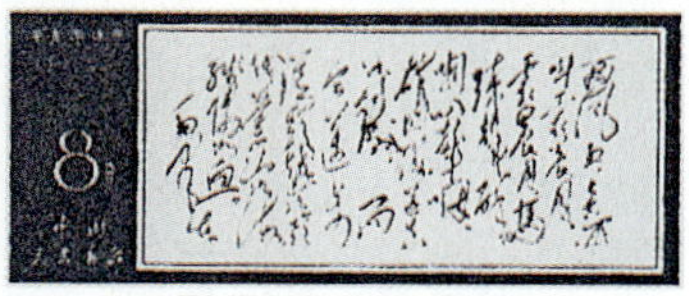
420 "Loushanguan Pass"

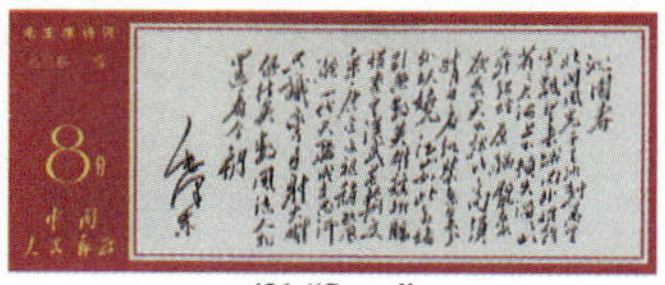
421 "Snow"

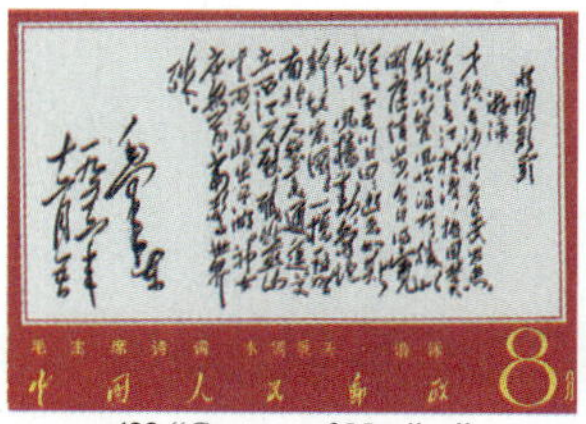
422 "Capture of Nanjing"

423 Mao Writing Poems at Desk

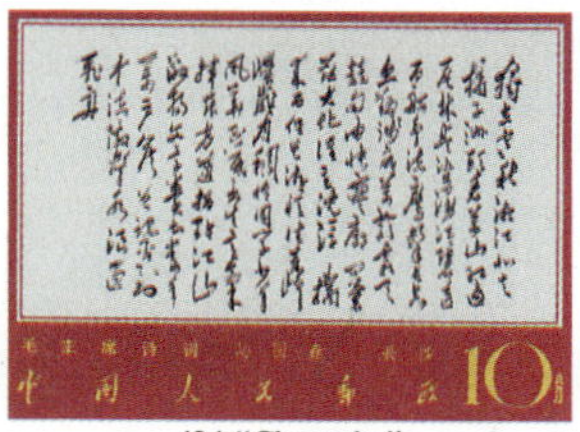
424 "Changsha"

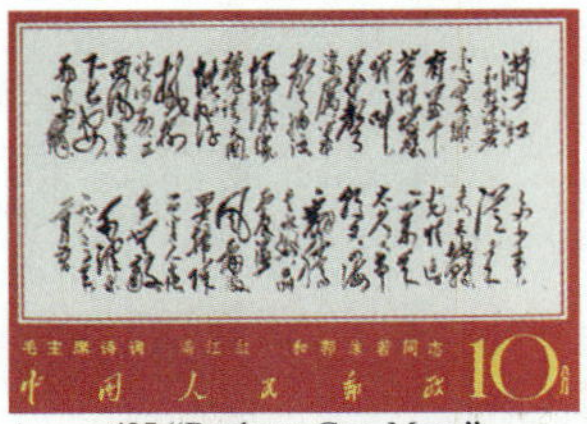
425 "Reply to Guo Moro"

1967. Poems of Mao Tse-tung.

2372	**412**	4f. black, yellow & red	18·00	20·00
2373	**413**	4f. black, yellow & red	55·00	14·50
2374	**414**	8f. black, yellow & red	55·00	10·50
2375	**415**	8f. black, yellow & red	46·00	15·00
2376	**416**	8f. black, yellow & red	£200	20·00
2377	**417**	8f. black, yellow & red	£130	20·00
2378	**418**	8f. black, yellow & red	£300	20·00
2379	**419**	8f. black, yellow & red	65·00	20·00
2380	**420**	8f. black, yellow & red	55·00	20·00
2381	**421**	8f. black, yellow & red	55·00	20·00
2382	**422**	8f. black, yellow & red	£150	20·00
2383	**423**	10f. multicoloured	22·00	20·00
2384	**424**	10f. black, yellow & red	24·00	18·00
2385	**425**	10f. black, yellow & red	29·00	15·00

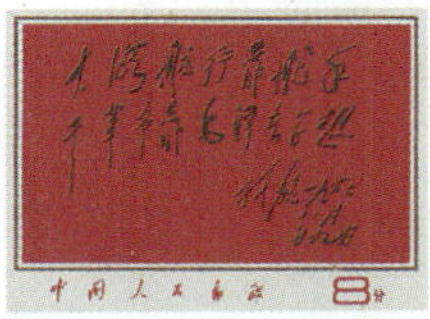
426 Epigram on Chairman Mao by Lin Piao

1967. Fleet Expansionists' Congress.
2386 **426** 8f. gold and red . . . . 40·00 8·75

427 Mao Tse-tung and Procession

1968. "Revolutionary Literature and Art" (1st issue). Multicoloured designs showing scenes from People's Operas.

2387	8f. Type **427**	44·00	6·75
2388	8f. "Raid on the White Tiger Regiment"	44·00	6·75
2389	8f. "Taking Tiger Mountain"	44·00	6·75
2390	8f. "On the Docks"	44·00	6·75
2391	8f. "Shachiapang"	44·00	6·75
2392	8f. "The Red Lantern" (vert)	44·00	6·75

428 "Red Detachment of Women" (ballet)

1968. "Revolutionary Literature and Art" (2nd issue). Multicoloured.

2393	8f. Type **428**	44·00	6·75
2394	8f. "The White-haired Girl" (ballet)	44·00	12·00
2395	8f. Mao Tse-tung, Symphony Orchestra and Chorus (50 × 36 mm)	44·00	12·00

429 Mao Tse-tung ("Unite still more closely")

1968. Mao's Anti-American Declaration.
2396 **429** 8f. brown, gold and red 50·00 12·00

430

431

432

433

434

1968. "Directives of Mao Tse-tung".

2397	**430**	8f. brown, red & yellow	£160	36·00
2398	**431**	8f. brown, red & yellow	£160	36·00
2399	**432**	8f. brown, red & yellow	£160	36·00
2400	**433**	8f. brown, red & yellow	£160	36·00
2401	**434**	8f. brown, red & yellow	£160	36·00

435 Inscription by Lin Piao. 26 July, 1965

1968. 41st Anniv of People's Liberation Army.
2402 **435** 8f. black, gold and red 12·00 5·50

436 "Chairman Mao goes to Anyuan" (Liu Chunhua)

1968. Mao's Youth.
2403 **436** 8f. multicoloured . . . . 25·00 7·00

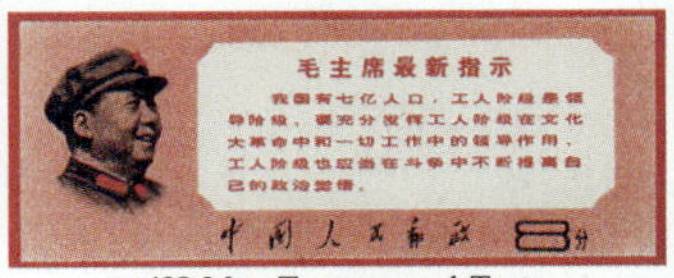
438 Mao Tse-tung and Text

1968. "Thoughts of Mao Tse-tung" (2nd issue).
2405 **438** 8f. brown and red . . . 55·00 19·00

439 Displaying "The Words of Mao Tse-tung"

1968. "The Words of Mao Tse-tung". No gum.
2406 **439** 8f. multicoloured . . . . 17·00 3·25

440 Yangtse Bridge

1968. Completion of Yangtse Bridge, Nanking. Multicoloured. No gum.

2407	4f. Type **440**	5·00	2·30
2408	8f. Buses on bridge	19·00	6·75
2409	8f. View of end portals	13·00	6·75
2410	10f. Aerial view	5·00	2·30

Nos. 2408/9 are larger, size 49 × 27 mm.

441 Li Yu-ho singing "I am filled with Courage and Strength"

1969. Songs from "The Red Lantern" Opera. Multicoloured. No gum.

2411	8f. Type **441**	8·50	8·00
2412	8f. Li Ti-mei singing "Hatred in my Heart"	48·00	11·50

442 Communist Party Building, Shanghai

1969. No gum.

2413	**442**	1½f. red, brown & lilac	70	70
2414	–	8f. brown, grn & cream	2·75	3·00
2415	–	8f. red and purple	70	40
2416	–	8f. brown and blue	1·30	70
2417	–	20f. blue, purple & red	2·00	1·50
2418	–	50f. brown and green	2·10	1·50

DESIGNS: "Historic Sites of the Revolution"; Size 27 × 22 mm—No. 2414, Pagoda Hill, Yenan; No. 2415, Gate of Heavenly Peace, Peking; No. 2418, Mao Tse-tung's house, Yenan. Size as T **442**—No. 2416, People's Heroes Monument, Peking; No. 2417, Conference Hall, Tsunyi.
See also Nos. 2455/65.

443 Rice Harvesters

1969. Agricultural Workers. Mult. No gum.

2419	4f. Type **443**	9·50	2·20
2420	8f. Grain harvest	11·50	1·90
2421	8f. Study Group with "Thoughts of Mao"	37·00	8·75
2422	10f. Red Cross worker with mother and child	9·50	1·90

444 Snow Patrol

445 Farm Worker

1969. Defence of Chen Pao Tao in the Ussur River. Multicoloured. No gum.

2423	8f. Type **444**	7·75	5·50
2424	8f. Guards by river (horiz)	7·75	5·50
2425	8f. Servicemen and Militia (horiz)	17·00	8·25
2426	35f. As No. 2424	7·75	6·75
2427	43f. Type **444**	7·75	6·75

1969. "The Chinese People" (woodcuts). No gum.

2428A	**445**	4f. purple and orange	55	45
2429A	–	8f. purple and orange	1·10	60
2430A	–	10f. green and orange	2·10	1·20

DESIGNS: 8f. Foundryman. 10f. Soldier.

446 Chin Hsun-hua in Water

447 Tractor-driver

1970. Heroic Death of Chin Hsun-hua in Kirin Border Floods. No gum.
2431 **446** 8f. black and red . . . . 19·00 15·00

1970. No gum.

2432	**447**	5f. black, red & orange	1·70	80
2433	–	1y. black and red	4·25	2·75

DESIGN—HORIZ: 1y. Foundryman.

448 Cavalry Patrol

449 "Yang Tse-jung, Army Scout"

1970. 43rd Anniv of People's Liberation Army. No gum.
2434 **448** 8f. multicoloured . . . . 7·00 5·00

1970. "Taking Tiger Mountain" (Revolutionary opera). Multicoloured. No gum.

2435	8f. (1) Type **449**	15·00	8·75
2436	8f. (2) "The patrol sets out" (horiz)	15·00	6·25
2437	8f. (3) "Leaping through the forest"	15·00	6·25
2438	8f. (4) "Li Yung-chi's farewell" (27 × 48 mm)	15·00	8·75
2439	8f. (5) "Yang Tse-jung in disguise" (27 × 48 mm)	15·00	6·25
2440	8f. (6) "Congratulating Yang Tse-jung" (horiz)	30·00	8·75

450 Soldiers in Snow

1970. 2nd Anniv of Defence of Chen Pao Tao. No gum.
2441 **450** 4f. multicoloured . . . . 3·00 2·20

451 Communard Standard

453 Workers and Great Hall of the People, Peking

452 Communist Party Building, Shanghai

1971. Cent of Paris Commune. Mult. No gum.

2442 **451** 4f. multicoloured . . . . 15·00 8·00
2443 – 8f. brown, pink and red 49·00 15·00
2444 – 10f. red, brn and pink 80·00 6·25
2445 – 22f. brown, red & pink 15·00 6·75

DESIGNS—HORIZ: 8f. Fighting in Paris, March 1871; 22f. Communards in Place Vendome. VERT: 10f. Commune proclaimed at the Hotel de Ville.

1971. 50th Anniv of Chinese Communist Party. Multicoloured. No gum.

2446 4f. (12) Type **452** . . . . . 8·00 2·30
2447 4f. (13) National Peasant Movement Inst., Canton 8·00 2·30
2448 8f. (14) Chingkang Mountains . . . . 7·75 2·30
2449 8f. (15) Conference Building, Tsunyi . . . . 7·75 2·30
2450 8f. (16) Pagoda Hill, Yenan 7·75 2·30
2452 8f. (18) Workers and Industry . . . . 16·00 3·25
2453 8f. (19) Type **453** . . . . . 16·00 3·25
2454 8f. (20) Workers and Agriculture . . . . . . 16·00 3·75
2451 22f. (17) Gate of Heavenly Peace, Peking . . . . . 16·00 3·25

SIZES: As Type **452**. Nos. 2447/2450 and 2451. As Type **453**. Nos. 2452/4.

454 National Peasant Movement Institute, Canton

455 Welcoming Bouquets

1971. Revolutionary Sites. Multicoloured. No gum.

2455 1f. Communist Party Building, Shanghai (vert) 20 20
2456 2f. Type **454** 20 20
2457 3f. Site of 1929 Congress, Kutien 25 20
2458 4f. Mao Tse-tung's house, Yenan 25 20
2459 8f. Gate of Heavenly Peace, Peking 25 25
2460 10f. Monument, Chingkang Mountains 35 25
2461 20f. River bridge, Yenan . . 45 25
2462 22f. Mao's birthplace, Shaoshan 70 35
2463 35f. Conference Building, Tsunyi . . . . 1·00 40
2464 43f. Start of the Long March, Chingkang Mountains . . . . 1·30 50
2465 52f. People's Palace, Peking 2·40 55

1971. "Afro-Asian Friendship" Table Tennis Tournament, Peking. Multicoloured. No gum.

2466 8f. (22) Type **455** . . . . . 5·00 1·30
2467 8f. (23) Group of players . . 5·00 1·30
2468 8f. (24) Asian and African players . . . . 5·00 1·30
2469 43f. (21) Tournament badge 10·00 2·30

456 Enver Hoxha making speech

1971. 30th Anniv of Albanian Worker's Party. Multicoloured. No gum.

2470 8f. (25) Type **456** . . . . . 10·00 5·75
2471 8f. (26) Party Headquarters 7·00 3·50
2472 8f. (27) Albanian flag, rifle and pick . . . . 7·00 3·50
2473 52f. (28) Soldier and Worker's Militia (horiz) 14·00 5·75

457 Conference Hall, Yenan

1972. 30th Anniv of Publication of "Yenan Forum's Discussions on Literature and Art". Multicoloured. No gum.

2474 8f. (33) Type **457** . . . . . 6·00 2·30
2475 8f. (34) Army choir . . . . 6·00 2·30
2476 8f. (35) "Brother and Sister" 6·00 2·30
2477 8f. (36) "Open-air Theatre" 6·00 2·30
2478 8f. (37) "The Red Lantern" (opera) . . . . 12·00 2·30
2479 8f. (38) "Red Detachment of Women" (ballet) . . . . 12·00 2·30

458 Ball Games

1972. 10th Anniv of Mao Tse-tungs's Edict on Physical Culture. Multicoloured. No gum.

2480 8f. (39) Type **458** . . . . . 7·00 1·50
2481 8f. (40) Gymnastics . . . . 7·00 1·50
2482 8f. (41) Tug-of-War . . . . 7·00 1·50
2483 8f. (42) Rock-climbing . . . 7·00 1·50
2484 8f. (43) High-diving . . . . 7·00 1·50

Nos. 2481/4 are size 26 × 36 mm.

460 Freighter "Fenglei"

1972. Chinese Merchant Shipping. Multicoloured.

2485 8f. (29) Type **460** . . . . . 8·75 2·50
2486 8f. (30) Tanker "Taching No. 30" . . . . 8·75 2·50
2487 8f. (31) Cargo-liner "Chang Seng" . . . . 8·75 2·50
2488 8f. (32) Dredger "Hsienfeng" . . . . . . 8·75 2·50

461 Championship Badge

462 Wang Chin-hsi, the "Iron Man"

1972. 1st Asian Table Tennis Championships, Peking. Multicoloured. No gum.

2489 8f. (45) Type **461** . . . . . 2·30 85
2490 8f. (46) Welcoming crowd (horiz) . . . . 2·30 85
2491 8f. (47) Game in progress (horiz) . . . . 2·00 85
2492 22f. (48) Players from three countries . . . . 2·50 1·70

1972. Wang Chin-hsi (workers' hero) Commem. No gum.

2493 **462** 8f. multicoloured . . . . 3·50 1·60

463 Cliff-edge Construction

464 Giant Panda eating Bamboo Shoots

1972. Construction of Red Flag Canal. Mult.

2494 8f. (49) Type **463** . . . . . 1·60 85
2495 8f. (50) "Youth" tunnel . . 1·60 85
2496 8f. (51) "Taoguan bridge" 1·60 85
2497 8f. (52) Cliff-edge canal . . 1·60 85

1973. China's Giant Pandas.

2498 **464** 4f. (61) multicoloured . . 13·50 5·25
2499 – 8f. (59) mult (horiz) . . 13·50 5·25
2500 – 8f. (60) mult (horiz) . . 13·50 5·25
2501 – 10f. (58) multicoloured 60·00 11·00
2502 – 20f. (57) multicoloured 32·00 8·00
2503 – 43f. (62) multicoloured 40·00 15·00

DESIGNS: 8f. to 43f. Different brush and ink drawings of pandas.

465 "New Power in the Mines" (Yang Shi-guang)

466 Girl dancing

1973. International Working Women's Day. Mult.

2504 8f. (63) Type **465** . . . . . 2·50 1·40
2505 8f. (64) "Woman Committee Member" (Tang Hsiaoming) . . . . 2·50 1·40
2506 8f. (65) "I am a Sea-gull" (Army telegraph line woman) (Pan Jiajun) . . 2·50 1·40

1973. Children's Day. Multicoloured.

2507 8f. (86) Type **466** . . . . . 1·60 1·30
2508 8f. (87) Boy musician . . . 1·60 1·30
2509 8f. (88) Boy with scarf . . . 1·60 1·30
2510 8f. (89) Boy with tambourine . . . . 1·60 1·30
2511 8f. (90) Girl with drum . . 1·60 1·30

467 Badge of Championships

468 "Hsi-erh"

1973. Asian, African and Latin-American Table Tennis Invitation Championships. Multicoloured.

2512 8f. (91) Type **467** . . . . . 2·30 1·20
2513 8f. (92) Visitors . . . . . . 2·30 1·20
2514 8f. (93) Player . . . . 2·30 1·20
2515 22f. (94) Guest players . . . 3·50 1·40

1973. Revolutionary Ballet "Hsi-erh" ("The White-haired Girl"). Multicoloured.

2516 8f. (53) Type **468** . . . . . 5·00 1·30
2517 8f. (54) Hsi-erh escapes from Huang (horiz) . . . . . . 5·00 1·30
2518 8f. (55) Hsi-erh meets Tachun (horiz) . . . . . . 5·00 1·30
2519 8f. (56) Hsi-erh becomes a soldier . . . . 5·00 1·30

469 Fair Building

1973. Chinese Exports Fair, Canton.

2520 **469** 8f. multicoloured . . . . 3·50 2·40

470 Mao's Birthplace, Shaoshan

471 Steam and Diesel Trains

1973. No gum.

2521 **470** 1f. green & light green 55 25
2522 – 1½f. red and yellow . . . 55 30
2523 – 2f. blue and green . . . 55 25
2524 – 3f. green and yellow . . 55 25
2525 – 4f. red and yellow . . . 55 25
2526 – 5f. brown and yellow . . 55 25
2527 – 8f. purple and flesh . . . 55 25
2528 – 10f. blue and flesh . . . 55 25
2529 – 20f. red and buff . . . . 1·30 25
2530 – 22f. violet and yellow . . 2·00 25
2531 – 35f. purple and yellow 2·75 85
2532 – 43f. brown and flesh 3·50 1·40
2533 – 50f. blue and mauve 4·25 2·20
2534 – 52f. brown and yellow 5·50 2·75
2535 **471** 1y. multicoloured . . . 2·10 60
2536 – 2y. multicoloured . . . 3·50 70

DESIGNS—As Type **470**: 1½f. National Peasant Movement Institute, Shanghai. 2f. National Institute, Kwangchow. 3f. Headquarters Building, Nanching uprising. 4f. Great Hall of the People, Peking. 5f. Wen Chia Shih. 8f. Gate of Heavenly Peace, Peking. 10f. Chingkang Mountains. 20f. Kutien Congress building. 22f. Tsunyi Congress building. 35f. Bridge, Yenan. 43f. Hsi Pai Po. 50f. "Fairy Gate", Lushan. 52f. People's Heroes Monument, Peking. As Type **471**: 2y. Trucks on mountain road.

472 "Phoenix" Pot

473 Dance Routine

1973. Archaeological Treasures. Multicoloured.

2537 4f. (66) Type **472** . . . . . 1·10 75
2538 4f. (67) Silver pot . . . . . 1·10 75
2539 8f. (68) Porcelain horse and groom . . . . 1·10 75
2540 8f. (69) Figure of woman . . 1·10 75
2541 8f. (70) Carved pedestals . . 1·10 75
2542 8f. (71) Bronze horse . . . 1·10 75
2543 8f. (72) Gilded "frog" . . . 1·10 75
2544 8f. (73) Lamp-holder figurine . . . . 1·10 75
2545 10f. (74) Tripod jar . . . . 1·10 90
2546 10f. (75) Bronze vessel . . . 1·10 90
2547 20f. (76) Bronze wine vessel 1·70 1·30
2548 52f. (77) Tray with tripod 3·25 2·75

1974. Popular Gymnastics. Multicoloured.

2549 8f. (1) Type **473** . . . . . . 8·00 3·00
2550 8f. (2) Rings exercise . . . 8·00 3·00
2551 8f. (3) Dancing on beam . . 8·00 3·00
2552 8f. (4) Handstand on parallel bars . . . . . . 8·00 3·00
2553 8f. (5) Trapeze exercise . . . 8·50 3·50
2554 8f. (6) Vaulting over horse 8·50 3·50

474 Lion Dance

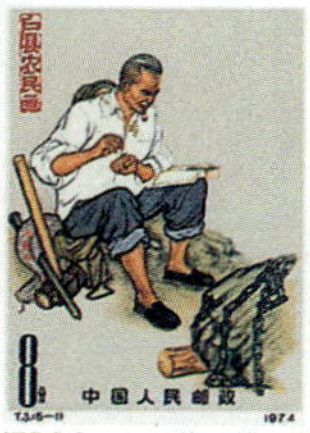

475 Man reading Book

1974. Acrobatics. Multicoloured.

2555 8f. (1) Type **474** . . . . . . 7·50 2·75
2556 8f. (2) Handstand on chairs 7·50 2·75
2557 8f. (3) Diabolo team (horiz) 7·50 2·75
2558 8f. Revolving jar (horiz) . . 8·00 2·75
2559 8f. (5) Spinning plates . . . 8·00 2·75
2560 8f. (6) Foot-juggling with parasol . . . . 8·00 2·75

1974. Huhsien Paintings. Multicoloured.

2561 8f. (1) Type **475** . . . . . . 2·00 1·30
2562 8f. (2) Mineshaft (23 × 57 mm) . . . . 2·00 1·30
2563 8f. (3) Workers hoeing field (horiz) . . . . 2·00 1·30
2564 8f. (4) Workers eating (horiz) . . . . 2·00 1·30
2565 8f. (5) Wheatfield landscape (57 × 23 mm) . . . . . . 2·30 1·30
2566 8f. (6) Harvesting (horiz) . . 2·30 1·30

476 Postman

1974. Centenary of UPU. Multicoloured.

2567 8f. (1) Type **476** . . . . . . 6·50 3·50
2568 8f. (2) People of five races 6·50 3·50
2569 8f. (3) Great Wall of China 6·50 3·50

477 Inoculating Children

1974. Country Doctors. Multicoloured.
2570 8f. (1) Type **477** . . . . . . 1·50 1·00
2571 8f. (2) On country visit (vert) . . . . 1·50 1·00
2572 8f. (3) Gathering herbs (vert) 1·50 1·00
2573 8f. (4) Giving acupuncture 1·50 1·00

478 Wang Chin-hsi, "The Iron Man"

1974. Chairman Mao's Directives on Industrial and Agricultural Teaching. Multicoloured. (a) "Learning Industry from Taching".
2574 8f. (1) Type **478** . . . . . . 1·30 95
2575 8f. (2) Pupils studying Mao's works . . . . 1·30 95
2576 8f. (3) Oil-workers sinking well . . . . 1·30 95
2577 8f. (4) Consultation with management . . . . . . 1·30 95
2578 8f. (5) Taching oilfield as development site . . . . 1·30 95

(b) "Learning Agriculture from Tachai".
2579 8f. (1) Tachai workers looking to future . . . . 1·30 95
2580 8f. (2) Construction workers 1·30 95
2581 8f. (3) Agricultural workers making field tests . . . . 1·30 95
2582 8f. (4) Trucks delivering grain to State granaries 1·30 95
2583 8f. (5) Workers going to fields . . . . 1·30 95

479 National Day Celebrations

480 Steel Worker, Taching

1974. 25th Anniv of Chinese People's Republic. Multicoloured. (a) National Day.
2584 8f. Type **479** . . . . 5·50 3·75

(b) Chairman Mao's Directives.
2585 8f. (1) Type **480** . . . . . . 1·80 1·60
2586 8f. (2) Agricultural worker, Tachai . . . . 1·80 1·60
2587 8f. (3) Coastal guard . . . . 1·80 1·60

481 Fair Building

1974. Chinese Exports Fair, Canton.
2588 **481** 8f. multicoloured . . . . 3·50 1·60

482 Revolutionary Monument, Permet

483 Capital Stadium

1974. 30th Anniv of Albania's Liberation. Mult.
2589 8f. Type **482** . . . . 3·50 1·60
2590 8f. Albanian patriots . . . 3·50 1·60

1974. Peking Buildings. No gum.
2591 **483** 4f. black and green . . . 16·00 20
2592 – 8f. black and blue . . . 35 20
DESIGN: 8f. Hotel Peking.

484 Water-cooled Turbine Generator

1974. Industrial Production. Multicoloured.
2593 8f. (78) Type **484** . . . . . 18·00 3·50
2594 8f. (79) Mechanical rice sprouts transplanter . . . 18·00 3·50
2595 8f. (80) Universal cylindrical grinding machine . . . . 18·00 3·50
2596 8f. (81) Mobile rock drill (vert) . . . . 18·00 3·50

485 Congress Delegates

1975. 4th National People's Congress, Peking. Multicoloured.
2597 8f. (1) Type **485** . . . . . . 3·50 1·40
2598 8f. (2) Flower-decked rostrum . . . . 3·50 1·40
2599 8f. (3) Farmer, worker, soldier and steel mill . . . 3·50 1·40

486 Teacher Studying

1975. Country Women Teachers. Multicoloured.
2600 8f. (1) Type **486** . . . . . . 8·75 2·75
2601 8f. (2) Teacher on rounds 8·75 2·75
2602 8f. (3) Open-air class . . . 8·75 2·75
2603 8f. (4) Primary class aboard boat . . . . 8·75 2·75

487 Broadsword

1975. "Wushu" (popular sport). Multicoloured.
2604 8f. (1) Type **487** . . . . . . 3·75 2·10
2605 8f. (2) Sword exercises . . . 3·75 2·10
2606 8f. (3) "Boxing" . . . . . . 3·75 2·10
2607 8f. (4) Leaping with spear 3·75 2·10
2608 8f. (5) Cudgel exercise . . . 3·75 2·10
2609 43f. (6) Cudgel versus spears (60 × 30 mm) . . . . . . 10·50 11·00

488 "Mass Revolutionary Criticism"

489 Parade of Athletes

1975. Criticism of Confucius and Liu Piao. Multicoloured.
2610 8f. (1) Type **488** . . . . . . 6·75 2·75
2611 8f. (2) "Leaders of the production brigade" . . . 6·75 2·75
2612 8f. (3) "The battle continues" (horiz) . . . . 6·75 2·75
2613 8f. (4) "Liberated slave – pioneer critic" (horiz) . . . 6·75 2·75

1975. 3rd National Games, Peking. Mult.
2614 8f. (1) Type **489** . . . . . . 1·20 85
2615 8f. (2) Athletes studying (horiz) . . . . 1·20 85
2616 8f. (3) Volleyball players (horiz) . . . . 1·20 85
2617 8f. (4) Athlete, soldier, farmer and worker . . . 1·20 85
2618 8f. (5) Various sports (horiz) 1·20 85
2619 8f. (6) Ethnic types and horse racing (horiz) . . . 1·20 85
2620 35f. (7) Children and divers 4·50 3·50

490 Members of Expedition

492 Children sticking Posters

491 "Studying Together"

1975. Chinese Ascent of Mount Everest. Mult.
2621 8f. (2) Type **490** 55 35
2622 8f. (3) Mountaineers with flag (horiz) 55 35
2623 43f. (1) View of Mount Everest (horiz) . . . . 1·20 85

1975. National Conference "Learning Agriculture from Tachai". Multicoloured.
2624 8f. (1) Type **491** . . . . . . 3·50 1·30
2625 8f. (2) "Promote Hard Work" . . . . 3·50 1·30
2626 8f. (3) Chinese combine-harvester . . . . 3·50 1·30

1975. "Children's Progress". Multicoloured.
2627 8f. (1) Girl and young boy 1·10 95
2628 8f. (2) Type **492** . . . . . . 1·10 95
2629 8f. (3) Studying . . . . . . 1·10 95
2630 8f. (4) Harvesting . . . . . . 1·10 95
2631 52f. (5) Tug-of-war . . . . 6·75 3·75

493 Ploughing Paddy Field

1975. Mechanised Farming. Multicoloured.
2632 8f. (1) Type **493** . . . . . . 2·20 1·30
2633 8f. (2) Mechanical rice seedlings transplanter . . 2·20 1·30
2634 8f. (3) Irrigation pump . . . 2·20 1·30
2635 8f. (4) Spraying cotton field 2·20 1·30
2636 8f. (5) Combine harvester 2·20 1·30

494 Bridge over Canal

1976. Completion of 4th Five-year Plan. Mult.
2637 8f. (1) Harvest scene . . . . 3·50 1·80
2638 8f. (2) Type **494** . . . . . . 3·50 1·80
2639 8f. (3) Fertilizer plant . . . 3·50 1·80
2640 8f. (4) Textile factory . . . 3·50 1·80
2641 8f. (5) Iron foundry . . . . 3·50 1·80
2642 8f. (6) Steam coal train . . 3·50 1·80
2643 8f. (7) Hydro-electric power station . . . . 3·50 1·80
2644 8f. (8) Shipbuilding . . . . 3·50 1·80
2645 8f. (9) Oil industry . . . . 3·50 1·80
2646 8f. (10) Pipe-line and harbour . . . . 3·50 1·80
2647 8f. (11) Diesel train on viaduct . . . . 4·75 1·80
2648 8f. (12) Crystal formation (scientific research) . . . 4·75 1·80
2649 8f. (13) Classroom (rural education) . . . . 4·75 1·80
2650 8f. (14) Workers' health centre . . . . 4·75 1·80
2651 8f. (15) Workers' flats . . . 5·50 1·80
2652 8f. (16) Department store . . 5·50 1·80

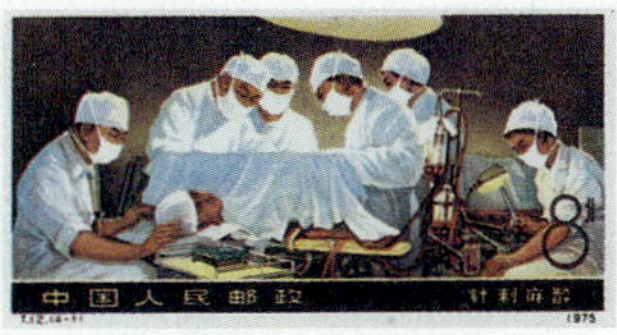
495 Heart Surgery

1976. Medical Services' Achievements. Mult.
2653 8f. (1) Type **495** . . . . . 3·50 1·00
2654 8f. (2) Restoration of tractor-driver's severed arm . . . . 3·50 1·00
2655 8f. (3) Exercise of fractured arm . . . . 3·50 1·00
2656 8f. (4) Cataract operation – patient threading needle 3·50 1·00

496 Students studying at "May 7" School

1976. 10th Anniv of Mao's "May 7 Directive". Multicoloured.
2657 8f. (1) Type **496** . . . . . . 1·80 1·40
2658 8f. (2) Students in agriculture . . . . 1·80 1·40
2659 8f. (3) Students in production team . . . . 1·80 1·40

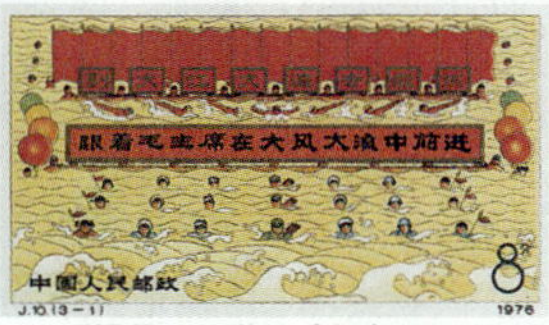
497 Formation of Swimmers

1976. 10th Anniv of Chairman Mao's Swim in Yangtse River. Multicoloured.
2660 8f. (1) Type **497** . . . . . . 2·00 1·20
2661 8f. (2) Swimmers crossing Yangtse . . . . 2·00 1·20
2662 8f. (3) Swimmers in surf . . 2·00 1·20
Nos. 2661/2 are smaller, 35 × 27 mm.

498 Students with Rosettes

1976. "Going to College". Multicoloured.
2663 8f. (1) Type **498** . . . . . . 2·40 1·20
2664 8f. (2) Study group . . . . 2·40 1·20
2665 8f. (3) On-site instructions 2·40 1·10
2666 8f. (4) Students operating computer . . . . 2·40 1·10
2667 8f. (5) Return of graduates from college . . . . . . 2·40 1·10

499 Electricity Lineswoman

501 Peasant arranging Student's Headband

500 Lu Hsun

1976. Maintenance of Electric Power Lines. Multicoloured.
2668 8f. (1) Type **499** . . . . . . 2·40 1·60
2669 8f. (2) Linesman replacing insulator . . . . 2·40 1·60
2670 8f. (3) Linesman using hydraulic lift . . . . 3·00 1·60
2671 8f. (4) Technician inspecting transformer . . . . . . 3·00 1·60

1976. 95th Birth Anniv of Lu Hsun (revolutionary leader). Multicoloured.
2672 8f. (1) Type **500** . . . . . . 5·25 1·70
2673 8f. (2) Lu Hsun sick, writing in bed . . . . 5·25 1·70
2674 8f. (3) Lu Hsun, workers and soldiers . . . . . . 5·25 1·70

1976. Students and Country Life. Multicoloured.
2675 4f. (1) Type **501** . . . . . . 1·10 55
2676 8f. (2) Student teaching farm woman (horiz) . . . . . 1·10 55
2677 8f. (3) Irrigation survey . . . 1·10 55
2678 8f. (4) Agricultural student testing wheat (horiz) . . . 1·10 55
2679 10f. (5) Student feeding lamb . . . . 1·90 75
2680 20f. (6) Frontier guards (horiz) . . . . 5·25 1·80

502 Mao Tse-tung's Birthplace

1976. Shaoshan Revolutionary Sites. Mult.
2681 4f. (1) Type **502** . . . . . . 1·30 85
2682 8f. (2) School building . . . 1·60 85
2683 8f. (3) Peasants' Association building . . . . 1·60 85
2684 10f. (4) Railway station . . 2·00 1·30

503 Chou En-lai

504 Statue of Lui Hu-lan

1977. 1st Death Anniv of Chou En-lai. Mult.
2685 8f. (1) Type **503** . . . . . . 1·50 70
2686 8f. (2) Chou En-lai making report . . . . 1·50 70
2687 8f. (3) Chou meeting "Iron Man" Wang Chin-hsi (horiz) . . . . 1·50 70
2688 8f. (4) Chou with provincial representatives (horiz) . . 3·50 70

1977. 30th Death Anniv of Lin Hu-lan (heroine and martyr). Multicoloured.
2689 8f. (1) Type **504** . . . . . . 5·25 2·50
2690 8f. (2) Text by Mao Tse-tung . . . . 5·25 2·50
2691 8f. (3) Lin Hu-lan and people . . . . 5·25 2·50

505 Revolutionaries and Text

1977. 30th Anniv of 1947 Taiwan Rising. Mult.
2692 8f. Type **505** . . . . 1·50 85
2693 10f. Three Taiwanese with banner . . . . 2·20 1·30

506 Weapon Maintenance

1977. Chinese Militiawomen. Multicoloured.
2694 8f. (1) Type **506** . . . . . . 5·00 2·75
2695 8f. (2) On horseback . . . . 5·00 2·75
2696 8f. (3) Directing traffic in tunnel . . . . 5·00 2·75

507 Sheep Rearing

508 Cadre Members

1977. Multicoloured.
2697 1f. Coal mining 30 30
2698 1½f. Type **507** 30 20
2699 2f. Exports 30 20
2700 3f. Forest and diesel-train 30 20
2701 4f. Hydro-electric power . . 30 20
2702 5f. Fishing 30 20
2703 8f. Agriculture 30 20
2704 10f. Radio tower and mail-vans 35 25
2705 20f. Steel production 40 25
2706 30f. Road transport 40 25
2707 40f. Textile manufacture . . 55 25
2708 50f. Tractor assembly . . . 65 25
2709 60f. Oil-rigs and setting sun 75 25
2710 70f. Railway viaduct, Yangtse Gorge . . . . . 1·20 35

1977. Promoting Tachai-type Developments. Mult.
2711 8f. (1) Type **508** . . . . . . 1·00 75
2712 8f. (2) Modern cultivation 1·00 75
2713 8f. (3) Reading wall newspaper . . . . 1·00 75
2714 8f. (4) Reclaiming land for agriculture . . . . 1·00 75

509 Party Leader addressing Workers

1977. "Taching-type" Industrial Conference. Mult.
2715 8f. (1) Type **509** . . . . . . 1·70 95
2716 8f. (2) Drilling for oil in snowstorm . . . . 1·70 95
2717 8f. (3) Man with banner over mass formation of workers . . . . 1·70 95
2718 8f. (4) Smiling workers and industrial scene . . . . . . 1·70 95

510 Mongolians Rejoicing

511 Rumanian Flag

1977. 30th Anniv of Inner Mongolian Autonomous Region. Multicoloured.
2719 8f. Type **510** 60 25
2720 10f. Mongolian industrial scene and iron ore train 65 35
2721 20f. Mongolian pasture . . 1·50 85

1977. Centenary of Rumanian Independence. Mult.
2722 8f. Type **511** 95 55
2723 10f. "The Battle of Smirdan" (Grigorescu) . . 95 75
2724 20f. Mihai Viteazu Memorial . . . . 2·20 1·50

512 Yenan and Floral Border

1977. 35th Anniv of Yenan Forum on Literature and Art. Multicoloured.
2725 8f. (1) Type **512** . . . . . . 1·00 60
2726 8f. (2) Hammer, sickle and gun . . . . 1·00 60

513 Chu Teh, National People's Congress Chairman

514 Soldier, Sailor and Airman under Banner of Mao Tse-tung

1977. 1st Death Anniv of Chu Teh.
2727 **513** 8f. (1) multicoloured . . 75 35
2728 – 8f. (2) multicoloured . . 75 35
2729 – 8f. (3) black, bl & gold 75 35
2730 – 8f. (4) black, bl & gold 75 35
DESIGNS—VERT: No. 2728, Chu Teh during his last session of Congress. HORIZ: No. 2729, Chu Teh at his desk. No. 2730, Chu Teh on horseback as Commander of People's Liberation Army.

1977. People's Liberation Army Day. Mult.
2731 8f. (1) Type **514** . . . . . . 1·80 95
2732 8f. (2) Soldiers in Ching-kang Mountains . . . . 1·80 95
2733 8f. (3) Guerrilla fighters returning to base . . . . 1·80 95
2734 8f. (4) Chinese forces crossing Yangtse River . . 1·80 95
2735 8f. (5) "The Steel Wall" (National Defence Forces) 1·80 95

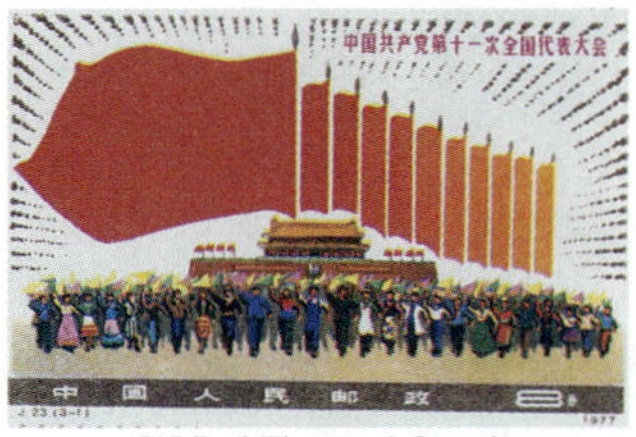
515 Red Flags and Crowd

1977. 11th National Communist Party Congress. Multicoloured.
2736 8f. (1) Type **515** . . . . . . 4·00 3·00
2737 8f. (2) Mao banner and procession . . . . 4·00 3·00
2738 8f. (3) Hammer and sickle banner and procession . . 4·00 3·00

516 Mao Tse-tung

1977. 1st Death Anniv of Mao Tse-tung. Mult.
2739 8f. (1) Type **516** . . . . . . 1·10 80
2740 8f. (2) Mao as young man 1·10 80
2741 8f. (3) Making speech . . . 1·10 80
2742 8f. (4) Mao broadcasting . . 1·10 80
2743 8f. (5) Mao with Chou En-lai and Chu Teh (horiz) 1·10 80
2744 8f. (6) Reviewing the army 1·10 80

517 Mao Memorial Hall

1977. Completion of Mao Memorial Hall, Peking. Multicoloured.
2745 8f. (1) Type **517** . . . . . . 2·50 1·50
2746 8f. (2) Commemoration text 2·50 1·50

518 Tractors transporting Oil-rig

1978. Development of Petroleum Industry. Mult.
2747 8f. (1) Type **518** 55 45
2748 8f. (2) Clearing wax from oil well 55 45
2749 8f. (3) Laying pipe-line . . . 55 45
2750 8f. (4) Tung Fang Hung oil refinery, Peking 55 45
2751 8f. (5) Loading a tanker, Taching 55 45
2752 20f. (6) Oil-rig and drilling ship "Exploration" . . . 1·60 80

519 Rifle Shooting from Sampan

1978. "Army and People are One Family". Multicoloured.
2753 8f. (1) Type **519** . . . . . . 1·60 1·30
2754 8f. (2) Helping with rice harvest . . . . 1·60 1·30

520 Great Banner of Chairman Mao

521 "Learn from Comrade Lei Feng" (Inscription by Mao Tse-tung)

1978. 5th National People's Congress. Mult.
2755 8f. (1) Type **520** . . . . . 1·00 75
2756 8f. (2) Constitution . . . . 1·00 75
2757 8f. (3) Emblems of modernization . . . . . 1·00 75

1978. Lei Feng (Communist fighter) Commem.
2758 **521** 8f. (1) gold and red . . . 1·60 1·30
2759 – 8f. (2) gold and red . . . 1·60 1·30
2760 – 8f. (3) multicoloured . . 1·60 1·30
DESIGNS: No. 2759, Inscription by Chairman Hua; No. 2760, Lei Feng reading Mao's works.

522 Hsiang Ching-yu (Women's Movement Pioneer)

523 Conference Emblem and Tien on Men Gate, Peking

1978. International Working Women's Day.
2761 **522** 8f. (1) black, red & gold 90 75
2762 – 8f. (2) black, red & gold 90 75
DESIGN: No. 2762, Yang Kai-hui (communist fighter).

1978. National Science Conference. Mult.
2763 8f. (1) Type **523** . . . . . . 1·00 80
2764 8f. (2) Flags . . . . 1·00 80
2765 8f. (3) Emblem, flag and globe . . . . 1·00 80
MS2765a 140 × 106 mm. Nos. 2763/2765. Imperf £350 £170

524 Launching a Radio-sonde

1978. Meteorological Services. Multicoloured.
2766 8f. (1) Type **524** 70 55
2767 8f. (2) Radar station 70 55
2768 8f. (3) Weather forecasting with computers 70 55
2769 8f. (4) Commune group observing sky 70 55
2770 8f. (5) Cloud-dispersing rockets 70 55

525 Galloping Horse

526 Football

1978. Galloping Horses.
2771 **525** 4f. (1) multicoloured . . 75 55
2772 – 8f. (2) multicoloured . . 75 55
2773 – 8f. (3) multicoloured . . 75 55
2774 – 10f. (4) multicoloured . . 75 55
2775 – 20f. (5) multicoloured . . 2·75 90
2776 – 30f. (6) multicoloured . . 2·50 1·20
2777 – 40f. (7) mult (horiz) . . 3·00 1·70
2778 – 50f. (8) mult (horiz) . . 3·75 1·90
2779 – 60f. (9) mult (horiz) . . 4·50 2·75
2780 – 70f. (10) mult (horiz) . . 5·00 3·50
MS2781 148 × 98 mm. 5y. multicoloured (82 × 32 mm) . . £200 £100
DESIGNS: No. 2772/80, various paintings of horses by Hsu Pei-hung.

1978. "Building up Strength for the Revolution". Multicoloured.
2782 8f. (2) Type **526** 50 40
2783 8f. (3) Swimming 50 40
2784 8f. (4) Gymnastics 50 40
2785 8f. (5) Running 50 40
2786 20f. (1) Group exercises . . 1·00 70
The 20f. is larger, 48 × 27 mm.

527 Material Feeder

1978. Chemical Industry Development. Fabric Production. Multicoloured.
2787 8f. (1) Type **527** 75 60
2788 8f. (2) Drawing-out threads 75 60
2789 8f. (3) Weaving 75 60
2790 8f. (4) Dyeing and printing 75 60
2791 8f. (5) Finished products . . 75 60

528 Conference Emblem

529 Grassland Improvement, Mongolia

1978. National Finance and Trade Conference. Multicoloured.

2792	8f. (1) Type **528**	50	40
2793	8f. (2) Inscription by Mao Tse-tung	50	40

1978. Progress in Animal Husbandry. Mult.

2794	8f. (1) Type **529**	1·30	60
2795	8f. (2) Sheep rearing by the Kazakhs	1·30	60
2796	8f. (3) Shearing sheep, Tibet	1·30	60

530 Automated loading of Burning Coke

1978. Iron and Steel Industry. Mult.

2797	8f. (1) Type **530**	80	50
2798	8f. (2) Checking molten iron	80	50
2799	8f. (3) Pouring molten steel	80	50
2800	8f. (4) Steel-rolling mill	80	50
2801	8f. (5) Loading steel train	80	50

531 Soldier

1978. Army Modernization. Multicoloured.

2802	8f. (1) Type **531**	1·00	50
2803	8f. (2) Soldier firing missile	1·00	50
2804	8f. (3) Amphibious landing	1·00	50

532 Cloth Toy Lion

1978. Arts and Crafts. Multicoloured.

2805	4f. (1) Type **532**	45	25
2806	8f. (2) Three-legged pot (vert)	45	25
2807	8f. (3) Lacquerware rhinoceros	45	25
2808	10f. (4) Embroidered kitten (vert)	45	30
2809	20f. (5) Basketware	65	50
2810	30f. (6) Cloissone pot (vert)	80	65
2811	40f. (7) Lacquerware plate and swan	1·10	85
2812	50f. (8) Boxwood carving (vert)	1·80	1·20
2813	60f. (9) Jade carving	2·20	1·50
2814	70f. (10) Ivory carving (vert)	2·30	1·80
MS2815	139 × 90 mm. 3y. Lacquerware panel "Flying Fairies" (85 × 36 mm)	£250	£140

533 Worker, Peasant and Intellectual

1978. 4th National Women's Congress.

2816	**533** 8f. multicoloured	1·60	90

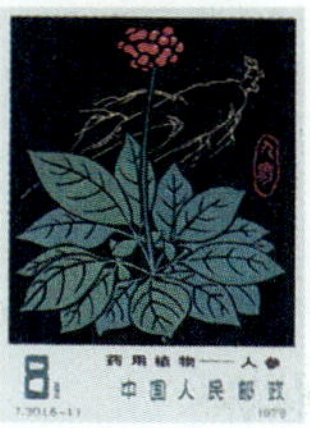

534 "Panax ginseng"

1978. Medicinal Plants. Multicoloured.

2817	8f. (1) Type **534**	45	25
2818	8f. (2) "Datura metel"	45	25
2819	8f. (3) "Belamcanda chinensis"	45	25
2820	8f. (4) "Platycodon grandiflorum"	45	25
2821	55f. (5) "Rhododendron dauricum"	2·50	80

535 Cogwheel, Grain, Rocket and Flag

1978. 9th National Trades Union Congress.

2822	**535** 8f. multicoloured	2·50	1·70

536 Emblem, Open Book and Flowers

1978. 10th National Congress of Communist Youth League.

2823	**536** 8f. multicoloured	2·00	1·10

537 Chinese and Japanese Children exchanging Gifts

1978. Signing of Chinese–Japanese Treaty of Peace and Friendship. Multicoloured.

2824	8f. Type **537**	65	35
2825	55f. Great Wall of China and Mt. Fuji	2·30	1·80

538 Hui, Han and Mongolian

1978. 20th Anniv of Ningsia Hui Autonomous Region. Multicoloured.

2826	8f. (1) Type **538**	1·00	80
2827	8f. (2) Coal loading machine, Holan colliery	1·00	80
2828	10f. (3) Irrigation and Chingtunghsia power station	1·00	80

539 Chinsha River Bridge, West Szechuan

540 Transplanting Rice Seedlings by Machine

1978. Highway Bridges. Multicoloured.

2829	8f. (1) Type **539**	45	35
2830	8f. (2) Hsinghong Bridge, Wuhsi	45	35
2831	8f. (3) Chiuhsikou Bridge, Fengdu	45	35
2832	8f. (4) Chinsha Bridge	45	35
2833	60f. (5) Shangyeh Bridge, Sanmen	3·25	1·30
MS2834	145 × 70 mm. 2y. Hsingkiang River bridge (horiz, 85 × 37 mm)	£250	£110

1978. Water Country Modernization. Mult.

2835	8f. (1) Type **540**	6·00	2·75
2836	8f. (2) Crop spraying	6·00	2·75
2837	8f. (3) Selecting seeds	6·00	2·75
2838	8f. (4) Canal-side village	6·00	2·75
2839	8f. (5) Delivering and storing grain	6·00	2·75

Nos. 2835/9 were issued together, se-tenant, forming a composite design.

541 Festivities

1978. 20th Anniv of Kwangsi Chuang Autonomous Region. Multicoloured.

2840	8f. (1) Type **541**	2·20	75
2841	8f. (2) Industrial complexes (vert)	2·20	75
2842	10f. (3) River scene (vert)	2·30	90

542 Tibetan Peasant reporting Mineralogical Discovery

1978. Mining Development. Multicoloured.

2843	4f. Type **542**	55	35
2844	8f. Miners with pneumatic drill	75	45
2845	10f. Open-cast mining	1·30	80
2846	20f. Electric mine train	1·70	1·10

543 Pair of Golden Pheasants on Rock

544 Einstein

1979. Golden Pheasants. Multicoloured.

2847	4f. Type **543**	1·30	65
2848	8f. Pheasant in flight	2·30	80
2849	45f. Pheasant looking for food	4·50	3·25

1979. Birth Centenary of Albert Einstein (physicist).

2850	**544** 8f. brown, gold & slate	2·50	1·70

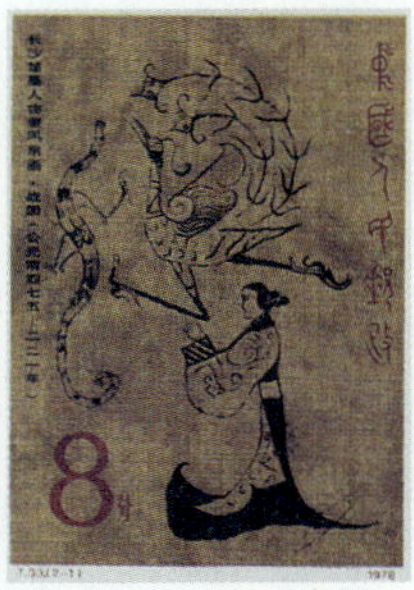

545 Woman, Monster and Phoenix

1979. Silk Paintings from a Tomb of the Warring States Period (475–221 B.C.). Multicoloured.

2851	8f. Type **545**	1·60	60
2852	60f. Man riding dragon	3·00	1·90

546 Jing Shan

547 Hammer and Sickle

1979. Peking Scenes. Multicoloured.

2853	1y. Type **546**	75	30
2854	2y. Summer Palace	1·60	60
2855	5y. Beihai Park	5·50	1·30

1979. 90th Anniv of International Labour Day.

2856	**547** 8f. multicoloured	1·10	80

548 Memorial Frieze

1979. 60th Anniv of May 4th Movement. Mult.

2857	8f. (1) Type **548**	80	50
2858	8f. (2) Girl and symbols of progress	80	50

549 Children of Different Races

1979. International Year of the Child. Mult.

2859	8f. I.Y.C. emblem and children with balloons	1·10	65
2860	60f. Type **549**	8·25	5·25

550 Spring over Great Wall

1979. The Great Wall. Multicoloured.

2861	8f. (1) Type **550**	1·20	85
2862	8f. (2) Summer over Great Wall	1·20	85
2863	8f. (3) Autumn over Great Wall	1·20	85
2864	60f. (4) Winter over Great Wall	6·75	5·00
MS2865	139 × 78 mm. 2y. Shanhaiguan, Great Wall	£110	65·00

551 Roaring Tiger

1979. Manchurian Tiger. Paintings by Liu Jiyou. Multicoloured.

2866	4f. Type **551**	1·10	70
2867	8f. Two young tigers	1·10	70
2868	60f. Tiger at rest	4·75	2·00

552 Mechanical Harvester

1979. Trades of the People's Communes. Mult.

2869	4f. (1) Type **552** (Agriculture)	1·10	95
2870	8f. (2) Planting a sapling (Forestry)	1·10	95

2871 8f. (3) Herding ducks (Stock raising) . . . . 1·10 95
2872 8f. (4) Basket weaving . . . 1·10 95
2873 10f. (5) Fishermen with handcarts of fish (Fishing) 1·90 1·30

里乔内第31届国际邮票博览会
1979年

(**553**) (½-size illustration)

1979. International Stamp Fair, Riccione. No. **MS**2865 optd with T **553** and new serial number (J 41 etc), in gold.
MS2874 2y. multicoloured (sold at 2y.50) £425 £300

554 Games' Emblem, Running, Volleyball and Weightlifting

1979. 4th National Games.
2875 **554** 8f. (1) multicoloured . . 65 50
2876 – 8f. (2) multicoloured . . 65 50
2877 – 8f. (3) black, grn & red 65 50
2878 – 8f. (4) black, red & grn 65 50
MS2879 57 × 62 mm. 2y. gold, green and vermilion . . . . 46·00 26·00
DESIGNS: No. 2876, Football, badminton, high jumping and ice dancing. 2877, Fencing, Skiing, gymnastics and diving. 2878, Motor cycling, table tennis, basketball and archery. 21 × 27 mm—2y. Games emblem.

555 National Flag and Mountains

556 National Emblem

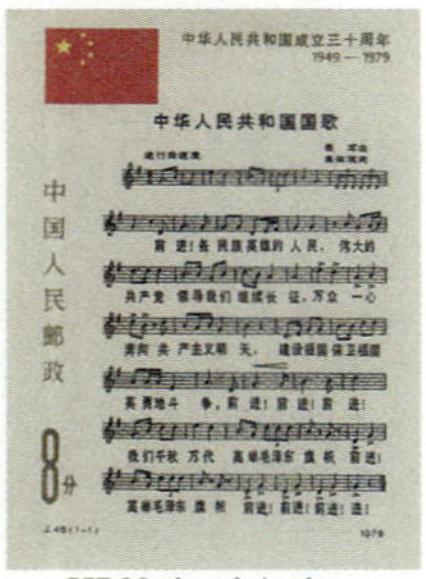

557 National Anthem

558 Dancers and Drummer

559 Tractor and Crop-spraying Antonov An-2

1979. 30th Anniv of People's Republic of China. Multicoloured.
2880 8f. (1) National flag and rainbow . . . . 1·80 1·30
2881 8f. (2) Type **555** . . . . . . 1·80 1·30
2882 8f. Type **556** . . . . 2·40 1·00
2884 8f. Type **557** . . . . 3·00 2·75
2885 8f. (1) Type **558** 70 30
2886 8f. (2) Dancers and tambourine player 70 30
2887 8f. (3) Dancers and banjo player 70 30
2888 8f. (4) Dancers and drummer 70 30
2889 8f. (1) Type **559** 80 45
2890 8f. (2) Computer and cogwheels 80 45
2891 8f. (3) Rocket, jet fighter and submarine 80 45
2892 8f. (4) Atomic symbols . . . 80 45
MS2883 67 × 75 mm. **556** 1y. multicoloured . . . . 46·00 26·00

560 Exhibition Emblem

561 Children with Model Aircraft

1979. National Exhibition of Juniors' Scientific and Technological Works.
2893 **560** 8f. multicoloured . . . . 1·00 60

1979. Study of Science from Childhood. Mult.
2894 8f. (1) Type **561** 65 50
2895 8f. (2) Girls with microscope and test tube 65 50
2896 8f. (3) Children with telescope 65 50
2897 8f. (4) Boy catching butterflies 65 50
2898 8f. (5) Girl noting weather readings 65 50
2899 60f. (6) Boys with model boat . . . . 3·00 1·60
MS2900 148 × 90 mm. 2y. Girl with book and space and undersea scenes £700 £300

562 Yu Shan

1979. Taiwan Views. Multicoloured.
2901 8f. (1) Type **562** 85 65
2902 8f. (2) Sun Moon Lake . . 85 65
2903 8f. (3) Chikan Tower . . 85 65
2904 8f. (4) Suao-Hualien highway 85 65
2905 55f. (5) Tian Xiang Falls . . 3·25 1·30
2906 60f. (6) Moonlight over Banping Mountain . . . 3·75 2·75

563 Symbols of Literature and Art

1979. 4th National Congress of Literary and Art Workers. Multicoloured.
2907 4f. Type **563** 75 50
2908 8f. Seals, hammer, sickle, rifle, atomic symbol and flowers . . . . 1·30 70

564 "Shaoshan" Type Electric Locomotive

1979. Railway Construction. Multicoloured.
2909 8f. (1) Type **564** . . . . . . 1·00 80
2910 8f. (2) Modern railway viaduct . . . . 1·00 80
2911 8f. (3) Goods train crossing bridge . . . . 1·00 80

565 "Chrysanthemum Petal"

1979. Camellias of Yunnan. Multicoloured.
2912 4f. (1) Type **565** 80 40
2913 8f. (2) "Lion Head" 80 40
2914 8f. (3) Camellia "Chrysantha (Hu) Tuyama" 80 40
2915 10f. (4) "Small Osmanthus Leaf" 80 40
2916 20f. (5) "Baby Face" . . . 1·50 65
2917 30f. (6) "Cornelian" . . . 2·50 85
2918 40f. (7) Peony Camellia . . 2·75 1·00
2919 50f. (8) "Purple Gown" . . 2·75 1·20
2920 60f. (9) "Dwarf Rose" . . . 2·75 1·50
2921 70f. (10) "Willow Leaf Spinel Pink" . . . . . . 3·00 1·60
MS2922 135 × 90 mm. 2y. "Red Jewellery" (85 × 36 mm) . . . . £140 70·00

566 (reduced—actual size 91 × 68 mm)

1979. People's Republic of China Stamp Exhibition, Hong Kong. No. **MS**2922 optd in margin with T **566**, in gold.
MS2923 2y. multicoloured . . . £250 £150

567 Dr. Bethune attending Wounded Soldier

1979. 40th Death Anniv of Dr. Norman Bethune. Multicoloured.
2924 8f. Type **567** . . . . 1·30 80
2925 70f. Bethune Memorial, Mausoleum of Martyrs, Shijiazhuang . . . . . . 1·90 1·50

568 Central Archives Hall

1979. International Archives Weeks. Mult.
2926 8f. (1) Type **568** 80 40
2927 8f. (2) Gold cabinet containing documents of Ming and Ching dynasties (vert) 80 40
2928 60f. (3) Imperial Archives Main Hall . . . . . . 5·50 1·90

569 Waterfall Cave, Home of Monkey King

570 Stalin

1979. Scenes from "Pilgrimage to the West" (Chinese classical novel). Multicoloured.
2929 8f. (1) Type **569** . . . . . 1·60 1·00
2930 8f. (2) Necha, son of Li, fighting Monkey . . . . 1·60 1·00
2931 8f. (3) Monkey in Mother Queen's peach orchard . . 1·60 1·00
2932 8f. (4) Monkey in alchemy furnace . . . . 1·60 1·00
2933 10f. (5) Monkey fighting White Bone Demon . . . 2·75 1·00
2934 20f. (6) Monkey extinguishing fire with palm-leaf fan . . . . . . 3·50 1·30
2935 60f. (7) Monkey fighting Spider Demon in Cobweb Cave . . . . 9·00 4·00
2936 70f. (8) Monkey on scripture-seeking route to India . . . . 9·75 4·50

1979. Birth Centenary of Stalin.
2937 **570** 8f. (1) brown . . . . . 1·30 1·00
2938 – 8f. (2) black . . . . . . 1·30 1·00
DESIGN: No. 2038, Stalin appealing for unity against Germany.

571 Peony

572 Meng Liang, "Hongyang Cave"

1980. Paintings of Qi Baishi.
2939 **571** 4f. (1) multicoloured . . 85 60
2940 – 4f. (2) multicoloured . . 85 60
2941 – 8f. (3) multicoloured . . 85 60
2942 – 8f. (4) black, blue & red 85 60
2943 – 8f. (5) multicoloured . . 85 60
2944 – 8f. (6) black, grey & red 85 60
2945 – 8f. (7) multicoloured . . 85 60
2946 – 8f. (8) multicoloured . . 85 60
2947 – 10f. (9) blk, yell and red 1·20 60
2948 – 20f. (10) grey, brn & blk 1·20 60
2949 – 30f. (11) multicoloured 1·80 1·00
2950 – 40f. (12) multicoloured 2·00 1·40
2951 – 50f. (13) blk, grey & red 3·50 1·80
2952 – 55f. (14) multicoloured 4·75 2·50
2953 – 60f. (15) blk, grey & red 6·50 3·50
2954 – 70f. (16) multicoloured 7·25 5·00
MS2955 120 × 86 mm. 2y. multicoloured . . . . £120 50·00
DESIGNS: No. 2940, Squirrels and grapes; 2941, Crabs and wine; 2942, Tadpoles in mountain spring; 2943, Chicks; 2944, Lotus; 2945, Red plum; 2946, River kingfisher; 2947, Bottle gourds; 2948, "The Voice of Autumn"; 2949, Wisteria; 2950, Chrysanthemums; 2951, Shrimps; 2952, Litchi; 2953, Cabbages and mushrooms; 2954, Peaches. 37 × 61 mm—**MS**2955, "Evergreen".

1980. Facial Make-up in Peking Operas. Mult.
2956 4f. (1) Type **572** . . . . . . 1·40 70
2957 4f. (2) Li Kui, "Black Whirlwind" . . . . . . 2·75 70
2958 8f. (3) Huang Gai, "Meeting of Heroes" . . . . 1·80 70
2959 8f. (4) Monkey King, "Havoc in Heaven" . . . 1·80 70
2960 10f. (5) Lu Zhishen, "Wild Boar Forest" . . . . . . 2·75 1·10
2961 20f. (6) Lian Po, "Reconciliation between the General and the Minister" . . . . 3·50 2·30
2962 60f. (7) Zhang Fei, "Reed Marsh" . . . . 10·50 4·25
2963 70f. (8) Dou Erdun, "Stealing the Emperor's Horse" . . . . 11·50 5·50

573 Chinese Olympic Committee Emblem

574 Bear Macaque

1980. Winter Olympic Games, Lake Placid. Multicoloured.
2964 8f. (1) Type **573** 75 35
2965 8f. (2) Speed skating 75 35
2966 8f. (3) Figure skating . . . 75 35
2967 60f. (4) Skiing . . . . 5·00 1·60

1980. New Year. Year of the Monkey.
2968 **574** 8f. red, black and gold £275 85·00

575 Klara Zetkin (journalist and politician)

1980. 70th Anniv of International Working Women's Day.
2969 **575** 8f. black, yellow & brn 1·30 90

576 Orchard

1980. Afforestation. Multicoloured.
2970 4f. Type **576** 45 25
2971 8f. Highway lined with trees 50 25
2972 10f. Aerial sowing by Antonov An-2 biplane . . 85 40
2973 20f. Factory amongst trees 1·30 65

577 Apsaras (celestial beings)

1980. 2nd National Conference of Chinese Scientific and Technical Association.
2974 **577** 8f. multicoloured . . . . 2·00 1·30

578 Freighter

1980. Mail Transport. Multicoloured.
2975 2f. Type **578** . . . . 1·40 1·10
2976 4f. Mail bus . . . . 1·40 1·10
2977 8f. Travelling post office coach . . . . 2·20 1·10
2978 10f. Tupolev Tu-154 airplane . . . . 3·00 1·80

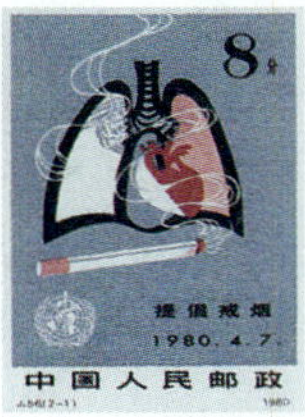
579 Cigarette damaging Heart and Lungs

1980. Anti-smoking Campaign. Multicoloured.
2979 8f. Type **579** 85 45
2980 60f. Face smoking and face holding flower in mouth, symbolising choice of smoking or health . . . . 6·00 3·00

580 Jian Zhen Memorial Hall, Yangzhou

1980. Return of High Monk Jian Zhen's Statue. Multicoloured.
2981 8f. (1) Type **580** . . . . . 2·75 70
2982 8f. (2) Statue of Jian Zhen (vert) . . . . 2·75 70
2983 60f. (3) Junk in which Jian Zhen travelled to Japan 17·00 7·25

581 Lenin

582 "Swallow Chick" Kite

1980. 110th Birth Anniv of Lenin.
2984 **581** 8f. brown, pink & green 1·60 90

1980. Kites. Multicoloured.
2985 8f. (1) Type **582** . . . . . 2·75 1·20
2986 8f. (2) "Slender swallow" kite . . . . 2·75 90
2987 8f. (3) "Semi-slender swallow" kite . . . . . 2·75 90
2988 70f. (4) "Dual swallows" kite . . . . 13·50 5·00

583 Hare running in Fright

1980. Scenes from "Gu Dong" (Chinese fairy tale). Multicoloured.
2989 8f. (1) Type **583** . . . . . 1·70 1·40
2990 8f. (2) Hare tells other animals "Gu Dong is coming" . . . . 1·70 1·40
2991 8f. (3) Lion asks "What is Gu Dong?" . . . . . . 1·70 1·40
2992 8f. (4) Animals discover sound of "Gu Dong" is made by falling papaya 1·70 1·40

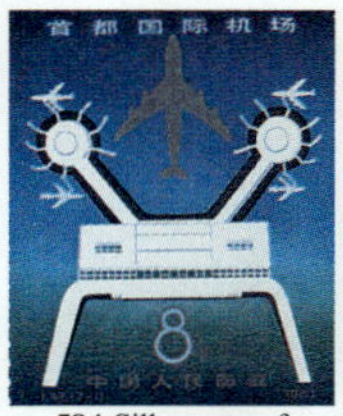
584 Silhouette of Ilyushin Il-86 Jetliner and Plan of Terminal Building

585 Stag

1980. Peking International Airport. Multicoloured.
2993 8f. Type **584** . . . . 1·30 80
2994 10f. Airplane and runway lights . . . . 1·80 1·30

1980. Sika Deer. Multicoloured.
2995 4f. Type **585** . . . . 1·10 95
2996 8f. Doe and fawn . . . . . 1·10 95
2997 60f. Herd . . . . 6·00 4·00

586 "White Lotus"

1980. Lotus Paintings by Yu Zhizhen. Mult.
2998 8f. (1) Type **586** . . . . . . 2·20 90
2999 8f. (2) "Rose-tipped Snow" 2·20 90
3000 8f. (3) "Buddha's Seat" . . 2·20 90
3001 70f. (4) "Variable Charming Face" . . . . 19·00 8·00
MS3002 70 × 144 mm. 1y. "Fresh Lotus on Rippling Waters" (48 × 88 mm) . . . . £130 70·00

587 Returned Pearl Cave and Sword-cut Stone

1980. Guilin Landscapes. Multicoloured.
3003 8f. (1) Type **587** . . . . . 1·40 80
3004 8f. (2) Distant view of three mountains . . . . . . 1·40 80
3005 8f. (3) Nine-horse Fresco Hill . . . . 1·40 80
3006 8f. (4) Egrets around the aged banyan . . . . . . 1·40 80
3007 8f. (5) Western Hills at sunset (vert) . . . . . 1·40 80
3008 8f. (6) Moonlight on the Lijiang River (vert) . . 1·40 80
3009 60f. (7) Springhead and ferry (vert) . . . . . . 10·50 3·25
3010 70f. (8) Scenic path at Yangshuo (vert) . . . . . 12·00 4·00

588 Exhibition Gateway

1980. China Exhibition in United States. Mult.
3011 8f. Type **588** 80 65
3012 70f. Great Wall and emblems of San Francisco, Chicago and New York . . . . 6·50 2·75

589 Burebista (founder-king) and Rumanian Flag

1980. 2050th Anniv of Dacian State.
3013 **589** 8f. multicoloured . . . . 2·00 1·30

590 "Sea of Clouds" (Liu Haisu)

1980. UNESCO Exhibition of Chinese Paintings and Drawings. Multicoloured.
3014 8f. (1) Type **590** . . . . . . 1·40 60
3015 8f. (2) "Black-naped Oriole and Magnolia" (Yu Feian) (vert) . . . . . . 1·40 60
3016 8f. (3) "Tending Bactrian Camels" (Wu Zuoren) . . 1·40 60

591 Quzi Tower in Spring

1980. Liu Yuan (Tarrying Garden), Suzhou. Mult.
3017 8f. (1) Type **591** . . . . . 4·50 2·75
3018 8f. (2) Yuancui Pavilion in Summer . . . . 4·50 2·75
3019 10f. (3) Hanbi Shanfang in Autumn . . . . 5·50 2·75
3020 60f. (4) Guanyun Peak in Winter . . . . 38·00 12·50

592 Xu Guangqi

593 Pistol-shooting

1980. Scientists of Ancient China. Multicoloured.
3021 8f. (1) Type **592** (agriculturalist and astronomer) . . . . . . 2·00 90
3022 8f. (2) Li Bing (hydraulic engineer) . . . . 2·00 90
3023 8f. (3) Jia Sixie (agronomist) 2·00 90
3024 60f. (4) Huang Daopo (textile expert) . . . . . 13·00 4·75

1980. 1st Anniv of Return to International Olympic Committee. Multicoloured.
3025 **593** 4f. (1) brown, yell & mve 45 20
3026 – 8f. (2) brown, yell & grn 80 30
3027 – 8f. (3) brown, yell & blue 80 30
3028 – 10f. (4) brown, yellow & orange . . . . 1·20 55
3029 – 60f. (5) multicoloured . . 5·00 1·70
DESIGNS: No. 3026, Gymnastics; No. 3027, Diving; No. 3028, Volleyball; No. 3029, Archery.

594 White Flag Dolphin

595 Cock

1980. White Flag Dolphin. Multicoloured.
3030 8f. Type **594** . . . . 2·40 40
3031 60f. Two dolphins . . . . . 4·75 1·60

1981. New Year. Year of the Cock.
3032 **595** 8f. multicoloured . . . . 6·25 3·25

596 Early Morning

1981. Scenes of Xishuang Banna. Multicoloured.
3033 4f. (1) Type **596** 70 45
3034 4f. (2) Mountain village of Dai nationality 70 45
3035 8f. (3) Rainbow over Lanchang River . . . . . 1·40 60
3036 8f. (4) Ancient Temple (vert) 1·40 60
3037 8f. (5) Moonlit night (vert) 1·40 60
3038 60f. (6) Phoenix tree in bloom (vert) . . . . . . 7·75 3·50

597 Flower Basket Lantern

1981. Palace Lanterns. Multicoloured.
3039 4f. (1) Type **597** . . . . . . 1·40 70
3040 8f. (2) Dragons playing with a pearl . . . . 1·70 95
3041 8f. (3) Dragon and phoenix 1·70 95
3042 8f. (4) Treasure bowl . . . 1·70 95
3043 20f. (5) Flower and birds . . 3·75 2·75
3044 60f. (6) Peony lantern painted with fishes . . . 12·50 7·75

598 Crossing the River

1981. Marking the Gunwale (Chinese fable). Multicoloured.
3045 8f. (1) Chinese text of story 1·20 80
3046 8f. (2) Type **598** . . . . . 1·20 80
3047 8f. (3) The sword drops in the water . . . . 1·20 80
3048 8f. (4) Making mark on gunwale . . . . 1·20 80
3049 8f. (5) Diving into river to recover sword . . . . . 1·20 80

599 Chinese Elm

600 Vase with Two Tigers (Song Dynasty)

1981. Miniature Landscapes (dwarf trees). Mult.
3050 4f. (1) Type **599** 70 55
3051 8f. (2) Juniper 70 55
3052 8f. (3) Maidenhair tree . . . 70 55
3053 10f. (4) Chinese Juniper (horiz) 70 55
3054 20f. (5) Wild Kaki persimmon (horiz) . . . . 1·40 1·00
3055 60f. (6) Single-seed juniper (horiz) . . . . 4·25 2·50

1981. Ceramics from Cizhou Kilns. Multicoloured.
3056 4f. (1) Type **600** 35 30
3057 8f. (2) Carved black glazed vase (Jin dynasty) (horiz) 85 70
3058 8f. (3) Amphora with apricot blossoms (modern) 85 70
3059 8f. (4) Jar with two phoenixes (Yuan dynasty) (horiz) 85 70
3060 10f. (5) Flat flask with dragon and phoenix (Yuan dynasty) (horiz) . . 1·40 70
3061 60f. (6) Vessel with tiger-shaped handles (modern) (horiz) . . . . 4·50 3·75

601 Giant Panda "Stamp"

603 Inscription by Chou En-lai

602 Qinchuan Bull

1981. People's Republic of China Stamp Exhibition, Japan. Multicoloured.
3062 8f. Type **601** 75 25
3063 60f. Cockerel and junk "stamps" . . . . 2·75 1·30

1981. Cattle. Multicoloured.
3064 4f. (1) Type **602** 60 45
3065 8f. (2) Binhu buffalo 60 45
3066 8f. (3) Yak 60 45
3067 8f. (4) Black and white dairy cattle 60 45
3068 10f. (5) Red pasture bull . . 90 60
3069 55f. (6) Simmental crossbreed bull . . . . . 4·75 2·30

1981. "To Deliver Mail for Ten Thousand Li, Has Bearing on Arteries and Veins of the Country".
3070 **603** 8f. multicoloured 80 20

604 ITU and WHO Emblems and Ribbons forming Caduceus

605 Safety in Building Construction

1981. World Telecommunications Day.
3071 **604** 8f. multicoloured 80 20

1981. National Safety Month. Multicoloured.
3072 8f. (1) Type **605** 70 45
3073 8f. (2) Mining safety 70 45
3074 8f. (3) Road safety 70 45
3075 8f. (4) Farming and forestry safety 70 45

606 Trunk Call Building

607 St. Bride Vase (Men's singles)

1981.
3076 **606** 8f. brown . . . . 1·00 55

1981. Chinese Team's Victories at World Table Tennis Championships. Multicoloured.
3077 8f. (3) Type **607** 30 20
3078 8f. (4) Iran Cup (Men's doubles) 30 20
3079 8f. (5) G. Geist Prize (Women's singles) 30 20
3080 8f. (6) W. J. Pope Trophy (Women's doubles) . . . 30 20
3081 8f. (7) Heydusek Prize (Mixed doubles) 30 20
3082 20f. (1) Swathling Cup (Men's team) . . . . . . 1·00 80
3083 20f. (2) Marcel Corbillon Cup (Women's team) . . 1·00 80

608 Hammer and Sickle

609 Five Veterans Peak

1981. 60th Anniv of Chinese Communist Party.
3084 **608** 8f. multicoloured 70 35

1981. Lushan Mountains. Multicoloured.
3085 8f. (1) Type **609** 70 50
3086 8f. (2) Hanpo Pass (horiz) 70 50
3087 8f. (3) Yellow Dragon Pool and Waterfall 70 50
3088 8f. (4) Sunlit Peak (horiz) 70 50
3089 8f. (5) Three-layer Spring . . 70 50
3090 8f. (6) Stone and pines (horiz) 70 50
3091 60f. (7) Dragon Head Cliff 8·00 3·50

610 Silver Ear ("Tremella fuciformis")

1981. Edible Mushrooms. Multicoloured.
3092 4f. (1) Type **610** 30 25
3093 8f. (2) Veiled stinkhorn ("Dictyophora indusiata") 60 35
3094 8f. (3) "Hericium erinaceus" 60 35
3095 8f. (4) "Russula rubra" . . 60 35
3096 10f. (5) Shii-take mushroom ("Lentinus edodes") . . . 85 35
3097 70f. (6) White button mushroom ("Agaricus bisporus") . . . . 3·75 1·80

611 Medal

612 Huangguoshu Waterfall

1981. Quality Month.
3098 **611** 8f. (1) silver, black and red 65 45
3099 8f. (2) gold, brown and red 65 45

1981.
3100 – 1f. green 20 20
3101 – 1½f. red 20 20
3102 – 2f. green 20 20
3103 **612** 3f. brown 20 20
3118 – 3f. dp brn, brn & lt brn 30 20
3104 – 4f. violet 20 20
3119 – 4f. mauve and lilac . . . 30 20
3105 – 5f. brown 20 20
3106 – 8f. blue 20 20
3107 – 10f. purple 20 20
3121 – 10f. brown 50 35
3108 – 20f. green 25 20
3122 – 20f. blue . . . . . . 1·00 70
3109 – 30f. brown 30 20
3110 – 40f. black 35 20
3111 – 50f. mauve 45 25
3112 – 70f. black 55 35
3113 – 80f. red 60 45
3114 – 1y. lilac 80 55
3115 – 2y. green . . . . . . 1·30 1·10
3116 – 5y. blue . . . . 3·00 2·20
DESIGNS—VERT: 1f. Xishuang Banna. 1½f. Huashan Mountain. 2f. Taishan Mountain. 4f. Palm trees, Hainan. 5f. Pagoda, Huqiu Hill, Suzhou. 8f. Great Wall. 10f. North-east Forest. HORIZ: 20f. Herding sheep on Tianshan Mountain. 30f. Sheep on grassland, Inner Mongolia. 40f. Stone Forest. 50f. Pagodas, Ban Pingshan Mountain, Taiwan. 70f. Mt. Zhumulangma. 80f. Seven Star Grotto, Guangdong. 1y. Gorge, Yangtze River. 2y. Guilin. 5y. Mt. Huangshan.

613 Stone Forest in Autumn

1981. Stone Forest. Multicoloured.
3125 8f. (1) Stone Forest in a mist 70 45
3126 8f. (2) Type **613** 70 45
3127 8f. (3) Pool in Stone Forest 70 45
3128 10f. (4) Dawn over Stone Forest (vert) 70 45
3129 70f. (5) Stone Forest by starlight (vert) . . . . . 5·50 4·75

614 Lu Xun as Youth

1981. Birth Centenary of Lu Xun (writer).
3130 **614** 8f. black, green & yell 70 35
3131 – 20f. blk, brn & dp brn 1·40 95
DESIGN: 20f. Lu Xun in later life.

615 Dr. Sun Yat-sen

1981. 70th Anniv of 1911 Revolution.
3132 **615** 8f. (1) multicoloured . . 70 35
3133 – 8f. (2) black, grn & yell 70 35
3134 – 8f. (3) black, pk & yell 70 35
DESIGNS: No. 3133, Grave of 72 Martyrs, Huang Hua Gate; No. 3134, Headquarters of Military Government of Hubei Province.

616 "Tree" symbolizing Co-ordination

1981. Asian Conference of Parliamentarians on Population and Development. Multicoloured.
3135 8f. Type **616** 30 25
3136 70f. Design symbolizing Enlightenment 80 65

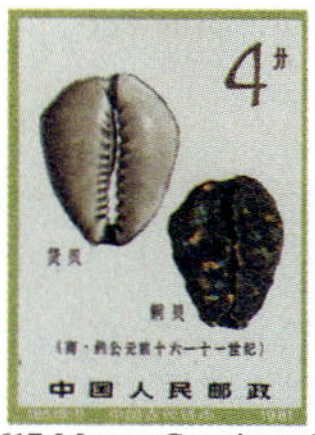

617 Money Cowrie and Cowrie-shaped Bronze Coin

1981. Ancient Chinese Coins (1st series). Minted before 221 B.C. Multicoloured.
3137 4f. (1) Type **617** 45 35
3138 4f. (2) Shovel coin 45 35
3139 8f. (3) Shovel coin inscribed "Li" 60 45
3140 8f. (4) Shovel coin inscribed "An Yi Er Jin" 60 45
3141 8f. (5) Knife coin inscribed "Qi Fa Ha" 60 45
3142 8f. (6) Knife coin inscribed "Jie Mo Zhi Fa Hua" . . 60 45
3143 60f. (7) Knife coin inscribed "Cheng Bai" . . . . . 2·50 1·10
3144 70f. (8) Circular coin with hole inscribed "Gong" . . 3·50 1·90
See also Nos. 3162/69.

618 Hands and Globe with IYDP Emblem

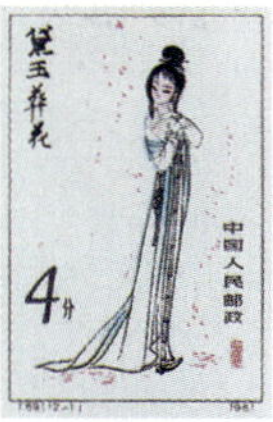

619 Daiyu

1981. International Year of Disabled Persons.
3145 **618** 8f. multicoloured 40 20

1981. The Twelve Beauties of Jinling from "A Dream of Red Mansions" by Cao Xueqin. Multicoloured. Designs showing paintings by Liu Danzhai.
3146 4f. (1) Type **619** 80 50
3147 4f. (2) Baochai chases butterfly 80 50
3148 8f. (3) Yuanchun visits parents 80 50
3149 8f. (4) Yingchun reading Buddhist sutras 80 50
3150 8f. (5) Tanchun forms poetry society 80 50
3151 8f. (6) Xichun painting . . . 80 50
3152 8f. (7) Xiangyun picking up necklace 80 50
3153 10f. (8) Liwan lectures her son . . . . 1·50 60
3154 20f. (9) Xifeng hatches plot 2·20 75
3155 30f. (10) Sister Qiao escapes 3·25 1·10
3156 40f. (11) Keqing relaxing . . 3·75 2·30
3157 80f. (12) Miaoyu serves tea 8·50 3·25
MS3158 139 × 78 mm. 2y. Baoyu and Daiyu reading (59 × 39 mm) 80·00 43·00

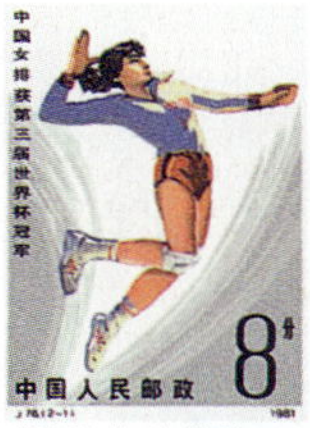

620 Volleyball Player

621 Dog

1981. Victory of Chinese Women's Team in World Cup Volleyball Championships. Multicoloured.
3159 8f. Type **620** 30 25
3160 20f. Player holding Cup . . 70 50

1982. New Year. Year of the Dog.
3161 **621** 8f. multicoloured . . . . 4·00 2·10

1982. Ancient Chinese Coins (2nd series). As T **617**. Multicoloured.
3162 4f. (1) Guilian ("Monster Mask") 60 35
3163 4f. (2) Shu shovel coin . . . 60 35
3164 8f. (3) Xia Zhuan shovel coin 60 35
3165 8f. (4) Han Dan shovel coin . 60 35
3166 8f. (5) Pointed-head knife coin 60 35
3167 8f. (6) Ming knife coin . . . 60 50
3168 70f. (7) Jin Hua knife coin 2·30 1·60
3169 80f. (8) Yi Liu Hua circular coin . . . . 3·00 2·10

622 Nie Er and Score of "March of the Volunteers"

1982. 70th Anniv of Nie Er (composer).
3170 **622** 8f. multicoloured 40 25

623 Dripping Water and Children

625 Building on Fire, Hoses and Fire Engine

624 Dr. Robert Koch and Laboratory Equipment

1982. Int Drinking Water and Sanitation Decade.
3171 **623** 8f. grey, orange & blue . . . 40 25

1982. Centenary of Discovery of Tubercle Bacillus.
3172 **624** 8f. multicoloured 40 25

1982. Fire Control. Multicoloured.
3173 8f. (1) Type **625** 55 25
3174 8f. (2) Chemical fire extinguisher 55 25

626 Solar System

1982. "Cluster of Nine Planets" (planetary conjunction).
3175 **626** 8f. multicoloured 70 25

627 "Hemerocallis flava" and "H. fulva"

628 Soong Ching Ling addressing First Plenary Session

1982. Medicinal Plants. Multicoloured.
3176 4f. (1) Type **627** 40 30
3177 8f. (2) "Fritillaria unibracteata" 40 30
3178 8f. (3) "Aconitum carmichaeli" 40 30
3179 10f. (4) "Lilium brownii" . . 40 30
3180 20f. (5) "Arisaema consanguineum" . . . 85 45
3181 70f. (6) "Paeonia lactiflora" 3·00 1·70
MS3182 138 × 70 mm. 2y. "Iris tectorum" and "Iris" spp. (82 × 35 mm) . . . . 14·00 8·50

1982. 1st Death Anniv of Soong Ching Ling (former Head of State). Multicoloured.
3183 8f. Type **628** 45 35
3184 20f. Portrait of Soong Ching Ling . . . . 1·60 1·30

629 Sable

1982. The Sable. Multicoloured.
3185 8f. Type **629** 85 45
3186 80f. Sable running . . . . 4·50 2·75

630 Census Emblem

631 Text, Emblem and Globe

1982. National Census.
3187 **630** 8f. multicoloured 30 20

1982. Second U.N. Conference on the Exploration and Peaceful Uses of Outer Space, Vienna.
3188 **631** 8f. multicoloured 30 20

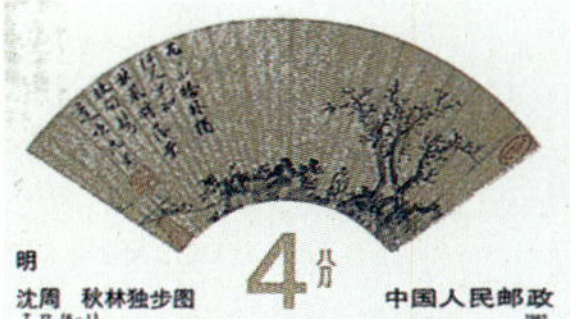
632 "Strolling Alone in Autumn Woods" (Shen Zhou)

1982. Fan Paintings of the Ming and Qing Dynasties. Multicoloured.
3189 4f. (1) Type **632** 40 25
3190 8f. (2) "Jackdaw on withered Tree" (Tang Yin) 75 50
3191 8f. (3) "Bamboos and Sparrows" (Zhou Zhimian) 75 50
3192 10f. (4) "Writing Poem under Pine" (Chen Hongshou and Bai Han) 75 50
3193 20f. (5) "Chrysanthemums" (Yun Shouping) . . . . 1·30 75
3194 70f. (6) "Masked Hawfinch, Grape Myrtle and Chinese Parasol" (Wang Wu) . . 3·50 2·40

633 Courier on Horseback (Wei-Jin period tomb mural, Jiayu Pass)

1982. 1st All-China Philatelic Federation Congress. Sheet 136 × 80 mm.
MS3195 **633** 1y. multicoloured 11·00 6·50

634 Society Emblem

635 Orpiment

1982. 60th Anniv of Chinese Geological Society.
3196 **634** 8f. gold, stone & black 30 20

1982. Minerals. Multicoloured.
3197 4f. Type **635** 20 20
3198 8f. Stibnite 20 20
3199 10f. Cinnabar 50 25
3200 20f. Wolframite 80 50

636 "12", Hammer and Sickle and Great Hall of the People

637 Hoopoe

1982. 12th National Communist Party Congress.
3201 **636** 8f. multicoloured 30 20

1982. Birds. Multicoloured.
3202 8f. (1) Type **637** 65 30
3203 8f. (2) Barn swallow 65 30
3204 8f. (3) Black-naped oriole 65 30
3205 20f. (4) Great tit . . . . . 1·20 60
3206 70f. (5) Great spotted woodpecker . . . . . . 4·00 3·00
MS3207 135 × 79 mm. 2y. Ashy minivet, magpie robin, Daurian redstart, red-flanked bluetail and little cuckoo . . . . 32·00 18·00

638 "Plum Blossom" (Guan Shanyue)

1982. 10th Anniv of Normalization of Diplomatic Relations with Japan. Multicoloured.
3208 8f. Type **638** 35 20
3209 70f. "Hibiscus" (Xiao Shufang) . . . . 1·00 80

639 Globe, Profiles and Ear of Wheat

640 Guo Moruo

1982. World Food Day.
3210 **639** 8f. multicoloured 30 25

1982. 90th Birth Anniv of Guo Moruo (writer). Multicoloured.
3211 8f. Type **640** 20 20
3212 20f. Guo Moruo writing . . 40 25

641 Head of Bodhisattva

642 Dr. D. S. Kotnis

1982. Sculptures of Liao Dynasty. Mult.
3213 8f. (1) Type **641** 45 35
3214 8f. (2) Bust of Bodhisattva 45 35
3215 8f. (3) Boy on lotus flower 45 35
3216 70f. (4) Bodhisattva . . . . 3·75 2·20
MS3217 129 × 80 mm. 2y. Head of Bodhisattva (different) (36 × 55 mm) . . . . 25·00 11·50

1982. 40th Death Anniv of Dr. D. S. Kotnis.
3218 **642** 8f. green and black . . . 45 20
3219 – 70f. lilac and black . . . 2·30 1·20
DESIGN: Dr. Kotnis in army uniform.

643 Couple holding Flaming Torch

644 Wine Container

1982. 11th National Communist Youth League Congress.
3220 **643** 8f. multicoloured 30 20

1982. Bronzes of Western Zhou Dynasty. Mult.
3221 4f. (1) Type **644** 80 45
3222 4f. (2) Cooking vessel . . . 80 45
3223 8f. (3) Food container . . . 95 45
3224 8f. (4) Cooking vessel with ox head and dragon design 95 45
3225 8f. (5) Ram-shaped wine container 95 45
3226 10f. (6) Wine jar . . . . . 1·60 50
3227 20f. (7) Food bowl . . . . 2·20 90
3228 70f. (8) Wine container . . . 8·25 3·00

645 "Pig" (Han Meilin)

646 Harp

1983. New Year. Year of the Pig.
3229 **645** 8f. multicoloured . . . . 4·50 3·50

1983. Stringed Musical Instruments.
3230 **646** 4f. (1) green and brown 1·40 60
3231 – 8f. (2) purple, grn & brn 1·60 70
3232 – 8f. (3) multicoloured . . 1·60 70
3233 – 10f. (4) multicoloured . . 2·00 85
3234 – 70f. (5) multicoloured . . 14·00 3·75
DESIGNS—VERT: 8f. (3231), Four string guitar; 10f. Four string lute; 70f. Three string lute. HORIZ: 8f. (3232), Qin.

647 "February 7" Monument, Jiangan

1983. 60th Anniv of Peking–Hankow Railway Workers' Strike.
3235 **647** 8f. (1) yellow, blk & grey 50 35
3236 – 8f. (2) stone, brown and lilac 50 35
DESIGN: No. 3236, "February 7" Memorial tower, Zhengzhou.

648 Zhang Gong attracted by Yingying's Beauty

1983. Scenes from "The Western Chamber" (musical drama) by Wang Shifu.
3237 **648** 8f. (1) multicoloured . . 1·80 80
3238 8f. (2) multicoloured . . 1·80 80
3239 10f. (3) multicoloured . . 3·50 1·60
3240 80f. (4) multicoloured . . 13·50 4·50
MS3241 130 × 80 mm. 2y. stone and black . . . . 70·00 32·00
DESIGNS: As T **648**—No. 3228, Zhang Gong and Yingying listening to music; 3239, Zhang Gong and Yingying's wedding; 3240, Zhang Gong and Yingying parting at Changting Pavilion; 27 × 48 mm—2y. Interrogation of Hongniang (Yingying's maid) Ming dynasty woodblock.

649 Karl Marx

650 Tomb, Mt. Qiaoshan, Huangling

1983. Death Centenary of Karl Marx.
3242 **649** 8f. grey and black . . . 30 20
3243 – 20f. lilac and black . . . 65 25
DESIGN: 20f. "Marx making Speech" (Wen Guozhang).

1983. Tomb of the Yellow Emperor. Mult.
3244 8f. Type **650** . . . . 1·00 40
3245 10f. Hall of Founder of Chinese Culture (horiz) 1·60 40
3246 20f. Xuanyuan cypress . . . 2·50 80

651 Messengers and Globe

1983. World Communications Year.
3247 **651** 8f. multicoloured 55 25

652 Chinese Alligator

1983. Chinese Alligator. Multicoloured.
3248 8f. Type **652** . . . . 1·00 45
3249 20f. Alligator and hatching eggs . . . . 1·90 75

653 "Scratching" (Wang Yani)

1983. Children's Paintings. Multicoloured.
3250 8f. (1) Type **653** 30 20
3251 8f. (2) "I Love the Great Wall" (Liu Zhong) . . . 30 20
3252 8f. (3) "Kitten" (Tang Axi) 30 20
3253 8f. (4) "The Sun, Birds, Flowers and Me" (Bu Hua) 30 20

654 Congress Hall

1983. 6th National People's Congress. Mult.
3254 8f. Type **654** 30 20
3255 20f. Score of National Anthem 95 40

655 Terracotta Soldiers

656 Sun Yujiao

1983. Terracotta Figures from Qin Shi Huang's Tomb. Multicoloured.
3256 8f. (1) Type **655** 75 50
3257 8f. (2) Heads figures 75 50
3258 10f. (3) Soldiers and horses 1·00 55
3259 70f. (4) Aerial view of excavation . . . . 5·75 3·00
MS3260 100 × 85 mm. 2y. Soldier leading horse (59 × 39 mm) . . 65·00 21·00

1983. Female Roles in Peking Opera. Mult.
3261 4f. (1) Type **656** 85 35
3262 8f. (2) Chen Miaochang . . 85 35
3263 8f. (3) Bai Suzhen 85 35
3264 8f. (4) Sister Thirteen . . . 85 35
3265 10f. (5) Qin Xianglian . . . 85 35
3266 20f. (6) Yang Yuhuan . . . 2·50 80
3267 50f. (7) Cui Yingying . . . 5·25 1·70
3268 80f. (8) Mu Guiying . . . 7·00 2·10

657 Li Bai (poet)

659 Games Emblem

658 Woman and Women working

1983. Poets and Philosophers of Ancient China. Paintings by Liu Lingcang. Multicoloured.
3269 8f. (1) Type **657** 55 25
3270 8f. (2) Du Fu (poet) 55 25
3271 8f. (3) Han Yu (philosopher) 55 25
3272 70f. (4) Liu Zongyuan (philosopher) . . . . . . 4·50 2·30

1983. 5th National Women's Congress.
3273 **658** 8f. multicoloured 30 20

1983. 5th National Games. Multicoloured.
3274 4f. (1) Type **659** 45 20
3275 8f. (2) Gymnastics 45 20
3276 8f. (3) Badminton 45 20
3277 8f. (4) Diving 45 20
3278 20f. (5) High jump . . . . 1·00 80
3279 70f. (6) Windsurfing . . . . 3·25 2·00

660 "One Child per Couple"

1983. Family Planning. Multicoloured.
3280 8f. (1) Type **660** 30 20
3281 8f. (2) "Population, cultivated fields and grain" 30 20

661 Hammer and Cogwheel as "10"

1983. 10th National Trade Union Congress.
3282 **661** 8f. multicoloured 30 20

662 Mute Swan

1983. Swans. Multicoloured.
3283 8f. (1) Type **662** 40 35
3284 8f. (2) Mute swans 40 35
3285 10f. Tundra swans 60 45
3286 80f. (4) Whooper swans in flight . . . . 2·75 2·00

663 Liu Shaoqi

1983. 85th Birth Anniv of Liu Shaoqi (former Head of State).
3287 **663** 8f. (1) multicoloured . . 55 45
3288 – 8f. (2) multicoloured . . 55 45
3289 – 8f. (3) brown, bl & gold 55 45
3290 – 8f. (4) brown, bl & gold 55 45
DESIGNS: No. 3288, Liu reading a speech; 3289, Liu making a speech; 3290, Liu meeting model worker Shi Chuanxiang.

664 $100 National Emblem Stamp, 1951

665 Mao Tse-tung in 1925

1983. National Stamp Exhibition, Peking. Mult.
3291 8f. Type **664** 30 20
3292 20f. North West China $1 Yanan Pagoda stamp, 1946 . . . . 70 30

1983. 90th Birth Anniv of Mao Tse-tung.
3293 **665** 8f. (1) multicoloured . . 30 25
3294 – 8f. (2) stone, brn & gold 30 25
3295 – 10f. (3) grey, brn & gold 70 25
3296 – 20f. (4) multicoloured . . 1·60 75
DESIGNS: No. 3294, Mao Tse-tung in Yanan, 1945. 3295, Mao Tse-tung inspecting Yellow River, 1952. 3296, Mao Tse-tung in library, 1961.

666 "Rat" (Zhan Tong)

667 Young Girl with Ball

1984. New Year. Year of the Rat.
3297 **666** 8f. black, yellow & red 3·00 1·20

1984. Child Welfare. Multicoloured.
3298 8f.+2f. Type **667** 30 25
3299 8f.+2f. Young boy with toy panda 30 25

668 Women with Dog

1984. Tang Dynasty Painting "Beauties wearing Flowers" by Zhou Fang. Details of scroll. Mult.
3300 8f. Type **668** 85 35
3301 10f. Women and Manchurian crane 85 40
3302 70f. Women, dog and Manchurian crane . . . . 5·75 2·30
MS3303 161 × 39 mm. 2y. Complete scroll (156 × 35 mm) . . . . . 85·00 44·00

669 "The Spring of Shanghai"

670 Ren Bishi

1984. Chinese Roses. Multicoloured.
3304 4f. (1) Type **669** 35 20
3305 8f. (2) "Rosy Dawn of the Pujiang River" 35 20
3306 8f. (3) "Pearl" 35 20
3307 10f. (4) "Black Whirlwind" 40 30
3308 20f. (5) "Yellow Flower in the Battlefield" 80 40
3309 70f. (6) "Blue Phoenix" . . 2·75 1·20

1984. 80th Birth Anniv of Ren Bishi (member of Communist Party Secretariat) (1st issue).
3310 **670** 8f. brown, black & pur 30 20
See also Nos. 3361/3.

671 Japanese Crested Ibis

1984. Japanese Crested Ibis. Multicoloured.
3311 8f. (1) Type **671** 55 20
3312 8f. (2) Ibis wading 55 20
3313 80f. (3) Ibis perching . . . 2·20 1·30

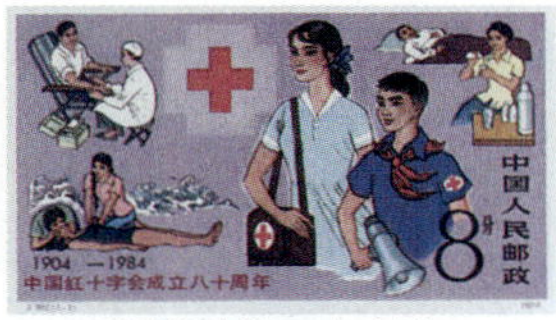
672 Red Cross Activities

1984. 80th Anniv of Chinese Red Cross Society.
3314 **672** 8f. multicoloured 30 20

673 Building Dam

1984. Gezhou Dam Project. Multicoloured.
3315 8f. Type **673** 30 20
3316 10f. View of dam and lock gates (vert) 40 30
3317 20f. Freighter in lock . . . 80 65

674 Inverted Image Tower and Yilang Pavilion

1984. Zhuo Zheng Garden, Suzhou. Mult.
3318 8f. (1) Type **674** 60 35
3319 8f. (2) Loquat Garden . . . 60 35
3320 10f. (3) Water court of Xiao Cang Lang 60 35
3321 70f. (4) Yuanxiang Hall and Yiyu Study . . . . 2·75 1·40

675 Pistol Shooting

1984. Olympic Games, Los Angeles. Multicoloured.
3322 4f. Type **675** 20 20
3323 8f. High jumping 20 20
3324 8f. Weightlifting 20 20
3325 10f. Gymnastics 25 20
3326 20f. Volley ball 30 25
3327 80f. Diving . . . . 1·30 40
MS3328 96 × 70 mm. 2y. Olympic rings and gymnasts (61 × 37 mm) 6·00 4·00

676 Calligraphy

677 Tianjin

1984. Art Works by Wu Changshuo. Mult.
3329 4f. (1) Type **676** 40 25
3330 4f. (2) "Pair of Peaches" . . 40 25
3331 8f. (3) "Lotus" 40 25
3332 8f. (4) "Wisteria" 40 25
3333 8f. (5) "Peony" 40 25
3334 10f. (6) "Autumn Chrysanthemum" . . . 75 45
3335 20f. (7) "Plum Blossom" . . . 1·00 60
3336 70f. (8) Seal and impression 3·25 2·30

1984. Luanhe River–Tianjin Water Diversion Project. Multicoloured.
3337 8f. Type **677** 20 20
3338 10f. Locks and canal (horiz) 30 20
3339 20f. Tunnel and sculpture 40 25

678 Chinese and Japanese Pagodas

1984. Chinese–Japanese Youth Friendship Festival. Multicoloured.
3340 8f. Type **678** 20 20
3341 20f. Girls watering shrub . . 30 20
3342 80f. Young people dancing 75 55

679 Factory Worker

1984. 35th Anniv of People's Republic. Mult.
3343 8f. (1) Type **679** 20 20
3344 8f. (2) Girl and rainbow . . 20 20
3345 8f. (4) Girl and symbols of science 20 20
3346 8f. (5) Soldier 20 20
3347 20f. (3) Flag and Manchurian cranes (36 × 50 mm) 45 30

680 Chen Jiageng

1984. 110th Birth Anniv of Chen Jiageng (educationist and patriot). Multicoloured.
3348 8f. Type **680** 30 20
3349 80f. Jimei School 55 35

681 The Maiden's Study

1984. Scenes from "Peony Pavilion" (drama) by Tang Xianzu. Paintings by Dai Dunbang. Multicoloured.
3350 8f. (1) Type **681** 50 40
3351 8f. (2) Du Liniang dreaming 50 40
3352 20f. (3) Du Liniang drawing self-portrait . . . . 1·00 75
3353 70f. (4) Du Liniang and Liu Mengmei married . . . . 4·00 3·00
MS3354 136 × 80 mm. 2y. Du Liniang and her maid, Chun Xiang in garden (85 × 57 mm) 31·00 12·50

682 Baoguo Temple

1984. Landscapes of Mt. Emei Shan. Mult.
3355 4f. (1) Type **682** 35 20
3356 8f. (2) Leiyin Temple . . . 40 30
3357 8f. (3) Hongchun Lawn 40 30
3358 10f. (4) Elephant Bath Pool 55 35
3359 20f. (5) Woyun Temple . . 95 75
3360 80f. (6) Shining Cloud Sea, Jinding . . . . 4·00 2·40

683 Ren Bishi

684 Flowers in Chinese Vase

1984. 80th Birth Anniv of Ren Bishi (2nd issue).
3361 **683** 8f. brown and purple . . 20 20
3362 – 10f. black and lilac . . . 30 20
3363 – 20f. black and brown . . 35 20
DESIGNS: 10f. Ren Bishi reading speech at Communist Party Congress; 20f. Ren Bishi saluting.

1984. Chinese Insurance Industry.
3364 **684** 8f. multicoloured 30 20

685 "Ox" (Yao Zhonghua)

687 Lotus of Good Luck

686 "Zunyi Meeting" (Liu Xiangping)

1985. New Year. Year of the Ox.
3365 **685** 8f. multicoloured 55 40

1985. 50th Anniv of Zunyi Meeting. Mult.
3366 8f. Type **686** 30 25
3367 20f. "Arrival of the Red Army in Northern Shaanxi" (Zhao Yu) . . . 75 60

1985. Festival Lanterns. Multicoloured.
3368 8f. (1) Type **687** 50 20
3369 8f. (2) Auspicious dragon and phoenix 50 20
3370 8f. (3) A hundred flowers blossoming 50 20
3371 70f. (4) Prosperity and affluence . . . . 2·75 1·20

688 Stylized Dove and Women's Open Hands

689 Hands reading Braille

1985. United Nations Decade for Women.
3372 **688** 20f. multicoloured . . . 30 20

1985. Welfare Fund for the Handicapped. Multicoloured.
3373 8f.+2f. (1) Type **689** . . . . 1·20 60
3374 8f.+2f. (2) Lips and sign language . . . . 1·20 60
3375 8f.+2f. (3) Learning to use artificial limb . . . . . . 1·20 60
3376 8f.+2f. (4) Stylized figure in wheelchair . . . . 1·20 60

690 "Green Calyx" Mei

691 Headquarters

1985. Mei Flowers. Multicoloured.
3377 8f. (1) Type **690** 30 20
3378 8f. (2) "Pendant" mei . . . 30 20
3379 8f. (3) "Contorted dragon" mei 30 20
3380 10f. (4) "Cinnabar" mei . . 40 20
3381 20f. (5) "Versicolor" mei . . 55 25
3382 80f. (6) "Apricot" mei . . . 2·50 95
MS3383 130 × 70 mm. 2y. "Duplicate" mei and "Condensed fragrance" mei (88 × 48 mm) 22·00 15·00

1985. 60th Anniv of All-China Trade Unions Federation.
3384 **691** 8f. multicoloured 30 20

692 Bird and Children

1985. International Youth Year.
3385 **692** 20f. multicoloured . . . 30 20

693 Giant Panda

694 Xian Xinghai (bust, Cao Chongen)

1985. Giant Panda. Multicoloured.
3386 8f. Type **693** 20 20
3387 20f. Giant panda (different) (horiz) 20 20
3388 50f. Giant panda (different) 45 30
3389 80f. Two giant pandas (horiz) 65 45
MS3390 74 × 80 mm. 3y. Giant panda and cub (39 × 58 mm) 4·00 3·00

1985. 80th Birth Anniv of Xian Xianghai (composer).
3391 **694** 8f. multicoloured 30 20

695 Agnes Smedley

696 Zheng He (navigator)

1985. American Journalists in China.
3392 **695** 8f. brown, stone and ochre 20 20
3393 – 20f. olive, grey and stone 30 20
3394 – 80f. purple, lilac and cream 70 45
DESIGNS: 20f. Anna Louise Strong; 80f. Edgar Snow.

1985. 580th Anniv of Zheng He's First Voyage to Western Seas. Multicoloured.
3395 8f. (1) Type **696** 20 20
3396 8f. (2) Zheng He on elephant 20 20
3397 20f. (3) Exchanging goods 45 35
3398 80f. (4) Bidding farewell . . 1·50 65

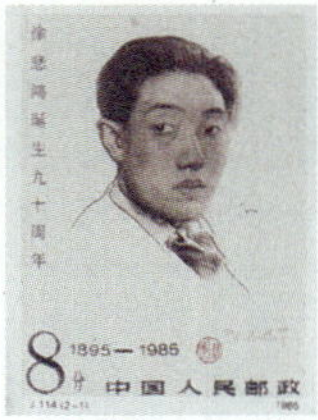
697 "Self-portrait"

1985. 90th Birth Anniv of Xu Beihong (artist). Multicoloured.
3399 8f. Type **697** 30 20
3400 20f. Xu Beihong at work . . 70 25

698 Lin Zexu

699 "Prosperity"

1985. Birth Bicentenary of Lin Zexu (statesman).
3401 **698** 8f. multicoloured 30 20
3402 – 80f. brown and black . . 60 25
DESIGN—55 × 23 mm. 80f. "Burning opium at Humen" (relief).

1985. 20th Anniv of Tibet Autonomous Region. Multicoloured.
3403 8f. Type **699** 20 20
3404 10f. "Celebration" 30 25
3405 20f. "Harvest 50 45

700 Chinese Army at Lugouqiao

1985. 40th Anniv of Victory over Japan.
3406 **700** 8f. black, brown & red 30 20
3407 – 80f. black, brown & red 30 20
DESIGN: 80f. Defending the Great Wall.

701 Cycling

1985. 2nd National Workers' Games, Peking. Multicoloured.
3408 8f. Type **701** 20 20
3409 20f. Hurdling 30 25

702 Gobi Oasis

1985. 30th Anniv of Xinjiang Uygur Autonomous Region. Multicoloured.
3410 8f. Type **702** 20 20
3411 10f. Oilfield and Lake Tianchi (54 × 26 mm) . . 20 20
3412 20f. Tianshan pasture . . . 30 25

703 Athletes and Silhouette of Woman

1985. 1st National Youth Games, Zhengzhou.
3413 **703** 8f. multicoloured 20 20
3414 – 20f. red, blue and black 40 35
DESIGN: 20f. Basketball players and silhouette of man.

704 Forbidden City (½-size illustration)

1985. 60th Anniv of Imperial Palace Museum.
3415 **704** 8f. (1) multicoloured . . 20 20
3416 – 8f. (2) multicoloured . . 20 20
3417 – 20f. (3) multicoloured . . 20 20
3418 – 80f. (4) multicoloured . . 50 45
DESIGNS: Nos. 3416/18, Different parts of Forbidden City.

705 Zou Taofen

706 Memorial Pavilion

1985. 90th Anniv of Zou Taofen (journalist).
3419 **705** 8f. black, brown & silver 20 20
3420 – 20f. black, green & silver 20 20
DESIGN: 20f. Premier Chou En-lai's inscription in memory of Zou Taofen.

1985. 50th Anniv of December 9th Movement.
3421 **706** 8f. multicoloured 30 20

707 "Tiger"

708 First Experimental Satellite

1986. New Year. Year of the Tiger.
3422 **707** 8f. multicoloured 55 40

1986. Space Research. Multicoloured.
3423 4f. (1) Type **708** 20 20
3424 8f. (2) Mil-Mi8 helicopters recovering satellites . . . 20 20
3425 8f. (3) Underwater launched rocket 20 20
3426 10f. (4) Rocket launched from land 30 20
3427 20f. (5) Dish aerial 30 20
3428 70f. (6) Satellite and diagram of orbit 70 40

709 Dong Biwu

710 Lin Boqu

1986. Birth Centenary of Dong Biwu (founder of Chinese Communist Party).
3429 **709** 8f. black and brown . . 20 20
3430 – 20f. black and brown . . 30 20
DESIGN: 20f. At meeting for ratification of U.N. Charter, Los Angeles, 1945.

1986. Birth Centenary of Lin Boqu (politician).
3431 **710** 8f. brown and black . . 20 20
3432 – 20f. brown and black . . 30 20
DESIGN: 20f. At Yanan.

711 He Long

1986. 90th Birth Anniv of He Long (politician).
3433 **711** 8f. black and brown . . 20 20
3434 – 20f. black and brown . . 30 20
DESIGN: 20f. On horse.

712 Skin Tents, Inner Mongolia

713 Comet and Earth

1986. Traditional Houses.
3435 **712** 1f. green, brown & grey 20 20
3436 – 1½f. brown, red & blue 20 20
3437 – 2f. brown and bistre . . 20 20
3438 – 3f. black and brown . . 20 20
3439 – 4f. red and black . . . 20 20
3439a – 5f. black, grey & green 20 20
3440 – 8f. grey, red and black 20 20
3441 – 10f. black and orange 20 20
3441b – 15f. black, grey & grn 20 20
3442 – 20f. grey, green & blk 20 20
3442b – 25f. black, grey & pink 30 20
3443 – 30f. lilac, blue & brown 30 20
3444 – 40f. brn, pur & stone 55 25
3445 – 50f. blue, mve & dp bl 55 30
3445b – 80f. black, grey & blue 50 20
3446 – 90f. black and red . . 80 50
3447 – 1y. brown and grey . . 90 60
3448 – 1y.10 blue, blk & brn 90 70
3448a – 1y.30 blk, grey & red 60 35
3448b – 1y.60 blue & black . . 75 35
3448c – 2y. black, grey & brown 80 35
DESIGNS: 1½f. Tibet. 2f. North-East China. 3f. Hunan. 4f. Jiangsu. 5f. Shandong. 8f. Peking. 10f. Yunnan. 15f. Guangxi. 20f. Shanghai. 25f. Ningxia. 30f. Anhui. 40f. North Shaanxi. 50f. Sichuan. 80f. Shanxi. 90f. Taiwan. 1y. Fujian. 1y.10, Zhejiang, 1y.30, Qinghai. 1y.60, Guizhou. 2y. Jiangxi.

1988. Appearance of Halley's Comet.
3449 **713** 20f. grey and blue . . . 30 25

714 Cranes

1986. Great White Crane. Multicoloured.
3450 8f. Type **714** 30 20
3451 10f. Crane flying (vert) . . . 30 20
3452 70f. Four cranes (vert) . . . 55 25
MS3453 159 × 51 mm. 2y. Group of cranes flying (116 × 27 mm) . . 7·00 4·00

715 Li Weihan

1986. 90th Birth Anniv of Li Weihan (politician). Each green and black.
3454 8f. Type **715** 20 20
3455 20f. Li Weihan at work . . 30 25

716 Stylized People on Dove

1986. International Peace Year.
3456 **716** 8f. multicoloured 35 25

717 Mao Dun

1986. 90th Birth Anniv of Mao Dun (writer). Each grey, black and brown.
3457 8f. Type **717** 20 20
3458 20f. Mao Dun and manuscript 30 25

718 Wang Jiaxiang

1986. 80th Birth Anniv of Wang Jiaxiang (first People's Republic ambassador to U.S.S.R.). Multicoloured.
3459 8f. Type **718** 20 20
3460 20f. Wang Jiaxiang at Yan'an 30 25

719 Flowers on Desk

1986. Teachers' Day.
3461 **719** 8f. multicoloured 30 20

720 "Magnolia sinensis"

1986. Magnolias. Multicoloured.
3462 8f. (1) Type **720** 30 30
3463 8f. (2) "Manglietia patungensis" 30 30
3464 70f. (3) "Alcimandra cathcartii" . . . . 2·40 2·10
MS3465 131 × 70 mm. 2y. "Manglietia grandis" and "Manglietiastrum sinicum" (58 × 48 mm) . . . . 11·50 7·00

721 Sun Yat-sen (120th birth anniv)

1986. 75th Anniv of 1911 Revolution. Leaders. Multicoloured.
3466 8f. Type **721** 20 20
3467 10f. Huang Xing (70th death anniv) 30 25
3468 40f. Zhang Taiyan (50th death anniv) . . . . . . 1·00 90

722 Bronze Tiger

1986. 2nd All-China Philatelic Federation Congress. Sheet 129 × 80 mm.
MS3469 **722** 2y. multicoloured 4·25 3·50

723 Dr. Sun Yat-sen

1986. 120th Birth Anniv of Dr. Sun Yat-sen. Sheet 82 × 136 mm.
MS3470 **723** 2y. multicoloured 7·75 6·50

724 Zhu De

1986. Birth Centenary of Marshal Zhu De.
3471 **724** 8f. brown 20 20
3472 – 20f. green 40 25
DESIGN: 20f. Making speech, 1950.

725 Archery

726 "Rabbit"

1986. Sport in Ancient China. Each grey, black and red.
3473 8f. (1) Type **725** 30 20
3474 8f. (2) Weiqi (horiz) 30 20
3475 10f. (3) Golf (horiz) 40 25
3476 50f. (4) Football . . . . . 3·00 1·70

1987. New Year. Year of the Rabbit.
3477 **726** 8f. multicoloured 35 25

727 Xu Xiake

728 Steller's Sea Eagle

1987. 400th Birth Anniv of Xu Xiake (explorer). Multicoloured.
3478 8f. Type **727** 45 30
3479 20f. Recording observations in cave . . . . 1·90 1·50
3480 40f. Climbing mountain . . 3·75 2·20

1987. Birds of Prey. Multicoloured.
3481 8f. (1) Black kite (horiz) . . 40 25
3482 8f. (2) Type **728** 40 25
3483 10f. (3) Himalayan griffon 45 25
3484 90f. (4) Upland buzzard (horiz) . . . . 5·25 1·00

729 Hawk Kite

1987. Kites. Multicoloured.
3485 8f. (1) Type **729** 50 20
3486 8f. (2) Centipede 50 20
3487 30f. (3) The Eight Diagrams 1·70 80
3488 30f. (4) Phoenix . . . . . . 1·70 80

730 Liao Zhongkai

731 "Eventful Years"

1987. 110th Birth Anniv of Liao Zhongkai (politician). Multicoloured.
3489 8f. Type **730** 20 20
3490 20f. Liao Zhongkai with wife 30 20

1987. 90th Birth Anniv of Ye Jianying (revolutionary and co-founder of People's Army). Portraits. Multicoloured.
3491 8f. Type **731** 35 30
3492 10f. "Founder of the State" 45 40
3493 30f. "Everywhere Green Hills" . . . . 1·70 1·50

732 Worshipping Bodhisattvas (Northern Liang Dynasty)

1987. Dunhuang Cave Murals (1st series). Mult.
3494 8f. Type **732** 40 20
3495 10f. Deer King Jataka (Northern Wei dynasty) 50 25
3496 20f. Heavenly musicians (Northern Wei dynasty) 1·40 60
3497 40f. Flying Devata (Northern Wei dynasty) 2·50 1·10
MS3498 142 × 93 mm. 2y. Mahasattva Jataka . . . . . . 25·00 12·00
See also Nos. 3553/6, 3682/5, 3811/**MS**3815, 3910/13 and 4131/**MS**4135.

733 "Happy Holiday" (Yan Qinghu)

1987. Children's Day. Childrens' drawings. Mult.
3499 8f. (1) Type **733** 20 20
3500 8f. (2) Children with doves and balloons (Liu Yuan) 30 20

734 Town

1987. Improvements in Rural Areas. Multicoloured.
3501 8f. (1) Type **734** 40 35
3502 8f. (2) Fresh foods (horiz) 40 35
3503 10f. (3) Feeding cattle (horiz) 60 50
3504 20f. (4) Outdoor cinema . . 1·10 95

735 Emblem

736 Globe

1987. Postal Savings.
3505 **735** 8f. turquoise, yell & red 30 20

1987. Centenary of Esperanto (invented language).
3506 **736** 8f. blue, black & green 25 20

737 Flag over Great Wall

1987. 60th Anniv of People's Liberation Army. Multicoloured.
3507 8f. (1) Type **737** 30 20
3508 8f. (2) Soldier and rocket launcher 30 20
3509 10f. (3) Sailor and submarine 70 30
3510 30f. (4) Pilot and jet fighters 1·40 75

738 Dove above Houses

1987. Int Year of Shelter for the Homeless.
3511 **738** 8f. multicoloured 25 20

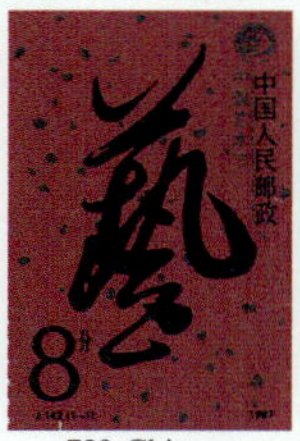

739 Chinese Character

740 Pan Gu inventing the Universe

1987. China Art Festival, Peking.
3512 **739** 8f. black, red and gold 25 20

1987. Folk Tales. Multicoloured.
3513 4f. (1) Type **740** 20 20
3514 8f. (2) Nu Wa creating human being 25 20
3515 8f. (3) Yi shooting nine suns 25 20
3516 10f. (4) Chang'e flying to the moon 35 20
3517 20f. (5) Kua Fu chasing the sun 70 30
3518 90f. (6) Jing Wei filling the sea . . . . 2·50 1·20

741 Sun rising behind Party Flag

1987. 13th National Communist Party Congress.
3519 **741** 8f. multicoloured 20 20

742 Yellow Crane Tower, Wuhan

1987. Ancient Buildings. Multicoloured.
3520 8f. (1) Type **742** 35 20
3521 8f. (2) Yue Yang Tower . . . 35 30
3522 10f. (3) Teng Wang Pavilion 40 35
3523 90f. (4) Peng Lai Pavilion 3·25 3·25
MS3524 129 × 93 mm. Nos. 3520/3 (sold at 1y.50) . . . . 13·50 9·00

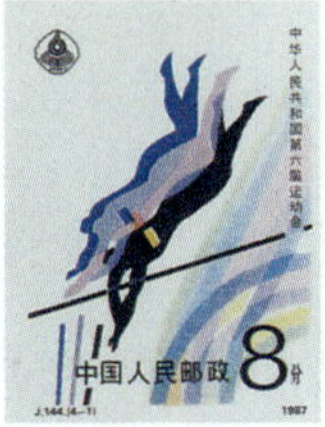

743 Pole Vaulting

1987. 6th National Games, Guangdong Province. Multicoloured.
3525 8f. (1) Type **743** 25 20
3526 8f. (2) Women's softball . . 25 20
3527 30f. (3) Weightlifting 55 30
3528 50f. (4) Diving 90 50

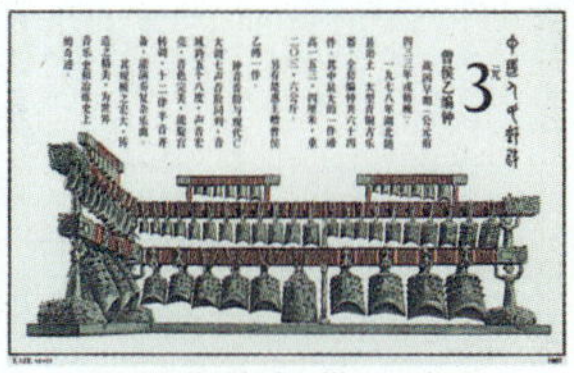

744 Bells (½-size illustration)

1987. Warring States Period (430 B.C.) Bronze Chime Bells from Tomb of Marquis Yi Zeng State, Hubei. Sheet 91 × 165 mm. No gum. Imperf.
MS3529 **744** 3y. multicoloured 6·75 4·75

745 Shi Jin practising Martial Arts

1987. Literature. "Outlaws of the Marsh" (1st series). Multicoloured.
3530 8f. Type **745** 35 20
3531 10f. Sagacious Lu uprooting willow tree 45 20
3532 30f. Lin Chon sheltering in temple of mountain spirit 1·50 75
3533 50f. Song Jian helping Chao Gai to escape . . . . . . 2·10 1·60
MS3534 139 × 87 mm. 2y. Outlaws with captured birthday gift(85 × 56 mm) . . . . . . 18·00 16·00
See also Nos. 3614/17, 3778/**MS**3782, 3854/7 and **MS**4252.

746 Dragon

747 Cai Yuanpri

1988. New Year. Year of the Dragon.
3535 **746** 8f. multicoloured 35 30

1988. 120th Birth Anniv of Cai Yuanpei (educationist). Multicoloured.
3536 8f. Type **747** 20 20
3537 20f. Cai Yuanpei seated in chair 25 20

748 Tao Zhu

1988. 80th Birth Anniv of Tao Zhu (Communist Party official). Multicoloured.
3538 8f. Type **748** 20 20
3539 20f. Tao Zhu (half-length portrait) 25 20

749 Harvest Festival

1988. Flourishing Rural Areas of China. Mult.
3540 8f. Type **749** 25 20
3541 10f. Couple with fish, flowers and chickens . . . 25 20
3542 20f. Couple making scientific study 45 30
3543 30f. Happy family 70 50

750 Flag and Rainbow

751 Wuzhi Mountain

1988. 7th National People's Congress.
3544 **750** 8f. multicoloured 20 20

1988. Establishment of Hainan Province. Mult.
3545 8f. Type **751** 20 10
3546 10f. Wanquan River 20 20
3547 30f. Beach 20 30
3548 1y.10 Bay and deer 55 45

752 Li Siguang (geologist)

1988. Scientists (1st series). Multicoloured.
3549 8f. Type **752** 20 15
3550 10f. Zhu Kezhen (meteorologist) 20 15
3551 20f. Wu Youxun (physicist) 20 15
3552 30f. Hua Luogeng (mathematician) 25 25
See also Nos. 3702/5 and 3821/4.

1988. Dunhuang Cave Murals (2nd series). As T **732**. Multicoloured.
3553 8f. (1) Hunting (Western Wei dynasty) 20 15
3554 8f. (2) Fighting (Western Wei dynasty) 20 15
3555 10f. (3) Farming (Northern Zhou dynasty) 25 15
3556 90f. (4) Building pagoda (Northern Zhou dynasty) 2·00 95

753 Healthy Trees and Hand holding back polluted Soil

1988. Environmental Protection. Multicoloured.
3557 8f. (1) Type **753** 20 15
3558 8f. (2) Doves in clean air and hand holding back polluted air 20 15
3559 8f. (3) Fishes in clean water and hand holding back polluted water 20 15
3560 8f. (4) Peaceful landscape and hand holding back noise waves 20 15

754 Large Dragon Stamps, 1878

1988. 110th Anniv of First Chinese Empire Stamps. Sheet 70 × 100 mm.
MS3561 **754** 3y. multicoloured 4·50 4·25

755 Games Emblem

1988. 11th Asian Games, Peking (1990) (1st issue). Multicoloured.
3562 8f. Type **755** 20 15
3563 30f. Games mascot 20 15
See also Nos. 3653/6 and 3695/3700.

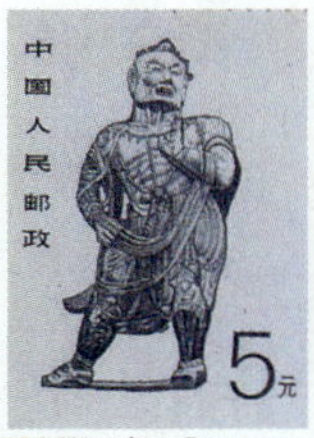

756 Warrior, Longmen Grotto, Henan

757 Peony

1988. Art of Chinese Grottoes.
3564 – 2y. brown & light brown 70 30
3565 **756** 5y. black and brown . . 1·40 45
3566 – 10y. brown and stone . . 2·50 95
3567 – 20y. black and brown . . 5·75 1·90
DESIGNS: 2y. Buddha, Yungang Grotto, Shanxi. 10y. Bodhisattva, Maijishan Grotto, Gansu. 20y. Woman with chickens, Dazu Grotto, Sichuan.
See also No. **MS**3639.

1988. 10th Anniv of Chinese–Japanese Treaty of Peace and Friendship. Multicoloured.
3568 8f. Type **757** 20 10
3569 1y.60 Cherry blossom . . . 85 45

758 Coal Wharf, Quinghuangdao

1988. Achievements of Socialist Construction (1st series). Multicoloured.
3570 8f. Type **758** 20 15
3571 10f. Ethylene works, Shangdong 20 15
3572 20f. Baoshan steel works, Shanghai 25 15
3573 30f. Television centre, Peking 25 25
See also Nos. 3691/22, 3678/81 and 3759/62.

759 Taishan Temple

1988. Mount Taishan Views. Multicoloured.
3574 8f. Type **759** 25 15
3575 10f. Ladder to Heaven . . . 35 25
3576 20f. Daguang Park 70 35
3577 90f. Sun Watching Peak . . 2·75 1·30

760 Liao Chengzhi

761 Cycling

1988. 80th Birth Anniv of Liao Chengzhi (Communist Party leader). Multicoloured.
3578 8f. Type **760** 20 15
3579 20f. Liao Chengzhi at work 20 15

1988. 1st National Peasant Games. Multicoloured.
3580 8f. Type **761** 20 15
3581 20f. Wushu 20 15

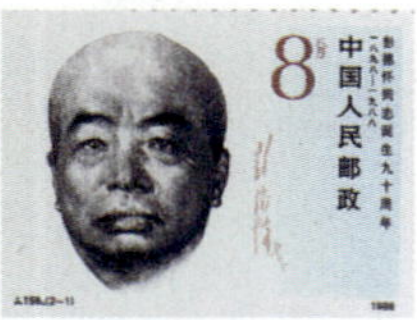
762 Peng Dehuai

1988. 90th Birth Anniv of General Peng Dehuai. Multicoloured.
3582 8f. Type **762** 20 15
3583 20f. In uniform 20 15

763 Battle against Lu Bu

1988. Literature. "Romance of the Three Kingdoms" by Luo Guanzhong (1st series). Multicoloured.
3584 8f. (1) Heroes become sworn brothers (horiz) 30 15
3585 8f. (2) Type **763** 30 25
3586 30f. (3) Fengyi Pavilion (horiz) 80 60
3587 50f. (4) Discussing heroes over wine . . . . 1·40 1·00
MS3588 182 × 65 mm. 3y. Guan Yu and retinue (157 × 37 mm) . . 18·00 13·00
See also Nos. 3711/14, 3807/10, 3944/**MS**3948 and 4315/**MS**4319.

764 People in Heart

765 Stag's Head

1988. International Volunteers' Day.
3589 **764** 20f. multicoloured . . . 25 15

1988. Pere David's Deer. Multicoloured.
3590 8f. Type **765** 25 15
3591 40f. Herd . . . . 1·20 85

766 Da Yi Pin

1988. Orchids. Multicoloured.
3592 8f. Type **766** 20 15
3593 10f. Dragon 25 25
3594 20f. Large phoenix tail . . . 45 35
3595 50f. Silver-edged black orchid . . . . 1·00 85
MS3596 119 × 85 mm. 2y. Red lotus petal (55 × 36 mm) . . . . . . 15·00 5·25

767 Snake

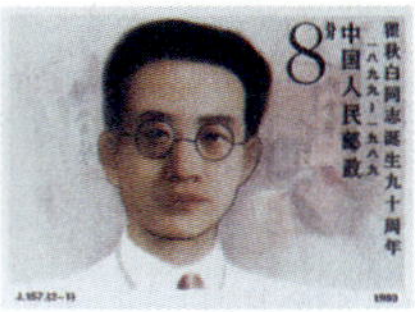
768 Qu Quibai

1989. New Year. Year of the Snake.
3597 **767** 8f. multicoloured 40 35

1989. 90th Birth Anniv of Qu Qiubai (writer). Multicoloured.
3598 8f. Type **768** 20 15
3599 20f. Qu Qiubai (half-length portrait) 25 15

769 Pheasant

1989. Brown Eared-pheasant. Multicoloured.
3600 8f. Type **769** 20 15
3601 50f. Two pheasants 35 35

770 "Heaven" (top section)

1989. Silk Painting from Han Tomb, Mawangdui, Changsha. Multicoloured.
3602 8f. Type **770** 25 15
3603 20f. "Earth" (central section) 25 25
3604 30f. "Underworld" (bottom section) 25 25
MS3605 90 × 165 mm. 5y. Complete painting. Imperf . . . . 4·75 3·00

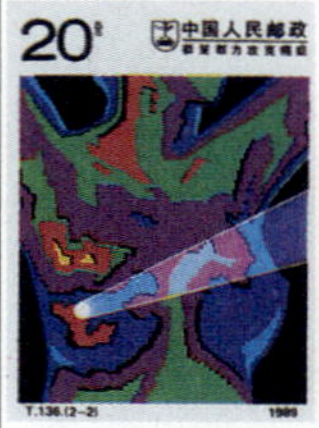
771 Diagnosis by Thermography

773 Children

772 Memorial Frieze

1989. Anti-cancer Campaign.
3606 **771** 8f. grey, red & black . . 25 25
3607 – 20f. multicoloured . . . 25 25
DESIGN: 8f. Crab and red crosses.

1989. 70th Anniv of May 4th Movement.
3608 **772** 8f. multicoloured 25 15

1989. 40th International Children's Day. Children's paintings. Multicoloured.
3609 8f.+4f. (1) Type **773** 20 15
3610 8f.+4f. (2) Child and penguins 20 15
3611 8f.+4f. (3) Child flying on bird 20 15
3612 8f.+4f. (4) Boy and girl playing ball 20 15

774 Globe, Doves and Lectern

1989. Cent of Interparliamentary Union.
3613 **774** 20f. multicoloured . . . 30 25

1989. Literature. "Outlaws of the Marsh" (2nd series). As T **745**. Multicoloured.
3614 8f. Wu Song killing tiger on Jingyang Ridge 20 15
3615 10f. Qin Ming riding through hail of arrows . . 20 15
3616 20f. Hua Rong shooting wild goose 30 25
3617 1y.30 Li Kui fighting Zhang Shun on sampan . . . . 1·50 50

775 Anniversary Emblem

1989. 10th Anniv of Asia–Pacific Telecommunity.
3618 **775** 8f. multicoloured 25 15

1989. Achievements of Socialist Construction (2nd series). As T **758**. Multicoloured.
3619 8f. International telecommunications building, Peking (vert) . . 20 15
3620 10f. Xi Qu coal mine, Gu Jiao 20 15
3621 20f. Long Yang Gorge hydro-electric power station, Qinghai 20 15
3622 30f. Da Yao Shan tunnel on Guangzhou–Heng Yang railway 25 15

776 Five Peaks of Mt. Huashan

1989. Mount Huashan. Multicoloured.
3623 8f. Type **776** 20 10
3624 10f. View from top of Mt. Huashan 20 10
3625 20f. Thousand Foot Precipice 30 15
3626 90f. Blue Dragon Ridge . . 90 60

777 "Fable of the White Snake" (stage design, Ye Qianyu)

1989. Contemporary Art. Multicoloured.
3627 8f. Type **777** 20 10
3628 20f. "Lijiang River in Fine Rain" (Li Keran) 25 15
3629 50f. "Marching Together" (oxen) (Wu Zuoren) . . . 60 45

778 Doves and 1949 $50 Stamp

780 Ribbons and Gate of Heavenly Peace, Peking

779 Lecturing in Temple of Apricot, Qufu

1989. 40th Anniv of Chinese People's Political Conference.
3630 **778** 8f. red, blue and black 25 15

1989. 2540th Birth Anniv of Confucius (philosopher). Multicoloured.
3631 8f. Type **779** 20 15
3632 1y.60 Confucius in ox-drawn cart 75 70
MS3633 74 × 106 mm. 3y. Confucius. No gum. Imperf . . 3·75 2·50

1989. 40th Anniv of People's Republic. Mult.
3634 8f. Type **780** 20 15
3635 10f. Flowers and ribbons . . 20 15
3636 20f. Stars and ribbons . . . 20 15
3637 40f. Buildings and ribbons 25 15
MS3638 120 × 84 mm. 3y. Gate of Heavenly Peace, Peking and revellers . . . . 2·10 1·60

1989. National Stamp Exhibition, Peking. Sheet 60 × 109 mm containing No. 3566.
MS3639 10y. sepia and cinnamon 19·00 13·00

781 Woman using Camera

1989. 150th Anniv of Photography.
3640 **781** 8f. multicoloured 25 15

782 Li Dazhao

1989. Birth Centenary of Li Dazhao (co-founder of Chinese Communist Party). Multicoloured.
3641 8f. Type **782** 20 15
3642 20f. Li Dazhao and script 25 25

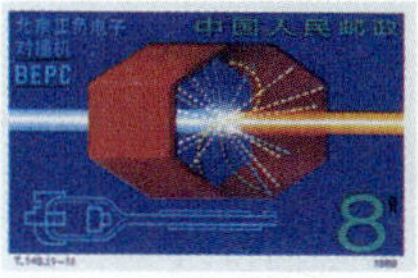
783 Diagram of Collider in Action

1989. Peking Electron-Positron Collider.
3643 **783** 8f. multicoloured 25 15

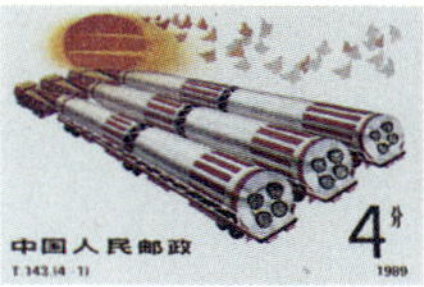
784 Rockets

1989. National Defence. Multicoloured.
3644 4f. Type **784** 20 15
3645 8f. Rocket on transporter 20 15
3646 10f. Rocket launch (vert) . . 20 15
3647 20f. Jettison of fuel tank . . 25 15

785 Spring Morning, Su Causeway

1989. West Lake, Hangzhou. Multicoloured.
3648 8f. Type **785** 20 15
3649 10f. Crooked Courtyard . . 20 15
3650 30f. Moon over Three Pools 25 25
3651 40f. Snow on Broken Bridge 35 25
MS3652 144 × 60 mm. 5y. West Lake (85 × 37 mm) . . . . 3·75 2·20

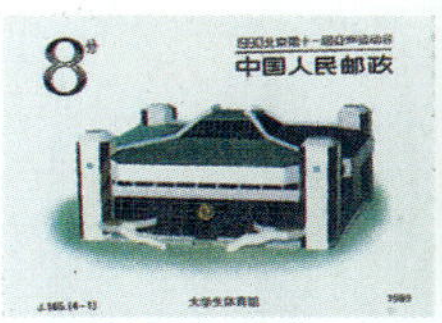

786 Peking College Gymnasium **787** Horse

1989. 11th Asian Games, Peking (1990) (2nd issue). Multicoloured.
3653 8f. Type **786** 20 15
3654 10f. Northern Suburbs swimming pool 20 15
3655 30f. Workers' Stadium . . . 20 15
3656 1y.60 Chaoyang Gymnasium 35 25

1990. New Year. Year of the Horse.
3657 **787** 8f. multicoloured 50 25

788 Narcissi **790** Emblem

789 Bethune and Medical Team in Canada

1990. Narcissi. Multicoloured.
3658 8f. Type **788** 20 15
3659 20f. Natural group of narcissi 20 15
3660 30f. Arrangement of narcissi 20 15
3661 1y.60 Arrangement (different) 50 45

1990. Birth Centenary of Norman Bethune (surgeon). Multicoloured.
3662 8f. Type **789** 20 15
3663 1y.60 Bethune and medical team in China 55 45

1990. 80th International Women's Day.
3664 **790** 20f. red, green and black 30 25

791 Birds flying above Trees

1990. Tree Planting Day. Multicoloured.
3665 8f. Type **791** 20 15
3666 10f. Trees in city 20 15
3667 20f. Great Wall and trees 20 15
3668 30f. Forest and field of wheat 25 15

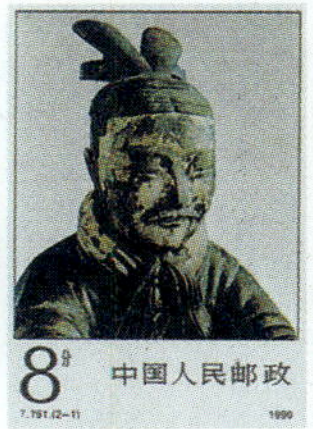

792 Ban Po Plate **794** Charioteer

793 Li Fuchun

1990. Pottery. Multicoloured.
3669 8f. Type **792** 20 15
3670 20f. Miao Di Gou dish . . 20 15
3671 30f. Ma Jia Yao jar 20 15
3672 50f. Ma Chang jar 25 15

1990. 90th Birth Anniv of Li Fuchun (politician). Multicoloured.
3673 8f. Type **793** 20 15
3674 20f. Li Fuchun (different) 25 25

1990. 10th Anniv of Discovery of Bronze Chariots in Emperor Qin Shi Huang's Tomb. Multicoloured.
3675 8f. Type **794** 20 10
3676 50f. Horse's head 35 25
MS3677 140 × 78 mm. 5y. Chariots (115 × 37 mm) . . . . 5·25 3·50

1990. Achievements of Socialist Construction (3rd series). As T **758**. Multicoloured.
3678 8f. Second automobile factory 20 15
3679 10f. Yizheng chemical and fibre company 20 15
3680 20f. Shengli oil field 25 15
3681 30f. Qinshan nuclear power station 25 15

1990. Dunhuang Cave Murals (3rd series). Sui Dynasty. As T **732**. Multicoloured.
3682 8f. Flying Devatas 20 15
3683 10f. Worshipping Bodhisattva (vert) 20 15
3684 30f. Saviour Avalokitesvara (vert) 45 25
3685 50f. Indra 70 50

795 Snow Leopard

1990. The Snow Leopard. Multicoloured.
3686 8f. Type **795** 25 15
3687 50f. Leopard stalking . . . 25 15

796 West Fujian Communications Bureau (Red Posts) 4p. Stamp

1990. 60th Anniv of Communist China Stamp Issues. Multicoloured.
3688 8f. Type **796** 20 15
3689 20f. Chinese Soviet Republic 1c. stamp 25 15

797 Zhang Wentian **798** Emblem

1990. 90th Birth Anniv of Zhang Wentian (revolutionary).
3690 8f. Type **797** 20 15
3691 20f. Zhang Wentian and Zunyi Meeting venue . . 25 15

1990. International Literacy Year.
3692 **798** 20f. multicoloured . . . 25 15

799 Great Wall, Film and Screen **801** Athletics

800 Olympic ring "Balloons" carrying Giant Panda

1990. 85th Anniv of Chinese Films.
3693 **799** 20f. multicoloured . . . 25 15

1990. "Sportphilex '90" International Stamp Exhibition, Peking. Sheet 79 × 110 mm.
MS3694 **800** 10y. multicoloured 16·00 10·50

1990. 11th Asian Games, Peking (3rd issue). Multicoloured.
3695 4f. Type **801** 20 15
3696 8f. Gymnastics 20 15
3697 10f. Martial arts 20 15
3698 20f. Volleyball 20 15
3699 30f. Swimming 25 15
3700 1y.60 Shooting 70 60
MS3701 190 × 130 mm. Nos. 3562/3, 3653/6 and 3695/3700 (sold at 7y.) 9·75 7·00

802 Zhang Yuzhe (astronomer)

1990. Scientists (2nd series). Multicoloured.
3702 8f. Lin Qiaozhi (gynaecologist) 20 15
3703 10f. Type **802** 20 15
3704 20f. Hou Debang (chemist) 25 15
3705 30f. Ding Ying (agronomist) 25 15

803 Towering Temple

1990. Mount Hengshan, Hunan Province. Mult.
3706 8f. Type **803** 20 15
3707 10f. Aerial view of mountain 20 15
3708 20f. Trees and buildings on slopes 25 15
3709 50f. Zhurong Peak 45 25

804 Gusu Post Office, Suzhou

1990. 3rd All-China Philatelic Federation Congress. Sheet 130 × 80 mm.
MS3710 **804** 2y. multicoloured 5·25 3·75

1990. Literature. "Romance of the Three Kingdoms" by Luo Guanzhong (2nd series). As T **763**. Multicoloured.
3711 20f. (1) Cao Cao leading night attack on Wuchao (horiz) 20 15
3712 20f. (2) Liu Bei calling at Zhuge Liang's thatched cottage 20 15
3713 30f. (3) General Zhao rescuing A Dou single-handedly (horiz) 25 25
3714 50f. (4) Zhang Fei repulsing attackers at Changban Bridge 45 25

805 Revellers listening to Music

1990. Painting "Han Xizai's Night Revels" by Gu Hongzhong. Multicoloured.
3715 50f. (1) Type **805** 55 45
3716 50f. (2) Drummer and dancers 55 45
3717 50f. (3) Women attending man with fan and man and women in alcove . . 55 45
3718 50f. (4) Women playing flutes and couple by painted screen 55 45
3719 50f. (5) Young couple and women attending seated man 55 45
Nos. 3715/19 were printed together, se-tenant, forming a composite design.

806 Sheep **808** Wreath on Wall and Last Verse of the "Internationale"

807 Yuzui (dam at Dujiang)

1991. New Year. Year of the Sheep.
3720 **806** 20f. multicoloured . . . 45 25

1991. Dujiangyan Irrigation Project. Mult.
3721 20f. Type **807** 20 10
3722 50f. Feishayan (weir) . . . 35 15
3723 80f. Baopingkou (diversion of part of River Minjiang through new opening in Yulei Mountain) 55 35

1991. 120th Anniv of Paris Commune.
3724 **808** 20f. multicoloured . . . 25 15

809 Apple **810** Saiga

1991. Family Planning. Multicoloured.
3725 20f. Type **809** 20 15
3726 50f. Child's and adult's hands within heart . . . 25 15

1991. Horned Ruminants. Multicoloured.
3727 20f. Type **810** 20 10
3728 20f. Takin 20 10
3729 50f. Argali 25 15
3730 2y. Ibex 50 35

811 Dancers **812** Map and Emperor Penguins

1991. 40th Anniv of Chinese Administration of Tibet. Multicoloured.
3731 25f. Type **811** 20 15
3732 50f. Rainbows over mountain road 25 25
MS3733 75 × 100 mm. 2y. Clouds and cranes around 1952 $400 Lhasa stamp (39 × 53 mm) . . 4·75 2·20

1991. 30th Anniv of Implementation of Antarctic Treaty.
3734 **812** 20f. multicoloured . . . 40 25

813 "Rhododendron delavayi"

1991. Rhododendrons. Multicoloured.
3735 10f. Type **813** 20 15
3736 15f. "Rhododendron molle" 20 15
3737 20f. "Rhododendron simsii" 20 15
3738 20f. "Rhododendron fictolacteum" 20 15
3739 50f. "Rhododendron agglutinatum" (vert) . . . 45 25
3740 80f. "Rhododendron fortunei" (vert) 70 45
3741 90f. "Rhododendron giganteum" (vert) 80 50
3742 1y.60 "Rhododendron rex" (vert) . . . . 1·30 85
MS3743 135 × 89 mm. 5y. "Rhododendron wardii" . . . 9·75 6·50

814 Pleasure Boat on Lake Nanhu (venue of first Party congress)

1991. 70th Anniv of Chinese Communist Party. Multicoloured.
3744 20f. Type **814** 20 15
3745 50f. Party emblem 25 25

815 Statue, Xuxian

1991. 2200th Anniv of Peasant Uprising led by Chen Sheng and Wu Guang.
3746 **815** 20f. black, brown and deep brown 25 15

816 Hanging Temple

1991. Mount Hengshan, Shanxi Province. Mult.
3747 20f. Type **816** 20 15
3748 20f. Snow-covered peak . . 20 15
3749 55f. "Shrine of Hengshan" carved in rock face . . . 45 25
3750 80f. Temples in Flying Stone Grotto 70 45

817 Mammoths and Man

1991. 13th International Union for Quaternary Research Conference, Peking.
3751 **817** 20f. multicoloured . . . 40 25

818 Pine Valley

1991. Chengde Royal Summer Resort. Mult.
3752 15f. Type **818** 20 10
3753 20f. Pavilions around lake 20 10
3754 90f. Maples and pavilions on islet 60 45
MS3755 130 × 70 mm. 2y. View of resort (88 × 39 mm) . . . . . 6·00 3·00

819 Chen Yi

820 Clasped Hands forming Heart

1991. 90th Birth Anniv of Chen Yi (co-founder of People's Army).
3756 20f. Type **819** 20 15
3757 50f. Verse "The Green Pine" written by Chen Yi . . . 25 25

1991. Flood Disaster Relief.
3758 **820** 80f. multicoloured . . . 35 25
The proceeds from the sale of No. 3758 were donated to the International Decade for Natural Disaster Reduction National Committee.

1991. Achievements of Socialist Construction (4th series). As T **758**. Multicoloured.
3759 20f. Luoyang glassworks . . 20 10
3760 25f. Urumchi chemical fertilizer works 20 15
3761 55f. Shenyang–Dalian expressway 20 15
3762 80f. Xichang satellite launching centre 25 25

821 Xu Xilin

1991. 80th Anniv of 1911 Revolution. Mult.
3763 20f. (1) Type **821** 20 15
3764 20f. (2) Qiu Jin 20 15
3765 20f. (3) Song Jiaoren . . . 20 15

822 Wine Pot and Warming Bowl, Song Dynasty

823 Tao Xingzhi

1991. Jingdezhen China. Multicoloured.
3766 15f. (1) Type **822** 20 15
3767 20f. (2) Blue and white porcelain vase, Yuan dynasty 20 15
3768 20f. (3) Covered jar with dragon design, Ming dynasty (horiz) 20 15
3769 25f. (4) Vase with flower design, Qing dynasty 20 15
3770 50f. (5) Modern plate with fish design 25 15
3771 2y. (6) Modern octagonal bowl (horiz) 55 35

1991. Birth Centenary of Tao Xingzhi (educationist). Each blue, grey and red.
3772 20f. Type **823** 20 15
3773 50f. Tao Xingzhi in traditional robes 25 25

824 Xu Xiangqian

1991. 90th Birth Anniv of Xu Xiangqian (revolutionary). Multicoloured.
3774 20f. Type **824** 20 15
3775 50f. In uniform 25 25

825 Emblem

826 Monkey

1991. 1st Women's World Football Championship, Guangdong Province. Multicoloured.
3776 20f. Type **825** 20 15
3777 50f. Player 25 25

1991. Literature. "Outlaws of the Marsh" (3rd series). As T **745**. Multicoloured.
3778 20f. (1) Dai Zong delivers forged letter from Liangshan Marsh 20 15
3779 25f. (2) Yi Zhangqing captures Stumpy Tiger Wang 20 15
3780 25f. (3) Mistress Gu rescues Xie brothers from Dengzhou jail 20 15
3781 90f. (4) Sun Li gains entrance to Zhu family manor in guise of military magistrate 90 50
MS3782 87 × 140 mm. 3y. Mount Liangshan warriors raiding execution compound (56 × 86 mm) 7·00 4·75

1992. New Year. Year of the Monkey. Paper-cut designs.
3783 **826** 20f. multicoloured . . . 20 15
3784 – 50f. black and red . . . 30 25
DESIGN: 50f. Magpies and plum blossom around Chinese character for monkey.

827 Black Stork

828 "Metasequoia glyptostroboides"

1992. Storks. Multicoloured.
3785 20f. Type **827** 25 15
3786 1y.60 White stork 70 60

1992. Conifers. Multicoloured.
3787 20f. Type **828** 20 15
3788 30f. "Cathaya argyrophylla" 20 15
3789 50f. "Taiwania flousiana" 25 25
3790 80f. "Abies beshanzuensis" 35 25

829 Madai Seabream

1992. Offshore Breeding Projects. Multicoloured.
3791 20f. Type **829** 20 15
3792 25f. Prawn 20 15
3793 50f. Farrer's scallops . . . 25 25
3794 80f. "Laminaria japonica" (seaweed) 30 25

830 River Crossing at Yanan

831 Flower and Landscape on Globe

1992. 50th Anniv of Publication of Mao Tse-tung's Talks at the Yanan Forum on Literature and Art.
3795 **830** 20f. black, orange & red 25 15

1992. World Environment Day. 20th Anniv of U. N. Environment Conference, Stockholm.
3796 **831** 20f. multicoloured . . . 30 25

832 Seven-spotted Ladybird

833 Basketball

1992. 19th International Entomology Congress, Peking. Insects. Multicoloured.
3797 20f. Type **832** 20 15
3798 30f. "Sympetrum croceolum" (dragonfly) 25 15
3799 50f. "Chrysopa septempunctata" (lacewing) 25 25
3800 2y. Praying mantis 80 45

1992. Olympic Games, Barcelona. Mult.
3801 20f. Type **833** 20 15
3802 25f. Gymnastics (horiz) . . 20 15
3803 50f. Diving (horiz) 25 25
3804 80f. Weightlifting 40 35
MS3805 91 × 68 mm. 5y. Marathon runners (53 × 36 mm) . . . . . 2·75 2·10

834 Emblem

835 Manchurian Cranes over Great Wall

1992. International Space Year.
3806 **834** 20f. multicoloured . . . 25 15

1992. Literature. "Romance of the Three Kingdoms" by Luo Guanzhong (3rd series). As T **763**. Multicoloured.
3807 20f. Zhuge Liang urging Zhang Zhao to join fight against Cao Cao (horiz) 20 15
3808 30f. Zhuge Liang's sarcastic goading of Sun Quan . . 20 15
3809 50f. Jiang Gan stealing forged letter from Zhou Yu (horiz) 25 25
3810 1y.60 Zhuge Liang and Lu Su in straw-covered boat under arrow attack . . . 45 35

1992. Dunhuang Cave Murals (4th series). Tang Dynasty. As T **732**. Multicoloured.
3811 20f. Bodhisattva (vert) . . . 20 15
3812 25f. Musical performance (vert) 20 15
3813 55f. Flight on a dragon . . 25 25
3814 80f. Emperor Wudi dispatching his envoy Zhang Qian to the western regions 40 35
MS3815 89 × 130 mm. 5y. Guanyin, Goddess of Mercy (48 × 66 mm) 3·00 2·10

1992. 20th Anniv of Normalization of Diplomatic Relations with Japan. Multicoloured.
3816 20f. Type **835** 20 15
3817 2y. Japanese and Chinese girls and dove 80 50

836 Statue of Mazu, Meizhou Islet

837 Party Emblem

1992. Mazu, Sea Goddess.
3818 **836** 20f. brown and blue . . 25 15

1992. 14th National Communist Party Congress.
3819 **837** 20f. multicoloured . . . 25 15

838 Jiao Yulu

839 Xiong Qinglai (mathematician) and Formula

1992. 70th Birth Anniv of Jiao Yulu (Party worker).
3820 **838** 20f. multicoloured . . . 25 15

1992. Scientists (3rd series). Multicoloured.
3821 20f. Type **839** 20 15
3822 30f. Tang Feifan (microbiologist) and medal 20 15
3823 50f. Zhang Xiaoqian (doctor) and hospital scene 25 15
3824 1y. Liang Sicheng (architect) and plan 30 25

840 Luo Ronghuan in Officer's Uniform

1992. 90th Birth Anniv of Luo Ronghuan (army leader). Multicoloured.
3825 20f. Type **840** 20 15
3826 50f. Luo Ronghuan as young man 25 25

841 State Arms

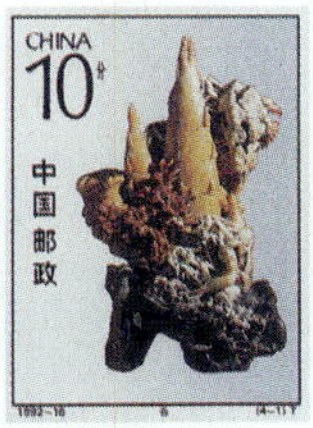

843 "Spring" (Zhou Baiqi)

842 Liu Bocheng in Officer's Uniform

1992. 10th Anniv of Constitution.
3827 **841** 20f. multicoloured . . . 25 15

1992. Birth Centenary of Liu Bocheng (army leader).
3828 **842** 20f. multicoloured . . . 20 15
3829 – 50f. deep green & green 25 25
DESIGN—VERT: 50f. Liu Bocheng as young man.

1992. Qingtian Stone Carvings. Multicoloured.
3830 10f. Type **843** 20 15
3831 20f. "Chinese Sorghum" (Lin Rukui) 20 15
3832 40f. "Harvest" (Zhang Aiting) 25 15
3833 2y. "Blooming Flowers and Full Moon" (Ni Dongfang) 45 25

844 Cock

845 Song Qing-ling

1993. New Year. Year of the Cock. Paper-cut designs by Cai Lanying.
3834 **844** 20f. red and black . . . 25 15
3835 – 50f. white, red & black 25 25
DESIGN: 50f. Flowers around Chinese character for rooster.

1993. Birth Centenary of Song Qing-ling (Sun Yat-sen's wife). Multicoloured.
3836 20f. Type **845** 20 15
3837 1y. Song Qing-ling with children 40 45

846 Bactrian Camel

1993. Bactrian Camel. Multicoloured.
3838 20f. Type **846** 25 15
3839 1y.60 Adult with young . . 50 45

847 Flag, Basket of Flowers and Streamers

1993. 8th National People's Congress, Peking.
3840 **847** 20f. multicoloured . . . 25 15

848 Players

849 Sportswomen

1993. Go.
3841 **848** 20f. multicoloured . . . 20 15
3842 – 1y.60 red, black & gold 45 35
DESIGN: 1y.60, "China Vogue" (black) and "linked stars" (white) formations on board.

1993. 1st East Asian Games, Shanghai. Mult.
3843 50f. Type **849** 20 15
3844 50f. Dong dong (mascot) . . 20 15
Nos. 3843/4 were printed together, se-tenant, forming a composite design of Shanghai Stadium.

850 Li Jishen

1993. Revolutionaries (1st series). Each brown and black.
3845 20f. Type **850** 20 15
3846 30f. Zhang Lan (vert) . . . 20 15
3847 50f. Shan Junru (vert) . . . 20 15
3848 1y. Huang Yanpei 25 15
See also Nos. 3888/91.

851 "Phyllostachys nigra"

1993. Bamboo. Multicoloured.
3849 20f. Type **851** 20 15
3850 30f. "Phyllostachys aureosulcata spectabilis" 20 15
3851 40f. "Bambusa ventricosa" 20 15
3852 1y. "Pseudosasa amabilis" 25 15
MS3853 100 × 73 mm. 5y. "Phyllostachys heterocycla pubescens" (50 × 36 mm) . . . 2·75 2·20

1993. Literature. "Outlaws of the Marsh" (4th series). As T **745**. Multicoloured.
3854 20f. Yin Tianxi and gang capturing Chai Jin . . . 20 15
3855 30f. Shi Qian stealing Xu Ning's armour 20 15
3856 50f. Xu Ning teaching use of barbed lance 25 25
3857 2y. Shi Xiu saving Lu Junyi from execution 55 45

852 Crater Lake in Winter

1993. Changbai Mountains. Multicoloured.
3858 20f. Type **852** 15 10
3859 30f. Mountain tundra in autumn 20 10
3860 50f. Waterfall in summer . . 25 15
3861 1y. Forest in spring 40 45

853 Games Emblem and Temple of Heaven

854 "Losana", Temple of Ancestors

1993. 7th National Games, Peking.
3862 **853** 20f. multicoloured . . . 25 15

1993. 1500th Anniv of Longmen Grottoes, Luoyang. Multicoloured.
3863 20f. Type **854** 15 10
3864 30f. "Sakyamuni", Middle Binyang Cave 20 15
3865 50f. "King of Northern Heavens" standing on Yaksha 25 15
3866 1y. "Bodhisattva", Guyang Cave 30 25
MS3867 150 × 57 mm. 5y. Temple of Ancestors (119 × 39 mm) . . . 3·00 1·70

855 Queen Bee and Workers on Comb

1993. The Honey Bee. Multicoloured.
3868 10f. Type **855** 20 15
3869 15f. Bee extracting nectar . . 20 15
3870 20f. Two bees on blossom 20 15
3871 2y. Two bees among flowers 55 70

856 Bowl, New Stone Age

1993. Lacquer Work. Multicoloured.
3872 20f. Type **856** 20 15
3873 30f. Duck-shaped container (from Marquis Yi's tomb), Warring States Period 20 15
3874 50f. Plate decorated with foliage (Zhang Cheng), Yuan Dynasty 25 25
3875 1y. Chrysanthemum-shaped container, Qing Dynasty 30 25

857 Mao Tse-tung in North Shaanxi

1993. Birth Centenary of Mao Tse-tung. Mult.
3876 20f. Type **857** 20 15
3877 1y. Mao in library 25 25
MS3878 83 × 137 mm. 5y. Mao and Great Wall (48 × 59 mm) . . . 2·20 2·20

858 Fan Painting of Bamboo and Rock

1993. 300th Birth Anniv of Zheng Banqiao (artist). Multicoloured.
3879 10f. Type **858** 20 15
3880 20f. Orchids 20 15
3881 20f. Orchids, bamboo and rock (scroll) (vert) . . . 20 15
3882 30f. Bamboo (scroll) (vert) 25 15
3883 50f. Chrysanthemum in vase 25 15
3884 1y.60 Calligraphy on fan . . 55 35

859 Yang Hucheng

860 Dog (folk toy, Hebei)

1993. Birth Centenary of General Yang Hucheng.
3885 **859** 20f. multicoloured . . . 25 15

1994. New Year. Year of The Dog.
3886 **860** 20f. multicoloured . . . 20 15
3887 – 50f. black, red & yellow 25 25
DESIGN: 50f. Dogs and flowers around Chinese character for dog.

861 Ma Xulun

1994. Revolutionaries (2nd series). Each brown and black.
3888 20f. Chen Qiyou (horiz) . . 20 10
3889 20f. Chen Shutong 20 10
3890 50f. Type **861** 25 15
3891 50f. Xu Deheng (horiz) . . 25 15

862 Great Siberian Sturgeon

1994. Sturgeons. Multicoloured.
3892 20f. Type **862** 20 15
3893 40f. Chinese sturgeon . . . 20 15
3894 50f. Chinese paddlefish . . . 25 15
3895 1y. Yangtze sturgeon . . . 35 25

863 Tree in Dunes

864 Ming Dynasty Three-legged Round Teapot

1994. "Making the Desert Green". Multicoloured.
3896 15f. Type **863** 15 10
3897 20f. Flower-covered dune . . 20 10
3898 40f. Forest of poplars . . . 25 15
3899 50f. Oasis 30 25

1994. Yixing Unglazed Teapots. Multicoloured.
3900 20f. Type **864** 15 10
3901 30f. Qing dynasty four-legged square teapot . . . 20 10
3902 50f. Qing dynasty patterned teapot 20 15
3903 1y. Modern teapot 30 25

865 Entrance Gate

1994. 70th Anniv of Huang-pu Military Academy.
3904 **865** 20f. multicoloured . . . 25 15

866 "100" and Olympic Rings

1994. Centenary of Int Olympic Committee.

3905	**866** 20f. multicoloured . . .	25	15

867 Tao Yuanming (poet)

1994. Writers. Each black, brown and red.

3906	20f. Type **867**	15	10
3907	30f. Cao Zhi (poet)	20	15
3908	50f. Sima Qian (historian)	25	15
3909	1y. Qu Yuan (poet)	30	15

1994. Dunhuang Cave Murals (5th series). Tang Dynasty Frescoes in Mogao Caves. As T **732**. Multicoloured.

3910	10f. Flying Devata	20	10
3911	20f. Vimalakirti on dais . .	20	15
3912	50f. Zhang Yichao's forces	25	15
3913	1y.60 Sorceresses	45	25

868 Zhaojun

1994. Marriage of Zhaojun (from Han court) and Monarch of Xiongnu. Multicoloured.

3914	20f. Type **868**	20	15
3915	50f. Journey to Xiongnu . .	30	20
MS3916	145 × 80 mm. 3y. Wedding ceremony (85 × 46 mm)	3·25	2·75

869 Emblem

870 Heaven's South Gate

1994. 6th Far East and South Pacific Games for the Disabled, Peking.

3917	**869** 20f. multicoloured . . .	20	15

1994. UNESCO World Heritage Site. Wulingyuan. Multicoloured.

3918	20f. Type **870**	20	10
3919	30f. Shentangwan	20	15
3920	50f. No. One Bridge (horiz)	25	25
3921	1y. Writing Brush Peak (horiz)	35	35
MS3922	135 × 80 mm. 3y. Picturesque Corridor (50 × 36 mm)	3·25	2·50

871 Jade Maiden Peak

1994. Mt. Wuyi. Multicoloured.

3923	50f. (1) Type **871**	25	15
3924	50f. (2) Nine Turns Brook	25	15
3925	50f. (3) Hanging Block . . .	25	15
3926	50f. (4) Elevated Meadow	25	15

Nos. 3923/6 were issued together, se-tenant, forming a composite design.

872 Examining Scroll

873 Whooping Crane

1994. Paintings by Fu Baoshi. Multicoloured.

3927	10f. Waterfall and river . .	20	15
3928	20f. Type **872**	20	15
3929	20f. Tree	20	15
3930	40f. Musicians	20	15
3931	50f. Wooded landscape . .	25	15
3932	1y. Scholars	30	15

1994. Cranes. Multicoloured.

3933	20f. Type **873**	25	15
3934	2y. Black-necked crane . . .	45	40

874 UPU Monument

1994. World Post Day. 120th Anniv of Universal Postal Union. Sheet 85 × 113 mm.

MS3935	**874** 3y. multicoloured	3·25	2·20

875 White Emperor's City

1994. Gorges of Yangtse River. Mult.

3936	10f. (1) Type **875**	20	10
3937	20f. (2) River steamer in Qutang Gorge	20	10
3938	20f. (3) Small boat in Wuxia Gorge	20	10
3939	30f. (4) Goddess Peak . . .	20	10
3940	50f. (5) Boats in Xiling Gorge	25	15
3941	1y. (6) Qu Yuan Memorial Hall	30	25
MS3942	140 × 78 mm. 5y. Panoramic view of river gorges (115 × 36 mm)	3·50	2·50

876 Rock Formation

1994. 4th All-China Philatelic Federation Congress, Peking. Sheet 120 × 85 mm.

MS3943	**876** 3y. multicoloured	2·20	1·70

1994. Literature. "Romance of the Three Kingdoms" by Luo Guanzhong (4th series). As T **763**. Multicoloured.

3944	20f. Cao Cao composing poem with lance in hand (horiz)	15	10
3945	30f. Liu Bei's wedding to sister of Sun Quan . . .	20	10
3946	50f. Ambush at Xiaoyaojin (horiz)	25	15
3947	1y. Lu Xun's forces destroying Liu Bei's camps	30	25
MS3948	182 × 65 mm. 5y. Battle of Chibi (175 × 36 mm)	5·25	4·25

877 Shenzhen

1994. Special Economic Zones. Multicoloured.

3949	50f. (1) Type **877**	15	10
3950	50f. (2) Zhuhai	15	10
3951	50f. (3) Shantou	15	10
3952	50f. (4) Xiamen	15	10
3953	50f. (5) Hainan	15	10

878 Dayan Pagoda, Cien Temple, Xian

879 Pig

1994. Pagodas. Each black, lightt brown and brown.

3954	20f. (1) Type **878**	20	15
3955	20f. (2) Zhenguo Pagoda, Kaiyuan Temple, Quanzhou	20	15
3956	50f. (3) Liuhe Pagoda, Kaihua Temple, Hangzhou	20	15
3957	2y. (4) Youguo Temple, Kaifeng	25	15
MS3958	139 × 90 mm. As Nos. 3954/7 but cream backgrounds	7·50	4·75

1995. New Year. Year of the Pig.

3959	**879** 20f. multicoloured . . .	25	15
3960	– 50f. black and red . . .	25	15

DESIGN: 50f. Chinese character ("pig") and pigs.

880 Willows beside River Songhua

1995. Winter in Jilin. Multicoloured.

3961	20f. Type **880**	20	10
3962	50f. Jade tree on hillside (vert)	25	15

881 Relief Map and Tropic of Cancer

1995. Mt. Dinghu. Multicoloured.

3963	15f. (1) Type **881**	20	15
3964	20f. (2) Ravine	20	15
3965	20f. (3) Monastery on hillside and forest-covered slopes	20	15
3966	2y.30 (4) Pair of silver pheasants in forest . . .	40	35

882 Summit Emblem

1995. United Nations World Summit for Social Development, Copenhagen.

3967	**882** 20f. multicoloured . . .	20	10

883 Snowy Owl

1995. Owls. Multicoloured.

3968	10f. Eagle owl	20	15
3969	20f. Long-eared owl	20	15
3970	50f. Type **883**	25	15
3971	1y. Eastern grass owls . . .	35	25

884 "Osmanthus fragrans thunbergii"

1995. Sweet Osmanthus. Multicoloured.

3972	20f. (1) Type **884**	15	10
3973	20f. (2) "Osmanthus fragrans latifolius" . . .	15	10
3974	50f. (3) "Osmanthus fragrans aurantiacus" . .	25	15
3975	1y. (4) "Osmanthus fragrans semperflorens"	40	35

885 Player

1995. World Table Tennis Championships, Tianjin. Multicoloured.

3976	20f. Type **885**	20	10
3977	50f. Stadium	25	15
MS3978	140 × 90 mm. Nos. 3976/7 (sold at 700f.)	22·00	16·00

No. **MS**3978 was issued to commemorate Chinese victory in all seven titles contested at the championships.

886 Ladies and Courtiers

1995. "Spring Outing" by Zhang Xuan. Details of the painting. Multicoloured.

3979	50f. (1) Type **886**	25	15
3980	50f. (2) Courtiers on horseback	25	15

Nos. 3979/80 were issued together, se-tenant, forming a composite design.

887 Donglu Play, Shanxi

1995. Shadow Play. Regional characters. Mult.

3981	20f. (1) Type **887**	20	15
3982	40f. (2) Luanxain play, Hebei	20	15
3983	50f. (3) Xiaoyi play, Shanxi	25	15
3984	50f. (4) Dayi play, Sichuan	25	15

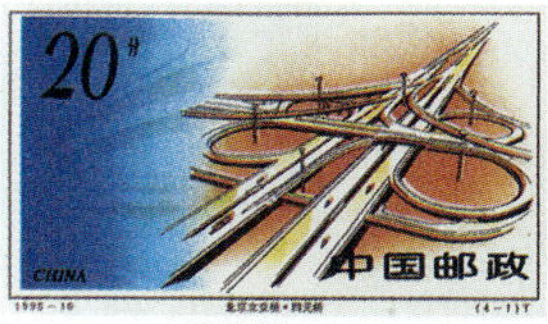

888 Siyuan

1995. Motorway Interchanges, Peking. Mult.

3985	20f. Type **888**	15	10
3986	30f. Tianningsi	20	10
3987	50f. Yuting	25	15
3988	1y. Anhui	35	25

890 Asian Elephants at River

1995. 20th Anniv of China–Thailand Diplomatic Relations. Multicoloured.

3990	1y. (1) Type **890**	25	15
3991	1y. (2) Asian elephants at river (face value at left)	25	15

Nos. 3990/1 were issued together, se-tenant, forming a composite design.

891 East and West Dongting Hills

1995. Lake Taihu. Multicoloured.
3992 20f. (1) Type **891** 15 10
3993 20f. (2) Tortoise Islet in spring 15 10
3994 50f. (3) Li Garden in summer 25 15
3995 50f. (4) Jichang Garden in autumn 25 15
3996 230f. (5) Plum Garden in winter 60 50
MS3997 122 × 81 mm. 500f. Stone tablet on Tortoise Islet inscribed "Beauty that nurtured Wu and Yue" by Liao Lun (88 × 59 mm) 3·25 2·50

893 Yucheng Post, Jiangsu

1995. "China'96" International Stamp Exhibition, Peking. Ancient Chinese Post Offices. Mult.
3999 20f. Type **893** 20 10
4000 50f. Jimingshan Post, Hebei 25 15
See also No.**MS**4108.

894 Hill Gate

1995. 1500th Anniv of Shaolin Temple, Henan. Multicoloured.
4001 20f. Type **894** 20 15
4002 20f. Pagoda Forest 20 15
4003 50f. Martial arts practice (detail of fresco, White Robe Hall) 20 15
4004 100f. Thirteen monks rescue the Prince of Qin (detail of fresco) 30 25

895 New Stone Age Jar

1995. Tibetan Culture. Multicoloured.
4005 20f. Type **895** 15 10
4006 30f. Helmet (7th century) . . 20 10
4007 50f. Celestial chart 25 15
4008 100f. Pearl and coral mandala 35 25

896 Koalas in Eucalyptus Tree

1995. Endangered Animals. Multicoloured.
4009 20f. Type **896** 20 10
4010 2y.90 Giant pandas amongst bamboo . . . . 1·10 85

897 Japanese Attack in North China, 7 July 1937

1995. 50th Anniv of End of Second World War and of War against Japan. Multicoloured.
4011 10f. (1) Type **897** 15 10
4012 20f. (2) Battle of Taier Village 15 10
4013 20f. (3) Battle at Great Wall 15 10
4014 50f. (4) Guerrillas 20 15
4015 50f. (5) Forces at Mangyo, Burma 20 15
4016 60f. (6) Airplane donated by overseas Chinese 25 15
4017 100f. (7) Liberation of Taiwan, October 1945 . . 30 15
4018 100f. (8) Crew on deck of battleship 30 25

898 Woman's Profile and Flags (equality)

899 Great Wall at Jinshanling Hill

1995. 4th World Conference on Women, Peking. Multicoloured.
4019 15f. Type **898** 15 10
4020 20f. Woman's profile and wheel of colours (development) 15 10
4021 50f. Woman's profile and dove (peace) 25 15
4022 60f. Dove and flower (friendship) 30 25

1995. International Stamp and Coin Exhibition, Peking. Sweet Osmanthus. Sheet 143 × 85 mm.
MS4023 Nos. 3972/5 (sold at 3y.) 5·25 4·00

1995. The Great Wall of China.
4024 – 5f. turquoise, bl & blk 20 20
4024a – 10f. black and green . . 20 20
4024b – 20f. black and lavender 20 20
4025 – 30f. black and yellow 20 15
4025a – 40f. black and pink . . 20 20
4026 – 50f. black, brn & yell 20 10
4027 **899** 60f. black and brown 20 15
4027a – 60f. black and yellow 20 20
4027b – 80f. multicoloured . . . 30 20
4028 – 100f. black and red . . 25 15
4029 – 150f. black and green 45 25
4031 – 200f. black and pink . . 55 35
4032 – 230f. black and green 60 45
4032a – 270f. mauve, blk & grn 90 70
4035 – 290f. black and blue . . 80 60
4036 – 300f. black and green 90 90
4036a – 320f. mve, blk & lav . 1·00 80
4037 – 420f. black and orange 1·20 1·20
4037a – 440f. light brown, black and brown . . . . . 1·40 1·40
4038 – 500f. black, brn & bl 1·50 1·50
4038a – 540f. black and blue . 1·50 1·50
4038b – 10y. multicoloured . . 3·00 3·00
4038c – 20y. multicoloured . . 6·50 6·50
4038d – 50y. grey, blk & grn . . 16·00 16·00
DESIGNS: 5f. Hushan section of wall; 10f. Wall at Jiumenkou Pass; 20f. Wall at Shanhaiguan; 30f. Wall at Huangya Pass; 40f. Jinshanling section of wall; 50f. Wall seen from Gubeikou; 60f. (4027a), Huanghua Tower and wall; 80f. Mutianyu section of wall; 100f. Wall seen from Badaling; 150f. Wall at Jurong Pass; 200f. Wall at Zijing Pass; 230f. Wall at Shanhaiguan Pass; 270f. Wall at Pingxingguan Pass; 290f. Laolongtou (end of wall); 300f. Wall at Niangziguan Pass; 320f. Wall at Desheng Pass; 420f. Wall at Pianguan Pass; 440f. Wall at Yanmen Pass; 500f. Bianjing Tower; 540f. Zhenbei Tower; 10y. Huama section; 20y. Wall at Sanguankou Pass; 50y. Wall at Jiayuguan Pass.

900 Dawn on Heavenly Terrace Peak

1995. The Jiuhua Mountains, Anhui. Mult.
4039 10f. (1) Type **900** 15 10
4040 20f. (2) Hall of Meditation (vert) 15 10
4041 20f. (3) Hall of the Mortal Body 15 10
4042 50f. (4) Sunset at Zhiyuan Temple 25 10
4043 50f. (5) Roc listening to Scriptures (rock formation) (vert) 25 10
4044 290f. (6) Phoenix pine . . . 70 45

901 Black and White Film

1995. Centenary of Motion Pictures. Mult.
4045 20f. Type **901** 20 10
4046 50f. Colour film 25 15

902 Flag and New York Headquarters

1995. 50th Anniv of UNO. Multicoloured.
4047 20f. Type **902** 20 10
4048 50f. Anniversary emblem and "flags" 25 15

903 Blessing Spot

1995. Sanqing Mountain. Multicoloured.
4049 20f. Type **903** 15 10
4050 20f. Spring Goddess 15 10
4051 50f. Music charm (vert) . . 25 15
4052 100f. Supernatural python (rock formation) (vert) . . 35 35

904 Central Mountain Temple and Huang Gai Peak

1995. Mount Song. Multicoloured.
4053 20f. Type **904** 15 10
4054 50f. Moonrise over Fawang Temple 20 10
4055 60f. Shaolin Temple in snow 25 15
4056 1y. Mountain ridge 35 25

905 Victoria Harbour

1995. Hong Kong. Multicoloured.
4057 20f. Type **905** 20 15
4058 50f. Central Plaza 20 15
4059 60f. Hong Kong Cultural Centre 25 15
4060 290f. Repulse Bay 55 35

906 Sun Zi

907 Rat

1995. "Art of War" (book) by Sun Zi. Mult.
4061 20f. Type **906** 15 10
4062 20f. Elaborating strategies 15 10
4063 30f. Capturing Ying 20 10
4064 50f. Battle at Ailing 25 15
4065 100f. Conference at Huangchi 35 25

1996. New Year. Year of the Rat. Mult.
4066 20f. Type **907** 20 10
4067 50f. Pattern and Chinese character 25 15

908 Speed Skating

1996. 3rd Asian Winter Games, Harbin. Mult.
4068 50f. Type **908** 25 15
4069 50f. Ice hockey 25 15
4070 50f. Figure skating 25 15
4071 50f. Skiing 25 15
Nos. 4068/71 were issued together, se-tenant, forming a composite design.

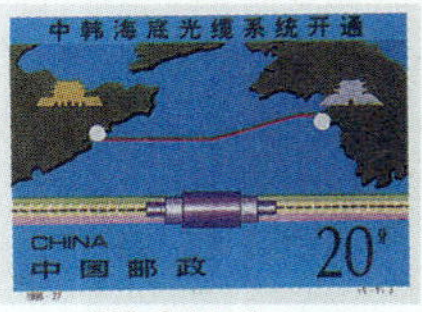
909 Cable Route

1996. Inaug of Korea–China Submarine Cable.
4072 **909** 20f. multicoloured . . . 25 10

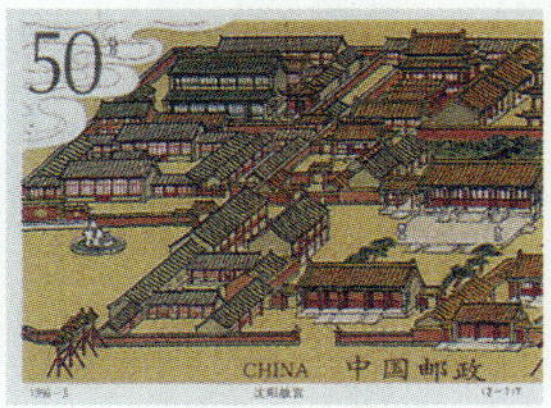
910 Palace Complex

1996. Shenyang Imperial Palace. Multicoloured.
4073 50f. Type **910** 25 15
4074 50f. Pagoda and buildings 25 15
Nos. 4073/4 were issued together, se-tenant, forming a composite design.

911 Tianjin Posts Bureau

1996. Cent of Chinese State Postal Service. Mult.
4075 10f. Type **911** 20 15
4076 20f. Former Directorate General of North China Posts building, Peking . . 20 15
4077 50f. Postal headquarters of Chinese Soviet Republic, Zhongshi, Jiangxi . . . 20 15
4078 100f. Present Peking postal complex 30 25
MS4079 153 × 83 mm. 1897 surcharged red revenue stamps (89 × 59 mm) . . . . 5·25 4·25

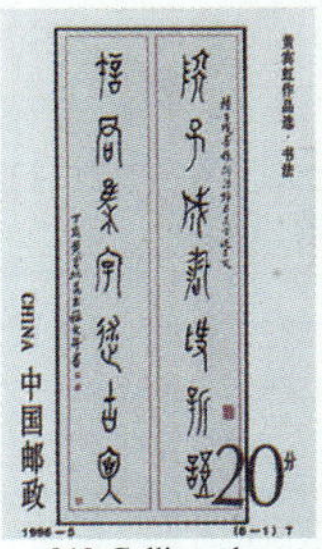
912 Calligraphy

1996. Paintings by Huang Binhong. Mult.
4080 20f. (1) Type **912** 20 15
4081 20f. (2) Mountain landscape 20 15
4082 40f. (3) Mount Qingcheng in rain 45 25
4083 50f. (4) View from Xiling . . 55 25
4084 50f. (5) Landscape 55 25
4085 230f. (6) Flowers . . . . . 2·40 1·20

913 Shenyang F-8 Jet Fighter

1996. Chinese Aircraft. Multicoloured.
4086 20f. (1) Type **913** 15 10
4087 50f. (2) Nanchang A-5 jet fighter 25 15
4088 50f. (3) Xian Y-7 transport 25 15
4089 100f. (4) Harbin Y-12 utility plane 35 35

914 Green Scenery of Lijing River

1996. Bonsai Landscapes. Multicoloured.
4090 20f. (1) Type **914** 20 15
4091 20f. (2) Glistening Divine Peak 20 15
4092 50f. (3) Melting snow fills the river 20 15
4093 50f. (4) Eagle Beak Rock 20 15
4094 100f. (5) Memorable Years 30 25
4095 100f. (6) Peaks rising in Rosy Clouds 30 25

915 Sago Cycad ("Cycas revoluta")

1996. Cycads. Multicoloured.
4096 20f. Type **915** 20 10
4097 20f. Panzhihua cycad ("Cycas panzhihuaensis") 20 10
4098 50f. Nepal cycad 25 15
4099 230f. Polytomous cycad 45 45

916 Great Wall of China at Jinshan Ridge

1996. 25th Anniv of China–San Marino Diplomatic Relations. Multicoloured.
4100 100f. Type **916** 40 35
4101 100f. Walled rampart, San Marino 40 35
Nos. 4100/1 were issued together, se-tenant, forming a composite design.

919 Paddy Agricultural Tool

1996. Hemudu Archaeological Site, Yuyao, Zhejiang. Multicoloured.
4104 20f. Type **919** 15 10
4105 50f. Building supports 25 10
4106 100f. Paddles 35 25
4107 230f. Dish engraved with two birds and sun 60 60

920 Bronze Tripod

1996. "China '96" International Stamp Exhibition, Peking (2nd issue). Sheet 77 × 140 mm.
MS4108 **920** 500f. multicoloured 6·25 4·25

921 Children rejoicing

922 "The Discus Thrower" (Miron)

1996. Children. Multicoloured.
4109 20f. Type **921** 15 10
4110 30f. Girls pushing child in wheelchair in rain 20 10
4111 50f. Expedition to Antarctica 25 15
4112 100f. Planting sapling 35 35

1996. Centenary of Modern Olympic Games.
4113 **922** 20f. multicoloured 15 15

923 "Land"

1996. Preserve Land. Designs showing Chinese characters. Multicoloured.
4114 20f. Type **923** 20 10
4115 50f. "Cultivation" 25 15

924 Jinglue Terrace

1996. Jinglue Terrace, Guangxi Zhuang. Mult.
4116 20f. Type **924** 20 10
4117 50f. Structure of Zhenwu Pavilion 25 15

925 Red Flag Car

1996. Motor Vehicles. Multicoloured.
4118 20f. Type **925** 20 15
4119 20f. Dongfeng two-door truck 20 15
4120 50f. Jiefang four-door truck 30 15
4121 100f. Peking four-wheel drive 45 25

926 Banbidian Village, Kaiping District

1996. 20th Anniv of Tangshan Earthquake. Development of New City. Multicoloured.
4122 20f. (1) Type **926** 15 10
4123 50f. (2) East Hebei Cement Works 25 15
4124 50f. (3) Earthquake memorials, Xinhua Road 25 15
4125 100f. (4) Bulk carrier in Jingtang Harbour 35 35

927 Emblem, Globe and "30"

1996. 30th Int Geological Conference, Peking.
4126 **927** 20f. multicoloured 25 15

928 Tianchi Lake

1996. Tianshan Mountains, Xinjiang.
4127 **928** 20f. (1) multicoloured 15 10
4128 – 50f. (2) multicoloured 25 15
4129 – 50f. (3) blue, mve & blk 25 15
4130 – 100f. (4) multicoloured 45 35
DESIGNS—VERT: No. 4128, Waterfalls; 4129, Snow-capped mountain peaks. HORIZ: No. 4130. Mountains and landscape.

1996. Dunhuang Cave Murals (6th series). As T **732**. Multicoloured.
4131 10f. Mount Wutai (Five Dynasties) (vert) 15 10
4132 20f. Li Shengtian, King of Khotan (Five Dynasties) (vert) 20 10
4133 50f. Guanyin, Goddess of Mercy, saves boat (Northern Song period) 25 15
4134 100f. Worshipping Bodhisattvas (Western Xia) 35 35
MS4135 95 × 135 mm. 500f. Goddess of Mercy with 1000 Hands (Yuan dynasty) (45 × 110 mm) 6·25 5·25

929 Tombs

1996. Emperors' Tombs of Western Xia Dynasty, Yinchuan, Ningxia Hui. Multicoloured.
4136 20f. Type **929** 20 10
4137 20f. Divine Gate ornament 20 10
4138 50f. Stone base from Stele Pavilion 25 15
4139 100f. Piece of stele from Shouling Tomb 40 25

930 Datong–Qinhuangdao Line

1996. Railways. Multicoloured.
4140 15f. Type **930** 15 10
4141 20f. Lanzhou–Xinjiang line 20 10
4142 50f. Peking–Kowloon line 25 15
4143 100f. Peking West railway station 30 25

931 Shang Dynasty Tortoise Shell

932 Ye Ting

1996. Ancient Archives. Multicoloured.
4144 20f. Type **931** 20 10
4145 20f. Han Dynasty wood slip inscribed with divinations on a marriage 20 10
4146 50f. Ming dynasty iron scroll conferring merit on General Li Wen 25 15
4147 100f. Qing dynasty diplomatic credentials (1905) 30 25

1996. Birth Cent of Ye Ting (revolutionary). Mult.
4148 20f. Type **932** 20 10
4149 50f. Ye Ting in uniform 25 15

933 Emblem

1996. 96th Interparliamentary Union Conference, Peking.
4150 **933** 20f. multicoloured 30 15

934 Transport and Telecommunications

1996. Pudong Area of Shanghai. Mult.
4151 10f. (1) Type **934** 15 10
4152 20f. (2) People's Bank of China branch, Lujiazui finance and business area 20 10
4153 20f. (3) Jinqiao export centre 20 10
4154 50f. (4) Garden of Advance Science and Technology, Zhangjiang 25 15
4155 60f. (5) Customs House, Waigaoqiao bonded area 25 15
4156 100f. (6) Apartment blocks 30 25
MS4157 161 × 75 mm. 500f. View of Pudong (89 × 44 mm) 6·25 5·25

935 Chinese Rocket "Long March"

1996. 47th Congress of International Astronautical Federation. Multicoloured.
4158 20f. Type **935** 20 10
4159 100f. Communications satellite 35 25

936 Singapore

1996. City Scenes. Multicoloured.
4160 20f. Type **936** 20 15
4161 290f. Panmen Gate, Suzhou 80 50

937 Red Army in Marshland

1996. 60th Anniv of Long March by Communist Army. Multicoloured.
4162 20f. Type **937** 35 20
4163 50f. Reunion of three armies 70 35

938 Two Gods

1996. Tianjin Clay Statuettes. Multicoloured.
4164 20f. (1) Type **938** 15 10
4165 50f. (2) Seated man blowing sugar figure 25 15
4166 50f. (3) Woman and child returning from fishing 25 15
4167 100f. (4) Women painting at table 30 25

939 Bank of China

1996. Economic Growth in Hong Kong. Mult.
4168 20f. Type **939** 15 10
4169 40f. Container terminal 20 10
4170 60f. Airplane taking off from Kai Tak Airport 25 15
4171 290f. Stock exchange 50 35

940 Emblem over Farmland

941 "Horse treading on Flying Swallow" (bronze) and Great Wall of China

1997. 1st National Agricultural Census.
4172 **940** 50f. multicoloured . . . 25 15

1997. Tourist Year.
4173 **941** 50f. multicoloured . . . 25 15

942 Chinese Lantern

943 "Pine on Mount Huangshan"

1997. New Year. Year of the Ox. Mult.
4174 50f. Type **942** 25 15
4175 150f. Ox 45 35

1997. Birth Centenary of Pan Tianshou (artist). Multicoloured.
4176 50f. (1) Type **943** 30 15
4177 50f. (2) "Rosy Clouds of Dawn" 30 15
4178 100f. (3) "Clearing Up after Mould Rains" 65 45
4179 100f. (4) "Chrysanthemum and Bamboo" 65 45
4180 150f. (5) "Sleeping Cat" . . 1·10 60
4181 150f. (6) "Corner of Lingyan Brook" . . . . 1·10 60

944 Tea Tree at Lancang, Yunnan

945 Celebration

1997. Tea. Multicoloured.
4182 50f. (1) Type **944** 20 10
4183 50f. (2) Statue of Lu Yu (author of "Classic of Tea") 20 10
4184 150f. (3) Tea grinder (Tang dynasty) (horiz) 45 35
4185 150f. (4) "Tea Party at Huishan" (Wen Zhenming) (horiz) 45 35

1997. 50th Anniv of Autonomous Region of Inner Mongolia. Multicoloured.
4186 50f. (1) Type **945** 20 15
4187 50f. (2) People of different cultures ("Unity") (horiz) 20 15
4188 200f. (3) Galloping horses ("Advance") (horiz) . . . 80 50

946 Lady Amherst's Pheasant

1997. Rare Pheasants. Multicoloured.
4189 50f. Type **946** 20 10
4190 540f. Common pheasant . . 1·20 95

947 Zengchong Drum Tower

948 Buddha and Attendant Bodhisattva (Northern Wei dynasty)

1997. Dong Architecture. Multicoloured.
4191 50f. (1) Type **947** 20 10
4192 50f. (2) Baier drum tower 20 10
4193 150f. (3) Wind and rain bridge over River Nanjiang (horiz) 45 25
4194 150f. (4) Wind and rain shelter in field (horiz) . . 45 25

1997. Maiji Grottoes, Gansu Province. Mult.
4195 50f. (1) Type **948** 20 10
4196 50f. (2) Attendant Bodhisattva and disciple (Northern Wei dynasty) 20 10
4197 100f. (3) Maid servant (Western Wei dynasty) . . 25 15
4198 150f. (4) Buddha (Western Wei dynasty) 35 25
4199 150f. (5) Attendant Bodhisattva (Northern Zhou dynasty) 35 25
4200 200f. (6) Provider (Song dynasty) 45 35

949 Sino-British Joint Declaration and Red Roses

1997. Return of Hong Kong to China. Mult.
4201 50f. Type **949** 30 15
4202 150f. Basic Law and mixed roses 80 50
MS4203 140 × 95 mm. 800f. Deng Xiaoping (55 × 46 mm) . . . . 2·75 2·20
MS4204 140 × 95 mm. 50y. As No. **MS**4203 . . . . 36·00 35·00

950 Taihuai Temple

1997. Ancient Temples, Wutai Mountain. Mult.
4205 40f. (1) Type **950** 20 10
4206 50f. (2) Great Hall, Nanchan Temple 20 10
4207 50f. (3) Eastern Hall, Foguang ("Buddhist Light") Temple 20 10
4208 150f. (4) Bronze Hall, Xiantong ("Revelation") Temple 35 25
4209 150f. (5) Bodhisattva Summit 35 25
4210 200f. (6) Zhenhai Temple . . 45 35

951 Tanks

1997. 70th Anniv of People's Liberation Army. Multicoloured.
4211 50f. (1) Type **951** 20 10
4212 50f. (2) Frigate flotilla . . . 20 10
4213 50f. (3) Jet fighter 20 10
4214 50f. (4) Ballistic missile . . . 20 10
4215 200f. (5) Tank, destroyer and jet fighters 60 45

952 Scene from "A Dream of Red Mansions" (carved by Jiang Yilin)

954 "Rosa rugosa"

953 Emblem

1997. Shoushan Stone Carvings. Mult.
4216 50f. (1) Type **952** 20 10
4217 50f. (2) "Rhinoceros basking in Sunshine" (Zhou Jinting) 20 10
4218 150f. (3) "Fragrance and Jade" 45 25
4219 150f. (4) "Li the Cripple, Han Zhongli and Lu Dongbin in drunken Joy" (Lin Fada) 45 25
MS4220 97 × 97 mm. 800f. Qianlong's chained seals (59 × 58 mm) . . . . 5·25 5·25

1997. 15th National Communist Party Congress.
4221 **953** 50f. multicoloured . . . 55 35

1997. Roses. Multicoloured.
4222 150f. Type **954** 55 35
4223 150f. "Aotearoa" of New Zealand 85 70
Nos. 4222/3 were issued together, se-tenant, forming a composite design.

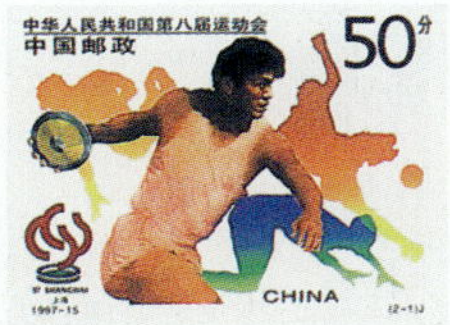

955 Putting the Shot and Athletes

1997. 8th National Games, Shanghai. Mult.
4224 50f. (1) Type **955** 20 15
4225 150f. Mascot and stadium 50 45
MS4226 140 × 90 mm. Nos. 4224/5 5·25 3·50

956 Hall of Prayer for Good Harvests

1997. Temple of Heaven, Peking. Mult.
4227 50f. (1) Type **956** 20 10
4228 50f. (2) Imperial Vault of Heaven 20 10
4229 150f. (3) Circular mound altar 40 25
4230 150f. (4) Hall of Abstinence 40 25

957 Sunrise

1997. Mount Huangshan. Sheet 190 × 150 mm containing T **957** and similar multicoloured designs.
MS4231 200f. (1) Type **957**; 200f. (2) Xihai (West Sea) Peaks; 200f. (3) Flying Rock in clouds; 200f. (4) Beihai (North Sea) Peaks (vert); 200f. (5) Yuping (Jade Screen) Peak (vert); 200f. (6) Dream of Flowering Brush Peak; 200f . . 8·00 4·25

958 Archers' Tower, Jar and Gate Tower

1997. Xi'an City Walls. Multicoloured.
4232 50f. (1) Type **958** 20 10
4233 50f. (2) Archers' Tower . . 20 10
4234 150f. (3) Watchtower . . . 45 35
4235 150f. (4) South-west corner tower 45 35

959 Diversion Canal

1997. Three Gorges Project (damming of Yangtse River). Multicoloured.
4236 50f. Type **959** 20 10
4237 50f. Dam under construction 20 10
Nos. 4236/7 were issued together, se-tenant, forming a composite design.

960 Temple of the Heavenly Queen

1997. Macao. Multicoloured.
4238 50f. Type **960** 20 15
4239 100f. Lianfeng (Lotus Peak) Temple 25 15
4240 150f. Great Sanba Archway (former facade of St. Paul's Church) 35 25
4241 200f. Songshan (Pine Hill) Lighthouse 55 35

961 Metallurgy in Ancient China

1997. Achievement in 1996 of Production of over 100,000,000 Tons of Steel a Year. Multicoloured.
4242 50f. Type **961** 20 15
4243 150f. Modern steel works 50 35

962 Digital Transmission

963 Cloth Tiger (Guo Qiuying)

1997. Telecommunications. Multicoloured.
4244 50f. (1) Type **962** 20 10
4245 50f. (2) Program-controlled switch and computer . . . 20 10
4246 150f. (3) Digital communication 40 35
4247 150f. (4) Mobile communication 40 35

1997. Literature. "Outlaws of the Marsh" (5th series). As T **745**. Multicoloured.
4248 40f. (1) Hu Yanzhuo tricks Guan Sheng 25 15
4249 50f. (2) Lu Junyi captures Shi Wengong 25 15
4250 50f. (3) Yan Qing wrestles with Qing Tianzhu . . . 25 15
4251 150f. (4) Hong Tianlei defeats government troops 70 50
MS4252 120 × 135 mm. 800f. Liangshan Heroes (59 × 89 mm) 3·50 3·25

1998. New Year. Year of the Tiger. Mult.
4253 50f. Type **963** 20 10
4254 150f. Chinese character . . 35 25

964 Keyuan Garden

1998. Villas and Gardens in Guangdong. Mult.
4255 50f. Type **964** 20 10
4256 50f. Liangyuan Garden . . 20 10
4257 100f. Qinghiu Garden . . . 30 25
4258 200f. Yuyin Villa 55 45

965 Deng Xiaoping

1998. 1st Death Anniv of Deng Xiaoping. Mult.
4259 50f. (1) Type **965** 20 10
4260 50f. (2) During Liberation War 20 10
4261 50f. (3) With Mao Tse-tung 20 10
4262 100f. (4) As Chairman of Military Commission . . 30 25
4263 150f. (5) Making speech . . 40 35
4264 200f. (6) In south China . . 55 45

966 Officers and Badge

1998. People's Police. Multicoloured.
4265 40f. (1) Type **966** 20 10
4266 50f. (2) Officers using computer and patrol officers using radio . . . 20 10
4267 50f. (3) Officer and elderly woman 20 10
4268 100f. (4) Officer on traffic control duty 40 25
4269 150f. (5) Officers on fire duty 50 35
4270 200f. (6) Border guards . . 65 45

967 State Arms

968 Chou En-lai on Horseback

1998. 9th National People's Congress, Peking.
4271 **967** 50f. multicoloured . . . 20 10

1998. Birth Centenary of Chou En-lai.
4272 **968** 50f. black, cream & red 20 10
4273 – 50f. black, cream & red 20 10
4274 – 150f. black, cream & red 50 35
4275 – 150f. multicoloured . . . 50 35
DESIGNS: No. 4273, Walking; 4274, Wearing floral decoration; 4275, Clapping.

969 Fangcao Lake

1998. World Heritage Site. Jiuzhaigou (nine-village valley). Multicoloured.
4276 50f. (1) Type **969** 20 10
4277 50f. (2) Wuhua Lake . . . 20 10
4278 150f. (3) Shuzheng Falls . . 50 35
4279 150f. (4) Nuorilang Falls . . 50 35
MS4280 150 × 85 mm. 800f. Long Lake . . . . 3·75 3·25

970 House on Stilts

1998. Dai Architecture, Xishuangbanna. Mult.
4281 50f. (1) Type **970** 20 10
4282 50f. (2) Ornamental well . . 20 10
4283 150f. (3) Pavilion and streamers 50 35
4284 150f. (4) Pagoda 50 35

971 Haikou

1998. Hainan Special Economic Zone. Mult.
4285 50f. (1) Type **971** 20 10
4286 50f. (2) Yangpu 20 10
4287 150f. (3) Sanya Phoenix International Airport . . 50 35
4288 150f. (4) Monument, Yalongwan 50 35

972 Yingtian Academy

1998. Ancient Academies. Multicoloured.
4289 50f. (1) Type **972** 20 10
4290 50f. (2) Songyang Academy 20 10
4291 150f. (3) Yuelu Academy . . 50 35
4292 150f. (4) Bailu Academy . . 50 35

973 University Buildings

1998. Centenary of Peking University.
4293 **973** 50f. multicoloured . . . 20 10

974 Congress Emblem

1998. 22nd UPU Congress, Peking (1999). Mult.
4294 50f. Type **974** 20 10
4295 540f. Emblem (vert) . . . . 1·90 1·20

975 Mountain Peaks

1998. Shennongjia (primitive forest). Mult.
4296 50f. (1) Type **975** 20 10
4297 50f. (2) River gorge 20 10
4298 150f. (3) Forest 50 35
4299 150f. (4) Grasslands 50 35

976 Great Hall of the People of Chongqing

1998. Chongqing. Multicoloured.
4300 50f. Type **976** 20 10
4301 150f. Chongqing port . . . 50 35

977 "Tiger"

1998. Paintings by He Xiangning. Mult.
4302 50f. Type **977** 20 10
4303 100f. "Lion" (vert) 40 25
4304 150f. "Plum Blossom" (vert) 50 35

978 Grasslands

1998. Xilingguole Grasslands, Inner Mongolia. Multicoloured.
4305 50f. (1) Type **978** 20 15
4306 50f. (2) Meadow steppe . . 20 15
4307 150f. (3) Forest of poplars and birches 65 35
MS4308 140 × 80 mm. 800f. Xilingguole River . . . . . . 2·50 2·20

979 Baishilazi

1998. Jingpo Lake, Heilonjiang. Multicoloured.
4309 50f. (1) Type **979** 20 10
4310 50f. (2) Pearl Gate 20 10
4311 50f. (3) Mt. Xiaogushan . . 20 10
4312 50f. (4) Diaoshuilou waterfall 20 10
Nos. 4309/12 were issued together, se-tenant, forming a composite design.

980 Wurzburg Palace, Germany

1998. World Heritage Sites. Multicoloured.
4313 50f. Type **980** 20 10
4314 540f. Puning Temple, Chengde . . . . 1·90 1·20

1998. Literature. "The Romance of the Three Kingdoms" by Luo Guanzhong (5th series). As T **763**. Multicoloured.
4315 50f. (1) Liu Bei appoints a Guardian for his Heir at Baidi City (horiz) 20 10
4316 50f. (2) Zhuge Liang leads his army home 20 10
4317 100f. (3) Funeral of Zhuge Liang (horiz) 40 25
4318 150f. (4) Three Kingdoms united under the reign of Jin 50 35
MS4319 181 × 65 mm. 800f. Stratagem of the Empty City 5·25 3·00

981 Wave and Houses

1998. Flood Relief Fund.
4320 **981** 50f. (+50f.) mult 50 45
No. 4320 includes the se-tenant premium-carrying tab shown in Type **981**. The premium was used to help the victims of floods in the Yangtse and Songhuajiang River areas.

982 Louvre Palace, Paris

1998. Ancient Palaces. Multicoloured.
4321 50f. Type **982** 20 10
4322 200f. Imperial Palace, Peking 65 45

983 Face

1998. Rock Paintings, Helan Mountains. Mult.
4323 50f. Type **983** 20 10
4324 100f. Hunting 40 25
4325 150f. Ox 50 35

984 Vase with Five Spouts (Northern Song Dynasty)

1998. Longquan Pottery. Multicoloured.
4326 50f. (1) Type **984** 30 15
4327 50f. (2) Vase with phoenix ears (Southern Song dynasty) 30 15
4328 50f. (3) Double gourd vase (Yuan dynasty) 30 15
4329 150f. (4) Ewer decorated with three fruits (Ming dynasty) 50 35

985 Meridian Gate

1998. Mausoleum of King Yandi, Yanling County, Hunan. Multicoloured.
4330 50f. Type **985** 20 10
4331 100f. Saluting Pavilion . . . 40 25
4332 150f. Tomb 50 35
MS4333 150 × 80 mm. Nos. 4330/3 2·30 1·90

986 Men discussing Campaign (Yi Rongsheng)

1998. 50th Anniv of Liberation War. Multicoloured.
4334 50f. (1) Type **986** 20 10
4335 50f. (2) Conquering Jinzhou (Ren Mengzhang, Zhang Hongzan, Li Shuji and Guang Tingbo) 20 10
4336 50f. (3) Battle of Huaihai (Chen Qi, Zhao Guangtao, Chen Jian and Wei Chuyu) 20 10
4337 50f. (4) Liberating Peking (Zhang Ruwei, Deng Jiaju, Wu Changjiang and Shen Yaoyi) 20 10
4338 150f. (5) Supporting the Front (Cui Kaixi) 50 35

987 Liu Shaoqi

1998. Birth Centenary of Liu Shaoqi (Chairman of the Republic, 1959–68).
4339 **987** 50f. (1) multicoloured . . 20 10
4340 – 50f. (2) black, buff and red 20 10
4341 – 50f. (3) multicoloured . . 20 10
4342 – 150f. (4) multicoloured 50 35
DESIGNS—VERT: No. 4340, Shaoqi at Seventh National Communist Party Congress. HORIZ: No. 4341, Presented with necklace of flowers while on diplomatic mission; 4342, Working at desk.

988 Chillon Castle, Lake Geneva, Switzerland

1998. Lakes. Multicoloured.
4343 50f. Type **988** 20 10
4344 540f. Bridge 24, Slender West Lake, Yangzhou . . 1·90 1·20

989 Canal Fork

1998. Lingqu Canal. Multicoloured.
4345 50f. Type **989** 20 10
4346 50f. Bridge over canal (vert) 20 10
4347 150f. Lock (vert) 50 35

990 Road into Macao

1998. Macao. Multicoloured.
4348 50f. Type **990** 20 10
4349 100f. Bridge and buildings 40 25
4350 150f. Macao Stadium . . . 50 35
4351 200f. Airport 65 45

991 Deng Xiaoping at Third Plenary Session

1998. 20th Anniv of Third Plenary Session of 11th Central Committee of Chinese Communist Party. Multicoloured.
4352 50f. Type **991** 20 10
4353 150f. Deng Xiaoping Theory and buildings 50 35

992 Emperor Angelfish

1998. 22nd Universal Postal Union Congress and "China '99" International Stamp Exhibition, Peking. Sheet 190 × 150 mm. containing T **992** and similar multicoloured designs.
MS4354 200f. (1) Type **992**; 200f. (2) Spotted coral grouper; 200f. (3) Blue-spotted butterflyfish; 200f. (4) Ear-spotted angelfish (vert); 200f. (5) Pennant coralfish (vert); 200f. (6) Emperor snapper; 200f. (7) Clown triggerfish; 200f. (8) Regal angelfish . . . . 6·75 5·75

993 Ceramic Rabbit (Zhang Chang)

1999. New Year. Year of the Rabbit. Multicoloured.
4355 50f. Type **993** 20 10
4356 150f. Chinese character ("Good Luck") 50 35

994 Ploughing

1999. Stone Carvings of Han Dynasty.
4357 **994** 50f. (1) green, cream and black 20 10
4358 – 50f. (2) brown, cream and black 20 10
4359 – 50f. (3) blue, cream and black 20 10
4360 – 50f. (4) brown, cream and black 50 35
4361 – 150f. (5) green, cream and black 50 35
4362 – 150f. (6) lilac, cream and black 50 35
DESIGNS: No. 4358, Weaving; 4359, Dancing; 4360, Carriage and outriders; 4361, Jing Ke's attempted assassination of Emperor Qinshihuang; 4362, Goddess Chang'e flying to moon.

995 Wine Vessel, Northern Song Dynasty

996 Peony and Globe

1999. Ceramics from the Jun Kiln, Henan. Multicoloured.
4363 80f. Type **995** 30 15
4364 100f. Wine vessel, Northern Song Dynasty (different) 40 25
4365 150f. Double-handled stove, Yuan Dynasty 50 35
4366 200f. Double-handled vase, Yuan Dynasty 65 45

1999. World Horticulture Fair, Kunming. Mult.
4367 80f. Type **996** 30 15
4368 200f. Exhibition halls and tree 65 45

997 Stag

1999. Red Deer. Multicoloured.
4369 80f. (1) Type **997** 30 15
4370 80f. (2) Doe and fawns . . . 30 15

998 Puji Temple

1999. Putuo Mountain, Lianhuayang. Mult.
4371 30f. Type **998** 10 10
4372 60f. Nantian Gate (vert) . . 20 10
4373 60f. Step beach 20 10
4374 80f. Pantuo Rock 30 15
4375 80f. Fanyin Cave (vert) . . 30 15
4376 280f. Fayu Temple 95 60

999 Nine Dragon Wall. Beihai (detail)

1999. "China 1999" International Stamp Exhibition, Peking (2nd issue). Sheet 174 × 68 mm.
MS4377 **999** 800f. multicoloured 4·25 2·50

1000 Fang Zhimin (sculpture)

1999. Birth Centenary of Fang Zhimin (revolutionary). Multicoloured.
4378 80y. Type **1000** 40 25
4379 80y. Full-length portrait of Fang Zhimin 40 25

1001 First Congress Building, Berne, Switzerland (1874)

1999. 22nd Universal Postal Union Congress, Peking (3rd issue). Multicoloured (except No. **MS**4382).
4380 80f. Type **1001** 30 15
4381 540f. 22nd Congress building, Peking . . . . 1·90 1·20
MS4382 85 × 150 mm. 800f. black and brown (Quotation in Chinese characters "Develops modern postal service to satisfy social demands" (by Pres. Jiang Zemin) (51 × 92 mm) . . . . 3·50 3·00

1002 UPU Emblem and Great Wall

1003 Emblem

1999. 125th Anniv of Universal Postal Union.
4383 **1002** 80f. multicoloured . . . 30 15

1999. International Year of the Elderly.
4384 **1003** 80f. multicoloured . . . 30 15

1004 Conference Hall

1999. 50th Anniv of Chinese People's Political Conference. Multicoloured.
4385 60f. Type **1004** 20 10
4386 80f. Mao Tse-tung and emblem (vert) 30 15

1005 Han Couple

1999. 50th Anniv of People's Republic. Ethnic Groups. Couples from different ethnic groups. Multicoloured.
4387 80f. (1) Type **1005** 30 15
4388 80f. (2) Mongolian 30 15
4389 80f. (3) Hui 30 15
4390 80f. (4) Tibetan 30 15
4391 80f. (5) Uygur 30 15
4392 80f. (6) Miao 30 15
4393 80f. (7) Yi 30 15
4394 80f. (8) Zhuang 30 15
4395 80f. (9) Bouyei 30 15
4396 80f. (10) Korean 30 15
4397 80f. (11) Manchu 30 15
4398 80f. (12) Dong 30 15
4399 80f. (13) Yao 30 15
4400 80f. (14) Bai 30 15
4401 80f. (15) Tujia 30 15
4402 80f. (16) Hani 30 15
4403 80f. (17) Kazak 30 15
4404 80f. (18) Dai 30 15
4405 80f. (19) Li 30 15
4406 80f. (20) Lisu 30 15
4407 80f. (21) Va 30 15
4408 80f. (22) She 30 15
4409 80f. (23) Gaoshan 30 15
4410 80f. (24) Lahu 30 15
4411 80f. (25) Sui 30 15
4412 80f. (26) Dongxiang 30 15
4413 80f. (27) Naxi 30 15
4414 80f. (28) Jingpo 30 15
4415 80f. (29) Kirgiz 30 15
4416 80f. (30) Tu 30 15
4417 80f. (31) Daur 30 15
4418 80f. (32) Mulam 30 15
4419 80f. (33) Qiang 30 15
4420 80f. (34) Blang 30 15
4421 80f. (35) Salar 30 15
4422 80f. (36) Maonan 30 15
4423 80f. (37) Gelao 30 15
4424 80f. (38) Xibe 30 15
4425 80f. (39) Achang 30 15
4426 80f. (40) Primi 30 15
4427 80f. (41) Tajik 30 15
4428 80f. (42) Nu 30 15
4429 80f. (43) Uzbek 30 15
4430 80f. (44) Russian 30 15
4431 80f. (45) Ewenki 30 15
4432 80f. (46) De'ang 30 15
4433 80f. (47) Bonan 30 15
4434 80f. (48) Yugur 30 15
4435 80f. (49) Gin 30 15
4436 80f. (50) Tatar 30 15
4437 80f. (51) Derung 30 15
4438 80f. (52) Oroqen 30 15
4439 80f. (53) Hezhen 30 15
4440 80f. (54) Monba 30 15
4441 80f. (55) Lhoba 30 15
4442 80f. (56) Jino 30 15

1006 Mt. Kumgang, North Korea

1999. 50th Anniv of China–North Korea Diplomatic Relations. Multicoloured.
4443 80f. (1) Type **1006** 30 15
4444 80f. (2) Mt. Lushan, China 30 15

1007 Children reading

1008 Early Cambrian Chengjiang Biota Fossil

1999. 10th Anniv of Project Hope (promotion of rural education).
4445 **1007** 80f. multicoloured . . . 30 15

1999. 50th Anniv of Chinese Academy of Sciences. Multicoloured.
4446 80f. (1) Type **1008** 30 15
4447 80f. (2) Underwater robot 30 15
4448 80f. (3) Head and mathematical equation (vert) 30 15
4449 80f. (4) Astronomical telescope (vert) 30 15

1009 Li Lisan

1011 Rongzhen in Uniform

1010 Sino-Portuguese Joint Declaration

1999. Birth Centenary of Li Lisan (trade unionist). Multicoloured.

4450 80f. Type **1009** 30 15
4451 80f. Li Lisan (different) . . 30 15

1999. Return of Macao to China. Multicoloured.

4452 80f. Type **1010** 30 15
4453 150f. Basic Law of Macao Special Region and Great Wall of China 50 35
MS4454 140 × 95 mm. 800f. Deng Xiaoping (59 × 59 mm) . . . . 4·25 3·50
MS4455 140 × 95 mm. 50y. As No. **MS**4454 . . . . 25·00 21·00

1999. Birth Centenary of Nie Rongzhen (revolutionary). Multicoloured.

4456 80f. Type **1011** 30 15
4457 80f. Rongzhen in chair . . . 30 15

1012 1961 8f. 1911 Revolution Stamp and Dr. Sun Yat-sen

1999. The Twentieth Century. Multicoloured.

4458 60f. (1) Type **1012** 20 10
4459 60f. (2) 1989 8f. May 4th Movement stamp 20 10
4460 80f. (3) 1991 20f. Chinese Communist Party stamp 30 15
4461 80f. (4) 1995 20f. (No. 4013) End of Second World War and of War against Japan stamp 30 15
4462 80f. (5) 1959 20f. People's Republic anniversary stamp and Mao Tse-tung 30 15
4463 200f. (6) 1989 20f. National Defence stamp 65 45
4464 260f. (7) 1996 500f. Pudong Area of Shanghai stamp 75 50
4465 280f. (8) Deng Xiaoping and fireworks (based on 1997 800f. Return of Hong Kong to China stamp) . . 85 60

1013 Chinese Dragon

1014 Welcoming the Spring Festival

2000. New Year. Year of the Dragon. Each black, gold and red.

4466 80f. Type **1013** 20 15
4467 2y.80 "The Sun Rising in the Eastern Sky" and Chinese character for dragon 85 60

2000. Spring Festival. Multicoloured.

4468 80f. Type **1014** 20 15
4469 80f. Bidding farewell to the outgoing year 20 15
4470 2y.80 Offering sacrifices to the God of Land 85 60
MS4471 124 × 84 mm. 8y. Family celebrations (90 × 59 mm) . . . 6·25 5·25

1015 Japanese Crested Ibis

2000. Wildlife. Sheet 146 × 213 mm containing T **1015** and similar vert designs. Multicoloured.
MS4472 30f. Type **1015**; 60f. Golden Kaiser-i-hind; 80f. Giant panda; 1y. Brown eared-pheasant; 1y.50 Chinese sturgeon; 2y. Snib-nosed monkey; 2y.60 White flag dolphin; 2y.80 Manchurian crane; 3y.70 Tiger; 5y.40 Chinese alligator 7·25 5·25

1016 Neolithic Jade Dragon

2000. Chinese Dragon Artefacts. Multicoloured.

4473 60f. (1) Type **1016** 20 15
4474 80f. (2) Dragon-shaped brooch, Warring States 30 15
4475 80f. (3) Eaves tile with carved dragon, Han Dynasty 30 15
4476 80f. (4) Coiled dragon on copper mirror, Tang Dynasty 30 15
4477 80f. (5) Bronze dragon, Jin Dynasty 30 15
4478 2y.80 (6) Dragon decoration from Qing Dynasty Red Sandalwood Throne . . . 85 60

1017 Wanxian Bridge

2000. Road Bridges over the Yangtze River. Mult.

4479 80f. (1) Type **1017** 20 15
4480 80f. (2) Huangshi 20 15
4481 80f. (3) Tongling 20 15
4482 2y.80 (4) Jiangyin 85 60

1018 Cangshan Mountain and Erhai Lake

2000. Landscapes of Dali, Yunnan Province. Mult.

4483 80f. (1) Type **1018** 20 15
4484 80f. (2) Three Pagodas, Chongsheng Temple . . . 20 15
4485 80f. (3) Jizu Mountain . . . 20 15
4486 2y.80 (4) Shibao Mountain 85 60

1019 Mulan weaving Cloth

2000. Literature. *Mulan* (folk tale). Multicoloured.

4487 80f. (1) Type **1019** 30 25
4488 80f. (2) Mulan dressed as male soldier 30 25
4489 80f. (3) Mulan on horseback 30 25
4490 80f. (4) Mulan resuming her female identity 30 25

1020 Good Luck Treasure Pagoda

2000. Taer Lamasery, Qinghai Province. Mult.

4491 80f. (1) Type **1020** 20 15
4492 80f. (2) Big Golden Tile Palace 20 15
4493 80f. (3) Big Scripture Hall 20 15
4494 2y.80 (4) Banqen Residence 85 60

1021 Li Fuchan and Cai Chang

2000. Birth Centenaries of Li Fuchan and Cai Chang (revolutionary couple).

4495 **1021** 80f. black, buff and brown 20 15

1022 "Entering a New Century" (Ling Lifei)

2000. New Millennium. Winning Entries in National Children's "Prospects in the New Century" Stamp Design Competition. Mult.

4496 30f. (1) Type **1022** 10 10
4497 60f. (2) "I Build a Bridge to Connect the Mainland with Taiwan" (Wang Yumeng) 20 15
4498 60f. (3) "Palace in a Tree" (Li Zhao) 20 15
4499 80f. (4) "Protecting the Earth" (Chen Zhuo) . . . 20 15
4500 80f. (5) "Communications in the New Century" (Qin Tian) 20 15
4501 80f. (6) "Space Travel" (Wang Yiru) 20 15
4502 2y.60 (7) "The Earth gets Younger" (Tian Yuan) . . 75 50
4503 2y.80 (8) "World Peace" (Song Zhili) 85 60

1023 Chen Yun

2000. 95th Birth Anniv of Chen Yun (revolutionary). Multicoloured.

4504 80f. (1) Type **1023** 20 15
4505 80f. (2) Chen Yun wearing white jacket and hat (vert) 20 15
4506 80f. (3) Chen Yun wearing black jacket (vert) 20 15
4507 2y.80 (4) Chen Yun 85 60

1024 He Pot (Chinese wine vessel)

2000. Pots. Multicoloured.

4508 80f. (1) Type **1024** 30 15
4509 80f. (2) Koumiss (fermented mare's milk flask) 30 15

Stamps in similar designs were issued by Kazakhstan.

1025 Great Peak

2000. Laoshan Mountain. Multicoloured.

4510 80f. (1) Type **1025** 20 15
4511 80f. (2) Yangkou Bay . . . 20 15
4512 80f. (3) Beijiu Lake 20 15
4513 2y.80 (4) Taiqing Palace . . 85 60
MS4514 153 × 82 mm. Nos. 4510/13 6·25 5·25

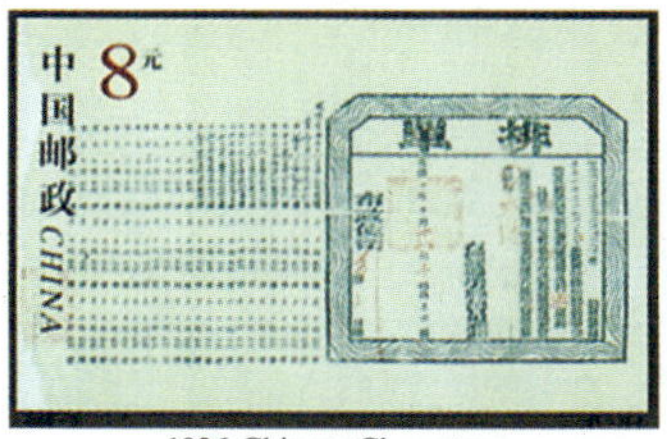

1026 Chinese Characters

2000. 5th Philatelic Federation Congress, Peking. Sheet 130 × 80 mm.
MS4515 **1026** 8y. multicoloured 6·25 5·25

1027 Grandma Carp telling a Story

2000. *Small Carp Leap Through Dragon Gate* (children's story). Multicoloured.

4516 80f. (1) Type **1027** 40 35
4517 80f. (2) Searching for Dragon Gate 40 35
4518 80f. (3) Uncle Crab helping Carp 40 35
4519 80f. (4) Carp leaping through Dragon Gate . . 40 35
4520 80f. (5) Aunt Swallow delivering a letter 40 35

1028 Financial Central District

2000. Shenzhen Special Economic Zone. Mult.

4526 80f. (1) Type **1028** 30 15
4527 80f. (2) China International New and Hi-Tech Achievement Fair Exhibition Centre 30 15
4528 80f. (3) Yantian Harbour . . 30 15
4529 80f. (4) Shenzhen Bay . . . 30 15
4530 2y.80 (5) Shekou Industrial District 85 60

1029 "2000" and Olympic Rings (½-size illustration)

2000. Olympic Games, Sydney. Sheet 122 × 82 mm.
MS4531 **1029** 8y. multicoloured 4·50 3·75

1030 Coconut Forest Bay, Hainan

2000. 40th Anniv of China–Cuba Diplomatic Relations. Multicoloured.

4532 80f. (1) Type **1030** 30 15
4533 80f. (2) Varadero beach, Matanzas, Cuba 30 15

Stamps in similar designs were issued by Cuba.

1031 Puppets

2000. Masks and Puppets. Multicoloured.

4534 80f. (1) Type **1031** 30 15
4535 80f. (2) Carnival masks . . 30 15

1032 "Eternal Fidelity" Palace Lamp

1033 Confucius

2000. Relics from Tomb of Liu Sheng. Multicoloured.

4536 80f. (1) Type **1032** 30 15
4537 80f. (2) Bronze pot with dragon design 30 15

4538	80f. (3) Boshan incense burner with gold inlay	30	15
4539	2y.80 (4) Rosefinch-shaped cup	85	60

2000. Ancient Thinkers. Each black, red and brown.

4540	60f. (1) Type **1033**	20	15
4541	80f. (2) Mencius	30	15
4542	80f. (3) Lao Zi	30	15
4543	80f. (4) Zhuang Zi	30	15
4544	80f. (5) Mo Zi	30	15
4545	2y.80 (6) Xun Zi	85	60

1034 Launch of *Shenzhou*

2000. Test Flight of *Shenzhou* (spacecraft). Mult.

4546	80f. Type **1034**	30	25
4547	80f. Orbiting Earth	30	25

1035 Meteorological Satellite

2000. 50th Anniv of World Meteorological Organization. Multicoloured.

4548	80f. (1) Type **1035**	30	15
4549	80f. (2) Meteorological equipment and Qinghai–Tibet plateau	30	15
4550	80f. (3) Computers and numbers	30	15
4551	2y.80 (4) Airplane and wind flow diagram	85	60

1036 Scarlet Kaffir Lily

1037 Jingshu Bell, Western Zhou Dynasty

2000. Flowers. Multicoloured.

4552	80f. (1) Type **1036**	30	15
4553	80f. (2) Noble clivia	30	15
4554	80f. (3) Golden striat kaffir lily	30	15
4555	2y.80 (4) White kaffir lily	85	60
MS4556	145 × 115 mm. Nos. 4552/5	7·25	6·00

2000. Ancient Bells. Multicoloured.

4557	80f. (1) Type **1037**	30	15
4558	80f. (2) Su chime bell, Spring and Autumn Period	30	15
4559	80f. (3) Jingyun bell, Tang Dynasty	30	15
4560	2y.80 (4) Qianlong bell, Qing Dynasty	85	60

1038 Sun, Moon and Observatory

1039 Snake

2001. New Millennium. Multicoloured.

4561	60f. (1) Type **1038**	20	15
4562	80f. (2) Globe and white dove	30	15
4563	80f. (3) Child's hands, leaf and World map (horiz)	30	15
4564	80f. (4) Silhouette of head and circuit board (horiz)	30	15
4565	2y.80 (5) Sun, stars and sundial	85	60

2001. New Year. Year of the Snake. Multicoloured.

4566	80f. Type **1039**	30	25
4567	2y.80 "Fortune Illuminates all Things" and Chinese character for snake	85	70

1040 Tang Qin

1041 Takin

2001. Chou (Clown) Roles in Peking Opera. Multicoloured.

4568	80f. (1) Type **1040**	30	25
4569	80f. (2) Liu Lihua	30	25
4570	80f. (3) Gao Lishi	30	25
4571	80f. (4) Jiang Gan	30	25
4572	80f. (5) Yang Xiangwu	30	25
4573	2y.80 (6) Shi Qian	85	70

2001. Wildlife (2nd series). Sheet 146 × 212 mm containing T **1041** and similar vert designs. Multicoloured.

MS4574	30f. Type **1041**; 60f. Chinese paddle-fish; 60f. Pere David's deer; 80f. Yangtze sturgeon; 80f. Ibex; 80f. Steller's sea eagle; 80f. Bactrian camel; 1y. Snow leopard; 2y.60 Sable; 5y.40 Saiga	11·50	9·50

1042 Zhouzhuang, Kunshan

2001. Ancient Towns, Taihu Lake Valley. Multicoloured.

4575	80f. (1) Type **1042**	30	25
4576	80f. (2) Tongli, Wujiang	30	25
4577	80f. (3) Wuzhen, Tongziang	30	25
4578	80f. (4) Nanxun, Huzhou	30	25
4579	80f. (5) Luzhi, Wuxian	30	25
4580	2y.80 (6) Xitang, Jiashan	1·00	85

1043 "Ying Ning"

2001. Classical Literature. *Strange Stories from a Chinese Studio* by Pu Songling. Multicoloured.

4581	60f. (1) Type **1043**	20	15
4582	80f. (2) "A Bao"	40	35
4583	80f. (3) "Mask of Evildoer"	40	35
4584	2y.80 (4) "Stealing Peach"	1·00	85
MS4585	144 × 85 mm. 8y. "A Taoist of Laoshan" (86 × 57 mm)	12·50	10·50

1044 Queen Mother (detail)

2001. Yongle Temple Murals, Shanxi. "Portrait of Paying Homage to Xianyuan Emperor". Multicoloured.

4586	60f. (1) Type **1044**	20	15
4587	80f. (2) Jade Lady presenting treasure	30	25
4588	80. (3) Celestial Worthy of the East	30	25
4589	2y.80 (4) Venus and Mercury	1·00	85

1045 Nanyan Hall in Autumn

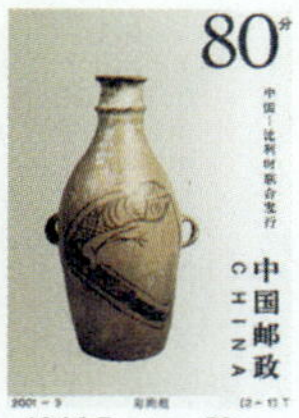

1046 Pottery Vase

2001. Mount Wudang, Hubei Province. Multicoloured.

4590	60f. (1) Type **1045**	20	15
4591	80f. (2) Zixiao Temple in winter	30	25
4592	80f. (3) Taizi slope in summer	30	25
MS4593	150 × 90 mm. 8y. Golden Crown and buildings in spring (47 × 72 mm)	9·00	7·50

2001. Chinese Pottery. Multicoloured.

4594	80f. (1) Type **1046**	30	25
4595	80f. (2) Teapot	30	25

1047 Dragon Boat Race

2001. Duanwu Dragon Boat Festival. Multicoloured.

4596	80f. (1) Type **1047**	30	25
4597	80f. (2) Vase, mobile and flowers	30	25
4598	2y.80 (3) Dragon's head and expulsion of five poisons	1·00	85

1048 Wang Jinmei

2001. Leaders of the Chinese Communist Party. Multicoloured.

4599	80f. (1) Type **1048**	30	25
4600	80f. (2) Zhao Shiyan	30	25
4601	80f. (3) Deng Enming	30	25
4602	80f. (4) Cai Hesen	30	25
4603	80f. (5) He Shuheng	30	25

1049 Party Flag

2001. 80th Anniv of Chinese Communist Party.

4604	**1049** 80f. red, yellow and black	30	25

1050 Emblem

2001. Choice of Beijing as 2008 Olympic Host City.

4605	**1050** 80f. multicoloured	50	45

1051 Yinlianzhuitan Waterfall

2001. Waterfalls. Multicoloured.

4606	80f. (1) Type **1051**	30	25
4607	80f. (2) Doupotang Waterfall (horiz)	30	25
4608	80f. (3) Dishuitan Waterfall	30	25
MS4609	124 × 84 mm. 8y. Huangguoshu Waterfall (39 × 59 mm)	6·25	5·25

1052 Pigeon Nest

2001. Beidaihe Summer Resort. Multicoloured.

4610	60f. (1) Type **1052**	20	15
4611	80f. (2) Umbrellas, Zhonghai Beach	30	25
4612	80f. (3) Sailing dinghies, Lianfeng Hill	30	25
4613	2y.80 Windsurfers, Tiger Stone	1·00	85

1053 "2001" and Emblem

2001. 21st World University Games, Beijing. Multicoloured.

4614	60f. Type **1053**	20	15
4615	80f. "2001" and sports pictograms	30	25
4616	2y.80 "2001" and globes	1·00	85

1054 Water Diversion Canal

2001. Datong River Diversion Project. Mult.

4617	80f. (1) Type **1054**	30	25
4618	80f. (2) Overland pipes, Xianming Gorge	30	25
4619	80f. (3) Canal tunnel	30	25
4620	2y.80 (4) Aqueduct, Zhuanglang River	1·00	85

1055 Wuhu Bridge over Yangtze River

2001. Wuhu Bridge. Multicoloured.

4621	80f. Type **1055**	30	25
4622	2y.80 Road section of Wuhu Bridge	1·00	85

1056 *Paphiopedilum malipoense*

2001. Orchids. Multicoloured.

4623	80f. (1) Type **1056**	30	25
4624	80f. (2) *Paphiopedilum dianthum*	30	25
4625	80f. (3) *Paphiopedilum markianum*	30	25
4626	2y.80 (4) *Paphiopedilum appletonianum*	1·00	85
MS4627	145 × 95 mm. Nos. 4623/6	7·25	6·00

1057 Mask of San Xing Dui

2001. Golden Masks. Multicoloured.
4628 80f. Type **1057** 40 35
4629 80f. Mask of Tutankhamun 40 35
Stamps in similar designs were also issued by Egypt.

1058 Emblem

2001. 9th Asia Pacific Economic Co-operation Conference, Shanghai.
4630 **1058** 80f. multicoloured . . . 30 25

1059 Ertan Hydroelectric Power Station (½-size illustration)

2001. Sheet 150 × 85 mm.
MS4631 **1059** 8y. multicoloured 3·75 3·25

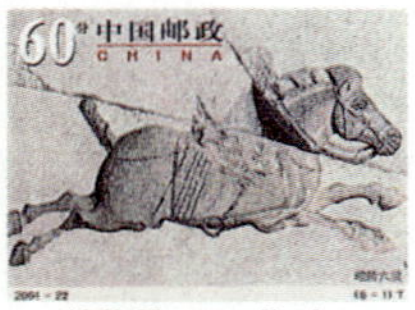

1060 Horse galloping

2001. Six Steeds (relief sculptures), Zhaoling Mausoleum. Multicoloured.
4632 60f. (1) Type **1060** 30 25
4633 80f. (2) Galloping 40 35
4634 80f. (3) Trotting 40 35
4635 80f. (4) With rider 40 35
4636 80f. (5) Trotting 40 35
4637 2y.80 (6) Galloping . . . . 1·30 1·00

1061 Chinese Junk

2001. Ancient Sailing Craft. Multicoloured.
4638 80f. Type **1061** 30 25
4639 80f. Portuguese caravel . . . 30 25
Stamps in the same design were issued by Portugal.

1062 Diving **1063** Liupanshan Mountains

2001. 9th National Games, Guangzhou. Mult.
4640 80f. Type **1062** 30 25
4641 2y.80 Volleyball . . . . . . 1·30 1·00
MS4642 140 × 90 mm. Nos. 4640/1 4·75 4·00

2001. Liupanshan Mountains. Multicoloured.
4643 80f. (1) Type **1063** 30 25
4644 80f. (2) Forest, Liangdianxia Gorge 30 25
4645 80f. (3) Old Dragon Pool, Jinghe River 30 25
4646 2y.80 (4) Wild Lotus Valley, West Gorge . . . . . . 1·30 1·00

1064 Lending an Umbrella by the Lake **1065** Emblem

2001. Tale of Xu Xian and the White Snake. Multicoloured.
4647 80f. (1) Type **1064** 30 25
4648 80f. (2) Stealing the Immortal Grass 30 25
4649 80f. (3) Flooding the Jinshan Hill 30 25
4650 2y.80 (4) Meeting at the Broken Bridge . . . . . 1·30 1·00

2001. China's Membership of World Trade Organization.
4651 **1065** 80f. multicoloured . . . 1·60 1·30

1066 Zheng's advancing Fleet

2001. 340th Anniv of Zheng Chenggong's Seizure of Formosa (Taiwan) from Dutch Colonists. Each drab, black and red.
4652 80f. (1) Type **1066** 30 25
4653 80f. (2) Populace offering troops food and water . . 30 25
4654 2y.80 Zheng viewing island 1·30 1·00

1067 Engineers and Route of Railway (½-size illustration)

2001. Construction of the Qinghai--Tibet Railway. Sheet 135 × 114 mm.
MS4655 **1067** 8y. multicoloured 6·25 5·25

1068 Horse **1069** "A Couple of Eagles"

2002. New Year. Year of the Horse. Multicoloured.
4656 80f. Type **1068** 40 35
4657 2y.80 Chinese character for horse . . . . 1·50 1·20

2002. Paintings by Badashanren. Multicoloured.
4658 60f. (1) Type **1069** 30 25
4659 80f. (2) "A Single Pine Tree" 40 35
4660 80f. (3) "Lotus Flowers" . . 40 35
4661 80f. (4) "Chrysanthemum in a Vase" 40 35
4662 2y.60 (5) "A Couple of Magpies on a Rock" . . 1·40 1·10
4663 2y.80 (6) "Landscape after Dong Yuan's Style" . . . 1·50 1·20

1070 Forest Protection **1071** Yellow-bellied Tragopan

2002. Environmental Protection. Multicoloured.
4664 5f. Maintaining low birth rate 10 10
4665 10f. Type **1070** 10 10
4666 30f. Mineral resources protection 20 15
4667 50f. Desert (desertification) control and prevention . . 20 15
4668 60f. Air pollution prevention 30 25
4670 80f. Water resources protection 40 35
4673 1y.50 Ocean protection . . . 85 70
4674 4y.50 Bird, globe and water (biodiversity protection) 1·40 1·10

2002. Birds. Multicoloured.
4674a 40f. Chinese monal pheasant 10 10
4675 80f. Type **1071** 40 35
4676 1y. Biddulph's ground jay 50 45
4676a 1y.20 Taiwan yuhina . . 20 10
4677 2y. Taiwan blue magpie . . 1·00 85
4680 4y.20 Przewalski's redstart 2·00 1·70
4682 5y. Yellow bellied tit . . . 1·60 1·30
4683 5y.40 Koslow's bunting . . 2·50 2·10
4684 6y. Yunnan nuthatch . . . 1·80 1·50

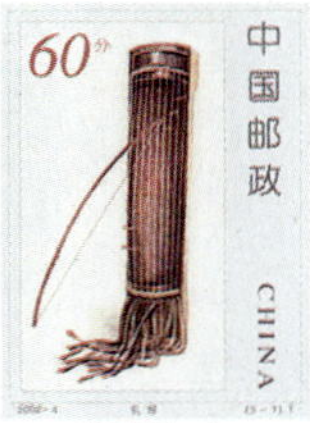

1072 Golden Camellia (*Camellia nitidissima*) **1073** Yaqin

2002. Flowers. Multicoloured.
4690 80f. Type **1072** 40 35
4691 80f. Cannonball tree flower (*Couroupita guianensis*) . . 40 35
Stamps showing similar subjects were issued by Malaysia.

2002. Stringed Musical Instruments. Multicoloured.
4692 60f. (1) Type **1073** 30 25
4693 80f. (2) Erhu 40 35
4694 80f. (3) Banhu 40 35
4695 80f. (4) Satar 40 35
4696 2y.80 (5) Matouqin . . . . 1·60 1·30

1074 "The Royal Carriage" (Yan Liben) (¼ size-illustration)

2002. Sheet 160 × 82 mm.
MS4697 **1074** 8y. multicoloured 3·50 3·00

1075 Wine Vessel

2002. Northern Song Dynasty Ceramics. Mult.
4698 60f. (1) Type **1075** 30 25
4699 80f. (2) Three-legged basin 35 30
4700 80f. (3) Bowl 35 30
4701 2y.80 (4) Dish . . . . . . 1·30 1·00

2001. Classical Literature. Strange Stories from a Chinese Studio by Pu Songling (2nd series). Vert designs as T **1043**. Multicoloured.
4702 60f. (1) "Xi Fangping" . . . 30 25
4703 80f. (2) "Pianpian" 35 30
4704 80f. (3) "Tian Qilang" . . . 35 30
4705 2y.80 (4) "Bai Qiulian" . . 1·30 1·00

1076 Wuliang Taoist Temple **1078** Ruyi (good luck symbol)

1077 Sifang Street

2002. Qianshan Mountain. Views of the mountain. Multicoloured.
4706 80f. (1) Type **1076** 35 30
4707 80f. (2) Maitreya peak . . . 35 30
4708 80f. (3) Longquan temple 35 30
4709 2y.80 (4) "Terrace of the Immortals" (peak) . . . 1·30 1·00
Nos. 4706/9 were issued together, se-tenant, forming a composite design.

2002. Lijiang City.
4710 **1077** 80f. red 30 25
4711 – 80f. green (vert) 30 25
4712 – 2y.80 blue . . . . . 1·30 1·00
MS4713 145 × 101 mm Nos. 4710/12 2·75 2·30
DESIGNS: 80f. Bridges over city river; 2y.80, Traditional Naxi house.

2002. Greetings Stamp.
4714 **1078** 80f. multicoloured . . . 50 45

1079 Footballer

2002. World Cup Football Championship, Japan and South Korea. Multicoloured.
4715 80f. Type **1079** 30 25
4716 2y. Players tackling 95 80

1080 Maota Pagoda Lighthouse **1082** "Avalokitesvara of the Sun and Moon"

1081 Lijia Gorge Hydro-electric Power Station

2002. Lighthouses.
4717 **1080** 80f. (1) black and green 30 25
4718 – 80f. (2) black and ochre 30 25
4719 – 80f. (3) black and grey 30 25
4720 – 80f. (4) black, brown and orange 30 25
4721 – 80f. (5) black and red 30 25
DESIGNS: 80f. (2) Jianxin pagoda lighthouse; 80f. (3) Huaniaoshan; 80f. (4) Laotieshan; 80f. (5) Lin'gao.

2002. Hydro-electric Power Generation and Water Control on the Yellow River. Multicoloured.
4722 80f. (1) Type **1081** 30 25
4723 80f. (2) Liujia Gorge Hydro-electric Power Station . . 30 25
4724 80f. (3) Qingtong Gorge dam 30 25
4725 80f. (4) Sanmen Gorge dam 30 25
MS4726 115 × 96 mm 8y. Xiaolangdi dam (39 × 59 mm) . . . . . . 3·25 2·75

2002. Stone Carvings, Dazu County, Sichuan Province. Multicoloured.
4727 80f. (1) Type **1082** 30 25
4728 80f. (2) Samantabhadra riding elephant, North Mountain 30 25
4729 80f. (3) Three Avatamasaka Sages, Holy Summit Mountain 30 25
4730 80f. (4) Man wearing headdress (statue), Cave of the Three Emperors, Stone Gate Mountain . . 30 25
MS4731 130 × 96 mm 8y. "Avalokitesvara of a Thousand Hands" (39 × 59 mm) . . . . 3·25 2·75

1083 *Ammopiptanthus mongolicus*

2002. Desert Plants. Multicoloured.
4732 80f. (1) Type **1083** 30 25
4733 80f. (2) *Calligonum rubicundum* 30 25
4734 80f. (3) *Hedysarum scoparium* 30 25
4735 2y. (4) *Tamarix leptostachys* 95 80

1084 Emperor Penguins

2002. Antarctica. Multicoloured.
4736 80f. Type **1084** 30 25
4737 80f. Aurora Australis . . . 30 25
4738 2y. Grove mountain, scientists and snowy sheathbill 95 80

1085 Shepherd on Horse-back, Sheep and Lakeside

2002. Qinghai Lake. Multicoloured.

4739	80f. Type **1085**	30	25
4740	80f. Bird island	30	25
4741	2y.80 Lake and mountain	1·30	1·00

1086 Huang Gonglue

1087 Bian Que

2002. Early 20th-century Generals. Multicoloured.

4742	80f. (1) Type **1086**	30	25
4743	80f. (2) Xu Jishen	30	25
4744	80f. (3) Cai Shengxi	30	25
4745	80f. (4) Wei Baqun	30	25
4746	80f. (5) Liu Zhidan	30	25

2002. Early Chinese Scientists.

4747 **1087**	80f. (1) grey and black	30	25
4748 –	80f. (2) grey and black	30	25
4749 –	80f. (3) grey and black	30	25
4750 –	80f. (4) stone and black	30	25

DESIGNS: 80f. (1) Type **1087**; 80f. (2) Lui Hui; 80f. (3) Su Song; 80f. (4) Song Yingxing.

1088 Xianshengmen Gate

1089 Large Family Gathering

2002. Yandang Mountain. Multicoloured.

4751	80f. (1) Type **1088**	30	25
4752	80f. (2) Dalongqiu waterfall and pond	30	25
4753	80f. (3) Beidou cave (horiz)	30	25
4754	80f. (4) Guanyin peak (horiz)	30	25

2002. Mid-autumn Festival. Multicoloured.

4755	80f. (1) Type **1089**	30	25
4756	80f. (2) Food and couple with daughter	30	25
4757	2y. (3) Courting couple with birds perched on knees	85	70

1090 Peng Zhen

1091 Bojnice Castle

2002. Birth Centenary of Peng Zhen (revolutionary leader).

4758 **1090**	80f. brown, cinnamon and black	30	25
4759 –	80f. sepia, cinnamon and black	30	25

DESIGNS: 80f. Type **1090**; 80f. In army uniform.

2002. Castles. Multicoloured.

4760	80f. Type **1091**	30	25
4761	80f. Congtai Pavilion, Handan	30	25

Nos. 4760/1 were issued together, se-tenant, forming a composite design.

Stamps of a similar design were issued by Slovakia.

1092 Immortal Maiden moved by Dong's Filial Love

1093 Flowers

2002. Tale of Dong Yong and the Seventh Immortal Maiden. Multicoloured.

4762	80f. (1) Type **1092**	30	25
4763	80f. (2) Seventh immortal maiden marrying Dong Yong	30	25
4764	80f. (3) Maiden weaving brocade to buy Dong Yong's freedom	30	25
4765	80f. (4) Everlasting love	30	25
4766	2y. (5) Maiden returned to Heaven leaving Dong Yong behind	85	70

2002. Greetings Stamp. Paper with fluorescent fibres.

4767 **1093**	80f. multicoloured	50	45

1094 Waterfalls on the Yellow River

2002. Hukou Waterfalls. Sheet 131 × 90 mm.

MS4768 **1094**	8y. multicoloured	3·25	2·50

1095 Shanxi History Museum

2002. Museums. Multicoloured.

4769	80f. (1) Type **1095**	30	25
4770	80f. (2) Shanghai	30	25
4771	80f. (3) Henan	30	25
4772	80f. (4) Tibet	30	25
4773	80f. (5) Tianjin Natural History museum	30	25

1096 Kung Fu

2002. Martial Arts. Multicoloured.

4774	80f. (1) Type **1096**	30	25
4775	80f. (2) Tae Kwon Do	30	25

1097 White-handed Gibbon (*Hylobates lar*)

1098 Goat

2002. Gibbons. Multicoloured.

4776	80f. (1) Type **1097**	30	25
4777	80f. (2) White-cheeked gibbon (*Hylobates leucogenys*)	30	25
4778	80f. (3) Black gibbon (*Hylobates concolor*)	30	25
4779	2y. (4) Hoolock gibbon (*Hylobates hoolock*)	85	70

2003. New Year. Year of the Goat. Multicoloured.

4780	80f. Type **1098**	25	20
4781	2y.80 Chinese character for goat	65	50

1099 "Five Boys wrestling for a Lotus"

2003. Yangliuqing New Year Pictures (woodcut prints). Multicoloured.

4782	80f. (1) Type **1099**	25	20
4783	80f. (2) "Zhong Kui" (vert)	25	20
4784	80f. (3) "Stealing the Herb of Immortality"	25	20
4785	2y. (4) "Wealth in a Jade Hall" (vert)	65	50

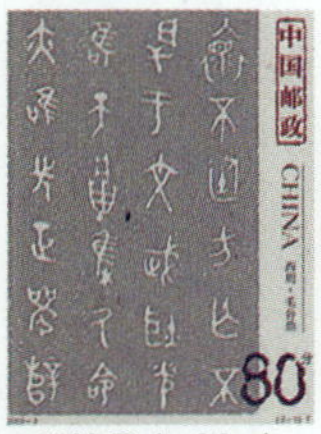

1100 Duke Mao's Tripod (Western Zhou dynasty)

1101 Knot

2003. Calligraphy. Seal Characters. Multicoloured.

4786	80f. Type **1100**	30	25
4787	80f. Carvings of Mount Tai (Qin dynasty)	30	25

2003. Greetings Stamp. Chinese Decorative Knot.

4788 **1101**	80f. multicoloured	30	25

1102 Lily (*Lilium taliense*)

2003. Greetings Stamps. Lilies. Multicoloured.

4789	60f. (1) Type **1102**	20	15
4790	80f. (2) *Lilium lanongense*	25	20
4791	80f. (3) *Lilium distichum*	25	20
4792	2y. (4) *Lilium lophophorum*	65	50
MS4793	140 × 95 mm. 8y. *Lilium leucanthum* (76 × 54 mm)	2·50	2·10

1103 Maple Bridge, Suzhou, Jiangsu Province

2003. Ancient Bridges. Multicoloured.

4794	80f. (1) Type **1103**	25	20
4795	80f. (2) Xiaoshang bridge, Linying, Henan province	25	20
4796	80f. (3) Lugouqiao bridge, Beijing	25	20
4797	80f. (4) Double Dragon bridge, Jianshui, Yunnan province	25	20

1104 Bell Tower, Xi'an

2003. Buildings. Multicoloured.

4798	80f. Type **1104**	25	20
4799	80f. Mosque, Isfahan	25	20

Stamps of the same design were issued by Iran.

1105 Giant Buddha (statue, Lingyun mountain, Leshan province)

2003. UNESCO World Heritage Sites. Sheet 145 × 90 mm.

MS4800 **1105**	8y. multicoloured	2·30	1·90

1106 Eight Diagram Buildings, Gulangyu Island

2003. Gulangyu Island, Fujian Province. Multicoloured.

4801	80f. Type **1106**	25	20
4802	80f. Sunlight rock	25	20
4803	2y. Shuzhuang park	65	50
MS4804	180 × 80 mm. Nos. 4801/3	1·60	1·30

Nos. 4801/3 were issued together, se-tenant, forming a composite design of the island.

2003. Classical Literature. Strange Stories from a Chinese Studio by Pu Songling (3rd series). As T **1043**. Multicoloured.

4805	10f. (1) "Xiang Yu"	20	15
4806	30f. (2) "Tiger of Zhaocheng"	20	15
4807	60f. (3) "Tian Qilang"	20	15
4808	80f. (4) "Ah Xiu"	30	25
4809	1y.50 (5) "Wang Gui'an"	50	45
4810	2y. (6) "Goddess"	65	50
MS4811	144 × 85 mm. 8y. "Princess of the Dongting Lake" (90 × 60 mm)	2·50	2·10

1107 "SARS" overprinted with Stop Sign

1109 Late Spring Cottage

1108 Meteorites descending

2003. Campaign to Control Severe Acute Respiratory Syndrome (SARS).

4812 **1107**	80f. multicoloured	20	15

2003. Meteorite Shower over Jilin Province, (8 March 1976). Multicoloured.

4813	80f. Type **1108**	20	15
4814	80f. Dispersal	20	15
4815	2y. Meteorite No. 1 (largest ever found)	65	50

2003. Master-of-Nets Garden, Suzhou. Multicoloured.

4816	80f. (1) Type **1109**	20	15
4817	80f. (2) Pavilion Greeting the Moon and Breeze	20	15
4818	80f. (3) Veranda of Bamboo	20	15
4819	2y. (4) Hall of Ten Thousand Volumes	65	50

Nos. 4816/19 were issued together, se-tenant, forming a composite design.

1110 Antelopes

2003. Endangered Species. Tibetan Antelope (Pantholops hodgsoni). Multicoloured.

4820 80f. Type **1110** 20 15
4821 2y. Female and fawn . . . 65 50

1111 Huangcheng (town)

2003. Kongtong Mountain, Gansu Province. Multicoloured.

4822 80f. (1) Type **1111** 20 15
4823 80f. (2) Playing the Zither Gorge 20 15
4824 80f. (3) Pagoda Courtyard 20 15
4825 2y. (4) Thunder Peak . . . 65 50

Nos. 4822/5 were issued together, se-tenant, forming a composite design.

1112 Junk (sailing ship)

1114 Ruyi Maid

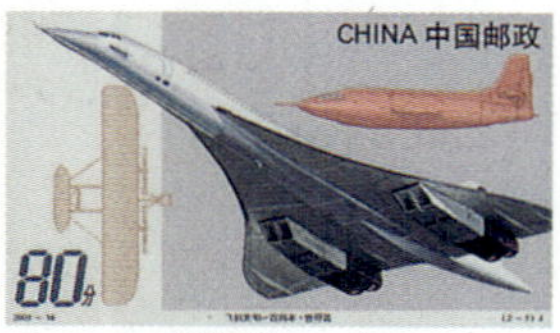
1113 Concorde

2003. Greetings Stamp. "Plain Sailing".

4826 **1112** 80f. multicoloured . . . 40 35

2003. Centenary of Powered Flight.

4827 80f. Type **1113** 20 15
4828 2y. Chinese aircraft 65 50

2003. Painted Statues, Jinci Temple, Shanxi Province. Multicoloured.

4829 80f. (1) Type **1114** 20 15
4830 80f. (2) Maid holding towel 20 15
4831 80f. (3) Maid carrying seal 20 15
4832 2y. (4) Maid smiling 65 50

1115 Dam and Reservoir

2003. Three Gorges Hydroelectric Project on Yangtze River. Multicoloured.

4833 80f. (1) Type **1115** 20 15
4834 80f. (2) Navigation locks . . 20 15
4835 2y. (3) Electricity pylons . . 65 50

1116 Wrestling

2003. Regional Traditional Sports. Multicoloured.

4836 80f. (1) Type **1116** 30 25
4837 80f. (2) Archery 30 25
4838 80f. (3) Horse racing 30 25
4839 80f. (4) Swinging 30 25
MS4840 120 × 80 mm Nos. 4836/40 1·60 1·30

1117 Tian'anmen Gate

2003.

4841 **1117** 80f. multicoloured . . . 40 35

1118 Mother tattooing Back

1119 Stylized Water

2003. 900th Birth Anniv of General Yue Fei (Pengju). Multicoloured.

4842 80f. Type **1118** 30 25
4843 80f. Wearing armour . . . 30 25
4844 2y. Reading 65 50

2003. Inauguration of Water Diversion Project. Sheet 126 × 80 mm.

MS4845 **1119** 8y. multicoloured 2·50 2·10

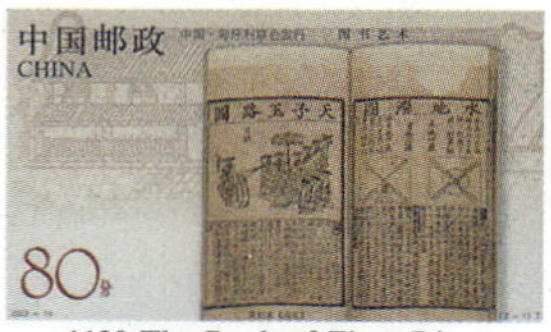
1120 The Book of Zhou Rites

2003. Ancient Books. Multicoloured.

4846 80f. Type **1120** 30 25
4847 80f. The Illuminated Chronicle 30 25

Stamps of a similar design were issued by Hungary.

1121 Climbing Mountain

1123 Swearing Brotherhood

1122 Astronaut and Satellite

2003. Double Ninth (ninth day of ninth month) Festival. Multicoloured.

4848 80f. (1) Type **1121** 30 25
4849 80f. (2) Looking at flowers 30 25
4850 2y. Playing chess and drinking tea 65 50

2003. 1st Chinese Manned Space Flight. Multicoloured.

4851 80f. Type **1122** 20 15
4852 1y. Astronaut and flag . . . 65 50

2003. Folk Tales. Liang Shanbo and Zhu Yingtai. Multicoloured.

4853 80f. (1) Type **1123** 20 15
4854 80f. (2) As classmates . . . 20 15
4855 80f. (3) Saying goodbye . . 20 15
4856 80f. (4) On terrace 20 15
4857 2y. Turning into butterflies 75 60

1124 Bronze Horse

2003. China 2003, 16th Asia International Stamp Exhibition.

4858 **1124** 80f. multicoloured . . . 30 25

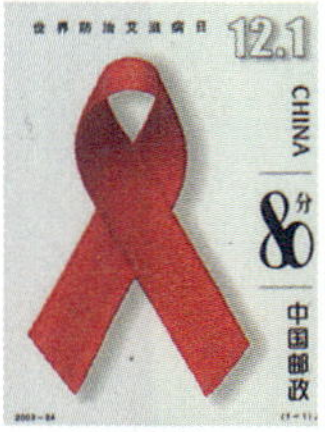
1125 Ribbon

2003. World AIDS Awareness Day.

4859 **1125** 80f. rose and black . . 30 25

1126 Seated in Deckchair

2003. 110th Birth Anniv of Mao Zedong (Communist Party Chairman). Each brown and black.

4860 80f. (1) Type **1126** 30 25
4861 80f. (2) Wearing coat and hat 30 25
4862 80f. (3) Seated on bench . . 30 25
4863 80f. (4) Writing 30 25

1127 Rectangular Dish

2003. Eastern Zhou Dynasty Bronze Ware. Multicoloured.

4864 60f. (1) Type **1127** 20 15
4865 60f. (2) Gui (round dish) . . 20 15
4866 80f. (3) Iron tripod 20 15
4867 80f. (4) Gourd-shaped ladle 20 15
4868 80f. (5) Animal shaped wine vessel (vert) 20 15
4869 80f. (6) Wine vessel (vert) 20 15
4870 1y. Square pot with applied decoration (vert) 40 35
4871 2y. Bronze tripod with dragon-shaped handle (vert) 65 50

1128 Monkey

2004. New Year. "Year of the Monkey".

4872 **1128** 80f. multicoloured . . . 20 15
MS4873 129 × 182 mm. No. 4872 × 6 9·50 7·75

1129 "Feelings of Pipa"

1130 Deng Yingchao

2004. Taohuawu New Year Pictures (woodcut prints). Multicoloured.

4874 80f. (1) Type **1129** 20 15
4875 80f. (2) "Kyliin bringing a Son" 20 15
4876 80f. (3) "Liu Hai playing with the Golden Toad" 20 15
4877 2y. (4) "Ten Beauties playing Football" 65 50
MS4878 159 × 90 mm. Nos. 4874/7 1·40 1·10

2004. Birth Centenary of Deng Yingchao (politician). Multicoloured.

4879 80f. Type **1130** 20 15
4880 80f. Wearing glasses 20 15

1131 "Harmony" Sculpture and Suzhou Industrial Park

2004. 10th Anniv of Suzhou Industrial Park.

4881 **1131** 80f. multicoloured . . . 20 15

A stamp of the same design was issued by Singapore.

1132 Red Crosses

2004. Centenary of China Red Cross Society.

4882 **1132** 80f. rose, black and gold 20 15

1133 "Trying to Learn the Handan Walk"

2004. Idioms. Multicoloured.

4883 80f. (1) Type **1133** 30 25
4884 80f. (2) "Lord Ye's love for Dragon" 30 25
4885 80f. (3) "Filling a Position in Yu Band" 30 25
4886 80f. (4) "When the Snipe and Clam Grapple" . . . 30 25

1134 Peacock

2004. Peafowl. Multicoloured.

4887 80f. Type **1134** 30 25
4888 80f. White peacock (vert) . . 30 25
MS4889 120 × 99 mm. 6y. Peahen and peacock with tail displayed (60 × 40 mm) . . . . 1·90 1·60

1135 Mouth of River

2004. Nanxi River, Zhejiang Province. Showing views of the river. Multicoloured.

4890 60f. (1) Type **1135** 20 15
4891 80f. (2) Trees and boat . . . 20 15
4892 80f. (3) Rock and small craft 20 15
4893 2y. (4) Small craft and inlets 50 45

Nos. 4890/3 were issued together, se-tenant, forming a composite design.

1136 Sengmao Peak

2004. Danxia Mountain, Guangdong Province. Views of the mountain. Multicoloured.
4894 60f. (1) Type **1136** 20 15
4895 80f. (2) Xianglong lake . . . 20 15
4896 80f. (3) Chahu peak 20 15
4897 2y. (4) Jinjiang river 50 45

1137 Sky Scrapers

2004. 20th Anniv of Economic and Technological Development Zones.
4898 **1137** 80f. multicoloured . . . 20 15

1138 Xianglong Farm

2004. Returning Emigrants Hometowns. Multicoloured.
4899 80f. (1) Type **1138** 30 25
4900 80f. (2) Jinan university . . 30 25
4901 80f. (3) Fuqing Rongqiao development zone 30 25
4902 80f. (4) Kaiping hometown 30 25

1139 "Fallen into Water"

1141 "Dragon Princess asking Liu to Deliver Letter"

1140 Ming Dynasty Decorated Arch, Xidi

2004. "Sima Guang breaking the Vat". Multicoloured.
4903 80f. (1) Type **1139** 20 15
4904 80f. (2) "Breaking the Vat" 20 15
4905 2y. (3) "Rescued" 75 60

2004. Ancient Villages, Anhui Province. Multicoloured.
4906 80f. (1) Type **1140** 30 25
4907 80f. (2) Curved roofs . . . 30 25
4908 80f. (3) Buildings and lake 30 25
4909 80f. (4) Moon, buildings and pond 30 25

2004. "Liu Delivers a Letter". Multicoloured.
4910 80f. (1) Type **1141** 20 15
4911 80f. (2) "Delivering letter to Dongting Lake" . . . 20 15
4912 80f. (3) "Family Reunion" 20 15
4913 80f. (4) "Mutual Love" . . 75 60

1142 "Eight Immortals Crossing the Sea" (½-size illustration)

2004. "Eight Immortals Crossing the Sea" (folk tale). Sheet 156 × 82 mm.
MS4914 **1142** 6y. multicoloured 1·90 1·60

1143 Temple of Heaven, Beijing

2004. Olympic Games, Athens 2004–Beijing 2008. Multicoloured.
4915 80f. Type **1143** 30 25
4916 80f. Parthenon, Athens . . . 30 25
Stamps of the same design were issued by Greece.

1144 Deng Xiaoping

2004. Birth Centenary of Deng Xiaoping (leader of China, 1978–89). Multicoloured.
4917 80f. Type **1144** 30 25
4918 80f. Saluting (horiz) . . . 30 25
MS4919 90 × 130 mm. 6y. Seated (50 × 60 mm) . . . . 1·90 1·60

1145 South China Tiger

2004. South China Tiger (*Panthera tigris amoyensis*). Multicoloured.
4920 80f. Type **1145** 20 15
4921 2y. Mother and cubs . . . 50 45

1146 Huairentang and Participants of First Meeting

1148 *Meconopsis lancifolia*

1147 Emperor Qianlong's Seal

2004. 50th Anniv of People's Congress. Multicoloured.
4922 80f. Type **1146** 20 15
4923 80f. Auditorium 20 15

2004. Bloodstone Seals. Multicoloured.
4924 80f. Type **1147** 20 15
4925 2y. Emperor Jiaquing's seals 50 45
Nos. 4924/5 were issued in se-tenant pairs within the sheet.

2004. *Meconopsis*. Multicoloured.
4926 80f. (1) Type **1148** 20 15
4927 80f. (2) *Meconopsis racemosa* 20 15
4928 80f. (3) *Meconopsis punicea* 20 15
4929 2y. *Meconopsis integrifolia* 50 45

1149 Bronze Age Cucuteni Pot

2004. Cultural Heritage. Multicoloured.
4930 80f. Type **1149** 20 15
4931 80f. Drum supported by phoenixes and tigers . . . 20 15
Stamps of the same design were issued by Romania.

1150 Flag

2004. National Symbols. Multicoloured.
4932 **1150** 80f. scarlet and lemon 20 15
4933 80f. multicoloured (vert) 20 15
DESIGN: No. 4933 Emblem.

1151 Forest, Xing'an Mountain

2004. Landscapes. Multicoloured.
4934 80f. (1) Type **1151** 20 15
4935 80f. (2) Yalu river basin . . 20 15
4936 80f. (3) Reefs, Yellow Sea 20 15
4937 80f. (4) Zhoushan archipelago 20 15
4938 80f. (5) Taiwan coastline . . 20 15
4939 80f. (6) Xisha Islands . . . 20 15
4940 80f. (7) Lake, trees and mountains, Southern Guangxi 20 15
4941 80f. (8) Rain forest, Southern Yunnan 20 15
4942 80f. (9) Mount Qomolangma 20 15
4943 80f. (10) Pamir mountains 20 15
4944 80f. (11) Badain Jaran desert 20 15
4945 80f. (12) Hulun Buir steppe 20 15
MS4946 230 × 146 mm. Nos. 4934/45 4·25 3·50

1152 Jinmao Tower, Shanghai

2004. Architecture. Multicoloured.
4947 80f. Type **1152** 20 15
4948 80f. Park Guell, Barcelona 20 15
Stamps of the same design were issued by Spain.

1153 Woodland

2004. "Festival of Brightness on the River". (painting by Zhang Zeduan). Sheet 236 × 120 mm containing T **1153** and similar horiz designs showing parts of the painting.
MS4949 60f. (1) Type **1153**; 80f. (2) Trees and people on horseback; 80f. (3) Boats at riverbank; 80f. (4) Passenger boats; 80f. (5) Bridge; 80f. (6) Houses and boats on river; 80f. (7) Trees, wagon and buildings; 1y. (8) Tower; 2y. (9) Town crossroads . . . . . . 2·50 2·20

1153a Bird

2004.
4949a **1153a** 80f. multicoloured . . 20 15

1154 Aiwan Pavilion, Changsha, Hunan Province

1155 Yi Ying Tablet

2004. Pavilions. Multicoloured.
4950 80f. (1) Type **1154** 20 15
4951 80f. (2) Pipa, Jiujiang, Jiangxi province 20 15
4952 80f. (3) Orchid, Shaoxing, Zhejiang province 20 15
4953 80f. (4) Zuiweng, Chuzhou, Anhui province 20 15

2004. Calligraphy. Zuoshu (official script). Showing inscribed tablets. Each black, silver and red.
4954 80f. (1) Type **1155** 20 15
4955 80f. (2) Zhang Qian 20 15
4956 80f. (3) Cao Quan 20 15
4957 80f. (4) Shimen ode 20 15

1156 Rooster

2005. New Year. "Year of the Rooster".
4958 **1156** 80f. multicoloured . . . 30 25

1157 Tower

2005. Completion of Gas Pipeline from Tarim to Baihe. Multicoloured.
4959 80f. Type **1157** 20 15
4960 3y. Pipeline 75 60

1158 North Gate, Taipei

2005. Taiwanese Architecture. Multicoloured.
4961 80f. (1) Type **1158** 20 15
4962 80f. (2) Confucius Temple, Tainan 20 15
4963 80f. (3) Longshan Temple, Lugang 20 15
4964 80f. (4) Erkunshen Fort, Tainan 20 15
4965 1y.50 (5) Matsu Temple, Penghu 40 35

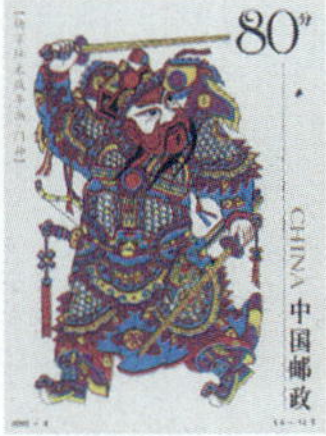
1159 "Door God"

1161 Great Wall

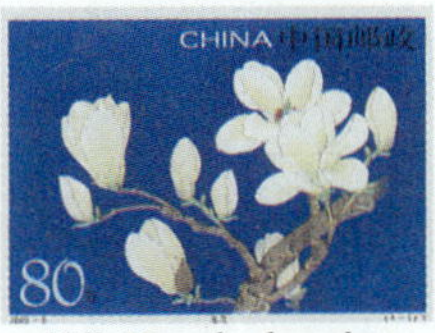
1160 *Magnolia dennudata*

2005. Yangjiabu New Year Pictures (woodcut prints). Multicoloured.
4966 80f. (1) Type **1159** 20 15
4967 80f. (2) "Abundance for Years Running" 20 15

4968 80f. (3) "Good News on New Year's Day" 20 15
4969 80f. (4) "Goddess strewing Flowers from Heaven" . . 20 15
MS4970 150 × 90 mm. Nos. 4966/9 1·50 1·20

2005. Magnolias. Multicoloured.
4971 80f. (1) Type **1160** 20 15
4972 80f. (2) *Magnolia delavayi* 20 15
4973 80f. (3) *Magnolia grandiflora* 20 15
4974 80f. (4) *Magnolia liliflora* . . 20 15

2005.
4975 **1161** 80f. multicoloured . . . 15 10

1162 Multicoloured Hands

2005. World Earth Day.
4976 **1162** 80f. multicoloured . . . 15 10

1163 Sunrise

2005. Jigong Mountains. Multicoloured.
4977 80f. (1) Type **1163** 15 10
4978 80f. (2) Garden in the clouds 15 10
4979 80f. (3) Moon pond 15 10
4980 80f. (4) Black Dragon waterfall 15 10

1164 "80" **1165** "Magnolias" (Chen Hongshou)

2005. 80th Anniv of Trade Union Federation.
4981 **1164** 80f. multicoloured . . . 15 10

2005. Paintings. Multicoloured.
4982 80f. Type **1165** 15 10
4983 80f. "Flower Vase in a Window Niche" (Ambrosius Bosschaert) 15 10
Stamps of a similar design were issued by Liechtenstein.

1166 Tiger Beach

2005. Dalian Coast. Multicoloured.
4984 80f. (1) Type **1166** 15 10
4985 80f. (2) Bangchui island . . 15 10
4986 80f. (3) Golden pebble beach 15 10
4987 80f. (4) Lushunkou 15 10

1167 Emblem

2005. Centenary of Fudan University.
4988 **1167** 80f. multicoloured . . . 15 10

1168 *Emperor's New Clothes* **1169** Zheng He

2005. Birth Bicentenary of Hans Christian Andersen (writer). Multicoloured.
4989 60f. (1) Type **1168** 15 10
4990 80f. (2) *The Little Mermaid* 15 10
4991 80f. (3) *Thumbelina* 15 10
4992 80f. (4) *The Little Match Girl* 15 10
4993 80f. (5) *The Ugly Duckling* . 15 10

2005. 600th Anniv of the Voyages of Zheng He (Ma Sanbao). Multicoloured.
4994 80f. (1) Type **1169** 15 10
4995 80f. (2) Map and pavilions 15 10
4996 80f. (3) Navigational instrument 15 10
MS4997 139 × 80 mm. 6y. Nine-masted "Treasure ship" (71 × 50 mm) . . . . 1·00 1·00
Stamps of a similar design were issued by Hong Kong and Macau.

1170 Southern Hall

2005. Centenary of Nantong Museum. Mult.
4998 80f. (1) Type **1170** 15 10
4999 80f. (2) Central Hall 15 10

1171 Red-crowned Crane and Chick

2005. Xianghai Nature Reserve. Multicoloured.
5000 80f. (1) Type **1171** 15 10
5001 80f. (2) Cranes in flight . . 15 10
5002 80f. (3) Ruddy shelduck . . 15 10
5003 80f. (4) Golden eagle . . . 15 10

1172 Yang Jingyu

2005. Generals (1st issue). Multicoloured.
5004 80f. (1) Type **1172** 15 10
5005 80f. (2) Zuo Quan 15 10
5006 80f. (3) Peng Xuefeng . . . 15 10
5007 80f. (4) Luo Binghui 15 10
5008 80f. (5) Guan Xiangying . . 15 10
See also Nos. 5022/31.

1173 Soldiers with Machine Guns

2005. 60th Anniv of End of World War II. Multicoloured.
5009 80f. (1) Type **1173** 15 10
5010 80f. (2) Soldier blowing bugle 15 10
5011 80f. (3) Normandy landings 15 10
5012 80f. (4) Capture of Berlin 15 10
MS5013 81 × 121 mm. 6p. Dove (vert) . . . . 1·00 1·00

1174 Celebration

2005. 40th Anniv of Tibet Autonomous Region.
5014 **1174** 80f. multicoloured . . . 15 10

1175 Early Actor

2005. Centenary of Chinese Cinema.
5015 **1175** 80f. multicoloured . . . 15 10

1176 Chinese Script

2005. "Five Happiness arrive".
5016 **1176** 80f. multicoloured . . . 15 10

1177 Golden Summit

2005. Fanjing Mountain Nature Reserve. Multicoloured.
5017 80f. (1) Type **1177** 15 10
5018 80f. (2) Mushroom Rock . . 15 10
5019 80f. (3) Broadleaf forest . . 15 10
5020 80f. (4) Heiwan River . . . 15 10

1178 Waterwheel, China

2005. Waterwheels and Windmills. Multicoloured.
5021 80f. (1) Type **1178** 15 10
5022 80f. (2) Windmill, Netherlands 15 10
Stamps of the same design were issued by Netherlands.

1179 Su Yu

2005. Generals (2nd issue). Each black, grey and red.
5023 80f. (1) Type **1179** 15 10
5024 80f. (2) Xu Haidong 15 10
5025 80f. (3) Huang Kecheng . . 15 10
5026 80f. (4) Chen Geng 15 10
5027 80f. (5) Tan Zheng 15 10
5028 80f. (6) Xiao Jinguang . . . 15 10
5029 80f. (7) Zhang Yunyi . . . 15 10
5030 80f. (8) Luo Ruiqing 15 10
5031 80f. (9) Wang Shusheng . . 15 10
5032 80f. (10) Xu Guangda . . . 15 10

1180 Horses

2005. "Goddess of the River Luo" (painting by Gu Kaizhi). Sheet 236 × 120 mm containing T **1180** and similar horiz designs showing parts of the painting.
MS5033 80f. (1) Type **1179**; 80f. (2) Goddess dancing, Cao Zhi and retinue; 80f. (3) Goddess, banners, hills and trees (60 × 30 mm.); 80f. (4) Goddess, trees and flowers (40 × 30 mm.); 80f. (5) Cao Zhi seated with retinue (60 × 30 mm.); 80f. (6) Goddess with scarf and Cao Zhi (60 × 30 mm.); 80f. (7) Goddess leaving (60 × 30 mm.); 80f. (8) Boat; 80f. (9) Cao Zhi seated with two attendants (40 × 30 mm.); 80f. (10) Cao Zhi leaving . . . . 2·20 2·20

1181 Musicians

2005. 50th Anniv of Xinjiang Uygur Autonomous Region. Multicoloured.
5034 80f. (1) Type **1181** 15 10
5035 80f. (2) Dancers 15 10
5036 80f. (3) Women carrying food 15 10
Nos. 5034/6 were issued together, se-tenant, forming a composite design.

1182 Stylized "10"

2005. 10th National Games, Jiangsu Province. Sheet 130 × 90 mm.
MS5037 **1182** 6y. multicoloured 1·00 1·00

1183 *Panthera pardus*

2005. Carnivores. Multicoloured.
5038 80f. Type **1183** 15 10
5039 80f. Puma concolor 15 10
Stamps of the same design were issued by Canada.

1185 Ceramics

2005. Chengtoushan Archaeological Site.
5041 **1185** 80f. multicoloured . . . 15 10

1187 Emblem

2005. Olympic Games, Beijing. Designs showing games emblem and mascots.

5043 80f. (1) Type **1187** 15 10
5044 80f. (2) Beibei 15 10
5045 80f. (3) Jingjing 15 10
5046 80f. (4) Huanhuan 15 10
5047 80f. (5) Yingying 15 10
5048 80f. (6) Nini 15 10

1188 Dog

2006. New Year. Year of the Dog.

5049 **1188** 80f. multicoloured . . . 25 15

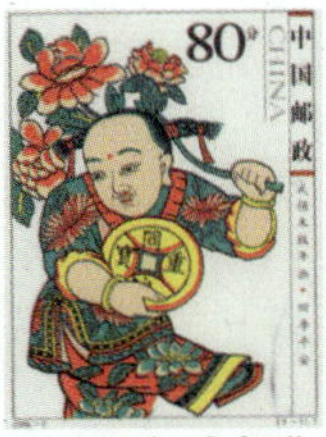

1189 "Being Safe all Year Round" **1190** Fish Lantern

2006. Wuqiang New Year Pictures (woodcut prints). Multicoloured.

5050 80f. (1) Type **1189** 15 10
5051 80f. (2) "Five blessings approach your door" . . 15 10
5052 80f. (3) "Flower of prosperity blossoms" . . 15 10
5053 80f. (4) "Lion rolling embroidered ball" . . . 15 10
MS5054 173 × 80 mm. Nos. 5050/3 1·00 1·00

2006. Chinese Lanterns. Multicoloured.

5055 80f. (1) Type **1190** 15 10
5056 80f. (2) Chinese white cabbage lantern 15 10
5057 80f. (3) Lotus lantern . . . 15 10
5058 80f. (4) Dragon and phoenix lantern 15 10
5059 1w.50 (5) Butterfly lantern 35 20

1191 Rainbow, Field and Animals **1193** *Ginkgo biloba*

1192 Yangdi

2006. Abolition of Agricultural Tax.

5060 **1191** 80f. multicoloured . . . 15 10

2006. Lijiang River. Multicoloured.

5061 80f. (1) Type **1192** 15 10
5062 80f. (2) Langshi 15 10
5063 80f. (3) Huangbu 15 10
5064 80f. (4) Xingping 15 10

Nos. 5061/4 were issued together, se-tenant, forming a composite design.

2006. Endangered Species. Trees. Multicoloured.

5065 80f. (1) Type **1193** 15 10
5066 80f. (2) *Glyptostrobus pensilis* 15 10
5067 80f. (3) *Davidia involucrate* 15 10
5068 80f. (4) *Liriodendron chinense* 15 10

1194 Pekinese

2006. Dogs. Multicoloured.

5069 (1) 80f. Type **1194** 15 10
5070 (2) 80f. Pug (vert) 15 10
5071 (3) 80f. Chow chow 15 10
5072 (4) 80f. Tibetan mastiff (vert) 15 10

1195 Gateway

2006. Qingcheng Mountain. Multicoloured.

5073 (1) 60f. Type **1195** 10 10
5074 (2) 80f. Path 15 10
5075 (3) 80f. Temple 15 10
5076 (4) 80f. Spring 15 10

1196 Sakyamuni

2006. Yungang Grottoes. Multicoloured.

5077 (1) 80f. Type **1196** 15 10
5078 (2) 80f. Bodhisattva of Offering 15 10
5079 (3) 80f. Head of Bodhisattva 15 10
5080 (4) 80f. Xieshi Bodhisattva 15 10
MS5081 80 × 120 mm. 6y. Sakyamuni (40 × 60 mm) . . . 1·50 1·50

1197 Green Dragon Mountain Stream

2006. Tianzhu Mountain. Multicoloured.

5082 (1) 60f. Type **1197** 10 10
5083 (2) 80f. Terrace 15 10
5084 (3) 80f. Sanzu Temple . . . 15 10
5085 (4) 80f. Qingtian Peak . . . 15 10

1198 Liang Xi (forestry)

2006. Scientists. Multicoloured.

5086 (1) 80f. Type **1198** 15 10
5087 (2) 80f. Mao Yisheng (bridges) 15 10
5088 (3) 80f. Yan Jici (physics) 15 10
5089 (4) 80f. Zhou Peiyuan (physics) 15 10

1199 Dagu Lighthouse

2006. Lighthouses. Multicoloured.

5090 (1) 80f. Type **1199** 15 10
5091 (2) 80f. Guishan 15 10
5092 (3) 80f. Wusongkou 15 10
5093 (4) 80f. Mulantou 15 10

Nos. 5090/3 were issued together, se-tenant, forming a composite design.

1200 Geospace Double Star Exploration

2006. 50th Anniv of Chinese Space Programme. Multicoloured.

5094 (1) 80f. Type **1200** 15 10
5095 (2) 80f. Shenzhou-VI manned space ship . . . 15 10

Nos. 5094/5 were issued together, se-tenant, forming a composite design.

1201 Empire Lasting Forever Gold Cup **1202** Gao Junyu

2006. Gold and Silver Ware. Multicoloured.

5096 (1) 80f. Type **1201** 15 10
5097 (2) 80f. Baroque tankard . . 15 10

Stamps of the same design were issued by Poland.

2006. Early Leaders of Chinese Communist Party. Each black and brown.

5098 (1) 80f. Type **1202** 15 10
5099 (2) 80f. Wang Hebo 15 10
5100 (3) 80f. Su Zhaozheng . . . 15 10
5101 (4) 80f. Peng Pai 15 10
5102 (5) 80f. Deng Zhongxia . . 15 10

1203 Crossing Kekexili

2006. Opening of Qinghai-Tibet Railway to Traffic. Multicoloured.

5103 (1) 80f. Type **1203** 15 10
5104 (2) 80f. Crossing Danggula mountains 15 10
5105 (3) 80f. Lhasa railway station 15 10

1204 Snow-covered Mountains and Kanasi Lake

2006. Kanasi Nature Reserve. Multicoloured.

5106 (1) 80f. Type **1204** 15 10
5107 (2) 80f. Trees, Crouching Dragon Bend 15 10
5108 (3) 80f. Deer and Celestial Bend 15 10
5109 (3) 80f. Trees in autumn, Moon Bend 15 10

1205 Cheng Heng's Seismometer and Seismograph

2006. Earthquake Awareness and Detection.

5110 **1205** 80f. multicoloured . . . 15 10

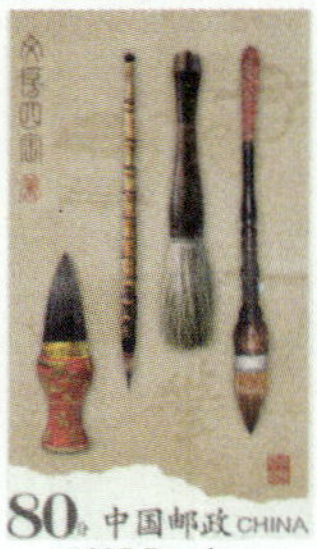

1207 Brushes

2006. Calligraphy. Multicoloured.

5115 (1) 80f. Type **1207** 15 10
5116 (2) 80f. Ink stick 15 10
5117 (3) 80f. Paper and book . . 15 10
5118 (4) 80f. Ink slab 15 10

1208 Emblem

2006. 50th Anniv of Returned Overseas Chinese Federation.

5119 **1208** 80f. multicoloured . . . 15 10

1209 Piano

2006. Musical Instruments. Multicoloured.

5120 80f. Type **1209** 15 10
5121 80f. Guqin 15 10

Stamps of a similar design were issued by Austria.

1210 "100"

2006. 100th Export Commodities Fair.

5122 **1210** 80f. multicoloured . . . 15 10

1211 Setting Out

2006. 70th Anniv of Long March by Communist Army. Multicoloured.

5123 (1) 80f. Type **1211** 15 10
5124 (2) 80f. Zunyi conference . . 15 10
5125 (3) 80f. On Luding Bridge 15 10
5126 (4) 80f. Crossing marshy grasslands 15 10
MS5127 120 × 90 mm. 6y. Joining forces in Jinggangshan (80 × 50 mm) . . . . 1·00 1·00

1212 Flags

2006. 15th Anniv of Diplomatic Relations with Association of Southeast Asian Nations.

5128 **1212** 80f. multicoloured . . . 15 10

1212a Fish

2006. New Year Stamps. Multicoloured.
5129 (1) 80f. Type **1212a** 15 10
5130 (2) 80f. 3y. Greetings . . . 50 30

1213 Emblem

2006. China-Africa Forum.
5131 **1213** 80f. multicoloured . . . 15 10

1214 Home of Sun Yat-sen

2006. 140th Birth Anniv of Sun Yat-sen. Multicoloured.
5132 (1) 80f. Type **1214** 15 10
5133 (2) 80f. Zhongshan Mausoleum 15 10
5134 (3) 80f. Dr.Sun Yat-sen Memorial Hall 15 10
5135 (4) 80f. 1y.50 Zhongshan University 25 15

1214a Chinese monal

2006. Birds. Multicoloured.
5135a 40f. Type **1214a** 10 10
5135b 1y.20 Taiwan 20 20

1215 Boy on Horseback

2006. "Steed" (scroll painting). Design showing parts of the painting. Multicoloured.
5136 (1) 80f. 1y.20 Type **1215** . . 20 10
5137 (2) 80f. 1y.20 Zhi Dun (monk), scholar and servant 20 10
Nos. 5136/7were issued together, se-tenant, forming a composite design of part of the painting.

1216 Wu Lanfu

2006. Birth Centenary of Wu Lanfu (Vice-Chairman of 5th CPPCC National Committee 1978–83).
5138 **1216** 1y.20 multicoloured . . 20 10

1217 High Speed Locomotive

2006. Railway Expansion. Multicoloured.
5139 (1) 80f. 1y.20 Type **1217** . . 20 10
5140 (2) 80f. 1y.20 Industrial transport train 20 10
5141 (3) 80f. 1y.20 Agricultural transport truck 20 10
5142 (4) 80f. 1y.20 Dockyard railway 20 10
MS5143 126 × 76 mm. 6y. High speed train (90 × 40 mm) . . . 1·00 1·00

1218 Dove and Emblems

2006. 110th Anniv of Postal Service.
5144 **1218** 1y.20 multicoloured . . 20 10

1219 Pig and Piglets

2007. New Year. Year of the Pig.
5145 **1219** 1y.20 multicoloured . . 20 10

1220 Emblem

1221 Ta Xue Xun Mei

2007. Changchun 2007–Asian Winter Games.
5146 **1220** 1y.20 multicoloured . . 20 10

2007. Shiwan Pottery. Multicoloured.
5147 (1) 80f. 1y.20 Type **1221** . . 20 10
5148 (2) 80f. 1y.20 Wang Zhaojun Chu Sai 20 10

1222 "Divine Birds of the Sun"

2007. Greetings Stamp.
5149 **1222** 1y.20 multicoloured . . 20 10

1223 Zuo Zuo Ti Dao

2007. Mianzhu Wood Engravings. Multicoloured.
5150 (1) 80f. 1y.20 Type **1223** . . 20 10
5151 (2) 80f. 1y.20 Mu Guiying 20 10
5152 (3) 80f. 1y.20 Shuang Xi Tong Zi 20 10
5153 (4) 80f. 1y.20 Zhang Xian She Gou 20 10

1224 Lin Xiangru

2007. Sheng Jue of Beijing Opera. Multicoloured.
5154 (1) 80f. Type **1224** 10 10
5155 (2) 80f. 1y.20 Song Shijie . . 20 10
5156 (3) 80f. 1y.20 Zhou Yu . . 20 10
5157 (4) 80f. 1y.20 Xu Xian . . . 20 10
5158 (5) 80f. 1y.20 Gao Chong 20 10
5159 (6) 80f. 1y.20 Ren Tanghui 20 10

1225 Mounted Messenger

2007. Postal Savings Bank.
5160 **1225** 1y.20 multicoloured . . 1·00 60

1226 "Look on Waterfall under Pine"

2007. Paintings by Li Keran. Multicoloured.
5161 (1) 1y.20 Type **1226** 30 10
5162 (2) 1y.20 "Thousands of Mountains turn Red" . . 30 10
5163 (3) 1y.20 "Looking on Picture" 30 10
5164 (4) 1y.20 "Setting Crane Free" 30 10
5165 (5) 1y.20 "Grazing Cattle in Pond" 30 10
5166 (6) 1y.20 "Raining in Jiangnan" 30 10

1227 Masks

2007. Centenary of Modern Chinese Theatre.
5167 **1227** 1y.20 multicoloured . . 1·00 60

1228 He Garden

2007. Yangzhou Gardens. Multicoloured.
5168 (1) 1y.20 Type **1228** 35 10
5169 (2) 1y.20 Ge Garden 35 10
5170 (3) 1y.20 Xu Garden 35 10

1229 Dragon Dance (Indonesia)

1229a Torch Relay Emblem

2007. Traditional Dances. Multicoloured.
5171 (1) 1y.20 Type **1229** 50 30
5172 (2) 1y.20 Lion dance (China) 50 30

Stamps of a similar design were issued by Indonesia.

2007. Personalised Stamp.
5172a **1229a** 1y.20 multicoloured 1·00 60

1230 Sports

2007. 60th Anniv of Inner Mongolian Autonomous Region. Multicoloured.
5173 (1) 1y.20 Type **1230** 50 30
5174 (2) 1y.20 Women performers 50 30
MS5175 120 × 70 mm. Nos. 5173/4 1·00 1·00

1231 Zhouling Mausoleum

1233 Father and Children

1232 Emblem

2007. Qing Dynasty Mausoleums. Multicoloured.
5176 (1) 1y.20 Type **1231** 35 10
5177 (2) 1y.20 Xiaoling 35 10
5178 (3) 1y.20 Tailing 35 10

2007. Centenary of Tongji University.
5179 **1232** 1y.20 multicoloured . .

2007. Kong Rong and the Pears (tale of unselfishness). Multicoloured. (a) Ordinary gum.
5180 (1) 1y.20 Type **1233** 35 10
5181 (2) 1y.20 Mother and children 25 10

(b) Self-adhesive.
5182 (1) 1y.20 As Type **1233** . . 35 10
5183 (2) 1y.20 As No. 5181 . . . 35 10
Nos. 5180/1 and 5182/3 were each issued together, se-tenant forming a composite design of father, mother and children.

1234 Chongqing

2007. Development of Chongqing. Multicoloured.
5184 (1) 1y.20 Type **1234** 50 30
5185 (2) 1y.20 Road interchange 50 30
Nos. 5184/5 were issued together, se-tenant, forming a composite design.

1235 Heilong Mountain

2007. Wudalianchi National Park. Multicoloured.
5186 (1) 1y.20 Type **1235** 35 10
5187 (2) 1y.20 Sanchi Pool . . . 35 10
5188 (3) 1y.20 Sea of Rock . . . 35 10

1236 Flag, Doves and 'Forever Blooming Bauhinia' (sculpture) (symbol of Hong Kong)

2007. 10th Anniv of Re-unification of Hong Kong and China. Multicoloured.
5189 (1) 1y.20 Type **1236** 35 10
5190 (2) 1y.20 'CEPA' 35 10
5191 (3) 1y.50 Towers and bridge 35 10
MS5191a 110 × 150 mm. Nos. 5189/91 and No. 1459 of Hong Kong . . . . 1·40 1·40

1237 Yang Shangkun

1238a Emblem

1238 San Panwei

2007. Birth Centenary of Yang Shangkun (president 1988–93). Multicoloured.
5192 (1) 1y.20 Type **1237** 50 30
5193 (2) 1y.20 As older man (*horiz*) 50 30

2007. Nanji Island Nature Reserves. Multicoloured.
5194 (1) 1y.20 Type **1238** 35 10
5195 (2) 1y.20 Longchuan reef . . 35 10
5196 (3) 1y.50 Da Sha'ao 35 10

2007. Personalised Stamp. 80th Anniv of People's Liberation Army (1st issue).
5197 **1238a** 1y.20 multicoloured 1·00 60
See also Nos. 5199/5202.

1239 Western Xia Dynasty Bronze Plate (½-size illustration. Actual size 61 × 40 mm)

2007. All China Philatelic Federation Congress. Sheet 121 × 80 mm.
MS5198 **1239** 6y. multicoloured 1·00 1·00

1240 Soldier, Sailor and Airman

1241 Beibei diving

2007. 80th Anniv of People's Liberation Army (2nd issue). Multicoloured.
5199 (1) 1y.20 Type **1240** 25 10
5200 (2) 1y.20 Soldier wearing fatigues 25 10
5201 (3) 1y.20 Soldier wearing helmet and flak jacket . . 25 10
5202 (4) 1y.20 Women soldiers 25 10

2007. Olympic Games, Beijing. Showing mascots. Multicoloured.
5203 (1) 1y.20 Type **1241** 30 10
5204 (2) 1y.20 Jingjing shooting 30 10
5205 (3) 1y.20 Yingying pole vaulting (athletics) 30 10
5206 (4) 1y.20 Nini playing volleyball 30 10
5207 (5) 1y.20 Huanhuan riding BMX cycle 30 10
5208 (6) 1y.20 Jingjing weightlifting 30 10
See also Nos. 5043/8.

1242 Hot Sea, Zaotong Valley

2007. Geothermal Volcanoes, Tengcheng. Mult.
5209 (1) 1y.20 Type **1242** 35 10
5210 (2) 1y.20 Group of volcanoes (vert) 35 10
5211 (3) 1y.20 Celestial Pillar Valley (vert) 35 10

1243 Da Chibi

2007. Jin Hu (Golden Lake). Multicoloured.
5212 (1) 1y.20 Type **1243** 50 30
5213 (2) 1y.20 Maoer Mountain 50 30

1244 Emblem

2007. Federation Internationale de Football Association Women's World Cup Football Championships, China.
5214 **1244** 1y.20 multicoloured . . 1·00 60

1245 Emblem

2007. Special Olympics Summer Games, China.
5215 **1245** 1y.20 multicoloured . . 1·00 60

1246 Zhang Fei Temple

2007. Historic Sites, Three Gorges. Multicoloured.
5216 (1) 1y.20 Type **1246** 25 10
5217 (2) 1y.20 Pagoda, Shibaozhai Village (vert) 25 10
5218 (3) 1y.20 Archway and street, Old Dachang (vert) 25 10
5219 (4) 1y.20 Quyuan's mausoleum 25 10

1247 First National Congress Site

2007. 17th Chinese Communist Party National Congress. Multicoloured.
5220 (1) 1y.20 Type **1247** 50 30
5221 (2) 1y.20 Site of Second Plenary Session 50 30
MS5222 135 × 87 mm. 6y. Dove (60 × 40 mm) . . . . 1·40 1·40

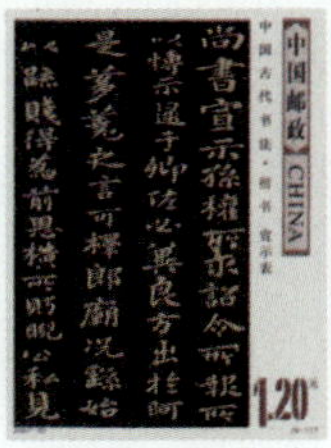

1248 'Proclamation'

2007. Calligraphy. Multicoloured.
5223 (1) 1y.20 Type **1248** . . . 30 10
5224 (2) 1y.20 'Zang Menglong' 30 10
5225 (3) 1y.20 'Sweet Spring at Jiucheng Palace' 30 10
5226 (4) 1y.20 Preface for 'Sacred Religion at Wild Goose Pagoda' 30 10
5227 (5) 1y.20 Yan Qinli stele . . 30 10
5228 (6) 1y.20 'Mysterious' . . . 30 10

1249 Mount Gongga (China)

2007. Mountains. Multicoloured.
5229 (1) 1y.20 Type **1249** 50 30
5230 (2) 1y.20 Popocatepetl (Mexico) 50 30
Stamps of a similar design were issued by Mexico.

1250 Satellite in Lunar Orbit

2007. Successful Maiden Flight of Cheng E 1.
5231 **1250** 1y.20 multicoloured . . 1·00 60

1251 Emblem

2007. EXPO 2010, Shanghai.
5232 **1251** (1) 1y.20 emerald, black and yellow 50 30
5233 – (2) 1y.20 blue, black and ultramarine . . . 50 30
DESIGNS: 5232, Type **1251**; 5233, Mascot.

1252 Agricultural University Gymnasium

2007. Olympic Games, Beijing. Venues. Mult.
5234 (1) 80f. Type **1252** 25 10
5235 (2) 1y.20 Laoshan mountain bike course 40 25
5236 (3) 1y.20 National indoor stadium 40 25
5237 (4) 1y.20 Peking university gymnasium 40 25
5238 (5) 1y.20 National aquatics centre 40 25
5239 (6) 1y.20 Qingdao Olympic sailing centre 40 25
MS5240 140 × 85 mm. 6y. National stadium (pentagon) (65 × 61 mm) 1·60 1·60
See also Nos. 5043/8 and 5203/8.

1253 Rat

2008. New Year. Year of the Rat.
5241 **1253** 1y.20 multicoloured . . 40 25

1254 *Gate Guardian General Standing with Cane*

1255 Zhang Fei

2008. Zhuxian New Year Wood Engravings. Multicoloured.
5242 1y.20 Type **1254** 40 25
5243 1y.20 *Give Her Son a Lecture* 40 25
5244 1y.20 *Come Back With Fruitful Result* 40 25
5245 1y.20 *Chivalrous Women* . . 40 25

2008. Jing Roles of Beijing Opera. Multicoloured.
5246 80f. Type **1255** 25 10
5247 1y.20 Xu Yanzhao 40 25
5248 1y.20 Bao Zheng 40 25
5249 1y.20 Lian Po 40 25
5250 1y.20 Cao Cao 40 25
5251 1y.20 Yang Yansi 40 25

1256 *Urocissa caerulea* (Formosan blue magpie)

2008. Birds. Sheet 145 × 171 mm containing T **1256** and similar vert designs. Multicoloured.
MS5252 1y.20 × 6, Type **1256**; *Emberiza koslowi* (Koslow's bunting); *Garrulax sukatschewi* (black-fronted laughing thrush); *Tragopan caboti* (Cabot's tragopan); *Chrysolophus pictus* (golden pheasant); *Podoces biddulphi* (Biddulph's ground jay) 2·50 2·50
The stamps and margins of **MS**5252 form a composite design.

1257 Profiles

2008. 11th National People's Congress.
5253 **1257** 1y.20 multicoloured . . 40 25

1258 Huanhuan carrying Torch

2008. Olympic Games, Beijing. Multicoloured.
5254 1y.20 Type **1258** 50 35
5255 3y. Relay torch (vert) . . . 50 35
MS5256 140 × 90 mm. Nos. 5254/5 1·00 1·00
Nos. 5257/8 have been left for self-adhesive stamps, not yet received.

MILITARY POST STAMPS

M 225

M 892 Armed Forces

1953.
M1593 **M 225** $800 yellow, red and orange . . . 90·00 46·00
M1594 $800 yellow, red and purple . . . £800
M1595 $800 yellow, red and blue £53000

Nos. M1593/5 were issued for the use of the Army, Air Force and Navy respectively.

1995. No gum.
M3998 M **892** 20f. multicoloured 8·50 1·30

POSTAGE DUE STAMPS

D 192

D 233

1950.
D1459 D **192** $100 blue 15 15
D1460 $200 blue 15 15
D1461 $500 blue 15 15
D1462 $800 blue 23·00 15
D1463 $1,000 blue 40 35
D1464 $2,000 blue 40 35
D1465 $5,000 blue 25 50
D1466 $8,000 blue 25 85
D1467 $10,000 blue 60 2·10

1954.
D1628 D **233** $100 red 2·10 20
D1629 $200 red 60 20
D1630 $500 red 2·10 20
D1631 $800 red 20 20
D1632 $1,600 red 20 20

CHINA—TAIWAN (FORMOSA)

A. CHINESE PROVINCE

The island of Taiwan was ceded by China to Japan in 1895 and was returned to China in 1945 after the defeat of Japan. From 1949 Taiwan was controlled by the remnants of the Nationalist Government under Chiang Kai-shek.

1945. 100 sen = 1 yen.
1947. 100 cents = 1 yuan (C.N.C.).

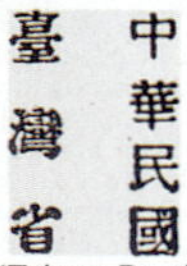
(**1**) "Taiwan Province, Chinese Republic"

1945. Optd as Type **1**. (a) On stamps as Nos. J1/3 of Japanese Taiwan. Imperf.
1 J **1** 3s. red 70 3·00
2 5s. green 80 55
3 10s. blue 1·20 55
4 30s. blue 4·00 5·00
5 40s. purple 4·50 4·00
6 50s. grey 3·75 3·75
7 1y. green 4·25 5·50

(b) On stamps of Japan. Imperf.
8 **87** 5y. olive (No. 424) 18·00 18·00
9 **88** 10y. purple (No. 334) 26·00 26·00

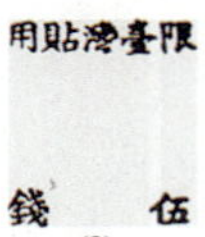
(**2**)

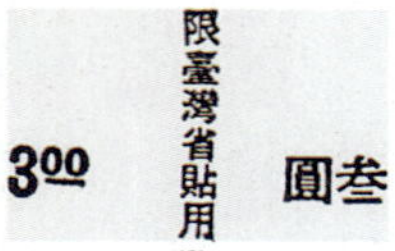
(**3**)

1946. Stamps of China surch as T **2** with two to four characters in lower line denoting value.
10 – 2s. on 2c. blue (No. 509) 20 90
11 – 5s. on 5c. orange (No. 513) 20 55
12 **60** 10s. on 4c. lilac 20 50
13 – 30s. on 15c. pur (No. 517) 20 55
19 **107** 50s. on $20 red 35 90
16 **58** 65s. on $20 green 40 1·90
15 – $1 on 20c. blue (No. 519) 20 1·30
17 **58** $1 on $30 brown 25 1·30
65 **60** $2 on 2½c. red 55 2·30
18 **58** $2 on $50 orange 45 55
20 **107** $3 on $100 red 20 50
77 **103** $5 on $40 orange 80 1·20
78 **107** $5 on $50 violet 80 30
79 $5 on $70 orange 70 2·75
80 $5 on $100 red 80 55
21 $5 on $200 green 20 50
67 **82** $10 on $3 yellow 2·00 3·25
82 **118** $10 on $150 blue 55 80
22 **107** $10 on $500 green 25 40
66 **72** $20 on 2c. green 80 80
71 **89** $20 on $3 red 2·50 2·10
83 **118** $20 on $250 violet 1·20 1·00
23 **107** $20 on $700 brown 80 70
68 **82** $50 on 50c. green 2·75 1·20
24 **107** $50 on $1,000 red 1·50 1·50
72 **89** $100 on $20 pink 1·20 55
73 **94** $100 on $20 red £700
25 **107** $100 on $3,000 blue 3·25 1·00
74 **94** $200 on $10 blue 2·00 1·20
70 **72** $500 on $30 purple 6·75 2·40
81 **107** $600 on $100 red 11·50 3·25
69 **82** $800 on $4 brown 6·00 4·75
85 **118** $1,000 on $20,000 red 2·50 2·00
75 **94** $5,000 on $10 blue 6·75 4·50
76 $10,000 on $20 red 11·00 3·75
84 **118** $200,000 on $3,000 blue £375 29·00

1946. Opening of National Assembly, Nanking. Issue of China surch as Type **3**.
26 **111** 70s. on $20 green 2·00 4·25
27 $1 on $30 blue 2·75 4·75
28 $2 on $50 brown 2·20 4·75
29 $3 on $100 red 2·75 4·75

4 President Chiang Kai-shek (note characters to right of head)

5 Entrance to Dr. Sun Yat-sen Mausoleum (note characters above face value)

1947. President's 60th Birthday.
30 **4** 70s. red 1·30 1·80
31 $1 green 1·80 2·75
32 $2 red 1·80 2·75
33 $3 green 1·80 2·75
34 $7 orange 2·20 3·25
35 $10 red 3·25 3·75

1947. 1st Anniv of Return of Government to Nanking.
36 **5** 50s. green 1·40 1·90
37 $3 blue 1·40 1·90
38 $7.50 red 1·40 1·90
39 $10 brown 1·40 1·90
40 $20 purple 1·40 1·90

For other stamps as Types **4** and **5**, but with different Chinese characters, see N.E. Provinces Types **7** and **9**.

1947. No gum.
41 **169** $1 brown 2·40 25
42 $2 brown 70 25
43 $3 green 70 25
44 $5 orange 70 25
45 $9 blue 70 25
46 $10 red 70 25
47 $20 green 70 35
59 $25 green 95 35
48 $50 purple 70 25
49 $100 blue 70 70
50 $200 brown 70 70
60 $5,000 orange 8·25 55
61 $10,000 green 9·50 2·75
62 $20,000 brown 9·75 3·00
63 $30,000 blue 11·50 80
64 $40,000 brown 10·00 70

6 Sun Yat-sen and Palms

(**7**)

1948. "Re-valuation" surcharges. Surch as T **7**.
51 **6** $25 on $100 blue 1·20 1·70
52 $300 on $3 green 80 35
53 $500 on $7.50 orange 1·20 55
54 $1,000 on 30c. grey 5·50 4·00
55 $1,000 on $3 green 3·50 55
56 $2,000 on $3 green 3·00 55
57 $3,000 on $3 green 4·25 1·10
58 $3,000 on $7.50 orange 65·00 2·30

1949. No value indicated. Stamps of China optd with five Chinese characters, similar to top line of T **2**.
86 **146** (–) Orange (Ord. postage) 1·20 15
87 **147** (–) Green (Air Mail) 5·00 2·50
88 **148** (–) Mauve (Express) 3·25 4·00
89 **149** (–) Red (Registration) 2·50 3·00

PARCELS POST STAMPS

1948. As Type P **112** of China, with six Chinese characters in the sky above the lorry.
P65 $100 green — 55
P66 $300 red — 55
P67 $500 olive — 55
P68 $1,000 black — 55
P69 $3,000 purple — 55

Parcels Post stamps were not on sale in unused condition.

POSTAGE DUE STAMPS

D 7

(D 8)

(D 9)

1948.
D51 D **7** $1 blue 1·10 4·00
D52 $3 blue 1·10 5·50
D53 $5 blue 1·10 4·25
D54 $10 blue 1·10 5·50
D55 $20 blue 1·10 4·25

1949. "Re-valuation" surcharges. Surch as Type D **8**.
D65 D **7** $50 on $1 blue 7·50 37·00
D66 $100 on $3 blue 7·50 10·50
D67 $300 on $5 blue 7·50 9·00
D68 $500 on $10 blue 7·50 8·50

1949. Handstamped with Type D **9**.
D86 **6** $1,000 on $3 green (No. 55) 16·00 16·00
D87 $3,000 on $3 green (No. 57) 24·00 24·00
D88 $5,000 orange (No. 60) 43·00 43·00

B. CHINESE NATIONALIST REPUBLIC

1949. 100 cents = 1 silver yuan (or New Taiwan Yuan).
Silver Yuan Surcharges.

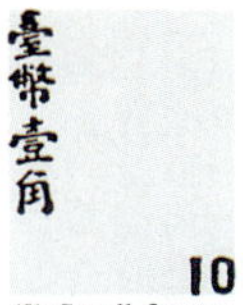
(**8**) Small figures

(**9**) Large figures

1949. Stamps of Taiwan Province surch. (a) With T **8**.
90 **6** 10c. on $50 purple 40·00 4·75

(b) As T **9** (figures at right).
91 **6** 2c. on $30,000 blue 36·00 23·00
92 10c. on $40,000 brown 45·00 23·00

(**10**)

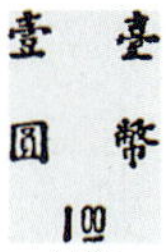
(**11**)

1949. Stamps of North Eastern Provinces (Manchuria), surch as T **10**.
93 **5** 2c. on $44 red 40·00 6·75
95 5c. on $44 red 55·00 11·50
96 10c. on $44 red 48·00 6·75
97 20c. on $44 red 60·00 8·00
98 30c. on $44 red 70·00 16·00
99 50c. on $44 red 85·00 21·00

1950. Surch as T **11** on stamp of China but with no indication of value.
100 **169** $1 on (–) green 90·00 4·75
101 $2 on (–) green £120 10·50
102 $5 on (–) green £1100 48·00
103 $10 on (–) green £1300 75·00
104 $20 on (–) green £3000 £450

1950. Stamps of China surch. (a) As T **8** (figure "5" at left).
105 **118** 5c. on $200,000 purple 4·50 2·75

(b) As T **9** (figures at left).
106 **118** 3c. on $30,000 brown 5·75 3·75
107 3c. on $40,000 green 7·75 4·50
108 3c. on $50,000 blue 6·50 3·75
108a 10c. on $4,000 grey 22·00 5·50
109 10c. on $6,000 purple 17·00 4·00
110 10c. on $20,000 red 13·00 3·25
110a 10c. on $2,000,000 orge 14·00 3·25
110b 20c. on $500,000 mauve 31·00 5·00
110c 20c. on $1,000,000 red 48·00 6·00
110d 30c. on $3,000,000 bistre 60·00 8·75
110e 50c. on $5,000,000 blue £110 8·75

GUM. All the following stamps to No. 616 were issued without gum except where otherwise stated.

12 Koxinga

1950. Rouletted. (a) Postage.
111 **12** 3c. grey 2·20 1·00
112 10c. brown 1·90 20
113 15c. yellow 11·50 5·75
114 20c. green 1·90 15
115 30c. red 40·00 12·00
116 40c. orange 3·25 20
117 50c. brown 6·00 45
118 80c. red 11·50 3·00
119 $1 violet 9·75 50
120 $1.50 green 44·00 6·75
121 $1.60 blue 45·00 90
122 $2 mauve 17·00 65
123 $5 turquoise 90·00 10·50

(b) Air. With character at each side of head.
124 **12** 60c. blue 13·50 7·25

13 Peasant and Ballot Box

15 Peasant and Scroll

1951. Division of Country into Self-governing Districts. Perf or imperf.
125A **13** 40c. red 11·50 50
126A $1 blue 18·00 1·50
127A $1.60 purple 28·00 2·50
128A $2 brown 45·00 6·00
MS128Ba 102 × 71 mm. **13** $2 green. Imperf £300 £325

1951. Silver Yuan surcharges. As T **169** of China but without value, surch.
129 $5 on (–) green 75·00 9·25
130 $10 on (–) green £300 7·25
131 $20 on (–) green £700 25·00
132 $50 on (–) green £700 80·00

1952. Land Tax Reduction. Perf or imperf.
133A **15** 20c. orange 6·75 1·00
134A 40c. green 10·00 85
135A $1 brown 18·00 4·25
136A $1.40 blue 24·00 2·50
137A $2 grey 55·00 33·00
138A $5 red 75·00 7·50

16 President and Rejoicing crowds

(**17**)

1952. 2nd Anniv of Re-election of Pres. Chiang Kai-shek. Flag in red and blue. Eight characters in scroll. Perf or imperf.
139A **16** 40c. red 8·00 50
140A $1 green 15·00 2·75
141A $1.60 orange 26·00 2·00
142A $2 blue 39·00 17·00
143A $5 purple 50·00 4·00

See also Nos. 151/6.

1952. Stamps of China surch. with T **17**.
144 **145** 3c. on 4c. grn (No. 1350) 3·75 3·25
145 3c. on 10c. lilac (No. 1351) 6·00 4·50
146 3c. on 20c. bl (No. 1353) 4·50 3·50
147 3c. on 50c. brown (No. 1354) 9·25 8·25

(**18**)

(**19**)

1953. T **169** of China, but without value, surch as T **18**.
148 $10 on (–) green £150 13·00
149 $20 on (–) green £400 23·00
150 $50 on (–) green £1500 £700

1953. 3rd Anniv of Re-election of Pres. Chiang Kai-shek. As T **16** but eleven characters in scroll. Flag in red and blue. Perf or imperf.
151A 10c. orange 13·00 1·70
152A 20c. green 15·00 1·70
153A 40c. red 16·00 1·40
154A $1.40 blue 37·00 3·50
155A $2 sepia 75·00 5·00
156A $5 purple £130 14·50

1953. Surch as T **19**.
157 **12** 3c. on $1 violet 1·30 1·10
158 10c. on 15c. yellow 8·00 1·30
159 10c. on 30c. red 2·50 95
160 20c. on $1.60 blue 2·75 75

20 Doctor, Nurses and Patients

21 Pres. Chiang Kai-shek

1953. Establishment of Anti-tuberculosis Assn. Cross of Lorraine in red. On paper with coloured network.
161 **20** 40c. brown on stone 10·50 75
162 $1.60 blue on turquoise 34·00 1·40
163 $2 green on yellow 46·00 1·50
164 $5 red on flesh 70·00 9·25

1953.
165 **21** 10c. brown 3·25 20
166 20c. purple 2·75 20
167 40c. green 2·75 20
168 50c. purple 6·00 30
169 80c. brown 15·00 2·00
170 $1 green 8·25 20
171 $1.40 blue 10·00 35
172 $1.60 red 10·00 20
173 $1.70 green 16·00 3·50
174 $2 brown 11·00 20
175 $3 blue £170 6·25
176 $4 turquoise 14·00 95
177 $5 red 13·00 50
178 $10 green 38·00 3·00
179 $20 purple 75·00 6·25

22 Silo Bridge over River Cho-Shui-Chi

23 Sapling, Tree and Plantation

1954. Completion of Silo Bridge. Various frames.

180	**22**	40c. red	15·00	60
181	–	$1.60 blue	85·00	1·20
182	**22**	$3.60 black	45·00	5·75
183	–	$5 mauve	£110	6·75

DESIGN: $1.60, $5, Silo Bridge.

1954. Afforestation Day.

184	**23**	40c. green	13·00	70
185	–	$10 violet	95·00	4·75
186	–	$20 red	34·00	1·10
187	–	$50 blue	60·00	5·75

DESIGNS: $10, Tree plantation and houses; $20, Planting seedling; $50, Map of Taiwan and tree.

24 Runner

25 Douglas DC-6 over City Gate, Taipeh

1954. Youth Day.

188	**24**	40c. blue	22·00	1·60
189		$5 red	70·00	9·50

1954. Air. 15th Anniv of Air Force Day.

190	**25**	$1 brown	13·50	1·00
191	–	$1.60 black	12·00	55
192	–	$5 blue	19·00	1·20

DESIGNS: $1.60, Republic F-84G Thunderjets over Chung Shang Bridge, Taipeh. $5, Doves over Chi Kan Lee (Fort Zeelandia) in Tainan City.

26 Refugees crossing Pontoon Bridge

27 Junk and Bridge

1954. Relief Fund for Chinese Refugees from North Vietnam.

193	**26**	40c.+10c. blue	24·00	4·25
194		$1.60+40c. purple	70·00	27·00
195		$5+$1 red	£110	£130

1954. 2nd Anniv of Overseas Chinese League.

196	**27**	40c. orange	16·00	50
197		$5 blue	13·00	3·75

28 "Chainbreaker"

(29)

1955. Freedom Day.

198	**28**	40c. green	3·50	55
199	–	$1 olive	16·00	6·75
200	–	$1.60 red	13·00	3·75

DESIGNS: $1, Soldier with torch and flag; $1.60, Torch and figures "1.23".

1955. Surch. as T **29**.

201	**12**	3c. on $1 violet	3·00	1·00
202		20c. on 40c. orange	3·25	85

31 Pres. Chiang Kai-shek and Sun Yat-sen Memorial Building

1955. 1st Anniv of President Chiang Kai-shek's Second Re-election.

203	**31**	20c. olive	3·25	30
204		40c. green	3·25	30
205		$2 red	8·75	1·10
206		$7 blue	14·00	1·90
MS206a		147 × 104 mm. Nos. 203/6. Imperf	£170	£130

(32)

33 Air Force Badge

1955. Nos. 116/18, 120 and 124 surch as T **32**. Nos. 212/14 have additional floral ornament below two characters at top.

207	**12**	10c. on 80c. red	3·25	30
208		10c. on $1.50 green	3·25	50
212		20c. on 40c. orange	4·00	30
213		20c. on 50c. brown	4·50	30
214		20c. on 60c. blue	5·00	1·20

1955. Armed Forces' Day.

209	**33**	40c. blue	4·75	50
210		$2 red	18·00	2·10
211		$7 green	19·00	1·80
MS211a		148 × 105 mm. Nos. 209/11. Imperf	£375	£300

35 Flags of U.N. and Taiwan

36 Pres. Chiang Kai-shek

1955. 10th Anniv of UNO.

215	**35**	40c. blue	2·75	35
216		$2 red	6·75	95
217		$7 green	8·00	2·00

1955. President's 69th Birthday. With gum.

218	**36**	40c. brown, blue and red	5·00	50
219		$2 blue, green and red	11·00	1·60
220		$7 green, brown and red	16·00	2·75
MS220a		148 × 105 mm. Nos. 218/20. Imperf. No gum	£130	90·00

37 Sun Yat-sen's Birthplace

(38)

1955. 90th Birth Anniv (1956) of Dr. Sun Yat-sen.

221	**37**	40c. blue	3·25	40
222		$2 brown	7·25	1·20
223		$7 red	10·50	2·10

1956. Nos. 1213 and 1211 of China surch as T **38**.

232B	**148**	3c. on (–) mauve	1·00	25
224	**146**	20c. on (–) orange I	55	25
304		20c. on (–) orange II	60	20

On No. 232 the characters are smaller and there are leaves on either side of the "3".

(I) Surch with Type **38**. (II) The characters are below the figures.

39 Old and Modern Postal Transport

40 Children at Play

1956. 60th Anniv of Postal Service.

225	**39**	40c. red	1·70	20
226		$1 blue	3·25	65
227		$1.60 brown	4·75	45
228		$2 green	7·00	95
MS228a		Two sheets, each 149 × 103 mm. No. 228 in red and in crimson. Imperf. Set of 2 sheets	95·00	70·00

1956. Children's Day.

229	**40**	40c. green	1·30	20
230		$1.60 blue	3·00	40
231		$2 red	4·75	95

42 Earliest and Latest Steam Locomotives

43 Pres. Chiang Kai-shek

1956. 75th Anniv of Chinese Railways.

233	**42**	40c. red	3·50	25
234		$2 blue	6·25	50
235		$8 green	8·75	1·70

1956. 70th Birthday of President Chiang Kai-shek. Various portraits of President. With gum.

236	**43**	20c. orange	3·50	20
237	–	40c. red	5·50	20
238	–	$1 blue	7·75	30
239	–	$1.60 purple	9·50	20
240	–	$2 brown	14·00	45
241	–	$8 turquoise	29·00	85

SIZES—$21\frac{1}{2} \times 30$ mm: 20c., 40c.; $26\frac{1}{2} \times 26\frac{1}{2}$ mm: $1, $1.60; $30 \times 21\frac{1}{2}$ mm: $2, $8.

(44)

(45)

46 Telecommunications Symbols

1956. No. 1212 of China surch with T **44**.

242	**147**	3c. on (–) green	1·00	25

1956. No. 1214 of China surch with T **45**.

243	**149**	10c. on (–) red	1·00	25

1956. 75th Anniv of Chinese Telegraph Service.

244	**46**	40c. blue	85	25
245		$1.40 red	1·40	25
246		$1.60 green	2·40	30
247		$2 brown	4·50	35

47 Map of China

48 Mencius with his Mother

1957. (a) Printed in one colour.

248	**47**	3c. blue	40	20
249		10c. violet	1·20	25
250		20c. orange	1·00	20
251		40c. red	1·20	20
252		$1 brown	2·00	20
253		$1.60 green	4·25	30

(b) With frames in blue.

268	**47**	3c. blue	20	20
269		10c. violet	55	20
270		20c. orange	75	20
271		40c. red	1·10	20
272		$1 brown	3·25	35
273		$1.60 green	3·75	25

1957. Mothers' Teaching.

254	**48**	40c. green	1·10	20
255	–	$3 brown	1·90	60

DESIGN: $3, Marshal Yueh Fei with his mother.

49 Chinese Scout Badges and Rosettes

1957. 50th Anniv of Boy Scout Movement, Jubilee Jamboree and Birth Centenary of Lord Baden-Powell (Founder).

256	**49**	40c. violet	75	25
257		$1 green	1·50	45
258		$1.60 blue	1·90	25

50 Globe, Radio Mast and Microphone

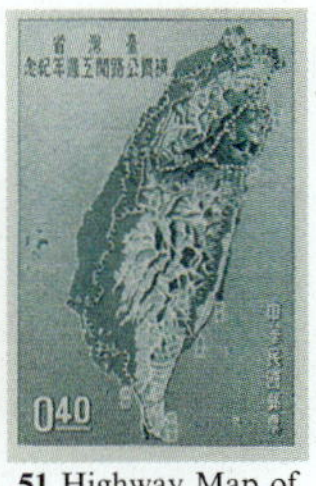
51 Highway Map of Taiwan

1957. 30th Anniv of Chinese Broadcasting Service.

259	**50**	40c. salmon	35	20
260		50c. mauve	85	30
261		$3.50 blue	1·60	60

1957. 1st Anniv of Taiwan Cross-Island Highway Project.

262	**51**	40c. green	2·50	30
263		$1.40 blue	5·50	1·50
264		$2 sepia	7·25	1·80

52 Freighter "Hai Min" and River Vessel "Kiang Foo"

1957. 85th Anniv of China Merchants' Steam Navigation Co.

265	**52**	40c. blue	50	20
266		80c. purple	1·00	70
267		$2.80 red	1·80	1·10

53 "Batocera lineolata" (longhorn beetle)

54 "Phalaenopsis amabilis"

1958. Insects. Multicoloured. With gum.

274	10c. Type **53**	1·00	40
275	40c. "Papilio maraho" (butterfly)	1·10	20
276	$1 Atlas moth	2·00	35
277	$1.40 "Erasmia pulchella" (moth)	3·25	65
278	$1.60 "Cheirotonus macleayi" (beetle)	4·25	40
279	$2 Great mormon (butterfly)	5·25	1·00

1958. Taiwan Orchids. Orchids in natural colours; backgrounds in colours given. With gum.

280	**54**	20c. brown	1·90	25
281	–	40c. violet	2·00	25
282	–	$1.40 purple	3·75	40
283	–	$3 blue	5·25	75

ORCHIDS—VERT: 40c. "Laeliacattleya"; $1.40, "Cycnoches chlorochilon klotzsch". HORIZ: $3, "Dendrobium phalaenopsis".

55 WHO Emblem

56 Presidential Mansion, Taipeh

1958. 10th Anniv of WHO.

284	**55**	40c. blue	40	20
285		$1.60 red	65	30
286		$2 purple	1·20	50

1958.

290a	**56**	$5 green	4·50	25
290b		$5.60 violet	4·50	50
290c		$6 orange	5·00	25
290d		$10 green	7·25	25
290e		$20 red	12·50	30
289		$50 brown	49·00	1·80
290		$100 blue	70·00	4·50

58 Ploughman

1958. 10th Anniv of Joint Commission on Chinese Rural Reconstruction.

291	**58**	20c. green	95	25
292		40c. black	1·20	25
293		$1.40 purple	2·30	25
294		$3 blue	3·75	65

59 President Chiang Kai-shek Reviewing Troops

1958. 72nd Birthday of President Chiang Kai-shek and National Day Review. With gum.

295	**59**	40c. multicoloured	1·00	40

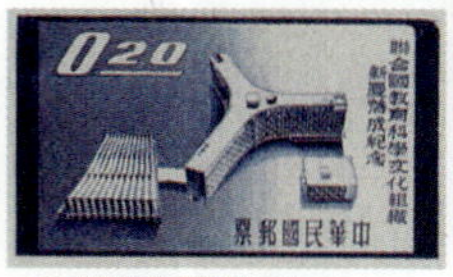

60 UNESCO Headquarters, Paris

61 Flame of Freedom encircling Globe

1958. Inaug of UNESCO Headquarters.
296 **60** 20c. blue 30 25
297 40c. green 50 25
298 $1.40 red 65 35
299 $3 purple 95 75

1958. 10th Anniv of Declaration of Human Rights.
300 **61** 40c. green 30 20
301 60c. sepia 35 20
302 $1 red 55 25
303 $3 blue 75 50

1958. No. 192 surch **350**.
305 $3.50 on $5 blue 4·00 1·60

64 The Constitution

65 Chu Kwang Tower, Quemoy

1958. 10th Anniv of Constitution.
306 **64** 40c. green 65 25
307 50c. purple 1·00 25
308 $1.40 red 1·90 30
309 $3.50 blue 3·50 85

1959.

310 **65** 3c. orange 30 20
311 5c. olive 50 25
312 10c. lilac 35 20
313 20c. blue 40 20
314 40c. brown 45 20
315 50c. turquoise 1·00 20
316 $1 red 1·00 20
317 $1.40 green 2·10 20
318 $2 myrtle 2·30 20
319 $2.80 mauve 4·75 65
320 $3 slate 3·50 20
See also Nos. 367/82f.

66 Slaty-backed Gull

67 ILO Emblem and Headquarters, Geneva

1959. Air. With gum.
321 **66** $8 black, blue and green 4·50 40

1959. 40th Anniv of ILO.
322 **67** 40c. blue 20 20
323 $1.60 brown 30 20
324 $3 green 75 30
325 $5 red 1·20 70

68 Scout Bugler

1959. 10th World Scout Jamboree, Manila.
326 **68** 40c. red 60 20
327 50c. blue 1·10 25
328 $5 green 2·20 75

69 Inscribed Rock on Mt. Tai-wu, Quemoy

1959. Defence of Quemoy (Kinmen) and Matsu Islands, 1958.
329 **69** 40c. brown 40 20
330 – $1.40 blue 70 20
331 – $2 green 1·70 25
332 **69** $3 blue 2·10 40
DESIGN—(41 × 23½ mm): $1.40, $2, Map of Taiwan, Quemoy and Matsu Islands.

70

1959. International Correspondence Week.
333 **70** 40c. blue 60 20
334 $1 red 70 30
335 $2 sepia 85 20
336 $3.50 red 1·10 70

71 National Science Hall

72 Confederation Emblem

1959. Inauguration of Taiwan National Science Hall. With gum.
337 **71** 40c. multicoloured 1·20 25
338 – $3 mult (different view) 2·50 75

1959. 10th Anniv of International Confederation of Free Trade Unions.
339 **72** 40c. green 30 20
340 $1.60 purple 65 35
341 $3 orange 1·20 65

73 Sun Yat-sen and Abraham Lincoln

74 "Bomb Burst" by Thunder Tiger Aerobatic Squadron

1959. 150th Birth Anniv of Lincoln. With gum.
342 **73** 40c. multicoloured 45 30
343 $3 multicoloured 1·00 40

1960. Air. Chinese Air Force Commem. With gum.
344 **74** $1 multicoloured 5·25 45
345 – $2 multicoloured 4·75 35
346 – $5 multicoloured 7·25 55
DESIGNS—HORIZ: (Various aerobatics): $2, Loop; $5, Diamond formation flying over jet fighter.

75 Night Delivery

1960. Introduction of "Prompt Delivery" and "Postal Launch" Services.
347 **75** $1.40 purple 1·20 25
348 $1.60 blue "Yu-Khi" (postal launch) 1·40 45

76 "Uprooted Tree"

79 Winged Tape-reel

77 Cross-Island Highway

1960. World Refugee Year. With gum.
349 **76** 40c. green, brown & black 55 20
350 $3 green, orange & black 1·10 45

1960. Inaug of Taiwan Cross-Island Highway.
351 **77** 40c. green 75 20
352 – $1 blue 2·40 30
353 – $2 purple 1·80 30
354 **77** $3 brown 2·50 40
MS354a 144 × 103 mm. Nos. 352 and 354. Imperf £160 65·00
DESIGN—VERT: $1, $2 Tunnels on Highway.

1960. Visit of Pres. Eisenhower. Nos. 331/2 optd **WELCOME U.S. PRESIDENT DWIGHT D. EISENHOWER 1960** in English and Chinese.
355 – $2 green 1·10 45
356 **69** $3 blue 1·50 50

1960. Phonopost (tape-recordings) Service.
357 **79** $2 red 1·50 1·50

80 "Flowers and Red-billed Blue Magpies" (after Hsiao Yung)

81 Youth Corps Flag and Summer Activities

1960. Ancient Chinese Paintings from Palace Museum Collection (1st series). With gum.
358 – $1 multicoloured 3·75 50
359 – $1.40 multicoloured 7·25 85
360 **80** $1.60 multicoloured 8·25 1·50
361 – $2 multicoloured 12·00 3·00
PAINTINGS—HORIZ: $1, "Two Riders" (after Wei Yen). $1.40, "Two Horses and Groom" (after Han Kan). $2, "A Pair of Green-winged Teals in a Rivulet" (after Monk Hui Ch'ung).
See also Nos. 451/4, 577/80 and 716/19.

1960. Youth Summer Activities.
362 **81** 50c. green 70 25
363 – $3 brown 1·10 55
DESIGN—HORIZ: $3, Youth Corps Flag and other summer activities.

82 "Forest Cultivation"

83 Chu Kwang Tower, Quemoy

1960. 5th World Forestry Congress, Seattle. Multicoloured. With gum.
364 $1 Type **82** 1·50 20
365 $2 "Forest Protection" (trees and sika deer) 2·20 70
366 $3 "Lumber Production" (cable railway) 3·00 50
MS366a 100 × 145 mm. Nos. 364/6 forming a composite design. Imperf. No gum 25·00 19·00

1960. As T **65** but redrawn.
367 **83** 3c. brown 30 20
382 10c. green 2·10 30
368 40c. violet 30 20
369 50c. orange 50 20
370 60c. purple 55 20
371 80c. green 55 20
372 $1 green 2·00 20
373 $1.20 green 1·20 20
374 $1.50 blue 1·60 20
375 $2 red 1·40 20
376 $2.50 blue 1·40 25
377 $3 green 2·00 20
378 $3.20 brown 4·50 20
379 $3.60 blue 4·50 55
382f $4 green 11·50 35
380 $4.50 red 6·75 80

84 Diving

85 Bronze Wine Vase (Shang Dynasty)

1960. Sports. With gum.
383 **84** 50c. brown, yellow & blue 90 20
384 – 80c. violet, yellow & purple 80 20
385 – $2 multicoloured 2·10 25
386 – $2.50 black and orange 2·30 50
387 – $3 multicoloured 3·50 60
388 – $3.20 multicoloured 4·50 75
DESIGNS: 80c. Discus-throwing; $2, Basketball; $2.50, Football; $3, Hurdling; $3.20, Sprinting.

1961. Ancient Chinese Art Treasures (1st series). With gum.
389 **85** 80c. multicoloured 2·30 20
390 – $1 indigo, blue and red 3·50 30
391 – $1.20 blue, brown & yellow 4·25 45
392 – $1.50 brown, blue & mauve 4·50 95
393 – $2 brown, violet and green 5·25 70
394 – $2.50 black, lilac and blue 8·50 1·20
DESIGNS: $1, Bronze cauldron (Chou); $1.20, Porcelain vase (Sung); $1.50, Jade perforated tube (Chou); $2, Porcelain jug (Ming); $2.50, Jade flower vase (Ming).
See also Nos. 408/13 and 429/34.

86 Farmer and Mechanical Plough

87 Mme. Chiang Kai-shek

1961. Agricultural Census.
395 **86** 80c. purple 1·00 20
396 $2 green 3·25 45
397 $3.20 red 4·75 35

1961. 10th Anniv (1960) of Chinese Women's Anti-Aggression League. With gum.
398 **87** 80c. black, red & turquoise 1·80 30
399 $1 black, red and green 3·50 60
400 $2 black, red and brown 3·75 65
401 $3.20 black, red and purple 5·50 1·30

88 Taiwan Lobster

89 Jeme Tien-yao and Locomotive

1961. Mail Order Service.
402 **88** $3 myrtle 4·25 40

1961. Birth Centenary of Jeme Tien-yao (railway engineer).
403 – 80c. violet 1·30 20
404 **89** $2 black 2·75 65
DESIGN: 80c. As Type **89** but locomotive heading right.

90 Pres. Chiang Kai-shek

91 Convair 880 Jetliner ("The Mandarin Jet"), Biplane and Flag

1961. 1st Anniv of Chiang Kai-shek's Third Term Inauguration. Multicoloured. With gum.
405 80c. Map of China (horiz) 2·00 25
406 $2 Type **90** 5·00 1·40
MS406a 139 × 100 mm. Nos. 405/6. Imperf. No gum 16·00 18·00

1961. 40th Anniv of Chinese Civil Air Service. With gum.
407 **91** $10 multicoloured 3·75 1·40

1961. Ancient Chinese Art Treasures (2nd issue). As T **85**. With gum.
408 80c. multicoloured 1·80 25
409 $1 blue, brown and bistre 3·50 50
410 $1.50 blue and salmon 4·50 1·20
411 $2 red, black and blue 7·50 75
412 $4 blue, sepia and red 9·75 1·40
413 $4.50 brown, sepia and blue 18·00 3·00
DESIGNS—VERT: 80c. Palace perfumer (Ching); $1, Corn vase (Warring States); $2, Jade tankard (Sung). HORIZ: $1.50, Bronze bowl (Chou); $4, Porcelain bowl (Southern Sung); $4.50, Jade chimera (Han).

92 Sun Yat-sen and Chiang Kai-shek

93 Lotus Lake

1961. 50th National Day. With gum.
414 **92** 80c. brown, blue and grey . . . 1·60 20
415 – $5 multicoloured . . . . . 4·00 1·60
MS415a 135 × 100 mm. Nos. 414/15 13·50 10·00
DESIGN—HORIZ: $5, Map and flag.

1961. Taiwan Scenery. Multicoloured. With gum.
416 80c. Pitan (Green Lake) (vert) 4·00 20
417 $1 Type **93** . . . . 8·50 80
418 $2 Sun-Moon Lake . . . . . 11·00 60
419 $3.20 Wulai Waterfall (vert) 14·50 1·20

94 Steel Furnace

95 Atomic Reactor, National Tsing Hwa University

1961. Taiwan Industries. With gum.
420 – 80c. indigo, brown & blue 1·90 25
421 **94** $1.50 multicoloured . . . 3·50 75
422 – $2.50 multicoloured . . . 4·75 70
423 – $3.20 indigo, brown & blue 6·50 70
DESIGNS—VERT: 80c. Oil refinery. $2.50, Aluminium manufacture. HORIZ: $3.20, Fertilizer plant.

1961. 1st Taiwan Atomic Reactor Inauguration. Multicoloured. With gum.
424 80c. Type **95** . . . . 1·90 20
425 $2 Interior of reactor . . . 5·00 1·50
426 $3.20 Reactor building (horiz) 5·25 1·10

96 Telegraph Wires and Microwave Reflector Pylons

97 Postal Segregating, Facing and Cancelling Machine

1961. 80th Anniv of Chinese Telecommunications. Multicoloured. With gum.
427 80c. Type **96** . . . . 1·20 20
428 $3.20 Microwave parabolic antenna (horiz) . . . 2·50 1·00

1962. Ancient Chinese Art Treasures (3rd issue). As T **85**. With gum.
429 80c. brown, violet and red . . 1·10 25
430 $1 purple, brown and blue . . 1·30 25
431 $2.40 blue, brown and red . . 14·00 85
432 $3 multicoloured . . . . . . 16·00 70
433 $3.20 red, green and blue . . 14·00 70
434 $3.60 multicoloured . . . . 22·00 90
DESIGNS—VERT: 80c. Jade topaz twin wine vessel (Chiang). $1, Bronze pouring vase (Warring States). $2.40, Porcelain vase (Ming). $3, Tsun bronze wine vase (Shang). $3.20, Porcelain jar (Ching). $3.60, Jade perforated disc (Han).

1962.
435 **97** 80c. purple . . . . 1·30 40

98 Mt. Yu Weather Station

99 Distribution of Milk and U.N. Emblem

1962. World Meteorological Day.
436 **98** 80c. brown 65 20
437 – $1 blue . . . . 1·60 40
438 – $2 green . . . . 2·20 85
DESIGNS—HORIZ: $1, Route-map of Typhoon Pamela. VERT: $2, Weather balloon passing globe.

1962. 15th Anniv of UNICEF.
439 **99** 80c. red 70 20
440 $3.20 green . . . . 2·10 65
MS440a 135 × 100 mm. Nos. 439/40. Imperf . . . . 13·50 4·00

100 Campaign Emblem

101 Yu Yu-jen (journalist)

1962. Malaria Eradication. With gum.
441 **100** 80c. red, green and blue 60 20
442 $3.60 brown, grn & dp brn . . . . 1·30 1·40

1962. "Elder Reporter" Yu Yu-jen Commemoration. With gum.
443 **101** 80c. sepia and pink . . . 1·80 25

102 Koxinga

103 Co-operative Emblem

1962. Tercentenary of Koxinga's Recovery of Taiwan. With gum.
444 **102** 80c. purple . . . . 1·60 25
445 $2 green . . . . 3·00 70

1962. 40th International Co-operative Day.
446 **103** 80c. brown 65 20
447 – $2 lilac . . . . 1·40 60
DESIGN: $2, Global handclasp.

104 UNESCO Symbols

105 Emperor T'ai Tsu (Ming Dynasty)

1962. UNESCO Activities Commem.
448 **104** 80c. mauve 55 20
449 – $2 lake . . . . 1·20 50
450 – $3.20 green . . . . 1·30 35
DESIGNS—HORIZ: $2, UNESCO emblem on open book. $3.20, Emblem linking hemispheres.

1962. Ancient Chinese Paintings from Palace Museum Collection (2nd series). Emperors. Multicoloured. With gum.
451 80c. T'ai Tsung (Tang) . . . 15·00 1·60
452 $2 T'ai Tsu (Sung) . . . . . 32·00 6·00
453 $3.20 Genghis Khan (Yuan) 43·00 6·75
454 $4 Type **105** . . . . 50·00 18·00

106 "Lions" Emblem and Activities

107 Pole Vaulting

1962. 45th Anniv of Lions International With gum.
455 **106** 80c. multicoloured . . . . 1·20 25
456 $3.60 multicoloured . . . 2·50 95
MS456a 100 × 75 mm. Nos. 455/6. Imperf. No gum . . . . 20·00 8·00

1962. Sports. With gum.
457 **107** 80c. brown, black & blue 1·00 20
458 $3.20 multicoloured . . . 2·20 55
DESIGN—HORIZ: $3.20, Rifle shooting.

108 Young Farmers

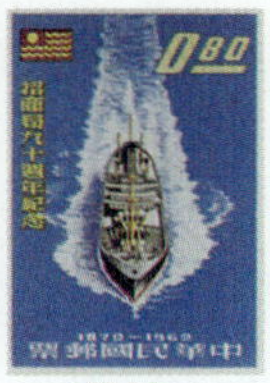

109 Liner

1962. 10th Anniv of Chinese 4-H Clubs.
459 **108** 80c. red 65 20
460 – $3.20 green . . . . 2·00 65
MS460a 135 × 100 mm. Nos. 459/60. Imperf . . . . 20·00 9·75
DESIGN: $3.20, 4-H Clubs emblem.

1962. 90th Anniv of China Merchants' Steam Navigation Co. Multicoloured. With gum.
461 80c. Type **109** . . . . . . 1·60 25
462 $3.60 Freighter "Hai Min" and Pacific route-map (horiz) . . . . 3·50 95

110 Harvesting

111 Youth, Girl, Torch and Martyrs Monument, Huang Hua Kang

1963. Freedom from Hunger. With gum.
463 **110** $10 multicoloured . . . . 5·00 95

1963. 20th Youth Day.
464 **111** 80c. purple 75 20
465 $3.20 green . . . . 2·00 60

112 Barn Swallows and Pagoda

113 Refugee in Tears

1963. 1st Anniv of Asian-Oceanic Postal Union. With gum. Multicoloured.
466 80c. Type **112** . . . . 4·25 50
467 $2 Northern gannet . . . . 5·50 90
468 $6 Manchurian crane and pine tree (vert) . . . . . . 11·00 2·75

1963. Refugees' Flight from Mainland.
469 **113** 80c. black . . . . 1·30 20
470 – $3.20 red . . . . 2·75 45
DESIGN—HORIZ: $3.20, Refugees on march.

114 Convair 880 over Tropic of Cancer Monument, Kiai

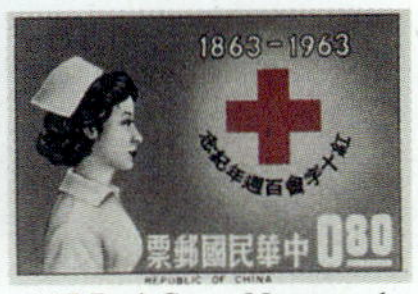

115 Red Cross Nurse and Emblem

1963. Air. Multicoloured. With gum.
471 $2.50 Suspension Bridge, Pitan (horiz) . . . . 6·00 20
472 $6 Type **114** . . . . 10·00 35
473 $10 Lion-head Mountain, Sinchu . . . . 13·00 70

1963. Red Cross Centenary. With gum.
474 **115** 80c. red and black . . . . 4·25 30
475 – $10 red, green and blue 9·00 2·75
DESIGN: $10, Globe and scroll.

116 Basketball

117 Freedom Torch

1963. 2nd Asian Basketball Championships, Taipeh.
476 **116** 80c. mauve . . . . 1·10 25
477 – $2 violet . . . . 2·20 75
DESIGN: $2, Hands reaching for inscribed ball.

1963. 15th Anniv of Declaration of Human Rights.
478 **117** 80c. green 80 40
479 – $3.20 red . . . . 1·60 80
DESIGN—HORIZ: $3.20, Human figures and scales of justice.

118 Country Scene

119 Dr. Sun Yat-sen and his Book "Three Principles of the People"

1963. "Good-People, Good-Deeds" Campaign. Multicoloured. With gum.
480 40c. Type **118** . . . . . . 2·40 30
481 $4.50 Lighting candle . . . . 5·75 2·10

1983. 10th Anniv of Land-to-Tillers Programme. With gum.
482 **119** $5 multicoloured . . . . 8·75 1·20

120 Torch of Liberty

121 Broadleaf Cactus

1964. 10th Anniv of Liberty Day.
483 **120** 80c. orange 60 20
484 – $3.20 blue . . . . 2·40 45
DESIGN—VERT: $3.20, Hands with broken manacles.

1964. Taiwan Cacti. Multicoloured. With gum.
485 80c. Type **121** . . . . 3·75 25
486 $1 Crab cactus . . . . 6·25 1·00
487 $3.20 Nopalxochia . . . . . 9·50 25
488 $5 Grizzly-Bear cactus . . . 10·00 1·30

122 Wu Chih-hwei (politician)

123 Chu Kwang Tower, Quemoy

1964. 99th Birth Anniv of Wu Chih-hwei (politician).
489 **122** 80c. brown . . . . 1·60 25

1964.
490 **123** 3c. purple 20 20
491 5c. green 20 20
492 10c. green 45 20
493 20c. green 25 20
494 40c. red 25 20
495 50c. purple 45 20
496 80c. orange 70 20
497 $1 violet 35 20
498 $1.50 purple . . . . . . 6·75 75
499 $2 purple 80 20
500 $2.50 blue . . . . 1·80 20
501 $3 grey . . . . 2·10 25
502 $3.20 blue . . . . 2·75 20
504 $4 green . . . . 3·50 20

124 Nurse and Florence Nightingale

125 Weir

1964. Nurses Day.
506 – 80c. violet . . . . 1·30 25
507 **124** $4 red . . . . 3·00 70
DESIGN—HORIZ: 80c. Nurses holding candlelight ceremony.

1964. Inaug of Shihmen Reservoir. With gum. Mult.
508 80c. Type **125** . . . . 2·10 20
509 $1 Irrigation channel . . . . 3·00 35
510 $3.20 Dam and powerhouse 6·50 50
511 $5 Main spillway . . . . . . 8·75 2·20

126 Ancient Ship and Modern Freighter

127 Bananas

1964. Navigation Day.
512 **126** $2 orange 75 20
513 $3.60 green . . . . 1·90 50

1964. Taiwan Fruits. Multicoloured. With gum.
514 80c. Type **127** . . . . 7·75 35
515 $1 Oranges . . . . 15·00 1·30
516 $3.20 Pineapples . . . . . . 21·00 80
517 $4 Water-melons . . . . . . 31·00 2·30

128 Lockheed Starfighters, "Tai Ho", "Tai Choa" and "Tai Tsung" (destroyers) and Artillery

129 Globe and Flags of Formosa and U.S.A.

1964. Armed Forces Day.
518 **128** 80c. blue . . . . 1·30 20
519 $6 purple . . . . 3·75 65

1964. New York World's Fair (1st issue). With gum.
520 **129** 80c. multicoloured . . . . 2·10 35
521 – $5 multicoloured . . . . 4·75 1·10
DESIGN—HORIZ: $5, Taiwan Pavilion at Fair.
See also Nos. 550/1.

130 Cowman holding Calf

131 Cycling

1964. Animal Protection.
522 **130** $2 purple . . . . 1·30 25
523 $4 blue . . . . 3·00 95

1964. Olympic Games, Tokyo.
524 **131** 80c. blue 75 20
525 – $1 red . . . . 1·50 25
526 – $3.20 green . . . . 2·10 40
527 – $10 violet . . . . 3·75 1·80
DESIGNS: $1, Runner breasting tape; $3.20, Gymnastics; $10, High jumping.

132 Hsu Kuang-chi (statesman)

133 Factory-bench ("Pharmaceutics")

1964. Famous Chinese.
528 **132** 80c. blue . . . . 2·40 25
See also Nos. 558/9, 586/7, 599, 606/9, 610, 738/40, 960 and 1072/7.

1964. Taiwan Industries. Multicoloured. With gum.
529 40c. Type **133** . . . . 2·00 25
530 $1.50 Loom ("Textiles") (horiz) . . . . 3·75 1·30
531 $2 Refinery ("Chemicals") . . 4·75 35
532 $3.60 Cement-mixer ("Cement") (horiz) . . . . 7·50 1·20

134 Dr. Sun Yat-sen (founder)

135 Mrs. Eleanor Roosevelt and "Human Rights" Emblem

1964. 70th Anniv of Kuomintang.
533 **134** 80c. green . . . . 2·20 30
534 $3.60 purple . . . . . . 4·25 90

1964. 16th Anniv of Declaration of Human Rights.
535 **135** $10 brown and violet . . 1·90 50

136 Law Code and Scales of Justice

137 Rotary Emblem and Mainspring

1965. 20th Judicial Day.
536 **136** 80c. red 50 20
537 $3.20 green 95 55

1965. 60th Anniv of Rotary International.
538 **137** $1.50 red 70 20
539 $2 green 70 25
540 $2.50 blue . . . . 1·30 45

138 "Double Carp"

139 Mme. Chiang Kai-shek

1965.
541 **138** $5 violet . . . . 13·50 60
542 $5.60 blue . . . . 12·00 3·75
543 $6 brown . . . . 11·50 1·30
544 $10 mauve . . . . 22·00 80
545 $20 red . . . . 27·00 1·20
546 $50 green . . . . 39·00 4·00
547 $100 red . . . . 70·00 6·50
See also Nos. 695/698ab.

1965. 15th Anniv of Chinese Women's Anti-Aggression League. With gum.
548 **139** $2 multicoloured . . . . 16·00 50
549 $6 multicoloured . . . . 28·00 4·00

140 Unisphere and Taiwan Pavilion, N.Y. Fair

1965. New York World's Fair (2nd issue). Multicoloured. With gum.
550 $2 Type **140** . . . . 25·00 85
551 $10 Peacock and various birds ("100 birds paying tribute to Queen Phoenix") 32·00 2·50

141 ITU Emblem and Symbols

1965. Centenary of ITU. Multicoloured. With gum.
552 80c. Type **141** 80 20
553 $5 ITU emblem and symbols (vert) . . . . 2·10 75

142 Madai Seabream

143 ICY Emblem

1965. Taiwan Fishes. Mult. With gum.
554 40c. Type **142** . . . . 2·50 35
555 80c. Silver pomfret . . . . 4·00 40
556 $2 Skipjack tuna (vert) . . . 6·75 1·20
557 $4 Moonfish . . . . 11·00 1·70

1965. Famous Chinese. Portraits as T **132**.
558 $1 red (Confucius) . . . . . 4·00 30
559 $3.60 blue (Mencius) . . . . 6·00 80

1965. Int Co-operation Year. Mult. With gum.
560 $2 Type **143** . . . . 1·10 25
561 $6 I.C.Y. emblem (horiz) . . 3·75 1·20

144 Road Crossing

145 Dr. Sun Yat-sen

1965. Road Safety.
562 **144** $1 purple . . . . 1·60 40
563 $4 red . . . . 2·50 95

1965. Birth Centenary of Dr. Sun Yat-sen. Multicoloured. With gum.
564 $1 Type **145** . . . . 3·50 25
565 $4 As T **145** but with portrait, etc., on right . . . 8·25 85
566 $5 Dr. Sun Yat-sen and flags (horiz) . . . . 12·50 2·20

146 Children with Firework

147 Lien Po, "Marshal and Prime Minister Reconciled"

1965. Chinese Folklore (1st Series). Multicoloured. With gum.
567 $1 Type **146** . . . . 6·75 40
568 $4.50 Dragon dance . . . . 8·75 1·40
See also Nos. 581/3 and 617.

1966. Painted Faces of Chinese Opera. Multicoloured. With gum.
569 $1 Type **147** . . . . 12·00 25
570 $3 Kuan Yu, "Reunion at Ku City" . . . . 16·00 55
571 $4 Chang Fei, "Long Board Slope" . . . . 26·00 85
572 $6 Buddha, "The Flower-scattering Angel" . . . . . 34·00 3·25

148 Pigeon holding Postal Emblem

149 "Fishing on a Snowy Day" (After artist of the "Five Dynasties")

1966. 70th Anniv of Chinese Postal Services. Multicoloured. With gum.
573 $1 Type **148** . . . . 2·20 25
574 $2 Postman by Chu memorial stone (horiz) . . . . 3·25 30
575 $3 Postal Museum (horiz) . . 3·75 40
576 $4 "Postman climbing" . . . 6·75 1·80

1966. Ancient Chinese Paintings from Palace Museum Collection (3rd series). With gum. Multicoloured.
577 $2.50 Type **149** . . . . . . 5·25 45
578 $3.50 "Calves on the Plain" . . 10·00 65
579 $4.50 "Snowscape" . . . . . 12·00 1·40
580 $5 "Magpies" (after Lin Ch'un) . . . . 17·00 1·80
Nos. 578/9 both after Sung artists.

1966. Chinese Folklore (2nd series). As T **146**. With gum. Multicoloured.
581 $2.50 Dragon boat racing (horiz) . . . . 14·00 40
582 $4 "Lady Chang O Flying to the Moon" (horiz) . . . . 7·75 45
583 $6 Lion Dance . . . . 4·75 85

150 Flags of Argentine and Chinese Republics

151 Lin Sen

1966. 150th Anniv of Argentine Republic's Independence. With gum.
584 **150** $10 multicoloured . . . . 3·75 65

1966. Birth Centenary of Lin Sen (statesman).
585 **151** $1 sepia . . . . 1·80 20

1966. Famous Chinese. Portraits as T **132**.
586 $2.50 sepia . . . . 3·25 35
587 $3.50 red . . . . 4·75 65
PORTRAITS: $2.50, General Yueh Fei. $3.50, Wen Tien-hsiang (statesman).

153 Bean Geese

154 Pres. Chiang Kai-shek

1966.
588 **153** $3.50 brown . . . . . . 1·00 25
589 $4 red 85 20
590 $4.50 green . . . . 1·60 25
591 $5 purple 90 20
592 $5.50 green . . . . 1·30 25
593 $6 blue . . . . 3·50 25
594 $6.50 violet . . . . 1·80 30
595 $7 black . . . . 1·20 20
596 $8 red . . . . 1·60 25

1966. President Chiang Kai-shek's re-election for 4th Term. With gum. Multicoloured.
597 $1 Type **154** . . . . 2·00 30
598 $5 President in Uniform . . . 5·50 1·50

1966. Famous Chinese. Portrait as T **132**.
599 $1 blue (Tsai Yuan-Pei, scholar) . . . . 1·90 25

155 Various means of Transport

156 Boeing 727-100 over Chilin Pavilion, Grand Hotel, Taipeh

1967. Development of Taiwan Communications. Multicoloured. With gum.
600 $1 Mobile postman and microwave station (vert) . . 1·20 20
601 $5 Type **155** . . . . 2·20 80

1967. Air. Multicoloured. With gum.
602 $5 Type **156** . . . . 3·25 25
603 $8 Boeing 727-100 over Palace Museum, Taipeh . . 4·75 55

157 Pres. Chiang Kai-shek

158 "God of Happiness" (wood carving)

1967. Chiang Kai-shek's 4th Presidential Term. With gum.
604 **157** $1 multicoloured . . . . 1·60 20
605 $4 multicoloured . . . . 3·00 80

1967. Famous Chinese. Poets. Portraits. As T **132**.
606 $1 black (Chu Yuan) . . . . 1·40 25
607 $2 brown (Li Po) . . . . . 3·25 30

608 $2.50 brown (Tu Fu) . . . . 4·00 50
609 $3 green (Po Chu-i) . . . . 6·00 45

1967. Famous Chinese. Portrait as T **132**.
610 $1 black (Chiu Ching, female revolutionary) . . . . . . 1·90 25

1967. Chinese Handicrafts. Multicoloured. With gum.
611 $1 Type **158** . . . . 2·30 45
612 $2.50 Vase and dish . . . . 3·50 70
613 $3 Chinese dolls . . . . . . 4·50 1·40
614 $5 Palace lanterns . . . . . 7·50 3·25

159 "WACL" on World Map **160** Muller's Barbet

1967. 1st World Anti-Communist League Conference, Taipei.
615 **159** $1 red 60 20
616 $5 blue . . . . 1·30 70

GUM. From No. 617 all stamps were issued with gum unless otherwise stated.

1967. Chinese Folklore (3rd series). Stilts Pastime. As T **146**.
617 $4.50 multicoloured . . . . 1·60 40
DESIGN: "The Fisherman and the Wood-cutter" (Chinese play on stilts).

1967. Taiwan Birds. Multicoloured.
618 $1 Type **160** . . . . 3·00 20
619 $2 Maroon oriole (horiz) . . . 5·00 25
620 $2.50 Japanese green pigeon (horiz) . . . . 8·00 75
621 $3 Formosan blue magpie (horiz) . . . . 8·00 40
622 $5 Crested serpent eagle . . . 10·00 75
623 $8 Mikado pheasant (horiz) 13·00 75

161 Chung Hsing Pagoda **162** Flags and China Park, Manila

1967. International Tourist Year. Multicoloured.
624 $1 Type **161** . . . . 1·40 20
625 $2.50 Yeh Liu National Park (coastal scene) (horiz) . . . 3·50 45
626 $4 Statue of Buddha (horiz) 4·25 65
627 $5 National Palace Museum, Taipei (horiz) . . . . . . 5·25 85

1967. China–Philippines Friendship.
628 **162** $1 multicoloured 65 20
629 $5 multicoloured . . . . 2·10 55

163 Chungshan Building, Yangmingshan **164** Taroko Gorge

1968.
630 **163** 5c. brown 30 20
631 10c. green 35 20
632 50c. purple 30 20
633 $1 red 35 20
634 $1.50 green . . . . 2·50 55
635 $2 purple 85 20
636 $2.50 blue 95 20
637 $3 blue . . . . 1·10 20
For redrawn design see Nos. 791/8.

1968. 17th Pacific Area Travel Association Conference, Taipei. Multicoloured.
638 $5 Type **164** . . . . 2·00 30
639 $8 Chungshan Building, Yangmingshan . . . . . . 2·50 35

165 Harvesting Sugar-cane **166** Vice-Pres. Cheng

1968. Sugar-cane Technologists Congress, Taiwan.
640 **165** $1 multicoloured . . . . 1·40 20
641 $4 multicoloured . . . . 3·00 55

1968. 3rd Death Anniv of Vice-Pres. Chen Cheng.
642 **166** $1 multicoloured . . . . 1·50 25

167 Bean Geese **168** Jade Cabbage (Ching Dynasty)

1968. 90th Anniv of Chinese Postage Stamps.
643 **167** $1 red . . . . 7·00 25
MS644 75 × 100 mm. **167** $3 green. Imperf . . . . 13·00 4·50

1968. Chinese Art Treasures, National Palace Museum (1st series). Multicoloured.
645 $1 Type **168** . . . . 1·70 20
646 $1.50 Jade battle-axe (Warring States period) . . 3·00 40
647 $2 Lung-ch'uan porcelain flower bowl (Sung dynasty) (horiz) . . . . 3·50 20
648 $2.50 Yung Cheng enamelled vase (Ching dynasty) . . 4·00 55
649 $4 Agate "fingered" flower-holder (Ching dynasty) (horiz) . . . . 4·75 55
650 $5 Sacrificial vessel (Western Chou) . . . . 5·25 80
See also Nos. 682/7 and 732/7.

169 WHO Emblem on "20" **170** Sun, Planets and "Rainfall"

1968. 20th Anniv of WHO.
651 **169** $1 green 40 20
652 $5 red . . . . 1·00 55

1968. International Hydrological Decade.
653 **170** $1 green and orange . . . 45 20
654 $4 blue and orange . . . 1·20 20

171 "A City of Cathay" (Section of hand-scroll painting)

1968. "A City of Cathay" (Scroll, Palace Museum) (1st series).
655 **171** $1 (1) multicoloured . . . 1·70 30
656 – $1 (2) multicoloured . . . 1·70 30
657 – $1 (3) multicoloured . . . 1·70 30
658 – $1 (4) multicoloured . . . 1·70 30
659 – $1 (5) multicoloured . . . 1·70 30
660 – $5 multicoloured . . . . 12·00 2·00
661 – $8 multicoloured . . . . 19·00 2·75
DESIGNS—As Type **171**: Nos. 655/9 together show panorama of the city ending with the palace. LARGER (61 × 32 mm). $5, City wall and gate; $8, Great bridge.
The five $1 stamps were issued together se-tenant in horiz strips, representing the last 11 feet of the 37 foot scroll, which is viewed from right to left as it is unrolled.
The stamps may be identified by the numbers given in brackets, which correspond to the numbers in the bottom right-hand corners of the stamps.
See also Nos. 699/703.

172 Map and Radio "Waves" **173** Human Rights Emblem

1968. 40th Anniv of Chinese Broadcasting Service.
662 **172** $1 grey, ultram & blue . . 50 20
663 – $4 red and blue . . . . . 1·10 25
DESIGN—VERT: $4, Stereo broadcast "waves".

1968. Human Rights Year.
664 **173** $1 multicoloured 55 20
665 $5 multicoloured . . . . 1·40 20

174 Harvesting Rice **175** Throwing the Javelin

1968. Rural Reconstruction.
666 **174** $1 brown, ochre & yellow 45 20
667 $5 bronze, green & yellow 1·20 70

1968. Olympic Games, Mexico. Multicoloured.
668 $1 Type **175** 45 20
669 $2.50 Weightlifting 70 20
670 $5 Pole-vaulting (horiz) . . . 1·20 30
671 $8 Hurdling (horiz) . . . . . 1·80 50

176 President Chiang Kai-shek and Main Gate, Whampoa Military Academy

1968. "President Chiang Kai-shek's Meritorious Services". Multicoloured.
672 $1 Type **176** 65 25
673 $2 Reviewing Northern Expedition Forces . . . . 1·00 35
674 $2.50 Suppression of bandits 2·50 95
675 $3.50 Marco Polo Bridge and Victory Parade, Nanking, 1945 . . . . 1·40 50
676 $4 Chinese Constitution . . . 1·60 60
677 $5 National flag . . . . . . 2·50 80
Each stamp bears the portrait of President Chiang Kai-shek as in Type **176**.

177 Cockerel **178** National Flag

1968. New Year Greetings. "Year of the Cock".
678 **177** $1 multicoloured . . . . 19·00 60
679 $4.50 multicoloured . . . 30·00 5·00

1968. 20th Anniv of Chinese Constitution.
680 **178** $1 multicoloured 60 20
681 $5 multicoloured . . . . 1·00 60

1969. Chinese Art Treasures, National Palace Museum (2nd series). Multicoloured as T **168**.
682 $1 Jade buckle (Ching dynasty) (horiz) . . . . . 1·00 20
683 $1.50 Jade vase (Sung dynasty) . . . . 2·00 30
684 $2 Cloisonne enamel teapot (Ching dynasty) (horiz) . . 1·60 20
685 $2.50 Bronze sacrificial vessel (Kuei) (horiz) . . . . . . 2·30 45
686 $4 Hsuan-te "heavenly ball" vase (Ming dynasty) . . . 2·75 65
687 $5 "Gourd" vase (Ching dynasty) . . . . 3·75 90

179 Servicemen and Savings Emblem

1969. 10th Anniv of Forces' Savings Services.
688 **179** $1 brown 30 20
689 $4 blue 90 45

180 Ti (flute)

1969. Chinese Musical Instruments. Mult.
690 $1 Type **180** 70 25
691 $2.50 Sheng (pipes) . . . . . 1·20 35
692 $4 P'i-p'a (lute) . . . . . . 1·60 60
693 $5 Cheng (zither) . . . . . . 1·80 35

181 Chungshan Building, Yangmingshan **182** "Double Carp"

1969. 10th Kuomintang Congress.
694 **181** $1 multicoloured 65 20

1969.
695ab **182** $10 blue . . . . 2·10 20
695c $14 red . . . . 2·50 10
696ab $20 brown . . . . . . 4·25 30
697ab $50 green . . . . . . 6·25 50
698ab $100 red . . . . 8·50 1·00
Type **182** is a redrawn version of Type **138**.

1969. "A City of Cathay" (scroll) (2nd series). As T **171**. Multicoloured.
699 $1 "Musicians" . . . . . . 1·00 20
700 $1 "Bridal chair" . . . . . 1·00 20
701 $2.50 Emigrants with ox-cart 2·40 75
702 $5 "Scroll gallery" . . . . . 4·25 70
703 $8 "Roadside cafe" . . . . . 7·50 1·00
Nos. 699/70 form a composite picture of a bridal procession.

184 ILO Emblem **185** "Food and Clothing"

1969. 50th Anniv of ILO.
704 **184** $1 blue 55 20
705 $8 red . . . . 1·40 45

1969. "Model Citizen's Life" Movement.
706 **185** $1 red 25 20
707 – $2.50 blue 60 30
708 – $4 green 75 35
DESIGNS: $2.50, "Housekeeping and Road Safety"; $4, "Schooling and Recreation".

186 Bean Geese over Mountains **187** Children and Symbols of Learning

1969. Air. Multicoloured.
709 $2.50 Type **186** . . . . . . 2·30 25
710 $5 Bean geese over sea . . . 4·00 45
711 $8 Bean geese over land (horiz) . . . . 5·75 60

1969. 1st Anniv of Nine-year Free Education System.
712 **187** $1 red 35 20
713 – $2.50 green 70 30
714 – $4 blue 90 35
715 **187** $5 brown . . . . 1·10 50
DESIGNS—VERT: $2.50 and $4, Children and school.

188 "Flowers and Ring-necked Pheasants", Ming dynasty (Lu Chih) — **189** "Charles Mallerin" Rose

1969. Ancient Chinese Paintings from Palace Museum Collection (4th series). "Birds and Flowers". Multicoloured.

716 $1 Type **188** 1·50 20
717 $2.50 "Bamboos and Ring-necked Pheasants" (Sung dynasty) 3·00 35
718 $5 "Flowers and Birds" (Sung dynasty) 7·25 60
719 $8 "Twin Manchurian Cranes and Flowers" (G. Castiglione, Ching dynasty) 8·50 1·00

1969. Roses. Multicoloured.

720 $1 Type **189** 1·10 25
721 $2.50 "Golden Sceptre" 3·25 25
722 $5 "Peace" 4·25 30
723 $8 "Josephine Bruce" 3·75 65

190 Launching Missile — **191** APU Emblem

1969. 30th Air Defence Day.

724 **190** $1 purple 1·40 25

1969. 5th Asian Parliamentarians' Union General Assembly. Taipeh.

725 **191** $1 red 40 20
726 $5 green 95 30

192 Pekingese Dogs — **193** Satellite and Earth Station

1969. New Year Greetings. "Year of the Dog".

727 **192** 50c. multicoloured 1·70 25
728 $4.50 multicoloured 8·25 1·80

1969. Inauguration of Satellite Earth Station, Yangmingshan.

729 **193** $1 multicoloured 60 20
730 $5 multicoloured 1·20 30
731 $8 multicoloured 2·00 55

1970. Chinese Art Treasures, National Palace Museum (3rd series). As T **168**. Multicoloured.

732 $1 Lacquer vase (Ching dynasty) 1·00 20
733 $1.50 Agate grinding-stone (Ching dynasty) (horiz) 1·40 25
734 $2 Jade carving (Ching dynasty) (horiz) 1·60 20
735 $2.50 "Shepherd and Ram" jade carving (Han dynasty) (horiz) 2·10 30
736 $4 Porcelain jar (Ching dynasty) 2·30 40
737 $5 "Bull" porcelain urn (Northern Sung dynasty) 3·25 65

1970. Famous Chinese. Portraits as T **132**.

738 $1 red 65 20
739 $2.50 green 95 25
740 $4 blue 1·60 35

PORTRAITS: $1, Hsuan Chuang (traveller). $2.50, Hua To (physician). $4, Chu Hsi (philosopher).

194 Taiwan Pavilion and EXPO Emblem — **195** Chungshan Building, Yangmingshan

1970. World Fair "EXPO 70", Osaka, Japan. Multicoloured.

741 $5 Type **194** 75 20
742 $8 Pavilion encircled by national flags 1·50 55

1970.

743 **195** $1 red 50 20

For redrawn design see No. 1039.

196 Rain-cloud, Palm and Recording Apparatus — **197** Martyrs' Shrine

1970. World Meteorological Day. Mult.

744 $1 Type **196** 40 20
745 $8 "Nimbus 3" satellite (horiz) 95 50

1970. Revolutionary Martyrs' Shrine. Mult.

746 $1 Type **197** 60 20
747 $8 Shrine gateway 1·70 50

198 General Yueh Fei ("Loyalty")

1970. Chinese Opera. "The Virtues". Opera characters. Multicoloured.

748 $1 Type **198** 1·40 25
749 $2.50 Emperor Shun tortured by stepmother ("Filial Piety") 2·40 40
750 $5 Chin Liang-yu "The Lady General" ("Chastity") 3·25 55
751 $8 Kuan Yu and groom ("Fidelity") 5·00 70

199 Three Horses at Play

1970. "One Hundred Horses" (handscroll by Lang Shih-ning (G. Castiglione)). Multicoloured.

752 $1 (1) Horses on plain 85 25
753 $1 (2) Horses on plain (different) 85 25
754 $1 (3) Horses playing 85 25
755 $1 (4) Horses on river bank 85 25
756 $1 (5) Horses crossing river 85 25
757 $5 Type **199** 7·75 75
758 $8 Groom roping horses 9·25 95

SERIAL NUMBERS. are indicated to aid identification of the above and certain other sets. For key to Chinese numerals see table at the beginning of CHINA.

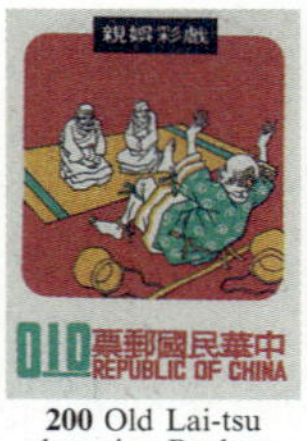
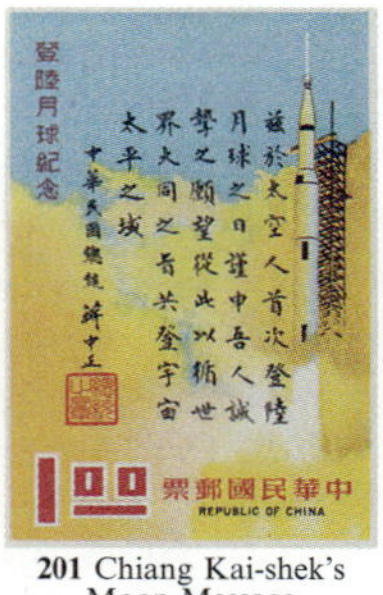

200 Old Lai-tsu dropping Buckets — **201** Chiang Kai-shek's Moon Message

1970. Chinese Folk-tales (1st series). Mult.

759 10c. Type **200** 20 15
760 10c. Yien-tsu disguised as a deer 20 15
761 10c. Hwang Hsiang with fan 20 15
762 10c. Wang Shiang fishing 20 15
763 10c. Chu Hsiu-chang reunited with mother 20 15
764 50c. Emperor Wen tasting mother's medicine 35 20
765 $1 Lu Chi dropping oranges 55 25
766 $1 Yang Hsiang fighting tiger 60 30

See also Nos. 817/24, 1000/7, 1064/7, 1210/13 and 1312/15.

1970. 1st Man on the Moon. Multicoloured.

767 $1 Type **201** 75 15
768 $5 "Apollo 11" astronauts (horiz) 1·10 35
769 $8 "First step on the Moon" 2·40 55

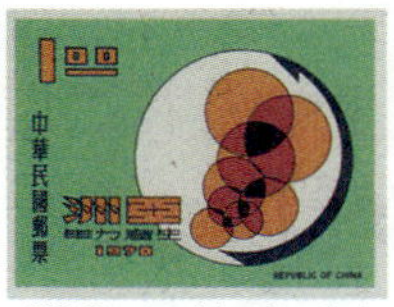

202 Productivity Symbol — **203** Flags of Taiwan and United Nations

1970. Asian Productivity Year.

770 **202** $1 multicoloured 50 15
771 $5 multicoloured 1·10 35

1970. 25th Anniv of United Nations.

772 **203** $5 multicoloured 1·60 50

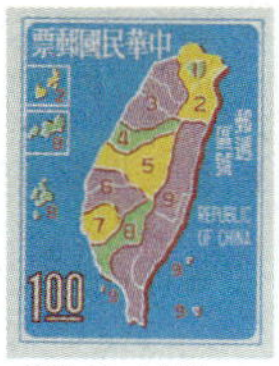

204 Postal Zone Map — **205** "Cultural Activities" (10th month)

1970. Postal Zone Numbers Campaign. Mult.

773 $1 Type **204** 65 15
774 $2.50 Postal Zone emblem (horiz) 1·10 35

1970. "Occupations of the Twelve Months" Hanging Scrolls. Multicoloured. (a) "Winter".

775 $1 Type **205** 2·75 40
776 $2.50 "School Buildings" (11th month) 6·25 90
777 $5 "Games in the Snow" (12th month) 10·00 1·10

(b) "Spring".

778 $1 "Lantern Festival" (1st month) 1·80 30
779 $2.50 "Apricots in Blossom" (2nd month) 4·00 65
780 $5 "Purification Ceremony" (3rd month) 6·00 80

(c) "Summer".

781 $1 "Summer Shower" (4th month) 1·80 30
782 $2.50 "Dragon boat Festival" (5th month) 4·00 65
783 $5 "Lotus Pond" (6th month) 6·00 80

(d) "Autumn".

784 $1 "Weaver Festival" (7th month) 2·20 35
785 $2.50 "Moon Festival" (8th month) 4·75 80
786 $5 "Chrysanthemum Blossom" (9th month) 7·50 95

The month numbers are given by the Chinese characters in brackets, which follow the face value on the stamps.

206 "Planned Family" — **207** Toy Pig

1970. Family Planning. Multicoloured.

787 $1 Type **206** 60 15
788 $4 "Family excursion" (vert) 1·50 40

1970. New Year Greetings. "Year of the Boar".

789 **207** 50c. multicoloured 2·30 20
790 $4.50 multicoloured 4·50 70

208 Chungshan Building, Yangmingshan — **209** Shin-bone Tibia

1971.

791 **208** 5c. brown 20 15
792 10c. green 20 15
793 50c. red 45 15
794 $1 red 50 15
795 $1.50 blue 75 25
796 $2 purple 1·30 20
797 $2.50 green 1·80 25
798 $3 blue 2·10 30

Type **208** is a redrawn version of Type **163**.

1971. Taiwan Shells. Multicoloured.

799 $1 Type **209** 75 15
800 $2.50 Kuroda's lyria 1·20 35
801 $5 "Conus stupa kuroda" 1·80 70
802 $8 Rumphius's slit shell 2·75 45

210 Savings Book and Certificate — **211** Chinese greeting African Farmer

1971. National Savings Campaign. Mult.

803 $1 Type **210** 50 15
804 $4 Hand dropping coin in savings bank 1·50 35

1971. 10th Anniv of Sino-African Technical Co-operation Committee. Multicoloured.

805 $1 Type **211** 45 15
806 $8 Rice-growing (horiz) 1·30 55

212 Red and White Flying Squirrel — **213** Pitcher delivering ball

1971. Taiwan Animals. Multicoloured.

807 $1 Taiwan macaque (vert) 50 15
808 $2 Type **212** 1·20 25
809 $3 Chinese pangolin 1·50 40
810 $5 Sika deer 2·00 55

1971. World Little League Baseball Championships, Taiwan. Multicoloured.

811 $1 Type **213** 30 15
812 $2.50 Players at base (horiz) 50 20
813 $4 Striker and catcher 80 25

(214) — **215** 60th Anniv Emblem and flag

1971. Victory of "Tainan Giants" in World Little League Baseball Championships, Williamsport (U.S.A.). Optd with T **214**.

814 **163** $1 red 30 15
815 $2.50 blue 55 20
816 $3 blue 45 25

1971. Chinese Folk-tales (2nd series). As T **200**. Multicoloured.

817 10c. Yu Hsun and elephant 20 15
818 10c. Tsai Hsun with mulberries 20 15
819 10c. Tseng Sun with firewood 20 15
820 10c. Kiang Keh and bandits 20 15
821 10c. Tsu Lu with sack of rice 20 15
822 50c. Meng Chung gathering bamboo shoots 30 20
823 $1 Tung Yung and wife 70 30
824 $1 Tzu Chien shivering with cold 70 30

1971. 60th National Day. Multicoloured.

825 $1 Type **215** 50 15
826 $2.50 National anthem, map and flag 85 15

827 $5 Pres. Chiang Kai-shek, constitution and flag . . . 1·00 35
828 $8 Dr. Sun Yat-sen, "Three Principles" and flag . . . 1·20 40

216 AOPU Emblem

1971. Asian-Oceanic Postal Union Executive Committee Session, Taipeh.
829 **216** $2.50 multicoloured . . . 55 15
830 $5 multicoloured 85 20

217 "White Frost Hawk"

1971. "Ten Prized Dogs" (paintings on silk by Lang Shih-ning (G. Castiglione)). Multicoloured.
831 $1 Type **217** 80 20
832 $1 "Black Dog with Snow-white Claws" . . . 3·00 15
833 $2 "Star-glancing Wolf" . . 1·30 20
834 $2 "Yellow Leopard" . . . 5·00 30
835 $2.50 "Golden-winged Face" 2·00 55
836 $2.50 "Flying Magpie" . . . 6·50 65
837 $5 "Young Black Dragon" 4·75 60
838 $5 "Heavenly Lion" . . . . 9·50 70
839 $8 "Young Grey Dragon" . 6·50 70
840 $8 "Mottle-coated Tiger" . . 12·00 80

218/221 Squirrels

1971. New Year Greetings. "Year of the Rat".
841 **218** 50c. multicoloured 80 20
842 **219** 50c. multicoloured 80 20
843 **220** 50c. multicoloured 80 20
844 **221** 50c. multicoloured 80 20
845 **218** $4.50 multicoloured . . . 4·25 50
846 **219** $4.50 multicoloured . . . 4·25 50
847 **220** $4.50 multicoloured . . . 4·25 50
848 **221** $4.50 multicoloured . . . 4·25 50
The four designs in each value were issued together, se-tenant, forming a composite design.

222 Flags of Taiwan and Jordan

1971. 50th Anniv of Hashemite Kingdom of Jordan.
849 **222** $5 multicoloured . . . . 1·50 25

223 Freighter "Hai King"

1971. Centenary of China Merchants Steam Navigation Company. Multicoloured.
850 **223** $4 blue, red and green . . 65 30
851 – $7 multicoloured . . . . 1·00 45
DESIGN—VERT: $7. Liner on Pacific.

224 Downhill Skiing

1972. Winter Olympic Games, Sapporo, Japan.
852 **224** $1 black, yellow and blue 25 15
853 – $5 black, orange & green 60 20
854 – $8 black, red and grey . . 80 25
DESIGNS: $5, Cross-country skiing; $8, Giant slalom.

225 Yung Cheng Vase

226 Doves

1972. Chinese Porcelain. (1st series). Ch'ing Dynasty. Multicoloured.
855 $1 Type **225** 85 15
856 $2 Kang Hsi jar . . . . . 1·40 25
857 $2.50 Yung Cheng jug . . . 1·90 30
858 $5 Chien Lung vase . . . 2·20 30
859 $8 Chien Lung jar . . . . 3·00 45
See also Nos. 914/18, 927/31 and 977/81.

1972. 10th Anniv of Asian-Oceanic Postal Union.
860 **226** $1 black and blue 45 20
861 $5 black and violet . . . 1·30 35

227 "Dignity with Self-Reliance" (Pres. Chiang Kai-shek)

229 First Day Covers

228 Mounted Messengers

1972.
862 **227** 5c. brown and yellow . . 25 15
863 10c. blue and orange . . 20 15
863b 20c. purple and green . . 25 15
864 50c. lilac and purple . . 30 15
865 $1 red and blue . . . 20 15
866 $1.50 yellow and blue . . 35 20
867 $2 violet, purple & orge 60 20
868 $2.50 green and red . . 95 25
869 $3 red and green 90 25

1972. "The Emperor's Procession" (Ming dynasty handscrolls). Multicoloured. (a) First issue.
870 $1 (1) Pagoda and crowds . . 65 20
871 $1 (2) Seven carriages 65 20
872 $1 (3) Emperor's coach . . . 65 20
873 $1 (4) Horsemen with flags 65 20
874 $1 (5) Horsemen and Emperor 65 20
875 $2.50 Type **228** . . . . . 2·50 20
876 $5 Guards . . . . 3·50 25
877 $8 Imperial sedan chair . . . 7·00 55

(b) Second issue.
878 $1 (1) Three ceremonial barges 70 20
879 $1 (2) Sedan chairs 70 20
880 $1 (3) Two ceremonial barges 70 20
881 $1 (4) Horsemen with mounted orchestra 70 20
882 $1 (5) Two carriages 70 20
883 $2.50 City gate . . . . . . 2·50 20
884 $5 Mounted orchestra . . . 3·75 25
885 $8 Ceremonial barge . . . . 3·75 50
Nos. 870/4 are numbered from right to left and Nos. 878/82 are numbered from left to right. They were each issued together, se-tenant, forming composite designs showing the departure of the procession from the palace and its return.
Nos. 875/7 and 883/5 show enlarged details from the scrolls.
See also Nos. 937/50 and 1040/7.

1972. Philately Day.
886 **229** $1 blue 25 15
887 $2.50 green 30 20
888 $8 red 55 25
DESIGNS—VERT: $2.50, Magnifying glass and stamps. HORIZ: $8, Magnifying glass, perforation-gauge and tweezers.

(230)

231 Emperor Yao

1972. Taiwan's Victories in Senior and Little World Baseball Leagues. Nos. 865/7 and 869 optd with T **230**.
889 **227** $1 red and blue 25 15
890 $1.50 yellow and blue . . 40 25
891 $2 violet, purple & orange 45 20
892 $3 red and green 45 25

1972. Chinese Cultural Heroes.
893 **231** $3.50 blue 55 30
894 – $4 red 65 15
895 – $4.50 violet 80 25
896 – $5 green 75 15
897 – $5.50 purple . . . . . 1·10 35
898 – $6 orange . . . . . . 1·20 30
899 – $7 brown . . . . . . 1·40 15
900 – $8 blue . . . . 1·60 20
DESIGNS: $4, Emperor Shun; $4.50, Yu the Great; $5, King T'ang; $5.50, King Weng; $6, King Wu; $7, Chou Kung; $8, Confucius.

1972. "ROCPEX" Philatelic Exhibition, Taipeh. Sheet 71 × 100 mm.
MS901 **227** Nos. 867 ($2) and 869 ($3) . . . . 5·75 2·20

232 Mountaineering

233 Microwave Systems and Electronic Sorting Machine

1972. 20th Anniv of China Youth Corps. Multicoloured.
902 $1 Type **232** 30 15
903 $2.50 Winter sport 50 15
904 $4 Diving 70 20
905 $8 Parachuting . . . . . 1·00 30

1972. Improvement of Communications.
906 **233** $1 red 25 15
907 – $2.50 blue 45 25
908 – $5 purple 80 40
DESIGNS—HORIZ: $2.50, Boeing 721-100 airliner and "Hai Mou" (container ship); $5, Diesel railcar and motorway.

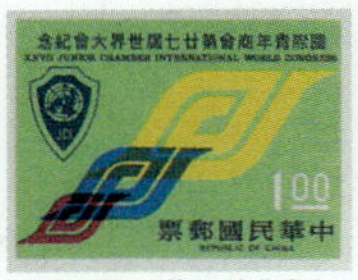

234 "Eyes" and J.C.I. Emblem

235 Cow and Calf

1972. 27th World Congress of Junior Chamber International, Taipeh.
909 **234** $1 multicoloured 30 15
910 $5 multicoloured 45 25
911 $8 multicoloured 60 40

1972. New Year Greetings. "Year of the Ox".
912 **235** 50c. black and red . . . . 1·80 35
913 $4.50 brown, red & yellow 4·00 90

1973. Chinese Porcelain (2nd series). Ming Dynasty. As T **225**. Multicoloured.
914 $1 Fu vase . . . . 1·00 15
915 $2 Floral vase . . . . . . 1·50 15
916 $2.50 Ku vase . . . . . . 1·80 30
917 $5 Hu flask . . . . 2·20 45
918 $8 Garlic-head vase . . . . 3·00 55

236 "Kicking the Shuttlecock"

237 Bamboo Sampan

1973. Chinese Folklore (1st series). Mult.
919 $1 Type **236** 50 15
920 $4 "The Fisherman and the Oyster-fairy" (horiz) . . . 95 20
921 $5 "Lady in a Boat" (horiz) 1·00 20
922 $8 "The Old Man and the Lady" . . . . 1·30 40
See also Nos. 982/3 and 1037/8.

1973. Taiwan Handicrafts (1st series). Mult.
923 $1 Type **237** 45 15
924 $2.50 Marble vase (vert) . . 75 15
925 $5 Glass plate 95 20
926 $8 Aborigine Doll (vert) . . . 1·20 40
See also Nos. 988/91.

1973. Chinese Porcelain (3rd series). Ming Dynasty. Horiz. designs as T **225**. Multicoloured.
927 $1 Dragon stem-bowl 75 25
928 $2 Dragon pot . . . . 1·10 25
929 $2.50 Covered jar with lotus decor . . . . 1·40 25
930 $5 Covered jar showing horses . . . . 1·80 50
931 $8 "Immortals" bowl . . . . 2·50 60

238 Contractors' Equipment

239 Pres. Chiang Kai-shek and Flag

1973. 12th Convention of International Federation of Asian and Western Pacific Contractors' Association.
932 **238** $1 multicoloured 30 15
933 – $5 blue and black 65 30
DESIGN—HORIZ: $5, Bulldozer.

1973. Inauguration of Pres. Chiang Kai-shek's 5th Term of Office.
934 **239** $1 multicoloured 50 25
935 $4 multicoloured . . . . 1·00 50

240 Lin Tse-hsu (statesman)

1973. Lin Tse-hsu Commemoration.
936 **240** $1 purple 60 20

1973. "Spring Morning in the Han Palace" (Ming dynasty handscroll). As T **228**. Mult. (a) First issue.
937 $1 (1) Palace gate 40 20
938 $1 (2) Feeding green peafowl 40 20
939 $1 (3) Emperor's wife 40 20
940 $1 (4) Ladies and pear tree 40 20
941 $1 (5) Music pavilion 40 20
942 $5 Giant rock (vert) . . . . 2·50 55
943 $8 Lady musicians (vert) . . 3·75 95

(b) Second issue.
944 $1 (6) Game with flowers . . 40 20
945 $1 (7) Leisure room 40 20
946 $1 (8) Ladies with teapots . . 40 20
947 $1 (9) Artist at work 40 20
948 $1 (10) Palace wall and guards 40 20
949 $5 Playing game at table (vert) . . . . 2·50 55
950 $8 Swatting insect (vert) . . . 3·75 95
Nos. 937/41 and 944/8 are numbered from right to left and were each issued together, se-tenant. When the two strips are placed side by side, they form a composite design showing the complete handscroll.
Nos. 942/3 and 949/50 show enlarged details from the scroll.

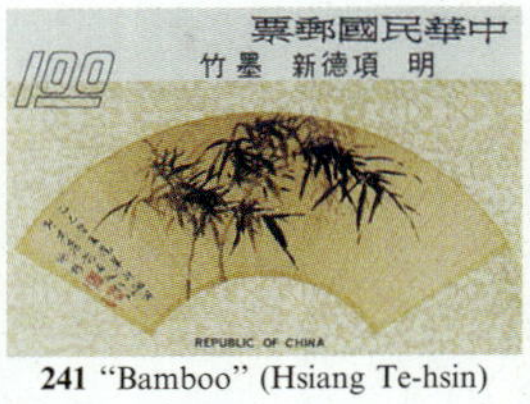

241 "Bamboo" (Hsiang Te-hsin)

1973. Ancient Chinese Fan Paintings (1st series). Multicoloured.
951 $1 Type **241** 55 15
952 $2.50 "Flowers" (Sun K'O-hung) 95 20
953 $5 "Landscape" (Ch'iu Ying) 1·40 40
954 $8 "Seated Figure and Tree" (Shen Chou) . . . . 2·00 50
See also Nos. 1052/5.

243 Emblem of World Series **245** Interpol Emblem

1973. Little League World Baseball Series. Taiwan Victory in Twin Championships.
955 **243** $1 blue, red and yellow 65 15
956 $4 blue, green & yellow 1·40 35

1973. 50th Anniv of International Criminal Police Organization (Interpol).
957 **245** $1 blue and orange 30 15
958 $5 green and orange 60 25
959 $8 purple and orange 80 45

1973. Famous Chinese. Portrait as T **132**.
960 $1 violet (Ch'iu Feng-chia (poet)) 75 25

246 Dam and Power Station

1973. Opening of Tsengwen Reservoir. Mult.
961 $1 Upper section of reservoir 25 15
962 $1 Middle section of reservoir 25 15
963 $1 Lower section of reservoir 25 15
964 $5 Type **246** (30 × 22 mm) 90 50
965 $8 Spillway (50 × 22 mm) 1·30 45
The $1 values together show complete map of reservoir (each 38 × 26 mm).

247 "Snow-dotted Eagle"

1973. Paintings of Horses. Multicoloured.
966 50c. Type **247** 70 25
967 $1 "Comfortable Ride" 1·00 25
968 $1 "Red Flower Eagle" 1·00 25
969 $1 "Cloud-running Steed" 1·00 25
970 $1 "Sky-running Steed" 1·00 25
971 $2.50 "Red Jade Steed" 2·75 50
972 $5 "Thunder-clap Steed" 4·50 65
973 $8 "Arabian Champion" 6·75 60
MS974 151 × 121 mm. Nos. 966/7 and 971/2. Imperf 34·00 11·50

248 Tiger **249** Road Tunnel Taroko Gorge

1973. New Year Greetings. "Year of the Tiger".
975 **248** 50c. multicoloured 85 20
976 $4.50 multicoloured 1·80 50

1974. Chinese Porcelain (4th series). Sung Dynasty. As T **225**. Multicoloured.
977 $1 Ko vase 55 15
978 $2 Kuan vase (horiz) 80 20
979 $2.50 Ju bowl (horiz) 1·10 30
980 $5 Kuan incense burner (horiz) 1·30 30
981 $8 Chun incense burner (horiz) 1·40 40

1974. Chinese Folklore (2nd series). As T **236**. Multicoloured.
982 $1 Balancing pot 50 15
983 $8 Magicians (horiz) 1·40 20

1974. Taiwan Scenery (1st series). Mult.
984 $1 Type **249** 60 15
985 $2.50 Luce Chapel, Tungai University 85 20
986 $5 Tzu En Pagoda, Sun Moon Lake 1·10 20
987 $8 Goddess of Mercy Statue, Keelung 1·40 25
See also Nos. 992/5.

1974. Taiwan Handicrafts (2nd series). As T **237**. Multicoloured.
988 $1 "Fighting Cocks" (brass) 40 15
989 $2.50 "Fruits" (jade) 60 25
990 $5 "Fisherman" (wood-carving) (vert) 85 30
991 $8 "Bouquet of Flowers" (plastic) (vert) 1·50 40

1974. Taiwan Scenery (2nd series). As T **249** but all horiz. Multicoloured.
992 $1 Dr. Sun Yat-Sen Memorial Hall. Taipeh 40 15
993 $2.50 Reaching-Moon Tower, Cheng Ching Lake 65 15
994 $5 Seashore, Lanyu 90 20
995 $8 Inter-island bridge, Penghu 1·20 25

250 Pres. Chiang Kai-shek **251** Long-distance Runner

1974. 50th Anniv of Chinese Military Academy.
996 **250** $1 mauve 30 15
997 – $14 blue 75 45
DESIGN—VERT: $14, Cadets on parade.

1974. 80th Anniv of International Olympic Committee.
998 **251** $1 blue, black & red 30 15
999 – $8 multicoloured 85 45
DESIGN: $8, Female relay runner.

1974. Chinese Folk tales (3rd series). As T **200**. Multicoloured.
1000 50c. Wen Yen-po retrieving ball 25 15
1001 50c. T'i Ying pleading for mercy 25 15
1002 50c. Wang Ch'i in battle 25 15
1003 50c. Wang Hua returning gold 25 15
1004 $1 Pu Shih offering sheep to the emperor 40 25
1005 $1 Szu Ma Kuang saving playmate from water-jar 40 25
1006 $1 Tung Yu at study 40 25
1007 $1 K'ung Yung selecting the smallest pear 40 25

252 "Crape Myrtle" (Wei Sheng)

1974. Ancient Chinese Moon-shaped Fan-paintings (1st series). Multicoloured.
1008 $1 Type **252** 35 15
1009 $2.50 "White Cabbage and Insects" (Hsu Ti) 65 25
1010 $5 "Hibiscus and Rock" (Li Ti) 1·00 25
1011 $8 "Pomegranates and Narcissus Fly-catcher" (Wu Ping) 1·70 50
See also Nos. 1068/71 and 1115/1118.

253 "The Battle of Marco Polo Bridge" **254** Chrysanthemum

1974. Armed Forces' Day.
1012 **253** $1 multicoloured 35 15
MS1013 108 × 147 mm. No. 1012 × 8 7·50 6·00

1974. Chrysanthemums.
1014 **254** $1 multicoloured 30 15
1015 – $2.50 multicoloured 60 30
1016 – $5 multicoloured 85 30
1017 – $8 multicoloured 1·30 25
DESIGNS: Nos. 1015/17, various chrysanthemums.

255 Chinese Pavilion **256** Steel Mill, Kaohsiung

1974. "Expo 74" World Fair, Spokane, Washington. Multicoloured.
1018 $1 Type **255** 30 15
1019 $8 Fairground map 70 45

1974. Major Construction Projects (1st series). Chinese inscr in single-line characters, figures of value solid.* Multicoloured.
1020 50c. Type **256** 20 15
1021 $1 Taiwan North link railway 30 15
1022 $2 Petrochemical works, Kaohsiung 20 15
1023 $2.50 TRA trunk line electrification 40 15
1024 $3 Taichung harbour (horiz) 30 15
1025 $3.50 Taoyuan international airport (horiz) 30 15
1026 $4 Taiwan North–south motorway (horiz) 30 15
1027 $4.50 Giant shipyard, Kaohsiung (horiz) 50 35
1028 $5 Su-ao port (horiz) 50 25
*The first series can also be distinguished by the Chinese and English inscr at the foot being in different colours; in the second and third series only one colour is used.
See also Nos. 1122a/1122i and 1145/1153.

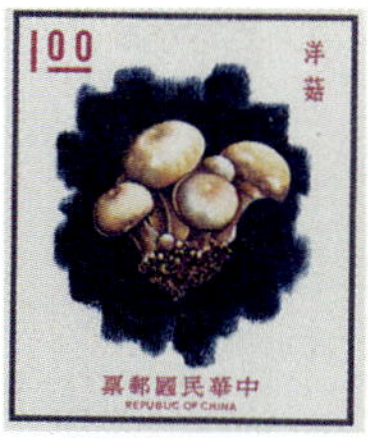

257 White Button Mushrooms **259** Chinese Hare

258 Baseball Strikers

1974. Edible Fungi. Multicoloured.
1029 $1 Type **257** 35 15
1030 $2.50 Oyster fungus 50 20
1031 $5 Veiled stinkhorn 95 25
1032 $8 Golden mushrooms 1·20 35

1974. Taiwan Triple Championship Victories in World Little League Baseball Series, U.S.A. Multicoloured.
1033 $1 Type **258** 30 15
1034 $8 Player and banners 70 35

1974. New Year Greetings. "Year of the Hare".
1035 **259** 50c. multicoloured 45 15
1036 $4.50 multicoloured 1·80 30

1975. Chinese Folklore (3rd series). As T **236**. Multicoloured.
1037 $4 Acrobat 75 35
1038 $5 Jugglers with diabolo 1·10 55

260 Chungshan Building, Yangmingshan **261** Sun Yat-sen Memorial Hall, Taipeh

1975.
1039 **260** $1 red 50 15
Type **260** is a redrawn version of Type **195**.

1975. "New Year Festivals" (handscroll by Ting Kuan-p'eng). As T **228**. Multicoloured.
1040 $1 (1) Greetings 40 15
1041 $1 (2) Entertainer 40 15
1042 $1 (3) Crowd and musicians 40 15
1043 $1 (4) Picnic 40 15
1044 $1 (5) Puppet show 40 15
1045 $2.50 New Year greetings 2·00 35
1046 $5 Children buying fireworks 3·25 55
1047 $8 Entertainer with monkey and dog 4·75 95
Nos. 1040/4 were issued together, se-tenant, forming a composite design.

1975. 50th Death Anniv of Dr. Sun Yat-sen.
1048 $1 Type **261** 30 15
1049 $4 Sun Yat-sen's handwriting 45 25
1050 $5 Bronze statue of Sun Yat-sen (vert) 65 25
1051 $8 Sun Yat-sen Memorial Hall, St. John's University, U.S.A 90 30

1975. Ancient Chinese Fan Paintings (2nd series). As T **241**. Multicoloured.
1052 $1 "Landscape" (Li Liu-fang) 45 15
1053 $2.50 "Landscape" (Wen Cheng-ming) 85 30
1054 $5 "Landscape" (Chou Ch'en) 1·20 40
1055 $8 "Landscape" (T'ang Yin) 1·80 40

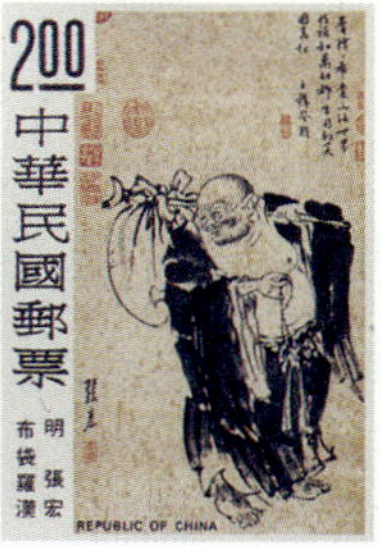

262 "Yuan-chin" Coin (Chou dynasty) **263** "Lohan, the Cloth-bag Monk" (Chang Hung)

1975. Ancient Chinese Coins (1st series). Mult.
1056 $1 Type **262** 35 15
1057 $4 "Pan-liang" coin (Chin dynasty) 80 20
1058 $5 "Five chu" coin (Han dynasty) 95 20
1059 $8 "Five chu" coin (Liang dynasty) 1·20 25
See also Nos. 1111/14 and 1184/7.

1975. Ancient Chinese Figure Paintings. Mult.
1060 $2 Type **263** 70 20
1061 $4 "Lao-tzu on buffalo" (Chao Pu-chih) 1·40 25
1062 $5 "Shih-te" (Wang-wen) 2·30 30
1063 $8 "Splashed-ink Immortal" (Liang K'ai) 3·00 40

1975. Chinese Folk-tales (4th series). As T **200**. Multicoloured.
1064 $1 Chu-Yin reading by light of fireflies 25 15
1065 $2 Hua Mu-lan going to battle disguised as a man 35 20
1066 $2 Ling Kou Chien living a humble life 45 25
1067 $5 Chou Ch'u defeating the tiger 95 35

1975. Ancient Chinese Moon-shaped Fan Paintings (2nd series). As T **252**. Multicoloured.
1068 $1 "Cherry-apple blossoms" (Lin Ch'un) 45 15
1069 $2 "Spring blossoms and a colourful butterfly" (Ma K'uei) 75 15
1070 $5 "Monkeys and deer" (I Yuan-chi) 95 30
1071 $8 "Tree sparrows among bamboo" (anon.) 2·40 55

1975. Famous Chinese. Martyrs of War against Japan. Portraits as T **132**.
1072 $2 red (Gen. Chang Tzu-chung) 25 15
1073 $2 brown (Maj.-Gen. Kao Chih-hang) 25 15
1074 $2 green (Capt. Sha Shih-chiun) 25 15
1075 $5 brown (Maj-Gen. Hsieh Chin-yuan) 35 15
1076 $5 blue (Lt. Yen Hai-wen) 35 15
1077 $5 blue (Lt.-Gen. Tai An-lan) 35 15

264 "Lotus Pond with Willows"

1975. Madame Chiang Kai-shek's Landscape Paintings (1st series). Multicoloured.
1078 $2 Type **264** 1·00 15
1079 $5 "Sun breaks through Mountain Clouds" 1·60 35
1080 $8 "A Pair of Pine Trees" 2·75 45
1081 $10 "Fishing and Farming" 3·75 75
See also Nos. 1139/1142 and 1727/30.

265 Rectangular Cauldron

266 Dragon, Nine-Dragon Wall, Peihai

1975. Ancient Bronzes (1st series). Mult.

1082	$2 Type **265**	30	15
1083	$5 Cauldron with "Phoenix" handles (horiz)	65	20
1084	$8 Flat jar (horiz)	95	25
1085	$10 Wine vessel	1·10	35

See also Nos. 1119/22.

1975. New Year Greetings. "Year of the Dragon".

1086 **266**	$1 multicoloured	50	20
1087	$5 multicoloured	1·30	60

267 Techi Dam

268 Biathlon

1975. Completion of Techi Reservoir. Mult.

1088	$2 Type **267**	30	15
1089	$10 Dam and reservoir	60	45

1976. Winter Olympic Games, Innsbruck. Mult.

1090	$2 Type **268**	30	15
1091	$5 Luge	50	25
1092	$8 Skiing	70	35

269 "Chin"

1976. Chinese Musical Instruments (1st series). Multicoloured.

1093	$2 Type **269**	35	15
1094	$5 "Se" (string instrument)	55	20
1095	$8 "Standing Kong-ho" (harp)	65	25
1096	$10 "Sleeping Kong-ho" (harp)	85	30

See also Nos. 1156/9.

270 Postman collecting Mail

1976. 80th Anniv of Chinese Postal Service. Multicoloured.

1097	$2 Type **270**	25	15
1098	$5 Mail-sorting systems (vert)	35	20
1099	$8 Mail transport (vert)	85	20
1100	$10 Traditional and modern post deliveries	75	25
MS1101	130 × 100 mm. Nos. 1097/1100	10·50	6·50

271 Pres. Chiang Kai-shek

1976. 1st Death Anniv of President Chiang Kai-shek. Multicoloured.

1102	$2 Type **271**	25	15
1103	$2 People paying homage (horiz)	25	15
1104	$2 Lying-in-state (horiz)	25	15
1105	$2 Start of funeral procession (horiz)	25	15
1106	$5 Roadside obeisance (horiz)	40	20
1107	$8 Altar, Tzuhu Guest-house (horiz)	50	30
1108	$10 Tzuhu Guest-house (horiz)	65	35

272 Chinese and U.S. Flags

273 "Kung Shou Pu" Coin (Shang/Chou Dynasties)

1976. Bicentenary of American Revolution.

1109 **272**	$2 multicoloured	25	15
1110	$10 multicoloured	70	45

1976. Ancient Chinese Coins (2nd series). Mult.

1111	$2 Type **273**	30	15
1112	$5 "Chien Tsu Pu" coin (Chao Kingdom)	65	20
1113	$8 "Yuan Tsu Pu" coin (Tsin Kingdom)	85	25
1114	$10 "Fang Tsu Pu" coin (Chin/Han Dynasties)	1·20	30

1976. Ancient Chinese Moon-shaped Fan-paintings (3rd series) As T **252**. Multicoloured.

1115	$2 "Hibiscus" (Li Tung)	55	15
1116	$5 "Lilies" (Lin Chun)	1·10	20
1117	$8 "Two Sika Deer, Mushrooms and Pine" (Mou Chung-fu)	1·50	30
1118	$10 "Wild Flowers and Japanese Quail" (Li An-chung)	3·25	45

1976. Ancient Bronzes (2nd series). As T **265**. Multicoloured.

1119	$2 Square cauldron	35	15
1120	$5 Round cauldron	75	15
1121	$8 Wine vessel	1·00	25
1122	$10 Wine vessel with legs	1·20	30

No. 1119 is similar to Type **265**, but has four characters at left only.

1976. Major Construction Projects (2nd series). Designs as Nos. 1020/8, but Chinese inscr in double-lined characters. Figures of value solid. Multicoloured.

1122a	$1 As No. 1021	35	15
1122b	$2 As No. 1023	35	15
1122c	$3 As No. 1024	30	15
1122d	$4 As No. 1026	30	15
1122e	$5 As Type **256**	30	15
1122f	$6 As No. 1025	35	20
1122g	$7 As No. 1027	40	20
1122h	$8 As No. 1022	45	25
1122i	$9 As No. 1028	50	30

See also Nos. 1145/53.

274 Chiang Kai-shek and Mother

1976. 90th Birth Anniv of President Chiang Kai-shek. Multicoloured.

1123	$2 Type **274**	30	15
1124	$5 Chiang Kai-shek	65	20
1125	$10 Chiang Kai-shek and Dr. Sun Yat-sen in railway carriage (horiz)	1·00	45

275 Chinese and KMT Flags

1976. 11th Kuomintang National Congress. Mult.

1126	$2 Type **275**	30	15
1127	$10 President Chiang Kai-shek and Dr. Sun Yat-sen	65	40
MS1128	111 × 87 mm. No. 1126/7. Perf	5·00	4·25

276 Brazen Serpent

277 "Bird and Plum Blossom" (Ch'en Hung-shou)

1976. New Year Greetings. "Year of the Snake".

1129 **276**	$1 multicoloured	50	15
1130	$5 multicoloured	1·60	25

1977. Ancient Chinese Paintings. "Three Friends of Winter".

1131	$2 Type **277**	85	20
1132	$8 "Wintry Days" (Yang Wei-chen)	2·30	40
1133	$10 "Rock and Bamboo" (Hsia Ch'ang)	3·00	45

278 Black-naped Orioles

1977. Taiwan Birds. Multicoloured.

1134	$2 Type **278**	45	15
1135	$8 River kingfisher	1·00	25
1136	$10 Pheasant-tailed jacana	1·60	35

279 Emblems of Industry and Commerce

1977. Industry and Commerce Census.

1137 **279**	$2 multicoloured	25	15
1138	$10 multicoloured	70	45

280 "Green Mountains rising into Clouds"

1977. Madame Chiang Kai-shek's Landscape Paintings (2nd series). Multicoloured.

1139	$2 Type **280**	75	20
1140	$5 "Boat amidst Spring's Beauty"	1·50	40
1141	$8 "Scholar beside the Rivulet"	2·30	40
1142	$10 "Green Water rising to meet the Bridge"	2·50	60

281 WACL Emblem

282 Steel Mill, Kaohsiung

1977. 10th World Anti-Communist League Conf.

1143 **281**	$2 multicoloured	25	15
1144	$10 multicoloured	65	45

1977. Major Construction Projects (3rd series). Designs as Nos. 1122a/i, but redrawn with double lined figures of value as in T **282**. Multicoloured.

1145	$1 Taiwan North link railway	35	15
1146	$2 TRA trunk line electrification	35	15
1147	$3 Taichung harbour (horiz)	30	15
1148	$4 Taiwan North–south highway (horiz)	25	15
1149	$5 Type **282**	30	15
1150	$6 Taoyuan international airport (horiz)	30	20
1151	$7 Giant shipyard, Kaohsiung (horiz)	40	20
1152	$8 Petrochemical works, Kaohsiung	45	25
1153	$9 Su-ao port (horiz)	50	30

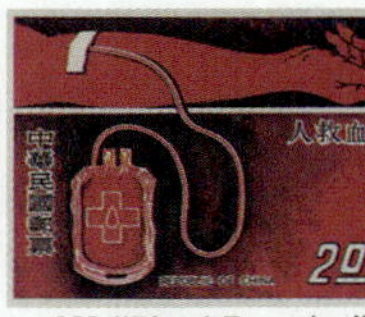

283 "Blood Donation"

1977. Blood Donation Movement.

1154 **283**	$2 red, black and yellow	25	15
1155 –	$10 red and black	70	45

DESIGN—VERT: $10, "Blood Transfusion".

284 San-hsien

285 "Idea leuconoe"

1977. Chinese Musical Instruments (2nd series). Multicoloured.

1156	$2 Type **284**	30	15
1157	$5 Tung-hsiao (wind instrument)	45	20
1158	$8 Yang-chin (xylophone)	55	25
1159	$10 Pai-hsiao (pipes)	85	35

1977. Taiwan Butterflies. Multicoloured.

1160	$2 Type **285**	40	20
1161	$4 Great orange-tip	75	30
1162	$6 "Stichophthalma howqua"	1·00	35
1163	$10 "Atrophaneura horishanus"	1·60	30

286 "National Palace Museum"

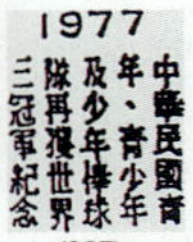

(287)

1977. Children's Drawings. Multicoloured.

1164	$1 Type **286**	25	15
1165	$2 "Festival of Sea Goddess"	30	20
1166	$4 "Boats on Lan-yu"	45	20
1167	$5 "Temple" (vert)	55	25

1977. Triple Championships of the 1977 Little League World Baseball Series. Nos. 1146 and 1152 optd with Type **287**.

1168	$2 multicoloured	25	15
1169	$8 multicoloured	70	30

288 Plate

289 Lions Club Emblem

1977. Ancient Chinese Carved Lacquer Ware (1st series). Multicoloured.

1170	$2 Type **288**	50	20
1171	$5 Bowl	75	20
1172	$8 Box	1·20	25
1173	$10 Three-tiered box	1·30	30

See also Nos. 1206/1209.

1977. 60th Anniv of Lions International.

1174 **289**	$2 multicoloured	25	15
1175	$10 multicoloured	65	40

290 "Cheng" Government Standard Mark

291 Human Figure and Diagram of Heart

1977. Standardization Movement.

1176 **290**	$2 multicoloured	55	15
1177	$10 multicoloured	1·70	30

1977. Prevention of Heart Disease Campaign.

1178 **291**	$2 multicoloured	25	15
1179	$10 multicoloured	65	45

292 White Horse

293 First Page of Constitution

1977. New Year Greetings. "Year of the Horse". Details from "One Hundred Horses" by Lang Shih-ning (Giuseppe Castiglione). Multicoloured.

1180	$1 Type **292**	50	15
1181	$5 Two Horses (horiz)	1·40	30

1977. 30th Anniv of Constitution. Mult.

1182	$2 Type **293**	25	15
1183	$10 President Chiang accepting constitution	65	30

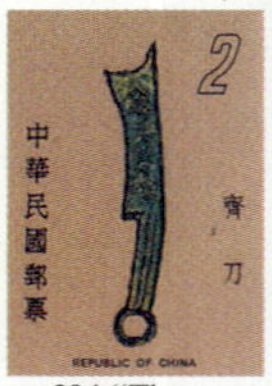
294 "Three-character" Knife (Chi State)

295 "Dragon" Stamp, 1878

1978. Ancient Chinese Coins (3rd series). Mult.

1184	$2 Type **294**	30	15
1185	$5 Longer sharp-headed knife (Yen State)	75	15
1186	$8 Sharp-headed knife (Yet State)	90	20
1187	$10 Chao or Ming knife	1·10	30

1978. Cent of Chinese Postage Stamp. Mult.

1188	$2 Type **295**	35	15
1189	$5 "Dr. Sun Yat-sen" stamp, 1941	55	25
1190	$10 "Chiang Kai-shek" stamp, 1958	80	40
MS1191	143 × 101 mm. Nos. 1188/1190	9·00	3·50

296 Dr. Sun Yat-sen Memorial Hall

1978. "Rocpex" Taipeh 1978 Philatelic Exhibition. Multicoloured.

1192	$2 Type **296**	25	15
1193	$10 "Dragon" and 1977 "New Year" stamps	65	35

297 Chiang Kai-shek as a Young Man

298 Section through Nuclear Reactor

1978. 3rd Death Anniv of Pres. Chiang Kai-shek. Multicoloured.

1194	$2 Type **297**	25	15
1195	$5 Chiang on horseback (horiz)	45	25
1196	$8 Chiang making speech (horiz)	60	40
1197	$10 Reviewing armed forces	80	50

1978. Nuclear Power Plant.

1198 **298**	$10 multicoloured	80	20

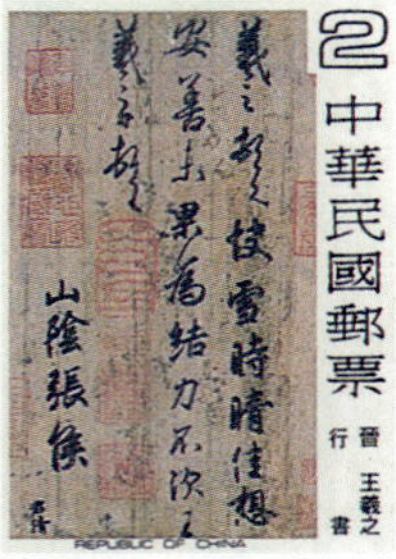
299 Letter by Wang Hsi-chih

300 Human Figure in Polluted Environment

1978. Chinese Calligraphy. Multicoloured.

1199	$2 Type **299**	75	20
1200	$4 Eulogy of Ni K'uan by Chu Sui-liang	1·90	20
1201	$6 Inscription on poem "Lake Tai" by Wen Cheng-ming	2·40	40
1202	$8 Autobiography by Huai-su	3·00	35
1203	$10 Poem by Ch'ang Piao	5·25	50

1978. Cancer Prevention.

1204 **300**	$2 green, yellow & red	30	15
1205	$10 blue, green & dp blue	60	35

1978. Ancient Chinese Carved Lacquer Ware (2nd series). As T **288**. Multicoloured.

1206	$2 Square box	30	15
1207	$5 Box on legs	45	15
1208	$8 Round box	60	20
1209	$10 Vase (vert)	85	30

1978. Chinese Folk-tales (5th series). As T **200**. Multicoloured.

1210	$1 Tsu Ti brandishing sword	25	15
1211	$2 Pan Ch'ao throwing down pen	50	20
1212	$2 Tien Tan's "Fire Bull Battle"	70	20
1213	$5 Liang Hung-yu as army drummer	1·00	25

1978. Triple Championships of the Little League World Baseball Series. Nos. 1148 and 1150 optd as T **287**, but with four lines of characters and dated 1978.

1214	$4 Taiwan North–south highway	25	15
1215	$6 Taoyuan international airport	50	30

302 Yellow Orange-tip

1978. Taiwan Butterflies. Multicoloured.

1216	$2 Type **302**	55	20
1217	$4 Two-brand crow	65	20
1218	$6 Common map butterfly	1·10	30
1219	$10 "Atrophaneura polyeuctes"	2·30	50

303 Jamboree Badge, Camp and Scout Salute

304 Tropical Tomatoes

1978. Taiwanese Boy Scouts' 5th Jamboree.

1220 **303**	$2 multicoloured	30	15
1221	$10 multicoloured	45	30

1978. Asian Vegetable Research and Development Centre. Multicoloured.

1222	$2 Type **304**	45	20
1223	$10 Tropical tomatoes (different)	1·20	45

305 Aerial View of Bridge

306 National Flag

1978. Opening of the Sino-Saudi Bridge. Mult.

1224	$2 Type **305**	40	15
1225	$6 Close-up of bridge	1·10	30

1978.

1226 **306**	$1 red and blue	20	15
1377	$1 red and blue	25	15
1378	$1.50 red, blue & yellow	40	15
1227	$2 red and blue	20	15
1379	$2 red, blue and yellow	25	15
1297	$3 red, blue and green	50	15
1380	$3 red and blue	30	15
1298	$4 red, blue and brown	55	20
1381	$4 red, blue and light blue	30	15
1228	$5 red, blue and green	30	15
1382	$5 red, blue and brown	30	15
1229	$6 red, blue and orange	35	20
1300	$7 red, blue and brown	55	20
1384	$7 red, blue and green	55	20
1230	$8 red, blue and green	50	25
1385	$8 red, blue & deep red	55	20
1386	$9 red, blue and green	70	20
1231	$10 red, blue and lt blue	75	30
1387	$10 red, blue and violet	70	25
1302	$12 red, blue and mauve	90	30
1389	$14 red, blue and green	1·30	40

The $1 values differ in the face value, which is printed in colour on No. 1226, whilst on No. 1377 it is white.

Nos. 1377/8, 1379, 1380, 1381, 1382 and the $6 to $14 values are as Type **306** but have solid background panel to face value and inscr.

307 "Imitation of the Three Sheep by Emperor Hsuan-tsung of the Ming Dynasty" (Emperor Kao-tsung)

308 Boeing 747-100 and Control Building

1978. New Year Greetings. "Year of the Sheep".

1232 **307**	$1 multicoloured	30	20
1233	$5 multicoloured	1·50	45

1978. Completion of Taoyuan International Airport. Multicoloured.

1234	$2 Type **308**	30	15
1235	$10 Passenger terminal building (horiz)	65	45

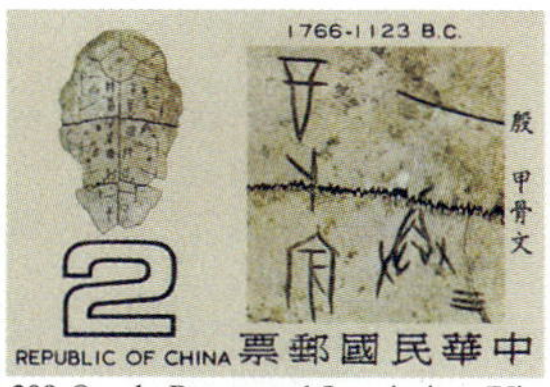
309 Oracle Bones and Inscription (Yin Dynasty)

1979. Origin and Development of Chinese Characters. Multicoloured.

1236	$2 Type **309**	60	15
1237	$5 "Leh-chi" cauldron and inscription (Spring and Autumn period)	1·10	25
1238	$8 Engraved seal and seal-style characters (Western Han dynasty)	1·70	45
1239	$10 Square plain-style characters inscribed on stone (Eastern Han dynasty)	2·50	75

310 Chihkan Tower, Tainan

1979. Tourism. Multicoloured.

1240	$2 Type **310**	30	15
1241	$5 Confucius Temple, Tainan	55	20
1242	$8 Koxinga Shrine, Tainan	80	25
1243	$10 Eternal Castle, Tainan	1·60	35

311/314 "Children Playing Games on a Winter Day" (⅔-size illustration)

1979. Sung Dynasty Painting.

1244 **311**	$5 multicoloured	2·50	45
1245 **312**	$5 multicoloured	2·50	45
1246 **313**	$5 multicoloured	2·50	45
1247 **314**	$5 multicoloured	2·50	45
MS1248	101 × 145 mm. Nos. 1244/7	23·00	11·50

Nos. 1244/7 were printed together, se-tenant, forming the composite design illustrated.

315 Lu Hao-tung (revolutionary)

316 White Jade Brush Washer (Ming dynasty)

1979. Famous Chinese.

1249 **315**	$2 blue	60	15

1979. Ancient Chinese Jade (1st series). Multicoloured.

1250	$2 Yellow jade brush holder embossed with clouds and dragons (Sung dynasty) (vert)	30	15
1251	$5 Type **316**	85	30
1252	$8 Dark green jade brush washer carved with clouds and dragons (Ch'ing dynasty)	1·10	45
1253	$10 Bluish jade washer in shape of lotus (Ch'ing dynasty)	1·80	60

See also Nos. 1291/4.

317 Plum Blossom

318 Houses

1979.

1254 **317**	$10 blue	1·70	20
1255	$20 brown	2·20	20
1255b	$40 red	2·20	20
1256	$50 green	4·50	25
1257	$100 red	6·25	80
1257b	$300 red and violet	19·00	3·25
1257c	$500 red and brown	32·00	5·25

The $300 and $500 are size 25 × 33 mm.

1979. Environmental Protection. Mult.

1258	$2 Type **318**	25	15
1259	$10 Rural scene (horiz)	85	35

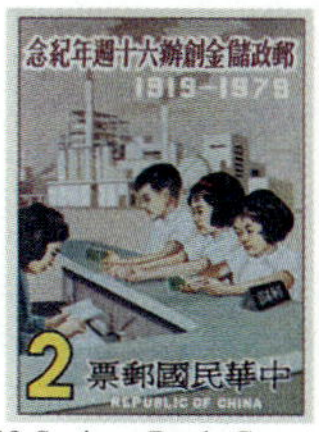
319 Savings Bank Counter

1979. 60th Anniv of Postal Savings Bank. Multicoloured.

1260	$2 Type **319**	25	15
1261	$5 Savings bank queue	35	20
1262	$8 Computer and savings book (horiz)	50	20
1263	$10 Money box and "tree" emblem (horiz)	70	25

320 Steere's Liocichla

1979. Birds. Multicoloured.
1264 $2 Swinhoe's pheasant . . . 45 15
1265 $8 Type **320** . . . . 1·00 25
1266 $10 Formosan yuhina . . . 1·20 35

321 Sir Rowland Hill

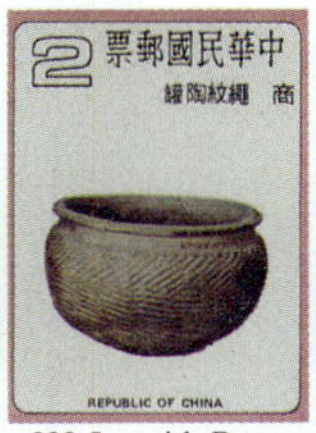
322 Jar with Rope Pattern

1979. Death Centenary of Sir Rowland Hill.
1267 **321** $10 multicoloured . . . 1·00 25

1979. Ancient Chinese Pottery. Multicoloured.
1268 $2 Type **322** (Shang dynasty) 35 15
1269 $5 Two handled jar (Shang dynasty) . . . . 1·00 20
1270 $8 Red jar with "ears" (Han dynasty) . . . . 1·80 20
1271 $10 Green glazed jar (Han dynasty) . . . . 2·10 25

323 Children and I.Y.C. Emblem

324 "Trees on a Winter Plain" (Li Ch'eng)

1979. International Year of the Child.
1272 **323** $2 multicoloured 30 15
1273 $10 multicoloured . . . 65 35

1979. Ancient Chinese Paintings. Mult.
1274 $2 Type **324** (Sung dynasty) 70 20
1275 $5 "Bamboo" (Wen T'ung, Sung dynasty) . . . . . 1·40 25
1276 $8 "Old Tree, Bamboo and Rock" (Chao Mengfu, Yuan dynasty) . . . . . 2·50 40
1277 $10 "Twin Pines" (Li K'an, Yuan dynasty) . . . . . 3·50 45

325 Taiwan Macaque

326 Competition Emblem and Symbols of Ten Trades

1979. New Year Greetings. "Year of the Monkey".
1278 **325** $1 multicoloured . . . . 1·00 20
1279 $6 multicoloured . . . . 3·00 50

1979. 10th National Vocational Training Competition, Taichung.
1280 **326** $2 multicoloured 25 15
1281 $10 multicoloured . . . 70 35

327 "75" and Rotary Emblem

328 Tunnel of Nine Turns

1980. 75th Anniv of Rotary International. Mult.
1282 $2 Type **327** 30 15
1283 $12 Anniversary emblem and symbols of Rotary's services (vert) 80 40

1980. Tourism. Scenic Spots on the East–West Cross-Island Highway. Multicoloured.
1284 $2 Type **328** 35 15
1285 $8 Mt. Hohuan (horiz) . . . 75 25
1286 $12 Bridge, Tien Hsiang . . 1·50 35

329 Shih Chien-ju (hero of revolution)

330 Chung-cheng Memorial Hall

1980. Famous Chinese.
1287 **329** $2 brown 30 15

1980. 5th Death Anniv of Chiang Kai-shek. Multicoloured.
1288 $2 Type **330** 25 15
1289 $8 Quotation of Chiang Kai-shek 40 20
1290 $12 Bronze statue of Chiang Kai-shek 55 40

1980. Ancient Chinese Jade (2nd series). As T **316**. Multicoloured.
1291 $2 Kuang (cup) decorated with dragons (Sung dynasty) (vert) 45 15
1292 $5 Dark green jade melon-shaped brush washer (Ming dynasty) 85 20
1293 $8 Bluish jade Po Monk's alms bowl (Ch'ing dynasty) . . . . 1·20 20
1294 $10 Yellow jade brush washer (Ch'ing dynasty) 1·50 25

331 Tzu-Ch'iang Squadron over Presidential Mansion

1980. Air. Multicoloured.
1303 $5 Type **331** 30 15
1304 $7 Boeing 747-100 airliner and insignia of CAL (state airline) 75 25
1305 $12 National Flag and Boeing 747-100 . . . . . 1·00 35

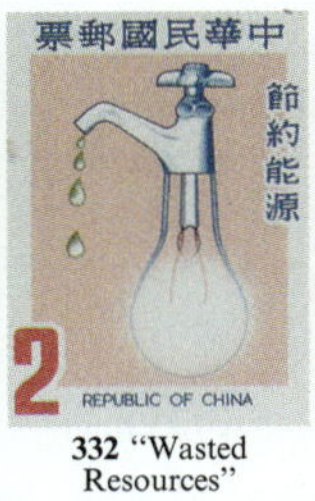
332 "Wasted Resources"

333 Military Official

1980. Energy Conservation.
1306 **332** $2 multicoloured 25 15
1307 $12 multicoloured . . . 75 45

1980. T'ang Dynasty Tri-coloured Pottery. Multicoloured.
1308 $2 Type **333** 55 15
1309 $5 Chickens . . . . 1·10 20
1310 $8 Horse . . . . 1·50 20
1311 $10 Camel . . . . 1·60 25

1980. Chinese Folk-tales (6th series). As T **200**. Multicoloured.
1312 $1 Grinding mortar into a needle 25 15
1313 $2 Returning lost articles . . 40 20
1314 $2 Wen Tien-hsiang in prison 60 20
1315 $5 Sending coal to poor during snow . . . . . . 1·10 25

334 TRA Trunk Line Electrification

335 Money Boxes within Ancient Chinese Coin

1980. Completion of Ten Major Construction Projects. Multicoloured.
1316 $2 Type **334** 40 15
1317 $2 Taichung Harbour . . . 40 15
1318 $2 Chiang Kai-shek International Airport . . 40 15
1319 $2 Integrated steel mill . . . 40 15
1320 $2 Sun Yat-sen National Freeway 40 15
1321 $2 Nuclear power plant . . 40 15
1322 $2 Petrochemical industrial zone in south 40 15
1323 $2 Su-ao Harbour 40 15
1324 $2 Kaohsiung Shipyard . . 40 15
1325 $2 Taiwan North Link Railway 40 15
MS1326 217 × 100 mm. Nos. 1316/25 11·50 9·25

1980. 10th National Savings Day. Mult.
1327 $2 Type **335** 40 15
1328 $12 Hand placing coin in money box . . . . 1·10 45

336/339 Landscape (⅔-size illustration)

1980. Painting by Ch'iu Ying.
1329 **336** $5 multicoloured . . . . 2·30 35
1330 **337** $5 multicoloured . . . . 2·30 35
1331 **338** $5 multicoloured . . . . 2·30 35
1332 **339** $5 multicoloured . . . . 2·30 35
MS1333 101 × 144 mm. Nos. 1329/32 18·00 14·00

Nos. 1329/32 were printed together, se-tenant, forming the composite design illustrated.

340 Cock

341 Heads, Flag and Census Form

1980. New Year Greetings. "Year of the Cock".
1334 **340** $1 multicoloured 75 15
1335 $6 multicoloured . . . . 2·50 40
MS1336 77 × 101 mm. Nos. 1334/5, each × 2 . . . . 10·50 8·25

See also No. 2047.

1980. Population and Housing Census. Mult.
1337 $2 Type **341** 25 20
1338 $12 Flag and buildings (horiz) 90 45

342 Central Weather Bureau

1981. Completion of Meteorological Satellite Ground Station, Taipei. Multicoloured.
1339 $2 "TIROS-N" weather satellite (vert) 30 15
1340 $10 Type **342** 90 45

343 "Happiness"

344 "Wealth"

345 "Longevity"

346 "Joy"

1981. New Year Calligraphy.
1341 **343** $5 gold, red and black 1·20 20
1342 **344** $5 gold, red and black 1·20 20
1343 **345** $5 gold, red and black 1·20 20
1344 **346** $5 gold, red and black 1·20 20

347 Candle and Siamese Twins

1981. International Year for Disabled Persons.
1345 **347** $2 multicoloured 25 15
1346 $10 multicoloured . . . 75 25

348 Mt. Ali

1981. Tourism. Multicoloured.
1347 $2 Type **348** 35 15
1348 $7 Oluanpi 80 20
1349 $12 Sun Moon Lake . . . . 1·40 30

349 "Children on River Bank"

1981. Children's Day. Children's Drawings. Mult.
1350 $1 Type **349** 15 15
1351 $2 "Cable-cars" 25 15
1352 $5 "Lobsters" 30 15
1353 $7 "Village" 35 20

350 Main Gate Chiang Kai-shek Memorial Hall

1981. 6th Death Anniv of Chiang Kai-shek.
1712 **350** 10c. red 25 15
1354 20c. violet 25 15
1714 30c. green 25 15
1355 40c. red 25 15
1356 50c. brown 25 15
1717 60c. blue 25 15

351 Brush Washer (Hsuan-te ware)

352 Electric and First Steam Locomotives

1981. Ancient Chinese Enamelware (1st series). Ming Dynasty Cloisonne Enamelware. Multicoloured.

1357 $2 Type **351** 45 15
1358 $5 Ritual vessel with ring handles (Chiang-ta'i ware) (vert) 85 20
1359 $8 Plate decorated with dragons (Wan-li ware) . . 1·10 20
1360 $10 Vase (vert) . . . . . . 1·40 25

See also Nos. 1438/41, 1472/5 and 1542/5.

1981. Centenary of Railway. Mult.

1361 $2 Type **352** 35 15
1362 $14 Side views of steam and electric locomotives (horiz) . . . . 1·30 45

353 "Liagore rubromaculata"

1981. Crabs. Multicoloured.

1363 $2 Type **353** 40 15
1364 $5 "Ranina ranina" (vert) 60 20
1365 $8 "Platymaia wyvillethomsoni" 80 25
1366 $14 "Lambrus nummifera" (vert) . . . . 1·30 30

354 Bureau Emblem

355 The Cowherd

1981. 40th Anniv of Central Weather Bureau.

1367 **354** $2 multicoloured 35 15
1368 $14 multicoloured . . . 1·10 45

1981. Fairy Tales. "The Cowherd and the Weaving Maid". Multicoloured.

1369 $2 Type **355** 45 15
1370 $4 The cowherd watching the weaving maid through rushes 70 20
1371 $8 The cowherd and the weaving maid on opposite sides of Heavenly River 1·20 25
1372 $14 The cowherd and the weaving maid meeting on bridge of magpies . . . . 2·10 50

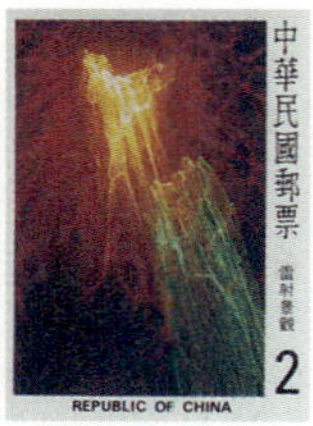

356 Laser Display

1981. Lasography Exhibition. Designs showing different laser displays.

1373 **356** $2 multicoloured 25 15
1374 – $5 multicoloured 30 20
1375 – $8 multicoloured 50 30
1376 – $14 multicoloured . . . 1·10 65

357 Goalkeeper catching Ball

359 Chinese Republic Anniv Emblem and "Stamps"

358 Officers watching Battle from Mound

1981. Athletics Day. Multicoloured.

1390 $5 Women soccer players 60 20
1391 $5 Type **357** 60 20

1981. 70th Anniv of Founding of Chinese Republic. Multicoloured.

1392 $2 Type **358** 25 15
1393 $2 Officer clenching fist and soldiers awaiting battle . . 25 15
1394 $2 Officer on horseback saluting 25 15
1395 $2 Attacking buildings . . . 25 15
1396 $3 Attacking fortifications 35 20
1397 $3 Dockside scene 35 20
1398 $8 Chiang Kai-shek 55 30
1399 $14 Sun Yat-sen . . . . . 1·00 40
MS1400 115 × 168 mm. Nos. 1392/9 8·00 2·50

1981. "Rocpex Taipei '81" International Stamp Exhibition.

1401 **359** $2 multicoloured 20 15
1402 $14 multicoloured . . . 65 30

360 Detail of Scroll

1981. Sung Dynasty painting "One Hundred Young Boys". Designs showing details of Scroll.

1403 **360** $2 (1) multicoloured . . 1·40 25
1404 – $2 (2) multicoloured . . 1·40 25
1405 – $2 (3) multicoloured . . 1·40 25
1406 – $2 (4) multicoloured . . 1·40 25
1407 – $2 (5) multicoloured . . 1·40 25
1408 – $2 (6) multicoloured . . 1·40 25
1409 – $2 (7) multicoloured . . 1·40 25
1410 – $2 (8) multicoloured . . 1·40 25
1411 – $2 (9) multicoloured . . 1·40 25
1412 – $2 (10) multicoloured . . 1·40 25

See note below No. 661 on identification of designs.

Nos. 1403/12 were printed together in se-tenant blocks of ten (5 × 2) within the sheet, each strip of five forming a composite design.

361 Dog

362 Information-using Services and Emblem

1981. New Year Greetings. "Year of the Dog".

1413 **361** $1 multicoloured . . . 85 15
1414 $10 multicoloured . . . 2·00 45
MS1415 78 × 102 mm. Nos. 1413/14, each × 2 . . . . 11·50 3·50

See also No. 2048.

1981. Information Week.

1416 **362** $2 multicoloured 45 20

363 Telephones of 1881 and 1981

364 Arrangement in Basket

1981. Centenary of Chinese Telecommunications Service. Multicoloured.

1417 $2 Map and hand holding telephone handset (vert) 25 15
1418 $3 Type **363** 30 20
1419 $8 Submarine cable map . . 50 20
1420 $18 Computer and telecommunication units (vert) 60 25

1982. Chinese Flower Arrangements. Mult.

1421 $2 Type **364** 25 15
1422 $3 Arrangement in jug . . . 35 20
1423 $8 Arrangement in vase . . 75 25
1424 $18 Arrangement in holder 1·40 40

365 Kuan Yu leaves for Cheng City

1982. Scenes from "The Ku Cheng Reunion" (opera). Multicoloured.

1425 $2 Type **365** 70 15
1426 $3 Chang Fei refuses to open city gates . . . . . 1·30 20
1427 $4 Chang Fei apologises to Kuan Yu . . . . 1·60 25
1428 $18 Liu Pei, Kuan Yu and Chang Fei are reunited 3·25 65

366 Dr. Robert Koch and Tubercle Bacillus

367 Chang Shih-liang (revolutionary)

1982. Centenary of Discovery of Tubercle Bacillus.

1429 **366** $2 multicoloured 30 20

1982. Famous Chinese.

1430 **367** $2 red 25 15

368 "Martyrs' Shrine"

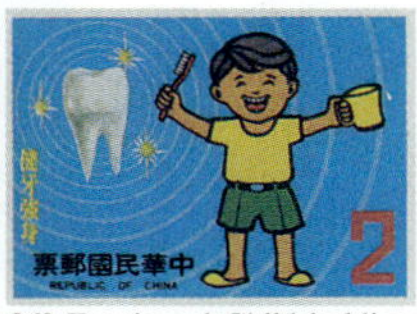

369 Tooth and Child holding Toothbrush and Mug

1982. Children's Day. Children's paintings.

1431 $2 Type **368** 45 15
1432 $3 "House Yard" 60 20
1433 $5 "Cattle Herd" 80 20
1434 $8 "A Sacrificial Ceremony for a Plentiful Year" . . . 1·10 25

1982. Dental Health. Multicoloured.

1435 $2 Type **369** 35 15
1436 $3 Methods of cleaning teeth 70 20
1437 $10 Dental check-up . . . . 1·40 30

1982. Ancient Chinese Enamelware (2nd series). As T **351**. Multicoloured.

1438 $2 Champleve cup and plate (Ch'ien-lung ware) 50 15
1439 $5 Cloisonne duck container (Ch'ien-lung ware) (vert) 95 20
1440 $8 Painted incense burner (K'ang-hsi period) . . . . 1·70 20
1441 $12 Cloisonne Tibetan lama milk-tea pot (Ch'ien-lung ware) (vert) . . . . . . 2·50 25

370 "Spring Dawn" (Meng Hao-jan)

1982. Chinese Classical Poetry (1st series). Tang Dynasty Poems. Multicoloured.

1442 $2 Type **370** . . . . 2·20 20
1443 $3 "On Looking for a Hermit and not Finding Him" (Chia Tao) . . . . 4·50 20
1444 $5 "Summer Dying" (Liu Yu-hsi) . . . . 6·75 40
1445 $18 "Looking at the Snow Drifts on South Mountains" (Tsu Yung) 10·50 90

See also Nos. 1476/9, 1524/7, 1594/7, 1866/9, 1910/13 and 2074/7.

371 Softball

1982. 5th World Women's Softball Championship, Taipeh.

1446 **371** $2 multicoloured 45 15
1447 $18 multicoloured . . . 1·30 45

372 Scouts on Rope Bridge, and Lord Baden-Powell

1982. 75th Anniv of Boy Scout Movement and 125th Birth Anniv of Lord Baden-Powell. Multicoloured.

1448 $2 Type **372** 25 15
1449 $18 Emblem, scouts making frame and camp 80 45

373 Tweezers holding Stamp

374 Carved Lion

1982. Philately Day. Multicoloured.

1450 $2 Type **373** 45 15
1451 $18 Examining stamp album with magnifying glass . . 1·30 45

1982. Tsu Shih Temple, Sanhsia. Multicoloured.

1452 $2 Type **374** 40 15
1453 $3 Lion brackets (horiz) . . 55 20
1454 $5 Carved sub-lintels in passageway 90 25
1455 $18 Temple roofs (horiz) . . 1·80 40

1982. Chinese Folk-tales (7th series). Stories from "36 Examples of Filial Piety" by Wu Yen-huan, As T **200**. Multicoloured.

1456 $1 Shao K'ang supporting his mother 30 15
1457 $2 Hsun Kuan leading soldier reinforcements to her father 50 20
1458 $3 Ku Yen-wu refusing to serve Ch'ing dynasty . . . 70 20
1459 $5 Ting Ch'un-liang caring for his paralysed father 1·30 25

375 Riding Horses

1982. 30th Anniv of China Youth Corps. Multicoloured.

1460 $2 Type **375** 15 15
1461 $3 Flag and water sport (vert) 25 15
1462 $18 Mountaineering 80 50

376 Lohan with Boy Attendant and Monkey

378 Pig

1982. Lohan (Buddhist Saint) Scroll Paintings by Liu Sung-nien. Multicoloured.

1463 $2 Type **376** . . . . 1·40 20
1464 $3 Monk presenting seated Lohan with scroll . . . . 2·40 30

1465 $18 Tribal king paying homage to seated Lohan 6·00 80
MS1466 140 × 102 mm. Nos. 1463/5 22·00 7·50
MS1467 No. **MS**1466 with vertical overprint in red left and right margins 26·00 19·00

1982. New Year. "Year of the Pig".
1468 **378** $1 multicoloured 1·20 15
1469 $10 multicoloured 2·75 50
MS1470 77 × 102 mm. Nos. 1468/9, each × 2 12·50 4·75
See also No. 2049.

1983. Ancient Chinese Enamelware (3rd series). Ch'ing Dynasty Enamelware. As T **351**. Multicoloured.
1472 $2 Square basin with rounded corners 40 15
1473 $3 Vase decorated with landscape panels (vert) 75 20
1474 $4 Blue teapot with flower pattern 1·20 25
1475 $18 Cloisonne elephant with vase on back (vert) 1·60 40

379 "Wan-hsi-sha" (Yen Shu)

380 Hsin-hsien Concealed Fall, Wawa Valley

1983. Chinese Classical Poetry (2nd series). Sung Dynasty Lyrical Poems. Multicoloured.
1476 $2 Type **379** 2·30 25
1477 $3 "Ch'ing-yu-an" (Ho Chu) 4·50 35
1478 $5 "Su-mu-che" (Fan Chung-yen) 6·00 40
1479 $11 "Hsing-hsiang-tzu" (Ch'ao Pu-chih) 9·50 60

1983. Landscapes. Multicoloured.
1480 $2 Type **380** 65 20
1481 $3 University Pond, Chitou Forest 1·10 30
1482 $18 Mount Jade (horiz) 1·50 45

381 Matteo Ricci and Astrolabe

1983. 400th Anniv of Matteo Ricci's (missionary) Arrival in China. Multicoloured.
1483 $2 Type **381** 40 15
1484 $18 Matteo Ricci and Great Wall 1·20 35

382 Wu Ching-heng (Chairman of development committee)

383 Hsu Hsien meets Pai Su-chen

1983. 70th Anniv of Mandarin Phonetic Symbols. Multicoloured.
1485 $2 Type **382** 40 15
1486 $18 Children studying symbols 1·20 35

1983. Fairy Tales. "Lady White Snake". Multicoloured.
1487 $2 Type **383** 35 15
1488 $3 Pai Su-chen steals Tree of Life 65 20
1489 $3 Confrontation with Fahai at Chin Shan Temple 1·00 30
1490 $18 Pai Su-chen is imprisoned beneath Thunder Peak Pagoda 1·70 50

384 Pot with Cord Pattern

385 Communication Emblems circling Globe

1983. Ancient Chinese Bamboo Carvings. Multicoloured.
1491 $2 Type **384** 50 15
1492 $3 Vase with Tao-t'ien motif 80 20
1493 $4 Carved mountain scene with figures 85 25
1494 $18 Brush-holder with relief showing ladies 2·30 40

1983. World Communications Year. Mult.
1495 $2 Type **385** 40 15
1496 $18 WCY emblem 80 35

386 Grouper

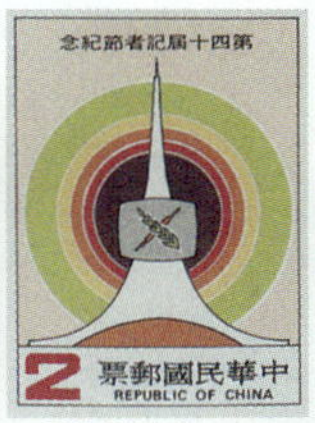
387 T.V. Screen, Antenna and Radio Waves

1983. Protection of Fishery Resources. Mult.
1497 $2 Type **386** 45 20
1498 $18 Lizardfish 1·70 45

1983. Journalists' Day.
1499 **387** $2 multicoloured 30 15

388 Yurt

389 Brown Shrike

1983. Mongolian and Tibetan Scenes.
1500 $2 Type **388** 50 15
1501 $3 Potala Palace 85 20
1502 $5 Sheep on prairie 1·00 25
1503 $11 Camel caravan 1·40 40

1983. 2nd East Asian Bird Protection Conference. Multicoloured.
1504 $2 Type **389** 55 20
1505 $18 Grey-faced buzzard-eagle 2·20 45

390 Pink Plum Blossom

391 Congress Emblem

1983. Plum Blossom. Multicoloured.
1506 $2 Type **390** 25 15
1507 $3 Red plum blossom 40 20
1508 $5 Plum blossom and pagoda 60 20
1509 $11 White plum blossom 1·10 25

1983. 38th Jaycees International World Congress. Multicoloured.
1510 $2 Type **391** 30 15
1511 $18 Emblems and globe 1·10 45

392 World Map as Heart

393 Rat

1983. 8th Asian-Pacific Cardiology Congress. Mult.
1512 $2 Type **392** 30 15
1513 $18 Heart and electrocardiogram 1·10 45

1983. New Year. "Year of the Rat".
1514 **393** $1 multicoloured 1·40 15
1515 $10 multicoloured 3·75 50
MS1516 78 × 103 mm. Nos. 1514/15, each × 2 26·00 6·25
See also No. 2038.

394 Mother and Child reading and Chin Ting Prize

1983. National Reading Week. Mult.
1517 $2 Type **394** 30 15
1518 $18 Chin Ting prize (for outstanding publications) books and father and son reading (vert) 1·00 35

395 Boeing 737 over Chiang Kai-shek Airport

396 Soldiers with Flags

1984. Air. 37th Anniv of Civil Aeronautics Administration. Multicoloured.
1519 $7 Type **395** 55 15
1520 $11 Boeing 747 over Chung-cheng Memorial Hall (horiz) 80 30
1521 $18 Boeing 737 over Sun Yat-sen Memorial Hall (horiz) 1·10 45

1984. World Freedom Day. Multicoloured.
1522 $2 Type **396** 30 15
1523 $18 Globe and people of the world 1·30 35

397 "Hsiao-liang-chou" (Kuan Yun-shih)

1984. Chinese Classical Poetry (3rd series). Yuan Dynasty Lyric Poems. Multicoloured.
1524 $2 Type **397** 2·40 25
1525 $3 "A Lady holds a fine fan of silk", "Tien-ching-sha" (Po P'u) 3·75 30
1526 $5 "Picnic under banana leaves "Ch'ing-chiang-yin" (Chang Ko-chin) 5·25 35
1527 $18 "Plum blossoms in the snowbound wilderness "Tien-ching-sha" (Shang Cheng-shu) 8·25 95

398 Forest Scene

400 Lin Chueh-min (revolutionary)

1984. Forest Resources. Multicoloured.
1528 $2 Type **398** 80 15
1529 $2 Reservoir and dam 80 15
1530 $2 Camp in forest 80 15
1531 $2 Wooded slopes 80 15
Nos. 1528/31 were printed together se-tenant, forming a composite design.

1984. Famous Chinese.
1536 **400** $2 green 30 15

401 Agency Emblem and Broadcasting Equipment

402 "Five Auspicious Tokens"

1984. 60th Anniv of Central News Agency. Mult.
1537 $2 Type **401** 25 15
1538 $10 Agency emblem and satellite communications 75 30

1984. 85th Birth Anniv of Chang Ta-chien (artist). Multicoloured.
1539 $2 Type **402** 1·30 20
1540 $5 "The God of Longevity" 3·50 20
1541 $18 "Lotus Blossoms in Ink Splash" 5·25 45

1984. Ancient Chinese Enamelware (4th series). Ch'ing Dynasty Enamelware. As T **351**. Mult.
1542 $2 Lidded cup and teapot on tray 40 15
1543 $3 Cloisonne wine vessel on phoenix (vert) 60 20
1544 $4 Yellow teapot with pink and blue chrysanthemum decoration 95 25
1545 $18 Cloisonne candle-holder on bird 1·30 40

403 Boeing 747-200 circling Globe

1984. Inauguration of China Airlines Global Service. Multicoloured.
1546 $2 Type **403** 20 15
1547 $7 Globe and Boeing 747-200 35 20
1548 $11 Boeing 747-200 over New York 55 30
1549 $18 Boeing 747-200 over Netherlands 90 50

404 Judo

1984. Olympic Games, Los Angeles. Mult.
1550 $2 Type **404** 25 15
1551 $5 Archery (vert) 40 20
1552 $18 Swimming 95 50

405 Container Ship "Ming Comfort"

406 "Gentiana arisanensis"

1984. 30th Navigation Day. Multicoloured.
1553 $2 Type **405** 75 15
1554 $18 "Prosperity" (tanker) 2·10 40

1984. Alpine Plants. Multicoloured.
1555 $2 Type **406** 40 15
1556 $3 "Epilobium nankotaiza nense" 70 20
1557 $5 "Adenophora uehatae" 95 30
1558 $18 "Aconitum fukutomei" 2·30 50

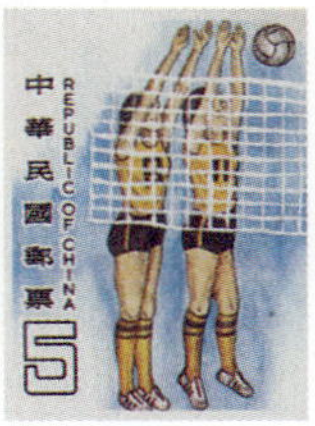

407 Scholars listening to Music
408 Volleyball Players

1984. Sung Dynasty Painting "The Eighteen Scholars". Multicoloured.
1559 $2 Type **407** . . . . 2·10 20
1560 $3 Scholars playing chess . . 3·25 20
1561 $5 Scholars writing . . . . 4·75 25
1562 $18 Scholars painting . . . 12·00 60

1984. Athletics Day. Multicoloured.
1563 $5 Type **408** 80 20
1564 $5 Volleyball player 80 20
Nos. 1563/4 were printed together, se-tenant, forming a composite design.

409 Union Emblem
410 1965 Confucius $1 Stamp

1984. 20th Anniv of Asian-Pacific Parliamentarians' Union.
1565 **409** $10 multicoloured . . . 65 20

1984. New Postal Museum Building, Taipeh. Multicoloured.
1566 $2 Type **410** 20 15
1567 $5 1933 Sun Yat-sen 5c. stamp 40 15
1568 $18 New Postal Museum building . . . . 1·00 50
MS1569 128 × 89 mm. Nos. 1566/8 8·25 1·80

411 Flag and Emblem
412 Commission Services

1984. Grand Alliance for China's Reunification Convention.
1570 **411** $2 multicoloured 40 15

1984. 30th Anniv of Vocational Assistance Commission for Retired Servicemen.
1571 **412** $2 multicoloured 40 15

413 Pine Tree
414 Ox

1984. Pine, Bamboo and Plum (1st series). Multicoloured.
1572 $2 Type **413** 25 15
1573 $8 Bamboo 65 20
1574 $10 Plum blossom 75 30
See also Nos. 1633/5, 1783/5 and 1845/7.

1984. New Year Greetings. "Year of the Ox".
1575 **414** $1 multicoloured 85 15
1576 $10 multicoloured . . . 2·75 30
MS1577 78 × 101 mm. Nos. 1575/6, each × 2 . . . . 7·00 2·10
See also No. 2039.

415 Legal Code Book and Scales
416 Ku-kang Lake and Pagoda, Quemoy

1985. Judicial Day.
1578 **415** $5 multicoloured 55 20

1985. Scenery of Quemoy and Matsu. Mult.
1579 $2 Type **416** 25 15
1580 $5 Kuang-hai stone, Quemoy 55 20
1581 $8 Sheng-li reservoir, Matsu 95 20
1582 $10 Tung-chu lighthouse, Matsu . . . . 1·30 25

417 Sir Robert Hart and 1878 3c. Stamp
418 Lo Fu-hsing

1985. 150th Anniv of Sir Robert Hart (founder of Chinese Postal Service).
1583 **417** $2 multicoloured 40 15

1985. Birth Centenary of Lo Fu-hsing (patriot).
1584 **418** $2 multicoloured 40 15

419 Tsou Jung
421 Lily

420 Main Gate, Chung-cheng Memorial Hall

1985. 80th Death Anniv of Tsou Jung (revolutionary).
1585 **419** $3 green 40 15

1985. 10th Death Anniv of President Chiang Kai-shek. Multicoloured.
1586 $2 Type **420** 25 15
1587 $8 Tzuhu, President Chiang's temporary resting place 95 20
1588 $10 President Chiang Kai-shek (vert) . . . . 1·20 30

1985. Mothers' Day. Multicoloured.
1589 $2 Type **421** 80 15
1590 $2 Carnation 80 15

422 View of Tunnel
423 Girl Guide saluting

1985. 1st Anniv of Kaohsiung Cross-harbour Tunnel.
1591 **422** $5 multicoloured 60 20

1985. 75th Anniv of Girl Guide Movement.
1592 **423** $2 multicoloured 25 15
1593 $18 multicoloured . . . 1·50 35

424 "Buxom is the Peach Tree..."

1985. Chinese Classical Poetry (4th series). Poems from "Book of Odes", edited by Confucius. Multicoloured.
1594 $2 Type **424** . . . . 1·00 20
1595 $5 "Thick grows that tarragon ..." . . . . . . 2·50 30
1596 $8 "Thick grow the rush leaves ..." . . . . 4·00 35
1597 $10 "... The snowflakes fly" 5·25 40

425 Wax Jambo

1985. Fruit. Multicoloured.
1598 $2 Type **425** 55 15
1599 $3 Guavas 85 20
1600 $5 Carambolas . . . . . . 1·20 20
1601 $8 Lychees . . . . 1·80 25

426 Dragon Boat
427 Lady of Rank, T'ang Dynasty

1985. Ch'ing Dynasty Ivory Carvings. Mult.
1602 $2 Type **426** 35 15
1603 $3 Carved landscape 50 20
1604 $5 Melon-shaped water container 80 25
1605 $18 Brush-holder (vert) . . 1·00 35

1985. 4th Asian Costume Conference. Chinese Costumes (1st series). Multicoloured.
1606 $2 Type **427** 70 15
1607 $5 Palace woman, Sung dynasty . . . . 1·30 20
1608 $8 Lady of rank, Yuan dynasty . . . . 2·20 20
1609 $11 Lady of rank, Ming dynasty . . . . 2·75 25
See also Nos. 1687/90, 1767/70, 1833/6, 1906/9 and 1973/6.

428 Bird feeding Chicks

1985. Social Welfare.
1610 **428** $2 multicoloured 40 15

429 North Gate, Taipeh
430 Oak Tree

1985. Historic Buildings (1st series). Mult.
1611 $2 Type **429** 25 15
1612 $5 San Domingo fort, Tamsui 55 20
1613 $8 Lung Shan Temple, Lukang 75 20
1614 $10 Confucius Temple, Changhua . . . . 1·10 25
See also Nos. 1700/3.

1985. Bonsai. Multicoloured.
1615 $2 Type **430** 25 15
1616 $5 Five-leaf pine 60 25
1617 $8 Lohan pine 85 35
1618 $18 Banyan . . . . 1·30 50

431 World Trade Centre and Sports Goods Logo
432 Flag, Map and Scenes of Peace

1985. Trade Shows. Multicoloured.
1619 $2 Type **431** 70 15
1620 $2 Toys and gifts logo (blue and red) 70 15
1621 $2 Electronics logo (blue) 70 15
1622 $2 Machinery logo (black and orange) 70 15
Nos. 1619/22 were printed together, se-tenant, forming a composite design depicting Taipeh World Trade Centre.

1985. 40th Anniv of Return of Taiwan to China. Multicoloured.
1623 $2 Type **432** 80 15
1624 $18 Chiang Kai-shek and triumphal arch . . . . . 1·90 45

433 Emblem
434 Sun Yat-sen

1985. 7th Asian Federation for the Mentally Retarded Conference, Taipeh.
1625 **433** $2 multicoloured 40 15
1626 $11 multicoloured . . . 1·20 30

1985. 120th Birth Anniv of Sun Yat-sen.
1627 **434** $2 multicoloured 45 15
1628 $18 multicoloured . . . 1·50 45

435 Tiger
436 Emblem

1985. New Year Greetings. "Year of the Tiger".
1629 **435** $1 multicoloured 55 15
1630 $10 multicoloured . . . 1·90 35
MS1631 77 × 101 mm. Nos. 1629/30, each × 2 . . . . 9·75 2·75
See also No. 2040.

1985. 50th Anniv of Postal Simple Life Insurance.
1632 **436** $2 multicoloured 40 15

437 Pine Tree

1986. Pine, Bamboo and Plum (2nd series). Multicoloured.
1633 $1 Type **437** 25 15
1634 $11 Bamboo 55 20
1635 $18 Plum blossom 80 20

438 Detail of Scroll

1986. Painting "Hermit Anglers on a Mountain Stream" by T'ang Yin. Designs showing details of the scroll. Multicoloured.
1636 $2 (1) Type **438** . . . . . 1·60 20
1637 $2 (2) Pavilions on bank . . 1·60 20
1638 $2 (3) Anglers in boats near waterfall . . . . 1·60 20

1639 $2 (4) Pavilions on stilts . . 1·60 20
1640 $2 (5) Anglers in boat near island . . . . 1·60 20

Nos. 1636/40 were printed together, forming a composite design.

See note below No. 661 on identification of designs in se-tenant strips.

439 Gladioli in Vase

440 Loading and unloading Boeing 747 Mail Plane

1986. Flower Arrangements (1st series). Mult.
1641 $2 Type **439** 30 20
1642 $5 Roses in double wicker holders 60 20
1643 $8 Roses and fern in pot on stand 75 20
1644 $10 Various flowers in large and small pots . . . . . 1·10 25

See also Nos. 1741/4.

1986. 90th Anniv of Post Office. Mult.
1645 $2 Type **440** 25 15
1646 $5 Postman on motorcycle (vert) 30 20
1647 $8 Customer at cash dispenser and clerk at savings bank computer terminal (vert) 50 20
1648 $10 Electronic sorting machine and envelopes circling globe 60 25
MS1649 130 × 100 mm. Nos. 1645/8 5·25 2·10

441 Chen Tien-hva (revolutionary writer)

442 Mountain shrouded in Mist

1986. Famous Chinese.
1650 **441** $2 violet 25 15

1986. Yushan National Park. Multicoloured.
1651 $2 Type **442** 45 15
1652 $5 People on mountain top 1·10 20
1653 $8 Snow covered mountain peak . . . . 1·50 25
1654 $10 Forest on mountain side 2·00 30

443 Hydro-electric Power Station

1986. Power Stations. Multicoloured.
1655 $2 Type **443** 35 15
1656 $8 Thermo-electric power station 65 20
1657 $10 Nuclear power station 95 30

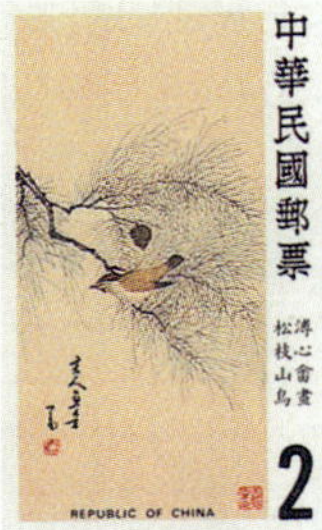
444 Taiwan Firecrest in Tree

446 Green-winged Macaw

445 Emblems

1986. Paintings by P'u Hsin-yu. Mult.
1658 $2 Type **444** . . . . 1·60 15
1659 $8 Landscape . . . . 3·50 25
1660 $10 Woman in garden . . . 4·50 35

1986. 25th Anniv of Asian Productivity Organization and 30th Anniv of China Productivity Centre.
1661 **445** $2 multicoloured 25 15
1662 $11 multicoloured . . . 90 30

1986. Protection of Intellectual Property.
1663 **446** $2 multicoloured 95 20

447 Starck's Damselfish ("Chrysiptera starcki")

(**448**)

1986. Coral Reef Fishes. Multicoloured.
1664 $2 Type **447** . . . . 2·30 1·40
1665 $2 Copper-banded butterflyfish ("Chelmon rostratus") . . . . 2·30 1·40
1666 $2 Pearl-scaled butterflyfish ("Chaetodon xanthurus") 2·30 1·40
1667 $2 Four-spotted butterflyfish ("Chaetodon quadrimaculatus") . . . . 2·30 1·40
1668 $2 Meyer's butterflyfish ("Chaetodon meyeri") . . 2·30 1·40
1669 $2 Japanese swallow ("Genicanthus semifasciatus") (female) 2·30 1·40
1670 $2 Japanese swallow ("Genicanthus semifasciatus") (male) . . 2·30 1·40
1671 $2 Blue-ringed angelfish ("Pomacanthus annularis") . . . . 2·30 1·40
1672 $2 Harlequin tuskfish ("Lienardella fasciata") 2·30 1·40
1673 $2 Undulate triggerfish ("Balistapus undulatus") 2·30 1·40

1986. 60th Anniv of Chiang Kai-shek's Northward Expedition. Nos. 1229 and 1386 surch as T **448**.
1674 **306** $2 on $6 red, bl & orge 25 15
1675 $8 on $9 red, bl & grn 50 30

449 Tzu Mu Bridge

450 Yingtai and Shanpo going to School

1986. Road Bridges. Multicoloured.
1676 $2 Type **449** 45 15
1677 $5 Chang Hung bridge over Hsiu-ku-luan-chi 80 20
1678 $8 Kuan Fu bridge over Hsintien River . . . . . 1·20 20
1679 $10 Kuan Tu bridge over Tanshui River . . . . . 2·00 25

1986. Folk Tales. "Love between Liang Shanpo and Chu Yingtai". Multicoloured.
1680 $5 Type **450** 70 15
1681 $5 Classmates 70 15
1682 $5 Yingtai and Shanpo by lake 70 15
1683 $5 Yingtai telling Shanpo she is to be married . . . 70 15
1684 $5 Ascending to heaven as butterflies 70 15

451 Children playing by Lake and Rainbow

452 Lady of Warring States Period

1986. Cleanliness and Courtesy. Mult.
1685 $2 Type **451** 35 20
1686 $8 Children helping others in street 75 25

1986. Chinese Costumes (2nd series). Mult.
1687 $2 Lady of rank, Shang dynasty 55 15
1688 $5 Type **452** . . . . 1·20 20
1689 $8 Empress's assembly dress, later Han dynasty . . . 1·70 20
1690 $10 Beribboned dress of lady of rank, Wei and Tsin dynasties . . . . . 2·50 25

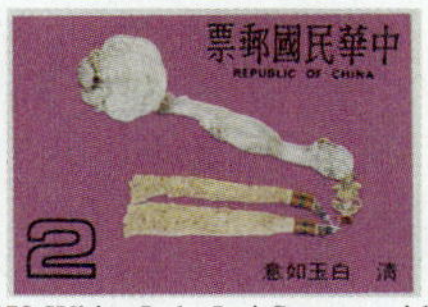
453 White Jade Ju-i Sceptre with Fish Decoration

1986. Ch'ing Dynasty Ju-i (1st series). Mult.
1691 $2 Type **453** 25 15
1692 $3 Coral ju-i sceptre with fungus motif 40 20
1693 $4 Redwood ju-i sceptre inlaid with precious stones 55 25
1694 $18 Gold-painted ju-i sceptre with three abundances (fruit) . . . . 1·50 40

See also Nos 1735/8.

454 Chiang Kai-shek and Books

1986. Birth Cent of Chiang Kai-shek. Mult.
1695 $2 Type **454** 45 15
1696 $5 Chiang Kai-shek, flag, map and crowd 75 20
1697 $8 Chiang Kai-shek, emblem and youths 90 20
1698 $10 Chiang Kai-shek, flags on globe and clasped hands . . . . 1·10 25
MS1699 120 × 90 mm. Nos. 1695/8 7·75 2·50

455 Erh-sha-wan Gun Emplacement, Keelung

456 Hare

1986. Historic Buildings (2nd series). Mult.
1700 $2 Chin-kuang-fu House, Pei-pu 35 15
1701 $5 Type **455** 70 20
1702 $8 Hsi T'ai fort 95 25
1703 $10 Matsu Temple, Peng-hu 1·40 30

1986. New Year Greetings. "Year of the Hare".
1704 **456** $1 multicoloured 50 15
1705 $10 multicoloured . . . 2·10 30
MS1706 78 × 102 mm. Nos. 1704/5, each × 2 . . . . 13·00 2·50

See also No. 2041.

457 Shrubs on Rock Formation

458 Glove Puppet

1987. Kenting National Park. Multicoloured.
1707 $2 Type **457** 40 15
1708 $5 Rocky outcrop 80 20
1709 $8 Sandy bay . . . . 1·20 20
1710 $10 Rocky bays . . . . . . 1·80 25

1987. Puppets. Multicoloured.
1721 $2 Type **458** 45 15
1722 $5 String puppet 90 25
1723 $18 Shadow show puppet 1·50 40

459 Envelope, Parcel and Globe

460 Wu Yueh (revolutionary)

1987. Speedpost Service.
1724 **459** $2 multicoloured 30 15
1725 $18 multicoloured . . . 1·10 45

1987. Famous Chinese.
1726 **460** $2 red 85 15

461 "Singing Creek with Bamboo Orchestra"

1987. Madame Chiang Kai-shek's Landscape Paintings (3rd series). Each black, stone and red.
1727 $2 Type **461** 55 15
1728 $5 "Mountains draped in Clouds" . . . . 1·50 20
1729 $5 "Vista of Tranquility" . . 2·20 25
1730 $10 "Mountains after a Snowfall" . . . . 2·75 40

462 Bodhisattva Head, Northern Wei Dynasty

463 View of Dam

1987. Ancient Chinese Stone Carvings. Mult.
1731 $5 Type **462** 65 30
1732 $5 Standing Buddha, Northern Ch'i dynasty . . 65 30
1733 $5 Bodhisattva head, T'ang dynasty 65 30
1734 $5 Seated Buddha, T'ang dynasty 65 30

1987. Ch'ing Dynasty Ju-i (2nd series). As T **453**. Multicoloured.
1735 $2 Silver ju-i sceptre with fungus decoration of pearls and precious stones 50 15
1736 $3 Gold ju-i sceptre with Eight Treasures decoration of pearls and precious stones 90 20
1737 $4 Gilt ju-i sceptre inlaid with precious stones and kingfisher feather . . . . 1·40 25
1738 $18 Gilt ju-i sceptre with wirework and inlaid with malachite . . . . 3·50 40

1987. Feitsui Reservoir Inauguration. Multicoloured.
1739 $2 Type **463** 40 15
1740 $18 View of reservoir . . . 1·60 50

1987. Flower Arrangements (2nd series). As T **439**. Multicoloured.
1741 $2 Roses and pine twig in holder 30 15
1742 $5 Flowers in pot 60 20
1743 $8 Tasselled pendant hanging from bamboo in vase 80 20
1744 $10 Pine in flask 95 25

464 Emblem

465 Soldiers firing from behind Barricades

1987. 70th Lions Clubs International Convention, Taipeh.
1745 **464** $2 multicoloured 35 15
1746 $18 multicoloured . . . 1·30 55

1987. 50th Anniv of Start of Sino-Japanese War. Multicoloured.
1747 $1 Type **465** 25 15
1748 $2 Chiang Kai-shek making speech from balcony 35 15
1749 $5 Crowd throwing money onto flag 40 20
1750 $6 Columns of soldiers and tanks on mountain road 50 20
1751 $8 General giving written message to Chiang Kai-shek 75 25
1752 $18 Pres. and Madame Chiang Kai-shek at front of crowd . . . . 1·00 40

466 Airplane flying to Left

467 Wang Yun-wu

1987. Air. Multicoloured.
1753 $9 Type **466** 60 30
1754 $14 Airplane 90 45
1755 $18 Airplane flying to right 1·20 55

1987. Birth Centenary (1988) of Wang Yun-wu (lexicographer).
1756 **467** $2 black 30 15

468 Trees on Islands and Fisherman

1987. Painting "After Chao Po-su's 'Red Cliff'" by Wen Cheng-ming. Designs showing details of the scroll. Multicoloured.
1757 $3 (1) Type **468** 80 20
1758 $3 (2) Tree and three figures on island 80 20
1759 $3 (3) House in walled enclosure on island . . . 80 20
1760 $3 (4) Figures in doorway of building and horse in stable 80 20
1761 $3 (5) Cliffs and sea 80 20
1762 $3 (6) Islets, trees and figures on shore 80 20
1763 $3 (7) Trees among cliffs . . 80 20
1764 $3 (8) People in sampan . . 80 20
1765 $3 (9) Building surrounded by trees and cliffs 80 20
1766 $3 (10) Cliffs, trees and waterfall 80 20

Nos. 1757/66 were printed together, se-tenant, forming a composite design.

See note below No. 661 on identification of designs in se-tenant strips.

469 Han Lady of Rank, Early Ch'ing Dynasty

470 Ta Chen Tian, Confucius Temple, Taichung

1987. Chinese Costumes (3rd series). Mult.
1767 $1.50 Type **469** 70 15
1768 $3 Manchu bannerman's wife, Ch'ing dynasty . . . 95 20
1769 $7.50 Woman's Manchu-style Ch'i-p'ao, early Republic period . . . . 1·50 25
1770 $18 Jacket and skirt, early Republic period . . . . . 3·00 40

1987. International Confucianism and the Modern World Symposium, Taipeh. Multicoloured.
1771 $3 Type **470** 40 20
1772 $18 Confucius and fresco . . 1·50 70

471 Dragon

472 Flag and Emblem as "40"

1987. New Year Greetings. "Year of the Dragon".
1773 **471** $1.50 multicoloured . . 55 15
1774 $12 multicoloured . . 2·10 30
MS1775 77 × 101 mm. Nos. 1773/4, each × 2 . . . . 9·75 2·10

See also No. 2042.

1987. 40th Anniv of Constitution. Mult.
1776 $3 Type **472** 25 15
1777 $16 "40" in national colours and emblem . . . . . . 1·00 60

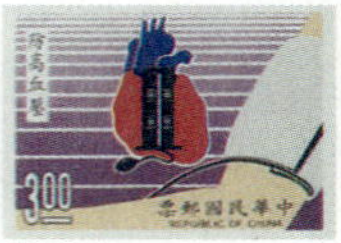
473 Sphygmomanometer

474 Plum

1988. Nat Health. Prevent Hypertension Campaign.
1778 **473** $3 multicoloured 35 15

1988. Flowers (1st series). Multicoloured.
1779 $3 Type **474** 95 15
1780 $7.50 Apricot . . . . 1·60 30
1781 $12 Peach . . . . 2·40 45
MS1782 119 × 80 mm. Nos. 1779/81 20·00 16·00

See also Nos. 1798/**MS**1801, 1809/**MS**1812 and 1829/**MS**1832.

475 Pine Tree

476 Modelled Dough Figurines

1988. Pine, Bamboo and Plum (3rd series). Multicoloured.
1783 $1.50 Type **475** 30 15
1784 $7.50 Bamboo 55 20
1785 $16 Plum blossom . . . . . 1·20 30

1988. Traditional Handicrafts. Multicoloured.
1786 $3 Type **476** 65 15
1787 $7.50 Blown sugar fish . . . 1·50 35
1788 $16 Sugar painting . . . . 2·30 75

477 Hsu Hsi-lin (revolutionary)

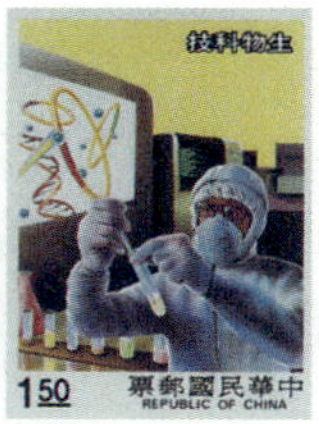
478 Bio-technology

1988. Famous Chinese.
1789 **477** $3 brown 50 20

1988. Science and Technology. Multicoloured.
1790 $1.50 Type **478** 25 15
1791 $3 Surveyors at oil field (energy) 30 15
1792 $7 Syringe piercing letter "B" (hepatitis control) . . 40 15
1793 $7.50 Mechanised production line (automation) 45 25
1794 $10 Satellite and computer terminal (information) . . 55 35
1795 $12 Laser (electro-optics) . . 65 40
1796 $16 Laboratory worker (materials) 85 55
1797 $16.50 Tin of fruit and technician (food technology) . . . . 1·10 65

1988. Flowers (2nd series). As T **474**. Mult.
1798 $3 Tree peony 50 15
1799 $7.50 Pomegranate . . . . 1·40 30
1800 $12 East Indian lotus . . . 2·20 45
MS1801 120 × 80 mm. Nos. 1798/1800 . . . . 11·50 9·25

479 Policemen on Point Duty and Motor Cycle

1988. Police Day. Multicoloured.
1802 $3 Type **479** 25 15
1803 $12 Communications operator and fire-fighters 70 45

480 Butler's Pigmy Frog

1988. Amphibians. Multicoloured.
1804 $1.50 Type **480** 70 15
1805 $3 Taipeh striped slender frog . . . . 1·10 25
1806 $7.50 "Microhyla inornata" 2·20 35
1807 $16 Tree frog . . . . 3·75 60

481 "60" on Map

1988. 60th Anniv of Broadcasting Corporation of China.
1808 **481** $3 multicoloured 35 15

1988. Flowers (3rd series). As T **474**. Mult.
1809 $3 Garden balsam 50 15
1810 $7.50 Sweet osmanthus . . 1·40 30
1811 $12 Chrysanthemum . . . . 2·20 45
MS1812 119 × 80 mm. Nos. 1809/11 10·50 6·50

482 Chiang Kai-shek and Soldiers

1988. 30th Anniv of Kinmen Bombardment. Multicoloured.
1813 $1.50 Type **482** 25 15
1814 $3 Chiang Kai-shek and soldier reporters 35 20
1815 $7.50 Soldiers firing howitzer 55 30
1816 $12 Tank battle 75 45

483 Basketball Player

1988. Sports Day. Multicoloured.
1817 $5 Type **483** 80 20
1818 $5 Two basketball players 80 20
1819 $5 Baseball hitter 80 20
1820 $5 Baseball catcher 80 20

484 Crater

1988. Yangmingshan National Park. Mult.
1821 $1.50 Type **484** 25 15
1822 $3 Lake 40 25
1823 $7.50 Mountains 90 35
1824 $16 Lake and mountains . . 1·30 50

485-88 "Lofty Mount Lu"

1988. Painting by Shen Chou.
1825 **485** $5 multicoloured . . . . 1·40 20
1826 **486** $5 multicoloured . . . . 1·40 20
1827 **487** $5 multicoloured . . . . 1·40 20
1828 **488** $5 multicoloured . . . . 1·40 20

Nos. 1825/8 were printed together, se-tenant, forming the composite design illustrated.

1988. Flowers (4th series). As T **474**. Mult.
1829 $3 Cotton rose hibiscus . . 50 15
1830 $7.50 Camellia . . . . . . 1·60 30
1831 $12 Narcissus . . . . 2·40 45
MS1832 120 × 80 mm. Nos. 1829/31 11·00 9·00

1988. Chinese Costumes (4th series). As T **469**. Multicoloured.
1833 $2 Nobleman with tall hat, Shang dynasty 60 15
1834 $3 Ruler with topknot, Warring States period . . 95 20
1835 $7.50 Male official with writing brush in hair, Wei-chin dynasty . . . . 1·50 35
1836 $12 Male court official with hanging brush on hat, late Northern dynasties . . . 2·50 60

489 Snake

490 Tai Ch'uan-hsien

1988. New Year Greetings. "Year of the Snake".
1837 **489** $2 multicoloured . . . . 1·70 25
1838 $13 multicoloured . . . 4·25 55
MS1839 77 × 101 mm. Nos. 1837/8, each × 2 . . . . 13·00 10·50

See also No. 2043.

1989. Birth Centenary (1990) of Tai Ch'uan-hsien (Civil Service reformer).
1840 **490** $3 black 50 20

491 Pres. Chiang Ching-kuo

1989. 1st Death Anniv of President Chiang Ching-Kuo. Multicoloured.
1841 $3 Type **491** 25 15
1842 $6 Chiang Ching-kuo, political rally and voters 40 25
1843 $7.50 Chiang Ching-kuo at docks 55 35
1844 $16 Chiang Ching-kuo with children 80 55

492 Pine Tree

1989. Pine, Bamboo and Plum (4th series). Multicoloured.
1845 $3 Type **492** 25 15
1846 $16.50 Bamboo . . . . . 1·20 25
1847 $21 Plum blossom . . . . . 1·40 35

493 Ni Ying-tien

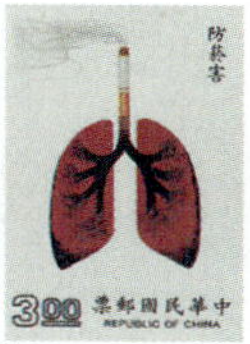
494 Lungs smoking

1989. 79th Death Anniv of Ni Ying-tien (revolutionary).
1848 **493** $3 black 30 15

1989. Anti-smoking Campaign.
1849 **494** $3 multicoloured 30 15

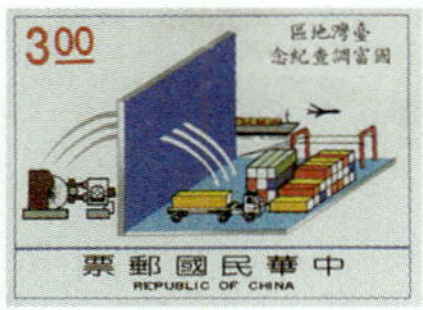

495 Mu Tou Yu Lighthouse **496** Distribution of Industrial Goods

1989. Lighthouses. White panel at foot. Mult.
1850 75c. Type **495** 25 15
1851 $2 Lu Tao lighthouse . . . 25 15
1852 $2.25 Pen Chia Yu lighthouse 25 15
1853 $3 Pitou Chiao lighthouse 35 20
1854 $4.50 Tungyin Tao lighthouse 40 15
1855 $6 Chilai Pi lighthouse . . . 60 25
1856 $7 Fukwei Chiao lighthouse 70 35
1857 $7.50 Hua Yu lighthouse . . 80 35
1858 $9 Oluan Pi lighthouse . . . 80 25
1859 $10 Kaohsiung lighthouse 95 50
1860 $10.50 Yuweng Tao lighthouse . . . . 1·00 35
1861 $12 Tungchu Tao lighthouse 1·20 50
1862 $13 Yeh Liu lighthouse . . 1·40 50
1863 $15 Tungchi Yu lighthouse 1·70 90
1864 $16.50 Chimei Yu lighthouse 1·60 75
For designs with blue panel at foot, see Nos. 2003/15.

1989. National Wealth Survey.
1865 **496** $3 multicoloured 40 15

497 "I once tended nine Fields of Orchids"

1989. Chinese Classical Poetry (5th series). Poems from "Ch'u Ts'u". Multicoloured.
1866 $3 Type **497** 30 15
1867 $7.50 "No grief is greater than parting" 80 40
1868 $12 "...living remote and neglected" . . . . . . 2·00 75
1869 $16 "The horse will not gallop into servitude" . . 2·50 95

498 Underground Train

1989. Completion of Taipeh Underground Section of Western Railway Line. Multicoloured.
1870 $3 Type **498** 45 15
1871 $16 Train in cutting . . . . 1·50 85

499 Blue Triangle

1989. Butterflies (1st series). Multicoloured.
1872 $2 Type **499** 30 15
1873 $3 Great mormon 80 20
1874 $7.50 Chequered swallowtail 1·90 25
1875 $9 Common rose . . . . . 2·30 35
See also Nos. 1902/5.

500 Pumpkin Teapot **501** Fan Chung-yen

1989. Teapots (1st series). Multicoloured.
1876 $2 Type **500** 55 15
1877 $3 Clay teapot . . . . . . 1·00 25
1878 $12 "Chopped wood" teapot 1·90 50
1879 $16 Clay pear teapot . . . 2·20 70
See also Nos. 1946/50.

1989. Birth Millenary of Fan Chung-yen (civil service reformer).
1880 **501** $12 multicoloured . . . 1·10 55

502 Trees and Right Side of Mountain

1989. Painting "Autumn Colours on the Ch'iao and Hua Mountains" by Ch'iao Mengfu. Designs showing details of the scroll. Multicoloured.
1881 $7.50 (1) Type **502** . . . . 1·80 50
1882 $7.50 (2) Left side of mountain and trees . . . 1·80 50
1883 $7.50 (3) Trees and house 1·80 50
1884 $7.50 (4) Mountain, trees and house . . . . 1·80 50
Nos. 1872/5 were printed together, se-tenant, forming a composite design.

503 Insured Groups and Family **504** Liwu River Gorge

1989. Social Welfare.
1885 **503** $3 multicoloured 30 15

1989. Taroko National Park. Multicoloured.
1886 $2 Type **504** 30 15
1887 $3 North Peak of Chilai, Taroko Mountain 35 25
1888 $12 Waterfalls 80 40
1889 $16 Chingshui Cliff . . . . 1·00 55

505 Horse **506** Yu Lu

1989. New Year Greetings. "Year of the Horse".
1890 **505** $2 multicoloured 45 20
1891 $13 multicoloured . . . 1·60 60
MS1892 78 × 102 mm. Nos. 1890/1, each × 2 . . . . 8·00 6·00
See also No. 2044.

1990. Door Gods. Multicoloured.
1893 $3 Type **506** . . . . 1·30 20
1894 $3 Shen Shu . . . . 1·30 20
1895 $7.50 Wei-ch'ih Ching-te (facing right) . . . . . . 2·75 45
1896 $7.50 Ch'in Shu-pao (facing left) . . . . 2·75 45

507 Lishan **508** Crystal containing Emblem and Industrial Symbols

1990. Tourism. Multicoloured.
1897 $2 Type **507** 35 20
1898 $18 Fir tree at Tayuling (vert) . . . . 1·70 95

1990. 40th Anniv of National Insurance.
1899 **508** $3 multicoloured 45 15

509 Harbour and Tanks

1990. Yung-An Hsiang Liquefied Natural Gas Terminal. Multicoloured.
1900 $3 Type **509** 35 15
1901 $16 Gas tanker and map showing pipeline route (vert) . . . . 1·20 60

510 African Monarch **511** Court Official, Northern Wei Period to T'ang Dynasty

1990. Butterflies (2nd series). Multicoloured.
1902 $2 Orange tiger 30 15
1903 $3 Type **510** 35 25
1904 $7.50 "Pieris canidia" . . . 85 35
1905 $9 Peacock . . . . 1·10 50

1990. Chinese Costumes (5th series). Mult.
1906 $2 Type **511** 25 15
1907 $3 Civil official in winged hat and green robe, Three Kingdoms period to Ming dynasty 50 15
1908 $7.50 Royal guard in bamboo hat, Yuan dynasty . . . . 1·10 30
1909 $12 Highest grade civil official in robe decorated with crane bird, Ming dynasty . . . . 1·60 60

512 "Spring Song at Midnight"

1990. Chinese Classical Poetry (6th series). Multicoloured.
1910 $3 Type **512** 65 25
1911 $7.50 Couple on river bank ("Summer Song at Midnight") . . . . 1·30 35
1912 $12 Girl washing clothes in river ("Autumn Song at Midnight") . . . . 2·20 50
1913 $16 Snow-bound river scene ("Winter Song at Midnight") . . . . 2·75 80

513 Japanese Black Pine

1990. Bonsai. Multicoloured.
1914 $3 Type **513** 35 20
1915 $6.50 "Ehretia microphylla" 55 30
1916 $12 "Buxus harlandii" . . . 85 60
1917 $16 "Celtis sinensis" . . . . 1·20 80

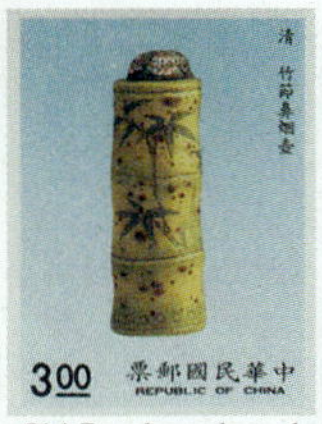

514 Bamboo-shaped Glass Snuff Bottle **516** Running

515 Taiwan Firecrest

1990. Snuff Bottles. Multicoloured.
1918 $3 Type **514** 25 15
1919 $6 Glass bottle with peony design 45 30
1920 $9 Melon-shaped amber bottle 70 50
1921 $16 White jade bottle . . . 1·20 90

1990. Birds. Multicoloured.
1922 $2 Type **515** 30 15
1923 $3 Formosan barwing . . . 30 15
1924 $7.50 White-eared sibia . . 65 20
1925 $16 Formosan yellow tit . . 1·50 55

1990. Sports. Multicoloured.
1926 $2 Type **516** 25 15
1927 $3 Long jumping 30 20
1928 $7 Pole vaulting 55 30
1929 $16 Hurdling . . . . 1·20 60

517 Curtiss Tomahawk II Fighters and Air Crews

1990. 50th Anniv of Arrival of "Flying Tigers" American Volunteer Group.
1930 **517** $3 multicoloured 80 20

518 Cats

1990. Children's Drawings. Multicoloured.
1931 $2 Type **518** 25 15
1932 $3 Common peafowl . . . 30 20
1933 $7.50 Chickens 60 30
1934 $12 Cattle market 90 50

519 National Theatre **520** Cowrie Shells

1990. Cultural Buildings in Chiang Kai-shek Memorial Park, Taipeh.
1935 **519** $3 orange, dp blue & bl 30 15
1936 – $12 mauve, violet & lilac 1·20 45
DESIGN: $12 National Concert Hall.

1990. Ancient Coins. "Shell" Money. Mult.
1937 $2 Type **520** 25 15
1938 $3 Oyster shell 30 20
1939 $6.50 Bone 40 30
1940 $7.50 Bronze 50 35
1941 $9 Jade 60 40

521 Sheep **522** Hu Shih

1990. New Year Greetings. "Year of the Sheep".
1942 **521** $2 multicoloured 55 15
1943 $13 multicoloured . . . 2·20 50
MS1944 77 × 101 mm. Nos. 1942/3, each × 2 . . . . 7·75 1·80
See also No. 2045.

1990. Birth Centenary of Hu Shih (written Chinese reformer).
1945 **522** $3 violet 30 15

523 Teapot with Dragon Spout and Handle **524** Happiness

1991. Teapots (2nd series). Multicoloured.
1946 $2 Blue and white teapot with phoenix design . . . 30 15
1947 $3 Type **523** 40 25
1948 $9 Teapot with floral design on lid and landscape on body 80 40
1949 $12 Rectangular teapot with passion flower design . . 1·10 50
1950 $16 Brown rectangular teapot with floral decoration . . . . 1·40 80

1991. Greetings Stamps. Gods of Prosperity. Multicoloured.
1951 $3 Type **524** 50 15
1952 $3 Wealth 50 15
1953 $7.50 Longevity (with white beard) . . . . 1·10 35
1954 $7.50 Joy . . . . 1·10 35

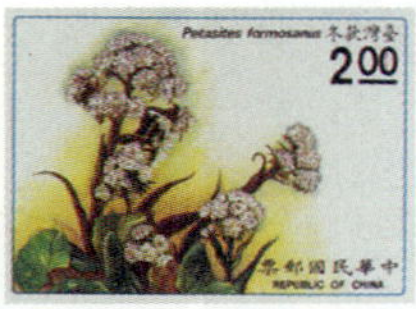

525 "Petasites formosanus"

526 Hsiung Cheng-chi (revolutionary)

1991. Plants (1st series). Multicoloured.
1955 $2 Type **525** 25 15
1956 $3 "Heloniopsis acutifolia" . . 30 15
1957 $7.50 "Disporum shimadai" . . 60 30
1958 $9 "Viola nagasawai" . . . 70 35
See also Nos. 1969/72, 1995/8 and 2026/9.

1991. Famous Chinese.
1959 **526** $3 blue 25 15

527 Agriculture

528 Bamboo Hobby-horse

1991. 80th Anniv (1992) of Founding of Chinese Republic. Multicoloured.
1960 $3 Type **527** 25 15
1961 $7.50 Industry 50 25
1962 $12 Dancer and leisure equipment 85 45
1963 $16 Transport and communications . . . . . 1·10 55

1991. Children's Games (1st series). Mult.
1964 $3 Type **528** 30 20
1965 $3 Woven-grass grasshoppers 30 20
1966 $3 Spinning tops 30 20
1967 $3 Windmills 30 20
MS1968 150 × 100 mm. Nos. 1964/7 5·50 1·70
See also No. 2056/**MS**2060 and 2120/**MS**2124.

1991. Plants (2nd series). As T **525**. Mult.
1969 $2 "Gaultheria itoana" . . . 25 15
1970 $3 "Lysionotus montanus" . . 35 20
1971 $7.50 "Leontopodium microphyllum" 95 25
1972 $9 "Gentiana flavo-maculata" . . . . 1·20 35

529 Male Official's Summer Court Dress

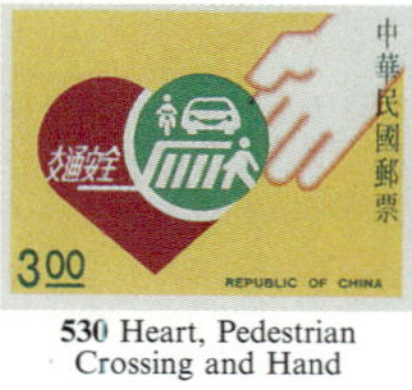

530 Heart, Pedestrian Crossing and Hand

1991. Chinese Costumes (6th series). Ch'ing Dynasty. Multicoloured.
1973 $2 Male official's winter court dress with dragon design 40 15
1974 $3 Type **529** 55 20
1975 $7.50 Male official's winter overcoat . . . . 1·20 30
1976 $12 Everyday skull-cap, jacket and travelling robe 1·90 45

1991. Road Safety. Multicoloured.
1977 $3 Type **530** 40 15
1978 $7.50 Hand, road and broken bottle ("Don't Drink and Drive") . . . 1·20 35

531 Ch'ing Dynasty Cloisonne Lion

532 Strawberries

1991. No value expressed. Multicoloured.
1979 (–) Type **531** 60 20
1980 (–) Cloisonne lioness . . . . 2·30 70
Nos. 1979/80 were sold at the prevailing rates for domestic ordinary and domestic prompt delivery letters.

1991. Fruits. Multicoloured.
1981 $3 Type **532** 30 15
1982 $7.50 Grapes 50 30
1983 $9 Mango 65 35
1984 $16 Sugar apple . . . . . . 1·10 60

533 Formosan Whistling Thrush

1991. River Birds. Multicoloured.
1985 $5 Type **533** 40 20
1986 $5 Brown dipper 40 20
1987 $5 Mandarins 40 20
1988 $5 Black-crowned night herons 40 20
1989 $5 Little egrets 40 20
1990 $5 Plumbeous redstarts . . 40 20
1991 $5 Little forktail 40 20
1992 $5 Grey wagtail 40 20
1993 $5 River kingfishers 40 20
1994 $5 Pied wagtails 40 20
Nos. 1985/94 were printed together, se-tenant, forming a composite design.

1991. Plants (3rd series). As T **525**. Mult.
1995 $3.50 "Rosa transmorrisonensis" . . . 35 15
1996 $5 "Impatiens devolii" . . . 55 20
1997 $9 "Impatiens uniflora" . . 85 35
1998 $12 "Impatiens taye-monii" 1·10 45

534 Rock Climbing

1991. International Camping and Caravanning Federation Rally, Fulung Beach. Multicoloured.
1999 $2 Type **534** 25 15
2000 $3 Fishing 35 20
2001 $7.50 Bird-watching 65 35
2002 $10 Boys with pail wading in water 95 55

1991. Lighthouses. As Nos. 1851/3 and 1855/64 but with blue panel at foot.
2003 50c. As No. 1863 . . . . . 20 15
2004 $1 As No. 1851 . . . . . . 25 20
2005 $3.50 As No. 1855 . . . . . 30 20
2006 $5 As No. 1856 . . . . . . 40 25
2007 $7 As No. 1853 . . . . . . 45 20
2008 $9 As No. 1858 . . . . . . 65 35
2009 $10 As No. 1859 . . . . . . 80 45
2010 $12 As No. 1861 . . . . . . 85 50
2011 $13 As No. 1852 . . . . . . 95 60
2012 $19 As No. 1857 . . . . . . 1·40 80
2013 $20 As No. 1862 . . . . . . 1·50 80
2014 $26 As No. 1860 . . . . . . 1·70 1·00
2015 $28 As No. 1864 . . . . . . 2·20 1·20

535 Peacock

536 Monkey

1991. "Peacocks" by Giuseppe Castiglione. Designs showing details of painting. Multicoloured.
2020 $5 Type **535** 60 20
2021 $20 Peacock displaying tail 2·40 80
MS2022 138 × 102 mm. No. 2021 3·50 1·10

1991. New Year Greetings. "Year of the Monkey".
2023 **536** $3.50 multicoloured . . 25 15
2024 $13 multicoloured . . . 1·20 60
MS2025 78 × 101 mm. Nos. 2023/4, each × 2 . . . . 4·75 1·70
See also No. 2046.

1991. Plants (4th series). As T **525**. Mult.
2026 $3.50 "Kalanchoe garambiensis" 30 15
2027 $5 "Pieris taiwanensis" . . . 45 20
2028 $9 "Pleione formosana" . . 70 40
2029 $12 "Elaeagnus oldhamii" 95 45

537 Scrolls

538 Peace in the Wake of Firecrackers

1992. International Book Fair, Taipeh. Mult.
2030 $3.50 Type **537** 30 15
2031 $5 Folded-leaves book . . . 45 20
2032 $9 Butterfly-bound books 75 35
2033 $15 Sewn books . . . . . 1·20 60

1992. Greetings Stamps. Nienhwas (paintings conveying wishes for the coming year). Mult.
2034 $5 Type **538** 35 20
2035 $5 Elephant with riders (Good fortune and satisfaction) 35 20
2036 $12 Children and five "birds" (Five blessings upon the house) 85 55
2037 $12 Children angling for large fish (Abundance for every year) 85 55

1992. Signs of Chinese Zodiac. As previous designs but with additional symbol in top left-hand corner.
2038 **393** $5 multicoloured 40 15
2039 **414** $5 multicoloured 40 15
2040 **435** $5 multicoloured 40 15
2041 **456** $5 multicoloured 40 15
2042 **471** $5 multicoloured 40 15
2043 **489** $5 multicoloured 40 15
2044 **505** $5 multicoloured 40 15
2045 **521** $5 multicoloured 40 15
2046 **536** $5 multicoloured 40 15
2047 **340** $5 multicoloured 40 15
2048 **361** $5 multicoloured 40 15
2049 **378** $5 multicoloured 40 15
MS2050 181 × 101 mm. Nos. 2038/49 6·50 2·30
Nos. 2038/49 were issued together in se-tenant blocks of 12 stamps within the sheet. The stamps are listed in order from right to left of the block.

539 Taiwan Red Cypress ("Chamaecyparis formosensis")

540 Mother and son (Spring)

1992. Forest Resources. Conifers. Mult.
2051 $5 Type **539** 40 10
2052 $5 Taiwan cypress ("Chamaecyparis taiwanensis") 40 10
2053 $5 Taiwan incense cedar ("Calocedrus formosana") 40 10
2054 $5 Ranta fir ("Cunninghamia konishii") 40 10
2055 $5 Taiwania ("Taiwania cryptomerioides") 40 10
Nos. 2051/5 were printed together, se-tenant, forming a composite design.

1992. Children's Games (2nd series). As T **528**. Multicoloured.
2056 $5 Walking on tin cans . . 55 20
2057 $5 Chopstick guns 40 10
2058 $5 Rolling hoops 55 20
2059 $5 Grass fighting 55 20
MS2060 150 × 101 mm. Nos. 2056/9 4·00 3·25

1992. Parent–Child Relationships. Mult.
2061 $3.50 Type **540** 35 20
2062 $5 Mother carrying child on back (summer) 55 25
2063 $9 Mother and child pushing toy rabbits (autumn) 75 40
2064 $10 Mother feeding child (winter) 95 45

港 香 一 覽 展 票 郵 華 中
(**541**) (½-size illustration)

1992. Chinese Stamps Exhibition, Hong Kong. Sheet as No. **MS**2060 but imperf, optd in margin with T **541** in magenta.
MS2065 150 × 101 mm. Nos. 2056/9 14·00 11·00

542 Vase decorated with Bats and Longevity Characters

543 Lion and Stone Pavilion

1992. Glassware decorated with Enamel. Mult.
2066 $3.50 Type **542** 25 15
2067 $5 Gourd-shaped vase decorated with landscape and children at play . . . 45 20
2068 $7 Vase with peony decoration 65 30
2069 $17 Vase showing mother teaching child to read . . 1·40 65

1992. Stone Lions from Lugouqiao Bridge.
2070 **543** $5 blue and brown . . . 50 20
2071 – $5 green and violet . . . 50 20
2072 – $12 orange and green . . 1·10 50
2073 – $12 violet and black . . 1·10 50
DESIGNS: No. 2071, Bridge and lioness with cub; 2070, Bridge parapet and lion; 2073, Bridge parapet and lioness with two cubs.

544 "People make Friends and are tied to Each Other as Roots to a Plant"

1992. Chinese Classical Poetry (7th series). Multicoloured.
2074 $3.50 Type **544** 25 15
2075 $5 Couple at window ("Conjugal love will last forever") 55 25
2076 $9 Couple in garden ("Man takes pains to uphold virtue/Till one's hair turns forever grey") 95 35
2077 $15 "Tartar horses lean toward the north wind" 1·40 55

545 Drummer and Crowd

546 "Two Birds perched on a Red Camellia Branch"

1992. Temple Fair. Multicoloured.
2078 $5 Type **545** 70 35
2079 $5 Man with basket dancing 70 35
2080 $5 Musicians 70 35
2081 $5 Man pushing cart . . . 70 35
2082 $5 Women and children . . 70 35
Nos. 2078/82 were printed together, se-tenant, forming a composite design.

1992. Ming Dynasty Silk Tapestries. Mult.
2083 $5 Type **546** 50 20
2084 $12 "Two Birds playing on a Peach Branch" . . . . 1·00 20
MS2085 111 × 88 mm. Nos. 2083/4 2·40 75

547 Cart in "The General and the Premier" **548** Steam Locomotive and Train

1992. Chinese Opera Props. Multicoloured.

2086	$3.50 Type **547**	40	20
2087	$5 Ship in "The Lucky Pearl"	55	25
2088	$9 Horse in "Chao-chun serves as an Envoy"	75	40
2089	$12 Sedan chair in "Escort to the Wedding"	95	50

1992. Alishan Mountain Railway. Mult.

2090	$5 Type **548**	45	15
2091	$15 Diesel locomotive and train	1·20	40

549 Chinese River Otter **550** Cock

1992. Mammals. Multicoloured.

2092	$5 Type **549**	55	20
2093	$5 Formosan flying fox	55	20
2094	$5 Formosan clouded leopard	55	20
2095	$5 Formosan black bear	55	20

1992. New Year Greetings. "Year of the Cock". Multicoloured.

2096	$3.50 Type **550**	35	20
2097	$13 Cock (facing left)	1·00	45
MS2098	78 × 101 mm. Nos. 2096/7, each × 2	3·00	2·40

北臺一覽展票郵賓律菲

PHILIPPINE STAMP EXHIBITION 1992 · TAIPEI

(551)

1992. Philippine Stamp Exhibition, Taipeh. No. **MS**2098 optd in margin with T **551**.

MS2099	78 × 101 mm. Nos. 2096/7, each × 2	3·00	2·40

552 Schall and Astronomical Instruments

1992. 400th Birth Anniv of Johann Adam Schall von Bell (missionary astronomer).

2100	**552** $5 multicoloured	30	15

553 Satisfaction for Every Year

1993. Greetings Stamps. Nienhwas (paintings conveying wishes for the coming year). Multicoloured.

2101	$5 Type **553**	45	20
2102	$5 Birds and flowers (Joy)	45	20
2103	$12 Butterfly and flowers (Happiness and longevity)	1·10	35
2104	$12 Flowers in vase (Wealth and peace)	1·10	35

554 Applying Enamel and Glass Decoration to Temple Roof

1992. International Traditional Crafts Exhibition, Taipeh. Multicoloured.

2105	$3.50 Type **554**	25	15
2106	$5 Ceremonial lantern	35	20
2107	$9 Pottery jars	65	40
2108	$15 Oil-paper umbrella	95	70

555 Pan Gu creating Universe

1993. The Creation. Multicoloured.

2109	$3.50 Type **555**	30	15
2110	$5 Pan Gu creating animals (horiz)	40	20
2111	$9 Nu Wa creating human beings (horiz)	70	45
2112	$19 Nu Wa mending the sky with smelted stone	1·40	85

556 Mandarins **557** Water Lily

1993. Lucky Animals (1st series).

2113	**556** $3.50 multicoloured	30	15
2114	– $5 multicoloured	40	25
2115	– $10 red and black	55	35
2116	– $15 multicoloured	1·20	80

DESIGNS: $5, Chinese unicorn; $10, Deer; $15, Crane.

See also Nos. 2151/4.

1993. Water Plants. Multicoloured.

2117	$5 Type **557**	45	20
2118	$9 Taiwan cow lily	80	40
2119	$12 Water hyacinth	1·00	55

1993. Children's Games (3rd series). As T **528**. Multicoloured.

2120	$5 Tossing sandbags	40	20
2121	$5 Bamboo dragonflies	40	20
2122	$5 Skipping	40	20
2123	$5 Duel of strength with rope passed round waists	40	20
MS2124	150 × 100 mm. Nos. 2120/3	3·00	2·40

北臺——覽展票郵亞利大澳

AUSTRALIAN STAMP EXHIBITION 1993 – TAIPEI

(558) (⅔-size illustration)

1993. Australian Stamp Exhibition, Taipeh. No. **MS**2124 optd in margin with T **558** in green and black.

MS2125	150 × 100 mm. Nos. 2120/3	3·25	2·50

國泰——覽展票郵華中

(559)

1993. Chinese Stamp Exhibition, Bangkok, Thailand. No. **MS**2124 optd with T **559**.

MS2126	150 × 100 mm. Nos. 2120/3	3·25	2·50

560 Ching-Kang-Chang Plateau (source)

1993. Yangtze River. Multicoloured.

2127	$3.50 Type **560**	30	15
2128	$3.50 Turn in river (Chinsha River)	30	15
2129	$5 Roaring Tiger Gorge (white water in narrow ravine)	40	20
2130	$5 Chutang Gorge (calm water in wide gorge)	40	20
2131	$9 Dragon Gate, Pawu and Titsui Gorges	80	45

561 Noise Pollution and Music

1993. Environmental Protection. Children's Drawings. Multicoloured.

2132	$5 Type **561**	40	20
2133	$17 Family looking out over green fields (vert)	1·20	80

562 Cup with Tou-Ts'ai Figures

1993. Ch'eng-hua Porcelain Cups of Ming Dynasty. Multicoloured.

2134	$3.50 Type **562**	30	15
2135	$5 Chicken decoration	40	20
2136	$7 Flowers and fruits of four seasons decoration	60	35
2137	$9 Dragon decoration	75	50

563 Graphic Design **564** Child on Father's Shoulders

1993. 32nd International Vocational Training Competition, Taipeh. Multicoloured.

2138	$3.50 Type **563**	25	15
2139	$5 Computer technology	30	20
2140	$9 Carpentry	65	40
2141	$12 Welding	80	60

1993. Parent–Child Relationships. Mult.

2142	$3.50 Type **564**	30	15
2143	$5 Father playing flute to child	40	20
2144	$9 Child reading to father	75	45
2145	$10 Father pointing at bird	80	50

565 Man carrying Scroll

1993. "Taipeh '93" Asian Stamp Exhibition. Sheet 139 × 97 mm containing T **565** and similar vert designs showing details of "Enjoying Antiquities" by Tu Chin. Multicoloured.

MS2146	$5 Type **565**; $5 Man examining antiquities; $5 Man sitting by table; $5 Woman tying bundle	2·75	1·30

566 Persimmons **567** Gymnastics

1993. Fruits. Multicoloured.

2147	$5 Type **566**	35	20
2148	$5 Peaches	35	20
2149	$12 Loquats	95	60
2150	$12 Papayas	95	60

1993. Lucky Animals (2nd series). As T **556**. Mult.

2151	$1 Blue dragon (representing Spring, wood and the East)	25	15
2152	$2.50 White tiger (Autumn, metal and the West)	35	15
2153	$9 Linnet (Summer, fire and the South)	70	35
2154	$19 Black tortoise (Winter, water and the North)	1·40	80

1993. Taiwan Area Games, Taoyuan. Mult.

2155	$5 Type **567**	35	20
2156	$5 Taekwondo	35	20

568 Stone Lion, New Park, Taipeh **569** Chick

1993. Stone Lions. Multicoloured.

2157	$3.50 Type **568**	25	15
2158	$5 Hsinchu City Council building	40	20
2159	$9 Temple, Hsinchu City	65	35
2160	$12 Fort Providentia, Tainan	95	50

1993. Mikado Pheasant. Multicoloured.

2161	$5 Type **569**	40	25
2162	$5 Mother and chicks	40	25
2163	$5 Immature male and female	40	25
2164	$5 Adults	40	25

Nos. 2161/4 were issued together, se-tenant, forming a composite design.

570 Dog **571** Scientist and Vegetables

1993. New Year Greetings. "Year of the Dog". Multicoloured.

2165	$3.50 Type **570**	25	15
2166	$13 Dog (facing left)	1·20	50
MS2167	78 × 102 mm. Nos. 2165/6, each × 2	2·00	1·10

1993. 20th Anniv of Asian Vegetable Research and Development Centre. Multicoloured.

2168	$5 Type **571**	35	20
2169	$13 Scientists and fields of crops	1·10	60

念紀展郵光國年二十八

日七十二至日一十二月二十

(572)

1993. "Kuo-kuang" Stamp Exhibition, Kaohsiung. No. **MS**2167 optd in margin with T **572** in red.

MS2170	78 × 102 mm. Nos. 2165/6, each × 2	2·30	1·30

573 Courtroom **574** Cutting Bamboo

1994. Inauguration of Taiwan Constitutional Court.

2171	**573** $5 multicoloured	40	20

1994. Traditional Paper Making. Multicoloured.

2172	$3.50 Type **574**	25	15
2173	$3.50 Cooking bamboo	25	15

2174 $5 Moulding bamboo pulp in wooden panels 45 25
2175 $5 Stacking wet paper for pressing 45 25
2176 $12 Drying paper 95 50

575 "Clivia miniata" **576** Wind Lion Lord

1994. Flowers. Multicoloured.
2177 $5 Type **575** 35 20
2178 $12 "Cymbidium sinense" 95 50
2179 $19 "Primula malacoides" 1·50 90

1994. Kinmen Wind Lion Lords.
2180 **576** $5 multicoloured 40 20
2181 – $9 multicoloured 70 35
2182 – $12 multicoloured . . . 95 45
2183 – $17 multicoloured . . . 1·20 65
DESIGNS: $9 to $17 Different Lion Lord statues.

577 Sailing Paper Boats **578** Playing Chess

1994. Children's Games (4th series). Mult.
2184 $5 Type **577** 40 20
2185 $5 Fighting with water-guns 40 20
2186 $5 Throwing paper plane . . 40 20
2187 $5 Human train 40 20
MS2188 125 × 80 mm. Nos. 2184/7 1·90 95

1994. Rural Pastimes. Multicoloured.
2189 $5 Type **578** 30 20
2190 $10 Playing the flute 80 35
2191 $12 Telling stories 95 50
2192 $19 Drinking tea . . . . . 1·50 80

579 Malaysian Night Heron and Chicks **580** Book with Hand on Cover

1994. Parent–Child Relationships. Birds with their Young. Multicoloured.
2193 $5 Type **579** 30 20
2194 $7 Little tern (horiz) . . . 55 25
2195 $10 Common noddy (horiz) 85 40
2196 $12 Muller's barbet . . . . 1·00 45

1994. Protection of Intellectual Property Rights. Multicoloured.
2197 $5 Type **580** 40 20
2198 $15 Head with locked computer disk as brain . . 1·20 60

581 Caring for the Young **582** Anniversary Emblem and Olympic Rings

1994. International Rotary Clubs Convention, Taipeh. "Towards an Harmonious Society". Multicoloured.
2199 $5 Type **581** 40 20
2200 $17 Caring for the aged . . 1·40 75

1994. Centenary of International Olympic Committee. Multicoloured.
2201 $5 Type **582** 40 20
2202 $15 Running, high jumping and weight-lifting . . . 1·20 60

583 Summit of Dah-pa Mountain **584** Chien Mu

1994. Shei-pa National Park. Multicoloured.
2203 $5 Type **583** 40 20
2204 $7 Shei-san Valley 60 25
2205 $10 Holy Ridge 90 40
2206 $17 Shiah-tsuei Pool . . . . 1·30 75

1994. Birth Centenary of Chien Mu (academic).
2207 **584** $5 multicoloured 40 20

585 Window

1994. International Year of the Family. Mult.
2208 $5 Type **585** 40 20
2209 $15 Globe and house . . . 1·20 60

586 Sueirenjy making Flame **587** Lin Yutang

1994. Invention Myths. Multicoloured.
2210 $5 Type **586** 40 20
2211 $10 Fushijy drawing Pa-kua characters 80 35
2212 $12 Shennungjy making pitchfork 95 50
2213 $15 Tsangjier inventing pictorial characters . . . 1·40 75

1994. Birth Centenary of Dr. Lin Yutang (essayist and lexicographer).
2214 **587** $5 multicoloured 40 20

588 Cheng Ho's Junk **589** Dr. Sun Yat-sen (founder)

1994. World Trade Week. Multicoloured.
2215 $5 Type **588** 40 20
2216 $17 Cheng Ho and route map around South Asia 1·20 60

1994. Centenary of Kuomintang Party. Mult.
2217 $5 Type **589** 40 20
2218 $19 Modern developments and voter placing slip in ballot box . . . . 1·40 70

590 Pig **591** Yen Chia-kan

1994. New Year Greetings. "Year of the Pig". Multicoloured.
2219 $3.50 Type **590** 30 20
2220 $13 Pig (facing left) . . . . 1·10 60
MS2221 78 × 101 mm. Nos. 2219/20, each × 2 . . . . 2·75 1·60

1994. 1st Death Anniv of Yen Chia-kan (President, 1974–78). Multicoloured.
2222 $5 Type **591** 40 20
2223 $15 Visiting farmers . . . . 1·20 60

592 Horse's Back **593** Begonia

1995. Traditional Architecture. Roof Styles. Mult.
2224 $5 Type **592** 40 20
2225 $5 Swallow's tail 40 20
2226 $12 Talisman (stove and bowl) 95 50
2227 $19 Cylinder-shaped brick 1·50 90

1995. Chinese Engravings. Flowers. Mult.
2228 $3.50 Type **593** 25 15
2229 $5 Rose 45 20
2230 $19 Flower . . . . 1·50 80
2231 $26 Climbing rose . . . . . 2·20 1·20
For these designs, but with the characters for the country name in a different order, see Nos. 2480/3.

594 Rotating Wheel of Pipes **595** Courtiers

1995. Irrigation Techniques from "Tian Gong Kai Wu" (encyclopaedia) by Sung Yin-shing. Multicoloured.
2232 $3.50 Type **594** 25 15
2233 $3.50 Donkey turning wheel to raise water 25 15
2234 $5 Pedal-driven device to raise water 45 25
2235 $12 Man turning wheel to raise water 95 50
2236 $13 Well . . . . 1·10 60

1995. "Beauties on an Outing" by Lee Gong-lin. Details of the painting. Multicoloured.
2237 $9 Type **595** 75 35
2238 $9 Courtier and beauty with child 75 35
2239 $9 Courtier with two beauties 75 35
2240 $9 Courtier 75 35
MS2241 110 × 80 mm. Nos. 2238/9 1·80 80
Nos. 2237/40 were issued together, se-tenant, forming a composite design.

596 Emblem and Landscape **597** Chinese Showy Lily

1995. Inaug of National Health Insurance Plan.
2242 **596** $12 multicoloured . . . 95 50

1995. Bulbous Flowers. Multicoloured.
2243 $5 Type **597** 35 20
2244 $12 Blood lily 80 50
2245 $19 Hyacinth . . . . 1·50 90

598 Opening Lines

1995. Chinese Calligraphy. "Cold Food Observance" (poem) by Su Shih.
2246 **598** $5 (1) multicoloured . . 55 25
2247 – $5 (2) multicoloured . . 55 25
2248 – $5 (3) multicoloured . . 55 25
2249 – $5 (4) multicoloured . . 55 25
Nos. 2246/9 were issued together, se-tenant, forming a composite design; the stamps are numbered in Chinese numerals to the right of the face value, from right to left.

599 Red Peony **600** Hand, Birds and Cracked Symbol

1995. Peonies. Paintings by Tsou I-kuei. Self-adhesive. Imperf.
2250 $5 Type **599** 50 20
2251 $5 Pink peony 50 20

1995. Anti-drugs Campaign. Multicoloured.
2252 $5 Type **600** 40 20
2253 $15 Arm and syringe forming cross . . . . . . 1·10 60

601 Old Hospital Building

1995. Centenary of National Taiwan University Hospital, Taipeh. Multicoloured.
2254 $5 Type **601** 50 20
2255 $19 New building . . . . . 1·50 80

602 Chichi Bay

1995. Tourism. East Coast National Scenic Area. Multicoloured.
2256 $5 Type **602** 40 20
2257 $5 Shihyuesan (rocky promontory) 40 20
2258 $12 Hsiaoyehlieu (eroded rocks) . . . . 1·10 50
2259 $15 Changhong Bridge . . . 1·40 70

603 Mating **604** Bird feeding on Branch

1995. The Cherry Salmon. Multicoloured.
2260 $5 Type **603** 40 20
2261 $7 Female digging redd . . 60 25
2262 $10 Fry hatching 80 45
2263 $17 Fry swimming . . . . . 1·50 70

1995. Chinese Engravings. Birds. Mult.
2264 $2.50 Type **604** 30 20
2265 $7 Bird on branch of peach tree 60 30
2266 $13 Bird preening . . . . . 1·10 50
2267 $28 Yellow bird . . . . . . 2·50 1·10
For these designs with different face values and the order of the characters in the country name changed, see Nos. 2532/7.

605 "Tubastraea aurea" **606** Pasteur

1995. Marine Life. Multicoloured.
2268 $3.50 Type **605** 30 20
2269 $3.50 "Chromodoris elizabethina" 30 20
2270 $5 "Spirobranchus giganteus corniculatus" 50 25
2271 $17 "Himerometra magnipinna" . . . . . . 1·40 65

1995. Death Cent of Louis Pasteur (chemist).
2272 **606** $17 multicoloured . . . 1·60 65

607 Porcelain Vase **608** Soldiers

1995. 70th Anniv of National Palace Museum. Multicoloured.
2273 $3.50 "Strange Peaks and Myriad Trees" (painting) (horiz) 25 15
2274 $3.50 Type **607** 25 15
2275 $5 X Fu-K'uei Ting bronze three-fronted vessel . . . 40 20
2276 $26 "The Fragrance of Flowers" (quatrain) (horiz) . . . . 2·00 95

1995. 50th Anniv of End of Sino-Japanese War. Multicoloured.
2277 $5 Type **608** 45 20
2278 $19 Taiwan flag, map and city . . . . 1·50 60
MS2279 78 × 102 mm. Nos. 2277/8 2·20 95

609 Common Green Turtle ("Chelonia mydas")

610 Scientists in Crop Field

1995. Year of the Sea Turtle. Multicoloured.
2280 $5 Type **609** 45 20
2281 $5 Loggerhead turtle ("Caretta caretta") . . . 45 20
2282 $5 Olive ridley turtle ("Lepidochelys olivacea") 45 20
2283 $5 Hawksbill turtle ("Eretmochelys imbricata") 45 20

1995. Centenary of Taiwan Agricultural Research Institute. Multicoloured.
2284 $5 Type **610** 55 20
2285 $28 Scientists in greenhouse growing anthuriums . . . 2·10 80

611 Rat

612 Escorting Bride to Ceremony

1995. New Year Greetings. "Year of the Rat". Multicoloured.
2286 $3.50 Type **611** 25 15
2287 $13 Rat (different) . . . . 1·20 45
MS2288 77 × 101 mm. Nos. 2286/7, each × 2 . . . . 2·75 1·20

1996. Traditional Wedding Ceremonies. Mult.
2289 $5 Type **612** 35 15
2290 $12 Honouring Heaven, Earth and ancestors . . . 1·00 40
2291 $19 Nuptial chamber . . . 1·80 75

613 Sharon Fruit

618 "Bougainvillea spectabilis"

614-17 "Scenic Dwelling at Chu-Ch'u"

1996. Chinese Engravings of Fruit by Hu Chen-yan.
2292 **613** $9 multicoloured . . . 70 25
2293 – $12 multicoloured . . . 1·10 40
2294 – $15 multicoloured . . . 1·30 50
2295 – $17 multicoloured . . . 1·50 55
DESIGNS: $12 to $17, Different fruits.
For other values with the order of the characters in the country name reversed see Nos. 2580/2.

1996. Painting by Wang Meng.
2296 **614** $5 multicoloured 45 20
2297 **615** $5 multicoloured 45 20
2298 **616** $5 multicoloured 45 20
2299 **617** $5 multicoloured 45 20
Nos. 2296/9 were issued together, se-tenant, forming the composite design illustrated.

1996. Flowering Vines. Multicoloured.
2300 $5 Type **618** 45 20
2301 $12 Wisteria . . . . 1·00 40
2302 $19 Wood rose . . . . . . 1·50 65

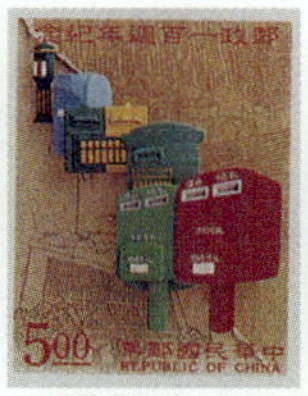
619 Postboxes

620 Lecture and University

1996. Centenary of Chinese State Postal Service. Multicoloured.
2303 $5 Type **619** 35 15
2304 $9 Weighing equipment . . 70 30
2305 $12 Postal transport 90 40
2306 $13 Modern technology . . 1·00 45
MS2307 78 × 101 mm. Nos. 2303/6 3·00 1·30

1996. Centenary of National Chiao Tung University.
2308 **620** $19 multicoloured . . . 1·50 60

621 Chimei Giant Lion

1996. Tourism. Penghu National Scenic Area. Multicoloured.
2309 $5 Type **621** 35 15
2310 $5 Chipei beach (sand-spit) 35 15
2311 $12 Tungpan Yu 90 40
2312 $17 Tingkou Yu . . . . . 1·30 65

622 Hand holding Family (charity)

1996. 30th Anniv of Tzu-Chi Foundation (Buddhist relief organization). Multicoloured.
2313 $5 Type **622** 40 20
2314 $19 Hospital patient in tulip petal (medicine) . . . . . 1·70 65

623 With National Flag

1996. Inauguration of First Directly-elected President. Designs showing President Lee Teng-Hui and Vice-President Lien Chan. Multicoloured.
2315 $3.50 Type **623** 25 15
2316 $5 Outside Presidential Office building 40 15
2317 $13 Asia-Pacific Operations Hub Project . . . . . . 1·10 45
2318 $15 Meeting public at celebrations . . . . . . 1·20 50
MS2319 124 × 80 mm. Nos. 2315/18 3·00 1·40

624 Monument

1996. South China Sea Archipelago. Pratas and Itu Aba Islands. Multicoloured.
2320 $5 Type **624** 45 15
2321 $12 Monument (different) . 1·40 55
MS2322 78 × 101 mm. Nos. 2320/1 1·90 70

625 Modern Gymnast and Cyclist

626 Feeding Silkworms

1996. Centenary of Modern Olympic Games. Multicoloured.
2323 $5 Type **625** 45 15
2324 $15 Ancient Greek athletes 1·30 50

1996. Silk Production Techniques from "Tian Gong Kai Wu" (encyclopaedia) by Sung Yin-shing. Multicoloured.
2325 $5 Type **626** 40 15
2326 $5 Picking out cocoons . . 40 15
2327 $7 Degumming raw silk . . 50 20
2328 $10 Reeling raw silk 80 40
2329 $13 Weaving silk . . . . . 1·10 45

627 Bamboo

628 Tou-kung Bracket

1996. Chinese Engravings. Plants. Mult.
2330 $1 Type **627** 35 15
2331 $10 Orchid 80 40
2332 $20 Plum tree . . . . . . 1·70 70

1996. Traditional Architecture. Roof Supports. Multicoloured.
2333 $5 Type **628** 50 20
2334 $5 Chiue-ti bracket 50 20
2335 $10 Bu-tong beam 85 35
2336 $19 Dye-tou structure . . . 1·50 60

629 "Princess Iron Fan" (1941)

1996. Chinese Film Production. Mult.
2337 $3.50 Type **629** 25 15
2338 $3.50 "Chin Shan Bi Xie" (1957) 25 15
2339 $5 "Oyster Girl" (1964) . . 50 25
2340 $19 "City of Sadness" (1989) . . . . 1·50 65

630 Children dancing

631 "Autumn Scene with Wild Geese"

1996. Winning Entries in Children's Stamp Design Competition. Multicoloured.
2341 $5 Type **630** 50 20
2342 $5 Children playing in park 50 20
2343 $5 Black and white spotted cat 50 20
2344 $5 Container ship 50 20
2345 $5 Children showering . . . 50 20
2346 $5 Chinese gods and crowd 50 20
2347 $5 Pair of peacocks 50 20
2348 $5 Flying horse and rainbow 50 20
2349 $5 Elephant 50 20
2350 $5 Man and striped animals 50 20
2351 $5 Painting paper lampshades 50 20
2352 $5 Flock of geese 50 20
2353 $5 Children joining hands in garden 50 20
2354 $5 Archer 50 20
2355 $5 Children on ostrich's back 50 20
2356 $5 New Year celebrations 50 20
2357 $5 Butterflies on bamboo plant 50 20
2358 $5 Goatherd 50 20
2359 $5 Water-lilies on pond . . 50 20
2360 $5 Cats eating fish 50 20

1996. 10th Asian International Stamp Exhibition, Taipeh. Ancient Paintings from National Palace Museum. Multicoloured.
2361 $5 Type **631** 45 15
2362 $7 "Reeds and Wild Geese" 65 25
2363 $13 "Wild Geese gathering on Shore of Reeds" . . . 1·10 40
2364 $15 "Wild Geese on Bank in Autumn" . . . . 1·30 50
MS2365 125 × 80 mm. Nos. 2361/4 3·50 1·40

632 Bar Code and Graph

633 Disabled Worker and Open Hands

1996. 50th Anniv of Merchants' Day. Mult.
2366 $5 Type **632** 50 20
2367 $26 Line graph and globe 2·30 95

1996. Caring for the Handicapped. Mult.
2368 $5 Type **633** 55 20
2369 $19 Disabled boy painting, emblems within honeycomb and hands forming heart (employment) . . . . . . 1·50 65

634 Ox

636 Early Porcelain Production

念紀展郵際國雄高年週百政郵
日七十二至日一十二月二十年五十八
635

1996. New Year Greetings. "Year of the Ox". Multicoloured.
2370 $3.50 Type **634** 35 20
2371 $13 Ox (different) . . . . 1·30 50
MS2372 78 × 101 mm. Nos. 2370/1, each × 2 . . . . 3·50 1·40

1996. Chinese Postal Service Centenary Stamp Exhibition, Kaohsiung. No. **MS**2372 optd in top margin with T **635** in magenta.
MS2373 78 × 101 mm. Nos. 2370/1, each × 2 . . . . 3·50 1·40

1997. Porcelain Production Techniques from "Tian Gong Kai Wu" (encyclopaedia) by Sung Yin-shing. Multicoloured.
2374 $5 Type **636** 45 20
2375 $5 Improved shaping . . . 45 20
2376 $7 Painting 65 25
2377 $10 Glazing 85 40
2378 $13 Firing . . . . 1·10 55

637 Dragons and Carp (from window, Longsan Temple, Lukang)

638 Peace Doves and Memorial

1997. (a) T **637**.
2379 **637** $50 red . . . . 4·25 1·70
2380 $60 blue . . . . 5·00 2·00
2381 $70 red . . . . 6·00 2·40
2382 $100 green . . . . . . 8·50 3·50

(b) As T **637** but with outer decorated frame. Size 25 × 33 mm.
2386 **637** $300 violet and blue . . 25·00 10·00
2387 $500 red and carmine . . 39·00 17·00
For $50 and $100 values in different colours and with the characters in the country name in reverse order see Nos. 2573/4.

1997. 50th Anniv of 228 Incident (civilian demonstration against government).
2390 **638** $19 multicoloured . . . 1·50 60

639 "Rhododendron x mucronatum"

640 River, Trees and Wildlife

1997. Shrubs. Multicoloured.
2391 $5 Type **639** 50 20
2392 $12 "Hibiscus rosa-sinensis" 1·10 40
2393 $19 "Hydrangea macrophylla" . . . . . . 1·60 60

1997. Protection of Water Resources. Mult.
2394 $5 Type **640** 45 20
2395 $19 Rivers and trees . . . . 1·60 60

641 Decorated Door

642 "Dorcus formosanus"

1997. Traditional Architecture. Mult.
2396 $5 Type **641** 45 20
2397 $5 Gable wall 45 20
2398 $10 Brick wall-carving . . . 95 40
2399 $19 Verandah . . . . . . 1·50 55

1997. Insects. Multicoloured.
2400 $5 Type **642** 40 20
2401 $7 Giant katydid 65 25
2402 $10 Philippine birdwing . . 90 40
2403 $17 Big-headed stick insect 1·50 60

643 Alunite

1997. Minerals. Multicoloured.
2404 $5 Type **643** 40 20
2405 $5 Aragonite 40 20
2406 $12 Energite . . . . 1·00 40
2407 $19 Hokutolite . . . . . . 1·40 55

644 Nanyashan Coastline

645 Train and Chingshuei Cliffs (northern loop)

1997. Tourism. North-east Coast National Scenic Area. Multicoloured.
2408 $5 Type **644** 45 20
2409 $5 Pitou Coastline (rocky shore) 45 20
2410 $12 Stone pillar, Nanya . . 90 35
2411 $19 Tsaoling historic trail 1·20 45

1997. Completion of Round-island Railway System. Multicoloured.
2412 $5 Type **645** 50 20
2413 $28 Train leaving tunnel (southern loop) . . . . . 1·80 60

646 Integrated Circuit and Communications Equipment

1997. Electronic Industry. Multicoloured.
2414 $5 Type **646** 45 20
2415 $26 Circuit board, portable computer, mobile phone and synthesized keyboard 2·30 85

647 Shaolinquan

1997. Martial Arts. Multicoloured.
2416 $5 Type **647** 40 20
2417 $5 Form and will boxing (vert) 40 20
2418 $9 Taijiquan 70 25
2419 $19 Eight diagrams boxing (vert) . . . . 1·40 55

648 "Hsi Hsiang Chi" (Wang Shih-fu)

649 Bitan Bridge over River Shindian

1997. Chinese Classical Opera. Multicoloured.
2420 $5 Type **648** 40 20
2421 $5 "Dan Daw Huei" (Kuan Han-chin) 40 20
2422 $12 "Han Guong Chiou" (Ma Jyi-yuan) 90 35
2423 $15 "Wu Tong Yu" (Bai Pu) . . . . 1·20 45

1997. Inauguration of Second Northern Freeway. Multicoloured.
2424 $5 Type **649** 40 15
2425 $19 Hsinchu Interchange . . 1·40 55

650 Badminton

651 Palm of Buddha

1997. Sports. Multicoloured.
2426 $5 Type **650** 40 20
2427 $12 Bowling . . . . 1·00 40
2428 $19 Lawn tennis . . . . . 1·40 60

1997. Classical Literature. "Journey to the West" (Ming dynasty novel). Multicoloured.
2429 $3.50 Type **651** 30 20
2430 $3.50 Pilgrimage of T'ang Monk 30 20
2431 $5 The Flaming Mountain 45 25
2432 $20 The Cobweb Cave . . . 1·40 55

652 Purple-crowned Lory

1997. Birds (1st series). Illustrations from the Ching dynasty Bird Manual. Multicoloured.
2433 $5 Type **652** 40 25
2434 $5 Green magpie (on branch with small orange flowers) 40 25
2435 $5 Blue-crowned hanging parrot (green bird with red throat and rump) . . 40 25
2436 $5 Niltavas sp. (two birds with orange breasts) . . . 40 25
2437 $5 Red-billed blue magpie (with long blue tail) . . 40 25
2438 $5 David's laughing thrush (on branch with red flowers) 40 25
2439 $5 Przewalski's rosefinch (on branch with orange-centred white flowers) . . 40 25
2440 $5 Common rosefinch (on branch with yellow flowers) 40 25
2441 $5 Mongolian trumpeter finch (on branch with white flowers and red hips) 40 25
2442 $5 Long-tailed minivets (two black and red birds) . . 40 25
2443 $5 Black-naped oriole (on branch with weeping leaves) 40 25
2444 $5 Yellow-headed buntings (two birds on branch with thorns and small pink flowers) 40 25
2445 $5 Bohemian waxwing (on branch with large blue flowers) 40 25
2446 $5 Mongolian trumpeter finches (two birds on branch with large pink flowers) 40 25
2447 $5 Chinese jungle mynah (with "bristles" above beak) 40 25
2448 $5 Java sparrow (with white patch on neck) 40 25
2449 $5 Long-tailed parakeet (on branch with small blue flowers) 40 25
2450 $5 Black-winged starling (by stream) 40 25
2451 $5 Cloven-feathered dove (two green and white birds) 40 25
2452 $5 Wryneck (on ground) . . 40 25

See also Nos. 2603/6, 2671/4, 2740/3, 2823/6 and 2929/32.

653 Tiger

654 Pres. Chiang

1997. New Year Greetings. "Year of the Tiger".
2453 **653** $3.50 multicoloured . . 25 15
2454 $13 multicoloured . . . 85 50
MS2455 78 × 101 mm. Nos. 2453/4, each × 2 . . . . 2·20 1·20

1998. 10th Death Anniv of Chiang Ching-kuo (President 1978–88).
2456 **654** $5 brown 35 20
2457 – $19 red . . . . 1·10 60
DESIGN—HORIZ: $19 Chiang and applauding crowd.

655 "Abundance"

656 "Gaillardia pulchella var. picta"

1998. Wishes for the Coming Year. Mult.
2458 $5 Type **655** 40 15
2459 $5 Flowers springing from lidded bowl ("Harmony") 40 15
2460 $12 Peonies in containers ("Honour and Wealth") 75 30
2461 $12 Flowers in vase and oranges in bowl ("Luck") 75 30

1998. Herbaceous Flowers. Multicoloured.
2462 $5 Type **656** 40 15
2463 $12 "Kalanchoe blossfeldiana" 85 40
2464 $19 "Portulaca oleracea var. granatus" . . . . 1·90 65

657 Horseman drawing Bow

1998. Painting by Liu Kuan-tao. Mult.
2465 $5 Type **657** 50 25
2466 $19 Kublai Khan and entourage on hunting expedition (63 × 40 mm) 1·60 60
MS2467 125 × 170 mm. Nos. 2465/6 2·10 85

658 "A Frog has only One Mouth"

1998. Children's Nursery Rhymes. Mult.
2468 $5 Type **658** 50 25
2469 $5 Mouse and cat ("A Little Mouse climbs an Oil Lamp") 50 25
2470 $12 Children and fireflies ("Fireflies") 85 50
2471 $19 Girl and egret carrying baskets ("Egrets") . . . 1·80 65

659 Cultural Symbols within Human Head

1998. 70th Anniv of Copyright Law.
2472 **659** $19 multicoloured . . . 1·90 65

660 "Chung K'uei Moving" (Kung Kai)

661 Emblem and Cherry Blossom

1998. Ancient Paintings of Chung K'uei (mythological figure). Multicoloured.
2473 $5 Type **660** 50 15
2474 $20 Chung K'uei dancing ("An Auspicious Occasion") . . . . 1·60 65

1998. 125th Anniv of International Law Association and 68th Conference, Taipeh.
2475 **661** $15 multicoloured . . . 1·30 50

662 Grain Barge

663 Begonia

1998. Ships and Vehicles from "Tian Gong Kai Wu" (encyclopaedia) by Sung Yin-shing. Multicoloured.
2476 $5 Type **662** 40 15
2477 $7 Six-oared ferry boat . . 65 25
2478 $10 One-wheel horse-drawn carriage 85 35
2479 $13 Man pushing one-wheel cart . . . . 1·00 50

1998. Chinese Engravings. Flowers. Designs as Nos. 2228/31 but with values changed and Chinese characters for the country name in reverse order as in T **663**. Multicoloured.
2480 $7 Type **663** 50 25
2481 $19 As No. 2229 . . . . . 1·60 65
2482 $20 As No. 2230 . . . . . 1·90 75
2483 $26 As No. 2231 . . . . . 1·90 75

664 Pao-yu visits Garden

1998. Classical Literature. "Red Chamber Dream" (novel) by Tsao Hsueh-Chin. Multicoloured.
2484 $3.50 Type **664** 40 15
2485 $3.50 Tai-yu burying flowers 40 15
2486 $5 Pao-chai playing with butterflies 65 35
2487 $5 Hsiang-yun in drunken sleep . . . . 1·20 60

665 Scout Badge (⅔-size illustration)

1998. 20th Asia-Pacific and Eighth China National Scout Jamboree, Pingtung University. Multicoloured.
2488 $5 Type **665** 40 15
2489 $5 Tents 40 15

666 Carved Base of Pillar

667 Table Tennis

1998. Traditional Architecture. Multicoloured.
2490 $5 Type **666** 50 25
2491 $5 Carved stone ramp ("spirit way") between staircases 50 25

2492 $10 Carved base (with fishes) of column 85 40
2493 $19 Carved stone drainage spout . . . . 1·30 60

1998. Sports. Multicoloured.
2494 $5 Type **667** 40 15
2495 $5 Table tennis player serving 40 15
2496 $7 Rugby player with ball 65 25
2497 $7 Rugby players 65 25
Stamps of the same value were issued together, se-tenant, forming a composite design.

668 "The Fox borrows the Tiger's Ferocity"

1998. Chinese Fables. Multicoloured.
2498 $5 Type **668** 40 25
2499 $5 "A Frog in a Well" . . . 40 25
2500 $12 "Adding Legs to a Drawing of a Snake" . . 1·00 40
2501 $19 "The Snipe and the Clam at a Deadlock" . . 1·60 60

670 Taiwushan

1998. Kinmen National Park. Multicoloured.
2508 $5 Type **670** 50 25
2509 $5 Kuningtou Cliff 50 25
2510 $12 Teyueh Tower and Huang Hui-huang's House, Shuitou . . . . . 1·20 40
2511 $19 Putou beach, Leihyu . . 1·80 60

671 Hodgson's Hawk Eagle ("Spizaetus nipalensis")

672 Mountain and Pavilions

1998. Birds (2nd series). Multicoloured.
2512 $5 Type **671** 40 15
2513 $5 Hodgson's hawk eagle in flight 40 15
2514 $5 Crested serpent eagle ("Spilornis cheela") on branch 40 15
2515 $5 Crested serpent eagle carrying snake 40 15
2516 $10 Black kite ("Milvus migrans") on rock . . . 85 35
2517 $10 Black kite in flight . . . 85 35
2518 $10 Indian black eagle ("Ictinaetus malayensis") on branch 85 35
2519 $10 Indian black eagle in flight 85 35
Nos. 2512/13, 2514/15, 2516/17 and 2518/19 respectively were issued together, se-tenant, each pair forming a composite design.

1998. Ching Dynasty Jade Mountain Carvings. Mult.
2520 $5 Type **672** 40 25
2521 $5 Men working in jade mine (horiz) 40 25
2522 $7 Men washing elephant (horiz) 65 25
2523 $26 Five men on a mountain . . . . 2·10 85
MS2524 132 × 102 mm. Nos. 2520/3 3·50 1·60

673 Rabbit

674 Butterfly and Pumpkin ("Many Descendants")

1998. New Year Greetings. "Year of the Rabbit". Multicoloured.
2525 $3.50 Type **673** 30 15
2526 $13 Rabbit (different) . . . 1·00 50
MS2527 78 × 102 mm. Nos. 2525/6, each × 2 . . . . 3·00 1·50

1999. Wishes for the Coming Year. Multicoloured.
2528 $5 Type **674** 50 15
2529 $5 Mandarins (ducks) and lotus flowers ("Good marriage that brings sons") 50 15
2530 $12 Egret ("Prosperity") . . 1·00 50
2531 $12 Goldfish and flowers ("Abundance") . . . . . 1·00 50

1999. Chinese Engravings. Birds and Plants. Designs as Nos. 2264/7 and 2330/1 but with values and Chinese characters for the country name in reverse order as in T **663**. Multicoloured.
2532 $1 Type **604** 30 15
2533 $3.50 As No. 2265 . . . . 40 25
2534 $5 As No. 2266 . . . . . 50 35
2535 $10 As No. 2267 . . . . . 85 40
2536 $12 Type **627** . . . . . . 1·30 60
2536a $20 As No. 2482 . . . . . 1·30 60
2537 $28 As No. 2331 . . . . . 1·90 75
2537a $34 As No. 2649 . . . . . 1·90 75

ALLIANCE '99 INT'L FAIR OF PRODUCTS & TRAVEL
Jan 30 - Feb. 1, 1999

臺北國際友邦商品暨旅遊展紀念
中華民國八十八年一月三十日至二月一日

(**675**)

1999. "Alliance '99" International Products and Travel Fair. No. **MS**2527 optd in margins with T **675**.
MS2538 78 × 102 mm. Nos. 2525/6, each × 2 . . . . 3·00 1·50

676 "Gloxinia"

677 Boy towing Toy Elephant

1999. Indoor Flowers. Multicoloured.
2539 $5 Type **676** 40 25
2540 $12 African violet 85 35
2541 $19 Flamingo flower . . . . 1·90 65

1999. Illustrations from "Joy in Peacetime" (Ching Dynasty book). Lantern Festival. Multicoloured.
2542 $5 Type **677** 50 25
2543 $5 Women, children and crane 50 25
2544 $7 Children playing with toy animals 85 35
2545 $26 Children playing . . . 2·10 65
MS2546 170 × 125 mm. Nos. 2542/5 4·50 1·50

678 Hanging Cylinder

679 "Baby Sleeps"

1999. Traditional Architecture. Decorative Features. Multicoloured.
2547 $5 Type **678** 50 25
2548 $5 Taishi screen 50 25
2549 $10 Xuanyu (gable decoration) 85 40
2550 $19 Wood carving . . . . . 1·70 60

1999. Nursery Rhymes. Multicoloured.
2551 $5 Type **679** 50 25
2552 $5 Mother comforting baby frightened by storm ("Be Brave") 50 25
2553 $12 Mother and baby rocking ("Rock, Rock, Rock") 85 40
2554 $19 Mother, baby, cat and flies ("Buggie Flies") . . . 1·70 60

680 Atayal Ancestor Festival

682 "Washing Cotton Yarn" (Liang Chenyu)

681 Nurses treating Patients

1999. Taiwan's Aboriginal Culture. Multicoloured.
2555 $5 Type **680** 75 60
2556 $5 Dancers with hip bells (Saisat Festival of the Dwarfs) 75 60
2557 $5 Circle of singers (Bunun Millet Harvest Song) . . 75 60
2558 $5 Line of singers in red coats (Tsou Victory Festival) 75 60
2559 $5 Dancers and millet biscuits mounted on board (Rukai Harvest Festival) 75 60
2560 $5 Men with bamboo poles (Paiwan Bamboo Festival) 75 60
2561 $5 Procession of men carrying yellow scarves (Puyuma Harvest Ceremony) 75 60
2562 $5 Line of women dancers with white headdresses (Ami Harvest Ceremony) 75 60
2563 $5 Launch of new fishing boat (Yami Boat Ceremony) 75 60

1999. Centenary of International Council of Nurses. Multicoloured.
2564 $5 Type **681** 50 25
2565 $17 Globe and nurse carrying tray . . . . . 1·40 40

1999. Chinese Classical Opera (Legends of the Ming Dynasty). Multicoloured.
2566 $5 Type **682** 50 25
2567 $5 "The Story of a Pipa" (Kaoming) 50 25
2568 $12 "The Story of Hung Fu" (Chang Fengyi) . . . 85 35
2569 $15 "Paiyueh Pavilion" (Shi Hui) . . . . 1·30 40
MS2570 139 × 90 mm. Nos. 2566/9 3·25 1·30

683 Coins

1999. 50th Anniv of Introduction of the Silver Yuan. Multicoloured.
2571 $5 Type **683** 50 25
2572 $25 Banknotes . . . . . . 2·10 1·00

684 Dragons and Carp (from window, Longsan Temple, Lukang)

685 Children giving Present

1999. (a) As Nos. 2379, 2382, 2386 and 2387 but with Chinese characters for the country name in reverse order, as in T **684**, and colours changed.
2573 **684** $50 green . . . . 4·25 2·50
2574 $100 brown . . . . . . 6·25 5·00

(b) as T **684** but with outer decorated frame. Size 25 × 33 mm.
2578 $300 red and blue . . . . . 21·00 12·50
2579 $500 red and brown . . . . 47·00 17·00

1999. Chinese Engravings of Fruit by Hu Chen-yan. Designs as Nos. 2292/4 but with Chinese characters for the country name in reverse order, and values changed. Multicoloured.
2580 50c. As Type **613** 30 25
2581 $6 As $12 . . . . 50 35
2582 $25 As $15 . . . . 2·10 65

1999. "Taipei" International Stamp Exhibition. As No. **MS**2570 but additionally inscr "TAIPEI INTERNATIONAL STAMP EXHIBITION 1999" (INVITATIONAL) in English and Chinese and with exhibition emblem.
MS2583 140 × 90 mm. Nos. 2566/9 3·25 1·30

1999. Fathers' Day. Multicoloured.
2584 $5 Type **685** 50 25
2585 $25 Father teaching boy to ride bike . . . . 2·10 1·00

686 Peony Lobster (Taiwanese Cuisine)

1999. Chinese Regional Dishes. Multicoloured.
2586 $5 Type **686** 40 15
2587 $5 Buddha jumps the wall (Fukien) (plate, teapot, jar and cups) 40 15
2588 $5 Flower hors d'oeuvres (Cantonese) 40 15
2589 $5 Dongpo pork (Kiangsu and Chekiang) (plate, bowl and double handled jar) 40 15
2590 $5 Stewed fish jaws (Shanghai) (plate decorated with strawberries) 40 15
2591 $5 Beggar's chicken (Hunan) (with folded napkin) . . . 40 15
2592 $5 Carp jumping over dragon's gate (Szechwan) (on silver platter) 40 15
2593 $5 Peking duck (Peking) (in silver dish) 40 15

687 Scuba Diving

1999. Outdoor Activities. Multicoloured.
2594 $5 Type **687** 40 25
2595 $6 Canoeing 50 35
2596 $10 Surfing 95 40
2597 $25 Windsurfing . . . . . 2·30 65

688 Stage and Audience

1999. Taiwanese Opera. Multicoloured.
2598 $5 Type **688** 40 25
2599 $6 Preparation in the dressing room 50 35
2600 $10 Two actresses 95 40
2601 $25 Actress as clown . . . 2·30 65

689 Collapsed Buildings

1999. Taiwan Earthquake Victims' Fund. Sheet 124 × 80 mm containing T **689** and similar horiz design.
MS2602 $25+$25 Type **689**; $25+$25 Hands joined over cracked ground . . . . 12·50 10·00

690 Yellow-headed Amazon

691 Dragon

1999. Birds (3rd series). Illustrations from the Ching Dynasty Bird Manual. Multicoloured.
2603 $5 Type **690** 40 25
2604 $5 Golden-winged parakeet 40 25
2605 $12 Grey parrot . . . . . 1·00 40
2606 $25 Chattering lory . . . . 2·30 65

1999. New Year Greetings "Year of the Dragon". Multicoloured.
2607 $3.50 Type **691** 30 15
2608 $13 Dragon (different) . . . 1·30 50
MS2609 78 × 102 mm. Nos 2634/4, each × 2 . . . . 3·25 1·50

692 ST-1 Communication Satellite over Earth

1999. Year 2000. Multicoloured.
2610 $5 Type **692** (information) 50 25
2611 $5 Deer and river (environmental protection) 50 25
2612 $12 Modern buildings and high-speed train (industry and economy) . . . . . 1·00 40
2613 $15 Dove and St. Peter's Basilica,Vatican City (peace) . . . . 1·40 60
MS2614 102 × 145 mm. Nos. 2610/13 3·50 1·70

1999. "Taipei 2000" International Stamp Exhibition. As No. **MS**2614 but additionally inscr "TAIPEI 2000 STAMP EXHIBITION" in English and Chinese and with exhibition emblem in the margin.
MS2615 102 × 146 mm. Nos. 2610/14 3·50 1·70

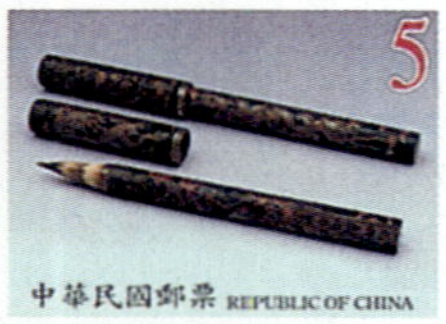
693 Emperor Chia-Ching's "Coloured Cloud Dragon" Writing Brushes (Ming Dynasty)

2000. Traditional Chinese Writing Equipment. Mult.
2616 $5 Type **693** 50 25
2617 $5 Emperor Lung Ching's "Imperial Dragon Fragrance" ink stick (Ming Dynasty) (vert) . . 50 25
2618 $7 "Clear Heart House" (calligraphy, Tsai Hsiang) (Sung Dynasty) (vert) . . 65 35
2619 $26 "Celadon Toad Inkstone" (Sung Dynasty) 2·50 85

694 Kaoping River Bridge Pylon

2000. Inauguration of Second Southern Freeway. Multicoloured.
2620 $5 Type **694** 65 25
2621 $12 Main junction, Tainan 1·30 40
MS2622 125 × 60 mm. $25 Road bridge over Kaoping River (79 × 29 mm) . . . . 2·75 90

695 Branch, Fields and Houses

2000. Seasonal Periods (1st series). Designs depicting the six seasonal periods of Spring. Multicoloured.
2623 $5 Type **695** ("Commencement of Spring") 50 25
2624 $5 Man ploughing fields in the rain ("Rain Water") 50 25
2625 $5 Forks of lightning, little egret and cattle egret ("Waking of Insects") . . 50 25
2626 $5 Men transplanting rice seedlings (Spring Equinox) 50 25
2627 $5 Basket of fruit and houses ("Pure Brightness") 50 25
2628 $5 Rain, farmer and river ("Grain Rain") 50 25
See also Nos. 2636/41, 2652/7 and 2675/80.

696 Shuanghsi River and School Gates, Waishuanghsi Campus

697 Three Heroes at Altar

2000. Centenary of Soochow University. Mult.
2629 $5 Type **696** 50 25
2630 $25 Justice statue, Soochow Law School, Taipeh campus and Ansu Hall, Waishuanghsi campus . . 2·50 1·00

2000. Classical Literature. *Romance of the Three Kingdoms* by Luo Guanzhong (1st series). Mult.
2631 $3.50 Type **697** 40 25
2632 $3.50 Guan Yu reading at night 40 25
2633 $5 Couple in cottage receiving guest 65 35
2634 $20 Arrows raining down on sampans . . . . 1·70 40
MS2635 140 × 100 mm. Nos. 2631/4 3·25 1·30
See also Nos. 2797/**MS**2801.

698 Crops and Mountains

2000. Seasonal Periods (2nd series). Designs depicting the six seasonal periods of Summer. Multicoloured.
2636 $5 Type **698** ("Commencement of Summer") 50 25
2637 $5 Water wheel and houses in rain ("Little Fullness") 50 25
2638 $5 Ears of grain and houses ("Husks of Grain") . . . 50 25
2639 $5 Insect on plant and houses (Summer Solstice) 50 25
2640 $5 Palm leaf fan and fields ("Lesser Heat") 50 25
2641 $5 Watermelons ("Great Heat") 50 25
Nos. 2636/41 were issued together, se-tenant, forming a composite design.

699 Chen Shui-bian and Lu Hsiu-lien

2000. Inauguration of Chen Shui-bian as 10th President and Lu Hsiu-lien as Vice-President. Mult.
2642 $5 Type **699** 50 15
2643 $5 Presidential Office building 50 15
MS2644 125 × 80 mm. Nos. 2642/3, each × 2 . . . . 2·10 65

700 Hsialiao

701 Taiwan Giant Sacred Tree

2000. Monuments Marking the Tropic of Cancer. Multicoloured.
2645 $5 Type **700** 40 25
2646 $12 Wuho . . . . 1·30 50
2647 $25 Chingpu . . . . 2·30 90

2000. Chinese Engravings of Fruit by Hu Chen-yan. As No. 2295 but with Chinese characters for the country name in reverse order, as in T **683**, and with value (2648) or new design changed.
2648 $32 multicoloured . . . . . 3·00 2·40
2649 $34 multicoloured . . . . . 3·25 2·75

2000. Sacred Trees. Multicoloured.
2650 $5 Type **701** 40 25
2651 $39 Sacred Sleeping Moon Tree . . . . 3·50 1·40

702 Grain drying

2000. Seasonal Periods (3rd series). Depicting the six seasonal periods of Autumn. Multicoloured.
2652 $5 Type **702** ("Commencement of Autumn") 50 25
2653 $5 Rick and village ("Bounds of Heat") . . . 50 25
2654 $5 Dew covered leaves ("White Dew") 50 25
2655 $5 Red leaves ("Autumn Equinox") 50 25
2656 $5 Bare tree ("Cold Dew") 50 25
2657 $5 Frost on plant ("Descent of Hoar Frost") 50 25
Nos. 2652/57 were issued together, se-tenant. forming a composite design.

2000. No. 1784 surch **350**.
2658 $3.50 on $7.50 multicoloured 40 25

704 Red Spider Lily

705 Seismograph and map of Taiwan

2000. Poisonous Plants. Multicoloured.
2659 $5 Type **704** 50 25
2660 $5 Odollam erberus-tree (*Cerbera manghas*) 50 25
2661 $12 Rosary pea . . . . . . 1·30 40
2662 $20 Oleander . . . . 2·10 75

2000. Earthquakes. Multicoloured.
2663 $5 Type **705** 40 25
2664 $12 Rescue workers . . . . 1·30 40
2665 $25 Earthquake drills . . . 2·75 1·00

706 *Anotogaster sieboldii*

2000. Dragonflies. Multicoloured.
2666 $5 Type **706** 50 25
2667 $5 *Lamelligomphus formosanus* (horiz) 50 25
2668 $12 *Neurothemis ramburii* (horiz) . . . . 1·40 40
2669 $12 *Trithemis festiva* . . . . 1·40 40
MS2670 135 × 80 mm. Nos. 2666/9 3·75 1·30

707 White's Thrush

2000. Birds 4th series). Illustrations from the Ching Dynasty Bird Manual. Multicoloured.
2671 $5 Type **707** 50 25
2672 $5 Brambling 50 25
2673 $12 Rothschild's mynah . . 1·30 40
2674 $25 Southern grackle . . . 2·50 75

708 Lake, Mountains and Bowl

2000. Seasonal Periods (4th series). Designs depicting the six seasonal periods of Winter. Multicoloured.
2675 $5 Type **708** ("Commencement of Winter") 50 25
2676 $5 Trees covered in snow ("Lesser Snow") 50 25
2677 $5 Mountains covered in snow ("Great Snow") . . 50 25
2678 $5 Rice balls in bowl ("Winter Solstice") . . . 50 25
2679 $5 Houses and tree branch covered in snow ("Lesser Cold") 50 25
2680 $5 Log cabin covered in snow ("Great Cold") . . 50 25
Nos. 2675/80 were issued together, se-tenant, forming a composite design.

709 Palace Lamp Boulevard and Classrooms

2000. 50th Anniv of Tamkang University. Mult.
2681 $5 Type **709** 50 25
2682 $25 Maritime Museum and "Scroll Plaza" (sculpture) 2·50 1·00

710 Snake

712 Cruise Ship and Buildings

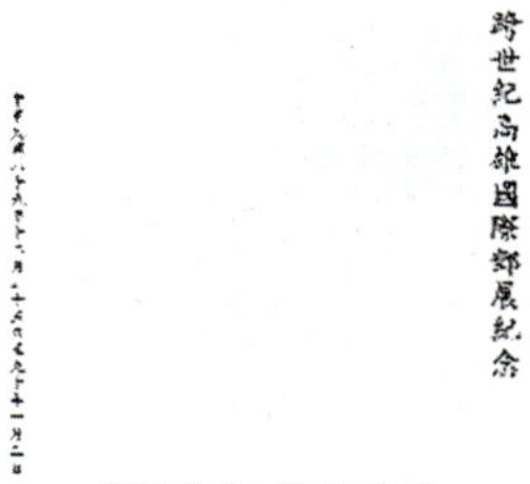
(**711**) (½-size illustration)

2000. New Year Greetings. "Year of the Snake". Multicoloured.
2683 $3.50 Type **710** 30 25
2684 $13 Snake (different) . . . 1·30 40

2000. "Turn of the Century" International Stamp Exhibition, Kaohsiung. As No. **MS**2685 optd with T **711** in the margin.
MS2685 78 × 102 mm. 2 × 3.50 multicoloured; 2 × $13 multicoloured . . . . 3·25 1·50

2001. "Three Small Links" (establishment of trade links between Kinmen, Xiamen, Matsu and Foochow). Multicoloured.
2687 $9 Type **712** 85 60
2688 $25 Cruise ship and monument . . . . 2·30 1·50

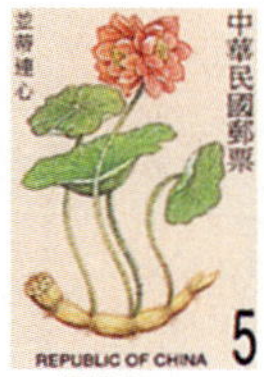
713 Lotus Blossoms ("Marital Bliss")

715 Apples

714 Aquarius

2001. Wishes for the Coming Year. Multicoloured.
2689 $5 Type **713** 50 35
2690 $5 Loganberries, lichees and walnuts ("Success in one's career") 50 35
2691 $12 Pomegranates ("Producing many offspring") . . . . 1·00 75
2692 $12 Peonies and pair of Chinese bulbuls ("Growing old together with wealth and high position") . . . . 1·00 75

2001. Signs of the Western Zodiac (1st series). Air Signs. Multicoloured.
2693 $5 Type **714** 50 25
2694 $12 Gemini . . . . 1·20 50
2695 $25 Libra . . . . 2·50 1·80
See also Nos. 2708/10, 2726/8 and 2755/7.

2001. Fruits (1st series). Multicoloured.
2696 $5 Type **715** 50 25
2697 $7 Guavas 75 25

2698	$12 Pears	1·20	40
2699	$25 Melons	2·50	75

See also Nos. 2732/5, 2785/8 and 2879/82.

716 Main Peak

2001. Mount Jade. Views of Mount Jade. Mult.

2700	$5 Type **716**	50	35
2701	$5 Western peak	50	35
2702	$12 Northern peak	1·20	85
2703	$25 Eastern peak	2·50	1·70

717 Girls playing with Ball ("Little Ball")

2001. Children's Playtime Rhymes. Multicoloured.

2704	$5 Type **717**	50	35
2705	$5 Children sitting in a circle ("Point to the Water Vat")	50	35
2706	$12 Boys dancing ("Pangolin")	1·20	85
2707	$25 Children playing ("Shake and Stamp")	2·50	1·70

2001. Signs of the Western Zodiac (2nd series). Earth Signs. As T **714**. Multicoloured.

2708	$5 Capricorn	50	25
2709	$12 Taurus	1·20	50
2710	$25 Virgo	2·50	1·80

718 Sakyamuni Buddha, Northern Wei Dynasty

2001. Ancient Statues of Buddha. Multicoloured.

2711	$5 Type **718**	50	35
2712	$9 Seated Buddha, Tang Dynasty	75	50
2713	$12 Mahavairocana Buddha, Sung Dynasty	1·30	85
MS2714	102 × 146 mm. Nos. 2711/13	3·25	2·50

719 Thresher

2001. Early Agricultural Implements. Multicoloured.

2715	$5 Type **719**	50	35
2716	$7 Ox plough	75	50
2717	$10 Bamboo baskets and yoke	95	65
2718	$25 Coir raincoat and hat	2·50	1·70

720 Mackay

721 Girl dancing, Globe and Emblem

2001. Death Centenary of George Leslie Mackay (missionary and educator).

2719	**720**	$25 multicoloured	2·10	1·70

2001. Kiwanis International (community organization) Convention, Taipeh. Multicoloured.

2720	$5 Type **721**	50	25
2721	$25 Mother and child within heart	2·10	1·40

722 Dragon

2001. Kites. Multicoloured.

2722	$5 Type **722**	40	35
2723	$5 Phoenix	40	35
2724	$5 Tiger	40	35
2725	$5 Fish	40	35

2001. Signs of the Western Zodiac (3rd series). Fire Signs. As T **714**. Multicoloured.

2726	$5 Aries	50	35
2727	$12 Leo	1·20	65
2728	$25 Sagittarius	2·30	1·50

723 Medium-Capacity Car

2001. Rapid Transit System, Taipeh. Multicoloured.

2729	$5 Type **723**	50	25
2730	$12 Passengers and tickets	1·40	60
MS2731	125 × 60 mm. $25 Chientan Station, Tamshui Line (84 × 42 mm)	2·75	1·30

2001. Fruits (2nd series). As T **715**. Multicoloured.

2732	$1 Plums	30	15
2733	$3.50 Tangerines	40	25
2734	$20 Longans	1·60	1·00
2735	$40 Grapefruit	3·50	2·40

724 Keeper and Monkeys ("Now Three, Now Four")

2001. Chinese Fables. Multicoloured.

2736	$5 Type **724**	50	35
2737	$5 Man selling weapons ("Selling the All Penetrating Sword and Unyielding Shield")	50	35
2738	$12 Farmer sitting under tree ("Waiting by the Tree for the Rabbit")	1·00	50
2739	$25 Old man and children ("An Old Fool Moves Mountains")	1·90	1·30

725 Japanese Waxwing

2001. Birds (5th series). Showing illustrations from the Ching Dynasty Bird Manual. Multicoloured.

2740	$5 Type **725**	50	35
2741	$5 Siberian rubythroat	50	35
2742	$12 White-rumped munia	1·00	50
2743	$25 Great barbet	1·90	1·30

726 Second Terminal, Chiang Kai-shek International Airport

2001. 90th Anniv of Republic of China. Multicoloured.

2744	$5 Type **726**	50	35
2745	$5 Computer screens, lap top computer, mobile phone and Globe	50	35
2746	$12 Dance, National Theatre	85	50
2747	$15 Dolphins	1·50	90

727 Flame, Karate, Javelin and Table Tennis

2001. National Games, Kaohsiung and Pingtung. Multicoloured.

2748	$5 Type **727**	50	25
2749	$25 Swimming, athletics, weightlifting and map	2·10	1·40

728 Pitcher

2001. 34th World Baseball Championship and 21st Asia Baseball Tournament. Multicoloured.

2750	$5 Type **728**	50	35
2751	$5 Batter	50	35
2752	$12 Catcher	1·00	65
2753	$20 Base runner	1·80	1·20
MS2754	120 × 85 mm. Nos. 2750/3	4·00	2·50

2001. Signs of the Western Zodiac (4th series). Water Signs. As T **714**. Multicoloured.

2755	$5 Pisces	50	35
2756	$12 Cancer	1·20	65
2757	$25 Scorpio	2·30	1·50

729 Mozhaonu holding Fan ("Thunder Storm")

2001. Taiwanese Puppet Theatre. (1st series). Showing puppets. Multicoloured.

2758	$5 Type **729**	50	25
2759	$6 Taiyangau ("Rising Winds, Surging Clouds")	65	35
2760	$10 Kuangdao ("Thunder Crazy Sword")	1·20	65
2761	$25 Chin Chia-chien ("Thunder Golden Light")	2·50	1·30

See also Nos. 2887/90.

730 Old School Building, Shuiyan Road, Taipeh

731 Horse

2001. Centenary of National Defence Medical Centre. Multicoloured.

2762	$5 Type **730**	50	25
2763	$25 New school building and medical staff	2·10	1·40

2001. New Year Greetings. "Year of the Horse". Multicoloured.

2764	$3.50 Type **731**	40	25
2765	$13 Horse (different)	1·30	85
MS2766	78 × 102 mm. Nos. 2764/5, each × 2	3·25	2·75

732 Yu Pin

2001. Birth Centenary of Yu Pin (religious leader).

2767	**732**	$25 multicoloured	2·30	1·60
MS2768		80 × 60 mm. $25 As No. 2767	2·30	1·80

733 Carnations

2001. Greetings Stamps. Multicoloured.

2769	$5 Type **733**	40	35
2770	$5 White lilies	40	35
2771	$5 Pink violas	40	35
2772	$5 Orange flowers with yellow centres	40	35
2773	$5 Pink flowers with five petals	40	35
2774	$5 Pink roses	40	35
2775	$5 Christmas tree decorations	40	35
2776	$5 Poinsettia	40	35
2777	$5 Purple ball-shaped flowers	40	35
2778	$5 Sunflowers	40	35

734 Students with Flags

2002. 50th Anniv of Fu Hsing Kang College (military university). Multicoloured.

2779	$5 Type **734**	50	25
2780	$25 University buildings and statue	2·10	1·40

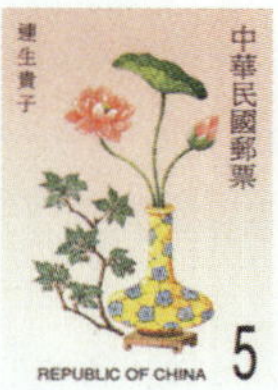

735 Vase containing Lotus Flower and Sweet Osmanthus ("Producing many offspring")

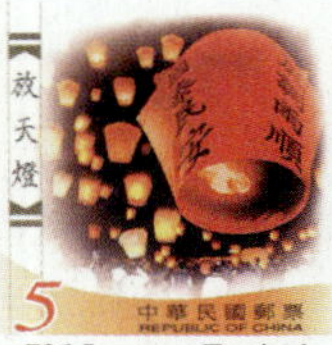

736 Lantern Festival (Pinghsi and Shihfen)

2002. Wishes for the Coming Year. Multicoloured.

2781	$5 Type **735**	50	25
2782	$5 Orchid and osmanthus plants ("Person of high morality")	50	25
2783	$12 Vase containing peonies and flowering crabapple ("Hall full of the rich and famous")	1·30	60
2784	$12 Vase containing roses ("Safe and peaceful in all four seasons")	1·30	60

2002. Fruits (3rd series). As T **715**. Multicoloured.

2785	$6 Avocados	50	40
2786	$10 Lychees	85	65
2787	$17 Dates	1·50	1·00
2788	$32 Passionfruit	3·00	2·10

2002. Traditional Folk Festivals (1st series). Multicoloured.

2789	$5 Type **736**	50	35
2790	$5 Fireworks display (Yanshui)	50	35
2791	$10 Matsu (sea goddess) procession (Peikang)	1·00	60
2792	$20 Dragon boat race	2·10	1·30

See also Nos. 2817/20.

737 Mountain in Winter

2002. Mount Hsueh. Views of Mount Hsueh. Multicoloured.

2793	$5 Type **737**	40	35
2794	$5 North ridge	40	35
2795	$12 Slopes in autumn	1·00	75
2796	$25 Glacial cirques (bowl-shaped depressions)	2·10	1·50

738 Three Heroes chasing Lu Bu

2002. Classical Literature. Romance of the Three Kingdoms by Luo Guanzhong (2nd series). Multicoloured.

2797	$3.50 Type **738**	40	25
2798	$3.50 Chao Yun	40	25
2799	$5 Dr. Hua Tuo operating on Guan Yu's arm	50	35
2800	$20 Chu-Ko Liang playing lute to repel invaders	2·10	1·30
MS2801	140 × 100 mm. Nos. 2797/800	3·50	2·10

739 Chinese Crested Tern (*Thalasseus bernsteini*)

2002. Endangered Species. Chinese Crested Tern. Two sheets, 240 × 160 mm (**MS**2802a) and 120 × 60 mm (**MS**2802b) containing T **739** and similar horiz designs. Multicoloured.

MS2802	(a) $5 × 10, Type **739**; Two Terns in flight; Tern flying (left); Landing on rock; Perched on rock with open beak; Feeding chick; Diving; Flying above rocks; On ground looking left; Adult and chick; On nest (b) $25 Tern in flight (80 × 30 mm) Set of 2 sheets	6·25	5·00

740 Bowl decorated with Lotus

741 Stock (*Matthiola incana*)

2002. Ching Dynasty Enamel Porcelain Bowls. Multicoloured.

2803	$5 Type **740**	40	35
2804	$5 Peacock	40	35
2805	$7 Peonies	65	50
2806	$32 Birds and bamboo	3·00	2·00

2002. Scented Flowers. Multicoloured.

2807	$5 Type **741**	40	35
2808	$12 Gardenia (*Gardenia jasminoides*)	1·00	85
2809	$25 Banana shrub (*Michelia figo*)	2·10	1·70

742 Bottle-nosed Dolphin (*Tursiops truncates*)

2002. Marine mammals. Multicoloured.

2810	$5 Type **742**	40	35
2811	$5 Humpback whale (*Megaptera novaeangliae*)	40	35
2812	$10 Killer whale (*Orcinus orca*)	85	65
2813	$25 Risso's dolphin (*Grampus griseus*)	2·50	2·00
MS2814	120 × 80 mm. As Nos. 2810/13	4·25	3·25

743 Player in Wheelchair

2002. International Paralympics Committee World Table Tennis Championships, Taipeh. Multicoloured.

2815	$5 Type **743**	50	35
2816	$5 Player using crutch	50	35

2002. Traditional Folk Festivals (2nd series). As T **736**. Multicoloured.

2817	$5 Water lanterns (Keelung)	40	35
2818	$5 Fireworks display (Touchengi)	40	35
2819	$10 Yimin (martyrs) procession (Taoyuan)	95	65
2820	$20 Burning the Prince's boat (Tungkang)	1·80	1·20

744 Republic of China and Vatican City Flags

2002. 60th Anniv of Republic of China—Vatican City Diplomatic Relations ($5). 80th Anniv of First Apostolic Delegate to Republic of China ($17). Multicoloured.

2821	$5 Type **744**	40	35
2822	$17 Celso Costantini (first apostolic delegate)	1·50	1·20

745 Vernal Hanging Parrot

2002. Birds (6th series). Illustrations from the Ching Dynasty Bird Manual. Multicoloured.

2823	$5 Type **745**	40	35
2824	$5 White-rumped munia	40	35
2825	$12 White-headed greenfinch	85	65
2826	$25 Yunnan greenfinch	1·90	1·40

746 Liang Shan-po and Chu Ying-tai (impromptu performance)

2002. Chinese Regional Opera. Multicoloured.

2827	$5 Type **746**	40	35
2828	$6 Hsueh Ting-shan and Fan Li-hua (indoor performance)	50	35
2829	$10 Hsueh Ping-kuei and Wang Pao-chuan (outdoor stage performance)	85	65
2830	$25 The Living Buddha Chikung (modern theatre)	2·10	1·40

747 Mother and Baby Koala

749 Goat

748 Knot

2002. Koalas at Taipei Municipal Zoo. Multicoloured.

2831	$5 Type **747**	40	25
2832	$5 Eating leaf	40	25
2833	$9 Resting	75	50
2834	$21 Mother with baby on back	1·70	1·20
MS2835	85 × 115 mm. Nos. 2831/4	3·25	2·20

2002. Greetings Stamps. Chinese Decorative Knots. Designs showing various knots (knot colours given). Multicoloured.

2836	$3.50 Type **748**	30	25
2837	$3.50 green, blue and yellow	30	25
2838	$3.50 red and yellow	30	25
2839	$3.50 orange and green	30	25
2840	$3.50 blue and straw	30	25
2841	$3.50 blue, mauve, green, red and yellow	30	25
2842	$3.50 red and yellow (different)	30	25
2843	$3.50 mauve and blue	30	25
2844	$3.50 pink and lavender	30	25
2845	$3.50 yellow and blue	30	25
2846	$5 Type **748**	40	35
2847	$5 As No. 2837	40	35
2848	$5 As 2838	40	35
2849	$5 As 2839	40	35
2850	$5 As 2840	40	35
2851	$5 As 2841	40	35
2852	$5 As 2842	40	35
2853	$5 As 2843	40	35
2854	$5 As 2844	40	35
2855	$5 As 2845	40	35
2856	$25 Type **748**	2·00	1·60
2857	$25 As 2837	2·00	1·60
2858	$25 As 2838	2·00	1·60
2859	$25 As 2839	2·00	1·60
2860	$25 As 2840	2·00	1·60
2861	$25 As 2841	2·00	1·60
2862	$25 As 2842	2·00	1·60
2863	$25 As 2843	2·00	1·60
2864	$25 As 2844	2·00	1·60
2865	$25 As 2845	2·00	1·60

2002. New Year Greetings. "Year of the Goat". Multicoloured.

2866	$3.50 Type **749**	30	25
2867	$13 Goat (different)	1·00	85
MS2868	78 × 102 mm. Nos. 2866/7, each × 2	2·75	2·20

750 "Street Scene on a Summer's Day" (Chen Cheng-po)

2002. Taiwanese Artists (1st series). Multicoloured.

2869	$5 Type **750**	40	35
2870	$5 "Girl in white dress" (Li Mei-shu) (vert)	40	35
2871	$10 "Courtyard with banana trees" (Liao Chi-chun) (vert)	85	65
2872	$20 "Sunrise" (Kuo Po-chuan)	1·70	1·30

See also Nos. 2939/42 and 2964/7.

中華郵政股份有限公司成立紀念
中華民國九十二年一月一日

(**751**) (½-size illustration)

2003. Inauguration of Chunghwa Post Co. (new postal service). No. **MS**2868 optd with T **751** in the margin.

MS2873	78 × 102 mm. 2 × $3.50 multicoloured, 2 × $13 multicoloured	2·75	2·20

752 WTO Emblem, Map and Buildings

2003. 1st Anniv of Membership of World Trade Organisation.

2874	**752**	$17 multicoloured	1·40	90

753 Main Peak in Spring

2003. Mount Nanhu. Views of Mount Nanhu. Multicoloured.

2875	$5 Type **753**	40	25
2876	$5 Glacial cirques	40	25
2877	$12 Lake and main peak	95	60
2878	$25 Snow-covered Mount Chungyang Chien	1·90	1·30

2003. Fruits (4th series). As T **715**. Multicoloured.

2879	$9 Rose apples	65	50
2880	$13 Kumquats	85	65
2881	$15 Lemons	95	75
2882	$34 Coconuts	2·10	1·70

754 Family

2003. "Caring Heart". Multicoloured.

2883	$5 Type **754** (family life)	40	25
2884	$5 Woman and wheelchair user (volunteers)	40	25
2885	$10 Fields and heart (care for the environment)	85	50
2886	$25 Child and dogs (care for animals)	2·00	1·30

755 Outdoor Performance ("Journey to the West")

2003. Taiwanese Puppet Theatre (2nd series). Multicoloured.

2887	$5 Type **755**	40	25
2888	$5 Television showing hand puppets	40	25
2889	$10 Theatre performance ("Mysteries of the Wolf Castle")	85	50
2890	$25 Film showing hand puppet ("Legend of the Sacred Stone")	2·00	1·30

756 Blue-tailed Bee-eater in Flight

2003. Endangered Species. Blue-tailed Bee-eaters (*Merops philippinus*). Multicoloured.

2891	$5 Type **756**	40	25
2892	$5 Five birds on branch	40	25
2893	$10 Sunbathing	85	50
2894	$20 Offering food to mate in nest	1·60	1·00
MS2895	135 × 80 mm. Nos. 2891/4	3·25	1·80

757 Wash Stand

758 Jhang Guo-lao riding Mule

2003. Taiwanese Furniture. Multicoloured.

2896	$5 Type **757**	40	25
2897	$5 Canopied bed	40	25
2898	$12 Taishi chair	95	60
2899	$20 Pahsien table	1·60	1·00

2003. Eight Immortals (1st series). Multicoloured.

2900	$5 Type **758**	40	25
2901	$5 Li Tie-guai riding fish	40	25
2902	$10 Han Jhong-li holding fan	85	50
2903	$25 Lyu Dong-bin wearing sword and carrying flywhisk	2·00	1·20

See also Nos. 2958/61.

759 *Vamuna virilis*

2003. Moths. Multicoloured.

2904	$5 Type **759**	40	25
2905	$5 *Antitrygodes divisaria perturbata*	40	25
2906	$12 *Sinna extrema*	95	60
2907	$20 *Thyas juno*	1·60	1·00

760 *Sympetrum eroticum ardens*

2003. Dragonflies. Multicoloured.

2908	$5 Type **760**	40	25
2909	$5 *Acisome panorpoides*	40	25
2910	$10 *Anax parthenope Julius* (horiz)	85	50
2911	$17 *Rhyothemis variegata aria* (horiz)	1·40	85
MS2912	80 × 135 mm. Nos. 2908/11	3·25	1·80

761 Two Cranes

2002. Greetings Stamps. Multicoloured.

2913	$3.50 Type **761**	30	15
2914	$3.50 Carved ducks	30	15
2915	$3.50 Decorative fish	30	15
2916	$3.50 Bamboo	30	15
2917	$3.50 Carved eagle	30	15
2918	$5 Vase and knot	40	25
2919	$5 Type **761**	40	25
2920	$5 As No. 2914	40	25
2921	$5 Three jars	40	25
2922	$5 Flowers in vase	40	25
2923	$5 Carved golden dragon	40	25
2924	$5 As No. 2915	40	25
2925	$5 As No. 2916	40	25
2926	$5 Child riding mythical animal	40	25
2927	$5 As No. 2917	40	25
2928	$12 As No. 2922	95	60

762 White-throated Laughing Thrush

2003. Birds (7th series). Showing illustrations from the Ching Dynasty Bird Manual. Multicoloured.

2929	$5 Type **762**	40	25
2930	$5 Great mynah	40	25
2931	$12 Yellow-legged button quail	95	60
2932	$25 Crested lark	2·00	1·20

763 Chungshan Park, Taichung

2003. Landscapes. Multicoloured.

2933	$5 Type **763**	40	25
2934	$5 Dongshan river, Ilan	40	25
2935	$11 Hills, Tianliao ("Moonscape")	85	50
2936	$20 Sansiantai coral reef, Chenggong ("Terrace of the Three Immortals")	1·60	1·00

764 Building Central Highway

2003. 25th Anniv of Veteran's Day. Multicoloured.

2937	$5 Type **764**	40	25
2938	$25 Veterans and retirement building	1·90	1·20

765 "Back Yard" (Lu Tie-jhou) **766** Monkey

2003. Taiwanese Artists (2nd series). Multicoloured.

2939	$5 Type **765**	40	25
2940	$5 "Jioufen, A Goldmine Town" (Lin Ke-gong)	40	25
2941	$10 "Leisure" (Chen Jin) (horiz)	85	50
2942	$20 "East Gate" (Li Ze-fan) (horiz)	1·70	1·00

2003. New Year Greetings. "Year of the Monkey". Multicoloured.

2943	$3.50 Type **766**	30	15
2944	$13 Monkey enclosed in heart	1·00	65
MS2945	78 × 102 mm. Nos. 2943/4, each × 2	2·75	1·60

767 Fumaroles and Spring, Yangmingshan Hot Springs

2003. Thermal Springs. Multicoloured.

2946	$5 Type **767**	40	25
2947	$5 Nanfangao bridge and cold spring, Suao	40	25
2948	$10 Shuei Huo Tang Yuan (water and gas) and hot spring, Guanziling	85	50
2949	$25 Lighthouse and hot spring, Green Island	2·00	1·20
MS2950	102 × 146 mm. Nos. 2946/9	3·75	2·20

768 Jhonggang Interchange

2004. Completion of National Highway Number Three. Multicoloured.

2951	$5 Type **768**	40	25
2952	$25 Cingshuei service area	1·90	1·20
MS2953	125 × 60 mm. $20 Cingshuei service area (enlarged) (80 × 30 mm)	1·70	85

769 *Lilium formosanum* **770** Stylized People enclosed in Heart

2004. Flowering Bulbs. Taiwan Flower Expo, Changhua (**MS**2957). Multicoloured.

2954	$5 Type **769**	40	25
2955	$5 Hippeastrum hybrid	40	25
2956	$12 Freesia hybrid	1·00	60
MS2957	102 × 146 mm. Nos. 2954/6	1·90	1·10

2004. Eight Immortals (2nd series). As T **758**. Multicoloured.

2958	$5 Han Siang-zih playing flute	40	25
2959	$5 He Sian-gu holding lotus blossom	40	25
2960	$10 Cao Guo-jiou holding tablet	85	50
2961	$25 Lan Cai-he holding flower basket	2·00	1·20

2004. Centenary of Taiwan Red Cross Society. Multicoloured.

2962	$5 Type **770**	40	25
2963	$5 Stylized Red Cross workers	40	25

Nos. 2962/3 were issued together, se-tenant, forming a composite design.

771 "Young Girl from Lu Kai" (Yan Shui-long)

2004. Taiwanese Artists (3rd series). Multicoloured.

2964	$5 Type **771**	40	25
2965	$5 "Old Street in Taipeh" (Yang Sang-lang) (horiz)	40	25
2966	$10 "Farmers" (Lee Shih-chiao) (horiz)	85	50
2967	$20 "Fish Shop" (Liu Chi-hsiang)	1·70	1·00

772 *Parantica sita niphonica*

2004. Butterflies. Multicoloured.

2968	$5 Type **772**	40	25
2969	$5 *Choaspes benjaminii formosanus*	40	25
2970	$17 *Junonia aimana*	1·50	85
2971	$20 *Artipe eryx horiella*	1·70	1·00

773 Outdoor Performance ("Eight General")

2004. Yijhen (folk activities). Multicoloured.

2972	$5 Type **773**	40	25
2973	$5 Martial arts display ("Song Jiang Battle Array")	40	25
2974	$11 Drum dance	85	50
2975	$25 Stilt walking	2·00	1·20

774 President Chen Shui-bian and Vice President Ms. Hsui-lien Annette Lu

2004. Inauguration of President Chen Shui-bian and Vice President Ms. Hsui-lien Annette Lu. Showing the president and vice president. Multicoloured.

2976	$5 Type **774**	40	25
2977	$5 Clasped hands	40	25
2978	$5 Festival	40	25
2979	$5 Train and Taipeh skyline	40	25
MS2980	125 × 60 mm. $12 Train and Taipeh skyline (different) (80 × 30 mm)	1·00	60

775 Harry Potter (Daniel Radcliffe) playing Quidditch (game)

2004. Harry Potter and the "Prisoner of Azkaban" (film based on book by J. K. Rowling). Two sheets, each 190 × 130 mm containing T **775** and similar horiz designs. Multicoloured.

MS2981	(a) $5 × 6, Type **775**; In the storm; Harry and Hermione Granger (Emma Watson) riding Buckbeak the Hippogriff; Harry and Hogwarts towers; Harry repelling Dementors; Harry with wand extended. (b) $5 × 6, Hedwig (Harry's owl) delivering Owl Post; Hedwig; Harry riding Buckbeak; Buckbeak; Harry and *Monster Book of Monsters*; Crookshanks (Hermione's cat)	8·50	5·00

776 Keelung Station

2004. Old Train Stations (1st series). Multicoloured.

2982	$5 Type **776**	40	25
2983	$5 Taipeh	40	25
2984	$15 Hsinchu	1·20	75
2985	$25 Taichung	2·00	1·30

See also Nos. 3062/5.

777 Iron Fort, Nangan

2004. Tourism. Matsu Islands. Multicoloured.

2986	$5 Type **777**	40	25
2987	$5 Cinbi village, Beigan	40	25
2988	$9 Fujheng village, Tungchu	75	50
2989	$25 Lienyuyikeng (virtuous woman's fjord), Tungyin	2·00	1·30

778 *Uca borealis*

2004. Crabs. Multicoloured.

2990	$3.50 Type **778**	30	15
2991	$3.50 *Uca formosensis*	30	15
2992	$5 *Uca arcuata*	40	25
2993	$25 *Uca latea*	2·00	1·30

779 Woman playing Lute (detail)

2004. ROCUPEX'04, International Stamp Exhibition, Taipei. Sheet 80 × 125 mm containing T **779** and similar vert design. Multicoloured.

MS2994	$5 Type **779**; $25 Seated scholar and standing woman	2·30	1·50

The stamps and margin of **MS**2994 form a composite design of "Listening to the Lute" (painting by Li Sing).

780 Sun Moon Lake

2004. TAIPEH 2005 International Stamp Exhibition. Sheet 103 × 146 mm containing T **780** and similar horiz design. Multicoloured.

MS2995	$5 Type **780**; $25 Mount Ali	2·30	1·50

781 Children riding Dove, Symbols of Peace and War (Yang Chih-yuan)

2004. International Day of Peace. Winning Design in Lions Club International Peace Poster Competition.

2996	**781** $15 multicoloured	1·20	75

782 Dear Daniel

2004. 30th Anniv of Hello Kitty (character created by Yamaguchi Yuko). Two sheets, each 130 × 100 containing T **782** and similar multicoloured designs.

MS2997	(a) $5 Type **782** (boyfriend); $15 Hello Kitty holding teacup. (b) $5 Hello Kitty and bird (60 × 40 mm); Dear Daniel wearing purple jacket (40 × 60 mm)	3·25	2·00

The stamps and margins of **MS**2997a form composite designs of a tea table and Taipeh 101 Tower and **MS**2997b a composite design of feeding the birds on the waterfront.

783 Ship

2004. Greetings Stamps. Multicoloured.
2998 $3.50 Type **783** ("Sea of smooth sailing") 30 15
2999 $3.50 Lions ("Two lions bring good fortune") . . 30 15
3000 $3.50 Goats ("Three suns (goats) of auspiciousness") 30 15
3001 $3.50 Vase of flowers ("Safety in all four seasons") 30 15
3002 $3.50 Stylised bats ("Five blessings at the door") . . 30 15
3003 $3.50 Fruit ("Six is silky smooth") 30 15
3004 $3.50 Couple ("Married for seven lives") 30 15
3005 $3.50 Embroidered panel and carving ("Eight immortals wish for your longevity") 30 15
3006 $3.50 Dragon ("Nine means success") 30 15
3007 $3.50 Food ("Ten is all round perfection") . . . 30 15
3008 $5 As Type **783** 40 25
3009 $5 As No. 2999 . . . . . . 40 25
3010 $5 As No. 3000 . . . . . . 40 25
3011 $5 As No. 3001 . . . . . . 40 25
3012 $5 As No. 3002 . . . . . . 40 25
3013 $5 As No. 3003 . . . . . . 40 25
3014 $5 As No. 3004 . . . . . . 40 25
3015 $5 As No. 3005 . . . . . . 40 25
3016 $5 As No. 3006 . . . . . . 40 25
3017 $5 As No. 3007 . . . . . . 40 25

784 University Building Facade and Old Medical College Gate

2004. 50th Anniv of Kaohsiung Medical University. Multicoloured.
3018 $5 Type **784** 40 25
3019 $5 Mosquito, snake, scholar and laboratory beaker . . 40 25

786 Women's Taekwondo

2004. Olympic Games, Athens (2nd series). Medal Winners. Multicoloured.
3024 $5 Type **786** (Chen Shih-hsin) (gold medal) 40 25
3025 $5 Men's Taekwondo (Chu Mu-yen) (gold medal) (horiz) 40 25
3026 $9 Archery team (men's silver medal and women's bronze medal) (horiz) . . 75 50
3027 $12 Medal winners 95 60

787 Black-billed Spoonbills in Flight

2004. Endangered Species. Black-billed Spoonbill (*Platalea minor*). Multicoloured.
3028 $2.50 Type **787** 20 15
3029 $2.50 Standing on one leg 20 15
3030 $15 With raised wings . . . 1·30 60
3031 $25 Feeding . . . . 2·00 1·20
MS3032 120 × 60 mm. $20 Six Spoonbills (80 × 30 mm) . . . 1·70 85
The stamp and margin of No. **MS**3032 form a composite design of Spoonbills and lake.

788 Yen Chai-kan **789** Decorated Lantern

2004. Birth Centenary of Yen Chai-kan (former president).
3033 **788** $12 multicoloured . . . 1·00 50

2004. New Year Greetings. "Year of the Rooster". Multicoloured.
3034 $3.50 Type **789** 30 15
3035 $13 Lanterns and stylised rooster . . . . 1·00 60
MS3036 110 × 76 mm. $5 Lanterns, rooster, hen and chicks (46 × 26 mm) 40 25

790 Prefecture Hall, Jhuluo

2004. 300th Anniv of Jhuluo (Chiaya). Multicoloured.
3037 $5 Type **790** 40 25
3038 $5 East Gate 40 25

791 Crane (1st rank)

2005. Cing Dynasty Official Court Dress Designs. Showing bird designs associated with court rank. Multicoloured.
3039 $3.50 Type **791** 20 15
3040 $3.50 Pheasant (2nd rank) 20 15
3041 $5 Peacock (3rd rank) . . . 30 25
3042 $25 Goose (4th rank) . . . 1·80 1·20

792

793

794

795

2005. Greetings Stamps. Internet Shorthand.
3043 **792** $5 multicoloured 30 25
3044 **793** $5 multicoloured 30 25
3045 **794** $5 multicoloured 30 25
3046 **795** $5 multicoloured 30 25

796 Map of Taiwan and Centenary Emblem

2005. Centenary of Rotary International. Mult.
3047 $5 Type **796** 30 25
3048 $12 Dove and emblem . . . 85 60

797 *Kandelia obovata*

2005. Mangroves. Multicoloured.
3049 $3.50 Type **797** 20 15
3050 $3.50 *Rhizophora stylosa* . . 20 15
3051 $5 *Avicennia marina* 30 25
3052 $5 *Lumnitzera racemosa* . . 30 25

798 Longshan Temple, Mengjia

2005. Architecture. Multicoloured.
3053 $5 Type **798** 30 25
3054 $5 Lin Ben Yuan's Garden, Banciao 30 25
3055 $13 Chaotian Temple, Beigang 85 65
3056 $15 Anping Fort, Tainan . . 95 75

799 Ceiling, Lognshan Temple

2005. TAIPEI 2005 International Stamp Exhibition (1st issue). Sheet 102 × 146 mm containing T **799** and similar multicoloured design.
MS3057 $5 Type **799**; $25 Puppets (horiz) . . . . 1·90 1·50
See also Nos. 3074 and **MS**3075.

800 *Rhinomuraena quaesita*

2005. Fish. Multicoloured.
3058 $5 Type **800** 30 25
3059 $5 *Pomacanthus semicirculatus* 30 25
3060 $12 *Forcipiger flavissimus* . . 75 60
3061 $25 *Pterois volitans* . . . . 1·60 1·30

2005. Old Train Stations (2nd series). As T **776**. Multicoloured.
3062 $5 Changhua 30 25
3063 $5 Chiayi 30 25
3064 $15 Tainan 95 75
3065 $25 Kaohsiung . . . . . . 1·60 1·30

801 Mayhem in Fengyi Pavilion

2005. Classical Literature. *Romance of the Three Kingdoms* by Luo Guanzhong (3rd series). Multicoloured.
3066 $3.50 Type **801** 20 15
3067 $3.50 Deterring the enemy 20 15
3068 $5 Releasing Tsao Tsao . . 30 25
3069 $20 A trick in the bag . . . 1·30 1·00
MS3070 140 × 100 mm. Nos. 3066/69 2·00 1·60

802 Clasped Hands **803** Albert Einstein

2005. Lifeline (telephone counselling service).
3071 **802** $12 multicoloured . . . 75 60

2005. Centenary of the Publication of "Special Theory of Relativity" by Albert Einstein.
3072 **803** $15 multicoloured . . . 95 75

804 Mickey holding Ship's Wheel (*Steamboat Willie*)

2005. Mickey Mouse (character created by Walt Disney). Two sheets, each 140 × 90 containing T **804** and similar vert designs showing films. Multicoloured.
MS3073 (a) $5 Type **804**; $25 As magician (*Fantasia*). (b) $5 Two Mickeys (*Prince and the Pauper*); $25 Decorating tree (*Twice Upon a Christmas*) . . . . 6·25 6·25

2005. TAIPEI 2005 International Stamp Exhibition (2nd issue).
3074 **802** $15 multicoloured . . . 95 75

2005. TAIPEI 2005 International Stamp Exhibition (3rd issue). Six sheets, each 103 × 146 mm containing T **803** and similar multicoloured designs.
MS3075 (a) Conservation (circular). $5 Type **803**; $25 Formosan rock monkey. (b) Technology (rectangular). $5 Microscope (29 × 37 mm); $25 DNA strands (37 × 29 mm). (c) Flora (triangular). $5 Flowers (52 × 32 mm); $25 Fruit (52 × 32 mm). (d) Festivals (rectangular). $5 Ear shooting ceremony (30 × 40 mm); $25 Dragon boat race (40 × 30 mm). (e) Cuisine (rectangular). $5 "Buddha jumping over wall" (40 × 30 mm); $25 Rice cakes (40 × 30 mm). (f) Ocean life (oval). $5 Angelfish (43 × 33 mm); $25 Coral (43 × 33 mm) . . . . . 1·90 1·90

2005. Classical Literature. Journey to the West (Ming dynasty novel). Multicoloured.
3076 $3.50 Type **804** 20 15
3077 $3.50 Baby in River 20 15
3078 $5 Making pass at Chang E 30 25
3079 $20 Taming Monster of River Flowing Sands . . 1·30 1·00
See also Nos. 2429/32.

808 "Loyalty and Filial Piety"

2005. Kaohsiung 2005 International Stamp Exhibition. Sheet 102 × 146 mm containing T **808** and similar multicoloured design.
MS3080 $5 Type **808**; $25 Ruyi sceptre (horiz) . . . . 50 5·00

809 Triwizard Cup

2005. Harry Potter and *The Goblet of Fire* (film based on book by J. K. Rowling). Two sheets, each 190 × 130 mm containing T **809** and similar horiz designs. Multicoloured.
MS3081 (a) $5 × 6, Type **809**; Harry underwater; Harry and Hungarian Horntail; Harry summons his Firebolt; Golden egg; Harry negotiates the maze. (b) $5 × 6, Hungarian Horntail; Harry riding his Firebolt; Nagini; Grindylow; Fawkes the phoenix; Merchieftainess . . . . 8·50 8·50

810 Siberian Husky

811 Dog

2005. Pets (1st series). Multicoloured.
3082 $3.50 Type **810** 20 15
3083 $5 Golden retriever 30 25
3084 $12 Himalayan cat . . . . 1·00 50
3085 $25 Scottish fold cat . . . 1·80 1·20
See also Nos. 3096/99, 3155/58 and 3183/6.

2006. New Year. Year of the Dog. Multicoloured.
3086 $3.50 Type **811** 20 15
3087 $13 Calligraphy and dog . . 85 65
MS3088 110 × 76 mm. $12 Three dogs (50 × 30 mm) . . . . . 1·00 1·00

812 Preparing Tea Set and Warming Pot

2006. Tea Ceremony. Multicoloured.
3089 $5 Type **812** 30 25
3090 $5 Placing leaves in pot and rinsing 30 25
3091 $5 Pouring hot water over pot and warming cups . . 30 25
3092 $5 Drying pot and pouring tea 30 25
3093 $5 Smelling and drinking brewed tea 30 25

813 Taipei 101 Tower

814 Juvenile and Parent

2006. Taipei 101 Tower (world's tallest building). Multicoloured.
3094 $5 Type **813** 30 25
3095 $12 Tower at night 75 60

2006. Pets (2nd series). As T **810**. Multicoloured.
3096 $2.50 Labrador 15 10
3097 $7 St. Bernard 40 30
3098 $10 Siamese cat 60 50
3099 $32 Persian cat . . . . . 1·90 1·40

2006. King Penguins (*Aptenodytes patagonicus*). Multicoloured.
3100 $5 Type **814** 30 25
3101 $5 Courtship 30 25
3102 $9 Swimming and diving (horiz) 55 45
3103 $12 Gliding and preening (horiz) 75 60
MS3104 120 × 60 mm $15 Five penguins (80 × 30 mm) 95 75

815 Storks

2006. Winning Entries in Children's Drawing Competition. Multicoloured.
3105 $5 Type **815** 30 25
3106 $5 Couple wearing striped tops and headdresses . . 30 25
3107 $5 Pheasants 30 25
3108 $5 Chinese opera characters 30 25
3109 $5 Fishermen 30 25
3110 $5 Giant marrows 30 25
3111 $5 Decorating lanterns . . . 30 25
3112 $5 Bridge 30 25
3113 $5 Steam train 30 25
3114 $5 Sunflowers 30 25
3115 $5 Aborigines 30 25
3116 $5 Children and ladder . . 30 25
3117 $5 Women wearing feathered headdresses and chickens 30 25
3118 $5 Musicians and dancers . 30 25
3119 $5 Mythical animals 30 25
3120 $5 Cats 30 25
3121 $5 Children riding cow . . . 30 25
3122 $5 Whale 30 25
3123 $5 Acrobats 30 25
3124 $5 Coach 30 25

816 *Diaphanes citrinus*

2006. Fireflies. Multicoloured.
3125 $5 Type **816** 30 25
3126 $5 *Pyrocoelia analis* 30 25
3127 $5 *Diaphanes formosus* . . . 30 25
3128 $5 *Diaphanes niveus* 30 25

817 Landscape and Roadway (½-size illustration)

2006. Completion of Nangang—Suao Section of National Highway Number Five. Sheet 125 × 55 mm.
MS3129 **817** $12 multicoloured 75 75

818 Winnie the Pooh and Piglet

2006. Winnie the Pooh (Walt Disney cartoon character (originally created by A. A. Milne)). Two sheets, each 140 × 90 mm containing T **818** and similar horiz designs. Multicoloured.
MS3130 (a) $5 Type **818**; $25 Pooh and Tigger fishing. (b) $5 Pooh pushing Piglet in wheel barrow; $25 Pooh, Piglet and Tigger floating in rubber ring Set of 2 sheets . . . . 2·00 2·00

819 Bag Outline containing Coastline

2006. Travel. Multicoloured.
3131 $3.50 Type **819** 20 15
3132 $3.50 Camera outline containing boat 20 15
3133 $3.50 Notebook outline containing bridge 20 15
3134 $3.50 Windsurfer outline containing rock 20 15
3135 $3.50 Heart outline containing steam train . . 20 15
3136 $5 As Type **819** 30 25
3137 $5 As No. 3132 . . . . . . 30 25
3138 $5 As No. 3133 . . . . . . 30 25
3139 $5 As No. 3134 . . . . . . 30 25
3140 $5 As No. 3135 . . . . . . 30 25

820 *Amphiron ocellaris*

2006. Fish. Multicoloured.
3141 $5 Type **820** 30 25
3142 $5 *Zanclus cornutus* 30 25
3143 $12 *Coris gaimard* 30 25
3144 $12 *Oxycirrhites typus* 30 25

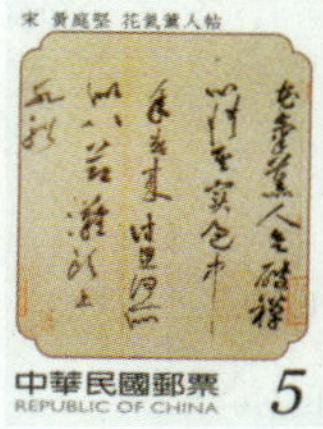

821 Poem in Seven-character Regulated Verse (Huang T'ing-Chien)

2006. Calligraphy and Bird Paintings. Multicoloured.
3145 $5 Type **821** 30 25
3146 $9 Calligraphy on silk (Mi Fu) 55 45
3147 $12 "Magpie and Hare" (detail) (Ts'ui Po) 75 60
3148 $15 "Magpie and Hare" (detail) (different) . . . 1·00 80
MS3149 76 × 142 mm. $12 As No. 3147; $15 As No. 3148 . . . 1·40 1·40
The stamps and margins of **MS**3149 form the painting "Magpie and Hare" (Ts'ui Po).

822 *Crocothemis servilia servilia*

2006. Dragonflies. Multicoloured.
3150 $5 Type **822** 30 25
3151 $5 *Orthetrum pruinosum neglectum* (vert) 30 25
3152 $12 *Diplacodes trivialis* (vert) 75 60
3153 $12 *Orthetrum sabina Sabina* 75 60
MS3154 80 × 135 mm. As Nos. 3150/3 . . . . 2·20 2·20
The stamps and margins of **MS**3154 form a composite design of river and meadow.

2006. Pets (3rd series). As T **810**. Multicoloured.
3155 $1 Yorkshire terrier 10 10
3156 $9 Pomeranian 55 45
3157 $10 Abyssinian cat 60 50
3158 $32 Norwegian forest cat . . 1·90 1·40

823 Hang Gliding

2006. Outdoor Activities. Multicoloured.
3159 $3.50 Type **823** 20 15
3160 $3.50 Paragliding (vert) . . 20 15
3161 $12 Micro-light 75 60
3162 $15 Parasailing (vert) . . . 95 75

824 Fairy Pitta

2006. Fairy Pitta (*Pitta nympha*). Multicoloured.
3163 $5 Type **824** 30 25
3164 $5 Perched on branch (vert) 30 25
3165 $12 Parent and nestlings . . 75 60
3166 $12 Catching insect (vert) . 75 60
MS3167 135 × 80 mm. As Nos. 3163/6 . . . . 2·20 2·20
The stamps and margins of **MS**3167 form a composite design of woodland glade.

2006. Marine Mammals. As T **742**. Multicoloured.
3168 $5 *Stenella attenuate* 30 25
3169 $5 *Stenella longirostris* . . . 30 25
3170 $10 *Feresa attenuate* 60 50
3171 $15 *Physter macrocephalus* 95 75
MS3172 135 × 80 mm. As Nos. 3168/71 . . . . 2·20 2·20

825 *Ludwigia octovalvis*

2006. Native Flowers. Multicoloured.
3173 $5 Type **825** 30 25
3174 $5 *Hygrophila pogonocalyx* (vert) 30 25
3175 $5 *Titanotrichum oldhamii* (vert) 30 25

826 Jongshan Building, Yangmingshan National Park

2006. Tourism. Multicoloured.
3176 $5 Type **826** 30 25
3177 $5 Taroko Gorge (vert) . . 30 25
3178 $9 Queen's Head rock, Yeliou (vert) 55 45
3179 $12 Sun Moon Lake 75 60

827 Pig

2006. New Year. Year of the Pig. Multicoloured.
3180 $3.50 Type **827** 20 15
3181 $13 Drums 85 65
MS3182 110 × 76 mm. $12 Piglets (50 × 30 mm) 75 75

2006. Pets (4th series). As T **810**. Multicoloured.
3183 50c. Border collie 10 10
3184 $13 Beagle 85 65
3185 $17 American shorthair cat 1·00 80
3186 $34 Maine coon cat . . . . 2·10 1·90

828 Locomotive 700T

2006. Inauguration of High Speed Railway. Multicoloured.
3187 $12 Type **828** 75 60
3188 $12 Hsinchu Station 75 60

829 *Phaius tankervilleae*

831 Heart and Stylized Couple

830 Earring

2007. Flowers. Orchids. Multicoloured.
3189 $3.50 Type **829** 20 15
3190 $5 *Spiranthes sinensis* . . . 30 25
3191 $12 *Vanda* 75 60
3192 $25 *Cattleya* . . . . 1·60 1·30

2007. Cing Dynasty Jewellery. Multicoloured.
3193 $5 Type **830** 30 25
3194 $5 Gilt hair pin 30 25
3195 $12 Fingernail guard . . . 75 60
3196 $25 Ring . . . . 1·60 1·30

2007. St. Valentine's Day.
3197 **831** $5 multicoloured 30 25
3198 $20 multicoloured . . . 1·30 1·00

832 Cilin (1st rank)

2007. Official Cing Dynasty Military Dress Designs. Designs associated with military rank. Multicoloured.
3199 $3.50 Type **832** 20 15
3200 $3.50 Lion (2nd rank) . . . 20 15

3201 $5 Leopard (3rd rank) . . . 30 25
3202 $25 Tiger (4th rank) . . . . 1·40 1·10

No. 3203 and Type 833 have been left for 'Memorial Museum' issued on 28 February 2007, not yet received.

834 Kanjin Bridge, Taoyuan

2007. Bridges. Multicoloured.
3204 $5 Type **834** 30 25
3205 $5 Fusing Bridge, Luofu . . 30 25
3206 $12 MacArthur Second Bridge, Taipei 65 50
3207 $15 Dajhih Bridge, Taipei 80 60

835 Lesser Panda (red panda)

2007. Lesser Panda (*Ailurus fulgens*). Multicoloured.
3208 $5 Type **835** 30 25
3209 $5 Asleep 30 25
3210 $10 Scratching (vert) 55 40
3211 $10 Foraging (vert) 55 40
MS3212 80 × 105 mm. $12 Pandas (40 × 50 mm) 65 65

836 Dharma Drum Monastery

837 Chung Tai Chan Monastery

838 Fo Guang Shan Monastery

839 Tzu Chi Foundation

2007. Buddhist Architecture.
3213 **836** $5 multicoloured 30 25
3214 **837** $5 multicoloured 30 25
3215 **838** $5 multicoloured 30 25
3216 **839** $5 multicoloured 30 25

840 Dahlia

2007. Greetings Stamps. Language of Flowers. Multicoloured.
3217 $3.50 Type **840** (gratitude) 20 15
3218 $3.50 Iris (trust) 20 15
3219 $3.50 Clematis and ladybirds (elegance) . . . 20 15
3220 $3.50 Tung blossom and moths (joy) 20 15
3221 $3.50 Rose (true love) . . . 20 15
3222 $3.50 Sunflower (adoration) 20 15
3223 $3.50 Bird of Paradise (happiness) 20 15
3224 $3.50 Lotus (purity) 20 15
3225 $3.50 Ox-eye daisy (vitality) 20 15
3226 $3.50 Balloon flower and dragon fly (chastity) . . . 20 15
3227 $5 As Type **840** 30 25
3228 $5 As No. 3215 . . . . . . 30 25
3229 $5 As No. 3216 . . . . . . 30 25
3230 $5 As No. 3217 . . . . . . 30 25
3231 $5 As No. 3218 . . . . . . 30 25
3232 $5 As No. 3219 . . . . . . 30 25
3233 $5 As No. 3220 . . . . . . 30 25
3234 $5 As No. 3221 . . . . . . 30 25
3235 $5 As No. 3222 . . . . . . 30 25
3236 $5 As No. 3223 . . . . . . 30 25

841 Rice Bucket and Shelves

2007. Food Utensils. Multicoloured.
3237 $5 Type **841** 30 25
3238 $5 Wooden steamer 30 25
3239 $12 Rice baskets, rattan and wood 65 50
3240 $12 Bowls, chopsticks and container 65 50

842 *Paphiopedilum*

843 Page, Pen, Flower and Rainbow

2007. Orchids. Multicoloured.
3241 $1 Type **842** 10 10
3242 $2.50 *Phalaenopsis Aphrodite* 10 10
3243 $10 *Dendrobium* 55 40
3244 $32 *Oncidium* . . . . 1·40 1·10

2007. 20th Anniv of Lifting of Martial Law.
3245 **843** $12 multicoloured . . . 65 50

844 *Balistoides conspicillum*

2007. Fish. Multicoloured.
3246 $5 Type **844** 30 25
3247 $5 *Nemateleotris magnifica* 30 25
3248 $12 *Paracanthurus hepatus* 65 50
3249 $25 *Cetoscarus bicolour* . . 1·40 1·10

845 Chiang Wei-shui

2007. Chiang Wei-shui (politician) Commemoration.
3250 **845** $25 deep brown . . . . 1·40 1·10

846 Taipei Tower and Map

2007. 1st Taiwan–African Heads of State Summit.
3251 **846** $12 multicoloured . . . 65 50

847 Horses and Attendants

2007. 'Eighteen Scholars of the T'ang' (painting by Emperor Hui-tsung). Sheet 236 × 120 mm containing T **847** and similar horiz designs showing parts of the painting.
MS3252 (1) $5 Type **847**; (2) $5 Riders, horses and attendants amongst trees; (3) $5 Laden horse, attendants and scholar; (4) $5 Central figure and three groups of scholars (51 × 30 mm.); (5) $5 Attendants preparing tea (36 × 30 mm.); (6) $5 Listening to music (36 × 30 mm.); (7) $5 Seated around table; (8) $5 Cranes; (9) $5 Raised platform (51 × 30 mm.); (10) $5 Trees, plants and inscription . . . . 2·00 2·00

The stamps of No. **MS**3252 were arranged in two horizontal strips of five stamps, the identification numbers given are from right to left (1/5) upper strip, (6/10) lower strip.

848 Doves and Envelope

2007. 'Feelings'.
3253 **848** $5 gold, silver and vermilion 30 25

849 *Marchia loebbeckei*

2007. Shells. Multicoloured.
3254 $5 Type **849** 30 25
3255 $5 *Harpa major* 30 25
3256 $12 *Cypraea aurantium* . . . 65 50
3257 $12 *Epitonium scalare* . . . 65 50

850 *Ascocentrum*

851 *Pericrocotus solaris* (grey-chinned minivet)

2007. Orchids. Multicoloured.
3258 $7 Type **850** 40 30
3259 $9 *Arundina graminifolia* . . 50 40
3260 $15 *Vanda teres* 80 60
3261 $20 *Epidendrum* . . . . . . 1·10 85

2007. Birds. Multicoloured.
3262 $3.50 Type **851** 20 15
3263 $5 *Parus varius* (varied tit) 30 25
3264 $12 *Luscinia calliope* (Siberian rubythroat) . . 65 50
3265 $25 *Phoenicurus auroreus* (Daurian redstart) . . . . 1·40 1·10

852 Speed Walking

2007. Leisure Sports. Multicoloured.
3266 $5 Type **852** 30 25
3267 $5 Cycling 30 25
3268 $12 Skate boarding 65 50
3269 $25 In-line skating . . . . 1·40 1·10

853 '100', Doves and Emblems

2007. Centenary of Scouting.
3270 **853** $12 multicoloured . . . 65 50

854 Rat

855 Lei Chen

2007. New Year. Year of the Rat. Multicoloured.
3271 $3.50 Type **854** 20 15
3272 $13 Rat (different) 70 55
MS3273 110 × 76 mm. $12 Decorated rats (64 × 40 mm)

2007. Personalities. Political Reformers.
3274 **855** $5 brown 20 15
3275 – $5 olive 20 15
3276 – $5 purple 20 15
3277 – $5 black 20 15
DESIGNS: 3274, Type **855**; 3275, Fu Jheng; 3276, Kuo Yu Sing; 3277, Huang Hsin Chieh.

856 Liou Family Compound in Shangfangliao, Sinpu, Hsinchu County

857 Lin Family Mansion in Banciao, Taipei County

858 Li Teng-fang Compound in Dasi, Taoyuan County

859 Siao Family Compound in Jiadong, Pingtung County

2008. Traditional Houses.
3278 **856** $5 multicoloured 20 15
3279 **857** $5 multicoloured 20 15
3280 **858** $5 multicoloured 20 15
3281 **859** $12 multicoloured . . . 65 50

860 *Dicrurus aeneus* (bronzed drongo)

861 Mirror Man

2008. Birds. Multicoloured.
3282 $1 Type **860** 10 10
3283 $2.50 *Lanius schach* (long-tailed shrike) 10 10
3284 $10 *Dendrocitta formosae* (grey treepie) 55 40
3285 $32 *Pycnonotus sinensis* (light-vented bulbul) . . . 1·40 1·10

2008. Regional Opera–Taiwanese Puppets (*The Scholar Knight of Yunjhou*).
3286 $5 Type **861** 20 15
3287 $5 Old Oddball 20 15
3288 $5 Shih Yan-wun 20 15
3289 $5 Dragon Lady of the Bitter Sea 20 15
MS3290 145 × 88 mm. Nos. 3286/9 90 90
The stamps and margins of **MS**3290 form a composite design.

862 *Plum Blossoms and Solitary Bird* (Pien Wen-Chin)

2008. Taipei 2008–Asian International Stamp Exhibition. Multicoloured.

3291		$5 Type **862**	30	25
3292		$9 *Apricot Blossoms and Peacocks* (Lu chi)	40	30
3293		$13 *Wild Duck by Brook* (Ch'en Lin)	70	55
3294		$15 *Bamboo and Shrike* (Li An-chung)	80	60
MS3295		145 × 102 mm. Nos. 3291/4	2·20	1·70

863 *Syrmaticus mikado* (mikado pheasant)

2008.

3296	**863**	$25 multicoloured	1·40	1·10

864 Sheldon

2008. Characters from *Finding Nemo* (film by Walt Disney/Pixar). Two sheets 140 × 90 mm containing each T **864** and similar multicoloured designs.

MS3297		(a) $5 × 5, Type **864**; Squirt; Tad; Nemo; Peach. (b) $5 × 5, Turtles; Dory (26 × 34 mm); Bubbles; Nemo (34 × 26 mm); Pearl	3·00	3·00

The stamps and margins of **MS**3297a/b, respectively, form composite designs.

POSTAGE DUE STAMPS

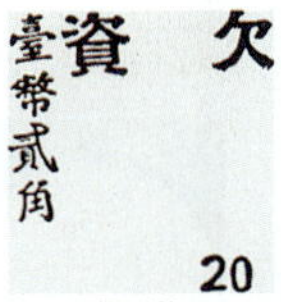

(D 12)

(D 15)

1950. Surch as Type D **12**.

D105	**6**	4c. on $100 blue	13·00	9·00
D106		10c. on $100 blue	25·00	16·00
D107		20c. on $100 blue	12·50	19·00
D108		40c. on $100 blue	39·00	50·00
D109		$1 on $100 blue	34·00	60·00

1951. No. 524 of China surch as Type D **15**.

D133		40c. on 40c. orange	13·50	19·00
D134		80c. on 40c. orange	13·50	19·00

(D 19)

D 43

1953. Revenue stamps as T **143** of China surch as Type D **19**.

D151		10c. on $50 blue	15·00	10·00
D152		20c. on $100 olive	15·00	15·00
D153		40c. on $20 brown	18·00	1·20
D154		80c. on $500 green	28·00	3·50
D155		100c. on $30 mauve	28·00	9·00

1956.

D236	D **43**	20c. red and blue	1·10	20
D237		40c. green and buff	1·60	20
D238		80c. brown and grey	3·25	30
D239		$1 blue and mauve	3·50	30

(D 97)

D 152

1961. Surch with Type D **97**.

D429	**56**	$5 on $20 red	2·20	75

1964. Surch as Type D **97**.

D490	**83**	10c. on 80c. green	25	20
D491		20c. on $3.60 blue	40	20
D492		40c. on $4.50 red	65	30

1966.

D588	D **152**	10c. brown and lilac	25	20
D589		20c. blue and yellow	45	20
D590		50c. ultram & blue	75	20
D591		$1 violet and flesh	55	20
D592		$2 green and blue	70	20
D593		$5 red and buff	1·50	35
D594a		$10 purple & mauve	8·00	1·00

D 399

1984.

D1532a	D **399**	$1 red and blue	10	10
D1533a		$2 yellow and blue	10	10
D1534		$3 green & mauve	25	20
D1535a		$5 blue and yellow	30	15
D1536		$5.50 mauve & bl	50	35
D1537		$7.50 yellow & vio	60	40
D1538b		$10 yellow and red	30	15
D1539		$20 blue and green	1·70	1·10

CHINA EXPEDITIONARY FORCE Pt. 1

Stamps used by Indian military forces in China.

12 pies = 1 anna; 16 annas = 1 rupee.

Stamps of India optd **C.E.F.**

1900. Queen Victoria.

C 1	**40**	3p. red	40	1·25
C 2	**23**	½a. green	75	30
C 3	–	1a. purple	4·25	1·50
C11	–	1a. red	40·00	8·00
C 4	–	2a. blue	3·00	9·00
C 5	–	2a.6p. green	2·75	13·00
C 6	–	3a. orange	2·75	16·00
C 7	–	4a. green (No. 96)	2·75	7·50
C 8	–	8a. mauve	2·75	20·00
C 9	–	12a. purple on red	17·00	16·00
C10	**37**	1r. green and red	27·00	29·00

1904. King Edward VII.

C12	**41**	3p. grey	7·50	7·50
C13	–	1a. red (No. 123)	7·50	70
C14	–	2a. lilac	14·00	2·75
C15	–	2a.6p. blue	3·25	5·00
C16	–	3a. orange	3·75	4·00
C17	–	4a. olive	8·50	17·00
C18	–	8a. mauve	8·00	7·50
C19	–	12a. purple on red	11·00	19·00
C20	–	1r. green and red	16·00	28·00

1909. King Edward VII.

C21		½a. green (No. 149)	1·75	1·50
C22		1a. red (No. 150)	3·25	30

1913. King George V.

C23	**55**	3p. grey	8·00	30·00
C24	**56**	½a. green	4·00	6·00
C25	**57**	1a. red	5·00	4·00
C26	**58**	1½a. brown (No. 163)	29·00	90·00
C27	**59**	2a. lilac	21·00	80·00
C28	**61**	2a.6p. blue	17·00	28·00
C29	**62**	3a. orange	32·00	£275
C30	**63**	4a. olive	29·00	£190
C32	**65**	8a. mauve	28·00	£375
C33	**66**	12a. red	28·00	£130
C34	**67**	1r. brown and green	75·00	£375

BRITISH RAILWAY ADMINISTRATION

1901. No. 121 of China surch **B.R.A. 5 Five Cents**.

BR133b	**32**	5c. on ½c. brown	£325	£100

CHRISTMAS ISLAND Pt. 1

Situated in the Indian Ocean about 600 miles south of Singapore. Formerly part of the Straits Settlements and then of the Crown Colony of Singapore, Christmas Island was occupied by the Japanese from 31 March 1942 until September 1945. It reverted to Singapore after liberation but subsequently became an Australian territory on 15 October 1958.

1958. 100 cents = 1 Malayan dollar.
1968. 100 cents = 1 Australian dollar.

1 Queen Elizabeth II

2 Map

1958. Type of Australia with opt and value in black.

1	**1**	2c. orange	55	80
2		4c. brown	60	30
3		5c. mauve	60	50
4		6c. blue	1·00	30
5		8c. sepia	1·75	50
6		10c. violet	1·00	30
7		12c. red	1·75	1·75
8		20c. blue	1·00	1·75
9		50c. green	1·75	1·75
10		$1 turquoise	1·75	1·75

1963.

11	**2**	2c. orange	1·25	35
12	–	4c. brown	50	15
13	–	5c. purple	50	20
14	–	6c. blue	30	35
15	–	8c. black	2·50	35
16	–	10c. violet	40	15
17	–	12c. red	40	25
18	–	20c. blue	1·00	20
19	–	50c. green	1·00	20
20	–	$1 yellow	1·75	35

DESIGNS—VERT: 4c. Moonflower; 5c. Robber crab; 8c. Phosphate train; 10c. Raising phosphate. HORIZ: 6c. Island scene; 12c. Flying Fish cove; 20c. Loading cantilever; 50c. Christmas Island frigate bird. LARGER (35 × mm): $1 White-tailed tropic bird.

1965. 50th Anniv of Gallipoli Landing. As T **184** of Australia, but slightly larger (22 × 34½ mm).

21		10c. brown, black and green	30	1·50

12 Golden-striped Grouper

1968. Fishes. Multicoloured.

22		1c. Type **12**	45	45
23		2c. Moorish idol	60	20
24		3c. Long-nosed butterflyfish	60	30
25		4c. Pink-tailed triggerfish	60	20
26		5c. Regal angelfish	60	20
27		9c. White-cheeked surgeonfish	60	40
28		10c. Lionfish	60	20
28a		15c. Saddle butterflyfish	5·50	2·50
29		20c. Ornate butterflyfish	1·50	55
29a		30c. Giant ghost pipefish	5·50	2·50
30		50c. Clown surgeonfish	1·75	1·50
31		$1 Meyer's butterflyfish	1·75	2·00

13 "Angel" (mosaic)

14 "The Ansidei Madonna" (Raphael)

1969. Christmas.

32	**13**	5c. multicoloured	20	30

1970. Christmas. Paintings. Multicoloured.

33		3c. Type **14**	20	15
34		5c. "The Virgin and Child, St. John the Baptist and an Angel" (Morando)	20	15

15 "The Adoration of the Shepherds" (attr to the School of Seville)

16 H.M.S. "Flying Fish" (survey ship), 1887

1971. Christmas. Multicoloured.

35		6c. Type **15**	30	50
36		20c. "The Adoration of the Shepherds" (Reni)	70	1·00

1972. Ships. Multicoloured.

37		1c. "Eagle" (merchant sailing ship), 1714	25	60
38		2c. H.M.S. "Redpole" (gunboat), 1890	30	70
39		3c. "Hoi Houw" (freighter), 1959	30	70
40		4c. "Pigot" (sailing ship), 1771	40	75
41		5c. "Valetta" (cargo-liner), 1968	40	75
42		6c. Type **16**	40	75
43		7c. "Asia" (sail merchantman), 1805	40	75
44		8c. "Islander" (freighter), 1929–60	45	80
45		9c. H.M.S. "Imperieuse" (armoured cruiser), 1888	65	70
46		10c. H.M.S. "Hecate" (coast defence turret ship), 1871	50	80
47		20c. "Thomas" (galleon), 1615	50	1·00
48		25c. Royal Navy sail sloop, 1864	50	1·75
49		30c. "Cygnet" (flute), 1688	50	1·00
50		35c. "Triadic" (freighter), 1958	50	1·00
51		50c. H.M.S. "Amethyst" (frigate), 1857	50	1·50
52		$1 "Royal Mary" (warship), 1643	70	1·75

No. 45 is inscribed "H.M.S. Imperious", No. 46 "H.M.S. Egeria" and No. 48 "H.M.S. Gordon", all in error.

17 Angel of Peace

19 Mary and Holy Child within Christmas Star

18 Virgin and Child, and Map

1972. Christmas. Multicoloured.

53		3c. Type **17**	15	40
54		3c. Angel of Joy	15	40
55		7c. Type **17**	20	50
56		7c. As No. 54	20	50

1973. Christmas.

57	**18**	7c. multicoloured	25	35
58		25c. multicoloured	75	1·00

1974. Christmas.

59	**19**	7c. mauve and grey	25	60
60		30c. orange, yellow and grey	75	2·50

20 "The Flight into Egypt"

21 Dove of Peace and Star of Bethlehem

1975. Christmas.

61	**20**	10c. yellow, brown and gold	25	35
62		35c. pink, blue and gold	50	1·75

1976. Christmas.

63	**21**	10c. red, yellow and mauve	15	45
64	–	10c. red, yellow and mauve	15	45
65	**21**	35c. violet, blue and green	20	55
66	–	35c. violet, blue and green	20	55

DESIGNS: Nos. 64 and 66 are "mirror-images" of Type **21**.

22 William Dampier (explorer)

1977. Famous Visitors. Multicoloured.

67		1c. Type **22**	15	80
68		2c. Captain de Vlamingh (explorer)	20	1·00
69		3c. Vice-Admiral MacLear	30	80

70 4c. Sir John Murray (oceanographer) 30 90
71 5c. Admiral Aldrich 30 40
72 6c. Andrew Clunies Ross (first settler) 30 60
73 7c. J. J. Lister (naturalist) . . 30 40
74 8c. Admiral of the Fleet Sir William May 35 70
75 9c. Henry Ridley (botanist) . . 40 1·75
76 10c. George Clunies Ross (phosphate miner) 55 55
77 20c. Captain Joshua Slocum (yachtsman) 50 75
78 45c. Charles Andrews (naturalist) 60 45
79 50c. Richard Hanitsch (biologist) . . . . 70 1·75
80 75c. Victor Purcell (scholar) 60 1·25
81 $1 Fam Choo Beng (educator) 60 1·25
82 $2 Sir Harold Spencer-Jones (astronomer) . . . . 65 2·00

23 Australian Coat of Arms on Map of Christmas Island

1977. Silver Jubilee.
83 **23** 45c. multicoloured 45 55

24 "A Partridge in a Pear Tree" **25** Abbott's Booby

1977. Christmas. "The Twelve Days of Christmas". Multicoloured.
84A 10c. Type **24** 10 20
85A 10c. "Two turtle doves" . . 10 20
86A 10c. "Three French hens" . . 10 20
87A 10c. "Four calling birds" . . 10 20
88A 10c. "Five gold rings" . . . 10 20
89A 10c. "Six geese a-laying" . . 10 20
90A 10c. "Seven swans a-swimming" 10 20
91A 10c. "Eight maids a-milking" 10 20
92A 10c. "Nine ladies dancing" 10 20
93A 10c. "Ten lords a-leaping" 10 20
94A 10c. "Eleven pipers piping" 10 20
95A 10c. "Twelve drummers drumming" 10 20

1978. 25th Anniv of Coronation.
96 – 45c. black and blue 45 75
97 – 45c. multicoloured 45 75
98 **25** 45c. black and blue 45 75
DESIGNS: No. 96, White Swan of Bohun; No. 97, Queen Elizabeth II.

26 "Christ Child" **27** Chinese Children

1978. Christmas Scenes from "The Song of Christmas". Multicoloured.
99 10c. Type **26** 15 20
100 10c. "Herald Angels" . . . 15 20
101 10c. "Redeemer" 15 20
102 10c. "Israel" 15 20
103 10c. "Star" 15 20
104 10c. "Three Wise Men" . . 15 20
105 10c. "Manger" 15 20
106 10c. "All He Stands For" . . 15 20
107 10c. "Shepherds Come" . . . 15 20

1979. International Year of the Child. Children of different races. Multicoloured, colours of inscr given.
108 20c. green (Type **27**) 30 45
109 20c. turquoise (Malay children) 30 45
110 20c. lilac (Indian children) . . 30 45
111 20c. red (European children) 30 45
112 20c. yellow ("Oranges and Lemons") 30 45

28 1958 2c. Definitive

1979. Death Centenary of Sir Rowland Hill. Multicoloured.
113 20c. Type **28** 25 40
114 20c. 1963 2c. map definitive 25 40
115 20c. 1965 50th Anniv of Gallipoli Landing 10c. commemorative 25 40
116 20c. 1964 4c. Pink-tailed triggerfish definitive 25 40
117 20c. 1969 Christmas 5c. . . . 25 40

29 Wise Men following Star

1979. Christmas. Multicoloured.
118 20c. Type **29** 20 30
119 55c. Virgin and Child 45 70

30 9th Green

1980. 25th Anniv of Christmas Island Golf Club. Multicoloured.
120 20c. Type **30** 35 50
121 55c. Clubhouse . . . . . . 40 1·00

31 Surveying

1980. Phosphate Industry (1st series). Multicoloured.
122 15c. Type **31** 15 30
123 22c. Drilling for samples . . 15 35
124 40c. Sample analysis 20 55
125 55c. Mine planning 25 60
See also Nos. 126/9, 136/9 and 140/3.

1980. Phosphate Industry (2nd series). As T **31**. Multicoloured.
126 15c. Jungle clearing 15 15
127 22c. Overburden removal . . 15 20
128 40c. Open cut mining 20 25
129 55c. Restoration 20 30

32 Angel with Harp **33** "Cryptoblepharus egeriae"

1980. Christmas. Multicoloured.
130 15c. Type **32** 10 25
131 15c. Angel with wounded soldier 10 25
132 22c. Virgin and Child 15 30
133 22c. Kneeling couple 15 30
134 60c. Angel with harp (different) 30 30
135 60c. Angel with children . . 20 30

1981. Phosphate Industry (3rd series). As T **31**. Multicoloured.
136 22c. Screening and Stockpiling 15 15
137 28c. Train loading 20 20
138 40c. Railing 25 25
139 60c. Drying 25 25

1981. Phosphate Industry (4th series). As T **31**. Multicoloured.
140 22c. Crushing 20 20
141 28c. Conveying 25 25
142 40c. Bulk storage 30 30
143 60c. "Consolidated Venture" (bulk carrier) loading . . . 35 35

1981. Reptiles. Multicoloured.
144 24c. Type **33** 20 20
145 30c. "Emoia nativitata" . . . 25 25
146 40c. "Lepidodactylus listeri" 30 30
147 60c. "Cyrtodactylus sp. nov." 35 35

34 Scene from Carol "Away in a Manger"

1981. Christmas.
148 **34** 18c. silver, dp blue & bl . . 30 50
149 – 24c. multicoloured 30 55
150 – 40c. multicoloured 35 65
151 – 60c. multicoloured 40 75
DESIGNS: 24c. to 60c. show various scenes from carol "Away in a Manger".

35 Reef Heron

1982. Birds. Multicoloured.
152 1c. Type **35** 70 30
153 2c. Common noddy ("Noddy") 70 30
154 3c. White-bellied swiftlet ("Glossy Swiftlet") 70 70
155 4c. Christmas Island imperial pigeon ("Imperial Pigeon") 70 70
156 5c. Christmas Island white-eye ("Silvereye") 80 70
157 10c. Island thrush ("Thrush") 70 70
158 25c. Red-tailed tropic bird ("Silver Bosunbird") . . . 1·25 60
159 30c. Emerald dove 80 70
160 40c. Brown booby 80 55
161 50c. Red-footed booby 80 55
162 65c. Christmas Island frigate bird ("Frigatebird") . . . 80 55
163 75c. White-tailed tropic bird ("Golden Bosunbird") . . 90 65
164 80c. Australian kestrel ("Nankeen Kestrel") (vert) 1·25 2·50
165 $1 Moluccan hawk owl ("Hawk-owl") (vert) . . . 2·50 3·00
166 $2 Australian goshawk ("Goshawk") (vert) . . . . 1·75 4·00
167 $4 Abbott's booby (vert) . . 3·00 3·25

36 Joseph **37** "Mirror" Dinghy and Club House

1982. Christmas. Origami Paper Sculptures. Mult.
168 27c. Type **36** 30 30
169 50c. Angel 45 45
170 75c. Mary and baby Jesus . . 65 65

1983. 25th Anniv of Christmas Island Boat Club. Multicoloured.
171 27c. Type **37** 20 30
172 35c. Ocean-going yachts . . . 20 35
173 50c. Fishing launch and cargo ship (horiz) 25 40
174 75c. Dinghy-racing and cantilever (horiz) 25 60

38 Maps of Christmas Island and Australia, Eastern Grey Kangaroo and White-tailed Tropic Bird

1983. 25th Anniv of Australian Territory. Mult.
175 24c. Type **38** 60 30
176 30c. Christmas Island and Australian flag 70 50
177 85c. Maps of Christmas Island and Australia, and Boeing 727 . . . . 1·50 1·75

39 Candle and Holly **40** Feeding on Leaf

1983. Christmas. Candles. Multicoloured.
178 24c. Type **39** 20 20
179 30c. Six gold candles 30 40
180 85c. Candles . . . . 70 1·50

1984. Red Land Crab. Multicoloured.
181 30c. Type **40** 25 30
182 40c. Migration 30 40
183 55c. Development stages . . 30 50
184 85c. Adult females and young 45 70

41 "Leucocoprinus fragilissimus" **42** Run-out

1984. Fungi. Multicoloured.
185 30c. Type **41** 20 55
186 40c. "Microporus xanthopus" 25 70
187 45c. "Hydropus anthidepes" ("Trogia anthidepas") . . 30 80
188 55c. "Haddowia longipes" . . 30 90
189 85c. "Phillipsia domingensis" 35 1·25

1984. 25th Anniv of Cricket on Christmas Island. Multicoloured.
190 30c. Type **42** 30 85
191 40c. Bowled-out . . . . . . 30 1·10
192 50c. Batsman in action . . . 35 1·50
193 85c. Fielder diving for catch 55 1·75

43 Arrival of Father Christmas

1984. Christmas and "Ausipex" International Stamp Exhibition, Melbourne. Sheet 100 × 100 mm containing T **43** and similar horiz designs. Multicoloured.
MS194 30c. Type **43**; 55c. Distribution of presents; 85c. Departure of Father Christmas 2·50 3·25

44 Robber Crab **45** "Once in Royal David's City"

1985. Crabs (1st series). Multicoloured.
195 30c. Type **44** . . . . 1·00 70
196 40c. Horn-eyed ghost crab . . 1·10 1·10
197 55c. Purple hermit crab . . . 1·50 1·60
198 85c. Little nipper . . . . . . 2·25 2·50

1985. Crabs (2nd series). As T **44**. Multicoloured.
199 33c. Blue crab . . . . 1·25 65
200 45c. Tawny hermit crab . . . 1·40 1·25
201 60c. Red nipper . . . . . . 1·75 2·00
202 90c. Smooth-handed ghost crab . . . . 2·50 3·00

1985. Crabs (3rd series). As T **44**. Multicoloured.
203 33c. Red crab . . . . 1·25 60
204 45c. Mottled crab . . . . . . 1·75 1·40
205 60c. Rock hopper crab . . . 2·50 2·50
206 90c. Yellow nipper . . . . . 3·00 3·50

1985. Christmas Carols. Multicoloured.
207 27c. Type **45** . . . . 1·00 1·40
208 33c. "While Shepherds Watched Their Flocks by Night" . . . . 1·10 1·50
209 45c. "Away in a Manger" . . 1·40 1·75
210 60c. "We Three Kings of Orient Are" . . . . 1·50 1·90
211 90c. "Hark the Herald Angels Sing" . . . . 1·60 2·00

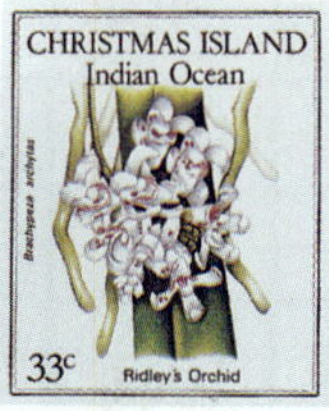

46 Halley's Comet over Christmas Island

47 Ridley's Orchid

1986. Appearance of Halley's Comet. Multicoloured.

212 33c. Type **46** 40 80
213 45c. Edmond Halley 45 1·10
214 60c. Comet and "Consolidated Venture" (bulk carrier) loading phosphate 50 2·25
215 90c. Comet over Flying Fish Cove 60 2·50

1986. Native Flowers. Multicoloured.

216 33c. Type **47** 50 55
217 45c. Hanging flower 30 85
218 60c. Hoya 30 1·50
219 90c. Sea hibiscus 35 2·00

1986. Royal Wedding. As T **112** of Ascension. Multicoloured.

220 33c. Prince Andrew and Miss Sarah Ferguson 45 50
221 90c. Prince Andrew piloting helicopter, Digby, Canada, 1985 95 1·75

48 Father Christmas and Reindeer in Speed Boat

1986. Christmas. Multicoloured.

222 30c. Type **48** 85 60
223 36c. Father Christmas and reindeer on beach 1·00 60
224 55c. Father Christmas fishing 1·50 1·50
225 70c. Playing golf 2·75 3·50
226 $1 Sleeping in hammock 2·75 4·00

49 H.M.S. "Flying Fish" and Outline Map of Christmas Island

1987. Centenary of Visits by H.M.S. "Flying Fish" and H.M.S. "Egeria". Multicoloured.

227 36c. Type **49** 40 75
228 90c. H.M.S. "Egeria" and outline map 70 2·50

50 Blind Snake

51 Children watching Father Christmas in Sleigh

1987. Wildlife. Multicoloured.

229 1c. Type **50** 40 90
230 2c. Blue-tailed skink 40 90
231 3c. Insectivorous bat 90 90
232 5c. Grasshopper 90 90
233 10c. Christmas Island fruit bat 90 90
234 25c. Gecko 1·00 1·00
235 30c. "Mantis religiosa" (mantid) 1·25 1·25
236 36c. Moluccan hawk owl ("Hawk-owl") 3·00 1·75
237 40c. Bull-mouth helmet 1·75 2·25
237a 41c. Nudibranch ("Phidiana" sp.) 1·25 70
238 50c. Textile or cloth of gold cone 1·75 2·25
239 65c. Brittle stars 1·40 1·25
240 75c. Regal angelfish 1·40 1·75
241 90c. "Appias paulina" (butterfly) 3·00 3·25
242 $1 "Hypolimnas misippus" (butterfly) 3·00 3·25
243 $2 Shrew 3·00 7·00
244 $5 Green turtle 3·25 7·00

1987. Christmas. Sheet 165 × 65 mm, containing T **51** and similar multicoloured designs.

MS245 30c. Type **51**; 37c. Father Christmas distributing gifts (48 × 22 mm); 90c. Children with presents (48 × 22 mm); $1 Singing carols 4·00 4·00

The stamps within No. **MS**245 form a composite design of a beach scene.

1988. Bicentenary of Australian Settlement. Arrival of First Fleet. As Nos. 1105/9 of Australia, but each inscribed "CHRISTMAS ISLAND Indian Ocean" and "AUSTRALIA BICENTENARY".

246 37c. Aborigines watching arrival of Fleet, Botany Bay 1·50 1·75
247 37c. Aboriginal family and anchored ships 1·50 1·75
248 37c. Fleet arriving at Sydney Cove 1·50 1·75
249 37c. Ship's boat 1·50 1·75
250 37c. Raising the flag, Sydney Cove, 26 January 1788 1·50 1·75

Nos. 246/50 were printed together, se-tenant, forming a composite design.

52 Captain William May

54 Beach Toys

53 Pony and Trap, 1910

1988. Cent of British Annexation. Mult.

251 37c. Type **52** 35 40
252 53c. Annexation ceremony 50 55
253 95c. H.M.S. "Imperieuse" (armoured cruiser) firing salute 90 95
254 $1.50 Building commemorative cairn 1·40 1·50

1988. Cent of Permanent Settlement. Mult.

255 37c. Type **53** 80 40
256 55c. Phosphate mining, 1910 1·00 55
257 70c. Steam locomotive, 1914 1·60 85
258 $1 Arrival of first aircraft, 1957 1·75 1·25

1988. Christmas. Toys and Gifts. Multicoloured.

259 32c. Type **54** 40 35
260 39c. Flippers, snorkel and mask 50 40
261 90c. Model soldier, doll and soft toys 1·10 1·10
262 $1 Models of racing car, lorry and jet aircraft 1·25 1·25

55 Food on Table ("Good Harvesting")

1989. Chinese New Year. Multicoloured.

263 39c. Type **55** 45 40
264 70c. Decorations ("Prosperity") 80 70
265 90c. Chinese girls ("Good Fortune") 1·10 90
266 $1 Lion dance ("Progress Every Year") 1·25 1·00

56 Sir John Murray

1989. 75th Death Anniv of Sir John Murray (oceanographer). Multicoloured.

267 39c. Type **56** 50 50
268 80c. Map of Christmas Island showing Murray Hill 1·25 95
269 $1 Oceanographic equipment 1·50 1·25
270 $1.10 H.M.S. "Challenger" (survey ship), 1872 1·75 1·50

57 Four Children

58 "Huperzia phlegmaria"

1989. Malay Hari Raya Festival. Multicoloured.

271 39c. Type **57** 55 50
272 55c. Man playing tambourine 80 70
273 80c. Girl in festival costume 1·25 1·00
274 $1.10 Christmas Island Mosque 1·60 1·40

1989. Ferns. Multicoloured.

275 41c. Type **58** 75 60
276 65c. "Asplenium polydon" 1·10 85
277 80c. Common bracken 1·40 1·00
278 $1.10 Birds-nest fern 1·60 1·40

59 Virgin Mary and Star

61 First Sighting, 1615

1989. Christmas. Multicoloured.

279 36c. Type **59** 60 40
280 41c. Christ Child in manger 60 45
281 80c. Shepherds and star 1·50 80
282 $1.10 Three Wise Men following star 1·60 1·10

1989. "Melbourne Stampshow '89". Nos. 237a and 242 optd with Stampshow logo.

283 41c. Nudibranch ("Phidiana sp.") 1·00 45
284 $1 "Hypolimnas misippus" (butterfly) 3·25 1·25

1990. 375th Anniv of Discovery of Christmas Island. Multicoloured.

285 41c. Type **61** 1·25 50
286 $1.10 Second sighting and naming, 1643 1·50 1·40

62 Miniature Tractor pulling Phosphate

1990. Christmas Island Transport. Multicoloured.

287 1c. Type **62** 15 20
288 2c. Phosphate train 40 40
289 3c. Diesel railcar No. 8802 (vert) 20 20
290 5c. Loading road train 40 40
291 10c. Trishaw (vert) 30 30
292 15c. Terex truck 65 65
293 25c. Articulated bus 30 30
294 30c. Cable passenger carriage (vert) 30 35
295 40c. Passenger barge (vert) 35 40
296 50c. Kolek (outrigger canoe) 55 55
297 65c. Flying Doctor aircraft and ambulance 3·75 1·50
298 75c. Commercial van 1·50 1·50
299 90c. Vintage lorry 1·50 1·75
300 $1 Water tanker 1·50 1·75
301 $2 Traction engine 2·50 3·25
302 $5 Steam locomotive No. 1 3·25 4·75

63 Male Abbott's Booby

1990. Abbott's Booby. Multicoloured.

303 10c. Type **63** 85 30
304 20c. Juvenile male 1·40 50
305 29c. Female with egg 1·60 55
306 41c. Pair with chick 2·25 70

MS307 122 × 68 mm. 41c. Male with wings spread; 41c. Male on branch; 41c. Female with fledgling 5·50 3·00

The three stamps within No. **MS**307 form a composite design and are without the WWF logo.

64 1977 Famous Visitors 9c. Stamp

1990. Centenary of Henry Ridley's Visit.

308 41c. Type **64** 55 75
309 75c. Ridley (botanist) in rainforest 85 2·00

1990. "New Zealand 1990" International Stamp Exhibition, Auckland. No. **MS**307 optd "**NZ 1990 WORLD STAMP EXHIBITION AUCKLAND, NEW ZEALAND, 24 AUGUST – 2 SEPTEMBER 1990**" in purple on the sheet margins.

MS310 122 × 68 mm. 41c. Male with wings spread; 41c. Male on branch; 41c. Female with fledgling 7·50 8·50

65 "Corymborkus veratrifolia"

66 "Islander" (freighter), 1898

1990. Christmas. Flowers. Multicoloured.

311 38c. Type **65** 1·10 70
312 43c. "Hoya aldrichii" 1·25 75
313 80c. "Quisqualis indica" 2·25 2·75
314 $1.20 "Barringtonia racemosa" 2·75 3·50

1990. "Birdpex '90" Stamp Exhibition, Christchurch. No. **MS**307 optd **BIRDPEX '90 NATIONAL PHILATELIC EXHIBITION UNIVERSITY OF CANTERBURY CHRISTCHURCH NZ 6—9 DEC 1990 IN CONJUCTION WITH THE 20TH INTERNATIONAL ORNITHOLOGICAL CONGRESS**.

MS315 122 × 68 mm. 41c. Male with wings spread; 41c. Male on branch; 41c. Female with fledgling 9·00 9·50

1991. Centenary of First Phosphate Mining Lease. Multicoloured.

316 43c. Type **66** 1·00 90
317 43c. Miners loading tipper wagons, 1908 1·00 90
318 85c. Shay steam locomotive No. 4, 1925 1·40 1·25
319 $1.20 Extracting phosphate, 1951 1·75 1·60
320 $1.70 Land reclamation, 1990 2·00 1·90

Nos. 316/20 were printed together, se-tenant, forming a composite forest design.

67 Teaching Children Road Safety

1991. Christmas Island Police Force. Multicoloured.

321 43c. Type **67** 1·50 1·00
322 43c. Traffic control 1·50 1·00
323 90c. Airport customs 2·25 3·25
324 $1.20 Police launch "Fregata Andrews" towing rescued boat 3·00 3·00

MS325 135 × 88 mm. Nos. 321/4 7·50 7·50

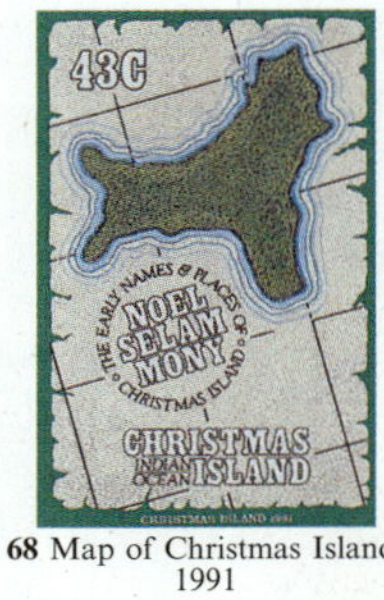

68 Map of Christmas Island, 1991

1991. Maps of Christmas Island. Multicoloured.

326 43c. Type **68** 1·00 65
327 75c. Goos Atlas, 1666 1·75 1·10
328 $1.10 De Manevillette, 1745 2·25 1·60
329 $1.20 Comberford, 1667 2·25 1·90

69 "Bruguiera gymnorrhiza"

1991. Local Trees. Multicoloured.

330	43c. Type **69**	1·00	65
331	70c. "Syzgium operculatum"	1·50	1·00
332	85c. "Ficus microcarpa"	1·75	1·25
333	$1.20 "Arenga listeri"	2·00	1·60

70 "Family round Christmas Tree" (S'ng Yen Luiw)

1991. Christmas. Children's Paintings. Mult.

334	38c. Type **70**	75	55
335	38c. "Opening Presents" (Liew Ann Nee)	75	55
336	38c. "Beach Party" (Foo Pang Chuan)	75	55
337	38c. "Christmas Walk" (Too Lai Peng)	75	55
338	38c. "Santa Claus and Christmas Tree" (Jesamine Wheeler)	75	55
339	43c. "Santa Claus fishing" (Ho Puay Ha)	75	60
340	$1 "Santa Claus in Boat" (Ng Hooi Hua)	1·50	1·50
341	$1.20 "Santa Claus surfing" (Yani Kawi)	1·75	1·75

71 Discussing Evacuation, 1942 **72** Snake's-head Cowrie

1992. 50th Anniv of Partial Evacuation. Mult.

342	45c. Type **71**	1·00	1·25
343	45c. Families waiting to embark	1·00	1·25
344	$1.05 Ferrying evacuees to "Islander"	2·50	2·75
345	$1.20 Departure of "Islander" (freighter)	2·75	3·00

1992. Shells. Multicoloured.

346	5c. Tiger cowrie	60	70
347	10c. Type **72**	80	70
348	15c. Scorpion conch	1·25	70
349	20c. Royal oak scallop	1·25	70
350	25c. Striped engina	1·25	70
351	30c. Prickly Pacific drupe	1·25	70
352	40c. Reticulate distorsio	1·25	75
353	45c. Tapestry turban	1·25	75
354	50c. Beautiful goblet	1·25	75
355	60c. Captain cone	1·50	80
356	70c. Layonkaire's turban	1·50	90
357	80c. Chirage spider conch	1·75	1·00
358	90c. Common delphinia	1·75	1·25
359	$1 Ceramic vase	1·75	1·50
360	$2 Partridge tun	1·40	1·75
361	$5 Strawberry drupe	3·50	3·75

73 Torpedoing of "Eidsvold"

1992. 50th Anniv of Sinkings of "Eidsvold" and "Nissa Maru". Multicoloured.

362	45c. Type **73**	1·50	75
363	80c. "Eidsvold" sinking	2·25	2·25
364	$1.05 "Nissa Maru" under attack	2·75	3·50
365	$1.20 "Nissa Maru" beached	2·75	3·75

1992. "Kuala Lumpur '92" International Philatelic Exhibition. No. 361 optd with exhibition symbol.

366	$5 Strawberry drupe	9·00	7·00

75 Jungle **76** Abbott's Booby

1992. Christmas. Multicoloured.

367	40c. Type **75**	90	1·25
368	40c. Red-tailed tropic bird and brown booby over rock	90	1·25
369	45c. Brown boobies on headland	90	1·25
370	$1.05 Red-tailed tropic bird, brown booby and cliffs	1·60	1·75
371	$1.20 Cliffs	1·60	1·75

Nos. 367/71 were printed together, se-tenant, forming a composite coastal design.

1993. Seabirds. Multicoloured.

372	45c. Type **76**	60	85
373	45c. Christmas Island frigate bird	60	85
374	45c. Common noddy	60	85
375	45c. White-tailed ("Golden Bosunbird") tropic bird	60	85
376	45c. Brown booby	60	85
MS377	140 × 70 mm. Nos. 372/6	2·75	4·00

Nos. 372/6 were printed together, se-tenant, forming a composite design.

77 Dolly Beach

1993. Scenic Views of Christmas Island. Mult.

378	85c. Type **77**	1·50	1·75
379	95c. Blow Holes	1·75	2·25
380	$1.05 Merrial Beach	1·90	2·50
381	$1.20 Rainforest	2·00	2·50

78 Turtle on Beach

1993. Christmas. Multicoloured.

382	40c. Type **78**	1·00	70
383	45c. Crabs and wave	1·00	70
384	$1 Christmas Island frigate bird and rainforest	2·25	3·25

79 Map of Christmas Island

1993. 350th Anniv of Naming of Christmas Island.

385	**79**	$2 multicoloured	3·00	3·50

80 Pekingese

1994. Chinese New Year ("Year of the Dog"). Multicoloured.

386	45c. Type **80**	1·00	1·40
387	45c. Mickey (Christmas Island dog)	1·00	1·40
MS388	106 × 70 mm. Nos. 386/7	2·50	3·50

81 Shay Locomotive No. 4

1994. Steam Locomotives. Multicoloured.

389	85c. Type **81**	1·75	1·75
390	95c. Locomotive No. 9	1·75	2·00
391	$1.20 Locomotive No. 1	2·00	2·25

82 "Brachypeza archytas" **83** Angel blowing Trumpet

1994. Orchids. Multicoloured.

392	45c. Type **82**	1·10	1·40
393	45c. "Thelasis capitata"	1·10	1·40
394	45c. "Corymborkis veratrifolia"	1·10	1·40
395	45c. "Flickingeria nativitatis"	1·10	1·40
396	45c. "Dendrobium crumenatum"	1·10	1·40

1994. Christmas. Multicoloured.

397	40c. Type **83**	80	60
398	45c. Wise Man holding gift	80	60
399	80c. Star over Bethlehem	1·75	2·50

84 Pig

1995. Chinese New Year ("Year of the Pig").

400	**84**	45c. multicoloured	75	60
401	–	85c. multicoloured	1·25	1·75
MS402		106 × 71 mm. Nos. 400/1	2·00	2·50

DESIGN: 85c. Pig (different).

85 Golfer playing Shot

1995. 40th Anniv of Christmas Island Golf Course.

403	**85**	$2.50 multicoloured	4·25	4·25

86 Father Christmas with Map on Christmas Island Frigate Bird

1995. Christmas. Multicoloured.

404	40c. Type **86**	80	60
405	45c. Father Christmas distributing presents	80	60
406	80c. Father Christmas waving goodbye	1·75	2·50

87 De Havilland D.H.98 Mosquito on Reconnaissance Mission

1995. 50th Anniv of End of Second World War. Each black, stone and red.

407	45c. Type **87**	95	95
408	45c. H.M.S. "Rother" (frigate)	95	95

88 Lemon-peel Angelfish

1995. Marine Life. Multicoloured.

412	20c. Pink-tailed triggerfish	15	20
413	30c. Japanese inflator-filefish ("Longnose filefish")	20	25
414	45c. Princess anthias	30	35
415	75c. Type **88**	55	60
416	85c. Moon wrasse	60	65
417	90c. Spotted boxfish	65	70
418	95c. Moorish idol	70	75
419	$1 Emperor angelfish	70	75
420	$1.20 Glass-eyed snapper ("Glass bigeye")	85	90

89 Rat with Drum

1996. Chinese New Year ("Year of the Rat"). Multicoloured.

425	45c. Type **89**	1·00	1·25
426	45c. Rat with tambourine	1·00	1·25
MS427	106 × 70 mm. Nos. 425/6	3·00	3·50

90 Christmas Island White-Eye ("White-eye") **91** Three Ships approaching Island

1996. Christmas Island Land Birds. Multicoloured.

428	45c. Type **90**	75	50
429	85c. Moluccan hawk owl ("Hawk-owl")	1·75	2·00

1996. Christmas. "I saw Three Ships" (carol). Multicoloured.

430	40c. Type **91**	75	60
431	45c. Madonna and Child with ships at anchor	75	60
432	80c. Ships leaving	1·60	2·10

1996. 300th Anniv of Willem de Vlamingh's Discovery of Christmas Island. As No. 1665 of Australia.

433	45c. multicoloured	1·00	1·50

92 Ox facing Right

1997. Chinese New Year ("Year of the Ox"). Multicoloured.

434	45c. Type **92**	1·00	1·00
435	45c. Ox facing left	1·00	1·00
MS436	106 × 70 mm. Nos. 434/5	2·00	2·50

93 Father Christmas reading Letter

1997. Christmas. Multicoloured.

437	40c. Type **93**	90	70
438	45c. Father Christmas carving wooden boat	90	70
439	80c. Father Christmas in sleigh	1·90	2·50

94 Tiger

1998. Chinese New Year ("Year of the Tiger"). Multicoloured.

440	45c. Type **94**	1·40	1·40
441	45c. Tiger with head facing left	1·40	1·40
MS442	106 × 70 mm. Nos. 440/1	3·00	3·25

95 Christmas Island Frigate Bird

1998. Marine Life. Multicoloured.

443	5c. Type **95**	20	30
444	5c. Four ambon chromis	20	30
445	5c. Three ambon chromis	20	30
446	5c. One pink anemonefish	20	30

447 5c. Three pink anemonefish 20 30
448 10c. Reef heron ("Eastern Reef Egret") 25 30
449 10c. Whitelined cod 25 30
450 10c. Pyramid butterflyfish 25 30
451 10c. Dusky parrotfish 25 30
452 10c. Spotted garden eel 25 30
453 25c. Sooty tern 30 35
454 25c. Stripe-tailed damselfish ("Scissortail sergeant") 30 35
455 25c. Thicklip wrasse 30 35
456 25c. Blackaxil chromis 30 35
457 25c. Orange anthias 30 35
458 45c. Brown booby 35 40
459 45c. Green turtle 35 40
460 45c. Pink anemonefish 35 40
461 45c. Blue sea star 35 40
462 45c. Kunie's chromodoris 35 40

Nos. 443/62 were printed together, se-tenant, with the backgrounds forming a composie design.

96 Orchid Tree

1998. Christmas. Flowering Trees. Multicoloured.
463 40c. Type **96** 60 50
464 80c. Flame tree 1·40 1·40
465 95c. Sea hibiscus 1·40 2·00

97 Leaping Rabbit

1999. Chinese New Year ("Year of the Rabbit"). Multicoloured.
466 45c. Type **97** 1·00 1·25
467 45c. Rabbit with pestle and mortar 1·00 1·25
MS468 106 × 70 mm. Nos. 466/7 2·00 2·50

98 Carnival Dragon (Fong Jason) (Community Arts Festival)

1999. Festivals. Children's Paintings. Mult.
469 45c. Type **98** 60 60
470 45c. Red crab holding Easter egg (Community Arts Festival, Siti Zanariah Zainal) 60 60
471 85c. Ghost and child (Tan Diana) (Hungry Ghost Festival) (vert) 95 1·10
472 $1.20 Walls of Mecca (Anwar Ramlan) (Hari Raya Haji Festival) (vert) 1·25 1·40

99 Santa Claus in Hammock

1999. Christmas. Multicoloured.
473 40c. Type **99** 80 70
474 45c. Santa Claus with Christmas pudding 80 70
475 95c. Santa Claus in sleigh pulled by Abbott's boobies 1·75 2·00

100 Chinese Dragon

2000. Chinese New Year ("Year of the Dragon"). Multicoloured.
476 45c. Type **100** 1·00 1·25
477 45c. Chinese dragon facing left 1·00 1·25
MS478 106 × 70 mm. Nos. 476/7 2·00 2·50

101 Yeow Jian Min

102 The Three Kings

2000. New Millennium. "Face of Christmas Island". Multicoloured.
479 45c. Type **101** 80 80
480 45c. Ida Chin (schoolgirl) 80 80
481 45c. Ho Tak Wah (elderly man) 80 80
482 45c. Thomas Faul and James Neill (young boys) 80 80
483 45c. Siti Sanniah Kawi (mother of three) 80 80

2000. Christmas. "We Three Kings" (carol). Mult.
484 40c. Type **102** 55 65
485 40c. Birds with Three Gifts 55 65
486 45c. Crabs with Three Gifts 55 65

103 Green Snake

2001. Chinese New Year ("Year of the Snake"). Mult.
487 45c. Type **103** 1·00 75
488 $1.35 Silver snake 2·00 2·25
MS489 106 × 70 mm. Nos. 487/8 3·00 3·00

104 *Chaetocalathus semisupinus*

2001. International Stamps. Fungi. Multicoloured.
490 $1 Type **104** 90 90
491 $1.50 *Pycnoporus sanguineus* 1·25 1·50

105 Rat

106 Imperial Pigeon

2002. Chinese New Year ("Year of the Horse"). Multicoloured.
492 5c. Type **105** 40 50
493 5c. Ox 40 50
494 5c. Tiger 40 50
495 5c. Rabbit 40 50
496 15c. Dragon 45 55
497 15c. Snake 45 55
498 15c. Horse (gold) 45 55
499 15c. Goat 45 55
500 25c. Monkey 55 65
501 25c. Cock 55 65
502 25c. Dog 55 65
503 25c. Pig 55 65
504 45c. Horse (purple) 60 70
505 $1.35 Horse (gold) 1·25 1·50
MS506 106 × 70 mm. Nos. 504/5 3·00 3·25

2002. Endangered Species. Christmas Island Birds. Multicoloured.
507 45c. Type **106** 90 90
508 45c. Christmas Island hawk owl 90 90
509 $1 Goshawk 1·50 1·50
510 $1.50 Thrush 1·90 1·90

107 Yellow Goat

2003. Chinese New Year ("Year of the Goat"). As T **107** plus designs as Nos. 492/503 with backgrounds in mauve and some values changed. Multicoloured.
511 10c. Type **105** 45 55
512 10c. Ox 45 55
513 10c. Tiger 45 55
514 10c. Rabbit 45 55
515 15c. Dragon 45 55
516 15c. Snake 45 55
517 15c. Horse 45 55
518 15c. Goat (animal in gold) 45 55
519 25c. Monkey 50 60
520 25c. Cock 50 60
521 25c. Dog 50 60
522 25c. Pig 50 60
523 50c. Type **107** 65 75
524 $1.50 Blue goat 1·60 1·90
MS525 105 × 70 mm. Nos. 523/4 2·50 3·00

Nos. 492/503 have red backgrounds.

108 Santa riding on Whale Shark

2003. Christmas. Multicoloured.
526 45c. Type **108** 90 90
527 50c. Santa sitting on green turtle and distributing gifts 90 90

109 Yellow Monkey

2004. Chinese New Year ("Year of the Monkey"). Plus designs as Nos. 492/503 in turquoise and blue with some values changed. Multicoloured.
528 10c. Rat 45 55
529 10c. Ox 45 55
530 10c. Tiger 45 55
531 10c. Rabbit 45 55
532 15c. Dragon 45 55
533 15c. Snake 45 55
534 15c. Horse 45 55
535 15c. Goat 45 55
536 25c. Monkey (animal in gold) 50 60
537 25c. Cock 50 60
538 25c. Dog 50 60
539 25c. Pig 50 60
540 50c. Type **109** 65 75
541 $1.45 Orange-brown monkey 1·60 1·90
MS542 105 × 70 mm. Nos. 540/1 2·75 3·25

110 Meyer's Butterflyfish

2004. Christmas Island Underwater. Multicoloured.
543 10c. Type **110** 30 40
544 10c. Whale shark 30 40
545 10c. Saddle butterflyfish 30 40
546 10c. Racoon butterflyfish 30 40
547 10c. Green turtles 30 40
548 25c. Clown triggerfish 35 45
549 25c. Pair of Emperor angelfish 35 45
550 25c. False Moorish idols 35 45
551 25c. Emperor angelfish (juvenile) 35 45
552 25c. Pyramid butterflyfish 35 45
553 25c. Bennett's butterflyfish 35 45
554 25c. Parrotfish with blue and yellow stripes 35 45
555 25c. Dotty triggerfish 35 45
556 25c. Divers observing fish 35 45
557 25c. Pair of butterflyfish 35 45
558 50c. Coral cod and powder-blue surgeonfish 65 75
559 50c. Emperor angelfish (adult) 65 75
560 50c. Harlequin filefish 65 75
561 50c. Pink Anemonefish 65 75
562 50c. Nudibranch 65 75

Nos. 543/62 were printed together, se-tenant, with the background forming a composite design showing a coral reef and schools of fish.

111 Rooster

2005. Chinese New Year ("Year of the Rooster"). Designs as Nos. 492/503 with backgrounds in vermilion and yellow with some values changed. Multicoloured.
563 10c. Rat 25 35
564 10c. Ox 25 35
565 10c. Tiger 25 35
566 10c. Rabbit 25 35
567 15c. Dragon 25 35
568 15c. Snake 25 35
569 15c. Horse 25 35
570 15c. Goat 25 35
571 25c. Monkey 35 45
572 25c. Cock (animal in red foil) 35 45
573 25c. Dog 35 45
574 25c. Pig 35 45
575 50c. Type **111** 60 70
576 $1.45 Rooster (with right foot raised under body) 1·60 1·75
MS577 105 × 70 mm. Nos. 575/6 2·50 2·75

2005. Taipei 2005 International Stamp Exhibition. No. **MS**577 optd **Taipei 2005 18th international Stamp Exhibition**.
MS578 105 × 70 mm. Nos. 575/6 2·75 3·00

113 Santa and Decorated Palm Tree

2005. Christmas. Multicoloured.
579 45c. Type **113** 75 60
580 90c. Santa in sleigh drawn by crabs 1·25 1·40

114 Purple Dog

2006. Chinese New Year ("Year of the Dog"). Multicoloured.
581 10c. Rat 25 35
582 10c. Ox 25 35
583 10c. Tiger 25 35
584 10c. Rabbit 25 35
585 15c. Dragon 25 35
586 15c. Snake 25 35
587 15c. Horse 25 35
588 15c. Goat 25 35
589 25c. Monkey 35 45
590 25c. Cock 35 45
591 25c. Dog (animal in copper foil) 35 45
592 25c. Pig 35 45
593 50c. Type **114** 60 70
594 $1.45 Leaping dog (in copper foil) 1·60 1·60
MS595 106 × 70 mm. Nos. 593/4 2·25 2·50

115 Mosque

2006. Heritage Buildings. Multicoloured.
596 50c. Type **115** 90 90
597 $1 Tai Pak Kong Temple 1·75 1·75
598 $1 Soon Tian Temple 1·75 1·75
599 $1.45 Tai Jin House 2·25 2·25

116 Orange Pig running

2007. Chinese New Year ('Year of the Pig'). T **116** and similar horiz designs plus designs as Nos. 492/503 with composite backgrounds showing pigs. Multicoloured. (a) Ordinary gum.
600 10c. Rat 15 15
601 10c. Ox 15 15
602 10c. Tiger 15 15
603 10c. Rabbit 15 15
604 15c. Dragon 20 20
605 15c. Snake 20 20
606 15c. Horse 20 20
607 15c. Goat 20 20
608 25c. Monkey 35 35
609 25c. Cock 35 35
610 25c. Dog 35 35
611 25c. Pig (animal in gold foil) 35 35
612 50c. Type **116** 65 65
613 $1.45 Yellow pig standing 1·90 1·90
MS614 106 × 70 mm. Nos. 612/13 2·50 2·50

(b) Circular sheet 170 × 170 mm containing designs as Nos. 426, 434, 440, 466, 476, 487, 504, 523, 540, 575, 593 and 612 but smaller, 33 × 23 mm, with some values changed. Self-adhesive.
MS615 50c. × 12 Rat with tambourine; As Type **92**; As Type **94**; As Type **97**; As Type **100**; As Type **103**; Horse (purple); As Type **107**; As Type **109**; As Type **111**; As Type **103**; As Type **116**; $1 8·00 8·00

No. **MS**615 commemorates the end of the 12-year cycle of Chinese New Year stamps.

117 Santa arriving by Speedboat

2007. Christmas. Multicoloured. (i) Domestic Mail.
616 45c. Type **117** 55 60
617 50c. Santa unloading net full of presents 70 75

(ii) International Post.
618 $1.10 Santa on beach distributing presents . . . 1·70 1·90

118 Rat

2007. Chinese New Year ('Year of the Rat'). Multicoloured.
619 10c. Rat (11.01pm–1.00am) (animal in gold foil) . . . 15 15
620 10c. Ox (1.01am–3.00am) . . 15 15
621 10c. Tiger (3.01am–5.00am) 15 15
622 10c. Rabbit (5.01am–7.00am) 15 15
623 10c. Dragon (7.01am–9.00am) 15 15
624 10c. Snake (9.01am–11.00am) 15 15
625 15c. Horse (11.01am–1.00pm) 20 20
626 15c. Pig (9.01pm–11.00pm) 20 20
627 25c. Goat (1.01pm–3.00pm) 35 35
628 25c. Monkey (3.01pm–5.00pm) 35 35
629 25c. Cock (5.01pm–7.00pm) 30 30
630 25c. Dog (7.01pm–9.00pm) 30 30
631 50c. Type **118** 65 65
632 $1.45 Calligraphy (in gold foil) . . . . 1·90 1·90
MS633 136 × 70 mm. Nos. 631/2 2·50 2·50
Nos. 619/30 show the zodiac's ruling hours.

CILICIA Pt. 16

A district in Asia Minor, occupied and temporarily controlled by the French between 1919 and 20 October 1921. The territory was then returned to Turkey.

40 paras = 1 piastre.

1919. Various issues of Turkey optd **CILICIE**. A. On No. 726 (surch Printed Matter stamp optd with Star and Crescent).
1 **15** 5pa. on 10pa. green . . . . 2·30 2·75

B. On 1901 issue optd with Star and Crescent.
2 **21** 1pi. blue (No. 543) . . . . 1·60 1·50
32 1pi. blue (No. 631) . . . . 1·70 2·75

C. On 1909 issue optd with Star and Crescent (No. 7 also optd as T **24**).
4 **28** 20pa. red (No. 572) . . . . 2·30 2·50
35 20pa. red (No. 643) . . . . 1·60 2·50
7 1pi. blue (No. 649) £950 £600
8 1pi. blue (No. 645) . . . . 7·50 8·00

D. On 1913 issue.
36 **30** 20pa. pink . . . . 1·80 2·30

E. On Pictorial issue of 1914.
37 **32** 2pa. purple . . . . 70 2·30
11 – 4pa. brown (No. 500) . . . 1·10 3·00
12 – 6pa. blue (No. 502) . . . 9·00 8·00
13 – 1¾pi. brown and grey (No. 507) . . . . . . 2·30 3·75

F. On Postal Anniv issue of 1916.
14 **60** 5pa. green . . . . £110 60·00
15 20pa. blue . . . . 1·90 3·00
40 1pi. black and violet . . . 2·00 1·50
17 5pi. black and brown . . . 1·90 3·75

G. On Pictorial issues of 1916 and 1917.
18 **73** 10pa. green . . . . 2·50 3·25
19 **76** 50pa. blue . . . . 7·00 3·50
41 **69** 5pi. on 2pa. blue (No. 914) 2·50 3·00
21 **63** 25pi. red on buff . . . . 2·75 3·50
22 **64** 50pi. red . . . . 2·50 3·00
23 50pi. blue . . . . 22·00 25·00

H. On Armistice issue of 1919 optd with T **81** of Turkey.
24 **76** 50pa. blue . . . . 8·25 5·00
25 **77** 2pi. blue and brown . . . 2·75 3·00
26 **78** 5pi. brown and blue . . . 12·00 4·75

1919. Various issues of Turkey optd **Cilicie**. A. On No. 726 (surch Printed Matter stamp optd with Star and Crescent).
46 **15** 5pa. on 10pa. green . . . . 1·40 2·00

B. On 1901 issue optd with Star and Crescent.
47 **21** 1pi. blue (No. 543) . . . . 1·30 90
48 1pi. blue (No. 631) . . . . 2·50 3·25
49 1pi. blue (No. 669) . . . . 70·00 55·00

C. On 1908 issue optd with T **24** and Star and Crescent.
50 **25** 20pa. red . . . . 11·00 3·75

D. On 1909 issue optd with Star and Crescent (No. 52 also optd as T **24**).
52a **28** 20pa. red (No. 643) £150 £120
52 20pa. red (No. 647) . . . . 2·00 3·50

E. On 1913 issue.
53 **30** 5pa. bistre . . . . 3·50 3·75
54 20pa. pink . . . . 1·30 3·00

F. On Pictorial issue of 1914.
55 **32** 2pa. purple . . . . 1·70 2·75
56 – 4pa. brown (No. 500) . . . 1·70 1·60

G. On Postal Anniv issue of 1916.
57 **60** 20pa. blue . . . . 1·10 1·60
58 1pi. black and violet . . . 1·10 1·30
59 5pi. black and brown . . . 2·30 2·75

H. On Pictorial issues of 1916 and 1917.
60 **72** 5pa. orange . . . . 2·30 3·50
61 **75** 1pi. blue . . . . 2·30 3·00
62 **69** 5pi. on 2pa. blue (No. 914) 7·50 6·75
63 **64** 50pi. green on yellow . . . 46·00 32·00

1919. Various issues of Turkey optd **T.E.O. Cilicie**. A. On No. 726 (surch Printed Matter stamp optd with Star and Crescent).
69 **15** 5pa. on 10pa. green . . . . 2·00 2·30

B. On 1892 issue optd with Star and Crescent and Arabic surch.
70 **15** 10pa. on 20pa. red (No. 630) . . . . 50 2·30

C. On 1909 issue optd with Star and Crescent.
71 **28** 20pa. red (No. 572) . . . . 2·75 3·00
72 20pa. red (No. 643) . . . . 2·30 2·75

D. On 1909 issue optd with Tougra and surch in Turkish.
73 **28** 5pa. on 2pa. green (No. 938) 90 50

E. On Pictorial stamp of 1914.
74 – 1pi. blue (No. 505) . . . . . 90 1·10

F. On Postal Anniv issue of 1916.
75 **60** 5pa. green . . . . £120 85·00
76 20pa. blue . . . . 80 1·10
77 1pi. black and violet . . . 1·90 2·30

G. On Postal Anniv issue of 1916 optd with Star and Crescent.
78 **60** 10pa. red (No. 654) 50 85

H. On Pictorial issues of 1916 and 1917.
79 **72** 5pa. orange 45 90
80 **73** 10pa. green . . . . 1·20 2·30
81 **74** 20pa. red 60 80
82 **77** 2pi. blue and brown . . . 2·00 1·70
83 **78** 5pi. brown and blue . . . 1·90 2·30
84 **69** 5pi. on 2pa. blue . . . . 7·50 7·75
85 **63** 25pi. red on buff . . . . 7·25 7·75
86 **64** 50pi. green on yellow . . . 75·00 60·00

I. On Charity stamp of 1917.
87 **65** 10pa. purple . . . . 2·00 2·30

1920. "Mouchon" key-type of French Levant surch **T.E.O. 20 PARAS**.
88 B 20pa. on 10c. red . . . . . 1·80 2·30

7

1920. Surch **OCCUPATION MILITAIRE Francaise CILICIE** and value.
89 **7** 70pa. on 5pa. red . . . . . 1·50 2·00
90 3½pi. on 5pa. red . . . . . 1·70 2·50

1920. Stamps of France surch **O.M.F. Cilicie** and new value.
100 **11** 5pa. on 2c. red . . . . . 30 2·00
101 **18** 10pa. on 5c. green 50 85
102 20pa. on 10c. red . . . . 50 1·10
103 1pi. on 25c. blue 65 85
104 **15** 2pi. on 15c. green . . . . 90 1·10
105 **13** 5pi. on 40c. red and blue . 1·20 2·30
106 10pi. on 50c. brown & lav 1·70 2·30
107 50pi. on 1f. red and green 2·30 3·00
108 100pi. on 5f. blue & yellow 22·00 24·00

1920. Stamps of France surch **O.M.F. Cilicie SAND. EST** and new value.
109 **11** 5pa. on 2c. red . . . . . 4·00 6·00
110 **18** 10pa. on 5c. green . . . . 5·25 6·00
111 20pa. on 10c. red . . . . 3·50 4·25
112 1pi. on 25c. blue . . . . 3·00 4·25
113 **15** 2pi. on 15c. green . . . . 10·50 10·50
114 **13** 5pi. on 40c. red and blue 60·00 60·00
115 20pi. on 1f. red and green 90·00 90·00

1921. Air. Nos. 104/5 optd **POSTE PAR AVION** in frame.
116 **15** 2pi. on 15c. green £7000
117 **13** 5pi. on 40c. red and blue £7000

POSTAGE DUE STAMPS

1919. Postage Due stamps of Turkey optd **CILICIE**.
D27 D **49** 5pa. brown . . . . . . 2·00 3·50
D28 D **50** 20pa. red . . . . 2·30 3·50
D29 D **51** 1pi. blue . . . . 6·50 7·00
D45 D **52** 2pi. blue . . . . 4·25 5·25

1919. Postage Due stamps of Turkey optd **Cilicie**.
D64 D **49** 5pa. brown . . . . . . 2·50 3·50
D65 D **50** 20pa. red . . . . 2·00 3·50
D66 D **51** 1pi. blue . . . . 5·75 7·00
D67 D **52** 2pi. blue . . . . 5·00 6·50

1921. Postage Due Stamps of France surch **O.M.F. Cilicie** and value.
D118 D **11** 1pi. on 10c. brown . . 6·25 8·00
D119 2pi. on 20c. olive . . 4·75 8·00
D120 3pi. on 30c. red . . 2·25 2·25
D121 4pi. on 50c. purple . . 4·75 7·75

CISKEI Pt. 1

The Republic of Ciskei was established on 4 December 1981, being constructed from tribal areas formerly part of the Republic of South Africa.

This independence did not receive international political recognition. We are satisfied, however, that the stamps had "de facto" acceptance for the carriage of mail outside Ciskei.

Ciskei was formally re-incorporated into South Africa on 27 April 1994.

100 cents = 1 rand.

1 Dr. Lennox Sebe, Chief Minister
2 Green Turaco

1981. Independence. Multicoloured.
1 5c. Type **1** 10 10
2 15c. Coat of arms 20 15
3 20c. Flag 30 30
4 25c. Mace 35 25

1981. Birds. Multicoloured.
5 1c. Type **2** 20 15
6 2c. Cape wagtail 20 15
7 3c. White-browed coucal . . 50 15
8 4c. Yellow-tufted malachite sunbird 20 15
9 5c. Stanley crane 20 15
10 6c. African red-winged starling 20 15
11 7c. Giant kingfisher 20 15
12 8c. Hadada ibis 30 15
13 9c. Black cuckoo 30 15
14 10c. Black-collared barbet . . 30 15
14a 11c. African black-headed oriole 55 30
14b 12c. Malachite kingfisher . . 1·10 30
14c 14c. Hoopoe . . . . 1·50 30
15 15c. African fish eagle . . . 30 30
15a 16c. Cape puff-back flycatcher . . . . 1·00 30
15b 18c. Long-tailed whydah . . 1·50 30
16 20c. Cape longclaw 40 30
16a 21c. Lemon dove . . . . . 1·50 60
17 25c. Cape dikkop 30 30
18 30c. African green pigeon . . 40 40
19 50c. Brown-necked parrot . . 60 60
20 1r. Narina's trogon . . . . 90 1·25
21 2r. Cape eagle owl . . . . . 1·75 2·50

3 Cecilia Makiwane (first Xhosa nurse)
4 Boom Sprayer

1982. Nursing. Multicoloured.
22 8c. Type **3** 15 10
23 15c. Operating theatre 30 30
24 20c. Matron lighting nurse's lamp (horiz) 40 40
25 25c. Nurses and patient (horiz) 50 50

1982. Pineapple Industry. Multicoloured.
26 8c. Type **4** 10 10
27 15c. Harvesting 20 25
28 20c. Despatch to cannery . . . 25 30
29 30c. Packing for local market 30 35

5 Brown Hare

1982. Small Mammals. Multicoloured.
30 8c. Type **5** 15 15
31 15c. Cape fox 25 25
32 20c. Cape ground squirrel . . 30 30
33 25c. Caracal 40 40

6 Assegai
7 Dusky Shark

1983. Trees (1st series). Multicoloured.
34 8c. Cabbage tree 15 10
35 20c. Type **6** 30 30
36 25c. Cape chestnut 35 35
37 40c. Outeniqua yellowwood . . 50 55
See also Nos. 52/5.

1983. Sharks. Multicoloured.
38 8c. Type **7** 15 15
39 20c. Sand tiger ("Ragged-tooth shark") 30 30
40 25c. Tiger shark (57 × 21 mm) 35 35
41 30c. Scalloped hammerhead (57 × 21 mm) 40 40
42 40c. Great white shark (57 × 21 mm) 50 50

8 Lovedale
9 White Drill Uniform

1983. Educational Institutions.
43 **8** 10c. lt brown, brown & black 10 10
44 – 20c. lt brown, brown & black 20 20
45 – 25c. brown, red and black . . 25 25
46 – 40c. lt brown, brown & black 40 45
DESIGNS: 20c. Fort Hare; 25c. Healdtown; 40c. Lennox Sebe.

1983. British Military Uniforms (1st series). 6th Warwickshire Regiment of Foot, 1821–27. Multicoloured.
47 20c. Type **9** 40 40
48 20c. Light Company privates 40 40
49 20c. Grenadier Company sergeants 40 40
50 20c. Undress blue frock coats 40 40
51 20c. Officer and field officer in parade order 40 40
See also Nos. 64/8 and 95/8.

1984. Trees (2nd series). As T **6**. Multicoloured.
52 10c. "Rhus chirindensis" . . . 15 15
53 20c. "Phoenix reclinata" . . . 25 35
54 25c. "Ptaeroxyon obliquum" 30 40
55 40c. "Apodytes dimidiata" . . 40 55

10 Sandprawn

1984. Fish-bait. Multicoloured.
56 11c. Type **10** 20 15
57 20c. Coral worm 30 30
58 25c. Bloodworm 35 35
59 30c. Red-bait 40 40

11 Banded Martin ("Banded Sand Martin")

1984. Migratory Birds. Multicoloured.

60	11c. Type **11**	25	20
61	25c. House martin	50	50
62	30c. Greater striped swallow	60	60
63	45c. Barn swallow ("European Swallow")	80	85

1984. British Military Uniforms (2nd series). Cape Mounted Rifles. As T **9**. Multicoloured.

64	25c. (1) Trooper in field and sergeant in undress uniforms, 1830	45	45
65	25c. (2) Trooper and sergeant in full dress, 1835	45	45
66	25c. (3) Officers in undress, 1830	45	45
67	25c. (4) Officers in full dress, 1827–34	45	45
68	25c. (5) Officers in full dress, 1834	45	45

The stamps are numbered as indicated in brackets.

12 White Steenbras

1985. Coastal Angling. Multicoloured.

69	11c. Type **12**	20	15
70	25c. Bronze seabream	30	30
71	30c. Kob	40	45
72	50c. Spotted grunt	70	80

13 Brownies holding Handmade Doll

1985. International Youth Year. 75th Anniv of Girl Guide Movement. Multicoloured.

73	12c. Type **13**	15	15
74	25c. Rangers planting trees	25	25
75	30c. Guides with flag	30	30
76	50c. Guides building fire	60	65

14 Furniture making

1985. Small Businesses. Multicoloured.

77	12c. Type **14**	15	10
78	25c. Dressmaking	30	30
79	30c. Welding	30	30
80	50c. Basketry	60	65

15 "Antelope"

16 Earth showing Africa

1985. Sail Troopships. Multicoloured.

81	12c. Type **15**	20	15
82	25c. "Pilot"	45	45
83	30c. "Salisbury"	45	45
84	50c. "Olive Branch"	80	85

1986. Appearance of Halley's Comet. Mult.

85	12c. (1) Earth showing South America	70	70
86	12c. (2) Type **16**	70	70
87	12c. (3) Stars and Moon	70	70
88	12c. (4) Moon and Milky Way	70	70
89	12c. (5) Milky Way and stars	70	70
90	12c. (6) Earth showing Australia	70	70
91	12c. (7) Earth and meteor	70	70
92	12c. (8) Meteor, Moon and comet tail	70	70
93	12c. (9) Comet head and Moon	70	70
94	12c. (10) Sun	70	70

Nos. 85/94 were issued in sheetlets of 10 stamps forming a composite design of the southern skies in April. Each stamp is inscribed with a number from "A1-10" to "A10-10". The first number is given in brackets in the listing to aid identification.

17 Fifer in Winter Dress

18 Welding Bicycle Frame

1986. British Military Uniforms (3rd series). 98th Regiment of Foot. Multicoloured.

95	14c. Type **17**	20	15
96	20c. Private in summer dress	30	30
97	25c. Grenadier in full summer dress	35	35
98	30c. Sergeant-major in full winter dress	50	50

1986. Bicycle Factory, Dimbaza. Multicoloured.

99	14c. Type **18**	20	15
100	20c. Spray-painting frame	30	30
101	25c. Installing wheelspokes	35	35
102	30c. Final assembly	50	50

19 President Dr. Lennox Sebe

1986. 5th Anniv of Independence. Multicoloured.

103	14c. Type **19**	15	15
104	20c. National Shrine, Ntaba kaNdoda	20	30
105	25c. Legislative Assembly, Bisho	20	35
106	30c. Automatic telephone exchange, Bisho	25	50

20 "Boletus edulis"

22 Wire Windmill

21 Nkone Cow and Calf

1987. Edible Mushrooms. Multicoloured.

107	14c. Type **20**	25	15
108	20c. "Macrolepiota zeyheri"	40	40
109	25c. "Termitomyces spp"	50	50
110	30c. "Russula capensis"	60	60

1987. Nkone Cattle. Multicoloured.

111	16c. Type **21**	20	15
112	20c. Nkone cow	25	30
113	25c. Nkone bull	30	35
114	30c. Herd of Nkone	40	55

1987. Homemade Toys. Multicoloured.

115	16c. Type **22**	20	15
116	20c. Rag doll	25	30
117	25c. Clay horse (horiz)	30	35
118	30c. Wire car (horiz)	40	55

23 Seven Birds

24 Bush Lily

1987. Folklore (1st series). Sikulume. Mult.

119	16c. Type **23**	20	15
120	20c. Cannibals chasing Sikulume	25	30
121	25c. Sikulume attacking the inabulele	30	35
122	30c. Chief Mangangezulu chasing Sikulume and his bride	40	55

See also Nos. 127/36, 153/6 and 161/4.

1988. Protected Flowers. Multicoloured.

123	16c. Type **24**	20	15
124	30c. Harebell	35	35
125	40c. Butterfly iris	40	40
126	50c. Vlei lily	60	65

25 Numbakatali crying and Second Wife feeding Black Crows

1988. Folklore (2nd series). Mbulukazi. Mult.

127	16c. Type **25**	30	35
128	16c. Numbakatali telling speckled pigeons of her childlessness	30	35
129	16c. Numbakatali finding children in earthenware jars	30	35
130	16c. Broad Breast sees Mbulukazi and brother at river	30	35
131	16c. Broad Breast asking to marry Mbulukazi	30	35
132	16c. Broad Breast and his two wives, Mbulukazi and her half-sister Mahlunguluza	30	35
133	16c. Mahlunguluza pushing Mbulukazi from precipice to her death	30	35
134	16c. Mbulukazi's ox tearing down Mahlunguluza's hut	30	35
135	16c. Ox licking Mbulukazi back to life	30	35
136	16c. Mahlunguluza being sent back to her father in disgrace	30	35

26 Oranges and Grafted Rootstocks in Nursery

1988. Citrus Farming. Multicoloured.

137	16c. Type **26**	20	15
138	30c. Lemons and inarching rootstock onto mature tree	40	40
139	40c. Tangerines and fruit being hand-picked	50	50
140	50c. Oranges and fruit being graded	60	65

27 "Amanita phalloides"

1988. Poisonous Fungi. Multicoloured.

141	16c. Type **27**	75	30
142	30c. "Chlorophyllum molybdites"	1·10	75
143	40c. "Amanita muscaria"	1·40	1·10
144	50c. "Amanita pantherina"	1·60	1·25

28 Kat River Dam

1989. Dams. Multicoloured.

145	16c. Type **28**	35	25
146	30c. Cata dam	55	50
147	40c. Binfield Park dam	65	65
148	50c. Sandile dam	70	80

29 Taking Eggs from Rainbow Trout

1989. Trout Hatcheries. Multicoloured.

149	18c. Type **29**	25	15
150	30c. Fertilized eyed trout ova and alevins	45	45
151	40c. Five-week-old fingerlings	55	55
152	50c. Adult male	60	65

30 Lion and Little Jackal killing Eland

1989. Folklore (3rd series). Little Jackal and the Lion. Multicoloured.

153	18c. Type **30**	20	15
154	30c. Little Jackal's children carrying meat to clifftop home	35	35
155	40c. Little Jackal pretending to be trapped	40	40
156	50c. Lion falling down cliff face	45	50

31 Cape Horse-cart

33 Handweaving on Loom

32 Mpunzikazi offering Food to Five Heads

1989. Animal-drawn Transport. Multicoloured.

157	18c. Type **31**	20	15
158	30c. Jubilee spider	35	35
159	40c. Ballantine half-tent ox-drawn wagon	40	40
160	50c. Voortrekker wagon	45	50

1990. Folklore (4th series). The Story of Makanda Mahlanu (Five Heads). Multicoloured.

161	18c. Type **32**	20	15
162	30c. Five Heads killing Mpunzikazi with his tail	35	35
163	40c. Mpunzanyana offering food to Five Heads	40	40
164	50c. Five Heads transformed into a man	45	50

1990. Handmade Carpets. Multicoloured.

165	21c. Type **33**	30	20
166	35c. Spinning	50	50
167	40c. Dyeing yarn	70	70
168	50c. Knotting carpet	70	70

34 Wooden Beam Plough, 1855

1980. Ploughs. Multicoloured.

169	21c. Type **34**	25	20
170	35c. Triple disc plough, 1895	40	40
171	40c. Reversible disc plough, 1895	50	50
172	50c. "Het Volk" double furrow plough, 1910	60	65

35 Prickly Pear Vendor

1990. Prickly Pear. Multicoloured.

173	21c. Type **35**	30	20
174	35c. Prickly pear bushes	50	50
175	40c. Whole and opened fruits	60	60
176	50c. Bushes in bloom	70	80

36 African Marsh Owl ("Marsh Owl")

37 Sao Bras (now Mossel Bay) on Map, 1500

1991. Owls. Multicoloured.

177	21c. Type **36**	1·10	40
178	35c. African scops owl ("Scops")	1·40	80
179	40c. Barn owl	1·75	1·00
180	50c. African wood owl ("Wood")	1·90	1·40

1991. Stamp Day. D'Ataide's Letter of 1501. Multicoloured.

181	25c. Type **37**	70	70
182	25c. Bartolomeo Dias's ship foundering off Cabo Tormentoso (now Cape of Good Hope) during voyage to India, 1500	70	70
183	25c. Captain Pedro d'Ataide landing at Sao Bras, 1601	70	70
184	25c. D'Ataide leaving letter relating death of Dias on tree	70	70
185	25c. Captain Joao da Nova finding letter, 1501	70	70

The inscriptions at the foot of Nos. 181 and 182 are transposed.

38 Comet Nucleus

1991. The Solar System. Multicoloured.

186	1c. Type **38**	20	15
187	2c. Trojan asteroids	20	15
188	5c. Meteoroids	20	15
189	7c. Pluto	30	15
190	10c. Neptune	30	15
191	20c. Uranus	50	20
192	25c. Saturn	60	20
193	30c. Jupiter	65	30
194	35c. Planetoids in asteroid belt	65	40
195	40c. Mars	80	50
196	50c. The Moon	80	70
197	60c. Earth	80	80
198	1r. Venus	1·00	1·25
199	2r. Mercury	1·60	2·00
200	5r. The Sun	2·25	3·25
MS201	197 × 93 mm. Nos. 186/200	10·00	10·00

39 Fort Armstrong and Xhosa Warrior

1991. 19th-century Frontier Forts. Multicoloured.

202	27c. Type **39**	30	30
203	45c. Keiskamma Hoek Post and Sir George Grey (governor of Cape Colony, 1854–58)	45	55
204	65c. Fort Hare and Xhosa Chief Sandile	55	70
205	85c. Peddie Cavalry Barracks and cavalryman	75	1·25

40 Cumulonimbus

1992. Cloud Formations. Multicoloured.

206	27c. Type **40**	40	25
207	45c. Altocumulus	55	65
208	65c. Cirrus	65	80
209	85c. Cumulus	75	1·10

41 "Intelsat VI" Communications Satellite

1992. International Space Year. Satellites over Southern Africa. Multicoloured.

210	35c. Type **41**	40	25
211	70c. "G P S Navstar" (navigation)	80	80
212	90c. "Meteosat" (meteorology)	1·10	1·10
213	1r.05 "Landsat VI" (Earth resources survey)	1·25	1·40

42 Universal Disc-harrow, 1914

1992. Agricultural Tools. Multicoloured.

214	35c. Type **42**	40	25
215	70c. Clod crusher and pulveriser, 1914	80	70
216	90c. Self-dump hay rake, 1910	1·10	95
217	1r.05 McCormick hay tedder, 1900	1·10	1·10

43 Mpekweni Sun Marine Resort

1992. Hotels. Multicoloured.

218	35c. Type **43**	40	25
219	70c. Katberg Protea Hotel	80	80
220	90c. Fish River Sun Hotel	1·10	1·10
221	1r.05 Amatola Sun Hotel, Amatole Mountains	1·10	1·25

44 Vasco da Gama, "Sao Gabriel" and Voyage round Cape of Good Hope, 1497

1993. Navigators. Multicoloured.

222	45c. Type **44**	65	30
223	65c. James Cook, H.M.S. "Endeavour" and first voyage, 1768–71	1·10	75
224	85c. Ferdinand Magellan, "Vitoria" and circumnavigation, 1519	1·25	90
225	90c. Sir Francis Drake, "Golden Hind" and circumnavigation, 1577–80	1·25	95
226	1r.05 Abel Tasman, "Heemskerk" and discovery of Tasmania, 1642	1·40	1·25

The ship on No. 222 is wrongly inscribed "San Gabriel", that on No. 224 "Victoria" and that on No. 226 "Heemskerck".

45 Island Canary

47 Jointed Cactus

46 Goshen Church (Moravian Mission), Whittlesea

1993. Cage Birds. Multicoloured.

227	45c. Type **45**	45	30
228	65c. Budgerigar	70	60
229	85c. Peach-faced lovebirds	90	80
230	90c. Cockatiel	95	85
231	1r.05 Gouldian finch	1·00	1·10

1993. Churches and Missions.

232 **46**	45c. stone, black and red	35	20
233 –	65c. blue, black and red	60	60
234 –	85c. brown, black and red	80	80
235 –	1r.05 yellow, black and red	90	1·00

DESIGNS: 65c. Kamastone Mission Church; 85c. Richie Thompson Memorial Church (Hertzog Mission), near Seymour; 1r.05, Bryce Ross Memorial Church (Pirie Mission), near Dimbaza.

1993. Invader Plants. Multicoloured.

236	45c. Type **47**	40	30
237	65c. Thorn apple	70	60
238	85c. Coffee weed	90	80
239	1r.05 Poisonous wild tobacco	1·00	1·00
MS240	98 × 125 mm. Nos. 236/9	2·75	2·75

48 "Losna" (steamer) (near Fish River), 1921

1994. Shipwrecks. Multicoloured.

241	45c. Type **48**	75	30
242	65c. "Catherine" (barque) (Waterloo Bay), 1846	1·25	60
243	85c. "Bennebroek" (East Indiaman) (near Mtana River), 1713	1·40	90
244	1r.05 "Sao Joao Baptista" (galleon) (between Fish and Kei Rivers), 1622	1·50	1·25

49 "Herman Steyn"

1994. Hybrid Roses. Multicoloured.

245	45c. Type **49**	35	30
246	70c. "Esther Geldenhuys"	60	60
247	95c. "Margaret Wasserfall"	80	80
248	1r.15 "Professor Fred Ziady"	1·00	1·00
MS249	149 × 114 mm. Nos. 245/8	2·50	2·75

COCHIN Pt. 1

A state of South West India. Now uses Indian stamps.

6 puttans = 5 annas.
12 pies = 1 anna; 16 annas = 1 rupee.

1 Emblems of State

1892. Value in "puttans".

5a **1**	½put. orange	2·50	1·50
2	1put. purple	3·00	2·75
3	2put. violet	2·00	2·25

3

5

1903. Value in "pies" or "puttans". With or without gum.

16 **3**	3pies. blue	1·50	10
17	½put. green (smaller)	1·25	40
18 **5**	1put. red	1·75	10
19 **3**	2put. violet	2·50	50

1909. Surch **2**. No gum.

22 **3**	2 on 3 pies. mauve	15	50

8 Raja Rama Varma I

10 Raja Rama Varma II

1911. Value in "pies" or "annas".

26 **8**	2p. brown	30	10
27	3p. blue	1·50	10
28	4p. green	1·75	10
29	9p. red	1·40	10
30	1a. orange	3·00	10
31	1½a. purple	7·50	45
32	2a. grey	7·50	40
33	3a. red	38·00	38·00

1916. Various frames.

35b **10**	2p. brown	1·60	10
36	4p. green	1·00	10
37	6p. brown	2·50	10
38	8p. brown	1·75	10
39	9p. red	20·00	35
40	10p. blue	6·00	10
41a	1a. orange	11·00	35
42	1½a. purple	3·75	20
43	2a. grey	4·25	10
44	2¼a. green	7·00	3·25
45	3a. red	12·00	35

1922. Surch with figure and words.

46 **8**	2p. on 3p. blue	40	30

1928. Surch **ONE ANNA ANCHAL & REVENUE** and value in native characters.

50 **10**	1a. on 2¼a. green	6·00	12·00

1932. Surch in figures and words both in English and in native characters.

51 **10**	3p. on 4p. green	1·25	1·40
52	3p. on 8p. brown	2·25	2·75
53	9p. on 10p. blue	1·50	3·25

18 Maharaja Rama Varma III

26 Maharaja Kerala Varma II

1933.

54 **18**	2p. brown	85	50
55	4p. green	60	10
56	6p. red	70	10
57	1a. orange	85	20
58	1a.8p. red	3·00	6·50
59	2a. grey	6·00	1·60
60	2¼a. green	1·75	30
61	3a. orange	5·50	1·60
62	3a.4p. violet	1·75	1·40
63	6a.8p. sepia	1·75	14·00
64	10a. blue	3·00	17·00

1934. Surch with figure and words.

65 **10**	6p. on 8p. brown	75	60
66	6p. on 10p. blue	1·75	2·00

1939. Optd **ANCHAL**.

74 **18**	1a. orange	75	1·60

1939. Surch in words only.

75 **18**	3p. on 1a.8p. red	£250	£100
77	6p. on 1a.8p. red	3·50	21·00

1943. Surch **SURCHARGED** and value in words.

79 **18**	3p. on 4p. green	7·00	4·00
76	3p. on 1a.8p. red	6·00	10·00
78	1a.3p. on 1a.8p. red	1·00	50

1943. Surch **ANCHAL SURCHARGED NINE PIES**.

84 **18**	9p. on 1a. orange	25·00	8·00

1943. Surch **ANCHAL** and value in words.

81a **18**	6p. on 1a. orange	£160	70·00
82	9p. on 1a. orange	£140	£130

1943.

85 **26**	2p. brown	3·50	4·50
87a	4p. green	3·75	5·50
88	6p. brown	3·75	10
89	9p. blue	45·00	1·25
90a	1a. orange	23·00	55·00
91	2¼a. green	27·00	2·50

1944. Surch with value in words only.

93 **26**	2p. on 6p. brown	75	4·00
94	3p. on 4p. green	7·00	10

96 3p. on 6p. brown . . . . . 1·00 20
97 4p. on 6p. brown . . . . . 5·00 12·00

1944. Surch **SURCHARGED** and value in words.
95 **26** 3p. on 4p. green . . . . . 5·50 10
92c 1a.3p. on 1a. orange . . . † £3750

1944. Surch **ANCHAL NINE PIES**.
92a **26** 9p. on 1a. orange . . . . 6·50 3·75

1944. Surch **ANCHAL SURCHARGED NINE PIES**.
92b **26** 9p. on 1a. orange . . . . 7·50 3·00

28 Maharaja Ravi Varma

29 Maharaja Ravi Varma

1944.
98 **28** 9p. blue . . . . 16·00 4·00
99 1a.3p. mauve . . . . . . 8·00 8·50
100 1a.9p. blue . . . . 9·50 16·00

1946. No gum.
101 **29** 2p. brown . . . . 2·75 20
102 3p. red 50 30
103 4p. green . . . . £2500 80·00
104 6p. brown . . . . 24·00 6·50
105 9p. blue . . . . 1·50 10
106 1a. orange . . . . 9·00 32·00
107 2a. black . . . . £120 8·50
108 3a. red . . . . 85·00 1·50
For No. 106, optd "U.S.T.C." or "T.-C." with or without surch, see Travancore-Cochin.

30 Maharaja Kerala Varma III

31 Chinese Nets

1948.
109 **30** 2p. brown . . . . 1·75 15
110 3p. red . . . . 1·00 15
111 4p. green . . . . 17·00 3·50
112 6p. brown . . . . 18·00 25
113 9p. blue . . . . 2·50 50
114 2a. black . . . . 65·00 2·50
115 3a. orange . . . . 70·00 1·00
116 3a.4p. violet . . . . . . 70·00 £350

1949.
117 **31** 2a. black . . . . 5·00 8·50
118 – 2¼a. green (Dutch palace) 2·75 9·50

SIX PIES

ആറു പൈ
(33)

1949. Surch as T **33**.
121 **29** 3p. on 9p. blue . . . . . 12·00 23·00
124a **30** 3p. on 9p. blue . . . . . 2·75 50
126 6p. on 9p. blue . . . . . 1·75 40
119 **28** 6p. on 1a.3p. mauve . . . 5·50 4·50
122 **29** 6p. on 1a.3p. mauve . . . 16·00 15·00
120 1a. on 1a.9p. blue . . . . 2·25 1·40
123 1a. on 1a.9p. blue . . . . 3·50 2·25

1949. Surch **SIX PIES** or **NINE PIES** only.
127 **29** 6p. on 1a. orange . . . . 65·00 £150
128 9p. on 1a. orange . . . . 95·00 £150

OFFICIAL STAMPS

1913. Optd **ON C G S**.
O1 **8** 3p. blue £120 10
O2 4p. green . . . . 9·00 10
O3a 9p. red . . . . 15·00 10
O4 1½a. purple . . . . 48·00 10
O5 2a. grey . . . . 13·00 10
O6 3a. red . . . . 55·00 45
O7 6a. violet . . . . 60·00 2·00
O8 12a. blue . . . . 40·00 7·00
O9 1½r. green . . . . 35·00 75·00

1919. Optd **ON C G S**.
O10 **10** 4p. green . . . . 4·00 10
O11 6p. brown . . . . 12·00 10
O26 8p. brown . . . . 7·00 10
O13 9p. red . . . . 65·00 10
O27 10p. blue . . . . 6·00 10
O15 1½a. purple . . . . 5·50 10
O28 2a. grey . . . . 40·00 25
O17 2¼a. green . . . . 13·00 15
O29 3a. red . . . . 8·50 20
O19 6a. violet . . . . 38·00 50
O19a 12a. blue . . . . 15·00 5·00
O19b 1½r. green . . . . 25·00 £120

1923. Official stamps surch in figures and words.
O32 **10** 6p. on 8p. brown . . . . 2·50 10
O33 6p. on 10p. blue . . . . 4·00 10
O20b **8** 8p. on 9p. red £130 20
O21 **10** 8p. on 9p. red . . . . . 70·00 10
O23 **8** 10p. on 9p. red . . . . . £1200 15·00
O22 **10** 10p. on 9p. red . . . . . 80·00 1·00

1933. Optd **ON C G S**.
O34 **18** 4p. green . . . . 4·25 10
O35 6p. red . . . . 3·75 10
O52 1a. orange . . . . 1·00 10
O37 1a.8p. red . . . . 1·50 30
O38 2a. grey . . . . 18·00 10
O39 2¼a. green . . . . 6·00 10
O53 3a. orange . . . . 3·00 1·75
O41 3a.4p. violet . . . . . . 1·50 15
O42 6a.8p. sepia . . . . . . 1·50 20
O43 10a. blue . . . . 1·50 1·00

1943. Official stamp surch **NINE PIES**.
O57 **10** 9p. on 1½a. purple . . . . £650 27·00

1943. Official stamps surch **SURCHARGED** and value in words.
O63 **18** 3p. on 4p. green . . . . . £170 60·00
O58 3p. on 1a.8p. red . . . . 5·50 30·00
O66 1a.3p. on 1a. orange . . . £300 £100
O61 1a.9p. on 1a.8p. red . . . 1·50 40

1943. Official stamps surch in words.
O62 **18** 3p. on 4p. green . . . . . 30·00 11·00
O64 3p. on 1a. orange . . . . 2·25 3·75
O65 9p. on 1a. orange . . . . £275 55·00
O59 9p. on 1a.8p. red . . . . £130 30·00
O60 1a.9p. on 1a.8p. red . . . 2·75 2·75

1944. Optd **ON C G S**.
O68 **26** 4p. green . . . . 40·00 7·00
O69b 6p. brown . . . . 1·00 10
O70 1a. orange . . . . £3000 60·00
O71 2a. black . . . . 7·00 1·00
O72 2¼a. green . . . . 4·25 1·10
O73a 3a. red . . . . 9·50 40

1944. Official stamps surch **SURCHARGED** and value in words.
O75 **26** 3p. on 4p. green . . . . . 5·00 40
O78 9p. on 6p. brown . . . . 4·50 40
O80 1a.3p. on 1a. orange . . . 3·75 10

1944. Official stamps surch in words.
O74 **26** 3p. on 4p. green . . . . . 3·50 10
O76 3p. on 1a. orange . . . . 26·00 7·50
O77 9p. on 6p. brown . . . . 11·00 3·50
O79 1a.3p. on 1a. orange . . . 13·00 2·75

1946. Optd **ON C G S**.
O81 **28** 9p. blue . . . . 3·00 10
O82 1a.3p. mauve . . . . . . 1·60 20
O83 1a.9p. blue . . . . 40 1·00

1948. Optd **ON C G S**.
O84 **29** 3p. red . . . . 1·25 10
O85 4p. green . . . . 30·00 7·00
O86 6p. brown . . . . 14·00 1·75
O87 9p. blue 75 10
O88 1a.3p. mauve . . . . . . 4·00 1·40
O89 1a.9p. blue . . . . 4·75 40
O90 2a. black . . . . 14·00 3·00
O91 2¼a. green . . . . 23·00 5·00

1949. Optd **ON C G S**.
O92 **30** 3p. red . . . . 1·25 15
O93 4p. green . . . . 1·50 40
O94 6p. brown . . . . 2·75 30
O95 9p. blue . . . . 3·25 10
O96 2a. black . . . . 2·75 15
O97 2¼a. green . . . . 3·25 6·50
O98 3a. orange . . . . 1·10 1·00
O99 3a.4p. violet . . . . . . 45·00 45·00

1949. Official stamps surch as T **33**.
O103 **30** 6p. on 3p. red . . . . . . 1·25 75
O104 9p. on 4p. green . . . . 75 3·00
O100 **28** 1a. on 1a.9p. blue . . . 60 70
O101 **29** 1a. on 1a.9p. blue . . . 23·00 17·00

1949. Optd **SERVICE**.
O105 **30** 3p. on 9p. (No. 125) . . 60 80

For later issues see **TRAVANCORE-COCHIN**.

COCHIN-CHINA Pt. 6

A former French colony in the extreme S. of Indo-China, subsequently incorporated into French Indo-China.

100 centimes = 1 franc.

1886. Stamps of French Colonies surch.
1 **J** 5 on 25c. brown on yellow . . £160 £120
2 5 on 2c. brown on yellow . . . 20·00 18·00
3 5 on 25c. brown on yellow . . . 23·00 15·00
4 5 on 25c. black on red . . . . 30·00 50·00
Nos. 1 and 4 are surcharged with numeral only; Nos. 2 and 3 are additionally optd **C. CH.**

COCOS (KEELING) ISLANDS Pt. 1

Islands in the Indian Ocean formerly administered by Singapore and transferred to Australian administration on 23 November 1955.

1963. 12 pence = 1 shilling;
20 shillings = 1 pound.
1966. 100 cents = 1 dollar (Australian).

5 Jukong (sailboat)

6 White Tern

1963.
1 – 3d. brown . . . . 1·00 1·50
2 – 5d. blue . . . . 1·50 80
3 – 8d. red . . . . 1·00 1·75
4 – 1s. green . . . . 1·00 75
5 **5** 2s. purple . . . . 9·00 2·75
6 **6** 2s.3d. green . . . . 12·00 2·75
DESIGNS—HORIZ (As Type **5**): 3d. Copra industry; 1s. Palms. (As Type **6**): 5d. Lockheed Super Constellation airliner. VERT (As Type **5**): 8d. Map of islands.

1965. 50th Anniv of Gallipoli Landing. As T **184** of Australia, but slightly larger (22 × 34½ mm).
7 5d. brown, black and green . . 60 45

With the introduction of decimal currency on 14 February 1966, Australian stamps were used in Cocos Islands until the 1969 issue.

7 Reef Clam

9 "Dragon", 1609

1969. Decimal Currency. Multicoloured.
8 1c. Lajonkaines turbo shell (vert) 30 60
9 2c. Elongate or small giant clam (vert) 75 80
10 3c. Type **7** 40 20
11 4c. Floral blenny (fish) 30 50
12 5c. "Porites cocosensis" (coral) 35 30
13 6c. Atrisignis flyingfish 75 75
14 10c. Buff-banded rail 75 70
15 15c. Java sparrow 75 30
16 20c. Red-tailed tropic bird . . 75 30
17 30c. Sooty tern 75 30
18 50c. Reef heron (vert) 75 30
19 $1 Great frigate bird (vert) . . 1·50 75

1976. Ships. Multicoloured.
20 1c. Type **9** 30 40
21 2c. H.M.S. "Juno", 1857 (horiz) 30 40
22 5c. H.M.S. "Beagle", 1836 (horiz) 30 40
23 10c. H.M.A.S. "Sydney", 1914 (horiz) 35 40
24 15c. S.M.S. "Emden", 1914 (horiz) 60 55
25 20c. "Ayesha", 1907 (horiz) . . 60 65
26 25c. T.S.S. "Islander", 1927 . . 60 75
27 30c. M.V. "Cheshire", 1951 . . 60 75
28 35c. Jukong (sailboat) (horiz) . 60 75
29 40c. C.S. "Scotia", 1900 (horiz) 60 75
30 50c. R.M.S. "Orontes", 1929 . 60 75
31 $1 Royal Yacht "Gothic", 1954 . . . . 75 1·00

10 Map of Cocos (Keeling) Islands, Union Flag, Stars and Trees

1979. Inauguration of Independent Postal Service and First Statutory Council. Multicoloured.
32 20c. Type **10** 20 40
33 50c. Council seat and jukong (sailboat) 25 85

11 Forceps Fish

12 "Peace on Earth"

1979. Fishes. Multicoloured.
34 1c. Type **11** . . . . 30 1·00
35 2c. Ornate butterflyfish . . . 30 30
36 5c. Barbier . . . . 50 1·25
37 10c. Meyer's butterflyfish . . 30 1·25
38 15c. Pink wrasse 30 30
39 20c. Clark's anemonefish . . 40 30
39a 22c. Undulate triggerfish . . 45 30
40 25c. Red-breasted wrasse . . 40 1·25
40a 28c. Guineafowl wrasse . . . 35 35
41 30c. Madagascar butterflyfish 40 45
42 35c. Cocos-Keeling angelfish 40 1·75
43 40c. Coral hogfish . . . . . 45 1·00
44 50c. Clown wrasse 85 75
45 55c. Yellow-tailed tamarin . . 50 1·50
45a 60c. Greasy grouper 50 75
46 $1 Palette surgeonfish . . . . 60 3·50
47 $2 Melon butterflyfish . . . 70 3·50

1979. Christmas. Multicoloured.
48 25c. Type **12** 25 40
49 55c. Atoll seascape ("Goodwill") 40 70

13 Star, Map of Cocos (Keeling) Islands and Island Landscape

1980. Christmas. Multicoloured.
50 15c. Type **13** 10 10
51 28c. The Three Kings 15 15
52 60c. Adoration 40 40

14 "Administered by the British Government, 1857"

15 "Eye of the Wind" and Map of Cocos (Keeling) Islands

1980. 25th Anniv of Territorial Status under Australian Administration. Multicoloured.
53 22c. Type **14** 15 15
54 22c. Arms of Ceylon 15 15
55 22c. Arms of Straits Settlements 15 15
56 22c. Arms of Singapore . . . 15 15
57 22c. Arms and flag of Australia 15 15

1980. "Operation Drake" (round the world expedition) and 400th Anniv of Sir Francis Drake's Circumnavigation of the World. Multicoloured.
58 22c. Type **15** 25 15
59 28c. Routes map (horiz) . . . 25 15
60 35c. Sir Francis Drake and "Golden Hind" 25 15
61 60c. Prince Charles (patron) and "Eye of the Wind" (brigantine) 45 30

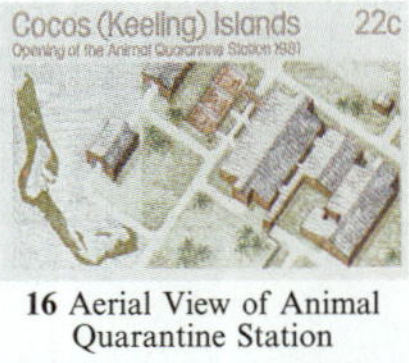

16 Aerial View of Animal Quarantine Station

1981. Opening of Animal Quarantine Station. Multicoloured.
62 22c. Type **16** 15 15
63 45c. Unloading livestock . . . 20 30
64 60c. Livestock in pen 20 35

17 Consolidated Catalina Flying Boat "Guba"

1981. Aircraft. Multicoloured.
65 22c. Type **17** 25 25
66 22c. Consolidated Liberator and Avro Lancastrian . . . 25 25
67 22c. Douglas DC-4 and Lockheed Constellation . . 25 25
68 22c. Lockheed Electra 25 25
69 22c. Boeing 727-100 airliners 25 25

18 Prince Charles and Lady Diana Spencer

1981. Royal Wedding.
70 **18** 24c. multicoloured 30 20
71 60c. multicoloured 50 60

19 "Angels we have heard on High"

1981. Christmas. Scenes and Lines from Carol "Angels we have heard on High". Multicoloured.
72 18c. Type **19** 10 10
73 30c. "Shepherds why this Jubilee?" 20 20
74 60c. "Come to Bethlehem and see Him" 35 35

20 "Pachyseris speciosa" and "Heliofungia actiniformis" (corals)

1981. 150th Anniv of Charles Darwin's Voyage. Multicoloured.
75 24c. Type **20** 25 15
76 45c. Charles Darwin in 1853 and "Pavona cactus" (coral) 40 30
77 60c. H.M.S. "Beagle", 1832, and "Lobophyllia hemprichii" (coral) 45 35
MS78 130 × 95 mm. 24c. Cross-section of West Island; 24c. Cross-section of Home Island 75 85

21 Queen Victoria

1982. 125th Anniv of Annexation of Cocos (Keeling) Islands to British Empire. Multicoloured.
79 24c. Type **21** 15 15
80 45c. Union flag 25 25
81 60c. Captain S. Fremantle (annexation visit, 1857) . . 30 35

22 Lord Baden-Powell

1982. 75th Anniv of Boy Scout Movement. Multicoloured.
82 27c. Type **22** 25 25
83 75c. "75" and map of Cocos (Keeling) Islands (vert) . . . 60 1·50

23 "Precis villida"

24 "Call His Name Immanuel"

1982. Butterflies and Moths. Multicoloured.
84 1c. Type **23** . . . . 1·00 60
85 2c. "Cephonodes picus" (horiz) 40 40
86 5c. "Macroglossum corythus" (horiz) . . . . 1·50 70
87 10c. "Chasmina candida" . . 40 40
88 20c. "Nagia linteola" (horiz) 40 65
89 25c. "Eublemma rivula" . . . 40 75
90 30c. "Eurrhyparodes tricoloralis" 40 65
91 35c. "Hippotion boerhaviae" (horiz) . . . . 1·50 75
92 40c. "Euploea core" 40 80
93 45c. "Psara hipponalis" (horiz) 50 80
94 50c. "Danaus chrysippus" (horiz) . . . . 60 1·25
95 55c. "Hypolimnas misippus" 60 70
96 60c. "Spodoptera litura" . . . 65 1·75
97 $1 "Achaea janata" . . . . . 2·75 2·75
98 $2 "Panacra velox" (horiz) . . 2·00 2·75
99 $3 "Utetheisa pulchelloides" (horiz) . . . . 2·75 2·75

1982. Christmas. Multicoloured.
100 21c. Type **24** 25 30
101 35c. "I bring you good tidings" 40 40
102 75c. "Arise and flee into Egypt" . . . . 1·00 1·25

25 "God will look after us" (Matt. 1:20)

26 Hari Raya Celebration

1983. Christmas. Extracts from New Testament. Multicoloured.
103 24c. Type **25** 30 45
104 24c. "Our baby King, Jesus" (Matthew. 2:2) 30 45
105 24c. "Your Saviour is born" (Luke. 2:11) 30 45
106 24c. "Wise men followed the Star" (Matthew. 2:9–10) . . 30 45
107 24c. "And worship the Lord" (Matthew. 2:11) 30 45

1984. Cocos-Malay Culture (1st series). Mult.
108 45c. Type **26** 45 35
109 75c. Melenggok dancing . . . 65 50
110 85c. Cocos-Malay wedding 75 55
See also Nos. 128/31.

27 Unpacking Barrel

1984. 75th Anniv of Cocos Barrel Mail. Multicoloured.
111 35c. Type **27** 40 25
112 55c. Jukong awaiting mail ship 75 50
113 70c. P & O mail ship "Morea" 85 55
MS114 125 × 95 mm. $1 Retrieving barrel . . . . 1·00 1·25

28 Captain William Keeling

29 Malay Settlement, Home Island

1984. 375th Anniv of Discovery of Cocos (Keeling) Islands. Multicoloured.
115 30c. Type **28** 60 40
116 65c. "Hector" . . . . 1·25 90
117 95c. Mariner's astrolabe . . . 1·50 1·25
118 $1.10 Map circa 1666 . . . . 1·60 1·50

1984. "Ausipex" International Stamp Exhibition, Melbourne. Multicoloured.
119 45c. Type **29** 75 50
120 55c. Airstrip, West Island . . 85 60
MS121 130 × 95 mm. $2 Jukongs (native craft) racing . . . . . 2·75 2·50

30 "Rainbow" Fish

32 Jukong-building

31 Cocos Islanders

1984. Christmas. Multicoloured.
122 24c. Type **30** 50 60
123 35c. "Rainbow" butterfly . . 1·10 1·40
124 55c. "Rainbow" bird . . . . 1·25 2·00

1984. Integration of Cocos (Keeling) Islands with Australia. Sheet 90 × 52 mm, containing T **31** and similar horiz design. Multicoloured.
MS125 30c. Type **31**; 30c. Australian flag on island . . . . 1·50 1·25

1985. Cocos-Malay Culture (2nd series). Handicrafts. Multicoloured.
126 30c. Type **32** 75 35
127 45c. Blacksmithing . . . . . 1·00 55
128 55c. Woodcarving . . . . . 1·25 65

33 C.S. "Scotia"

1985. Cable-laying Ships. Multicoloured.
129 33c. Type **33** . . . . 1·50 40
130 65c. C.S. "Anglia" . . . . . 2·25 1·60
131 80c. C.S. "Patrol" . . . . . 2·25 2·25

34 Red-footed Booby

35 Mantled Top

1985. Birds of Cocos (Keeling) Islands. Mult.
132 33c. Type **34** . . . . 1·75 2·25
133 60c. Nankeen night heron (juvenile) (horiz) . . . . . 2·00 2·50
134 $1 Buff-banded rail (horiz) 2·25 2·50
Nos. 132/4 were issued together, se-tenant, forming a composite design.

1985. Shells and Molluscs. Multicoloured.
135 1c. Type **35** . . . . 60 1·25
136 2c. Rang's nerite . . . . . . 60 1·25
137 3c. Jewel box . . . . 60 1·25
138 4c. Money cowrie . . . . . . 1·00 1·25
139 5c. Purple Pacific drupe . . . 60 1·25
140 10c. Soldier cone . . . . . . 70 1·25
141 15c. Merlin-spike auger . . . 2·00 1·25
142 20c. Pacific strawberry cockle 2·00 1·50
143 30c. Lajonkaire's turban . . 2·00 1·50
144 33c. Reticulate mitre . . . . 2·25 1·50
145 40c. Common spider conch 2·25 1·50
146 50c. Fluted giant clam or scaled tridacna . . . . . . 2·25 1·75
147 60c. Minstrel cowrie . . . . 2·25 2·25
148 $1 Varicose nudibranch . . . 3·25 3·25
149 $2 Tesselated nudibranch . . 3·50 4·25
150 $3 Hamincea cymballum . . 4·25 4·75

36 Night Sky and Palm Trees

1985. Christmas. Sheet 121 × 88 mm, containing T **36** and similar horiz designs.
MS151 27c. × 4 multicoloured 2·00 2·75
The stamps within No. **MS**151 show a composite design of the night sky seen through a grove of palm trees. The position of the face value on the four stamps varies. Type **36** shows the top left design. The top right stamp shows the face value at bottom right, the bottom left at top left and the bottom right at top right.

37 Charles Darwin, c. 1840

38 Coconut Palm and Holly Sprigs

1986. 150th Anniv of Charles Darwin's Visit. Multicoloured.
152 33c. Type **37** 70 60
153 60c. Map of H.M.S. "Beagle's" route, Australia to Cocos Islands . . . . . 1·25 2·25
154 $1 H.M.S. "Beagle" . . . . 1·75 2·75

1986. Christmas. Multicoloured.
155 30c. Type **38** 60 70
156 90c. Nautilus shell and Christmas tree bauble . . . 2·00 3·00
157 $1 Tropical fish and bell . . 2·00 3·00

39 Jukong

1987. Sailing Craft. Multicoloured.
158 36c. Type **39** . . . . 1·10 1·60
159 36c. Ocean racing yachts . . 1·10 1·60
160 36c. "Sarimanok" (replica of early dhow) . . . . 1·10 1·60
161 36c. "Ayesha" (schooner) . . 1·10 1·60
Nos. 158/61 were printed together, se-tenant, each strip forming a composite background design.

40 Beach, Direction Island

1987. Cocos Islands Scenes. Multicoloured.
162 70c. Type **40** . . . . 1·40 1·40
163 90c. Palm forest, West Island 1·75 2·00
164 $1 Golf course . . . . 2·75 3·00

41 Radio Transmitter and Palm Trees at Sunset

1987. Communications. Multicoloured.
165 70c. Type **41** . . . . 1·25 1·50
166 75c. Boeing 727-100 airliner at terminal . . . . 1·50 1·75
167 90c. "Intelsat 5" satellite . . 1·75 2·25
168 $1 Airmail letter and globe 2·00 2·25

42 Batik Printing

1987. Cocos (Keeling) Islands Malay Industries. Multicoloured.
169 45c. Type **42** . . . . 1·25 1·50
170 65c. Jukong building . . . . 1·75 2·00
171 75c. Copra production . . . 2·00 2·25

43 Hands releasing Peace Dove and Map of Islands

44 Coconut Flower

1987. Christmas. Multicoloured.
172 30c. Type **43** 40 40
173 90c. Local children at Christmas party . . . . . 1·25 1·90
174 $1 Island family and Christmas star . . . . . . 1·50 1·90

1988. Bicentenary of Australian Settlement. Arrival of First Fleet. As Nos. 1105/9 of Australia but each inscr "COCOS (KEELING) ISLANDS" and "AUSTRALIA BICENTENARY".
175 37c. Aborigines watching arrival of Fleet, Botany Bay . . . . 2·00 2·00
176 37c. Aboriginal family and anchored ships . . . . . . 2·00 2·00
177 37c. Fleet arriving at Sydney Cove . . . . 2·00 2·00
178 37c. Ship's boat . . . . . . 2·00 2·00
179 37c. Raising the flag, Sydney Cove, 26 January 1788 . . 2·00 2·00
Nos. 175/9 were printed together, se-tenant, forming a composite design.

1988. Life Cycle of the Coconut. Multicoloured.
180 37c. Type **44** 50 40
181 65c. Immature nuts . . . . . 75 1·00
182 90c. Coconut palm and mature nuts . . . . 1·10 1·75
183 $1 Seedlings . . . . 1·25 1·75
MS184 102 × 91 mm. Nos. 180/3 . . 4·00 4·50

45 Copra 3d. Stamp of 1963

46 "Pisonia grandis"

1988. 25th Anniv of First Cocos (Keeling) Islands Stamps. Each showing stamp from 1963 definitive set.
185 **45** 37c. green, black and blue 1·25 1·25
186 – 55c. green, black and brown . . . . 1·75 1·50
187 – 65c. blue, black and lilac 1·90 2·50
188 – 70c. red, black and grey . . 1·90 2·50
189 – 90c. purple, black and grey 2·25 2·75
190 – $1 green, black and brown 2·25 2·75
DESIGNS: 55c. Palms 1s.; 65c. Lockheed Super Constellation airplane 5d.; 70c. Map 8d.; 90c. "Jukong" (sailboat) 2s.; $1 White tern 2s.3d.

1988. Flora. Multicoloured.
191 1c. Type **46** 50 80
192 2c. "Cocos nucifera" 50 80
193 5c. "Morinda citrifolia" . . . 1·00 90
194 10c. "Cordia subcordata" . . 70 90
195 30c. "Argusia argentea" . . . 1·00 1·25
196 37c. "Calophyllum inophyllum" . . . . 1·50 1·00
197 40c. "Barringtonia asiatica" 1·00 1·25
198 50c. "Caesalpinia bonduc" . . 1·25 3·00
199 90c. "Terminalia catappa" . . 1·75 4·00
200 $1 "Pemphis acidula" . . . . 1·75 2·50
201 $2 "Scaevola sericea" . . . . 2·50 2·50
202 $3 "Hibiscus tiliaceus" . . . 3·50 3·75

1988. "Sydpex '88" National Stamp Exhibition, Sydney. Sheet 78 × 85 mm. Multicoloured.
MS203 As No. 202 . . . . . . 4·25 5·00

47 Beach at Sunset

1988. Christmas.
204 **47** 32c. multicoloured 80 50
205 90c. multicoloured . . . . 1·75 2·75
206 $1 multicoloured . . . . 2·00 2·75

48 Captain P. G. Taylor

49 Jukong and Star

1989. 50th Anniv of First Indian Ocean Aerial Survey.
207 **48** 40c. multicoloured 80 60
208 – 70c. multicoloured . . . . 1·75 2·50
209 – $1 multicoloured . . . . . 2·00 2·50
210 – $1.10 blue, lilac and black 2·25 2·75

DESIGNS: 70c. Consolidated Catalina flying boat "Guba" and crew; $1 "Guba" over Direction Islands; $1.10, Unissued Australia 5s. stamp commemorating flight.

1989. Christmas.
211 **49** 35c. multicoloured 80 60
212 80c. multicoloured . . . . 2·50 3·00
213 $1.10 multicoloured . . . 2·50 3·00

50 H.M.A.S. "Sydney" (cruiser)

1989. 75th Anniv of Destruction of German Cruiser "Emden". Multicoloured.
214 40c. Type **50** . . . . 1·75 1·75
215 70c. "Emden" . . . . 2·00 2·00
216 $1 "Emden's" steam launch 2·25 2·25
217 $1.10 H.M.A.S. "Sydney" (1914) and crest . . . . 2·25 2·25
MS218 145 × 90 mm. Nos. 214/7 7·50 7·50

51 Xanthid Crab

1990. Cocos Islands Crabs. Multicoloured.
219 45c. Type **51** . . . . 1·75 75
220 75c. Ghost crab . . . . . . 2·50 2·00
221 $1 Red-backed mud crab . . 2·75 2·25
222 $1.30 Coconut crab (vert) . . 3·00 3·00

52 Captain Keeling and "Hector", 1609

1990. Navigators of the Pacific.
223 **52** 45c. mauve . . . . . . 2·75 1·25
224 – 75c. mauve and blue . . . 3·00 3·25
225 – $1 mauve and stone . . . 3·50 3·75
226 – $1.30 mauve and buff . . 4·25 5·00
DESIGNS: 75c. Captain Fitzroy and H.M.S. "Beagle", 1836; $1 Captain Belcher and H.M.S. "Samarang", 1846; $1.30, Captain Fremantle and H.M.S. "Juno", 1857.

1990. "New Zealand 1990" International Stamp Exhibition, Auckland. No. 188 optd with logo and **NEW ZEALAND 1990 24 AUG 2 SEP AUCKLAND**.
228 70c. red, black and grey . . 4·25 4·00
MS229 127 × 90 mm. As Nos. 194, 199 and 201, but self-adhesive 8·00 8·00

1990. No. 187 surch **$5**.
230 $5 on 65c. blue, black and lilac . . . . 18·00 18·00

55 Cocos Atoll from West and Star

58 Beaded Sea Star

1990. Christmas. Multicoloured.
231 40c. Type **55** . . . . 80 1·25
232 70c. Cocos atoll from south 1·75 2·75
233 $1.30 Cocos atoll from east 3·00 3·50

1990. Nos. 140/1, 143 and 146/7 surch **POSTAGE PAID** plus additional words as indicated.
236 (1c.) on 30c. Lajonkaire's turban (**LOCAL**) . . . . 2·00 2·75
235 (43c.) on 10c. Soldier cone (**MAINLAND**) . . . . . 1·40 2·00
237 70c. on 60c. Minstrel cowrie (**ZONE 1**) . . . . . . 1·50 2·75
238 80c. on 50c. Fluted giant clam or scaled tridacna (**ZONE 2**) . . . . . . 1·75 3·50
239 $1.20 on 15c. Marlin-spike auger (**ZONE 5**) . . . . . 2·00 3·75

1991. Starfish and Sea Urchins. Multicoloured.
240 45c. Type **58** . . . . 1·25 75
241 75c. Feather star . . . . . 2·00 2·25
242 $1 Slate pencil urchin . . . 2·00 2·25
243 $1.30 Globose sea urchin . . 2·75 3·25

59 Cocos Islands

1991. Malay Hari Raya Festival. Multicoloured.
244 45c. Type **59** . . . . 1·00 65
245 75c. Island house . . . . . 1·75 2·25
246 $1.30 Islands scene . . . . . 2·50 3·25

60 Child praying

1991. Christmas. Multicoloured.
247 38c. Type **60** . . . . 1·25 80
248 43c. Child dreaming of Christmas Day . . . . . . 1·25 80
249 $1 Child singing . . . . . . 2·50 2·50
250 $1.20 Child fascinated by decorations . . . . 2·75 4·00
MS251 118 × 74 mm. 38c., 43c., $1, $1.20, Local children's choir 7·00 8·00
The four values in No. **MS**251 form a composite design.

61 "Lybia tessellata"

1992. Crustaceans. Multicoloured.
252 5c. Type **61** . . . . 90 1·10
253 10c. "Pilodius areolatus" . . 1·40 1·40
254 20c. "Trizopagurus strigatus" 1·60 1·60
255 30c. "Lophozozymus pulchellus" . . . . 2·00 2·00
256 40c. "Thalamitoides quadridens" . . . . 2·00 2·00
257 45c. "Calcinus elegans" (vert) 2·00 2·00
258 50c. "Clibarius humilis" . . . 2·25 2·25
259 60c. "Trapezia rufopunctata" (vert) . . . . 2·50 2·50
260 80c. "Pylopaguropsis magnimanus" (vert) . . 2·75 3·00
261 $1 "Trapezia ferruginea" (vert) . . . . 2·75 3·00
262 $2 "Trapezia guttata" (vert) 3·75 4·50
263 $3 "Trapezia cymodoce" (vert) . . . . 4·25 4·50

62 "Santa Maria"

64 R.A.F. Supermarine Spitfires on Island Airstrip

63 Buff-banded Rail searching for Food

1992. 500th Anniv of Discovery of America by Columbus.
264 **62** $1.05 multicoloured . . . 3·00 3·50

1992. Endangered Species. Buff-banded Rail. Mult.
265 10c. Type **63** 70 85
266 15c. Banded rail with chick 90 1·10
267 30c. Two rails drinking . . . 1·25 1·40
268 45c. Rail and nest . . . . . 1·50 1·60
MS269 165 × 78 mm. 45c. Two rails by pool; 85c. Chick hatching; $1.20, Head of rail . . . . . . 9·00 9·00

1992. 50th Anniv of Second World War. Mult.
270 45c. Type **64** . . . . 2·50 1·40
271 85c. Mitsubishi A6M Zero-Sen aircraft bombing Kampong . . . . 3·75 3·75
272 $1.20 R.A.F. Short Sunderland flying boat . . 4·75 5·00

65 Waves breaking on Reef

66 "Lobophyllia hemprichii"

1992. Christmas. Multicoloured.
273 40c. Type **65** . . . . 1·50 80
274 80c. Direction Island . . . . 3·25 3·50
275 $1 Moorish idols (fish) and coral . . . . 3·25 3·50

1993. Corals. Multicoloured.
276 45c. Type **66** 75 55
277 85c. "Pocillopora eydouxi" 1·25 1·75
278 $1.05 "Fungia scutaria" . . 1·75 2·00
279 $1.20 "Sarcophyton sp" . . . 1·75 2·25

67 Plastic 5r. Token

68 Primary School Pupil

1993. Early Cocos (Keeling) Islands Currency. Multicoloured.
280 45c. Type **67** . . . . 1·60 80
281 85c. 1968 1r. plastic token . . 2·25 2·50
282 $1.05 1977 150r. commemorative gold coin 2·75 3·00
283 $1.20 1910 plastic token . . . 2·75 3·50

1993. Education. Multicoloured.
284 5c. Type **68** 50 85
285 45c. Secondary school pupil 1·25 60
286 85c. Learning traditional crafts . . . . 2·25 2·25
287 $1.05 Learning office skills 2·75 3·50
288 $1.20 Seaman training . . . 3·25 3·75

69 Lifeboat and Crippled Yacht

1993. Air-Sea Rescue. Multicoloured.
289 45c. Type **69** . . . . 2·50 1·40
290 85c. Israeli Aircraft Industry Westwind Seascan (aircraft) 3·50 3·75
291 $1.05 "R.J. Hawke" (ferry) 4·00 5·00
MS292 135 × 61 mm. Nos. 289/91 10·00 11·00

70 Peace Doves

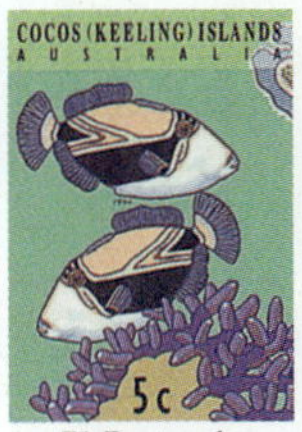

71 Rectangle Triggerfish and Coral

1993. Christmas.
293 **70** 40c. multicoloured . . . . 1·75 80
294 80c. multicoloured . . . . 3·00 3·50
295 $1 multicoloured . . . . . 3·00 3·50

1994. Transfer of Postal Service to Australia Post. Multicoloured.
296 5c. Type **71** 35 45
297 5c. Three rectangle triggerfish and map section 35 45
298 5c. Two rectangle triggerfish and map section 35 45
299 5c. Two rectangle triggerfish, map section and red coral 35 45
300 5c. Rectangle triggerfish with red and brown corals . . . 35 45
301 10c. Green turtles on beach 35 45
302 10c. Two green turtles . . . 35 45
303 10c. Crowd of young green turtles 35 45
304 10c. Green turtle and map section 35 45
305 10c. Green turtle, pyramid butterflyfish and map section 35 45
306 20c. Three pyramid butterflyfish and map section 55 65
307 20c. Pyramid butterflyfish with brown coral 55 65
308 20c. Two pyramid butterflyfish and coral . . 55 65

309	20c. Three pyramid butterflyfish and coral	55	65
310	20c. Coral, pyramid butterflyfish and map section	55	65
311	45c. Jukongs with map of airport	60	70
312	45c. Two jukongs with red or blue sails and map section	60	70
313	45c. Jukong in shallows	60	70
314	45c. Two jukongs with red or yellow sails and map section	60	70
315	45c. Two jukongs, one with blue jib, and map section	60	70

Nos. 296/315 were printed together, se-tenant, with the backgrounds forming a composite map.

72 Prabu Abjasa Puppet

73 Angel playing Harp

1994. Shadow Puppets. Multicoloured.

316	45c. Type **72**	65	50
317	90c. Prabu Pandu	1·25	1·50
318	$1 Judistra	1·40	1·50
319	$1.35 Abimanju	1·50	2·50

1994. Seasonal Festivals. Multicoloured.

320	40c. Type **73**	50	50
321	45c. Wise Man holding gift	55	50
322	80c. Mosque at night	1·00	1·75

74 White-tailed Tropic Bird and Blue-faced Booby ("Masked Booby")

1995. Sea-birds of North Keeling Island. Multicoloured.

323	45c. Type **74**	75	50
324	85c. Great frigate bird and white tern	1·00	1·50
MS325	106 × 70 mm. Nos. 323/4	1·75	2·50

75 Yellow Crazy Ant

76 Saddle Butterflyfish

1995. Insects. Multicoloured.

326	45c. Type **75**	1·00	1·25
327	45c. Aedes mosquito	1·00	1·25
328	45c. Hawk moth	1·00	1·25
329	45c. Scarab beetle	1·00	1·25
330	45c. Lauxaniid fly	1·00	1·25
331	$1.20 Common eggfly (butterfly)	1·50	1·75

Nos. 326/30 were printed together, se-tenant, forming a composite design.

1995. Marine Life. Multicoloured.

332	5c. Redspot wrasse	10	10
333	30c. Blue-throated triggerfish ("Gilded triggerfish")	20	25
334	40c. Type **76**	30	35
335	45c. Arc-eyed hawkfish	60	60
335a	45c. Wideband fusilier	30	35
335b	45c. Striped surgeonfish	30	35
335c	45c. Orangeband surgeonfish	30	35
335d	45c. Indo-Pacific sergeant	30	35
335e	70c. Crowned squirrelfish	50	55
336	75c. Orange-pine unicornfish	55	60
337	80c. Blue tang	60	65
338	85c. Juvenile twin-spotted wrasse ("Humpback wrasse")	60	65
339	90c. Threadfin butterflyfish	65	70
339a	95c. Sixstripe wrasse	70	75
340	$1 Bluestripe snapper	70	75
341	$1.05 Longnosed butterflyfish	75	80
342	$1.20 Freckled hawkfish	85	90
343	$2 Powder-blue surgeonfish	1·40	1·50
343a	$5 Goldback anthias	3·50	3·75

77 Members of Malay Community

78 Black Rhinoceros with Calf

1996. Hari Raya Puasa Festival. Multicoloured.

344	45c. Type **77**	65	60
345	75c. Beating drums	1·25	1·75
346	85c. Preparing festival meal	1·25	1·75

1996. Cocos Quarantine Station. Multicoloured.

347	45c. Type **78**	2·00	1·25
348	50c. Alpacas	1·25	1·50
349	$1.05 Boran cattle	2·00	2·50
350	$1.20 Ostrich with chicks	2·50	3·00

79 Dancers and Tambourine

80 "Wrapped Present" (Lazina Brian)

1997. Hari Raya Puasa Festival. Multicoloured.

351	45c. Type **79**	65	60
352	75c. Girl clapping and sailing dinghies	1·00	1·60
353	85c. Dancers on beach and food	1·25	1·60

1998. Hari Raya Puasa Festival. Paintings by children. Multicoloured.

354	45c. Type **80**	80	90
355	45c. "Mosque" (Azran Jim)	80	90
356	45c. "Cocos Malay Woman" (Kate Gossage)	80	90
357	45c. "Yacht" (Matt Harber)	80	90
358	45c. "People dancing" (Rakin Chongkin)	80	90

81 Preparing Food on Beach

1999. Hari Raya Puasa Festival. Multicoloured.

359	45c. Type **81**	65	75
360	45c. Woman with child and jukongs on beach	65	75
361	45c. Jukongs and palm fronds	65	75
362	45c. Two men watching jukongs	65	75
363	45c. Jukong and white flowers	65	75

82 Jukong (Cocos sailing boat)

1999. Island Wildlife. Multicoloured.

364	5c. Type **82**	50	60
365	5c. Bennett's and ornate butterflyfish	50	60
366	5c. Green and hawksbill turtles	50	60
367	5c. Yellow-tailed anemonefish and various butterflyfish	50	60
368	5c. Hump-headed wrasse	50	60
369	10c. Yacht, Direction Island	50	60
370	10c. Black-backed butterflyfish	50	60
371	10c. Moorish idols	50	60
372	10c. "Pseudoanthias cooperi" (fish)	50	60
373	10c. Red-tailed tropic birds	50	60
374	25c. Blue-faced booby	65	75
375	25c. Lesser wanderer (butterfly)	65	75
376	25c. Lesser and greater frigate birds	65	75
377	25c. "Hippotion velox" (moth)	65	75
378	25c. Common eggfly (butterfly)	65	75
379	45c. White tern	75	85
380	45c. Red-tailed tropic bird and great frigate bird	75	85
381	45c. Chinese rose	75	85
382	45c. Meadow argus (butterfly)	75	85
383	45c. Sea hibiscus	75	85

Nos. 364/83 were printed together, se-tenant, with the backgrounds forming a composite design.

83 Ratma Anthoney

2000. New Millennium. "Face of Cocos (Keeling) Islands". Multicoloured.

384	45c. Type **83**	60	70
385	45c. Nakia Haji Dolman (schoolgirl)	60	70
386	45c. Muller Eymin (elderly man)	60	70
387	45c. Courtney Press (toddler)	60	70
388	45c. Mhd Abu-Yazid (school boy)	60	70

84 Little Nipper (crab)

2000. Endangered Species. Crabs of Cocos (Keeling) Islands. Multicoloured.

389	5c. Type **84**	25	35
390	5c. Purple crab	25	35
391	45c. Smooth-handed ghost crab	55	65
392	45c. Horn-eyed ghost crab	55	65

85 Loggerhead Turtle

2002. Turtles. Multicoloured.

393	45c. Type **85**	95	95
394	45c. Hawksbill turtle	95	95
395	45c. Leatherback turtle	95	95
396	45c. Green turtle	95	95

86 Eastern Reef Egret

2003. Shoreline Birds. Multicoloured.

397	50c. Type **86**	1·10	1·10
398	50c. Sooty tern	1·10	1·10
399	50c. Ruddy turnstone	1·10	1·10
400	50c. Whimbrel	1·10	1·10

Nos. 397/400 were printed together, se-tenant, forming a composite background design of a shoreline.

87 Queen Elizabeth II and Cocos Malay Musicians

2004. 50th Anniv of Royal Tour to Australia. Visit of Queen Elizabeth II to Cocos (Keeling) Islands. Multicoloured.

401	50c. Type **87**	1·00	1·00
402	50c. Queen and *Gothic* (liner acting as Royal Yacht)	1·00	1·00
403	$1 Queen and Clunies Ross (Oceania) House	1·75	1·75
404	$1.45 Queen and model jukong (Cocos sailing boat)	2·00	2·00
MS405	135 × 72 mm. Nos. 401/4	5·25	5·25

88 Blacktip Reef Shark

2005. Reef Sharks. Multicoloured.

406	50c. Type **88**	1·00	1·00
407	50c. Two Grey reef sharks	1·00	1·00
408	$1 Two Blacktip reef sharks near atoll	1·75	1·75
409	$1.45 Grey reef shark	2·00	2·00

89 Frigate Bird

2006. Coral Reefs. Multicoloured.

410	10c. Type **89**	15	15
411	10c. Booby	15	15
412	10c. Sooty terns	15	15
413	10c. White terns	15	15
414	10c. Rufous night-heron	15	15
415	25c. Threadfin butterflyfish	35	35
416	25c. Saddle butterflyfish	35	35
417	25c. Orangeband surgeonfish	35	35
418	25c. Manta ray	35	35
419	25c. Scrawled butterflyfish	35	35
420	25c. Blue tang	35	35
421	25c. Picasso triggerfish and wrasse	35	35
422	25c. Turtle	35	35
423	25c. Moorish Idol	35	35
424	25c. Longnose butterflyfish	35	35
425	50c. Seychelles butterflyfish	65	65
426	50c. Powderblue surgeonfish	65	65
427	50c. Orange-lined triggerfish and starfish	65	65
428	50c. Unidentified striped fish	65	65
429	50c. Bicoloured angelfish	65	65

Nos. 410/29 were printed together, se-tenant, forming a composite background design showing a coral reef and atoll.

90 Oriental Moonsnail

2007. Living Shells. Multicoloured.

430	50c. Type **90**	70	70
431	50c. Pearly nautilus	70	70
432	$1 Partridge tun	1·40	1·40
433	$1.45 Giant clam	2·00	2·00

91 Chinese Pond Heron

2008. Visiting Birds. Multicoloured.

434	50c. Type **91**	65	65
435	50c. Black-winged stilt	65	65
436	$1 White-breasted waterhen	1·40	1·40
437	$1.45 Saunders' tern	2·00	2·00

OFFICIAL STAMPS

1991. No. 182 surch **OFFICIAL PAID MAINLAND.**

O1	(43c.) on 90c. Coconut palm and mature nuts	†	90·00

No. O1 was not sold to the public in unused condition.

COLOMBIA — Pt. 20

A republic in the N.W. of South America. Formerly part of the Spanish Empire, Colombia became independent in 1819. The constituent states became the Granadine Confederation in 1858. The name was changed to the United States of New Granada in 1861, and the name Colombia was adopted later the same year.

100 centavos = 1 peso.

Prices. For the early issues prices in the used column are for postmarked copies, pen-cancellations are generally worth less.

1

3

1859. Imperf.

1	1	2½c. green	70·00	80·00
2		5c. blue	70·00	70·00
8		5c. slate	55·00	45·00
9		10c. yellow	45·00	40·00
5		20c. blue	70·00	48·00
6		1p. red	48·00	80·00

1861. Imperf.

11	3	2½c. black	£1000	£400
12		5c. yellow	£160	£120
13		10c. blue	£650	£120
14		20c. red	£350	£150
15		1p. red	£800	£250

4 5 6

1862. Imperf.

16	4	10c. blue	£140	70·00
17		20c. red	—	£500
18		50c. green	£100	85·00
19		1p. lilac	£350	£225

1862. Imperf.

21	5	5c. orange	55·00	42·00
24		10c. blue	90·00	13·50
23		20c. red	£130	35·00
25		50c. green	£150	£110

1863. Imperf.

26	6	5c. orange	42·00	32·00
27		10c. blue	32·00	13·50
28		20c. red	65·00	32·00
29		50c. green	55·00	32·00
30		1p. mauve	£275	£110

7 8 9

1865. Imperf.

31	7	1c. red	8·00	8·00
32	8	2½c. black on lilac	20·00	13·50
33	9	5c. orange	35·00	17·00
34		10c. violet	40·00	6·00
35		20c. blue	45·00	13·50
37		50c. green	60·00	32·00
38		1p. red	70·00	13·50

10 12 19

1865. Imperf.

39	10	25c. black on blue	45·00	35·00
40		50c. black on yellow	35·00	40·00
41		1p. black on red	£110	£100

1866. Imperf. Various Arms Designs.

44	12	5c. orange	42·00	25·00
45	–	10c. lilac	13·00	6·00
46	–	20c. blue	27·00	15·00
47	–	50c. green	10·50	10·50
48	–	1p. red	60·00	20·00
49	–	5p. black on green	—	£130
50	–	10p. black on red	£275	£120

1868. Arms (various frames) inscr "ESTADOS UNIDOS DE COLOMBIA". Imperf.

51	19	5c. yellow	60·00	42·00
52		10c. lilac	1·25	70
54		20c. blue	1·25	45
55		50c. green	1·25	85
57		1p. red	3·00	1·25

24 25

26 27

28 30

1869. Imperf.

58	24	2½c. black on violet	3·50	1·40

1870. Imperf.

59a	25	1c. green	3·00	2·10
60		1c. red	2·10	2·10
61	26	2c. brown	45	45
62	27	5c. orange	55	35
65a	28	10c. mauve	55	25
67		25c. black on blue	6·50	6·00
87		25c. green	15·00	15·00

1870. Different frames. Imperf.

69	30	5p. black on green	5·00	4·25
71		10p. black on red	5·50	3·25

See also Nos. 118/19.

32 Andean Condor 33 35

1876. Imperf.

84	32	5c. violet	5·75	1·90
85	33	10c. brown	90	25
86	–	20c. blue	1·10	35

DESIGN: 20c. As Type 33 but with different frame.

1881. Imperf.

93	35	1c. green	2·75	1·75
99		2c. red	80	65
100		5c. blue	1·75	45
101		10c. purple	1·25	85
97		20c. black	1·40	55

39 40

1881. Imperf.

102	39	1c. black on green	1·25	1·25
103		2c. black on rose	1·25	1·25
104		5c. black on lilac	1·75	75

1883. Inscr "CORREOS NACIONALES DE LOS E.E. U.U. DE COLOMBIA".

106a	40	1c. yellow on green	35	35
107		2c. red on pink	45	45
109		5c. blue on blue	45	25
111		10c. orange on yellow	25	25
112		20c. mauve on lilac	35	35
113		50c. brown on buff	90	90
114		1p. red on blue	3·00	55
115		5p. brown on yellow	2·50	2·25
116		10p. black on red	5·50	6·50

1886. Perf.

118	30	5p. brown	1·25	1·00
119		10p. black on lilac	1·25	1·00

42 43 Gen. Sucre

44 Bolivar 46 Gen. Nerino

1886.

120	42	1c. green	1·75	60
121	43	2c. red on pink	75	75
124	44	5c. blue on blue	2·10	15
125	–	10c. orange (Pres. Nunez)	1·40	25
126	46	20c. violet on lilac ("REPULICA")	90	35
137		20c. violet on lilac ("REPUBLICA")	1·10	50
130	42	50c. brown on buff	40	45
132		1p. mauve	2·10	1·00
133		5p. brown	8·50	5·00
134		5p. black	10·00	7·50
135		10p. black on pink	16·00	4·25

See also Nos. 162/4a.

48 51 50

1890.

143	48	1c. green on green	2·50	85
144	51	2c. red on pink	70	50
145	50	5c. blue on blue	55	20
147	51	10c. brown on yellow	55	20
148		20c. violet	1·60	1·60

See also Nos. 149, etc.

53 54 55

58 61 75

1892.

149b	48	1c. red on yellow	15	10
150	53	2c. red on rose	9·00	9·00
151a		2c. green	15	10
152a	50	5c. black on brown	6·50	20
153	54	5c. brown on brown	20	20
155	51	10c. brown on red	20	20
156	55	20c. brown on blue	20	20
159	42	50c. violet on lilac	35	20
161	58	1p. blue on green	85	20
162	42	5p. red on pink	9·00	1·25
164		10p. blue	7·50	1·25

1898.

171	61	1c. red on yellow	25	25
172		5c. brown on brown	25	25
173		10c. brown on red	3·25	1·25
174		50c. blue on lilac	1·00	75

For stamps showing map of Panama and inscr "COLOMBIA" see Panama Nos. 5/18.

For provisionals issued at Cartagena during the Civil War, 1899–1902, see list in Stanley Gibbons Stamp Catalogue Part 20 (South America).

1902. Arms in various frames. Imperf or perf.

259	75	½c. brown	85	85
260		1c. green	2·50	2·10
192		2c. black on red	15	15
261		2c. blue	60	35
193		4c. red on green	15	15
194		4c. blue on green	20	20
195		5c. green on green	15	15
196		5c. blue on blue	10	10
262		5c. red	60	60
197		10c. black on pink	15	15
263		10c. mauve	85	25
198		20c. brown on brown	15	15
199		20c. blue on brown	20	20
200		50c. green on red	45	45
201		50c. blue on red	1·50	1·50
202		1p. purple on brown	25	25

82 85 River Magdalena

1903. Imperf or perf.

203	82	5p. green on blue	9·00	4·25
204		10p. green on green	9·00	9·00
205		50p. orange on red	45·00	42·00
206		100p. blue on red	38·00	35·00

Nos. 205/6 are larger (31 × 38 mm).

1902. Imperf or perf.

212	85	2c. green	80	80
213		2c. blue	80	80
214		2c. red	10·00	10·00
215	–	10c. red	50	50
216	–	10c. pink	50	50
219	–	10c. orange	8·00	8·00
242	–	10c. blue on brown	1·75	1·75
243	–	10c. blue on green	5·00	4·25
247	–	10c. blue on red	2·50	2·50
245	–	10c. blue on lilac	13·00	13·00
220	–	20c. violet	40	40
221	–	20c. blue	3·25	3·25
224	–	20c. red	12·00	12·00

DESIGNS: 10c. Iron Quay, Savanilla, with eagle above; 20c. Hill of La Popa.

88 Gunboat "Cartagena" 89 Bolivar

90 General Pinzon 91 92

1903. Imperf or perf.

225	88	5c. blue	2·10	2·10
226		5c. brown	3·25	3·25
227	89	50c. green	5·00	5·00
228		50c. brown	4·25	4·25
230		50c. orange	4·25	4·25
231		50c. red	3·25	3·25
233	90	1p. brown	90	65
234		1p. red	90	90
235		1p. blue	3·50	3·25
237	91	5p. brown	6·00	6·00
238		5p. purple	3·75	3·75
239		5p. green	6·00	6·00
240	92	10p. green	6·50	6·00
241		10p. purple	14·00	14·00

93 96

97 98 President Marroquin

1902.

248	93	1c. green on yellow	20	20
249		2c. red on pink	20	20
250		5c. blue	20	20
251		10c. brown on yellow	20	20
252		20c. mauve on pink	10	10
253		50c. red on green	1·00	1·25
254		1p. black on yellow	3·25	2·50
255		5p. blue on blue	20·00	15·00
256		10p. brown on pink	14·00	11·00

1904.

270	96	½c. yellow	55	10
274		1c. green	40	10
278		2c. red	40	10
281		5c. blue	1·00	10
283		10c. violet	45	20
284		20c. black	75	15
286	97	1p. brown	13·00	1·60
287	98	5p. black and red	38·00	30·00
288		10p. black and blue	42·00	32·00

102 Camilo Torres 104 Narino demanding Liberation of Slaves

1910. Centenary of Independence.

345	102	½c. black and purple	35	20
346	–	1c. green	35	10
347	–	2c. red	35	10
348	–	5c. blue	1·00	25
349	–	10c. purple	6·50	5·00
350	–	20c. brown	12·00	7·50
351	104	1p. purple	75·00	22·00
352	–	10p. lake	£300	£200

DESIGNS—As Type 102: 1c. P. Salavarrieta; 2c. Narino; 5c. Bolivar; 10c. Caldas; 20c. Santander. As Type 104: 10p. Bolivar resigning.

110 C. Torres 113 Arms 111 Boyaca Monument

123 La Sabana Station

112 Cartagena

1917. Portraits as T **110**.

357	**110**	½c. yellow (Caldas)	10	15
358		1c. green (Torres)	10	10
393	**113**	1½c. brown	45	45
359	**110**	2c. red (Narino)	10	10
380	**113**	3c. red on yellow	20	10
394		3c. blue	20	15
360	**110**	4c. purple (Santander)	45	10
395		4c. blue (Santander)	20	10
361		5c. blue (Bolivar)	2·50	20
396		5c. red (Bolivar)	2·50	15
397	**113**	8c. blue	20	15
362	**110**	10c. grey (Cordoba)	2·50	20
398		10c. blue (Cordoba)	6·50	35
363	**111**	20c. red	1·40	25
399	**113**	30c. bistre (Caldas)	7·00	25
400	**123**	40c. brown	14·00	4·50
364	**112**	50c. red	1·60	25
606		50c. red (San Pedro Alejandrino)	8·25	3·75
365a	**110**	1p. blue (Sucre)	10·00	40
366		2p. orange (Cuervo)	12·00	25
367		5p. grey (Ricaurte)	35·00	10·00
401		5p. violet (Ricaurte)	3·50	35
368	**113**	10p. brown	35·00	8·50
402		10p. green	5·00	90

For similar 40c. see No. 541.

1918. Surch **Especie Provisional** and value.

374	**96**	0.00½c. on 20c. black	70	10
376		0.03c. on 10c. violet	1·40	35

115

124

1918.

378	**115**	3c. red	75	10

1918. Air. No. 359 optd **1er Servicio Postal Aereo 6-18-19.**

379		2c. red	£2500	£1600

1920. As T **75**, **96** and **113** but with "PROVISIONAL" added in label across design.

381	**96**	½c. yellow	1·10	20
382		1c. green	55	10
383		2c. red	55	20
384	**113**	3c. green	40	20
385	**96**	5c. blue	90	25
386		10c. violet	5·00	1·25
387		10c. blue	8·50	4·00
388		20c. green	6·00	3·25
389	**75**	50c. red	7·50	2·50

1921. No. 360 surch **PROVICIONAL $003.**

390		$0.03 on 4c. purple	65	20

1921. No. 360 surch **PROVISIONAL $0.03.**

392		$0.03 on 4c. purple	2·75	75

1924.

403	**124**	1c. red	75	25
404		3c. blue	65	25

1925. Large fiscal stamps surch **CORREOS 1 CENTAVO** or optd **CORREOS PROVISIONAL**.

405		1c. on 3c. brown	55	10
406		4c. purple	55	25

127

129 Death of Bolivar (after P. A. Quijano)

1926.

410	**127**	1c. green	40	10
411		4c. blue	40	10

1930. Death Centenary of Bolivar.

412	**129**	4c. black and blue	25	10

132

133 Galleon

1932. Air. Optd **CORREO AEREO.**

413	**132**	5c. yellow	3·25	3·25
414		10c. purple	80	25
415		15c. green	1·40	1·40
416		20c. red	80	45
417		30c. blue	80	25
418		40c. lilac	1·60	55
419		50c. olive	3·50	2·50
420		60c. brown	3·50	2·50
421		80c. green	10·00	8·50
422	**133**	1p. blue	8·50	5·00
423		2p. red	26·00	19·00
424		3p. mauve	55·00	50·00
425		5p. olive	75·00	65·00

These and similar stamps without the "CORREO AEREO" overprint were issues of a private air company and are not listed in this catalogue.

1932. Nos. 395 and 399 surch.

427		1c. on 4c. blue	20	10
428		20c. on 30c. bistre	7·00	20

137 Oil Wells

138 Coffee Plantation

140 Gold Mining

141 Columbus

1932. 1c. is vert, 8c. is horiz.

429	–	1c. green (Emeralds)	85	10
430	**137**	2c. red (Oil)	85	10
431	**138**	5c. brown (Coffee)	85	10
432	–	8c. blue (Platinum)	7·50	25
485	**140**	10c. yellow (Gold)	6·50	10
486	**141**	20c. blue	21·00	60

142 Coffee

143 Gold

1932. Air.

435	**142**	5c. brown and orange	45	20
436	–	10c. black and red	85	20
437	–	15c. violet and green	40	15
438	–	15c. violet and red	5·00	15
439	–	20c. green and red	85	10
440	–	20c. olive and green	4·00	20
441	**142**	30c. brown and blue	3·25	10
442	–	40c. bistre and violet	1·60	10
443	–	50c. brown and green	13·00	1·25
444	–	60c. violet and brown	2·50	25
445	**142**	80c. brown and green	15·00	65
446	**143**	1p. bistre and blue	13·00	70
447		2p. bistre and red	14·00	1·90
448	–	3p. green and violet	21·00	7·00
449	–	5p. green and olive	50·00	19·00

DESIGNS—As Type **142**: 10c., 50c. Cattle; 15c., 60c. Oil Wells; 20c., 40c. Bananas. As Type **143**: 3p., 5p. Emeralds.

144 Pedro de Heredia

148 Coffee Plantation

147 Oil Wells

151 Allegory of 1935 Olympiad

1934. 400th Anniv of Cartagena.

451	**144**	1c. green	1·50	55
452		5c. brown	2·50	55
453		8c. blue	1·50	55

1934. Air. 4th Centenary of Cartagena. Surch **CARTAGENA 1533 1933** and value.

454	–	10c. on 50c. brown and green (No. 443)	3·50	3·50
455	**142**	15c. on 80c. brn & grn	3·50	3·50
456	**143**	20c. on 1p. bis & bl	5·50	6·00
457		30c. on 2p. bistre and red	6·00	6·00

1934.

458	**147**	2c. red	10	10
459	**148**	5c. brown	3·50	10
460	–	10c. orange	17·00	10

DESIGN: 10c. Gold miner facing left.

1935. 3rd National Olympiad. Inscr "III OLIMPIADA BARRANQUILLA 1935".

461	–	2c. orange and green	75	25
462	–	4c. green	75	25
463	**151**	5c. yellow and brown	75	20
464	–	7c. red	1·75	1·50
465	–	8c. mauve and black	1·75	1·50
466	–	10c. blue and brown	1·75	1·10
467	–	12c. blue	1·75	1·90
468	–	15c. red and blue	4·25	3·00
469	–	18c. yellow and purple	5·00	5·00
470	–	20c. green and violet	5·00	3·25
471	–	24c. blue and green	6·00	4·25
472	–	50c. orange and blue	6·00	3·75
473	–	1p. blue and olive	60·00	38·00
474	–	2p. blue and green	£100	70·00
475	–	5p. blue and violet	£300	£250
476	–	10p. blue and black	£650	£500

DESIGNS—VERT: 2c. Footballers; 4c. Discus thrower; 1p. G.P.O.; 2p. "Flag of the Race" Monument; 5p. Arms; 10p. Andean condor. HORIZ: 7c. Runners; 8c. Tennis player; 10c. Hurdler; 12c. Pier; 15c. Athlete; 18c. Baseball; 20c. Seashore; 24c. Swimmer; 50c. Aerial view of Barranquilla.

152 Nurse and Patients

1935. Obligatory Tax. Red Cross.

477	**152**	5c. red and green	1·75	45

1935. Surch **12 CENTAVOS.**

478		12c. on 1p. blue (No. 365a)	4·25	1·25

154 Simon Bolivar

155 Tequendama Falls

1937.

487	**154**	1c. green	10	10
488	**155**	10c. red	10	10
489		12c. blue	3·75	1·25

156 Footballer

157 Discus Thrower

1937. 4th National Olympiad.

490	**156**	3c. green	80	55
491	**157**	10c. red	3·25	1·60
492	–	1p. black	30·00	24·00

DESIGN: 1p. Runner (20½ × 27 mm).

159 Exhibition Palace

161 Mother and Child

1937. Barranquilla Industrial Exhibition.

493	**159**	5c. purple	1·60	25
494	–	15c. blue	6·00	3·25
495	–	50c. brown	17·00	6·00

DESIGNS—HORIZ: 15c. Stadium. VERT: 50c. "Flag of the Race" Monument.

1937. Obligatory Tax. Red Cross.

509	**161**	5c. red	1·40	55

1937. Surch in figures and words.

510	**156**	1c. on 3c. green	60	55
511	**155**	2c. on 12c. blue	30	30
512	–	5c. on 8c. blue (No. 432)	35	25
513	–	5c. on 8c. blue (No. 397)	35	25
514	**155**	10c. on 12c. blue	4·25	85

164 Entrance to Church of the Rosary

166 "Bochica" (Indian god)

1938. 400th Anniv of Bogota.

515	–	1c. green	15	15
516	**164**	2c. red	15	10
517	–	5c. black	20	10
518	–	10c. brown	40	25
519	**166**	15c. blue	3·25	90
520	–	20c. mauve	3·25	90
521	–	1p. brown	30·00	25·00

DESIGNS—VERT: 1c. "Calle del Arco" ("Street of the Arch") Old Bogota; 5c. Bogota Arms; 10c. G. J. de Quesada. HORIZ (larger): 20c. Convent of S. Domingo; 1p. First Mass on Site of Bogota.

168 Proposed P.O., Bogota

1939. Obligatory Tax. P.O. Rebuilding Fund.

522	**168**	¼c. blue	10	10
564		¼c. purple	10	10
523		½c. red	10	10
524		1c. violet	10	10
567		1c. orange	10	10
525		2c. green	25	10
526		20c. brown	3·25	30

1939. Air. Surch **5 cts** or **15 cts** and bar.

527		5c. on 20c. (No. 439)	25	20
528		5c. on 40c. (No. 442)	25	20
530		15c. on 30c. (No. 441)	60	15
531		15c. on 40c. (No. 442)	1·10	25

171 Bolivar

172 Coffee Plantation

173 Arms of Colombia

174 Columbus

175 Caldas

176 La Sabana Station

1939.

533	**171**	1c. green	10	10
535	**172**	5c. brown	10	10
536		5c. blue	10	10
538	**173**	15c. blue	1·40	10
539	**174**	20c. black	17·00	30
540	**175**	30c. olive	5·50	40
541	**176**	40c. brown	28·00	14·00

For similar 40c. see No. 400.

178 Proposed New P.O., Bogota

1940. Obligatory Tax. P.O. Rebuilding Fund.

542	**178**	¼c. blue	10	10
543		½c. red	10	10
544		1c. violet	10	10
545		2c. green	15	10
546		20c. brown	1·60	25

179 "Arms and the Law"

180 Bridge at Boyaca

1940. Death Centenary of Gen. Santander.

547	–	1c. olive	20	20
548	**179**	2c. red	25	15
549	–	5c. brown	25	20
550	–	8c. red	90	40
551	–	10c. yellow	45	40
552	–	15c. blue	1·10	55
553	–	20c. green	1·40	60
554	**180**	50c. violet	2·50	2·10
555	–	1p. red	11·00	10·00
556	–	2p. orange	35·00	32·00

DESIGNS—VERT: 1c. Gen. Santander; 5c. Medallion of Santander by David; 8c. Santander's statue, Cucuta; 15c. Church at Rosario. HORIZ: 10c. Santander's birthplace, Rosario; 20c. Battlefield at Paya; 1p. Death of Santander; 2p. Victorious Army at Zamora.

181 Tobacco Plant

182 Santander

183 Garcia Rovira

184 General Sucre

185 "Protection"

1940.

557	**181**	8c. green and red	45	30
558	**182**	15c. blue	80	25
559	**183**	20c. grey	4·00	25
560	–	40c. brown (Galan)	2·50	40
561	**184**	1p. black	11·00	1·25
562		1p. violet	2·50	70

1940. Obligatory Tax. Red Cross Fund.

563	**185**	5c. red	25	15

186 Pre-Colombian Monument

187 Proclamation of Independence

1941. Air.

568	**186**	5c. grey	25	10
691		5c. yellow	20	10
742		5c. blue	35	15
747		5c. red	35	15
569	–	10c. orange	25	10
692	–	10c. red	20	10
743	–	10c. blue	35	20
570		15c. red	25	10
693	–	15c. blue	20	10
571	–	20c. green	40	10
694	–	20c. violet	20	10
745	–	20c. blue	45	25
749	–	20c. red	45	25
572	**186**	30c. blue	40	10
695		30c. green	35	10
750		30c. red	75	10
573	–	40c. purple	1·60	10
696	–	40c. grey	55	10
574	–	50c. green	1·60	10
697	–	50c. red	65	10
575	–	60c. purple	1·60	10
698	–	60c. olive	85	10
576	**186**	80c. olive	4·00	35
699		80c. brown	1·25	10
577	**187**	1p. black and blue	4·00	20
700		1p. brown and olive	3·00	35
578	–	2p. black and red	8·00	1·25
701	–	2p. blue and green	3·75	55
579	**187**	3p. black and violet	14·00	4·00
702		3p. black and red	7·00	3·50
580	–	5p. black and green	35·00	17·00
703	–	5p. green and sepia	20·00	8·00

DESIGNS: As Type **186**: 10c., 40c. "El Dorado" Monument; 15c., 50c. Spanish Fort, Cartagena; 20c., 60c. Street in Old Bogota. As Type **187**: 2p., 5p. National Library, Bogota.

188 Arms of Palmira

189 Home of Jorge Isaacs (author)

1942. 8th National Agricultural Exn, Palmira.

581	**188**	30c. red	5·00	70

1942. Honouring J. Isaacs.

582	**189**	50c. green	3·25	35

190 Peace Conference Delegates

1942. 40th Anniv of Wisconsin Peace Treaty ending Civil War.

583	**190**	10c. orange	3·25	45

1943. Surch **$ 0.0½ MEDIO CENTAVO**.

584	**168**	½c. on 1c. violet	10	10
585		½c. on 2c. green	10	10
586		½c. on 20c. brown	20	20

1944. Surch **5 Centavos**.

587	5c. on 10c. orge (No. 460)	20	15

193 National Shrine

194 San Pedro, Alejandrino

1944.

592	**193**	30c. olive	2·10	1·25
593	**194**	50c. red	2·10	1·25

1944. Surch with new values in figures and words.

594	**172**	1c. on 5c. brn (No. 535)	15	15
595		2c. on 5c. brn (No. 535)	15	15

195 Banner

199 Manuel Murillo Toro

196 Viceroy Solis Building

1944. 75th Anniv of General Benefit Institution of Cundinamarca.

596	**195**	2c. blue and yellow	10	10
597	–	5c. blue and yellow	10	10
598	–	20c. black and green	95	75
599	–	40c. black and red	4·25	3·25
600	**196**	1p. black and red	8·50	6·50
MS601		100 × 87 mm. Nos. 596/600. Imperf	8·50	8·50

DESIGNS: As T **195**: 5c. Arms of the Institution; 20c. Manuel Murillo Toro. As T **196**: 40c. St. Juan de Dios Maternity Hospital.

1944.

602	**199**	5c. olive	35	20

201 Proposed P.O., Bogota

(**202** Stalin, Roosevelt and Churchill)

1945. Obligatory Tax. P.O. Rebuilding Fund.

609	**201**	½c. blue	10	10
610		½c. brown	10	10
611		½c. red	10	10
612		½c. mauve	10	10
613		1c. violet	10	10
614		1c. orange	10	10
615		1c. green	10	10
616		2c. green	10	10
617a		20c. brown	80	10

1945. Victory. Optd with T **202**.

618	**172**	5c. brown	25	15

203 Clock Tower, Cartagena

204 Fort San Sebastian Cartagena

1945.

621	**203**	50c. green	2·50	80

1945. Air.

622	**204**	5c. grey	20	10
623	–	10c. orange	20	10
624	–	15c. red	20	10
625	**204**	20c. green	25	10
626	–	30c. blue	35	10
627	–	40c. red	55	10
628	**204**	50c. green	70	15
629	–	60c. purple	3·25	80
630	–	80c. grey	5·00	55
631	–	1p. blue	5·00	55
632	–	2p. red	7·50	2·40

DESIGNS—As Type **204**: 10c., 30c., 60c. Tequendama Falls; 15c., 40c., 80c. Santa Marta. HORIZ (larger): 1p., 2p. Capitol, Bogota.

207 Sierra Nevada of Santa Maria

1945. 25th Anniv of 1st Air Mail Service in America.

633	**207**	20c. green	1·25	60
634	–	30c. blue	1·25	60
635	–	50c. red	1·25	60

DESIGNS: 30c. Junkers F-13 seaplane "Tolima"; 50c. San Sebastian Fortress, Cartagena.

1946. Surch **1** above **UN CENTAVO**.

636	**138**	1c. on 5c. brown	15	15

209 Gen. Sucre

211 Map of South America

212 Bogota Observatory

1946.

638	**209**	1c. blue and brown	20	10
639		2c. red and violet	20	10
640		5c. blue and olive	20	10
641		9c. red and green	45	35
642		10c. orange and blue	35	25
643		20c. orange and black	45	25
644		30c. green and red	45	25
645		40c. red and green	45	25
646		50c. violet and purple	45	25

The 5c. to 50c. are larger (23½ × 32 mm).

1946. Obligatory Tax. Red Cross Fund. Optd with red cross.

647	**172**	5c. brown (No. 535)	25	20

1946.

648	**211**	15c. blue	25	10

1946.

649	**212**	5c. brown	10	10
650		5c. blue	10	10

213 Andres Bello

214 Joaquin de Cayzedo y Cuero

1946. 80th Death Anniv of Andres Bello (poet and teacher).

651	**213**	3c. brown (postage)	25	15
652		10c. orange	40	10
653		15c. black	55	10
654		5c. blue (air)	25	15

1946.

655	**214**	2p. turquoise	5·00	45
656		2p. green	65	20

215 Proposed New P.O., Bogota

217 Coffee Plant

1946. Obligatory Tax. P.O. Rebuilding Fund.

657	**215**	3c. blue	15	10

1946. 5th Central American and Caribbean Games, Barranquilla. As No. 621 optd **V JUEGOS C. A. Y DEL C. 1946.**

658	50c. red	2·50	1·60

1947.

659	**217**	5c. multicoloured	35	10

218 "Masdevallia Nicterina"

220 Antonio Narino

1947. Colombian Orchids. Multicoloured.

660	1c. Type **218**	10	10
661	2c. "Miltonia vexillaria"	10	10
662	5c. "Cattleya dowiana aurea"	45	20
663	5c. "Cattleya chocoensis"	45	20
664	5c. "Odontoglossum crispum"	45	20
665	10c. "Cattleya labiata trianae"	65	15

1947. Obligatory Tax. Optd **SOBRETASA** in fancy letters.

666	**183**	20c. grey (No. 559)	4·25	1·75
676	**141**	20c. blue (No. 486)	25·00	17·00

1947. 4th Pan-American Press Conf, Bogota.

667	**220**	5c. blue on blue (post)	25	15
668	–	10c. brown on blue	35	15
669	–	5c. blue on blue (air)	20	10
670	–	10c. red on blue	35	20

PORTRAITS: No. 668, A. Urdaneta y Urdaneta; 669, F. J. de Caldas; 670, M. del Socorro Rodriguez.

222 Arms of Colombia and Cross

223 J. C. Mutis and J. J. Triana

224 M. A. Caro and R. J. Cuervo

1947. Obligatory Tax. Red Cross Fund.

671	**222**	5c. lake	20	10
704		5c. red	20	10

1947.

673	**223**	25c. green	35	15
675	**224**	3p. purple	45	10

225 Bogota Cathedral

1948. 9th Pan-American Congress, Bogota. Inscr as in T **225**.

677	**225**	5c. brown (postage)	15	10
678	–	10c. orange	25	20
679	–	15c. blue	25	20
MS679a		91 × 91 mm. 50c. slate. Imperf	1·75	1·75

DESIGNS: 10c. National Capitol; 15c. Foreign Office; 50c. Map of North America and Arms of Bogota.

680	–	5c. brown (air)	15	10
681	–	15c. blue	35	25
MS681a		91 × 91 mm. 50c. brown. Imperf	1·75	1·75

DESIGNS: 5c. Chancellery; 15c. Raphael Court, Capitol; 50c. Map of South America and Arms of Colombia.

1948. Obligatory Tax. Savings Bank stamps surch **COLOMBIA SOBRETASA 1 CENTAVO**. Various designs.

682	1c. on 5c. brown	10	10
683	1c. on 10c. violet	10	10

684 1c. on 25c. red 10 10
685 1c. on 50c. blue 10 10

1948. Optd **C** (= "CORREOS"). No gum.
686 **168** 1c. orange 10 10

1948. Optd **CORREOS**.
687 **201** 1c. olive 10 10
688 2c. green 10 10
689 20c. brown 20 10

232 Simon Bolivar

234 Carlos Martinez Silva

233 Proposed New P.O., Bogota

1948.
690 **232** 15c. green 35 15

1948. Obligatory Tax. P.O. Rebuilding Fund.
705 **233** 1c. red 10 10
706 2c. green 10 10
707 3c. blue 10 10
708 5c. grey 10 10
709 10c. violet 20 10
See also Nos. 756 and 758/62.

1949.
710 **234** 40c. red 35 10

235 Julio Garavito Armero

236 Dr. Juan de Dios Carrasquilla

1949. J. G. Armero (mathematician).
711 **235** 4c. green 25 15

1949. 75th Anniv of National Agricultural Society.
712 **236** 5c. bistre 20 10

237 Arms of Colombia

238 Allegory of Justice

1949. New Constitution.
713 **237** 15c. blue (postage) . . . 20 10
714 **238** 5c. green (air) 15 10
715 – 10c. orange 15 10
DESIGN: 10c. Allegory of Constitution.

239 Tree and Congress Emblem

240 F. J. Cisneros

1949. 1st Forestry Congress, Bogota.
716 **239** 5c. olive 20 10

1949. 50th Death Anniv of Francisco Javier Cisneros (engineer).
717 **240** 50c. blue and brown . . . 1·00 50
718 50c. violet and green . . . 1·00 50
719 50c. yellow and purple . . 1·00 50

241 Mother and Child

1950. Red Cross Fund. Surch with new value and date as in T **241**.
720 **241** 5 on 2c. multicoloured . . 80 35

1950. Obligatory Tax. Optd **SOBRETASA**.
721 **172** 5c. blue 15 10

243 "Masdevallia Chimaera"

244 Santo Domingo Post Office

244a Globe

1950. 75th Anniv of UPU. (a) Inscr "1874 UPU 1949".
722 **243** 1c. brown (postage) . . . 30 10
723 – 2c. violet 30 10
724 – 3c. mauve 10 10
725 – 4c. green 20 10
726 – 5c. orange 35 10
727 – 11c. red . . . . 1·60 75
728 **244** 18c. blue 80 40
DESIGNS—VERT: 3c. "Cattleya labiata trianae"; 4c. "Masdevallia nicterina"; 5c. "Cattleya dowiana aurea". HORIZ: 2c. "Odontoglossum crispum"; 11c. "Miltonia vexillaria".

(b) Imperf.
MS728a 90 × 90 mm. 50c. yellow (postage) . . . . 1·25 1·50

(c) Imperf.
MS728b 90 × 90 mm. 50c. slate (air) 1·25 1·50

245 Antonio Baraya (patriot)

246 Farm

1950.
729 **245** 2c. red 10 10

1950.
730 **246** 5c. red and buff 30 15
731 5c. green and turquoise 30 15
732 5c. blue and light blue . . 30 15

247 Arms of Bogota

248 Map and Badge

1950.
733 **247** 5p. green . . . . 1·60 10
734 – 10p. orange (Arms of Colombia) . . . . 2·40 15

1951. 60th Anniv of Colombian Society of Engineers.
735 **248** 20c. red, yellow and blue 35 15

249 Arms of Colombia and Cross

250 Fray Bartolome de Las Casas

1951. Obligatory Tax. Red Cross Fund.
736 **249** 5c. red 20 15
737 **250** 5c. red 20 15
738 5c. green and red 20 10

251 D. G. Valencia

254 Dr. Nicolas Osorio

1951. 8th Death Anniv of D. G. Valencia (poet and orator).
739 **251** 25c. black 40 10

1951. Surch **1 centavo**.
740 **233** 1c. on 3c. blue 10 10

1951. Nationalization of Barranca Oilfields. Optd **REVERSION CONCESION MARES 25 Agosto 1951.**
741 **147** 2c. red 10 10

1952. Colombian Doctors.
751 **254** 1c. blue 10 10
752 – 1c. blue (P. Martinez) . . 10 10
753 – 1c. bl (E. Uriocoechea) . . 10 10
754 – 1c. blue (Jose M. Lombana) 10 10

255 Proposed New P.O., Bogota

256 Manizales Cathedral

1952.
755 **255** 5c. blue 15 10
756 **233** 20c. brown . . . . 8·00 10
757 **201** 25c. grey . . . . 12·00 1·60
758 **233** 25c. green 20 10
759 – 50c. orange . . . . . . 25·00 14·00
760 – 1p. red 55 25
761 – 2p. purple . . . . 27·00 2·50
762 – 2p. violet 65 10
DESIGN: 50c. to 2p. Similar to T **233** but larger, $24\frac{1}{2} \times 19$ mm.
Owing to a shortage of postage stamps the above obligatory tax types were issued for ordinary postal use.

1952. Obligatory Tax. No. 759 surch.
763 8c. on 50c. orange 15 10

1952. Centenary of Manizales.
764 **256** 23c. black and blue . . . 25 15

1952. 1st Latin-American Congress of Iron Specialists. Surch **1952 1' CONFERENCIA SIDERURGICA LATINO-AMERICANA.** and new value.
765 **223** 15c. on 25c. green (postage) 30 20
766 **186** 70c. on 80c. red (air) . . 75 25

258 Queen Isabella and Columbus Monument

1953. 500th Birth Anniv of Isabella the Catholic.
767 **258** 23c. black and blue . . . 35 35

1953. Air. Optd **CORREO AEREO** or surch also.
768 **233** 5c. on 8c. blue 15 10
769 15c. on 20c. brown . . . 25 10
770 15c. on 25c. green 65 10
771 25c. green 30 10

1953. Air. Optd **AEREO**.
772 **155** 10c. red 15 10

EXTRA RAPIDO. Stamps bearing this overprint or inscription were used to prepay the additional cost of air carriage of inland mail handled by the National Postal Service from 1953 to 1964. Subsequently remaining stocks of these stamps were used for other classes of correspondence. Since the 1920s regular air service for inland and foreign mail has been provided by the Air Postal Service, a separate undertaking which is administered by the Avianca airline and for which the regular air stamps are used.

1953. Air. No. 727 surch **CORREO EXTRA RAPIDO 5 5**.
773 5c. on 11c. red 20 10

262

1953. Air. Fiscal stamps optd as in T **262** or surch also.
774 **262** 1c. on 2c. green 10 10
775 50c. red 10 10

263

1953. Air. Real Estate Tax stamps optd as in T **263**.
776 **263** 5c. red 15 10
777 20c. brown 20 10

1953. Surch.
778 – 40c. on 1p. red (No. 760) 45 10
779 **214** 50c. on 2p. green 45 10

266 Don M. Ancizar

267 Map of South America

1953. Colombian Chorographical Commission Centenary. Portraits inscr as in T **266**.
780 **266** 14c. red and black . . . 40 30
781 – 23c. blue and black . . . 35 20
782 – 30c. sepia and black . . 35 15
783 – 1p. green and black . . . 15 10
PORTRAITS: 23c. J. J. Triana; 30c. M. Ponce de Leon; 1p. A. Codazzi.

1953. 2nd National Philatelic Exhibition, Bogota. Real Estate Tax stamps surch as in T **267**.
784 **267** 5c. on 5p. mult (post) . . 35 15
785 – 15c. on 10p. multicoloured (air) . . 40 25
DESIGN: 15c. Map of Colombia.

1953. Air. Optd **CORREO EXTRA-RAPIDO** or surch also.
786 **233** 2c. on 8c. blue 10 10
787 10c. violet 15 10

269 Fountain, Tunja

271 Map of Colombia

270 Pastelillo Fort, Cartagena

1954. Air.
788 – 5c. purple 30 10
789 – 10c. black 20 10
790 – 15c. red 20 10
791 – 15c. vermilion 20 10
792 – 20c. brown 30 10
793 – 25c. blue 30 10
794 – 25c. purple 30 10
795 – 30c. brown 15 10
796 – 40c. blue 25 10
797 – 50c. purple 25 10
798 **269** 60c. sepia 35 10
799 – 80c. lake 25 20
800 – 1p. black and blue . . . 1·40 20
801 **270** 2p. black and green . . . 3·75 25
802 – 3p. black and red . . . . 5·00 55

803 – 5p. green and brown . . . 7·00 1·40
804 **271** 10p. olive and red . . . . 8·50 3·50
DESIGNS. As Type **269**—VERT: 5c., 30c. Galeras volcano, Pasto; 15c. red, 50c. Bolivar Monument, Boyaca; 15c. vermilion, 25c. (2) Sanctuary of the Rocks, Narino; 20c., 80c. Nevado del Ruiz Mts., Manizales; 40c. J. Isaacs Monument, Cali. HORIZ: 10c. San Diego Monastery, Bogota. As Type **270**—HORIZ: 1p. Girardot Stadium, Medellin; 3p. Santo Domingo Gateway and University, Popayan. As Type **271**—HORIZ: 5p. Sanctuary of the Rocks, Narino.

1954. Surch.
805 **266** 5c. on 14c. red & black 30 15
806 **256** 5c. on 23c. black & blue 30 15

272 Andean Condor carrying Shield

273

1954. Air.
807 **272** 5c. purple 50 20

1954. 400th Anniv of Franciscan Community in Colombia.
808 **273** 5c. brown, green & sepia 25 15

1954. Obligatory Tax. Red Cross Fund. No. 807 optd with cross and bar in red.
809 **272** 5c. purple . . . . 1·60 40

275 Soldier, Flag and Arms of Republic

1954. National Army Commemoration.
810 **275** 5c. blue (postage) 20 10
811 15c. red (air) 30 10

276

1954. 7th National Athletic Games, Cali. Inscr "VII JUEGOS ATLETICOS", etc.
812 – 5c. blue (postage) 15 10
813 **276** 10c. red 25 10
814 – 15c. brown (air) 25 15
815 **276** 20c. green 60 35
DESIGN: 5c., 15c. Badge of the Games.

277

278 Saint's Convent and Cell, Cartagena

1954. 50th Anniv of Colombian Academy of History.
816 **277** 5c. green and blue 20 10

1954. Death Tercentenary of San Pedro Claver.
817 **278** 5c. deep green (postage) 15 10
MS818 121 × 130 mm. No. 817 but printed in green . . . . 1·75 1·75

819 – 15c. deep brown (air) . . . 15 10
MS820 121 × 130 mm. No. 819 but printed in brown . . . . . . 1·75 1·75
DESIGN: 15c. San Pedro Claver Church, Cartagena.

279 Mercury

280 Archbishop Mosquera

1954. 1st International Fair, Bogota.
821 **279** 5c. orange (postage) . . . 25 10
822 15c. blue (air) 25 10
823 50c. red ("EXTRA RAPIDO") 30 10

1954. Air. Death Cent of Archbishop Mosquera.
824 **280** 2c. green 10 10

281 Virgin of Chiquinquira

1954. Air.
825 **281** 5c. mult (brown frame) 10 10
826 5c. mult (violet frame) . . 10 10

282 Tapestry presented by Queen Margaret of Austria

1954. Tercentenary of Senior College of Our Lady of the Rosary, Bogota.
827 **282** 5c. black & orge (postage) 25 15
828 – 10c. blue 25 15
829 – 15c. brown 35 15
830 – 20c. brown and black . . 60 25
MS831 125 × 131 mm. Nos. 827/30 in new colours . . . . 3·25 3·50

832 **282** 15c. black & red (air) . . 35 15
833 – 20c. blue 55 15
834 – 25c. brown 55 15
835 – 50c. red and black . . . 85 30
MS836 125 × 131 mm. Nos. 832/5 in new colours . . . . 3·25 3·50
DESIGNS—VERT: Nos. 828, 833, Friar Cristobal de Torres (founder). HORIZ: Nos. 829, 834, Cloisters and statue; 830, 835, Chapel and coat of arms.

283 Paz de Rio Steel Works

284 J. Marti

1954. Inauguration of Paz del Rio Steel Plant.
837 **283** 5c. black & bl (postage) 15 10
838 20c. black & green (air) 70 45

1955. Birth Cent of Marti (Cuban revolutionary).
839 **284** 5c. red (postage) 15 10
840 – 15c. green (air) 25 10

285 Badge, Flags and Korean Landscape

1955. Colombian Forces in Korea.
841 **285** 10c. purple (postage) . . 25 10
842 20c. green (air) 25 15

286 Merchant Marine Emblem

287 M. Fidel Suarez

1955. Greater Colombia Merchant Marine Commemoration. Inscr as in T **286**.
843 **286** 15c. green (postage) . . . 20 10
844 – 20c. violet 85 15
MS845 125 × 131 mm. Nos. 810, 841, 843/4 in new colours . . . . . 3·25 3·50

846 **286** 25c. black (air) 35 10
847 – 50c. green . . . . 1·40 15
MS848 125 × 131 mm. Nos. 125 × 131 mm. Nos. 811, 842, 846/7 in new colours . . . . . 3·25 3·50
DESIGN—HORIZ: 20, 50c. "City of Manizales" (freighter) and skyscrapers.

1955. Air. Birth Centenary of Marco Fidel Suarez (President, 1918–21).
849 **287** 10c. blue 15 10

288 San Pedro Claver feeding Slaves

1955. Obligatory Tax. Red Cross Fund and 300th Anniv of San Pedro Claver.
850 **288** 5c. purple and red 25 10

289 Hotel Tequendama and San Diego Church

1955.
851 **289** 5c. blue and light blue (postage) 15 10
852 15c. lake and pink (air) 25 10

290 Bolivar's Country House

1955. 50th Anniv of Rotary International.
853 **290** 5c. blue (postage) 15 10
854 15c. red (air) 25 10

291 Belalcazar, De Quesada and Balboa

1955. 7th Postal Union Congress of the Americas and Spain. Inscr as in T **291**.
855 **291** 2c. brn & grn (postage) 10 10
856 – 5c. brown and blue . . . 15 10
857 – 23c. black and blue . . . 2·25 50
MS858 120 × 130 mm. Nos. 855/7 in slightly different colours (sold at 50c.) . . . . 3·25 3·50

859 – 15c. black and red (air) 15 10
860 – 20c. black and brown . . . 25 10

862 – 2c. black and brown ("EXTRA RAPIDO") . . 10 10
863 – 5c. sepia and yellow 15 10
864 – 1p. brown and slate . . . . 12·00 5·50
865 – 2p. black and violet . . . . 7·50 6·50
MS861 120 × 130 mm. Nos. 859/60 in slightly different colours (sold at 50c.) . . . . 3·25 3·50

DESIGNS—HORIZ: 2c. (No. 855), Type **291**; 2c. (No. 862), Atahualpa, Tisquesuza, Montezuma; 5c. (No. 856), San Martin, Bolivar and Washington; 5c. (No. 863), King Ferdinand, Queen Isabella and coat of arms; 15c. O'Higgins, Santander and Sucre; 20c. Marti, Hidalgo and Petion; 23c. Columbus, "Santa Maria", "Pinta" and "Nina"; 1p. Artigas, Lopez and Murillo; 2p. Calderon, Baron de Rio Branco and De La Mar.

292 J. E. Caro

293 Salamanca University

1955. Death Cent of Jose Eusebio Caro (poet).
866 **292** 5c. brown (postage) . . . 10 10
867 15c. green (air) 25 10

1955. Air. 700th Anniv of Salamanca University.
868 **293** 20c. brown 15 10

294 Gold Mining, Narino

1956. Regional Industries. Inscr "DEPARTAMENTO", "PROVIDENCIA" (No. 874), "INTENDENCIA" (2p. to 5p.) or "COMISARIA" (10p.).
869 – 2c. green and red 10 10
870 – 3c. black and purple . . . 10 10
871 – 3c. brown and blue . . . 10 10
872 – 3c. violet and green . . . 10 10
873 – 4c. black and green . . . 30 10
874 – 5c. black and blue . . . 20 10
875 – 5c. slate and red 30 10
876 – 5c. olive and brown . . . 30 10
877 – 5c. brown and olive . . . 25 10
878 – 5c. brown and blue . . . 30 10
879 – 10c. black and yellow . . 25 10
880 – 10c. brown and green . . 20 10
881 – 10c. brown and blue . . 20 10
882 – 15c. black and blue . . 25 10
883 – 20c. blue and brown . . 30 10
884 – 23c. red and blue 35 15
885 – 25c. black and olive . . 35 15
886 **294** 30c. brown and blue . . . 30 10
887 – 40c. brown and purple . . 10 10
888 – 50c. black and green . . 30 10
889 – 60c. green and sepia . . . 25 10
890 – 1p. slate and purple . . . 90 10
891 – 2p. brown and green . . . 1·90 25
892 – 3p. black and red . . . . 1·75 35
893 – 5p. blue and brown . . . 4·00 25
894 – 10p. green and brown . . 9·50 3·00
DESIGNS—As Type **294**. HORIZ: 2c. Barranquilla naval workshops, Atlantico; 4c. Fishing, Cartagena Port, Bolivar; 5c. (No. 875) View of Port, San Andres; 5c. (No. 876) Cocoa, Cauca; 5c. (No. 877) Prize cattle, Cordoba; 23c. Rice harvesting, Huila; 25c. Bananas, Magdalena; 40c. Tobacco, Santander; 50c. Oil wells of Catatumbo, Norte de Santander; 60c. Cotton harvesting, Tolima. VERT: 3c. (3), Allegory of Industry, Antioquia; 5c. (No. 874) Map of San Andres Archipelago; 5c. (No. 878) Steel plant, Boyaca; 10c. (3), Coffee, Caldas; 15c. Cathedral at Sal Salinas de Zipaquira, Cundinamarca; 20c. Platinum and map, Choco. LARGER (37½ × 27 mm)—HORIZ: 1p. Sugar factory, Valle del Cauca; 2p. Cattle fording river, Meta; 3p. Statue and River Amazon, Leticia; 5p. Landscape, La Guajira. VERT: 10p. Rubber tapping, Vaupes.

295 Henri Dunant and S. Samper Brush

1956. Obligatory Tax. Red Cross Fund.
895 **295** 5c. brown 20 10

1956. Air. No. 783 optd **EXTRA-RAPIDO**.
896 1p. green and black 25 10

297 Columbus and Lighthouse

1956. Columbus Memorial Lighthouse.
897 **297** 3c. black (postage) . . . 15 10
898 15c. blue (air) 20 10
899 3c. green ("EXTRA RAPIDO") 15 10

298 Altar of St. Elisabeth and Sarcophagus of Jimenez de Quesada, Primada Basilica, Bogota

299 St. Ignatius of Loyola

1956. 700th Anniv of St. Elisabeth of Hungary.
900 **298** 5c. purple (postage) . . . 15 10
901 15c. brown (air) 30 15

1956. 400th Death Anniv of St. Ignatius of Loyola.
902 **299** 5c. blue (postage) 15 10
903 5c. brown (air) 20 10

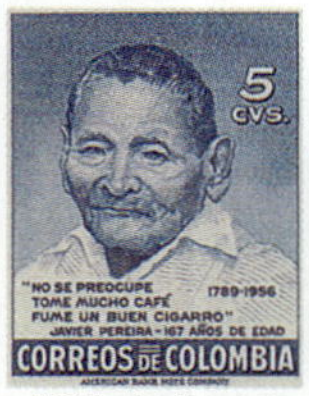
300 Javier Pereira

302 Dairy Farm

1956. Pereira Commemoration.
904 **300** 5c. blue (postage) 10 10
905 20c. red (air) 10 10

1957. Air. No. 874 optd **EXTRA-RAPIDO**.
906 5c. black and blue 20 10

1957. Air. As No. 580 (colours changed) optd **EXTRA-RAPIDO**.
907 5p. black and buff . . . . . 6·00 3·75

1957. 25th Anniv of Agricultural Credit Bank.
908 **302** 1c. olive (postage) 10 10
909 – 2c. brown 10 10
910 – 5c. blue 15 10
911 **302** 5c. orange (air) 15 10
912 – 10c. green 25 20
913 – 15c. black 25 10
914 – 20c. red 40 30
915 – 5c. brown ("EXTRA RAPIDO") 15 10

DESIGNS: 2c., 10c. Farm tractor; 5c. (No. 910), 15c. Emblem of agricultural prosperity; 5c. (No. 915), Livestock; 20c. Livestock.

303 Racing Cyclist

1957. Air. 7th Round Colombia Cycle Race.
916 **303** 2c. brown 15 15
917 5c. blue 25 25

304 Arms and Gen. Rayes (founder)

305 Father J. M. Delgado

1957. 50th Anniv of Military Cadet School.
918 **304** 5c. blue (postage) 15 10
919 – 10c. orange 20 10
MS920 130 × 120 mm. Nos. 918/19 in slightly different colours . . 9·50 9·50
921 **304** 15c. red (air) 20 10
922 – 20c. brown 30 10

DESIGN: 10c., 20c. Arms and Military Cadet School.

1957. Father Delgado Commemoration.
923 **305** 2c. lake (postage) 10 10
924 10c. blue (air) 15 10

306 St. Vincent de Paul with Children

308 Fencer

307 Signatories to Bogota Postal Convention of 1838, and UPU Monument, Berne

1957. Centenary of Colombian Order of St. Vincent de Paul.
925 **306** 1c. green (postage) . . . 10 10
926 5c. red (air) 15 10

1957. 14th UPU Congress, Ottawa and International Correspondence Week.
927 **307** 5c. green (postage) . . . 15 10
928 10c. grey 15 10
929 15c. brown (air) 20 10
930 25c. blue 20 10

1957. 3rd S. American Fencing Championships.
931 **308** 4c. purple (postage) . . . 20 10
932 20c. brown (air) 35 10

309 Discovery of Hypsometry by F. J. de Caldas

1958. International Geophysical Year.
933 **309** 10c. black (postage) . . . 30 10
934 25c. green (air) 45 10
935 1p. violet ("EXTRA RAPIDO") 15 10

310 Nurses with Patient, and Ambulance

1958. Obligatory Tax. Red Cross Fund.
936 **310** 5c. red and black 15 10

1958. Nos. 882 and 884 surch.
937 5c. on 15c. black and blue . . 10 10
938 5c. on 23c. red and blue . . 25 20

1958. Air. No. 888 optd **AEREO**.
939 50c. black and green 20 10

313 Father R. Almanza and San Diego Church, Bogota

1958. Father Almanza Commemoration.
940 **313** 10c. lilac (postage) . . . 10 10
941 25c. grey (air) 30 10
942 10c. green ("EXTRA RAPIDO") 10 10

1958. Nos. 780/2 surch **CINCO** (5c.) or **VEINTE** (20c.).
943 **266** 5c. on 14c. red & black 15 10
944 – 5c. on 30c. sepia & black 10 10
945 – 20c. on 23c. blue & blk 25 15

315 Msr. Carrasquilla and Rosario College, Bogota

1959. Birth Centenary of Msr. R. M. Carrasquilla.
946 **315** 10c. brown (postage) . . 15 10
947 25c. red (air) 20 10
948 1p. blue 60 20

1959. Surch **20c.** and ornament.
949 **258** 20c. on 23c. black & bl 25 15

1959. As No. 826 but with "CORREO EXTRA RAPIDO" obliterated.
950 **281** 5c. multicoloured 10 10

1959. No. 794 surch.
951 10c. on 25c. purple 15 10

318 Luz Marina Zuluaga ("Miss Universe 1959")

320 J. E. Gaitan (political leader)

1959. "Miss Universe 1959" Commemoration.
952 **318** 10c. mult (postage) . . . 10 10
953 1p.20 mult (air) 65 45
954 5p. mult ("EXTRA RAPIDO") . . . . . . 25·00 24·00

1959. No. 873 surch.
955 2c. on 4c. black and green . . 30 10

1959. J. E. Gaitan Commem. Nos. 956 and 958 are surch on T **320**.
956 **320** 10c. on 3c. grey 15 10
957 30c. purple 25 15
958 2p. on 1p. black ("EXTRA RAPIDO") 60 25

1959. Air. Surch.
960 **269** 50c. on 60c. sepia . . . . 5·00 30

323 Capitol, Bogota

324 Santander

1959.
961 **323** 2c. brn & blue (postage) 10 10
962 3c. violet and black . . . 10 10
963 **324** 5c. brown and yellow . . 15 10
964 – 5c. ultramarine & blue . . 15 10
965 – 10c. black and red 15 10
966 **324** 10c. black and green . . . 15 10
967 – 35c. black and grey (air) 1·75 10

PORTRAIT (as Type **324**): Nos. 964/5, 967, Bolivar.

1959. Air. Unification of Airmail Rates. Optd **UNIFICADO** within outline of aeroplane.
968 **299** 5c. brown 15 10
969 **302** 5c. orange 35 35
970 **306** 5c. red 20 20
971 **155** 10c. red (No. 772) 10 10
972 – 10c. black (No. 789) . . . 20 10
973 **304** 15c. red 30 10
974 – 20c. brown (No. 792) . . 20 10
975 – 20c. brown (No. 922) . . 10 10
976 **308** 20c. brown 25 15
977 – 25c. blue (No. 793) . . . 25 10
978 – 25c. purple (No. 794) . . 25 10
979 **313** 25c. grey 25 10
980 **315** 25c. red 30 10
981 – 30c. brown (No. 795) . . 20 10
982 **269** 50c. on 60c. sepia (No. 960) 15 10
983 **315** 1p. blue 35 10
984 **318** 1p.20 multicoloured . . . 45 35
985 **270** 2p. black and green . . . 2·10 20
986 – 3p. black & red (No. 802) 7·00 45
987 – 5p. grn & brn (No. 803) 7·50 45
988 **271** 10p. olive and red . . . . 9·50 1·60

326 Colombian 2½c. stamp of 1859 and Postman with Mule

328 2c. Air Stamp of 1918, Junkers F-13 "Colombia" and Lockheed Constellation

327 Tete-beche 5c. stamps of 1859

1959. Colombian Stamp Cent. Inscr "1859 1959".
989 **326** 5c. grn & orge (postage) 20 15
990 – 10c. blue and lake 40 15
991 **326** 15c. green and red 35 10
992 – 25c. brown and blue . . . 2·25 1·25
993 – 25c. red and brown (air) 40 20
994 – 50c. blue and red 55 20
995 – 1p.20 brown and green . . 2·10 1·25
996 – 10c. lilac and bistre ("EXTRA RAPIDO") 20 10
MS997 74 × 70 mm. **327** 5c. blue on pink (sold at 5p.) . . . . . . 13·00 15·00

DESIGNS—VERT: Colombian stamps of 1859 (except No. 993): No. 990, 5c. and river steamer; 992, 10c. and steam locomotive "Cordoba"; 993, Postal decree of 1859 and Pres. M. Ospina; 996, 10c. and map of Colombia. HORIZ: No. 994, 20c. and Junkers F-13 seaplane "Colombia"; 995, 1p. and Lockheed Constellation airliner over valley.

1959. Air. 40th Anniv of Colombian "AVIANCA" Air Mail Services.
998 **328** 35c. red, black and blue 15 10
999 – 60c. black and green . . . 25 15
MS1000 90 × 50 mm. Two 1p. stamps in designs of Nos. 998/9 but in different colours . . . . 4·00 4·25
MS1001 Sheets as last but containing two 1p.50 stamps in different colours and inscr "EXTRA RAPIDO" . . . . 4·00 4·25

DESIGN: 60c. As Type **328** but without Colombian 2c. stamp.

329 Eldorado Airport, Bogota

331 A. von Humboldt (after J. K. Stieler)

1960. Air.
1002 **329** 35c. orange and black 45 20
1003 60c. red and grey . . . 35 35
1004 1p. blue and grey ("EXTRA RAPIDO") 1·00 45

1960. Death Centenary of Alexander von Humboldt (naturalist). Animals.
1005 – 5c. brn & turq (postage) 10 10
1006 **331** 10c. sepia and red . . . 10 10
1007 – 20c. purple and yellow 20 10
1008 – 35c. brown (air) 45 10
1009 – 1p.30 brown and red . . 1·25 90
1010 – 1p.45 lemon and blue . . 1·00 45

DESIGNS—VERT: 5c. Two-toed sloth; 20c. Long-haired spider monkey. HORIZ: 35c. Giant anteater; 1p.30, Nine-banded armadillo; 1p.45, "Blue" parrotfish.

332 "Anthurium andreanum"

333 Refugee Family

1960. Colombian Flowers.
1011 **332** 5c. mult (postage) . . . 20 10
1012 A 20c. yellow, green & sep 10 10
1013 B 5c. multicoloured (air) 10 10
1014 5c. multicoloured 10 10
1015 A 10c. yellow, green & bl 10 10
1016 C 20c. multicoloured . . . 10 10
1017 D 25c. multicoloured . . . 35 10
1018 C 35c. multicoloured . . . 25 10
1019 B 60c. multicoloured . . . 35 20
1020 **332** 60c. multicoloured . . . 35 10
1021 1p.45 multicoloured . . 90 35
1022 C 5c. multicoloured ("EXTRA RAPIDO") 10 10
1023 D 10c. multicoloured . . . 10 10
1024 **332** 1p. multicoloured . . . 90 55
1025 A 1p. yellow, green & sepia 90 55
1026 B 1p. multicoloured . . . 90 55
1027 C 1p. multicoloured . . . 90 55
1028 D 1p. multicoloured . . . 90 55
1029 C 2p. multicoloured . . . 1·60 80

FLOWERS: A, "Espelitia grandiflora"; B, "Passiflora mollissima"; C, Odontoglossum luteo purpureum"; D, "Stanhopea tigrina".

1960. Air. World Refugee Year.
1030a **333** 60c. grey and green . . 15 15

1960. Air. 8th Pan-American Highway Congress (1st issue). Sheet 46 × 56 mm.
MS1031 **339** 2p.50 brown and blue 5·00 5·00
See also Nos. 1056/60.

334 Lincoln Statue, Washington

335 "House of the Flower Vase"

1960. 150th Birth Anniv of Abraham Lincoln.
1032 **334** 20c. blk & mve (postage) 15 10
1033 40c. black & brown (air) 45 25
1034 60c. black and red . . . 25 10

1960. 150th Anniv of Independence.
1035 – 5c. brn & grn (postage) 10 10
1036 **335** 20c. purple and brown 15 10
1037 – 20c. yellow, blue & mve 10 15
1038 – 5c. multicoloured (air) 15 10
1039 – 5c. sepia and violet . . . 15 10
1040 – 35c. multicoloured . . . 20 10
1041 – 60c. green and brown . . 40 10
1042 – 1p. green and red . . . 35 20
1043 – 1p.20 indigo and blue . . 35 20
1044 – 1p.30 black and orange 35 20
1045 – 1p.45 multicoloured . . 65 55
1046 – 1p.65 brown and green 45 35
MS1047 90 × 75 mm. As designs of postage and air stamps but in new colours. 50c. As No. 1037; 50c. As No. 1038; 1p. As No. 1040; 1p. As No. 1035 (Extra Rapido) . . . 3·50 4·00
DESIGNS—VERT: No. 1035, Cartagena coins of 1811–13; 1038, Arms of Cartagena; 1037, Arms of Mompos; 1043, Statue of A. Galan. HORIZ: No. 1039, J. Camacho, J. T. Lozano and J. M. Pey; 1040, 1045, Colombian Flag; 1041, A. Rosillo, A. Villavicencio and J. Caicedo; 1042, B. Alvares and J. Gutierrez; 1044, Front page of "La Bagatela" (newspaper); 1046, A. Santos, J. A. Gomez and L. Mejia.

336 St. Luisa de Marillac and Sanctuary

337 St. Isidro Labrador (after G. Vasquez)

1960. Obligatory Tax. Red Cross Fund.
1048 **336** 5c. red and brown . . . 20 10
1049 – 5c. red and blue 20 10
DESIGN: No. 1049, H. Dunant and battle scene.

1960. St. Isidro Labrador Commem (1st issue).
1050 **337** 10c. mult (postage) . . . 10 10
1051 – 20c. multicoloured . . . 15 10
1052 **337** 35c. multicoloured (air) 20 10
MS1053 90 × 60 mm. As designs of postage stamps but in slightly different colours. 1p.50 As T **337**; 1p.50 As No. 1051 (Extra Rapido) 6·00 6·00
DESIGN: 20c. "The Nativity" (after Vasquez).
See also Nos. 1126/8.

338 U.N. Headquarters, New York

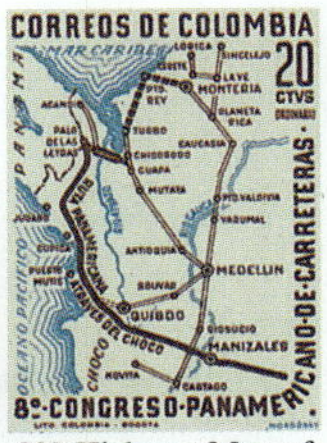

339 Highway Map of Northern Colombia

1960. U.N. Day.
1054 **338** 20c. red and black . . . 15 10
MS1055 55 × 49 mm. **338** 50c. green and chocolate. Imperf . . . . 2·25 2·50

1961. 8th Pan-American Highway Congress.
1056 **339** 20c. brn & bl (postage) 30 25
1057 10c. purple & green (air) 30 25
1058 20c. red and blue 30 25
1059 30c. black and green . . 30 25
1060 10c. blue and green ("EXTRA RAPIDO") 30 25

340 Alfonso Lopez (statesman)

341 Text from Resolution of Confederated Cities

1961. 75th Birth Anniv of Alfonso Lopez (President, 1934–38 and 1941–45).
1061 **340** 10c. brn & red (postage) 15 10
1062 20c. brown and violet . . 15 10
1063 35c. brown & blue (air) 35 10
1064 10c. brown and green ("EXTRA RAPIDO") 15 10
MS1065 74 × 60 mm. **340** 1p. brown and violet . . . . 2·75 2·75

1961. 50th Anniv of Valle del Cauca.
1066 – 10c. mult (postage) . . . 10 10
1067 **341** 20c. brown and black . . 15 10
1068 – 35c. brown & olive (air) 30 10
1069 – 35c. brown & green . . . 30 10
1070 – 1p.30 sepia and purple 35 15
1071 – 1p.45 green and brown 35 15
1072 – 10c. brown and olive ("EXTRA RAPIDO") 15 10
DESIGNS—HORIZ: 10c. (No. 1066), La Ermita Church, bridge and arms of Cali; 35c. (No. 1068), St. Francis' Church, Cali; 1p.30, Conservatoire; 1p.45, Agricultural College, Palmira. VERT: 10c. (No. 1072), Aerial view of Cali; 35c. (No. 1069), University emblem.

342 Arms and View of Cucuta

345 Arms of Barranquilla

1961. 50th Anniv of North Santander.
1073 – 20c. mult (postage) . . . 15 10
1074 **342** 20c. multicoloured . . . 15 10
1075 – 35c. green & bistre (air) 45 10
1076 – 10c. purple & green ("EXTRA RAPIDO") 15 10
DESIGNS—HORIZ: No. 1073, Arms of Ocana and Pamplona; 1075, Panoramic view of Cucuta. VERT: No. 1076, Villa del Rosario, Cucuta.

1961. Air. Optd **Aereo** (1077) or **AEREO** (others) and airplane or surch also.
1077 **332** 5c. multicoloured 10 10
1078 – 5c. brown & turquoise (No. 1005) 10 10
1079 – 10c. on 20c. purple and yellow (No. 1007) . . 10 10

1961. Atlantico Tourist Issue.
1080 – 10c. mult (postage) . . . 10 10
1081 **345** 20c. red, blue and yellow 15 10
1082 – 20c. multicoloured . . . 15 10
1083 – 35c. sepia and red (air) 45 10
1084 – 35c. red, yellow & green 35 10
1085 – 35c. blue and gold . . . 65 10
1086 – 1p.45 brown and green 45 20
MS1087 90 × 76 mm. As designs of postage and air stamps but in new colours: 35c. As T **345**; 40c. As No. 1080; 1p. As No. 1084; 1p. As No. 1088 . . . . 3·75 3·75
1088 – 10c. yellow and brown ("EXTRA RAPIDO") 15 10
MS1089 90 × 76 mm. As designs of postage and air stamps but in new colours: 50c. As No. 1085; 50c. As No. 1083; 50c. As No. 1082; 50c. As No. 1088 . . . . 3·75 3·75
DESIGNS—VERT: No. 1080, Arms of Popayan; 1082, Arms of Bucaramanga; 1083, Courtyard of Tourist Hotel; 1087, Holy Week procession, Popayan. HORIZ: No. 1084, View of San Gill; 1085, Barranquilla Port; 1086, View of Velez.

346 Nurse M. de la Cruz

347 Boxing

1961. Red Cross Fund. Cross in red.
1090 **346** 5c. brown 15 10
1091 5c. purple 15 10

1961. 4th Bolivarian Games. Inscr as in T **347**. Multicoloured.
1092 20c. Type **347** (postage) . . 20 10
1093 20c. Basketball 10 10
1094 20c. Running 10 10
1095 25c. Football 20 10
1096 35c. Diving (air) 25 10
1097 35c. Tennis 25 10
1098 1p.45 Baseball 35 15
1099 10c. Statue and flags ("EXTRA RAPIDO") . . 10 10
1100 10c. Runner with Olympic torch ("EXTRA RAPIDO") 10 10
MS1101 74 × 106 mm. mult. 50c. Statue and flags; 50c. Baseball; 1p. Football; 1p. Basketball . . . 3·75 3·75

348 "SEM" Emblem and Mosquito

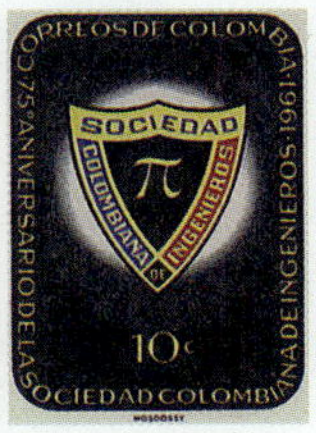

349 Society Emblem

1962. Malaria Eradication.
1102 **348** 20c. red & ochre (post) 15 15
1103 – 50c. blue and ochre . . . 15 15
1104 **348** 40c. red & yellow (air) 15 15
1105 – 1p.45 blue and grey . . 40 40
1106 – 1p. blue and green ("EXTRA RAPIDO") 2·75 2·75
DESIGN: 50c., 1p., 1p.45, Campaign emblem and mosquito.

1962. 6th National Engineers' Congress, 1961 and 75th Anniv of Colombian Society of Engineers.
1107 **349** 10c. mult (postage) . . . 20 20
1108 – 5c. red and blue (air) . . 10 10
1109 – 10c. brown and green . . 30 15
1110 – 15c. brown and purple . . 25 15
1111 **349** 2p. multicoloured ("EXTRA RAPIDO") 1·60 90
DESIGNS: No. 1108, A. Ramos and Engineering Faculty, Cauca University, Popayan; 1109, M. Triana, A. Arroyo and Monserrate cable and funicular railway; 1110, D. Sanchez and first Society H.Q., Bogota.

350 OEA Emblem

351 Mother Voting and Statue of Policarpa Salavarrieta

1962. 70th Anniv of Organization of American States (OEA). Flags multicoloured; background colours given.
1112 **350** 25c. red & blk (postage) 15 10
MS1113 41 × 45 mm. **350** 2p.50 yellow and black . . . . . . 3·00 3·00
1114 35c. blue & black (air) . . . 15 10

1962. Women's Franchise.
1115 **351** 5c. black, grey and brown (postage) . . . 10 10
1116 10c. black, grey and blue 15 10
1117 5c. blk, grey & pink (air) 10 10
1118 35c. black, grey & buff 25 10
1119 45c. black, grey & green 25 10
1120 45c. black, grey & mauve 25 10

353 Scouts in Camp

354 St. Isidro Labrador (after G. Vasquez)

1962. 30th Anniv of Colombian Boy Scouts and 25th Anniv of Colombian Girl Scouts. As T **353** but without "EXTRA RAPIDO".
1121 **353** 10c. brn & turq (postage) 10 10
1122 15c. brown & red (air) 25 10
1123 – 40c. lake and red 15 10
1124 – 1p. blue and Salmon . . 30 15
1125 **353** 1p. violet & yellow ("EXTRA RAPIDO") 3·50 3·25
DESIGN: 40c., 1p. Girl Scouts.

1962. St. Isidro Labrador Commem (2nd issue).
1126 **354** 10c. multicoloured . . . 10 10
1127 – 10c. mult (air—"EXTRA RAPIDO") 10 10
1128 **354** 2p. multicoloured . . . 2·50 1·50
DESIGN: 10c. (No. 1127), "The Nativity" (after G. Vasquez).

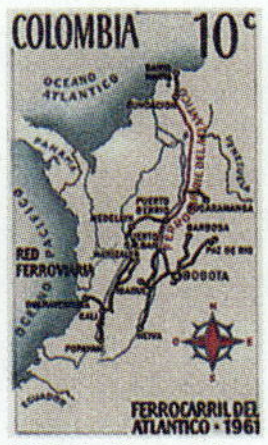

355 Railway Map

356 Posthorn

1962. Completion of Colombia Atlantic Railway.
1129 **355** 10c. red, green and olive (postage) 30 20
1130 – 5c. myrtle & sepia (air) 30 10
1131 **355** 10c. red, turq & bistre 30 20
1132 – 1p. brown and purple . . 4·50 45
1133 – 5p. brown, blue & grn ("EXTRA RAPIDO") 10·00 4·50
DESIGNS—HORIZ: 5c. 1854 steam and 1961 diesel locomotives; 1, 5p. Pres. A. Parra and R. Magdalena railway bridge.

1962. 50th Anniv of Postal Union of the Americas and Spain.
1134 **356** 20c. gold & bl (postage) 15 10
1135 – 50c. gold & green (air) 30 10
1136 **356** 60c. gold and purple . . 20 10
DESIGN: 50c. Posthorn, dove and map.

357 Virgin of the Mountain, Bogota

358 Centenary Emblem

1963. Ecumenical Council, Vatican City.
1137 **357** 60c. mult (postage) . . . 20 10
1138 – 60c. red, yell & gold (air) 10 10
DESIGN: No. 1138, Pope John XXIII.

1963. Obligatory Tax. Red Cross Centenary.
1139 **358** 5c. red and bistre . . . 10 10

359 Hurdling and Flags

1963. Air. South American Athletic Championships, Cali.
1140 **359** 20c. multicoloured . . . 15 10
1141 80c. multicoloured . . . 15 10

360 Bolivar Monument

1963. Air. Centenary of Pereira.
1142 **360** 1p.90 brown and blue . . 10 10

361 Tennis Player **363** Veracruz Church

362 Pres. Kennedy and Alliance Emblem

1963. Air. 30th South American Tennis Championships, Medellin.
1143 **361** 55c. multicoloured . . . 25 10

1963. Air. "Alliance for Progress".
1144 **362** 10c. multicoloured . . . 10 10

1964. Air. National Pantheon, Veracruz Church. Multicoloured.
1145 1p. Type **363** 25 10
1146 2p. "The Crucifixion" . . . 35 20

364 Cartagena

1964. Air. Cartagena Commemoration.
1147 **364** 3p. multicoloured . . . 80 55

365 Eleanor Roosevelt

1964. Air. 15th Anniv of Declaration of Human Rights.
1148 **365** 20c. brown and olive . . 10 10

366 A. Castilla (composer and founder) and Music

1964. Air. Tolima Conservatoire Commem.
1149 **366** 30c. turquoise & bistre 20 10

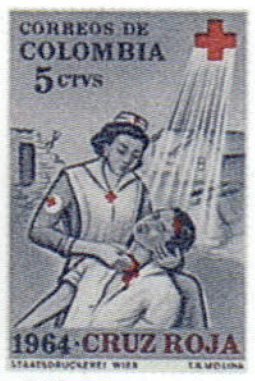

367 Manuel Mejia and Coffee Growers' Flag Emblem **368** Nurse with Patient

1965. Manuel Mejia Commemoration.
1150 **367** 25c. brn & red (postage) 10 10
1151 – 45c. sepia & brown (air) 15 10
1152 – 5p. black and green . . 1·60 30
1153 – 10p. black and blue . . 2·10 25

DESIGNS: 45c. Gathering coffee-beans; 5p. Mule transport; 10p. Freighter "Manuel Mejia" at Buenaventura Port. Each design includes a portrait of M. Mejia, director of the National Coffee Growers' Association.

1965. Obligatory Tax. Red Cross Fund.
1154 **368** 5c. blue and red 10 10

369 ITU Emblem and "Waves" **370** Orchid ("Cattleya trianae")

1965. Air. Centenary of ITU.
1155 **369** 80c. indigo, red and blue 15 10

1965. Air. 5th Philatelic Exhibition, Bogota.
1156 **370** 20c. multicoloured . . . 20 10

371 Satellites, Telegraph Pole and Map

1965. Air. Cent of Colombian Telegraphs. Mult.
1157 60c. Type **371** 15 10
1158 60c. Statue of Pres. Murrillo Toro, Bogota (vert) . . . 15 10

372 Junkers F-13 Seaplane "Colombia" (1920)

1965. Air. "History of Colombian Aviation". Multicoloured.
1159 5c. Type **372** 10 10
1160 10c. Dornier Wal Do-J (1924) 10 10
1161 20c. Dornier Do-B Merkur seaplane (1926) 20 10
1162 50c. Ford 5-AT Trimotor (1932) 20 10
1163 60c. De Havilland Gipsy Moth (1930) 30 10
1164 1p. Douglas DC-4 (1947) . . 35 10
1165 1p.40 Douglas DC-3 (1944) 20 15
1166 2p.80 Lockheed Constellation (1951) . . . 45 30
1167 3p. Boeing 720B jet liner (1961) 65 55
See also No. E1168.

373 Badge, and Car on Mountain Road

1966. Air. 25th Anniv (1965) of Colombian Automobile Club.
1168 **373** 20c. multicoloured . . . 10 10

374 J. Arboleda (writer)

1966. Julio Arboleda Commemoration.
1169 **374** 5c. multicoloured 10 10

375 Red Cross and Children as Nurse and Patient

1966. Obligatory Tax. Red Cross Fund.
1170 **375** 5c.+5c. mult 10 10

376 16th-century Galleon

1966. History of Maritime Mail. Multicoloured.
1171 5c. Type **376** 20 10
1172 15c. Riohacha brigantine (1850) 35 15
1173 20c. Uraba schooner 35 15
1174 40c. Steamer and barge, Magdalena, 1900 . . . . 65 15
1175 50c. Modern freighter . . . 1·90 1·00

377 Hogfish

1966. Fishes. Multicoloured.
1176 80c. Type **377** (postage) . . 30 10
1177 10p. Spotted electric ray . . 4·75 3·25
1178 2p. Pacific flyingfish (air) . . 15 20
1179 2p.80 Blue angelfish 50 30
1180 20p. King mackerel . . . . 8·75 5·75

378 Arms of Colombia, Venezuela and Chile **379** C. Torres (patriot)

1966. Visits of Chilean and Venezuelan Presidents.
1181 **378** 40c. mult (postage) . . . 10 10
1182 1p. multicoloured (air) 25 10
1183 1p.40 multicoloured . . 25 10

1967. Famous Colombians.
1184 **379** 25c. vio & yell (postage) 10 10
1185 – 60c. purple and yellow 10 10
1186 – 1p. green and yellow . . 35 10
1187 – 80c. blue & yellow (air) 15 10
1188 – 1p.70 black and yellow 30 10

PORTRAITS: 60c. J. T. Lozano (naturalist); 80c. Father F. R. Mejia (scholar); 1p. F. A. Zea (writer); 1p.70, J. J. Casas (diplomat).

380 Map of Signatory Countries

1967. "Declaration of Bogota".
1189 **380** 40c. mult (postage) . . . 15 10
1190 60c. multicoloured . . . 15 10
1191 3p. multicoloured (air) 30 15

381 "Monochaetum" and Bee

1967. National Orchid Congress and Tropical Flora and Fauna Exhibition, Medellin. Multicoloured.
1192 25c. Type **381** (postage) . . 10 10
1193 2p. "Passiflora vitifolia" and butterfly 45 35
1194 1p. "Cattleya dowiana" (vert) (air) 15 10
1195 1p.20 "Masdevallia coccinea" (vert) 10 10
1196 5p. "Catasetum macrocarpum" and bee 55 10
MS1197 100 × 150 mm. Nos. 1194/6 4·00 3·50

382 Nurse's Cap **383** Lions Emblem

1967. Obligatory Tax. Red Cross Fund.
1198 **382** 5c. red and blue 10 10

1967. 50th Anniv of Lions International.
1199 **383** 10p. mult (postage) . . . 1·40 35
1200 25c. multicoloured (air) 15 10

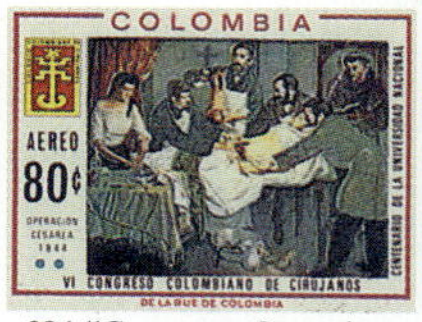

384 "Caesarean Operation, 1844" (from painting by Grau) **385** SENA Emblem

1967. Air. 6th Colombian Surgeons' Congress, Bogota and Centenary of National University.
1201 **384** 80c. multicoloured . . . 15 10

1967. 10th Anniv of National Apprenticeship Service.
1202 **385** 5p. black, gold and green (postage) . . . . . . 1·25 20
1203 2p. black, gold and red (air) 20 10

386 Calima Diadem **387** Radio Antenna

1967. Administrative Council of UPU Consultative Commission of Postal Studies. Main design and lower inscr in brown and gold.
1204 **386** 1p.60 pur (postage) . . . 15 10
1205 – 3p. blue 35 10
1206 – 30c. red (air) 20 10
1207 – 5p. red 90 20
1208 – 20p. violet . . . . . 7·00 4·25
MS1209 92 × 92 mm. Nos. 1206/7 but in new colours. Imperf . . 1·75 1·75

DESIGNS (Colombian archaeological treasures) VERT: 30c. Chief's head-dress; 5p. Cauca breastplate; 20p. Quimbaya jug. HORIZ: 3p. Tolima anthropomorphic figure and postal "pigeon on globe" emblem.

1968. "21 Years of National Telecommunications Services". Inscr "1947–1968".
1210 **387** 50c. mult (postage) . . . 15 10
1211 – 1p. multicoloured . . . 30 10
1212 – 50c. mult (air) 15 10
1213 – 1p. yellow, grey & blue 30 10

DESIGNS: No. 1211, Communications network; 1212, Diagram; 1213, Satellite.

388 The Eucharist **389** "St. Augustine" (Vasquez)

1968. 39th International Eucharistic Congress, Bogota (1st issue).
1214 **388** 60c. mult (postage) . . . 15 10
1215 80c. multicoloured (air) 15 10
1216 3p. multicoloured . . . 35 10

1968. 39th International Eucharistic Congress, Bogota (2nd Issue). Multicoloured.
1217 25c. Type **389** (postage) . . 10 10
1218 60c. "Gathering Manna" (Vasquez) 10 10
1219 1p. "Betrothal of the Virgin and St. Joseph" (B. de Figueroa) 10 10
1220 5p. "La Lechuga" (Jesuit Statuette) 25 20
1221 10p. "Pope Paul VI" (painting by Franciscan Missionary Mothers) . . 55 10
1222 80c. "The Last Supper" (Vasquez) (horiz) (air) . . 15 10
1223 1p. "St. Francis Xavier's Sermon" (Vasquez) . . . 25 10
1224 2p. "Elijah's Dream" (Vasquez) 10 10
1225 3p. As No. 1220 . . . . 25 10
1226 20p. As No. 1221 . . . . 3·25 90
MS1227 91 × 90 mm. Nos. 1220/1. Imperf . . . . 1·60 1·60

390 Pope Paul VI

391 University Arms

1968. Pope Paul's Visit to Colombia. Multicoloured.
1228 25c. Type **390** (postage) . . 15 10
1229 80c. Reception podium (horiz) (air) 15 10
1230 1p.20 Pope Paul giving Blessing 10 10
1231 1p.80 Cathedral, Bogota . . 10 15

1968. Centenary of National University.
1232 **391** 80c. mult (postage) . . . 10 10
1233 – 20c. red, green and yellow (air) 10 10
DESIGN: 20c. Mathematical symbols.

392 Antioquia 2½c. Stamp of 1858

393 Institute Emblem and Split Leaf

1968. Centenary of First Antioquia Stamps.
1234 **392** 30c. blue and green . . . 10 10
MS1235 59 × 79 mm. 5p. blue and bistre . . . . 2·25 2·50
See also Nos. 1249/50.

1969. 25th Anniv (1967) of Inter-American Agricultural Sciences Institute.
1236 **393** 20c. mult (postage) . . . 10 10
1237 1p. multicoloured (air) 15 10

394 Pen and Microscope

1969. Air. 20th Anniv of University of the Andes.
1238 **394** 5p. multicoloured . . . 45 10

395 Von Humboldt and Andes (Quindio Region)

1969. Air. Birth Bicentenary of Alexander von Humboldt (naturalist).
1239 **395** 1p. green and brown . . 15 10

396 Junkers F-13 Seaplane and Map

397 Red Cross

1969. Air. 50th Anniv of 1st Colombian Airmail Flight. Multicoloured.
1240 1p. Type **396** 25 15
1241 1p.50 Boeing 720B and globe 30 10
MS1242 93 × 92 mm. Two 15p. designs as Nos. 1240/1 but colours changed. Imperf . . . . 2·50 3·00
See also Nos. 1249/50.

1969. Obligatory Tax. Colombian Red Cross.
1243 **397** 5c. red and violet . . . 10 10

398 "The Battle of Boyaca" (J. M. Espinosa)

1969. 150th Anniv of Independence. Mult.
1244 20c. Type **398** (postage) . . 15 10
1245 30c. "Liberation Army crossing Pisba Pass" (F. A. Caro) 15 10
1246 2p.30 "Entry into Santa Fe" (I. Castillo-Cervantes) (air) 20 20

399 Institute Emblem

400 Cranial Diagram

1969. Air. 20th Anniv of Colombian Social Security Institute.
1247 **399** 20c. green and black . . 10 10

1969. Air. 13th Latin-American Neurological Congress, Bogota.
1248 **400** 70c. multicoloured . . . 20 10

401 Junkers F-13 Seaplane and Puerto Colombia

402 Child posting Christmas Card

1969. Air. 50th Anniv of "Avianca" Airline. Multicoloured.
1249 2p. Type **401** 40 10
1250 3p.50 Boeing 720B and globe 35 25
MS1251 93 × 91 mm. As Nos. 1249/50 but face values changed to 3p.50 and 5p. Imperf 2·50 3·00

1969. Air. Christmas. Multicoloured.
1252 60c. Type **402** 15 10
1253 1p. Type **402** 15 10
1254 1p.50 Child with Christmas presents 45 10

403 "Poverty"

405 National Sports Institute Emblem

404 Dish Aerial and Ancient Head

1970. Colombian Social Welfare Institute and 10th Anniv of Children's Rights Law.
1255 **403** 30c. multicoloured . . . 10 10

1970. Air. Opening of Satellite Earth Station, Choconta.
1256 **404** 1p. black, red & green 40 10

1970. Air. 9th National Games, Ibague (1st issue).
1257 **405** 1p.50 black, yell & grn 25 15
1258 – 2p.30 multicoloured . . 15 20
DESIGN: 2p.30, Dove and rings (Games emblem).
See also No. 1265.

406 Exhibition Emblem

1970. Air. 2nd Fine Arts Biennial, Medellin.
1259 **406** 30c. multicoloured . . . 10 10

407 Dr. E. Santos (founder) and Buildings

1970. Air. 30th Anniv (1969) of Territorial Credit Institute.
1260 **407** 1p. black, yellow & grn 15 10

408 U.N. Emblem, Scales and Dove

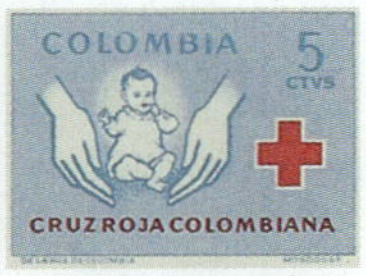

409 Hands protecting Child

1970. Air. 25th Anniv of United Nations.
1261 **408** 1p.50 yellow, bl & ultram 20 10

1970. Obligatory Tax. Colombian Red Cross.
1262 **409** 5c. red and blue 10 10

410 Theatrical Mask

1970. Latin-American University Theatre Festival. Manizales.
1263 **410** 30c. brown, orange & blk 10 10

411 Postal Emblem, Letter and Stamps

1970. Philatelic Week.
1264 **411** 2p. multicoloured . . . 30 10

412 Discus-thrower and Ibague Arms

1970. 9th National Games, Ibague (2nd issue).
1265 **412** 80c. brown, green & yell 20 10

413 "St. Teresa" (B. de Figueroa)

414 Int Philatelic Federation Emblem

1970. St. Teresa of Avila's Elevation to Doctor of the Universal Church. No. 1267 optd **AEREO**.
1266 **413** 2p. mult (postage) . . . 10 10
1267 2p. mult (air) 30 10

1970. Air. "EXFILCA 70" Stamp Exhibition, Caracas, Venezuela.
1268 **414** 10p. multicoloured . . . 1·50 20

415 Chicha Maya Dance

416 Stylized Athlete

1970. Folklore Dances and Costumes. Mult.
1269 1p. Type **415** (postage) . . . 35 10
1270 1p.10 Currulao dance . . . 35 10
1271 60c. Napanga costume (air) 20 15
1272 1p. Joropo dance 20 10
1273 1p.30 Guabina dance . . . 30 10
1274 1p.30 Bambuco dance . . . 20 10
1275 1p.30 Cumbia dance 20 10
MS1276 Two sheets each 80 × 110 mm. Face values and colours changed. (a) 2p.50 As No. 1271; 2p.50 As No. 1272; 5p. As No. 1273. (b) 4p. As No. 1270; 4p. As No. 1274; 4p. As No. 1275 Pair . . . . 7·00 7·00
In MS1276 "AERO" is omitted from the design.

1971. Air. 6th Pan-American Games, Cali (1st issue).
1277 **416** 1p.50 multicoloured . . 35 45
1278 – 2p. orange, green & blk 35 40
DESIGN: 2p. Games emblem.

417 G. Alzate Avendano

1971. Air. 10th Anniv of Gilberto Alzate Avendano (politician).
1279 **417** 1p. multicoloured . . . 15 25

418 Priest's House, Guacari

1971. 400th Anniv of Guacari (town).
1280 **418** 1p. multicoloured . . . 25 10

419 Commemorative Medal

1971. Air. Centenary of Bank of Bogota.
1281 **419** 1p. gold, brown & green 40 20

420 Sports Centre

421 Weightlifting

1971. Air. 6th Pan-American Games (2nd issue) and "EXFICALI 71" Stamp Exhibition, Cali. Mult.
1282 1p.30 Type **420** (yellow emblem) 40 30
1283 1p.30 Football 40 30
1284 1p.30 Wrestling 40 30
1285 1p.30 Cycling 40 30
1286 1p.30 Volleyball 40 30
1287 1p.30 Diving 40 30
1288 1p.30 Fencing 40 30
1289 1p.30 Type **420** (green emblem) 40 30
1290 1p.30 Sailing 40 30
1291 1p.30 Show-jumping 40 30
1292 1p.30 Athletics 40 30
1293 1p.30 Rowing 40 30
1294 1p.30 Cali emblem 40 30
1295 1p.30 Netball 40 30
1296 1p.30 Type **420** (blue emblem) 40 30
1297 1p.30 Stadium 40 30
1298 1p.30 Baseball 40 30
1299 1p.30 Hockey 40 30
1300 1p.30 Type **421** 40 30
1301 1p.30 Medals 40 30
1302 1p.30 Boxing 40 30
1303 1p.30 Gymnastics 40 30
1304 1p.30 Rifle-shooting 40 30
1305 1p.30 Type **420** (red emblem) 40 30

422 "Bolivar at Congress" (after S. Martinez-Delgado)

1971. 150th Anniv of Great Colombia Constituent Assembly, Rosario del Cucuta.
1306 **422** 80c. multicoloured . . . 15 10

423 "Battle of Carabobo" (M. Tovar y Tovar)

1971. Air. 150th Anniv of Battle of Carabobo.
1307 **423** 1p.50 multicoloured . . 15 15

424 CIME Emblem

1972. 20th Anniv of Inter-Governmental Committee on European Migration.
1308 **424** 60c. black and grey . . . 25 10

425 ICETEX Symbol

1972. 20th Anniv of Institute of Educational Credit and Technical Training Abroad.
1309 **425** 1p.10 brown and green 20 10

426 Rev. Mother Francisca del Castillo

1972. 300th Birth Anniv of Reverend Mother Francisca J. del Castillo.
1310 **426** 1p.20 multicoloured . . 20 10

427 Soldier and Frigate "Almirante Padilla"

1972. 20th Anniv of Colombian Troops' Participation in Korean War.
1311 **427** 1p.20 multicoloured . . 1·25 15

428 Hat and Ceramics

429 "Maxillaria triloris" (orchid)

1972. Colombian Crafts and Products. Mult.
1312 1p.10 Type **428** (postage) . . 30 10
1313 50c. Woman in shawl (air) 30 10
1314 1p. Male doll 20 10
1315 3p. Female doll 20 25

1972. 10th National Stamp Exhibition and 7th World Orchid-growers' Congress, Medellin. Mult.
1316 20p. Type **429** (postage) . . 5·00 25
1317 1p.30 "Mormodes rolfeanum" (orchid) (horiz) (air) 15 10

430 Uncut Emeralds and Pendant

432 Congo Dance

431 Pres. Narino's House

1972. Colombian Emeralds.
1318 **430** 1p.10 multicoloured . . 30 10

1972. 400th Anniv of Leyva (town).
1319 **431** 1p.10 multicoloured . . 30 10

1972. Air. Barranquilla International Carnival.
1320 **432** 1p.30 multicoloured . . 10 10

433 Island Scene

435 "Pres. Laureano Gomez" (R. Cubillos)

1972. 150th Anniv of Annexation of San Andres and Providencia Islands.
1321 **433** 60c. multicoloured . . . 20 10

1972. Air. No. 1142 surch.
1322 **360** 1p.30 on 1p.90 brn and bl 20 15

1972. Air. Pres. Gomez Commemoration.
1323 **435** 1p.30 multicoloured . . 20 10

436 Postal Administration Emblem

1972. National Postal Administration.
1324 **436** 1p.10 green 15 10

437 Colombian Family

1972. "Social Front for the People" Campaign.
1325 **437** 60c. orange 10 10

438 Pres. Guillermo Valencia

439 Benito Juarez

1972. Air. Pres. Valencia Commemoration.
1326 **438** 1p.30 multicoloured . . 25 10

1972. Air. Death Centenary of Benito Juarez (Mexican statesman).
1327 **439** 1p.50 multicoloured . . 20 10

440 "La Rebeca" Monument

441 "350" and Arms of Bucaramanga

1972. Air. "La Rebeca" Monument, Centenary Park, Bogota.
1328 **440** 80c. multicoloured . . . 25 30
1329 1p. multicoloured . . . 20 10

1972. Air. 350th Anniv of Bucaramanga (city).
1330 **441** 5p. multicoloured . . . 30 10

442 University Buildings

443 League Emblems

1973. Air. 350th Anniv of Javeriana University.
1331 **442** 1p.30 brown and green 25 10
1332 1p.50 brown and blue . . 25 10

1973. 40th Anniv of Colombian Radio Amateurs League.
1333 **443** 60c. red, dp blue & blue 15 10

444 Tamalameque Vessel

445 "Battle of Maracaibo" (M. F. Rincon)

1973. Inauguration of Museum of Pre-Colombian Antiques, Bogota. Multicoloured.
1334 60c. Type **444** (postage) . . 25 10
1335 1p. Tairona axe-head . . . 45 10
1336 1p.10 Muisca jug 30 10
1337 1p. As No. 1335 (air) . . . 40 35
1338 1p.30 Sinu vessel 20 10
1339 1p.70 Quimbaya vessel . . . 25 20
1340 3p.50 Tumaco figurine . . . 50 30

1973. Air. 150th Anniv of Naval Battle of Maracaibo.
1341 **445** 10p. multicoloured . . . 3·25 30

446 Banknote Emblem

1973. Air. 50th Anniv of Republican Bank.
1342 **446** 2p. multicoloured . . . 25 10

1973. Air. No. 1306 optd **AEREO**.
1343 **422** 80c. multicoloured . . . 15 10

448 "Pres. Ospina" (after C. Leudo)

449 Arms of Toro

1973. Air. 50th Anniv of Ministry of Communications.
1344 **448** 1p.50 multicoloured . . 20 10

1973. Air. 400th Anniv of Toro.
1345 **449** 1p. multicoloured . . . 15 10

450 Bolivar at Bombona

1973. Air. 150th Anniv of Battle of Bombona.
1346 **450** 1p.30 multicoloured . . 20 10

451 "General Narino" (after J. M. Espinosa)

452 Young Child

1973. 150th Death Anniv of General Antonio Narino.
1347 **451** 60c. multicoloured . . . 15 10

1973. Child Welfare Campaign.
1348 **452** 1p.10 multicoloured . . 20 10

453 Fiscal Emblem

1974. 50th Anniv of Republic's General Comptrollership.
1349 **453** 80c. black, brown & bl . . . 15 10

454 Copernicus

455 Andes Communications and Map

1974. Air. 500th Birth Anniv of Copernicus.
1350 **454** 2p. multicoloured . . . 20 15

1974. Air. Meeting of Communications Ministers, Andean Group, Cali.
1351 **455** 2p. multicoloured . . . 10 15

456 Laura Montoya and Cross

457 Television Set with Inravision Emblem

1974. Birth Centenary of Revd. Mother Laura Montoya (missionary).
1352 **456** 1p. multicoloured . . . 15 10

1974. Air. 20th Anniv of Inravision (National Institute of Radio and Television).
1353 **457** 1p.30 black, brn & orge . . 20 10

458 Athlete

1974. 10th National Games, Pereira.
1354 **458** 2p. brown, red & yellow . . 20 10

459 Rivera and Statue

1974. 50th Anniv of Novel "La Voragine".
1355 **459** 10p. multicoloured . . . 35 15

460 Aquatic Emblem

1974. Air. 2nd World Swimming Championships, Cali (1975).
1356 **460** 4p.50 blue, turq & blk . . 30 15

461 Condor Emblem

1974. Air. Centenary of Bank of Colombia.
1357 **461** 1p.50 multicoloured . . 20 10

462 Tailplane

1974. Air.
1358 **462** 20c. brown 10 10

463 UPU "Letter"

1974. Air. Centenary of Universal Postal Union (1st issue).
1359 **463** 20p. red, blue & black . . 1·10 30
See also Nos. 1363/6.

464 General Jose Maria Cordoba

465 "Progress and Expansion"

1974. Air. 150th Anniv of Battles of Junin and Ayacucho.
1360 **464** 1p.30 multicoloured . . 20 10

1974. Centenary of Colombian Insurance Company.
1361 **465** 1p.10 mult (postage) . . 20 10
1362 3p. mult (air) 35 10

466 White-tailed Trogon and U.P.U. "Letter"

467 La Quiebra Tunnel

1974. Air. Centenary of U.P.U. (2nd issue). Colombian Birds. Multicoloured.
1363 1p. Type **466** 75 40
1364 1p.30 Red-billed toucan (horiz) 75 50
1365 2p. Andean cock of the rock (horiz) . . . . 1·50 50
1366 2p.50 Scarlet macaw . . . . 1·50 60
Nos. 1364/6 also depict the U.P.U. "letter".

1974. Centenary of Antioquia Railway.
1367 **467** 1p.10 multicoloured . . 90 35

468 Boy with Ball

1974. Christmas. Multicoloured.
1368 80c. Type **468** 10 10
1369 1p. Girl with racquet . . . 10 15

469 "Protect the Trees"

1975. Air. Colombian Ecology. Multicoloured.
1370 1p. Type **469** 20 10
1371 6p. "Protect the Amazon" . . 20 15

470 "Wood No. 1" (R. Roncancio)

1975. Air. Colombian Art. Multicoloured.
1372 2p. Type **470** . . . . . . 1·00 30
1373 3p. "The Market" (M. Diaz Vargas) (vert) . . . . . . 1·75 30
1374 4p. "Child with Thorn" (G. Vazquez) (vert) . . . 15 10
1375 5p. "The Annunciation" (Santaferena School) (vert) 45 30

471 Gold Cat

1975. Pre-Colombian Archaeological Discoveries. Sinu Culture. Multicoloured.
1376 80c. Type **471** (postage) . . 20 10
1377 1p.10 Gold necklace 20 10
1378 2p. Nose pendant (air) . . . 40 10
1379 10p. "Alligator" staff ornament . . . . 2·10 35

472 Marconi and "Elettra" (steam yacht)

473 Santa Marta Cathedral

1975. Birth Centenary of Guglielmo Marconi (radio pioneer).
1380 **472** 3p. multicoloured . . . 75 10

1975. 450th Anniv of Santa Marta. Multicoloured.
1381 80c. Type **473** (postage) . . 10 10
1382 2p. "El Rodadero" (sea-front), Santa Marta (horiz) (air) 20 10

474 Maria de J. Paramo (educationalist)

475 Pres. Nunez

1975. International Women's Year.
1383 **474** 4p. multicoloured . . . 25 10

1975. 150th Birth Anniv of President Rafael Nunez.
1384 **475** 1p.10 multicoloured . . 15 10

476 Arms of Medellin

479 Sugar Cane

1975. 300th Anniv of Medellin.
1385 **476** 1p. multicoloured . . . 25 10
See also Nos. 1386, 1388, 1394, 1404, 1419, 1434, 1481/3, 1672/4, 1678/9, 1752, 1758, 1859 and 1876.

1976. Centenary of Reconstruction of Cucuta City. As T **476**.
1386 1p.50 multicoloured 30 10

1976. Surch.
1387 **471** 1p.20 on 80c. mult . . . 15 10

1976. Arms of Cartagena. As T **476**.
1388 1p.50 multicoloured 20 10

1976. 4th Cane Sugar Export and Production Congress, Cali.
1389 **479** 5p. green and black . . 45 10

480 Bogota

1976. Air. Habitat. U.N. Conference on Human Settlements. Multicoloured.
1390 10p. Type **480** . . . . . . 1·10 35
1391 10p. Barranquilla . . . . . 1·10 35
1392 10p. Cali . . . . 1·10 35
1393 10p. Medellin . . . . 1·10 35

1976. Arms of Ibague. As T **476**.
1394 1p.20 multicoloured 15 10

481 University Emblem and "90"

482 M. Samper

1976. Air. 90th Anniv of Colombia University.
1395 **481** 5p. multicoloured . . . 20 10

1976. Air. 150th Birth Anniv of Miguel Samper (statesman and writer).
1396 **482** 2p. multicoloured . . . 20 10

483 Early Telephone

484 "Callicore sp."

1976. Air. Telephone Centenary.
1397 **483** 3p. multicoloured . . . 20 10

1976. Colombian Fauna and Flora. Multicoloured.
1398 3p. Type **484** 75 10
1399 5p. "Morpho sp." (butterfly) 1·25 20
1400 20p. Black anthurium (plant) . . . . 1·10 25

485 Purace Indians, Cauca

486 Rotary Emblem

1976.
1401 **485** 1p.50 multicoloured . . 10 10

1976. 50th Anniv of Colombian Rotary Club.
1402 **486** 1p. multicoloured . . . 10 10

487 Boeing 747 Jumbo Jet

1976. Air. Inaug of Avianca Jumbo Jet Service.
1403 **487** 2p. multicoloured . . . 15 10

1976. 535th Anniv of Tunja City Arms. As T **476**.
1404 1p.20 multicoloured 15 10

488 "The Signing of Declaration of Independence" (left-hand detail of painting, Trumbull)
489 Police Handler and Dog

1976. Bicentenary of American Revolution.
1405 **488** 30p. multicoloured . . . 1·75 1·10
1406 – 30p. multicoloured . . . 1·75 1·10
1407 – 30p. multicoloured . . . 1·75 1·10
DESIGNS: Nos. 1406/7 show different portions of the painting.

1976. National Police.
1408 **489** 1p.50 multicoloured . . 25 10

490 Franciscan Convent

1976. Air. 150th Anniv of Panama Congress.
1409 **490** 6p. multicoloured . . . 20 20

491 Head of Columbia

1977. Air. Opening of Philatelic Museum, Medellin. Sheet 130 × 105 mm.
MS1410 **491** 25p. blue, orange and yellow . . . . 5·00 5·50

1977. Surch.
1411 **475** 2p. on 1p.10 mult (postage) 25 10
1412 – 2p. on 1p.20 mult (No. 1404) 20 10
1413 **489** 2p. on 1p.50 mult . . . 20 10
1414 **487** 3p. on 2p. mult (air) . . 15 10

494 Coffee Plant and Beans
495 Coffee Grower with mule

493 Postal Museum, Bogota

1977. Opening of Postal Museum, Bogota. Sheet 130 × 106 mm.
MS1415 **493** 25p. multicoloured 1·50 1·75

1977. Air. Coffee Production.
1416 **494** 3p. multicoloured . . . 15 10
1416a 3p.50 multicoloured . . 20 10

1977. Air. 50th Anniv of National Federation of Coffee Growers.
1417 **495** 10p. multicoloured . . . 20 15

496 Beethoven and Score of Ninth Symphony

1977. Air. 150th Anniv of Beethoven.
1418 **496** 8p. multicoloured . . . 25 15

1977. Arms of Popayan. As T **476**.
1419 5p. multicoloured 30 15

497 Mother feeding Baby
498 Wattled Jacana and "Eichhornia crassipes"

1977. Nutrition Campaign.
1420 **497** 2p. multicoloured . . . 15 10
1420a 2p.50 multicoloured . . 80 10

1977. Colombian Birds and Plants. Multicoloured.
1421 10p. Type **498** (postage) . . 2·25 50
1422 20p. Plum-throated cotinga and "Pyrostegia venusta" 2·50 60
1423 5p. Crimson-mantled woodpecker and "Meriania" (air) . . . . 1·50 50
1424 5p. American purple gallinule and "Nymphaea" . . . . . . 1·50 50
1425 10p. Pampadour cotinga and "Cochlospermum orinocense" . . . . . . 2·75 60
1426 10p. Northern royal flycatcher and "Jacaranda copaia" . . . . 2·75 60

499 Games Emblem
500 "La Cayetana" (E. Grau)

1977. Air. 13th Central American and Caribbean Games, Medellin (1978).
1427 **499** 6p. multicoloured . . . 25 10

1977. Air. 20th Anniv of Female Suffrage. Multicoloured.
1428 8p. Type **500** 20 20
1429 8p. "Nayade" (Beatriz Gonzalez) 20 20

501 "Judge Francisco Antonio Moreno y Escandon" (J. Gutierrez)

1977. Air. Bicentenary of National Library. Mult.
1430 20p. Type **501** 55 10
1431 25p. "Viceroy Manuel de Guiror" (unknown artist) 55 20

502 "Fidel Cano" (Francisco Cano)
503 Abacus and Alphabet

1977. 90th Anniv of "El Espectador" Magazine by Fidel Cano.
1432 **502** 4p. multicoloured . . . 20 10

1977. Popular Education.
1433 **503** 3p. multicoloured . . . 15 10

1977. Arms of Barranquilla. As T **476**.
1434 5p. multicoloured 30 15

504 Dr. F. L. Acosta
505 Cauca University Arms

1977. Air. Birth Centenary of Dr. Federico Lleras Acosta (veterinary surgeon).
1435 **504** 5p. multicoloured . . . 30 10

1977. Air. 150th Anniv of Cauca University.
1436 **505** 5p. multicoloured . . . 25 10

506 "Cudecom" Building, Bogota
508 "Cattleya triannae"

1977. Air. 90th Anniv of Society of Colombian Engineers.
1437 **506** 1p.50 multicoloured . . 10 10

1977. Air. No. 1364 surch **$2.00**.
1438 2p. on 1p.30 multicoloured 90 25

1978.
1439 **508** 2p.50 multicoloured . . 25 10
1439a 3p. multicoloured . . . 25 10

509 Tayronan Lost City
510 "Creator of Energy" (A. Betancourt)

1978. Air.
1440 **509** 3p.50 multicoloured . . 35 10

1978. Air. 150th Anniv of Antioquia University Law School.
1441 **510** 4p. multicoloured . . . 20 10

511 Column of the Slaves
512 "Catalina"

1978. Air. 150th Anniv of Ocana Convention.
1442 **511** 2p.50 multicoloured . . 15 10

1978. Air. 150th Anniv of Cartagena University.
1443 **512** 4p. multicoloured . . . 20 10

513 Running

1978. 13th Central American and Caribbean Games, Medellin. Multicoloured.
1444 10p. Type **513** 35 25
1445 10p. Basketball 35 25
1446 10p. Baseball 35 25
1447 10p. Boxing 35 25
1448 10p. Cycling 35 25
1449 10p. Fencing 35 25
1450 10p. Football 35 25
1451 10p. Gymnastics 35 25
1452 10p. Judo 35 25
1453 10p. Weightlifting 35 25
1454 10p. Wrestling 35 25
1455 10p. Swimming 35 25
1456 10p. Tennis 35 25
1457 10p. Shooting 35 25
1458 10p. Volleyball 35 25
1459 10p. Water polo 35 25

514 "Sigma 2" (A. Herran)
515 Human Figure from Gold Pendant

1978. Centenary of Bogota Chamber of Commerce.
1460 **514** 8p. multicoloured . . . 20 20

1978. Air. Tolima Culture.
1461 **515** 3p.50 multicoloured . . 20 20

516 "Apotheosis of the Spanish Language" (Left-hand detail of mural, L. A. Acuna)

1978. Air. Millenary of Castilian Language. Multicoloured.
1462 11p. Type **516** 55 50
1463 11p. Central detail 55 50
1464 11p. Right-hand detail . . . 55 50
Nos. 1462/4 were issued together, se-tenant, forming a composite design.

517 Presidential Guard

1978. Air. 50th Anniv of Presidential Guard Battalion.
1465 **517** 9p. multicoloured . . . 25 25

518 Human Figure
519 General Tomas Cipriano de Mosquera

1978. Air. Muisca Culture.
1466 **518** 3p.50 multicoloured . . 20 10

1978. Death Centenary of General Tomas Cipriano de Mosquera (statesman).
1467 **519** 6p. multicoloured . . . 20 20

520 El Camarin de Carmen, Bogota
521 Gold Owl Ornament

1978. Air. "Espamer '78" Stamp Exhibition, Bogota.
1468 **520** 30p. multicoloured . . . 1·75 20
MS1469 126 × 96 mm. **520** 50p. multicoloured . . . . 2·75 3·00

1978. Air. Calima Culture.
1470 **521** 3p.50 multicoloured . . 20 10
1470a 4p. multicoloured . . . 25 10

522 "Virgin and Child" (Gregorio Vasquez)
523 Church and Bullring

1978. Air. Christmas.
1471 **522** 2p.50 multicoloured . . 10 10

1978. Air. Manizales Fair.
1472 **523** 7p. multicoloured . . . 25 15

524 Frog in beaten Gold
525 Children playing Hopscotch

1979. Air. Quimbaya Culture.
1473 **524** 4p. multicoloured . . . 15 10

1979. Air. International Year of the Child. Multicoloured.
1474 8p. Type **525** 30 10
1475 12p. Child in sou'wester and oilskins 20 20
1476 12p. Child at blackboard (horiz) 20 20

526 Anthurium
528 "Jimenez de Quesada" (after C. Leudo)

527 Rio Prado Hydro-electric Barrage

1979. Anthurium Flowers from Narino. Multicoloured, background colours given.
1477 **526** 3p. light green 25 10
1478 3p. red 25 10
1479 3p. green 25 10
1480 3p. blue 25 10

1979. Arms. As T **476**. Multicoloured.
1481 4p. Sogamoso 45 10
1482 10p. Socorro 20 15
1483 10p. Santa Cruz y San Gil de la Nueva Baeza . . . 20 15

1979. Air. Tourism. Multicoloured.
1484 5p. Type **527** 35 10
1485 7p. River Amazon 60 30
1486 8p. Tomb, San Agustin Archaeological Park . . . 25 20
1487 14p. San Fernando Fort, Cartagena 45 35

1979. Air. 400th Death Anniv of Gonzalo Jimenez de Quesada (conquistador).
1488 **528** 20p. multicoloured . . . 1·60 65

529 Hill and First Stamps of Great Britain and Colombia

1979. Air. Death Centenary of Sir Rowland Hill.
1489 **529** 15p. multicoloured . . . 25 25

530 "Uribe" (after Acevedo Bernal)

1979. 65th Death Anniv of General Rafael Uribe Uribe (statesman).
1490 **530** 8p. multicoloured . . . 30 15

531 "Village" (Leonor Alarcon)

1979. 20th Anniv of Community Works Boards.
1491 **531** 15p. multicoloured . . . 85 30

532 Three Kings and Soldiers

1979. Air. Christmas. Multicoloured.
1492 3p. Type **532** 75 40
1493 3p. Nativity 75 40
1494 3p. Shepherds 75 40

533 River Magdalena Bridge and Avianca Emblem
534 Gold Nose Pendant

1979. Air. 350th Anniv of Barranquilla and 60th Anniv of Avianca National Airline.
1495 **533** 15p. multicoloured . . . 25 15

1980. Air. Tairona Culture.
1496 **534** 3p. multicoloured . . . 25 10

535 "Boy playing Flute" (Judith Leyster)
536 Antonio Jose de Sucre

1980. Air. 2nd International Music Competition, Ibague.
1497 **535** 6p. multicoloured . . . 30 10

1980. Air. 150th Death Anniv of General Antonio Jose de Sucre.
1498 **536** 12p. multicoloured . . . 20 15

537 "The Watchman" (Edgar Negret)

1980. Air. Modern Sculpture.
1499 **537** 25p. multicoloured . . . 1·40 1·25

538 Television Screen

1980. Inaug of Colour Television in Colombia.
1500 **538** 5p. multicoloured . . . 25 10

539 Bullfighting Poster (H. Courttin)
540 "Learn to Write"

1980. Tourism. Festival of Cali.
1501 **539** 5p. multicoloured . . . 35 15

1980. The Alphabet.
1502 **540** 4p. black, brown & grn 25 10
1503 – 4p. multicoloured . . . 25 10
1504 – 4p. brown, blk & lt brn 25 10
1505 – 4p. multicoloured . . . 40 15
1506 – 4p. brown, black & grn 25 10
1507 – 4p. black and turquoise 25 10
1508 – 4p. black and green . . 25 10
1509 – 4p. mauve, black & grn 40 15
1510 – 4p. black and blue . . . 25 10
1511 – 4p. black and green . . 25 10
1512 – 4p. green, black & brown 25 10
1513 – 4p. multicoloured . . . 25 10
1514 – 4p. brown, black & grn 25 10
1515 – 4p. multicoloured . . . 25 10
1516 – 4p. yellow, black & grn 25 10
1517 – 4p. black, brown & yell 25 10
1518 – 4p. brown, black & turq 25 10
1519 – 4p. brown, black & grn 25 10
1520 – 4p. brown, black & grn 25 10
1521 – 4p. yellow, black & turq 25 10
1522 – 4p. green, black & blue 40 15
1523 – 4p. brown, black & grn 25 10
1524 – 4p. green, black & lt grn 25 10
1525 – 4p. multicoloured . . . 25 10
1526 – 4p. multicoloured . . . 25 10
1527 – 4p. brown, black & grn 25 10
1528 – 4p. multicoloured . . . 40 15
1529 – 4p. multicoloured . . . 25 10
1530 – 4p. brown, black & grn 25 10
1531 – 4p. brown and black . . 25 10

DESIGNS: No. 1503, "a" Eagle; 1504, "b" Buffalo; 1505, "c" Andean Condor; 1506, "ch" Chimpanzee; 1507, "d" Dolphin; 1508, "e" Elephant; 1509, "f" Greater Flamingo; 1510, "g" Seagull; 1511, "h" Hippopotamus; 1512, "i" Iguana; 1513, "j" Giraffe; 1514, "k" Koala; 1515, "l" Lion; 1516, "ll" Llama; 1517, "m" Blackbird; 1518, "n" Otter; 1519, Gnu; 1520, "o" Bear; 1521, "p" Pelican; 1522, "q" Resplendent Quetzal; 1523, "r" Rhinoceros; 1524, "s" Grasshopper; 1525, "t" Tortoise; 1526, "u" Magpie; 1527, "v" Viper; 1528, "w" Wagon with animals; 1529, "x" Fox playing xylophone; 1530, "y" Yak; 1531, "z" Fox.

541 "Miraculous Virgin" (statue, Real del Sarte)

1980. Air. 150th Anniv of Apparition of Holy Virgin to Sister Catalina Labouri Gontard in Paris.
1532 **541** 12p. multicoloured . . . 45 15

542 "Country Scene, San Gil" (painting, Luis Roncancio)

1980. Air. Agriculture.
1533 **542** 12p. multicoloured . . . 1·00 30

543 Villavicencio Song Festival

1980. Tourism. Festivals. Multicoloured.
1534 5p. Type **543** 30 15
1535 9p. Vallenato festival . . . 15 15

544 Gustavo Uribe Ramirez and "Samanea saman"

1980. 12th Death Anniv of Gustavo Uribe Ramirez (ecologist).
1536 **544** 10p. multicoloured . . . 35 15

545 Narino Palace

1980. Narino Palace (Presidential residence).
1537 **545** 5p. multicoloured . . . 30 10

546 Monument to First Pioneers, Armenia

1980. City of Armenia.
1538 **546** 5p. multicoloured . . . 30 10

547 Olaya Herrera (after Miguel Diaz Varges)

549 Athlete with Torch

548 "Simple Simon"

1980. Air. Birth Centenary of Dr. Enrique Olaya Herrera (President, 1930–34).
1539 **547** 20p. multicoloured . . . 45 25

1980. Air. Christmas. Illustrations to stories by Rafael Pombo. Multicoloured.
1540 4p. Type **548** 25 15
1541 4p. "The Cat's Seven Lives" 25 15
1542 4p. "The Walking Tadpole" 25 15

1980. 11th National Games, Neiva.
1543 **549** 5p. multicoloured . . . 20 10

550 Golfers

551 Crab pierced by Sword

1980. Air. 28th World Golf Cup, Cajica.
1544 **550** 30p. multicoloured . . . 2·10 1·50

1980. 20th Anniv of Colombian Anti-cancer League.
1545 **551** 10p. multicoloured . . . 35 20

552 "Justice" and University Emblem

1980. 50th Anniv of Refounding of Pontifical Xavier University Law Faculty.
1546 **552** 20p. multicoloured . . . 25 30

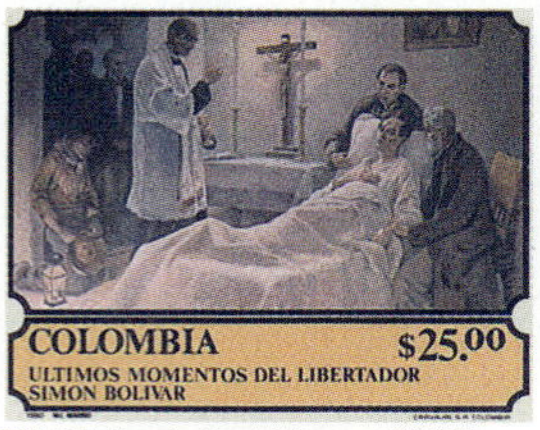

553 "Bolivar's Last Moments" (Marcos Leon Marino)

1980. 150th Death Anniv of Simon Bolivar. Multicoloured.
1547 25p. Type **553** (postage) . . 45 35
1548 6p. Bolivar and his last proclamation (air) 25 25

554 St. Pedro Claver

555 Statue of Bird, San Agustin

1981. Air. 400th Birth Anniv of St. Pedro Claver.
1549 **554** 15p. multicoloured . . . 20 30

1981. Air. Archaeological Discoveries. Mult.
1550 7p. Type **555** 30 15
1551 7p. Hypogeum (funeral chamber), Tierradentro 30 15
1552 7p. Hypogeum, Tierradentro (different) 30 15
1553 7p. Statue of man, San Agustin 30 15

556 "Square Abstract" (Omar Rayo)

1981. Air. 4th Biennial Arts Exhibition, Medellin. Multicoloured.
1554 20p. Type **556** 30 20
1555 25p. "Flowers" (Alejandro Obregon) 40 30
1556 50p. "Child with Hobby Horse" (Fernando Botero) 1·50 1·25

557 Diver

1981. Air. 8th South American Swimming Championships, Medellin.
1557 **557** 15p. multicoloured . . . 25 30

558 Santamaria Bull Ring

1981. Air. 50th Anniv of Santamaria Bull Ring, Bogota.
1558 **558** 30p. multicoloured . . . 1·50 80

559 Mariano Ospina Perez (after Delio Ramirez)

1981. Presidents of Colombia (1st series). Multicoloured.
1559 5p. Type **559** 25 10
1560 5p. Eduardo Santos (after Ines Acevedo) 25 10
1561 5p. Miguel Abadia Mendez (after Gomez Compuzano) 25 10
1562 5p. Jose Vicente Concha (after Acevedo Bernal) . . 25 10
1563 5p. Carlos E. Restrepo . . . 25 10
1564 5p. Rafael Reves (after Acevedo Bernal) 25 10
1565 5p. Santiago Perez 25 10
1566 5p. Manuel Murillo Toro (after Moreno Otero) . . 25 10
1567 5p. Jose Hilario Lopez . . . 25 10
1568 5p. Jose Maria Obando . . 25 10
See also Nos. 1569/78, 1579/88, 1599/1608, 1615/24 and 1634/43.

1981. Presidents of Colombia (2nd series). Multicoloured.
1569 7p. Type **559** . . . . . . 2·75 35
1570 7p. As No. 1560 . . . . . 2·75 35
1571 7p. As No. 1561 . . . . . 2·75 35
1572 7p. As No. 1562 . . . . . 2·75 35
1573 7p. As No. 1563 . . . . . 2·75 35
1574 7p. As No. 1564 . . . . . 2·75 35
1575 7p. As No. 1565 . . . . . 2·75 35
1576 7p. As No. 1566 . . . . . 2·75 35
1577 7p. As No. 1567 . . . . . 2·75 35
1578 7p. As No. 1568 . . . . . 2·75 35

1981. Presidents of Colombia (3rd series). As T **559**. Multicoloured.
1579 7p. Pedro Alcantara Herran 2·10 20
1580 7p. Mariano Ospina Rodriguez (after Coriolando Leudo) . . . 2·10 20
1581 7p. Tomas Cipriano de Mosquera . . . . 2·10 20
1582 7p. Santos Gutierrez . . . . 2·10 20
1583 7p. Aquileo Parra (after Constancio Franco) . . . 2·10 20
1584 7p. Rafael Nunez . . . . . 2·10 20
1585 7p. Marco Fidel Suarez (after Jesus Maria Duque) 2·10 20
1586 7p. Pedro Nel Ospina (after Coriolano Leudo) . . . . 2·10 20
1587 7p. Enrique Olaya Herrera (after M. Diaz Vargas) . . 2·10 20
1588 7p. Alfonso Lopez Pumarejo (after Luis F. Uscategui) 2·10 20

560 Crossed-legged Figure

1981. Air. Quimbaya Culture. Multicoloured.
1589 9p. Type **560** 40 15
1590 9p. Seated figure 40 15
1591 9p. Printing block and print 40 15
1592 9p. Clay pot 40 15

561 Fruit

1981. Air. Fruit. Designs showing fruit.
1593 **561** 25p. multicoloured . . . 2·10 1·40
1594 – 25p. multicoloured . . . 2·10 1·40
1595 – 25p. multicoloured . . . 2·10 1·40
1596 – 25p. multicoloured . . . 2·10 1·40
1597 – 25p. multicoloured . . . 2·10 1·40
1598 – 25p. multicoloured . . . 2·10 1·40
Nos. 1593/8 were issued together in se-tenant blocks of six forming a composite design.

1981. Presidents of Colombia (4th series). As T **559**. Multicoloured.
1599 7p. Manuel Maria Mallarino 1·00 15
1600 7p. Santos Acosta . . . . . 1·00 15
1601 7p. Eustorgio Salgar . . . . 1·00 15
1602 7p. Julian Trujillo . . . . . 1·00 15
1603 7p. Francisco Javier Zaldua (after Francisco Valles) 1·00 15
1604 7p. Jose Eusebio Otalora (after Ricardo Moros) . . 1·00 15
1605 7p. Miguel Antonio Caro 1·00 15
1606 7p. Manuel A. Sanclemente (after Epifanio Garay) . . 1·00 15
1607 7p. Laureano Gomez (after Jose Bascones) . . . . . 1·00 15
1608 7p. Guillermo Leon Valencia (after Luis Angel Rengifo) . . . . 1·00 15

562 "Comunero tearing down Edict" (Manuela Beltran)

1981. Air. Bicentenary of Comuneros Uprising.
1609 **562** 20p. multicoloured . . . 25 30

563 Jose Maria Villa and West Bridge

564 Restrepo (after R. Acevedo Bernal)

1981. West Bridge, Santa Fe de Antioquia.
1610 **563** 60p. multicoloured . . . 65 10

1981. Air. Birth Centenary of Jose Manuel Restrepo (historian).
1611 **564** 35p. multicoloured . . . 35 15

565 Anniversary Emblem

566 Los Nevados National Park

1981. 50th Anniv of Caja Agraria (peasants' bank).
1612 **565** 15p. multicoloured . . . 15 10

1981. Los Nevados National Park.
1613 **566** 20p. multicoloured . . . 20 10

567 Andres Bello

568 Squatting Figure

1981. Birth Centenary of Andres Bello (poet).
1614 **567** 18p. multicoloured . . . 20 15

1981. Presidents of Colombia (5th series). As T **559**. Multicoloured.
1615 7p. Bartolome Calvo (after Miguel Diaz Vargas) . . 60 15
1616 7p. Sergio Camargo 60 15
1617 7p. Jose Maria Rojas Garrido 60 15
1618 7p. J. M. Campo Serrano (after H. L. Brown) . . . 60 15
1619 7p. Eliseo Payan (after R. Moros Urbina) 60 15
1620 7p. Carlos Holguin (after Coriolano Leudo) 60 15
1621 7p. Jose Manuel Marroquin (after Rafael Tavera) . . 60 15
1622 7p. Ramon Gonzalez Valencia (after Jose Maria Vidal) 60 15
1623 7p. Jorge Holguin (after M. Salas Yepes) 60 15
1624 7p. Ruben Piedrahita Arango 60 15

1981. Air. Calima Culture. Multicoloured.
1625 9p. Type **568** 80 15
1626 9p. Vessel with two spouts 80 15
1627 9p. Human-shaped vessel with two spouts 80 15
1628 9p. Pot 80 15

569 1c. Stamp of 1881

1981. Air. Centenary of Admission to UPU.
1629 **569** 30p. green and pink . . 30 20
MS1630 100×70 mm. 50p. multicoloured (2, 5, 10 and 20c. stamps of 1881). Imperf . . . 1·75 2·00

570 Girl with Water Jug

1981. Colombian Solidarity.
1631 **570** 30p. brown, blk & orge 70 30
1632 – 30p. brown, blk & orge 70 30
1633 – 30p. brown, blk & orge 70 30
DESIGNS: No. 1632, Baby with basket; 1633, Boy sitting on wheelbarrow.

1982. Presidents of Colombia (6th series). As T **559**. Multicoloured.
1634 7p. Simon Bolivar 50 15
1635 7p. Francisco de Paula Santander 50 15
1636 7p. Joaquin Mosquera (after C. Franco) 50 15
1637 7p. Domingo Caicedo . . . 50 15
1638 7p. Jose Ignacio de Marquez (after C. Franco) 50 15
1639 7p. Juan de Dios Aranzazu 50 15
1640 7p. Jose de Obaldia (after Jesus M. Duque) 50 15
1641 7p. Guillermo Quintero Calderon (after Silvano Cuellar) 50 15
1642 7p. Carlos Lozano y Lozano (after Helio Ramierz) . . 50 15
1643 7p. Roberto Urdaneta Arbelaez (after Jose Bascones Agneto) 50 15

571 Solano Bay, Choco

1982. Air. Tourism. Multicoloured.
1644 20p. Type **571** 25 30
1645 20p. Tota Lake, Boyaca . . 25 30
1646 20p. Corrales, Boyaca . . . 25 30

572 America Cup Player

1982. Air. World Cup Football Chamoionship, Spain. Sheet 179×150 mm containing T **572** and similar vert designs showing players and badges of Colombian football clubs stadium (h). Multicoloured.
MS1647 9p.×15 (a) Type **572**; (b) Atletico Bucaramanga; (c) Deportivo Cali; (d) Once Caldas; (e) Cucuta Deportivo; (f) Atletico Junior; (g) Independiente Medellin; (h) Barranquilla stadium; (i) Millonarios; (j) Atletico Nacional; (k) Deportivo Pereira; (l) Atletico Quindio; (m) Independiente Santa Fe; (n) Deportes Tolima; (o) Union Magdalena . . . . 3·50 3·25

573 Gun Club Emblem

1982. Air. Centenary of Bogota Gun Club.
1648 **573** 20p. multicoloured . . . 25 15

574 Flower Arrangement in Basket

576 Capitalization Certificate

575 Zoomorphic Figure (crocodile)

1982. Country Flowers. Designs showing flower arrangements. Multicoloured.
1649 7p. Type **574** 75 15
1650 7p. Pink arrangement in basket 75 15
1651 7p. Red roses in pot 75 15
1652 7p. Lilac and white arrangement in basket . . 75 15
1653 7p. Orange and yellow arrangement in basket . . 75 15
1654 7p. Mixed arrangement in vase 75 15
1655 7p. Pink roses in vase . . . 75 15
1656 7p. Daisies in pot 75 15
1657 7p. Bouquet of yellow roses 75 15
1658 7p. Pink and yellow arrangement 75 15

1982. Air. Tairona Culture.
1659 **575** 25p. gold, black & brown 90 35
1660 – 25p. gold, black & mve 90 35
1661 – 25p. gold, black & green 90 35
1662 – 25p. gold, black & mve 90 35
1663 – 25p. gold, black & blue 90 35
1664 – 25p. gold, black & red 90 35
DESIGNS—VERT: No. 1660, Anthropomorphic figure with crest; 1661, Anthropomorphic figure with two crests; 1662, Anthropozoomorphic figure; 1663, Anthropozoomorphic figure with elaborate headdress; 1664, Pectoral.

1982. 50th Anniv of Central Mortgage Bank.
1665 **576** 9p. green and black . . 35 20

577 State Governor's Palace, Pereira

1982. Air. Pereira City.
1666 **577** 35p. multicoloured . . . 35 20

578 Biplane and Badge

1982. Air. American Air Forces Co-operation.
1667 **578** 18p. multicoloured . . . 25 15

579 St. Thomas Aquinas

580 St. Theresa of Avila (after Zurbaran)

1982. St. Thomas Aquinas Commemoration.
1668 **579** 5p. multicoloured . . . 15 10

1982. 400th Death Anniv of St. Theresa of Avila.
1669 **580** 5p. multicoloured . . . 15 10

581 St. Francis of Assisi (after Zurbaran)

583 Gabriel Garcia Marquez

582 Magdalena River

1982. 800th Birth Anniv of St. Francis of Assisi.
1670 **581** 5p. multicoloured . . . 15 10

1982. Air. Tourism.
1671 **582** 30p. multicoloured . . . 2·25 70

1982. Town Arms. As T **476**. Multicoloured.
1672 10p. Buga 25 10
1673 16p. Rionegro 45 15
1674 23p. Honda 25 20

1982. Award of Nobel Prize for Literature to Gabriel Garcia Marquez.
1675 **583** 7p. grey & grn (postage) 25 15
1676 25p. grey & blue (air) . . 20 10
1677 30p. grey and brown . . 25 10

1983. Town Arms. As T **476**. Multicoloured.
1678 10p. San Juan de Pasto . . 30 15
1679 20p. Santa Fe de Bogota . . 25 10

584 "Liberty Fort" (drawing in National Archives)

1983. Air. San Andres Archipelago.
1680 **584** 25p. multicoloured . . . 25 10

585 Open Book

1983. Bicentenary of First Girls' School, Santa Fe de Bogota.
1681 **585** 9p. grey, black & gold 25 15

586 Sunset

1983. Air. Las Gaviotas Ecological Centre.
1682 **586** 12p. multicoloured . . . 15 10

587 Self-portrait

588 Radio Bands

1983. Death Centenary of Jose Maria Espinosa (artist).
1683 **587** 9p. multicoloured . . . 20 10

1983. Air. 50th Anniv of Radio Amateurs League.
1684 **588** 12p. multicoloured . . . 35 20

589 "Dona Rangel de Cuellas donating Territory" (Marcos L. Marino)

590 Bolivar

1983. 250th Anniv of Cucuta.
1685 **589** 9p. multicoloured . . . 30 15

1983. Birth Bicentenary of Simon Bolivar.
1686 **590** 9p. mult (postage) . . . 25 10
1687 – 30p. yell, bl & red (air) 35 25
1688 – 100p. multicoloured . . 1·25 85
DESIGNS—HORIZ: 30p. Bolivar as national flag. VERT: 100p. Bolivar and flag.

591 Porfirio Barba Jacob (after Frank Linas)

592 "Passiflora laurifolia"

1983. Birth Centenary of Porfirio Barba Jacob.
1689 **591** 9p. brown and black . . 20 10

1983. Bicentenary of Royal Botanical Expedition from Spain to South America. Multicoloured.
1690 9p. Type **592** (postage) . . . 20 10
1691 9p. "Cinchona lanceifolia" 20 10
1692 60p. "Cinchona cordifolia" 65 15
1693 12p. "Cinchona ovalifolia" (air) 30 15
1694 12p. "Begonia guaduensis" 30 15
1695 40p. "Begonia urticae" . . . 1·10 80

593 Plaza de la Aduana

1983. Air. 450th Anniv of Cartagena. Mult.
1696 12p. Type **593** 30 15
1697 35p. Cartagena buildings and monuments 80 20

594 "Dawn in the Andes" (Alejandro Obregon)

595 Scout Badge

1983.

1698 **594** 20p. mult (postage) . . . 75 25
1699 30p. mult (air) . . . . . 1·25 35

1983. Air. 75th Anniv of Boy Scout Movement.
1700 **595** 12p. multicoloured . . . 20 15

596 Santander

597 Coffee

1984. Francisco de Paula Santander (President of New Granada, 1832–37).
1701 **596** 12p. green 25 15
1702 12p. blue 25 15
1703 12p. red 25 15

1984. Air. Exports.
1704 **597** 14p. purple & green . . 10 10

598 Admiral Jose Prudencio Padilla

1984. Anniversaries. Multicoloured.
1705 10p. Type **598** (birth bicentenary) 75 20
1706 18p. Luis A. Calvo (composer, birth cent) . . 35 15
1707 20p. Diego Fallon (writer, 150th birth anniv) 35 15
1708 20p. Candelario Obeso (writer, death cent) . . . 1·00 30
1709 22p. Luis Eduardo Lopez de Mesa (writer, birth centenary) 45 15

599 Rainbow over Countryside

600 Stylized Globe on Stand

1984. Marandua, City of the Future.
1710 **599** 15p. mult (postage) . . . 30 15
1711 30p. mult (air) 20 20

1984. Air. 45th Congress of Americanists, Bogota.
1712 **600** 45p. multicoloured . . . 30 30

601 Nativity and Children playing

602 Maria Concepcion Loperena

1984. Christmas.
1713 **601** 12p. mult (postage) . . . 25 10
1714 14p. mult (air) 30 10

1985. 150th Birth Anniv of Maria Concepcion Loperena (Independence heroine).
1715 **602** 12p. multicoloured . . . 35 25

603 Dove, Map and Members' Flags

604 Mejia and Farman F.40 Type Biplane

1985. Air. Contadora Group.
1716 **603** 40p. multicoloured . . . 40 25

1985. Birth Centenary of Gonzalo Mejia (airport architect).
1717 **604** 12p. multicoloured . . . 20 10

605 "Married Couple" (Pedro nel Gomez)

1985.

1718 **605** 37p. mult (postage) . . . 25 10
1719 40p. mult (air) 40 25

606 Capybara

607 Straight-billed Woodcreepers

1985. Fauna. Multicoloured. (a) Mammals.
1720 12p. Type **606** (postage) . . 15 10
1721 15p. Ocelot 35 25
1722 15p. Spectacled bear 35 25
1723 20p. Mountain tapir 35 25

(b) Birds.

1724 14p. Lineated woodpeckers (air) 60 40
1725 20p. Type **607** 60 25
1726 50p. Coppery-bellied pufflegs . . . . 1·40 70
1727 55p. Blue-crowned motmots 1·60 80

608 Scenery and Gardel

609 "Gloria" (cadet ship), "Caldas" (frigate) and Naval Officer

1985. 50th Death Anniv of Carlos Gardel (singer).
1728 **608** 15p. multicoloured . . . 20 10

1985. Air. 50th Anniv of Almirante Padilla Naval College.
1729 **609** 20p. multicoloured . . . 1·25 45

610 Group of Colombians

611 Alphabet Tree

1985. Air. National Census.
1730 **610** 20p. multicoloured . . . 35 25

1985. National Education Year.
1731 **611** 15p. multicoloured . . . 30 15

612 Boy Playing Flute to Toys

613 Pumarejo

1985. Christmas. Multicoloured.
1732 15p. Type **612** (postage) . . 25 15
1733 20p. Girl looking at dressed tree (air) 30 20

1986. Air. Birth Centenary of Alfonso Lopez Pumarejo (President, 1934–38 and 1942–45).
1734 **613** 24p. multicoloured . . . 30 15

614 Cyclists and Countryside

615 Carranza (after Carlos Dupuy)

1986. Air. "Coffee and Cycling, Pride of Colombia".
1735 **614** 60p. multicoloured . . . 45 25

1986. Eduardo Carranza (poet) Commemoration.
1736 **615** 18p. multicoloured . . . 20 15

616 Hand reaching for Sun

617 Northern Pudu

1986. Centenary of External University.
1737 **616** 18p. multicoloured . . . 30 20

1986. Air.
1738 **617** 50p. multicoloured . . . 60 35

618 Ricaurte and Birth Place, Leiva

1986. Birth Bicentenary of Gen. Antonio Ricaurte (Independence hero).
1739 **618** 18p. multicoloured . . . 20 15

619 Pope and Arms

620 Couple and Satellite

1986. Air. Visit of Pope John Paul II (1st issue).
1740 **619** 24p. multicoloured . . . 35 20
See also Nos. 1745/**MS**1747.

1986. Air. World Communications Day.
1741 **620** 50p. multicoloured . . . 60 35

621 Silva and Illustration of "Nocturne"

622 Girl and Doves

1986. 90th Death Anniv of Jose Asuncion Silva (poet).
1742 **621** 18p. multicoloured . . . 20 15

1986. Air. International Peace Year.
1743 **622** 55p. multicoloured . . . 65 40

623 Martinez

624 Pope and Medellin Cathedral

1986. 10th Death Anniv of Fernando Gomez Martinez (politician and founder of "El Colombiano" newspaper).
1744 **623** 24p. multicoloured . . . 30 20

1986. Air. Visit of Pope John Paul II (2nd issue). Multicoloured.
1745 55p. Type **624** 50 45
1746 60p. Pope giving blessing in Bogota 50 45
MS1747 80 × 12 mm. 200p. Pope praying before painting "Virgin of Chiquinquira" (49 × 39 mm) . . 2·50 90

625 Montejo

626 Computer Portrait of Bach

1986. Air. Birth Centenary of Enrique Santos Montejo (journalist and editor of "El Tiempo").
1748 **625** 25p. multicoloured . . . 30 20

1986. Air. Composers' Birth Anniversaries (1985). Multicoloured.
1749 70p. Type **626** (300th anniv) 65 60
1750 100p. "The Permanency of Baroque" (300th annivs of Handel and Bach and 400th anniv of H. Schutz) 75 55

627 De La Salle (founder) and National Colours

1986. Air. Centenary of Brothers of Christian Schools in Colombia.
1751 **627** 25p. multicoloured . . . 30 15

628 Convent of Mercy

1986. 450th Anniv of Santiago de Cali.
1752 20p. Arms (as T **476**) . . . 15 10
1753 25p. Type **628** 15 10

629 Piece of Coal and National Colours

630 Castro Silva

1986. Air. Completion of El Cerrejon Coal Complex.
1754 **629** 55p. multicoloured . . . 40 40

1986. Birth Centenary (1985) of Jose Vincente Castro Silva (Principal of Senior College of the Rosary).
1755 **630** 20p. multicoloured . . . 25 15

631 "The Five Signatories" (detail, R. Vasquez)

1986. Air. Centenary of Constitution. Mult.
1756 25p. Type **631** 30 20
MS1757 120 × 81 mm. 200p. Rafael Nunez (President 1880s and 1890s), Miguel Antonio Caro (National Council of Delegates chairman, 1886; President 1894–98) and Presidential Palace, Bogota (49 × 39 mm) . . . . . 2·50 2·50

1986. Arms of Antioquia. As T **476**.
1758 55p. multicoloured 20 10

632 Garcia Lorca

1986. Air. 50th Death Anniv of Federico Garcia Lorca (poet).
1759 **632** 60p. multicoloured . . . 35 25

633 Symbolic Prism

634 Maya

1986. Centenary of Fine Art Faculty and 50th Anniv of Architecture Faculty at National University.
1760 **633** 40p. multicoloured . . . 20 30

1986. 6th Death Anniv of Rafael Maya (poet and critic).
1761 **634** 25p. multicoloured . . . 30 20

635 Andean Condor

636 "Thanks! Friends of the World"

1986.
1762 **635** 20p. blue 35 20
1763 25p. blue 35 20

1986. Air. Thanks for Help after Devastation of Armero by Volcanic Eruption, 1985.
1767 **636** 50p. multicoloured . . . 60 35

637 Mestiza Virgin (from crib at Pasto)

638 Left-hand Side of Mural

1986. Air. Christmas.
1768 **637** 25p. multicoloured . . . 30 15

1987. Air. 450th Anniv of Popayan City. "The Apotheosis of Popayan" by Ephram Martinez Zambrano. Multicoloured.
1769 100p. Type **638** . . . . . . 1·40 75
1770 100p. Right-hand side of mural . . . . 1·40 75
Nos. 1769/70 were printed together, se-tenant, forming a composite design.

639 Uribe Mejia

640 "Conversion of St. Augustine of Hippo"

1987. Birth Centenary (1986) of Pedro Uribe Mejia (coffee industry pioneer).
1771 **639** 25p. multicoloured . . . 30 15

1987. Air. 1600th Anniv of Conversion of St. Augustine.
1772 **640** 30p. multicoloured . . . 10 10

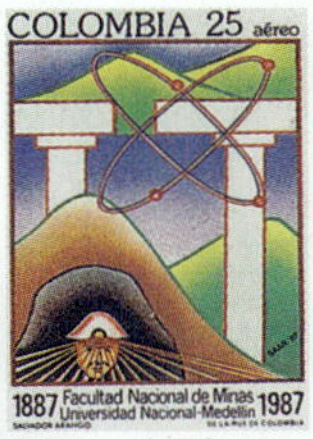

641 Atomic Diagram, Pit Props and Miner in Shaft

642 St. Barbara's Church

1987. Air. Centenary of National Mines Faculty of National University, Medellin.
1773 **641** 25p. multicoloured . . . 10 10

1987. 450th Anniv of Mompox City.
1774 **642** 500p. multicoloured . . 2·50 2·50

643 Hawk-headed Parrot

644 White Horse

1987. Fauna.
1775 **643** 30p. green (postage) . . 90 25
1776 – 30p. purple 45 20
1777 – 30p. red (air) 90 25
1778 – 35p. brown 15 20
DESIGNS—HORIZ: No. 1776, Boutu; 1778, South American red-lined turtle. VERT: No. 1777, Greater flamingo.
See also Nos. 1807/9, 1815/17, 1823/6 and 1855/8.

1987. Air. Pure-bred Horses. Multicoloured.
1779 60p. Type **644** 45 35
1780 70p. Black horse 45 35

645 Mastheads, Fidel Cano (founder), Luis Cano, Luis Gabriel Cano Isaza and Alfonso Cano Isaza (editors)

1987. Air. Cent of "El Espectador" (newspaper).
1781 **645** 60p. multicoloured . . . 25 15

646 Isaacs and Scene from "Maria"

1987. 150th Birth Anniv of Jorge Isaacs (writer).
1782 **646** 70p. multicoloured . . . 25 10

648 Mutis and Illustration of "Condor"

1987. 33rd Death Anniv of Aurelio Martinez Mutis (poet).
1785 **648** 90p. multicoloured . . . 1·25 55

649 Houses forming House

650 Family and Dish Aerial

1987. Air. International Year of Shelter for the Homeless.
1786 **649** 60p. multicoloured . . . 65 35

1987. Social Security and Communications.
1787 **650** 35p. multicoloured . . . 30 20

651 Flags

652 Nativity Scene in Globe

1987. Air. 1st Meeting of Eight Latin-American Presidents of Contadora and Lima Groups, Acapulco, Mexico.
1788 **651** 80p. multicoloured . . . 55 55

1987. Air. Christmas.
1789 **652** 30p. multicoloured . . . 30 15

653 Houses, Telephone Wires and Dials

1987. Air. Rural Telephone Network.
1790 **653** 70p. multicoloured . . . 35 10

654 Mountain Sanctuaries

655 Flower (Life)

1988. Air. 450th Anniv of Bogota (1st issue).
1791 **654** 70p. multicoloured . . . 25 70
See also Nos. 1803/4.

1988. 40th Anniv of Declaration of Human Rights (1st issue).
1792 **655** 30p. green 10 10
1793 – 35p. red 10 10
1794 – 40p. lilac 15 10
1795 – 40p. blue 10 10
DESIGNS—VERT: No. 1793, Road (Freedom of choice). HORIZ: 1794, Circle of children (Freedom of association); 1795, Couple on bench (Communication).
See also Nos. 1840/1.

657 Mask

1988. Air. Gold Museum, Bogota. Multicoloured.
1796 70p. Type **657** 30 30
1797 80p. Votive figure 60 30
1798 90p. Human figure 85 65

658 Pasto Cathedral

659 Waterfall

1988. 450th Anniv of Pasto.
1799 **658** 60p. multicoloured . . . 40 20

1988. Centenary of Bogota Water Supply and Sewerage Organization.
1800 **659** 100p. multicoloured . . 35 10

660 Score and Composers

661 M. Currea de Aya

1988. Centenary (1987) of National Anthem by Rafael Nunez and Oreste Sindici.
1801 **660** 70p. multicoloured . . . 25 25

1988. Birth Centenary of Maria Currea de Aya (women's rights pioneer).
1802 **661** 80p. multicoloured . . . 25 10

662 Modern Bogota

664 College

1988. Air. 450th Anniv of Bogota (2nd issue). Multicoloured.
1803 80p. Type **662** 55 30
1804 90p. Street in old Bogota (horiz) 60 30

1988. Fauna. As T **643**.
1807 35p. brown 25 15
1808 35p. green 25 15
1809 40p. orange 25 15

DESIGNS—HORIZ: No. 1807, Crab-eating racoon; 1808, Caribbean monk seal; 1809, Giant otter.

1988. Centenary of Return of Society of Jesus to St. Bartholomew's Senior College.
1810 **664** 120p. multicoloured . . 35 20

665 Eduardo Santos

666 Mother and Children

1988. Personalities. Multicoloured.
1811 80p. Type **665** (birth centenary) (postage) . . . 45 25
1812 90p. Jorge Alvarez Lleras (astronomer) 45 25
1813 80p. Zipa Tisquesusa (16th-century Indian chief) (air) 45 25

1988. Air. Christmas.
1814 **666** 40p. multicoloured . . . 15 10

1988. Fauna. As T **643**.
1815 40p. grey (postage) 15 10
1816 45p. violet 75 25
1817 45p. blue (air) 75 25
DESIGNS—HORIZ: No. 1815, American manatee; 1816, Masked trogon. VERT: No. 1817, Blue-bellied curassow.

667 Andres Bello College

1988.
1818 **667** 115p. multicoloured . . 35 20

668 Building and Nieto Caballero

669 Gomez

1989. Air. Birth Centenary of Agustin Nieto Caballero (educationalist).
1819 **668** 100p. multicoloured . . 30 15

1989. Air. Birth Centenary of Laureano Gomez (President, 1950–53).
1820 **669** 45p. multicoloured . . . 15 10

670 Map

1989. Air. International Coffee Organization.
1821 **670** 110p. multicoloured . . 30 15

671 Modern Flats, Recreation Area and Hands holding Brick

1989. Air. 12th Habitat U.N. Conference on Human Settlements, Cartagena.
1822 **671** 100p. multicoloured . . 20 10

1989. Fauna. As T **643**.
1823 40p. brown (postage) . . . 10 10
1824 45p. black 75 25
1825 55p. brown 15 10
1826 45p. blue (air) 10 10
DESIGNS—HORIZ: No. 1823, White-tailed deer; 1824, Harpy eagle; 1826, Blue discus. VERT: No. 1825, False anole.

672 Emblem

1989. 25th Anniv of Adpostal (postal administration).
1827 **672** 45p. multicoloured . . . 10 10

673 Hands

675 "Simon Bolivar" (Pedro Jose Figueroa)

674 Fruit, Coffee Beans and Mountains

1989. Air. Bicentenary of French Revolution.
1828 **673** 100p. multicoloured . . 20 10

1989. Air. Philexfrance 89 International Stamp Exhibition, Paris. Sheet 145 × 110 mm containing T **674** and similar multicoloured designs.
MS1829 110p. Type **674**; 110p. Fruit, flowers and mountains; 110p. Wildlife and snow-capped mountain peak (41 × 26 mm); 110p. Man with basket of fruit floating over fields; 110p. River valley; 110p. Gemstones, gold and industry (41 × 25 mm); 110p. Fishes and seashore (41 × 26 mm) 1·40 1·40

1989. 170th Anniv of Liberation Campaign. Multicoloured.
1830 40p. Type **675** (postage) . . 10 10
1831 40p. "Santander" (Figueroa) 10 10
1832 45p. "Bolivar and Santander during the Campaign for the Plains" (J. M. Zamora) (46 × 37 mm) . . 10 10
1833 45p. "From Boyaca to Santa Fe" (left-hand detail) (Francisco de P. Alvarez) (29 × 36 mm) 10 10
1834 45p. Right-hand detail (29 × 36 mm) 10 10
1835 45p. Mounted officer and foot soldiers (left-hand detail) (31 × 51 mm) . . . 35 10
1836 45p. Mounted officer (centre detail) (33 × 51 mm) . . . 35 10
1837 45p. Mounted soldiers with flag (right-hand detail) (31 × 51 mm) 35 35
MS1838 119 × 79 mm. 250p. "The Lancers" (sculpture by R. Arenas Betancur) (49 × 39 mm) (air) 55 55
Nos. 1833/4 and 1835/7 (showing details of triptych by A. de Santa Maria) were issued together, se-tenant, each forming a composite design.

676 Founder's House

1989. 450th Anniv of Tunja.
1839 **676** 45p. multicoloured . . . 10 10

1989. Human Rights (2nd issue). As T **655**.
1840 45p. brown (postage) . . . 10 10
1841 55p. green (air) 15 10
DESIGNS—HORIZ: 45p. Musicians (Culture). VERT: 55p. Family.

677 Healthy Children and Shadowy Figures

678 Gold Ornaments of Quimbaya, Calima and Tolima

1989. Air. Anti-drugs Campaign.
1842 **677** 115p. multicoloured . . 25 15

1989. Air. America. Pre-Columbian Crafts. Multicoloured.
1843 115p. Type **678** 25 15
1844 130p. Indian making pot and Sinu ceramic figure (horiz) 25 15

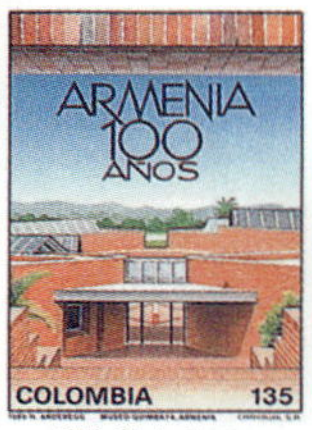

679 Quimbaya Museum

680 Mantilla

1989. Centenary of Armenia City.
1845 **679** 135p. multicoloured . . 25 15

1989. Air. 45th Death Anniv of Joaquin Quijano Mantilla (chronicler).
1846 **680** 170p. multicoloured . . 75 20

681 Boeing 767 and Globe

682 "The Fathers of the Fatherland leaving Congress" (R. Acevedo Bernal)

1989. Air.
1847 **681** 130p. multicoloured . . 45 15

1989. Air. 170th Anniv of Creation of First Republic of Colombia (1851) and 168th Anniv of its Constitution (others). Multicoloured.
1848 130p. Type **682** 55 15
1849 130p. "Church of the Rosary, Cucuta" (Carmelo Fernandez) . . 55 15
1850 130p. Republic's arms . . . 55 15
1851 130p. "Bolivar at Congress of Angostura" (46 × 36 mm) (Tito Salas) 55 15

683 Nativity (Barro-Raquira clay figures)

684 "Plaza de la Aduana" (H. Lemaitre)

1989. Air. Christmas.
1852 **683** 55p. multicoloured . . . 40 10

1990. Air. Presidential Summit, Cartagena.
1853 **684** 130p. multicoloured . . 60 40

685 Headphones on Marble Head

687 "Espeletia hartwegiana"

686 Cuervo Borda and National Museum

1990. Air. 50th Anniv of Colombia National Radio.
1854 **685** 150p. multicoloured . . 30 15

1990. Fauna. As T **643**.
1855 50p. grey 10 10
1856 50p. purple 10 10
1857 60p. brown 15 10
1858 60p. brown 60 20
DESIGNS: No. 1855, Grey fox; 1856, Common poison-arrow frog; 1857, Pygmy marmoset; 1858, Sun-bittern.

1990. Air. Velez City Arms. As T **476**.
1859 60p. multicoloured 15 10

1990. Air. Birth Centenary (1989) of Teresa Cuervo Borda (artist).
1860 **686** 60p. multicoloured . . . 15 10

1990. Multicoloured.
1861 60p. Type **687** 15 10
1862 60p. "Ceiba pentandra" (horiz) 15 10
1863 70p. "Ceroxylon quindiuense" 15 10
1864 70p. "Tibouchina lepidota" 15 10

688 Theatrical Masks

689 Statue, Bogota

1990. Air. 2nd Iberian-American Theatre Festival, Bogota.
1865 **688** 150p. gold, brown & orge 60 15

1990. 150th Death Anniv of Francisco de Paula Santander (President of New Granada, 1832–37). Multicoloured.
1866 50p. Type **689** (postage) . . 40 10
1867 60p. Gateway of National Pantheon (air) 40 10
1868 60p. "General Santander with the Constitution" (Jose Maria Espinosa) . . 40 10
1869 70p. Santander, organizer of public education (after F. S. Guitierrez) 40 10
1870 70p. "The Postal Carrier" (Jose Maria del Castillo) (horiz) 40 10
MS1871 109 × 89 mm. 5000p. "Santander on Death Bed" (Luis Garcia Hevia) (49 × 39 mm) . . 6·00 6·00

690 Postmen

1990. Air. 150th Anniv of the Penny Black.
1872 **690** 150p. multicoloured . . 30 15

691 Cadet, Arms and School

693 Graph

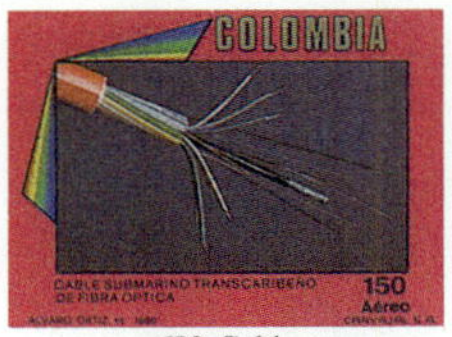

692 Cable

1990. 50th Anniv of General Santander Police Cadets School.
1873 **691** 60p. multicoloured . . . 15 10

1990. Air. Trans-Caribbean Submarine Fibre Optic Cable.
1874 **692** 150p. multicoloured . . 60 15

1990. Air. 50th Anniv of I.F.I.
1875 **693** 60p. multicoloured . . . 15 10

1990. Arms of Cartago. As T **476**.
1876 50p. multicoloured 35 10

694 Player's Legs

1990. Air. World Cup Football Championship, Italy. Sheet 120 × 90 mm.
MS1877 **694** 500p. multicoloured 30 30

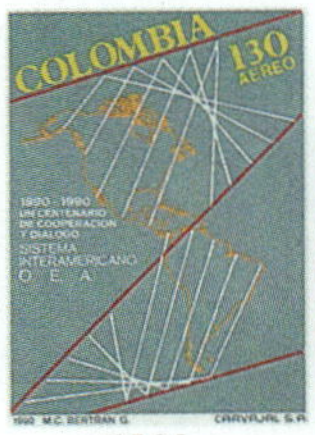

695 Map **696** Women on Beach

1990. Air. 10th Anniv of Organization of American States.
1878 **695** 130p. multicoloured . . 55 15

1990. La Guajira.
1879 **696** 60p. multicoloured . . . 15 10

697 Indian wearing Gold Ornaments **698** St. John Bosco (founder) and Boys

1990. Air. 50th Anniv of Gold Museum, Bogota.
1880 **697** 170p. multicoloured . . 35 20

1990. Centenary of Salesian Brothers in Colombia.
1881 **698** 60p. multicoloured . . . 15 10

699 Brown Pelican, Roseate Spoonbills and Dolphins

1990. Air. America. Natural World. Multicoloured.
1882 150p. Type **699** . . . . . . 1·00 30
1883 150p. Land animals and Salvin's curassows . . . . 1·00 30

700 Christ Child **701** Monastery

1990. Air. Christmas.
1884 **700** 70p. multicoloured . . . 15 10

1990. Air. Monastery of Nostra Senhora de las Lajas, Ipiales.
1885 **701** 70p. multicoloured . . . 15 10

702 Titles and Abstract **703** Christ of the Miracles, Buga Church

1991. Air. Bicentenary of "La Prensa".
1886 **702** 170p. multicoloured . . 30 15

1991.
1887 **703** 70p. multicoloured . . . 15 10

704 "Anaea syene" **705** Humpback Whale leaping from Water

1991. Butterflies. Multicoloured.
1888 70p. Type **704** (postage) . . 15 10
1889 70p. "Callithea philotima" (horiz) 15 10
1890 80p. "Thecla coronata" . . 15 10
1891 80p. "Agrias amydon" (horiz) (air) 15 10
1892 170p. "Morpho rhetenor" (horiz) 30 15
1893 190p. "Heliconius longarenus ernestus" (horiz) 35 20

1991. Air. Marine Mammals. Multicoloured.
1894 80p. Type **705** 15 10
1895 170p. Humpback whale diving 60 15
1896 190p. Amazon dolphins (horiz) 65 20

706 National Colours

1991. New Constitution.
1897 **706** 70p. multicoloured . . . 15 10
See also No. 1914.

707 Dario Echandia Olaya (after Delio Ramirez) **708** Girardot (after Jose Maria Espinosa)

1991. 2nd Death Anniv of Dario Echandia Olaya.
1898 **707** 80p. multicoloured . . . 15 10

1991. Birth Bicent of Colonel Atanasio Girardot.
1899 **708** 70p. multicoloured . . . 15 10

709 Galan **710** Stone Statue of God, San Agustin

1991. 2nd Death Anniv of Luis Carlos Galan Sarmiento (politician).
1900 **709** 80p. multicoloured . . . 15 10

1991. Pre-Columbian Art. Multicoloured.
1901 80p. Type **710** (postage) . . 15 10
1902 90p. Burial vessel, Tierradentro 15 10
1903 90p. Statue, San Agustin (air) 15 10
1904 210p. Gold flyingfish, San Agustin (horiz) 50 20

711 Sailfish

1991.
1905 **711** 830p. multicoloured . . 2·50 1·00

712 Cloisters of St. Augustine's, Tunja

1991. Architecture. Multicoloured.
1906 80p. Type **712** (postage) . . 15 10
1907 90p. Bridge, Chia 15 10
1908 90p. Roadside chapel, Pamplona (vert) (air) . . 15 10
1909 190p. Church of the Conception, Santa Fe de Bogota (vert) 60 20

713 "Santa Maria" **714** Lleras Camargo (after Rafael Salas)

1991. Air. America. Voyages of Discovery. Mult.
1910 90p. Type **713** 35 20
1911 190p. Amerindians and approaching ship 85 30

1991. 1st Death Anniv of Alberto Lleras Camargo (President, 1945–46 and 1958–62).
1912 **714** 80p. multicoloured . . . 15 10

715 Police Officers, Transport, Emblem and Flag

1991. Centenary of Police.
1913 **715** 80p. multicoloured . . . 30 10

1991. Air. New Constitution (2nd issue). As No. 1897 but new value and additionally inscr "SANTAFE DE BOGOTA. D.C. Julio 4 de 1991".
1914 90p. multicoloured 15 10

716 Member Nations' Flags **717** First Government Building, Sogamoso

1991. Air. 5th Group of Rio Presidential Summit, Cartagena.
1915 **716** 190p. multicoloured . . 30 15

1991.
1916 **717** 80p. multicoloured . . . 10 10

718 "Adoration of the Kings" (Baltazar de Figueroa) **719** D. Turbay Quintero

1991. Air. Christmas.
1917 **718** 90p. multicoloured . . . 15 10

1992. Diana Turbay Quintero (journalist) Commemoration.
1918 **719** 80p. multicoloured . . . 10 10

720 Hand holding Posy of Flowers **721** Cut Flowers

1992. Air. 8th U.N. Conference on Trade and Development Session, Cartagena.
1919 **720** 210p. multicoloured . . 35 20

1992. Air. Exports.
1920 90p. Type **721** 15 10
1921 210p. Fruits and nuts (horiz) 35 20

722 Statue of General Santander, Barranquilla (R. Verlet) **723** Music, Book and Paint Brush

1992. Birth Bicentenary of General Francisco de Paula Santander. Multicoloured.
1922 80p. Type **722** (postage) . . 10 10
1923 190p. Francisco de Paula Santander (after Sergio Trujillo Magnenat) (air) 30 15
MS1924 120 × 90 mm. 950p. "Battle of Boyaca, 1819" (Martin Tovar) (50 × 40 mm) . . . . 1·20 1·20

1992. Air. Copyright Protection.
1925 **723** 190p. multicoloured . . 30 15

725 Lievano Aguirre **726** Enrique Low Murtra (1st anniv)

1992. 10th Death Anniv of Indalecio Lievano Aguirre (ambassador to United Nations).
1928 **725** 80p. multicoloured . . . 10 10

1992. Death Anniversaries of Justice Ministers. Multicoloured.
1929 100p. Type **726** 15 10
1930 110p. Rodrigo Lara Bonilla (8th anniv) 20 10

727 Town Arms and Rings

1992. 14th National Games, Barranquilla.
1931 **727** 110p. multicoloured . . 20 10

728 Landscape

729 Athlete and Olympic Rings

1992. Air. 2nd U.N. Conference on Environment and Development, Rio de Janeiro. Paintings by Roberto Palomino. Multicoloured.
1932 230p. Type **728** 35 20
1933 230p. Birds in trees 35 20

1992. Air. Olympic Games, Barcelona.
1934 **729** 110p. multicoloured . . 20 10

730 "Discovery of America by C. Columbus" (Dali)

1992. Air. America. Multicoloured.
1935 230p. Type **730** 80 30
1936 260p. "America Magic, Myth and Legend" (Al. Vivero) . . . . 1·00 75

731 American Crocodile

1992. Endangered Animals. Multicoloured.
1937 100p. Type **731** 15 10
1938 100p. Andean condor (vert) . . 45 30

732 Maria Lopez de Escobar (founder)

734 Map of the Americas

733 Avianca Colombia McDonnell Douglas MD-83

1992. 50th Anniv of House of Mother and Child.
1939 **732** 100p. mult (postage) . . 15 10
1940 110p. mult (air) 20 10

1992. Air.
1941 **733** 110p. multicoloured . . 20 10

1992. Meeting of First Ladies of the Americas and the Caribbean, Cartagena.
1942 **734** 100p. multicoloured . . 15 10

735 "Zenaida" (Ana Mercedes Hoyos)

1992. 500th Anniv of Discovery of America by Columbus. Paintings.
1943 **735** 100p. mult (postage) . . 15 10
1944 – 110p. multicoloured . . 20 10
1946 – 110p. mult (air) 20 10
1947 – 230p. multicoloured . . 35 20
1948 – 260p. green and violet 40 20
MS1945 Two sheets. (a) 120 × 90 mm. 400p. multicoloured; (b) 90 × 120 mm. 440p. mult 1·30 1·30
DESIGNS: 110p. (1944), "Study for 1/500" (Beatriz Gonzalez); 110p. (1946), "Blue Eagle" (Alejandro Obregon); 230p. "Cantileo" (Luis Luna); 260p. "Maize" (Antonio Caro); 400p. "Great Curtain" (Luis Caballero); 440p. "Homage to Guatavita" (Alejandro Obegoin).

736 Recycling

1992.
1949 **736** 100p. multicoloured . . 15 10

737 Front Curtain

1992. Air. Columbus Theatre.
1950 **737** 230p. multicoloured . . 35 20

739 "Nativity" (Carlos Alfonso Mendez)

1992. Christmas. Children's Drawings. Mult.
1952 100p. Type **739** (postage) . . 15 10
1953 110p. Kings approaching stable (Catalina del Valle) (air) 20 10

740 G. Lara

748 Footballers

742 Campaign Emblem

1992. Air. 10th Death Anniv of Gloria Lara (ambassador to the United Nations).
1954 **740** 230p. multicoloured . . 40 20

1993. Lions Club International Amblyopia Prevention Campaign.
1956 **742** 100p. multicoloured . . 15 10

1993. Air. America Cup Football Championship, Ecuador.
1962 **748** 220p. multicoloured . . 35 20

749 Prisoners

1993. Bicentenary of French Declaration of Human Rights. Multicoloured.
1963 150p. Type **749** (postage) . . 25 15
1964 150p. The elderly 25 15
1965 200p. The infirm 35 20
1966 200p. Children 35 20
1968 220p. Women (air) 35 20
1969 220p. The poor 35 20
1970 460p. Environmental protection . . . . 1·00 40
1971 520p. Immigrants . . . . . 1·10 45
MS1967 101 × 88 mm. 800p. Woman releasing dove (29 × 39 mm) . . 70 70

750 Amerindian (Jose Luis Correal)

752 Green-winged Macaw ("Papagayo")

751 Emblem and Flags

1993. Air. International Year of Indigenous Peoples.
1972 **750** 460p. multicoloured . . 70 35

1993. Air. World Cup Football Championship, U.S.A. (1994) (1st issue).
1973 **751** 220p. multicoloured . . 35 20
See also Nos. 2006/9.

1993. The Amazon. Multicoloured.
1974 150p. Type **752** (postage) . . 60 40
1975 150p. Anaconda 20 10
1976 220p. Water-lilies (air) . . . 35 20
1977 220p. Ipecacuanha flower 35 20
MS1978 120 × 90 mm. 880p. Amerindian on river and detail of map (horiz) 75 75

753 Cotton-headed Tamarin

755 Nativity

754 Alberto Pumarejo (politician)

1993. Air. America. Endangered Animals. Mult.
1979 220p. Type **753** 35 20
1980 220p. American purple gallinule 60 30
1981 460p. Andean cock of the rock 90 40
1982 520p. American manatee . . 80 40

1993. Famous Colombians. Multicoloured.
1983 150p. Type **754** 20 10
1984 150p. Lorencita Villegas de Santos (First Lady, 1938–42) 20 10
1985 150p. Meliton Rodriguez (photographer) 20 10
1986 150p. Tomas Carrasquilla (writer) 20 10

1993. Christmas. Multicoloured.
1987 200p. Type **755** (postage) . . 30 15
1988 220p. Shepherd (air) 35 20

756 San Andres y Providencia

1993. Tourism. Multicoloured.
1989 220p. Type **756** 35 20
1990 220p. Cocuy National Park 35 20
1991 220p. La Cocha Lake . . . 35 20
1992 220p. Waterfall, La Macarena mountains . . 35 20
1993 460p. Chicamocha (vert) . . 70 35
1994 460p. Sierra Nevada de Santa Marta (vert) . . . 70 35
1995 520p. Embalse de Penol (vert) 80 40
See also No. E1996.

757 Museum Entrance

759 Yellow-eared Conure

1993. 170th Anniv of National Museum.
1997 **757** 150p. multicoloured . . 20 10

1994. Birds. Multicoloured.
1999 180p. Type **759** (postage) . . 70 45
2000 240p. Bogota rail 90 60
2001 270p. Toucan barbets (horiz) (air) . . . . 1·10 70
2002 560p. Cinnamon teals (horiz) . . . . 2·10 1·40

760 Emblem

1994. Air. International Decade for Natural Disaster Reduction. National Disaster Prevention System.
2003 **760** 630p. blue, yellow & red 95 50

762 Escriva de Balaguer

1994. Air. Beatification of Josemaria Escriva de Balaguer (founder of Opus Dei).
2005 **762** 560p. multicoloured . . 85 45

763 Trophy and Player and Emblem on Flag

1994. World Cup Football Championship, U.S.A. (2nd issue). Multicoloured.
2006 180p. Type **763** (postage) . . 25 15
MS2007 121 × 90 mm. 1110p. Player helping opponent to feet and emblem . . . . 2·10 2·10

2008 270p. Match scene, trophy and emblem (air) 40 20
2009 560p. Trophy, emblem, ball and national colours (vert) 85 45

764 Flagpoles

765 "Self-portrait"

1994. Air. 4th Latin American Presidential Summit, Cartagena.
2011 **764** 630p. multicoloured . . 95 50
See also No. E2010.

1994. Birth Centenary of Ricardo Rendon (painter).
2012 **765** 240p. black 30 15

766 Biplane and William Knox Martin

1994. Air. 75th Anniv of First Airmail Flight.
2013 **766** 270p. multicoloured . . 35 20

767 Emblem

1994. 40th Anniv of Radio and Television Network.
2014 **767** 180p. multicoloured . . 25 15

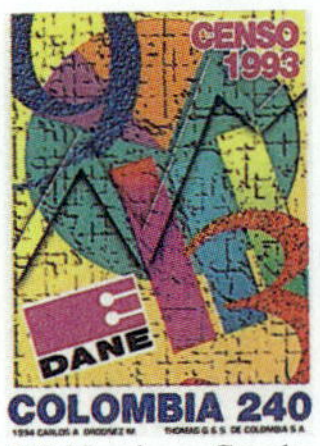

768 Numbers, Graphs and Pie Chart

770 Horse and Bicycle

1994. 1993 Census.
2015 **768** 240p. multicoloured . . 30 15

1994. Air. America. Postal Transport. Mult.
2017 **770** 270p. multicoloured . . 35 20
See also No. E2018.

771 Founders and Pi Symbol

1994. Centenary of Colombian Society of Engineers.
2019 **771** 180p. multicoloured . . 25 15

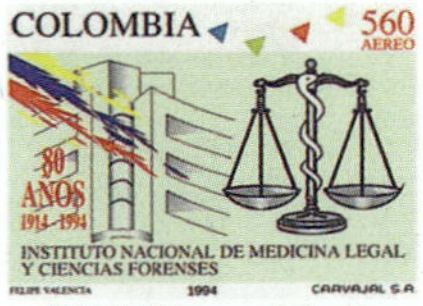

772 Building and Scales

1994. Air. 80th Anniv of National Institute of Legal Medicine and Forensic Sciences.
2020 **772** 560p. multicoloured . . 75 40

773 Three Wise Men

1994. Air. Christmas.
2021 **773** 270p. multicoloured . . 35 20
See also No. E2022.

774 1921 SCADTA 30c. Stamp

775 Common Iguana

1995. Air. 75th Anniv (1994) of Sociedad Colombo-Alemana de Transportes Aereos (SCADTA) (private air company contracted to carry mail).
2023 **774** 330p. pink, brown & blk 60 25

1995. Air. Flora and Fauna. Multicoloured.
2024 650p. Type **775** 85 45
2025 650p. Iguana facing left . . 85 45
2026 750p. Forest (left detail) . . 1·00 50
2027 750p. Forest (right detail) 1·00 50
Stamps of the same value were issued together in se-tenant pairs, each pair forming a composite design.

776 1920 10c. Stamp

1995. Air. 75th Anniv of Compania Colombiana de Navagacion Aerea (private air company contracted to carry mail).
2028 **776** 330p. multicoloured . . 45 25

778 Jose Miguel Pey

1995. Colombian Patriots. Multicoloured.
2030 270p. Type **778** (revolutionary) 35 20
2031 270p. Jorge Tadeo Lozana (zoologist and revolutionary) 35 20
2032 270p. Antonio Narino (journalist and politician) 35 20
2033 270p. Camilo Torres (lawyer and revolutionary) . . . 35 20
2034 270p. Jose Fernandez Madrid (doctor and revolutionary) 35 20
2035 270p. Jose Maria del Castillo y Rada (lawyer) 35 20
2036 270p. Custodio Garcia Rovira (revolutionary) . . 35 20
2037 270p. Antonio Villavicencio (revolutionary) 35 20
2038 270p. Liborio Mejia (lawyer and historian) 35 20
2039 270p. Rafael Urdaneta (diplomat) 35 20
2040 270p. Juan Garcia del Rio (writer and politician) . . 35 20
2041 270p. Gen. Jose Maria Melo 35 20
2042 270p. Gen. Tomas Herrera 35 20
2043 270p. Froilan Largacha (acting President, Feb–June 1863) 35 20
2044 270p. Salvader Camacho Roldan (writer) 35 20
2045 270p. Gen. Ezequiel Hurtado (acting President, Apr–Aug 1884) 35 20
2046 270p. Dario Echandia Olaya (lawyer) 35 20
2047 270p. Alberto Lleras Camargo (President, 1945–46) 35 20
2048 270p. Gen. Gustavo Rojas Pinilla (President, 1953–57) 35 20
2049 270p. Carlos Lleras Restrepo (President, 1966–70) 35 20

779 Farmers on Hillside

1995. Air. 50th Anniv of FAO.
2050 **779** 750p. multicoloured . . 1·00 50

780 Bello

781 Fireman

1995. Air. 25th Anniv of Andres Bello (scholar and writer). Agreement on Intellectual Co-operation.
2051 **780** 650p. multicoloured . . 85 45

1995. Air. Centenary of Fire Brigade of Bogota.
2052 **781** 330p. multicoloured . . 45 25

782 Emblem

783 Anniversary Emblem

1995. Air. 50th Anniv of National Chamber of Commerce.
2053 **782** 330p. multicoloured . . 45 25

1995. Air. 50th Anniv of UNO.
2054 **783** 750p. multicoloured . . 45 25

784 Emblem

786 Obando (after Efrain Martinez)

1995. Air. 1st Pacific Ocean Games, Cali.
2055 **784** 750p. multicoloured . . 1·00 50

1995. Birth Bicentenary of General Jose Maria Obando.
2057 **786** 220p. multicoloured . . 25 15

787 San Filipe de Barajas Castle

1995. Air. 11th Non-aligned Countries' Conference, Cartagena de Indias.
2058 **787** 650p. multicoloured . . 80 40

788 Estela Lopez Pomareda in "Maria", Charlie Chaplin and Jackie Coogan

1995. Air. Centenary of Motion Pictures.
2059 **788** 330p. black and brown 40 20

789 Harvesting Poppies for Opium

790 Anniversary Emblem

1995. Air. World Campaign against Drug Trafficking. Multicoloured.
2060 330p. Type **789** 40 20
2061 330p. Manacled hands (horiz) 40 20

1995. Air. 25th Anniv of Andean Development Corporation.
2062 **790** 650p. multicoloured . . 80 40

792 Madre-Monte

1995. Air. Myths and Legends (1st issue). Multicoloured.
2065 750p. Type **792** 90 45
2066 750p. La Llorana 90 45
2067 750p. El Mohan (river spirit) 90 45
2068 750p. Alligator man 90 45
Nos. 2065/8 were issued together, se-tenant, in sheetlets in which the background colour gradually changes down the sheet; each design therefore occurs in four slightly different colours.
See also Nos. 2085/8.

793 Holy Family

1995. Christmas. Stained Glass Windows from Chapel of the Apostles, Bogota School. Mult.
2069 220p. Type **793** (postage) . . 25 15
2070 330p. Nativity (air) 40 20

794 Asuncion Silva

1996. Air. Death Centenary of Jose Asuncion Silva (poet).
2071 **794** 400p. multicoloured . . 50 25

795 Painting by Luz Maria Tobon Mesa **796** Salavarrieta (after Jose Maria Espinosa)

1996. Air. Providence Island.
2072 **795** 800p. multicoloured . . 1·00 50

1996. Air. Birth Bicentenary of Policarpa Salavarrieta.
2073 **796** 900p. multicoloured . . 1·10 55

797 De Greiff (Ricardo Rendon) **799** Santa Maria la Antigua del Darien

1996. 1st Death Anniv of Leon De Greiff (poet).
2074 **797** 400p. black 50 25

1996. Town Arms. Multicoloured.
2076 400p. Type **799** 50 25
2077 400p. San Sebastian de Mariquita 50 25
2078 400p. Marinilla 50 25
2079 400p. Santa Cruz de Mompox 50 25

801 Medellin Cathedral

1996. Air.
2081 **801** 400p. multicoloured . . 50 25

803 Mosquera Courtyard

1996. 150th Anniv of National Capitol, Bogota.
2083 **803** 400p. multicoloured . . 50 25

804 National Archive, Bogota

1996. Air.
2084 **804** 400p. multicoloured . . 50 25

1996. Air. Myths and Legends (2nd issue). Multicoloured.
2085 900p. The Creation of Koguin . . . . 1·10 55
2086 900p. Yonna Wayu . . . . 1·10 55
2087 900p. Jaguar-man . . . . . 1·10 55
2088 900p. Lord of the Animals 1·10 55

805 Anniversary Emblem

1996. Air. 25th Anniv of Regional Centre for the Development of Books in Latin America and Caribbean.
2089 **805** 800p. brn, blk & dp brn 95 50

806 Guitar and Notes **808** Golf Course

807 Jorge Isaacs and Pump

1996. 50th Anniv of Society of Colombian Authors and Composers.
2090 **806** 400p. multicoloured . . 50 25

1996. Air. Pioneers of Petroleum Industry. Multicoloured.
2091 800p. Type **807** 95 50
2092 800p. Francisco Burgos Rubio and refinery (at night) 95 50
2093 800p. Diego Martinez Camargo and drilling tower 95 50
2094 800p. Prisciliano Cabrales Lora and drilling platform 1·25 60
2095 800p. Manuel Maria Palacio and firefighting tug . . . 1·25 90
2096 800p. Roberto de Mares and refinery 95 50
2097 800p. General Virgilio Barco Maldonado and workmen 95 50
2098 800p. Workmen and Ecopetrol (state petroleum industry) emblem 95 50

1996. Air. 50th Anniv of Colombian Golf Federation.
2099 **808** 400p. multicoloured . . 50 25

809 Pre-Columban Pendant, Malagana Treasure

1996. "Exfilbo '96" National Stamp Exn, Bogota.
2100 **809** 400p. multicoloured . . 50 25

810 Theatre Curtain (detail, Guillermo Vallejo)

1996. 30th Anniv of Founders Theatre, Manizales. Sheet 120 × 90 mm containing T **810** and similar multicoloured design.
MS2101 4000p. Type **810**; 4000p. Detail showing settlers with animals (horiz) . . . . 6·00 6·00

811 Postman delivering Letter

1996. Christmas. The Annunciation. Mult.
2102 400p. Type **811** (postage) . . 50 25
2103 400p. Woman reading letter and postman (air) 50 25

813 Cemetery, Mompox

1996. UNESCO World Heritage Sites. Mult.
2106 400p. Type **813** 50 25
2107 400p. San Agustin Archaeological Park . . . 50 25
2108 400p. Palace of the Inquisition, Cartagena . . 50 25
2109 400p. Underground tomb, Tierradentro Archaeological Park . . . 50 25

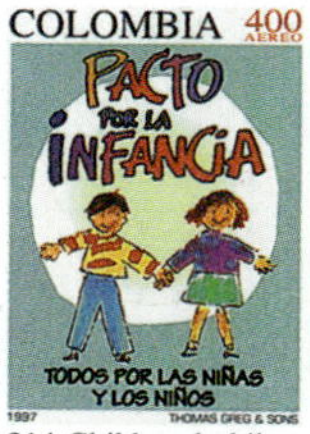

814 Children holding Hands **815** Hurtado

1997. Air. Children's Rights.
2110 **814** 400p. multicoloured . . 45 25

1997. 2nd Death Anniv of Alvaro Gomez Hurtado (lawyer and politician).
2111 **815** 400p. black and blue . . 45 25

816 Film Reels and Harbour Tower **817** Emblem

1997. Air. Centenary of Colombian Cinema and 53rd International Union of Film Archives Congress, Cartagena de Indias.
2112 **816** 800p. multicoloured . . 90 45

1997. Air. 50th Anniv (1996) of State Social Security.
2113 **817** 400p. multicoloured . . 45 25

818 Hand holding Mobile Phone

1997. Air. Centenary (1996) of Ericsson Company in Colombia.
2114 **818** 900p. multicoloured . . 90 45

819 Cattle

1997. Air. Cordoba Cattle Fair.
2115 **819** 400p. multicoloured . . 30 15

820 "Maria Varilla in the Clouds" (William Vive)

1997. Porro National Festival, San Pelayo.
2116 **820** 400p. multicoloured . . 30 15

821 Typewriter

1997. 50th Anniv of Bogota Journalists' Association.
2117 **821** 400p. multicoloured . . 30 15

822 Museum Buildings

1997. Air. 1st Anniv of Numismatic Museum at State Mint, Bogota.
2118 **822** 800p. multicoloured . . 65 35

823 Palm

1997. Air. Vegetable Ivory Palm Production Project.
2119 **823** 900p. multicoloured . . 70 35

824 Barco

1997. Virgilio Barco (President, 1986–90) Commem.
2120 **824** 500p. multicoloured . . 40 20

825 Straightening Contorted Tree and Healthy Couple

1997. Air. 50th Anniv of Colombian Society of Orthopaedic Surgery and Traumatology.
2121 **825** 1000p. multicoloured . . 80 40

826 Luis Carlos Lopez (poet)

1997. Air. Personalities. Multicoloured.
2122 500p. Type **826** 40 20
2123 500p. Aurelio Arturo (poet) 40 20
2124 500p. Enrique Perez Arbelaez (botanist and historian) 40 20
2125 500p. Jose Maria Gonzalez Benito (mathematician and astronomer) 40 20
2126 500p. Jose Manuel Rivas Sacconi (philologist and diplomat) 40 20
2127 500p. Eduardo Lemaitre Roman (historian and journalist) 40 20
2128 500p. Diojenes Arrieta (journalist and politician) 40 20
2129 500p. Gabriel Turbay Abunader (politician and diplomat) 40 20
2130 500p. Guillermo Echavarria Misas (aviation pioneer) 40 20
2131 500p. Juan Friede Alter (historian) 40 20
2132 500p. Fabio Lozano Torrijos (diplomat) . . . 40 20
2133 500p. Lino de Pombo (engineer and diplomat) 40 20
2134 500p. Cacica Gaitana (Indian resistance leader) 40 20
2135 500p. Josefa Acevedo de Gomez (writer) 40 20
2136 500p. Domingo Bioho (Black leader) 40 20
2137 500p. Soledad Acosta de Samper (historian) 40 20
2138 500p. Maria Cano Marquez (workers' leader) 55 30
2139 500p. Manuel Quintin Lame (native leader) 40 20
2140 500p. Ezequiel Uricoechea (linguist and naturalist) 40 20
2141 500p. Juan Rodriguez Freyle (chronicler) 40 20
2142 500p. Gerardo Reichel-Dolmatoff (archaeologist) 40 20
2143 500p. Ramon de Zubiria (educationist) 40 20
2144 500p. Esteban Jaramillo (economist) 40 20
2145 500p. Pedro Fermin de Vargas (economist) . . . 40 20

827 National Flag, Dove and Children playing

1997. Peace. Multicoloured.
2146 500p. Type **827** (postage) . . 40 20
2147 1100p. Children holding hands in ring (air) 85 45

828 Postman on Moped

1997. America. The Postman. Multicoloured.
2148 500p. Type **828** (postage) . . 40 20
2149 1100p. Postman raising envelope to night sky (air) 85 45

829 Pregnant Women

830 Dove Emblem

1998. Air. 50th Anniv of WHO Safe Motherhood.
2150 **829** 1100p. multicoloured . . 65 35

1998. Air. 4th Bolivarian Stamp Exhibition, Santafe de Bogota.
2151 **830** 1000p. orange and blue 60 30

831 Gaitan

832 Colombian Flag and Map of the Americas

1998. 50th Death Anniv of Jorge Eliecer Gaitan.
2152 **831** 500p. multicoloured . . . 30 15

1998. Air. 50th Anniv of Organization of American States.
2153 **832** 1000p. multicoloured . . 60 30

833 Cogs

1998. 50th Anniv of Santander Industrial University.
2154 **833** 500p. multicoloured . . . 30 15

834 "Gloria" (cadet ship) and Dolphins

1998. Air. International Year of the Ocean.
2155 **834** 1100p. multicoloured . . 65 35

835 Football Boot

1998. Air. World Cup Football Championship, France. Multicoloured.
2156 1100p. Type **835** 65 35
2157 1100p. Ball 65 35
2158 1100p. Goalkeeper's glove 65 35
Nos. 2156/8 were issued together, se-tenant, forming a composite design.

836 University Arms

1998. 75th Anniv of Colombia Free University.
2159 **836** 500p. black and red . . 30 15

837 "Bolivar Condor" (sculpture, R. Arenas Betancur) and Cathedral

1998. 150th Anniv of Manizales.
2160 **837** 500p. multicoloured . . 30 15

838 Gold Coin, Tairona Culture

839 Borrero

1998. 75th Anniversaries. Multicoloured.
2161 500p. Type **838** (National Bank) 30 15
2162 500p. Gold sheaf of corn, Malagana Culture (Comptroller-General's Office) 30 15
2163 500p. Gold mask, Quimbaya Culture (Banking Superintendent's Office) 30 15

1998. 1st Death Anniv of Misael Pastrana Borrero (President, 1970–74).
2164 **839** 500p. multicoloured . . 30 15

840 The Andes and University Campus

1998. 50th Anniv of University of the Andes, Bogota.
2165 **840** 500p. black and yellow 30 15

841 Woman panning for Gold, and Cherubs

843 Academy of Languages Arms

842 Bochica

1998. Christmas. Multicoloured.
2166 500p. Type **841** (postage) . . 30 15
2167 1000p. Three kings, camel and star (air) 60 30
2168 1000p. Nativity 60 30
Nos. 2167/8 were issued together, se-tenant, forming a composite design.

1998. Air. Muisca Mythology. Multicoloured.
2169 1000p. Type **842** 60 30
2170 1000p. Chiminigua 60 30
2171 1000p. Bachue and Huitica 60 30
Nos. 2169/71 were issued together, se-tenant, forming a composite design.

1998. Arms of Colombian Academies. Mult.
2172 500p. Type **843** 30 15
2173 500p. Medicine 30 15
2174 500p. Law 30 15
2175 500p. History 30 15
2176 500p. Physical and Natural Sciences 30 15
2177 500p. Economics 30 15
2178 500p. Ecclesiastical History 30 15

844 Soledad Roman de Nunez (First Lady, 1880–82 and 1884–94)

845 Lopez (after G. Ricci)

1999. America (1998). Famous Women. Mult.
2179 600p. Type **844** (postage) . . 35 20
2180 1200p. Bertha Hernandez de Ospina (politician) (air) 70 35

1999. Birth Bicentenary of Jose Hilario Lopez (President, 1849–53).
2181 **845** 1000p. multicoloured . . 60 30

846 Green Turtle

1999. Turtles. Multicoloured.
2182 1300p. Type **846** 80 50
2183 1300p. Leatherback turtle ("Dermochelys coriacea") 80 40
2184 1300p. Hawksbill turtle ("Eretmochelys imbricata") 80 40
Nos. 2182/4 were issued together, se-tenant, forming a composite design.

847 Colombian and Japanese Suns across the Pacific

1999. 70 Years of Japanese Emigration to Colombia.
2185 **847** 1300p. multicoloured (yellow sun at left) . . 80 40
2186 1300p. multicoloured (red sun at left) . . . 80 40
Nos. 2185/6 were issued together, se-tenant, forming a composite design.

848 Medal

850 Zuleta Angel

849 Crucifix above Pamplona

1999. 900th Anniv of Sovereign Military Order of Malta.
2187 **848** 1200p. multicoloured . . 70 35

1999. 450th Anniv of Pamplona.
2188 **849** 1000p. multicoloured . . 60 30

1999. Birth Centenary of Eduardo Zuleta Angel (politician and diplomat).
2189 **850** 600p. multicoloured . . 35 20

851 Colombian Olympic Committee Emblem

1999. 13th Pan-American Games, Winnipeg. Mult.
2190 1200p. Type **851** 70 35
2191 1200p. Running (facing right) 70 35
2192 1200p. Weightlifting (facing left) 70 35
2193 1200p. Cycling (facing right) 70 35
2194 1200p. Shooting (facing left) 70 35
2195 1200p. Roller blading (facing right) 70 35
2196 1200p. Running (facing left) 70 35
2197 1200p. Weightlifting (facing right) 70 35
2198 1200p. Cycling (facing left) 70 35
2199 1200p. Shooting (facing right) 70 35
2200 1200p. Roller blading (facing left) 70 35

852 Robles

854 Flowers leaving Hands

853 "125" and Emblem

1999. 150th Birth Anniv of Luis A. Robles.
2201 **852** 600p. multicoloured . . 35 20

1999. 125th Anniv of Universal Postal Union. Each lilac, violet and gold.
2202 1000p. Type **853** 60 30
2203 1300p. Emblem 85 45

1999. America. A New Millennium without Arms. Multicoloured.
2204 1200p. Type **854** 75 40
2205 1200p. Flowers moving towards hands 75 40
Nos. 2204/5 were issued together, se-tenant, forming a composite design.

855 Landscape

1999. 40th Anniv of International Development Bank. Multicoloured.
2206 1000p. Type **855** 60 30
2207 1000p. Landscape, sunbeams and red fruits 60 30
Nos. 2206/7 were issued together, se-tenant, forming a composite design.

856 Nativity

1999. Christmas. Multicoloured.
2208 600p. Type **856** 35 20
2209 600p. Angel and Three Wise Men 35 20
Nos. 2208/9 were issued together, se-tenant, forming a composite design.

857 Emblem

858 Rainbow, Globe and "2000"

1999. Centenary of Invention of Aspirin (drug).
2210 **857** 600p. multicoloured . . 35 20

2000. New Millennium. Multicoloured.
2211 1000p. Type **858** 60 30
2212 1000p. Man with Colombian flag and dove 60 30

859 University Arms

2000. 50th Anniv of Medellin University.
2213 **859** 1000p. multicoloured . . 60 30

860 Faria Bermudez

2000. 20th Death Anniv (1999) of Father Jose Rafael Faria Bermudez.
2214 **860** 1300p. brown and black 85 45

861 Pianist and Score

2000. Religious Music Festival, Popayan.
2215 **861** 1000p. multicoloured . . 60 40

862 Stylized Figures forming Olympic Rings

2000. Olympic Games, Sydney.
2216 **862** 1000p. multicoloured . . 60 40

863 Male and Female Symbols under Umbrella

2000. A.I.D.S. Awareness Campaign.
2217 **863** 1000p. multicoloured . . 60 40

864 Weather Vane

2000. 50th Anniv of World Meteorological Society.
2218 **864** 1000p. multicoloured . . 60 40

865 Footprints

2000. National Birth Register.
2219 **865** 1000p. multicoloured . . 60 40

866 "Archangel" (Fernando Botero)

2001. Botero Foundation, Bogota. Multicoloured.
2220 650p. Type **866** 40 25
2221 650p. "Gypsy with Tamborine" (Jean Baptiste Camille Corot) 40 25
2222 650p. "Vera Sergine Renoir" (Pierre-Auguste Renoir) 40 25
2223 650p. "Man on Horse" (Botero) 40 25
2224 650p. "Mother Superior" (Botero) 40 25
2225 650p. "Town" (Botero) . . 40 25
2226 650p. "Flowers" (Botero) 40 25
2227 650p. "Cezanne" (Botero) 40 25
2228 650p. "The Patio" (Botero) 40 25
2229 650p. "Absinthe Drinker at Grenelle" (Henri Toulouse-Lautrec) 40 25
2230 650p. "The Pequeno Valley" (Jean Baptiste Camille Corot) 40 25
2231 650p. "The Studio" (Botero) 40 25

867 Children enclosed in Circle

868 Girl and Dove

2001. Children's Day.
2232 **867** 1100p. multicoloured . . 65 30

2001. 150th Anniv of the Abolition of Slavery.
2233 **868** 1100p. multicoloured . . 65 30

869 Emblem, River Boat and River

870 Football and Club Emblems

2001. 500th Anniv of Discovery of Magdalena River.
2234 **869** 1100p. multicoloured . . 65 30

2001. Copa America Football Championships.
2235 **870** 1900p. multicoloured . . 1·10 55

871 Waterfall, Woman and Wildlife

2001. America. Cultural Heritage. Los Katios National Park.
2236 **871** 2100p. multicoloured . . 1·20 60

872 Children encircling Globe

2001. United Nations Year of Dialogue among Civilizations.
2237 **872** 650p. multicoloured . . 40 20

873 "Reclining Woman" (sculpture, Fernando Botero)

2001.
2238 **873** 1100p. multicoloured . . 65 30

874 Man and Christmas Tree (Diego Rivera)

2001. Christmas.
2239 **874** 1100p. multicoloured . . 65 30

875 Cartegna de Indias and Vanessa Mendoza Bustos

2002. Miss Colombia, 2001–2002. Multicoloured.
2240 800p. Type **875** 50 25
2241 800p. Miss Colombia and St Francis of Assisi church, Quibdo 50 25

876 Stylized Figures and "BOGOTA 2002"

2002. 7th South American Games, Bogota.
2242 **876** 2100p. red, yellow and black . . . . 1·30 65

877 Frigate Bird, Islands and Marine Fauna

2002. Nature. Sheet 140 × 162 mm containing T **877** and similar horiz designs. Multicoloured.
MS2243 2300p. × 8, Type **877**; Condors and mountain; Whales, reptiles, birds and cliffs; Horse rider, birds, animals and mountain peak; Monkeys and birds; Macaws; Flamingos and otter; Egret, jaguar tapir, giant lily pads and manatee . . . . 11·00 11·00
No. **MS**2243 forms a composite design.

878 Flower and Girl (Diana Tovar Reyes)

2002. Children's Day.
2244 **878** 1400p. multicoloured . . 90 45

879 Postal Emblem

2002. New Emblem of Colombia Post.
2245 **879** 800p. ultramarine, red and yellow 50 25

880 Ruddy Duck (*Oxyura jamicensis*)

2002.
2246 **880** 3900p. multicoloured . . 2·50 1·20

881 Harlequin Poison Dart Frog (*Dendrobates histrionicus*)

2002. Amphibians. Sheet 120 × 80 mm containing T **881** and similar horiz design. Multicoloured.
MS2247 7200p. × 2, Type **881**; Tree frog (*Hyla crepitans*) . . . . . 4·50 4·50

882 Flambeau Butterfly (*Dryas iulia*)

2002. Butterflies. Sheet 117 × 71 mm containing T **882** and similar multicoloured design.
MS2248 13700p. × 2, Type **882**; Banded orange heliconian (*Dryadula phaetusa*) (vert) . . . 8·50 8·50

883 Boy wearing Prosthetic Leg

2002. 25th Anniv of Integral Rehabilitation Centre of Colombia (CIREC).
2249 **883** 1000p. multicoloured . . 60 30

884 Narino Chest Decoration

2002. Pre-Colombian Art. Multicoloured.
2250 800p. Type **884** 50 25
2251 800p. Narino disc 50 25
2252 1400p. Calima diadem with raised decoration 50 25
2253 1400p. Calima collar 50 25
2254 2100p. Tairona anthropomorphic chest decoration 50 25
2255 2100p. Tairona circular chest decoration 50 25

885 Doctors

2002. Centenary of Society of Surgeons, San Jose Hospital, Bogota. Multicoloured.
2256 800p. Type **885** 50 25
2257 800p. San Jose hospital . . 50 25

886 Consuelo Araujo Noguera

2002. 1st Death Anniv of Consuelo Araujo Noguera "La Cacica" (journalist and politician).
2258 **886** 1400p. multicoloured . . 90 45

887 "End to Violence" and Stylized Woman

2002. Regional Conference of U N I (international trade union organisation), Rio de Janeiro.
2259 **887** 1000p. multicoloured . . 60 30

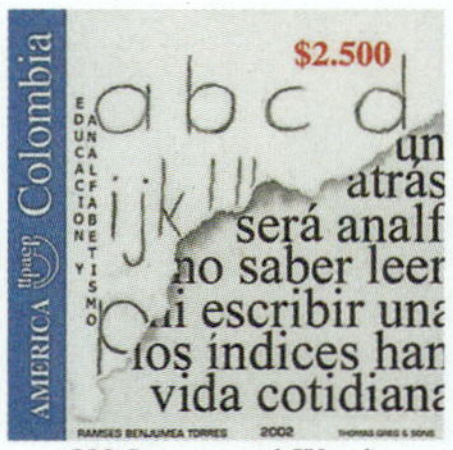

888 Letters and Words

2002. America. Education and Literacy Campaign. Each black, blue and orange.
2260 2500p. Type **888** . . . . . 1·60 80
2261 2500p. Person wearing eye-patch reading . . . . . . 1·60 80

889 Nativity

2002. Christmas.
2262 **889** 800p. multicoloured . . 50 25

890 "Critical Moments during Independence" (detail, Pedro Nel Gomez)

2002. Centenary of Academy of History. Multicoloured.
2263 800p. Type **890** 50 25
2264 800p. Horse riders with spears ("Critical Moments during Independence", detail) 50 25
2265 800p. Slaves, woman feeding baby ("Critical Moments during Independence", detail) 50 25
2266 800p. Forest ("Cafetal", Gonzalo Ariza) 50 25
2267 800p. Horse riders ("Battle of Palonegro", Marco Tobon Mejia) 50 25
2268 800p. "Jaguar hunting" (Noe Leon) 50 25
2269 800p. Bathers ("I sail across", Pedro Nel Gomez) 50 25
2270 800p. "Colombia Murdered" (Sebastian Villalaz) . . . 50 25
2271 800p. "The Women" (Jose Rodriguez) 50 25
2272 800p. Man with beard ("Santander Plaza" (detail, Juan Cardenas)) 50 25
2273 800p. Carriage ("Santander Plaza") 50 25
2274 800p. Horse and couple ("Santander Plaza") . . . 50 25
Nos. 2263/5 and 2272/4 were respectively issued together, se-tenant, forming a composite design of the painting named.

891 "Marching Soldiers" (Eladio Rubio)

2002. Centenary of Peace Treaty at end of Thousand Days' War.
2275 **891** 1600p. multicoloured . . 1·00 50

892 Man wearing Yellow Hat and Carnival Float

2003. Negros y Blancos Carnival, Pasto. Multicoloured.
2276 1000p. Type **892** 45 20
2277 1000p. Procession 45 20
2278 1200p. Float with hands and fish 55 25

893 Buildings and Buses

2003. TransMilenio (transport system).
2279 **893** 1000p. multicoloured . . 45 20

894 City Arms

895 *Montastraea annularis*, *Acropora cervicornis* and *Diploria strigosa*

2003. Departments (1st issue). Caldas. Multicoloured.
2280 1200p. Type **894** 55 25
2281 1200p. Government building, Manizales (49 × 39 mm) 55 25
2282 1200p. "Capesinos" (Alpio Jaramillo) 55 25
2283 2400p. Parochial Church, Salamina . . . . 1·00 50
2284 2400p. "Neira" (David Manzur) (49 × 39 mm) . . 1·00 50
2285 2400p. La Enea Chapel, Manizales . . . . 1·00 50
2286 2800p. Verde lake, Villamaria . . . . 1·20 60
2287 2800p. Aguadas (49 × 39 mm) . . . . . . 1·20 60
2288 2800p. Carnival del Diablo 1·20 60
2289 4100p. Miner, Marmato . . 1·80 90
2290 4100p. "Mariposa del eje cafetero" (Maripaz Jaramillo) (49 × 39 mm) 1·80 90
2291 4100p. Old town, Pacora . . 1·80 90
See also No. 2295/2306, 2307/18, 2349/60, 2362/73, 2381/92, 2415/26, 2444/56, 2461/72, 2473/84 and 2492/2503.

2003. Rosario Island. Corals.
2292 **895** 1000p. multicoloured . . 45 20

896 *Hapalopsittaca fuertesi* (bird)

2003.
2293 **896** 1000p. multicoloured . . 45 20

897 *Masdevallia ignea*

2003. Orchids. Four sheets containing T **897** and similar multicoloured designs.
MS2294 (a) 151 × 120 mm. 2400p. × 2, Type **897**; *Miltoniopisis vexillaria* (56 × 44 mm); (b) 151 × 120 mm. 2800p. × 2, *Odontoglossum crispum* (56 × 44 mm); *Masdevallia macrura*; (c) 99 × 170 mm. 5000p. × 2, *Cimbidium*; *Oncidium obryzatum*; (d) 151 × 120 mm. 7000p. × 2, *Cattleya dowiana*; *Cattleya trianaei* (50 × 50 mm) Set of 4 sheets . . . . 14·00 14·00

2003. Departments (2nd issue). Huila. As T **894**. Multicoloured.
2295 1200p. Arms 55 25
2296 1200p. Government building, Neiva (49 × 39 mm) 55 25
2297 1200p. "La Gaijana" (Phillippe Massonat) . . . 55 25
2298 2400p. Bordonnes waterfall, Isnos . . . . 1·00 50
2299 2400p. San Augustin archaeological park (49 × 39 mm) . . . . . . 1·00 50
2300 2400p. Lavapatas fountain, San Augustin . . . . . . 1·00 50
2301 2800p. La Tatacoa desert, Villavieja . . . . 1·20 60
2302 2800p. Ceiba de La Libertad (49 × 39 mm) . . . . . . 1·20 60
2303 2800p. Hat maker, Suaza . . 1·20 60
2304 4100p. Senora de los Delores, Aipe . . . . . . 1·80 90
2305 4100p. "Paisje" (Mario Ayerbe) (49 × 39 mm) . . 1·80 90
2306 4100p. Dancers . . . . . . 1·80 90

2003. Departments (3rd issue). Santander. As T **894**. Multicoloured.
2307 1200p. Historical center, Barichara 55 25
2308 1200p. Ophthalmic Foundation, Bucaramanga (49 × 39 mm) 55 25
2309 1200p. "Quebrada de las Nieves" (Humberto Ballesteros) 55 25
2310 2400p. International piano festival poster . . . . . . 1·00 50
2311 2400p. *Cristo Petrolero* (sculpture), oil refinery, Barrancabermeja (49 × 39 mm) . . . . . . 1·00 50
2312 2400p. Parochial church, San Andres . . . . . . 1·00 50
2313 2800p. Gustavo Cote Uribe (writer) . . . . 1·20 60
2314 2800p. Commercial Club, Bucaramanga (49 × 39 mm) . . . . . . 1·20 60
2315 2800p. "Oriente Colobiano" Carnival, Bucaramanga 1·20 60
2316 4100p. Historical centre, Albania . . . . 1·80 90
2317 4100p. Chicamocha river gorge, Cepita (49 × 39 mm) . . . . . . 1·80 90
2318 4100p. "Entreguerras" (Beatriz Gonzalez) . . . . 1·80 90

898 Tree and Players

2003. El Tejo (national ball game). Multicoloured.
2319 2400p. Type **898** . . . . . 1·20 60
2320 2400p. Two players . . . . 1·20 60
2321 2400p. Trophy (40 × 40 mm) 1·20 60
Nos. 2319/20 were issued together, se-tenant, forming a composite design.

899 Hawk, Sloth, Kinkajou, Humming Bird and Anteater

2003. America. Flora and Fauna. Multicoloured.
2322 1600p. Type **899** 70 35
2323 1600p. Opossum, toucan, leopard, butterfly and armadillo 70 35

900 Emblem and Building Facade

2003. 117th Anniv of Universad Externado de Colombia. Sheet 120 × 90 mm containing T **900** and similar horiz design. Multicoloured.
MS2324 1200p. Type **900**; Emblem and building (different) 55 55
The stamps and background of No. **MS**2324 form a composite design.

901 Military Arms

2003. 50th Anniv of End of Korean War. Multicoloured.
2325 1200p. Type **901** 55 25
2326 1200p. National arms . . . 55 25
2327 1200p. Navy arms 55 25
2328 1200p. Air Force arms . . . 55 25
2329 1200p. Map of Korea . . . 55 25

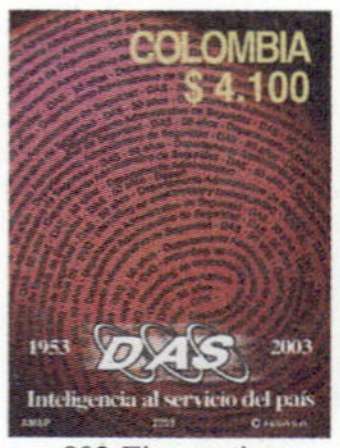

902 Fingerprint

903 General Ramon Quinones

2003. 50th Anniv of DAS (security department). Sheet 120 × 90 mm.
MS2330 **902** 4100p. multicoloured 1·80 90

2003. General Ramon Arturo Rincon Quinones Commemoration.
2331 **903** 1000p. multicoloured . . 45 20

904 Shepherd and Sheep

2003. Christmas. Multicoloured.
2332 1000p. Type **904** 45 20
2333 1000p. Tree, star, airplane and rabbit 45 20
2334 1000p. Hares and dog . . . 45 20
2335 1000p. Sleigh, angel, reindeer and horse . . . 45 20
2336 1000p. Sheep, child, swan and house 45 20
2337 1000p. Leaves, cowboy, duck and Red Indian . . 45 20

905 El Dorado Ceremony (engraving) (Teodoro de Bry)

2004. Laguna de Guatavita (site of legend of El Dorado (cult of the Muisca Indians)). Multicoloured.
2338 2800p. Type **905** . . . . . 1·40 70
2339 2800p. Laguna de Guatavita (painting) (M. Maria Paz) 1·40 70
2340 2800p. Laguna de Guatavita (painting) (Gonzalo Ariza) 1·40 70
2341 2800p. Laguna de Guatavita (painting) (A. Humboldt Thibault/F. Schoell) . . . 1·40 70
2342 2800p. Laguna de Guatavita 1·40 70
2343 2800p. Laguna de Guatavita (engraving) (Eustacio Barreto) . . . . 1·40 70
MS2344 120 × 90 mm. 1700p. Prow of Balsa Muisca (gold raft (ritual object found in lake)); 2000p. Stern of raft (vert) . . . . . . 2·00 2·00

906 Locomotive 2-8-2 (painting) (Ferrando Acuna)

2004. Railways. Multicoloured.
2345 1100p. Type **906** 55 25
2346 1100p. Locomotive 4-8-0 (painting) (Ferrando Acuna) 55 25
2347 1300p. Locomotive 2-6-2 (painting) (Gustavo Arias de Greiff) 65 30
2348 1300p. Locomotive 4-6-2 (painting) (Gustavo Arias de Greiff) 65 30

2004. Departments (4th issue). Tolima. As T **894**. Multicoloured.
2349 2000p. Nevado del Tolima 1·00 50
2350 2000p. Arms (25 × 39 mm) 1·00 50
2351 2000p. "Ambalema" (Price) 1·00 50
2352 2000p. Pots . . . . 1·00 60
2353 2000p. Icononzo Waterfall (25 × 39 mm) . . . . . . 1·00 50
2354 2000p. Armita Church, Mariquita . . . . 1·00 50
2355 2000p. "Matachos" (Jorge Elias Triana) . . . . . . 1·00 50
2356 2000p. Panoptico de Ibague (25 × 39 mm) . . . . . . 1·00 50
2357 2000p. Alberto Castilla Conservatory, Ibague . . 1·00 50
2358 2000p. Magdalena river, Pescadores . . . . 1·00 50
2359 2000p. "Calarca Cheiftain" (painting) (Dario Ortiz Vidales) (25 × 39 mm) . . 1·00 50
2360 2000p. Tolima Museum of Art, Ibague . . . . . . 1·00 50

907 Anniversary Emblem

2004. 5th Anniv of Maloka Theme Park.
2361 **907** 1100p. multicoloured . . 55 25

2004. Departments (5th issue). Narino. As T **894**. Multicoloured.
2362 1100p. Galeras volcano, San Juan de Pasto 55 25
2363 1100p. Gen. Antonio Narino (25 × 39 mm) 55 25
2364 1100p. Ministry of Interior, San Juan de Pasto . . . 55 25
2365 1100p. Fields, Catambuco 55 25
2366 1100p. Our Lady of Lajas Sanctuary, Ipiales (25 × 39 mm) 55 25
2367 1100p. Sandona 55 25
2368 1100p. "Galleria de Espejos" (painting) (Homero Aguilar) 55 25
2369 1100p. Varnishers (1853) (25 × 39 mm) 55 25
2370 1100p. "Palmas Doradas" (painting) (Maria Moran) 55 25
2371 1100p. El Morro (archaeological site), Tumaco 55 25
2372 1100p. Virgin de la Playa Sanctuary, San Pablo (25 × 39 mm) 55 25
2373 1100p. "Fiesta de negros y blancos" (painting) (Manuel Estrada) 55 25

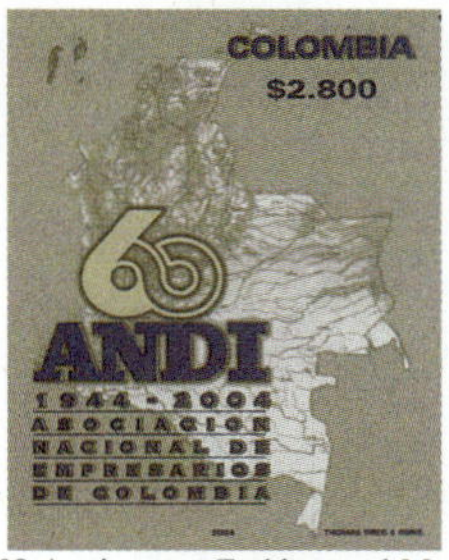

908 Anniversary Emblem and Map

2004. 60th Anniv of ANDI (National Association of Industrialists).
2374 **908** 2800p. bistre, indigo and olive . . . . 1·40 70
2375 2800p. indigo and bistre 1·40 70

909 Olympic Rings and Flame

2004. Olympic Games, Athens.
2376 **909** 4400p. multicoloured . . 2·20 1·10

910 Centenary Emblem

2004. Centenary of FIFA (Federation Internationale de Football).
2377 **910** 3500p. multicoloured . . 1·80 90

911 Women

2004. 50th Anniv of Women's Citizenship.
2378 **911** 1500p. multicoloured . . 55 25

912 Emblem

913 Microphone

2004. 50th Anniv of Federal Commission of Electricity (CFE).
2379 **912** 1300p. multicoloured . . 65 30

2004. 50th Anniv of Colombian Association of Speakers (ACL).
2380 **913** 1700p. multicoloured . . 85 40

2004. Departments (6th issue). Choco. As T **894**. Multicoloured.
2381 3000p. Arms . . . . 1·50 75
2382 3000p. Quibdo (48 × 38 mm) 1·50 75
2383 3000p. Indigenous girls dancing . . . . 1·50 75
2384 3000p. San Pacho festival 1·50 75
2385 3000p. Carasquilla College, Quibdo (48 × 38 mm) . . 1·50 75
2386 3000p. Woman and child (Manuel Maria Paz) . . . 1·50 75
2387 3000p. Boating on San Juan river, Canoa . . . . . 1·50 75
2388 3000p. Women in river (Migdonio Luna Salazar) (48 × 38 mm) . . . . . . 1·50 75

2389 3000p. Our Lady of Rosario Sanctury, Condoto . . . 1·50 75
2390 3000p. Utria Cove . . . . . 1·50 75
2391 3000p. Bellavista Church, Bojaya (48 × 38 mm) . . . 1·50 75
2392 3000p. Goldsmith, Acandi 1·50 75

914 Child and Footballs

2004. National Games.
2393 **914** 7000p. multicoloured . . 3·50 1·70

915 Hammerhead Sharks

2004. America. Environmental Protection. Mult.
2394 5000p. Type **915** . . . . . 2·40 2·50
2395 5000p. Humpback whale . . 2·40 2·50

916 Angel and Child on Swing

2004. Christmas. Multicoloured.
2396/2404 2800p. × 9, Type **916**; Angel and Mary; Figure climbing steps in tree; Mary with Halo; Mary holding flowers; Emperor; Joseph and Mary riding donkey; Bethlehem; The Nativity . . . . . . 12·00 12·00

917 Buckle

2005. Pre-Hispanic Gold Artefacts (1st issue). Multicoloured.
2405 1200p. Type **917** 60 30
2406 1200p. Collar 60 30
See also Nos. 2408/9.

918 Emblem, Town and Mountains

2005. Centenary of Rotary International.
2407 **918** 3100p. multicoloured . . 1·50 75

2005. Pre-Hispanic Gold Artefacts (2nd issue). As T **917**. Multicoloured.
2408 1800p. Articulated collar . . 90 45
2409 1800p. Cuff 90 45

919 Inscr "Protographium tyastes panamensis"

2005. Butterflies. Sheet 138 × 86 mm containing T **919** and similar horiz designs. Multicoloured.
MS2410 4600p. × 3, Type **919**; *Dismorphia zaela*; *Actinote ozomene* . . . . 6·75 6·75
The stamps and margins of **MS**2410 form a composite design.

920 Pectoral Decoration (Quinbaya)

2005. 60th Anniv of FENALCO.
2411 **920** 1200p. multicoloured . . 60 30

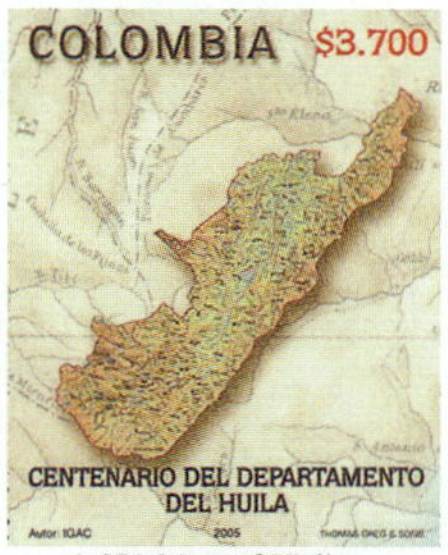

921 Map of Huila

2005. Centenary of Huila Department. Sheet 110 × 140 mm containing T **921** and similar vert design. Multicoloured.
MS2412 3700p. × 2, Type **921**; Map showing position . . . . . . 1·80 1·80
The stamps and margins of **MS**2412 form a composite design.

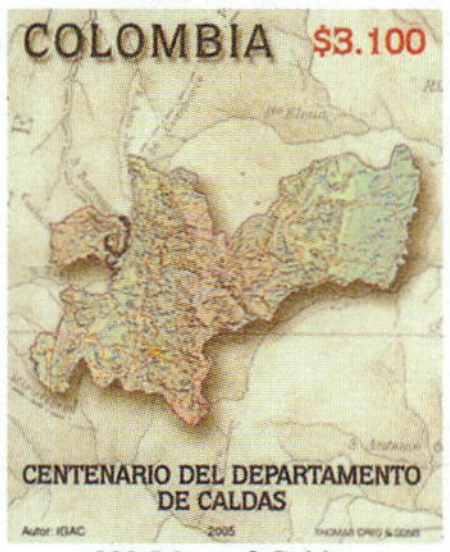

922 Map of Caldas

2005. Centenary of Caldas Department. Sheet 110 × 140 mm containing T **922** and similar vert design. Multicoloured.
MS2413 3100p. × 2, Type **922**; Map showing position . . . . . . 1·50 1·50
The stamps and margins of **MS**2413 form a composite design.

923 Map of Atlantico

2005. Centenary of Atlantico Department. Sheet 138 × 86 mm containing T **923** and similar vert design. Multicoloured.
MS2414 4200p. × 2, Type **923**; Map showing position . . . . . . 2·00 2·00
The stamps and margins of **MS**2414 form a composite design.

2005. Departments (7th issue). San Andres and Santa Catalina. As T **894**. Multicoloured.
2415 1200p. San Andres archipelago 60 30
2416 1200p. Arms (48 × 38 mm) 60 30
2417 1200p. Johnny cay 60 30
2418 1200p. Cangrejo cay 60 30
2419 1200p. Craftsman (48 × 38 mm) 60 30
2420 1200p. Cultural Centre, San Andres 60 30
2421 1200p. Morgan's head, Santa Catalina 60 30
2422 1200p. Island beach (48 × 38 mm) 60 30
2423 1200p. Island architecture 60 30
2424 1200p. Cove, San Andreas 60 30
2425 1200p. Bautista Church, San Andreas (48 × 38 mm) . . 60 30
2426 1200p. Panorama 60 30

924 *Mutisia clematis*

2005. 50th Anniv of Botanical Gardens, Bogota.
2427 **924** 1400p. multicoloured . . 70 35

925 Sport (detail) (Guillermo Arriaga)

2005. Bolivarianos Games.
2428 **925** 3500p. multicoloured . . 1·70 80

926 University Building

2005. 50th Anniv of University de los Andes Past Students Association.
2429 **926** 2000p. multicoloured . . 95 50

927 Globe

2005. International Ozone Layer Protection Day.
2430 **927** 2000p. multicoloured . . 95 45

928 Don Quixote reading

2005. 400th Anniv of "Don Quixote de la Mancha" (novel by Miguel de Cervantes).
2431 1300p. Type **928** 60 30
2432 1300p. Wearing hat (vert) 60 30
2433 1300p. Facing right (vert) 60 30

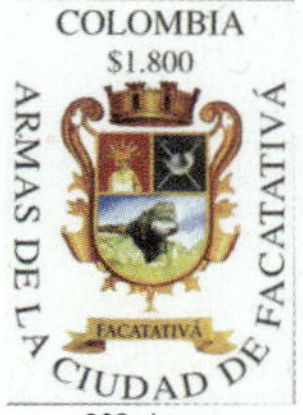

929 Arms

2005. Facatativa City Arms.
2434 **929** 1800p. multicoloured . . 85 45

930 Bank Building

2005. 50th Anniv of Colpatria Bank.
2435 **930** 1200p. multicoloured . . 60 30

932 Statue

2005. 50th Anniv of Escuela de Lanceros (military training school).
2437 **932** 10000p. multicoloured 2·75 1·40

933 Clasped Hands

2005. 50th Anniv of Latin Union.
2438 **933** 5000p. multicoloured . . 2·40 1·20

934 Globe as Bauble

2005. Christmas.
2439 **934** 3100p. multicoloured . . 1·50 75

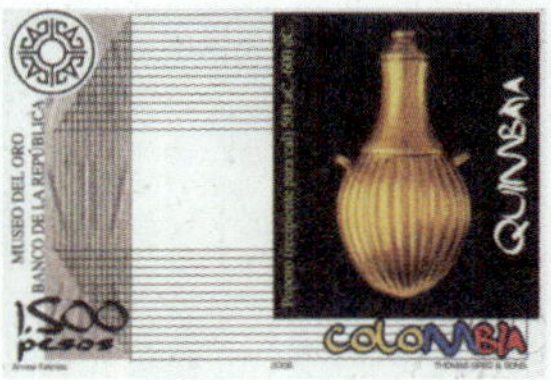

934b Gold Poporo

2006. Gold Museum. Multicoloured.
2441 1500p. Type **934b** 70 35
2442 1500p. Narrow poporo . . . 70 35

935 "Impresion de los Derechos del Hombre" (Luis Cancino)

2006. 60th Anniv of Colombian Journalism.
2443 **935** 2000p. multicoloured . . 55 30

2006. Department (8th issue) Quindo. As Type **894**. Multicoloured.
2444 3300p. "Paso del Quindio" (painting) (1836) (48 × 38 mm) . . . . . . 1·60 80
2445 3300p. Gold statue (22 × 38 mm) . . . . . . 1·60 80
2446 3300p. Coffee growing, Quimbaya (48 × 38 mm) 1·60 80
2447 3300p. Harvesting coffee, Pijao (48 × 38 mm) . . . 1·60 80
2448 3300p. Valle de Cocora (22 × 38 mm) . . . . . . 1·60 80
2449 3300p. Botanical garden, Calarca (48 × 38 mm) . . 1·60 80
2450 3300p. Cultural centre, Armenia (48 × 38 mm) . . 1·60 80
2451 3300p. Statue, Armenia (22 × 38 mm) . . . . . . 1·60 80
2452 3300p. Cemetery, Circasia (48 × 38 mm) . . . . . 1·60 80
2453 3300p. Panorama (48 × 38 mm) . . . . . . 1·60 80
2454 3300p. San Jose Temple, Genova (22 × 38 mm) . . 1·60 80
2455 3300p. "Fundacion de Armenia" (painting) (48 × 38 mm) . . . . . . 1·60 80

936 "50", Olive Wreath and Face

2006. 50th Anniv (2005) of Italian Cultural Institute, Bogota. Multicoloured.

2457	1300p. Type **936**	60	30
2458	1300p. "50", olive wreath and face (different) . . .	60	30

937 Pope John Paul II

939 Fryderyk Chopin

938 Francis Xavier

2006. Pope John Paul II Commemoration.

2459	**937**	4800p. multicoloured . .	2·30	1·20

2006. 500th Birth Anniv of Saint Francis Xavier.

2460	**938**	4500p. multicoloured . .	2·10	1·10

2006. Department (9th issue). Valle del Cauca. As Type **894**. Multicoloured.

2461	1300p. Landscape (1852) (48 × 38 mm)	60	30
2462	1300p. Arms (22 × 38 mm)	60	30
2463	1300p. Panorama, Sevilla (48 × 38 mm)	60	30
2464	1300p. Lake Calima, El Darién (48 × 38 mm) . . .	60	30
2465	1300p. Hermitage, Santiago de Cali. (22 × 38 mm) . .	60	30
2466	1300p. Port, Buenaventura (48 × 38 mm)	60	30
2467	1300p. Railway station, Palmira (48 × 38 mm) . .	60	30
2468	1300p. Sugar cane (22 × 38 mm)	60	30
2469	1300p. Salsa dancers (48 × 38 mm)	60	30
2470	1300p. Museum, El Cerrito (48 × 38 mm)	60	30
2471	1300p. Basilica (22 × 38 mm)	60	30
2472	1300p. Panorama, Valle del Cauca (48 × 38 mm) . . .	60	30

2006. Department (10th issue). Boyaca. As Type **894**. Multicoloured.

2473	2000p. Bolivar Plaza, Tunja (48 × 38 mm)	95	50
2474	2000p. Arms (22 × 38 mm)	95	50
2475	2000p. Campo de Boyaca (1851) (48 × 38 mm) . . .	95	50
2476	2000p. Bolivar monument, Campo de Boyaca (48 × 38 mm)	95	50
2477	2000p. Alter, Virgen de Chiquinquira (22 × 38 mm)	95	50
2478	2000p. Panorama, Garagoa (48 × 38 mm)	95	50
2479	2000p. Los Libertadores Plaza, Duitama (48 × 38 mm)	95	50
2480	2000p. Emeralds (22 × 38 mm)	95	50
2481	2000p. Plaza, Villa de Leyva (48 × 38 mm)	95	50
2482	2000p. Sierra Nevada del Cocuy (48 × 38 mm) . . .	95	50
2483	2000p. Temple of the sun, Sogamoso (22 × 38 mm)	95	50
2484	2000p. El Salitre Hacienda, Paipa (48 × 38 mm) . . .	95	50

2006. Fryderyk Franciszek (Frederic) Chopin (composer and musician) Commemoration.

2485	**939**	5300p. multicoloured . .	2·50	1·30

940 Mascot and Emblem

2006. Central American and Caribbean Games.

2486	**940**	2000p. multicoloured . .	1·10	55

941 Alberto Camargo (painting by G. Camacho)

2006. Birth Centenary of Alberto Lleras Camargo (politician and diplomat).

2487	**941**	1300p. multicoloured . .	70	35
2488		3300p. multicoloured . .	1·80	90

942 *Birth of Jesus* (painting attributed to Rubens School)

2006. Christmas.

2489	**942**	1300p. multicoloured . .	70	35
2490		3300p. multicoloured . .	1·80	90

943 Left Hand

2006. America. Energy Conservation. Sheet 120 × 90 mm containing T **943** and similar vert design. Multicoloured.

MS2491 5000p. × 2, Type **943**; Right hand . . . . 5·50 5·50

The stamps and margins of **MS**2491 form a composite design.

2007. Department (11th issue). Sucre. As Type **894**. Multicoloured.

2492	3300p. Arms (30 × 40 mm)	1·80	90
2493	3300p. San Francisco de Asis Cathedral, Sincelejo (50 × 40 mm)	1·80	90
2494	3300p. Beach, Tolu (1851) (30 × 40 mm)	1·80	90
2495	3300p. Cattle, Ganaderia (30 × 40 mm)	1·80	90
2496	3300p. Bull fight, Corralejas (50 × 40 mm)	1·80	90
2497	3300p. Parroquial Temple, Corazal (30 × 40 mm) . .	1·80	90
2498	3300p. Sheet music (30 × 40 mm)1	80	90
2499	3300p. La Fandanguera (50 × 40 mm)	1·80	90
2500	3300p. Fisherman, Caimilo (30 × 40 mm)	1·80	90
2501	3300p. Palms, Sincelejo (30 × 40 mm)	1·80	90
2502	3300p. Weaving, Sampues (50 × 40 mm)	1·80	90
2503	3300p. Hammocks, Morroa (30 × 40 mm)	1·80	90

944 General Jose Maria Cordova, Soldiers and Arms

2007. General Jose Maria Cordova Military School.

2504	**944**	10000p. multicoloured	5·50	2·75

945 Robert Baden Powell and Scouts

2007. Centenary of Scouting. Multicoloured.

2505	1500p. Type **945**	80	40
2506	1500p. Scout camp (21st World Scout Jamboree)	80	40
2507	1500p. Emblem and Robert Baden Powell	80	40
2508	1500p. Emblem and badger footprint (75th (2006) anniv of Colombia scouts)	80	40

946 '120' and Newsvendor

2007. 120th Anniv of *El Espectador*. Sheet 120 × 90 mm containing T **946** and similar horiz design. Multicoloured.

MS2509 4500p. × 2, Type **946**; Early front page (vert) . . . . 5·00 5·00

947 Emblem

948 Emblem

2007. Pan American Games.

2510	**947**	3700p. multicoloured . .	2·00	1·00

No. 2510 was issued together, se-tenant, forming a composite design of a runner when viewed across the sheet.

2007. International Spanish Language Congress.

2511	**948**	5300p. multicoloured . .	3·00	1·50

PRIVATE AIR COMPANIES

The "LANSA" and Avianca Companies operated inland and foreign air mail services on behalf of the Government and issued the following stamps. Later only the Avianca Company performed this service and the regular air stamps were used on the mail without overprints.

Similar issues were also made by Compania Colombiana de Navegacion Aerea during 1920. These are very rare and will be found listed in the Stanley Gibbons Stamp Catalogue, Part 20 (South America).

A. "LANSA" (Lineas Aereas Nacionales Sociedad Anonima).

1 Wing

1950. Air.

1	**1**	5c. yellow	15	10
2		10c. red	25	15
3		15c. blue	25	10
4		20c. green	40	25
5		30c. purple	1·25	1·25
6		60c. brown	1·50	1·75

With background network colours in brackets.

7	**1**	1p. grey (buff)	6·00	7·50
8		2p. blue (green)	8·50	9·50
9		5p. red (red)	29·00	29·00

The 1p. was also issued without the network.

1950. Air. Nos. 691/7 and 700/3 optd **L**.

10	5c. yellow	15	10
11	10c. red	15	10
12	15c. blue	15	10
13	20c. violet	15	10
14	30c. green	15	15
15	40c. grey	3·50	15
16	50c. red	55	15
17	1p. purple and green	4·25	1·75
18	2p. blue and green	8·50	3·25
19	3p. black and red	8·50	9·50
20	5p. turquoise and sepia . . .	28·00	28·00

1951. As Nos. 696/703 but colours changed and optd **L**.

21	40c. orange	90	55
22	50c. blue	90	55
23	60c. grey	90	45
24	80c. red	75	45
25	1p. red and vermilion	3·75	3·75
26	2p. blue and red	4·50	4·50
27	3p. green and brown	8·25	7·25
28	5p. grey and yellow	21·00	23·00

B. Avianca Company.

1950. Air. Nos. 691/703 optd **A**.

1	5c. yellow	10	10
2	10c. red	15	10
3	15c. blue	10	10
4	20c. violet	20	10
5	30c. green	15	10
6	40c. grey	45	10
7	50c. red	25	10
8	60c. olive	75	15
9	80c. brown	1·40	15
10	1p. purple and green	1·60	15
11	2p. blue and green	5·00	1·60
12	3p. black and red	8·50	7·50
13	5p. turquoise and sepia . . .	25·00	22·00

1951. Air. As Nos. 696/703 but colours changed and optd **A**.

14	40c. orange	4·50	25
15	50c. blue	6·25	25
16	60c. grey	1·75	15
17	80c. red	60	15
18	1p. red and vermilion	2·10	15
19	1p. brown and green	2·25	35
20	2p. blue and red	2·10	35
21	3p. green and brown	4·50	90
22	5p. grey and yellow	8·25	90

The 60c. also comes with the **A** in the centre.

All values except the 2p. and 3p. exist without the overprint.

ACKNOWLEDGEMENT OF RECEIPT STAMPS

AR 60

AR 100

1894.

AR169	AR **60**	5c. red	2·50	2·10

1902. Similar to Type AR **60**. Imperf or perf.

AR265	5c. blue	12·00	12·00
AR211	10c. blue on blue	90	90

1903. No. 197 optd **Habilitado Medellin A R**.

AR258	**75**	10c. black on pink . .	13·00	

1904. No. 262 optd **A R**.

AR266	**75**	5c. red	21·00	21·00

1904.

AR290	AR **100**	5c. blue	7·50	3·50

AR 106 A. Gomez

AR 117 Map of Colombia

1910.

AR354	AR **106**	5c. green & orge	6·00	15·00

1917. Inscr "AR".

AR371	**123**	4c. brown	12·50	11·00
AR372	AR **117**	5c. brown	5·00	4·00

OFFICIAL STAMPS

1937. Optd **OFICIAL**.

O496	–	1c. green (No. 429) . .	10	10
O497	**137**	2c. red (No. 430) . . .	20	20
O498	–	5c. brown (No. 431) . .	10	10
O499	–	10c. orge (No. 485) . .	25	20
O500	**156**	12c. blue	90	25
O501	**141**	20c. blue	1·40	65
O502	**110**	30c. bistre	2·10	65
O503	**123**	40c. brown	22·00	14·00
O504	**112**	50c. red	1·75	80
O505	**110**	1p. blue	14·00	6·00
O506		2p. orange	15·00	6·00
O507		5p. grey	50·00	50·00
O508	**57**	10p. brown	£110	£110

REGISTRATION STAMPS

R 12

R 32

1865. Imperf.
R42 R **12** 5c. black . . . . 90·00 45·00

1865. Type similar to R **12**, but letter "R" in star. Imperf.
R43 5c. black . . . . £100 50·00

1870. Imperf.
R73 R **32** 5c. black . . . . 2·50 2·50

1870. Type similar to R **32** but with "R" in centre and inscr "REJISTRO". Imperf.
R74 5c. black . . . . 1·10 90

1881. Eagle and arms in oval frame, inscr "RECOMENDADA" at foot. Imperf or pin-perf.
R105 10c. lilac . . . . 30·00 30·00

R 42

R 48

1883. Perf.
R117 R **42** 10c. red on orange . . 80 1·00

1899.
R141 R **48** 10c. red . . . . 5·00 3·50
R166 10c. brown . . . . . 1·40 75

R 85

1902. Imperf or perf.
R264 R **85** 10c. purple . . . . . 4·00 4·00
R207 20c. red on blue . . . 80 80
R208 20c. blue on blue . . . 1·25 1·25

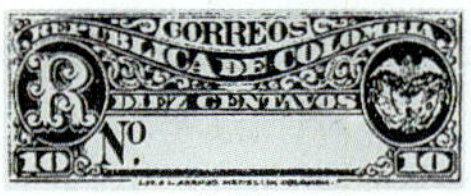
R 94

1902. Perf.
R257 R **94** 10c. purple . . . . . 19·00 19·00

R 99

1904.
R289 R **99** 10c. purple . . . . . 13·00 35

R **105** Execution of 24 February, 1810

1910.
R353 R **105** 10c. black and red . . 20·00 50·00

R **114** Puerto Colombia

1917.
R369 R **114** 4c. blue and green . . 35 3·25
R370 – 10c. blue . . . . . 7·50 25
DESIGN: 10c. Tequendama Falls.

R **127**

1925.
R409 R **127** (10c.) blue . . . . . 9·50 1·75

1932. Air. Air stamps of 1932 optd **R**.
R426 **132** 20c. red . . . . 6·00 4·25
R450 – 20c. green & red (439) 6·00 75

SPECIAL DELIVERY STAMPS

E **118** Express Messenger

1917.
E373 E **118** 5c. green . . . . . . 5·00 4·25

E **310**

1958. Air.
E936 E **310** 25c. red and blue . . 25 15

1959. Air. Unification of Air Mail Rates. Optd **UNIFICADO** within outline of airplane.
E989 E **310** 25c. red and blue . . 45 10

E **361** Boeing 720B on Back of "Express" Letter

1963. Air.
E1143 E **361** 50c. black & red . . 20 10

1966. Air. "History of Colombian Aviation". As T **372**. Inscr "EXPRESO". Multicoloured.
E1168 80c. Boeing 727 jetliner (1966) 10 15

E **647** Numeral

1987.
E1783 E **647** 25p. green and red 25 15
E1784 30p. green and red 25 15

E **663** Sailfish "Istiaphorus amaricanus"

1988. No Value expressed.
E1805 E **663** (A) blue . . . . . . 2·25 1·10
E1806 (B) blue 75 15

E **724** Black & Chestnut Eagle

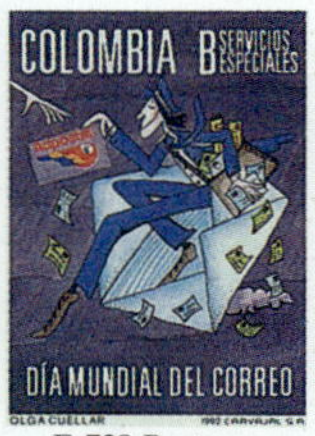
E **738** Postman climbing out of Envelope

1992. No value expressed. Multicoloured.
E1926 B (200p.) Type E **724** . . 1·00 50
E1927 A (950p.) Spectacled bear 2·50 75

1992. World Post Day. No value expressed.
E1951 E **738** B (200p.) mult . . . 35 20

E **741** "Three Musicians"

1993. Fernando Botero (painter) Commemoration. No value expressed.
E1955 E **741** B multicoloured . . 35 20

E **743** Parading "Virgin of the Sorrows"

1993. Popayan Holy Week. No value expressed.
E1957 E **743** B multicoloured . . 35 20

E **744** Mother and Child

E **745** Mother House, Pasto

1993. 90th Anniv of Pan-American Health Organization. No value expressed.
E1958 E **744** B multicoloured . . 35 20

1993. Centenary of Franciscan Convent of Mary Immaculate. No value expressed.
E1959 E **745** B multicoloured . . 35 20

E **746** Stamps, Magnifying Glass and Tweezers

E **747** Cano

1993. 18th National Stamp Exhibition. No value expressed.
E1960 E **746** B multicoloured . . 35 20

1993. 7th Death Anniv of Guillermo Cano (newspaper editor).
E1961 E **747** 250p. multicoloured 40 20

1993. Tourism. As T **756**. Multicoloured.
E1996 250p. Otun Lake (vert) . . 35 20

E **758** Marie Poussepin (founder)

E **761** Biplane

1994. Order of Sisters of the Presentation.
E1998 E **758** 300p. multicoloured 45 25

1994. 75th Anniv of Air Force.
E2004 E **761** 300p. multicoloured 45 25

1994. 4th Latin American Presidential Summit, Cartagena. As T **764**. Multicoloured.
E2010 300p. Setting sun over harbour walls 45 25

E **769** Emblem

1994. International Year of The Family.
E2016 E **769** 300p. multicoloured 40 20

1994. American Postal Transport. As T **770**. Multicoloured.
E2018 300p. Men carrying "stamps" depicting van, ship and aircraft 40 20

1994. Christmas. As T **773**. Multicoloured.
E2022 300p. Nativity 40 20

E **777** Championship Advertising Poster and Gold Ornament

1995. B.M.X. World Championship, Melgar.
E2029 E **777** 400p. multicoloured 55 30

E **785** Bicycle

1995. World Cycling Championships, Bogota and Boyaca.
E2056 E **785** 400p. multicoloured 50 25

E **791** Hands protecting Lake and Marine Angelfish

E **798** Emblem on Cross

1995. America. Environmental Protection. Multicoloured.
E2063 400p. Type E **791** 50 25
E2064 400p. Hands protecting tree 50 25

1996. 400th Anniv of Order of St. John of God in Colombia.
E2075 E **798** 500p. multicoloured 60 30

E **800** Trains

1996. Inauguration (1995) of Medellin Underground Railway.
E2080 E **800** 500p. multicoloured 1·50 75

E **802** Runners

1996. Olympic Games, Atlanta. Centenary of Modern Olympic Games.
E2082 E **802** 500p. multicoloured . . . 60 30

E **812** Fruit Seller

1996. America. Traditional Costumes.
E2104 500p. Type E **812** 60 30
E2105 500p. Fisherman 60 30

TOO LATE STAMPS

L **47**

L **59**

1888. Perf.
L136 L **47** 2½c. black on lilac . . 4·00 1·50

1892. Perf.
L167 L **59** 2½c. blue on red . . . 4·00 3·25

L **86**

L **107**

1902. Imperf or perf.
L209 L **86** 5c. violet on red . . . 45 45

1914. Perf.
L355 L **107** 2c. brown . . . . . . 8·50 6·00
L356 5c. green . . . . . . 8·50 6·00

COMORO ISLANDS Pt. 6, Pt. 12

An archipelago N.W. of Madagascar comprising Anjouan, Great Comoro, Mayotte and Moheli. A French colony from 1891, Mayotte became an Overseas Department of France in December 1974, the remaining islands forming the Independent State of Comoro.

100 centimes = 1 franc.

1 Anjouan Bay

2 Native Woman

6 Mutsamudu Village

1950.
1 **1** 10c. blue (postage) . . . . . 10 2·50
2 50c. green 10 25
3 1f. brown 75 60
4 **2** 2f. green . . . . 1·00 1·00
5 – 5f. violet . . . . 1·50 2·00
6 6f. purple . . . . 1·50 2·00
7 – 7f. red . . . . 1·70 1·50
8 – 10f. green . . . . 1·70 60
9 – 11f. blue . . . . 1·80 2·30
10 – 15f. brown 60 45
11 – 20f. red 55 65
12 – 40f. indigo and blue . . . . 13·00 13·50

13 **6** 50f. red and green (air) . . . 3·00 2·50
14 – 100f. brown and red . . . . 2·75 4·25
15 – 200f. red, green and violet . . 29·00 24·00
DESIGNS (as Type **1**)—HORIZ: 7f., 10f., 11f. Mosque at Moroni; 40f. Coelacanth. VERT: 15f., 20f. Ouani Mosque, Anjouan. (As Type **6**)—HORIZ: 100f. Natives and Mosque de Vendredi; 200f. Ouani Mosque, Anjouan (different).

1952. Military Medal Cent. As T **48** of Cameroun.
16 15f. blue, yellow and green . . 25·00 32·00

1954. Air. 10th Anniv of Liberation. As T **52** of Cameroun.
17 15f. red and brown . . . . . 15·00 46·00

9 Village Pump

1956. Economic and Social Development Fund.
18 **9** 9f. violet . . . . 60 3·50

10 "Human Rights"

1958. 10th Anniv of Declaration of Human Rights.
19 **10** 20f. green and blue . . . . 2·75 10·00

1959. Tropical Flora. As T **58** of Cameroun. Mult.
20 10f. "Colvillea" (horiz) . . . . 1·10 3·00

11 Radio Station, Dzaoudzi

1960. Inaug of Comoro Broadcasting Service.
21 **11** 20f. green, violet and red . . 1·40 2·50
22 – 25f. green, brown and blue . . 1·10 1·90
DESIGN: 25f. Radio mast and map.

12 Bull-mouth Helmet

12a Giant Clam

1962. Multicoloured. (a) Postage. Sea Shells.
23 50c. Type **12** . . . . 40 2·30
24 1f. Common harp . . . . . . 75 2·30
25 2f. Ramose murex . . . . . . 1·10 3·75
26 5f. Giant green turban . . . . 2·30 4·50
27 20f. Scorpion conch . . . . . 5·75 14·50
28 25f. Trumpet triton . . . . . 8·00 17·00

(b) Air. Marine Plants.
29 100f. Type **12a** . . . . 3·25 13·50
30 500f. Stoney coral . . . . . . 12·50 50·00

1962. Malaria Eradication. As T **70** of Cameroun.
31 25f.+5f. red . . . . 90 7·75

1962. Air. 1st Trans-Atlantic T.V. Satellite Link. As Type F **23** of Andorra.
32 25f. mauve, purple and violet 1·50 1·10

14 Emblem in Hands and Globe

14a Centenary Emblem

1963. Freedom from Hunger.
33 **14** 20f. green and brown . . . 1·40 9·50

1963. Red Cross Centenary.
34 **14a** 50f. red, grey and green . . 3·25 12·50

15 Globe and Scales of Justice

16 Tobacco Pouch

1963. 15th Anniv of Declaration of Human Rights.
35 **15** 15f. green and red . . . . . 4·75 10·50

1963. Handicrafts. (a) Postage. As T **17**.
36 **16** 3f. ochre, red and green . . 1·80 3·75
37 – 4f. myrtle, purple & orange . 1·80 4·00
38 – 10f. brown, green & chest . 1·60 4·50

(b) Air. Size 27 × 48 mm.
39 – 65f. red, brown and green . . 2·30 7·25
40 – 200f. pink, red & turq . . . 5·25 11·00
DESIGNS: 4f. Perfume-burner; 10f. Lamp bracket; 65f. Baskets; 200f. Filigree pendant.

16a "Philately"

17 Pirogue

1964. "PHILATEC 1964" International Stamp Exhibition, Paris.
41 **16a** 50f. red, green and blue . . 1·20 8·75

1964. Native Craft. Multicoloured.
42 15f. Type **17** (postage) . . . . 3·25 4·50
43 30f. Boutre felucca . . . . . 4·25 7·75

44 50f. Mayotte pirogue (air) . . 2·50 7·00
45 85f. Schooner . . . . 4·50 7·00
Nos. 44/5 are larger, 27 × 48½ mm.

18 Boxing (Ancient bronze plaque)

19 Medal

1964. Air. Olympic Games, Tokyo.
46 **18** 100f. green, brown & choc 5·75 15·00

1964. Air. Star of Grand Comoro.
47 **19** 500f. multicoloured . . . . 10·00 34·00

20 "Syncom" Communications Satellite, Telegraph Poles and Morse Key

1965. Air. Centenary of ITU.
48 **20** 50f. blue, green and grey . . 5·25 27·00

21 Great Hammerhead

1965. Marine Life.
49 – 1f. green, orange and violet 2·50 3·25
50 **21** 12f. black, blue and red . . 3·25 4·00
51 – 20f. red and green . . . . . 4·00 4·50
52 – 25f. brown, red and green 5·50 4·25
DESIGNS—VERT: 1f. Spiny lobster; 25f. Spotted grouper. HORIZ: 20f. Scaly turtle.

21a Rocket "Diamant"

1966. Air. Launching of 1st French Satellite.
53 **21a** 25f. lilac, blue and violet 3·00 6·00
54 – 30f. lilac, violet and blue 3·25 6·50
DESIGN: 30f. Satellite "A1".

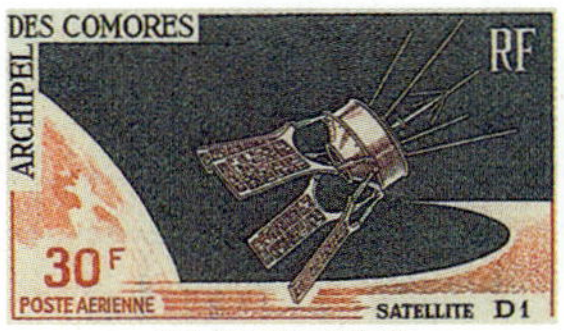

21b Satellite "D1"

1966. Air. Launching of Satellite "D1".
55 **21b** 30f. purple, green & orange 1·10 2·30

22 Lake Sale

1966. Comoro Views. Multicoloured.
56 15f. Type **22** (postage) . . . . 75 3·25
57 25f. Itsandra Hotel, Moroni 1·20 2·00
58 50f. The Battery, Dzaoudzi (air) . . . . 1·80 4·75
59 200f. Ksar Fort, Mutsamudu (vert) . . . . 3·50 7·50
Nos. 58/9 are larger, 48 × 27 mm and 27 × 48 mm respectively.

23 Anjouan Sunbird

1967. Birds. Multicoloured.
60 2f. Type **23** (postage) . . . . 6·00 5·75
61 10f. Madagascar malachite kingfisher . . . . 5·25 7·25
62 15f. Mascarene fody . . . . . 10·00 9·00
63 30f. Courol . . . . 21·00 23·00
64 75f. Madagascar paradise flycatcher (vert) (27 × 48 mm) (air) . . . . 12·00 16·00
65 100f. Blue-cheeked bee eater (vert) (27 × 48 mm) . . . . 10·00 22·00

24 Nurse tending Child

25 Slalom Skiing

1967. Comoro Red Cross.
66 **24** 25f.+5f. purple, red & grn 2·75 4·50

1968. Air. Winter Olympic Games, Grenoble.
67 **25** 70f. brown, blue and green 4·25 5·25

26 Bouquet, Sun and WHO Emblem

1968. 20th Anniv of WHO.
68 **26** 40f. red, violet and green . . 80 1·40

27 Powder-blue Surgeonfish

28 Human Rights Emblem

1968. Fishes.
69 **27** 20f. bl, yell & red (postage) 4·50 7·00
70 – 25f. blue, orange & turq . . 5·25 8·50
71 – 50f. ochre, blue & pur (air) 6·25 8·00
72 – 90f. ochre, green & emer . . 9·00 11·00
DESIGNS—As T **27**: 25f. Emperor angelfish. 48 × 27 mm: 50f. Moorish idol; 90f. Oriental sweetlips.

1968. Human Rights Year.
73 **28** 60f. green, brown & orange 2·75 5·50

29 Swimming

1968. Air. Olympic Games, Mexico.
74 **29** 65f. multicoloured . . . . . 2·75 6·00

30 Prayer Mat and Worshipper

1969. Msoila Prayer Mats.
75 **30** 20f. red, green and violet . . 1·20 3·25
76 – 30f. green, violet and red . . 1·40 3·50
77 – 45f. violet, red and green . . 3·00 5·75
DESIGNS: As Type **30**, but worshipper stooping (30f.) or kneeling upright (45f.).

31 Vanilla Flower

1969. Flowers. Multicoloured.
78 10f. Type **31** (postage) . . . . 3·00 2·75
79 15f. Ylang-ylang blossom . . 3·00 2·75
80 50f. "Heliconia" (vert) (air) . . 4·25 4·75
81 85f. Tuberose (vert) . . . . . 5·50 7·00
82 200f. Orchid (vert) . . . . . 10·00 9·25

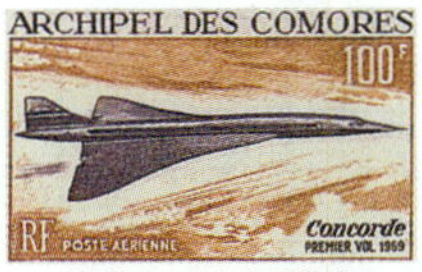

32 Concorde in Flight

1969. Air. 1st Flight of Concorde.
83 **32** 100f. purple and brown . . 10·00 27·00

33 ILO Building, Geneva

1969. 50th Anniv of ILO.
84 **33** 5f. grey, green and orange 2·30 3·25

34 Poinsettia

1970. Flowers.
85 **34** 25f. multicoloured . . . . . 3·75 3·00

1970. New UPU Headquarters Building, Berne. As T **156** of Cameroun.
86 65f. brown, green and violet 3·75 6·00

35 "EXPO" Panorama

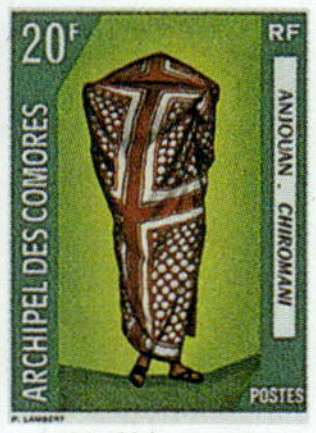

36 Chiromani Costume, Anjouan

1970. Air. World Fair "EXPO 70", Osaka, Japan. Multicoloured.
87 60f. Type **35** . . . . 4·25 3·75
88 90f. Geisha and map of Japan 5·25 4·50

1970. Comoro Costumes. Multicoloured.
89 20f. Type **36** . . . . 3·25 2·75
90 25f. Bouiboui, Great Comoro 3·75 4·25

37 Mosque de Vendredi, Moroni

38 Great Egret

1970.
91 **37** 5f. turquoise, green and red 3·50 3·50
92 10f. violet, green & purple 3·00 3·75
93 40f. brown, green and red 4·00 4·00

1971. Birds. Multicoloured.
94 5f. Type **38** . . . . 2·50 3·50
95 10f. Comoro olive pigeon . . 3·00 3·25
96 15f. Green-backed heron . . 3·50 3·75
97 25f. Comoro blue pigeon . . . 3·00 3·75
98 35f. Humblot's flycatcher . . . 4·25 5·50
99 40f. Allen's gallinule . . . . . 6·50 6·00

39 Sunset, Moutsamoudou (Anjouan)

40 Map of Comoro Archipelago

1971. Air. Comoro Landscapes. Multicoloured.
100 **39** 15f. multicoloured . . . . 2·50 2·30
101 – 20f. multicoloured . . . . 3·00 2·50
102 – 65f. multicoloured . . . . 3·25 3·00
103 – 85f. multicoloured . . . . 3·75 3·75
104 **40** 100f. brown, green & bl . . 9·25 7·25
DESIGNS—(As Type **39**): 20f. Sada village (Mayotte); 65f. Ruined palace, Iconi (Great Comoro); 85f. Offshore islands; Moumatchoua (Moheli).
See also Nos. 124/8, 132/6, 157/60 and 168/71.

41 "Pyrostegia venusta"

42 Lithograph Cone

1971. Tropical Plants. Multicoloured.
105 1f. Type **41** (postage) . . . . 2·50 2·50
106 3f. "Allamanda cathartica" (horiz) . . . . 2·75 2·50
107 20f. "Plumeria rubra" . . . 4·75 3·75
108 60f. "Hibiscus schizopetalous" (air) . . . 4·25 4·25
109 85f. "Acalypha sanderii" . . 9·25 7·75
The 60 and 85f. are 27 × 48 mm.

1971. Sea Shells. Multicoloured.
110 5f. Type **42** . . . . 2·75 2·50
111 10f. Lettered cone . . . . . 3·50 3·25
112 20f. Princely cone . . . . . 3·75 4·00
113 35f. Polished nerite . . . . . 6·00 3·00
114 60f. Serpent's-head cowrie . . 9·50 4·25

1971. 1st Death Anniv of Charles de Gaulle. Designs as Nos. 1937 and 1940 of France.
115 20f. black and purple . . . . 3·50 5·00
116 35f. black and purple . . . . 3·50 5·50

44 Mural, Airport Lounge

1972. Air. Inauguration of New Airport, Moroni.
117 **44** 65f. multicoloured . . . . 1·70 2·50
118 – 85f. multicoloured . . . . 2·30 3·25
119 – 100f. green, brown & blue 4·00 4·50
DESIGNS: 85f. Mural similar to T **44**; 100f. Airport Buildings.

45 Eiffel Tower, Paris and Telecommunications Centre, Moroni

1972. Air. Inauguration of Paris–Moroni Radio-Telephone Link.
120 **45** 35f. red, purple & blue . . 3·00 2·50
121 – 75f. red, violet and blue . . 3·00 2·50
DESIGN: 75f. Telephone conversation.

46 Underwater Spear-fishing

1972. Air. Aquatic Sports.
122 **46** 70f. red, green and blue . . 9·50 8·00

47 Pasteur, Crucibles and Microscope

1972. 150th Birth Anniv of Louis Pasteur.
123 **47** 65f. blue, brown & orange 5·50 6·25

1972. Air. Anjouan Landscapes. (a) As T **39**. Multicoloured.
124 20f. Fortress wall, Cape Sima 3·00 2·30
125 35f. Bambao Palace . . . . 3·25 2·50
126 40f. Palace, Domoni . . . . 2·50 2·50
127 60f. Gomajou Island . . . . 3·50 4·25

(b) As T **40**.
128 – 100f. green, blue & brown 7·75 9·00
DESIGN: 100f. Map of Anjouan.

48 Pres. Said Mohamed Cheikh

50 Bank

1973. Air. Said Mohamed Cheikh, President of Comoro Council, Commemoration.
129 **48** 20f. multicoloured . . . . 3·00 3·50
130 35f. multicoloured . . . . 3·25 3·75

1973. Air. International Coelacanth Study Expedition. No. 72 surch **Mission Internationale pour l'etude du Coelacanthe** and value.
131 120f. on 90f. brn, grn & emer 17·00 8·25

1973. Great Comoro Landscapes. (a) Postage. As T **39**. Multicoloured.
132 10f. Goulaivoini . . . . . . 3·75 2·30
133 20f. Mitsamiouli . . . . . . 4·00 2·50
134 35f. Foumbouni . . . . . . 4·75 3·00
135 50f. Moroni . . . . 5·75 3·75

(b) Air. As Type **40**.
136 – 135f. purple, green & violet 16·00 8·75
DESIGN—VERT: 135f. Map of Great Comoro.

1973. Moroni Buildings. Multicoloured.
137 5f. Type **50** . . . . 3·25 3·25
138 15f. Post Office . . . . . . 3·00 3·50
139 20f. Prefecture . . . . 3·75 3·00

51 Volcanic Eruption

1973. Air. Karthala Volcanic Eruption (Sept 1972).
140 **51** 120f. multicoloured . . . . 16·00 11·00

52 Dr. G. A. Hansen

54 Zaouiyat Chaduli Mosque

53 Pablo Picasso (artist)

1973. Air Centenary of Hansen's Identification of Leprosy Bacillus.
141 **52** 100f. green, purple & blue 4·75 5·50

1973. Air. 500th Birth Anniv of Nicolas Copernicus. As T **52**.
142 150f. purple, blue & ultram 6·75 7·75
DESIGN: 150f. Copernicus and solar system.

1973. Air. Picasso Commemoration.
143 **53** 200f. multicoloured . . . . 20·00 11·50
MS144 100 × 131 mm. **53** 100f. multicoloured . . . . 12·00 12·50

1973. Mosques. Multicoloured.
145 20f. Type **54** . . . . 2·30 4·00
146 35f. Salimata Hamissi Mosque (horiz) . . . . . 3·00 3·00

55 Star and Ribbon

1974. Air. Order of the Star of Anjouan.
147 **55** 500f. gold, blue & brown 20·00 22·00

56 Said Omar Ben Soumeth (Grand Mufti of the Comoros)

1974. Air. Multicoloured.
148 135f. Type **56** . . . . 6·00 4·00
149 200f. Ben Soumeth seated (vert) . . . . 8·25 6·75

57 Doorway of Mausoleum

1974. Mausoleum of Shaikh Said Mohamed.
150 **57** 35f. brown, black & green 3·50 4·00
151 – 50f. brown, black & green 4·25 4·00
DESIGN: 50f. Mausoleum.

58 Wooden Combs **59** Mother and Child

1974. Comoro Handicrafts (1st series). Mult.
152 15f. Type **58** . . . . 1·90 3·25
153 20f. Three-legged table . . . 3·00 3·25
154 35f. Koran lectern (horiz) . . 4·75 4·00
155 75f. Sugar-cane press (horiz) 7·75 5·75
See also Nos. 164/7.

1974. Comoros Red Cross Fund.
156 **59** 35f.+10f. brown & red . . 2·75 4·50

1974. Air. Mayotte Landscapes. (a) As T **39**. Multicoloured.
157 20f. Moya beach . . . . . . 3·25 3·00
158 35f. Chiconi . . . . 3·50 3·50
159 90f. Mamutzu harbour . . . 6·75 5·50

(b) As T **40**.
160 120f. green and blue . . . . 7·25 7·00
DESIGN—VERT: 120f. Map of Mayotte.

60 UPU Emblem and Globe

1974. Centenary of Universal Postal Union.
161 **60** 30f. red, brown and green 4·00 3·50

61 Boeing 707 taking off

1975. Inauguration of Direct Moroni–Hahaya–Paris Air Service.
162 **61** 135f. blue, green and red 10·50 9·75

62 Rotary Emblem, Moroni Clubhouse and Map

1975. Air. 70th Anniv of Rotary International and 10th Anniv of Moroni Rotary Club.
163 **62** 250f. multicoloured . . . . 14·00 12·50

63 Bracelet

1975. Comoro Handicrafts (2nd series).
164 **63** 20f. brown and purple . . 3·50 3·50
165 – 35f. brown and green . . 3·25 3·75
166 – 120f. brown and blue . . . 7·50 6·75
167 – 135f. brown and red . . 10·50 8·00
DESIGNS: 35f. Diadem; 120f. Sabre; 125f. Dagger.

1975. Moheli Landscapes. (a) Postage. As T **39**. Multicoloured.
168 30f. Mohani Village . . . . 4·50 3·75
169 50f. Djoezi Village . . . . . 5·50 4·25
170 55f. Chirazian tombs . . . . 7·00 5·00

(b) Air. As T **40**.
171 230f. green, blue and brown 20·00 12·50
DESIGN: 230f. Map of Moheli.

64 Coelacanth and Skin-diver

1975. Coelacanth Expedition.
172 **64** 50f. bistre, blue & brown 10·50 7·50

65 Tambourine-player

1975. Folklore Dances. Multicoloured.
173 100f. Type **65** . . . . 70·00 70·00
174 150f. Dancers with tambourines . . . . 70·00 70·00

66 Athlete and Athens, 1896 Motifs

1976. Olympic Games, Munich (1972) and Montreal (1976). Multicoloured.
175 20f. Type **66** (postage) . . . 10 10
176 25f. Running 30 10
177 40f. Athlete and Paris, 1900 motif 45 20
178 75f. High-jumping 95 50
179 100f. Exercises and World's Fair, St. Louis, 1904 motif (air) . . . . 1·00 65
180 500f. Gymnast on bars . . . 5·25 2·75
MS181 91 × 120 mm. 400f. Olympic stadium, Montreal . . . . . . 4·75 2·75

67 Government House, Flag and Map

1976. 1st Anniv of Independence. Multicoloured.
182 **67** 30f. multicoloured 60 25
183 50f. multicoloured . . . . 1·00 40

68 Agricultural Scene and U.N. Stamp

1976. 25th Anniv of U.N. Postal Services. Multicoloured.
184 15f. Type **68** (postage) . . . 10 10
185 30f. Surgery scene and U.N. W.H.O. stamp 30 10
186 50f. Village scene and UNICEF stamp 55 30
187 75f. Telecommunications satellite and U.N. I.T.U. stamp 80 35
188 200f. Concorde, airship "Graf Zeppelin" and U.N. ICAO stamp (air) . . . . . 2·20 90
189 400f. Lufthansa jet airliner and U.N. U.P.U. stamp . . 4·00 2·10
MS190 104 × 104 mm. 500f. Ring of people with letters on globe (53 × 35 mm) . . . . 4·50 1·80

69 Copernicus, and Rocket on Launch-pad

1976. "Success of Operation Viking", and Bicentenary of American Revolution. Multicoloured.
191 5f. Type **69** (postage) 20 10
192 10f. Einstein, Sagan and Young (horiz) 20 10
193 25f. "Viking" orbiting Mars 35 10
194 35f. Vikings' discovery of America (horiz) 75 25
195 100f. U.S. flag and Mars landing . . . . 1·40 50
196 500f. First colour photograph of Martian terrain (horiz) (air) . . . . 7·50 2·50
MS197 116 × 82 mm. 400f. "Viking" on Mars (41 × 59 mm) . . . . 4·50 1·60

70 U.N. Headquarters, New York and Flags

1976. 1st Anniv of Comoro Islands Admission to United Nations.
198 **70** 40f. multicoloured 60 30
199 50f. multicoloured 85 40

71 President Lincoln and Bombardment of Fort Sumter

1976. Bicentenary of American Revolution. Showing various battle scenes of American Civil War. Multicoloured.
200 10f. Type **71** (postage) . . . 10 10
201 30f. General Beauregard and Bull Run (vert) 35 20
202 50f. General Johnston and Antietam 45 40
203 100f. General Meade and Gettysburg (air) . . . . . 1·20 60
204 200f. General Sherman and Chattanooga (vert) . . . . 1·80 1·10
205 400f. General Pickett and Appomattox . . . . 3·75 2·00
MS206 110 × 76 mm. 500f. Surrender of General Lee to General Grant (59 × 41 mm) . . . . 4·50 2·75

72 Andean Condor **74** Giffard's Dirigible, 1851 and French Locomotive, 1837

73 Wolf

1976. "Endangered Animals" (1st series). Multicoloured.
207 15f. Type **72** (postage) . . . 35 10
208 20f. Tiger cat (horiz) 55 10
209 35f. Leopard . . . . 1·00 25
210 40f. White rhinoceros (horiz) 1·30 45
211 75f. Mountain nyala . . . . 2·75 55
212 400f. Orang-utan (horiz) (air) 6·75 1·50
MS213 78 × 100 mm. 500f. Indri (lemur) (38 × 56 mm) . . . . . 6·75 1·90

1977. "Endangered Animals" (2nd series). Mult.
214 10f. Type **73** (postage) . . . 10 10
215 30f. Aye-aye 45 10
216 40f. Banded duiker 95 25
217 50f. Giant tortoise . . . . . 1·20 25
218 200f. Ocelot (air) . . . . . . 2·75 90
219 400f. Galapagos penguin ("Manchot des Galapagos") . . . . 6·00 1·70
MS220 96 × 76 mm. 500f. Sumatran tiger (56 × 38 mm) . . . . . . 7·50 1·90

1977. History of Communications. Airships and Railways. Multicoloured.
221 20f. Type **74** (postage) . . . 30 10
222 25f. Santos-Dumont's airship "Ballon No. 6" (1906) and Brazilian steam locomotive (19th century) 35 10
223 50f. Russian airship "Astra" (1914) and "Trans-Siberian Express" (1905) 75 25
224 75f. British airship R-34 (1919) and "Southern Belle" pullman express (1910–25) . . . . 1·00 30
225 200f. U.S. Navy airship "Los Angeles" (1930) and Pacific locomotive (1930) (air) . . 2·30 80
226 500f. German airship "Hindenburg", 1933, and "Rheingold" express, 1933 5·75 1·90
MS227 100 × 80 mm. 500f. Airship "Graf Zeppelin" and locomotive "Nord-Express" (54 × 35 mm) 5·50 2·10

75 Koch, Morgan, Fleming, Muller and Waksman (medicine)

1977. Nobel Prize Winners. Multicoloured.
228 30f. Type **75** (postage) . . . 50 10
229 40f. Michelson, Bragg, Raman and Zernike (physics) 60 15
230 50f. Tagore, Yeats, Russell and Hemingway (literature) 80 25
231 100f. Rontgen, Becquerel, Planck, Lawrence and Einstein (physics) . . . . . 2·10 35
232 200f. Ramsey and Marie Curie (chemistry), Banting and Hench (medicine) and Perrin (physics) (air) . . . 2·50 90
233 400f. Dunant, Briand, Schweitzer and Martin Luther King (peace) . . . 5·50 1·70
MS234 94 × 64 mm. 500f. Alfred Nobel (50 × 41 mm) . . . . . 5·50 1·90
The 200f. wrongly attributes the chemistry prize to all those depicted and gives the date 1913 instead of 1911 for Marie Curie. On the 50 and 100f. names are wrongly spelt.

76 "Clara, Ruben's Daughter"

1977. 400th Birth Anniv of Peter Paul Rubens (1st issue). Multicoloured.
235 20f. Type **76** (postage) . . . 25 10
236 25f. "Suzanne Fourment" . . 30 10
237 50f. "Venus in front of Mirror" 75 25
238 75f. "Ceres" 95 30
239 200f. "Young Girl with Blond Hair" (air) . . . . 2·30 75
240 500f. "Helene Fourment in Wedding Dress" . . . . . 6·25 1·90
MS241 110 × 86 mm. 500f. "Self-portrait" (31 × 47 mm) . . . . 5·50 2·00
See also Nos. 407/10.

77 Queen Elizabeth II, Westminster Abbey and Guards

1977. Air. Silver Jubilee of Queen Elizabeth II.
242 **77** 500f. multicoloured . . . . 5·00 1·80
MS243 114 × 86 mm. 1000f. multicoloured . . . . 9·50
DESIGN: 1000f. State coach.

79 Swordfish

1977. Fishes. Multicoloured.
256 30f. Type **79** (postage) . . . 45 15
257 40f. Oriental sweetlips . . . 90 20
258 50f. Lionfish . . . . 1·30 40
259 100f. Racoon butterflyfish . . 2·75 70
260 200f. Clown anemonefish (air) 3·75 90
261 400f. Black-spotted puffer . . 6·75 2·30
MS262 80 × 100 mm. 500f. Coelacanth (46 × 37 mm) . . . 6·00 2·10

80 Jupiter Lander

1977. Space Research. Multicoloured.
263 30f. Type **80** (postage) . . . 30 10
264 50f. Uranus probe (vert) . . 50 10
265 75f. Venus probe 85 30
266 100f. Space shuttle (vert) . . 1·00 40
267 200f. "Viking 3" (air) . . . . 2·10 75
268 400f. "Apollo–Soyuz" link (vert) . . . . 4·25 1·60
MS269 101 × 75 mm. 500f. Allegory of the Sun (50 × 41 mm) . . . 5·50 1·90

1977. Air. First Paris–New York Commercial Flight of Concorde. No. 188 optd **Paris-New-York - 22 nov. 1977.**
270 200f. multicoloured . . . . . 4·25 2·75

82 Allen's Gallinule

1978. Birds. Multicoloured.
271 15f. Type **82** (postage) . . . 30 15
272 20f. Blue-cheeked bee eater 45 20
273 35f. Madagascar malachite kingfisher 65 25
274 40f. Madagascar paradise flycatcher . . . . 1·10 35
275 75f. Anjouan sunbird . . . . 1·80 40
276 400f. Great egret (air) . . . . 8·25 2·00
MS277 76 × 88 mm. 500f. Mascarene fody (47 × 33 mm) . . . . . . 6·50 2·10

83 Greek Ball Game and Modern Match

1978. World Cup Football Championship, Argentina. Multicoloured.
278 30f. Type **83** (postage) . . . 30 10
279 50f. Breton football 50 15
280 75f. 14th-century London game 75 30
281 100f. 18th-century Italian game . . . . 1·00 40
282 200f. 19th-century English game (air) . . . . 2·10 75
283 400f. English cup-tie, 1891 . . 4·25 1·60
MS284 120 × 70 mm. 500f. English cup-tie final, 1902 . . . . . . 5·00 1·90

84 "Oswolt Krel"

1978. 450th Death Anniv of Albrecht Durer (artist) (1st issue). Multicoloured.
286 20f. Type **84** (postage) . . . 10 10
287 25f. "Elspeth Tucher" . . . 30 10
288 50f. "Hieronymus Holzshuher" 60 25
289 75f. "Young Girl" 85 30
290 200f. "Emperor Maximilian I" (air) . . . . 2·20 80
291 500f. "Young Girl" (detail) 5·00 1·90
MS292 90 × 75 mm. 500f. "Self-portrait" (41 × 50 mm) . . . . 5·50 2·00
See also Nos. 411/15.

85 Bach

1978. Composers. Multicoloured.
293 30f. Type **85** (postage) . . . 55 20
294 40f. Mozart 85 20
295 50f. Berlioz . . . . 1·00 30
296 100f. Verdi . . . . 2·40 50
297 200f. Tchaikovsky (air) . . . 3·25 75
298 400f. Gershwin . . . . . . 5·25 1·70
MS299 100 × 79 mm. 500f. Beethoven (150th death anniv) 6·75 2·00

Following a revolution on 13 May 1978, it was announced that sets showing Butterflies or commemorating the 25th Anniversary of the Coronation of Queen Elizabeth II, 10th World Telecommunications Day and Aviation History had not been placed on sale in the islands and were not valid for postage there.

86 Rowland Hill, Locomotive "Adler" and Saxony 3pf. Stamp, 1860

1978. Death Centenary of Sir Rowland Hill. Multicoloured.
300 20f. Type **86** (postage) . . . 20 10
301 30f. Penny-farthing and Netherlands 5c. stamp, 1852 . . . . 40 10
302 40f. Early letter-box and 2d. blue 70 10
303 75f. Pony Express and U.S. stamp, 1847 . . . . . . 95 30
304 200f. Airship and French 20c. stamp, 1863 (air) . . . . 1·90 65
305 400f. Postman and Basel $2\frac{1}{2}$r. stamp, 1845 . . . . . . 4·00 90
MS306 110 × 79 mm. 500f. Early Comoro Isalnds stamps (53 × 35 mm) . . . . 4·75 2·00

87 Interpreting Meteorological Satellite Photographs

1978. European Space Agency. Multicoloured.
307 10f. Type **87** (postage) . . . 10 10
308 25f. Writing weather forecast 30 10
309 35f. Aiding wrecked ship . . 35 10
310 50f. Telecommunications as teaching aid 55 20
311 100f. Boeing 727 landing (air) 1·00 30
312 500f. Space shuttle . . . . . 4·75 1·60
MS313 108 × 77 mm. 500f. Satellite over map of Africa (59 × 38 mm) 5·25 2·30

1978. Argentina's Victory in World Cup Football Championship. Nos. 278/284 optd **REP. FED. ISLAMIQUE DES COMORES 1 ARGENTINE 2 HOLLANDE 3 BRESIL.**
314 **83** 30f. mult (postage) 45 25
315 – 50f. multicoloured 45 40
316 – 75f. multicoloured 55 55
317 – 100f. multicoloured . . . . 1·20 1·10
318 – 200f. multicoloured (air) . . 1·80 45
319 – 400f. multicoloured . . . . 3·75 90
MS320 120 × 70 mm. 500f. multicoloured . . . . 4·50 2·50

89 Philidor, Anderssen and Steinitz

1979. Chess Grand Masters. Multicoloured.
321 40f. Type **89** (postage) . . . 45 10
322 100f. Venetian players and pieces . . . . 1·00 25
323 500f. Alekhine, Spassky and Fischer (air) . . . . . . 4·75 1·60

90 Galileo and "Voyager 1"

1979. Exploration of the Solar System. Mult.
324 20f. Type **90** (postage) . . . 10 10
325 30f. Kepler and "Voyager 2" 30 10
326 40f. Copernicus and "Voyager 1" 45 20
327 100f. Huygens and "Voyager 2" . . . . 1·00 30
328 200f. Herschel and "Voyager 2" (air) . . . . 1·80 60
329 400f. Leverrier and "Voyager 2" . . . . 3·75 1·20

91 Kayak

1979. Olympic Games, Moscow (1980). Mult.
330 10f. Type **91** (postage) . . . 10 10
331 25f. Swimming 30 10
332 35f. Archery 35 10
333 50f. Pole vault 45 20
334 75f. Long jump 80 35
335 500f. High jump (air) . . . . 4·50 1·60

92 "Charaxes defulvata"

1979. Fauna. Multicoloured.
336 30f. Type **92** . . . . 1·70 35
337 50f. Courol . . . . 3·50 90
338 75f. Blue-cheeked bee eater 5·00 1·60

1979. Optd or surch **REPUBLIQUE FEDERALE ISLAMIQUE DES COMORES**. (a) Birds, Nos. 271/275.
339 15f. Type **82** 30 25
340 50f. on 35f. Madagascar malachite kingfisher . . . 50 50
341 50f. on 20f. Blue-cheeked bee eater . . . . 1·10 1·00
342 50f. on 40f. Madagascar paradise flycatcher . . . . 1·10 1·00
343 200f. on 75f. Anjouan sunbird . . . . 3·25 3·25

(b) World Cup, Nos. 278/282.
344 1f. on 100f. Italian game (postage) 10 10
345 2f. on 75f. London game . . 10 10
346 3f. on 30f. Type **83** 10 10
347 50f. Breton football 85 50
348 200f. English game (air) . . . 2·00 1·90

1979. Nos. 293/7 surch or optd **Republique Federale Islamique des Comores.**
349 – 5f. on 100f. Verdi (post) . . 55 10
350 **85** 30f. J. S. Bach . . . . . . 1·10 35
351 – 40f. Mozart . . . . 1·40 45
352 – 50f. Berlioz . . . . 2·30 75
353 – 50f. on 200f. Tchaikovsky (air) . . . . 3·25 1·00

94 State Coach

1979. 25th Anniv of Coronation of Queen Elizabeth II. Multicoloured.
354 5f. on 25f. Type **94** (postage) 10 10
355 10f. Drum Major 30 25
356 50f. on 40f. Queen carrying orb and sceptre 65 65
357 100f. St. Edward's Crown . . 1·40 1·40
358 50f. on 200f. Herald reading Proclamation (air) . . . . 1·00 1·00
Nos. 354/8 were only valid for postage overprinted as in Type **94**.

95 "Papilio dardanus-cenea stoll"

1979. Butterflies. Multicoloured.
359 5f. on 20f. Type **95** 30 10
360 15f. "Papilio dardanus–brown" 45 25
361 30f. "Chrysiridia croesus" . . 65 50
362 50f. "Precis octavia" . . . . 1·40 1·10
363 75f. "Bunaea alcinoe" . . . 2·20 1·70
Nos. 359/63 were only valid for postage overprinted as in Type **95**.

96 Otto Lilienthal and Glider

1979. History of Aviation. Multicoloured.
364 30f. Type **96** (postage) . . . 45 45
365 50f. Wright Brothers 65 65
366 50f. on 75f. Louis Bleriot . . 75 75
367 100f. Claude Dornier . . . . 1·40 1·30
368 200f. Charles Lindbergh (air) 2·20 2·10

Nos. 364/8 were only valid for postage overprinted as in Type **96**.

97 Tobogganing **98** Lychees

1979. International Year of the Child (1st issue). Multicoloured.
369 20f. Astronauts (postage) . . 10 10
370 30f. Type **97** 30 10
371 40f. Painting 45 20
372 100f. Locomotive "Rocket", 1829, and toy train . . . . 1·00 30
373 200f. Football (air) . . . . . 1·90 50
374 400f. Canoeing . . . . . . 4·00 1·10
See also Nos. 389/90.

1979. Fruit. Multicoloured.
375 60f. Type **98** 85 30
376 70f. Papaws . . . . 1·00 45
377 100f. Avocado pears . . . . 1·30 50
378 125f. Bananas . . . . 1·60 80

101 Rotary Emblem and Village Scene

1979. Air. Rotary International.
388 **101** 400f. multicoloured . . . 6·25 3·75

102 Mother and Child on Boat **103** Basketball

1979. Air. International Year of the Child (2nd issue). Multicoloured.
389 200f.+30f. Type **102** . . . . 3·50 2·75
390 250f. Mother and baby . . . 3·50 2·20

1979. Indian Ocean Olympic Games.
391 **103** 200f. multicoloured . . . 2·20 1·30

1979. Various stamps optd **REPUBLIQUE FEDERALE ISLAMIQUE DES COMORES**.
(a) Air. Apollo–Soyuz Space Test Project (Appendix).
392 100f. Presidents Brezhnev and Ford with astronauts . . . 1·20 1·20
393 200f. Space link-up . . . . . 2·40 2·30
(b) Bicentenary of American Revolution (Appendix).
394 25f. Fremont, Kit Carson and dancing Indian 30 25
395 35f. D. Boone, Buffalo Bill and wagon train 40 35
396 75f. H. Wells, W. Fargo and stagecoach ambush 85 80
(c) Winter Olympic Games, Innsbruck (Appendix).
397 35f. Speed skating 40 35
(d) Telephone Centenary (Appendix).
398 75f. Philip Reis 85 80
(e) Air. Olympic Games, Munich and Montreal.
399 100f. multicoloured (No. 179) 1·20 1·20
(f) U.N. Postal Services.
400 75f. mult (No. 187) 85 80
(g) Endangered Animals.
401 35f. mult (No. 209) 40 35
402 40f. mult (No. 210) 45 45
(h) Nobel Prize Winners.
403 100f. mult (No. 231) . . . . 1·20 1·20
(i) Rubens.
404 25f. mult (No. 236) 30 25
(j) Durer.
405 25f. mult (No. 287) 30 25
406 75f. mult (No. 289) 85 80

105 "Profile Head of Old Man"

1979. 400th Birth Anniv of Peter Paul Rubens (artist) (2nd issue). Multicoloured.
407 25f. Type **105** 30 10
408 35f. "Young Girl with Flag" 45 10
409 50f. "Isabelle d'Este, Margave of Mantua" . . . 80 15
410 75f. "Philip IV, King of Spain" 95 25

106 "Portrait of Young Girl"

1979. 450th Death Anniv of Albrecht Durer (artist) (2nd issue). Multicoloured.
411 20f. "Self-portrait" (postage) 20 15
412 30f. "Young Man" 30 15
413 40f. Type **106** 45 15
414 100f. "Jerome" (air) 95 25
415 200f. "Jacob Muffel" . . . . 2·00 40

107 Satellite and Receiving Station

1979. 10th World Telecommunications Day. Multicoloured.
416 75f. Satellites 85 30
417 100f. Two satellites . . . . . 1·00 40
418 200f. Type **107** . . . . 2·10 90

108 Pirogue

1980. Handicrafts. Multicoloured.
419 60f. Type **108** 95 25
420 100f. Anjouan puppet . . . . 1·30 50

109 Sultan Said Ali

1980. Sultans. Multicoloured.
421 40f. Type **109** 50 20
422 60f. Sultan Ahmed 75 25

110 Dimadjou Dispensary

1980. Air. 75th Anniv of Rotary International and 15th Anniv of Moroni Rotary Club (100f.).
423 100f. Type **110** . . . . 1·10 50
424 260f. Concorde airplane . . . 2·75 1·20

111 Sherlock Holmes and Sir Arthur Conan Doyle

1980. 50th Death Anniv of Sir Arthur Conan Doyle (writer).
425 **111** 200f. multicoloured . . . 3·75 1·40

112 Grand Mosque and Holy Ka'aba, Mecca

1980. 1350th Anniv of Occupation of Mecca by Mohammed.
426 **112** 75f. multicoloured 85 45

113 Dome of the Rock

1980. Year of the Holy City, Jerusalem.
427 **113** 60f. multicoloured 75 40

114 Kepler, Copernicus

1980. 50th Anniv of Discovery of Pluto.
428 **114** 400f. violet, red & mauve 5·00 2·50

115 Avicenna

1980. Birth Millenary of Avicenna (physician and philosopher).
429 **115** 60f. multicoloured 95 45

116 Mermoz, Dabry, Gimie and Seaplane "Comte da la Vaulx"

1980. 50th Anniv of First South Atlantic Flight.
430 **116** 200f. multicoloured . . . 3·75 2·10

1981. Various stamps surch.
431 15f. on 200f. multicoloured (No. 425) (postage) 30 25
432 20f. on 75f. mult (No. 426) 40 35
433 40f. on 125f. mult (No. 378) 90 90
434 60f. on 75f. mult (No. 338) 1·70 1·20
435 30f. on 200f. multicoloured (No. 430) (air) 70 70

118 Team posing with Shield

1981. World Cup Football Championship, Spain (1982). Multicoloured.
436 60f. Footballers coming on Field (vert) 55 10
437 75f. Type **118** 75 25
438 90f. Captains shaking hands 1·00 25
439 100f. Tackle . . . . 1·00 45
440 150f. Players hugging after goal (vert) . . . . 1·70 55
MS441 104 × 80 mm. 500f. Team with cup (vert) . . . . 4·50 1·50

119 "Bowls and Pot"

1981. Birth Centenary of Pablo Picasso. Mult.
442 40f. "Dove and Rainbow" . . 50 10
443 70f. "Still-life on Chest of Drawers" 90 20
444 150f. "Studio with Plaster Head" . . . . 1·70 55
445 250f. Type **119** . . . . . . 2·75 80
446 500f. "Red Tablecloth" . . . 5·50 1·60

120 "Apollo" Launch

1981. Conquest of Space. Multicoloured.
447 50f. Type **120** 50 10
448 75f. Space Shuttle launch . . 65 25
449 100f. Space Shuttle releasing fuel tank . . . . 1·00 30
450 450f. Space Shuttle in orbit 4·50 1·50
MS451 104 × 79 mm. 500f. Space shuttle and carrier aircraft . . 4·50 1·60

121 Buckingham Palace

1981. British Royal Wedding. Multicoloured.
452 125f. Type **121** . . . . . . 1·20 30
453 200f. Highgrove House . . . 1·80 65

454 450f. Caernarvon Castle . . . 3·75 1·40
MS455 132 × 97 mm. As Nos. 452/4 but inscriptions and values in magenta . . . . 5·00 2·20

1981. Design as Type O **99** but inscr "POSTES 1981".
456 5f. green, black & brn . . . 10 10
457 15f. green, black & yell . . . 10 10
458 25f. green, black & red . . . 30 10
459 35f. green, black & lt grn . . . 45 25
460 75f. green, black & blue . . . 95 40

1981. Various stamps surch.
461 **114** 5f. on 400f. violet, red and mauve (postage) . . 25 25
462 – 20f. on 90f. mult (No. 438) 45 40
463 – 45f. on 100f. mult (No. 377) . . . . . . 1·20 1·10
464 – 45f. on 100f. mult (No. 420) . . . . . . 1·20 1·10
465 – 10f. on 70f. mult (No. 443) (air) 25 25
466 **110** 10f. on 100f. mult 45 40
467 **102** 50f. on 200f.+30f. mult 1·20 1·10
468 – 50f. on 260f. mult (No. 424) . . . . . . 1·20 1·10

123 Mercedes, 1914

1981. 75th Anniv of French Grand Prix Motor Race. Multicoloured.
469 20f. Type **123** 30 10
470 50f. Delage, 1925 . . . . . 60 15
471 75f. Rudi Caracciola 90 25
472 90f. Stirling Moss . . . . . 1·00 40
473 150f. Maserati, 1957 . . . . 1·70 50
MS474 107 × 86 mm. 500f. Mechanics replacing car tyres (vert) . . . . 6·75 1·70

124 Scouts preparing to Sail

1981. 75th Anniv of Boy Scout Movement. Multicoloured.
475 50f. Type **124** 50 25
476 75f. Paddling pirogue 80 40
477 250f. Sailing felucca . . . . 2·50 85
478 350f. Scouts looking out to sea from boat . . . . . . 3·50 1·20
MS479 78 × 102 mm. 500f. Lord Baden-Powell . . . . 5·25 1·80

125 Goethe

1982. 150th Death Anniv of Goethe (poet).
480 **125** 75f. multicoloured 75 35
481 350f. multicoloured . . . 3·50 1·00

126 Princess of Wales

1982. 21st Birthday of Princess of Wales.
482 **126** 200f. multicoloured . . . 1·90 60
483 – 300f. multicoloured . . . 3·00 90
MS484 112 × 80 mm. 500f. multicoloured . . . . 5·00 1·70
DESIGNS: 300, 500f. Different portraits.

1982. Birth of Prince William of Wales. Nos. 452/4 optd **NAISSANCE ROYALE 1982**.
485 125f. Type **121** . . . . 1·30 60
486 200f. Highgrove House . . . 2·10 90
487 450f. Caernarvon Castle . . . 4·00 2·20
MS488 132 × 97 mm. As Nos. 485/7 but inscriptions and values in magenta . . . . 5·75 5·50

1982. World Cup Football Championship Winners. Nos. 436/40 optd.
489 60f. Type **117** 60 25
490 75f. Team posing with shield (horiz) 75 30
491 90f. Captains shaking hands (horiz) 85 45
492 100f. Tackle (horiz) . . . . . 1·00 45
493 150f. Players hugging after goal . . . . 1·50 65
MS494 104 × 80 mm. 500f. As No. 489 . . . . 4·50 2·75
OVERPRINTS: 60f., 150f. **ITALIE - ALLEMAGNE (R.F.A.) 3 - 1.**; 75f., 90f., 100f. **ITALIE 3 ALLEMAGNE (R.F.A.) 1.**

129 Boy playing Trumpet

1982. Norman Rockwell Paintings. Multicoloured.
495 60f. Type **129** 75 25
496 75f. Sleeping porter 75 25
497 100f. Couple listening to early radio . . . . 1·20 25
498 150f. Children playing leapfrog . . . . 1·70 45
499 200f. Tramp cooking sausages . . . . 2·30 55
500 300f. Boy talking to clown 3·25 95

130 Sultan Said Mohamed Sidi

1982. Sultans. Multicoloured.
501 30f. Type **130** 35 10
502 60f. Sultan Ahmed Abdallah 75 10
503 75f. Sultan Salim (horiz) . . 85 25
504 300f. Sultans Said Mohamed Sidi and Ahmed Abdallah (horiz) . . . . 3·25 1·30

131 Montgolfier Brothers' Balloon, 1783

1983. Air. Bicentenary of Manned Flight. Mult.
505 100f. Type **131** . . . . 1·20 45
506 200f. Vincenzo Lunardi's balloon over London, 1784 1·80 70
507 300f. Blanchard and Jeffries crossing the Channel, 1785 3·00 95
508 400f. Henri Giffard's steam-powered dirigible airship, 1852 (horiz) . . . . 4·25 1·40
MS509 79 × 103 mm. 500f. Balloon used for carrying post, 1870 . . 5·50 1·70

132 Type "470" Dinghy

1983. Air. Pre-Olympic Year. Multicoloured.
510 150f. Type **132** . . . . 1·50 55
511 200f. "Flying Dutchman" . . 1·80 70
512 300f. Type "470" (different) 3·00 85
513 400f. "Finn" class dinghies 4·25 1·40
MS514 103 × 80 mm. 500f. Soling yachts . . . . 5·25 1·70

133 Lake Ziani

1983. Landscapes. Multicoloured.
515 60f. Type **133** 65 30
516 100f. Sunset . . . . 1·00 50
517 175f. Chiromani (vert) . . . 1·70 75
518 360f. Itsandra beach . . . . 3·25 1·40
519 400f. Anjouan . . . . 4·50 1·80

134 Moheli

1983. Portraits. Multicoloured.
520 30f. Type **134** 35 25
521 35f. "Mask of Beauty" . . . 55 25
522 50f. Mayotte 55 25

135 Pure-bred Arab

1983. Horses. Multicoloured.
523 75f. Type **135** 80 25
524 100f. Anglo-Arab . . . . . . 1·10 30
525 125f. Lipizzan . . . . 1·40 50
526 150f. Tennessee . . . . . . 1·60 50
527 200f. Appaloosa . . . . . . 2·00 75
528 300f. Pure-bred English . . . 3·25 1·00
529 400f. Clydesdale . . . . . . 4·25 1·40
530 500f. Andalusian . . . . . . 5·50 1·70

136 "Double Portrait"

1983. 500th Birth Anniv of Raphael. Mult.
531 100f. Type **136** . . . . 1·10 45
532 200f. Fresco detail . . . . . 2·40 80
533 300f. "St. George and the Dragon" . . . . 3·50 1·00
534 400f. "Balthazar Castiglione" 4·75 1·40

137 Symbols of Development

1984. Air. International Conference on Development of Comoros.
535 **137** 475f. multicoloured . . . 4·75 2·40

138 Basketball

1984. Air. Olympic Games, Los Angeles. Mult.
536 60f. Type **138** 45 25
537 100f. Basketball (different) . . 95 40
538 165f. Basketball (different) . . 1·40 65
539 175f. Baseball (horiz) . . . . 1·50 75
540 200f. Baseball (different) (horiz) . . . . 1·80 80
MS541 104 × 80 mm. 500f. Basketball (different) (horiz) . . 6·00 1·50

139 "William Fawcett"

1984. Transport. Multicoloured. (a) Ships.
542 100f. Type **139** . . . . 1·10 40
543 150f. "Lightning" . . . . . 1·80 60
544 200f. "Rapido" . . . . 2·30 90
545 350f. "Sindia" . . . . 3·75 1·40

(b) Automobiles.
546 100f. De Dion Bouton and Trepardoux, 1885 . . . . 1·50 40
547 150f. Benz "Victoria", 1893 2·20 70
548 200f. Colombia electric, 1901 2·75 90
549 350f. Fiat, 1902 . . . . . . 4·50 1·40

140 Barn Swallows

1985. Air. Birth Bicentenary of John J. Audubon (ornithologist). Multicoloured.
550 100f. Type **140** . . . . 1·00 40
551 125f. Northern oriole . . . . 1·30 55
552 150f. Red-shouldered hawk (horiz) . . . . 1·60 70
553 500f. Red-breasted sapsucker (horiz) . . . . 5·50 2·20

1985. International Exhibitions. Nos. **MS**451, **MS**474, **MS**479, **MS**509 and **MS**514 optd.
MS554 Five sheets. (a) 500f. **MOPHILA'85 HAMBOURG**; (b) 500f. **TSUKUBA EXPO '85**; (c) 500f. **ARENTINA'85 BUENOS AIRES**; (d) 500f. **ITALIA '85 ROMA** and emblem; 500f. **OLYMPHILEX '85 LAUSANNE** and emblem . . . . 6·75 3·00

142 Harbours

1985. Air. "Philexafrique" Stamp Exhibition, Lome, Togo (1st issue). Multicoloured.

555	200f. Type **142**	2·50	1·60
556	200f. Scouts walking along road	2·50	1·60

See also Nos. 576/7.

143 Victor Hugo (novelist, death centenary)

1985. Anniversaries. Multicoloured.

557	100f. Type **143**	1·30	40
558	200f. Jules Verne (novelist) (80th death anniv)	2·20	80
559	300f. Mark Twain (150th birth anniv)	3·25	1·20
560	450f. Queen Elizabeth, the Queen Mother (85th birth anniv) (vert)	4·50	1·70
561	500f. Statue of Liberty (centenary) (vert)	5·00	2·10

The 200f. and 300f. also commemorate International Youth Year.

144 Map and Flag on Sun

1985. Air. 10th Anniv of Independence.

562	**144**	10f. multicoloured	20	10
563		15f. multicoloured	30	10
564		125f. multicoloured	1·80	70
565		300f. multicoloured	4·25	1·60

145 Arthritic Spider Conch

1985. Shells. Multicoloured.

566	75f. Type **145**	1·00	30
567	125f. Silver conch	1·50	45
568	200f. Costate tun	2·50	75
569	300f. Elephant's snout	3·75	1·20
570	450f. Orange spider conch	5·50	1·80

146 U.N. Emblem and Map of Islands

1985. 10th Anniv of Membership of UNO.

571	**146**	5f. multicoloured	10	10
572		30f. multicoloured	20	10
573		75f. multicoloured	70	30
574		125f. multicoloured	1·30	50
575		400f. multicoloured	3·75	1·90

147 Runners ("Youth")

1985. Air. "Philexafrique" Stamp Exhibition, Lome, Togo (2nd issue). Multicoloured.

576	250f. Type **147**	2·50	1·40
577	250f. Earth mover and road construction ("Development")	2·50	1·40

148 Globe, Galleon, Wright Type A Biplane and Rocket Capsule

1985. 20th Anniv of Moroni Rotary Club.

578	**148**	25f. multicoloured	30	10
579		75f. multicoloured	80	40
580		125f. multicoloured	1·30	50
581		500f. multicoloured	4·50	2·30

149 "Astraeus hygrometricus"

1985. Fungi. Multicoloured.

582	75f. "Boletus edulis"	1·20	30
583	125f. "Sarcoscypha coccinea"	1·50	50
584	200f. "Hypholoma fasciculare"	2·50	80
585	350f. Type **149**	3·75	1·30
586	500f. "Armillariella mellea"	5·25	2·10

150 Sikorsky S-43 Amphibian

1985. Air. 50th Anniv of Union des Transports Aeriennes. Multicoloured.

587	25f. Type **150**	25	10
588	75f. Douglas DC-9 airplane and camel	65	30
589	100f. Douglas DC-4, DC-6, Nord 2501 Noratlas and De Havilland Heron 2 aircraft	1·00	55
590	125f. Maintenance	1·30	70
591	1000f. Emblem and Latecoere 28, Sikorsky S-43, Douglas DC-10 and Boeing 747-200 aircraft (35 × 47 mm)	11·00	5·50
MS592	Two sheets each 131 × 110 mm. (a) Nos. 587/9; (b) Nos. 590/1	3·25	2·30

151 Edmond Halley, Comet and "Giotto" Space Probe

1986. Air. Appearance of Halley's Comet. Multicoloured.

593	125f. Type **151**	1·20	50
594	150f. Giacobini-Zinner comet, 1959	1·50	65
595	225f. J. F. Encke and Encke comet, 1961	2·30	95
596	300f. Computer enhanced picture of Bradfield comet, 1980	2·75	1·20
597	450f. Halley's comet and "Planet A" space probe	4·50	2·10

152 Footballers

1986. Air. World Cup Football Championship, Mexico. Designs showing footballers.

598	**152**	125f. multicoloured	1·20	50
599	–	210f. multicoloured	1·90	90
600	–	500f. multicoloured	4·75	2·20
601	–	600f. multicoloured	5·50	2·50

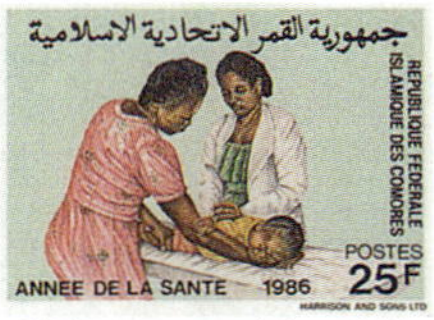

153 Doctor examining Child

1986. World Health Year. Multicoloured.

602	25f. Type **153**	30	10
603	100f. Doctor weighing child	1·00	65
604	200f. Nurse innoculating baby	2·10	1·30

154 Ndzoumara (wind instrument) 155 Server

1986. Musical Instruments. Multicoloured.

605	75f. Type **154**	80	40
606	125f. Ndzedze (string instrument)	1·20	60
607	210f. Gaboussi (string instrument)	2·00	90
608	500f. Ngoma (drums)	5·00	2·00

1987. Air. Tennis as 1988 Olympic Games Discipline. Multicoloured.

609	150f. Type **155**	1·60	55
610	250f. Player preparing shot	2·75	95
611	500f. Player being lobbed	5·00	1·90
612	600f. Players each side of net	6·25	2·30

156 On Tree Branch

1987. Air. Endangered Animals. Mongoose-Lemur. Multicoloured.

613	75f. Type **156**	1·60	40
614	100f. Head of mongoose-lemur with ruff	2·10	55
615	125f. Mongoose-lemur on rock	3·50	90
616	150f. Head of mongoose-lemur without ruff	4·00	1·40

157 Women working in Field

1987. Woman and Development. Multicoloured.

617	75f. Type **157**	80	30
618	125f. Woman picking musk seeds (vert)	1·70	50
619	1000f. Woman making basket	9·50	4·00

158 Men's Downhill

1987. Air. Winter Olympic Games, Calgary (1988). Multicoloured.

620	150f. Type **158**	1·20	55
621	225f. Ski jumping	2·00	90
622	500f. Women's slalom	4·75	2·00
623	600f. Men's luge	5·50	2·50

159 Didier Daurat, Raymond Vanier and "Air Bleu"

1987. Air. Aviation. Multicoloured.

624	200f. Type **159**	2·00	80
625	300f. Letord 4 Lorraine and route map (1st regular airmail service, Paris–Le Mans–St. Nazaire, 1918)	2·75	1·10
626	500f. Morane Saulnier Type H and route map (1st airmail flight, Villacoublay–Pauillac, 1913)	4·75	1·90
627	1000f. Henri Pequet flying Humber-Sommer biplane (1st aerophilately exn, Allahabad) (36 × 49 mm)	9·50	3·25

160 Ice Skating

1988. Multicoloured. (a) Winter Olympic Games, Calgary.

628	75f. Type **160** (postage)	60	15
629	125f. Speed skating	95	40
630	350f. Two-man bobsleigh	3·00	85
631	400f. Biathlon (air)	3·75	1·10
MS632	116 × 75 mm. 750f. Slalom	6·75	1·40

(b) Olympic Games, Seoul.

633	100f. Relay (postage)	95	25
634	150f. Showjumping	1·50	45
635	500f. Pole-vaulting	4·50	1·30
636	600f. Football (air)	5·50	1·50
MS637	116 × 75 mm. 750f. Running	6·75	1·50

161 Kiwanis International Emblem and Hand supporting Figures

1988. Child Health Campaigns. Multicoloured.

638	75f. Type **161**	75	30
639	125f. Kiwanis emblem, wheelchair and crutch	1·10	50
640	210f. Kiwanis emblem and man with children (country inscr in black)	1·90	85
641	210f. As No. 640 but country inscr in white	2·00	85
642	425f. As No. 639	4·00	1·80
643	425f. As No. 639 but with Lions International emblem	3·75	1·80
644	500f. Type **161**	5·00	2·30
645	500f. As Type **161** but with Rotary emblem	5·00	2·40

162 Throwing the Discus — **163** Columbus and "Santa Maria"

1988. Olympic Games, Barcelona (1992) (1st issue). Multicoloured.
646 75f. Type **162** (postage) . . . 60 15
647 100f. Rowing (horiz) 95 25
648 125f. Cycling (horiz) . . . . 1·20 40
649 150f. Wrestling (horiz) . . . 1·40 55

650 375f. Basketball (air) . . . . 3·50 1·00
651 600f. Tennis . . . . 5·50 1·20
MS652 90 × 75 mm. 750f. Marathon . . . 7·25 1·50
See also Nos. 709/MS715 . . .
See also Nos. 709/14.

1988. 500th Anniv (1992) of Discovery of America by Columbus. Multicoloured.
653 75f. Type **163** (postage) . . . 60 25
654 125f. Martin Alonzo Pinzon and "Pinta" . . . . 1·20 30
655 150f. Vicente Yanez Pinzon and "Nina" . . . . 1·40 45
656 250f. Search for gold . . . . 2·20 70

657 375f. Wreck of "Santa Maria" (air) . . . . . . 3·50 1·00
658 450f. Preparation for fourth voyage . . . . 4·25 1·10
MS659 99 × 68 mm. 750f. Columbus landing at Samana Cay . . . . 7·25 1·50

1988. Nos. 641, 643 and 645 (125 and 400f. with colours changed) surch.
660 75f. on 210f. multicoloured 75 45
661 125f. on 425f. multicoloured 1·00 60
662 200f. on 425f. multicoloured 1·70 80
663 300f. on 500f. multicoloured 2·75 1·20
664 400f. on 500f. multicoloured 3·75 1·90

1988. Olympic Games Medal Winners for Tennis. Nos. 609/12 optd.
665 150f. Optd **Medalle d'or Seoul Miloslav Mecir (Tchec.)** . . 1·50 70
666 250f. Optd **Medaille d'argent Seoul Tim Mayotte (U.S.A)** 2·50 1·50
667 500f. Optd **Medaille d'or Seoul Steffi Graf (R.F.A.)** 4·50 2·75
668 600f. Optd **Medaille d'argent Seoul Gabriela Sabatini (Argentine)** 5·50 3·50

166 Alberto Santos-Dumont and "14 bis"

1988. Air. Aviation Pioneers.
669 **166** 100f. purple . . . . . . 1·20 45
670 – 150f. mauve . . . . . . 1·70 60
671 – 200f. black . . . . . . 2·00 80
672 – 300f. brown . . . . . . 2·75 1·50
673 – 500f. blue . . . . . . 4·75 2·40
674 – 800f. green . . . . . . 7·50 3·00
DESIGNS: 150f. Wright Type A and Orville and Wilbur Wright; 200f. Louis Bleriot and Bleriot XI; 300f. Farman Voisin No. 1 bis and Henri Farman; 500f. Gabriel and Charles Voisin and Voisin "Boxkite"; 800f. Roland Garros and Morane Saulnier Type I.

167 Galileo Galilei — **168** Yuri Gagarin (cosmonaut) and Daughters

1988. Appearance of Halley's Comet. Mult.
675 200f.+10f. Type **167** (postage) 2·00 45
676 200f.+10f. Nicolas Copernicus . . . . . . 2·00 45
677 200f.+10f. Johannes Kepler 2·00 45
678 200f.+10f. Edmond Halley . . 2·00 45
679 200f.+10f. Japanese "Planet A" space probe . . . . . 2·00 45
680 200f.+10f. American "Ice" space probe . . . . . . 2·00 45
681 200f.+10f. "Planet A" space probe (different) . . . . . 2·00 45
682 200f.+10f. Russian "Vega" space probe . . . . 2·00 45
MS683 100 × 75 mm. 750f. Space probe and Halley (41 × 35 mm) (air) . . . . 7·25 1·50

1988. Personalities. Multicoloured.
684 150f. Type **168** (20th death anniv) (postage) . . . . 1·30 40
685 300f. Henri Dunant (founder of Red Cross) (125th anniv of Red Cross Movement) 2·75 85
686 400f. Roger Clemens (baseball player) . . . . . 3·50 1·10
687 500f. Gary Kasparov (chess player) (air) . . . . . . 5·50 1·10
688 600f. Paul Harris (founder of Rotary International) (birth centenary) . . . . 5·50 1·20
MS689 104 × 84 mm. 750f. John F. Kennedy (American statesman) (25th death anniv) (29 × 41 mm) 7·25 1·50

169 Alain Prost (racing driver) and Formula 1 Racing Car

1988. Cars, Trains and Yachts. Multicoloured.
690 75f. Type **169** (postage) . . . 1·50 45
691 125f. George Stephenson (railway engineer), "Rocket" and Borsig Class 05 steam locomotive, 1935, Germany . . . . 1·30 25
692 500f. Ettore Bugatti (motor manufacturer) and Aravis "Type 57" . . . . 4·75 1·10
693 600f. Rudolph Diesel (engineer) and German Class V200 diesel locomotive . . . . 5·50 1·30
694 750f. Dennis Conner and "Stars and Stripes" (America's Cup contender) (air) . . . . 7·00 1·60
695 1000f. Michael Fay and "New Zealand" (America's Cup contender) . . . . . 9·25 2·00
MS696 131 × 85 mm. 1000f. Enzo Ferrari (motor manufacturer) and Formula 1 racing car (50 × 35 mm) 10·00 1·80

170 "Papilio nireus aristophontes" (female)

1989. Scouts, Butterflies and Birds. Multicoloured.
697 50f. Type **170** (postage) . . . 55 10
698 75f. "Papilio nireus aristophontes" (male) . . . 85 15
699 150f. "Charaxes fulvescens separanus" . . . . 1·70 40
700 375f. Bronze mannikin . . . 4·00 70
701 450f. "Charaxes castor comoranus" (air) . . . . . 4·50 90
702 500f. Madagascar white-eye 5·00 1·10
MS703 116 × 92 mm. 750f. Red forest fody and "Charaxes paradoxa" . . . . 9·00 1·80

171 Aussat "K3" and N. Uphoff (individual dressage)

1989. Satellites and Olympic Games Medal Winners for Equestrian Events. Multicoloured.
704 75f. Type **171** (postage) . . . 70 15
705 150f. "Brasil sat" and P. Durand (individual show jumping) . . . . 1·30 40
706 375f. "ECS 4" and J. Martinek (modern pentathlon) . . . . 3·50 75
707 600f. "Olympus 1" and M. Todd (cross-country) (air) . . . . 5·50 1·40
MS708 97 × 67 mm. 750f. Satellite and horses . . . . 6·75 1·50

172 Running

1989. Olympic Games, Barcelona (1992) (2nd issue). Multicoloured.
709 75f. Type **172** (postage) . . . 75 25
710 150f. Football . . . . 1·50 45
711 300f. Tennis . . . . 2·75 60
712 375f. Baseball . . . . 3·50 80

713 500f. Gymnastics (air) . . . 4·50 1·10
714 600f. Table tennis . . . . . 5·50 1·40
MS715 90 × 75 mm. 750f. Show jumping . . . . 6·75 1·50

173 Dr. Joseph-Ignace Guillotin and Guillotine

1989. Bicentenary of French Revolution. Mult.
716 75f. Type **173** (postage) . . . 80 25
717 150f. Soldiers with cannon (Battle of Valmy) and Gen. Kellermann . . . . 1·70 40
718 375f. Jean Cottereau (Chouan) and Vendeens . . 3·50 70
719 600f. Invasion of Les Tuileries (air) . . . . . . 5·75 1·60
MS720 113 × 67 mm. 1000f. Jacques Necker and storming of the Bastille . . . . 8·75 2·75

1989. Various stamps surch.
721 25f. on 250f. mult (No. 656) (postage) 35 10
722 150f. on 200f. mult (No. 532) 1·30 55
723 150f. on 200f. mult (No. 558) 1·30 55
724 150f. on 200f. mult (No. 604) 1·30 55
725 5f. on 250f. multicoloured (No. 390) (air) 10 10
726 25f. on 250f. mult (No. 610) 25 20
727 50f. on 250f. mult (No. 576) 45 25
728 50f. on 250f. mult (No. 577) 45 25
729 150f. on 200f. mult (No. 511) 1·40 55
730 150f. on 200f. mult (No. 555) 1·40 55
731 150f. on 200f. mult (No. 556) 1·40 55
732 150f. on 200f. black (No. 671) . . . . 1·40 55

175 Airport Pavilion

1990.
733 **175** 5f. orange, brown & red 10 10
734 10f. orange, brown & bl 10 10
735 25f. orange, brown & grn 10 10
736 – 50f. black and red 45 25
737 – 75f. black and blue . . . 75 25
738 – 150f. black and green . . 1·40 45
DESIGNS: 50 to 150f. Federal Assembly.

176 Player challenging Goalkeeper

1990. Air. World Cup Football Championship, Italy (1st issue). Multicoloured.
739 75f. Type **176** 95 40
740 150f. Player heading ball . . 1·50 70
741 500f. Overhead kick . . . . 4·25 2·30
742 1000f. Player evading tackle 9·00 2·10
See also Nos. 743/8.

177 Brazilian Player

1990. World Cup Football Championship, Italy (2nd issue). Multicoloured.
743 50f. Type **177** (postage) . . . 45 10
744 75f. English player 75 25
745 100f. West German player . . 95 30
746 150f. Belgian player . . . . 1·40 45

747 375f. Italian player (air) . . . 3·50 1·10
748 600f. Argentinian player . . . 5·50 1·40
MS749 100 × 80 mm. 750f. Argentine and Italian players . . . . . . 6·75 1·40

178 U.S. Space Telescope

1990. Multicoloured.
750 75f. Type **178** (postage) . . . 75 25
751 150f. Pope John Paul II and Mikhail Gorbachev, 1989 1·50 35
752 200f. Kevin Mitchell (San Francisco Giants baseball player) . . . . 2·00 45
753 250f. De Gaulle and Adenauer, 1962 . . . . . 2·20 50
754 300f. "Titan 2002" space probe . . . . 2·75 70
755 375f. French TGV Atlantique express train and Concorde airplane . . . . 3·75 1·00
756 450f. Gary Kasparov (World chess champion) and Anderssen v Steinitz chess match (air) . . . . 4·50 1·10
757 500f. Paul Harris (founder of Rotary International) and symbols of health, hunger and humanity . . . . . . 4·50 80
MS758 97 × 68 mm. 1000f. Lunar module and crew of "Apollo 11" (47 × 35 mm) . . . . 8·75 1·50

179 Edi Reinalter (skiing, 1948) — **180** Dish Aerial, Moroni Volo-volo

1990. Winter Olympics, Albertville (1992). Medal Winners at previous Games. Multicoloured.
759 75f. Type **179** (postage) . . . 55 25
760 100f. Canada (ice hockey, 1924) 95 30
761 375f. Baroness Gratia Schimmelpenninck van der Oye (skiing, 1936) (air) . . 3·25 1·00
762 600f. Hasu Haikki (ski jumping, 1948) . . . . . . 5·50 1·00
MS763 72 × 87 mm. 750f. Berger and Engelmann (ice skating, 1924) (36 × 41 mm) . . . . 6·75 1·40

1991.
764 **180** 75f. multicoloured . . . 85 20
765 150f. multicoloured . . . 1·60 55
766 225f. multicoloured . . . 2·20 80
767 300f. multicoloured . . . 3·00 1·10
768 500f. multicoloured . . . 4·50 1·40

181 Emblem and Leaves

1991. Indian Ocean Commission Conference.

769	**181**	75f. multicoloured	75	25
770		150f. multicoloured	1·20	80
771		225f. multicoloured	2·00	1·20

182 De Gaulle and Battle of Koufra, 1941

183 Emblem and Stylized View of Exhibition

1991. 50th Anniv of World War II. Multicoloured.

772	125f. Type **182** (postage)	1·70	30
773	150f. Errol Flynn in "Adventures in Burma"	1·50	50
774	300f. Henry Fonda in "The Longest Day"	3·25	90
775	375f. De Gaulle and Battle of Britain, 1940	3·50	75
776	450f. Humphrey Bogart in "Sahara" (air)	4·50	1·00
777	500f. De Gaulle and Battle of Monte Cassino, 1944	4·50	90
MS778	121 × 91 mm. 1000f. De Gaulle and "Normandie-Niemen" aircraft, 1943	10·50	2·30

1991. "Telecom '91" Int Telecommunications Exhibition, Geneva. Multicoloured.

779	75f. Type **183**	1·20	55
780	150f. Emblem (horiz)	1·70	1·30

184 Weather Space Station "Columbus"

1991. Anniversaries and Events. Multicoloured.

781	100f. Type **184** (postage)	1·00	25
782	150f. Gandhi (43rd death anniv)	1·60	40
783	250f. Henri Dunant (founder of Red Cross) (90th anniv of award of Nobel Peace Prize)	2·40	60
784	300f. Wolfgang Amadeus Mozart (composer, death bicentenary)	3·00	70
785	375f. Brandenburg Gate (bicent and second anniv of fall of Berlin Wall)	4·00	95
786	400f. Konrad Adenauer (German Chancellor) signing new constitution (25th death anniv)	4·00	95
787	450f. Elvis Presley (entertainer, 14th death anniv) (air)	5·00	1·00
788	500f. Ferdinand von Zeppelin (airship pioneer, 75th death anniv)	5·00	1·00

185 Cep

1992. Fungi and Shells. Multicoloured.

789	75f. Type **185** (postage)	80	25
790	125f. Textile cone	1·30	45
791	150f. Puff-ball	1·60	55
792	150f. Bull-mouth helmet (shell)	1·60	60
793	500f. Map cowrie (air)	5·75	1·60
794	600f. Scarlet elf cups	5·75	1·10
MS795	100 × 70 mm. 750f. "Nautilus pompilius" (shell)	8·25	1·80

186 Ham (chimpanzee) on "Mercury" flight, 1960

1992. Space Research. Multicoloured.

796	75f. Type **186** (postage)	90	25
797	125f. "Mars Observer" space probe	1·30	35
798	150f. Felix (cat) and "Veronique" rocket, 1963	1·60	65
799	150f. "Mars Rover" and "Marsokod" space vehicles	1·70	70
800	500f. "Phobos" project (air)	5·25	1·40
801	600f. Laika (dog) and "Sputnik 2" flight, 1957	6·25	1·60
MS802	112 × 80 mm. 1000f. "Viking" space vehicle (29 × 41 mm)	9·25	2·10

187 "Endeavour" (space shuttle), Capt. James Cook and H.M.S. "Endeavour"

1992. Space and Nautical Exploration. Mult.

803	75f. Type **187** (postage)	90	20
804	100f. "Cariane" space microphone, Sir Francis Drake and "Golden Hind"	1·30	25
805	150f. Infra-red astronomical observation device, John Smith and "Susan Constant"	1·70	40
806	225f. Space probe "B", Robert F. Scott and "Discovery"	2·20	70
807	375f. "Magellan" (Venus space probe), Ferdinand Magellan and ship (air)	4·00	95
808	500f. "Newton" (satellite), Vasco da Gama and "Sao Gabriel"	6·25	2·75
MS809	112 × 77 mm. 1000f. "Hermes-Columbus" (spacescraft), Christopher Columbus and fleet	9·75	2·10

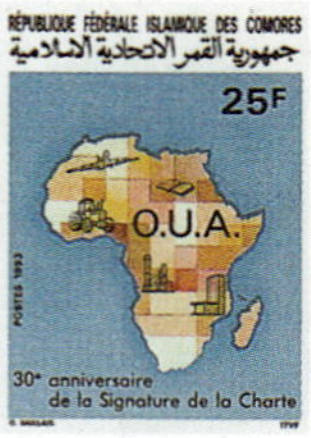

188 Map

189 Footballers

1993. 30th Anniv of Organization of African Unity.

810	**188**	25f. multicoloured	10	10
811		50f. multicoloured	45	25
812		75f. multicoloured	90	50
813		150f. multicoloured	1·50	1·10

1993. World Cup Football Championship, U.S.A. (1994).

814	**189**	25f. multicoloured	30	15
815		75f. multicoloured	75	25
816		100f. multicoloured	1·00	40
817		150f. multicoloured	1·40	55

190 ITU Emblem

1993. World Telecommunications Day. "Telecommunications and Human Development".

818	**190**	50f. multicoloured	45	25
819		75f. multicoloured	75	25
820		100f. multicoloured	1·00	40
821		150f. multicoloured	1·50	80

191 Edaphosaurus

1994. Prehistoric Animals. Multicoloured.

822	75f. Type **191**	55	25
823	75f. Moschops	55	25
824	75f. Kentrosaurus	55	25
825	75f. Compsognathus	55	25
826	75f. Sauroctonus	55	25
827	75f. Ornitholestes	55	25
828	75f. Styracosaurus	55	25
829	75f. Acanthopholis	55	25
830	150f. Edmontonia	85	25
831	150f. Struthiomimus	85	25
832	150f. Diatryma	85	25
833	150f. Uintatherium	85	25
834	450f. Dromiceiomimus	3·00	90
835	450f. Iguanodon	3·00	90
836	525f. Synthetoceras	3·50	90
837	525f. Euryapteryx	3·50	90
MS838	149 × 106 mm. 1200f. Tyrannosaurus rex (41 × 59 mm)	9·50	2·75

192 "Hibiscus syriacus"

1994. Plants. Multicoloured.

839	75f. Type **192**	45	25
840	75f. Cashew nut	45	25
841	75f. Butter mushroom	45	25
842	150f. "Pyrostegia venusta" (flower)	95	25
843	150f. Manioc (root)	95	25
844	150f. "Lycogala epidendron" (fungus)	95	25
845	525f. "Allamanda cathartica" (flower)	3·50	1·00
846	525f. Cacao (nut)	3·50	1·00
847	525f. "Clathrus ruber" (fungus)	4·00	1·20

193 Purple-tip ("Colotis zoe")

1994. Insects. Multicoloured.

848	75f. Type **193**	45	25
849	75f. "Charaxes comoranus" (butterfly)	45	25
850	75f. "Hypurgus ova" (beetle)	45	25
851	150f. Death's-head hawk moth ("Acherontia atropos")	95	30
852	150f. "Verdant hawk moth ("Euchloron megaera")	95	30
853	150f. "Onthophagus catta" (beetle)	95	30
854	450f. African monarch ("Danaus chrysippus") (butterfly)	3·50	90
855	450f. "Papilio phorbanta" (butterfly)	3·50	90
856	450f. "Echinosoma bolivari" (beetle)	3·50	90

OFFICIAL STAMPS

O **99** Comoro Flag

1979.

O379	O **99**	5f. grn, blk & azure	10	10
O380		10f. grn, blk & grey	10	10
O381		20f. grn, blk & stone	10	10
O382		30f. green, blk & bl	35	10
O383		40f. grn, blk & yell	65	25
O384		60f. grn, blk & lt grn	50	25
O384a		75f. grn, blk & lt grn	45	25
O385		100f. grn, blk & yell	1·10	60
O386	–	100f. mult	80	50
O386a	–	125f. mult	1·30	70
O387	–	400f. mult	3·50	1·70

DESIGNS: Nos. O386, O386a, O387, Pres. Cheikh.

POSTAGE DUE STAMPS

D **9** Mosque in Anjouan

D **10** Coelacanth

1950.

D16	D **9**	50c. green	10	5·25
D17		1f. brown	10	5·50

1954.

D18	D **10**	5f. sepia and green	15	5·75
D19		10f. violet and brown	3·50	5·50
D20		20f. indigo and blue	95	6·75

D **78** Pineapple

1977. Multicoloured.

D244	1f. Hibiscus (horiz)	10	10
D245	2f. Type D **78**	10	10
D246	5f. White butterfly (horiz)	10	10
D247	10f. Chameleon (horiz)	10	10
D248	15f. Banana flower (horiz)	10	10
D249	20f. Orchid (horiz)	10	10
D250	30f. "Allamanda cathartica" (horiz)	40	10
D251	40f. Cashew nuts	70	10
D252	50f. Custard apple	75	10
D253	100f. Breadfruit (horiz)	1·40	40
D254	200f. Vanilla (horiz)	3·25	95
D255	500f. Ylang-ylang flower (horiz)	7·75	2·10

APPENDIX

The following stamps have either been issued in excess of postal needs or have not been available to the public in reasonable quantities at face value. Such stamps may later be given full listing if there is evidence of regular postal use.

1975.

Various stamps optd **ETAT COMORIEN** or surch also.

Birds issue (No. 60). 10f. on 2f.

Fishes issue (No. 71). Air 50f.

Birds issue (No. 99). 40f.

Comoro Landscapes issue (Nos. 102/4). Air 75f. on 65f., 100f. on 85f., 100f.

Tropical Plants issue (Nos. 105/9). Postage 5f. on 1f., 5f. on 3f.; Air 75f. on 60f., 100f. on 85f.

Seashells issue (No. 114). 75f. on 60f.

Aquatic Sports issue (No. 122). Air 75f. on 70f.

Anjouan Landscapes issue (Nos. 126/8). Air 40f., 75f. on 60f., 100f.

Said Mohamed Cheikh issue (Nos. 129/30). Air 20f., 35f.

Great Comoro Landscapes issue (Nos. 134 and 136). Postage 35f.; Air 200f. on 135f.

Moroni Buildings issue (No. 139). 20f.

Karthala Volcano issue (No. 140). Air 200f. on 120f.

Hansen issue (No. 141). Air 100f.

Copernicus issue (No. 142). Air 400f. on 150f.

Picasso issue (No. 143). Air 200f.

Mosques issue (Nos. 145/6). 15f. on 20f., 25f. on 35f.

Star of Anjouan issue (No. 147). 500f.

Said Omar Ben Soumeth issue (Nos. 148/9). Air 100f. on 135f., 200f.

Shaikh Said Mohamed issue (No. 150). 30f. on 35f.

Handicrafts issue (Nos. 153/5). 20f., 30f. on 35f., 75f.

Mayotte Landscapes issue (Nos. 157/60). Air 10f. on 20f., 30f. on 35f., 100f. on 90f., 200f. on 120f.

UPU Centenary issue (No. 161). 500f. on 30f.

Air Service issue (No. 162). Air 100f. on 135f.

Rotary issue (No. 163). Air 400f. on 250f.

Handicrafts issue (Nos. 164/7). 15f. on 20f., 30f. on 35f., 100f. on 120f., 200f. on 135f.

Moheli Landscapes issue (Nos. 168/71). Postage 30f., 50f., 50f. on 55f.; Air 200f. on 230f.

Coelacanth issue (No. 172). 50f.

Folk-dances issue (Nos. 173/4). 100f., 100f. on 150f.

Apollo–Soyuz Space Test Project. Postage 10, 30, 50f.; Air 100, 200, 400f. Embossed on gold foil. Air 1500f.

1976.

Bicent of American Revolution. Postage 15, 25, 35, 40, 75f.; Air 500f. Embossed on gold foil: Air 1000f.

Winter Olympic Games, Innsbruck. Postage 5, 30, 35, 50f.; Air 200, 400f. Embossed on gold foil. Air 1000f.

Children's Stories. Postage 15, 30, 35, 40, 50f.; Air 400f.

Telephone Centenary. Postage 10, 25, 75f.; Air 100, 200, 500f.

Bicentenary of American Revolution (Early Settler and Viking Space Rocket). Embossed on gold foil. Air 1500f.

Bicent of American Revolution (J. F. Kennedy and Apollo). Embossed on gold foil. Air 1500f.

1978.

World Cup Football Championship, Argentina. Embossed on gold foil. Air 1000f.

Death Centenary of Sir Rowland Hill. Embossed on gold foil. Air 1500f.

Argentina's World Cup Victory. Optd on World Cup issue. Air 1000f.

1979.

International Year of the Child. Embossed on gold foil. Air 1500f.

1988.

Rotary International. Embossed on gold foil. Air 1500f.

1989.

Scouts, Butterflies and Birds. Embossed on gold foil. Air 1500f.

Satellites and Olympic Winners. Embossed on gold foil. Air 1500f.

Bicentenary of French Revolution. Embossed on gold foil. Air 1500f.

1990.

World Cup Football Championship. Embossed on gold foil. Air 1500f.

Winter Olympic Games, Albertville (1992). Embossed on gold foil. Air 1500f.

1991.

Birth Centenary of Charles De Gaulle (1990). Embossed on gold foil. Air 1500f.

1992.

Olympic Games, Barcelona. Boxing. Embossed on gold foil. Air 1500f.

CONFEDERATE STATES OF AMERICA Pt. 22

Stamps issued by the seceding states in the American Civil War.

1 Jefferson Davis

2 T. Jefferson

1861. Imperf.
1 **1** 5c. green £180 £110
3 **2** 10c. blue £180 £130

3 Jackson

4 Jefferson Davis

1862. Imperf.
4 **3** 2c. green £450 £475
5 **1** 5c. blue . . . . £120 80·00
6 **2** 10c. red £900 £350

1862. Imperf.
7 **4** 5c. blue . . . . 11·50 16·00

5 Jackson

6 Jefferson Davis

9 Washington

1863. Imperf or perf (10c.).
9 **5** 2c. red . . . . 60·00 £250
10 **6** 10c. blue (TEN CENTS) . . . £500 £350
12 10c. blue (10 CENTS) . . . 14·50 18·00
14 **9** 20c. green . . . . 32·00 £225

CONGO (BRAZZAVILLE) Pt. 6, Pt. 12

Formerly Middle Congo. An independent republic within the French Community.

1 "Birth of the Republic"

1959. 1st Anniv of Republic.
1 **1** 25f. multicoloured 75 25

1960. 10th Anniv of African Technical Co-operation Commission. As T **62** of Cameroun.
2 50f. lake and green 95 75

1960. Air. Olympic Games. No. 276 of French Equatorial Africa optd with Olympic rings and **XVIIe OLYMPIADE 1960 REPUBLIQUE DU CONGO 250F**.
3 250f. on 500f. blue, black & grn 8·75 8·25

2 Pres. Youlou

3 U.N. Emblem, map and Flag

1960.
4 **2** 15f. green, red and turquoise 45 25
5 85f. blue and red . . . . . . 1·80 65

1961. Admission into UNO.
6 **3** 5f. multicoloured 30 10
7 20f. multicoloured 45 25
8 100f. multicoloured . . . . . 1·90 1·20

4 "Thesium tencio"

1961. Air.
9 – 100f. purple, yellow & green 3·00 1·70
10 – 200f. yellow, turq & brown 5·25 2·50
11 **4** 500f. yellow, myrtle & brown 14·50 6·25
FLOWERS: 100f. "Helicrysum mechowiam"; 200f. "Cogniauxia podolaena".

1961. Air. Foundation of "Air Afrique" Airline. As T **69** of Cameroun.
12 50f. purple, myrtle and green 1·50 80

6 Rainbow Runner

7 Brazzaville Market

1961. Tropical Fish.
13 **6** 50c. multicoloured 30 10
14 – 1f. brown and green 30 10
15 – 2f. brown and blue 30 15
15a – 2f. red, brown and green . . 70 40
16 **6** 3f. green, orange and blue 40 25
17 – 5f. sepia, brown and green 70 40
18 – 10f. brown and turquoise . . 1·40 40
18a – 15f. purple, green & violet 2·40 1·40
FISH: 1, 2f. (No. 15), Sloan's viperfish ("Chauliodus sloanei"); 2f. (No. 15a), Fishes pursued by squid; 5f. Giant marine hatchetfish; 10f. Long-toothed fangtooth; 15f. Johnson's deep sea angler.

1962.
19 **7** 20f. red, green and black . . 75 45

1962. Malaria Eradication. As T **70** of Cameroun.
20 25f.+5f. brown 95 90

8 "Yang-tse" (freighter) loading Timber, Pointe Noire

1962. Air. International Fair, Pointe Noire.
21 **8** 50f. multicoloured . . . . . 1·50 1·00

1962. Sports. As T **12** of Central African Republic.
22 20f. sepia, red & blk (postage) 45 30
23 50f. sepia, red and black . . . 95 60
24 100f. sepia, red and black (air) 2·50 1·50
DESIGNS—HORIZ: 20f. Boxing; 50f. Running. VERT: (26 × 47 mm): 100f. Basketball.

1962. Union of African and Malagasy States. 1st Anniv. As No. 328 of Cameroun.
25 **72** 30f. violet . . . . 1·20 75

1962. Freedom from Hunger. As T **76** of Cameroun.
26 25f.+5f. turquoise, brn & bl 95 90

9 Town Hall, Brazzaville and Pres. Youlou

1963. Air.
27 **9** 100f. multicoloured £170 £140

9a "Costus spectabilis" (K. Schum)

10 King Makoko's Gold Chain

1963. Air. Flowers. Multicoloured.
28 100f. Type **9a** . . . . 4·00 2·10
29 250f. "Acanthus montanus T. anders" . . . . 7·75 3·75

1963. Air. African and Malagasy Posts and Telecommunications Union. As T **18** of Central African Republic.
30 85f. red, buff and violet . . . 1·50 80

1963. Space Telecommunications. As Nos. 37/8 of Central African Republic.
31 25f. blue, orange and green . . 75 45
32 100f. violet, brown and blue 1·70 1·30

1963. Folklore and Tourism.
33 **10** 10f. bistre and black 40 25
34 – 15f. multicoloured 55 30
DESIGN: 15f. Kebekebe mask.
See also Nos. 45/6 and 62/4.

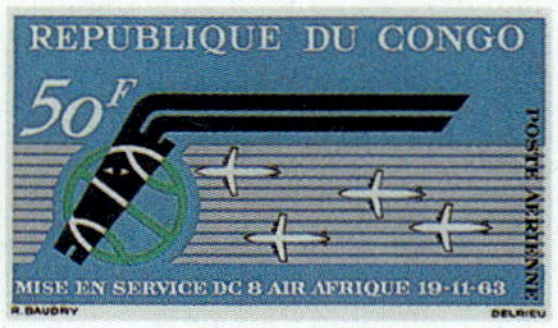

11 Airline Emblem

1963. Air. 1st Anniv of "Air Afrique", and Inaug of DC-8 Service.
35 **11** 50f. multicoloured 95 65

12 Liberty Square, Brazzaville

1963. Air.
36 **12** 25f. multicoloured 85 55
See also No. 56.

1963. Air. European-African Economic Convention. As T **24** of Central African Republic.
37 50f. multicoloured . . . . . . 1·30 90

1963. 15th Anniv of Declaration of Human Rights. As T **26** of Central African Republic.
38 25f. blue, turquoise & brown 80 45

13 Statue of Hathor, Abu Simbel

1964. Air. Nubian Monuments.
39 **13** 10f.+5f. violet & brown . . 75 45
40 25f.+5f. brown & turq . . . 95 65
41 50f.+5f. turquoise & brn . . 1·90 1·40

14 Barograph

1964. World Meteorological Day.
42 **14** 50f. brown, blue & green . . 1·00 80

15 Machinist

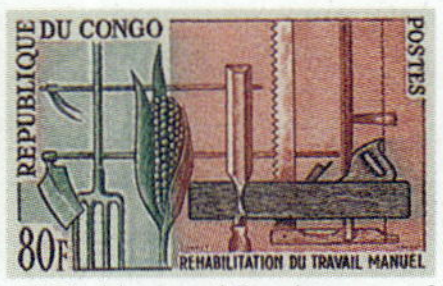

16 Emblem and Implements of Manual Labour

1964. "Technical Instruction".
43 **15** 20f. brown, mauve & turq 75 45

1964. Manual Labour Rehabilitation.
44 **16** 80f. green, red and sepia . . 1·20 80

17 Diaboua Ballet

19 Wood Carving

18 Tree-felling

1964. Folklore and Tourism. Multicoloured.
45 30f. Type **17** . . . . 1·10 55
46 60f. Kebekebe dance (vert) . . 2·10 1·00

1964. Air.
47 **18** 100f. brown, red and green 2·20 1·00

1964. Congo Sculpture.
48 **19** 50f. sepia and red . . . . . 1·40 75

20 Students in Classroom

1964. Development of Education.
49 **20** 25f. red, purple and blue . . 75 45

1964. Air. 5th Anniv of Equatorial African Heads of State Conference. As T **31** of Central African Republic.
50 100f. multicoloured . . . . . 1·50 90

21 Sun, Ears of Wheat, and Globe within Cogwheel

1964. Air. Europafrique.
51 **21** 50f. yellow, blue and red . . 1·00 70

22 Stadium, Olympic Flame and Throwing the Hammer

1964. Air. Olympic Games, Tokyo. Sport and flame orange.
52 **22** 25f. violet and brown . . . 55 25
53 – 50f. purple and olive 95 55
54 – 100f. green and brown . . . 2·10 1·10
55 – 200f. olive and red . . . . 3·75 2·20
MS55a 191 × 100 mm. Nos. 52/5 9·50 9·00
DESIGNS—Stadium, Olympic Flame and: VERT: 50f. Weightlifting; 100f. Volleyball. HORIZ: 200f. High-jumping.

1964. 1st Anniv of Revolution and National Festival. As T **12** but inscr "1er ANNIVERSAIRE DE LA REVOLUTION FETE NATIONALE 15 AOUT 1964".
56 20f. multicoloured 55 25

23 Posthorns, Envelope and Radio Mast

1964. Air. Pan-African and Malagasy Posts and Telecommunications Congress, Cairo.
57 **23** 25f. sepia and red 55 40

1964. French, African and Malagasy Co-operation. As T **88** of Cameroun.
58 25f. brown, green and red . . 75 45

24 Dove, Envelope and Radio Mast

1965. Establishment of Posts and Telecommunications Office, Brazzaville.
59 **24** 25f. multicoloured 55 30

25 Town Hall, Brazzaville and Arms

1965. Air.
60 **25** 100f. multicoloured . . . . 1·50 70

26 "Europafrique"

1965. Air. Europafrique.
61 **26** 50f. multicoloured . . . . . 1·00 70

27 African Elephant

29 Pres. Massamba-Debat

28 Cadran de Breguet's Telegraph and "Telstar"

1965. Folklore and Tourism.
62 – 15f. purple, green and blue 1·20 70
63 **27** 20f. black, blue and green 1·20 70
64 – 85f. multicoloured . . . . 3·75 4·00
DESIGNS—VERT: 15f. Bushbuck; 85f. Dancer on stilts.

1965. Air. Centenary of ITU.
65 **28** 100f. brown and blue . . . 2·50 1·10

1965. Portrait in sepia.
66 **29** 20f. yellow, green & brown 30 15
66a 25f. green, turquoise & brn 45 25
66b 30f. orange, turq & brn . . 45 25

30 Sir Winston Churchill

1965. Air. Famous Men.
67 – 25f. on 50f. sepia and red 75 70
68 **30** 50f. sepia and green . . . . 1·50 1·40
69 – 80f. sepia and blue . . . . 2·40 2·20
70 – 100f. sepia and yellow . . 3·00 2·75
MS70a 106 × 145 mm. Nos. 67/70 5·00 5·00
PORTRAITS: 25f. Lumumba; 80f. Pres. Boganda; 100f. Pres. Kennedy.

31 Pope John XXIII

1965. Air. Pope John Commemoration.
71 **31** 100f. multicoloured . . . . 2·00 1·40

32 Athletes and Map of Africa

33 Natives hauling Log

1965. 1st African Games, Brazzaville. Inscr "PREMIERS JEUX AFRICAINS". Mult.
72 25f. Type **32** 55 40
73 40f. Football (34½ × 34½ mm) 95 45
74 50f. Handball (34½ × 34½ mm) 95 55
75 85f. Running (34½ × 34½ mm) 1·30 75
76 100f. Cycling (34½ × 34½ mm) 1·80 1·40
MS76a 137 × 169 mm. Nos. 72/6 8·75 8·25

1965. Air. National Unity.
77 **33** 50f. brown and green . . . 95 60

34 "World Co-operation"

1965. Air. International Co-operation Year.
78 **34** 50f. multicoloured . . . . . 1·20 85

35 Arms of Congo

37 Trench-digging

36 Lincoln

1965.
79 **35** 20f. multicoloured 55 25

1965. Air. Death Centenary of Abraham Lincoln.
80 **36** 90f. multicoloured . . . . . 1·50 70

1966. Village Co-operative.
81 **37** 25f. multicoloured 45 25

1966. National Youth Day. As T **37** but showing youth display.
82 30f. multicoloured 55 40

38 De Gaulle and Flaming Torch

1966. Air. 22nd Anniv of Brazzaville Conference.
83 **38** 500f. brown, red & green . . 34·00 25·00

39 Weaving

40 People and Clocks

1966. World Festival of Negro Arts, Dakar. Multicoloured.
84 30f. Type **39** 75 35
85 85f. Musical Instrument (horiz) 1·90 85
86 90f. Mask . . . . 2·00 1·20

1966. Establishment of Shorter Working Day.
87 **40** 70f. multicoloured . . . . . 1·20 45

41 WHO Building

1966. Inaug of WHO Headquarters, Geneva.
88 **41** 50f. violet, yellow and blue 95 50

42 Satellite "D1" and Brazzaville Tracking Station

1966. Air. Launching of Satellite "D1".
89 **42** 150f. black, red and green 2·75 1·50

43 St. Pierre Claver Church

44 Volleyball

1966.
90 **43** 70f. multicoloured . . . . . 1·20 60

1966. Sports.
91 **44** 1f. brown, bistre and blue 10 10
92 – 2f. brown, green and blue 20 10
93 – 3f. brown, lake and green 30 20
94 – 5f. brown, blue and green 30 20
95 – 10f. violet, turquoise & grn 55 25
96 – 15f. brown, violet and lake 75 35
DESIGNS—VERT: 2f. Basketball; 5f. Sportsmen; 10f. Athlete; 15f. Football. HORIZ: 3f. Handball.

45 Jules Rimet Cup and Globe

46 Corn, Atomic Emblem and Map

1966. World Cup Football Championship, England.
97 **45** 30f. multicoloured . . . . . 1·00 50

1966. Air. Europafrique.
98 **46** 50f. multicoloured 95 60

47 Pres. Massamba-Debat and Presidential Palace, Brazzaville

1966. Air. 3rd Anniv of Congolese Revolution. Multicoloured.
99 25f. Type **47** 40 25
100 30f. Robespierre and Bastille, Paris 55 25
101 50f. Lenin and Winter Palace, St. Petersburg . . . . . . 1·30 40
MS102 132 × 160 mm. Nos. 99/101 2·20 2·10

1966. Air. Inauguration of DC-8F Air Services. As T **54** of Central African Republic.
103 30f. yellow, black and violet 75 25

48 Dr. Albert Schweitzer

1966. Air. Schweitzer Commemoration.
104 **48** 100f. multicoloured . . . . 2·50 1·20

49 View of School

1966. Inaug of Savorgnan de Brazza High School.
105 **49** 30f. multicoloured 75 30

50 Pointe-Noire Railway Station

51 Silhouette of Congolese, and UNESCO Emblem

1966.
106 **50** 60f. red, brown and green 1·30 80

1966. 20th Anniv of UNESCO.
107 **51** 90f. blue, brown & green 1·50 90

52 Balumbu Mask

53 Cancer "The Crab", Microscope and Pagoda

1966. Congolese Masks.
108 **52** 5f. sepia and red 40 20
109 – 10f. brown and blue . . . 50 20
110 – 15f. blue, sepia & brown 60 25
111 – 20f. multicoloured 95 30
MASKS: 10f. Kuyu; 15f. Bakwele; 20f. Bateke.

1966. Air. 9th Int Cancer Congress, Tokyo.
112 **53** 100f. multicoloured . . . . 1·70 1·20

54 Sociable Weaver

55 Medal, Ribbon and Map

1967. Air. Birds. Multicoloured.
113 50f. Type **54** . . . . 1·60 60
114 75f. European bee eater . . . 3·25 1·10
115 100f. Lilac-breasted roller . . 3·25 1·10
116 150f. Regal sunbird . . . . . 4·00 2·30
117 200f. South African crowned crane . . . . 7·25 2·75
118 250f. Secretary bird . . . . . 8·75 3·25
119 300f. Black-billed turaco . . 13·00 6·00

1967. "Companion of the Revolution" Order.
120 **55** 20f. multicoloured 55 35

56 Learning the Alphabet (Educational Campaign)

57 Mahatma Gandhi

1967. Education and Sugar Production Campaigns. Multicoloured.
121 25f. Type **56** 75 50
122 45f. Cutting sugar-cane . . . 1·20 60

1967. Gandhi Commemoration.
123 **57** 90f. black and blue . . . . 2·00 80

58 Prisoner's Hands in Chains

59 Ndumba, Lady of Fashion

1967. Air. African Liberation Day.
124 **58** 500f. multicoloured . . . . 10·00 4·00

1967. Congolese Dolls. Multicoloured.
125 5f. Type **59** 30 10
126 10f. Fruit seller 45 20
127 25f. Girl pounding saka-saka 50 25
128 30f. Mother and child . . . 60 25

60 Congo Scenery

61 "Europafrique"

1967. International Tourist Year.
129 **60** 60f. red, orange and green 95 60

1967. Europafrique.
130 **61** 50f. multicoloured 95 45

62 "Sputnik 1" and "Explorer 6"

1967. Air. Space Exploration.
131 **62** 50f. blue, violet & brown 75 40
132 – 75f. lake and slate . . . . 1·20 55
133 – 100f. blue, red & turquoise 2·00 1·00
134 – 200f. red, blue and lake . . 3·00 1·90
DESIGNS: 75f. "Ranger 6" and "Lunik 2"; 100f. "Mars 1" and "Mariner 4"; 200f. "Gemini" and "Vostok".

63 Brazzaville Arms

1967. 4th Anniv of Congo Revolution.
135 **63** 30f. multicoloured 75 45

1967. Air. 5th Anniv of African and Malagasy Posts and Telecommunications Union. As T **66** of Central African Republic.
136 100f. green, red and brown 1·50 80

64 Jamboree Emblem, Scouts and Tents

1967. Air. World Scout Jamboree, Idaho.
137 **64** 50f. blue, brown & chestnut 85 30
138 – 70f. red, green and blue . . 1·30 60
DESIGN: 70f. Saluting hand, Jamboree camp and emblem.

65 Sikorsky S-43 Amphibian and Map

1967. Air. 30th Anniv of Aeromaritime Airmail Link.
139 **65** 30f. multicoloured 75 45

66 Dove, Human Figures and U.N. Emblem

67 Young Congolese

1967. U.N. Day and Campaign in Support of U.N.
140 **66** 90f. multicoloured . . . . 1·70 85

1967. 21st Anniv of UNICEF.
141 **67** 90f. black, blue & brown 1·70 85

68 Albert Luthuli (winner of Nobel Peace Prize) and Dove

70 Arms of Pointe Noire

69 Global Dance

1968. Luthuli Commemoration.
142 **68** 30f. brown and green . . . 75 50

1968. Air. "Friendship of the Peoples".
143 **69** 70f. brown, green & blue 1·00 55

1968.
144 **70** 10f. multicoloured 50 30

71 "Old Man and His Grandson" (Ghirlandaio)

1968. Air. Paintings. Multicoloured.
145 30f. Type **71** 70 45
146 100f. "The Horatian Oath" (J.-L. David) (horiz) . . . 2·20 1·00
147 200f. "The Negress with Peonies" (Bazille) (horiz) 4·75 3·00
See also Nos. 209/13.

72 "Mother and Child"

73 Diesel Train crossing Mayombe Viaduct

1968. Mothers' Festival.
148 **72** 15f. black, blue and red . . 55 40

1968.
149 **73** 45f. lake, blue and green 2·00 70

74 Beribboned Rope

1968. Air. 5th Anniv of Europafrique.
150 **74** 50f. multicoloured . . . . 1·00 50

75 Daimler, 1889

1968. Veteran Motor Cars. Multicoloured.
151 5f. Type **75** (postage) 45 25
152 20f. Berliet, 1897 . . . . . 85 45
153 60f. Peugeot, 1898 . . . . . 1·70 70
154 80f. Renault, 1900 . . . . . 2·30 1·10
155 85f. Fiat, 1902 . . . . . 3·25 1·90
156 150f. Ford, 1915 (air) . . . . 4·50 2·20
157 200f. Citroen . . . . 4·75 2·10

1968. Inauguration of Petroleum Refinery, Port Gentil, Gabon. As T **80** of Central African Republic.
158 30f. multicoloured 95 35

76 Dr. Martin Luther King **78** Robert Kennedy

77 "The Barricade" (Delacroix)

1968. Air. Martin Luther King Commemoration.
159 **76** 50f. black, green & emerald 1·20 40

1968. Air. 5th Anniv of Revolution Paintings. Multicoloured.
160 25f. Type **77** . . . . 1·90 75
161 30f. "Destruction of the Bastille" (H. Robert) . . . 1·90 75

1968. Air. Robert Kennedy Commemoration.
162 **78** 50f. black, green and red 95 45

79 "Tree of Life" and WHO Emblem

1968. 20th Anniv of WHO.
163 **79** 25f. red, purple and green 55 40

80 Start of Race

1968. Air. Olympic Games, Mexico.
164 **80** 5f. brown, blue and green 30 10
165 – 20f. green, brown & blue 45 25
166 – 60f. brown, green and red 95 60
167 – 85f. brown, red and slate 2·00 80
DESIGNS—VERT: 20f. Football; 60f. Boxing. HORIZ: 85f. High-jumping.

1968. Air. "Philexafrique" Stamp Exn, Abidjan (1969) (1st issue). As T **86** of Central African Republic.
168 100f. multicoloured . . . . . 3·00 2·10

DESIGN: 100f. "G. de Gueidan writing" (N. de Largilliere).

1969. Air. "Philexafrique" Stamp Exhibition, Abidjan, Ivory Coast (2nd issue). As T **138** of Cameroun.
169 50f. green, brown & mauve 2·00 1·90
DESIGN: 50f. Pointe-Noire harbour, lumbering and Middle Congo stamp of 1933.

1969. Air. Birth Bicentenary of Napoleon Bonaparte. As T **144** of Cameroun. Multicoloured.
170 25f. Battle of Rivoli (C. Vernet) . . . . 1·30 60
171 50f. "Battle of Marengo" (Pahou) . . . . 1·90 90
172 75f. "Battle of Friedland" (H. Vernet) . . . . 3·00 1·50
173 100f. "Battle of Jena" (Thevenin) . . . . 4·50 1·60

81 "Che" Guevara

1969. Air. Ernesto "Che" Guevara (Latin-American revolutionary) Commemoration.
174 **81** 90f. brown, orange & lake 1·20 60

82 Doll and Toys

1969. Air. International Toy Fair, Nuremberg.
175 **82** 100f. slate, mauve & orange . . . . 1·70 85

83 Beribboned Bar

1969. Air. Europafrique.
176 **83** 50f. violet, black & turq . . 85 35

1969. 5th Anniv of African Development Bank. As T **146** of Cameroun.
177 25f. brown, red and green . . 45 25
178 30f. brown, green and blue 45 25

84 Astronauts

1969. Air. 1st Man on the Moon. Sheet 65 × 51 mm containing T **84** and similar vert design.
MS179 1000f. Type **84**; 1000f. Lunar module . . . . 39·00 39·00

85 Modern Bicycle

1969. Cycles and Motor-cycles.
180 **85** 50f. purple, orange & brn 1·20 45
181 – 75f. black, lake & orange 1·50 45
182 – 80f. green, blue & purple 1·70 70
183 – 85f. green, slate & brown 1·90 90
184 – 100f. multicoloured . . . . 2·50 1·00
185 – 150f. brown, red & black 3·50 1·20
186 – 200f. pur, dp grn & grn . . 5·00 2·00
187 – 300f. green, purple & blk 8·75 3·00
DESIGNS: 75f. "Hirondelle" cycle; 80f. Folding cycle; 85f. "Peugeot" cycle; 100f. "Excelsior Manxman" motor-cycle; 150f. "Norton" motor-cycle; 200f. "Brough Superior" motor-cycle; 300f. "Matchless and N.I.G.-J.A.P.S." motor-cycle.

86 Series ZE Diesel-electric Train entering Mbamba Tunnel

1969. African International Tourist Year. Mult.
188 40f. Type **86** . . . . 1·80 60
189 60f. Series ZE diesel-electric train crossing the Mayombe (horiz) . . . . 3·00 90

87 Mortar Tanks

1969. Loutete Cement Works.
190 **87** 10f. slate, brown and lake 30 10
191 – 15f. violet, blue & brown 50 20
192 – 25f. blue, brown and red 55 25
193 – 30f. blue, violet & ultram 60 25
MS194 170 × 101 mm. Nos. 190/3 3·00 3·00
DESIGNS—VERT: 15f. Mixing tower; 25f. Cableway. HORIZ: 30f. General view of works.

1969. 10th Anniv of A.S.E.C.N.A. As T **150** of Cameroun.
195 100f. brown . . . . 2·00 90

88 Harvesting Pineapples

1969. 50th Anniv of ILO.
196 **88** 25f. brown, green & blue 40 30
197 – 30f. slate, purple and red 55 30
DESIGN: 30f. Operating lathe.

89 Textile Plant

1970. "SOTEXCO" Textile Plant, Kinsoundi.
198 **89** 15f. black, violet & green 40 25
199 – 20f. green, red and purple 40 25
200 – 25f. brown, blue & lt blue 60 25
201 – 30f. brown, red and slate 60 30
DESIGNS: 20f. Spinning machines; 25f. Printing textiles; 30f. Checking finished cloth.

90 Linzolo Church **91** Artist at work

1970. Buildings.
202 **90** 25f. green, brown & blue 75 25
203 – 90f. brown, green & blue 1·20 40
DESIGN: HORIZ: 90f. Cosmos Hotel, Brazzaville.

1970. Air. "Art and Culture".
204 **91** 100f. brown, plum & grn 2·00 70
205 – 150f. plum, lake & green 3·00 1·20
206 – 200f. brown, choc & ochre 4·00 2·10
DESIGNS: 150f. Lesson in wood-carving; 200f. Potter at wheel.

92 Diosso Gorges

1970. Tourism.
207 **92** 70f. purple, brown & grn 1·30 40
208 – 90f. purple, green & brown 2·00 60
DESIGN: 90f. Foulakari Falls.

1970. Air. Paintings. As T **71**. Multicoloured.
209 150f. "Child with Cherries" (J. Russell) . . . . 3·75 1·60
210 200f. "Erasmus" (Holbein the younger) . . . . 5·50 2·10
211 250f. "Silence" (Bernadino Luini) . . . . 5·75 2·50
212 300f. "Scenes from the Scio Massacre" (Delacroix) . . 7·50 3·50
213 500f. "Capture of Constantinople" (Delacroix) . . . . 12·00 4·75

93 Aurichalcite

1970. Air. Minerals. Multicoloured.
214 100f. Type **93** . . . . 4·75 1·90
215 150f. Dioptase . . . . 6·50 2·50

94 "Volvaria esculenta"

1970. Mushrooms. Multicoloured.
216 5f. Type **94** 65 35
217 10f. "Termitomyces entolomoides" 95 50
218 15f. "Termitomyces microcarpus" . . . . . . 1·50 75
219 25f. "Termitomyces aurantiacus" . . . . . . 2·50 1·10
220 30f. "Termitomyces mammiformis" . . . . . . 4·25 1·70
221 50f. "Tremella fuciformis" . . 7·00 1·90

95 Laying Cable **96** Mother feeding Child

1970. Laying of Coaxial Cable, Brazzaville–Pointe Noire.
222 **95** 25f. buff, brown and blue 1·00 45
223 – 30f. brown and green . . . 1·30 75
DESIGN: 30f. Diesel locomotive and cable-laying gang.

1970. New U.P.U. Headquarters Building, Berne. As T **156** of Cameroun.
224 30f. purple, slate and plum 75 45

1970. Mothers' Day. Multicoloured.
225 85f. Type **96** 95 40
226 90f. Mother suckling baby . . 1·20 60

97 U.N. Emblem and Trygve Lie

1970. 25th Anniv of United Nations.
227 **97** 100f. blue, indigo and lake 1·30 90
228 – 100f. lilac, red and lake . . 1·30 90
229 – 100f. green, turq & lake . . 1·30 90
MS230 130 × 100 mm. Nos. 227/9 6·00 5·75
DESIGNS—VERT: No. 228, as Type **97**, but with portrait of Dag Hammarskjold. HORIZ: No. 229, as Type **97**, but with portrait of U Thant and arrangement reversed.

98 Lenin in Cap **100** Karl Marx

99 "Brillantaisia vogeliana"

1970. Air. Birth Centenary of Lenin.
231 **98** 45f. brown, yellow & grn 1·00 55
232 – 75f. brown, red and blue 1·80 80
DESIGN: 75f. Lenin seated (after Vassiliev).

1970. "Flora and Fauna". Multicoloured.
(a) Flowers. Horiz designs.
233 1f. Type **99** 60 35
234 2f. "Plectranthus decurrens" 60 35
235 3f. "Myrianthemum mirabile" 45 35
236 5f. "Connarus griffonianus" 1·10 35
(b) Insects. Vert designs.
237 10f. "Sternotomis variabilis" 1·60 55
238 15f. "Chelorrhina polyphemus" . . . . . . 2·50 55
239 20f. "Metopodontus savagei" 2·50 70

1970. Air. Founders of Communism.
240 **100** 50f. brown, green & red 1·30 45
241 – 50f. brown, blue and red 1·30 45
DESIGN: No. 241, Friedrich Engels.

101 Kentrosarus

1970. Prehistoric Creatures. Multicoloured.
242 15f. Type **101** . . . . 1·50 65
243 20f. Dinotherium (vert) . . . 3·00 1·00
244 60f. Brachiosaurus (vert) . . 5·00 1·20
245 80f. Arsinoitherium . . . . . 6·00 2·50

102 "Mikado 141" Steam Locomotive, 1932

1970. Locomotives of Congo Railways (1st series).
246 **102** 40f. black, green & purple 2·20 1·00
247 – 60f. black, green & blue 2·50 1·20
248 – 75f. black, red and blue 4·00 1·70
249 – 85f. red, green & orange 5·75 2·50
DESIGNS: 60f. Super-Golwe steam locomotive, 1947; 75f. Alsthom Series BB 1100 diesel locomotive, 1962; 85f. Diesel locomotive No. BB BB 302, 1969.
See also Nos. 371/4.

103 Lilienthal's Glider, 1891

1970. Air. History of Flight and Space Travel.
250 **103** 45f. brown, blue and red 85 30
251 – 50f. green and brown . . 90 45
252 – 70f. brown, red and blue 1·30 60
253 – 90f. brown, olive & blue 1·50 85
DESIGNS: 50f. Lindbergh's "Spirit of St. Louis", 1927; 70f. "Sputnik I"; 90f. First man on the Moon, 1969.

104 "Wise Man"

1970. Air. Christmas. Stained-glass Windows, Brazzaville Cathedral. Multicoloured.
254 100f. Type **104** . . . . . . 1·50 60
255 150f. "Shepherd" . . . . . . 2·00 90
256 250f. "Angels" . . . . . . 3·50 1·60
MS257 152 × 116 mm. Nos. 254/6 8·00 8·00

105 "Cogniauxia padolaena" **106** Marilyn Monroe

1971. Tropical Flowers. Multicoloured.
258 1f. Type **105** 20 25
259 2f. "Celosia cristata" 30 25
260 5f. "Plumeria acutifolia" . . . 30 25
261 10f. "Bauhinia variegata" . . 90 40
262 15f. "Euphorbia pulcherrima 1·30 70
263 20f. "Thunbergia grandiflora" 2·30 60
See also D264/9.

1971. Air. Great Names of the Cinema.
270 **106** 100f. brown, blue & grn 6·50 75
271 – 150f. mauve, blue & pur 6·50 1·00
272 – 200f. brown and blue . . 6·50 1·30
273 – 250f. plum, blue & green 6·50 1·60
PORTRAITS: 150f. Martine Carol; 200f. Eric K. von Stroheim; 250f. Sergei Eisenstein.

107 "Carrying the Cross" (Veronese)

1971. Air. Easter. Religious Paintings. Mult.
274 100f. Type **107** . . . . . . 1·70 80
275 150f. "Christ on the Cross" (Burgundian School c. 1500) (vert) . . . 2·75 1·00
276 200f. "Descent from the Cross" (Van der Weyden) 3·75 1·20
277 250f. "The Entombment" (Flemish School c. 1500) (vert) . . . . 4·50 1·80
278 500f. "The Resurrection" (Memling) (vert) . . . . . 9·50 3·25

108 Telecommunications Map

1971. Air. Pan-African Telecommunications Network.
279 **108** 70f. multicoloured 95 30
280 85f. multicoloured . . . . 1·30 40
281 90f. multicoloured . . . . 1·80 70

109 Global Emblem

1971. Air. World Telecommunications Day.
282 **109** 65f. multicoloured 95 45

110 Green Night Adder **111** Afro-Japanese Allegory

1971. Reptiles. Multicoloured.
283 5f. Type **110** 45 25
284 10f. African egg-eating snake (horiz) 65 25
285 15f. Flap-necked chameleon 1·10 35
286 20f. Nile crocodile (horiz) . . 1·80 45
287 25f. Rock python (horiz) . . 2·20 90
288 30f. Gaboon viper . . . . . 2·75 90
289 40f. Brown house snake (horiz) . . . . 3·25 1·00
290 45f. Jameson's mamba . . . 4·50 1·20

1971. Air. "Philatokyo 1971" Stamp Exn, Tokyo.
291 **111** 75f. black, mauve & violet 1·20 75
292 – 150f. brown, red & purple 1·80 1·10
DESIGN: 150f. "Tree of Life", Japanese girl and African in mask.

112 "Pseudimbrasia deyrollei"

1971. Caterpillars. Multicoloured.
293 10f. Type **112** 80 35
294 15f. "Bunaca alcinoe" (vert) 1·10 50
295 20f. "Epiphora vacuna ploetzi" . . . . 1·90 65
296 25f. "Imbrasia eblis" . . . . 3·00 1·00
297 30f. "Imbrasia dione" (vert) 4·75 1·50
298 40f. "Holocera angulata" . . 6·50 1·90

113 Japanese Scout **114** Olympic Torch

1971. World Scout Jamboree, Asagiri, Japan (1st issue). On foil.
299 **113** 90f. silver (postage) . . . 3·00 1·90
300 – 90f. silver . . . . 3·00 1·90
301 – 90f. silver . . . . 3·00 1·90
302 – 90f. silver . . . . 3·00 1·90
303 – 1000f. gold (air) . . . . . 27·00 25·00
DESIGNS—VERT: No. 300, French Scout; 301, Congolese Scout; 302, Lord Baden-Powell. HORIZ: No. 303, Scouts and Lord Baden-Powell.
See also Nos. 306/9.

1971. Air. Olympic Games, Munich.
304 **114** 150f. red, green & purple 2·00 1·10
305 – 350f. violet, green & brn 5·00 2·50
DESIGN—HORIZ: 350f. Sporting cameos within Olympic rings.

115 Scout Badge, Dragon and Congolese Wood-carving

1971. Air. World Scout Jamboree, Asagiri, Japan (2nd issue).
306 **115** 85f. purple, brown & grn 1·10 30
307 – 90f. brown, violet & lake 1·30 40
308 – 100f. green, red & brown 1·50 60
309 – 250f. brown, red & green 3·00 1·30
DESIGNS—HORIZ: 250f. Congolese mask, geisha and scout badge. VERT: 90f. African and Japanese mask; 100f. Japanese woman and African.

116 Running

1971. Air. 75th Anniv of Modern Olympic Games.
310 **116** 75f. brown, blue and red 85 35
311 – 85f. brown, blue and red 95 45
312 – 90f. brown and violet . . 1·20 60
313 – 100f. brown and blue . . 1·50 60
314 – 150f. brown, red & green 2·50 1·00
DESIGNS: 85f. Hurdling; 90f. Various events; 100f. Wrestling; 150f. Boxing.

117 "Cymothae sangaris"

1971. Butterflies. Multicoloured.
315 30f. Type **117** . . . . 1·40 60
316 40f. "Papilio dardanus" (vert) 2·50 90
317 75f. "Iolaus timon" . . . . . 4·00 1·70
318 90f. "Papilio phorcas" (vert) 5·75 2·75
319 100f. "Euchloron megaera" 7·50 3·50

118 African and European Workers

1971. Racial Equality Year.
320 **118** 50f. multicoloured . . . . 1·30 45

119 De Gaulle and Congo 1966 Brazzaville Conference Stamp

1971. Air. 1st Death Anniv of General De Gaulle.
321 **119** 500f. brown, green & red 18·00 16·00
322 – 1000f. red & grn on gold 27·00 25·00
323 – 1000f. red & grn on gold 27·00 25·00
DESIGNS—VERT (29 × 38 mm): No. 322, Tribute by Pres. Ngouabi; 323, De Gaulle and Cross of Lorraine.

1971. Air. 10th Anniv of African and Malagasy Posts and Telecommunications Union. Similar to T **184** of Cameroun. Multicoloured.
324 100f. U.A.M.P.T. H.Q. and Congolese woman . . . . 1·50 75

1971. Inauguration of Brazzaville–Pointe Noire Cable Link. Surch **REPUBLIQUE POPULAIRE DU CONGO INAUGURATION DE LA LIAISON COXIALE 18-11-71** and new value.
325 **95** 30f. on 25f. buff, brn & bl 55 40
326 – 40f. on 30f. brown and green (No. 223) 95 50

121 Congo Republic Flag and Allegory of Revolution

1971. Air. 8th Anniv of Revolution.
327 **121** 100f. multicoloured . . . 2·00 70

122 Congolese with Flag

1971. Air. 2nd Anniv of Congolese Workers' Party, and Adoption of New National Flag. Multicoloured.
328 30f. Type **122** 55 25
329 40f. National flag . . . . . 1·20 45

123 Map and Emblems

125 Book Year Emblem

124 Lion

1971. "Work–Democracy–Peace".
330 **123** 30f. multicoloured 35 25
331 40f. multicoloured 45 25
332 100f. multicoloured . . . 1·20 45

1972. Wild Animals.
333 **124** 1f. brown, blue & green 25 10
334 – 2f. brown, green and red 45 10
335 – 3f. brown, orge and red 65 25
336 – 4f. brown, blue & violet 80 30
337 – 5f. brown, green and red 1·00 45
338 – 20f. brown, blue & orge 2·40 75
339 – 30f. green, emer & brn . . 3·25 90
340 – 40f. black, green and blue 4·75 1·30
DESIGNS—HORIZ: 2f. African elephants; 3f. Leopard; 4f. Hippopotamus; 20f. Potto; 30f. De Brazza's monkey. VERT: 5f. Gorilla; 40f. Pygmy chimpanzee.

1972. Air. International Book Year.
341 **125** 50f. green, yellow & red 95 45

126 Team Captain with Cup

127 Girl with Bird

1973. Air. Congolese Victory in Africa Football Cup. Multicoloured.
342 100f. Type **126** . . . . 1·70 85
343 100f. Congolese team (horiz) 1·70 85

1973. Air. U.N. Environmental Conservation Conference, Stockholm.
344 **127** 85f. green, blue & orange 2·00 1·10

128 Miles Davis

1973. Air. Famous Negro Musicians.
345 **128** 125f. multicoloured . . . 3·25 1·00
346 – 140f. red, lilac & mauve 3·25 1·00
347 – 160f. green, emer & orge 4·00 1·50
348 – 175f. purple, red & blue 4·00 1·50
DESIGNS: 140f. Ella Fitzgerald; 160f. Count Basie; 175f. John Coltrane.

129 Hurdling

1973. Air. Olympic Games, Munich (1972).
349 **129** 100f. violet and mauve . . 1·50 70
350 – 150f. violet and green . . 2·00 1·00
351 – 250f. red and blue . . . . 3·50 1·90
DESIGNS—VERT: 150f. Pole-vaulting. HORIZ: 250f. Wrestling.

130 Oil Tanks, Djeno

1973. Air. Oil Installations, Pointe Noire.
352 **130** 180f. indigo, red & blue 3·00 1·70
353 – 230f. black, red and blue 3·75 1·70
354 – 240f. purple, blue & red 4·50 1·90
355 – 260f. black, red and blue 6·75 2·50
DESIGNS—VERT: 230f. Oil-well head; 240f. Drill in operation. HORIZ: 260f. Off-shore oil-rig.

131 Lunar Module and Astronaut on Moon

1973. Air. Moon Flight of "Apollo 17".
356 **131** 250f. multicoloured . . . 4·25 2·20

132 "Telecommunications"

1973. Air. World Telecommunications Day.
357 **132** 120f. multicoloured . . . 2·10 95

133 Copernicus and Solar System

1973. Air. 500th Birth Anniv of Copernicus (astronomer).
358 **133** 50f. green, blue & lt blue 1·00 55

134 Rocket and African Scenes

1973. Air. Centenary of World Meteorological Organization.
359 **134** 50f. multicoloured . . . . 1·50 70

135 WHO Emblem

137 General View of Brewery

136 "Study of a White Horse"

1973. 25th Anniv of WHO. Multicoloured.
360 40f. Type **135** 55 25
361 50f. Design similar to T **135** (horiz) 75 25

1973. Air. Paintings by Delacroix. Multicoloured.
362 150f. Type **136** . . . . 2·75 1·80
363 250f. "Sleeping Lion" . . . . 5·25 2·75
364 300f. "Tiger and Lion" . . . 6·25 3·00
See also Nos. 384/6 and 437/40.

1973. Congo Brewers' Association. Views of Kronenbourg Brewery.
365 **137** 30f. blue, red & lt blue . . 50 30
366 – 40f. grey, orange & red 55 30
367 – 75f. blue, red and black 1·00 45
368 – 85f. multicoloured . . . . 1·50 75
369 – 100f. multicoloured . . . 1·70 1·00
370 – 250f. green, brown & red 3·25 1·90
DESIGNS: 40f. Laboratory; 75f. Regulating vats; 85f. Control console; 100f. Bottling plant; 250f. Capping bottles.

1973. Locomotives of Congo Railways (2nd series). As T **102**. Multicoloured.
371 30f. Golwe steam locomotive c. 1935 . . . . 1·50 65
372 40f. Diesel-electric locomotive, 1935 . . . . . 2·30 85
373 75f. Whitcomb diesel-electric locomotive, 1946 . . . . . 3·75 1·50
374 85f. Alsthom Series CC200 diesel-electric locomotive, 1973 . . . . 4·50 1·60

138 Stamp Map, Album, Dancer and Oil Rig

1973. Air. International Stamp Exhibition, Brazzaville and 10th Anniv of Revolution.
375 **138** 30f. grey, lilac & brown 1·20 35
376 – 40f. red, brown & purple 65 40
377 **138** 100f. blue, brown & pur 2·75 1·00
378 – 100f. lilac, purple & red 1·70 1·00
DESIGNS: 40f., 100f. Map, album and Globes.

139 President Marien Ngouabi

1973. Air.
379 **139** 30f. multicoloured 45 10
380 40f. multicoloured 45 15
381 75f. multicoloured . . . . 1·00 45

1973. Pan-African Drought Relief. No. 236 surch **100F SECHERESSE SOLIDARITE AFRICAINE**.
382 100f. on 5f. multicoloured . . 1·70 75

1973. 12th Anniv of African and Malagasy Posts and Telecommunications Union. As T **216** of Cameroun.
383 100f. violet, blue and purple 1·50 70

1973. Air. Europafrique. As T **136**. Multicoloured.
384 100f. "Wild Dog" . . . . . 3·25 1·60
385 100f. "Lion and Leopard" . . 3·25 1·60
386 100f. "Adam and Eve in Paradise" . . . . 3·25 1·60
Nos. 384/6 are details taken from J. Brueghel's "Earth and Paradise".

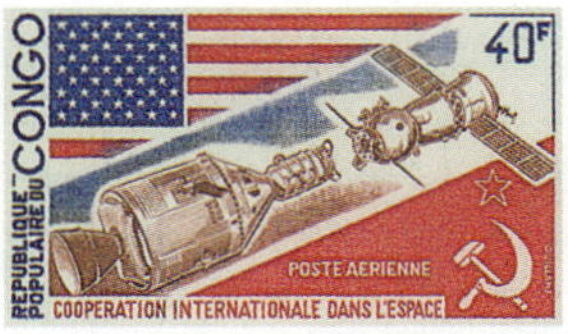

141 "Apollo" and "Soyuz" Spacecraft

1973. Air. International Co-operation in Space.
387 **141** 40f. brown, red & blue . . 50 35
388 – 80f. blue, red and green 1·10 60
DESIGN: 80f. Spacecraft docked.

142 UPU Monument and Satellite

1973. Air. UPU Day.
389 **142** 80f. blue & ultramarine 1·00 40

1973. Air. "Skylab" Space Laboratory. As T **141**.
390 30f. green, brown and blue 50 25
391 40f. green, red and orange . . 60 25
DESIGNS: 30f. Astronauts walking outside "Skylab"; 40f. "Skylab" and "Apollo" spacecraft docked.

143 Hive and Bees

1973. "Labour and Economy".
392 **143** 30f. green, blue and red 90 25
393 40f. green, blue & green 1·30 30

144 Congo Family and Emblems

1973. 10th Anniv of World Food Programme.
394 **144** 30f. brown and red . . . 45 25
395 – 40f. orange, green & blue 60 25
396 – 100f. brown, green & orge 1·20 60
DESIGNS—HORIZ: 40f. Ears of corn and emblems. VERT: 100f. Ear of corn, granary and emblems.

145 Goalkeeper

146 Runners

1973. Air. World Football Cup Championship, West Germany (1974). (1st issue).
397 **145** 40f. green, dp brn & brn 55 25
398 – 100f. green, red & violet 1·70 85
DESIGN: 100f. Forward.
See also Nos. 403 and 408.

1973. Air. 2nd African Games, Lagos, Nigeria.
399 **146** 40f. red, green & brown 60 25
400 100f. green, red & brown 1·80 85

147 Pres. John F. Kennedy

148 Map and Flag

1973. Air. 10th Death Anniv of President Kennedy.
401 **147** 150f. black, gold & blue 2·00 1·10

1973. Air. 4th Anniv of Congo Workers' Party.
402 **148** 40f. multicoloured 55 25

149 Players seen through Goalkeeper's Legs

1974. Air. World Cup Football Championship, West Germany (2nd issue).
403 **149** 250f. green, red & brown 3·50 2·20

150 Globe, Flags and Names of Dead Astronauts

1974. Air. Conquest of Space.
404 **150** 30f. brown, blue & red . . 35 25
405 – 40f. multicoloured 60 40
406 – 100f. brown, blue & red 1·40 90
DESIGNS: 40f. Gagarin and Shepard; 100f. Leonov in space, and Armstrong on Moon.

151 A. Cabral

152 Spacecraft docking

1974. 1st Death Anniv of Cabral (Guinea-Bissau guerilla leader).
407 **151** 100f. purple, red & blue 1·00 65

1974. Air. West Germany's Victory in World Cup Football Championship. As T **149**.
408 250f. brown, pink and blue 3·75 2·20
DESIGN: Footballers within ball.

1974. Air. Soviet-American Space Co-operation.
409 **152** 200f. blue, violet and red 2·30 1·20
410 – 300f. blue, brown & red 3·50 1·70
DESIGN—HORIZ: 300f. Spacecraft on segments of globe.

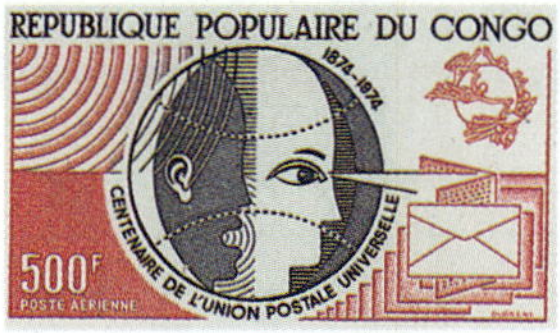

153 "Sound and Vision"

1974. Air. Centenary of UPU.
411 **153** 500f. black and red . . . 6·75 3·50

154 Felix Eboue and Cross of Lorraine

1974. 30th Death Anniv of Eboue ("Free French" Leader).
412 **154** 30f. multicoloured 75 45
413 40f. multicoloured . . . . 1·20 70

155 Lenin

1974. Air. 30th Death Anniv of Lenin.
414 **155** 150f. orange, red & green 2·20 1·10

1974. Birth Centenary of Churchill. As T **154**. Multicoloured.
415 200f. Churchill and Order of the Garter . . . . 2·75 1·50

1974. Birth Centenary of Guglielmo Marconi (radio pioneer). As T **154**. Multicoloured.
416 200f. Marconi and early apparatus . . . . 2·50 1·40

1974. Air. Centenary of Berne Convention. No. 411 surch **9 OCTOBRE 1974 300F**.
417 **153** 300f. on 500f. blk & red 3·75 2·20

157 Pineapple

1974. Congolese Fruits. Multicoloured.
418 30f. Type **157** 65 40
419 30f. Bananas 70 45
420 30f. Safous 70 50
421 40f. Avocado pears . . . . . 1·10 50
422 40f. Mangoes . . . . 1·10 50
423 40f. Papaya . . . . 1·10 50
424 40f. Oranges . . . . 1·10 50

158 Gen. Charles De Gaulle

1974. 30th Anniv of Brazzaville Conference.
425 **158** 100f. brown and green . . 3·75 2·20

1974. 10th Anniv of Central African Customs and Economic Union. As Nos. 734/5 of Cameroun.
426 40f. mult (postage) 60 25
427 100f. multicoloured (air) . . 1·20 60

159 George Stephenson (railway pioneer) and Early and Modern Locomotives (½-size illustration)

1974. 150th Anniv (1975) of Public Railways.
428 **159** 75f. olive and green . . . 3·00 1·10

160 Irish Setter

1974. Dogs. Multicoloured.
429 30f. Type **160** . . . . 1·10 60
430 40f. Borzoi . . . . 1·30 60
431 75f. Pointer . . . . 2·75 1·10
432 100f. Great Dane . . . . . 3·75 1·10

1974. Cats. As T **160**. Multicoloured.
433 30f. Havana chestnut . . . . 1·10 60
434 40f. Red Persian . . . . . . 1·30 60
435 75f. British blue . . . . . . 2·75 1·10
436 100f. Serval . . . . 3·75 1·10

1974. Air. Impressionist Paintings. As T **136**. Mult.
437 30f. "The Argenteuil Regatta" (Monet) . . . . 1·70 75
438 40f. "Seated Dancer" (Degas) (vert) . . . . 1·80 90
439 50f. "Girl on Swing" (Renoir) (vert) . . . . . . 2·75 1·30
440 75f. "Girl in Straw Hat" (Renoir) (vert) . . . . . . 3·50 1·90

161 National Fair

1974. Air. National Fair, Brazzaville.
441 **161** 30f. multicoloured 85 45

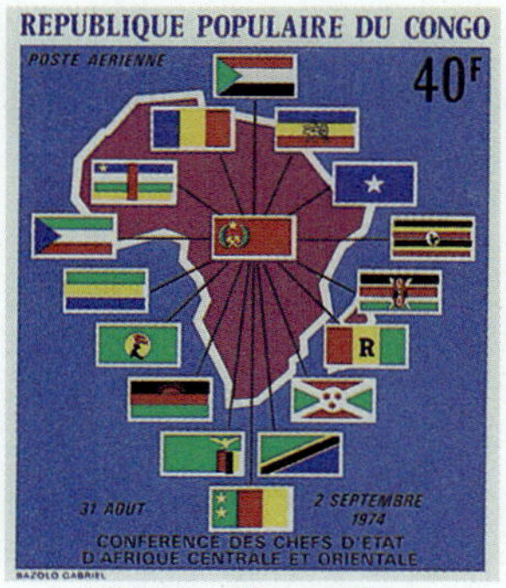

162 African Map and Flags

1974. Air. African Heads-of-State Conference, Brazzaville.
442 **162** 40f. multicoloured 75 45

163 Flags and Dove

1974. 5th Anniv of Congo Labour Party.
443 **163** 30f. red, yellow & green 45 25
444 – 40f. brown, red & yellow 80 30
DESIGN: 40f. Hands holding flowers and hammer.

164 U Thant and U.N. Headquarters Building

1975. 1st Death Anniv of U Thant (U.N. Secretary-General).
445 **164** 50f. multicoloured 75 45

1975. 1st Death Anniv of Paul G. Hoffman (U.N. Programme for Underdeveloped Countries administrator). As T **164**. Multicoloured.
446 50f. Hoffman and U.N. "Laurel Wreath" (vert) . . 75 45

166 Workers and Development

1975. National Economic Development.
447 **166** 40f. multicoloured 60 40

167 Mao Tse-tung and Map of China

1975. 25th Anniv (1974) of Chinese People's Republic.
448 **167** 75f. red, mauve & blue . . 3·75 1·50

168 Woman with Hoe

1975. 10th Anniv of Revolutionary Union of Congolese Women.
449 **168** 40f. multicoloured 60 30

169 Paris–Brussels Line, 1890 (½-size illustration)

1975. Air. Railway History. Multicoloured.
450 50f. Type **169** . . . . . . 1·90 70
451 75f. Santa Fe Line, 1880 . . 3·25 1·00

170 "Five Weeks in a Balloon"

1975. Air. 70th Anniv of Jules Verne (novelist). Multicoloured.
452 40f. Type **170** . . . . . . 1·50 60
453 50f. "Around the World in 80 Days" . . . . 1·80 1·10

171 Line-up of Team

1975. Victory of Cara Football Team in Africa Cup. Multicoloured.
454 30f. Type **171** 40 25
455 40f. Receiving trophy (vert) 60 30

172 1935 Citroen and Notre Dame Cathedral, Paris

1975. Veteran Cars. Multicoloured.
456 30f. Type **172** . . . . . . 1·00 50
457 40f. 1911 Alfa Romeo and St. Peter's Rome . . . . 1·30 50
458 50f. 1926 Rolls Royce and Houses of Parliament, London . . . . 1·60 70
459 75f. 1893 C. F. Duryea and Manhattan skyline, New York . . . . 3·00 1·00

173 "Soyuz" Spacecraft

1975. Air. "Apollo–Soyuz" Space Test Project.
460 **173** 95f. black, red & brown 1·10 60
461 – 100f. black, violet & blue 1·30 75
DESIGN: 100f. "Apollo" Spacecraft.

174 Tipoye Carriage

1975. Traditional Congo Transport. Multicoloured.
462 30f. Type **174** 85 45
463 40f. Pirogue 1·00 75

175 "Raising the Flag"

1975. 2nd Anniv of Institutions of Popular Tasks.
464 **175** 30f. multicoloured 55 25

176 Conference Hall

1975. 3rd Anniv of Congolese National Conference.
465 **176** 40f. multicoloured 60 30

177 Fishing with Wooden Baskets

1975. Traditional Fishing. Multicoloured.
466 30f. Type **177** 65 25
467 40f. Fishing with line (vert) 70 35
468 60f. Fishing with spear (vert) 95 35
469 90f. Fishing with net 1·20 80

178 Chopping Firewood **179** "Esanga"

1975. Domestic Chores. Multicoloured.
470 30f. Type **178** 65 30
471 30f. Pounding meal 65 30
472 40f. Preparing manioc (horiz) 90 30

1975. Traditional Musical Instruments. Mult.
473 30f. Type **179** 75 25
474 40f. "Kalakwa" 1·00 35
475 60f. "Likembe" 1·40 60
476 75f. "Ngongui" 1·70 75

180 "Dzeke" Money Cowrie

1975. Ancient Congolese Money.
477 **180** 30f. ochre, brown & red 55 30
478 – 30f. ochre, violet & brn 55 30
478a **180** 35f. orange and brown 80 35
478b – 35f. red, bistre and violet 80 35
479 – 40f. brown and blue 80 30
480 – 50f. blue and brown 95 45
481 – 60f. brown and green 1·10 60
482 – 85f. green and red 1·80 70
DESIGNS: 30, 35 (478b) f. "Okengo" iron money; 40f. Gallic coin (60 B.C.); 50f. Roman coin (37 B.C.); 60f. Danubian coin (2nd century B.C.); 85f. Greek coin (4th century B.C.).

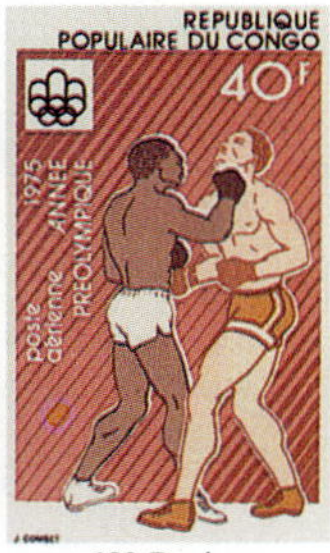

181 Dr. Schweitzer **183** Boxing

182 "Moschops"

1975. Birth Centenary of Dr. Albert Schweitzer.
483 **181** 75f. green, mauve & brn 1·50 70

1975. Prehistoric Animals. Multicoloured.
484 55f. Type **182** 1·70 75
485 75f. "Tyrannosaurus" 2·50 75
486 95f. "Cryptocleidus" 4·50 1·10
487 100f. "Stegosauras" 6·00 1·50

1975. Air. Olympic Games, Montreal (1976). Multicoloured.
488 40f. Type **183** 45 25
489 50f. Basketball 60 45
490 85f. Cycling (horiz) 1·00 55
491 95f. High jumping (horiz) 1·20 55
492 100f. Throwing the javelin (horiz) 1·50 70
493 150f. Running (horiz) 2·20 95

184 Alexander Fleming (biochemist) (20th Death Anniv)

1975. Celebrities.
494 **184** 60f. black, green and red 1·70 80
495 – 95f. black, blue and red 1·70 80
496 – 95f. green, red and lilac 2·30 1·10
DESIGNS: No. 495, Clement Ader (aviation pioneer) (50th death anniv); 496, Andre Marie Ampere (physicist) (birth bicent).

185 U.N. Emblem with Laurel Wreaths

1975. 30th Anniv of UNO.
497 **185** 95f. blue, red and green 1·30 65

186 Map of Africa and Sportsmen

1975. Air. 10th Anniv of 1st African Games, Brazzaville.
498 **186** 30f. multicoloured 75 35

187 Chained Women and Broken Link

1975. International Women's Year. Multicoloured.
499 35f. Type **187** 65 35
500 60f. Global handclasp 90 50

188 Pres. Ngouabi and Crowd with Flags

1975. 6th Anniv of Congolese Workers' Party. Multicoloured.
501 30f. Type **188** (postage) 55 25
502 35f. "Echo"–P.C.T. "man" with roll of newsprint and radio waves (36 × 27 mm) 55 25
503 60f. Party members with flag (26 × 38 mm) (air) 75 45

189 River Steamer "Alphonse Fondere"

1976. Air. Old-time Ships. Multicoloured.
504 5f. Type **189** 20 15
505 10f. Paddle-steamer "Hamburg", 1839 30 15
506 15f. Paddle-steamer "Gomer", 1831 30 15
507 20f. Paddle-steamer "Great Eastern", 1858 45 15
508 30f. Type **189** 55 25
509 40f. As 10f. 70 35
510 50f. As 15f. 95 60
511 60f. As 20f. 1·20 60
512 95f. River steamer "J.M. White II" 1878 1·90 1·00

190 "The Peasant Family" (L. le Nain)

1976. Air. Europafrique. Paintings. Multicoloured.
513 60f. Type **190** 1·40 50
514 80f. "Boy with spinning Top" (Chardin) 1·60 80
515 95f. "Venus and Aeneas" (Poussin) 2·20 80
516 100f. "The Sabines" (David) 2·40 1·00

191 Alexander Graham Bell and Early Telephone

1976. Telephone Centenary.
517 **191** 35f. brown, light brown and yellow (postage) 55 25
518 60f. red, mve & pink (air) 95 35

192 Fruit Market

1976. Market Scenes. Multicoloured.
519 35f. Type **192** 55 25
520 60f. Laying out produce 1·20 60

193 Congolese Woman **194** Pole-vaulting

1976. Congolese Women's Hair-styles.
521 **193** 35f. multicoloured 50 25
522 – 60f. multicoloured 85 25
523 – 95f. multicoloured 1·30 40
524 – 100f. multicoloured 1·50 45
DESIGNS: 60f. to 100f. Various Congolese Women's hair-styles.

1976. 1st Central African Games, Yaounde. Multicoloured.
525 60f. Type **194** (postage) 75 30
526 95f. Long-jumping 1·30 60
527 150f. Running (air) 1·70 90
528 200f. Throwing the discus 2·75 1·20

195 Kob **196** Saddle-bill Storks ("Jabirus")

1976. Congolese Fauna. Multicoloured.
529 5f. Type **195** 50 10
530 10f. African buffaloes 55 10
531 15f. Hippopotami 85 35
532 20f. Warthog 1·20 45
533 25f. African elephants 1·30 50

1976. Birds. Multicoloured.
534 5f. Type **196** 95 30
535 10f. Shining-blue kingfisher ("Martin-Pecheur") (37 × 37 mm) 1·50 50
536 20f. Crowned cranes ("Grues Couronnees") (37 × 37 mm) 2·40 65

197 OAU Building on Map **198** Cycling

1976. Air. 13th Anniv of OAU.
537 **197** 60f. multicoloured 75 35

1976. Central African Games, Libreville. Mult.
538 35f. Type **198** 35 10
539 60f. Handball 60 25
540 80f. Running 1·00 45
541 95f. Football 1·30 60

199 "Nymphaea mierantha"

1976. Tropical Flowers. Multicoloured.
542 5f. Type **199** 20 10
543 10f. "Heliotrope" 35 10
544 15f. "Strelitzia reginae" 55 20

200 Pioneers' Emblem

1976. National Pioneers Movement.
545 **200** 35f. multicoloured 45 25

201 "Spirit of 76" (detail, A. M. Willard)

1976. Bicent of American Revolution. Mult.
546 100f. Type **201** . . . . 1·00 30
547 125f. Destruction of George III's statue . . . . 1·20 45
548 150f. Gunners-Battle of Princeton . . . . 1·60 60
549 175f. Wartime generals . . . 1·90 70
550 200f. Surrender of Gen. Burgoyne, Saratoga . . . 2·20 90
MS551 114 × 77 mm. 500f. "Battle of Lexington" (detail, W. Wollen) 5·50 2·20

202 Pirogue Race

1977. Pirogue Racing. Multicoloured.
552 35f. Type **202** 55 25
553 60f. Race in progress . . . . 1·00 55

203 Butter Catfish

1977. Freshwater Fishes. Multicoloured.
554 10f. Type **203** 40 10
555 15f. Big-eyed catfish 75 10
556 25f. Citharinid 95 25
557 35f. Mbessi mormyrid . . . 1·30 45
558 60f. "Mongandza" . . . . . 2·75 70

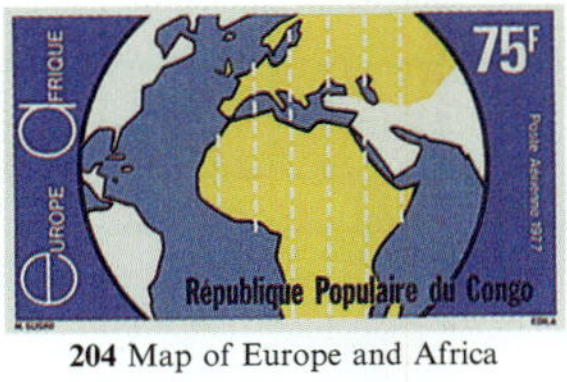

204 Map of Europe and Africa

1977. Air. Europafrique.
559 **204** 75f. multicoloured 95 60

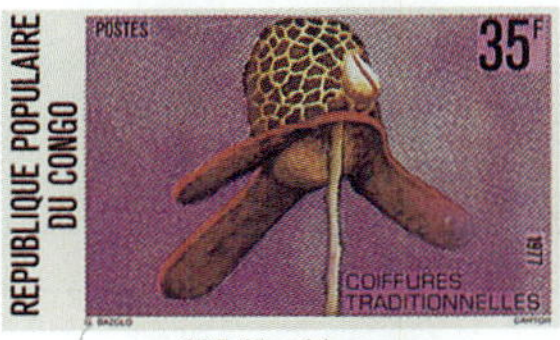

205 Headdress

1977. Traditional Headdresses. Multicoloured.
560 35f. Type **205** (postage) . . . 45 35
561 60f. Headdress with tail . . . 95 55
562 250f. Two headdresses (air) 3·00 1·80
563 300f. Headdresses with beads 3·50 2·20

206 Wrestling

1977. Bondjo Wrestling.
564 – 25f. multicoloured 45 10
565 **206** 40f. multicoloured 55 25
566 – 50f. multicoloured 75 45
DESIGNS—VERT: 25f., 50f. Different wrestling scenes.

207 "Schwaben", 1911

1977. History of the Zeppelin. Multicoloured.
567 40f. Type **207** (postage) . . . 50 25
568 60f. "Viktoria Luise", 1913 75 45
569 100f. "Bodensee" . . . . . . 1·10 45
570 200f. "Graf Zeppelin" . . . 2·00 70
571 300f. "Graf Zeppelin II" . . 3·50 1·00
MS572 104 × 92 mm. 500f. "Graf Zeppelin" LZ127 (different) (air) 6·75 2·20

208 Rising Sun of "Revolution"

1977. 14th Anniv of Revolution.
573 **208** 40f. multicoloured 55 25

209 "Flow of Trade"

1977. Air. GATT Trade Convention, Lome.
574 **209** 60f. black and red 95 45

210 Hugo and Scene from "Hunchback of Notre Dame"

1977. 175th Birth Anniv of Victor Hugo.
575 **210** 35f. brown, red and blue 55 35
576 – 60f. green, drab and blue 85 35
577 – 100f. brown, blue & red 1·50 60
DESIGNS: 60f. Scene from "Les Miserables"; 100f. Scene from "The Toilers of the Sea".

211 Newton and Constellations

1977. Air. 250th Death Anniv of Isaac Newton.
578 **211** 140f. mauve, green & brn 2·20 1·10

212 Mao Tse-tung

1977. 1st Death Anniv of Mao Tse-tung.
579 **212** 400f. gold and red . . . . 8·75 6·25

213 Rubens

1977. 400th Birth Anniv of Peter Paul Rubens.
580 **213** 600f. gold and blue . . . 9·50 6·75

214 Child leading Blind Person

1977. Fight Against Blindness.
581 **214** 35f. multicoloured 60 45

215 Paul Kamba and Records

1977. Paul Kamba (musician) Commemoration.
582 **215** 100f. multicoloured . . . 1·00 60

216 Trajan Vuia and his Vuia No. 1

1977. Aviation History. Multicoloured.
583 60f. Type **216** 55 25
584 75f. Bleriot and Bleriot XI over Channel 70 25
585 100f. Roland Garros and Morane Saulnier Type 1 95 55
586 200f. Lindbergh and "Spirit of St. Louis" . . . . . . 2·20 70
587 300f. Tupolev Tu-144 . . . . 3·00 90
MS588 116 × 91 mm. 500f. Lindbergh and "Spirit of St. Louis" over SS "Mauritania" 5·75 2·10

217 General de Gaulle

1977. Historic Personalities, and Silver Jubilee of Queen Elizabeth II. Multicoloured.
589 200f. Type **217** . . . . 2·20 45
590 200f. King Baudouin of Belgium . . . . 2·50 60
591 250f. Queen and Prince Philip in open car . . . . 2·30 90
592 300f. Queen Elizabeth . . . . 3·00 95
MS593 110 × 91 mm. 500f. Royal Family on balcony after Coronation (50 × 37 mm) (air) 5·50 1·90

218 Ambete Statue

1978. Congolese Sculpture.
594 **218** 35f. lake, brown & green 60 30
595 – 85f. brown, green & lake 1·30 75
DESIGN: 85f. Babembe statue.

219 "The Apostle Simon"

1978. 400th Birth Anniv of Peter Paul Rubens (2nd issue). Multicoloured.
596 60f. Type **219** 95 25
597 140f. "The Duke of Lerma" 1·50 40
598 200f. "Madonna and Saints" 2·20 65
599 300f. "The Artist and his Wife" . . . . 3·25 85
MS600 106 × 123 mm. 500f. "The Farm at Laeken" . . . . . . 6·00 2·10

220 Pres. Ngouabi making Speech

1978. 1st Death Anniv of President Marien Ngouabi.
601 **220** 35f. black, yellow & red 40 25
602 – 60f. multicoloured 55 45
603 – 100f. black, yellow & red 1·00 60
DESIGNS—HORIZ: 60f. Pres. Ngouabi at his desk. VERT: 100f. Portrait of Pres. Ngouabi.

221 Ferenc Puskas (Hungary)

1978. World Cup Football Championship, Argentina. Famous Players. Multicoloured.
604 60f. Type **221** 55 25
605 75f. Giacinto Facchetti (Italy) 75 25
606 100f. Bobby Moore (England) . . . . 1·00 45
607 200f. Raymond Kopa (France) . . . . 2·30 80
608 300f. Pele (Brazil) . . . . . 3·25 95
MS609 137 × 100 mm. 500f. Franz Beckenbauer (West Germany) 6·25 2·10

222 Pearl S. Buck (Literature, 1938)

1978. Nobel Prize Winners. Multicoloured.
610 60f. Type **222** 60 25
611 75f. Fridtjof Nansen and camp scene (Peace) 75 25
612 100f. Henri Bergson and "Elan Vita" (Literature) . . 1·00 50
613 200f. Alexander Fleming and penicillin (Medicine) . . . 2·00 90
614 300f. Gerhart Hauptmann and hands with book (Literature) . . . . 2·75 90
MS615 118 × 81 mm. 500f. Jean Henri Dunant (Peace, 1901) . . 6·00 2·75

223 Purple Heron **224** Okapi

1978. Air. Birds. Multicoloured.
616 65f. Mallard . . . . 1·20 60
617 75f. Type **223** . . . . 1·20 60
618 150f. Great reed warbler . . 3·00 1·10
619 240f. Hoopoe . . . . 4·50 1·90

1978. Endangered Animals. Multicoloured.
620 35f. Type **224** 85 35
621 60f. African buffalo (horiz) 1·70 50
622 85f. Black rhinoceros (horiz) 3·00 60
623 150f. Chimpanzee . . . . . 4·75 1·10
624 200f. Hippopotamus (horiz) 6·00 1·90
625 300f. Kob . . . . 9·25 2·30

225 Clenched Fist, Emblem and Crowd

1978. 11th World Youth and Students Festival, Havana, Cuba.
626 **225** 35f. multicoloured 55 40

226 Pyramids, Egypt

1978. The Seven Wonders of the Ancient World. Multicoloured.
627 35f. Type **226** 45 10
628 50f. Hanging Gardens of Babylon (vert) 45 10
629 60f. Statue of Zeus, Olympia (vert) 60 25
630 95f. Colossos of Rhodes (vert) 80 45
631 125f. Mausoleum, Halicarnassus (vert) . . . 1·20 45
632 150f. Temple of Artemis, Ephesus . . . . 1·60 55
633 200f. Pharos, Alexandria (vert) . . . . 2·00 60
634 300f. Map showing sites of the Seven Wonders . . . . 3·00 90

1978. 25th Anniv of Queen Elizabeth's Coronation. Nos. 591/**MS**593 optd **ANNIVERSAIRE DU COURONNEMENT 1953–1978**. Multicoloured.
635 250f. Queen and Prince Philip in open car . . . . 2·50 1·20
636 300f. Queen Elizabeth . . . 3·00 1·50
MS637 110 × 91 mm. 500f. Royal family on balcony after Coronation . . . . 4·50 3·50

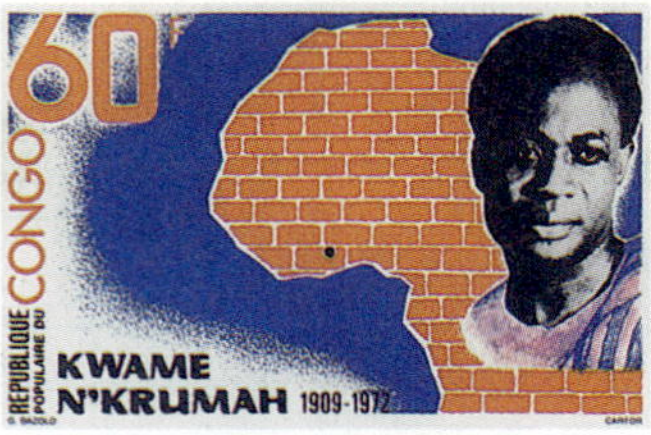

228 Kwame Nkrumah and Map of Africa

1978. Kwame Nkrumah (Ghanaian statesman) Commemoration.
638 **228** 60f. multicoloured 75 45

229 Hunting Wild Pigs

1978. Multicoloured.
639 35f. Type **229** . . . . 1·50 30
640 50f. Smoking fish 75 45
641 60f. Hunter with kill (vert) 2·30 40
642 140f. Woman hoeing (vert) 1·50 60

1978. Air. "Philexafrique" Stamp Exhibition, Libreville, Gabon (1st issue) and International Stamp Fair, Essen, West Germany. As T **237** of Benin. Multicoloured.
643 100f. Peregrine Falcon and Wurttemberg 1851 1k. stamp . . . . 2·00 1·40
644 100f. Leopard and Congo 1978 240f. stamp . . . . 2·00 1·40
See also Nos. 668/9.

230 Basket Weaving **232** Satellites, Antennae and Map of Africa

231 "Kalchreut"

1978. Occupations. Multicoloured.
645 85f. Type **230** 85 40
646 90f. Wood sculpture . . . . 1·00 60

1978. 450th Death Anniv of Albrecht Durer (artist). Multicoloured.
647 65f. Type **231** 65 30
648 150f. "Elspeth Tucher" . . . 1·40 60
649 250f. "Grasses" . . . . . . 2·40 90
650 350f. "Self-portrait" . . . . 3·50 1·10

1978. Air. Pan African Telecommunications.
651 **232** 100f. red, green & orange 1·30 70

1978. World Cup Winners Nos. 604/**MS**609 optd with names of past winners.
652 60f. multicoloured 55 25
653 75f. multicoloured 75 45
654 100f. multicoloured 95 60
655 200f. multicoloured . . . . . 2·20 80
656 300f. multicoloured . . . . . 3·00 1·40
MS657 137 × 100 mm. 500f. multicoloured . . . . 5·50 3·50
DESIGNS: 60f. **1962 VAINQUEUR: BRESIL**; 75f. **1966 VAINQUEUR GRANDE BRETAGNE**; 100f. **1970 VAINQUEUR ALLEMAGNE (RFA)**; 300f. **1978 VAINQUEUR ARGENTINA**; 500f. **ARGENTINE-PAYS BAS 3-1 25 juin 1978.**

234 Diseased Heart, Blood Pressure Graph and Circulation Diagram

1978. World Hypertension Year.
658 **234** 100f. brown, red & turq 1·20 60

235 Road to the Sun

1978. 9th Anniv of Congolese Workers' Party.
659 **235** 60f. multicoloured 60 25

236 Captain Cook and Native Feast

1979. Death Bicentenary of Captain James Cook. Multicoloured.
660 65f. Type **236** 75 25
661 150f. Easter Island monuments . . . . 1·80 40
662 250f. Hawaiian canoes . . . 2·75 80
663 350f. H.M.S. "Resolution" and H.M.S. "Adventure" at anchor . . . . 3·75 1·30

237 Pres. Ngouabi

1979. 2nd Anniv of Assassination of President Ngouabi.
664 **237** 35f. multicoloured 35 10
665 60f. multicoloured 55 25

238 IYC Emblem and Child

1979. International Year of the Child.
666 **238** 45f. multicoloured 45 25
667 75f. multicoloured 85 30

239 "Solanum torvum" and Earthenware Jars

1979. "Philexafrique" Stamp Exhibition, Libreville, Gabon (2nd issue).
668 **239** 60f. multicoloured . . . . 1·40 1·00
669 – 150f. orange, brn & grn 2·75 1·90
DESIGN: 150f. UPU emblem, Concorde airplane, postal runner and diesel locomotive.

240 Rowland Hill, Diesel Locomotive and German 5m. Stamp, 1900

1979. Death Centenary of Sir Rowland Hill. Multicoloured.
670 65f. Type **240** 75 10
671 100f. Steam locomotive and French "War Orphans" stamp of 1917 . . . . . . 1·00 45
672 200f. Diesel locomotive and U.S. Columbus stamp of 1893 . . . . 2·30 65
673 300f. Steam locomotive and England–Australia "First Aerial Post" vignette . . . 3·00 95
MS674 102 × 77 mm. 500f. Electric locomotive, Concorde and Middle Congo 45c. stamp, 1933 . . . 6·00 2·40

241 Pres. Salvador Allende

1979. Salvador Allende (former President of Chile) Commemoration.
675 **241** 100f. multicoloured . . . 1·00 55

242 "The Teller of Legends"

1979. African Folk Tales as Part of Children's Education.
676 **242** 45f. multicoloured 75 45

243 Handball Players **244** Map of Africa filled with Heads

1979. Marien Ngouabi Handball Cup. Mult.
677 45f. Type **243** 50 25
678 75f. Handball players 95 45
679 250f. Cup on map of Africa, player and Marien Ngouabi (vert) (22 × 37 mm) . . . . . . 2·40 1·20

1979. Air. 5th Pan-African Youth Conference, Brazzaville.
680 **244** 45f. multicoloured 55 25
681 75f. multicoloured 95 45

245 "Madonna with Joseph and Five Angels" (woodcut)

1979. 450th Death Anniv (1978) of Albrecht Durer (artist) (2nd issue). Sheet 89 × 115 mm.
MS682 **245** 500f. brown and green 6·25 2·20

246 Congo Map and Flag

1979. 16th Anniv of Revolution.
683 **246** 50f. multicoloured 55 25

247 Abala Peasant Woman

1979. Air.
684 **247** 150f. multicoloured . . . 2·00 1·00

248 IYC Emblem and Child

1979. International Year of the Child (2nd issue). Sheet 110 × 85 mm.
MS685 **248** 250f. multicoloured 2·75 1·20

249 Bach and Musical Instruments

1979. Personalities. Multicoloured.
686 200f. Type **249** . . . . 2·30 90
687 200f. Albert Einstein and astronauts on the Moon 2·30 90

250 Yoro

1979. Yoro Fishing Port. Multicoloured.
688 45f. Type **250** 60 25
689 75f. Yoro at night 95 45

251 Moukoukoulou Dam and Power Station

1979. Moukoukoulou Hydro-electric Power Station.
690 **251** 20f. multicoloured 45 25
691 45f. multicoloured 95 45

1979. Air. 10th Anniv of "Apollo 11" Moon Landing. Optd **ALUNISSAGE APOLLO XI JUILLET 1969**.
692 – 80f. blue, red and green (No. 388) 90 85
693 **173** 95f. blk, red & crimson 1·00 95
694 – 100f. brown, blue and red (No. 406) . . . . . . 1·00 95
695 – 100f. black, violet and blue (No. 461) . . . . 1·00 95
696 – 300f. blue, brown and red (No. 410) . . . . . 2·75 2·50

253 Fencer

1979. Air. Pre-Olympic Year (1st issue) Multicoloured.
697 65f. Runner, map of Africa and Olympic rings (horiz) 60 10
698 100f. Boxer (horiz) . . . . . 1·00 45
699 200f. Type **253** . . . . 2·00 60
700 300f. Footballer (horiz) . . . 3·00 80
701 500f. Olympic emblem . . . 4·75 1·70
See also Nos. 716/9.

254 ASECNA Emblem and Douglas DC-10

1979. 20th Anniv of ASECNA (African Air Safety Organization).
702 **254** 100f. multicoloured . . . 1·10 60

255 Party Emblem Workers and Flowers

1979. 10th Anniv of Congolese Workers' Party.
703 **255** 45f. multicoloured 55 25

256 Cross-country Skiing **257** Emblem and Globe

1979. Air. Winter Olympic Games, Lake Placid (1980). Multicoloured.
704 40f. Type **256** 40 10
705 60f. Slalom 70 25
706 200f. Ski-jump . . . . 2·00 75
707 350f. Downhill skiing (horiz) 3·50 1·40
708 500f. Skier (vert, 31 × 46 mm) 4·75 1·90

1980. 15th Anniv of National Posts and Telecommunications Office.
709 **257** 45f. multicoloured 45 25
710 95f. multicoloured 95 35

1980. Air. Winter Olympic Games Medal Winners. Nos. 704/8 optd with names of winners.
711 40f. Cross-country skiing . . 40 10
712 60f. Slalom 70 25
713 200f. Ski jump . . . . 2·00 85
714 350f. Downhill skiing . . . . 3·50 1·60
715 500f. Skier . . . . 4·75 2·20
OVERPRINTS: 40f. **VAINQUEUR ZIMIATOV U.R.S.S.**; 60f. **VAINQUEUR MOSERPROELL Autriche**; 200f. **VAINQUEUR TOMANEN Finlande**; 350f. **VAINQUEUR STOCK AUTRICHE**; 500f. **VAINQUEURS STENMARK-WENZEL**.

259 Long jump **260** Pope John Paul II

1980. Air. Olympic Games, Moscow.
716 **259** 75f. multicoloured 85 10
717 – 150f. mult (horiz) . . . . 1·50 40
718 – 250f. multicoloured . . . 2·30 60
719 – 350f. multicoloured . . . 3·25 75
MS720 103 × 78 mm. 500f. multicoloured (horiz) . . . . . 4·75 2·10
Nos. 717/**MS**720 show different view of the long jump.

1980. Papal Visit.
721 **260** 100f. multicoloured . . . 2·00 70

261 Rotary Emblem

1980. 75th Anniv of Rotary International.
722 **261** 150f. multicoloured . . . 1·50 55

262 Glass Works

1980. Pointe Noire Glass Works. Multicoloured.
723 30f. Type **262** 30 25
724 35f. Glass works (different) 55 45

263 Claude Chappe and Semaphore Tower

1980. Claude Chappe Commemoration.
725 **263** 200f. multicoloured . . . 2·50 1·50

264 Real Madrid Stadium

1980. Air. World Cup Football Championship, Spain (1982). Multicoloured.
726 60f. Type **264** 55 10
727 75f. Real Zaragoza 75 25
728 100f. Atletico de Madrid . . 1·00 45
729 150f. Valencia C.F. . . . . . 1·40 40
730 175f. R.C.D. Espanol . . . . 2·00 45
MS731 104 × 79 mm. 250f. F.C. Barcelona stadium . . . . . . 2·20 1·10

265 Floating Quay

1980. Port of Mossaka. Multicoloured.
732 45f. Type **265** 45 25
733 90f. Aerial view of port . . . 1·00 55

266 "Crucifixion"

1980. Air. Paintings by Rembrandt. Multicoloured.
734 65f. "Adoration of the Shepherds" (detail) (horiz) 65 25
735 100f. "Entombment" (horiz) 1·00 45
736 200f. "Christ at Emmaus" (horiz) . . . . 2·00 60
737 300f. "Annunciation" . . . . 3·00 80
738 500f. Type **266** . . . . . . 5·50 1·40

267 Jacques Offenbach (composer) **268** "Papilio dardanus"

1980. Air. Death Anniversaries. Multicoloured.
739 100f. Albert Camus (writer) (20th anniv) . . . . . . 1·30 65
740 150f. Type **267** (centenary) 2·20 1·40

1980. Butterflies. Multicoloured.
741 5f. Type **268** 45 10
742 15f. "Kallima aethiops" . . . 90 20
743 20f. "Papilio demodocus" . . 90 25
744 60f. "Euphaedra" . . . . . 2·40 60
745 90f. "Hypolimnas misippus" 4·50 75
MS746 120 × 80 mm. 300f. "Charaxes smaragdalis" . . . 15·00 10·00

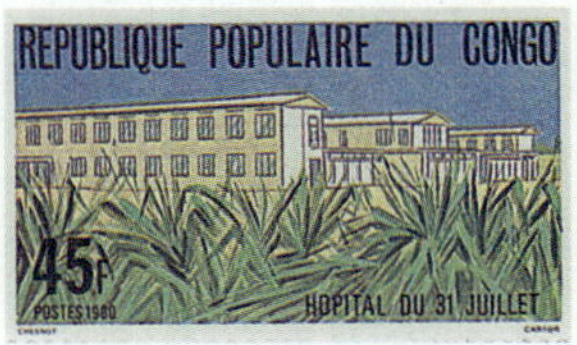

269 Hospital

1980. "31 July" Hospital.
747 **269** 45f. multicoloured 60 25

270 Man presenting Human Rights Charter

1980. 32nd Anniv of Human Rights Convention. Multicoloured.
748 350f. Type **270** . . . . 3·00 1·60
749 500f. Man breaking chains 4·50 2·50

271 Raffia Dancing Skirts

1980. Air. Traditional Dancing Costumes. Mult.
750 250f. Type **271** . . . . . . 3·00 1·10
751 300f. Tam-tam dancers (vert) 3·25 1·70
752 350f. Masks . . . . 4·25 2·20

272 Clenched Fists, Flag and Dove **273** Coffee and Cocoa Trees on Map of Congo

1980. 17th Anniv of Revolution. Multicoloured.
753 75f. Citizens and State emblem (36 × 23 mm) . . . 75 35
754 95f. Type **272** 95 45
755 150f. Dove carrying state emblem (36 × 23 mm) . . . 1·40 80

1980. Coffee and Cocoa Day. Multicoloured.
756 45f. Type **273** 50 25
757 95f. Coffee and cocoa beans 1·00 60

274 Cut Logs

1980. Forest Exploitation. Multicoloured.
758 70f. Type **274** 80 45
759 75f. Lorry with logs 80 45

275 President Neto

1980. 1st Death Anniv of President Neto.
760 **275** 100f. multicoloured . . . 95 45

276 Olive-bellied Sunbird ("Souimanga Olivatre")

1980. Birds. Multicoloured.
761 45f. Type **276** 85 45
762 75f. Red-crowned bishop ("Travailleur a Tete Rouge") . . . . 1·00 40
763 90f. Moorhen ("Poule d'Eauafricaine") . . . . . 1·40 55
764 150f. African pied wagtail ("Alouette Canelle") . . . 2·20 70
765 200f. Yellow-mantled whydah (vert) . . . . 3·00 1·40
766 250f. "Geai-bleu" (vert) . . . 3·50 1·60
MS767 148 × 105 mm. Nos. 761/6 26·00 18·00

277 Conference Emblem

1980. World Tourism Conference, Manila.
768 **277** 100f. multicoloured . . . 95 55

278 Child Writing

1980. Return to School.
769 **278** 50f. multicoloured 55 25

279 The First House

1980. Brazzaville Centenary.
770 **279** 45f. ochre, grey & brown 50 25
771 – 65f. lt brown, brn & orge 75 45
772 – 75f. multicoloured . . . . 1·00 60
773 – 150f. multicoloured . . . 1·80 1·20
774 – 200f. multicoloured . . . 2·30 1·70
DESIGNS: 65f. First native village; 75f. The old Town Hall; 150f. Brazzaville from the Bacongo Promontory, 1912; 200f. Meeting between Savorgnan de Brazza (explorer) and Makoko (local chieftain).

280 Cataracts

1980. The River Congo. Multicoloured.
775 80f. Type **280** . . . . 1·00 55
776 150f. Bridge at Djoue . . . . 1·80 80

1980. Air. Olympic Medal Winners. Nos. 716/19 optd.
777 75f. **DOMBROWSKI (RDA)** 75 45
778 150f. **SANEIEV (URSS)** . . 1·40 80
779 250f. **SIMEONI (IT)** . . . . 2·40 1·20
780 350f. **THOMPSON (GB)** . . 3·50 1·70
MS781 103 × 78 mm. 500f. **UUDMAE (URSS)** . . . . . 4·75 4·25

282 Stadium and Sportsmen

1980. Revolutionary Stadium. Heroes of Congolese Sport.
782 **282** 60f. multicoloured 75 45

283 New Railway Bridge

1980. Realignment of Railway.
783 **283** 75f. multicoloured 95 45

284 Mangoes

1980. Loudima Fruit Station. Multicoloured.
784 10f. Type **284** 30 10
785 25f. Oranges 50 10
786 40f. Lemons 60 25
787 85f. Mandarins . . . . . . 1·10 40

1980. 5th Anniv of African Posts and Telecommunications Union. As T **269** of Benin.
788 100f. multicoloured 95 45

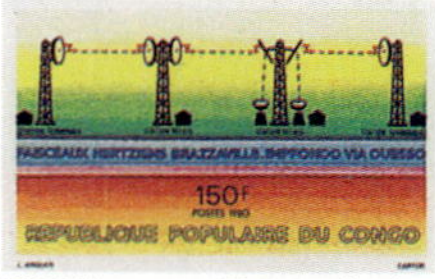

285 Microwave Communication

1980. Communications. Multicoloured.
789 75f. Moungouni Earth Station (36 × 36 mm) . . . 75 40
790 150f. Type **285** . . . . 1·50 55

286 Presentation of Marien Ngouabi Handball Cup

1981. African Handball Champions. Mult.
791 100f. Type **286** . . . . 1·30 40
792 150f. Team members . . . . 1·50 70

287 Pres. Sassou-Nguesso

1981. President Sassou-Nguesso.
793 **287** 45f. multicoloured 45 20
794 75f. multicoloured 70 25
795 100f. multicoloured . . . 95 50

288 Space Shuttle

1981. Conquest of Space. Multicoloured.
796 100f. "Luna 17" . . . . . . 1·00 25
797 150f. Type **288** . . . . 1·50 40
798 200f. Satellite and space shuttle . . . . 1·90 60
799 300f. Space shuttle approaching landing strip 2·75 85
MS800 103 × 79 mm. 500f. Space shuttle launch . . . . 5·00 1·70

289 Head and Dove **290** Twin Palm Tree

1981. Anti-Apartheid Campaign.
801 **289** 100f. blue 95 40

1981. The Twin Palm Tree of Louingui.
802 **290** 75f. multicoloured . . . . 1·00 45

291 Bird approaching Snare

1981. Traditional Snares and Traps. Mult.
803 5f. Type **291** 10 10
804 10f. Bird in snare (vert) . . . 10 10
805 15f. Rodent approaching snare 35 20
806 20f. Rodent in snare 35 20
807 30f. Sprung trap 45 30
808 35f. Deer approaching trap 45 30

292 Human Figure and Caduceus

1981. World Telecommunications Day.
809 **292** 120f. multicoloured . . . 1·30 40

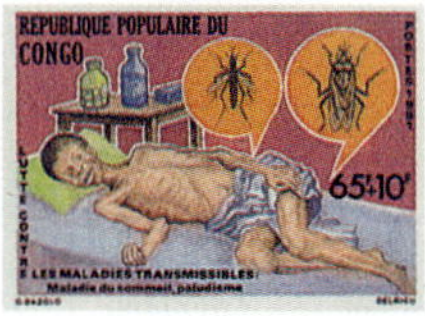

293 Sleeping Sickness and Malaria Victim

1981. Campaign against Transmissible Diseases. Multicoloured.
810 40f.+5f. Doctor, nurse, patients and mosquito . . 60 25
811 65f.+10f. Type **293** . . . . . 1·00 60

294 Collecting Rubber

1981. Rubber Extraction. Multicoloured.
812 50f. Tapping rubber tree . . 60 25
813 70f. Type **294** 95 45

295 Helping a Disabled Person

1981. International Year of Disabled People.
814 **295** 45f. blue, purple & red . . 45 25
815 – 75f.+5f. multicoloured . . 95 60
DESIGN: 75f. Disabled people superimposed on globe.

296 "The Studio"

1981. Air. Birth Centenary of Pablo Picasso. Multicoloured.
816 100f. Type **296** . . . . 1·20 45
817 150f. "Landscape Land and Sea" . . . . 1·80 60
818 200f. "The Studio at Cannes" 2·30 80
819 300f. "Still-life with Water Melon" . . . . 4·00 1·20
820 500f. "Large Still-life" . . . 6·50 2·00

297 King Maloango and Mausoleum

1981. Mausoleum of King Maloango. Mult.
821 75f. Mausoleum 75 25
822 150f. Type **297** . . . . 1·50 60

298 Prince Charles, Lady Diana Spencer and Coach

1981. Wedding of Prince of Wales. Mult.

823	100f. Type **298**	1·00	50
824	200f. Couple and Landau	1·90	70
825	300f. Couple and horses	3·00	1·10
MS826	103 × 78 mm. 400f. Couple and ornament	4·00	1·50

299 Preparing Food

1981. World Food Day.

827 **299**	150f. multicoloured	1·70	70

300 Bird carrying Letter

1981. Universal Postal Union Day.

828 **300**	90f. blue, red and grey	95	30

301 Guardsman

1981. Royal Guard.

829 **301**	45f. multicoloured	60	25

302 Spraying Cassava

1981. Campaign for the Control of Cassava Beetle.

830 **302**	75f. multicoloured	1·20	40

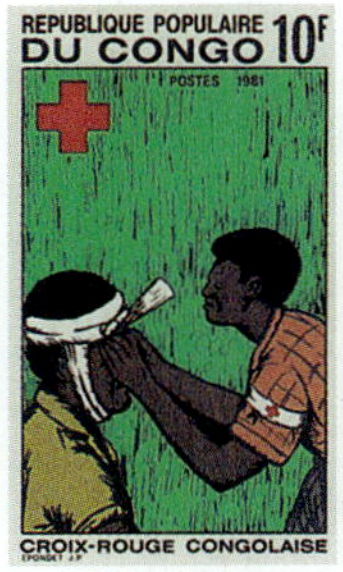

303 Bandaging a Patient

305 Fetish

304 Brazza's Tree

1981. Red Cross. Multicoloured.

831	10f. Type **303**	10	10
832	35f. Inoculating a young girl	45	25
833	60f. Nurse and villagers	65	40

1981. Tree of Brazza.

834 **304**	45f. multicoloured	85	25
835	75f. multicoloured	1·10	35

1981. Fetishes.

836 **305**	15f. multicoloured	10	10
837 –	25f. multicoloured	30	10
838 –	45f. multicoloured	45	10
839 –	50f. multicoloured	60	25
840 –	60f. multicoloured	75	45

DESIGNS: 25f. to 60f. Different fetishes.

306 Bangou Caves

1981. Bangou Caves.

841 **306**	20f. multicoloured	45	25
842	25f. multicoloured	45	25

307 "Congolese Coiffure"

1982. Ivory Sculptures by R. Engongodzo. Multicoloured.

843	25f. Type **307**	35	10
844	35f. "Congo Coiffure" (different)	40	10
845	100f. "King Makoko, his Queen and Counsellor" (horiz)	1·00	45

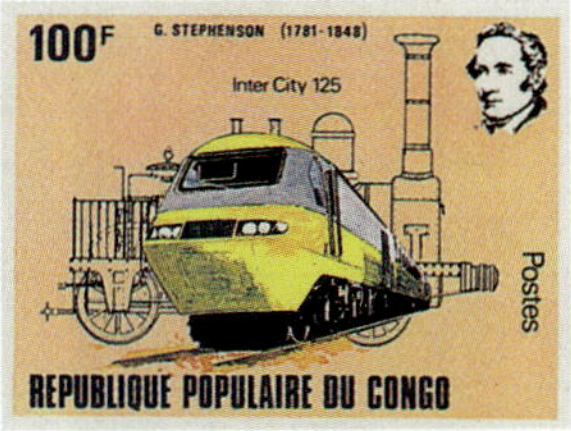

308 "Patentee" and Inter-City 125 Express Train, Great Britain

1982. Birth Bicentenary (1981) of George Stephenson (railway engineer). Multicoloured.

846	100f. Type **308**	1·00	45
847	150f. "Hikari" express train, Japan	1·60	55
848	200f. Advanced Passenger Train (APT), Great Britain	2·20	70
849	300f. TGV 001 locomotive, France	3·25	1·10

309 Scout with Binoculars

1982. 75th Anniv of Boy Scout Movement. Multicoloured.

850	100f. Type **309**	1·00	35
851	150f. Scout reading map	1·50	45
852	200f. Scout talking to village woman	1·90	60
853	300f. Scouts on rope bridge	2·75	80
MS854	96 × 70 mm. 500f. Scouts (horiz)	5·25	1·50

310 Franklin D. Roosevelt

1982. Anniversaries. Multicoloured.

855	150f. Type **310** (birth cent)	1·60	55
856	250f. George Washington on horseback (250th birth anniv)	2·20	80
857	350f. Johann von Goethe (writer) (150th death anniv)	3·25	1·00

311 Princess of Wales and Candles

1982. 21st Birthday of Princess of Wales. Mult.

858	200f. Type **311**	2·10	60
859	300f. Princess and "21"	2·75	80
MS860	112 × 80 mm. 500f. Princess within picture frame	4·75	1·50

312 Road Building

1982. Five Year Plan. Multicoloured.

861	60f. Type **312**	85	45
862	100f. Telecommunications	1·20	60
863	125f. Operating theatre equipment	1·50	70
864	150f. Hydro-electric project	2·00	95

313 Dish Antenna

1982. ITU Delegates' Conference, Nairobi.

865 **313**	300f. multicoloured	3·00	1·40

314 Mosque, Medina

1982. Air. 1350th Death Anniv of Mohammed.

866 **314**	400f. multicoloured	4·25	1·90

315 WHO Regional Office

1982. World Health Organization Regional Office, Brazzaville.

867 **315**	125f. multicoloured	1·20	60

316 Mother feeding Baby

1982. Health Campaign.

868 **316**	100f. multicoloured	1·00	55

1982. Birth of Prince William of Wales. Nos. 823/**MS**826 optd **NAISSANCE ROYALE 1982**.

869	100f. multicoloured	95	50
870	200f. multicoloured	1·80	90
871	300f. multicoloured	2·75	1·40
MS872	103 × 78 mm. 400f. multicoloured	3·75	3·50

318 Dr. Robert Koch and Bacillus

1982. Centenary of Discovery of Tubercle Bacillus.

873 **318**	250f. multicoloured	3·25	1·40

1982. World Cup Football Championship Results. Nos. 724/28 optd.

874	60f. **EQUIPE QUATRIEME FRANCE**	45	25
875	75f. **EQUIPE TROISIEME POLOGNE**	75	45
876	100f. **EQUIPE SECONDE ALLEMAGNE (RFA)**	1·00	60
877	150f. **EQUIPE VAINQUEUR/ITALIE**	1·40	70
878	175f. **ITALIE–ALLEMAGNE (RFA) 3 1**	2·00	90
MS879	104 × 79 mm. 250f. As No. 878	2·50	2·30

320 Pres. Sassou-Ngeusso and Prize

1982. Award of 1980 Simba Prize to Pres. Sassou-Nguesso.

880 **320**	100f. multicoloured	95	45

321 Turtle

1982. Turtles.

881 **321**	30f. multicoloured	50	25
882 –	45f. multicoloured	85	45
883 –	55f. multicoloured	1·00	65

DESIGNS: 45, 55f. Different turtles.

322 Amelia Earhart and "Friendship"

1982. 50th Anniv of Amelia Earhart's Transatlantic Flight.

884 **322**	150f. lt brown, grn & brn	1·80	90

323 "La Malafoutier" **324** Grey Parrots nesting in Hole in Tree

1982.
885 **323** 100f. multicoloured . . . 1·20 40

1982. Birds' Nests. Multicoloured.
886 40f. Type **324** 95 25
887 75f. Palm tree and nest . . . 1·60 45
888 100f. Nest hanging from branch . . . . 2·40 60

325 Map of Network

1982. Hertzian Wave Network.
889 **325** 45f. multicoloured 45 25
890 60f. multicoloured 55 25
891 95f. multicoloured . . . . 1·00 40

326 Council Headquarters, Brussels

1983. 30th Anniv of Customs Co-operation Council.
892 **326** 100f. multicoloured . . . 95 45

327 Marien N'Gouabi Mausoleum

1983.
893 **327** 60f. multicoloured . . . . 1·00 25
894 80f. multicoloured 85 45

328 Raffia Weaving

1983.
895 **328** 150f. multicoloured . . . 1·50 70

329 Chess Pieces

1983. Chess Pieces Carved by R. Engongonzo. Multicoloured.
896 40f. Type **329** 45 25
897 60f. Close-up of white pawn, king, queen and bishop . . 75 45
898 95f. Close-up of black rook, bishop, queen and king . . 1·40 70

330 Blacksmiths

1983.
899 **330** 45f. multicoloured 55 25

331 Study for "The Transfiguration"

1983. Easter. 500th Birth Anniv of Raphael. Multicoloured.
900 200f. Type **331** . . . . 2·30 60
901 300f. "Deposition from the Cross" (horiz) . . . . . . 3·25 85
902 400f. "Christ in his Glory" 4·00 1·20

332 Comb **333** "Pila ovata"

1983. Traditional Combs. Multicoloured.
903 30f. Type **332** 35 10
904 70f. Comb (different) 90 25
905 85f. Three combs . . . . . . 1·00 60

1983. Shells. Multicoloured.
905a 25f. Charonia lampas . . .
906 35f. Type **333** 90 35
907 65f. True achatina . . . . . 1·30 50

334 Windsurfing

1983. Air. Pre-Olympic Year.
908 **334** 100f. multicoloured . . . 95 30
909 – 200f. mult (horiz) . . . . 1·80 60
910 – 300f. multicoloured . . . 2·75 85
911 – 400f. multicoloured . . . 3·75 1·20
MS912 104 × 80 mm. 500f. multicoloured (horiz) . . . . 4·50 1·50
DESIGNS: 200 to 500f. Various windsurfing scenes.

335 Montgolfier Balloon, 1783 **336** Hands holding Gun and Pick

1983. Air. Bicentenary of Manned Flight. Mult.
913 100f. Type **335** . . . . 1·50 25
914 200f. Montgolfier balloon "Le Flesselles", 1784 . . . 2·50 60
915 300f. Auguste Piccard's stratosphere balloon "F.N.R.S.", 1931 . . . . 3·25 85
916 400f. Modern hot-air balloon 4·50 1·20
MS917 79 × 100 mm. 500f. Paris siege balloon, 1870 . . . . . . 5·75 1·80

1983. 20th Anniv of Revolution.
918 **336** 60f. multicoloured 45 25
919 100f. multicoloured . . . 95 45

337 Mgr. A. Carrie and Church of the Sacred Heart, Loango

1983. Centenary of Evangelism. Multicoloured.
920 150f. Type **337** . . . . 1·60 70
921 250f. Mgr. Augouard and St. Joseph's Church, Linzolo . . . . 2·75 1·20

338 Thunbergia

1984. Flowers. Multicoloured.
922 5f. Type **338** 10 10
923 15f. Bougainvillaea (horiz) . . 35 10
924 20f. Anthurium 45 10
925 45f. Allamanda (horiz) . . . 80 25
926 75f. Hibiscus . . . . 1·20 60

339 "Virgin and Child with St. John"

1984. Air. Christmas. Paintings by Botticelli. Multicoloured.
927 150f. Type **339** . . . . 1·50 55
928 350f. "Virgin and Child" (St. Barnabas) . . . . . . 3·25 1·20
929 500f. "Virgin and Child" . . 5·00 1·70

340 "Vase of Flowers" (Manet)

1984. Air. Paintings. Multicoloured.
930 100f. Type **340** . . . . 1·00 35
931 200f. "The Small Holy Family" (Raphael) . . . . 1·90 65
932 300f. "La Belle Jardiniere" (detail) (Raphael) . . . . 2·75 1·00
933 400f. "The Virgin of Lorette" (Raphael) . . . . 3·75 1·40
934 500f. "Richard Wagner" (Giuseppe Tivoli) . . . . . 4·75 1·70

341 Peace Dove

1984. 34th Anniv of World Peace Council.
935 **341** 50f. multicoloured 45 25
936 100f. multicoloured . . . 95 45

342 Judo

1984. Air. Olympic Games, Los Angeles. Mult.
937 45f. Type **342** 45 10
938 75f. Judo (different) (horiz) 75 25
939 150f. Wrestling (horiz) . . . 1·50 50
940 175f. Fencing (horiz) . . . . 1·60 60
941 350f. Fencing (different) (horiz) . . . . 3·50 1·20
MS942 103 × 80 mm. 500f. Boxing 4·75 2·30

343 Mushroom Cloud

1984. Campaign against Weapons of Mass Destruction.
943 **343** 200f. black, brown & orge 1·80 70

344 Rice

1984. Agriculture. Multicoloured.
944 10f. Type **344** 10 10
945 15f. Pineapples 10 10
946 60f. Manioc (vert) 60 25
947 100f. Palms (vert) . . . . . 1·20 45

345 Congress Palace

1984. Chinese–Congolese Co-operation.
948 **345** 60f. multicoloured 55 25
949 100f. multicoloured . . . 95 40

346 Loulombo Station

1984. 50th Anniv of Congo Railways. Mult.
950 10f. Type **346** 20 10
951 25f. Chinese workers' camp at Les Bandas 40 30
952 125f. "50" forming bridge and tunnel . . . . 1·70 1·00
953 200f. Headquarters building 3·75 1·40

347 Alsthom CC203 Diesel Locomotive

1984. Transport. Multicoloured. (a) Locomotives.

954	100f. Type **347**	1·20	45
955	150f. Alsthom BB 103 diesel	1·80	65
956	300f. Diesel locomotive No. BB BB 301	3·75	1·40
957	500f. BB420 diesel train "L'Eclair"	5·25	2·00
	(b) Ships.		
958	100f. Pusher tug	1·20	45
959	150f. Pusher tug (different)	1·60	65
960	300f. Buoying boat	3·25	1·40
961	500f. "Saint" (freighter)	5·25	2·10

348 Giant Ground Pangolin

1984. Animals. Multicoloured.

962	30f. Type **348**	2·40	70
963	70f. Bat	5·25	1·30
964	85f. African civet	6·75	1·80

Nos. 962/4 are inscribed "1983".

349 Fish in Basket

1984. World Fisheries Year. Multicoloured.

965	5f. Type **349**	35	10
966	20f. Casting nets	50	10
967	25f. Fishes	50	10
968	40f. Men pulling nets in	85	40
969	55f. Boat net and fishes	1·40	55

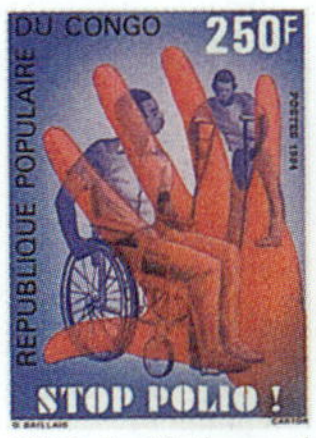

350 Polio Victims and Hand **351** M'bamou Palace Hotel, Brazzaville

1984. Anti-polio Campaign. Multicoloured.

970	250f. Type **350**	2·75	1·20
971	300f. Polio victims within target	3·25	1·70

1984.

972 **351**	60f. multicoloured	45	25
973	100f. multicoloured	95	25

352 S. van den Berg, Windsurfing

1984. Air. Olympic Games Yachting Gold Medal Winners. Multicoloured.

974	100f. Type **352**	1·00	40
975	150f. U.S.A., "Soling" class (horiz)	1·50	60
976	200f. Spain, "470" dinghy (horiz)	2·00	90
977	500f. U.S.A., "Flying Dutchman" two-man dinghy	4·50	2·00

353 Floating Logs

1984. Floating Logs on River Congo. Mult.

978	60f. Type **353**	60	25
979	100f. Logs and boat on river	1·40	55

354 "The Holy Family" **355** "Zonocerus variegatus"

1985. Air. Christmas. Multicoloured.

980	100f. Type **354**	1·00	40
981	200f. "Virgin and Child" (G. Bellini) (horiz)	1·90	85
982	400f. "Virgin and Child with Angels" (Cimabue)	3·75	1·70

1985.

983 **355**	125f. multicoloured	1·60	55

1985. International Exhibitions. Nos. **MS**800, **MS**854, **MS**912 and **MS**917 optd.
MS984 (a) 500f. **TSUKUBA EXPO '85**; (b) 500f. **Italia'85 ROME** and emblem; (c) 500f. **OLYMPHILEX '85 LAUSANNE** and emblem; (d) 500f. **MOPHILA '85 HAMBOURG** . . . 5·50 5·50

357 Black-headed Grosbeaks

1985. Air. Birth Bicentenary of John J. Audubon (ornithologist). Multicoloured.

985	100f. Type **357**	1·00	45
986	150f. Scarlet ibis	1·60	65
987	200f. Red-tailed hawk (horiz)	2·30	90
988	350f. Labrador duck	4·00	1·50

358 Funeral Procession

1985. Burial of Teke Chief.

989 **358**	225f. multicoloured	2·30	1·00

359 Mother weighing Child

1985. "Philexafrique" Stamp Exhibition, Lome, Togo (1st issue). Multicoloured.

990	200f. Type **359**	2·75	2·00
991	200f. Boy writing and man ploughing field	2·75	2·00

See also Nos. 1004/5.

360 "Trichoscypha acuminata" **361** Brazzaville Lions Club Pennant

1985. Fruits. Multicoloured.

992	5f. Type **360**	10	10
993	10f. "Aframomum africanum"	10	10
994	125f. "Gambeya lacuurtiana"	1·30	60
995	150f. "Landolphia jumelei"	1·70	80

1985. 30th Anniv of Lions Club.

996 **361**	250f. multicoloured	2·75	1·00

362 Moscow Kremlin, Soldier and Battlefield

1985. 40th Anniv of End of World War II.

997 **362**	60f. multicoloured	60	25

363 Doves forming Heart

1985. Air. 25th Anniv of U.N. Membership.

998 **363**	190f. multicoloured	1·80	85

365 Girl Guide with Yellow-bellied Wattle-eye (International Youth Year)

1985. Anniversaries and Events. Multicoloured.

999	150f. Type **365**	1·60	65
1000	250f. Jacob Grimm (folklorist) and scene from "Snow White and the Seven Dwarfs" (birth bicentenary) (International Youth Year)	2·30	1·10
1001	350f. Johann Sebastian Bach (composer) and organ (300th birth anniv) (European Music Year)	3·00	1·30
1002	450f. Queen Elizabeth, the Queen Mother (85th birthday) (vert)	3·75	1·70
1003	500f. Statue of Liberty (centenary) (vert)	4·75	2·10

366 Construction Equipment within Heads and Building

1985. "Philexafrique" Stamp Exhibition, Lome, Togo (2nd issue). Multicoloured.

1004	250f. Type **366**	2·75	2·00
1005	250f. Loading mail at airport	2·75	2·00

367 Emblem and Rainbow

1985. Air. 40th Anniv of UNO.

1006 **367**	180f. multicoloured	1·80	70

368 "Coprinus"

1985. Fungi. Multicoloured.

1007	100f. Type **368**	1·60	40
1008	150f. "Cortinarius"	2·30	65
1009	200f. "Armillariella mellea"	3·00	75
1010	300f. "Dictyophora"	3·75	1·20
1011	400f. "Crucibulum vulgare"	5·50	1·70

369 "Virgin and Child" (Gerard David)

1985. Air. Christmas. Multicoloured.

1012	100f. Type **369**	1·00	35
1013	200f. "Adoration of the Magi" (Hieronymus Bosch)	1·90	70
1014	400f. "Virgin and Child" (Anthony Van Dyck) (horiz)	3·75	1·60

370 Edmond Halley and Computer Picture of Comet

1986. Air. Appearance of Halley's Comet. Multicoloured.

1015	125f. Type **370**	1·00	45
1016	150f. West's Comet, 1976 (vert)	1·60	55
1017	225f. Ikeya-Seki Comet, 1965 (vert)	2·30	85
1018	300f. "Giotto" space probe and comet trajectory	2·75	1·10
1019	350f. Comet and "Vega" space probe	2·75	1·30

371 President planting Sapling **372** Boys and Hoops with Handles

1986. National Tree Day. Multicoloured.
1020 60f. Type **371** 50 25
1021 200f. Map, tree and production of oxygen and carbon dioxide . . . . . 2·10 85

1986. Children's Hoop Races. Multicoloured.
1022 5f. Type **372** 10 10
1023 10f. Boy with hoop on string 10 10
1024 60f. Boys racing with hoops (horiz) 75 25
MS1025 150 × 200 mm. Nos. 1022/4 1·60 1·60

373 Cosmos-Frantel Hotel

1986. Air.
1026 **373** 250f. multicoloured . . . 2·30 1·00

375 Emptying Rubbish into Dustbin **376** Woman carrying Basket on Head

1986. World Environment Day. Multicoloured.
1030 60f. Type **375** 60 25
1031 125f. Woman dumping rubbish in street . . . . 1·30 50

1986. Traditional Methods of Carrying Goods. Multicoloured.
1032 5f. Type **376** 10 10
1033 10f. Woman carrying basket at back held by rope from head 10 10
1034 60f. Man carrying wood on shoulder 75 50

377 Footballers

1986. Air. World Cup Football Championship, Mexico.
1035 **377** 150f. multicoloured . . . 1·40 60
1036 – 250f. multicoloured . . . 2·50 1·00
1037 – 440f. multicoloured . . . 4·00 1·70
1038 – 600f. multicoloured . . . 6·25 2·40
DESIGNS: 250f. to 600f. Various football scenes.

378 Sisters tending Patients

1986. Centenary of Sisters of St. Joseph of Cluny Mission.
1039 **378** 230f. multicoloured . . . 2·75 1·50

379 Programme Emblem **380** Emblem

1986. International Communications Development Programme.
1040 **379** 40f. multicoloured . . . 45 25
1041 60f. multicoloured . . . 55 45
1042 100f. multicoloured . . . 1·00 60

1986. International Peace Year.
1043 **380** 100f. blue, grn & lt grn 1·00 50

381 Foodstuffs

1986. World Food Day. Multicoloured.
1044 75f. Type **381** 80 45
1045 120f. Woman spoon-feeding child . . . . 1·30 60

382 Woman holding Child and Windmill with Medical Symbols **383** Douglas DC-10 and "25" on Map

1986. UNICEF Child Survival Campaign. Multicoloured.
1046 15f. Type **382** 10 10
1047 30f. Children (horiz) 30 25
1048 70f. Woman and child . . . 90 50

1986. Air. 25th Anniv of Air Afrique.
1049 **383** 200f. multicoloured . . . 2·10 95

384 Lenin **386** "Virgin and Child"

385 Men's Slalom

1986. 27th U.S.S.R. Communist Party Congress.
1050 **384** 100f. multicoloured . . . 1·40 60

1986. Air. Winter Olympic Games, Calgary (1988). Multicoloured.
1051 150f. Type **385** . . . . . . 1·40 60
1052 250f. Four-man bobsleigh (vert) . . . . 2·50 1·00
1053 440f. Ladies cross-country skiing (vert) . . . . . . 4·00 1·50
1054 600f. Ski-jumping . . . . . 6·00 2·30

1986. Air. Christmas. Paintings by Rogier van der Weyden. Multicoloured.
1055 250f. Type **386** . . . . . . 2·30 1·00
1056 440f. "Nativity" . . . . . . 4·25 1·70
1057 500f. "Virgin of the Pink" 5·00 1·70

387 "Osteolaemus tetraspis"

1987. Air. Crocodiles. Multicoloured.
1058 75f. Type **387** . . . . 1·90 40
1059 100f. "Crocodylus cataphractus" . . . . . . 2·30 60
1060 125f. "Osteolaemus tetraspis" (different) . . . 2·75 75
1061 150f. "Crocodylus cataphractus" (different) 3·25 1·30

388 Pres. Sassou-Nguesso and Map **389** Traditional Marriage Ceremony

1987. Election of Pres. Sassou-Nguesso as Chairman of Organization of African Unity.
1062 **388** 30f. multicoloured . . . 30 10
1063 45f. multicoloured . . . 45 10
1064 75f. multicoloured . . . 80 30
1065 120f. multicoloured . . . 1·30 45

1987.
1066 **389** 5f. multicoloured 10 10
1067 15f. multicoloured . . . 20 10
1068 20f. multicoloured . . . 30 10

390 "Sputnik"

1987. Air. 30th Anniv of First Artificial Space Satellite.
1069 **390** 60f. multicoloured . . . 55 25
1070 240f. multicoloured . . . 2·40 1·40

391 Starting Back-stroke Race

1987. Air. Olympic Games, Seoul (1988) (1st issue). Swimming. Multicoloured.
1071 100f. Type **391** 95 40
1072 200f. Freestyle . . . . . . 1·80 75
1073 300f. Breast-stroke . . . . 2·75 1·10
1074 400f. Butterfly . . . . . . 3·75 1·50
MS1075 104 × 80 mm. 750f. Start of women's race . . . . 6·25 4·00
See also Nos. 1121/**MS**1125.

392 Blue Lake, National Route 2

1987.
1076 **392** 5f. multicoloured 10 10
1077 15f. multicoloured . . . 10 10
1078 75f. multicoloured . . . 1·00 50
1079 120f. multicoloured . . . 1·50 75

393 Flags and Pres. Ngouabi **395** Emblem

394 "Precis almanta"

1987. 10th Death Anniv of President Marier Ngouabi.
1080 **393** 75f. multicoloured . . . 80 20
1081 120f. multicoloured . . . 1·30 40

1987. Butterflies. Multicoloured.
1082 75f. "Precis epicleli" . . . . 1·00 35
1083 120f. "Deilephila nerii" . . 1·70 55
1084 450f. "Euryphene senegalensis" . . . . . . 5·00 1·70
1085 550f. Type **394** . . . . . . 6·50 2·40

1987. African Men of Science Congress.
1086 **395** 15f. multicoloured . . . 10 10
1087 90f. multicoloured . . . 90 60
1088 230f. multicoloured . . . 2·30 95

396 Fist and Broken Manacle **397** Hands putting Money into Pot within Map

1987. Anti-Apartheid Campaign. Multicoloured.
1089 60f. Type **396** 60 25
1090 240f. Chain forming outline of map, Nelson Mandela and bars (26 × 38 mm) . . 2·50 1·20

1987. African Fund.
1091 **397** 25f. multicoloured . . . 30 10
1092 50f. multicoloured . . . 45 10
1093 70f. multicoloured . . . 80 25

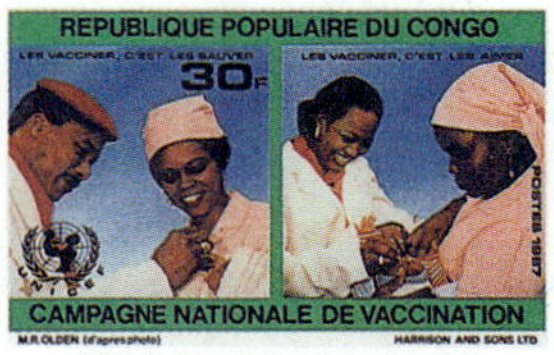

398 Babies being Vaccinated

1987. National Vaccination Campaign. Mult.
1094 30f. Type **398** (postage) . . 30 10
1095 45f. Doctor vaccinating child (vert) 75 45
1096 500f. Queue waiting for vaccination (air) . . . . 5·25 3·50

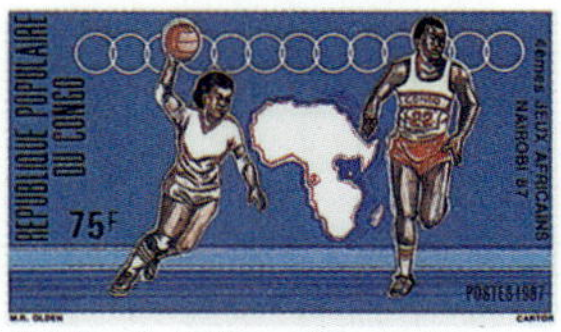

399 Handball Player, Map and Runner

1987. 4th African Games, Nairobi.
1097 **399** 75f. multicoloured . . . 80 50
1098 120f. multicoloured . . . 1·30 75

400 Follereau

1987. 10th Death Anniv of Raoul Follereau (leprosy pioneer).
1099 **400** 120f. multicoloured . . . 1·60 75

401 Coubertin and Greece 1896 1d. Stamp

1987. Air. 50th Death Anniv of Pierre de Coubertin (founder of modern Olympic games). Multicoloured.
1100 75f. Type **401** 80 30
1101 120f. Runners and France 1924 10c. stamp . . . . . 1·20 45
1102 350f. Congo 1964 100f. stamp and hurdler . . . . 3·50 1·40
1103 600f. High jumper and Congo 1968 85f. stamp 5·50 2·30

402 Basket of Produce and Hands holding Ears of Wheat

1987. 40th Anniv of FAO.
1104 **402** 300f. multicoloured . . . 2·75 1·50

403 Hillside Farming and Produce within "2000"

1987. "Food Self-sufficiency by Year 2000".
1105 **403** 20f. multicoloured . . . 30 10
1106 55f. multicoloured . . . 70 20
1107 100f. multicoloured . . . 1·00 55

404 Simon Kimbangu

406 Writer crossing through "Apartheid"

405 Lenin inspecting Parade in Red Square

1987. Birth Centenary of Simon Kimbangu (founder of Church of Jesus Christ on Earth). Multicoloured.
1108 75f. Type **404** 75 30
1109 120f. Kimbangu feeding grey parrot . . . . 1·20 50
1110 240f. Kimbanguiste Temple, Nkamba (horiz) . . . . . 2·75 1·50
MS1111 160 × 100 mm. Nos. 1108/10 5·50 4·25

1988. 70th Anniv of Russian Revolution.
1112 **405** 75f. multicoloured . . . 1·80 85
1113 120f. multicoloured . . . 2·40 1·40

1988. African Anti-Apartheid Writers.
1114 **406** 15f. multicoloured . . . 10 10
1115 60f. multicoloured . . . 55 25
1116 75f. multicoloured . . . 80 45

407 Schweitzer and Hospital

1988. Air. 75th Anniv of Arrival at Lambarene of Dr. Albert Schweitzer (missionary).
1117 **407** 240f. multicoloured . . . 3·00 1·40

408 Samuel Morse

1988. 150th Anniv of Morse Telegraph. Mult.
1118 90f. Type **408** 90 40
1119 120f. Morse and telegraph equipment . . . . 1·20 60

409 Banknote and Field within "10"

1988. 10th Anniv of International Agricultural Development Fund.
1120 **409** 240f. multicoloured . . . 2·30 1·10

1988. Air. Olympic Games, Seoul (2nd issue). Modern Pentathlon. As T **391**. Multicoloured.
1121 75f. Swimming 80 30
1122 170f. Cross-country running (vert) . . . . 1·80 60
1123 200f. Shooting . . . . . . 2·00 75
1124 600f. Horse-riding . . . . . 5·50 2·10
MS1125 104 × 80 mm. 750f. Fencing 7·00 3·00

411 Eucalyptus Plantation, Brazzaville

412 Hands holding Gun and Pick

1988. Anti-desertification Campaign. Mult.
1126 5f. Type **411** 40 10
1127 10f. Stop sign and man chopping down tree . . . 40 10

1988. 25th Anniv of Revolution. Multicoloured.
1128 75f. Type **412** 80 30
1129 75f. People tending crops . . . 80 30
1130 120f. Pres. Sassou-Nguesso holding aubergine . . . . 1·00 45

413 Yoro Fishing Village

1988.
1131 35f. Type **413** 45 25
1132 40f. Place de la Liberte . . 45 25

414 People on Map and Jet Fighters attacking Virus

1988. 1st International Day against AIDS.
1133 **414** 60f. multicoloured . . . 45 25
1134 – 75f. multicoloured . . . 75 45
1135 – 180f. black, red & blue 1·80 90
DESIGNS: 75f. Virus consisting of healthy and infected people; 180f. Globe and laurel branches.

415 Pres. Sassou-Nguesso addressing Crowd

1989. 10th Anniv of 5 February Movement. Multicoloured.
1136 75f. Type **415** 80 30
1137 120f. Pres. Sassou-Nguesso and symbols of progress 1·00 55

416 Emblems

1989. 40th Anniv of Declaration of Human Rights.
1138 **416** 120f. multicoloured . . . 1·00 55
1139 350f. multicoloured . . . 2·75 1·50

417 Bari

1989. Air. World Cup Football Championship, Italy (1990) (1st issue). Multicoloured.
1140 75f. Type **417** 75 30
1141 120f. Rome . . . . 1·20 45
1142 500f. Florence . . . . . . 5·00 1·60
1143 550f. Naples . . . . 5·50 1·90
See also Nos. 1174/7.

418 "Storming of the Bastille" (detail, J. P. Houel)

1989. Air. "Philexfrance 89" International Stamp Exhibition. Multicoloured.
1144 300f. Type **418** (bicent of French revolution) . . . 3·00 1·30
1145 400f. "Eiffel Tower" (G. Seurat) (centenary of Eiffel Tower (1986)) . . . 4·00 1·50

419 Astronaut and Landing Module

1989. Air. 20th Anniv of First Manned Landing on Moon. Multicoloured.
1146 400f. Type **419** . . . . . . 4·00 1·50
1147 400f. Astronaut on lunar surface . . . . 4·00 1·50

420 Marien Ngouabi

1989. 50th Birth Anniv (1988) of Marien Ngouabi (President, 1969–77).
1148 **420** 240f. black, yell & mve 2·30 85

421 Henri Dunant (founder), Volunteer with Child and Anniversary Emblem
422 Emblem on Dove

1989. 125th Anniv (1988) of Red Cross.
1149 75f. Type **421** (postage) . . 1·00 45
1150 120f. Emblem, Dunant and Congolese Red Cross station (air) . . . . . . 1·20 60

1989. 25th Anniv of Organization of African Unity.
1151 **422** 120f. multicoloured . . . 1·20 40

423 "Opuntia phaeacantha"

1989. Cacti. Multicoloured.
1152 35f. Type **423** 35 10
1153 40f. "Opuntia ficus-indica" 50 10
1154 60f. "Opuntia erinacea" (horiz) 75 20
1155 75f. "Opuntia rufida" . . . 1·10 35
1156 120f. "Opuntia leptocaulis" (horiz) . . . . 1·50 50
MS1157 55 × 79 mm. 220f. "Opuntia compresa" (30 × 39 mm) . . . 3·75 2·30

424 Banknote, Coins and Woman

1989. 25th Anniv of African Development Bank.
1158 **424** 75f. multicoloured . . . 85 45
1159 120f. multicoloured . . . 1·20 40

425 Ice Dancing

1989. Winter Olympic Games, Albertville (1992) (1st issue). Multicoloured.
1160 75f. Type **425** 60 20
1161 80f. Cross-country skiing . . 60 30
1162 100f. Speed skating . . . . 1·00 35
1163 120f. Luge . . . . 1·20 50
1164 200f. Slalom . . . . 2·00 65
1165 240f. Ice hockey . . . . . 2·20 80
1166 400f. Ski jumping . . . . . 3·75 1·30
MS1167 80 × 62 mm. 500f. Four-man bobsleigh (31 × 36 mm) . . 4·50 2·50
See also Nos. 1245/**MS**1247.

426 Doctor examining Patient
427 Emblem and People with raised Fists

1989. 40th Anniv of WHO. Multicoloured.
1168 60f. Type **426** 80 45
1169 75f. Blood donation (vert) . . . 1·00 70

1989. 20th Anniv of Congolese Workers' Party.
1170 **427** 75f. multicoloured . . . 80 45
1171 120f. multicoloured . . . 1·30 45

1990. Local Health Campaigns. Nos. 1168/9 optd **NOTRE PLANETE, NOTRE SANTE PENSER GLOBALEMENT AGIR LOCALEMENT.**
1172 60f. multicoloured 80 60
1173 75f. multicoloured . . . . . 1·00 85

429 Footballers

430 Family supporting Open Book

1990. Air. World Cup Football Championship, Italy (2nd issue). Designs showing footballers.
1174 **429** 120f. multicoloured . . . 1·20 40
1175 – 240f. multicoloured . . . 2·40 90
1176 – 500f. multicoloured . . . 4·50 1·70
1177 – 600f. multicoloured . . . 5·50 2·10

1990. International Literacy Year.
1178 **430** 75f. black, yellow & blue 80 45

431 Ramblas, Barcelona

1990. Olympic Games, Barcelona (1992) (1st issue). Multicoloured.
1179 100f. Type **431** (postage) . . 95 35
1180 150f. Yachting (horiz) . . . 1·30 45
1181 200f. Yachting (different) (horiz) . . . . 1·90 60
1182 240f. Market stalls, Barcelona (horiz) . . . . 2·10 90
1183 350f. Harbour, Barcelona (horiz) (air) . . . . . . 1·40 3·25
1184 500f. Monument, Barcelona 3·25 4·25
MS1185 90 × 117 mm. 750f. Barcelona Cathedral . . . . . 6·75 1·70
See also Nos. 1328/**MS**1334.

432 Turtle Dove ("Tourterelle des bois")

1990. Birds. Multicoloured.
1186 25f. Type **432** 35 20
1187 50f. Dartford warbler ("Fauvette Pitchou") (vert) 60 35
1188 70f. Common kestrel ("Faucon Crecerelle") (vert) . . . . 1·00 60
1189 150f. Grey parrot ("Perroquet Gris") (vert) 1·90 1·30

433 Mondo Mask

435 Sunflower

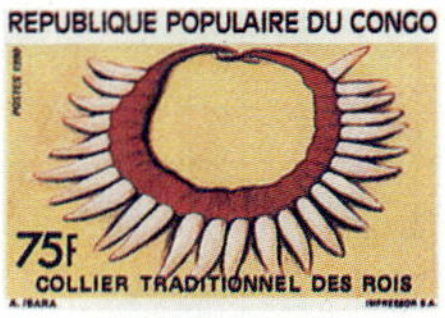

434 Necklace

1990. Dance Masks. Multicoloured.
1190 120f. Type **433** . . . . . . 1·20 70
1191 360f. Bapunu mask . . . . 3·50 1·50
1192 400f. Kwele mask . . . . . 4·00 1·70

1990. Traditional Royal Necklaces. Multicoloured.
1193 75f. Type **434** 80 45
1194 100f. Money cowrie necklace 1·10 80

1990. Flowers. Multicoloured.
1195 30f. Type **435** 30 10
1196 45f. "Cassia alata" (horiz) 45 25
1197 75f. Opium poppy 80 30
1198 90f. "Acalypha sanderil" . . 1·00 45

436 Hot-air Balloon dropping Envelopes on Africa

437 The Blusher

1991. Air. 10th Anniv of Pan-African Postal Union. Multicoloured.
1199 60f. Type **436** 55 40
1200 120f. Envelopes on map of Africa . . . . 1·00 60

1991. Fungi. Multicoloured.
1201 30f. Type **437** 35 10
1202 45f. "Catathelasma imperiale" 45 30
1203 75f. Caesar's mushroom . . 85 35
1204 90f. Royal boletus . . . . 1·00 45
1205 120f. Deer mushroom . . . 1·30 45
1206 150f. "Boletus chrysenteron" 1·80 65
1207 200f. Horse mushroom . . . 2·40 85
MS1208 79 × 70 mm. 350f. "Boletus versipellis" (39 × 31 mm) . . . 6·00 2·10

438 Type Dr-16 Diesel Locomotive, Finland

1991. Trains. Multicoloured.
1209 60f. Type **438** 65 20
1210 75f. TGV express, France 75 30
1211 120f. Suburban S-350 electric railcar, Italy . . . 1·30 40
1212 200f. Type DE 24000 diesel locomotive, Turkey . . . 2·20 75
1213 250f. DE 1024 diesel-electric locomotive, Germany . . 3·25 1·00
MS1214 90 × 65 mm. 350f. "ETR-450", Italy (31 × 39 mm) 6·00 1·50

439 Canoe, Palm Tree and Setting Sun

440 Congolese Woman

1991. International African Tourism Year. Multicoloured.
1215 75f. Type **439** 80 45
1216 120f. Zebra and map of Africa . . . . 1·30 75

1991.
1217 **440** 15f. blue 10 10
1218 30f. green 30 10
1219 60f. yellow 35 25
1220 75f. mauve 55 30
1221 120f. brown . . . . . . 1·00 50

441 Christopher Columbus (after Sebastian del Pombo)

442 "Kalanchoe pinnata"

1991. 500th Anniv (1992) of Discovery of America by Columbus. Multicoloured.
1222 20f. Type **441** 35 10
1223 35f. Christopher Columbus 35 10
1224 40f. Christopher Columbus (different) 45 35
1225 55f. "Santa Maria" 65 35
1226 75f. "Nina" 90 35
1227 150f. "Pinta" . . . . 1·70 85
1228 200f. Arms and signature of Columbus . . . . 2·20 1·00

1991. Medicinal Plants. Multicoloured.
1229 15f. "Ocimum viride" (horiz) 10 10
1230 20f. Type **442** 30 10
1231 30f. "Euphorbia hirta" (horiz) 30 10
1232 60f. "Catharantheus roseus" 50 35
1233 75f. "Bidens pilosa" 70 45
1234 100f. "Brillantasia patula" 1·20 60
1235 120f. "Cassia occidentalis" 1·30 95

443 Route Map

1991. Centenary of Trans-Siberian Railway. Mult.
1236 120f. Type **443** . . . . . 1·50 75
1237 240f. Russian Class N steam locomotive superimposed on map . . . . 3·00 1·50

444 Honey fungus

1991. Scouts, Butterflies and Fungi. Mult.
1238 35f. "Euphaedra eusemoides" (butterfly) (postage) 55 35
1239 40f. Type **444** 65 35
1240 75f. "Palla decius" (butterfly) 85 35
1241 80f. "Kallima ansorgei" (butterfly) . . . . 1·10 40
1242 500f. "Cortinarius speciocissimus" (fungus) (air) . . . . 4·50 1·40
1243 600f. "Graphium illyris" (butterfly) . . . . 5·50 1·50
MS1244 99 × 68 mm. 750f. "Volvariella bombycina" (fungus) 5·75 2·75

445 Ice Hockey

1991. Air. Winter Olympic Games, Albertville (1992) (2nd issue). Multicoloured.
1245 120f. Type **445** . . . . . 1·50 70
1246 300f. Speed skating . . . . 3·25 1·00
MS1247 117 × 72 mm. 750f. Slalom skiing . . . . 7·50 1·80

446 "Telecom 91"

1991. "Telecom 91" World Telecommunications Exhibition, Geneva. Multicoloured.
1248 75f. Type **446** 80 45
1249 120f. Stylized view of exhibition (vert) . . . . . 1·30 75

447 Beetle and Peanuts

448 Woman drinking at Waterfall

1991. Harmful Insects. Multicoloured.
1250 75f. Type **447** 90 45
1251 120f. Stag beetle (horiz) . . 1·40 60
1252 200f. Beetle and coffee . . . 2·20 1·00
1253 300f. Goliath beetle . . . . 3·25 1·70

1991. "Water is Life".
1254 **448** 75f. multicoloured . . . 80 45

449 Pintail

450 Breaking Chain and Hand holding Dove

1991. Wild Ducks. Multicoloured.
1255 75f. Type **449** 95 45
1256 120f. Eider (vert) . . . . . 1·40 60
1257 200f. Common shoveler (vert) . . . . 2·10 1·10
1258 240f. Mallard . . . . 2·75 1·40

1991. 30th Anniv of Amnesty International. Multicoloured.
1259 40f. Candle, barbed wire and sun 45 25
1260 75f. Type **450** 80 45
1261 80f. Boy holding human rights banner and soldiers threatening boy (horiz) . . 1·00 55

451 1891 5c. on 1c. "Commerce" stamp

1991. Centenary of Congolese Stamps.
1262 **451** 75f. green and brown . . 80 60
1263 – 120f. dp brn, grn & brn 1·50 1·10
1264 – 240f. multicoloured . . . 2·75 1·90
1265 – 500f. multicoloured . . . 5·00 3·50
DESIGNS: 120f. 1900 1c. "Leopard in ambush" stamp; 240f. 1959 25f. "Birth of the Republic" stamp; 500f. "Commerce", "Leopard" and "Republic" stamps.

452 Ferrari "512 S"

1991. Cars and Space. Multicoloured.
1266 35f. Type **452** (postage) . . 35 10
1267 40f. Vincenzo Lancia and Lancia "Stratos" 45 10
1268 75f. Airship "Graf Zeppelin", Maybach "Type 12" car and Wilhelm Maybach 85 45
1269 80f. Mars space probe . . . 85 45

1270 500f. "Magellan" space probe over Venus (air) . . 5·00 1·10
1271 600f. "Ulysses" space probe photographing sun spot 6·25 1·30
MS1272 125 × 87 mm. 750f. Crew of "Apollo 11" (60 × 42 mm) . . 7·25 2·20

453 Small Blue

1991. Butterflies. Multicoloured.
1273 75f. Type **453** . . . . . . 1·00 45
1274 120f. Charaxes . . . . . . 1·30 65
1275 240f. Leaf butterfly (vert) . . 2·50 1·20
1276 300f. Butterfly on orange (vert) . . . . 3·25 2·10

454 General De Gaulle

1991. De Gaulle and Africa. Multicoloured.
1277 75f. Type **454** . . . . . . 1·00 50
1278 120f. De Gaulle, soldiers and Free French flag (vert) . . . . 1·30 75
1279 240f. De Gaulle making speech, Brazzaville, 1940 2·50 1·50

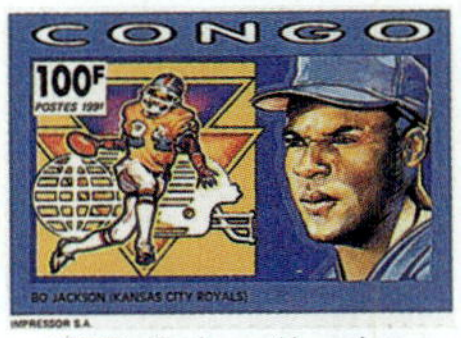

455 Bo Jackson (American footballer)

1991. Celebrities and International Organizations. Multicoloured.
1280 100f. Type **455** . . . . . 1·00 35
1281 150f. Nick Faldo (golfer) . . 1·50 35
1282 200f. Rickey Henderson and Barry Bonds (baseball players) . . . . 2·00 55
1283 240f. Gary Kasparov (World chess champion) 2·75 60
1284 300f. Starving child and Lions International and Rotary International emblems . . . . 3·00 70
1285 350f. Wolfgang Amadeus Mozart (composer) . . . 3·75 80
1286 400f. De Gaulle and Churchill visiting the Eastern Front, 1944 . . . 4·50 90
1287 500f. Henry Dunant (founder of Red Cross) 5·00 1·10
MS1288 106 × 74 mm. 750f. President De Gaulle (35 × 51 mm) 8·75 3·00

456 Painting

1991. Paintings. Multicoloured.
1289 75f. Type **456** 80 40
1290 120f. Couple in silhouette (vert) . . . . 1·30 60

457 Diana Monkey

1991. Primates. Multicoloured.
1291 30f. Type **457** 35 10
1292 45f. Chimpanzee 45 10
1293 60f. Gelada (vert) 85 15
1294 75f. Hamadryas baboon (vert) . . . . 1·10 35
1295 90f. Pigtail macaque (vert) 1·40 50
1296 120f. Gorilla (vert) . . . . 1·70 50
1297 240f. Mandrill (vert) . . . 3·50 80
MS1298 99 × 67 mm. 250f. Young gorilla (31 × 39 mm) . . . . . 4·00 1·40

458 "Sputnik 2" and Laika (space dog)

1992. Celebrities, Anniversaries and Events. Mult.
1299 50f. Type **458** (35th anniv of space flight) (postage) . . 85 25
1300 75f. Martin Luther King (Nobel Peace Prize winner, 1964) and Gandhi 85 25
1301 120f. Meteosat "MOP-2" and "ERS-1" satellites, globe and stern trawler ("Europe-Africa") . . . . 1·30 40
1302 300f. Konrad Adenauer (German statesman, 25th death anniv) and crowd before Brandenburg Gate (3rd anniv of opening of Berlin Wall) . . . . . . 2·75 75
1303 240f. "Graf Zeppelin", Ferdinand von Zeppelin (75th death anniv) and Maybach Zeppelin motor car (air) . . . . 3·00 85
1304 500f. Pope and globe (Papal visit to Africa) . . . . . . 5·50 1·40
MS1305 97 × 75 mm. 600f. Elvis Presley (entertainer, 15th death anniv) . . . . 6·25 2·30

459 Juan de la Cosa and Map

460 Secretary Bird

1992. "Genova 92" International Thematic Stamp Exhibition. Multicoloured.
1306 75f. Type **459** . . . . 1·10 35
1307 95f. Martin Alonso Pinzon and astrolabe . . . . . . 1·30 35
1308 120f. Alonso de Ojeda and hourglass . . . . 2·00 35
1309 200f. Vicente Yanez Pinzon and sun clock . . . . . . 2·75 50
1310 250f. Bartholomew Columbus and quadrant 3·75 60
MS1311 55 × 81 mm. 400f. Christopher Columbus (40 × 31 mm) . . . . 6·50 1·50

1992. Birds. Multicoloured.
1312 60f. Type **460** . . . . 1·20 35
1313 75f. Saddle-bill stork . . . 1·50 35
1314 120f. Wattled crane . . . . 2·00 35
1315 200f. Black-headed heron . . 3·50 60
1316 250f. Greater flamingo . . . 4·50 85
MS1317 60 × 84 mm. 400f. South African crowned crane (39 × 31 mm) . . . . 6·75 1·60

461 Lion

462 "Madonna of the Grand Duke" (Raphael)

1992. Big Cats. Multicoloured.
1318 45f. Type **461** 55 55
1319 60f. Tiger 65 60
1320 75f. Lynx 75 70
1321 95f. Caracal 85 80
1322 250f. Ocelot . . . . 2·40 2·20
MS1323 90 × 64 mm. 400f. Cheetah (31 × 39 mm) . . . . 7·50 1·80

1992. Christmas. Multicoloured.
1324 95f. Type **462** . . . . 1·20 50
1325 200f. "Madonna of the Book" (Sandro Botticelli) 2·50 90
1326 250f. "Carondelet Madonna" (Fra Bartolommeo) . . . . 3·00 1·70
MS1327 59 × 81 mm. 400f. "Madonna of the Chair" (Raphael) (31 × 39 mm) . . . . 4·50 2·40
No. 1325 is wrongly inscribed "Boticelli" and No. 1326 "Bartolomeo".

463 Baseball and Towers of Church of the Holy Family

464 N. Mishkutienok and A. Dmitriev (Unified Team)

1992. Olympic Games, Barcelona (2nd issue). Multicoloured.
1328 75f. Type **463** (postage) . . 80 20
1329 100f. Running and "The Muses" (Eusebio Arnau) 1·00 35
1330 150f. Hurdling and painted dome (Miguel Barcelo) of Market Theatre . . . . . 1·50 45
1331 200f. High jumping and Sant Pau hospital . . . . 2·20 75
1332 400f. Putting the shot and "Miss Barcelona" (Joan Miro) (air) . . . . . . 3·75 90
1333 500f. Table tennis and "Don Juan of Austria" (galley) 5·00 1·30
MS1334 104 × 80 mm. 750f. Tennis and Church of the Holy Family (Gaudi) (29 × 50 mm) . . . . 7·25 1·50

1992. Winter Olympic Games Gold Medal Winners. Multicoloured.
1335 150f. Type **464** (pairs figure skating) (postage) . . . . 1·40 35
1336 200f. Austrian team (four-man bobsleighing) . . . . 1·80 55
1337 500f. Gunda Niemann (Germany, women's speed skating) (air) . . . . . . 5·00 1·10
1338 600f. Bjorn Daehlie (Norway, 50 km cross-country skiing) . . . . . . 6·25 1·30
MS1339 118 × 83 mm. 750f. Alberto Tomba (Italy, giant slalom) (35 × 50 mm) . . . . 7·25 1·70
No. 1338 is wrongly inscribed "Blorn Daehlle".

465 African Red-tailed Buzzard ("Charognard")

467 Topi

466 Overhead Volley

1993. Birds of Prey. Multicoloured.
1340 45f. Type **465** 90 35
1341 75f. Ruppell's griffon ("Vautour") . . . . . . 1·40 60
1342 120f. Verreaux's eagle ("Aigle") . . . . 2·20 1·00

1993. World Cup Football Championship, U.S.A. (1994).
1343 **466** 75f. multicoloured . . . 1·30 50
1344 – 95f. multicoloured . . . 1·40 75
1345 – 120f. multicoloured . . . 2·20 95
1346 – 200f. multicoloured . . . 3·25 1·40
1347 – 250f. multicoloured . . . 3·75 1·90
MS1348 87 × 61 mm. 400f. multicoloured . . . . 6·75 3·25
DESIGNS: 95f. to 400f. Different footballing scenes.

1993. Animals. Multicoloured.
1349 60f. Type **467** 80 15
1350 75f. Grant's gazelle . . . . 1·20 15
1351 95f. Quagga . . . . 1·40 30
1352 120f. Leopard . . . . 1·90 30
1353 200f. African buffalo . . . 2·75 45
1354 250f. Hippopotamus . . . . 3·50 45
1355 300f. Hooded vulture . . . 4·25 45
1356 350f. Lioness and cub . . . 4·75 75
Nos. 1349/56 were issued together, se-tenant, forming a composite design.

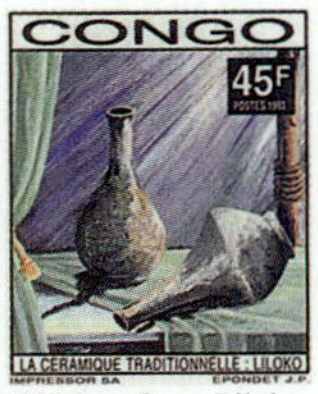

468 Jars from Liloko

1993. Traditional Pottery. Multicoloured.
1357 45f. Type **468** 60 30
1358 75f. Jug from Mbeya . . . 95 50
1359 120f. Jar from Mbeya . . . 1·40 85

470 Show Jumping

1993. Summer Olympic Games, Atlanta (1996) and Winter Olympic Games, Lillehammer, Norway (1994). Multicoloured.
1366 50f. Type **470** (postage) . . 1·10 30
1367 75f. Cycling . . . . 1·10 15
1368 120f. Two-man dinghy . . . 1·10 30
1369 240f. Fencing . . . . 2·10 60
1370 300f. Hurdling (air) . . . . 2·20 85
1371 400f. Figure skating . . . . 2·50 85
1372 500f. Basketball . . . . . . 3·50 1·20
1373 600f. Ice hockey . . . . . . 4·25 1·20
MS1374 Two sheets. (a) 101 × 71 mm. 750f. Running; (b) 138 × 101 mm. 750f. Skiing . . 7·50 1·50

471 "Hibiscus schizopetalus"

1993. Wild Flowers. Multicoloured.
1375 75f. Type **471** 95 25
1376 95f. "Pentas lanceolata" . . 1·30 45
1377 120f. "Ricinus communis" . . 2·20 45
1378 200f. "Delonix regia" . . . 3·75 85
1379 250f. "Stapelia gigantea" . . 4·50 1·40

OFFICIAL STAMPS

O 68 Arms

1968.
O142 **O 68** 1f. multicoloured . . . 10 10
O143 2f. multicoloured . . . 10 10
O144 5f. multicoloured . . . 10 10
O145 10f. multicoloured . . 30 15
O146 25f. multicoloured . . 30 25
O147 30f. multicoloured . . 70 25
O148 50f. multicoloured . . 95 35
O149 85f. multicoloured . . 2·30 90
O150 100f. multicoloured . . 2·50 1·40
O151 200f. multicoloured . . 3·50 2·30

POSTAGE DUE STAMPS

D 7 Letter-carrier

1961. Transport designs.
D19 **D 7** 50c. bistre, red & blue 10 10
D20 – 50c. bistre, purple & bl 10 10
D21 – 1f. brown, red & green 10 10
D22 – 1f. green, red and lake 10 10
D23 – 2f. brown, green & bl . . 10 10
D24 – 2f. brown, green & bl . . 10 10
D25 – 5f. sepia and violet . . 30 25
D26 – 5f. sepia and violet . . 30 25

D27 – 10f. brown, blue & grn . . . 75 70
D28 – 10f. brown and green . . 75 70
D29 – 25f. brown, blue & turq . 1·60 1·50
D30 – 25f. black and blue . . . 1·60 1·50

DESIGNS: D20, Holste Broussard monoplane; D21, Hammock-bearers; D22, "Land Rover" car; D23, Pirogue; D24, River steamer of 1932; D25, Cyclist; D26, Motor lorry; D27, Steam locomotive, 1932; D28, Diesel locomotive; D29, Seaplane of 1935; D30, Boeing 707 airliner.

1971. Tropical Flowers. Similar to T **105**, but inscr "Timbre-Taxe". Multicoloured.
D264 1f. Stylized bouquet 25 20
D265 2f. "Phaeomeria magnifica" 30 25
D266 5f. "Millettia laurentii" . . 35 30
D267 10f. "Polianthes tuberosa" 50 45
D268 15f. "Pyrostegia venusta" 80 75
D269 20f. "Hibiscus rosa sinensis" . . . . 1·10 1·00

D **374** Passion Flower

1986. Flowers and Fruit. Multicoloured.
D1027 5f. Type D **374** 20 20
D1028 10f. Canna lily 40 35
D1029 15f. Pineapple 45 40

APPENDIX

The following stamps have either been issued in excess of postal needs or have not been available to the public in reasonable quantities at face value. Such stamps may later be given full listing if there is evidence of regular postal use.

All embossed on gold foil

1991.

Scout and Butterfly. Air 1500f.

Winter Olympic Games, Albertville (1992). Air 1500f.

1992.

Olympic Games, Barcelona. Air 1500f.

CONGO DEMOCRATIC REPUBLIC (EX ZAIRE) Pt. 14

In May 1997 Zaire changed its name to the Democratic Republic of Congo after President Mobutu and his Government was overthrown by a rebellion led by Laurent Kabila.

New Currency

July 1998. 100 cents = 1 Congolese franc.

273 Mother Teresa

274 Diana Princess of Wales

1998. 1st Death Anniv of Mother Teresa (founder of Missionaries of Charity).
1494 50000z. Type **273** . . . . . 1·25 80
MS1495 69 × 99 mm. 325000z. Praying . . . . 7·50 7·50

1998. 1st Death Anniv of Diana, Princess of Wales. Multicoloured.
1496 50000z. Type **274** . . . . . 1·10 80
1497 50000z. Wearing white jacket with blue collar . . 1·10 80
1498 50000z. Wearing large hat 1·10 80
1499 50000z. Wearing white top with blue dots . . . . . 1·10 80
1500 50000z. Wearing neck scarf 1·10 80
1501 50000z. Wearing pearl necklace . . . . 1·10 80
1502 100000z. Wearing tiara . . . 2·10 1·60
1503 100000z. Wearing black top 2·10 1·60
1504 100000z. Resting head on hands . . . . 2·10 1·60
1505 100000z. Wearing cream top 2·10 1·60
1506 125000z. Wearing red and black dress . . . . 2·50 2·00
1507 125000z. Wearing cream jacket . . . . 2·50 2·00
1508 125000z. Profile . . . . . . 2·50 2·00
1509 125000z. Wearing tiara . . . 2·50 2·00
MS1510 Two sheets each 70 × 100 mm. (a) 400000z. Carrying bouquet; (b) 400000z. Wearing evening dress (31 × 47 mm) . . . . 9·00 9·00

275 Building

1999. Independence. Multicoloured.
1511 25c. Type **275** 50 50
1512 50c. Coat of Arms 95 95
1513 75c. Making speech . . . . 1·40 1·40
1514 1f.25 Procession . . . . . . 2·40 2·40
1515 3f. Crowd and man breaking chains . . . . . 5·50 5·50
MS1516 Two sheets each 90 × 120 mm. (a) 2f.50 Crossed weapons, handshake and tractor; (b) 3f.50 Crossed weapons, handshake and tractor . . . . 10·00 10·00

Nos. 1511/**MS**1516 also exist imperforate.

276 Men fighting in Boat

1999. *Outlaws of the Marsh* (Chinese literature). Multicoloured.
1517 1f.45 Type **276** . . . . . . 1·10 1·10
1518 1f.45 Men fighting in blacksmith's shop . . . . 1·10 1·10
1519 1f.45 Men gathered around tree . . . . 1·10 1·10
1520 1f.45 Men writing . . . . . 1·10 1·10
1521 1f.50 Crowds fighting . . . 1·10 1·25
1522 1f.50 Man pulling tree from ground . . . . 1·10 1·25
1523 1f.50 Man threatening other man with sword . . . . . 1·10 1·25
1524 1f.50 Man climbing over balcony . . . . 1·10 1·25
1525 1f.60 Men outside fort . . 1·25 1·25
1526 1f.60 Man in snow storm . . 1·25 1·25
1527 1f.60 Man killing tiger . . . 1·25 1·25
1528 1f.60 Man reading writing on wall . . . . 1·25 1·25
1529 1f.70 Crowds fighting . . . 1·25 1·40
1530 1f.70 Man drawing sword . . 1·25 1·40
1531 1f.70 Man jumping from balcony . . . . 1·25 1·40
1532 1f.70 Man lifting other man 1·25 1·40
1533 1f.80 Archer on horseback 1·40 1·40
1534 1f.80 Men sitting round table eating . . . . . . 1·40 1·40
1535 1f.80 Joust . . . . 1·40 1·40
1536 1f.80 Man tearing scroll . . 1·40 1·40
MS1537 Four sheets each 110 × 75 mm. (a) 10f. Man falling into river (83 × 55 mm); (b) 10f. Men fighting among reeds (83 × 55 mm); (c) 10f. Horsemen outside burning Fort; (d) 10f. Man dead on floor, horseman and prisoner . . . . 16·00 16·00

277 Rat

1999. Chinese Horoscope. Multicoloured.
1538 78c. Type **277** 85 40
1539 78c. Ox 85 40
1540 78c. Tiger 85 40
1541 78c. Rabbit 85 40
1542 78c. Dragon 85 40
1543 78c. Snake 85 40
1544 78c. Horse 85 40
1545 78c. Goat 85 40
1546 78c. Monkey 85 40
1547 78c. Cockerel 85 40
1548 78c. Dog 85 40
1549 78c. Pig 85 40

278 Okapi

279 Four-coloured Bush Shrike (*Telophorus quadricolor*)

2000. Flora and Fauna. Multicoloured.
1550 1f. Type **278** 55 55
1551 1f. Common kestrel 55 55
1552 1f. Giraffe and rainbow . . 55 55
1553 1f. Giraffe 55 55
1554 1f. Mandrill 55 55
1555 1f. Savannah baboon . . . 55 55
1556 1f. Leopard 55 55
1557 1f. Birdwing butterflies . . . 55 55
1558 1f. Hippopotamus 55 55
1559 1f. Hadada ibis 55 55
1560 1f. Water lilies 55 55
1561 1f. Steenbok 55 55
1562 7f.80 Lion (47 × 34 mm) . . 3·75 2·75
MS1563 76 × 106 mm. 10f. Warthog (41 × 56 mm) . . . . 4·00 4·00

Nos. 1550/61 were issued together, se-tenant, forming a composite design.

2000. Flora and Fauna of Africa. Multicoloured.
1564 1f. Type **279** 45 35
1565 1f.50 Leopard (*Panthera pardus*) 70 55
1566 1f.50 Sun 80 80
1567 1f.50 *Pieris citrina* (butterfly) 80 80
1568 1f.50 European bee eater (*Merops apiaster*) 80 80
1569 1f.50 Red-backed shrike (*Lanius collurio*) 80 80
1570 1f.50 Village weaver (*Ploceus cucullatus*) 80 80
1571 1f.50 *Charaxes pelias* . . . 80 80
1572 1f.50 Green charaxes (*Charaxes eupale*) 80 80
1573 1f.50 Giraffe (*Giraffa camelopardalis*) 80 80
1574 1f.50 Bushbaby (*Galago moholi*) 80 80
1575 1f.50 *Strelitzia reginae* (flower) 80 80
1576 1f.50 Thomson's gazelle (*Gazella thomsoni*) 80 80
1577 1f.50 Hoopoe (*Upupa epops*) 80 80
1578 2f. Puku (*Kobus vardoni*) . . 95 95
1579 2f. Protomedia (*Colotis protomedia*) 95 95
1580 3f. Ground pangolin (*Smutsia temminckii*) . . . 1·40 1·40
1581 3f. *Cararina abyssinica* (flower) . . . . 1·40 1·40
MS1582 Two sheets each 106 × 76 mm. (a) 10f. Cape eland (*Taurotragus oryx*); (b) 10f. Hippopotamus (*Hippopotamus amphibious*) . . . . 8·00 8·00

Nos. 1566/1577 were issued together, se-tenant, forming a composite design.

280 Leopard Cat (*Felis bengalensis*)

2000. Wild Cats and Dogs. Multicoloured.
1583 1f.50 Type **280** 80 80
1584 1f.50 African golden cat (*Felis aurata*) 80 80
1585 1f.50 Caracal (*Felis caracal*) 80 80
1586 1f.50 Puma (*Felis concolor*) 80 80
1587 1f.50 Black-footed cat (*Felis nigripes*) 80 80
1588 1f.50 Lion (*Panthera leo*) . . 80 80
1589 1f.50 Clouded leopard (*Neofelis nebulosa*) 80 80
1590 1f.50 Margay (*Felis wiedii*) 80 80
1591 1f.50 Cheetah (*Acinonyx jubatus*) 80 80
1592 1f.50 Spainsh lynx (*Felis pardina*) 80 80
1593 1f.50 Jaguarundi (*Felis yagouarundi*) 80 80
1594 1f.50 Serval (*Felis serval*) . . 80 80
1595 2f. Black-backed jackal (*Canis mesomelas*) . . . . 1·00 1·00
1596 2f. Bat-eared fox (*Otocyon megalotis*) . . . . . . 1·00 1·00
1597 2f. Bush dog (*Speothos venaticus*) . . . . 1·00 1·00
1598 2f. Coyote (*Canis latrans*) 1·00 1·00
1599 2f. Dhole (*Cuon alpinus*) . . 1·00 1·00
1600 2f. Fennec fox (*Fennecus zerda*) . . . . 1·00 1·00
1601 2f. Grey fox (*Urocyon cinereoargenteus*) . . . . 1·00 1·00
1602 2f. Wolf (*Canis lupus*) . . . 1·00 1·00
1603 2f. Kit fox (*Vulpes macrotis*) 1·00 1·00
1604 2f. Maned wolf (*Chrysocyon brachyurus*) . . . . . . 1·00 1·00
1605 2f. Racoon-dog (*Nyctereutes procyonoides*) . . . . . . 1·00 1·00
1606 2f. Red fox (*Vulpes vulpes*) 1·00 1·00
MS1607 Two sheets each 106 × 76 mm. (a) 10f. Leopard (*Panthera pardus*); (b) 10f. Arctic fox (*Alopex lagops*) . . . . . 8·00 8·00

281 "2000" and Mountains

2000. New Millennium.
1608 **281** 4f.50 multicoloured . . . 1·00 1·00
1609 9f. multicoloured . . . . 1·90 1·90
1610 15f. multicoloured . . . 3·25 3·25

282 Egyptian Goose (*Alopochen aegyptiacus*)

283 Golden-shouldered Parrot (*Psephotus chrysopterygius*)

2000. Birds of the Congo. Multicoloured.
1611 3f. Type **282** 10 10
1612 3f. Ardeola ibis 10 10
1613 4f.50 Black-collared barbet (*Lybius torquatus*) 15 10
1614 4f.50 Namaqua dove (*Oena capensis*) 15 10
1615 9f. Great blue turaco (*Corythaeola cristata*) (inscr "Corythaelo") . . . 30 15
1616 9f. Common kestrel (*Falco tinnunculus*) 30 15
MS1617 Four sheets. (a) 95 × 97 mm. 9f. × 6, Red bishop (*Euplectes orix*); Red-collared whydah (*Euplectis ardens*); African golden oriole (*Oriolus auratus*); Village weaver (*Ploceus cucullatus*); Zebra waxbill (*Amandava subflava*); Scarlet-chested sunbird (*Nectarina senegalensis*). (b) 95 × 99 mm. 9f. × 6; Blue-breasted kingfisher (*Halcyon malimbica*) (inscr "Haleyon malimbicus"); *Tachymarptis melba*; African fish eagle (*Haliaeetus vocifer*); Purple heron (*Ardea purpurea*); Whale-headed stork (*Baleaniceps rex*); South African crowned crane (*Balearica regulorum*). (c) 110 × 85 mm. 15f. African jacana (*Actophilornis africanus*) (horiz). (d) 85 × 110 mm. 20f. Lesser pied kingfisher (*Ceryle rudis*) (horiz) Set of 4 sheets . . . . 4·75 4·75

2000. Parrots. Multicoloured.
1618 4f.50 Type **283** 15 10
1619 8f. Blue-fronted amazon (*Amazona aestiva*) 15 10
1620 8f.50 *Are nobilis cumanensis* 25 10
1621 9f. Peach-faced lovebird (*Agapornis roseicollis*) . . 30 15
MS1622 Four sheets. (a) 143 × 181 mm. 5f. × 9, Scarlet macaw (*Ara macao*); *Neophema elegans*; Vernal hanging parrot (*Loriculus vernalis*); Sun conure (*Aratinga solstialis*); Black-headed caique (*Piontes melanocephala*); *Bolborhynchus lineola*; Chestnut-fronted macaw (*Ara severa*); *Psephotus chrysoptergius dissimilas*; Military macaw (*Ara miltaris*). (b) 143 × 181 mm. 5f. × 9, *Eos squamata*; Golden conure *Aratinga guarouba*); *Aratinga aurea*; Dusky lory (*Pseudeos fuscata*); Fischer's lovebird (*Agapornis fischeri*); *Aratinga nana*; *Aratinga mitrata*; Rainbow lory (*Trichoglossus haematodus*); Sulphur-crested cockatoo (*Cacatua galerita*). (c) 79 × 109 mm. 15f. *Opopsitta diophthalma*. (d) 103 × 74 mm. 15f. Yellow and blue macaw (*Ara ararauna*) (inscr "ararrauna") (horiz) Set of 4 sheets . . . . 2·75 2·75

284 White-tailed Goldenthroat (*Polytmus guainumbi*) (inscr "Lophornis ornata")

2000. Hummingbirds. Multicoloured.

1623	8f.50 Type **284**	30	15
1624	9f. Hummingbird (inscr "Polytrus guauvunibi")	30	15

MS1625 Three sheets. (a) 145 × 103 mm. 4f.50 × 9, White-tipped sicklebill (*Eutoxeres aquila*) (inscr "Ertoxeres"); Long-tailed sylph (*Aglaiocerus kingi*) (inscr "Aglaiolepus kinde"); Ruby-throated hummingbird (*Archilochus colubris*) (inscr "calobris"); Streamertail (*Trochilus polytmus*) (inscr "Trochlus polytaus"); Rainbow bearded thornbill (*Chalcostigma herrani*) (inscr "Chaliostigna"); Sword-billed hummingbird (*Ensifera*); Ruby topaz hummingbird (*Chrysolampis mosquitus*) (inscr "Chrysolampus"); *Phaethornis syrmatophorus* (inscr "Phorethornus"); Bee hummingbird (*Calypte helenae*) (inscr "Calypre hetervare"). (b) 110 × 84 mm. 15f. Collared Inca (*Coeligena torquata*) (inscr "torgoata"). (c) 111 × 85 mm. 20f. Violet sabrewing (*Campylopterus hemileucurus*) (inscr "hemileicurus") Set of 3 sheets 2·50 2·50

CONGO (KINSHASA) Pt. 14

This Belgian colony in Central Africa became independent in 1960. There were separate issues for the province of Katanga (q.v.).

In 1971 the country was renamed ZAIRE and later issues will be found under that heading.

1967. 100 sengi = 1 (li)kuta; 100 (ma)kuta = 1 zaire.

1960. Various stamps of Belgian Congo optd **CONGO** or surch also. (a) Flowers issue of 1952. Multicoloured.

360	10c. "Dissotis"	20	10
361	10c. on 15c. "Protea"	20	10
362	20c. "Vellozia"	20	10
363	40c. "Ipomoea"	20	10
364	50c. on 60c. "Euphorbia"	20	10
365	50c. on 75c. "Ochna"	20	10
366	1f. "Hibiscus"	20	10
367	1f.50 "Schizoglossum"	20	10
368	2f. "Ansellia"	20	10
369	3f. "Costus"	40	10
370	4f. "Nymphaea"	40	20
371	5f. "Thunbergia"	40	10
372	6f.50 "Thonningia"	60	10
373	8f. "Gloriosa"	80	20
374	10f. "Silene"	1·25	20
375	20f. "Aristolochia"	2·50	55
376	50f. "Eulophia"	14·00	3·75
377	100f. "Cryptosepalum"	24·00	6·25

(b) Wild Animals issue of 1959.

378	10c. brown, sepia and blue	15	10
379	20c. blue and red	15	10
380	40c. brown and blue	15	10
381	50c. multicoloured	15	10
382	1f. black, green & brown	15	10
383	1f.50 black and yellow	20	10
384	2f. black, brown and red	30	10
385	3f.50 on 3f. blk, pur & slate	35	10
386	5f. brown, green and sepia	50	15
387	6f.50 brown, yellow and blue	65	15
388	8f. bistre, violet and brown	80	30
389	10f. multicoloured	1·00	35

(c) Madonna.

390	**102** 50c. brown, ochre & chest	50	50

(d) African Technical Co-operation Commission. Inscr in French or Flemish.

391	**103** 3f.50 on 3f. sal & slate	40	40

106 Congo Map

1960. Independence Commemoration.

392	**106** 20c. bistre	10	10
393	50c. red	10	10
394	1f. green	10	10
395	1f.50 brown	10	10
396	2f. mauve	10	10
397	3f.50 violet	10	10
398	5f. blue	15	10
399	6f.50 black	20	10
400	10f. orange	30	20
401	20f. blue	50	30

107 Congo Flag and People breaking Chain **109** Pres. Kasavubu

1961. 2nd Anniv of Congo Independence Agreement. Flag in yellow and blue.

402	**107** 2f. violet	10	10
403	3f.50 red	10	10
404	6f.50 brown	20	10
405	10f. green	25	15
406	20f. mauve	45	30

1961. Coquilhatville Conf. Optd **CONFERENCE COQUILHATVILLE AVRIL-MAI-1961**.

407	**106** 20c. bistre	60	60
408	50c. red	60	60
409	1f. green	60	60
410	1f.50 brown	60	60
411	2f. mauve	60	60
412	3f.50 violet	60	60
413	5f. blue	60	60
414	6f.50 black	60	60
415	10f. orange	60	60
416	20f. blue	60	60

1961. 1st Anniv of Independence. Inscr as in T **109**. Portraits and inscriptions in sepia.

417	**109** 10c. yellow	10	10
418	20c. red	10	10
419	40c. turquoise	10	10
420	50c. salmon	10	10
421	1f. lilac	10	10
422	1f.50 brown	10	10
423	2f. green	10	10
424	– 3f.50 mauve	15	10
425	– 5f. grey	1·75	15
426	– 6f.50 blue	30	10
427	– 8f. olive	35	10
428	– 10f. blue	75	10
429	– 20f. orange	75	15
430	– 50f. blue	1·40	30
431	– 100f. green	2·50	50

DESIGNS—HORIZ: 3f.50 to 8f. Pres. Kasavubu and map of Congo Republic. VERT: 10f. to 100f. Pres. Kasavubu in full uniform and outline map.

1961. Re-opening of Parliament. Optd **REOUVERTURE du PARLEMENT JUILLET 1961**.

432	**109** 10c. yellow	10	10
433	20c. red	10	10
434	40c. turquoise	10	10
435	50c. salmon	30	20
436	1f. lilac	30	20
437	1f.50 brown	80	70
438	2f. green	80	70
439	– 5f. grey (No. 425)	80	70
440	– 10f. violet (No. 428)	80	85

111 Dag Hammarskjold **112** Campaign Emblem

1962. Dag Hammarskjold Commemoration.

441	**111** 10c. brown and grey	10	10
442	20c. blue and grey	10	10
443	30c. bistre and grey	10	10
444	40c. blue and grey	10	10
445	50c. red and grey	10	10
446	3f. olive and grey	2·50	1·60
447	6f.50 violet and grey	70	50
448	8f. brown and grey	80	60

MS448a 65 × 90 mm. **111** 25f. brown and grey. Imperf 3·75 3·75

1962. Malaria Eradication.

449	**112** 1f.50 brown, black & yell	10	10
450	2f. turq, brown & green	30	15
451	6f.50 lake, black & blue	15	10

1962. 2nd Anniv of Independence. No. **MS**448a optd **2 EME ANNIVERSAIRE DE L'INDEPENDANCE**, etc. in green.

MS451a 65 × 90 mm. **111** 25f. brown and grey. Imperf 1·75 1·75

1962. Reorganization of Aboula Ministry. Optd **"Paix, Travail, Austerite..., C. ADOULA 11 juillet 1962.**

452	**111** 10c. brown and grey	10	10
453	20c. blue and grey	10	10
454	30c. bistre and grey	10	10
455	40c. blue and grey	10	10
456	50c. red and grey	1·25	50
457	3f. olive and grey	15	10
458	6f.50 violet and grey	20	10
459	8f. brown and grey	30	15

114

1963. 1st Participation in UPU Congress.

460	**114** 2f. violet	1·40	1·00
461	4f. red	10	10
462	7f. blue	20	10
463	20f. green	30	15

115 Emblem, Bears and Tractor

1963. Freedom from Hunger.

464	**115** 5f.+2f. violet & mauve	15	10
465	9f.+4f. green & yellow	30	20
466	12f.+6f. violet & blue	35	25
467	20f.+10f. green & red	1·75	1·60

116 Whale-headed Stork

1963. Protected Birds.

468	– 10c. multicoloured	15	10
469	– 20c. blue, black and red	15	10
470	– 30c. black, brown & grn	15	10
471	– 40c. black, orange & grey	15	10
472	**116** 1f. black, green & brown	30	15
473	– 2f. blue, brown and red	7·00	1·25
474	– 3f. black, pink and green	55	20
475	– 4f. blue, green and red	55	20
476	– 5f. black, red and blue	85	20
477	– 6f. black, bistre & violet	7·00	1·25
478	– 7f. indigo, blue & turq	1·25	20
479	– 8f. blue, yellow & orange	1·40	20
480	– 10f. black, red and blue	1·40	20
481	– 20f. black, red & yellow	2·50	30

BIRDS—VERT: 10c. Eastern white pelicans ("Pelicans"); 30c. African open-bill stork ("Bec-Duvert"); 2f. Marabou stork ("Marabout"); 4f. Congo peafowl ("Paon Congolais"); 6f. Secretary bird ("Serpentaire"); 8f. Sacred ibis ("Ibis Sacre"). HORIZ: 20c. Crested guineafowl ("Pintables de Schouteden"); 40c. Abdim's stork ("Cigoon a Ventre Blanc"); 3f. Greater flamingos ("Flamants Roses"); 5f. Hartlaub's duck ("Canards de Hartlaub"); 7f. Black-casqued hornbill ("Calaos"); 10f. South African crowned cranes ("Grue Cauronnse"); 20f. Saddle-bill stork ("Jabiru d'Afrique").

117 Strophanthus ("S. sarmentosus") **118** "Reconciliation"

1963. Red Cross Centenary. Cross in red.

482	**117** 10c. green and violet	10	10
483	A 20c. blue and red	10	10
484	**117** 30c. red and green	10	10
485	A 40c. violet and blue	10	10
486	**117** 5f. lake and olive	10	10
487	A 7f. purple and orange	10	10
488	B 9f. olive	20	10
489	20f. violet	1·60	70

DESIGNS—VERT: A, "Cinchona ledgeriana". HORIZ: B, Red Cross nurse.

1963. "National Reconciliation".

490	**118** 4f. multicoloured	90	30
491	5f. multicoloured	10	10
492	9f. multicoloured	15	10
493	12f. multicoloured	20	10

119 Kabambare Sewer, Leopoldville

1963. European Economic Community Aid.

494	**119** 20c. multicoloured	10	10
495	A 30c. multicoloured	10	10
496	B 50c. multicoloured	10	10
497	**119** 3f. multicoloured	90	35
498	A 5f. multicoloured	10	10
499	B 9f. multicoloured	15	10
500	A 12f. multicoloured	15	10

DESIGNS: A, Tractor and bridge on plan; B, Construction of Ituri Road.

120 N'Djili Airport, Leopoldville

1963. "Air Congo" Commemoration.

501	**120** 2f. multicoloured	10	10
502	– 5f. multicoloured	10	10
503	**120** 6f. multicoloured	90	40
504	– 7f. multicoloured	10	10
505	**120** 30f. multicoloured	25	15
506	– 50f. multicoloured	40	25

DESIGN: 5f., 7f., 50f. Mailplane and control tower.

1963. 15th Anniv of Declaration of Human Rights. Optd **10 DECEMBRE 1948 10 DECEMBRE 1963 15e anniversaire DROITS DE L'HOMME**.

507	**114** 2f. violet	10	10
508	4f. red	10	10
509	7f. blue	20	20
510	20f. green	20	20

122 Student in Laboratory

1964. 10th Anniv of Lovanium University. Mult.

511	50c. Type **122**	10	10
512	1f.50 University buildings	10	10
513	8f. Atomic and nuclear reactor symbols	1·75	1·60
514	25f. University arms and buildings	20	15
515	30f. Type **122**	20	20
516	60f. As 1f.50	40	30
517	75f. As 8f.	50	50
518	100f. As 25f.	70	60

MS518a 141 × 70 mm. 20f. (Type **122**), 30f. (As 8f.), 100f. As 25f. Imperf 2·75 2·75

1964. Various stamps surch over coloured metallic panels. (a) Stamps of Belgian Congo surch **REPUBLIQUE DU CONGO** and value.

519	– 1f. on 20c. (No. 340)	10	10
520	– 2f. on 1f.50 (No. 306)	6·25	2·25
521	– 5f. on 6f.50 (No. 348)	15	15
522	– 8f. on 6f.50 (No. 311)	60	25

(b) Stamps of Congo (Kinshasa) surch.

523	– 1f. on 20c. (No. 379)	10	10
524	– 1f. on 6f.50 (No. 372)	10	10
525	– 2f. on 1f.50 (No. 367)	10	10
530	**109** 3f. on 20c.	25	20
531	4f. on 40c.	25	20
526	– 5f. on 6f.50 (No. 387)	45	20
528	**106** 6f. on 6f.50	30	20
529	7f. on 20c.	40	25

125 Pole-vaulting

1964. Olympic Games, Tokyo.

532	**125** 5f. sepia, grey and red	10	10
533	– 7f. violet, red and green	80	40
534	– 8f. brown, yellow & blue	10	10
535	**125** 10f. purple, blue & purple	10	10
536	– 20f. brown, green & orge	20	20
537	– 100f. brown, mauve & grn	80	20

MS537a 135 × 85 mm. 21, 31 and 100f. As Nos. 535/7 but new colours. Imperf 4·50 4·50

DESIGNS—VERT: 7f., 20f. Throwing the javelin. HORIZ: 8f., 100f. Hurdling.

OCCUPATION OF STANLEYVILLE. During the occupation of Stanleyville from 5 August to 24 November, 1964, stocks of a number of contemporary issues were overprinted **REPUBLIQUE POPULAIRE** and issued by the rebel authorities.

126 National Palace

1964. National Palace, Leopoldville.

538	**126** 50c. mauve and blue	10	10
539	1f. blue and purple	10	10
540	2f. brown and violet	10	10
541	3f. green and brown	10	10
542	4f. orange and blue	10	10
543	5f. violet and green	10	10
544	6f. brown and orange	10	10
545	7f. olive and brown	10	10
546	8f. red and blue	2·00	35
547	9f. violet and red	10	10

548 10f. brown and green . . 10 10
549 20f. blue and brown . . . 10 10
550 30f. red and green 15 10
551 40f. blue and purple . . . 25 10
552 50f. brown and green . . 35 10
553 100f. black and orange . . 65 15

127 Pres. Kennedy

128 Rocket and Unisphere

1964. Pres. Kennedy Commemoration.
554 **127** 5f. blue and black 10 10
555 6f. purple and black . . . 10 10
556 9f. brown and black . . . 10 10
557 30f. violet and black . . . 30 10
558 40f. green and black . . . 2·00 60
559 60f. brown and black . . 50 25
MS559a 64 × 76 mm. **127** 150f. grey and red . . . . 2·25 2·25
See also No. **MS**630.

1965. New York World's Fair.
560 **128** 50c. purple and black . . 10 10
561 1f.50 blue and violet . . . 10 10
562 2f. brown and green . . . 10 10
563 10f. green and red 70 40
564 18f. blue and brown . . . 10 10
565 27f. red and green 25 10
566 40f. grey and red 40 15

129 Football

1965. 1st African Games, Leopoldville.
567 – 5f. black, brown & blue 10 10
568 **129** 6f. red, black and blue . . 10 10
569 – 15f. black, green & orange 10 10
570 – 24f. black, green & mve 20 10
571 **129** 40f. blue, black & turq . . 1·25 45
572 – 60f. purple, black & blue 45 15
SPORTS—VERT: 5f., 24f. Basketball; 15f., 60f. Volleyball.

130 Telecommunications Satellites

1965. Centenary of ITU. Multicoloured.
573 6f. Type **130** 10 10
574 9f. Telecommunications satellites (different view) . . 10 10
575 12f. Type **130** 10 10
576 15f. As 9f. 10 10
577 18f. Type **130** . . . . 1·00 30
578 20f. As 9f. 15 10
579 30f. Type **130** 25 10
580 40f. As 9f. 30 10

131 Parachutist and troops landing

1965. 5th Anniv of Independence.
581 **131** 5f. brown and blue . . . 10 10
582 6f. brown and orange . . 10 10
583 7f. brown and green . . . 45 20
584 9f. brown and mauve . . 10 10
585 18f. brown and yellow . . 15 10

132 Matadi Port

1965. International Co-operation Year.
586 **132** 6f. blue, black & yellow 10 10
587 – 8f. brown, black & blue 10 10
588 – 9f. turq, black & brown 10 10
589 **132** 12f. mauve, black & grey 80 30
590 – 25f. olive, black and red 20 10
591 – 60f. grey, black & yellow 40 10
DESIGNS: 8f., 25f. Katanga mines; 9f., 60f. Tshopo Barrage, Stanleyville.

133 Medical Care

1965. Congolese Army.
592 **133** 2f. blue and red 10 10
593 5f. brown, red and pink 10 10
594 – 6f. brown and blue . . . 10 10
595 – 7f. green and yellow . . . 10 10
596 – 9f. brown and green . . . 10 10
597 – 10f. brown and green . . 40 40
598 – 18f. violet and red 15 10
599 – 19f. brown & turquoise 60 40
600 – 20f. brown and blue . . . 15 10
601 – 24f. multicoloured 20 15
602 – 30f. multicoloured 25 10
DESIGNS—HORIZ: 6f., 9f. Feeding child; 7, 18f. Bridge-building. VERT: 10f., 20f. Building construction; 19f. Telegraph line maintenance; 24f., 30f. Soldier and flag.

1966. World Meteorological Day. Nos. 590/1 optd **6e Journee Meteorologique Mondiale / 23.3.66** (on coloured metallic panel) and WMO Emblem.
603 25f. olive, black and red . . 75 45
604 60f. grey, black and yellow 75 50

135 Carved Stool and Head

1966. World Festival of Negro Arts, Dakar.
605 **135** 10f. black, red and grey 10 10
606 – 12f. black, green & blue 10 10
607 – 15f. black, blue & purple 15 10
608 – 53f. black, red and blue 1·10 90
DESIGNS—VERT: 12f. Statuettes; 53f. Statuettes of women. HORIZ: 15f. Woman's head and carved goat.

136 Pres. Mobutu and Fish Workers

1966. Pres. Mobutu Commemoration.
609 **136** 2f. brown and blue . . . 10 10
610 – 4f. brown and red 10 10
611 – 6f. brown and olive . . . 65 60
612 – 8f. brown and turquoise 10 10
613 – 10f. brown and lake . . . 10 10
614 – 12f. brown and violet . . 10 10
615 – 15f. brown and green . . 10 10
616 – 24f. brown and mauve . . 20 15
DESIGNS (Pres. Mobutu and): 4f. Harvesting pyrethrum; 6f. Building construction; 8f. Winnowing maize; 10f. Cotton-picking; 12f. Harvesting fruit; 15f. Picking coffee-beans; 24f. Harvesting pineapples.

137 Pres. Mobutu and Workers rolling up Sleeves ("Retroussons les manches!)

1904.
MS617 **137** 128 × 95 mm. 15f. brown, blue and red (block of four) 75 75

1966. Inaug of WHO Headquarters, Geneva. Nos. 550/3 optd **O.M.S. Geneve 1966** and WHO Emblem.
618 **126** 30f. red and green 70 70
619 40f. blue and purple . . . 70 70
620 50f. brown and green . . 75 75
621 100f. black and orange . . 75 75

139 Footballer

1966. World Cup Football Championship.
622 **139** 10f. green, violet & brown 10 10
623 – 30f. green, violet & purple 25 20
624 – 50f. brown, blue & green 85 80
625 – 60f. gold, sepia & green 45 40
DESIGNS: 30f. Two footballers; 50f. Three footballers; 60f. Jules Rimet Cup and football.

1966. World Cup Football Championship Final. Nos. 622/5 optd **FINALE ANGLETERRE - ALLEMAGNE 4 - 2**.
626 **139** 10f. green, violet & brown 25 45
627 – 30f. green, violet & purple 80 1·40
628 – 50f. brown, blue & green 1·25 1·75
629 – 60f. gold, sepia and green 1·40 2·25

141 President Kennedy

1966. Kennedy Commemoration (2nd issue). Two sheets each 65 × 78 mm.
MS630 **141** 150f. brown; 150f. blue 7·00 7·00

1967. 4th African Unity Organization (O.U.A.) Conf, Kinshasa. Nos. 538/43 surch **4e Sommet OUA KINSHASA du 11 au 14 - 9 - 67** and value.
631 **126** 1k. on 2f. 10 10
632 3k. on 5f. 10 10
633 5k. on 4f. 20 15
634 6k.60 on 1f. 25 20
635 9k.60 on 50c. 40 25
636 9k.80 on 3f. 50 40

143 "OUA" Emblem

1904.
MS637 **143** 50k. ("0.5z.") red, black and blue (77 × 80 mm) . . . . 2·00 2·00

144 Congolese blowing Horn

1967. EXPO 70 World Fair, Montreal. Sheet 90 × 76 mm.
MS638 **144** 50k. maroon . . . . 2·00 2·00

1967. New Constitution. Nos. 609/10 and 592 surch **1967 NOUVELLE CONSTITUTION** with coloured metallic panel obliterating old value.
639 **136** 4k. on 2f. 20 15
640 **133** 5k. on 2f. 20 15
641 – 21k. on 4f. 90 70

1967. 1st Congolese Games, Kinshasa. Nos. 567 and 569 surch **1ers Jeux Congolais 25/6 au 2/7/67 Kinshasa** and value.
642 1k. on 5f. 10 10
643 9.6k. on 15f. 50 50

1967. 1st Flight by Air Congo BAC "One-Eleven". No. 504 surch **1er VOL BAC ONE ELEVEN 14/5/67** and value.
644 9.6k. on 7f. 70 20

1968. World Children's Day (8.10.67). Nos. 586 and 588 surch **JOURNEE MONDIALE DE L'ENFANCE 8 - 10 - 67** and new value.
645 **132** 1k. on 6f. 10 10
646 9k. on 9f. 50 50

1968. International Tourist Year (1967). Nos. 538, 541 and 544 surch **Annee Internationale du Tourisme 24-10-67** and new value.
647 **126** 5k. on 50c. 20 20
648 10k. on 6f. 40 40
649 15k. on 3f. 60 60

1968. (a) No. 540 surch.
650 **126** 1k. on 2f. 10 10

(b) Surch (coloured panel obliterating old value, and new value surch on panel. Panel colour given first, followed by colour of new value). (i) Nos. 538 and 542.
651 **126** 2k. on 50c. (bronze and black) 10 10
652 2k. on 50c. (blue and white) 10 10
653 9.6k. on 4f. (black and white) 50 45

(ii) No. 609.
654 **136** 10k. on 2f. (black and white) 55 10

152 Leaping Leopard

1968.
655 **152** 2k. black on green . . . 15 10
656 9.6k. black on red 65 15

1968. As Nos. 609, etc, but with colours changed and surch in new value.
657 **136** 15s. on 2f. brown & blue 10 10
658 – 1k. on 6f. brown & chest 10 10
659 – 3k. on 10f. brown & grn 10 10
660 – 5k. on 12f. brown & orge 20 15
661 – 20k. on 15f. brown & grn 70 50
662 – 50k. on 24f. brown & pur 1·90 1·25

154 Human Rights Emblem

1968. Human Rights Year.
663 **154** 2k. green and blue . . . 10 10
664 9.6k. red and green . . . 40 25
665 10k. brown and lilac . . . 40 25
666 40k. violet and brown . . 1·50 1·10

1969. 4th O.C.A.M. (Organization Commune Africaine et Malgache) Summit Meeting, Kinshasa. Nos. 663/6 with colours changed optd **4EME SOMMET OCAM 27-1-1969 KINSHASA** and emblem.
667 **154** 2k. brown and green . . . 10 10
668 9.60k. green and pink . . 40 25
669 10k. blue and grey . . . 40 25
670 40k. violet and blue . . . 1·50 1·10

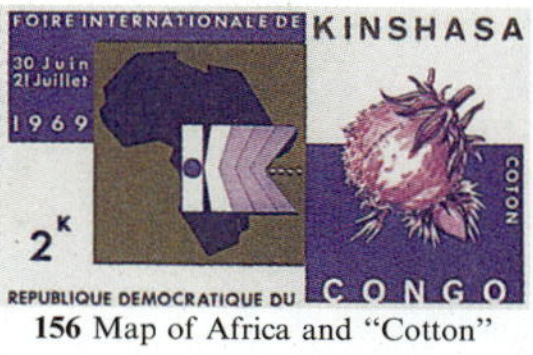

156 Map of Africa and "Cotton"

1969. International Fair, Kinshasa (1st Issue).
671 **156** 2k. multicoloured 10 10
672 – 6k. multicoloured 30 30
673 – 9.6k. multicoloured . . . 40 20

674 – 9.8k. multicoloured . . . 40 35
675 – 11.6k. multicoloured . . . 50 50
DESIGNS: Map of Africa and: 6k. "Copper"; 9.6k. "Coffee"; 9.8k. "Diamonds"; 11.6k. "Palm-oil".

157 Fair Entrance

1969. Inaug of Int Fair, Kinshasa (2nd issue).
676 **157** 2k. purple and gold . . . 10 10
677 – 3k. blue and gold 10 10
678 – 10k. green and gold . . . 40 40
679 – 25k. red and gold . . . . 1·00 85
DESIGNS: 3k. "Gecomin" (mining company) pavilion; 10k. Administration building; 25k. African Unity Organization pavilion.

158 Congo Arms

159 Pres. Mobutu

1969.
680 **158** 10s. red and black 10 10
681 15s. blue and black . . . 10 10
682 30s. green and black . . . 10 10
683 60s. purple and black . . 10 10
684 90s. bistre and black . . 10 10
685 **159** 1k. multicoloured 10 10
686 2k. multicoloured 10 10
687 3k. multicoloured 15 10
688 5k. multicoloured 15 15
689 6k. multicoloured 20 15
690 9.6k. multicoloured . . . 30 25
691 10k. multicoloured . . . 40 30
692 20k. multicoloured . . . 80 60
693 50k. multicoloured . . . 2·00 1·75
694 100k. multicoloured . . . 4·00 3·50

160 "The Well-sinker" (O. Bonnevalle)

1969. 50th Anniv of International Labour Organization. Paintings. Multicoloured.
695 3k. Type **160** 15 15
696 4k. "Cocoa Production" (J. van Noten) 20 15
697 8k. "The Harbour" (C. Meunier) (vert) 70 25
698 10k. "The Poulterer" (H. Evenepoel) 45 35
699 15k. "Industry" (C. Meunier) 85 50

161 "Adoration of the Magi" (Rubens)

1969. Christmas. Sheet 86 × 85 mm.
MS700 **161** 50k. purple . . . . . 1·75 1·75

162 Pres. Mobutu, Map and Flag

1970. 10th Anniv of Independence.
701 **162** 10s. multicoloured 10 10
702 90s. multicoloured 10 10
703 1k. multicoloured 10 10
704 2k. multicoloured 10 10
705 7k. multicoloured 25 15
706 10k. multicoloured . . . 40 25
707 20k. multicoloured . . . 80 50

1970. Surch. (a) National Palace series.
708 **126** 10s. on 1f. 10 10
709 20s. on 2f. 10 10
710 30s. on 3f. 10 10
711 40s. on 4f. 10 10
712 60s. on 7f. 80 75
713 90s. on 9f. 80 75
714 1k. on 6f. 15 10
715 3k. on 30f. 80 75
716 4k. on 40f. 15 10
717 5k. on 50f. . . . . . . 2·00 1·90
718 10k. on 100f. 90 75

(b) Congolese Army series.
719 90s. on 9f. (No. 596) 15 10
720 1k. on 7f. (No. 595) 15 10
721 2k. on 24f. (No. 601) 15 10

(c) Pres. Mobutu series.
722 **136** 20s. on 2f. 15 10
723 – 40s. on 4f. (No. 610) . . 15 10
724 – 1k. on 12f. (No. 614) . . 80 70
725 – 2k. on 24f. (No. 616) . . 15 10

164 I.T.U. Headquarters, Geneva

1970. United Nations Commemorations.
726 **164** 1k. olive, green and pink 10 10
727 – 2k. grey, green and orange 10 10
728 – 6k.60 red, pink and blue 25 25
729 **164** 9k.60 multicoloured . . . 30 30
730 – 9k.80 sepia, brown and bl 35 35
731 – 10k. sepia, brown and lilac 35 35
732 – 11k. sepia, brown and pink 40 40
DESIGNS AND EVENTS: 1k., 9k.60, (ITU World Day); 2k., 6k.60, New UPU Headquarters, Berne (Inauguration); 9k.80, 10k., 11k. U.N. Headquarters, New York (25th anniversary).

165 Pres. Mobutu and Independence Arch

1970. 5th Anniv of "New Regime".
733 **165** 2k. multicoloured 10 10
734 10k. multicoloured . . . 45 35
735 20k. multicoloured . . . 85 80

166 "Apollo 11"

1970. Visit of "Apollo 11" Astronauts to Kinshasa.
736 **166** 1k. blue, black and red 10 10
737 – 2k. violet, black and red 10 10
738 – 7k. black, orange and red 25 25
739 – 10k. black, pink and red 35 35
740 – 30k. black, green and red 1·00 1·00
DESIGNS: 2k. Astronauts on Moon; 7k. Pres. Mobutu decorating wives; 10k. Pres. Mobutu with astronauts; 30k. Astronauts after splashdown.

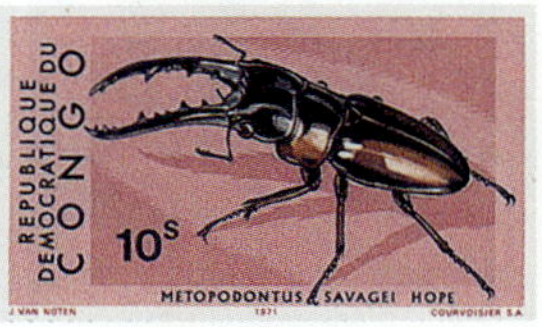

167 "Metopodontus savagei"

1971. Insects. Multicoloured.
741 10s. Type **167** 25 15
742 50s. "Cicindela regalis" . . . 25 15
743 90s. "Magacephala catenulata" 25 15
744 1k. "Stephanorrhina guttata" 25 15
745 2k. "Pupuricenus congoanus" 25 15
746 3k. "Sagra tristis" 50 25
747 5k. "Steraspis subcalida" . . 1·75 80
748 10k. "Mecosaspis explanata" 2·40 1·25
749 30k. "Goliathus meleagris" 5·75 3·25
750 40k. "Sternotomis virescens" 8·25 4·75

168 "Colotis protomedia"

1971. Butterflies and Moths. Multicoloured.
751 10s. Type **168** 25 15
752 20s. "Rhodophitus simplex" 25 15
753 70s. "Euphaedra overlaeti" 25 15
754 1k. "Argema bouvieri" . . . 25 15
755 3k. "Cymothoe reginae-elisabethae" 50 25
756 5k. "Miniodes maculifera" 1·40 60
757 10k. "Salamis temora" . . . 1·90 90
758 15k. "Eronia leda" . . . . 3·75 1·60
759 25k. "Cymothoe sangaris" . . 5·00 2·50
760 40k. "Euchloron megaera" . . 8·00 4·50

169 "Four Races" around Globe

170 Pres. Mobutu and Obelisk

1971. Racial Equality Year.
761 **169** 1k. multicoloured 10 10
762 4k. multicoloured 15 15
763 5k. multicoloured 20 20
764 10k. multicoloured . . . 40 40

1971. 4th Anniv of Popular Revolutionary Movement (MPR).
765 **170** 4k. multicoloured 15 15

171 "Hypericum bequaertii"

1971. Tropical Plants. Multicoloured.
766 1k. Type **171** 35 15
767 4k. "Dissotis brazzae" . . . 70 30
768 20k. "Begonia wollast" . . . 3·50 1·50
769 25k. "Cassia alata" . . . . . 4·50 1·90

172 ITU Emblem (International Telecommunications Day)

1971. "Telecommunications and Space". Mult.
770 1k. Type **172** 10 10
771 3k. Dish aerial (Satellite Earth Station, Kinshasa) 15 15
772 6k. Map of Pan-African telecommunications network 30 30

173 Savanna Monkey

1971. Congo Monkeys. Multicoloured.
773 10s. Type **173** 30 15
774 20s. Moustached monkey (vert) 30 15
775 70s. De Brazza's monkey . . 45 35
776 1k. Yellow baboon 45 25
777 3k. Pygmy chimpanzee (vert) 75 50
778 5k. Black mangabey (vert) . . 1·75 1·25
779 10k. Owl-faced monkey . . . 3·25 2·40
780 15k. Diana monkey . . . . 5·25 3·50
781 25k. Western black-and-white colobus (vert) . . . . . 9·00 6·00
782 40k. L'Hoest's monkey (vert) 12·00 8·50

174 Hotel Inter-Continental

1971. Opening of Hotel Inter-Continental, Kinshasa.
783 **174** 2k. multicoloured 10 10
784 12k. multicoloured . . . 50 50

175 "Reader"

1971. Literacy Campaign. Multicoloured.
785 50s. Type **175** 10 10
786 2k.50 Open book and abacus 20 10
787 7k. Symbolic alphabet . . . 45 35

For later issues see **ZAIRE**.

COOK ISLANDS Pt. 1

A group of islands in the South Pacific under New Zealand control, including Aitutaki, Niue, Penrhyn and Rarotonga. Granted self-government in 1965.

See also issues for Aitutaki and Penrhyn Island.

1892. 12 pence = 1 shilling;
20 shillings = 1 pound.
1967. 100 cents = 1 dollar.

1

1892.
1 **1** 1d. black . . . . 27·00 26·00
2 1½d. mauve . . . . 40·00 38·00
3 2½d. blue . . . . 40·00 38·00
4 10d. red £140 £130

2 Queen Makea Takau

3 White Tern or Torea

1893.
11ba **3** ½d. blue . . . . 5·50 8·00
28 ½d. green . . . . 2·75 3·25
13 **2** 1d. brown . . . . 19·00 19·00
12 1d. blue . . . . 5·00 5·00
29 1d. red . . . . 4·00 3·00
43 1½d. mauve . . . . 12·00 4·00
15a **3** 2d. brown . . . . 9·50 8·00
16a **2** 2½d. red . . . . 20·00 9·00
32 2½d. blue . . . . 3·75 7·00
9 5d. black . . . . 20·00 15·00
18a **3** 6d. purple . . . . 19·00 25·00
19 **2** 10d. green . . . . 18·00 48·00
46 **3** 1s. red . . . . 27·00 95·00

1899. Surch **ONE HALF PENNY**.
21 **2** ½d. on 1d. blue . . . . . . 32·00 42·00

1901. Optd with crown.
22 **2** 1d. brown £180 £140

1919. New Zealand stamps (King George V) surch **RAROTONGA** and value in native language in words.
56 **62** ½d. green . . . . 40 1·00
47 **53** 1d. red . . . . 1·00 3·00
57 **62** 1½d. brown 50 75
58 2d. yellow . . . . 1·50 1·75
48a 2½d. blue . . . . 2·00 2·25
49a 3d. brown . . . . 2·50 2·00
50c 4d. violet . . . . 1·75 4·25
51a 4½d. green . . . . 1·75 8·00
52a 6d. red . . . . 1·75 5·50
53 7½d. brown . . . . 1·50 5·50
54a 9d. green . . . . 2·00 15·00
55a 1s. red . . . . 2·75 18·00

9 Captain Cook landing

17 Harbour, Rarotonga and Mt. Ikurangi

1920. Inscr "RAROTONGA".

81	**9**	½d. black and green	4·50	8·50
82	–	1d. black and red	6·00	2·25
72	–	1½d. black and blue	8·50	8·50
83	–	2½d. brown and blue	6·00	24·00
73	–	3d. black and brown	2·25	5·50
84	**17**	4d. green and violet	10·00	16·00
74	–	6d. brown and orange	3·00	8·50
75	–	1s. black and violet	5·00	17·00

DESIGNS—VERT: 1d. Wharf at Avarua; 1½d. Captain Cook (Dance); 2½d. Te Po, Rarotongan chief; 3d. Palm tree. HORIZ: 6d. Huts at Arorangi; 1s. Avarua Harbour.

1921. New Zealand stamps optd **RAROTONGA**.

76	F **4**	2s. blue	27·00	55·00
77		2s.6d. brown	19·00	50·00
78		5s. green	27·00	65·00
79		10s. red	75·00	£120
80		£1 red	£120	£200

1926. "Admiral" type of New Zealand optd **RAROTONGA**.

90	**71**	2s. blue	10·00	40·00
92		3s. mauve	16·00	42·00

1931. No. 77 surch **TWO PENCE**.

93	2d. on 1½d. black and blue	9·50	2·75

1931. Arms type of New Zealand optd **RAROTONGA**.

95	F **6**	2s.6d. brown	10·00	22·00
96		5s. green	19·00	55·00
97		10s. red	38·00	95·00
98		£1 pink	95·00	£160

20 Captain Cook landing

22 Double Maori Canoe

1932. Inscribed "COOK ISLANDS".

106	**20**	½d. black and green	1·00	4·50
138	–	1d. black and red	2·00	1·00
108	**22**	2d. black and brown	1·50	50
140	–	2½d. black and blue	1·00	2·00
110	–	4d. black and blue	1·50	50
111	–	6d. black and orange	1·75	2·25
105	–	1s. black and violet	13·00	22·00

DESIGNS—VERT: 1d. Captain Cook. HORIZ: 2½d. Natives working cargo; 4d. Port of Avarua; 6d. R.M.S. "Monowai"; 1s. King George V.

1935. Jubilee. As 1932 optd **SILVER JUBILEE OF KING GEORGE V. 1910-1935.**

113	1d. red	60	1·40
114	2½d. blue	1·50	2·50
115	6d. green and orange	3·75	6·00

1936. Stamps of New Zealand optd **COOK ISLANDS.**

116	**71**	2s. blue	13·00	45·00
131w	F **6**	2s.6d. brown	24·00	24·00
117	**71**	3s. mauve	13·00	70·00
132	F **6**	5s. green	11·00	24·00
133w		10s. red	60·00	90·00
134		£1 pink	65·00	£100
135w		£3 green	60·00	£160
98b		£5 blue	£200	£325

1937. Coronation. T **106** of New Zealand optd **COOK IS'DS.**

124	**106**	1d. red	40	80
125		2½d. blue	80	1·40
126		6d. orange	80	60

29 King George VI

30 Native Village

1938.

143	**29**	1s. black and violet	3·00	2·50
128	**30**	2s. black and brown	18·00	13·00
145	–	3s. blue and green	38·00	32·00

DESIGN—HORIZ: 3s. Native canoe.

32 Tropical Landscape

34 Ngatangiia Channel, Rarotonga

1940.

130	**32**	3d. on 1½d. black & purple	75	60

1946. Peace. Peace stamps of New Zealand of 1946 optd **COOK ISLANDS**.

146	**132**	1d. green	30	10
147	–	2d. purple	30	50
148	–	6d. brown and red	1·00	1·25
149	**139**	8d. black and red	60	1·25

1949.

150	**34**	½d. violet and brown	10	1·25
151	–	1d. brown and green	3·50	2·25
152	–	2d. brown and red	2·00	2·25
153	–	3d. green and blue	2·75	2·00
154	–	5d. green and violet	6·00	1·50
155	–	6d. black and red	5·50	2·75
156	–	8d. olive and orange	55	3·75
157	–	1s. blue and brown	4·25	3·75
158	–	2s. brown and red	3·00	13·00
159	–	3s. blue and green	14·00	24·00

DESIGNS—HORIZ: 1d. Captain Cook and map of Hervey Is; 2d. Rarotonga and Rev. John Williams; 3d. Aitutaki and palm trees; 5d. Rarotonga Airfield; 6d. Penrhyn village; 8d. Native hut. VERT: 1s. Map and statue of Capt. Cook; 2s. Native hut and palms; 3s. "Matua" (inter-island freighter).

1953. Coronation. As Types of New Zealand but inscr "COOK ISLANDS".

160	**164**	3d. brown	1·00	85
161	**166**	6d. grey	1·25	1·50

1960. No. 154 surch **1/6**.

162	1s.6d. on 5d. green and violet	75	40

45 Tiare Maori

52 Queen Elizabeth II

55 "Tiare Taporo"

56 Eclipse and Palm

1963.

163	**45**	1d. green and yellow	45	65
164	–	2d. red and yellow	20	50
165	–	3d. yellow, green and violet	70	65
166	–	5d. blue and black	8·00	2·25
167	–	6d. red, yellow and green	1·00	60
168	–	8d. black and blue	4·25	1·50
169	–	1s. yellow and green	1·00	60
170	**52**	1s.6d. violet	2·75	2·00
171	–	2s. brown and blue	1·75	1·00
172	–	3s. black and green	1·75	1·75
173	**55**	5s. brown and blue	13·00	4·00

DESIGNS—VERT (As Type **45**): 2d. Fishing god; 8d. Long-tailed tuna. HORIZ (As Type **45**): 3d. Frangipani (plant); 5d. White tern ("Love Tern"); 6d. Hibiscus; 1s. Oranges. (As Type **55**): 2s. Island scene; 3s. Administration Centre, Mangaia.

1965. Solar Eclipse Observation, Manuae Island.

174	**56**	6d. black, yellow and blue	20	10

57 N.Z. Ensign and Map

1965. Internal Self-government.

175	**57**	4d. red and blue	20	10
176	–	10d. multicoloured	20	15
177	–	1s. multicoloured	20	15
178	–	1s.9d. multicoloured	50	1·25

DESIGNS: 10d. London Missionary Society Church; 1s. Proclamation of Cession, 1900; 1s.9d. Nikao School.

1966. Churchill Commemoration. Nos. 171/3 and 175/7 optd **In Memoriam SIR WINSTON CHURCHILL 1874 – 1965.**

179	**57**	4d. red and blue	1·00	30
180	–	10d. multicoloured	2·00	45
181	–	1s. multicoloured	2·00	65
182	–	2s. brown and blue	2·00	1·50
183	–	3s. black and green	2·00	1·50
184	**55**	5s. brown and blue	2·25	2·00

1966. Air. Various stamps optd **Airmail** and Douglas DC-3 airplane or surch in addition.

185	–	6d. red, yell & grn (No. 167)	1·25	20
186	–	7d. on 8d. blk & bl (No. 168)	2·00	25
187	–	10d. on 3d. green and violet (No. 165)	1·00	15
188	–	1s. yellow and green (No. 169)	1·00	15
189	**52**	1s.6d. violet	1·50	1·25
190	–	2s.3d. on 3s. black and green (No. 172)	1·00	65
191	**55**	5s. brown and blue	1·75	1·50
192	–	10s. on 2s. brown and blue (No. 171)	1·75	14·00
193	–	£1 pink (No. 134)	13·00	17·00

63 "Adoration of the Magi" (Fra Angelico)

1966. Christmas. Multicoloured.

194a	1d. Type **63**	10	10
195a	2d. "The Nativity" (Memling)	20	10
196a	4d. "Adoration of the Wise Men" (Velazquez)	30	15
197a	10d. "Adoration of the Wise Men" (H. Bosch)	30	20
198a	1s.6d. "Adoration of the Shepherds" (J. de Ribera)	40	35

68 Tennis and Queen Elizabeth II

1967. 2nd South Pacific Games, Noumea. Mult.

199	½d. Type **68** (postage)	10	10
200	1d. Basketball and Games emblem	10	10
201	4d. Boxing and Cook Islands Team badge	10	10
202	7d. Football and Queen Elizabeth II	20	15
203	10d. Running and Games Emblem (air)	20	15
204	2s.3d. Running and Cook Islands' Team badge	25	65

1967. Decimal currency. Various stamps surch.

205	**45**	1c. on 1d.	45	1·50
206	–	2c. on 2d. (No. 164)	10	10
207	–	2½c. on 3d. (No. 165)	20	10
209	**57**	3c. on 4d.	15	10
210	–	4c. on 5d. (No. 166)	10·00	30
211	–	5c. on 6d. (No. 167)	15	10
212	**56**	5c. on 6d.	5·00	1·25
213	–	7c. on 8d. (No. 168)	30	10
214	–	10c. on 1s. (No. 169)	15	10
215	**52**	15c. on 1s.6d.	2·00	1·00
216	–	30c. on 3s. (No. 172)	24·00	4·50
217	**55**	50c. on 5s.	4·00	1·25
218	–	$1 and 10s. on 10d. (No. 176)	17·00	5·50
219	–	$2 on £1 (No. 134)	55·00	75·00
220	–	$6 on £3 (No. 135)	£100	£140
221	–	$10 on £5 (No. 98)	£150	£170

75 Village Scene, Cook Islands 1d. Stamp of 1892 and Queen Victoria

1967. 75th Anniv of First Cook Islands Stamps. Multicoloured.

222	1c. (1d.) Type **75**	10	10
223	3c. (4d.) Post Office, Avarua, Rarotonga and Queen Elizabeth II	15	10
224	8c. (10d.) Avarua, Rarotonga and Cook Islands 10d. stamp of 1892	30	15
225	18c. (1s.9d.) "Moana Roa", (inter-island ship), Douglas DC-3 aircraft, map and Captain Cook	1·40	30
MS226	134×109 mm. Nos. 222/5	1·75	2·75

The face values are expressed in decimal currency and in the Sterling equivalent.

79 Hibiscus

81 Queen Elizabeth and Flowers

1967. Flowers. Multicoloured.

227A	½c. Type **79**	10	10
228A	1c. "Hibiscus syriacus"	10	10
229A	2c. Frangipani	10	10
230A	2½c. "Clitoria ternatea"	20	10
231B	3c. "Suva Queen"	40	10
232A	4c. Water lily (wrongly inscribed "Walter Lily")	70	1·00
233B	4c. Water lily	2·50	10
234B	5c. "Bauhinia bipinnata rosea"	30	10
235B	6c. Yellow hibiscus	30	10
236B	8c. "Allamanda cathartica"	30	10
237B	9c. Stephanotis	30	10
238B	10c. "Poinciana regia flamboyant"	30	10
239A	15c. Frangipani	40	10
240B	20c. Thunbergia	3·50	1·50
241A	25c. Canna lily	80	30
242A	30c. "Euphorbia pulcherrima poinsettia"	65	50
243A	50c. "Gardinia taitensis"	1·00	55
244B	$1 Queen Elizabeth II	1·25	80
245B	$2 Queen Elizabeth II	2·25	1·50
246A	$4 Type **81**	1·50	4·25
247A	$6 Type **81**	1·75	5·50
247cA	$8 Type **81**	5·00	16·00
248A	$10 Type **81**	3·25	12·00

97 "Ia Orana Maria"

1967. Gauguin's Polynesian Paintings.

249	**97**	1c. multicoloured	10	10
250	–	3c. multicoloured	15	10
251	–	5c. multicoloured	20	10
252	–	8c. multicoloured	25	10
253	–	15c. multicoloured	50	15
254	–	22c. multicoloured	65	20
MS255		156×132 mm. Nos. 249/54	1·75	1·50

DESIGNS: 3c. "Riders on the Beach"; 5c. "Still Life with Flowers" and inset portrait of Queen Elizabeth; 8c. "Whispered Words"; 15c. "Maternity"; 22c. "Why are you angry?".

98 "The Holy Family" (Rubens)

100 "Matavai Bay, Tahiti" (J. Barralet)

1967. Christmas. Renaissance Paintings.

256	**98**	1c. multicoloured	10	10
257	–	3c. multicoloured	10	10
258	–	4c. multicoloured	10	10
259	–	8c. multicoloured	20	15
260	–	15c. multicoloured	35	15
261	–	25c. multicoloured	40	15

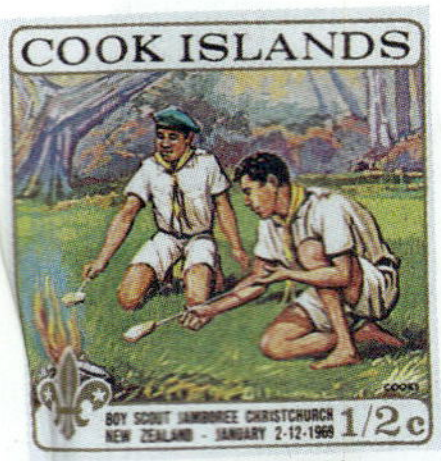DESIGNS: 3c. "The Epiphany" (Durer); 4c. "The Lucca Madonna" (J. van Eyck); 8c. "The Adora-tion of the Shepherds" (J. da Bassano); 15c. "The Nativity" (El Greco); 25c. "The Madonna and Child" (Correggio).

1968. Hurricane Relief. Nos. 231, 233, 251, 238, 241 and 243/4 optd **HURRICANE RELIEF PLUS** and premium.

262 3c.+1c. multicoloured 15 15
263 4c.+1c. multicoloured 15 15
264 5c.+2c. multicoloured 15 15
265 10c.+2c. multicoloured . . . 15 15
266 25c.+5c. multicoloured . . . 20 20
267 50c.+10c. multicoloured . . . 25 30
268 $1+10c. multicoloured . . . 35 50

On No. 264 silver blocking obliterates the design area around the lettering.

1968. Bicentenary of Captain Cook's First Voyage of Discovery.

269 **100** $\frac{1}{2}$c. mult (postage) 10 10
270 – 1c. multicoloured 15 10
271 – 2c. multicoloured 30 20
272 – 4c. multicoloured 40 20
273 – 6c. multicoloured (air) . . 45 25
274 – 10c. multicoloured 45 25
275 – 15c. multicoloured 50 35
276 – 25c. multicoloured 60 55

DESIGNS—VERT: 1c. "Island of Huaheine" (John Cleveley); 2c. "Town of St. Peter and St. Paul, Kamchatka" (J. Webber); 4c. "The Ice Islands" (Antarctica: W. Hodges). HORIZ: 6c. "Resolution" and "Discovery" (J. Webber); 10c. "The Island of Tahiti" (W. Hodges); 15c. "Karakakooa, Hawaii" (J. Webber); 25c. "The Landing at Middleburg" (J. Sherwin).

102 Dinghy-sailing

1968. Olympic Games, Mexico. Multicoloured.

277 1c. Type **102** 10 10
278 5c. Gymnastics 10 10
279 15c. High-jumping 25 10
280 20c. High-diving 25 10
281 30c. Cycling 60 20
282 50c. Hurdling 50 25

103 "Madonna and Child" (Titian)

1968. Christmas. Multicoloured.

283 1c. Type **103** 10 10
284 4c. "The Holy Family of the Lamb" (Raphael) 15 10
285 10c. "The Madonna of the Rosary" (Murillo) 25 10
286 20c. "Adoration of the Magi" (Memling) 40 10
287 30c. "Adoration of the Magi" (Ghirlandaio) 45 10
MS288 114 × 177 mm. Nos. 283/7 1·25 1·60

104 Campfire Cooking

1969. Diamond Jubilee of New Zealand Scout Movement and 5th National (New Zealand) Jamboree. Multicoloured.

289 $\frac{1}{2}$c. Type **104** 10 10
290 1c. Descent by rope 10 10
291 5c. Semaphore 15 10
292 10c. Tree-planting 20 10
293 20c. Constructing a shelter . . 25 15
294 30c. Lord Baden-Powell and island scene 45 25

105 High Jumping

1969. 3rd South Pacific Games, Port Moresby. Multicoloured.

295 $\frac{1}{2}$c. Type **105** 10 40
296 $\frac{1}{2}$c. Footballer 10 40
297 1c. Basketball 50 40
298 1c. Weightlifter 50 40
299 4c. Tennis-player 50 50
300 4c. Hurdler 50 50
301 10c. Javelin-thrower 55 50
302 10c. Runner 55 50
303 15c. Golfer . . . . 1·75 1·50
304 15c. Boxer . . . . 1·75 1·50
MS305 174 × 129 mm. Nos. 295/304 7·50 6·00

106 Flowers, Map and Captain Cook ($\frac{1}{2}$-size illustration)

1969. South Pacific Conference, Noumea. Mult.

306 5c. Premier Albert Henry . . 20 20
307 10c. Type **106** 80 40
308 25c. Flowers, map and arms of New Zealand 30 40
309 30c. Queen Elizabeth II, map and flowers 30 40

107 "Virgin and Child with Saints Jerome and Dominic" (Lippi)

1969. Christmas. Multicoloured.

310 1c. Type **107** 10 10
311 4c. "The Holy Family" (Fra Bartolomeo) 10 10
312 10c. "The Adoration of the Shepherds" (A. Mengs) . . 15 10
313 20c. "Madonna and Child with Saints" (Robert Campin) 25 20
314 30c. "The Madonna of the Basket" (Correggio) . . . 25 30
MS315 132 × 97 mm. Nos. 310/14 1·00 1·50

108 "The Resurrection of Christ" (Raphael)

115 Mary, Joseph, and Christ in Manger

110 The Royal Family

1970. Easter.

316 **108** 4c. multicoloured 10 10
317 – 8c. multicoloured 10 10
318 – 20c. multicoloured 15 10
319 – 25c. multicoloured 20 10
MS320 132 × 162 mm. Nos. 316/19 1·25 1·25

DESIGNS: "The Resurrection of Christ" by Dirk Bouts (8c.), Altdorfer (20c.), Murillo (25c.).

1970. "Apollo 13". Nos. 233, 236, 239/40, 242 and 245/6 optd **KIA ORANA APOLLO 13 ASTRONAUTS Te Atua to Tatou Irinakianga.**

321 4c. multicoloured 10 10
322 8c. multicoloured 10 10
323 15c. multicoloured 10 10
324 20c. multicoloured 40 15
325 30c. multicoloured 20 20
326 $2 multicoloured 50 90
327a $4 multicoloured . . . . . 1·00 2·75

1970. Royal Visit to New Zealand. Multicoloured.

328 5c. Type **110** 50 30
329 30c. Captain Cook and H.M.S. "Endeavour" . . . 2·00 1·75
330 $1 Royal Visit commemorative coin . . . 3·00 3·00
MS331 145 × 97 mm. Nos. 328/30 9·50 10·00

1970. 5th Anniv of Self-Government. Nos. 328/30 optd **FIFTH ANNIVERSARY SELF-GOVERNMENT AUGUST 1970.**

332 **110** 5c. multicoloured 40 15
333 – 30c. multicoloured 80 35
334 – $1 multicoloured . . . . 1·00 90

On No. 332, the opt is arranged in one line around the frame of the stamp.

1970. Surch **FOUR DOLLARS $4.00.**

335a **81** $4 on $8 multicoloured 1·25 1·75
336a $4 on $10 multicoloured 1·25 1·50

1970. Christmas. Multicoloured.

337 1c. Type **115** 10 10
338 4c. Shepherds and Apparition of the Angel 10 10
339 10c. Mary showing Child to Joseph 15 10
340 20c. The Wise Men bearing Gifts 20 20
341 30c. Parents wrapping Child in swaddling clothes . . . 25 35
MS342 100 × 139 mm. Nos. 337/41 1·00 1·50

1971. Surch **PLUS 20c UNITED KINGDOM SPECIAL MAIL SERVICE.**

343 30c.+20c. (No. 242) 30 50
344 50c.+20c. (No. 243) . . . . 1·00 1·75

The premium of 20c. was to prepay a private delivery service fee in Great Britain during the postal strike. The mail was sent by air to a forwarding address in the Netherlands. No. 343 was intended for ordinary airmail $\frac{1}{2}$ oz. letters, and No. 344 included registration fee.

117 Wedding of Princess Elizabeth and Prince Philip

1971. Royal Visit of Duke of Edinburgh. Multicoloured.

345 1c. Type **117** 30 50
346 4c. Queen Elizabeth, Prince Philip, Prince Charles and Princess Anne at Windsor 75 1·10
347 10c. Prince Philip sailing . . 1·25 1·25
348 15c. Prince Philip in polo gear . . . . 1·25 1·25
349 25c. Prince Philip in naval uniform, and Royal Yacht, "Britannia" . . . . . . 1·50 2·00
MS350 168 × 122 mm. Nos. 345/9 6·50 10·00

1971. 4th South Pacific Games, Tahiti. Nos. 238, 241 and 242 optd **Fourth South Pacific Games Papeete** and emblem or surch also.

351 10c. multicoloured 10 10
352 10c.+1c. multicoloured . . . 10 10
353 10c.+3c. multicoloured . . . 10 10
354 25c. multicoloured 15 10
355 25c.+1c. multicoloured . . . 15 10
356 25c.+3c. multicoloured . . . 15 10
357 30c. multicoloured 15 10
358 30c.+1c. multicoloured . . . 15 10
359 30c.+3c. multicoloured . . . 15 10

The stamps additionally surch 1c. or 3c. helped to finance the Cook Islands' team at the games.

1971. Nos. 230, 233, 236/7 and 239 surch **10c.**

360 10c. on 2$\frac{1}{2}$c. multicoloured . . 15 25
361 10c. on 4c. multicoloured . . 15 25
362 10c. on 8c. multicoloured . . 15 25
363 10c. on 9c. multicoloured . . 15 25
364 10c. on 15c. multicoloured . . 15 25

121 "Virgin and Child" (Bellini)

123 St. John

1971. Christmas.

365 **121** 1c. multicoloured 10 20
366 – 4c. multicoloured 10 20
367 – 10c. multicoloured 25 10
368 – 20c. multicoloured 50 20
369 – 30c. multicoloured 50 40
MS370 135 × 147 mm. Nos. 365/9 2·00 3·25
MS371 92 × 98 mm. 50c. + 5c. "The Holy Family in a Garland of Flowers" (Jan Brueghel and Pieter van Avont) (41 × 41 mm) . . . 75 1·40

DESIGNS: Various paintings of the "Virgin and Child" by Bellini. Similar to Type **121**.

1972. 25th Anniv of South Pacific Commission. No. 244 optd **SOUTH PACIFIC COMMISSION FEB. 1947 – 1972.**

372 $1 multicoloured 40 75

1972. Easter. Multicoloured.

373 5c. Type **123** 10 10
374 10c. Christ on the Cross . . 10 10
375 30c. Mary, Mother of Jesus 25 40
MS376 79 × 112 mm. Nos. 373/5 forming triptych of "The Crucifixion" . . . . 1·00 2·25

1972. Hurricane Relief. (a) Nos. 239, 241 and 243 optd **HURRICANE RELIEF PLUS** and premium.

379 15c.+5c. multicoloured . . . 20 20
380 25c.+5c. multicoloured . . . 20 20
382 50c.+10c. multicoloured . . . 25 25

(b) Nos. 373/5 optd **Hurricane Relief Plus** and premium.

377 5c.+2c. multicoloured 15 15
378 10c.+2c. multicoloured . . . 15 15
381 30c.+5c. multicoloured . . . 20 20

126/7 Rocket heading for Moon

1972. Apollo Moon Exploration Flights. Mult.

383 5c. Type **126** 20 15
384 5c. Type **127** 20 15
385 10c. Lunar module and astronaut 20 15
386 10c. Astronaut and experiment 20 15
387 25c. Command capsule and Earth 25 20
388 25c. Lunar Rover 25 20
389 30c. Sikorsky Sea King helicopter . . . . 1·00 40
390 30c. Splashdown . . . . . 1·00 40
MS391 83 × 205 mm. Nos. 383/90 4·50 6·00

These were issued in horizontal se-tenant pairs of each value, forming one composite design.

1972. Hurricane Relief. Nos. 383/390 surch **HURRICANE RELIEF Plus** and premium.

392 5c.+2c. multicoloured 10 10
393 5c.+2c. multicoloured 10 10
394 10c.+2c. multicoloured . . . 10 10
395 10c.+2c. multicoloured . . . 10 10
396 25c.+2c. multicoloured . . . 15 15
397 25c.+2c. multicoloured . . . 15 15
398 30c.+2c. multicoloured . . . 25 15
399 30c.+2c. multicoloured . . . 25 15
MS400 83 × 205 mm. No. **MS**391 surch 3c. on each stamp . . . 2·50 3·50

129 High-jumping

130 "The Rest on the Flight into Egypt" (Caravaggio)

1972. Olympic Games, Munich. Multicoloured.

401 10c. Type **129** 20 10
402 25c. Running 40 15
403 30c. Boxing 40 20
MS404 88 × 78 mm. 50c. + 5c. Pierre de Coubertin . . . . 1·00 2·00
MS405 84 × 133 mm. Nos. 401/3 1·25 2·00

1972. Christmas. Multicoloured.

406 1c. Type **130** 10 10
407 5c. "Madonna of the Swallow" (Guercino) . . . 25 10
408 10c. "Madonna of the Green Cushion" (Solario) . . . 35 10
409 20c. "Madonna and Child" (di Credi) 55 20
410 30c. "Madonna and Child" (Bellini) 85 30
MS411 141 × 152 mm. Nos. 406/10 3·25 4·00
MS412 101 × 82 mm. 50c. + 5c. "The Holy Night" (Correggio) (31 × 43 mm) . . . . 75 1·50

131 Marriage Ceremony

133 "Noli me Tangere" (Titian)

132 Taro Leaf

1972. Royal Silver Wedding. Each black and silver.
413 5c. Type **131** 25 15
414 10c. Leaving Westminster Abbey 35 25
415 15c. Bride and bridegroom (40 × 41 mm) 45 50
416 30c. Family group (67 × 40 mm) 55 75

1973. Silver Wedding Coinage.
417 **132** 1c. gold, mauve and black 10 10
418 – 2c. gold, blue and black 10 10
419 – 5c. silver, green and black 10 10
420 – 10c. silver, blue and black 20 10
421 – 20c. silver, green and black 30 10
422 – 50c. silver, mauve and black 50 15
423 – $1 silver, blue and black 75 30
DESIGNS—HORIZ (37 × 24 mm): 2c. Pineapple; 5c. Hibiscus. (46 × 30 mm): 10c. Oranges; 20c. White tern; 50c. Striped bonito. VERT: (32 × 55 mm): $1 Tangaroa.

1973. Easter. Multicoloured.
424 5c. Type **133** 15 10
425 10c. "The Descent from the Cross" (Rubens) 20 10
426 30c. "The Lamentation of Christ" (Durer) 25 10
MS427 132 × 67 mm. Nos. 424/6 55 1·25

1973. Easter. Children's Charity. Designs as Nos. 424/6 in separate miniature sheets 67 × 87 mm, each with a face value of 50c. + 5c.
MS428 As Nos. 424/6 Set of 3 sheets 1·00 1·75

134 Queen Elizabeth II in Coronation Regalia

137 The Annunciation

136 Tipairua

1973. 20th Anniv of Queen Elizabeth's Coronation.
429 **134** 10c. multicoloured 50 90
MS430 64 × 89 mm. 50c. as 10c. 2·50 2·25

1973. 10th Anniv of Treaty Banning Nuclear Testing. Nos. 234, 236, 238 and 240/2 optd **TENTH ANNIVERSARY CESSATION OF NUCLEAR TESTING TREATY.**
431 5c. multicoloured 10 10
432 8c. multicoloured 10 10
433 10c. multicoloured 10 10
434 20c. multicoloured 15 15
435 25c. multicoloured 20 15
436 30c. multicoloured 20 15

1973. Maori Exploration of the Pacific. Sailing Craft. Multicoloured.
437 ½c. Type **136** 10 10
438 1c. Wa'a Kaulua 10 10
439 1½c. Tainui 15 10
440 5c. War canoe 30 15
441 10c. Pahi 40 15
442 15c. Amatasi 60 65
443 25c. Vaka 75 80

1973. Christmas. Scene from a 15th-century Flemish "Book of Hours". Multicoloured.
444 1c. Type **137** 10 10
445 5c. The Visitation 10 10
446 10c. Annunciation to the Shepherds 10 10
447 20c. Epiphany 15 10
448 30c. The Slaughter of the Innocents 20 15
MS449 121 × 128 mm. Nos. 444/8 55 1·40
See also No. **MS**454.

138 Princess Anne

140 "Jesus carrying the Cross" (Raphael)

139 Running

1973. Royal Wedding. Multicoloured.
450 25c. Type **138** 20 10
451 30c. Captain Mark Phillips 25 10
452 50c. Princess Anne and Captain Phillips 30 15
MS453 119 × 100 mm. Nos. 450/2 55 35

1973. Christmas. Children's Charity. Designs as Nos. 444/8 in separate miniature sheets 50 × 70 mm, each with a face value of 50c. + 5c.
MS454 As Nos. 444/8 Set of 5 sheets 75 80

1974. British Commonwealth Games, Christchurch. Multicoloured.
455 1c. Diving (vert) 10 10
456 3c. Boxing (vert) 10 10
457 5c. Type 139 . . . . 10 10
458 10c. Weightlifting 10 10
459 30c. Cycling 40 25
MS460 115 × 90 mm. 50c. Discobolus 40 55

1974. Easter. Multicoloured.
461 5c. Type **140** 10 20
462 10c. "The Holy Trinity" (El Greco) 15 20
463 30c. "The Deposition of Christ" (Caravaggio) . . . 25 30
MS464 130 × 70 mm. Nos. 461/3 1·50 70

1974. Easter. Children's Charity. Designs as Nos. 461/3 in separate miniature sheets 59 × 87 mm, each with a face value of 50c. + 5c.
MS465 As Nos. 461/3 Set of 3 sheets 70 1·40

141 Grey Bonnet

142 Queen Elizabeth II

1974. Sea Shells. Multicoloured.
466 ½c. Type **141** 30 10
467 1c. Common Pacific vase . . 30 10
468 1½c. True heart cockle . . . 30 10
469 2c. Terebellum conch 30 10
470 3c. Bat volute 45 10
471 4c. Gibbose conch 50 10
472 5c. Common hairy triton . . 50 10
473 6c. Serpent's head cowrie . . 50 2·00
474 8c. Granulate frog shell . . . 60 10
475 10c. Fly-spotted auger . . . 60 10
476 15c. Episcopan mitre 70 20
477 20c. Butterfly moon . . . . 1·00 20
478 25c. Royal oak scallop . . . 1·00 2·50
479 30c. Soldier cone . . . . . 1·00 30
480 50c. Textile or cloth of gold cone . . . . 8·50 4·50
481 60c. Red-mouth olive . . . . 8·50 4·50
482 $1 Type **142** . . . . 3·00 4·50
483 $2 Type **142** . . . . 1·75 2·25
484 $4 Queen Elizabeth II and sea shells (60 × 39 mm) . . 2·50 7·00
485 $6 As $4 (60 × 39 mm) . . . 16·00 7·00
486 $8 As $4 (60 × 39 mm) . . . 21·00 9·00
487 $10 As $4 (60 × 39 mm) . . . 23·00 9·00

143 Footballer and Australasian Map

1974. World Cup Football Championship, West Germany. Multicoloured.
488 25c. Type **143** 20 10
489 50c. Map and Munich Stadium 35 25
490 $1 Footballer, stadium and World Cup 55 45
MS491 89 × 100 mm. Nos. 488/90 1·00 2·75

144 Obverse and Reverse of Commemorative $2.50 Silver Coin

146 "Madonna of the Goldfinch" (Raphael)

1974. Bicentenary of Captain Cook's Second Voyage of Discovery.
492 **144** $2.50 silver, black and violet . . . . 12·00 7·00
493 – $7.50 silver, black and green . . . . 20·00 13·00
MS494 73 × 73 mm. Nos. 492/3 35·00 48·00
DESIGN: $7.50, As Type **144** but showing $7.50 coin.

145 Early Stamps of Cook Islands

1974. Centenary of UPU. Multicoloured.
495 10c. Type **145** 25 15
496 25c. Old landing strip, Rarotonga, and stamp of 1898 . . . . 35 40
497 30c. Post Office, Rarotonga, and stamp of 1920 . . . . 40 40
498 50c. UPU emblem and stamps 40 65
MS499 118 × 79 mm. Nos. 495/8 1·00 1·75

1974. Christmas. Multicoloured.
500 1c. Type **146** 10 10
501 5c. "The Sacred Family" (Andrea del Sarto) 20 10
502 10c. "The Virgin adoring the Child" (Correggio) 25 10
503 20c. "The Holy Family" (Rembrandt) 40 20
504 30c. "The Virgin and Child" (Rogier van der Weyden) 50 30
MS505 114 × 133 mm. Nos. 500/4 1·40 2·25

147 Churchill and Blenheim Palace

1974. Birth Centenary of Sir Winston Churchill. Multicoloured.
506 5c. Type **147** 15 10
507 10c. Churchill and Houses of Parliament 15 10
508 25c. Churchill and Chartwell 25 20
509 30c. Churchill and Buckingham Palace 25 25
510 50c. Churchill and St. Paul's Cathedral 30 50
MS511 108 × 114 mm. Nos. 506/10 1·25 1·00

1974. Christmas. Children's Charity. Designs as Nos. 500/504 in separate miniature sheets 53 × 69 mm, each with a face value of 50c. + 5c.
MS512 As Nos. 500/4 Set of 5 sheets 1·00 1·00

148 Vasco Nunez de Balboa and Discovery of Pacific Ocean (1513)

1975. Pacific Explorers. Multicoloured.
513 1c. Type **148** 15 10
514 5c. Fernando de Magellanes and map (1520) 65 20
515 10c. Juan Sebastian del Cano and "Vitoria" (1520) . . . 1·25 20
516 25c. Friar Andres de Urdaneta and ship (1564–67) . . . . 2·25 75
517 30c. Miguel Lopez de Legazpi and ship (1564–67) . . . . 2·25 80

149 "Apollo" Capsule

1975. "Apollo–Soyuz" Space Project. Mult.
518 25c. Type **149** 45 15
519 25c. "Soyuz" capsule 45 15
520 30c. "Soyuz" crew 50 15
521 30c. "Apollo" crew 50 15
522 50c. Cosmonaut within "Soyuz" 55 25
523 50c. Astronauts within "Apollo" 55 25
MS524 119 × 119 mm. Nos. 518/23 1·50 1·00
These were issued in horizontal se-tenant pairs of each value, forming one composite design.

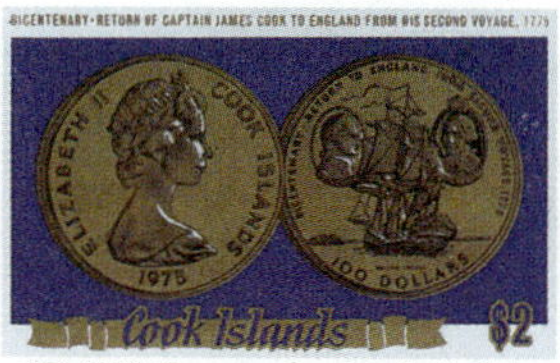

150 $100 Commemorative Gold Coin

1975. Bicentenary of Captain Cook's 2nd Voyage.
525 **150** $2 brown, gold and violet 2·50 1·75

151 Cook Islands' Flag and Map

1975. 10th Anniv of Self-government.
526 5c. Type **151** 40 10
527 10c. Premier Sir Albert Henry and flag (vert) 45 10
528 25c. Rarotonga and flag . . 80 30

1975. Christmas. Multicoloured.
529 6c. Type **152** 20 10
530 10c. "Madonna in the Meadow" (Raphael) . . . 20 10
531 15c. "Madonna of the Oak" (att. Raphael) 30 10
532 20c. "Adoration of the Shepherds" (J. B. Maino) 30 15
533 35c. "The Annunciation" (Murillo) 50 20
MS534 110 × 124 mm. Nos. 529/33 1·10 90

152 "Madonna by the Fireside" (R. Campin)

1975. Christmas. Children's Charity. Designs as Nos. 529/33 in separate miniature sheets 53 × 71 mm, each with a face value of 75c. + 5c.
MS535 As Nos. 529/33 Set of 5 sheets . . . . 1·10 1·25

153 "Entombment of Christ" (Raphael)

1976. Easter. Multicoloured.
536 7c. Type **153** 30 10
537 15c. "Pieta" (Veronese) 50 15
538 35c. "Pieta" (El Greco) 75 25
MS539 144 × 55 mm. Nos. 536/8 1·50 85

1976. Easter. Children's Charity. Designs as Nos. 536/8 in separate miniature sheets 69 × 69 mm, each with a face value of 60c. + 5c.
MS540 As Nos. 536/8 Set of 3 sheets 1·10 1·40

154 Benjamin Franklin and H.M.S. "Resolution"

1976. Bicent of American Revolution. Mult.
541 $1 Type **154** 6·00 1·50
542 $2 Captain Cook and H.M.S. "Resolution" 8·00 2·50
MS543 118 × 58 mm. $3 Cook, Franklin and H.M.S. "Resolution" (74 × 31 mm) 13·00 6·50

1976. Visit of Queen Elizabeth to U.S.A. Nos. 541/2 optd **Royal Visit July 1976.**
544 **154** $1 multicoloured 4·00 1·50
545 – $2 multicoloured 6·00 2·50
MS546 $3 Cook, Franklin and H.M.S. "Resolution" 7·00 5·50

156 Hurdling

157 "The Visitation"

1976. Olympic Games, Montreal. Multicoloured.
547 7c. Type **156** 20 10
548 7c. Hurdling (value on left) 20 10
549 15c. Hockey (value on right) 40 15
550 15c. Hockey (value on left) 40 15
551 30c. Fencing (value on right) 40 15
552 30c. Fencing (value on left) 40 15
553 35c. Football (value on right) 40 20
554 35c. Football (value on left) 40 20
MS555 104 × 146 mm. Nos. 547/54 3·50 2·00

1976. Christmas. Renaissance Sculptures. Mult.
556 6c. Type **157** 10 10
557 10c. "Adoration of the Shepherds" 10 10
558 15c. "Adoration of the Shepherds" (different) 15 10
559 20c. "The Epiphany" 20 20
560 35c. "The Holy Family" 25 25
MS561 116 × 110 mm. Nos. 556/60 1·00 1·75

1976. Christmas. Children's Charity. Designs as Nos. 556/60 in separate miniature sheets 66 × 80 mm, each with a face value of 75c. + 5c.
MS562 As Nos. 556/60 Set of 5 sheets 1·10 1·10

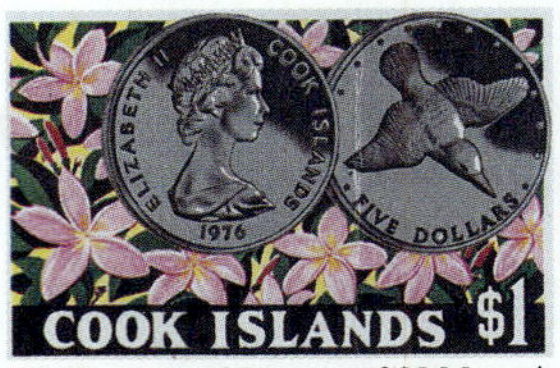
158 Obverse and Reverse of $5 Mangaia Kingfisher Coin

1976. National Wildlife and Conservation Day.
563 **158** $1 multicoloured 1·00 1·00

159 Imperial State Crown

1977. Silver Jubilee. Multicoloured.
564 25c. Type **159** 40 50
565 25c. The Queen with regalia 40 50
566 50c. Westminster Abbey 50 65
567 50c. Coronation coach 50 65
568 $1 The Queen and Prince Philip 80 90
569 $1 Royal Visit, 1974 80 90
MS570 130 × 136 mm. As Nos. 564/9 (borders and "COOK ISLANDS" in a different colour) 2·25 2·00

160 "Christ on the Cross"

161 "Virgin and Child" (Memling)

1977. Easter. 400th Birth Anniv of Rubens. Multicoloured.
571 7c. Type **160** 35 10
572 15c. "Christ on the Cross" 55 15
573 35c. "The Deposition of Christ" 1·10 30
MS574 118 × 65 mm. Nos. 571/3 1·40 1·60

1977. Easter. Children's Charity. Designs as Nos. 571/3 in separate miniature sheets 60 × 79 mm, each with a face value of 60c. + 5c.
MS575 As Nos. 571/3 Set of 3 sheets 1·00 1·00

1977. Christmas. Multicoloured.
576 6c. Type **161** 25 10
577 10c. "Madonna and Child with Saints and Donors" (Memling) 25 10
578 15c. "Adoration of the Kings" (Geertgen) 35 10
579 20c. "Virgin and Child with Saints" (Crivelli) 45 15
580 35c. "Adoration of the Magi" (16th century Flemish school) 60 20
MS581 118 × 111 mm. Nos. 576/80 1·40 1·75

1977. Christmas. Children's Charity. Designs as Nos. 576/80 in separate miniature sheets 69 × 69 mm, each with a face value of 75c. + 5c.
MS582 As Nos. 576/80 Set of 5 sheets 1·00 1·25

162 Obverse and Reverse of $5 Cook Islands Swiftlet Coin

1977. National Wildlife and Conservation Day.
583 **162** $1 multicoloured 1·00 65

163 Captain Cook and H.M.S. "Resolution" (from paintings by N. Dance and H. Roberts)

1978. Bicent of Discovery of Hawaii. Mult.
584 50c. Type **163** 1·00 60
585 $1 Earl of Sandwich and Cook landing at Owhyhee (from paintings by Thomas Gainsborough and J. Cleveley) 1·45 75
586 $2 Obverse and reverse of $200 coin and Cook monument, Hawaii 1·60 1·25
MS587 118 × 95 mm. Nos. 584/6 5·00 7·50

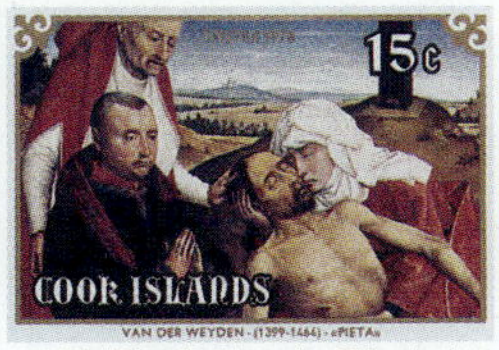
164 "Pieta" (Van der Weyden)

1978. Easter. Paintings from the National Gallery, London. Multicoloured.
588 15c. Type **164** 40 25
589 35c. "The Entombment" (Michelangelo) 50 40
590 75c. "The Supper at Emmaus" (Caravaggio) 75 65
MS591 114 × 96 mm. Nos. 588/90 1·50 2·00

1978. Easter. Children's Charity. Designs as Nos. 588/90 in separate miniature sheets, 85 × 72 mm, each with a face value of 60c. + 5c.
MS592 As Nos. 588/90 Set of 3 sheets 1·10 1·10

165 Queen Elizabeth II

169 "The Virgin and Child" (Van Der Weyden)

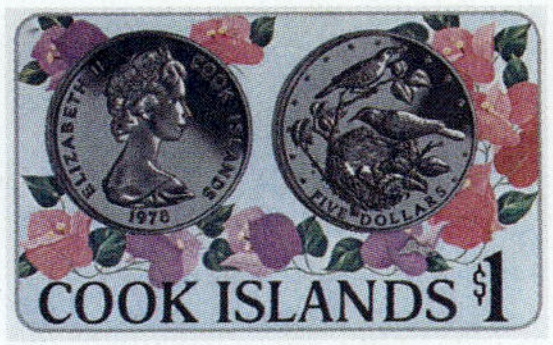
168 Obverse and Reverse of Cook Islands Warblers $5 Coin

1978. 25th Anniv of Coronation. Multicoloured.
593 50c. Type **165** 25 30
594 50c. The Lion of England 25 30
595 50c. Imperial State Crown 25 30
596 50c. Statue of Tangaroa (god) 25 30
597 70c. Type **165** 25 30
598 70c. Sceptre with Cross 25 30
599 70c. St. Edward's Crown 25 30
600 70c. Rarotongan staff god 25 30
MS601 103 × 142 mm. Nos. 593/600* 1·00 1·50
*In No. **MS**601 the designs of Nos. 595 and 599 are transposed.

1978. Nos. 466, 468, 473/4 and 478/82 surch.
602 5c. on 1½c. True heart cockle 60 10
603 7c. on ½c. Type **141** 65 15
604 10c. on 6c. Serpent's-head cowrie 70 15
605 10c. on 8c. Granulate frog shell 70 15
606 15c. on ½c. Type **141** 70 20
607 15c. on 25c. Royal oak scallop 70 20
608 15c. on 30c. Soldier cone 70 20
609 15c. on 50c. Textile or cloth of gold cone 70 20
610 15c. on 60c. Red-mouth olive 70 20
611 17c. on ½c. Type **141** 90 25
612 17c. on 50c. Textile or cloth of gold cone 90 25

1978. 250th Birth Anniv of Captain James Cook. Nos. 584/6 optd **1728 250th ANNIVERSARY OF COOK'S BIRTH 1978.**
613 50c. Type **163** 2·00 75
614 $1 Earl of Sandwich and Cook landing at Owhyhee 2·25 1·00
615 $2 $200 commemorative coin and Cook monument, Hawaii 2·50 2·00
MS616 Nos. 613/15 14·00 17·00

1978. National Wildlife and Conservation Day.
617 **168** $1 multicoloured 1·00 1·00

1978. Christmas. Paintings. Multicoloured.
618 15c. Type **169** 45 15
619 17c. "The Virgin and Child" (Crivelli) 45 20
620 35c. "The Virgin and Child" (Murillo) 80 35
MS621 107 × 70 mm. Nos. 618/20 1·50 1·50

1979. Christmas. Children's Charity. Designs as Nos. 618/20 in separate miniature sheets 57 × 87 mm, each with a face value of 75c. +5c.
MS622 As Nos. 618/20 Set of 3 sheets 1·00 1·00

170 Virgin with Body of Christ

171 "Captain Cook" (James Weber)

1979. Easter. Details of Painting "Descent" by Gaspar de Crayar. Multicoloured.
623 10c. Type **170** 25 10
624 12c. St. John 30 20
625 15c. Mary Magdalene 35 25
626 20c. Weeping angels 45 30
MS627 83 × 100 mm. As Nos. 623/6, but each with a charity premium of 2c. 65 75
Stamps from No. **MS**627 are slightly smaller, 32 × 40 mm, and are without borders.

1979. Death Bicentenary of Captain Cook. Mult.
628 20c. Type **171** 40 20
629 30c. H.M.S. "Resolution" 50 35
630 35c. H.M.S. "Royal George" (ship of the line) 50 45
631 50c. "Death of Captain Cook" (George Carter) 55 60
MS632 78 × 112 mm. Nos. 628/31 1·75 1·25
Stamps from No. **MS**632 have black borders.

172 Post-Rider

174 Brother and Sister

1979. Death Centenary of Sir Rowland Hill. Mult.
633 30c. Type **172** 15 20
634 30c. Mail coach 15 20
635 30c. Automobile 15 20
636 30c. Diesel train 15 20
637 35c. "Cap-Hornier" (full-rigged ship) 15 20
638 35c. River steamer 15 20
639 35c. "Deutschland" (liner) 15 20
640 35c. "United States" (liner) 15 20
641 50c. Balloon "Le Neptune" 25 25
642 50c. Junkers F13 airplane 25 25
643 50c. Airship "Graf Zeppelin" 25 25
644 50c. Concorde 25 25
MS645 132 × 104 mm. Nos. 633/44 3·75 4·00

1979. Nos. 466, 468 and 481 surch.
646 6c. on ½c. Type **141** 20 30
647 10c. on 1½c. Cockle shell 25 20
648 15c. on 60c. Olive shell 40 40

1979. International Year of the Child. Mult.
649 30c. Type **174** 25 25
650 50c. Boy with tree drum 40 40
651 65c. Children dancing 50 50
MS652 102 × 75 mm. As Nos. 649/51, but each with a charity premium of 5c. 1·00 1·50
Designs for stamps from No. **MS**652 are as Nos. 649/51 but have IYC emblem in red.

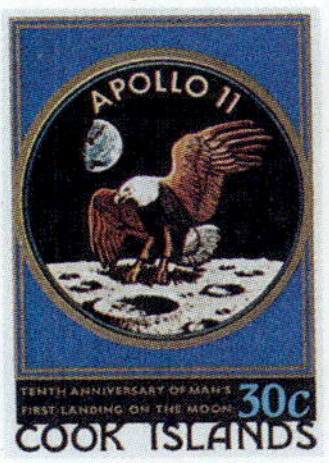
175 "Apollo 11" Emblem

177 Glass Christmas Tree Ornaments

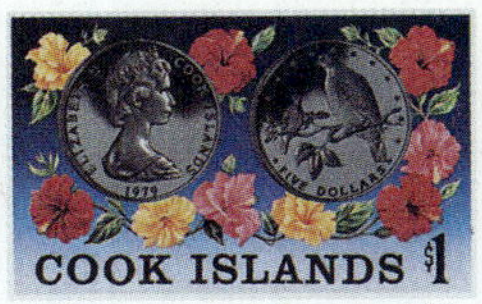
176 Obverse and Reverse of $5 Rarotongan Fruit Dove Coin

1979. 10th Anniv of "Apollo 11" Moon Landing. Multicoloured.
653 30c. Type **175** 40 60
654 50c. "Apollo 11" crew 50 80

655 60c. Neil Armstrong on the Moon . . . . 65 1·00
656 65c. Splashdown recovery . . 70 1·10
MS657 119 × 105 mm. Nos. 653/6 2·75 2·50

1979. National Wildlife and Conservation Day.
658 **176** $1 multicoloured . . . . 1·60 2·50

1979. Christmas. Multicoloured.
659 6c. Type **177** (postage) . . . 10 10
660 10c. Hibiscus and star . . . 10 10
661 12c. Poinsettia, bells and candle 15 10
662 15c. Poinsettia leaves and Tiki (god) 15 15
663 20c. Type **177** (air) 20 15
664 25c. As No. 660 . . . . . . 25 20
665 30c. As No. 661 . . . . . . 30 25
666 35c. As No. 662 . . . . . . 35 30

1980. Christmas. As Nos. 659/66 but with charity premium.
667 6c.+2c. Type **177** (postage) 10 10
668 10c.+2c. Hibiscus and star . . 15 15
669 12c.+2c. Poinsettia, bells and candle 15 20
670 15c.+2c. Poinsettia leaves and Tiki (god) 15 20
671 20c.+4c. Type **177** (air) . . . 15 25
672 25c.+4c. As No. 660 . . . . 15 25
673 30c.+4c. As No. 661 . . . . 20 30
674 35c.+4c. As No. 662 . . . . 25 35

178 "Flagellation"

181 Queen Elizabeth the Queen Mother

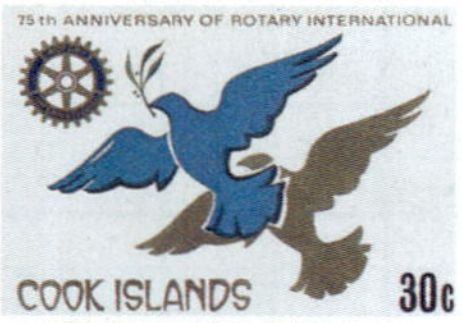

179 Dove with Olive Twig

1980. Easter. Illustrations by Gustav Dore. Each gold and brown.
675 20c. Type **178** 25 30
676 20c. "Crown of Thorns" . . 25 30
677 30c. "Jesus Insulted" 35 35
678 30c. "Jesus Falls" 35 35
679 35c. "The Crucifixion" . . . 40 35
680 35c. "The Descent from the Cross" 40 35
MS681 120 × 110 mm. As Nos. 675/80, but each with a charity premium of 2c. . . . . 1·10 1·50

1980. Easter. Children's Charity. Designs as Nos. 675/80 in separate miniature sheets 60 × 71 mm, each with a face value of 75c. + 5c.
MS682 As Nos. 675/80 Set of 6 sheets . . . . 1·00 1·50

1980. 75th Anniv of Rotary International. Mult.
683 30c. Type **179** 35 35
684 35c. Hibiscus flower 40 40
685 50c. Ribbons 50 50
MS686 72 × 113 mm. Nos. 683/5, but each with a charity premium of 3c. 1·10 1·50

1980. "Zeapex 80" International Stamp Exhibition, Auckland. Nos. 633/44 optd **ZEAPEX STAMP EXHIBITION—AUCKLAND 1980** and New Zealand 1865 1s. Stamp.
687 30c. Type **172** 35 25
688 30c. Mail coach 35 25
689 30c. Automobile 35 25
690 30c. Diesel train 35 25
691 35c. "Cap-Hornier" (full-rigged ship) 40 30
692 35c. River steamer 40 30
693 35c. "Deutschland" (liner) . . 40 30
694 35c. "United States" (liner) 40 30
695 50c. Balloon "Le Neptune" 60 35
696 50c. Junkers "F13" airplane 60 35
697 50c. Airship"Graf Zeppelin" 60 35
698 50c. Concorde 60 35
MS699 132 × 104 mm. Nos. 687/98 6·00 6·00

1980. "Zeapex '80" International Stamp Exhibition, Auckland. As No **MS**681 but containing stamps without charity premium of 2c. optd *"Zeapex '80 Auckland + 10c"* in black on gold background.
MS700 120 × 110 mm. Nos. 675/80 (sold at $1.80) . . . . 1·00 1·75
Stamps from No. **MS**700 are unaffected by the overprint which appears on the sheet margin.

1980. 80th Birthday of the Queen Mother.
701 **181** 50c. multicoloured . . . . 1·00 1·00
MS702 64 × 78 mm. **181** $2 multicoloured . . . . 1·25 1·75

182 Satellites orbiting Moon

1980. 350th Death Anniv of Johannes Kepler (astronomer). Multicoloured.
703 12c. Type **182** 50 35
704 12c. Space-craft orbiting Moon 50 35
705 50c. Space-craft orbiting Moon (different) . . . . . 1·00 80
706 50c. Astronaut and Moon vehicle . . . . 1·00 80
MS707 122 × 122 mm. Nos. 703/6 2·75 2·75

183 Scene from novel "From the Earth to the Moon"

184 "Siphonogorgia"

1980. 75th Death Anniv of Jules Verne (author).
708 **183** 20c. multicoloured 45 35
709 – 20c. multicoloured 45 35
710 – 30c. multicoloured (mauve background) 55 45
711 – 30c. multicoloured (blue background) 55 45
MS712 121 × 122 mm. Nos. 708/11 2·75 2·25
DESIGNS: Showing scenes from the novel "From the Earth to the Moon".

1980. Corals (1st series). Multicoloured.
713 1c. Type **184** 30 30
714 1c. "Pavona praetorta" . . . 30 30
715 1c. "Stylaster echinatus" . . 30 30
716 1c. "Tubastraea" 30 30
717 3c. "Millepora alcicornis" . . 30 30
718 3c. "Junceella gemmacea" . . 30 30
719 3c. "Fungia fungites" 30 30
720 3c. "Heliofungia actiniformis" 30 30
721 4c. "Distichopora violacea" . 30 30
722 4c. "Stylaster" 30 30
723 4c. "Gonipora" 30 30
724 4c. "Caulastraea echinulata" 30 30
725 5c. "Ptilosarcus gurneyi" . . 30 30
726 5c. "Stylophora pistillata" . . 30 30
727 5c. "Melithaea squamata" . . 30 30
728 5c. "Porites andrewsi" . . . 30 30
729 6c. "Lobophyllia bemprichii" 30 30
730 6c. "Palauastrea ramosa" . . 30 30
731 6c. "Bellonella indica" . . . 30 30
732 6c. "Pectinia alcicornis" . . 30 30
733 8c. "Sarcophyton digitatum" 30 30
734 8c. "Melithaea albitincta" . . 30 30
735 8c. "Plerogyra sinuosa" . . . 30 30
736 8c. "Dendropyllia gracilis" . . 30 30
737 10c. As Type **184** 30 30
738 10c. As No. 714 . . . . . . 30 30
739 10c. As No. 715 . . . . . . 30 30
740 10c. As No. 716 . . . . . . 30 30
741 12c. As No. 717 . . . . . . 30 30
742 12c. As No. 718 . . . . . . 30 30
743 12c. As No. 719 . . . . . . 30 30
744 12c. As No. 720 . . . . . . 30 30
745 15c. As No. 721 . . . . . . 30 30
746 15c. As No. 722 . . . . . . 30 30
747 15c. As No. 723 . . . . . . 30 30
748 15c. As No. 724 . . . . . . 30 30
749 20c. As No. 725 . . . . . . 35 30
750 20c. As No. 726 . . . . . . 35 30
751 20c. As No. 727 . . . . . . 35 30
752 20c. As No. 728 . . . . . . 35 30
753 25c. As No. 729 . . . . . . 35 30
754 25c. As No. 730 . . . . . . 35 30
755 25c. As No. 731 . . . . . . 35 30
756 25c. As No. 732 . . . . . . 35 30
757 30c. As No. 733 . . . . . . 40 30
758 30c. As No. 734 . . . . . . 40 30
759 30c. As No. 735 . . . . . . 40 30
760 30c. As No. 736 . . . . . . 40 30
761 35c. Type **184** 45 35
762 35c. As No. 714 . . . . . . 45 35
763 35c. As No. 715 . . . . . . 45 35
764 35c. As No. 716 . . . . . . 45 35
765 50c. As No. 717 . . . . . . 65 75
766 50c. As No. 718 . . . . . . 65 75
767 50c. As No. 719 . . . . . . 65 75
768 50c. As No. 720 . . . . . . 65 75
769 60c. As No. 721 . . . . . . 75 75
770 60c. As No. 722 . . . . . . 75 75
771 60c. As No. 723 . . . . . . 75 75
772 60c. As No. 724 . . . . . . 75 75
773 70c. As No. 725 . . . . . . 2·50 75
774 70c. As No. 726 . . . . . . 2·50 75
775 70c. As No. 727 . . . . . . 2·50 75
776 70c. As No. 728 . . . . . . 2·50 75
777 80c. As No. 729 . . . . . . 2·50 80
778 80c. As No. 730 . . . . . . 2·50 80
779 80c. As No. 731 . . . . . . 2·50 80
780 80c. As No. 732 . . . . . . 2·50 80
781 $1 As No. 733 . . . . . . 3·75 1·00
782 $1 As No. 734 . . . . . . 3·75 1·00
783 $1 As No. 735 . . . . . . 3·75 1·00
784 $1 As No. 736 . . . . . . 3·75 1·00
785 $2 As No. 723 . . . . . . 12·00 3·00
786 $3 As No. 720 . . . . . . 12·00 3·00
787 $4 As No. 726 . . . . 4·50 15·00
788 $6 As No. 715 . . . . 6·00 19·00
789 $10 As No. 734 . . . . . . 27·00 40·00
Nos. 761/74 are 30 × 40 mm, and Nos. 785/9, which include a portrait of Queen Elizabeth II in each design, are 55 × 35 mm.
See also Nos. 966/94.

185 Annunciation

187 Prince Charles

186 "The Crucifixion" (from book of Saint-Amand)

1980. Christmas. Scenes from 13th-century French Prayer Books. Multicoloured.
801 15c. Type **185** 25 15
802 30c. The Visitation 35 25
803 40c. The Nativity 45 30
804 50c. The Epiphany 60 40
MS805 89 × 114 mm. Nos. 801/4 1·50 1·50

1981. Christmas. Children's Charity. Designs as Nos. 801/4 in separate miniature sheets 55 × 68 mm, each with a face value of 75c +5c. Imperf.
MS806 As Nos. 801/4 Set of 4 sheets 1·50 1·50

1981. Easter. Illustrations from 12th-century French Prayer Books. Multicoloured.
807 15c. Type **186** 30 30
808 25c. "Placing in Tomb" (from book of Ingeburge) 35 35
809 40c. "Mourning at the Sepulchre" (from book of Ingeburge) 45 45
MS810 72 × 116 mm. As Nos. 807/9, but each with a charity premium of 2c. . . . . 1·00 1·00

1981. Easter. Children's Charity. Designs as Nos. 807/9 in separate miniature sheets 64 × 53 mm, each with a face value of 75c. + 5c. Imperf.
MS811 As Nos. 807/9 Set of 3 sheets 1·10 1·10

1981. Royal Wedding. Multicoloured.
812 $1 Type **187** . . . . 50 1·10
813 $2 Prince Charles and Lady Diana Spencer . . . . . 60 1·40
MS814 106 × 59 mm. Nos. 812/13 1·10 2·50

188 Footballers

1981. World Cup Football Championship, Spain (1982). Designs showing footballers. Mult.
815 20c. Type **188** 40 20
816 20c. Figures to right of stamp 40 20
817 30c. Figures to left 50 30
818 30c. Figures to right 50 30
819 35c. Figures to left 50 35
820 35c. Figures to right 50 35
821 50c. Figures to left 65 45
822 50c. Figures to right 65 45
MS823 180 × 94 mm. As Nos. 815/22, but each with a charity premium of 3c. . . . . 6·50 8·50
The two designs of each value were printed together, se-tenant, in horizontal pairs throughout the sheet, forming composite designs.

1981. International Year for Disabled Persons. Nos. 812/13 surch **+5c**.
824 $1+5c. Type **187** . . . . . . 55 1·75
825 $2+5c. Prince Charles and Lady Diana Spencer . . . 70 2·50
MS826 106 × 59 mm. $1 + 10c, $2 + 10c. As Nos. 824/5 . . . . . 1·00 4·00

190 "Holy Virgin with Child"

1982. Christmas. Details of Paintings by Rubens. Multicoloured.
827 8c. Type **190** 55 20
828 15c. "Coronation of St. Catherine" 65 35
829 40c. "Adoration of the Shepherds" 90 80
830 50c. "Adoration of the Magi" 1·00 1·00
MS831 86 × 110 mm. As Nos. 827/30, but each with a charity premium of 3c. . . . . 3·50 4·00

1982. Christmas. Children's Charity. Designs as Nos. 827/30 in separate miniature sheets 62 × 78 mm, each with a face value of 75c. +5c.
MS832 As Nos. 827/30 Set of 4 sheets . . . . 3·50 4·00

191 Princess of Wales (inscr "21st Birthday")

1982. 21st Birthday of Princess of Wales. Multicoloured.
833 $1.25 Type **191** . . . . . . 2·25 1·50
834 $1.25 As Type **191**, but inscr "1 July 1982" . . . . . . 2·25 1·50
835 $2.50 Princess (inscr "21st Birthday") (different) . . . 3·00 2·25
836 $2.50 As No. 835, but inscr "1 July 1982" . . . . . . 3·00 2·25
MS837 92 × 72 mm. $1.25, Type **191**; $2.50, As No. 835. Both inscribed "21st Birthday 1 July 1982" . . . . 7·00 4·50

1982. Birth of Prince William of Wales (1st issue). Nos. 812/13 optd.
838 $1 Type **187** . . . . 1·50 1·25
839 $1 Type **187** . . . . 1·50 1·25
840 $2 Prince Charles and Lady Diana Spencer . . . . . 2·50 2·00
841 $2 Prince Charles and Lady Diana Spencer . . . . . 2·50 2·00
MS842 106 × 59 mm. Nos. 812/13 optd **21 JUNE 1982. ROYAL BIRTH** . . . . 4·00 4·00
OPTS: Nos. 838 and 840, **ROYAL BIRTH 21 JUNE 1982**; 839 and 841, **PRINCE WILLIAM OF WALES**.

1982. Birth of Prince William of Wales (2nd issue). As Nos. 833/6 but with changed inscriptions. Multicoloured.
843 $1.25 As Type **191**, inscribed "Royal Birth" . . . . . . 2·25 1·00
844 $1.25 As Type **191**, inscribed "21 June 1982" . . . . . 2·25 1·00
845 $2.50 As No. 835, inscribed "Royal Birth" . . . . 2·75 1·50
846 $2.50 As No. 835, inscribed "21 June 1982" . . . . . 2·75 1·50
MS847 92 × 73 mm. $1.25, As Type **191**; $2.50, As No. 835. Both inscribed "Royal Birth 21 June 1982". . . . . 6·00 2·75

193 "The Accordionist" (inscr "Serenade")

194 Franklin D. Roosevelt

1982. Norman Rockwell (painter) Commemoration. Multicoloured.
848 5c. Type **193** 15 10
849 10c. "Spring" (inscr "The Hikers") 20 15
850 20c. "The Doctor and the Doll" 25 25
851 30c. "Home from Camp" . . 25 30

1982. Air. American Anniversaries. Multicoloured.
852 60c. Type **194** . . . . 1·25 80
853 80c. Benjamin Franklin . . . 1·50 1·00
854 $1.40 George Washington . . 1·75 2·25
MS855 116 × 60 mm. Nos. 852/4 4·75 3·00

ANNIVERSARIES: 60c. Roosevelt (birth centenary); 80c. "Articles of Peace" negotiations bicentenary; $1.40, Washington (250th birth anniv).

195 "Virgin with Garlands" (detail, Rubens) and Princess Diana with Prince William

1982. Christmas.
856 **195** 35c. multicoloured . . . . 1·75 70
857 – 48c. multicoloured . . . . 2·25 1·50
858 – 60c. multicoloured . . . . 2·50 2·00
859 – $1.70 multicoloured . . . 3·50 6·00
MS860 104 × 83 mm. 60c. × 4. Designs, each 27 × 32 mm, forming complete painting "Virgin with Garlands" . . . . . . 7·00 8·50
DESIGNS: 48c. to $1.70, Different details from Ruben's painting "Virgin with Garlands".

196 Princess Diana and Prince William

1982. Christmas. Birth of Prince William of Wales. Children's Charity. Sheet 73 × 59 mm.
MS861 **196** 75c. + 5c. multicoloured 2·75 4·00
No. **MS**861 comes with 4 different background designs showing details from painting "Virgin with Garlands" (Rubens).

197 Statue of Tangaroa

198 Scouts using Map and Compass

1983. Commonwealth Day. Multicoloured.
862 60c. Type **197** 70 50
863 60c. Rarotonga oranges . . . 70 50
864 60c. Rarotonga Airport . . . 70 50
865 60c. Prime Minister Sir Thomas Davis 70 50

1983. 75th Anniv of Boy Scout Movement and 125th Anniv of Lord Baden-Powell (founder). Multicoloured.
866 12c. Type **198** 55 20
867 12c. Hiking 55 20
868 36c. Campfire cooking . . . 80 40
869 36c. Erecting tent 80 40
870 48c. Hauling on rope . . . . 1·00 55
871 48c. Using bos'n's chair . . . 1·00 55
872 60c. Digging hole for sapling 1·00 70
873 60c. Planting sapling . . . . 1·00 70
MS874 161 × 132 mm. As Nos. 866/73, but each with a premium of 2c. . . . . 3·00 3·50

1983. 15th World Scout Jamboree, Alberta, Canada. Nos. 866/73 optd **XV WORLD JAMBOREE** (Nos. 875, 877, 879, 881) or **ALBERTA, CANADA 1983** (others).
875 12c. Type **198** 60 20
876 12c. Hiking 60 20
877 36c. Campfire cooking . . . 90 40
878 36c. Erecting tent 90 40
879 48c. Hauling on rope . . . . 1·10 55
880 48c. Using bos'n's chair . . . 1·10 55
881 60c. Digging hole for sapling 1·25 70
882 60c. Planting sapling . . . . 1·25 70
MS883 161 × 132 mm. As Nos. 875/82, but each with a premium of 2c. . . . . 2·75 3·25

1983. Various stamps surch.
884 – 18c. on 8c. mult (No. 733) 75 50
885 – 18c. on 8c. mult (No. 734) 75 50
886 – 18c. on 8c. mult (No. 735) 75 50
887 – 18c. on 8c. mult (No. 736) 75 50
888 – 36c. on 15c. mult (No. 745) . . . . . . 1·25 85
889 – 36c. on 15c. mult (No. 746) . . . . . . 1·25 85
890 – 36c. on 15c. mult (No. 747) . . . . . . 1·25 85
891 – 36c. on 15c. mult (No. 748) . . . . . . 1·25 85
892 – 36c. on 30c. mult (No. 757) . . . . . . 1·25 85
893 – 36c. on 30c. mult (No. 758) . . . . . . 1·25 85
894 – 36c. on 30c. mult (No. 759) . . . . . . 1·25 85
895 – 36c. on 30c. mult (No. 760) . . . . . . 1·25 85
896 **184** 36c. on 35c. mult . . . . 1·25 85
897 – 36c. on 35c. mult (No. 762) . . . . . . 1·25 85
898 – 36c. on 35c. mult (No. 763) . . . . . . 1·25 85
899 – 36c. on 35c. mult (No. 764) . . . . . . 1·25 85
900 – 48c. on 25c. mult (No. 753) . . . . . . 1·50 1·25
901 – 48c. on 25c. mult (No. 754) . . . . . . 1·50 1·25
902 – 48c. on 25c. mult (No. 755) . . . . . . 1·50 1·25
903 – 48c. on 25c. mult (No. 756) . . . . . . 1·50 1·25
904 – 72c. on 70c. mult (No. 773) . . . . . . 2·50 1·75
905 – 72c. on 70c. mult (No. 774) . . . . . . 2·50 1·75
906 – 72c. on 70c. mult (No. 775) . . . . . . 2·50 1·75
907 – 72c. on 70c. mult (No. 776) . . . . . . 2·50 1·75
908 – 96c. on $1.40 multicoloured (No. 854) 2·00 2·00
909 – 96c. on $2 mult (No. 813) 8·50 5·50
910 – 96c. on $2.50 mult (No. 835) . . . . . . 3·00 3·00
911 – 96c. on $2.50 mult (No. 836) . . . . . . 3·00 3·00
912 – $5.60 on $6 mult (No. 788) . . . . . . 23·00 18·00
913 – $5.60 on $10 mult (No. 789) . . . . . . 23·00 18·00

202 Union Flag

1983. Cook Islands Flags and Ensigns. Multicoloured.
914 6c. Type **202** (postage) . . . 70 70
915 6c. Group Federal flag . . . 70 70
916 12c. Rarotonga ensign . . . 85 85
917 12c. Flag of New Zealand . . 85 85
918 15c. Cook Islands' flag (1973–79) 85 85
919 15c. Cook Islands' National flag 85 85
920 20c. Type **202** (air) 85 85
921 20c. Group Federal flag . . . 85 85
922 30c. Rarotonga ensign . . . 95 95
923 30c. Flag of New Zealand . . 95 95
924 35c. Cook Islands' flag (1973–1979) . . . . . . 1·00 1·00
925 35c. Cook Islands' National flag . . . . 1·00 1·00
MS926 Two sheets, each 132 × 120 mm. (a) Nos. 914/19. (b) Nos. 920/5. P 13 . . . . 3·50 4·75

203 Dish Aerial, Satellite Earth Station

204 "La Belle Jardiniere"

1983. World Communications Year.
927 – 36c. multicoloured 75 80
928 – 48c. multicoloured 90 95
929 **203** 60c. multicoloured . . . . 1·25 1·50
930 – 96c. multicoloured . . . . 1·90 3·25
MS931 90 × 65 mm. $2 multicoloured . . . . 2·25 2·75
DESIGNS: 36, 48, 96c. Various satellites.

1983. Christmas. 500th Birth Anniv of Raphael. Multicoloured.
932 12c. Type **204** 80 55
933 18c. "Madonna and Child with five Saints" . . . . . 1·10 70
934 36c. "Madonna and Child with St. John" . . . . . 1·75 1·75
935 48c. "Madonna of the Fish" 2·25 2·25
936 60c. "Madonna of the Baldacchino" . . . . . . 2·75 3·75
MS937 139 × 113 mm. As Nos. 932/6, but each with a premium of 3c. . . . . 2·00 2·50

1983. Christmas. 500th Birth Anniv of Raphael. Children's Charity. Designs as Nos. 932/6 in separate miniature sheets 66 × 82 mm., each with a face value of 85c. + 5c.
MS938 As Nos. 932/6 Set of 5 sheets 4·50 3·75

205 Montgolfier Balloon, 1783

1984. Bicentenary (1983) of Manned Flight. Mult.
939 36c. Type **205** 50 50
940 48c. Ascent of Adorne, Strasbourg, 1784 . . . . . 60 60
941 60c. Balloon driven by sails, 1785 . . . . 75 90
942 72c. Ascent of man on horse, 1798 . . . . 90 1·25
943 96c. Godard's aerial acrobatics, 1850 . . . . . 1·00 1·60
MS944 104 × 85 mm. $2.50, Blanchard and Jeffries crossing Channel, 1785 . . . . 1·50 2·25
MS945 122 × 132 mm. As Nos. 939/43, but each with a premium of 5c. . . . . . . 1·50 2·25

206 Cuvier's Beaked Whale

1984. Save the Whale. Multicoloured.
946 10c. Type **206** 50 50
947 18c. Risso's dolphin 75 75
948 20c. True's beaked whale . . . 75 75
949 24c. Long-finned pilot whale 80 80
950 30c. Narwhal 90 90
951 36c. White whale . . . . . . 1·10 1·10
952 42c. Common dolphin . . . 1·40 1·40
953 48c. Commerson's dolphin . . 1·60 1·60
954 60c. Bottle-nosed dolphin . . 1·90 1·90
955 72c. Sowerby's beaked whale 2·00 2·00
956 96c. Common porpoise . . . 2·50 2·50
957 $2 Boutu . . . . 3·25 3·25

207 Athens, 1896

208 "Siphonogorgia"

1984. Olympic Games, Los Angeles. Multicoloured.
958 18c. Type **207** 60 40
959 24c. Paris, 1900 . . . . . . 65 45
960 36c. St. Louis, 1904 . . . . 75 55
961 48c. London, 1948 . . . . . 85 65
962 60c. Tokyo, 1964 . . . . . . 95 75
963 72c. Berlin, 1936 . . . . . . 1·00 90
964 96c. Rome, 1960 . . . . . . 1·10 1·00
965 $1.20 Los Angeles, 1930 . . . 1·25 1·25

1984. Corals (2nd series). New designs and Nos. 785/9 surch. Multicoloured.
966 1c. Type **208** 30 10
967 2c. "Millepora alcicornis" . . 30 10
968 3c. "Distichopora violacea" . 40 10
969 5c. "Ptilosarcus gurneyi" . . 45 10
970 10c. "Lobophyllia bemprichii" 50 10
971 12c. "Sarcophyton digitatum" 60 15
972 14c. "Pavona praetorta" . . 60 15
973 18c. "Junceella gemmacea" . 70 20
974 20c. "Stylaster" 70 20
975 24c. "Stylophora pistillata" . 70 20
976 30c. "Palauastrea ramosa" . 1·00 25
977 36c. "Melithaea albitincta" . 1·25 30
978 40c. "Stylaster echinatus" . 1·25 30
979 42c. "Fungia fungites" . . . 1·25 35
980 48c. "Gonipora" . . . . . . 1·25 35
981 50c. "Melithaea squamata" . 1·75 45
982 52c. "Bellonella indica" . . 1·75 60
983 55c. "Plerogyra sinuosa" . . 1·75 65
984 60c. "Tubastraea" . . . . . 1·90 70
985 70c. "Heliofungia actiniformis" . . . . . . 2·00 85
986 85c. "Caulastraea echinulata" 2·25 1·00
987 96c. "Porites andrewsi" . . . 2·50 1·10
988 $1.10 "Pectinia alcicornis" . . 2·50 1·40
989 $1.20 "Dendrophyllia gracilis" . . . . 2·50 1·50
990 $3.60 on $2 "Gonipora" (55 × 35 mm) . . . . . . 5·50 4·00
991 $4.20 on $3 "Heliofungia actiniformis" (55 × 35 mm) 6·00 5·00
992 $5 on $4 "Stylophora pistillata" (55 × 35 mm) . . 6·50 5·50
993 $7.20 on $6 "Stylaster echinatus" (55 × 35 mm) . . 8·50 8·50
994 $9.60 on $10 "Melithaea albitincta" (55 × 35 mm) . . 10·00 10·00

1984. Olympic Gold Medal Winners. Nos. 963/5 optd.
995 72c. Berlin, 1936 (optd **Equestrian Team Dressage Germany**) 60 65
996 96c. Rome, 1960 (optd **Decathlon Daley Thompson Great Britain**) 80 85
997 $1.20 Los Angeles, 1930 (optd **Four Gold Medals Carl Lewis U.S.A.**) . . . . 1·00 1·10

211 Captain Cook's Cottage, Melbourne

1984. "Ausipex" International Stamp Exhibition, Melbourne. Multicoloured.
998 36c. Type **211** . . . . . . 2·00 1·50
999 48c. H.M.S. "Endeavour" careened for Repairs" (Sydney Parkinson) . . . 3·25 2·50
1000 60c. "Cook's landing at Botany Bay" (E. Phillips Fox) . . . . 3·50 3·25
1001 $2 "Captain James Cook" (John Webber) . . . . . 4·25 4·25
MS1002 140 × 100 mm. As Nos. 998/1001, but each with a face value of 90c. . . . . . . 7·50 7·50

1984. Birth of Prince Henry. Nos. 812 and 833/6 variously optd or surch also (No. 1007).
1003 $1.25 Optd **Commemorating-15 Sept. 1984** (No. 833) 1·75 1·50
1004 $1.25 Optd **Birth H.R.H. Prince Henry** (No. 834) 1·75 1·50
1005 $2.50 Optd **Commemorating-15 Sept. 1984** (No. 835) 2·50 2·75
1006 $2.50 Optd **Birth H.R.H. Prince Henry** (No. 836) 2·50 2·75
1007 $3 on $1 Optd **Royal Birth Prince Henry 15 Sept. 1984** (No. 812) . . . . . 4·50 5·00

213 "Virgin on Throne with Child" (Giovanni Bellini)

214 Downy Woodpecker

1984. Christmas. Multicoloured.
1008 36c. Type **213** . . . . . . 1·90 40
1009 48c. "Virgin and Child" (anonymous, 15th century) . . . . 2·00 60
1010 60c. "Virgin and Child with Saints" (Alvise Vivarini) 2·25 80
1011 96c. "Virgin and Child with Angels" (H. Memling) . . 2·50 1·60
1012 $1.20 "Adoration of Magi" (G. Tiepolo) . . . . . . 2·75 2·00
MS1013 120 × 113 mm. As Nos. 1008/12, but each with a premium of 5c. . . . . 4·25 3·25

1984. Christmas. Designs as Nos. 1008/12 in separate miniature sheets 62 × 76 mm, each with a face value of 95c. + 5c.
MS1014 As Nos. 1008/12 Set of 5 sheets . . . . 5·00 5·50

1985. Birth Bicentenary of John J. Audubon (ornithologist). Designs showing original paintings. Multicoloured.
1015 30c. Type **214** . . . . . . 2·50 1·25
1016 55c. Black-throated blue warbler . . . . 2·75 1·75
1017 65c. Yellow-throated warbler . . . . 3·00 2·25
1018 75c. Chestnut-sided warbler 3·25 2·75
1019 95c. Dickcissel . . . . . . 3·25 3·00
1020 $1.15 White-crowned sparrow . . . . 3·25 3·50
MS1021 Three sheets, each 76 × 75 mm. (a) $1.30, Red-cockaded woodpecker. (b) $2.80, Seaside sparrow. (c) $5.30, Zenaida dove Set of 3 sheets 13·00 8·50

215 "The Kingston Flyer" (New Zealand)

1985. Famous Trains. Multicoloured.

1022 20c. Type **215** 30 50
1023 55c. Class 625 locomotive (Italy) 40 85
1024 65c. Gotthard electric locomotive (Switzerland) 45 90
1025 75c. Union Pacific diesel locomotive No. 6900 (U.S.A.) 50 1·10
1026 95c. Canadian National "Super Continental" type diesel locomotive (Canada) 50 1·25
1027 $1.15 TGV express train (France) 50 1·50
1028 $2.20 "The Flying Scotsman" (Great Britain) 55 2·50
1029 $3.40 "Orient Express" 60 3·75

No. 1023 is inscribed "640" in error.

216 "Helena Fourment" (Peter Paul Rubens) **217** "Lady Elizabeth 1908" (Mabel Hankey)

1985. International Youth Year. Multicoloured.

1030 55c. Type **216** 3·50 2·75
1031 65c. "Vigee-Lebrun and Daughter" (E. Vigee-Lebrun) 3·75 3·25
1032 75c. "On the Terrace" (Renoir) 4·00 3·50
1033 $1.30 "Young Mother Sewing" (M. Cassatt) 5·00 7·50
MS1034 103 × 106 mm. As Nos. 1030/3, but each with a premium of 10c. 8·50 5·50

1985. Life and Times of Queen Elizabeth the Queen Mother. Designs showing paintings. Multicoloured.

1035 65c. Type **217** 40 50
1036 75c. "Duchess of York, 1923" (Savely Sorine) 45 60
1037 $1.15 "Duchess of York, 1925" (Philip de Laszlo) 55 85
1038 $2.80 "Queen Elizabeth, 1938" (Sir Gerald Kelly) 1·40 2·25
MS1039 69 × 81 mm. $5.30, As $2.80 2·50 3·50

For these designs in a miniature sheet, each with a face value of 55c., see No. **MS**1079.

218 Albert Henry (Prime Minister, 1965–78) **219** Golf

1985. 20th Anniv of Self-government. Mult.

1040 30c. Type **218** 1·00 60
1041 50c. Sir Thomas Davis (Prime Minister, 1978–April 1983 and from November 1983) 1·40 1·25
1042 65c. Geoffrey Henry (Prime Minister, April–November 1983) 1·75 1·75
MS1043 134 × 70 mm. As Nos. 1040/2, but each with a face value of 55c. 1·75 2·00

1985. South Pacific Mini Games, Rarotonga. Multicoloured.

1044 55c. Type **219** 4·00 3·50
1045 65c. Rugby 4·00 4·00
1046 75c. Tennis 5·50 6·00
MS1047 126 × 70 mm. Nos. 1044/6, but each with a premium of 10c. 11·00 13·00

220 Sea Horse, Gearwheel and Leaves **221** "Madonna of the Magnificat"

1985. Pacific Conference, Rarotonga.

1048 **220** 55c. black, gold and red 1·25 65
1049 – 65c. black, gold and violet 1·40 80
1050 – 75c. black, gold and green 1·60 1·10
MS1051 126 × 81 mm. As Nos. 1048/50, but each with a face value of 50c. 1·60 2·00

No. 1048 shows the South Pacific Bureau for Economic Co-operation logo and is inscribed "S.P.E.C. Meeting, 30 July–1 August 1985, Rarotonga". No. 1049 also shows the S.P.E.C. logo, but is inscribed "South Pacific Forum, 4–6 August 1985, Rarotonga". No. 1050 shows the Pacific Islands Conference logo and the inscription "Pacific Islands Conference, 7–10 August 1985, Rarotonga".

1985. Christmas. Virgin and Child Paintings by Botticelli. Multicoloured.

1052 55c. Type **221** 2·50 1·25
1053 65c. "Madonna with Pomegranate" 2·75 1·25
1054 75c. "Madonna and Child with Six Angels" 3·00 1·60
1055 95c. "Madonna and Child with St. John" 3·25 2·00
MS1056 90 × 104 mm. As Nos. 1052/5, but each with a face value of 50c. 6·00 3·75

1985. Christmas. Virgin and Child Paintings by Botticelli. Square designs (46 × 46 mm) as Nos. 1052/5 in separate miniature sheets, 50 × 51 mm, with face values of $1.20, $1.45, $2.20 and $2.75. Imperf.

MS1057 As Nos. 1052/5 Set of 4 sheets 9·00 11·00

222 "The Eve of the Deluge" (John Martin) **223** Queen Elizabeth II

1986. Appearance of Halley's Comet. Paintings. Multicoloured.

1058 55c. Type **222** 1·50 1·25
1059 65c. "Lot and his Daughters" (Lucas van Leyden) 1·60 1·40
1060 75c. "Auspicious Comet" (from treatise c. 1857) 1·75 1·50
1061 $1.25 "Events following Charles I" (Herman Saftleven) 2·50 2·25
1062 $2 "Ossian receiving Napoleonic Officers" (Anne Louis Girodet-Trioson) 3·25 3·00
MS1063 130 × 100 mm. As Nos. 1058/62, but each with a face value of 70c. 5·50 7·00
MS1064 84 × 63 mm. $4 "Halley's Comet of 1759 over the Thames" (Samuel Scott) 8·50 9·50

1986. 60th Birthday of Queen Elizabeth II. Designs showing formal portraits.

1065 **223** 95c. multicoloured 1·50 1·50
1066 – $1.25 multicoloured 1·75 1·75
1067 – $1.50 multicoloured 2·00 2·00
MS1068 Three sheets, each 44 × 75 mm. As Nos. 1065/7, but with face values of $1.10, $1.95 and $2.45 Set of 3 sheets 10·00 11·00

224 U.S.A. 1847 Franklin 5c. Stamp and H.M.S. "Resolution" at Rarotonga

1986. "Ameripex '86" International Exhibition, Chicago. Multicoloured.

1069 $1 Type **224** 5·50 3·75
1070 $1.50 Chicago 3·50 4·25
1071 $2 1975 definitive $2, Benjamin Franklin and H.M.S. "Resolution" 6·50 5·50

225 Head of Statue of Liberty **226** Miss Sarah Ferguson

1986. Centenary of Statue of Liberty. Multicoloured.

1072 $1 Type **225** 75 85
1073 $1.25 Hand and torch of Statue 90 1·10
1074 $2.75 Statue of Liberty 2·00 2·50

1986. Royal Wedding. Multicoloured.

1075 $1 Type **226** 1·25 1·25
1076 $2 Prince Andrew 2·00 2·50
1077 $3 Prince Andrew and Miss Sarah Ferguson (57 × 31 mm) 2·50 3·50

1986. "Stampex '86" Stamp Exhibition, Adelaide. No. **MS**1002 optd **Stampex 86 Adelaide**.

MS1078 90c. × 4 multicoloured 7·50 6·50

The "Stampex '86" exhibition emblem is also overprinted on the sheet margin.

1986. 86th Birthday of Queen Elizabeth the Queen Mother. Designs as Nos. 1035/8 in miniature sheet, 91 × 116 mm, each with a face value of 55c. Multicoloured.

MS1079 55c. × 4. As Nos. 1035/8 8·50 8·00

228 "Holy Family with St. John the Baptist and St. Elizabeth"

1986. Christmas. Paintings by Rubens. Mult.

1080 55c. Type **228** 2·00 1·00
1081 $1.30 "Virgin with the Garland" 3·00 2·75
1082 $2.75 "Adoration of the Magi" (detail) 6·00 7·00
MS1083 140 × 100 mm. As Nos. 1080/2, but each size 36 × 46 mm with a face value of $2.40 12·00 13·00
MS1084 80 × 70 mm. $6.40. As No. 1081 but size 32 × 50 mm 12·00 13·00

1986. Visit of Pope John Paul II to South Pacific. Nos. 1080/2 surch **FIRST PAPAL VISIT TO SOUTH PACIFIC POPE JOHN PAUL II NOV 21-24 1986.**

1085 55c.+10c. Type **228** 2·75 2·00
1086 $1.30+10c. "Virgin with the Garland" 3·50 2·50
1087 $2.75+10c. "Adoration of the Magi" (detail) 6·00 3·75
MS1088 140 × 100 mm. As Nos. 1085/7, but each size 36 × 46 mm with a face value of $2.40 + 10c. 14·00 13·00
MS1089 80 × 70 mm. $6.40+50c. As No. 1086 but size 32 × 50 mm 14·00 13·00

1987. Various stamps surch. (a) On Nos. 741/56, 761/76 and 787/8.

1090 10c. on 15c. "Distichopora violacea" 20 20
1091 10c. on 15c. "Stylaster" 20 20
1092 10c. on 15c. "Gonipora" 20 20
1093 10c. on 15c. "Caulastraea echinulata" 20 20
1094 10c. on 25c. "Lobophyllia bemprichii" 20 20
1095 10c. on 25c. "Palauastrea ramosa" 20 20
1096 10c. on 25c. "Bellonella indica" 20 20
1097 10c. on 25c. "Pectinia alcicornis" 20 20
1098 18c. on 12c. "Millepora alcicornis" 25 25
1099 18c. on 12c. "Junceella gemmacea" 25 25
1100 18c. on 12c. "Fungia fungites" 25 25
1101 18c. on 12c. "Heliofungia actiniformis" 25 25
1102 18c. on 20c. "Ptilosarcus gurneyi" 25 25
1103 18c. on 20c. "Stylophora pistillata" 25 25
1104 18c. on 20c. "Melithaea squamata" 25 25
1105 18c. on 20c. "Porites andrewsi" 25 25
1106 55c. on 35c. Type **184** 40 45
1107 55c. on 35c. "Pavona praetorta" 40 45
1108 55c. on 35c. "Stylaster echinatus" 40 45
1109 55c. on 35c. "Tubastraea" 40 45
1110 65c. on 50c. As No. 1098 45 50
1111 65c. on 50c. As No. 1099 45 50
1112 65c. on 50c. As No. 1100 45 50
1113 65c. on 50c. As No. 1101 45 50
1114 65c. on 60c. As No. 1090 45 50
1115 65c. on 60c. As No. 1091 45 50
1116 65c. on 60c. As No. 1092 45 50
1117 65c. on 60c. As No. 1093 45 50
1118 75c. on 70c. As No. 1102 55 60
1119 75c. on 70c. As No. 1103 55 60
1120 75c. on 70c. As No. 1104 55 60
1121 75c. on 70c. As No. 1105 55 60
1122 $6.40 on $4 "Stylophora pistillata" 4·50 4·75
1123 $7.20 on $6 "Stylaster echinatus" 5·00 5·25

(b) On Nos. 812/13.

1124 $9.40 on $1 Type **187** 15·00 16·00
1125 $9.40 on $2 Prince Charles and Lady Diana Spencer 15·00 16·00

(c) On Nos. 835/6.

1126 $9.40 on $2.50 Princess of Wales (inscribed "21st Birthday") 15·00 16·00
1127 $9.40 on $2.50 As No. 1126, but inscribed "1 July 1982" 15·00 16·00

(d) On Nos. 966/8, 971/2, 975, 979/80, 982 and 987/9.

1128 5c. on 1c. Type **208** 20 20
1129 5c. on 2c. "Millepora alcicornis" 20 20
1130 5c. on 3c. "Distichopora violacea" 20 20
1131 5c. on 12c. "Sarcophyton digitatum" 20 20
1132 5c. on 14c. "Pavona praetorta" 20 20
1133 18c. on 24c. "Stylophora pistillata" 25 25
1134 55c. on 52c. "Bellonella indica" 40 45
1135 65c. on 42c. "Fungia fungites" 45 50
1136 75c. on 48c. "Gonipora" 55 60
1137 95c. on 96c. "Porites andrewsi" 70 75
1138 95c. on $1.10 "Pectinia alcicornis" 70 75
1139 95c. on $1.20 "Dendrophyllia gracilis" 70 75

(e) On Nos. 998/1001.

1140 $1.30 on 36c. Type **211** 2·00 2·00
1141 $1.30 on 48c. "The "Endeavour" careened for Repairs" (Sydney Parkinson) 2·00 2·00
1142 $1.30 on 60c. "Cook's landing at Botany Bay" (E. Phillips Fox) 2·00 2·00
1143 $1.30 on $2 "Captain James Cook" (John Webber) 2·00 2·00

(f) On Nos. 1065/7.

1144 **223** $2.30 on 95c. mult 7·00 8·00
1145 – $2.80 on $1.25 mult 7·00 8·00
1146 – $2.80 on $1.50 mult 7·00 8·00

(g) On Nos. 1075/7.

1147 $2.80 on $1 Type **226** 6·00 6·50
1148 $2.80 on $2 Prince Andrew 6·00 6·50
1149 $2.80 on $3 Prince Andrew and Miss Sarah Ferguson (57 × 31 mm) 6·00 6·50

1987. Various stamps surch.

1150 $2.80 on $2 "Gonipora" (No. 785) 3·00 3·25
1151 $5 on $3 "Heliofungia actiniformis" (No. 786) 5·00 5·50
1152 $9.40 on $10 "Melithaea albitincta" (No. 789) 8·00 9·00
1153 $9.40 on $1 Type **187** (No. 838) 8·00 9·00
1154 $9.40 on $1 Type **187** (No. 839) 8·00 9·00
1155 $9.40 on $2 Prince Charles and Lady Diana Spencer (No. 840) 8·00 9·00
1156 $9.40 on $2 Prince Charles and Lady Diana Spencer (No. 841) 8·00 9·00
MS1157 106 × 59 mm. $9.20 on $1 Type **187**; $9.20 on $2 Prince Charles and Lady Diana Spencer 12·00 15·00

1987. Hurricane Relief. Various stamps surch **HURRICANE RELIEF** and premium. (a) On Nos. 1035/8.
1158 65c.+50c. Type **217** . . . . 1·00 1·00
1159 75c.+50c. "Duchess of York, 1923" (Savely Sorine) . . . . 1·10 1·10
1160 $1.15+50c. "Duchess of York, 1925" (Philip de Laszlo) . . . . 1·40 1·50
1161 $2.80+50c. "Queen Elizabeth, 1938" (Sir Gerald Kelly) . . . . . . 2·50 3·25
MS1162 69 × 81 mm. $5.30 + 50c. As $2.80 + 50c. . . . . 5·00 6·50

(b) On Nos. 1058/62.
1163 55c.+50c. Type **222** 85 85
1164 65c.+50c. "Lot and his Daughters" (Lucas van Leyden) 90 90
1165 75c.+50c. "Auspicious Comet" (from treatise c. 1587) . . . . . 1·10 1·10
1166 $1.50+50c. "Events following Charles I" (Herman Saftleven) . . . 1·40 1·50
1167 $2+50c. "Ossian receiving Napoleonic Officers" (Anne Louis Girodet-Trioson) . . . . 2·00 2·50

(c) On Nos. 1065/7.
1168 **223** 95c.+50c. mult . . . . 1·25 1·25
1169 – $1.25+50c. mult . . . . 1·50 1·50
1170 – $1.50+50c. mult . . . . 1·60 1·60
MS1171 Three sheets, each 44 × 75 mm. As Nos. 1168/70, but with face values of $1.10 + 50c., $1.95 + 50c., $2.45 + 50c. Set of 3 sheets . . . . 12·00 14·00

(d) On Nos. 1069/71.
1172 $1+50c. Type **224** . . . . 4·00 4·00
1173 $1.50+50c. Chicago . . . . 2·25 2·75
1174 $2+50c. 1975 definitive $2, Benjamin Franklin and H.M.S. "Resolution" . . 4·25 4·25

(e) On Nos. 1072/4.
1175 $1+50c. Type **225** . . . . 1·00 1·25
1176 $1.25+50c. Hand and torch of Statue . . . . 1·25 1·50
1177 $2.75+50c. Statue of Liberty 2·25 3·00

(f) On Nos. 1075/7.
1178 $1+50c. Type **226** . . . . 1·25 1·25
1179 $2+50c. Prince Andrew . . 2·00 2·25
1180 $3+50c. Prince Andrew and Miss Sarah Ferguson (57 × 31 mm) . . . . 2·75 3·25

(g) On Nos. 1080/2.
1181 55c.+50c. Type **228** 85 85
1182 $1.30+50c. "Virgin with the Garland" . . . . 1·50 1·75
1183 $2.75+50c. "The Adoration of the Magi" (detail) . . . 2·50 3·00
MS1184 140 × 100 mm. As Nos. 1181/3, but each size 36 × 46 mm with a face value of $2.40 + 50c. . . . . 13·00 15·00
MS1185 80 × 70 mm. $6.40 + 50c. As No. 1182, but size 32 × 50 mm. 8·50 9·50

(h) On Nos. 1122, 1134/7 and 1150/1.
1186 55c.+25c. on 52c. "Bellonella indica" . . . 80 80
1187 65c.+25c. on 42c. "Fungia fungites" 90 90
1188 75c.+25c. on 48c. "Gonipora" . . . . . . 1·00 1·00
1189 95c.+25c. on 96c. "Porites andrewsi" . . . . 1·25 1·25
1190 $2.80+50c. on $2 "Gonipora" . . . . . . 3·50 3·50
1191 $5+50c. on $3 "Heliofungia actiniformis" . . . . . . 5·50 6·00
1192 $6.40+50c. on $4 "Stylophora pistillata" . . 7·00 8·00

1987. Royal Ruby Wedding. Nos. 484 and 787 optd **ROYAL WEDDING FORTIETH ANNIVERSARY.**
1193 $4 Queen Elizabeth II and sea shells . . . . 5·50 5·50
1194 $4 Queen Elizabeth II and "Stylophora pistillata" . . 5·50 5·50

233 "The Holy Family" (Rembrandt)

1987. Christmas. Different paintings of the Holy Family by Rembrandt.
1195 **233** $1.25 multicoloured . . 2·50 2·25
1196 – $1.50 multicoloured . . 3·00 2·50
1197 – $1.95 multicoloured . . 4·50 4·50
MS1198 100 × 140 mm. As Nos. 1195/7, but each size 47 × 36 mm with a face value of $1.15 . . . . 7·00 8·50
MS1199 70 × 80 mm. $6 As Nos. 1196, but size 40 × 31 mm 9·50 11·00

234 Olympic Commemorative $50 Coin

1988. Olympic Games, Seoul. Multicoloured.
1200 $1.50 Type **234** . . . . . . 4·50 2·50
1201 $1.50 Olympic torch and Seoul Olympic Park . . . 4·50 2·50
1202 $1.50 Steffi Graf playing tennis and Olympic medal 4·50 2·50
MS1203 131 × 81 mm. $10 Combined design as Nos. 1200/2, but measuring 114 × 47 mm. . . 11·00 12·00
Nos. 1200/2 were printed together, se-tenant, forming a composite design.

1988. Olympic Tennis Medal Winners, Seoul. Nos. 1200/2 optd.
1204 $1.50 Type **234** (optd **MILOSLAV MECIR CZECHOSLOVAKIA GOLD MEDAL WINNER MEN'S TENNIS**) . . . . 4·00 2·25
1205 $1.50 Olympic torch and Seoul Olympic Park (optd **TIM MAYOTTE UNITED STATES GABRIELA SABATINI ARGENTINA SILVER MEDAL WINNERS**) . . 4·00 2·25
1206 $1.50 Steffi Graf playing tennis and Olympic medal (optd **GOLD MEDAL WINNER STEFFI GRAF WEST GERMANY**) . . 4·00 2·25
MS1207 131 × 81 mm. $10 Combined design as Nos. 1200/2, but measuring 114 × 47 mm (optd **GOLD MEDAL WINNER SEOUL OLYMPIC GAMES STEFFI GRAF – WEST GERMANY**) . . . . 12·00 11·00

236 "Virgin and Child"

1988. Christmas.
1208 **236** 70c. multicoloured . . . 3·00 2·00
1209 – 85c. multicoloured . . . 3·25 2·25
1210 – 95c. multicoloured . . . 3·50 2·50
1211 – $1.25 multicoloured . . 4·25 3·25
MS1212 80 × 100 mm. $6.40, multicoloured (45 × 60 mm) . . 8·50 11·00
DESIGNS: 85c., 95c., $1.25, Various versions of the "Virgin and Child" by Durer.

237 "Apollo 11" leaving Earth

1989. 20th Anniv of First Manned Landing on Moon. Multicoloured.
1213 40c. Type **237** . . . . . . 1·75 1·75
1214 40c. Lunar module over Moon . . . . 1·75 1·75
1215 55c. Aldrin stepping onto Moon . . . . 2·00 2·00
1216 55c. Astronaut on Moon . . 2·00 2·00
1217 65c. Working on lunar surface . . . . 2·25 2·25
1218 65c. Conducting experiment 2·25 2·25
1219 75c. "Apollo 11" leaving Moon . . . . 2·25 2·25
1220 75c. Splashdown in South Pacific . . . . 2·25 2·25
MS1221 108 × 91 mm. $4.20, Astronauts on Moon . . . . . 5·50 6·50

238 Rarotonga Flycatcher

1989. Endangered Birds of the Cook Islands. Multicoloured.
1222 15c. Type **238** (postage) . . 2·00 2·00
1223 20c. Pair of Rarotonga flycatchers . . . . 2·00 2·00
1224 65c. Pair of Rarotonga fruit doves . . . . 2·75 2·75
1225 70c. Rarotonga fruit dove 2·75 2·75
MS1226 Four sheets, each 70 × 53 mm. As Nos. 1222/5, but with face values of $1, $1.25, $1.50, $1.75 and each size 50 × 32 mm (air) Set of 4 sheets 11·00 12·00

239 Villagers

1989. Christmas. Details from "Adoration of the Magi" by Rubens. Multicoloured.
1227 70c. Type **239** . . . . . . 1·40 1·40
1228 85c. Virgin Mary . . . . . 1·60 1·60
1229 95c. Christ Child . . . . . 1·75 2·00
1230 $1.50 Boy with gift . . . . 2·00 3·00
MS1231 85 × 120 mm. $6.40, "Adoration of the Magi" (45 × 60 mm) . . . . 12·00 14·00

240 Reverend John Williams and L.M.S. Church

1990. Christianity in the Cook Islands. Multicoloured.
1232 70c. Type **240** 85 85
1233 85c. Mgr. Bernardine Castanie and Roman Catholic Church . . . . 1·00 1·10
1234 95c. Elder Osborne Widstoe and Mormon Church . . 1·10 1·40
1235 $1.60 Dr. J. E. Caldwell and Seventh Day Adventist Church . . . . 1·90 2·25
MS1236 90 × 90 mm. As Nos. 1232/5, but each with a face value of 90c. . . . . 4·75 6·50

241 "Woman writing a Letter" (Terborch) **243** Queen Elizabeth the Queen Mother

242 Sprinting

1990. 150th Anniv of the Penny Black. Designs showing paintings. Multicoloured.
1237 85c. Type **241** . . . . . . 1·50 1·25
1238 $1.15 "George Gisze" (Holbein the Younger) . . 1·75 1·75
1239 $1.55 "Mrs. John Douglas" (Gainsborough) . . . . . 2·25 2·50
1240 $1.85 "Portrait of a Gentleman" (Durer) . . . . 2·75 3·00
MS1241 82 × 150 mm. As Nos. 1237/40, but each with a face value of $1.05 . . . . 9·00 11·00

1990. Olympic Games, Barcelona, and Winter Olympic Games, Albertville (1992) (1st issue). Multicoloured.
1242 $1.85 Type **242** . . . . . . 5·50 5·50
1243 $1.85 Cook Islands $50 commemorative coin . . . 5·50 5·50
1244 $1.85 Skiing . . . . 5·50 5·50
MS1245 109 × 52 mm. $6.40, As Nos. 1242/4, but size 80 × 26 mm. 14·00 15·00
See also Nos. 1304/10.

1990. 90th Birthday of Queen Elizabeth the Queen Mother.
1246 **243** $1.85 multicoloured . . 6·00 5·00
MS1247 66 × 101 mm. **243** $6.40, multicoloured . . . . 12·00 14·00

244 "Adoration of the Magi" (Memling)

1990. Christmas. Religious Paintings. Mult.
1248 70c. Type **244** . . . . . . 2·00 1·75
1249 85c. "Holy Family" (Lotto) 2·25 1·90
1250 95c. "Madonna and Child with Saints John and Catherine" (Titian) . . . 2·50 2·25
1251 $1.50 "Holy Family" (Titian) . . . . 4·00 6·00
MS1252 98 × 110 mm. $6.40, "Madonna and Child enthroned, surrounded by Saints" (Vivarini) (vert) . . . . 12·00 13·00

1990. "Birdpex '90" Stamp Exhibition, Christchurch, New Zealand. No. **MS**1226 optd **Birdpex '90.**
MS1253 Four sheets, each 70 × 53 mm. As Nos. 1222/5, but with face values of $1, $1.25, $1.50, $1.75 and each size 50 × 32 mm Set of 4 sheets . . 16·00 18·00

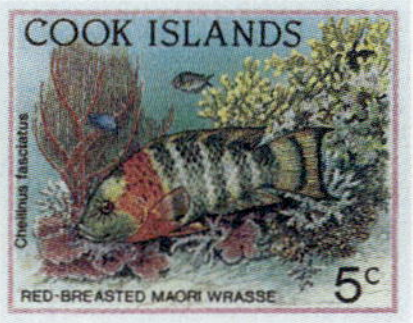

246 Columbus (engraving by Theodoro de Bry) **249** Red-breasted Wrasse

248 "Adoration of the Child" (G. delle Notti)

1991. 500th Anniv (1992) of Discovery of America by Columbus (1st issue).
1254 **246** $1 multicoloured . . . . 3·25 3·00
See also No. 1302.

1991. 65th Birthday of Queen Elizabeth II. No. 789 optd **65TH BIRTHDAY.**
1255 $10 "Melithaea albitincta" 14·00 15·00

1991. Christmas. Religious Paintings. Mult.
1256 70c. Type **248** . . . . . . 2·50 1·75
1257 85c. "The Birth of the Virgin" (B. Murillo) . . . 2·75 2·00
1258 $1.15 "Adoration of the Shepherds" (Rembrandt) 3·25 3·25
1259 $1.50 "Adoration of the Shepherds" (L. le Nain) 4·75 7·00
MS1260 79 × 103 mm. $6.40, "Madonna and Child" (Lippi) (vert) . . . . 12·00 13·00

1992. Reef Life (1st series). Multicoloured with white borders.
1261 5c. Type **249** . . . . . . 1·00 75
1262 10c. Blue sea star . . . . . 1·00 75
1263 15c. Bicoloured angelfish ("Black and gold angelfish") . . . . 1·25 85
1264 20c. Spotted pebble crab . . 1·25 1·00
1265 25c. Black-tipped grouper ("Black-tipped cod") . . . 1·25 1·00
1266 30c. Spanish dancer . . . . 1·25 1·00
1267 50c. Regal angelfish . . . . 1·25 1·25
1268 80c. Big-scaled soldierfish ("Squirrel fish") . . . . . 1·50 1·50
1269 85c. Red pencil sea urchin 4·25 2·75

1270 90c. Red-spotted rainbowfish 4·75 2·75
1271 $1 Cheek-lined wrasse 4·75 2·75
1272 $2 Long-nosed butterflyfish 6·00 4·50
1273 $3 Red-spotted rainbowfish 4·75 6·00
1274 $5 Blue sea-star 5·50 8·00
1275 $7 "Pygoplites diacanthus" 11·00 14·00
1276 $10 Spotted pebble crab 15·00 16·00
1277 $15 Red pencil sea urchin 21·00 23·00

The 25, 50c., $1 and $2 include a silhouette of the Queen's head.

For designs in a larger size, 40 × 30 mm, and with brown borders, see Nos. 1342/52.

250 Tiger

1992. Endangered Wildlife. Multicoloured.

1279 $1.15 Type **250** 1·25 1·25
1280 $1.15 Indian elephant 1·25 1·25
1281 $1.15 Brown bear 1·25 1·25
1282 $1.15 Black rhinoceros 1·25 1·25
1283 $1.15 Chimpanzee 1·25 1·25
1284 $1.15 Argali 1·25 1·25
1285 $1.15 Heaviside's dolphin 1·25 1·25
1286 $1.15 Eagle owl 1·75 1·25
1287 $1.15 Bee hummingbird 1·75 1·25
1288 $1.15 Puma 1·25 1·25
1289 $1.15 European otter 1·25 1·25
1290 $1.15 Red kangaroo 1·25 1·25
1291 $1.15 Jackass penguin 1·75 1·25
1292 $1.15 Asian lion 1·25 1·25
1293 $1.15 Peregrine falcon 1·75 1·25
1294 $1.15 Persian fallow deer 1·25 1·25
1295 $1.15 Key deer 1·25 1·25
1296 $1.15 Alpine ibex 1·25 1·25
1297 $1.15 Mandrill 1·25 1·25
1298 $1.15 Gorilla 1·25 1·25
1299 $1.15 "Vanessa atalanta" (butterfly) 1·25 1·25
1300 $1.15 Takin 1·25 1·25
1301 $1.15 Ring-tailed lemur 1·25 1·25

251 Columbus and Landing in New World

1992. 500th Anniv of Discovery of America by Columbus (2nd issue).

1302 **251** $6 multicoloured 7·50 8·00
MS1303 128 × 84 mm. $10 As T **251**, but detail of landing party only (40 × 29 mm) 7·00 8·50

252 Football and $50 Commemorative Coin

1992. Olympic Games, Barcelona (2nd issue). Multicoloured.

1304 $1.75 Type **252** 2·50 2·50
1305 $1.75 Olympic gold medal 2·50 2·50
1306 $1.75 Basketball and $10 coin 2·50 2·50
1307 $2.25 Running 3·50 3·50
1308 $2.25 $10 and $50 coins 3·50 3·50
1309 $2.25 Cycling 3·50 3·50
MS1310 155 × 91 mm. $6.40, Javelin throwing 14·00 15·00

253 Festival Poster

255 "Worship of Shepherds" (Parmigianino)

1992. 6th Festival of Pacific Arts, Rarotonga. Multicoloured.

1311 80c. Type **253** 2·00 2·00
1312 85c. Seated Tangaroa carving 2·00 2·00
1313 $1 Seated Tangaroa carving (different) 2·25 2·25
1314 $1.75 Standing Tangaroa carving 3·00 4·00

1992. Royal Visit by Prince Edward. Nos. 1311/14 optd **ROYAL VISIT**.

1315 80c. Type **253** 2·50 2·50
1316 85c. Seated Tangaroa carving 2·50 2·50
1317 $1 Seated Tangaroa carving (different) 2·75 2·75
1318 $1.75 Standing Tangaroa carving 4·50 5·00

1992. Christmas. Religious Paintings by Parmigianino. Multicoloured.

1319 70c. Type **255** 1·00 1·00
1320 85c. "Virgin with Long Neck" 1·25 1·25
1321 $1.15 "Virgin with Rose" 1·50 1·75
1322 $1.90 "St. Margaret's Virgin" 2·75 3·75
MS1323 86 × 102 mm. $6.40, As 85c. but larger (36 × 46 mm) 11·00 12·00

256 Queen in Garter Robes

258 "Virgin with Child" (Filippo Lippi)

257 Coronation Ceremony

1992. 40th Anniv of Queen Elizabeth II's Accession. Multicoloured.

1324 80c. Type **256** 1·75 1·50
1325 $1.15 Queen at Trooping the Colour 2·00 2·00
1326 $1.50 Queen in evening dress 2·75 3·00
1327 $1.95 Queen with bouquet 3·00 3·50

1993. 40th Anniv of Coronation. Multicoloured.

1328 $1 Type **257** 3·00 2·00
1329 $2 Coronation photograph by Cecil Beaton 4·50 4·00
1330 $3 Royal family on balcony 7·00 6·00

1993. Christmas. Religious Paintings. Mult.

1331 70c. Type **258** 80 80
1332 85c. "Bargellini Madonna" (Lodovico Carracci) 95 95
1333 $1.15 "Virgin of the Curtain" (Rafael Sanzio) 1·40 1·60
1334 $2.50 "Holy Family" (Agnolo Bronzino) 3·25 3·75
1335 $4 "Saint Zachary Virgin" (Parmigianino) (32 × 47 mm) 4·00 5·50

259 Skiing, Flags and Ice Skating (½-size illustration)

1994. Winter Olympic Games, Lillehammer.

1336 **259** $5 multicoloured 8·00 8·50

260 Cup on Logo with German and Argentinian Players

1994. World Cup Football Championship, U.S.A.

1337 **260** $4.50 multicoloured 6·00 7·50

261 Neil Armstrong taking First Step on Moon

1994. 25th Anniv of First Manned Moon Landing. Multicoloured.

1338 $2.25 Type **261** 3·75 3·75
1339 $2.25 Astronaut on Moon and view of Earth 3·75 3·75
1340 $2.25 Astronaut and flag 3·75 3·75
1341 $2.25 Astronaut with reflection in helmet visor 3·75 3·75

1994. Reef Life (2nd series). As Nos. 1261 and 1263/71, but each 40 × 30 mm and with brown borders.

1342 5c. Type **249** 60 70
1344 15c. Bicoloured angelfish 70 75
1345 20c. Spotted pebble crab 85 85
1346 25c. Black-tipped grouper 90 90
1347 30c. Spanish dancer 90 90
1348 50c. Regal angelfish 1·10 1·10
1349 80c. Big-scaled soldierfish 1·25 1·25
1350 85c. Red pencil sea urchin 1·25 1·25
1351 90c. Red-spotted rainbowfish 1·25 1·25
1352 $1 Cheek-lined wrasse 1·40 1·40

262 Actors in Outrigger Canoe

1994. Release of "The Return of Tommy Tricker" (film shot in Cook Islands). Scenes from film. Multicoloured.

1359 85c. Type **262** 1·10 1·25
1360 85c. Male and female dancers 1·10 1·25
1361 85c. European couple on beach 1·10 1·25
1362 85c. Aerial view of island 1·10 1·25
1363 85c. Two female dancers 1·10 1·25
1364 85c. Cook Islands couple on beach 1·10 1·25
1364a 90c. Type **262** 75 1·10
1364b 90c. As No. 1360 75 1·10
1364c 90c. As No. 1361 75 1·10
1364d 90c. As No. 1362 75 1·10
1364e 90c. As No. 1363 75 1·10
1364f 90c. As No. 1364 75 1·10

263 "The Virgin and Child" (Morales)

1994. Christmas. Religious Paintings. Mult.

1365 85c. Type **263** 2·00 2·00
1366 85c. "Adoration of the Kings" (Gerard David) 2·00 2·00
1367 85c. "Adoration of the Kings" (Foppa) 2·00 2·00
1368 85c. "The Madonna and Child with St. Joseph and Infant Baptist" (Baroccio) 2·00 2·00
1369 $1 "Madonna with Iris" (Durer) 2·00 2·00
1370 $1 "Adoration of the Shepherds" (Le Nain) 2·00 2·00
1371 $1 "The Virgin and Child" (school of Leonardo) 2·00 2·00
1372 $1 "The Mystic Nativity" (Botticelli) 2·00 2·00

264 Pirates ("Treasure Island")

1994. Death Centenary of Robert Louis Stevenson (author). Multicoloured.

1373 $1.50 Type **264** 3·00 3·00
1374 $1.50 Duel ("David Balfour") 3·00 3·00
1375 $1.50 Mr. Hyde, ("Dr. Jekyll and Mr. Hyde") 3·00 3·00
1376 $1.50 Rowing boat and sailing ship ("Kidnapped") 3·00 3·00

265 U.N. and National Flags with Peace Doves

1995. 50th Anniv of United Nations.

1377 **265** $4.75 multicoloured 4·75 7·00

266 Queen Elizabeth the Queen Mother and Coat of Arms

1995. 95th Birthday of Queen Elizabeth the Queen Mother.

1378 **266** $5 multicoloured 11·00 9·00

267 German Delegation signing Unconditional Surrender at Rheims

1995. 50th Anniv of End of Second World War. Multicoloured.

1379 $3.50 Type **267** 8·00 8·00
1380 $3.50 Japanese delegation on U.S.S. "Missouri", Tokyo Bay 8·00 8·00

1995. 50th Anniv of FAO. As T **265**. Mult.

1381 $4.50 FAO and U.N. emblems 4·75 7·00

268 Green Turtle

1995. Year of the Sea Turtle. Multicoloured.

1382 85c. Type **268** 1·75 1·60
1383 $1 Hawksbill turtle 2·00 1·75
1384 $1.75 Green turtle on beach 3·00 3·25
1385 $2.25 Young hawksbill turtles hatching 3·75 4·00

269 Emblem and Throwing the Discus

1996. Olympic Games, Atlanta. Multicoloured.

1386 85c. Type **269** 1·50 1·50
1387 $1 Athlete with Olympic Torch 1·75 1·75
1388 $1.50 Running 2·50 2·50
1389 $1.85 Gymnastics 2·75 2·75
1390 $2.10 Ancient archery 3·00 3·00
1391 $2.50 Throwing the javelin 3·00 3·00

270 Queen Elizabeth II

1996. 70th Birthday of Queen Elizabeth II. Multicoloured.
1392 $1.90 Type **270** . . . . . . 2·75 2·75
1393 $2.25 Wearing tiara . . . . 3·25 3·25
1394 $2.75 In Garter robes . . . 3·50 3·50
MS1395 103 × 152 mm. Designs as Nos. 1392/4, but each with a face value of $2.50 . . . . 15·00 15·00

1997. 28th South Pacific Forum. Nos. 1364a/f optd **28th South Pacific Forum** (Nos. 1396, 1399/1400) or **12–22 September 1997** (Nos. 1397/8 and 1401). Multicoloured.
1396 90c. Type **262** . . . . . . 1·00 1·25
1397 90c. As No. 1360 . . . . . 1·00 1·25
1398 90c. As No. 1361 . . . . . 1·00 1·25
1399 90c. As No. 1362 . . . . . 1·00 1·25
1400 90c. As No. 1363 . . . . . 1·00 1·25
1401 90c. As No. 1364 . . . . . 1·00 1·25

272 "Lampides boeticus" (female)

1997. Butterflies. Multicoloured.
1402 5c. Type **272** 10 10
1403 10c. "Vanessa atalanta" . . 15 15
1404 15c. "Lampides boeticus" (male) 20 20
1405 20c. "Papilio godeffroyi" . . 25 25
1406 25c. "Danaus hamata" . . . 25 25
1407 30c. "Xois sesara" 30 30
1408 50c. "Vagrans egista" . . . 45 45
1409 70c. "Parthenos sylvia" . . 70 70
1410 80c. "Hyblaea sanguinea" . 80 85
1411 85c. "Melanitis leda" . . . 80 85
1412 90c. "Ascalapha odorata" . 85 90
1413 $1 "Precis villida" 90 95
1414 $1.50 "Parthenos sylvia" . . 1·25 1·40
1415 $2 "Lampides boeticus" (female) . . . . 1·50 1·60
1416 $3 "Precis villida" . . . . 2·20 2·30
1417 $4 "Melanitis leda" . . . . 3·00 3·25
1418 $5 "Vagrans egista" . . . . 3·75 4·00
1419 $7 "Hyblaea sanguinea" . . 5·25 5·50
1420 $10 "Vanessa atalanta" . . 7·25 7·50
1421 $15 "Papilio godeffroyi" . . 11·00 11·50

The 70c. and $1 include an outline portrait of Queen Elizabeth II. Nos. 1414/21 are larger, 41 × 25 mm, with the Queen's portrait included on the $4 to $15.

273 Queen Elizabeth and Prince Philip

1997. Golden Wedding of Queen Elizabeth and Prince Philip.
1424 **273** $2 multicoloured . . . . 2·75 2·50
MS1425 76 × 102 mm. **273** $5 multicoloured . . . . 8·00 8·00

274 Diana, Princess of Wales

277 Lady Elizabeth Bowes-Lyon

1998. Diana, Princess of Wales Commemoration.
1426 **274** $1.15 multicoloured . . . 1·25 1·25
MS1427 70 × 100 mm. $3.50, Princess Diana and guard of honour . . . . 3·25 4·50

1998. Children's Charities. No. **MS**1427 surch **+$1 CHILDREN'S CHARITIES**.
MS1428 70 × 100 mm. $3.50 + $1 Princess Diana and guard of honour . . . . 3·50 4·50

1999. New Millennium. Nos. 1311/14 optd **KIA ORANA THIRD MILLENNIUM**.
1429 80c. Type **253** 65 65
1430 85c. Seated Tangaroa carving 70 70
1431 $1 Seated Tangaroa carving (different) 80 80
1432 $1.75 Standing Tangaroa carving . . . . 1·40 1·75

2000. Queen Elizabeth the Queen Mother's 100th Birthday.
1433 **277** $4.50 brown and blue . . 4·25 4·25
1434 – $4.50 brown and blue . . 4·25 4·25
1435 – $4.50 multicoloured . . 4·25 4·25
1436 – $4.50 multicoloured . . 4·25 4·25
MS1437 73 × 100 mm. $6 multicoloured . . . . 4·75 6·00
DESIGNS: 1434, Lady Elizabeth Bowes-Lyon as young woman; 1435, Queen Mother wearing green outfit; 1436, Queen Mother wearing pearl earrings and necklace; **MS**1437, Queen Mother in blue hat and plum jacket.

278 Ancient Greek Runner on Urn

2000. Olympic Games, Sydney. Multicoloured.
1438 $1.75 Type **278** . . . . . . 1·75 2·00
1439 $1.75 Modern runner . . . . 1·75 2·00
1440 $1.75 Ancient Greek archer . 1·75 2·00
1441 $1.75 Modern archer . . . . 1·75 2·00
MS1442 99 × 90 mm. $3.90, Olympic torch in Cook Islands . . . . 2·75 3·50

2001. Suwarrow Wildlife Sanctuary. Nos. 1279/90 surch **80c SUWARROW SANCTUARY**.
1443 80c. on $1.15 Heavisides's dolphin . . . . 95 1·10
1444 80c. on $1.15 Eagle owl . . 95 1·10
1445 80c. on $1.15 Bee hummingbird . . . . . . 95 1·10
1446 80c. on $1.15 Puma . . . . 95 1·10
1447 80c. on $1.15 European otter . . . . 95 1·10
1448 80c. on $1.15 Red kangaroo 95 1·10
1449 90c. on $1.15 Type **250** . . 95 1·10
1450 90c. on $1.15 Indian elephant . . . . 95 1·10
1451 90c. on $1.15 Brown bear . 95 1·10
1452 90c. on $1.15 Black rhinoceros . . . . 95 1·10
1453 90c. on $1.15 Chimpanzee 95 1·10
1454 90c. on $1.15 Argali . . . . 95 1·10

2002. Christmas. Nos. 1248/51 and 1256/9 optd **CHRISTMAS 2002** or surch.
1455 20c. on 70c. Type **244** . . . 35 40
1456 20c. on 70c. Type **248** . . . 35 40
1457 80c. on $1.15 "Adoration of the Shepherds" (Rembrandt) . . . . . . 1·00 1·00
1458 85c. "Holy Family" (Lotto) 1·10 1·25
1459 85c. "The Birth of the Virgin" (B. Murillo) . . . 1·10 1·25
1460 90c. on $1.50 "Adoration of the Shepherds" (L. le Nain) . . . . 1·25 1·25
1461 95c. "Madonna and Child with Saints John and Catherine" (Titian) . . . 1·25 1·25
1462 $1 on $1.50 "The Holy Family" (Titian) . . . . 1·40 1·40

2003. Nos. 1414/19 surch.
1463 20c. on $1.50 *Parthenos Sylvia* 35 40
1464 80c. on $2 *Lampides boeticus* (female) 35 40
1465 85c. on $3 *Precis villida* . . 1·00 1·00
1466 85c. on $4 *Melanitis leda* . . 1·10 1·25
1467 90c. on $5 *Vagrans egista* . 1·10 1·25
1468 90c. on $7 *Hyblaea sanguinea* . . . . 1·10 1·25

282 Statue of Liberty's Torch and Cook Islands Flag

2003. "United We Stand". Support for Victims of 11 September 2001 Terrorist Attacks.
MS1469 75 × 109 mm. **282** 90c. × 4 multicoloured . . . . 4·00 4·50

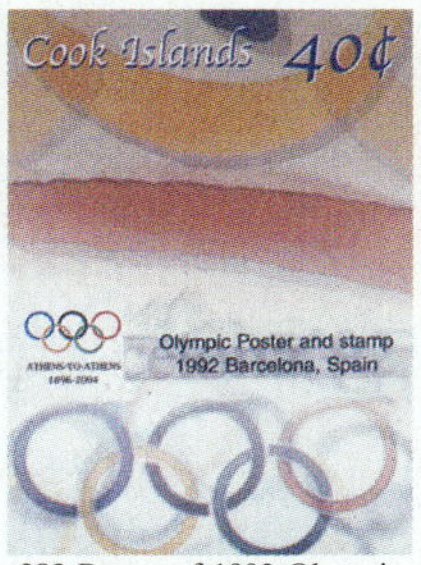

283 Poster of 1992 Olympic Games, Barcelona

2004. Olympic Games, Athens, Greece. Multicoloured.
1470 40c. Type **283** 60 65
1471 60c. "The Pancration" (Greek art) (horiz) . . . . 90 1·00
1472 $1 Cycling (horiz) . . . . . 2·00 2·25
1473 $2 Gold medal, Berlin, 1936 2·50 2·75

284 Cook Islands Warbler ("Cook Islands Reed Warbler")

2005. Endangered Birds of the Cook Islands. Four sheets, each 95 × 132 mm, containing T **284** and similar horiz designs. Multicoloured.
MS1474 (a) 80c. × 4 Type **284**. (b) 90c. × 4 Mangaia kingfisher. (c) $1.15 × 4 Rarotonga starling. (d) $1.95 × 4 Cook Islands swiftlet ("Atiu Swiftlet") . . . . 20·00 22·00

285 Pope John Paul II

2005. Pope John Paul II Commemoration.
1475 **285** $1.35 multicoloured . . 1·90 1·90

2005. Olympic Gold Medal Winners, Athens (2004). Nos. 1470/3 optd.
1476 40c. "Poster of 1992 Olympic Games, Barcelona" (optd with Type A) 60 65
1477 40c. "Poster of 1992 Olympic Games, Barcelona" (optd with Type B) 60 65
1478 40c. "Poster of 1992 Olympic Games, Barcelona" (optd with Type C) 60 65
1479 40c. "Poster of 1992 Olympic Games, Barcelona" (optd with Type D) 60 65
1480 40c. "Poster of 1992 Olympic Games, Barcelona" (optd with Type E) 60 65
1481 60c. "The Pancration" (Greek art) (horiz) (optd with Type A) 70 80
1482 60c. "The Pancration" (Greek art) (horiz) (optd with Type B) 70 80
1483 60c. "The Pancration" (Greek art) (horiz) (optd with Type C) 70 80
1484 60c. "The Pancration" (Greek art) (horiz) (optd with Type D) 70 80
1485 60c. "The Pancration" (Greek art) (horiz) (optd with Type E) 70 80
1486 $1 Cycling (horiz) (optd with Type A) . . . . . 1·50 1·60
1487 $1 Cycling (horiz) (optd with Type B) . . . . . 1·50 1·60
1488 $1 Cycling (horiz) (optd with Type C) . . . . . 1·50 1·60
1489 $1 Cycling (horiz) (optd with Type D) . . . . . 1·50 1·60
1490 $1 Cycling (horiz) (optd with Type E) . . . . . 1·50 1·60
1491 $2 Gold medal, Berlin, 1936 (optd with Type A) . . . 2·50 2·75
1492 $2 Gold medal, Berlin, 1936 (optd with Type B) . . . 2·50 2·75
1493 $2 Gold medal, Berlin, 1936 (optd with Type C) . . . 2·50 2·75
1494 $2 Gold medal, Berlin, 1936 (optd with Type D) . . . 2·50 2·75
1495 $2 Gold medal, Berlin, 1936 (optd with Type E) . . . 2·50 2·75
OVERPRINTS (all with four gold stars): Type A **DWIGHT PHILLIPS Men's LONG JUMP USA 35**; Type B **XING HUINA Women's 10,000m CHINA 32**; Type C **IAN THORPE Men's 200m FREESTYLE AUSTRALIA 17**; Type D **MIZUKI NOGUCHI Women's Marathon JAPAN 16**; Type E **YVONNE BOENISCH Women's 57kg JUDO GERMANY 14**.

287 Black-lined Maori Wrasse

288 Hawksbill Turtle

289 Red-spot Rainbow Fish, Smooth Sea Star and Black tipped Cod (½-size illustration)

2007. Wildlife of the South Pacific. Multicoloured.
(a) Size 39 × 25 mm.
1496 5c. Type **287** 10 15
1497 10c. Pair of blue lorikeets on palm frond 15 20
1498 20c. *Tubastrea aurea* (daisy coral) 30 35
1499 30c. Three ocean sunfish . . 40 45
1500 40c. *Lampides boeticus* (butterfly) (female) . . . 45 50
1501 50c. Pair of Rarotonga starlings 55 60
(b) Size 48 × 27 mm. Frames and inscriptions in gold.
1502 80c. Mangaia kingfishers . . 75 80
1503 80c. Cook Islands reed-warblers 75 80
1504 80c. As No. 1501 . . . . . 75 80
1505 80c. Matiu swiftlet 75 80
1506 90c. *Lampides boeticus* (butterfly) (male) . . . . 1·00 1·10
1507 90c. *Vagrans egista* (butterfly) . . . . 1·00 1·10
1508 90c. *Melantis leda* (butterfly) 1·00 1·10
1509 90c. As No. 1500 . . . . . 1·00 1·10
1510 $1 As No. 1498 . . . . . . 1·10 1·25
1511 $1 *Stylaster elegans* (hydroid coral) . . . . 1·10 1·25
1512 $1 *Fromia monilis* (sea star) 1·10 1·25
1513 $1 *Choriaster granulatus* (smooth sea star) . . . . . 1·10 1·25
1514 $1.10 Black tipped cod . . . 1·40 1·50
1515 $1.10 Red-spot rainbow fish 1·40 1·50
1516 $1.10 As Type **287** . . . . 1·40 1·50
1517 $1.10 Longnose butterflyfish 1·40 1·50
1518 $1.20 As No. 1499 . . . . 2·00 2·10
1519 $1.20 Three ocean sunfish, two feeding on floating weeds . . . . 2·00 2·10
1520 $1.20 Diver and ocean sunfish . . . . 2·00 2·10
1521 $1.20 Four ocean sunfish, one swimming towards camera with mouth open 2·00 2·10
1522 $2 As No. 1497 . . . . . . 2·25 2·40
1523 $2 Two young blue lorikeets in tree hole . . . . 2·25 2·40
1524 $2 Pair of blue lorikeets and white hibiscus flowers . . 2·25 2·40
1525 $2 Pair of blue lorikeets perched on plant . . . . 2·25 2·40
(c) Horiz designs as T **288**. Multicoloured.
1526 $3 Type **288** . . . . 3·50 3·75
1527 $3 Leatherback turtle . . . 3·50 3·75
1528 $3 Green turtle . . . . . . 3·50 3·75
1529 $3 Olive Ridley turtle . . . 3·50 3·75
1530 $5 Sowerby's whale . . . . 5·00 5·25
1531 $5 Cuvier's beaked whale . . 5·00 5·25
1532 $5 Bottle-nosed dolphin . . 5·00 5·25
1533 $5 Commerson's dolphin . . 5·00 5·25
(d) Horiz designs as T **289**. Multicoloured.
1534 $7.50 Type **289** . . . . . . 9·50 10·00
1535 $10 *Lampides boeticus* (male and female) and *Melantis leda* butterflies . . . . 12·75 13·00
1536 $15 Matiu swiftlet, Cook Islands reed-warbler and blue lorikeets . . . . . 17·00 18·00
No. 1510 is wrongly inscr 'Smooth Sea Star *Choriaster granulatus*'.

OFFICIAL STAMPS

1975. Nos. 228, etc, optd **O.H.M.S.** or surch also.
O 1 1c. multicoloured . . . . .
O 2 2c. multicoloured . . . . .

O 3 3c. multicoloured
O 4 4c. multicoloured
O 5 5c. on 2½c. multicoloured
O 6 8c. multicoloured
O 7 10c. on 6c. multicoloured
O 8 18c. on 20c. multicoloured
O 9 25c. on 9c. multicoloured
O 10 30c. on 15c. multicoloured
O 11 50c. multicoloured
O 12 $1 multicoloured
O 13 $2 multicoloured
O 14 $4 multicoloured
O 15 $6 multicoloured
O1/15 Set of 15 † 7·00

These stamps were only sold to the public cancelled-to-order and not in unused condition.

1978. Nos. 466/7, 474, 478/81, 484/5, 542 and 568/9 optd **O.H.M.S.** or surch also.

O16 – 1c. mult (No. 467) 80 10
O17 **141** 2c. on ½c. multicoloured 80 10
O18 – 5c. on ½c. multicoloured 90 10
O19 – 10c. on 8c. mult (No. 474) 1·00 10
O20 – 15c. on 50c. mult (No. 480) 1·25 10
O21 – 18c. on 60c. mult (No. 481) 1·25 15
O22 – 25c. mult (No. 478) 1·50 20
O23 – 30c. mult (No. 479) 1·50 25
O24 – 35c. on 60c. mult (No. 481) 1·50 30
O25 – 50c. mult (No. 480) 2·00 35
O26 – 60c. mult (No. 481) 2·25 45
O27 – $1 mult (No. 568) 5·00 65
O28 – $1 mult (No. 569) 5·00 65
O29 – $2 mult (No. 542) 7·00 2·25
O30 – $4 mult (No. 484) 13·00 2·25
O31 – $6 mult (No. 485) 13·00 3·50

1985. Nos. 786/8, 862/5, 969/74, 976, 978, 981, 984/6 and 988/9 optd **O.H.M.S.** or surch also.

O32 5c. "Ptilosarcus gurneyi" 50 60
O33 10c. "Lobophyllia bemprichii" 50 60
O34 12c. "Sarcophyton digitatum" 5·00 75
O35 14c. "Pavona praetorta" 5·00 75
O36 18c. "Junceella gemmacea" 5·00 75
O37 20c. "Stylaster" 60 60
O38 30c. "Palauastrea ramosa" 60 60
O39 40c. "Stylaster echinatus" 60 60
O40 50c. "Melithaea squamata" 6·50 90
O41 55c. on 85c. "Caulastraea echinulata" 70 70
O42 60c. "Tubastraea" 70 80
O43 70c. "Heliofungia actiniformis" 6·50 1·10
O46 75c. on 60c. Type **197** 3·00 1·00
O47 75c. on 60c. Rarotonga oranges 3·00 1·00
O48 75c. on 60c. Rarotonga Airport 3·00 1·00
O49 75c. on 60c. Prime Minister Sir Thomas Davis 3·00 1·00
O44 $1.10 "Pectinia alcicornis" 1·60 1·10
O45 $2 on $1.20 "Dendrophyllia gracilis" 3·25 2·00
O50 $5 on $3 "Heliofungia actiniformis" 17·00 5·00
O51 $9 on $4 "Stylophora pistillata" 8·50 10·00
O52 $14 on $6 "Stylaster echinatus" 12·50 14·00
O53 $18 on $10 "Melithaea albitincta" 18·00 18·00

1995. Nos. 1261/6 optd **O.H.M.S.**

O54 5c. Type **249** 40 75
O55 10c. Blue sea star 40 75
O56 15c. Bicoloured angelfish 50 75
O57 20c. Spotted pebble crab 55 80
O58 25c. Black-tipped grouper 60 70
O59 30c. Spanish dancer 60 70
O60 50c. Regal angelfish 80 80
O61 80c. Big-scaled soldierfish 1·25 1·25
O62 85c. Red pencil sea urchin 1·25 1·25
O63 90c. Red-spotted rainbowfish 1·25 1·25
O64 $1 Cheek-lined wrasse 1·50 1·50
O65 $2 Long-nosed butterflyfish 2·25 2·50
O66 $3 Red-spotted rainbowfish 3·75 4·00
O67 $5 Blue sea star 4·50 5·00
O68 $7 "Pygoplites diacanthus" 6·50 7·50
O69 $10 Spotted pebble crab 8·00 9·50

COSTA RICA Pt. 15

A republic of Central America. Independent since 1821.

1863. 8 reales = 1 peso.
1881. 100 centavos = 1 peso.
1901. 100 centimos = 1 colon.

1

8 General P. Fernandez

14 Pres. Soto

1863.

1 **1** ½r. blue 30 1·00
3 2r. red 1·50 1·80
4 4r. green 15·00 15·00
5 1p. orange 38·00 38·00

1881. Surch.

6 **1** 1c. on ½r. blue 2·75 7·75
8 2c. on ½r. blue 3·00 3·50
9 5c. on ½r. blue 6·75 12·50

1882. Surch **U.P.U.** and value.

10 **1** 5c. on ½r. blue 60·00
11 10c. on 2r. red 70·00
12 20c. on 4r. green £275

1883.

13 **8** 1c. green 3·00 1·50
14 2c. red 3·00 1·50
15 5c. violet 30·00 1·90
16 10c. orange £130 12·00
17 40c. blue 1·90 3·00

1887.

18 **14** 5c. violet 5·75 40
19 10c. orange 3·25 2·40

1887. Fiscal stamps similar to T **8** and **14** optd **CORREOS**.

20 1c. red 4·25 3·00
21 5c. brown 5·75 3·00

17 Pres. Soto

19

1889. Various frames.

22 **17** 1c. brown 35 45
23 2c. green 35 45
24 5c. orange 45 35
25 10c. lake 40 35
26 20c. green 30 35
27 50c. red 1·10 85
28 1p. blue 1·20 85
29 2p. violet 6·00 4·75
30 5p. olive 22·00 11·50
31 10p. black 90·00 60·00

1892. Various frames.

32 **19** 1c. blue 30 40
33 2c. orange 30 40
34a 5c. mauve 30 25
35 10c. green 80 35
36 20c. red 12·00 15
37 50c. blue 4·00 2·75
38 1p. green on yellow 95 80
39 2p. red on grey 2·75 85
40 5p. blue on blue 1·90 85
41a 10p. brown on buff 6·50 5·00

29 Juan Santamaria

31 Puerto Limon

1901. Various designs dated "1900".

42 **29** 1c. black and green 3·00 30
43 – 2c. black and red 25 15
52 – 4c. black and purple 1·70 70
44 **31** 5c. black and blue 3·00 30
53 – 6c. black and olive 7·25 4·00
45 – 10c. black and brown 3·00 35
46 – 20c. black and lake 21·00 25
54 – 25c. brown and lilac 16·00 30
47 – 50c. blue and red 5·00 95
48 – 1col. black and olive £100 3·50
49 – 2col. black and red 15·00 3·00
50 – 5col. black and brown 70·00 3·50
51 – 10col. red and green 27·00 3·00

DESIGNS—VERT: 2c. Juan Mora F; 4c. Jose M. Canas; 6c. Julian Volio; 10c. Braulio (wrongly inscr "BRANLIO") Carrillo; 25c. Eusebio Figueroa; 50c. Jose M. Castro; 1col. Puente de Birris; 2col. Juan Rafael Mora; 5col. Jesus Jimenez. HORIZ: 20c. National Theatre; 10col. Arms.

1905. No. 46 surch **UN CENTIMO** in ornamental frame.

55 1c. on 20c. black and lake 55 50

43 Juan Santamaria

44 Juan Mora

1907. Dated "1907".

57 **43** 1c. blue and brown 4·00 40
58 **44** 2c. black and green 2·10 30
69 – 4c. blue and red 12·00 2·50
60 – 5c. blue and orange 3·00 30
71 – 10c. black and blue 19·00 1·00
72 – 20c. black and olive 26·00 5·00
63 – 25c. slate and lavender 3·00 3·00
74 – 50c. blue and red 55·00 25·00
75 – 1col. black and brown 21·00 19·00
76 – 2col. green and red £150 95·00

PORTRAITS: 4c. Jose M. Canas. 5c. Mauro Fernandez. 10c. Braulio Carrillo. 20c. Julian Volio. 25c. Eusebio Figueroa. 50c. Jose M. Castro. 1col. Jesus Jimenez. 2col. Juan Rafael Mora.

53 Juan Santamaria

54 Julian Volio

1910. Various frames.

77 **53** 1c. brown 10 10
78 – 2c. green (Juan Mora F.) 25 10
79 – 4c. red (Jose M. Canas) 30 20
80 – 5c. orange (Mauro Fernandez) 95 10
81 – 10c. blue (B. Carrillo) 25 10
82 **54** 20c. olive 40 20
83 – 25c. purple (Eusebio Figueroa) 12·50 1·20
84 – 1col. brown (Jesus Jimenez) 50 50

1911. Optd **1911** between stars.

85 **29** 1c. black and green 1·90 95
86 **43** 1c. blue and brown 95 40
88 **44** 2c. black and green 1·20 65

1911. Optd **Habilitado 1911**.

93 4c. black and purple (No. 52) 1·00 10
90 5c. blue and orange (No. 60) 1·50 20
91 10c. black and blue (No. 71) 49·00 5·75

59 Liner "Antilles"

62

1911. Surch **Correos Un centimo** or **Correos S 5 centimos**.

94 **59** 1c. on 10c. blue 35 25
96 1c. on 25c. violet 35 20
97 1c. on 50c. brown 50 40
98 1c. on 1c. brown 50 40
99 1c. on 5c. red 80 55
100 1c. on 10c. brown 1·10 70
101 5c. on 5c. orange 40 25

1912. Surch **Correos Dos centimos 2**.

102 **62** 2c. on 5c. brown 3·25 2·00
109 2c. on 10c. blue 95·00 80·00
104 2c. on 50c. red 44·00 19·00
105 2c. on 1c. brown 1·30 80
112 2c. on 2c. red 80 60
107 2c. on 5c. green 6·00 3·00
108 2c. on 10col. purple 4·75 3·00

67 Plantation and Administration Building

1921. Centenary of Coffee Cultivation.

115 **67** 5c. black and blue 2·75 2·75

68 Simon Bolivar

69

1921.

116 **68** 15c. violet 55 20

1921. Cent of Independence of Central America.

117 **69** 5c. violet 90 40

70 Juan Mora and Julio Acosta

1921. Centenary of Independence.

118 **70** 2c. black and orange 1·30 1·30
119 3c. black and green 1·30 1·30
120 6c. black and red 2·20 2·20
121 15c. black and blue 4·00 4·00
122 30c. black and brown 5·50 5·50

1922. Coffee Publicity. Nos. 77/81 and 116 optd with sack inscr "CAFE DE COSTA RICA".

123 **53** 1c. brown 30 10
124 – 2c. green 30 10
125 – 4c. red 30 10
126 – 5c. orange 1·50 40
127 – 10c. blue 60 40
128 **68** 15c. violet 3·50 2·10

1922. Optd **CORREOS 1922**.

129 **69** 5c. violet 55 40

1922. Surch with red cross and **5c.**

130 5c.+5c. orange (No. 80) 70 30

1923. Optd **COMPRE UD. CAFE DE COSTA RICA** in circular frame.

131 5c. orange (No. 80) 2·30 70

77 Jesus Jimenez (statesman)

81 Coffee-growing

80 National Monument

1923. Birth Centenary of J. Jimenez.

132 **77** 2c. brown 30 30
133 4c. green 35 30
134 5c. blue 50 30
135 20c. red 60 40
136 1col. violet 80 75

1923.

137 **80** 1c. purple 15 10
138 **81** 2c. yellow 40 10
139 – 4c. green 70 35
140 – 5c. blue 1·30 10
141 – 5c. green 35 10
142 – 10c. brown 2·50 10
143 – 10c. red 45 10
144 – 12c. red 9·00 2·50
145 – 20c. blue 9·75 65
146 – 40c. orange 10·00 2·30
147 – 1col. olive 2·20 80

All the above are inscr "U.P.U. 1923." except the 10c. and 12c. which are inscr "1921 EN COMMEMORACION DEL PRIMER CONGRESO POSTAL", etc.

DESIGNS—HORIZ: 5c. P.O., San Jose; 10c. Columbus and Isabella I; 12c. "Santa Maria"; 20c. Columbus landing at Cariari; 40c. Map of Costa Rica. VERT: 4c. Banana-growing; 1col. M. Gutierrez.

85 Don R. A. Maldonado y Velasco

86 Map of Guanacaste

1924.

148 **85** 2c. green 45 20

For 3c. green see No. 211 and for other portraits as T **85** see Nos. 308/12.

1924. Cent of Province of Nicoya (Guanacaste).

149 **86** 1c. red 35 10
150 2c. purple 35 10
151 5c. green 35 10
152 10c. orange 2·30 50
153 – 15c. blue 80 50
154 – 20c. grey 1·60 85
155 – 25c. brown 2·30 1·50

DESIGN: 15c., 20c., 25c. Church at Nicoya.

88 Discus Thrower

93 Arms and Curtiss "Jenny"

1925. Inscr "JUEGOS OLIMPICOS". Imperf or perf.

156 **88** 5c. green 1·60 2·30
157 – 10c. red 1·60 2·30
158 – 20c. blue 3·50 4·00

DESIGNS—VERT: 10c. Trophy. HORIZ: 20c. Parthenon.

1926. Surch with values in ornamental designs.
159 3c. on 5c. (No. 140) 30 10
160 6c. on 10c. (No. 142) 35 25
161 30c. on 40c. (No. 146) . . . 1·30 35
162 45c. on 1col. (No. 147) . . . 1·50 45

1926. Surch with value between bars.
163 10c. on 12c. red (No. 144) . . 1·10 30

1926. Air.
164 **93** 20c. blue . . . . 2·75 60

94 Heredia Normal School

1926. Dated "1926".
165 – 3c. blue 55 10
166 – 6c. brown 55 20
167 **94** 30c. orange . . . . 1·40 35
168 – 45c. violet . . . . 3·75 1·40
DESIGNS: 3c. St. Louis College, Cartago; 6c. Chapui Asylum, San Jose; 45c. Ruins of Ujarras.

1928. Lindbergh Good Will Tour of Central America. Surch with aeroplane, **LINDBERGH ENERO 1928** and new value.
169 10c. on 12c. red (No. 144) . . 4·75 4·75

1928. Surch **5 5**.
170 **68** 5c. on 15c. violet 20 10

1929. Surch **CORREOS** and value.
171 **62** 5c. on 2col. red 55 10
173 13c. on 40c. green 30 15

98 Post Office

103 Juan Rafael Mora

1930. Types of 1923 reduced in size and dated "1929" as T **98**.
174 – 1c. purple (as No. 137) . . 20 10
175 **98** 5c. green 20 10
176 – 10c. red (as No. 143) . . . 55 10

1930. Air. No. O178 surch **CORREO 1930 AEREO**, Bleriot XI airplane and new value.
177 **O 95** 8c. on 1col. 70 60
178 20c. on 1col. . . . . . 1·00 65
179 40c. on 1col. . . . . . 2·10 1·60
180 1col. on 1col. . . . . . 3·00 2·00

1930. Air. Optd **CORREO AEREO** (No. 181) or **Correo Aereo** (others) or surch also.
182 **62** 5c. on 10c. brown 35 25
181 – 10c. red (No. 143) . . . . 1·60 25
183 **62** 20c. on 50c. blue 45 25
184 40c. on 50c. blue 55 25
185 1col. orange . . . . 1·80 45

1931.
186 **103** 13c. red 55 10

1931. Air. Fiscal stamps (Arms design) inscr "TIMBRE 1929" (or "1930", 3col.), surch **Habilitado 1931 Correo Aereo** and new value.
190 2col. on 2col. green . . . . . 36·00 36·00
191 3col. on 5col. brown . . . . 36·00 36·00
192 5col. on 10col. black . . . . 36·00 36·00

1932. Air. Telegraph stamp optd with wings inscr **CORREO CR AEREO**.
193 **62** 40c. green . . . . 2·50 35

106

1932. 1st National Philatelic Exhibition.
194 **106** 3c. orange 15 10
195 5c. green 40 25
196 10c. red 50 25
197 20c. blue 70 40
See also Nos. 231/4.

107 Ryan Brougham over La Sabana Airport, San Jose

1934. Air.
198 **107** 5c. green 20 20
507 5c. deep blue 40 20
508 5c. pale blue 40 20
199 10c. red 20 20
509 10c. green 40 20
510 10c. turquoise 40 20
200 15c. brown 40 20
511 15c. red 50 20
201 20c. blue 40 20
202 25c. orange 55 20
512 35c. violet . . . . 1·30 20
203 40c. brown . . . . 1·70 20
204 50c. black 70 20
205 60c. yellow . . . . 1·40 20
206 75c. violet . . . . 2·75 50
207 – 1col. red . . . . 1·50 20
208 – 2col. blue . . . . 5·75 1·00
209 – 5col. black . . . . 5·75 5·00
210 – 10col. brown . . . . . . 8·75 8·50
DESIGN: 1, 2, 5, 10col. Allegory of the Air Mail.

1934.
211 **85** 3c. green 15 10

109 Nurse at Altar

111 Our Lady of the Angels

1935. Costa Rican Red Cross Jubilee.
212 **109** 10c. red . . . . 7·00 25

1935. 300th Anniv of Apparition of Our Lady of the Angels.
213 – 5c. green 20 20
214 **111** 10c. red 35 20
215 – 30c. orange 50 20
216 – 45c. violet . . . . 1·20 60
217 **111** 50c. black . . . . 2·00 1·10
DESIGNS: 5c., 30c. Aerial view of Cartago; 45c. Allegory of the Apparition.

112 Cocos Island

1936.
218 **112** 4c. brown 35 10
219 8c. violet 50 20
220 25c. orange 60 20
221 35c. brown 80 20
222 40c. brown . . . . 1·10 30
223 50c. yellow . . . . 1·20 60
224 2col. green . . . . 9·75 9·25
225 5col. green . . . . 29·00 23·00

113 Cocos Island and Fleet of Columbus

1936.
226 **113** 5c. green 25 20
227 10c. red 45 20

114 Airplane over Mt. Poas

1937. Air. 1st Annual Fair.
228 **114** 1c. black 40 35
229 2c. brown 40 35
230 3c. violet 40 35

1937. 2nd National Philatelic Exhibition. As T **106**, but inscr "DICIEMBRE 1937".
231 **106** 2c. purple 35 10
232 3c. black 35 10
233 5c. green 35 10
234 10c. orange 35 10
MS234a 164 × 101 mm. Nos. 231/4. Imperf . . . . 1·10 1·10

115 Tunny

116 Native and Donkey carrying Bananas

117 Puntarenas

1937. National Exhibition, San Jose (1st Issue).
235 **115** 2c. black (postage) . . . 35 10
236 **116** 5c. green 50 10
237 – 10c. red 80 20

238 **117** 2c. black (air) 15 10
239 5c. green 20 10
240 20c. blue 30 10
241 1col.40 brown . . . . . . 2·40 2·40
DESIGN—As Type **116**: 10c. Coffee gathering.

118 Purple Guaria Orchid "Carrleya skinneri"

119 National Bank

1938. National Exhibition, San Jose (2nd Issue).
242 **118** 1c. violet & grn (postage) 50 10
243 3c. brown 30 10

244 **119** 1c. violet (air) 10 10
245 3c. red 10 10
246 10c. red 30 10
247 75c. brown . . . . 2·40 1·80
DESIGN—As Type **118**: 3c. Cocoa-bean.

1938. No. 145 optd **1938**.
248 20c. blue . . . . 1·40 25

121 La Sabana Airport

1940. Air. Opening of San Jose Airport.
249 **121** 5c. green 20 20
250 10c. red 20 20
251 25c. blue 20 20
252 35c. brown 20 20
253 60c. orange 40 40
254 85c. violet . . . . 1·20 1·00
255 2col.35 green . . . . . . 6·00 5·75

1940. No. 168 variously surch **15 CENTIMOS** in ornamental frame.
256 15c. on 45c. violet 50 20
There are five distinct varieties of this surcharge.

1940. Pan-American Health Day. Unissued stamps prepared for the 8th Pan-American Child Welfare Congress optd **DIA PANAMERICANO DE LA SALUD 2. DICIEMBRE 1940**. (a) Postage. Allegorical design.
261 5c. green 25 20
262 10c. red 35 20
263 20c. blue 80 45
264 40c. brown . . . . 1·60 1·50
265 55c. orange . . . . 3·25 2·50

(b) Air. View of Duran Sanatorium.
266 10c. red 20 20
267 15c. violet 20 20
268 25c. blue 45 40
269 35c. brown 65 55
270 60c. green . . . . 1·00 80
271 75c. olive . . . . 2·50 2·20
272 1col.35 orange . . . . . . 8·00 6·25
273 5col. brown . . . . 42·00 42·00
274 10col. mauve £140 £110

1940. Air. Pan-American Aviation Day. Surch **AERO Aviacion Panamericana Dic. 17 1940** and value.
275 15c. on 50c. yellow 85 85
276 30c. on 50c. yellow 85 85

1941. Surch **15 CENTIMOS 15**.
277 **112** 15c. on 25c. orange . . . 45 45
278 15c. on 35c. brown . . . 45 45
279 15c. on 40c. brown . . . 45 45
280 15c. on 2col. green . . . 45 45
281 15c. on 5col. green . . . 90 90

131 Stadium and Flag

132 Football Match

1941. Central American and Caribbean Football Championship.
282 **131** 5c. green (postage) . . . 65 25
283 10c. orange 45 25
284 15c. red 70 35
285 25c. blue 80 50
286 40c. brown . . . . 3·00 1·20
287 50c. violet . . . . 4·00 1·90
288 75c. orange . . . . 6·25 5·50
289 1col. red . . . . 11·50 11·00
290 **132** 15c. red (air) 80 25
291 30c. blue 90 25
292 40c. brown 90 35
293 50c. violet . . . . 1·30 80
294 60c. green . . . . 1·60 90
295 75c. yellow . . . . 2·75 1·50
296 1col. mauve . . . . 4·50 4·50
297 1col.40 red . . . . 9·25 9·25
298 2col. green . . . . 21·00 18·00
299 5col. black . . . . 50·00 40·00

1941. Air. Costa Rica–Panama Boundary Treaty. Optd **Mayo 1941 Tratado Limitrofe Costa Rica – Panama** or surch also.
300 **107** 5c. on 20c. blue 10 10
301 15c. on 20c. blue 10 10
302 40c. on 75c. violet 35 10
303 – 65c. on 1col. red (No. 207) 60 50
304 – 1col.40 on 2col. blue (No. 208) . . . . . . 3·50 3·25
305 – 5col. black (No. 209) . . 12·00 12·00
306 – 10col. brown (No. 210) . . 14·50 14·00

1941. As Type **85** but with new portraits.
308 – 3c. orange 25 10
309 – 3c. purple 25 10
310 – 3c. red 25 10
310a – 3c. blue 25 10
311 – 5c. violet 25 10
312 – 5c. black 25 10
PORTRAITS: 3c. (Nos. 308/10) C. G. Viquez. 3c. (No. 310a) Mgr. B. A. Thiel. 5c. J. J. Rodriguez.

136 New Decree and Restored University

1941. Restoration of National University.
313 – 5c. green (postage) . . . 40 20
314 **136** 10c. orange 40 20
315 – 15c. red 60 20
316 **136** 25c. blue 90 35
317 – 50c. brown . . . . 5·75 2·30

318 **136** 15c. red (air) 20 20
319 – 30c. blue 35 20
320 **136** 40c. orange 40 35
321 – 60c. blue 50 40
322 **136** 1col. violet . . . . 2·00 2·00
323 – 2col. black . . . . 5·00 5·00
324 **136** 5col. purple . . . . 16·00 16·00
DESIGN—(Nos. 313, 315, 317, 319, 321 and 323): The original Decree and University.

1941. Surch.
325 5c. on 6c. brn (No. 166) . . 35 10
326 15c. on 20c. blue (No. 248) . 65 20

139 "V", Torch and Flags

140 Francisco Morazan

1942. War Effort.

327	**139**	5c. red	30	10
328		5c. orange	30	10
329		5c. green	30	10
330		5c. blue	30	10
331		5c. violet	30	10

1942. Portraits and dates.

332	A	1c. lilac (postage)	10	10
333	B	2c. black	10	10
334	C	3c. blue	10	10
335	D	5c. turquoise	10	10
336		5c. green	10	10
337	**140**	15c. red	10	10
338	E	25c. blue	60	15
339	F	50c. violet	1·80	60
340	G	1col. black	3·50	1·70
341	H	2col. orange	5·25	3·25
341a	I	5c. brown (air)	10	10
342	A	10c. red	10	10
342a		10c. olive	10	10
342b	J	15c. violet	10	10
343	K	25c. blue	10	45
344	L	30c. brown	20	10
345	D	40c. blue	25	10
346		40c. red	25	10
347	**140**	45c. purple	45	25
348	M	45c. black	20	10
349	E	50c. green	1·70	20
350		50c. orange	40	20
351	N	55c. purple	35	30
352	F	60c. blue	60	20
353		60c. green	20	10
354	G	65c. red	90	25
355		65c. blue	25	20
356	O	75c. green	60	35
357	H	85c. orange	1·10	45
358		85c. violet	1·50	60
359	P	1col. black	1·50	35
360		1col. red	60	20
361	Q	1col.05 sepia	80	50
362	R	1col.15 brown	2·00	1·70
363		1col.15 green	2·75	1·20
364	B	1col.40 violet	3·00	2·30
365		1col.40 yellow	1·70	1·50
366	C	2col. black	4·75	1·20
367		2col. olive	1·50	45

PORTRAITS: A, J. Mora Fernandez. B, B. Carranza. C, T. Guardia. D, M. Aguilar. E, J. M. Alfaro. F, F. M. Oreamuno. G, J. M. Castro. H, J. R. Mora. I, S. Lara. J, C. Duran. K, A. Esquivel. L, V. Herrera. M, J. R. de Gallegos. N, P. Fernandez. O, B. Soto. P, J. M. Montealegre. Q, B. Carrillo. R, J. Jimenez.

1943. Air. Optd **Legislacion Social 15 Setiembre 1943**.

368		5col. black (No. 209)	4·50	3·00
369		10col. brown (No. 210)	5·50	3·25

142 San Ramon

143 Allegory of Flight

1944. Centenary of San Ramon.

370	**142**	5c. green (postage)	10	10
371		10c. orange	10	10
372		15c. red	30	10
373		40c. grey	1·20	65
374		50c. blue	2·20	1·20
375	**143**	10c. orange (air)	10	10
376		15c. red	10	10
377		40c. blue	40	10
378		45c. red	40	35
379		60c. green	55	40
380		1col. brown	1·40	85
381		1col.40 grey	8·75	5·50
382		5col. violet	24·00	16·00
383		10col. black	70·00	60·00

1944. Ratification of Costa Rica and Panama Boundary Treaty. Optd **La entrevista ... 1944**.

384	**139**	5c. orange	15	10
385		5c. green	15	10
386		5c. blue	15	10
387		5c. violet	15	10

1944. Air. No. 207 optd **1944**.

388		1col. red	1·80	75

1945. Air. Official Air stamps of 1934 optd **1945** in oblong network frame.

389	**107**	5c. green	75	70
390		10c. red	75	75
391		15c. brown	75	75
392		20c. blue	55	50
393		25c. orange	75	75
394		40c. brown	45	45
395		50c. black	75	75
396		60c. yellow	1·40	1·20
397		75c. violet	1·10	1·00
398	–	1col. red (No. O220)	1·10	1·00
399	–	2col. blue (No. O221)	8·50	6·25
400	–	5col. black (No. O222)	9·50	8·50
401	–	10col. brown (No. O223)	15·00	11·50

1945. Air stamps. Telegraph stamps as Type **62** optd **CORREO AEREO 1945** and bar.

402	**62**	40c. green	25	10
403		50c. blue	30	10
404		1col. orange	90	40

148 Mauro Fernandez

149 Coffee Gathering

1945. Birth Centenary of Fernandez.

405	**148**	20c. green	30	10

1945.

406	**149**	5c. black and green	20	10
407		10c. black and orange	20	10
408		20c. black and red	40	15

150 Florence Nightingale and Nurse Cavell

1945. Air. 60th Anniv of National Red Cross Society.

409	**150**	1col. black	90	50

1946. Air. Central American and Caribbean Football Championship. As Type **132**, but inscribed "FEBRERO 1946".

410	**132**	25c. green	1·10	65
411		30c. orange	1·10	65
412		55c. blue	1·40	65

1946. Surch **15 15**.

413	**148**	15c. on 20c. green	25	10

152 San Juan de Dios Hospital

153 Ascension Esquivel

1946. Air. Centenary of San Juan de Dios Hospital.

414	**152**	5c. black and green	10	10
415		10c. black and brown	10	10
416		15c. black and red	10	10
417		25c. black and blue	10	10
418		30c. black and orange	45	25
419		40c. black and olive	10	10
420		50c. black and violet	35	25
421		60c. black and green	65	60
422		75c. black and brown	50	40
423		1col. black and blue	65	35
424		2col. black and brown	1·00	80
425		3col. black and purple	2·10	2·00
426		5col. black and yellow	2·50	2·50

1947. Air. Former Presidents.

427	–	2col. black and blue	1·60	1·20
428	**153**	3col. black and red	2·50	1·60
429	–	5col. black and green	4·00	2·10
430	–	10col. black and orange	7·00	5·25

PORTRAITS: 2col. Rafael Iglesias. 5col. Cleto Gonzalez Viquez. 10col. Ricardo Jimenez.

1947. No. O228 optd **CORREOS 1947**.

431	**57**	5c. green	10	10

1947. Air. Nos. 410/2 surch **Habilitado para C 0.15 Decreto No. 16 de 28 abril de 1947**.

432	**132**	15c. on 25c. green	1·00	80
433		15c. on 30c. orange	1·00	80
434		15c. on 55c. blue	1·00	80

156 Columbus at Cariari

158 Franklin D. Roosevelt

1947. Air.

435	**156**	25c. black and green	25	10
436		30c. black and blue	30	10
437		40c. black and orange	40	10
438		45c. black and violet	55	15
439		50c. black and red	60	10
440		65c. black and brown	1·80	90

1947. Air. Stamps of 1942 surch **C0.15**.

441	E	15c. on 50c. orange	30	25
442	F	15c. on 60c. green	30	25
443	O	15c. on 75c. green	30	25
444	P	15c. on 1col. red	45	35
445	Q	15c. on 1col.5 sepia	30	25

1947.

446	**158**	5c. green (postage)	10	10
447		10c. red	10	10
448		15c. blue	15	10
449		25c. orange	30	25
450		30c. red	60	35
451		15c. green (air)	10	10
452		30c. red	10	10
453		45c. brown	10	10
454		65c. orange	25	10
455		75c. blue	35	10
456		1col. green	50	35
457		2col. black	1·40	1·10
458		5col. red	2·75	2·50

159 Miguel de Cervantes Saavedra

1947. 400th Birth Anniv of Cervantes.

459	**159**	30c. blue	45	10
460		55c. red	65	40

160 Steam Locomotive "Maria Cecilia"

1947. Air. 50th Anniv of Pacific Electric Railway.

461	**160**	35c. black and green	2·50	55

161 National Theatre

162 Rafael Iglesias

1948. Air. 50th Anniv of National Theatre.

462	**161**	15c. black and blue	20	10
463		20c. black and red	20	10
464	**162**	35c. black and green	40	10
465	**161**	45c. black and violet	45	15
466		50c. black and red	45	15
467		75c. black and purple	1·10	80
468		1col. black and green	2·10	1·10
469		2col. black and lake	3·25	1·60
470	**162**	5col. black and yellow	5·25	3·75
471		10col. black and blue	12·00	7·50

1948. Air. Surch **HABILITADO PARA C 0.35**.

472	**156**	35c. on 40c. blk & orge	1·20	50

1949. Air. 125th Anniv of Annexation of Guanacaste. Nos. 361, 409, 363 and 365 variously surch **1824-1949 125 Aniversario de la Anexion Guanacaste** and value.

473	Q	35c. on 1col. 5 sepia	30	10
474	**150**	50c. on 1col. black	50	40
475	R	55c. on 1col.15 green	65	55
476	B	55c. on 1col.40 yellow	70	50

165 Globe and Dove

1950. Air. 75th Anniv of UPU (1949).

477	**165**	15c. red	10	10
478		25c. blue	30	30
479		1col. green	50	40

166 Battle of El Tejar, Cartago

167 Capture of Limon

169 Bull

1950. Air. Inscr "GUERRA DE LIBERACION NACIONAL 1948".

480	**166**	15c. black and red	10	10
481	**167**	20c. black and green	10	10
482	–	25c. black and blue	30	10
483	–	35c. black and brown	35	10
484	–	55c. black and violet	65	10
485	–	75c. black and orange	1·10	35
486	–	80c. black and grey	1·10	50
487	–	1col. black and orange	1·50	60

DESIGNS—VERT: 80c., 1col. Dr. C. L. Valverde. HORIZ: 25c. La Lucha Ranch; 35c. Trench of San Isidro Battalion; 55c., 75c. Observation post.

1950. Air. National Agriculture and Industries Fair. Centres in black.

488	**169**	1c. green	20	20
489	A	2c. blue	20	20
490	B	3c. brown	20	20
491	C	5c. blue	20	20
492	**169**	10c. green	20	20
493	A	30c. violet	20	20
494	D	45c. orange	20	20
495	C	50c. grey	40	20
496	B	65c. blue	40	20
497	D	80c. red	90	65
498	**169**	2col. orange	2·50	1·70
499	A	3col. blue	6·00	4·25
500	C	5col. red	7·75	6·50
501	D	10col. red	7·75	6·50

DESIGNS—VERT: A, Fishing; B, Pineapple; C, Bananas; D, Coffee.

170 Queen Isabella and Caravels

1952. Air. 500th Anniv of Isabella the Catholic.

502	**170**	15c. red	25	10
503		20c. orange	50	10
504		25c. blue	75	10
505		55c. green	2·50	25
506		2col. violet	4·75	50

1953. Air. Surch **15 15** within ornaments.

513	**158**	15c. on 30c. red	30	10
514		15c. on 45c. brown	30	10
515		15c. on 65c. orange	30	10

1953. Air. Surch **HABILITADO PARA CINCO CENTIMOS 1953**.

515a	**155**	5c. on 30c. blk & blue	1·50	1·30
516		5c. on 40c. blk & orge	25	25
517		5c. on 45c. blk & vio	25	25
518		5c. on 65c. blk & brn	25	25

173

1953. Fiscal stamps surch as in T **173**.

519	**173**	5c. on 10c. green	25	10

174 "Vegetable Oil"

(175)

1954. Air. National Industries. Centres in black.

520		5c. red (Type **174**)	15	10
520a		5c. blue (Type **174**)	25	10

521 10c. indigo (Pottery) 20 10
521a 10c. blue (Pottery) 25 10
522 15c. green (Sugar) 15 10
522a 15c. yellow (Sugar) 25 10
523 20c. violet (Soap) 15 10
524 25c. lake (Timber) 20 10
525 30c. lilac (Matches) 55 40
526 35c. purple (Textiles) . . . 25 15
527 40c. black (Leather) 55 35
528 45c. green (Tobacco) . . . 1·00 40
529 50c. purple (Confectionery) . . 65 15
530 55c. yellow (Canning) . . . 50 15
531 60c. brown (General industries) . . . . 1·20 65
532 65c. red (Metals) . . . . . 1·50 95
533 75c. violet (Pharmaceutics) . 2·20 80
533a 75c. red (as No. 533) . . . 50 35
533b 80c. violet (as No. 533) . . 1·00 80
534 1col. turq (Paper) 65 40
535 2col. mauve (Rubber) . . . 2·10 1·20
536 3col. green (Aircraft) . . . 3·00 1·90
537 5col. black (Marble) . . . . 4·50 1·50
538 10col. yellow (Beer) . . . . 13·00 9·50

1955. Fiscal stamps optd for postal use as in T **175**.
539 **175** 5c. on 2c. green 15 10
540 15c. on 2c. green 20 10

176 Rotary Emblem over Central America

177 Map of Costa Rica

1956. Air. 50th Anniv Rotary International.
542 **176** 10c. green 10 10
543 – 25c. blue 10 10
544 – 40c. brown 45 35
545 – 45c. red 30 20
546 – 60c. purple 40 30
547 – 2col. orange . . . . . . 1·10 60
DESIGNS: 25c. Emblem, hand and boy; 40c., 2col. Emblem and hospital; 45c. Emblem, leaves and Central America; 60c. Emblem and lighthouse.

1957. Air. Centenary of War of 1856–67.
548 **177** 5c. blue 20 20
549 – 10c. green 20 20
550 – 15c. orange 20 20
551 – 20c. brown 30 20
552 – 25c. blue 30 20
553 – 30c. violet 45 20
554 – 35c. red 45 20
555 – 40c. black 45 20
556 – 45c. red 50 20
557 – 50c. blue 55 20
558 – 55c. ochre . . . . 1·10 20
559 – 60c. red 80 30
560 – 65c. red . . . . 1·00 30
561 – 70c. yellow . . . . 1·20 35
562 – 75c. green . . . . 1·10 35
563 – 80c. sepia . . . . 1·30 40
564 – 1col. black . . . . 1·50 40
DESIGNS: 10c. Map of Guanacaste; 15c. Wartime inn; 20c. Santa Rosa house; 25c. Gen. D. J. M. Quiros; 30c. Old Presidential Palace; 35c. Minister D. J. B. Calvo; 40c. Dr. Luis Molina; 45c. Gen. D. J. J. Mora; 50c. Gen. D. J. M. Canas; 55c. Juan Santamaria Monument; 60c. National Monument; 65c. A. Vallerriestra; 70c. Pres. R. Castilla Marquesado of Peru; 75c. San Carlos Fortress; 80c. Vice-President D. F. M. Oreamuno of Costa Rica; 1col. Pres. D. J. R. Mora of Costa Rica.

1958. Obligatory Tax. Christmas. Nos. 489 and 521a surch **SELLO DE NAVIDAD PRO - CIUDAD DE LOS NINOS 5 5**.
565 A 5c. on 2c. black & blue . . 20 20
566 – 5c. on 10c. black & blue . . 40 20

179 Pres. Gonzalez Viquez

180 Pres. R. J. Oreamuno and Electric Locomotive No. 31

1959. Air. Birth Centenaries of Presidents Gonzalez (1958) and Oreamuno (1959).
567 **179** 5c. blue and pink 15 10
568 – 10c. slate and red . . . 15 10
569 – 15c. black and slate . . . 15 10
570 – 20c. brown and red . . . 40 10
571 – 35c. blue and purple . . 15 10
572 – 55c. violet and brown . . 40 15
573 – 80c. blue 50 40
574 **180** 1col. lake and orange . . 80 50
575 – 2col. lake and black . . . 1·80 1·50
DESIGNS—As Type **179**: 10c. Pres. Oreamuno. As Type **180**: Pres. Gonzalez and: 15c. Highway bridge; 55c. Water pipe-line; 80c. National Library. Pres. Oreamuno and: 20c. Puntarenas Quay; 35c. Post Office, San Jose. 2col. Both presidents and open book inscr "PROBIDAD" ("Honesty").

181 Father Flanagan

182 Goal Attack

1959. Obligatory Tax. Christmas. Inscr "SELLO DE NAVIDAD".
576 **181** 5c. green 55 20
577 – 5c. mauve 55 20
578 – 5c. olive 55 20
579 – 5c. black 55 20
PAINTINGS: No. 577, "Girl with braids" (after Modigliani). No. 578, "Boy with a clubfoot" (after Ribera). No. 579, "The boy blowing on charcoal" (after "El Greco").

1960. Air. 3rd Pan-American Football Games.
580 **182** 10c. blue 25 25
581 – 25c. blue 25 25
582 – 35c. red 30 30
583 – 50c. brown 40 30
584 – 85c. turquoise . . . . . 1·00 80
585 – 5col. purple . . . . . . 2·30 2·30
MS585a 139 × 80 mm. 2col. blue (as 35c.). Imperf . . . . 5·00 5·00
DESIGNS: 25c. Player heading ball; 35c. Defender tackling forward; 50c. Referee bouncing ball; 85c. Goalkeeper seizing ball; 5col. Player kicking high ball.

183 "Uprooted Tree"

184 Prof. J. A. Facio

1960. Air. World Refugee Year.
586 **183** 35c. blue and yellow . . . 35 25
587 85c. black and pink . . . 65 55

1960. Birth Centenary of Professor Justo A. Facio.
588 **184** 10c. red 20 20

185 "OEA" and Banner

1960. Air. 6th and 7th Chancellors' Reunion Conference, Organization of American States, San Jose. Multicoloured.
589 25c. Type **185** 15 15
590 35c. "OEA" within oval chains 35 35
591 55c. Clasped hands and chains 50 40
592 5col. Flags in form of flying bird . . . . 3·25 3·00
593 10col. "OEA" on map of Costa Rica, and flags . . . 5·25 4·50
MS593a 124 × 76 mm. 2col. "OEA" and map of Americas. Imperf . . . 3·00 3·00

186 St. Louise de Marillac, Sister of Charity and Children

1960. Air. 300th Death Anniv of St. Vincent de Paul.
594 **186** 10c. green 20 20
595 – 25c. lake 20 20
596 – 50c. blue 20 20
597 – 1col. bistre 40 35
598 – 5col. sepia . . . . 2·20 1·70
DESIGNS—HORIZ: St. Vincent de Paul, and: 25c. Two-storey building; 1col. Modern building; 50c. As Type **186**, but scene shows Sister at bedside. VERT: 5col. Stained-glass window picturing St. Vincent de Paul with children.

187 Father Peralta

1960. Obligatory Tax. Christmas. Inscr "SELLO DE NAVIDAD".
599 **187** 5c. brown 50 20
600 – 5c. orange 50 20
601 – 5c. red 50 20
602 – 5c. blue 50 20
DESIGNS: No. 600, "Girl" (after Renoir); No. 601, "The Drinkers" (after Velasquez); No. 602, "Children Singing" (sculpture, after Zuniga).

188 Running

1960. Air. Olympics Game, Rome. Centres and inscriptions in black.
603 1c. yellow (T **188**) 10 10
604 2c. blue (Diving) 10 10
605 3c. red (Cycling) 10 10
606 4c. yellow (Weightlifting) . . 20 10
607 5c. green (Tennis) 20 10
608 10c. red (Boxing) 20 10
609 25c. turquoise (Football) . . 20 10
610 85c. mauve (Basketball) . . . 1·20 80
611 1col. grey (Baseball) . . . . 1·40 1·10
612 10col. lavender (Pistol-shooting) . . . . 11·00 8·00
MS612a 100 × 65 mm. 5col. multicoloured (27 × 27 mm) (Romulus and Remus statue) 6·00 6·00

1961. Air. 15th World Amateur Baseball Championships. No. 533a optd **XV Campeonato Mundial de Beisbol de Aficionados** or surch also.
613 25c. on 75c. black and red 25 15
614 75c. black and red 60 15

190 M. Aguilar

191 Prof. M. Obregon

1961. Air. 1st Continental Lawyers' Conference.
615 **190** 10c. blue 25 20
616 – 10c. purple 25 20
617 – 25c. violet 25 20
618 – 25c. sepia 25 20
PORTRAITS: No. 616, A. Brenes. No. 617, A. Gutierrez. No. 618, V. Herrera.
See also Nos. 628/31.

1961. Air. Birth Centenary of Obregon.
619 **191** 10c. turquoise 30 20

192 Granary (FAO)

1961. Air. United Nations Commemoration.
620 **192** 10c. green 10 10
621 – 20c. orange 10 10
622 – 25c. slate 10 10
623 – 30c. blue 10 10
624 – 35c. red 90 20
625 – 45c. violet 35 15
626 – 85c. blue 70 55
627 – 10col. black . . . . . . 5·25 4·50
MS627a 100 × 65 mm. 5col. blue 3·25 3·25
DESIGNS: 20c. "Medical Care" (WHO); 25c. Globe and workers (ILO); 30c. Globe and communications satellite "Correo 1B" (ITU); 35c. Compass and rocket (WMO); 45c. "The Thinker" (statue) and open book (UNESCO); 85c. Douglas DC-6 airliner and globe (ICAO); 5col. "United Nations covering the world"; 10col. "Spiderman" on girder (International Bank).

1961. Air. 9th Central American Medical Congress. As T **190** but inscr "NOVENO CONGRESO MEDICO", etc.
628 10c. violet 20 15
629 10c. turquoise 20 15
630 25c. sepia 25 15
631 25c. purple 25 15
PORTRAITS: No. 628, Dr. E. J. Roman. No. 629, Dr. J. M. S. Alfaro. No. 630, Dr. A. S. Llorente. No. 631, Dr. J. J. U. Giralt.

1961. Obligatory Tax. Children's City Christmas issue. No. 522 surch **SELLO DE NAVIDAD PRO-CIUDAD DE LOS NINOS 5 5**.
632 5c. on 10c. black and green 35 20

1962. Air. Surch in figures.
633 10c. on 15c. black and green (No. 522) 15 10
634 25c. on 15c. black and green (No. 522) 15 15
635 35c. on 50c. black and purple (No. 529) 30 15
636 85c. on 80c. blue (No. 573) 90 75

1962. Air. 2nd Central American Philatelic Convention. Optd **II CONVENCION FILATELICA CENTROAMERICANA SETIEMBRE 1962**.
637 30c. blue (No. 623) 55 40
638 2col. red and black (No. 575) 1·60 1·20

1962. Air. No. 522 surch **C 0.10**.
639 10c. on 15c. black & green 15 15

1962. Air. Fiscal stamps as T **175** optd **CORREO AEREO** and surch with new value for postal use.
640 25c. on 2c. green 10 10
641 35c. on 2c. green 15 15
642 45c. on 2c. green 35 25
643 85c. on 2c. green 65 50

198 "Virgin and Child" (after Bellini)

199 Jaguar

1962. Obligatory Tax. Christmas.
644 **198** 5c. sepia 65 20
645 A 5c. green 65 20
646 B 5c. blue 65 20
647 C 5c. red 65 20
DESIGNS: A, "Angel with Violin" (after Mellozo); B, Mgr. Ruben Odio; C, "Child's Head" (after Rubens).
See also Nos. 674/7.

1963. Air.
648 – 5c. brown and olive . . . 25 15
649 – 10c. blue and orange . . 25 15
650 **199** 25c. yellow and blue . . . 40 15
651 – 30c. brown and green . . 65 40
652 – 35c. brown and bistre . . 1·00 40
653 – 40c. blue and green . . . 1·20 55
654 – 85c. black and green . . 3·75 55
655 – 5col. brown and green . . 11·50 4·00
ANIMALS (As Type **199**): 5c. Paca. 10c. Bairds tapir. 30c. Ocelot. 35c. White-tailed deer. 40c. American manatee. 85c. White-throated capuchin. 5col. White-lipped peccary.

200 Arms and Campaign Emblem

202 Anglo-Costa Rican Bank

1963. Air. Malaria Eradication.
656 **200** 25c. red 15 10
657 35c. brown 25 15
658 45c. blue 35 25
659 85c. green 65 45
660 1col. blue . . . . 1·10 60

1963. Obligatory Tax Fund for Children's Village. Nos. 644/7 surch **1963 10 CENTIMOS**.
661 **198** 10c. on 5c. sepia 40 20
662 A 10c. on 5c. green 40 20
663 B 10c. on 5c. blue 40 20
664 C 10c. on 5c. red 40 20

1963. Anglo-Costa Rican Bank Centenary.
665 **202** 10c. blue 20 20

203 ½ real Stamp of 1863 and Sail Merchantman "William le Lacheur"

1963. Air. Stamp Centenary.
666 **203** 25c. blue and purple . . . 15 10
667 – 2col. orange and grey . . 1·80 1·30

668 – 3col. green and ochre . . 3·00 2·10
669 – 10col. brown and green 10·50 6·00
MS669a 60 × 100 mm. 5col. blue, brown, green and light brown. Perf or imperf . . . . 4·50 4·50
DESIGNS: 2col. 2 reales stamp of 1863 and Postmaster-General R. B. Carrillo; 3col. 4 reales stamp of 1863 and mounted postman and pack-mule of 1839; 5col. ½ real, 2 reales, 4 reales, and 1 peseta stamp of 1863 (as in Nos. 666/9); 10col. 1 peso stamp of 1863 and mule-drawn mail van.

1963. Unissued animal designs as T **199**. Surch.
670 10c. on 1c. brown and green 1·10 30
671 25c. on 2c. sepia and brown 1·10 30
672 35c. on 3c. brown and green 1·50 30
673 85c. on 4c. brown and lake 2·75 60
ANIMALS: 1c. Tamandua. 2c. Grey fox. 3c. Nine-banded armadillo. 4c. Giant anteater.

1963. Obligatory Tax. Christmas. As Nos. 644/7 but inscr "1963" and new colours.
674 **198** 5c. blue 45 20
675 A 5c. red 45 20
676 B 5c. black 45 20
677 C 5c. sepia 45 20

205 Pres. Orlich (Costa Rica)

206 Puma (clay statuette)

1963. Air. Presidential Reunion, San José. Portraits in sepia.
678 **205** 25c. purple 25 20
679 – 30c. mauve 25 20
680 – 35c. ochre 25 20
681 – 85c. blue 45 20
682 – 1col. brown 50 30
683 – 3col. green . . . . . . 2·30 1·60
684 – 5col. slate . . . . . . 3·00 2·30
PRESIDENTS: 30c. Rivera (Salvador). 35c. Ydigoras (Guatemala). 85c. Villeda (Honduras). 1col. Somoza (Nicaragua). 3col. Chiari (Panama). 5col. Kennedy (U.S.A.).

1963. Air. Archaeological Discoveries.
685 **206** 5c. turquoise and green 20 20
686 – 10c. turquoise and yellow 20 20
687 – 25c. sepia and red 20 20
688 – 30c. turquoise and buff 25 20
689 – 35c. green and salmon . . 25 20
690 – 45c. brown and blue . . . 25 20
691 – 50c. brown and blue . . . 40 20
692 – 55c. brown and green . . 55 20
693 – 75c. brown and buff . . . 55 20
694 – 85c. brown and yellow . . 1·40 1·40
695 – 90c. brown and yellow . . 1·80 1·80
696 – 1col. brown and blue . . 1·10 35
697 – 2col. turquoise & yellow 1·60 65
698 – 3col. brown and green . . 5·50 1·00
699 – 5col. brown & yellow . . 5·50 5·50
700 – 10col. green and mauve 9·00 9·00
DESIGNS—HORIZ: 10c. Ceremonial stool; 1col. Twin beakers; 2col. Alligator. VERT: 25c. Man (statuette); 30c. Dancer; 35c. Vase; 45c. Deity; 50c. Frog; 55c. "Eagle" bell; 75c. Multi-limbed deity; 85c. Kneeling effigy; 90c. "Bird" jug; 3col. Twin-tailed lizard; 5col. Child; 10col. Stone effigy of woman.

207 Flags

210 Mgr. R. Odio and Children

1964. Air. "Centro America".
701 **207** 30c. multicoloured 80 25

1964. Air. Surch.
702 – 5c. on 30c. (No. 688) . . 55 25
703 **207** 15c. on 30c. 55 25
704 – 15c. on 85c. (No. 694) . . 55 25
See Nos. 745/9.

1964. Paris Postal Conf. No. 695 surch **C 0.15 CONFERENCIA POSTAL DE PARIS - 1864**.
705 15c. on 90c. brn & yellow . . 25 20

1964. Obligatory Tax. Christmas. Inscr "SELLO DE NAVIDAD", etc.
706 **210** 5c. brown 40 20
707 A 5c. blue 40 20
708 B 5c. purple 40 20
709 C 5c. green 40 20
DESIGNS: A, Teacher and child; B, Children at play; C, Children in class.

211 A. Gonzalez F.

213 Handfuls of Grain

1965. Air. 50th Anniv of National Bank.
710 **211** 35c. green . . . . 3·25 25

1965. Air. 75th Anniv of Chapui Hospital. No 697 surch **75 ANIVERSARIO ASILO CHAPUI 1890–1965**.
711 2col. turquoise and yellow . . 1·40 75

1965. Air. Freedom from Hunger.
712 – 15c. black, grey & brown 25 20
713 **213** 35c. black and buff . . . 25 20
714 – 50c. green and blue . . . 25 20
715 – 1col. silver, black & green 40 25
DESIGNS—HORIZ: 15c. Map and grain silo; 1col. Douglas DC-8 airliner over map. VERT: 50c. Children and population graph.

214 National Children's Hospital

215 L. Briceno B.

1965. Christmas Charity. Obligatory Tax. Inscr "SELLO DE NAVIDAD", etc.
716 **214** 5c. green 25 20
717 A 5c. brown 25 20
718 B 5c. red 25 20
719 C 5c. blue 25 20
DESIGNS—As Type **214**: A, Father Casiano; B, Poinsettia. DIAMOND: C, Father Christmas with children.

1965. Air. Incorporation of Nicoya District.
720 **215** 5c. slate, black & brown 40 20
721 – 10c. slate and blue . . . 40 20
722 – 15c. slate and bistre . . . 40 20
723 – 35c. slate and blue . . . 40 20
724 – 50c. violet and grey . . . 55 20
725 – 1col. slate and ochre . . . 1·20 40
DESIGNS: 10c. Nicoya Church; 15c. Incorporation scroll; 35c. Map of Guanacaste Province; 50c. Provincial dance; 1col. Guanacaste map and produce.

216 Running

217 Pres. John F. Kennedy and "Mercury" Space Capsule encircling Globe

1965. Air. Olympic Games (1964). Mult.
726 5c. Type **216** 15 15
727 10c. Cycling 15 15
728 40c. Judo 15 15
729 65c. Handball 25 15
730 80c. Football 40 15
731 1col. Olympic torches 50 35
MS731a 68 × 95 mm. No. 731 (× 2) in different colours. Perf or imperf 3·25 3·25

1965. Air. 2nd Death Anniv of Pres. Kennedy. Multicoloured.
732 45c. Type **217** 25 15
733 55c. Kennedy in San Jose Cathedral (vert) 35 20
734 85c. President with son (vert) 55 40
735 1col. Facade of White House, Washington (vert) 65 45
MS735a 68 × 94 mm. No. 735 (× 2) in different colours. Perf or imperf 1·20 1·20

218 Fire Engine

219 Angel

1966. Air. Centenary of Fire Brigade.
736 **218** 5c. red and black 35 15
737 – 10c. red and yellow . . . 40 15
738 – 15c. black and red 60 15
739 – 35c. yellow and black . . 1·00 25
740 – 50c. red and blue . . . . 2·10 45
DESIGNS—VERT: 10c. Fire engine of 1866; 15c. Firemen with hoses; 35c. Brigade badge; 50c. Emblem of Central American Fire Brigades Confederation.

1966. Obligatory Tax. Christmas. Inscr "SELLO DE NAVIDAD", etc.
741 **219** 5c. blue 25 20
742 – 5c. red (Trinkets) 25 20
743 – 5c. green (Church) . . . 25 20
744 – 5c. brown (Reindeer) . . 25 20

1966. Air. (a) Surch with new value.
745 – 15c. on 30c. (No. 688) . . . 15 15
746 – 15c. on 45c. (No. 690) . . . 15 15
747 – 35c. on 75c. (No. 693) . . . 20 15
748 – 35c. on 55c. (No. 733) . . . 20 15
749 – 50c. on 85c. (No. 734) . . . 40 15

(b) Revenue stamps (as T **175**) surch **CORREOS DE COSTA RICA AEREO** and value.
750 15c. on 5c. blue 15 10
751 35c. on 10c. red 25 15
752 50c. on 20c. red 40 25

221 Central Bank, San Jose

222 Telecommunications Building, San Pedro

1967. Obligatory Tax. Social Plan for Postal Workers.
753 10c. blue 25 20
DESIGN—as Type **221** (34 × 26 mm.): 10c. Post Office, San José.

1967. Air. 50th Anniv of Central Bank.
754 **221** 5c. green 25 20
755 15c. brown 25 20
756 35c. red 25 20

1967. Air. Costa Rican Electrical Industry.
757 – 5c. black 25 20
758 **222** 10c. mauve 25 20
759 – 15c. orange 25 20
760 – 25c. blue 25 20
761 – 35c. green 25 20
762 – 50c. brown 35 25
DESIGNS—VERT: 5c. Electric pylons; 15c. Central Telephone Exchange, San José. HORIZ: 25c. La Garita Dam; 35c. Rio Macho Reservoir; 50c. Cachi Dam.

223 "Chondrorhyncha aromatica"

224 OEA Emblem and Split Leaf

1967. Air. University Library. Orchids. Mult.
763 5c. Type **223** 10 10
764 10c. "Miltonia endresii" . . . 40 25
765 15c. "Stanhopea cirrhata" . . 40 25
766 25c. "Trichopilia suavis" . . 85 25
767 35c. "Odontoglossum schlieperianum" 85 25
768 50c. "Cattleya skinneri" . . . 1·10 25
769 1col. "Cattleya dowiana" . . . 3·00 80
770 2col. "Odontoglossum chiriquense" . . . . 4·50 1·50

1967. Air. 25th Anniv of Inter-American Institute of Agricultural Science.
771 **224** 50c. ultramarine & blue 25 15

225 Madonna and Child

226 LACSA Emblem

1967. Obligatory Tax. Christmas.
772 **225** 5c. green 25 20
773 5c. mauve 25 20
774 5c. blue 25 20
775 5c. turquoise 25 20

1967. Air. 20th Anniv (1966) of LACSA (Costa Rican Airlines). Multicoloured.
776 40c. Type **226** 20 15
777 45c. LACSA emblem and jetliner (horiz) 25 15
778 50c. Wheel and emblem . . . 25 20

227 Church of Solitude

228 Scouts in Camp

1967. Air. Churches and Cathedrals (1st series).
779 **227** 5c. green 10 10
780 – 10c. blue 10 10
781 – 15c. purple 10 10
782 – 25c. ochre 10 10
783 – 30c. brown 10 10
784 – 35c. blue 25 10
785 – 40c. orange 25 10
786 – 45c. green 25 10
787 – 50c. olive 35 10
788 – 55c. brown 35 10
789 – 65c. mauve 60 25
790 – 75c. sepia 65 35
791 – 80c. yellow . . . . 1·20 40
792 – 85c. purple . . . . 1·40 40
793 – 90c. green . . . . 1·40 65
794 – 1col. slate . . . . 1·10 35
795 – 2col. green . . . . 5·25 1·80
796 – 3col. orange . . . . . . 7·50 3·00
797 – 5col. blue . . . . 7·50 3·00
798 – 10col. red . . . . 9·25 4·50
DESIGNS: 10c. Santo Domingo Basilica, Heredia; 15c. Tilaran Cathedral; 25c. Alajuela Cathedral; 30c. Church of Mercy; 35c. Our Lady of the Angels Basilica; 40c. San Rafael Church, Heredia; 45c. Ruins, Ujarras; 50c. Ruins of Parish Church, Cartago; 55c. San Jose Cathedral; 65c. Parish Church, Puntarenas; 75c. Orosi Church; 80c. Cathedral of San Isidro the General; 85c. San Ramon Church; 90c. Church of the Forsaken; 1col. Coronado Church; 2col. Church of St. Teresita; 3col. Parish Church, Heredia; 5col. Carmelite Church; 10col. Limon Cathedral.
See also Nos. 918/33.

1968. Air. Golden Jubilee (1966) of Scout Movement in Costa Rica. Multicoloured.
799 15c. Scout on traffic control (vert) 15 10
800 25c. Scouts tending campfire (vert) 25 15
801 35c. Scout badge and flags (vert) 40 20
802 50c. Type **228** 65 35
803 65c. First scout troop on parade (1916) 80 40

1968. Air. 3rd National Philatelic Exhibition, San Jose. Sheet No. **MS**669a optd **III EXPOSICION FILATELICA NACIONAL 2–4 AGOSTO 1968 COSTA RICA 68** in three lines.
MS804 60 × 100 mm. 5col. blue, brown, green and light brown. Perf or imperf . . . . 13·50 13·50

229 "Madonna and Child"

230 Running

1968. Christmas Charity. Obligatory Tax.
805 **229** 5c. black 25 20
806 5c. purple 25 20
807 5c. brown 25 20
808 5c. red 25 20

1969. Air. Olympic Games, Mexico. Mult.
809 30c. Type **230** 10 10
810 40c. Woman breasting tape . . 10 10
811 55c. Boxing 25 15
812 65c. Cycling 35 15
813 75c. Weightlifting 35 15
814 1col. High-diving 40 25
815 3col. Rifle-shooting . . . . . 1·60 1·00

231 Exhibition Emblem

232 Arms of San Jose

1969. Air. "Costa Rica 69" Philatelic Exn.
816 **231** 35c. multicoloured 15 10
817 40c. multicoloured 15 10
818 50c. multicoloured 25 15
819 2col. multicoloured . . . . 1·00 55

1969. Coats of Arms. Multicoloured.
820 15c. Type **232** 30 10
821 35c. Cartago 30 10
822 50c. Heredia 35 10
823 55c. Alajuela 35 10
824 65c. Guanacaste 55 25
825 1col. Puntarenas . . . . . . 3·50 35
826 2col. Limon . . . . 4·00 55

233 ILO Emblem

234 Map on Football

1969. Air. 50th Anniv of ILO.

827	**233**	35c. turquoise and black	25	10
828		50c. red and black	25	15

1969. Air. 4th CONCACAF Football Championships. Multicoloured.

829		65c. Type **234**	35	15
830		75c. Goalmouth melee	35	20
831		85c. Players with ball	40	35
832		1col. Two players with ball	55	40

235 Madonna and Child

236 Stylized Crab

1969. Christmas. Charity. Obligatory Tax.

833	**235**	5c. turquoise	25	20
834		5c. lake	25	20
835		5c. blue	25	20
836		5c. orange	25	20

1970. Air. 10th Inter-American Cancer Congress, San Jose.

837	**236**	10c. black and mauve	25	20
838		15c. black and yellow	25	20
839		50c. black and orange	25	20
840		1col.10 black and green	55	20

238 Costa Rican stamps and Magnifier

239 Japanese Vase and Flowers

1970. Air. "Costa Rica 70" Philatelic Exhibition.

843	**238**	1col. red and blue	1·10	20
844		2col. mauve and blue	1·20	55

1970. Air. Expo 70. Multicoloured.

845		10c. Type **239**	10	10
846		15c. Ornamental cart (horiz)	10	10
847		35c. Sun tower (horiz)	40	10
848		40c. Tea-ceremony (horiz)	50	10
849		45c. Coffee-picking	50	10
850		55c. View of Earth from Moon	50	10

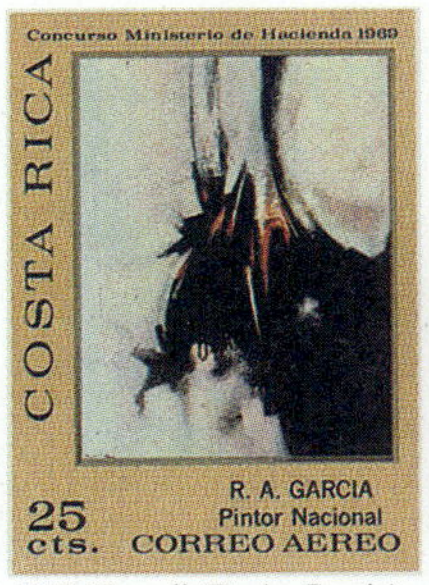

240 "Irazu" (R. A. Garcia)

241 "Holy Child"

1970. Air. Costa Rican Paintings. Mult.

851		25c. Type **240**	80	35
852		45c. "Escazu Valley" (M. Bertheau)	80	35
853		80c. "Estuary Landscape" (T. Quiros)	1·30	60
854		1col. "The Other Face" (C. Valverde)	1·30	65
855		2col.50 "Madonna" (L. Daell) (vert)	2·75	2·10

1970. Christmas Charity. Obligatory Tax.

856	**241**	5c. mauve	35	20
857		5c. brown	35	20
858		5c. olive	35	20
859		5c. violet	35	20

242 Costa Rican Arms of 21 October 1964

243 National Theatre, San Jose

1971. Air. Various Costa Rican Coats of Arms (with dates). Multicoloured.

860		5c. Type **242**	40	20
861		10c. 27 November 1906	40	20
862		15c. 29 September 1848	50	20
863		25c. 21 April 1840	50	20
864		35c. 22 November 1824	65	20
865		50c. 2 November 1824	75	20
866		1col. 6 March 1824	80	30
867		2col. 10 May 1823	1·60	85

1971. Air. OEA General Assembly. San Jose.

868	**243**	2col. purple	40	35

244 J. M. Delgado and M. J. Arce (Salvador)

1971. Air. 150th Anniv of Central American Independence. Multicoloured.

869		5c. Type **244**	20	20
870		10c. M. Larreinaga and M. A. de la Cerda (Nicaragua)	20	20
871		15c. J. C. del Valle and D. de Herrera (Honduras)	20	20
872		35c. P. Alvarado and F. del Castillo (Costa Rica)	20	20
873		50c. A. Larrazabal and P. Molina (Guatemala)	20	20
874		1col. ODECA flag (vert)	20	20
875		2col. ODECA emblem (vert)	40	40

ODECA = Organization of Central American States.

245 Cradle on "PAX"

246 Federation Emblem

1971. Christmas Charity. Obligatory Tax.

876	**245**	10c. orange	25	20
877		10c. brown	25	20
878		10c. green	25	20
879		10c. blue	25	20

1971. Air. 50th Anniv of Costa Rican Football Federation.

880	**246**	50c. multicoloured	35	20
881		60c. multicoloured	35	20

247 "Children of the World"

248 Guanacaste Tree

1972. Air. 25th Anniv of UNICEF.

882	**247**	50c. multicoloured	25	15
883		1col.10 multicoloured	40	25

1972. Air. Bicentenary of Liberia City.

884	**348**	green, brown and emerald	40	20
885	–	brown and green	40	20
886	–	brown and black	40	20
887	–	Scarlet, black and buff	40	20

DESIGNS;— HORIZ: 40c. Hermitage, Liberia; 55c. Rincon Brujo Petroglyphs. VERT: 60c. Painted head sculpture.

250 Farmer's Family and Farm

251 Inter-American Stamp Exhibitions

1972. Air. 30th Anniv of OEA Institute of Agricultural Sciences (IICA).

892	**250**	20c. multicoloured	35	20
893	–	45c. multicoloured	35	20
894	–	50c. yellow, green & blk	35	20
895	–	10col. multicoloured	2·75	1·80

DESIGNS—HORIZ: 45c. Cattle. VERT: 50c. Tree-planting; 10col. Agricultural worker and map.

1972. Air. "Exfilbra 72" Stamp Exhibition.

896	**251**	50c. brown and orange	15	15
897		2col. violet and blue	40	35

252 Madonna and Child

253 First Book printed in Costa Rica

1972. Christmas Charity. Obligatory Tax.

898	**252**	10c. red	25	20
899		10c. lilac	25	20
900		10c. blue	25	20
901		10c. green	25	20

1972. Air. International Book Year. Mult.

902		20c. Type **253**	40	20
903		50c. National Library, San Jose (horiz)	40	20
904		75c. Type **253**	40	20
905		5col. As 50c.	2·00	1·00

254 View near Irazu

255 Madonna and Child

1972. Air. American Tourist Year. Mult.

906		5c. Type **254**	35	20
907		15c. Entrance to Culebra Bay	35	20
908		20c. Type **254**	35	20
909		25c. As 15c.	35	20
910		40c. Manuel Antonio Beach	35	20
911		45c. Costa Rican Tourist Institute emblem	35	20
912		50c. Lindora Lake	35	20
913		60c. Post Office Building, San Jose (vert)	35	20
914		80c. As 40c.	40	20
915		90c. As 45c.	40	20
916		1col. As 50c.	40	20
917		2col. As 60c.	75	50

1973. Air. Churches and Cathedrals (2nd series). As Nos. 779/94 but colours changed.

918	**227**	5c. grey	20	20
919	–	10c. green	20	20
920	–	15c. orange	20	20
921	–	25c. brown	20	20
922	–	30c. purple	20	20
923	–	35c. violet	20	20
924	–	40c. green	20	20
925	–	45c. brown	20	20
926	–	50c. red	20	20
927	–	55c. blue	25	20
928	–	65c. black	30	20
929	–	75c. red	30	20
930	–	80c. green	30	20
931	–	85c. lilac	35	25
932	–	90c. red	35	25
933	–	1col. blue	35	25

1973. Obligatory Tax. Christmas Charity.

934	**255**	10c. red	25	20
935		10c. purple	25	20
936		10c. black	25	20
937		10c. brown	25	20

256 Flame Emblem

257 OEA Emblem

1973. Air. 25th Anniv of Declaration of Human Rights.

938	**256**	50c. red and blue	25	20

1973. Air. 25th Anniv of Organization of American States.

939	**257**	20c. red and blue	25	20

258 J. Vargas Calvo

260 Telephone Centre, San Pedro

1974. Air. Costa Rican Composers. Mult.

940		20c. Type **258**	40	20
941		20c. Alejandro Monestel	40	20
942		20c. Julio Mata	40	20
943		60c. Julio Fonseca	40	20
944		2col. Rafael Chaves	90	35
945		5col. Manuel Gutierrez	2·10	1·20

1974. Air. Fiscal stamps as Type **175** (but without surcharge) optd **HABILITADO PARA CORREO AEREO.**

946		50c. brown	15	10
947		1col. violet	35	15
948		2col. orange	75	40
949		5col. green	1·80	1·60

1974. Air. 25th Anniv of Costa Rican Electrical Institute. Multicoloured.

950		50c. Type **260**	15	10
951		65c. Control Room, Rio Macho (horiz)	25	15
952		85c. Power house, Rio Macho	35	15
953		1col.25 Cachi Dam, Rio Macho (horiz)	40	20
954		2col. Institute H.Q. building	80	40

261 "Exfilmex" Emblem

262 Couple on Map

1974. Air. "Exfilmex" Stamp Exhibition, Mexico City.

955	**261**	65c. green	15	10
956		3col. pink	65	40

1974. Air. 25th Anniv of 4-S Clubs.

957	**262**	20c. emerald and green	40	20
958	–	50c. multicoloured	40	20

DESIGN. 50c. Young agricultural workers.

263 Brenes Mesen

264 Child's and Adult's Hands

1974. Air. Birth Centenary of Roberto Brenes Mesen (educator).

959	**263**	20c. black and brown	15	10
960	–	85c. black and red	25	15
961	–	5col. brown and black	1·60	90

DESIGNS—VERT: 85c. Brenes Mesen's "Poems of Love and Death". HORIZ: 5col. Brenes Mesen's hands.

1974. Air. 50th Anniv of Costa Rican Insurance Institute.

962	–	20c. multicoloured	10	10
963	–	50c. multicoloured	10	10
964	**264**	65c. multicoloured	10	10
965	–	85c. multicoloured	10	10
966	–	1col.25 black and gold	30	10
967	–	2col. multicoloured	55	25
968	–	2col.50 multicoloured	65	40
969	–	20col. multicoloured	4·25	4·25

DESIGNS—HORIZ: 20c. R. Jimenez Oreamuno and T. Soley Guell (founders); 50c. Spade ("Harvest Insurance"). VERT: 85c. Paper boat within hand ("Marine Insurance"); 1col.25, Institute emblem; 2col. Arm in brace ("Workers' Rehabilitation"); 2col.50, Hand holding spanner ("Risks at Work"); 20col. House in protective hands ("Fire Insurance").

265 WPY Emblem

266 "Boys eating Cakes" (Murillo)

1974. Air. World Population Year.
970 **265** 2col. red and blue 50 25

1974. Obligatory Tax. Christmas.
971 **266** 10c. red 30 20
972 – 10c. purple 30 20
973 – 10c. black 30 20
974 – 10c. blue 30 20
DESIGNS: No. 972, "The Beautiful Gardener" (Raphael); No. 973, "Maternity" (J. R. Bonilla); No. 974, "The Prayer" (J. Reynolds).

267 Oscar J. Pinto (football pioneer)

268 "Mormodes buccinator"

1974. Air. 1st Central American Olympic Games, Guatemala (1973). Each grey and blue.
975 20c. Type **267** 10 10
976 50c. D. A. Montes de Oca (shooting champion) . . . 10 10
977 1col. Eduardo Garnier (promoter of athletics) . . 50 20

1975. Air. 1st Central American Orchids Exhibition. Multicoloured.
978 25c. Type **268** 65 20
979 25c. "Gongora claviodora" 65 20
980 25c. "Masdevallia ephippium" 65 20
981 25c. "Encyclia spondiadum" 65 20
982 65c. "Lycaste skinneri alba" 1·60 20
983 65c. "Peristeria elata" . . . . 1·60 20
984 65c. "Miltonia roezelii" . . . 1·60 20
985 65c. "Brassavola digbyana" 1·60 20
986 80c. "Epidendrum mirabile" 2·30 35
987 80c. "Barkeria lindleyana" 2·30 35
988 80c. "Cattleya skinneri" . . . 2·30 35
989 80c. "Sobralia macrantha splendens" . . . . . . 2·30 35
990 1col.40 "Lycaste cruenta" . . 2·75 40
991 1col.40 "Oncidium obryzatum" . . . . 2·75 40
992 1col.40 "Gongora armeniaca" 2·75 40
993 1col.40 "Sievekingia suavis" 2·75 40
994 1col.75 "Hexisea imbricata" 1·60 40
995 2col.15 "Warcewiczella discolor" . . . . 1·60 55
996 2col.50 "Oncidium kramerianum" . . . . . . 2·75 1·10
997 3col.25 "Cattleya dowiana" 3·25 1·40

269 Emblem of Costa Rica Radio Club

1975. Air. 16th Convention of Radio Amateurs Federation of Central America and Panama, San Jose.
998a **269** 1col. purple and black 45 10
999 – 1col.10 red and blue . . 75 25
1000 – 2col. blue and black . . 1·40 40
DESIGNS—VERT: 1col.10, Federation emblem within "V" of Flags. HORIZ: 2col. Federation emblem.

270 Nicoyan Beach

1975. Air. 150th Anniv of Annexation of Nicoya. Multicoloured.
1001 25c. Type **270** 15 10
1002 75c. Cattle-drive 25 20
1003 1col. Colonial church . . . 35 20
1004 3col. Savannah riders (vert) 1·00 85

271 3c. Philatelic Exhibition Stamp of 1932

1975. Air. 6th National Philatelic Exhibition, San Jose.
1005 **271** 2col.20 orange & black 40 35
1006 – 2col.20 green and black 40 35
1007 – 2col.20 red and black . . 40 35
1008 – 2col.20 blue and black 40 35
DESIGNS: Stamps of 1932. No. 1006, 5c. stamp; No. 1007, 10c. stamp; No. 1008, 20c. stamp.

272 IWY Emblem

273 U.N. Emblem

1975. Air. International Women's Year.
1009 **272** 40c. red and blue 10 10
1010 1col.25 blue and black 40 20

1975. Air. 30th Anniv of United Nations.
1011 **273** 10c. blue and black . . . 20 20
1012 – 60c. multicoloured . . . 20 20
1013 – 1col.20 multicoloured . . 30 20
DESIGNS—HORIZ: 60c. General Assembly. VERT: 1col.20, U.N. Headquarters, New York.

274 "The Visitation"

275 "Children with Tortoise" (F. Amighetti)

1975. Air. "The Christmas Tradition". Paintings by Jorge Gallardo. Multicoloured.
1014 50c. Type **274** 35 20
1015 1col. "The Nativity and the Comet" 50 20
1016 5col. "St. Joseph in his workshop" . . . . 1·80 75

1975. Obligatory Tax. Christmas. Children's Village. Multicoloured.
1017 **275** 10c. brown 30 20
1018 – 10c. purple 30 20
1019 – 10c. grey 30 20
1020 – 10c. blue 30 20
DESIGNS: No. 1018, "The Virgin of the Carnation" (Da Vinci); No. 1019, "Happy Dreams" (child in bed—Sonia Romero); No. 1020, "Child with Pigeon" (Picasso).

276 Schoolboy and Flags

277 Prof. A. M. Brenes Mora

1976. Air. 20th Anniv of "20–30" Youth Clubs in Costa Rica.
1021 **276** 1col. multicoloured . . . 25 15

1976. Birth Centenary (1970) of Professor A. M. Brenes Mora (botanist).
1022 **277** 1col. violet (postage) . . 50 20
1023 – 5c. multicoloured (air) 50 20
1024 – 30c. multicoloured . . . 50 20
1025 – 55c. multicoloured . . . 50 20
1026 – 2col. multicoloured . . . 1·00 40
1027 – 10col. multicoloured . . 4·50 2·75
DESIGNS: 5c. "Quercus breneseii"; 30c. "Maxillaria albertii"; 55c. "Calathea brenesii"; 2col. "Brenesia costaricensis"; 10col. "Philodendron brenesii".
No. 1023 is wrongly inscribed "brenessi".

278 Open Book as "Flower"

281 Early and Modern Telephones

280 Mounted Postman with Pack Mule

1976. Air. Costa Rican Literature. Mult.
1028 15c. Type **278** 20 20
1029 1col.10 Reader with "T.V. eye" 20 20
1030 5col. Book and flag (horiz) 1·00 80

1976. Centenary (1974) of UPU.
1032 **280** 20c. black and yellow . . 35 20
1033 – 50c. multicoloured . . . 35 20
1034 – 65c. multicoloured . . . 35 20
1035 – 85c. multicoloured . . . 35 20
1036 – 2col. black and blue . . 80 45
DESIGNS—HORIZ: 50c., 5c. UPU stamp of 1882; 65c., 10c. UPU stamp of 1882; 85c., 20c. UPU stamp of 1882. VERT: 2col. UPU Monument, Berne.

1976. Telephone Centenary.
1037 **281** 1col.60 black and blue 40 20
1038 – 2col. black, brown & grn 50 20
1039 – 5col. black and yellow 1·20 1·00
DESIGNS: 2col. Costa Rica's first telephone; 5col. Alexander Graham Bell.

282 Emblems and Costa Rica 2c. Stamp of 1901 with Centre Inverted

1976. Air. 7th National Philatelic Exhibition.
1040 **282** 50c. multicoloured . . . 15 15
1041 1col. multicoloured . . . 15 15
1042 2col. multicoloured . . . 40 15
MS1043 75 × 60 mm. 5col. As T **282** but with stamp in centre of design. Imperf or perf . . . . 2·75 2·75

283 Emblem of Comptroller General

284 "Girl in Wide-brimmed Hat" (Renoir)

1976. Air. 25th Anniv of Comptroller General.
1044 **283** 35c. blue and black . . . 10 10
1045 – 2col. black, brown & bl 55 40
DESIGN—VERT: 2col. Amadeo Quiros Blanco (1st Comptroller).

1976. Obligatory Tax. Christmas.
1046 **284** 10c. lake 30 20
1047 – 10c. purple 30 20
1048 – 10c. slate 30 20
1049 – 10c. blue 30 20
DESIGNS: No. 1047, "Virgin and Child" (Hans Memling); No. 1048, "Meditation" (Floria Pinto de Herrero); No. 1049, "Gaston de Mezerville" (Lolita Zeller de Peralta).

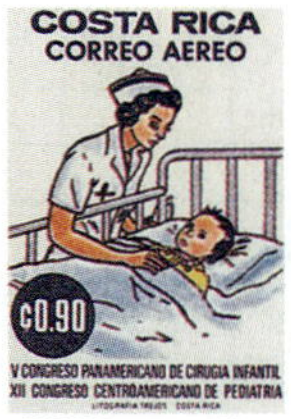

285 Nurse tending Child

286 "LACSA" encircling Globe

1976. Air. 5th Pan-American Children's Surgery Congress. Multicoloured.
1050 90c. Type **285** 25 15
1051 1col.10 National Children's Hospital (horiz) 40 25

1976. Air. 30th Anniv of LACSA Airline. Mult.
1052 1col. Type **286** 25 15
1053 1col.20 Route-map of LACSA services 40 20
1054 3col. LACSA emblem and Costa Rican flag . . . . 1·10 70

287 Boston Tea Party

1976. Air. Bicent of American Revolution. Mult.
1055 2col.20 Type **287** 40 35
1056 5col. Declaration of Independence . . . . . . 1·00 75
1057 10col. Ringing the Independence Bell (vert) 1·80 1·50

288 Boruca Textile

289 Tree of Guanacaste

1977. Air. National Handicrafts Project. Mult.
1058 75c. Type **288** 15 15
1059 1col.50 Decorative handicraft in wood . . . 35 15

1977. Air. 50th Anniv of Rotary Club, San Jose.
1060 **289** 40c. green, blue and yellow 20 10
1061 – 50c. black, blue and yellow 15 10
1062 – 60c. black, blue and yellow 15 10
1063 – 3col. multicoloured . . . 1·00 60
1064 – 10col. black, blue and yellow . . . . 3·50 2·50
DESIGNS—VERT: 50c. Felipe J. Alvarado (founder); 10col. Paul Harris, founder of Rotary International. HORIZ: 60c. Dr. Blanco Cervantes Hospital; 3col. Map of Costa Rica.

290 Juana Pereira

291 Alonso de Anguciana de Gamboa

1977. Air. 50th Anniv of Coronation of Our Lady of the Angels (Patron Saint of Costa Rica).
1065 50c. Type **290** 20 20
1066 1col. First church of Our Lady of the Angels (horiz) 20 20
1067 1col.10 Our Lady of the Angels 20 20
1068 1col.25 Our Lady's crown 30 20

1977. Air. 400th Anniv of Foundation of Esparza.
1069 **291** 35c. purple, mve & blk 10 10
1070 – 75c. brown, red & black 15 10
1071 – 1col. dp bl, bl & blk . . 35 15
1072 – 2col. green and black . . 65 40
DESIGNS: 75c. Church of Esparza; 1col. Our Lady of Candelaria, Patron Saint of Esparza; 2col. Diego de Artieda y Chirino.

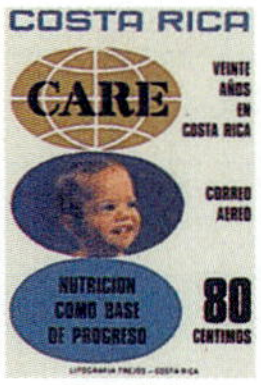

292 Child

293 Institute Emblem

1977. Air. 20 Years of "CARE" in Costa Rica. Multicoloured.
1073 80c. Type **292** 25 15
1074 1col. Soya beans (horiz) 40 15

1977. Air. 25th Anniv of Hispanic Cultural Institute of Costa Rica. Multicoloured.
1075 50c. Type **293** 50 15
1076 1col.40 First map of the Americas, 1540 (40 × 30 mm) 1·00 40

294 "Our Lady of Mercy Church" (R. Ulloa)

295 Health Ministry on Map

1977. Air. Mystical Paintings. Multicoloured.
1077 50c. Type **294** 40 20
1078 1col. "Christ" (F. Pinto de Herrero) 40 20
1079 5col. "St. Francis and the Birds" (L. Gonzalez de Saenz) 1·80 75

1977. Air. 50th Anniv of Health Ministry.
1080 **295** 1col.40 multicoloured 40 15

296 "Child's Head" (Rubens)

297 Weaving

1977. Obligatory Tax. Christmas.
1081 **296** 10c. red 30 20
1082 – 10c. blue 30 20
1083 – 10c. green 30 20
1084 – 10c. purple 30 20
DESIGNS: No. 1082, "Tenderness" (Cristina Fournier); No. 1083, "Abstraction" (Amparo Cruz); No. 1084, "Mariano Goya" (Francisco de Goya).

1978. Air. 21st Congress of Confederation of Latin American Tourist Organizations. Multicoloured.
1085 50c. Type **297** 15 15
1086 1col. Picnic 30 15
1087 2col. Beach scene 95 20
1088 5col. Fruit market 1·80 85
1089 10col. Lake scene 2·40 1·90

298 Reader with Book

299 Jose de San Martin

1978. National Literacy Campaign.
1090 **298** 50c. blue, black & orge 25 20

1978. Air. Birth Bicent of Jose de San Martin.
1091 **299** 5col. multicoloured 1·30 80

300 Globe

301 "XXX"

1978. Air. 50th Anniv of Pan-American Institute of Geography and History.
1092 **300** 5col. blue, gold & lt blue 1·20 65

1978. Air. 30th Anniv of Central American University Confederation.
1093 **301** 80c. blue 25 15

302 Emblems

1978. Air. 6th Inter-American Philatelic Exn, Buenos Aires.
1094 **302** 2col. turq, gold & blk 55 40

1978. Air. 50th Anniv of 1st PanAm Flight in Costa Rica. Nos. 994/6 optd **"50 Aniversario del primer vuelo de PAN AM en Costa Rica 1928 – 1978"**.
1095 1col.75 "Hexisea imbricata" 50 35
1096 2col.15 "Warcewiczella discolor" 65 40
1097 2col.50 "Oncidium kramerianum" 90 50

1978. Air. 50th Anniv of Lindbergh's Visit to Costa Rica. Nos. 994/6 optd **"50 Aniversario de la visita de Lindbergh a Costa Rica 1928 – 1978"**.
1098 1col.75 "Hexisea imbricata" 1·30 35
1099 2col.15 "Warcewiczella discolor" 1·60 40
1100 2col.50 "Oncidium kramerianum" 2·00 50

1978. Air. Carlos Maria Ulloa Hospital Centenary. Nos. 964 and 968 surch **"Centenario del Asilo Carlos Maria Ulloa 1878 – 1978"** and new value.
1101 50c. on 65c. multicoloured 15 15
1102 2col. on 2col.50 mult 55 25

306 Star over Map of Costa Rica

308 "Christmas Winds" (L. F. Chacon)

1978. Air. Christmas.
1103 **306** 50c. blue and black 20 15
1104 1col. mauve and black 20 15
1105 5col. red and black 1·40 65

1978. Air. Nos. 982/5 and 995/6 surch.
1106 50c. on 65c. "Lycaste skinneri alba" 60 55
1107 50c. on 65c. "Peristeria elata" 60 55
1108 50c. on 65c. "Miltonia roezelii" 60 55
1109 50c. on 65c. "Brassavola digbyana" 60 55
1110 1col.20 on 2col.15 "Warcewiczella discolor" 1·30 55
1111 2col. on 2col.50 "Oncidium kramerianum" 1·30 55

1978. Obligatory Tax. Christmas. Children's Village.
1112 **308** 10c. slate 30 20
1113 10c. red 30 20
1114 – 10c. mauve 30 20
1115 – 10c. blue 30 20
DESIGN: Nos. 1114/15, "Girl playing with Kite" (sculpture by Nester Zeledon).

309 "The Flying Men", Chorotega Ritual

310 Domingo Rivas

1978. Air. 500th Anniv of Gonzalo Fernandez de Oviedo (first chronicler of Spanish Indies).
1116 **309** 85c. multicoloured 20 20
1117 – 1col.20 blue and black 20 20
1118 – 10col. multicoloured 2·10 2·10
DESIGNS—HORIZ: 1col.20, Oviedo giving his "History of Indies" to Duke of Calabria. VERT: 10col. Lord of Oviedo's coat of arms.

1978. Air. Centenary of San Jose Cathedral.
1119 **310** 1col. blue and black 15 15
1120 – 20col. multicoloured 3·75 3·75
DESIGN: 20c. San Jose Cathedral.

311 Cocos Island

1979. Air. Presidential Visit to Cocos Island. Mult.
1121 90c. Type **311** 30 15
1122 2col.10 Cocos Island (different) 75 40
1123 3col. Cocos Island (different) 1·10 55
1124 5col. Moon over Cocos Island (vert) 1·80 1·10
1125 10col. Commemorative plaque and people with flag (vert) 3·50 2·75
MS1126 139 × 102 mm. Nos. 1121/5 12·00 12·00

312 Shrimp

1979. Air. Conservation of Marine Fauna. Multicoloured.
1127 60c. Type **312** 20 20
1128 85c. Mahogany snapper 20 20
1129 1col.80 Yellow corvina 50 20
1130 3col. Lobster 75 40
1131 10col. Frigate mackerel 2·50 2·40

313 Hungry Nestlings (Song Thrushes)

1979. Air. International Year of the Child.
1132 **313** 1col. multicoloured 70 15
1133 2col. multicoloured 1·60 65
1134 20col. multicoloured 11·00 5·75

315 Microwave Transmitters, Mt. Hazu

1979. Air. 30th Anniv of Costa Rican Electricity Institute. Multicoloured.
1136 1col. Arenal Dam 20 20
1137 5col. Type **315** 1·10 70

316 Sir Rowland Hill and Penny Black

1979. Air. Death Centenary of Sir Rowland Hill.
1138 – 5col. mauve and blue 1·20 55
1139 **316** 10col. blue and black 2·50 1·20
DESIGN: 5col. Sir Rowland Hill and first Costa Rican stamp.

317 "Waiting" (Hernan Gonzalez)

318 "Danaus plexippus"

1979. Air. National Sculpture Competition. Multicoloured.
1140 60c. Type **317** 15 15
1141 1col. "The Heroes of Misery" (Juan Ramon Bonilla) 20 15
1142 2col.10 "Bullocks" (Victor M. Bermudez) (horiz) 55 20
1143 5col. "Chlorite Head" (Juan Rafael Chacon) 1·50 1·10
1144 20col. "Motherhood" (Francisco Zuniga) 5·00 2·50

1979. Air. Butterflies. Multicoloured.
1145 60c. Type **318** 2·10 35
1146 1col. "Phoebis philea" 4·25 35
1147 1col.80 "Rothschildia sp." 6·50 55
1148 2col.10 "Prepona omphale" 8·50 75
1149 2col.60 "Marpesia marcella" 8·50 1·50
1150 4col.05 "Morpho cypris" 12·50 2·50

319 "Green House" (M. Murillo)

320 Jose Joaquin Rodriguez Zeledon

1979. Air. 30th Anniv of SOS Children's Villages. Children's Paintings. Multicoloured.
1151 2col.50 Type **319** 55 40
1152 5col. "Four houses" (L. Varela) 1·20 65
1153 5col.50 "Blue house" (M. Perez) 1·60 95

1979. Air. Costa Rican Presidents (1st series).
1154 **320** 10c. blue 10 10
1155 – 60c. purple 15 10
1156 – 85c. red 25 15
1157 – 1col. orange 35 15
1158 – 2col. brown 65 40
DESIGNS: 60c. Rafael Iglesias Castro; 85c. Ascension Esquivel Ibarra; 1col. Cleto Gonzalez Viquez; 2col. Ricardo Jimenez Oreamuno.
See also Nos. 1180/4 and 1256/60.

321 Holy Family

322 Boy leaning on Tree

1979. Air. Christmas.
1159 **321** 1col. multicoloured 20 15
1160 1col.60 multicoloured 50 25

1979. Obligatory Tax. Christmas. Children's Village.
1161 **322** 10c. blue 25 20
1162 10c. orange 25 20
1163 10c. mauve 25 20
1164 10c. green 25 20

323 Tree

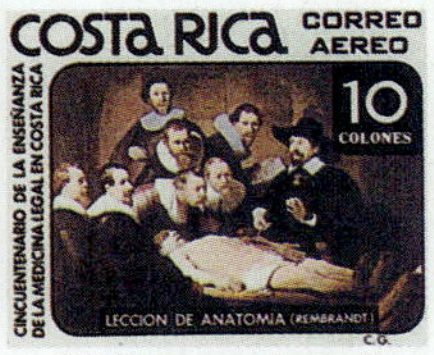

324 "Anatomy Lesson" (Rembrandt)

1980. Air. Reafforestation.
1165 **323** 1col. brown, blue & grn 15 15
1166 3col.40 brown, ol & grn 60 45

1980. Air. 50th Anniv of Legal Medical Teaching in Costa Rica.
1167 **324** 10col. multicoloured 4·00 1·70

325 Rotary Anniversary Emblem

326 Puerto Limon

1980. 75th Anniv of Rotary International.
1168 **325** 2col.10 green, yellow and black 35 25
1169 5col. multicoloured 95 65

1980. Air. 14th International Symposium on Remote Sensing of the Environment. Multicoloured.
1170 2col.10 Type **326** 35 25
1171 5col. Gulf of Nicoya, Guanacaste 95 65

327 Football

328 Poas Volcano

1980. Air. Olympic Games, Moscow. Mult.
1172 1col. Type **327** 40 15
1173 3col. Cycling . . . . . . 7·75 55
1174 4col.05 Baseball . . . . . . 7·75 75
1175 20col. Swimming . . . . . 7·75 5·25

1980. Air. 10th Anniv of National Parks Service.
1176 1col. Type **328** 20 15
1177 2col.50 Beach at Cahuita . . 50 40

329 Jose Maria Zeledon Brenes (lyric writer)

330 Exhibition Emblem

1980. Air. National Anthem. Multicoloured.
1178 1col. Type **329** 20 15
1179 10col. Manuel Maria Gutierrez (composer) . . 1·70 1·40

1980. Air. Costa Rican Presidents (2nd series). As T **320**.
1180 1col. red 20 10
1181 1col.60 turquoise 35 15
1182 1col.80 brown 40 15
1183 2col.10 green 45 20
1184 3col. lilac 70 45
DESIGNS: 1col. Alfredo Gonzalez; 1col.60, Federico Tinoco; 1col.80, Francisco Aguilar; 2col.10, Julio Acosta; 3col. Leon Cortes.

1980. Air. 8th National Stamp Exhibition.
1185 **330** 5col. multicoloured . . . 85 60
1186 20col. multicoloured . . 3·50 2·75

331 Fruit

332 "Giant Poro" (Jorge Carvajal)

1980. Air. Costa Rican Produce. Mult.
1187 10c. Type **331** 15 10
1188 60c. Chocolate 20 15
1189 1col. Coffee 35 15
1190 2col.10 Bananas 65 20
1191 3col.40 Flowers . . . . . 1·10 45
1192 5col. Cane sugar . . . . . 1·20 65

1980. Air. Paintings. Multicoloured.
1193 1col. Type **332** 30 15
1194 2col.10 "Secret Look" (Rolando Cubero) 50 25
1195 2col.45 "Consuelo" (Fernando Carballo) (31 × 32 mm) 65 35
1196 3col. "Volcano" (Lola Fernandez) 75 40
1197 4col.05 "Hearing Mass" (Francisco Amighetti) . . 1·10 50

333 "Madonna and Child" (Raphael)

334 Boy on Swing

1980. Air. Christmas. Multicoloured.
1198 1col. Type **333** 35 25
1199 10col. "Madonna, Jesus and St. John" (Raphael) . . . 2·40 1·80

1980. Obligatory Tax. Christmas. Children's Village.
1200 **334** 10c. red 25 20
1201 10c. yellow 25 20
1202 10c. blue 25 20
1203 10c. green 25 20

335 New Harbour, Caldera

336 Harpy Eagle

1980. Air. "Paying your Taxes Means Progress". Multicoloured.
1204 1col. Type **335** 25 15
1205 1col.30 Juan Santamaria International Airport (32 × 25 mm) 40 15
1206 2col.10 River Frio railway bridge 70 35
1207 2col.60 Highway to Colon City (25 × 32 mm) 75 40
1208 5col. Regional postal centre, Huetar . . . . 1·30 75

1980. Air. Fauna. Multicoloured.
1209 2col.10 Type **336** . . . . . 1·40 35
1210 2col.50 Scarlet macaw . . . 1·90 45
1211 3col. Puma . . . . . . 2·50 55
1212 5col.50 Black-handed spider monkey . . . . 5·00 1·10

337 Monge and Magazine "Repertorio Americano"

1980. Air. Birth Centenary of Joaquin Garcia Monge.
1213 **337** 1col.60 blue, yell & red 25 15
1214 3col. blue, lt bl & red . . 55 40

338 Arms of Aserri

339 Rodrigo Facio Brenes (rector)

1981. Air. Cornea Bank.
1215 **338** 1col. multicoloured . . . 20 15
1216 1col.80 multicoloured . . 50 20
1217 5col. blue . . . . 1·40 75
DESIGNS: 1col.80, Eye; 5col. Abelardo Rojas (founder).

1981. Air. 40th Anniv of University of Costa Rica and 20th Anniv of Medical School.
1218 – 5c. multicoloured 15 10
1219 – 10c. multicoloured . . . 15 10
1220 – 50c. multicoloured . . . 15 10
1221 – 1col.30 multicoloured . . 20 10
1222 – 3col.40 multicoloured . . 50 35
1223 **339** 4col.05 grn, bl & dp bl 65 40
DESIGNS: HORIZ: 5c. Medical-surgical clinic; 10c. Physiology lesson; 50c. Medical School and Dr. Antonia Pena Chavarria (first Dean); 1col.30, School of Music and Fine Arts; 3col.40, Carlos Monge Alfaro Library.

340 Ass-drawn Mail Van, 1857

1981. Air. 150th Birth Anniv of Heinrich von Stephan (founder of UPU).
1224 – 1col. lt blue, grn & bl . . 20 15
1225 **340** 2col.10 yell, red & brn 50 20
1226 – 10col. grey, mve & grn 2·20 1·50
DESIGNS: 1col. Mail carried by mule, 1839; 10col. Carrying mail to Sarapiqui, 1858.

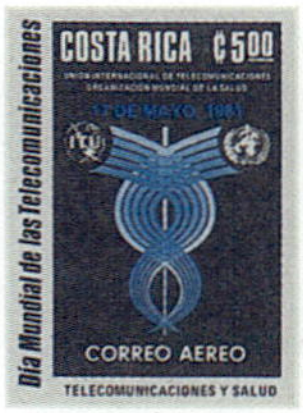

341 ITU and WHO Emblems and Ribbons forming Caduceus

342 Sts. Peter and Paul

1981. Air. World Telecommunications Day.
1227 **341** 5col. blue and black . . 1·00 65
1228 25col. multicoloured . . 5·00 4·25

1981. Air. Centenary of Consecration of Bernardo August Thiel as Bishop of San Jose. Mult.
1229 1col. Type **342** 15 10
1230 1col. St. Vincent de Paul . . 15 10
1231 1col. Death of St. Joseph . . 15 10
1232 1col. Archangel St. Michael 15 10
1233 1col. Holy Family 15 10
1234 2col. Bishop Thiel 45 30

343 Juan Santamaria (national hero)

344 Potter

1981. Air. Homage to the Province of Alajuela. Multicoloured.
1235 1col. Type **343** (150th birth anniv) 20 15
1236 2col.45 Alajuela Cathedral 35 30

1981. Air. Banco Popular and the Development of the Community. Multicoloured.
1237 15c. Type **344** 15 10
1238 1col.60 Building construction 20 15
1239 1col.80 Farming 20 15
1240 2col.50 Fishermen 25 15
1241 3col. Nurse and patient . . 40 15
1242 5col. Rural guard 75 25

345 Leon Fernandez Bonilla (founder)

346 Disabled Person in Wheelchair holding Scales of Justice

1981. Air. National Archives. Multicoloured.
1243 1col.40 Type **345** 25 20
1244 2col. Arms of National Archives 35 20
1245 3col. University of Santo Tomas (horiz) 45 35
1246 3col.50 Model of new archives' building (horiz) 55 35

1981. Air. International Year of Disabled Persons.
1247 – 1col. multicoloured . . . 35 15
1248 **346** 2col.60 deep orange, orange and black . . . 80 15
1249 – 10col. multicoloured . . 3·50 80
DESIGNS—VERT: 1col. Steps and disabled person in wheelchair. HORIZ: 10col. Healthy person helping disabled towards the sun.

347 FAO Emblem

348 Boy in Pedal-car

1981. Air. World Food Day.
1250 **347** 5col. multicoloured . . . 40 25
1251 10col. multicoloured . . 80 55

1981. Obligatory Tax. Christmas. Children's Village.
1252 **348** 10c. red 25 20
1253 10c. orange 25 20
1254 10c. blue 25 20
1255 10c. green 25 20

1981. Air. Costa Rican Presidents (3rd series) As T **320**.
1256 1col. red 40 40
1257 2col. orange 40 40
1258 3col. green 50 40
1259 5col. blue 95 65
1260 10col. blue . . . . 1·90 1·50
DESIGNS: 1c. Rafael Angel Calderon Guardia; 2col. Teodoro Picado Milchalski; 3col. Jose Figueres Ferrer; 5col. Otilio Ulate Blanco; 10col. Mario Echandi Jimenez.

349 Arms of Bar Association

1982. Air. Centenary of Bar Association.
1261 **349** 1col. blue and black . . 15 15
1262 – 2col. multicoloured . . . 15 15
1263 – 20col. green and black 2·20 1·40
DESIGNS—VERT: 2col. Eusebio Figueroa (first president of Association). HORIZ: 20col. Bar Association building.

350 Housing

1982. Air. Costa-Rican Progress. Mult.
1264 95col. Type **350** 10 10
1265 1col.15 Farmers' fairs . . . 10 10
1266 1col.45 Grade and high schools 10 10
1267 1col.65 National plan for drinking water 15 10
1268 1col.80 Rural health 15 10
1269 2col.10 Playgrounds 20 10
1270 2col.35 National Theatre Square 30 10
1271 2col.60 Dish aerial (International and national telephone system) 30 10
1272 3col. Electric railway to Atlantic coast 40 10
1273 4col.05 Irrigation at Guanacaste 40 35

351 Fountain, Central Park

352 Saint's Stone

1982. Air. Bicentenary of Alajuela. Mult.
1274 5col. Type **351** 50 25
1275 10col. Juan Santamaria Historical and Cultural Museum (horiz) . . . . . 1·00 45
1276 15col. Christ of Esquipulas Church . . . . 1·50 1·10
1277 20col. Mgr. Estevan Lorenzo de Tristan . . . 2·00 1·30
1278 25col. Padre Juan Manuel Lopez del Corral . . . . 2·40 1·60

1982. Air. 50th Anniv of Perez Zeledon County. Multicoloured.
1279 10c. Type **352** 10 10
1280 50c. Monument to Mothers 10 10
1281 1col. Pedro Perez Zeledon 10 10
1282 1col.25 San Isidro Labrador Church 10 10
1283 3col.50 Municipal building (horiz) 30 20
1284 4col.25 County arms 45 20

1982. Air. Nos. 1070 and 1207 surch.
1285 3col. on 75c. red and black 30 20
1286 5col. on 2col.60 mult . . . 50 20

1982. Air. 9th National Stamp Exhibition. Nos. 1005/8 surch **IX EXPOSICION FILATELICA - 1982** and new value.
1287 **271** 8col.40 on 2col.20 orange and black . . . 55 40
1288 – 8col.40 on 2col.20 green and black 55 40
1289 – 8col.40 on 2col.20 red and black 55 40
1290 – 8col.40 on 2col.20 blue and black 55 40
1291 **271** 9col.70 on 2col.20 orange and black . . . 65 55
1292 – 9col.70 on 2col.20 green and black 65 55
1293 – 9col.70 on 2col.20 red and black 65 55
1294 – 9col.70 on 2col.20 blue and black 65 55

355 Dr Robert Koch and Cross of Lorraine

356 Student at Lathe

1982. Air. Centenary of Discovery of Tubercle Bacillus.

1295 – 1col.50 red and black . . 15 15
1296 **355** 3col. grey and black . . 30 15
1297 – 3col.30 multicoloured . . 30 15

DESIGNS: 1col.50, Koch and anti-T.B. Campaign emblem; 3col.30, Koch and Ministry of Public Health Building, San Jose.

1982. Obligatory Tax. Christmas. Children's Village.

1298 **356** 10c. red 25 20
1299 10c. grey 25 20
1300 10c. violet 25 20
1301 10c. blue 25 20

357 Blood Donors Association Emblem

358 Migration Committee Emblem

1982. Air. 7th Pan-American Blood Donors Congress. Multicoloured.

1302 **357** 30col. multicoloured . . 1·90 1·30
1303 – 50col. red, blue & black 3·00 2·00

DESIGN: 50col. Congress emblem.

1982. Air. 30th Anniv of Intergovernmental Migration Committee.

1304 **358** 8col.40 lt blue, bl & blk 50 20
1305 – 9col.70 blue and black 70 35
1306 – 11col.70 mult 75 35
1307 – 13col.05 bl, blk & grey 90 45

DESIGNS—HORIZ: 11col.70, Emblem and handshake; 13col.05, Emblem within double-headed arrow. VERT: 9col.70, Emblem.

359 "St. Francis" (El Greco)

360 Pope John Paul II

1983. Air. 800th Birth Anniv (1982) of St. Francis of Assisi.

1308 **359** 4col.80 brown, blk & bl 45 20
1309 – 7col.40 brn, blk & grey 65 20

DESIGN: 7col.40, Portrait of Francis by unknown artist.

1983. Air. Papal Visit.

1310 **360** 5col. brown, yell & bl . . 2·30 20
1311 10col. brown, grn & bl 2·30 45
1312 15col. brown, mve & bl 5·25 70

361 WCY Emblem

362 Egg

1983. World Communications Year.

1313 **361** 10c. multicoloured . . . 30 20
1314 50c. multicoloured . . . 30 20
1315 10col. multicoloured . . 1·20 30

1983. 1st World Conference on Human Rights, Alajuela (1982).

1316 **362** 20col. grey and black . . 2·10 95

363 UPU Monument, Berne, and 1883 2c. Stamp

1983. Centenary of U.P.U. Membership.

1317 **363** 3col. yellow, red & blk 1·10 30
1318 – 10col. yellow, bl & blk 2·20 45

DESIGN: 10col. Central Post Office, San Jose, and 1883 40c. stamp.

364 "Alliance Building, San Jose" (Cristina Fournier)

365 Bolivar (after Francisco Zuniga)

1983. Centenary of French Alliance (French language-teaching association).

1319 **364** 12col. multicoloured . . 1·80 55

1983. Air. Birth Bicentenary of Simon Bolivar.

1320 **365** 10col. multicoloured . . 95 20

1983. Nos. 1308/9 surch.

1321 10c. on 4col.80 brown, black and blue 20 20
1321a 50c. on 4col.80 brown, black and blue 20 20
1322 1col.50 on 7col.40 brown, black and grey 20 20
1323 3col. on 7col.40 brown, black and grey 20 20

367 Repairing Wheelchair

368 Three Kings

1988. Obligatory Tax. Christmas. Children's Village.

1324 **367** 10c. red 25 20
1325 10c. orange 25 20
1326 10c. blue 25 20
1327 10c. green 25 20

1983. Christmas. Multicoloured.

1328 1col.50 Type **368** 20 15
1329 1col.50 Holy Family and Shepherds 20 15
1330 1col.50 People bearing gifts 20 15

Nos. 1328/30 were printed together, se-tenant, forming a composite design.

369 Fisherman

370 Resplendent Quetzal ("Quetzal")

1983. Fisheries Development.

1331 **369** 8col.50 multicoloured . . 80 30

1984. Birds. Multicoloured.

1332 10c. Type **370** 55 20
1333 50c. Red-legged honey-creeper ("Mielero Patirrojo") (horiz) 55 20
1334 1col. Clay-coloured thrush ("Mirlo Pardo") (horiz) 55 20
1335 1col.50 Blue-crowned motmot ("Momotode Diadema Azul") 55 20
1336 3col. Green violetear ("Colibri orejivioloceo verde") . . . . 1·40 25
1337 10col. Blue and white swallow ("Golondirina Azul y Blanca") (horiz) 4·75 35

371 Jose Joaquin Mora

1984. 1856 Campaign Heroes. Multicoloured.

1339 50c. Type **371** 10 10
1340 1col.50 Pancha Carrasco . . 15 10
1341 3col. Juan Santamaria (horiz) 30 20
1342 8col.50 Juan Rafael Mora Porras 95 60

372 Jesus Bonilla Chavarria

373 Necklace Bead

1984. Musicians.

1343 **372** 3col. 50 violet and black 30 20
1344 – 5col. red and black . . . 45 30
1345 – 12col. green and black 1·20 90
1346 – 13col. yellow and black 1·30 1·00

DESIGNS: 5col. Benjamin Gutierrez; 12col. Pilar Jimenez; 13col. Jose Daniel Zuniga.

1984. Jade Museum Artifacts. Multicoloured.

1347 4col. Type **373** 80 25
1348 7col. Seated figure . . . . 1·60 40
1349 10col. Ceramic dish (horiz) 2·00 50

374 Basketball Players

375 Street Scene

1984. Olympic Games, Los Angeles. Mult.

1350 1col. Type **374** 10 10
1351 8col. Swimming 65 15
1352 11col. Cycling 90 40
1353 14col. Running . . . . . . 1·20 65
1354 20col. Boxing . . . . 1·60 1·20
1355 30col. Football . . . . . . 2·50 1·50

1984. Centenary of Public Street Lighting.

1356 **375** 6col. multicoloured . . . 55 40

376 Emblem and National Independence Monument

1984. 10th National Philatelic Exhibition. Mult.

1357 10col. Type **376** 90 55
1358 10col. Emblem and Juan Mora Fernandez statue 90 55

MS1359 116 × 86 mm. Nos. 1357/8, each × 2 . . . . 12·00 12·00

377 National Coat of Arms

378 Child on Tricycle

1984.

1360 **377** 100col. blue . . . . . . 8·00 3·75
1361 100col. yellow . . . . . 8·00 3·75

1984. Obligatory Tax. Christmas. Children's Village.

1362 **378** 10c. violet 25 25

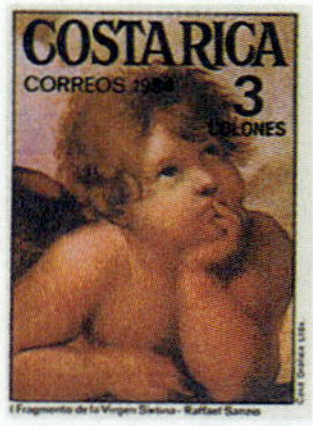

379 "Sistine Virgin" (detail, Raphael)

380 Cyclists

1984. Christmas. Multicoloured.

1363 3col. Type **379** 25 25
1364 3col. "Sistine Virgin" (detail) (different) 25 25

1984. 20th Costa Rica Cycle Race.

1365 **380** 6col. multicoloured . . . 55 30

381 Emblem and 1968 Scouting Jubilee Stamp

1985. International Youth Year.

1366 **381** 11col. multicoloured . . 1·60 55

382 Workers' Monument (Francisco Zuniga)

383 U.N. Emblem and 1935 Red Cross Jubilee Stamp

1985. "National Values".

1367 **382** 6col. mauve and black 80 30
1368 – 11col. yell, blk & bl . . 1·30 50
1369 – 13col. multicoloured . . 1·40 55
1370 – 30col. multicoloured . . 4·50 1·20

DESIGNS—As T **382**. 11col. First printing press (Freedom of speech); 13col. Dove, flag and globe (Neutrality); 65 × 35 mm—30col. Nos. 1367/9.

1985. Centenary of Costa Rican Red Cross.

1371 **383** 3col. red, brown & blk 1·60 25
1372 – 5col. black, red and grey 2·40 25

DESIGN: 5col. U.N. Emblem and 1946 Red Cross Society stamp.

384 Hands holding "S"

385 "Brassia arcuigera"

1985. 50th Anniv of Saprissa Football Club.

1373 **384** 3col. mauve and green 25 15
1374 – 3col. black and mauve 25 15
1375 – 6col. mauve, brn & grn 50 25

DESIGNS: As T **384**—Hands holding football; 34 × 26 mm—6col. Ricardo Saprissa and Saprissa Stadium.

1985. Orchids. Multicoloured.

1376 6col. Type **385** . . . . . . 1·30 55
1377 6col. "Encyclia peraltensis" 1·30 55
1378 6col. "Maxillaria especie" 1·30 55
1379 13col. "Oncidium turialbae" 1·50 1·10
1380 13col. "Trichopilia marginata" . . . . 1·50 1·10
1381 13col. "Stanhopea ecornuta" 1·50 1·10

386 1940 25c. Stamp and Hand holding Tweezers

387 Hands reaching out to Child

1985. 11th National Stamp Exhibition.
1382 **386** 20col. bl, ultram & pink . . . 1·20 55

1985. Obligatory Tax. Christmas. Children's Village.
1383 **387** 10c. brown 40 25

388 Children looking at Star

1985. Christmas.
1384 **388** 3col. multicoloured . . . 20 10

390 Costa Rica Lyceum **391** Land and Cattle College Project

1986. Centenary of Free Compulsory Education.
1390 **390** 3col. brown & lt brown . . . 15 10
1391 30col. brown and pink . . . 1·60 80
DESIGN: 30col. Mauro Fernandez Acuna (education Minister).

1986. 27th Annual Inter-American Development Bank Assembly, San Jose. Multicoloured.
1392 10col. Type **391** 50 25
1393 10col. Bank emblem 50 25
1394 10col. Cape Blanco fisherman 50 25

392 Francisco J. Orlich Bolmarcich **393** Pique (mascot)

1986. Former Presidents of Costa Rica.
1395 **392** 3col. green 40 15
1396 – 3col. green 40 15
1397 – 3col. green 40 15
1398 – 3col. green 40 15
1399 – 3col. green 40 15
1400 – 6col. brown 65 15
1401 – 6col. brown 65 15
1402 – 6col. brown 65 15
1403 – 6col. brown 65 15
1404 – 6col. brown 65 15
1405 – 10col. orange 95 25
1406 – 10col. orange 95 25
1407 – 10col. orange 95 25
1408 – 10col. orange 95 25
1409 – 10col. orange 95 25
1410 – 11col. grey . . . . . . 1·30 40
1411 – 11col. grey . . . . . . 1·30 40
1412 – 11col. grey . . . . . . 1·30 40
1413 – 11col. grey . . . . . . 1·30 40
1414 – 11col. grey . . . . . . 1·30 40
1415 – 13col. brown . . . . . 1·60 40
1416 – 13col. brown . . . . . 1·60 40
1417 – 13col. brown . . . . . 1·60 40
1418 – 13col. brown . . . . . 1·60 40
1419 – 13col. brown . . . . . 1·60 40
DESIGNS: Nos. 1395, 1400, 1405, 1410, 1415, Type **392**; 1396, 1401, 1406, 1411, 1416, Jose Joaquin Trejos Fernandez; 1397, 1402, 1407, 1412, 1417, Daniel Oduber Quiros; 1398, 1403, 1408, 1413, 1418, Rodrigo Carazo Odio; 1399, 1404, 1409, 1414, 1419, Luis Alberto Monge Alvarez.

1986. World Cup Football Championship. Mexico.
1420 **393** 1col. multicoloured . . . 30 15
1421 – 1col. multicoloured . . . 30 15
1422 – 4col. multicoloured . . . 1·40 15
1423 – 6col. pur, brn & black . . 2·00 25
1424 – 11col. pur, red & blk . . 4·00 40
DESIGNS:—VERT: No. 1420, 1422, Type **393**. HORIZ: No. 1421, 1423, Footballs and players; 1424, Footballs and players (different).

394 Emblem and "Peace" **395** Gold Artefact

1986. International Peace Year. Each bearing the Year emblem and "Peace" in various languages (first language given in brackets).
1425 **394** 5col. blue and brown (Hoa Binh) 55 25
1426 – 5col. blue and brown (Vrede) 55 25
1427 – 5col. blue and brown (Pace) 55 25

1986. Exhibits in Gold Museum. Mult.
1428 6col. Type **395** 40 25
1429 6col. Figure with three-lobed base 40 25
1430 6col. Frog 40 25
1431 6col. Centipede 40 25
1432 6col. Two monkeys in sun . . 40 25
1433 13col. Figure with dragon-head arms 80 40
1434 13col. Two monkeys 80 40
1435 13col. Animal-shaped figure . . 80 40
1436 13col. Sun with ball pendant . . 80 40
1437 13col. Figure within frame . . 80 40

396 Child **397** Fork-lift Truck and Airplane (Osvaldo Andres Gonzalez Vega)

1986. Obligatory Tax. Christmas. Children's Village.
1438 **396** 10c. brown 25 25

1986. Air. 40th Anniv of LACSA (national airline). Children's Drawings. Multicoloured.
1439 1col. Airplane flying over house and van (Adriana Elias Hidalgo) 50 15
1440 7col. Type **397** . . . . . 3·50 30
1441 16col. Airplane, letters and photographs (David Valverde Rodiguez) . . . 8·00 75

398 Lattice-winged Bat **399** Extracting Snake's Venom (detail of mural, Francisco Amighetti)

1986. Flora and Fauna. Bats and Frogs. Multicoloured.
1442 2col. Type **398** 15 15
1443 3col. Common long-tongued bat 30 15
1444 4col. White bat 40 15
1445 5col. Group of white bats . . 50 15
1446 6col. "Agalychnis callidryas" (frog) 65 25
1447 10col. "Dendrobates pumilio" (frog) . . . . . 1·10 25
1448 11col. "Hyla ebraccata" (frog) . . . . 1·10 40
1449 20col. "Phyllobates lugubris" (frog) . . . . . 2·00 65
MS1450 60 × 70 mm. 50 col. "Agalychris callidryas" (frog) on arum flower . . . . 1·00 1·00

1987. National Science and Technology Day.
1451 **399** 8col. multicoloured . . . 3·00 20

400 Statuette **401** Arms of San Jose Province

1987. Centenary of National Museum. Pre-Colombian Art. Multicoloured.
1452 8col. Type **400** 40 25
1453 8col. Jug in form of human figure 40 25
1454 8col. Vase in form of human figure 40 25
1455 8col. Stone jar 40 25
1456 8col. Pot with human-type legs and arms 40 25
1457 15col. Bowl (horiz) 65 25
1458 15col. Carving of animal defeating human (horiz) . . 65 25
1459 15col. Flask (horiz) 65 25

1987. 250th Anniv of San Jose.
1460 **401** 20col. multicoloured . . 95 50
1461 – 20col. red, black & bl . . 95 50
1462 – 20col. red, black & bl . . 95 50
DESIGNS: Nos. 1461, Donkey cart in cobbled street; 1462, View down street.

402 16th-century Map of Audiencia, Guatemala

1987. Columbus Day.
1463 **402** 30col. brown and yellow . . 2·30 65

403 Map by Bartholomew Columbus, 1503 **404** Cross and Doves

1987. 500th Anniv (1992) of Discovery of America by Columbus (1st issue). Each brown and yellow.
1464 4col. Type **403** 25 25
1465 4col. 16th-century map of Costa Rica 25 25
See also Nos. 1480, 1496, 1521 and 1538/40.

1987. Obligatory Tax. Christmas, Children's Village.
1466 **404** 10c. blue and brown . . 25 25

405 "Village Scene" (Fausto Pacheco) **406** Pres. Arias and National Flag

1987. International Year of Shelter for the Homeless.
1467 **405** 1col. multicoloured . . . 55 25

1987. Award of Nobel Peace Prize to Pres. Oscar Arias Sanchez.
1468 **406** 10col. multicoloured . . 1·60 30

407 Green Turtle **408** Anniversary Emblem

1988. 17th Annual General Assembly of International Union for Nature Conservation. Multicoloured.
1469 5col. Type **407** 50 15
1470 5col. Golden toad on leaf . . 50 15
1471 5col. Emperor (butterfly) . . 50 15

1988. 125th Anniv of Red Cross.
1472 **408** 30col. red and blue . . . 1·40 65

409 Man with Pen and Radio (Adult Education) **410** Symbols of Bank Activities

1988. Costa Rica–Liechtenstein Cultural Co-operation.
1473 **409** 18col. red, brown & grn . . 1·90 25
1474 – 20col. multicoloured . . 1·90 25
DESIGN: 20col. Headphones on books (radio broadcasts).

1988. 125th Anniv of Anglo–Costa Rican Bank.
1475 **410** 3col. blue, red & yellow . . 25 15

411 Games Emblem **412** Roman Macava and Curtiss "Robin"

1988. Olympic Games, Seoul. Multicoloured.
1476 25col. Type **411** 80 50
1477 25col. Games mascot . . . 80 50

1988. Airmail Pioneers.
1478 **412** 10col. multicoloured . . 50 15

413 School Courtyard **414** Amerindian Necklace

1988. Centenary of Girls' High School.
1479 **413** 10col. brown & yellow . . 40 25

1988. 500th Anniv (1992) of Discovery of America by Columbus (2nd issue).
1480 **414** 4col. multicoloured . . . 25 25

415 Dengo and College **416** Former Observation Tower

1988. Birth Centenary of Omar Dengo (Director of Heredia Teachers' College).
1481 **415** 10col. brown, grey & bl . . 30 25

1988. Cent of National Meteorological Institute.
1482 **416** 2col. multicoloured . . . 65 25

417 "Eschweilera costarricensis" **418** Map of France and Costa Rican National Monument

1989. Flowers. Multicoloured.
1483 5col. Type **417** 25 25
1484 10col. "Heliconia wagneriana" 30 25
1485 15col. "Heliconia lophocarpa" 55 25
1486 20col. "Aechmea magdalenae" 65 25

1487 25col. "Psammisia ramiflora" 80 25
1488 30col. Passion flower . . . 1·10 25

1989. Bicentenary of French Revolution.
1489 **418** 30col. black, blue & red 1·40 50

419 Sugar Mill

420 Corn Grinder

1989. 151st Anniv of Grecia County.
1490 **419** 10col. multicoloured . . 65 25

1989. America. Pre-Columbian Artefacts. Mult.
1491 50col. Type **420** . . . . . . 2·40 1·20
1492 100col. Granite sphere, 1500 A.D. . . . . 4·75 1·80

422 Orchid

423 Dr. Henri Pittier (first Director)

1989. "100 Years of Democracy" Presidents' Summit.
1493 **422** 10col. multicoloured . . 1·50 25

1989. Centenary of National Geographical Institute.
1494 **423** 18col. multicoloured . . 65 25

424 Teacher and Children

425 Pre-Columbian Gold Frog and Spanish Coin

1989. Obligatory Tax. Christmas. Children's Village.
1495 **424** 1col. blue, green & black 25 25

1989. 500th Anniv (1992) of Discovery of America by Columbus (3rd issue).
1496 **425** 4col. multicoloured . . . 25 15

426 "Exporting Coffee" (painting in theatre by Jose Villa)

427 Football in Cube

1990. Centenary of National Theatre.
1497 **426** 5col. multicoloured . . . 65 25

1990. World Cup Football Championship, Italy.
1498 **427** 5col. multicoloured . . . 25 15

428 "50 U"

1990. 50th Anniv of University of Costa Rica.
1499 **428** 18col. multicoloured . . 65 25

429 "Education Democracy Peace"

431 Painting by Juan Ramirez

1990. Patriotic Symbols.
1500 **429** 100col. blue and black 2·10 90
1501 – 200col. multicoloured . . 4·50 1·40
1502 – 500col. multicoloured . . 9·75 4·75
DESIGNS: 200col. Map of Costa Rica in national colours; 500col. State arms.

1991. Air. No. 1491 optd **LEY 7097 CORREO AEREO**.
1503 **420** 50col. multicoloured . . 1·60 55

1990. Costa Rican Coffee.
1504 **431** 50col. multicoloured . . 2·10 50

432 Penny Black

433 Heredia Hospital

1990. 150th Anniv of the Penny Black.
1505 **432** 50col. black and blue . . 1·80 50

1990. Hospital Centenaries.
1506 **433** 50col. blue, orge & grn 1·20 30
1507 – 100col. orange, bl & grn 2·50 65
DESIGN: 100col. National Psychiatric Hospital.

434 Yellow-bark Tree ("Tabebuia ochracea")

436 "Banana Picker" (Alleardo Villa, Ceiling of Grand Staircase)

1990. America. The Natural World. Mult.
1508 18col. Scarlet macaw ("Ara macao") 55 15
1509 18col. Buffon's macaw ("Ara ambigua") 55 15
1510 24col. Carao tree ("Cassia grandis") 80 40
1511 24col. Type **434** 80 40

1990. Obligatory Tax. Children's Village. No. 1490 optd **LEY 7157 PRO-CIUDAD DE LOS NINOS 1990**.
1512 **419** 10col. multicoloured . . 30 25

1991. Air. Paintings in National Theatre.
1516 **436** 30col. multicoloured . . 1·40 40

437 Costa Rica and Panama Flags and Seals

439 Route of First Voyage on Stone Globe

1991. 50th Anniv of Costa Rica–Panama Boundary Treaty.
1517 **437** 10col. multicoloured . . 25 15
1518 – 10col. black and blue . . 25 15
1519 – 10col. blue, brown & blk 25 15
DESIGNS: No. 1518. Presidents meeting: 1519, Map.

1991. Air. "Exfilcori '91" National Stamp Exhibition. No. 1501 optd **Aereo EXFILCORI '91**.
1520 200col. multicoloured . . . 7·00 1·80

1991. 500th Anniv (1992) of Discovery of America by Columbus (4th issue).
1521 **439** 4col. red, black and blue 80 15

1991. Air. Centenary of Basketball. No. 1474 optd **CENTENARIO DEL BALONCESTO CORREO AEREO**.
1522 20col. multicoloured . . . . 2·75 80

1991. Nos. 1482 and 1342 surch.
1523 **416** 1col. on 2col. mult . . . 30 15
1524 – 3col. on 8col.50 mult . . 30 15

443 Dr. Rafael Angel Calderon Guardia Hospital

444 Child praying

1991. Air. 50th Anniv of Social Security Administration.
1525 **443** 15col. multicoloured . . 1·30 30

1991. Obligatory Tax. Christmas. Children's Village.
1526 **444** 10col. blue 90 25

445 "La Poesia" (Vespaciano Bignami)

446 Benito Serrano Jimenez

1992. Air. Paintings in National Theatre.
1527 **445** 35col. multicoloured . . 3·25 80

1992. Former Presidents of Supreme Court of Justice. Multicoloured.
1528 5col. Type **446** 25 15
1529 5col. Luis Davila Solera . . 25 15
1530 5col. Fernando Baudrit Solera 25 15
1531 5col. Alejandro Alvarado Garcia 25 15

447 Oxcart

448 Dr. Solon Nunez Frutos (public health pioneer)

1992. 25th Anniv of National Directorate of Community Development.
1532 **447** 15col. multicoloured . . 1·50 30

1992.
1533 **448** 15col. black and red . . 95 30

449 Total Solar Eclipse

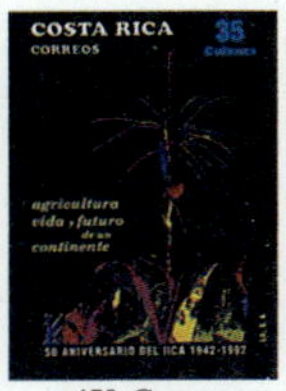

450 Crops

1992. International Space Year. Mult.
1534 45col. Type **449** . . . . . . 1·60 50
1535 45col. Post office building and total eclipse . . . . 1·60 50
1536 45col. Partial eclipse . . . . 1·60 50

1992. 50th Anniv of Inter-American Institute for Agricultural Co-operation.
1537 **450** 35col. multicoloured . . 1·40 40

451 "Nina"

452 Waterfall

1992. Air. 500th Anniv of Discovery of America by Columbus (5th issue). Multicoloured.
1538 45col. Type **451** 80 50
1539 45col. "Santa Maria" . . . 80 50
1540 45col. "Pinta" 80 50

1992. 450th Anniv of Discovery of Coco Island. Multicoloured.
1541 2col. Type **452** 20 10
1542 15col. View of cliffs from sea 40 15

453 Drilling

454 American Chameleon

1992. Obligatory Tax. Christmas. Children's Village.
1543 **453** 10col. red 25 15

1992. America. Coco Island Fauna. Mult.
1544 15col. Type **454** . . . . . . 1·20 25
1545 35col. Cocos finch . . . . . 2·75 40

1992. Centenary of Limon. No. 1500 optd **CENTENARIO DE LIMON**.
1546 **429** 100col. blue and black 2·00 95

456 "Allegory of the Fine Arts" (detail, R. Fontana)

457 Emblem

1993. Paintings in National Theatre.
1547 **456** 20col. multicoloured . . 80 25

1993. Air. International Arts Festival.
1548 **457** 45col. multicoloured . . 1·40 50

1993. No. 1494 surch.
1549 **423** 5col. on 18col. mult . . 40 15

459 Common Dolphin

460 Emblem

1993. Dolphins. Multicoloured.
1550 10col. Type **459** 90 25
1551 20col. Striped dolphins . . . 1·80 25

1993. 40th Anniv of Civil Service Statute.
1552 **460** 5col. multicoloured . . . 30 25

461 Anniversary Emblem

462 Communication Zone

1993. 50th Anniv of Chamber of Industry.
1553 **461** 45col. multicoloured . . 1·40 90

1993. 25th Anniv of University of Costa Rica School of Communication and Sciences.
1554 **462** 20col. black, red & blue 50 30

463 "Passiflora vitifolia"

1993. Tropical Rainforest Flora. Mult.
1555 2col. Type **463** 30 15
1556 35col. "Gurania megistantha" 90 55

464 Campaigners

465 Association Emblem

1993. 50th Anniv of Guaranteed Social Rights.
1557 **464** 20col. multicoloured . . 50 30

1993. 15th International Customs Officers' Associations Congress.
1558 **465** 45col. multicoloured . . 1·10 75

466 Carpentry

467 Dish Aerial

1993. Obligatory Tax. Christmas. Children's Village.
1559 **466** 10col. multicoloured . . 25 15

1993. Air. 30th Anniv of Costa Rican Electrical Institute's Responsibility for Development of Telecommunications.
1560 **467** 45col. multicoloured . . 1·10 75

468 Prof. Castro

469 Assembly Hall

1993. Birth Centenary of Miguel Angel Castro Carazo (founder of Commercial School).
1561 **468** 20col. red and blue . . . 65 30

1993. 150th Anniv of Costa Rica University Faculty of Law.
1562 **469** 20col. multicoloured . . 50 30

470 "The Dancer" (Adriatico Froli)

471 Mural (Luis Feron)

1994. National Theatre.
1563 **470** 20col. multicoloured . . 50 30

1994. Air. 150th Anniv of Ministry of Government and Police.
1564 **471** 45col. multicoloured . . 1·10 75

472 Flamingo Tongue

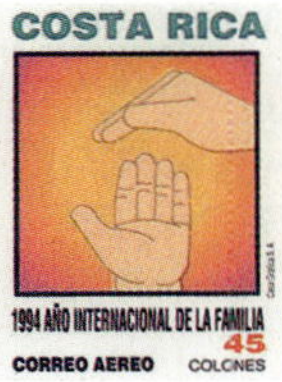

473 Hands forming Shelter

1994. Marine Animals. Multicoloured.
1565 5col. Type **472** 30 15
1566 10col. "Ophioderma rubicundum" 50 15
1567 15col. Black-barred soldierfish 75 25
1568 20col. King angelfish . . . 95 30
1569 35col. Creole-fish . . . . . 1·60 55
1570 45col. "Tubastraea coccinea" . . . . 2·10 75
1571 50col. "Acanthaster planci" 2·40 80
1572 55col. "Ocypode sp." . . . 2·75 90
1573 70col. Speckled balloon-fish 3·75 1·10
MS1574 60 × 70 mm. 100col. "Thalassoma lucasnum" . . . 4·75 4·75

1994. Air. International Year of the Family.
1575 **473** 45col. multicoloured . . 1·10 1·10

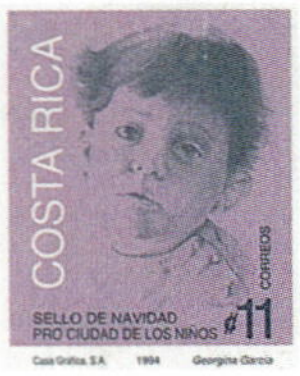

474 Child

1994. Obligatory Tax. Christmas. Children's Village.
1576 **474** 11col. green and lilac . . 15 15

475 Courier

1994. America. Postal Transport. Details of an illustration from "Album de Figueroa". Each orange, light orange and blue.
1577 20col. Type **475** 30 30
1578 20col. Rear of pack ox . . . 30 30
Nos. 1577/8 were issued together in se-tenant pairs with intervening label, each strip forming a composite design.

476 "Federico" (Luis Delgado)

477 Antonio Jose de Sucre (President of Bolivia. 1826–28)

1995. 90th Anniv of Rotary International.
1579 **476** 20col. multicoloured . . 90 40

1995. Anniversaries. Multicoloured.
1580 10col. Type **477** (birth bicentenary) 25 25
1581 30col. Jose Marti (poet and Cuban revolutionary) (death centenary) 65 65

478 "Rider" (sculpture, Nestor Varela)

480 "The Boy and the Cloud" (Francisco Amighetti)

1995. 50th Anniv of Guanacaste Institute.
1582 **478** 50col. green, blk & gold 1·10 1·10

1995. No. 1561 surch **5**.
1583 **468** 5col. on 20col. red & bl 25 25

1995. 50th Anniv of UNO.
1584 **480** 5col. multicoloured . . . 25 25

481 Woman holding Baby

482 "January"

1995. Obligatory Tax. Christmas. Children's Village.
1585 **481** 12col. multicoloured . . 55 25
MS1586 95 × 90 mm. No. 1585 plus 5 labels illustrating printing stages 3·50 3·50

1995. 13th National Stamp Exn. Seasonal paintings by Lola Fernandez. Multicoloured.
1587 50col. Type **482** . . . . . . 1·10 1·10
1588 50col. "November" . . . . 1·10 1·10

483 Jabiru

1995. America. Environmental Protection. Multicoloured.
1589 30col. Type **483** 65 65
1590 40col. Coastline 90 90
1591 40col. Woodland and lake 90 90
1592 50col. Leaf-cutting ant . . . 1·20 1·20
MS1593 100 × 70 mm. Nos. 1589/92 6·00 6·00

484 Steam Locomotive

1996. Postcards from Limon. Multicoloured.
1594 30col. Type **484** 65 65
1595 30col. Freighter at quay . . 65 65
1596 30col. View of Port Moin 65 65
1597 30col. "Fruitsellers" (Diego Villalobos) 65 65
1598 30col. "Calypso" (Jorge Esquivel) 65 65

485 Douglas DC-3

1996. Air. 50th Anniv of LACSA (national airline). Multicoloured.
1599 5col. Type **485** 25 25
1600 10col. Curtiss C-46 Commando 25 25
1601 20col. Beechcraft 40 40
1602 30col. Douglas DC-6B . . . 65 65
1603 35col. B.A.C. One Eleven 75 75
1604 40col. Convair CV 440 Metropolitan 90 90
1605 45col. Lockheed L.188 Electra 95 95
1606 50col. Boeing 727-200 . . . 1·10 1·10
1607 55col. Douglas DC-8 . . . 1·20 1·20
1608 60col. Airbus Industrie A320 1·30 1·30

486 Mosque, Synagogue and Christian Church

1996. 3000th Anniv of Jerusalem.
1609 **486** 30col. multicoloured . . 65 45

487 Maria del Milagro Paris and Francisco Rivas

1996. Olympic Games, Atlanta. Costa Rican Swimmers. Multicoloured.
1610 5col. Type **487** 15 10
1611 5col. Sylvia Poll and Federico Yglesias 15 10
1612 5col. Claudia Poll and Alfredo Cruz 15 10
Nos. 1610/12 were issued together, se-tenant, forming a composite design of a swimming pool.

488 Juana del Castillo (wife of Jose Maria Castro)

489 Water Droplet and Leaves

1996. 175th Anniv of Independence. Mult.
1613 30col. Type **488** 55 40
1614 30col. Juan Mora (President, 1849–59) 55 40
1615 30col. Jose Maria Castro (President, 1847–49 and 1866–68) 55 40
1616 30col. Pacifica Fernandez (wife of Juan Mora) . . . 55 40

1996. "Water is Life". 35th Anniv of Aqueducts and and Sewers.
1617 **489** 15col. multicoloured . . 30 25

490 "Christmas Carol" (J. M. Sanchez)

491 "Countrywomen" (Gonzalo Morales)

1996. Obligatory Tax. Christmas. Children's Village.
1618 **490** 14col. red and yellow . . 55 25

1996. America. Traditional Costumes. Mult.
1619 45col. Type **491** 90 55
1620 45col. "Lemon Black" (Manuel de la Cruz Gonzalez) (horiz) 90 55

492 Procession passing Palm-topped Wall

494 Child and Man listening to Radio

493 Class, 1930s

1997. Entrance of the Saints, San Ramon. Details of a painting by Jorge Carvajal. Multicoloured.
1621 30col. Type **492** 55 30
1622 30col. Church on hill behind procession 55 30
1623 30col. Procession passing beneath tree 55 30
Nos. 1621/3 were issued together, se-tenant, forming a composite design of the painting.

1997. Centenary of School of Fine Arts.
1624 **493** 50col. multicoloured . . 1·10 45

1997. 50th Anniv of Radio Nederland.
1625 **494** 45col. multicoloured . . 80 50

495 Postmen

1997. America. The Postman. 14th National Stamp Exhibition.
1626 **495** 30col. multicoloured . . 40 30

496 Church (Roberto Cambronero)

497 Antonio Obando Chan (bust, Olger Villegas)

1997. Bicentenary of Church of the Immaculate Conception, Heredia.
1627 **496** 50col. multicoloured . . 1·10 60

1997. Obligatory Tax. Christmas. Children's Village.
1628 **497** 15col. multicoloured . . 30 30

498 Arche de la Defense and Ball

1998. World Cup Football Championship, France.
1629 **498** 50col. black, blue & red 1·10 80

499 Figueres demolishing Fort Bellavista's Walls

1998. 50th Anniv of Second Republic. Mult.
1630 10col. Type **499** 50 20
1631 30col. Pres. Jose Figueres . . 75 20
1632 45col. Type **499** . . . . . . 1·10 20
1633 50col. Sledgehammer destroying wall . . . . . 1·20 30
MS1634 120 × 91 mm. Nos. 1631 and 1633 . . . . 1·80 1·80

500 "Caligo memnon"

1998. Butterflies. Multicoloured.
1635 10col. Type **500** 30 20
1636 15col. Emperor 30 30
1637 20col. Orange swallowtail 50 35
1638 30col. Malachite 75 55
1639 35col. Great southern white 90 65
1640 40col. "Parides iphidamas" 95 75
1641 45col. "Smyrna blonfildia" 1·10 80
1642 50col. "Callicore pitheas" 1·20 90
1643 55col. Orion . . . . 1·40 1·00
1644 60col. Monarch . . . . . . 1·50 1·20

501 "Generation of Knowledge" (Julio Escamez)

502 Carmen Lyra (writer)

1998. 25th Anniv of National University, Heredia.
1645 **501** 50col. multicoloured . . 1·20 80

1998. America. Famous Women.
1646 **502** 50col. orange, brown and ochre 65 45

503 Poinsettias

504 Gandhi

1998. Obligatory Tax. Christmas. Children's Village. Multicoloured (except No. 1649).
1647 16col. Poinsetta (gold background) 40 40
1648 16col. Type **503** 40 40
1649 16col. Berries on branch (green, black and red) . . 40 40

1998. 50th Death Anniv of Mahatma Gandhi.
1650 **504** 50col. multicoloured . . 1·00 60

505 South American Red-lined Turtle

1998. 50th Anniv of International Nature Protection Union. Turtles. Multicoloured.
1651 60col. Type **505** . . . . . . 1·50 1·50
1652 70col. Mexican red turtle ("Rhinoclemmys pulcherrima") . . . . . . 1·60 1·60
1653 70col. Snapping turtle ("Chelydra serpentina") 1·60 1·60

506 Common Morel

1999. Fungi. Multicoloured.
1654 50col. Type **506** 90 90
1655 50col. Cep (*Boletus edulis*) 90 90

507 Boy

1999. 50th Anniv of SOS Children's Villages.
1656 **507** 50col. multicoloured . . 1·00 55

508 Man minding Cart outside Telephone Box

509 Sanabria Martinez

1999. 50th Anniv of National Electricity Corporation.
1657 **508** 75col. multicoloured . . 65 45

1999. Birth Centenary of Victor Sanabria Martinez (Archbishop of San Jose).
1658 **509** 300col. violet . . . . . 2·50 2·10

510 Elderly Woman with Children (poster, Fernando Francia)

512 Village and Children

511 Woman helping Children

1999. International Year of the Elderly.
1659 **510** 50col. multicoloured . . 40 30

1999. 50th Anniv of Supreme Elections Tribunal.
1660 **511** 70col. multicoloured . . 65 45

1999. Obligatory Tax. Christmas. Children's Village.
1661 **512** 17col. multicoloured . . 25 25

513 Granados

1999. Carmen Granados Death Commemoration.
1662 **513** 50col. multicoloured . . 50 30

514 Woman holding Head

515 Globe

1999. America. A New Millennium without Arms. Multicoloured.
1663 50col. Type **514** 40 30
1664 70col. Man 65 40

1999. 125th Anniv of Universal Postal Union.
1665 **515** 75col. multicoloured . . 75 45

516 Orchid

1999. "Philexfrance 99" International Stamp Exhibition, Paris. Multicoloured.
1666 300col. Type **516** . . . . . 2·75 1·80
1667 300col. Orchid and Eiffel Tower . . . . 2·75 1·80

517 Jaguar

2000. 50th Anniv of Central Bank of Costa Rica. Multicoloured.
1668 60col. Type **517** 80 60
1669 60col. Scorpion 80 60
1670 60col. Bat 80 60
1671 60col. Crab 80 60
1672 60col. Dragon 80 60
1673 90col. Obverse and reverse of ½-escudo gold coin, 1825 . . . . 1·40 1·00
1674 90col. Obverse and reverse of ½-unze gold coin, 1850 1·40 1·00
1675 90col. Obverse and reverse of ½-peso silver coin, 1850 1·40 1·00
1676 90col. Obverse and reverse of 20 pesos gold coin, 1873 . . . . 1·40 1·00
1677 90col. Obverse and reverse of 1-colon coin, 1900 . . 1·40 1·00

518 Taekwondo

519 Rafael Calderon Guardia

2000. Olympic Games, Sydney. Multicoloured.
1678 60col. Type **518** 65 40
1679 60col. Cycling 65 40
1680 60col. Swimming 65 40
1681 60col. Football 65 40
1682 70col. Running 75 50
1683 70col. Boxing 75 50
1684 70col. Gymnastics 75 50
1685 70col. Tennis 75 50

Stamps of the same value were issued together, se-tenant, in blocks of four stamps, each block forming the composite design of a map of Australia with the sport appearing within the outline of the map.

2000. Birth Centenary of Rafael Angel Calderon Guardia (politician).
1686 **519** 100col. blue 80 30

520 "Fisherman in Cojimar"

2000. Birth Centenary of Max Jiminez (artist). Multicoloured.
1687 50col. Type **520** 60 40
1688 50col. "Adamant" 60 40

521 Child's Face

522 Family

2000. Obligatory Tax. Christmas. Children's Village.
1689 **521** 20col. green 30 30
1690 20col. red 30 30
1691 20col. blue 30 30
1692 20col. brown 30 30

2000. AIDS Awareness. Multicoloured.
1693 60col. Type **522** 55 30
1694 90col. Man between blocks of colour . . . . 1·10 60

523 Nativity Scene

2000. Christmas.
1695 **523** 100col. multicoloured . . 1·10 80

524 Cocos Cuckoo (*Coccyzus ferruginous*)

2001. America. UNESCO. World Heritage Sites. Coco Island. Birds. Multicoloured.
1696 95col. Type **524** . . . . . . 1·60 1·20
1697 115col. Cocos finch (*Pinaroloxias inornata*) . . 1·90 1·60

525 Cart and Windmill (½-size illustration)

2001. 150th Anniv of Costa Rica–Netherlands Co-operation Treaty.
1698 **525** 65col. multicoloured . . 65 50

2001. No. 1502 surch.
1699 65col. on 500col. multicoloured 65 55
1700 80col. on 500col. multicoloured 80 70
1701 95co. on 500col. multicoloured 95 80

2001. No. 1602 surch **C5.00**.
1702 5col. on 30col. multicoloured 25 15

528 Guaria Turrialba (*Cattleya dowiana*)

2001. Spain–Costa Rican Stamp Exhibition, San Jose. Orchids. Multicoloured.
1703 65col. Type **528** 80 65
1704 65col. "Trichophilia" . . . 80 65

529 Boy pushing Furniture on Barrow

2001. Child Labour Eradication Campaign.
1705 **529** 100col. multicoloured . . 1·10 80

530 Child holding Stamp and Magnifier

2001. Obligatory Tax. Christmas. Children's Village. Multicoloured, colour of right-hand title panel given.
1706 **530** 21col. violet 30 30
1707 21col. green 30 30
1708 21col. red 30 30
1709 21col. yellow 30 30

531 Steam Locomotive and Tomas Guardia

2001. Tomas Guardia (former President and railway pioneer) Commemoration.
1710 **531** 65col. multicoloured . . 80 55

2002. No. 1501 surch **65**.
1711 65col. on 200col. multicoloured 65 50

534 National Team Members (½-size illustration)

2002. World Cup Football Championship, Japan and South Korea.
1712 **534** 65col. multicoloured . . 65 50

535 Group Emblem

536 Children and Globe

2002. 16th Rio Group Conference, San Jose.
1713 **535** 65col. blue and green . . 75 50

2002. America. Literacy Campaign. Multicoloured.
1714 65col. Type **536** 75 40
1715 100col. Woman reading Braille . . . . 1·10 65
Nos. 1714/15 have Braille letters embossed at lower edge.

537 Bridge

2002. Inauguration of Bridge over River Tempisque.
1716 **537** 95c. multicoloured . . . 1·10 80

538 Two Women and Man

2002. Centenary of Pan American Health Organization. Multicoloured.
1717 10cols. Type **538** 25 10
1718 10cols. Centenary emblem 25 10
1719 10cols. Woman and child 25 10
1720 10cols. Boy and man . . . 25 10
1721 50cols. As No. 1718 . . . . 55 40
Nos. 1717/20 were issued together, se-tenant, forming a composite design.

539 World Trade Centre, New York, U.S.A.

2002. 1st Anniv of Attack on World Trade Centre, New York.
1722 **539** 110cols. multicoloured 1·20 1·10
No. 1722 has Braille letters embossed at lower edge.

540 *Lirope tetraphylla* (inscr "tetraphyla")

2002. Uvita Island. Multicoloured.
1723 75cols. Type **540** . . . . . 1·20 1·20
1724 75cols. *Ulva lactuca* . . . . 1·20 1·20
1725 75cols. *Cittarium pica* . . . 1·20 1·20
1726 75cols. *Gorgona flabellum* . . 1·20 1·20
Nos. 1723/6 are embossed with Braille letters.

541 Laughing Child

2002. Obligatory Tax. Christmas. Children's Village. Multicoloured, colour of title panel given.
1727 **541** 22col. violet 30 30
1728 22col. blue 30 30
1729 22col. orange 30 30
1730 22col. green 30 30

542 *Archocentrus sajica*

2003. America. Fauna. Multicoloured.
1731 110col. Type **542** . . . . . 2·00 1·20
1732 110col. *Asatheros diquis* . . 2·00 1·20
Nos. 1731/2 are embossed with Braille letters.

543 Small Island

2003. 25th Anniv of Coco Island National Park. Multicoloured.
1733 75c. Type **543** . . . . . . 1·20 75
1734 75c. Bay and coastline . . . 1·20 75
Nos. 1733/4 are embossed with Braille letters.

544 Franklin Ramon Chang-Diaz

2003. Franklin Ramon Chang-Diaz (astronaut). Multicoloured.
1735 75col. Type **544** . . . . . . 1·50 1·10
1736 75col. *Phanaeus changdiazi* 1·50 1·10
Nos. 1735/6 were issued together, se-tenant, each pair forming a composite design. Nos. 1735/6 are embossed with Braille letters.

545 Cocori and Turtle

2003. *Cocori* (children's story written by Joaquin Gutierrez and illustrated by Hugo Diaz). Multicoloured.
1737 25col. Type **545** 50 30
1738 25col. Cocori looking into water 50 30
1739 25col. Toucan 50 30
1740 25col. Girl and Cocori . . . 50 30
1741 25col. Cocori and bird . . . 50 30
1742 25col. With father and animals 50 30
1743 25col. With monkey and turtle 50 30
1744 25col. Monkey with raised paws, turtle and Cocori 50 30
1745 25col. With mother 50 30
1746 25col. Picking flowers with mother 50 30
Nos. 1737/46 are embossed with Braille letters.

546 Jose Maria Zeledon Brenes (lyricist)

547 Pope John Paul II

2003. Centenary of National Anthem Lyrics. Multicoloured.
1747 75col. Type **546** . . . . . 1·40 85
1748 75col. Text (50 × 35 mm) . . 1·40 85
Nos. 1747/8 were issued together, se-tenant, forming a composite design.

2003. 25th Anniv of Pontificate of Pope John Paul II.
1749 **547** 130col. multicoloured . . 2·50 1·80

548 Children and Star

2003. Obligatory Tacol. Christmas. Children's Village. Multicoloured, colour of title panel given.
1750 **548** 23col. mauve 40 20
1751 23col. green 40 20
1752 23col. vermilion 40 20
1753 23col. yellow 40 20

549 Charles Lindbergh and *Spirit of St. Louis*

2003. 75th Anniv of Charles Lindbergh's Arrival in Costa Rica.
1754 **549** 110col. multicoloured . . 2·10 1·60
No. 1754 is embossed with Braille letters.

550 Ruins and Wall

2003. Guayabo de Turrialba Archaeological Site.
1755 **550** 110col. multicoloured . . 2·10 1·60
No. 1755 is embossed with Braille letters.

551 *Tetranema floribundum*

2004. America. Native Fauna and Flora. Trees. Multicoloured.
1756 75col. Type **551** . . . . . . 1·40 85
1757 75col. *Ceiba pentandra* . . . 1·40 85
1758 90col. *Ceiba pentandra* (different) . . . . 1·80 1·20
1759 110col. *Tetrenema gamboanum* . . . . . . 2·10 1·40

552 Arenal Volcano

2004. Volcanoes. Multicoloured.
1760 85col. Type **552** . . . . . . 1·70 1·00
1761 120col. Irazu . . . . 2·40 1·70
1762 140col. Poas . . . . 2·50 1·80

554 Miguel Rodriguez and Members Flags

2004. Inauguration of Miguel Angel Rodriguez as President of Organization of American States (OES).
1767 **554** 120col. multicoloured . . 2·40 1·75

555 Three Kings

2004. Obligatory Tacol. Christmas. Children's Village. Multicoloured, colour of title panel given.
1768 **555** 25col. yellow 50 30
1769 25col. green 50 30
1770 25col. violet 50 30
1771 25col. magenta 50 30

556 Centenary Emblem

2004. Centenary of FIFA (Federation Internationale de Football). Multicoloured.
1772 140p. Type **556** . . . . . . 2·50 1·80
1773 140p. Player and ball . . . 2·50 1·80

557 Frog

2005. Centenary of Rotary International. Mult.
1774 140p. Type **557** . . . . . . 2·50 1·80
1775 140p. Centenary emblem . . 2·50 1·80
1776 140p. Butterfly . . . . . . 2·50 1·80

558 Albert Einstein

2005. International Year of Physics.
1777 **558** 95col. scarlet . . . . . 1·90 1·30
1778 – 95col. brown . . . . . 1·90 1·30
DESIGN: No. 1778 Max Planck.

559 Pope Benedict XVI   **560** *Passiflora vitifolia*

2005. Pope Benedict XVI and Pope John Paul II. Each brown and ochre.
1779 140p. Type **559** . . . . . . 2·50 1·80
1780 140p. Pope John Paul II . . 2·50 1·80

2005. National Parks. Multicoloured.
1781 85p. Type **560** . . . . . . 1·70 1·00
1782 85p. *Dryas iulia moderata* 1·70 1·00
1783 85p. *Potos flavus* . . . . . 1·70 1·00

561 Child using Computer

2005. America. Struggle against Poverty.
1784 **561** 140p. olive and black . . 2·50 1·80
1785 – 140p. yellow and black 2·50 1·80
1786 – 140p. ochre and black 2·50 1·80
DESIGNS: No. 1785, Carpenter; 1786, Doctor.

562 Children   **563** Acrobats (sculpture)

2005. Obligatory Tax. Christmas. Children's Village. Multicoloured, colour of face value given.
1787 **562** 28col. white 50 30
1788 28col. ochre 50 30
1789 28col. brown 50 30
1790 28col. red 50 30

2006. Air. International Arts Festival.
1791 **563** 120col. multicoloured . . 2·40 1·70

564 Players (½-size illustration)

2006. Centenary of Club Sport Cartaginees.
1792 **564** 85col. multicoloured . . 1·70 1·30

565 Juan Raphael Mora (president 1849–59) and National Monument.

2006. 150th Anniv of "National Campaign" (to overthrow William Walker's mercenary army). Sheet 90×182 mm containing T **565** and similar horiz designs. Ochre and brown.
MS1793 85col.×5, Type **565**; Juan Santamaria monument and Meson de Guerra; Map of Central America (49×39 mm); General Jose Maria Cañias and Casa Santa Rosa; Luis Molina (ambassador to Washington) and Joaquin Bernardo Calvo (chancellor) 5·50 5·50
The stamps of **MS**1793 form a composite design.

566 Players

2006. World Cup Football Championship, Germany.
1794 **566** 120col. multicoloured . . 2·40 1·70

567 Globe as Electric Plug

2006. America. Energy Conservation.
1795 **567** 155col. multicoloured . . 2·70 2·10

568 *Sula sula*

2006. Isla del Coco National Park. Multicoloured.
1796 180col. Type **568** . . . . . 2·60 2·00
1797 180col. *Mycteroperca olfax* 2·60 2·00
1798 180col. *Zanclus cornutus* . . 2·60 2·00
1799 180col. *Eretmochelys imbricaas* . . . . 2·60 2·00
1800 180col. *Tursiops truncates* 2·60 2·00
1801 180col. *Myripristis berndti* 2·60 2·00
1802 180col. *Dendroica petechia aureola* . . . . 2·60 2·00
1803 180col. *Carcharhinus limbatus* . . . . 2·60 2·00
1804 180col. *Anous stolidus* . . . 2·60 2·00
1805 180col. *Acarus rubroviolaceus* . . . . 2·60 2·00

569 Jose Ferrer

2006. Birth Centenary of Jose Figueres Ferrer (president of Costa Rica, 1948—1949, 1953—1958 and 1970—1974.). Multicoloured.
1806 115col. Type **569** . . . . . 1·50 1·10
MS1807 89×60 mm. 1000col. As No. 1806. Imperf . . . . . . 12·00 12·00

570 *Bixa orellana*

2006. Forest Fruiting Trees. Multicoloured.
1808 155col. Type **570** . . . . . 2·50 1·80
1809 155col. *Garcinia intermedia* 2·50 1·80
1810 155col. *Hymenaea courbaril* 2·50 1·80

571 Flag

2006. Centenary of National Symbols. Mult.
1811 155col. Type **571** . . . . . 2·50 1·80
1812 155col. Arms . . . . 2·50 1·80

572 Child

2006. Obligatory Tax. Christmas. Children's Village. Multicoloured, colour of border given.
1813 **572** 32col. bistre 55 35
1814 32col. ochre 55 35
1815 32col. green 55 35
1816 32col. yellow 55 35

573 Francisco Orlich

2007. Birth Centenary of Francisco Jose Orlich Bolmarcich (president, 1962–66).
1817 **573** 115cols. multicoloured 1·50 1·10

574 *Guarianthe skinneri*

2007. Orchids. Multicoloured.
1818 180cols. Type **574** . . . . . 2·60 2·00
1819 180cols. Inscr 'Galenandra arundinis' . . . . 2·60 2·00
1820 180cols. *Encyclia ossenbachiana* . . . . . . 2·60 2·00
1821 180cols. *Dracula inexperata* 2·60 2·00
1822 180cols. *Guarianthe skinneri* (different) . . . . 2·60 2·00
1823 180cols. *Kefersteinia retanae* 2·60 2·00
1824 180cols. Inscr 'Corianthes kaiseriana' . . . . 2·60 2·00
1825 180cols. *Psychopsis krameriana* . . . . 2·60 2·00
1826 180cols. *Chonroscaphe yamilethae* . . . . 2·60 2·00
1827 180cols. *Cattleya dowiana* 2·60 2·00
MS1828 90×60 mm.1000cols. *Brassia suavissima*. Imperf . . 12·00 12·00

575 Giovanni Melchior Bosco (Don Bosco) (founder)   **576** Frog-shaped Gold Pendant

2007. Centenary of the Salesian Society in Costa Rica.
1829 **575** 110cols. multicoloured 1·20 90

2007. Pre-Colombian Art. Multicoloured.
1830 155cols. Type **576** . . . . . 2·50 1·80
1831 155cols. Bird-shaped jade pendant . . . . 2·50 1·50
1832 155cols. Carved stone panel (*horiz*) . . . . 2·50 1·80
1833 155cols. Ceramic burner with lizard . . . . 2·50 1·80
1834 155cols. Male stone figure 2·50 1·80

577 Students and Teacher

2007. America. Education for All. Multicoloured.
1835 115cols. Type **577** . . . . . 2·50 1·80
1836 155cols. Family . . . . . . 2·50 1·80

578 Space Walk by Ramon Chang-Diaz (Costa Rican born astronaut and plasma specialist)

2007. Plasma Technology. Multicoloured.
1837 240cols. Type **578** . . . . . 4·75 3·50
1838 240cols. Plasma symbol . . 4·75 3·50

579 La Negrita (statue)

2007. La Negrita (Costa Rica's patron saint), Basilica Virgin de Los Angeles, Cartago. Multicoloured.
1839 115cols. Type **579** . . . . . 2·50 1·80
1840 115cols. Enclosed in reliquary . . . . 2·50 1·80
Nos. 1839/40 were issued together, *se-tenant*, forming a composite background design.
No. **MS**1841 has been left for miniature sheet not yet received.

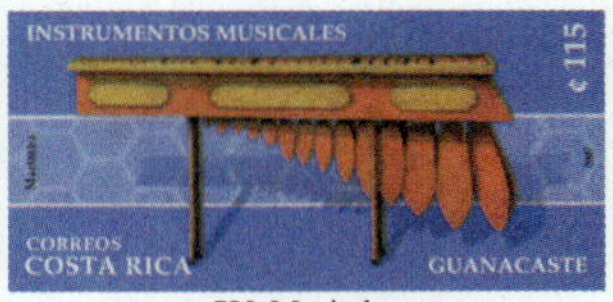

580 Marimba

2007. Musical Instruments. Multicoloured.
1842 115cols. Type **580** . . . . . 2·50 1·80
1843 115cols. Quijongo (*vert*) . . 2·50 1·80
MS1841 100×150 mm. 1000cols. Shrine (75×115 mm) . . . . . 12·00 12·00

Nos. 1844/7 and Type **581** have been left for 'National Parks', issued on 17 August 2007, not yet received.

582 Cyclist

2007. Special Olympic Games, Shanghai. Mult.
1848 240cols. Type **582** . . . . . 4·75 3·50
1849 240cols. Swimmer . . . . . 4·75 3·50
1850 240cols. Runner . . . . . . 4·75 3·50

583 *Por qe Tio Conejo las orejas largas* (Why has Tio Conejo such long ears?)

2007. *Cuentos de mia Tía Panchita* (Tales of My Aunt Panchita) (children's stories by Carmen Lyra (Maria Isabela Carvajal)). Two sheets containing T **583** and similar multicoloured designs.
MS1851 94×40 mm. 100cols×4, Type **583**; *La Mica* (the monkey); *Uvieta* (the grapevine); *Tio Conejo y los caites de su abuela* (Tio Conejo and his grandmother's shoes) . . . . 8·00 8·00
MS1852 90×60 mm.1000cols. *De como Tio Conejo salio de un apuro* (Tio Conejo left in a hurry) (79×49 mm.) . . . . 12·00 12·00
The stamps and margins of **MS**1851 form a composite design.

EXPRESS DELIVERY STAMPS

E 237 New UPU Headquarters Building and Emblem

1970. Air. New UPU Headquarters Building.

E841	E 237	35c. multicoloured	55	25
E842		60c. multicoloured	70	25

In Type E 237 "ENTREGA INMEDIATA" is in the form of a perforated tab.

No. E842 has the same main design, but the tab is inscr "EXPRES".

E 249 Winged Letter

1972.

E888	E 249	75c. brown & red	35	35
E889		75c. green & red	35	35
E890		75c. mauve & red	1·60	75
E891		1col.50 blue & red	50	40

E 279 Concorde

1976.

E1031	E 279	1col. multicoloured	50	40
E1135	–	2col. multicoloured	80	45
E1136	–	2col. multicoloured	75	45
E1137	–	4col. multicoloured	65	40

Nos. E1135/7 is as Type E 279, but inscribed "EXPRESS".

OFFICIAL STAMPS

Various issues optd **OFICIAL** except where otherwise stated.

1883. Stamps of 1883.

O35	8	1c. green	1·20	55
O36		2c. red	1·20	50
O22		5c. violet	7·25	3·00
O23		10c. orange	9·75	4·00
O38		40c. blue	1·20	50

1887. Stamps of 1887.

O39	14	5c. violet	12·00	3·50
O40		10c. orange	85	50

1889. Stamps of 1889.

O41	17	1c. brown	20	10
O42		2c. blue	20	10
O43		5c. orange	20	10
O44		10c. lake	20	10
O45		20c. green	30	10
O46		50c. red	1·30	1·30

1892. Stamps of 1892.

O47	19	1c. blue	25	15
O48		2c. orange	25	15
O49		5c. mauve	25	15
O50		10c. green	3·00	1·40
O51		20c. red	20	10
O52		50c. blue	60	55

1901. Stamps of 1901 (Nos. 42/48).

O53	1c. black and green	40	40
O54	2c. black and red	40	40
O61	4c. black and purple	1·40	1·30
O55	5c. black and blue	40	30
O62	6c. black and olive	1·60	1·60
O56	10c. black and brown	75	75
O57	20c. black and lake	1·10	1·10
O63	25c. brown and lilac	9·50	9·75
O58	50c. blue and red	7·75	3·75
O59	1col. black and olive	16·00	9·75

1903. Stamp of 1901 optd **PROVISORIO OFICIAL**.

O60	2c. black & red (No. 43)	2·75	2·75

1908. Stamps of 1907 (Nos. 57/76).

O77	1c. blue and brown	10	10
O78	2c. black and green	10	10
O79	4c. blue and red	10	10
O80	5c. blue and orange	10	10
O81	10c. black and blue	1·20	75
O82	25c. slate and lavender	30	20
O83	50c. blue and red	55	50
O84	1col. black and brown	1·20	1·10

1917. Stamps of 1910 optd **OFICIAL 15-VI-1917**.

O115	5c. orange (No. 80)	35	35
O116	10c. blue (No. 81)	20	20

1920. No. 82 surch **OFICIAL 15 CENTIMOS**.

O117	15c. on 20c. olive	55	55

1921. Official stamps of 1908 optd **1921–22** or surch also.

O123	4c. blue & red (No. O79)	40	40
O124	6c. on 1c. blue & brown (No. O77)	50	50
O125	20c. on 25c. slate and lavender (No. O82)	55	50
O126	50c. blue & red (No. O83)	2·40	2·00
O127	1col. black & brn (No. O84)	4·50	3·75

1921. No. O115 surch **10 CTS.**

O128	10c. on 5c. orange	45	40

1923. Stamps of 1923.

O137	77	2c. brown	10	10
O138		4c. green	10	10
O139		5c. blue	30	30
O140		20c. red	20	20
O141		1col. violet	45	45

O 95

1926.

O169	O 95	2c. black and blue	20	20
O231		2c. black and lilac	10	10
O170		3c. black and red	20	20
O232		3c. black and brown	10	10
O171		4c. black and blue	20	20
O233		4c. black and red	10	10
O172		5c. black and green	20	20
O173		6c. black and yellow	10	10
O235		8c. black and brown	10	10
O174		10c. black and red	20	20
O175		20c. black and green	20	20
O237		20c. black and blue	10	10
O176		30c. black and orange	20	20
O238		40c. black and orange	20	20
O177		45c. black and brown	20	20
O239		55c. black and lilac	30	30
O178		1col. black and lilac	35	35
O240		1col. black and brown	30	30
O241		2col. black and blue	65	65
O242		5col. black & yellow	3·00	3·00
O243		10col. blue and black	21·00	21·00

1934. Air. Air stamps of 1934.

O211	107	5c. green	20	20
O212		10c. red	20	20
O213		15c. brown	45	45
O214		20c. blue	75	75
O215		25c. orange	75	75
O216		40c. brown	90	75
O217		50c. black	90	75
O218		60c. yellow	1·10	90
O219		75c. violet	1·10	90
O220	–	1col. red	3·00	1·50
O221	–	2col. blue	6·25	4·50
O222	–	5col. black	8·75	7·75
O223	–	10col. brown	11·00	11·00

1936. Stamps of 1936.

O228	113	5c. green	20	20
O229		10c. red	20	20

POSTAGE DUE STAMPS

D 42

D 64

1903.

D55	D 42	5c. blue	6·75	1·10
D56		10c. brown	6·75	1·00
D57		15c. green	3·50	1·80
D58		20c. red	4·75	1·80
D59		25c. blue	4·75	2·30
D60		30c. brown	6·00	2·50
D61		40c. olive	6·75	2·50
D62		50c. red	6·75	2·40

1915.

D115	D 64	2c. orange	1·20	55
D116		4c. blue	1·20	55
D117		8c. green	1·20	55
D118		10c. violet	1·20	55
D119		20c. brown	1·20	55

CRETE Pt. 3

Former Turkish island in the E. Mediterranean under the joint protection of Gt. Britain, France, Italy and Russia from 1898 to 1908, when the island was united to Greece. This was recognized by Turkey in 1913. Greek stamps now used.

100 lepta = 1 drachma.

1 Hermes

2 Hera

3 Prince George of Greece

4 Talos

1900.

1	1	1l. brown	65	20
12		1l. yellow	55	55
2	2	5l. green	1·25	20
3	3	10l. red	2·00	20
4	2	20l. red	7·75	1·25
13		20l. orange	4·00	70
15	3	25l. blue	8·00	65
14	1	50l. blue	11·00	11·50
16		50l. lilac	26·00	16·00
17	4	1d. violet	26·00	16·00
18	–	2d. brown	8·00	6·00
19	–	5d. black and green	8·00	7·00

DESIGNS (as Type 4): 2d. Minos; 5d. St. George and Dragon.

ΠΡΟΣΩΡΙΝΟΝ
(7) ("Provisional")

1900. Optd as T 7.

5	3	25l. blue	2·00	1·40
6	1	50l. lilac	1·40	80
7	4	1d. violet	9·50	4·00
8	–	2d. brown (No. 18)	26·00	16·00
9	–	5d. black & green (No. 19)	60·00	70·00

1904. Surch **5** twice.

20	2	5 on 20l. orange	3·25	75

10 Rhea

12 Prince George of Greece

16 Europa and Jupiter

1905.

21	10	2l. lilac	1·40	30
22	–	5l. green	4·00	30
23	12	10l. red	4·00	30
24	–	20l. green	4·00	75
25	–	25l. blue	5·00	70
26	–	50l. brown	3·75	3·50
27	16	1d. sepia and red	65·00	50·00
28	–	3d. black and orange	45·00	28·00
29	–	5d. black and olive	32·00	13·50

DESIGNS—As Type 10: 5l. Europa; 20l. Miletus; 25l. Triton; 50l. Ariadne. As Type 16: 3d. Minos ruins. 44 × 28½ mm: 5d. Mt. Ida.

19 High Commissioner A. T. A. Zaimis

1907. Various designs.

30	19	25l. black and blue	35·00	1·40
31	–	1d. black and green	9·00	6·25

DESIGN—HORIZ: (larger): 1d. Landing of Prince George of Greece at Suda.

21 Hermes

ΕΛΛΑΣ
(22)
("Greece")

1908. Optd as T 22 in various sizes and styles.

32	1	1l. brown	40	20
33	10	2l. lilac	40	20
34	–	5l. green (No. 22)	55	20
35	3	10l. red	80	40
36	21	10l. red	2·40	65
37	–	20l. green (No. 24)	4·50	65
38	19	25l. black and blue	10·00	1·40
63	–	25l. blue (No. 25)	3·00	55
39	–	50l. brown (No. 26)	5·00	5·00
40	16	1d. sepia and red	65·00	55·00
52	–	1d. black & grn (No. 31)	11·00	11·00
41	–	2d. brown (No. 18)	9·50	9·50
42	–	3d. black & orge (No. 28)	40·00	28·00
43	–	5d. black & olive (No. 29)	40·00	24·00

1909. Optd with T 7 and 22 or surch with new value also.

44	1	1l. yellow (No. 12)	1·10	1·10
45	D 8	1l. red (No. D10)	1·10	1·10
46		2 on 20l. red (No. D73)	1·10	1·10
47		2 on 20l. red (No. D13)	1·10	1·10
48	2	5 on 20l. red (No. 4)	80·00	80·00
49		5 on 20l. orange (No. 13)	1·10	1·10

OFFICIAL STAMPS

O 21

1908.

O32	O 21	10l. red	15·00	1·40
O33		30l. blue	30·00	2·50

In the 30l. the central figures are in an oval frame.

1908. Optd with T 22.

O44	O 21	10l. red	16·00	1·40
O45		30l. blue	30·00	1·40

POSTAGE DUE STAMPS

D 8

1901.

D10	D 8	1l. red	45	50
D11		5l. red	1·10	40
D12		10l. red	1·10	25
D13		20l. red	1·50	70
D14		40l. red	12·00	11·00
D15		50l. red	12·00	11·00
D16		1d. red	12·00	11·00
D17		2d. red	13·00	11·00

1901. Surch "1 drachma" in Greek characters.

D18	D 8	1d. on 1d. red	8·75	8·00

1908. Optd with T 22.

D70	D 8	1l. red	25	30
D45		5l. red	1·00	20
D72		10l. red	55	25
D47		20l. red	2·50	80
D74		40l. red	8·00	7·50
D75		50l. red	11·00	10·00
D76		1d. red	18·00	18·00
D51		1d. on 1d. red (No. D18)	9·50	9·50
D52		2d. red	18·00	18·00

REVOLUTIONARY ASSEMBLY, 1905

In March, a revolt in favour of union with Greece began, organized by Venizelos with headquarters at Theriso, South of Canea. The revolt collapsed in November 1905.

V 1

V 2 Crete enslaved

1905. Imperf.

V1	V 1	5l. red and green	13·50	7·00
V2		10l. green and red	13·50	7·00
V3		20l. blue and red	13·50	7·00

V4		50l. green and violet	13·50	7·00
V5		1d. red and blue	13·50	7·00

1905.

V 6	V 2	5l. orange	40	1·10
V 7		10l. grey	40	1·10
V 8		20l. mauve	1·05	2·10
V 9		50l. blue	2·75	4·25
V10	–	1d. violet and red	4·25	4·25
V11	–	2d. brown and green	4·25	5·00

DESIGN: 1, 2d. King George of Greece.

CROATIA Pt. 3

Part of Hungary until 1918 when it became part of Yugoslavia. In 1941 it was proclaimed an independent state but in 1945 it became a constituent republic of the Federal People's Republic of Yugoslavia.

In 1991 Croatia became independent.

April 1941. 100 paras = 1 dinar.
Sept 1941. 100 banicas = 1 kuna.
1991. 100 paras = 1 dinar.
1994. 100 lipa = 1 kuna.

(1)

(2)

1941. Stamps of Yugoslavia optd as T 1 ("Independent Croat State").

1	99	50p. orange	1·00	2·25
2		1d. green	1·00	2·25
3		1d.50 red	1·00	1·00
4		2d. mauve	1·00	1·75
5		3d. brown	2·50	4·50
6		4d. blue	2·50	5·00
7		5d. blue	2·50	5·00
8		5d.50 violet	2·50	5·50

1941. Stamps of Yugoslavia optd as T 2.

9	99	25p. black	20	30
10		50p. orange	20	30
11		1d. green	20	30
12		1d.50 red	20	30
13		2d. pink	20	60
14		3d. brown	20	90
15		4d. blue	25	1·00
16		5d. blue	40	1·00
17		5d.50 violet	40	1·25
18		6d. blue	50	1·75
19		8d. brown	80	2·00
20		12d. violet	90	2·50
21		16d. purple	1·00	3·00
22		20d. blue	1·25	3·50
23		30d. pink	2·00	5·50

(3)

(4)

1941. Stamps of Yugoslavia surch as T 3.

24	99	1d. on 3d. brown	15	40
25		2d. on 4d. blue	15	40

1941. Founding of Croatian Army. Nos. 414/26 of Yugoslavia optd with T 4.

25a	99	25p. black		
25b		50p. orange		
25c		1d. green		
25d		1d.50 red		
25e		2d. pink		
25f		3d. brown		
25g		4d. blue		
25h		5d. blue		
25i		5d.50 violet		
25j		6d. blue		
25k		8d. brown		
25l		12d. violet		
25m		16d. purple		
25n		20d. blue		
25o		30d. pink		
		Set of 15	£150	£375

Sold at double face value.

1941. Stamps of Yugoslavia optd as T 2 but without shield.

26	109	1d.50+1d.50 black	5·00	10·00
27	–	4d.+3d. brown (No. 457)	5·00	10·00

1941. Postage Due stamps of Yugoslavia optd **NEZAVISNA DRZAVA HRVATSKA FRANCO.**

28	D 56	50p. violet	20	30
29		2d. blue	30	60
30		5d. orange	30	60
31		10d. brown	35	90

7 Mt. Ozalj

8 Banja Luka

1941.

32	7	25b. red	25	25
33	–	50b. green	10	10
34	–	75b. olive	10	10
35	–	1k. green	10	10
36	–	1k.50 green	10	10
37	–	2k. red	10	10
38	–	3k. red	10	10
39	–	4k. blue	10	10
40	–	5k. black	75	75
41	–	5k. blue	10	10
42	–	6k. olive	10	10
43	–	7k. orange	10	10
44	–	8k. brown	10	10
45	–	10k. violet	40	30
46	–	12k. brown	50	50
47	–	20k. brown	40	30
48	–	30k. brown	55	50
49	–	50k. green	1·00	1·00
50	8	100k. violet	1·60	2·25

DESIGNS: 50b. Waterfall at Jajce; 75b. Varazdin; 1k. Mt. Velebit; 1k.50, Zelenjak; 2k. Zagreb Cathedral; 3k. Church at Osijek; 4k. River Drina; 5k. (No. 40), Konjic Bridge; 5k. (No. 41), Modern building at Zemun; 6k. Dubrovnik; 7k. R. Save in Slavonia; 8k. Mosque at Sarajevo; 10k. Lake Plitvice; 12k. Klis Fortress near Split; 20k. Hvar; 30k. Harvesting in Syrmia; 50k. Senj.

9 Croat (Sinj) Costume

10 Emblems of Germany, Croatia and Italy

1941. Red Cross.

51	9	1k.50+1k.50 blue	35	60
52	–	2k.+2k. brown	35	70
53	–	5k.+4k. red	85	1·75

COSTUMES: 2k. Travnik. 4k. Turopolje.

1941. Eastern Volunteer Fund.

54	10	4k.+2k. blue	1·00	2·75

11 Glider

(12)

1942. Aviation Fund. Glider in flight as T 11.

55	11	2k.+2k. brown (vert)	40	60
56	–	2k.50+2k.50 green	60	1·00
57	–	3 k+3k. red (vert)	75	1·25
58	–	4k.+4k. blue	85	1·90

DESIGNS—HORIZ: 2k.50, Glider (different); 4k. Seaplane glider. VERT: 3k. Boy with model glider.

1942. 1st Anniv of Croat Independence. Optd with T 12.

59	2k. brown (as No. 37)	15	35
60	5k. red (as No. 40)	25	70
61	10k. green (as No. 45)	40	1·00

1942. Banja Luka Philatelic Exhibition. Inscr "F.I." in top right corner.

62	8	100k. violet	1·40	3·75

1942. Surch **0.25kn** and bar.

63	0.25k. on 2k. red (No. 37)	20	50

14 Trumpeters

15 Sestine (Croatia)

1942. National Relief Fund.

64	14	3k.+1k. red	40	1·00
65	–	4k.+2k. brown	60	1·10
66	–	5k.+5k. blue	80	1·90

DESIGNS—HORIZ: 4k. Procession beneath triumphal archways. VERT: 5k. Mother and child.

1942. Red Cross Fund. Peasant girls in provincial costumes.

67	15	1k.50+50b. brown	60	1·25
68	–	3k.+1k. violet	60	1·25
69	–	4k.+2k. blue	80	1·75
70	–	10k.+5k. bistre	1·00	2·10
71	15	13k.+6k. red	2·00	4·50

COSTUMES: 3k. Slavonia. 4k. Bosnia. 10k. Dalmatia.

15a Red Cross Sister

16 M. Gubec

1942. Charity Tax. Red Cross Fund. Cross in red.

71a	15a	1k. green	20	60

1942. Croat ("Ustascha") Youth Fund.

72	16	3k.+6k. red	25	70
73	–	4k.+7k. brown	25	70
MS73a		5k.+20k. blue (perf or imperf)	7·00	16·00

DESIGNS—VERT: Dr. A. Starcevic; 5k. Trumpet and flag.

17

19 Arms of Zagreb

1943. Labour Front. Vert designs showing workers as T 17.

74	17	2k.+1k. brown and olive	1·50	3·25
75	–	3k.+3k. brown & purple	1·50	3·25
76	–	7k.+4k. brown & grey	1·50	3·25

1943. 7th Centenary of Foundation of Zagreb.

77	19	3k.50 (+ 6k.50) blue	1·10	3·75

1943. Pictorial designs as T 8, but with views surrounded by frame line.

78	3k.50 brown	35	40
79	12k.50 black	35	70

DESIGNS: 3k.50, Trakoscan Castle; 12k.50, Veliki Tabor.

21 A. Pavelic

22 Krsto Frankopan

1943. Croat ("Ustascha") Youth Fund.

80	21	5k.+3k. red	15	65
81		7k.+5k. green	15	65
MS81a	21	12k.+8k. blue (perf or imperf)	8·50	20·00

1943. Famous Croats.

82	–	1k. blue	15	30
83	22	2k. olive	15	30
84	–	3k.50 red	15	50

PORTRAITS: 1k. Katarina Zrinska. 3k.50, Peter Zrinski.

23 Croat Sailor and Motor Torpedo Boats

1943. Croat Legion Relief Fund.

85	23	1k.+50b. green	10	25
86	–	2k.+1k. red	10	25
87	–	3k.50+1k.50 blue	10	25
88	–	9k.+4k.50 brown	10	25
MS88a		1k.+0k.50 blue; 2k.+1k. green; 3k.50+1k.50 blue; 9k.+4k.50 brown (perf or imperf)	2·50	5·00

DESIGNS: 2k. Pilot and Heinkel bomber; 3k.50, Infantrymen; 9k. Mechanized column.

24 St. Mary's Church and Cistercian Monastery, 1650

1943. Philatelic Exhibition, Zagreb.

89	24	18k.+9k. blue	1·40	4·00
MS89a		99 × 132 mm. 24 18k.+9k. black	5·00	12·00

1943. Return of Sibenik to Croatia. Optd **HRVATSKO MORE 8, IX. 1943.**

90	24	18k.+9k. blue	3·25	9·00

26 Nurse and Patient

26a

1943. Red Cross Fund.

91	–	1k.+50b. blue	20	50
92	–	2k.+1k. red	20	50
93	–	3k.50+1k.50 blue	20	50
94	26	8k.+3k. brown	20	50
95		9k.+4k. green	20	50
96	–	10k.+5k. violet	30	75
97	26	12k.+6k. blue	30	90
98	–	12k.50+6k. brown	50	1·25
99	26	18k.+8k. orange	75	1·90
100		32k.+12k. grey	1·25	2·75

DESIGN: 1k., 2k., 3k.50, 10k., 12k.50, Mother and children.

1943. Charity Tax. Red Cross Fund. Cross in red.

100a	26a	2k. blue	20	50

27 A. Pavelic

28 Ruder Boskovic

1943.

101	27	25b. red	10	15
105		50b. blue	10	15
102		75b. green	10	15
106		1k. green	10	15
107		1k.50 violet	10	15
108		2k. red	10	15
109		3k. red	10	15
110		3k.50 blue	10	15
111		4k. purple	10	15
103		5k. blue	10	15
112		8k. brown	10	15
113		9k. red	10	15
114		10k. purple	10	15
115		12k. brown	10	15
116		12k.50 black	10	15
117		18k. brown	10	15
104		32k. brown	10	15
118		50k. green	10	15
119		70k. orange	30	60
120		100k. violet	70	1·40

The design of the 25b., 75b., 5k., and 32k. is 20½ × 26 mm, the rest are 22 × 28 mm.

1943. Honouring Ruder Boskovic (astronomer).

121	28	3k.50 red	15	35
122		12k.50 purple	30	50

29 Posthorn

30 St. Sebastian

1944. Postal and Railway Employees' Relief Fund.

123	29	7k.+3k.50 brn, red & bis	20	40
124	–	16k.+8k. blue	20	50
125	–	24k.+12k. red	30	70
126	–	32k.+16k. black & red	65	1·10

DESIGNS—VERT: 16k. Dove, airplane and globe; 24k. Mercury. HORIZ: 32k. Winged wheel.

1944. War Invalids' Relief Fund.
127 **30** 7k.+3k.50 mauve & red . . 20 50
128 – 16k.+8k. green 25 70
129 – 24k.+12k. yell, brn & red 25 70
130 – 32k.+16k. blue . . . . . . 45 1·10
DESIGNS—HORIZ: 16k. Blind man and cripple; 32k. Death of Peter Svacic, 1094. VERT: 24k. Mediaeval statuette.

31 The Legion in Action

32 Jure-Ritter Francetic

1944. Croat Youth Fund. No. 134 perf, others imperf.
131 **31** 3k.50+1k.50 brown 10 15
132 – 12k.50+6k.50 blue 10 15
134 **32** 12k.50+287k.50 black . . . 3·50 11·50
133 18k.+9k. brown 10 15
DESIGN: No. 132, Sentries on the Drina.

33

1944. Labour Front. Inscr "D.R.S.".
135 **33** 3k.50+1k. red 10 20
136 – 12k.50+6k. brown 40 65
137 – 18k.+9k. blue 15 35
138 – 32k.+16k. green 15 35
MS138a 74 × 100 mm. 32k.+16k. (as No. 138) brown on yellow . . 1·50 4·50
DESIGNS: 12k.50, Digging; 18k. Instruction; 32k. "On Parade".

34 Bombed Home

35 War Victim

1944. Charity Tax. War Victims.
138b **34** 1k. green 10 15
138c **35** 2k. red 10 15
138d 5k. green 10 15
138e 10k. blue 15 35
138f 20k. brown 40 85

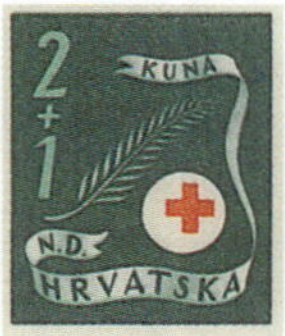

36

37 Storm Division Soldiers

1944. Red Cross. Cross in red.
139 **36** 2k.+1k. green 10 30
140 3k.50+1k.50 red 15 40
141 12k.50+6k. blue 20 50

1945. Creation of Croatian Storm Division on 9th October 1944.
142 **37** 50k.+50k. red and grey . . 42·00 £100
143 – 70k.+70k. sepia & grey . . 42·00 £100
144 – 100k.+100k. bl & grey . . 42·00 £100
MS144a 216 × 134 mm. Nos. 142/4 £600 £1400
DESIGNS: 70k. Storm Division soldiers in action; 100k. Divisional emblem.

38

39

1945. Postal Employees' Fund.
145 **38** 3k.50+1k.50 grey 10 20
146 – 12k.50+6k. purple 10 30
147 – 24k.+12k. green 15 35
148 – 50k.+25k. purple 20 60
MS148a 99 × 110 mm. 100k.+50k. red . . . . 4·00 8·00

DESIGNS: 12k.50, Telegraph linesman; 24k. Telephone switchboard; 50k. The postman calls.

1945. Labour Day.
149 **39** 3k.50 brown . . . . 20 1·25

40 Interior of Zagreb Cathedral

41 Statue of the Virgin and Shrine

1991. Obligatory Tax. Workers' Fund. Mass for Croatia. Perf or imperf.
150 **40** 1d.20 gold and black . . . 40 40

1991. Obligatory Tax. Workers' Fund. 700th Anniv of Shrine of the Virgin, Trsat. Perf or imperf.
151 **41** 1d.70 multicoloured . . . 50 50

42 State Arms

43 Members of Parliament

1991. Obligatory Tax. Workers' Fund. Rally in Ban Jelacic Square, Zagreb. Perf or imperf.
152 **42** 2d.20 multicoloured . . . 50 50
See also No. 170.

1991. Obligatory Tax. Workers' Fund. First Multi-party Session of Croatian Parliament, 30 May 1990. Perf or imperf.
153 **43** 2d.20 multicoloured . . . 50 50

44 Sud Aviation Caravelle Jetliner over Zagreb Cathedral and Dubrovnik

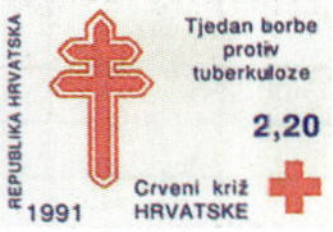

45 Anti-tuberculosis Emblem

1991. Air.
154 **44** 1d. blue, black and red . . 30 30
155 – 2d. multicoloured 30 30
156 – 3d. multicoloured 30 30
DESIGNS: 2d. Bell tower and ruins of Diocletian's Palace, Split; 3d. Sud Aviation Caravelle jetliner over Zagreb Cathedral and Pula amphitheatre.

1991. Obligatory Tax. Anti-tuberculosis Week.
157 **45** 2d.20 red and blue 30 30

46 Ban Jelacic Statue

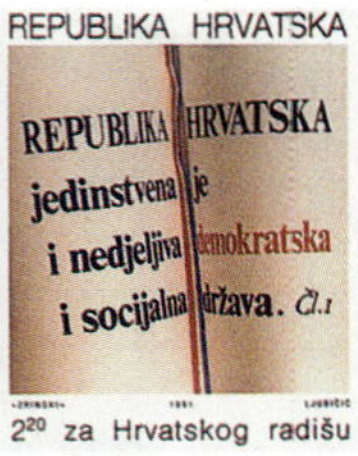

48 First Article of Constitution in Croatian

1991. Obligatory Tax. Workers' Fund. Re-erection of Ban Josip Jelacic Equestrian Statue, Zagreb. Perf or imperf.
158 **46** 2d.20 multicoloured . . . 50 50

1991. No. 150 surch **4⁰⁰ HPT** and posthorn.
159 **40** 4d. on 1d.20 gold & blk . . 35 35

1991. Obligatory Tax. Workers' Fund. 1st Anniv of New Constitution. Multicoloured. Perf or imperf.
160 2d.20 Type **48** 30 30
161 2d.20 Text in English 80 80
162 2d.20 Text in French 80 80
163 2d.20 Text in German . . . 80 80
164 2d.20 Text in Russian . . . 80 80
165 2d.20 Text in Spanish 80 80

49 Book of Croatian Independence

50 17th-century Crib Figures, Kosljun Monastery, Krk

1991. Recognition of Independence.
166 **49** 30d. multicoloured . . . . 1·10 1·10

1991. Christmas.
167 **50** 4d. multicoloured 60 60

51 "VUKOVAR" and Barbed Wire

52 Ban Josip Jelacic

1992. Obligatory Tax. Vukovar Refugees' Fund.
168 **51** 2d.20 brown and black . . 40 40

1992. No. 151 surch **2⁰⁰ HPT** and posthorn.
169 **41** 20d. on 1d.70 mult . . . . 3·00 3·00

1992. As No. 152, but redrawn with new value and "HPT" emblem replacing obligatory tax inscr at foot.
170 **42** 10d. multicoloured 30 30

1992. Obligatory Tax. Famous Croatians. Multicoloured.
171 4d.+2d. Type **52** 35 35
172 4d.+2d. Dr. Ante Starcevic (founder of Party of the Right) 30 30
173 7d.+3d. Stjepan Radic (founder of Croation Peasant Party) 30 30

53 Olympic Rings

54 Osijek Cathedral on Paper Dart

1992. Winter Olympic Games, Albertville, France.
174 **53** 30d. multicoloured 80 80

1992. Air.
175 **54** 4d. multicoloured 25 20

55 Knin

56 Statue of King Tomislav, Zagreb

1992. Croatian Towns (1st series).
176 **55** 6d. multicoloured 15 15
177 – 7d. multicoloured 15 15
178 – 20d. blue, red and yellow 75 75
179 – 30d. multicoloured 40 40
180 – 45d. multicoloured 75 75
181 – 50d. multicoloured 75 75
182 – 300d. multicoloured . . . 2·50 2·50
DESIGNS: 7d. Von Eltz Castle, Lukovar; 20d. St. Francis's Church, Ilok; 30d. Dr. Ante Starcevic Street, Gospic; 45d. Rector's Palace, Dubrovnik; 50d. St. Jakov's Cathedral, Sibenik; 300d. Sokak houses, Beli Manastir.
See also Nos. 208/14, 382/7, 523/4, 636 and 639.

1992.
183 **56** 10d. green 20 20

57 Red Cross Emblems on Globe

58 Map of Croatia on Red Cross

1992. Obligatory Tax. Red Cross Week.
184 **57** 3d. red and black 20 20

1992. Obligatory Tax. Solidarity Week.
185 **58** 3d. red and black 20 20

59 Central Railway Station, Zagreb

1992. Centenary of Zagreb Central Railway Station.
186 **59** 30d. multicoloured 35 35

60 Society Imprint

61 Bishop Josip Strossmayer (patron) and Academy Building

1992. 150th Anniv of Matica Hrvatska (Croatian language society).
187 **60** 20d. gold and red 25 25

1992. 125th Anniv of Croatian Academy of Sciences and Arts.
188 **61** 30d. multicoloured 35 35

62 Olympic Rings on Computer Pattern

1992. Olympic Games, Barcelona. Mult.
189 40d. Type **62** 35 35
190 105d. Rings and symbolic sports 65 65

63 Bellflowers

64 Blue Rock Thrush

1992. Flowers. Multicoloured.
191 30d. Type **63** 25 25
192 85d. Degenia (vert) 50 50

1992. Environmental Protection. Mult.
193 40d. Type **64** 25 25
194 75d. Red-spot snake 50 50

65 15th-century Carrack, Dubrovnik

66 "Madonna of Bistrica"

1992. Europa. 500th Anniv of Discovery of America by Columbus (1st issue).
195 **65** 30d. multicoloured 30 30
196 – 75d. black and red 75 75
DESIGN: 75d. "Indian Horseman" (bronze statue in Chicago by Ivan Mestrovic).
See also Nos. 198/9.

1992. Obligatory Tax. Fund for National Shrine to Madonna of Bistrica.
197 **66** 5d. gold and blue 20 20

1992. Europa. 500th Anniv of Discovery of America by Columbus (2nd issue). As Nos. 195/6, but new face values and with additional CEPT posthorns emblem.
198 **65** 60d. multicoloured 50 50
199 – 130d. black, red and gold (as No. 196) . . . . . . 1·10 1·10

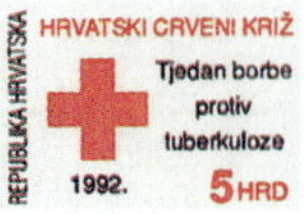

67 Red Cross

69 Dove and Coat of Arms

68 "25"

1992. Obligatory Tax. Anti-tuberculosis Week.
200 **67** 5d. red and black 20 20

1992. Croatian Language Anniversaries. Mult.
201 40d. Type **68** (25th anniv of Croatian Language Declaration) 25 25
202 130d. "100" (centenary of Croatian "Orthography" by Dr. I. Broz) 45 45

1992. 750th Anniv of Grant of Royal City Charter to Samobor.
203 **69** 90d. multicoloured 35 35

70 Remains of Altar Screen from Uzdolje Church

71 St. George and the Dragon

1992. 1100th Anniv of Duke Mucimir's Donation (judgement in ecclesiastical dispute).
204 **70** 60d. multicoloured 25 25

1992. Obligatory Tax. Croatian Anti-cancer League.
205 **71** 15d. multicoloured 20 20
See also No. 255.

72 Seal of King Bela IV

1992. 750th Anniv of Zagreb's Charter from King Bela IV.
206 **72** 180d. multicoloured . . . 50 50

73 "Croatian Christmas" (Ljubo Babic)

1992. Christmas.
207 **73** 80d. multicoloured 25 25

74 Former Town Hall, Vinkovci

75 Lorkovic

1992. Croatian Towns (2nd series). Mult.
208 100d. Type **74** 25 20
209 200d. Castle, Pazin (vert) . . 35 30
210 500d. Jelacic Square, Slavonski Brod 80 75
211 1000d. Town Hall, Jelacic Square, Varazdin . . . . . 1·25 1·00
212 2000d. Zorin cultural centre, Karlovac . . . . 1·40 1·25
213 5000d. St. Donat's Church and St. Stosija's Cathedral belltower, Zadar (vert) . . 1·60 1·50
214 10000d. Pirovo peninsula and Franciscan monastery, Vis 3·00 2·75

1992. Death Centenary of Blaz Lorkovic (political economist).
218 **75** 250d. multicoloured . . . 50 50

76 Coiled National Colours

77 Bunic-Vucic

1992. 150th Anniv of "Kolo" (literary Magazine).
219 **76** 300d. multicoloured . . . 60 60

1992. 400th Birth Anniv of Ivan Bunic-Vucic (poet).
220 **77** 350d. multicoloured . . . 65 65

78 Ljudevit Gaj Square, Krapina

1993. 800th Anniv of Krapina.
221 **78** 300d. multicoloured . . . 60 60

79 Tesla

1993. 50th Death Anniv of Nikola Tesla (physicist).
222 **79** 250d. multicoloured . . . 50 50

80 Quinquerez ("self-portrait")

1993. Death Cent of Ferdo Quiquerez (painter).
223 **80** 100d. multicoloured . . . 25 25

81 Red Deer

1993. Animals of the Kapacki Rit Swamp. Multicoloured.
224 500d. Type **81** 70 70
225 550d. White-tailed sea eagle 80 80

82 Sulentic ("self-portrait")

1993. Birth Centenary of Zlatko Sulentic (painter).
226 **82** 350d. multicoloured . . . 45 45

83 Kursalon, Lipik

1993. Centenary of Lipik Spa.
227 **83** 400d. multicoloured . . . 45 45

84 Kovacic (statue, Vojin Bakic)

1993. 50th Death Anniv of Ivan Goran Kovacic (writer).
228 **84** 200d. multicoloured . . . 30 30

85 Minceta Fortress, Dubrovnik

1993. 59th P.E.N. Literary Congress, Dubrovnik.
229 **85** 800d. multicoloured . . . 1·00 1·00

86 Ivan Kakaljevic (writer)

87 Mask and Split Theatre

1993. 150th Anniv of First Speech in Croatian Language made to Croatian Parliament.
230 **86** 500d. multicoloured . . . 45 45

1993. Centenary of Split Theatre.
231 **87** 600d. multicoloured . . . 45 45

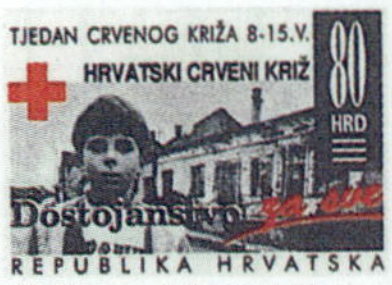

88 Boy and Ruined House

89 Pag in 16th Century

1993. Obligatory Tax. Red Cross Week.
232 **88** 80d. black and red 20 20

1993. 550th Anniv of Refoundation of Pag.
233 **89** 800d. multicoloured . . . 60 60

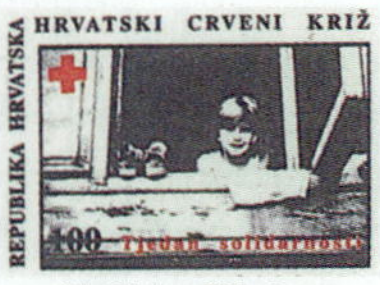

90 Dove

91 Girl at Window

1993. 1st Anniv of Croatia's Membership of U.N.
234 **90** 500d. multicoloured . . . 40 40

1993. Obligatory Tax. Solidarity Week.
235 **91** 100d. black and red . . . 20 20

92 "In the Cafe" (Ivo Dulcic)

1993. Europa. Contemporary Art. Mult.
236 700d. Type **92** 40 40
237 1000d. "The Waiting Room" (Miljenko Stancic) 60 60
238 1100d. "Two Figures" (Lijubo Ivancic) 80 80

93 "Homodukt" (Milivoj Bijelic)

1993. 45th Art Biennial, Venice. Mult.
239 250d. Type **93** 25 25
240 600d. "Snails" (Ivo Dekovic) 45 45
241 1000d. "Esa carta de mi flor" (Zeljko Kipke) 70 70

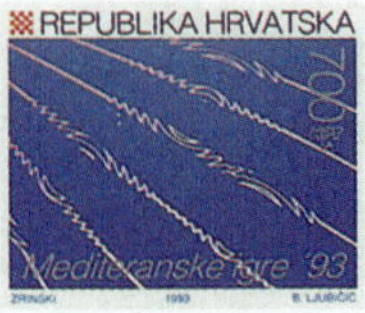

94 Symbolic Running Track

1993. 12th Mediterranean Games, Roussillon (Languedoc), France.
242 **94** 700d. multicoloured . . . 45 45

95 "Slavonian Oaks"

1993. 150th Birth Anniv of Adolf Waldinger (painter).
243 **95** 300d. multicoloured . . . 25 25

96 Battle of Krbava, 1493

1993. Anniversaries of Famous Battles. 16th-century engravings.
244 800d. Type **96** 50 50
245 1300d. Battle of Sisak, 1593 90 90

97 Krleza (after Marija Ujevic)

1993. Birth Centenary of Miroslav Krleza (writer).
246 **97** 400d. multicoloured . . . 30 30

98 Cardinal Stepinac

99 Croatian Postman

1993. Obligatory Tax. Cardinal Stepinac Foundation.
247 **98** 150d. black, mauve & gold 20 20

1993. 1st Anniv of Croatia's Membership of Universal Postal Union.
248 **99** 1800d. multicoloured . . . 85 85

100 Paljetak

1993. Birth Centenary of Vlaho Paljetak (singer-songwriter).
249 **100** 500d. multicoloured . . . 30 30

101 Peter Zrinski and Krsto Frankopan

1993. Obligatory Tax. Zrinski-Frankopan Foundation.
250 **101** 200d. blue and grey . . . 20 20

102 "Freedom of Croatia" (central motif of 1918 stamp)

1993. Stamp Day.
251 **102** 600d. multicoloured . . . 30 30

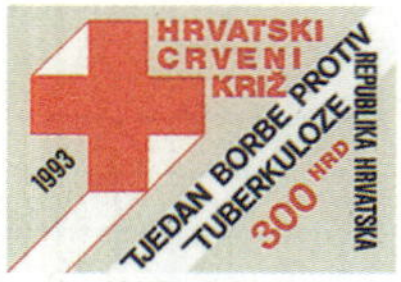

103 Red Cross

1993. Obligatory Tax. Anti-tuberculosis Week.
252 **103** 300d. green, black & red 20 20

104 Antonio Magini's Map of Istria, 1620

105 Smiciklas

1993. 50th Anniv of Incorporation of Istria, Rijeka and Zadar into Croatia.
253 **104** 2200d. multicoloured . . 80 80

1993. 150th Birth Anniv of Tadija Smiciklas (historian).
254 **105** 800d. black, gold and red 30 30

1993. Obligatory Tax. Croatian Anti-cancer League.
255 **71** 400d. multicoloured . . . 20 20

106 Allegory of Birth of Croatian History on Shores of the Adriatic

1993. Centenary of National Archaeological Museum, Split.
256 **106** 1000d. multicoloured . . 40 40

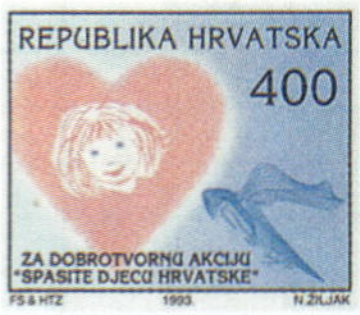

107 Girl In Heart

108 Croatian and French Flags and Soldiers

1993. Obligatory Tax. Save Croatian Children Fund.
257 **107** 400d. red, blue and black 20 20

1993. 50th Anniv of Uprising of 13th Pioneer Battalion, Villefranche-de-Rouergue, France.
258 **108** 3000d. multicoloured . . 95 95

109 Tomic

110 Astronomical Diagram

1993. 150th Birth Anniv of Josip Eugen Tomic (writer).
259 **109** 900d. brown, green & red 30 30

1993. 850th Anniv of Publication of "De Essentiis" by Herman Dalmatin.
260 **110** 1000d. multicoloured . . 30 30

111 Christmas on the Battlefield

112 Skiers

1993. Christmas. Multicoloured.
261 1000d. Type **111** 35 35
262 4000d. "Nativity" (fresco, St. Mary's Church, Dvigrad) . . . . 1·40 1·40

1993. Cent of Competitive Skiing in Croatia.
263 **112** 1000d. multicoloured . . 35 35

113 Decorations and Badge

1993. 125th Anniv of Croatian Militia.
264 **113** 1100d. multicoloured . . 35 35

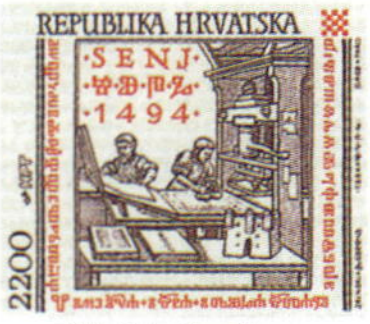

114 Printing Press

1994. 500th Anniv of Printing of First Croatian Book (a Glagolitic missal), Senj.
265 **114** 2200d. brown and red . . 70 70

115 Skier

1994. Winter Olympic Games, Lillehammer, Norway.
266 **115** 4000d. multicoloured . . 1·10 1·10

116 Iguanodon

117 Masthead

1994. Croatian Dinosaur Fossils from West Istria. Multicoloured.
267 2400d. Type **116** 60 60
268 4000d. Iguanodon, skeleton and map . . . . 1·00 1·00
Nos. 267/8 were issued together, se-tenant, forming a composite design.

1994. 150th Anniv of "Zora Dalmatinska" (literary periodical).
269 **117** 800d. multicoloured . . . 30 30

118 University, Emperor Leopold I's Seal and Vice-chancellor's Chain

119 Wolf

1994. 325th Anniv of Croatian University, Zagreb.
270 **118** 2200d. multicoloured . . 70 70

1994. Planet Earth Day.
271 **119** 3800d. multicoloured . . 1·25 1·25

120 Safety Signs and Worker wearing Protective Clothing

121 Globe and Map

1994. 75th Anniv of ILO and 50th Anniv of Philadelphia Declaration (social charter).
272 **120** 1000d. multicoloured . . 40 40

1994. Obligatory Tax. Red Cross Week.
273 **121** 500d. black, stone & red 20 20

122 Flying Man (17th-century idea by Faust Vrancic)

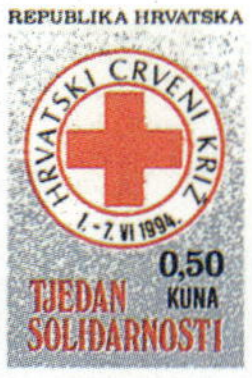

123 Red Cross

1994. Europa. Inventions. Multicoloured.
274 3800d. Type **122** . . . . . . 1·25 1·25
275 4000d. Quill and pencil writing surname (technical pencil by Slavoljub Penkala, 1906) (32 × 23 mm) . . . . 1·25 1·25

1994. Obligatory Tax. Solidarity Week.
276 **123** 50l. red, black and grey 20 20

124 Croatian Iris

125 Petrovic

1994. Flowers. Multicoloured.
277 2k.40 Type **124** 75 75
278 4k. Meadow saffron . . . . 1·25 1·25

1994. 1st Death Anniv of Drazen Petrovic (basketball player).
279 **125** 1k. multicoloured 35 35

126 Plitvice Lakes

1994. 150th Anniv of Tourism in Croatia. Multicoloured.
280 80l. Type **126** 20 20
281 1k. River Krka 25 25
282 1k.10 Kornati Islands 40 40
283 2k.20 Kopacki Trscak ornithological reserve . . . 70 70
284 2k.40 Opatija Riviera 80 80
285 3k.80 Brijuni Islands . . . . 1·25 1·25
286 4k. Trakoscan Castle, Zagorje . . . . 1·40 1·40

127 Baranovic at Keyboard

128 Monstrance

1994. Musical Anniversaries.
287 **127** 1k. multicoloured 35 35
288 – 2k.20 silver, black & red 65 65
289 – 2k.40 multicoloured . . . 80 80
DESIGNS—VERT: 1k. Type **127** (birth centenary of Kresimir Baranovic (composer and conductor/director of Croatian National Theatre Opera, Zagreb, 1915–40)); 2k.20, Vatroslav Lisinski (composer, 175th birth anniv). HORIZ: 2k.40, Score and harp player (350th anniv of Pauline song-book).

1994. Obligatory Tax. Ludbreg Shrine.
290 **128** 50l. multicoloured 20 20

129 Men dressed in Croatian and American Colours

130 Mother and Children

1994. Centenary of Croatian Brotherhood in U.S.A.
291 **129** 2k.20 multicoloured . . . 70 60

1994. Obligatory Tax. Save Croatian Children Fund.
292 **130** 50l. multicoloured 20 20

131 Family

132 St. George and the Dragon

1994. International Year of the Family.
293 **131** 80l. multicoloured 30 30

1994. Obligatory Tax. Croatian Anti-Cancer League.
294 **132** 50l. multicoloured 20 20

133 Pope John Paul II and his Arms

134 Franjo Bucar (Committee member, 1920–46)

1994. Papal Visit.
295 **133** 1k. multicoloured 35 35

1994. Cent of International Olympic Committee.
296 **134** 1k. multicoloured 40 40

135 Red Cross on Leaf

136 The Little Prince (book character)

1994. Obligatory Tax. Anti-tuberculosis Week.
297 **135** 50l. red, green & black . . 20 20

1994. 50th Death Anniv of Antoine de Saint-Exupery (writer).
298 **136** 3k.80 multicoloured . . . 1·00 1·00

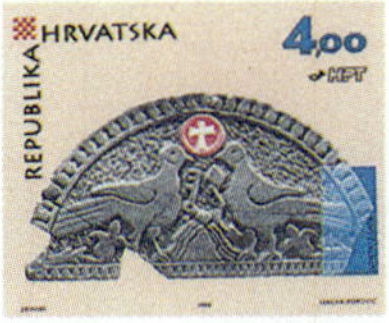
137 "Resurrection" (lunette, Gati, Omis)

1994. 13th International Convention on Christian Archaeology, Split and Porec.
299 **137** 4k. multicoloured . . . . 1·10 1·10

138 "Still Life with Fruits and Basket" (Marino Tartaglia)

1994. Paintings. Multicoloured.
300 2k.40 Type **138** 60 60
301 3k.80 "In the Park" (Milan Steiner) 95 95
302 4k. "Self-portrait" (Vilko Gecan) . . . . 1·25 1·25

139 Plan of Fortress

1994. Obligatory Tax. 750th Anniv of Slavonski Brod.
303 **139** 50l. yellow, black & red 20 20

140 IOC Centenary Emblem and Flame

1994. Obligatory Tax. National Olympic Committee. Designs incorporating either the National Olympic Committee emblem or the International Olympic Committee centenary emblem.
304 50l. Type **140** 20 20
305 50l. As T **140** but with National Olympic Committee emblem 20 20
306 50l. Tennis and national emblem (vert) 20 20
307 50l. Football and centenary emblem (vert) 20 20
308 50l. As No. 306 but with centenary emblem (vert) . . 20 20
309 50l. As No. 307 but with national emblem (vert) . . 20 20
310 50l. Basketball and centenary emblem (vert) 20 20
311 50l. Handball and national emblem (vert) 20 20
312 50l. As No. 310 but with national emblem (vert) . . 20 20
313 50l. As No. 311 but with centenary emblem (vert) . . 20 20
314 50l. Kayaks and national emblem (vert) 20 20
315 50l. Water polo and centenary emblem (vert) . . 20 20
316 50l. As No. 314 but with centenary emblem (vert) . . 20 20
317 50l. As No. 315 but with national emblem (vert) . . 20 20
318 50l. Running and centenary emblem (vert) 20 20
319 50l. Gymnastics and national emblem (vert) 20 20
320 50l. As No. 318 but with national emblem (vert) . . 20 20
321 50l. As No. 319 but with centenary emblem (vert) . . 20 20

141 Cover of "Gazophylacium"

142 St. Mark's Church and Gas Lamp

1994. 400th Birth Anniv of Ivan Belostenec (lexicographer).
322 **141** 2k.20 multicoloured . . . 70 70

1994. 900th Annivs of Zagreb (323/5) and Zagreb Bishopric (326). Multicoloured.
323 1k. Type **142** 30 30
324 1k. Street scene from early film, Maxi Cat (cartoon character) and left side of Zagreb Exchange 30 30
325 1k. Right side of Zagreb Exchange, S. Penkala's biplane and Cibona building 30 30
326 4k. 15th-century bishop's crosier and 17th-century view of Zagreb by Valvasor . . . . 1·00 1·00
MS327 79 × 59 mm. 13k.50 Penkala's biplane and street scene from early film (23 × 47 mm) 3·50 3·50

Nos. 323/6 were issued together, se-tenant, forming a composite design.

143 "Epiphany" (relief, Vrhovac Church)

1994. Christmas.
328 **143** 1k. multicoloured 35 30

144 "Translation of the Holy House" (Giovanni Battista Tiepolo)

145 Modern Tie

1994. 700th Anniv of St. Mary's Sanctuary, Loreto.
329 **144** 4k. multicoloured . . . . 1·10 1·10

1995. Ties. Multicoloured.
330 1k.10 Type **145** 25 25
331 3k.80 English dandy, 1810 . . 80 80
332 4k. Croatian soldier, 1630 . . 85 85
MS333 109 × 88 mm. Nos. 330/2 2·00 2·00

146 St. Catherine's Church and Monastery, Zagreb, and Jesuit

1995. Monasteries. Multicoloured.
334 1k. Type **146** (350th anniv) 20 20
335 2k.40 St. Paul's Monastery, Visovac, and Franciscan monk (550th anniv) . . . 50 50

147 Istrian Short-haired Hunting Dog

1995. Dogs. Multicoloured.
336 2k.20 Type **147** 50 50
337 2k.40 Posavinian hunting dog 50 50
338 3k.80 Istrian wire-haired hunting dog . . . . 1·00 1·00

148 Rowing

1995. Obligatory Tax. National Olympic Committee. Multicoloured.
339 50l. Type **148** 15 15
340 50l. Petanque 15 15
341 50l. Monument to Drazen Petrovic, Olympic Park, Lausanne 15 15
342 50l. Tennis 15 15
343 50l. Basketball 15 15

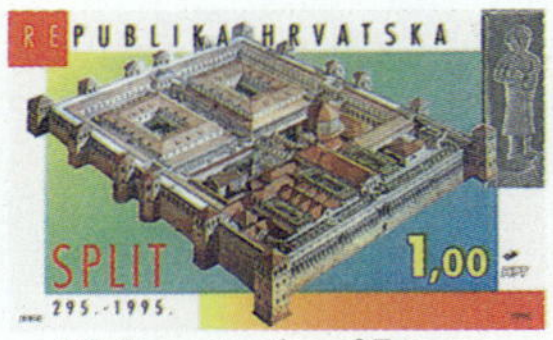
149 Reconstruction of Emperor Diocletian's Palace

1995. 1700th Anniv of Split. Multicoloured.
344 1k. Type **149** 20 20
345 2k.20 "Split Harbour" (Emanuel Vidovic) 40 40
346 4k. View of city and bust of Marko Marulic (Ivan Mestrovic) 80 80
MS347 90 × 60 mm. 13k.40 Aerial view (23 × 47 mm) . . . . . . 2·75 2·75

150 Player

151 Woman's Head

1995. World Handball Championship, Iceland.
348 **150** 4k. multicoloured 80 80

1995. Obligatory Tax. Red Cross Week.
349 **151** 50l. black and red 15 15

152 Storm Clouds and Clear Sky

1995. Europa. Peace and Freedom. Mult.
350 2k.40 Type **152** 50 50
351 4k. Angel (detail of sculpture, Francesco Robba) 80 80

153 Shadow behind Cross

1995. 150th Anniv of July Riots (352) and 50th Anniv of Croatian Surrender at Bleiburg (353). Multicoloured.
352 1k.10 Type **153** 25 25
353 3k.80 Sunrise behind cross . . 80 80

154 Arms and Hand holding Rose

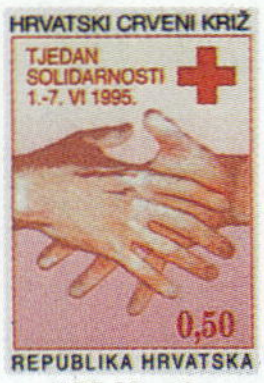
155 Hands

1995. Independence Day.
354 **154** 1k.10 multicoloured . . . 25 25

1995. Obligatory Tax. Solidarity Week.
355 **155** 50l. multicoloured 15 15

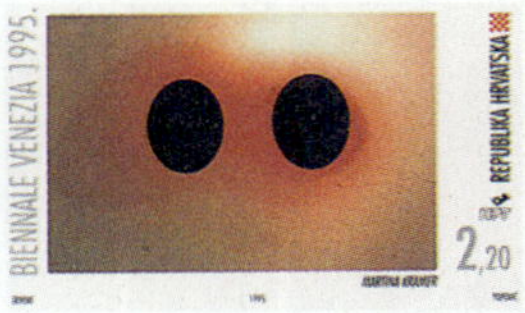
156 "Installation" (detail) (Martina Kramer)

1995. 46th Art Biennale, Venice. Work by Croatian artists. Multicoloured.
356 2k.20 Type **156** 45 45
357 2k.40 "Paracelsus Paraduchamps" (Mirk Zrinscak) (vert) 50 50
358 4k. "Shadows/136" (Goran Petercol) 80 80

157 "St. Antony" (detail of polyptych by Ljubo Babic, St. Antony's Sanctuary, Zagreb)

1995. 800th Birth Anniv of St. Antony of Padua.
359 **157** 1k. multicoloured 20 20

158 Loggerhead Turtle

1995. Animals. Multicoloured.
360 2k.40 Type **158** 60 60
361 4k. Bottle-nosed dolphin . . 90 90

159 Osijek Cathedral

160 "Croatian Pieta"

1995. Obligatory Tax. Restoration of Sts. Peter and Paul's Cathedral, Osijek.
362 **159** 65l. multicoloured 15 15

1995. Obligatory Tax. "Holy Mother of Freedom" War Memorial.
363 **160** 65l. on 50l. blk, red & bl 70 70
364 – 65l. black, red and blue 15 15
365 – 65l. blue and yellow . . 15 15

DESIGN: 65l. Projected memorial church.

Nos. 364/5 were not issued without surcharge.

161 Town and Fortress

1995. Liberation of Knin.
366 **161** 1k.30 multicoloured . . . 30 30

162 Electric Power Plant

1995. Centenary of Jaruga Hydro-electric Power Station, River Krka.
367 **162** 3k.60 multicoloured . . . 75 75

163 Postman

1995. Stamp Day.
368 **163** 1k.30 multicoloured . . . 30 30

165 Suppe and Heroine of "The Fair Galatea" (operetta)

1995. Death Centenary of Franz von Suppe (composer).
370 **165** 6k.50 multicoloured . . . 1·40 1·40

166 Petrinja Fortress (after Valvasor) and Cavalrymen

167 Ivo Tijardovic

1995. 400th Anniv of Habsburg Capture of Petrinja.
371 **166** 2k.20 multicoloured . . . 45 45

1995. Composers' Anniversaries. Mult.
372 1k.20 Type **167** (birth centenary) 25 25
373 1k.40 Lovro von Matacic (10th death) 30 30
374 6k.50 Jakov Gotovac (birth centenary) . . . . 1·40 1·40

168 Herman Bolle (architect, 150th birth)

1995. Anniversaries. Multicoloured.
375 1k.30 Type **168** 30 30
376 2k.40 Izidor Krsnjavi (artist and art administrator, 150th birth) 50 50
377 3k.60 Gala curtain by Vlaho Bukovac (cent of National Theatre) 75 75

169 Children in Nest

170 Left-hand Detail of Curtain

1995. Obligatory Tax. Save Croatian Children Fund.
378 **169** 65l. multicoloured 15 15

1995. Obligatory Tax. Centenary of National Theatre, Zagreb. Details of gala curtain by Vlaho Bukovac. Multicoloured.
379 65l. Type **170** 15 15
380 65l. Central detail 15 15
381 65l. Right-hand detail 15 15
Nos. 379/81 were issued together, se-tenant, forming a composite design.

171 Zagrebacka Street, Bjelovar

1995. Croatian Towns (3rd series). Mult.
382 1k. Type **171** 20 20
383 1k.30 St. Peter and St. Paul's Cathedral, Osijek (vert) . . 30 30
384 1k.40 Castle, Cakovec (vert) 30 30
385 2k.20 Rovinj 45 45
386 2k.40 Korcula 50 50
387 3k.60 Town Hall, Zupanja 75 75

172 "50"

1996. 50th Anniversaries. Multicoloured.
395 3k.60 Type **172** (UNO) . . . 75 75
396 3k.60 "5" and "FAO" within biscuit forming "50" (FAO) 75 75

173 Spiro Brusina (zoologist)

174 Birds flying through Sky

1995. Anniversaries. Multicoloured.
397 1k. Type **173** (150th birth) . . 20 20
398 2k.20 Bogoslav Sulek (philologist, death cent) . . 45 45
399 6k.50 Faust Vrancic's "Dictionary of Five European Languages" (400th anniv of publication) . . . . 1·40 1·40

1995. Obligatory Tax. Anti-drugs Campaign.
400 **174** 65l. multicoloured 15 15

175 Breast Screening

176 Hands reading Braille

1995. Obligatory Tax. Croatian Anti-cancer League. Breast Screening Campaign.
401 **175** 65l. multicoloured 15 15

1995. Centenary of Institute for Blind Children, Zagreb.
402 **176** 1k.20 red, yellow & black 25 25

177 Animals under Christmas Tree

1995. Christmas.
403 **177** 1k.30 multicoloured . . . 30 30

178 Polo, Animals in Boat and Court of Kublai Khan

1995. 700th Anniv of Marco Polo's Return from China.
404 **178** 3k.60 multicoloured . . . 75 75

179 Hrvatska Kostajnica

180 Lectionary of Bernardin of Split, 1495 (first printed book using Cakavian dialect)

1995. Liberated Towns. Multicoloured.
405 20l. Type **179** 10 10
406 30l. Slunj 10 10
407 50l. Gracac 10 10
408 1k.20 Drnis (vert) 25 25
409 6k.50 Glina . . . . 1·40 1·40
410 10k. Obrovac (vert) . . . . . 2·00 2·00

1995. Incunabula. Multicoloured.
420 1k.40 Type **180** 30 30
421 3k.60 Callipers and last page of "Spovid Opcena" (manual for confessors), 1496 (first book printed in Croatia) 75 75

181 Crucifix

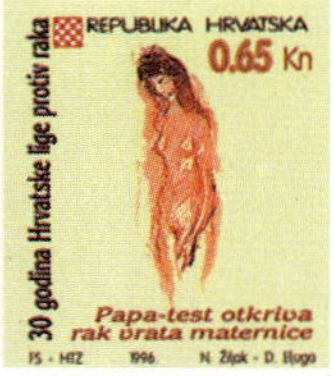

182 Breast Cancer Campaign

1996. Events and Anniversaries. Mult.
422 1k.30 St. Marko Krizevcanin (detail of mosaic (Ante Starcevic), St. Marko's Church, Zagreb) (canonization) 30 30
423 1k.30 Type **181** (700th anniv of veneration of miraculous crucifix, St. Guido's Church, Rijeka) 30 30
424 1k.30 Ivan Merz (teacher and Catholic youth worker, birth centenary) 30 30

1996. Obligatory Tax. 30th Anniv of Anti-cancer League.
425 **182** 65l. multicoloured 15 15

183 Eugen Kvaternik (125th anniv of Rakovica Uprising)

184 Madonna and Child and Church

1996. Anniversaries. Multicoloured.
426 1k.20 Type **183** 25 25
427 1k.40 Ante Starcevic (founder of Part of the Right, death centenary) (vert) 30 30
428 2k.20 Stjepan Radic (founder of Croatian Peasant Party) (125th birth anniv and 75th anniv of Peasant Republic constitution) (vert) 45 45
429 3k.60 Collage (75th anniv of Labin Republic) (vert) . . 75 75

1996. Obligatory Tax. St. Mary of Bistrica Sanctuary.
430 **184** 65l. multicoloured 15 15

185 Julije Domac (founder) and Culture

1996. Centenary of Pharmacology Institute, University of Zagreb.
431 **185** 6k.50 multicoloured . . . 1·40 1·40

186 Score

187 Cvijeta Zuzoric (beauty)

1996. Music Anniversaries. Multicoloured.
432 2k.20 Type **186** (400th birth anniv of Vinko Jelic, composer) 45 45
433 2k.20 "O" over musical bars (150th anniv of "Love and Malice" (first Croatian opera) by Vatroslav Lisinski) 45 45
434 2k.20 Josip Slavenski (composer, birth cent) . . 45 45
435 2k.20 "Lijepa nasa domovino" (birth bicent of Antun Mihanovic and 175th birth anniv of Josip Runjanin (composers of National Anthem)) 45 45

1996. Europa. Famous Women. Mult.
436 2k.20 Type **187** 45 45
437 3k.60 Ivana Brlic-Mazuranic (writer) 75 75

188 Olympic Rings

189 Nikola Subic Zrinski of Sziget (Ban of Croatia)

1996. Obligatory Tax. National Olympic Committee.
438 **188** 65l. multicoloured 15 15

1996. 16th and 17th-century Members of Zrinski and Frankopan Families. Multicoloured.
439 1k.30 Type **189** 30 30
440 1k.40 Nikola Zrinski (Ban of Croatia) 30 30
441 2k.20 Petar Zrinski (Ban of Croatia) 45 45
442 2k.40 Katarina Zrinski (wife of Petar and sister of Fran Krsto Frankopan) 50 50
443 3k.60 Fran Krsto Frankopan (writer and revolutionary) 75 75
MS444 117 × 172 mm. Nos. 439/43 2·10 2·10

190 Child outside House

191 Soldier carrying Child

1996. Obligatory Tax. Red Cross Fund.
445 **190** 65l. black and red 15 15

1996. 5th Anniv of National Guard.
446 **191** 1k.30 multicoloured . . . 30 30

192 Istrian Bluebell

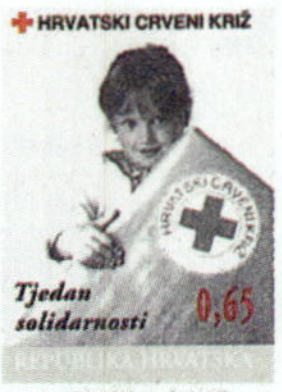

193 Child with Red Cross Parcel

1996. Flowers. Multicoloured.
447 2k.40 Type **192** 45 45
448 3k.60 Dubrovnik corn-flower 75 75

1996. Obligatory Tax. Solidarity Week.
449 **193** 65l. black and red 15 15

194 Football

1996. European Football Championship, England.
450 **194** 2k.20 black and red . . . 45 45

195 Konscak's Map of California

196 Children sitting outside House

1996. 250th Anniv of Father Ferdinand Konscak's Expedition to Lower California.
451 **195** 2k.40 multicoloured . . . 45 45

1996. Obligatory Tax. Save Croatian Children Fund.
452 **196** 65l. multicoloured 15 15

197 Anniversary Emblem

198 Man holding Dumb-bell and Falcon

1996. Obligatory Tax. 800th Anniv of Osijek.
453 **197** 65l. blue, orange & grey 15 15

1996. 150th Birth Anniv of Josip Fon (founder of Croatian Falcon gymnastics society).
454 **198** 1k.40 multicoloured . . . 30 30

199 Olympic Colours and Rings

200 Cathedral

1996. Olympic Games, Atlanta, and Centenary of Modern Olympics.
455 **199** 3k.60 multicoloured . . . 75 75

1996. Obligatory Tax. Restoration of Dakovo Cathedral.
456 **200** 65l. multicoloured 15 15

201 "Church Tower"

202 Crucifix

1996. Obligatory Tax. 1700th Anniv of Split.
457 **201** 65l. ultramarine and blue 15 15

1996. Obligatory Tax. Vukovar.
458 **202** 65l. multicoloured 15 15

203 Lighted Candle, Shell and Lilies

204 Tweezers holding Stamp

1996. Obligatory Tax. Anti-drugs Campaign.
459 **203** 65l. multicoloured 15 15

1996. Stamp Day. 5th Anniv of Issue of First Postage Stamp by Independent Croatia.
460 **204** 1k.30 multicoloured . . . 30 30

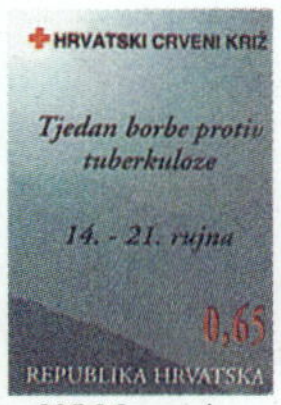

205 Mountains

206 St. Elias's Chapel, Zumberak

1996. Obligatory Tax. Anti-tuberculosis Week.
461 **205** 65l. multicoloured 15 15

1996. 700th Anniv of First Written Reference to Zumberak.
462 **206** 2k.20 multicoloured . . . 45 45

207 Illuminated Page

208 Fishes and Spear

1996. Early Middle Ages. Multicoloured.
463 1k.20 Type **207** (900th anniv of "Vekenega's Book of Gospels") 25 25
464 1k.40 Gottschalk (Benedictine abbot) (1150th anniv of Gottschalk's visit to Duke of Trpimir) 30 30

1996. Millenary of First Written Reference to Fishing in Croatia.
465 **208** 1k.30 multicoloured . . . 30 30

209 Gjuro Pilar (geologist, 150th anniv)

1996. Scientists' Birth Anniversaries. Mult.
466 2k.40 Type **209** 50 50
467 2k.40 Frane Bulic (archaeologist, 150th anniv) 50 50
468 2k.40 Ante Sercer (otolaryngologist, cent) . . 50 50

210 Sir Frederick Banting and Charles Best (discoverers)

1996. Obligatory Tax. Croatian Diabetic Council. 75th Anniv of Discovery of Insulin.
469 **210** 65l. gold, yellow & black 15 15

211 Laws of Dominican Nuns, Zadar

1996. 600th Anniv of Founding of Dominican General High School (university), Zadar.
470 **211** 1k.40 multicoloured . . . 30 30

212 "Rain" (Menci Crncic)

1996. 20th-century Paintings. Multicoloured.
471 1k.30 Type **212** 30 30
472 1k.40 "Peljesac-Korcula Channel" (Mato Medovic) 30 30
473 3k.60 "Pink Dream" (Vlaho Bukovac) 75 75

213 "Mother of God of Remete", Zagreb

214 Children of Different Races

1996. Obligatory Tax.
474 **213** 65l. multicoloured 15 15

1996. 50th Anniv of UNICEF.
475 **214** 3k.60 multicoloured . . . 75 75

215 Sts. Peter's and Paul's Cathedral

216 Nativity

1996. 800th Anniv of First Written Reference to Osijek. Multicoloured.
476 2k.20 Type **215** 45 45
477 2k.20 Riverbank and view down street 45 45

1996. Christmas.
478 **216** 1k.30 multicoloured . . . 30 30

217 Bond and Bank

218 Mihanovic

1996. Anniversaries. Multicoloured.
479 2k.40 Type **217** (150th anniv of founding of First Croatian Savings Bank, Zagreb) 50 50
480 3k.60 Frontispiece (bicent of publication of "The Principles of the Corn Trade" by Josip Sipus) . . 75 75

1997. Obligatory Tax. Birth Bicentenary (1996) of Antun Mihanovic.
481 **218** 65l. multicoloured 15 15

219 "Professor Baltazar" (Zagreb School of Animated Film)

1997. Centenary of Croatian Films. Mult.
482 1k.40 Oktavijan Miletic (cameraman and director) filming "Vatroslav Lisinski" (first Croatian sound film), 1944 . . . . . 30 30
483 1k.40 Type **219** 30 30
484 1k.40 Mirjana Bohanev-Vidovic and Relja Basic in "Who Sings Means No Harm", 1970 . . . . . . 30 30

220 Dr. Ante Starcevic's House

221 Don Quixote and Windmill

1997. Obligatory Tax.
485 **220** 65l. multicoloured 15 15

1997. Birth Anniversaries. Multicoloured.
486 2k.20 Type **221** (450th anniv of Miguel de Cervantes (author of "Don Quixote")) 45 45
487 3k.60 Metal type (600th anniv of Johannes Gutenberg (inventor of printing)) (horiz) 75 75

222 Woman

223 "Big Joseph" by Vladimir Nazor (illus. Sasa Santel)

1997. Obligatory Tax. Croatian Anti-cancer League.
488 **222** 65l. multicoloured 15 15

1997. Europa. Tales and Legends.
489 – 1k.30 multicoloured . . . 30 30
490 **223** 3k.60 red, black & gold 75 75
DESIGNS—HORIZ: 1k.30, Elves from "Stribor's Forest" by Ivana Brlic-Mazuranic (illus. Cvijeta Job).

224 Noble Pen Shell

225 Comforting Hand

1997. Molluscs and Insects. Multicoloured.
491 1k.40 Type **224** 30 30
492 2k.40 "Radziella styx" (cave beetle) 50 50
493 3k.60 Giant tun 75 75

1997. Obligatory Tax. Red Cross Week.
494 **225** 65l. multicoloured 15 15

226 Pres. Franjo Tudjman

1997. 5th Anniv of Croatia's Membership of United Nations.
495 **226** 6k.50 multicoloured . . . 1·40 1·40

227 Ludwig Zamenhof (inventor)

1997. Croatian Esperanto (invented language) Conference.
496 **227** 1k.20 multicoloured . . . 25 25

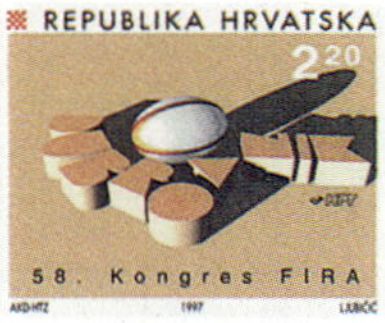

228 Congress Emblem

1997. 58th Congress of International Amateur Rugby Federation, Dubrovnik.
497 **228** 2k.20 multicoloured . . . 40 40

229 "Vukovar" (Zlatko Atac) (¾-size illustration)

1997. Rebuilding of Vukovar.
498 **229** 6k.50 multicoloured . . . 1·25 1·25

230 King Petar Svacic (1095–97)

1997. Kings of Croatia. Multicoloured.
499 1k.30 Type **230** (900th death anniv) 25 25
500 2k.40 King Stjepan Drzislav (996–97) 45 45

231 16th-century Dubrovnik Courier (after Nicole de Nicolai) **232** Tennis

1997. Stamp Day.
501 **231** 2k.30 multicoloured . . . 45 45

1997. Olympic Medal Winners. Mult.
502 1k. Type **232** (Goran Ivanisevic—bronze (singles and doubles), Barcelona 1992) 20 20
503 1k.20 Basketball (silver, Barcelona 1992) 25 25
504 1k.40 Water polo (silver, Atlanta 1996) (27 × 31 mm) 25 25
505 2k.20 Handball (gold, Atlanta 1996) (27 × 31 mm) 40 40

233 Turkish Attack on Sibenik, 1647

1997. Defence of Sibenik. Multicoloured.
506 1k.30 Type **233** (350th anniv of defence against the Turks) 25 25
507 1k.30 Air attack on Sibenik, 1991 . . . . 25 25

234 Frane Petric (philosopher) **235** Parliamentary Session (after Ivan Zasche) and Ivan Kukuljevic (politician)

1997. Anniversaries. Multicoloured.
508 1k.40 Type **234** (400th death anniv) 25 25
509 1k.40 "Madonna and Child" (detail from the polyptich of St. Michael in Franciscan Church, Cavtat) (500th anniv of first recorded work of Vicko Lovrin (artist)) 25 25
510 1k.40 Frano Krsinic (sculptor, birth cent) . . . 25 25
511 1k.40 Dubravko Dujsin (actor, 50th death anniv) 25 25

1997. Anniversaries. Multicoloured.
512 2k.20 Type **235** (150th anniv of promulgation of Croatian as official language) 40 40
513 3k.60 Zagreb and elevation of school (centenary of Croatian Grammar School, Zadar) 70 70

236 Primordial Elephant

1997. Palaeontological Finds. Multicoloured.
514 1k.40 Type **236** 25 25
515 2k.40 Fossil of "Viviparus novskaensis" (periwinkle) 45 45

237 "Painter in the Pond" (Nikola Masic)

1997. Paintings. Multicoloured.
516 1k.30 Type **237** 25 25
517 2k.20 "Angelus" (Emanuel Vidovic) 40 40
518 3k.60 "Tree in the Snow" (Slava Raskaj) 70 70

238 Child Jesus in the Stable **239** "Electra" by Sophocles

1997. Christmas. Multicoloured.
519 1k.30 Type **238** 25 25
520 3k.60 "Birth of Jesus" (Isidor Krsnjavi) (33 × 59 mm) . . 70 70

1997. Literary Anniversaries. Multicoloured.
521 1k. Type **239** (400th anniv of publication of collected translations by Dominko Zlataric) 20 20
522 1k.20 Closed book (300th birth anniv of Filip Grabovac and 250th anniv of publication of his "Best of Folk Speech and the Illyric or Croatian Language") 25 25

240 Ilok **241** Score and Varazdin (Baroque Evenings)

1998. Croatian Towns (4th series).
523 **240** 5k. violet, brown & red 95 95
524 – 10k. brown, violet & red 2·00 2·00
DESIGN: 10k. Dubrovnik.

1998. Europa. National Festivals. Mult.
531 1k.45 Type **241** 30 30
532 4k. Dubrovnik (Summer Festival) 75 75

242 Olympic Rings and Japanese Red Sun

1998. Winter Olympic Games, Nagano, Japan.
533 **242** 2k.45 multicoloured . . . 45 45

243 Jelacics Flag and Battle near Moor (lithograph)

1998. Historical Events of 1848. Mult.
534 1k.60 Type **243** 30 30
535 1k.60 "Croatian Assembly in Session" (Dragutin Weingartner) 30 30
536 4k. Ban Josip Jelacic (after Ivan Zasche) (21 × 31 mm) 75 75

244 Mimara **245** Caesar's Mushroom

1998. Birth Centenary of Ante Topic Mimara (art collector).
537 **244** 2k.65 multicoloured . . . 50 50

1998. Fungi. Multicoloured.
538 1k.30 Type **245** 25 25
539 1k.30 Saffron milk cup ("Lactarius deliciosus") . . 25 25
540 7k.20 "Morchella conica" . . 1·40 1·40

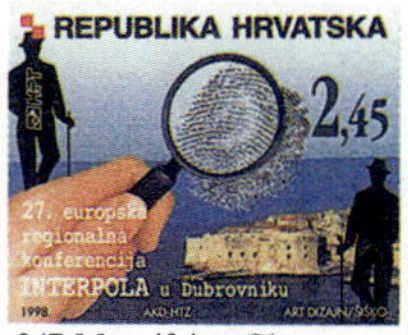

246 Stepinac **247** Magnifying Glass over Fingerprint and Dubrovnik

1998. Birth Centenary of Cardinal Alojzije Stepinac (Archbishop of Zagreb).
541 **246** 1k.50 multicoloured . . . 30 30

1998. 27th European Regional Conference of Interpol, Dubrovnik.
542 **247** 2k.45 multicoloured . . . 50 50

248 *Falkusa* (fishing boat)

1998. "Espo '98" World's Fair, Lisbon. Sheet 97 × 80 mm.
MS543 **248** 14k.85 multicoloured 2·60 2·60

249 Football

1998. World Cup Football Championship, France.
544 **249** 4k. multicoloured 75 75

250 Title Page of "Slavonic Fairy"

1998. Writers' Anniversaries. Multicoloured.
545 1k.20 Type **250** (450th birth anniv of Juraj Barakovic (poet)) 25 25
546 1k.50 Milan Begovic (50th death anniv) 30 30
547 1k.60 Mate Balota (birth centenary) 30 30
548 2k.45 Antun Gustav Matos (125th birth anniv) 50 50
549 2k.65 Matija Antun Relkovic (death bicentenary) 50 50
550 4k. Antun Branko Simic (birth centenary) 75 75

251 Text on Water

1998. 19th Danube Countries Conference, Osijek.
551 **251** 1k.80 multicoloured . . . 35 35

252 Betlheim

1998. Birth Centenary of Dr. Stjepan Betlheim (psychoanalyst).
552 **252** 1k.50 multicoloured . . . 30 30

253 Team Member

1998. Winning of Bronze Medal by Croatia in World Cup Football Championship. Sheet 112 × 82 mm containing T **253** and similar horiz design. Multicoloured.
MS553 4k. × 4, Composite design of Croatian World Cup Squad 3·00 3·00

254 Liburnian Sewn Boat (1st century B.C.)

1998. Croatian Ships. Multicoloured.
554 1k.20 Type **254** 25 25
555 1k.50 Condura (11th–12th centuries) 30 30
556 1k.60 Ragusan (Dubrovnik) carrack (16th century) . . 30 30
557 1k.80 Istrian bracera 35 35
558 2k.45 River Neretva sailing barge 50 50
559 2k.65 Barque 50 50
560 4k. "Vila Velebita" (sail/steam cadet ship) 75 75
561 7k.20 "Amorela" (car ferry) 1·40 1·40
562 20k. "King Petar Kresimir IV" (missile corvette) . . . 3·75 3·75

255 Mail Coach and Posthorn

1998. Stamp Day. 150th Anniv of Creation of Croatian Supreme Postal Administration.
563 **255** 1k.50 multicoloured . . . 30 30

256 Font and Cathedral

1998. 700th Anniv of Sibenik Bishopric and Proclamation of Sibenik as a Free Borough.
564 **256** 4k. multicoloured 75 75

257 Pope John Paul II

1998. 2nd Papal Visit.
565 **257** 1k.50 multicoloured . . . 30 30

258 Horse Tram, Osijek

1998. Transport. Multicoloured.
566 1k.50 Type **258** 30 30
567 1k.50 First motor car in Zagreb, 1901 . . . . . . 30 30
568 1k.50 Electric train, Karlovac–Rijeka line (125th anniv) 30 30
569 1k.50 Aerial view of Ostrovica–Delnice section of Zagreb–Rijeka motorway 30 30
570 7k.20 Zagreb funicular railway (19 × 23 mm) . . . 1·40 1·40

259 "Adoration of the Shepherds" (detail, from breviary "Officinum Virginis" illus by Klovic)

1998. Christmas. 500th Birth Anniv of Julije Klovic (artist).
571 **259** 1k.50 multicoloured . . . 30 30

260 Ibrisimovic

1998. 300th Death Anniv of Father Luka Ibrisimovic (revolutionary).
572 **260** 1k.90 multicoloured . . . 35 35

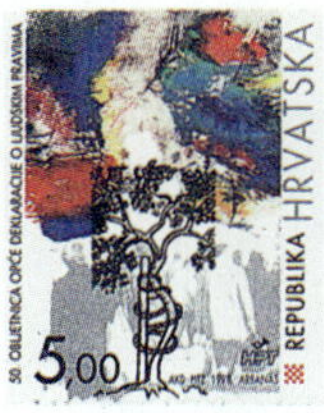

261 Distorted Tree bound to Stake

262 "Cypress" (Frano Simunovic)

1998. 50th Anniv of Universal Declaration of Human Rights.
573 **261** 5k. multicoloured 95 95

1998. 20th-century Art. Multicoloured.
574 1k.90 "Paromlin Road" (Josip Vanista) (horiz) . . 35 35
575 2k.20 Type **262** 40 40
576 5k. "Coma" (interactive video installation, Dalibor Martinis) 95 95

263 Flags

264 Haulik

1999. Zagreb Fair.
577 **263** 1k.80 multicoloured . . . 35 35

1999. 130th Death Anniv of Cardinal Juraj Haulik (first Archbishop of Zagreb).
578 **264** 5k. multicoloured 95 95

265 Mljet Island National Park

1999. Europa. Parks and Gardens. Multicoloured.
579 1k.80 Type **265** 30 30
580 5k. River Lonja Basin Nature Park 85 85

266 Viper

1999. The Orsini's Viper. Multicoloured.
581 2k.20 Type **266** 35 35
582 2k.20 Viper on alert 35 35
583 2k.20 Two vipers 35 35
584 2k.20 Viper's head 35 35

267 Anniversary Emblem

268 Orlando's Pillar with Mask

1999. 50th Anniv of Council of Europe.
585 **267** 2k.80 multicoloured . . . 45 45

1999. 19th Foundation of European Carnival Cities Convention, Dubrovnik.
586 **268** 2k.30 multicoloured . . . 40 40

269 1 Kreutzer Coin, 1849

1999. 150th Anniv of Minting of Jelacic Kreutzer (587) and Fifth Anniv of Croatian Kuna (588). Multicoloured.
587 2k.30 Type **269** 40 40
588 5k. One kuna coin 85 85

270 Vladimir Nazor (writer)

1999. Anniversaries. Multicoloured.
589 1k.80 Type **270** (50th death anniv) 30 30
590 2k.30 Ferdo Livadic (composer, birth bicentenary) 40 40
591 2k.50 Ivan Rendic (sculptor, 150th birth anniv) 45 45
592 2k.80 Milan Lenuci (urban planner, 150th birth anniv) 45 45
593 3k.50 Vjekoslav Klaic (historian, 150th birth anniv) 60 60
594 4k. Emilij Laszowski (historian, 50th death anniv) 70 70
595 5k. Antun Kanizlic (religious writer and poet, 300th birth anniv) 85 85

271 Basilica and Mosaics of Bishop Euphrasius, St. Maurus and Fish

1999. Euphrasian Basilica, Porec.
596 **271** 4k. multicoloured 70 70

272 Swimming, Diving and Rowing

1999. 2nd World Military Gamzes, Zagreb.
597 **272** 2k.30 multicoloured . . . 40 40

273 Reconstruction of Woman, Skull Fragments and Stone Tools

1999. Centenary of Discovery of Remains of Early Man in Krapina. Multicoloured.
598 1k.80 Type **273** 30 30
599 4k. Dragutin Gorjanovic-Kramberger (palaeontologist and discoverer of remains) and bone fragments 70 70
Nos. 598/9 were issued together, se-tenant, forming a composite design.

274 UPU Emblem and Clouds

1999. World Post Day. 125th Anniv of Universal Postal Union.
600 **274** 2k.30 multicoloured . . . 40 40

275 Lace, "Jesus expelling the Merchants from the Temple" (detail of fresco, Ivan Ranger), and Angel, St. Mary's Church

1999. 600th Anniv of Founding of Paulist Monastery of the Blessed Virgin Mary in Lepoglava. Multicoloured.
601 5k. Type **275** 85 85
602 5k. Altar angel and facade of St. Mary's Church 85 85
603 5k. St. Elizabeth (statue), detail of choir gallery and lace 85 85

276 Josip Jelacic, Ban of Croatia (after C. Lanzelli)

1999. 150th Anniv of Composing of the Jelacic March by Johann Strauss, the Elder.
604 **276** 3k.50 multicoloured . . . 60 60

277 Cloud and Chemical Symbol for Ozone

1999. World Ozone Layer Protection Day.
605 **277** 5k. multicoloured 85 85

278 Pazin Grammar School

1999. School Anniversaries. Multicoloured.
606 2k.30 Type **278** (centenary) 40 40
607 3k.50 Pozega Grammar School (300th anniv) . . . 60 60

279 Hebrang

280 "Madonna of the Rose- garden" (Blaz Jurjev of Trogir)

1999. Birth Cent of Andrija Hebrang (politician).
608 **279** 1k.80 multicoloured . . . 30 10

1999. "Croats—Christianity, Culture, Art" Exhibition, Vatican City.
609 **280** 5k. multicoloured 85 85

281 "Nativity for my Children" (plaster relief, Mila Wood)

1999. Christmas.
610 **281** 2k.30 multicoloured . . . 35 35

282 "Winter Landscape" (Gabrijel Jurkic)

1999. Modern Art. Multicoloured.
611 2k.30 Type **282** 35 35
612 3k.50 "Klek" (Oton Postruznik) 55 55
613 5k. "Stone Table" (Ignjat Job) (vert) 75 75

283 Tudjman

284 Angel

1999. Death Commem of President Franjo Tudjman.
614 **283** 2k.30 black and red . . . 35 35
615 5k. blue, black and red 75 75

2000. Holy Year 2000.
616 **284** 2k.30 multicoloured . . . 35 35

285 Woman's Face

286 Latin Text, Building and Archbishop Stjepan Cosmi (founder)

2000. St. Valentines Day.
617 **285** 2k.30 multicoloured . . . 35 35

2000. 300th Anniv of Split Grammar School.
618 **286** 2k.80 multicoloured . . . 40 40

287 Typewriter

288 "The Lamentation" (Andrija Medulic)

2000. Centenary of Association of Croatian Writers.
619 **287** 2k.30 black and red . . . 35 35

2000. Anniversaries. Multicoloured.
620 1k.80 Type **288** (artist, 500th birth anniv) 30 30
621 2k.30 Matija Petar Katancic (poet, 250th birth anniv) 35 35
622 2k.80 Marija Ruzicka-Strozzi (actress, 150th birth anniv) 40 40
623 3k.50 Statue of Marko Marulic (writer, 550th birth anniv) 55 55
624 5k. "Madonna with the Child and Saints" (Blaz Jurjev Trogiranin) (artist, 550th death anniv) (47 × 25 mm) 75 75

289 Map of Croatia and European Union Stars

2000. Europa. 50th Anniv of Schuman Plan (proposal for pooling the coal and steel industries of France and West Germany). Multicoloured.
625 2k.30 Type **289** 35 35
626 5k. "Building Europe" (vert) 75 75

290 Flag

2000. 10th Anniv of Independence.
627 **290** 2k.30 multicoloured . . . 35 35

291 Pavilion Building

2000. "EXPO 2000" World's Fair, Hanover. Sheet 100 × 74 mm.
MS628 **291** 14k.40 multicoloured 1·60 1·60

292 *Micromeria croatica*

2000. Flowers. Multicoloured.
629 3k.50 Type **292** 55 55
630 5k. *Geranium dalmaticum* . . 75 75

293 Statute and Postcard of Kastav

2000. 600th Anniv of the Kastav Statute.
631 **293** 1k.80 multicoloured . . . 30 30

294 Blanusa Gospel and "2000"

2000. World Mathematics Year.
632 **294** 3k.50 multicoloured . . . 55 55

295 Angels (fresco), St. George's Church, Purga

2000. 300th Birth Anniv of Ivan Ranger (artist).
633 **295** 1k.80 multicoloured . . . 30 30

296 Stone Tablet

2000. 900th Anniv of Baska Stone Tablet (early Croatian written record). Sheet 95 × 67 mm.
MS634 **296** 16k.70 multicoloured 3·00 3·00

297 Latin Text

2000. 800th Birth Anniv of Toma, Archdeacon of Split.
635 **297** 3k.50 black, silver and blue 55 55

298 Vis

2000. Croatian Towns (5th series).
636 – 2k.30 multicoloured . . 40 40
639 **298** 3k.50 multicoloured . . 60 60
639a – 3k.50 multicoloured . . 60 60
640 – 5k. multicoloured . . 90 90
DESIGNS: 2k.30, Makarska; 3k.50, Rijeka; 5k. Virovitica.

299 Austrian Empire 1850 9k. Stamp and Postmark

2000. World Post Day. Multicoloured.
641 2k.30 Type **299** (150th anniv of first stamp in territory of Croatia) 40 40
642 2k.30 Automatic sorting machine (introduction of automatic sorting system) 40 40

300 Basketball, Football, Handball, Water-polo and Tennis Balls

2000. Olympic Games, Sydney.
643 **300** 5k. multicoloured 85 85

301 "Nativity" (relief, Church of the Blessed Virgin Mary, Ogulin)

2000. Christmas.
644 **301** 2k.30 multicoloured . . . 40 40

302 "Korcula" (Vladimir Varlaj)

2000. Paintings (1st series). Multicoloured.
645 1k.80 Type **302** 30 30
646 2k.30 "Brusnik" (Duro Tiljak) 40 40
647 5k. "Boats" (Ante Kastelancic) 85 85
See also Nos. 675/7, 711/13, 746/48, 779/8, 826/8 and 872/4.

303 White Dove, Ship and Village

2001. New Millennium.
648 **303** 2k.30 multicoloured . . . 40 40

304 Charles the Great (statue)

2001. 1200th Anniv of the Coronation of Charlemagne as Emperor of the Romans. Sheet 92 × 78 mm.
MS649 **304** 14k.40 multicoloured 1·60 1·60

305 Scene from *Radmio and Ljubmir* (poem)

2001. 500th Death Anniv of Dzore Drzic (playwright).
650 **305** 2k.80 multicoloured . . . 45 45

306 Black Rider (comic strip character)

2001. Birth Centenary of Andrija Maurovic (comic strip illustrator).
651 **306** 5k. multicoloured 85 85

307 Goran Ivanisevic

2001. Croatian Sporting Victories. Multicoloured.
652 2k.50 Type **307** (Wimbledon Men's Champion) 40 40
653 2k.80 Janica Kostelic (Alpine Skiing World Cup Women's Champion) . . . 45 45

308 Olive Tree, Kastel Stafilic

2001.
654 **308** 1k.80 multicoloured . . . 30 30

309 Water (green splash to left)

2001. Europa. Water Resources. Multicoloured.
655 3k.50 Type **309** 60 60
656 5k. Water (blue splash to right) 85 85
Nos. 655/6 were issued together, se-tenant, forming a composite design.

310 Poster (Mikele Janko)

2001. World No Smoking Day.
657 **310** 2k.50 multicoloured . . . 40 40

311 Apollo (*Parnassius apollo*)

2001. Butterflies. Multicoloured.
658 2k.50 Type **311** 40 40
659 2k.80 Scarce large blue (*Maculinea teleius*) 45 45
660 5k. False ringlet (*Coenonympha oedippus*) . . 85 85

312 Vukovar

2001.
661 **312** 2k.80 multicoloured . . . 45 45

313 Statues and Flames

2001. Trsteno Arboretum. Sheet 95 × 76 mm.
MS662 **313** 14k.40 multicoloured 1·60 1·60

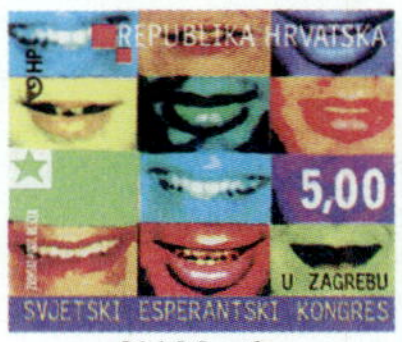

314 Mouths

2001. World Esperanto Congress, Zagreb.
663 **314** 5k. multicoloured 85 85

315 Woman and Wall

2001. 50th Anniv of United Nations Commissioner for Refugees (No. 664) and I.O.M. International Organization for Migration (No. 665). Mult.
664 1k.80 Type **315** 30 30
665 5k. Refugees and 50IOM . . 85 85

316 Perforated Blocks of Colour

2001. Stamp Day.
666 **316** 2k.50 multicoloured . . . 40 40

317 Croatian Sheep Dog

2001. Dog Breeds. Multicoloured.
667 1k.80 Type **317** 35 35
668 5k. Dalmatian 90 90

318 Head of "Our Lady of Konavle" (statue) **319** Children encircling Globe

2001. 10th Anniv of Republic of Croatia.
669 **318** 2k.30 multicoloured . . . 40 40

2001. U.N. Year of Dialogue among Civilizations.
670 **319** 5k. multicoloured 90 90

320 Klis (16th-century)

2001. Fortresses (1st series). Multicoloured.
671 1k.80 Type **320** 35 35
672 2k.50 Ston (14th-century) . . 45 45
673 3k.50 Sisak (16th-century) . . 60 60
See also Nos. 675/7, 705/7, 734/6, 776/8, 817/19, 867/9 and 908/10.

321 Adoration of the Magi (altarpiece), The Visitation of Mary Church, Cucerje **323** Lavoslav Ruzicka, (Chemistry, 1939)

322 "Amphitheatre Ruins" (Vjekoslav Parac)

2001. Christmas.
674 **321** 2k.30 multicoloured . . . 40 40

2001. Paintings (2nd series). Multicoloured.
675 2k.50 Type **322** 45 45
676 2k.50 "Maternite du Port-Royal" (Leo Junek) . . . 45 45
677 5k. "Nude with a Baroque Figure" (Slavko Sohaj) (vert) 90 90

2001. Nobel Prize Winners. Multicoloured.
678 2k.80 Type **323** 45 25
679 3k.50 Vladimir Prelog (Chemistry, 1975) 60 60
680 5k. Ivo Andric (Literature, 1961) 90 90

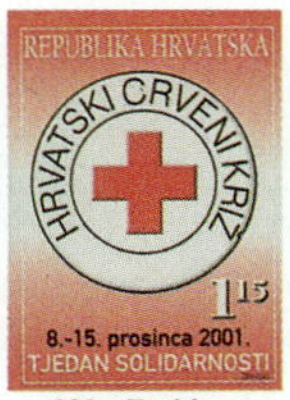

323a Emblem

2001. Obligatory Tax. Solidarity Week.
680a **323a** 1k.15 vermilion and black 30 30

324 Ivan Gucetic

2002. Anniversaries. Multicoloured.
681 1k.80 Type **324** (writer, 500th death anniv) 35 35
682 2k.30 Dobrisa Cesaric (writer, birth centenary) 40 40
683 2k.50 Juraj Rattkay (historian, 350th anniv of publication of *Memoria Regum et Banorum Regnorum Dalmatia, Croatiae et Sclavoniae Ab Origine sua usque ad praesentem Annum 1652 deducta* (history of Croatia)) 45 45
684 2k.80 Franjo Vranjanin Laurana (sculptor, 500th death anniv) 50 50
685 3k.50 Augustin Kazotic (Bishop of Zagreb, 300th anniv of beatification) . . . 65 65
686 5k. Matko Laginja (politician and writer, 150th birth anniv) 95 95

325 Skier

2002. Winter Olympic Games, Salt Lake City, U.S.A.
687 **325** 5k. multicoloured 95 95

326 Barcode and "Reaper" (drawing, Robert Franges Mihanovic)

2002. 150th Anniv of Croatian Chamber of Economy.
688 **326** 2k.50 multicoloured . . . 45 45

327 9th-century Gable bearing Prince Trpimir's Name (detail, altar partition, Rizinice Church)

2002. 1150th Anniv of Prince Trpimir's Deed of Gift of Land to Archbishop of Salona. Sheet 116 × 59 mm.
MS689 **327** 14k.40 multicoloured 2·75 2·75

328 Kuharic

2002. Cardinal Franjo Kuharic (Archbishop of Zagreb) Commemoration.
690 **328** 2k.30 multicoloured . . . 2·75 2·75

329 "Divan"

2002. 80th Death Anniv of Vlaho Bukovac (artist).
691 **329** 5k. multicoloured 95 95
A stamp in a similar design was issued by Czech Republic.

330 Arms

2002. 750th Anniv of Royal Borough of Krizevci.
692 **330** 1k.80 multicoloured . . . 35 35

331 Facade

2002. Centenary of Post Office Building, Varazdin.
693 **331** 2k.30 multicoloured . . . 40 40

332 Clown with Umbrella

2002. Europa. Circus. Multicoloured.
694 **332** 3k.50 multicoloured . . . 65 65
695 5k. multicoloured 90 95

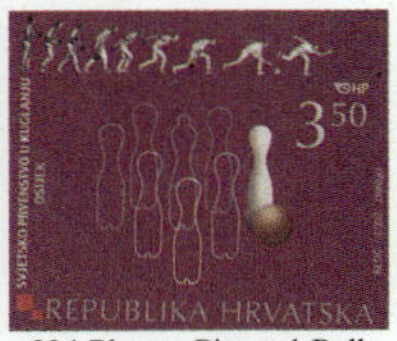

333 Stylised Player and Ball **334** Player, Pin and Ball

2002. World Cup Football Championships, Japan and South Korea. Multicoloured.
696 3k.50 Type **333** 65 65
697 5k. Stylised player ball at right 90 90

2002. World Ten-pin Bowling Championship, Osijek.
698 **334** 3k.50 multicoloured . . . 65 65

335 Common Oak (*Quercus robur*) **336** Mouse and Moon

2002. Trees. Multicoloured.
699 1k.80 Type **335** 35 35
700 2k.50 Sessile oak (*Quercus petraea*) 45 45
701 2k.80 Holly oak (*Quercus ilex*) 50 50

2002. 15th World Animated Film Festival, Zagreb.
702 **336** 5k. multicoloured 90 90

337 Pag Lacework **338** Slavonic Script

2002. Lace-making. Multicoloured.
703 3k.50 Type **337** 65 65
704 5k. Liedekerke lacework and statue of lace-maker . . . 90 90
Stamps of a similar design were issued by Belgium.

2002. Fortresses (2nd series). As T **320**. Multicoloured.
705 2k.50 Skocibuha family summer villa, Sipan (16th-century) 45 45
706 2k.50 Nehaj (16th-century) 45 45
707 5k. Veliki Tabor (16th-century) 90 90

2002. Centenary of Krk Slavic Academy.
708 **338** 4k. black and red 70 70

339 Child's Face and Emblem

2002. Children's Telephone Helpline.
709 **339** 2k.30 multicoloured . . . 40 40

340 "Our Lady and the Saints" (detail) (polyptych, Nikola Bozidarevic), Dance Church, Dubrovnik

2002. Christmas.
710 **340** 2k.30 multicoloured . . . 40 40

2002. Paintings (3rd series). As T **322**. Multicoloured.
711 2k.50 "Girl in the Boat" (Milivoj Uzelac) (vert) . . . 45 45
712 2k.50 "Flowers on the Window" (Antun Motika) (vert) 45 45
713 5k. "On the Drava River" (Krsto Hededusic) 90 90

340a Elderly Woman receiving Red Cross Parcel

2002. Obligatory Tax. Solidarity Week.
713a **340a** 1k.15 multicoloured . . 30 30

341 Zagreb Cathedral

343 Column Capitals, Bell Tower, St. Mary's Church, Zadar

342 Pavao Vitezovic

2002. 150th Anniv of Zagreb Archbishopric.
714 **341** 2k.80 multicoloured . . . 50 50

2002. 350th Birth Anniv of Pavao Ritter Vitezovic (writer).
715 **342** 2k.30 multicoloured . . . 40 40

2002. 900th Anniv of Accession Hungarian King Koloman to Croatian Throne.
716 **343** 3k.50 multicoloured . . . 60 60

344 Kosjenka (Regoc)

2003. Fairy Stories. Showing characters from stories by Ivana Brlic Mazuranic. Multicoloured.
717 2k.30 Type **344** 40 40
718 2k.80 Malik Tintilinic (Suma Striborova) 50 50

345 Heart enclosed in Jigsaw Puzzle

2003. St. Valentine's Day.
719 **345** 2k.30 multicoloured . . . 40 40

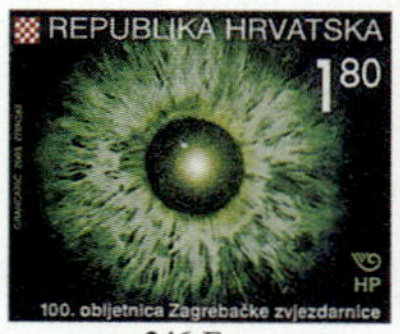

346 Eye

347 Players and Coach

2003. Centenary of Zagreb Astronomical Observatory (1k.80). 150th Anniv of Meteorological Measurements and 50th Anniv of Meteorological Station on Zavizan (3k.50). Multicoloured.
720 1k.80 Type **346** 30 30
721 3k.50 Eye and lightening . . 65 65

2003. Croatia, World Handball Champions, Portugal 2003. Sheet 112 × 83 mm containing T **347** and similar vert designs showing team.
MS722 4k. Type **347**; 4k. Eight players; 4k. Six players; 4k. Four players . . . . 3·00 3·00

348 Building Facade and Monks

349 Page from Missal

2003. 500th Anniv of the Paulist (White Friars) Secondary School, Lepoglava.
723 **348** 5k. multicoloured 90 90

2003. 600th Anniv of Duke Hrvoje's Glagolitic Missal (illuminated book).
724 **349** 5k. multicoloured 90 90

350 Prosthetic Leg

2003. Anti-Landmine Campaign.
725 **350** 2k.30 multicoloured . . . 40 40

351 Janica Kostelic

2003. World Cup Alpine Skiing Gold Medallists, St. Moritz 2003. Multicoloured.
726 3k.50 Type **351** 60 60
727 3k.50 Ivica Kosteli 60 60

352 Antun Soljan (poet, tenth anniv)

2003. Death Anniversaries. Multicoloured.
728 1k.80 Type **352** 30 30
729 2k.30 Hanibal Lucic (poet, 450th anniv) 40 40
730 5k. Federiko Benkovic (artist, 250th anniv) 90 90

353 St. Jerome

2003. 550th Anniv of St. Jerome Papal Institutions, Rome.
731 **353** 2k.80 multicoloured . . . 50 50

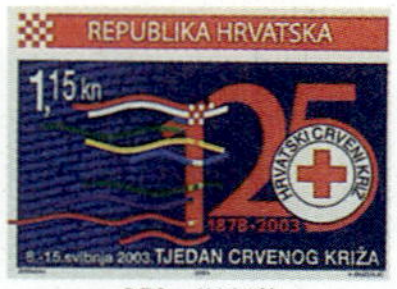

353a "125"

2003. Obligatory Tax. Red Cross Week. 125th Anniv of Croatian Red Cross.
731a **353a** 1k.15 multicoloured . . 25 25

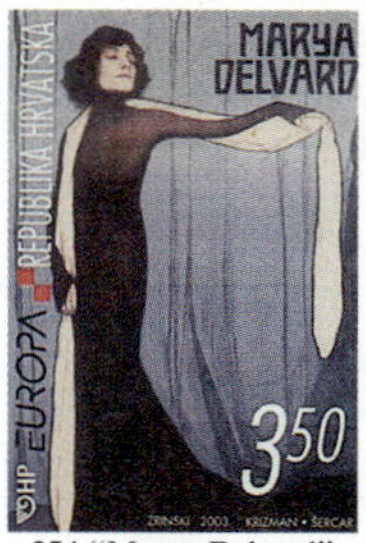

354 "Marya Delvard" (Tomislav Krizman)

2003. Europa. Poster Art. Multicoloured.
732 3k.50 Type **354** 50 60
733 5k. "The Firebird" (Boris Bucan) (35 × 35 mm) . . . 90 90

2003. Fortresses (3rd series). As T **320**. Multicoloured.
734 1k.80 Kostajnica, (15th-century) 30 30
735 2k.80 Slavonski, Brod (18th-century) 50 50
736 5k. Minceta, Dubrovnik (15th-century) 90 90

355 Pope John Paul II

2003. Pope John Paul II's Third Visit to Croatia.
737 **355** 2k.30 multicoloured . . . 40 40

356 Squirrel (*Sciurus vulgaris*)

2003. Fauna. Multicoloured.
738 2k.30 Type **356** 40 40
739 2k.80 Dormouse (*Glis glis*) 50 50
740 3k.50 Beaver (*Castor fiber*) 60 60

357 Cope

2003. King Ladislaus' Cope (11th-century). Sheet 95 × 70 mm.
MS741 **357** 1k. multicoloured . . 20 20

358 Letter Box, Envelopes and Stamp

2003. Stamp Day. 50th Anniv of Post Museum, Zagreb.
742 **358** 2k.30 multicoloured . . . 40 40

358a "tjedan borbe protiv TBC"

2003. Obligatory Tax. Anti-Tuberculosis Week.
742a **358a** 1k.15 vermilion and green 25 25

359 Vines and Paths

2003. UNESCO World Heritage Site. Primosten Vineyard. Sheet 110 × 78 mm.
MS743 **359** 10k. multicoloured 1·80 1·80

360 Mother of Mercy (statue) and Nativity Church, Varaldin

2003. 300th Anniv of Ursuline Religious Order in Croatia.
744 **360** 2k.50 multicoloured . . . 45 45

361 Three Wise Men

2003. Christmas.
745 **361** 2k.30 multicoloured . . . 40 40

2003. Paintings (4th series). As T **322**. Multicoloured.
746 1k.80 "Flower Girl II" (Slavko Kopac) 30 30
747 3k.50 "Dry Stone Wall" (Oton Gliha) (vert) 60 60
748 3k.50 "Pont Des Art" (Josip Racic) (vert) 60 60

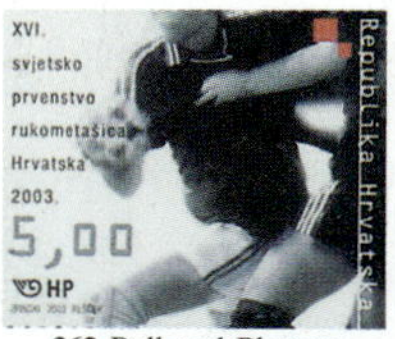

362 Ball and Players

2003. 16th Women's World Handball Championships.
749 **362** 5k. multicoloured 90 90

362a Snow-covered House and Tree

2003. Obligatory Tax. Solidarity Week.
749a **362a** 1k.15 multicoloured . . 25 25

363 Josip Hatze

364 Manuscript Page

2004. Musical Anniversaries. Multicoloured.
750 5k. Type **363** (125th birth anniv of Josip Hatze (composer)) 90 90
751 5k. Violin bridge and strings (50th anniv of Zagreb Soloists ensemble) 90 90

2004. 600th Anniv of Hval's Manuscript.
752 **364** 2k.30 multicoloured . . . 40 40

365 Stylized Boxing Ring

2004. European Boxing Championship, Pula.
753 **365** 2k.80 multicoloured . . . 50 50

366 Adult Heron

2004. Purple Heron (*Ardea purourea*). Mult.
754 5k. Type **366** 90 90
755 5k. Adult and chick 90 90
756 5k. Adults flying 90 90
757 5k. Adult in reed bed 90 90

367 Frontispiece of "De Regno Dalmatiae et Croatie"

369 Martyrdom of St. Domnius and Ivan Lucic

368 Wild Flowers

2004. Anniversaries. Multicoloured.
758 2k.30 Type **367** (writer and historian) (400th birth anniv) 40 40
759 3k.50 Antun Vrancic (writer) (500th birth anniv) 65 65
760 3k.50 St. Jerome (sculpture) (Andrija Alesi) (500th death anniv) 65 65
761 10k. Frontispiece Croatian grammar (Bartol Kasic) (400th anniv of first publication) . . . . 1·80 1·80

2004. Risnjak National Park. Sheet 99 × 74 mm.
MS762 **368** 10k. multicoloured 1·80 1·80

2004. 700th Anniv of the Martyrdom of St. Domnius.
763 **369** 3k.50 multicoloured . . . 65 65

369a Elderly man and Child

2004. Obligatory Tax. Red Cross Week.
763a **369a** 1k.15 multicoloured . . 25 25

370 Toboggan, Skater, Ski Poles and Skis

2004. Europa. Holidays. Multicoloured.
764 3k.50 Type **370** 65 65
765 3k.50 Deck chair, beach ball and sunglasses 65 65

371 Football and Emblem

372 Dog Rose (*Rosa canina*)

2004. Centenary of FIFA (Federation Internationale de Football Association).
766 **371** 2k.50 multicoloured . . . 45 45

2004. Medicinal Plants. Multicoloured.
767 2k.30 Type **372** 40 40
768 2k.80 Sweet violet (*Viola odorata*) 50 50
769 3k.50 Peppermint (*Mentha piperita*) 65 65

373 Puppets forming "UNIMA"

2004. World UNIMA (puppeteers) Conference, Opatija. International Puppetry Festival, Rijeka.
770 **373** 3k.50 multicoloured . . . 65 65

374 Multicoloured Football

2004. European Football Championship 2004, Portugal.
771 **374** 3k.50 multicoloured . . . 65 65

375 Mostar Bridge

2004. Reconstruction of Ottoman Bridge at Mostar.
772 **375** 3k.50 multicoloured . . . 65 65

376 Discus Throwing

2004. Olympic Games, Athens.
773 **376** 3k.50 multicoloured . . . 65 65

377 Building Facade

2004. Centenary of Post Office, Zagreb.
774 **377** 2k.30 multicoloured . . . 40 40

377a Hand-washing

2004. Obligatory Tax. Anti-Tuberculosis Week.
774a **377a** 1k.15 multicoloured . . 20 20

378 Andrija Miosic

2004. 300th Birth Anniv of Father Andrija Kacic Miosic (writer).
775 **378** 2k.80 multicoloured . . . 40 40

2004. Fortresses (4th series). As T **320**. Multicoloured.
776 3k.50 Dubovac (15th-century) 65 65
777 3k.50 Valpovo (15th–18th century) 65 65
778 3k.50 Gripe (17th-century) . . 65 65

2004. Paintings (5th series). As T **322**. Multicoloured.
779 2k.30 "Parisian Suburb" (Juraj Plancic) (vert) . . . 40 40
780 2k.30 "Noon in Supetar" (Jerolim Mise) (vert) . . . 40 40
781 2k.30 "Self-portrait" (Miroslav Kraljevic) (vert) 40 40

379 Christmas Wheat

2004. Christmas.
782 **379** 2k.30 multicoloured . . . 40 40

379a Children, Red Cross Parcel and Elderly Woman

2004. Obligatory Tax. Solidarity Week.
782a **379a** 1k.15 multicoloured . . 20 20

380 Antun and Stjepan Radic (founders)

2004. Centenary of Croatian Peoples Peasants' Party (HPSS).
783 **380** 7k.20 turquoise and black 1·40 1·40

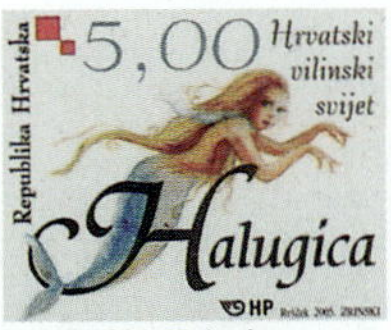

381 Halugica

2005. Fairy Stories. Showing characters from stories by Vladimir Nazor. Multicoloured.
784 5k. Type **381** 95 95
785 5k. Longbeard Mannikin ("Grujo the Pioneer") . . . 95 95

382 " " and Circuit Board

2005. World Conferences on Information Technology, Geneva and Tunis.
786 **382** 2k.80 multicoloured . . . 50 50

383 Livia Drusilla (Oxford—Opuzen Livia) (statue)

2005. Roman Archaeological Site, Narona. Joint British—Croatian Roman Exhibitions, 2004—2005. Sheet 110 × 71 mm.
MS787 **383** 10k. multicoloured 1·80 1·80

384 Circle enclosing Square

2005. EXPO 2005 World Exhibition, Aichi, Japan. Sheet 97 × 80 mm.
MS788 **384** 10k. vermilion and silver 1·80 1·80

385 Pope John Paul II

2005. Pope John Paul II Commemoration.
789 **385** 2k.30 multicoloured . . . 40 40

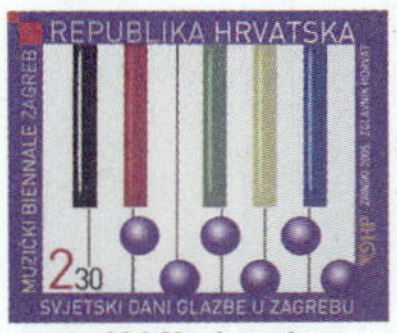

386 Keyboard

387 Ladybird (*Coccinella septempunctata*)

2005. Croatian Music. Multicoloured.
790 2k.30 Type **386** (Music Biennale (festival), Zagreb) 40 40
791 2k.30 Stjepan Sulek (composer) 40 40

2005. Insects. Multicoloured.
792 1k.80 Type **387** 35 35
793 2k.30 *Rosalia alpine* 40 40
794 3k.50 Stag beetle (*Lucanus cervus*) 65 65

388 Tank

2005. 10th Anniv of Military Action.
795 **388** 1k.80 multicoloured . . . 35 35

389 Josip Buturac

2005. Birth Centenary of Josip Buturac (historian and writer).
796 **389** 2k.80 multicoloured . . . 50 50

389a Kiss

2005. Obligatory Tax. Red Cross Week.
796a **389a** 1k.15 multicoloured . . 20 20

390 Bread

2005. Europa. Gastronomy. Multicoloured.
797 3k.50 Type **390** 65 65
798 3k.50 Glass of wine 65 65

391 Rock, Sea and Cliff

2005. Tourism. Multicoloured.
799 1k.80 Type **391** 50 50
800 1k.80 Branches, cliff and sea 50 50
801 1k.80 Sea and rock 50 50
802 1k.80 Canoe, rock and sea 50 50
803 1k.80 Sea surrounding rock 50 50
804 3k.50 Trees 50 50
805 3k.50 Trees and cliff 50 50
806 3k.50 Cliff and rocks 50 50
807 3k.50 Cliff and sunken rocks 50 50
808 3k.50 Rock point and sea . . 50 50

392 Kresimir Cosic

393 Coral surrounding Sponge

2005. 10th Death Anniv of Kresimir Cosic (basketball player).
809 **392** 3k.50 multicoloured . . . 65 65

2005. Endangered Species.
810 **393** 3k.50 multicoloured . . . 65 65

394 Building Facade

2005. Varazdinske Toplice Spa.
811 **394** 1k.80 multicoloured . . . 50 50

395 St. Florian (statue)

2005. International Fire Brigade Olympics, Varazdin.
812 **395** 2k.30 multicoloured . . . 40 40

2005. 50th Anniv of Europa Stamps. As T **65**. Multicoloured.
813 7k.20 As No. 195 . . . . . 1·30 1·30
814 8k. Stylized bird . . . . . . 1·50 1·50
MS815 92 × 78 mm. Nos. 813/14 2·75 2·75

396 Morse Code Machine

2005. 155th Anniv of First Overhead Telegraph Lines.
816 **396** 2k.30 multicoloured . . . 40 40

396a Running

397 Adam Baltazar Krcelic (writer) (290th birth anniv)

2005. Obligatory Tax. Anti-Tuberculosis Week.
816a **396a** 1k.15 multicoloured . . 20 20

2005. Fortresses (5th series). As T **320**. Multicoloured.
817 1k. Ilok (14th—15th-century) 20 20
818 3k.50 Motovun (13th—15th-century) (vert) . . . 65 65
819 3k.50 St. Nicholas Fortress, Sibenik (16th-century) . . 65 65

2005. Personalities. Multicoloured.
820 1k. Type **397** 20 20
821 2k.30 Dragutin Tadijanovic (writer) (100th birthday) . . 40 40
822 2k.30 Augustin (Tin) Ujevic (writer) (50th death anniv) 40 40
823 2k.80 "Madonna and Child" (Juraj Culinovic) (400th death anniv (2004)) 55 55

398 "Our Lady with Child and Saints" (detail)

2005. Christmas. Ordinary or self-adhesive gum.
824 **398** 2k.30 multicoloured . . . 40 40

2005. Paintings (6th series). As T **322**. Multicoloured.
826 1k.80 "Zader" (Edo Mutric) 50 50
827 5k. "Meander" (Julije Knifer) 85 85
828 10k. "Drawing" (Miroslav Sutej) (vert) . . . . 1·60 1·60

399 Team and Trophy

2005. Croatia—Winner of Davis Cup (tennis championship)—2005.
829 **399** 5k. multicoloured 85 85

399a Elderly Man receiving Red Cross Parcel

2005. Obligatory Tax. Solidarity Week.
829a **379a** 1k.15 multicoloured . . 20 20

400 Boris Papndopulo

2006. Musicians' Birth Centenaries. Multicoloured.
830 1k.80 Type **400** 50 50
831 2k.30 Milo Cipra 40 40
832 2k.80 Ivan Brkanovic 65 65

401 Crossed Skies

2006. Winter Olympic Games, Turin.
833 **401** 3k.50 multicoloured . . . 65 65

402 "Self-portrait with Velvet Cap with Plume"

2006. 400th Birth Anniv of Rembrandt Harmenszoon Van Rijn (Rembrandt) (artist).
834 **402** 5k. multicoloured 85 85

403 Josip Kozarac (writer) (death centenary)

2006. Anniversaries. Multicoloured.
835 1k. Type **403** 20 20
836 1k. Andrija Ljudevit Adamic (entrepreneur) (240th birth anniv) 20 20
837 5k. Ljubo Karaman (art historian) (120th birth anniv) 85 85
838 7k.20 Vanja Radaus (artist and writer) (birth centenary) . . . . 1·30 1·30

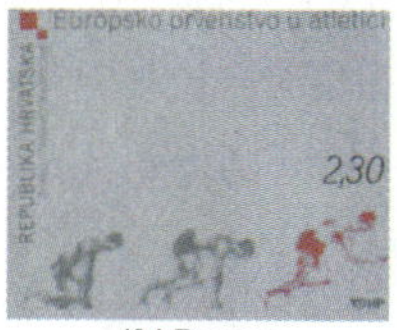

404 Runner

2006. European Athletics Championship, Göteburg.
839 **404** 2k.30 multicoloured . . . 40 40

405 Stylized Player

2006. World Cup Football Championship, Germany.
840 **405** 2k.80 multicoloured . . . 65 65

406 Crowd and Part of Flag

2006. Tourism. Designs showing parts of the Croatian flag. Multicoloured.
841 1k.80 Type **406** . . . . . . 1·20 1·20
842 1k.80 Crowd and part of flag (larger) . . . . 1·20 1·20
843 1k.80 Crowd and part of flag (large red square) . . . . 1·20 1·20
844 1k.80 Crowd and part of flag (large white square) . . . 1·20 1·20
845 1k.80 Flag and crowd (two raised arms) . . . . 1·20 1·20
846 3k.50 Flag creased . . . . . 2·20 2·20
847 3k.50 Flag (one raised arm) 2·20 2·20
848 3k.50 Flag . . . . 2·20 2·20
849 3k.50 Flag and crowd (several raised arms and cap) . . . . 2·20 2·20
850 3k.50 Small part of flag and crowd . . . . 2·20 2·20

407 Boy carrying Red Cross Bag

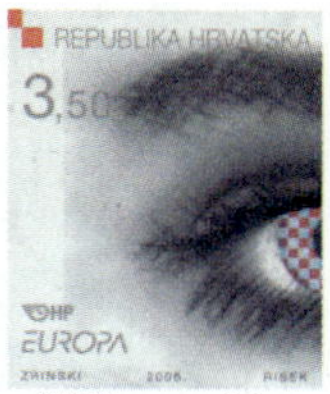

408 Eye containing Squares

2006. Obligatory Tax. Red Cross Week.
851 **407** 1k.15 multicoloured . . . 1·00 1·00

2006. Europa. Integration. Multicoloured.
852 3k.50 Type **408** . . . . . . 2·10 2·10
853 3k.50 Eye containing stars . . 2·10 2·10
Nos. 852/3 were issued together, se-tenant, forming a composite design of an eye.

409 Little Tern

2006. Little Tern (*Sterna albifrons*). Multicoloured.
854 5k. Type **409** . . . . 3·00 3·00
855 5k. Diving . . . . 3·00 3·00
856 5k. Facing right . . . . . . 3·00 3·00
857 5k. Sitting on eggs . . . . . 3·00 3·00

410 Elmore (1905)

2006. Centenary of Croatian Motor Club (HAK).
858 **410** 5k. multicoloured . . . . 3·00 3·00

411 *Nymphaea alba*

2006. Flora. Multicoloured.
859 2k.30 Type **411** . . . . . . 1·40 1·40
860 2k.80 *Nuphar lutea* . . . . . 1·70 1·70
861 3k.50 *Menyanthes trifoliate* 2·20 2·20

412 Nikola Tesla

2006. 150th Birth Anniv of Nikola Tesla (scientist).
862 **412** 3k.50 multicoloured . . . 2·20 2·20

413 Clock Tower

2006. 250th Anniv of Bjelovar.
863 **413** 2k.80 multicoloured . . . 1·60 1·60

414 Post Box

415 "Tjedan borbe protiv TBC-a"

2006. Statehood.
864 **414** 2k.30 multicoloured . . . 1·40 1·40

2006. Obligatory Tax. Anti-Tuberculosis Week.
865 **415** 1k.15 multicoloured . . . 1·00 1·00

416 Synagogue and Menorah

2006. Bicentenary of Jewish Community, Zagreb.
866 **416** 5k. multicoloured . . . . 3·00 3·00

2006. Fortresses (6th series). As T **320**. Mult.
867 1k. Sudurad, Sipan (16th-century) 95 95
868 1k. St Mary of Mercy, Vrboska (16th-century) . . 95 95
869 7k.20 Francopan Citadel, Ogulin (16th-century) . . 2·40 2·40

417 "DAN BIJELOG STAPA 2006"

2006. White Stick Day.
869 **417** 1k.80 black and vermillion 1·10 1·10
No. 869 has "White Cane Safety Day" embossed in Braille on its surface.

418 "Nativity" (Pantaleone)

419 Santa on Skis

2006. Christmas. Ordinary or self-adhesive gum.
870 **418** 2k.30 multicoloured . . . 1·00 1·00

2006. Paintings (7th series). As T **322**. Mult.
872 1k. "Still Life" (Vladimir Becic) . . . . 1·20 1·20
873 1k.80 "Composition Tyma 3" (Ivan Picelj) . . . . . . 1·70 1·70
874 10k. "Self Portrait Hunter" (Nasta Rojc) (vert) . . . . 7·00 7·00

2006. Obligatory Tax. Solidarity Week.
875 **419** 1k.15 multicoloured . . . 1·00 1·00

420 Emblem

421 Orko

2007. 400th Anniv of Classical Gymnasium, Zagreb.
876 **420** 5k. multicoloured . . . . 3·00 3·00

2007. Fairy Stories. Multicoloured.
877 2k.30 Type **421** . . . . 1·40 1·40
878 2k.30 Macic ("Grujo the Pioneer") . . . . 1·40 1·40

422 Building Facade

2007. 400th Anniv of National and University Library, Zagreb.
879 **422** 5k. multicoloured . . . . 3·00 3·00

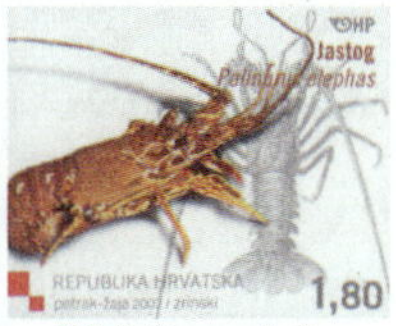

423 *Palinurus elephas*

2007. Fauna. Multicoloured.
880 1k.80 Type **423** . . . . . . 1·20 1·20
881 2k.30 *Nephrops norvegicus* . . 1·40 1·40
882 2k.80 *Astacus astacus* . . . . 1·60 1·60

424 Istrian Ox

2007. Autochthonous Breeds. Multicoloured.
883 2k.80 Type **424** . . . . . . 1·60 1·60
884 3k.50 Posavina horse . . . . 1·70 1·70
885 5k. Dalmatian donkey . . . 3·00 3·00

425 Emblem

2007. Europa. Centenary of Scouting. Multicoloured.
886 3k.50 Type **425** . . . . . . 2·30 2·30
887 3k.50 Neckerchief . . . . . 2·30 2·30

426 Andrija Mohorovicic

2007. Anniversaries. Multicoloured.
888 5k. Type **426** (mathematician and seismologist) (150th birth anniv) . . . . 3·00 3·00
889 7k.20 Duro Baglivi (medical scientist) (300th birth anniv) . . . . 4·50 4·50

427 Team Members

428 Red Cross, Red Crescent and Proposed New Emblems

2007. Croatia–World Water Polo Champions, Melbourne 2007 Sheet 105 × 68 mm containing T **427** and similar vert designs. Multicoloured.
MS890 5k. × 3, Type **427**; Ten team members; Flag and team members 9·25 9·25
The stamps and margins of **MS**890 form a composite design of the winning team and trainers.

2007. Obligatory Tax. Red Cross Week.
891 **428** 1k.15 multicoloured . . . 1·00 1·00

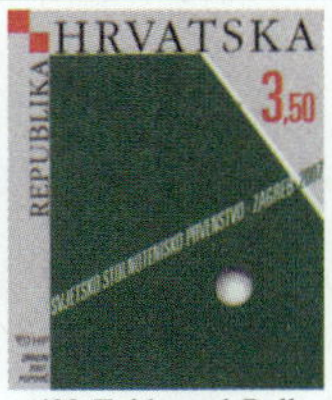

429 Table and Ball

2007. World Table Tennis Championship, Zagreb–2007.
892 **429** 3k.50 multicoloured . . . 2·30 2·30

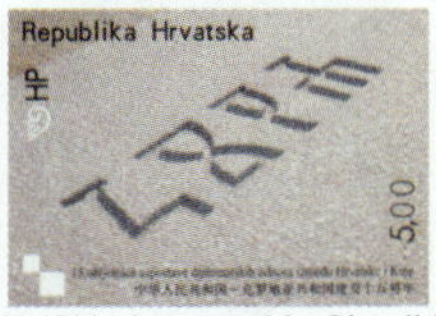

430 'China' engraved in Glagolitic Script

2007. 15th Anniv of Croatia–China Diplomatic Relations. Multicoloured.
893 5k. Type **430** . . . . 3·25 3·25
894 5k. 'Hrvatska' written in Chinese script . . . . . . 3·25 3·25

431 Women in Window (17th-century Trompe L'Oeil)

432 Lake and Cliff

2007. Centenary of City Museum, Zagreb.
895 **431** 2k.30 multicoloured . . . 1·50 1·50

2007. Red Lake. Sheet 112 × 72 mm.
MS896 **432** 10k. multicoloured 6·25 6·25
The stamp and margins of **MS**896 form a composite design of the Red Lake and surrounding area.

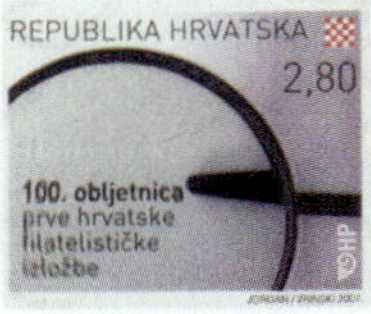

433 Magnifying Glass

433a "Tjedan borbe protiv TBC-a"

2007. Centenary of First National Philatelic Exhibition.
897 **433** 2k.80 multicoloured . . . 1·75 1·75

2007. Obligatory Tax. Anti-Tuberculosis Week.
897a **433a** 1k.15 multicoloured . . 1·00 1·00

434 Sv. Ivan na pucini (St. John at open sea)

2007. Lighthouses. Multicoloured.
898 5k. Type **434** . . . . 3·25 3·25
899 5k. Savudrija . . . . 3·25 3·25
900 5k. Porer . . . . 3·25 3·25

435 Fragment of Statute

436 Omis

2007. 500th Anniv of Veprinac Statute (oldest Croatian legal document).
901 **435** 2k.70 multicoloured . . . 1·75 1·75

2007. Towns.
902 **436** 1k.80 brown, bistre and vermilion . . . . . . 1·20 1·20
903 – 2k.30 brown, rose and vemilion (horiz) . . . . 1·40 1·40
904 – 2k.80 multicoloured . . . 1·60 1·60
DESIGNS: 1k.80 Type **436**; 2k.30 Koprivnica; 2k.80 Krk.

437 Blanka Vlasic

2007. Blanka Vlasic. Women's High Jump World Champion–2007.
905 **437** 2k.30 multicoloured . . . 1·50 1·50

438 Nativity (painting, Bishop's Palace, Pozega)

439 Marija Zagorka

2007. Christmas. Ordinary or self-adhesive gum.
906 **438** 2k.30 multicoloured . . . 1·60 1·60

2007. 50th Death Anniv of Marija Juric Zagorka (writer).
907 **439** 7k.20 multicoloured . . . 4·75 4·75

2007. Paintings (8th series). As T **322**. Mult.
908 2k.80 *Area by the River Sava* (Branko Senoa) . . . . . 1·50 1·50
909 5k. *Bridgeport* (Ivan Benokovic) . . . . 3·25 3·35
910 5k. *Pegasus's Garden* (Ferdinand Kulmer) . . . 3·25 3·25

440 Angel (Vedran Damjanovic Maglica)

2007. New Year.
911 **440** 1k.80 multicoloured . . . 1·25 1·25

441 Gifts

2007. Obligatory Tax. Solidarity Week.
912 **441** 1k.15 multicoloured . . . 1·00 1·00

442 Igor Kuljeric

2008. Croatian Composers. Multicoloured.
913 2k.30 Type **442** (70th birth anniv) . . . . 1·50 1·50
914 2k.30 Krsto Odak (120th birth anniv) . . . . 1·50 1·50

443 Marija Zagorka

2008. 250th Anniv of *Arithmetika Horvatszka* (mathematical handbook).
915 **443** 3k.50 multicoloured . . . 2·25 2·25

444 Steam Locomotive MAV 651/JZ 31

2008. Steam Locomotives made by MAV Gepgyar, Budapest. Multicoloured.
916 5k. Type **444** . . . . 3·25 3·25
917 5k. MAV 601/JZ 32 . . . . 3·25 3·25

2008. Towns. As T **436**. Multicoloured .
918 7k.20 St Nicholas Church, Cavtat . . . . 4·75 4·75

445 Stylized Athletes

2008. Olympic Games, Beijing.
919 **445** 5k. multicoloured . . . . 3·25 3·25

446 *Hellborus niger* (Christmas rose)

2008. Flora. Multicoloured.
920 1k.80 Type **446** . . . . . . 1·25 1·25
921 2k.80 *Onosma stellulata* (star flower) . . . . 1·50 1·50
922 3k.50 *Lonicera glutinosa* (honeysuckle) . . . . . . 2·25 2·25

Nos. 923/5 and Type **447** have been left for 'Personalities', issued on 22 April 2008, not yet received.

Nos. 926/35 and Type **448** have been left for 'Greetings', issued on 25 April 2008, not yet received.

Nos. 936 and Type **449** have been left for 'Red Cross', issued on 8 May 2008, not yet received.

450 Volkswagen *Beetle*

2008.
937 **450** 2k.30 multicoloured . . . 1·50 1·50

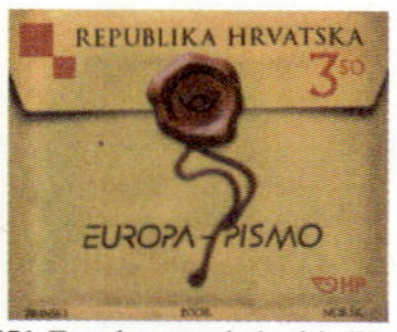

451 Envelope sealed with Wax

2008. Europa. The Letter. Multicoloured.
938 3k.50 Type **451** . . . . . . 2·30 2·30
939 5k. Airmail envelope . . . . 3·00 3·00
No. 939 has the outline of an aircraft embossed at upper right.

452 Footballs

2008. European Football Championships, Austria and Switzerland.
940 **452** 3k.50 multicoloured . . . 2·30 2·30

453 Sails

2008. *Adris.*
941 **453** 2k.30 multicoloured . . . 1·50 1·50

454 Ivan Vucetica

2008. 150th Birth Anniv of Ivan Vucetica (fingerprint identification pioneer). Sheet 112 × 73 mm.
MS942 454 10k. multicoloured 6·25 6·25
The stamp and margins of **MS**942 form a composite design.

OFFICIAL STAMPS

O 11

O 12

1942.
O55 **O 11** 25b. red 10 10
O56 50b. grey 10 10
O57 75b. green 10 10
O58 1k. brown 10 10
O59 2k. blue 10 10
O60 3k. red 10 10
O61 3k.50 red 10 10
O62 4k. purple 10 10
O63 5k. blue 20 40
O64 6k. violet 10 10
O65 10k. green 10 10
O66 12k. red 15 30
O67 12k.50 orange 10 10
O68 20k. blue 20 40
O69 **O 12** 30k. grey and brown . . . 15 30
O70 40k. grey and violet . . 15 30
O71 50k. grey and red . . . 50 1·00
O72 100k. salmon & black . . 50 1·00

POSTAGE DUE STAMPS

1941. Nos. D259/63 of Yugoslavia optd **NEZAVISNA DRZAVA HRVATSKA** in three lines above a chequered shield.
D26 **D 10** 50p. violet 20 40
D27 1d. red 20 40
D28 2d. blue . . . . 6·00 12·50
D29 5d. orange . . . . . . 65 1·25
D30 10d. brown . . . . . . 3·00 8·00

D 9

D 15

1941.
D51 **D 9** 50b. red 15 45
D52 1k. red 15 45
D53 2k. red 20 60
D54 5k. red 35 90
D55 10k. red . . . . 50 1·25

1942.
D67 **D 15** 50b. olive and blue . . 15 30
D68 1k. olive and blue . . . 15 35
D69 2k. olive and blue . . . 15 35
D76 4k. olive and blue . . . 10 20
D70 5k. olive and blue . . . 20 40
D78 6k. olive and blue . . . 10 55
D79 10k. blue and indigo . . 15 50
D80 15k. blue and indigo . . 15 50
D72 20k. blue and indigo . . 80 1·60

SERBIAN POSTS IN CROATIA

100 paras = 1 dinar.

REPUBLIC OF SRPSKA KRAJINA

Following Croatia's declaration of independence from Yugoslavia on 30 May 1991 fighting broke out between Serb inhabitants, backed by units of the Yugoslav Federal Army, and Croatian forces. By January 1992, when a ceasefire sponsored by the United Nations and the European Community became effective, the Croatian Serbs and their allies controlled 30% of the country organized into the districts of the Krajina, Western Slavonia and Eastern Slavonia. These were declared peace-keeping zones under United Nations supervision and the Yugoslav Army withdrew. In 1993 the Serbs proclaimed the Republic of Srpska Krajina, covering all three areas, and elections for a separate president and parliament were held in January 1994.

K **1** Stag, Kopacevo Marsh

K **3** Coat of Arms

1993.
K1 K **1** 200d. green and yellow . . 25 25
K2 – 500d. black and red . . . 65 65
K3 – 1000d. green and yellow 1·40 1·40
K4 – 1000d. green and yellow 1·40 1·40
K5 – 2000d. black and red . . 3·00 3·00
DESIGNS: No. K2, Krka Monastery; K3, Town walls, Knin; K4, Ruined house, Vukovar; K5, Coat of arms.
For 100000d. in same design as No. K2 see No. K12.

1993. Issued at Knin. Nos. 2594/5 of Yugoslavia surch.
K6 5000d. on 3d. black and red 65 65
K7 10000d. on 2d. blue and red 65 65

1993.
K8 K **3** A blue and red 45 45
No. K8 was sold at the internal letter rate.

K **4** Citadel, Knin

A

(K 5)

K **6** Helmet and Swords

1993.
K 9 K **4** 5000d. green and red . . 10 10
K10 – 10000d. green and red 15 15
K11 – 50000d. blue and red . . 75 75
K12 – 100000d. blue and red 1·50 1·50
DESIGNS: 10000d. Heron, Kopacevo Marsh; 50000d. Icon and church, Vukovar; 100000d. Krka Monastery.

Currency Reform

1993. No. K8 surch with Type K **5** (Cyrillic letter "D").
K13 K **3** "D" on A blue and red 40 40
No. K13 was sold at the new internal letter rate.

1993. Nos. K9/12 surch with Type K **5** (Cyrillic letter "D").
K14 K **4** "D" on 5000d. grn & red 45 45
K15 – "D" on 10000d. green and red 85 85
K16 – "D" on 50000d. blue and red . . . . 2·50 2·50
K17 – "D" on 100000d. blue and red . . . . 8·50 8·50

1993.
K18 K **6** R blue . . . . 1·10 1·10
No. K18 was sold at the internal registered letter rate.

K **7** St. Simeon

1994. Serb Culture and Tradition. Mult.
K19 50p. Type K **7** 80 80
K20 80p. Krajina coat of arms (vert) . . . . 1·25 1·25
K21 1d. "The Vucedol Dove" (carving) (vert) . . . . . 1·75 1·75

K **8** Cup-and-saucer

K **9** Krka Monastery

1994. Climbing Plants. Multicoloured.
K22 30p. Type K **8** 60 60
K23 40p. "Dipladenia" 85 85
K24 60p. Black-eyed Susan . . . 1·25 1·25
K25 70p. Climbing rose . . . . 1·50 1·50

1994.
K26 K **9** 5p. red 10 10
K27 – 10p. brown 20 20
K28 – 20p. green 40 40
K29 – 50p. red 55 55
K30 – 60p. violet 70 70
K31 – 1d. blue . . . . 2·25 2·25
DESIGNS: 10p. Carin; 20p. Vukovar; 50p. Monument, Batina; 60p. Ilok; 1d. Lake, Plitvice.

K **10** "The Flower of Life" (memorial to Jasenovac Concentration Camp victims)

K **11** "A" over Mosaic

1995. 50th Anniv of End of Second World War.
K32 K **10** 60p. multicoloured . . 1·40 1·40

1995.
K33 K **11** A red 30 30
No. K33 was sold at the internal letter rate.

K **12** Krcic Waterfall, Knin

1995.
K34 K **12** 10p. blue 10 10
K35 – 20p. ochre 10 10
K36 – 40p. red 20 20
K37 – 2d. blue . . . . 1·10 1·10
K38 – 5d. brown . . . . . . 2·75 2·75
DESIGNS: 20p. Benkovac; 40p. Citadel, Knin; 2d. Petrinja; 5d. Pakrac.

In May 1995 the Croatian army occupied Western Slavonia and in August 1995 the Krajina and these areas were reincorporated into the Republic of Croatia. The only surviving part of the Serbian territories, Eastern Slavonia, was, by agreement, placed under temporary United Nations administration in November 1995 and was subsequently called Sremsko Baranjska Oblast (Srem and Baranya Region).

SREMSKO BARANJSKA OBLAST

K **13** Common Cormorant ("Phalacrocorax carbo"), Kopacevo Marsh

1995. Protected Species. Multicoloured.
K39 80p. Type K **13** 90 90
K40 80p. Chamois, Lika 90 90

K **14** St. Dimitriev's Church, Dalj

K **15** Vukovar Marina, River Danube

1995. Churches (1st series).
K41 K **14** 5p. green 10 10
K42 – 10p. red 15 15
K43 – 30p. mauve 35 35
K44 – 50p. brown 80 80
K45 – 1d. blue . . . . 1·10 1·10
DESIGNS: 10p. St. Peter and St. Paul's Church, Bolman; 30p. St. Nicholas's Church, Mirkovci; 50p. St. Nicholas's Church, Tenja; 1d. St. Nicholas's Church, Vukovar.
See also Nos. K48/53.

1996. River Danube Co-operation.
K46 K **15** 1d. multicoloured . . . 1·50 1·50

K **16** The Worker's Hall, Vukovar

K **17** Archangel Church, Darda

1996.
K47 K **16** A red 30 30
No. K47 was sold at the internal letter rate.

1996. Churches (2nd series).
K48 K **17** 10p. brown 10 10
K49 – 50p. violet 10 10
K50 – 1d. green 15 15
K51 – 2d. green 45 45
K52 – 5d. blue . . . . . . 1·90 1·90
K53 – 10d. blue . . . . . . 3·75 3·75
DESIGNS: 50p. St. George's Church, Knezevo; 1 d St. Nicholas's Church, Jagodnjak; 2d. Archangel Gabriel's Church, Brsadin; 5d. St. Stephen's Church, Borovo Selo; 10d. St. Nicholas's Church, Pacetin.

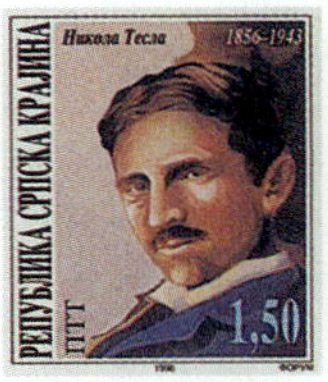
K **18** Nikola Tesla

K **19** Milica Stojadinovic-Srpkinja (1830–78) (poetess)

1996. 140th Birth Anniv of Nikola Tesla (inventor).
K54 K **18** 1d.50 multicoloured . . 1·50 1·50

1996. Europa, Famous Women, Mult.
K55 1d.50 Type K **19** . . . . . 2·50 2·50
K56 1d.50 Mileva Marie-Einstein (1875–1948) (mathematician) . . . . . 2·50 2·50

K **20** Jasna Sekaric (Olympic gold medal winner)

K **21** Milutin Milankovic

1996. Centenary of Modern Olympic Games.
K57 K **20** 1d.50 multicoloured . . 1·25 1·25

1996. Milutin Milankovic (geophysicist) Commemoration (1879–1958).
K58 K **21** 1d.50 multicoloured . . 1·25 1·25

K **22** "Madonna and Child" (icon)

K **23** Pigeon

1996. Christmas.
K59 K **22** 1d.50 multicoloured . . 1·25 1·25

1997. Domestic Pets. Multicoloured.
K60 1d. Type K **23** 50 50
K61 1d. Budgerigar 50 50
K62 1d. Cat 50 50
K63 1d. Black labrador 50 50

1997. No. K18 surch or optd (No. K67) with crosses obliterating former name.
K64 K **6** 10p. on R blue 10 10
K65 20p. on R blue 10 10
K66 30p. on R blue 15 15
K67 R (90p.) blue 40 40
K68 1d. on R blue 30 30
K69 1d.50 on R blue 60 60
K70 2d. on R blue 80 80
K71 5d. on R blue . . . . 1·50 1·50
K72 10d. on R blue . . . . 3·75 3·75
K73 20d. on R blue . . . . 9·00 9·00

K **25** St. Peter and St. Paul's Cathedral, Orolik

K **26** Prince Marko and The Turks

1997. Restoration of Orthodox Church, Ilok.
K74 K **25** 50p.+50p. blue 35 35
K75 – 60p.+50p. mauve . . . 35 35
K76 – 1d.20+50p. red 55 55
DESIGNS: 60p. St. George's Church, Tovarnik; 1d.20, Church, Negoslavci.

1997. Europa. Tales and Legends. Mult.
K77 1d. Type K **26** 70 70
K78 1d. Emperor Trajan 70 70

The postal administration of the Srem and Baranya Region was reincorporated into that of the Republic of Croatia on 19 May 1997. Eastern Slavonia was returned to Croatian control on 15 January 1998.

CUBA Pt. 15

An island in the W. Indies, ceded by Spain to the United States in 1898. A republic under U.S. protection until 1901 when the island became independent. The issues to 1871, except Nos. 13, 14, 19, 20/7, 32, 44 and 48, were for Puerto Rico also.

1855. 8 reales plata fuerte (strong silver reales) = 1 peso.
1866. 100 centimos = 1 escudo.
1871. 100 centimos = 1 peseta.
1881. 100 milesimas = 100 centavos = 1 peso.
1898. 100 cents = 1 U.S. dollar.
1899. 100 centavos = 1 peso.

SPANISH COLONY

1

5

1855. Imperf.
6 **1** ½r. green . . . . 6·25 85
9 ½r. blue . . . . 3·50 80
10 1r. green . . . . 3·25 80
11 2r. red . . . . 15·00 3·25
Nos. 10/11 optd **HABILITADO POR LA NACION** were issues of Philippines (Nos. 44/5).

1855. No. 11a surch **Y ¼**.
12 **1** Y¼ on 2r. red . . . . £200 65·00

1862. Imperf.
13 **5** ¼r. black on buff . . . . . . 19·00 20·00

6

7

1864. Imperf.
14 **6** ¼r. black on buff . . . . 16·00 18·00
15 ½r. green . . . . 4·00 80
16 ½r. green on pink . . . . 10·00 2·10
17 1r. blue on brown . . . . 3·75 80
18b 2r. red . . . . 20·00 4·75

1866. Dated "1866". Imperf.
19 **7** 5c. mauve . . . . 33·00 29·00
20 10c. blue . . . . 3·25 80
21 20c. green . . . . 1·40 80
22 40c. pink . . . . 8·75 7·00

1866. No. 14 optd **66**. Imperf.
23 **6** ¼r. black on buff . . . . . . 60·00 70·00

1867. Dated "1867". Perf.
24 **7** 5c. mauve . . . . 38·00 19·00
25 10c. blue . . . . 19·00 1·30
26 20c. green . . . . 12·00 1·80
27 40c. pink . . . . 13·50 8·75

9

11

1868. Dated "1868".
28 **9** 5c. lilac . . . . 18·00 10·50
29 10c. blue . . . . 3·50 1·70
30 20c. green . . . . 6·00 3·25
31 40c. pink . . . . 14·50 7·50

1868. Nos. 28/31 optd **HABILITADO POR LA NACION**.
36 **9** 5c. lilac . . . . 60·00 32·00
37 10c. blue . . . . 60·00 32·00
38 20c. green . . . . 60·00 32·00
39 40c. pink . . . . 60·00 32·00

1869. Dated "1869".
32 **9** 5c. pink . . . . 37·00 14·00
33 10c. brown . . . . 3·50 1·70
34 20c. orange . . . . 6·25 2·20
35 40c. lilac . . . . 32·00 10·50

1869. Nos. 32/5 optd **HABILITADO POR LA NACION**.
40 **9** 5c. pink . . . . £120 38·00
41 10c. brown . . . . 50·00 34·00
42 20c. orange . . . . 44·00 34·00
43 40c. lilac . . . . 70·00 34·00

1870.
44 **11** 5c. blue . . . . £140 60·00
45 10c. green . . . . 2·40 85
46 20c. brown . . . . 2·75 85
47 40c. pink . . . . £180 35·00

12

13

1871. Dated "1871".
48 **12** 12c. lilac . . . . 18·00 10·50
49a 25c. blue . . . . 2·00 85
50 50c. green . . . . 2·20 85
51 1p. brown . . . . 30·00 8·25

1873.
52 **13** 12½c. green . . . . 27·00 14·00
53 25c. grey . . . . 2·20 85
54 50c. brown . . . . 1·60 85
55 1p. brown . . . . £275 44·00

1874. Dated "1874".
56 **12** 12½c. brown . . . . 17·00 8·00
57 25c. blue 85 55
58 50c. lilac . . . . 1·50 80
59 1p. red . . . . £190 60·00

14

15

1875.
60 **14** 12½c. mauve 90 90
61 25c. blue 40 35
62 50c. green 50 40
63 1p. brown . . . . 7·75 5·00

1876. Inscr "ULTRAMAR 1876".
64 **15** 12½c. green . . . . 1·80 1·50
65a 25c. lilac . . . . 1·40 30
66 50c. blue 75 40
67 1p. black . . . . 8·25 3·75

1877. Inscr "CUBA 1877".
68 **15** 10c. green . . . . 25·00
69 12½c. lilac . . . . 4·75 2·20
70 25c. green 60 50
71 50c. black 60 50
72 1p. brown . . . . 26·00 13·00

1878. Inscr "CUBA 1878".
73 **15** 5c. blue 55 50
74 10c. black . . . . 60·00
75a 12½c. bistre . . . . 3·50 1·70
76 25c. green 25 20
77 50c. green 35 20
78 1p. red . . . . 9·75 4·75

1879. Inscr "CUBA 1879".
79 **15** 5c. black 55 25
80 10c. orange . . . . £120 75·00
81 12½c. pink 55 25
82 25c. blue 45 25
83 50c. grey 45 25
84 1p. bistre . . . . 15·00 9·75

1880. "Alfonso XII" key-type inscr "CUBA 1880".
85 X 5c. green 35 20
86 10c. red . . . . 70·00
87 12½c. lilac 35 20
88 25c. lilac 35 20
89 50c. brown 35 20
90 1p. brown . . . . 5·25 2·75

1881. "Alfonso XII" key-type inscr "CUBA 1881".
91 X 1c. green 25 20
92 2c. pink . . . . 37·00
93a 2½c. bistre 50 35
94 5c. lilac 25 20
95 10c. brown 35 20
96 20c. brown . . . . 5·25 4·25

1882. "Alfonso XII" key-type inscr "CUBA".
97 X 1c. green 35 35
98 2c. pink . . . . 2·20 35
118 2½c. brown 35 20
119 2½c. mauve 35 25
100 5c. lilac . . . . 2·20 50
123 5c. grey . . . . 2·20 45
101 10c. brown 55 20
126 10c. blue . . . . 1·30 85
121 20c. brown . . . . 13·00 2·75
122 20c. lilac . . . . 12·50 4·00

1883. 1882 issue optd or surch with fancy pattern.
103 X 5c. lilac . . . . 1·90 1·30
106 5 on 5c. lilac . . . . . 1·60 1·00
104 10c. brown . . . . 5·00 4·50
107 10 on 10c. brown . . . . 2·20 1·60
105 20c. brown . . . . £130 35·00
111 20 on 20c. brown . . . . 25·00 21·00
The surcharges exist in four different patterns.

1890. "Baby" key-type inscr "ISLA DE CUBA".
135 Y 1c. brown . . . . 12·00 6·25
147 1c. grey . . . . 7·25 3·50
159 1c. blue . . . . 3·00 35
169 1c. purple 80 25
136 2c. blue . . . . 6·50 2·10
148 2c. brown . . . . 1·40 50
160 2c. pink . . . . 35·00 10·00
170 2c. red . . . . 7·25 75
137 2½c. green . . . . 8·75 4·00
149 2½c. orange . . . . 41·00 9·25
161 2½c. mauve . . . . 2·75 25
171 2½c. pink 65 20
138 5c. grey 70 60
150 5c. green 90 40
172 5c. blue 45 20
139 10c. brown . . . . 2·50 75
151 10c. pink . . . . 1·50 40
173 10c. green . . . . 2·10 20
140 20c. purple 75 60
152 20c. blue . . . . 8·50 7·50
162 20c. brown . . . . 22·00 9·50
174 20c. lilac . . . . 15·00 5·25
175 40c. brown . . . . 27·00 11·50
176 80c. brown . . . . 49·00 18·00

1898. "Curly Head" key-type inscr "CUBA 1898 Y 99".
183 Z 1m. brown 20 15
184 2m. brown 20 15
185 3m. brown 20 15
186 4m. brown . . . . 3·50 1·40
187 5m. brown 20 15
188 1c. purple 20 15
189 2c. green 20 15
190 3c. brown 20 15
191 4c. orange . . . . 10·50 3·50
192 5c. pink 70 15
193 6c. blue 20 15
194 8c. brown 75 35
195 10c. red 80 35
196 15c. grey . . . . 3·50 35
197 20c. purple 45 15
198 40c. mauve . . . . 1·80 35
199 60c. black . . . . 2·00 35
200 80c. brown . . . . 11·50 7·25
201 1p. green . . . . 11·50 7·25
202 2p. blue . . . . 22·00 7·25

OFFICIAL STAMPS

1860. As Nos. O50/3 of Spain but without full points after "OFICIAL" and "ONZAS" or "LIBRA". Imperf.
O12 ½o. black on yellow . . . . — 34·00
O13 1o. black on pink . . . . . — 34·00
O14 4o. black on green . . . . . — £180
O15 1l. black on blue . . . . . — £425
The face values of Nos. O12/15 are expressed in onzas (ounces) or libra (pound), referring to the maximum weight for which each value could prepay postage.

PRINTED MATTER STAMPS

All Printed Matter stamps are key-types inscribed "CUBA IMPRESOS".

1888. "Alfonso XII".
P129 X ½m. black 55 15
P130 1m. black 55 20
P131 2m. black 55 20
P132 3m. black . . . . 1·00 80
P133 4m. black . . . . 1·90 1·50
P134 8m. black . . . . 7·25 3·50

1890. "Baby".
P141 Y ½m. brown 60 45
P142 1m. brown 60 45
P143 2m. brown . . . . 1·00 80
P144 3m. brown . . . . 1·00 80
P145 4m. brown . . . . 7·50 5·50
P146 8m. brown . . . . 7·50 5·50

1892. "Baby".
P153 Y ½m. lilac 40 30
P154 1m. lilac 40 30
P155 2m. lilac 40 30
P156 3m. lilac . . . . 1·50 30
P157 4m. lilac . . . . 3·50 1·70
P158 8m. lilac . . . . 7·75 3·00

1894. "Baby".
P163 Y ½m. pink 20 20
P164 1m. pink 60 20
P165 2m. pink 60 20
P166 3m. pink . . . . 1·70 80

P167 4m. pink . . . . 3·00 1·00
P168 8m. pink . . . . 6·00 3·75

1896. "Baby".
P177 Y ½m. green 20 20
P178 1m. green 20 20
P179 2m. green 20 20
P180 3m. green . . . . 2·50 80
P181 4m. green . . . . 5·50 4·00
P182 8m. green . . . . 10·00 6·00

UNITED STATES ADMINISTRATION

1899. Stamps of United States of 1894 surch **CUBA** and value.
246 1c. on 1c. green (No. 283) . . 4·50 35
247 2c. on 2c. red (No. 270) . . . 8·50 65
248 2½c. on 2c. red (No. 270) . . 4·25 70
249 3c. on 3c. violet (No. 271) . . 8·50 1·50
250 5c. on 5c. blue (No. 286) . . 12·00 1·70
251 10c. on 10c. brown (No. 289) 21·00 5·50

29 Statue of Columbus

1899.
307 **29** 1c. green . . . . 1·70 20
308 – 2c. red . . . . 1·20 20
303 – 3c. purple . . . . 3·75 15
304 – 5c. blue . . . . 3·75 15
310 – 10c. brown . . . . 3·25 50
DESIGNS: 2c. Palms; 3c. Statue of "La India" (Woman); 5c. Liner "Umbria" (Commerce); 10c. Ploughing Sugar Plantation.

POSTAGE DUE STAMPS

1899. Postage Due stamps of United States of 1894 surch **CUBA** and value.
D253 **D 87** 1c. on 1c. red . . . . 38·00 4·50
D254 2c. on 2c. red . . . . 38·00 4·50
D255 5c. on 5c. red . . . . 38·00 4·50
D256 10c. on 10c. red . . . 23·00 2·10

SPECIAL DELIVERY STAMP

1899. No. E283 of United States surch **CUBA. 10c. de PESO.**
E252 **E 46** 10c. on 10c. blue . . . £160 85·00

INDEPENDENT REPUBLIC

1902. Surch **UN CENTAVO HABILITADO OCTUBRE 1902** and figure **1**.
306 1c. on 3c. purple (No. 303) 2·00 50

36 Major-General Antonio Maceo

37 B. Maso

1907.
311 **36** 50c. black and slate . . . 1·20 80
318 50c. black and violet . . . 1·70 50

1910.
312 **37** 1c. violet and green 85 25
320 1c. green . . . . 1·00 25
313 – 2c. green and red . . . . 1·50 25
321 – 2c. red . . . . 1·00 25
314 – 3c. blue and violet . . . . 1·20 25
315 – 5c. green and blue . . . . 16·00 85
322 – 5c. blue . . . . 2·00 25
316 – 8c. violet and olive . . . . 1·20 35
323 – 8c. black and olive . . . . 2·00 65
317 – 10c. blue and sepia . . . . 7·25 70
319 – 1p. black and slate . . . 8·00 4·25
324 – 1p. black . . . . 5·25 2·10
PORTRAITS: 2c. M. Gomez. 3c. J. Sanguily. 5c. I. Agramonte. 8c. C. Garcia. 10c. Mayia. 1p. C. Roloff.

40 Map of W. Indies

43 Gertrudis Gomez de Avellaneda

1914.
325 **40** 1c. green . . . . 2·10 25
326 2c. red 70 25
328 3c. violet . . . . 4·50 35
329 5c. blue . . . . 6·50 25
330 8c. olive . . . . 5·25 65
331 10c. brown . . . . 9·50 35
332 10c. olive . . . . 11·00 50
333 50c. orange . . . . 70·00 9·25
334 $1 slate . . . . £100 22·00

1914. Birth Centenary of Gertrudis Gomez de Avellaneda (poetess).
335 **43** 5c. blue . . . . 13·00 4·50

44 Jose Marti

47

1917.
336 **44** 1c. green 75 25
337 – 2c. red (Gomez) 80 25
338 – 3c. violet (La Luz) 85 25
339 – 5c. blue (Garcia) 80 25
349a – 8c. brown (Agramonte) 3·00 25
341 – 10c. brown (Palma) . . . 2·50 25
342 – 20c. green (Saco) . . . . 14·50 1·70
343 – 50c. red (Maceo) . . . . 14·50 75
344 – 1p. black (Cespedes) . . . 14·50 75

1927. 25th Anniv of Republic.
352 **47** 25c. violet . . . . 13·00 3·75

48 PN 9 Flying Boat over Havana Harbour

1927. Air.
353 **48** 5c. blue . . . . 3·50 1·70

49 T. Estrada Palma

1928. 6th Pan-American Conference.
354 **49** 1c. green 50 30
355 – 2c. red 50 30
356 – 5c. blue . . . . 1·20 45
357 – 8c. brown . . . . 2·50 1·10
358 – 10c. brown . . . . 1·10 75
359 – 13c. orange . . . . 1·70 75
360 – 20c. olive . . . . 2·10 90
361 – 30c. purple . . . . 4·25 75
362 – 50c. red . . . . 6·75 2·75
363 – 1p. black . . . . 13·50 6·25
DESIGNS: 2c. Gen. G. Machado; 5c. El Morro, Havana; 8c. Railway Station, Havana; 10c. President's Palace; 13c. Tobacco plantation; 20c. Treasury Secretariat; 30c. Sugar Mill; 50c. Havana Cathedral; 1p. Galician Immigrants' Centre, Havana.

1928. Air. Lindbergh Commemoration. Optd **LINDBERGH FEBRERO 1928**.
364 **48** 5c. red . . . . 3·50 1·50

51 The Capitol, Havana

52 Hurdler

1929. Inauguration of Capitol.
365 **51** 1c. green 35 30
366 2c. red 40 30
367 5c. blue 55 40
368 10c. brown . . . . 1·00 50
369 20c. purple . . . . 3·75 2·40

1930. 2nd Central American Games, Havana.
370 **52** 1c. green 60 60
371 2c. red 60 70
372 5c. blue 85 70
373 10c. brown . . . . 1·60 1·60
374 20c. purple . . . . 12·50 4·25

1930. Air. Surch **CORREO AEREO NACIONAL** and value.
375 **47** 10c. on 25c. violet . . . . 3·00 1·70

54 Fokker Super Trimotor over Beach

1931. Air.
376 **54** 5c. green 50 15
377 8c. red . . . . 3·25 1·00
378 10c. blue 50 15
379 15c. red . . . . 1·10 30
380 20c. brown . . . . 1·10 15
381 30c. purple . . . . 1·70 20
382 40c. orange . . . . 3·75 45
383 50c. green . . . . 4·25 50
384 1p. black . . . . 6·75 1·10

55 Ford "Tin Goose" over Forest

1931. Air.
385 **55** 5c. purple 40 15
386 10c. black 40 15
387 20c. red . . . . 3·00 90
388 20c. pink . . . . 1·80 50
389 50c. blue . . . . 5·00 95
390 50c. turquoise . . . . . . 2·50 1·00

56 Mangos of Baragua

57 Battle of Mal Tiempo

1933. 35th Anniv of War of Independence.
391 **56** 3c. brown . . . . 1·10 25
392 **57** 5c. blue . . . . 1·00 40
393 – 10c. green . . . . 2·50 40
394 – 13c. red . . . . 2·75 1·00
395 – 20c. black . . . . 5·25 3·00
DESIGNS—HORIZ: 10c. Battle of Coliseo; 13c. Maceo, Gomez and Zayas. VERT: 20c. Campaign Monument.

1933. Establishment of Revolutionary Govt. Stamps of 1917 optd **GOBIERNO REVOLUCIONARIO 4-9-1933** or surch also.
396A **44** 1c. green . . . . 4·00 25
397A – 2c. on 3c. vio (No. 338) 4·00 25

59 Dr. Carlos J. Finlay

61 Map of Caribbean

1934. 101st Birth Anniv of C. J. Finlay ("yellow-fever" researcher).
398 **59** 2c. red . . . . 1·00 25
399 5c. blue . . . . 1·90 55

1935. Air. Havana–Miami "Air Train". Surch **PRIMER TREN AEREO INTERNACIONAL. 1935 O'Meara y du Pont + 10 cts.** Imperf or perf.
400 **54** 10c.+10c. red . . . . . 4·25 4·25

1936. Free Port of Matanzas. Inscr as in T **61**. Perf or imperf (same prices).
401 **61** 1c. green (postage) 35 25
402 – 2c. red 55 25
403 – 4c. purple 95 25
404 – 5c. blue . . . . 1·40 25
405 – 8c. brown . . . . 2·50 70
406 – 10c. green . . . . 2·75 70
407 – 20c. brown . . . . 5·00 2·50
408 – 50c. slate . . . . 9·25 3·50
409 – 5c. violet (air) 75 30
410 – 10c. orange . . . . 1·00 45
411 – 20c. green . . . . 3·50 2·00
412 – 50c. black . . . . 8·50 3·50
DESIGNS—POSTAGE: 2c. Matanzas Bay and Free Zone; 4c. "Rex" (liner) in Mantanzas Bay; 5c. Ships in the Free Zone; 8c. Bellamar Caves; 10c. Yumuri Valley; 20c. Yumuri River; 50c. Sailing ship and steamer. AIR: 5c. Aerial panorama; 10c. Airship "Macon" over Concord Bridge; 20c. Airplane "Cuatro Vientos" over Matanzas; 50c. San Severino Fortress.

63 President J. M. Gomez

64 Gen. J. M. Gomez Monument

1936. Inauguration of Gomez Monument.
413 **63** 1c. green . . . . 1·20 25
414 **64** 2c. red . . . . 1·80 30

65 "Peace and Labour"

66 Maximo Gomez Monument

1936. Inaug of Maximo Gomez Monument.
415 **65** 1c. green (postage) 35 25
416 **66** 2c. red 45 25
417 – 4c. purple 55 25
418 – 5c. blue . . . . 3·00 75
419 – 8c. olive . . . . 3·50 90
420 – 5c. violet (air) . . . . . . 2·00 1·00
421 – 10c. brown . . . . 3·50 1·00
DESIGNS—VERT: 4c. Flaming torch; 8c. Dove of Peace. HORIZ: 5c. (No. 418) Army of Liberation; 5c. (No. 420) Lightning; 10c. "Flying Wing".

68 Caravel and Sugar Cane

1937. 400th Anniv of Cane Sugar Industry.
422 – 1c. green . . . . 1·00 40
423 – 2c. red 50 25
424 **68** 5c. blue . . . . 1·00 40
DESIGNS (each with caravel in upper triangle). HORIZ: 2c. Early sugar mill; 5c. Modern sugar mill.

69 Mountain View (Bolivia)

70 Camilo Henriquez (Chile)

1937. American Writers and Artists Assn.
424a – 1c. green (postage) . . . 70 70
424b **69** 1c. green 70 70
424c – 2c. red 70 70
424d – 2c. red 70 70
424e **70** 3c. violet . . . . 1·40 1·40
424f – 3c. violet . . . . 1·40 1·40
424g – 4c. brown . . . . 1·50 1·50
424h – 4c. brown . . . . 3·00 3·00
424i – 5c. blue . . . . 1·70 1·70
424j – 5c. blue . . . . 1·70 1·70
424k – 8c. green . . . . 8·00 8·00
424l – 8c. green . . . . 2·50 2·00
424m – 10c. brown . . . . 2·75 2·75
424n – 10c. brown . . . . 2·75 2·75
424o – 25c. lilac . . . . 34·00 28·00
424p – 5c. red (air) . . . . . . 6·25 6·25
424q – 5c. red . . . . 6·25 6·25
424r – 10c. blue . . . . 6·25 6·25
424s – 10c. blue . . . . 6·25 6·25
424t – 20c. green . . . . 9·00 9·00
424u – 20c. green . . . . 9·00 9·00
DESIGNS—VERT: No. 424a, Arms of the Republic (Argentina); No. 424c, Arms (Brazil); No. 424f, Gen. F. de Paula Santander (Colombia); No. 424g, Autograph of Jose Marti (Cuba); No. 424j, Juan Montalvo (Ecuador); No. 424k, Abraham Lincoln (U.S.A.); No. 4241, Quetzal and scroll (Guatemala); No. 424m, Arms (Haiti); No. 424n, Francisco Morazan (Honduras); No. 424r, Inca gate, Cuzco (Peru); No. 424s, Atlacatl (Indian warrior) (El Salvador); No. 424t, Simon Bolivar (Venezuela); No. 424u, Jose Rodo (Uruguay). HORIZ: No. 424d, River scene (Canada); No. 424h, National Monument (Costa Rica); No. 424i, Columbus Lighthouse (Dominican Republic); No. 424o, Ships of Columbus; No. 424p, Arch (Panama); No. 424q, Carlos Lopez (Paraguay).

1937. Centenary of Cuban Railway. Surch **1837 1937 PRIMER CENTENARIO FERROCARRIL EN CUBA** and value either side of an early engine and coach.
425 **47** 10c. on 25c. violet . . . . 11·50 3·25

1938. Air. 25th Anniv of D. Rosillo's Overseas Flight from Key West to Havana. Optd **1913 1938 ROSILLO Key West-Habana**.
426 **48** 5c. orange . . . . 3·50 2·10

74 Pierre and Marie Curie

75 Allegory of Child Care

1938. International Anti-cancer Fund. 40th Anniv of Discovery of Radium.
427 **74** 2c.+1c. red . . . . 3·00 1·30
428 5c.+1c. blue . . . . 3·00 1·40

1938. Obligatory Tax. Anti-T.B. Fund.
429 **75** 1c. green . . . . 1·60 25

76 Native and Cigar

80 Calixto Garcia

1939. Havana Tobacco Industry.
430 **76** 1c. green 35 25
431 – 2c. red 45 25
432 – 5c. blue 90 30
DESIGNS: 2c. Cigar, globe and wreath of leaves; 5c. Tobacco plant and box of cigars.

1939. Air. Experimental Rocket Post. Optd **EXPERIMENTO DEL COHETE Postal ANO DE 1939**.
433 **55** 10c. green . . . . 40·00 7·75

1939. Birth Centenary of Gen. Calixto Garcia. Perf or imperf.
434 **80** 2c. red 55 25
435 – 5c. blue 90 40
DESIGN: 5c. Garcia on horseback.

82 Nurse and Child

83 Gonzalo de Quesada and Union Flags

84 Rotarian Symbol, Flag and Tobacco Plant

1939. Obligatory Tax. Anti-T.B.
436 **82** 1c. red 90 25

1940. 50th Anniv of Pan-American Union.
437 **83** 2c. red 95 40

1940. Rotary International Convention.
438 **84** 2c. red . . . . 1·70 85

85 Lions, Emblem, Flag and Palms

86 Dr. Gutierrez

1940. Lions International Convention, Havana.
439 **85** 2c. red . . . . 1·70 85

1940. Centenary of Publication of First Cuban Medical Review.
440 **86** 2c. red 85 40
441 5c. blue . . . . 1·20 40
MS442 127 × 177 mm. Two each of Nos. 440/1. Imperf (sold at 25c.) 4·75 4·00
See also Nos. **MS**560/1.

87 Sir Rowland Hill and G.B. 1d. of 1840 and Cuba Issues of 1855 and 1899

1940. Air. Centenary of 1st Adhesive Postage Stamps.
443 **87** 10c. brown . . . . 3·25 2·10
MS444 128 × 178 mm. No. 443 in block of four. Imperf (sold at 60c.) 15·00 15·00

88 "Health" protecting Children

89 Heredia and Niagara Falls

1940. Obligatory Tax. Children's Hospital and Anti-T.B. Funds.
445 **88** 1c. blue 90 25

1940. Air. Death Centenary of J. M. Heredia y Campuzaono (poet).
446 – 5c. green . . . . 2·25 1·10
447 **89** 10c. grey . . . . 2·75 1·60
DESIGN: 5c. Heredia and palms.

90 General Moncada and Sword

91 Moncada riding into Battle

1941. Birth Centenary of H. Moncada.
448 **90** 3c. brown . . . . 1·20 45
449 **91** 5c. blue . . . . 1·20 45

92 Mother and Child

95 "Labour, Wealth of America"

1941. Obligatory Tax. Anti-T.B.
450 **92** 1c. brown 90 25

1942. American Democracy. Imperf or perf.
451 – 1c. green 25 20
452 – 3c. brown 35 20
453 **95** 5c. blue 55 25
454 – 10c. mauve . . . . 1·40 60
455 – 13c. red . . . . 2·50 1·00
DESIGNS: 1c. Western Hemisphere; 3c. Cuban Arms and portraits of Maceo, Bolivar, Juarez and Lincoln; 10c. Tree of Fraternity, Havana; 13c. Statue of Liberty.

98 Gen. Ignacio Agramonte Loynaz

99 Rescue of Sanguily

1942. Birth Centenary of Gen. I. A. Loynaz.
456 **98** 3c. brown 85 40
457 **99** 5c. blue . . . . 1·70 50

100 "Victory"

102 "Unmask Fifth Columnists"

1942. Obligatory Tax. Red Cross Fund.
458 **100** ½c. orange 40 25
459 ½c. grey 55 25

1942. Obligatory Tax. Anti-T.B. Fund. Optd **1942**.
460 **92** 1c. red . . . . 1·00 30

1943. Anti-Fifth Column.
461 **102** 1c. green 50 25
462 – 3c. red 95 25
463 – 5c. blue 95 30
464 – 10c. brown . . . . 3·25 95
465 – 13c. purple . . . . 4·75 2·10
DESIGNS—HORIZ: (45 × 25 mm.) 5c. Woman in snake's coils ("The Fifth Column is like the Serpent — destroy it"); 10c. Men demolishing column with battering-ram ("Fulfil your patriotic duty by destroying the Fifth Column").
Type **102**. 13c. Woman with monster "Don't be afraid of the Fifth Column. Attack it". VERT: Girl with finger to lips "Be Careful! The Fifth Column is spying on you".

105 Eloy Alfaro, Flags of Ecuador and Cuba and Scroll of Independence

1943. Birth Centenary of E. Alfaro (former President of Ecuador).
466 **105** 3c. green . . . . 1·10 40

106 "The Long Road to Retirement"

107 "Health" Protecting Child

1943. Postal Employees' Retirement Fund.
467 **106** 1c. green 60 40
470 3c. red . . . . 1·10 50
471 5c. blue 95 50

1943. Obligatory Tax. Anti-tuberculosis.
473 **107** 1c. brown 90 25

108 Columbus

109 Discovery of Tobacco

1944. 450th Anniv of Discovery of America.
474 **108** 1c. green (postage) . . . 30 20
475 – 3c. brown 40 20
476 – 5c. blue 65 25
477 **109** 10c. violet . . . . 2·75 75
478 – 13c. red . . . . 3·75 1·70
479 – 5c. olive (air) 95 40
480 – 10c. grey . . . . 2·10 70
DESIGNS—VERT: 3c. Bartolome de las Casas; 5c. (No. 476), Statue of Columbus. HORIZ: 5c. (No. 479) Mountains of Gibara; 10c. (No. 480), Columbus Lighthouse; 13c. Columbus at Pinar del Rio.

110 Carlos Roloff

111 American Continents and Brazilian "Bull's Eyes" stamps

1944. Birth Centenary of Major-Gen. Roloff.
481 **110** 3c. violet . . . . 1·00 30

1944. Cent of 1st American Postage stamps.
482 **111** 3c. brown . . . . 1·30 55

112 Society Seal

113 Governor Las Casas and Bishop Penalver

1945. 150th Anniv of Economic Society of Friends of Havana.
483 **112** 1c. green 40 20
484 **113** 2c. red 95 30

115 Old Age Pensioners

1945. Postal Employees' Retirement Fund.
485 **115** 1c. green 60 40
487 2c. red . . . . 1·00 40
489 5c. blue . . . . 2·50 40

116 Valdes

1946. Death Centenary of Gabriel de la Concepcion Valdes (poet).
491 **116** 2c. red . . . . 1·10 20

117 Manuel Marquez Sterling

118 Red Cross and Globe

1946. Founding of "Manuel Marquez Sterling" Professional School of Journalism.
492 **117** 2c. red . . . . 1·80 20

1946. 80th Anniv of International Red Cross.
493 **118** 2c. red . . . . 1·20 40

119 Prize Cattle and Dairymaid

120 Franklin D. Roosevelt

1947. National Cattle Show.
494 **119** 2c. red . . . . 1·60 50

1947. 2nd Death Anniv of Pres. Roosevelt.
495 **120** 2c. red . . . . 1·80 50

121 Antonio Oms and Pensioners

1947. Postal Employees' Retirement Fund.
496 **121** 1c. green 40 40
497 2c. red 40 40
498 5c. blue . . . . 1·70 70

122 Marta Abreu

1947. Birth Centenary of M. Abreu (philanthropist).
499 **122** 1c. green 50 20
500 – 2c. red 80 20
501 – 5c. blue . . . . 1·30 30
502 – 10c. violet . . . . 2·75 60
DESIGNS: 2c. Allegory of Charity; 5c. Monument; 10c. Allegory of Patriotism.

123 Dr. G. A. Hansen and Isle of Pines

1948. Int Leprosy Relief Congress, Havana.
503 **123** 2c. red . . . . 1·00 30

124 Council of War

1948. Air. 50th Anniv of War of Independence.
504 **124** 8c. black and yellow . . . 1·80 80

1948. Air. American Air Mail Society Convention, Havana. Sheet **MS**444 optd **CONVENCION MAYO 21-22-23 1948 AMERICAN AIR MAIL SOCIETY** in blue across block of four.
MS505 128 × 178 mm. No. 443 in block of four. Imperf (sold at 60c.) 16·00 14·00

125 Woman and Child

126 Death of Marti

1948. Postal Employees' Retirement Fund.
506 **125** 1c. green 40 25
507 2c. red 45 25
508 5c. blue 1·20 35

1948. 50th Death Anniv of Jose Marti.
509 **126** 2c. red 80 25
510 – 5c. blue 2·30 40
DESIGN: 5c. Marti disembarking at Playitas.

127 Gathering Tobacco

129 Antonio Maceo

1948. Havana Tobacco Industry.
511 **127** 1c. green 35 30
512 – 2c. red 50 30
513 – 5c. blue 85 30
DESIGNS: 2c. Girl with box of cigars and flag; 5c. Cigar and shield.
This set comes again redrawn with smaller designs of 21 × 25 mm.

1948. Birth Centenary of Gen. Maceo.
514 – 1c. green 20 15
515 **129** 2c. red 30 20
516 – 5c. blue 50 20
517 – 8c. brown and black 80 40
518 – 10c. green and brown 80 35
519 – 20c. blue and red 3·00 1·20
520 – 50c. blue and red 5·25 2·75
521 – 1p. violet and black 10·00 4·00
DESIGNS—VERT: 1c. Equestrian statue of Maceo; 5c. Mausoleum at El Cacahual. HORIZ: 8c. Maceo and raised swords; 10c. Maceo leading charge; 20c. Maceo at Peralejo; 50c. Declaration at Baragua; 1p. Death of Maceo at San Pedro.

131 Symbol of Medicine

132 Morro Castle and Lighthouse

1948. 1st Pan-American Pharmaceutical Congress.
522 **131** 2c. red 1·80 45

1949. Centenary of El Morro Lighthouse.
523 **132** 2c. red 1·80 45

133 Jagua Castle

1949. Centenary of Newspaper "Hoja Economica" and Bicentenary of Jagua Fortress.
524 **133** 1c. green 70 30
525 2c. red 1·40 30

134 M. Sanguily

135 Isle of Pines

1949. Birth Centenary of Manuel Sanguily y Garritte (poet).
526 **134** 2c. red 60 30
527 5c. blue 1·90 30

1949. 20th Anniv of Return of Isle of Pines to Cuba.
528 **135** 5c. blue 2·50 95

136 Ismael Cespedes

137 Woman and Child

1949. Postal Employees' Retirement Fund.
529 **136** 1c. green 70 30
530 2c. red 70 30
531 5c. blue 1·70 40

1949. Obligatory Tax. Anti-tuberculosis.
532 **137** 1c. blue 60 25
547 1c. red 60 25
No. 547 is dated "1950".

138 Enrique Collazo

139 E. J. Varona

1950. Birth Centenary of Gen. Collazo.
533 **138** 2c. red 65 20
534 5c. blue 1·80 40

1950. Birth Centenary of Varona (writer).
535 **139** 2c. red 40 20
536 5c. blue 2·00 20

1950. National Bank Opening. No. 512 optd **BANCO NACIONAL DE CUBA INAUGURACION 27 ABRIL 1950**.
540 2c. red 1·40 30

1950. 75th Anniv of U.P.U. Optd **U.P.U. 1874 1949**.
541 **127** 1c. green 30 20
542 – 2c. pink (As No. 512) 40 20
543 – 5c. blue (As No. 513) 70 30

142 Balanzategui, Pausa and Railway Crash

143 F. Figueredo

1950. Postal Employees' Retirement Fund.
544 **142** 1c. green 1·40 60
545 2c. red 1·40 60
546 5c. blue 4·00 95

1951. Postal Employees' Retirement Fund.
548 **143** 1c. green 1·20 15
549 2c. red 1·20 15
550 5c. blue 2·75 15

144 Foundation Stone

145 Narciso Lopez

1951. Obligatory Tax. P.O. Rebuilding Fund.
551 **144** 1c. violet 90 25

1951. Centenary of Cuban Flag.
552 – 1c. red, bl & grn (postage) 55 35
553 **145** 2c. black and red 65 35
554 – 5c. red and blue 1·60 50
555 – 10c. red, blue and violet 2·75 75
556 – 5c. red, blue & olive (air) 1·60 45
557 – 8c. red, blue and brown 2·75 60
558 – 25c. red, blue and black 4·00 1·90
DESIGNS—VERT: 1c. Miguel Teurbe Tolon; 5c. (No. 554) Emilia Teurbe Tolon; 8c. Raising the flag; 10c. Flag; 25c. Flag and El Morro lighthouse. HORIZ: 5c. (No. 556) Lopez landing at Cardenas.

147 Clara Maass, Newark Memorial and Las Animas, Havana, Hospitals

1951. 50th Death Anniv of Clara Maass (nurse).
559 **147** 2c. red 2·10 45

1951. 50th Anniv of Discovery of Cause of Yellow-fever by Dr. Carlos J. Finley, and to honour Martyrs of Science. Sheet **MS**442 optd **50 ANIVERSARIO DESCUBRIMIENTO AGENTE TRANSMISOR**, etc., across block of four.
MS560 127 × 177 mm. Two each of Nos. 440/1. Imperf (sold at 25c.) (postage) 5·75 5·00
Optd as last but with aeroplane motif and CORREO AERO in addition.
MS561 127 × 177 mm. Two each of Nos. 440/1 Imperf (sold at 25c.) (air) 11·00 8·50

148 Capablanca (after E. Valderrama)

149 Chessboard showing end of Capablanca v. Lasker

1951. 30th Anniv of Jose Capablanca's Victory in World Chess Championship.
562 **148** 1c. orge & grn (postage) 3·50 70
563 – 2c. brown and red 4·25 1·30
564 E **150** 5c. blue and black 8·50 2·00
565 **149** 5c. yellow & green (air) 4·75 85
566 – 8c. purple and blue 8·25 1·30
567 **148** 25c. sepia & brown 14·50 3·25
DESIGN—VERT: 2c., 8c. Capablanca playing chess.

151 Dr. A. Guiteras Holmes

152 Morrillo Fortress

1951. 16th Death Anniv of Dr. A. Guiteras Holmes in skirmish at Morrillo.
568 **151** 1c. green (postage) 40 20
569 – 2c. red 70 30
570 **152** 5c. blue 1·40 50
571 **151** 5c. mauve (air) 1·80 1·20
572 – 8c. green 2·50 1·60
573 **152** 25c. black 4·75 3·00
MS574 Two sheets 125 × 133 mm. each containing Nos. 568/73 (each sold at 60c.)
(a) Stamps in green 42·00 42·00
(b) Stamps in brown 17·00 17·00
DESIGNS—HORIZ: 2, 8c. Guiteras framing social laws.

153 Mother and Child

154 Christmas Emblems

1951. Obligatory Tax. Anti-tuberculosis.
575 **153** 1c. brown 55 25
576 1c. red 55 25
577 1c. green 55 25
578 1c. blue 55 25

1951. Christmas Greetings.
579 **154** 1c. red and green 2·75 30
580 2c. green and red 3·25 60

155 Jose Maceo

156 General Post Office

157 Isabella the Catholic

1952. Birth Centenary of Gen. Maceo.
581 **155** 2c. brown 55 20
582 5c. blue 1·20 20

1952. Obligatory Tax. P.O. Rebuilding Fund.
583 **156** 1c. blue 40 15
584 1c. red 75 25

1952. 5th Birth Centenary of Isabella the Catholic.
585 **157** 2c. red (postage) 1·60 40
586 25c. purple (air) 3·75 1·20
MS587 Two sheets each 108 × 108 mm containing Nos. 585/6. (a) 2c. indigo and 25c. carmine. (b) 2c. carmine and 25c. indigo 30·00 30·00

1952. As No. 549 surch with new value. (a) Postage.
588 **143** 10c. on 2c. brown 1·70 50
(b) Air. Optd **AEREO** in addition.
589 **143** 5c. on 2c. brown 90 40
590 8c. on 2c. brown 1·80 40
591 10c. on 2c. brown 1·80 40
592 25c. on 2c. brown 2·75 1·40
593 50c. on 2c. brown 9·25 2·50
594 1p. on 2c. brown 21·00 10·00

159 Proclamation of Republic

160 Statue, Havana University

1952. 50th Anniv of Republic.
595 **159** 1c. black & grn (postage) 20 15
596 – 2c. black and red 30 15
597 – 5c. black and blue 40 15
598 – 8c. black and brown 65 15
599 – 20c. black and olive 1·60 40
600 – 50c. black and orange 3·25 90
601 – 5c. green & violet (air) 40 15
602 **160** 8c. green and red 65 15
603 – 10c. green and blue 1·60 40
604 – 25c. green and purple 2·30 1·10
DESIGNS—HORIZ:—POSTAGE: 2c. Estrada Palma and Estevez Romero; 5c. Barnet, Finlay, Guiteras and Nunez; 8c. The Capitol; 20c. Map showing central highway; 50c. Sugar factory. AIR: 5c. Rural school; 10c. Presidential Palace; 25c. Banknote.

162 Seaplane and Route of Flight

164 Coffee Beans

1952. Air. 39th Anniv of Florida–Cuba flight by A. Parla.
605 **162** 8c. black 1·40 55
606 – 25c. blue 4·00 1·70
MS607 Four sheets each 111 × 92 mm. Nos. 605/6 each in blue and in green 65·00 65·00
DESIGN—HORIZ: 25c. Agustin Parla Orduna and Curtiss A-1 seaplane.

1952. Bicentenary of Coffee Cultivation.
608 **164** 1c. green 55 25
609 – 2c. red 1·00 30
610 – 5c. green and blue 1·70 35
DESIGNS: 2c. Plantation worker and map; 5c. Coffee plantation.

165 Col. C. Hernandez

1952. Postal Employees' Retirement Fund.
611 **165** 1c. green (postage) 35 30
612 2c. red 55 30
613 5c. blue 65 30
614 8c. black 1·70 45
615 10c. red 1·70 45
616 20c. brown 6·50 3·50
617 5c. orange (air) 80 30
618 8c. green 80 30
619 10c. brown 1·00 30
620 15c. green 2·00 70
621 20c. turquoise 2·50 95
622 25c. red 2·00 95
623 30c. violet 5·25 2·30
624 45c. mauve 5·25 3·25
625 50c. blue 3·00 2·30
626 1p. yellow 11·00 4·75

166 A. A. De La Campa

167 Statue, Havana University

168 Dominguez, Estebanez and Capdevila (defence lawyers)

1952. 81st Anniv of Execution of Eight Rebel Medical Students.
627 **166** 1c. black & grn (postage) 30 15
628 – 2c. black and red 60 25
629 – 3c. black and violet 75 25
630 – 5c. black and blue 80 50
631 – 8c. black and sepia 1·60 50
632 – 10c. black and brown 1·30 45
633 – 13c. black and purple 2·50 70
634 – 20c. black and olive 4·00 1·20
635 **167** 5c. blue and indigo (air) 1·40 40
636 **168** 25c. green and orange 4·00 1·40
PORTRAITS: 2c. C. A. de la Torre. 3c. A. Bermudez. 5c. E. G. Toledo. 8c. A. Laborde. 10c. J. De M. Medina. 13c. P. Rodriguez. 20c. C. Verdugo.

169 Child's Face

170 Christmas Tree

1952. Obligatory Tax. Anti- tuberculosis.
637 **169** 1c. orange 90 25
638 1c. red 90 25
639 1c. green 90 25
640 1c. blue 90 25

1952. Christmas.
641 **170** 1c. red and green 4·75 1·70
642 3c. green and violet 4·75 1·70

171 Marti's Birthplace

172 Dr. Rafael Montoro

1953. Birth Centenary of Jose Marti.
643 **171** 1c. brn & grn (postage) 40 15
644 – 1c. brown and green 40 15
645 – 3c. brown and violet 45 15
646 – 3c. brown and violet 45 15
647 – 5c. brown and blue 80 15
648 – 5c. brown and blue 80 15
649 – 10c. black and brown 1·60 40
650 – 10c. black and brown 1·60 40
651 – 13c. brown and green 2·75 85
652 – 13c. brown and green 2·75 1·00
653 – 5c. black & red (air) 45 15
654 – 5c. black and red 45 15
655 – 8c. black and green 1·20 15
656 – 8c. black and green 1·20 15
657 – 10c. red and blue 2·75 50
658 – 10c. blue and red 2·75 50
659 – 15c. black and violet 1·90 1·00
660 – 15c. black and violet 1·90 1·00
661 – 25c. red and brown 5·00 1·30
662 – 25c. red and brown 5·00 1·30
663 – 50c. blue and yellow 8·00 2·75
DESIGNS—HORIZ: No. 644, Marti before Council of War; No. 645, Prison wall; No. 647, "El Abra" ranch; No. 652, First edition of "Patria"; No. 656, House of Maximo Gomez, Montecristi; No. 658, Marti as an orator; No. 663, "Fragua Martiana" (modern building). VERT: No. 646, Marti in prison; No. 648, Allegory of Marti's poems; No. 649, Marti and Bolivar Statue, Caracas; No. 650, Marti writing; No. 651, Revolutionaries' meeting-place; No. 653, Marti in Kingston, Jamaica; No. 654, Marti in Ibor City; No. 655, Manifesto of Montecristi; No. 657, Marti's portrait; No. 659, Marti's first tomb; No. 660, Obelisk at Des Rios; No. 661, Monument in Havana; No. 662, Marti's present tomb.

1953. Birth Centenary of Montoro (statesman).
664 **172** 3c. purple 1·60 30

173 Dr. F. Carrera Justiz

174 Lockheed Constellation

1953.
665 **173** 3c. red 2·00 30

1953. Air.
666 **174** 8c. brown 1·10 20
667 15c. red 2·10 65
668 – 2p. brown and green 25·00 9·25
670 – 2p. myrtle and blue 18·00 6·50
669 – 5p. brown and blue 48·00 16·00
671 – 5p. myrtle and red 39·00 15·00
DESIGN: Nos. 668/71, Constellation facing right.

1953. No. 512 surch.
672 3c. on 2c. red 1·60 25

176 Congress Building

177

1953. 1st Int Accountancy Congress, Havana.
673 **176** 3c. blue (postage) 80 40
674 – 8c. red (air) 2·10 65
675 – 25c. green 3·25 1·10
DESIGNS: 8c. Congress building and "Cuba"; 25c. Aerial view of building and airplane.

1953. Obligatory Tax. Anti-T.B.
676 **177** 1c. red 60 25

178 M. Coyula Llaguno

179 Postal Employees' Retirement Association Flag

1954. Postal Employees' Retirement Fund. Inscr "1953".
677 **178** 1c. green (postage) 35 15
678 – 3c. red 35 15
679 **179** 5c. blue 1·00 15
680 – 8c. red 1·90 40
681 – 10c. sepia 3·00 60
682 – 5c. blue (air) 60 25
683 – 8c. purple 80 25
684 – 10c. orange 1·40 30
685 **179** 1p. grey 8·25 6·75
PORTRAITS—VERT: Nos. 678, 680, F.L.C. Hensell; Nos. 681, 683, A. G. Rojas; No. 684, G. H. Saez. HORIZ: No. 682, M. C. Llaguno.

180 Jose Marti

181 Hauling Sugar

1954. Portraits. Roul. (No. 1180a/b) or perf. (others).
686 **180** 1c. green 35 15
990 1c. red 50 15
1680 1c. blue 25 10
687 – 2c. red (Gomez) 35 15
991 – 2c. olive (Gomez) 55 15
1681 – 2c. green (Gomez) 25 10
688 – 3c. violet (de la Luz Caballero) 35 15
1180a – 3c. orange (Caballero) 1·20 15
689 – 4c. mauve (Aldama) 40 15
690 – 5c. blue (Garcia) 50 15
691 – 8c. lake (Agramonte) 75 15
692 – 10c. sepia (Palma) 75 15
693 – 13c. red (Finlay) 1·10 15
1180b – 13c. brown (Finlay) 1·80 40
694 – 14c. grey (Sanchez) 1·40 15
695 – 20c. olive (Saco) 2·20 40
1682 – 20c. violet (Saco) 1·50 50
696 – 50c. ochre (Maceo) 3·75 40
697 – 1p. orange (Cespedes) 7·25 45

1954. Air. Sugar Industry.
698 – 5c. green 40 15
699 – 8c. brown 1·10 50
700 **181** 10c. green 1·10 50
701 – 15c. brown 2·50 50
702 – 20c. blue 1·10 15
703 – 25c. red 80 15
704a – 30c. purple 3·00 1·00
705 – 40c. blue 4·25 1·20
706 – 45c. violet 3·50 2·00
707 – 50c. blue 3·50 1·30
708 – 1p. blue 9·25 2·75
DESIGNS—VERT: 5c. Sugar cane; 1p. A. Reinoso. HORIZ: 8c. Sugar harvesting; 15c. Train load of sugar cane; 20c. Modern sugar factory; 25c. Evaporators; 30c. Stacking sugar in sacks; 40c. Loading sugar on ship; 45c. Oxen hauling cane; 50c. Primitive sugar factory.

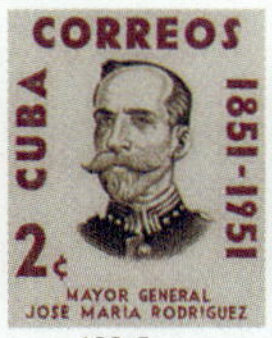

182 Jose M. Rodriguez

183 View of Sanatorium

1954. Birth Centenary of Rodriguez.
709 **182** 2c. sepia and lake 80 25
710 – 5c. sepia and blue 2·40 50
DESIGN: 5c. Rodriguez on horseback.

1954. General Batista Sanatorium.
711 **183** 3c. blue (postage) 95 45
712 9c. green (air) 2·10 85

184

185 Father Christmas

186 Maria Luisa Dolz

1954. Obligatory Tax. Anti-T.B.
713 **184** 1c. red 90 25
714 1c. green 90 25
715 1c. blue 90 25
716 1c. violet 90 25

1954. Christmas Greetings.
717 **185** 2c. green and red 5·75 1·20
718 4c. red and green 5·75 1·20

1954. Birth Centenary of Maria Dolz (educationist).
719 **186** 4c. blue (postage) 95 40
720 12c. mauve (air) 1·80 70

187 Boy Scouts and Cuban Flag

189 Major-Gen. F. Carrillo

188 P. P. Harris and Rotary Emblem

1954. 3rd National Scout Camp.
721 **187** 4c. green 1·30 40

1955. 50th Anniv of Rotary International.
722 **188** 4c. blue (postage) 1·60 30
723 12c. red (air) 1·80 85

1955. Birth Centenary of Carrillo.
724 **189** 2c. blue and red 50 25
725 – 5c. sepia and blue 90 40
DESIGN: 5c. Half-length portrait.

190 1855 Stamp and "La Volanta"

1955. Centenary of First Cuban Postage Stamps and 50th Anniv of First Republican Stamps.
726 – 2c. blue & pur (postage) 75 15
727 **190** 4c. green and buff 1·00 40
728 – 10c. red and blue 3·00 75
729 – 14c. orange and green 6·50 1·80
730 – 8c. green & blue (air) 90 35
731 – 12c. red and green 1·00 35
732 – 24c. blue and red 1·80 1·00
733 – 30c. brown & orange 4·00 1·60
DESIGNS (a) With 1855 stamp: 2c. Old Square and Convent of St. Francis; 10c. Havana in 19th century; 14c. Captain-General's residence and Plaza de Armas; (b) With 1855 and 1905 stamps: 8c. Palace of Fine Arts; 12c. Plaza de la Fraternidad; 24c. Aerial view of Havana; 30c. Plaza de la Republica.

191 Maj.-Gen. Menocal

192 Mariel Bay

1955. Postal Employees' Retirement Fund.
734 **191** 2c. green (postage) 80 15
735 – 4c. mauve 90 25
736 – 10c. blue 1·40 50
737 – 14c. grey 3·25 1·20
738 **192** 8c. green and red (air) 1·20 25
739 – 12c. blue and brown 1·60 70
740 – 1p. ochre and green 9·00 2·75
DESIGNS—As Type **191**: HORIZ: 4c. Gen. E. Nunez; 14c. Dr. A. de Bustamante. VERT: 10c. J. Gomez. As Type **192**: HORIZ: 12c. Varadero Beach; 1p. Vinales Valley.

193 Cuban Academy

194 Route of 1914 Flight

1955. Air. Centenary of Tampa, Florida.
741 **193** 12c. brown and red 2·20 60

1955. Air. 35th Death Anniv of Crocier (aviator).
742 **194** 12c. green and red 90 50
743 – 30c. mauve and green 3·00 75
DESIGN: 30c. Crocier in aircraft cockpit.

195

196 Wright Flyer 1

1955. Obligatory Tax. Anti-T.B.
744 **195** 1c. orange 90 25
745 1c. yellow 90 25
746 1c. blue 90 25
747 1c. mauve 90 25

1955. Air. Int Philatelic Exhibition, Havana.
748 **196** 8c. black, red and blue 1·20 60
749 – 12c. black, green and red 2·75 85
750 – 24c. black, violet & red 8·50 3·25
751 – 30c. black, blue & orange 7·25 4·25
752 – 50c. black olive & orange 9·75 5·00
MS753 175 × 140 mm. Nos. 748/52 in new colours 34·00 34·00
DESIGNS: 12c. Lindbergh's airplane "Spirit of St. Louis"; 24c. Airship "Graf Zeppelin"; 30c. Lockheed Super Constellation airplane; 50c. Convair Delta Dagger airplane.

197 Wild Turkey

198 Expedition Disembarking

1955. Christmas Greetings.
754 **197** 2c. green and red 5·25 2·10
755 4c. lake and green 5·25 2·20

1955. Birth Centenary of General Nunez.
756 – 4c. lake (postage) 1·20 85
757 – 8c. blue and red (air) 1·80 70
758 **198** 12c. green and brown 2·75 1·10
DESIGNS—VERT: ($22\frac{1}{2} \times 32\frac{1}{2}$ mm.): 4c. Portrait of Nunez. HORIZ: As Type **198**: 8c. "Three Friends" (tug).

199 Bishop P. A. Morell de Santa Cruz

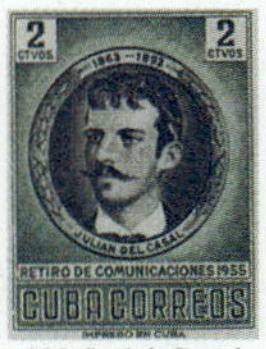

200 J. del Casal

1956. Bicentenary of Cuban Postal Service.
759 – 4c. blue & brn (postage) 1·20 45
760 **199** 12c. green & brown (air) 2·10 50
PORTRAIT: 4c. F. C. de la Vega.

1956. Postal Employees' Retirement Fund.
761 **200** 2c. black & grn (postage) 35 15
762 – 4c. black and mauve 55 15
763 – 10c. black and blue 1·00 15
764 – 14c. black and violet 1·30 15
765 – 8c. black & brown (air) 1·30 15

766 – 12c. black and ochre 2·20 20
767 – 30c. black and blue 4·00 1·50
PORTRAITS: 4c. Luisa Perez de Zambrana. 8c. Gen. J. Sanguily. 10c. J. Clemente Zenea. 12c. Gen. J. M. Aguirre. 14c. J. J. Palma. 30c. Col. E. Fonts Sterling.

201 Victor Munoz

202 Mother and Baby

1956. Munoz Commemoration.
768 **201** 4c. brown and green 1·20 45

1956. Air. Mothers' Day.
769 **202** 12c. blue and red 4·00 35

203 Aerial View of Temple

204 Gundlach's Hawk

1956. Masonic Grand Lodge of Cuba Temple, Havana.
770 – 4c. blue (postage) 1·40 45
771 **203** 12c. green (air) 2·75 50
DESIGN: 4c. Ground level view of Temple.

1956. Air. Birds.
772 – 8c. blue 50 20
773 – 12c. grey 7·50 40
783 – 12c. green 1·50 45
774 **204** 14c. olive 1·70 25
775 – 19c. brown 1·10 55
776 – 24c. mauve 1·30 55
777 – 29c. green 1·90 55
778 – 30c. brown 2·30 85
779 – 50c. slate 4·25 1·10
780 – 1p. red 6·50 2·30
784 – 1p. blue 5·75 5·75
781 – 2p. purple 13·00 4·25
785 – 2p. red 17·00 15·00
782 – 5p. red 35·00 8·75
786 – 5p. purple 37·00 33·00
DESIGNS—HORIZ: 8c. Wood duck; 12c. (2) Plain pigeon; 29c. Goosander; 30c. Northern bobwhite; 2p. (2) Northern jacana. VERT: 19c. Herring gull; 24c. American white pelican; 50c. Great blue heron; 1p. (2) Common caracara; 5p. (2) Ivory-billed woodpecker.

205 H. de Blanck

207 Church of Our Lady of Charity

1956. Air. Birth Centenary of H. De Blanck (composer).
787 **205** 12c. blue 1·80 50

1956. Air. Inaug of Philatelic Club of Cuba Building. No. 776 but colour changed and surch **Inauguracion Edificio Club Filatelico de la Republica de Cuba Julio 13 de 1956** and value.
788 – 8c. on 24c. orange 2·50 85

1956. Inscr "NTRA. SRA. DE LA CARIDAD", etc.
789 – 4c. blue & yell (postage) 1·00 40
790 **207** 12c. green & red (air) 2·10 70
MS791 76 × 77 mm. Nos. 789/90 12·50 10·50
DESIGN: 4c. Our Lady of Charity over landscape.

208

209

1956. Air. 250th Birth Anniv of Benjamin Franklin.
792 **208** 12c. brown 2·10 70

1956. "Grito de Yara" (War of Independence). Commem.
793 **209** 4c. sepia and green 1·00 40

(210)

211

1956. Air. 12th Inter-American Press Assn. Meeting. As No. 781 but colour changed and surch with T **210**.
794 – 12c. on 2p. grey 3·00 1·20

1956. Obligatory Tax. Anti-T.B.
795 **211** 1c. red 90 25
796 1c. green 90 25
797 1c. blue 90 25
798 1c. brown 90 25

212

213 Prof. R. G. Menocal

1956. Christmas Greetings.
799 **212** 2c. red and green 3·75 1·60
800 4c. green and red 3·75 1·80

1956. Birth Centenary of Prof. R. G. Menocal.
801 **213** 4c. brown 95 40

214a Martin M. Delgado

215 Scouts around Camp Fire

1957. Birth Centenary of Delgado (patriot).
802 **214a** 4c. green 95 40

1957. Birth Centenary of Lord Baden-Powell.
803 **215** 4c. green & red (postage) 1·30 50
804 – 12c. slate (air) 2·50 95
DESIGN—VERT: 12c. Lord Baden-Powell.

216 "The Art Critics" (Melero)

217 Hanabanilla Falls

1957. Postal Employees' Retirement Fund.
805 – 2c. green & brn (postage) 60 15
806 **216** 4c. red and brown 1·20 40
807 – 10c. olive and brown 1·80 60
808 – 14c. blue and brown 1·50 45
809 **217** 8c. blue and red (air) 80 15
810 – 12c. green and red 3·25 40
811 – 30c. olive and violet 3·75 65
DESIGNS—HORIZ: As Type **216** (Paintings): 2c. "The Blind" (Vega); 10c. "Carriage in the Storm" (Menocal); 14c. "The Convalescent" (Romanach); As Type **217**: 12c. Sierra de Cubitas; 30c. Puerto Boniato.

218 Posthorn Emblem of Cuban Philatelic Society

219 Juan F. Steegers

1957. Stamp Day. Cuban Philatelic Exn.
812 **218** 4c. bl, brn & red (postage) 95 40
813 – 12c. brn, yell & grn (air) 1·90 50
DESIGN: 12c. Philatelic Society Building, Havana.

1957. Birth Centenary of Steegers (fingerprint pioneer).
814 **219** 4c. blue (postage) 95 40
815 – 12c. brown (air) 1·90 50
DESIGN: 12c. Thumbprint.

220 Baseball Player

221 Nurse Victoria Bru Sanchez

1957. Air. Youth Recreation. Centres in brown.
816 **220** 8c. green on green 1·70 50
817 – 12c. lilac on lavender 2·50 60
818 – 24c. blue on blue 3·50 1·70
819 – 30c. flesh on orange 5·25 2·10
DESIGNS—12c. Ballet dancer; 24c. Diver; 30c. Boxers.

1957. Nurse Victoria Bru Sanchez Commem.
820 **221** 4c. blue 1·20 40

222 J. de Aguero leading Patriots

223 Youth with Dogs and Cat

1957. Joaquin de Aguero (patriot) Commem.
821 **222** 4c. green (postage) 95 40
822 – 12c. blue (portrait) (air) 2·10 50

1957. 50th Anniv of Band of Charity (for prevention of cruelty to animals).
823 **223** 4c. green (postage) 1·80 70
824 – 12c. brown (air) 3·25 70
DESIGN: 12c. Jeanette Ryder (founder).

224 Col. R. Manduley del Rio (patriot)

225 J. M. Heredia y Girard

1957. Col. R. Manduley del Rio. Commem.
825 **224** 4c. green 2·75 2·10

1957. Air. J. M. Heredia y Girard (poet). Commem.
826 **225** 8c. violet 1·10 40

226 Palace of Justice, Havana

1957. Inauguration of Palace of Justice.
827 **226** 4c. grey (postage) 1·30 50
828 12c. green (air) 2·10 60

227 Army Leaders of 1856

228 J. R. Gregg

1957. Centenary of Cuban Army of Liberation.
829 **227** 4c. brown and green 95 40
830 4c. brown and blue 95 40
831 4c. brown and pink 95 40
832 4c. brown and yellow 95 40
833 4c. brown and lilac 95 40

1957. Air. Gregg (shorthand pioneer) Commem.
834 **228** 12c. green 2·10 95

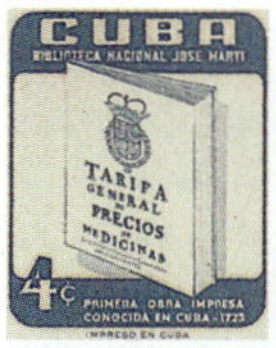

229 Cuba's First Publication, 1723

230 Jose Marti Public Library

1957. "Jose Marti" Public Library. Inscr "BIBLIOTECA NACIONAL".
835 **229** 4c. slate (postage) 1·30 50
836 – 8c. blue (air) 60 30
837 **230** 12c. sepia 2·40 60
DESIGN—VERT: As Type **230**: 8c. D. F. Caneda, first Director.

231 U.N. Emblem and Map of Cuba

1957. Air. U.N. Day.
838 **231** 8c. brown and green 1·10 30
839 12c. green and red 1·60 70
840 30c. mauve and blue 3·75 1·60

232 Fokker Trimotor "General New" and Map

1957. Air. 30th Anniv of Inaug of Air Mail Services between Havana and Key West, Florida.
841 **232** 12c. blue and purple 2·50 1·00

233

235 Courtyard

1957. Obligatory Tax. Anti-tuberculosis.
842 **233** 1c. red 90 25
843 1c. green 90 25
844 1c. blue 90 25
845 1c. grey 90 25

1957. Centenary of 1st Cuban Teachers' Training College.
846 **235** 4c. brn & grn (postage) 1·30 50
847 – 12c. buff and blue (air) 1·40 50
848 – 30c. sepia and red 2·50 70
DESIGNS—VERT: 12c. School facade. HORIZ: 30c. General view of school.

236 Street Scene, Trinidad

237 Christmas Crib

1957. Postal Employees' Retirement Fund.
849 **236** 2c. brown & bl (postage) 30 15
850 – 4c. green and brown 65 15
851 – 10c. sepia and red 1·10 30
852 – 14c. green and red 1·60 25
853 – 8c. black and red (air) 65 30
854 – 12c. black and brown 1·30 40
855 – 30c. brown and grey 2·50 65
DESIGNS—VERT: 4c. Sentry-box on old wall of Havana; 10c. Calle Padre Pico (street), Santiago de Cuba; 12c. Sancti Spiritus Church; 14c. Church and street scene, Camaguey. HORIZ: 8c. "El Viso" Fort, El Caney; 30c. Concordia Bridge, Matanzas.

1957. Christmas. Multicoloured centres.
856 **237** 2c. sepia 3·00 1·20
857 4c. black 3·00 1·30

239 Dayton Hedges and Textile Factories

240 Dr. F. D. Roldan

1958. Dayton Hedges (founder of Cuban Textile Industry) Commemoration.
858 **239** 4c. blue (postage) . . . . 2·10 1·00
859 8c. green (air) . . . . . . 2·10 1·00

1958. Dr. Francisco D. Roldan (physiotherapy pioneer) Commemoration.
861 **240** 4c. green . . . . 1·30 40

241 "Diario de la Marina" Building

1958. 125th Anniv of "Diario de la Marina" Newspaper.
862 – 4c. olive (postage) . . . . 1·00 95
863 **241** 29c. black (air) . . . . . 3·50 1·60
PORTRAIT—VERT: 4c. J. I. Rivero y Alonso (journalist).

242 Map of Cuba showing Postal Routes of 1756

243 Gen. J. M. Gomez

1958. Stamp Day and National Philatelic Exhibition, Havana. Inscr as in T **242**.
864 **242** 4c. myrtle, buff and blue (postage) 95 40
865 – 29c. indigo, buff and blue (air) . . . . 3·75 1·40
DESIGN: 29c. Ocean map showing sea-post routes of 1765.

1958. Birth Centenary of Gen. J. M. Gomez.
866 **243** 4c. blue (postage) . . . . 1·30 50
867 – 12c. myrtle (air) . . . . . 2·00 70
DESIGN: 12c. Gomez at Arroyo Blanco.

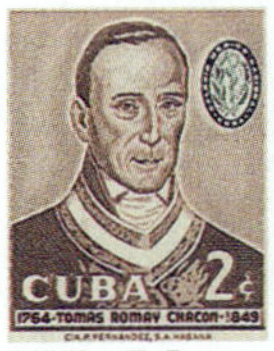

244 Dr. T. Romay Chacon

245 Dr. C. de la Torre

246 Painted Polymita

1958. Famous Cubans. Portraits as T **244**. (a) Doctors. With emblem of medicine.
868 2c. brown and green 70 30
869 4c. black and green 70 30
870 10c. red and green 70 30
871 14c. blue and green 85 30

(b) Lawyers. With emblem of law.
872 2c. sepia and red 70 30
873 4c. black and red 75 30
874 10c. green and red 75 30
875 14c. blue and red 95 30

(c) Composers. With lyre emblem of music.
876 2c. brown and blue 70 30
877 4c. purple and blue 70 30
878 10c. green and blue 80 30
879 14c. red and blue 95 30
PORTRAITS—Doctors: 2c. Type **244**. 4c. A. A. Aballi. 10c. F. G. del Valle. 14c. V. A. de Castro. Lawyers: 2c. J. M. G. Montes. 4c. J. A. G. Lanuza. 10c. J. B. H. Barreiro. 14c. P. G. Llorente. Composers: 2c. N. R. Espadero. 4c. I. Cervantes. 10c. J. White. 14c. B. de Salas.

1958. Birth Cent of De la Torre (archaeologist).
880 **245** 4c. blue (postage) . . . . 1·60 50
881 **246** 8c. red, yellow & blk (air) 6·75 40
882 – 12c. sepia on green . . . 9·25 2·30
883 – 30c. green on pink . . . 13·50 2·75
DESIGNS—As Type **246**: 12c. "Megalocnus rodens"; 30c. "Perisphinctes spinatus" (ammonite).

247 Felipe Poey (naturalist)

248 "Papilio caiguanabus" (butterfly)

1958. Poey Commemoration. Designs as T **247/8** inscr "1799–FELIPE POEY–1891".
884 – 2c. blk & lav (postage) . . 65 25
885 **247** 4c. sepia . . . . 1·00 35
886 **248** 8c. multicoloured (air) . . 1·60 60
887 – 12c. orange, black & grn 1·80 60
888 – 14c. multicoloured . . . . 4·50 90
889 – 19c. multicoloured . . . . 5·75 1·20
890 – 24c. multicoloured . . . . 6·75 1·20
891 – 29c. blue, brown & black 9·75 1·50
892 – 30c. brown, green & blk 14·00 2·20
DESIGNS—VERT: 2c. Cover of Poey's book; 12c. "Teria gundlachia"; 14c. "Teria ebriola"; 19c. "Nathalis felicia" (all butterflies). HORIZ: 24c. Tobacco fish; 29c. Butter hamlet; 30c. Tattler sea bass (all fishes).

249 Theodore Roosevelt

250 National Tuberculosis Hospital

1958. Birth Centenary of Roosevelt.
893 **249** 4c. green (postage) . . . 1·00 35
894 – 12c. sepia (air) . . . . . 1·60 45
DESIGN—HORIZ: 12c. Roosevelt leading Rough Riders at San Juan 1898.

1958. Obligatory Tax. Anti-T.B.
895 **250** 1c. brown 45 25
896 1c. green 45 25
897 1c. red 45 25
898 1c. grey 45 25

251 UNESCO Headquarters, Paris

252 "Cattleyopsis lindenii" (orchid)

1958. Air. Inaug of UNESCO Headquarters.
899 **251** 12c. green . . . . 1·40 45
900 – 30c. blue . . . . 2·75 1·50
DESIGN: 30c. Facade composed of letters "UNESCO" and map of Cuba.

1958. Christmas. Orchids. Multicoloured.
901 2c. Type **252** . . . . . . 3·50 1·20
902 4c. "Oncidium guibertianum" 3·50 1·20

253 "The Revolutionary"

254 Gen. A. F. Crombet

1959. Liberation Day.
903 **253** 2c. black and red 70 30

1959. Gen. Crombet Commemoration.
904 **254** 4c. myrtle 95 35

255 Postal Notice of 1765

256 Hand Supporting Sugar Factory

1959. Air. Stamp Day and National Philatelic Exhibition, Havana.
905 **255** 12c. sepia and blue . . . 1·40 35
906 – 30c. blue and sepia . . . 2·30 1·30
DESIGN: 30c. Administrative postal book of St. Cristobal, Havana, 1765.

1959. Agricultural Reform.
907 **256** 2c.+1c. blue and red (postage) 95 20
908 – 12c.+3c. green and red (air) . . . . 2·10 70
DESIGN (42 × 30 mm.): 12c. Farm workers and factory plant.

257 Red Cross Nurse

1959. "For Charity".
909 **257** 2c.+1c. red 50 25

1959. Air. American Society of Travel Agents Convention, Havana. No. 780 (colour changed) surch **CONVENCION ASTA OCTUBRE 17 1959 12c.** and bar.
910 12c. on 1p. green . . . . . . 2·40 1·20

259 Teresa Garcia Montes (founder)

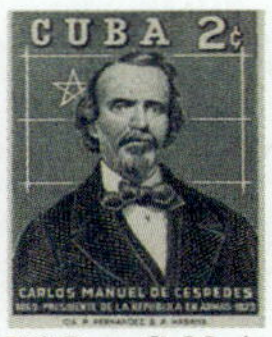

260 Pres. C. M. de Cespedes

1959. Musical Arts Society Festival, Havana.
911 **259** 4c. brown (postage) . . . 1·40 50
912 – 12c. green (air) . . . . . 2·40 65
DESIGN—HORIZ: 12c. Society Headquarters, Havana.

1959. Cuban Presidents.
913 2c. slate (Type **260**) 60 20
914 2c. green (Betancourt) . . . 60 20
915 2c. violet (Calvar) 60 20
916 2c. brown (Maso) 60 20
917 4c. red (Spotorno) 85 30
918 4c. brown (Palma) 85 30
919 4c. black (F. J. de Cespedes) 85 30
920 4c. violet (Garcia) 85 30

261 Rebel Attack at Moncada Barracks

264 Pres. T. Estrada Palma Monument

1960. 1st Anniv of Cuban Revolution.
921 **261** 1c. grn, red & bl (postage) 20 15
922 – 2c. green, sepia and blue 95 15
923 – 10c. green, red and blue 2·30 85
924 – 12c. green, purple & blue 3·00 60
925 – 8c. green, red & bl (air) 2·30 40
926 – 12c. green, purple & brn 2·50 35
927 – 29c. red, black & green 4·00 1·20
DESIGNS: 2c. Rebels disembarking from "Granma"; 8c. Battle of Santa Clara; 10c. Battle of the Uvero; 12c. postage, "The Invasion" (Rebel and map of Cuba); 12c. air, Rebel Army entering Havana; 29c. Passing on propaganda ("Clandestine activities in the towns").

1960. Surch **HABILITADO PARA** and value (No. 932 without **PARA**).
928 **256** 2c. on 2c.+1c. blue and red (postage) . . . . . . 1·40 30
929 – 2c. on 4c. mve (No. 689) 1·00 50
930 – 2c. on 5c. blue (690) . . . 1·00 50
931 – 2c. on 13c. red (693) . . . 1·00 50
932 – 10c. on 20c. olive (342) 1·80 70
933 – 12c. on 12c.+3c. green and red (908) (air) . . . 2·30 85

1960. Surch in figures.
934 – 1c. on 4c. (No. 869) (postage) 60 30
935 – 1c. on 4c. (No. 873) . . . 60 30
936 – 1c. on 4c. (No. 877) . . . 60 30
937 **245** 1c. on 4c. blue 60 30
938 1c. on 4c. (No. 902) . . . 80 40
939 **254** 1c. on 4c. myrtle 60 30
940 **260** 1c. on 4c. brown 60 30
941 – 2c. on 14c. (No. 694) . . . 1·20 30
942 **54** 12c. on 40c. orge (air) . . 2·30 85
943 – 12c. on 45c. (No. 706) . . 2·30 85

1960. Postal Employees' Retirement Fund.
944 **264** 1c. brn & blue (postage) 30 15
945 – 2c. green and red 40 15
946 – 10c. brown and red . . . 1·10 30
947 – 12c. green and violet . . . 1·60 60
948 – 8c. grey and red (air) . . 95 30
949 – 12c. blue and red . . . . 1·60 30
950 – 30c. violet and red . . . 3·50 1·60
MONUMENTS—VERT: 2c. "Mambi Victorioso"; 8c. Marti; 10c. Marta Abreu; 12c. (No. 947) Agramonte; 12c. (No. 949) Heroes of Cacarajicara. HORIZ: 30c. Dr. C. de la Torriente.

(265)

266 Pistol-shooting

1960. Air. Stamp Day and National Philatelic Exn, Havana. Nos. 772/3 in new colours optd with T **265**.
951 8c. yellow 85 50
952 12c. red . . . . 2·30 85
MS953 128 × 178 mm. No. 403 in block of four . . . . 22·00 22·00

1960. Olympic Games.
954 – 1c. vio (Sailing) (postage) 60 30
955 **266** 2c. orange 70 30
956 – 8c. blue (Boxing) (air) . . 1·00 30
957 – 12c. red (Running) . . . 1·40 60
MS958 79 × 91 mm. Nos. 954/5 each in blue. Imperf . . . . 8·00 8·00

267 C. Cienfuegos and View of Escolar

1960. 1st Death Anniv of Cienfuegos (revolutionary leader). Centre multicoloured.
959 **267** 2c. sepia . . . . 1·80 30

268 Air Stamp of 1930, Ford "Tin Goose" Airplane and "Sputnik"

1960. Air. 80th Anniv of National Airmail Service. Centre multicoloured.
960 **268** 8c. violet . . . . 4·25 2·50

270 Ipomoea

271 Tobacco Plant and Bars of "Christmas Hymn"

1960. Christmas. Inscr "NAVIDAD 1960–61". (a) T **270**.
961 1c. multicoloured 85 85
962 2c. multicoloured . . . . . . 1·10 1·10
963 10c. multicoloured . . . . . 2·75 3·00

(b) As T **271**.
964a/d 1c. multicoloured . . . . 2·10 1·80
965a/d 2c. multicoloured . . . . 3·50 3·50
966a/d 10c. multicoloured . . . . 8·25 8·00
DESIGNS: As T **271** (same for each value) a, T **271**. b, Mariposa. c, Lignum-vitae. d, Coffee plant.
Prices are for single stamps.

272

1960. Sub-industrialized Countries Conference.
967 **272** 1c. black, yellow and red (postage) 30 15
968 – 2c. multicoloured 30 15
969 – 6c. red, black and cream 2·00 70

970 – 8c. multicoloured (air) 70 15
971 – 12c. multicoloured 2·00 15
972 – 30c. red and grey 2·50 85
973 – 50c. multicoloured 3·00 1·10
DESIGNS—HORIZ: 2c. Graph and symbols; 6c. Cogwheels; 12c. Workers holding lever; 30c. Maps. VERT: 8c. Hand holding machete; 50c. Upraised hand.

273 J. Menendez

274 Jose Marti and "Declaration of Havana"

1961. Jesus Menendez Commemoration.
974 **273** 2c. sepia and green 85 30

1961. Air. Declaration of Havana.
975 **274** 8c. red, black and yellow 1·60 1·10
976 12c. violet, black & buff 2·30 1·80
977 30c. brown, black & blue 5·25 4·75
MS978 103 × 80 mm. Nos. 975/7. No gum. Imperf 11·50 11·50
The above were issued with part of background text of the declaration in English, French and Spanish. Prices the same for each language.

275 U.N. Emblem within Dove of Peace

1961. 15th Anniv of U.N.O.
979 **275** 2c. brn & grn (postage) 45 20
980 10c. green and purple 1·60 60
MS981 102 × 64 mm. Nos. 979/80. No gum. Imperf 3·50 3·50

982 8c. red and yellow (air) 70 30
983 12c. blue and orange 2·00 60
MS984 102 × 64 mm. Nos. 982/3. No gum. Imperf 7·50 7·50

276 10c. Revolutionary Label of 1874 and "CUBA MAMBISA" "Postmark"

1961. Stamp Day. Inscr "24 DE ABRIL DIA DEL SELLO".
985 **276** 1c. red, green and black 30 15
986 – 2c. orange, slate & black 40 15
987 – 10c. turq, red & black 1·60 50
DESIGNS: 2c., 50c. stamp of 1907 and "CUBA REPUBLICANA" "postmark"; 10c., 2c. stamp of 1959 and "CUBA REVOLUCIONARIA" "postmark".

1961. May Day. Optd **PRIMERO DE MAYO 1961 ESTAMOS VENCIENDO**.
988 **273** 2c. sepia and green 1·60 30

278

1961. "For Peace and Socialism".
989 **278** 2c. multicoloured 1·40 30
No. 989 is lightly printed on back with pattern of wavy lines and multiple inscr "CORREOS CUBA" in buff.

1961. Air. Surch **HABILITADO PARA 8 cts.**
992 **174** 8c. on 15c. red 95 50
993 **54** 8c. on 20c. brown 95 50

1961. 1st Official Philatelic Exhibition. No. 987 optd **primera exposicion filatelica oficial oct. 7-17, 1961.**
994 10c. turq, red and black 1·90 50

281 Book and Lamp

1961. Education Year.
995 **281** 1c. red, black and green 15 15
996 2c. red, black and blue 15 15
997 10c. red, black and violet 90 25
998 12c. red, black & orange 1·60 60
The 2, 10 and 12c. show the letters "U", "B" and "A" on the book forming the word "CUBA".

282 "Polymita sulfurosa flammulata"

283 "Polymita picta fulminata"

1961. Christmas. Inscr "NAVIDAD 1961–62". Multicoloured. (a) Various designs as T **282**.
999 1c. Type **282** 50 20
1000 2c. Cuban grassquit (vert) 2·10 60
1001 10c. "Othreis toddi" (horiz) 3·00 1·20

(b) Various designs as T **283**.
1002a/d 1c. Snails (horiz) 50 20
1003a/d 2c. Birds (vert) 2·10 60
1004a/d 10c. Butterflies (horiz) 3·00 1·20
DESIGNS: No. 1002a, Type **283**; 1002b, "Polymita p. nigrofasciata"; 1002c, "Polymita p. fuscolimbata"; 1002d, "Polymita p. roseolimbata"; 1003a, Cuban macaw; 1003b, Cuban trogon; 1003c, Bee hummingbird; 1003d, Ivory-billed woodpecker; 1004a, "Uranidia boisduvalii"; 1004b, "Phoebis avellaneda"; 1004c, "Phaloe cubana"; 1004d, "Papoilio gundlacchianus".
Prices are for single stamps.

284 Castro Emblem

285 Hand with Machete

1962. 3rd Anniv of Cuban Revolution. Emblem in yellow, red, grey and blue. Colours of background and inscriptions given.
1005 **284** 1c. grn & pink (postage) 85 40
1006 2c. black and orange 1·70 50
1007 8c. brown & blue (air) 85 30
1008 12c. ochre and green 1·90 60
1009 30c. violet and yellow 2·50 1·00

1962. Air. 1st Anniv of Socialist Republic's First Sugar Harvest.
1010 **285** 8c. sepia and red 75 15
1011 12c. black and lilac 2·00 50

286 Armed Peasant and Tractor

1962. National Militia.
1012 **286** 1c. black and green 30 20
1013 – 2c. black and blue 60 30
1014 – 10c. black and orange 2·10 60
DESIGNS: 2c. Armed worker and welder; 10c. Armed woman and sewing-machinist.

287 Globe and Music Emblem

1962. Air. International Radio Service. Inscr and aerial yellow; musical notation black; lines on globe brown, background colours given.
1015 **287** 8c. grey 95 30
1016 12c. blue 1·90 60
1017 30c. green 2·75 1·40
1018 1p. lilac 5·75 3·75

288 Soldiers, Aircraft and Burning Ship

1962. 1st Anniv of "Playa Giron" (Sea Invasion Attempt of Cuban Exiles).
1019 **288** 2c. multicoloured 35 15
1020 3c. multicoloured 35 20
1021 10c. multicoloured 2·40 65

289 Arrival of First Mail from the Indies

1962. Stamp Day.
1022 **289** 10c. black and red on cream 3·00 90

290 Clenched Fist Salute

1962. Labour Day.
1023 **290** 2c. black on buff 30 15
1024 3c. black on red 60 25
1025 10c. black on blue 2·10 70

291 Wrestling

1962. National Sports Institute (I.N.D.E.R.) Commemoration. As T **291**. On cream paper.
1026a/e 1c. brown and red 30 20
1027a/e 2c. red and green 30 20
1028a/e 3c. blue and red 1·20 20
1029a/e 9c. purple and blue 75 30
1030a/e 10c. orange and purple 80 30
1031a/e 13c. black and red 85 45
DESIGNS: No. 1026a, Type **291**; 1026b, Weight-lifting; 1026c, Gymnastics; 1026d, Judo; 1026e, Throwing the discus; 1027a, Archery; 1027b, Roller skating; 1027c, Show jumping; 1027d, Ninepin bowling; 1027e, Cycling; 1028a, Rowing (coxed four); 1028b, Speed boat; 1028c, Swimming; 1028d, Kayak; 1028e, Yachting; 1029a, Football; 1029b, Tennis; 1029c, Baseball; 1029d, Basketball; 1029e, Volleyball; 1030a, Underwater fishing; 1030b, Shooting; 1030c, Model airplane flying; 1030d, Water polo; 1030e, Boxing; 1031a, Pelota; 1031b, Sports stadium; 1031c, Jai alai; 1031d, Chess; 1031e, Fencing.
Prices are for single stamps.

292 A. Santamaria and Soldiers

1962. 9th Anniv of "Rebel Day".
1032 **292** 2c. lake and blue 60 40
1033 – 3c. blue and lake 1·10 60
DESIGN: 3c. Santamaria and children.

293 Dove and Festival Emblem

1962. World Youth Festival, Helsinki.
1034 **293** 2c. multicoloured 85 30
1035 – 3c. multicoloured 1·40 60
MS1036 91 × 52 mm. Nos. 1034/5. Imperf 5·75 5·75

DESIGN: 3c. As Type **293** but with "clasped hands" instead of dove.

294 Czech 5k. "Praga 1962" stamp of 1961

1962. Air. International Stamp Exn, Prague.
1037 **294** 31c. multicoloured 4·25 1·80
MS1038 150 × 123 mm. No. 1037 10·50 10·50

295 Rings and Boxing Gloves

1962. 9th Central American and Caribbean Games, Jamaica.
1039 **295** 1c. ochre and red 15 15
1040 – 2c. ochre and blue 15 15
1041 – 3c. ochre and purple 15 15
1042 – 13c. ochre and green 1·90 80
DESIGNS: Rings and: 2c. Tennis rackets; 3c. Baseball bats; 13c. Rapiers and mask.

296 "Cuban Women"

1962. 1st Cuban Women's Federation National Congress.
1043 **296** 9c. red, green and black 95 30
1044 – 13c. black, blue & green 2·10 70
DESIGN—VERT: 13c. Mother and child, and Globe.

297 Running

1962. 1st Latin-American University Games. Multicoloured.
1045 1c. Type **297** 30 15
1046 2c. Baseball 65 20
1047 3c. Netball 1·00 25
1048 13c. Globe 2·00 55

298 Microscope and Parasites

1962. Malaria Eradication. Mult.
1049 1c. Type **298** 45 25
1050 2c. Mosquito and pool 45 25
1051 3c. Cinchona plant and formulae 1·60 40

299 Cuban Boa

300 Cuban Night Lizard

1962. Christmas. Inscr "NAVIDAD 1962–63". Multicoloured. (a) Various designs as T **299**.
1052 2c. Type **299** 50 20
1053 3c. "Cubispa turquino" (vert) 85 70
1054 10c. Jamacian long-tongued bat . . . . 3·25 1·70

(b) Various designs as T **300**.
1055a/d 2c. Reptiles 50 20
1056a/d 3c. Insects (vert) 85 70
1057a/d 10c. Mammals . . . . . 3·25 1·70

DESIGNS: No. 1055a, Type **300**; 1055b, Knight anole; 1055c, Wright's ground boa; 1055d, Cuban ground iguana; 1056a, "Chrysis superba"; 1056b, "Essosthutha roberto"; 1056c, "Hortensia conciliata"; 1056d, "Lachnopus argus"; 1057a, Desmarest's hutia; 1057b, Prehensile-tailed hutia; 1057c, Cuban solenodon; 1057d, Desmarest's hutia (white race).
Prices are for single stamps.

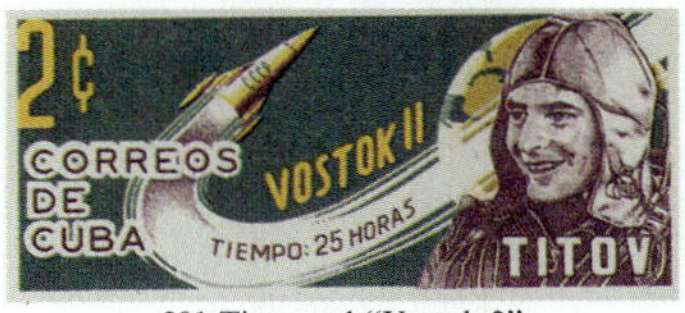

301 Titov and "Vostok 2"

1963. Cosmic Flights (1st issue).
1058 – 1c. blue, red and yellow 30 15
1059 **301** 2c. green, purple & yell 60 25
1060 – 3c. violet, red & yellow 60 20

DESIGNS: 1c. Gagarin and "Vostok 1"; 3c. Nikolaev, Popovich and "Vostoks 3 and 4".
See also Nos. 1133/4.

302 Attackers

1963. 6th Anniv of Attack on Presidential Palace.
1061 **302** 9c. black and red 90 15
1062 – 13c. purple and blue . . 1·10 40
1063 – 30c. green and red . . . 2·75 90

DESIGNS: 13c. Rodriguez, C. Servia, Machado and Westbrook; 30c. J. Echeverria and M. Mora.

303 Baseball

1963. 4th Pan-American Games, Sao Paulo.
1064 **303** 1c. green . . . . 1·00 30
1065 – 13c. red (Boxing) . . . . 2·75 55

304 "Mask" Letter Box

1963. Stamp Day.
1066 **304** 3c. black and brown . . 80 25
1067 – 10c. black and violet . . 2·00 50

DESIGN: 10c. 19th-century Post Office, Cathedral Place, Havana.

305 Revolutionaries and Statue

1963. Labour Day. Multicoloured.
1068 3c. Type **305** 45 15
1069 13c. Celebrating Labour Day . . . . 1·80 85

306 Child

1963. Children's Week.
1070 **306** 3c. brown and blue . . . 50 20
1071 30c. red and blue . . . . 2·50 95

307 Ritual Effigy

308 "Breaking chains of old regime"

1963. 60th Anniv of Montane Anthropological Museum.
1072 **307** 2c. brown and salmon 70 20
1073 – 3c. purple and blue . . . 85 30
1074 – 9c. grey and red . . . . 1·60 50

DESIGNS—HORIZ: 3c. Carved chair; VERT: 9c. Statuette.

1963. 10th Anniv of "Rebel Day".
1075 **308** 1c. black and pink . . . 20 15
1076 – 2c. purple and lt blue . . 20 15
1077 – 3c. sepia and lilac . . . 20 15
1078 – 7c. purple and green . . 30 15
1079 – 9c. purple and yellow . . 70 40
1080 – 10c. green and ochre . . 2·00 60
1081 – 13c. blue and buff . . . 3·00 1·10

DESIGNS: 2c. Palace attack; 3c. "The Insurrection"; 7c. "Strike of April 9th" (defence of radio station); 9c. "Triumph of the Revolution" (upraised flag and weapons); 10c. "Agrarian Reform and Nationalization" (artisan and peasant); 13c. "Victory of Giron" (soldiers in battle).

309 Star Apple

310 "Roof and Window"

1963. Cuban Fruits. Multicoloured.
1082 1c. Type **309** 20 15
1083 2c. Chiromoya 20 15
1084 3c. Cashew nut 30 20
1085 10c. Custard apple . . . . 1·90 60
1086 13c. Mango . . . . 2·50 1·90

1963. 7th Int Architects Union Congress, Havana.
1087 3c. multicoloured 40 20
1088 3c. multicoloured 40 20
1089 3c. black, blue and bistre . . 40 20
1090 3c. multicoloured 40 20
1091 13c. multicoloured . . . . 1·60 70
1092 13c. multicoloured . . . . 1·60 70
1093 13c. red, olive and black . . 1·60 70
1094 13c. multicoloured . . . . 1·60 70

DESIGNS—VERT: No. 1087, Type **310**; Nos. 1090/2, Symbols of building construction as Type **310**. HORIZ: Nos. 1089/90 and 1093, Sketches of urban buildings; No. 1094, as Type **310** (girders and outline of house).

311 Hemingway and Scene from "The Old Man and the Sea"

1963. Ernest Hemingway Commemoration.
1095 **311** 3c. brown and blue . . . 55 15
1096 – 9c. turquoise and mauve 1·40 20
1097 – 13c. black and green . . 2·40 70

DESIGNS—Hemingway and: 9c. Scene from "For Whom the Bell Tolls"; 13c. Residence at San Francisco de Paula, near Havana.

312 "Zapateo" (dance) after V. P. de Landaluze

1964. 50th Anniv of National Museum.
1098 **312** 2c. multicoloured 15 10
1099 – 3c. multicoloured 65 15
1100 – 9c. multicoloured 90 50
1101 – 13c. black and violet . . 1·90 85

DESIGNS—VERT: (32 × 42½ mm.): 3c. "The Rape of the Mulattos" (after C. Enriquez); 9c. Greek amphora; 13c. "Dilecta Mea" (bust, after J. A. Houdon).

313 B. J. Borrell (revolutionary)

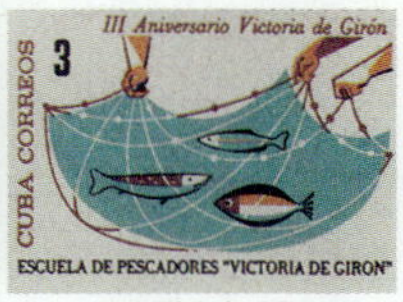

314 Fish in Net

1964. 5th Anniv of Revolution.
1102 **313** 2c. black, orange & grn 30 15
1103 – 3c. black, orange & red 55 20
1104 – 10c. black, orange & pur 1·00 40
1105 – 13c. black, orange & bl 2·00 85

PORTRAITS: 3c. M. Salado. 10c. O. Lucero. 13c. S. Gonzalez (revolutionaries).

1964. 3rd Anniv of Giron Victory.
1106 **314** 3c. multicoloured 30 15
1107 – 10c. black, grey & bistre 70 40
1108 – 13c. slate, black & orge 2·10 85

DESIGNS—HORIZ: 10c. Victory Monument. VERT: 13c. Fallen eagle.

315 V. M. Pera (1st Director of Military Posts, 1868–71)

1964. Stamp Day.
1109 **315** 3c. blue and brown . . . 40 15
1110 – 13c. green and lilac . . . 2·00 60

DESIGN: 13c. Cuba's first (10c.) military stamp.

316 Symbolic "1"

317 Chinese Monument, Havana

1964. Labour Day.
1111 **316** 3c. multicoloured 30 15
1112 – 13c. multicoloured . . . 1·40 70

DESIGN: 13c. As Type **316** but different symbols within "1".

1964. Cuban–Chinese Friendship.
1113 **317** 1c. multicoloured 30 15
1114 – 2c. red, olive and black 55 15
1115 – 3c. multicoloured . . . . 1·10 20

DESIGNS—HORIZ: 2c. Cuban and Chinese. VERT: 3c. Flags of Cuba and China.

318 Globe

1964. U.P.U. Congress, Vienna.
1116 **318** 13c. brown, green & red 80 30
1117 – 30c. black, bistre & red 1·70 75
1118 – 50c. black, blue and red 3·50 1·20

DESIGNS: 30c. H. von Stephan (founder of U.P.U.); 50c. U.P.U. Monument, Berne.

319 Mutton Snapper

1964. Popular Savings Movement. Mult.
1119 1c. Type **319** 40 15
1120 2c. Cow 60 15
1121 13c. Poultry . . . . 2·50 60

320 "Rio Jibacoa"

1964. Cuban Merchant Fleet. Multicoloured.
1122 1c. Type **320** 30 15
1123 2c. "Camilo Cienfuegos" . . 50 15
1124 3c. "Sierra Maestra" 70 20
1125 9c. "Bahia de Siguanea" . . 1·70 70
1126 10c. "Oriente" . . . . . . 4·25 1·20

321 Vietnamese Fighter

322 Raul Gomez Garcia and Poem

1964. "Unification of Vietnam" Campaign. Mult.
1127 2c. Type **321** 25 15
1128 3c. Vietnamese shaking hands across map 35 15
1129 10c. Hand and mechanical ploughing 80 20
1130 13c. Vietnamese, Cuban and flags . . . . 2·20 60

1964. 11th Anniv of "Rebel Day".
1131 **322** 3c. black, red and ochre 40 15
1132 – 13c. multicoloured . . . 2·40 50

DESIGN: 13c. Inscr "LA HISTORIA ME ABSOLVERA" (Castro's book).

1964. Cosmic Flights (2nd issue). As T **301**.
1133 9c. yellow, violet and red . . 1·20 50
1134 13c. yellow, red and green 3·00 85

DESIGNS: 9c. "Vostok-5" and Bykovksy; 13c. "Vostok-6" and Tereshkova.

323 Start of Race

1964. Olympic Games, Tokyo.
1135 – 1c. yellow, blue and purple 30 15
1136 – 2c. multicoloured 30 15
1137 – 3c. brown, black & red 30 15
1138 **323** 7c. violet, blue and orange 70 20
1139 – 10c. yellow, purple & bl 1·40 70
1140 – 13c. multicoloured . . . 2·75 1·10

DESIGNS—VERT: 1c. Gymnastics; 2c. Rowing; 3c. Boxing. HORIZ: 10c. Fencing; 13c. Games symbols.

325 Satellite and Globe

326 Rocket and part of Globe

1964. Cuban Postal Rocket Experiment. 25th Anniv Various rockets and satellites. (a) Horiz. designs as T **325**.
1141 **325** 1c. multicoloured 20 15
1142 – 2c. multicoloured 60 15
1143 – 3c. multicoloured 85 40
1144 – 9c. multicoloured . . . . 2·30 85
1145 – 13c. multicoloured . . . 3·00 1·90

(b) Horiz. designs as T **326**.
1146a/d – 1c. multicoloured . . . 20 15
1147a/d – 2c. multicoloured . . . 60 15
1148a/d – 3c. multicoloured . . . 85 40
1149a/d – 9c. multicoloured . . . 2·30 85
1150a/d – 13c. multicoloured . . . 3·00 1·90

(c) Larger 44 × 28 mm.
1151 – 50c. green and black . . . 10·50 3·00
MS1152 110 × 74 mm. As No. 1151 (different) . . . . 20·00 20·00

DESIGN: 50c. Cuban Rocket Post 10c. Stamp of 1939.
Nos. 1141 and 1146, 1142 and 1147, 1143 and 1148, 1144 and 1149, 1145 and 1150 were printed together in five sheets of 25, each comprising four stamps as Type **325** plus five se-tenant stamp-size labels inscribed overall "1939 COHETE POSTAL CUBANO 25 ANIVERSARIO 1964" forming a centre cross and four blocks of four different stamps as Type **326** in each corner. The four-stamp design incorporates different subjects, which together form a composite design around a globe.
Prices are for single stamps.

1964. 1st Three-Manned Space Flight. As No. 1151 but colours changed. Optd **VOSJOD-1 octubre 12 1964 PRIMERA TRIPULACION DEL ESPACIO** and large rocket.
1153 50c. green and brown . . . 4·75 1·80

328 Lenin addressing Meeting

1964. 40th Death Anniv of Lenin.
1154 **328** 3c. black and orange . . 30 20
1155 – 13c. red and violet . . . 90 35
1156 – 30c. black and blue . . . 1·80 80
DESIGNS—HORIZ: 13c. Lenin mausoleum. VERT: 30c. Lenin and hammer and sickle emblem.

329 Leopard

1964. Havana Zoo Animals. Multicoloured.
1157 1c. Type **329** 30 15
1158 2c. Indian elephant (vert) . . 30 15
1159 3c. Red deer (vert) 30 15
1160 4c. Eastern grey kangaroo 30 15
1161 5c. Lions 40 15
1162 6c. Eland 35 15
1163 7c. Common zebra 35 15
1164 8c. Striped hyena 65 15
1165 9c. Tiger 65 15
1166 10c. Guanaco 80 15
1167 13c. Chimpanzees 80 15
1168 20c. Collared Peccary . . . 1·10 25
1169 30c. Common racoon (vert) 1·50 55
1170 40c. Hippopotamus . . . . 3·00 90
1171 50c. Brazilian tapir . . . . 4·00 1·20
1172 60c. Dromedary (vert) . . . 4·50 1·50
1173 70c. American Bison . . . . 4·50 1·60
1174 80c. Asiatic black bear (vert) 5·75 1·90
1175 90c. Water buffalo . . . . 5·75 2·40
1176 1p. Roe deer at Zoo Entrance . . . . 8·25 2·40

330 Jose Marti

1964. "Liberators of Independence". Multicoloured. Each showing portraits and campaigning scenes.
1177 1c. Type **330** 15 15
1178 2c. A. Maceo 35 15
1179 3c. M. Gomez 70 40
1180 13c. C. Garcia . . . . . . 1·90 85

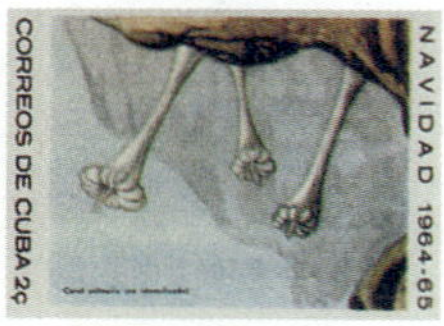

331 Dwarf Cup Coral

332 Small Flower Coral

1964. Christmas. Inscr "NAVIDAD 1964–65". Multicoloured. (a) As T **331**.
1181 2c. Type **331** 65 30
1182 3c. Sea anemone . . . . . 1·10 60
1183 10c. Stone lily . . . . . . 1·90 1·10

(b) As T **332**.
1184a/d 2c. Coral 65 30
1185a/d 3c. Jellyfish . . . . . . 1·10 60
1186a/d 10c. Sea stars and urchins . . . . 1·90 1·10
DESIGNS: No. 1184a, Type **332**; 1184b, Elkhorn coral; 1184c, Dense moosehorn coral; 1184d, Yellow brain coral; 1185a, Portuguese man-of-war; 1185b, Moon jellyfish; 1185c, Thimble jellyfish; 1185d, Upside-down jellyfish; 1186a, Big-spined sea-urchin; 1186b, Edible sea urchin; 1186c, Caribbean brittle star; 1186d, Reticulated sea star.
Prices are for single stamps.

333 Dr. Tomas Romay

334 Map of Latin America and Part of Declaration

1964. Birth Bicentenary of Dr. Tomas Romay (scientist).
1187 **333** 1c. black and bistre . . . 40 15
1188 – 2c. sepia and brown . . 40 15
1189 – 3c. brown and bistre . . 60 20
1190 – 10c. black and bistre . . 2·10 50
DESIGNS—VERT: 2c. First vaccination against smallpox. HORIZ: 3c. Dr. Romay and extract from his treatise on the vaccine; 10c. Dr. Romay's statue.

1964. 2nd Declaration of Havana. Mult.
1191 3c. Type **334** 75 50
1192 13c. Map of Cuba and native receiving revolutionary message . . 2·75 1·60
The two stamps have the declaration superimposed in tiny print across each horiz. row of five stamps, thus requiring strips of five to show the complete declaration.

335 "Maritime Post" (diorama)

1965. Inauguration of Cuban Postal Museum. Mult.
1193 13c. Type **335** . . . . . 4·25 1·10
1194 30c. "Insurgent Post" (diorama) . . . . . . 3·25 1·80
MS1195 127 × 76 mm. Two sheets. Nos. 1193/4 but with blue instead of yellow frames. Imperf . . . 9·25 9·25

336 "Sondero" (schooner)

1965. Cuban Fishing Fleet. Multicoloured. Fishing crafts.
1196 1c. Type **336** 15 15
1197 2c. "Omicron" 30 15
1198 3c. "Victoria" 45 15
1199 9c. "Cardenas" 65 30
1200 10c. "Sigma" . . . . . . 3·50 85
1201 13c. "Lambda" . . . . . . 5·75 1·40

337 Lydia Doce

1965. International Women's Day. Multicoloured.
1202 3c. Type **337** . . . . . . 1·00 40
1203 13c. Clara Zetkin . . . . . 1·60 85

338 Jose Antonio Echeverria University City

1965. "Technical Revolution". Inscr "REVOLUCION TECNICA".
1204 **338** 3c. black, brown and chestnut 90 25
1205 – 13c. multicoloured . . . . 4·50 70
DESIGN: 13c. Scientific symbols.

339 Leonov

1965. "Voskhod 2", Space flight.
1206 **339** 30c. brown and blue . . 2·50 95
1207 – 50c. blue and magenta 4·75 1·90
DESIGN: 50c. Beliaiev, Leonov and "Voskhod 2".

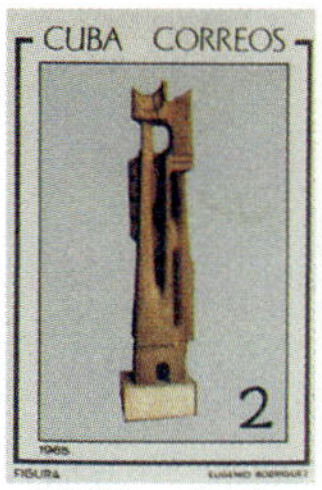

340 "Figure" (after E. Rodrigues)

341 Lincoln Statue, Washington

1965. National Museum Treasures. Mult.
1208 2c. Type **340** (27 × 42 mm) 30 15
1209 3c. "Landscape with sunflowers" (V. Manuel) (31 × 42 mm) 50 20
1210 10c. "Abstract" (W. Lam) (42 × 31 mm) . . . . . . 1·30 50
1211 13c. "Children" (E. Ponce) (39 × 33½ mm) . . . . . 2·30 95

1965. Death Centenary of Abraham Lincoln.
1212 – 1c. brown, grey and yellow 15 15
1213 – 2c. ultramarine & blue 30 15
1214 **341** 3c. black, red and blue 95 40
1215 – 13c. black, orange & bl 2·10 70
DESIGNS—HORIZ: 1c. Cabin at Hodgenville, Kentucky (Lincoln's birthplace); 2c. Lincoln Monument, Washington. VERT: 13c. Abraham Lincoln.

342 18th-century Mail Ship and Old Postmarks (bicent of Maritime Mail)

1965. Stamp Day.
1216 **342** 3c. bistre and red . . . 2·50 25
1217 – 13c. red, black and blue 2·50 70
DESIGN: 13c. Cuban; 10c. "Air Train" stamp of 1935 and glider train over Capitol, Havana.

343 Sun and Earth's Magnetic Pole

1965. International Quiet Sun Year. Multicoloured.
1218 1c. Type **343** 30 15
1219 2c. I.Q.S.Y. emblem (vert) 30 15
1220 3c. Earth's magnetic fields 60 15
1221 6c. Solar rays 70 20
1222 30c. Effect of solar rays on various atmospheric layers 2·50 70
1223 50c. Effect of solar rays on satellite orbits . . . . . 3·25 1·70
MS1224 94 × 70 mm. No. 1223. Imperf . . . . 7·75 7·75
Nos. 1221/3 are larger, 47 × 20 mm. or 20 × 47 mm. (30c.).

344 Telecommunications Station

1965. Centenary of I.T.U. Multicoloured.
1225 1c. Type **344** 15 10
1226 2c. Satellite (vert) 15 10
1227 3c. "Telstar" 30 10
1228 10c. "Telstar" and receiving station (vert) . . . . . . 1·10 25
1229 30c. I.T.U. emblem . . . . 3·00 1·10

345 Festival Emblem and Flags

1965. World Youth and Students Festival. Multicoloured.
1230 13c. Type **345** . . . . . . 1·40 40
1231 30c. Soldiers of three races and flags . . . . 2·75 70

346 M. Perez (pioneer balloonist), Balloon and Satellite

1965. Matias Perez Commemoration.
1232 **346** 3c. black and red . . . . 1·80 1·20
1233 – 13c. black and blue . . . 2·75 1·20
DESIGN: 13c. As Type **346**, but with rockets in place of satellite.

347 Rose (Europe)

1965. Flowers of the World. Multicoloured.
1234 1c. Type **347** 15 10
1235 2c. Chrysanthemum (Asia) 30 10
1236 3c. Strelitzia (Africa) 30 10
1237 4c. Dahlia (N. America) . . 30 10
1238 5c. Orchid (S. America) . . 1·40 30
1239 13c. "Grevillea banksii" (Oceania) . . . . . . 3·00 1·20
1240 30c. "Brunfelsia nitida" (Cuba) . . . . 4·25 2·10

348 Swimming

1965. First National Games.
1241 **348** 1c. multicoloured 20 10
1242 – 2c. multicoloured 30 10
1243 – 3c. black, red and grey 70 30
1244 – 30c. black, red and grey 2·50 95
SPORTS: 2c. Basketball. 3c. Gymnastics. 30c. Hurdling.

349 Anti-tank gun

1965. Museum of the Revolution. Mult.
1245 1c. Type **349** 15 10
1246 2c. Tank 15 10
1247 3c. Bazooka 30 10
1248 10c. Rebel Uniform 95 30
1249 13c. Launch "Granma" and compass . . . . 2·75 60

350 C. J. Finlay

351 "Anetia numidia" (butterfly)

1965. 50th Death Anniv of Carlos J. Finlay (malaria researcher).
1250 – 1c. black, green & blue 15 10
1251 – 2c. brown, ochre and black 15 10
1252 **350** 3c. brown and black . . 30 15
1253 – 7c. black and lilac . . 40 15
1254 – 9c. bronze and black . . 70 30

1255 – 10c. black and blue . . . 1·80 40
1256 – 13c. multicoloured . . . 2·75 85

DESIGNS—HORIZ: 1c. Finlay's signature. VERT: 2c. Yellow fever mosquito; 7c. Finlay's microscope; 9c. Dr. C. Delgado; 10c. Finlay's monument; 13c. Finlay demonstrating his theories, after painting by Valderrama.

1965. Cuban Butterflies. Multicoloured.

1257 2c. Type **351** 30 10
1258 2c. "Carathis gortynoides" 30 10
1259 2c. "Hymenitis cubana" . . 30 10
1260 2c. "Eubaphe heros" . . . 30 10
1261 2c. "Dismorphia cubana" . . 30 10
1262 3c. "Siderone nemesis" . . . 35 15
1263 3c. "Syntomidopsis variegata" 35 15
1264 3c. "Ctenuchidia virgo" . . 35 15
1265 3c. "Lycorea ceres" . . . 35 15
1266 3c. "Eubaphe disparilis" . . 35 15
1267 13c. "Anetia cubana" . . . 1·80 75
1268 13c. "Prepona antimache" 1·80 75
1269 13c. "Sylepta reginalis" . . 1·80 75
1270 13c. "Chlosyne perezi" . . . 1·80 75
1271 13c. "Anaea clytemnestra" 1·80 75

1965. "Conquest of Space" Philatelic Exhibition, Havana. Sheet 94 × 65 mm containing stamp as No. 1223 but inscr "EXHIBICION FILATELICA CONQUISTA DEL ESPACIO".

MS1272 50c. multicoloured . . . 14·50 14·50

352 20c. Coin of 1962

1965. 50th Anniv of Cuban Coinage. Mult.

1273 1c. Type **352** 25 10
1274 2c. 1p. coin of 1934 . . . . 25 10
1275 3c. 40c. coin of 1962 . . . . 25 15
1276 8c. 1p. coin of 1915 . . . . 65 25
1277 10c. 1p. coin of 1953 . . . 1·50 50
1278 13c. 20p. coin of 1915 . . . 2·20 60

353 Oranges

1965. Tropical Fruits. Multicoloured.

1279 1c. Type **353** 20 10
1280 2c. Custard-apples 20 10
1281 3c. Papayas 20 20
1282 4c. Bananas 30 10
1283 10c. Avocado pears 50 15
1284 13c. Pineapples 85 70
1285 20c. Guavas . . . . 2·20 70
1286 50c. Mameys . . . . 4·50 1·20

354 Northern Oriole **355** Painted Bunting

1965. Christmas. Vert. designs showing bird life.
(a) As T **354**. Multicoloured.

1287 3c. Type **354** . . . . 2·10 1·80
1288 5c. Scarlet tanager . . . . . 2·30 2·30
1289 13c. Indigo bunting . . . . 5·25 4·25

(b) As T **355**.

1290a/d 3c. multicoloured . . . . 2·10 1·80
1291a/d 5c. multicoloured . . . . 2·30 2·30
1292a/d 13c. multicoloured . . . 5·25 4·25

DESIGNS: No. 1290a, Type **355**; 1290b, American redstart; 1290c, Blackburnian warbler; 1290d, Rose-breasted grosbeak; 1291a, Yellow-throated warbler; 1291b, Blue-winged warbler; 1291c, Prothonotary warbler; 1291d, Hooded warbler; 1292a, Blue-winged teal; 1292b, Wood duck; 1292c, Common shoveler; 1292d, Black-crowned night heron.

Prices are for single stamps.

356 Hurdling

1965. 7th Anniv of International Athletics, Havana. Multicoloured.

1293 1c. Type **356** 15 10
1294 2c. Throwing the discus . . 25 10
1295 3c. Putting the shot 60 15
1296 7c. Throwing the javelin . . 60 30
1297 9c. High-jumping 85 40
1298 10c. Throwing the hammer 1·70 70
1299 13c. Running . . . . 2·30 1·00

357 Shark–sucker

1965. National Aquarium. Multicoloured.

1300 1c. Type **357** 25 10
1301 2c. Skipjack/Bonito tuna . . 25 10
1302 3c. Sergeant major 60 10
1303 4c. Sailfish 70 15
1304 5c. Nassau grouper 70 25
1305 10c. Mutton snapper . . . 1·00 40
1306 13c. Yellow-tailed snapper 3·75 1·00
1307 30c. Squirrelfish . . . . . 5·75 1·70

358 A. Voisin, Cuban and French Flags

1965. 1st Death Anniv of Prof. Andre Voisin (scientist).

1308 **358** 3c. multicoloured 85 30
1309 – 13c. multicoloured . . . 2·10 60

DESIGN: 13c. Similar to Type **358** but with microscope and plant in place of cattle.

359 Skoda Omnibus

1965. Cuban Transport. Multicoloured.

1310 1c. Type **359** 15 10
1311 2c. Ikarus omnibus 15 10
1312 3c. Leyland omnibus . . . 25 10
1313 4c. Russian-built Type TEM-4 diesel locomotive . . . . 3·00 55
1314 7c. French-built BB. 69,000 diesel locomotive . . . . 3·00 60
1315 10c. Tug "R.D.A." . . . . 1·80 40
1316 13c. Freighter "13 de Marzo" . . . . 2·75 70
1317 20c. Ilyushin IL-18 airliner 3·00 1·10

360 Infantry Column

1966. 7th Anniv of Revolution. Mult.

1318 1c. Type **360** 25 10
1319 2c. Soldier and tank 20 10
1320 3c. Sailor and torpedo-boat 85 10
1321 10c. MiG-21 jet fighter . . 1·80 50
1322 13c. Rocket missile . . . . 2·30 85

SIZES—As Type **360**: 2c., 3c. HORIZ: (38½ × 23½ mm): 10c., 13c.

361 Conference Emblem

1966. Tricontinental Conference, Havana.

1323 **361** 2c. multicoloured 15 10
1324 – 3c. multicoloured 30 15
1325 – 13c. multicoloured . . . 1·70 60

DESIGNS: 3c., 13c. As Type **361** but re-arranged.

362 Guardalabarca Beach

1966. Tourism. Multicoloured.

1326 1c. Type **362** 25 10
1327 2c. La Gran Piedra (mountain resort) 25 15
1328 3c. Guama, Las Villas (country scene) 75 25
1329 13c. Waterfall, Soroa (vert) 3·25 70

363 Congress Emblem and "Treating Patient" (old engraving)

1966. Medical and Stomachal Congresses, Havana. Multicoloured.

1330 3c. Type **363** 55 10
1331 13c. Congress emblem and children receiving treatment . . . . 2·75 60

364 Afro-Cuban Doll

1966. Cuban Handicrafts. Multicoloured.

1332 1c. Type **364** 15 10
1333 2c. Sombreros 15 10
1334 3c. Vase 20 10
1335 7c. Gourd lampshades . . . 20 15
1336 9c. Rare-wood lampstand 65 25
1337 10c. "Horn" shark (horiz) 1·00 40
1338 13c. Painted polymita shell necklace and earrings (horiz) . . . . 2·00 85

365 "Chelsea College" (after Canaletto)

1966. National Museum Exhibits. Inscr "1966". Multicoloured.

1339 1c. Ming Dynasty vase (vert) 15 10
1340 2c. Type **365** 70 10
1341 3c. "Portrait of a Young Girl" (after Goya) (vert) 60 30
1342 13c. Portrait of Fayum (vert) . . . . 2·50 85

366 Cosmonauts in Training **367** Tank in Battle

1966. 5th Anniv of 1st Manned Space Flight. Multicoloured.

1343 1c. Tsiolkovsky and diagram (horiz) 15 10
1344 2c. Type **366** 15 10
1345 3c. Gagarin, rocket and globe (horiz) 30 10
1346 7c. Nikolaev and Popovich 50 15
1347 9c. Tereshkova and Bykovsky (horiz) 70 30
1348 10c. Komarov, Feoktistov and Yegorov (horiz) . . . 95 40
1349 13c. Leonov in space (horiz) 1·90 70

1966. 5th Anniv of Giron Victory.

1350 **367** 2c. black, green and bistre 15 10
1351 – 3c. black, blue and red 70 10
1352 – 9c. black, brown & grey 30 15
1353 – 10c. black, blue and green . . . . 1·40 15
1354 – 13c. black, brown and blue . . . . 2·40 85

DESIGNS: 3c. "Houston" (freighter) sinking; 9c. Disabled tank and poster-hoarding; 10c. Young soldier; 13c. Operations map.

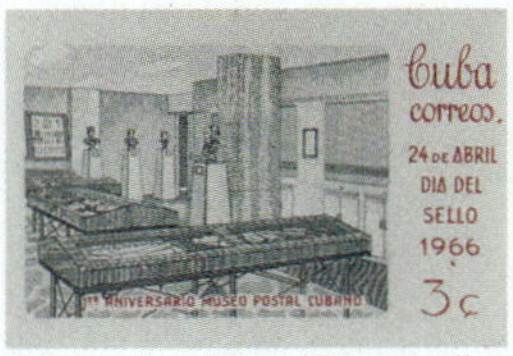

368 Interior of Postal Museum (1st Anniv)

1966. Stamp Day.

1355 **368** 3c. green and red . . . . 1·00 10
1356 – 13c. brown, black & red 2·75 80

DESIGN: 13c. Stamp collector and Cuban 2c. stamp of 1959.

369 Bouquet and Anvil **370** W.H.O. Building

1966. Labour Day. Multicoloured.

1357 2c. Type **369** 15 10
1358 3c. Bouquet and Machete 30 10
1359 10c. Bouquet and Hammer 70 30
1360 13c. Bouquet and parts of globe and cogwheel . . . 1·90 1·00

1966. Inaug of W.H.O. Headquarters, Geneva.

1361 **370** 2c. black, green & yell 15 10
1362 – 3c. black, blue and yellow 60 15
1363 13c. black, yellow and blue . . . . 2·00 70

DESIGNS (W.H.O. Building on): 3c. Flag; 13c. Emblem.

371 Athletics **372** Makarenko Pedagogical Institute

1966. 10th Central American and Caribbean Games.

1364 **371** 1c. sepia and green . . . 15 10
1365 – 2c. sepia and orange . . 25 10
1366 – 3c. brown and yellow . . 35 10
1367 – 7c. blue and mauve . . 35 15
1368 – 9c. black and blue . . . 65 25
1369 – 10c. black and brown . . 1·10 25
1370 – 13c. blue and red . . . . 2·75 70

DESIGNS—HORIZ: 2c. Rifle-shooting. VERT: 3c. Baseball; 7c. Volleyball; 9c. Football; 10c. Boxing; 13c. Basketball.

1966. Educational Development.

1371 **372** 1c. black and green . . . 15 10
1372 – 2c. black, ochre & yellow 15 10
1373 – 3c. black, ultram & bl 25 10
1374 – 10c. black, brown & grn 75 25
1375 – 13c. multicoloured . . . 1·90 60

DESIGNS: 2c. Alphabetization Museum; 3c. Lamp (5th anniv of National Alphabetization Campaign); 10c. Open-air class; 13c. "Farmers' and Workers' Education".

373 "Agrarian Reform"

1966. Air. "Conquests of the Revolution". Multicoloured.
1376 1c. Type **373** 15 10
1377 2c. "Industrialisation" . . . 15 10
1378 3c. "Urban Reform" . . . 40 15
1379 7c. "Eradication of Unemployment" 40 15
1380 9c. "Education" 75 30
1381 10c. "Public Health" . . . 1·70 30
1382 13c. Paragraph from Castro's book, "La Historia me Absolvera" 2·20 50

374 Workers with Flag

1966. 12th Revolutionary Workers' Union Congress, Havana.
1383 **374** 3c. multicoloured . . . . 1·00 30

375 Flamed Cuban Liguus

377 Arms of Pinar del Rio

376 Pigeon and Breeding Pen

1966. Cuban Shells. Multicoloured.
1384 1c. Type **375** 30 10
1385 2c. Measled cowrie 40 15
1386 3c. West Indian fighting conch 60 25
1387 7c. Rough American scallops 70 30
1388 9c. Crenate liguus 85 30
1389 10c. Atlantic trumpet triton 1·60 50
1390 13c. Archer's Cuban liguus 3·25 1·00

1966. Pigeon-breeding. Multicoloured.
1391 1c. Type **376** 40 15
1392 2c. Pigeon and time-clock 40 15
1393 3c. Pigeon and pigeon-loft 40 25
1394 7c. Pigeon and breeder tending pigeon-loft . . . 85 30
1395 9c. Pigeon and pigeon-yard 85 40
1396 10c. Pigeon and breeder placing message in capsule 2·50 60
1397 13c. Pigeons in flight over map of Cuba ($44\frac{1}{2} \times 28$ mm) . . . . . 4·00 1·00

1966. National and Provincial Arms. Mult.
1398 1c. Type **377** 15 10
1399 2c. Arms of Havana 25 10
1400 3c. Arms of Matanzas . . . 25 15
1401 4c. Arms of Las Villas . . . 30 15
1402 5c. Arms of Camaguey . . . 60 25
1403 9c. Arms of Oriente . . . . 1·00 50
1404 13c. National Arms (26 × 44 mm) . . . . . . 2·30 60

378 "Queen" and Simultaneous Games

379 Emblem and Chessboard (Capablanca—Lasker game, 1914)

1966. 17th Chess Olympiad, Havana.
1405 – 1c. black and green . . . 25 10
1406 – 2c. black and blue . . . 25 10
1407 – 3c. black and red 40 15
1408 – 9c. black and ochre . . . 80 30
1409 **378** 10c. black and mauve . . 1·90 30
1410 – 13c. black, blue & turq 2·75 85
MS1411 77 × 61 mm. **379** 30c. black, blue and yellow. Imperf . . . 12·00 12·00
DESIGNS—VERT: 1c. "Pawn"; 2c. "Rook". 3c. "Knight"; 9c. "Bishop". HORIZ: 13c. Olympiad Emblem and "King".

380 Lenin Hospital

1966. Cuban–Soviet Friendship. Mult.
1412 2c. Type **380** 15 10
1413 3c. World map and "Havana" (tanker) . . . 30 10
1414 10c. Cuban and Soviet technicians . . . . 1·00 30
1415 13c. Cuban fruit-pickers and Soviet tractor technicians 2·00 95

381 A. Roldan and Music of "Fiesta Negra"

1966. Song Festival.
1416 **381** 1c. brown, black & grn 15 10
1417 – 2c. brown, black & mve 25 10
1418 – 3c. brown, black & blue 25 10
1419 – 7c. brown, black & vio 65 15
1420 – 9c. brown, black & yell 65 25
1421 – 10c. brn, blk & orge . . 2·40 50
1422 – 13c. brown, black & bl 3·25 1·00
CUBAN COMPOSERS AND WORKS: 2c. E. S. de Fuentes and "Tu" (habanera, Cuban dance). 3c. M. Simons and "El Manisero". 7c. J. Anckermann and "El arroyo que murmura". 9c. A. G. Caturla and "Pastoral Lullaby". 10c. E. Grenet and "Ay Mama Ines". 13c. E. Lecuona and "La Comparsa" (dance).

382 Bacteriological Warfare

1966. "Genocide in Viet-Nam". Mult.
1423 2c. Type **382** 30 10
1424 3c. Gas warfare 50 15
1425 13c. "Conventional" bombing . . . . 2·75 70

383 A. L. Fernandez ("Nico") and Beach Landing

1966. 10th Anniv of 1956 Revolutionary Successes. Portrait in black and brown.
1426 **383** 1c. brown and green . . 15 10
1427 – 2c. brown and purple . . 15 10
1428 – 3c. brown and purple . . 15 10
1429 – 7c. brown and blue . . . 25 15
1430 – 9c. brown and turquoise 60 15
1431 – 10c. brown and olive . . 2·10 60
1432 – 13c. brown and orange 2·00 95
HEROES AND SCENES: 2c. C. Gonzalez and beach landing. 3c. J. Tey and street fighting. 7c. T. Aloma and street fighting. 9c. O. Parellada and street fighting. 10c. J. M. Marquez and beach landing. 13c. F. Pais and trial scene.

384 Globe and Recreational Activities

1966. International Leisure Time and Recreation Seminar. Multicoloured.
1433 3c. Type **384** 15 10
1434 9c. Clock, eye and world map . . . . 1·40 30
1435 13c. Seminar poster . . . . 1·90 70

385 Arrow and Telecommunications Symbols

1966. 1st National Telecommunications Forum. Multicoloured.
1436 3c. Type **385** 60 10
1437 10c. Target and satellites . . 3·00 30
1438 13c. Shell and satellites ($28\frac{1}{2} \times 36$ mm) . . . . . 4·50 85
MS1439 161 × 116 mm. Nos. 1436/8 (sold at 30c.) . . . . 12·00 12·00

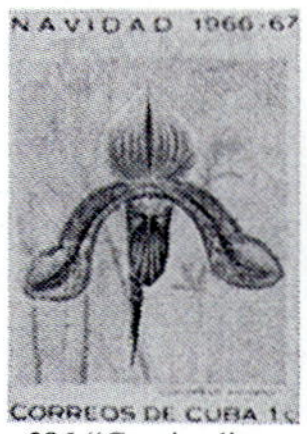

386 "Cypripedium eurilochus"

387 "Cattleya speciosissima"

1966. Christmas. Orchids. Multicoloured.
(a) As T **386**.
1440 1c. Type **386** 75 15
1441 3c. "Cypripedium hookerae volunteanum . . . . . . 1·10 40
1442 13c. "Cypripedium stonei" . 4·00 1·60
(b) As T **387**.
1443a/d 1c. multicoloured 75 15
1444a/d 3c. multicoloured . . . . 1·10 40
1445a/d 13c. multicoloured . . . 4·00 1·60
DESIGNS: No. 1443a, Type **387**; 1443b, "Cattleya mendelli"; 1443c, "Cattleya trianae"; 1443d, "Cattleya labiata"; 1444a, "Cypripedium morganiae"; 1444b, "Cattleya" "Countess of Derby"; 1444c, "Cattleya gigas"; 1444d, "Cypripedium stonei"; 1445a, "Cattleya mendelli" "Countess of Montrose"; 1445b, "Oncidium macranthum"; 1445c, "Cattleya aurea"; 1445d, "Laelia anceps".
Prices are for single stamps.

388 Flag and Hands ("1959—Liberation")

1966. 8th Anniv of Revolution. Mult.
1446 3c. Type **388** 25 10
1447 3c. Clenched fist ("1960—Agrarian Reform") . . . 25 10
1448 3c. Hands holding pencil ("1961—Education") . . 25 10
1449 3c. Hand protecting plant ("1965—Agriculture") . . 25 10
1450 13c. Head of Rodin's statue, "The Thinker", and arrows ("1962—Planning") (vert) . . . . 1·50 50
1451 13c. Hands moving lever ("1963—Organization") (vert) . . . . 1·50 50
1452 13c. Hand holding plant within cogwheel ("1964—Economy") (vert) . . . 1·50 50
1453 13c. Hand holding rifle-butt, and part of globe ("1966—Solidarity") (vert) 1·50 50

389 "Spring" (after J. Arche)

1967. National Museum Exhibits. Paintings (1st series). Multicoloured.
1454 1c. "Coffee-pot" (A. A. Leon) (vert) 30 10
1455 2c. "Peasants" (E. Abela) (vert) 50 15
1456 3c. Type **389** 70 25
1457 13c. "Still Life" (Amelia Pelaez) (vert) . . . . . . 2·10 1·00
1458 30c. "Landscape" (G. Escalante) . . . . . 5·75 2·10
See also Nos. 1648/54, 1785/91, 1871/7, 1900/6, 2005/11, 2048/54, 2104/9, 2180/5, 2260/5, 2346/51, 2430/5, 2530/5, 2620/5, 2685/90, 2816/21, 3218/23 and 3229/34.

390 Menelao Mora, Jose A. Echeverria and Attack on Presidential Palace

1967. National Events of 13 March 1957.
1459 **390** 3c. green and black . . . 15 10
1460 – 13c. brown and black . . 2·50 85
1461 – 30c. blue and black . . . 2·30 95
DESIGNS ($36\frac{1}{2} \times 24\frac{1}{2}$ mm.): 13c. Calixto Sanchez and "Corynthia" landing; 30c. Dionisio San Roman and Cienfuegos revolt.

391 "Homo habilis"

1967. "Prehistoric Man". Multicoloured.
1462 1c. Type **391** 30 10
1463 2c. "Australopithecus" . . . 50 10
1464 3c. "Pithecanthropus erectus" 50 15
1465 4c. Peking man 70 25
1466 5c. Neanderthal man . . . 1·00 30
1467 13c. Cro-Magnon man carving ivory tusk . . . . 3·50 70
1468 20c. Cro-Magnon man painting on wall of cave 7·25 1·10

392 Victoria

1967. Stamp Day. Carriages. Multicoloured.
1469 3c. Type **392** 30 20
1470 9c. Volanta . . . . 1·70 50
1471 13c. Quitrin . . . . 2·50 95

393 Cuban Pavilion

1967. "Expo 67", Montreal.
1472 **393** 1c. multicoloured 30 10
1473 – 2c. multicoloured 30 10
1474 – 3c. multicoloured 45 15
1475 – 13c. multicoloured . . . 2·40 95
1476 – 20c. multicoloured . . . 2·75 1·00

DESIGNS: 2c. Bathysphere, satellite and met. balloon ("Man as Explorer"); 3c. Ancient rock-drawing and tablet ("Man as Creator"); 13c. Tractor, ear of wheat and electronic console ("Man as Producer"); 20c. Olympic athletes ("Man in the Community").

394 "Eugenia malaccencis"

395 "Giselle"

1967. 150th Anniv of Cuban Botanical Gardens. Multicoloured.
1477 1c. Type **394** 15 10
1478 2c. "Jacaranda filicifolia" . . 15 10
1479 3c. "Coroupita guianensis" 35 10
1480 4c. "Spathodea campanulata" 35 15
1481 5c. "Cassia fistula" 75 25
1482 13c. "Plumieria alba" . . . 2·20 70
1483 20c. "Erythrina poeppigiana" . . . . . . 3·75 85

1967. Int Ballet Festival, Havana. Mult.
1484 1c. Type **395** 30 10
1485 2c. "Swan Lake" 30 10
1486 3c. "Don Quixote" 40 15
1487 4c. "Calaucan" . . . . . . 2·20 55
1488 13c. "Swan Lake" (different) 3·25 1·00
1489 20c. "Nutcracker" . . . . . 3·75 1·40

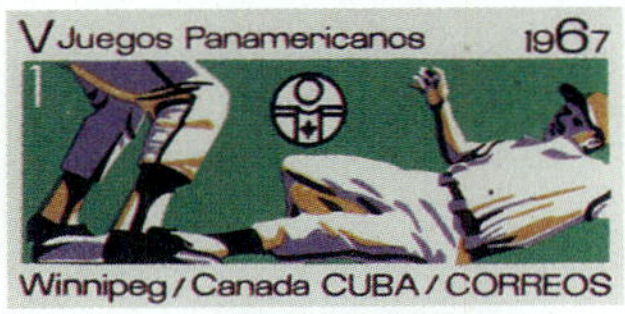

396 Baseball

1967. 5th Pan-American Games, Winnipeg. Mult.
1490 1c. Type **396** 15 10
1491 2c. Swimming 30 10
1492 3c. Basketball (vert) 40 10
1493 4c. Gymnastics (vert) . . . 70 15
1494 5c. Water-polo (vert) . . . 80 25
1495 13c. Weight-lifting . . . . . 2·40 50
1496 20c. Hurling the javelin . . 3·75 95

397 L. A. Turcios Lima, Map and OLAS Emblem

1967. 1st Conference of Latin-American Solidarity Organization (OLAS), Havana.
1497 13c. black, red and blue . . 1·60 60
1498 13c. black, red and brown 1·60 60
1499 13c. black, red and lilac . . 1·60 60
1500 13c. black, red and green . . 1·60 60
DESIGNS: No. 1497, Type **397**; No. 1498, Fabricio Ojidia; No. 1499, L. de La Puente Uceda; No. 1500, Camilo Torres; Martyrs of Guatemala, Venezuela, Peru and Colombia respectively. Each with map and OLAS emblem.

398 "Portrait of Sonny Rollins" (Alan Davie)

1967. "Contemporary Art" (Havana Exn from the Paris "Salon de Mayo"). Various designs showing modern paintings. Sizes given in millimetres. Multicoloured.
1501 1c. Type **398** 25 10
1502 1c. "Twelve Selenites" (F. Labisse) (39 × 41) . . 25 10
1503 1c. "Night of the Drinker" (F. Hundertwasser) (53 × 41) 25 10
1504 1c. "Figure" (Mariano) (48 × 41) 25 10
1505 1c. "All-Souls" (W. Lam) (45 × 41) 25 10
1506 2c. "Darkness and Cracks" (A. Tapies) (37 × 54) . . . 50 15
1507 2c. "Bathers" (G. Singier) (37 × 54) 50 15
1508 2c. "Torso of a Muse" (J. Arp) (37 × 46) 50 15
1509 2c. "Figure" (M. W. Svanberg) (57 × 54) . . . 50 15
1510 2c. "Oppenheimer's Information" (Erro) (37 × 41) 50 15
1511 3c. "Where Cardinals are Born" (Max Ernst) (37 × 52) . . . . 1·20 25
1512 3c. "Havana Landscape" (Portocarrero) (37 × 41) 1·20 25
1513 3c. "EG 12" (V. Vasarely) (37 × 42) . . . . 1·20 25
1514 3c. "Frisco" (A. Calder) (37 × 50) . . . . 1·20 25
1515 3c. "The Man with the Pipe" (Picasso) (37 × 52) 1·20 25
1516 4c. "Abstract Composition" (S. Poliakoff) (36 × 50) . . 1·40 65
1517 4c. "Painting" (Bram van Velde) (36 × 68) . . . . . 1·40 65
1518 4c. "Sower of Fires" (detail, Matta) (36 × 47) . . . . . 1·40 65
1519 4c. "The Art of Living" (R. Magritte) (36 × 50) . . 1·40 65
1520 4c. "Poem" (J. Miro) (36 × 56) . . . . 1·40 65
1521 13c. "Young Tigers" (J. Messagier) (50 × 33) . . 3·75 2·20
1522 13c. "Painting" (Vieira da Silva) (50 × 36) . . . . . 3·75 2·20
1523 13c. "Live Cobra" (P. Alechinsky) (50 × 35) 3·75 2·20
1524 13c. "Stalingrad" (detail, A. Jorn) (50 × 46) . . . . 3·75 2·20
1525 30c. "Warriors" (E. Pignon) (55 × 32) . . . . 14·00 9·00
MS1526 128 × 90 mm. 50c. "Cloister" (mural representing the "Salon de Mayo" pictures). Imperf . . . . 10·00 10·00

399 Common Octopus

1967. World Underwater Fishing Championships. Multicoloured.
1527 1c. Green moray 15 10
1528 2c. Type **399** 15 10
1529 3c. Great barracuda 15 10
1530 4c. Bull shark 60 15
1531 5c. Spotted Jewfish . . . . 1·30 30
1532 13c. Chupare stingray . . . 2·75 95
1533 20c. Green turtle . . . . . 5·25 1·10

400 "Sputnik 1"

1967. Soviet Space Achievements. Mult.
1534 1c. Type **400** 15 10
1535 2c. "Lunik 3" 15 10
1536 3c. "Venusik" 15 10
1537 4c. "Cosmos" 30 10
1538 5c. "Mars 1" 50 15
1539 9c. "Electron 1, 2" 60 30
1540 10c. "Luna 9" 95 60
1541 13c. "Luna 10" . . . . . . 2·10 85
MS1542 164 × 132 mm. Nos. 1534/1. Imperf . . . . 13·00 13·00

401 "Storming the Winter Palace" (from painting by Sokolov, Skalia and Miasnikova)

1967. 50th Anniv of October Revolution. Paintings. Multicoloured.
1543 1c. Type **401** 15 10
1544 2c. "Lenin addressing 2nd Soviet Congress" (Serov) (48 × 36) 15 10
1545 3c. "Lenin in the year 1919" (Nalbandian) (35 × 37) . . 35 15
1546 4c. "Lenin explaining the GOELRO Map" (Schmatko) (48 × 36) . . . 35 25
1547 5c. "Dawn of the Five-Year Plan" construction work (Romas) (50 × 36) . . . . 3·00 45
1548 13c. "Kusnetzkroi steel Furnace No. 1" (Kotov) (36 × 51) . . . . 2·40 70
1549 30c. "Victory Jubilation" (Krivonogov) (50 × 36) . . 3·25 1·10

402 Royal Force Castle, Havana

1967. Historic Cuban Buildings. Multicoloured.
1550 1c. Type **402** 15 10
1551 2c. Iznaga Tower, Trinidad ($26\frac{1}{2} \times 47\frac{1}{2}$) 15 10
1552 3c. Castle of Our Lady of the Angels, Cienfuegos ($41\frac{1}{2} \times 29$) 55 10
1553 4c. Church of St. Francis of Paula, Havana ($41\frac{1}{2} \times 29$) 55 10
1554 13c. Convent of St. Francis, Havana (39 × 13) . . . . . 2·75 60
1555 30c. Morro Castle, Santiago de Cuba (43 × 26) . . . . 4·00 1·10

403 Ostrich

404 Golden Pheasant

1967. Christmas. Birds of Havana Zoo. Mult.
(a) As T **403**.
1556 1c. Type **403** . . . . . . 1·40 70
1557 3c. Hyacinth macaw . . . . 1·90 1·10
1558 13c. Greater flamingoes . . 3·75 2·10

(b) As T **404**.
1559a/d 1c. multicoloured . . . . 1·40 70
1560a/d 3c. multicoloured . . . . 1·90 1·10
1561a/d 13c. multicoloured . . . 3·75 2·10
DESIGNS: No. 1559a, Type **404**; 1559b, White stork; 1559c, Crowned crane; 1559d, Emu; 1560a, Grey parrot; 1560b, Chattering lory; 1560c, Keel-billed toucan; 1560d, Sulphur-crested cockatoo; 1561a, American white pelican, 1561b, Egyptian goose; 1561c, Mandarin; 1561d, Black swan.
Prices are for single stamps.

405 "Che" Guevara

1968. Major Ernesto "Che" Guevara Commem.
1562 **405** 13c. black and red . . . 3·50 60

406 Man and Tree ("Problems of Artistic Creation, Scientific and Technical Work")

1968. Cultural Congress, Havana. Mult.
1563 3c. Chainbreaker cradling flame ("Culture and Independence") (vert) . . 15 10
1564 3c. Hand with spanner and rifle ("Integral Formation of Man") (vert) 15 10
1565 13c. Demographic emblems ("Intellectual Responsibility") (vert) . . 1·40 50
1566 13c. Hand with communications emblems ("Culture and Mass-Communications Media") (vert) . . . . 1·70 60
1567 30c. Type **406** . . . . . . 2·30 1·10

407 Canaries

1968. Canary-breeding.
1568 **407** 1c. multicoloured 15 10
1569 – 2c. multicoloured 15 10
1570 – 3c. multicoloured 30 20
1571 – 4c. multicoloured 30 25
1572 – 5c. multicoloured 60 30
1573 – 13c. multicoloured . . . 3·25 70
1574 – 20c. multicoloured . . . 4·50 95
DESIGNS: Canaries and breeding cycle—mating, eggs, incubation and rearing young.

408 "The Village Postman" (after J. Harris)

1968. Stamp Day. Multicoloured.
1575 13c. Type **408** . . . . . . 2·10 60
1576 30c. "The Philatelist" (after G. Sciltian) . . . . 3·00 95

409 Nurse tending Child ("Anti-Polio Campaign")

1968. 20th Anniv of W.H.O.
1577 **409** 13c. black, red and olive 2·10 70
1578 – 30c. black, blue & olive 2·75 1·00
DESIGN: 30c. Two doctors ("Hospital Services").

410 "Children"

1968. International Children's Day.
1579 **410** 3c. multicoloured . . . . 1·00 30

411 "Cuatro Vientos" and Route Map

1968. 35th Anniv of Seville–Camaguey Flight by Barberan and Collar. Multicoloured.
1580 13c. Type **411** . . . . . . 2·10 50
1581 30c. Captain M. Barberan and Lieut. J. Collar . . . 2·75 70

412 "Canned Fish"

1968. Cuban Food Products. Multicoloured.
1582 1c. Type **412** 20 15
1583 2c. "Milk Products" 25 15
1584 3c. "Poultry and Eggs" . . 40 30
1585 13c. "Cuban Rum" . . . . 2·50 60
1586 20c. "Canned Shell-fish" . . 3·00 95

413 Siboney Farmhouse

1968. 15th Anniv of Attack on Moncada Barracks. Multicoloured.
1587 3c. Type **413** 15 10
1588 13c. Map of Santiago de Cuba and assault route 1·90 70
1589 30c. Students and school buildings (on site of Moncada Barracks) . . . 3·00 1·00

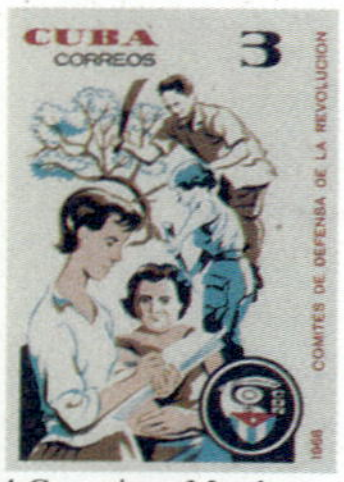

414 Committee Members and Emblem

1968. 8th Anniv of Revolutionary Defence Committee.
1590 **414** 3c. multicoloured . . . . 1·60 15

415 Che Guevara and Rifleman

1968. Day of the Guerrillas.
1591 **415** 1c. black, green & gold 15 10
1592 – 3c. black, brown & gold 15 15
1593 – 9c. multicoloured . . . 50 15
1594 – 10c. black, green and gold . . . . 1·10 30
1595 – 13c. black, pink & gold 2·10 85
DESIGNS—"Che" Guevara and: 3c. Machine-gunners; 9c. Riflemen; 10c. Soldiers cheering; 13c. Map of Caribbean and South America.

416 C. M. de Cespedes and Broken Wheel

1968. Centenary of Cuban War of Independence. Multicoloured.
1596 1c. Type **416** 15 15
1597 1c. E. Betances and horsemen 15 15
1598 1c. I. Agramonte and monument 15 15
1599 1c. A. Maceo and "The Protest" 15 15
1600 1c. J. Marti & patriots . . . 15 15
1601 3c. M. Gomez and "Invasion" 20 15
1602 3c. J. A. Mella and declaration 20 15
1603 3c. A. Guiteras and monument 20 15
1604 3c. A. Santamaria and riflemen 20 15
1605 3c. F. Pais & graffiti 20 15
1606 9c. J. Echeverria and students . . . . 1·00 25
1607 13c. C. Cienfuegos and rebels . . . . 2·40 85
1608 30c. "Che" Guevara and Castro addressing meeting 2·75 1·30

417 "The Burning of Bayamo" (J. E. Hernandez Giro)

1968. National Philatelic Exhibition, Bayamo-Manzanillo. Sheet 137 × 84 mm.
MS1609 **417** 50c. multicoloured 7·75 6·75

418 Parade of Athletes, Olympic Flag and Flame

1968. Olympic Games, Mexico. Multicoloured.
1610 1c. Type **418** 20 10
1611 2c. Basketball (vert) 15 10
1612 3c. Throwing the hammer (vert) 15 10
1613 4c. Boxing 15 10
1614 5c. Water-polo 35 10
1615 13c. Pistol-shooting . . . . 2·40 45
1616 30c. Calendar-stone (32½ × 50 mm) . . . . . 3·75 70
MS1617 125 × 84 mm. 50c. Runners and flags (50 × 30 mm). Imperf 12·00 12·00

419 Crop-spraying

1968. Civil Activities of Cuban Armed Forces. Multicoloured.
1618 3c. Type **419** 15 10
1619 9c. "Che Guevara" Brigade 50 15
1620 10c. Road-building Brigade 80 25
1621 13c. Agricultural Brigade . . 1·70 70

420 "Manrique de Lara's Family" (J.-B. Vermay)

1968. 150th Anniv of San Alejandro Painting School. Multicoloured.
1622 1c. Type **420** 15 15
1623 2c. "Seascape" (L. Romanach) (48 × 37) 15 15
1624 3c. "Wild Cane" (A. Rodriguez) (40 × 48) 35 25
1625 4c. "Self-portrait" (M. Melero) (40 × 50) . . 35 25
1626 5c. "The Lottery List" (J. J. Tejada) (48 × 37) . . . . 1·10 35
1627 13c. "Portrait of Nina" (A. Menocal) (40 × 50) . . 3·25 55
1628 30c. "Landscape" (E. S. Chartrand) (54 × 37) . . . 5·00 90
MS1629 63 × 97 mm. 50c. "The Siesta" (G. Gollazo) (48 × 37 mm) 7·50 6·50

421 Cuban Flag and Rifles

1969. 10th Anniv of "The Triumph of the Rebellion".
1630 **421** 13c. multicoloured . . . 1·80 60

422 Gutierrez and Sanchez

1969. Cent of Villaclarenos Patriots Rebellion.
1631 **422** 3c. multicoloured 90 20

423 Mariana Grajales, Rose and Statue

1969. Cuban Women's Day.
1632 **423** 3c. multicoloured . . . . 1·00 25

424 Cuban Pioneers

1969. Cuban Pioneers and Young Communist Unions. Multicoloured.
1633 3c. Type **424** 30 15
1634 13c. Young Communists . . 1·80 80

425 Guaimaro Assembly

1969. Centenary of Guaimaro Assembly.
1635 **425** 3c. brown and sepia . . 90 25

426 "The Postman" (J. C. Cazin)

1969. Cuban Stamp Day. Multicoloured.
1636 13c. Type **426** . . . . . 2·00 50
1637 30c. "Portrait of a Young Man" (George Romney) (36 × 44 mm) . . . . . . 3·25 70

427 Agrarian Law, Headquarters, Eviction of Family, and Tractor

1969. 10th Anniv of Agrarian Reform.
1638 **427** 13c. multicoloured . . . 1·90 70

428 Hermit Crab in West Indian Chank

1969. Crustaceans. Multicoloured.
1639 1c. Type **428** 15 10
1640 2c. Spiny shrimp 30 10
1641 3c. Spiny lobster 30 10
1642 4c. Blue crab 40 15
1643 5c. Land crab 40 20
1644 13c. Freshwater prawn . . . 2·75 45
1645 30c. Pebble crab . . . . . 4·00 80

429 Factory and Peasants

1969. 50th Anniv of I.L.O. Mult.
1646 3c. Type **429** 40 15
1647 13c. Worker breaking chain 1·90 70

430 "Flowers" (R. Milian)

1969. National Museum Paintings (2nd series). Multicoloured.
1648 1c. Type **430** 15 10
1649 2c. "The Annunciation" (A. Eiriz) 15 10
1650 3c. "Factory" (M. Pogolotti) 1·00 20
1651 4c. "Territorial Waters" (L. M. Pedro) 25 15
1652 5c. "Miss Sarah Gale" (John Hoppner) 25 15
1653 13c. "Two Women wearing Mantillas" (I. Zuloaga) 1·90 70
1654 30c. "Virgin and Child" (F. Zurbaran) . . . . . 2·75 90
SIZES—HORIZ: 2c. As No. 1648. VERT: 3c. As No. 1648. 4c. 40 × 44 mm; 5c. and 30c. 40 × 46 mm; 13c. 38 × 42 mm.

431 Television Cameras and Emblem

1969. Cuban Radiodiffusion Institute. Mult.
1655 3c. Type **431** 35 20
1656 13c. Broadcasting tower and "Globe" . . . . 1·90 80
1657 1p. TV Reception diagram 4·50 1·70

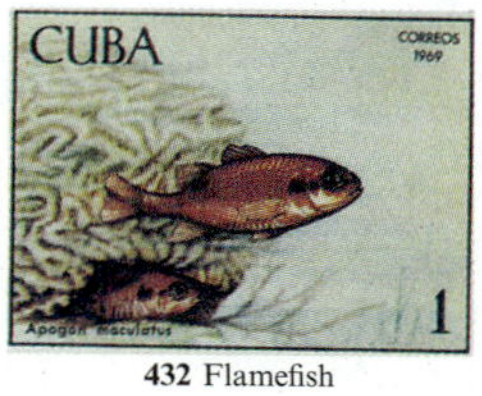

432 Flamefish

1969. Cuban Pisciculture. Multicoloured.
1658 1c. Type **432** 15 10
1659 2c. Spanish hogfish 15 10
1660 3c. Yellow-tailed damselfish 35 10
1661 4c. Royal gramma 35 20
1662 5c. Blue chromis 55 25
1663 13c. Black-barred soldierfish 3·50 45
1664 30c. Man-of-war fish (vert) 4·75 80

433 "Cuban Film Library"

1969. 10th Anniv of Cuban Cinema Industry. Multicoloured.

1665	1c. Type **433**	15	10
1666	3c. "Documentaries"	25	20
1667	13c. "Cartoons"	2·50	50
1668	30c. "Full-length Features"	2·75	55

434 "Napoleon in Milan". (A. Appiani (the Elder))

1969. Paintings in Napoleonic Museum, Havana. Multicoloured.

1669	1c. Type **434**	15	10
1670	2c. "Hortensia de Beauharnais" (F. Gerard)	20	10
1671	3c. "Napoleon-First Consul" (J. B. Regnault)	20	15
1672	4c. "Elisa Bonaparte" (R. Lefevre)	45	20
1673	5c. "Napoleon planning the Coronation" (J. G. Vibert)	70	30
1674	13c. "Corporal of Cuirassiers" (J. Meissonier)	3·25	65
1675	30c. "Napoleon Bonaparte" (R. Lefevre)	4·00	85

SIZES—VERT: 2c. 42½ × 55 mm; 3c. 46 × 56½ mm; 4c., 13c., 44 × 63 mm; 30c. 45½ × 60 mm. HORIZ: 5c. 64 × 47 mm.

435 Baseball Players

1969. Cuba's Victory in World Amateur Baseball Championships, Dominican Republic.

1676	**435**	13c. multicoloured	2·00	50

436 Von Humboldt, Book and American Eel

1969. Birth Bicentenary of Alexander von Humboldt. Multicoloured.

1677	3c. Type **436**	15	10
1678	13c. Night monkey	2·30	75
1679	30c. Andean condors	3·75	65

437 Ancient Egyptians in Combat

1969. World Fencing Championships, Havana. Multicoloured.

1683	1c. Type **437**	15	10
1684	2c. Roman Gladiators	15	10
1685	3c. Norman and Viking	25	10
1686	4c. Medieval tournament	30	15
1687	5c. French musketeers	50	20
1688	13c. Japanese samurai	2·40	45
1689	30c. Mounted Cubans, War of Independence	3·75	70

MS1690 66 × 98 mm. 50c. Modern fencing. Imperf . . . 10·00 10·00

438 Militiaman

1969. 10th Anniv of National Revolutionary Militias.

1691	**438**	3c. multicoloured	1·00	25

439 Major Cienfuegos and Wreath on Sea

1969. 10th Anniv of Disappearance of Major Camilo Cienfuego.

1692	**439**	13c. multicoloured	2·00	50

440 Strawberries and Grapes

1969. Agriculture and Livestock Projects. Multicoloured.

1693	1c. Type **440**	20	15
1694	1c. Onion and asparagus	20	15
1695	1c. Rice	20	15
1696	1c. Bananas	20	15
1697	3c. Pineapple (vert)	40	40
1698	3c. Tobacco plant (vert)	40	40
1699	3c. Citrus fruits (vert)	40	40
1700	3c. Coffee (vert)	40	40
1701	3c. Rabbits (vert)	40	40
1702	10c. Pigs (vert)	40	25
1703	13c. Sugar-cane	2·30	60
1704	30c. Bull	3·25	85

441 Stadium and Map of Cuba (2nd National Games)

1969. Sporting Events of 1969. Multicoloured.

1705	1c. Type **441**	20	10
1706	2c. Throwing the discus (9th Anniv Games)	20	10
1707	3c. Running (Barrientos commemoration) (vert)	20	10
1708	10c. Basketball (2nd Olympic Trial Games) (vert)	40	25
1709	13c. Cycling (6th Cycle Race) (vert)	3·00	60
1710	30c. Chessmen and Globe (7th Capablanca Int. Chess Tournament, Havana) (vert)	4·25	90

442 "Plumbago capensis"

443 "Petrea volubilis"

1969. Christmas. Flowers. (a) As T **442**. Mult.

1711	1c. Type **442**	30	15
1712	3c. "Turnera ulmifolia"	90	25
1713	13c. "Delonix regia"	2·10	90

(b) As T **443**.

1714a/d	1c. multicoloured	30	15
1715a/d	3c. multicoloured	90	25
1716a/d	13c. multicoloured	2·10	90

DESIGNS: No. 1714a, Type **443**; 1714b, "Clitoria ternatea"; 1714c, "Duranta repens"; 1714d, "Ruellia tuberosa"; 1715a, "Thevetia peruviana"; 1715b, "Hibiscus elatus"; 1715c, "Allamanda cathartica"; 1715d, "Cosmos sulphureus"; 1716a, "Nerium oleander" (wrongly inscr "Neriun"); 1716b, "Cordia sebestena"; 1716c, "Lochnera rosea"; 1716d, "Jatropha integerrima".
Prices are for single stamps.

444 River Snake

1969. Swamp Fauna. Multicoloured.

1717	1c. Type **444**	10	10
1718	2c. Banana frog	10	10
1719	3c. Giant tropical gar (fish)	15	10
1720	4c. Dwarf hutia (vert)	15	10
1721	5c. Alligator	15	15
1722	13c. Cuban Amazon (vert)	4·25	45
1723	30c. Red-winged blackbird (vert)	5·25	70

445 "Jibacoa Beach" (J. Hernandez)

446 Yamagua

1970. Tourism. Multicoloured.

1724	1c. Type **445**	10	10
1725	3c. "Trinidad City" (J. Hernandez)	15	15
1726	13c. Santiago de Cuba (A. Alonzo)	1·90	80
1727	30c. Vinales Valley (J. Hernandez)	2·75	95

1970. Medicinal Plants. Multicoloured.

1728	1c. Type **446**	25	10
1729	3c. Albahaca Morada	25	10
1730	10c. Curbana	35	15
1731	13c. Romerillo	1·90	70
1732	30c. Marilope	2·50	85
1733	50c. Aguedita	3·50	1·00

447 Weightlifting

1970. 11th Central American and Caribbean Games. Multicoloured.

1734	1c. Type **447**	15	10
1735	3c. Boxing	15	10
1736	10c. Gymnastics	25	15
1737	13c. Athletics	1·90	65
1738	30c. Fencing	2·75	90

MS1739 85 × 128 mm. 50c. Baseball. Imperf . . . 9·75 9·75

448 "Enjoyment of Life"

1970. "EXPO 70" World Fair, Osaka, Japan. Multicoloured.

1740	1c. Type **448**	15	10
1741	2c. "Uses of nature" (vert)	20	10
1742	3c. "Better Living Standards"	30	25
1743	13c. "International Co-operation" (vert)	2·30	55
1744	30c. Cuban Pavilion	3·25	80

449 Oval Pictograph, Ambrosio Cave

1970. 30th Anniv of Cuban Speleological Society.

1745	**449**	1c. red and brown	10	10
1746	–	2c. black and brown	15	10
1747	–	3c. red and brown	15	10
1748	–	4c. black and brown	20	15
1749	–	5c. black, red and brown	30	25
1750	–	13c. black and brown	1·90	60
1751	–	30c. red and brown	4·00	65

DESIGNS—HORIZ: (42 × 32½ mm): 2c. Cave 1, Punta del Este, Isle of Pines; 5c. As 2c. (different); 30c. Stylized fish, Cave 2, Punta del Este. VERT: 3c. Stylized mask, Pichardo Cave, Sierra de Cubitas; 4c. Conical complex, Ambrosio Cave, Varadero; 13c. Human face, Garcia Robiou Cave, Catalina de Guines.

450 J. D. Blino, Balloon and Spacecraft

1970. Aviation Pioneers. Multicoloured.

1752	3c. Type **450**	80	15
1753	13c. A. Theodore, balloon and satellite	2·75	70

451 "Lenin in Kazan" (O. Vishniakov) (½-size illustration)

1970. Birth Centenary of Lenin. Paintings. Mult.

1754	1c. Type **451**	10	10
1755	2c. "Lenin's Youth" (Prager)	10	10
1756	3c. "The 2nd Socialist Party Congress" (Vinogradov)	15	10
1757	4c. "The First Manifesto" (Golubkov)	25	15
1758	5c. "The First Day of Soviet Power" (Babasiuk)	25	20
1759	13c. "Lenin in the Smolny Institute" (Sokolov)	2·20	50
1760	30c. "Autumn in Gorky" (Varlamov)	2·75	65

MS1761 79 × 112 mm. 50c. "Lenin and Gorky" (N. Barkakov) (45 × 43 mm). Imperf . . . 10·50 10·50

SIZES: 4, 5c. As Type **451**: 2, 3, 13, 30c. 70 × 34 mm.

452 "The Letter" (J. Archer)

1970. Cuban Stamp Day. Paintings. Mult.

1762	13c. Type **452**	2·40	50
1763	30c. "Portrait of a Cadet" (anonymous) (35 × 49 mm)	3·00	65

453 Da Vinci's Anatomical Drawing, Earth and Moon

1970. World Telecommunications Day.

1764	**453**	30c. multicoloured	2·75	50

454 Vietnamese Fisherman

1970. 80th Birthday of Ho Chi Minh (North Vietnamese leader). Multicoloured.

1765	1c. Type **454**	10	10
1766	3c. Cultivating rice-fields	40	10
1767	3c. Two Vietnamese children	40	10
1768	3c. Children entering air-raid shelter	40	10
1769	3c. Camouflaged machine-shop	55	10
1770	3c. Rice harvest	55	15
1771	13c. Pres. Ho Chi Minh	2·75	70

SIZES: Nos. 1766/7, 33 × 44½ mm, Nos. 1768, 1770, 33½ × 46 mm, No. 1769, 35 × 42 mm, No. 1771, 34½ × 39½ mm.

455 Tobacco Plantation and "Eden" Cigar band

1970. "Cuban Cigar Industry". Multicoloured.

1772	3c. Type **455**	15	10
1773	13c. 19 th century cigar factory and "El Mambi" band	1·70	70
1774	30c. Packing cigars (19th-century) and "Gran Pena" band	2·75	1·00

456 Cane crushing Machinery

1970. Cuban Sugar Harvest Target. "Over 10 million Tons". Multicoloured.

1775	1c. Type **456**	15	10
1776	2c. Sowing and crop-spraying	15	10
1777	3c. Cutting sugar-cane	20	10
1778	10c. Ox-cart and diesel-electric locomotive	4·75	45
1779	13c. Modern cane cutting machine	1·50	25
1780	30c. Cane-cutters and globe (vert)	2·20	70
1781	1p. Sugar warehouse	4·00	1·90

457 P. Figueredo and National Anthem (original version)

1970. Death Centenary of Pedro Figueredo (composer of National Anthem). Multicoloured.

1782	3c. Type **457**	25	15
1783	20c. 18 98 version of anthem	2·20	60

458 Cuban Girl, Flag and Federation Badge

1970. 10th Anniv of Cuban Women's Federation.

1784	**458** 3c. multicoloured	85	50

459 "Peasant Militia" (S. C. Moreno)

1970. National Museum Paintings (3rd series). Multicoloured.

1785	1c. Type **459**	15	15
1786	2c. "Washerwoman" (A. Fernandez)	15	15
1787	3c. "Puerta del Sol, Madrid" (L. P. Alcazar)	15	15
1788	4c. "Fishermen's Wives" (J. Sorolla)	15	15
1789	5c. "Portrait of a Lady" (T. de Keyser)	15	15
1790	13c. "Mrs. Edward Foster" (Lawrence)	2·00	50
1791	30c. "Tropical Gipsy" (V. M. Garcia)	3·25	80

SIZES—HORIZ: 2c., 3c. 46 × 42 mm. SQUARE. 4c. 41 × 41 mm. VERT: 5c., 13c., 30c. 39 × 46 mm.

460 Crowd in Jose Marti Square, Havana (½-size illustration)

1970. 10th Anniv of Havana Declaration.

1792	**460** 3c. blue, red & black	60	15

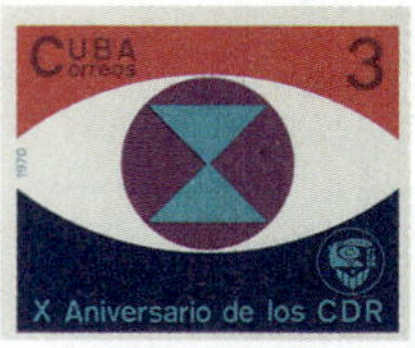

461 C. D. R. Emblem

1970. 10th Anniv of Revolution Defence Committees.

1793	**461** 3c. multicoloured	75	25

462 Laboratory, Emblem and Microscope

1970. 39th A.T.A.C. (Sugar Technicians Assn) Conference.

1794	**462** 30c. multicoloured	2·75	70

463 Helmeted Guineafowl

1970. Wildlife. Multicoloured.

1795	1c. Type **463**	75	15
1796	2c. Black-billed whistling duck	80	15
1797	3c. Common pheasant	1·00	15
1798	4c. Mourning dove	1·10	15
1799	5c. Northern bobwhite	1·20	20
1800	13c. Wild boar	2·10	1·10
1801	30c. White-tailed deer	3·50	1·50

464 "Black Magic Parade" (M. Puente)

1970. Afro-Cuban Folklore Paintings. Mult.

1802	1c. Type **464**	15	10
1803	3c. "Zapateo Hat Dance" (V. L. Landaluze)	30	15
1804	10c. "Los Hoyos Conga Dance" (D. Ravenet)	80	45
1805	13c. "Climax of the Rumba" (E. Abela)	2·20	70

SIZES—HORIZ: 10c. 45 × 44 mm. VERT: 3, 13c. 37 × 49 mm.

465 Common Zebra on Road Crossing

1970. Road Safety Week. Multicoloured.

1806	3c. Type **465**	90	15
1807	9c. Prudence the Bear on point duty	1·30	25

466 Letter "a" and Abacus

1970. International Education Year. Mult.

1808	13c. Type **466**	2·00	25
1809	30c. Microscope and cow	2·75	70

467 Cuban Blackbird **468** Cuban Pygmy Owl

1970. Christmas. Birds. Multicoloured. (a) As T **467**.

1810	1c. Type **467**	85	40
1811	3c. Oriente warbler	1·80	60
1812	13c. Zapata sparrow	2·50	1·10

(b) As T **468**.

1813a/d	1c. multicoloured	85	40
1814a/d	3c. multicoloured	1·80	60
1815a/d	13c. multicoloured	2·50	1·10

DESIGNS: No. 1813a, Type **468**; 1813b, Cuban tody; 1813c, Cuban green woodpecker; 1813d, Zapata wren; 1814a, Cuban solitaire; 1814b, Blue-grey gnatcatcher; 1814c, Cuban vireo; 1814d, Yellow-headed warbler; 1815a, Hook-billed kite; 1815b, Gundlach's hawk; 1815c, Blue-headed quail dove; 1815d, Cuban conure. Prices are for single stamps.

469 School Badge and Cadet Colour-party

1970. "Camilo Cienfuegos" Military School.

1816	**469** 3c. multicoloured	1·00	20

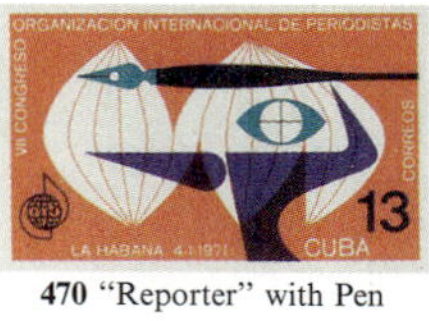

470 "Reporter" with Pen

1971. 7th Journalists International Organization Congress, Havana.

1817	**470** 13c. multicoloured	1·80	50

471 Lockheed 8A Sirius

1971. 35th Anniv of Camaguey–Seville Flight by Menendez Pelaez. Multicoloured.

1818	13c. Type **471**	2·40	25
1819	30c. Lieut. Menendez Pelaez and map	2·75	65

472 Meteorological Class **473** Games Emblem

1971. World Meteorological Day. Multicoloured.

1820	1c. Type **472**	10	10
1821	3c. Hurricane map (40 × 36 mm)	15	10
1822	8c. Meteorological equipment	85	20
1823	30c. Weather radar systems (horiz)	4·00	1·20

1971. 6th Pan-American Games, Cali, Colombia. Multicoloured.

1824	1c. Type **473**	15	10
1825	2c. Athletics	15	10
1826	3c. Rifle-shooting (horiz)	15	10
1827	4c. Gymnastics	15	10
1828	5c. Boxing	15	10
1829	13c. Water-polo (horiz)	2·00	40
1830	30c. Baseball (horiz)	2·50	70

474 Paris Porcelain, 19th-century

1971. Porcelain and Mosaics in Metropolitan Museum, Havana. Multicoloured.

1831	1c. Type **474**	10	10
1832	3c. Mexican pottery bowl, 17th-century	10	10
1833	10c. 19th-century Paris porcelain (similar to T **474**)	30	15
1834	13c. "Colosseum" Italian mosaic, 19th-century	1·80	25
1835	20c. 17th-century Mexican pottery dish (similar to 3c.)	1·80	70
1836	30c. "St. Peter's Square" (Italian mosaic 19th-cent.)	2·30	85

SIZES—VERT: 3c. 46 × 54 mm. 10c. as Type **474**. 20c. 43 × 49 mm. HORIZ: 13c., 30c. 50 × 33 mm.

475 Mother and Child **476** Cosmonaut in Training

1971. 10th Anniv of Cuban Infant Centres.

1837	**475** 3c. multicoloured	60	15

1971. 10th Anniv of First Manned Space Flight. Multicoloured.

1838	1c. Type **476**	15	10
1839	2c. Speedometer test	15	10
1840	3c. Medical examination	15	10
1841	4c. Acceleration tower	15	10
1842	5c. Pressurisation test	25	10
1843	13c. Cosmonaut in gravity chamber	1·80	40
1844	30c. Crew in flight simulator	2·50	85
MS1845	100 × 63 mm. 50c. Yuri Gagarin. Imperf	8·25	8·25

477 Cuban and Burning Ship

1971. 10th Anniv of Giron Victory.
1846 **477** 13c. multicoloured . . . 2·00 60

478 Sailing Packet "Windsor Castle" attacked by French Privateer Brig "Jeune Richard" (1807)

1971. Stamp Day. Multicoloured.
1847 13c. Type **478** . . . . . . 2·50 60
1848 30c. Mail steamer "Orinoco", 1851 . . . . 3·75 80

479 Transmitter and Hemispheres

1971. 10th Anniv of Cuban International Broadcasting Services.
1849 **479** 3c. multicoloured 30 15
1850 50c. multicoloured . . . 3·75 90

480 "Cattleya skinnerii"

482 Larvae and Pupae

481 Loynaz del Castillo and "Invasion Hymn"

1971. Tropical Orchids (1st series). Mult.
1851 1c. Type **480** 15 10
1852 2c. "Vanda hibrida" 15 10
1853 3c. "Cypripedium callossum" 15 10
1854 4c. "Cypripedium glaucophyllum" 15 10
1855 5c. "Vanda tricolor" 20 10
1856 13c. "Cypripedium mowgh" 2·10 50
1857 30c. "Cypripedium solum" 4·25 95
See also Nos. 1908/14 and 2012/18.

1971. Birth Centenary of Enrique Loynaz del Castillo (composer).
1858 **481** 3c. multicoloured 75 20

1971. Apiculture. Multicoloured.
1859 1c. Type **482** 15 10
1860 3c. Working bee 15 10
1861 9c. Drone 50 15
1862 13c. Defending the hive . . 2·75 40
1863 30c. Queen bee . . . . . . 4·25 1·00

483 "The Ship" (Lydia Rivera)

1971. Exhibition of Children's Drawings. Havana. Multicoloured.
1864 1c. Type **483** 15 10
1865 3c. "Little Train" (Yuri Ruiz) 75 10
1866 9c. "Sugar-cane Cutter" (Horacio Carracedo) . . . 15 15
1867 10c. "Return of Cuban Fisherman" (Angela Munoz and Lazaro Hernandez) 40 15
1868 13c. "The Zoo" (Victoria Castillo) . . . . 1·60 40
1869 20c. "House and Garden" (Elsa Garcia) . . . . . . 2·50 70
1870 30c. "Landscape" (Orestes Rodriguez) (vert) . . . . 2·75 1·10
SIZES: 9c., 13c. 45 × 35 mm, 10c. 45 × 38 mm, 20c. 47 × 42 mm, 30c. 39 × 49 mm.

1971. National Museum Paintings (4th series). As T **459**. Multicoloured.
1871 1c. "St. Catherine of Alexandria" (Zurbaran) 10 10
1872 2c. "The Cart" (F. Americo) (horiz) 15 10
1873 3c. "St. Christopher and the Child" (J. Bassano) . . . 15 10
1874 4c. "Little Devil" (R. Portocarrero) 20 10
1875 5c. "Portrait of a Lady" (N. Maes) 30 15
1876 13c. "Phoenix" (R. Martinez) . . . . . . 1·80 50
1877 30c. "Sir William Pitt" (Gainsborough) . . . . . 2·75 85
SIZES: 1, 3c. 30 × 56 mm, 2c. 48 × 37 mm, 4, 5c. 37 × 49 mm, 13, 30c. 39 × 49 mm.

485 Bonefish

1971. Sport Fishing. Multicoloured.
1878 1c. Type **485** 25 25
1879 2c. Great amberjack 25 25
1880 3c. Large-mouthed black bass 25 25
1881 4c. Dolphin (fish) 40 25
1882 5c. Atlantic tarpon 50 25
1883 13c. Wahoo . . . . 2·50 70
1884 30c. Blue marlin . . . . . 4·25 1·20

486 Ball within "C"

1971. World Amateur Baseball Championships. Multicoloured.
1885 3c. Type **486** 25 20
1886 1p. Hand holding globe within "C" . . . . 5·00 2·00

487 "Dr. F. Valdes Dominguez" (artist unknown)

1971. Centenary of Medical Students' Execution. Multicoloured.
1887 3c. Type **487** 30 15
1888 13c. "Students Execution" (M. Mesa) (62 × 47 mm) 1·50 50
1889 30c. "Captain Federico Capdevila" (unknown artist) . . . . 2·50 70

488 American Kestrel

1971. Death Centenary of Ramon de la Sagra (naturalist). Cuban Birds. Multicoloured.
1890 1c. Type **488** 40 15
1891 2c. Cuban pygmy owl . . . 40 15
1892 3c. Cuban trogon 60 15
1893 4c. Great lizard cuckoo . . 65 25
1894 5c. Fernandina's flicker . . 85 25
1895 13c. Stripe-headed tanager (horiz) . . . . 1·50 45
1896 30c. Red-legged thrush (horiz) . . . . 3·00 90
1897 50c. Cuban emerald and ruby-throated hummingbirds (56 × 30 mm) . . . . . . 6·25 1·80

489 Baseball Player and Global Emblem

1971. Cuba's Victory in World Amateur Baseball.
1898 **489** 13c. multicoloured . . . 1·60 70

490 "Children of the World"

1971. 25th Anniv of UNICEF.
1899 **490** 13c. multicoloured . . . 2·10 85

1972. National Museum Paintings (5th series). As T **459**. Multicoloured.
1900 1c. "The Reception of Ambassadors" (V. Carpaccio) 10 10
1901 2c. "Senora Malpica" (G. Collazo) 15 10
1902 3c. "La Chorrera Fortress" (E. Chartrand) 15 10
1903 4c. "Creole Landscape" (C. Enriquez) 15 10
1904 5c. "Sir William Lemon" (G. Romney) 15 10
1905 13c. "La Tajona Beach" (H. Cleenewek) . . . . . 2·10 50
1906 30c. "Valencia Beach" (J. Sorolla y Bastida) . . 3·50 1·20
SIZES: 1c., 3c. 51 × 33 mm, 2c. 28 × 53 mm, 4c., 5c. 36 × 44 mm, 13c., 30c. 43 × 34 mm.

492 "Capitol" Stamp of 1929 (now Natural History Museum)

1972. 10th Anniv of Academy of Sciences.
1907 **492** 13c. purple and yellow 1·80 60

1972. Tropical Orchids (2nd series). As T **480**. Multicoloured.
1908 1c. "Brasso Cattleya sindorossiana" 15 10
1909 2c. "Cypripedium doraeus" 15 10
1910 3c. "Cypripedium exul" . . 15 10
1911 4c. "Cypripedium rosydawn" 15 10
1912 5c. "Cypripedium champolliom" 15 10
1913 13c. "Cypripedium bucolique" . . . . 2·20 85
1914 30c. "Cypripedium sullanum" . . . . 2·75 1·00

493 "Eduardo Agramonte" (F. Martinez)

1972. Death Centenary of Dr. E. Agramonte (surgeon and patriot).
1915 **493** 3c. multicoloured 50 25

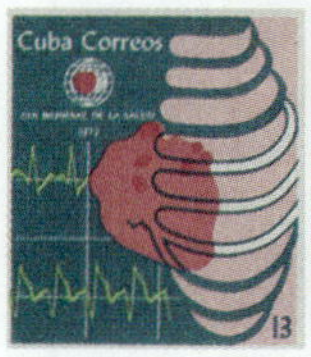

494 Human Heart and Thorax

496 "Vincente Mora Pera" (Postmaster General, War of Independence) (R. Loy)

495 "Sputnik 1"

1972. World Health Day.
1916 **494** 13c. multicoloured . . . 1·60 60

1972. "History of Space". Multicoloured.
1917 1c. Type **495** 25 10
1918 2c. "Vostok 1" 25 10
1919 3c. Valentina Tereshkova in capsule 25 10
1920 4c. A. Leonov in space . . . 25 10
1921 5c. "Lunokhod 1" moon Vehicle 25 10
1922 13c. Linking of "Soyuz" capsules . . . . 1·90 40
1923 30c. Dobrovolsky, Volkov and Pataiev, victims of "Soyuz 11" disaster . . . 2·30 70

1972. Stamp Day. Multicoloured.
1924 13c. Type **496** . . . . . . 1·50 60
1925 30c. Mambi Mailcover of 1897 (48 × 39 mm) . . . . 2·40 70

497 Cuban Workers

498 Jose Marti and Ho Chi Minh

1972. Labour Day.
1926 **497** 3c. multicoloured 75 30

1972. 3rd Symposium on Indo-China War. Multicoloured.
1927 3c. Type **498** 30 15
1928 13c. Bombed house (38 × 29 mm) . . . . . . 1·30 35
1929 30c. Symposium emblem . . 1·60 45

1972. Paintings from the Metropolitan Museum, Havana (6th series). As T **430**. Multicoloured.
1930 1c. "Salvador del Muro" (J. del Rio) 15 10
1931 2c. "Louis de las Casas" (J. del Rio) 15 10
1932 3c. "Christopher Columbus" (anonymous) 15 10
1933 4c. "Tomas Gamba" (V. Escobar) 30 10
1934 5c. "Maria Galarraga" (V. Escobar) 30 10
1935 13c. "Isabella II of Spain" (F. Madrazo) . . . . . . 1·60 40
1936 30c. "Carlos III of Spain" (M. Melero) . . . . . . 2·10 70
SIZES—VERT: (35 × 44 mm) 1930/34, (34 × 52 mm) 1935/6.

500 Children in Boat

1972. Children's Song Competition.
1937 **500** 3c. multicoloured 95 30

501 Ilyushin Il-18, Map and Flags

1972. Air. 1st Anniv of Havana–Santiago de Chile Air Service.
1938 **501** 25c. multicoloured . . . 2·50 85

502 Tarpan

1972. Thoroughbred Horses. Multicoloured.
1939 1c. Type **502** 25 10
1940 2c. Kertag 25 10
1941 3c. Creole 25 10
1942 4c. Andalusian 25 10
1943 5c. Arab 25 10
1944 13c. Quarter-horse . . . . 2·40 70
1945 30c. Pursang . . . . 2·75 1·00

503 Frank Pais

1972. 15th Death Anniv of Frank Pais.
1946 **503** 13c. multicoloured . . . 1·40 60

504 Athlete and Emblem

1972. Olympic Games, Munich.
1947 **504** 1c. orange and brown . . 25 10
1948 – 2c. purple, blue & orge 25 10
1949 – 3c. green, yellow & blk 25 10
1950 – 4c. bl, yell & brn 25 10
1951 – 5c. red, black & yellow 25 10
1952 – 13c. lilac, green & blue 1·60 40
1953 – 30c. blue, red and green 2·10 70
MS1954 58½ × 75 mm. 50c. multicoloured. Imperf . . . . 5·00 5·00
DESIGNS—HORIZ: 2c. "M" and boxing; 3c. "U" and weightlifting; 4c. "N" and fencing; 5c. "I" and rifle-shooting; 13c. "C" and running; 30c. "H" and basketball; 50c. Gymnastics.

505 "Landscape with Tree-trunks" (D. Ramos)

1972. International Hydrological Decade. Mult.
1955 1c. Type **505** 15 10
1956 3c. "Cyclone" (T. Lorenzo) 15 10
1957 8c. "Vineyards" (D. Ramos) 65 15
1958 30c. "Forest and Stream" (A. R. Morey) (vert) . . . 2·00 70

506 "Papilio thoas oviedo"

1972. Butterflies from the Gundlach Collection. Multicoloured.
1959 1c. Type **506** 15 10
1960 2c. "Papilio devilliers" . . . 15 10
1961 3c. "Papilio polixenes polixenes" 15 10
1962 4c. "Papilio androgeus epidaurus" 15 10
1963 5c. "Papilio cayguanabus" 20 10
1964 13c. "Papilio andraemon hernandezi" . . . . . 4·75 1 10
1965 30c. "Papilio celadon" . . . 6·25 1 40

507 "In La Mancha" (A. Fernandez)

1972. 425th Birth Anniv of Cervantes. Paintings by A. Fernandez. Multicoloured.
1966 3c. Type **507** 15 10
1967 13c. "Battle with the Wine Skins" (horiz) . . . . . 1·80 60
1968 30c. "Don Quixote of La Mancha" . . . . 1·90 70
MS1969 76 × 116 mm. 50c. "Scene from Don Quixote" (J. M. Carbonero) (47 × 29 mm) . . . 4·00 4·00

508 E. "Che" Guevara and Map of Bolivia

1972. 5th Anniv of Guerrillas' Day. Mult.
1970 3c. Type **508** 15 10
1971 13c. T. "Tania" Bunke and map of Bolivia . . . . . 1·80 50
1972 30c. G. "Inti" Peredo and map of Bolivia . . . . . 2·00 50

509 "Abwe" (shakers)

1972. Traditional Musical Instruments. Mult.
1973 3c. Type **509** 15 10
1974 13c. "Bonko enchemiya" (drum) . . . . 1·80 60
1975 30c. "Iya" (drum) . . . . . 1·90 70

510 Cuban 2c. Stamp of 1951

1972. National Philatelic Exhibition, Matanzas. Multicoloured.
1976 13c. Type **510** . . . . . . 2·00 60
1977 30c. Cuban 25c. airmail stamp of 1951 . . . . . 2·40 70

511 Viking Longship

1972. Maritime History. Ships Through the Ages. Multicoloured.
1978 1c. Type **511** 25 10
1979 2c. Caravel (vert) 25 10
1980 3c. Galley 25 10
1981 4c. Galleon (vert) 30 20
1982 5c. Clipper 85 20
1983 13c. Steam packet . . . . . 4·25 95
1984 30c. Atomic ice-breaker "Lenin" and Adelie penguins (55 × 29 mm) . . 7·75 1·70

512 Lion of St. Mark

1972. UNESCO "Save Venice" Campaign. Multicoloured.
1985 3c. Type **512** 15 10
1986 13c. Bridge of Sighs (vert) 1·60 60
1987 30c. St. Mark's Cathedral 2·10 1·20

513 Baseball Coach (poster)

516 "Gertrude G. de Avellaneda" (A. Esquivel)

515 Bronze Medal, Women's 100 m

1972. "Cuba, World Amateur Baseball Champions of 1972".
1988 **513** 3c. violet and orange . . 1·00 25

1972. Sports events of 1972. Posters.
1989 – 1c. multicoloured 25 10
1990 – 2c. multicoloured 25 10
1991 **513** 3c. black, orange & grn 25 10
1992 – 4c. red, black and blue 25 10
1993 – 5c. orge, bl & lt bl . . . 25 10
1994 – 13c. multicoloured . . . 1·40 70
1995 – 30c. vio, blk & bl . . . 2·00 1·00
DESIGNS AND EVENTS: 1c. Various sports (10th National Schoolchildren's Games); 2c. Pole vaulting (Barrientos Memorial Athletics); 3c. As Type **513**, but inscr changed to read "XI serie nacional de beisbol aficionado" and colours changed (11th National Amateur Baseball Series); 4c. Wrestling (Cerro Pelado International Wrestling Championships); 5c. Foil (Central American and Caribbean Fencing Tournament); 13c. Boxing (Giraldo Cordova Boxing Tournament); 30c. Fishes (Ernest Hemingway National Marlin Fishing Contest).

1972. Cuban Successes in Olympic Games, Munich. Multicoloured.
1996 1c. Type **515** 25 10
1997 2c. Bronze (women's 4 × 100 m relay) 25 10
1998 3c. Gold (boxing, 54 kg) . . 25 10
1999 4c. Silver (boxing, 81 kg) . . 25 10
2000 5c. Bronze (boxing, 51 kg) 25 10
2001 13c. Gold (boxing, 67 kg) 1·40 70
2002 30c. Gold (boxing, 81 kg) and Silver Cup (boxing Teofilo Stevenons) . . . . 2·00 1·00
MS2003 65 × 90 mm. 50c. Bronze medal, Basketball. Imperf . . . 5·00 5·00

1973. Death Centenary of Gertrude Gomez de Avellaneda (poetess).
2004 **516** 13c. multicoloured . . . 1·80 60

1973. National Museum Paintings (6th series). As T **459**. Multicoloured.
2005 1c. "Bathers in the Lagoon" (C. Enriquez) (vert) . . . 25 10
2006 2c. "Still Life" (W. C. Heda) (vert) 25 10
2007 3c. "Scene of Gallantry" (V. de Landaluse) (vert) . . 25 10
2008 4c. "Return at Evening" (C. Troyon) (vert) 25 10
2009 5c. "Elizabetta Mascagni" (F. X. Fabre) (vert) . . . 25 10
2010 13c. "The Picador" (E. de Lucas Padilla) . . . . . 1·30 70
2011 30c. "In the Garden" (J. A. Morell) (vert) . . . . . . 1·90 1·00

1973. Tropical Orchids (3rd series). As Type **480**. Multicoloured.
2012 1c. "Dendrobium" (hybrid) 15 10
2013 2c. "Cypripedium exul. O' Brien" 25 10
2014 3c. "Vanda miss. Joaquin" 25 10
2015 4c. "Phalaenopsis schilleriana Reichb" . . . 25 10
2016 5c. "Vanda gilbert tribulet" 30 10
2017 13c. "Dendrobium" (hybrid) (different) . . . . 2·40 60
2018 30c. "Arachnis catherine" 2·75 95

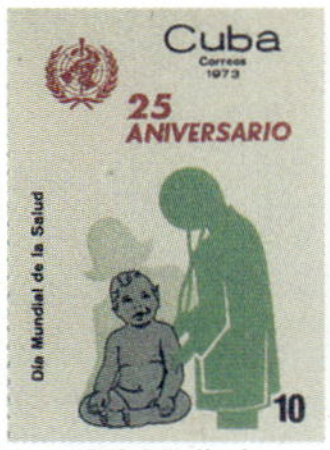

518 Medical Examination

520 "Soyuz" Rocket on Launch-pad

519 Children and Vaccine

1973. 25th Anniv of W.H.O.
2019 **518** 10c. multicoloured . . . 1·00 40

1973. Freedom from Polio Campaign.
2020 **519** 3c. multicoloured 60 30

1973. Cosmonautics Day. Russian Space Exploration. Multicoloured.
2021 1c. Type **520** 25 10
2022 2c. "Luna 1" in moon orbit (horiz) 25 10
2023 3c. "Luna 16" leaving moon 25 10
2024 4c. "Venus 7" probe (horiz) 25 10
2025 5c. "Molniya 1" communications satellite 25 10
2026 13c. "Mars 3" probe (horiz) 1·60 95
2027 30c. Research ship "Kosmonavt Yury Gargarin" (horiz) . . . . 4·75 1·20

521 Santiago de Cuba Postmark, 1839

1973. Stamp Day. Multicoloured.
2028 13c. Type **521** . . . . . . 1·80 60
2029 30c. "Havana" postmark, 1760 . . . . 1·90 70

522 "Ignacio Agramonte" (A. Espinosa)

1973. Death Centenary of Maj.-Gen. Ignacio Agramonte.
2030 **522** 13c. multicoloured . . . 1·30 60

523 Copernicus' Birthplace and Instruments

1973. 500th Birth Anniv of Copernicus. Mult.
2031 3c. Type **523** 15 10
2032 13c. Copernicus and "spaceship" . . . . . . 1·30 60
2033 30c. "De Revolutionibus Orbium Celestium" and Frombork Tower . . . . 2·50 85
MS2034 84 × 78 mm. 50c. Copernicus statue, Warsaw (vert) 5·25 5·00

524 Emblem of Basic Schools

1973. Educational Development.
2035 **524** 13c. multicoloured . . . 1·30 30

525 Jersey Breed

526 Festival Emblem

1973. Cattle Breeds. Multicoloured.
2036 1c. Type **525** 25 10
2037 2c. Charolais 25 10
2038 3c. Creole 25 10
2039 4c. Swiss 30 10
2040 5c. Holstein 30 10
2041 13c. St. Gertrude's . . . . 1·30 30
2042 30c. Brahman Cebu . . . . 2·75 60

1973. 10th World Youth and Students' Festival, East Berlin.
2043 **526** 13c. multicoloured . . . 1·30 25

527 Siboney Farmhouse

529 "Amalia de Sajonia" (J. K. Rossler)

528 Midshipman and Destroyer

1973. 20th Anniv of Revolution. Mult.
2044 3c. Type **527** 30 30
2045 13c. Moncada Barracks . . 1·30 40
2046 30c. Revolution Square, Havana . . . . 2·10 60

1973. 10th Anniv of Revolutionary Navy.
2047 **528** 3c. multicoloured 80 30

1973. National Museum Paintings (7th series). Multicoloured.
2048 1c. Type **529** 15 10
2049 2c. "Interior" (M. Vicens) (horiz) 15 10
2050 3c. "Margaret of Austria" (J. Pantoja de la Cruz) . . 20 10
2051 4c. "Syndic of the City Hall" (anon) 20 10
2052 5c. "View of Santiago de Cuba" (J. H. Giro) (horiz) 20 10
2053 13c. "The Catalan" (J. J. Tejada) . . . . 1·50 50
2054 30c. "Guayo Alley" (J. J. Tejada) . . . . 2·00 60

530 "Spring"

1973. Centenary of World Meteorological Organization. Paintings by J. Madrazo. Mult.
2055 8c. Type **530** 60 15
2056 8c. "Summer" 60 15
2057 8c. "Autumn" 60 15
2058 8c. "Winter" 60 15

531 Weightlifting

532 "Erythrina standleyana"

1973. 27th Pan-American World Weightlifting Championships, Havana. Designs showing various stages of weightlifting exercise.
2059 **531** 1c. multicoloured 15 10
2060 – 2c. multicoloured 15 10
2061 – 3c. multicoloured 15 10
2062 – 4c. multicoloured 15 10
2063 – 5c. multicoloured 15 10
2064 – 13c. multicoloured . . . 1·30 50
2065 – 30c. multicoloured . . . 2·30 1·00

1973. Wild Flowers (1st series). Mult.
2066 1c. Type **532** 15 10
2067 2c. "Lantana camara" . . . 15 10
2068 3c. "Canavalia maritima" . . 15 10
2069 4c. "Dichromena colorata" . . 15 10
2070 5c. "Borrichia arborescens" . 15 10
2071 13c. "Anguria pedata" . . . 1·60 70
2072 30c. "Cordia sebestena" . . 2·75 1·00
See also Nos. 2152/6.

533 Congress Emblem

1973. 8th World Trade Union Congress, Varna, Bulgaria.
2073 **533** 13c. multicoloured . . . 1·20 30

534 Ballet Dancers

535 True Fasciate Liguus

1973. 25th Anniv of Cuban National Ballet.
2074 **534** 13c. lt blue, bl & gold 1·60 30

1973. Shells. Multicoloured.
2075 1c. Type **535** 25 10
2076 2c. Guitart's liguus 25 10
2077 3c. Wharton's Cuban liguus 25 10
2078 4c. Angela's Cuban liguus 25 10
2079 5c. Yellow-banded liguus . . 25 10
2080 13c. "Liguus blainianus" . . 2·75 95
2081 30c. Ribbon liguus . . . . 3·50 1·10

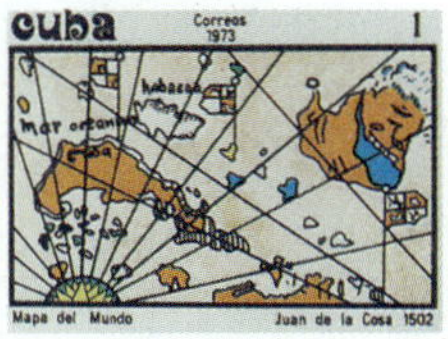

536 Juan de la Cosa's Map, 1502

1973. Maps of Cuba. Multicoloured.
2082 1c. Type **536** 15 10
2083 3c. Ortelius's map, 1572 . . 20 10
2084 13c. Bellini's map, 1762 . . 1·40 20
2085 40c. Cartographic survey map, 1973 . . . . 1·80 80

537 1c. Stamp of 1960 (No. 921)

1974. 15th Anniv of Revolution. Revolution stamps of 1960. Multicoloured.
2086 1c. Type **537** 15 10
2087 3c. 2c. stamp 25 10
2088 13c. 8c. air stamp . . . . . 3·75 50
2089 40c. 12c. air stamp . . . . 2·10 70

538 "Head of a Woman" (F. Ponce de Leon)

1974. Paintings in Camaguey Museum. Mult.
2090 1c. Type **538** 25 10
2091 3c. "Mexican Children" (J. Arche) 25 10
2092 8c. "Portrait of a Young Woman" (A. Menocal) 30 15
2093 10c. "Mulatto Woman with Coconut" (L. Romanach) 1·00 30
2094 13c. "Head of Old Man" (J. Arburu) . . . . 1·60 50

539 A. Cabral

540 "Lenin" (after J. V. Kosmin)

1974. 1st Death Anniv of Amilcar Cabral (Guinea-Bissau guerilla leader).
2095 **539** 13c. multicoloured . . . 1·20 20

1974. 50th Anniv of Lenin's Death.
2096 **540** 30c. multicoloured . . . 2·40 70

541 Games Emblem

542 "C. M. de Cespedes" (after F. Martinez)

1974. 12th Central American and Caribbean Games, Santo Domingo. Multicoloured.
2097 1c. Type **541** 20 10
2098 2c. Throwing the javelin . . 20 10
2099 3c. Boxing 20 10
2100 4c. Baseball player (horiz) 20 10
2101 13c. Handball player (horiz) 1·30 25
2102 30c. Volleyball (horiz) . . . 1·90 70

1974. Death Centenary of Carlos M. de Cespedes (patriot).
2103 **542** 13c. multicoloured . . . 1·10 25

543 "Portrait of a Man" (J. B. Vermay)

544 "Comecon" Headquarters Building, Moscow

1974. National Museum Paintings (8th series). Multicoloured.
2104 1c. Type **543** 25 10
2105 2c. "Nodriza" (C. A. Van Loo) 25 10
2106 3c. "Cattle by a River" (R. Morey) (46 × 32 mm) 25 10
2107 4c. "Village Landscape" (R. Morey) (46 × 32 mm) 25 10
2108 13c. "Faun and Bacchus" (Rubens) . . . . 1·10 30
2109 30c. "Playing Patience" (R. Madrazo) . . . . . . 2·00 70

1974. 25th Anniv of Council for Mutual Economic Aid.
2110 **544** 30c. multicoloured . . . 1·70 70

545 Jose Marti and Lenin

1974. Visit of Leonid Brezhnev (General Secretary of Soviet Communist Party). Multicoloured.
2111 13c. Type **545** . . . . . . 1·60 40
2112 30c. Brezhnev with Castro 1·70 70

546 "Martian Crater"

1974. Cosmonautics Day. Science Fiction paintings by Sokolov. Multicoloured.
2113 1c. Type **546** 20 10
2114 2c. "Fiery Labyrinth" . . . 20 10
2115 3c. "Amber Wave" 20 10
2116 4c. "Space Navigators" . . . 20 15
2117 13c. "Planet in the Nebula" 1·60 20
2118 30c. "The World of the Two Suns" . . . . 2·75 60
See also Nos. 2196/201.

547 Cuban Letter of 1874

1974. Centenary of U.P.U.
2119 **547** 30c. multicoloured . . . 2·00 85

1974. Stamp Day. Postal Markings of Pre-Stamp Exhibition. As T **521**. Multicoloured.
2120 1c. "Havana" postmark . . 20 10
2121 3c. "Matanzas" postmark 30 10
2122 13c. "Trinidad" postmark 1·20 25
2123 20c. "Guana Vacoa" postmark . . . . 1·80 30

548 Congress Emblem

1974. 18th Sports' Congress of "Friendly Armies".
2124 **548** 3c. multicoloured 70 25

549 "Eumaeus atala atala" (butterfly)

1974. 175th Birth Anniv of Felipe Poey (naturalist). Multicoloured.
2125 1c. Type **549** 25 10
2126 2c. "Pineria terebra" (shell) 25 10
2127 3c. Reef butterflyfish . . . 25 10
2128 4c. "Eurema dina dina" (butterfly) 80 25
2129 13c. "Hemitrochus fuscolabiata" (shell) . . . 2·75 60
2130 30c. Bicoloured damsel-fish 3·50 70
MS2131 92 × 66 mm. 50c. "Apogon binotatus" (fish). Imperf . . . 6·75 6·75

550 A. Mompo and 'Cello

1974. 50th Anniv of Havana Philharmonic Orchestra. Leading Personalities. Multicoloured.
2132 1c. Type **550** 20 10
2133 3c. C. P. Sentenat and piano 20 10
2134 5c. P. Mercado and trumpet 20 10
2135 10c. P. Sanjuan and emblem 1·10 20
2136 13c. R. Ondina and flute . . 1·40 30

551 "Heliconia humilis"

552 Boxers and Global Emblem

1974. Garden Flowers. Multicoloured.
2137 1c. Type **551** 25 10
2138 2c. "Anthurium andraeanum" 25 10
2139 3c. "Canna generalis" . . . 25 10
2140 4c. "Alpinia purpurata" . . 30 10
2141 13c. "Gladiolus grandiflorus" . . . . . . 1·70 25
2142 30c. "Amomum capitatum" 4·50 85

1974. World Amateur Boxing Championships.
2143 **552** 1c. multicoloured 20 15
2144 – 3c. multicoloured 30 15
2145 – 13c. multicoloured . . . 1·30 25
DESIGNS: 3c., 13c. Stages of Boxing matches similar to Type **552**.

553 Mauritius Dodo ("Dodo")

555 "Suriana maritima"

554 Salvador Allende

1974. Extinct Birds. Multicoloured.
2146 1c. Type **553** 35 10
2147 3c. Cuban macaw ("Ara de Cuba") 35 10
2148 8c. Passenger pigeon ("Paloma Migratoria") . . 75 25
2149 10c. Moa . . . . 2·40 45
2150 13c. Great auk ("Gran Alca") . . . . 3·00 70

1974. 1st Death Anniv of Pres. Allende of Chile.
2151 **554** 13c. multicoloured . . . 1·20 50

1974. Wild Flowers. (2nd series). Mult.
2152 1c. Type **555** 25 10
2153 3c. "Cassia ligustrina" . . . 25 10
2154 8c. "Flaveria linearis" . . . 35 20
2155 10c. "Stachytarpheta jamaicensis" . . . . . . 1·90 25
2156 13c. "Bacopa monnieri" . . 3·25 75

556 Flying Model Airplane

557 Indians playing Ball

1974. 10th Anniv of Civil Aeronautical Institute. Multicoloured.
2157 1c. Type **556** 25 10
2158 3c. Parachutist 25 10
2159 8c. Glider in flight (horiz) 35 15
2160 10c. Antonov An-2 biplane spraying crops (horiz) . . 1·10 40
2161 13c. Ilyushin Il-62M in flight (horiz) . . . . 1·70 40

1974. History of Baseball in Cuba. Mult.
2162 1c. Type **557** 15 10
2163 3c. Players of 1874 (First official game) 15 10
2164 8c. Emilio Sabourin 30 15
2165 10c. Modern players (horiz) (44 × 27 mm) . . . . . 1·00 25
2166 13c. Latin-American Stadium, Havana (horiz) (44 × 27 mm) . . . . . . 1·60 30

558 Stamp, Cachet and Horseman

1974. Cent of "Mambi" Revolutionary Stamp.
2167 **558** 13c. multicoloured . . . 1·20 25

559 Comecon Headquarters Building, Moscow and Emblem

1974. 16th Socialist Countries' Customs Conference.
2168 **559** 30c. blue and gold . . . 1·70 55

560 Maj. Camilo Cienfuegos (revolutionary)

1974. 15th Anniv of Disappearance of Cienfuegos
2169 **560** 3c. multicoloured 60 25

561 Miner's Helmet

1974. 8th World Mining Congress.
2170 **561** 13c. multicoloured . . . 1·20 30

562 Oil Refinery

1974. 15th Anniv of Cuban Petroleum Institute.
2171 **562** 3c. multicoloured 60 15

563 Earth Station

1974. Inauguration of "Inter-Sputnik" Satellite Earth Station. Multicoloured.
2172 3c. Type **563** 20 10
2173 13c. Satellite and aerial . . 1·00 15
2174 1p. Satellite and flags . . . 2·75 1·10

564 Emblems and Magnifying Glass

1974. 10th Anniv of Cuban Philatelic Federation.
2175 **564** 30c. multicoloured . . . 1·90 60

565 "Mercury"

566 F. Joliot-Curie (1st president) (Picasso)

1974. 4th National Stamp Exhibition, Havana. Sheet 85 × 68 mm.
MS2176 **565** 50c. multicoloured 5·00 5·00

1974. 25th Anniv of World Peace Congress.
2177 **566** 30c. multicoloured . . . 2·40 60

567 R. M. Villena

1974. 75th Birth Anniv of Ruben Martinez Villena (revolutionary).
2178 **567** 3c. red and yellow . . . 55 15

568 Boxing Trophy

1975. Cuban Victories in World Amateur Boxing Championships. Sheet 109 × 74 mm. Imperf.
MS2179 **568** 50c. multicoloured 5·00 5·00

569 "The Word" (M. Pogolotti)

1975. National Museum Paintings (9th series). Multicoloured.
2180 1c. Type **569** 15 10
2181 2c. "The Silk-Cotton Tree" (H. Cleenewerk) 15 10
2182 3c. "Landscape" (G. Collazo) 15 10
2183 5c. "Still Life" (F. Peralta) 20 10
2184 13c. "Maria Wilson" (F. Martinez) (vert) . . . 1·20 30
2185 30c. "The Couple" (M. Fortunay) . . . . . 2·20 60

570 Bouquet and Woman's Head

1975. International Woman's Year.
2186 **570** 13c. multicoloured . . . 1·20 30

571 Skipjack Tuna and Fishing-boat

1975. Cuban Fishing Industry. Mult.
2187 1c. Type **571** 25 10
2188 2c. Blue-finned tunny . . . 25 10
2189 3c. Nassau grouper 25 10
2190 8c. Silver hake 25 15
2191 13c. Prawn . . . . 1·10 60
2192 30c. Lobster . . . . 3·25 95

572 Nickel

1975. Cuban Minerals. Multicoloured.
2193 3c. Type **572** 30 15
2194 13c. Copper . . . . 1·30 25
2195 30c. Chromium . . . . . . 2·20 60

1975. Cosmonautics Day. Science Fiction paintings. As T **546**. Multicoloured.
2196 1c. "Cosmodrome" 15 10
2197 2c. "Exploration craft" (vert) 15 10
2198 3c. "Earth eclipsing the Sun" 15 10
2199 5c. "On the Threshold" . . 30 10
2200 13c. "Astronauts on Mars" 1·20 20
2201 30c. "Astronauts' view of Earth" . . . . 2·00 50

573 Letter and "Correos" Postmark

1975. Stamp Day. Multicoloured.
2202 3c. Type **573** 15 10
2203 13c. Letter and steamship postmark . . . . 1·20 25
2204 30c. Letter and "N.A." postmark . . . . 1·80 50

574 Hoisting Red Flag over Reichstag, Berlin

1975. 30th Anniv of "Victory over Fascism".
2205 **574** 30c. multicoloured . . . 1·90 50

575 Sevres Vase

1975. National Museum Treasures. Mult.
2206 1c. Type **575** 15 10
2207 2c. Meissen "Shepherdess and Dancers" 15 10
2208 3c. Chinese Porcelain Dish—"Lady with Parasol" (horiz) 20 10
2209 5c. Chinese Bamboo Screen—"The Phoenix" 30 10
2210 13c. "Allegory of Music" (F. Boucher) . . . . . . 1·20 25
2211 30c. "Portrait of a Lady" (L. Toque) . . . . 1·70 50
MS2212 61 × 104 mm. 50c. Park scene—"El Columpio" (H. Roberts) (25 × 39 mm) . . 4·75 4·50

576 Coloured Balls and Globe "Man"

1975. International Children's Day.
2213 **576** 3c. multicoloured 40 10

577 Cuban Vireo

1975. Birds (1st series). Multicoloured.
2214 1c. Type **577** 25 10
2215 2c. Cuban screech owl . . . 25 10
2216 3c. Cuban conure 25 10
2217 5c. Blue-headed quail dove 50 15
2218 13c. Hook-billed kite . . . 2·30 50
2219 30c. Zapata rail . . . . . . 3·25 95
See also Nos. 2301/6.

578 View of Centre

1973. 10th Anniv of National Scientific Investigation Centre.
2220 **578** 13c. multicoloured . . . 1·10 20

579 Commission Emblem and Drainage Equipment

1975. Int Commission on Irrigation and Drainage.
2221 **579** 13c. multicoloured . . . 1·10 20

580 "Cedrea mexicana" **581** Women cultivating Young Plants

1975. Reafforestation. Multicoloured.
2222 1c. Type **580** 15 10
2223 3c. "Swietonia mahagoni" 30 10
2224 5c. "Calophyllum brasiliense" 30 10
2225 13c. "Hibiscus tiliaceus" . . 90 30
2226 30c. "Pinus caribaea" . . . 1·40 50

1975. 15th Anniv of Cuban Women's Federation.
2227 **581** 3c. multicoloured 40 15

582 Conference Emblem and Broken Chains **583** Baseball

1975. International Conference on the Independence of Puerto Rico.
2228 **582** 13c. multicoloured . . . 80 25

1975. 7th Pan-American Games, Mexico. Mult.
2229 1c. Type **583** 20 10
2230 3c. Boxing 20 10
2231 5c. Handball 20 10
2232 13c. High jumping . . . . 1·20 30
2233 30c. Weightlifting . . . . 1·70 40
MS2234 77×91 mm. 50c. Games emblem and Sun disc. Imperf 4·25 4·25

584 Emblem and Crowd

1975. 15th Anniv of Revolutionary Defence Committees.
2235 **584** 3c. multicoloured 40 15

585 Institute Emblem

1975. 15th Anniv of Cuban "Friendship Amongst the Peoples" Institute.
2236 **585** 3c. multicoloured 25 15

586 Silver 1 Peso Coin, 1913

1975. 15th Anniv of Nationalization of Bank of Cuba. Multicoloured.
2237 13c. Type **586** 90 30
2238 13c. 1 peso banknote, 1934 90 30
2239 13c. 1 peso banknote, 1946 90 30
2240 13c. 1 peso banknote, 1964 90 30
2241 13c. 1 peso banknote, 1973 90 30

587 "La Junta", Cuba's first locomotive, 1837

1975. "Evolution of Railways". Multicoloured.
2242 1c. Type **587** 15 10
2243 3c. Steam locomotive "M. M. Prieto", 1920 . . . . 25 10
2244 5c. Russian-built Type TEM-4 diesel locomotive 25 10
2245 13c. Hungarian-built Type DVM-9 diesel locomotive . . . . 2·50 30
2246 30c. Russian-built Type M-62K diesel locomotive . . . . 3·00 60

588 Bobbins and Flag

1975. Textile Industry.
2247 **588** 13c. multicoloured . . . 1·00 20

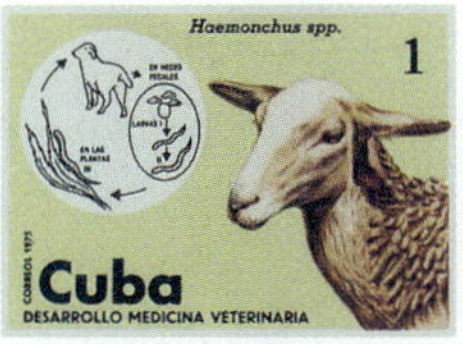

589 Sheep and Diagram

1975. Development of Veterinary Medicine. Animals and Disease Cycles. Multicoloured.
2248 1c. Type **589** 20 10
2249 2c. Dog 20 10
2250 3c. Cockerel 20 10
2251 5c. Horse 20 10
2252 13c. Pig . . . . 1·10 30
2253 30c. Ox . . . . 2·00 50

590 Manuel Ascunce Domenech **592** Communists with Flags inside Figure "1"

591 "Irrigation"

1975. Manuel Domenech Educational Detachment.
2254 **590** 3c. multicoloured 30 15

1975. Agriculture and Water-supply.
2255 **591** 13c. multicoloured . . . 1·00 25

1976. 1st Cuban Communist Party Congress. Multicoloured.
2256 3c. Type **592** 15 10
2257 13c. Workers with banner (horiz) 90 30
2258 30c. Jose Marti and Cuban leaders (horiz) . . . . . 1·20 40

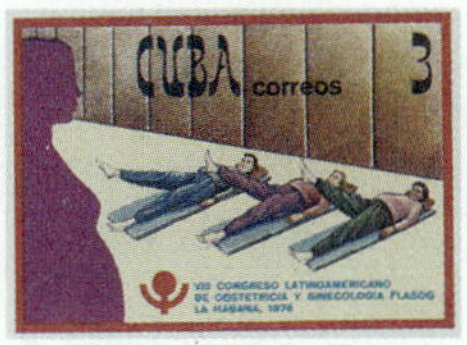

593 Pre-natal Exercises

1976. 8th Latin-American Obstetrics and Gynaecology Congress, Havana.
2259 **593** 3c. multicoloured 50 15

594 "Seated Woman" (V. Manuel) **595** Conference Emblem and Building

1976. National Museum Paintings (10th series). Multicoloured.
2260 1c. Type **594** 15 10
2261 2c. "Garden" (S. Rusinol) (horiz) 15 10
2262 3c. "Guadalquivir River" (M. Barron y Carrillo) (horiz) 20 10
2263 5c. "Self-portrait" (Jan Steen) 20 10
2264 13c. "Portrait of Woman" (L. M. van Loo) . . . . 1·10 20
2265 30c. "La Chula" (J. A. Morell) (27×44 mm) . . 1·80 40

1976. Socialist Communications Ministers' Conference, Havana.
2266 **595** 13c. multicoloured . . . 1·10 20

596 American Foxhound

1976. Hunting Dogs. Multicoloured.
2267 1c. Type **596** 20 10
2268 2c. Labrador retriever . . . 20 10
2269 3c. Borzoi 20 10
2270 5c. Irish setter 20 15
2271 13c. Pointer . . . . 1·10 25
2272 30c. Cocker Spaniel . . . . 2·00 40

597 Flags, Arms and Anthem

1976. Socialist Constitution, 1976.
2273 **597** 13c. multicoloured . . . 1·10 30

598 Ruy Lopez Segura

1976. History of Chess. Multicoloured.
2274 1c. Type **598** 15 10
2275 2c. Francois Philidor . . . 15 10
2276 3c. Wilhelm Steinitz 20 10
2277 13c. Emanuel Lasker . . . 1·50 25
2278 30c. Jose Raul Capablanca 1·60 55

599 Radio Aerial and Map

1976. 15th Anniv of Cuban International Broadcasting Services.
2279 **599** 50c. multicoloured . . . 1·60 70

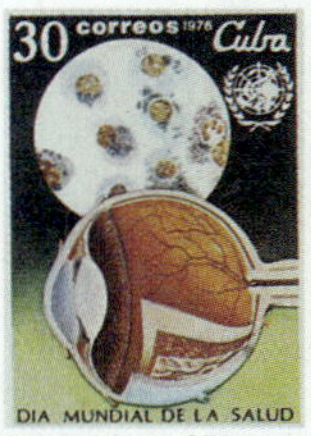

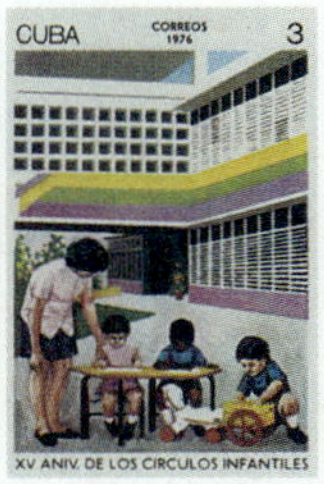

600 Section of Human Eye and Microscope Slide **601** Children in Creche

1976. World Health Day.
2280 **600** 30c. multicoloured . . . 1·20 50

1976. 15th Anniv of Infant Welfare Centres.
2281 **601** 3c. multicoloured 50 15

602 Y. Gagarin in Space-suit

1976. 15th Anniv of First Manned Space Flight. Multicoloured.
2282 1c. Type **602** 15 10
2283 2c. V. Tereshkova and rockets 15 10
2284 3c. Cosmonaut on "space walk" (vert) 20 10
2285 5c. Spacecraft and Moon (vert) 30 10
2286 13c. Spacecraft in manoeuvre (vert) 90 25
2287 30c. Space link . . . . . . 1·40 30

603 Cuban Machine-gunner

1976. 15th Anniv of Giron Victory. Mult.
2288 3c. Type **603** 20 10
2289 13c. Cuban pilot and Lockheed F-80 Shooting Star fighter attacking ship 80 25
2290 30c. Cuban soldier wielding rifle (vert) . . . . . . 1·50 45

604 Heads of Farmers

1976. 15th Anniv of National Association of Small Farmers (ANAP).
2291 **604** 3c. multicoloured 50 10

605 Volleyball

1976. Olympic Games, Montreal. Mult.
2292 1c. Type **605** 15 10
2293 2c. Basketball 15 10
2294 3c. Long-jumping 15 10
2295 4c. Boxing 20 10
2296 5c. Weightlifting 20 10
2297 13c. Judo 90 30
2298 30c. Swimming . . . . . 1·40 50
MS2299 100 × 80 mm. 50c. Otter emblem. Imperf . . . . 3·75 3·75

606 Modern Secondary School

1976. Rural Secondary Schools.
2300 **606** 3c. black and red 50 10

607 Oriente Warbler

1976. Birds (2nd series). Multicoloured.
2301 1c. Type **607** 30 10
2302 2c. Cuban pygmy owl . . . 30 10
2303 3c. Fernandina's flicker . . 30 20
2304 5c. Cuban tody 85 25
2305 13c. Gundlach's hawk . . . 1·70 40
2306 30c. Cuban trogon . . . . 3·50 1·00

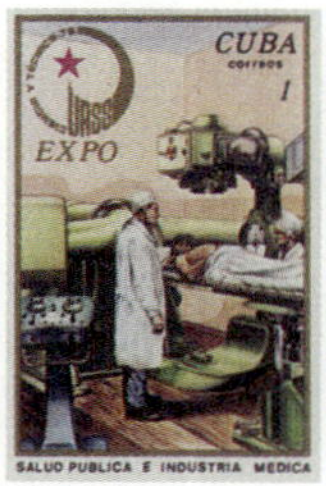

608 Medical Treatment **609** "El Inglesito"

1976. "Expo", Havana. Soviet Science and Technology. Multicoloured.
2307 1c. Type **608** 15 10
2308 3c. Child and deer ("Environmental Protection") 15 10
2309 10c. Cosmonauts on launch pad ("Cosmos Investigation") 40 30
2310 30c. Tupolev Tu-144 airplane ("Soviet Transport") (horiz) . . . 2·10 60

1976. Death Cent of Henry M. Reeve (patriot).
2311 **609** 13c. multicoloured . . . 55 20

610 "G. Collazo" (J. Dabour)

1976. Cuban Paintings. Multicoloured.
2312 1c. Type **610** 15 10
2313 2c. "The Art Lovers" (G. Collazo) (horiz) . . . 15 10
2314 3c. "The Patio" (G. Collazo) 15 10
2315 5c. "Cocotero" (G. Collazo) 15 10
2316 13c. "New York Studio" (G. Collazo) (horiz) . . . 50 20
2317 30c. "Emelinz Collazo" (G. Collazo) (horiz) . . . 1·70 60

611 School Activities

1976. 10th Anniv of "Camilo Cienfuegos" Military School.
2318 **611** 3c. multicoloured 30 15

612 "Imias" (freighter)

1976. Development of Cuban Merchant Marine. Multicoloured.
2319 1c. Type **612** 30 15
2320 2c. "Comandante Camilo Cienfuegos" (freighter) . . 30 15
2321 3c. "Comandante Pinares" (cargo liner) 30 15
2322 5c. "Vietnam Heroico" (cargo liner) 60 25
2323 13c. "Presidente Allende" (ore carrier) . . . . . . 1·90 60
2324 30c. "XIII Congreso" (bulk carrier) . . . . 3·75 1·00

613 Emblem and part of Cine Film

1976. 8th International Cinematographic Festival of Socialist Countries, Havana.
2325 **613** 3c. multicoloured 30 15

614 Scene from "Apollo"

1976. 5th International Ballet Festival, Havana. Multicoloured.
2326 1c. Type **614** 15 10
2327 2c. "The River and the Forest" (vert) 15 10
2328 3c. "Giselle" 15 10
2329 5c. "Oedipus Rex" (vert) . . 20 10
2330 13c. "Carmen" (vert) . . . 90 25
2331 30c. "Vital Song" (vert) . . 1·60 35

615 Soldier and Sportsmen

1976. 3rd Military Games.
2332 **615** 3c. multicoloured 40 15

616 "Granma"

1976. 20th Anniv of "Granma" Landings.
2333 **616** 1c. multicoloured 15 10
2334 – 3c. multicoloured 15 10
2335 – 13c. multicoloured . . . 80 25
2336 – 30c. multicoloured . . . 1·30 55
DESIGNS: 3c. to 30c. Different scenes showing guerrillas.

617 "Cuban Landscape" (F. Cavada)

1976. 5th National Philatelic Exhibition. Sheet 90 × 100 mm.
MS2337 **617** 50c. multicoloured 5·00 4·75

618 Volleyball

1976. Cuban Victories in Montreal Olympic Games. Multicoloured.
2338 1c. Type **618** 15 10
2339 2c. Hurdling 15 10
2340 3c. Running 15 10
2341 8c. Boxing 20 15
2342 13c. Winning race 65 25
2343 30c. Judo . . . . 1·40 50
MS2344 69 × 101 mm. 50c. As No. 2341 . . . . 4·00 3·00

619 "Golden Cross Inn" (S. Scott)

1977. National Museum Paintings (11th series). Multicoloured.
2345 1c. Type **619** 15 10
2346 3c. "Portrait of a Man" (J. Verspronck) (vert) . . 15 10
2347 5c. "Venetian Landscape" (F. Guardi) 15 10
2348 10c. "Valley Corner" (H. Cleenewerck) (vert) 45 15
2349 13c. "F. Xaviera Paula" (anon) (vert) 65 30
2350 30c. "F. de Medici" (C. Allori) (vert) . . . . 1·60 50
The vert designs are slightly larger, 27 × 43 mm.

620 Motor Bus

1977. Rural Transport.
2351 **620** 3c. multicoloured 65 15

621 Map of Cuba

1977. Constitution of Popular Government.
2352 **621** 13c. multicoloured . . . 55 20

622 Cuban Green Woodpecker

1977. Cuban Birds. Multicoloured.
2353 1c. Type **622** 50 25
2354 4c. Cuban grassquit 60 25
2355 10c. Cuban blackbird . . . 1·20 30
2356 13c. Zapata wren . . . . . 1·80 35
2357 30c. Bee hummingbird . . . 3·50 85

623 Mechanical Scoop and Emblem

1977. Air. 6th Latin-American and Caribbean Sugar Exporters Meeting, Havana.
2358 **623** 13c. multicoloured . . . 60 20

624 Fire-mouthed Cichlid

1977. Fish in Lenin Park Aquarium, Havana. Multicoloured.
2359 1c. Type **624** 15 10
2360 3c. Tiger barb 15 10
2361 5c. Koi carp 15 10
2362 10c. Siamese fightingfish . . 25 15
2363 13c. Freshwater angelfish (vert) . . . . 1·10 20
2364 30c. Buenos Aires tetra . . 2·30 50

625 "Sputnik 1" and East German Stamp

1977. 20th Anniv of 1st Artificial Satellite. Multicoloured.
2365 1c. Type **625** 20 15
2366 3c. "Luna 16" and Hungarian stamp 20 15
2367 5c. "Cosmos" and North Korean stamp 20 15
2368 10c. "Sputnik 3" and Polish stamp 30 20
2369 13c. Earth, Moon and Yugoslav stamp 95 30
2370 30c. Earth, Moon and Cuban stamp . . . . . . 1·60 50
MS2371 95 × 76 mm. 50c. "Sputnik 1" and Russian stamp. Imperf 3·75 3·50

626 Antonio Maria Romeu

1977. Cuban Musicians. Multicoloured.
2372 3c. Type **626** (postage) . . . 30 10
2373 13c. Jorge Ankerman (air) 80 25

627 "Hibiscus rosa sinensis"

1977. Birth Centenary of Dr. Juan Tomas Roig (botanist). Cuban Flowers. Multicoloured.
2374 1c. Type **627** (postage) . . . 15 10
2375 2c. "Nerium oleander" . . . 15 10
2376 5c. "Allamanda cathartica" 15 10
2377 10c. "Pelargonium zonale" 30 15
2378 13c. "Caesalpinia pulcherrima" (air) 70 15
2379 30c. "Catharanthus roseus" 1·40 45
MS2380 71 × 92 mm. 50c. Dr. J. T. Roig (33 × 40 mm) . . . . 3·50 3·00

628 Horse-drawn Fire Engine

1977. Fire Prevention Week. Multicoloured.
2381 1c. Type **628** 15 10
2382 2c. Horse-drawn fire engine (different) 15 10
2383 6c. Early motor fire pump 20 10
2384 10c. Modern motor fire pump 40 15
2385 13c. Turntable-ladder . . . 75 30
2386 30c. Heavy rescue vehicle . . 1·60 40

629 20th Anniversary Medal

1977. National Decorations.
2387 **629** 1c. mult (postage) . . . 20 10
2388 – 3c. multicoloured 20 15
2389 – 13c. multicoloured (air) 65 20
2390 – 30c. multicoloured . . . 1·20 45
DESIGNS: 3c. to 30c. Various medals and ribbons.

630 "Portrait of Mary"
631 Boxing

1977. Painting by Jorge Arche. Mult.
2391 1c. Type **630** (postage) . . . 15 10
2392 3c. "Jose Marti" 15 10
2393 5c. "Portrait of Aristides" 15 10
2394 10c. "Bathers" (horiz) . . . 40 15
2395 13c. "My Wife and I" (air) 50 15
2396 30c. "The Game of Dominoes" (horiz) . . . 1·30 50
MS2397 64 × 79 mm. 50c. "Self-portrait" . . . . 3·25 3·25

1977. Military Spartakiad. Multicoloured.
2398 1c. Type **631** (postage) . . . 15 10
2399 3c. Volleyball 15 10
2400 5c. Parachuting 15 10
2401 10c. Running 30 15
2402 13c. Grenade-throwing (air) 50 15
2403 30c. Rifle-shooting (horiz) 1·20 50

632 Che Guevara

1977. Air. 10th Anniv of Guerrilla Heroes Day.
2404 **632** 13c. multicoloured . . . 80 25

633 Curtiss A-1 Seaplane and Parla Stamp of 1952

1977. 50th Anniv of Cuban Air Mail. Mult.
2405 1c. Type **633** (postage) . . . 15 10
2406 2c. Ford 5-AT trimotor airplane and Havana–Key West cachet 15 10
2407 5c. Flying boat "American Clipper" and first flight cachet 15 10
2408 10c. Douglas DC-4 and Havana-Madrid cachet . . 45 15
2409 13c. Lockheed Super Constellation and Havana–Mexico cachet (air) 80 15
2410 30c. Ilyushin Il-18 and Havana–Prague cachet . . 1·60 70

634 Cruiser "Aurora"

1977. 60th Anniv of Russian Revolution.
2411 **634** 3c. black, red and gold 15 10
2412 – 13c. black, red and gold 35 20
2413 – 30c. gold, red and black 1·30 50
DESIGNS: 13c. Lenin and flags; 30c. Hammer and sickle with scenes of technology.

635 "The Adoration of the Magi" (detail)

1977. Air. 400th Birth Anniv of Peter Paul Rubens. Sheet 85 × 115 mm.
MS2414 **635** 50c. multicoloured 3·75 3·75

636 Cat

1977. Felines in Havana Zoo. Multicoloured.
2415 1c. Type **636** (postage) . . . 15 10
2416 2c. Leopard (black race) . . 15 10
2417 8c. Puma 15 15
2418 10c. Leopard 90 25
2419 13c. Tiger (air) . . . . . . 1·10 25
2420 30c. Lion . . . . 1·50 55

637 Cienfuegos Uprising

1977. 20th Anniv of Martyrs of the Revolution. Multicoloured.
2421 3c. Type **637** (postage) . . . 15 10
2422 20c. Attack on the Presidential Palace . . . 80 30
2423 13c. Landing from the "Corynthia" (air) 60 25

638 Clinic, Havana

1977. 75th Anniv of Pan-American Health Organization.
2424 **638** 13c. multicoloured . . . 60 15

639 Map of Cuba and Units of Measurement

1977. International System of Measurement.
2425 **639** 3c. multicoloured 30 10

640 University Building and Coat of Arms

1978. 250th Anniv of Havana University. Multicoloured.
2426 3c. Type **640** (postage) . . . 20 10
2427 13c. University building and crossed sabres (air) . . . 60 25
2428 30c. Student crowd and statue 90 50

641 "Jose Marti" (A. Menocal)
642 "Seated Woman" (R. Madrazo)

1978. Air. 125th Anniv of Jose Marti (patriot).
2429 **641** 13c. multicoloured . . . 65 15

1978. National Museum Paintings (12th series). Multicoloured.
2430 1c. Type **642** (postage) . . . 15 10
2431 4c. "Girl" (J. Sorolla) . . . 15 10
2432 6c. "Landscape with Figures" (J. Pilliment) (horiz) 15 10
2433 10c. "The Cow" (E. Abela) (horiz) 50 15
2434 13c. "El Guadalquivir" (M. Barron) (horiz) (air) 85 25
2435 30c. "H. E. Ridley" (J. J. Masquerier) 95 50

643 Patrol Boat, Frontier Guard and Dog

1978. 15th Anniv of Frontier Troops.
2436 **643** 13c. multicoloured . . . 1·30 30

644 Cuban Solitaire

1978. Cuban Birds. Multicoloured.
2437 1c. Type **644** (postage) . . . 45 10
2438 4c. Cuban gnatcatcher . . . 50 10
2439 10c. Oriente warbler . . . . 1·30 20
2440 13c. Zapata sparrow (air) 1·50 50
2441 30c. Cuban macaw and ivory-billed woodpecker (vert) . . . . 2·30 1·10

645 "Antonio Maceo" (A. Melero)
646 "Intercosmos" Satellite

1978. Air. Centenary of Baragua Protest.
2442 **645** 13c. multicoloured . . . 60 30

1978. Cosmonautics Day. Multicoloured.
2443 1c. Type **646** (postage) . . . 15 10
2444 2c. "Luna 24" (horiz) . . . 15 10
2445 5c. "Venus 9" 30 10
2446 10c. "Cosmos" (horiz) . . . 30 20
2447 13c. "Venus 10" (horiz) (air) 60 15
2448 30c. "Lunokhod 2" (36 × 46 mm) . . . . . . 1·00 50

647 Smiling Worker and Emblem

1978. 9th World Federation of Trade Unions Congress, Prague.
2449 **647** 30c. red and black . . . 85 45

648 Parliament Building, Budapest and 1919 Hungarian Stamp

1978. Air "Socfilex" Stamp Exhibition, Budapest.
2450 **648** 30c. multicoloured . . . 1·40 55

649 "Melocactus guitarti"

1978. Cactus Flowers. Multicoloured.
2451 1c. Type **649** (postage) . . . 20 10
2452 4c. "Leptocereus wrightii" 20 10
2453 6c. "Opuntia militaris" . . . 20 10
2454 10c. "Cylindropuntia hystrix" 50 20
2455 13c. "Rhodocactus cubensis" (air) 75 30
2456 30c. "Harrisia taetra" . . . 1·20 50

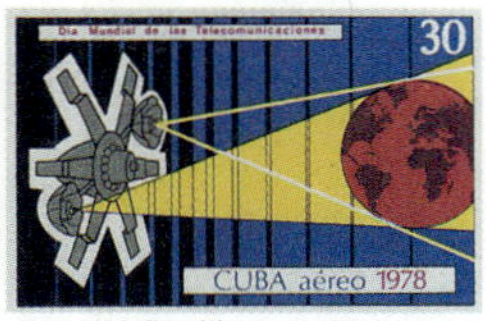

650 Satellite and Globe

1978. Air. World Telecommunications Day.
2457 **650** 30c. multicoloured . . . 1·00 45

651 Africans and O.A.U. Emblem

1978. Air. 15th Anniv of Organization of African Unity.
2458 **651** 30c. multicoloured . . . 85 45

652 "Niven, Wales" (G.H. Russell)

1978. Air. Capex 78 International Philatelic Exhibition, Toronto. Sheet 69 × 93 mm.
MS2459 **652** 50c. multicoloured 3·00 3·00

653 Clown Barb

1978. Fish in Lenin Park Aquarium, Havana. Multicoloured.
2460 1c. Type **653** (postage) . . . 15 10
2461 4c. Flame tetra 15 10
2462 6c. Guppy 15 10
2463 10c. Dwarf gourami 35 15
2464 13c. Veil-tailed goldfish (air) 70 20
2465 30c. Brown discus . . . . . 1·40 50

654 Basketball

655 Moncada Fortress

1978. 13th Central American and Caribbean Games. Multicoloured.
2466 1c. Type **654** (postage) . . . 20 10
2467 3c. Boxing 20 10
2468 5c. Weightlifting 20 10
2469 10c. Fencing (horiz) 35 15
2470 13c. Volleyball (air) 50 25
2471 30c. Running . . . . 1·00 45

1978. 25th Anniv of Attack on Moncada Fortress. Multicoloured.
2472 3c. Type **655** (postage) . . . 20 10
2473 13c. Soldiers with rifles (air) 40 15
2474 30c. Dove and flags 90 35

656 Prague

1978. 11th World Youth and Students' Festival, Havana. Multicoloured.
2475 3c. Type **656** (postage) . . . 20 10
2476 3c. Budapest 20 10
2477 3c. Berlin 20 10
2478 3c. Bucharest 20 10
2479 3c. Warsaw 20 10
2480 13c. Moscow (air) 55 15
2481 13c. Vienna 55 15
2482 13c. Helsinki 55 15
2483 13c. Sofia 55 15
2484 13c. Berlin 55 15
2485 30c. Havana (46 × 36 mm) 1·20 30

657 Marching Soldiers with Flag

659 "Marina" (Venetian fishing vessel) A. Brandeis)

658 "Pargo"

1978. 5th Anniv of Young Workers Army.
2486 **657** 3c. multicoloured 25 10

1978. Fishing Fleet. Multicoloured.
2487 1c. Type **658** (postage) . . . 15 10
2488 2c. Fish-processing ship . . 15 10
2489 5c. Shrimp fishing boat . . 15 10
2490 10c. Stern trawler 40 15
2491 13c. "Mar Carbide" (air) . . 85 25
2492 30c. Refrigeration and processing ship . . . . . 1·60 60

1978. Air. PRAGA 78 International Philatelic Exhibition. Sheet 83 × 109 mm.
MS2493 **659** 50c. multicoloured 3·00 3·00

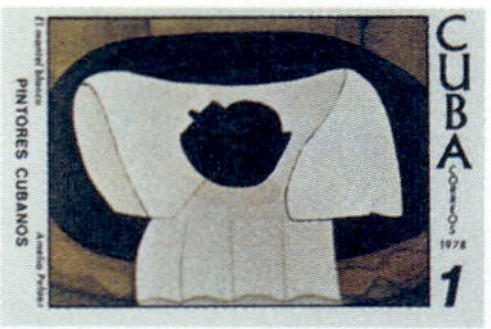

660 "The White Coat" (Pelaez del Casal)

1978. Painting by Amelia Pelaez del Casal. Multicoloured.
2494 1c. Type **660** (postage) . . . 15 10
2495 3c. "Still Life with Flowers" 15 10
2496 6c. "Women" 15 10
2497 10c. "Fish" 35 15
2498 13c. "Flowering Almond" (air) 50 15
2499 30c. "Still Life in Blue" . . 1·10 45
MS2500 63 × 80 mm. 50c. "Portrait of Amelia" (L. Romanach) . . 3·25 3·00

661 Letters, Satellite and Globe

1978. Air 20th Anniv of Organization for Communication Co-operation between Socialist Countries.
2501 **661** 30c. multicoloured . . . 1·00 35

662 Postcard

1978. Air. 6th National Stamp Exhibition. Sheet 105 × 66 mm. Imperf.
MS2502 **662** 50c. multicoloured 3·00 3·00

663 Hand

1978. Air. International Anti-Apartheid Year.
2503 **663** 13c. black, pink & mve 1·30 1·10

664 White Rhinoceros

1978. Animals in Havana Zoo. Multicoloured.
2504 1c. Type **664** (postage) . . . 20 10
2505 4c. Okapi (vert) 20 10
2506 6c. Mandrill 20 10
2507 10c. Giraffe (vert) 50 15
2508 13c. Cheetah (air) 70 30
2509 30c. African elephant (vert) 1·50 65

665 "Grand Pas de Quatre"

1978. 30th Anniv of National Ballet Company. Multicoloured.
2510 3c. Type **665** (postage) . . . 20 10
2511 13c. "Giselle" (air) 65 25
2512 30c. "Genesis" . . . . . . 1·30 40

666 Hibiscus

668 Fidel Castro and Soldier

667 Julius and Ethel Rosenberg

1978. Pacific Flowers.
2513 **666** 1c. mult (postage) . . . 15 10
2514 – 4c. multicoloured 15 10
2515 – 6c. multicoloured 20 10
2516 – 10c. multicoloured . . . 40 15
2517 – 13c. mult (air) 65 25
2518 – 30c. multicoloured . . . 1·30 40
DESIGNS: 4c. to 30c. Different flowers.

1978. Air. 25th Death Anniv of Julius and Ethel Rosenberg (American Communists).
2519 **667** 13c. multicoloured . . . 50 15

1979. 20th Anniv of Revolution. Mult.
2520 3c. Type **668** 15 15
2521 13c. Symbols of industry . . 40 15
2522 1p. Flag, flame and globe 2·75 1·10

669 Julio Mella

1979. 50th Death Anniv of J. A. Mella.
2523 **669** 13c. multicoloured . . . 45 15

670 Blue-headed Quail Dove

1979. Doves and Pigeons. Multicoloured.
2524 1c. Type **670** 35 15
2525 3c. Key West quail dove . . 40 15
2526 7c. Grey-faced quail dove 40 15
2527 8c. Ruddy quail dove . . . 50 20
2528 13c. White-crowned pigeon 95 25
2529 30c. Plain pigeon . . . . . 1·90 70

671 "Genre Scene" (D. Teniers)

1979. National Museum Paintings (13th series). Multicoloured.
2530 1c. Type **671** 15 10
2531 3c. "Arrival of Spanish Troops" (J. Meissonier) 15 10
2532 6c. "A Joyful Gathering" (Sir David Wilkie) . . . 25 10
2533 10c. "Capea" (E. de Lucas Padilla) 35 10
2534 13c. "Teatime" (R. Madrazo) (vert) . . . 65 20
2535 30c. "Peasant in front of a Tavern" (Adriaen van Ostade) . . . . 1·40 40

672 "Nymphaea capensis"

673 "20" Flag and Film Frames

1979. Aquatic Flowers. Multicoloured.
2536 3c. Type **672** 15 10
2537 10c. "Nymphaea ampla" . . 30 15
2538 13c. "Nymphaea coerulea" 50 20
2539 30c. "Nymphaea rubra" . . 1·20 40

1979. 20th Anniv of Cuban Cinema.
2540 **673** 3c. multicoloured 30 10

674 Rocket Launch

1979. Cosmonautics Day. Multicoloured.

2541 1c. Type **674** 15 10
2542 4c. "Soyuz" 15 10
2543 6c. "Salyut" 30 10
2544 10c. "Soyuz" and "Salyut" link-up 40 10
2545 13c. "Soyuz" and "Salyut" 70 15
2546 30c. Parachute and capsule 1·50 40
MS2547 67 × 91 mm. 50c. Design similar to 10c . . . . 3·00 3·00

675 Hands and Globe

1979. 6th Non-Aligned Countries Summit Conference. Multicoloured.

2548 3c. Type **675** 20 10
2549 13c. "6" ("Against Colonialism") 40 15
2550 30c. Joined coin and globe ("A New Economic Order") . . . . 1·10 35

676 Cuna Indian Tapestry, Panama

1979. 20th Anniv of "House of the Americas" Museum.

2551 **676** 13c. multicoloured . . . 40 20

677 Farmer holding Title Deed

1979. 20th Anniv of Agrarian Reform.

2552 **677** 3c. multicoloured 30 10

678 "The Party" (J. Pascin)

1979. Philaserdica 79 Philatelic Exhibition, Sofia, Bulgaria. Sheet 104 × 52 mm.

MS2553 **678** 50c. multicoloured 3·00 3·00

679 "Eulepidotis rectimargo"

1979. Cuban Nocturnal Butterflies. Mult.

2554 1c. Type **679** 15 10
2555 4c. "Othreis materna" . . . 15 10
2556 6c. "Noropsis hieroglyphica" 35 15
2557 10c. "Heterochroma sp." . . 35 15
2558 13c. "Melanchroia regnatrix" 75 20
2559 30c. "Attera gemmata" . . 1·80 45

680 Children's Heads

1979. Air. International Year of the Child.

2560 **680** 13c. multicoloured . . . 80 15

681 "Avenue du Maine, Paris"

1979. 10th Death Anniv of Victor Manuel Garcia (painter). Multicoloured.

2561 1c. Type **681** 15 10
2562 3c. "Portrait of Enmita" . . 15 10
2563 6c. "Rio San Juan, Matanzas" 15 10
2564 10c. "Landscape with Woman carrying Hay" . . 25 15
2565 13c. "Still-life with Vase" . . 35 15
2566 30c. "Street by Night" . . . 1·30 45
MS2567 64 × 81 mm. 50c. "Self-portrait" . . . . 3·00 3·00

682 Clenched Fists, Dove and Bombs

1979. 30th Anniv of World Peace Council.

2568 **682** 30c. multicoloured . . . 85 35

683 Lighthouse and Fireworks

1979. Air. "Carifesta 79" Festival, Havana.

2569 **683** 13c. multicoloured . . . 60 15

684 Wrestling

1979. Pre-Olympics, Moscow 1980. Mult.

2570 1c. Type **684** 15 10
2571 4c. Boxing 15 10
2572 6c. Volleyball 15 10
2573 10c. Rifle-shooting 20 15
2574 13c. Weightlifting 45 25
2575 30c. High jump . . . . . . 1·20 35

685 "Rosa eglanteria"

686 Council Emblem

1979. Roses. Multicoloured.

2576 1c. Type **685** 20 10
2577 2c. "Rosa centifolia anemonoides" 20 10
2578 3c. "Rosa indica vulgaris" 20 10
2579 5c. "Rosa eglanteria var. punicea" 20 10
2580 10c. "Rosa sulfurea" . . . 20 15
2581 13c. "Rosa muscosa alba" 45 15
2582 20c. "Rosa gallica purpurea velutina, Parva" 90 30

1979. 30th Anniv of Council of Mutual Economic Aid.

2583 **686** 13c. multicoloured . . . 40 15

687 Games Emblem and Activities

1979. Air. "Universiada 79" 10th World University Games, Mexico City.

2584 **687** 13c. green, gold & turq 60 15

688 Conventions Palace

1979. Air. 6th Non-Aligned Countries Summit Conference, Havana.

2585 **688** 50c. multicoloured . . . 1·50 95

689 Sir Rowland Hill and Casket containing Freedom of the City of London

1979. Air. Death Centenary of Sir Rowland Hill.

2586 **689** 30c. multicoloured . . . 1·20 30

690 Ford 5-AT Trimotor

1979. 50th Anniv of Cuban Airlines. Mult.

2587 1c. Type **690** 15 10
2588 2c. Sikorsky S-38 flying boat 15 10
2589 3c. Douglas DC-3 . . . . . 30 10
2590 4c. Ilyushin Il-18 . . . . . 30 10
2591 13c. Yakovlev Yak-40 . . . 75 25
2592 40c. Ilyushin Il-62M . . . . 2·00 50

691 Rumanian "New Constitution" Stamp of 1948

1979. Air. "Socfilex 79" Stamp Exhibition, Bucharest.

2593 **691** 30c. multicoloured . . . 1·10 50

692 Camilo Cienfuegos

1979. 20th Anniv of Disappearance of Camilo Cienfuegos (revolutionary).

2594 **692** 3c. multicoloured 25 10

693 Alvaro Reinoso and Sugar Cane

1979. 15th Anniv of Sugar Cane Institute and 150th Birth Anniv of Alvaro Reinoso.

2595 **693** 13c. multicoloured . . . 60 15

694 Chimpanzees

1979. Young Zoo Animals. Multicoloured.

2596 1c. Type **694** 25 10
2597 2c. Leopards 25 10
2598 3c. Fallow deer 25 10
2599 4c. Lions 25 10
2600 5c. Brown bears 25 10
2601 13c. Eurasian red squirrels 40 25
2602 30c. Giant pandas 95 40
2603 50c. Tigers . . . . 1·80 85

695 Ground Receiving Station

1979. Air. 50th Anniv of International Radio Consultative Committee.

2604 **695** 30c. multicoloured . . . 1·10 30

696 "Rhina oblita"

1980. Insects. Multicoloured.

2605 1c. Type **696** 15 10
2606 5c. "Odontocera josemartii" (vert) 15 10
2607 6c. "Pinthocoelium columbinum" 15 10
2608 10c. "Calosoma splendida" (vert) 35 10
2609 13c. "Homophileurus cubanus" (vert) 75 25
2610 30c. "Heterops dimidiata" (vert) . . . . 1·50 65

697 Weightlifting

1980. Olympic Games, Moscow. Multicoloured.

2611 1c. Type **697** 15 10
2612 2c. Shooting 15 10
2613 5c. Javelin 15 10
2614 6c. Wrestling 15 10
2615 8c. Judo 20 10
2616 10c. Running 20 15
2617 13c. Boxing 45 25
2618 30c. Volleyball . . . . . . 1·30 60
MS2619 94 × 79 mm. 50c. Misha the bear (mascot) (27 × 35 mm) . . 2·50 2·20

698 "Oak Trees" (Henry Joseph Harpignies)

1980. National Museum Paintings (14th series). Multicoloured.

2620	1c. Type **698**	15	10
2621	4c. "Family Reunion" (Willem van Mieris) (horiz)	15	10
2622	6c. "Poultry" (Melchior de Hondecoeter)	15	10
2623	9c. "Innocence" (Williams A. Bouguereau)	55	15
2624	13c. "Venetian Scene II" (Michele Marieschi) (horiz)	70	25
2625	30c. "Spanish Country-women" (Joaquin Dominguez Bequer)	1·50	55

699 "Malvern Hall" (John Constable)

1980. London 1980 International Stamp Exhibition. Sheet 104 × 51 mm.

MS2626	**699** 50c. multicoloured	3·00	3·00

700 Intercosmos Emblem

1980. Intercosmos Programme. Mult.

2627	1c. Type **700**	15	10
2628	4c. Satellite and globe (Physics)	15	10
2629	6c. Satellite and dish aerial (Communications)	15	10
2630	10c. Satellite, grid lines and map (Meteorology)	35	15
2631	13c. Staff of Aesculapius, rocket and satellites (Biology and Medicine)	45	25
2632	30c. Surveying Satellite	1·50	55

701 Cuban Stamps of 1955 and 1959 (½-size illustration)

1980. 125th Anniv of Cuban Stamps.

2633	**701** 30c. blue, red & lt blue	1·00	50

702 "Bletia purpurea"

1980. Orchids. Multicoloured.

2634	1c. Type **702**	20	10
2635	4c. "Oncidium leiboldii"	20	10
2636	6c. "Epidendrum cochieatum"	20	10
2637	10c. "Cattleyopsis lindenii"	50	10
2638	13c. "Encyclia fucata"	90	25
2639	30c. "Encyclia phoenicea"	2·00	60

703 Bottle-nosed Dolphin

1980. Marine Mammals. Multicoloured.

2640	1c. Type **703**	40	10
2641	3c. Humpback whale (vert)	40	10
2642	13c. Cuvier's beaked whale	1·20	15
2643	30c. Caribbean monk seal	3·00	60

704 Houses

705 Pitcher

1980. "Moncada" Programme. Mult.

2644	3c. Type **704**	15	10
2645	13c. Refinery	30	15

ANNIVERSARIES: 3c. Urban Reform (20th Anniv). 13c. Foreign industry (20th Anniv).

1980. Copper Handicrafts. Multicoloured.

2646	3c. Type **705**	15	10
2647	13c. Wine container (38 × 26 mm)	55	25
2648	30c. Two handled pitcher	1·10	40

706 Emblem, Flag and Roses

707 "Clotilde in her Garden" (J. Sorolla y Bastida)

1980. 20th Anniv of Cuban Women's Federation.

2649	**706** 3c. multicoloured	30	15

1980. Espamer 80 Stamp Exhibition, Madrid. Sheet 91 × 53 mm.

MS2650	**707** 50c. multicoloured	3·00	3·00

708 Flags

1980. 20th Anniv of 1st Havana Declaration.

2651	**708** 13c. multicoloured	40	25

709 Building Galleon "Nuesta Sra. de Atocha", 1620

1980. Cuban Shipbuilding. Multicoloured.

2652	1c. Type **709**	15	10
2653	3c. Building ship of the line "El Rayo", 1749	15	10
2654	7c. Building ship of the line "Santisima Trinidad", 1769	15	10
2655	10c. "Santisima Trinidad" at sea, 1805 (vert)	45	10
2656	13c. Building steamships "Colon" and "Congreso", 1851	95	15
2657	30c. Cardenas and Chullima shipyards	1·60	50

710 Arnaldo Tamayo

1980. Air. 1st Cuban–Soviet Space Flight.

2658	**710** 13c. multicoloured	40	15
2659	30c. multicoloured	1·20	40

711 U.N. General Assembly

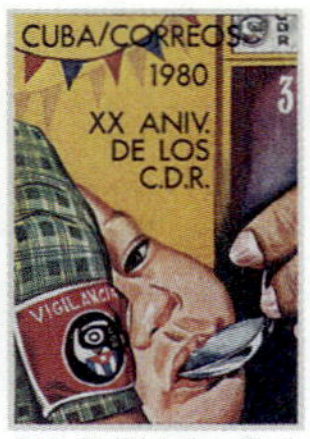

712 Child being Fed

1980. 20th Anniv of Fidel Castro's First Speech at the United Nations.

2660	**711** 13c. multicoloured	45	15

1980. 20th Anniv of Revolution's Defence Committees.

2661	**712** 3c. multicoloured	25	15

713 "Portrait of a Lady" (Ludger Tom Ring, the younger)

1980. 49th International Philatelic Federation Congress, Essen. Sheet 94 × 54 mm.

MS2662	**713** 50c. multicoloured	3·00	2·75

714 Inspection Locomotive

1980. Early Locomotives. Multicoloured.

2663	1c. Type **714**	20	10
2664	2c. Inspection locomotive, Chaparra Sugar Company	20	10
2665	7c. Fireless locomotive, San Francisco Sugar Mill	20	10
2666	10c. Saddle-tank locomotive, Australia Estate	40	10
2667	13c. Steam locomotive	70	15
2668	30c. Oil-fired locomotive, 1909, Smith Comas Estate	1·70	55

715 "Roncali" Lighthouse, San Antonio

1980. Lighthouses (1st series). Multicoloured.

2669	3c. Type **715**	15	10
2670	13c. Jagua, Cienfuegos	55	25
2671	30c. Punta Maisi, Guantanamo	1·30	40

See also Nos. 2746/8, 2859/61 and 2920/2.

716 Bronze Medal

1980. Cuban Olympic Medal Winners. Mult.

2672	13c. Type **716**	40	15
2673	30c. Silver medal	90	25
2674	50c. Gold medal	1·80	70

717 "Pancratium arenicolum"

719 Congress Emblem

718 Locomotive "La Junta", 1840s

1980. Forest Flowers. Multicoloured.

2675	1c. Type **717**	15	10
2676	4c. "Urechites lutea"	15	10
2677	6c. "Solanum elaegnifolium"	20	10
2678	10c. "Hamelia patens"	45	10
2679	13c. "Morinda royoc"	70	25
2680	30c. "Centrosema virginianum"	1·90	50

1980. 7th National Stamp Exhibition. Sheet 100 × 49 mm.

MS2681	**718** 50c. multicoloured	3·00	3·00

1980. 2nd Communist Party Congress. Mult.

2682	3c. Type **719**	15	10
2683	13c. Dish aerial and factories (Industry)	30	15
2684	30c. Gymnast, reader and elderly man resting (Recreation)	90	25

720 "Lady Mayo" (Anton van Dyck)

1981. National Museum Paintings (15th series). Multicoloured.

2685	1c. Type **720**	15	10
2686	6c. "La Hilandera" (Giovanni B. Piazzeta)	15	10
2687	10c. "Daniel Collyer" (Francis Cotes)	40	10
2688	13c. "Gardens of Palma de Mallorca" (Santiago Rusinol) (horiz)	50	25
2689	20c. "Landscape with Road and Houses" (Frederick W. Watts) (horiz)	80	30
2690	50c. "Landscape with Sheep" (Jean F. Millet) (horiz)	1·70	70

721 Short-finned Mako

1981. Fishes. Multicoloured.

2691	1c. Type **721**	20	10
2692	3c. Opah	20	10
2693	10c. Sailfish	40	15
2694	13c. Oceanic sunfish (vert)	1·50	25
2695	30c. Dolphin and flying-fish	95	40
2696	50c. White marlin	1·70	90

722 Saving Ball

1981. World Cup Football Championship, Spain (1982). (1st issue). Multicoloured.
2697 1c. Diving for ball (horiz) . . . 15 10
2698 2c. Passing ball (horiz) . . . 15 10
2699 3c. Running with ball (horiz) 15 10
2700 10c. Type **722** 35 15
2701 13c. Heading ball 35 15
2702 50c. Tackle (horiz) . . . . 1·50 85
MS2703 94 × 55 mm. 1p. Spanish flag and football . . . . 4·00 4·00
See also Nos. 2775/**MS**2782.

723 Mother, Child, Boots and Toy Train

724 Jules Verne, Konstantin Tsiolkovsky and Sergei Korolev

1981. 20th Anniv of Kindergartens.
2704 **723** 3c. multicoloured 60 10

1981. 20th Anniv of First Man in Space. Mult.
2705 1c. Type **724** 15 10
2706 2c. Yuri Gagarin (first man in space) (horiz) 15 10
2707 3c. Valentina Tereshkova (first woman in space) (horiz) 15 10
2708 5c. Aleksandr Leonov (first space walker) (horiz) . . . 15 10
2709 13c. Crew of "Voskhod I" (horiz) 35 15
2710 30c. Ryumen and Popov (horiz) 85 40
2711 50c. Tamayo and Romanenko (crew of Soviet–Cuban flight) . . . 1·90 70

725 Jet Fighters and Rocket

1981. 20th Anniv of Defeat of Invasion Attempt by Cuban Exiles. Multicoloured.
2712 3c. Type **725** (Defence and Air Force Day) 15 10
2713 13c. Hand waving machine-pistol (Victory at Giron) 35 25
2714 30c. Book and flags (Proclamation of Revolution's socialist character) (horiz) 85 55

726 Reynold Garcia Garcia (leader of attack), Barracks and Children

1981. 25th Anniv of Attack on Goicuria Barracks.
2715 **726** 3c. multicoloured 40 15

727 Tractor and Women planting Crops

1981. 20th Anniv of National Association of Small Farmers.
2716 **727** 3c. multicoloured 40 15

728 Austrian Stag Stamp, 1959

1981. WIPA 81 International Stamp Exhibition, Vienna. Sheet 103 × 50 mm.
MS2717 **728** 50c. multicoloured 2·50 2·50

729 Canelo

1981. Fighting Cocks. Multicoloured.
2718 1c. Type **729** 15 10
2719 3c. Cenizo (horiz) 15 10
2720 7c. Blanco 20 10
2721 13c. Pinto 40 10
2722 30c. Giro (horiz) . . . . . 1·00 40
2723 50c. Jabao . . . . 1·80 70

730 Anniversary Emblem

731 "Mother and Child" (wood-engraving by Zlatka Dabov)

1981. 20th Anniv of Ministry of the Interior.
2724 **730** 13c. multicoloured . . . 30 15

1981. 1300th Anniv of Bulgarian State and Bulgaria 81 International Stamp Exhibition. Sheet 58 × 92 mm.
MS2725 **731** 50c. black, silver and gold . . . . 2·20 2·20

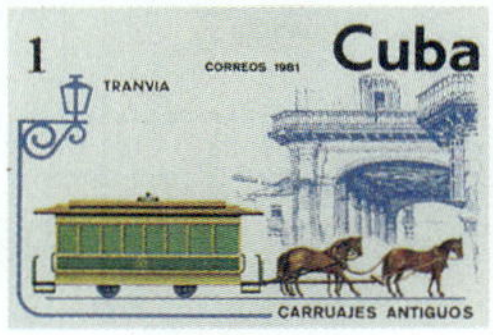

732 Tram

1981. Horse-drawn Vehicles. Multicoloured.
2726 1c. Type **732** 15 10
2727 4c. Village bus 15 10
2728 9c. Brake 20 10
2729 13c. Landau 30 10
2730 30c. Phaeton . . . . 1·10 45
2731 50c. Hearse . . . . 2·00 75

733 "House in the Country" (Maria Cardidad de la O)

735 Gymnasts

734 Sandinista Guerrilla and Map of Nicaragua

1981. International Year of Disabled People.
2732 **733** 30c. multicoloured . . . 1·10 30

1981. 20th Anniv of Sandinista National Liberation Front.
2733 **734** 13c. multicoloured . . . 40 20

1981. 20th Anniv of State Organizations. Mult.
2734 3c. Type **735** (National Sports and Physical Recreation Institute) . . . 15 10
2735 13c. "RHC", radio waves and map (Radio Havana) 35 25
2736 30c. Arrows ("Mincex" Foreign Trade Ministry) 1·10 40

736 Carlos J. Finlay, Mosquito and Theory

1981. Centenary of Biological Vectors Theory.
2737 **736** 13c. multicoloured . . . 80 25

737 Arms of Non-aligned Countries, Manacled Hands and Hands releasing Dove

1981. 20th Anniv of Non-aligned Countries Movement.
2738 **737** 50c. multicoloured . . . 1·70 95

738 White Horse

1981. Horses. Multicoloured.
2739 1c. Type **738** 15 10
2740 3c. Brown horse 15 10
2741 8c. Bucking white horse . . 15 10
2742 13c. Horse being broken-in 35 25
2743 30c. Black horse . . . . . 1·10 45
2744 50c. Herd of horses (horiz) 1·70 70

739 "Idyll in a Tea House" (Kitagawa Utamaro)

1981. Philatokyo 81 International Stamp Exhibition. Sheet 92 × 58 mm.
MS2745 **739** 50c. multicoloured 2·50 2·50

1981. Lighthouses (2nd series). As T **715**. Mult.
2746 3c. Piedras del Norte . . . 15 10
2747 13c. Punta Lucrecia 40 15
2748 40c. Guano del Este . . . . 1·70 60

740 "Flor de Cuba Sugar Mill"

1981. 80th Anniv of Jose Marti National Library. Lithographs by Eduardo Laplante. Multicoloured.
2749 3c. Type **740** 15 10
2750 13c. "El Progreso Sugar Mill" 30 15
2751 30c. "Santa Teresa Sugar Mill" . . . . 1·00 60

741 Pablo Picasso and Cuban Stamp

1981. Birth Centenary of Pablo Picasso (artist).
2752 **741** 30c. multicoloured . . . 1·10 35

742 Sailing Ship

1981. Espamer 81 International Stamp Exhibition, Buenos Aires. Sheet 96 × 54 mm.
MS2753 **742** 1p. multicoloured 4·00 3·75

743 "Napoleon in Coronation Regalia" (Anon.)

1981. 20th Anniv of Napoleonic Museum. Mult.
2754 1c. Type **743** 15 10
2755 3c. "Napoleon with Landscape" (J. H. Vernet) (horiz) 15 10
2756 10c. "Bonaparte in Egypt" (Eduard Detaille) . . . 30 25
2757 13c. "Napoleon on Horseback" (Hippolyte Bellange) (horiz) 30 25
2758 30c. "Napoleon in Normandy" (Bellange) (horiz) . . . . 1·00 50
2759 50c. "Death of Napoleon" (Anon) . . . . 1·70 85

744 Revolutionaries

745 Cuban Emerald ("Zun-Zun")

1981. 25th Anniversaries. Multicoloured.
2760 3c. Type **744** (30th November insurrection) 15 10
2761 20c. Soldier (Revolutionary Armed Forces) 35 15
2762 1p. Launch "Granma" (disembarkation of revolutionary forces) 4·00 1·40

1981. Fauna.
2763 **745** 1c. blue 50 10
2764 – 2c. green 70 25
2765 – 5c. brown 15 25
2766 – 20c. red 70 25
2767 – 35c. lilac 1·30 40
2768 – 40c. grey 1·90 60
DESIGNS: 2c. Cuban conure ("Catey"); 5c. Desmarest's hutia; 20c. Cuban solenodon; 35c. American manatee; 40c. Crocodile.

746 Ortiz (after Jorge Arche y Silva)

747 Conrado Benitez

1981. Birth Centenary of Fernando Ortiz (folklorist). Multicoloured.
2769 3c. Type **746** 15 10
2770 10c. Idol (pendant) 30 15
2771 30c. Arara drum 1·20 45
2772 50c. Thunder god (Chango carving) 1·80 70

1981. 20th Anniv of Literacy Campaign. Mult.
2773 5c. Type **747** 25 15
2774 5c. Manuel Ascunce 25 15

748 Goalkeeper

749 Lazaro Pena (trade union delegate)

1982. World Cup Football Championship, Spain (2nd issue). Multicoloured.
2775 1c. Type **748** 15 10
2776 2c. Footballers 15 10
2777 5c. Heading ball 15 10
2778 10c. Kicking ball 25 15
2779 20c. Running for ball (horiz) 65 25
2780 40c. Tackle (horiz) 1·30 60
2781 50c. Shooting for goal 1·70 95
MS2782 62 × 109 mm. 1p. Feet and football (31 × 39 mm) 4·25 4·25

1982. 10th World Trade Unions' Congress, Havana.
2783 **749** 30c. multicoloured 95 50

750 "Euptoieta hegesia hegesia"

1982. Butterflies. Multicoloured.
2784 1c. Type **750** 15 10
2785 4c. "Metamorpha stelenes insularis" 15 10
2786 5c. "Helicantus charithanius ramsdeni" 15 10
2787 20c. "Phoebis avellaneda" 1·20 30
2788 30c. "Hamadryas ferox diasia" 1·90 50
2789 50c. "Marpesia eleuchea eleuchea" 3·50 90

751 Lobster

1982. Exports.
2790 – 3c. green 15 10
2791 **751** 4c. red 15 10
2792 – 6c. blue 20 10
2793 – 7c. orange 30 10
2794 – 8c. lilac 30 10
2795 – 9c. grey 30 15
2796 – 10c. lilac 40 15
2797 – 30c. brown 60 25
2798 – 50c. red 1·70 50
2799 – 1p. brown 3·25 1·30
DESIGNS—HORIZ: 3c. Sugar; 6c. Tinned fruit; 7c. Agricultural machinery; 8c. Nickel. VERT: 9c. Rum; 10c. Coffee; 30c. Citrus fruit; 50c. Cigars; 1p. Cement.

752 "Greenland" (cottage tulip)

1982. Tulips. Multicoloured.
2800 1c. Type **752** 15 10
2801 3c. "Mariette" (Lily-flowered tulip) 20 10
2802 8c. "Ringo" (triumph) 20 15
2903 20c. "Black Tulip" (Darwin) 50 25
2804 30c. "Jewel of Spring" (Darwin hybrid) 1·20 40
2805 50c. "Orange Parrot" (parrot tulip) 1·60 70

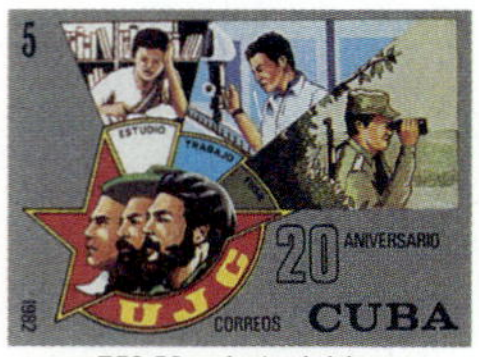

753 Youth Activities

1982. 20th Anniv of Communist Youth Union.
2806 **753** 5c. multicoloured 25 15

754 "Mars" Satellite

1982. Cosmonautics Day. Second United Nations Conference on Exploration and Peaceful Uses of Outer Space. Multicoloured.
2807 1c. Type **754** 15 10
2808 3c. "Venera" satellite 15 10
2809 6c. "Salyut–Soyuz" link-up 20 10
2810 20c. "Lunokhod" moon vehicle 40 15
2811 30c. "Venera" with heatshield 1·10 30
2812 50c. "Kosmos" satellite 1·70 60

755 Letter from British Postal Agency, Havana, to Vera Cruz

1982. Stamp Day. Multicoloured.
2813 20c. Type **755** 65 20
2814 30c. Letter from French postal agency, Havana, to Tampico, Mexico 1·10 25

756 Map of Cuba and Wave Pattern

757 "Portrait of Young Woman" (Jean Greuze)

1982. 20th Anniv of Cuban Broadcasting and Television Institute.
2815 **756** 30c. multicoloured 85 25

1982. National Museum Paintings (16th series). Multicoloured.
2816 1c. Type **757** 15 10
2817 3c. "Procession in Brittany" (Jules Breton) (46 × 36 mm) 15 10
2818 9c. "Landscape" (Jean Piliment) (horiz) 20 15
2819 20c. "Towards Evening" (William Bourgueran) 50 20
2820 30c. "Tiger" (Delacroix) (horiz) 1·00 30
2821 40c. "The Chair" (Wilfredo Lam) 1·60 40

758 Steamship "Louisiane" at St. Nazaire

1982. Philexfrance 82 International Stamp Exhibition, Paris. Sheet 110 × 60 mm.
MS2822 **758** 1p. multicoloured 4·50 4·50

759 Hurdling and 1930 Sports Stamp

1982. "Deporfilex '82" Stamp and Coin Exhibition, Havana.
2823 **759** 20c. multicoloured 1·20 40
See also No. **MS**2840.

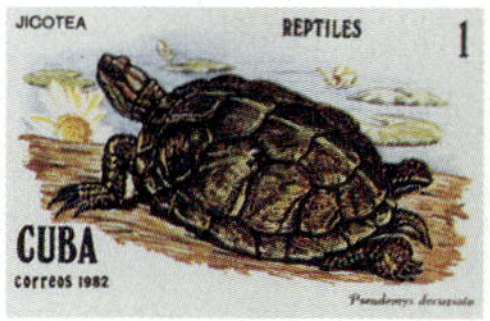

760 Tortoise

1982. Reptiles. Multicoloured.
2824 1c. Type **760** 15 10
2825 2c. Snake 15 10
2826 3c. Cuban crocodile 20 10
2827 20c. Iguana 70 25
2828 30c. Lizard 1·10 35
2829 50c. Snake 2·00 50

761 Georgi Dimitrov

763 Baseball

762 Dr. Robert Koch and Bacillus

1982. Birth Centenary of Georgi Dimitrov (Bulgarian statesman).
2830 **761** 30c. multicoloured 95 25

1982. Centenary of Discovery of Tubercle Bacillus.
2831 **762** 20c. multicoloured 1·00 25

1982. 14th Central American and Caribbean Games, Havana. Multicoloured.
2832 1c. Type **763** 15 10
2833 2c. Boxing 15 10
2834 10c. Water polo 30 15
2835 20c. Javelin 70 35
2836 35c. Weightlifting 1·10 50
2837 50c. Volleyball 1·70 60

764 "Eichornia crassipes"

1982. 20th Anniv of Hydraulic Development Plan.
2838 5c. Type **764** 30 15
2839 20c. "Nymphaea alba" 80 25

765 Crocodile Mascot

1982. Deporfilex 82 Stamp and Coin Exhibition, Havana (2nd issue). Sheet 77 × 52 mm.
MS2840 **765** 1p. multicoloured 4·25 4·25

766 Hand holding Gun

1982. Namibia Day.
2841 **766** 50c. multicoloured 1·60 95

767 Goal

768 "Devil" (V. P. Landaluse)

1982. World Cup Football Championship Finalists. Multicoloured.
2842 5c. Type **767** 15 10
2843 20c. Heading ball 65 35
2844 30c. Tackle 95 40
2845 50c. Saving goal 1·70 80

1982. 20th Anniv of National Folk Ensemble. Multicoloured.
2846 20c. Type **768** 70 30
2847 30c. "Epiphany festival" (V.P. Landaluze) (horiz) 1·00 50

769 Prehistoric Owl

1982. Prehistoric Animals. Multicoloured.
2848 1c. Type **769** 60 20
2849 5c. "Crocodylus rhombifer" (horiz) 15 10
2850 7c. Prehistoric eagle 2·75 40
2851 20c. "Geocapromys colombianus" (horiz) 60 25
2852 35c. "Megalocnus rodens" 1·00 60
2853 50c. "Nesophontes micrus" (horiz) 1·40 85

770 Che Guevara

1982. 15th Death Anniv of "Che" Guevara (guerrilla fighter).
2854 **770** 20c. multicoloured . . . 80 25

771 Christopher Columbus, "Santa Maria" and Map of Cuba

1982. 490th Anniv of Discovery of America by Columbus. Multicoloured.
2855 5c. Type **771** 95 25
2856 20c. "Santa Maria" (vert) 1·10 35
2857 35c. Caravel "Pinta" (vert) 1·80 65
2858 50c. Caravel "Nina" (vert) 2·20 85

1982. Lighthouses (3rd series). As T **715**. Multicoloured.
2859 5c. Cayo Jutias 70 10
2860 20c. Cayo Paredon Grande 1·90 20
2861 30c. Morro, Santiago de Cuba . . . . 2·50 50

772 George Washington (anonymous painting)

1982. 250th Birth Anniv of George Washington. Multicoloured.
2862 5c. Type **772** 20 10
2863 20c. Portrait of Washington by Daniel Huntington . . 65 25

773 Paddle-steamer "Almendares"

1982. 8th National Stamp Exhibition, Ciego de Avila. Sheet 110 × 60 mm.
MS2864 **773** 1p. multicoloured 4·25 4·25

774 Steam Locomotive (1917) and Boating Lake

1982. 10th Anniv of Lenin Park, Havana.
2865 **774** 5c. multicoloured 50 15

775 Capablanca as Child and Chess King

1982. 40th Death Anniv of Jose Capablanca (chess player). Multicoloured.
2866 5c. Type **775** 20 15
2867 20c. Capablanca and rook 90 25
2868 30c. Capablanca and knight 1·20 45
2869 50c. Capablanca and queen 1·90 70

776 Lenin, Marx, Russian Arms and Kremlin Tower

1982. 60th Anniv of U.S.S.R.
2870 **776** 30c. multicoloured . . . 1·10 20

777 Methods of Communications

1983. World Communications Year (1st issue).
2871 **777** 20c. multicoloured . . . 65 20
See also Nos. 2929/33.

778 Birthplace and Birth Centenary Stamp

1983. 130th Birth Anniv of Jose Marti (writer).
2872 **778** 5c. multicoloured 25 15

779 Throwing the Javelin

780 "Che" Guevara and Radio Waves

1983. Olympic Games, Los Angeles (1984). Multicoloured.
2873 1c. Type **779** 15 10
2874 5c. Volleyball 20 10
2875 6c. Basketball 20 10
2876 20c. Weightlifting 70 25
2877 30c. Wrestling . . . . . . 1·00 50
2878 50c. Boxing . . . . 1·60 70
MS2879 94 × 54 mm. 1p. Judo (28 × 36 mm) . . . . 4·50 4·50

1983. 25th Anniv of Radio Rebelde.
2880 **780** 20c. multicoloured . . . 60 25

781 Karl Marx

1983. Death Centenary of Karl Marx.
2881 **781** 30c. multicoloured . . . 95 50

782 Charles's Hydrogen Balloon

783 "Vostok 1"

1983. Bicentenary of Manned Flight. Mult.
2882 1c. Type **782** 15 10
2883 3c. Montgolfier balloon . . 15 10
2884 5c. Montgolfier balloon "Le Gustave" 15 10
2885 7c. Eugene Godard's quintuple "acrobatic" balloon 30 10
2886 30c. Montgolfier unmanned balloon . . . . 1·80 70
2887 50c. Charles Green's balloon "Royal Vauxhall" . . . . 2·00 95
MS2888 89 × 60 mm. 1p. Jose Domingo Blino (first Cuban balloonist) (28 × 36 mm) . . . 4·00 4·00

1983. Cosmonautics Day. Multicoloured.
2889 1c. Type **783** 15 10
2890 4c. French "D1" satellite . . 20 10
2891 5c. "Mars 2" 25 10
2892 20c. "Soyuz" 65 25
2893 30c. Meteorological satellite 95 45
2894 50c. Intercosmos programme 1·50 70

784 Letter sent by First International Airmail Service

1983. Stamp Day. Multicoloured.
2895 20c. Type **784** 65 25
2896 30c. Letter sent by first Atlantic airmail service . . 1·10 30

785 Weasel

1983. Brasiliana 83 International Stamp Exhibition, Rio de Janeiro. 50th Death Anniv of Santos Dumont (Brazilian aviator). Sheet 101 × 71 mm.
MS2897 **785** 1p. multicoloured 5·00 5·00

786 Jose Rafael de las Heras

1983. Birth Bicentenary of Simon Bolivar. Mult.
2898 5c. Type **786** 25 15
2899 20c. Simon Bolivar 60 25

787 J. L. Tasende, Abel Santamaria and B. L. Santa Coloma

1983. 30th Anniv of Attack on Moncada Fortress. Multicoloured.
2900 5c. Jose Marti and fortress (horiz) 15 10
2901 20c. Type **787** 65 25
2902 30c. Symbol of Castro's book "History Will Absolve Me" 85 45

789 Weightlifting

1983. 9th Pan-American Games, Caracas. Mult.
2904 1c. Type **789** 15 10
2905 2c. Volleyball 15 10
2906 3c. Baseball 25 10
2907 20c. High jump 65 25
2908 30c. Basketball 95 45
2909 40c. Boxing . . . . 1·50 70

790 "Harbour" (Claude Vernet)

1983. Centenary of French Alliance (French language-teaching association).
2910 **790** 30c. multicoloured . . . 2·30 70

791 Salvador Allende and burning Presidential Palace

1983. 10th Death Anniv of Salvador Allende (President of Chile).
2911 **791** 20c. multicoloured . . . 65 25

792 Regional Peasants Committee

1983. 25th Anniv of Peasants in Arms Congress.
2912 **792** 5c. multicoloured 20 10

793 "Portrait of a Young Man"

1983. 500th Birth Anniv of Raphael. Mult.
2913 1c. "Girl with Veil" 15 10
2914 2c. "The Cardinal" 15 10
2915 5c. "Francesco M. della Rovere" 25 10
2916 20c. Type **793** 65 25
2917 30c. "Magdalena Doni" . . 95 50
2918 50c. "La Fornarina" . . . . 1·50 85

794 Quality Seal and Exports

1983. State Quality Seal.
2919 **794** 5c. multicoloured 20 10

1983. Lighthouses (4th series). As T **715**. Multicoloured.
2920 5c. Carapachibey, Isle of Youth 15 10
2921 20c. Cadiz Bay 65 35
2922 30c. Punta Gobernadora . . 1·60 70

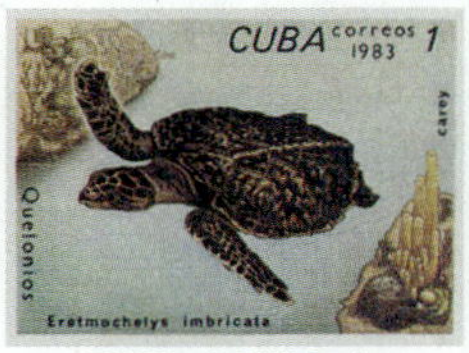

795 Hawksbill Turtle

1983. Turtles. Multicoloured.
2923 1c. Type **795** 15 10
2924 2c. "Lepidochelys kempi" 15 10
2925 5c. "Chrysemys decusata" 20 10
2926 20c. Loggerhead turtle . . . 65 25
2927 30c. Green turtle . . . . . 1·10 40
2928 50c. "Dermochelys coriacea" 2·20 85

796 Bell's Gallow Frame and Modern Telephones

1983. World Communications Year (2nd issue). Multicoloured.

2929 1c. Type **796** 15 10
2930 5c. Telegram and airmail envelopes and U.P.U. emblem 25 10
2931 10c. Satellite and antenna 35 15
2932 20c. Telecommunications satellite and dish aerial . . 65 25
2933 30c. Television and Radio Commemorative plaque and tower block 95 40

797 Cuban Stamps of 1933 and 1965

1983. 150th Birth Anniv of Carlos J. Finlay (malaria researcher).

2934 **797** 20c. multicoloured . . . 75 20

798 "Jatropha angustifolia"

799 Tobacco Flowers

1983. Flora and Fauna. Multicoloured. (a) Flowers.

2935 5c. Type **798** 40 15
2936 5c. "Cochlospermum vitifolium" 40 15
2937 5c. "Tabebuia lepidota" . . 40 15
2938 5c. "Kalmiella ericoides" . . 40 15
2939 5c. "Jatropha integerrima" 40 15
2940 5c. "Melocactus actinacanthus" 40 15
2941 5c. "Cordia sebestana" 40 15
2942 5c. "Tabernaemontana apoda" 40 15
2943 5c. "Lantana camera" . . . 40 15
2944 5c. "Cordia gerascanthus" 40 15
2945 5c. "Opuntia dillenii" . . . 40 15
2946 5c. "Euphorbia podocarpifolia" 40 15
2947 5c. "Dinema cubincola" . . 40 15
2948 5c. "Guaiacum officinale" 40 15
2949 5c. "Magnolia cubensis" . . 40 15

(b) Birds.

2950 5c. Bee hummingbird . . . 40 15
2951 5c. Northern mockingbird 40 15
2952 5c. Cuban tody 40 15
2953 5c. Cuban Amazon 40 15
2954 5c. Zapata wren 40 15
2955 5c. Brown pelican 40 15
2956 5c. Great red-bellied woodpecker 40 15
2957 5c. Red-legged thrush . . . 40 15
2958 5c. Cuban conure 40 15
2959 5c. Eastern meadowlark . . 40 15
2960 5c. Cuban grassquit 40 15
2961 5c. White-tailed tropic bird 40 15
2962 5c. Cuban solitaire 40 15
2963 5c. Great lizard cuckoo . . 40 15
2964 5c. Cuban gnatcatcher . . . 40 15
MS2965 Two sheets each 95 × 55 mm. (a) 1p. "Hedychium coronarium" (flower); (b) 1p. Cuban trogon "Priotelus temnurus" . . . . 10·50 10·50

1983. Flowers.

2966 **799** 60c. green . . . . 1·90 60
2967 – 70c. red . . . . 2·30 70
2968 – 80c. blue . . . . 2·50 85
2969 – 90c. violet . . . . 3·75 1·10

DESIGNS: 70c. Lily; 80c. Mariposa; 90c. Orchid.

800 Flag and Plan of El Jigue Battlefield

1983. 25th Anniv of Revolution (1st issue). Multicoloured.

2970 5c. Type **800** 15 10
2971 20c. Flag and railway tracks at Santa Clara . . . . . 3·00 1·00

801 Flag and Revolutionaries

1983. 25th Anniv of Revolution (2nd issue). Multicoloured.

2972 20c. Type **801** 65 30
2973 20c. "25" and star 65 30
2974 20c. Workers and Cuban Communist Party emblem 65 30

802 Lazaro Gonzalez, CTC Emblem and 15th Congress Flag

1984. 45th Anniv of Revolutionary Workers' Union.

2975 **802** 5c. multicoloured 20 15

803 "Ixias balice balice"

1984. Butterflies. Multicoloured.

2976 1c. Type **803** 15 15
2977 2c. "Phoebis avellaneda avellaneda" 15 15
2978 3c. "Anthocaris sara sara" 15 15
2979 5c. "Victorina superba superba" 15 15
2980 20c. "Heliconius cydno cydnides" 80 25
2981 30c. "Parides gundlachianus calzadillae" . . . . . 1·40 65
2982 50c. "Catagramma sorana sorana" . . . . 2·40 90

804 Clocktower and Russian Stamps of 1924–25

1984. 60th Death Anniv of Lenin.

2983 **804** 30c. multicoloured . . . 1·10 20

805 Risso's Dolphin

1984. Whales and Dolphins. Multicoloured.

2984 1c. Type **805** 25 15
2985 2c. Common dolphin . . . 25 15
2986 5c. Sperm whale (horiz) . . 25 15
2987 6c. Spotted dolphin 25 15
2988 10c. False killer whale (horiz) 80 15
2989 30c. Bottle-nosed dolphin 1·40 30
2990 50c. Humpback whale (horiz) . . . . 2·20 60

806 Sandino and Crowd holding Banner

1984. 50th Death Anniv of Augusto C. Sandino.

2991 **806** 20c. multicoloured . . . 65 20

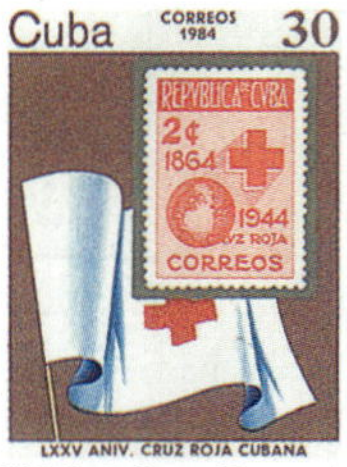

807 Red Cross Flag and Stamp of 1946

1984. 75th Anniv of Cuban Red Cross.

2992 **807** 30c. multicoloured . . . 1·10 30

808 Scene from Cartoon Film

1984. 25th Anniv of Cuban Cinema.

2993 **808** 20c. multicoloured . . . 85 30

809 "Brownea grandiceps"

1984. Caribbean Flowers. Multicoloured.

2994 1c. Type **809** 10 10
2995 2c. "Couroupita guianensis" 10 10
2996 5c. "Triplaris surinamensis" 15 10
2997 20c. "Amherstia nobilis" . . 85 30
2998 30c. "Plumieria alba" . . . 1·20 50
2999 50c. "Delonix regia" . . . . 2·20 90

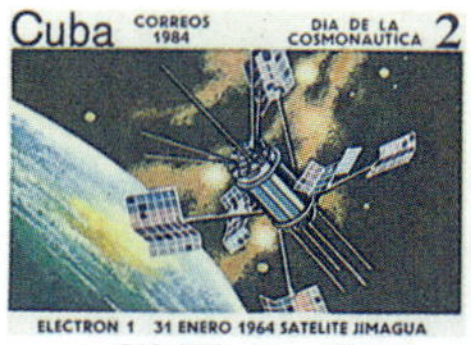

810 "Electron 1"

1984. Cosmonautics Day. Multicoloured.

3000 2c. Type **810** 10 10
3001 3c. "Electron 2" 10 10
3002 5c. "Intercosmos 1" 15 10
3003 10c. "Mars 5" 45 15
3004 30c. "Soyuz 1" . . . . . . 1·20 50
3005 50c. Soviet–Bulgarian space flight, 1979 . . . . . . 2·20 90
MS3006 98 × 53 mm. 1p. "Luna" (vert) . . . . 1·70 1·70

811 Mexican Mail Runner

1984. Stamp Day. Multicoloured.

3007 20c. Type **811** 85 30
3008 30c. Egyptian boatman . . 1·20 50

Nos. 3007/8 show details of mural by R. R. Radillo in Havana Stamp Museum.

See also Nos. 3097/8, 3170/1, 3336/7 and 3619/20.

812 "Buenos Aires" (mail steamer)

1984. Espana 84 International Stamp Exhibition, Madrid. Sheet 110 × 64 mm.

MS3009 **812** 1p. multicoloured 4·00 3·50

813 Basketball

1984. Pre-Olympics.

3010 **813** 20c. multicoloured . . . 1·10 30

814 Pink Roses

816 Saver and Pile of Coins

815 Workers in Field

1984. Mothers' Day. Multicoloured.

3011 20c. Type **814** 85 30
3012 20c. Red roses 85 30

1984. 25th Anniv of Land Reform Act.

3013 **815** 5c. multicoloured 35 10

1984. 1st Anniv of People's Saving Bank.

3014 **816** 5c. multicoloured 35 10

817 Locomotive

1984. Locomotives. Multicoloured.

3015 1c. Type **817** 15 10
3016 4c. Locomotive No. 73 . . . 20 10
3017 5c. Locomotive (different) 25 10
3018 10c. Locomotive (different) 45 15
3019 30c. Locomotive No. 350 . . 1·30 40
3020 50c. Locomotive No. 495 . . 2·20 80

818 Cuban stamp of 1877 1902

1984. 19th Universal Postal Union Congress Philatelic Salon, Hanburg. Sheet 97 × 67 mm.

MS3021 **818** 1p. multicoloured 4·00 3·50

819 Baron de Coubertin and Runner with Olympic Flame

1984. 90th Anniv of Int Olympic Committee.
3022 **819** 30c. multicoloured . . . 1·20 50

820 Baby with Toy Dog

1984. Children's Day.
3023 **820** 5c. multicoloured 25 10

821 Wrestling

822 Emilio Roig de Leuchsenring

1984. Olympic Games, Los Angeles. Mult.
3024 1c. Type **821** 10 10
3025 3c. Throwing the discus . . 10 10
3026 5c. Volleyball 15 10
3027 20c. Boxing 85 30
3028 30c. Basketball . . . . . 1·20 50
3029 50c. Weightlifting . . . . 2·20 90
MS3030 76 × 55 mm. 1p. Baseball 4·75 4·50

1984. 20th Death Anniv of Emilio Roig de Leuchsenring.
3031 **822** 5c. multicoloured 35 10

823 Men's Volleyball

1984. Friendship Tournament. Mult.
3032 3c. Type **823** 10 10
3033 5c. Women's volleyball . . . 20 10
3034 8c. Water polo 30 10
3035 30c. Boxing 85 30

824 Cow in Pasture

1984. Cattle. Multicoloured.
3036 2c. Type **824** 10 10
3037 3c. Cuban Carib 10 10
3038 5c. Charolaise (vert) 15 10
3039 30c. Cuban Cebu (vert) . . 1·10 30
3040 50c. White-udder cow . . . 1·90 65

825 Emu

1984. Ausipex 84 International Stamp Exhibition, Melbourne. Sheet 57 × 83 mm.
MS3041 **825** 1p. multicoloured 4·25 4·00

826 Polymita

1984. Cuban Wildlife. Multicoloured.
3042 1c. Type **826** 10 10
3043 2c. Cuban solenodon . . . 10 10
3044 3c. "Alsophis cantherigerus" (snake) 10 10
3045 4c. "Osteopilus septentrionalis" (frog) . . 15 10
3046 5c. Bee hummingbirds . . . 60 15
3047 10c. Bushy-tailed hutia . . . 35 15
3048 30c. Cuban tody . . . . . 2·50 95
3049 50c. Peach-faced lovebird . . 4·00 1·20

827 King Ferdinand and Queen Isabella

1984. "Espamer '85" International Stamp Exhibition, Havana. Multicoloured.
3050 5c. Type **827** 10 10
3051 20c. Columbus departing from Palos de Moguer . . 1·30 80
3052 30c. "Santa Maria", "Pinta" and "Nina" . . . . . . 1·90 1·40
3053 50c. Columbus arriving in America . . . . 1·00 70

828 Balwin tank Locomotive No. 498

1984. 75th Anniv of Havana—Santiago de Cuba Railway and Ninth National Stamp Exhibition, Santiago de Cuba. Sheet 108 × 75 mm.
MS3054 **828** 1p. multicoloured 4·00 3·25

829 Flag and Soldier

1984. 25th Anniv of National Militia.
3055 **829** 5c. multicoloured 25 10

830 Cienfuegos

1984. 25th Anniv of Disappearance of Camilo Cienfuegos (revolutionary).
3056 **830** 5c. multicoloured 35 10

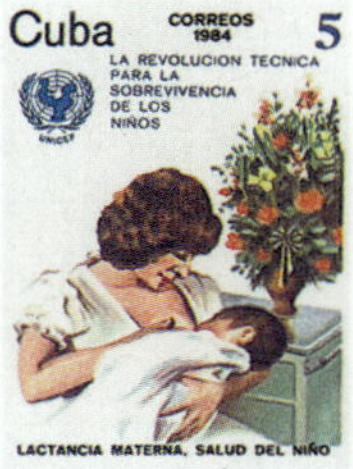

831 Mother breast-feeding Baby

1984. Infant Survival Campaign.
3057 **831** 5c. multicoloured 35 15

832 Morgan, 1909

1984. Cars. Multicoloured.
3058 1c. Type **832** 10 10
3059 2c. Austin, 1922 . . . . . 10 10
3060 5c. Dion-Bouton, 1903 . . . 10 10
3061 20c. "T" Ford, 1908 . . . . 80 15
3062 30c. Karl Benz, 1885 . . . 1·30 30
3063 50c. Karl Benz, 1910 . . . 2·40 65

833 18th-century Letters and Museum Emblem

1985. 20th Anniv of Cuban Postal Museum.
3064 **833** 20c. multicoloured . . . 65 25

834 Celia Sanchez (after E. Escobedo)

1985. 5th Death Anniv of Celia Sanchez (revolutionary).
3065 **834** 5c. multicoloured 35 15

835 Pigeon

1985. "Porto-1985" International Pigeon Exhibition, Oporto, Portugal.
3066 **835** 20c. multicoloured . . . 1·10 25

836 Chile (1962)

1985. World Cup Football Championship, Mexico (1986) (1st issue). Multicoloured.
3067 1c. Type **836** 10 10
3068 2c. England (1966) 10 10
3069 3c. Mexico (1970) 10 10
3070 4c. West Germany (1974) . . 15 10
3071 5c. Argentina (1978) 15 15
3072 30c. Spain (1982) . . . . . 1·20 50
3073 50c. Sweden (1958) . . . . 1·90 65
MS3074 84 × 64 mm. 1p. Footballers (39 × 31 mm) . . . . 3·50 2·75
See also Nos. 3135/**MS**41.

837 Pteranodon

1985. Baconao Valley National Park. Prehistoric Animals (1st series). Multicoloured.
3075 1c. Type **837** 35 15
3076 2c. Brontosaurus 35 15
3077 4c. Iguanodontus 35 15
3078 5c. Estegosaurus 35 15
3079 8c. Monoclonius 50 15
3080 30c. Corythosaurus . . . . 1·60 50
3081 50c. Tyrannosaurus . . . . 3·00 75
See also Nos. 3264/9.

838 Uruguay 1911 and Argentina 1921 Congress Stamps and Emblem (½-size illustration)

1985. 13th Postal Union of the Americas and Spain Congress, Havana.
3082 **838** 20c. multicoloured . . . 2·75 75

839 Indians playing Football

1985. Espamer '85 International Stamp Exhibition, Havana. Multicoloured.
3083 1c. Type **839** 15 15
3084 2c. Indian sitting by fire . . 15 15
3085 5c. Fishing with nets and spears 45 15
3086 20c. Making pottery 45 25
3087 30c. Hunting with spears . . 70 40
3088 50c. Decorating canoe and paddle . . . . 3·00 80
MS3089 91 × 51 mm. 1p. Women cooking (25 × 36 mm) . . . . 5·75 5·25
See also Nos. 3264/9.

840 Spaceship circling Moon

1985. Cosmonautics Day. Multicoloured.
3090 2c. Type **840** 10 10
3091 3c. Spaceships 10 10
3092 10c. Cosmonauts meeting in space 35 10
3093 13c. Cosmonauts soldering in space 50 15
3094 20c. "Vostok II" and Earth 60 25
3095 50c. "Lunayod I" crossing moon crater . . . . . . 2·00 65

841 Lenin's Tomb

842 Peonies

1985. 12th World Youth and Students' Festival, Moscow.
3096 **841** 30c. multicoloured . . . 70 50

1985. Stamp Day. As T **811**. Multicoloured.
3097 20c. Roman soldier and chariot 70 25
3098 30c. Medieval nobleman and monks 95 40

1985. Mothers' Day. Multicoloured.
3099 1c. Type **842** 10 10
3100 4c. Carnations 10 10
3101 5c. Dahlias 15 10
3102 13c. Roses 45 10
3103 20c. Roses (different) . . . 70 15
3104 50c. Tulips . . . . 1·70 55

843 Guiteras and Aponte

1985. 50th Death Anniv of Antonio Guiteras and Carlos Aponte (revolutionaries).
3105 **843** 5c. multicoloured 25 10

844 Star, "40" and Soldier with Flag

1985. 40th Anniv of End of Second World War.
3106 **844** 5c. multicoloured 15 15
3107 – 20c. multicoloured . . . 55 30
3108 – 30c. red, yellow & violet 95 45
DESIGNS: 20c. "40" and Soviet Memorial, Berlin-Treptow; 30c. Dove within "40".

845 Andean Condor

1985. Argentina 85 International Stamp Exhibition, Buenos Aires. Sheet 64 × 81 mm.
MS3109 **845** 1p. multicoloured 4·25 4·00

846 Daimler, 1885

1985. Centenary of the Motor Cycle. Multicoloured.
3110 2c. Type **846** 10 10
3111 5c. Kayser tricycle, 1910 . . 15 10
3112 10c. Fanomovil, 1925 . . . 35 10
3113 30c. Mars "A 20", 1926 . . 1·10 25
3114 50c. Simson "BSW", 1936 . 2·00 55

847 La Plata and Hermanos Ameijeiras Hospitals

1985. Development of Health Care since the Revolution.
3115 **847** 5c. multicoloured 25 10

848 Flowers and Soldier with Gun

1985. 25th Anniv of Federation of Cuban Women.
3116 **848** 5c. multicoloured 25 10

849 Athletes and Emblem

1985. World University Games, Kobe, Japan.
3117 **849** 50c. multicoloured . . . 1·50 55

850 Crowd, Flags and Statue

1985. 25th Anniv of First Havana Declaration.
3118 **850** 5c. multicoloured 35 15

851 Roman Cargo Ship

1985. Italia 85 International Stamp Exhibition, Rome. Sheet 97 × 62 mm.
MS3119 **851** 1p. multicoloured 4·25 3·50

852 Emblem in "25"

1985. 25th Anniv of Committees for Defence of the Revolution.
3120 **852** 5c. multicoloured 25 10

853 Cherub Angelfish

1985. Fishes. Multicoloured.
3121 1c. Type **853** 25 15
3122 3c. Rock beauty 25 15
3123 5c. Four-eyed butterflyfish 25 15
3124 10c. Reef butterflyfish . . . 45 25
3125 20c. Spot-finned butterflyfish 1·00 50
3126 50c. Queen angelfish . . . . 2·50 1·60

854 Cuban and Party Flags and Central Committee Building

856 U.N. Building, New York, and Emblem

855 Spain 1930 25c. and Cuba 1942 1c. Columbus Stamps

1985. 20th Anniv of Cuban Communist Party and Third Party Congress.
3127 **854** 5c. multicoloured 35 15

1985. Exfilna 85 International Stamp Exhibition, Madrid. Sheet 99 × 61 mm.
MS3128 **855** 1p. multicoloured 4·25 3·50

1985. 40th Anniv of U.N.O.
3129 **856** 20c. multicoloured . . . 80 25

857 Old Square and Arms

1985. UNESCO World Heritage. Old Havana. Multicoloured.
3130 2c. Type **857** 20 15
3131 5c. Real Fuerza Castle . . . 20 15
3132 20c. Havana Cathedral . . . 80 25
3133 30c. Captain General's Palace . . . . 1·30 40
3134 50c. El Templete . . . . . 2·10 55

858 Footballers

860 Ministry Emblem

859 Red Flags and Emblem

1986. World Cup Football Championship, Mexico (2nd issue).
3135 **858** 1c. multicoloured 10 10
3136 – 4c. multicoloured 10 10
3137 – 5c. multicoloured 15 10
3138 – 10c. multicoloured . . . 25 15
3139 – 30c. multicoloured . . . 95 30
3140 – 50c. multicoloured . . . 1·50 55
MS3141 94 × 50 mm. 1p. mult . . 4·00 3·50
DESIGNS: 4c. to 1p. Various footballing scenes.

1986. 3rd Cuban Communist Party Congress, Havana. Multicoloured.
3142 5c. Type **859** 10 10
3143 20c. Red and national flags 1·10 25

1986. 25th Anniv of Ministry of Interior Trade.
3144 **860** 5c. multicoloured 25 10

861 People practising Sports

862 "Tecomaria capensis"

1986. 25th Anniv of National Sports Institute.
3145 **861** 5c. multicoloured 25 10

1986. Exotic Flowers. Multicoloured.
3146 1c. Type **862** 10 10
3147 3c. "Michelia champaca" . . 15 10
3148 5c. "Thunbergia grandiflora" 15 10
3149 8c. "Dendrobium phalaenopsis" 25 10
3150 30c. "Allamanda violacea" 95 25
3151 50c. "Rhodocactus bleo" . . 1·60 40

863 Gundlach and Red-winged Blackbird

1986. 90th Death Anniv of Juan C. Gundlach (ornithologist). Multicoloured.
3152 1c. Type **863** 25 15
3153 3c. Olive-capped warbler . . 25 15
3154 7c. La Sagra's flycatcher . . 40 30
3155 9c. Yellow warbler 50 30
3156 30c. Grey-faced quail dove 2·00 1·20
3157 50c. Common flicker . . . 3·50 2·00

864 Pioneers and "25"

865 Gomez and Statue

1986. 25th Anniv of Jose Marti Pioneers.
3158 **864** 5c. multicoloured 25 10

1986. 150th Birth Anniv of Maximo Gomez.
3159 **865** 20c. multicoloured . . . 80 25

866 Nursery Nurse with Children

867 "Vostok" and Korolev (designer)

1986. 25th Anniv of Children's Day Care Centres.
3160 **866** 5c. multicoloured 35 10

1986. 25th Anniv of First Man in Space. Multicoloured.
3161 1c. Type **867** 10 10
3162 2c. Yuri Gargarin (first man in space) and "Vostok" 10 10
3163 5c. Valentina Tereshkova (first woman in space) and "Vostok" 15 10
3164 20c. "Salyut" space station 50 15
3165 30c. Capsule descending with parachute 70 25
3166 50c. "Soyuz" rocket on launch pad . . . . . . 1·50 55
MS3167 95 × 70 mm. 100p. Tsoilkovsky (scientist) . . . . 4·00 3·25

868 National Flag and 1981 Stamp

869 Reels as National Flag and Globe and Tape forming "25"

1986. 25th Anniv of Socialist State (1959) and Victory at Giron. Multicoloured.
3168 5c. Type **868** 15 10
3169 20c. Flags and arms 95 15

1986. Stamp Day. As T **811** showing details of mural by R. R. Radillo in Havana Stamp Museum. Multicoloured.
3170 20c. Early mail coach . . . 65 15
3171 30c. Express rider 85 25

1986. 25th Anniv of Radio Havana Cuba.
3172 **869** 5c. multicoloured 35 10

870 "Stourbridge Lion", U.S.A., 1829

1986. Expo '86 World's Fair, Vancouver. Railway Locomotives. Multicoloured.
3173 1c. Type **870** 10 10
3174 4c. "Rocket", Great Britain, 1829 . . . . 10 10
3175 5c. First Russian locomotive, 1845 . . . . 15 10
3176 8c. Marc Seguin's locomotive, France, 1830 25 15

3177 30c. First Canadian locomotive, 1836 . . . . 65 30
3178 50c. Steam locomotive, Belgium Grand Central Railway, 1872 . . . . . 1·60 40
MS3179 92 × 54 mm. 1p. Locomotive "La Junta", 1840s, Cuba . . . . 4·25 4·00

871 Hand holding Machete and Farmer ploughing and driving Tractor

1986. 25th Anniv of National Association of Small Farmers.
3180 **871** 5c. multicoloured 35 10

872 Dove and Arms on Coin

1986. International Peace Year.
3181 **872** 30c. multicoloured . . . 85 25

873 Emblem

1986. 25th Anniv of Ministry of the Interior.
3182 **873** 5c. multicoloured 35 15

874 King

1986. 18th Death Anniv of Martin Luther King (human rights campaigner).
3183 **874** 20c. multicoloured . . . 85 20

875 Bonifacio Byrne

1986. 50th Death Anniv of Bonifacio Byrne (poet).
3184 **875** 5c. multicoloured 25 10

876 Dove, Pen Nib and Paint Brush

877 Sandino and Pres. Ortega of Nicaragua

1986. 25th Anniv of National Union of Cuban Writers and Artists.
3185 **876** 5c. multicoloured 25 10

1986. 25th Anniv of Sandinista Movement of Nicaragua.
3186 **877** 20c. multicoloured . . . 65 20

878 Tanker, Tupolev Tu-154 and Lorry

1986. 25th Anniv of Ministry of Transport.
3187 **878** 5c. multicoloured 50 25

879 Sportsmen and Emblem

1986. 5th Central American and Caribbean University Games, Havana.
3188 **879** 20c. multicoloured . . . 85 20

880 Cuban Revolutionaries' 1897 2c. Stamp

1986. Stockholmia 86 International Stamp Exhibition. Sheet 111 × 70 mm containing T **880** and similar vert design. Multicoloured.
MS3189 50c. Type **880**; 50c. Sweden 1885 10ore. Stamp . . . . . . 4·00 3·00

881 Map

1986. 25th Anniv of Non-Aligned Countries Movement.
3190 **881** 50c. multicoloured . . . 1·70 40

882 "Cattleya hardyana"

1986. Orchids. Multicoloured.
3191 1c. Type **882** 10 10
3192 4c. "Brassolaeliocattleya" "Horizon Flight" 15 10
3193 5c. "Phalaenopsis" "Margit Moses" 15 15
3194 10c. "Laeliocattleya" "Prism Palette" 25 15
3195 30c. "Phalaenopsis violacea" 95 30
3196 50c. "Disa uniflora" . . . . 1·60 50

883 Mayan House and Jade Statue (Belize)

1986. Latin American History. Pre-Columbian Culture (1st series). Multicoloured.
3197 1c. Type **883** 10 10
3198 1c. Inca vessel and Gateway of the Sun, Tiahuanacu (Bolivia) 10 10
3199 1c. Spain 1930 1p. stamp of Columbus and 500th anniv of Columbus's discovery of America emblem 10 10
3200 1c. Diaguitan duck-shaped pitcher and ruins, Pucara de Quitor (Chile) 10 10
3201 1c. Archaeological park, San Augustin and Quimbayan statuette (Columbia) . . . 10 10
3202 5c. Moler memorial and Chorotega decorated earthenware statue (Costa Rica) 15 10
3203 5c. Tabaco idol and typical aboriginal houses (Cuba) 15 10
3204 5c. Spain 1930 40c. stamp of Martin Pinzon and anniversary emblem . . . 15 10
3205 5c. Typical houses and animal shaped seat (Dominica) 15 10
3206 5c. Tolita statue and Ingapirca fort (Ecuador) 15 10
3207 10c. Maya vase and Tikal temple (Guatemala) . . 25 15
3208 10c. Copan ruins and Maya idol (Honduras) 25 15
3209 10c. Spain 1930 30c. stamp of Vincent Pinzon and anniversary emblem . . . 25 15
3210 10c. Chichen-Itza temple and Zapoteca urn (Mexico) 25 15
3211 10c. Punta de Zapote idols and Ometepe ceramic (Nicaragua) 25 15
3212 20c. Tonosi ceramic and Barrile monolithic sculptures (Panama) . . . 60 25
3213 20c. Machu Picchu ruin and Inca figure (Peru) 60 25
3214 20c. Spain 1930 10p. stamp of Columbus and Pinzon brothers and anniversary emblem 60 25
3215 20c. Typical aboriginal dwellings and triangular stone carving (Puerto Rico) 60 25
3216 20c. Santa Ana female figure and Santo Domingo cave (Venezuela) 60 25
See also Nos. 3276/95, 3371/90, 3458/77, 3563/82, 3666/85 and 3769/88.

884 Medal and Soldier with Rifle

1986. 50th Anniv of Formation International Brigades in Spain.
3217 **884** 30c. multicoloured . . . 80 30

885 "Two Children" (Gutierrez de la Vega)

1986. National Museum Paintings (17th series). Multicoloured.
3218 2c. Type **885** 10 10
3219 4c. "Sed" (Jean-Gorges Vibert) (horiz) 10 10
3220 6c. "Virgin and Child" (Niccolo Abbate) 15 10
3221 10c. "Bullfight" (Eugenio de Lucas Velazquez) (horiz) 25 15
3222 30c. "The Five Senses" (Anon) (horiz) 95 30
3223 50c. "Meeting at Thomops Castle" (Jean Louis Ernest) (horiz) . . . . . 1·60 55

886 People and "Granma"

1986. 30th Annivs of "Granma" Landings (5c.) and Revolutionary Armed Forces (20c.). Multicoloured.
3224 5c. Type **886** 40 10
3225 20c. Soldier, rifle and flag 1·30 15

887 Scholars and "Che" Guevara

1986. 25th Anniv of Scholarship Programme.
3226 **887** 5c. multicoloured 25 10

888 Man learning to write and Sanmarti

890 "Gitana" (Joaquin Sorolla)

889 Map and Revolutionaries

1986. 25th Anniv of Literacy Campaign.
3227 **888** 5c. multicoloured 25 10

1987. 30th Anniv of Attack on La Plata Garrison.
3228 **889** 5c. multicoloured 25 10

1987. National Museum Paintings (18th series). Multicoloured.
3229 3c. Type **890** 10 10
3230 5c. "Sir Walter Scott" (Sir John W. Gordon) 15 10
3231 10c. "Farm Meadows" (Alfred de Breanski) (horiz) 35 15
3232 20c. "Still Life" (Isaac van Duynen) (horiz) 85 25
3233 30c. "Landscape with Figures" (Francesco Zuccarelli) (horiz) 95 30
3234 40c. "Waffle Seller" (Ignacio Zuloaga) . . . . 1·40 50

891 Palace, Delivery Van and Echeverria

1987. 30th Anniv of Attack on Presidential Palace.
3235 **891** 5c. multicoloured 25 10

892 Lazarus Ludwig Zamenhof (inventor) and Russia 1927 14k. Stamp

1987. Centenary of Esperanto (invented language).
3236 **892** 30c. multicoloured . . . 85 30

893 1956 Cuban Postal Service Bicentenary Stamps

1987. 10th National Stamp Exhibition, Holguin. Sheet 85 × 61 mm.
MS3237 **893** 1p. multicoloured 1·70 1·70

894 Badge and Slogan

1987. 25th Anniv and 5th Congress of Youth Communist League.
3238 **894** 5c. multicoloured 25 10

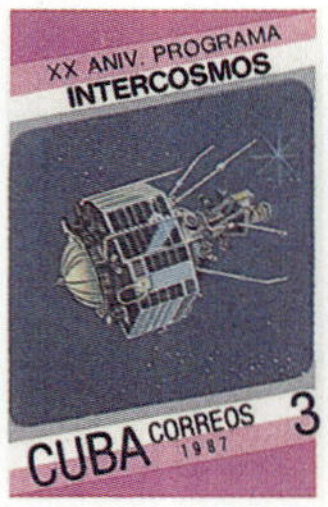

895 "Intercosmos I" Satellite

897 Dahlias

896 Cover with Postal Fiscal Stamp, 1890

1987. Cosmonautics Day. 20th Anniv of Intercosmos Programme. Multicoloured.
3239 3c. Type **895** 10 10
3240 5c. "Intercosmos II" 15 10
3241 10c. "TD" 25 15
3242 20c. "Cosmos 93" 65 25
3243 30c. "Molniya" 85 30
3244 50c. "Vostok 3" . . . . . 1·40 55
MS3245 65 × 85 mm. 1p. Rocket and "Vostok 3" (31 × 39 mm) . . . 4·00 3·00

1987. Stamp Day. Multicoloured.
3246 30c. Type **896** . . . . . . 1·10 25
3247 50c. Cover with bisect, 1869 1·80 50

1987. Mothers' Day. Multicoloured.
3248 3c. Type **897** 10 10
3249 5c. Roses 15 10
3250 10c. Roses in basket 25 15
3251 13c. Decorative dahlias . . 35 15
3252 30c. Cactus dahlias 80 25
3253 50c. Roses (different) . . . 1·30 50

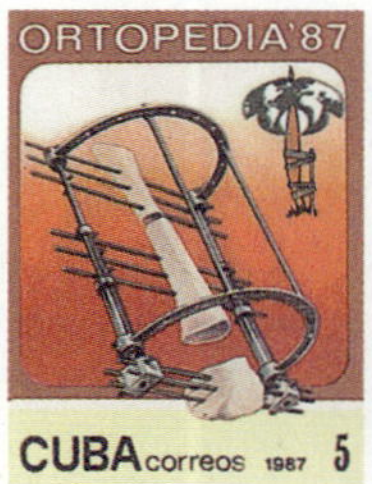

898 Fractured Femur Immobilised in Frame

899 Emblem

1987. "Orthopedia '87" Portuguese and Spanish Speaking Countries' Orthopedists Meeting, Havana.
3254 **898** 5c. multicoloured 25 10

1987. 25th Anniv of Cuban Broadcasting and Television Institute.
3255 **899** 5c. multicoloured 25 10

900 Battle Monument, Sierra Maestra Mountains

1987. 30th Anniv of Battle of El Uvero.
3256 **900** 5c. multicoloured 25 10

901 Messenger with Pack Llamas and 1868 Stamp (Bolivia)

1987. Capex '87 International Stamp Exhibition, Toronto. 19th-century Mail Carriers as depicted on cigarette cards. Multicoloured.
3257 3c. Type **901** 10 10
3258 5c. Postman and motor car and 1900 stamp (France) 15 10
3259 10c. Messenger on elephant and 1883 stamp (Siam) . . 25 15
3260 20c. Messenger on camel and 1879 stamp (Egypt) 50 25
3261 30c. Mail troika and stamp (Russia) 80 25
3262 50c. Messenger on horseback and stamp (Indo-China) . . . . . . 1·30 50
MS3263 67 × 71 mm. 1p. Messenger on horseback and stamp (Cuba) (31 × 39 mm) . . . . 4·00 3·75

902 Model of Prehistoric Animal

1987. Prehistoric Valley, Baconao National Park (2nd series). Designs showing various exhibits.
3264 **902** 3c. multicoloured 15 10
3265 – 5c. multicoloured 25 15
3266 – 10c. multicoloured . . . 45 15
3267 – 20c. multicoloured . . . 95 25
3268 – 35c. multicoloured . . . 1·60 30
3269 – 40c. multicoloured . . . 1·70 40

903 Pais and Rafael Maria Mendive Popular University Buildings

1987. 30th Death Anniv of Frank Pais (teacher and student leader).
3270 **903** 5c. multicoloured 25 10

904 Flags and Sportsmen

1987. 10th Pan-American Games, Indianapolis.
3271 **904** 50c. multicoloured . . . 1·50 40

905 Memorial

1987. 30th Anniv of Cienfuegos Uprising.
3272 **905** 5c. multicoloured 25 10

906 "The Post in Denmark, 1887"

1987. Hafnia 87 International Stamp Exhibition, Copenhagen. Sheet 85 × 60 mm.
MS3273 **906** 1p. multicoloured 4·00 3·00

907 Port of La Coruna

1987. Espamer 87 International Stamp Exhibition, La Coruna, Spain. Sheet 108 × 70 mm.
MS3274 **907** 1p. multicoloured 4·00 3·25

908 Coins and 1968 Independence War Centenary 30c. Stamp

1987. 20th Anniv of Heroic Guerilla Fighters Day.
3275 **908** 50c. multicoloured . . . 1·30 50

909 Tehuelche Man and Red-crowned Ant-tanager (Argentina)

1987. Latin American History (2nd series). Multicoloured.
3276 1c. Type **909** 15 15
3277 1c. Red-billed toucan and Tibirica man (Brazil) . . 15 15
3278 1c. Spain 1930 5c. stamp of La Rabida Monastery and 500th anniv of Columbus's discovery of America emblem 15 15
3279 1c. Andean condor and Lautaro man (Chile) . . . 15 15
3280 1c. Calarca man and hoatzin (Colombia) 15 15
3281 5c. Cuban trogon and Hatuey man (Cuba) . . . 45 15
3282 5c. Scaly-breasted ground dove and Enriquillo man (Dominican Republic) . . 45 15
3283 5c. Spain 1930 30c. stamp of departure from Palos and anniversary emblem . . . 45 15
3284 5c. Toucan barbet and Ruminahui man (Ecuador) 45 15
3285 5c. Resplendent quetzal and Tecum Uman man (Guatemala) 45 15
3286 10c. Anacaona woman and limpkin (Haiti) 70 15
3287 10c. Lempira man and slaty flowerpiercer (Honduras) 70 15
3288 10c. Spain 1930 10p. Columbus stamp and anniversary emblem . . . 70 15
3289 10c. Northern royal flycatcher and Cuauhtemoc woman (Mexico) 70 15
3290 10c. Painted redstart and Nicarao man (Nicaragua) 70 15
3291 20c. Andean cock of the rock and Atahualpa man (Peru) . . . . 1·10 40
3292 20c. Atlactl man and red-tailed hawk (El Salvador) 1·10 40
3293 20c. Spain 1930 10p. stamp of arrival in America and anniversary emblem . . . 1·10 40
3294 20c. Abayuba man and red-breasted plantcutter (Uruguay) . . . . 1·10 40
3295 20c. Guaycaypuro man and blue and yellow macaw (Venezuela) . . . . 1·10 40

910 1950 2c. Train Stamp

1987. 150th Anniv of Cuban Railway. Designs showing Cuban stamps.
3296 **910** 3c. red, brown & black 10 10
3297 – 5c. multicoloured 15 10
3298 – 10c. multicoloured . . . 25 15
3299 – 20c. multicoloured . . . 50 15
3300 – 35c. multicoloured . . . 1·00 30
3301 – 40c. multicoloured . . . 1·20 40
MS3302 Two sheets. (a) 106 × 67 mm. 1p. multicoloured; (b) 207 × 165 mm. Nos. 3296/3301. Imperf . . . . 4·00 3·75
DESIGNS: 5c. 1965 7c. "BB.69,000" diesel locomotive stamp; 10c. 1975 1c. French-built "La Junta" locomotive stamp; 20c. 1975 3c. M. M. Prieto" locomotive stamp; 35c. 1980 10c. locomotive stamp; 40c. 1980 13c. locomotive stamp.

911 Satellites and Russia 1927 14k. Stamp

1987. 70th Anniv of Russian Revolution.
3303 **911** 30c. multicoloured . . . 85 25

912 "Landscape" (Domingo Ramos)

1988. 170th Anniv of San Alejandro Arts School, Havana. Multicoloured.
3304 1c. Type **912** 10 10
3305 2c. "Portrait of Rodriguez Morey" (Eugenio Gonzalez Olivera) 10 10
3306 3c. "Landscape with Malangas and Palm Trees" (Valentin Sanz Carta) 15 10
3307 5c. "Ox-carts" (Eduardo Morales) 15 15
3308 10c. "Portrait of Elena Herrera" (Armando Menocal) (vert) 35 15
3309 30c. "The Rape of Dejanira" (Miguel Melero) (vert) 75 25
3310 50c. "The Card Player" (Leopoldo Romanach) . . 1·20 50

913 "Boletus satanas"

915 Mario Munoz Santiago Monument, de Cuba

914 Radio Operator, Satellite and Caribe Ground Station

1988. Poisonous Mushrooms. Multicoloured.
3311 1c. Type **913** 10 10
3312 2c. "Amanita citrina" . . . 15 10
3313 3c. "Tylopilus felleus" . . . 25 15
3314 5c. "Paxillus involutus" . . 25 15
3315 10c. "Inocybe patouillardii" 60 25

3316 30c. "Amanita muscaria" 1·60 55
3317 50c. "Hypholoma fasciculare" 2·50 1·10

1988. 30th Anniv of Radio Rebelde.
3318 **914** 5c. multicoloured 25 10

1988. 30th Anniv of Mario Munoz Third Front.
3319 **915** 5c. multicoloured 25 15

916 Frank Pais Memorial and Eternal Flame

917 Red Roses

1988. 30th Anniv of Frank Pais Second Eastern Front.
3320 **916** 5c. multicoloured 25 15

1988. Mothers' Day. Multicoloured.
3321 1c. Type **917** 10 10
3322 2c. Pale pink roses 10 10
3323 3c. Daisies 10 10
3324 5c. Dahlias 15 10
3325 13c. White roses 25 15
3326 35c. Carnations 80 25
3327 40c. Pink roses 95 30

918 "Gorizont" Satellite

1988. Cosmonautics Day. Multicoloured.
3328 2c. Type **918** 10 10
3329 3c. "Mir"–"Kvant" link 10 10
3330 4c. "Signo 3" 10 10
3331 5c. Mars space probe 15 10
3332 10c. "Phobos" 25 15
3333 30c. "Vega" space probe 70 25
3334 50c. Spacecraft 1·20 50
MS3335 95 × 60 mm. 1p. Spacecraft (different) (31 × 39 mm) 4·00 3·75

1988. Stamp Day. As T **811**. Details of mural by R. R. Radillo in Havana Stamp Museum. Mult.
3336 30c. Telegraphist and mail coach 95 30
3337 50c. Carrier pigeon 1·60 50

919 Storage Tanks, Products, Sugar Cane and Laboratory Equipment

1988. 25th Anniv of ICIDCA (Cuban Institute for Research on Sugarcane Byproducts).
3338 **919** 5c. multicoloured 25 10

920 Havana–Madrid, 1948

1988. Cubana Airlines Transatlantic Flights. Mult.
3339 2c. Type **920** 10 10
3340 4c. Havana–Prague, 1961 10 10
3341 5c. Havana–Berlin, 1972 15 10
3342 10c. Havana–Luanda, 1975 25 15
3343 30c. Havana–Paris, 1983 85 25
3344 50c. Havana–Moscow, 1987 1·50 50

921 "Furst Menschikoff" and 1917 20p. Finnish Stamp

1988. Finlandia 88 International Stamp Exhibition, Helsinki. Sheet 93 × 51 mm.
MS3345 **921** 1p. multicoloured 3·50 3·25

922 Steam Train (½-size illustration)

1988. Postal Union of the Americas and Spain Colloquium on "America" Postage Stamps, Havana.
3346 **922** 20c. multicoloured 1·30 30

923 "Megasoma elephas"

1988. Beetles. Multicoloured.
3347 1c. Type **923** 10 10
3348 3c. "Platycoelia flavoscutellata" (vert) 10 10
3349 4c. "Plusiotis argenteola" 10 10
3350 5c. "Hetersoternus oberthuri" 15 10
3351 10c. "Odontotaenius zodiacus" 35 15
3352 35c. "Chrysophora chrysochlora" (vert) 1·10 30
3353 40c. "Phanaeus leander" 1·40 50

924 Chess Pieces

1988. Birth Centenary of Jose Capablanca (chess master). Multicoloured.
3354 30c. Type **924** 70 30
3355 40c. Juan Corzo, Capablanca and flags (1901 Cuban Championship) (horiz) 95 30
3356 50c. Emanuel Lasker and Capablanca (1921 World Championship) (horiz) 1·00 40
3357 1p. Checkmate in 1921 game with Lasker 2·50 90
3358 3p. "J. R. Capablanca" (E. Valderrama) 7·75 2·40
3359 5p. Chess pieces, flag, globe and Capablanca 14·00 4·50
MS3360 6 sheets, 58 × 88 mm (b, c) or 89 × 60 mm (others). (a) 30c. 1951 1c. Capablanca stamp; 30c. As No. 3354 but 29 × 36 mm; (b) 40c. 1951 5c. chess stamp; 40c. As No. 3355 but 36 × 27 mm; (c) 50c. 1951 5c. chess stamp; 50c. As No. 3356 but 36 × 28 mm; (d) 1p. 1951 2c. Capablanca stamp; 1p. As No. 3357 but 29 × 36 mm; (e) 3p. 1951 25c. Capablanca stamp; 3p. As No. 3358 but 28 × 36 mm; (f) 5p. 1951 8c. Capablanca stamp; 3p. As No. 3359 but 29 × 36 mm 60·00 55·00

925 Sun and Fortress

1988. 35th Anniv of Assault on Moncada Fortress.
3361 **925** 5c. red, yellow & black 25 10

926 Czechoslovakia 1920 20h. Stamp

1988. Praga 88 International Stamp Exhibition and 70th Anniv of First Czechoslovak Stamps. Sheet 91 × 52 mm.
MS3362 **926** 1p. multicoloured 3·50 3·25

927 Camilo Cienfuegos, "Che" Guevara and Map

1988. 30th Anniv of Rebel Invasion Columns.
3363 **927** 5c. multicoloured 15 10

928 Emblem

1988. 30th Anniv of "Revista Internacional" (magazine).
3364 **928** 30c. multicoloured 1·10 30

929 Locomotive "Northumbrian", 1831

1988. Railway Development. Multicoloured.
3365 20c. Type **929** 50 25
3366 30c. Locomotive "E. L. Miller", 1834 1·00 40
3367 50c. "La Junta" (Cuba's first locomotive, 1840s) 2·20 80
3368 1p. Electric railcar 4·00 1·20
3369 2p. Russian-built M-62K diesel locomotive 7·25 2·75
3370 5p. Diesel railcar set 16·00 7·75

930 Arms and Jose de San Martin (Argentina)

1988. Latin-American History (3rd series). Mult.
3371 1c. Type **930** 10 10
3372 1c. Arms and M. A. Padilla (Bolivia) 10 10
3373 1c. 1944 10c. Discovery of America stamp 10 10
3374 1c. Arms and A. de Silva Xavier, "Tiradentes" (Brazil) 10 10
3375 1c. Arms and Bernardo O'Higgins (Chile) 10 10
3376 5c. A. Narino and arms (Colombia) 10 10
3377 5c. Arms and Jose Marti (Cuba) 10 10
3378 5c. 1944 13c. Discovery of America stamp 10 10
3379 5c. Arms and Juan Pablo Duarte (Dominican Republic) 10 10
3380 5c. Arms and Antonio Jose de Sucre (Ecuador) 10 10
3381 10c. Manuel Jose Arce and arms (El Salvador) 25 10
3382 10c. Arms and Jean Jacques Dessalines (Haiti) 25 10
3383 10c. 1944 5c. Discovery of America airmail stamp 25 10
3384 10c. Miguel Hidalgo and arms (Mexico) 25 10
3385 10c. Arms and J. Dolores Estrada (Nicaragua) 25 10
3386 20c. Jose E. Diaz and arms (Paraguay) 35 15
3387 20c. Arms and Francisco Bolognesi (Peru) 35 15
3388 20c. 1944 10c. Discovery of America airmail stamp 35 15
3389 20c. Arms and Jose Gervasio Artigas (Uruguay) 35 15
3390 20c. Simon Bolivar and arms (Venezuela) 35 15

931 Maces and Governor's Palace

1988. 20th Anniv of Havana Museum.
3391 **931** 5c. multicoloured 25 10

932 Ballerinas and Mute Swan

1988. 40th Anniv of National Ballet (3392) and 150th Anniv of Grand Theatre, Havana (3393). Multicoloured.
3392 5c. Type **932** 50 15
3393 5c. Theatre, 1838 and 1988 50 15

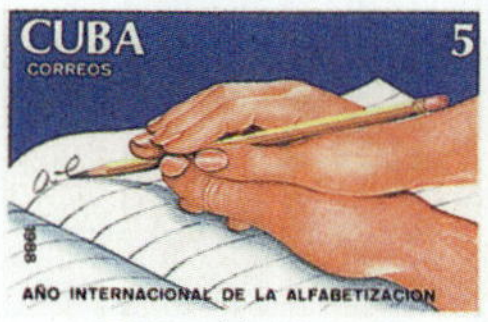

933 Practising Letters

1988. International Literacy Year.
3394 **933** 5c. multicoloured 25 10

934 Emblem

1988. 40th Anniv of Declaration of Human Rights.
3395 **934** 30c. multicoloured 1·10 30

935 Ernesto Che Guevara Plaza

1988. 30th Anniv of Battle of Santa Clara.
3396 **935** 30c. multicoloured 1·10 30

936 National Flag forming "30"

1989. 30th Anniv of Revolution.
3397 **936** 5c. multicoloured 10 10
3398 20c. multicoloured 55 15
3399 30c. gold, blue and red 75 25
3400 50c. gold, blue and red 1·50 50

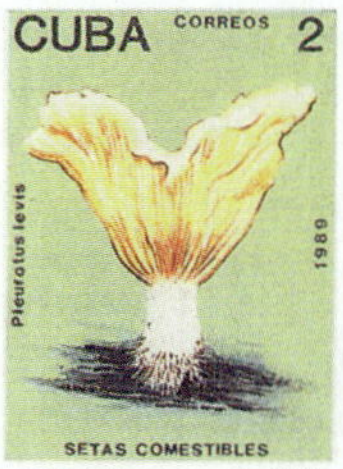

937 "Pleurotus levis"

1989. Edible Mushrooms. Multicoloured.
3401 2c. Type **937** 10 10
3402 3c. "Pleurotus floridanus" 15 10
3403 5c. "Amanita caesarea" 20 15
3404 10c. "Lentinus cubensis" (horiz) 45 15
3405 40c. "Pleurotus ostreatus" (red) 1·60 40
3406 50c. "Pleurotus ostreatus" (brown) 1·70 50

938 India River Post, 1858

1989. India 89 International Stamp Exhibition, New Delhi. Sheet 91 × 51 mm.
MS3407 **938** 1p. multicoloured 3·50 3·25

939 1982 30c. Cuban Stamp

1989. 50th Anniv of Revolutionary Workers' Union.
3408 **939** 5c. multicoloured 25 10

940 "Metamorpho dido"

1989. Butterflies. Multicoloured.
3409 1c. Type **940** 10 10
3410 3c. "Callithea saphhira" . . 10 10
3411 5c. "Papilio zagreus" . . . 15 10
3412 10c. "Mynes sestia" 25 15
3413 30c. "Papilio dardanus" . . 1·20 30
3414 50c. "Catagranma sorana" 2·10 65

941 Footballer **942** "30" and Arms

1989. World Cup Football Championship, Italy (1990).
3415 **941** 1c. multicoloured 10 10
3416 – 3c. multicoloured 10 10
3417 – 5c. multicoloured 10 10
3418 – 10c. multicoloured . . . 15 10
3419 – 30c. multicoloured . . . 85 15
3420 – 50c. multicoloured . . . 1·50 30
MS3421 62 × 50 mm. 1p. multicoloured (39 × 31 mm) . . 3·50 2·75
DESIGNS: 3c. to 1p. Various footballers.

1989. 30th Anniv of National Revolutionary Police.
3422 **942** 5c. multicoloured 25 15

943 "Zodiac" Rocket and 1934 Australian Cover

1989. Cosmonautics Day. Rocket Post (1st series). Multicoloured.
3423 1c. Type **943** 10 10
3424 3c. Rocket and cover from India to Poland, 1934 . . . 10 10
3425 5c. Rocket and 1934 English cover 15 10
3426 10c. "Icarus" rocket and 1935 Dutch cover 20 15
3427 40c. "La Douce France" rocket and 1935 French cover 95 40
3428 50c. Rocket and 1939 Cuban cover . . . . . . 1·20 55
See also Nos. 3516/21.

1989. Stamp Day. As T **811**. Details of mural by R. R. Radillo in Havana Stamp Museum. Mult.
3429 30c. Mail coach 70 30
3430 50c. 18th-century sailing packet . . . . 5·50 2·00

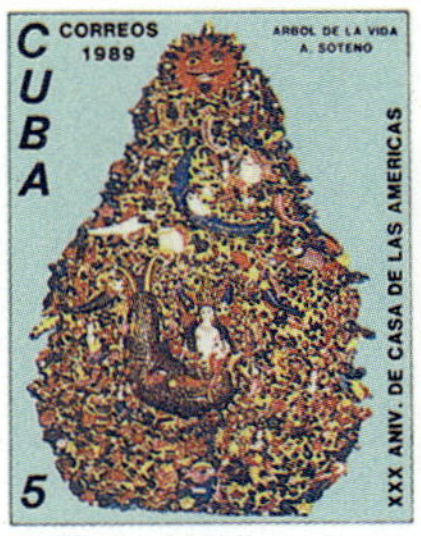

944 "Tree of Life" (A. Soteno)

1989. 30th Anniv of "House of the Americas" Museum, Havana.
3431 **944** 5c. multicoloured 25 10

945 Bulgaria 1l. Stamp

1989. Bulgaria 89 International Stamp Exhibition, Sofia. Sheet 90 × 50 mm.
MS3432 **945** 1p. green, vermillion and black . . . . 4·00 2·75

946 Coded Envelope

1989. Post Codes.
3433 **946** 5c. multicoloured 25 10

947 Tobacco Flowers **948** Signing Decree

1989. Mothers' Day. Perfumes and Flowers. Mult.
3434 1c. Type **947** 10 10
3435 3c. Violets 10 10
3436 5c. Mariposa 15 10
3437 13c. Roses 30 15
3438 30c. Jasmine 85 25
3439 50c. Orange-flower . . . . 1·50 55

1989. 30th Anniv of Agrarian Reform Law.
3440 **948** 5c. multicoloured 25 10

949 "40" and Headquarters Building, Moscow

1989. 40th Anniv of Council for Mutual Economic Aid.
3441 **949** 30c. multicoloured . . . 1·10 15

950 Tower of Juche Idea, Pyongyang

1989. 13th World Youth and Students' Festival, Pyongyang.
3442 **950** 30c. multicoloured . . . 1·10 15

951 "Rouger de Lisle singing The Marseillaise" (Pils)

1989. Philexfrance 89 International Stamp Exhibition, Paris. Sheet 96 × 56 mm.
MS3443 **951** 1p. multicoloured 3·50 2·75

952 Toco Toucan

1989. Brasiliana '89 Stamp Exhibition. Rio de Janeiro. Birds. Multicoloured.
3444 1c. Type **952** 25 10
3445 3c. Chestnut-bellied heron 25 10
3446 5c. Scarlet ibis 35 10
3447 10c. White-winged trumpeter 45 15
3448 35c. Harpy eagle . . . . . 1·60 50
3449 50c. Amazonian umbrellabird . . . . . . 2·20 75

953 "El Fenix" (galleon)

1989. Cuban Sailing Ships. Multicoloured.
3450 1c. Type **953** 10 10
3451 3c. "Triunfo" (ship of the line) 10 10
3452 5c. "El Rayo" (ship of the line) 15 10
3453 10c. "San Carlos" (ship of the line) 35 15
3454 30c. "San Jose" (ship of the line) . . . . 1·30 30
3455 50c. "San Genaro" (ship of the line) . . . . 2·10 55

954 Carved Stone and Men in Dugout Canoe

1989. America. Pre-Columbian Cultures. Mult.
3456 5c. Type **954** 25 10
3457 20c. Cave painters 70 30

955 Domingo F. Sarmiento and "Govenia utriculata" (Argentina)

1989. Latin American History (4th series). Multicoloured.
3458 1c. Type **955** 10 10
3459 1c. Machado de Assis and "Laelia grandis" (Brazil) 10 10
3460 1c. El Salvador 1892 1p. Columbus stamp 10 10
3461 1c. Jorge Isaacs and "Cattleya trianae" (Colombia) 10 10
3462 1c. Alejo Carpentier and "Cochleanthes discolor" (Cuba) 10 10
3463 5c. "Oxalis adenophylla" and Pablo Neruda (Chile) 15 10
3464 5c. Pedro H. Urena and "Epidendrum fragrans" (Dominican Republic) . . 15 10
3465 5c. El Salvador 1893 2p. City of Isabela stamp . . 15 10
3466 5c. Juan Montalvo and "Miltonia vexillaria" (Ecuador) 15 10
3467 5c. "Odontoglossum rossii" and Miguel A. Asturias (Guatemala) 15 10
3468 10c. "Laelia anceps" and Jose C. del Valle (Honduras) 30 15
3469 10c. "Laelia ancepes alba" and Alfonso Reyes (Mexico) 30 15
3470 10c. El Salvador 1893 5p. Columbus Statue stamp 30 15
3471 10c. "Brassavola acaulis" and Ruben Dario (Nicaragua) 30 15
3472 10c. Belisario Porras and "Pescatorea cerina" (Panama) 30 15
3473 20c. Ricardo Palma and "Coryanthes leucocorys" (Peru) 50 20
3474 20c. Eugenio Maria de Hostos and "Guzmania berteroniana" (Puerto Rico) 50 20
3475 20c. El Salvador 1893 10p. Departure from Palos stamp 50 20
3476 20c. "Cypella herbertii" and Jose E. Rodo (Uruguay) 50 20
3477 20c. "Cattleya mossiae" and Romulo Gallegos (Venezuela) 50 20

956 Cienfuegos and Flag

1989. 30th Anniv of Disappearance of Camilo Cienfuegos (revolutionary).
3478 **956** 5c. multicoloured 25 10

957 Church Tower

1989. 475th Anniv of Trinidad City.
3479 **957** 5c. multicoloured 15 10

958 "Outskirts of Niza" (E. Boudin)

1989. Paintings in National Museum. Mult.
3480 1c. "Family Scene" (Antoine Faivre) 10 10
3481 2c. "Flowers" (Emile J. H. Vernet) 10 10
3482 5c. "Judgement of Paris" (Charles Le Brun) 15 10
3483 20c. Type **958** 75 15
3484 30c. "Portrait of Sarah Bernhardt" (G. J. V. Clairin) (36 × 46 mm) 95 20
3485 50c. "Fishermen in Harbour" (C. J. Vernet) 1·90 55

959 Archery

1989. 11th Pan-American Games, Havana (1st issue). Multicoloured.

3486	5c. Type **959**	20	10
3487	5c. Shooting	20	10
3488	5c. Fencing	20	10
3489	5c. Cycling	20	10
3490	5c. Water polo	20	10
3491	20c. Lawn tennis (vert)	55	25
3492	30c. Swimming (vert)	95	25
3493	35c. Diving (vert)	1·20	30
3494	40c. Hockey	1·30	30
3495	50c. Basketball (vert)	1·90	65

See also Nos. 3584/93 and 3621/30.

960 Front Page

1989. Centenary of "Golden Age" (children's magazine compiled by Jose Marti).

3496 **960**	5c. blue, black and red	35	10

961 "Almendares" (paddle-steamer)

1990. 25th Anniv of Postal Museum. Mult.

3497	5c. Type **961**	15	10
3498	30c. Mail train	2·75	80

962 Cave Painters (½-size illustration)

1990. 50th Anniv of Speleological Society.

3499 **962**	30c. multicoloured	1·70	30

963 Player No. 11 and Colosseum

964 Baseball

1990. World Cup Football Championship, Italy. Multicoloured.

3500	5c. Type **963**	10	10
3501	5c. Player No. 10	10	10
3502	5c. Player No. 8	10	10
3503	10c. Goalkeeper	20	10
3504	30c. Player No. 11 and arch	1·10	30
3505	50c. Player	1·80	55
MS3506	94 × 62 mm. 1p. Goalkeeper catching ball (39 × 31 mm)	3·00	2·75

1990. Olympic Games, Barcelona (1992) (1st issue). Multicoloured.

3507	1c. Type **964**	10	10
3508	4c. Running	10	10
3509	5c. Basketball	15	10
3510	10c. Volleyball	40	15
3511	30c. Wrestling (horiz)	95	30
3512	50c. Boxing	1·70	65
MS3513	88 × 48 mm. 1p. High jumping (39 × 31 mm)	3·50	2·75

See also Nos. 3604/**MS**3619 and 3692/**MS**3698.

965 Tower of Babel, Dove and Globe

1990. 75th Esperanto Congress, Havana.

3514 **965**	30c. multicoloured	1·10	30

966 Skiing

1990. Winter Olympic Games, Albertville (1992). Sheet 91 × 50 mm.

MS3515 **966**	1p. multicoloured	4·00	2·75

1990. Cosmonautics Day. Rocket Post (2nd series). As T **943**. Multicoloured.

3516	1c. 1932 Austrian Cover and "U12" rocket	10	10
3517	2c. 1933 German cover, rocket and liner	10	10
3518	3c. 1934 Netherlands cover, "NRB" rocket and windmill	15	10
3519	10c. 1935 Belgian cover and rocket	20	15
3520	30c. 1935 Yugoslavian cover and "JUG1" rocket	95	15
3521	50c. 1936 U.S.A. cover and rocket	1·70	55

1990. Stamp Day. As T **811**. Showing details of mural by R. R. Radillo in Havana Stamp Museum. Multicoloured.

3522	30c. Russian-built Type TEM-4 diesel locomotive leaving station	2·50	65
3523	50c. De Havilland Comet 1 airplane	1·50	40

967 Flag and Globe

1990. Centenary of Labour Day.

3524 **967**	5c. multicoloured	85	15

968 Penny Black with Maltese Cross Cancellation

1990. Stamp World London 90 International Stamp Exhibition. Sheet 95 × 51 mm.

MS3525 **968**	1p. multicoloured	1·40	1·40

969 Hill and Penny Black

1990. 150th Anniv of the Penny Black. Mult.

3526	2c. Type **969**	10	10
3527	3c. Twopenny blue	10	10
3528a	5c. G.B. 1855 4d. stamp	1·10	60
3529	10c. G.B. 1847 1s. embossed stamp	20	15
3530	30c. G.B. paid hand-stamp	1·10	15
3531	50c. Twopenny blues on cover to Malta	1·90	55

970 Celia Sanchez (after O. Yanes)

1990. 70th Birth Anniv of Celia Sanchez Manduley (revolutionary).

3532 **970**	5c. multicoloured	45	15

971 Flags and Ho Chi Minh

1990. Birth Centenary of Ho Chi Minh (Vietnamese leader).

3533 **971**	50c. multicoloured	1·50	40

972 Hogfish and Sample Analysis

1990. 25th Anniv of Oceanology Institute. Mult.

3534	5c. Type **972**	10	10
3535	30c. "Arrecife coralino" and research vessel	1·00	30
3536	50c. Lobster and diver collecting samples	1·70	40

973 "Banara minutiflora"

974 Windsurfing

1990. 5th Latin American Botanical Congress. Multicoloured.

3537	3c. Type **973**	10	10
3538	5c. "Oplonia nannophylla"	10	10
3539	10c. "Jacquinia brunnescens"	40	15
3540	30c. "Rondeletia brachycarpa"	1·20	20
3541	50c. "Rondeletia odorata"	1·90	70

1990. Tourist Sports. Multicoloured.

3542	5c. Type **974**	10	10
3543	10c. Underwater fishing (horiz)	40	20
3544	30c. Sea fishing (horiz)	1·10	20
3545	40c. Shooting	1·80	70

975 "The Flute of Pan" (detail)

1990. Paintings by A. G. Menocal in National Museum. Multicoloured.

3546	5c. Type **975**	20	20
3547	20c. "Shepherd"	65	30
3548	50c. "Ganymede"	1·90	50
3549	1p. "Venus Anadiomena"	2·75	1·10
MS3550	101 × 128 mm. Nos. 3546/9	6·00	5·75

976 Great Crested Grebe

1990. "New Zealand 90" International Stamp Exhibition, Auckland. Birds. Multicoloured.

3551	2c. Type **976**	20	10
3552	3c. Weka rail	20	10
3553	5c. Kea	20	15
3554	10c. Bush wren	45	20
3555	30c. Grey butcher bird	1·40	40
3556	50c. Parson bird	2·40	85
MS3557	81 × 55 mm. 1p. Brown Kiwi ("Apteryx australis mantelli") (wrongly inscr "Aptery") (39 × 31 mm)	5·00	4·75

977 Lighthouse

1990. 8th U.N.O. Congress on Crime Prevention and Treatment of Delinquents.

3558 **977**	50c. red, blue and silver	1·90	50

978 Caravel and Shoreline

1990. America. The Natural World. Mult.

3559	5c. Type **978**	30	20
3560	20c. Christopher Columbus and native village	1·10	40

979 Cameraman

1990. 40th Anniv of Cuban Television.

3561 **979**	5c. multicoloured	40	15

980 Steam Locomotive No. 1712 and Havana Railway Station

1990. 30th Anniv of Nationalization of Railways.

3562 **980**	50c. multicoloured	3·25	1·00

981 Flag and Couple (Argentina)

1990. Latin-American History (5th series). Multicoloured.

3563	1c. Type **981**	10	10
3564	1c. Flag and couple (Bolivia)	10	10
3565	1c. Argentina 1892 5c. Discovery of America stamp	10	10
3566	1c. Flag and couple (Colombia)	10	10
3567	1c. Flag and couple (Costa Rica)	10	10
3568	5c. Flag and couple (Cuba)	20	10
3569	5c. Flag and couple (Chile)	20	10
3570	5c. Dominican Republic 1900 ½c. Columbus stamp	20	10
3571	5c. Flag and couple (Ecuador)	20	10
3572	5c. Flag and couple (El Salvador)	20	10
3573	10c. Flag and couple (Guatemala)	35	15
3574	10c. Flag and couple (Mexico)	35	15
3575	10c. Puerto Rico 1893 3c. Discovery of America stamp	35	15
3576	10c. Flag and couple (Nicaragua)	35	15
3577	10c. Flag and couple (Panama)	35	15
3578	20c. Flag and couple (Paraguay)	65	20
3579	20c. Flag and couple (Peru)	65	20
3580	20c. El Salvador 1894 10p. Columbus stamp	65	20
3581	20c. Flag and couple (Puerto Rico)	65	20
3582	20c. Flag and couple (Venezuela)	65	20

982 Player

983 Boxing

1990. 11th World Pelota Championship.
3583 **982** 30c. multicoloured . . . 1·40 50

1990. 11th Pan-American Games, Havana (1991) (2nd issue). As T **959**. Multicoloured.
3584 5c. Kayaking 20 10
3585 5c. Rowing 20 10
3586 5c. Yachting 20 10
3587 5c. Judo 20 10
3588 5c. Show jumping 20 10
3589 10c. Table tennis 35 20
3590 20c. Gymnastics (vert) . . . 65 30
3591 30c. Baseball (vert) . . . . 1·00 30
3592 35c. Basketball (vert) . . . 1·20 40
3593 50c. Football (vert) . . . . 1·80 95

1990. 16th Central American and Caribbean Games, Mexico. Multicoloured.
3594 5c. Type **983** 10 10
3595 30c. Baseball . . . . 1·20 30
3596 50c. Volleyball . . . . . . 2·10 60

984 "Chioides marmorosa"

986 Long Jumping

985 Guerra Aguiar and 1966 3c. Stamp

1991. Butterflies. Multicoloured.
3597 2c. Type **984** 35 10
3598 3c. "Composia fidelissima" 35 10
3599 5c. "Danaus plexippus" . . 35 10
3600 10c. "Hypolimnas misippus" 55 20
3601 30c. "Hypna iphigenia" . . 1·80 30
3602 50c. "Hemiargus ammon" 2·75 60

1991. 1st Death Anniv of Jose Guerra Aguiar (founder of Cuban Postal Museum).
3603 **985** 5c. multicoloured 50 20

1991. Olympic Games, Barcelona (1992) (2nd issue). Multicoloured.
3604 1c. Type **986** 10 10
3605 2c. Throwing the javelin . . 10 10
3606 3c. Hockey 20 10
3607 5c. Weightlifting 20 15
3608 40c. Cycling . . . . 1·40 40
3609 50c. Gymnastics . . . . . 1·90 60
MS3610 59 × 80 mm. 1p. Torch bearer (31 × 39 mm) . . . . . 3·75 3·25

987 Yuri Gagarin and "Vostok"

988 Statue and Flag

1991. 30th Anniv of First Man in Space. Mult.
3611 5c. Type **987** 10 10
3612 10c. "Soyuz" and Y. Romanenko 20 10
3613 10c. "Salyut" space station and A. Tamayo 20 10
3614 30c. "Mir" space station (left half) . . . . 1·10 20
3615 30c. "Mir" space station (right half) . . . . 1·10 20
3616 50c. Launch of "Buran" space shuttle . . . . . . 1·70 60

Nos. 3612/13 and 3614/15 respectively were issued together, se-tenant, forming composite designs.

1991. 30th Anniversaries. Multicoloured.
3617 5c. Type **988** (proclamation of Socialism) 10 10
3618 50c. Playa Giron (invasion attempt by Cuban exiles) 2·20 95

1991. Stamp Day. Designs as T **811** showing details of mural by R. R. Radillo in Havana Stamp Museum. Multicoloured.
3619 30c. Rocket (vert) . . . . . 1·10 40
3620 50c. Dish aerial . . . . . . 1·90 50

1991. 11th Pan-American Games, Havana (3rd series). As T **959**. Multicoloured.
3621 5c. Volleyball (vert) 10 10
3622 5c. Synchronized swimming (vert) 10 10
3623 5c. Weightlifting (vert) . . . 10 10
3624 5c. Baseball (vert) 10 10
3625 5c. Gymnastics (vert) . . . 10 10
3626 10c. Ten-pin bowling . . . 35 20
3627 20c. Boxing (vert) 65 30
3628 30c. Running . . . . 1·00 30
3629 35c. Wrestling . . . . . . 1·20 40
3630 50c. Judo . . . . 1·80 60

989 Simon Bolivar and Map

1991. 165th Anniv of Panama Congress.
3631 **989** 50c. multicoloured . . . 2·20 70

990 Dirigible Balloon Design and Jean-Baptiste Meusnier

1991. Espamer '91 Iberia–Latin America Stamp Exhibition, Buenos Aires. Airships. Mult.
3632 5c. Type **990** 20 10
3633 10c. First steam-powered dirigible airship and Henri Giffard 40 20
3634 20c. Paul Hanlein and first airship with gas-powered motor 75 40
3635 30c. "Deutschland" (first airship with petrol motor) and Karl Wolfert . . . . 1·00 60
3636 50c. David Schwarz and first rigid aluminium airship 1·80 1·00
3637 1p. Ferdinand von Zeppelin and airship "Graf Zeppelin" . . . . 3·50 2·00
No. 3637 is inscr "Hindenburg".

992 Cayo Largo

1991. Tourism. Multicoloured.
3645 20c. Type **992** 65 20
3646 20c. Varadero 65 20
3647 30c. San Carlos de la Cabana Fortress (horiz) 1·10 40
3648 30c. Castillo de los Tres Reyes del Morro (horiz) 1·10 40

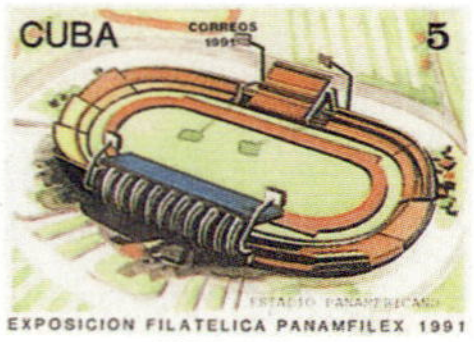

993 Stadium

1991. Panamfilex 1991 Pan-American Stamp Exhibition. Multicoloured.
3649 5c. Type **993** 20 10
3650 20c. Baragua swimming-pool complex 65 40
3651 30c. Ramon Fonst hall . . . 90 60
3652 50c. Reynaldo Paseiro cycle-track . . . . 1·70 1·00
MS3653 89 × 50 mm. 1p. Sports Centre (39 × 31 mm) . . . . . 3·75 3·50

994 "Kataoka Dengoemon Takafusa" (Utagawa Kuniyoshi)

1991. Phila Nippon '91 International Stamp Exhibition, Tokyo. Multicoloured.
3654 5c. Type **994** 20 10
3655 10c. "Night Walk" (Hosoda Eishi) 40 20
3656 20c. "Courtesans" (Torii Kiyonaga) 75 40
3657 30c. "Conversation" (Kitagawa Utamaro) . . . 1·00 50
3658 50c. "Inari-bashi Bridge" (Ando Hiroshige) . . . . 1·80 95
3659 1p. "On the Terrace" (Torii Kiyonaga) . . . . 3·50 2·00

995 Figure Skating

1991. Winter Olympic Games, Albertville. Sheet 60 × 80 mm.
MS3660 **995** 1p. multicoloured 3·75 3·50

996 Statue of Jose Marti

1991. 4th Cuban Communist Party Congress.
3661 **996** 5c. multicoloured 20 10
3662 – 50c. black, blue and red 1·90 60
DESIGN: 50c. Party emblem.

997 Christopher Columbus and Pinzon Brothers

1991. America. Voyages of Discovery. Mult.
3663 5c. Type **997** 30 10
3664 20c. "Santa Maria", "Nina" and "Pinta" . . . . . . 1·40 30

998 Marti (after F. Martinez)

1991. Centenary of Publication of "The Simple Verses" by Jose Marti.
3665 **998** 50c. multicoloured . . . 2·20 50

999 Julian Aguirre and Charango (Argentina)

1991. Latin-American History (6th series). Music. Multicoloured.
3666 1c. Type **999** 10 10
3667 1c. Eduardo Caba and antara (pipes) (Bolivia) . . 10 10
3668 1c. Chile 1853 10c. stamp 10 10
3669 1c. Heitor Villalobos and trumpet with gourd resonator (Brazil) 10 10
3670 1c. Guillermo Uribe-Holguin and cununo macho (drum) (Colombia) . . . 10 10
3671 5c. Claves (sticks) and Miguel Failde (Cuba) . . 20 10
3672 5c. Enrique Soro and Araucanian kultrum (Chile) 20 10
3673 5c. Chile 1903 10c. on 30c. stamp 20 10
3674 5c. Rondador (xylophone) and Segundo L. Moreno (Ecuador) 20 10
3675 5c. Marimba and Ricardo Castillo (Guatemala) . . . 20 10
3676 10c. Vihuela and Carlos Chavez (Mexico) 45 20
3677 10c. Luis A. Delgadillo and maracas (Nicaragua) . . . 45 20
3678 10c. Chile 1906 2c. stamp 45 20
3679 10c. Alfredo de Saint-Malo and mejorana (Panama) 45 20
3680 10c. Jose Asuncion Flores and harp (Paraguay) . . . 45 20
3681 20c. Daniel Alomia and quena (flute) (Peru) . . . 90 30
3682 20c. Cuatro (guitar) and Juan Morell y Campos (Puerto Rico) 90 30
3683 20c. Chile 1905 10c. stamp 90 30
3684 20c. Eduardo Fabini and tamboril (drums) (Uruguay) 90 30
3685 20c. Cuatro (guitar) and Juan V. Lecuna (Venezuela) 90 30

1000 Mascot

1991. 1st Jose Marti Pioneers Congress.
3686 **1000** 5p. multicoloured . . . 40 20

1001 Toussaint L'Ouverture (revolutionary leader)

1991. Bicentenary of Haitian Revolution.
3687 **1001** 50c. multicoloured . . . 2·20 50

1002 "35", Stars and Soldier

1991. 35th Anniversaries. Multicoloured.
3688 5c. Type **1002** (Revolutionary Armed Forces) 30 20
3689 50c. Launch "Granma" (disembarkation of revolutionary forces) (vert) . . . . 2·20 50

1003 Agramonte (after F. Martinez)

1991. 150th Birth Anniv of Ignacio Agramonte (poet).
3690 **1003** 5c. multicoloured . . . 35 10

1004 Skiing

1992. Winter Olympic Games, Albertville (3rd issue). Sheet 77 × 63 mm.
MS3691 **1004** 1p. multicoloured 3·75 3·25

1005 Table Tennis and Plan of Montjuic Complex

1992. Olympic Games, Barcelona (3rd issue). Mult.
3692 3c. Type **1005** 10 10
3693 5c. Handball and Vall d'Hebron complex 20 10
3694 10c. Shooting and Badalona complex 35 15
3695 20c. Long jumping and Montjuic complex (vert) 65 20
3696 35c. Judo and Diagonal complex . . . . 1·40 50
3697 50c. Fencing and Montjuic complex . . . . 1·80 50
MS3698 62 × 77 mm. 100c. Gymnastics and plan of Barcelona (31 × 39 mm) . . . . 3·75 3·25

1006 Flooded Terraces and Dead Trees

1992. Environmental Protection. Mult.
3699 5c. Type **1006** 30 10
3700 20c. Whale and dead fish in polluted sea 65 30
3701 35c. Satellite picture of ozone levels over Antarctica and gas mask in polluted air . . . . . 1·40 50
3702 40c. Rainbows, globe, doves and nuclear explosion . . 1·50 50

1007 Blue Angelfish

1992. Fishes. Multicoloured.
3703 5c. Type **1007** 20 10
3704 10c. Jackknife-fish 20 15
3705 20c. Blue tang 70 20
3706 30c. Sergeant-major . . . . 1·20 30
3707 50c. Yellow-tailed damselfish 2·10 60

1008 Boxer

1992. Dogs. Multicoloured.
3708 5c. Type **1008** 10 10
3709 10c. Great dane 20 10
3710 20c. German shepherd . . . 70 20
3711 30c. Short-haired, long-haired and wire-haired dachshunds . . . . 1·20 30
3712 35c. Dobermann . . . . . 1·20 40
3713 40c. Fox terrier . . . . . 1·50 40
3714 50c. Poodle . . . . 1·90 60
MS3715 52 × 81 mm. 1p. Bichon fries (32 × 40 mm) . . . . . . 4·50 3·50

1009 Badge

1992. 30th Anniv and Sixth Congress of Youth Communist League.
3716 **1009** 5c. multicoloured . . . 40 15

1010 Jose Marti

1992. Centenary of Cuban Revolutionary Party.
3717 **1010** 5c. multicoloured . . . 30 10
3718 50c. multicoloured . . . 1·90 60

1011 Columbus Sighting Land

1992. America. 500th Anniv of Discovery of America by Columbus. Multicoloured.
3719 5c. Type **1011** 35 15
3720 20c. Columbus landing at San Salvador . . . . . . 1·00 30

1012 Alhambra, Sierra Nevada

1992. Granada 92 International Philatelic Exhibition. Designs showing views of the Alhambra. Multicoloured.
3721 5c. Type **1012** 10 10
3722 10c. Sunset 20 10
3723 20c. Doorway and arches . . 85 20
3724 30c. Courtyard of the Lions 1·40 30
3725 35c. Bedroom . . . . 1·70 50
3726 50c. View of Albaicin from balcony . . . . 2·30 60

1013 Facade and Plate

1992. 50th Anniv of La Bodeguita del Medio (restaurant).
3727 **1013** 50c. multicoloured . . . 1·90 60

1014 "Cattleya hibrida"

1992. 40th Anniv of Soroa Orchid Garden. Mult.
3728 3c. Type **1014** 20 10
3729 5c. "Phalaenopsis sp." . . . 20 10
3730 10c. "Cattleyopsis lindenii" 20 15
3731 30c. "Bletia purpurea" . . . 1·10 30
3732 35c. "Oncidium luridum" 1·20 40
3733 40c. "Vanda hibrida" . . . 1·50 50

1015 Hummingbird

1992. The Bee Hummingbird. Multicoloured.
3734 5c. Type **1015** 50 20
3735 10c. Perched on twig . . . 70 20
3736 20c. Perched on twig with flowers . . . . 1·50 20
3737 30c. Hovering over flower 2·50 40

1016 Guardalavaca Beach

1992. Tourism. Multicoloured.
3738 10c. Type **1016** 35 20
3739 20c. Hotel Bucanero 75 20
3740 30c. View of Havana . . . 1·40 50
3741 50c. Varadero beach . . . . 2·00 60

1017 Eligio Sardinas

1992. Olymphilex '92 International Olympic Stamps Exhibition, Barcelona. Designs showing Cuban sportsmen. Multicoloured.
3742 5c. Type **1017** 20 10
3743 35c. Ramon Fonst (fencer) 1·20 40
3744 40c. Sergio "Pipian" Martinez (cyclist) . . . . 1·40 50
3745 50c. Martin Dihigo (baseball player) . . . . 1·90 70

1018 Columbus before Queen Isabella

1992. Expo 92 World's Fair, Seville. Sheet 95 × 76 mm.
MS3746 **1018** 1p.50 multicoloured 5·00 4·75

1019 Alvarez Cabral

1992. Genova '92 International Thematic Stamp Exhibition. Explorers and their ships. Multicoloured.
3747 5c. Type **1019** 20 10
3748 10c. Alonso Pinzon 35 20
3749 20c. Alonso de Ojeda . . . 75 20
3750 30c. Amerigo Vespucci . . . 1·20 40
3751 35c. Henry the Navigator 1·40 40
3752 40c. Bartolomeu Dias . . . 1·70 50
MS3753 92 × 53 mm. 1p. Columbus's fleet (31 × 39 mm) 4·50 4·25

1020 High Jumping

1992. 6th World Athletics Cup, Havana. Mult.
3754 5c. Type **1020** 20 10
3755 20c. Throwing the javelin 70 20
3756 30c. Throwing the hammer 1·10 30
3757 40c. Long jumping (vert) . . 1·50 50
3758 50c. Hurdling (vert) . . . . 1·90 60
MS3759 64 × 84 mm. 1p. Relay race (39 × 31 mm) . . . . 3·75 2·75

1021 Men's High Jump (Gold) and Women's Discus (Gold)

1992. Cuban Olympic Games Medal Winners. Multicoloured.
3760 5c. Type **1021** 20 10
3761 5c. Men's 4 × 400 m relay (silver) and men's discus (bronze) 20 10
3762 5c. Men's 4 × 100 m relay and women's high jump and 800 m (bronze) . . . 20 10
3763 20c. Baseball (gold) 70 20
3764 20c. Boxing (7 gold and 2 silver) 70 20
3765 20c. Women's volleyball (gold) 70 20
3766 50c. Men's judo (bronze) and women's judo (gold, silver and 2 bronze) . . . 1·90 60
3767 50c. Greco-roman (gold and 2 bronze) and freestyle (gold and bronze) wrestling . . . . 1·90 60
3768 50c. Fencing (silver, bronze) and weightlifting (silver) 1·90 60

1022 Christopher Columbus and Queen Isabella the Catholic

1992. Latin-American History (7th series). Multicoloured.
3769 1c. Type **1022** 10 10
3770 1c. Columbus at Rabida Monastery 10 10
3771 1c. Columbus presenting plans to King Ferdinand and Queen Isabella . . . 10 10
3772 1c. Columbus before Salamanca Council . . . 10 10
3773 1c. Departure from Palos . . 10 10
3774 5c. Fleet stopping off at Canary Islands 20 10
3775 5c. Columbus reassuring crew 20 10
3776 5c. Sighting of land 20 10
3777 5c. Columbus landing . . . 20 10
3778 5c. Columbus's encounter with Amerindians 20 10
3779 10c. "Santa Maria" grounded off Hispaniola 35 20
3780 10c. Arrival of "Nina" at Palos 35 20
3781 10c. Columbus's procession through Barcelona . . . 35 20
3782 10c. Columbus before King and Queen 35 20
3783 10c. Departure from Cadiz on second voyage 35 20

3784 20c. King and Queen welcoming Columbus . . 85 30
3785 20c. Fleet leaving on third voyage . . 85 30
3786 20c. Columbus's deportation in chains from Hispaniola 85 30
3787 20c. Fleet embarking on fourth voyage 85 30
3788 20c. Death of Columbus at Valladolid 85 30

1023 Chacon

1024 Sanctuary of Our Lady of Charity, Cobre

1992. Birth Centenary of Jose Maria Chacon y Calvo (historian).
3789 **1023** 30c. multicoloured . . . 1·40 50

1992. Churches. Multicoloured.
3790 5c. Type **1024** 20 10
3791 20c. St. Mary's Church, Rosario . . . . 1·00 20
3792 30c. Church of the Holy Spirit, Havana . . . . . 1·40 30
3793 50c. Guardian of the Holy Angel Church, Pena Pobre, Havana . . . . . 2·75 40

1025 Diagram of Engine and Truck

1993. Development of Diesel Engine. Each showing an engine at a different stage of cycle. Multicoloured.
3794 5c. Type **1025** 10 10
3795 10c. Motor car 20 10
3796 30c. Tug 90 50
3797 40c. Diesel locomotive . . . 3·75 1·40
3798 50c. Tractor . . . . 1·50 85
MS3799 81 × 61 mm. 1p. Rudolph Diesel (80th death anniv) (39 × 31 mm) . . . . 3·75 2·50

1026 Player

1993. Davis Cup Men's Team Tennis Championship. Designs showing tennis players. Multicoloured.
3800 5c. Type **1026** 20 20
3801 20c. Double-handed backhand 65 30
3802 30c. Serve . . . . 1·00 50
3803 35c. Stretched forehand (horiz) . . . . 1·10 60
3804 40c. Returning drop shot (horiz) . . . . 1·40 70
MS3805 50 × 79 mm. 1p. Forehand (39 × 31 mm) . . . . 3·25 3·00

1027 Pedro Emilio Roux

1993. Scientists. Multicoloured.
3806 3c. Type **1027** (bacteriologist) 10 10
3807 5c. Carlos Finlay (biologist) 20 10
3808 10c. Ivan Petrovich Pavlov (physiologist) 35 20
3809 20c. Louis Pasteur (chemist) 65 30
3810 30c. Santiago Ramon y Cajal (histologist) . . . . 1·00 50
3811 35c. Sigmund Freud (psychiatrist) . . . . . . 1·10 60
3812 40c. Wilhelm Roentgen (physicist) . . . . 1·30 70
3813 50c. Joseph Lister (surgeon) 1·70 85
MS3814 67 × 52 mm. 1p. Robert Koch (bacteriologist) (vert) . . 3·25 3·00

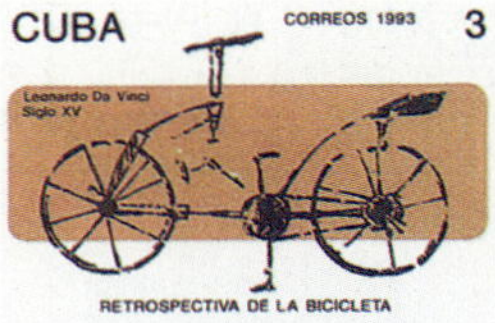

1028 Bicycle Design by Leonardo da Vinci

1993. Bicycles. Multicoloured.
3815 3c. Type **1028** 10 10
3816 5c. Draisiana hobby-horse 20 10
3817 10c. Michaux boneshaker 50 20
3818 20c. Starley penny-farthing 1·00 25
3819 30c. Lawson "Safety" bicycle . . . . 1·50 50
3820 35c. Modern bicycle . . . . 1·70 60

1029 "Valencian Fishwives"

1993. Paintings by Joaquin Sorolla in the National Museum. Multicoloured.
3821 3c. "Child eating Melon" (vert) 10 10
3822 5c. Type **1029** 20 10
3823 10c. "Regatta" 40 20
3824 20c. "Peasant Girl" 70 30
3825 40c. "Summertime" . . . . 1·40 70
3826 50c. "By the Sea" . . . . . 1·90 85

1030 "Four Winds" and Statue of Barberan and Collar

1993. 60th Anniv of Seville (Spain)–Camaguey (Cuba) Flight by Mariano Barberan and Joacuin Collar.
3827 **1030** 30c. multicoloured . . . 1·10 50

1031 Northern Jacana

1993. Brasiliana '93 International Stamp Exhibition, Rio de Janeiro. Water Birds. Multicoloured.
3828 3c. Type **1031** 10 10
3829 5c. Great blue heron (27 × 44 mm) 20 10
3830 10c. Black-necked stilt . . . 35 20
3831 20c. Black-crowned night heron 65 30
3832 30c. Sandhill crane (27 × 44 mm) . . . . . . 1·00 50
3833 50c. Limpkin . . . . 1·80 85

1032 Fidel Castro and Text

1993. Anniversaries. Multicoloured.
3834 5c. Type **1032** (40th anniv of publication of "History Will Absolve Me") . . . 15 10
3835 5c. Jose Marti (140th birth anniv) and Rafael M. Mendive (vert) 15 10
3836 5c. Carlos M. de Cespedes and broken wheel (125th anniv of Yara Proclamation) 15 10
3837 5c. Moncada Barracks (40th anniv of attack on barracks) 15 10

1033 "Sedum allantoides"

1034 Devillier's Swallowtail

1993. Cienfuegos Botanical Garden. Mult.
3838 3c. Type **1033** 10 10
3839 5c. "Heliconia caribaea" . . 20 10
3840 10c. "Anthurium andraeanum" 40 20
3841 20c. "Pseudobombax ellipticum" 75 30
3842 35c. "Ixora coccinea" . . . 1·20 60
3843 50c. "Callistemon specious" 2·10 85

1993. Bangkok 1993 International Stamp Exhibition. Butterflies. Multicoloured.
3844 3c. Type **1034** 15 10
3845 5c. Giant brimstone 20 15
3846 20c. Great southern white 75 30
3847 30c. Buckeye . . . . 1·10 50
3848 35c. White peacock . . . . 1·20 50
3849 50c. African monarch . . . 1·80 85

1035 Greater Flamingo

1036 Simon Bolivar

1993. America. Endangered Animals. Mult.
3850 5c. Type **1035** 30 15
3851 50c. Roseate spoonbill . . . 1·90 85

1993. Latin-American Integration. Mult.
3852 50c. Type **1036** . . . . . . 1·50 85
3853 50c. Jose Marti . . . . . . 1·50 85
3854 50c. Benito Juarez . . . . . 1·50 85
3855 50c. Che Guevara . . . . . 1·50 85
Nos. 3852/5 were issued together, se-tenant, forming a composite design.

1037 Swimming

1993. 17th Central American and Caribbean Games, Ponce, Puerto Rico. Multicoloured.
3856 5c. Type **1037** 10 10
3857 10c. Pole vaulting 20 15
3858 20c. Boxing 75 30
3859 35c. Gymnastics (parallel bars) (vert) . . . . . . 1·20 50
3860 50c. Baseball (vert) . . . . 1·80 85
MS3861 49 × 80 mm. 1p. Basketball (40 × 32 mm) . . . . 4·25 2·50

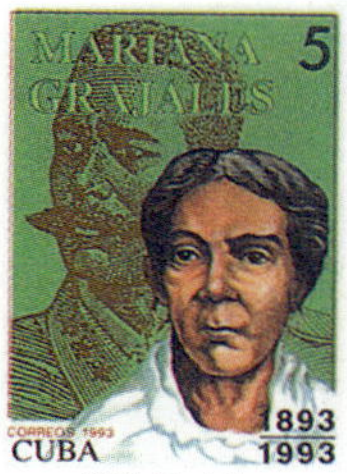

1038 Grajales

1039 Tchaikovsky

1993. Death Centenary of Mariana Grajales.
3862 **1038** 5c. multicoloured . . . 35 10

1993. Death Centenary of Pyotr Tchaikovsky (composer). Multicoloured.
3863 5c. Type **1039** 20 10
3864 20c. Ballerina in "Swan Lake" 70 30
3865 30c. Statue of Tchaikovsky 1·00 50
3866 50c. Tchaikovsky Museum (horiz) . . . . 1·40 85

1040 Flag, Dove and Broken Chains

1041 Players Challenging for Ball

1994. 35th Anniv of Revolution.
3867 **1040** 5c. multicoloured . . . 35 10

1994. World Cup Football Championship, U.S.A.
3868 **1041** 5c. multicoloured . . . 20 10
3869 – 20c. multicoloured . . . 65 30
3870 – 30c. multicoloured . . . 95 50
3871 – 35c. multicoloured . . . 1·00 50
3872 – 40c. multicoloured . . . 1·40 60
3873 – 50c. multicoloured . . . 1·50 85
MS3874 90 × 57 mm. 1p. multicoloured (39 × 31 mm) . . 3·25 2·50
DESIGNS: 20c. to 1p. Various footballing scenes.

1042 Blue Persian

1994. Cats. Multicoloured.
3875 5c. Type **1042** 20 20
3876 10c. Havana 65 20
3877 20c. Maine coon 95 40
3878 30c. British blue shorthair 1·00 50
3879 35c. Black and white bicolour Persian . . . . 1·40 50
3880 50c. Golden Persian . . . . 1·50 85
MS3881 49 × 80 mm. 1p. Abyssinian (39 × 31 mm) . . . . 4·50 2·50

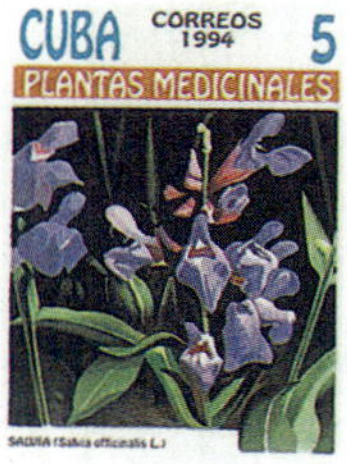

1043 Sage

1994. Medicinal Plants. Multicoloured.
3882 5c. Type **1043** 20 10
3883 10c. Aloe 30 20
3884 20c. Sunflower 70 30
3885 30c. False chamomile . . . 1·00 50
3886 40c. Pot marigold . . . . . 1·40 60
3887 50c. Large-leaved lime . . . 1·70 85

1044 London Public Transport, 1860

1994. Carriages. Multicoloured.
3888 5c. Type **1044** 20 10
3889 10c. Coach of King Fernando VII and Maria Luisa of Spain 30 20
3890 30c. French Louis XV style coach . . . . 1·10 50
3891 35c. Queen Isabel II of Spain's gala-day coach . . 1·20 50
3892 40c. Empress Catherine II of Russia's summer carriage 1·50 60
3893 50c. Havana cab (68 × 27 mm) . . . . 1·80 85

1045 Caribbean Edible Oyster

1994. Aquaculture. Multicoloured.
3894 5c. Type **1045** 35 20
3895 20c. "Cardisoma guanhumi" (crab) 65 30
3896 30c. Red-breasted tilapia . . 95 50

3897	35c. "Hippospongia lachne" (sponge)	1·10	50
3898	40c. "Panulirus argus" (crustacean)	1·40	60
3899	50c. Common carp	1·70	85

1046 Ancient Greek Athletes and Olympic Flag

1994. Centenary of International Olympic Committee. Multicoloured.

3900	5c. Type **1046**	20	10
3901	30c. Olympic flag and world map in Olympic colours	95	50
3902	50c. Olympic flag and flame	1·70	85

1047 Michael Faraday (discoverer of electricity)

1994. Scientists. Multicoloured.

3903	5c. Type **1047**	20	10
3904	10c. Marie Sklodowska-Curie (co-discoverer of radium)	30	20
3905	20c. Pierre Curie (co-discoverer of radium)	75	30
3906	30c. Albert Einstein (formulated Theory of Relativity)	1·10	60
3907	40c. Max Planck (physicist)	1·50	60
3908	50c. Otto Hahn (chemist)	1·90	85

1048 "Opuntia dillenii"

1994. Cacti. Multicoloured.

3909	5c. Type **1048**	20	10
3910	10c. "Opuntia millspaughii" (vert)	35	20
3911	30c. "Leptocereus santamarinae"	75	50
3912	35c. "Pereskia marcanoi"	1·20	50
3913	40c. "Dendrocereus nudiflorus" (vert)	1·70	60
3914	50c. "Pilocereus robinii"	1·90	85

1049 Rocket and 1939 10c. Rocket Post Stamp

1994. 2nd Spanish--Cuban Stamp Exhibition. Sheet 51 × 75 mm.

MS3915	**1049** 1p. multicoloured	3·75	2·50

1050 Rough Collies

1994. Dogs. Multicoloured.

3916	5c. Type **1050**	30	20
3917	20c. American cocker spaniels	75	30
3918	30c. Dalmatians	1·00	50
3919	40c. Afghan hounds	1·50	60
3920	50c. English cocker spaniels	1·80	85

1051 "Carpilius corallinus" (crab)

1994. Cayo Largo. Multicoloured.

3921	15c. Type **1051**	45	20
3922	65c. Shore and Cayman Islands ground iguana (vert)	2·50	1·00
3923	75c. House and brown pelican	2·75	1·20
3924	1p. Fence and common green turtle	3·75	1·70

1052 Cienfuegos

1994. 35th Anniv of Disappearance of Camilo Cienfuegos (revolutionary).

3925	**1052** 15c. multicoloured	90	20

1053 Yellow-edged Grouper

1994. Caribbean Animals. Multicoloured.

3926	10c. Type **1053**	45	20
3927	15c. Spotted eagle ray (vert)	45	20
3928	15c. Sailfish	45	20
3929	15c. Greater flamingoes (vert)	45	20
3930	65c. Bottle-nosed dolphin	2·50	1·00
3931	65c. Brown pelican (vert)	2·50	1·00

1054 Douglas DC-3

1994. 50th Anniv of I.C.A.O.

3932	**1054** 65c. multicoloured	2·20	1·00

1055 Bronze Statues of Deer

1994. 55th Anniv of Havana Zoo. Mult.

3933	15c. Type **1055**	35	20
3934	65c. Green-winged macaw	1·80	1·00
3935	75c. Eurasian goldfinch	2·10	1·20

1056 Boy with Stockbook

1994. 30th Anniv of Cuban Philatelic Federation.

3936	**1056** 15c. multicoloured	55	20

1057 Anole

1994. Reptiles. Multicoloured.

3937	15c. Type **1057**	35	20
3938	65c. Dwarf gecko	1·80	1·00
3939	75c. Curly-tailed lizard	2·00	1·20
3940	85c. Dwarf gecko (different)	2·20	1·40
3941	90c. Anole	2·50	1·60
3942	1p. Dwarf gecko (different)	2·75	1·70

1058 Cover and Spanish Mail Packet (18th-century sea mail)

1059 Cover of "Postal History of Cuba" by Jose Guerra Aguiar

1994. America. Postal Transport. Mult.

3943	15c. Type **1058**	35	20
3944	65c. Cover and messenger on horseback (19th-century rebel post) (horiz)	1·90	1·00

1995. 30th Anniv of Postal Museum.

3945	**1059** 15c. multicoloured	55	20

1060 Jose Marti and Flag

1995. Centenary of War of Independence.

3946	**1060** 15c. multicoloured	55	20

1061 Boxing

1063 1855 Cuba and Puerto Rico ½r. Stamp

1062 Siboney Cow

1995. 12th Pan-American Games, Mar del Plata, Argentina. Multicoloured.

3947	10c. Type **1061**	20	15
3948	15c. Weightlifting	35	20
3949	65c. Volleyball	1·50	95
3950	75c. Wrestling (horiz)	1·80	1·10
3951	85c. Baseball (horiz)	2·10	1·20
3952	90c. High jumping (horiz)	2·20	1·30

1995. 50th Anniv of F.A.O.

3953	**1062** 75c. multicoloured	1·80	1·10

1995. Postal Anniversaries.

3954	**1063** 15c. blue and black	35	20
3955	– 65c. multicoloured	1·50	95

DESIGNS: 15c. Type **1063** (140th anniv of first Cuban postage stamp); 65c. Colonial-style letterbox and letter (140th anniv of domestic postal service).

1064 Queen Angelfish

1995. 35th Anniv of National Aquarium. Mult.

3956	10c. Type **1064**	35	10
3957	15c. Shy hamlet	45	20
3958	65c. Porkfish	1·90	85
3959	75c. Red-spotted hawk-fish	2·20	95
3960	85c. French angelfish	2·75	1·40
3961	90c. Blue tang	2·75	1·40

1065 Portrait of Marti and Death Scene

1995. Death Centenary of Jose Marti (revolutionary). Multicoloured.

3962	15c. Type **1065**	35	15
3963	65c. Marti and Maximo Gomez in boat	1·60	95
3964	75c. Marti and Montecristi Declaration	1·80	1·20
3965	85c. Marti, Antonio Maceo and Gomez	2·20	1·30
3966	90c. Mausoleum and casket (vert)	2·30	1·40

1066 Maceo

1995. Centenary of Battle of Peralejo and 150th Birth Anniv of Antonio Maceo (revolutionary).

3967	**1066** 15c. multicoloured	70	20

1067 Gulf Fritillary

1995. Butterflies. Multicoloured.

3968	10c. Type **1067**	35	10
3969	15c. "Eunica tatila"	35	20
3970	65c. "Melete salacia"	1·60	95
3971	75c. Cuban clearwing	1·80	1·20
3972	85c. Palmira sulphur	2·20	1·30
3973	90c. Cloudless sulphur	2·30	1·40

1068 Supermarine Spitfire (Great Britain)

1995. 2nd World War Combat Planes. Mult.

3974	10c. Type **1068**	35	10
3975	15c. Ilyushin Il-2 (Russia)	35	20
3976	65c. Curtiss P-40 (United States)	1·60	95
3977	75c. Messerschmitt ME-109 (Germany)	1·80	1·20
3978	85c. Morane Saulnier 406 (France)	2·20	1·30

1069 Lecuona

1070 Horse in Stable

1995. Birth Cent of Ernesto Lecuona (composer).
3979 **1069** 15c. multicoloured . . . 55 20

1995. Singapore '95 International Stamp Exhibition. Arab Horses. Multicoloured.
3980 10c. Type **1070** 45 10
3981 15c. Two greys (horiz) . . . 45 20
3982 65c. Tethered horse . . . . 2·00 95
3983 75c. Horse in field . . . . . 2·40 1·20
3984 85c. Mare and foal . . . . 2·75 1·30
3985 90c. Grey galloping in field 2·75 1·40

1071 China P.R. 1995 20f. Stamp

1995. Beijing 1995 International Stamp and Coin Exhibition. Sheet 89 × 58 mm.
MS3986 **1071** 50c. multicoloured 1·40 1·20

1072 Wrestling

1995. Olympic Games, Atlanta (1996) (1st issue). Multicoloured.
3987 10c. Type **1072** 25 10
3988 15c. Weightlifting 35 20
3989 65c. Volleyball . . . . . . 1·60 95
3990 75c. Running . . . . 1·80 1·20
3991 85c. Baseball . . . . 2·20 1·30
3992 90c. Judo . . . . 2·30 1·40
MS3993 75 × 60 mm. 1p. Boxing (31 × 39 mm) . . . . 3·50 2·40
See also Nos. 4052/**MS**4057.

1073 Acana Factory

1995. 400th Anniv of Sugar Production in Cuba. Paintings by Eduardo Laplante. Multicoloured.
3994 15c. Type **1073** . . . . . . 2·75 45
3995 65c. Manaca factory . . . . 1·70 85

1074 Flag and Anniversary Emblem

1995. 50th Anniv of U.N.O.
3996 **1074** 65c. multicoloured . . . 1·60 95

1075 Lion

1076 St. Clare of Assisi's Convent

1995. Animals from Havana Zoological Gardens. Multicoloured.
3997 10c. Type **1075** 35 10
3998 15c. Grevy's zebra (horiz) 35 20
3999 65c. Orang-utan . . . . . . 1·60 95
4000 75c. Indian elephant (horiz) 1·80 1·20
4001 85c. Eurasian red squirrel (horiz) . . . . 2·20 1·30
4002 90c. Common racoon (horiz) 2·30 1·40

1995. 50th Anniv of UNESCO World Heritage Sites. Multicoloured.
4003 65c. Type **1076** . . . . . . 1·60 95
4004 75c. St. Francis of Assisi's Monastery church . . . . 1·80 1·20

1077 "Bletia patula"

1078 Greta Garbo

1995. Orchids. Multicoloured.
4005 40c. Type **1077** . . . . . . 1·00 65
4006 45c. "Galeandra beyrichii" 1·10 65
4007 50c. "Vanilla dilloniana" . . 1·30 75
4008 65c. "Macradenia lutescens" 1·60 95
4009 75c. "Oncidium luridum" 1·80 1·20
4010 85c. "Ionopsis utricularioides" . . . . . 2·30 1·30

1995. Centenary of Motion Pictures. Designs showing film stars (except No. 4015). Mult.
4011 15c. Type **1078** 35 15
4012 15c. Marlene Dietrich . . . 35 15
4013 15c. Marilyn Monroe . . . 35 15
4014 15c. Charlie Chaplin . . . 35 15
4015 15c. Lumiere Brothers (inventors of cine camera) 35 15
4016 15c. Vittorio de Sica 35 15
4017 65c. Humphrey Bogart . . . 1·60 95
4018 75c. Rita Montaner . . . . 1·80 1·20
4019 85c. Cantinflas . . . . . . 2·20 1·30

1079 Capitol

1995. 4th Spanish—Cuban Stamp Exhibition. Sheet 90 × 65 mm.
MS4020 **1079** 1p. multicoloured 3·50 2·40

1080 Great Red-bellied Woodpecker

1995. America. Environmental Protection. Mult.
4021 15c. Type **1080** 40 20
4022 65c. Cuban tody . . . . . 1·80 95

1081 Alfonso Goulet and Francisco Crombet Ballon

1995. Death Centenaries of Generals killed during War of Independence (1st issue). Mult.
4023 15c. Type **1081** 45 20
4024 15c. Jesus Calvar, Jose Guillermo Moncada and Tomas Jordan 45 20
4025 15c. Francisco Borrero and Francisco Inchaustegui . . 45 20
Nos. 4023/5 were issued together, se-tenant, forming a composite design of the national flag behind the portraits.
See also Nos. 4089/91 and 4162/3.

1082 Least Tern and Aerial View

1083 Carlos de Cespedes

1995. Coco Key. Multicoloured.
4026 10c. Type **1082** 25 10
4027 15c. White ibis and beach 35 20
4028 45c. Stripe-headed tanager and villas . . . . 1·10 65
4029 50c. Red-legged thrush and apartments . . . . . . 1·30 75
4030 65c. Northern mocking-bird and villas around pool . . 1·60 95
4031 75c. Greater flamingo and couple in pool . . . . . 1·80 1·20

1996. Independence Fighters.
4032 – 10c. orange 25 10
4033 **1083** 15c. green 35 20
4034 – 65c. blue . . . . 1·60 95
4035 – 75c. red . . . . 1·80 1·20
4036 – 85c. green . . . . . . 2·00 1·30
4037 – 90c. brown . . . . . . 2·30 1·40
4040 – 1p.05 mauve . . . . . 2·75 1·70
4041 – 2p.05 brown . . . . . 5·50 3·25
4042 – 3p. brown . . . . . . 7·50 4·75
DESIGNS: 10c. Serafin Sanchez; 65c. Jose Marti; 75c. Antonio Maceo; 85c. Juan Gualberto Gomez; 90c. Quintin Bandera; 1p.05, Ignacio Agramonte; 2p.05, Maximo Gomez; 3p. Calixto Garcia.

1084 "Che" Guevara and Emblem

1996. 30th Anniv of Organization of Solidarity of Peoples of Africa, Asia and Latin America.
4053 **1084** 65c. multicoloured . . . 35 20

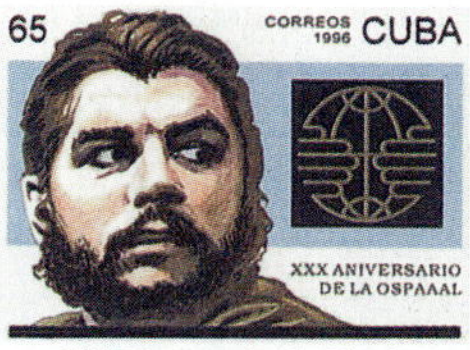

1085 Leonardo da Vinci

1996. Scientists. Multicoloured.
4046 10c. Type **1085** 25 10
4047 15c. Mikhail Lomonosov (aerodromic machines) . . 35 20
4048 65c. James Watt (steam engine) . . . . 1·60 95
4049 75c. Guglielmo Marconi (first radio transmitter) . . 1·80 1·20
4050 85c. Charles Darwin (theory of evolution) . . . . . 2·20 1·30

1086 Athletics

1996. Olympic Games, Atlanta (2nd issue). Multicoloured.
4052 10c. Type **1086** 25 10
4053 15c. Weightlifting 20 10
4054 65c. Judo . . . . 1·60 95
4055 75c. Wrestling (horiz) . . . 1·80 1·20
4056 85c. Boxing (horiz) . . . . 2·20 1·30
MS4057 59 × 80 mm. 1p. Baseball (31 × 39 mm) . . . . 3·50 2·40

1087 Cierva C.4 Autogyro

1996. Espamer Spanish–Latin American and "Aviation and Space" Stamp Exhibitions, Seville, Spain. Multicoloured.
4058 15c. Type **1087** 35 20
4059 65c.35 2-L airplane . . . . 1·70 95
4060 75c. C-201 Alcotan airplane 2·00 1·20
4061 85c. CASA C-212 Aviocar 2·30 1·30
MS4062 94 × 60 mm. 1p. Old Post Office and Gold Tower (40 × 30 mm) . . . . 3·50 2·40

1088 Belted Kingfisher

1996. Death Centenary of Juan Gundlach (ornithologist). Birds. Multicoloured.
4063 10c. Type **1088** 25 10
4064 15c. American redstart . . . 35 20
4065 65c. Common yellowthroat 1·60 95
4066 75c. Painted bunting . . . . 1·80 1·20
4067 85c. Cedar waxwing . . . . 2·20 1·30
MS4068 90 × 49 mm. 1p. Cuban vireo ("Vireo gundlachi") (36 × 28 mm) . . . . 3·50 2·40

1089 Yuri Gagarin (cosmonaut)

1090 National Flag and Hand holding Gun

1996. 35th Anniv of First Man in Space. Mult.
4069 15c. Type **1089** 35 20
4070 65c. Globes and "Vostok I" (spaceship) (horiz) . . . . 1·60 95

1996. 35th Anniversaries. Multicoloured.
4071 15c. Type **1090** (victory at Giron) 40 20
4072 65c. Flags and "35" (Declaration of Socialist character of the Revolution) . . . . . . 1·80 95

1091 "Bahama"

1996. CAPEX'96 International Stamp Exhibition, Toronto, Canada. 18th-century Ships of the Line built in Cuban Yards. Multicoloured.
4073 10c. Type **1091** 25 10
4074 15c. "Santissima Trinidad" 35 20
4075 65c. "Principe de Asturias" 1·60 95
4076 75c. "San Pedro de Alcantara" . . . . 1·80 1·20
4077 85c. "Santa Ana" . . . . . . 2·00 1·30
MS4078 90 × 50 mm. 1p. "San Genaro" (39 × 31 mm) . . . . 2·50 2·40

1092 Cuban Tody

1996. Caribbean Animals. Multicoloured.
4079 10c. Type **1092** 25 10
4080 15c. Purple-throated carib ("Eulampis jugularis") . . 35 20
4081 15c. Wood duck ("Aix sponsa") 35 20
4082 15c. Spot-finned butterflyfish 35 20
4083 65c. "Popilio cresphontes" (butterfly) . . . . 1·60 95
4084 65c. Indigo hamlet . . . . 1·60 95

1093 "Epidendrum porpax"

1996. Orchids. Multicoloured.
4085 5c. Type **1093** 25 10
4086 10c. "Cyrtopodlium punctatum" 35 15
4087 15c. "Polyrrhiza lindeni" . . 35 20

1094 Charging into Battle and Maceo

1996. Death Cent of General Jose Maceo.
4088 **1094** 15c. multicoloured . . . 55 20

1996. Death Centenaries of Generals killed during War of Independence (2nd issue). As T **1081**. Multicoloured.
4089 15c. Esteban Tamayo and Angel Guerra 40 20
4090 15c. Juan Fernandez Ruz, Jose Maria Aguirre and Serafin Sanchez 40 20
4091 15c. Juan Bruno Zayas and Pedro Vargas Sotomayor 40 20
Nos. 4089/91 were issued together, se-tenant, forming a composite design.

1095 "Jacaranda arborea" and Coast, Santiago de Cuba

1996. Tourism and Flowers. Multicoloured.
4092 15c. Type **1095** 35 20
4093 65c. "Begonia bissei" and San Pedro de la Roca Fort . . . . 1·60 95
4094 75c. "Byrsonima crassifolia" and Baconao Park, Santiago de Cuba (vert) 1·80 1·10
4095 85c. "Pereskia zinniiflora" and Sanctuary, Cobre (vert) . . . . 2·00 1·30

1096 Baldwin Locomotive No. 1112, 1878

1996. Steam Railway Locomotives. Mult.
4096 10c. Type **1096** 25 10
4097 15c. American locomotive No. 1302, 1904 . . . . . 35 20
4098 65c. Baldwin locomotive No. 1535, 1906 . . . . . 1·60 95
4099 75c. Rogers locomotive, 1914 . . . . 1·80 1·10
4100 90c. Baldwin locomotive, 1920 . . . . 2·20 1·30

1097 Free Negroes, 19th-century

1098 Children

1996. America. Costumes. Multicoloured.
4101 15c. Type **1097** 40 20
4102 65c. Guayabera couple, 20th-century . . . . . . 1·80 95

1996. 50th Anniv of UNICEF.
4103 **1098** 15c. multicoloured . . . 55 20

1099 Capablanca and Pieces

1996. 75th Anniv of Jose Raul Capablanca's First World Championship Victory. Mult.
4104 15c. Type **1099** 35 20
4105 65c. Capablanca and tournament . . . . 1·60 95
4106 75c. Globe on king and Capablanca . . . . . . 1·80 1·20
4107 85c. Capablanca as boy playing chess . . . . . . 2·00 1·30
4108 90c. Capablanca playing in tournament . . . . 2·20 1·40

1100 Flag and "Granma"

1101 Monument, Santiago de Cuba

1996. 40th Anniversaries of "Granma" Landings (15c.) and Revolutionary Armed Forces (65c.). Multicoloured.
4109 15c. Type **1100** 35 15
4110 65c. "40", flag and soldier with rifle . . . . 2·50 1·40

1996. Death Centenary of General Antonio Maceo. Multicoloured.
4111 10c. Type **1101** 25 10
4112 15c. Maceo 45 20
4113 15c. Memorial of Maceo's disembarkation, Duaba (horiz) 45 20
4114 65c. "Fall of Antonio Maceo" (detail, A. Menocal) (horiz) . . . 2·50 1·40
4115 75c. Maceo, Panchito Gomez Toro and monument, San Pedro (horiz) . . . . 2·75 1·70

1102 Women's Judo and Gold Medal (Driulis Gonzalez)

1996. Cuban Medal Winners at Olympic Games, Atlanta. Multicoloured.
4116 10c. Type **1102** 25 10
4117 10c. Freestyle wrestling and bronze medal 25 10
4118 15c. Weightlifting and gold medal (Pablo Lara) . . . 45 20
4119 15c. Greco-Roman wrestling and gold medal (Feliberto Aguilera) 45 20
4120 15c. Fencing and silver medal 45 20
4121 15c. Swimming and silver medal 45 20
4122 65c. Women's volleyball and gold medal . . . . . . 2·50 1·40
4123 65c. Boxing and gold medal (Maikro Romero, Hector Vinent, Ariel Hernandez and Felix Savon) . . . . 2·50 1·40
4124 65c. Women's running and silver medal . . . . . . 2·50 1·40
4125 65c. Baseball and gold medal . . . . 2·50 1·40

1103 Rat

1996. Chinese New Year. Year of the Rat.
4126 **1103** 15c. multicoloured . . . 80 30

1104 Minho Douro, Portugal

1996. Espamer '98 Spanish–Latin American Stamp Exhibition, Havana. Railway Locomotives. Multicoloured.
4127 15c. Type **1104** 45 20
4128 65c. Vulcan Iron Works, Brazil . . . . 2·30 1·30
4129 65c. Baldwin, Dominican Republic . . . . 2·30 1·30
4130 65c. Alco, Panama . . . . 2·30 1·30
4131 65c. Baldwin, Puerto Rico 2·30 1·30
4132 65c. Slaughter Gruning Co, Spain . . . . 2·30 1·30
4133 75c. Yorkshire Engine Co, Argentine Republic . . . 2·75 1·50
4134 75c. Porter, Chile . . . . . 2·75 1·50
4135 75c. Locomotive, Paraguay 2·75 1·50
4136 75c. Locomotive No. 12, Mexico . . . . 2·75 1·50
MS4137 105 × 85 mm. 1p. Baldwin, Cuba (36 × 29 mm) . . . . . 3·75 3·50

1105 Seal-point Siamese

1107 Dromedary

1106 "Romance del Palmar", 1938

1997. Hong Kong '97 International Stamp Exhibition. Cats. Multicoloured.
4138 10c. Type **1105** 35 10
4139 15c. Burmese 45 20
4140 15c. Japanese bobtail (horiz) 45 20
4141 65c. Singapura (horiz) . . . 2·30 1·30
4142 75c. Korat (horiz) . . . . . 2·75 1·50
MS4143 90 × 107 mm. 1p. Blue-point Siamese (39 × 31 mm) . . . . 3·50 3·25

1997. Centenary of Cuban Films. Mult.
4144 15c. Type **1106** 45 20
4145 65c. "Memorias del Subdesarrollo", 1968 (vert) . . . . 2·20 1·20

1997. Zoo Animals. Multicoloured.
4146 10c. Type **1107** 35 10
4147 15c. White rhinoceros . . . 45 20
4148 15c. Giant panda 45 20
4149 75c. Orang-utan . . . . . . 2·40 1·30
4150 90c. European bison . . . . 2·75 1·60

1108 Ox

1997. Chinese New Year. Year of the Ox.
4151 **1108** 15c. multicoloured . . . 65 30

1109 Menelao Mora and Palace

1997. 40th Anniv of Attack on Presidential Palace.
4152 **1109** 15c. multicoloured . . . 85 20

1110 Players

1997. World Cup Football Championship, France (1998).
4153 **1110** 10c. multicoloured . . . 35 10
4154 – 15c. multicoloured (red face value) 45 20
4155 – 15c. multicoloured (mauve face value) 45 20
4156 – 65c. multicoloured . . . 2·40 1·30
4157 – 75c. multicoloured . . . 2·75 1·60
MS4158 108 × 88 mm. 1p. multicoloured (39 × 31 mm) . . 3·25 3·00
DESIGNS: 15c. to 1p. Footballer (different).

1111 Youths with Flags and Emblem

1997. 35th Anniv of Communist Youth Union.
4159 **1111** 15c. multicoloured . . . 85 20

1112 "Caledonia"

1997. Stamp Day. Postal Services. Mult.
4160 15c. Type **1112** (170th anniv of maritime service) . . . 55 30
4161 65c. Fokker F.10A Super Trimotor airplane (70th anniv of international airmail) . . . . 2·20 1·20

1113 Adolfo del Castillo and Enrique del Junco Cruz-Munoz

1997. Death Centenaries of Generals killed during War of Independence (3rd issue).
4162 15c. Type **1113** 45 20
4163 15c. Alberto Rodriguez Acosta and Mariano Sanchez Vaillant 45 20
Nos. 4162/3 were issued together, se-tenant, forming a composite design.

1114 Black-bordered Orange

1997. Butterflies. Multicoloured.
4164 10c. Type **1114** 35 10
4165 15c. Bush sulphur ("Eurema dina") 45 20
4166 15c. Zebra ("Colobura dirce") 45 20
4167 65c. Red admiral . . . . . 2·20 1·20
4168 85c. "Kricogonia castalia" 2·75 1·30

1115 Luperon

1116 Royal Palms

1997. Death Cent of Gen. Gregorio Luperon.
4169 **1115** 65c. multicoloured . . . 2·10 1·20

1997. 150th Anniv of Chinese Presence in Cuba.
4170 **1116** 15c. multicoloured . . . 1·10 60

1117 National Flag and United Nations Emblem

1997. 50th Anniv of Cuban United Nations Association.
4171 **1117** 65c. multicoloured . . . 2·10 1·20

1118 Rainbow and Dove holding Olive Branch

1997. 14th World Youth and Students Festival, Cuba. Multicoloured.
4172 10c. Type **1118** 30 10
4173 15c. "Alma Mater" (statue) 40 20
4174 15c. Children on play apparatus (vert) 40 20
4175 65c. Che Guevara . . . . . 2·10 1·20
4176 75c. Statue and tower . . . 2·50 1·30

1119 Pharos of Alexandria

1997. Seven Wonders of the Ancient World. Mult.
4177 10c. Type **1119** 20 10
4178 15c. Egyptian pyramids . . 40 20
4179 15c. Hanging Gardens of Babylon 40 20
4180 15c. Colossus of Rhodes . . 40 20
4181 65c. Mausoleum of Halicarnassus . . . . . . 2·10 1·20
4182 65c. Statue of Zeus at Olympia . . . . 2·10 1·20
4183 75c. Temple of Artemis at Ephesus . . . . 2·30 1·30

1120 Pais and Testamonial of Fidel Castro

1997. 40th Death Anniv of Frank Pais (revolutionary).
4184 **1120** 15c. multicoloured . . . 50 20

1121 Mahatma Gandhi, Indian Flag and State Arms

1122 Saffron Finch ("Sicalis flaveola")

1997. 50th Anniv of Indian Independence.
4185 **1121** 15c. multicoloured . . . 50 20

1997. Birds of the Caribbean. Multicoloured.
4186 15c. Type **1122** 40 20
4187 15c. Red-headed barbet ("Eubucco bourcierii") . . 40 20
4188 15c. Cuban Amazon ("Amazona leucocephala") 40 20
4189 15c. Blue-crowned trogon ("Trogon curucui") . . . 40 20
4190 65c. Blue-throated goldentail ("Hylocharis eliciae") . . 1·90 1·10
4191 65c. Yellow-crowned Amazon ("Amazona ochrocephala") . . . . . 1·90 1·10
4192 75c. Eurasian goldfinch ("Carduelis carduelis") . . 2·10 1·20

1123 Franz Liszt and Memorial Stone commemorating his first Concert when Aged Nine

1997. Composers. Multicoloured.
4193 10c. Type **1123** 40 20
4194 15c. Johann Sebastian Bach and original manuscript score of Sonata in G minor for violin 40 30
4195 15c. Frederic Chopin and birthplace, Zelazowa Wola, Poland 40 30
4196 15c. Ludwig van Beethoven and Karntnerther Theatre where he presented the Ninth Symphony Mass in D major 40 30
4197 65c. Ignacio Cervantes and detail of score of "La Solitaria" (dance) . . . . 1·10 95
4198 75c. Wolfgang Amadeus Mozart and detail of score of first attempt at choral composition . . . 1·80 1·10

1124 Cuban Solitaire and Valle de Vinales

1997. Tourism. Multicoloured.
4199 10c. Type **1124** 40 20
4200 15c. Cuban crow and Cape Jutia 40 30
4201 65c. Olive-caped warbler and Soroa Falls (vert) . . 1·70 95
4202 75c. Giant kingbird and San Juan River (vert) . . . . 1·80 1·10

1125 "Hibiscus elatus" ("Majagua")

1997. Caribbean Flowers. Multicoloured.
4203 15c. Type **1125** 40 25
4204 15c. Rose periwinkle ("Vicaria") 40 25
4205 15c. Geiger tree ("Vomitel") 40 25
4206 15c. Bur marigold ("Romerillo") 40 25
4207 65c. Minnie root ("Salta perico") . . . . 1·70 95
4208 75c. Marilope . . . . 1·80 95

1126 Facade

1127 Congress Emblem

1997. 50th Anniv of Oriente University.
4209 **1126** 15c. multicoloured . . . 50 30

1997. 5th Cuban Communist Party Congress and 30th Death Anniv of Ernesto "Che" Guevara (revolutionary). Multicoloured.
4210 15c. Type **1127** 40 25
4211 65c. Che Guevara and letter from Guevara to Fidel Castro . . . . 1·70 95
4212 75c. Portrait of Che Guevara . . . . 1·80 95

1128 19th-century Post Box and Postman

1130 Soviet Flag, Lenin and "Aurora" (cruiser)

1129 Australopithecus, South Africa

1997. America. The Postman. Multicoloured.
4213 15c. Type **1128** 40 25
4214 65c. 20th-century post boxes and postman . . . . . . 1·60 85

1997. Prehistoric Man. Multicoloured.
4215 10c. Type **1129** 35 20
4216 15c. Pithecanthropus, Java 45 25
4217 15c. Sinanthropus, China . . 45 25
4218 15c. Neanderthal man . . . 45 25
4219 65c. Cro-Magnon man . . . 1·80 95
4220 75c. Oberkassel man, Germany . . . . 2·00 1·10

1997. 80th Anniv of Russian Revolution.
4221 **1130** 75c. multicoloured . . . 2·10 1·20

1131 "John Bull", 1831

1997. Railway Locomotives. Multicoloured.
4222 10c. Type **1131** 25 10
4223 15c. Baldwin steam locomotive, 1910–13 . . . 35 20
4224 15c. Locomotive "Old Ironsides", 1832, U.S.A. 35 20
4225 65c. Russian-built Type TEM-4.1 diesel locomotive, 1970 . . . . 1·60 95
4226 75c. Russian-built Type TE-114k diesel locomotive, 1975 . . . . 1·80 1·10
No. 4222 is inscribed "1830".

1132 National Flag and Capitol, Havana

1997. 50th Anniv of U.N. Conference on Trade and Employment, Havana.
4227 **1132** 65c. multicoloured . . . 1·60 85

1133 Garcia and 1970 30c. Stamp

1997. Birth Centenary of Victor Manuel Garcia (painter).
4228 **1133** 15c. multicoloured . . . 50 30

1134 Havana Cathedral and Pope John Paul II

1998. Papal Visit. Multicoloured.
4229 65c. Type **1134** . . . . . . 2·40 1·10
4230 75c. Our Lady of Charity Cathedral (vert) . . . . 2·75 1·10
MS4231 110 × 85 mm. 50c. Pres. Fidel Castro meeting Pope on visit to Vatican (31 × 39 mm); 50c. Pope giving blessing (31 × 39 mm) . . 3·50 2·50

1135 Menendez

1136 Players

1998. 50th Death Anniv of Jesus Menendez (labour leader).
4232 **1135** 15c. multicoloured . . . 55 30

1998. World Cup Football Championship, France. Multicoloured.
4233 10c. Type **1136** 50 20
4234 15c. Player in purple shirt lying on ground and player in red and white stripes 80 30
4235 15c. Player in yellow and black strip 80 30
4236 65c. Player in blue shirt tackling player in red and white strip (horiz) . . . . 2·50 1·10
4237 65c. Player in red and blue strip fending off player in light blue strip (horiz) . . 2·50 1·10
MS4238 111 × 88 mm. 1p. Crowd behind player No. 11 (39 × 31 mm) 4·00 3·00

1137 Isabel Rubio Diaz

1138 Revee

1998. Death Centenary of Captain Isabel Rubio Diaz (founder of mobile military hospital during War of Independence).
4239 **1137** 15c. multicoloured . . . 60 30

1998. Death Centenary of Brigadier General Vidal Ducasse Revee (revolutionary).
4240 **1138** 15c. multicoloured . . . 60 30

1139 Radio Operator and Che Guevara

1998. Communicators' Day. 40th Anniv of Radio Rebelde.
4241 **1139** 15c. multicoloured . . . 60 30

1140 Shand Mason & Co Horse-drawn Fire Engine, 1901 (Havana)

1998. Fire Engines. Multicoloured.
4242 10c. Type **1140** 35 20
4243 15c. Horse-drawn personnel and equipment vehicle, 1905 (Havana Municipal Service) 40 25
4244 15c. American–French Fire Engine Co vehicle, 1921 (Guanabacoa) 50 25
4245 65c. Chevrolet 6400 fire engine, 1952 (used throughout Cuba) . . . . 1·60 95
4246 75c. American-French-Foamite Co fire engine, 1956 (Havana) . . . . . 1·80 1·10

1141 Monument and Antonio Maceo (revolutionary)

1998. 120th Anniv of Baragua Protest (against slavery).
4247 **1141** 15c. multicoloured . . . 60 30

1142 Flags, Soldiers and Tank

1143 Tiger

1998. 10th Anniv of Victory of Angolan Government and Cuban Forces in Defence of Cuito Cuanavale, Angola.
4248 **1142** 15c. multicoloured . . . 60 30

1998. Chinese New Year. Year of the Tiger.
4249 **1143** 15c. multicoloured . . . 60 30

1144 Chihuahua ("Tatiana Vasti de Nino Angelo")

1998. Champion Dogs. Multicoloured.
4250 10c. Type **1144** 30 20
4251 15c. Beagle ("Danco") . . . 40 30
4252 15c. Mexican naked hound ("Xolot del Mictlan") . . 40 30
4253 65c. German spaniel ("D'Milican Nalut Aiwa") 2·10 1·30
4254 75c. Chow-chow ("Yoki II") 2·50 1·40

1145 Ancestor of Chimpanzee

1998. Evolution of the Chimpanzee. Multicoloured.
4255 10c. Type **1145** 45 20
4256 15c. Head and skull of "Pan troglodytes blumenbach" 50 30
4257 15c. Chimpanzee and hand and foot 50 30
4258 65c. Mother with infant and new-born chimp . . . . 2·50 1·40
4259 75c. On branch and distribution map . . . . 2·75 1·40

1146 Postman on Bicycle

1998. Juvalex 98 International Youth Stamp Exhibition, Luxembourg. Sheet 111 × 82 mm.
MS4260 **1146** 1p. multicoloured 4·75 3·75

1147 Skate

1998. Deep Sea Fishes. Multicoloured.
4261 15c. Type **1147** 55 30
4262 15c. Gulper ("Eurypharynx pelecanoides") 55 30
4263 65c. "Caulophryne" sp. . . 2·75 1·30
4264 75c. Sloan's viperfish . . . 3·00 1·40

1148 Garcia Lorca

1998. Birth Cent of Federico Garcia Lorca (poet).
4265 **1148** 75c. multicoloured . . . 3·00 1·40

1149 Crab

1150 Diana, Princess of Wales

1998. International Year of the Ocean. Mult.
4266 65c. Type **1149** . . . . . . 2·40 1·30
4267 65c. Fishes . . . . 2·40 1·30

1998. Diana, Princess of Wales Commemoration. Multicoloured.
4268 10c. Type **1150** 40 20
4269 10c. Wearing patterned dress 40 20
4270 10c. Wearing yellow and pink jacket 40 20
4271 15c. Wearing checked jacket 55 30
4272 15c. Wearing red jacket . . 55 30
4273 65c. Wearing white jacket 2·75 1·30
4274 75c. Wearing purple jacket 3·00 1·40

1151 Abel Santamaria

1998. 45th Anniv of Attack on Moncada Barracks. Multicoloured.
4275 15c. Type **1151** 55 30
4276 65c. Jose Marti . . . . . . 2·75 1·20

1152 The Crystal Palace, London (Great Exhibition, 1851)

1998. "Expo 2000" World's Fair, Hanover, Germany.
4277 **1152** 15c. multicoloured . . . 55 30
4278 – 15c. multicoloured . . . 55 30
4279 – 15c. multicoloured . . . 55 30
4280 – 15c. black, red & yellow 55 30
4281 – 65c. multicoloured . . . 2·75 1·20
4282 – 75c. multicoloured . . . 3·00 1·40
DESIGNS—HORIZ: No. 4277, Type **1152**; 4278, Atomium, Brussels (International Exhibition, 1958); 4280, Map and flag of Germany; 4282, Twipsy (mascot) on globe and fireworks. VERT: No. 4279, Twipsy; 4281, Eiffel Tower, Paris (Exhibition, 1889).

1153 Baseball

1998. 18th Central American and Caribbean Games, Maracaibo, Venezuela.
4283 **1153** 15c. multicoloured . . . 55 20

1154 Kim Il Sung and Pyongyang Landmarks

1998. 50th Anniv of Korean People's Democratic Republic (North Korea).
4284 **1154** 75c. multicoloured . . . 3·00 1·40

1155 Japanese Bust

1998. Cent of First Japanese Immigrant to Cuba.
4285 **1155** 75c. multicoloured . . . 3·00 1·40

1156 "Coelogyne flaccida"

1157 Buildings and Emblem

1998. 30th Anniv of National Botanical Garden. Orchids. Multicoloured.
4286 10c. Type **1156** 40 20
4287 15c. "Dendrobium fimbriatum" 55 30
4288 15c. Bamboo orchid ("Arundina graminifolia") 55 30
4289 65c. "Bletia patula" . . . . 2·50 1·10
4290 65c. Nun's orchid ("Phaius tankervilliaea") . . . . . 2·50 1·10

1998. 5th Congress of Revolution Defence Committees.
4291 **1157** 15c. multicoloured . . . 55 20

1158 Knight Anole and Archway, Gibara

1998. World Tourism Day. Views of Holguin. Multicoloured.
4292 10c. Type **1158** 40 20
4293 15c. Water lizard, Mirador de Mayabe 55 30
4294 65c. Water chameleon, Guardalavaca Beach (horiz) . . . . 2·50 1·10
4295 75c. Stone lizard, Pinares de Mayari (horiz) . . . . . 3·00 1·40

1159 Bernarda Toro (Manana)

1160 Two Conures

1998. America. Famous Women. Independence Activists. Multicoloured.
4296 65c. Type **1159** . . . . . . 2·50 1·10
4297 75c. Maria Cabrales . . . . 3·00 1·40

1998. The Cuban Conure. Multicoloured.
4298 10c. Type **1160** 40 20
4299 15c. Head of conure 55 30
4300 65c. Conure on branch . . . 2·50 1·10
4301 75c. Conure and leaves . . 3·00 1·40

1161 "Swan Lake"

1998. 50th Anniv of Cuban National Ballet.
4302 **1161** 15c. blue 55 20
4303 – 65c. multicoloured . . . 2·75 1·20
DESIGN: 65c. "Giselle".

1162 Apartment Building on O'Farrill and Goicuria Streets, Havana, and Victims

1998. 40th Death Anniv of Rogelia Perea, Angel Ameijeiras and Pedro Gutierrez (revolutionaries).
4304 **1162** 15c. multicoloured . . . 55 20

1163 Capt. Braulio Coroneaux (revolutionary) and Tank

1998. 40th Anniv of Battle of Guisa.
4305 **1163** 15c. multicoloured . . . 55 20

1164 Family holding Hands and United Nations Emblem

1165 Garcia Iniguez

1998. 50th Anniv of Universal Declaration of Human Rights.
4306 **1164** 65c. multicoloured . . . 2·50 1·20

1998. Death Centenary of Major-General Calixto Garca Iniguez (independence fighter).
4307 **1165** 65c. multicoloured . . . 2·30 1·20

1166 Varela and San Carlos Seminary, Havana

1998. 145th Death Anniv of Felix Varela (philosopher and Vicar-General of New York).
4308 **1166** 75c. multicoloured . . . 2·30 1·40

1167 Carlos Manuel de Cespedes

1998. Cent of Cuban War of Independence. Mult.
4309 15c. Type **1167** 40 20
4310 15c. Ignacio Agramonte Loynaz 40 20
4311 15c. Maximo Gomez Baez 40 20
4312 15c. Jose Maceo Grajales . . 40 20
4313 15c. Salvador Cisneros Betancourt 40 20
4314 15c. Calixto Garcia Iniguez 40 20
4315 15c. Adolfo Flor Crombet 40 20

4316 15c. Serafin Sanchez Valdivia 40 20
4317 65c. Jose Marti Perez . . . 1·40 95
4318 75c. Antonio Maceo Grajales . . . . 1·60 95

1168 Revolutionaries and Map

1998. 40th Anniv of Capture of Palma Soriano by Revolutionaries.
4319 **1168** 15c. multicoloured . . . 55 20

1169 "Granma" Landings

1999. 40th Anniv of Revolution. Multicoloured.
4320 65c. Type **1169** . . . . . . 2·10 1·20
4321 65c. Camilo Cienfuegos and Fidel Castro . . . . . . 2·10 1·20
4322 65c. Castro and white doves 2·10 1·20

1170 Police Car and Motor Cycle

1999. 40th Anniv of National Revolutionary Police.
4323 **1170** 15c. multicoloured . . . 60 20

1171 Workers' Rally

1172 Rabbit

1999. 60th Anniv of Revolutionary Workers' Union.
4324 **1171** 15c. multicoloured . . . 55 20

1999. Chinese New Year. Year of the Rabbit.
4325 **1172** 75c. multicoloured . . . 2·10 1·40

1173 Lenin

1999. 75th Death Anniv of Vladimir Ilich Lenin (Russian statesman).
4326 **1173** 75c. multicoloured . . . 2·50 1·40

1174 Ornithosuchus

1999. Prehistoric Animals. Multicoloured.
4327 10c. Type **1174** 40 25
4328 15c. Bactrosaurus 55 30
4329 15c. Saltopus 55 30
4330 65c. Protosuchus . . . . . 2·30 1·10
4331 75c. Mussaurus . . . . . . 2·50 1·30

1175 Damaso Perez Prado

1999. Cuban Musicians. Multicoloured.
4332 5c. Type **1175** 20 10
4333 15c. Benny More 70 30
4334 15c. Chano Pozo 70 30
4335 35c. Miguelito Valdes . . . 1·40 60
4336 65c. Bola de Nieve . . . . 2·75 1·20
4337 75c. Rita Montaner . . . . 2·75 1·40

1176 Bolivar

1177 Emblem

1999. Centenary of Simon Bolivar's Visit to Cuba. Multicoloured.
4338 65c. Type **1176** . . . . . . 2·40 1·20
4339 65c. Simon Bolivar House and statue, Havana . . . 2·40 1·20

1999. 40th Anniv of State Security Department of the Ministry of the Interior.
4340 **1177** 65c. multicoloured . . . 2·30 1·20

1178 Giant Panda

1999. China 99 International Stamp Exhibition, Peking. Sheet 109 × 82 mm.
MS4341 **1178** 1p. multicoloured 4·25 2·10

1179 Postal Rocket

1999. Stamp Day.
4342 15c. Type **1179** (60th anniv) 45 20
4343 65c. Rider on horse (130th anniv of rebel postal service) . . . . 2·00 85

1180 Painting by Roberto Matta

1999. 40th Anniv of House of the Americas (cultural organization).
4344 **1180** 65c. multicoloured . . . 2·30 85

1181 Steam Locomotive

1999. iBRA 99 International Stamp Exhibition, Nuremberg. Sheet 86 × 109 mm.
MS4345 **1181** 1p. multicoloured 1·40 1·40

1182 Castro drafting Reform Law

1999. 40th Anniv of Agrarian Reform Law.
4346 **1182** 65c. multicoloured . . . 1·40 85

1183 Royal Gramma

1999. Birth Bicentenary of Felipe Poey (naturalist). Fishes. Multicoloured.
4347 5c. Type **1183** 20 10
4348 15c. Peppermint basslet . . 45 20
4349 65c. Golden hamlet ("Hypoplectrus gummigutta") . . . . . 2·00 85
4350 65c. Dusky damselfish ("Stegastes dorsopunicans") . . . . 2·00 85
MS4351 84 × 110 mm. 1p. Poey and shy hamlet ("Hypoplectrus guttavarius") (vert) . . . . . 4·25 2·10

1184 "1814" (engraving, Jean Louis Meissonier)

1999. Philexfrance 99 International Stamp Exhibition, Paris. Sheet 85 × 110 mm.
MS4352 **1184** 1p. multicoloured . 4·25 2·10

1185 Baseball

1999. 13th Pan-American Games, Winnipeg, Canada. Multicoloured.
4353 15c. Type **1185** 40 20
4354 65c. Volleyball (vert) . . . . 1·90 85
4355 75c. Boxing . . . . 2·20 95

1186 "Victory of Wioming" (Gao Hong)

1999. 50th Anniv of People's Republic of China. Paintings. Multicoloured.
4356 5c. Type **1186** 20 10
4357 15c. "Nanchang Revolt" (Cai Lang) 40 30
4358 40c. "Red Army crossing Marsh" (Gao Quan) . . . 1·30 65
4359 65c. "Occupation of Presidential Palace" (Cheng Yifei and Wei Jingahan) . . . . . . 2·00 1·90
4360 75c. "Founding of the Republic Ceremony" (Dong Xiwen) . . . . . 2·30 1·30

1187 "Morning Glory" (Qi Baishi)

1999. "China 1999" International Stamp Exhibition, Peking. Chinese Paintings. Multicoloured.
4361 5c. Type **1187** 20 10
4362 5c. "Three Galloping Horses" (Xu Beihong) . . 20 10
4363 15c. "Hunan Woman" (Fu Baoshi) 45 30
4364 15c. "Village of Luxun" (Wu Guanzhong) 45 30
4365 15c. "Crossing" (Huangzhou) 45 30
4366 40c. "Pine Tree" (He Xiangning) . . . . 1·30 70
4367 65c. "Sleeping Woman" (Jin Shangyi) . . . . 2·00 95
4368 75c. "Poetic Scene in Xun Yang" (Chen Yifei) . . . 2·20 1·20

1188 Heinrich von Stephan (founder) and Emblem

1999. 125th Anniv of Universal Postal Union.
4369 **1188** 75c. multicoloured . . . 2·10 1·20

1189 Havana Fortress and *Antia numidia*

1999. World Tourism Day. Butterflies and Views of Havana. Multicoloured.
4370 10c. Type **1189** 30 20
4371 15c. Cathedral and black swallowtail 40 30
4372 65c. St. Francis of Assisi Convent and flambeau . . 1·90 95
4373 75c. National Senate and *Eueides cleobaea* . . . . 2·10 1·20

1190 Map of Germany on Globe

1999. "EXPO 2000" World's Fair, Hanover. Mult.
4374 5c. Type **1190** 20 10
4375 15c. Twipsy (mascot) (vert) 40 30
4376 15c. Exhibition site, Philadelphia, 1876 . . . . 40 30
4377 15c. Exhibition site, Osaka, 1970 . . . . 40 30
4378 65c. Exhibition site, Hanover . . . . 2·00 95
4379 75c. Exhibition site, Montreal, 1967 . . . . . 2·30 1·20

1191 Fokker F.27 Friendship

1999. 70th Anniv of Cuban Airlines. Multicoloured.
4380 15c. Type **1191** 40 20
4381 15c. Douglas DC-10 . . . . 40 30
4382 65c. Airbus Industrie A320 1·90 95
4383 75c. Douglas DC-3 . . . . 2·10 1·20

1192 Atomic Cloud and Feral Rock Pigeon

1194 Cienfuegos

1193 MINFAR Headquarters

1999. America. A New Millennium without Arms. Multicoloured.
4384 15c. Type **1192** 40 25
4385 65c. Globe and dove . . . . 2·00 1·20

1999. 40th Anniversaries. Multicoloured.
4386 15c. Type **1193** (Ministry of Revolutionary Armed Forces) 40 25
4387 65c. Militia members (National Revolutionary Militia) . . . . 2·00 1·20

1999. 40th Anniv of Disappearance of Major Camilo Cienfuegos (revolutionary).
4388 **1194** 15c. multicoloured . . . 1·20 30

1195 Vieja Plaza

1999. 9th Latin American Summit of Heads of State and Government, Havana. Multicoloured.
4389 65c. Type **1195** . . . . . . 1·90 95
4390 75c. San Francisco de Asis Plaza . . . . 2·10 2·10
MS4391 109 × 85 mm. 1p. Armas Plaza (37 × 31 mm) . . . . . 4·75 2·10

1196 Steam Locomotive

1999. 12th Cuban Philatelic Federation Congress. Sheet 110 × 85 mm.
MS4392 **1196** 1p. multicoloured 4·25 2·10

1197 Hemingway and Fisherman

1999. Birth Cent of Ernest Hemingway (writer).
4393 **1197** 65c. multicoloured . . . 2·10 95

1198 Villena

1999. Birth Centenary of Ruben Martinez Villena (revolutionary).
4394 **1198** 15c. multicoloured . . . 50 30

1199 Romay Chacon

1999. 150th Death Anniv of Tomas Romay Chacon (scientist).
4395 **1199** 65c. multicoloured . . . 2·10 95

1200 Dragon

2000. Chinese New Year. "Year of the Dragon".
4396 **1200** 15c. multicoloured . . . 50 30

1201 "Hot Rumba"

2000. Paintings by Concepcion Ferrant. Mult.
4397 10c. Type **1201** 30 25
4398 15c. "Cachumba" 40 30
4399 65c. "House of the babalao" 1·60 1·20
4400 75c. "Tata Cunengue" . . . 1·80 1·30

1202 *Helcyra superba*

2000. "BANGKOK 2000" International Stamp Exhibition. Butterflies. Multicoloured.
4401 10c. Type **1202** 30 20
4402 15c. *Pantaporia punctata* . . 40 30
4403 15c. *Neptis themis* 40 30
4404 65c. *Curetis acuta* . . . . . 1·70 1·20
4405 75c. *Chrysozephyrus ataxus* 2·00 1·40

1203 World Map

2000. Group of 77 South Summit, Havana.
4406 **1203** 75c. multicoloured . . . 2·10 1·40

1204 Lenin

2000. 130th Birth Anniv of Vladimir Ilich Lenin.
4407 **1204** 75c. multicoloured . . . 2·10 1·40

1205 Cuba and Puerto Rico 1855 1r. Stamp

2000. Stamp Day. Multicoloured.
4408 65c. Type **1205** (145th anniv of first Cuba and Puerto Rico stamp) . . . . 1·70 1·20
4409 90c. Jaime Gonzalez Crocier (airmail pioneer), airplane and cover (70th anniv of the airmail service) . . . 2·30 1·50

1206 Commander Guevara and Map

2000. 35th Anniv of Visit of "Che" Guevara (guerrilla fighter) to Congo.
4410 **1206** 65c. multicoloured . . . 1·80 1·20

1207 Captain San Luis

2000. 60th Birth Anniv of Eliseo Reyes Rodriguez ("Captain San Luis").
4411 **1207** 65c. multicoloured . . . 1·80 1·20

1208 Baldwin Locomotive, 1882

2000. "Stamp Show 2000" International Stamp Exhibition, London. Steam Locomotives. Mult.
4412 5c. Type **1208** 10 10
4413 10c. Baldwin locomotive, 1895 . . . . 30 20
4414 15c. Baldwin locomotive, 1912 . . . . 40 30
4415 65c. Alco locomotive, 1919 1·70 1·20
4416 75c. Alco locomotive, 1925 2·00 1·40
MS4417 104 × 85 mm. 1p. Henschel locomotive, 1920 (38 × 28 mm) 3·00 2·20

1209 Henri Giffard and Steam-powered Dirigible Airship

2000. WIPA 2000 International Stamp Exhibition, Vienna. Airship Development. Multicoloured.
4418 10c. Type **1209** 30 20
4419 15c. Albert and Gaston Tissander and airship (vert) 45 30
4420 50c. Charles Renard, Arthur Krebs and *La France* (airship) . . . . 1·40 85
4421 65c. Pierre and Paul Lebaudy and airship . . . 1·80 1·20
4422 75c. August von Perseval and airship . . . . 2·10 1·40
MS4423 85 × 108 mm. 1p. Ferdinand von Zeppelin and LZ-1 (first Zeppelin airship) (39 × 31 mm) 3·00 2·20

1210 Emblem

2000. 2nd World Meeting of "Friendship and Solidarity with Cuba", Havana.
4424 **1210** 65c. multicoloured . . . 1·60 1·40

1211 Caballero

2000. Birth Bicentenary of Jose de la Luz y Caballero (educator).
4425 **1211** 65c. multicoloured . . . 1·60 1·40

1212 Music Score, Roldan and Violin

2000. Birth Centenary of Amadeo Roldan (musician and conductor).
4426 **1212** 65c. multicoloured . . . 1·60 1·40

1213 Mother holding Child ("Child of El Senor Don Pomposo")

2000. *The Golden Age* (children's magazine by Jose Marti). Designs illustrating stories featured in the magazines. Multicoloured.
4427 5c. Type **1213** 10 10
4428 10c. Child with doll ("The Black Doll") 30 20
4429 15c. Child reading ("Mischevious Child") . . 50 30
4430 50c. "The Nightingale" (Hans Christian Andersen) . . . . . . 1·80 1·20
4431 65c. Frontispiece . . . . . 2·30 1·40
4432 75c. "The Enchanted Prawn" (Edourd R. L. Laboulaye) . . . . . . 2·75 1·70
MS4433 121 × 156 mm. As Nos. 4427/32 but smaller (36 × 29 mm) . . . . 5·75 5·25

1214 Members' Flags

2000. 20th Anniv of Latin American Association for Integration (A.L.A.D.I.).
4434 **1214** 65c. multicoloured . . . 1·70 1·40

1215 Touch Bearer

2000. Olymphilex 2000 Stamp Exhibition, Sydney. Sheet 110 × 86 mm.
MS4435 **1215** 1p. multicoloured 2·50 1·90

1216 Running

2000. Olympic Games, Sydney. Multicoloured.
4436 5c. Type **1216** 10 10
4437 15c. Football 50 30

4438 65c. Baseball . . . . 2·30 1·20
4439 75c. Cycling . . . . 2·75 1·40

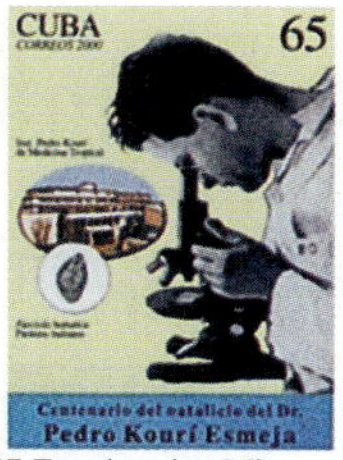

1217 Esmeja using Microscope

2000. Birth Centenary of Dr. Pedro Kouri Esmeja (tropical disease and parasitology pioneer).
4440 **1217** 65c. multicoloured . . . 1·70 1·40

1218 Women and Flag

2000. 40th Anniv of Federation of Cuban Women.
4441 **1218** 15c. multicoloured . . . 50 35

1219 18th-century Sailing Packet

2000. "Espana 2000" World Stamp Exhibition, Madrid. Multicoloured.
4442 10c. Type **1219** 30 20
4443 15c. Statue, La Cibeles Plaza, Madrid and Spain 1850 6c. stamp 50 30
4444 15c. Crystal Palace, Madrid (venue) and 1850 cover 50 30
4445 65c. Palace of Communications, Madrid and set of Spain 1850 stamps . . . . 2·30 1·40
4446 75c. Galician Centre, Havana with Cuba and Puerto Rica 1855 ½r. stamp . . . . 2·50 1·70
MS4447 111 × 88 mm. 100c. Queen Isabella II of Spain (31 × 39 mm) 3·50 3·00

1220 Senen Casas Reguerio Railway Station, Santiago de Cuba

2000. 20th Congress of Pan-American Railways.
4448 **1220** 65c. multicoloured . . . 1·80 1·50

1221 Coconut Forest Bay, Hainan, China

2000. 40th Anniv of Cuba–China Diplomatic Relations. Joint issue with China. Multicoloured.
4449 15c. Type **1221** 50 40
4450 15c. Varadero beach, Matanzas, Cuba 50 40
Nos. 4449/50 were issued together, se-tenant, forming a composite design.

1222 Hawksbill Turtle (*Eretmochelys imbricata*), Guardalavaca

2000. World Tourism Day. Diving Sites. Mult.
4451 10c. Type **1222** 30 20
4452 15c. Nassau grouper (*Epinephelus striatus*), El Colony 40 30
4453 65c. French angelfish (*Pomacanthus paru*), Santa Lucia (horiz) . . . . . . 1·90 1·30
4454 75c. Black margate (*Anisotremus surinamensis*), Maria la Gorda (horiz) . . . . . . 2·10 1·40

1223 House and People Gardening

1224 Emblem, Heart-shaped Globe and Family

2000. 40th Anniv of Committees for Defense of the Revolution (CDR).
4455 **1223** 15c. multicoloured . . . 50 35

2000. America. Anti-A.I.D.S. Campaign. Mult.
4456 15c. Type **1224** 50 35
4457 65c. Emblem, heart-shaped globe and couple . . . . 2·10 1·40

1225 Soldiers carrying Flags

2000. 25th Anniv of Cuban International Mission to Angola.
4458 **1225** 75c. multicoloured . . . 2·10 1·70

1226 Humboldt and Guesthouse, Trinidad

2000. Bicentennial of Friedrich Wilhelm Heinrich Alexander von Humboldt's Visit to Cuba. Mult.
4459 15c. Type **1226** 50 35
4460 65c. Humboldt, frontispiece of *On the Island of Cuba* (political essay) and Humboldt House, Havana 2·10 1·40

1227 *Polymita picta iolimbata*

2000. New Millennium. Snails. Multicoloured.
4461 65c. Type **1227** . . . . . . 2·10 1·40
4462 65c. *Polymita picta roseolimbata* . . . . . . 2·10 1·40
4463 65c. *Polymita picta picta* . . 2·10 1·40
4464 65c. *Polymita picta nigrolimbata* . . . . . . 2·10 1·40
4465 65c. *Polymita versicolor* . . 2·10 1·40
Nos. 4461/4 were issued together, se-tenant, forming a composite design.

1228 Dragon

2001. New Year. Year of the Dragon.
4466 **1228** 15c. multicoloured . . . 85 45

1229 Mandarin Duck (*Aix galericulata*)

2001. Birds. Hong Kong 2001 International Stamp Exhibition. Multicoloured.
4467 5c. Type **1229** 10 10
4468 10c. Golden pheasant (*Chrysolophus pictus*) (inscr "Chryysolophus") 30 20
4469 15c. Grey heron (*Ardea cinerea*) 50 30
4470 65c. Red Jungle-fowl (*Gallus gallus*) . . . . 2·30 1·40
4471 75c. Collared dove (*Streptotelia decaocto*) . . 2·50 1·70
MS4472 111 × 85 mm. 1p. Common crane (*Grus grus*) (32 × 40 mm) 3·25 2·30

1230 Sports Centre

2001. 40th Anniv of INDER (National Institute for Sport, Physical Education and Recreation).
4473 **1230** 65c. multicoloured . . . 2·10 1·40

1231 Refugees

2001. 50th Anniv of United Nations High Commissioner for Refugees.
4474 **1231** 65c. multicoloured . . . 2·00 1·30

1232 James Miholland's Locomotive

2001. Steam Locomotives. Multicoloured.
4475 10c. Type **1232** 30 20
4476 15c. Theodore Sheffler's fire-less steam locomotive . . 40 30
4477 40c. Adams and Price's chain driven locomotive 1·20 75
4478 65c. Peckett and Sons' Bulan . . . . 2·00 1·40
4479 75c. W. G. Bagnall's fire-less steam locomotive . . . . 2·30 1·70

1233 Anniversary Emblem and Lighthouse 2001

2001. 105th Inter-Parliamentary Union Conference, Havana.
4480 **1233** 65c. multicoloured . . . 2·20 1·40

1234 "Bombardeo del 15 Abril" (Servando Cabrera)

2001. 40th Anniv of Bay of Pigs (Playa Giron).
4481 **1234** 65c. multicoloured . . . 2·10 1·40

1235 Cats

2001. Cats and Dogs. Showing cats, dogs and animal societies' emblems. Multicoloured.
4482 10c. Type **1235** 30 20
4483 15c. Fighting dogs 40 30
4484 15c. German shepherd, boxer and puppy 40 30
4485 65c. Spaniel and collies . . 1·90 1·30
4486 75c. Snarling dog, cats, and puppy . . . . 2·30 1·40

1236 Anniversary Emblem

2001. 40th Anniv of Radio Havana Cuba.
4487 **1236** 65c. multicoloured . . . 2·00 1·40

1237 Boats (engraving, Frederic Mialhe)

2001. Cuba 2001 International Tourism Convention, Havana.
4488 **1237** 65c. multicoloured . . . 2·00 1·40

1238 St. Michael's Cathedral, Brussels

1239 Sniffer Dog and Handler

2001. Belgica 2001 International Stamp Exhibition, Brussels. Multicoloured.
4489 5c. Type **1238** 20 10
4490 10c. Sablon Church (horiz) 30 20
4491 15c. Royal Palace (horiz) . . 50 40

4492 65c. Basilica of the Sacred Heart, Koekelberg (horiz) 2·00 1·40
4493 75c. Atomium (model of an iron crystal) Exhibition Centre . . . . 2·30 1·70
MS4494 107 × 83 mm. 100c. Kings Residence, Grand Place, Brussels (32 × 40 mm) . . . . 3·00 2·20

2001. 40th Anniv of Ministry of Interior.
4495 **1239** 65c. multicoloured . . . 1·80 1·40

1240 Locomotive *JR 500*

2001. Japanese Locomotives. Philanippon '01 International Stamp Exhibition, Tokyo. Multicoloured.
4496 5c. Type **1240** 10 10
4497 10c. Locomotive *JR 700* . . 30 20
4498 15c. Locomotive *MAX 1* . . 40 30
4499 65c. Locomotive *MAX 2* . . 1·90 1·30
4500 75c. Locomotive *300* . . . . 2·10 1·40
MS4501 78 × 110 mm. 100c. Locomotive *Zero* (40 × 32 mm) 3·00 1·90

1241 Mount Titano and St. Marino (statue)

2001. 1700th Anniv of Founding of San Marino.
4502 **1241** 75c. multicoloured . . . 2·20 1·40

1242 Tench (*Tinca tinca*)

2001. Aquatics Breeding Programme. Multicoloured.
4503 5c. Type **1242** 10 10
4504 10c. Common frog (*Rana temporaria*) 30 20
4505 15c. Blue land crab (*Cardisoma guanhumi*) . . 40 30
4506 65c. Common mussel (*Mytilus edulis*) . . . . . 1·90 1·30
4507 75c. Spotted tilapia (*Tilapia mariae*) . . . . 2·10 1·40
MS4508 86 × 111 mm. 1p. White-clawed crayfish (*Potamobius pallipes*) (40 × 32 mm) . . . . 3·00 3·00

1243 Anniversary Emblem and Ernesto "Che" Guevara

2001. 40th Anniv of Recycling.
4509 **1243** 65c. multicoloured . . . 2·00 1·30

1244 Valle de Vinales, Pinar del Rio

2001. Tourism. Multicoloured.
4510 10c. Type **1244** 25 15
4511 15c. Trindad de Cuba 40 20
4512 65c. Playa Sirena (beach), Cayo Largo del Sur . . . 1·90 1·30
4513 75c. Morro-Cabana (castle), Havana . . . . 2·10 1·40

1245 Children encircling Globe

2001. United Nations Year of Dialogue Among Civilizations.
4514 **1245** 65c. multicoloured . . . 2·00 1·40

1246 *Tetramicra malpighiarum* (orchid)

2001. America. UNESCO World Heritage Sites. Desamarco del Granma National Park. Multicoloured.
4515 15c. Type **1246** 40 20
4516 65c. *Liggus vittatus* (shell) 1·90 1·40

1247 Building

2001. Centenary of José Marti National Library.
4517 **1247** 15c. multicoloured . . . 45 30

1248 Torso and Head

1249 Eduardo Chibas

2001. 25th Anniv of Cuban Airliner Explosion over Barbados. Showing parts of painting. Multicoloured.
4518 5c. Type **1248** 10 10
4519 10c. Dove 25 15
4520 15c. Pregnant woman . . . 40 20
4521 50c. Stylized birds . . . . . 1·40 95
4522 65c. Star and houses . . . . 1·90 1·30
Nos. 4518/22 were issued together, se-tenant, forming a composite design.

2001. 50th Death Anniv of Eduardo Chibas (politician).
4523 **1249** 65c. multicoloured . . . 2·00 1·30

1250 Napoleon on Horseback and Map of Battle of Eylau (inscr "Elyeau")

2001. 40th Anniv of Napoleon Museum, Havana. Showing Napoleon and battles maps.
4524 10c. Type **1250** 30 15
4526 10c. Battle of Marengo . . 30 15
4527 65c. Battle of Waterloo . . 1·90 1·30
4528 75c. Battle of Abukin . . . 2·10 1·40

1251 Pablo de la Torriente

1253 Tyrone Power

1252 Mosaic Pigeon (3013-67-HM)

2001. Birth Centenary of Pablo de la Torriente (writer).
4529 **1251** 75c. multicoloured . . . 2·20 1·40

2001. 4th Pigeon Fanciers Federation Congress. Multicoloured.
4530 65c. Type **1252** . . . . . . 1·80 85
4531 65c. Emperor (2241-55-ME) 1·80 85
4532 65c. Bronzed (338-59-HE) 1·80 85
4533 65c. Mosaic (1561-66-HM) 1·80 85
4534 65c. Dark emperor (2021-61-ME) . . . . 1·80 85

2001. Actors. Multicoloured.
4535 5c. Type **1253** 20 10
4536 10c. Steve McQueen 30 15
4537 10c. Ava Gardner 30 15
4538 15c. Rita Hayworth 40 20
4539 15c. James Dean 40 20
4540 15c. Marilyn Monroe . . . 40 20
4541 65c. Natalie Wood . . . . 1·90 85
4542 65c. Rock Hudson . . . . 1·90 85
4543 75c. Richard Burton . . . . 2·10 1·30
MS4544 150 × 185 mm. Nos. 4535/43 6·75 5·75

1254 Bamboo and Horse

2002. Year of the Horse.
4545 **1254** 15c. multicoloured . . . 45 30

1255 Cigars and Hat

2002. 4th Habano (cigar) Festival, Havana. Multicoloured.
4546 5c. Type **1255** 20 10
4547 10c. Smoking cigar 30 15
4548 15c. Wax seal and map . . 40 20
4549 65c. Stamps, Punch and crossed swords . . . . . 1·90 85
4550 75c. Flag, tobacco plants and Alejandro Robaina (5th anniv of "Vegas Robaina" (cigar manufacturer)) . . . . . 2·10 95
MS4551 118 × 91 mm. 1p. Fidel Castro, map and star (40 × 32 mm) 3·00 1·90

1256 Profile, Dove holding Envelope and Computer (½-size illustration)

2002. 2nd UPAEP Information Technology Workshop.
4552 **1256** 65c. multicoloured . . . 2·10 1·30

1257 Map Reading

1259 Two Football Players (Brazil in foreground)

1258 Soldiers, Demonstrators, Industry and Computers

2002. Pioneer Explorers (scouts). Multicoloured.
4553 5c. Type **1257** 20 10
4554 15c. Tying knots 40 20
4555 50c. Cooking over campfire 1·40 70
4556 65c. Lighting campfire . . . 1·90 85
4557 75c. Orienteering . . . . . 2·10 95

2002. 40th Anniv of Young Communists Union.
4558 **1258** 15c. multicoloured . . . 40 30

2002. World Cup Football Championships, Japan and South Korea. Showing two players and flag, player in foreground given. Multicoloured.
4559 15c. Type **1259** 40 20
4560 15c. Spain 40 20
4561 15c. France 40 20
4562 15c. Germany 40 20
4563 15c. Korean Republic . . . 40 20
4564 65c. Argentina . . . . . . 1·90 85
4565 75c. Italy . . . . 2·10 95
4566 85c. Japan . . . . 2·30 1·10

1260 NH Parque Central Hotel, Havana

2002. Spanish–Cuban Philatelic Exhibition, Havana. Sheet 110 × 84 mm.
MS4567 **1260** 1p. multicoloured 3·00 2·00

1261 Bust and Experimental Agricultural Building, Santiago de las Vegas

2002. 125th Birth Anniv of Juan Thomas Roig (botanist). Multicoloured.
4568 5c. Type **1261** 20 10
4569 10c. Juan Roig's house and bust 30 15
4570 15c. Tobacco plant and Roig 40 20
4571 50c. Roig (sculpture) and *Allophyllum roiggi* . . . . 1·40 70
4572 65c. Botanical dictionary and Roig . . . . 1·90 85

1262 Table with Wine and Cigars

2002. Expovid 2002 International Wine Festival, Havana. Multicoloured.
4573 15c. Type **1262** 20 10
4574 65c. Glass of white wine and barrels 1·90 85
4575 75c. Glass of red wine and vineyard 2·10 95

1263 Hands, Heart and Leaf

1264 *Amanita junquillea*

2002. 10th Anniv of MediCuba Switzerland (humanitarian organization).
4576 **1263** 75c. multicoloured 2·20 1·40

2002. Fungi. Multicoloured.
4577 5c. Type **1264** 20 10
4578 15c. *Lepiota puellaris* 40 20
4579 45c. *Cortinarius cumatillis* 1·20 60
4580 65c. *Pholiota adipose* (inscr "Pholliota") 1·90 85
4581 75c. Shaggy ink cap (*Coprinus comatus*) 2·10 95

1265 Nicolas Guillen

2002. Birth Centenary of Nicolas Guillen (poet).
4582 **1265** 65c. multicoloured 1·90 1·30

1266 "Dockers" (painting)

2002. Birth Centenary of Marcelo Pogolotti (artist).
4583 **1266** 15c. multicoloured 55 30

1267 Agostinho Neto and Map of Africa

2002. 80th Birth Anniv of Agostinho Neto (first president of independent Angola).
4584 **1267** 65c. multicoloured 1·90 1·30

1268 Grey plover (*Pluvialis squatarola*) (inscr "Calidris minutilla")

2002. Espana 2002 International Stamp Exhibition. Birds. Multicoloured.
4585 5c. Type **1268** 20 10
4586 10c. Greater yellow-legs (*Tringa melanoleuca*) (inscr "melanoleucas") 30 15
4587 15c. Semi-palmated plover (*Charadius semipalmatus*) 40 20
4588 65c. Least sandpiper (*Calidris minutilla*) (inscr "Pluvialis squatarola") 1·90 95
4589 75c. Ruddy turnstone (*Arenaria interpres*) 2·10 1·30
MS4590 110 × 87 mm. 1p. Sora crake (*Porzana Carolina*) (40 × 32 mm) 2·75 1·90

1269 Photographer and War Scene

2002. 3rd International War Correspondents' Conference.
4591 **1269** 65c. multicoloured 1·90 95

1270 Ernesto "Che" Guevara

2002. 35th Death Anniv of Ernesto "Che" Guevara (revolutionary). Multicoloured.
4592 5c. Type **1270** 20 10
4593 10c. Face 30 15
4594 15c. Smoking 50 30
4595 50c. Speaking 1·60 75
4596 65c. Facing left 1·90 85
4597 75c. Seated facing right 2·30 1·10
MS4598 200 × 161 mm. Nos. 4592/7 6·75 5·25

1271 Emblem, Teacher and Pupil

2002. UPAEP. Literacy Campaign. Multicoloured.
4599 15c. Type **1271** 50 30
4600 65c. School, flag, children and computer 1·90 95

1272 Mercury Monterrey (1957)

2002. Cars. Multicoloured.
4601 5c. Type **1272** 20 10
4602 5c. Pontiac Catalina (1956) 30 15
4603 15c. Cadillac Fleetwood (1959) 50 30
4604 65c. Hudson Hornet (1951) 1·90 95
4605 75c. Chevrolet Bel Air (1957) 2·30 1·20
4606 85c. Mercedes Benz 190 SL (1957) 2·50 1·40

1273 G. Mesa

1274 Statuette and Emblem

2002. 15th Intercontinental Cup Baseball Championship. Showing players. Multicoloured.
4607 5c. Type **1273** 20 10
4608 15c. A. Pacheco 50 30
4609 50c. O. Linares 1·60 75
4610 65c. O. Kindelan 1·90 95
4611 75c. L. Ulacia 2·30 1·40

2002. 4th Havana International Trade Fair.
4612 **1274** 65c. multicoloured 1·90 95

1275 G. and R. Stephenson's *Rocket*

2002. Steam Locomotives. Multicoloured.
4613 5c. Type **1275** 20 10
4614 15c. Early locomotive (inscr "Miller") 50 30
4615 50c. *Vulcan* 1·60 75
4616 65c. *Consolidation* 1·90 95
4617 75c. *Mikado* 2·30 1·40

A brief description of each locomotive is given in the enlarged margin above or below the relevant stamp.

1276 Corp de Ballet

2002. 40th Anniv of Ballet de Camaguey (dance company). Multicoloured.
4618 65c. Type **1276** 1·90 95
4619 75c. Principal dancers 2·30 1·40

1277 Centenary Emblem and Surgeon General Wyman

2002. Centenary of PanAmerican Health Organization.
4620 **1277** 65c. multicoloured 1·90 95

1278 "Emi Cosinca" (painting)

2002. Birth Centenary of Wilfred Lam (artist). Paintings. Multicoloured.
4621 15c. Type **1278** 50 30
4622 45c. "Yo say" 1·60 75
4623 65c. "Retro de H. H." 1·90 95
4624 75c. "Mujer Sentada" 2·30 1·40

1279 Dulce Loynaz

2002. Birth Centenary of Dulce M. Loynaz (writer).
4625 **1279** 65c. multicoloured 1·90 1·30

1280 Bottle-nose Dolphin (*Tursiops truncates*)

2002. National Philately Championship. Sheet 84 × 111 mm.
MS4626 **1280** 1p. multicoloured 3·00 2·40

1281 Red Deer (*Cervus elaphus*) and Irish Elk (*Megaloceros*) (½-size illustration)

2002. Prehistoric Animals. Prehistoric animals and their modern counterparts. Multicoloured.
4627 5c. Type **1281** 20 10
4628 10c. Gelada baboon (*Theropithecus gelada*) and baboon (*Papio anubis*) 30 15
4629 15c. Black rhinoceros (*Diceros bicornis*) and woolly rhinoceros (*Coelodonta*) 50 30
4630 45c. Dire wolf (*Canis dirus*) and wolf (*Canis lupus*) 1·30 75
4631 65c. Grizzly bear (*Ursus arctos*) and cave bear (*Ursus spelaeus*) 1·90 95
4632 75c. Saber-toothed tiger (*Smilodon*) and lion (*Panthera leo*) 2·30 1·40

1282 Goat

2003. New Year. "Year of the Goat". Multicoloured.
4633 15c. Type **1282** 50 30
4634 15c. Goat facing left (red background) 50 30

1283 "Flores Amaraillas" (Amelia Pelaez)

1284 Jose Marti's Birthplace

2003. 185th Anniv of San Alejandro Art School. Multicoloured.
4635 5c. Type **1283** 20 10
4636 15c. "Harlequin" (Rene Portocarrero) 40 20
4637 65c. Abstract (Mario Carrreno) (horiz) 1·80 95
4638 75c. Figures (Servando Cabrera) 2·10 1·10

2003. 150th Birth Anniv of Jose Marti (writer and revolutionary). Multicoloured.
4639 15c. Type **1284** 40 20
4640 65c. "Los Antillos libres..." and clouds (horiz) 1·80 95
4641 65c. Unfinished letter to Manuel Mercado, 18 May 1985 1·80 95
4642 75c. Jose Marti 2·10 1·10
MS4643 84 × 109 mm. 1p. Jose Marti (40 × 32 mm) 3·00 2·40

1285 Men seated around Table

2003. Habana (cigar) Festival, Havana. Multicoloured.
4644 15c. Type **1285** 40 20
4644a 15c. Woman with cigar box 40 20
4645 50c. Growing tobacco and hands rolling cigar (46 × 46 mm) . . . . . 1·30 75
4646 65c. Building faÇade (5th anniv of "Trinidad" (cigar manufacturer)) (46 × 46 mm) . . . . . 1·80 95
4647 75c. Man seated on stamp, palm and office (46 × 46 mm) . . . . . 2·10 1·10
MS4648 125 × 98 mm. 1p. Aboriginal smoking cigar (32 × 40 mm) . . . . 3·00 2·40

1286 Fidel Castro

2003. 40th Anniv of Radio Rebelde.
4649 **1286** 65c. multicoloured . . . 1·80 95

1287 Felix Varela

1288 Mario Munoz

2003. 150th Death Anniv of Felix Varela (priest and reformer).
4650 **1287** 65c. multicoloured . . . 1·80 95

2003. 45th Anniv of Mario Munoz Monroy Third Eastern Front.
4651 **1288** 15c. multicoloured . . . 50 30

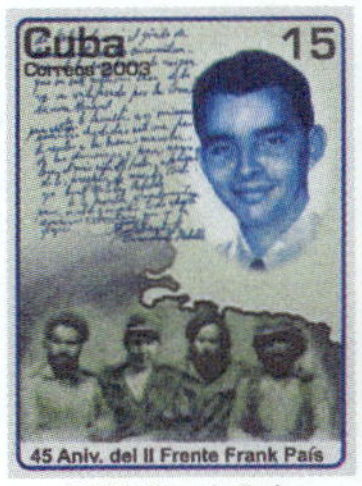

1289 Frank Pais

1290 "El pensamiento" (Manuel Mendive)

2003. 45th Anniv of Frank Pais M26J Urban Front.
4652 **1289** 15c. multicoloured . . . 50 30

2003. 16th World Sexology Congress, Havana.
4653 **1290** 65c. multicoloured . . . 1·80 95

1291 Container Ship

2003. Transport. Multicoloured.
4654 5c. Type **1291** 20 10
4655 10c. Lorry 30 15
4656 15c. Locomotive pulling container truck 40 20
4657 65c. Lorry at airport . . . . 1·80 95
4658 75c. Aircraft and lorry . . . 2·10 1·10

1292 *Nymphaea ampla* and *Lepisosteus tristoechus*

1294 Barrack Facade

1293 Kayaking

2003. Flora and Fauna. Multicoloured.
4659 5c. Type **1292** 20 10
4660 10c. Stripe-headed tanager (*Spindalis zena pretre*) and *Magnolia grandiflora* . . . 30 15
4661 15c. *Lillium candicum* and *Polymita picta* 40 20
4662 65c. *Stralitzia regale* and *Solenodon cubanus* . . . . 1·80 95
4663 75c. *Hibiscus rosa sinesis* and Bee hummingbird (*Mellisuga helenae*) (inscr "Mellysuga") . . . . . . 2·10 1·10
MS4664 112 × 85 mm. 1p. Woolly mammoth (*Mammuthus primigenius*) (40 × 32 mm) . . . 3·00 2·40

2003. Pan American Games. Multicoloured.
4665 5c. Type **1293** 20 10
4666 15c. Judo 40 20
4667 50c. Athletics . . . . 1·30 75
4668 65c. Volleyball . . . . . . 1·80 95

2003. 50th Anniv of Assault on Moncada Barracks, Santiago de Cuba. Multicoloured.
4669 15c. Type **1294** 40 20
4670 65c. Fidel Castro . . . . . 1·80 95

1295 Flat Truck

2003. Railways. Multicoloured.
4671 5c. Type **1295** (Cuba) (c. 1930) 20 10
4672 10c. Crane (USA) (1920) . . 30 15
4673 15c. General Electric Co. BB120/120E (USA) (1925) 40 20
4674 65c. DVM-9-Ganz (Hungary) (1969) . . . . 1·80 95
4675 75c. American Locomotive Co. 2-6-0 (USA) (1905) 2·10 1·10

1296 Flowers in Desert (⅗-size illustration)

2003. United Nations Covention to Combat Desertification (UNCCD) Conference, Havana.
4676 **1296** 65c. multicoloured . . . 2·50 95

1297 Snowy Owl (*Nyctea scandiaca*)

2003. Bangkok 2003 International Stamp Exhibition. Fauna. Multicoloured.
4677 5c. Type **1297** 20 10
4678 10c. Puffin (*Fratercula artica*) 30 15
4679 15c. Gannet (*Sula bassana*) 40 20
4680 65c. Polar bear and cub (*Ursus maritimus*) . . . . 1·80 95
4681 75c. Arctic fox (*Alopex lagopus*) . . . . 2·10 1·10
MS4682 86 × 108 mm. 1p. Harp seal pup (*Pagolphilus groenlandicus*) 3·50 3·00

1298 *Gardenia jasminoides* and Silver-spot (*Dione juno*)

2003. Butterflies and Flowers. Multicoloured.
4683 5c. Type **1298** 20 10
4684 15c. *Chrysanthemus sinence* and *Apatura ilia* 40 20
4685 65c. *Hibiscus rosa sinensis* and peacock (*Inachis io*) 1·80 95
4686 75c. *Althea rosea* and *Marpesia iole* . . . . . . 2·10 1·10
MS4687 111 × 87 mm. 1p. *Zantedeschia aethiopica* and monarch (*Danaus plexippus*) (32 × 40 mm) . . . . 3·50 3·00

1299 Cuban Conure (*Aratinga euops*) (inscr "eops")

2003. Ecotourism. Multicoloured.
4688 10c. Type **1299** 20 10
4689 15c. Cuban green woodpecker (*Xiphiopicus percussus*) 40 20
4690 65c. Cuban grassquit (*Tiaris canora*) . . . . 1·80 95
4691 75c. Cuban trogon (*Priotelus temnurus*) . . . . 2·10 1·10

1300 Young Crocodile and Eggs

2003. Crocodiles (*Crocodylus rhombifer*). Multicoloured.
4692 15c. Type **1300** 40 20
4693 15c. Adult 40 20
4694 65c. Adult eating bird . . . 1·80 95
4695 75c. Head . . . . 2·10 1·10

1301 Cuban Green Woodpecker (*Xiphiopicus percussus*)

2003. America. Flora and Fauna. Multicoloured.
4696 15c. Type **1301** 40 20
4697 65c. *Encyclia phoenicea* . . 2·10 1·10

1302 Antonio Munoz

2003. Baseball World Cup Championship—2003, Cuba. Multicoloured.
4698 5c. Type **1302** 20 10
4699 10c. Lourdes Gourriel . . . 20 10
4700 15c. Lazaro Vargas 40 20
4701 15c. Jorge Valdes 40 20
4702 65c. Lazaro Valle . . . . . 1·80 95
4703 75c. Javier Mendez . . . . 2·10 1·10
MS4704 110 × 86 mm. 1p. Players (32 × 40 mm) . . . . 3·50 3·00

1303 Alicia Alonso as *Giselle*

2003. Ballet Anniversaries. Multicoloured.
4705 65c. Type **1303** (60th anniv of Alicia Alonso's performance as *Giselle*) 2·10 95
4706 65c. National Ballet Company (55th anniv) (horiz) . . . . 2·10 95

1304 Wright Brothers and *Wright Flyer*

2003. Centenary of Powered Flight. Multicoloured.
4707 5c. Type **1304** 20 10
4708 15c. Pitcairn PA-5 (1928) . . 40 20
4709 65c. Estearman C-3MB (1927) . . . . 1·80 95
4710 75c. Douglas M-2 (1926) . . 2·10 1·10

1305 Partisans

2004. 45th Anniv of Revolution.
4711 **1305** 65c. multicoloured . . . 1·60 1·10

1306 Rowing Boats and Emblem (½-size illustration)

2004. 15th Anniv of ExpoCuba.
4712 **1306** 65c. multicoloured . . . 1·60 1·10

1307 Baseball and Parthenon (½-size illustration)

2004. Olympic Games, Athens. Multicoloured.
4713 10c. Type **1307** 20 10
4714 15c. Early runners (amphora) and modern women runners 30 15
4715 65c. Modern boxers and early athlete . . . . . 1·80 95
4716 75c. Early charioteer and modern show-jumper . . 2·10 1·10

1308 Monkey

1309 Julio Mella

2004. New Year. Year of the Monkey. Multicoloured, background colour given.
4717 15c. Type **1308** (lilac) . . . 50 30
4718 15c. Monkey (orange) . . . 50 30

2004. 75th Death Anniv of Julio Antonio Mella (revolutionary).
4719 **1309** 65c. multicoloured . . . 1·60 1·10

1310 San Pablo College and Jose Marti

2004. Jose Marti (writer and revolutionary) Commemoration. Multicoloured.
4720 5c. Type **1310** 20 10
4721 5c. Mariano Marti (father) 20 10
4722 5c. Leonor Perez (mother) 20 10
4723 10c. With Fermin Dominguez 30 15
4724 10c. As young man and Havana jail 30 15
4725 15c. Wearing prison uniform and Fragua Martiana Museum 40 20
4726 15c. "El Abra", Isla de Pinos and Jose Marti . . 40 20
4727 15c. Guanabacoa Grammar School and Jose Marti seated with his son . . . 40 20
4728 65c. Emperado building and Jose Marti holding son 1·80 95
4729 75c. "La Jatia" and Jose Marti . . . . 2·10 1·10

1311 San Juan de Dios Church

2004. 490th Anniv of Santa Maria del Puerto del Principe.
4730 **1311** 15c. multicoloured . . . 50 30

1312 Tram and Conductor

2004. Trams. Multicoloured.
4731 5c. Type **1312** 20 10
4732 10c. Tram No. 276 . . . . 30 15
4733 15c. Tram with two doors 40 20
4734 65c. Grey tram . . . . . . 1·80 95
4735 75c. Smaller orange tram . . 2·10 1·10
MS4736 110 × 81 mm. $1 Green tram (40 × 32 mm) . . . . . . 3·00 2·40

1313 Mexico Cathedral

2004. Bi-National (Cuba—Mexico) Philatelic Exhibition. Sheet 81 × 100 mm.
MS4737 **1313** $1 multicoloured 3·00 2·40

1314 Burgos Pointer

2004. Espana 2004 International Stamp Exhibition. Dogs. Multicoloured.
4738 5c. Type **1314** 20 10
4739 10c. Small Spanish hound 30 15
4740 15c. Malloquin bulldog . . 40 20
4741 65c. Catalan sheepdog . . . 1·80 95
4742 75c. Pyrenean mastiff . . . 2·10 1·10
MS4743 103 × 82 mm. $1 Spanish mastiff . . . . 2·50 1·90

1315 Cascarita and Julio Cuevas (singers)

2004. 40th Anniv of Egrem Record Company. Singers. Multicoloured.
4744 10c. Type **1315** 30 15
4745 15c. Carlos Puebla 40 20
4746 65c. Benny More . . . . . 1·80 95
4747 75c. Compay Segundo . . . 2·10 1·10

1316 Police Cars

2004. 45th Anniv of State Security Department.
4748 **1316** 15c. multicoloured . . . 50 30

1317 Children and Fidel Castro playing Chess

2004. National Sports Olympiad. Sheet 111 × 86 mm.
MS4749 **1317** $1 multicoloured 2·50 1·90

1318 "Antonio Nunez Jimenez" (Oswaldo Guayasamin)

1320 Maria Teresa Mora

1319 Footballer

2004. 10th Anniv of Antonio Nunez Jimenez Foundation for Nature and Man.
4750 **1318** 65c. multicoloured . . . 2·10 1·10

2004. Centenary of FIFA (Federation Internationale de Football Association). Multicoloured.
4751 10c. Type **1319** 30 15
4752 15c. Goalkeeper 40 20
4753 65c. No. 10 player . . . . 1·80 95
4754 75c. No. 3 player . . . . . 2·10 1·10

2004. 80th Anniv of International Chess Federation. Multicoloured.
4755 15c. Type **1320** 40 20
4756 65c. Jose Raul Capablanca (horiz) . . . . 1·80 95
4757 75c. Ernesto "Che" Guevara 2·10 1·10

1321 Corundum

2004. Minerals. Multicoloured.
4758 5c. Type **1321** 20 10
4759 10c. Thenardite 30 15
4760 15c. Uranium 40 20
4761 65c. Realgar . . . . 1·80 95
4762 75c. Fluoride . . . . 2·10 1·10
MS4763 861 × 112 mm. $1 Copper 3·00 2·40

1322 Budgerigars

2004. Pets. Multicoloured.
4764 5c. Type **1322** 20 10
4765 10c. Fish 30 15
4766 15c. Dogs 40 20
4767 65c. Cats . . . . 1·80 95
4768 75c. Finches . . . . 2·10 1·10
MS4769 105 × 82 mm. $1 Horse (40 × 32 mm) . . . . 3·50 3·00

1323 Building Facade

2004. 25th Anniv of Convention Centre.
4770 **1323** 65c. multicoloured . . . 2·10 1·20

1324 Lockheed Constellation

2004. 75th Anniv of Cubana Airline. Multicoloured.
4771 15c. Type **1324** 40 20
4772 65c. Ilyushin IL62M . . . . 1·80 95
4773 75c. Airbus 330 . . . . . . 2·10 1·10

1325 Coastline, Map of Cuba and Tern

2004. America. Environmental Protection. Mult.
4774 15c. Type **1325** 50 30
4775 65c. Fish, reef and map . . 2·10 1·10

2004. Marine Mammals. Multicoloured.
4776 5c. Type **1326** 20 10
4777 10c. *Lagenorhynchus obliquidens* 30 15
4778 15c. *Stenella attenuate* . . . 40 20
4779 65c. *Grampus griseus* . . . . 1·80 95
4780 75c. *Tursiops truncates* . . . 2·10 1·10
MS4781 110 × 86 mm. $1 *Orcinus orca* (40 × 32 mm) . . . . . . 3·50 3·00

1327 Camilo Cienfuegos

2004. 45th Anniv of Disappearance of Camilo Cienfuegos (revolutionary).
4782 **1327** 65c. multicoloured . . . 2·10 1·30

1328 Locomotive ALCO No. 48 4-6-0 (Agramonte) (1906)

2004. Centenary of Railway Stations. Multicoloured.
4783 15c. Type **1328** 40 20
4784 65c. BLW No. 57 4-6-0 (Aguacate) (1907) . . . . 1·80 95
4785 75c. ALCO No. 7 4-4-0 (Guira De Melina) (1903) 2·10 1·10

1329 Panorama Hotel

2004. Philatelic Congress. 40th Anniv of Cuban Philatelic Federation. Sheet 85 × 110 mm.
MS4786 **1329** $1 multicoloured 2·50 1·90

1330 El Templete (monument) (site of founding of Havana)

2004. 485th Anniv of San Cristobal de la Habana. Multicoloured.
4787 15c. Type **1330** 40 20
4788 65c. Preaching under ceiba tree (painting) . . . . . 1·80 95
4789 75c. Founding of Havana (painting) . . . . 2·10 1·10

1331 Building Facade

2004. 40th Anniv of Latin American Parliament.
4790 **1331** 65c. multicoloured . . . 1·90 1·20

1332 Ministry Building and Raul Roa (minister 1959—73)

2004. 45th Anniv of Ministry of Foreign Affairs.
4791 **1332** 65c. multicoloured . . . 1·90 1·20

1333 Alejo Carpentier

2004. Birth Centenary of Alejo Carpentier (writer).
4792 **1333** 65c. multicoloured . . . 1·90 1·20

1334 Rey Vicente Anglada

2004. 130th Anniv of Official Baseball Championships. Showing players. Multicoloured.
4793 5c. Type **1334** 20 10
4794 10c. Braudilio Vincent . . . 30 15
4795 15c. Rogelio Garcia 40 20
4796 65c. Luis Casanova . . . . 1·80 95
4797 75c. Victor Mesa . . . . . 2·10 1·10
MS4798 111 × 87 mm. $1 Martin Dihigo (32 × 40 mm) . . . . . 3·00 2·40

1335 Mayor de Trinidad Plaza and 1865 Trinidad—Barcelona Letter

2005. Tourism and Postal History. 40th Anniv of Postal Museum. Multicoloured.
4799 15c. Type **1335** 40 20
4800 65c. Caridad del Cobre Sanctuary and 1861 El Cobre—Santiago de Cuba letter . . . . 2·10 1·10
4801 75c. Matanzas Cathedral and 1848 Matanzas—Havana letter . . . . . . 2·40 1·40

1336 Rooster

2005. New Year. The Year of the Rooster. Multicoloured.
4802 15c. Type **1336** 50 30
4803 15c. Rooster jumping . . . 50 30

1337 Woman, Child and Symbols of Communication (½-size illustration)

2005. 5th Anniv of Ministry of Information and Communications.
4804 **1337** 65c. multicoloured . . . 2·10 1·10

1338 Miguel de Cervantes

2005. 400th Anniv of "The Ingenious Hidalgo Don Quixote of La Mancha" (novel written by Miguel de Cervantes y Saavedra).
4805 **1338** 65c. multicoloured . . . 2·10 1·10

1339 Carnotaurus

2005. Pre-Historic Animals. Multicoloured. Litho.
4806 5c. Type **1339** 20 10
4807 10c. Oviraptor 30 15
4808 30c. Parasaurlophus . . . . 1·00 50
4809 65c. Sauropelta . . . . . 2·10 1·10
4810 90c. Iguanodon . . . . . 2·40 1·20
MS4811 110 × 86 mm.1p. Velociraptor (40 × 32 mm) . . 2·50 1·90

1340 Bacunayagua Bridge

2005. Bridges. Multicoloured.
4812 10c. Type **1340** 30 15
4813 15c. La Concordia 40 20
4814 50c. El Triunfo . . . . . . 1·70 85
4815 65c. Yayabo . . . . 2·10 1·10
4816 75c. Canimar . . . . 2·40 1·40
MS4817 110 × 86 mm.1p. Plaza (40 × 32 mm) . . . . 2·50 1·90

1341 *Amazona ochrocephala* and *Amazona leucocephala*

2005. Parrots. Multicoloured.
4818 5c. Type **1341** 20 10
4819 10c. *Agapornis personata* and *Agapornis fischeri* . . 30 15
4820 15c. *Cactua galerita* and *Cacatua leadbeateri* . . . 40 20
4821 65c. *Psittacula krameri* and *Psittacula himalayana* (vert) . . . . 2·10 1·10
4822 75c. *Aratinga guarouba* and *Aratinga euops* . . . . . 2·40 1·40
MS4823 86 × 110 mm.1p. *Ara macao* (32 × 40 mm) . . . . 2·50 1·90

1342 Telephone Handsets

2005. 10th Anniv (2004) of ETECSA.
4824 **1342** 90c. multicoloured . . . 2·50 1·10

1343 Cat

2005. Cats. Multicoloured.
4825 5c. Type **1343** 20 10
4826 10c. Washing (*vert*) 30 15
4827 40c. Hunting 60 30
4828 65c. Two cats . . . . 1·80 95
4829 75c. Mother and kitten . . 2·10 1·10
MS4830 91 × 100 mm. 1p.Two kittens (32 × 40 mm) . . . . . 3·00 2·40

1344 Plaza de la Revolution, Cuba and Canadian Parliamentary Building

2005. 60th Anniv of Cuba–Canada Diplomatic Relations.
4831 **1344** 65c. multicoloured . . . 1·80 95

1345 Manatee (As No. 2767)

1346 Waterfall

2005. Fauna.
4832 **1345** 15c. brown 40 20
4833 – 65c. carmine . . . . . 1·80 95
4834 – 75c. green . . . . . . 2·10 1·10
4835 – 90c. blue . . . . . . 2·50 1·90
DESIGNS: 15c.Type 1345; 65c. Cuban conure (As No. 2764); 75c. Crocodile (As No. 2768); 90c. Cuban emerald (As Type **745**).

2005. World Water Day.
4836 **1346** 90c. multicoloured . . . 2·50 1·90

1347 Yacht ('Balandro')

2005. Fishing and Merchant Shipping. Multicoloured.
4837 10c. Type **1347** 30 15
4838 20c. Schooner ('Goleta') . . 35 15
4839 30c. Bonito fishing boat ('Bonitero') . . . . 1·00 50
4840 45c. Shrimp boat ('Cameronero') . . . . . 1·10 55
4841 90c. Lobster boat ('Langostero') . . . . . 2·50 1·10
MS4842 81 × 102 mm. 1p. Ferry ('Transbordador') (40 × 32 mm) 1·50 1·90

1348 1855 ½r. Stamp (No. 1) and San Francisco de Asis Convent

2005. 150th Anniv of First Stamp. Multicoloured.
4843 15c. Type **1348** 40 20
4844 65c. 1855 1r. Stamp (No. 2) and Castillo de los Tres Reyes del Morro, Havana 2·10 1·10
4845 75c. 1855 2r. Stamp (No. 3) and first colonial Postal building . . . . 2·40 1·40

1349 People

2005. Social Security for All.
4846 **1349** 65c. multicoloured . . . 2·10 1·10

1350 Locomotive DSB B 40, 1869

2005. Locomotives. Multicoloured.
4847 5c. Type **1350** 20 10
4848 10c. Great Northern locomotive, 1902 . . . . 20 10
4849 15c. 2-8-2T Minaret locomotive, 1929 . . . . 40 20
4850 15c. 0-4-2T C. F. White locomotive, 1885 . . . . 40 20
4851 2p.05 WP FP7A 805D locomotive . . . . 4·75 3·75
MS4852 111 × 86 mm. 1p. Inscr 'XIV No. 4 Krauss & Co, 1884' (40 × 32 mm) . . . . 2·50 1·90

1351 Maximo Gomez

2005. Death Centenary of Maximo Gomez y Baez (military commander).
4853 **1351** 1p.05 multicoloured . . 2·50 1·90

1352 Castillo del Morro and Flower

2005. 490th (2004) Anniv of Foundation of Santiago de Cuba. Multicoloured.
4854 75c. Type **1352** . . . . . . 2·40 1·40
MS4855 111 × 86 mm. 1p. Casa de Diego Velaquez de Cuellar (Spanish conquistador, governor of Cuba 1511–1524) (40 × 32 mm) 2·50 1·90

1353 Elephant

1355 Cuban Flag and Son Dancers

1354 Flags and Emblem

2005. National Zoo. Multicoloured.
4856 10c. Type **1353** 20 10
4857 15c. Cheetah (horiz) 40 20
4858 50c. Water buffalo (horiz) 1·75 85
4859 65c. Giraffe . . . . 2·10 1·10
4860 75c. Lion . . . . 2·40 1·10
MS4861 111 × 87 mm. 1p. Zebra (40 × 32 mm) . . . . 2·50 1·90

2005. Venezuela 2005–Festival of Youth and Students.
4862 **1354** 65c. multicoloured . . . 2·10 1·10

2005. National Dances. Multicoloured.
4863 65c. Type **1355** . . . . . . 2·10 1·10
4864 65c. Brazilian flag and Samba dancers . . . . . 2·10 1·10
Stamps of a similar design were issued by Brazil.

1356 Arnaldo Tamayo Mendez

2005. 25th Anniv of Joint Cuba–Russia Space Flight. Multicoloured.
4865 90c. Type **1356** . . . . . . 2·40 1·20
4866 90c. Yuri Romanenko . . . 2·40 1·20
Nos. 4865/6 were issued together, se-tenant, forming a composite background design.

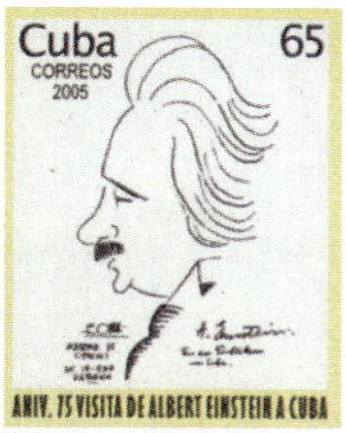

1357 Albert Einstein (sketch)

2005. 25th Anniv of Albert Einstein's Visit to Cuba. Multicoloured.
4867 **1357** 65c. black and yellow 2·10 1·10
4868 – 75c. multicoloured . . . 2·40 1·40
DESIGNS: 65c. Type **1357**; 75c. Einstein writing.

1358 Emblem, Presidential Palace and Fidel Castro (½-size illustration. Actual size 71 × 30 mm)

2005. 45th Anniv of Committee for the Defence of the Revolution.
4869 **1358** 50c. multicoloured . . . 1·70 85

1359 Great Wall, China and Castillo de los Tres Reyes del Morro, Cuba

2005. 45th Anniv of Cuba–China Diplomatic Relations. Multicoloured.
4870 15c. Type **1359** 40 20
4871 15c. Presidents Hu Jintao and Fidel Castro 40 20

1360 Starving Children

2005. America. Struggle against Poverty. Multicoloured.
4872 50c. Type **1360** . . . . . . 1·75 80
4873 75c. Mother and child . . . 2·40 1·40

1361 Saragossa College and Jose Marti, 1871

2005. Jose Marti (writer and revolutionary) Commemoration. Multicoloured.
4874 5c. Type **1361** 20 10
4875 5c. With Fermin Dominguez and Principal Theatre, Saragossa, 1872 . . . . . 20 10
4876 5c. Central College, Madrid, 1871 . . . . 20 10
4877 10c. Victor Hugo's house, Paris, 1872 . . . . 30 15
4878 10c. Moneda No. 12, Mexico City, 1875 . . . . 30 15
4879 15c. School, Guatemala City, 1876 . . . . 40 20
4880 15c. Plaza de Guardiola, Mexico City, 1894 . . . . 40 20
4881 15c. San Idefonso No. 40, Mexico City, 1894 . . . . 40 20
4882 65c. Plaza Bolivar, Caracas, 1885 . . . . 2·10 1·10
4883 75c. Santa Maria College, Caracas, 1893 . . . . . 2·40 1·40
MS4884 1121 × 82 mm. 1p. Speaking to Martinez Ybor's tobacco workers, Tampa, 1892 (40 × 32 mm) . . . . 2·50 1·90

1362 Inscr 'Gelderlander'

2005. Horses. Multicoloured.
4885 10c. Type **1362** 30 15
4886 15c. Inscr 'Arabe' 40 20
4887 50c. Quarter horse . . . . 1·70 85
4888 65c. Inscr 'Cimarrones' . . 2·10 1·10
4889 75c. Lipizzaner . . . . . . 2·40 1·40
MS4890 103 × 79 mm. 1p. Holstein (32 × 40 mm) . . . . 2·50 1·90

1363 Flag, Emblem, Globe, Computer and Family

2005. World Information Society Summit, Tunis.
4891 **1363** 75c. multicoloured . . . 2·40 1·40

1364 1855 Y¼. Stamp (No. 4) and Cover

2005. 150th Anniv of First Local Delivery, Havana. Multicoloured.
4892 15c. Type **1364** 40 20
4893 65c. 1862 ¼r. Stamp (No. 13) and Colonial mailbox . . . . 2·10 1·10

1365 Prisoners

2005.
4894 **1365** 65c. multicoloured . . . 2·10 1·10

1366 1962 5p. of Spain Stamp and Castillo de la Real Fuerza

2005. 50th Anniv of Europa Stamps. Multicoloured.
4895 1p.30 Type **1366** . . . . . 2·90 1·50
4896 2p.05 1961 1p. of Spain and Santisima Trinidad Church . . . . 4·75 2·50
4897 2p.55 1968 3p.50 of Spain and Castillo de Morro, Santiago de Cuba . . . . 6·00 3·00
4898 3p.90 1964 5p. of Spain and San Cristobal Cathedral, Havana . . . . 9·00 4·50
MS4899 121 × 97 mm. Nos. 4895/8 22·00 16·00

1367 Silver and Ebony Cross

2005. Jewellery. Multicoloured.
4900 5c. Type **1367** 20 10
4901 10c. Silver pendant 30 15
4902 45c. Silver and garnet necklace . . . . 1·10 55
4903 65c. Silver and ruby pendant 2·10 1·10
4904 75c. Silver, amber and ebony pendan . . . . . 2·40 1·40
MS4905 111 × 86 mm. 1p. Gold, diamond and black enamel pendant (32 × 40 mm) . . . . 2·50 1·90

1368 Institute Building

2005. 45th Anniv of Instituto Cubano de Amistad con los Pueblos (the Cuban Institute for Friendship with the People).
4906 **1368** 1p.05 multicoloured . . 2·00 1·00

1369 *Clathrus cancellatus*

2005. Fungi and Snails. Multicoloured.
4907 10c. Type **1369** 30 15
4908 20c. *Polymita picta* 60 30
4909 30c. *Lepiota puellaris* . . . 1·00 50
4910 65c. *Polymita muscarum* . . 2·10 1·10
4911 75c. *Clitocybe infundibuliformis* . . . . 2·40 1·40
MS4912 111 × 86 mm. 1p. *Polymita versicolor* (40 × 32 mm) . . . . 2·50 1·90

1370 Hotel Facade

2005. 130th Anniv of Hotel Inglaterra.
4913 **1370** 65c. multicoloured . . . 2·10 1·10

1371 Pug ('Carlino') **1372** Emblems

2006. New Year. The Year of the Dog. Multicoloured.
4914 15c. Type **1371** 40 20
4915 15c. Shih Tzu 40 20

2006. 40th Anniv of Organizacion de Solidaridad con los Pueblos de Asia, Africa y America Latina (Organization of Solidarity with the People of Asia, Africa and Latin America).
4916 **1372** 65c. multicoloured . . . 2·10 1·10

1373 Cuba No. 8 Player

2006. World Cup Football Championships, Germany. Designs showing Cuban footballers. Multicoloured.
4917 15c. Type **1373** 40 20
4918 45c. No. 5 player . . . . . 1·10 55
4919 65c. Player wearing red and white strip . . . . 2·10 1·10
4920 75c. No. 4 player . . . . . 2·40 1·40

1374 Cover and Post Rider

2006. 250th Anniv of Cuban Postal Service. Multicoloured.
4921 75c. Type **1374** . . . . . . 2·40 1·40
4922 2p.05 Ship and cover . . . 4·75 2·50
MS4923 86 × 112 mm. 1p. *El Ritmo Cubano* (statue) (F. Gelabert) (Havana 06 International Philatelic Exhibition) (40 × 32 mm) 2·50 1·90

1375 Maria del Carmen Wastewater Treatment Plant

2006. 30th Anniv of OPEC Development Fund.
4924 **1375** 75c. multicoloured . . . 2·40 1·40

1376 Congregation receiving Mass at Higher Institute of Physical Training, Santa Clara and Pope John Paul II (½-size illustration. Actual size 71 × 30 mm)

2006. 1st Death Anniv of Pope John Paul II. Designs showing Pope John Paul II saying Mass. Multicoloured.
4925 65c. Type **1376** . . . . . . 2·10 1·10
4926 75c. Plaza Ignacio Agramonte, Camaguey (46 × 30 mm) . . . . . . 2·40 1·40
4927 90c. Plaza Antonio Maceo, Santiago de Cuba (46 × 30 mm) . . . . . . 2·50 1·10
4928 1p.05 Pope John Paul II and congregation receiving Mass at Plaza Jose Marti, Havana . . . . 2·50 1·90

1377 Teodoro Perez's House, Cayo Hueso, 1893

2006. 10th Anniv of Jose Marti Cultural Society. Sheet 111 × 82 mm.
MS4929 **1377** 1p. multicoloured 2·50 1·90

1378 Flag, Rifle and Fatigues

2006. 45th Anniv of Bay of Pigs (Playa Giron).
4930 **1378** 65c. multicoloured . . . 2·10 1·10

2006. Jose Marti (writer and revolutionary) Commemoration. As T **1361**. Multicoloured.
4931 5c. 116 West Street, New York, Gonzalo de Quesada and Jose Marti, 1893 . . . . 20 10
4932 5c. Hotel de Madame Griffou, New York, 1890 20 10
4933 10c. 324 Classon Ave, New York and Jose Marti seated with his son, 1885 30 15
4934 10c. Masonic Temple, New York, 1888 . . . . 30 15
4935 15c. Cajobabo Beach, Oriente and Gomez inscribed on stone 40 20
4936 15c. Marti inscribed on stone and Dos Rios, Oriente 40 20
4937 75c. Hardman Hall, New York, 1891 . . . . 2·40 1·40
4938 85c. 120 Front Street, New York, 1891 . . . . 2·50 1·50
4939 90c. Jose Marti seated with Maria Mantilla and Bath Beach, Long Island, 1890 2·50 1·10
Nos. 4935/6 were issued together, se-tenant, forming a composite design.

1379 Yangchuanosaurus

2006. Pre-historic Animals. Multicoloured.
4940 5c. Type **1379** 20 10
4941 10c. Spinosaurus 30 15
4942 30c. Pachycephalosaurus . . 1·00 50
4943 35c. Muttaburrasaurus . . . 1·20 60
4944 65c. Stegosaurus . . . . . 2·10 1·10
4945 1p.05 Saichania . . . . . . 2·50 1·90
MS4946 109 × 88 mm. 1p. Stenonychosaurus (32 × 40 mm) 2·50 1·90

1380 Statue and Flags

2006. 45th Anniv of Ministry of Interior.
4947 **1380** 75c. multicoloured . . . 2·40 1·40

1381 Chickens

2006. Domesticated Fowl. Multicoloured.
4948 5c. Type **1381** 20 10
4949 15c. Guinea fowl 40 20
4950 15c. Turkeys 40 20
4951 45c. Geese . . . . 1·10 55
4952 50c. Golden pheasant . . . 1·70 85
4953 75c. Peacock . . . . 2·40 1·40
MS4954 109 × 88 mm. 1p. Duck (40 × 32 mm) . . . . 2·50 1·50

1382 *Cerro Pelado*

2006. 40th Anniv of Voyage of *Cerro Pelado* taking Cuban Athletes to Central American and Caribbean Games, Puerto Rico. Multicoloured.
4955 65c. Type **1382** . . . . . . 2·10 1·10
4956 75c. Athletes in cargo crate 2·40 1·40
4957 85c. Disembarking . . . . 2·50 1·50

1383 Centre Building

2006. 20th Anniv of Biotech Centre.
4958 **1383** 65c. multicoloured . . . 2·10 1·10

1384 *Pucho y sus Perrerias* (½-size illustration. Actual size 71 × 30 mm)

2006. Cartoons by Virgillo Martinez. Multicoloured.
4959 15c. Type **1384** 40 20
4960 65c. *Cucho* . . . . 2·10 1·10

1385 Granville Gee Bee R2

2006. Aircraft. Multicoloured.
4961 10c. Type **1385** 30 15
4962 15c. Comte AC-4 Gentleman 40 20
4963 15c. Bucker Jungmann . . . 40 20
4964 50c. Mustang TF 51 . . . . 1·70 85
4965 75c. Spitfire Supermarine MK . . . . 2·40 1·40
4966 85c. Lavochkin La-9 (Inscr ‘Lavochkine’) . . . . . . 2·50 1·50
MS4967 111 × 85 mm. 1p. Bucker Jungmann (different) (40 × 32 mm). Imperf . . . . . 2·50 1·90

1386 Bulldog

2006. Dogs. Multicoloured.
4968 5c. Type **1386** 20 10
4969 10c. American cocker spaniel 30 15
4970 15c. Sharpei 40 20
4971 20c. Airedale terrier 60 30
4972 35c. Pomeranian . . . . . 1·20 60
4973 2p.05 Dalmatian . . . . . 4·75 2·50
MS4974 86 × 112 mm. 1p. Whippet (32 × 40 mm) . . . . 2·50 1·90

1387 ‘Che’ Guevara and Emblem

2006. 45th Anniv of Recycling. Multicoloured.
4975 15c. Type **1387** 40 20
4976 65c. Flags and ‘45’ . . . . 2·10 1·10

1388 Statue and Cuban Coat of Arms

2006. 7th Cuban–Spanish Philatelic Exhibition. Sheet 86 × 111 mm containing T **1388** and similar vert design. Multicoloured.
MS4977 50c. × 2, Type **1388**; Statue and Spanish coat of arms . . . 3·25 2·10

1389 Emblem and Buildings

2006. 14th Non-Aligned Movement Summit.
4978 **1389** 65c. multicoloured . . . 2·10 1·10

1390 Pedro Santacilia (Cuban poet), Casa de Mexico, Habana Vieja and Benito Juarez (½-size illustration. Actual size 71 × 30 mm)

2006. Birth Bicentenary of Benito Juarez.
4979 **1390** 65c. multicoloured . . . 2·10 1·10

1391 Rio Hanabanilla

2006. Espana 06 International Philatelic Exhibition, Malaga. Multicoloured.
4980 5c. Type **1391** 20 10
4981 10c. Laguna Boconao . . . 30 15
4982 15c. Sierra de la Gran Piedra 40 20
4983 20c. Valle de los Ingenios 60 30
4984 50c. Laguno del Tesoro . . 1·70 85
4985 75c. Sierra Maestra . . . . 2·40 1·40
MS4986 111 × 85 mm. 1p. Villa de Vinales (40 × 32 mm) . . . . . 2·50 1·90

1392 Horses

2006. Animals in the Service of Man. Multicoloured.
4987 5c. Type **1392** 20 10
4988 15c. Camels 40 20
4989 30c. Goats . . . . 1·00 50
4990 40c. Llamas . . . . 1·20 60
4991 50c. Cats . . . . 1·70 85
4992 1p.05 Elephants . . . . . . 2·50 1·90
MS4993 111 × 87 mm. 1p. Dogs (40 × 32 mm) . . . . 2·50 1·90

1393 Solar Panels

2006. America. Energy Conservation. Multicoloured.
4994 65c. Type **1393** . . . . . . 2·10 1·10
4995 65c. Hydro-electric generator 2·10 1·10
4996 65c. Oil field . . . . 2·10 1·10
4997 65c. Wind turbines . . . . 2·10 1·10

1394 Luis and Sergio Saíz Montes de Oca

2006. 20th Anniv of Saiz Brothers Association of Young Writers and Artists.
4998 **1394** 75c. multicoloured . . . 2·40 1·40

1395 Alicia Alonso and Igor Youskevitch

2006. 20th International Ballet Festival, Havana. Multicoloured.
4999 75c. Type **1395** . . . . . . 2·40 1·40
5000 85c. Alicia Alonso . . . . . 2·50 1·50

1396 Stephenson’s *Rocket* and Inter-city Diesel Electric Locomotive

2006. Belgica 06 International Juvenile Philatelic Exhibition. Locomotives.
5001 5c. Type **1396** 20 10
5002 10c. Turbine locomotive and diesel electric 30 15
5003 15c. *Shinkasen* electric locomotive and *City of Los Angeles* diesel electric 40 20
5004 65c. Steam and diesel locomotives . . . . . . 2·10 1·10
5005 75c. TEE integrated diesel electric locomotive and *TGV*electric . . . . . . 2·40 1·40
5006 85c. Electric monorail locomotive, Brisbane and first monorail, Wuppertal, 1901 . . . . 2·50 1·50
MS5007 102 × 94 mm. Size 40 × 32 mm. 50c. × 2,. Steam locomotive; Diesel locomotive 3·25 2·10

1397 Emblem

2006. Telefood.
5008 **1397** 75c. multicoloured . . . 2·40 1·40

1398 Horse-drawn Ambulance, Brazil, 1899

2006. Fire Fighting and Rescue Equipment. Multicoloured.
5009 5c. Type **1398** 20 10
5010 10c. Merry Weather pump, England, 1898 . . . . . 30 15
5011 20c. Laurin & Klement appliance, Czech Republic, 1910 . . . . . 60 30
5012 45c. Motor cycle appliance, UK, 1925 . . . . 1·10 55
5013 90c. Ladder, Germany, 1930 2·50 1·10
MS5014 87 × 102 mm. 1p. Fire-fighter (32 × 40 mm) . . . . . 2·50 1·90

1399 Frank Pais (revolutionary)

2006. 50th Anniv of Santiago de Cuba Uprising.
5015 **1399** 65c. multicoloured . . . 2·10 1·10

1400 Tank and Medal

2006. 50th Anniversaries. Multicoloured.
5016 65c. Type **1400** (Revolutionary Armed Forces) . . . . 2·10 1·10
5017 65c. *Granma* (landing of revolutionary fighters) . . 2·10 1·10

1401 Flag, Jose Marti and Emblem

2006. 30th Anniv of People Power.
5018 **1401** 75c. multicoloured . . . 2·40 1·40

1402 Globe and Camera

2006. 20th Anniv of Film and Television School.
5019 **1402** 75c. multicoloured . . . 2·40 1·40

1403 Gonzalo de Queseda y Arostegui and Gonzalo De Queseda y Miranda (founder) (½-size illustration. Actual size 71 × 30 mm)

2006. 55th Anniv of Fragua Martiana Museum.
5020 **1403** 90c. multicoloured . . . 2·50 1·10

1404 Students raising Flag

2006. 45th Anniv of Literacy Campaign.
5021 **1404** 65c. multicoloured . . . 2·10 1·10

1405 Birthplace and Ignacio Agramonte y Loinaz

2006. 165th Birth Anniv of Ignacio Agramonte y Loinaz (revolutionary leader).
5022 **1405** 65c. multicoloured . . . 2·10 1·10

EXPRESS MAIL STAMPS

E **34**

1900. As Type E **34**, but inscr "immediata".
E306 E **34** 10c. orange . . . . . 37·00 12·50

1902. Inscr "inmediata".
E307 E **34** 10c. orange . . . . . 2·00 1·00

E **39** J. B. Zayas

1910.
E320 E **39** 10c. blue and orange 13·00 3·50

E **41** Bleriot XI and Morro Castle

1914.
E352 E **41** 10c. blue . . . . . . 12·50 20

E **62** Mercury

1936. Free Port of Matanzas. Inscr as T **61**. Perf or imperf (same prices).
E409 E **62** 10c. purple (express) 4·00 1·70
E413 – 15c. blue (air express) 4·00 2·75
DESIGN: 15c. Maya Lighthouse.

E **67** "Triumph of the Revolution"

1936. Maximo Gomez Monument.
E422 E **67** 10c. orange . . . . . 4·50 2·00

E **71** Temple of Quetzalcoatl (Mexico)

1937. American Writers and Artists Association.
E424v E **71** 10c. orange . . . . . 6·00 5·00
E424w – 10c. orange . . . . . 6·00 5·00
DESIGN: No. 424w, Ruben Dario (Nicaragua).

E **114**

1945.
E485 E **114** 10c. brown . . . . . 3·75 50

E **146** Government House, Cardenas

1951. Centenary of Cuban Flag.
E559 E **146** 10c. red, blue & orge 8·00 1·20

E **150** Capablanca Club, Havana

1951. 30th Anniv of Jose Capablanca's Victory in World Chess Championship.
E568 E **150** 10c. purple & green 20·00 4·75

1952. As No. 549 surch **10c E. ESPECIAL**.
E595 **143** 10c. on 2c. brown . . . 5·50 1·30

E **161** National Anthem and Arms E **176** Roseate Tern

1952. 50th Anniv of Republic.
E605 E **161** 10c. blue & orange . . 2·75 1·00

1952. Postal Employees' Retirement Fund. Inscr "ENTREGA ESPECIAL".
E627 **165** 10c. olive . . . . . . 5·00 2·20

1953.
E673 E **176** 10c. blue . . . . . . 4·50 1·30

1954. Postal Employees' Retirement Fund. Portrait of G. H. Saez as No. 684, inscr "ENTREGA ESPECIAL".
E686 10c. olive . . . . 4·25 1·10

1955. Postal Employees' Retirement Fund. Vert portrait (F. Varela) as T **191**, inscr "ENTREGA ESPECIAL".
E741 10c. lake . . . . 3·75 1·10

1956. Postal Employees' Retirement Fund. Vert portrait (J. J. Milanes) as T **200**, inscr "ENTREGA ESPECIAL".
E768 10c. black and red . . . . 5·50 75

1957. Postal Employees' Retirement Fund. As T **216** but inscr "ENTREGA ESPECIAL".
E812 10c. turquoise & brown . . 4·00 1·30
PAINTING: 10c. "Yesterday" (Cabrera).

1957. Postal Employees' Retirement Fund. As T **236** but inscr "ENTREGA ESPECIAL".
E856 10c. violet and brown . . . 2·50 1·10
DESIGN—HORIZ: 10c. Statue of Gen. A. Maceo, Independence Park, Pinar del Rio.

E **238** Motor-cyclist in Havana

1958.
E858 E **238** 10c. blue . . . . . . 2·50 1·00
E954 10c. violet . . . . . 3·00 1·00
E955 10c. orange . . . . . 3·00 95
E859 20c. green . . . . . 2·50 1·00

1958. Poey Commem. As Nos. 890/2 but inscr "ENTREGA ESPECIAL".
E893 10c. multicoloured . . . . 5·50 2·75
E894 20c. red, blue and black . . 18·00 11·50
DESIGNS—HORIZ: Fish: 10c. Black-finned snapper; 20c. Spotted mosquitofish.

1960. Surch **HABILITADO ENTREGA ESPECIAL 10c.**
E961 **55** 10c. on 20c. pink . . . . 2·40 50
E962 10c. on 50c. turquoise . . 2·40 50

1962. Stamp Day. As T **289** but inscr "ENTREGA ESPECIAL".
E1023 10c. brown & bl on yell 7·00 1·70
DESIGN: 10c. 18th-century sailing packet.

E **991** Great Red-bellied Woodpecker

1991. Birds. Multicoloured.
E3638 45c. Type E **991** . . . . 1·80 50
E3639 50c. Cuban solitaire . . . 1·90 60
E3640 2p. Cuban trogon . . . . 7·25 2·50
E3641 4p. Cuban grassquit . . . 14·50 4·25
E3642 5p. Ivory-billed woodpecker . . . . . 18·00 5·25
E3643 10p. Cuban amazon (horiz) . . . . . . 35·00 7·75
E3644 16p.45 Bee hummingbird (horiz) . . . . 55·00 16·00

POSTAGE DUE STAMPS

D **42**

1914.
D336 D **42** 1c. red . . . . 4·25 85
D338 2c. red . . . . 6·75 1·00
D340 5c. red . . . . 7·75 1·20

CUNDINAMARCA Pt. 20

One of the states of the Granadine Confederation. A Department of Colombia from 1886, now uses Colombian stamps.

100 centavos = 1 peso.

1 2

1870. Imperf.
1 **1** 5c. blue . . . . 2·75 2·75
2 **2** 10c. red . . . . 10·00 10·00

3 4

1877. Imperf.
5 **3** 10c. red . . . . 1·25 1·25
6 **4** 20c. green . . . . 2·25 2·25
7 – 50c. mauve . . . . 3·00 3·00
8a – 1p. brown . . . . 5·00 5·00
The 50c. and 1p. are in larger Arms designs.

11 13

1884. Imperf.
14 **11** 5c. blue 50 60

1885. Imperf.
17 **13** 5c. blue 30 30
18 10c. red . . . . 1·50 1·50
19 10c. red on lilac 90 90
20 20c. green . . . . 1·25 1·25
21 50c. mauve . . . . 1·75 1·75
22 1p. brown . . . . 2·00 2·00

14 15

1904. Imperf or perf. Various frames.
23 **14** 1c. orange 15 15
24 2c. blue 15 15
35 2c. grey 45 45
25 **15** 3c. red 20 20
26 5c. green 20 20
27 10c. brown 20 20
28 15c. pink 25 25
29 20c. blue on green 20 20
32 20c. blue 40 40
42 40c. blue 30 30
30 50c. mauve 25 25
31 1p. green 25 25
The illustrations show the main type. The frames and position of the arms in Type **15** differ for each value.

REGISTRATION STAMP

R **17**

1904. Imperf or perf.

R46	R 17	10c. brown	75	75

CURACAO Pt. 4

A Netherlands colony consisting of two groups of islands in the Caribbean Sea, N. of Venezuela. Later part of Netherlands Antilles.

100 cents = 1 gulden.

1

2

4

1873.

13	1	2½c. green	5·50	8·75
7		3c. bistre	55·00	£120
14		5c. red	12·50	12·50
26		10c. blue	70·00	18·00
27		12½c. yellow	£140	60·00
22		15c. brown	32·00	20·00
23		25c. brown	55·00	8·75
24		30c. grey	42·00	50·00
17		50c. lilac	2·40	3·00
29		1g.50 indigo and blue	£110	90·00
12		2g.50 mauve and bistre	48·00	40·00

1889.

37	2	1c. grey	1·60	1·75
38		2c. mauve	1·60	1·75
39		2½c. green	5·50	4·00
40a		3c. brown	6·25	5·50
41		5c. red	24·00	2·00

1891. Surch **25 CENT**.

42	1	25c. on 30c. grey	17·00	15·00

1892.

43	4	10c. blue	1·60	1·60
44		12½c. green	19·00	8·00
45		15c. red	3·25	3·25
46		25c. brown	£110	6·50
47		30c. grey	3·25	8·00

1895. Surch **2½ cent** (No. 48) or **2½ CENT** (No. 50).

48	1	2½c. on 10c. blue	15·00	9·50
50		2½c. on 30c. grey	£140	6·25

1899. 1898 stamps of Netherlands surch **CURACAO** and value.

51	12	12½c. on 12½c. blue	28·00	8·75
52		25c. on 25c. blue and red	2·40	2·25
53	13	1g.50 on 2½g. lilac	22·00	22·00

9

10

11

1903.

54	9	1c. olive	2·00	1·50
55a		2c. brown	14·50	4·00
56		2½c. green	6·00	60
57		3c. orange	9·75	6·25
58		5c. red	9·75	60
59		7½c. grey	30·00	7·25
60	10	10c. slate	15·00	2·50
61		12½c. blue	2·00	65
62		15c. brown	18·00	13·50
63		22½c. olive and brown	18·00	14·00
64		25c. violet	18·00	3·00
65		30c. brown	40·00	16·00
66		50c. brown	36·00	10·00
67	11	1½g. brown	40·00	32·00
68		2½g. blue	38·00	32·00

12

13

14

15

1915.

69	12	½c. lilac	1·75	1·75
70		1c. olive	30	40
71		1½c. blue	30	20
72		2c. brown	1·40	1·25
73		2½c. green	1·10	25
74		3c. yellow	2·50	1·90
75		3c. green	3·00	2·75
76		5c. red	2·10	25
77		5c. green	4·00	2·75
78		5c. mauve	2·10	25
79c	12	7½c. bistre	1·25	20
80	13	10c. red	18·00	3·50
81	12	10c. lilac	5·50	5·50
82		10c. red	4·50	1·90
83	13	12½c. blue	3·00	1·00
84		12½c. red	2·50	2·00
85		15c. olive	90	1·60
86		15c. blue	5·00	2·75
87		20c. blue	8·00	3·00
88		20c. olive	3·00	2·25
89		22½c. orange	3·00	3·00
90		25c. mauve	4·00	1·60
91		30c. slate	4·00	1·60
92		35c. slate and orange	4·00	5·75
93a	14	50c. green	5·50	40
94		1½g. violet	16·00	13·50
95		2½g. red	25·00	22·00

1918.

96	15	1c. black on buff	7·25	3·75

1919. Surch **5 CENT**.

97	13	5c. on 12½c. blue	4·50	2·50

17 Queen Wilhelmina

20

1923. Queen's Silver Jubilee.

98	17	5c. green	1·10	2·50
99		7½c. green	1·90	2·50
100		10c. red	3·00	4·50
101		20c. grey	3·00	4·50
102		1g. purple	35·00	21·00
103		2g.50 black	70·00	£180
104		5g. brown	90·00	£225

1927. Unissued Marine Insurance stamps, as Type M 22 of Netherlands, inscr "CURACAO", surch **FRANKEERZEGEL** and value.

105		3c. on 15c. green	35	35
106		10c. on 60c. red	35	35
107		12½c. on 75c. brown	35	35
108		15c. on 1g.50 blue	2·75	2·75
109		25c. on 2g.25 brown	6·00	6·00
110		30c. on 4½g. black	13·50	10·50
111		50c. on 7½g. red	7·25	7·00

1928.

112	20	6c. orange	1·50	35
113		7½c. orange	65	55
114		10c. red	1·50	55
115		12½c. brown	1·50	1·25
116		15c. blue	1·50	55
117		20c. blue	5·50	90
118		21c. green	9·00	10·00
119		25c. purple	3·50	2·25
120		27½c. black	11·50	12·50
121		30c. green	5·50	1·10
122		35c. black	2·00	1·10

1929. Air. Surch **LUCHTPOST** and value.

123	13	50c. on 12½c. red	14·00	14·00
124		1g. on 20c. blue	14·00	14·00
125		2g. on 15c. olive	40·00	42·00

1929. Surch **6 ct.** and bars.

126	20	6c. on 7½c. orange	1·60	1·25

23

24a

1931. Air.

126a	23	10c. green	20	20
126b		15c. slate	45	20
127		20c. red	1·00	25
127a		25c. olive	90	1·00
127b		30c. yellow	45	45
128		35c. blue	1·10	1·10
129		40c. green	75	55
130		45c. orange	2·10	2·10
130a		50c. red	1·00	65
131		60c. purple	75	45
132		70c. black	6·50	2·10
133		1g.40 brown	4·00	4·75
134		2g.80 bistre	4·50	5·25

1931. Surch.

134a	12	1½ on 2½c. green	3·50	3·25
135		2½ on 3c. green	1·10	95

1933. 400th Birth Anniv of William I of Orange.

136	24a	6c. orange	1·60	1·25

25 Frederik Hendrik

26 "Johannes van Walbeeck"

1934. 300th Anniv of Dutch Colonization. Inscr "1634 1934".

137	–	1c. black	1·10	1·25
138	–	1½c. mauve	85	35
139	–	2c. orange	1·10	1·25
140	25	2½c. green	90	1·40
141		5c. brown	90	1·10
142		6c. blue	85	35
143	–	10c. red	2·10	1·25
144	–	12½c. brown	6·25	6·25
145	–	15c. blue	1·90	1·50
146	26	20c. black	3·00	2·50
147		21c. brown	11·00	14·00
148		25c. green	11·50	11·50
149	–	27½c. purple	13·50	16·00
150	–	30c. red	11·50	7·00
151	–	50c. yellow	11·50	11·50
152	–	1g.50 blue	48·00	52·00
153	–	2g.50 green	50·00	55·00

PORTRAITS: 1c. to 2c. Willem Usselinx. 10c. to 15c. Jacob Binckes. 27½c. to 50c. Cornelis Evertsen, the younger. 1g.50, 2g.50, Louis Brion.

1934. Air. Surch **10 CT.**

154	23	10c. on 20c. red	21·00	16·00

27

28 Queen Wilhelmina

1936.

155A	27	1c. brown	30	20
156A		1½c. blue	30	20
157A		2c. orange	30	20
158A		2½c. green	30	20
159A		5c. red	30	20

1936.

160	28	6c. purple	75	20
161		10c. red	1·10	20
162		12½c. green	1·60	90
163		15c. blue	1·40	55
164		20c. orange	1·40	55
165		21c. black	2·50	2·75
166		25c. red	1·60	1·10
167		27½c. brown	3·25	3·75
168		30c. bistre	75	35
169		50c. green	3·50	35
170		1g.50 brown	23·00	12·50
171a		2g.50 red	18·00	13·00

29 Queen Wilhelmina

30 Dutch Flags and Arms

1938. 40th Anniv of Coronation.

172	29	1½c. violet	20	30
173		6c. red	85	75
174		15c. blue	1·60	1·25

1941. Air. Prince Bernhard Fund to equip Dutch Forces. Centres in red, blue and orange.

175	30	10c.+10c. red	18·00	16·00
176		15c.+25c. blue	25·00	20·00
177		20c.+25c. brown	25·00	20·00
178		25c.+25c. violet	25·00	20·00
179		30c.+50c. orange	25·00	20·00
180		35c.+50c. green	25·00	20·00
181		40c.+50c. brown	25·00	20·00
182		50c.+1g. blue	25·00	20·00

31 Queen Wilhelmina

33 Aruba

1941.

248	31	6c. violet	1·50	2·00
184a		10c. red	2·40	1·10
185		12½c. green	2·75	1·10
251		15c. blue	1·50	2·40
187		20c. orange	1·90	90
188		21c. grey	4·50	2·10
254		25c. red	20	20
255		27½c. brown	1·50	1·60
256		30c. bistre	1·75	1·10
257		50c. green	2·10	20
192		50c. green (21 × 26 mm)	16·00	55
193		1½g. brown (21 × 26 mm)	21·00	1·40
194		2½g. purple (21 × 26 mm)	21·00	1·40

See also Nos. 258/61.

1942.

195	–	1c. brown and violet	25	25
196	–	1½c. green and blue	25	25
197	–	2c. brown and black	1·25	35
198	–	2½c. yellow and green	25	25
199	33	5c. black and red	1·00	25
200	–	6c. blue and purple	60	60

DESIGNS—HORIZ: 1c. Bonaire. 2c. Saba. 2½c. St. Maarten. 6c. Curacao. VERT: 1½c. St. Eustatius.

34 Queen Wilhelmina and Douglas DC-2 over Atlantic Ocean

35 Dutch Royal Family

1942. Air.

201	34	10c. blue and green	35	35
202	–	15c. green and red	45	35
203	–	20c. green and brown	55	35
204	–	25c. brown and blue	50	35
205	–	30c. violet and red	55	35
206	34	35c. green and violet	90	55
207	–	40c. brown and green	1·10	55
208	–	45c. black and red	65	35
209	–	50c. black and violet	1·60	35
210	–	60c. blue and brown	1·60	90
211	34	70c. blue and brown	2·00	90
212	–	1g.40 green and blue	11·00	1·75
213	–	2g.80 blue & ultramarine	16·00	2·50
214	–	5g. green and purple	27·00	13·00
215	–	10g. brown and green	35·00	20·00

DESIGNS: 15, 40c., 1g.40, Fokker airplane "Zilvermeeuw" over coast. 20, 45c., 2g.80, Map of Netherlands West Indies. 25, 50c., 5g. Side view of Douglas DC-2 airplane. 30, 60c., 10g. Front view of Douglas DC-2 airplane.

1943. Birth of Princess Margriet.

216	35	1½c. orange	30	30
217		2½c. red	30	30
218		6c. black	1·00	65
219		10c. blue	1·00	80

1943. Air. Dutch Prisoners of War Relief Fund. Nos. 212/15 surch **Voor Krijgsgevangenen** and new value.

220		40c.+50c. on 1g.40 green & bl	6·25	4·75
221		45c.+50c. on 2g.80 blue & ult	4·25	4·50
222		50c.+75c. on 5g. green & pur	6·25	4·50
223		60c.+100c. on 10g. brn & grn	6·25	4·75

37 Princess Juliana

38 Map of Netherlands

1944. Air. Red Cross Fund. Cross in red; frame in red and blue.

224	37	10c.+10c. brown	2·10	1·60
225		15c.+25c. green	2·00	1·60
226		20c.+25c. black	2·00	1·75
227		25c.+25c. grey	2·00	1·75
228		30c.+50c. purple	2·00	1·75
229		35c.+50c. brown	2·00	1·75
230		40c.+50c. green	2·00	2·00
231		50c.+100c. violet	2·00	2·00

1946. Air. Netherlands Relief Fund. Value in black.

232	38	10c.+10c. orange & grey	1·10	1·25
233		15c.+25c. grey and red	1·25	1·25
234		20c.+25c. orange & grn	1·25	1·25
235		25c.+25c. grey & violet	1·25	1·25
236		30c.+50c. buff & green	1·25	1·40
237		35c.+50c. orange & red	1·25	1·40

238		40c.+75c. buff & blue	1·25	1·60
239		50c.+100c. buff & violet	1·25	1·60

1946. Air. National Relief Fund. As T **38** but showing map of Netherlands Indies and inscr "CURACAO HELPT ONZEOOST". Value in black.

240		10c.+10c. buff & violet	1·10	1·25
241		15c.+25c. buff & blue	1·25	1·25
242		20c.+25c. orange & red	1·25	1·25
243		25c.+25c. buff & green	1·25	1·25
244		30c.+50c. grey & violet	1·25	1·40
245		35c.+50c. orange & grn	1·25	1·40
246		40c.+75c. grey & red	1·25	1·60
247		50c.+100c. orange & grey	1·25	1·60

1947. Size 25 × 31½ mm.

258	**31**	1½g. brown	3·50	1·10
259		2½g. purple	45·00	10·75
260		5g. olive	£100	£150
261		10g. orange	£125	£275

40 Aeroplane and Posthorn

41 Douglas DC-2 and Waves

1947. Air.

262	**40**	6c. black	35	15
263		10c. red	35	15
264		12½c. purple	50	15
265		15c. blue	50	30
266		20c. green	65	35
267		25c. orange	65	20
268		30c. violet	90	35
269		35c. red	90	55
270		40c. green	90	55
271		45c. violet	1·10	80
272		50c. red	1·10	20
273		60c. blue	1·25	55
274		70c. brown	2·75	1·10
275	**41**	1g.50 black	2·00	80
276		2g.50 red	13·50	3·50
277		5g. green	21·00	7·00
278		7g.50 blue	65·00	55·00
279		10g. violet	50·00	17·00
280		15g. red	80·00	65·00
281		25g. brown	75·00	55·00

1947. Netherlands Indies Social Welfare Fund. Surch **NIWIN** and value.

282	**28**	1½c.+2½c. on 6c. purple	90	90
283		2½c.+5c. on 10c. red	90	90
284		5c.+7½c. on 15c. blue	90	90

43

45 Queen Wilhelmina

1948. Portrait of Queen Wilhelmina.

285	**43**	6c. purple	1·00	1·10
286		10c. red	1·00	1·50
287		12½c. green	1·00	90
288		15c. blue	1·00	1·10
289		20c. orange	1·00	2·00
290		21c. black	1·00	2·00
291		25c. mauve	35	20
292		27½c. brown	20·00	17·00
293		30c. olive	18·00	1·25
294		50c. green	16·00	20
295		1g.50c. brn (21½ × 28½ mm)	28·00	7·50

1948. Golden Jubilee.

296	**45**	6c. orange	65	65
297		12½c. blue	65	65

46 Queen Juliana

47

1948. Accession of Queen Juliana.

298	**46**	6c. red	55	55
299		12½c. green	55	55

1948. Child Welfare Fund. Inscr "VOOR HET KIND".

300	**47**	6c.+10c. brown	2·40	1·60
301	–	10c.+15c. red	2·40	1·60
302	–	12½c.+20c. green	2·40	1·60
303	**47**	15c.+25c. blue	2·40	1·75
304	–	20c.+30c. brown	2·40	1·90
305	–	25c.+35c. violet	2·40	2·00

DESIGNS—10, 20c. Native boy in straw hat. 12½, 25c. Curly-haired girl.

POSTAGE DUE STAMPS

For stamps as Nos. D42/61 and D96/105 in other colours see Postage Due stamps of Netherlands Indies and Surinam.

D 3

D 5

1889.

D42C	D **3**	2½c. black and green	2·40	2·75
D43C		5c. black and green	1·60	1·60
D44C		10c. black and green	24·00	21·00
D45C		12½c. black and green	£275	£140
D46C		15c. black and green	16·00	14·00
D47C		20c. black and green	7·00	7·00
D48C		25c. black and green	£140	£110
D49C		30c. black and green	8·50	7·25
D50C		40c. black and green	8·50	7·25
D51C		50c. black and green	30·00	23·00

1892.

D52C	D **5**	2½c. black and green	35	30
D53C		5c. black and green	65	55
D54C		10c. black and green	1·50	50
D55A		12½c. black and green	1·90	1·25
D56C		15c. black and green	2·40	1·25
D57A		20c. black and green	3·00	1·25
D58C		25c. black and green	1·40	95
D59A		30c. black and green	21·00	12·00
D60A		40c. black and green	25·00	12·50
D61A		50c. black and green	40·00	13·50

1915.

D 96a	D **5**	2½c. green	55	55
D 97a		5c. green	55	55
D 98a		10c. green	55	50
D 99a		12½c. green	1·40	1·50
D100a		15c. green	1·40	1·50
D101a		20c. green	55	1·00
D102a		25c. green	20	10
D103a		30c. green	2·10	2·40
D104		40c. green	2·50	3·00
D105a		50c. green	1·75	2·25

For later issues see **NETHERLANDS ANTILLES**.

CYPRUS Pt. 1

An island in the East Mediterranean. A British colony, which became a republic within the British Commonwealth in 1960.

1880. 12 pence = 1 shilling.
1881. 40 paras = 1 piastre; 180 piastres = 1 pound.
1955. 1000 mils = 1 pound.
1983. 100 cents = 1 pound.
2008. 100 cents = 1 euro.

1880. Stamps of Great Britain (Queen Victoria) optd **CYPRUS**.

1	**7**	½d. red	£110	£100
2	**5**	1d. red	14·00	38·00
3	**41**	2½d. mauve	3·00	10·00
4	–	4d. green (No. 153)	£130	£225
5	–	6d. grey (No. 161)	£500	£650
6	–	1s. green (No. 150)	£700	£450

1881. Stamps of Great Britain (Queen Victoria) surch with new values.

9	**5**	½d. on 1d. red	45·00	65·00
10		30 paras on 1d. red	£120	85·00

7

13

1881.

31	**7**	½pi. green	7·00	1·25
40		½pi. green and red	4·00	1·25
32		30pa. mauve	6·50	9·00
41		30pa. mauve and green	2·00	2·00
33		1pi. red	14·00	4·00
42		1pi. red and blue	6·50	1·25
34		2pi. blue	14·00	1·75
43		2pi. blue and purple	9·00	1·25
35a		4pi. olive	18·00	28·00
44		4pi. olive and purple	17·00	8·00
21		6pi. grey	60·00	17·00
45		6pi. brown and green	16·00	23·00
46		9pi. brown and red	19·00	23·00
22		12pi. brown	£180	40·00
47		12pi. brown and black	19·00	60·00
48		18pi. grey and brown	50·00	55·00
49		45pi. purple and blue	95·00	£150

1882. Surch.

25	**7**	½pi. on ½pi. green	£150	6·50
24		30pa. on 1pi. red	£1500	£110

1903. As T **7** but portrait of King Edward VII.

60		5pa. brown and black	1·00	·25
61		10pa. orange and green	4·25	·00
50		½pi. green and red	6·50	·25
51		30pa. violet and green	13·00	3·50
64		1pi. red and blue	9·00	·00
65		2pi. blue and purple	10·00	·75
66		4pi. brown and purple	18·00	9·50
67		6pi. brown and green	22·00	15·00
68		9pi. brown and red	45·00	8·50
69		12pi. brown and black	29·00	45·00
70		18pi. black and brown	40·00	12·00
71		45pi. purple and blue	95·00	£140

1912. As T **7** but portrait of King George V.

74b		10pa. orange and green	2·25	1·25
86		10pa. grey and yellow	13·00	8·00
75		½pi. green and red	2·00	30
76		30pa. violet and green	3·00	1·50
88		30pa. green	7·00	1·25
77		1pi. red and blue	4·75	1·75
90		1pi. violet and red	3·50	4·00
91		1½pi. yellow and black	9·00	5·50
78		2pi. blue and purple	6·50	2·00
93		2pi. red and blue	13·00	23·00
94		2¾pi. blue and purple	8·00	9·00
79		4pi. olive and purple	4·25	4·75
80		6pi. brown and green	4·00	9·00
81		9pi. brown and red	30·00	26·00
82		12pi. brown and black	21·00	48·00
83		18pi. black and brown	32·00	40·00
84		45pi. purple and blue	95·00	£140
100		10s. green and red on yellow	£375	£750
101		£1 purple and black on red	£1200	£2250

1924.

103	**13**	¼pi. grey and brown	1·25	50
104		½pi. black	4·50	12·00
118		½pi. green	2·25	1·00
105		¾pi. green	2·50	1·00
119		¾pi. black	3·00	50
106		1pi. purple and brown	2·00	1·25
107		1½pi. orange and black	2·25	11·00
120		1½pi. red	4·00	1·00
108		2pi. red and green	2·75	17·00
121		2pi. yellow and black	11·00	3·25
122		2½pi. blue	3·75	1·00
109		2¾pi. blue and purple	3·25	4·00
110		4pi. olive and purple	3·75	4·00
111		4½pi. blk & orge on green	3·50	4·25
112		6pi. brown and green	3·75	7·00
113		9pi. brown and purple	6·50	4·50
114		12pi. brown and black	10·00	60·00
115		18pi. black and orange	20·00	5·00
116		45pi. purple and blue	48·00	38·00
117		90pi. grn & red on yellow	£100	£200
102		£1 purple & black on red	£300	£750
117a		£5 black on yellow	£3000	£7000

14 Silver coin of Amathus, 6th-century B.C.

1928. 50th Anniv of British Rule. Dated "1878 1928".

123	**14**	¾pi. violet	2·75	1·50
124	–	1pi. black and blue	3·00	1·50
125	–	1½pi. red	4·50	2·00
126	–	2½pi. blue	3·50	2·25
127	–	4pi. brown	7·00	8·00
128	–	6pi. blue	10·00	25·00
129	–	9pi. purple	8·00	12·00
130	–	18pi. black and brown	23·00	26·00
131	–	45pi. violet and blue	40·00	48·00
132	–	£1 blue and brown	£225	£300

DESIGNS—VERT: 1pi. Philosopher Zeno; 2½pi. Discovery of body of St. Barnabas; 4pi. Cloister, Abbey of Bella Paise; 9pi. Tekke of Umm Haram; 18pi. Statue of Richard I, Westminster; 45pi. St. Nicholas Cathedral, Famagusta, (now Lala Mustafa Pasha Mosque); £1 King George V. HORIZ: 1½pi. Map of Cyprus; 6pi. Badge of Cyprus.

24 Ruins of Vouni Palace

30 St. Sophia Cathedral, Nicosia (now Selimiye Mosque)

1934.

133	**24**	¼pi. blue and brown	1·25	1·00
134	–	½pi. green	1·50	1·00
135	–	¾pi. black and violet	2·50	40
136	–	1pi. black and brown	2·25	1·80
137	–	1½pi. red	2·25	1·25
138	–	2½pi. blue	4·00	1·75
139	**30**	4½pi. black and red	4·00	4·25
140	–	6pi. black and blue	10·00	16·00
141	–	9pi. brown and violet	10·00	6·50
142	–	18pi. black and green	45·00	38·00
143	–	45pi. green and black	85·00	70·00

DESIGNS—HORIZ: ½pi. Small Marble Forum, Salamis; ¾pi. Church of St. Barnabas and St. Hilarion, Peristerona; 1pi. Roman theatre, Soli; 1½pi. Kyrenia Harbour; 2½pi. Kolossi Castle; 45pi. Forest scene, Troodos. VERT: 6pi. Bayraktar Mosque, Nicosia; 9pi. Queen's Window, St. Hilarion Castle; 18pi. Buyuk Khan, Nicosia.

The ¼pi. to 2½pi. values have a medallion portrait of King George V.

1935. Silver Jubilee. As T **13** of Antigua.

144		¾pi. blue and grey	3·00	1·50
145		1½pi. blue and red	4·75	2·50
146		2½pi. brown and blue	4·25	1·50
147		9pi. grey and purple	18·00	22·00

1937. Coronation. As T **2** of Aden.

148		¾pi. grey	1·50	75
149		1½pi. red	2·00	1·50
150		2½pi. blue	2·75	2·50

36 Map of Cyprus

37 Othello's Tower, Famagusta

38 King George VI

1938.

151	–	¼pi. blue and brown	1·00	40
152	–	½pi. green	1·50	30
152a	–	½pi. violet	2·25	40
153	–	¾pi. black and violet	17·00	1·00
154	–	1pi. orange	1·75	25
155	–	1½pi. red	5·50	1·50
155a	–	1½pi. violet	1·75	55
155ab	–	1½pi. green	3·50	80
155b	–	2pi. black and red	2·00	25
156	–	2½pi. blue	35·00	2·50
156a	–	3pi. blue	2·75	40
156b	–	4pi. blue	3·00	60
157	**36**	4½pi. grey	1·75	25
158	–	6pi. black and blue	2·50	1·00
159	**37**	9pi. black and purple	2·75	40
160	–	18pi. black and olive	11·00	1·00
161	–	45pi. green and black	32·00	3·75
162	**38**	90pi. mauve and black	29·00	6·50
163	–	£1 red and blue	60·00	25·00

DESIGNS: 2pi. Peristerona Church; 3pi., 4pi. Kolossi Castle. All other values except 4½pi., 9pi., 90pi. and £1 have designs as 1934 issue but portrait of King George VI.

1946. Victory. As T **9** of Aden.

164		1½pi. violet	30	10
165		3pi. blue	30	30

1948. Silver Wedding. As T **10/11** of Aden.

166		1½pi. violet	75	40
167		£1 blue	50·00	70·00

1949. U.P.U. As T **20/23** of Antigua.

168		1½pi. violet	60	1·25
169		2pi. red	1·50	1·50
170		3pi. blue	1·00	1·00
171		9pi. purple	1·00	2·75

1953. Coronation. As T **13** of Aden.

172		1½pi. black and green	1·50	10

39 Carobs

42 Mavrovouni Copper Pyrites Mine

49 St. Hilarion Castle

53 Arms of Byzantium, Lusignan, Ottoman Empire and Venice

1955.

173	**39**	2m. brown	30	40
174	–	3m. violet	30	15
175	–	5m. orange	1·75	10
176	**42**	10m. brown and green	2·00	10
177	–	15m. olive and blue	3·75	45
178	–	20m. brown and blue	1·50	15
179	–	25m. turquoise	3·50	60
180	–	30m. black and lake	3·00	10
181	–	35m. brown and turquoise	2·00	40
182	–	40m. green and brown	2·00	60
183	**49**	50m. blue and brown	2·00	30
184	–	100m. mauve and green	13·00	60

185 – 250m. blue and brown . . 13·00 10·00
186 – 500m. slate and purple . . 32·00 12·00
187 **53** £1 lake and slate . . . . . 26·00 45·00
DESIGNS—As Type **39**: 3m. Grapes; 5m. Oranges. As Type **42**: 15m. Troodos Forest; 20m. Beach of Aphrodite; 25m. 5th-century B.C. coin of Paphos; 30m. Kyrenia; 35m. Harvest in Mesaoria; 40m. Famagusta harbour. As Type **49**: 100m. Hala Sultan Tekke; 250m. Kanakaria Church. As Type **53**: 500m. Coins of Salamis, Paphos, Citium and Idalium.

ΚΥΠΡΙΑΚΗ
ΔΗΜΟΚΡΑΤΙΑ
KIBRIS
CUMHURIYETI
(54)

55 Map of Cyprus

1960. Nos. 173/87 optd as T **54** ("CYPRUS REPUBLIC" in Greek and Turkish).
188 **39** 2m. brown 20 75
189 – 3m. violet 20 15
190 – 5m. orange . . . . 1·00 10
191 **42** 10m. brown and green . . 1·00 10
192 – 15m. olive and blue . . . 2·00 10
193 – 20m. brown and blue . . 1·75 1·50
194 – 25m. turquoise . . . . . . 1·75 1·75
195 – 30m. black and lake . . . 1·75 10
196 – 35m. brown and turquoise 1·75 70
197 – 40m. green and brown . . 2·00 2·50
198 **49** 50m. blue and brown . . . 2·00 60
199 – 100m. mauve and green . . 9·00 1·00
200 – 250m. blue and brown . . 28·00 4·50
201 – 500m. slate and purple . . 40·00 22·00
202 **53** £1 lake and slate . . . . . 48·00 50·00

1960. Constitution of Republic.
203 **55** 10m. sepia and green . . . 30 10
204 30m. blue and brown . . . 65 10
205 100m. purple and slate . . 2·00 2·00

56 Doves

1962. Europa.
206 **56** 10m. purple and mauve . . 10 10
207 40m. blue and cobalt . . . 20 15
208 100m. emerald and green 20 20

57 Campaign Emblem

1962. Malaria Eradication.
209 **57** 10m. black and green . . . 15 15
210 30m. black and brown . . 30 15

63 St. Barnabas's Church

1962.
211 – 3m. brown and orange . . 10 30
212 – 5m. purple and green . . . 10 10
213 – 10m. black and green . . . 15 10
214 – 15m. black and purple . . 50 15
215 **63** 25m. brown and chestnut 60 20
216 – 30m. blue and light blue 20 10
217 – 35m. green and blue . . . 35 10
218 – 40m. black and blue . . . 1·25 1·75
219 – 50m. bronze and bistre . . 50 10
220 – 100m. brown and bistre . . 3·50 30
221 – 250m. black and brown . . 13·00 2·25
222 – 500m. brown and green . . 19·00 9·00
223 – £1 bronze and grey . . . . 17·00 30·00
DESIGNS—VERT: 3m. Iron Age jug; 5m. Grapes; 10m. Bronze head of Apollo; 15m. Selimiye Mosque, Nicosia; 35m. Head of Aphrodite; 100m. Hala Sultan Tekke; 500m. Mouflon. HORIZ: 30m. Temple of Apollo Hylates; 40m. Skiing, Troodos; 50m. Salamis Gymnasium; 250m. Bella Paise Abbey; £1 St. Hilarion Castle.

72 Europa "Tree"

1963. Europa.
224 **72** 10m. blue and black . . . 1·75 20
225 40m. red and black . . . . 9·00 2·00
226 150m. green and black . . 27·00 6·00

73 Harvester **75** Wolf Cub in Camp

1963. Freedom from Hunger.
227 **73** 25c. ochre, sepia and blue 30 25
228 – 75m. grey, black and lake 1·75 1·00
DESIGN: 75m. Demeter, Goddess of Corn.

1963. 50th Anniv of Cyprus Scout Movement and 3rd Commonwealth Scout Conference, Platres. Multicoloured.
229 3m. Type **75** 10 20
230 20m. Sea Scout 35 10
231 150m. Scout with Mouflon 1·00 2·50
MS231a 110 × 90 mm. Nos. 229/31 (sold at 250m.) Imperf £100 £180

79 Children's Centre, Kyrenia

1963. Centenary of Red Cross. Multicoloured.
232 10m. Nurse tending child (vert) 50 15
233 100m. Type **79** . . . . 2·00 3·50

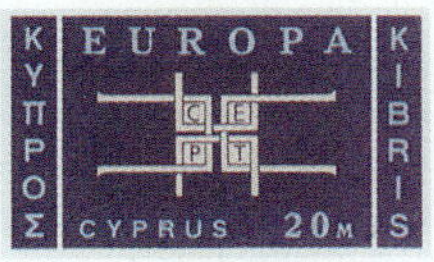

80 "Co-operation" (emblem)

1963. Europa.
234 **80** 20m. buff, blue and violet 2·50 40
235 30m. grey, yellow and blue 2·50 40
236 150m. buff, blue and brown . . . . 26·00 9·00

1964. U.N. Security Council's Cyprus Resolution, March 1964. Nos. 2 3 etc. optd with U.N. emblem and **1964**.
237 10m. black and green 15 10
238 30m. blue and light blue . . 20 10
239 40m. black and blue . . . 25 30
240 50m. bronze and bistre . . . 25 10
241 100m. brown and bistre . . . 25 50

82 Soli Theatre

1964. 400th Birth Anniv of Shakespeare. Mult.
242 15m. Type **82** 70 15
243 35m. Curium Theatre 70 15
244 50m. Salamis Theatre 70 15
245 100m. Othello Tower, and scene from "Othello" . . . 1·10 2·25

86 Running **89** Europa "Flower"

1964. Olympic Games, Tokyo.
246 **86** 10m. brown, black & yell 10 10
247 – 25m. brown, black and slate 20 10
248 – 75m. brown, black and chest 35 65
MS248a 110 × 90 mm. Nos. 246/8 (sold at 250m.) Imperf . . . . 6·00 15·00
DESIGNS—HORIZ: 25m. Boxing; 75m. Charioteers.

1964. Europa.
249 **89** 20m. brown and ochre . . . 1·50 10
250 30m. ultramarine and blue 1·50 10
251 150m. olive and green . . 18·00 5·50

90 Dionysus and Acme

1964. Cyprus Wines. Multicoloured.
252 10m. Type **90** 30 10
253 40m. Silenus (satyr) (vert) . . 65 1·25
254 50m. Commandaria wine (vert) 65 10
255 100m. Wine factory . . . . 1·50 2·00

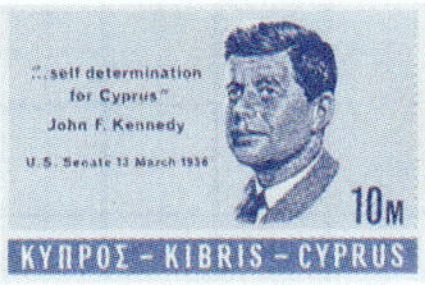

94 President Kennedy

1965. President Kennedy Commemoration.
256 **94** 10m. blue 10 10
257 40m. green 25 35
258 100m. red 30 35
MS258a 110 × 90 mm. Nos. 256/8 (sold at 250m.) Imperf . . . . 3·25 8·00

95 "Old Age" **98** I.T.U. Emblem and Symbols

1965. Introduction of Social Insurance Law.
259 **95** 30m. drab and green . . . 15 10
260 – 45m. green, blue and ultramarine 20 10
261 – 75m. brown and flesh . . . 1·25 2·50
DESIGNS—(As Type **95**): 45m. "Accident". LARGER (23 × 48 mm): 75m. "Maternity".

1965. Centenary of I.T.U.
262 **98** 15m. black, brown & yell 75 20
263 60m. black, grn & lt grn 7·50 3·25
264 75m. black, indigo & bl . . 8·50 4·75

99 I.C.Y. Emblem

1965. International Co-operation Year.
265 **99** 50m. brown and green . . 75 10
266 100m. purple and green . . 1·25 50

100 Europa "Sprig"

1965. Europa.
267 **100** 5m. black, brown & orge 50 10
268 45m. black, brown & grn 7·00 1·50
269 150m. black, brn & grey 13·00 3·75

1966. U.N. General Assembly's Cyprus Resolution. Nos. 211, 213, 216 and 221 optd **U.N. Resolution on Cyprus 18 Dec. 1965**.
270 3m. brown and orange . . . 10 50
271 10m. black and green 10 10
272 30m. blue and light blue . . 15 15
273 250m. black and brown . . . 80 2·25

102 Discovery of St. Barnabas's Body

1966. 1900th Death Anniv of St. Barnabas.
274 **102** 15m. multicoloured . . . 10 10
275 – 25m. drab, black and blue 15 10
276 – 100m. multicoloured . . . 45 2·00
MS277 110 × 91 mm. 250m. multicoloured (imperf) . . . . 3·50 13·00

DESIGNS—HORIZ: 25m. St. Barnabas's Chapel; 250m. "Privileges of Cyprus Church". VERT: 100m. St. Barnabas (icon).

1966. No. 211 surch **5M**.
278 5m. on 3m. brown & orange 10 10

107 General K. S. Thimayya and U.N. Emblem

1966. General Thimayya Commemoration.
279 **107** 50m. black and brown . . 30 10

108 Europa "Ship" **113** Silver Coin of Evagoras I

109 Stavrovouni Monastery

1966. Europa.
280 **108** 20m. green and blue . . . 40 10
281 30m. purple and blue . . 40 10
282 150m. bistre and blue . . 3·25 3·00

1966. Multicoloured.
283 3m. Type **109** 40 10
284 5m. Church of St. James, Trikomo 10 10
285 10m. Zeno of Citium (marble bust) 15 10
286 15m. Minoan wine ship of 700 B.C. (painting) 15 10
287 20m. Type **113** . . . . . . 1·25 1·00
288 25m. Sleeping Eros (marble statue) 30 10
289 30m. St. Nicholas Cathedral, Famagusta 50 20
290 35m. Gold sceptre from Curium 50 30
291 40m. Silver dish from 7th century 70 30
292 50m. Silver coin of Alexander the Great 90 10
293 100m. Vase, 7th century B.C. 4·00 15
294 250m. Bronze ingot-stand . . 1·00 40
295 500m. "The Rape of Ganymede" (mosaic) . . . 2·75 70
296 £1 Aphrodite (marble statue) 2·25 6·50
DESIGNS—VERT (As Type **109**): 5m. and 10m. HORIZ (As Type **113**): 15m., 25m. and 50m. VERT (As Type **113**): 30m., 35m., 40m. and 100m.
Nos. 294/6 are as Type **113** but larger, 28 × 40 mm.

123 Power Station, Limassol **124** Cogwheels

1967. First Development Programme. Mult.
297 10m. Type **123** 10 10
298 15m. Arghaka-Maghounda Dam (vert) 15 10
299 35m. Troodos Highway (vert) 20 10
300 50m. Hilton Hotel, Nicosia (vert) 20 10
301 100m. Famagusta Harbour (vert) . . . . 20 1·10

1967. Europa.
302 **124** 20m. olive, grn & lt grn 30 10
303 30m. violet, lilac and mauve 30 10
304 150m. sepia, brn chestnut 2·25 2·25

125 Throwing the Javelin

1967. Athletic Games, Thessalonika. Multicoloured.
305 15m. Type **125** 20 10
306 35m. Running 20 35
307 100m. High-jumping . . . . 30 1·00
MS308 110 × 90 mm. 250m. Running (amphora) and Map of Eastern Mediterranean (imperf) . . . . 1·25 6·50

127 Ancient Monuments

1967. International Tourist Year. Multicoloured.
309 10m. Type **127** 10 10
310 40m. Famagusta Beach . . . 15 90
311 50m. Hawker Siddeley Comet-4 at Nicosia Airport 15 10
312 100m. Skier and youth hostel 20 95

128 Saint Andrew Mosaic

129 "The Crucifixion" (icon)

1967. Centenary of St Andrew's Monastery.
313 **128** 25m. multicoloured . . . 10 10

1967. Cyprus Art Exhibition, Paris.
314 **129** 50m. multicoloured . . . 10 10

130 The Three Magi

131 Human Rights Emblem over Stars

1967. 20th Anniv of UNESCO.
315 **130** 75m. multicoloured . . . 20 20

1968. Human Rights Year. Multicoloured.
316 50m. Type **131** 10 10
317 90m. Human Rights and U.N. emblems 30 70
MS318 95 × 75½ mm. 250m. Scroll of Declaration . . . . 60 4·75

134 Europa "Key"

1968. Europa.
319 **134** 20m. multicoloured . . . 25 10
320 30m. multicoloured . . . 25 10
321 150m. multicoloured . . . 1·00 2·25

135 U.N. Children's Fund Symbol and Boy drinking Milk

1968. 21st Anniv of UNICEF.
322 **135** 35m. brown, red and black 10 10

136 Aesculapius

137 Throwing the Discus

1968. 20th Anniv of W.H.O.
323 **136** 50m. black, green and olive 10 10

1968. Olympic Games, Mexico. Multicoloured.
324 10m. Type **137** 10 10
325 25m. Sprint finish 10 10
326 100m. Olympic Stadium (horiz) . . . . 20 1·25

138 I.L.O. Emblem

141 Europa Emblem

139 Mercator's Map of Cyprus, 1554

1969. 50th Anniv of I.L.O.
327 **138** 50m. brown and blue . . 15 10
328 90m. brown, black and grey 15 55

1969. 1st International Congress of Cypriot Studies.
329 **139** 35m. multicoloured . . . 20 30
330 – 50m. multicoloured . . . 20 10
DESIGN: 50m. Blaeu's map of Cyprus, 1635.

1969. Europa.
331 **141** 20m. multicoloured . . . 30 10
332 30m. multicoloured . . . 30 10
333 150m. multicoloured . . . 1·00 2·00

142 European Roller ("Roller")

1969. Birds of Cyprus. Multicoloured.
334 5m. Type **142** 40 15
335 15m. Audouin's gull 60 15
336 20m. Cyprus warbler 60 15
337 30m. Jay ("Cyprus Jay") (vert) 60 15
338 40m. Hoopoe (vert) 65 30
339 90m. Eleonora's falcon (vert) 1·50 5·00

143 "The Nativity" (12th-century wall painting)

1969. Christmas. Multicoloured.
340 20m. Type **143** 15 10
341 45m. "The Nativity" (14th-century wall painting) 15 20
MS342 110 × 90 mm. 250m. "Virgin and Child between Archangels Michael and Gabriel" (6th–7th-century Mosaic) (imperf) 3·00 12·00

146 Mahatma Gandhi

1970. Birth Centenary of Mahatma Gandhi.
343 **146** 25m. blue, drab and black 50 10
344 75m. brown, drab and black 75 65

147 "Flaming Sun"

1970. Europa.
345 **147** 20m. brown, yell & orge 30 10
346 30m. blue, yellow & orge 30 10
347 150m. purple, yell & orge 1·00 2·50

148 Gladioli

149 I.E.Y. Emblem

1970. Nature Conservation Year. Multicoloured.
348 10m. Type **148** 10 10
349 50m. Poppies 15 10
350 90m. Giant fennel . . . . . 50 1·40

1970. Anniversaries and Events.
351 **149** 5m. black and brown . . 10 10
352 – 15m. multicoloured . . . 10 10
353 – 75m. multicoloured . . . 15 75
DESIGNS AND EVENTS: 5m. International Education Year. HORIZ: 15m. Mosaic (50th General Assembly of International Vine and Wine Office); 75m. Globe, dove and U.N. emblem (25th anniv of United Nations).

152 Virgin and Child

153 Cotton Napkin

1970. Christmas. Wall-painting from Church of Panayia Podhythou, Galata. Multicoloured.
354 25m. Archangel (facing right) 15 20
355 25m. Type **152** 15 20
356 25m. Archangel (facing left) 15 20
357 75m. Virgin and Child between Archangels (42 × 30 mm) 15 30

1971. Multicoloured.
358 3m. Type **153** 30 35
359 5m. Saint George and Dragon (19th-century bas-relief) 10 10
360 10m. Woman in festival costume 15 50
361 15m. Archaic Bichrome Kylix (cup) (horiz) 20 10
362 20m. A pair of donors (Saint Mamas Church) 35 65
363 25m. "The Creation" (6th-century mosaic) . . . 30 10
364 30m. Athena and horse-drawn chariot (4th-century B.C. terracotta) (horiz) . . 30 10
365 40m. Shepherd playing pipe (14th-century fresco) . . . 1·00 1·00
366 50m. Hellenistic head (3rd-century B.C.) 80 10
367 75m. "Angel" (mosaic detail), Kanakaria Church . . . . 2·00 1·00
368 90m. Mycenaean silver bowl (horiz) . . . . 2·00 2·25
369 250m. Moufflon (detail of 3rd-century mosaic) (horiz) 1·50 30
370 500m. Ladies and sacred tree (detail 6th-century amphora) (horiz) . . . . . 1·00 30
371 £1 Horned god from Enkomi (12th-century bronze statue) . . . . 1·75 45
SIZES: 24 × 37 mm or 37 × 24 mm 10m. to 90m., 41 × 28 mm or 28 × 41 mm 250m. to £1.

154 Europa Chain

1971. Europa.
372 **154** 20m. blue, ultram & blk 25 10
373 30m. green, myrtle & blk 25 10
374 150m. yellow, grn & blk 1·10 3·00

155 Archbishop Kyprianos

1971. 150th Anniv of Greek War of Independence. Multicoloured.
375 15m. Type **155** 10 10
376 30m. "Taking the Oath" (horiz) 10 10
377 100m. Bishop Germanos, flag and freedom-fighters . . . 20 50

156 Kyrenia Castle

1971. Tourism. Multicoloured.
378 15m. Type **156** 10 10
379 25m. Gourd on sunny beach (vert) 10 10
380 60m. Mountain scenery (vert) 20 60
381 100m. Church of Saint Evlalios, Lambousa . . . 20 65

157 Madonna and Child in Stable

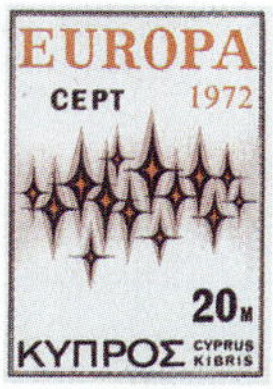

159 "Communications"

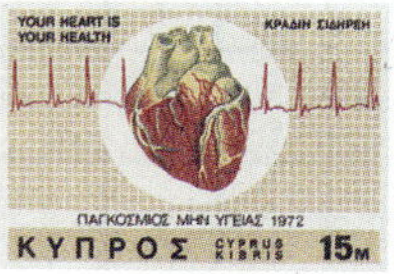

158 Heart

1971. Christmas. Multicoloured.
382 10m. Type **157** 10 10
383 50m. The Three Wise Men 15 35
384 100m. The Shepherds 20 35

1972. World Heart Month.
385 **158** 15m. multicoloured . . . 10 10
386 50m. multicoloured . . . 20 45

1972. Europa.
387 **159** 20m. orange, sepia & brn 40 15
388 30m. orange, ultram & bl 40 15
389 150m. orge, myrtle & grn 2·50 4·50

160 Archery

1972. Olympic Games, Munich. Multicoloured.
390 10m. Type **160** 25 10
391 40m. Wrestling 35 15
392 100m. Football . . . . . . 75 1·75

161 Stater of Marion

162 Bathing the Child Jesus

1972. Ancient Coins of Cyprus (1st series).
393 **161** 20m. blue, black and silver 20 10
394 – 30m. blue, black and silver 20 10
395 – 40m. brown, blk & silver 20 20
396 – 100m. pink, black and silver . . . . 60 1·00
COINS: 30m. Stater of Paphos; 40m. Stater of Lapithos; 100m. Stater of Idalion.
See also Nos. 486/9.

1972. Christmas. Detail of mural in Holy Cross Church, Agiasmati. Multicoloured.
397 10m. Type **162** 10 10
398 20m. The Magi 10 10
399 100m. The Nativity 15 30
MS400 100 × 90 mm. 250m. Showing the mural in full (imperf) . . . 1·10 4·50

163 Mount Olympus, Troodos

1973. 29th International Ski Federation Congress. Multicoloured.
401 20m. Type **163** 10 10
402 100m. Congress emblem . . . 25 35

164 Europa "Posthorn"

1973. Europa.
403 **164** 20m. multicoloured . . . 25 10
404 30m. multicoloured . . . 25 10
405 150m. multicoloured . . . 1·50 3·50

165 Archbishop's Palace, Nicosia

1973. Traditional Architecture. Multicoloured.
406 20m. Type **165** 10 10
407 30m. House of Hajigeorgajis Cornessios, Nicosia (vert) 10 10
408 50m. House at Gourri, 1850 (vert) 15 10
409 100m. House at Rizokarpaso, 1772 . . . . 40 85

1973. No. 361 surch **20M**.
410 20m. on 15m. multicoloured 15 15

167 Scout Emblem

168 Archangel Gabriel

1973. Anniversaries and Events.
411 **167** 10m. green and brown . . 20 10
412 – 25m. blue and lilac . . . 20 10
413 – 35m. olive, stone and green 20 25
414 – 50m. blue and indigo . . 20 10
415 – 100m. brown and sepia 50 80
DESIGNS AND EVENTS—VERT: 10m. (60th anniv of Cyprus Boy Scouts); 50m. Airline emblem (25th anniv of Cyprus Airways); 100m. Interpol emblem (50th anniv of Interpol). HORIZ: 25m. Outlines of Cyprus and the E.E.C. (Association of Cyprus with "Common Market"); 35m. F.A.O. emblem (10th anniv of F.A.O.).

1973. Christmas. Murals from Araka Church. Multicoloured.
416 10m. Type **168** 10 10
417 20m. Madonna and Child . . 10 10
418 100m. Araka Church (horiz) 40 75

169 Grapes

170 "The Rape of Europa" (Silver Stater of Marion)

1974. Products of Cyprus. Multicoloured.
419 25m. Type **169** 10 15
420 50m. Grapefruit 20 70
421 50m. Oranges 20 70
422 50m. Lemons 20 70

1974. Europa.
423 **170** 10m. multicoloured . . . 15 10
424 40m. multicoloured . . . 40 30
425 150m. multicoloured . . . 1·40 2·75

171 Title Page of A. Kyprianos' "History of Cyprus" (1788)

174 "Refugees"

1974. 2nd International Congress of Cypriot Studies. Multicoloured.
426 10m. Type **171** 10 10
427 25m. Solon (philososopher) in mosaic (horiz) 15 10
428 100m. "Saint Neophytos" (wall painting) 60 75
MS429 111 × 90 mm. 250m. Ortelius' map of Cyprus and Greek Islands, 1584. Imperf . . . . 1·25 5·00

1974. Obligatory Tax. Refugee Fund. No. 359 surch **REFUGEE FUND** in English, Greek and Turkish and **10M**.
430 10m. on 5m. multicoloured 10 10

1974. U.N. Security Council Resolution 353. Nos. 360, 365, 366 and 369 optd **SECURITY COUNCIL RESOLUTION 353 20 JULY 1974**.
431 10m. multicoloured 25 10
432 40m. multicoloured 30 60
433 50m. multicoloured 30 10
434 250m. multicoloured . . . . 70 3·00

1974. Obligatory Tax. Refugee Fund.
435 **174** 10m. black and grey . . . 10 10

175 "Virgin and Child between Two Angels", Stavros Church

1974. Christmas. Church Wall-paintings. Mult.
436 10m. Type **175** 10 10
437 50m. "Adoration of the Magi", Ayios Neophytos Monastery (vert) 20 10
438 100m. "Flight into Egypt", Ayios Neophytos Monastery 25 45

176 Larnaca–Nicosia Mail-coach, 1878

1975. Anniversaries and Events.
439 **176** 20m. multicoloured . . . 25 10
440 – 30m. blue and orange . . 25 60
441 **176** 50m. multicoloured . . . 25 10
442 – 100m. multicoloured . . . 40 1·40
DESIGNS AND EVENTS—HORIZ: 20m., 50m. Centenary of Universal Postal Union. VERT: 30m. "Disabled Persons" (8th European Meeting of International Society for the Rehabilitation of Disabled Persons); 100m. Council flag (25th anniv of Council of Europe).

177 "The Distaff" (M. Kashalos)

178 Red Cross Flag over Map

1975. Europa. Multicoloured.
443 20m. Type **177** 25 40
444 30m. "Nature Morte" (C. Savva) 25 50
445 150m. "Virgin and Child of Liopetri" (G. P. Georghiou) 40 80

1975. Anniversaries and Events. Multicoloured.
446 25m. Type **178** 20 10
447 30m. Nurse and lamp (horiz) 20 10
448 75m. Woman's steatite idol (horiz) 20 90
EVENTS: 25m.25th anniv of Red Cross; 30m. International Nurses' Day; 75m. International Women's Year.

179 Submarine Cable Links

181 Human-figured Vessel, 19th-century

1976. Telecommunications Achievements.
449 **179** 50m. multicoloured . . . 30 10
450 – 100m. yellow, vio & lilac 35 90
DESIGN—HORIZ: 100m. International subscriber dialling.

1976. Surch **10M**.
451 **153** 10m. on 3m. multicoloured 20 70

1976. Europa. Ceramics. Multicoloured.
452 20m. Type **181** 20 10
453 60m. Composite vessel, 2100–2000 B.C. 50 80
454 100m. Byzantine goblet . . . 90 1·75

182 Self-help Housing

1976. Economic Reactivation. Multicoloured.
455 10m. Type **182** 10 10
456 25m. Handicrafts 15 20
457 30m. Reafforestation 15 20
458 60m. Air communications . . 30 55

183 Terracotta Statue of Youth

184 Olympic Symbol

1976. Cypriot Treasures.
459 **183** 5m. multicoloured 10 80
460 – 10m. multicoloured . . . 10 60
461 – 20m. red, yellow and black 20 60
462 – 25m. multicoloured . . . 20 10
463 – 30m. multicoloured . . . 20 10
464 – 40m. green, brown & blk 30 55
465 – 50m. lt brown, brn & blk 30 10
466 – 60m. multicoloured . . . 30 20
467 – 100m. multicoloured . . . 40 50
468 – 250m. blue, grey and black . . . . 50 1·75
469 – 500m. black, brown & grn 60 2·00
470 – £1 multicoloured . . . . 1·00 2·25
DESIGNS—VERT: 10m. Limestone head (23 × 34 mm); 20m. Gold necklace from Lambousa (24 × 37 mm); 25m. Terracotta warrior (24 × 37 mm); 30m. Statue of a priest of Aphrodite (24 × 37 mm); 250m. Silver dish from Lambousa (28 × 41 mm); 500m. Bronze stand (28 × 41 mm); £1 Statue of Artemis (28 × 41 mm). HORIZ: 40m. Bronze tablet (37 × 24 mm); 50m. Mycenaean crater (37 × 24 mm); 60m. Limestone sarcophagus (37 × 24 mm); 100m. Gold bracelet from Lambousa (As Type **183**).

1976. Olympic Games, Montreal.
471 **184** 20m. red, black and yellow 10 10
472 – 60m. multicoloured (horiz) 20 30
473 – 100m. multicoloured (horiz) 30 35
DESIGNS: 60m. and 100m. Olympic symbols (different).

185 "George Washington" (G. Stuart)

186 Children in Library

1976. Bicentenary of American Revolution.
474 **185** 100m. multicoloured . . . 40 30

1976. Anniversaries and Events.
475 **186** 40m. multicoloured . . . 15 15
476 – 50m. brown and black . . 15 10
477 – 80m. multicoloured . . . 30 60
DESIGNS AND EVENTS: 40m. Type **186** (Promotion of Children's books); 50m. Low-cost housing (HABITAT Conference, Vancouver); 80m. Eye protected by hands (World Health Day).

187 Archangel Michael

188 "Cyprus 74" (wood engraving by A. Tassos)

1976. Christmas. Multicoloured.
478 10m. Type **187** 10 10
479 15m. Archangel Gabriel . . . 10 10
480 150m. The Nativity 45 80
Designs show icons from Ayios Neophytis Monastery.

1977. Refugee Fund.
481 **188** 10m. black 20 10
See also Nos. 634 and 892 (after No. 728).

189 "View of Prodhromos" (A. Diamantis)

1977. Europa. Paintings. Multicoloured.
482 20m. Type **189** 20 10
483 60m. "Springtime at Monagroulli" (T. Kanthos) 30 55
484 120m. "Old Port, Limassol" (V. Ioannides) . . . . . . 60 2·00

190 500m. Stamp of 1960

192 Archbishop Makarios in Ceremonial Robes

191 Bronze Coin of Emperor Trajan

1977. Silver Jubilee.
485 **190** 120m. multicoloured . . . 30 30

1977. Ancient Coins of Cyprus (2nd series).
486 **191** 10m. black, gold and blue 15 10
487 – 40m. black, silver and blue 30 30
488 – 60m. black, silver & orge 35 35
489 – 100m. black, gold and green 50 95
DESIGNS: 40m. Silver tetradrachm of Demetrios Poliorcetes; 60m. Silver tetradrachm of Ptolemy VIII; 100m. Gold octadrachm of Arsinoe II.

1977. Death of Archbishop Makarios. Mult.
490 20m. Type **192** 15 10
491 60m. Archbishop in doorway 20 10
492 250m. Head and shoulders portrait . . . . 50 1·10

193 Embroidery, Pottery and Weaving

1977. Anniversaries and Events. Multicoloured.
493 20m. Type **193** 10 10
494 40m. Map of Mediterranean 15 20
495 60m. Gold medals 20 20
496 80m. Sputnik 20 85
DESIGNS COMMEMORATE: 20m. Revitalization of handicrafts; 40m. "Man and the Biosphere" Programme in the Mediterranean region; 60m. Gold medals won by Cypriot students in the Orleans Gymnasiade; 80m. 60th anniv of Russian Revolution.

194 "Nativity"

1977. Christmas. Children's Paintings Mult.
497 10m. Type **194** 10 10
498 40m. "The Three Kings" . . 10 10
499 150m. "Flight into Egypt" . . 25 80

195 Demetrios Libertis

1978. Cypriot Poets.
500 **195** 40m. brown and bistre . . 10 10
501 – 150m. grey, black and red 30 80
DESIGN: 150m. Vasilis Michaelides.

196 Chrysorrhogiatissa Monastery Courtyard
197 Archbishop of Cyprus, 1950–1977

1978. Europa. Architecture. Multicoloured.
502 25m. Type **196** 15 10
503 75m. Kolossi Castle 25 35
504 125m. Municipal Library, Paphos . . . . 45 1·50

1978. Archbishop Makarios Commem. Mult.
505 15m. Type **197** 15 20
506 25m. Exiled in Seychelles, 9 March 1956–28 March 1957 . . . . 15 20
507 50m. President of the Republic 1960–1977 . . . 20 25
508 75m. "Soldier of Christ" . . 20 30
509 100m. "Fighter for Freedom" 25 35
MS510 100 × 80 mm. 300m. "The Great Leader" (imperf) . . . . 1·00 2·50

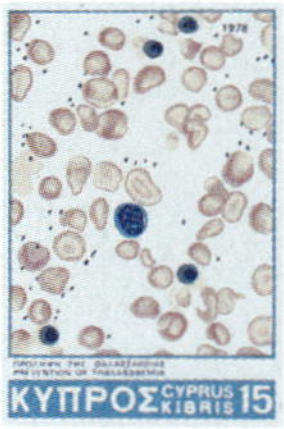

198 Affected Blood Corpuscles (Prevention of Thalassaemia)
199 Icon Stand

1978. Anniversaries and Events.
511 **198** 15m. multicoloured . . . 10 10
512 – 35m. multicoloured . . . 15 10
513 – 75m. black and grey . . . 20 30
514 – 125m. multicoloured . . . 35 80
DESIGNS—VERT: 35m. Aristotle (sculpture) (2300th death anniv). HORIZ: 75m. "Heads" (Human Rights); 125m. Wright brothers and Wright Flyer I (75th anniv of Powered Flight).

1978. Christmas.
515 **199** 15m. multicoloured . . . 10 10
516 – 35m. multicoloured . . . 15 10
517 – 150m. multicoloured . . . 40 60
DESIGNS: 35m., 150m. Different icon stands.

200 Aphrodite (statue from Soli)

1979. Goddess Aphrodite (1st issue). Multicoloured.
518 75m. Type **200** 25 10
519 125m. Aphrodite on shell (detail from Botticelli's "Birth of Venus") 35 25
See also Nos. 584/5.

201 Van, Larnaca–Nicosia Mail-coach and Envelope

1979. Europa. Communications. Multicoloured.
520 25m. Type **201** 20 10
521 75m. Radar, satellite and early telephone 30 20
522 125m. Aircraft, ship and envelopes . . . . 85 1·50

202 Peacock Wrasse

1979. Flora and Fauna. Multicoloured.
523 25m. Type **202** 15 10
524 50m. Black partridge (vert) 70 60
525 75m. Cedar (vert) 45 30
526 125m. Mule . . . . 50 1·25

203 I.B.E. and UNESCO Emblems
204 "Jesus" (from Church of the Virgin Mary of Arakas, Lagoudhera)

1979. Anniversaries and Events.
527 **203** 15m. multicoloured . . . 10 10
528 – 25m. multicoloured . . . 10 10
529 – 50m. black, brown and ochre 20 15
530 – 75m. multicoloured . . . 25 10
531 – 100m. multicoloured . . . 30 20
532 – 125m. multicoloured . . . 30 75
DESIGNS AND COMMEMORATIONS—VERT: 15m. Type **203** (50th anniv of International Bureau of Education); 125m. Rotary International emblem and "75" (75th anniv). HORIZ: 25m. Graphic design of dove and stamp album (20th anniv of Cyprus Philatelic Society); 50m. Lord Kitchener and map of Cyprus (Cyprus Survey Centenary); 75m. Child's face (International Year of the Child); 100m. Graphic design of footballers (25th anniv of U.E.F.A. European Football Association).

1979. Christmas. Icons. Multicoloured.
533 15m. Type **204** 10 10
534 35m. "Nativity" (Church of St Nicholas, Famagusta District) (29 × 41 mm) . . . 10 10
535 150m. "Holy Mary" (Church of the Virgin Mary of Arakas) 25 45

205 1880 $\frac{1}{2}$d. Stamp with "969" (Nicosia) Postmark

1980. Centenary of Cyprus Stamps. Multicoloured.
536 40m. Type **205** 10 10
537 125m. 1880 $2\frac{1}{2}$d. stamp with "974" (Kyrenia) postmark 15 20
538 175m. 1880 1s. stamp with "942" (Larnaca) postmark 15 25
MS539 105 × 85 mm. 500m. 1880 $\frac{1}{2}$d., 1d., $2\frac{1}{2}$d., 4d., 6d. and 1s. stamps (90 × 75 mm). Imperf 70 85

206 St. Barnabas (patron saint of Cyprus)
208 Gold Necklace, Arsos (7th-century B.C.)

207 Sailing

1980. Europa. Personalities. Multicoloured.
540 40m. Type **206** 15 10
541 125m. Zeno of Citium (founder of Stoic philosophy) 30 20

1980. Olympic Games, Moscow. Multicoloured.
542 40m. Type **207** 10 10
543 125m. Swimming 20 20
544 200m. Gymnastics 25 25

1980. Archaeological Treasures.
545 **208** 10m. multicoloured . . . 30 1·00
546 – 15m. multicoloured . . . 30 1·00
547 – 25m. multicoloured . . . 30 30
548 – 40m. multicoloured . . . 40 75
549 – 50m. multicoloured . . . 40 10
550 – 75m. multicoloured . . . 1·25 1·50
551 – 100m. multicoloured . . . 65 15
552 – 125m. multicoloured . . . 65 1·00
553 – 150m. multicoloured . . . 75 15
554 – 175m. multicoloured . . . 75 1·25
555 – 200m. multicoloured . . . 75 30
556 – 500m. multicoloured . . . 75 1·50
557 – £1 multicoloured . . . . 1·00 1·25
558 – £2 multicoloured . . . . 1·75 2·00
DESIGNS—HORIZ: 15m. Bronze cow, Vouni Palace (5th-cent B.C.); 40m. Gold finger-ring, Enkomi (13th-cent B.C.); 500m. Stone bowl, Khirokitia (6th-millennium B.C.). VERT: 25m. Amphora, Salamis (6th-cent B.C.); 50m. Bronze cauldron, Salamis (8th-cent B.C.); 75m. Funerary stele, Marion (5th-cent B.C.). 100m. Jug (15–14th-cent B.C.); 125m. Warrior (terracotta) (6th–5th-cent B.C.); 150m. Lions attacking bull (bronze relief), Vouni Palace (5th-cent B.C.); 175m. Faience rhyton, Kition (13th-cent B.C.); 200m. Bronze statue of Ingot God, Enkomi (12th-cent B.C.); £1 Ivory plaque, Salamis (7th-cent B.C.); £2 "Leda and the Swan" (mosaic), Kouklia (3rd-cent A.D.).

209 Cyprus Flag

1980. 20th Anniv of Republic of Cyprus. Multicoloured.
559 40m. Type **209** 10 10
560 125m. Signing Treaty of Establishment (41 × 29 mm) 20 15
561 175m. Archbishop Makarios 35 25

210 Head and Peace Dove

1980. International Day of Solidarity with Palestinian People.
562 **210** 40m. black and grey . . . 20 20
563 – 125m. black and grey . . 35 35
DESIGN: 125m. Head and dove with olive branch.

211 Pulpit, Tripiotis Church, Nicosia
212 Folk Dancing

1980. Christmas. Multicoloured.
564 25m. Type **211** 10 10
565 100m. Holy Doors, Panayia Church Paralimni 15 20
566 125m. Pulpit, Ayios Lazaros Church, Larnaca 15 20

1981. Europa. Folklore, showing folk-dancing from paintings by T. Photiades.
567 **212** 40m. multicoloured . . . 30 10
568 – 175m. multicoloured . . . 60 50

213 Self-portrait
214 "Ophrys kotschyi"

1981. 500th Anniv of Leonardo da Vinci's Visit. Multicoloured.
569 50m. Type **213** 40 10
570 125m. "The Last Supper" (50 × 25 mm) 70 40
571 175m. Cyprus lace and Milan Cathedral 95 60

1981. Cypriot Wild Orchids. Multicoloured.
572 25m. Type **214** 40 60
573 50m. "Orchis punctulata" . . 50 70
574 75m. "Ophrys argolica elegans" 55 80
575 150m. "Epipactis veratrifolia" 65 90

215 Heinrich von Stephan

1981. Anniversaries and Events.
576 **215** 25m. dp green, grn & bl 15 10
577 – 40m. multicoloured . . . 15 10
578 – 125m. black, red and green 30 25
579 – 150m. multicoloured . . . 35 30
580 – 200m. multicoloured . . . 70 80

DESIGNS AND COMMEMORATIONS: 25m. Type **137** (150th birth anniv of Heinrich von Stephan (founder of U.P.U.); 40m. Stylised man holding dish of food (World Food Day); 125m. Stylised hands (International Year for Disabled People); 150m. Stylised building and flower (European Campaign for Urban Renaissance); 200m. Prince Charles, Lady Diana Spencer and St. Paul's Cathedral (Royal Wedding).

216 "The Lady of the Angels" (from Church of the Transfiguration of Christ, Palekhori)

217 "Louomene" (Aphrodite bathing) (statue, 250 B.C.)

1981. Christmas. Murals from Nicosia District Churches. Multicoloured.
581 25m. Type **216** 20 10
582 100m. "Christ Pantokrator" (Church of Madonna of Arakas, Lagoudera) (vert) 60 20
583 125m. "Baptism of Christ" (Church of Our Lady of Assinou, Nikitari) 70 30

1982. Aphrodite (Greek goddess of love and beauty) Commemoration (2nd issue). Mult.
584 125m. Type **217** 55 45
585 175m. "Anadyomene" (Aphordite emerging from the waters) (Titian) 70 65

218 Naval Battle with Greek Fire, 985 A.D.

1982. Europa. Historic Events. Multicoloured.
586 40m. Type **218** 75 10
587 175m. Conversion of Roman Proconsul Sergius Paulus to Christianity, Paphos, 45 A.D. . . . . 1·00 2·50

219 "XP" (monogram of Christ) (mosaic)

1982. World Cultural Heritage. Multicoloured.
588 50m. Type **219** 20 10
589 125m. Head of priest-king of Paphos (sculpture) (24 × 37 mm) 40 25
590 225m. Theseus (Greek god) (mosaic) 60 95

1982. No. 550 surch **100**.
591 100m. on 75m. Funerary stele, Marion (5th-century B.C.) 50 50

221 Cyprus and Stylised "75"

1982. 75th Anniv of Boy Scout Movement. Multicoloured.
592 100m. Type **221** 35 20
593 125m. Lord Baden-Powell . . 40 40
594 175m. Camp-site 40 90

222 Holy Communion, The Bread

1982. Christmas.
595 **222** 25m. multicoloured . . . 10 10
596 – 100m. gold and black . . 30 15
597 – 250m. multicoloured . . . 70 1·50
DESIGN—VERT: 100m. Holy Chalice. HORIZ: 250m. Holy Communion, The Wine.

223 Cyprus Forest Industries' Sawmill

1983. Commonwealth Day. Multicoloured.
598 50m. Type **223** 10 10
599 125m. "Ikarios and the Discovery of Wine" (3rd-century mosaic) . . . 20 25
600 150m. Folk-dancers, Commonwealth Film and Television Festival, 1980 25 35
601 175m. Royal Exhibition Building, Melbourne (Commonwealth Heads of Government Meeting, 1981) 25 40

224 Cyprosyllabic Inscription (6th-century B.C.)

1983. Europa. Multicoloured.
602 50m. Type **224** 40 10
603 200m. Copper ore, ingot (Enkomi 1400–1250 B.C.) and bronze jug (2nd century A.D.) . . . . . . 1·10 2·40

225 "Pararge aegeria"

1983. Butterflies. Multicoloured.
604 60m. Type **225** 25 20
605 130m. "Aricia agestis" . . . 45 25
606 250m. "Glaucopsyche melanops" . . . . 85 2·50

1983. Nos. 545/56 surch.
607 1c. on 10m. Type **208** . . . . 35 1·00
608 2c. on 15m. Bronze cow, Vouni Palace (5th-century B.C.) (horiz) . . . . . . 35 1·25
609 3c. on 25m. Amphora, Salamis (6th-century B.C.) 35 1·00
610 4c. on 40m. Gold finger-ring, Enkomi (13th-century B.C.) (horiz) . . . . 40 1·00
611 5c. on 50m. Bronze cauldron, Salamis (8th-century B.C.) 50 50
612 6c. on 75m. Funerary stele, Marion (5th-century B.C.) 50 1·00
613 10c. on 100m. Jug (15th–14th-century B.C.) 50 40
614 13c. on 125m. Warrior (Terracotta) (6–5th-cent B.C.) 50 50
615 15c. on 150m. Lions attacking bull (bronze relief), Vouni Palace (5th-century B.C.) (horiz) 50 55
616 20c. on 200m. Bronze statue of Ingot God, Enkomi (12th-century B.C.) 50 65
617 25c. on 175m. Faience rhyton, Kition (13th-century B.C.) . . . . 55 1·10
618 50c. on 500m. Stone bowl, Khirokitia (6th-millenium B.C.) (horiz) . . . . 75 2·00

227 View of Power Station

228 St Lazaros Church, Larnaca

1983. Anniversaries and Events. Multicoloured.
619 3c. Type **227** 10 20
620 6c. W.C.Y. logo 15 15
621 13c. "Sol Olympia" (liner) and "Polys" (tanker) . . . 30 35
622 15c. Human Rights emblem and map of Europe . . . 20 25
623 20c. Nicos Kazantzakis . . . 20 75
624 25c. Makarios in church . . 25 75

COMMEMORATIONS: 3c. 30th anniv of Cyprus Electricity Authority; 6c. World Communications Year; 13c. 25th anniv of International Maritime Organization; 15c. 35th anniv of Universal Declaration of Human Rights; 20c. Birth centenary; 25c. 70th birth anniv.

1983. Christmas. Church Towers. Multicoloured.
625 4c. Type **228** 15 10
626 13c. St. Varvara Church, Kaimakli, Nicosia 40 35
627 20c. St. Ioannis Church, Larnaca . . . . 70 1·50

229 Waterside Cafe, Larnaca

1984. Old Engravings. Each brown and black.
628 6c. Type **229** 15 15
629 20c. Bazaar at Larnaca (39 × 25 mm) 40 85
630 30c. Famagusta Gate, Nicosia (39 × 25 mm) . . . . . . 65 1·50
MS631 110 × 85 mm. 75c. "The Confession" (St. Lazarus Church, Larnaca) . . . . 1·25 2·00

230 C.E.P.T. 25th Anniversary Logo

1984. Europa.
632 **230** 6c. lt green, green & blk 40 10
633 15c. lt blue, blue & black 70 2·00

1984. Obligatory Tax. Refugee Fund. As T **188** but new value and dated "1984".
634 1c. black 10 10

231 Running

1984. Olympic Games, Los Angeles. Multicoloured.
635 3c. Type **231** 15 10
636 4c. Olympic column 15 20
637 13c. Swimming 45 75
638 20c. Gymnastics . . . . . . 60 1·50

232 Prisoners-of-War

1984. 10th Anniv of Turkish Landings in Cyprus. Multicoloured.
639 15c. Type **232** 40 45
640 20c. Map and burning buildings 50 55

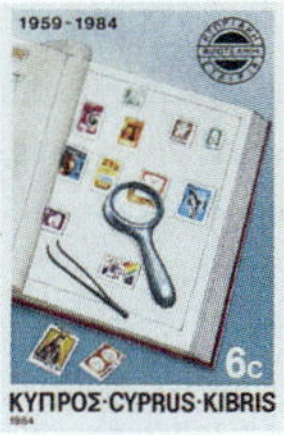

233 Open Stamp Album (25th Anniv of Cyprus Philatelic Society)

234 St. Mark (miniature from 11th-century Gospel)

1984. Anniversaries and Events. Multicoloured.
641 6c. Type **233** 30 20
642 10c. Football in motion (horiz) (50th anniv of Cyprus Football Association) 45 30
643 15c. "Dr. George Papanicolaou" (medical scientist) (birth centenary) 60 50
644 25c. Antique map of Cyprus and ikon (horiz) (International Symposia on Cartography and Medieval Paleography) . . . . . . 1·00 2·00

1984. Christmas. Illuminated Gospels. Mult.
645 4c. Type **234** 25 10
646 13c. Beginning of St. Mark's Gospel 45 50
647 20c. St. Luke (miniature from 11th-century Gospel) . . . 70 2·00

235 Autumn at Platania, Troodos Mountains

1985. Cyprus Scenes and Landscapes. Mult.
648 1c. Type **235** 20 60
649 2c. Ayia Napa Monastery . . 20 60
650 3c. Phini Village–panoramic view 20 60
651 4c. Kykko Monastery 20 30
652 5c. Beach at Makronissos, Ayia Napa 20 20
653 6c. Village street, Omodhos (vert) 30 20
654 10c. Panoramic sea view . . 45 30
655 13c. Windsurfing 55 25
656 15c. Beach at Protaras . . . 75 25
657 20c. Forestry for development (vert) . . . . 1·00 50
658 25c. Sunrise at Protaras (vert) 1·25 1·00
659 30c. Village house, Pera . . . 1·50 1·25
660 50c. Apollo Hylates Sanctuary, Curium . . . . 2·50 1·75
661 £1 Snow on Troodos Mountains (vert) . . . . . 4·00 3·00
662 £5 Personification of Autumn, House of Dionyssos, Paphos (vert) 14·00 15·00

236 Clay Idols of Musicians (7/6th century B.C.)

1985. Europa. European Music Year. Mult.
663 6c. Type **236** 50 35
664 15c. Violin lute, flute and score from the "Cyprus Suite" . . . . 90 2·25

237 Cyprus Coat of Arms (25th Anniv of Republic)

238 "The Visit of the Madonna to Elizabeth" (Lambadistis Monastery, Kalopanayiotis)

1985. Anniversaries and Events.
665 **237** 4c. multicoloured 15 15
666 – 6c. multicoloured 15 15
667 – 13c. multicoloured . . . . 25 1·00
668 – 15c. black, green and orange . . . . 1·00 1·25
669 – 20c. multicoloured . . . . 30 1·75
DESIGNS—HORIZ (43 × 30 mm): 6c. "Barn of Liopetri" (detail) (Pol. Georghiou) (30th anniv of EOKA Campaign); 13c. Three profiles (International Youth Year); 15c. Solon Michaelides (composer and conductor) (European Music Year). VERT—(as T **237**): 20c. U.N. Building, New York, and flags (40th anniv of United Nations Organization).

1985. Christmas. Frescoes from Cypriot Churches. Multicoloured.
670 4c. Type **238** 20 10
671 13c. "The Nativity" (Lambadistis Monastery, Kalopanayiotis) 50 65
672 20c. "Candlemas-day" (Asinou Church) . . . . . 70 2·00

239 Figure from Hellenistic Spoon Handle

1986. New Archaeological Museum Fund. Multicoloured.
673 15c. Type **239** 45 45
674 20c. Pattern from early Ionian helmet and foot from statue 60 75
675 25c. Roman statue of Eros and Psyche 65 95
676 30c. Head of statue . . . . . 75 1·10
MS677 111 × 90 mm. Nos. 673/6 (sold at £1) . . . . 12·00 16·00
No. 676 also commemorates the 50th anniv of the Department of Antiquities.

240 Cyprus Moufflon and Cedars

1986. Europa. Protection of Nature and the Environment. Multicoloured.
678 7c. Type **240** 35 30
679 17c. Greater flamingos ("Flamingos") at Larnaca Salt Lake . . . . 1·40 2·75

241 Cat's-paw Scallop

1986. Sea Shells. Multicoloured.
680 5c. Type **241** 30 15
681 7c. Atlantic trumpet triton . . 35 15
682 18c. Purple dye murex . . . 60 70
683 25c. Yellow cowrie . . . . . 1·00 2·00

1986. Nos. 653 and 655 surch.
684 7c. on 6c. Village street, Omodhos (vert) 40 30
685 18c. on 13c. Windsurfing . . 1·10 70

243 Globe Outline Map of Cyprus and Barn Swallows (Overseas Cypriots' Year)

1986. Anniversaries and Events. Multicoloured.
686 15c. Type **243** . . . . 1·00 45
687 18c. Halley's Comet over Cyprus beach (40 × 23 mm) 1·25 2·00
688 18c. Comet's tail over sea and Edmond Halley (40 × 23 mm) . . . . . . 1·25 2·00
Nos. 687/8 were printed together, se-tenant, forming a composite design.

244 Pedestrian Crossing

1986. Road Safety Campaign. Multicoloured.
689 5c. Type **244** 65 30
690 7c. Motor cycle crash helmet 70 30
691 18c. Hands fastening car seat belt . . . . 1·50 3·00

245 "The Nativity" (Church of Panayia tou Araka)

1986. Christmas. International Peace Year. Details of Nativity frescoes from Cypriot churches. Multicoloured.
692 5c. Type **245** 25 15
693 15c. Church of Panayia tou Moutoulla 65 30
694 17c. Church of St. Nicholas tis Steyis . . . . 75 2·00

246 Church of Virgin Mary, Asinou

1987. Troodos Churches on the World Heritage List. Multicoloured.
695 15c. Type **246** . . . . 70 1·10
696 15c. Fresco of Virgin Mary, Moutoulla's Church . . . 70 1·10
697 15c. Church of Virgin Mary, Podithou . . . . 70 1·10
698 15c. Fresco of Three Apostles, St. Ioannis Lampadistis Monastery . . 70 1·10
699 15c. Annunciation fresco, Church of the Holy Cross, Pelentriou . . . . 70 1·10
700 15c. Fresco of Saints, Church of the Cross, Ayiasmati . . 70 1·10
701 15c. Fresco of Archangel Michael and Donor, Pedoula's Church of St. Michael . . . . 70 1·10
702 15c. Church of St. Nicolaos, Steyis . . . . 70 1·10
703 15c. Fresco of Prophets, Church of Virgin Mary, Araka . . . . 70 1·10

247 Proposed Central Bank of Cyprus Building

1987. Europa. Modern Architecture.
704 **247** 7c. multicoloured 50 30
705 – 18c. black, grey and green 1·10 2·00
DESIGN: 18c. Headquarters complex, Cyprus Telecommunications Authority.

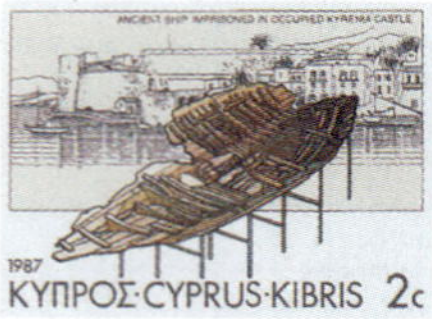

248 Remains of Ancient Ship and Kyrenia Castle

1987. Voyage of "Kyrenia II" (replica of ancient ship). Multicoloured.
706 2c. Type **248** 35 20
707 3c. "Kyrenia II" under construction, 1982–5 . . . 45 90
708 5c. "Kyrenia II" at Paphos, 1986 . . . . 75 20
709 17c. "Kyrenia II" at New York, 1986 . . . . 1·75 90

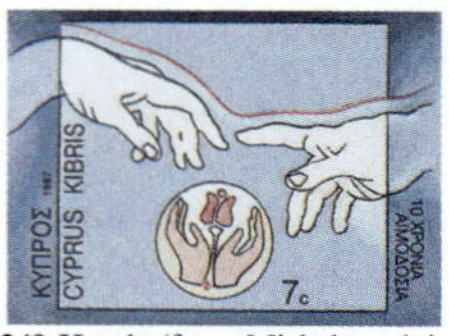

249 Hands (from Michelangelo's "Creation") and Emblem

1987. Anniversaries and Events. Multicoloured.
710 7c. Type **249** (10th anniv of Blood Donation Co-ordinating Committee) . . 50 25
711 15c. Snail with flowered shell and countryside (European Contryside Campaign) . . 1·10 40
712 20c. Symbols of ocean bed and Earth's crust ("Troodos '87" Ophiolites and Oceanic Lithosphere Symposium) . . . . 1·40 3·00

250 Nativity Crib

1987. Christmas. Traditional Customs. Mult.
713 5c. Type **250** 35 15
714 15c. Door knocker decorated with foliage . . . . 1·10 35
715 17c. Bowl of fruit and nuts 1·25 2·00

251 Flags of Cyprus and E.E.C.

1988. Cypriot–E.E.C. Customs Union. Mult.
716 15c. Type **251** . . . . 80 1·50
717 18c. Outline maps of Cyprus and E.E.C. countries . . . 80 80

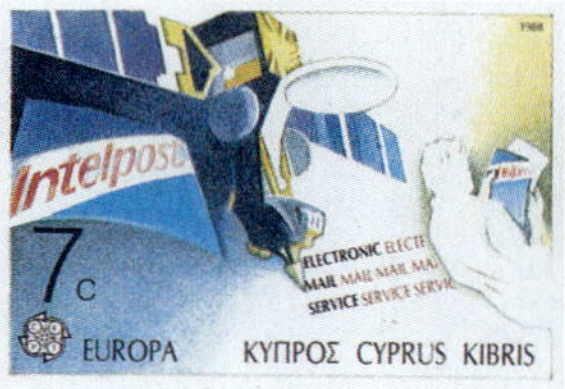

252 Intelpost Telefax Terminal

1988. Europa. Transport and Communications. Multicoloured.
718 7c. Type **252** . . . . 75 1·25
719 7c. Car driver using mobile telephone . . . . 75 1·25
720 18c. Nose of Cyprus Airways airliner and greater flamingos . . . . 2·50 3·00
721 18c. Boeing 739 airliner in flight and greater flamingos 2·50 3·00

253 Sailing

255 "Cyprus 74" (wood-engraving by A. Tassos)

254 Conference Emblem

1988. Olympic Games, Seoul. Multicoloured.
722 5c. Type **253** 30 20
723 7c. Athletes at start 35 40
724 10c. Shooting 40 70
725 20c. Judo . . . . 90 1·50

1988. Non-Aligned Foreign Ministers' Conference, Nicosia.
726 **254** 1c. black, blue and green 10 10
727 – 10c. multicoloured 45 70
728 – 50c. multicoloured . . . . 2·75 2·50
DESIGNS: 10c. Emblem of Republic of Cyprus; 50c. Nehru, Tito, Nasser and Makarios.

1988. Obligatory Tax. Refugee Fund. Variously dated.
892 **255** 1c. black and grey 10 10

1988. No. 651 surch **15c**.
730 15c. on 4c. Kykko Monastery 1·75 1·25

256 "Presentation of Christ at the Temple" (Church of Holy Cross tou Agiasmati)

257 Human Rights Logo

1988. Christmas. Designs showing frescoes from Cypriot churches. Multicoloured.
731 5c. Type **256** 25 20
732 15c. "Virgin and Child" (St. John Lampadistis Monastery) 55 25
733 17c. "Adoration of the Magi" (St. John Lampadistis Monastery) . . . . 80 1·75

1988. 40th Anniv of Universal Declaration of Human Rights.
734 **257** 25c. lt blue, dp blue & bl 90 1·25

258 Basketball

1989. 3rd Small European States' Games, Nicosia. Multicoloured.
735 1c. Type **258** 30 15
736 5c. Javelin 30 15
737 15c. Wrestling 65 20
738 18c. Athletics . . . . 85 1·00
MS739 109 × 80 mm. £1 Angel and laurel wreath (99 × 73 mm). Imperf 6·00 6·50

259 Lingri Stick Game

1989. Europa. Children's Games. Multicoloured.
740 7c. Type **259** . . . . 1·10 1·50
741 7c. Ziziros . . . . 1·10 1·50
742 18c. Sitsia . . . . 1·25 1·60
743 18c. Leapfrog . . . . 1·25 1·60

260 "Universal Man"

1989. Bicentenary of the French Revolution.
744 **260** 18c. multicoloured . . . . 1·00 60

261 Stylized Human Figures

262 Worker Bees tending Larvae

1989. Centenary of Interparliamentary Union (15c.) and 9th Non-Aligned Summit Conference, Belgrade (30c.). Multicoloured.
745 15c. Type **261** 65 40
746 30c. Conference logo . . . . 1·10 1·10

1989. Bee-keeping. Multicoloured.
748 3c. Type **262** 30 25
749 10c. Bee on rock-rose flower 70 50
750 15c. Bee on lemon flower . . 95 50
751 18c. Queen and worker bees 1·10 1·75

263 Outstretched Hand and Profile (aid for Armenian earthquake victims)

264 Winter (detail from "Four Seasons")

1989. Anniversaries and Events. Multicoloured.

752 3c. Type **263** 30 1·25
753 5c. Airmail envelope (Cyprus Philatelic Society F.I.P. membership) 45 10
754 7c. Crab symbol and daisy (European Cancer Year) 75 1·40
755 17c. Vegetables and fish (World Food Day) 1·10 1·40

1989. Roman Mosaics from Paphos. Multicoloured.

756 1c. Type **264** 30 1·25
757 2c. Personification of Crete (32 × 24 mm) 40 1·25
758 3c. Centaur and Maenad (24 × 32 mm) 50 1·25
759 4c. Poseidon and Amymone (32 × 24 mm) 70 1·40
760 5c. Leda 70 20
761 7c. Apollon 80 25
762 10c. Hermes and Dionysos (24 × 32 mm) 1·00 30
763 15c. Cassiopeia 1·75 45
764 18c. Orpheus (32 × 24 mm) 1·75 50
765 20c. Nymphs (24 × 32 mm) 2·00 75
766 25c. Amazon (24 × 32 mm) 2·00 80
767 40c. Doris (32 × 24 mm) 3·00 1·50
768 50c. Heracles and the Lion (39 × 27 mm) 3·00 1·50
769 £1 Apollon and Daphne (39 × 27 mm) 4·50 3·00
770 £3 Cupid (39 × 27 mm) 10·00 12·00

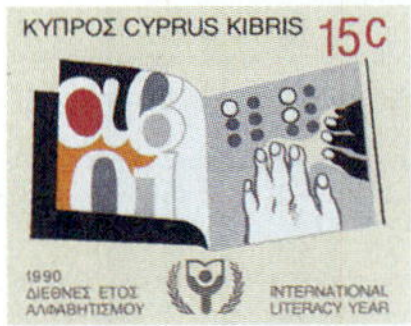

265 Hands and Open Book (International Literacy Year)

1990. Anniversaries and Events. Multicoloured.

771 15c. Type **265** 55 50
772 17c. Dove and profiles (83rd Inter-Parliamentary Conference, Nicosia) 65 90
773 18c. Lions International emblem (Lions Europa Forum, Limassol) 75 90

266 District Post Office, Paphos

1990. Europa. Post Office Buildings. Mult.

774 7c. Type **266** 1·40 25
775 18c. City Centre Post Office, Limassol 1·60 3·00

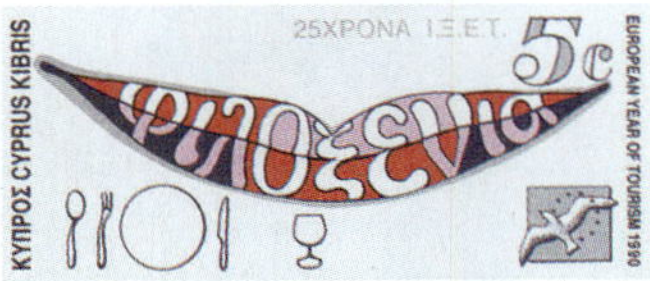

267 Symbolic Lips (25th anniv of Hotel and Catering Institute)

1990. European Tourism Year. Multicoloured.

776 5c. Type **267** 25 25
777 7c. Bell tower, St. Lazarus Church (1100th anniv) 30 25
778 15c. Butterflies and woman 2·25 45
779 18c. Birds and man 2·50 4·25

268 Sun (wood carving)

269 "Chionodoxa lochiae"

1990. 30th Anniv of Republic. Multicoloured.

780 15c. Type **268** 65 45
781 17c. Bulls (pottery design) 75 60
782 18c. Fishes (pottery design) 85 70
783 40c. Tree and birds (wood carving) 2·50 4·75
MS784 89 × 89 mm. £1 30th Anniversary emblem. Imperf 3·75 6·50

1990. Endangered Wild Flowers. Book illustrations by Elektra Megaw. Multicoloured.

785 2c. Type **269** 55 1·40
786 3c. "Pancratium maritimum" 55 1·40
787 5c. "Paeonia mascula" 75 20
788 7c. "Cyclamen cyprium" 80 25
789 15c. "Tulipa cypria" 1·60 30
790 18c. "Crocus cyprius" 1·75 3·50

270 "Nativity"

271 Archangel

1990. Christmas. 16th-century Icons. Mult.

791 5c. Type **270** 50 20
792 15c. "Virgin Hodegetria" 1·40 30
793 17c. "Nativity" (different) 1·60 3·50

1991. 6th-century Mosaics from Kanakaria Church. Multicoloured.

794 5c. Type **271** 20 15
795 15c. Christ Child 75 20
796 17c. St. James 1·50 1·75
797 18c. St. Matthew 1·75 2·25

272 "Ulysses" Spacecraft

1991. Europa. Europa in Space. Multicoloured.

798 7c. Type **272** 90 20
799 18c. "Giotto" and Halley's Comet 1·60 2·50

273 Young Cyprus Wheatear

1991. Cyprus Wheatear. Multicoloured.

800 5c. Type **273** 80 40
801 7c. Adult bird in autumn plumage 85 40
802 15c. Adult male in breeding plumage 1·25 50
803 30c. Adult female in breeding plumage 1·75 3·50

274 Mother and Child with Tents

1991. 40th Anniv of U.N. Commission for Refugees. Each deep brown, brown and silver.

804 5c. Type **274** 25 15
805 15c. Three pairs of legs 90 65
806 18c. Three children 1·10 2·50

275 The Nativity

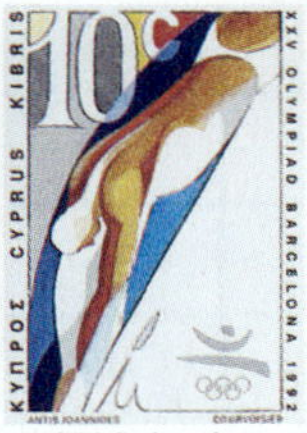

276 Swimming

1991. Christmas. Multicoloured.

808 5c. Type **275** 30 15
809 15c. Saint Basil 70 40
810 17c. Baptism of Jesus 1·00 1·75

1992. Olympic Games, Barcelona. Multicoloured.

811 10c. Type **276** 60 35
812 20c. Long jump 1·00 70
813 30c. Running 1·40 1·40
814 35c. Discus 1·60 2·50

277 World Map and Emblem ("EXPO '92" Worlds Fair, Seville)

1992. Anniversaries and Events. Multicoloured.

815 20c. Type **277** 1·60 80
816 25c. European map and football (10th under-16 European Football Championship) 1·75 1·10
817 30c. Symbols of learning (inauguration of University of Cyprus) 1·75 3·00

278 Compass Rose and Map of Voyage

1992. Europa. 500th Anniv of Discovery of America by Columbus. Multicoloured.

818 10c. Type **278** 1·10 1·40
819 10c. "Departure from Palos" (R. Balaga) 1·10 1·40
820 30c. Fleet of Columbus 1·50 2·00
821 30c. Christopher Columbus 1·50 2·00

Nos. 818/19 and 820/1 were each issued together, se-tenant, forming composite designs.

279 "Chamaeleo chamaeleon"

1992. Reptiles. Multicoloured.

822 7c. Type **279** 65 30
823 10c. "Lacerta laevis troodica" (lizard) 85 45
824 15c. "Mauremys caspica" (turtle) 1·25 80
825 20c. "Coluber cypriensis" (snake) 1·40 2·50

280 Minoan Wine Ship of 7th Century B.C. and Modern Tanker

1992. 7th International Maritime and Shipping Conference, Nicosia.

826 **280** 50c. multicoloured 3·00 3·00

281 "Visitation of the Virgin Mary to Elizabeth", Church of the Holy Cross, Pelendri

282 School Building and Laurel Wreath

1992. Christmas. Church Fresco Paintings. Mult.

827 7c. Type **281** 50 25
828 15c. "Virgin and Child Enthroned", Church of Panayia tou Araka 85 65
829 20c. "Virgin and Child", Ayios Nicolaos tis Stegis Church 1·25 2·25

1993. Centenary of Pancyprian Gymnasium (secondary school).

830 **282** 10c. multicoloured 75 60

283 "Motherhood" (bronze sculpture, Nicos Dymiotis)

1993. Europa. Comtemporary Art. Multicoloured.

831 10c. Type **283** 75 50
832 30c. "Motherhood" (painting, Christoforos Savva) (horiz) 1·50 2·25

284 Women Athletes (13th European Cup for Women)

1993. Anniversaries and Events. Multicoloured.

833 7c. Type **284** 40 30
834 10c. Scout symbols (80th anniv of Scouting in Cyprus) (vert) 55 40
835 20c. Water-skier, dolphin and gull (Moufflon Encouragement Cup) (inscr "Mufflon") 10·00 10·00
835a 20c. Water-skier, dolphin and seabird (inscr "Moufflon") 95 95
836 25c. Archbishop Makarios III and monastery (80th birth anniv) 1·40 2·00

285 Red Squirrelfish

1993. Fish. Multicoloured.

837 7c. Type **285** 50 25
838 15c. Red scorpionfish 75 55
839 20c. Painted comber 85 85
840 30c. Grey triggerfish 1·60 2·50

286 Conference Emblem

1993. 12th Commonwealth Summit Conference.

841 **286** 35c. brown and ochre 1·60 1·90
842 40c. brown and ochre 1·90 2·40

287 Ancient Sailing Ship and Modern Coaster

1993. "Maritime Cyprus '93" International Shipping Conference, Nicosia.

843 **287** 25c. multicoloured 1·40 1·40

288 Cross from Stavrovouni Monastery

290 Symbols of Disability (Persons with Special Needs Campaign)

289 Copper Smelting

1993. Christmas. Church Crosses. Multicoloured.
844 7c. Type **288** 40 25
845 20c. Cross from Lefkara . . 1·00 75
846 25c. Cross from Pedoulas (horiz) . . . . 1·25 2·25

1994. Europa. Discoveries. Ancient Copper Industry. Multicoloured.
847 10c. Type **289** 50 35
848 30c. Ingot, ancient ship and map of Cyprus . . . . . 1·25 2·00

1994. Anniversaries and Events. Multicoloured.
849 7c. Type **290** 50 25
850 15c. Olympic rings in flame (Centenary of International Olympic Committee) . . . 75 55
851 20c. Peace doves (World Gymnasiade, Nicosia) . . . 90 80
852 25c. Adults and unborn baby in tulip (International Year of the Family) . . . . . . 1·25 2·25

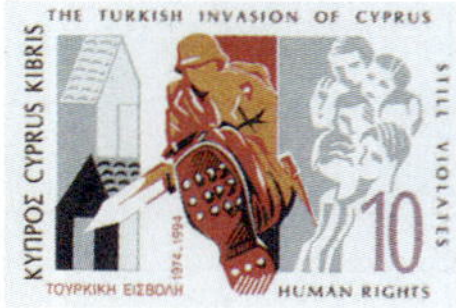

291 Houses, Soldier and Family

1994. 20th Anniv of Turkish Landings in Cyprus. Multicoloured.
853 10c. Type **291** 50 40
854 50c. Soldier and ancient columns . . . . 2·00 3·25

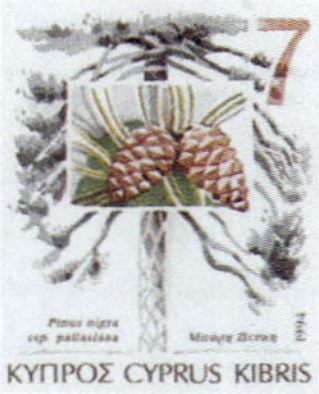

292 Black Pine

1994. Trees. Multicoloured.
855 7c. Type **292** 50 25
856 15c. Cyprus cedar 75 55
857 20c. Golden oak 90 80
858 30c. Strawberry tree . . . . 1·40 2·50

293 Airliner, Route Map and Emblem

1994. 50th Anniv of I.C.A.O.
859 **293** 30c. multicoloured . . . . 2·00 2·00

294 "Virgin Mary" (detail) (Philip Goul)

295 Woman from Paphos wearing Foustani

1994. Christmas. Church Paintings. Multicoloured.
860 7c. Type **294** 60 25
861 20c. "The Nativity" (detail) (Byzantine) . . . . 1·40 70
862 25c. "Archangel Michael" (detail) (Goul) . . . . . 1·60 2·75

1994. Traditional Costumes. Multicoloured.
863 1c. Type **295** . . . . 40 1·25
864 2c. Bride from Karpass . . . 55 1·25
865 3c. Woman from Paphos wearing sayia . . . . . . 60 1·25
866 5c. Woman from Messaoria wearing foustani . . . . . 70 1·25
867 7c. Bridegroom 75 20
868 10c. Shepherd from Messaoria 90 40
869 15c. Woman from Nicosia in festive costume . . . . . . 1·75 40
870 20c. Woman from Karpass wearing festive sayia . . . 1·75 50
871 25c. Woman from Pitsillia . . 1·90 60
872 30c. Woman from Karpass wearing festive doupletti 1·90 70
873 35c. Countryman . . . . . . 1·90 1·25
874 40c. Man from Messaoria in festive costume . . . . . . 2·25 1·75
875 50c. Townsman . . . . . . 2·25 2·00
876 £1 Townswoman wearing festive sarka . . . . 3·25 3·25

296 "Hearth Room" Excavation, Alassa, and Frieze

297 Statue of Liberty, Nicosia (left detail)

1995. 3rd International Congress of Cypriot Studies, Nicosia. Multicoloured.
877 20c. Type **296** 75 75
878 30c. Hypostyle hall, Kalavasos, and Mycenaean amphora . . . . 1·00 1·75
MS879 110 × 80 mm. £1 Old Archbishop's Palace, Nicosia (107 × 71 mm). Imperf . . . . 3·50 5·00

1995. 40th Anniv of Start of E.O.K.A. Campaign. Different details of the statue. Multicoloured.
880 20c. Type **297** . . . . 1·10 1·40
881 20c. Centre detail (face value at top right) . . . . . . 1·10 1·40
882 20c. Right detail (face value at bottom right) . . . . . 1·10 1·40
Nos. 880/2 were printed together, se-tenant, forming a composite design.

298 Nazi Heads on Peace Dove over Map of Europe

299 Symbolic Figure holding Healthy Food

1995. Europa. Peace and Freedom. Multicoloured.
883 10c. Type **298** . . . . 1·00 50
884 30c. Concentration camp prisoner and peace dove 2·25 3·25

1995. Healthy Living. Multicoloured.
885 7c. Type **299** 30 25
886 10c. "AIDS" and patients (horiz) 70 60
887 15c. Drug addict (horiz) . . . 75 60
888 20c. Smoker and barbed wire 95 1·50

300 European Union Flag and European Culture Month Logo

1995. European Culture Month and "Europhilex '95" International Stamp Exhibition, Nicosia. MS891 blue, yellow and stone or multicoloured (others).
889 20c. Type **300** 55 60
890 25c. Map of Europe and Cypriot church . . . . . 70 1·25
MS891 95 × 86 mm. 50c. Peace dove (42 × 30 mm); 50c. European Cultural Month symbol (42 × 30 mm) . . . . 6·00 7·00

301 Peace Dove with Flags of Cyprus and United Nations

1995. Anniversaries and Events. Multicoloured.
893 10c. Type **301** (50th anniv of United Nations) 50 35
894 15c. Hand pushing ball over net (cent of volleyball) (vert) 85 50
895 20c. Safety pin on leaf (European Nature Conservation Year) (vert) 95 80
896 25c. Clay pigeon contestant (World Clay Target Shooting Championship) 1·10 2·25

302 Reliquary from Kykko Monastery

303 Family (25th anniv of Pancyprian Organization of Large Families)

1995. Christmas.
897 **302** 7c. multicoloured 40 25
898 – 20c. multicoloured 90 60
899 – 25c. multicoloured . . . . 1·40 2·00
DESIGNS: 20, 25c. Different reliquaries of Virgin and Child from Kykko Monastery.

1996. Anniversaries and Events. Multicoloured.
900 10c. Type **303** 50 35
901 20c. Film camera (centenary of cinema) . . . . 1·25 70
902 35c. Silhouette of parent and child in globe (50th anniv of UNICEF) . . . . . . 1·75 1·75
903 40c. "13" and Commonwealth emblem (13th Conference of Commonwealth Speakers and Presiding Officers) . . 1·75 2·75

304 Maria Synglitiki

306 Watermill

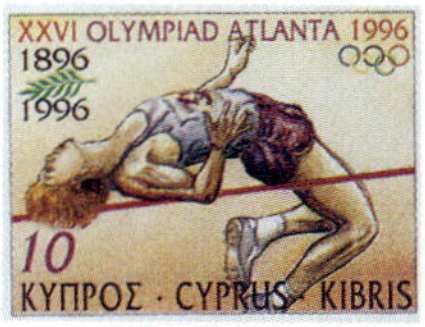

305 High Jump

1996. Europa. Famous Women. Multicoloured.
904 10c. Type **304** 75 30
905 30c. Queen Caterina Cornaro 1·75 2·50

1996. Centennial Olympic Games, Atlanta. Multicoloured.
906 10c. Type **305** 75 30
907 20c. Javelin . . . . 1·25 65
908 25c. Wrestling . . . . 1·40 1·10
909 30c. Swimming . . . . . . 1·60 2·50

1996. Mills. Multicoloured.
910 10c. Type **306** 70 40
911 15c. Olivemill 85 50
912 20c. Windmill . . . . 1·00 90
913 25c. Handmill . . . . 1·10 2·00

307 Icon of Our Lady of Iberia, Moscow

1996. Cyprus–Russia Joint Issue. Orthodox Religion. Multicoloured.
914 30c. Type **307** . . . . 1·75 2·00
915 30c. Stravrovouni Monastery, Cyprus . . . . 1·75 2·00
916 30c. Icon of St. Nicholas, Cyprus . . . . 1·75 2·00
917 30c. Voskresenskie Gate, Moscow . . . . 1·75 2·00

308 "The Nativity" (detail)

1996. Christmas. Religious Murals from Church of The Virgin of Asinou. Multicoloured.
918 7c. Type **308** 60 25
919 20c. "Virgin Mary between the Archangels Gabriel and Michael" . . . . 1·50 60
920 25c. "Christ bestowing Blessing" (vert) . . . . . 1·90 2·50

309 Basketball

1997. Final of European Basketball Cup.
921 **309** 30c. multicoloured . . . . 2·25 2·00

310 "The Last Supper"

1997. Easter. Religious Frescoes from Monastery of St. John Lambadestis. Multicoloured.
922 15c. Type **310** 80 50
923 25c. "The Crucifixion" . . . 95 1·50

311 Kori Kourelleni and Prince

1997. Europa. Tales and Legends. Multicoloured.
924 15c. Type **311** 90 40
925 30c. Digenis and Charon . . 1·50 2·50

312 "Oedipoda miniata" (grasshopper)

1997. Insects. Multicoloured.
926 10c. Type **312** 60 30
927 15c. "Acherontia atropos" (hawk moth) 85 40
928 25c. "Daphnis nerii" (hawk moth) . . . . 1·40 1·10
929 35c. "Ascalaphus macaronius" (owl-fly) . . . 1·60 2·25

313 Archbishop Makarios III and Chapel

1997. 20th Death Anniv of Archbishop Makarios III.
930 **313** 15c. multicoloured . . . . 1·00 50

314 The Nativity

1997. Christmas. Byzantine Frescos from the Monastery of St. John Lambadestis. Mult.
931 10c. Type **314** 50 25
932 25c. Three Kings following the star . . . . 1·60 70
933 30c. Flight into Egypt . . . 1·75 2·50

315 Green Jasper

1998. Minerals. Multicoloured.
934 10c. Type **315** 50 30
935 15c. Iron pyrite 70 45
936 25c. Gypsum 90 90
937 30c. Chalcedony . . . . . . 1·25 2·00

316 Players competing for Ball

1998. World Cup Football Championship, France.
938 **316** 35c. multicoloured . . . . 1·75 1·40

317 Cataclysmos Festival, Larnaca

1998. Europa. Festivals. Multicoloured.
939 15c. Type **317** . . . . 1·25 40
940 30c. House of Representatives, Nicosia (Declaration of Independence) . . . . . . 1·75 2·50

318 Mouflon Family Group **319** Flames and Globe Emblem

1998. Endangered Species. Cyprus Mouflon. Mult.
941 25c. Type **318** . . . . 1·00 1·25
942 25c. Mouflon herd . . . . . 1·00 1·25
943 25c. Head of ram . . . . . 1·00 1·25
944 25c. Ram on guard . . . . . 1·00 1·25

1998. 50th Anniv of Universal Declaration of Human Rights.
959 **319** 50c. multicoloured . . . . 1·25 1·60

320 World "Stamp" and Magnifying Glass

1998. World Stamp Day.
960 **320** 30c. multicoloured . . . . 1·60 1·60

321 "The Annunciation" **322** "Pleurotus eryngii"

1998. Christmas. Multicoloured.
961 10c. Type **321** 55 20
962 25c. "The Nativity" . . . . 1·25 65
963 30c. "The Baptism of Christ" 1·40 2·25
MS964 102 × 75 mm. Nos. 961/3 2·75 3·25

1999. Mushrooms of Cyprus. Multicoloured.
965 10c. Type **322** 40 30
966 15c. "Lactarius deliciosus" 70 40
967 25c. "Sparassis crispa" . . . 1·00 90
968 30c. "Morchella elata" . . . 1·25 2·00

323 Pair of Moufflons at Tripylos Reserve

1999. Europa. Parks and Gardens. Multicoloured.
969 15c. Type **323** . . . . 1·00 50
970 30c. Turtles on beach at Lara Reserve . . . . 1·75 2·00

324 Council of Europe Building, Emblem and Flags

1999. 50th Anniv of Council of Europe.
971 **324** 30c. multicoloured . . . . 1·50 1·50

325 Temple of Hylates Apollo, Kourion

1999. Cyprus–Greece Joint Issue. 4000 Years of Greek Culture. Multicoloured.
972 25c. Type **325** . . . . 1·25 1·50
973 25c. Mycenaean pot depicting warriors . . . . 1·25 1·50
974 25c. Mycenaean crater depicting horse . . . . . 1·25 1·50
975 25c. Temple of Apollo, Delphi . . . . 1·25 1·50

326 Paper Aeroplane Letters and U.P.U. Emblem

1999. 125th Anniv of Universal Postal Union. Multicoloured.
976 15c. Type **326** . . . . 1·00 50
977 35c. "125" and U.P.U. emblem . . . . 1·50 2·00

327 Container Ship and Cypriot Flag

1999. "Maritime Cyprus '99" Conference. Sheet 103 × 80 mm, containing T **327** and similar horiz designs. Multicoloured.
MS978 25c. Type **327**; 25c. Binoculars and chart; 25c. Stern of container ship; 25c. Tanker . . 3·50 4·00

328 Cypriot Refugee Fund Stamps and Barbed Wire (⅔-size illustration)

1999. 25th Anniv of Turkish Landings in Cyprus. Sheet 110 × 75 mm. Imperf.
MS979 **328** 30c. multicoloured 1·50 2·25

329 Angel **330** Woman's Silhouette with Stars and Globe

1999. Christmas. Multicoloured.
980 10c. Type **329** 55 10
981 25c. The Three Kings . . . . 1·25 60
982 30c. Madonna and child . . 1·40 2·25

2000. Miss Universe Beauty Contest, Cyprus. Sheet 80 × 65 mm, containing T **330** and similar vert design. Multicoloured.
MS983 15c. Type **330**; 35c. Statue of Aphrodite and apple . . . . . 2·00 2·00

331 Necklace, 4500–4000 B.C. **332** "Building Europe"

2000. Jewellery. Multicoloured.
984 10c. Type **331** 35 30
985 15c. Gold earrings, 3rd-cent B.C. 55 40
986 20c. Gold earring from Lampousa, 6th–7th-cent . . 65 50
987 25c. Brooch, 19th-cent 65 60
988 30c. Gold cross, 6th–7th-cent 85 75
989 35c. Necklace, 18th–19th-cent 90 85
990 40c. Gold earring, 19th-cent 1·40 95
991 50c. Spiral hair ring, 4th–5th-cent B.C. . . . . . . 1·50 1·25
992 75c. Gold-plated silver plaques from Gialia, 700–600 B.C. (horiz) . . . . . 2·00 2·00
993 £1 Gold frontlet from Egkomi, 14th–13th-cent B.C. (horiz) . . . . 4·00 2·75
994 £2 Gold necklace from Egkomi, 13th-cent B.C. (horiz) . . . . 6·50 6·00
995 £3 Buckles, 19th-cent (horiz) 9·00 9·00

2000. Europa.
996 **332** 30c. multicoloured . . . . 1·50 1·50

333 "50", Cross and Map of Cyprus

2000. 50th Anniv of Red Cross in Cyprus.
997 **333** 15c. multicoloured . . . . 1·50 80

334 Flame, Map of Cyprus and Broken Chain **335** Weather Balloon, Map and Satellite

2000. 45th Anniv of Struggle for Independence.
998 **334** 15c. multicoloured . . . . 1·50 80

2000. 50th Anniv of World Meteorological Organization.
999 **335** 30c. multicoloured . . . . 2·00 2·00

336 Monastery of Antifontis, Kalograia **337** Council of Europe Emblem

2000. Greek Orthodox Churches in Northern Cyprus.
1000 **336** 10c. brown and red . . . 70 25
1001 – 15c. dp green & green 1·00 35
1002 – 25c. dp violet & violet 1·40 90
1003 – 30c. red and grey . . . 1·50 2·25
DESIGNS—VERT: 15c. Church of St. Themonianos, Lysi. HORIZ: 25c. Church of Panagia Kanakaria, Lytrhagkomi; 30c. Church of Avgasida Monastery, Milia.

2000. 50th Anniv of European Convention of Human Rights.
1004 **337** 30c. multicoloured . . . 1·75 1·75

338 Archery **339** "The Annunciation"

2000. Olympic Games, Sydney. Multicoloured.
1005 10c. Type **338** 60 25
1006 15c. Gymnastics 80 35
1007 25c. Diving . . . . 1·25 80
1008 35c. Trampolining . . . . . 1·50 2·25

2000. Christmas. Gold Gospel Covers. Multicoloured.
1009 10c. Type **339** 65 25
1010 25c. "The Nativity" . . . . 1·50 70
1011 30c. "The Baptism of Christ" . . . . 1·60 1·75

340 "25" and Commonwealth Symbol

2001. 25th Anniv of Commonwealth Day.
1012 **340** 30c. multicoloured . . . 1·75 1·75

341 Silhouette, Dove and Barbed Wire

2001. 50th Anniv of United Nations High Commissioner for Refugees.
1013 **341** 30c. multicoloured . . . 1·75 2·00

342 Pavlos Liasides

2001. Birth Centenary of Pavlos Liasides (poet).
1014 **342** 13c. chocolate, ochre & brown . . . . 1·00 60

343 Bridge over River Diarizos

2001. Europa. Cypriot Rivers. Multicoloured.
1015 20c. Type **343** . . . . . . 1·00 50
1016 30c. Mountain torrent, River Akaki . . . . . . 1·50 2·00

344 *Pathenope massena*

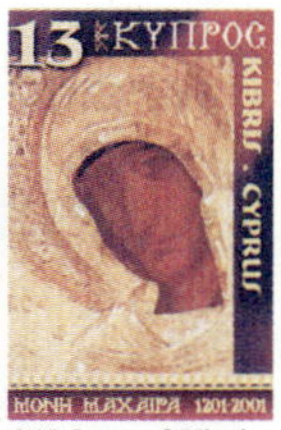

345 Icon of Virgin Mary

2001. Crabs. Multicoloured.
1017 13c. Type **344** 60 20
1018 20c. *Calappa granulata* . . 1·00 70
1019 25c. *Ocypode cursor* . . . 1·25 1·00
1020 30c. *Pagurus bernhardus* . . 1·60 1·75

2001. Christmas. 800th Anniv of Macheras Monastery. Multicoloured.
1021 13c. Type **345** 45 20
1022 25c. Macheras Monastery 1·25 65
1023 30c. Ornate gold crucifix . . 1·60 1·75

346 Loukis Akritas

2001. Loukis Akritas (writer) Commemoration.
1024 **346** 20c. green and brown . . 1·25 80

347 Tortoiseshell and White Cat

2002. Cats. Multicoloured.
1025 20c. Type **347** . . . . . . 1·25 1·40
1026 20c. British blue . . . . . 1·25 1·40
1027 25c. Tortoiseshell and white 1·25 1·40
1028 25c. Red and silver tabby 1·25 1·40

348 Acrobat on Horseback

350 Mother Teresa

349 *Myrtus communis*

2002. Europa. Circus. Multicoloured.
1029 20c. Type **348** . . . . . . 1·00 50
1030 30c. Clown on high wire . . 1·50 1·75

2002. Medicinal Plants. Multicoloured.
1031 13c. Type **349** 65 30
1032 20c. *Lavandula stoechas* . . 1·00 70
1033 25c. *Capparis spinosa* . . . 1·25 1·00
1034 30c. *Ocimum basilicum* . . . 1·50 1·75

2002. Mother Teresa (founder of Missionaries of Charity) Commemoration.
1035 **350** 40c. multicoloured . . . 2·50 2·00

351 Blackboard on Easel

2002. International Teachers' Day. Multicoloured.
1036 13c. Type **351** . . . . . . 1·00 1·00
1037 30c. Computer . . . . . . 1·75 2·00

352 Agate Seal-stone (5th century B.C.)

2002. "Cyprus - Europhilex '02", Stamp Exhibition, Nicosia. Cypriot Antiquities showing Europa. Multicoloured.
1038 20c. Type **352** . . . . . . 1·10 1·25
1039 20c. Silver coin of Timochares (5th–4th century B.C.) . . . . . . 1·10 1·25
1040 20c. Silver coin of Stasioikos (5th century B.C.) . . . . 1·10 1·25
1041 30c. Clay lamp (green backgound) (2nd century A.D.) . . . . 1·50 1·75
1042 30c. Statuette of Europa on the Bull (7th–6th century B.C.) . . . . 1·50 1·75
1043 30c. Clay lamp (purple backgound) (1st century B.C.) . . . . 1·50 1·75
MS1044 105 × 71 mm. 50c. Statue of Aphrodite with maps of Crete and Cyprus; 50c. "Europa on the Bull" (painting by Francesco di Giogio) 6·00 6·50

353 "Nativity"

2002. Christmas. Details from "Birth of Christ" (wall painting), Church of Metamorphosis Sotiros, Palechori. Multicoloured.
1045 13c. Type **353** 65 20
1046 25c. "Three Wise Men" . . 1·25 65
1047 30c. "Birth of Christ" (complete painting) (38 × 38 mm) . . . . . . 1·75 1·75

354 Triumph Roadster 1800, 1946

2003. International Historic Car Rally. Multicoloured.
1048 20c. Type **354** . . . . . . 1·40 1·50
1049 25c. Ford model T, 1917 . . 1·40 1·50
1050 30c. Baby Ford Y 8hp, 1932 1·40 1·50

355 "POSTER IS ART"

356 Mediterranean Horseshoe Bat in Flight

2003. Europa. Poster Art.
1051 **355** 20c. multicoloured . . . 70 50
1052 – 30c. multicoloured . . . 1·25 1 50

2003. Endangered Species. Mediterranean Horseshoe Bat. Multicoloured.
1053 25c. Type **356** . . . . . . 1·10 1 25
1054 25c. Head of bat (facing forwards) . . . . 1·10 1·25
1055 25c. Bats roosting . . . . . 1·10 1·25
1056 25c. Head of bat (facing sideways, mouth open) . . 1·10 1·25

357 Stylized Owl

358 Eleonora's Falcon

2003. 7th Conference of European Ministers of Education, Nicosia.
1057 **357** 30c. multicoloured . . . 1·50 1·50

2003. Birds of Prey. Multicoloured.
1058 20c. Type **358** . . . . . . 1·00 1·25
1059 20c. Eleonora's falcon in flight . . . . 1·00 1·25
1060 25c. Imperial eagle . . . . 1·10 1·40
1061 25c. Imperial eagle in flight 1·10 1·40
1062 30c. Little owl . . . . . . 1·25 1·50
1063 30c. Little owl in flight and eggs in nest . . . . . . 1·25 1·50

359 Constantinos Spyridakis (historian, author and Minister of Education 1965–70)

2003. Birth Centenaries.
1064 **359** 5c. black and drab . . . 40 50
1065 – 5c. blackish olive and green 40 50
DESIGN: 23 × 31 mm—No. 1065, Tefkros Anthias (poet).

360 Three Angels

2003. Christmas. Multicoloured.
1066 13c. Type **360** 65 20
1067 30c. Three Wise Men . . . 1·25 75
1068 40c. Nativity (37 × 59 mm) 1·75 2·00
Nos. 1066/7 show details from icon of Nativity in Church of Virgin Mary, Kourdali. No. 1068 shows the complete painting.

361 Stylized Footballer

362 Stylized Footballer

2004. Centenary of FIFA (Federation Internationale de Football Association).
1069 **361** 30c. multicoloured . . . 1·50 1·50

2004. 50th Anniv of UEFA (Union of European Football Associations).
1070 **362** 30c. multicoloured . . . 1·50 1·50

363 Flags of New Member Countries

2004. Enlargement of the European Union.
1071 **363** 30c. multicoloured . . . 1·50 1·50

364 Yiannos Kranidiotis and EU Emblem

2004. 5th Death Anniv of Yiannos Kranidiotis (politician).
1072 **364** 20c. multicoloured . . . 1·00 70

365 Sailing Boat and Ancient Amphitheatre

2004. Europa. Holidays. Multicoloured.
1073 20c. Type **365** 75 50
1074 30c. Family at seaside and statue . . . . 1·25 1·50

366 Horse Racing

2004. Olympic Games, Athens. Ancient Olympic sports. Multicoloured.
1075 13c. Type **366** 50 35
1076 20c. Running 70 50
1077 30c. Diving . . . . 1·00 90
1078 40c. Discus . . . . 1·40 1·75

367 Dolphin

2004. Mammals. Multicoloured.
1079 20c. Type **367** . . . . . . 1·00 1·00
1080 20c. Dolphin (blue background) . . . . . . 1·00 1·00
1081 30c. Fox (white background) 1·40 1·40
1082 30c. Fox (green background) 1·40 1·40
1083 40c. Hare (white background) . . . . . . 1·60 1·60
1084 40c. Hare (yellow background) . . . . . . 1·60 1·60

368 Choir of Angels

2004. Christmas. Multicoloured.
1085 13c. Type **368** 65 20
1086 30c. Three Wise Men . . . 1·50 75
1087 40c. Annunciation to the Shepherds (37 × 60 mm) 1·75 2·00
MS1088 63 × 84 mm. £1 Virgin and Child (38 × 38 mm) . . . . . 4·00 4·50

369 Georgios Philippou Pierides

370 Carolina Pelendritou and Medal

2004. Intellectual Personalities. Multicoloured.
1089 5c. Type **369** 50 50
1090 5c. Emilios Chourmouzios (wearing tie) 50 50

2004. Obligatory Tax. Refugee Fund. As T **255** but inscr "2003" or "2004".
1091 **255** 1c. black and grey . . . 10 10
1092 1c. black and grey . . . 10 10

2005. Carolina Pelendritou's Gold Medal for 100 Metres Swimming at Paralympic Games, Athens (2004).
1093 **370** 20c. multicoloured . . . 1·00 70

371 Emblem

372 "The Entrance" (Kyriacos Koulli)

2005. Centenary of Rotary International.
1094 **371** 40c. multicoloured . . . 1·25 1·40

2005. 50th Anniv of EOKA Struggle.
1095 **372** 50c. multicoloured . . . 1·75 1·90

373 Table with Fish, Casserole, Wine, Garlic, Tomato and Bread
374 German Shepherd Dog and Police Dog with Handler

2005. Europa. Gastronomy. Multicoloured.
1096 20c. Type **373** 75 50
1097 30c. Table with coffee, cheese, cocktail and desserts . . . . 1·25 1·50

2005. Dogs in Man's Life. Multicoloured.
1098 13c. Type **374** 70 30
1099 20c. Hungarian Vizsla and hunter with dog . . . . . 1·10 70
1100 30c. Labrador and man with guide dog . . . . . . 1·50 1·10
1101 40c. Dalmatian and boy with pet dog . . . . . . 1·75 1·90

375 Angel appearing to Shepherds

2005. Christmas. Multicoloured.
1102 13c. Type **375** 60 25
1103 30c. Holy Family and shepherds . . . . 1·40 85
1104 40c. Virgin Mary and Jesus Christ (37 × 59 mm) . . . 1·60 1·75
Nos. 1102/3 show details from icon "Birth of Christ" and No. 1104 shows icon of the "Virgin Mary Karmiotissa".

376 1964 30c. Flower Stamp

2006. 50th Anniv of First Europa Stamp. Sowing Cyprus Europa stamps. Multicoloured.
MS1105 94 × 84 mm. 30c. Type **376**; 30c. 1962 40m. doves stamp; 30c. 1963 40m. tree stamp; 30c. 1963 150m. CEPT stamp . . . . . . 4·75 5·00
The stamps within No. **MS**1105 have composite background designs.

377 "25" and Hand Stamp

2006. 25th Anniv of the Postal Museum, Nicosia.
1106 **377** 25c. multicoloured . . . 1·00 75

378 Self-portrait and "The Anatomy Lesson of Dr. Nicolaes Tulp"

2006. 400th Birth Anniv of Rembrandt (artist).
1107 **378** 40c. multicoloured . . . 2·00 2·00

379 Footballer kicking Ball

2006. World Cup Football Championship, Germany.
1108 **379** 50c. multicoloured . . . 2·00 2·00

380 Stamna or Kouza (Pitcher) Dance, Cyprus

2006. Folk Dances. Sheet 100 × 70 mm containing T **380** and similar horiz design. Multicoloured.
MS1109 40c. Type **380**; 40c. Nati dance, Himachal Pradesh, India 3·25 3·50
Stamps in similar designs were issued by India.

381 Stylized Hand and Swallow
382 *Elaeagnus angustifolia* (olive)

2006. Europa. Integration. Multicoloured, background colour given.
1110 **381** 30c. green . . . . 1·25 50
1111 40c. pink . . . . 1·50 1·75

2006. Cyprus Fruits. Multicoloured.
1112 20c. Type **382** . . . . . . 1·00 50
1113 25c. *Mespilus germanica* (medlar) (horiz) . . . . . 1·00 55
1114 60c. *Opuntia ficus barbarica* (prickly pear) . . . . . . 2·75 3·25

383 Flowers and Silhouettes

2006. Transplants.
1115 **383** 13c. multicoloured . . . 75 60

384 Bedford Water Carrier, 1997

2006. Fire Engines. Multicoloured.
1116 13c. Type **384** 75 30
1117 20c. Hino fire engine, 1994 1·00 70
1118 50c. Bedford fire engine with turntable ladder, 1959 . . 2·50 2·75

385 Nicos Nicolaides
386 Wood-carved Iconostasis (Arsenios), 1868

2006. 50th Death Anniv of Nicos Nicolaides (writer).
1119 **385** 5c. multicoloured 30 25

2006. Christmas. Showing carvings from Agiou Eleftheriou Church, Nicosia. Multicoloured.
1120 13c. Type **386** 70 25
1121 30c. Christ on the Cross from top of iconostasis 1·40 1·25
1122 40c. Stone bas-relief showing cross, spear and sponge 1·60 1·75

387 *Antedon mediterranea* (feather star)

2007. Echinodermata of Cyprus. Multicoloured.
1123 25c. Type **387** . . . . . . 1·25 1·25
1124 25c. *Centrostephanus longispinus* (sea urchin) . . 1·25 1·25
1125 25c. *Astropecten jonstoni* (starfish) . . . . 1·25 1·25
1126 25c. *Ophioderma longicaudum* (brittle star) 1·25 1·25

388 St. Zenon the Postman (illustration reduced. Actual size 75 × 65 mm)

2007. St. Zenon the Postman. Sheet 75 × 65 mm. Imperf.
MS1127 **388** £1 multicoloured . . 5·00 5·50

2007. Obligatory Tax. Refugee Fund. As T **255** but inscr '2007'.
1127a **255** 1c. black and grey . . . 10 10

389 Triumph Daytona T100R, 1972

2007. Old Motorcycles. Multicoloured.
1128 13c. Type **389** 70 25
1129 20c. Matchless G3L, 1941 1·25 70
1130 40c. BSAWM20, 1940 . . . 1·75 1·25
1131 60c. Ariel Red Hunter NH 359, 1939 . . . . 2·00 2·50

390 Emblem
391 Ear of Wheat and Scout Badge

2007. 50th Anniv of the Treaty of Rome.
1132 **390** 30c. multicoloured . . . 1·10 1·25

2007. Europa. Centenary of Scouting.
1133 **391** 30c. multicoloured . . . 1·25 1·40
1134 40c. multicoloured . . . 1·50 1·60

392 '50' and Stylized Figures

2007. 50th Anniv of Social Insurance. Multicoloured.
1135 40c. Type **392** (inscr in Greek) . . . . 1·50 1·60
1136 40c. Stylized figures (at left) and '50' (inscr '50 YEARS OF SOCIAL INSURANCE' in English) . . . . 1·50 1·60
Nos. 1135/6 were issued together, se-tenant, forming a composite design.

393 Pygmy Hippopotamus, 10000 BC

2007. Cyprus through the Ages (1st series). Multicoloured.
1137 25c. Type **393** . . . . . . 1·10 1·25
1138 25c. Stone vessel, 7000 BC 1·10 1·25
1139 25c. Ruins of Choirokoitia settlement of 7000 BC . . 1·10 1·25
1140 25c. Figurine of a woman, 3000 BC . . . . 1·10 1·25
1141 25c. Terracotta vessel, 2000 BC . . . . 1·10 1·25
1142 25c. Greek inscription on a bronze skewer, 1000 BC 1·10 1·25
1143 25c. Bird-shaped vessel, 800 BC . . . . 1·10 1·25
1144 25c. Map of 1718 showing the ancient Kingdoms of Cyprus in the first millennium BC . . . . . 1·10 1·25

394 Limassol District Administration Building

2007. Neoclassical Buildings of Cyprus. Multicoloured.
1145 13c. Type **394** 80 75
1146 15c. National Bank of Greece Building, Nicosia 90 80
1147 20c. Archaeological Research Unit's Building, Nicosia . . . . 1·10 95
1148 30c. National Art Gallery Building, Nicosia . . . . 1·25 1·00
1149 40c. Paphos Municipal Library Building . . . . 1·40 1·25
1150 50c. Office Building of A. G. Leventis Foundation, Nicosia . . . . 1·75 1·75
1151 £1 Limassol Municipal Library Building . . . . 3·75 3·75
1152 £3 Phaneromeni Gymnasium Building, Nicosia . . . . 8·50 9·50

395 Virgin Mary and Christ Child

2007. Christmas.Designs showing murals taken from Chapel of St. Themonianus, Lysi. Multicoloured.
1153 13c. Type **395** 65 20
1154 30c. Archangel Gabriel . . . 1·40 1·10
1155 40c. Christ Pantocrator (34 × 44 mm) . . . . . . 1·75 2·00

Currency change: 100 cents = 1 euro

396 'Aphrodite' (statue)

2008. Adoption of the Euro Currency. Sheet 100 × 62 mm containing T **396** and similar square design. Multicoloured.
MS1156 €1 Type **396**; €1 'Sleeping Lady' Statuette of Malta . . . . 5·00 5·00
A similar miniature sheet was issued by Malta.

397 'Cyprus 74' (wood-engraving by A. Tassos)

398 Pink Anemone

2008. Obligatory Tax. Refugee Fund. Design as T **255** but denominated in cents and euros as T **397**. Inscr '2008'.

1157 **255**	2c. black and grey	15	15

2008. *Anemone coronaria*. Multicoloured.

1158	26c. Type **398**	80	70
1159	34c. White anemone	1·00	90
1160	51c. Red anemone	1·60	1·60
1161	68c. Mauve anemone	1·90	2·25

TURKISH CYPRIOT POSTS

After the inter-communal clashes during December 1963, a separate postal service was established on 6 January 1964, between some of the Turkish Cypriot areas, using handstamps inscribed "KIBRIS TURK POSTALARI". During 1964, however, an agreement was reached between representatives of the two communities for the restoration of postal services. This agreement to which the United Nations representatives were a party, was ratified in November 1966 by the Republic's Council of Ministers. Under the scheme postal servcies were provided for the Turkish Cypriot communities in Famagusta, Limassol, Lefka and Nicosia, staffed by Turkish Cypriot employees of the Cypriot Department of Posts.

On 8 April 1970, 5m. and 15m. locally produced labels, originally designated "Social Aid Stamps", were issued by the Turkish Cypriot community and these can be found on commercial covers. These local stamps are outside the scope of this catalogue.

On 29 October 1973 Nos. 1/7 were placed on sale, but were again used only on mail between the Turkish Cypriot areas.

Following the intervention by the Republic of Turkey in July 1974 these stamps replaced issues of the Republic of Cyprus in that part of the island, north and east of the Attila Line, controlled by the Autonomous Turkish Cypriot Administration.

1974. 1000 mils = 1 pound.
1978. 100 kurus = 1 lira.
2005. 100 yeni kurus = 1 yeni lira.

1 50th Anniversary Emblem

1974. 50th Anniv of Republic of Turkey.

1 –	3m. multicoloured	30·00	30·00
2 –	5m. multicoloured	60	40
3 –	10m. multicoloured	50	20
4 **1**	15m. red and black	2·50	1·50
5 –	20m. multicoloured	70	20
6 –	50m. multicoloured	2·00	1·50
7 –	70m. multicoloured	16·00	16·00

DESIGNS—VERT: 3m. Woman sentry; 10m. Man and woman with Turkish flags; 20m. Ataturk statue, Kyrenia Gate, Nicosia; 50m. "The Fallen". HORIZ: 5m. Military parade, Nicosia; 70m. Turkish flag and map of Cyprus.

1975. Proclamation of the Turkish Federated State of Cyprus. Nos. 3 and 5 surch **KIBRIS TURK FEDERE DEVLETI 13.2.1975** and value.

8	30m. on 20m. multicoloured	75	1·00
9	100m. on 10m. multicoloured	1·25	2·00

3 Namik Kemal's Bust, Famagusta

1975. Multicoloured.

10	3m. Type **3**	15	40
11	10m. Ataturk Statue, Nicosia	25	10
12	15m. St. Hilarion Castle	35	20
13	20m. Ataturk Square, Nicosia	45	20
14	25m. Famagusta Beach	45	30
15	30m. Kyrenia Harbour	55	10
16	50m. Lala Mustafa Pasha Mosque, Famagusta (vert)	60	10
17	100m. Interior, Kyrenia Castle	80	90
18	250m. Castle walls, Kyrenia	1·00	2·25
19	500m. Othello Tower, Famagusta (vert)	1·50	4·50

See also Nos. 36/8.

4 Map of Cyprus

1975. "Peace in Cyprus". Multicoloured.

20	30m. Type **4**	20	15
21	50m. Map, laurel and broken chain	25	20
22	150m. Map and laurel-sprig on globe (vert)	65	1·00

5 "Pomegranates" (I. V. Guney)

1975. Europa. Paintings. Multicoloured.

23	90m. Type **5**	1·40	1·40
24	100m. "Harvest Time" (F. Direkoglu)	1·40	1·40

1976. Nos. 16/17 surch.

25	10m. on 50m. multicoloured	35	70
26	30m. on 100m. multicoloured	35	80

7 "Expectation" (ceramic statuette)

9 Olympic Symbol "Flower"

8 Carob

1976. Europa. Multicoloured.

27	60m. Type **7**	60	80
28	120m. "Man in Meditation"	80	1·60

1976. Export Products. Fruits. Multicoloured.

29	10m. Type **8**	15	10
30	25m. Mandarin	20	10
31	40m. Strawberry	25	25
32	60m. Orange	35	65
33	80m. Lemon	40	2·00

1976. Olympic Games, Montreal. Multicoloured.

34	60m. Type **9**	25	20
35	100m. Olympic symbol and doves	35	25

10 Kyrenia Harbour

11 Liberation Monument, Karaeglanoglu (Ay Georghios)

1976. Multicoloured.

36	5m. Type **10**	40	15
37	15m. St. Hilarion Castle	40	15
38	20m. Ataturk Square, Nicosia	40	15

1976. Liberation Monument.

47 **11**	30m. blue, pink and black	15	20
48 –	150m. red, pink and black	35	45

DESIGN: 150m. Liberation Monument (different view).

12 Hotel, Salamis Bay

1977. Europa. Multicoloured.

49	80m. Type **12**	65	80
50	100m. Kyrenia Port	75	80

13 Pottery

14 Arap Ahmet Pasha Mosque, Nicosia

1977. Handicrafts. Multicoloured.

51	15m. Type **13**	10	10
52	30m. Pottery (vert)	10	10
53	125m. Basketware	30	50

1977. Turkish Buildings in Cyprus. Multicoloured.

54	20m. Type **14**	10	10
55	40m. Paphos Castle (horiz)	10	10
56	70m. Bekir Pasha aqueduct (horiz)	15	20
57	80m. Sultan Mahmut library (horiz)	15	25

15 Namik Kemal (bust) and House, Famagusta

1977. Namik Kemal (patriotic poet). Multicoloured.

58	30m. Type **15**	15	15
59	140m. Namik Kemal (portrait) (vert)	35	60

16 Old Man and Woman

17 Oratory in Buyuk Han, Nicosia

1978. Social Security.

60 **16**	150k. black, yellow and blue	10	10
61 –	275k. black, orange and green	15	15
62 –	375k. black, blue and orange	25	20

DESIGNS: 275k. Injured man with crutch; 375k. Woman with family.

1978. Europa. Multicoloured.

63	225k. Type **17**	85	30
64	450k. Cistern in Selimiye Mosque, Nicosia	1·25	70

18 Motorway Junction

1978. Communications. Multicoloured.

65	75k. Type **18**	15	10
66	100k. Hydrofoil	15	10
67	650k. Boeing 720 at Ercan Airport	50	35

19 Dove with Laurel Branch

20 Kemal Ataturk

1978. National Oath.

68 **19**	150k. yellow, violet and black	10	10
69 –	225k. black, red and yellow	10	10
70 –	725k. black, blue and yellow	20	20

DESIGNS—VERT: 225k. "Taking the Oath". HORIZ: 725k. Symbolic dove.

1978. Ataturk Commemoration.

71 **20**	75k. turquoise & dp turq	10	10
72	450k. pink and brown	15	15
73	650k. blue and light blue	20	25

1979. Nos. 30/3 surch.

74	50k. on 25k. Mandarin	10	10
75	1l. on 40m. Strawberry	15	10
76	3l. on 60m. Orange	15	10
77	5l. on 80m. Lemon	35	15

22 Gun Barrel with Olive Branch and Map of Cyprus

1979. 5th Anniv of Turkish Peace Operation in Cyprus. Sheet 72 × 52 mm. Imperf.

MS78 **22**	15l. black, blue and green	80	1·25

23 Postage Stamp and Map of Cyprus

24 Microwave Antenna

1979. Europa. Communications. Multicoloured.

79	2l. Type **23**	20	10
80	3l. Postage stamps, building and map	20	10
81	8l. Telephones, Earth and satellite	70	30

1979. 50th Anniv of International Consultative Radio Committee.

82 **24**	2l. multicoloured	20	10
83	5l. multicoloured	20	10
84	6l. multicoloured	25	15

25 School Children

26 Lala Mustafa Pasha Mosque, Magusa

1979. International Year of the Child. Mult.

85	1½l. Type **25**	25	15
86	4½l. Children and globe (horiz)	40	20
87	6l. College children	60	20

1980. Islamic Commemorations. Multicoloured.

88	2½l. Type **26**	10	10
89	10l. Arap Ahmet Pasha Mosque, Lefkosa	30	15
90	20l. Mecca and Medina	50	20

COMMEMORATIONS: 2½l. 1st Islamic Conference in Turkish Cyprus; 10l. General Assembly of World Islam Congress; 20l. Moslem Year 1400 AH.

27 Ebu-Su'ud Efendi (philosopher)

28 Omer's Shrine, Kyrenia

1980. Europa. Personalities. Multicoloured.

91	5l. Type **27**	20	10
92	30l. Sultan Selim II	70	40

1980. Ancient Monuments.

93 **28**	2½l. blue and stone	10	10
94 –	3½l. green and pink	10	10
95 –	5l. brown on green	15	10
96 –	10l. mauve and green	20	10
97 –	20l. blue and yellow	35	25

DESIGNS: 3½l. Entrance gate, Famagusta; 5l. Funerary monuments (16th-century), Famagusta; 10l. Bella Paise Abbey, Kyrenia; 20l. Selimiye Mosque, Nicosia.

29 Cyprus 1880 6d. Stamp

30 Dome of the Rock

1980. Cyprus Stamp Centenary.
98 **29** $7\frac{1}{2}$l. black, brown and green 20 10
99 – 15l. brown, dp blue & bl 25 10
100 – 50l. black, red and grey . . 65 60
DESIGNS—HORIZ: 15l. Cyprus 1960 Constitution of the Republic 30m. commemorative stamp. VERT: 50l. Social Aid local, 1970.

1980. Palestinian Solidarity. Multicoloured.
101 15l. Type **30** 30 15
102 35l. Dome of the Rock (horiz) 70 30

31 Extract from World Muslim Congress Statement in Turkish

32 "Ataturk" (F. Duran)

1981. Day of Solidarity with Islamic Countries.
103 **31** 1l. buff, red and brown . . 15 75
104 – 35l. light green, black green 55 1·00
DESIGN: 35l. Extract in English.

1981. Ataturk Stamp Exhibition, Lefkosa.
105 **32** 10l. multicoloured 25 35

33 Folk-dancing

35 Wild Convolvulus

34 "Kemal Atatürk" (I. Calli)

1981. Europa. Folklore. Multicoloured.
106 10l. Type **33** 40 15
107 30l. Folk-dancing (different) 60 35

1981. Birth Centenary of Kemal Atatürk. Sheet 70 × 95 mm. Imperf.
MS108 **34** 150l. multicoloured . . 1·10 1·25

1981. Flowers. Multicoloured.
109 1l. Type **35** 10 10
110 5l. Persian cyclamen (horiz) 10 10
111 10l. Spring mandrake (horiz) 10 10
112 25l. Corn poppy 15 10
113 30l. Wild arum (horiz) . . . 15 10
114 50l. Sage-leaved rock rose . . 20 20
115 100l. "Cistus salviaefolius L." 30 30
116 150l. Giant fennel (horiz) . . 50 90

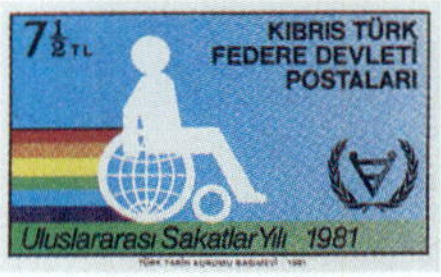

36 Stylised Disabled Person in Wheelchair

1981. Commemorations. Multicoloured.
117 $7\frac{1}{2}$l. Type **36** 25 35
118 10l. Heads of people of different races, peace dove and barbed wire (vert) . . 35 55
119 20l. People of different races reaching out from globe, with dishes (vert) 50 85
COMMEMORATIONS: $7\frac{1}{2}$l. International Year for Disabled Persons; 10l. Anti-Apartheid publicity; 20l. World Food Day.

37 Turkish Cypriot and Palestinian Flags

1981. Palestinian Solidarity.
120 **37** 10l. multicoloured 45 60

38 Prince Charles and Lady Diana Spencer

39 Charter issued by Sultan Abdul Aziz to Archbishop Sophronios

1981. Royal Wedding.
121 **38** 50l. multicoloured . . . . 1·00 85

1982. Europa (CEPT). Sheet 83 × 124 mm containing T **39** and similar vert design. Mult.
MS122 30l. × 2. Type **39**; 70l. × 2, Turkish forces landing at Tuzla, 1571 . . . . 4·50 5·00

40 Buffavento Castle

42 Cross of Lorraine, Koch and Bacillus (Centenary of Koch's Discovery of Tubercle Bacillus)

41 "Wedding" (A. Orek)

1982. Tourism. Multicoloured.
123 5l. Type **40** 10 10
124 10l. Windsurfing (horiz) . . . 15 10
125 15l. Kantara Castle (horiz) 25 15
126 30l. Shipwreck (300 B.C.) (horiz) 60 40

1982. Art (1st series). Multicoloured.
127 30l. Type **41** 15 30
128 50l. "Carob Pickers" (O. Nazim Selenge) (vert) 30 70
See also Nos. 132/3, 157/8, 176/7, 185/6, 208/9, 225/7, 248/50, 284/5, 315/16, 328/9, 369/70, 436/7, 567/8, 629/30 and 654/5.

1982. Anniversaries and Events. Multicoloured.
129 10l. Type **42** . . . . 1·00 40
130 30l. Spectrum on football pitch (World Cup Football Championships, Spain) . . 1·75 1·10
131 70l. "75" and Lord Baden-Powell (75th Anniv of Boy Scout movement and 125th birth anniv) (vert) . . . . 2·25 4·00

43 "Calloused Hands" (Salih Oral)

45 First Turkish Cypriot 10m. Stamp

44 Old Map of Cyprus by Piri Reis

1983. Art (2nd series). Multicoloured.
132 30l. Type **43** . . . . 75 1·40
133 35l. "Malya–Limassol Bus" (Emin Cizenel) . . . . . . 75 1·40

1983. Europa. Sheet 82 × 78 mm containing T **44** and similar horiz design. Multicoloured.
MS134 100l. Type **44**; 100l. Cyprus as seen from "Skylab" . . . . 30·00 15·00

1983. Anniversaries and Events. Multicoloured.
135 15l. Type **45** 90 50
136 20l. "Turkish Achievements in Cyprus" (horiz) 90 60
137 25l. "Liberation Fighters" . . 1·00 80
138 30l. Dish aerial and telegraph pole (horiz) . . . . 1·25 1·50
139 50l. Dove and envelopes (horiz) . . . . 2·75 3·75
EVENTS: 15, 20, 25l. T.M.T. (25th anniv of Turkish Cypriot Resistance Organization); 30, 50l. World Communications Year.

46 European Bee Eater

1983. Birds of Cyprus. Multicoloured.
140 10l. Type **46** . . . . 80 1·25
141 15l. Eurasian goldfinch . . . 1·00 1·25
142 50l. European robin . . . . 1·25 1·50
143 65l. Golden oriole . . . . . 1·40 1·50

1983. Establishment of Republic. Nos. 109, 111/12 and 116 optd **Kuzey Kibris Turk Cumhuriyeti 15.11.1983**, or surch also.
144 10l. Spring mandrake 20 15
145 15l. on 1l. Type **35** 30 15
146 25l. Corn poppy 40 25
147 150l. Giant fennel . . . . . 2·25 3·25

48 C.E.P.T. 25th Anniversary Logo

1984. Europa.
148 **48** 50l. yellow, brown and black . . . . 2·25 3·00
149 100l. lt blue, blue & black 2·25 3·00

49 Olympic Flame

50 Ataturk Cultural Centre

1984. Olympic Games, Los Angeles. Multicoloured.
150 10l. Type **49** 15 10
151 20l. Olympic events within rings (horiz) 35 25
152 70l. Martial arts event (horiz) 60 1·75

1984. Opening of Ataturk Cultural Centre, Lefkosa.
153 **50** 120l. stone, black and brown . . . . 1·25 1·75

52 Turkish Cypriot Flag and Map

1984. 10th Anniv of Turkish Landings in Cyprus. Multicoloured.
154 20l. Type **52** 50 25
155 70l. Turkish Cypriot flag within book . . . . 1·00 2·00

53 Burnt and Replanted Forests

1984. World Forestry Resources.
156 **53** 90l. multicoloured . . . . 1·25 1·75

54 "Old Turkish Houses, Nicosia" (Cevdet Cagdas)

1984. Art (3rd series). Multicoloured.
157 20l. Type **54** 50 40
158 70l. "Scenery" (Olga Rauf) 1·10 2·00

55 Kemal Ataturk, Flag and Crowd

56 Taekwondo Bout

1984. 1st Anniv of Turkish Republic of Northern Cyprus. Multicoloured.
159 20l. Type **55** 50 40
160 70l. Legislative Assembly voting for Republic (horiz) 1·10 2·00

1984. Int Taekwondo Championship, Girne.
161 **56** 10l. black, brown and grey 40 25
162 – 70l. multicoloured . . . . 1·60 2·50
DESIGN: 70l. Emblem and flags of competing nations.

57 "Le Regard"

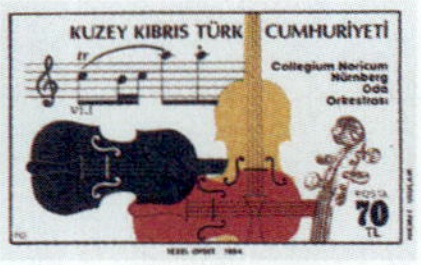

58 Musical Instruments and Music

1984. Exhibition by Saulo Mercader (artist). Multicoloured.
163 20l. Type **57** 30 25
164 70l. "L'equilibre de L'esprit" (horiz) . . . . 1·10 2·25

1984. Visit of Nurnberg Chamber Orchestra.
165 **58** 70l. multicoloured . . . . 1·50 2·25

59 Dr. Fazil Kucuk (politician)

61 George Frederick Handel

60 Goat

1985. 1st Death Anniv of Dr. Fazil Kucuk (politician). Multicoloured.
166 20l. Type **59** 30 30
167 70l. Dr. Fazil Kucuk reading newspaper . . . . 95 2·00

1985. Domestic Animals. Multicoloured.
168 100l. Type **60** 55 30
169 200l. Cow and calf 90 80
170 300l. Ram . . . . 1·25 2·00
171 500l. Donkey . . . . 2·00 3·25

1985. Europa. Composers.
172 **61** 20l. purple, green & lt grn 2·00 2·50
173 – 20l. purple, brown and pink . . . . 2·00 2·50
174 – 100l. purple, blue & lt blue 2·50 3·00
175 – 100l. purple, brn & lt brn 2·50 3·00
DESIGNS: No. 173, Giuseppe Domenico Scarlatti; 174, Johann Sebastian Bach; 175, Buhurizade Mustafa Itri Efendi.

1985. Art (4th series). As T **54**. Mult.
176 20l. "Village Life" (Ali Atakan) 60 50
177 50l. "Woman carrying Water" (Ismet V. Guney)) 1·40 2·50

62 Heads of Three Youths

1985. International Youth Year. Multicoloured.
178 20l. Type **62** 75 40
179 100l. Dove and globe . . . . 4·00 4·50

63 Parachutist (Aviation League)

65 Karagoz Show Puppets

64 Griffon Vulture

1985. Anniversaries and Events.
180 **63** 20l. multicoloured . . . . 1·75 45
181 – 50l. black, brown and blue 2·00 1·25
182 – 100l. brown . . . . 1·75 2·75
183 – 100l. multicoloured . . . . 1·75 2·75
184 – 100l. multicoloured . . . . 2·25 2·75
DESIGNS—VERT: No. 181, Louis Pasteur (Centenary of Discovery of Rabies vaccine); 182, Ismet Inonu (Turkish statesman) (birth centenary (1984)). HORIZ: 183, "40" in figures and symbolic flower (40th anniv of United Nations Organization); 184, Patient receiving blood transfusion (Prevention of Thalassaemia).

1986. Art (5th series). As T **54**. Mult.
185 20l. "House with Arches" (Gonen Atakol) 50 30
186 100l. "Ataturk Square" (Yalkin Muhtaroglu) . . . 1·75 1·75

1986. Europa. Protection of Nature and the Environment. Sheet 82 × 76 mm, containing T **64** and similar horiz design. Multicoloured.
MS187 100l. Type **64**; 200l. Litter on Cyprus landscape . . . . . . 10·00 7·50

1986. Karagoz Folk Puppets.
188 **65** 100l. multicoloured . . . . 2·25 2·50

66 Old Bronze Age Composite Pottery

1986. Archaeological Artefacts. Cultural Links with Anatolia. Multicoloured.
189 10l. Type **66** 55 20
190 20l. Late Bronze Age bird jug (vert) 95 30
191 50l. Neolithic earthenware pot . . . . 1·75 2·00
192 100l. Roman statue of Artemis (vert) . . . . . . 2·25 3·50

67 Soldiers, Defence Force Badge and Ataturk (10th anniv of Defence Forces)

69 Prince Andrew and Miss Sarah Ferguson

68 Guzelyurt Dam and Power Station

1986. Anniversaries and Events. Multicoloured.
193 20l. Type **67** . . . . 1·25 30
194 50l. Woman and two children (40th anniv of F.A.O.) . . 1·40 1·40
195 100l. Football and world map (World Cup Football Championship, Mexico) (horiz) . . . . 3·75 4·25
196 100l. Orbit of Halley's Comet and "Giotto" space probe (horiz) . . . . 3·75 4·25

1986. Modern Development (1st series). Mult.
197 20l. Type **68** . . . . 1·25 30
198 50l. Low cost housing project, Lefkosa . . . . . 1·40 1·40
199 100l. Kyrenia Airport . . . . 3·25 4·25
See also Nos. 223/4 and 258/63.

1986. 60th Birthday of Queen Elizabeth II and Royal Wedding. Multicoloured.
200 100l. Queen Elizabeth II . . 2·00 2·75
201 100l. Type **69** . . . . 2·00 2·75

70 Locomotive No. 11 and Trakhoni Station

1986. Cyprus Railway. Multicoloured.
202 50l. Type **70** . . . . 3·75 2·75
203 100l. Locomotive No. 1 . . . 4·25 4·75

1987. Nos. 94, 96/7 and 113 optd **Kuzey Kibris Turk Cumhuriyeti** or surch also (No. 205).
204 10l. mauve and green 50 70
205 15l. on 3½l. green and pink 50 70
206 20l. blue and yellow 55 75
207 30l. multicoloured . . . . . 70 1·10

1987. Art (6th series). As T **54**. Mult.
208 50l. "Shepherd" (Feridun Isiman) . . . . 1·25 1·25
209 125l. "Pear Woman" (Mehmet Uluhan) . . . . 1·75 3·00

72 Modern House (architect A. Vural Behaeddin)

1987. Europa. Modern Architecture. Multicoloured.
210 50l. Type **72** . . . . 1·00 30
211 200l. Modern house (architect Necdet Turgay) . . . . . 1·75 3·25

73 Kneeling Folk Dancer

74 Regimental Colour (1st anniv of Infantry Regiment)

1987. Folk Dancers. Multicoloured.
212 20l. Type **73** 80 20
213 50l. Standing male dancer . . 90 40
214 200l. Standing female dancer 2·00 1·75
215 1000l. Woman's headdress . . 4·75 6·50

1987. Anniversaries and Events. Multicoloured.
216 50l. Type **74** . . . . 1·75 1·00
217 50l. President Denktash and Turgut Ozal (1st anniv of Turkish Prime Minister's visit) (horiz) . . . . 1·75 1·00
218 200l. Emblem and Crescent (5th Islamic Summit Conference, Kuwait) . . . 3·00 4·25
219 200l. Emblem and laurel leaves (Membership of Pharmaceutical Federation) (horiz) . . . . 3·00 4·25

75 Ahmet Belig Pasha (Egyptian judge)

76 Tourist Hotel, Girne

1987. Turkish Cypriot Personalities.
220 **75** 50l. brown and yellow . . 65 40
221 – 50l. multicoloured 65 40
222 – 125l. multicoloured . . . . 1·50 3·00
DESIGNS: 50l. (No. 221) Mehmet Emin Pasha (Ottoman Grand Vizier); 125l. Mehmet Kamil Pasha (Ottoman Grand Vizier).

1987. Modern Development (2nd series). Mult.
223 150l. Type **76** . . . . 1·50 1·50
224 200l. Dogu Akdeniz University . . . . 1·75 2·25

1988. Art (7th series). As T **54**. Mult.
225 20l. "Woman making Pastry" (Ayhan Mentes) (vert) . . 50 30
226 50l. "Chair Weaver" (Osman Guvenir) 75 75
227 150l. "Woman weaving a Rug" (Zekai Yesiladali) (vert) . . . . 1·75 4·00

77 "Piyale Pasha" (tug)

1988. Europa. Transport and Communications. Multicoloured.
228 200l. Type **77** . . . . 2·25 75
229 500l. Dish aerial and antenna tower, Selvilitepe (vert) . . 3·00 4·50
No. 229 also commemorates the 25th anniv of Bayrak Radio and Television Corporation.

78 Lefkosa

79 Bulent Ecevit

1988. Tourism. Multicoloured.
230 150l. Type **78** 80 80
231 200l. Gazi-Magusa . . . . . 90 1·00
232 300l. Girne . . . . 1·50 2·00

1988. Turkish Prime Ministers. Multicoloured.
233 50l. Type **79** 60 85
234 50l. Bulent Ulusu 60 85
235 50l. Turgut Ozal 60 85

80 Red Crescent Members on Exercise

1988. Civil Defence.
236 **80** 150l. multicoloured . . . . 1·75 1·75

81 Hodori the Tiger (Games mascot) and Fireworks

1988. Olympic Games, Seoul. Multicoloured.
237 200l. Type **81** . . . . 1·40 1·00
238 250l. Athletics . . . . 1·60 1·25
239 400l. Shot and running track with letters spelling "SEOUL" . . . . 2·25 2·00

82 Sedat Simavi (journalist)

83 "Kemal Atatürk" (I. Calli)

1988. Anniversaries and Events.
240 **82** 50l. green 25 25
241 – 100l. multicoloured 75 45
242 – 300l. multicoloured . . . . 80 1·00
243 – 400l. multicoloured . . . . 2·00 2·00
244 – 400l. multicoloured . . . . 1·25 2·00
245 – 600l. multicoloured . . . . 2·75 2·75
DESIGNS—HORIZ: No. 241, Stylised figures around table and flags of participating countries (International Girne Conferences); 244, Presidents Gorbachev and Reagan signing treaty (Summit Meeting). VERT: No. 242, Cogwheels as flowers (North Cyprus Industrial Fair); 243, Globe (125th anniv of International Red Cross); 245, "Medical Services" (40th anniv of W.H.O.).

1988. 50th Death Anniv of Kemal Atatürk. Sheet 72 × 102 mm, containing T **83** and similar vert designs. Multicoloured.
MS246 250l. Type **83**; 250l. "Kemal Atatürk" (N. Ismail); 250l. In army uniform; 250l. In profile 3·25 3·25

84 Abstract Design

1988. 5th Anniv of Turkish Republic of Northern Cyprus. Sheet 98 × 76 mm. Imperf.
MS247 **84** 500l. multicoloured . . 2·25 2·25

1989. Art (8th series). As T **54**. Mult.
248 150l. "Dervis Pasa Mansion, Lefkosa" (Inci Kansu) . . 90 60
249 400l. "Gamblers' Inn, Lefkosa" (Osman Guvenir) 1·75 2·25
250 600l. "Mosque, Paphos" (Hikmet Ulucam) (vert) . . 2·50 3·00

85 Girl with Doll

1989. Europa. Children's Games. Multicoloured.
251 600l. Type **85** . . . . 2·25 1·25
252 1000l. Boy with kite . . . . 2·50 3·75

86 Meeting of Presidents Vassiliou and Denktash

1989. Cyprus Peace Summit, Geneva, 1988.
253 **86** 500l. red and black . . . . 1·25 1·25

87 Chukar Partridge

1989. Wildlife. Multcoloured.
254 100l. Type **87** 65 25
255 200l. Cyprus hare 70 35
256 700l. Black partridge . . . . 2·50 2·00
257 2000l. Red fox . . . . 3·00 4·00

88 Road Construction

1989. Modern Development (3rd series). Mult.
258 100l. Type **88** 25 15
259 150l. Laying water pipeline (vert) 30 20
260 200l. Seedling trees (vert) . . 40 30
261 450l. Modern telephone exchange (vert) . . . . . 1·00 1·00
262 650l. Steam turbine power station (vert) . . . . . . 1·25 1·75
263 700l. Irrigation reservoir . . 1·50 1·75

89 Unloading "Polly Pioneer" (freighter) at Quayside (15th anniv of Gazi Magusa Free Port)

1989. Anniversaries.
264 **89** 100l. multicoloured 70 20
265 – 450l. black, blue and red 80 80
266 – 500l. black, yellow and grey 80 80
267 – 600l. black, red and blue 2·25 2·25
268 – 1000l. multicoloured . . . 3·50 4·50
DESIGNS—VERT (26 × 47 mm): 450l. Airmail letter and stylized bird (25th anniv of Turkish Cypriot postal service). HORIZ (as T **89**): 500l. Newspaper and printing press (centenary of "Saded" newspaper); 600l. Statue of Aphrodite, lifebelt and seabird (30th anniv of International Maritime Organization); 1000l. Soldiers (25th anniv of Turkish Cypriot resistance).

90 Erdal Inonu

91 Mule-drawn Plough

1989. Visit of Professor Erdal Inonu (Turkish politician).
269 **90** 700l. multicoloured . . . . 80 1·00

1989. Traditional Agricultural Implements. Mult.
270 150l. Type **91** 30 25
271 450l. Ox-drawn threshing sledge 75 85
272 550l. Olive press (vert) . . . . 90 1·25

92 Smoking Ashtray and Drinks

1990. World Health Day. Multicoloured.
273 200l. Type **92** . . . . 1·00 40
274 700l. Smoking cigarette and heart . . . . 2·25 3·00

93 Yenierenkoy Post Office

1990. Europa. Post Office Buildings. Mult.
275 1000l. Type **93** . . . . 1·75 75
276 1500l. Ataturk Meydani Post Office . . . . 2·50 3·50
MS277 105 × 72 mm. Nos. 275/6 × 2 . . . . 7·50 8·00

94 Song Thrush

96 Amphitheatre, Soli

95 Two Football Teams

1990. World Environment Day. Birds. Mult.
278 150l. Type **94** . . . . 2·25 65
279 300l. Blackcap . . . . 3·00 90
280 900l. Black redstart . . . . . 4·50 3·50
281 1000l. Chiff-chaff . . . . . 4·50 3·50

1990. World Cup Football Championship, Italy. Multicoloured.
282 300l. Type **95** 75 50
283 1000l. Championship symbol, globe and ball . . . . . . 2·50 3·50

1990. Art (9th series). As T **54**. Multicoloured.
284 300l. "Abstract" (Filiz Ankacc) 40 25
285 1000l. Wooden sculpture (S. Tekman) (vert) . . . . 1·25 1·50

1990. Tourism. Multicoloured.
286 150l. Type **96** 40 20
287 1000l. Swan mosaic, Soli . . 1·75 2·50

97 Kenan Evren and Rauf Denktas

1990. Visit of President Kenan Evren of Turkey.
288 **97** 500l. multicoloured . . . . 1·00 1·00

98 Road Signs and Heart wearing Seat Belt

1990. Traffic Safety Campaign. Multicoloured.
289 150l. Type **98** . . . . 1·25 30
290 300l. Road signs, speeding car and spots of blood . . . 1·50 50
291 1000l. Traffic lights and road signs . . . . 3·75 4·50

99 Yildirim Akbulut

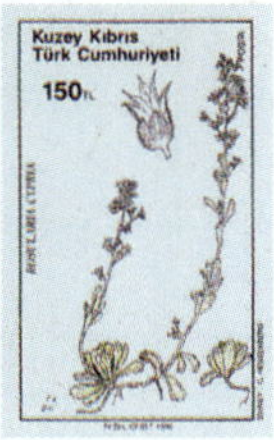
100 "Rosularia cypria"

1990. Visit of Turkish Prime Minister Yildrim Akbulut.
292 **99** 1000l. multicoloured . . . 1·10 1·10

1990. Plants. Multicoloured.
293 150l. Type **100** 70 20
294 200l. "Silene fraudratrix" . . 80 30
295 300l. "Scutellaria sibthorpii" 90 35
296 600l. "Sedum lampusae" . . 1·40 85
297 1000l. "Onosma caespitosum" 1·50 2·25
298 1500l. "Arabis cypria" . . . 2·25 4·00

101 Kemal Ataturk at Easel (wood carving)

1990. International Literacy Year. Multicoloured.
299 300l. Type **101** . . . . 1·25 35
300 750l. Globe, letters and books 2·50 3·25

1991. Nos. 189, 212 and 293 surch.
301 **66** 250l. on 10l. multicoloured . . . . . 1·50 1·50
302 **73** 250l. on 20l. multicoloured . . . . . 1·50 1·50
303 **100** 500l. on 150l. multicoloured . . . . . 2·00 2·25

103 "Ophrys lapethica"

104 "Hermes" (projected shuttle)

1991. Orchids (1st series). Multicoloured.
304 250l. Type **103** . . . . 1·25 60
305 500l. "Ophrys kotschyi" . . . 2·25 2·75
See also Nos. 311/14.

1991. Europa. Europe in Space. Sheet 78 × 82 mm, containing T **104** and similar vert design. Multicoloured.
MS306 2000l. Type **104**; 2000l. "Ulysses" (satellite) . . . . . 9·00 9·00

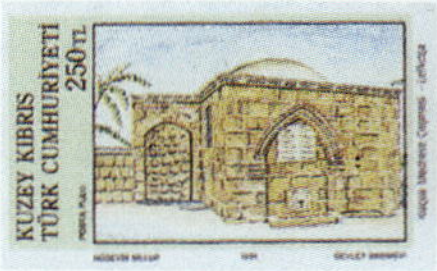
105 Kucuk Medrese Fountain, Lefkosa

106 Symbolic Roots (Year of Love to Yunus Emre)

1991. Fountains. Multicoloured.
307 250l. Type **105** 55 15
308 500l. Cafer Pasa fountain, Magusa 75 30
309 1500l. Sarayonu Square fountain, Lefkosa . . . . 1·50 1·60
310 5000l. Arabahmet Mosque fountain, Lefkosa . . . . 3·75 6·00

1991. Orchids (2nd series). As T **103**. Mult.
311 100l. "Serapias levantina" . . 85 20
312 500l. "Dactylorhiza romana" 2·25 50
313 2000l. "Orchis simia" . . . . 3·75 4·00
314 3000l. "Orchis sancta" . . . 4·25 5·00

1991. Art (10th series). As T **54**. Mult.
315 250l. "Hindiler" (S. Cizel) (vert) . . . . 2·00 50
316 500l. "Dusme" (A. Mene) (vert) . . . . 2·50 2·50

1991. Anniversaries and Events.
317 **106** 250l. yellow, black and mauve 25 25
318 – 500l. multicoloured . . . 45 60
319 – 500l. multicoloured . . . 45 60
320 – 1500l. multicoloured . . . 5·00 5·00
DESIGNS—VERT: No. 318, Mustafa Cagatay commemoration; 319, University building (5th anniv of Eastern Mediterranean University). HORIZ: No. 320, Mozart (death bicentenary).

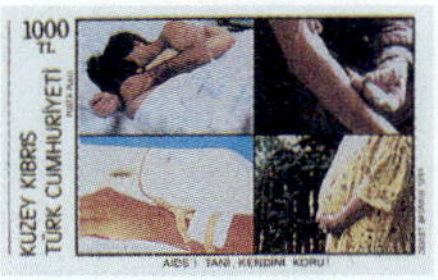
107 Four Sources of Infection

1991. "AIDS" Day.
321 **107** 1000l. multicoloured . . . 2·50 2·00

108 Lighthouse, Gazimagusa

1991. Lighthouses. Multicoloured.
322 250l. Type **108** . . . . 2·25 65
323 500l. Ancient lighthouses, Girne harbour . . . . . . 3·00 1·25
324 1500l. Modern lighthouse, Girne harbour . . . . . . 5·00 6·00

109 Elephant and Hippopotamus Fossils, Karaoglanoglu

1991. Tourism (1st series). Multicoloured.
325 250l. Type **109** . . . . 2·00 55
326 500l. Roman fish ponds, Lambusa . . . . 2·25 80
327 1500l. Roman remains, Lambusa . . . . 3·50 4·50
See also Nos. 330/3 and 351/2.

1992. Art (11th series). As T **54**, but 31 × 49 mm. Multicoloured.
328 500l. "Ebru" (A. Kandulu) 1·00 25
329 3500l. "Street in Lefkosa" (I. Tatar) . . . . 4·00 5·00

1992. Tourism (2nd series). As T **109**. Mult.
330 500l. Bugday Camii, Gazimagusa 80 80
331 500l. Clay pigeon shooting 80 80
332 1000l. Salamis Bay Hotel, Gazimagusa . . . . 1·50 1·50
333 1500l. Casino, Girne (vert) 2·50 3·25

110 Fleet of Columbus and Early Map

1992. Europa. 500th Anniv of Discovery of America by Columbus. Sheet 80 × 76 mm, containing T **110** and similar horiz design. Multicoloured.
MS334 1500l. Type **110**; 3500l. Christopher Columbus and signature . . . . 4·00 4·25

111 Green Turtle

1992. World Environment Day. Sea Turtles. Sheet 105 × 75 mm, containing T **111** and similar horiz design. Multicoloured.
MS335 1000l. × 2, Type **111**; 1500l. × 2, Loggerhead turtle . . . . 6·50 6·50

112 Gymnastics

113 New Generating Station, Girne

1992. Olympic Games, Barcelona. Multicoloured.
336 500l. Type **112** 80 90
337 500l. Tennis 80 90
338 1000l. High jumping (horiz) 1·00 1·25
339 1500l. Cycling (horiz) . . . . 4·50 4·50

1992. Anniversaries and Events (1st series). Multicoloured.
340 500l. Type **113** 50 50
341 500l. Symbol of Housing Association (15th anniv) 50 50
342 1500l. Domestic animals and birds (30th anniv of Veterinary Service) . . . . 3·50 3·75
343 1500l. Cat (International Federation of Cat Societies Conference) . . . . 3·50 3·75

114 Airliner over Runway

1992. Anniversaries and Events (2nd series). Multicoloured.
344 1000l. Type **114** (17th anniv of civil aviation) . . . . . 2·00 2·00
345 1000l. Meteorological instruments and weather (18th anniv of Meteorological Service) . . 2·00 2·00
346 1200l. Surveying equipment and map (14th anniv of Survey Department) . . . 2·75 3·00

115 Zubiye

1992. International Conference on Nutrition, Rome. Turkish Cypriot Cuisine. Multicoloured.
347 2000l. Type **115** . . . . . 1·50 1·50
348 2500l. Cicek Dolmasi . . . . 1·75 1·75
349 3000l. Tatar Boregi . . . . 2·00 2·25
350 4000l. Seftali Kebabi . . . . 2·25 2·50

1993. Tourism (3rd series). As T **109**. Mult.
351 500l. St. Barnabas Church and Monastery, Salamis . . 50 15
352 10000l. Ancient pot . . . . . 5·00 6·00

116 Painting by Turksal Ince **117** Olive Tree, Girne

1993. Europa. Contemporary Art. Sheet 79 × 69 mm, containing T **116** and similar vert design. Multicoloured.
MS353 2000l. Type **116**; 3000l. Painting by Ilkay Onsoy . . . 1·75 2·50

1993. Ancient Trees. Multicoloured.
354 500l. Type **117** 45 15
355 1000l. River red gum, Kyrenia Gate, Lefkosa . . 80 40
356 3000l. Oriental plane, Lapta 1·75 2·00
357 4000l. Calabrian pine, Cinarli 2·00 2·25

118 Traditional Houses **119** National Flags turning into Doves

1993. Arabahmet District Conservation Project, Lefkosa. Multicoloured.
358 1000l. Type **118** . . . . . 1·00 40
359 3000l. Arabahmet street . . . 2·50 3·25

1993. 10th Anniv of Proclamation of Turkish Republic of Northern Cyprus.
360 **119** 500l. red, black and blue 30 30
361 – 500l. red and blue 30 30
362 – 1000l. red, black and blue 40 30
363 – 5000l. multicoloured . . . 1·75 3·00
DESIGNS—HORIZ: No. 361, National flag forming figure "10"; No. 362, Dove carrying national flag; No. 363, Map of Cyprus and figure "10" wreath.

120 Kemal Ataturk **121** "Soyle Falci" (Goral Ozkan)

1993. Anniversaries. Multicoloured.
364 500l. Type **120** (55th death anniv) 30 30
365 500l. Stage and emblem (30th anniv of Turkish Cypriot theatre) (horiz) 30 30
366 1500l. Branch badges (35th anniv of T.M.T. organization) (horiz) . . . 30 50
367 2000l. World map and computer (20th anniv of Turkish Cypriot news agency) (horiz) . . . . . . 1·75 1·75
368 5000l. Ballet dancers and Caykovski'nin (death centenary) (horiz) . . . . 5·50 5·50

1994. Art (12th series). Multicoloured.
369 1000l. Type **121** 30 20
370 6500l. "IV. Hareket" (sculpture) (Senol Ozdevrim) . . . . 1·50 2·25

122 Dr. Kucuk and Memorial

1994. 10th Death Anniv of Dr. Fazil Kucuk (politician).
371 **122** 1500l. multicoloured . . . 70 85

123 Neolithic Village, Girne

1994. Europa. Archaeological Discoveries. Sheet 73 × 79 mm, containing T **123** and similar horiz design. Multicoloured.
MS372 8500l. Type **123**; 8500l. Neolithic man and implements 6·00 6·00

124 Peace Doves and Letters over Pillar Box **125** World Cup Trophy

1994. 30th Anniv of Turkish Cypriot Postal Service.
373 **124** 50000l. multicoloured . . 3·00 4·50

1994. World Cup Football Championship, U.S.A. Multicoloured.
374 2500l. Type **125** 50 25
375 10000l. Footballs on map of U.S.A. (horiz) . . . . . . 1·75 2·50

126 Peace Emblem

1994. 20th Anniv of Turkish Landings in Cyprus.
376 **126** 2500l. yellow, green and black 40 30
377 – 5000l. multicoloured . . . 60 60
378 – 7000l. multicoloured . . . 80 1·00
379 – 8500l. multicoloured . . . 1·10 1·50
DESIGNS—HORIZ: 5000l. Memorial; 7000l. Sculpture; 8500l. Peace doves forming map of Cyprus and flame.

127 Cyprus 1934 4½ pi. Stamp and Karpas Postmark

1994. Postal Centenary. Multicoloured.
380 1500l. Type **127** 20 20
381 2500l. Turkish Cypriot Posts 1979 Europa 2l. and Gazimagusa postmark . . 40 30
382 5000l. Cyprus 1938 6pi. and Bey Keuy postmark . . . 70 90
383 7000l. Cyprus 1955 100m. and Aloa postmark . . . . 1·00 1·50
384 8500l. Cyprus 1938 18pi. and Pyla postmark . . . . . . 1·25 2·00

128 Trumpet Triton

1994. Sea Shells. Multicoloured.
385 2500l. Type **128** 45 30
386 12500l. Mole cowrie . . . . 1·25 1·75
387 12500l. Giant tun . . . . . 1·25 1·75

1994. Nos. 280, 295, 315 and 317 surch.
388 1500l. on 250l. Type **106** . . 15 10
389 2000l. on 900l. Black redstart 2·75 90
390 2500l. on 250l. "Hindiler" (Sizel) 30 30
391 3500l. on 300l. "Scutellaria sibthorpii" . . . . 2·50 2·75

130 Donkeys on Mountain

1995. European Conservation Year. Multicoloured.
392 2000l. Type **130** 30 20
393 3500l. Coastline 30 30
394 15000l. Donkeys in field . . . 1·50 2·50

131 Peace Dove and Globe

1995. Europa. Peace and Freedom. Sheet 72 × 78 mm, containing T **131** and similar horiz design. Mult.
MS395 15000l. Type **131**; 15000l. Peace doves over map of Europe 3·75 4·00

132 Sini Katmeri

1995. Turkish Cypriot Cuisine. Multicoloured.
396 3500l. Type **132** 20 20
397 10000l. Kolokas musakka and bullez kizartma . . . 55 65
398 14000l. Enginar dolmasi . . . 90 1·60

133 "Papilio machaon"

1995. Butterflies. Multicoloured.
399 3500l. Type **133** 30 15
400 4500l. "Charaxes jasius" . . . 35 20
401 15000l. "Cynthia cardui" . . 1·00 1·40
402 30000l. "Vanessa atalanta" 1·75 2·50

134 Forest

1995. Obligatory Tax. Forest Regeneration Fund.
403 **134** 1000l. green and black . . 3·75 40

135 Beach, Girne

1995. Tourism. Multicoloured.
404 3500l. Type **135** 30 20
405 7500l. Sail boards 50 45
406 15000l. Ruins of Salamis (vert) . . . . 1·00 1·25
407 20000l. St. George's Cathedral, Gazimagusa (vert) . . . . 1·00 1·25

136 Suleyman Demirel and Rauf Denktas

1995. Visit of President Suleyman Demirel of Turkey.
408 **136** 5000l. multicoloured . . . 50 50

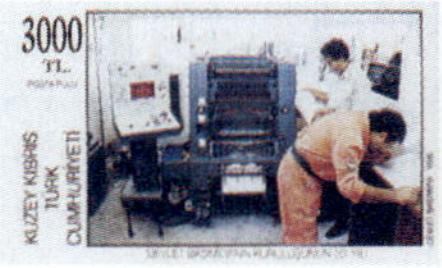

137 Stamp Printing Press **138** Kultegin Epitaph and Sculpture

1995. Anniversaries.
409 **137** 3000l. multicoloured . . . 40 40
410 – 3000l. multicoloured . . . 40 40
411 – 5000l. multicoloured . . . 70 70
412 – 22000l. ultram, bl & blk 1·00 1·75
413 – 30000l. multicoloured . . 1·40 2·25
414 – 30000l. multicoloured . . 1·40 2·25
DESIGNS—HORIZ: No. 409, Type **137** (20th anniv of State Printing Works); 410, Map of Turkey (75th anniv of Turkish National Assembly); 411, Louis Pasteur (chemist) and microscope (death centenary); 412, United Nations anniversary emblem (50th anniv); 413, Guglielmo Marconi (radio pioneer) and dial (centenary of first radio transmissions). VERT: No. 414, Stars and reel of film (centenary of cinema).

1995. Centenary of Deciphering of Orhon Epitaphs. Multicoloured.
415 5000l. Type **138** 85 50
416 10000l. Epitaph and tombstone . . . . 1·50 2·00

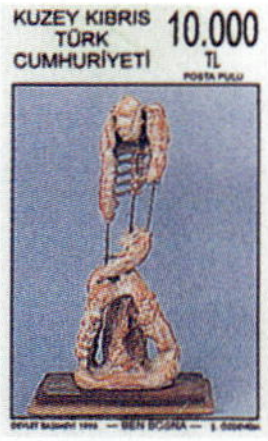

139 "Bosnia" (sculpture) **140** Striped Red Mullet

1996. Support for Moslems in Bosnia and Herzegovina.
417 **139** 10000l. multicoloured . . 1·50 1·75

1996. Fish. Multicoloured.
418 6000l. Type **140** . . . . . . 1·00 30
419 10000l. Peacock wrasse . . . 1·25 45
420 28000l. Common two-banded seabream . . . . 2·25 2·50
421 40000l. Dusky grouper . . . 2·75 3·50

141 Palm Trees **142** Beria Remzi Ozoran

1996. Tourism. Multicoloured.
422 100000l. Type **141** . . . . 1·00 30
423 150000l. Pomegranate . . . . 1·50 55

424 250000l. Ruins of Bella Paise Abbey (horiz) . . . . . . 2·00 2·50
425 500000l. Traditional dancers (horiz) . . . . 4·25 4·75

1996. Europa. Famous Women. Multicoloured.
426 15000l. Type **142** . . . . . . 1·25 25
427 50000l. Kadriye Hulusi Hacibulgur . . . . 2·50 3·50

143 Established Forest

1996. World Environment Day. Sheet 72 × 78 mm, containing T **143** and similar horiz design. Multicoloured.
MS428 50000l. Type **143**; 50000l. Conifer plantation . . . . . . 7·50 7·50

144 Basketball

1996. Olympic Games, Atlanta. Sheet 105 × 74 mm, containing T **144** and similar horiz designs. Multicoloured.
MS429 15000l. Type **144**; 15000l. Discus throwing; 50000l. Javelin throwing; 50000l. Volleyball . . 3·50 4·25

145 Symbolic Footballs

1996. European Football Championship, England. Multicoloured.
430 15000l. Type **145** . . . . . . 1·25 65
431 35000l. Football and flags of participating nations . . . 2·25 2·75

146 Houses on Fire (Auxiliary Fire Service)
147 "Amanita phalloides"

1996. Anniversaries and Events. Multicoloured.
432 10000l. Type **146** . . . . . . 1·00 40
433 20000l. Colour party (20th anniv of Defence Forces) (vert) . . . . 1·10 55
434 50000l. Children by lake (Nasreddin-Hoca Year) . . 1·40 1·60
435 75000l. Flowers (Children's Rights) . . . . 1·75 2·50

1997. Art (13th series). As T **121**. Multicoloured.
436 25000l. "City" (Lebibe Sonuc) (horiz) . . . . . . 1·25 50
437 70000l. "Woman opening Letter" (Ruzen Atakan) (horiz) . . . . 2·50 3·25

1997. Fungi. Multicoloured.
438 15000l. Type **147** 75 30
439 25000l. "Morchella esculenta" 1·10 1·25
440 25000l. "Pleurotus eryngii" 1·10 1·25
441 70000l. "Amanita muscaria" 2·00 3·25

148 Flag on Hillside

150 Prime Minister Necmettin Erbakan of Turkey

149 Mother and Children playing Leapfrog

1997. Besparmak Mountains Flag Sculpture.
442 **148** 60000l. multicoloured . . . 2·00 2·00

1997. Europa. Tales and Legends. Multicoloured.
443 25000l. Type **149** . . . . . . 1·50 30
444 70000l. Apple tree and well 2·50 3·25

1997. Visit of the President and the Prime Minister of Turkey.
445 15000l. Type **150** 50 30
446 80000l. President Suleyman Demirel of Turkey (horiz) 2·25 3·00

151 Golden Eagle

152 Coin of Sultan Abdulaziz, 1861–76

1997. Birds of Prey. Multicoloured.
447 40000l. Type **151** . . . . . . 1·50 1·50
448 40000l. Eleonora's falcon . . 1·50 1·50
449 75000l. Common kestrel . . . 2·25 2·50
450 100000l. Western honey buzzard . . . . 2·50 2·75

1997. Rare Coins. Multicoloured.
451 25000l. Type **152** 55 20
452 40000l. Coin of Sultan Mahmud II, 1808–39 . . . 70 45
453 75000l. Coin of Sultan Selim II, 1566–74 . . . . . . 1·25 1·50
454 100000l. Coin of Sultan Mehmed V, 1909–18 . . . 1·50 2·25

153 Open Book and Emblem

1997. Anniversaries.
455 **153** 25000l. multicoloured . . 65 20
456 – 40000l. multicoloured . . 1·00 30
457 – 100000l. black, red and stone . . . . 2·50 2·25
458 – 150000l. multicoloured . . 3·25 3·50
DESIGNS—HORIZ: 25000l. Type **153** (centenary of Turkish Cypriot Scouts); 40000l. Guides working in field (90th anniv of Turkish Cypriot Guides); 150000l. Rudolph Diesel and first oil engine (centenary of the diesel engine). VERT: 100000l. Couple and symbols (AIDS prevention campaign).

154 Ahmet and Ismet Sevki

1998. Ahmet and Ismet Sevki (photographers) Commemoration. Multicoloured.
459 40000l. Type **154** 75 25
460 105000l. Ahmet Sevki (vert) 2·00 3·00

155 "Agrion splendens" (dragonfly)

156 Wooden Double Door

1998. Useful Insects. Multicoloured.
461 40000l. Type **155** 80 25
462 65000l. "Ascalaphus macaronius" (owl-fly) . . . 1·25 40
463 125000l. "Podalonia hirsuta" 2·25 2·50
464 150000l. "Rhyssa persuasoria" . . . . 2·50 3·00

1998. Old Doors.
465 **156** 115000l. multicoloured . . 2·25 2·50
466 – 140000l. multicoloured . . 2·25 2·50
DESIGN: 140000l. Different door.

157 Legislative Assembly Building (Republic Establishment Festival)

1998. Europa. Festivals. Multicoloured.
467 40000l. Type **157** 75 25
468 150000l. Globe, flags and map (Int Children's Folk Dance Festival) (vert) . . . 4·00 4·00

158 Marine Life

1998. International Year of the Ocean.
469 **158** 40000l. multicoloured . . 1·00 40
470 – 90000l. multicoloured . . 2·00 2·50
DESIGN: 90000l. Different underwater scene.

159 Prime Minister Mesut Yilmaz of Turkey

1998. Prime Minister Yilmaz's Visit to Northern Cyprus.
471 **159** 75000l. multicoloured . . 1·75 2·00

160 Pres. Suleyman Demirel of Turkey

162 Deputy Prime Minister Bulent Ecevit

161 Victorious French Team

1998. President Demirel's "Water for Peace" Project.
472 75000l. Type **160** . . . . . . 1·25 50
473 175000l. Turkish and Turkish Cypriot leaders with inflatable water tank (horiz) . . . . 2·50 3·50

1998. World Cup Football Championship, France. Multicoloured.
474 75000l. Type **161** . . . . . . 1·25 50
475 175000l. World Cup trophy (vert) . . . . 2·50 3·50

1998. Visit of the Deputy Prime Minister of Turkey.
476 **162** 200000l. multicoloured . . 2·00 2·25

163 Itinerant Tinsmiths

1998. Local Crafts. Multicoloured.
477 50000l. Type **163** 45 25
478 75000l. Basket weaver (vert) 65 35
479 130000l. Grinder sharpening knife (vert) . . . . 1·25 1·25
480 400000l. Wood carver . . . . 3·50 4·50

164 Stylised Satellite Dish

165 Dr. Fazil Kucuk

1998. Anniversaries. Multicoloured (except No. 483).
481 50000l. Type **164** 80 30
482 75000l. Stylised birds and "15" . . . . 1·25 1·40
483 75000l. "75" and Turkish flag (red, black and orange) . . 1·25 1·40
484 175000l. Scroll, "50" and quill pen (vert) . . . . . . 2·00 3·00
MS485 72 × 78 mm. 75000l. As No. 482; 75000l. Map of Northern Cyprus . . . . 2·50 3·00
ANNIVERSARIES: No. 481, 35th anniv of Bayrak Radio and Television; 482, **MS**485, 15th anniv of Turkish Republic of Northern Cyprus; 483, 75th anniv of Turkish Republic; 484, 50th anniv of Universal Declaration of Human Rights.

1999. 15th Death Anniv of Dr. Fazil Kucuk (politician).
486 **165** 75000l. multicoloured . . 1·25 1·25

166 Otello

1999. Performance of Verdi's Opera Otello in Cyprus. Sheet 78 × 74 mm, containing T **166** and similar vert design. Multicoloured.
MS487 200000l. Type **166**; 200000l. Desdemona dead in front of fireplace . . . . 3·25 3·00

167 "Malpolon monspessulanus insignitus" (Montepellier)

1999. Snakes. Multicoloured.
488 50000l. Type **167** 75 30
489 75000l. "Hierophis jugularis" 1·00 45
490 195000l. "Vipera lebetina lebetina" (levantine viper) 1·75 2·00
491 220000l. "Natrix natrix" (grass snake) . . . . . . 1·75 2·00

168 Entrance to Cave

1999. Europa. Parks and Gardens. Incirli Cave. Multicoloured.
492 75000l. Type **168** . . . . . . 1·25 25
493 200000l. Limestone rocks inside cave (vert) . . . . . 2·50 3·00

169 Peace Dove and Map of Cyprus

1999. 25th Anniv of Turkish Landings in Cyprus. Multicoloured.
494 150000l. Type **169** . . . . . 2·00 1·50
495 250000l. Peace dove, map of Cyprus and sun . . . . . 2·50 3·00

170 Air Mail Envelope and Labels

1999. Anniversaries and Events. Multicoloured.
496 75000l. Type **170** (35th anniv of Turkish Cypriot Posts) 65 25
497 225000l. "125" and U.P.U. emblem (125th anniv of U.P.U.) . . . . 1·50 1·75
498 250000l. Total eclipse of the Sun, August 1999 . . . . 2·00 2·25

171 Turkish Gateway, Limassol

1999. Destruction of Turkish Buildings in Southern Cyprus. Each light brown and brown.
499 75000l. Type **171** 60 25
500 150000l. Mosque, Evdim . . 85 40
501 210000l. Bayraktar Mosque, Lefkosa . . . . 1·10 75
502 1000000l. Kebir Mosque, Baf (vert) . . . . 5·00 7·00

172 Mobile Phone

2000. New Millennium. Technology.
503 **172** 75000l. black, green and blue 70 20
504 – 150000l. black and blue 90 25
505 – 275000l. multicoloured . . 1·60 1·75
506 – 300000l. multicoloured . . 2·00 2·25
DESIGNS: 150000l. "Hosgeldin 2000"; 275000l. Computer and "internet" in squares; 300000l. Satellite over Earth.

173 Beach Scene

2000. Holidays. Multicoloured.
507 300000l. Type **173** . . . . . 1·75 1·90
508 340000l. Deck-chair on sea-shore . . . . 1·75 1·90

174 "Building Europe"

2000. Europa. Sheet 77 × 68 mm, containing T **174** and similar vert design. Multicoloured.
MS509 300000l. Type **174**; 300000l. Map of Europe with flower creating Council of Europe emblem and map of Cyprus . . 3·50 4·00

175 Bellapais Abbey

176 Pres. Ahmet Sezer of Turkey

2000. 4th International Bellapais Music Festival. Multicoloured.
510 150000l. Type **175** . . . . . 1·00 50
511 350000l. Emblem (vert) . . . 2·25 2·50

2000. Visit of President Ahmet Sezer of Turkey.
512 **176** 150000l. multicoloured . . 1·50 1·25

177 Olympic Torch and Rings

179 Grasshopper on Cactus

2000. Olympic Games, Sydney. Multicoloured.
513 125000l. Type **177** . . . . . 1·25 50
514 200000l. Runner (horiz) . . . 2·00 2·25

2000. No. 418 surch **50000 LIRA POSTA PULU**.
515 50000l. on 6000l. Type **140** 1·50 75

2000. Nature. Insects and Flowers. Multicoloured.
516 125000l. Type **179** 70 25
517 200000l. Butterfly on flower 1·10 45
518 275000l. Bee on flower . . . 1·40 1·25
519 600000l. Snail on flower . . . 2·75 3·25

180 Traditional Kerchief

2000. Traditional Handicrafts. Kerchiefs.
520 **180** 125000l. multicoloured . . 70 30
521 – 200000l. multicoloured . . 1·10 55
522 – 265000l. multicoloured . . 1·40 1·40
523 – 350000l. multicoloured . . 2·00 2·50
DESIGNS: 200000l. to 350000l. Different kerchiefs.

181 Lusignan House, Lefkosa

2001. Restoration of Historic Buildings. Mult.
524 125000l. Type **181** . . . . . 1·25 50
525 200000l. The Eaved House, Lefkosa . . . . 2·00 2·50

182 "Cuprum Kuprum Bakir Madeni" (Inci Kansu)

2001. Modern Art. Multicoloured.
526 125000l. Type **182** . . . . . 1·00 30
527 200000l. "Varolus" (Emel Samioglu) . . . . 1·60 45
528 350000l. "Ask Kuslara Ucar" (Ozden Selenge) (vert) . . 2·25 2·50
529 400000l. "Suyun Yolculugu" (Ayhatun Atesin) . . . . 2·25 2·50

183 Degirmenlik Reservoir

184 Atomic Symbol and X-ray

2001. Europa. Water Resources. Multicoloured.
530 200000l. Type **183** . . . . . 1·00 30
531 500000l. The Waters of Sinar 1·75 2·25

2001. World Environment Day. Radiation. Mult.
532 125000l. Type **184** 60 20
533 450000l. Radiation symbol and x-ray of hand . . . . 1·75 2·25

185 Ottoman Policeman, 1885

186 MG TF Sports Car, 1954

2001. Turkish Cypriot Police Uniforms. Multicoloured.
534 125000l. Type **185** . . . . . 1·00 40
535 200000l. Colonial policeman, 1933 . . . . 1·75 60
536 500000l. Mounted policeman, 1934 . . . . 2·50 2·25
537 750000l. Policewoman, 1983 3·25 3·75

2001. Classic Cars. Multicoloured.
538 175000l. Type **186** 75 30
539 300000l. Vauxhall 14, 1948 1·25 50
540 475000l. Bentley, 1922 . . . 1·75 1·75
541 600000l. Jaguar XK 120, 1955 . . . . 2·00 2·25

187 Graduate at Top of Steps and College Names

2001. Anniversaries.
542 **187** 200000l. multicoloured . . 1·40 1·40
543 – 200000l. black, mauve and brown . . . . 1·40 1·40
DESIGNS—HORIZ: No. 542, Type **187** (Centenary of Higher Education). VERT: No. 543, Book cover of *The Genocide Files* by Harry Scott Gibbons (anniversary of publication).

188 Chef mincing Logs into Letters (U. Karsu)

189 Turtle

2002. Caricatures. Multicoloured.
544 250000l. Type **188** . . . . . 1·00 40
545 300000l. Overfed people drinking from inflated cow, and starving children (M. Kayra) (horiz) . . . . 1·10 55
546 475000l. Can of cola parachuting down to pregnant African woman (S. Gazi) . . . . 1·50 1·50
547 850000l. Artist painting trees in city (M. Tozaki) . . . . 2·50 3·25

2002. Tourism. Underwater Scenes. Multicoloured.
548 250000l. Type **189** . . . . . 1·00 35
549 300000l. Starfish on rock . . 1·10 50
550 500000l. Fish in rocks . . . 1·60 1·60
551 750000l. Part of wreck . . . 2·25 2·75

190 Stilt-walker

192 Woman in White Tunic and Trousers

191 Turkish Football Team

2002. Europa. Circus. Sheet 79 × 72 mm, containing T **190** and similar vert design. Multicoloured.
MS552 600000l. Type **190**; 600000l. Child on high wire . . . . . . 4·00 4·50

2002. World Cup Football Championship, Japan and Korea (2002). Multicoloured.
553 300000l. Type **191** . . . . . 1·00 30
554 1000000l. Football Stadium, World Cup Trophy and footballer . . . . 2·75 3·25

2002. Traditional Costumes. Multicoloured.
555 250000l. Type **192** . . . . . 1·00 35
556 300000l. Man wearing grey jacket . . . . 1·10 55
557 425000l. Man in blue jacket and trousers . . . . 1·75 1·50
558 700000l. Woman in yellow tunic . . . . 2·50 3·00

193 "Accident by Bridge"

2002. Children's Paintings. Multicoloured.
559 300000l. Type **193** . . . . . 1·25 60
560 600000l. "Burning House" (vert) . . . . 2·50 3·00

194 Sureyya Ayhan (athlete)

195 Oguz Karayel (footballer) (70th birth anniv)

2002. Sporting Celebrities. Multicoloured.
561 300000l. Type **194** . . . . . 1·00 40
562 1000000l. Grand Master Park Jung-tae (taekwon-do) . . 2·50 3·25

2002. Celebrities' Anniversaries. Multicoloured.
563 100000l. Type **195** 45 15
564 175000l. Mete Adanir (footballer) (40th birth anniv) 70 30
565 300000l. M. Necati Ozkan (30th death anniv) . . . . 1·25 80
566 575000l. Osman Turkay (astronomer) (1st death anniv) (horiz) . . . . . . 2·25 2·75

196 Untitled Painting by Salih Bayraktar

197 Tree containing Meadow and Forest in Polluted Industrial Landscape

2003. Art (14th series). Multicoloured.
567 250000l. Type **196** . . . . . 1·00 50
568 1000000l. Untitled painting of woman's head (Feryal Suukan) . . . . 2·50 2·75

2003. Europa. Poster Art. Sheet 78 × 72 mm, containing T **197** and similar vert design. Multicoloured.
MS569 600000l. Type **197**; 600000l. Question mark containing wildlife in polluted landscape . . . . . 2·50 2·75

198 Cyprus Wheatear

2003. World Environment Day. Birds. Multi.
570 100000l. Type **198** 50 30
571 300000l. Cyprus warbler . . 1·00 60
572 500000l. Pygmy cormorant (vert) . . . . 1·50 1·50
573 600000l. Greater flamingo (vert) . . . . 1·60 1·75

199 Carved Wooden Chest

2003. Wooden Chests. Multicoloured.
574 250000l. Type **199** 50 25
575 300000l. Chest carved with circular designs 60 30
576 525000l. Chest carved with turquoise-blue figures . . 1·00 1·00
577 1000000l. Chest carved with flower heads and white birds . . . . 1·75 2·25

200 *ladiolus triphyllus*

2003. Flowers. Multicoloured.
578 150000l. Type **200** 30 20
579 175000l. *Tulipa cypria* 50 45
580 500000l. *Ranunculus asiaticus* 1·00 1·50
581 525000l. *Narcissus tazetta* . . 1·00 1·50

201 Kemal Ataturk and Flag of Turkish Republic of Northern Cyprus

2003. Political Anniversaries. Multicoloured.
582 3000000l. Type **201** (20th anniv of proclamation of Turkish Republic of Northern Cyprus) . . . . 3·25 3·50
583 3000000l. Kemal Atatürk and Turkish flag (80th anniv of Republic of Turkey) . . . 3·25 3·50

202 Horse-drawn Plough and Modern Farm Machinery

2003. Anniversaries. Multicoloured.
584 300000l. Type **202** (60th anniv of International Federation of Agricultural Producers) 50 40
585 500000l. Emblem (40th anniv of Lions Clubs in Cyprus) 90 1·10

203 Post Office and Pillar Box

2004. 40th Anniv of Turkish Cyprus Postal Services. Multicoloured.
586 250000l. Type **203** 40 25
587 1500000l. Globe and winged envelopes . . . . 2·00 2·25

204 Beach and Harbour Scenes

2004. Europa. Holidays. Sheet 72 × 75 mm containing T **204** and similar horiz design. Multicoloured.
MS588 600000l. Type **204**; 600000l. Seated woman with drink and beachside cafe . . . . 2·50 3·00

205 Pack Animals and Caravanserai

2004. Silk Road.
589 **205** 300000l. multicoloured . . 1·00 70

206 *Salvia veneris*

208 Footballer

207 Inside Stadium

2004. Plants. Multicoloured.
590 250000l. Type **206** 40 25
591 300000l. *Phlomis cypria* . . . 50 30
592 5000000l. *Pimpinella cypria* . . 90 90
593 6000000l. *Rosularia cypria* . . 1·10 1·25

2004. 50th Anniv of UEFA (Union of European Football Associations). Multicoloured.
594 300000l. Type **207** 60 30
595 1000000l. View from top of stadium . . . . 1·90 2·00

2004. Olympic Games, Athens. Multicoloured.
596 300000l. Type **208** 65 65
597 300000l. Boxing and horse riding 65 65
598 500000l. Weight lifting and gymnastics . . . . 1·00 1·10
599 500000l. Pole vaulting and tennis . . . . 1·00 1·10
Nos. 596/7 and 598/9, respectively, were each printed together, se-tenant, with the backgrounds forming composite designs.

(New Currency. 100 yeni kurus = 1 yeni lira)

209 Students Celebrating

2005. Anniversaries. Multicoloured.
600 15yhr. Type **209** (25th anniv of Eastern Mediterranean University, Gazimagusa) . . 35 60
601 30yhr. Eye and outlines of stamps (25th anniv of Cyprus Turkish Philatelic Association) 65 30
602 50yhr. Turtle emblem and outline map (w-ww.studyinnorthcyprus.org) 95 1·10

210 Stylized Dinghy

211 Boy and Girl in Orchard (Elmaziye Demirci)

2005. Tourism. Multicoloured.
603 10yhr. Type **210** 20 20
604 1ytl. Temple ruins, setting sun and windsurfer . . . . 1·50 1·60

2005. Children's Paintings. Multicoloured.
605 25yhr. Type **211** 55 45
606 50yhr. Couple (Elcim Oztemiz) . . . . 1·10 1·25

212 Brick Oven and Table laden with Food

213 *Dianthus cyprius*

2005. Europa. Gastronomy. Multicoloured.
607 60yhr. Type **212** 80 95
608 60yhr. Table laden with food and wine 80 95
MS609 113 × 77 mm. Nos. 607/8, each × 2 . . . . 2·75 3·25

2005. Endemic and Medicinal Plants. Multicoloured.
610 15yhr. Type **213** 35 25
611 25yhr. *Delphinium caseyi* . . 50 35
612 30yhr. *Brassica hilarionis* . . 55 40
613 50yhr. *Limonium albidum ssp. Cyprium* . . . . 95 1·10

214 Olive Branches and Sun Umbrellas

215 Ercan Airport

2005. Cultural and Art Activities. Multicoloured.
614 10yhr. Type **214** (International Olive Festival, Girne) 20 20
615 25yhr. Lala Mustafa Pasa Mosque and musical notes (International Culture and Art Festival, Gazimagusa) 50 35
616 50yhr. Folk dancers and Kyrenia Gate (International Folk Dances Festival, Lefkosa) . . . . 85 1·10
617 1ytl. Masks and stage (International Cyprus Theatre Festival) . . . . . 1·50 1·50

2005. Developments. Multicoloured.
618 50yhr. Type **215** . . . . . . 95 1·10
619 1ytl. Emblem and Middle East Technical University Northern Cyprus Campus, Guzelyurt (horiz) . . . . . 1·50 1·60

216 Outline Map of Cyprus

217 *Helianthemum obtusifolium*

2006. 50th Anniv of First Europa Stamp. Multicoloured.
620 1ytl.40 Type **216** . . . . . . 2·00 2·25
621 1ytl.40 View of Cyprus from satellite orbiting Earth . . 2·00 2·25
MS622 83 × 78 mm. Nos. 620/1 4·00 4·50
No. **MS**622 also exists imperforate.

2006. Wild Flowers. Multicoloured.
623 15yhr. Type **217** 35 25
624 25yhr. *Iris sisyrhinchium* (horiz) 50 35
625 40yhr. *Ranunculus asiaticus* (horiz) . . . . 80 1·00
626 50yhr. *Crocus veneris* (horiz) 95 1·10
627 60yhr. *Anemone coronaria* (horiz) . . . . 1·00 1·20
628 70yhr. *Cyclamen persicum* . . 1·10 1·30

218 "Adaption of a Woman's Figure to an Amphora" (ceramic by Semral Oztan)

2006. Art (15th series). Multicoloured.
629 55yhr. Type **218** . . . . . . 1·00 1·25
630 60yhr. "Female Figures" (Mustafa Hasturk) . . . 1·00 1·25

219 Birds (Selma Gürani)

220 Dr. Fazil Kucuk

2006. Europa. Integration. Showing winning entries in thematic drawing competition for high school students. Multicoloured.
631 70ykr. Type **219** . . . . . . 1·25 1·25
632 70ykr. Pregnant woman and flags of many nations (Suzan zcan) . . . . 1·25 1·25
MS633 78 × 72 mm. Nos. 631/2. Perf or imperf . . . . 2·50 2·50

2006. Birth Centenary of Dr. Fazil Kucuk (Deputy President (1959–73) of Republic of Cyprus).
634 **220** 40ykr. multicoloured . . . 1·25 80

221 Mustafa Kemal Ataturk

222 World Cup Trophy and Map of Germany

2006. 125th Birth Anniv of Mustafa Kemal Ataturk (first President (1923–38) of Turkey).
635 1ytl. Multicoloured . . . . . 2·00 2·00

2006. World Cup Football Championship, Germany. Multicoloured.
636 50ykr. Type **222** 75 75
637 1ytl. Football, player and Brandenburg Gate, Berlin 2·25 2·25

223 Lapwing

224 Trees ("Protect our Forests against Fire")

2006. Birds. Multicoloured.
638 40ykr. Type **223** 80 70
639 50ykr. Mallard 90 80
640 60ykr. Kingfisher . . . . . . 1·10 1·00
641 1ytl. Black-winged stilt . . . 2·00 2·25

2006. Anniversaries and Events. Multicoloured.
642 50ykr. Type **224** . . . . . . 1·00 75
643 1ytl.50 Yachts (Eastern Mediterranean Yacht Rally) . . . . 2·25 2·50

225 Naci Talat

226 Skeletal Leaf

2006. 15th Death Anniv of Naci Talat (former General Secretary of Turkish Cypriot Republican Turkish Party).
644 **225** 70ykr. multicoloured . . . 1·00 1·00

2007. International Conference on Environment: Survival and Sustainability, Lefkosa. Mult.
645 50ykr. Type **226** . . . . . . 1·00 75
646 80ykr. Red globe and parched ground . . . . . 1·40 1·40

227 Ewer

2007. Antique Household Utensils. Multicoloured.
647 70ykr. Type **227** . . . . . . 1·00 1·00
648 80ykr. Coal iron . . . . . . 1·40 1·40
649 1ytl.50 Oil lamp (vert) . . . 2·25 2·25
650 2ytl. Coffee pot on stove (vert) . . . . 3·50 3·50

228 Scout and Camp in Countryside

229 Painting by Osman Keten

2007. Europa. Centenary of Scouting. Multicoloured.
651 80ykr. Type **228** . . . . . . 1·75 1·75
652 80ykr. Three scouts playing music . . . . 1·75 1·75
MS653 79 × 73 mm. Nos. 651/2. Imperf . . . . 3·50 3·75

2007. Art (16th series). Multicoloured.
654 50ykl. Type **229** . . . . . . 1·00 80
655 70ykl. 'FRAGMENT CITY INTEGRI CITY' (Senih Cavusoglu) (horiz) . . . . 1·25 1·25

230 Chair-caner

2007. Crafts. Multicoloured.
656 40ykr. Type **230** 70 70
657 65ykr. Barrow man 90 90
658 70ykr. Cobbler . . . . 1·00 1·00
659 1ytl. Shoeshine man . . . . 1·75 1·75

231 Post Pigeon and Pigeon carrying Letter

2007. Post Office Past and Present. Multicoloured.
660 50ykr. Type **231** . . . . . . 1·00 80
661 60ykr. Mounted postman and early motor vehicles . . . 1·25 90
662 1ytl. Postman on bicycle and wall letterbox (horiz) . . . 2·00 2·00
663 1ytl.25 Modern postman on moped and postbox (horiz) 2·25 2·50

CYRENAICA Pt. 8

Part of the former Italian colony of Libya, N. Africa. Allied Occupation, 1942–49. Independent Administration, 1949–52. Then part of independent Libya.

Stamps optd **BENGASI** formerly listed here will be found under Italian P.O.s in the Turkish Empire, Nos. 169/70.

100 centesimi = 1 lira.

Stamps of Italy optd **CIRENAICA**.

1923. Tercent of Propagation of the Faith.
1 **66** 20c. orange and green . . . 4·00 18·00
2 30c. orange and red . . . 4·00 18·00
3 50c. orange and violet . . . 2·75 20·00
4 1l. orange and blue . . . . 2·75 26·00

1923. Fascist March on Rome stamps.
5 **77** 10c. green . . . . 4·25 7·25
6 30c. violet . . . . 4·25 7·50
7 50c. red . . . . 4·25 8·25
8 **74** 1l. blue . . . . 4·25 21·00
9 2l. brown . . . . 4·25 25·00
10 **75** 5l. black and blue . . . . . 4·25 35·00

1924. Manzoni stamps (Nos. 155/60).
11 **77** 10c. black and purple . . . 5·00 20·00
12 – 15c. black and green . . . . 5·00 20·00
13 – 30c. black . . . . 5·00 20·00
14 – 50c. black and brown . . . 5·00 20·00
15 – 1l. black and blue . . . . . 40·00 £150
16 – 5l. black and purple £400 £1300

1925. Holy Year stamps.
17 – 20c.+10c. brown & green . . 2·50 11·50
18 **81** 30c.+15c. brown & choc . . 2·50 13·00
19 – 50c.+25c. brown & violet . . 2·50 11·50
20 – 60c.+30c. brown and red . . 2·50 15·00
21 – 1l.+50c. purple and blue . . 2·50 20·00
22 – 5l.+2l.50 purple and red . . 2·50 30·00

1925. Royal Jubilee stamps.
23 **82** 60c. red . . . . 30 5·25
24 1l. blue . . . . 50 5·25
24a 1l.25 blue . . . . 2·50 11·00

1926. St. Francis of Assisi stamps.
25 **83** 20c. green . . . . 1·50 6·50
26 – 40c. violet . . . . 1·50 6·50
27 – 60c. red . . . . 1·50 11·50
28 – 1l.25 blue . . . . 1·50 18·00
29 – 5l.+2l.50 olive (as No. 196) 4·25 35·00

6

8

1926. Colonial Propaganda.
30 **6** 5c.+5c. brown . . . . 60 4·00
31 10c.+5c. olive . . . . 60 4·00
32 20c.+5c. green . . . . 60 4·00
33 40c.+5c. red . . . . 60 4·00
34 60c.+5c. orange . . . . . . 60 4·00
35 1l.+5c. blue . . . . 60 6·50

1927. 1st National Defence stamps of Italy optd **CIRENAICA**.
36 **89** 40+20c. black & brown . . 1·75 15·00
37 – 60+30c. brown and red . . 1·75 15·00
38 – 1l.25+60c. black & blue . . 1·75 30·00
39 – 5l.+2l.50 black & green . . 2·75 40·00

1927. Volta Centenary stamps of Italy optd **Cirenaica**.
40 **90** 20c. violet . . . . 5·00 18·00
41 50c. orange . . . . 6·50 11·50
42 1l.25 blue . . . . 10·00 26·00

1928. 45th Anniv of Italian–African Society.
43 **8** 20c.+5c. green . . . . 1·60 5·25
44 30c.+5c. red . . . . 1·60 5·25
45 50c.+10c. violet . . . . . . 1·60 9·25
46 1l.25+20c. blue . . . . . . 1·75 10·50

Stamps of Italy optd **CIRENAICA**. Colours changed in some instances.

1929. 2nd National Defence stamps.
47 **89** 30c.+10c. black & red . . . 3·00 10·50
48 50c.+20c. grey & lilac . . . 3·00 12·50
49 1l.25+50c. blue & brown . . 3·75 20·00
50 – 5l.+2l. black & green . . . 3·75 35·00

1929. Montecassino stamps (No. 57 optd **Cirenaica**).
51 **104** 20c. green . . . . 3·75 8·25
52 – 25c. red . . . . 3·75 8·25
53 – 50c.+10c. red . . . . . . 3·75 10·00
54 – 75c.+15c. brown . . . . . 3·75 10·00
55 **104** 1l.25+25c. purple . . . . . 7·25 16·00
56 – 5l.+1l. blue . . . . 7·25 20·00
57 – 10l.+2l. brown . . . . . . 7·25 26·00

1930. Marriage of Prince Humbert and Princess Marie Jose stamps.
58 **109** 20c. green . . . . 1·00 3·00
59 50c.+10c. red . . . . . . 80 4·00
60 1l.25+25c. red . . . . . . 80 9·25

1930. Ferrucci stamps (optd **Cirenaica**).
61 **114** 20c. violet . . . . 1·60 1·60
62 – 25c. green . . . . 1·60 1·60
63 – 50c. black . . . . 1·60 3·25
64 – 1l.25 blue . . . . 1·60 6·50
65 – 5l.+2l. red . . . . 5·00 13·00

1930. 3rd National Defence stamps.
66 **89** 30c.+10c. turq & grn . . . 13·00 16·00
67 – 50c.+10c. purple & green . . 13·00 20·00
68 – 1l.25+30c. lt brown & brn 13·00 30·00
69 – 5l.+11.50 green and blue . . 42·00 65·00

13

17 Columns of Leptis

1930. 25th Anniv (1929) of Italian Colonial Agricultural Institute.
70 **13** 50c.+20c. brown . . . . . 2·25 10·00
71 1l.25+20c. blue . . . . . . 2·25 10·00
72 1l.75+20c. green . . . . . 2·25 12·00
73 2l.55+50c. violet . . . . . 3·25 20·00
74 5l.+1l. red . . . . 3·25 28·00

1930. Virgil Bimillenary stamps optd **CIRENAICA**.
75 **118** 15c. violet . . . . 85 4·00
76 – 20c. brown . . . . 85 2·00
77 – 25c. green . . . . 85 1·50
78 – 30c. brown . . . . 85 2·00
79 – 50c. purple . . . . 85 1·50
80 – 75c. red . . . . 85 3·00
81 – 1l.25 blue . . . . 85 4·00
82 – 5l.+1l.50 purple . . . . . 3·00 21·00
83 – 10l.+2l.50 brown . . . . . 3·00 32·00

1931. St. Anthony of Padua stamps optd **Cirenaica** (75c., 5l.) or **CIRENAICA** (others).
84 **121** 20c. brown . . . . 1·25 8·25
85 – 25c. green . . . . 1·25 3·25
86 – 30c. brown . . . . 1·25 3·25
87 – 50c. purple . . . . 1·25 3·25
88 – 75c. grey (as No. 308) . . 1·25 8·25
89 – 1l.25 blue . . . . 1·25 16·00
90 – 5l.+2l.50 brn (as No. 310) 3·50 38·00

1932. Air stamps of Tripolitania optd **Cirenaica**.
91 **18** 50c. red 65 30
92 60c. orange . . . . 4·00 8·00
93 80c. purple . . . . 4·00 11·50

1932. Air stamps of Tripolitania of 1931 optd **CIRENAICA** and bars.
94 **18** 50c. red . . . . 1·00 1·00
95 80c. purple . . . . 5·25 12·00

1932. Air.
96 – 50c. violet . . . . 3·25 10
97 – 75c. red . . . . 5·00 5·00
98 – 80c. blue . . . . 5·00 10·00
99 **17** 1l. black . . . . 1·60 10
100 2l. green . . . . 2·00 5·00
101 5l. red . . . . 3·75 10·00
DESIGN—VERT: 50c. to 80c. Arab on Camel.

18 "Graf Zeppelin"

1933. Air. "Graf Zeppelin". Inscr "CROCIERA ZEPPELIN".
102 **18** 3l. brown . . . . 5·75 55·00
103 – 5l. violet . . . . 5·75 55·00
104 – 10l. green . . . . 5·75 £110
105 – 12l. blue . . . . 5·75 £120
106 **18** 15l. red . . . . 5·75 £120
107 – 20l. black . . . . 5·75 £140
DESIGNS: 5l., 12l. "Graf Zeppelin" and Roman galley; 10l., 20l. "Graf Zeppelin" and giant archer.

19 Air Squadron

1933. Air. Balbo Transatlantic Mass Formation Flight by Savoia Marchetti S-55X Flying Boats.
108 **19** 19l.75 blue and green . . . 11·50 £300
109 44l.75 blue and red . . . . 11·50 £300

1934. Air. Rome–Buenos Aires Flight. T **17** (new colours) optd with Savoia Marchetti S-71 airplane and **1934-XII PRIMO VOLO DIRETTO ROMA = BUENOS-AYRES TRIMOTORE "LOMBARDI-MAZZOTTI"** or surch also.
110 **17** 2l. on 5l. brown . . . . . 2·00 32·00
111 3l. on 5l. green . . . . . 2·00 32·00
112 5l. brown . . . . 2·00 35·00
113 10l. on 5l. pink . . . . . 2·25 35·00

21 Arab Horseman

1934. 2nd International Colonial Exn, Naples.
114 **21** 5c. brn & grn (postage) . . 2·75 9·00
115 10c. black and brown . . . 2·75 9·00
116 20c. blue and red . . . . 2·75 7·50
117 50c. brown and violet . . . 2·75 7·50
118 60c. blue and brown . . . 2·75 9·75
119 1l.25 green and blue . . . 2·75 16·00
120 – 25c. orange & blue (air) . . 2·75 9·00
121 – 50c. blue and green . . . . 2·75 7·50
122 – 75c. orange and brown . . 2·75 7·50
123 – 80c. green and brown . . . 2·75 9·00
124 – 1l. green and red . . . . . 2·75 10·00
125 – 2l. brown and blue . . . . 2·75 16·00
DESIGNS: 25 to 75c. Arrival of Caproni Ca 101 mail plane; 80c. to 2l. Caproni Ca 101 mail plane and Venus of Cyrene.

22

1934. Air. Rome–Mogadiscio Flight.
126 **22** 25c.+10c. green . . . . . 3·25 5·00
127 50c.+10c. brown . . . . . 3·25 5·00
128 75c.+15c. red . . . . . . 3·25 5·00
129 80c.+15c. black . . . . . 3·25 5·00
130 1l.+20c. brown . . . . . . 3·25 5·00
131 2l.+20c. blue . . . . . . 3·25 5·00
132 3l.+25c. violet . . . . . . 16·00 42·00
133 5l.+25c. orange . . . . . 16·00 42·00
134 10l.+30c. purple . . . . . 16·00 42·00
135 25l.+2l. green . . . . . . 16·00 42·00

OFFICIAL AIR STAMP

1934. Optd **SERVIZIO DI STATO** and crown.
O136 **22** 25l.+2l. red £1600 £1100

For stamps of British Occupation see under British Occupation of Italian Colonies.

CZECH REPUBLIC Pt. 5

Formerly part of Czechoslovakia, a federation dissolved on 31 December 1992 when the constituent republics became separate states.

100 haleru = 1 koruna.

1 State Arms

1993.
1 **1** 3k. multicoloured 25 20

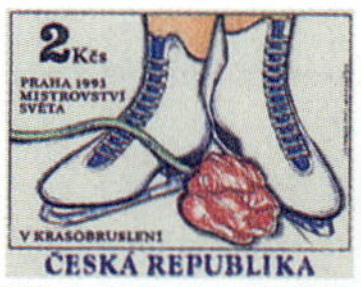

2 Skater's Boots and Tulip

3 Pres. Vaclav Havel

1993. Ice Skating Championships, Prague.
2 **2** 2k. multicoloured 20 15

1993.
3 **3** 2k. purple, blue & mauve . . 10 15
3a 3k.60 violet, mauve & blue 30 15

4 St. John and Charles Bridge, Prague

1993. 600th Death Anniv of St. John of Nepomuk (patron saint of Bohemia).
4 **4** 8k. multicoloured 85 45

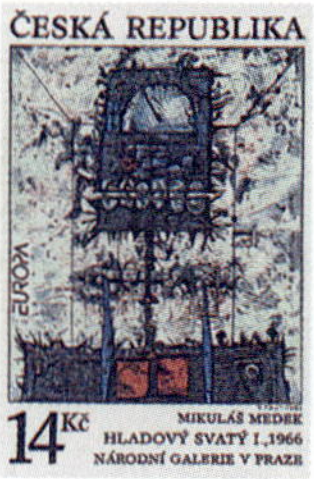

5 "Hladovy Svaty I" (Mikulas Medek)

1993. Europa. Contemporary Art.
5 **5** 14k. multicoloured . . . . . 7·50 2·40

6 Church of Sacred Heart, Prague

1993.
6 **6** 5k. multicoloured . . . . . . 1·50 45
See also No. 45.

7 Brevnov Monastery

1993. UNESCO World Heritage Site. Millenary of Brevnov Monastry, Prague.
7 **7** 4k. multicoloured 40 25

8 Weightlifter

9 Town Hall Tower and Cathedral of St. Peter and St. Paul

1993. Junior Weightlifting Championships, Cheb.
8 **8** 6k. multicoloured 55 35

1993. 750th Anniv of Brno.
9 **9** 8k. multicoloured . . . . . . 1·90 70

10 Sts. Cyril and Methodius

12 Ceske Budejovice

11 State Arms

1993. 1130th Anniv of Arrival of Sts. Cyril and Methodius in Moravia.
10 **10** 8k. multicoloured 75 30

1993. Sheet 76×90 mm.
MS11 **11** 8k. ×2 multicoloured 2·75 2·75

1993. Towns.
12 **12** 1k. brown and red 10 10
13 – 2k. red and blue 10 10
14 – 3k. blue and red 15 10
15 – 3k. blue and red 25 20
16 – 5k. green and brown 50 15
17 – 6k. green and yellow 60 30
18 – 7k. brown and green 60 35
20 – 8k. violet and yellow 40 30
21 – 10k. green and red 55 35
23 – 20k. red and blue . . . . 1·10 90
26 – 50k. brown and green . . . 30 1·60
DESIGNS—VERT: 2k. Usti nad Labem; 3k. (15) Brno; 5k. Pilsen; 6k. Slanyi; 7k. Antonin Dvorak Theatre, Ostrava; 8k. Olomouc; 10k. Hradec Kralove; 20k. Prague; 50k. Opava. HORIZ: 3k. (14) Cesky Krumlov (UNESCO World Heritage Site).

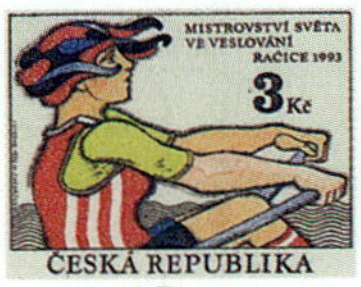

13 Rower

14 August Sedlacek (historian, 150th anniv)

1993. World Rowing Championships, Racice.
27 **13** 3k. multicoloured 25 30

1993. Birth Anniversaries.
28 **14** 2k. buff, blue and green . . 15 15
29 – 3k. buff, blue and violet . . 30 20
DESIGN: 3k. Eduard Cech (mathematician, centenary).

15 Pedunculate Oak

17 St. Nicholas

16 "Composition" (Joan Miro)

1993. Trees. Multicoloured.
30 5k. Type **15** 35 20
31 7k. Hornbeam 50 30
32 9k. Scots pine 70 45

1993. Art (1st series). Multicoloured.
33 11k. Type **16** . . . . 2·10 1·25
34 14k. "Green Corn Field with Cypress" (Vincent van Gogh) . . . . 3·50 1·50
See also Nos. 62/4, 116/18, 140/2, 174/6, 200/1, 221/2, 252/4, 282/4, 312/14, 350/2, 385/7, 393, 416/18, 449/451, 457, 485/7 and 521/3.

1993. Christmas.
35 **17** 2k. multicoloured 25 10

18 "Strahov Madonna"

1993. Christmas.
36 **18** 9k. multicoloured . . . . . 3·00 90

19 "Family" (C. Littasy-Rollier)

20 Kubelik

1994. International Year of the Family.
37 **19** 2k. multicoloured 10 10

1994. 54th Death Anniv of Jan Kublik (composer and violinist).
38 **20** 3k. yellow and black 25 10

21 Voltaire (writer, 300th anniv)

1994. Birth Anniversaries.
39 **21** 2k. purple, grey & mauve 15 25
40 – 6k. black, blue and green . . 45 25
DESIGN: 6k. Georg Agricola (mineralogist, 500th anniv).

22 Athletes

23 Marco Polo and Fantasy Animal

1994. Winter Olympic Games, Lillehammer, Norway.
41 **22** 5k. multicoloured 40 30

1994. Europa. Discoveries. Marco Polo's Journeys to the Orient. Multicoloured.
42 14k. Type **23** . . . . 1·10 1·25
43 14k. Marco Polo and woman on fantasy animals . . . . 1·10 1·25

24 Benes

26 Crayon Figures

25 Cubist Flats by Josef Chochol, Prague

1994. 110th Birth Anniv of Edvard Benes (President of Czechoslovakia 1935–38 and 1945–48).
44 **24** 5k. violet and purple . . . 40 20

1994. UNESCO World Heritage Sites. Mult.
45 8k. Market place, Telc . . . . 1·10 60
46 9k. Type **25** . . . . 1·25 75
No. 45 is similar to Type **6**.

1994. For Children.
47 **26** 2k. multicoloured 10 10

27 "Stegosaurus ungulatus"

1994. Prehistoric Animals. Multicoloured.
48 2k. Type **27** 20 10
49 3k. "Apatosaurus excelsus" . . 30 10
50 5k. "Tarbosaurus bataar" (vert) 50 30

28 Statue of Liberty holding Football

29 Flag of Prague Section

1994. World Cup Football Championship, U.S.A.
51 **28** 8k. multicoloured 75 45

1994. 12th Sokol (sports organization) Congress, Prague.
52 **29** 2k. multicoloured 10 15

30 Olympic Flag and Flame

1994. Centenary of Int Olympic Committee.
53 **30** 7k. multicoloured 60 40

31 Stylized Carrier Pigeons

1994. 120th Anniv of Universal Postal Union.
54 **31** 11k. multicoloured 90 80

32 Common Stonechat

33 NW, 1900

1994. Birds. Multicoloured.
55 3k. Type **32** 20 15
56 5k. Common rosefinch 30 25
57 14k. Bluethroat . . . . 1·25 75

1994. Racing Cars. Multicoloured.
58 2k. Type **33** 15 15
59 3k. L & K, 1908 . . . . . . 25 15
60 9k. Praga, 1912 . . . . 70 45

34 Angel

35 Emblem

1994. Christmas.
61 **34** 2k. multicoloured 10 10

1994. Art (2nd series). As T **16**.
62 7k. black and buff 50 55
63 10k. multicoloured 95 10
64 14k. multicoloured . . . . . 1·60 1·10
DESIGNS—VERT: 7k. "The Old Man and the Woman" (Lucas van Leyden); 10k. "Moulin Rouge" (Henri de Toulouse-Lautrec); 14k. "Madonna of St. Vitus".

1995. 20th Anniv of World Tourism Organization.
65 **35** 8k. blue and red 70 45

36 E.U. and Czech Republic Flags

37 Engraver's Transposition of 1918 Czechoslovakia 2h. Newspaper Stamp

1995. Association Agreement with European Union.
66 **36** 8k. multicoloured 70 45

1995. Czech Stamp Production.
67 **37** 3k. blue, grey and red . . . 25 20

38 Johannes Marcus Marci

39 Jiri Voskovec (actor and dramatist)

1995. Birth Anniversaries.
68 **38** 2k. sepia, stone & brown . . 20 10
69 – 5k. multicoloured 35 30
70 – 7k. purple, grey & mauve 70 35
DESIGNS: 2k. Type **38** (academic, 400th anniv); 5k. Ferdinand Peroutka (journalist and dramatist, centenary); 7k. Premysl Pitter (founder of Youth Care Centre, centenary).

1995. 90th Birth Anniversaries of Members of the Liberated Theatre, Prague. Caricatures from posters by Adolf Hoffmeister.
71 **39** 3k. black, yellow & orange 25 10
72 – 3k. black, yellow & green 25 10
73 – 3k. black, yellow & blue . . 25·00 10
DESIGNS: No. 72, Jan Werich (dramatist and actor); 73, Jaroslav Jezek (composer) (anniv 1996).

40 Church and Buildings

41 Buff-tailed Bumble Bee

1995. Townscapes.
75 **40** 40h. brown and pink . . . 10 10
76 – 60h. brown and stone . . . 10 10
DESIGN: 60h. Buildings, church and archway.

1995. European Nature Conservation Year. Endangered Insects. Multicoloured.
84 3k. Type **41** 25 10
85 5k. Praying mantis 40 30
86 6k. Banded agrion 55 30

42 Sandstone Arch, Labske Piskovce

1995. Rock Formations. Multicoloured.
87 8k. Stone Organ (basalt columns), Central Bohemia 85 60
88 9k. Type **42** 85 70

43 Rose and Women's Profiles

1995. Europa. Peace and Freedom. Multicoloured.
89 9k. Type **43** 85 40
90 14k. Butterfly, girl and profiles of ageing woman . . . . . 1·10 70

44 Cat

46 Wrestlers

45 Early Steam Train leaving Chocen Tunnel

1995. For Children.
91 **44** 3k.60 multicoloured 40 25

1995. 150th Anniv of Olomouc–Prague Railway.
92 **45** 3k. black, brown & blue . . 35 10
93 – 9k.60 black, brown & red 70 40
DESIGN: 9k.60. Crowd welcoming arrival of first train at Prague.

1995. World Greco-Roman Wrestling Championship, Prague.
94 **46** 3k. brown, stone and red . . 40 10

47 Violinist and Washerwoman (Vladimir Rencin)

49 Houses around smiling Sun

48 Voskovec, Wencih and Jezek (poster, Adolf Hoffmeister)

1995. Cartoons. Cartoons by named artists. Multicoloured.
95 3k. Type **47** 20 10
96 3k.60 Angel and naked man (Vladimir Jiranek) 30 10
97 5k. Champagne cork flying through ringmaster's hoop (Jiri Sliva) 40 30

1995. 70th Anniv of the Liberated Theatre, Prague, and 90th Birth Anniv of Founding Members (2nd issue). Sheet 61 × 81 mm.
MS98 **48** 22k. yellow and black 1·75 1·60

1995. 25th Anniv of SOS Children's Villages.
99 **49** 3k. multicoloured 25 10

50 Gothic Window

51 Rontgen and X-Ray Tube

1995. Architectural Styles.
101 **50** 2k.40 red and green . . . 10 10
102 – 3k. green and blue 25 10
103 – 3k.60 violet and green . . 35 10
104 – 4k. blue and red 30 15
105 – 4k.60 mauve and green . . 40 10
107 – 9k.60 blue and mauve . . 70 45
108 – 12k.60 brown and blue . . 85 45
109 – 14k. green and mauve . . 1·25 55
DESIGNS: 3k. Secession window; 3k.60, Roman window; 4k. Classicist doorway; 4k.60, Rococo window; 9k.60, Renaissance doorway; 12k.60, Cubist window; 14k. Baroque doorway.

1995. Centenary of Discovery of X-Rays by Wilhelm Rontgen.
113 **51** 6k. buff, black & violet . . 55 25

52 Emblem

1995. 50th Anniv of U.N.O.
114 **52** 14k. multicoloured . . . . 1·25 65

53 Christmas Tree

55 Stamp Design by Jaroslav Benda

54 Allegory of Music

1995. Christmas.
115 **53** 3k. multicoloured 25 20

1995. Art (3rd series). As T **16**.
116 6k. black, blue and buff . . . 45 45
117 9k. multicoloured 75 60
118 14k. multicoloured . . . . 1·25 90
DESIGNS: 6k. "Parisienne" (Ludek Marold); 9k. "Bouquet" (J. K. Hirschely); 14k. "Portrait of the Sculptor Josef Malinsky" (Antonin Machek).

1996. Cent of Czech Philharmonic Orchestra.
119 **54** 3k.60 multicoloured . . . 30 30

1996. Tradition of Czech Stamp Production.
120 **55** 3k.60 multicoloured . . . 30 20

56 Mencikova and Chessmen

1996. 90th Birth Anniv of Vera Mencikova (chess champion).
121 **56** 6k. black, buff and red . . 50 30

57 Woman with Bowl of Easter Eggs

58 Sudek and Camera

1996. Easter.
122 **57** 3k. multicoloured 25 20

1996. Birth Cent of Josef Sudek (photographer).
123 **58** 9k.60 buff, black & grey 80 45

59 Jiri Guth-Jarkovsky (first President of National Olympic Committee) and Stadium

61 Garden Dormouse

60 Jan (John the Blind)

1996. Centenary of Modern Olympic Games.
124 **59** 9k.60 multicoloured . . . 80 45

1996. Bohemian Kings of the Luxembourg Dynasty.
125 **60** 14k. blue, grey & purple 1·25 90
126 – 14k. green, grey & purple 1·25 90
127 – 14k. green, grey & purple 1·25 90
128 – 14k. blue, grey & purple 1·25 90
DESIGNS: No. 126, Karel (Charles IV, Holy Roman Emperor); 127, Vaclav IV; 128, Sigismund.

1996. Nature Conservation. Mammals. Sheet 119 × 138 mm containing T **61** and similar vert designs. Multicoloured.
MS129 3k.60 Type **61**; 5k. × 2 Forest dormouse; 6k. × 2 European souslik; 8k. × 2 Northern birch mouse . . . . 1·75 2·25

62 Ema Destinnova (singer)

63 Entering Stage as Pierrot

1996. Europa. Famous Women.
130 **62** 8k. lilac, black & mauve 70 50

1996. Birth Bicentenary of Jean Gasparde Deburau (mime actor).
131 **63** 12k. multicoloured 90 50

64 Throwing the Javelin

65 Boy and Girl on Cat

1996. Olympic Games, Atlanta.
132 **64** 3k. multicoloured 25 10

1996. For Children.
133 **65** 3k. multicoloured 25 10

66 St. John of Nepomuk's Church, Zelena Hora

68 Black Horse

67 Boy playing Flute and Flowers forming Butterfly

1996. Tourist Sites. Multicoloured.
134 8k. Type **66** (UNESCO World Heritage Site) . . . 65 50
135 9k. Prague Loretto 75 60

1996. 50th Anniv of UNICEF.
136 **67** 3k. multicoloured . . . . 2·25 10

1996. Kladruby Horses. Multicoloured.
137 3k. Type **68** 25 10
138 3k. White horse 25 10

69 Havel

1996. 60th Birthday of President Vaclav Havel. Sheet 79 × 100 mm.
MS139 **69** 6k. × 2 blue and red 95 95

1996. Art (4th series). As T **16**. Multicoloured.
140 9k. "Eden" (Josef Vachal) . . 65 60
141 11k. "Breakfast with Egg" (Georg Flegel) (vert) . . . 90 75
142 20k. "Baroque Chair" (Endre Nemes) (vert) . . . . . . 1·50 1·10

70 Brahe

1996. 450th Birth Anniv of Tycho Brahe (astronomer).
143 **70** 5k. multicoloured 40 30

71 Letov S-1

72 Nativity

1996. Biplanes. Multicoloured.
144 7k. Type **71** 55 15
145 8k. Aero A-11 . . . . . . 65 20
146 10k. Avia BH-21 . . . . . . 80 35

1996. Christmas.
147 **72** 3k. multicoloured 25 10

73 Czechoslovakia 1920 Stamp Design of V. Brunner

74 Easter Symbols

1997. Czech Stamp Production.
148 **73** 3k.60 blue and red 25 10

1997. Easter.
149 **74** 3k. multicoloured 25 10

75 Dog's-tooth Violet

76 Girl and Cats ("Congratulations")

1997. Endangered Plants. Multicoloured.
150 3k.60 Type **75** 25 10
151 4k. Bog arum 35 10
152 5k. Lady's slipper 35 10
153 8k. Dwarf bearded iris 70 30

1997. Greetings Stamp.
154 **76** 4k. multicoloured 30 10

77 St. Adalbert

78 Prince Bruncvik, Neomenie and Lion

1997. Death Millenary of St. Adalbert (Bishop of Prague).
155 **77** 7k. lilac 55 40

1997. Europa. Tales and Legends. Multicoloured.
156 8k. Type **78** 65 50
157 8k. King Wenceslas IV watching Zito the Magician in cart pulled by cocks 65 50

79 Ark of the Torah, Old-New Synagogue (east side)

80 Objects d'Art from Rudolf II's Collection

1997. Jewish Monuments in Prague. Each black, blue and red.
158 8k. Type **79** 70 50
159 10k. Grave of Rabbi Loew (Chief Rabbi of Prague), Old Jewish Cemetery 75 60

1997. "Rudolf II and Prague" Exhibition, Prague. Sheet 117 × 91 mm containing T **80** and similar vert design. Each black, red and green.
MS160 6k. Type **80**; 8k. Rudolf IV and Muses; 10k. Arcimboldo (court painter) 1·60 1·50

81 Rakosnicek (cartoon character) and Rowan Berries

1997. For Children.
161 **81** 4k.60 multicoloured 40 10

82 Krizik and Arc Lamp

1997. 150th Birth Anniv of Frantisek Krizik (electrical engineer).
162 **82** 6k. pink, blue and red 45 20

83 Swimmer

1997. European Swimming and Diving Championships, Prague.
163 **83** 11k. black, buff & blue 75 40

84 Mrs. Muller and Svejk in Wheelchair

1997. 110th Anniv of "Fortunes of the Good Soldier Svejk" (novel by Jaroslav Hasek). Illustrations by Josef Lada. Multicoloured.
164 4k. Type **84** 35 15
165 4k.60 Lt. Lukas and Col. Kraus von Zillergut with stolen dog 35 15
166 6k. Svejk smoking pipe 40 35

85 Prague Castle

1997. "Praga 1998" International Stamp Exhibition. Multicoloured.
167 15k. Type **85** 1·00 75
168 15k. View of Prague Old Town 1·00 75
MS169 99 × 119 mm. Nos. 167/8 plus two half stamp-size labels 2·00 2·40
See also No. **MS**182.

86 Post Bus, 1928

1997. Historic Service Vehicles. Multicoloured.
170 4k. Type **86** 30 10
171 4k.60 Skoda Sentinel lorry, 1924 30 20
172 8k. Tatra fire engine, 1933 60 45

87 Carp, Candle, Fir, Apple and Nut

88 Olympic Rings and Ice Hockey Puck

1997. Christmas.
173 **87** 4k. multicoloured 30 10

1997. Art (5th series). As T **16**.
174 7k. multicoloured 35 15
175 12k. green and black 1·00 75
176 16k. multicoloured 1·10 1·10
DESIGNS—HORIZ: 7k. "Landscape with Chateau in Chantilly" (Antonin Chittussi). VERT: 12k. "The Prophets came out of the Desert" (Frantisek Bilek); 16k. "Parisian Second-hand Booksellers" (T. F. Simon).

1998. Winter Olympic Games, Nagano, Japan.
177 **88** 7k. multicoloured 45 25

89 Jakub Obvrovsky's 1920 Design

90 Pres. Vaclav Havel

1998. Czech Stamp Production.
178 **89** 12k.60 brown and green 90 50

1998.
179 **90** 4k.60 green and red 40 10
179a 5k.40 blue and brown 40 10
179b 6k.40 agate and blue 30 15

91 Cupid and Heart

92 Slalom

1998. St. Valentine's Day.
180 **91** 4k. multicoloured 30 10

1998. World Skibob Championships, Spindleruv Mlyn.
181 **92** 8k. multicoloured 60 30

93 Vysehrad (1938 stamp design)

94 Chick in Egg Shell

1998. "Praga 1998" International Stamp Exhibition (2nd issue). 50th Anniv of First Prague Stamp Exhibition. Sheet 149 × 105 mm.
MS182 **93** 2 × 30k. blue 4·00 3·75

1998. Easter.
183 **94** 4k. multicoloured 30 10

95 Observatory Building and Telescope Dome

1998. Centenary of Ondrejov Observatory.
184 **95** 4k.60 yellow, black & red 40 30

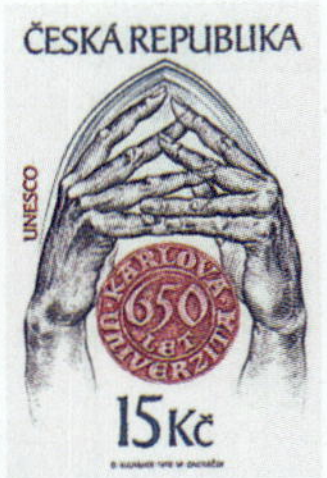

96 Hands forming Arch and Seal

97 Player celebrating

1998. 650th Anniv of Charles University and New Town, Prague. Sheet 120 × 92 mm containing T **96** and similar vert designs. Each black, red and blue.
MS185 15k. Type **96**; 22k. Charles IV (Holy Roman Emperor and King of Bohemia) and plan of Prague; 23k. Groin vault, St. Vitus's Cathedral 4·00 3·25

1998. Czech Gold Medal for Ice Hockey, Winter Olympic Games, Nagano. Sheet 106 × 88 mm.
MS186 **97** 23k. multicoloured 1·75 1·50

98 Grey Partridge

99 Book and Copyright Symbol

1998. Endangered Species. Multicoloured.
187 4k.60 Type **98** 40 30
188 4k.60 Black grouse ("Lyrurus tetrix") 40 60
189 8k. White deer ("Cervus elphus") 50 30
190 8k. Elk ("Alces alces") 50 45

1998. World Book and Copyright Day.
191 **99** 10k. multicoloured 75 30

100 The King's Ride, Moravia

1998. Europa. National Festivals. Multicoloured.
192 11k. Type **100** 75 55
193 15k. Carnival masks 1·10 70

101 Devil Musicians

102 Frantisek Kmoch (composer)

1998. For Children. Multicoloured.
194 4k. Type **101** 30 10
195 4k.60 Water sprite riding catfish 35 10

1998. Anniversaries. Multicoloured.
196 4k. Type **102** (150th birth anniv) 30 10
197 4k.60 Frantisek Palacky (historian, birth bicent) 40 30
198 6k. Rafael Kubelik (conductor, 2nd death anniv) 45 30

103 Prague Barricades, June 1848

1998. 150th Anniv of 1848 Revolutions.
199 **103** 15k. multicoloured 1·10 60

1998. Art (6th series). As T **16**. Multicoloured.
200 22k. "Amorpha-Two-coloured Fugue" (Frantisek Kupka) 1·50 1·10
201 23k. "Flight" (Paul Gauguin) 1·50 1·25

104 St. Barbara's Cathedral, Kutna Hora

1998. World Heritage Sites. Multicoloured.
202 8k. Type **104** 60 30
203 11k. Chateau Valtice 90 45

105 Soldiers with Flags

106 Capricorn

1998. 80th Anniv of Founding of Czechoslovak Republic. Paintings by Vojtech Preissig. Mult.
204 4k.60 Type **105** 40 10
205 5k. Soldiers marching 40 30
206 12k.60 Flags in Mala Street, Prague 1·00 60

1998. Signs of the Zodiac.
206a – 40h green, brown & blk 10 10
207 **106** 1k. yellow, red and black 10 10
208 – 2k. black, lilac and blue 10 10
209 – 5k. red, black and yellow 40 10
210 – 5k.40 green, black & brn 40 10
211 – 8k. red, black & purple 50 30
212 – 9k. green, black & orge 60 30

213 – 10k. yellow, blue & black 75 30
214 – 12k. orange, blue & black 85 50
216 – 17k. multicoloured . . . 75 45
217 – 20k. violet, black & brn 1·40 70
218 – 26k. multicoloured . . . 1·10 65
DESIGNS: 40h. Pisces; 2k. Virgo; 5k. Taurus; 5k.40; Scorpio; 8k. Cancer; 9k. Libra; 10k. Aquarius; 12k. Leo; 17k. Gemini; 20k. Sagittarius; 26k. Aries.

107 People following Star

1998. Christmas. Multicoloured.
219 4k. Type **107** 25 15
220 6k. Angel with trumpet over village (vert) 50 90

1998. Art (7th series). As T **16**. Multicoloured.
221 15k. Section of "The Greater Cycle" (Jan Preisler) . . . 1·10 90
222 16k. "Spinner" (Josef Navratil) (vert) . . . . . 1·40 1·00

108 1929 2k.50 Prague Stamp

1999. Czech Stamp Production.
223 **108** 4k.60 multicoloured . . . 40 20

109 Cat

110 Ornate Cockerel

1999. Cats. Multicoloured.
224 4k.60 Type **109** 35 15
225 5k. Cat with kitten 35 25
226 7k. Two cats 60 30

1999. Easter.
227 **110** 3k. multicoloured 25 10

111 Hoopoe

1999. Nature Conservation. Multicoloured.
228 4k.60 Type **111** 40 25
229 4k.60 European bee eater ("Merops apiaster") . . . 40 40
230 5k. "Euphydryas maturna" 40 25
231 5k. Rosy underwing ("Catocala electa") 40 25

112 Emblem

1999. Admission of Czech Republic into North Atlantic Treaty Organization.
232 **112** 4k.60 blue and red . . . 40 20

113 Emblem and Sky

1999. 50th Anniv of Council of Europe.
233 **113** 7k. multicoloured 55 20

114 Josef Rossler-Orovsky (co-founder)

1999. Centenary of Czech Olympic Committee.
234 **114** 9k. multicoloured 65 40

115 Sumava National Park

1999. Europa. Parks and Gardens. Multicoloured.
235 11k. Type **115** 85 50
236 17k. Podyji National Park . . 1·25 75

116 "Ferda the Ant, Pytlik the Beetle and The Proud Ladybird"

117 Chain Bridge Stadlec

1999. For Children. Birth Centenary of Ondrej Sekora (children's writer).
237 **116** 4k.60 multicoloured . . . 30 10

1999. Bridges. Multicoloured.
238 8k. Type **117** 60 40
239 11k. Wooden bridge, Cernvir (horiz) 85 55

118 King Wenceslas I handing over Grant and Miners

1999. 750th Anniv of Granting of Jihlava Mining Rights.
240 **118** 8k. multicoloured 60 30

119 "UPU", Globe and Emblem

121 Priessnitz and Treatments

120 Barrande and Trilobites

1999. 125th Anniv of Universal Postal Union.
241 **119** 9k. black, blue and green 60 45

1999. Birth Bicentenary of Joachim Barrande (French geologist and palaeontologist). Sheet 106 × 77 mm containing T **120** and similar horiz design. Each green, brown and black.
MS242 13k. Type **120**; 31k. *Deiphon forbesi*, *Ophioceras simplex* and *Carolincrinus barrandei* (trilobites) 3·00 2·00

1999. Birth Bicent of Vincenc Priessnitz (folk healer).
243 **121** 4k.60 multicoloured . . . 30 10

122 Woman

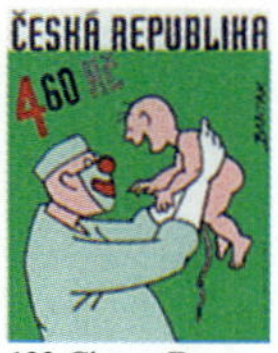

123 Clown Doctor and Laughing New-born Baby

1999. Folk Art. Beehives. Multicoloured.
244 4k.60 Type **122** 20 15
245 5k. St. Joseph with Infant Jesus 35 25
246 7k. Sweeper 65 25

1999. Graphic Humour of Miroslav Bartak. Multicoloured.
247 4k.60 Type **123** 25 10
248 5k. Dog disobeying No Smoking and No Dogs sign 40 30
249 7k. Night sky seeping in under window 65 30

124 "Mother of God" (altar painting)

1999. Beuron School (art movement). Sheet 108 × 166 mm containing T **124** and similar vert design showing paintings in St. Gabriel's Church, Prague. Multicoloured.
MS250 11k. Type **124**; 13k. "Jesus the Pantocrater" (painting in vault of apse) . . . . 1·75 1·40

125 Baby Jesus with Sheep and Lamb

127 Czechoslovakia 1938 1k.+50h. Child Welfare Stamp

126 Brmo, 1593 (after Willenberg)

1999. Christmas.
251 **125** 3k. multicoloured 25 10

1999. Art (8th series). As T **16**. Multicoloured.
252 13k. "Red Orchid" (Jindrich Styrsky) (vert) 90 70
253 17k. "Landscape with Marsh" (Julius Marak) (vert) . . . . 1·25 95
254 26k. "Monument" (Frantisek Hudecek) (vert) . . . . . 1·60 1·40

2000. "Brno 2000" Stamp Exhibition. Multicoloured.
255 5k. Type **126** 35 25
MS256 80 × 100 mm. 50k. St. James's Church (vert) . . . 3·25 2·40

2000. Czech Stamp Production.
257 **127** 5k.40 multicoloured . . . 40 25

128 Kutna Hora Coat of Arms and 14th-century Miners

129 Masaryk

2000. 700th Anniv of Granting of Royal Mining Rights to Kutn Hora.
258 **128** 5k. multicoloured 40 25

2000. 150th Birth Anniv of Tomas Masaryk (President of Czechoslovakia, 1918--35). Sheet 60 × 85 mm.
MS259 **129** 17k. blue, ultramarine and red . . . . 1·25 1·00

130 Animal-shaped Cake and Painted Eggs

131 "Winner" (statue, Stursa) and Prague Castle Tower)

2000. Easter.
260 **130** 5k. multicoloured 40 30

2000. Prague, European City of Culture. Sheet 166 × 109 mm containing T **131** and similar multicoloured designs.
MS261 9k. Type **131**; 11k. King David (wooden statue), Na Karlove Church; 17k. King Charles IV statue and Prague Castle (50 × 40 mm) . . . . . 2·50 3·00

132 Vitezslav Nezval (poet) (centenary)

134 "Building Europe"

133 Steam Locomotive, 1900

2000. Birth Anniversaries.
262 **132** 5k. blue, lilac and violet 40 25
263 – 8k. mauve, red and violet 50 35
DESIGN: 8k. Gustav Mahler (composer, 140th anniv).

2000. Conference of European Ministers of Transport, Prague. Railways. Sheet 114 × 112 mm containing T **133** and similar horiz design. Multicoloured.
MS264 8k. Type **133**; 15k. T371 electric locomotive, 2000 . . . 1·60 1·50

2000. Europa.
265 **134** 9k. multicoloured 60 40

135 Alarm Clock and Bird

137 *Geastrum pouzarii*

136 Fermat's Great Theorem

2000. International Children's Day.
266 **135** 5k.40 multicoloured . . . 40 25

2000. World Mathematics Year.
267 **136** 7k. multicoloured 45 40

2000. Endangered Fungi. Multicoloured.
268 5k. Type **137** 20 25
269 5k. Devil's boletus (*Boletus satanas*) 20 25
270 5k.40 *Verpa bohemica* . . . 30 30
271 5k.40 *Morchella pragensis* . . 30 30

138 Old Town Bridge Tower

2000. Historic Buildings. Multicoloured.
272 9k. Type **138** 35 55
273 11k. St. Nicolas's Church . . 45 55
274 13k. Municipal Hall 55 65

139 Leaves

2000. Annual International Monetary Fund and World Bank Group Meeting, Prague.
275 **139** 7k. multicoloured 55 40

140 Chariot Racing (detail from amphora)

2000. Olympic Games, Sydney.
276 **140** 9k. red, black and green 60 50
277 – 13k. multicoloured . . . 90 65
DESIGN: 13k. Canoeing and Czech flag.

141 Northern Goshawk and Common Pheasant (Autumn) **142** Nativity

2000. Hunting and Gamekeeping. Multicoloured.
278 5k. Type **141** 20 30
279 5k. Deer (winter) 20 45
280 5k.40 Mallard and ducklings (spring) 25 30
281 5k.40 Deer (summer) 25 30

2000. Art (9th series). As T **16**. Multicoloured.
282 13k. "St. Luke the Evangelist" (Master Theodoricus) (vert) 90 65
283 17k. "Simon with the Infant Jesus" (Petr Jan Brandl) (vert) . . . . 1·10 75
284 26k. "Brunette" (Alfons Mucha) (vert) . . . . . . 1·60 1·40

2000. Christmas.
285 **142** 5k. multicoloured 40 25

143 Cat **144** Czechoslovakia 1951 5c. Stamp

2000. Old and New Millennia. Multicoloured.
286 9k. Type **143** 60 50
287 9k. Magician pulling rabbit from hat 60 50

2001. Czech Stamp Production. 150th Birth Anniv of Alois Jirasek (writer).
288 **144** 5k.40 multicoloured . . . 40 25

145 Jan Amos Komensky (Comenius) (philosopher) **146** Cockerel and Woman

2001.
289 **145** 9k. black, red and brown 60 50

2001. Easter.
290 **146** 5k.40 multicoloured . . . 40 25

147 Church, Jakub u Kutne Hory

2001. Czech Architecture. Sheet 113 × 85 mm containing T **147** and similar vert designs. Each orange, green and black.
MS291 13k. Type **147**; 17k. Bucovice Chateau; 31k. The Dancing House, Prague . . . . 4·25 3·25

148 "Allegory of Art" (fresco, Vaclav Vavincec Reiner)

2001. Baroque Art. Sheet 146 × 117 mm.
MS292 **148** 50k. multicoloured 3·25 3·00

149 Pond

2001. Europa. Water Resources.
293 **149** 9k. lilac and black 60 45

150 Players **151** Maxipes Fik riding Bicycle

2001. Men's European Volleyball Championship, Ostrava.
294 **150** 12k. multicoloured . . . 1·00 65

2001. International Children's Day. *Vecernicek* (cartoon created by Rudolf Cechura).
295 **151** 5k.40 multicoloured . . . 1·00 25

152 Frantisek Skroup (composer) **153** Cats

2001. Birth Anniversaries. Multicoloured.
296 5k.40 Type **152** (bicentenary) 35 25
297 16k. Frantisek Halas (poet, centenary) . . . . 1·10 60

2001. Greetings Stamp. "Congratulations".
298 **153** 5k.40 multicoloured . . . 40 25

154 West Highland White Terrier

2001. Dogs. Multicoloured.
299 5k.40 Type **154** 35 25
300 5k.40 Beagle 35 25
301 5k.40 Golden retriever . . . 35 25
302 5k.40 German shepherd . . . 35 25

155 Fennec Fox (*Fennecus zerda*)

2001. Zoo Animals. Multicoloured.
303 5k.40 Type **155** 35 25
304 5k.40 Lesser panda (*Ailurus fulgens*) 35 25
305 5k.40 Siberian tiger (*Panthera tigris altaica*) 35 25
306 5k.40 Orang-utan (*Pongo pygmaeus*) 35 25

156 Emblem **157** Windmill, Kuzelov

2001. "Dialogue between Civilizations".
307 **156** 9k. multicoloured 60 40

2001. Mills. Multicoloured.
308 9k. Type **157** 50 50
309 14k.40 Water mill, Strehom 80 70

158 Kromeriz Chateau

2001. UNESCO World Heritage Sites. Mult.
310 12k. Type **158** 75 60
311 14k. Holasovice village . . . 70 70

2001. Art (10th series). As T **16**.
312 12k. black, buff and blue . . 80 75
313 17k. multicoloured . . . . . 1·25 90
314 26k. multicoloured . . . . . 1·90 1·50
DESIGNS—VERT: 12k. "The Annunciation of the Virgin Mary" (Michael Jindrich Rentz); 17k. "Sans-Souci Bar in Nimes" (Cyril Bouda); 26k. "The Goose Keeper" (Vaclav Brozik).

159 Christmas Tree and Half Moon carrying Gifts **160** 1938 2k. Stamp

2001. Christmas.
315 **159** 5k.40 multicoloured . . . 40 25

2002. 40th Death Anniv of Max Svabinsky (stamp designer).
316 **160** 5k.40 multicoloured . . . 40 30

161 Skier **162** Ski Jumper

2002. Winter Paralympic Games, Salt Lake City, U.S.A.
317 **161** 5k.40 multicoloured . . . 40 25

2002. Winter Olympic Games, Salt Lake City, U.S.A.
318 **162** 12k. multicoloured . . . 80 65

163 Girl with Easter Egg and Boy with Easter Sticks

2002. Easter.
319 **163** 5k.40 multicoloured . . . 25 15

164 Jaromir Vejvoda, Josef Poncar and Karel Vacek

2002. Composers' Birth Centenaries.
320 **164** 9k. black, red and violet 40 25

2002. No. 318 optd **ALES VALENTA ZLATA MEDAILE**.
321 **162** 12k. multicoloured . . . 50 30

166 "Divan" (Vlaho Bukovac)

2002.
322 **166** 17k. multicoloured . . . 70 45
A stamp in a similar design was issued by Croatia.

167 Circus Tent, Clown and Lion

2002. Europa. Circus.
323 **167** 9k. multicoloured 40 25

168 "Piano Keys–Lake" (Frantisek Kupka) **169** Mole and Butterfly

2002. Art. Sheet 148 × 105 mm, containing T **168** and similar vert design. Multicoloured.
MS324 23k. Type **168**. 31k. "Man with Broken Nose" (bust) (Auguste Rodin) . . . . 2·10 2·10

2002. For Children.
325 **169** 5k.40 multicoloured . . . 25 15

170 Pearl Oysters **171** Hus

2002. Nature Conservation.
326 **170** 9k. multicoloured 40 25

2002. Jan Hus (clergyman and preacher) Commemoration.
327 **171** 9k. multicoloured 40 25

172 *Maculinea nausithous*

2002. Endangered Species. Butterflies. Sheet 109 × 65 mm, containing T **172** and similar horiz designs. Multicoloured.
MS328 5k.40, Type **172**; 5k.40, *Maculinea alcon*; 9k. *Maculinea teleius*; 9k. *Maculinea arion* . . 1·10 70

173 Pansy

174 Zatopek

2002. Flowers.
329 50h. Cornflower 10 10
335 **173** 6k.40 multicoloured . . . 30 15
336 6k.50 Dahlia 25 15

2002. 80th Birth Anniv of Emil Zatopek (athlete).
340 **174** 9k. multicoloured 45 25

175 Chateau, Litomysl, Bohemia

2002. UNESCO World Heritage Sites. Mult.
341 12k. Type **175** 50 30
342 14k. Holy Trinity Column, Olumouc, Moravia (vert) 60 35

176 Angel, St. Nicholas with Basket of Gifts, and Devil

177 Star and Christmas Tree

2002. St Nicholas.
343 **176** 6k.40 multicoloured . . . 30 15

2002. Christmas.
344 **177** 6k.40 multicoloured . . . 30 15

178 Emblem

179 17th-century Armchair

2002. North Atlantic Treaty Organization Summit Meeting, Prague.
345 **178** 9k. azure, red and blue 40 25

2002. Antique Furniture. Multicoloured.
346 6k.40 Type **179** 30 15
347 9k. Sewing table, 1820 . . . 40 25
348 12k. Thonet dressing table, 1860 . . . . 50 30
349 17k. Armchair, 1923 . . . . 75 45

2002. Art (11th series). As T **16**.
350 12k. black and blue 50 30
351 20k. multicoloured 85 50
352 26k. multicoloured . . . . . 1·10 65
DESIGNS—HORIZ: 12k. "Forlorn Woman" (Jarsolav Panuska). VERT: 20k. "St. Wenceslas" (stained glass window) (Mikolas Ales); 26k. "Young Man with Lute" (Jan Peter Molitor).

180 Lion (statue, Josef Max)

2003. 10th Anniv of Czech Republic. Sheet 78 × 118 mm.
MS353 **180** 25k. brown, blue and red 1·10 1·10

181 Czechoslovakia 1937 2k.50 Stamp

182 Jaroslav Vrchlicky

2003. Czech Stamp Production. Jan C. Vondrous (stamp designer) and K. Seizinger (engraver) Commemoration.
354 **181** 6k.40 multicoloured . . . 30 15

2003. 150th Birth Anniversaries. Multicoloured.
355 6k.40 Type **182** (writer) . . . 30 15
356 8k. Josef Thomayer (physician and writer) . . . 35 20

183 Easter Egg

184 Rose and Prague

2003. Easter.
357 **183** 6k.40 multicoloured . . . 25 15

2003.
358 **184** 6k.40 multicoloured . . . 25 15

185 18th-century netted Lace

186 Poster for film *La Dolce Vita* (Karel Vaca)

2003. Traditional Crafts. Lace.
359 **185** 6k.40 multicoloured . . . 25 15
360 – 9k. red, deep blue and blue 35 20
DESIGN: 9k. Bobbin lace.

2003. Europa. Poster Art.
361 **186** 9k. multicoloured 35 20

187 Dragon Rocks and Trosky Castle, North-eastern Bohemia

2003. Natural Heritage. Multicoloured.
362 12k. Type **187** 50 30
363 14k. Punkva river caves, Brno 60 35

188 Jonathon (dog), Mach, Sebestova and Telephone (illustration from *The Boy Mach and the Girl Sebestova* (book) (Milos Maourek))

189 Stone Tower, Klet, South Bohemia

2003. For Children.
364 **188** 6k.40 multicoloured . . . 25 15

2003. Viewing Towers. Multicoloured.
365 6k.40 Type **189** 25 15
366 6k.40 Metal tower, Slovanka, Jablonec and Nisou . . . 25 15

190 Electric Train

2003. Centenary of First Tabor–Bechyne Electric Railway.
367 **190** 10k. multicoloured . . . 45 30

191 Marksman with Rifle

2003. European Marksmanship Championships, Plzen and Brno.
368 **191** 9k. multicoloured 35 20

192 Josef Dubrovsky

193 President Vaclav Klaus

2003. 250th Birth Anniv of Josef Dubrovsky (linguist).
369 **192** 9k. multicoloured 35 20

2003. (1st issue).
370 **193** 6k.40 stone, blue and mauve 25 15
See also No. 384, 424 and 542.

194 Siamese Fighting Fish (*Betta splendens*)

2003. Aquarium Fish. Sheet 176 × 115 mm containing T **194** and similar multicoloured designs.
MS371 12k. Type **194**; 14k. Freshwater angelfish (*Pterophyllum scalare*); 16k. Goldfish (*Carassius auratus*) (55 × 46 mm); 20k. Blue discus (*Symphysodon aequifasciatus*) (55 × 46 mm) . . . . 2·75 1·60

195 19th-century Anatolian Prayer Carpet

2003. Oriental Carpets. Multicoloured.
372 9k. Type **195** 35 20
373 12k. 18th-century Islamic carpet 50 30

196 Carving, Porta Coeli Monastery, Predklasteri

2003. Brno 2005 International Stamp Exhibition.
374 **196** 6k.50 multicoloured . . . 25 15

197 Red Kite (*Milvus milvus*)

2003. Birds of Prey. Multicoloured.
375 6k.50 Type **197** 25 15
376 8k. Peregrine falcon (*Falco peregrinus*) 35 20
377 9k. Booted eagle (*Hieraaetus pennatus*) 35 20

198 Wooden Fire Engine (1822)

2003. Fire Engines. Multicoloured.
378 6k.50 Type **198** 25 15
379 9k. Engine (1933) 35 20
380 12k. CSA 8/AVIA Daewoo (2002) 50 30

2003. As T **184** but with colour changed.
381 **184** 6k.50 multicoloured . . . 25 15

199 Hand-made Metal Lantern, Novy Svet, Prague

200 Snow-covered Christmas Tree

2003.
382 **199** 9k. multicoloured 35 20

2003. Christmas.
383 **200** 6k.50 multicoloured . . . 25 15

2003. President Vaclav Klaus (2nd issue). As T **193**.
384 **193** 6k.50 blue and lilac . . . 25 15

2003. Art (12th series). As T **16**. Multicoloured.
385 17k. "Poor Countryside" (Max Svabinsky) 70 45
386 20k. "Autumn in Veltrusy" (Antonín Slavícek) (vert) 85 50
387 26k. "Eleonore from Toledo" (Angola Brozino) (vert) . . 1·10 65

201 Czechoslovakia 1970 1k.80 Stamp

202 Water-powered Hammer, Lniste

2004. Czech Stamp Production. Jivi Svengsbir (designer and engraver) Commemoration.
388 **201** 6k.50 multicoloured . . . 25 15

2004. Iron Works. Multicoloured.
389 6k.50 Type **202** 25 15
390 17k. Iron furnace, Stara Hut u Adamova 75 45

203 Assumption of the Virgin Mary Church, Brno

2004.
391 **203** 17k. multicoloured . . . 70 45

204 Family

205 Players

2004. Easter.
392 **204** 6k.40 multicoloured . . . 25 15

2004. Art (13th series). As T **16**. Multicoloured.
393 26k. multicoloured . . . . . 1·10 65
DESIGNS—VERT: 26k. "Prometheus" (Antonin Prochazka).

2004. World Ice Hockey Championship, Prague and Ostrava.
394 **205** 12k. multicoloured . . . 50 30

206 Stars

2004. Accession to European Union.
395 **206** 9k. blue, yellow and deep blue 35 20

207 New Members Flags and EU Stars

2004. Enlargement of European Union.
396 **207** 9k. multicoloured 40 25

208 Bedrich Smetana

2004. Operatic Composers' Anniversaries. Multicoloured.
397 6k.50 Type **208** 25 15
398 8k. Antoniin Dvorak (death centenary) 35 20
399 10k. Leos Janacek (150th birth) 45 25

209 Family by River

2004. Europa. Holidays.
400 **209** 9k. multicoloured 35 20

210 Toad (illustration from *The Wind in the Willows* (children's book, Kenneth Graham)

211 Radegast (sculpture) (Albin Polsek)

2004. For Children.
401 **210** 6k.50 multicoloured . . . 30 20

2004. Brno 2005 International Stamp Exhibition (2nd issue).
402 **211** 6k.50 multicoloured . . . 60 35

212 Svata Hora (Holy Mountain), Pribram

2004. Tourism. Places of Pilgrimage. Multicoloured.
403 12k. Type **212** 55 35
404 14k. Svaty Hostyn, Bystrice Pod Hostynem 60 35

213 Athlete holding Javelin

214 Cyclist

2004. Paralympic Games, Athens 2004.
405 **213** 6k.50 multicoloured . . . 30 20

2004. Olympic Games, Athens 2004.
406 **214** 9k. multicoloured 40 25

215 Petrarch

2004. 700th Birth Anniv of Francesco Petrarca (Petrarch) (poet).
407 **215** 14k. multicoloured . . . 60 35

216 Tree in Winter

218 18th-century Music Teacher and Child

217 Budgerigars (*Melopsittacus undulates*)

2004. Tree Conservation. Multicoloured.
408 6k.50 Type **216** 30 20
409 8k. Tree in leaf 35 20

2004. Parrots. Sheet 115 × 168 mm containing T **217** and similar horiz designs. Multicoloured.
MS410 12k. Type **217**; 14k. Masked lovebird (*Agapornis personata*); 16k. Rose-ringed parakeet (*Psittacula krameri*); Green-winged macaw (*Ara chloroptera*) . . . 2·00 2·00

2004. 230th Anniv of Introduction of Compulsory Education.
411 **218** 6k.50 ochre, black and vermilion 30 20

219 Perambulator (1880)

220 Apple, Candle and Leaves

2004. Early Perambulators. Multicoloured.
412 12k. Type **219** 55 35
413 14k. Pram (1890) 60 35
414 16k. Pram (1900) 70 40

2004. Christmas.
415 **220** 6k.50 multicoloured . . . 30 20

2004. Art (14th series). As T **16**. Multicoloured.
416 20k. "On the Outskirts of Cesky Raj" (Alois Bubak) 85 60
417 22k. "The Long, the Broad and the Sharpsight" (Hanus Schwaiger) (vert) 90 65
418 26k. "Spring" (Vojtech Hynais) (vert) . . . . . . 1·20 70

221 Czechoslovakia 1960 60h. Stamp

222 "Moon Landscape" (drawing)

2005. Czech Stamp Production. Jaroslav Svab (stamp designer) and Jan Mracek (engraver) Commemorations.
419 **221** 6k.50 multicoloured . . . 30 20

2005. 60th Death Anniv of Petr Ginz (artist and Auschwitz victim). First Anniv of Colombia Space Shuttle Accident. Sheet 76 × 116 mm.
MS420 **222** 31k. multicoloured 1·40 1·40

223 Gate with Peacock and Trumpeter

224 Lily

2005.
421 **223** 7k.50 multicoloured . . . 35 20

2005.
422 **224** 7k.50 multicoloured . . . 35 20

225 "Granny"

2005. *Babicka* (The Grandmother) novel by Bozena Nemcova.
423 **225** 7k.50 multicoloured . . . 35 20

2005. President Vaclav Klaus (3rd issue). As T **193**.
424 **193** 7k.50 brown and magenta 35 20

226 Easter Egg

227 Fuchsia

2005. Easter.
425 **226** 7k.50 multicoloured . . . 35 20

2005. Flower.
426 **227** 19k. multicoloured . . . 90 60

228 St. Prokop's Basilica, Trebic

229 Bohuslav Brauner

2005. Tourism. Multicoloured.
427 14k. Type **228** 60 35
428 16k. Tugendhaft Villa, Brno (horiz) 70 40

2005. Birth Anniversaries. Multicoloured.
429 7k.50 Type **229** (150th) (chemist) 35 20
430 12k. Adalbert Stifter (200th) (artist and writer) 55 35
431 19k. Mikulas Dacicky (450th) (writer) 90 60

230 Roast Duck, Dumplings and Glass of Beer

2005. Europa Gastronomy.
432 **230** 9k. multicoloured 35 15

231 Peace Monument and Napoleon I

2005. Bicentenary of Battle of Austerlitz. Brno 2005 International Stamp Exhibition. Multicoloured.
433 19k. Type **231** 90 60
MS434 141 × 112 mm. 30k. "Napoleon I before the Battle of Austerlitz" (L. F. Lejune) (55 × 45 mm) . . . . 1·30 1·30

232 Kremilek and Vochomurka (cartoon characters)

234 Player

233 Emblem

2005. For Children.
435 **232** 7k.50 multicoloured . . . 30 20

2005. International Year of Physics.
436 **233** 12k. multicoloured . . . 55 35

2005. European Baseball Championships.
437 **234** 9k. multicoloured 40 30

235 Butterfly and Flowers (*Viola lutea sudetica* and *Hedysarum hedysaroides*)

2005. Endangered Species. Krkonose Mountains Fauna and Flora. Sheet 114 × 170 mm containing T **235** and similar multicoloured designs.
MS438 12k. Type **235**; 14k.White-throated dipper (*Cinclus cinclus*) and *Leucojum vernum*; 15k. *Salamandra salamandra*, *Primula minima* and Alpine shrew (*Sorex alpinus*) (44 × 55 mm); 22k. *Pneumonanthe asclepiadea*, *Aeschna coerulea* and Bluethroat (*Luscinia svecica svecica*) (44 × 55 mm) . . . . 3·00 3·00
The stamps and margin of No. **MS**438 were printed together, se-tenant, forming a composite design.

236 Franciscan Monastery Bell, Benesov and Assumption of Virgin Mary Church Bell, Havlickuv Brod

237 John Deere (1923)

2005. Bells.
439 **236** 7k.50 multicoloured . . . 35 20
440 – 9k. green and black . . . 40 30
441 – 12k. violet and black . . 55 35
DESIGNS: Type **236**; 9k. St. Jon and St. Paul Church, Dobrs; 12k. St Wenceslas Cathedral, Olomouc.

2005. Tractors. Multicoloured.
442 7k.50 Type **237** 35 20
443 9k. Lanz Bulldog (1921) . . . 40 30
444 18k. Skoda (1937) 85 55

238 Emblem

240 The Nativity

239 Stone and Player

2005. World Information Society Summit, Tunis.
445 **238** 9k. orange and violet . . 40 30

2005. Curling.
446 **239** 17k. multicoloured . . . 80 50

2005. Christmas. Multicoloured.
447 7k.50 Type **240** 35 20
448 9k. Three Magi (horiz) . . . 40 30

2005. Art (15th series). As T **16**. Multicoloured.
449 22k. "Summer Landscape" (Adolf Kosarek) . . . . . 1·00 65
450 25k. "Deinotherium" (Zdenek Burian) . . . . 1·20 70
451 26k. "Poplars near Velke Nemcice" (Alois Kalvoda) 1·20 70

241 Prague Castle (Czechoslovakia 1968 30h. Stamp)

242 Bouquet

2005. Czech Stamp Production. Jaroslav Lukavsky (stamp designer) and Ladislav Jirka (engraver) Commemoration.
452 **241** 7k.50 multicoloured . . . 35 20

2005. Greetings Stamps.
453 **242** 10k. multicoloured . . . 45 35

243 Hibiscus

244 Ice Hockey Players

2005.
454 **243** 11k. multicoloured . . . 55 35

2006. Winter Paralympic Games, Turin.
455 **244** 7k.50 multicoloured . . . 35 20

245 Women Skiers

2006. Winter Olympic Games, Turin.
456 **245** 9k. multicoloured . . . . 1·20 70

2006. Art (16th series). As T **16**. Multicoloured.
457 25k. multicoloured . . . . . 1·20 70
DESIGN: 25k. "Madonna of Zbraslav" (iccn) (40 × 50 mm).

246 Frantisek Josef Gerstner (mathematician) (250th birth anniv)

247 Daffodil

2006. Anniversaries. Multicoloured.
458 11k. Type **246** 55 35
459 12k. Jaroslav Jezek (composer) (birth centenary) 55 35
460 19k. Sigmund Freud (psychoanalyst) (150th birth anniv) 80 50

Nos. 460a and Type **246a** have been left for 'Wine' (value 12k.), issued on the 22nd February 2006, not yet recieved.

2006.
461 **247** 24k. multicoloured . . . 1·10 65

2006. K. Neumannova–Gold Medallist–Winter Olympic Games, Turin. No. 456 optd **K. NEUMANNOVA ZLATA MEDALLE**.
462 **248** 9k. multicoloured 40 30

249 Chicken and Easter Egg

251 Rose as Violinist

250 Monastery, Osek

2006. Easter.
463 **249** 7k.50 multicoloured . . . 35 20

2006. Tourism. Multicoloured.
464 12k. Type **250** 55 35
465 15k. Rock formation, Kokorinsko 70 40

2006. Greetings Stamp.
466 **251** 7k.50 multicoloured . . . 35 20

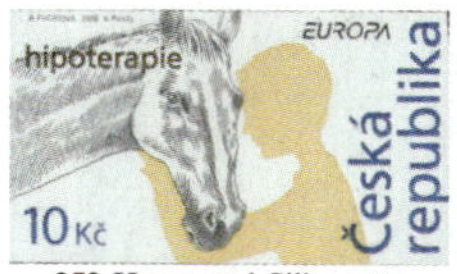

252 Horse and Silhouette

2006. Europa. Integration. Multicoloured.
467 10k. Type **252** (hippotherapy) 45 35
468 20k. Dog and silhouette (canistherapy) 90 70

253 Rumcajs and Family

254 Premysl Otakar I

2006. Rumcajs (cartoon by Vaclav Ctvrtek).
469 **253** 7k.50 multicoloured . . . 1·10 65

2006. Premyslid Dynasty Hereditary Kings. Sheet 112 × 165 mm containing T **254** and similar vert designs. Each claret, purple and slate.
MS470 12k. Type **254**; 14k. Vaclav (Wenceslas) I; 15k. Premysl Otakar II; 22k. Vaclav (Wenceslas) II; 28k Vaclav (Wenceslas) III . . . . 13·00 13·00

255 Gilded Brooch (1904)

256 Kamenice River Narrows

2006. Bohemian Jewellery. Multicoloured.
471 15k. Type **255** . . . . 2·10 1·40
472 18k. Garnet encrusted pendant (1930) . . . . . . 2·40 1·50

2006. Czech-Switzerland National Park.
473 **256** 19k. multicoloured . . . 2·60 1·50

257 *Gymnocalycium denudatum*

259 Multicoloured Tree

258 Prague Castle (mosaic) (Giovanni Castrucci) (½-size illustration)

2006. Cacti. Multicoloured.
474 7k.50 Type **257** . . . . . . 1·10 65
475 7k.50 *Obregonia denegrii* . . 1·10 65
476 10k. *Astrophytum asterias* . . 1·40 75
477 10k. *Cintia knizei* . . . . . 1·40 75

2006. PRAGA 2008 (1st issue). Sheet 105 × 141 mm.
MS478 **258** 35k. multicoloured 4·75 4·75
See also No. 481 and 488.

2006. Ecology.
479 **259** 7k.50 multicoloured . . . 1·10 65

260 Robin and Candle

261 Statue and Railings, Vrtbovska Gardens

2006. Christmas Congratulations.
480 **260** 7k.50 multicoloured . . . 1·10 65

2006. PRAGA 2008 International Stamp Exhibition (2nd issue).
481 **261** 7k.50 multicoloured . . . 1·10 65

262 Church of the Virgin Mary, Broumov

2006. Folk Architecture. Churches.
482 7k.50 Type **262** . . . . . . 1·10 65
483 19k. Church of St. Andrew, Hodslavice . . . . 2·60 1·50

263 The Nativity

2006. Christmas.
484 **263** 7k.50 multicoloured . . . 1·10 65

2006. Art (17th series). As T **16**. Multicoloured.
485 22k. multicoloured . . . . . 3·50 2·10
486 22k. multicoloured . . . . . 3·50 2·10
487 22k. multicoloured . . . . . 3·50 2·10
DESIGNS: 22k. "Still Life with Fruit" (Jan Davidz de Heem) (40 × 50 mm); 25k. "Montenegrin Madonna" (Jaroslav Cermak) (40 × 50 mm); 28k. "Pod suchym skalim" (Frantisek Kavan).

264 Exhibition Emblem

2006. PRAGA 2008 International Stamp Exhibition (3rd issue).
488 **264** 7k.50 magenta and ultramarine . . . . . . 1·10 65

265 Frana Sramek

2007. Personalities. Multicoloured.
489 7k.50 Type **265** (writer) (130th birth anniv) . . . . 1·10 65
490 19k. Kerl Slavoj Amerling (scientist) (birth bicentenary) . . . . 2·60 1·50

266 Emblem

2007. 300th Anniv of Technical University, Prague.
491 **266** 9k. multicoloured . . . . 1·20 70

267 Josef Slavik (violinist) (As Type **227**)

268 Angel with Infected Wing and Cancer Cell

2007. Czech Stamp Production. Josef Liesler (stamp designer) Commemoration.
492 **267** 7k.50 multicoloured . . . 1·10 65

2007. Oncological Disease Prevention.
493 **268** 7k.50 multicoloured . . . 1·10 65

269 Snake

271 Pieta

270 "Girl with a Puppet" (Utagawa Kunisada)

2007. 2nd Prize Winner in Design-a-Stamp Competition.
494 **269** 12k. multicoloured . . . 1·90 1·10

2007. Asian Art. Multicoloured.
495 12k. Type **270** . . . . 1·20 70
496 24k. "Siva, Parvati and Ganesa" (under painting on glass) . . . . 3·75 2·50

2007. Easter.
497 **271** 7k.50 multicoloured . . . 1·10 65

272 Langweil's Model of Prague

2007. Praga International Stamp Exhibition (1st issue). 750th Anniv of Lesser Prague.
498 **272** 7k.50 multicoloured . . . 1·10 65
See also No. 502.

273 Bouquet

274 Hall (J. Hoffman (architect))

2007. Congratulations.
499 **273** 11k. multicoloured . . . 1·75 95

2007. Stoclet Palace, Brussels. Multicoloured.
500 20k. Type **274** . . . . 2·75 1·60
501 35k. Palace exterior . . . . 4·75 3·25

275 Emblem

2007. Praga International Stamp Exhibition (2nd issue).
502 **275** 11k. multicoloured . . . 1·75 95

276 Jurkovic House, Luhacovice

2007. Tourism. Spa Resorts. Multicoloured.
503 12k. Type **276** . . . . 1·90 1·10
504 15k. Gocar Pavilion, Bohdanec . . . . 2·10 1·40

277 Cyclamen

278 Scouts

2007. Flowers. Multicoloured.
505 1k. Type **277** 20 10
506 23k. Geranium . . . . 3·50 2·10

2007. Europa. Centenary of Scouting.
507 **278** 11k. multicoloured . . . 1·75 95

279 Fast Arrows

2007. For Children. Birth Centenary of Jaroslav Foglar (creator of Fast Arrows (children's cartoon series)).
508 **279** 7k.50 multicoloured . . . 1·10 65

280 Gothic Stove

281 Vaclav Hollar (Jan Meyssens)

2007. Traditional Stoves. Multicoloured.
509 7k.50 Type **280** . . . . . . 1·10 65
510 12k. Renaissance stove . . . 1·75 1·10

2007. 400th Birth Anniv of Wenceslaus Hollar Bohemus (Vaclav Hollar) (artist). Sheet 116 × 121 mm.
MS511 **281** 35k. multicoloured 5·00 5·00

282 Charles Bridge, Prague

2007. Praga 2008, International Stamp Exhibition (3rd issue). 650th Anniv of Charles Bridge, Prague. Sheet 155 × 101 mm.
MS512 **282** 45k. multicoloured 6·25 6·25
The stamp and margins of **MS**512 form a composite design of Charles Bridge.

283 Film Projection (Victor Ponrepo's Blue Pike Cinema)

2007. Centenary of First Cinema, Prague.
513 **283** 7k.50 multicoloured . . . 1·10 65

284 *Ophrys holosericea*

286 Indian Cress

285 Teacher and Pupil

2007. Nature Protection. White Carpathian Mountains and Orchid Meadows—UNESCO Biosphere Reservation. Sheet 166 × 114 mm containing T **284** and similar multicoloured designs.
MS514 9k. Type **284** 10k.*Colias myrmidone* and *Anacamptis pyramidalis*; 11k.*Ophrys apifera*; 12k. *Coracias garrulus* and *Gymnadenia densiflora* (54 × 44 mm) 6·00 6·00
The stamps and margins of **MS**514 form a composite design of a mountain meadow.

2007. 350th Anniv of Opera Didactica Omnia (educational treatise by Jan Amos Komensky).
515 **285** 12k. gold, black and magenta . . . . 1·75 1·10

2007.
516 **286** 15k. multicoloured . . . 2·10 1·30

287 Water Tower, Karvina

289 The Nativity

288 Emil Holub

2007. Water Towers. Multicoloured.
517 7k.50 Type **287** . . . . . . 1·10 65
518 18k. Water tower, Pilsen . . 3·25 1·90

2007. 160th Birth Anniv of Emil Holub (explorer).
519 **288** 11k. green and carmine 1·75 1·10

2007. Christmas.
520 **289** 7k.50 multicoloured . . . 1·20 75

2007. Art (18th series). As T **16**. Multicoloured.
521 22k. multicoloured . . . . . 3·50 2·10
522 25k. multicoloured . . . . . 4·25 3·50
523 28k. multicoloured . . . . . 4·75 2·75
DESIGNS: 22k. 'Vrbicany Castle' (Amalie Manesova) (50 × 40 mm); 25k. 'Way to Bechyne Castle' (Otakar Lebeda) (40 × 50 mm); 28k. 'Montmartre' (Sobeslav Hippolyt Pinkas) (50 × 40 mm).

290 Gaillardia

291 Traffic Lights

2007.
524 **290** 2k.50 multicoloured . . . 1·00 60

2007. Entry of Czech Republic into Schengen Area (European Union area without border controls)–21 December 2007.
525 **291** 10k. multicoloured . . . 1·60 95

292 Emblem

293 *Zbraslav* Steam Locomotive (As No. 946)

2007. Praga International Stamp Exhibition (4th issue).
526 **292** 18k. green and blue . . . 3·00 1·80

2008. Czech Stamp Production. Frantisek Hudecek (stamp designer) and Bohdan Roule (engraver) Commemoration.
527 **293** 10k. multicoloured . . . 1·60 95

294 Karel Klosterman

295 Rose

2008. Personalities. Multicoloured.
528 11k. Type **294** (writer) (160th birth anniv) . . . . 1·75 1·10
529 14k. Josef Kajetan (playwright and writer) (birth bicentenary) . . . . 1·90 1·10

2008. Greetings Stamp.
530 **223** 10k. multicoloured . . . 1·50 90

2008.
531 **295** 10k. multicoloured . . . 1·50 90

295a Glass and Grapes

2008. Greetings Stamp.
532 **295a** 17k. multicoloured . . . 2·40 1·50

296 King Jiri **297** Globe as Tree

2008. 550th Anniv of Election of Jiri of Podebrady as King of Bohemia.

533 **296**	12k. plum, blue and ultramarine	1·75	1·10

2008. International Year of Planet Earth.

534 **297**	18k. multicoloured	3·00	1·80

298 *Mourning Christ*

2008. Easter.

535 **298**	10k. multicoloured	1·50	90

299 *Bath Servant Suzanna carrying King Wenceslas IV over River Vltava* (J. Navratil)

2008. Praga 2008 International Stamp Exhibition.

536 **299**	10k. multicoloured	1·50	90

300 Gerbera **301** Azalea

2008. Flowers.

537 **300**	21k. multicoloured	2·75	1·60

2008. Flowers.

538 **301**	3k. multicoloured	1·00	60

302 Decorated Globe **303** TV Tower and Hotel Jested

2008. 350th Anniv of *Orbis Pictus* (World in Pictures) (children's encyclopedia) by Jan Amos Komensky.

539 **302**	10k. multicoloured	1·50	90

2008. Tourism. Multicoloured.

540	12k. Type **303**	1·60	95
541	15k. Hradec Kralove	2·50	1·50

2008. President Vaclav Klaus (4th issue). As T **193**.

542	10k. indigo, blue and magenta	1·50	90

304 Astronomical Theodolite (made by Reichenbach Ertel), c.1830 **305** Early and Modern Player

2008. Centenary of National Technical Museum. Multicoloured.

543	10k. Type **304**	1·50	90
544	14k. JAWA 750 sports car (designed for 1000 Czechoslovak Miles Competion), 1935 (horiz)	1·90	1·10
545	18k. Siegfried Marcus petrol combustion engine (made by Märky, Bromovsky-Schultz works, Adamov), 1889	3·00	1·80

2008. Centenary of Czechoslovak Ice Hockey.

546 **305**	17k. multicoloured	2·40	1·50

306 Script

2008. Europa. The Letter.

547 **306**	17k. indigo, black and vermilion	2·40	1·50

307 Doggy and Kitty

2008. For Children. *The Doggy and Kitty's Tales, How They Kept Their House and About Many Other Things* by Josef Capek.

548 **307**	10k. multicoloured	1·60	95

308 *Alcedo atthis* (kingfisher)

2008. Nature Protection. Trebonsko–UNESCO Biosphere Reservation. Sheet 167 × 116 mm containing T **308** and similar multicoloured designs.

MS549	10k. Type **308**; 12k. *Lutra lutra* (otter) and *Spirea salicifolia* (willowleaf meadowsweet) (54 × 44 mm); 14k. *Haliaeetus albicilla* (white-tailed eagle) (54 × 44 mm); 18k. *Netta rufina* (red-crested pochard) and *Nymphaea alba* (water lily) (54 × 44 mm)	8·00	8·00

The stamps and margins of **MS**549 form a composite design of a pond and its inhabitants.

309 Pavilion, Ledeburk Garden, Prague

2008. Praga 2008 International Stamp Exhibition. Sheet 150 × 114 mm.

MS550 **309**	51k. multicoloured	3·75	3·75

The stamp and margins of **MS**550 form a composite design of the gardens.

CZECHOSLOVAK ARMY IN SIBERIA Pt. 5

During the War of 1914–18 many Czech and Slovak soldiers in the Austro-Hungarian armies surrendered to the Russian Army. After the war many of these formed an army in Siberia and fought the Bolshevists. They issued stamps for their own postal service and these were also sold to the public on the Siberian Railway.

100 kopeks = 1 rouble.

1 Church in Irkutsk **3** Sentry

1919. Imperf.

1 **1**	25k. red	15·00	22·00
2 –	50k. green	40·00	40·00
3 **3**	1r. red	40·00	45·00

DESIGN: 50k. Armoured train "Orlik".

1920. Perf.

4 **1**	25k. red	15·00	15·00
5 –	50k. green (as No. 2)	35·00	38·00
6 **3**	1r. brown	40·00	38·00

4 Lion of Bohemia

1919.

7 **4**	(25k.) red and blue	2·75

1920. No. 7 optd **1920.**

8 **4**	(25k.) red and blue	7·00

1920. No. 8 surch.

9 **4**	2(k.) red and blue	20·00
10	3(k.) red and blue	20·00
11	5(k.) red and blue	20·00
12	10(k.) red and blue	20·00
13	15(k.) red and blue	20·00
14	25(k.) red and blue	20·00
15	35(k.) red and blue	20·00
16	50(k.) red and blue	20·00
17	1r. red and blue	20·00

CZECHOSLOVAKIA Pt. 5

Formed in 1918 by the Czechs of Bohemia and Moravia and the Slovaks of northern Hungary (both part of Austro-Hungarian Empire). Occupied by Germany in 1939 (see note after No. 393c); independence restored 1945.

On 31 December 1992 the Czech and Slovak Federative Republic was dissolved, the two constituent republics becoming independent as the Czech Republic and Slovakia.

100 haleru = 1 koruna.

1 **2** Hradcany, Prague

1918. Roul.

1 **1**	10h. blue	13·50	15·00
2	20h. red	13·50	15·00

1918. (a) Imperf.

4 **2**	3h. mauve	10	10
9	30h. olive	25	10
10	40h. orange	25	10
12	100h. brown	65	10
14	400h. violet	1·40	25

(b) Imperf or perf.

5 **2**	5h. green	10	10
6	10h. red	10	10
7	20h. green	10	10
8	25h. blue	10	10
13	200h. blue	1·10	10

3

1919. Imperf or perf.

3 **3**	1h. brown	10	10
38	5h. green	10	10
39	10h. green	10	10
40	15h. red	10	10
41	20h. red	10	10
28	25h. purple	10	10
49	30h. mauve	35	10
11	50h. purple	25	10
30	50h. blue	25	10
50	60h. orange	25	10
32	75h. green	65	10
33	80h. green	1·10	10
34	120h. black	1·10	40
35	300h. green	3·50	40
36	500h. brown	2·10	35
37	1000h. purple	11·50	80

6 **7**

1919. 1st Anniv of Independence and Czechoslovak Legion Commemoration.

61 **6**	15h. green	10	10
62	25h. brown	10	10
63	50h. blue	10	10
64 **7**	75h. grey	10	10
65	100h. brown	10	10
66	120h. violet on yellow	10	10

1919. Charity. Stamps of Austria optd **POSTA CESKOSLOVENSKA 1919**. A. Postage stamp issue of 1916.

67 **49**	3h. violet	10	40
68	5h. green	10	40
69	6h. orange	50	60
70	10h. purple	60	90
71	12h. blue	60	60
72 **60**	15h. red	10	10
73	20h. green	10	10
75	25h. blue	10	25
76	30h. violet	10	25
77 **51**	40h. green	10	25
78	50h. green	10	25
79	60h. blue	10	25
80	80h. brown	10	25
81	90h. purple	45	60
82	1k. red on yellow	30	40
83aa **52**	2k. blue	1·40	2·10
85aa	3k. red	5·25	7·00
87 a	4k. green	13·00	14·00
89 a	10k. violet	£350	£300

B. Air stamps of 1918 optd **FLUGPOST** or surch also.

91 **52**	1k.50 on 2k. mauve	90·00	80·00
92	2k.50 on 3k. yellow	£120	£110
93	4k. grey	£650	£500

C. Newspaper stamp of 1908. Imperf.

94 N **43**	10h. red	£1500	£1500

D. Newspaper stamps of 1916. Imperf.

95 N **53**	2h. brown	10	25
96	4h. green	25	35
97	6h. blue	25	30
98	10h. orange	3·00	4·50
99	30h. red	1·50	1·50

E. Express Newspaper stamps of 1916.

100 N **54**	2h. red on yellow	26·00	25·00
101	5h. green on yellow	£1200	£900

F. Express Newspaper stamps of 1917.

102 N **61**	2h. red on yellow	10	15
103	5h. green on yellow	10	15

G. Postage Due stamps of 1908.

104 D **44**	2h. red	£5000	£3500
105	4h. red	21·00	21·00
106	6h. red	11·00	8·00
108	14h. red	45·00	4·00
109	25h. red	35·00	32·00
110	30h. red	£350	£275
111	50h. red	£800	£700

H. Postage Due stamps of 1916.

112 D **55**	5h. red	10	10
113	10h. red	15	20
114	15h. red	15	20
115	20h. red	1·90	2·40
116	25h. red	1·00	1·50
117	30h. red	40	80
118	40h. red	1·00	1·50
119	50h. red	£400	£250
120 D **56**	1k. blue	9·00	7·00
121	5k. blue	30·00	30·00
122	10k. blue	£325	£250

I. Postage Due stamps of 1916 (optd **PORTO** or surch **15** also).

123 **36**	1h. black	21·00	17·00
124 –	15h. on 2h. violet	95·00	85·00

J. Postage Due stamps of 1917 (surch **PORTO** and value).

125 **50**	10h. on 24h. blue	70·00	75·00
126	15h. on 36h. violet	40	60
127	20h. on 54h. orange	85·00	90·00
128	50h. on 42h. brown	40	65

1919. Various stamps of Hungary optd **POSTA CESKOSLOVENSKA 1919**. A. Postage stamp issue of 1900 ("Turul" type).

129 **7**	1f. grey	£2250	£1600
130	2f. yellow	3·50	5·25
131	3f. orange	38·00	25·00
132	6f. olive	4·25	5·25
133	50f. lake on blue	55	60

134		60f. green on red	40·00	35·00
135		70f. brown on green	£2250	£1600

B. Postage stamp issue of 1916 ("Harvester" and "Parliament" types).

136	18	2f. brown (No. 245)	10	10
137		3f. red	10	10
138		5f. green	10	10
139		6f. blue	45	60
140		10f. red (No. 250)	90	1·25
141		10f. red (No. 243)	£300	£200
142		15f. purple (No. 251)	10	25
143		15f. purple (No. 244)	£170	£110
144		20f. brown	7·00	9·00
145		25f. blue	55	60
146		35f. brown	7·00	10·50
147		40f. green	1·90	2·00
148	19	50f. purple	55	65
149		75f. green	45	50
150		80f. green	90	1·10
151		1k. red	1·25	1·25
152		2k. brown	7·00	10·50
153		3k. grey and violet	35·00	35·00
154		5k. lt brown & brown	85·00	65·00
155		10k. mauve and brown	£1200	£850

C. Postage stamp issue of 1918 ("Charles" and "Zita" types).

156	27	10f. red	10	10
157		20f. brown	25	30
158		25f. blue	1·50	1·10
159	28	40f. green	2·75	2·50
160		50f. purple	38·00	26·00

D. War Charity stamps of 1916.

161	20	10+2f. red	30	60
162	–	15+2f. lilac (No. 265)	45	90
163	22	40+2f. red	6·75	3·75

E. Postage stamps of 1919 ("Harvester" type inscr "MAGYAR POSTA").

164	30	10f. red (No. 305)	7·50	9·00
165		20f. brown	£5500	£6500

F. Newspaper stamp of 1900.

166	N 9	2f. orange (No. N136)	10	30

G. Express Letter stamp of 1916.

167	E 18	2f. olive & red (No. E245)	10	30

H. Postage Due stamps of 1903 with figures in black.

170	D 9	1f. green (No. D170)	£1300	£1000
173		2f. green	£650	£550
174		5f. green	£1400	£1100
168		12f. green	£5000	£4000
172		50f. green	£325	£225

I. Postage Due stamps of 1915 with figures in red.

176	D 9	1f. green (No. D190)	£150	£110
177		2f. green	60	50
178		5f. green	9·00	14·00
179		6f. green	1·50	1·75
180		10f. green	30	45
181		12f. green	1·90	2·40
182		15f. green	5·25	9·00
183		20f. green	70	1·10
184		30f. green	30·00	38·00

9 President Masaryk

10

11 Allegories of Republic

12 Hussite

13

1920.

185	9	125h. blue	60	20
186		500h. black	2·75	2·00
187		1000h. brown	4·50	4·25

1920.

188	10	5h. blue	10	10
189		5h. violet	10	10
190		10h. green	10	10
191		10h. olive	10	10
192		15h. brown	10	10
196	11	20h. red	10	10
193b	10	20h. orange	10	10
197	11	25h. brown	10	10
194a	10	25h. green	10	10
198	11	30h. purple	10	10
195	10	30h. purple	10	10
199	11	40h. brown	4·00	10
200		50h. red	10	10
201		50h. green	10	10
202		60h. blue	10	10
203	12	80h. violet	10	25
204		90h. sepia	30	50
205	13	100h. green	40	10
206	11	100h. brown	45	10
227	13	100h. red on yellow	2·00	10
207	11	150h. red	3·00	70
208		185h. orange	1·25	20
209	13	200h. purple	70	10
228		200h. blue on yellow	6·00	10
210	11	250h. green	2·25	45
211	13	300h. red	1·50	10
229		300h. purple on yellow	5·25	10
212		400h. brown	4·25	55
213		500h. green	5·25	55
214		600h. purple	7·00	55

1920. Air. Surch with airplane and value. Imperf or perf.

215	2	14k. on 200h. blue (No. 13)	15·00	25·00
216	3	24k. on 500h. brn (No. 36)	38·00	38·00
220		28k. on 1000h. pur (No. 37)	38·00	32·00

1920. Red Cross Fund. Surch with new value in emblem.

221	2	40h.+20h. yellow	80	95
222	3	60h.+20h. green	80	95
223	9	125h.+25h. blue	2·25	2·75

1922. Surch with airplane and value.

224	13	50 on 100h. green	1·50	2·25
225		100 on 200h. purple	3·75	3·75
226		250 on 400h. brown	6·00	8·00

18 President Masaryk, after portrait by M. Savatimsky

20

23a

1923. 5th Anniv of Republic.

230	18	50h. (+50h.) green	90	65
231		100h. (+100h.) red	1·25	1·10
232		200h. (+200h.) blue	6·25	6·50
233		300h. (+300h.) brown	7·50	8·00

1925.

234	20	40h. orange	75	20
235		50h. green	1·50	10
236		60h. purple	1·90	10
237	18	1k. red	90	10
238		2k. blue	3·00	30
245		3k. brown	6·75	10
240		5k. green	1·75	30

The 1, 2 and 3k. (which with the 5k. differ slightly in design from the haleru values) come in various sizes, differing in some cases in the details of the designs.

1925. International Olympic Congress. Optd **CONGRES OLYMP. INTERNAT. PRAHA 1925.**

246	18	50h. (+50h.) green	5·25	10·00
247		100h. (+100h.) red	8·25	14·00
248		200h. (+200h.) blue	50·00	90·00

1926. 8th All-Sokol Display, Prague. Optd **VIII. SLET VSESOKOLSKY PRAHA 1926.**

249	18	50h. (+50h.) green	4·25	6·00
250		100h. (+100h.) red	4·25	6·00
251		200h. (+200h.) blue	20·00	21·00
252		300h. (+300h.) brown	32·00	45·00

1926.

254b	23a	50h. green	10	10
254c		60h. purple	60	10
254d		1k. red	25	10

25 Karluv Tyn Castle

26 Strahov

27 Pernstyn Castle

28 Orava Castle

30 Hradcany, Prague

1926. Perf or imperf × perf.

267	25	20h. red	25	10
268	27	30h. green	10	10
258	28	40h. brown	50	10
259	25	1k.20 purple	35	45
270	26	1k.20 purple	35	10
271	25	1k.50 red	35	10
272	27	2k. green	25	10
263	30	2k. blue	75	10
273	25	2k.50 blue	5·25	25
273a	–	2k.50 blue	35	10
273b	28	3k. brown	45	10
264a	30	3k. red	1·75	10
265	–	4k. purple	5·25	65
277	–	5k. green	7·50	1·10

DESIGNS—As T **25/28**: 2k.50 (No. 273a), Statue of St. Wenceslas, Prague. As T **30**: 4, 5k. Upper Tatra.

32 Hradek Castle

33 Pres. Masaryk

1928. 10th Anniv of Independence.

278	32	30h. black	10	10
279	–	40h. brown	10	10
280	–	50h. green	15	15
281	–	60h. red	15	25
282	–	1k. red	25	20
283	–	1k.20 purple	35	65
284	–	2k. blue	40	65
285	–	2k.50 blue	1·25	1·75
286	33	3k. sepia	1·00	1·25
287	–	5k. violet	1·25	2·25

DESIGNS—HORIZ: 40h. Town Hall, Levoca; 50h. Telephone Exchange, Prague; 60h. Village of Jasina; 1k. Hluboka Castle; 1k.20, Pilgrim's House, Velehrad; 2k.50, The Grand Tatra. VERT: 2k. Brno Cathedral; 5k. Town Hall, Prague.

34 National Arms

35 St. Wenceslas on Horseback

1929. Perf or imperf × perf.

287a	34	5h. blue	10	10
287b		10h. brown	10	10
288		20h. red	10	10
289		25h. green	10	10
290		30h. purple	10	10
291a		40h. brown	10	10

1929. Death Millenary of St. Wenceslas.

293	35	50h. green	15	10
294	–	60h. violet	30	10
295	–	2k. blue	65	35
296	–	3k. brown	95	25
297	–	5k. purple	3·00	2·50

DESIGNS: 2k. Foundation of St. Vitus's Church; 3k., 5k. Martyrdom of St. Wenceslas.

36 Brno Cathedral

1929.

298	36	3k. brown	1·10	10
299	–	4k. blue	3·50	60
300	–	5k. green	3·00	35
301	–	10k. violet	7·50	3·00

DESIGNS: 4k. Tatra Mountains; 5k. Town Hall, Prague; 10k. St. Nicholas Church, Prague.

38

39

1930.

302a	38	50h. green	10	10
303		60h. purple	45	10
304		1k. red	10	10

See also No. 373.

1930. 80th Birthday of President Masaryk.

305	39	2k. green	70	35
306		3k. red	1·10	35
307		5k. blue	3·00	2·40
308		10k. black	6·00	4·75

40 Fokker F.IXD

41 Smolik S.19

1930. Air.

394	40	30h. violet	10	10
309		50h. green	10	20
310		1k. red	25	30
311	41	2k. green	45	70
312		3k. purple	1·40	95
313	–	4k. blue	85	90
314	–	5k. brown	2·75	1·90
315	–	10k. blue	4·00	5·25
316	–	20k. violet	5·00	5·00

DESIGNS—As Type **41**: 4, 5k. Smolik S.19 with tree in foreground; 10, 20k. Fokker F.IXD over Prague.

43 Krumlov

44 Dr. Miroslav Tyrs

1932. Views.

317	–	3k.50 purple (Krivoklat)	1·25	1·00
318	–	4k. blue (Orlik)	1·40	60
319	43	5k. green	2·25	60

1932. Birth Centenary of Dr. Tyrs, founder of the "Sokol" Movement.

320	44	50h. green	30	10
321		1k. red	80	10
322	–	2k. blue	5·00	40
323	–	3k. brown	8·00	50

On the 2k. and 3k. the portrait faces left.

46 Dr. M. Tyrs

47 Church and Episcopal Palace, Nitra

1933.

324	46	60h. violet	10	10

1933. 1100th Anniv of Foundation of 1st Christian Church at Nitra.

325	47	50h. green	30	10
326	–	1k. red (Church gateway)	3·25	25

49 Frederick Smetana

50 Consecrating Colours at Kiev

1934. 50th Death Anniv of Smetana.

327	49	50h. green	10	10

1934. 20th Anniv of Czechoslovak Foreign Legions.

328	50	50h. green	20	10
329	–	1k. red	25	10
330	–	2k. blue	1·75	25
331	–	3k. brown	2·25	30

DESIGNS—HORIZ: 1k. French battalion enrolling at Bayonne. VERT: 2k. Standard of the Russian Legion; 3k. French, Russian and Serbian legionaries.

52 Antonin Dvorak

53 "Where is my Fatherland?"

1934. 30th Death Anniv of Dvorak.

332	52	50h. green	10	10

1934. Centenary of Czech National Anthem.

333	53	1k. purple	30	20
334		2k. blue	80	40

54 Autograph portrait of Pres. Masaryk

55

1935. 85th Birthday of President Masaryk.

335	54	50h. green	15	10
336		1k. red	30	10
337	55	2k. blue	1·00	35
338		3k. brown	2·10	50

See also No. 374.

56 Czech Monument, Arras

57 Gen. M. R. Stefanik

1935. 20th Anniv of Battle of Arras.

339	56	1k. red	40	10
340		2k. blue	95	45

1935. 16th Death Anniv of Gen. Stefanik.

341	57	50h. green	10	10

58 St. Cyril and St. Methodius

59 J. A. Komensky (Comenius)

60 Dr. Edward Benes

60a Gen. M. R. Stefanik

61 Pres. Masaryk

1935. Prague Catholic Congress.

342	58	50h. green	15	10
343		1k. red	25	10
344		2k. blue	95	45

1935.

345	59	40h. blue	10	10
346	60	50h. green	10	10
390	60a	50h. green	10	10
347		60h. violet	10	10
391		60h. blue	7·00	14·00
348	61	1k. purple	10	10
395		1k. purple	10	10

No. 390 differs from No. 341 in having an ornament in place of the word "HALERU".

No. 348 has "1 Kc" in value tablets, No. 395 "1 K".

62 Symbolic of Infancy

63 K. H. Macha

1936. Child Welfare.

349	–	50h.+50h. green	25	35
350	62	1k.+50h. red	40	55
351	–	2k.+50h. blue	1·10	1·50

DESIGN: 50h., 2k. Grandfather, mother and child from centre of Type **62** (enlarged).

1936. Death Centenary of Macha (poet).

352	63	50h. green	10	10
353		1k. red	30	10

64 Banska Bystrica

65 Podebrady

1936.

354	–	1k.20 purple	10	10
355	64	1k.50 red	10	10
355a	–	1k.60 olive	10	10
356	–	2k. green	10	10
357	–	2k.50 blue	10	10
358	–	3k. brown	10	10
359	–	3k.50 violet	70	45
360	65	4k. violet	30	10
361	–	5k. green	30	10
362	–	10k. blue	55	45

DESIGNS—As Type **64**: 1k.20, Palanok Castle; 1k.60, St. Barbara's Church, Kutna Hora; 2k. Zvikov (Klingden Berg) Castle; 2k.50, Strecno Castle; 3k. Hruba Skala Castle (Cesky Raj); 3k.50, Slavkov Castle; 5k. Town Hall, Olomouc ($23\frac{1}{2}\times29\frac{1}{2}$ mm). As Type **65**: 10k. Bratislava and Danube.

66 President Benes

1937.

363	66	50h. green	10	10

67 Mother and Child

68 "Lullaby"

1937. Child Welfare.

364	67	50h.+50h. green	30	50
365		1k.+50h. red	40	65
366	68	2k.+1k. blue	90	1·50

69 Czech Legionaries

70 Prague

1937. 20th Anniv of Battle of Zborov.

367	69	50h. green	15	10
368		1k. red	15	10

1937. 16th Anniv of Founding of Little Entente.

369	70	2k. green	45	10
370		2k.50 blue	70	50

71 J. E. Purkyne

73 Peregrine Falcon

72a Gen. Stefanik Memorial

1937. 150th Birth Anniv of J. E. Purkyne (physiologist).

371	71	50h. green	10	10
372		1k. red	15	10

1937. Mourning for Pres. Masaryk. As T **38** and **55**, but panels of T **55** dated "14.IX.1937".

373	38	50h. black	10	10
374	55	2k. black	25	10

1937. Labour Congress, Prague. Optd **B.I.T. 1937.**

375	66	50h. green	15	10
376	64	1k.50 red	15	10
377	–	2k. green (No. 356)	35	60

1937. Philatelic Exhibition, Bratislava. (a) Sheet 150 × 110 mm.

MS377a		50h. blue (Poprad Lake, Tatra Mountains); 1k. red (as T **72a**)	1·50	2·25

(b) Sheet 150 × 165 mm containing 25 of No. N368.

MS377b	N 67	10h. red	2·25	12·00

1938. 10th International Sokol Display, Prague.

378	73	50h. green	15	10
379		1k. red	15	10

74 Pres. Masaryk and Slovak Girl

75 Czech Legionaries at Bachmac

1938. Child Welfare and Birthday of Late President Masaryk.

380	74	50h.+50h. green	30	50
381	74	1k.+50h. red	40	65
MS381a		71 × 91 mm. Memorial sheet **74**; 2k.+3k. black. Imperf	2·40	3·50

1938. 20th Anniv of Battles in Russia, Italy and France. Inscr "1918 1938".

382	75	50h. green	20	10
383	–	50h. green	10	10
384	–	50h. green	10	10

DESIGNS: Czech Legionaries at Doss Alto (No. 383) and at Vouziers (No. 384).

76 J. Fugner

77 Armament Factories, Pilsen

1938. 10th Sokol Summer Games.

385	76	50h. green	10	10
386		1k. red	10	10
387		2k. blue	15	10

1938. Provincial Economic Council Meeting, Pilsen.

388	77	50h. green	10	10

77a Vysehrad

78 St. Elizabeth's Cathedral, Kosice

1938. Prague Philatelic Exhibition.

MS388a		148 × 105 mm. 50h. blue (T **77a**); 1k. red (Hradcany, Prague)	3·25	3·50

1938. Kosice Cultural Exhibition.

389	78	50h. green	10	10

79 "Peace"

80 Jasina

1938. 20th Anniv of Czech Republic.

392	79	2k. blue	15	10
393		3k. brown	35	10
MS393a		71 × 90 m. 2k. (+8k.) blue (T **79**)	2·25	3·50

1939. Inauguration of Slovak Parliament. No. 362 surcharged **Otvorenie slovenskeho snemu 18.1.1939** and **300 h** between bars.

393b		300h. on 10k. blue	55	3·00

No. 393b was only issued in Slovakia but was withdrawn prior to the establishment of the Slovak state. The used price is for cancelled to order stamps.

1939. Inaug of Carpatho-Ukrainian Parliament.

393c	80	3k. blue	10·00	65·00

The used price is for cancelled-to-order.

From mid-1939 until 1945, Czechoslovakia was divided into the German Protectorate of Bohemia and Moravia and the independent state of Slovakia. Both these countries issued their own stamps. Germany had already occupied Sudetenland where a number of unauthorized local issues were made at Asch, Karlsbad, Konstantinsbad, Hiklasdorf, Reichenberg-Maffersdorf and Rumburg. Hungary occupied Carpatho-Ukraine and the stamps of Hungary were used there. In 1945, upon liberation, stamps of Czechoslovakia were once again issued.

81 Clasped Hands

82 Arms and Soldier

1945. Kosice Issue. Imperf.

396	81	1k.50 purple	1·50	2·00
397	82	2k. red	20	25
398		5k. green	2·00	1·75
399		6k. blue	45	40
400	81	9k. red	25	35
401		13k. brown	65	70
402		20k. blue	1·40	1·40
MS402a		132 × 120 mm. Nos. 397/9	3·50	4·25

83 Arms and Linden Leaf

84 Linden Leaf and Buds

85 Linden Leaf and Flower

1945. Bratislava Issue. Imperf.

403	83	50h. green	10	10
404		1k. purple	10	10
405		1k.50 red	10	10
406		2k. blue	10	10
407		2k.40 red	30	30
408		3k. brown	10	10
409		4k. green	15	10
410		6k. violet	15	10
411		10k. brown	30	20

1945. Prague Issue.

412	84	10h. black	10	10
413		30h. brown	10	10
414		50h. green	10	10
415		60h. blue	10	10
416	85	60h. blue	10	10
417		80h. red	10	10
418		120h. red	10	10
419		300h. purple	10	10
420		500h. green	10	10

86 Pres. Masaryk

87 Staff Capt. Ridky

1945. Moscow Issue. Perf.

421	86	5h. violet	10	10
422		10h. yellow	10	10
423		20h. brown	10	10
424		50h. green	10	10
425		1k. red	10	10
426		2k. blue	10	10

1945. War Heroes.

427	87	5h. grey	10	10
428	–	10h. brown	10	10
429	–	20h. red	10	10
430	–	25h. red	10	10
431	–	30h. violet	15	10
432	–	40h. brown	10	10
433	–	50h. green	10	10
434	–	60h. violet	15	10
435	87	1k. red	10	10
436	–	1k.50 red	10	10
437	–	2k. blue	10	10
438	–	2k.50 violet	10	10
439	–	3k. brown	10	10
440	–	4k. mauve	10	10
441	–	5k. green	10	10
442	–	10k. blue	15	10

PORTRAITS: 10h., 1k.50, Dr. Novak. 20h., 2k. Capt. O. Jaros. 25h., 2k.50, Staff Capt. Zimprich. 30h., 3k. Lt. J. Kral. 40h., 4k. J. Gabcik (parachutist). 50h., 5k. Staff Capt. Vasatko. 60h., 10k. Fr. Adamek.

88 Allied Flags

89 Russian Soldier and Slovak Partisan

1945. 1st Anniv of Slovak Rising.

443	88	1k.50 red	10	10
444	–	2k. blue	10	10
445	89	4k. brown	20	25
446	–	4k.50 violet	20	25
447	–	5k. green	25	40
MS447a		148 × 210 mm. Nos. 443/7	32·00	42·00

DESIGNS—VERT: 2k. Banska Bystrica. HORIZ: 4k.50, Sklabina; 5k. Strecno and partisan.

90 Pres. Masaryk

91 Pres. Benes

92

1945.

452	–	30h. purple	10	10
448	90	50h. brown	10	10
453	91	60h. blue	15	10
449	–	80h. green	10	10
454	–	1k. orange	10	10
455	90	1k.20 red	15	10
456		1k.20 mauve	10	10
450	91	1k.60 green	15	10
457	–	2k.40 red	15	10
458	91	3k. purple	20	10
459	90	4k. blue	15	10
460		5k. green	20	10
461	91	7k. black	25	10
462	–	10k. blue	55	10
451	90	15k. purple	50	10
462a	–	20k. brown	85	10

PORTRAIT: 30h., 80h., 1k., 2k.40, 10k., 20k. Gen. M. R. Stefanik.

1945. Students' World Congress, Prague.
463 **92** 1k.50+1k.50 red 10 10
464 2k.50+2k.50 blue 20 20

93 J. S. Kozina Monument

94 St. George and Dragon

1945. Execution of Jan Stadky Kozina, 1695.
465 **93** 2k.40 red 15 10
466 4k. blue 20 25

1946. Victory.
467 **94** 2k.40+2k.60 red 15 15
468 4k.+6k. blue 20 15
MS468a 79 × 91 mm. T **94** 4k.+6k. blue . . . . 90 1·00

94a Lockheed Constellation over Charles Bridge, Prague

1946. Air. 1st Prague–New York Flight.
468b **94a** 24k. blue on buff . . . 90 85
See also Nos. 475/6.

95 Capt. F. Novak and Westland Lysander

96 Lockheed Constellation over Bratislava

1946. Air.
469 **95** 1k.50 red 15 10
470 5k.50 blue 35 15
471 9k. purple 60 20
472 **96** 10k. green 50 35
473 **95** 16k. violet 80 30
474 **96** 20k. blue 80 50
475 **94a** 24k. red . . . . 1·00 75
476 50k. blue . . . . 2·00 1·25

97 K. H. Borovsky

98 Brno

1946. 90th Death Anniv of Borovsky (Independence advocate).
477 **97** 1k.20h. grey 10 10

1946.
478 **98** 2k.40 red 40 15
479 – 7k.40 violet (Hodonin) (horiz) 20 10
MS479a 69 × 89 mm. No. 478 . . 90 70

100 Emigrants

101 President Benes

1946. Repatriation Fund.
480 – 1k.60+1k.40 brown . . . 55 55
481 **100** 2k.40+2k.60 red 20 25
482 – 4k.+4k. blue 30 45
DESIGNS: 1k.60, Emigrants' departure; 4k. Emigrants' return.

1946. Independence Day.
483 **101** 60h. blue 10 10
484 1k.60 green 10 10
485 3k. purple 10 10
486 8k. purple 20 10

102 Flag and Symbols of Transport, Industry, Agriculture and Learning

103 St. Adalbert

1947. "Two Year Plan".
487 **102** 1k.20 green 10 10
488 2k.40 red 10 10
489 4k. blue 50 20

1947. 950th Death Anniv of St. Adalbert (Bishop of Prague).
490 **103** 1k.60 black 45 45
491 2k.40 red 65 60
492 5k. green . . . . 1·00 40

104 "Grief"

105 Rekindling Flame of Remembrance

1947. 5th Anniv of Destruction of Lidice.
493 **104** 1k.20 black 30 30
494 1k.60 black 45 45
495 **105** 2k.40 mauve 55 45

106 Congress Emblem

107 Pres. Masaryk

1947. Youth Festival.
496 **106** 1k.20 purple 45 25
497 4k. grey 45 15

1947. 10th Death Anniv of Pres Masaryk.
498 **107** 1k.20 black on buff . . . 15 10
499 4k. blue on cream 25 25

108 Stefan Moyses

109 "Freedom"

1947. 150th Birth Anniv of Stefan Moyses (Slavonic Society Organizer).
500 **108** 1k.20 purple 15 10
501 4k. blue 25 25

1947. 30th Anniv of Russian Revolution.
502 **109** 2k.40 red 30 15
503 4k. blue 50 15

110 Pres. Benes

1948.
504 **110** 1k.50 brown 10 10
505 2k. purple (19 × 23 mm) . . . 10 10
506 5k. blue (19 × 23 mm) . . . 15 10

111 "Athletes paying Homage to Republic"

115 Dr. J. Vanicek

1948. 11th Sokol Congress, Prague. (a) 1st issue.
507 **111** 1k.50 brown 10 10
508 3k. red 15 10
509 5k. blue 40 10

(b) 2nd issue. Inscr "XI. VSESOKOLSKY SLET V PRAZE 1948".
515 **115** 1k. green 10 10
516 – 1k.50 brown 15 10
517 – 2k. blue 15 10
518 **115** 3k. purple 20 10
PORTRAIT: 1k.50, 2k. Dr. J. Scheiner.

112 Charles IV

113 St. Wenceslas and Charles IV

1948. 600th Anniv of Charles IV University, Prague.
510 **112** 1k.50 brown on buff . . . 10 10
511 **113** 2k. brown on buff 15 10
512 3k. red on buff 15 10
513 **112** 5k. blue on buff 20 20

114 Insurgents

117 Fr. Palacky and Dr. F. L. Rieger

1948. Centenary of Abolition of Serfdom.
514 **114** 1k.50 black 10 10

1948. Cent of Constituent Assembly at Kromeriz.
519 **117** 1k.50 violet on buff . . . 10 10
520 3k. purple on buff 15 10

118 J. M. Hurban

119 President Benes

1948. Centenary of Slovak Insurrection.
521 **118** 1k.50 brown 10 10
522 – 3k. red (L. Stur) 10 10
523 – 5k. blue (M. Hodza) . . . 20 20

1948. Death of President Benes.
524 **119** 8k. black 10 10

120 "Independence"

121 President Gottwald

1948. 30th Anniv of Independence.
525 **120** 1k.50 blue 15 10
526 3k. red 20 15

1948.
772 **121** 15h. green 35 10
773 20h. brown 45 10
526a 1k. green 20 10
774 1k. lilac . . . . 1·10 10
527 1k.50 brown 20 10
528b 3k. red 30 10
775 3k. black 80 10
529 5k. blue 55 10
530 20k. violet (23 × 30 mm) . . 60 10
MS530a 66 × 99 mm. 30k. red (T **121**) . . . . 3·50 3·25
See also No. 538.

122 Czech and Russian Workers

123 Girl and Birds

1948. 5th Anniv of Russian Alliance.
531 **122** 3k. red 10 10

1948. 30th Anniv of First Czechoslovak Stamps. Imperf.
MS531a 70 × 90 mm. 10k. blue (T **2**) 2·00 1·75

1948. Child Welfare.
532 – 1k.50+1k. purple 30 10
533 – 2k.+1k. blue 15 10
534 **123** 3k.+1k. red 25 10
DESIGNS: 1k.50, Boy and birds; 2k. Mother and child.

124 V. I. Lenin

125 Pres. Gottwald Addressing Rally

1949. 25th Death Anniv of Lenin.
535 **124** 1k.50 purple 30 10
536 5k. blue 30 25

1949. 1st Anniv of Gottwald Government.
537 **125** 3k. brown 10 10

1949. As T **121** (23 × 30 mm) but inscr "UNOR 1948".
538 **121** 10k. green 35 25

126 P. O. Hviezdoslav

127 Mail Coach and Steam Train

1949. Poets.
539 **126** 50h. purple 10 10
540 – 80h. red 10 10
541 – 1k. green 10 10
542 – 2k. blue 30 10
543 – 4k. purple 30 10
544 – 8k. black 45 10
PORTRAITS: 80h. V. Vancura. 1k. J. Sverma. 2k. J. Fucik. 4k. J. Wolker. 8k. A. Jirasek.

1949. 75th Anniv of U.P.U.
545 **127** 3k. red . . . . 1·00 1·00
546 – 5k. blue 60 35
547 – 13k. green . . . . 1·60 40
DESIGNS: 5k. Mounted postman and mail van; 13k. Sailing ship and Douglas DC-2 airliner.

128 Girl Agricultural Worker

130 Industrial Worker

1949. 9th Meeting of Czechoslovak Communist Party.
548 **128** 1k.50 green 45 50
549 – 3k. red 25 25
550 **130** 5k. blue 45 50
DESIGN—HORIZ: 3k. Workers and flag.

131 F. Smetana and National Theatre, Prague

132 A. S. Pushkin

1949. 125th Birth Anniv of Smetana (composer).
551 **131** 1k.50 green 15 10
552 5k. blue 65 30

1949. 150th Birth Anniv of A. S. Pushkin (poet).
553 **132** 2k. green 25 25

133 F. Chopin and Warsaw Conservatoire

134 Globe and Ribbon

1949. Death Centenary of Chopin (composer).
554 **133** 3k. red 45 25
555 8k. purple 45 50

1949. 50th Sample Fair, Prague.
556 **134** 1k.50 purple 25 25
557 5k. blue 80 75

135 Zvolen Castle

1949.
558 **135** 10k. lake 60 10

1949. Air. Nos. 469/76 surch.
559 **95** 1k. on 1k.50 red 15 10
560 3k. on 5k.50 blue 25 10
561 6k. on 9k. purple 40 10
562 7k.50 on 16k. violet . . . 50 25
563 **96** 8k. on 10k. green 50 55
564 12k.50 on 20k. blue . . . 90 45
565 **94a** 15k. on 24k. red . . . . 2·25 75
566 30k. on 50k. blue . . . . 1·75 75

137 Mediaeval Miners

138 Modern Miner

1949. 700th Anniv of Czechoslovak Mining Industry and 150th Anniv of Miners' Laws.
567 **137** 1k.50 violet 50 40
568 **138** 3k. red . . . . 5·25 1·90
569 – 5k. blue . . . . 4·00 1·50
DESIGN—HORIZ: 5k. Miner with cutting machine.

139 Carpenters

140 Dove and Buildings

1949. 2nd T.U.C., Prague. Inscr 1949".
570 **139** 1k. green . . . . 3·00 1·25
571 – 2k. purple (Mechanic) . . 1·90 50

1949. Red Cross Fund. Inscr "CS CERVENY KRIZ".
572 **140** 1k.50h.+50h. red . . . . 3·50 1·60
573 – 3k.+1k. red . . . . . . 3·50 1·60
DESIGN—VERT: 3k. Dove and globe.

141 Mother and Child

142 Joseph Stalin

1949. Child Welfare Fund. Inscr "DETEM 1949".
574 **141** 1k.50+50h. grey . . . . . 3·25 1·10
575 – 3k.+1k. red . . . . . . 4·75 1·75
DESIGN: 3k. Father and child.

1949. 70th Birth Anniv of Joseph Stalin.
576 **142** 1k.50 green on buff . . . 75 40
577 – 3k. purple on buff . . . . 4·00 1·50
PORTRAIT: 3k. Stalin facing left.

143 Skier

144 Efficiency Badge

1950. Tatra Cup Ski Championship.
578 **143** 1k.50 blue . . . . 2·75 1·00
579 **144** 3k. red and buff . . . . . 2·75 1·00
580 **143** 5k. blue . . . . 1·90 85

145 V. Mayakovsky

1950. 20th Death Anniv of Mayakovsky (poet).
581 **145** 1k.50 purple . . . . . . 2·10 1 10
582 3k. red . . . . 1·75 80

146 Soviet Tank Driver and Hradcany, Prague

1950. 5th Anniv of Republic (1st issue).
583 **146** 1k.50 green 25 20
584 – 2k. purple 95 80
585 – 3k. red 20 10
586 – 5k. blue 40 20
DESIGNS: 2k. "Hero of Labour" medal; 3k. Workers and Town Hall; 5k. "The Kosice Programme" (part of text).

147 Factory and Workers

1950. 5th Anniv of Republic (2nd issue).
587 **147** 1k.50 green . . . . 1·40 75
588 – 2k. brown . . . . 1·75 55
589 – 3k. red 90 35
590 – 5k. blue 90 30
DESIGNS: 2k. Crane and Tatra Mts; 3k. Labourer and tractor; 5k. Three workers.

148 S. K. Neumann

1950. 75th Birth Anniv of S. K. Neumann (writer)
591 **148** 1k.50 blue 25 10
592 3k. purple . . . . 1·10 85

149 Bozena Nemcova

150 "Liberation of Colonial Nations"

1950. 130th Birth Anniv of Bozena Nemcova (authoress).
593 **149** 1k.50 blue . . . . 1·25 80
594 7k. purple 25 20

1950. 2nd International Students' World Congress, Prague. Inscr "II KONGRES MSS".
595 **150** 1k.50 green 15 10
596 – 2k. purple . . . . 1·50 1·25
597 – 3k. red 20 25
598 – 5k. blue 40 50
DESIGNS—HORIZ: 2k. Woman, globe and dove ("Fight for Peace"); 3k. Group of students ("Democratisation of Education"); 5k. Students and banner ("International Students, Solidarity").

151 Miner, Soldier and Farmer

152 Z. Fibich

1950. Army Day.
599 **151** 1k.50 blue 90 75
600 – 3k. red 25 35
DESIGN: 3k. Czechoslovak and Russian soldiers.

1950. Birth Centenary of Fibich (composer).
601 **152** 3k. red . . . . 1·40 1·40
602 8k. green 25 15

153 "Communications"

154 J. G. Tajovsky

1950. 1st Anniv of League of Postal, Telephone and Telegraph Employees.
603 **153** 1k.50 brown 25 15
604 3k. red 65 65

1950. 10th Death Anniv of J. Gregor Tajovsky (writer).
605 **154** 1k.50 brown 85 70
606 5k. blue 85 55

155 Reconstruction of Prague

1950. Philatelic Exhibition, Prague.
607 **155** 1k.50 blue 35 20
608 3k. red 60 55
MS608a 120 × 101 mm. No. 607 in imperf block of four . . . . . 27·00 20·00

156 Czech and Russian Workers

1950. Czechoslovak–Soviet Friendship.
609 **156** 1k.50 brown 55 25
610 5k. blue 75 50

157 Dove (after Picasso)

1951. Czechoslovak Peace Congress.
611 **157** 2k. blue . . . . 5·00 2·75
612 3k. red . . . . 3·00 1·60

158 Julius Fucik

159 Mechanical Hammer

1951. Peace Propaganda.
613 **158** 1k.50 grey 50 35
614 5k. blue . . . . 1·90 1·75

1951. Five Year Plan (heavy industry).
615 **159** 1k.50 black 10 10
616 – 3k. brown 15 10
617 **159** 4k. blue 65 50
DESIGN—HORIZ: 3k. Installing machinery.

160 Industrial Workers

161 Karlovy Vary

1951. International Women's Day.
618 **160** 1k.50 olive 25 10
619 – 3k. red . . . . 2·40 65
620 – 5k. blue 50 10
DESIGNS: 3k. Woman driving tractor; 5k. Korean woman and group.

1951. Air. Spas.
621 **161** 6k. green . . . . 2·25 75
622 – 10k. purple . . . . 2·25 95
623 – 15k. blue . . . . 5·50 75
624 – 20k. brown . . . . 7·00 2·25
DESIGNS—Ilyushin Il-12 airplane over: 10k. Piestany; 15k. Marianske Lazne; 20k. Silac.

162 Miners

163 Ploughing

1951. Mining Industry.
625 **162** 1k.50 black 80 60
626 3k. purple 10 15

1951. Agriculture.
627 **163** 1k.50 brown 50 65
628 – 2k. green (Woman and cows) . . . . 1·75 1·40

164 Tatra Mountains

165 Partisan and Soviet Soldier

1951. Recreation Centres. Inscr "ROH".
629 **164** 1k.50 green 20 10
630 – 2k. brown 90 70
631 – 3k. red 25 10
DESIGNS: 2k. Beskydy Mts; 3k. Krkonose Mts.

1951. 30th Anniv of Czechoslovak Communist Party. Inscr "30 LET" etc.
635 – 1k.50 grey 95 25
632 – 2k. brown 25 10
633 **165** 3k. red 30 10
636 – 5k. blue . . . . 1·90 90
634 – 8k. black 70 30
DESIGNS—HORIZ: 1k.50, 5k. Gottwald and Stalin; 8k. Marx, Engels, Lenin and Stalin. VERT: 2k. Factory militiaman.

167 Dvorak

168 Gymnast

1951. Prague Musical Festival.
637 **167** 1k. brown 25 10
638 – 1k.50 grey (Smetana) . . 1·25 55
639 **167** 2k. brown . . . . 1·25 60
640 – 3k. purple (Smetana) . . 25 15

1951. 9th Sokol Congress.
641 **168** 1k. green 55 20
642 – 1k.50 brown (Woman discus thrower) 55 25
643 – 3k. red (Footballers) . . . 1·25 25
644 – 5k. blue (Skier) . . . . . 3·25 1·25

1951. 10th Death Anniv of Bohumir Smeral. As T **154**, but portrait of Smeral.
645 1k.50 grey 45 40
646 3k. purple 45 15

170 Scene from "Fall of Berlin"

172 A. Jirasek

173 "Fables and Fates" (M. Ales)

1951. International Film Festival, Karlovy Vary. Inscr "SE SOVETSKYM FILMEM", etc.
647 **170** 80h. red . . . 35 25
648 – 1k.50 grey . . . 35 25
649 **170** 4k. blue . . . 1·10 75
DESIGN: 1k.50, Scene from "The Great Citizen".

1951. 30th Death Anniv of J. Hybes (politician). As T **154**, but portrait of Hybes.
650 1k.50 brown . . . 10 10
651 2k. red . . . 1·00 35

1951. Birth Centenary of Jirasek (author).
652 **172** 1k.50 black . . . 40 10
653 **173** 3k. red . . . 40 10
654 – 4k. black . . . 40 10
655 **172** 5k. blue . . . 1·90 1·10
DESIGN—As Type **173**: 4k. "The Region of Tabor" (M. Ales).

174 Miner and Pithead

176 Soldiers Parading

1951. Miner's Day.
656 **174** 1k.50 brown . . . 15 10
657 – 3k. red (miners drilling) . . . 15 10
658 **174** 5k. blue . . . 1·25 95

1951. Army Day. Inscr "DEN CS ARMADY 1951".
659 **176** 80h. brown . . . 25 20
660 – 1k. green . . . 25 25
661 – 1k.50 black . . . 40 25
662 – 3k. purple . . . 40 25
663 – 5k. blue . . . 1·60 60
DESIGNS—VERT: 1k. Gunner and field-gun; 1k.50, Pres. Gottwald; 3k. Tank driver and tank; 5k. Two pilots and aircraft.

178 Stalin and Gottwald

179 P. Jilemnicky

1951. Czechoslovak–Soviet Friendship.
664 **178** 1k.50 black . . . 10 10
665 – 3k. red . . . 15 10
666 **178** 4k. blue . . . 1·25 45
DESIGN ($23\frac{1}{2}\times31$ mm): 3k. Lenin, Stalin and Russian soldiers.

1951. 50th Birth Anniv of Jilemnicky (writer).
667 **179** 1k.50 purple . . . 20 15
668 2k. blue . . . 70 35

180 L. Zapotocky

181 J. Kollar

1952. Birth Centenary of Zapotocky (socialist pioneer).
669 **180** 1k.50 red . . . 10 15
670 4k. black . . . 1·00 35

1952. Death Centenary of Kollar (poet).
671 **181** 3k. red . . . 10 10
672 5k. blue . . . 1·00 50

182 Lenin Hall, Prague

183 Dr. E. Holub and Negro

1952. 40th Anniv of 6th All-Russian Party Conference.
673 **182** 1k.50 red . . . 10 25
674 5k. blue . . . 1·00 60

1952. 50th Death Anniv of Dr. Holub (explorer).
675 **183** 3k. red . . . 40 25
676 5k. blue . . . 2·00 1·40

184 Electric Welding

1952. Industrial Development.
677 **184** 1k.50 black . . . 35 15
678 – 2k. brown . . . 1·40 50
679 – 3k. red . . . 15 10
DESIGNS: 2k. Foundry; 3k. Chemical plant.

185 Factory-worker and Farm-girl

186 Young Workers

1952. International Women's Day.
680 **185** 1k.50 blue on cream . . . 1·00 40

1952. International Youth Week.
681 **186** 1k.50 blue . . . 10 10
682 – 2k. green . . . 15 10
683 **186** 3k. red . . . 1·60 65
DESIGN: 2k. Three heads and globe.

187 O. Sevcik

188 J. A. Komensky (Comenius)

1952. Birth Centenary of Sevcik (musician).
684 **187** 2k. brown . . . 70 45
685 3k. red . . . 15 15

1952. 360th Birth Anniv of Komensky (educationist).
686 **188** 1k.50 brown . . . 1·25 50
687 11k. blue . . . 25 10

189 Anti-fascist

190 Woman and Children

1952. "Fighters Against Fascism" Day.
688 **189** 1k.50 brown . . . 10 10
689 2k. blue . . . 1·00 50

1952. Child Welfare.
690 **190** 2k. purple on cream . . . 1·25 1·10
691 3k. red on cream . . . 15 15

191 Combine Harvester

1952. Agriculture Day.
692 **191** 1k.50 blue . . . 1·90 1·10
693 2k. brown . . . 25 25
694 – 3k. red (Combine drill) . . . 25 25

192 May Day Parade

1952. Labour Day.
695 **192** 3k. red . . . 30 35
696 4k. brown . . . 1·40 80

193 Russian Tank and Crowd

1952. 7th Anniv of Liberation.
697 **193** 1k.50 red . . . 60 50
698 5k. blue . . . 1·75 1·40

194 Boy Pioneer and Children

195 J. V. Myslbek

1952. International Children's Day.
699 **194** 1k.50 brown . . . 10 10
700 2k. green . . . 1·40 70
701 – 3k. red (Pioneers and teacher) . . . 15 10

1952. 30th Death Anniv of Myslbek (sculptor).
702 **195** 1k.50 brown . . . 10 10
703 2k. brown . . . 1·10 1·00
704 – 8k. green . . . 15 10
DESIGN: 8k. "Music" (statue).

196 Beethoven

197 "Rebirth of Lidice"

1952. International Music Festival, Prague. No. 706 inscr "PRAZSKE JARO 1952", etc.
705 **196** 1k.50 brown . . . 30 25
706 – 3k. lake . . . 30 25
707 **196** 5k. blue . . . 1·60 90
DESIGN—HORIZ: 3k. The House of Artists.

1952. 10th Anniv of Destruction of Lidice.
708 **197** 1k.50 black . . . 10 10
709 5k. blue . . . 90 55

198 Jan Hus

199 Bethlehem Chapel, Prague

1952. Renovation of Bethlehem Chapel and 550th Anniv of Installation of Hus as Preacher.
710 **198** 1k.50 brown . . . 10 10
711 **199** 3k. brown . . . 10 10
712 **198** 5k. black . . . 1·10 75

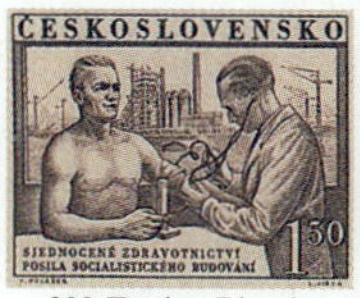

200 Testing Blood-pressure

201 Running

1952. National Health Service.
713 **200** 1k.50 brown . . . 25 80
714 – 2k. violet . . . 30 10
715 **200** 3k. red . . . 70 10
DESIGN—HORIZ: 2k. Doctor examining baby.

1952. Physical Culture Propaganda.
716 **201** 1k.50 brown . . . 2·00 35
717 – 2k. green (Canoeing) . . . 50 85
718 – 3k. brown (Cycling) . . . 3·25 45
719 – 4k. blue (Ice hockey) . . . 15 2·25

202 F. L. Celakovsky

1952. Death Centenary of Celakovsky (poet).
720 **202** 1k.50 sepia . . . 1·60 10
721 2k. green . . . 40 85

203 M. Ales

204 Mining in 17th Century

1952. Birth Centenary of Mikulas Ales (painter) (1st issue).
722 **203** 1k.50 green . . . 2·25 20
723 6k. brown . . . 1·25 1·75
See also Nos. 737/8.

1952. Miner's Day.
724 **204** 1k. brown . . . 10 70
725 – 1k.50 blue . . . 10 1·00
726 – 2k. black . . . 10 10
727 – 3k. brown . . . 15 10
DESIGNS: 1k.50, Mining machinery; 2k. Petr Bezruc Mine, Ostrava; 3k. Mechanical excavator.

205 Jan Zizka

206 "Fraternization" (after Pokorny)

1952. Army Day.
728 **205** 1k.50 red . . . 15 10
729 **206** 2k. brown . . . 15 10
730 – 3k. red . . . 15 10
731 **205** 4k. black . . . 1·75 70
DESIGNS: 3k. Soldiers marching with flag.

207 R. Danube, Bratislava

1952. National Philatelic Exhibition, Bratislava.
732 **207** 1k.50 brown . . . 10 10
MS732a 100 × 75 mm. 2k. red (Partisan Memorial); 3k. blue (Soviet Army Memorial) . . . 95·00 26·00

208 Lenin, Stalin and Revolutionaries

1952. 35th Anniv of Russian Revolution.
733 **208** 2k. brown . . . 1·25 80
734 3k. red . . . 10 10

209 Nurses and Red Cross Flag

211 Flags

210 Matej Louda z Chlumu (Hussite Warrior)

1952. 1st Czechoslovak Red Cross Conference.

735	**209**	2k. brown	1·25	55
736		3k. red	15	10

1952. Birth Centenary of Mikulas Ales (2nd issue).

737	**210**	2k. brown	25	10
738	–	3k. black	65	10

DESIGN: 3k. "Trutnov" (warrior fighting dragon).

1952. Peace Congress, Vienna.

739	**211**	3k. red	20	10
740		4k. blue	1·40	70

212 "Dove of Peace" (after Picasso)

213 Smetana Museum, Prague

1953. 2nd Czechoslovak Peace Congress, Prague.

741	**212**	1k.50 sepia	10	10
742	–	4k. blue	10	35

DESIGN: 4k. Workman, woman and child (after Lev Haas).

1953. 75th Birth Anniv of Prof. Z. Nejedly (museum founder).

743	**213**	1k.50 brown	10	10
744	–	4k. black	1·40	65

DESIGN: 4k. Jirasek Museum, Prague.

214 Marching Soldiers

215 M. Kukucin

1953. 5th Anniv of Communist Govt.

745	**214**	1k.50 blue	15	10
746	–	3k. red	15	10
747	–	8k. brown	2·00	80

DESIGNS—VERT: 3k. Pres. Gottwald addressing meeting. HORIZ: 8k. Stalin, Gottwald and crowd with banners.

1953. Czech Writers and Poets.

748	**215**	1k. grey	10	10
749	–	1k.50 brown	10	10
750	–	2k. lake	10	10
751	–	3k. brown	50	40
752	–	5k. blue	1·90	75

PORTRAITS—VERT: 1k.50, J. Vrchlicky. 2k. E. J. Erben. 3k. V. M. Kramerius. 5k. J. Dobrovsky.

216 Torch and Open Book

217 Woman Revolutionary

1953. 10th Death Anniv of Vaclavek (writer).

753	**216**	1k. brown	1·50	50
754	–	3k. brown (Vaclavek)	15	10

1953. International Women's Day.

755	–	1k.50 blue	15	10
756	**217**	2k. red	1·00	50

DESIGN—VERT: 1k.50, Mother and baby.

218 Stalin

219 Pres. Gottwald

1953. Death of Stalin.

757	**218**	1k.50 black	35	20

1953. Death of President Gottwald.

758	**219**	1k.50 black	20	10
759		3k. black	20	10
MS759a		67 × 100 mm. 5k. black (T **219**)	2·75	2·25

220 Pecka, Zapotocky and Hybes

1953. 75th Anniv of 1st Czech Social Democratic Party Congress.

760	**220**	2k. brown	25	10

221 Cyclists

1953. 6th International Cycle Race.

761	**221**	3k. blue	60	30

222 1890 May Day Medal

223 Marching Crowds

1953. Labour Day.

762	**222**	1k. brown	1·75	85
763	–	1k.50 blue	10	10
764	**223**	3k. red	20	10
765	–	8k. green	25	10

DESIGNS—As Type **222**: 1k.50, Lenin and Stalin; 8k. Marx and Engels.

224 Hydro-electric Barrage

225 Seed-drills

1953.

766	**224**	1k.50 green	95	40
767	–	2k. blue	20	10
768	–	3k. brown	20	10

DESIGNS—VERT: 2k. Welder and blast furnaces, Kuncice, HORIZ: 3k. Gottwald Foundry, Kuncice.

1953.

769	**225**	1k.50 brown	20	10
770	–	7k. green (Combine harvester)	1·60	1·10

226 President Zapotocky

229

1953.

776	**226**	30h. blue	60	10
780	**229**	30h. blue	55	10
777	**226**	60h. red	30	10
781	**229**	60h. pink	1·10	10

227 J. Slavik

228 L. Janacek

1953. Prague Music Festival. (a) 120th Death Anniv of Slavik (violinist).

778	**227**	75h. blue	60	10

(b) 25th Death Anniv of Janacek (composer).

779	**228**	1k.60 brown	1·25	10

230 Charles Bridge, Prague

1953.

782a	**230**	5k. grey	4·50	10

231 J. Fucik

232 Book, Carnation and Laurels

1953. 10th Death Anniv of Julius Fucik (writer).

783	**231**	40h. black	20	10
784	**232**	60h. mauve	50	25

233 Miner and Banner

234 Volley ball

1953. Miner's Day.

785	**233**	30h. black	20	10
786	–	60h. purple	1·25	50

DESIGN: 60h. Miners and colliery shafthead.

1953. Sports.

787	**234**	30h. red	2·10	1·40
788	–	40h. purple	3·75	70
789	–	60h. purple	3·75	70

DESIGNS—HORIZ: 40h. Motor cycling. VERT: 60h. Throwing the javelin.

235 Hussite Warrior

236 "Friendship" (after T. Bartfay)

1953. Army Day.

790	**235**	30h. sepia	25	10
791	–	60h. red	30	20
792	–	1k. red	1·75	1·25

DESIGNS: 60h. Soldier presenting arms; 1k. Czechoslovak Red Army soldiers.

1953. Czechoslovak–Korean Friendship.

793	**236**	30h. sepia	2·50	1·10

237 Hradcany, Prague and Kremlin, Moscow

1953. Czechoslovak–Soviet Friendship: Inscr "MESIC CESKOSLOVENSKO SOVETSKEHO", etc.

794	**237**	30h. black	1·00	55
795	–	60h. brown	1·25	75
796	–	1k.20 blue	2·50	1·40

DESIGNS: 60h. Lomonosov University, Moscow; 1k.20, "Stalingrad" tug, Lenin Ship-Canal.

238 Ema Destinnova (Opera Singer)

239 National Theatre, Prague

1953. 70th Anniv of National Theatre, Prague.

797	**238**	30h. black	95	80
798	**239**	60h. brown	25	10
799	–	2k. sepia	2·25	80

PORTRAIT—As Type **238**: 2k. E. Vojan (actor).

240 J. Manes (painter)

241 Vaclav Hollar (etcher)

1953.

800	**240**	60h. lake	25	10
801		1k.20 blue	1·50	95

1953. Inscr "1607 1677".

802	**241**	30h. black	25	10
803	–	1k.20 black	1·25	55

PORTRAIT: 1k.20, Hollar and engraving tools.

242 Leo Tolstoy

243 Class 498.0 Steam Locomotive

1953. 125th Birth Anniv of Tolstoy (writer).

804	**242**	60h. green	15	10
805		1k. brown	1·40	40

1953.

806	**243**	60h. blue and brown	65	25
807	–	1k. blue and brown	1·60	90

DESIGN: 1k. Ilyushin Il-12 (30th anniv of Czech airmail services).

244 Lenin (after J. Lauda)

245 Lenin Museum, Prague

1954. 30th Death Anniv of Lenin.

808	**244**	30h. sepia	45	10
809	**245**	1k.40 brown	1·75	1·25

246 Gottwald Speaking

247 Gottwald Mausoleum, Prague

248 Gottwald and Stalin (after relief by O. Spaniel)

1954. 25th Anniv of 5th Czechoslovak Communist Party Congress. Inscr "1929 1954".
810 **246** 60h. brown 30 10
811 – 2k.40 lake . . . . 3·75 1·40
DESIGN: 2k.40, Revolutionary and flag.
See also No. **MS**2917.

1954. 1st Anniv of Deaths of Stalin and Gottwald.
812 **247** 30h. sepia 25 20
813 **248** 60h. blue 30 10
814 – 1k.20h. lake . . . . . . 1·75 85
DESIGN—HORIZ: As Type **247**: 1k.20h. Lenin-Stalin Mausoleum, Moscow.

249 Girl and Sheaf of Corn

250 Athletics

1954.
815 – 15h. green 25 10
816 – 20h. lilac 30 10
817 – 40h. brown 45 10
818 – 45h. blue 45 10
819 – 50h. green 30 10
820 – 75h. blue 30 10
821 – 80h. brown 30 10
822 **249** 1k. green 65 10
823 – 1k.20 blue 30 10
824 – 1k.60 black . . . . . . 2·25 10
825 – 2k. brown . . . . 1·90 10
826 – 2k.40 blue . . . . 2·25 10
827 – 3k. red . . . . 1·50 10
DESIGNS: 15h. Labourer; 20h. Nurse; 40h. Postwoman; 45h. Foundry worker; 50h. Soldier; 75h. Metal worker; 80h. Mill girl; 1k.20, Scientist; 1k.60, Miner; 2k. Doctor and baby; 2k.40 Engine-driver; 3k. Chemist.

1954. Sports.
828 **250** 30h. sepia . . . . 2·25 85
829 – 80h. green . . . . 6·50 3·50
830 – 1k. blue . . . . 1·40 60
DESIGNS—HORIZ: 80h. Hiking. VERT: 1k. Girl diving.

251 Dvorak

252 Prokop Divis (physicist)

1954. Czechoslovak Musicians. Inscr as in T **251**.
831 **251** 30h. brown . . . . 1·00 25
832 – 40h. red (Janacek) . . . . 1·40 25
833 – 60h. blue (Smetana) . . . 80 15

1954. Bicentenary of Invention of Lightning Conductor by Divis.
834 **252** 30h. black 25 10
835 75h. brown . . . . 1·25 40

253 Partisan

254 A. P. Chekhov

1954. 10th Anniv of Slovak National Uprising. Inscr "1944–29. 8–1954".
836 **253** 30h. red 20 10
837 – 1k.20 bl (Woman partisan) . . . . . . 1·10 90

1954. 50th Death Anniv of Chekhov (playwright).
838 **254** 30h. green 20 10
839 45h. brown . . . . 1·25 50

255 Soldiers in Battle

257 J. Neruda

256 Farm Workers in Cornfield

1954. Army Day. 2k. inscr "ARMADY 1954".
840 **255** 60h. green 20 10
841 – 2k. brown . . . . 1·25 1·10
DESIGN: 2k. Soldier carrying girl.

1954. Czechoslovak–Russian Friendship.
842 **256** 30h. brown 15 10
843 – 60h. blue 25 10
844 – 2k. salmon . . . . 1·75 1·40
DESIGNS: 60h. Factory workers and machinery; 2k. Group of girl folk dancers.

1954. Czechoslovak Poets.
845 **257** 30h. blue 50 15
846 – 60h. red . . . . 1·50 30
847 – 1k.60 purple 40 15
PORTRAITS—VERT: 60h. J. Jesensky. 1k.60 J. Wolker.

258 Ceske Budejovice

1954. Czechoslovak Architecture. Background in buff.
848 – 30h. black (Telc) 90 10
849 – 60h. brown (Levoca) . . . 45 10
850 **258** 3k. blue . . . . 1·75 1·40

259 President Zapotocky

260 "Spirit of the Games"

1954. 70th Birthday of Zapotocky.
851 **259** 30h. sepia 45 10
852 60h. blue 20 10
MS852a 65 × 100 mm 2k. red (as T **259**) . . . . 8·00 4·75
See also Nos. 1006/7.

1955. 1st National Spartacist Games (1st issue). Inscr as in T **260**.
853 **260** 30h. red . . . . 1·50 40
854 – 45h. black & blue (Skier) 4·25 30
See also Nos. 880/2.

261 University Building

1955. 35th Anniv of Comenius University, Bratislava. Inscr as in T **261**.
855 **261** 60h. green 30 10
856 – 75h. brown . . . . 1·75 55
DESIGN: 75h. Comenius Medal (after O. Spaniel).

262 Cesky Krumlov

1955. Air.
857 **262** 80h. green . . . . 1·10 20
858 – 1k.55 sepia . . . . 1·50 35
859 – 2k.35 blue . . . . 1·50 15
860 – 2k.75 purple . . . . . . 2·75 30
861 – 10k. blue . . . . 5·25 1·25
DESIGNS: 1k.55, Olomouc; 2k.35, Banska Bystrica; 2k.75, Bratislava; 10k. Prague.

263 Skoda Motor Car

264 Russian Tank-driver

1955. Czechoslovak Industries.
862 **263** 45h. green 70 50
863 – 60h. blue 15 10
864 – 75h. black 25 10
DESIGNS: 60h. Shuttleless jet loom; 75h. Skoda Machine-tool.

1955. 10th Anniv of Liberation. Inscr as in T **264**.
865 – 30h. blue 25 10
866 **264** 35h. brown . . . . 1·25 55
867 – 60h. red 25 10
868 – 60h. black 25 10
DESIGNS—VERT: 30h. Girl and Russian soldier; No. 867, Children and Russian soldier. HORIZ: No. 868, Stalin Monument, Prague.

265 Agricultural Workers

266 "Music and Spring"

1955. 3rd Trades' Union Congress. Inscr as in T **265**.
869 – 30h. blue 15 10
870 **265** 45h. green . . . . 1·25 55
DESIGN: 30h. Foundry worker.

1955. International Music Festival, Prague. Inscr as in T **266**.
871 **266** 30h. indigo and blue . . . 35 10
872 – 1k. blue and pink . . . . 1·25 1·25
DESIGN: 1k. "Music" playing a lyre.

267 A. S. Popov (60th anniv of radio discoveries)

268 Folk Dancers

1955. Cultural Anniversaries. Portraits.
873 – 20h. brown 20 10
874 – 30h. black 20 10
875 – 40h. green 70 15
876 – 60h. black 45 10
877 **267** 75h. purple . . . . 1·40 50
878 – 1k.40 black on yellow . . 35 25
879 – 1k.60 blue 35 20
PORTRAITS: 20h. Jakub Arbes (writer). 30h. Jan Stursa (sculptor). 40h. Elena Marothy-Soltesova (writer). 60h. Josef V. Sladek (poet). 1k.40 Jan Holly (poet). 1k.60 Pavel J. Safarik (philologist).

1955. 1st National Spartacist Games (2nd issue). Inscr as in T **268**.
880 – 20h. blue 85 40
881 **268** 60h. green 25 10
882 – 1k.60 red 90 25
DESIGNS: 20h. Girl athlete; 1k.60, Male athlete.

269 "Friendship"

270 Ocova Woman, Slovakia

1955. 5th World Youth Festival, Warsaw.
883 **269** 60h. blue 35 10

1955. National Costumes (1st series).
884 **270** 60h. sepia, rose and red 10·00 7·00
885 – 75h. sepia, orange & lake 5·75 5·00
886 – 1k.60 sepia, blue & orge 10·00 5·50
887 – 2k. sepia, yellow and red 13·00 5·50
DESIGNS: 75h. Detva man, Slovakia; 1k.60, Chodsko man, Bohemia; 2k. Hana woman, Moravia.
See also Nos. 952/5 and 1008/11.

271 Swallowtail

1955. Animals and Insects.
888 – 20h. black and blue . . . 55 10
889 – 30h. brown and red . . . 55 10
890 – 35h. brown and buff . . . 1·10 15
891 **271** 1k.40 black and yellow . . 5·25 1·90
892 – 1k.50 black and green . . 55 15
DESIGNS: 20h. Common carp; 30h. Stag beetle; 35h. Grey partridge; 1k.50, Brown hare.

272 Tabor

1955. Towns of Southern Bohemia.
893 **272** 30h. purple 20 10
894 – 45h. red 75 55
895 – 60h. green 20 10
TOWNS: 45h. Prachatice; 60h. Jindrichuv Hradec.

273 Motor Cyclists and Trophy

273a Round Chapel

1955. 30th Int Motor Cycle Six-Day Trial.
896 **273** 60h. purple . . . . 2·40 25

1955. Prague International Philatelic Exhibition. Sheets 145 × 111 mm.
MS896a 30h. black (T **273a**); 45h. black (Brick tower); 60h. lake (fountain); 75h. lake (Winter Palace); 1k.60 black (Hradcany, 50 × 31 mm) . . . . 27·00 27·00
MS896b As above but imperf . . 65·00 65·00

274 Soldier and Family

275 Hans Andersen

1955. Army Day. Inscr as in T **274**.
897 **274** 30h. brown 25 10
898 – 60h. grn (Tank attack) . . 1·75 1·25

1955. Famous Writers. Vert portraits.
899 **275** 30h. red 15 10
900 – 40h. blue (Schiller) . . . 2·10 80
901 – 60h. purple (Mickiewicz) 25 10
902 – 75h. blk (Walt Whitman) 50 10

276 Railway Viaduct

1955. Building Progress. Inscr "STAVBA SOCIALISMU".
903 **276** 20h. green 30 25
904 – 30h. brown 30 10
905 – 60h. blue 30 10
906 – 1k.60 red 55 10
DESIGNS: 30h. Train crossing viaduct; 60k. Train approaching tunnel; 1k.60, Housing project, Ostrava.

277 "Electricity"

278 Karlovy Vary

1956. Five Year Plan. Inscr "1956–1960".
907 **277** 5h. brown 25 10
908 – 10h. black 25 10
909 – 25h. red 25 10
910 – 30h. green 25 10
911 – 60h. blue 35 10
DESIGNS—HORIZ: 10h. "Mining"; 25h. "Building"; 30h. "Agriculture"; 60h. "Industry".

1956. Czechoslovak Spas (1st series).
912 **278** 30h. green . . . . 1·40 25
913 – 45h. brown . . . . 1·25 35
914 – 75h. purple . . . . 6·25 3·50
915 – 1k.20 blue 90 15
SPAS: 45h. Marianske Lazne; 75h. Piestany; 1k.20, Vysne Ruzbachy, Tatra Mountains.

279 Jewellery

280 "We serve our People" (after J. Cumpelik)

1956. Czechoslovak Products.
916 **279** 30h. green 25 10
917 – 45h. blue (Glassware) . . 4·75 2·75
918 – 60h. purple (Ceramics) . . 1·00 10
919 – 75h. black (Textiles) . . . 25 10

1956. Defence Exhibition.
920 **280** 30h. brown 20 10
921 – 60h. red 20 10
922 – 1k. blue . . . . 3·25 3·25
DESIGNS: 60h. Liberation Monument, Berlin; 1k. "Tank Soldier with Standard" (after T. Schor).

281 Cyclists

282 Discus Thrower, Hurdler and Runner

1956. Sports Events of 1956.
923 **281** 30h. green and blue . . . 2·75 20
924 – 45h. blue and red . . . . 1·10 20
925 – 60h. blue and buff . . . . 1·50 45
926 **282** 75h. brown and yellow . . 1·00 20
927 – 80h. purple & lavender . . 1·00 20
928 **282** 1k.20 green & orange . . 95 35
DESIGNS—As Type **281**. VERT: 30h. T **281** (9th International Cycle Race); 45h. Basketball players (5th European Women's Basketball Championship, Prague). HORIZ: 60h. Horsemen jumping (Pardubice Steeplechase); 80h. Runners (International Marathon, Kosice). T **282**: 75h., 1k.20, (16th Olympic Games, Melbourne).

283 Mozart

284

1956. Bicentenary of Birth of Mozart and Prague Music Festival. Centres in black.
929 **283** 30h. yellow . . . . 1·00 70
930 – 45h. green . . . . 14·50 9·50
931 – 60h. purple 55 10
932 – 1k. salmon . . . . 1·60 45
933 – 1k.40 blue . . . . 2·75 90
934 – 1k.60 lemon . . . . . . 1·00 15
DESIGNS: 45h. J. Myslivecek; 60h. J. Benda; 1k. "Bertramka" (Mozart's villa); 1k.40, Mr. and Mrs. Dushek; 1k.60, Nostic Theatre.

1956. 1st National Meeting of Home Guard.
935 **284** 60h. blue 90 20

285 J. K. Tyl

286 Naval Guard

1956. Czech Writers (1st issue).
936 – 20h. purple (Stur) 70 10
937 – 30h. blue (Sramek) . . . 35 10
938 **285** 60h. black 25 10
939 – 1k.40 pur (Borovsky) . . 4·50 2·40
See also Nos. 956/9.

1956. Frontier Guards' Day.
940 **286** 30h. blue . . . . 1·10 40
941 – 60h. green 15 10
DESIGN: 60h. Military guard and watchdog.

287 Picking Grapes

1956. National Products.
942 **287** 30h. lake 25 10
943 – 35h. green 30 25
944 – 80h. blue 60 15
945 – 95h. brown . . . . 1·50 1·60
DESIGNS—VERT: 35h. Picking hops. HORIZ: 80h. Fishing; 95h. Logging.

288 "Kladno", 1855

1956. European Freight Services Timetable Conference. Railway engines.
946 – 10h. brown . . . . 1·25 10
947 **288** 30h. black 75 10
948 – 40h. green . . . . 3·50 15
949 – 45h. purple . . . . 19·00 9·50
950 – 60h. blue 75 10
951 – 1k. blue . . . . 1·25 15
DESIGNS—VERT: 10h. "Zbraslav", 1846. HORIZ: 40h. Class 534, 1945; 45h. Class 556.0, 1952; 60h. Class 477.0, 1955; 1k. Class E499.0 electric locomotive, 1954.

1956. National Costumes (2nd series). As T **270**.
952 30h. sepia, red and blue . . . 2·25 70
953 1k.20 sepia, blue and red . . 2·25 15
954 1k.40 brown, yellow & red 4·00 1·90
955 1k.60 sepia, green & red . . 2·40 30
DESIGNS: 30h. Slovacko woman; 1k.20, Blata woman; 1k.40, Cicmany woman, 1k.60, Novohradsko woman.

1957. Czech Writers (2nd issue). As T **285**. On buff paper.
956 15h. brown (Olbracht) . . . 30 10
957 20h. green (Toman) 30 10
958 30h. sepia (Salda) 30 10
959 1k.60 blue (Vansova) 55 10

289 Forestry Academy, Banska Stiavnica

1957. Towns and Monuments Anniversaries.
960 – 30h. blue 20 10
961 **289** 30h. purple 20 10
962 – 60h. red 40 10
963 – 60h. brown 40 10
964 – 60h. green 30 10
965 – 1k.25 black . . . . 3·50 1·40
DESIGNS: No. 960, Kolin; 962, Uherske Hradiste; 963, Charles Bridge, Prague; 964, Karlstejn Castle; 965, Moravska Trebova.

290 Girl Harvester

1957. 3rd Collective Farming Agricultural Congress, Prague.
966 **290** 30h. turquoise 70 10

291 Komensky's Mausoleum

292 J. A. Komensky (Comenius)

1957. 300th Anniv of Publication of Komensky's "Opera Didactica Omnia".
967 **291** 30h. brown 40 10
968 – 40h. green 40 10
969 **292** 60h. brown . . . . 1·90 1·10
970 – 60h. red 55 10
DESIGNS: As Type **291**: 40h. Komensky at work; 1k. Illustration from "Opera Didactica Omnia".

293 Racing Cyclists

1957. Sports Events of 1957.
971 **293** 30h. purple and blue . . . 35 10
972 60h. green and bistre . . 1·60 1·40
973 – 60h. violet and brown . . 35 10
974 – 60h. purple and brown . . 35 10
975 – 60h. black and green . . 35 10
976 – 60h. black and blue . . 1·00 10
DESIGNS—HORIZ: Nos. 971/2 (10th Int Cycle Race); 973, Rescue squad (Mountain Rescue Service); 975, Archer (World Archery Championships, Prague). VERT: 974, Boxers (European Boxing Championships, Prague); 976, Motor Cyclists (32nd Int Motor Cycle Six-Day Trial).

294 J. B. Foerster

1957. Int Music Festival Jubilee. Musicians.
977 – 60h. violet (Stamic) . . . 25 10
978 – 60h. black (Laub) 25 10
979 – 60h. blue (Ondricek) . . . 25 10
980 **294** 60h. sepia 25 10
981 – 60h. brown (Novak) . . . 90 10
982 – 60h. turquoise (Suk) . . . 25 10

295 J. Bozek (founder)

296 Young Collector Blowing Posthorn

1957. 250th Anniv of Polytechnic Engineering Schools, Prague.
983 **295** 30h. black 15 10
984 – 60h. brown 35 10
985 – 1k. purple 35 15
986 – 1k.40 violet 50 15
DESIGNS—VERT: 60h. F. J. Gerstner; 1k. R. Skuhersky. HORIZ: 1k.40, Polytechnic Engineering Schools Building, Prague.

1957. Junior Philatelic Exn, Pardubice.
987 **296** 30h. orange and green . . 50 10
988 – 60h. blue and brown . . . 2·10 1·25
DESIGN: 60h. Girl sending letter by pigeon.

297 "Rose of Friendship and Peace"

298 Karel Klic and Printing Press

1957. 15th Anniv of Destruction of Lidice.
989 – 30h. black 35 10
990 **297** 60h. red and black . . . 1·00 35
DESIGN: 30h. Veiled woman.

1957. Czech Inventors.
991 **298** 30h. black 15 10
992 – 60h. blue 35 10
DESIGN: 60h. Joseph Ressel and propeller.

299 Chamois

300 Marycka Magdonova

1957. Tatra National Park.
993 **299** 20h. black and green . . 65 45
994 – 30h. brown and blue . . 65 10
995 – 40h. blue and brown . . . 1·25 30
996 – 60h. green and yellow . . 50 10
997 – 1k.25 black and ochre . . 1·25 1·25
DESIGNS—VERT: 30h. Brown bear. HORIZ: 40h. Gentian; 60h. Edelweiss; 1k.25 (49 × 29 mm), Tatra Mountains.

1957. 90th Birthday of Petr Bezruc (poet).
998 **300** 60h. black and red . . . 50 10

301 Worker with Banner

303 Television Tower and Aerials

302 Tupolev Tu-104A and Paris–Prague–Moscow Route

1957. 4th World T.U.C., Leipzig.
999 **301** 75h. red 50 15

1957. Air. Opening of Czechoslovak Airlines.
1000 **302** 75h. blue and red . . . 80 10
1001 – 2k.35 blue and yellow . . 95 10
DESIGN: 2k.35, "Prague–Cairo–Beirut–Damascus".

1957. Television Development.
1002 **303** 40h. blue and red . . . 25 10
1003 – 60h. brown and green . . 30 10
DESIGN: 60h. Family watching television.

304 Youth, Globe and Lenin

1957. 40th Anniv of Russian Revolution.
1004 **304** 30h. red 20 10
1005 – 60h. blue 35 10
DESIGN: 60h. Lenin, refinery and Russian emblem.

1957. Death of President Zapotocky. As T **259** but dated "19 XII 1884–13 XI 1957".
1006 30h. black 10 10
1007 60h. black 25 10
MS1007a 70 × 100 mm. 2k. black (as 1006). Imperf . . . . 2·40 2·00

1957. National Costumes (3rd series). As T **270**.
1008 45h. sepia, red and blue . . 2·75 1·25
1009 75h. sepia, red and green . . 1·90 80
1010 1k.25 sepia, red & yellow . . 2·75 65
1011 1k.95 sepia, blue and red . . 3·25 2·10
DESIGNS—VERT: 45h. Pilsen woman; 75h. Slovacko man; 1k.25, Hana woman; 1k.95, Tesin woman.

305 Artificial Satellite ("Sputnik 2")

306 Figure Skating (European Championships, Bratislava)

1957. International Geophysical Year. Showing globe and dated "1957–1958".
1012 – 30h. brown and yellow 1·40 45
1013 – 45h. brown and blue . . 30 25
1014 **305** 75h. red and blue . . . 2·00 65
DESIGNS—HORIZ: 30h. Radio-telescope and observatory. VERT: 45h. Lomnicky Stit meteorological station.

1958. Sports Events of 1958.
1015 **306** 30h. purple 90 20
1016 – 40h. blue 30 20
1017 – 60h. brown 30 10
1018 – 80h. violet . . . . . 1·40 65
1019 – 1k.60 green 50 15
EVENTS: 40h. Canoeing (World Canoeing Championships, Prague); 60h. Volleyball (European Volleyball Championships, Prague); 80h. Parachuting (4th World Parachute-jumping Championship, Bratislava); 1k.60, Football (World Cup Football Championship, Stockholm).

307 Litomysl Castle (birthplace of Nejedly)

309 Jewellery

308 Soldiers guarding Shrine of "Victorious February"

1958. 80th Birthday of Nejedly (musician).
1020 **307** 30h. green 20 10
1021 – 60h. brown 20 10
DESIGN—HORIZ: 60h. Bethlehem Chapel, Prague.

1958. 10th Anniv of Communist Govt.
1022 – 30h. blue and yellow . . 25 10
1023 **308** 60h. brown and red . . 25 10
1024 – 1k.60 green and orange 35 10
DESIGNS—VERT: 30h. Giant mine-excavator. HORIZ: 1k.60, Combine-harvester.

1958. Brussels International Exhibition. Inscr "Bruxelles 1958".
1025 **309** 30h. red and blue . . . 25 10
1026 – 45h. red and lilac . . . 60 10
1027 – 60h. violet and green . . 25 10
1028 – 75h. blue and orange . . 1·10 80
1029 – 1k.20 green and red . . 60 10
1030 – 1k.95 brown and blue . . 70 15
DESIGNS—VERT: 45h. Toy dolls; 60h. Draperies; 75h. Kaplan turbine; 1k.20, Glassware. HORIZ: (48½ × 29½ mm), 1k.95, Czech pavilion.

310 George of Podebrady and his Seal

1958. National Exhibition of Archive Documents. Inscr as in T **310**.
1031 **310** 30h. red 35 10
1032 – 60h. violet 35 10
DESIGN: 60h. Prague, 1628 (from engraving).

311 Hammer and Sickle

1958. 11th Czech Communist Party Congress and 15th Anniv of Czech–Soviet Friendship Treaty. 45h. inscr as in T **311** and 60h. inscr "15. VYROCI UZAVRENI".
1033 **311** 30h. red 20 10
1034 – 45h. green 20 10
1035 – 60h. blue 20 10
DESIGNS: 45h. Map of Czechoslovakia, with hammer and sickle; 60h. Atomic reactor, Rez (near Prague).

312 "Towards the Stars" (after sculpture by G. Postnikov)

313 Pres. Novotny

1958. Cultural and Political Events. 45h. inscr "IV. KONGRES MEZINARODNI", etc, and 60h. inscr "I. SVETOVA ODBOROVA", etc.
1036 **312** 30h. red 70 40
1037 – 45h. purple 20 25
1038 – 60h. blue 20 10
DESIGNS—VERT: 45h. Three women of different races and globe (4th Int Democratic Women's Federation Congress, Vienna). HORIZ: 60h. Boy and girl with globes (1st World T.U. Conference of Working Youth, Prague). Type **312** represents the Society for the Dissemination of Cultural and Political Knowledge.

1958.
1039 **313** 30h. violet 45 10
1039a 30h. purple . . . . . 3·50 1·00
1040 60h. red 45 10

314 Telephone Operator

316 "The Poet and the Muse" (after Max Svabinsky)

315 Karlovy Vary (600th Anniv)

1958. Communist Postal Conference, Prague. Inscr as in T **314**.
1041 **314** 30h. sepia and brown . . 30 10
1042 – 45h. black and green . . 30 30
DESIGN: 45h. Aerial mast.

1958. Czech Spas (2nd series).
1043 **315** 30h. lake 10 10
1044 – 40h. brown 10 10
1045 – 60h. green 15 10
1046 – 80h. sepia 30 10
1047 – 1k.20 blue 45 15
1048 – 1k.60 violet . . . . . 1·10 65
SPAS: 40h. Podebrady; 60h. Marianske Lazne (150th Anniv); 80h. Luhacovice; 1k.20, Strbske Pleso; 1k.60, Trencianske.

1958. 85th Birthday of Dr. Max Svabinsky (artist).
1049 **316** 1k.60 black . . . . . . 3·25 80

317 S. Cech

319 Parasol Mushroom

318 Children's Hospital, Brno

1958. Writers' Anniversaries.
1050 – 30h. red (Julius Fucik) 25 10
1051 – 45h. violet (Gustav K. Zechenter) 95 45
1052 – 60h. blue (Karel Capek) 15 10
1053 **317** 1k.40 black 50 10

1958. National Stamp Exn, Brno. Inscr as in T **318**.
1054 **318** 30h. violet 20 10
1055 – 60h. red 20 10
1056 – 1k. sepia 45 10
1057 – 1k.60 myrtle . . . . . 1·60 1·50
DESIGNS: 60h. New Town Hall, Brno; 1k. St. Thomas's Church, Red Army Square; 1k.60, (50 × 28½ mm), Brno view.

1958. Mushrooms.
1058 **319** 30h. buff, green & brown 40 20
1059 – 40h. buff, red & brown 45 20
1060 – 60h. red, buff and black 55 25
1061 – 1k.40 red, green & brn 65 35
1062 – 1k.60 red, green & blk 5·25 2·00
DESIGNS—VERT: 40h. Cep; 60h. Red cap; 1k.40, Fly agaric; 1k.60, Boot-lace fungus.

320 Children sailing

322 Garlanded Woman ("Republic") with First Czech Stamp

321 Bozek's Steam Car of 1815

1958. Inauguration of UNESCO Headquarters Building, Paris. Inscr "ZE SOUTEZE PRO UNESCO".
1063 **320** 30h. red, yellow & blue 20 10
1064 – 45h. red and blue . . . 50 10
1065 – 60h. blue, yellow & brn 20 10
DESIGNS: 45h. Mother, child and bird; 60h. Child skier.

1958. Czech Motor Industry Commemoration.
1066 **321** 30h. violet and yellow 65 10
1067 – 45h. brown and green . . 50 10
1068 – 60h. green and orange 65 10
1069 – 80h. red and green . . . 50 10
1070 – 1k. brown and green . . 50 10
1071 – 1k.25 green & yellow . . 1·60 75
DESIGNS: 45h. "President" car of 1897; 60h. Skoda "450" car; 80h. Tatra "603" car; 1k. Skoda "706" motor coach; 1k.25, Tatra "III" and Praga "VS 3" motor trucks in Tibet.

1958. 40th Anniv of 1st Czech Postage Stamps.
1072 **322** 60h. blue 25 10

323 Ice Hockey Goalkeeper

1959. Sports Events of 1959.
1073 – 20h. brown and grey . . 30 10
1074 – 30h. brown & orange . . 30 10
1075 **323** 60h. blue and green . . 30 10
1076 – 1k. lake and yellow . . . 30 10
1077 – 1k.60 violet and blue . . 45 10
1078 – 2k. brown and blue . . . 1·60 1·25
DESIGNS: 20h. Ice hockey player (50th anniv of Czech Ice Hockey Association); 30h. Throwing the javelin; 60h. (Type **323**) World Ice Hockey Championships, 1959; 1k. Hurdling; 1k.60, Rowing; 2k. High jumping.

324 U.A.C. Emblem

325 "Equal Rights"

1959. 4th National Unified Agricultural Co-operatives Congress, Prague.
1079 **324** 30h. lake and blue . . . 20 10
1080 – 60h. blue and yellow . . 40 10
DESIGN: 60h. Artisan shaking hand with farmer.

1959. 10th Anniv of Declaration of Human Rights.
1081 **325** 60h. green 15 10
1082 – 1k. sepia 25 10
1083 – 2k. blue . . . . 1·40 55
DESIGNS: 1k. "World Freedom" (girl with Dove of Peace); 2k. "Freedom for Colonial Peoples" (native woman with child).

326 Girl with Doll

327 F. Joliot-Curie (scientist)

1959. 10th Anniv of Young Pioneers' Movement.
1084 **326** 30h. blue and yellow . . 30 10
1085 – 40h. black and blue . . 30 25
1086 – 60h. black and purple . . 30 10
1087 – 80h. brown and green . . 30 25
DESIGNS: 40h. Boy hiker; 60h. Young radio technician; 80h. Girl planting tree.

1959. 10th Anniv of Peace Movement.
1088 **327** 60h. purple . . . . . . 1·40 40

328 Man in outer space and Moon Rocket

329 Pilsen Town Hall

1959. 2nd Czech Political and Cultural Knowledge Congress, Prague.
1089 **328** 30h. blue 90 35

1959. Centenary of Skoda Works and National Stamp Exhibition, Pilsen. Inscr "PLZEN 1959".
1090 **329** 30h. brown 15 10
1091 – 60h. violet and green . . 15 10
1092 – 1k. blue 25 20
1093 – 1k.60 black & yellow . . 1·25 1·00
DESIGNS: 60h. Part of steam turbine; 1k. St. Bartholomew's Church, Pilsen; 1k.60, Part of SR-1200 lathe.

330 Congress Emblem and Industrial Plant

1959. 4th Trades Union Congress, Prague.

1094	**330**	30h. red and yellow . .	20	10
1095	–	60h. olive and blue . . .	20	10

DESIGN: 60h. Dam.

331 Zvolen Castle

1959. Slovak Stamp Exhibition, Zvolen.

1096	**331**	60h. olive and yellow . .	35	10

332 F. Benda (composer)

1959. Cultural Anniversaries.

1097	**332**	15h. blue	20	10
1098	–	30h. red	20	10
1099	–	40h. green	30	10
1100	–	60h. brown	30	10
1101	–	60h. black	55	10
1102	–	80h. violet	30	10
1103	–	1k. brown	30	10
1104	–	3k. brown	1·40	1·10

PORTRAITS: 30h. Vaclav Klicpera (dramatist); 40h. Aurel Stodola (engineer); 60h. (1100) Karel V. Rais (writer); 60h. (1101) Haydn (composer); 80h. Antonin Slavicek (painter); 1k. Petr Bezruc (poet). 3k. Charles Darwin (naturalist).

333 "Z" Pavilion

1959. Int Fair, Brno. Inscr "BRNO 6-20. IX. 1959".

1105	–	30h. purple & yellow . .	15	10
1106	–	60h. blue	15	10
1107	**333**	1k.60 blue & yellow . .	45	10

DESIGNS: 30h. View of Fair; 60h. Fair emblem and world map.

334 Revolutionary (after A. Holly)

1959. 15th Anniv of Slovak National Uprising and 40th Anniv of Republic. Inscr "1944 29.8.1959".

1108	**334**	30h. black & mauve . .	15	10
1109	–	60h. red	20	10
1110	–	1k.60 blue & yell . . .	40	10

DESIGNS—VERT: 60h. Revolutionary with upraised rifle (after sculpture "Forward" by L. Snopka). HORIZ: 1k.60, Factory, sun and linden leaves.

335 Moon Rocket

1959. Landing of Russian Rocket on Moon.

1111	**335**	60h. red and blue . . .	1·25	25

336 Lynx

1959. 10th Anniv of Tatra National Park. Inscr "1949 TATRANSKY NARODNY PARK 1959".

1112	–	30h. black and grey . .	65	10
1113	–	40h. brown & turquoise	65	10
1114	**336**	60h. red & yellow . . .	90	10
1115	–	1k. brown & blue . . .	2·00	75
1116	–	1k.60 brown	1·75	10

DESIGNS—HORIZ: 30h. Alpine marmots; 40h. European bison; 1k. Wolf; 1k.60, Red deer.

337 Stamp Printing Works, Peking

1959. 10th Anniv of Chinese People's Republic.

1117	**337**	30h. red and green . . .	25	10

338 Bleriot XI Monoplanes at First Czech Aviation School

1959. Air. 50th Anniv of 1st Flight by Jan Kaspar.

1118	**338**	1k. black and yellow . .	15	10
1119	–	1k.80 black & blue . .	75	10

DESIGN: 1k.80, Jan Kaspar and Bleriot XI in flight.

339 Great Spotted Woodpecker

341 Exercises

340 Tesla and Electrical Apparatus

1959. Birds.

1120	**339**	20h. multicoloured . . .	85	15
1121	–	30h. multicoloured . . .	85	15
1122	–	40h. multicoloured . . .	2·10	1·10
1123	–	60h. multicoloured . . .	85	15
1124	–	80h. multicoloured . . .	85	20
1125	–	1k. red, blue & black . .	85	20
1126	–	1k.20 brn, blue & blk . .	1·10	40

BIRDS: 30h. Blue tit; 40h. Eurasian nuthatch; 60h. Golden oriole; 80h. Eurasian goldfinch; 1k. Northern bullfinch; 1k.20, River kingfisher.

1959. Radio Inventors.

1127	**340**	25h. black and red . . .	1·10	20
1128	–	30h. black and brown . .	15	10
1129	–	35h. black and lilac . . .	20	10
1130	–	60h. black and blue . .	25	10
1131	–	1k. black and green . .	20	10
1132	–	2k. black and bistre . .	80	85

INVENTORS (each with sketch of invention): 30h. Aleksandr Popov; 35h. Edouard Branly; 60h. Guglielmo Marconi; 1k. Heinrich Hertz; 2k. Edwin Armstrong.

1960. 2nd National Spartacist Games (1st issue). Inscr as in T **341**.

1133	**341**	30h. brown and red . .	1·10	10
1134	–	60h. blue & light blue . .	45	25
1135	–	1k.60 brown & bistre . .	70	30

DESIGNS: 60h. Skiing; 1k.60, Basketball.

See also Nos. 1160/2.

342 Freighter "Lidice"

1960. Czech Ships.

1136	–	30h. green and red . . .	80	15
1137	–	60h. red and turquoise	25	10
1138	–	1k. violet and yellow . .	80	25
1139	**342**	1k.20 purple and green	1·75	90

SHIPS: 30h. Dredger "Praha Liben"; 60h. Tug "Kharito Latjev"; 1k. River boat "Komarno".

343 Ice Hockey

1960. Winter Olympic Games. Inscr as in T **343**.

1140	**343**	60h. sepia and blue . . .	45	25
1141	–	1k.80 black & green . .	3·75	2·10

DESIGN: 1k.80, Skating pair.

See also Nos. 1163/5.

344 Trencin Castle **345** Lenin

1960. Czechoslovak Castles.

1142		5h. blue (Type **344**)	15	10
1143		10h. black (Bezdez)	15	10
1144		20h. orange (Kost)	25	10
1145		30h. green (Pernstejn) . . .	25	10
1146		40h. brn (Kremnica) . . .	25	10
1146a		50h. black (Krivoklat) . . .	25	10
1147		60h. red (Karestejn) . . .	45	10
1148		1k. purple (Smolenice) . .	30	10
1149		1k.60 blue (Kokorin) . . .	65	10

1960. 90th Birth Anniv of Lenin.

1150	**345**	60h. olive	85	25

346 Soldier and Child

1960. 15th Anniv of Liberation.

1151	**346**	30h. lake and blue . . .	30	10
1152	–	30h. green and lavender	25	10
1153	–	30h. red and pink . . .	25	10
1154	–	60h. blue and buff . . .	25	10
1155	–	60h. purple and green . .	25	10

DESIGNS—VERT: No. 1152, Solider with liberated political prisoner; 1153, Child eating pastry. HORIZ: No. 1154, Welder; 1155, Tractor-driver.

347 Smelter

1960. Parliamentary Elections.

1156	**347**	30h. red and grey . . .	15	10
1157	–	60h. green and blue . .	20	10

DESIGN: 60h. Country woman and child.

348 Red Cross Woman with Dove

1960. 3rd Czechoslovak Red Cross Congress.

1158	**348**	30h. red and blue . . .	10	10

349 Fire-prevention Team with Hose

1960. 2nd Firemen's Union Congress.

1159	**349**	60h. blue and pink . . .	35	10

1960. 2nd National Spartacist Games (2nd issue). As T **341**.

1160	30h. red and green	40	10
1161	60h. black and pink	40	10
1162	1k. blue and orange	60	25

DESIGNS: 30h. Ball exercises; 60h. Stick exercises; 1k. Girls with hoops.

1960. Olympic Games, Rome. As Type **343**.

1163	1k. black and orange . . .	50	25
1164	1k.80 black and red	1·25	25
1165	2k. black and blue	2·00	85

DESIGNS: 1k. Sprinting; 1k.80, Gymnastics; 2k. Rowing.

350 Czech 10k. Stamp of 1936

1960. National Philatelic Exn, Bratislava (1st issue).

1166	–	60h. black and yellow . .	40	10
1167	**350**	1k. black and blue . . .	90	10

DESIGN: 60h. Hand of philatelist holding stamp Type **350**.

See also Nos. 1183/4.

351 Stalin Mine, Ostrava-Hermanice **352** V. Cornelius of Vsehra (historian)

1960. 3rd Five Year Plan (1st issue).

1168	**351**	10h. black and green . .	25	10
1169	–	20h. lake and blue . . .	25	10
1170	–	30h. blue and red . . .	25	10
1171	–	40h. green and lilac . . .	25	10
1172	–	60h. blue and yellow . .	25	10

DESIGNS: 20h. Hodonin Power Station; 30h. Klement Gottwald Iron Works, Kuncice; 40h. Excavator; 60h. Naphtha refinery.

See also Nos. 1198/1200.

1960. Cultural Anniversaries.

1173	**352**	10h. black	20	10
1174	–	20h. brown	30	10
1175	–	30h. red	40	10
1176	–	40h. green	45	10
1177	–	60h. violet	50	10

PORTRAITS: 20h. K. M. Capek Chod (writer); 30h. Hana Kvapilova (actress); 40h. Oskar Nedbal (composer); 60h. Otakar Ostricil (composer).

353 Zlin Trener 6 flying upside-down

1960. 1st World Aviation Aerobatic Championships, Bratislava.

1178	**353**	60h. violet and blue . .	90	25

354 "New Constitution"

1960. Proclamation of New Constitution.

1179	**354**	30h. blue and red . . .	25	10

355 Worker with "Rude Pravo"

1960. Czechoslovak Press Day (30h.) and 40th Anniv of Newspaper "Rude Pravo".
1180 – 30h. blue and orange . . 10 10
1181 **355** 60h. black and red . . . 20 10
DESIGN—HORIZ: (inscr "DEN TISKU"): 30h. Steel-workers with newspaper.

356 Globes

1960. 15th Anniv of W.F.T.U.
1182 **356** 30h. blue and bistre . . 25 10

357 Mail Coach and Ilyushin Il-18B

1960. Air. National Philatelic Exhibition, Bratislava (2nd issue).
1183 **357** 1k.60 blue and grey . . 2·50 1·40
1184 – 2k.80 green & cream . . 4·00 2·00
DESIGN: 2k.80, MIL Mi-4 helicopter over Bratislava.

358 Mallard

1960. Water Birds.
1185 – 25h. black and blue . . 50 10
1186 – 30h. black and green . . 1·10 20
1187 – 40h. black and blue . . 70 20
1188 – 60h. black and pink . . 80 20
1189 – 1k. black and yellow . . 1·25 20
1190 **358** 1k.60 black and lilac . . 2·40 1·60
BIRDS—VERT: 25h. Black-crowned night heron; 30h. Great crested grebe; 40h. Northern lapwing; 60h. Grey heron. HORIZ: 1k. Greylag goose.

359 "Doronicum clusii tausch"

1960. Flowers. Inscr in black.
1191 **359** 20h. yellow, orge & grn 50 10
1192 – 30h. red and green . . . 65 20
1193 – 40h. yellow and green . . 65 20
1194 – 60h. pink and green . . 70 20
1195 – 1k. blue, violet & green 1·00 35
1196 – 2k. yellow, green & pur 2·40 1·25
FLOWERS: 30h. "Cyclamen europaeum L"; 40h. "Primula auricula L"; 60h. "Sempervivum mont L"; 1k. "Gentiana clusil perr, et song"; 2k. "Pulsatilla slavica reuss".

360 A. Mucha (painter and stamp designer)

361 Automatic Machinery

1960. Stamp Day and Birth Centenary of Mucha.
1197 **360** 60h. blue 70 10

1961. 3rd Five Year Plan (2nd issue).
1198 **361** 20h. blue 10 10
1199 – 30h. red 20 10
1200 – 60h. green 20 10
DESIGNS: 30h. Turbo-generator and control desk; 60h. Excavator.

362 Motor Cyclists (Int Grand Prix, Brno)

1961. Sports Events of 1961.
1201 **362** 30h. blue and mauve . . 20 10
1202 – 30h. red and blue . . . 20 10
1203 – 40h. black and red . . . 35 10
1204 – 60h. purple and blue . . 35 10
1205 – 1k. blue and yellow . . 35 10
1206 – 1k.20 green & salmon . . 35 10
1207 – 1k.60 brown and red . . 1·60 1·00
DESIGNS—VERT: 30h. (No. 1202), Athletes with banners (40th anniv of Czech Physical Culture); 60h. Figure skating (World Figure Skating Championships, Prague); 1k. Rugger (35th anniv of rugby football in Czechoslovakia); 1k.20, Football (60th anniv of football in Czechoslovakia); 1k.60, Running (65th anniv of Bechovice–Prague Marathon Race). HORIZ: 40h. Rowing (European Rowing Championships, Prague).

363 Exhibition Emblem

365 J. Mosna

364 "Sputnik 3"

1961. "PRAGA 1962" Int Stamp Exn (1st issue).
1208 **363** 2k. red and blue . . . . 2·00 20
See also Nos. 1250/6, 1267/70, 1297/1300 and 1311/15.

1961. Space Research (1st series).
1209 – 20h. red and violet . . . 50 10
1210 **364** 30h. blue and buff . . . 50 10
1211 – 40h. red and green . . . 45 15
1212 – 60h. violet and yellow 30 10
1213 – 1k.60 blue and green . . 50 10
1214 – 2k. purple and blue . . . 1·50 1·00
DESIGNS—VERT: 20h. Launching cosmic rocket; 40h. Venus rocket. HORIZ: 60h. "Lunik 1"; 1k.60, "Lunik 3" and Moon; 2k. Cosmonaut (similar to T **366**).
See also Nos. 1285/90 and 1349/54.

1961. Cultural Anniversaries.
1215 **365** 60h. green 30 10
1216 – 60h. black 40 10
1217 – 60h. blue 40 10
1218 – 60h. red 30 10
1219 – 60h. brown 30 10
PORTRAITS: No. 1216, J. Uprka (painter); 1217, P. O. Hviezdoslav (poet); 1218, A. Mrstik (writer); 1219, J. Hora (poet).

366 Man in Space

1961. World's 1st Manned Space Flight.
1220 **366** 60h. red and turquoise 55 10
1221 3k. blue and yellow . . . 2·00 50

367 Kladno Steel Mills

368 "Instrumental Music"

1961.
1222 **367** 3k. red 85 10

1961. 150th Anniv of Prague Conservatoire.
1223 **368** 30h. sepia 30 10
1224 – 30h. red 35 10
1225 – 60h. blue 30 10
DESIGNS: No. 1224, Dancer; 1225, Girl playing lyre.

369 "People's House" (Lenin Museum), Prague

1961. 40th Anniv of Czech Communist Party.
1226 **369** 30h. brown 25 10
1227 – 30h. blue 25 10
1228 – 30h. violet 25 10
1229 – 60h. red 25 10
1230 – 60h. myrtle 25 10
1231 – 60h. red 25 10
DESIGNS—HORIZ: No. 1227, Gottwald's Museum, Prague. VERT: No. 1228, Workers in Wenceslas Square, Prague; 1229, Worker, star and factory plant; 1230, Woman wielding hammer and sickle; 1231, May Day procession, Wenceslas Square.

370 Manasek Doll

371 Gagarin waving Flags

1961. Czech Puppets.
1232 **370** 30h. red and yellow . . 20 10
1233 – 40h. sepia & turquoise 20 10
1234 – 60h. blue and salmon . . 20 10
1235 – 1k. green and blue . . . 20 10
1236 – 1k.60 red and blue . . . 1·25 35
PUPPETS: 40h. "Dr. Faustus and Caspar"; 60h. "Spejbl and Hurvinek"; 1k. Scene from "Difficulties with the Moon" (Askenazy); 1k.60, "Jasanek" of Brno.

1961. Yuri Gagarin's (first man in space) Visit to Prague.
1237 **371** 60h. black and red . . . 25 10
1238 – 1k.80 black and blue . . 45 10
DESIGN: 1k.80, Yuri Gagarin in space helmet, rocket and dove.

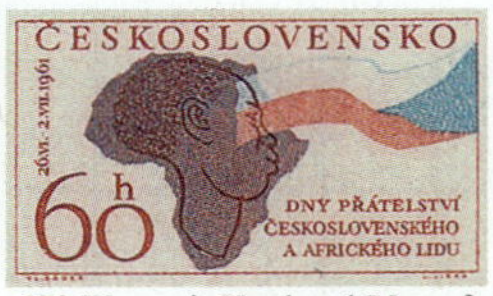

372 Woman's Head and Map of Africa

1961. Czecho-African Friendship.
1239 **372** 60h. red and blue . . . 25 10

373 Map of Europe and Fair Emblem

1961. Int Trade Fair, Brno. Inscr "M.V.B. 1961".
1240 **373** 30h. blue and green . . 15 10
1241 – 60h. green & salmon . . 25 10
1242 – 1k. brown and blue . . . 25 10
DESIGNS—VERT: 60h. Horizontal drill. HORIZ: 1k. Scientific discussion group.

374 Clover and Cow

375 Prague

1961. Agricultural Produce.
1243 – 20h. purple and blue . . 15 10
1244 **374** 30h. ochre and purple 15 10
1245 – 40h. orange and brown 15 10
1246 – 60h. bistre and green . . 20 10
1247 – 1k.40 brown & choc . . 40 10
1248 – 2k. blue and purple . . . 1·40 50
DESIGNS: 20h. Sugar beet, cup and saucer; 40h. Wheat and bread; 60h. Hops and beer; 1k.40, Maize and cattle; 2k. Potatoes and factory.

1961. 26th Session of Red Cross Societies League Governors' Council, Prague.
1249 **375** 60h. violet and red . . . 1·00 10

376 Orlik Dam

1961. "Praga 1962" International Stamp Exhibition (2nd and 3rd issues).
1250 **376** 20h. black and blue . . 75 30
1251 – 30h. blue and red . . . 45 10
1252 – 40h. blue and green . . 75 30
1253 – 60h. slate and bistre . . 75 30
1267 – 1k. purple and green . . 55 50
1254 – 1k.20 green and pink . . 90 45
1268 – 1k.60 brown and violet 95 65
1269 – 2k. black and orange . . 1·50 1·10
1255 – 3k. blue and yellow . . . 1·60 45
1256 – 4k. violet and orange . . 2·25 1·25
1270 – 5k. multicoloured . . . 22·00 17·00
DESIGNS—As Type **376**: 30h. Prague; 40h. Hluboka Castle from lake; 60h. Karlovy Vary; 1k. Pilsen; 1k.20, North Bohemian landscape; 1k.60, High Tatras; 2k. Iron-works, Ostrava-Kuncice; 3k. Brno; 4k. Bratislava. (50 × 29 mm): 5k. Prague and flags.

377 Orange-tip

1961. Butterflies and Moths. Multicoloured.
1257 15h. Type **377** 35 10
1258 20h. Southern festoon . . . 50 10
1259 30h. Apollo 90 25
1260 40h. Swallowtail 90 25
1261 60h. Peacock . . . . 1·10 25
1262 80h. Camberwell beauty . . 1·25 25
1263 1k. Clifden's nonpareil . . . 1·25 25
1264 1k.60 Red admiral . . . . 1·40 40
1265 2k. Brimstone . . . . . . 2·75 1·90

378 Congress Emblem and World Map

1961. 5th W.F.T.U. Congress, Moscow.
1266 **378** 60h. blue and red . . . 45 10

379 Racing Cyclists (Berlin–Prague–Warsaw Cycle Race)

380 K. Kovarovic (composer, centenary of birth)

1962. Sports Events of 1962.
1271 **379** 30h. black and blue . . 25 10
1272 – 40h. black and yellow . . 20 10

1273 – 60h. grey and blue . . . 30 10
1274 – 1k. black and pink . . . 30 10
1275 – 1k.20 black and green 30 10
1276 – 1k.60 black and green 1·40 55
DESIGNS: 40h. Gymnastics (15th World Gymnastics Championships, Prague); 60h. Figure Skating (World Figure Skating Championships, Prague); 1k. Bowling (World Bowling Championships, Bratislava); 1k.20, Football (World Cup Football Championship, Chile); 1k.60, Throwing the discus (7th European Athletic Championships, Belgrade).
See also No. 1306.

1962. Cultural Celebrities and Anniversaries.
1277 **380** 10h. brown 10 10
1278 – 20h. blue 10 10
1279 – 30h. brown 10 10
1280 – 40h. purple 15 10
1281 – 60h. black 15 10
1282 – 1k.60 myrtle 40 10
1283 – 1k.80 blue 50 10
DESIGNS—As Type **380**: 20h. F. Skroup (composer); 30h. Bozena Nemcova (writer); 60h. Rod of Aesculapius and Prague Castle (Czech Medical Association Cent); 1k.60, L. Celakovsky (founder, Czech Botanical Society). HORIZ: (41 × 22½ mm): 40h. F. Zaviska and K. Petr; 1k.80, M. Valouch and J. Hronec. (These two commemorate Czech Mathematics and Physics Union Cent).

381 Miner holding Lamp

1962. 30th Anniv of Miners' Strike, Most.
1284 **381** 60h. blue and red . . . 25 10

382 "Man Conquers Space" **384** Dove and Nest

383 Indian and African Elephants

1962. Space Research (2nd series).
1285 **382** 30h. red and blue . . . 25 10
1286 – 40h. blue and orange . . 25 10
1287 – 60h. blue and pink . . . 25 10
1288 – 80h. purple and green . . 60 10
1289 – 1k. blue and yellow . . . 25 25
1290 – 1k.60 green and yellow 1·40 60
DESIGNS—VERT: 40h. Launching of Soviet rocket; 1k. Automatic station on Moon. HORIZ: 60h. "Vostok-II"; 80h. Multi-stage automatic rocket; 1k.60, Television satellite station.

1962. Animals of Prague Zoos.
1291 – 20h. black & turquoise 55 10
1292 – 30h. black and violet . . 55 10
1293 – 60h. black and yellow . . 65 10
1294 **383** 1k. black and green . . 95 10
1295 – 1k.40 black and mauve 1·00 25
1296 – 1k.60 black and brown 2·10 1·10
ANIMALS—VERT: 20h. Polar bear; 30h. Chimpanzee; 60h. Bactrian camel. HORIZ: 1k.40, Leopard; 1k.60, Wild horses.

1962. Air. "Praga 1962" International Stamp Exhibition (4th issue).
1297 **384** 80h. multicoloured . . . 50 25
1298 – 1k.40 red, blue & black 2·00 2·75
1299 – 2k.80 multicoloured . . 3·25 2·75
1300 – 4k.20 multicoloured . . 4·75 2·75
DESIGNS: 1k.40, Dove; 2k.80, Flower and bird; 4k.20, Plant and bird. All designs feature "Praga 62" emblem. The 80h. and 2k.80 are inscr in Slovakian and the others in Czech.

385 Girl of Lidice **386** Klary's Fountain, Teplice

1962. 20th Anniv of Destruction of Lidice and Lezaky.
1301 **385** 30h. black and red . . . 35 10
1302 – 60h. black and blue . . . 35 10
DESIGN: 60h. Flowers and Lezaky ruins.

1962. 1200th Anniv of Discovery of Teplice Springs.
1303 **386** 60h. green and yellow . . 45 10

387 Campaign Emblem **388** Swimmer with Rifle

1962. Malaria Eradication.
1304 **387** 60h. red and black . . . 15 10
1305 – 3k. blue and black . . . 1·25 65
DESIGN: 3k. Campaign emblem and dove (different).

1962. Czechoslovakia's Participation in World Cup Football Championship Final, Chile. As No. 1275 but inscr "CSSR VE FINALE" and new value.
1306 1k.60 green and yellow . . . 1·25 20

1962. 2nd Military Spartacist Games. Inscr as in T **388**.
1307 **388** 30h. myrtle and blue . . 15 10
1308 – 40h. violet and yellow 20 10
1309 – 60h. brown and green . . 25 10
1310 – 1k. blue and red 30 10
DESIGNS: 40h. Soldier mounting obstacle; 60h. Footballer; 1k. Relay Race.

389 "Sun" and Field (Socialized Agriculture)

1962. "Praga 1962" Int Stamp Exn (5th issue).
1311 **389** 30h. multicoloured . . . 3·00 1·10
1312 – 60h. multicoloured . . . 80 25
1313 – 80h. multicoloured . . . 3·50 2·40
1314 – 1k. multicoloured . . . 3·50 2·75
1315 – 1k.40 multicoloured . . . 3·50 2·75
MS1315a 96 × 75 mm. 5k. multicoloured (View of Prague with Exhibition emblem) (perf or imperf) . . . . 16·00 16·00
DESIGNS—VERT: 60h. Astronaut in "spaceship"; 1k.40, Children playing under "tree". HORIZ: 80h. Boy with flute, and peace doves; 1k. Workers of three races. All have "Praga 62" emblem.

390 Swallow, "Praga 62" and Congress Emblems

1962. F.I.P. Day (Federation Internationale de Philatelie).
1316 **390** 1k.60 multicoloured . . 4·75 4·00

391 Zinkovy Sanatorium and Sailing Dinghy **392** Cruiser "Aurora"

1962. Czech Workers' Social Facilities.
1317 – 30h. black and blue . . 20 10
1318 **391** 60h. sepia and ochre . . 25 10
DESIGN—HORIZ: 30h. Children in day nursery, and factory.

1962. 45th Anniv of Russian Revolution.
1319 **392** 30h. sepia and blue . . . 10 10
1320 60h. black and pink . . . 25 10

393 Astronaut and Worker

1962. 40th Anniv of U.S.S.R.
1321 **393** 30h. red and blue . . . 25 10
1322 – 60h. black and pink . . 30 10
DESIGN—VERT: 60h. Lenin.

394 Crane ("Building Construction")

1962. 12th Czech Communist Party Congress, Prague.
1323 **394** 30h. red and yellow . . 25 10
1324 – 40h. blue and yellow . . 25 10
1325 – 60h. black and pink . . 25 10
DESIGNS—VERT: 40h. Produce ("Agriculture"). HORIZ: 60h. Factory plants ("Industry").

395 Stag Beetle **396** Table Tennis (World Championships, Prague)

1962. Beetles. Multicoloured.
1326 20h. Caterpillar-hunter (horiz) 25 10
1327 30h. Cardinal beetle (horiz) 25 10
1328 60h. Type **395** 25 10
1329 1k. Great dung beetle (horiz) 85 10
1330 1k.60 Alpine longhorn beetle 1·25 35
1331 2k. Blue ground beetle . . . 3·00 1·40

1963. Sports Events of 1963.
1332 **396** 30h. black and green . . 25 10
1333 – 60h. black and orange 25 10
1334 – 80h. black and blue . . 25 10
1335 – 1k. black and violet . . 30 10
1336 – 1k.20 black and brown 30 20
1337 – 1k.60 black and red . . 90 20
DESIGNS: 60h. Cycling (80th Anniv of Czech Cycling); 80h. Skiing (1st Czech Winter Games); 1k. Motor-cycle dirt track racing (15th Anniv of "Golden Helmet" Race, Pardubice); 1k.20, Weightlifting (World Championships, Prague); 1k.60, Hurdling (1st Czech Summer Games).

397 Industrial Plant **398** Guild Emblem

1963. 15th Anniv of "Victorious February" and 5th T.U. Congress.
1338 **397** 30h. red and blue . . . 15 10
1339 – 60h. red and black . . . 15 10
1340 – 60h. black and red . . . 15 10
DESIGNS—VERT: No. 1339, Sun and campfire. HORIZ: No. 1340, Industrial plant and annual "stepping stones".

1963. Cultural Anniversaries.
1341 **398** 20h. black and blue . . 10 10
1342 – 30h. red 10 10
1343 – 30h. red and blue . . . 10 10
1344 – 60h. black 15 10
1345 – 60h. purple and blue . . 15 10
1346 – 60h. myrtle 15 10
1347 – 1k.60 brown 45 10
DESIGNS—VERT: No. 1341 (Artist's Guild cent); 1342, E. Urx (journalist); 1343, J. Janosik (national hero); 1344, J. Palkovic (author); 1346, Woman with book, and children (cent of Slovak Cultural Society, Slovenska Matice); 1347, M. Svabinsky (artist, after self-portrait). HORIZ: 1345, Allegorical figure and National Theatre, Prague (80th anniv).

399 Young People

1963. 4th Czech Youth Federation Congress, Prague.
1348 **399** 30h. blue and red . . . 25 10

1963. Space Research (3rd series). As T **364** but inscr "1963" at foot.
1349 30h. purple, red & yellow 15 10
1350 50h. blue and turquoise . . 25 10
1351 60h. turquoise & yellow . . 25 10
1352 1k. black and brown 55 10
1353 1k.60 sepia and green . . . 40 10
1354 2k. violet and yellow . . . 1·60 75
MS1354a 84 × 70 mm. 3k. orange and green (Spacecraft and Mars). Imperf . . . . 7·00 4·00
DESIGNS—HORIZ: 30h. Rocket circling Sun; 50h. Rockets and Sputniks leaving Earth; 60h. Spacecraft and Moon; 1k. "Mars 1" rocket and Mars; 1k.60, Rocket heading for Jupiter; 2k. Spacecraft returning from Saturn.

400 TV Cameras and Receiver

1963. 10th Anniv of Czech Television Service. Inscr as in T **400**.
1355 **400** 40h. blue and orange . . 20 10
1356 – 60h. red and blue . . . 20 10
DESIGN—VERT: 60h. TV transmitting aerial.

401 Broadcasting Studio and Receiver

1963. 40th Anniv of Czech Radio Service. Inscr as in T **401**.
1357 **401** 30h. purple and blue . . 15 10
1358 – 1k. purple & turquoise 25 10
DESIGN—VERT: 1k. Aerial mast, globe and doves.

402 Ancient Ring and Moravian Settlements Map **404** Singer

403 Tupolev Tu-104A

1963. 1100th Anniv of Moravian Empire.
1359 **402** 30h. black and green . . 20 10
1360 – 1k.60 black and yellow 40 10
DESIGN: 1k.60, Ancient silver plate showing falconer with hawk.

1963. 40th Anniv of Czech Airlines.
1361 **403** 80h. violet and blue . . 80 20
1362 – 1k.80 blue and green . 1·50 45
DESIGN: 1k.80, Ilyushin Il-18B.

1963. 60th Anniv of Moravian Teachers' Singing Club.
1363 **404** 30h. red 35 10

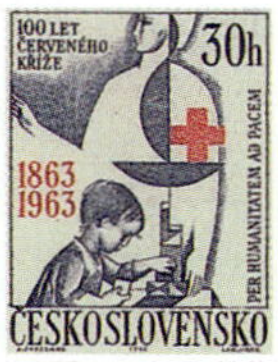

405 Nurse and Child **406** Wheatears and Kromeriz Castle

1963. Centenary of Red Cross.
1364 **405** 30h. blue and red . . . 35 10

1963. National Agricultural Exhibition.
1365 **406** 30h. green and yellow . . 35 10

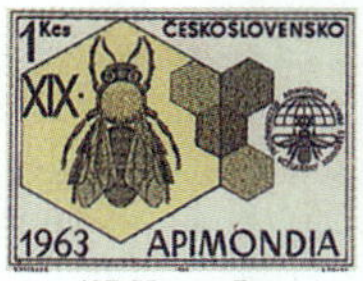

407 Honey Bee, Honeycomb and Congress Emblem

409 "Modern Fashion"

408 "Vostok 5" and Bykovsky

1963. 19th International Bee-keepers' Congress ("Apimondia '63").
1366 **407** 1k. brown and yellow . . 45 10

1963. 2nd "Team" Manned Space Flights.
1367 **408** 80h. pink and blue . . . 35 10
1368 – 2k.80 blue and purple . . 2·25 25
DESIGN: 2k.80, "Vostok 6" and Valentina Tereshkova.

1963. Liberec Consumer Goods Fair.
1369 **409** 30h. black and mauve 35 10

410 Portal of Brno Town Hall

411 Cave and Stalagmites

1963. Brno International Fair.
1370 **410** 30h. purple and blue . . 25 10
1371 – 60h. blue and salmon . . 30 10
DESIGN: 60h. Tower of Brno Town Hall.

1963. Czech Scenery. (a) Moravia.
1372 **411** 30h. brown and blue . . 25 10
1373 – 80h. brown and pink . . 40 10
(b) Slovakia.
1374 – 30h. blue and green . . . 30 10
1375 – 60h. blue, green & yellow 30 10
DESIGNS: No. 1373, Macocha Chasm; 1374, Pool, Hornad Valley; 1375, Waterfall, Great Hawk Gorge.

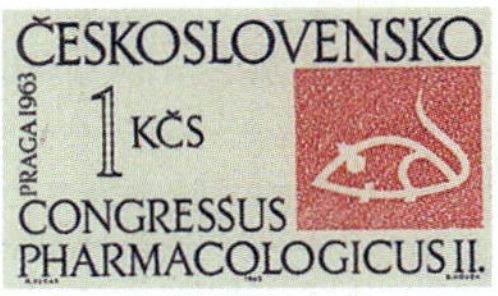

412 Mouse

1963. 2nd International Pharmacological Congress, Prague.
1376 **412** 1k. red and black . . . 45 10

413 Blast Furnace

1963. 30th International Foundry Congress, Prague.
1377 **413** 60h. black and blue . . 25 10

414 "Aid for Farmers Abroad"

1963. Freedom from Hunger.
1378 **414** 1k.60 sepia 45 10

415 Dolls

416 Canoeing

1963. UNESCO. Folk Art. Multicoloured.
1379 60h. Type **415** 15 10
1380 80h. Rooster 25 10
1381 1k. Vase of flowers 35 20
1382 1k.20 Detail of glass-painting "Janosik and his Men" 35 10
1383 1k.60 Stag 35 20
1384 2k. Horseman . . . . . . 2·75 1·10

1963. Olympic Games, Tokyo, 1964, and 50th Anniv of Czech Canoeing (30h.).
1385 **416** 30h. blue and green . . 30 10
1386 – 40h. brown and blue . . 30 10
1387 – 60h. lake and yellow . . 25 10
1388 – 80h. violet and red . . 30 20
1389 – 1k. blue and red 30 20
1390 – 1k.60 ultram & blue . . 1·50 70
DESIGNS: 40h. Volleyball; 60h. Wrestling; 80h. Basketball; 1k. Boxing; 1k.60, Gymnastics.

417 Linden Tree

418 "Human Reason and Technology."

1963. 20th Anniv of Czech–Soviet Treaty of Friendship.
1391 **417** 30h. brown and blue . . 15 10
1392 – 60h. red and green . . . 15 10
DESIGN: 60h. Hammer and sickle, and star.

1963. Technical and Scientific Knowledge Society Congress.
1393 **418** 60h. violet 35 10

419 Chamois

420 Figure Skating

1963. Mountain Animals.
1394 **419** 30h. multicoloured . . . 65 15
1395 – 40h. multicoloured . . . 65 30
1396 – 60h. sepia, yellow & grn 1·00 35
1397 – 1k.20 multicoloured . . 1·00 15
1398 – 1k.60 multicoloured . . 1·40 40
1399 – 2k. brown, orge & grn 4·00 2·25
ANIMALS: 40h. Ibex; 60h. Mouflon; 1k.20, Roe deer; 1k.60, Fallow deer; 2k. Red deer.

1964. Sports Events of 1964.
1400 **420** 30h. violet and yellow 15 10
1401 – 80h. blue and orange . . 15 10
1402 – 1k. brown and lilac . . 80 20
DESIGNS—VERT: 30h. Type **420** (Czech Students' Games); 1k. Handball (World Handball Championships). HORIZ: 80h. Cross-country skiing (Students' Games).

421 Ice Hockey

423 Magura Hotel, Zdiar, High Tatra

422 Belanske Tatra Mountains, Skiers and Tree

1964. Winter Olympic Games, Innsbruck.
1403 **421** 1k. purple and turquoise 75 30
1404 – 1k.80 green & lavender 1·00 55
1405 – 2k. blue and green . . . 2·50 2·10
DESIGNS—VERT: 1k.80, Tobogganing. HORIZ: 2k. Ski jumping.

1964. Tourist Issue.
1406 **422** 30h. purple and blue . . 20 10
1407 – 60h. blue and red . . . 30 10
1408 – 1k. brown and olive . . 55 10
1409 – 1k.80 green and orange 1·00 35
DESIGNS: 60h. Telc (Moravia) and motorcamp; 1k. Spis Castle (Slovakia) and angler; 1k.80, Cesky Krumlov (Bohemia) and sailing dinghies. Each design includes a tree.

1964. Trade Union Recreation Hotels.
1410 **423** 60h. green and yellow . . 20 10
1411 – 80h. blue and pink . . . 20 10
DESIGN: 80h. "Slovak Insurrection" Hotel, Lower Tatra.

424 Statuary (after Michelangelo)

1964. UNESCO Cultural Anniversaries.
1412 **424** 40h. black and green . . 20 10
1413 – 60h. black and red . . . 20 10
1414 – 1k. black and blue . . . 45 15
1415 – 1k.60 black and yellow 45 10
DESIGNS—HORIZ: 40h. Type **424** (400th death anniv of Michelangelo); 60h. Bottom, "Midsummer Night's Dream" (400th birth anniv of Shakespeare); 1k.60, King George of Podebrady (500th anniv of his mediation in Europe). VERT: 1k. Galileo Galilei (400th birth anniv).

425 Yuri Gagarin

1964. "Space Exploration". On cream paper.
1416 **425** 30h. blue and black . . 55 15
1417 – 60h. red and green . . . 30 10
1418 – 80h. violet and lake . . 55 20
1419 – 1k. violet and blue . . 85 25
1420 – 1k.20 bronze and red . . 55 25
1421 – 1k.40 turq & black . . 1·25 55
1422 – 1k.60 turq & violet . . 3·75 1·25
1423 – 2k. red and blue 85 25
ASTRONAUTS—HORIZ: 60h. Titov; 80h. Glenn; 1k.20, Popovich and Nikolaev. VERT: 1k. Carpenter; 1k.40, Schirra; 1k.60, Cooper; 2k. Tereshkova and Bykovsky.

426 Campanula

427 Miner of 1764

1964. Wild Flowers.
1424 **426** 60h. purple, orge & grn 1·50 10
1425 – 80h. multicoloured . . . 1·50 10
1426 – 1k. blue, pink & green 1·50 40
1427 – 1k.20 multicoloured . . 60 30
1428 – 1k.60 violet & green . . 80 40
1429 – 2k. red, turq & violet . . 4·75 1·90
FLOWERS: 80h. Musk thistle; 1k. Chicory; 1k.20, Yellow iris; 1k.60, Marsh gentian; 2k. Common poppy.

1964. Czech Anniversaries.
1430 – 30h. black and yellow . . 25 10
1431 – 60h. red and blue . . . 50 10
1432 **427** 60h. sepia and green . . 25 10
DESIGNS—HORIZ: (30½ × 22½ mm): 30h. Silesian coat of arms (stylized) (150th Anniv of Silesian Museum, Opava). (41½ × 23 mm): 60h. (No. 1431), Skoda ASC-16 fire engine (Centenary of Voluntary Fire Brigades); 60h. (No. 1432), (Bicentenary of Banska Stiavnica Mining School).

428 Cine-film "Flower"

429 Hradcany, Prague and Black-headed Gulls

1964. 14th Int Film Festival, Karlovy Vary.
1433 **428** 60h. black, blue & red 1·60 10

1964. 4th Czech Red Cross Congress, Prague.
1434 **429** 60h. violet and red . . . 45 10

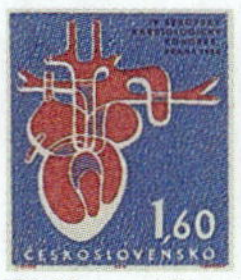

430 Human Heart

431 Slovak Girl and Workers

1964. 4th European Cardiological Congress, Prague.
1435 **430** 1k.60 red and blue . . . 1·00 10

1964. 20th Anniv of Slovak Rising and Dukla Battles.
1436 **431** 30h. red and brown . . 10 10
1437 – 60h. blue and red . . . 10 10
1438 – 60h. sepia and red . . . 10 10
DESIGNS: No. 1437, Armed Slovaks; 1438, Soldiers in battle at Dukla Pass.

432 Hradcany, Prague

433 Cycling

1964. Millenary of Prague.
1439 **432** 60h. brown & mauve . . 45 10
MS1439a 76 × 99 mm. 5k. red (Charles Bridge and City). Imperf 2·75 2·40

1964. Olympic Games, Tokyo. Multicoloured.
1440 60h. Type **433** 40 20
1441 80h. Throwing the discus and pole vaulting (vert) 45 20
1442 1k. Football (vert) 45 20
1443 1k.20 Rowing (vert) 55 35
1444 1k.60 Swimming 90 35
1445 2k.80 Weightlifting . . . . 4·00 2·40

433a "Voskhod", Astronauts and Globe

1964. Three-manned Space Flight of October 12–13.
MS1445a **433a** 3k. blue and lilac 5·75 4·25

434 Common Redstart

435 Brno Engineering Works (150th Anniv)

1964. Birds. Multicoloured.
1446 30h. Type **434** 35 10
1447 60h. Green woodpecker . . 65 10
1448 80h. Hawfinch 90 25
1449 1k. Black woodpecker . . . 90 30
1450 1k.20 European robin . . . 90 35
1451 1k.60 Eurasian roller . . . 1·40 90

1964. Czech Engineering.
1452 **435** 30h. brown 10 10
1453 – 60h. green and salmon . . 25 10
DESIGN: 60h. Class T334.0 diesel-hydraulic shunter.

436 "Dancing Girl"

437 Mountain Rescue Service (10th Anniv)

1965. 3rd National Spartacist Games.
1454 **436** 30h. red and blue . . . 10 10
See also Nos. 1489/92.

1965. Sports Events of 1965.
1455 **437** 60h. violet and blue . . 20 10
1456 – 60h. lake and orange . . 20 10
1457 – 60h. green and red . . . 20 10
1458 – 60h. green and yellow . . 20 10
SPORTS: No. 1456, Exercising with hoop (1st World Artistic Gymnastics Championships, Prague); 1457, Cycling (World Indoor Cycling Championships, Prague); 1458, Hurdling (Czech University Championships, Brno).

438 Domazlice

439 Exploration of Mars

1965. 700th Annivs of Six Czech Towns, and 20th Anniv of Terezin Concentration Camp (No. 1465).
1459 **438** 30h. violet and yellow 20 10
1460 – 30h. violet and blue . . 20 10
1461 – 30h. blue and olive . . . 20 10
1462 – 30h. sepia and olive . . 20 10
1463 – 30h. green and buff . . . 20 10
1464 – 30h. slate and drab . . . 20 10
1465 – 30h. red and black . . . 20 10
TOWNS: No. 1460, Beroun; 1461, Zatec; 1462, Policka; 1463, Lipnik and Becvou; 1464, Frydek-Mistek; 1465, Terezin concentration camp.

1965. Int Quiet Sun Years and Space Research.
1466 – 20h. purple and red . . 25 10
1467 – 30h. yellow and red . . 25 10
1468 – 60h. blue and yellow . . 25 10
1469 – 1k. violet & turquoise . . 50 10
1470 – 1k.40 slate and salmon 50 25
1471 **439** 1k.60 black and pink . . 50 25
1472 – 2k. blue & turquoise . . 1·40 1·25
DESIGNS—HORIZ: 20h. Maximum sun-spot activity; 30h. Minimum sun-spot activity ("Quiet Sun"); 60h. Moon exploration; 1k.40, Artificial satellite and space station; 2k. Soviet "Kosmos" and U.S. "Tiros" satellites. VERT: 1k. Space-ships rendezvous.

440 Horse Jumping (Amsterdam, 1928)

1965. Czechoslovakia's Olympic Victories.
1473 **440** 20h. brown and gold . . 20 10
1474 – 30h. violet and green . . 20 10
1475 – 60h. blue and gold . . . 20 10
1476 – 1k. brown and gold . . 40 20
1477 – 1k.40 green and gold . . 85 55
1478 – 1k.60 black and gold . . 85 55
1479 – 2k. red and gold 85 25
DESIGNS (each with city feature): 30h. Throwing the discus (Paris, 1900); 60h. Marathon (Helsinki, 1952); 1k. Weightlifting (Los Angeles, 1932); 1k.40, Gymnastics (Berlin, 1936); 1k.60, Rowing (Rome, 1960); 2k. Gymnastics (Tokyo, 1964).

441 Leonov in Space

1965. Space Achievements.
1480 **441** 60h. purple and blue . . 15 20
1481 – 60h. blue and mauve . . 15 20
1482 – 3k. purple and blue . . . 1·40 1·10
1483 – 3k. blue and mauve . . 1·40 1·10
DESIGNS: No. 1481, Grissom, Young and "Gemini 3"; 1482, Leonov leaving spaceship "Voskhod 2"; 1483, "Gemini 3" on launching pad at Cape Kennedy.

442 Soldier

1965. 20th Anniv of Liberation. Inscr "20 LET CSSR".
1484 **442** 30h. olive, black & red 20 10
1485 – 30h. violet, blue & red 20 10
1486 – 60h. black, red & blue 25 10
1487 – 1k. violet, brown & orge 50 20
1488 – 1k.60 multicoloured . . 85 40
DESIGNS: 30h. (No. 1485), Workers; 60h. Mechanic; 1k. Building worker; 1k.60, Peasant.

443 Children's Exercises

1965. 3rd National Spartacist Games.
1489 **443** 30h. blue and red . . . 15 10
1490 – 60h. brown and blue . . 20 10
1491 – 1k. blue and yellow . . . 30 10
1492 – 1k.60 red and brown . . 35 25
DESIGNS: 60h. Young gymnasts; 1k. Women's exercises; 1k.60, Start of race.

444 Slovak "Kopov"

1965. Canine Events.
1493 **444** 30h. black and red . . . 40 10
1494 – 40h. black & yellow . . 40 10
1495 – 60h. black and red . . 50 10
1496 – 1k. black and red . . 95 10
1497 – 1k.60 black & yellow . . 60 25
1498 – 2k. black and orange . . 2·10 1·10
DOGS: 30h. Type **444**; 1k. Poodle (Int Dog-breeders' Congress, Prague); 40h. German sheepdog; 60h. Czech "fousek" (retriever), (both World Dog Exn, Brno); 1k.60, Czech terrier; 2k. Afghan hound (both Plenary Session of F.C.I.—Int Federation of Cynology, Prague).

445 U.N. Emblem

1965. U.N. Commem and Int Co-operation Year.
1499 **445** 60h. brown & yellow . . 20 10
1500 – 1k. blue and turquoise 45 10
1501 – 1k.60 red and gold . . . 45 30
DESIGNS: 60h. T **445** (The inscr reads "Twentieth Anniversary of the signing of the U.N. Charter"); 1k. U.N. Headquarters ("20th Anniv of U.N."); 1k.60, I.C.Y. emblem.

446 "SOF" and Linked Rings

1965. 20th Anniv of World Federation of Trade Unions.
1502 **446** 60h. red and blue . . . 35 10

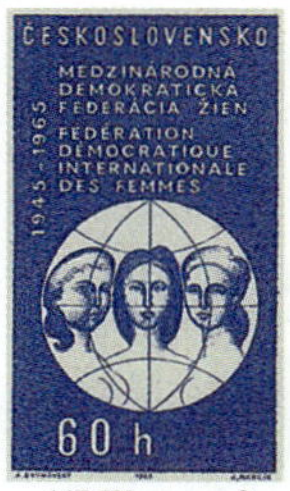

447 Women of Three Races

448 Children's House

1965. 20th Anniv of International Democratic Women's Federation.
1503 **447** 60h. blue 35 10

1965. Prague Castle (1st series). Inscr "PRAHA HRAD".
1504 **448** 30h. green 20 10
1505 – 60h. sepia 25 10
DESIGN—VERT: 60h. Mathias Gate.
See also Nos. 1572/3, 1656/7, 1740/1, 1827/8, 1892/3, 1959/60, 2037/8, 2103/4, 2163/4, 2253/4, 2305/6, 2337/8, 2404/5, 2466/7, 2543/4, 2599/2600, 2637/8, 2685/6, 2739/40, 2803/4, 2834/5, 2878/9, 2950/1, 2977/8 and 3026/7.

449 Marx and Lenin

450 Jan Hus

1965. 6th Organization of Socialist Countries' Postal Ministers Conference, Peking.
1506 **449** 60h. red and gold . . . 25 10

1965. Various Anniversaries and Events (1st issue).
1507 **450** 60h. black and red . . . 25 10
1508 – 60h. blue and red . . . 25 10
1509 – 60h. lilac and gold . . . 25 10
1510 – 1k. blue and orange . . 30 10
DESIGNS—VERT: No. 1507, T **450** (reformer, 550th death anniv); 1508, G. J. Mendel (publication cent in Brno of his study of heredity). HORIZ: (30½ × 23 mm): No. 1509, Jewellery emblems ("Jablonec 65" Jewellery Exn); 1510, Early telegraph and telecommunications satellite (I.T.U. cent).

451 "Lady at her Toilet" (after Titian)

1965. Culture. Sheet 75 × 99 mm.
MS1511 **451** 5k. multicoloured 3·50 3·00

1965. Various Anniversaries and Events (2nd issue). As T **450**.
1512 30h. black and green . . . 15 10
1513 30h. black and brown . . . 15 10
1514 60h. black and red 20 10
1515 60h. brown on cream . . . 20 10
1516 1k. black and orange . . . 20 10
DESIGNS—As Type **450**. HORIZ: No. 1512, L. Stur (nationalist, 150th birth anniv); 1513, J. Navratil (painter, death cent). VERT: No. 1514, B. Martinu (composer, 75th birth anniv). LARGER—VERT: (23½ × 30½ mm): No. 1515, Allegoric figure (Academia Istropolitana, Bratislava, 500th anniv). HORIZ: (30 × 22½ mm): No. 1516, Emblem (IUPAC Macromolecular Symposium, Prague).

452 "Fourfold Aid"

454 Levoca

453 Dotterel

1965. Flood Relief.
1517 **452** 30h. blue 15 10
1518 – 2k. black and olive . . . 70 40
DESIGN—HORIZ: 2k. Rescue by boat.

1965. Mountain Birds. Multicoloured.
1519 30h. Type **453** 60 10
1520 60h. Wallcreeper (vert) . . . 60 10
1521 1k.20 Redpoll 65 30
1522 1k.40 Golden eagle (vert) . . 1·10 35
1523 1k.60 Ring ousel 90 40
1524 2k. Spotted nutcracker (vert) 2·00 1·50

1965. Czech Towns. (a) Size 23 × 19 mm.
1525 **454** 5h. black and yellow . . 10 10
1526 – 10h. blue and bistre . . 20 10
1527 – 20h. sepia and blue . . . 10 10
1528 – 30h. blue and green . . 20 10
1529 – 40h. sepia and blue . . . 20 10
1530 – 50h. black and buff . . . 25 10
1531 – 60h. red and blue . . . 30 10
1532 – 1k. violet and green . . 35 10

(b) Size 30½ × 23½ mm.
1533 – 1k.20 olive and blue . . . 30 10
1534 – 1k.60 blue and yellow . . . 55 10
1535 – 2k. bronze and green . . . 70 10
1536 – 3k. purple & yellow . . . 85 10
1537 – 5k. black and pink . . . . 1·60 10
TOWNS: 10h. Jindrichuv Hradec; 20h. Nitra; 30h. Kosice; 40h. Hradec Kralove; 50h. Telc; 60h. Ostrava; 1k. Olomouc; 1k.20, Ceske Budejovice; 1k.60, Cheb; 2k. Brno; 3k. Bratislava; 5k. Prague.

455 Coltsfoot

457 "Music"

456 Panorama of "Stamps"

1965. Medicinal Plants. Multicoloured.
1538 30h. Type **455** 25 10
1539 60h. Meadow saffron . . . 45 10
1540 80h. Common poppy . . . 50 10
1541 1k. Foxglove 60 15
1542 1k.20 Arnica . . . . 1·00 25
1543 1k.60 Cornflower 75 35
1544 2k. Dog rose . . . . 3·00 1·50

1965. Stamp Day.
1545 **456** 1k. red and green . . . 3·75 3·50

1966. 70th Anniv of Czech Philharmonic Orchestra.
1546 **457** 30h. black and gold . . 55 25

458 Pair Dancing

1966. Sports Events of 1966. (a) European Figure Skating Championships, Bratislava.
1547 **458** 30h. red and pink . . . 15 10
1548 – 60h. emerald and green 20 10
1549 – 1k.60 brown & yellow . . 40 20
1550 – 2k. blue and turquoise 2·50 35
DESIGNS: 60h. Male skater leaping; 1k.60, Female skater leaping; 2k. Pair-skaters taking bows.

(b) World Volleyball Championships, Prague.
1551 – 60h. red and buff 20 10
1552 – 1k. violet and blue . . . 25 10
DESIGNS—VERT: 60h. Player leaping to ball; 1k. Player falling.

459 S. Sucharda (sculptor)

460 "Ajax", 1841, Austria

1966. Cultural Anniversaries.
1553 **459** 30h. green 15 10
1554 – 30h. blue 15 10
1555 – 60h. red 20 10
1556 – 60h. brown 20 10

PORTRAITS: No. 1553, Type **459** (birth centenary); 1554, Ignac J. Pesina (veterinary surgeon, birth bicentenary); 1555, Romain Rolland (writer, birth centenary); 1556, Donatello (sculptor, 500th death anniv).

1966. Railway Locomotives.
1557 **460** 20h. brown on cream . . 40 10
1558 – 30h. violet on cream . . 40 10
1559 – 60h. purple on cream . . 40 15
1560 – 1k. blue on cream . . . 75 15
1561 – 1k.60 blue on cream . . 80 15
1562 – 2k. red on cream . . . . 3·25 1·25
LOCOMOTIVES: 30h. "Karlstejn", 1865; 60h. Class 423.0 steam locomotive, 1946; 1k. Class 498.0 steam locomotive, 1946; 1k.60, Class S699.0 electric locomotive, 1964; 2k. Class T699.0 diesel locomotive, 1964.

461 Dancer

1966. Centenary of Bedrich Smetana's "Bartered Bride" (opera). Sheet 84 × 106 mm.
MS1563 **461** 3k. red, blue and deep blue . . . . 3·00 2·40

462 Brown Trout

1966. World Angling Championships, Svit. Mult.
1564 30h. Type **462** 30 10
1565 60h. Eurasian perch (horiz) 50 10
1566 1k. Common (Mirror) carp (horiz) 65 10
1567 1k.20 Northern pike (horiz) 65 15
1568 1k.40 European grayling (horiz) . . . . 1·00 25
1569 1k.60 European eel (horiz) 3·00 1·00

463 "Solidarity of Mankind" **465** Belvedere Palace

464 W.H.O. Building

1966. 20th Anniv of UNESCO.
1570 **463** 60h. black and yellow . . 25 10

1966. Inaug of W.H.O. Headquarters, Geneva.
1571 **464** 1k. ultramarine and blue 45 10

1966. Prague Castle (2nd series).
1572 **465** 30h. blue 20 10
1573 – 60h. black and yellow . . 35 20
MS1574 75 × 97½ mm. 5k. multicoloured . . . . 2·75 3·00
DESIGN: 60h. Wood triptych, "Virgin and Child" (St. George's Church).
See also Nos. 1656/**MS**1658 and 1740/**MS**1742.

467 Scarce Swallowtail

1966. Butterflies and Moths. Multicoloured.
1575 30h. Type **467** 40 10
1576 60h. Moorland clouded yellow 70 10
1577 80h. Lesser purple emperor 70 20
1578 1k. Apollo 70 25
1579 1k.20 Scarlet tiger moth . . 1·40 35
1580 2k. Cream-spot tiger moth 4·50 1·90

468 Flags

1966. 13th Czechoslovakian Communist Party Congress.
1581 **468** 30h. red and blue . . . 20 10
1582 – 60h. red and blue . . . 20 10
1583 – 1k.60 red and blue . . . 65 10
DESIGNS: 60h. Hammer and sickle; 1k.60, Girl.

469 Indian Village

1966. "North American Indians". Centenary of Naprstek's Ethnographic Museum, Prague.
1584 **469** 20h. blue and orange . . 20 10
1585 – 30h. black and brown . . 20 10
1586 – 40h. sepia and blue . . . 20 10
1587 – 60h. green and yellow . . 25 10
1588 – 1k. purple and green . . 35 10
1589 – 1k.20 blue and mauve 50 20
1590 – 1k.40 multicoloured . . 1·25 60
DESIGNS—VERT: 30h. Tomahawk; 40h. Haida totem poles; 60h. Katchina, "good spirit" of Hopi tribe; 1k.20, Dakote calumet (pipe of peace); 1k.40, Dakota Indian chief. HORIZ: 1k. Hunting American bison.

470 Atomic Symbol

1966. Centenary of Czech Chemical Society.
1591 **470** 60h. black and blue . . 35 10

471 "Guernica", after Picasso (½-size illustration)

1966. 30th Anniv of International Brigade's War Service in Spain.
1592 **471** 60h. black and blue . . 1·75 1·75

472 Pantheon, Bratislava **473** Fair Emblem

1966. Cultural Anniversaries.
1593 **472** 30h. lilac 20 10
1594 – 60h. blue 25 10
1595 – 60h. green 25 10
1596 – 60h. brown 25 10
DESIGNS: Type **472** (21st anniv of liberation of Bratislava); 1594, L. Stur (Slovak leader) and Devin Castle; 1595, Nachod (700th anniv); 1596, Arms, globe, books and view of Olomouc (400th anniv of State Science Library).

1966. Brno International Fair.
1597 **473** 60h. black and red . . . 25 10

474 "Atomic Age" **475** Olympic Coin

1966. Jachymov (source of pitch-blende).
1598 **474** 60h. black and red . . . 35 10

1966. 70th Anniv of Olympic Committee.
1599 **475** 60h. black and gold . . 20 10
1600 – 1k. blue and red . . . 85 20
DESIGN: 1k. Olympic flame and rings.

476 Missile Carrier, Tank and Mikoyan Gurevich MiG-21D Fighter

1966. Military Manoeuvres.
1601 **476** 60h. black and yellow . . 35 10

477 Moravian Silver Thaler (reverse and obverse) **480** Eurasian badger

479 First Space Rendezvous

1966. Brno Stamp Exhibition.
1602 **477** 30h. black and red . . . 30 10
1603 – 60h. black and orange 30 10
1604 – 1k.60 black and green 85 30
MS1605 75 × 100 mm. 5k. multicoloured . . . . 3·25 3·25
DESIGNS—HORIZ: 60h. "Mercury"; 1k.60, Brno buildings and crest.

1966. Space Research.
1606 **479** 20h. violet and green . . 30 10
1607 – 30h. green and orange 30 10
1608 – 60h. blue and mauve . . 30 10
1609 – 80h. purple and blue . . 30 10
1610 – 1k. black and violet . . 30 10
1611 – 1k.20 red and blue . . . 1·40 55
DESIGNS: 30h. Satellite and "back" of Moon; 60h. "Mariner 4" and first pictures of Mars; 80h. Satellite making "soft" landing on Moon; 1k. Satellite, laser beam and binary code; 1k.20, "Telstar", Earth and tracking station.

1966. Game Animals. Multicoloured.
1612 30h. Type **480** 20 10
1613 40h. Red deer (vert) 25 10
1614 60h. Lynx 30 10
1615 80h. Brown hare 40 25
1616 1k. Red fox 50 25
1617 1k.20 Brown bear (vert) . . 50 30
1618 2k. Wild boar . . . . . . 3·75 1·10

481 "Spring" (V. Hollar)

1966. Art (1st series).
1619 **481** 1k. black . . . . 5·50 2·25
1620 – 1k. multicoloured . . . 3·25 2·25
1621 – 1k. multicoloured . . . 3·50 2·75
1622 – 1k. multicoloured . . . 3·25 2·25
1623 – 1k. multicoloured . . . 28·00 20·00

PAINTINGS: No. 1620, "Mrs. F. Wussin" (J. Kupecky); 1621, "Snowy Owl" (K. Purkyne); 1622, "Bouquet" (V. Spale); 1623, "Recruit" (L. Fulla).
See also Nos. 1669, 1699/1703, 1747, 1753, 1756, 1790/4, 1835/8, 1861/5, 1914/18, 1999/2003, 2067/71, 2134/9, 2194/8, 2256/60, 2313/16, 2375/9, 2495/9, 2549/53, 2601/5, 2655/9, 2702/6, 2757/61, 2810/14, 2858/62, 2904/8, 2954/6, 3000/2, 3044/7, 3077/81 and 3107/9.

482 "Carrier Pigeon"

1966. Stamp Day.
1624 **482** 1k. blue and yellow . . . 1·10 90

483 "Youth" (5th Czech Youth Federation Congress) **484** Distressed Family

1967. Czech Congresses.
1625 **483** 30h. red and blue . . . 20 10
1626 – 30h. red and yellow . . 20 10
DESIGN: No. 1626, Rose and T.U. emblem (6th Trade Union Congress).

1967. "Peace for Viet-Nam".
1627 **484** 60h. black and salmon 25 10

485 Jihlava

1967. International Tourist Year.
1628 **485** 30h. purple 15 10
1629 – 40h. red 15 10
1630 – 1k.20 blue 40 30
1631 – 1k.60 black . . . . . 1·90 50
DESIGNS—As Type **485**: 40h. Brno. (76 × 30 mm): 1k.20, Bratislava; 1k.60, Prague.

486 Black-tailed Godwit

1967. Water Birds. Multicoloured.
1632 30h. Type **486** 25 10
1633 40h. Common shoveler (horiz) 35 10
1634 60h. Purple heron 35 10
1635 80h. Penduline tit 70 25
1636 1k. Pied avocet 70 25
1637 1k.40 Black stork . . . . 1·50 40
1638 1k.60 Tufted duck (horiz) 2·75 1·75

487 Sun and Satellite

1967. Space Research.
1639 **487** 30h. red and yellow . . 15 10
1640 – 40h. blue and grey . . 15 10
1641 – 60h. green and violet . . 25 10
1642 – 1k. blue and mauve . . 25 10
1643 – 1k.20 black and blue . . 40 25
1644 – 1k.60 lake and grey . . 1·75 45
DESIGNS: 40h. Space vehicles in orbit; 60h. "Man on the Moon" and orientation systems; 1k. "Exploration of the planets"; 1k.20, Lunar satellites; 1k.60, Lunar observatory and landscape.

488 Gothic Art (after painting by Theodoric)

1967. World Fair, Montreal. Multicoloured.
1645 30h. Type **488** 15 10
1646 40h. Jena Codex—ancient manuscript, "Burning of John Hus" 15 10
1647 60h. Lead crystal glass . . . 20 10
1648 80h. "The Shepherdess and the Chimney Sweep" (Andersen's Fairy Tales), after painting by J. Trnka 30 10
1649 1k. Atomic diagram ("Technical Progress") . . 35 25
1650 1k.20 Dolls by P. Rada ("Ceramics") . . . . . . 1·75 95
MS1651 95 × 75 mm. 3k. Montreal skyline . . . . 3·00 2·75

489 Bicycle Wheels and Dove

1967. Sports Events of 1967.
1652 **489** 60h. black and red . . . 20 10
1653 – 60h. black & turquoise 20 10
1654 – 60h. black and blue . . 20 10
1655 – 1k.60 black and violet 1·50 45
DESIGNS—HORIZ: Type **489** (20th Warsaw–Berlin–Prague Cycle Race): No. 1654, Canoeist in kayak (5th World Canoeing Championships). VERT: No. 1653, Basketball players (World Women's Basketball Championships); 1655, Canoeist (10th World Water-slalom Championships).

1967. Prague Castle (3rd series). As Type **465**.
1656 30h. lake 20 10
1657 60h. slate 50 10
MS1658 75 × 95 mm. 5k. multicoloured . . . . 2·00 3·00
DESIGNS: 30h. "Golden Street"; 60h. St. Wenceslas' Hall. SMALLER (30½ × 50 mm)—5k. "The Glory of Christ" (Bohemian 11th-century illuminated manuscript).

490 "PRAZSKE 1967" **491** Synagogue Curtain (detail)

1967. Prague Music Festival.
1659 **490** 60h. violet and green . . 25 10

1967. Jewish Culture.
1660 **491** 30h. red and blue . . . 20 10
1661 – 60h. black and green . . 25 10
1662 – 1k. blue and mauve . . 35 10
1663 – 1k.20 red and brown . . 50 10
1664 – 1k.40 black and yellow 50 10
1665 – 1k.60 green and yellow 3·75 2·75
DESIGNS: 60h. Printers' imprint (1530); 1k. Mikulov jug (1801); 1k.20, "Old-New" Synagogue, Prague (1268); 1k.40, Jewish memorial candelabra, Pinkas Synagogue (1536) (The memorial is for Czech victims of Nazi persecution); 1k.60, David Gans' tombstone (1613).

492 Lidice Rose **493** "Architecture"

1967. 25th Anniv of Destruction of Lidice.
1666 **492** 30h. black and red . . . 25 10

1967. 9th Int Architects' Union Congress, Prague.
1667 **493** 1k. black and gold . . . 35 10

494 Petr Bezruc

1967. Birth Centenary of Petr Bezruc (poet).
1668 **494** 60h. black and red . . . 25 10

1967. Publicity for "Praga 68" Stamp Exhibition. As Type **481**. Multicoloured.
1669 2k. "Henri Rousseau" (self-portrait) . . . . 2·40 1·40

495 Skalica

1967. Czech Towns.
1670 **495** 30h. blue 20 10
1671 – 30h. lake (Presov) . . . 20 10
1672 – 30h. green (Pribram) . . 20 10

496 Thermal Fountain and Colonnade, Karlovy Vary

1967. Postal Employees' Games.
1673 **496** 30h. violet and gold . . 25 10

497 Ondrejov Observatory and Universe

1967. 13th Int Astronomic Union Congress, Prague.
1674 **497** 60h. silver, blue & purple 1·75 35

498 "Miltonia spectabilis" **500** Military Vehicles

499 Eurasian Red Squirrel

1967. Botanical Garden Flowers. Multicoloured.
1675 20h. Type **498** 25 10
1676 30h. Cup and saucer plant 25 10
1677 40h. "Lycaste deppei" . . . 25 15
1678 60h. "Glottiphyllum davisii" 40 10
1679 1k. Painter's palette 60 25
1680 1k.20 "Rhodocactus bleo" 60 40
1681 1k.40 "Dendrobium phalaenopsis" . . . . . 2·40 65

1967. Fauna of Tatra National Park.
1682 **499** 30h. black, orge & yell 35 10
1683 – 60h. black and buff . . . 35 10
1684 – 1k. black and blue . . . 40 15
1685 – 1k.20 black, yell & grn 60 15
1686 – 1k.40 black, yell & pink 85 25
1687 – 1k.60 black, orge & yell 3·00 1·10
DESIGNS: 60h. Wild cat; 1k. Stoat; 1k.20, Hazel dormouse; 1k.40, West European hedgehog; 1k.60, Pine marten.

1967. Army Day.
1688 **500** 30h. green 25 10

501 Prague Castle ("PRAGA 62") **503** Pres. Novotny

1967. Air. "PRAGA 1968" Int Stamp Exhbition (1st issue).
1689 **501** 30h. multicoloured . . . 15 10
1690 – 60h. multicoloured . . . 25 20
1691 – 1k. multicoloured . . . 25 20
1692 – 1k.40 multicoloured . . 35 25
1693 – 1k.60 multicoloured . . 35 35
1694 – 2k. multicoloured . . . 55 25
1695 – 5k. multicoloured . . . 2·50 2·10
DESIGNS (Sites of previous Int Stamp Exns): 60h. Selimiye Mosque, Edirne ("ISTANBUL 1963"); 1k. Notre Dame, Paris ("PHILATEC 1964"); 1k.40, Belvedere Palace, Vienna ("WIPA 1965"); 1k.60, Capitol, Washington ("SIPEX 1965"); 2k. Amsterdam ("AMPHILEX 1967"). (40 × 55 mm): 5k. Prague ("PRAGA 1968").
See also Nos. 1718/20, 1743/8, 1749/54 and 1756.

502 Cruiser "Aurora"

1967. 50th Anniv of October Revolution.
1696 **502** 30h. red and black . . . 10 10
1697 – 60h. red and black . . . 15 10
1698 – 1k. red and black . . . 15 10
DESIGNS—VERT: 60h. Hammer and sickle emblems; 1k. "Reaching hands".

1967. Art (2nd series). As T **481**. Multicoloured.
1699 60h. "Conjurer with Cards" (F. Tichy) 25 25
1700 80h. "Don Quixote" (C. Majernik) 25 25
1701 1k. "Promenade in the Park" (N. Grund) 55 55
1702 1k.20 "Self-Portrait" (P. J. Brandl) 55 55
1703 1k.60 "Epitaph to Jan of Jeren" (Czech master) . . 4·25 4·25
All in National Gallery, Prague.

1967.
1704 **503** 2k. green . . . . 1·25 10
1705 3k. brown . . . . 1·75 10

504 Letov L-13 Glider

1967. Czech Aircraft. Multicoloured.
1706 30h. Type **504** 15 10
1707 60h. Letov L-40 Meta-Sokol 20 10
1708 80h. Letov L-200 Morava 20 10
1709 1k. Letov Z-37 Cmelak crop-sprayer 45 10
1710 1k.60 Zlin Z-526 Trener Master 55 10
1711 2k. Aero L-29 Delfin jet trainer . . . . 1·75 65

505 Czech Stamps of 1920

1967. Stamp Day.
1712 **505** 1k. lake and silver . . . 1·75 1·40

506 "CESKOSLOVENSKO 1918–1968"

1968. 50th Anniv of Republic (1st issue).
1713 **506** 30h. red, blue & ultram 70 25
See also Nos. 1780/1.

507 Skater and Stadium

1968. Winter Olympic Games, Grenoble.
1714 **507** 60h. black, yell & ochre 15 10
1715 – 1k. brown, bistre & blue 30 10
1716 – 1k.60 black, grn & lilac 55 10
1717 – 2k. black, blue & yellow 1·10 50
DESIGNS: 1k. Bobsleigh run; 1k.60, Ski jump; 2k. Ice hockey.

508 Charles Bridge, Prague, and Charles's Hydrogen Balloon **509** Industrial Scene and Red Sun

1968. Air. "PRAGA 1968" International Stamp Exhibition (2nd issue). Multicoloured.
1718 60h. Type **508** 45 15
1719 1k. Royal Summer-house, Belvedere, and William Henson's "Aerial Steam Carriage" 70 25
1720 2k. Prague Castle and airship 80 55

1968. 20th Anniv of "Victorious February".
1721 **509** 30h. red and blue . . . 10 10
1722 – 60h. red and blue . . . 15 10
DESIGN: 60h. Workers and banner.

510 Battle Plan **511** Human Rights Emblem

1968. 25th Anniv of Sokolovo Battles.
1723 **510** 30h. red, blue & green 45 10

1968. Human Rights Year.
1724 **511** 1k. red . . . . 1·10 30

512 Liptovsky Mikulas (town) and Janko Kral (writer)

1968. Various Commemorations.
1725 **512** 30h. green 25 10
1726 – 30h. blue and orange . . 25 10
1727 – 30h. red and gold . . . 25 10
1728 – 30h. purple 25 10
1729 – 1k. multicoloured . . . 40 10
DESIGNS—VERT: No. 1726, Allegorical figure of woman (150th anniv of Prague National Museum); 1727, Girl's head (cent of Prague National Theatre); 1728, Karl Marx (150th anniv of birth); 1729, Diagrammatic skull (20th anniv of W.H.O.).

513 "Radio" (45th anniv)

1968. Czech Radio and Television Annivs.
1730 **513** 30h. black, red and blue 20 10
1731 – 30h. black, red and blue 20 10
DESIGN: No. 1731, "Television" (15th anniv).

514 Athlete and Statuettes

515 Pres. Svoboda

1968. Olympic Games, Mexico. Multicoloured.
1732 30h. Type **514** 15 10
1733 40h. Runner and seated figure (Quetzalcoatl) . . . 20 10
1734 60h. Netball and ornaments 25 10
1735 1k. Altar and Olympic emblems 35 10
1736 1k.60 Football and ornaments 50 20
1737 2k. Prague Castle and key 70 55

1968.
1738 **515** 30h. blue 10 10
1738a 50h. green 10 10
1739 60h. red 25 10
1739a 1k. red 30 10

1968. Prague Castle (4th series). As Type **465**.
1740 30h. multicoloured 25 10
1741 60h. black, green & red . . 25 10
MS1742 75 × 95 mm. 5k. multicoloured . . . . 2·50 2·50
DESIGN: 30h. "Bretislav I" (from tomb in St. Vitus' Cathedral); 60h. Knocker on door of St. Wenceslas' Chapel. SMALLER (30½ × 51 mm)—5k. "St. Vitus" (detail of mosaic).

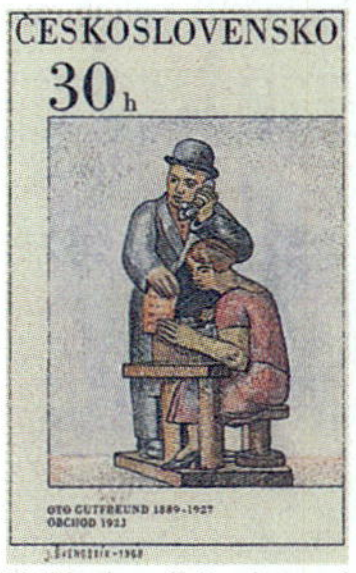

516 "Business" (sculpture by O. Gutfreund)

1968. "PRAGA 1968" Int Stamp Exn (3rd Issue). Multicoloured.
1743 30h. Type **516** 20 10
1744 40h. Broadcasting building, Prague 20 10
1745 60h. Parliament Building . . 20 20
1746 1k.40 "Prague" (Gobelin tapestry by Jan Bauch) . . 50 25
1747 2k. "The Cabaret Artiste" (painting by F. Kupka) (size 40 × 50 mm) . . . . 1·90 1·40
1748 3k. Presidential standard . . 50 45

1968. "PRAGA 1968" Int Stamp Exn (4th issue).
1749 30h. green, yellow & grey 20 10
1750 60h. violet, gold & green . . 20 10
1751 1k. indigo, pink and blue . . 30 20
1752 1k.60 multicoloured 55 25
1753 2k. multicoloured . . . . . 1·10 90
1754 3k. black, blue, pink & yell 1·25 35
DESIGNS—As Type **516**: 30h. St. George's Basilica, Prague Castle; 60h. Renaissance fountain; 1k. Dvorak's Museum; 1k.60, "Three Violins" insignia (18th-cent house); 3k. Prague emblem of 1475. As Type **481**: 2k. "Josefina" (painting by Josef Manes, National Gallery, Prague).

517 View of Prague

1968. "PRAGA 1968" (5th issue—50th Anniv of Czechoslovak Stamps). Sheet 73 × 111½ mm.
MS1755 **517** 10k. multicoloured 4·00 4·25

1968. "PRAGA 1968" (6th issue—F.I.P. Day). As T **481**.
1756 5k. multicoloured . . . . . 4·25 3·50
DESIGN: 5k. "Madonna of the Rosary" (detail from painting by Albrecht Durer in National Gallery, Prague).

518 Horse-drawn Coach on Rails "Hannibal" (140th Anniv of Ceske–Budejovice–Linz Railway)

1968. Railway Anniversaries.
1757 **518** 60h. multicoloured . . . 30 15
1758 – 1k. multicoloured . . . 85 25
DESIGN: 1k. Early steam locomotive "Johann Adolf" and modern electric locomotive (centenary of Ceske–Budejovice–Pilsen Railway).

519 Symbolic "S"

1968. 6th Int Slavonic Congress, Prague.
1759 **519** 30h. red and blue . . . 55 10

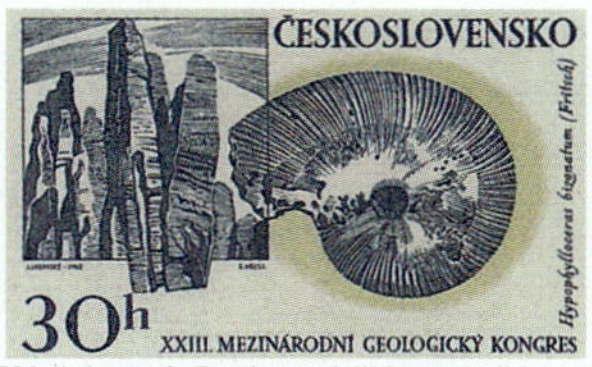

520 Adrspach Rocks and "Hypophylloceras bizonatum" (ammonite)

1968. 23rd Int Geological Congress, Prague.
1760 **520** 30h. black and yellow . . 20 10
1761 – 60h. black and mauve 20 10
1762 – 80h. black, pink & lav 25 10
1763 – 1k. black and blue . . . 35 10
1764 – 1k.60 black and yellow 1·40 55
DESIGNS: 60h. Basalt columns and fossilised frog; 80h. Bohemian "Paradise" and agate; 1k. Tatra landscape and "Chlamys gigas" shell; 1k.60, Barrandien (Bohemia) and limestone.

521 M. J. Hurban and Standard-bearer

1968. 120th Anniv of Slovak Insurrection and 25th Anniv of Slovak National Council.
1765 **521** 30h. blue 10 10
1766 – 60h. red 10 10
DESIGN: 60h. Partisans (120th anniv of Slovak Insurrection).

522 "Man and Child" (Jiri Beutler, aged 10)

1968. Munich Agreement. Drawings by children in Terezin concentration camp. Multicoloured.
1767 30h. Type **522** 20 10
1768 60h. "Butterflies" (Kitty Brunnerova, aged 11) . . 30 10
1769 1k. "The Window" (Jiri Schlessinger, aged 10) . . 45 10
The 1k. is larger (40 × 22 mm).

523 Banska Bystrica

525 Ernest Hemingway

524 National Flag

1968. Arms of Czech Regional Capitals (1st series). Multicoloured.
1770 60h. Type **523** 20 10
1771 60h. Bratislava 20 10
1772 60h. Brno 20 10
1773 60h. Ceske Budejovice . . . 20 10
1774 60h. Hradec Kralove . . . 20 10
1775 60h. Kosice 20 10
1776 60h. Ostrava 20 10
1777 60h. Pilsen 20 10
1778 60h. Usti nad Labem . . . 20 10
1779 1k. Prague (vert) 75 10
See also Nos. 1855/60, 1951/6, 2106/8 and 2214/15.

1968. 50th Anniv of Republic (2nd issue).
1780 **524** 30h. deep blue & blue 20 10
1781 – 60h. multicoloured . . . 20 10
MS1782 76 × 100 mm. 5k. red . . 3·00 3·25
DESIGN: 60h. Prague and Bratislava within outline "map" 5k. As T **6**.

1968. UNESCO. "Cultural Personalities of the 20th century in Caricature" (1st series).
1783 **525** 20h. black and red . . . 15 10
1784 – 30h. multicoloured . . . 15 10
1785 – 40h. red, black & lilac 15 10
1786 – 60h. black, green & bl 15 10
1787 – 1k. black, brn & yell . . 45 10
1788 – 1k.20 black, vio & red 50 20
1789 – 1k.40 black, brn & orge 1·40 45
PERSONALITIES: 30h. Karel Capek (dramatist); 40h. George Bernard Shaw; 60h. Maxim Gorky; 1k. Picasso; 1k.20, Taikan Yokoyama (painter); 1k.40, Charlie Chaplin.
See also Nos. 1829/34.

1968. Art (3rd series). As T **481**. Paintings in National Gallery, Prague. Multicoloured.
1790 60h. "Cleopatra II" (J. Zrzavy) 50 30
1791 80h. "The Black Lake" (J. Preisler) 70 50
1792 1k.20 "Giovanni Francisci as a Volunteer" (P. Bohun) . . . . . . 1·40 1·10
1793 1k.60 "Princess Hyacinth" (A. Mucha) 90 45
1794 3k. "Madonna and Child" (altar detail, Master Paul of Levoca) . . . . . . 4·00 3·50

526 "Cinder Boy"

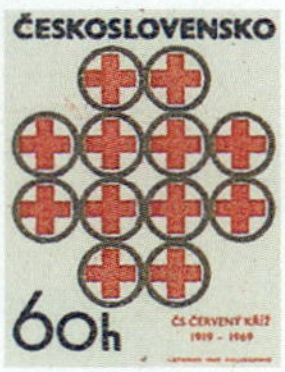

528 Red Crosses forming Cross

527 5h. and 10h. Stamps of 1918

1968. Slovak Fairy Tales. Multicoloured.
1795 30h. Type **526** 15 10
1796 60h. "The Proud Lady" . . 25 10
1797 80h. "The Knight who ruled the World" 30 10
1798 1k. "Good Day, Little Bench" 40 15
1799 1k.20 "The Enchanted Castle" 45 15
1800 1k.80 "The Miraculous Hunter" . . . . 2·00 50

1968. Stamp Day and 50th Anniv of 1st Czech Stamps.
1801 **527** 1k. gold and blue . . . 1·40 1·25

1969. 50th Anniv of Czech Red Cross and League of Red Cross Societies.
1802 **528** 60h. red, gold and sepia 25 10
1803 – 1k. red, blue and black 45 20
DESIGN: 1k. Red Cross symbols within heart-shaped "dove".

529 I.L.O. Emblem

530 Wheel-lock Pistol, c. 1580

1969. 50th Anniv of Int Labour Organization.
1804 **529** 1k. black and grey . . . 25 10

1969. Early Pistols. Multicoloured.
1805 30h. Type **530** 15 10
1806 40h. Italian horse-pistol, c. 1600 . . . . . 20 10
1807 60h. Kubik wheel-lock carbine, c. 1720 . . . . . 20 10
1808 1k. Flint-lock pistol, c. 1760 30 10
1809 1k.40 Lebeda duelling pistols, c. 1830 . . . . . 50 20
1810 1k.60 Derringer pistols, c. 1865 . . . . . 1·60 35

531 University Emblem and Symbols (50th Anniv of Brno University)

1969. Anniversaries.
1811 **531** 60h. black, blue & gold 20 10
1812 – 60h. blue 20 10
1813 – 60h. multicoloured 20 10
1814 – 60h. black and red . . . 20 10
1815 – 60h. red, silver & blue 20 10
1816 – 60h. black and gold . . 2·50 10
DESIGNS and ANNIVERSARIES: No. 1812, Bratislava Castle, open book and head of woman (50th Anniv Comenius University, Bratislava); 1813, Harp and symbolic eagle (50th Anniv Brno Conservatoire); 1814, Theatrical allegory (50th Anniv Slovak National Theatre (1970); 1815, Arms and floral emblems (Slovak Republican Council, 50th Anniv); 1816, Grammar school and allegories of Learning (Zniev Grammar School. Cent).

532 Veteran Cars of 1900–05

1969. Motor Vehicles. Multicoloured.
1817 30h. Type **532** 40 10
1818 1k.60 Veteran Cars of 1907 70 20
1819 1k.80 Prague Buses of 1907 and 1967 . . . . 1·75 85

533 "Peace" (after L. Guderna) (½-size illustration)

1969. 20th Anniv of Peace Movement.
1820 **533** 1k.60 multicoloured . . 55 25

534 Engraving by H. Goltzius

1969. Horses. Works of Art.
1821 **534** 30h. sepia on cream . . 25 10
1822 – 80h. purple on cream . . 25 10
1823 – 1k.60 slate on cream . . 40 20
1824 – 1k.80 black on cream . . 40 25
1825 – 2k.40 mult on cream . . 2·50 65
DESIGNS—HORIZ: 80h. Engraving by M. Merian. VERT: 1k.60, Engraving by V. Hollar; 1k.80, Engraving by A. Durer; 2k.40, Painting by J. E. Ridinger.

535 Dr. M. R. Stefanik as Civilian and Soldier

1969. 50th Death Anniv of General Stefanik.
1826 **535** 60h. red 35 10

536 "St. Wenceslas" (mural detail, Master of Litomerice, 1511)

1969. Prague Castle (5th series). Multicoloured.
1827 3k. Type **536** . . . . 2·10 1·40
1828 3k. Coronation Banner of the Czech Estates, 1723 2·10 1·40
See also Nos. 1892/3, 1959/60, 2037/8, 2103/4, 2163/4, 2253/4, 2305/6, 2337/8, 2404/5, 2466/7, 2543/4, 2599/600 and 2637/8.

1969. UNESCO. "Cultural Personalities of the 20th Century in Caricature" (2nd series). Designs as Type **525**.
1829 30h. black, red and blue . . 10 10
1830 40h. black, violet & blue . . 15 10
1831 60h. black, red & yellow . . 15 10
1832 1k. multicoloured 30 10
1833 1k.80 black, blue & orge . . 40 10
1834 2k. black, yellow & green 2·00 60
DESIGNS: 30h. P. O. Hviezdoslav (poet); 40h. G. K. Chesterton (writer); 60h. V. Mayakovsky (poet); 1k. Henri Matisse (Painter); 1k.80, A. Hrdlicka (anthropologist); 2k. Franz Kafka (novelist).

537 "Music"

538 Astronaut, Moon and Aerial View of Manhattan

1969. "Woman and Art". Paintings by Alfons Mucha. Multicoloured.
1835 30h. Type **537** 30 10
1836 60h. "Painting" 35 10
1837 1k. "Dance" 50 10
1838 2k.40 "Ruby and Amethyst" (40 × 51 mm) . . . . . 2·00 1·10

1969. Air. 1st Man on the Moon. Multicoloured.
1839 60h. Type **538** 20 10
1840 3k. "Eagle" module and aerial view of J. F. Kennedy Airport, New York . . . . 2·40 1·10

539 Soldier and Civilians

1969. 25th Anniv of Slovak Rising and Battle of Dukla.
1841 **539** 30h. bl & red on cream 10 10
1842 – 30h. grn & red on cream 10 10
DESIGN: No. 1842, General Svoboda and partisans.

540 Ganek (½-size illustration)

1969. 20th Anniv of Tatra National Park.
1843 **540** 60h. purple 15 10
1844 – 60h. blue 15 10
1845 – 60h. green 15 10
1846 – 1k.60 multicoloured . . 1·75 45
1847 – 1k.60 multicoloured . . 45 15
1848 – 1k.60 multicoloured . . 45 15
DESIGNS: No. 1844, Mala Valley; 1845, Bielovodska Valley. (SMALLER 40 × 23 mm): 1846, Velka Valley and gentian; 1847, Mountain stream, Mala Valley and gentian; 1848, Krivan Peak and autumn crocus.

541 Bronze Belt Fittings (8th–9th century)

1969. Archaeological Discoveries in Bohemia and Slovakia. Multicoloured.
1849 20h. Type **541** 15 10
1850 30h. Decoration showing masks (6th–8th century) 15 10
1851 1k. Gold Earrings (8th–9th century) 25 10
1852 1k.80 Metal Crucifix (obverse and reverse) (9th century) 50 25
1853 2k. Gilt ornament with figure (9th century) . . . 1·75 50

542 "Focal Point"—Tokyo

1969. 16th U.P.U. Congress, Tokyo.
1854 **542** 3k.20 multicoloured . . 1·60 1·00

1969. Arms of Czech Regional Capitals (2nd series). As T **523**. Multicoloured.
1855 50h. Bardejov 20 10
1856 50h. Hranice 20 10
1857 50h. Kezmarok 20 10
1858 50h. Krnov 20 10
1859 50h. Litomerice 20 10
1860 50h. Manetin 20 10

1969. Art (4th series). As T **481**. Multicoloured.
1861 60h. "Great Requiem" (F. Muzika) 55 50
1862 1k. "Resurrection" (Master of Trebon) 55 50
1863 1k.60 "Crucifixion" (V. Hloznik) 55 50
1864 1k.80 "Girl with Doll" (J. Bencur) 55 75
1865 2k.20 "St. Jerome" (Master Theodoric) . . . . . . 2·75 2·10

543 Emblem and "Stamps"

1969. Stamp Day.
1866 **543** 1k. purple, gold & blue 1·50 1·10

544 Ski Jumping

1970. World Skiing Championships, High Tatras. Multicoloured.
1867 50h. Type **544** 20 10
1868 60h. Cross-country skiing 20 10
1869 1k. Ski jumper "taking off" 20 10
1870 1k.60 Woman skier . . . . 1·10 35

545 J. A. Comenius (300th Death Anniv)

1970. UNESCO. Anniversaries of World Figures.
1871 **545** 40h. black 15 10
1872 – 40h. grey 25 10
1873 – 40h. brown 25 10
1874 – 40h. red 15 10
1875 – 40h. red 15 10
1876 – 40h. brown 15 10
DESIGNS: No. 1872, Ludwig van Beethoven (composer, birth bicent); 1873, Tosef Manes (artist, 150th birth anniv); 1874, Lenin (birth cent); 1875, Friedrich Engels (150th birth anniv); 1876, Maximilian Hell (astronomer, 250th birth anniv).

546 Bells

1970. World Fair, Osaka, Japan. "Expo 70". Multicoloured.
1877 50h. Type **546** 15 10
1878 80h. Heavy Machinery . . . 25 10
1879 1k. Beehives (folk sculpture) 25 10
1880 1k.60 "Angels and Saints" (17th-century icon) . . . 45 35
1881 2k. "Orlik Castle, 1787" (F. K. Wolf) 50 35
1882 3k. "Fujiyama" (Hokusai) 2·40 80
Nos. 1880/2 are larger, 51 × 37 mm.

547 Town Hall, Kosice

549 Lenin

548 "Autumn, 1955"

1970. 25th Anniv of Kosice Reforms.
1883 **547** 60h. blue, gold & red . . 35 10

1970. Paintings by Joseph Lada. Multicoloured.
1884 60h. Type **548** 20 10
1885 1k. "The Magic Horse" (vert) 40 10
1886 1k.80 "The Water Demon" (vert) 45 20
1887 2k.40 "Children in Winter, 1943" . . . . 2·00 55

1970. Birth Centenary of Lenin.
1888 **549** 30h. red and gold . . . 10 10
1889 – 60h. black and gold . . 10 10
DESIGN: 60h. Lenin (bareheaded).

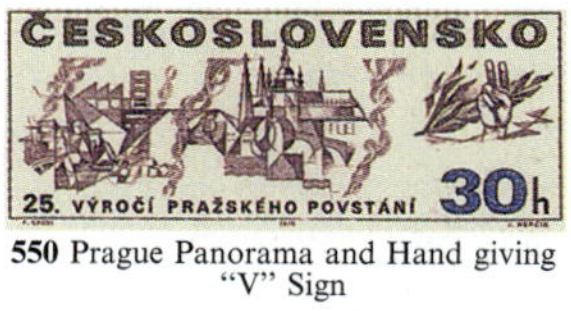

550 Prague Panorama and Hand giving "V" Sign

1970. 25th Anniv of Prague Rising and Liberation of Czechoslovakia.
1890 **550** 30h. purple, gold & blue 20 10
1891 – 30h. green, gold & red 20 10
DESIGN: No. 1891, Soviet tank entering Prague.

1970. Prague Castle. Art Treasures (6th series). As Type **536**. Multicoloured.
1892 3k. "Hermes and Athena" (painting by B. Spranger) 1·90 1·75
1893 3k. "St. Vitus" (bust) . . . 1·90 1·75

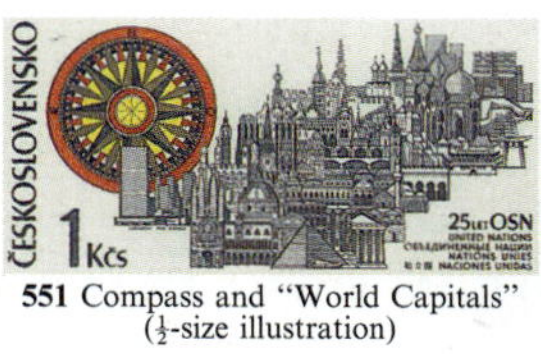

551 Compass and "World Capitals" (½-size illustration)

1970. 25th Anniv of United Nations.
1894 **551** 1k. multicoloured . . . 45 25

552 Thirty Years War Cannon and "Baron Munchausen"

1970. Historic Artillery. Multicoloured.
1895 30h. Type **552** 15 10
1896 60h. Hussite bombard and St. Barbara 15 10
1897 1k.20 Austro-Prussian War field-gun and Hradec Kralove 45 10
1898 1k.80 Howitzer (1911) and Verne's "Colombiad" . . 75 25
1899 2k.40 Mountain-gun (1915) and "Good Soldier Schweik" . . . . 1·50 50

553 "Rude Pravo"

554 "Golden Sun", Bridge-tower, Prague

1970. 50th Anniv of "Rude Pravo" (newspaper).
1900 **553** 60h. red, drab & black 20 10

1970. Ancient Buildings and House-signs from Prague, Brno and Bratislava. Multicoloured.
1901 40h. Type **554** 15 10
1902 60h. "Blue Lion" and Town Hall tower, Brno 25 10
1903 1k. Gothic bolt and Town Hall tower, Bratislava . . 25 10
1904 1k.40 Coat of arms and Michael Gate, Bratislava 1·90 35
1905 1k.60 "Moravian Eagle" and Town Hall gate, Brno 40 20
1906 1k.80 "Black Sun", "Green Frog" and bridge-tower, Prague 60 20

555 World Cup Emblem and Flags

1970. World Cup Football Championship, Mexico. Multicoloured.
1907 20h. Type **555** 10 10
1908 40h. Two players and badges of Germany and Uruguay 15 10
1909 60h. Two players and badges of England and Czechoslovakia . . . 20 10
1910 1k. Three players and badges of Rumania and Czechoslovakia 30 10
1911 1k.20 Three players and badges of Brazil and Italy 50 10
1912 1k.80 Two players and badges of Brazil and Czechoslovakia . . . . 1·75 30

556 "S.S.M." and Flags

557 Dish Aerial

1970. 1st Congress of Czechoslovak Socialist Youth Federation.
1913 **556** 30h. multicoloured . . . 35 10

1970. Art (5th series). As T **481**. Multicoloured.
1914 1k. "Mother and Child" (M. Galanda) 25 25
1915 1k.20 "The Bridesmaid" (K. Svolinsky) 50 35
1916 1k.40 "Walk by Night" (F. Hudecek) 50 40

1917 1k.80 "Banska Bystrica Market" (detail, D. Skutecky) 65 45
1918 2k.40 "Adoration of the Kings" (Vysehrad Codex) 2·10 2·40

1970. "Intercosmos". Space Research Programme. Multicoloured.
1919 20h. Type **557** 10 10
1920 40h. Experimental satellite 15 10
1921 60h. Meteorological satellite 20 10
1922 1k. Astronaut ("medical research") 25 10
1923 1k.20 Solar research 30 10
1924 1k.60 Rocket on Launch-pad . . . . 1·25 40

558 "Adam and Eve with Archangel Michael" (16th-century)

1970. Slovak Icons. Multicoloured.
1925 60h. Type **558** 20 25
1926 1k. "Mandylon" (16th-century) (horiz) . . 30 30
1927 2k. "St. George slaying the Dragon" (18th-century) (horiz) 50 50
1928 2k.80 "St. Michael the Archangel" (18th-century) 2·50 2·10

559 Czech 5h. Stamps of 1920

1970. Stamp Day.
1929 **559** 1k. red, black & green 90 85

560 "Songs from the Walls" (frontispiece, K. Stika)

561 Saris Church

1971. Czechoslovak Graphic Art (1st series).
1930 **560** 40h. brown 15 10
1931 – 50h. multicoloured . . . 20 10
1932 – 60h. grey 20 10
1933 – 1k. grey 25 10
1934 – 1k.60 black & cream . . 45 10
1935 – 2k. multicoloured . . . 1·75 50
DESIGNS: 50h. "The Fruit Trader" (C. Bouda); 60h. "Moon searching for Lilies-of-the-valley" (J. Zrzavy); 1k. "At the End of the Town" (K. Sokol); 1k.60, "Summer" (V. Hollar); 2k. "Shepherd and Gamekeeper, Orava Castle" (P. Bohun).
See also Nos. 2026/30, 2079/82, 2147/50 and 2202/5.

1971. Regional Buildings.
1936 – 50h. multicoloured . . 10 10
1936a – 1k. black, red & blue 20 10
1937 **561** 1k.60 black, vio & grn 45 10
1938 – 2k. multicoloured . . . 55 10
1939 – 2k.40 multicoloured . . 55 10
1940 – 3k. multicoloured . . . 70 10
1941 – 3k.60 multicoloured . . 85 10
1942 – 5k. multicoloured . . . 95 10
1943 – 5k.40 multicoloured . . 95 10
1944 – 6k. multicoloured . . . 1·40 10
1945 – 9k. multicoloured . . . 2·10 10
1946 – 10k. multicoloured . . 1·75 15
1947 – 14k. multicoloured . . 2·25 10
1948 – 20k. multicoloured . . 3·00 50
DESIGNS—HORIZ: 50h., 3k.60, Church, Chrudimsko; 2k.40, House, Jicinsko, 5k.40, Southern Bohemia baroque house, Posumavi; 10k. Wooden houses, Liptov; 14k. House and belfry, Valassko; 20k. Decorated house, Cicmany. (22 × 19 mm): 3k. Half-timbered house, Melnicko; 6k. Cottages, Orava; 9k. Cottage, Turnovsko. VERT: (19 × 22 mm): 1k. Ornamental roofs, Horacko; 2k. Bell-tower, Hornsek; 5k. Watch-tower, Nachodsko.

562 "The Paris Commune" (allegory) (½-size illustration)

1971. UNESCO. World Annivs. Multicoloured.
1949 1k. Type **562** 30 25
1950 1k. "World Fight against Racial Discrimination" (allegory) 30 25

1971. Arms of Czech Regional Capitals (3rd series). As Type **523**. Multicoloured.
1951 60h. Ceska Trebova 15 10
1952 60h. Karlovy Vary 15 10
1953 60h. Levoca 15 10
1954 60h. Trutnov 15 10
1955 60h. Uhersky Brod 15 10
1956 60h. Zilina 15 10

563 Chorister

564 Lenin

1971. 50th Annivs. Multicoloured.
1957 30h. Type **563** (Slovak Teachers' Choir) 20 10
1958 30h. Edelweiss, ice-pick and mountain (Slovak Alpine Organisation) (19 × 48 mm) 20 10

1971. Prague Castle (7th series). Art Treasures. As Type **536**. Multicoloured.
1959 3k. brown, buff and black 2·10 1·90
1960 3k. multicoloured . . . . . 2·10 1·90
DESIGNS: No. 1959, "Music" (16th-century wall painting); 1960, Head of 16th-century crozier.

1971. 50th Anniv of Czech Communist Party.
1961 30h. Type **564** 10 10
1962 40h. Hammer and sickle emblems 10 10
1963 60h. Clenched fists 15 10
1964 1k. Emblem on pinnacle . . 20 10

565 "50" Star Emblem

1971. 14th Czech Communist Party Congress. Multicoloured.
1965 30h. Type **565** 10 10
1966 60h. Clenched fist, worker and emblems (vert) . . . 15 10

566 Common Pheasant

1971. World Hunting Exn, Budapest. Mult.
1967 20h. Type **566** 45 10
1968 60h. Rainbow trout 15 10
1969 80h. Mouflon 20 10
1970 1k. Chamois 20 10
1971 2k. Red deer 45 20
1972 2k.60 Wild boar . . . . . 3·00 65

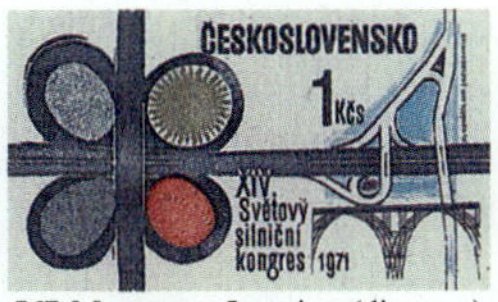
567 Motorway Junction (diagram)

1971. World Road Congress.
1973 **567** 1k. multicoloured . . . 25 10

568 Class T478.3 Diesel Locomotive

569 Gymnasts

1971. Cent of Prague C.K.D. Locomotive Works.
1974 **568** 30h. black, red & blue 10 10

1971. 50th Anniv of Proletarian Physical Federation.
1975 **569** 30h. multicoloured . . . 10 10

570 "Procession" (from "The Miraculous Bamboo Shoot" by K. Segawa)

1971. Biennial Exhibition of Book Illustrations for Children, Bratislava. Multicoloured.
1976 60h. "Princess" (Chinese Folk Tales, E. Bednarova) (vert) 20 10
1977 1k. "Tiger" (Animal Fairy Tales, Hanak) (vert) . . . 20 10
1978 1k.60 Type **570** 55 25

571 Coltsfoot and Canisters

1971. International Pharmaceutical Congress, Prague. Medicinal Plants and Historic Pharmaceutical Utensils. Multicoloured.
1979 30h. Type **571** 10 10
1980 60h. Dog rose and glass jars 15 10
1981 1k. Yellow pheasant's-eye and hand scales 25 10
1982 1k.20 Common valerian, pestle and mortar 40 10
1983 1k.80 Chicory and crucibles 55 20
1984 2k.40 Henbane and grinder 1·40 50

573 "Co-operation in Space"

1971. "Intersputnik" Day.
1997 **573** 1k.20 multicoloured . . 35 10

574 "The Krompachy Revolt" (J. Nemcik) (½-size illustration)

1971. 50th Anniv of The Krompachy Revolt.
1998 **574** 60h. multicoloured . . . 35 10

1971. Art (6th issue). As Type **481**. Multicoloured.
1999 1k. "Waiting" (I. Weiner-Kral) 40 35
2000 1k.20 "The Resurrection" (unknown 14th century artist) 40 35
2001 1k.40 "Woman with Jug" (M. Bazovsky) 55 40
2002 1k.80 "Woman in National Costume" (J. Manes) . . 70 50
2003 2k.40 "Festival of the Rosary" (Durer) . . . . 2·40 2·50

575 Wooden Dolls and Birds

576 Ancient Greek Runners

1971. 25th Anniv of UNICEF. Czech and Slovak Folk Art. Multicoloured.
2004 60h. Type **575** (frame and UNICEF emblem in bl) 15 10
2005 60h. Type **575** (frame and UNICEF emblem in black) . . . . 2·75 1·40
2006 80h. Decorated handle . . . 20 10
2007 1k. Horse and rider 20 10
2008 1k.60 Shepherd 35 20
2009 2k. Easter eggs and rattle 50 25
2010 3k. Folk hero . . . . 2·10 60

1971. 75th Anniv of Czechoslovak Olympic Committee and 1972 Games at Sapporo and Munich. Multicoloured.
2011 30h. Type **576** 10 10
2012 40h. High Jumper 10 10
2013 1k.60 Skiers 50 10
2014 2k.60 Discus-throwers, ancient and modern . . . 1·75 65

577 Posthorns

1971. Stamp Day.
2015 **577** 1k. multicoloured . . . 35 10

578 Figure Skating

1972. Winter Olympic Games, Sapporo, Japan. Multicoloured.
2016 40h. Type **578** 10 10
2017 50h. Skiing 15 10
2018 1k. Ice hockey 50 10
2019 1k.60 Bobsleighing . . . . 1·10 45

579 Sentry

580 Book Year Emblem

1972. 30th Annivs.
2020 – 30h. black and brown . . 10 10
2021 – 30h. black, red & yellow 10 10
2022 **579** 60h. multicoloured . . . 20 10
2023 – 60h. black, red & yellow 20 10
ANNIVERSARIES: No. 2020, Child and barbed wire (Terezin Concentration Camp); 2021, Widow and buildings (Destruction of Lezaky); 2022, Type **579** (Czechoslovak Unit in Russian Army); 2023, Hand and ruined building (Destruction of Lidice).

1972. International Book Year.
2024 **580** 1k. black and red . . . 35 10

581 Steam Locomotive No. 2 and Class E499.0 Electric Locomotive

582 Cycling

1972. Centenary of Kosice–Bohumin Railway.
2025 **581** 30h. multicoloured . . . 35 10

1972. Czechoslovak Graphic Art (2nd series). As Type **560**. Multicoloured.
2026 40h. "Pasture" (V. Sedlacek) 10 10
2027 50h. "Dressage" (F. Tichy) 15 10
2028 60h. "Otakar Kubin" (V. Fiala) 20 15
2029 1k. "The Three Kings" (E. Zmetak) 30 25
2030 1k.60 "Toilet" (L. Fulla) . . 1·40 1·25

1972. Olympic Games, Munich. Multicoloured.
2031 50h. Type **582** 10 10
2032 1k.60 Diving 35 20
2033 1k.80 Kayak-canoeing . . . 40 25
2034 2k. Gymnastics . . . . . . 1·25 45

583 Players in Tackle

1972. World and European Ice Hockey Championships, Prague. Multicoloured.
2035 60h. Type **583** 25 10
2036 1k. Attacking goal 45 10

1972. Prague Castle (8th series). Roof Decorations. As T **536**. Multicoloured.
2037 3k. Bohemian Lion emblem (roof boss), Royal Palace 1·00 80
2038 3k. "Adam and Eve" (bracket), St. Vitus Cathedral . . . . 2·50 2·50

1972. Czech Victory in Ice Hockey Championships. Nos. 2035/6 optd.
2039 **583** 60h. multicoloured . . . 7·00 7·00
2040 – 1k. multicoloured . . . 7·00 7·00
OVERPRINTS: 60h. **CSSR MISTREM SVETA**. 1k. **CSSR MAJSTROM SVETA**.

585 Frantisek Bilek (sculptor, birth centenary)

586 Workers with Banners

1972. Cultural Anniversaries.
2041 **585** 40h. multicoloured . . . 10 10
2042 – 40h. multicoloured . . . 10 10
2043 – 40h. green, yellow & blue 10 10
2044 – 40h. multicoloured . . . 10 10
2045 – 40h. violet, blue & green 10 10
2046 – 40h. green, brown & orge 10 10
DESIGNS: No. 2042, Antonin Hudecek (painter, birth cent); 2043, Janko Kral (poet, 150th birth anniv); 2044, Ludmila Podjavorinska (writer, birth cent); 2045, Andrej Sladkovic (painter, death cent); 2046, Jan Preisler (painter, birth cent).

1972. 8th Trade Union Congress, Prague.
2047 **586** 30h. violet, red & yellow 10 10

587 Wire Coil and Cockerel

1972. Slovak Wireworking. Multicoloured.
2048 20h. Type **587** 10 10
2049 60h. Aeroplane and rosette 15 10
2050 80h. Dragon and gilded ornament 20 10
2051 1k. Steam locomotive and pendant 55 10
2052 2k.60 Owl and tray 75 55

588 "Jiskra" (freighter)

1972. Czechoslovak Ocean-going Ships. Mult.
2053 50h. Type **588** 25 10
2054 60h. "Mir" (freighter) . . . 30 10
2055 80h. "Republika" (freighter) 35 10
2056 1k. "Kosice" (tanker) . . . 40 10
2057 1k.60 "Dukla" (freighter) 60 10
2058 2k. "Kladno" (freighter) . . 1·60 40
Nos. 2056/8 are size 49 × 30 mm.

589 "Hussar" (ceramic tile)

1972. "Horsemanship". Ceramics and Glass. Multicoloured.
2059 30h. Type **589** 10 10
2060 60h. "Turkish Janissary" (enamel on glass) 15 10
2061 80h. "St. Martin" (painting on glass) 25 10
2062 1k.60 "St. George" (enamel on glass) 45 10
2063 1k.80 "Nobleman's Guard, Bohemia" (enamel on glass) 55 10
2064 2k.20 "Cavalryman, c. 1800" (ceramic tile) . . . . . . 1·60 50

590 Revolutionary and Red Flag

1972. 55th Anniv of Russian October Revolution and 50th Anniv of U.S.S.R.
2065 **590** 30h. multicoloured . . . 10 10
2066 – 60h. red and gold . . . 15 10
DESIGN: 60h. Soviet star emblem.

1972. Art (7th issue). As T **481**.
2067 1k. multicoloured 70 45
2068 1k.20 multicoloured 95 55
2069 1k.40 brown and cream . . 95 65
2070 1k.80 multicoloured . . . . 1·00 1·00
2071 2k.40 multicoloured . . . . 2·10 2·25
DESIGNS: 1k. "Nosegay" (M. Svabinsky); 1k.20, "St. Ladislav fighting a Nomad" (14th century painter); 1k.40, "Lady with Fur Cap" (V. Hollar); 1k.80, "Midsummer Night's Dream" (J. Liesler); 2k.40, "Self-portrait" (P. Picasso).

591 Warbler feeding young European Cuckoo

1972. Songbirds. Multicoloured.
2072 60h. Type **591** 40 15
2073 80h. European cuckoo . . . 50 15
2074 1k. Black-billed magpie . . 50 15
2075 1k.60 Northern bullfinch (30 × 23 mm) 65 25
2076 2k. Eurasian goldfinch (30 × 23 mm) . . . . . . 1·10 35
2077 3k. Song thrush (30 × 23 mm) . . . . . . 5·00 1·40

592 "Thoughts into Letters"

1972. Stamp Day.
2078 **592** 1k. black, gold & pur . . 45 40

1973. Czechoslovak Graphic Art (3rd series). As Type **560**. Multicoloured.
2079 30h. "Flowers in the Window" (J. Grus) . . . 10 10
2080 60h. "Quest for Happiness" (J. Balaz) 15 10
2081 1k.60 "Balloon" (K. Lhotak) 45 20
2082 1k.80 "Woman with Viola" (R. Wiesner) . . . . . . 1·50 25

593 "Tennis Player"

594 Red Star and Factory Buildings

1973. Sports Events. Multicoloured.
2083 30h. Type **593** 35 10
2084 60h. Figure skating 20 10
2085 1k. Spartakaid emblem . . . 35 10
EVENTS: 30h. 80th anniv of lawn tennis in Czechoslovakia; 60h. World Figure Skating Championships, Bratislava; 1k. 3rd Warsaw Pact Armies Summer Spartakiad.

1973. 25th Anniv of "Victorious February" and People's Militia (60h.).
2086 **594** 30h. multicoloured . . . 10 10
2087 – 60h. blue, red & gold . . 15 10
DESIGN: 60h. Militiaman and banners.

595 Jan Nalepka and Antonin Sochar

1973. Czechoslovak Martyrs during World War II.
2088 **595** 30h. black, red and gold on cream 10 10
2089 – 40h. black, red and green on cream 15 10
2090 – 60h. black, red and gold on cream 15 10
2091 – 80h. black, red and green on cream 15 10
2092 – 1k. black, pink and green on cream . . . 20 10
2093 – 1k.60 black, red and silver on cream . . . 1·25 50
DESIGNS: 40h. Evzen Rosicky and Mirko Nespor; 60h. Vlado Clementis and Karol Smidke; 80h. Jan Osoha and Josef Molak; 1k. Marie Kuderikova and Jozka Jaburkova; 1k.60, Vaclav Sinkule and Eduard Urx.

596 Russian "Venera" Space-probe

1973. Cosmonautics' Day. Multicoloured.
2094 20h. Type **596** 10 10
2095 30h. "Cosmos" satellite . . 10 10
2096 40h. "Lunokhod" on Moon 10 10
2097 3k. American astronauts Grissom, White and Chaffee . . . . 1·00 70
2098 3k.60 Russian cosmonaut Komarov, and crew of "Soyuz II" . . . . . . 1·10 1·40
2099 5k. Death of Yuri Gagarin (first cosmonaut) . . . 4·25 4·00
Nos. 2094/6 are size 40 × 23 mm.

597 Radio Aerial and Receiver

598 Czechoslovak Arms

1973. Telecommunications Annivs. Multicoloured.
2100 30h. Type **597** 10 10
2101 30h. T.V. colour chart . . . 10 10
2102 30h. Map and telephone . . 10 10
ANNIVERSARIES: No. 2100, 50th anniv of Czech broadcasting; 2101, 20th anniv of Czechoslovak television service; 2102, 20th anniv of nationwide telephone system.

1973. Prague Castle (9th series). As Type **536**. Multicoloured.
2103 3k. Gold seal of Charles IV 1·75 2·00
2104 3k. Rook showing Imperial Legate (from "The Game and Playe of Chesse" by William Caxton) 90 60

1973. 25th Anniv of May 9th Constitution.
2105 **598** 60h. multicoloured . . . 10 10

1973. Arms of Czech Regional Capitals (4th series). As T **523**.
2106 60h. multicoloured (Mikulov) 20 10
2107 60h. multicoloured (Smolenice) 20 10
2108 60h. black and gold (Zlutice) 20 10

599 "Learning."

600 Tulip

1973. 400th Anniv of Olomouc University.
2109 **599** 30h. multicoloured . . . 10 10

1973. Olomouc Flower Show. Multicoloured.
2110 60h. Type **600** 95 55
2111 1k. Rose 75 25
2112 1k.60 Anthurium 35 20
2113 1k.80 Iris 40 25
2114 2k. Chrysanthemum . . . . 1·75 2·25
2115 3k.60 Boat orchid . . . . . 1·10 30
Nos. 2112/13 and 2115 are smaller, size 23 × 50 mm.

601 Irish Setter

1973. 50th Anniv of Czechoslovak Hunting Organization. Hunting Dogs. Multicoloured.
2116 20h. Type **601** 10 10
2117 30h. Czech whisker 10 10
2118 40h. Bavarian mountain bloodhound 10 10
2119 60h. German pointer . . . 15 10
2120 1k. Golden cocker spaniel 20 10
2121 1k.60 Dachshund . . . . . 2·00 60

602 "St. John the Baptist" (M. Svabinsky)

603 Congress Emblem

1973. Birth Centenary of Max Svabinsky (artist and designer).
2122 **602** 20h. black and green . . 10 10
2123 – 60h. black and yellow . . 20 10
2124 – 80h. black 25 25
2125 – 1k. green 25 25
2126 – 2k.60 multicoloured . . 2·10 1·90
DESIGNS: 60h. "August Noon"; 80h. "Marriage of True Minds"; 1k. "Paradise Sonata 1"; 2k.60, "The Last Judgement" (stained glass window).

1973. 8th World Trade Union Congress, Varna, Bulgaria.
2127 **603** 1k. multicoloured . . . 10 10

604 Tupolev Tu-104A over Bitov Castle

1973. 50th Anniv of Czechoslovak Airlines. Multicoloured.
2128 30h. Type **604** 10 10
2129 60h. Ilyushin Il-62 and Bezdez Castle 15 10
2130 1k.40 Tupolev Tu-134A and Orava Castle 40 10
2131 1k.90 Ilyushin Il-18 and Veveri Castle 55 20
2132 2k.40 Ilyshin Il-14P and Pernstejn Castle . . . . . 2·75 60
2133 3k.60 Tupolev Tu-154 and Trencin Castle 70 25

1973. Art (8th series). As Type **481**.
2134 1k. multicoloured . . . . . 1·75 1·60
2135 1k.20 multicoloured . . . . 1·75 1·60
2136 1k.80 black and buff 65 50
2137 2k. multicoloured 75 65
2138 2k.40 multicoloured 90 75
2139 3k.60 multicoloured . . . . 1·10 1·25
DESIGNS: 1k. "Boy from Martinique" (A. Pelc); 1k.20, "Fortitude" (M. Benka); 1k.80, Self-portrait (Rembrandt); 2k. "Pierrot" (B. Kubista); 2k.40, "Ilona Kubinyiova" (P. Bohun); 3k.60, Madonna and Child" (unknown artist, c. 1350).

605 Mounted Postman

1973. Stamp Day.
2140 **605** 1k. multicoloured . . . 25 25

606 "CSSR 1969–1974"

607 Bedrich Smetana (composer) (150th birth anniv)

1974. 5th Anniv of Federal Constitution.
2141 **606** 30h. red, blue and gold 10 10

1974. Celebrities' Birth Anniversaries.
2142 **607** 60h. multicoloured . . . 20 10
2143 – 60h. multicoloured . . . 20 10
2144 – 60h. brown, blue & red 20 10
DESIGNS AND ANNIVERSARIES: No. 2143, Josef Suk (composer, birth anniv); 2144, Pablo Neruda (Chilean poet, 70th birth anniv).

608 Council Building, Moscow

1974. 25th Anniv of Communist Bloc Council of Mutual Economic Assistance.
2145 **608** 1k. violet, red & gold . . 10 10

609 Exhibition Allegory

1974. "BRNO 74" National Stamp Exhibition (1st issue).
2146 **609** 3k.60 multicoloured . . 80 25

1974. Czechoslovak Graphic Art (4th series). As T **560**. Inscr "1974". Multicoloured.
2147 60h. "Tulips" (J. Broz) . . . 20 10
2148 1k. "Structures" (O. Dubay) 30 10
2149 1k.60 "Golden Sun-Glowing Day" (A. Zabransky) . . 55 15
2150 1k.80 "Artificial Flowers" (F. Gross) . . . . 1·50 35

610 Oskar Benes and Vaclav Prochazka

1974. Czechoslovak Partisan Heroes. Mult.
2151 30h. Type **610** 10 10
2152 40h. Milos Uher and Anton Sedlacek 10 10
2153 60h. Jan Hajecek and Marie Sedlackova 15 10
2154 80h. Jan Sverma and Albin Grznar 20 10
2155 1k. Jaroslav Neliba and Alois Hovorka 30 10
2156 1k.60 Ladislav Exnar and Ludovit Kukorelli . . . . 1·50 25

611 "Water—Source of Energy"

1974. International Hydrological Decade. Mult.
2157 60h. Type **611** 55 30
2158 1k. "Water for Agriculture" 55 30
2159 1k.20 "Study of the Oceans" 55 30
2160 1k.60 Decade emblem . . . 60 30
2161 2k. "Keeping water pure" 1·75 2·00

612 "Telecommunications"

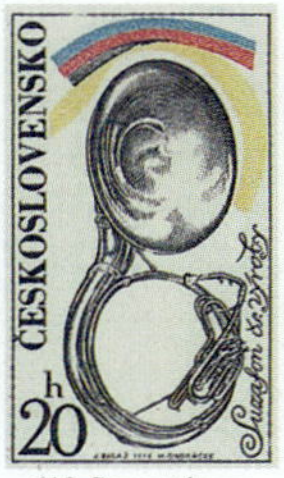

613 Sousaphone

1974. Inauguration of Czechoslovak Satellite Telecommunications Earth Station.
2162 **612** 30h. multicoloured . . . 25 10

1974. Prague Castle (10th series). As Type **536**. Multicoloured.
2163 3k. "Golden Cockerel", 17th-century enamel locket . . . . 1·75 1·90
2164 3k. Bohemian glass monstrance, 1840 . . . . 1·75 1·90

1974. Musical Instruments. Multicoloured.
2165 20h. Type **613** 15 10
2166 30h. Bagpipes 15 10
2167 40h. Benka violin 20 10
2168 1k. Sauer pyramid piano . . 30 15
2169 1k.60 Hulinsky tenor quinton . . . . 1·25 30

614 Child and Flowers (book illustration)

615 "Stamp Collectors"

1974. 25th International Children's Day.
2170 **614** 60h. multicoloured . . . 10 10

1974. "BRNO 74" National Stamp Exhibition (2nd issue). Multicoloured.
2171 30h. Type **615** 10 10
2172 6k. "Rocket Post" . . . . . 2·00 1·25

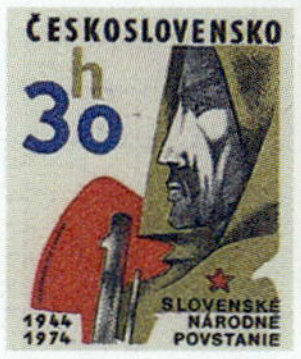

616 Slovak Partisan

617 "Hero and Leander"

1974. Czechoslovak Anniversaries. Multicoloured.
2173 30h. Type **616** 15 10
2174 30h. Folk-dancer 15 10
2175 30h. Actress holding masks 15 10
EVENTS: No. 2173, 30th anniv of Slovak Uprising; 2174, 25th anniv of Slovak SLUK Folk Song and Dance Ensemble; 2175, 25th anniv of Bratislava Academy of Music and Dramatic Arts.

1974. Bratislava Tapestries. "Hero and Leander" (1st series). Multicoloured.
2176 2k. Type **617** . . . . . . 1·50 1·25
2177 2k.40 "Leander Swimming across the Hellespont" . . 1·50 1·75
See also Nos. 2227/8 and 2281/2.

618 "Soldier on Guard"

620 Posthorn and Old Town Bridge Tower, Prague

619 U.P.U. Emblem and Postilion

1974. Old Shooting Targets. Multicoloured.
2178 30h. Type **618** 15 10
2179 60h. "Pierrot and Owl", 1828 . . . . 20 15
2180 1k. "Diana awarding Marksman's Crown", 1832 . . . . 30 15
2181 1k.60 "Still Life with Guitar", 1839 . . . . . 45 40
2182 2k.40 "Stag", 1834 . . . . 70 60
2183 3k. "Turk and Giraffe", 1831 . . . . 2·75 2·75

1974. Centenary of Universal Postal Union. Mult.
2184 30h. Type **619** 10 10
2185 40h. Early mail coach . . . 10 10
2186 60h. Early railway carriage 35 10
2187 80h. Modern mobile post office 25 10
2188 1k. Ilyushin Il-14 mail plane 60 10
2189 1k.60 Dish aerial, earth station . . . . 1·00 35

1974. Czechoslovak Postal Services.
2190 **620** 20h. multicoloured . . . 10 10
2191 – 30h. red, blue & brn . . 10 10
2192 – 40h. multicoloured . . . 10 10
2193 – 60h. orange, yell & bl . . 15 10
DESIGNS: 30h. P.T.T. emblem within letter; 40h. Postilion; 60h. P.T.T. emblem on dove's wing.
See also No. 2900.

1974. Art (9th series). As Type **481**. Multicoloured.
2194 1k. "Self-portrait" (L. Kuba) 80 70
2195 1k.20 "Frantisek Ondricek" (V. Brozik) 80 70
2196 1k.60 "Pitcher with Flowers" (O. Khubin) . . 80 70
2197 1k.80 "Woman with Pitcher" (J. Alexy) . . . 80 70
2198 2k.40 "Bacchanalia" (K. Skreta) . . . . 2·00 2·40

621 Stylized Posthorn

1974. Stamp Day.
2199 **621** 1k. multicoloured . . . 25 10

622 Winged Emblem

1975. Coil Stamps.
2200 **622** 30h. blue 10 10
2201 60h. red 15 10

1975. Czechoslovak Graphic Art (5th series). Engraved Hunting Scenes. As T **560**.
2202 60h. brown & cream 25 10
2203 1k. brown and cream . . . 30 15
2204 1k.60 brown & green . . . 45 25
2205 1k.80 brown & lt brown . . 1·75 50
DESIGNS: 60h. "Still Life with Hare" (V. Hollar); 1k. "The Lion and the Mouse" (V. Hollar); 1k.60, "Deer Hunt" (detail, P. Galle); 1k.80, "Grand Hunt" (detail, J. Callot).

623 "Woman"

624 Village Family

1975. International Women's Year.
2206 **623** 30h. multicoloured . . . 10 10

1975. 30th Anniv of Razing of 14 Villages. Multicoloured.
2207 60h. Type **624** 20 10
2208 1k. Women and flames . . . 25 10
2209 1k.20 Villagers and flowers 40 10

625 "Little Queens" (Moravia)

1975. Czechoslovak Folk Customs. Multicoloured.
2210 60h. Type **625** 60 60
2211 1k. Shrovetide parade, Slovakia 60 60
2212 1k.40 "Maid Dorothea" (play) 60 60
2213 2k. "Morena" effigy, Slovakia . . . . 1·40 1·40

1975. Arms of Czech Regional Capitals (5th series). As T **523**.
2214 60h. black, gold and red . . 25 10
2215 60h. multicoloured 25 10
ARMS: No. 2214, Nymburk. 2215, Znojmo.

626 Partisans at Barricade (½-size illustration)

1975. Czechoslovak Anniversaries.
2216 **626** 1k. multicoloured . . . 30 20
2217 – 1k. sepia and cream . . 30 20
2218 – 1k. multicoloured . . . 30 20
DESIGNS and ANNIVERSARIES: No. 2216, Type **626** (30th anniv of Czech Rising); 2217, Liberation celebrations (30th anniv of Liberation by Soviet Army); 2218, Czech–Soviet fraternity (5th anniv of Czech–Soviet Treaty).

627 Youth Exercises

1975. National Spartacist Games.
2219 **627** 30h. purple, bl & pink 10 10
2220 – 60h. red, lilac & yellow 15 10
2221 – 1k. violet, red & yell . . 25 20
DESIGNS: 60h. Children's exercises; 1k. Adult exercises.

628 Siamese Tigerfish and Lined Seahorse

1975. Aquarium Fishes. Multicoloured.

2222	60h. Type **628**	15	10
2223	1k. Siamese fighting fish and freshwater angelfish	30	10
2224	1k.20 Veil-tailed goldfish	65	15
2225	1k.60 Clown anemone-fish and butterflyfish	75	25
2226	2k. Yellow-banded angelfish, palette surgeonfish and semicircle angelfish	3·50	65

1975. Bratislava Tapestries. "Hero and Leander" (2nd series). As T **617**. Multicoloured.

2227	3k. "Leander's Arrival"	90	70
2228	3k.60 "Hermione"	2·25	2·40

629 "Pelicans" (N. Charushin)

1975. Biennial Exhibition of Book Illustrations for Children, Bratislava. Multicoloured.

2229	20h. Type **629**	10	10
2230	30h. "Sleeping Hero" (L. Schwarz)	10	10
2231	40h. "Horseman" (V. Munteau)	15	10
2232	60h. "Peacock" (K. Ensikat)	20	10
2233	80h. "The Stone King" (R. Dubravec)	70	35

630 "CZ-150" Motor Cycle (1951)

1975. Czechoslovak Motor Cycles. Multicoloured.

2234	20h. Type **630**	15	10
2235	40h. "Jawa 250", 1945	20	10
2236	60h. "Jawa 175", 1935	25	10
2237	1k. Janatka "ITAR", 1921	30	15
2238	1k.20 Michi "Orion", 1903	25	10
2239	1k.80 Laurin and Klement, 1898	1·60	40

631 "Solar Radiation" **632** President Gustav Husak

1975. Co-operation in Space Research.

2240	**631**	30h. violet, yellow & red	15	10
2241	–	60h. red, lilac & yellow	20	10
2242	–	1k. purple, yell & blue	25	10
2243	–	2k. multicoloured	55	10
2244	–	5k. multicoloured	3·00	2·75

DESIGNS—HORIZ: 60h. "Auroa Borealis"; 1k. Cosmic radiation measurement; 2k. Copernicus and solar radiation. VERT (40×50 mm): 5k. "Apollo-soyuz" space link.

1975.

2245	**632**	30h. blue	10	10
2246		60h. red	15	10

633 Oil Refinery

1975. 30th Anniv of Liberation. Multicoloured.

2247	30h. Type **633**	15	10
2248	60h. Atomic power complex	15	10
2249	1k. Underground Railway, Prague	40	10
2250	1k.20 Laying oil pipelines	30	15
2251	1k.40 Combine-harvesters and granary	30	20
2252	1k.60 Building construction	1·10	35

1975. Prague Castle. Art Treasures (11th series). As T **536**. Multicoloured.

2253	3k. Late 9th-century gold earring	95	75
2254	3k.60 Leather Bohemian Crown case, 1347	1·90	2·00

634 General Svoboda

1975. 80th Birthday of General Ludvik Svoboda. Sheet 76×96 mm.

MS2255	**634**	10k. multicoloured	11·50	11·50

1975. Art (10th series). As T **481**.

2256	1k. red, brown and black	75	75
2257	1k.40 multicoloured	75	75
2258	1k.80 multicoloured	75	75
2259	2k.40 multicoloured	1·10	1·25
2260	3k.40 multicoloured	1·75	1·60

PAINTINGS—VERT: 1k. "May" (Z. Sklenar); 1k.40, "Girl in National Costume" (E. Nevan); 2k.40, "Fire" (J. Capek); 3k.40, "Prague, 1828" (V. Morstadt). HORIZ: 1k.80, "Liberation of Prague" (A. Cermakova).

635 Posthorn Motif

1975. Stamp Day.

2261	**635**	1k. multicoloured	35	25

636 Frantisek Halas (poet)

1976. Celebrities' Anniversaries.

2262	**636**	60h. multicoloured	15	10
2263	–	60h. multicoloured	15	10
2264	–	60h. multicoloured	30	10
2265	–	60h. blue, red & yellow	15	10
2266	–	60h. multicoloured	15	10

DESIGNS AND ANNIVERSARIES—HORIZ: No. 2262, Type **636** (75th birth anniv); 2266, Ivan Krasko (poet, birth cent). VERT: No. 2263, Wilhelm Pieck (German statesman, birth cent); 2264, Frantisek Lexa (Egyptologist, birth cent); 2265, Jindrich Jindrich (ethnographer, birth cent).

637 Ski Jumping

1976. Winter Olympic Games, Innsbruck. Mult.

2267	1k. Type **637**	20	10
2268	1k.40 Figure skating	30	20
2269	1k.60 Ice hockey	1·25	30

638 Throwing the Javelin

1976. Olympic Games, Montreal. Multicoloured.

2270	2k. Type **638**	45	20
2271	3k. Relay-racing	80	30
2272	3k.60 Putting the shot	3·00	1·10

639 Table Tennis Player **640** Star Emblem and Workers

1976. European Table Tennis Championships, Prague and 50th Anniv of Organized Table Tennis in Czechoslovakia.

2273	**639**	1k. multicoloured	35	10

1976. 15th Czechoslovak Communist Party Congress, Prague. Multicoloured.

2274	30h. Type **640**	10	10
2275	60h. Furnace and monolith	15	10

641 Microphone and Musical Instruments **642** Hammer, Sickle and Red Flags

1976. Cultural Events and Anniversaries.

2276	**641**	20h. multicoloured	10	10
2277	–	20h. multicoloured	10	10
2278	–	20h. multicoloured	10	10
2279	–	30h. multicoloured	10	10
2280	–	30h. violet, red & blue	10	10

DESIGNS—HORIZ: No. 2276, Type **641** (50th anniv of Czechoslovak Radio Symphony Orchestra); 2278, Stage revellers (30th anniv of Nova Scena Theatre, Bratislava); 2279, Folk dancers, Wallachia (International Folk Song and Dance Festival, Straznice). VERT: No. 2277, Ballerina, violin and mask (30th anniv of Prague Academy of Music and Dramatic Art); 2280, Film "profile" (20th Film Festival, Karlovy Vary).

1976. Bratislava Tapestries. "Hero and Leander" (3rd series). As T **617**. Multicoloured.

2281	3k. "Hero with Leander's body"	2·00	1·25
2282	3k.60 "Eros grieving"	85	60

1976. 55th Anniv of Czechoslovak Communist Party.

2283	**642**	30h. blue, gold and red	15	10
2284	–	60h. multicoloured	20	10
MS2285		100×90 mm. 6k. multicoloured	2·75	3·00

DESIGN—VERT: (23×40 mm) 60h. Hammer and Sickle on flag. HORIZ (50×30 mm)—6k. Flag and commemorative inscription.

643 Manes Hall, Czechoslovakia Artists' Union

1976. Air. "PRAGA 78" International Stamp Exhibition (1st issue). Prague Architecture. Multicoloured.

2286	60h. Type **643**	35	10
2287	1k.60 Congress Hall, Julius Fucik Park	40	20
2288	2k. Powder Tower, Old Town (vert)	70	25
2289	2k.40 Charles Bridge and Old Bridge Tower	55	25
2290	4k. Old Town Square and Town Hall (vert)	85	30
2291	6k. Prague Castle and St. Vitus Cathedral (vert)	3·50	1·00

See also 2313/16, 2326/30, 2339/42, 2349/52, 2358/62, 2389/93, 2407/12, 2413/17, 2420/3 and **MS**2424/5.

644 "Warship" (Frans Huys) **645** "UNESCO" Plant

1976. Ship Engravings.

2292	**644**	40h. blk, cream & drab	35	10
2293	–	60h. blk, cream & grey	35	10
2294	–	1k. black, cream & grn	60	10
2295	–	2k. black, cream & blue	1·25	45

DESIGNS: 60h. "Dutch Merchantman" (V. Hollar); 1k. "Ship at Anchor" (N. Zeeman); 2k. "Galleon under Full Sail" (F. Chereau).

1976. 30th Anniv of UNESCO.

2296	**645**	2k. multicoloured	95	55

646 "Protected Child"

1976. European Security and Co-operation Conference, Helsinki. Sheet 114×167 mm containing two stamps as T **646**.

MS2297	6k. ×2 blue, yellow and red	5·00	5·00

647 Merino Ram **648** "Stop Smoking"

1976. "Bountiful Earth" Agricultural Exhibition, Ceske Budejovice. Multicoloured.

2298	30h. Type **647**	15	10
2299	40h. Berna-Hana Cow	15	10
2300	1k.60 Kladruby stallion	45	10

1976. W.H.O. Campaign against Smoking.

2301	**648**	2k. multicoloured	90	40

649 Postal Code Emblem **650** "Guernica 1937" (I. Weiner-Kral)

1976. Coil Stamps. Postal Code Campaign.

2302	**649**	30h. green	10	10
2303	–	60h. red	15	10

DESIGN: 60h. Postal map.

1976. 40th Anniv of International Brigades in Spanish Civil War.

2304	**650**	5k. multicoloured	1·25	55

1976. Prague Castle. Art Treasures (12th series). As T **536**. Multicoloured.

2305	3k. "Prague Castle, 1572" (F. Hoogenberghe)	2·00	1·90
2306	3k.60 "Satyrs" (relief from summer-house balustrade)	60	70

651 Common Zebra with Foal

1976. Dvurkralove Wildlife Park. Multicoloured.
2307 10h. Type **651** 15 10
2308 20h. African elephant, calf and cattle egret (vert) . . 50 15
2309 30h. Cheetah 15 10
2310 40h. Giraffe and calf (vert) 15 10
2311 60h. Black rhinoceros . . . 20 10
2312 3k. Bongo with offspring (vert) . . . . 2·00 65

1976. "PRAGA 1978" International Stamp Exhibition (2nd series). Art (11th series). As T **481**. Multicoloured.
2313 1k. "Flowers in Vase" (P. Matejka) 80 55
2314 1k.40 "Oleander Blossoms" (C. Bouda) . . . . . . 1·10 80
2315 2k. "Flowers in Vase" (J. Brueghel) . . . . . . 1·75 1·40
2316 3k.60 "Tulips and Narcissi" (J. R. Bys) 80 80

652 Postilion, Postal Emblem and Satellite

1976. Stamp Day.
2317 **652** 1k. blue, mauve & gold 25 10

653 Ice Hockey

654 Arms of Vranov

1977. 6th Winter Spartakiad of Warsaw Pact Armies. Multicoloured.
2318 60h. Type **653** 25 10
2319 1k. Rifle shooting (Biathlon) 30 10
2320 1k.60 Ski jumping . . . . . 1·40 45
2321 2k. Slalom 50 25

1977. Coats of Arms of Czechoslovak Towns (1st series). Multicoloured.
2322 60h. Type **654** 15 10
2323 60h. Kralupy and Vltavou 15 10
2324 60h. Jicin 15 10
2325 60h. Valasske Mezirici . . . 15 10
See also Nos. 2511/14, 2612/15, 2720/3, 2765/7, 2819/21 and 3017/20.

655 Window, Michna Palace

656 Children Crossing Road

1977. "PRAGA 78" International Stamp Exhibition (3rd issue). Historic Prague Windows. Multicoloured.
2326 20h. Type **655** 10 10
2327 30h. Michna Palace (different) 10 10
2328 40h. Thun Palace 10 10
2329 60h. Archbishop's Palace . . 15 10
2330 5k. Church of St. Nicholas 2·25 65

1977. 25th Anniv of Police Aides Corps.
2331 **656** 60h. multicoloured . . . 10 10

657 Cyclists at Warsaw (starting point)

658 Congress Emblem

1977. 30th Anniv of Peace Cycle Race. Mult.
2332 30h. Type **657** 15 10
2333 60h. Cyclists at Berlin . . . 20 10
2334 1k. Cyclists at Prague (finishing point) 85 25
2335 1k.40 Cyclists and modern buildings 40 15

1977. 9th Trade Unions Congress.
2336 **658** 30h. gold, red & carmine 10 10

1977. Prague Castle (13th series). As T **536**.
2337 3k. multicoloured . . . . . 1·10 1·25
2338 3k.60 green, gold & black 1·90 1·60
DESIGNS: 3k. Onyx cup, 1350 (St. Vitus Cathedral); 3k.60, Bronze horse, 1619 (A. de Vries).

659 French Postal Rider, 19th-century

1977. "PRAGA 78" International Stamp Exhibition (4th issue). Multicoloured.
2339 60h. Type **659** 15 10
2340 1k. Austrian postal rider, 1838 . . . . 30 10
2341 2k. Austrian postal rider, c. 1770 . . . . . . 50 25
2342 3k.60 German postal rider, 1700 . . . . 2·25 80

660 Coffee Pots

661 Mlada Boleslav Headdress

1977. Czechoslovak Porcelain.
2343 **660** 20h. multicoloured . . . 10 10
2344 – 30h. multicoloured . . . 10 10
2345 – 40h. multicoloured . . . 15 10
2346 – 60h. multicoloured . . . 20 10
2347 – 1k. blue, grn & violet . . 25 10
2348 – 3k. blue, gold and red 2·10 60
DESIGNS: 30h. Vase; 40h. Amphora; 60h. Jug, beaker, cup and saucer; 1k. Plate and candlestick; 3k. Coffee pot, cup and saucer.

1977. "PRAGA 78" International Stamp Exhibition (5th issue). Regional Headdresses. Multicoloured.
2349 1k. Type **661** 75 80
2350 1k.60 Vazek . . . . 3·50 3·50
2351 3k.60 Zavadka 75 80
2352 5k. Belkovice . . . . 1·25 1·10

662 V. Bombova's Illustrations of "Janko Gondashik and the Golden Lady"

1977. 6th Biennial Exhibition of Children's Book Illustrators, Bratislava. Multicoloured.
2353 40h. Type **662** 10 10
2354 60h. "Tales of Amur" (G. Pavlishin) 15 10
2355 1k. "Almgist et Wiksel" (U. Lofgren) 25 10
2356 2k. "Alice in Wonderland" and "Through the Looking Glass" (Nicole Claveloux) 75 25
2357 3k. "Eventyr" (J. Trnka) . . 2·25 65

663 Airships LZ-5 and "Graf Zeppelin"

664 UNESCO Emblem, Violin and Doves

1977. Air. "PRAGA 1978" International Stamp Exhibition (6th issue). Early Aviation. Mult.
2358 60h. Type **663** 15 10
2359 1k. Clement Ader's monoplane "Eole", Etrich Holubice and Dunne D-8 30 10
2360 1k.60 Jeffries and Blanchard balloon, 1785 . . . . . . 40 15
2361 2k. Lilienthal biplane glider, 1896 . . . . 50 15
2362 4k.40 Jan Kaspar's Bleriot XI over Prague . . . . . 3·50 85

1977. Congress of UNESCO International Music Council.
2363 **664** 60h. multicoloured . . . 10 10

665 "Peace"

1977. European Co-operation for Peace. Mult.
2364 60h. Type **665** 15 30
2365 1k.60 "Co-operation" . . . 40 45
2366 2k.40 "Social Progress" . . 1·50 60

666 Yuri Gagarin

1977. Space Research. Multicoloured.
2367 20h. S. P. Koroliov (space technician, launch of first satellite) 10 10
2368 30h. Type **666** (first man in space) 10 10
2369 40h. Aleksei Leonov (first space walker) 10 10
2370 1k. Neil Armstrong (first man on the Moon) . . . 25 10
2371 1k.60 "Salyut" and "Skylab" space stations 1·25 35

667 Revolutionaries and Cruiser "Aurora"

668 "Wisdom"

1977. 60th Anniv of Russian Revolution, and 55th Anniv of U.S.S.R. Multicoloured.
2372 30h. Type **667** 15 10
2373 30h. Russian woman, Kremlin, rocket and U.S.S.R. arms 15 10

1977. 25th Anniv of Czechoslovak Academy of Science.
2374 **668** 3k. multicoloured . . . 70 30

1977. Art (12th series). As Type **481**.
2375 2k. multicoloured 75 80
2376 2k.40 multicoloured . . . . 2·50 2·75
2377 2k.60 stone and black . . . 2·10 1·60
2378 3k. multicoloured . . . . . 1·00 1·00
2379 5k. multicoloured . . . . . 1·00 1·00
DESIGNS: 2k. "Fear" (J. Mudroch); 2k.40, "Portrait of Jan Francis" (P. M. Bohun); 2k.60, "Self Portrait" (V. Hollar); 3k. "Portrait of a Girl" (L. Cranach); 5k. "Cleopatra" (Rubens).

669 "Bratislava, 1574" (G. Hoefnagel)

1977. Historic Bratislava (1st series). Mult.
2380 3k. Type **669** . . . . . . 1·90 2·00
2381 3k.60 Bratislava Arms, 1436 1·10 80
See also Nos. 2402/3, 2500/1, 2545/6, 2582/3, 2642/3, 2698/9, 2736/7, 2793/4, 2842/3, 2898/9, 2952/3, 2997/8 and 3034/5.

670 Posthorn and Stamps

1977. Stamp Day.
2382 **670** 1k. multicoloured . . . 25 10

671 Z. Nejedly (historian)

674 Modern Coins

672 Civilians greeting Armed Guards

1978. Cultural Anniversaries. Multicoloured.
2383 30h. Type **671** (birth cent) 10 10
2384 40h. Karl Marx (160th birth anniv) 10 10

1978. 30th Annivs of "Victorious February" and National Front. Multicoloured.
2385 1k. Type **672** 20 10
2386 1k. Intellectual, peasant woman and steel worker 20 10

1978. Soviet–Czechoslovak Space Flight. No. 2368 optd **SPOLECNY LET SSSR*CSSR**.
2387 30h. red 20 15
2388 3k.60 blue . . . . 4·25 4·50

1978. 650th Anniv of Kremnica Mint and "PRAGA 1978" International Stamp Exhibition (7th issue). Multicoloured.
2389 20h. Type **674** 10 10
2390 40h. Culture medal, 1972 (Jan Kulich) 10 10
2391 1k.40 Charles University Medal, 1948 (O, Spaniel) 2·40 35
2392 3k. Ferdinand I medal, 1563 (L. Richter) 80 40
2393 5k. Gold florin of Charles Robert, 1335 . . . . . . 95 50

675 Tyre Marks and Ball

676 Hands supporting Globe

1978. Road Safety.
2394 **675** 60h. multicoloured . . . 10 10

1978. 9th World Federation of Trade Unions Congress, Prague.
2395 **676** 1k. multicoloured . . . 25 10

677 Putting the Shot

1978. Sports.
2396 – 30h. multicoloured . . . 15 10
2397 **677** 40h. multicoloured . . . 15 10
2398 – 60h. multicoloured . . . 70 15
2399 – 1k. multicoloured . . . 35 10
2400 – 2k. yellow, blue & red 55 25
2401 – 3k.60 multicoloured . . 1·75 85

DESIGNS AND EVENTS—HORIZ: 70th anniv of bandy hockey: 30h. Three hockey players, World Ice Hockey Championships; 60h. Tackle in front of goal; 2k. Goalmouth scrimmage. VERT: European Athletics Championships, Prague: 1k. Pole vault; 3k.60, Running.

1978. Historic Bratislava (2nd series). As T **669**.
2402 3k. green, violet and red . . 1·25 1·40
2403 3k.60 multicoloured . . . . 2·75 2·50
DESIGNS: 3k. "Bratislava" (Orest Dubay); 3k.60, "Fishpond Square, Bratislava" (Imro Weiner-Kral).

1978. Prague Castle (14th series). As T **536**.
2404 3k. yellow, black & green 95 80
2405 3k.60 multicoloured . . . . 3·25 2·50
DESIGNS: 3k. Memorial to King Premysl Otakar II, St. Vitus Cathedral; 3k.60, Portrait of King Charles IV (Jan Ocka).

678 Ministry of Posts, Prague

1978. 14th COMECON Meeting, Prague.
2406 **678** 60h. multicoloured . . . 10 10

679 Palacky Bridge

1978. "PRAGA 78" International Stamp Exhibition (8th issue). Prague Bridges. Multicoloured.
2407 20h. Type **679** 10 10
2408 40h. Railway bridge 55 10
2409 1k. Bridge of 1st May . . . 25 10
2410 2k. Manes Bridge 45 15
2411 3k. Svatopluk Cech Bridge . 55 30
2412 5k.40 Charles Bridge . . . 3·50 95

680 St. Peter and other Apostles **681** Dancers

1978. "PRAGA 78" International Stamp Exhibition (9th issue). Prague Town Hall Astronomical Clock. Multicoloured.
2413 40h. Type **680** 15 10
2414 1k. Astronomical clock face 20 15
2415 2k. Centre of Manes's calendar 35 15
2416 3k. "September" (grape harvest) . . . . 2·10 70
2417 3k.60 "Libra" (sign of the Zodiac) . . . . 1·25 25
MS2418 89 × 125 mm. 10k. Manes's calendar (48 × 38 mm) . . . . 10·50 12·50

1978. 25th Vychodna Folklore Festival.
2419 **681** 30h. multicoloured . . . 10 10

682 Gottwald Bridge

1978. "PRAGA 78" International Stamp Exhibition (10th issue). Modern Prague. Multicoloured.
2420 60h. Type **682** 65 10
2421 1k. Powder Gate Tower and Kotva department store 25 10
2422 2k. Ministry of Posts . . . 55 25
2423 6k. Prague Castle and flats 2·10 1·10

683 "Old Prague and Charles Bridge" (V. Morstadt)

1978. "PRAGA 1978" International Stamp Exhibition (11th issue). Sheet 96 × 74 mm.
MS2424 **683** 20k. multicoloured 10·50 12·50

684 Detail of "The Flaying of Marsyas" (Titian)

1978. "PRAGA 1978" International Stamp Exhibition (12th issue). Sheet 108 × 165 mm containing T **684** and similar vert design showing detail of painting.
MS2425 10k. Type **684**; 10k. King Midas . . . . 11·50 13·00

685 Fair Buildings **686** "Postal Newspaper Service" (25th Anniv)

1978. 20th International Engineering Fair, Brno.
2426 **685** 30h. multicoloured . . . 10 10

1978. Press, Broadcasting and Television Days.
2427 **686** 30h. green, blue & orge 10 10
2428 – 30h. multicoloured . . . 10 10
2429 – 30h. multicoloured . . . 10 10
DESIGNS: No. 2428, Microphone, newspapers, camera and Ministry of Information and Broadcasting; 2429, Television screen and Television Centre, Prague (25th anniv of Czechoslovak television).

687 Horses falling at Fence

1978. Pardubice Steeplechase. Multicoloured.
2430 10h. Type **687** 10 10
2431 20h. Sulky racing 10 10
2432 30h. Racing horses 15 10
2433 40h. Passing the winning post 15 10
2434 1k.60 Jumping a fence . . . 40 20
2435 4k.40 Jockey leading a winning horse . . . . . 2·50 90

688 Woman holding Arms of Czechoslovakia

1978. 60th Anniv of Independence.
2436 **688** 60h. multicoloured . . . 10 10

689 "Still Life with Flowers" (J. Bohdan)

1978. 30th Anniv of Slovak National Gallery, Bratislava. Multicoloured.
2437 2k.40 Type **689** 80 55
2438 3k. "Dream in a Shepherd's Hut" (L. Fulla) (horiz) . . 80 70
2439 3k.60 "Apostle with Censer" (detail, Master of the Spis Chapter) . . . . 3·75 3·50

690 Violinist and Bass Player (J. Konyves) **692** Council Building, Moscow

691 Alfons Mucha and design for 1918 Hradcany Stamp

1978. Slovak Ceramics.
2440 **690** 20h. multicoloured . . . 10 10
2441 – 30h. blue and violet . . 10 10
2442 – 40h. multicoloured . . . 10 10
2443 – 1k. multicoloured . . . 20 10
2444 – 1k.60 multicoloured . . 1·60 25
DESIGNS: 30h. Horseman (J. Franko); 40h. Man in Kilt (M. Polasko); 1k. Three girl singers (I. Bizmayer); 1k.60, Miner with axe (F. Kostka).

1978. Stamp Day.
2445 **691** 1k. multicoloured . . . 25 10

1979. Anniversaries.
2446 – 30h. brown, grn & orge 10 10
2447 – 60h. multicoloured . . . 15 10
2448 **692** 1k. multicoloured . . . 20 10
DESIGNS—HORIZ: 30h. Girl's head and ears of wheat (30th anniv of Unified Agricultural Co-operatives); 60h. Czechoslovakians and doves (10th anniv of Czechoslovak Federation). VERT: 1k. Type **692** (30th anniv of Council of Economic Mutual Aid).

693 "Soyuz 28"

1979. 1st Anniv of Russian–Czech Space Flight. Multicoloured.
2449 30h. Type **693** 15 10
2450 60h. A. Gubarev and V. Remek (vert) 15 10
2451 1k.60 J. Romanenko and G. Grechko 45 10
2452 2k. "Salyut 6" space laboratory . . . . 1·90 40
2453 4k. "Soyuz 28" touch down (vert) 85 40
MS2454 75 × 95 mm. 10k. Gubarev and Remek waving (38 × 54 mm) 5·00 5·00

694 "Campanula alpina" **695** Stylized Satellite

1979. 25th Anniv of Mountain Rescue Service. Multicoloured.
2455 10h. Type **694** 10 10
2456 20h. "Crocus scepusiensis" 10 10
2457 30h. "Dianthus glacialis" 10 10
2458 40h. Alpine hawkweed . . 15 10
2459a 3k. "Delphinium oxysepalum" . . . . . 1·25 50

1979. Anniversaries.
2460 **695** 10h. multicoloured . . . 10 10
2461 – 20h. multicoloured . . . 10 10
2462 – 20h. blue, orge & lt bl 10 10
2463 – 30h. blue, gold & red . 10 10
2464 – 30h. red, blue & blk . . 10 10
2465 – 60h. multicoloured . . 15 10
DESIGNS AND EVENTS—HORIZ: No. 2460, Type **695** 30th anniv of Telecommunications Research. 46 × 19 mm: (No. 2461), Artist and model (30th anniv of Academy of Fine Arts, Bratislava); 2462, Student and technological equipment (40th anniv of Slovak Technical University, Bratislava); 2463, Musical instruments and Bratislava Castle (50th anniv of Radio Symphony Orchestra, Bratislava); 2464, Pioneer's scarf and I.Y.C. emblem (30th anniv of Young Pioneer Organization and International Year of the Child); 2465, Adult and child with doves (30th anniv of Peace Movement).

1979. Prague Castle (15th series). As T **536**. Multicoloured.
2466 3k. Burial crown of King Premysl Otakar II . . . . 2·40 2·40
2467 3k.60 Portrait of Miss B. Reitmayer (Karel Purkyne) . . . . 1·25 1·00

696 Arms of Vlachovo Brezi **697** Healthy and Polluted Forests

1979. Animals in Heraldry. Multicoloured.
2468 30h. Type **696** 10 10
2469 60h. Jesenik (bear and eagle) 15 10
2470 1k.20 Vysoke Myto (St. George and the dragon) 30 10
2471 1k.80 Martin (St. Martin on horseback) . . . . 1·60 40
2472 2k. Zebrak (half bear, half lion) 40 10

1979. Man and the Biosphere. Multicoloured.
2473 60h. Type **697** 15 15
2474 1k.80 Clear and polluted water 45 30
2475 3k.60 Healthy and polluted urban environment . . . 2·50 85
2476 4k. Healthy and polluted pasture 95 40

698 Numeral and Printed Circuit **699** Industrial Complex

1979. Coil Stamps.
2477 – 50h. red 15 10
2478 **698** 1k. brown 20 10
2478a – 2k. green 50 25
2478b – 3k. purple 80 35
DESIGNS: Numeral and—50h. Dish aerial; 2k. Airplane; 3k. Punched tape.

1979. 35th Anniv of Slovak Uprising.
2479 **699** 30h. multicoloured . . . 10 10

700 Illustration by Janos Kass

1979. International Year of the Child and Biennial Exhibition of Children's Book Illustrations, Bratislava. Designs showing illustrations by artists named. Multicoloured.
2480 20h. Type **700** 10 10
2481 40h. Rumen Skorcev . . . 15 10
2482 60h. Karel Svolinsky . . . 15 10
2483 1k. Otto S. Svend 30 10
2484 3k. Tatyana Mavrina . . . 1·90 45

701 Modern Bicycles

1979. Historic Bicycles. Multicoloured.

2485	20h. Type **701**	15	10
2486	40h. Bicycles, 1910	15	10
2487	60h. "Ordinary" and tricycle, 1886	15	10
2488	2k. "Bone-shakers", 1870	45	25
2489	3k.60 Drais cycles, 1820	2·50	65

702 Bracket Clock (Jan Kraus)

1979. Historic Clocks. Multicoloured.

2490	40h. Type **702**	10	10
2491	60h. Rococo clock	15	10
2492	80h. Classicist clock	1·60	35
2493	1k. Rococo porcelain clock (J. Kandler)	25	10
2494	2k. Urn-shaped clock (Dufaud)	45	25

1979. Art (13th series). As T **481**.

2495	1k.60 multicoloured	65	55
2496	2k. multicoloured	75	60
2497	3k. multicoloured	1·00	70
2498	3k.60 multicoloured	2·75	2·75
2499	5k. yellow and black	1·10	1·25

DESIGNS: 1k.60, "Sunday by the River" (Alois Moravec); 2k. "Self-portrait" (Gustav Mally); 3k. "Self-portrait" (Ilja Jefimovic Repin); 3k.60, "Horseback Rider" (Jan Bauch); 5k. "Village Dancers" (Albrecht Durer).

1979. Historic Bratislava (3rd issue). As T **669**. Multicoloured.

2500	3k. "Bratislava, 1787" (L. Janscha)	1·10	90
2501	3k.60 "Bratislava, 1815" (after stone engraving by Wolf)	2·50	2·40

703 Postmarks, Charles Bridge and Prague Castle

1979. Stamp Day.

2502	**703** 1k. multicoloured	25	10

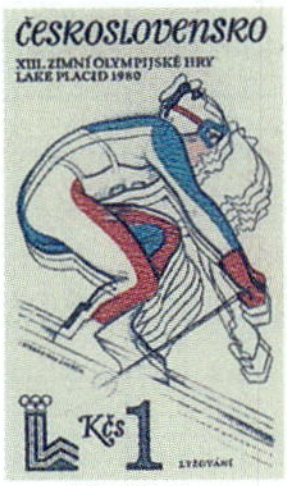

704 Skiing

1980. Winter Olympic Games, Lake Placid.

2503	**704** 1k. multicoloured	25	10
2504	– 2k. red, pink & blue	1·60	40
2505	– 3k. multicoloured	1·00	55

DESIGNS: 2k. Ice skating; 3k. Four-man bobsleigh.

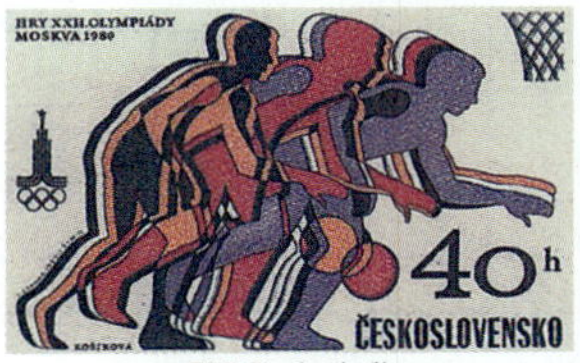

705 Basketball

1980. Olympic Games, Moscow. Multicoloured.

2506	40h. Type **705**	15	10
2507	1k. Swimming	25	10
2508	2k. Hurdles	2·40	40
2509	3k.60 Fencing	85	35

706 Marathon

1980. 50th International Peace Marathon, Kosice.

2510	**706** 50h. multicoloured	10	10

1980. Arms of Czech Towns (2nd series). As T **654**.

2511	50h. blue, black and gold	15	10
2512	50h. black and silver	15	10
2513	50h. multicoloured	15	10
2514	50h. gold, black and blue	15	10

DESIGNS: No. 2511, Bystrice nad Pernstejnem; 2512, Kunstat; 2513, Rozmital pod Tremsinem; 2514, Zlata Idka.

707 Bratislava Opera House and Bakovazena as King Lear

708 Tragic Mask

1980. 60th Anniv of Slovak National Theatre, Bratislava.

2515	**707** 1k. blue, yellow & orange	25	10

1980. 50th Anniv of Theatrical Review "Jiraskuv Hronov".

2516	**708** 50h. multicoloured	10	10

709 Mouse in Space

710 Police Parade Banner

1980. "Intercosmos" Space Programme.

2517	**709** 50h. blue, black and red	15	10
2518	– 1k. multicoloured	30	10
2519	– 1k.60 violet, blk & red	2·25	50
2520	– 4k. multicoloured	1·00	35
2521	– 5k. blue, black & purple	1·50	50
MS2522	75 × 94 mm. 10k. multicoloured	5·00	5·00

DESIGNS—VERT: 1k. Weather map and satellite; 1k.60, "Inter-sputnik" T.V. transmission; 4k. Survey satellite and camera. HORIZ: 5k. Czech-built satellite station; 10k. "Intercosmos" emblem.

1980. 35th Anniv of National Police Corps.

2523	**710** 50h. gold, red & blue	10	10

711 Lenin

712 Flag, Flowers and Prague Buildings

1980. 110th Birth Anniv of Lenin and 160th Birth Anniv of Engels.

2524	**711** 1k. brown, red & grey	20	10
2525	– 1k. blue and brown	20	10

DESIGN: No. 2525, Engels.

1980. Anniversaries. Multicoloured.

2526	50h. Type **712**	15	10
2527	1k. Child writing "Mir" (peace)	20	10
2528	1k. Czech and Soviet arms	20	10
2529	1k. Flowers, flags and dove	20	10

ANNIVERSARIES: No. 2526, 35th anniv of May uprising; 2527, 35th anniv of Liberation; 2528, 10th anniv of Czech–Soviet Treaty; 2529, 25th anniv of Warsaw Pact.

713 Gymnast

1980. National Spartakiad.

2530	– 50h. black, red & blue	10	10
2531	**713** 1k. multicoloured	20	10

DESIGN—HORIZ: 50h. Opening parade of athletes.

714 U.N. Emblem

1980. 35th Anniv of United Nations. Sheet 109 × 165 mm.

MS2532	**714** 4k. × 2 multicoloured	3·50	3·50

715 "Gerbera jamesonii"

716 "Chod Girl"

1980. Olomuc and Bratislava Flower Shows. Multicoloured.

2533	50h. Type **715**	15	15
2534	1k. "Aechmea fasciata"	1·75	40
2535	2k. Bird of paradise flower	35	25
2536	4k. Slipper orchid	85	40

1980. Graphic Cut-outs by Cornelia Nemeckova.

2537	**716** 50h. multicoloured	15	10
2538	– 1k. mauve, brown & red	25	10
2539	– 2k. multicoloured	45	25
2540	– 4k. multicoloured	2·50	70
2541	– 5k. blue, mauve & lt bl	1·10	50

DESIGNS: 1k. "Punch with his dog"; 2k. "Dandy cat with Posy"; 4k. Lion and Moon ("Evening Contemplation"); 5k. Dancer and piper ("Wallacchian Dance").

717 Map of Czechoslovakia and Family

718 Heads

1980. National Census.

2542	**717** 1k. multicoloured	25	10

1980. Prague Castle (16th series). As T **536**. Multicoloured.

2543	3k. Gateway of Old Palace	2·40	2·75
2544	4k. Armorial lion	1·10	75

1980. Historic Bratislava (4th issue). As T **669**. Multicoloured.

2545	3k. "View across the Danube" (J. Eder)	2·40	2·75
2546	4k. "The Old Royal Bridge" (J. A. Lantz)	1·10	75

1980. 10th Anniv of Socialist Youth Federation.

2547	**718** 50h. blue, orange & red	10	10

1980. "Essen '80" International Stamp Exhibition. Sheet 129 × 78 mm containing No. 2365 × 2 optd **DEN CSSR / 3 / MEZINARODNI VELETRH ZNAMEK / ESSEN 80 / TSCHECHOSLOWAKISCHER TAG** and **80 / 3. Internationale / Briefmarken-Messe / Essen / 1980** with Exhibition emblems in red.

MS2548	1k.60 × 2 multicoloured	17·00	17·00

1980. Paintings (14th series). As T **481**.

2549	1k. buff, blue and brown	1·25	1·00
2550	2k. multicoloured	2·00	2·10
2551	3k. red, brown and green	55	45
2552	4k. multicoloured	65	55
2553	5k. green, buff and black	85	80

DESIGNS—VERT: 1k. "Pavel Jozef Safarik" (Jozef B. Klemens); 2k. "Peasant Revolt" (mosaic, A. Podzemma); 3k. Bust of Saint from Lucivna Church; 5k. "Labour" (sculpture, Jan Stursa). HORIZ: 4k. "Waste Heaps" (Jan Zrzavy).

719 Carrier Pigeon

1980. Stamp Day.

2554	**719** 1k. black, red & blue	25	10

720 Five Year Plan Emblem

721 Invalid and Half-bare Tree

1981. 7th Five Year Plan.

2555	**720** 50h. multicoloured	10	10

1981. International Year of Disabled Persons.

2556	**721** 1k. multicoloured	25	10

722 Landau, 1800

723 Jan Sverma (partisan)

1981. Historic Coaches in Postal Museum.

2557	**722** 50h. yellow, black & red	20	10
2558	– 1k. yellow, black & grn	30	10
2559	– 3k.60 lt blue, blk & bl	2·00	40
2560	– 5k. stone, black & red	1·25	35
2561	– 7k. yellow, black & blue	1·50	65

DESIGNS: 1k. Mail coach, c. 1830–40; 3k.60, Postal sleigh, 1840; 5k. Mail coach and four horses, 1860; 7k. Coupe carriage, 1840.

1981. Celebrities' Anniversaries. Multicoloured.

2562	50h. Type **723** (80th birth anniv)	25	10
2563	50h. Mikulas Schneider-Trnavsky (composer) (birth cent)	35	10
2564	50h. Juraj Hronec (mathematician) (birth cent)	25	10
2565	50h. Josef Hlavka (architect) (150th birth anniv)	25	10
2566	1k. Dimitri Shostakovich (composer) (75th birth anniv)	60	10
2567	1k. George Bernard Shaw (dramatist) (125th birth anniv)	60	10
2568	1k. Bernardo Bolzano (philosopher) (birth bicent)	1·50	25
2569	1k. Wolfgang Amadeus Mozart (composer) (225th birth anniv)	75	15

724 Yuri Gagarin

1981. 20th Anniv of First Manned Space Flight. Sheet 108 × 165 mm.

MS2570	**724** 6k. × 2 multicoloured	5·00	5·00

725 Party Member with Flag

1981. 60th Anniv of Czechoslovak Communist Party. Multicoloured.

2571 50h. Type **725** 10 15
2572 1k. Symbols of progress and hands holding flag 20 15
2573 4k. Party member holding flag bearing symbols of industry (vert) 80 40

726 Hammer and Sickle

1981. 16th Czechoslovak Communist Party Congress. Multicoloured.

2574 50h. Type **726** 10 10
2575 1k. "XVI" and Prague buildings 25 10

1981. "WIPA 1981" International Stamp Exhibition, Vienna. Sheet 150 × 104 mm.

MS2576 No. 2561 × 4 . . . . . 21·00 21·00

727 Fallow-plough **728** Man, Woman and Dove

1981. 90th Anniv of Agricultural Museum.

2577 **727** 1k. multicoloured . . . 25 10

1981. Elections to Representative Assemblies.

2578 **728** 50h. red, stone & blue 10 10

729 "Uran" (Tatra Mountains) and "Rudy Rijen" (Bohemia)

1981. Achievements of Socialist Construction (1st series). Multicoloured.

2579 80h. Type **729** (Trade Union recreational facilities) . . 25 10
2580 1k. Prague–Brno–Bratislava expressway 30 10
2581 2k. Jaslovske Bohunice nuclear plant 50 25

See also Nos. 2644/6, 2695/7, 2753/5 and 2800/2.

1981. Historic Bratislava (5th issue). As T **669**. Multicoloured.

2582 3k. "Bratislava, 1760" (G. B. Probst) . . . . . 2·75 2·75
2583 4k. "Grassalkovichov Palace, 1815" (C. Bschor) 80 70

730 "Guernica"

1981. 45th Anniv of International Bridges in Spain and Birth Centenary of Pablo Picasso (artist). Sheet 90 × 76 mm.

MS2584 **730** 10k. multicoloured 3·75 3·75

731 Puppets **732** Map

1981. 30th National Festival of Amateur Puppetry Ensembles, Chrudim.

2585 **731** 2k. multicoloured . . . 45 30

1981. National Defence. Multicoloured.

2586 40h. Type **732** (Defence of borders) 10 10
2587 50h. Emblem of Civil Defence Organization (30th Anniv) (vert) . . . 15 10
2588 1k. Emblem of Svazarm (Organization for Co-operation with Army, 30th anniv) (28 × 23 mm) 25 10

733 Edelweiss, Climbers and Lenin

1981. 25th International Youth Climb of Rysy Peaks.

2589 **733** 3k.60 multicoloured . . 85 40

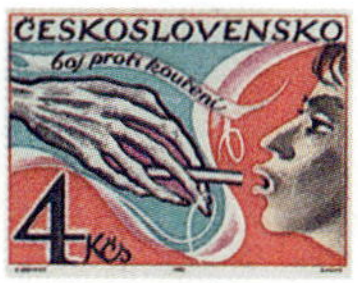

734 Illustration by Albin Brunovsky **736** Skeletal Hand removing Cigarette

735 Gorilla Family

1981. Biennial Exhibition of Book Illustrations for Children, Bratislava. Multicoloured.

2590 50h. Type **734** 15 15
2591 1k. Adolf Born 30 20
2592 2k. Vive Tolli 60 25
2593 4k. Etienne Delessert . . . 90 40
2594 10k. Suekichi Akaba . . . . 3·00 1·25

1981. 50th Anniv of Prague Zoo. Multicoloured.

2595 50h. Type **735** 30 10
2596 1k. Lion family 35 15
2597 7k. Przewalski's horses . . . 2·75 1·50

1981. Anti-smoking Campaign.

2598 **736** 4k. multicoloured . . . 1·75 85

1981. Prague Castle (17th series). As T **536**. Multicoloured.

2599 3k. Fragment of Pernstejn terracotta from Lobkovic Palace (16th century) . . 90 45
2600 4k. St. Vitus Cathedral (19th century engraving by J. Sembera and G. Dobler) . . . . 2·25 2·75

1981. Art (15th series). As T **481**.

2601 1k. multicoloured . . . . . 3·50 3·25
2602 2k. brown 60 50
2603 3k. multicoloured 80 65
2604 4k. multicoloured 90 70
2605 5k. multicoloured . . . . . 1·10 1·60

DESIGNS: 1k. "View of Prague from Petrin Hill" (V. Hollar); 2k. "Czech Academy of Arts and Sciences Medallion" (Otakar Spaniel); 3k. South Bohemian embroidery (Zdenek Sklenar); 4k. "Peonies" (A. M. Gerasimov); 5k. "Figure of a Woman Standing" (Picasso).

737 Eduard Karel (engraver)

1981. Stamp Day.

2606 **737** 1k. yellow, red and blue 25 10

738 Lenin **739** Player kicking Ball

1982. 70th Anniv of 6th Russian Workers' Party Congress, Prague.

2607 **738** 2k. red, gold and blue 55 25
MS2608 107 × 83 mm. No. 2607 × 4 6·50 6·50

1982. World Cup Football Championship, Spain. Multicoloured.

2609 1k. Type **739** 20 15
2610 3k.60 Heading ball 75 40
2611 4k. Saving goal . . . . . . 2·50 65

740 Hrob **741** Conference Emblem

1982. Arms of Czech Towns (3rd series). Multicoloured.

2612 50h. Type **740** 20 10
2613 50h. Mlada Boleslav 20 10
2614 50h. Nove Mesto and Metuji 20 10
2615 50h. Trencin 20 10

See also Nos. 2720/3, 2765/7, 2819/21 and 3017/20.

1982. Tenth World Federation of Trade Unions Congress, Havana.

2616 **741** 1k. multicoloured . . . 25 10

742 Workers and Mine

1982. 50th Anniv of Great Strike at Most (coalminers' and general strike).

2617 **742** 1k. multicoloured . . . 25 10

743 Locomotives of 1922 and 1982

1982. 60th Anniv of International Railways Union.

2618 **743** 6k. multicoloured . . . 1·75 70

744 Worker with Flag **745** Georgi Dimitrov

1982. 10th Trade Unions Congress, Prague.

2619 **744** 1k. multicoloured . . . 25 10

1982. Birth Centenary of Georgi Dimitrov (Bulgarian statesman).

2620 **745** 50h. multicoloured . . . 10 10

746 Girl with Flowers

1982. 10th International Exhibition of Children's Art, Lidice. Sheet 165 × 108 mm.

MS2621 **746** 2k. × 6 multicoloured 14·00 14·00

747 "Euterpe" (Crispin de Passe) **749** Child's Head, Rose and Barbed Wire (Lidice)

748 Girl with Doves

1982. Engravings with a Music Theme.

2622 **747** 40h. black, gold & brown 15 10
2623 – 50h. black, gold & red 20 10
2624 – 1k. black, gold & brown 30 15
2625 – 2k. black, gold & blue 50 25
2626 – 3k. black, gold & green 2·40 70

DESIGNS: 50h. "The Sanguine Man" (Jacob de Gheyn); 1k. "The Crossing of the Red Sea" (Adriaen Collaert); 2k. "Wandering Musicians" (Rembrandt); 3k. "Beggar with Viol" (Jacques Callot).

1982. Second Special Session of United Nations General Assembly on Disarmament, New York. Sheet 165 × 108 mm.

MS2627 **748** 6k. × 2 multicoloured 12·50 12·50

1982. 40th Anniv of Destruction of Lidice and Lezaky. Multicoloured.

2628 1k. Type **749** 30 10
2629 1k. Hands and barbed wire (Lezaky) 30 10

750 Memorial and Statue of Jan Zizka

1982. 50th Anniv of National Memorial, Prague.

2630 **750** 1k. multicoloured . . . 25 10

751 Satellite Orbits around Earth

1982. Second United Nations Conference on Research and Peaceful Uses of Outer Space, Vienna. Sheet 165 × 108 mm.

MS2631 **751** 5k. × 2 multicoloured 12·50 12·50

752 Krivoklat Castle

1982. Castles. Multicoloured.

2632 50h. Type **752** 20 10
2633 1k. Interior and sculptures at Krivoklat Castle . . . 35 15
2634 2k. Nitra Castle 65 30
2635 3k. Archaeological finds from Nitra Castle . . . . 1·00 40
MS2636 105 × 125 mm. Nos. 2632/5 3·00 3·00

1982. Prague Castle (18th series). As T **536**.

2637 3k. brown and green . . . . 2·40 70
2638 4k. multicoloured . . . . . 1·25 95

DESIGNS: 3k. "St. George" (statue by George and Martin of Kluz, 1372); 4k. Tomb of Prince Vratislav I, Basilica of St. George.

753 Ferry "Kamzik" in Bratislava Harbour

1982. Danube Commission. Multicoloured.

2639 3k. Type **753** 80 30
2640 3k.60 "TR 100" tug at Budapest . . . . 1·00 40
MS2641 Two sheets, each 127 × 127 mm. (a) No. 2639 × 4; (b) No. 2640 × 4 . . . . . . 20·00 20·00

1982. Historic Bratislava (6th issue). As T **669**.

2642 3k. black and red . . . . . 1·90 85
2643 4k. multicoloured . . . . . 2·10 1·25

DESIGNS: 3k. "View of Bratislava with Steamer"; 4k. "View of Bratislava with Bridge".

754 Agriculture

1982. Achievements of Socialist Construction (2nd series). Multicoloured.
2644 20h. Type **754** 10 10
2645 1k. Industry 35 10
2646 3k. Science and technology . . 95 45
See also Nos. 2695/7, 2753/5 and 2800/2.

755 "Scientific Research"

1982. 30th Anniv of Academy of Sciences.
2647 **755** 6k. multicoloured . . . 1·10 55

756 Couple with Flowers and Silhouette of Rider

1982. 65th Anniv of October Revolution and 60th Anniv of U.S.S.R. Multicoloured.
2648 50h. Type **756** 15 10
2649 1k. Cosmonauts and industrial complex 20 10

757 "Jaroslav Hasek" (writer) (Jose Malejovsky)

759 President Husak

758 Jaroslav Goldschmied (engraver) and Engraving Tools

1982. Sculptures. Multicoloured.
2650 1k. Type **757** 30 10
2651 2k. "Jan Zrzavy" (patriot) (Jan Simota) 55 25
2652 4k.40 "Leos Janacek" (composer) (Milos Axman) . . . . 1·10 55
2653 6k. "Martin Kukucin" (patriot) (Jan Kulich) . . 1·50 75
2654 7k. "Peaceful Work" (detail) (Rudolf Pribis) . . . . 3·00 1·25

1982. Art (16th series). As T **481**. Multicoloured.
2655 1k. "Revolution in Spain" (Josef Sima) . . . . . 1·60 95
2656 2k. "Woman drying Herself" (Rudolf Kremlicka) . . . . . . 2·50 2·25
2657 3k. "The Girl Bride" (Dezider Milly) . . . . 1·60 90
2658 4k. "Oil Field Workers" (Jan Zelibsky) . . . . 1·60 1·25
2659 5k. "The Birds Lament" (Emil Filla) . . . . . . 1·75 1·50

1983. Stamp Day.
2660 **758** 1k. multicoloured . . . 25 10

1983. 70th Birthday of President Husak.
2661 **759** 50h. blue 10 10
See also No. 2911.

760 Jaroslav Hasek (writer)

761 Armed Workers

1983. Celebrities' Anniversaries.
2662 **760** 50h. green, blue & red 15 15
2663 – 1k. brown, blue & red 25 15
2664 – 2k. multicoloured . . . 45 25
2665 – 5k. black, blue & red . 1·40 50
DESIGNS: Type **760** (birth centenary); 1k. Julius Fucik (journalist) (80th birth and 40th death annivs); 2k. Martin Luther (church reformist) (500th birth anniv); 5k. Johannes Brahms (composer) (150th birth anniv).

1983. Anniversaries. Multicoloured.
2666 50h. Type **761** (35th anniv of "Victorious February") 15 10
2667 1k. Family and agriculture and industrial landscapes (35th anniversary of National Front) 25 15

762 Radio Waves and Broadcasting Emblem

763 Ski Flyer

1983. Communications. Multicoloured.
2668 40h. Type **762** (60th anniv of Czech broadcasting) . . 15 10
2669 1k. Television emblem (30th anniv of Czech television) 20 10
2670 2k. W.C.Y. emblem and "1983" (World Communications Year) (40 × 23 mm) 45 25
2671 3k.60 Envelopes, Aero A-10 aircraft and mail vans (60th anniv of airmail and 75th anniv of mail transport by motor vehicles) (49 × 19 mm) . . 1·00 50

1983. 7th World Ski Flying Championships, Harrachov.
2672 **763** 1k. multicoloured . . . 25 10

764 A. Gubarev and V. Remek

1983. 5th Anniv of Soviet-Czechoslovak Space Flight. Sheet 109 × 165 mm.
MS2673 **764** 10k. × 2 multicoloured 14·00 14·00

765 Emperor Moth and "Viola sudetica"

1983. Nature Protection. Multicoloured.
2674 50h. Type **765** 20 10
2675 1k. Water lilies and edible frogs 40 15
2676 2k. Red crossbill and cones 1·60 40
2677 3k.60 Grey herons . . . . 1·60 50
2678 5k. Lynx and "Gentiana asclepiadea" . . . . . . 1·50 45
2679 7k. Red deer . . . . 3·25 1·50

766 Ivan Stepanovich Kbnev

1983. Soviet Army Commanders. Multicoloured.
2680 50h. Type **766** 15 10
2681 1k. Andrei Ivanovich Yeremenko 25 15
2682 2k. Rodion Yakovlevich Malinovsky 55 25

767 Dove

768 "Rudolf II" (Adrian de Vries)

1983. World Peace and Life Congress, Prague.
2683 **767** 2k. multicoloured . . . 45 40
MS2684 108 × 83 mm. No. 2683 × 4 9·25 9·25

1983. Prague Castle (19th series).
2685 **768** 4k. multicoloured . . . 1·40 1·00
2686 – 5k. orange, blk & red . . 85 1·00
DESIGN: 5k. Kinetic relief with timepiece by Rudolf Svoboda.

769 Mounted Messenger (Oleg K. Zotov)

1983. 9th Biennial Exhibition of Book Illustration for Children.
2687 **769** 50h. multicoloured . . . 15 10
2688 – 1k. multicoloured . . . 25 10
2689 – 4k. multicoloured . . . 95 40
2690 – 7k. red and black . . . 1·40 55
MS2691 115 × 133 mm. Nos. 2687/90 4·50 4·00
DESIGNS: 1k. Boy looking from window at birds in tree (Zbigniew Rychlicki); 4k. "Hansel and Gretel" (Lisbeth Zwerger); 7k. Three young negroes (Antonio P. Domingues).

770 Ilyushin Il-62 and Globe

1983. World Communications Year and 60th Anniv of Czechoslovak Airlines.
2692 **770** 50h. red, purple & pink 15 10
2693 – 1k. purple, red & pink 30 10
2694 – 4k. purple, red & pink 1·90 85
DESIGNS—VERT: 1k. Ilyushin Il-62 and envelope. HORIZ: 4k. Ilyushin Il-62 and Aero A-14 biplane.

1983. Achievements of Socialist Construction (3rd series). As T **754**.
2695 50h. Surveyor 15 10
2696 1k. Refinery 30 10
2697 3k. Hospital and operating theatre 75 50

1983. Historic Bratislava (7th series). As T **669**.
2698 3k. green, red and black . . 1·75 70
2699 4k. multicoloured . . . . 1·75 70
DESIGNS: 3k. Sculptures by Viktor Tilgner; 4k. "Mirbachov Palace" (Julius Schubert).

771 National Theatre, Prague

772 "Soldier with Sword and Shield" (Hendrik Goltzius)

1983. Czechoslovak Theatre Year.
2700 **771** 50h. brown 15 10
2701 – 2k. green 55 25
DESIGN: 2k. National Theatre and Tyl Theatre, Prague.

1983. Art (17th series), showing works from the National Theatre, Prague. As Type **481**.
2702 1k. multicoloured . . . . . 1·25 90
2703 2k. multicoloured . . . . . 2·75 90
2704 3k. yellow, black and blue 1·00 60
2705 4k. multicoloured . . . . . 1·00 60
2706 5k. multicoloured . . . . . 1·00 60

DESIGNS: 1k. "Zalov" (lunette detail by Mikolas Ales); 2k. "Genius" (stage curtain detail, Vojtech Hynais); 3k. "Music" and "Lyrics" (ceiling drawings, Frantisek Zenisek); 4k. "Prague" (detail from President's box, Vaclav Brozik); 5k. "Hradcany Castle (detail from President's box, Julius Marak).

1983. Period Costume from Old Engravings. Multicoloured.
2707 40h. Type **772** 15 10
2708 50h. "Warrior with Sword and Lance" (Jacob de Gheyn) 15 10
2709 1k. "Lady with Muff" (Jacques Callot) 30 10
2710 4k. "Lady with Flower" (Vaclav Hollar) . . . . . 1·10 40
2711 5k. "Gentleman with Cane" (Antoine Watteau) . . . 2·25 80

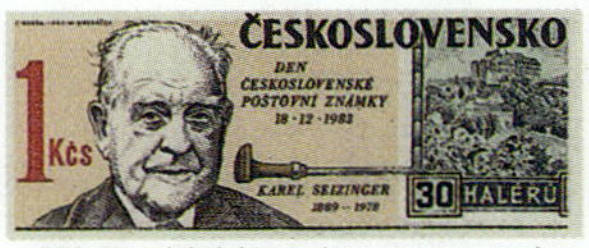

773 Karel Seizinger (stamp engraver)

1983. Stamp Day.
2712 **773** 1k. multicoloured . . . 25 10

774 National Flag, with Bratislava and Prague Castles

775 Council Emblem

1984. 15th Anniv of Czechoslovak Federation.
2713 **774** 50h. multicoloured . . . 10 10

1984. 35th Anniv of Council for Mutual Economic Aid.
2714 **775** 1k. multicoloured . . . 25 25

776 Cross-country Skiing

1984. Winter Olympic Games, Sarajevo. Mult.
2715 2k. Type **776** 45 25
2716 3k. Ice hockey 70 40
2717 5k. Biathlon . . . . . . 1·50 65
MS2718 110 × 99 mm. No. 2716 × 4 8·00 8·00

777 Olympic Flag, Ancient Greek Athletes and Olympic Flame

1984. 90th Anniv of International Olympic Committee.
2719 **777** 7k. multicoloured . . . 1·25 55

1984. Arms of Czech Towns (4th series). As T **740**. Multicoloured.
2720 50h. Turnov 30 10
2721 50h. Kutna Hora 30 10
2722 1k. Milevsko 45 25
2723 1k. Martin 45 25

778 "Soyuz" and Dish Aerials

779 Vendellin Opatrny

1984. "Interkosmos" International Space Flights. Multicoloured.
2724 50h. Type **778** 20 10
2725 1k. "Salyut"–"Soyuz" complex 35 15
2726 2k. Cross-section of orbital station 55 25
2727 4k. "Salyut" taking pictures of Earth's surface 75 50
2728 5k. "Soyuz" returning to Earth . . . . 1·00 65

1984. Anti-fascist Heroes.
2729 **779** 50h. black, red & blue 20 10
2730 – 1k. black, red & blue . . 30 10

2731 – 2k. black, red & blue . . 55 25
2732 – 4k. black, red & blue . . 1·10 40
DESIGNS: 1k. Ladislav Novomesky; 2k. Rudolf Jasiok; 4k. Jan Nalepka.

780 Musical Instruments

781 Telecommunications Building

1984. Music Year.
2733 **780** 50h. lt brown, gold & brn 20 10
2734 – 1k. multicoloured . . . 25 10
DESIGN: 1k. Organ pipes.

1984. Central Telecommunications Building, Bratislava.
2735 **781** 2k. multicoloured . . . 55 25

1984. Historic Bratislava (8th series). As T **669**. Multicoloured.
2736 3k. Arms of Vintners' Guild 1·25 85
2737 4k. Painting of 1827 Skating Festival . . . . 1·25 85

782 Doves, Globes and U.P.U. Emblem

783 Jack of Spades (16th century)

1984. 110th Anniv of Universal Postal Union. Sheet 165 × 108 mm.
MS2738 **782** 5k. × 4 multicoloured 16·00 16·00

1984. Prague Castle (20th series). As T **768**. Multicoloured.
2739 3k. Weather cock, St. Vitus Cathedral 75 80
2740 4k. King David playing psaltery (initial from Roudnice Book of Psalms) . . . . 1·40 1·25

1984. Playing Cards. Multicoloured.
2741 50h. Type **783** 20 10
2742 1k. Queen of Spades (17th century) 35 10
2743 2k. Nine of Hearts (18th century) 50 25
2744 3k. Jack of Clubs (18th century) 85 35
2745 5k. King of Hearts (19th century) . . . . 1·25 55

784 Family and Industrial Complex

1984. 40th Anniv of Slovak Uprising.
2746 **784** 50h. multicoloured . . . 10 10

785 Soldiers with Banner

1984. 40th Anniv of Battle of Dukla Pass.
2747 **785** 2k. multicoloured . . . 45 25

786 High Jumping

1984. Olympic Games, Los Angeles. Mult.
2748 1k. Type **786** 30 15
2749 2k. Cycling 50 25
2750 3k. Rowing 70 40
2751 5k. Weightlifting . . . . . 1·10 55
MS2752 107 × 95 mm. Nos. 2748/51 5·00 5·00

1984. Achievements of Socialist Construction (4th series). As T **754**. Multicoloured.
2753 1k. Telephone handset and letters (Communications) 40 10
2754 2k. Containers on railway trucks and river barge (Transport) 75 30
2755 3k. Map of Transgas pipeline 65 45
MS2756 157 × 105 mm. No. 2755 × 3 . . . . 5·00 5·00

1984. Art (18th series). As T **481**. Multicoloured.
2757 1k. "Milevsky River" (Karel Stehlik) 40 75
2758 2k. "Under the Trees" (Viktor Barvitius) 80 90
2759 3k. "Landscape with Flowers" (Zolo Palugyay) 1·25 60
2760 4k. Illustration of king from Vysehrad Codex . . . . 1·60 80
2761 5k. "Kokorin" (Antonin Manes) . . . . 2·00 95

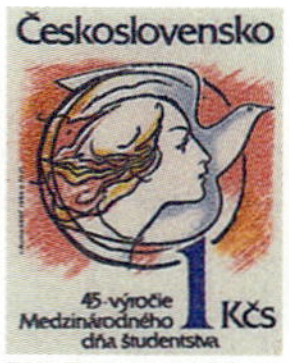

787 Dove and Head of Girl

788 Zapotocky

1984. 45th Anniv of International Students Day.
2762 **787** 1k. multicoloured . . . 25 10

1984. Birth Centenary of Antonin Zapotocky (politician).
2763 **788** 50h. multicoloured . . . 10 10

789 Bohumil Heinz (engraver) and Hands engraving

1984. Stamp Day.
2764 **789** 1k. multicoloured . . . 25 25

1985. Arms of Czech Towns (5th series). As T **740**. Multicoloured.
2765 50h. Kamyk nad Vltavou 30 10
2766 50h. Havirov 30 10
2767 50h. Trnava 30 10

790 "Art and Pleasure" (Jan Simota)

792 Helmet, Mail Shirt and Crossbow

791 View of Trnava

1985. Centenary of Prague University of Applied Arts.
2768 **790** 3k. multicoloured . . . 60 40

1985. 350th Anniv of Trnava University.
2769 **791** 2k. multicoloured . . . 35 20

1985. Exhibits from Military Museum. Mult.
2770 50h. Type **792** 15 10
2771 1k. Cross and star of Za vitezstvi order 30 10
2772 2k. Avia B-534 airplane and "Soyuz 28" (horiz) . . . 70 25

793 Lenin reading

1985. 115th Birth Anniv of Lenin.
MS2773 **793** 2k. × 6 multicoloured 4·50 3·00

794 U.N. Emblem and Stylized Dove

1985. 40th Anniv of United Nations Organization and International Peace Year (1986).
MS2774 **794** 6k. × 4 multicoloured 14·00 14·00

795 State Arms and Crowd

796 State Arms and Soldiers with National Flag

1985. 40th Anniv of Kosice Reforms.
2775 **795** 4k. multicoloured . . . 70 40

1985. 40th Anniv of National Security Forces.
2776 **796** 50h. multicoloured . . . 10 10

797 Automatic Optical Platform and Comet Trajectory

1985. Space Project "Vega" (research into Venus and Halley's Comet). Sheet 106 × 96 mm.
MS2777 **797** 5k. × 2 multicoloured 10·50 10·50

798 Emblem and Ice Hockey Players

1985. World and European Ice Hockey Championships, Prague.
2778 **798** 1k. multicoloured . . . 25 10

799 Pieces on Chessboard

802 Tennis

1985. 80th Anniv of Czechoslovak Chess Organization.
2779 **799** 6k. multicoloured . . . 1·50 70

800 Freedom Fighters and Prague

1985. Anniversaries. Multicoloured.
2780 1k. Type **800** (40th anniv of May uprising) 20 10
2781 1k. Workers shaking hands, flags and industrial motifs (15th anniv of Czechoslovak–Soviet Treaty) 20 10
2782 1k. Girl giving flowers to soldier, Prague Castle and tank (40th anniv of liberation) 20 10
2783 1k. Soldiers and industrial motifs (30th anniv of Warsaw Pact) 20 10

1985. Czechoslovak Victory in Ice Hockey Championships. No. 2778 optd **CSSR MISTREM SVETA**.
2784 **798** 1k. multicoloured . . . 5·25 5·00

1985. National Spartakiad. Multicoloured.
2785 50h. Type **802** 15 10
2786 1k. Gymnasts performing with ribbons (48 × 19 mm) 20 10

803 Study for "Fire" and "Republic" (Josef Capek)

1985. Anti-fascist Artists. Multicoloured.
2787 50h. Type **803** 15 10
2788 2k. "Geneva Conference on Disarmament" and "Prophecy of Three Parrots" (Frantisek Bidlo) 45 25
2789 4k. "Unknown Conscript" and "The almost peaceful Dove" (Antonin Pelc) . . 70 40

804 Girl holding Dove and Olive Branch

1985. 10th Anniv of European Security and Co-operation Conference, Helsinki. Sheet 107 × 135 mm.
MS2790 **804** 7k. × 4 multicoloured 11·50 11·50

805 Moscow Buildings and Young People holding Doves

1985. 12th World Youth and Students' Festival, Moscow.
2791 **805** 1k. multicoloured . . . 25 10

806 Figures on Globe

807 Rocking Horse (Kveta Pacovska)

1985. 40th Anniv of World Federation of Trade Unions.
2792 **806** 50h. multicoloured . . . 10 10

1985. Historic Bratislava (9th series). As T **669**.
2793 3k. lt brown, green & brown 70 75
2794 4k. black, green and red . . 1·00 1·10
DESIGNS: 3k. Tapestry (Elena Holeczyova); 4k. Pottery.

1985. 10th Biennial Exhibition of Book Illustrations for Children, Bratislava. Mult.
2795 1k. Type **807** 20 10
2796 2k. Elves (Gennady Spirin) 35 20
2797 3k. Girl, butterfly and flowers (Kaarina Kaila) 65 30
2798 4k. Boy shaking hands with hedgehog (Erick Ingraham) 80 40
MS2799 95 × 128 mm. Nos. 2795/8 5·00 5·00

1985. Achievements of Socialist Construction (5th series). As T **754**. Multicoloured.
2800 50h. Mechanical excavator 10 10
2801 1k. Train and map of Prague underground railway 30 15
2802 2k. Modern textile spinning equipment 35 25

808 Gateway to First Courtyard

809 Jug (4th century)

1985. Prague Castle (21st series).
2803 **808** 2k. black, blue & red . . 50 30
2804 – 3k. multicoloured . . . 1·10 40
DESIGN: 3k. East side of Castle.

1985. Centenary of Prague Arts and Crafts Museum. Glassware. Multicoloured.
2805 50h. Type **809** 10 10
2806 1k. Venetian glass container (16th century) 20 10
2807 2k. Bohemian glass with hunting scene (18th century) 40 25
2808 4k. Bohemian vase (18th century) 65 40
2809 6k. Bohemian vase (c. 1900) 1·40 65

1985. Art (19th series). As T **481**. Multicoloured.
2810 1k. "Young Woman in Blue Dress" (Josef Ginovsky) 1·60 1·00
2811 2k. "Lenin on Charles Bridge" (Martin Sladky) 1·60 1·00
2812 3k. "Avenue of Poplars" (Vaclav Rabas) . . . . . 1·60 1·00
2813 4k. "Beheading of St. Dorothea" (Hans Baldung Grien) . . . . . 1·60 1·00
2814 5k. "Jasper Schade van Westrum" (Frans Hals) 1·60 1·00

810 Bohdan Roule (engraver) and Engraving Plate

1985. Stamp Day.
2815 **810** 1k. multicoloured . . . 25 10

811 Peace Dove and Olive Twig

1986. International Peace Year. Multicoloured.
2816 **811** 1k. multicoloured . . . 25 10

812 Victory Statue Prague

813 Zlin Z-50LS Airplane, Locomotive "Kladno" and Rock Drawing of Chariot

1986. 90th Anniv of Czech Philharmonic Orchestra.
2817 **812** 1k. black, brown & vio 25 10

1986. "Expo '86" International Transport and Communications Exhibition, Vancouver.
2818 **813** 4k. multicoloured . . . 70 40

1986. Arms of Czech Towns (6th series). As T **740**. Multicoloured.
2819 50h. Vodnany 25 10
2820 50h. Zamberk 25 10
2821 50h. Myjava 25 10

814 Banner, Industry and Hammer and Sickle

1986. 17th Communist Party Congress, Prague. Multicoloured.
2822 50h. Type **814** 10 10
2823 1k. Buildings, hammer and sickle and star 25 10

815 Couple, Banner and Star

1986. 65th Anniv of Czechoslovakian Communist Party. Multicoloured.
2824 50h. Type **815** 10 10
2825 1k. Workers, banner and hammer and sickle . . . 25 10

816 Map and Stylized Man

1986. National Front Election Programme.
2826 **816** 50h. multicoloured . . . 10 10

817 Emblem and Crest on Film

1986. 25th Int Film Festival, Karlovy Vary.
2827 **817** 1k. multicoloured . . . 25 10

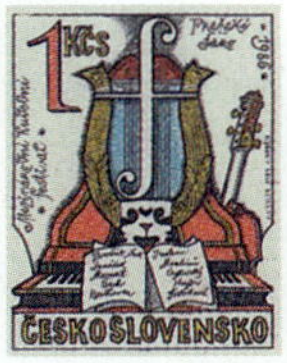

818 Musical Instruments

819 Ilyushin Il-86 and Airspeed Envoy II

1986. 40th Anniv of Prague Spring Music Festival.
2828 **818** 1k. multicoloured . . . 25 10

1986. 50th Anniv of Prague–Moscow Air Service.
2829 **819** 50h. multicoloured . . . 10 10

820 Sports Pictograms

1986. 90th Anniv of Czechoslovak Olympic Committee.
2830 **820** 2k. multicoloured . . . 45 25

821 Map and Goalkeeper

1986. World Cup Football Championship, Mexico.
2831 **821** 4k. multicoloured . . . 80 55

822 Globe, Net and Ball

1986. Women's World Volleyball Championship, Prague.
2832 **822** 1k. multicoloured . . . 35 10

823 Emblem

1986. "Praga '88" Stamp Exhibition, Prague (1st issue) and 60th Anniv of International Philatelic Federation. Sheet 110 × 82 mm containing T **823** and two labels.
MS2833 **823** 20k. multicoloured 14·00 14·00

824 Funeral Pendant

825 Wooden Cock, Slovakia

1986. Prague Castle (22nd series).
2834 **824** 2k. multicoloured . . . 55 50
2835 – 3k. orange, brown & bl 65 65
DESIGN: 3k. "Allegory of Blossoms" (sculpture, Jaroslav Horejc).

1986. 40th Anniv of UNICEF. Toys. Mult.
2836 10h. Type **825** 10 10
2837 20h. Wooden soldier on hobby horse, Bohemia . . 10 10
2838 1k. Rag doll, Slovakia . . . 15 10
2839 2k. Doll 35 10
2840 3k. Mechanical bus 50 25

826 Registration Label and Mail Coach

1986. Centenary of Registration Label.
2841 **826** 4k. multicoloured . . . 60 30

1986. Historic Bratislava (10th series). As T **669**.
2842 3k. black, red and blue . . 60 55
2843 4k. black, red and green . . 75 70
DESIGNS: 3k. Sigismund Gate, Bratislava Castle; 4k. "St. Margaret with a Lamb" (relief from Castle).

827 Eagle Owl

1986. Owls. Multicoloured.
2844 50h. Type **827** 25 10
2845 2k. Long-eared owl 55 25
2846 3k. Tawny owl 55 40
2847 4k. Barn owl 70 50
2848 5k. Short-eared owl . . . . 1·50 60

828 Curtain of D 37 Theatre (Vladimir Sychra)

1986. 50th Anniv of Formation of International Brigades in Spain. Sheet 165 × 108 mm.
MS2849 **828** 5k. × 2 multicoloured 14·00 14·00
See also Nos. 2880/4, **MS**2833, 2900, **MS**2903, 2923/**MS**2927, 2929, **MS**2933, 2934/**MS**2938, 2940/**MS**2944, **MS**2945, **MS**2946, **MS**2947, **MS**2948 and **MS**2949.

829 Type "Kt8" Articulated Tram and 1920s' Prague Tram

1986. Rail Vehicles. Multicoloured.
2850 50h. Type **829** 20 10
2851 1k. Series E 458.1 electric shunting engine and 1882–1913 steam locomotive . . 30 10
2852 3k. Series T 466.2 diesel locomotive and 1900–24 steam locomotive 70 35
2853 5k. Series M 152.0 railcar and 1930–35 railbus . . . 95 60

830 "The Circus Rider" (Jan Bauch)

1986. Circus and Variety Acts on Paintings. Multicoloured.
2854 1k. Type **830** . . . . 1·25 25
2855 2k. "The Ventriloquist" (Frantisek Tichy) . . . . 1·50 35
2856 3k. "In the Circus" (Vincent Hloznik) . . . . 1·45 55
2857 6k. "Clown" (Karel Svolinsky) . . . . 1·75 1·25

1986. Art (20th series). As T **481**. Multicoloured.
2858 1k. "The Czech Lion, May 1918" (Vratislav H. Brunner) . . . . . . 1·50 65
2859 2k. "Boy with Mandolin" (Jozef Sturdik) . . . . . 1·40 75
2860 3k. "The Metra Building" (Frantisek Gross) 80 80
2861 4k. "Maria Maximiliana of Sternberk" (Karel Skreta) 80 95
2862 5k. "Adam and Eve" (Lucas Cranach) . . . . 1·10 1·10

831 Brunner and Stamps of 1920

1986. Stamp Day. Birth Centenary of Vratislav Hugo Brunner (stamp designer).
2863 **831** 1k. multicoloured . . . 25 10

832 Bicyclists

1987. World Cross-country Cycling Championships, Mlada Boleslav.
2864 **832** 6k. multicoloured . . . 95 55

833 Pins and Ball

1987. 50th Anniv of Czechoslovakian Bowling Federation.
2865 **833** 2k. multicoloured . . . 35 25

834 Gold Stars of Heroes of C.S.S.R. and of Socialist Labour

1987. State Orders and Medals.
2866 **834** 50h. red, black & gold 10 10
2867 – 2k. multicoloured . . . 30 25
2868 – 3k. multicoloured . . . 55 40
2869 – 4k. multicoloured . . . 70 55
2870 – 5k. multicoloured . . . 95 60
DESIGNS: 2k. Order of Klement Gottwald; 3k. Order of the Republic; 4k. Order of Victorious February; 5k. Order of Labour.

835 Poplar Admiral

1987. Butterflies and Moths. Multicoloured.
2871 1k. Type **835** 20 10
2872 2k. Eyed hawk moth . . . 45 25

2873 3k. Large tiger moth 75 40
2874 4k. Viennese emperor moth 1·00 40

836 Emblem

1987. Nuclear Power Industry.
2875 **836** 5k. multicoloured . . . 80 55

837 Emblem

839 Stained Glass Window, St. Vitus's Cathedral (Frantisek Sequens)

1987. 11th Trades Union Congress, Prague.
2876 **837** 1k. multicoloured . . . 10 10

1987. 20th Anniv of "Interkosmos" Space Programme. Sheet 165 × 104 mm.
MS2877 **838** 10k. × 2 multicoloured 5·00 5·00

1987. Prague Castle (23rd series). Multicoloured.
2878 2k. Type **839** 45 40
2879 3k. Arms (mural), New Land Rolls Hall, Old Royal Palace 75 55
See also Nos. 2950/1 and 2977/8.

840 Telephone, 1894

1987. "Praga 88" Int Stamp Exhibition (2nd issue). Technical Monuments. Multicoloured.
2880 3k. Type **840** 45 35
2881 3k. Mail Van, 1924 . . . . 45 35
2882 4k. Tank locomotive "Archduke Charles" 1907 90 35
2883 4k. Prague tram, 1900 . . . 90 35
2884 5k. Steam roller, 1936 . . . 90 55
See also Nos. 2900, 2923/6, 2929/32 2934/7 and 2940/3.

841 "When the Fighting Ended" (Pavel Simon)

843 Chickens in Kitchen (Asun Balzola)

842 Prague Town Hall Clock and Theory of Functions Diagram

1987. 45th Anniv of Destruction of Lidice and Lezaky. Multicoloured.
2885 1k. Type **841** 25 10
2886 1k. "The End of the Game" (Ludmila Jirincova) . . . 25 10

1987. 125th Anniv of Union of Czech Mathematicians and Physicists. Multicoloured.
2887 50h. Type **842** 10 10
2888 50h. J. M. Petzval, C. Strouhal and V. Iarnik 10 10
2889 50h. Trajectory of Brownian motion and earth fold diagram 10 10

1987. 11th Biennial Exhibition of Book Illustrations for Children, Bratislava. Designs showing illustrations by artists named. Multicoloured.
2890 50h. Type **843** 35 15
2891 1k. Cranes with egg at railway points (Frederic Clement) 45 15
2892 2k. Birds on nest (Elzbieta Gaudasinska) 35 25
2893 4k. Couple looking over rooftops (Marija Lucija Stupica) 35 30
MS2894 97 × 130 mm. No. 2892 × 2 plus label . . . . 1·60 1·60

844 Barbed Wire, Flames and Menorah

1987. 40th Anniv of Terezin Memorial.
2895 **844** 50h. multicoloured . . . 10 10

845 "OSS" and Communications Equipment

1987. 30th Anniv of Organization of Socialist Countries' Postal Administrations.
2896 **845** 4k. multicoloured . . . 70 10

846 Purkyne and Microtome

1987. Birth Bicentenary of Jan Evangelista Purkyne (physiologist).
2897 **846** 7k. multicoloured . . . 1·25 70

1987. Historic Bratislava (11th series). As T **669**.
2898 3k. buff, black and blue . . 50 50
2899 4k. black and brown . . . . 1·00 1·00
DESIGNS: 3k. Detail of projecting window by Vyzdoby; 4k. "View of Bratislava" (engraving, Hans Mayer).

848 Postilion

849 Symbols of Industry, Lenin and Red Flag

1987. "Praga '88" International Stamp Exhibition (3rd issue).
2900 **848** 1k. multicoloured . . . 25 10

1987. 70th Anniv of Russian Revolution (2901) and 65th Anniv of USSR (2902). Multicoloured.
2901 50h. Type **849** 15 10
2902 50h. Hammer and sickle . . 15 10

1987. "Praga '88" International Stamp Exhibition (4th issue). Sheet 101 × 100 mm.
MS2903 **838** 10k. × 4 multicoloured 14·50 14·50

1987. Art (21st series). As T **481**.
2904 1k. multicoloured 70 25
2905 2k. multicoloured 90 70
2906 3k. multicoloured . . . . . 1·25 75
2907 4k. black, blue and red . . 90 90
2908 5k. multicoloured . . . . . 1·25 1·00
DESIGNS: 1k. "Enclosure of Dreams" (Kamil Lhotak); 2k. "Tulips" (Ester Simerova-Martincekova); 3k. "Bohemian Landscape" (triptych, Josef Lada); 4k. "Accordion Player" (Josef Capek); 5k. "Self-portrait" (Jiri Trnka).

850 Obrovsky and Detail of 1919 Stamp

1987. Stamp Day. 105th Birth Anniv of Jakub Obrovsky (designer).
2909 **850** 1k. multicoloured . . . 10 10

851 "Czechoslovakia", Linden Tree and Arms

1988. 70th Anniv of Czechoslovakia.
2910 **851** 1k. multicoloured . . . 10 10

1988. 75th Birthday of President Husak.
2911 **759** 1k. brown and red . . . 10 10

852 Ski Jumping and Ice Hockey

1988. Olympic Games, Calgary and Seoul. Mult.
2912 50h. Type **852** 10 10
2913 1k. Basketball and football 15 10
2914 6k. Throwing the discus and weightlifting 90 40

853 Red Flags and Klement Gottwald Monument, Pecky

1988. 40th Annivs of "Victorious February" (2915) and National Front (2916). Multicoloured.
2915 50h. Type **853** 10 10
2916 50h. Couple and detail of "Czech Constitution, 1961" (Vincent Hloznik) 10 10
MS2917 87 × 99 mm. 50h. × 2 multicoloured (Type **853**); 60h. × 2 sepia (Type **246**) . . . . . 2·50 2·50

854 Laurin and Klement Car, 1914

1988. Historic Motor Cars. Multicoloured.
2918 50h. Type **854** 10 10
2919 1k. Tatra "NW" type B, 1902 . . . . 15 10
2920 2k. Tatra "NW" type E, 1905 . . . . 40 20
2921 3k. Tatra "12 Normandie", 1929 . . . . 55 25
2922 4k. "Meteor", 1899 . . . . 75 40

855 Praga Post Office and Velka Javorina T.V. Transmitter

1988. "Praga '88" International Stamp Exhibition (5th issue) and 70th Anniv of Postal Museum. Multicoloured.
2923 50h. Type **855** 10 10
2924 1k. Mlada Boleslav telecommunications centre and Carmelite Street post office, Prague 30 10
2925 2k. Prague 1 and Bratislava 56 post offices 45 25
2926 4k. Malta Square, Prague, and Prachatice post offices 90 40
MS2927 108 × 80 mm. Nos. 2924/5 each × 2 . . . . 3·50 3·50

856 Woman with Linden Leaves as Hair and Open Book

857 Strahov Monastery

1988. 125th Anniv of Slovak Cultural Society.
2928 **856** 50h. multicoloured . . . 10 10

1988. "Praga '88" International Stamp Exhibition (6th issue). National Literature Memorial, Strahov Monastery. Multicoloured.
2929 1k. Type **857** 15 10
2930 2k. Open book and celestial globe 35 20
2931 5k. Illuminated initial "B", scrolls and decorative binding 80 50
2932 7k. Astrological signs, Strahov, illuminated book and globe . . . . . . 1·50 1·10
MS2933 125 × 79 mm. Nos. 2929/32 4·00 4·00

858 Waldstein Garden Fountain

1988. "Praga '88" International Stamp Exhibition (7th issue). Prague Fountains.
2934 **858** 1k. black, lilac & blue 15 10
2935 – 2k. multicoloured . . . 35 20
2936 – 3k. black, orange & lilac 55 35
2937 – 4k. black, orange & grn 65 45
MS2938 79 × 125 mm. Nos. 2934/7 3·50 3·50
DESIGNS: 2k. Old Town Square; 3k. Charles University; 4k. Courtyard, Prague Castle.

859 Washington Capitol and Moscow Kremlin

1988. Soviet–American Strategic Arms Limitation Talks, Moscow. Sheet 110 × 106 mm.
MS2939 **859** 4k. multicoloured 2·40 2·40

1988. "Praga '88" (8th issue). Thematic Philately Day. As No. **MS**2903 but inscr "DEN NAMETOVE FILATELIE" at top.
MS2940 **838** 10k. × 4 multicoloured 10·00 10·00

860 Trade Unions Central Recreation Centre

1988. "Praga '88" International Stamp Exhibition (9th issue). Present-day Prague. Multicoloured.
2941 50h. Type **860** 10 10
2942 1k. Koospol foreign trade company 20 10
2943 2k. Motol teaching hospital 40 10
2944 4k. Palace of Culture . . . 75 25
MS2945 Two sheets, each 148 × 96 mm. (a) Nos. 2941 × 2 and 2944 × 2; (b) Nos. 2942/3 each × 2 . . . . 1·60 1·60

861 Alfons Mucha (designer of first stamps)

1988. "Praga '88" International Stamp Exhibition (10th issue). 70th Anniv of First Czechoslovak Stamps. Sheet 82 × 96 mm.
MS2946 **861** 5k. × 2 multicoloured 2·40 2·40

862 "Turin, Monte Superag" (detail, Josef Navratil)

1988. "Praga '88" International Stamp Exhibition (11th issue). Postal Museum. Sheet 108 × 165 mm.
MS2947 **862** 5k. × 2 multicoloured 3·25 3·25

863 Ariadne

1988. "Praga '88" (12th issue). Prague National Gallery. Sheet 108 × 165 mm containing T **863** and similar vert design showing details of "Bacchus and Ariadne" by Sebastian Ricci.
MS2948 10k. Type **863**; 10k. Bacchus . . . . 5·00 5·00

864 King George

1988. "Praga '88" International Stamp Exhibition (13th issue). King George of Podebrady's Religious Peace Plans. Sheet 106 × 133 mm.
MS2949 **864** 1k.60 × 4 black and yellow . . . . 5·00 5·00

1988. Prague Castle (24th series). As T **839**. Multicoloured.
2950 2k. 17th-century pottery jug 30 35
2951 3k. "St. Catherine" (Paolo Veronese) 45 55

1988. Historic Bratislava (12th series). As T **669**. Multicoloured.
2952 3k. Hlavne Square (detail of print by R. Alt-Sandman) 45 40
2953 4k. Ferdinand House . . . 50 55

1988. Art (22nd series). As T **481**.
2954 2k. multicoloured 40 40
2955 6k. brown, black and blue 1·25 1·10
2956 7k. multicoloured . . . . . 1·75 1·50
DESIGNS: 2k. "Field Workers carrying Sacks" (Martin Benka); 6k. "Woman watching Bird" (Vojtech Preissig); 7k. "Leopard attacking Horseman" (Eugene Delacroix).

865 Benda and Drawings

1988. Stamp Day. 106th Birth Anniv of Jaroslav Benda (stamp designer).
2957 **865** 1k. multicoloured . . . 10 10

866 Emblem **867** Globe and Truck

1989. 20th Anniv of Czechoslovak Federal Socialist Republic.
2958 **866** 50h. multicoloured . . . 10 10

1989. Paris–Dakar Rally. Multicoloured.
2959 50h. Type **867** 10 10
2960 1k. Globe and view of desert on truck side . . . 15 10
2961 2k. Globe and truck (different) 30 15
2962 4k. Route map, turban and truck 50 25

868 Taras G. Shevchenko **870** Dove and Pioneers

869 "Republika" (freighter)

1989. Birth Anniversaries.
2963 **868** 50h. multicoloured . . . 15 10
2964 – 50h. multicoloured . . . 15 10
2965 – 50h. brown and green . . 15 10
2966 – 50h. brown and green . . 15 10
2967 – 50h. black, brn & dp brn 15 10
2968 – 50h. multicoloured . . . 15 10
DESIGNS: No. 2963, Type **868** (Ukrainian poet and painter, 175th anniv); 2964, Modest Petrovich Musorgsky (composer, 150th anniv); 2965, Jan Botto (poet, 160th anniv); 2966, Jawaharlal Nehru (Indian statesman, cent); 2967, Jean Cocteau (writer and painter, centenary); 2968, Charlie Chaplin (actor, centenary).

1989. Shipping.
2969 **869** 50h. grey, red and blue 15 10
2970 – 1k. multicoloured . . . 20 10
2971 – 2k. multicoloured . . . 25 10
2972 – 3k. grey, red and blue 35 20
2973 – 4k. multicoloured . . . 40 25
2974 – 5k. multicoloured . . . 45 35
DESIGNS: 1k. "Pionyr" (trawler); 2k. "Brno" (tanker); 3k. "Trinec" (container ship); 4k. "Orlik" (container ship); 5k. "Vltava" (tanker) and communications equipment.

1989. 40th Anniv of Young Pioneer Organization.
2975 **870** 50h. multicoloured . . . 10 10

1989. Art (23rd series). Sheet 110 × 86 mm containing vert designs as T **481** showing details of "Festival of Rose Garlands" by Albrecht Durer.
MS2976 10k. × 2 multicoloured 3·50 3·50

1989. Prague Castle (25th series). As T **839**.
2977 2k. brown, yellow and red 20 20
2978 3k. multicoloured 40 35
DESIGNS: 2k. King Kard of Bohemia (relief by Alexandra Colin from Archduke Ferdinand I's mausoleum); 3k. "Self-portrait" (V. V. Reiner).

871 Bastille, Crowd and Flag

1989. Bicentenary of French Revolution. Sheet 73 × 98 mm.
MS2979 **871** 5k. black, red and blue 80 80

872 White-tailed Sea Eagle

1989. Endangered Species.
2980 **872** 1k. multicoloured . . . 15 25

873 Fire-bellied Toads

1989. Endangered Amphibians. Multicoloured.
2981 2k. Type **873** 30 25
2982 3k. Yellow-bellied toad . . 45 35
2983 4k. Alpine newts 85 55
2984 5k. Carpathian newts . . . 1·10 60

874 Dancers

1989. 40th Anniv of Slovak Folk Art Collective.
2985 **874** 50h. multicoloured . . . 10 10

875 Horsemen and Mountains

1989. 45th Anniv of Slovak Rising.
2986 **875** 1k. multicoloured . . . 10 10

876 "Going Fishing" (Hannu Taina) **877** "Nolanea verna"

1989. 12th Biennial Exhibition of Book Illustrations for Children. Multicoloured.
2987 50h. Type **876** 10 10
2988 1k. "Donkey Rider" (Aleksandur Aleksov) . . 15 10
2989 2k. "Animal Dreams" (Jurgen Spohn Zapadny) 25 15
2990 4k. "Scarecrow" (Robert Brun) 40 25
MS2991 100 × 143 mm. No. 2990 × 2 . . . . 1·25 1·25

1989. Poisonous Fungi.
2992 **877** 50h. brown, deep brown and green 10 10
2993 – 1k. multicoloured . . . 20 10
2994 – 2k. green and brown . . 35 25
2995 – 3k. brown, yellow & red 45 35
2996 – 5k. multicoloured . . . 65 55
DESIGNS: 1k. Death cap; 2k. Destroying angel; 3k. "Cortinarius orellanus"; 5k. "Galerina marginata".

1989. Historic Bratislava (13th series). As T **669**.
2997 3k. multicoloured 35 40
2998 4k. black, red and green . . 55 50
DESIGNS: 3k. Devin Fortress and flower; 4k. Devin Fortress and pitcher.

878 Jan Opletal (Nazi victim)

1989. 50th Anniv of International Students Day.
2999 **878** 1k. multicoloured . . . 10 10

1989. Art (24th series). As T **481**. Multicoloured.
3000 2k. "Nirvana" (Anton Jasusch) 25 25
3001 4k. "Dusk in the Town" (Jakub Schikaneder) (horiz) 50 50
3002 5k. "Bakers" (Pravoslav Kotik) (horiz) 80 70

879 Bearded Falcon Stamp, Pens and Bouda

1989. Stamp Day. 5th Death Anniv of Cyril Bouda (stamp designer).
3003 **879** 1k. brown, yellow & red 10 10

880 Practising Alphabet **881** Tomas Masaryk (first President)

1990. International Literacy Year.
3004 **880** 1k. multicoloured . . . 10 10

1990. Birth Anniversaries. Multicoloured.
3005 50h. Type **881** (140th anniv) 10 10
3006 50h. Karel Capek (writer, centenary) 10 10
3007 1k. Vladimir Ilyich Lenin (120th anniv) 15 10
3008 2k. Emile Zola (novelist, 150th anniv) 30 15
3009 3k. Jaroslav Heyrovsky (chemist, centenary) . . . 35 20
3010 10k. Bohuslav Martinu (composer, centenary) . . 1·10 65

882 Pres. Vaclav Havel **883** Players

1990.
3011 **882** 50h. ultram, bl & red . . 10 10

1990. Men's World Handball Championship.
3012 **883** 50h. multicoloured . . . 10 10

884 Snapdragon **885** Pope John Paul II

1990. Flowers. Multicoloured.
3013 50h. Type **884** 10 10
3014 1k. "Zinnia elegans" 15 10
3015 3k. Tiger flower 35 25
3016 5k. Madonna lily 55 40

1990. Arms of Czech Towns (7th series). As T **740**. Multicoloured.
3017 50h. Bytca 10 10
3018 50h. Podebrady 10 10
3019 50h. Sobeslav 10 10
3020 50h. Prostejov 10 10

1990. Papal Visit.
3021 **885** 1k. brown, yellow & red 10 10

886 Woman holding Flags **887** Twopenny Blue

1990. 45th Anniv of Liberation.
3022 **886** 1k. multicoloured . . . 10 10

1990. 150th Anniv of Penny Black. Sheet 102 × 94 mm.
MS3023 **887** 7k. multicoloured 1·25 1·25

888 Footballers **889** Victory Signs

1990. World Cup Football Championship, Italy.
3024 **888** 1k. multicoloured . . . 10 10

1990. Free General Election.
3025 **889** 1k. multicoloured . . . 10 10

1990. Prague Castle (26th series). As T **824**.
3026 2k. multicoloured 50 40
3027 3k. green, dp green & red 70 65
DESIGNS: 2k. Jewelled glove (from reliquary of St. George); 3k. Seal of King Premysl Otakar II of Bohemia.

890 Map of Europe and Branch

1990. 15th Anniv of European Security and Co-operation Conference, Helsinki.
3028 **890** 7k. multicoloured . . . 80 55

891 Milada Horakova

1990. 40th Anniv of Execution of Milada Horakova.
3029 **891** 1k. multicoloured . . . 10 10

892 Poodles

1990. "Inter Canis" Dog Show, Brno. Mult.
3030 50h. Type **892** 10 10
3031 1k. Afghan hound, Irish wolfhound and greyhound 15 10
3032 4k. Czech terrier, bloodhound and Hanoverian bearhound 40 30
3033 7k. Cavalier King Charles, cocker and American cocker spaniels 65 50

1990. Historic Bratislava (14th series). As T **669**.
3034 3k. black and red 40 35
3035 4k. multicoloured 65 55
DESIGNS: 3k. Coin; 4k. "M. R. Stefanik" (J. Mudroch).

893 Horses jumping

1990. Centenary of Pardubice Steeplechase. Mult.
3036 50h. Type **893** 10 10
3037 4k. Horses galloping 45 35

894 Alpine Marmot

1990. Mammals. Multicoloured.
3038 50h. Type **894** 10 10
3039 1k. European wild cat . . . 10 10
3040 4k. Eurasian beaver 45 30
3041 5k. Common long-eared bat 60 40

895 European Flag

1990. Helsinki Pact Civic Gathering, Prague.
3042 **895** 3k. blue, yellow & gold 35 30

896 Snow-covered Church

1990. Christmas.
3043 **896** 50h. multicoloured . . . 10 10

1990. Art (25th series). As T **481**. Multicoloured.
3044 2k. multicoloured 40 35
3045 3k. black, brown & blue . . 50 40
3046 4k. multicoloured 60 60
3047 5k. multicoloured 70 75
DESIGNS—HORIZ: 2k. "Krucemburk" (Jan Zrzavy). VERT: 3k. "St. Agnes" (detail of sculpture, Josef Vaclav Myslbek); 4k. "Slovene in his Homeland" (detail, Alfons Mucha); 5k. "St. John the Baptist" (detail of sculpture, Auguste Rodin).

897 Karel Svolinsky (stamp designer) and "Czechoslovakia"

1990. Stamp Day.
3048 **897** 1k. purple, lilac & blue 10 10

898 Judo Throw

899 Svojsik

1991. European Judo Championships, Prague.
3049 **898** 1k. multicoloured . . . 10 10

1991. 80th Anniv of Czechoslovak Scout Movement and 115th Birth Anniv of A. B. Svojsik (founder).
3050 **899** 3k. multicoloured . . . 35 10

900 Jan Hus preaching

901 Alois Senefelder

1991. Anniversaries.
3051 **900** 50h. brown, stone & red 10 10
3052 – 1k. multicoloured . . . 10 10
3053 – 5k. multicoloured . . . 60 30
DESIGNS AND EVENTS: 50h. Type **900** (600th anniv of Bethlehem Chapel, Prague); 40 × 23 mm: 1k. Estates Theatre, Prague (re-opening) and Mozart (death bicent); 49 × 20 mm: 5k. Paddle-steamer "Bohemia" (150th anniv of boat excursions in Bohemia).

1991. Birth Anniversaries.
3054 **901** 1k. green, brown & red 20 10
3055 – 1k. black, green & red 20 10
3056 – 1k. blue, mauve & red 20 10
3057 – 1k. violet, blue and red 20 10
3058 – 1k. brown, orange & red 20 10
DESIGNS: No. 3054, Type **901** (inventor of lithography, 220th anniv); 3055, Andrej Kmet (naturalist, 150th anniv); 3056, Jan Masaryk (politician, 105th anniv); 3057, Jaroslav Seifert (composer, 90th anniv); 3058, Antonin Dvorak (composer, 150th anniv).

902 "Magion II" Satellite and Earth

903 Exhibition Pavilion, 1891

1991. Europa. Europe in Space.
3059 **902** 6k. blue, black & red . . 70 50

1991. Cent of International Exhibition, Prague.
3060 **903** 1k. blue, grey & mauve 10 10

904 Bearded Penguins, Map and Flag

1991. 30th Anniv of Antarctic Treaty.
3061 **904** 8k. multicoloured . . . 90 55

905 Blatna Castle

906 Jan Palach

1991. Castles. Multicoloured.
3062 50h. Type **905** . . . . . . 10 1·00
3063 1k. Bouzov 10 10
3064 3k. Kezmarok 40 25

1991. Jan Palach Scholarship.
3065 **906** 4k. black 35 30

907 Rip

908 "The Frog King" (Binette Schroeder)

1991. Beauty Spots.
3066 **907** 4k. red, blue & yellow 45 40
3067 – 4k. purple, green & blk 45 40
DESIGN: No. 3067, Krivan.

1991. 13th Biennial Exhibition of Book Illustrations for Children. Multicoloured.
3068 1k. Type **908** 10 10
3069 2k. "Pinocchio" (Stasys Eidrigevicius) 25 15

909 Hlinka

910 "Prague Jesus Child" (Maria-Victoria Church)

1991. 53rd Death Anniv of Father Andrej Hlinka (Slovak nationalist).
3070 **909** 10k. black . . . . 1·25 55

1991. Prague and Bratislava. Multicoloured.
3071 3k. Type **910** 45 40
3072 3k. St. Elisabeth's Church, Bratislava 45 40

911 "Gagea bohemica"

912 Boys in Costume

1991. Nature Protection. Flowers. Multicoloured.
3073 1k. Type **911** 10 10
3074 2k. "Aster alpinus" 20 20
3075 5k. "Fritillaria meleagris" 55 40
3076 11k. "Daphne eneorum" . . 1·25 75

1991. Art (26th series). As T **481**. Multicoloured.
3077 2k. "Family at Home" (Max Ernst) 20 20
3078 3k. "Milenci" (Auguste Renoir) 30 30
3079 4k. "Christ" (El Greco) . . 75 40
3080 5k. "Coincidence" (Ladislav Guderna) 85 55
3081 7k. "Two Japanese Women" (Utamaro) . . . . 1·10 80

1991. Christmas.
3082 **912** 50h. multicoloured . . . 10 10

913 Martin Benka (stamp designer) and Slovakian 1939 Stamp

1991. Stamp Day.
3083 **913** 2k. red, black & orange 35 10

914 Biathlon

916 Player

915 Comenius

1992. Winter Olympic Games, Albertville.
3084 **914** 1k. multicoloured . . . 10 10

1992. 400th Birth Anniv of Jan Komensky (Comenius) (educationist). Sheet 63 × 76 mm.
MS3085 **915** 10k. multicoloured 1·75 1·75

1992. World Ice Hockey Championship, Prague and Bratislava.
3086 **916** 3k. multicoloured . . . 35 35

917 Traffic Lights

1992. Road Safety Campaign.
3087 **917** 2k. multicoloured . . . 45 20

918 Tower, Seville Cathedral

1992. "Expo '92" World's Fair, Seville.
3088 **918** 4k. multicoloured . . . 25 25

919 Amerindian, "Santa Maria" and Columbus

1992. Europa. 500th Anniv of Discovery of America by Columbus.
3089 **919** 22k. multicoloured . . . 2·50 1·90

920 J. Kubis and J. Gabcik

1992. Free Czechoslovak Forces in World War II. Multicoloured.
3090 1k. Type **920** (50th anniv of assassination of Reinhard Heydrich) 10 10
3091 2k. Spitfires (air battles over England, 1939–45) . . . 20 10
3092 3k. Barbed wire and soldier (Tobruk, 1941) 25 15
3093 6k. Soldiers (Dunkirk, 1944–45) 90 25

921 Tennis Player

922 Nurse's Hats and Red Cross

1992. Olympic Games, Barcelona.
3094 **921** 2k. multicoloured . . . 35 10

1992. Red Cross.
3095 **922** 2k. multicoloured . . . 25 10

923 Player

924 Crawling Cockchafer

1992. European Junior Table Tennis Championships, Topolcany.
3096 **923** 1k. multicoloured . . . 10 10

1992. Beetles. Multicoloured.
3097 1k. Type **924** 10 10
3098 2k. "Ergates faber" 20 10
3099 3k. "Meloe violaceus" . . . 25 10
3100 4k. "Dytiscus latissimus" . . 30 45

925 Troja Castle

1992.

3101	**925**	6k. multicoloured . . .	60	45
3102	–	7k. black and lilac . . .	70	60
3103	–	8k. multicoloured . . .	90	75

DESIGNS—VERT: 7k. "St. Martin" (sculpture, G. R. Donner), Bratislava Cathedral. HORIZ: 8k. Lednice Castle.

926 Double Head and Posthorns

927 Anton Bernolak and Georgius Fandly

1992. Post Bank.

3104	**926**	20k. multicoloured . . .	1·75	70

1992. Bicentenary of Slovak Education Assn.

3105	**927**	5k. multicoloured . . .	55	30

928 Cesky Krumlov

929 Organ

1992.

3106	**928**	3k. brown and red . . .	35	10

1992. Art (27th series). As T **481**.

3107		6k. black and brown	50	50
3108		7k. multicoloured	65	70
3109		8k. multicoloured	1·00	90

DESIGNS—VERT: 6k. "The Old Raftsman" (Koloman Sokol); 8k. "Abandonned" (Toyen). HORIZ: 7k. "Still Life with Grapes" (Georges Braque).

1992. Christmas.

3110	**929**	2k. multicoloured . . .	10	10

930 Jindra Schmidt (engraver)

1992. Stamp Day.

3111	**930**	2k. multicoloured . . .	10	10

NEWSPAPER STAMPS

N 4

N 67 Dove

N 94 Messenger

1918. Imperf.

N24	N **4**	2h. green	10	10
N25		5h. green	10	10
N26		6h. red	10	10
N27		10h. lilac	10	10
N28		20h. blue	10	10
N29		30h. brown	10	10
N30		50h. orange	10	10
N31		100h. brown	45	10

1925. Surch with new value and stars.

N249	N **4**	5 on 2h. green	60	55
N250		5 on 6h. red	35	85

1926. Newspaper Express stamps optd **NOVINY** or surch also.

N251	E **4**	5h. on 2h. pur on yell	10	10
N253		5h. green on yellow . .	45	25
N254		10h. brown on yellow	10	10

1934. Optd **O.T.**

N332	N **4**	10h. lilac	10	10
N333		20h. blue	10	10
N334		30h. brown	15	10

1937. Imperf.

N364	N **67**	2h. brown	10	10
N365		5h. blue	10	10
N366		7h. orange	10	10
N367		9h. green	10	10
N368		10h. lake	10	10
N369		12h. blue	10	10
N370		20h. green	10	10
N371		50h. brown	10	15
N372		1k. olive	10	10

1946. Imperf.

N467	N **94**	5h. blue	10	10
N468		10h. red	10	10
N469		15h. green	10	10
N470		20h. green	10	10
N471		25h. purple	10	10
N472		30h. brown	10	10
N473		40h. red	10	10
N474		50h. brown	10	10
N475		1k. grey	10	10
N476		5k. blue	10	10

EXPRESS NEWSPAPER STAMPS

E 4

1918. Imperf. On yellow or white paper.

E24	E **4**	2h. purple	10	10
E25		5h. green	10	10
E26		10h. brown	45	45

OFFICIAL STAMPS

O 92

O 103

1945.

O463	O **92**	50h. green	10	10
O464		1k. blue	10	10
O465		1k.20 purple	15	10
O466		1k.50 red	10	10
O467		2k.50 blue	15	10
O468		5k. purple	20	30
O469		8k. red	30	45

1947.

O490	O **103**	60h. red	10	10
O491		80h. olive	10	10
O492		1k. blue	10	10
O493		1k.20 purple	10	10
O494		2k.40 red	10	10
O495		4k. blue	15	10
O496		5k. purple	15	30
O497		7k.40 violet	20	30

PERSONAL DELIVERY STAMPS

P 66

1937. For Prepayment. "V" in each corner.

P363	P **66**	50h. blue	20	35

1937. For Payment on Delivery. "D" in each corner.

P364	P **66**	50h. red	20	35

P 95

1946.

P469	P **95**	2k. blue	20	20

POSTAGE DUE STAMPS

D 4

1919. Imperf.

D24	D **4**	5h. olive	10	10
D25		10h. olive	10	10
D26		15h. olive	10	10
D27		20h. olive	10	10
D28		25h. olive	10	10
D29		30h. olive	25	10
D30		40h. olive	25	25
D31		50h. olive	25	10
D32		100h. brown	1·25	10
D33		250h. orange	6·00	1·10
D34		400h. red	8·25	1·10
D35		500h. green	3·00	25
D36		1000h. violet	3·00	35
D37		2000h. blue	16·00	75

1922. Postage stamps surch **DOPLATIT** and new value. Imperf or perf.

D229	**2**	10 on 3h. mauve	10	10
D224a		20 on 3h. mauve	10	10
D230		30 on 3h. mauve	10	10
D257	**3**	30 on 15h. red	1·75	30
D231	**2**	40 on 3h. mauve	10	10
D258	**3**	40 on 15h. red	35	25
D225		50 on 75h. green	25	25
D262		60 on 50h. purple	3·00	1·50
D263		60 on 50h. blue	3·50	1·90
D232		60 on 75h. green	40	10
D226		60 on 80h. green	35	10
D227		100 on 80h. green . . .	30	10
D233		100 on 120h. black . . .	90	10
D264	**2**	100 on 400h. violet . . .	55	10
D265	**3**	100 on 1000h. purple . .	1·10	30
D228	**2**	200 on 400h. violet . . .	55	25

1924. Postage Due stamp surch.

D249	D **4**	10 on 5h. olive	10	10
D250		20 on 5h. olive	10	10
D251		30 on 15h. olive	10	10
D252		40 on 15h. olive	10	10
D253		50 on 250h. orange . .	60	10
D234		50 on 400h. red	55	10
D254		60 on 250h. orange . .	90	20
D235		60 on 400h. red	2·10	60
D255		100 on 250h. orange . .	1·25	25
D236		100 on 400h. red . . .	1·25	25
D256		200 on 500h. green . .	3·00	1·75

1926. Postage stamps optd **DOPLATIT** or surch also.

D266	**13**	30 on 100h. green . . .	10	10
D279	**11**	40 on 185h. orange . . .	10	10
D267	**13**	40 on 200h. purple . . .	10	10
D268		40 on 300h. red	1·10	25
D280	**11**	50 on 20h. red	10	10
D281		50 on 150h. red	25	10
D269	**13**	50 on 500h. green . . .	55	10
D282	**11**	60 on 25h. brown . . .	25	25
D283		60 on 185h. orange . . .	25	10
D270	**13**	60 on 400h. brown . . .	45	10
D278	**11**	100h. brown	55	20
D284		100 on 25h. brown . . .	60	10
D271	**13**	100 on 600h. purple . . .	1·75	35

D 34

D 94

1928.

D285	D **34**	5h. red	10	10
D286		10h. red	10	10
D287		20h. red	10	10
D288		30h. red	10	10
D289		40h. red	10	10
D290		50h. red	10	10
D291		60h. red	10	10
D292		1k. blue	10	10
D293		2k. blue	35	10
D294		5k. blue	60	10
D295		10k. blue	1·25	10
D296		20k. blue	2·40	10

1946.

D467	D **94**	10h. blue	10	10
D468		20h. blue	10	10
D469		50h. blue	15	10
D470		1k. red	30	10
D471		1k.20 red	35	10
D472		1k.50 red	40	10
D473		1k.60 red	45	10
D474		2k. red	60	10
D475		2k.40 red	65	10
D476		3k. red	1·00	10
D477		5k. red	1·60	10
D478		6k. red	2·25	10

D 257

D 258

1954.

D845	D **257**	5h. green	10	10
D846		10h. green	10	10
D860		30h. green	10	10
D861		50h. green	15	10
D849		60h. green	15	10
D850		95h. green	35	10
D863	D **258**	1k. violet	25	10
D864		1k.20 violet	30	10
D865		1k.50 violet	45	10
D854		1k.60 violet	40	10
D855		2k. violet	75	10
D866		3k. violet	1·50	30
D867		5k. violet	2·00	45

D 572 Stylized Plant

1971.

D1985	–	10h. pink and blue	10	10
D1986	–	20h. blue & purple	10	10
D1987	–	30h. pink & green	10	10
D1988	–	60h. green & pur . .	15	10
D1989	–	80h. blue & orange	20	10
D1990	–	1k. green & red . .	25	10
D1991	–	1k.20 orange & grn	30	10
D1992	–	2k. red and blue . .	55	20
D1993	–	3k. yellow & black	95	20
D1994	–	4k. blue & brown	1·10	30
D1995	D **572**	5k.40 lilac and red	1·60	35
D1996	–	6k. yellow and red	2·00	45

DESIGNS: Various stylized plants as Type D **572**.

INDEX

investment

"If I could buy just one stamp..."

Investment Director Adrian Roose tackles the impossible question.

I'm often asked this question. "If you could buy just one stamp which would it be?"

Well... If you are looking for a single rare stamp to invest in then consider this item. It's returned almost 7.2% per annum over the last 10 years. There's no reason to suspect it won't offer the same returns over the next 10 years.

I've long been fascinated with the Great Britain SG121.

When I first joined Stanley Gibbons 14 years ago I followed the company training programme, working in different departments building up my knowledge.

I sat with the reference collection to study shade differences. I swotted up, reading reference books.

One of the first reference books I read was an invaluable little book stating how many of each Great Britain stamp had been printed.

It was worn and many pages were torn but in a supply and demand driven market the information it held was like the Holy Grail to me.

And one stamp always stood out. The Great Britain SG121.

It had, by far, the lowest print run of any Queen Victoria British stamp. Yet it wasn't the most expensive. Far from it, it looked distinctly undervalued.

I've watched over the years as this stamp has become more appreciated amongst collectors. They are beginning to realise how few of these stamps are available in top quality mint condition.

The Catalogue price is up from £7,500 to £20,000 in 10 years. A 166% increase in Catalogue prices.

If you'd bought the SG121 from us 10 years ago you wouldn't be taking the guaranteed minimum return of a 60% capital gain on your original investment (exit route 1).

We would have advised you to take exit route 2.

We'd be buying back the stamp for £15,000 (75% of Catalogue).

That equates to an almost 7.2% p.a. (compound) over 10 years.

Or (exit route 3) you could have placed it in our auction with 0% commission and potentially done even better.

I firmly believe this level of increase is just the start and the forthcoming years will see similar, if not better, increases.

How rare is this stamp? Approx 67,000 were printed. Compare that to a Penny Black, the world's first postage stamp. Probably the most famous stamp in the world. Over 68,000,000 Penny Blacks were printed.

We have staff scouring auctions the world over. They are permanently looking for rare stamps of the highest quality to offer to the collectors on our database.

Other staff travel the country on road-shows talking to the public and valuing their collections in the hope of finding quality stamps to offer to our clientele.

However despite our staff being permanently on the lookout this is the first Great Britain SG121 we have been able to offer in over 9 months...

This article is an extract from one of our investment newsletters. To subscribe *FREE* to this service visit: *www.stanleygibbons.com/fn*

STANLEY GIBBONS
The Home of Philately since 1856

AN IMPORTANT MESSAGE TO YOU

Dear Catalogue User,

As a collector and Stanley Gibbons catalogue user for many years myself, I am only too aware of the need to provide you with the information you seek in an accurate, timely and easily accessible manner.

Naturally, I have my own views on where changes could be made, but one thing I learned long ago is that we all have different opinions and requirements.

I would therefore be most grateful if you would complete the form overleaf and return it to me (or send your answers on a separate sheet if you prefer not to cut the page out of your catalogue).

If you would like the form to be sent to you by email, let me know at hjefferies@stanleygibbons.co.uk

Very many thanks for your help.

Yours sincerely,

Hugh Jefferies,
Editor.

Questionnaire

Please complete and return it to:

Hugh Jefferies *(Catalogue Editor)*
Stanley Gibbons Limited
7 Parkside, Ringwood
Hampshire BH24 2LE
United Kingdom

or

email: *hjefferies@stanleygibbons.co.uk*

2009 STAMPS OF THE WORLD

1. Level of detail

Do you feel that the level of detail in this catalogue is:

a) too specialised ☐
b) about right ☐
c) inadequate ☐

2. Frequency of issue

How often would you purchase a new edition of this catalogue?

a) Annually ☐
b) Every two years ☐
c) Every three to five years ☐
d) Less frequently ☐

3. Design and Quality

How would you describe the layout and appearance of this catalogue?

a) Excellent ☐
b) Good ☐
c) Adequate ☐
d) Poor ☐

4. *How important to you are the prices given in the catalogue*:

a) Important ☐
b) Quite important ☐
c) Of little interest ☐
d) Of no interest ☐

5. *Would you be interested in an electronic version of this catalogue?*

a) Yes ☐
b) Maybe ☐
c) No ☐

6. *Is there anything you would like to see in this catalogue that is not currently included?* ....

....
....
....
....
....
....
....

7. *Would you like us to let you know when the next edition of this catalogue is due to be published? If so please give your contact details below.*

Name: ....
Address:..
....
....
....
Email: ....
Telephone: ....

8. *Are there any other Stanley Gibbons Catalogues which you would like to be informed of when published.*

1.
2.
3.

Many thanks for your comments.

COLLECT
STAMPS OF THE WORLD
STAMPS

From Stanley Gibbons, THE WORLD'S LARGEST STAMP STOCK

Priority order form – Four easy ways to order

Phone:
020 7836 8444
Overseas: +44 (0)20 7836 8444

Fax:
020 7557 4499
Overseas: +44 (0)20 7557 4499

Email:
lmourne@stanleygibbons.co.uk

Post: Lesley Mourne,
Stamp Mail Order Department
Stanley Gibbons Ltd, 399 Strand
London, WC2R 0LX, England

Customer Details ____________________

Account Number ____________________

Name ____________________

Address ____________________

____________________ Postcode ____________________

Country ____________________ Email ____________________

Tel No ____________________ Fax No ____________________

Payment details

Registered Postage & Packing £3.60

I enclose my cheque/postal order for £ ____________________ in full payment.
Please make cheques/postal orders payable to Stanley Gibbons Ltd.
Cheques must be in £ sterling and drawn on a UK bank

Please debit my credit card for £____________________ in full payment.
I have completed the Credit Card section below.

Card Number ☐☐☐☐☐☐☐☐☐☐☐☐☐☐☐☐

CVC Number ☐☐☐

Start Date (Switch & Amex) ☐☐☐☐

Expiry Date ☐☐☐☐

Issue No (Switch) ☐☐

Signature ____________________ Date ____________________

COLLECT
STAMPS OF THE WORLD
STAMPS

From Stanley Gibbons, THE WORLD'S LARGEST STAMP STOCK

Condition (mint/UM/used)	Country	SG No.	Description	Price	Office use only
			POSTAGE & PACKAGING	£3.60	
			GRAND TOTAL		

Minimum price. The minimum catalogue price quoted is 10p. For individual stamps, prices between 10p and 95p are provided as a guide for catalogue users. The lowest price charged for individual stamps or sets purchased from Stanley Gibbons Ltd is £1

Please complete payment, name and address details overleaf